# THE
# SPORTS
# ENCYCLOPEDIA:
# PRO FOOTBALL

# THE SPORTS ENCYCLOPEDIA: PRO FOOTBALL

## 14TH EDITION
## The Modern Era
## 1960—1995

Revised and Updated

by
DAVID S. NEFT,
RICHARD M. COHEN
and
RICK KORCH

St. Martin's Griffin
New York

To Richard M. "Dick" Cohen 1938-1991
He spent much of his life researching sports history,
but he always believed that the best was yet to come.

ISBN 0-312-14424-5

First St. Martin's Griffin Edition: August 1996
10  9  8  7  6  5  4  3  2  1

Books are available in quantity for promotional or premium use. Write to Director of Special Sales, St. Martin's Press, 175 Fifth Avenue, New York, N.Y. 10010, for information on discounts and terms, or call toll-free (800) 221-7945. In New York, call (212) 674-5151 (ext. 645).

# Contents

## 1980-1995 New Challenges, New Triumphs 393

## Leaders and Features 781

# Preface

*Pro Football, The Modern Era* is a complete statistical record of professional football from 1960 to the present. All years prior to 1960 may be found in the companion book, *Pro Football, The Early Years*. The authors have also produced other sports reference books and encyclopedia histories.

Within each period the fan has the opportunity to guage football history in a much better perspective. In each period the authors have included statistical matter and text, arranged in an easy-to-follow year-by-year and division-by-division format. In addition, there are register sections, championship games, Super Bowls, single-season leaders by category and lifetime leaders by category, as well as a host of other featured material, all of which serves to make *Pro Football, The Modern Era* the most complete book of its kind.

For the authors, who could not have undertaken this project alone, there are many individuals and former professional players to thank, whose assistance was necessary in helping to make this book a reality. Their contributions are extensive and range from supplying demographic information to some of the color as it actually took place on the field. To these individuals, the authors express their deep appreciation that finally there is a book where you can "go and look it up."

Chief consultants in preparation of the written manuscripts —
Jordan A. Deutsch, John G. Hogrogian, Bob Carroll

Director of research and coordinator for earlier editions —
Roland T. Johnson

Special consultants —
John G. Hogrogian, Jim Campbell, Michael Neft

Pro Football Hall of Fame —
Joe Horrigan, research librarian, who made available not only his facility but also his endless knowledge, time and cooperation in seeing this book to its fruition.
Don Smith, public relations director

Stan Grosshandler — An independent contributor who coordi-

nated and served as liaison with the following former professional players:

Chuck Bednarik
Jack Christiansen
Dutch Clark
Charlie Conerly
Jack Cronin
Ed Danowski
Art DeCarlo
Art Donovan
Benny Friedman
Buckets Goldenberg
Otto Graham
Pat Harder
Mel Hein
Clarke Hinkle
Crazy Legs Hirsch

Dick Hoerner
Henry Jordan
Don Kindt
Joe Kopcha
Dante Lavelli
Jim Mutscheller
Ernie Nevers
Curly Oden
Johnny Sisk
Hank Soar
Ken Strong
Y.A. Tittle
Em Tunnell
Alex Wojciechowicz

Elias Sports Bureau —
Seymour Siwoff
Steve Hirdt

Independent contributors
Bob Allen
Mark Swayne
Irving D. Shapiro
Jason A. Schweinsberg

Joel Bussert
John Crelli
Terence J. Troup

University of Rhode Island Library — inter-library loan department

The Notre Dame International Sports and Games Research Collection —
Jethro Kyles, curator
Herb Juliano, curator until 1982

The authors' wives (a special thanks for once again displaying their faith and cooperation throughout the project) —
Naomi Neft, Nancy Cohen and Jacquie Korch

# Codes and Explanations

In each section of the book, unfamiliar abbreviations and bold facing may be shown. The following, by section, is an explanation of this matter:

## Yearly Sections

**Age** — The age shown for each player is as of Sept. 1 of that year.

**Traded Players** — Shown only on the team which the player played for most, along with a "from" or "to" reference.

**Bold Facing** — Indicates league leaders.

**Team Name Line** — Shown alongside the name of each team is the team Won-Lost-Tied record and the head coaches.

**Home team Indication** — In a team's game-by-game scores, certain opponents apppear in uppercase. That means that the opponent played at the team's home park.

**Opponent's Score** — In a team's game-by-game scores, the opponent's score always appears in the right-hand column.

**Rosters** — Attempts to include, in a year, only those who actually play in a league game. The limitations of data, however, may have accidently included men who did not get into a league game.

**Position Abbreviations** — (Applies to all sections.) If a man played more than one position, the listing is in order of amount played at each position:

BB — Blocking Back
C — Center
DB — Defensive back
DE — Defensive end
DG — Defensive guard
DT — Defensive tackle
NT — Nose tackle
FB — Fullback
FL — Flanker
G — Offensive and defensive guard
HB — Halfback
K — Punter or placekicker (and did not play any other position in a particular year
LB — Linebacker
MG — Middle guard
OG — Offensive guard
OE — Offensive end
OT — Offensive tackle
QB — Quarterback
RB — Running back
T — Offensive and defensive tackle
TB — Tailback
TE — Tight end
WB — Wingback
WR — Wide receiver

**Career Interruptions** — Fully explained, but covers only a full year or career end interruption.

**Team Abbreviations** — (Applies to all sections)

Akr — Akr
Atl — Atlanta
Arz — Arizona
Bal — Baltimore
Bkn — Brooklyn
Bos — Boston
Buf — Buffalo
Can — Canton

Car — Carolina
Chi — Chicago Bears
ChiB — Chicago Bears and Chicago Staleys
ChiC — Chicago Cardinals
ChiT — Chicago Tigers
Cin — Cincinnati
Cle — Cleveland
Col — Columbus
C-T — Chicago Cardinals-Pittsburgh Steelers (merged)
C-S — Cincinnati Reds and St. Louis Gunners
Dal — Dallas
Day — Dayton
Dec — Decatur
Den — Denver
Det — Detroit
Dul — Duluth
Eva — Evansville
Fra — Frankford
GB — Green Bay
Ham — Hammond
Har — Hartford
Hou — Houston
Ind — Indianapolis
Jax — Jacksonville
KC — Kansas City
Ken — Kenosha
LA — Los Angeles
Lou — Louisville
Mia — Miami
Mil — Milwaukee
Min — Minnesota or Minneapolis
Mun — Muncie
NE — New England
NO — New Orleans
Nwk — Newark
NYB — New York Bulldogs
NYG — New York Giants
NYJ — New York Jets
NYT — New York Titans
NYY — New York Yankees
Oak — Oakland
Oor — Oorang (Marion, Ohio)
Ora — Orange
Phi — Philadelphia
Pit — Pittsburgh
Phx — Phoenix
P-P — Philadelphia Eagles-Pittsburgh Steelers (merged)
Port — Portsmouth
Pott — Pottsville
Prov — Providence
Rac — Racine
Raid — Los Angeles Raiders
RI — Rock Island
Roch — Rochester
SD — San Diego
Sea — Seattle
SF — San Francisco
SI — Staten Island
StL — St. Louis
TB — Tampa Bay
Was — Washington

## Championship Section

**Giveaways** — Passes that were intercepted and fumbles lost

**Takeaways** — Passes intercepted and opposing fumbles recovered

Note: These two categories apply to team statsitics only

**TAP** — Indicates Tackled Attempting to Pass

9

## Register Section

Players have been assigned to the various register sections according to what time period they played in most

**Register sections, by period, are divided into an alphabetical register and then into various statistical registers. In the alphabetical register, alongside each player's name are one or more reference numbers (1, 2, 3, 4, 5). These reference numbers are to serve as guides where to find the player's statistical record (if there is no reference number, it means the player did not have enough minimum statistics to rate a ranking). The following are the reference numbers and their identification:**

> 1 — Passing
> 2 — Rushing and receiving
> 3 — Punt returns and kickoff returns
> 4 — Punting
> 5 — Kicking

Some of the unfamiliar information which appears in each alphabetical register is as follows:

Last name, Use name (name player was known as), nicknames which appear in parentheses ( ):

> Payton, Walter (Sweetness)

If a player used a name other than that he was "born as", his real name is indicated in parentheses ( ) after the last name. Such as in the case of Rocky Thompson:

> Thompson (born Symonds), Rocky

**Weight** — Average weight for career

**HC** — Indicates, for year or years, that the player was a head coach

**PC** — Indicates, for year or years, that the player was a head coach while actively playing

**League abbreviations** —

A — American Football League
AA — All-American Football Conference

**Other Major-League Sports** — Certain players also played professional basketball or major-league baseball. The basketball information is indicated with the league in abbreviations:

NBL — National Basketball League
NBA — National Basketball Association
BAA — Basketball Association of America
ABL — American Basketball League
ABA — American Basketball Association

**Career Interruptions** — If an abbreviation other than a league follows the year played, it means that only a full year was missed or a career ended because of certain prevailing reasons. The codes and explanations are as follows:

AA — Injured in automobile accident
AJ — Arm injury
BA — Broken arm
BC — Broken collarbone
BG — Broken finger
BH — Broken bone in hand
BL — Broken leg
BN — Broken ankle
BQ — Broken neck
BW — Broken or dislocated wrist
CFL — Played in Canadian Football League
CJ — Concussion
DR — Suspended for drug use
EJ — Elbow injury
FJ — Foot or heel injury
GJ — Groin injury
HJ — Hand injury
HO — Holdout
IJ — Eye injury
IL — Illness
JJ — Injury (type of injury unknown)
KJ — Knee injury
LJ — Leg or thigh injury (including Achilles' tendon)
MS — Military service
NJ — Ankle injury
PJ — Hip injury
RJ — Finger injury
SJ — Shoulder injury or shoulder separation
SL — Suspended by commissioner
TJ — Stomach or abdomen injury
USFL — Played in USFL
VR — Voluntarily retired
WFL — Played in World Football League
XJ — Back injury

| Use Name (Nickname) - Positions | Team by Year | See Section | Hgt. | Wgt. | College | Int | Pts |
|---|---|---|---|---|---|---|---|
| Agajanian, Ben (The Toeless Wonder) K | 45Phi 45Pit 47-48LA-AA 49NYG 53LA 54-57NYG 60LA-A 61DalA 61GB 62OakA 64SD-A | 5 | 6' | 215 | New Mexico | | 655 |
| Ameche, Alan (The Horse) FB | 55-60Bal | 2 | 6' | 218 | Wisconsin | | 264 |
| Armstrong, Neil OE-DB | 47-51Phi 52CFL HC78-81ChiB | 2 | 6'2" | 189 | Oklahoma State | 6 | 66 |
| Austin, Bill OG-T | 49-50NYG 51-52MS 53-57NYG HC66-68Pit HC70Was | | 6'1" | 223 | Oregon State | 1 | |
| Barnes, Larry FB-DE | 57SF 60OakA | 5 | 6'1" | 228 | Colorado State | | 55 |
| Barnett, Tom HB-DB | 59-60Pit | 2 | 5'11" | 190 | Purdue | | 12 |
| Barry, AL OG | 54GB 55-56MS 57GB 58-59NYG 60LA-A | | 6'2" | 230 | Southern Calif. | | |
| Baugh, Sammy QB-TB-DB | 37-52Was HC60-61NY-A HC64HouA | 12 4 | 6'2" | 182 | Texas Christian | 28 | 55 |
| Beatty, Ed C | 55-56SF 57-61Pit 61Was | | 6'3" | 229 | Mississippi | | |
| Beck, Ken DT-DE | 59-60GB | | 6'2" | 245 | Texas A&M | | |
| Bednarik, Chuck LB-C | 49-61Phi | | 6'3" | 233 | Pennsylvania | 20 | 6 |
| Bell, Eddie DB | 55-59Phi 59CFL 60NY-A | | 6'1" | 212 | Pennsylvania | 11 | 6 |
| Bernardi, Frank DB-HB | 55-57ChiC 60DenA | 3 | 5'9" | 181 | Colorado | 4 | 12 |
| Bernet, Ed OE | 55Pit 60DalA | 2 | 6'3" | 203 | S.M.U. | | 6 |
| Bettis, Tom LB | 55-61GB 62Pit 63ChiB HC77KC | | 6'2" | 228 | Purdue | 1 | |
| Bielski, Dick OE-FB | 55-59Phi 60-61Dal 62-63Bal | 2 5 | 6'1" | 224 | Maryland | | 208 |
| Biscaha, Joe OE | 59NYG 60BosA | | 6'1" | 190 | Richmond | | |
| Bishop, Bill DT-OT | 52-60ChiB 61Min | | 6'4" | 248 | North Texas State | 2 | 6 |
| Boll, Don OT-OG | 53-59Was 60NYG | 2 | 6'3" | 203 | S.M.U. | | 6 |
| Borden, Nate DE | 55-59GB 60-61Dal 62BufA | | 6' | 234 | Indiana | | |
| Boydston, Max OE | 55-58ChiC 60-61DalA 62OakA | 2 | 6'2" | 210 | Oklahoma | | 48 |
| Braatz, Tom LB-OE | 57Was 58LA 58-59Was 60Dal | | 6'1" | 216 | Marquette | 2 | |
| Brettschneider, Carl LB | 56-59ChiC 60-63Det | | 6'1" | 223 | Iowa State | 3 | |
| Brewster, Darrell (Pete) OE | 52-58Cle 59-60Pit | 2 | 6'3" | 210 | Purdue | | 126 |
| Brito, Gene DE-OE | 51-53Was 54CFL 55-58Was 59-60LA | 2 | 6'1" | 226 | Loyola Marymount | 1 | 12 |
| Brookshier, Tom DB | 53Phi 54-55MS 56-61Phi | | 6' | 196 | Colorado | 20 | |
| Brown, Ed QB-DB | 54-61ChiB 62-65Pit 65Bal | 12 4 | 6'2" | 209 | San Francisco | | 94 |
| Brown, Hardy LB-DB-FB | 48BknAA 49ChiAA 50Bal 50Was 51-56SF 56ChiC 60DenA | 5 | 6' | 193 | Tulsa | 13 | 43 |
| Brown, Paul | HC46-49CleAA HC50-62Cle HC68-69CinA HC70-75Cin | | | | Miami-Ohio | | |
| Brown, Ray DB-QB | 58-60Bal | 4 | 6'2" | 195 | Mississippi | 13 | |
| Brown, Rosey OT | 53-65NYG | | 6'3" | 249 | Morgan State | | |
| Brubaker, Dick OE-DE | 55,57ChiC 60BufA | 2 | 6' | 202 | Ohio State | | 6 |
| Brueckman, Charlie LB | 58Was 60LA-A | | 6'2" | 223 | Pittsburgh | | |
| Bruney, Fred DB | 53SF 54-55MS 56SF 56-57Pit 58LA 60-62BosA HC85Phi | 3 | 5'10" | 184 | Ohio State | 15 | 6 |
| Bullough, Hank OG-LB | 55GB 56-57MS 58GB HC78NE HC85-86Buf | | 6' | 230 | Michigan State | | |
| Campbell, Dick LB | 58-60Pit | | 6'1" | 227 | Marquette | 3 | |
| Campbell, Marion DT-DE-OT | 54-55SF 56-61Phi HC74-76Atl HC83-85Phi HC87-89Atl | | 6'3" | 250 | Georgia | 3 | |
| Campbell, Stan OG | 52Det 53-54MS 55-58Det 59-61Phi 62OakA | | 6' | 226 | Iowa State | | |
| Carmichael, AL HB | 53-58GB 60-61DenA | 23 | 6'1" | 192 | Southern Calif. | | 84 |
| Carpenter, Ken HB-OE | 50-53Cle 60DenA | 23 | 6' | 195 | Oregon State | 1 | 108 |
| Carpenter, Lew HB-FB-FL-OE-DB | 53-55Det 56MS 57-58Cle 59-63GB | 23 | 6'1" | 209 | Arkansas | | 126 |
| Carson, Johnny OE | 54-59Was 60HouA | 2 | 6'3" | 202 | Georgia | | 90 |
| Cassady, Hopalong HB-FL | 56-61Det 62Cle 62Phi 63Det | 23 | 5'10" | 183 | Ohio State | | 144 |
| Chorovich, Dick OT | 55-56Bal 60LA-A | | 6'4" | 260 | Miami-Ohio | | |
| Christiansen, Jack DB-HB | 51-58Det HC63-67SF | 3 | 6'1" | 190 | Colorado State | 46 | 78 |
| Churchwell, Don OT-DT | 59Was 60OakA | | 6'1" | 253 | Mississippi | | |
| Clarke, Leon OE-FL | 56-59LA 60-62Cle 63Min | 2 | 6'4" | 232 | Southern Calif. | | 114 |
| Clatterbuck, Bobby QB | 54-57NYG 60LA-A | 12 | 6'3" | 195 | Houston | | 6 |
| Collins, Ray DT-OT | 52-53SF 54NYG 55-59CFL 60-61DalA | | 5'11" | 238 | Lousiana State | | |
| Cone, Fred FB-K | 51-57GB 60Dal | 2 5 | 5'11" | 199 | Clemson | | 494 |
| Consright, Bil (Red) C-LB-OE-DE | 37-38ChiB 39-42Cle 43Was 43Bkn 44Cle HC62OakA | | 6'1" | 203 | Oklahoma | 4 | 6 |
| Conner, Clyde OE | 56-63SF | 2 | 6'2" | 193 | U. of Pacific | | 108 |
| Connolly, Ted OG | 54SF 55MS 56-62SF 63Cle | | 6'3" | 240 | Tulsa, Santa Clara | | |
| Cronin, Gene DE-OG-LB | 56-59Det 60Dal 61-62Was | | 6'2" | 229 | U. of Pacific | 1 | |
| Cross, Bob OT-DT | 52ChiB 53MS 54-55LA 56-57SF 58-59ChiC 60BosA | | 6'4" | 248 | Kilgore J.C. | | |
| Crow, Lindon DB | 55-57ChiC 58-60NYG 61-64LA | 3 | 6'1" | 195 | Southern Calif. | 38 | 20 |
| D'Agostino, Frank OG-OT | 56Phi 60NY-A | | 6'1" | 245 | Auburn | | |
| Davis, Milt DB | 57-60Bal | | 6'1" | 188 | U.C.L.A. | 27 | 18 |
| DeCarlo, Art DB-OE | 53Pit 54-55MS 56-57Was 57-60Bal | | 6'2" | 196 | Georgia | 7 | |
| Derby, Dean DB-HB | 57-61Pit 61-62Min | | 6' | 187 | Washington | 21 | 21 |
| Dimmick, Tom C-OT-LB | 56Phi 60DalA | | 6'6" | 253 | Houston | | |
| Dittrich, John OG | 56ChiC 57-58MS 59GB 60DalA 61BufA | | 6'1" | 236 | Wisconsin | | |
| Dooley, Jim OE-FL-HB-DB | 52-54ChiB 55MS 56-57ChiB 58BN 59-62ChiB HC68-71ChiB | 2 | 6'4" | 198 | Miami (Fla.) | 5 | 96 |
| Doran, Jim OE-DE | 51-59Det 60-61Dal | 2 | 6'2" | 201 | Iowa State | 1 | 150 |
| Dorow, Al QB | 54-56Was 57Phi 58-59CFL 60-61NY-A 62BufA | 12 | 6' | 193 | Michigan State | | 96 |
| Doyle, Dick DB | 55Pit 60DenA | | 6' | 193 | Ohio State | 2 | |
| Drulis, Chuck LB-OG | 42ChiB 43-44MS 45-49ChiB 50GB HC61StL | | 5'10" | 216 | Temple | 4 | |
| Dublinski, Tom QB | 52-54Det 56-57CFL 58NYG 60DenA | 12 | 6'2" | 197 | Utah | | 6 |
| Dupre, L.G. (Long Gone) HB | 55-59Bal 60-61Dal | 2 4 | 5'11" | 190 | Baylor | | 108 |
| Fears, Tom OE-DB | 48-56LA HC67-70NO | 2 5 | 6'2" | 213 | U.C.L.A. | 2 | 249 |
| Felton, Ralph LB-FB | 54-60Was 61-62BufA | 5 | 5'11" | 210 | Maryland | 7 | 19 |
| Ferguson, Howie FB | 53-58GB 60LA-A | 2 | 6'2" | 214 | none | | 78 |
| Filchock, Frankie TB-QB-DB-HB | 38Pit 38-41Was 42-43MS 44-45Was 46NYG 47-49DE 50Bal HC60-61DenA | 12 | 5'11" | 193 | Indiana | 1 | 18 |
| Fry, Bob OT-OG | 53LA 54-55MS 56-59LA 60-64Dal | | 6'4" | 235 | Kentucky | | |
| Fuller, Frank DT-OG-C-DE | 53,55,57-58LA 59ChiC 60-62StL 63Phi | | 6'4" | 244 | Kentucky | | 2 |
| Gain, Bob DT-DE-OT-LB | 52Cle 53MS 54-64Cle | | 6'3" | 256 | Kentucky | 1 | 9 |
| George, Bill LB-OG-DT | 52-65ChiB 66LA | 5 | 6'2" | 237 | Wake Forest | 18 | 26 |
| Gibron, Abe OG-DG | 49BufAA 50-56Cle 56-57Phi 58-59ChiB HC72-74ChiB | | 5'11" | 243 | Purdue | | |
| Gifford, Frank HB-FL-DB | 52-60NYG 61VR 62-64NYG | 123 5 | 6'1" | 197 | Southern Calif. | 1 | 484 |
| Gilmer, Harry QB-HB-DB | 48-52Was 53JJ 54Was 55-56Det HC65-66Det | 12 | 6' | 169 | Alabama | 5 | 12 |
| Glick, Gary DB-HB | 56-59Pit 59-61Was 61Bal 63SD-A | 5 | 6'2" | 195 | Colorado State | 14 | 65 |
| Gob, Art DE | 59-60Was 60LA-A | | 6'4" | 230 | Pittsburgh | | 2 |
| Gordon, Bobby DB | 58ChiC 60HouA | 4 | 6' | 195 | Tennessee | 5 | |
| Graham, Otto QB-DB | 46-49CleAA 50-55Cle HC66-68Was 45-46played in N.B.L. | 12 | 6'1" | 196 | Northwestern | 7 | 276 |
| Grant, Bud OE-DE | 51-52Phi 53CFL HC67-83,85Min 49-51 played in N.B.A. | 2 | 6'3" | 199 | Minnesota | | 42 |
| Griffin, Bob LB-C | 53-57LA 61DenA 61StL | | 6'3" | 235 | Arkansas | 1 | 2 |
| Groza, Lou (The Toe) OT-DT-K | 46-49CleAA 50-59Cle 60VR 61-67Cle | 5 | 6'3" | 240 | Ohio State | | 1608 |
| Guy, Buzz OG-DT-OT | 58-59NYG 60Dal 61HouA 61DenA | | 6'3" | 248 | Duke | | |
| Halas, George OE-DE | PC20Dec PC21-28ChiB HC29,33-42ChiB 43-45MS HC46-55, 58-67ChiB | | 6' | 175 | Illinois | | 68 |
| Hanner, Dave (Hawg) DT | 52-64GB | | 6'2" | 257 | Arkansas | 4 | 2 |

| Use Name (Nickname) - Positions | Team by Year | See Section | Hgt. | Wgt. | College | Int | Pts |
|---|---|---|---|---|---|---|---|
| Hansen, Wayne LB-C-OG-OT-DT | 50-58ChiB 60Dal | | 6'2" | 231 | Texas-El Paso | 6 | 6 |
| Harris, Jimmie DB | 57Phi 58LA 60DalA 61Dal | | 6'1" | 178 | Oklahoma | 11 | 6 |
| Hatley, John OG-DT | 53ChiB 54-55ChiC 60DenA | | 6'3" | 249 | Sul Ross State | | |
| Hauser, Art DT-OG | 54-57LA 59ChiC 59NYG 60BosA 61DenA | | 6' | 237 | Xavier-Ohio | | 6 |
| Hecker, Norb DB-OE | 51-53LA 54CFL 55-57Was HC66-68Atl | | 6'2" | 193 | Baldwin-Wallace | 28 | 20 |
| Heinrich, Don QB | 54-59NYG 60Dal 62OakA | 12 | 6' | 182 | Washington | | 30 |
| Helluin, Jerry DT | 52-53Cle 54-57GB 60HouA | | 6'2" | 272 | Tulane | 1 | 6 |
| Henke, Ed DE-LB-OG-DG-OT-DT | 49LA-AA 51-52SF 53-54MS 55CFL 56-60SF 61-63StL | | 6'3" | 227 | Southern Calif. | | |
| Herchman, Bill DT | 56-59SF 60-61Dal 62HouA | | 6'2" | 246 | Texas Tech | 1 | 6 |
| Hickey, Red OE-DE | 41Cle 42-44MS 45Cle 46-48LA HC59-63SF | 2 | 6'2" | 204 | Arkansas | | 96 |
| Hill, Harlon OE-DB | 54-61ChiB 62Pit 62Det | 2 | 6'3" | 199 | Florence State | 3 | 240 |
| Holovak, Mike FB-LB | 46LA 47-48ChiB HC61-68BosA | 2 | 6'1" | 213 | Boston College | 1 | 36 |
| Howell, Jim Lee OE-DE | 37-42NYG 43-45MS 46-48NYG HC54-60NYG | 2 | 6'6" | 210 | Arkansas | | 42 |
| Howton, Billy OE | 52-58GB 59Cle 60-63Dal | 2 | 6'2" | 191 | Rice | | 366 |
| Hudson, Bob LB-DB-OE | 51-52NYG 53-55Phi 56VR 57-58Phi 59Was 60DalA 60-61DenA | | 6'4" | 225 | Clemson | 19 | |
| Hughes, Ed DB | 54-55LA 56-58NYG HC71Hou | | 6'1" | 184 | N. Carolina State, Tulsa | 3 | |
| Ivy, Pop DE-OE | 40Pit 40-42ChiC 43-44MS 45-47ChiC HC58-59ChiC HC60-61StL HC62-63HouA | 2 | 6'3" | 208 | Oklahoma | 3 | 20 |
| Jackson, Charlie DB | 58ChiC 60DalA | | 5'11" | 180 | S.M.U. | 1 | |
| Jessup, Bill OE-FL | 51-52SF 53MS 54SF 55HJ 56-58SF 60DenA | 2 4 | 6'1" | 195 | Southern Calif. | | 42 |
| Johnson, Bill C-LB | 48-49SF-AA 50-56SF HC76-78Cin | | 6'3" | 228 | Tyler J.C. | 2 | 6 |
| Johnson, Harvey LB-BB-FB-G | 46-49NY-AA 51NYY HC68BufA HC71Buf | 5 | 5'11" | 212 | William & Mary | 1 | 262 |
| Johnson, Jack DB | 57-59ChiB 60-61BufA 61DalA | 4 | 6'3" | 198 | Miami (Fla.) | 8 | |
| Johnson, Joe HB-DE-FL | 54-58GB 60-61BosA | 2 | 6' | 185 | Boston College | | 48 |
| Jones, Jim DB-FB | 58LA 61OakA | | 6'1" | 204 | Washington | | |
| Joyce, Don DE-DT | 51-53ChiC 54-60Bal 61Min 62DenA | | 6'3" | 253 | Tulane | 1 | |
| Karilivacz, Carl DB | 53-57Det 58NYG 59-60LA | | 6' | 188 | Syracuse | 13 | 12 |
| Kinard, Billy DB-HB | 56Cle 57-58GB 60BufA | | 6' | 189 | Mississippi | 4 | 6 |
| King, Don OT-DT | 54Cle 55CFL 56Phi 56GB 60DenA | | 6'3" | 260 | Kentucky | 2 | |
| Knafelc, Gary OE | 54ChiC 54-62GB 63SF | 2 | 6'4" | 217 | Colorado | | 138 |
| Konovsky, Bob OG-DE-OT | 56-58ChiC 60ChiB 61DenA | | 6'2" | 246 | Wisconsin | | |
| Krouse, Ray DT-DE-OT | 51-55NYG 56-57Det 58-59Bal 60Was | | 6'3" | 263 | Maryland | | |
| Krutko, Larry FB | 58-60Pit | 2 | 6' | 220 | West Virginia | | 24 |
| Kuchta, Frank C-LB | 58-59Was 60DenA | | 6'2" | 225 | Notre Dame | | |
| Kuharich, Joe G-LB | 40-41ChiC 42-44MS 45ChiC HC52ChiC HC54-58Was HC64-68Phi | 5 | 5'11" | 195 | Notre Dame | 1 | 12 |
| Landry, Tom DB-HB-QB | 49NY-AA 50-55NYG HC60-88Dal | 12 4 | 6'1" | 191 | Texas | 32 | 36 |
| Lane, Night Train DB-OE | 52-53LA 54-59ChiC 60-65Det | | 6'1" | 194 | Western Neb. C.C. | 68 | 50 |
| Lansford, Buck OG-OT | 55-57Pit 58-60LA | | 6'2" | 232 | Texas | | |
| Larson, Paul QB | 57ChiC 60OakA | | 5'11" | 183 | California | | |
| Lary, Yale DB-K | 52-53Det 54-55MS 56-64Det | 34 | 6' | 187 | Texas A&M | 50 | 36 |
| Layne, Bobby QB | 48ChiB 49NYB 50-58Det 58-62Pit | 12 5 | 6'1" | 201 | Texas | | 372 |
| LeBaron, Eddie QB | 52-53Was 54CFL 55-59Was 60-63Dal | 12 4 | 5'9" | 166 | U. of Pacific | | 60 |
| Lewis, Woodley DB-OE-HB | 50-55LA 56-59ChiC 60Dal | 23 | 6' | 193 | Oregon | 26 | 108 |
| Lipscomb, Big Daddy DT-DE | 53-55LA 56-60Bal 61-62Pit died May 10, 1963 | | 6'6" | 284 | none | 1 | 2 |
| Long, Bob LB-DE | 55-59Det 60-61LA 62Dal | | 6'3" | 232 | U.C.L.A. | 7 | 2 |
| Macon, Eddie HB-DB | 52-53ChiB 54-59CFL 60OakA | 2 | 6' | 177 | U. of Pacific | 9 | 36 |
| Mains, Gil DT-DE | 54-61Det | | 6'2" | 243 | Murray State | | |
| Mangum, Pete LB | 54NYG 60DenA | | 6' | 219 | Mississippi | | |
| Marchetti, Gino DE-DT-OT | 52Dal 53-64Bal 65VR 66Bal | | 6'4" | 244 | San Francisco | 1 | 20 |
| Marchibroda, Ted QB | 54-56Pit 57ChiC HC75-79Bal HC93-95Ind | 12 | 5'10" | 178 | St. Boneventure, Detroit | | 18 |
| Martin, Jim LB-OG-DE-OT-K | 50Cle 51-61Det 62VR 63Bal 64Was | 5 | 6'2" | 227 | Notre Dame | 6 | 434 |
| Mathews, Ray HB-OE-FL-DB | 51-59Pit 60Dal | 123 | 6' | 190 | Clemson | 2 | 261 |
| Matson, Ollie HB-FB-DB-FL | 52ChiC 53MS 54-58ChiC 59-62LA 63Det 64-66Phi | 23 | 6'2" | 210 | San Francisco | 3 | 438 |
| Matuszak, Marv LB-OG | 53Pit 54MS 55-56Pit 57-58SF 58GB 59-61Bal 62-63BufA 64DenA | | 6'3" | 232 | Tulsa | 14 | |
| McCabe, Richie DB | 55Pit 56MS 57-58Pit 59Was 60-61BufA | | 6'1" | 185 | Pittsburgh | 9 | 6 |
| McCafferty, Don OE-DE | 46NYG HC70-72Bal HC73Det | | 6'4" | 220 | Ohio State | | 6 |
| McClairen, Jack OE | 55-60Pit | 2 | 6'4" | 213 | Bethune-Cookman | | 18 |
| McClung, Willie OT-DT | 55-57Pit 58-59Cle 60-61Det | | 6'2" | 250 | Florida A&M | | |
| McCormack, Mike OT-DG-DT | 51NYY 52-53MS 54-62Cle HC73-75Phi HC80-81Bal HC82Sea | | 6'4" | 246 | Kansas | 1 | |
| McElhenny, Hugh (The King) HB | 52-60SF 61-62Min 63NYG 64Det | 23 | 6'1" | 197 | Washington | | 360 |
| McHan, Lamar QB | 54-58ChiC 59-60GB 61-63Bal 63SF 64CFL | 12 | 6'1" | 201 | Arkansas | | 72 |
| McInhenny, Don HB | 56Det 57-59GB 60-61Dal 61SF | 23 | 6' | 197 | S.M.U. | | 84 |
| McPeak, Bill DE | 49-57Pit HC61-65Was | | 6'1" | 206 | Pittsburgh | | 6 |
| Meilinger, Steve OE | 56-57Was 58GB 59BA 60GB 61Pit 61StL | 2 | 6'2" | 227 | Kentucky | | 48 |
| Michaels, Walt LB | 51GB 52-61Cle 63NY-A HC77-82NYJ | | 6' | 231 | Washington & Lee | 11 | 12 |
| Middleton, Dave OE-HB-FL | 55-60Det 61Min | 2 | 6'1" | 194 | Auburn | | |
| Miller, Johnny OT-DT-DE | 56Was 57MS 58-59Was 60GB | | 6'5" | 253 | Boston College | | 2 |
| Miller, Paul DE-C | 54-57LA 60-61DalA 62SD-A | | 6'2" | 226 | Louisiana State | 1 | |
| Modzelewski, Dick (Little Mo) DT | 53-54Was 55Pit 56-63NYG 64-66Cle HC77Cle | | 6' | 258 | Maryland | | 4 |
| Moegle, Dick DB-HB | 55-59SF 60Pit 61Dal | 2 | 6' | 190 | Rice | 28 | 42 |
| Morris, Jack DB | 58-60LA 60Pit 61Min | 5 | 6' | 189 | Oregon | 8 | 30 |
| Mutscheller, Jim OE-DE | 64-61Bal | 2 | 6'1" | 213 | Notre Dame | | 240 |
| Myhra, Steve OG-LB-K | 57-61Bal | 5 | 6'1" | 237 | North Dakota | | 312 |
| Nagler, Gern OE | 53ChiC 54MS 55-58ChiC 59Pit 60-61Cle | 2 | 6'2" | 190 | Santa Clara | | 168 |
| Nix, Doyle DB | 55GB 56-57MS 58-59Was 60LA-A 61DalA | | 6'1" | 191 | S.M.U. | 16 | 6 |
| Nixon (born Nicksick), Mike DB-HB-WB | 35Pit 42Bkn HC59-61Was HC65Pit | | 5'11" | 181 | Pittsburgh | 23 | 2 |
| Nolan, Dick DB | 54-57NYG 58ChiC 59-61NYG 62Dal HC68-75SF HC78-80NO | | 6'1" | 185 | Maryland | 23 | 2 |
| Noll, Chuck LB-OG-C | 53-59Cle HC69-91Pit | | 6'1" | 218 | Dayton | 8 | 14 |
| North, John OE-DB | 48-49BalAA 50Bal HC73-75NO | 2 | 6'2" | 199 | Vanderbilt | 1 | 36 |
| Norton, Jerry DB-HB | 54-58Phi 59ChiC 60-61StL 62Dal 63-64GB | 234 | 5'11" | 195 | S.M.U. | 35 | 42 |
| Nutter, Buzz C-LB | 54-60Bal 61-64Pit 65Bal | | 6'4" | 230 | Virginia Tech | | |
| O'Connell, Tom QB | 53ChiB 54-55MS 56-57Cle 60-61BufA | 12 | 5'11" | 187 | Illinois | | 26 |
| Olszewski, Johnny (Johnny O) FB-HB | 53-57ChiC 58-60Was 61Det 62DenA | 2 | 5'" | 200 | California | | 114 |
| O'Neil, Bob OG-DE | 56-57Pit 61NY-A | | 6'1" | 229 | Notre Dame | | |
| Palumbo, Sam LB-C | 55-56Cle 57GB 60BufA | | 6'2" | 226 | Notre Dame | 1 | |
| Panfil, Ken OT-DT | 56-58LA 59ChiC 60-62StL | | 6'6" | 262 | Purdue | | |
| Parker, Buddy BB-LB-FB-DB | 35-36Det 37-43ChiC HC49ChiC HC51-56Det HC57-64Pit | 2 | 6' | 193 | Centenary | 2 | 28 |
| Patera, Jack LB-OG | 55-57Bal 58-59ChiC 60-61Dal HC76-82Sea | | 6'1" | 234 | Oregon | 6 | |

# Pre-1960 Players & Coaches

(Who overlap into the Modern Era)

| Use Name (Nickname) - Positions | Team by Year | See Section | Hgt. | Wgt. | College | Int | Pts |
|---|---|---|---|---|---|---|---|
| Pellington, Bill LB-OG | 53-64Bal | | 6'2" | 234 | Rutgers | 21 | 6 |
| Perry, Jerry DT-DE-OT-OG | 54Det 55MS 56-59Det 60-62StL | 5 | 6'4" | 237 | California | | 190 |
| Perry, Joe FB-DB | 48-49SF-AA 50-60SF 61-62Bal 63SF | 23 | 6' | 203 | Compton J.C. | 1 | 513 |
| Peters, Volney DT-PT-DE | 62-63ChiC 54-57Was 58Phi 60LA-A 61OakA | | 6'4" | 237 | Southern Calif. | | 6 |
| Pitts, Hugh LB | 56LA 60HouA | | 6'2" | 223 | Texas Christian | 3 | |
| Podoley, Jim HB-OE | 57-60Was 61JJ | 2 | 6'2" | 200 | Central Michigan | | 78 |
| Powell, Charley DE-LB-OE | 52-53SF 54MS 55-57SF 58-59 retired for pro boxing career 60-61OakA | | 6'2" | 226 | none | | 2 |
| Pricer, Billy FB | 57-60Bal 61DalA | 2 | 5'10" | 208 | Oklahoma | | 18 |
| Putnam, Duane OG-LB | 52-59LA 60Dal 61Cle 62LA | | 6' | 228 | U. of Pacific | | |
| Ramsey, Buster OG-LB | 46-51ChiC HC60-61BufA | | 6'1" | 219 | William & Mary | 7 | 2 |
| Rauch, Johnny QB-DB | 49NYB 50-51NYY 51Phi HC66-68OakA HC69BufA HC69-70Buf | 1 | 6' | 197 | Georgia | 2 | 6 |
| Rechichar, Bert DB-LB-HB-OE-K | 52Cle 53-59Bal 60Pit 61NY-A | 345 | 6'1" | 209 | Tennessee | 31 | 179 |
| Renfro, Ray FL-HB | 52-63Cle | 23 | 6'1" | 190 | North Texas | | 330 |
| Renfro, Will DT-DE-OT | 57-59Was 60Pit 61Phi | | 6'5" | 233 | Memphis State | | |
| Reynolds, Billy HB | 53-54Cle 55-56MS 57Cle 58Pit 60OakA | 23 | 5'10" | 195 | Pittsburgh | | 42 |
| Richardson, Jess DT | 53-56Pit 57JJ 58-61Phi 62-64BosA | | 6'2" | 261 | Alabama | 1 | |
| Richter, Les LB | 54-62LA | 5 | 6'3" | 238 | California | 16 | 193 |
| Riley, Lee DB | 55Det 56,58-59Phi 60NYG 61-62NY-A | 3 | 6'1" | 192 | Detroit | 23 | |
| Robustelli, Andy DE | 51-55LA 56-64NYG | | 6'1" | 230 | Arnold | 2 | 32 |
| Romine, Al DB-HB | 55,58GB 60DenA 61BosA | | 6'2" | 191 | North Alabama | 4 | |
| Rote, Kyle OE-HB | 51-61NYG | 2 | 6' | 199 | S.M.U. | | 312 |
| Rote, Tobin QB | 50-56GB 57-59Det 60-62CFL 64SD-A 66DenA | 12 | 6'3" | 211 | Rice | | 228 |
| Rush, Clive OE | 53FGB HC69BosA HC70Bos | 2 4 | 6'2" | 197 | Miami-Ohio | | |
| Rymkus, Lou OT-DT | 43Was 44-45MS 46-49CleAA 50-51Cle HC60HouA | | 6'4" | 231 | Notre Dame | 1 | 12 |
| Saban, Lou LB-FB | 46-49CleAA HC60-61BosA HC62-65BufA HC67-69DenA HC70-71Den HC72-76Buf | 5 | 6' | 202 | Indiana | 13 | 27 |
| St. Clair, Bob OT | 53-63SF 64FJ | | 6'9" | 263 | Tulsa, San Francisco | | |
| Schmidt, Joe LB | 53-65Det HC67-72Det | | 6'1" | 220 | Pittsburgh | 24 | 18 |
| Schnelker, Bob OE | 53Phi 64-60NYG 61Min 61Pit | 2 | 6'3" | 214 | Bowling Green | | 204 |
| Schrader, Jim C-OT | 54Was 55MS 56-61Was 62-64Phi | | 6'2" | 244 | Notre Dame | | |
| Scott, Tom DB-DE | 53-58Phi 59-64NYG | | 6'2" | 219 | Virginia | 8 | 18 |
| Scudero, Scooter DB-HB | 54-58Was 60Pit | 23 | 5'10" | 173 | San Francisco | 10 | 18 |
| Sears. Jimmy HB-DB | 54ChiC 55-56MS 57-58ChiC 60LA-A 61DenA | 23 | 5'11" | 183 | Southern Calif. | 2 | 18 |
| Sewell, Harley OG-LB | 53-62Det 63LA | | 6'1" | 230 | Texas | 1 | 6 |
| Shaw, Buck | HC46-49SF-AA HC50-54SF HC58-60Phi | | | | Notre Dame | | |
| Sherman, Allie QB-DB | 43P-P 44-47Phi HC61-68NYG | 12 | 5'11" | 170 | Brooklyn | 2 | 24 |
| Sherman, Will DB-HB | 52Dal 54-60LA 61Min | | 6'2" | 197 | St. Mary's | 29 | 24 |
| Shula, Don DB-HB | 51-52Cle 53-56Bal 57Was HC63-69Bal HC70-95Mia | | 5'11" | 190 | John Carroll | 21 | |
| Simerson, John C-OT | 57-58Phi 58Pit 60HouA 61BosA | | 6'3" | 257 | Purdue | | |
| Skorich, Nick G-LB | 46-48Pit HC61-63Phi HC71-74Cle | | 5'9" | 197 | Cincinnati | | |
| Spencer, Ollie OT-OG-C | 53Det 54-55MS 56Det 57-58GB 59-61Det 63OakA | | 6'2" | 245 | Kansas | | |

| Use Name (Nickname) - Positions | Team by Year | See Section | Hgt. | Wgt. | College | Int | Pts |
|---|---|---|---|---|---|---|---|
| Spinney, Art OG-DE-OE | 50Bal 51-52MS 53-60Bal | | 6' | 230 | Boston College | | |
| Stanfel, Dick OG | 52-55Det 56-58Was HC80NO | | 6'2" | 236 | San Francisco | | |
| Stits, Bill DB-HB | 54-56Det 57-58SF 59Was 59-61NYG | 23 | 6' | 194 | U.C.L.A. | 15 | 6 |
| Striegel, Bill OG-OT-LB | 59Phi 60BosA 60OakA | | 6'2" | 235 | U. of Pacific | | |
| Stroud, Jack OG-OT | 53-64NYG | | 6'1" | 235 | Tennessee | | |
| Sugar, Leo DE | 54-59ChiC 60StL 61Phi 62Det | | 6'1" | 214 | Purdue | 1 | 18 |
| Summerall, Pat DE-OE-K | 52Det 53-57ChiC 58-61NYG | 5 | 6'4" | 228 | Arkansas | | 563 |
| Sumner, Charlie DB | 55ChiB 56-57MS 58-60ChiB 61-62Min | | 6'1" | 194 | William & Mary | 21 | 6 |
| Sutherin, Don DB | 59NYG 59-60Pit | | 5'10" | 193 | Ohio State | 1 | |
| Sutton, Ed HB-DB | 57-59Was 60NYG | 2 | 6'1" | 205 | North Carolina | 1 | 60 |
| Svare, Harland (Swede) LB-OT | 53-54LA 55-60NYG HC62-65LA HC71-73SD | | 6' | 214 | Washington State | 9 | 6 |
| Taseff, Carl DB-HB | 51Cle 52MS 53-61Bal 61Phi 62BufA | 23 | 5'11" | 192 | John Carroll | 20 | 48 |
| Taylor, Hugh (Bones) OE | 47-54Was HC65HouA | 2 | 6'4" | 194 | Oklahoma City | | 348 |
| Temp, Jim DE | 58-60GB | | 6'4" | 245 | Wisconsin | 1 | |
| Thomas, Jessee DB | 55-57Bal 60LA-A | | 5'10" | 180 | Michigan State | 4 | 6 |
| Tittle, Y.A. (Ya-Ya, The Bald Eagle) QB | 48-49BalAA 50Bal 51-60SF 61-64NYG | 12 | 6' | 192 | Louisiana State | | 234 |
| Toneff, Bob DT-DG-DE-OT-OG | 52SF 53MS 54-58SF 59-64Was | | 6'2" | 260 | Notre Dame | 2 | |
| Triplett, Mel FB | 55-60NYG 61-62Min | 2 | 6'1" | 215 | Toledo | | 108 |
| Tunnell, Em (Emlen the Gremlin) DB-HB | 48-58NYG 59-61GB | 3 | 6'1" | 193 | Iowa | 79 | 60 |
| Turner, Bulldog C-LB-OG-OT-HB | 40-52ChiB HC62NY-A | | 6'1" | 237 | Hardion-Simmons | 16 | 24 |
| Van Brocklin, Norm (The Dutchman) QB | 49-57LA 58-60Phi HC61-66Min HC68-74Atl | 12 4 | 6'1" | 199 | Oregon | | 66 |
| Waller, Ron HB | 55-58LA 59KJ 60LA-A HC73SD | 23 | 5'11" | 180 | Maryland | | 54 |
| Wallner, Fred LB-OG | 51-52ChiC 53MS 54-55ChiC 60HouA | | 6'2" | 231 | Notre Dame | 3 | |
| Walston, Bobby OE-FL-HB-K | 51-62Phi | 2 5 | 6' | 190 | Georgia | | 881 |
| Waterfield, Bob QB-DB | 45Cle 46-52LA HC60-62LA | 12 45 | 6'1" | 196 | U.C.L.A. | 20 | 573 |
| Weatherall, Jim DT-OT | 55-57Phi 58Was 59-60Det | | 6'4" | 245 | Oklahoma | | |
| Weber, Chuck LB-DE-OG | 55-56Cle 56-58ChiC 59-61Phi | | 6'1" | 229 | West Chester | 10 | 6 |
| Webster, Alex (Big Red) HB-FB | 55-64NYG HC69-73NYG | 2 | 6'3" | 218 | N. Carolina State | | 336 |
| Wegert, Ted HB | 55-56Phi 60NY-A 60DenA 60BufA | 2 | 5'11" | 202 | none | | 30 |
| Wells, Billy HB | 54Was 55MS 56-57Was 57Pit 58Phi 60BosA | 23 | 5'9" | 176 | Michigan State | | 54 |
| Wietecha, Ray C-LB | 53-62NYG | | 6'1" | 225 | Northwestern | 1 | |
| Wilkins, Roy LB-DE | 58-59LA 60-61Was | | 6'3" | 224 | Georgia | | |
| Williams, Fred DT-OG | 52-63ChiB 64-65Was | | 6'4" | 249 | Arkansas | 2 | |
| Williams, Jerry HB-DB | 49-52LA 53-54Phi HC69-71Phi | 23 | 5'10" | 175 | Washington State | 15 | 108 |
| Wilson, Billy OE-FL | 51-60SF | 2 | 6'3" | 191 | San Jose State | | 294 |
| Wilson, George OE-DE | 37-46ChiB HC57-64Det 39-40 played in N.B.L. HC66-69MiaA | 2 | 6'1" | 199 | Northwestern | 3 | 108 |
| Wilson, Jerry LB-DE | 59-60Phi 60SF | | 6'3" | 238 | Auburn | | |
| Wilson, Tom (Touchdown Tommy) HB-FB | 56-61LA 62Cle 63Min | 23 | 6' | 203 | none | | 144 |
| Womble, Roye HB-FL | 54-57Bal 60LA-A | 2 | 6' | 185 | North Texas State | | 54 |
| Wren, Junior DB | 56-59Cle 60Pit 61NY-A | 4 | 6' | 192 | Missouri | 14 | 8 |
| Youngelman, Sid DT-DE | 55SF 56-58Phi 59Cle 60-61NY-A 62-63BufA | | 6'3" | 257 | Alabama | | |
| Zucco, Vic DB | 57-60ChiB | 3 | 6' | 187 | Michigan State | 8 | 6 |

Lifetime Statistics- Players from Pre-1960 Section 1 — **PASSING**

(All men with 25 or more passing attempts)

| Name | Years | Att. | Comp. | Comp. Pct. | Yards | Yds./ Att. | TD | Int. | Pct. Int. |
|---|---|---|---|---|---|---|---|---|---|
| Sammy Baugh | 37-52 | 2995 | 1693 | 56.5 | 21886 | 7.3 | 188 | 203 | 6.8 |
| Ed Brown | 54-65 | 1987 | 949 | 47.8 | 15600 | 7.9 | 102 | 138 | 6.9 |
| Bobby Clatterbuck | 54-57,60 | 149 | 77 | 51.7 | 1032 | 6.9 | 8 | 9 | 6.0 |
| Al Dorow | 54-57,60-62 | 1207 | 572 | 47.4 | 7708 | 6.4 | 64 | 93 | 7.7 |
| Tom Dublinski | 52-54,58,60 | 177 | 93 | 52.5 | 1300 | 7.3 | 8 | 13 | 7.3 |
| Frankie Filchock | 38-41,44-46,50 | 677 | 342 | 50.5 | 4921 | 7.3 | 47 | 79 | 11.7 |
| Frank Gifford | 52-60,62-64 | 63 | 29 | 46.0 | 823 | 13.1 | 14 | 6 | 9.5 |
| Harry Gilmer | 48-52,54-56 | 579 | 263 | 45.4 | 3786 | 6.5 | 23 | 45 | 7.8 |
| Otto Graham | 46-55 | 2626 | 1464 | 55.8 | 23584 | 9.0 | 174 | 135 | 5.1 |
| Don Heinrich | 54-60,62 | 406 | 164 | 40.4 | 2287 | 5.6 | 17 | 23 | 5.7 |
| Tom Landry | 49-55 | 47 | 11 | 23.4 | 172 | 3.7 | 1 | 7 | 14.9 |
| Bobby Layne | 48-62 | 3700 | 1814 | 49.0 | 26768 | 7.2 | 196 | 243 | 6.6 |
| Eddie LeBaron | 52-53,55-63 | 1796 | 897 | 49.9 | 13399 | 7.5 | 104 | 141 | 7.9 |
| Ted Marchibroda | 54-57 | 385 | 172 | 44.7 | 2169 | 5.6 | 16 | 29 | 7.5 |
| Ray Mathews | 51-60 | 51 | 19 | 37.3 | 350 | 6.9 | 2 | 2 | 3.9 |
| Lamar McHan | 54-64 | 1351 | 610 | 45.2 | 9449 | 7.0 | 72 | 108 | 8.0 |
| Tom O'Connell | 53,56-57,60-61 | 423 | 204 | 48.2 | 3261 | 7.7 | 21 | 34 | 8.0 |
| Johnny Rauch | 49-51 | 170 | 70 | 41.2 | 959 | 5.6 | 8 | 9 | 5.3 |
| Tobin Rote | 50-50,63-64,66 | 2907 | 1329 | 45.7 | 18850 | 6.5 | 148 | 191 | 6.6 |
| Allie Sherman | 43-47 | 135 | 66 | 48.9 | 823 | 6.1 | 9 | 9 | 6.7 |
| Y.A. Tittle | 48-64 | 4395 | 2427 | 55.2 | 33070 | 7.5 | 242 | 248 | 5.6 |
| Norm Van Brocklin | 49-60 | 2895 | 1553 | 53.6 | 23611 | 8.2 | 173 | 178 | 6.1 |
| Bob Waterfield | 45-52 | 1617 | 813 | 50.3 | 11849 | 7.3 | 98 | 127 | 7.9 |

Lifetime Statistics- Players from Pre-1960 Section 2 - **RUSHING and RECEIVING**

(All men with 25 or more rushing attempts or 10 or more receptions)

| | | RUSHING | | | | RECEIVING | | | |
|---|---|---|---|---|---|---|---|---|---|
| Name | Years | Att. | Yards | Avg. | TD | Rec. | Yards | Avg. | TD |
| Alan Ameche | 55-60 | 964 | 4045 | 4.2 | 40 | 101 | 733 | 7.3 | 4 |
| Tom Barnett | 59-60 | 81 | 263 | 3.2 | 1 | 7 | 52 | 7.4 | 1 |
| Sammy Baugh | 37-52 | 318 | 324 | 1.0 | 9 | 1 | 0 | 0.0 | 0 |
| Ed Bernet | 55-60 | | | | | 26 | 325 | 12.5 | 1 |
| Dick Bielski | 55-63 | 80 | 229 | 2.9 | 2 | 107 | 1305 | 12.2 | 10 |
| Max Boydston | 55-58,60-62 | | | | | 97 | 1328 | 13.7 | 8 |
| Darrell Brewster | 52-60 | | | | | 210 | 3758 | 17.9 | 21 |
| Gene Brito | 51-53,55-60 | | | | | 47 | 618 | 13.1 | 2 |
| Ed Brown | 54-65 | 265 | 920 | 3.6 | 14 | | | | |
| Dick Brubaker | 55,57,60 | | | | | 13 | 200 | 15.4 | 1 |
| Al Carmichael | 53-58,60-61 | 222 | 947 | 4.3 | 4 | 112 | 1633 | 14.6 | 8 |
| Ken Carpenter | 50-53,60 | 242 | 1199 | 5.0 | 11 | 71 | 823 | 11.6 | 6 |
| Lew Carpenter | 53-55,57-63 | 468 | 2025 | 4.3 | 16 | 87 | 782 | 9.0 | 4 |
| Johnny Carson | 54-60 | | | | | 173 | 2591 | 15.0 | 15 |
| Hopalong Cassady | 56-63 | 316 | 1229 | 3.9 | 6 | 111 | 1601 | 14.4 | 18 |
| Leon Clarke | 56-63 | 1 | -4 | -4.0 | 0 | 141 | 2215 | 15.7 | 18 |
| Bobby Clatterbuck | 54-57,60 | 29 | -27 | -0.9 | 1 | | | | |
| Fred Cone | 51-57,60 | 347 | 1156 | 3.3 | 12 | 75 | 852 | 11.4 | 4 |
| Clyde Connor | 56-63 | | | | | 203 | 2643 | 13.0 | 18 |
| Jim Dooley | 52-54,56-57,59-62 | 1 | 0 | 0.0 | 0 | 211 | 3172 | 15.0 | 16 |
| Jim Doran | 51-61 | 3 | 57 | 19.7 | 0 | 212 | 3667 | 17.3 | 24 |
| Al Dorow | 54-57,60-62 | 284 | 864 | 3.1 | 16 | | | | |
| Tom Dublinski | 52-54,58,60 | 28 | 118 | 4.2 | 1 | | | | |
| L.G. Dupre | 55-61 | 476 | 1761 | 3.7 | 11 | 104 | 1131 | 10.9 | 7 |
| Tom Fears | 48-56 | 5 | 15 | 3.0 | 0 | 400 | 5397 | 13.5 | 38 |
| Howie Ferguson | 53-58,60 | 670 | 2558 | 3.8 | 10 | 148 | 1247 | 8.4 | 3 |
| Frankie Filchock | 38-41,44-46,50 | 477 | 1478 | 3.1 | 6 | 8 | 88 | 11.0 | 0 |
| Frank Gifford | 52-60,62-64 | 840 | 3609 | 4.3 | 34 | 367 | 5434 | 14.8 | 43 |
| Harry Gilmer | 48-52,54-56 | 201 | 923 | 4.6 | 1 | 20 | 220 | 11.0 | 1 |
| Otto Graham | 46-55 | 405 | 882 | 2.2 | 44 | | | | |
| Bud Grant | 51-52 | | | | | 56 | 997 | 17.8 | 7 |
| Don Heinrich | 54-60,62 | 27 | 24 | 0.9 | 5 | | | | |
| Red Hickey | 41,45-48 | 7 | 7 | 1.0 | 1 | 75 | 1288 | 17.2 | 16 |
| Harlon Hill | 54-62 | 12 | 103 | 8.6 | 0 | 233 | 4717 | 20.2 | 40 |
| Mike Holovak | 46-48 | 136 | 720 | 5.3 | 6 | 13 | 155 | 11.9 | 0 |
| Jim Lee Howell | 37-42,46-47 | | | | | 61 | 921 | 15.1 | 7 |
| Billy Howton | 52-63 | 5 | 29 | 5.8 | 0 | 503 | 8459 | 16.8 | 61 |
| Pop Ivy | 40-42,45-47 | | | | | 53 | 513 | 9.7 | 1 |
| Bill Jessup | 51-52,54,56-58,60 | 1 | -5 | -5.0 | 0 | 61 | 994 | 16.3 | 7 |
| Joe Johnson | 54-58,60-61 | 93 | 376 | 4.0 | 0 | 84 | 920 | 11.0 | 8 |
| Gary Knafelc | 54-63 | | | | | 154 | 2162 | 14.0 | 23 |
| Larry Krutko | 58-60 | 96 | 331 | 3.4 | 4 | 14 | 108 | 7.7 | 0 |
| Tom Landry | 49-55 | 36 | 131 | 3.6 | 1 | 6 | 109 | 18.2 | 0 |
| Bobby Layne | 48-62 | 611 | 2451 | 4.0 | 25 | | | | |
| Eddie LeBaron | 52-53,55-63 | 202 | 650 | 3.2 | 9 | | | | |
| Woodley Lewis | 50-60 | 47 | 188 | 4.0 | 0 | 123 | 1885 | 15.3 | 12 |
| Eddie Macon | 52-53,60 | 70 | 324 | 4.6 | 2 | 14 | 49 | 3.5 | 2 |
| Ted Marchibroda | 53,55-57 | 50 | 176 | 3.5 | 3 | | | | |

## Lifetime Statistics- Players from Pre-1960    Section 2 - RUSHING and RECEIVING
### (All men with 25 or more rushing attempts or 10 or more receptions)

| Name | Years | Att. | Yards | Avg. | TD | Rec. | Yards | Avg. | TD |
|---|---|---|---|---|---|---|---|---|---|
| Ray Mathews | 51-60 | 300 | 1057 | 3.5 | 5 | 233 | 3963 | 17.0 | 34 |
| Ollie Matson | 52,54-66 | 1170 | 5173 | 4.4 | 40 | 222 | 3285 | 14.8 | 23 |
| Jack McClairen | 55-60 | | | | | 85 | 1253 | 14.7 | 3 |
| Hugh McElhenny | 52-64 | 1124 | 5281 | 5.7 | 38 | 264 | 3247 | 12.3 | 20 |
| Lamar McHan | 54-63 | 239 | 849 | 3.6 | 12 | 0 | 1 | — | 0 |
| Don McIlhenny | 56-61 | 414 | 1581 | 3.8 | 7 | 70 | 655 | 9.4 | 7 |
| Steve Meilinger | 56-58,60-61 | 1 | 6 | 6.0 | 0 | 60 | 863 | 14.4 | 8 |
| Dave Middleton | 55-61 | 67 | 210 | 3.1 | 2 | 183 | 2966 | 16.2 | 17 |
| Dick Moegle | 55-61 | 60 | 310 | 5.2 | 6 | 8 | 185 | 23.1 | 0 |
| Jim Mutscheller | 54-61 | | | | | 220 | 3684 | 16.7 | 40 |
| Gern Nagler | 53,55-61 | | | | | 196 | 3119 | 15.9 | 28 |
| John North | 48-50 | | | | | 38 | 784 | 20.6 | 5 |
| Jerry Norton | 54-64 | 47 | 341 | 7.3 | 1 | 11 | 125 | 11.4 | 1 |
| Tom O'Connell | 53,56-57,60-61 | 67 | 27 | 0.4 | 4 | | | | |
| Johnny Olszewski | 53-62 | 837 | 3320 | 4.0 | 16 | 104 | 988 | 9.5 | 3 |
| Buddy Parker | 35-43 | 180 | 489 | 2.7 | 4 | 40 | 378 | 9.5 | 0 |
| Joe Perry | 49-63 | 1929 | 9723 | 5.0 | 71 | 260 | 2021 | 7.8 | 12 |
| Jim Podoley | 57-60 | 209 | 746 | 3.6 | 2 | 78 | 1461 | 18.7 | 11 |
| Billy Pricer | 57-61 | 97 | 316 | 3.3 | 2 | 15 | 115 | 7.7 | 1 |
| Ray Renfro | 52-63 | 137 | 682 | 5.0 | 4 | 281 | 5508 | 19.6 | 50 |
| Billy Reynolds | 53-54,57-58,60 | 176 | 585 | 3.3 | 7 | 24 | 252 | 10.5 | 0 |
| Kyle Rote | 51-61 | 231 | 871 | 3.8 | 4 | 300 | 4797 | 16.0 | 48 |
| Tobin Rote | 50-59,63-64,66 | 635 | 3128 | 4.9 | 37 | 2 | 28 | 14.0 | 1 |
| Clive Rush | 53 | 1 | -6 | -6.0 | 0 | 14 | 190 | 13.6 | 0 |

| Name | Years | Att. | Yards | Avg. | TD | Rec. | Yards | Avg. | TD |
|---|---|---|---|---|---|---|---|---|---|
| Bob Schnelker | 53-61 | | | | | 211 | 3667 | 17.4 | 33 |
| Scooter Scudero | 54-58,60 | 43 | 139 | 3.2 | 0 | 6 | 62 | 10.3 | 1 |
| Jimmy Sears | 54,57-58,60-61 | 34 | 119 | 3.5 | 1 | 18 | 253 | 14.1 | 2 |
| Allie Sherman | 43-47 | 92 | -44 | -0.5 | 4 | | | | |
| Bill Stits | 54-61 | 49 | 165 | 3.4 | 0 | 8 | 69 | 8.6 | 0 |
| Ed Sutton | 57-60 | 282 | 1109 | 3.9 | 9 | 14 | 237 | 16.9 | 1 |
| Carl Taseff | 51,53-62 | 60 | 283 | 4.7 | 3 | 19 | 193 | 10.2 | 1 |
| Hugh Taylor | 47-54 | 1 | 7 | 7.0 | 0 | 272 | 5233 | 19.2 | 58 |
| Y.A. Tittle | 48-64 | 372 | 1245 | 3.3 | 39 | 1 | 4 | 4.0 | 0 |
| Mel Triplett | 55-62 | 685 | 2856 | 4.2 | 14 | 43 | 439 | 10.2 | 4 |
| Norm Van Brocklin | 49-60 | 105 | 40 | 0.4 | 11 | | | | |
| Ron Waller | 55-58,60 | 294 | 1569 | 5.3 | 8 | 44 | 443 | 10.1 | 1 |
| Bobby Walston | 51-62 | 4 | 12 | 3.0 | 0 | 311 | 5363 | 17.2 | 46 |
| Bob Waterfield | 45-52 | 75 | 21 | 0.3 | 13 | 3 | 19 | 6.3 | 0 |
| Alex Webster | 55-64 | 1196 | 4638 | 3.9 | 39 | 240 | 2679 | 11.2 | 7 |
| Ted Wegert | 55-56,60 | 109 | 408 | 3.7 | 4 | 14 | 131 | 9.4 | 1 |
| Billy Wells | 54,56-58,60-61 | 361 | 1384 | 3.8 | 5 | 57 | 725 | 12.7 | 2 |
| Jerry Williams | 49-54 | 172 | 910 | 5.3 | 10 | 91 | 1278 | 14.0 | 5 |
| Billy Wilson | 51-60 | | | | | 407 | 5902 | 14.5 | 49 |
| George Wilson | 37-46 | | | | | 111 | 1342 | 12.1 | 15 |
| Tom Wilson | 56-63 | 508 | 2553 | 5.0 | 18 | 61 | 617 | 10.1 | 5 |
| Royce Womble | 54-57,60 | 91 | 266 | 2.9 | 0 | 79 | 917 | 11.6 | 9 |

## Lifetime Statistics- Players from Pre-1960    Section 2 - PUNT RETURNS and KICKOFF RETURNS
### (All men with 25 or more punt returns or 25 or more kickoff returns)

| Name | Years | Att. | Yards | Avg. | TD | Rec. | Yards | Avg. | TD |
|---|---|---|---|---|---|---|---|---|---|
| Frank Bernardi | 55-57,60 | 39 | 362 | 10.1 | 1 | 4 | 101 | 25.3 | 0 |
| Fred Bruney | 53,56-62 | 53 | 265 | 5.0 | 0 | 18 | 421 | 23.4 | 0 |
| Al Carmichael | 53-58,60-61 | 122 | 912 | 7.5 | 0 | 191 | 4798 | 25.1 | 2 |
| Ken Carpenter | 50-53,60 | 34 | 370 | 10.9 | 1 | 41 | 895 | 21.8 | 0 |
| Lew Carpenter | 53-55,57-63 | 28 | 339 | 12.1 | 0 | 34 | 686 | 20.2 | 0 |
| Hopalong Cassady | 56-63 | 43 | 341 | 7.9 | 0 | 77 | 1594 | 20.7 | 0 |
| Jack Christiansen | 51-58 | 85 | 1084 | 12.8 | 8 | 59 | 1329 | 22.5 | 0 |
| Lindon Crow | 55-64 | 25 | 134 | 5.4 | 0 | | | | |
| Frank Gifford | 52-60,62-64 | 25 | 121 | 4.8 | 0 | 23 | 594 | 25.8 | 0 |
| Yale Lary | 52-53,56-64 | 126 | 758 | 6.0 | 3 | 22 | 495 | 22.5 | 0 |
| Woodley Lewis | 50-60 | 138 | 1026 | 7.4 | 3 | 137 | 3325 | 24.3 | 1 |
| Ray Mathews | 51-60 | 61 | 779 | 12.8 | 3 | 42 | 1069 | 25.5 | 0 |
| Ollie Matson | 52,54-66 | 65 | 595 | 9.2 | 3 | 144 | 3746 | 26.0 | 6 |
| Hugh McElhenny | 52-64 | 126 | 920 | 7.3 | 2 | 83 | 1921 | 23.1 | 0 |
| Don McIlhenny | 56-61 | 1 | 0 | 0.0 | 0 | 30 | 747 | 24.9 | 0 |
| Jerry Norton | 54-64 | 46 | 147 | 3.2 | 0 | 14 | 415 | 29.6 | 1 |

| Name | Years | Att. | Yards | Avg. | TD | Rec. | Yards | Avg. | TD |
|---|---|---|---|---|---|---|---|---|---|
| Joe Perry | 48-63 | | | | | 33 | 758 | 23.0 | 1 |
| Bert Rechichar | 52-61 | 85 | 311 | 3.7 | 0 | 23 | 448 | 19.5 | 0 |
| Ray Renfro | 52-63 | 40 | 225 | 5.6 | 0 | 9 | 154 | 17.1 | 0 |
| Billy Reynolds | 53-54,57-58,60 | 99 | 530 | 5.4 | 0 | 40 | 985 | 24.6 | 0 |
| Lee Riley | 55-56,58-61 | 48 | 249 | 5.2 | 0 | 32 | 764 | 23.9 | 0 |
| Scooter Scudero | 54-58,60 | 68 | 458 | 6.7 | 1 | 44 | 1143 | 26.0 | 1 |
| Jimmy Sears | 54,57-58,60-61 | 24 | 195 | 8.1 | 0 | 50 | 1169 | 23.4 | 0 |
| Bill Stits | 54-61 | 40 | 305 | 7.6 | 0 | 27 | 621 | 23.0 | 0 |
| Carl Taseff | 51,53-62 | 117 | 850 | 7.3 | 2 | 45 | 1019 | 22.6 | 0 |
| Em Tunnell | 48-61 | 258 | 2209 | 8.6 | 5 | 46 | 1215 | 26.4 | 1 |
| Ron Waller | 55-58,60 | 57 | 165 | 2.9 | 0 | 48 | 1146 | 23.9 | 0 |
| Billy Wells | 54,56-58,60 | 57 | 427 | 7.5 | 0 | 55 | 1267 | 23.0 | 0 |
| Jerry Williams | 49-54 | 51 | 277 | 5.4 | 0 | 20 | 476 | 23.8 | 0 |
| Tom Wilson | 56-63 | 3 | 28 | 9.3 | 0 | 62 | 1689 | 27.2 | 1 |
| Vic Zucco | 57-60 | 37 | 176 | 4.8 | 0 | 12 | 304 | 25.3 | 0 |

## Lifetime Statistics - Players from Pre-1960    Section 4 - PUNTING
### (All men with 25 or more punts)

| Name | Years | No. | Avg. |
|---|---|---|---|
| Sammy Baugh | 39-52 | 338 | 44.9 |
| Ed Brown | 54-65 | 493 | 40.5 |
| Ray Brown | 58-60 | 95 | 39.2 |
| L.G. Dupre | 55-61 | 29 | 35.4 |
| Bobby Gordon | 58-60 | 55 | 38.0 |

| Name | Years | No. | Avg. |
|---|---|---|---|
| Bill Jessup | 51-52,54,56-58,60 | 75 | 41.0 |
| Jack Johnson | 57-61 | 30 | 35.2 |
| Tom Landry | 49-55 | 389 | 40.9 |
| Yale Lary | 52-53,56-64 | 503 | 44.3 |
| Eddie LeBaron | 52-53,55-63 | 171 | 40.9 |
| Jerry Norton | 54-64 | 358 | 43.8 |

| Name | Years | No. | Avg. |
|---|---|---|---|
| Bert Rechichar | 52-61 | 38 | 37.7 |
| Clive Rush | 53 | 60 | 37.7 |
| Norm Van Brocklin | 49-60 | 523 | 42.9 |
| Bob Waterfield | 45-52 | 315 | 42.2 |
| Junior Wren | 56-61 | 36 | 36.3 |

## Lifetime Statistics - Players from Pre-1960    Section 5 - KICKING
### (All men with 10 or more PAT or field goal attempts)

| Name | Years | PAT | PAT Att. | PAT Pct. | FG | FG Att. | FG Pct. |
|---|---|---|---|---|---|---|---|
| Ben Agajanian | 45,47-49,53-57,60-62,64 | 343 | 351 | 98 | 104 | 204 | 51 |
| Larry Barnes | 57,60 | 37 | 39 | 95 | 6 | 25 | 24 |
| Dick Bielski | 55-63 | 58 | 62 | 94 | 26 | 65 | 40 |
| Hardy Brown | 48-56,60 | 25 | 30 | 83 | 0 | 1 | 0 |
| Fred Cone | 51-57,60 | 221 | 237 | 93 | 59 | 102 | 58 |
| Tom Fears | 48-56 | 12 | 14 | 86 | 1 | 4 | 25 |
| Ralph Felton | 54-62 | 16 | 17 | 94 | 1 | 2 | 50 |
| Bill George | 52-66 | 14 | 15 | 93 | 4 | 8 | 50 |
| Frank Gifford | 52-60,62-64 | 10 | 11 | 91 | 2 | 7 | 29 |
| Gary Glick | 56-61,63 | 26 | 29 | 90 | 9 | 25 | 36 |
| Lou Groza | 46-59,61-67 | 810 | 834 | 97 | 264 | 481 | 55 |
| Harvey Johnson | 46-49,51 | 178 | 180 | 99 | 28 | 52 | 54 |

| Name | Years | PAT | PAT Att. | PAT Pct. | FG | FG Att. | FG Pct. |
|---|---|---|---|---|---|---|---|
| Joe Kuharich | 40-41,45 | 12 | 13 | 92 | 0 | 4 | 0 |
| Bobby Layne | 48-62 | 120 | 124 | 97 | 34 | 50 | 68 |
| Jim Martin | 50-61,63-64 | 158 | 169 | 93 | 92 | 192 | 48 |
| Jack Morris | 58-61 | 15 | 15 | 100 | 3 | 8 | 38 |
| Steve Myhra | 57-61 | 180 | 189 | 95 | 44 | 91 | 48 |
| Jerry Perry | 54,56-62 | 92 | 96 | 96 | 32 | 58 | 55 |
| Bert Rechichar | 52-61 | 62 | 68 | 91 | 31 | 78 | 40 |
| Les Richter | 54-62 | 106 | 109 | 97 | 27 | 55 | 53 |
| Lou Saban | 46-49 | 21 | 22 | 95 | 0 | 2 | 0 |
| Pat Summerall | 52-61 | 257 | 265 | 97 | 100 | 212 | 47 |
| Bobby Walston | 51-62 | 365 | 384 | 95 | 80 | 157 | 51 |
| Bob Waterfield | 42-52 | 315 | 336 | 94 | 60 | 110 | 55 |

# 1960-1969
# From 12 to 26

The established National Football League faced yet another challenge from a rival league in the 1960's, but unlike the previous tests, this one produced far-reaching changes in the NFL. It eventually resulted in a two-fold increase in the number of teams, the adoption of many innovations to attract new fans, much-improved salaries and retirement benefits for the players, a big expansion of television coverage and the establishment of a Super Bowl championship game which attracted as much attention as baseball's World Series. Inevitably, these changes turned professional football into a big business for owners and players alike.

Having survived the challenge from the All-American Football Conference in the late 1940's, the NFL prepared to do battle with the new American Football League. The first step was to find a new commissioner to replace Bert Bell, under whose leadership the NFL had prospered for 13 years. When the owners reached a stalemate between the two primary candidates, 33-year-old Alvin (Peter) Rozelle was accepted by both factions as a compromise. In 1957 Rozelle had been named general manager of the Los Angeles Rams and one of his more noteworthy trades during the three-year stint was the acquisition of four-time All-Pro halfback Ollie Matson from the Chicago Cardinals in exchange for the rights to nine Ram players.

In an effort to head off the AFL's colonization of virgin football territory, the NFL decided to test two of the more promising areas by placing a club in Dallas beginning in 1960 and another in Minnesota to begin play in 1961. In addition, the desperate financial condition of the Cardinals and the desirability of St. Louis as an NFL city persuaded chairman of the board Violet Bidwill Wolfner and her husband, managing director Walter Wolfner, to move the team after 62 years in Chicago.

Meanwhile, the AFL laid plans for starting play in 1960, trying to avoid the pitfalls which caused the demise of three separate leagues using the same name earlier in the century. The AFL representatives and their cities were chief organizer Lamar Hunt, Dallas; William H. Sullivan, Boston; Ralph C. Wilson, Buffalo; Bob Howsam, Denver; K.S. (Bud) Adams, Houston; Barron Hilton, Los Angeles; Max Winter and William Boyer, Minneapolis-St. Paul; and Harry Wismer, New York City. Several of these men had been frustrated in attempts to buy NFL franchises previously.

When Minnesota was granted an NFL franchise, Winter and Boyer decided they had a better future in the more established league and thus withdrew from the AFL. The vacancy opened the door for an Oakland group headed by Y.C. (Chet) Soda and it included Ed McGah, Robert Osborne and Wayne Valley. The Raiders became the last of the original eight AFL teams to begin play in 1960 and eventually one of the more successful ones. Despite competition from NFL teams in Dallas, Los Angeles and New York, the AFL owners decided to stay in those cities, although the former two were later abandoned in favor of untested cities.

The AFL set out to differentiate its games from the NFL contests by adding several innovations. The new league adopted a rule for conversions whereby a team could elect to run or pass the ball across the goal line for two points as an alternative to the traditional one-point placekick used in the NFL. This added a new dimension of excitement and strategy to a play which had become nearly automatic. The AFL owners also decided to put the players' names on the backs of the jerseys and to make the scoreboard clock official, instead of having an official on the field keep the correct time as was done in the NFL. Both of these rules made the game more accessible to the average fan.

Joe Foss, a former pilot and South Dakota governor, was appointed as the first commissioner of the AFL, and a draft of college players similar to the one held annually by the NFL was

scheduled. The competition for players was expected to cause sharp increases in player salaries, just as it had done during the previous challenge from the AAFC. Because of the tempting offers made to college seniors, several players signed contracts with both leagues and soon found themselves as subjects of court battles.

The AFL won its first court cast over a player when a Los Angeles court declared Billy Cannon's contract with the Rams invalid, freeing him to sign with Houston. The Louisiana State University halfback had been the first player selected in the 1960 NFL draft, and his defection to the upstart AFL signalled the beginning of a long and costly bidding war between the two leagues. In the same year, however, Southern Methodist quarterback Don Meredith signed with the NFL's new entry in Dallas, the Cowboys, instead of with Hunt's Dallas Texans. In 1961 end Willard Dewveall became the first player to voluntarily switch leagues when he joined Houston of the AFL after playing out his option with the Chicago Bears.

The AFL received its biggest shot in the arm in 1965 when Sonny Werblin, who had taken over a shaky New York franchise from the league after Wismer had gone bankrupt in 1963, signed quarterbacks Joe Namath and John Huarte to sizeable contracts. Namath received a $225,000 bonus, an annual salary of $25,000 for three years, and no-cut and no-trade clauses in his contract, as the bidding war reached new heights. Although the cost seemed high at the time, Werblin proved himself to be a shrewd businessman, because Namath provided the charisma which made the important New York franchise a financial success and gave the league a degree of legitimacy previously unattained in th eyes of the New York media and many of the football fans across the country. As a measure of Namath's appeal, his first regular-season appearance in a Jet uniform attracted a crowd of 52,680 to Rice Stadium, where the Oilers were playing their first regular-season game after attracting an average of only 20,000 the previous year at Jeppeson Stadium. Three years later, Namath struck another blow for AFL pride when he predicted an AFL victory in Super Bowl III and then proceeded to direct the Jets to a win over the heavily favored Colts, giving the AFL its first Super Bowl triumph.

Although the New York franchise had floundered in its early years under the leadership of Wismer, Werblin wasted little time in upgrading the team. He hired Weeb Ewbank, a former Baltimore head coach, as his field boss in 1963 and the following year moved the team from the rundown Polo Grounds to new Shea Stadium, where it immediately set AFL attendance records. Werblin had a show-business background and he proved adept at utilizing that experience to attract new fans. Commissioner Foss also played a key role in preserving the franchise when he decided to have the league run the operation until the syndicate headed by Werblin came on the scene.

Another major reason behind the AFL's success was its ability to sell itself to a major television network at its inception. Under a contract signed with the American Broadcasting company, each AFL team received $150,000, and this needed revenue kept the league afloat when it otherwise might have folded. During the early years of its existence, the AFL suffered from a lack of superstars, poor attendance, the high cost of signing top draft choices and, in some cases, inadequate stadia. Attendance in the first year averaged only 16,500 but by 1962 began to climb steadily.

While the AFL may have had a shortage of quality players in its initial years, the games didn't lack for excitement or unpredictability. Most AFL teams used a wide-open, passing style which produced a lot of scoring. Although the defenses sometime seemed invisible, the style of play appealed immensely to the average fan. In the very first year Denver's Lionel Taylor caught 92 passes, and in 1964 George Blanda attempted 505

passes and Houston Teammate Charley Hennigan caught 101 of them for a total of 1,546 yards. Although Johnny Morris of the NFL's Chicago Bears caught 93 passes that same year, the older league with its stronger defenses couldn't quite match its young challenger when it came to high-scoring football.

When the Dallas Texans found their future growth limited by the presence of the NFL Cowboys and attendance figures below expectations, Hunt moved them to Kansas City after winning the 1962 AFL championship. As an inducement, Kansas City mayor H. Roe Bartle offered to enlarge Municipal Stadium and rent it to the team at $1 per year for the first two seasons, in addition to promising three times as many season tickets as the Texans sold in Dallas. With St. Louis the nearest competitor 250 miles away, Hunt saw a much brighter future in Kansas City, which became the AFL's first team in the Midwest.

The Los Angeles Chargers were actually the first AFL franchise to move to a new city, heading south for San Diego after their first year of play, in which they won the AFL's Western Division. Only 9,928 fans witnessed their title-clinching victory over Denver in 1960, and the club lost a total of $900,000 that first year. Those figures, combined with an enthusiastic appeal by San Diego officials, convinced Hilton to move the team without delay to the 34,000-seat Balboa Stadium.

Unknown to Commissioner Foss, AFL owners held a secret draft in 1961, hoping to sign the premium college players before the NFL teams held their draft. But when Foss learned of the plan, he declared the secret draft void and insisted another one be held. This infuriated Wismer, who had drafted Syracuse fullback Ernie Davis at the secret draft but saw Buffalo pick him at the official draft. Wismer tried to effect Foss' ouster but a majority of the owners backed the commissioner. While the competition for college seniors was fierce, the AFL refrained from signing established players currently under contract to NFL teams.

Rozelle convinced NFL owners that their interests would be better served if they united and sold the television rights to their games to one network in a single package. Such a plan brought added stability to the league, because the weaker clubs were able to share equally in the television revenue. Rozelle went before Congress in 1961 and convinced that body to pass a bill legalizing single-network contracts by professional sports leagues. He was rewarded the next year by being given a new five-year contract.

In 1962 a U.S. District judge ruled against the AFL's charges of monopoly by the NFL in the areas of expansion, player signings and television contracts, and the U.S. Fourth Circuit Court of Appeals refused to overturn that decision a year later. Meanwhile, both leagues competed for the spectators' dollars, the AFL instituting in 1961 a post-season All-Star game which got television exposure and the NFL experimenting in 1962 with a pre-season doubleheader involving four teams that drew a capacity house at Cleveland. The AFL had an all-Texas championship game in 1962 that went into a second overtime period before the Texans finally beat the Oilers in front of a full house of 37,981.

In 1963 the NFL was rocked by a gambling scandal which threatened the credibility of the entire league. Acting decisively, Rozelle suspended Green Bay's "Golden Boy" Paul Hornung and Detroit's defensive star Alex Karras for betting on football games in which they were not involved. In addition, five Detroit players — Joe Schmidt, Wayne Walker, John Gordy, Gary Lowe and Sam Williams — were fined $2,000 each for betting and the Lions' management was fined $4,000. Both players were reinstated 11 months later, but Rozelle's action served to maintain the public's faith in the integrity of the sport.

While Werblin was taking control of the AFL's New York franchise (changing its name from Titans to Jets) and Hunt was moving his team to Kansas City (changing its name from Texans to Chiefs), Al Davis left his job as an assistant coach at San Diego at age 33 to become the general manager and head coach at Oakland. With the Raiders finishing 2-12 and 1-13 in the

previous two seasons, Davis' task seemed formidable, but·he somehow blended several free agents and rookies with the holdovers and produced a team which went 10-4 and fell only one game short of the Western Division title. That season was only the beginning of what would prove to be a very successful career for Davis.

The survival of the AFL took a giant step in 1964 when Foss signed a five-year television contract with NBC for $36 million, guaranteeing each team $900,000 per year from television rights alone. The NFL also signed a new television contract, getting $14.1 million from CBS for the next two years of regular-season games. The new contract also permitted for the first time the telecasts of several games during prime time and also the telecasts of other games in the area of a team playing at home on a given Sunday.

With both leagues now having a measure of security because of the television revenue, they looked toward opening up new markets. They expanded into the Deep South for the first time in 1965, the NFL awarding a franchise to Atlanta and the AFL adding Miami, with both teams scheduled to begin league play in 1966. Following the same trend, New Orleans was slated to join the NFL in 1967.

While Kansas City's Hunt and Dallas' Tex Schramm were secretly discussing a merger, the war between the two leagues over signing players escalated in 1966 when placekicker Pete Gogolak played out his option with the Buffalo Bills and then signed with the NFL's New York Giants. The AFL interpreted this move as a deliberate attempt to lure away its top players, and Davis, who had replaced Foss as AFL commissioner in April 1966 after three impressive years at Oakland, set out to retaliate. The aggressive 36-year-old league boss began efforts to sign top NFL players, forcing the NFL owners to seriously consider a truce in the war. The two leagues spent an estimated $7 million on draft choices alone in 1966, including $1 million by Green Bay for running backs Donny Anderson and Jim Grabowski.

To the surprise of nearly everyone, Rozelle announced on June 8, 1966 a merger agreement between the two leagues, with the AFL paying $26 million for the added financial security of joining the stable NFL. The two sides agreed to a championship game between the two leagues beginning with the 1966 season. Starting in 1967, a common draft and inter-league pre-season games were scheduled. Expansion to 26 teams by 1968 and a total merger of the two leagues into one unit by 1970 was planned. Rozelle was chosen as commissioner of the two leagues and, with the goal of a merger agreement behind him, Davis resigned his post with the AFL and returned to Oakland as managing general partner. Milt Woodward was appointed AFL president until the two leagues realigned under one banner.

At the first common draft in 1967, the AFL demonstrated its uncanny ability to assess young talent — an ability that would later prove to be a major factor in its quick rise to equality with the NFL teams. The AFL drafted such future stars as Bob Griese, Gene Upshaw, George Webster and Floyd Little, while the best the NFL could do was Mel Farr and Charles (Bubba) Smith, the No. 1 choice in the entire draft. Rozelle announced at that draft that "futures" (players whose college class had graduated but who still had a year of eligibility left) no longer could be drafted.

The AFL also had some success in inter-league games during the 1967 pre-season, Denver beating Detroit 13-7 for the first AFL triumph and defending AFL champion Kansas City embarrassing Chicago 66-27. The regular season started on an explosive note, as four kickoffs were returned for touchdowns on the opening weekend. For the season, 14 touchdowns were scored on kickoff returns, including a record four by Green Bay rookie Travis Williams and three by Chicago's Gale Sayers. Both players had record-breaking kickoff return averages — Williams 41.1 and Sayers 37.7. There also was a single-season record of nine ties during that exciting 1967 season.

Cincinnati was granted a franchise to join the AFL in 1968, and the team chose the same nickname (Bengals) that was used by the Cincinnati team in the old AFL of 1941. Former Cleveland

coach Paul Brown was the leader of a group which bought the franchise, and he became its first head coach. Although his fellow owners weren't overly generous in the veteran allocation draft which supplied 40 players to the Bengals, Brown and player personnel director Al LoCasale used the draft wisely, building the Bengals into the first expansion team ever to win a division title in its third year of existence.

Two of the greatest names in NFL coaching annals retired in early 1968 — George Halas and Vince Lombardi. For Halas, 73, it was the fourth and final retirement after 40 years of professional coaching in Chicago, where he had owned a team since 1921. His coaching record was an impressive 320-147-30, giving him the most victories of any coach in NFL history. Lombardi resigned at the pinnacle of his career, having won five NFL championships during his nine-year reign at Green Bay and the frist two Super Bowls during his last two years. After one year in the sole capacity of general manager of the Packers, Lombardi took up a new challenge as part-owner, general manager and head coach of Washington in 1969 — a challenge that would be cut short by cancer after one season.

While AFL owners and players had agreed upon a pension increase in early 1968, the NFL was less sucessful. The resulting dispute prompted the NFL Players Association to declare a strike in July, and a compromise was reached only a few days before training camps were scheduled to open. The television networks learned just how powerful the influence of the football viewers had become when NBC switched at the appointed hour from its coverage of a close game between the Jets and the Raiders to begin a dramatic special of "Heidi." Enraged football fans jammed the network's switchboard, becoming even more upset when they learned that Oakland had scored two touchdowns in 17 seconds during the final minute of the game. Television had indeed created a "monster" that would have to be accommodated even further in the near future.

The AFL gained in respectability by leaps and bounds after the 1968 regular season had ended. PRO FOOTBALL WEEKLY announced the first-ever All-Pro team combining AFL and NFL players, and the AFL captured 10 of 22 positions. While Earl Morrall led the Baltimore Colts to an NFL title as a replacement for the injured Johnny Unitas, a young Joe Namath was making headlines with three touchdown passes in a 27-23 win over Oakland for the AFL championship. Because the AFL hadn't come close in either of the first two Super Bowl games, nobody gave the brash, voung Jets much of a chance against the once-beaten Colts. When Namath was quoted a few days before the game as saying that the Jets would beat Baltimore, the statement was interpreted as a typical example of Super bowl "hype." Namath fulfilled his promise on Super Bowl Sunday, however, completing 17 of 28 passes for 206 yards as the Jets defeated the Colts 16-7. It was a momentous day for the AFL, and four underdogs everywhere.

When the excitement surrounding Super Bowl III began to subside, the NFL and AFL owners began deliberations on the realignment of the two leagues under one roof. The procedure wasn't as simple as some owners had expected. Many NFL owners were determined to maintain the separate identities of the two leagues within one organization. Some AFL owners also were willing to accept this plan, until Paul Brown and several other owners (New York's Phil Iselin, Denver's Gerald Phipps and Miami's Joe Robbie insisted that the AFL could never achieve parity with the NFL as long as the teams in the NFL outnumbered their AFL counterparts 16 to 10.

Once the NFL owners realized that a 16-10 split of the teams would not be approved, they had to decide which three teams would move to the AFL. At first, none of the owners wanted to move, fearing that their reputation and attendance would suffer and that they would lose important rivalries. The New York Giants and the San Francisco 49ers were exempted from switching to the AFL by the terms of the original merger agreement, because it was deemed essential that they be in a different conference from their next-door neighbors, the New

York Jets and the Oakland Raiders. Reasons for not joining the AFL seemed to be numerous, while reasons for switching were hard to find.

In a non-stop meeting that lasted nearly 36 hours, the owners finally agreed on a new alignment, with Baltimore, Cleveland and Pittsburgh moving to the AFL. Baltimore owner Carroll Rosenbloom had taken the initiative, agreeing to move his Colts to the AFL, and Cleveland's Art Modell followed Rosenbloom's lead. Modell wanted Pittsburgh to join him in a new division of the realigned American Conference and, after some hesitation, Steeler bosses Art and Dan Rooney agreed. The move by Baltimore and Cleveland came as a surprise to many fans because the clubs were two of the NFL's better teams at that time. While Pittsburgh had been a member of the NFL since 1933, its switch was less surprising in light of its five consecutive losing seasons.

Al Davis, who had been a thorn in the sides of NFL owners during his two-month tenure as AFL commissioner prior to the merger agreement, didn't win any new friends when he prolonged the marathon realignment session an additional 12 hours by insisting upon knowing the exact alignment of the 13 remaining NFL teams before giving his ratification vote. Nevertheless, the meeting adjourned without an agreement on the new setup of the 13 NFL teams, forcing the approval of the overall realignment plan to be postponed.

Two divisional arrangements came within one vote of the unanimous approval needed at that May 9-10 meeting in 1969. The first had the Vikings, Redskins, Cardinals, Giants and Eagles in the Eastern Division; the Cowboys, Packers, Bears and Lions in the Central; the Rams, 49ers, Saints and Falcons in the Western. The second plan had the Cowboys, Redskins, Cardinals and Giants in the East; the Packers, Bears, Lions and Saints in the Central; the Vikings, Rams, 49ers, Falcons And Eagles in the West. The First proposal was closer to the alignment eventually adopted, needing only a reversal of the Vikings' and Cowboys' positions.

Because the NFL owners never were able to agree on an equitable divisional setup for their 13 teams, Rozelle eventually submitted five plans and had one drawn in a lottery.

The financial aspects of the merger agreement included an $18 million indemnity payment by the AFL, which also gave the NFL an $8 million franchise fee paid by the Cincinnati owners to join the league. On the other hand, the AFL was getting assets estimated at a value of $55 million in the form of the three NFL teams which joined the AFL teams. In addition, the 13 NFL clubs agreed to pay each of the three teams who switched to the AFL approximately $2.5 million as compensation for the move.

The persistence of the AFL owners in demanding an equal share of the pie virtually guaranteed the equality of the two factions within a relatively short period of time. While the existence of the AFL vanished along with the decade, just as it had arisen from nowhere at the beginning of the 1960's, the memory of the league lingered on. The rivalry between the NFL and AFL was continued as an NFC-AFC rivalry, although the divisions had been blurred by the realignment. More than a decade after the initial merger agreement, the controversy between NFC and AFC factions continued to rage. The spirit and innovations of the American Football League pervaded professional football long after its disappearance, making the sport a more popular attraction than ever.

The end of the decade also provided some touchy decisions for Rozelle. The commissioner signed a three-year contract with the ABC television network for weekly telecasts of Monday night football games, while some observers feared that overexposure might result. Whereas the armchair quarterback had previously been limited to weekends for most of his football viewing, he now would have the opportunity to witness a football game as a prime-time "production." More importantly, the move of pro football to prime-time television meant large-scale advertising revenue and, as a result, more money in the coffers of the individual teams. Inevitably, this increase in revenue would be

reflected in the salary demands of the players. Taken to its conclusion, the rapid spread in television exposure meant that the networks would have more control and the average fan less influence over the development of the sport.

Having dealt decisively with the gambling scandal in 1963, Rozelle faced a lesser but still noteworthy decision in 1969 when Namath was reportedly linked to several underworld figures through his part-ownership of a New York City nightclub. When Rozelle gave Namath the ultimatum of either selling his interest in the business or being suspended, Namath "retired" from football in a fit of pique. Although Namath was charged with "guilt by association" rather than any illegal activities, Rozelle was clearly within his broad authority as outlined in the league's constitution and by-laws and the standard player contract. Faced with the prospect of losing a substantial sum of money through a forfeited football contract and the possible loss of endorsements, Namath reconsidered his "retirement," choosing instead to sell his interest in Bachelors III and return to football.

Progress in the area of racial equality was achieved more quickly in professional football circles than in the surrounding environment, but some vestiges of foot-dragging were evident during the 1960's. Washington became the last NFL team to end the color barrier when it drafted Heisman Trophy winner Ernie Davis of Syracuse in 1962. Before the season started, the Redskins traded Davis to Cleveland for Bobby Mitchell, a black who became one of the league's leading receivers. Other blacks signed by the Redskins that year where Ron Hatcher, Leroy Jackson and John Nisby. After the 1965 season, several players in New Orleans for the AFL All-Star game charged that they were discriminated against, so the game was moved to Houston. In 1968 Merlin Briscoe of the Denver Broncos became the first black in pro football history to play regularly at quarterback, when an injury to the regular quarterback forced the rookie from Omaha to take over. Briscoe was traded to Buffalo the following year and he became a wide receiver.

A number of rule changes were adopted during the 1960's many of which made the game easier for the average fan to follow. The color of the officials' penalty flags was changed from white to gold, the uprights of the goal post were lengthened to a minimum of 20 feet above the crossbar and were painted gold, and the playing field was rimmed with a white border six feet wide. The major rule changes affecting the conduct of the game made it illegal for a player to grab the facemask of an opponent and required kicking shoes to be of standard production and not modified in any manner.

As the 1960's drew to a close, the emphasis on wide-open offensive football was beginning to change to a more conservative style of ball-control offense and short passes, as zone defenses became increasingly effective. While the influx of soccer-style kickers had accompanied a surge in the number of field goals, the number of touchdowns per game dropped significantly near the end of the decade. With 26 teams united under one organization and attendance booming, pro football was ready to begin a new era.

## ALL-NFL TEAM OF THE 1960's

### OFFENSE

| Name | Position |
|------|----------|
| Del Shofner | Split End |
| Charley Taylor | Split End |
| Gary Collins | Flanker |
| Boyd Dowler | Flanker |
| John Mackey | Tight End |
| Bob Brown | Tackle |
| Forrest Gregg | Tackle |
| Ralph Neely | Tackle |
| Gene Hickerson | Guard |
| Jerry Kramer | Guard |
| Howard Mudd | Guard |
| Jim Ringo | Center |
| Sonny Jurgensen | Quarterback |
| Bart Starr | Quarterback |
| Johnny Unitas | Quarterback |
| John David Crow | Halfback |
| Paul Hornung | Halfback |
| Leroy Kelly | Halfback |
| Gale Sayers | Halfback |
| Jim Brown | Fullback |
| Jim Taylor | Fullback |
| Jim Bakken | Kicker |
| Don Chandler | Punter |

### DEFENSE

| Name | Position |
|------|----------|
| Doug Atkins | End |
| Willie Davis | End |
| David (Deacon) Jones | End |
| Alex Karras | Tackle |
| Bob Lilly | Tackle |
| Merlin Olsen | Tackle |
| Dick Butkus | Linebacker |
| Larry Morris | Linebacker |
| Ray Nitschke | Linebacker |
| Tommy Nobis | Linebacker |
| Dave Robinson | Linebacker |
| Herb Adderley | Cornerback |
| Lem Barney | Cornerback |
| Bobby Boyd | Cornerback |
| Eddie Meador | Safety |
| Larry Wilson | Safety |
| Willy Wood | Safety |

## ALL-AFL TEAM OF THE 1960's

### OFFENSE

| Name | Position |
|------|----------|
| Lance Alworth | Flanker |
| Don Maynard | End |
| Fred Arbanas | Tight End |
| Ron Mix | Tackle |
| Jim Tyrer | Tackle |
| Ed Budde | Guard |
| Billy Shaw | Guard |
| Jim Otto | Center |
| Joe Namath | Quarterback |
| Clem Daniels | Running Back |
| Paul Lowe | Running Back |
| George Blanda | Kicker |
| Jarrel Wilson | Punter |

### DEFENSE

| Name | Position |
|------|----------|
| Jerry Mays | End |
| Gerry Philbin | End |
| Houston Antwine | Tackle |
| Tom Sestak | Tackle |
| Bobby Bell | Linebacker |
| George Webster | Linebacker |
| Nick Buoniconti | Linebacker |
| Willie Brown | Cornerback |
| Dave Grayson | Cornerback |
| Johnny Robinson | Safety |
| George Saimes | Safety |

(Both teams were chosen by the Pro Football Hall of Fame Selection Committee).

# 1960 N.F.L. Mara's Compromise

After four days of meetings and twenty-one deadlocked ballots, the league owners had still not elected a new commissioner to succeed the late Bert Bell. With the older owners supporting acting commissioner Austin Gunsel and the young owners supporting San Francisco attorney Marshall Leahy, New York Giant vice-president Wellington Mara presented an acceptable compromise candidate. He nominated Pete Rozelle, thirty-three-year-old general manager of the Los Angeles Rams. and the other owners quickly confirmed the young man as commissioner. Like Bell, Rozelle faced the challenge of a new league, the American Football League, at the start of his administration, but the NFL was strong enough at this time also to expand, shifting the Cardinals to St. Louis, putting a new team in Dallas this year, and granting Minneapolis-St. Paul a franchise for 1961. The new league would drive player salaries up, but the NFL owners had no worries about their league surviving.

## EASTERN CONFERENCE

**Philadelphia Eagles**—The Eagles hardly looked like champions when they lost to Cleveland on opening day and barely beat the new Dallas team 27-25 the next week. But the club slowly gained momentum and by mid-season was battling the Giants and Browns for the Eastern lead. They eliminated the Giants by beating them 17-10 and 31-23 in back-to-back games, while the Browns eliminated themselves with three mid-season losses. Quarterback Norm Van Brocklin moved the team with his passes, but reserve depth was the key to the title drive. When fullback Clarence Peaks was sidelined, rookie Ted Dean filled in splendidly, and when injuries depleted the linebacking corps, center Chuck Bednarik moved over to defense. The thirty-five-year-old Bednarik was the story of the year, playing most of the game while starring at center and middle linebacker.

**Cleveland Browns**—The Browns opened their year with an impressive 41-24 rout of the Eagles, but the Philadelphia club evened the score three weeks later with a 31-29 squeaker. Then, while the Eagles went on a hot streak, the Browns ran into trouble in mid-season. The Giants came to Cleveland in early November and held Jimmy Brown and Bobby Mitchell to a total of six yards rushing. The 17-13 New York victory was their sixth in a row over the Browns. After the Browns edged the Cards 28-27, a 14-10 loss to Pittsburgh and a 17-17 tie with the Cards put them too far behind the Eagles to catch up. But one element of satisfaction did come from the strong finale, a 48-34 victory over the Giants at Yankee Stadium.

**New York Giants**—A good early-season showing kept the Giants in the Eastern race into November, but the aging New York squad was barely holding together with paste and string. A bad knee sidelined Alex Webster for most of the year, elbow and leg troubles made Chuck Conerly's availability a week-to-week affair, and an injured shoulder put Jim Katcavage out of action for the last half of the season. The Eagles, holding a slim half-game lead, came to Yankee Stadium in mid-November and beat the New Yorkers 17-10. The biggest loss of the day, however, was halfback Frank Gifford, knocked unconscious with a concussion by Chuck Bednarik's vicious tackle. Another loss in Philadelphia made the Giants' chances slim, and a tie with the fledgling Cowboys ended their hopes completely.

**St. Louis Cardinals**—The team's move to St. Louis had an immediate effect, as the Cards beat the Rams 43-21 to open their new history. Long-time losers in Chicago, these new Cardinals moved up to fourth place in the East behind an improved defense and versatile offense. The defensive line, led by Frank Fuller, put strong pressure on enemy passers, while the mobile linebacking crew of Bill Koman, Dale Meinert, and Ted Bates improved with experience. In the secondary, Jerry Norton starred at safety, while rookie Larry Wilson broke into the lineup as a cornerback. John Roach was the third new starting quarterback in three years, but the main forces in the offensive resurgence were end Sonny Randle and halfback John David Crow.

**Pittsburgh Steelers**—After beating the new Dallas Cowboys to start the season, the Steelers won only once in their next seven games, with only a matching effort by the Redskins keeping them from dropping to the bottom of the East. Injuries plagued the Steelers along the way. Bobby Layne hurt his throwing hand, a bad leg slowed John Henry Johnson, and various physical ills bothered Jimmy Orr, Mike Sandusky, and Mike Henry. Flanker Buddy Dial stayed healthy and was the main offensive threat with his speed on long passes. The defense slacked off a bit, due partly to the retirement of All-Pro cornerback Jack Butler, but still was no pushover. Starting in late November, the Steelers drove back to respectabiltiy with a three-game win streak, crippling the Browns' title hopes 14-10, locking Washington into the basement 22-10, and ending the Eagles' nine-game win streak 27-21.

**Washington Redskins**—The Redskin defense sprang some major leaks in the secondary, but they were nothing compared to the leaks in the offensive line. Quarterback Ralph Guglielmi watched a flood of defensive linemen pour in on him every Sunday, forcing him either to hurry his pass or hang onto the ball and get smashed to the ground. The ends he was throwing to, Bill Anderson and Joe Walton, did not have good speed, and fullback Don Bosseler, the leading rusher, was no sprinter, so the Redskins scored 16 points or less in eight of their nine losses.

## WESTERN CONFERENCE

**Green Bay Packers**—After a close five-team race, the Packers emerged from the fray with their first Western title since 1944. They did not back into the crown but won it by taking their last three contests, two of which included head-to-head victories over the Bears and the '49ers. The Packers again were national news, and their biggest star was halfback Paul Hornung, who grabbed headlines with his unprecedented point production. As a runner, he had a nose for the end zone; as a kicker, his toe churned out points with field goals and extra points. After twelve games Hornung had set a new season's scoring record of 176 points.

**Detroit Lions**—With their defense jelling into a top unit, the Lions won their last four games to capture second place in the West. Rookie tackle Roger Brown joined Alex Karras, Darris McCord, and Bill Glass in a powerful front line, while Carl Brettschneider came from the Cardinals to complete the linebacking trio with Joe Schmidt and Wayne Walker. Another ex-Card, Night Train Lane, tightened up a secondary that already featured Yale Lary, Dick LeBeau, and Gary Lowe. Newcomers also helped the offense, as ex-Cleveland quarterback Jim Ninowski and freshman end Gail Cogdill made the pass a vital weapon in the Detroit attack again.

**San Francisco '49ers**—In a turn-about in the club's image, the defense carried the '49ers through the season. The young secondary of Abe Woodson, Jerry Mertens, Eddie Dove, and Dave Baker melded into a fine unit, while veterans Matt Hazeltine and Leo Nomellini anchored the linebacking front line units. The offense, however, bucked and sputtered, relying more than usual on Tommy Davis' field goals to bail it out. Head coach Red Hickey did experiment with the shotgun formation, with both ends split, a flanker and two wingbacks up near the line of scrimmage, and a quarterback all alone in the backfield, five yards back from the center. With the mobile John Brodie beating out Y. A. Tittle for the quarterback slot, the new formation often caught enemy defenses by surprise.

**Baltimore Colts**—Playing with a fractured vertebra in his back, Johnny Unitas still had his Colts at the head of the West. In mid-November, Baltimore held a one-game lead over Green Bay and had just won three straight games, apparently on the way to a third straight Western title. But when a torn Achilles tendon ended fullback Alan Ameche's career in mid-season, the Colt running game withered away and died. With only Unitas' passing to Ray Berry and Lenny Moore to worry about, enemy defenses concentrated solely on rushing the fragile Unitas and blanketing his receivers.

**Chicago Bears**—Neither Zeke Bratkowski nor Ed Brown had impressed at quarterback, fullback Rick Casares was slowing up, and the ends had no speed, but the Bears had scrapped their way to a 5-3-1 record, a half game behind the first-place Colts, by late November. The defense, led by Bill George and Doug Atkins, had kept the Bears in the race with several strong efforts through the fall. But the visions of championships dancing in George Halas' head were just so many sugar plums. The Packers just about killed any Bear hopes with a 41-13 drubbing two weeks from the end of the year, and the last two games turned into a nightmare, with a 42-0 beating by Cleveland and a 36-0 loss to Detroit.

**Los Angeles Rams**—It would have made great newspaper copy for new head coach Bob Waterfield and new general manager Elroy "Crazy Legs" Hirsch, great players in the salad days of the early 1950s, to lead the Rams back to glory, but it wasn't to be. Four losses right at the start established the Rams as also-rans in the West and prompted Waterfield to shake his club up. Young Frank Ryan began sharing the quarterback job with Billy Wade, Ollie Matson was shifted to a flanker position where his main duties were blocking and receiving, and Del Shofner became a defensive back after losing his offensive end job to rookie Carroll Dale. Although the Rams did beat the Packers and Colts down the stretch, the season was a troubled one all around.

**Dallas Cowboys**—Former New York assistant Tom Landry came in as head coach and tried to combine young talent with a coating of experienced players. For quarterbacks, Landry traded for little Eddie LeBaron and got rookie Don Meredith in the expansion draft, but the offense they commanded was practically invisible. Of the other players, end Jim Doran and linebacker Jerry Tubbs showed the most, with the roster in general an arid stretch of mediocrity. A perfect record of losses seemed inevitable for the Cowboys until they visited New York in December and gained a 31-31 tie with the Giants.

## FINAL TEAM STATISTICS

### OFFENSE

| | BALT. | CHI. | CLEVE. | DALL. | DET. | G.BAY | L.A. | N.Y. | PHIL. | PITT. | ST.L. | S.F. | WASH. |
|---|---|---|---|---|---|---|---|---|---|---|---|---|---|
| **FIRST DOWNS:** | | | | | | | | | | | | | |
| Total | 227 | 183 | 219 | 180 | 192 | 237 | 194 | 202 | 190 | 198 | 229 | 201 | 166 |
| by Rushing | 64 | 83 | 107 | 57 | 89 | 135 | 76 | 81 | 54 | 81 | 127 | 90 | 83 |
| by Passing | 143 | 90 | 96 | 105 | 88 | 86 | 101 | 107 | 121 | 104 | 89 | 96 | 71 |
| by Penalty | 20 | 10 | 16 | 18 | 15 | 16 | 17 | 14 | 15 | 13 | 13 | 15 | 12 |
| **RUSHING:** | | | | | | | | | | | | | |
| Number | 345 | 373 | 383 | 312 | 392 | 463 | 343 | 406 | 351 | 411 | 484 | 413 | 415 |
| Yards | 1289 | 1639 | 1930 | 1049 | 1714 | 2150 | 1449 | 1440 | 1134 | 1623 | 2356 | 1681 | 1313 |
| Average Yards | 3.7 | 4.4 | 5.0 | 3.4 | 4.4 | 4.6 | 4.2 | 3.5 | 3.2 | 3.9 | 4.9 | 4.1 | 3.2 |
| Touchdowns | 10 | 11 | 18 | 6 | 19 | 29 | 9 | 10 | 9 | 9 | 13 | 9 | 9 |
| **PASSING:** | | | | | | | | | | | | | |
| Attempts | 392 | 324 | 264 | 354 | 333 | 279 | 335 | 322 | 331 | 285 | 285 | 336 | 274 |
| Completions | 196 | 146 | 160 | 163 | 166 | 137 | 177 | 156 | 177 | 139 | 126 | 174 | 147 |
| Completion Pct. | 50.0 | 45.1 | 60,6 | 46.0 | 49.8 | 49.1 | 52.8 | 48.4 | 53.5 | 48.8 | 44.2 | 51.8 | 53.6 |
| Gross Yards | 3164 | 2130 | 2343 | 2388 | 2022 | 1993 | 2188 | 2385 | 2957 | 2511 | 1990 | 1866 | 1816 |
| Yards Lost Tackled | 208 | 304 | 299 | 284 | 344 | 118 | 366 | 131 | 141 | 89 | 179 | 287 | 385 |
| Net Yards | 2956 | 1826 | 2044 | 2104 | 1678 | 1875 | 1822 | 2254 | 2816 | 2422 | 1811 | 1579 | 1431 |
| Avg. Yds per Att (Gs) | 8.1 | 6.6 | 8.9 | 6.7 | 6.1 | 7.1 | 6.5 | 7.4 | 8.9 | 8.8 | 7.0 | 5.6 | 6.6 |
| Avg. Yds per Com (Gs) | 16.1 | 14.6 | 14.6 | 14.7 | 12.2 | 14.5 | 12.4 | 15.3 | 16.7 | 18.1 | 15.8 | 10.7 | 12.4 |
| Touchdowns | 26 | 13 | 22 | 17 | 6 | 9 | 19 | 20 | 29 | 20 | 20 | 11 | 9 |
| Interceptions | 24 | 32 | 5 | 33 | 21 | 13 | 22 | 23 | 20 | 21 | 25 | 12 | 23 |
| Percent Intercepted | 6.1 | 9.9 | 1.9 | 9.3 | 6.3 | 4.7 | 6.6 | 7.1 | 6.0 | 7.4 | 8.8 | 3.6 | 8.4 |
| **PUNTING:** | | | | | | | | | | | | | |
| Number | 52 | 64 | 55 | 60 | 64 | 49 | 64 | 49 | 60 | 64 | 44 | 65 | 60 |
| Average Distance | 38.5 | 39.7 | 42.0 | 42.0 | 43.8 | 41.2 | 42.3 | 39.2 | 43.1 | 44.2 | 44.9 | 44.3 | 42.1 |
| **PUNT RETURNS:** | | | | | | | | | | | | | |
| Number | 23 | 27 | 21 | 23 | 31 | 26 | 25 | 31 | 28 | 30 | 30 | 24 | 15 |
| Yards | 127 | 182 | 208 | 175 | 227 | 172 | 129 | 209 | 119 | 183 | 232 | 217 | 65 |
| Average Yards | 5.5 | 6.7 | 9.9 | 7.6 | 7.3 | 6.6 | 5.2 | 6.7 | 4.3 | 6.1 | 7.7 | 9.0 | 4.3 |
| Touchdowns | 0 | 0 | 0 | 0 | 0 | 0 | 1 | 0 | 0 | 0 | 0 | 0 | 0 |
| **KICKOFF RETURNS:** | | | | | | | | | | | | | |
| Number | 47 | 47 | 45 | 69 | 43 | 35 | 40 | 41 | 52 | 44 | 45 | 43 | 62 |
| Yards | 1030 | 1055 | 900 | 1264 | 916 | 852 | 941 | 894 | 973 | 964 | 1045 | 1167 | 1363 |
| Average Yards | 21.9 | 22.4 | 20.0 | 18.3 | 21.3 | 24.3 | 23.5 | 21.8 | 18.7 | 21.9 | 23.2 | 27.1 | 22.0 |
| Touchdowns | 1 | 0 | 1 | 0 | 0 | 0 | 0 | 0 | 0 | 0 | 0 | 1 | 0 |
| **INTERCEPTION RETURNS:** | | | | | | | | | | | | | |
| Number | 30 | 10 | 31 | 15 | 19 | 22 | 23 | 22 | 30 | 16 | 21 | 20 | 15 |
| Yards | 297 | 111 | 624 | 97 | 365 | 358 | 362 | 294 | 341 | 130 | 178 | 141 | 189 |
| Average Yards | 9.9 | 11.1 | 20.1 | 6.5 | 19.2 | 16.3 | 15.7 | 13.4 | 11.4 | 8.1 | 8.5 | 7.1 | 12.6 |
| Touchdowns | 0 | 0 | 6 | 0 | 2 | 1 | 3 | 2 | 0 | 0 | 0 | 0 | 0 |
| **PENALTIES:** | | | | | | | | | | | | | |
| Number | 51 | 83 | 49 | 62 | 68 | 64 | 64 | 48 | 57 | 61 | 46 | 63 | 69 |
| Yards | 504 | 707 | 534 | 600 | 726 | 578 | 625 | 460 | 544 | 606 | 456 | 604 | 713 |
| **FUMBLES:** | | | | | | | | | | | | | |
| Number | 24 | 18 | 20 | 22 | 13 | 18 | 17 | 49 | 24 | 27 | 42 | 14 | 29 |
| Number Lost | 12 | 10 | 12 | 17 | 9 | 12 | 9 | 26 | 10 | 14 | 22 | 4 | 15 |
| **POINTS:** | | | | | | | | | | | | | |
| Total | 288 | 194 | 362 | 177 | 239 | 332 | 265 | 271 | 321 | 240 | 288 | 208 | 178 |
| PAT Attempts | 37 | 25 | 46 | 23 | 28 | 41 | 31 | 32 | 40 | 28 | 34 | 21 | 19 |
| PAT Made | 35 | 23 | 44 | 21 | 26 | 41 | 31 | 32 | 39 | 27 | 33 | 21 | 19 |
| FG Attempts | 19 | 16 | 20 | 13 | 24 | 28 | 22 | 26 | 20 | 19 | 25 | 35 | 23 |
| FG Made | 9 | 7 | 12 | 6 | 13 | 15 | 14 | 13 | 14 | 11 | 15 | 19 | 15 |
| Percent FG Made | 47.4 | 43.8 | 60.0 | 46.2 | 54.2 | 53.6 | 63.6 | 50.0 | 70.0 | 57.9 | 60.0 | 54.3 | 65.2 |
| Safeties | 2 | 0 | 0 | 0 | 3 | 0 | 0 | 1 | 0 | 0 | 3 | 2 | 0 |

### DEFENSE

| | BALT. | CHI. | CLEVE. | DALL. | DET. | G.BAY | L.A. | N.Y. | PHIL. | PITT. | ST.L. | S.F. | WASH. |
|---|---|---|---|---|---|---|---|---|---|---|---|---|---|
| **FIRST DOWNS:** | | | | | | | | | | | | | |
| Total | 195 | 202 | 208 | 216 | 204 | 199 | 221 | 183 | 205 | 224 | 158 | 180 | 223 |
| by Rushing | 86 | 94 | 92 | 106 | 87 | 74 | 87 | 79 | 117 | 90 | 56 | 82 | 77 |
| by Passing | 98 | 84 | 102 | 97 | 94 | 110 | 114 | 89 | 81 | 120 | 93 | 89 | 126 |
| by Penalty | 11 | 24 | 14 | 13 | 23 | 15 | 20 | 15 | 7 | 14 | 9 | 9 | 20 |
| **RUSHING:** | | | | | | | | | | | | | |
| Number | 379 | 403 | 405 | 447 | 360 | 350 | 419 | 396 | 449 | 414 | 344 | 363 | 362 |
| Yards | 1591 | 1679 | 1643 | 2242 | 1348 | 1285 | 1718 | 1267 | 2200 | 1493 | 1212 | 1587 | 1502 |
| Average Yards | 4.2 | 4.2 | 4.1 | 5.0 | 3.7 | 3.7 | 4.1 | 3.2 | 4.9 | 3.6 | 3.5 | 4.4 | 4.1 |
| Touchdowns | 17 | 17 | 10 | 20 | 9 | 7 | 16 | 8 | 14 | 13 | 8 | 13 | 9 |
| **PASSING:** | | | | | | | | | | | | | |
| Attempts | 298 | 291 | 319 | 293 | 354 | 365 | 339 | 297 | 283 | 361 | 300 | 293 | 321 |
| Completions | 144 | 146 | 163 | 146 | 175 | 192 | 168 | 142 | 139 | 184 | 156 | 140 | 169 |
| Completion Pct. | 48.3 | 50.2 | 51.1 | 49.8 | 49.4 | 52.6 | 49.6 | 47.8 | 49.1 | 51.0 | 52.0 | 47.8 | 52.6 |
| Gross Yards | 2068 | 1808 | 2370 | 2305 | 2275 | 2432 | 2510 | 2010 | 1984 | 3075 | 2147 | 2001 | 2768 |
| Yards Lost Tackled | 342 | 420 | 207 | 175 | 226 | 275 | 155 | 177 | 157 | 284 | 330 | 183 | 204 |
| Net Yards | 1726 | 1388 | 2163 | 2130 | 2049 | 2157 | 2355 | 1833 | 1827 | 2791 | 1817 | 1818 | 2564 |
| Avg. Yds per Att (Gs) | 6.9 | 6.2 | 7.4 | 7.9 | 6.4 | 6.7 | 7.4 | 6.8 | 7.0 | 8.5 | 7.2 | 6.8 | 8.6 |
| Avg. Yds per Com (Gs) | 14.4 | 12.4 | 14.5 | 15.8 | 13.0 | 12.7 | 14.9 | 14.2 | 14.3 | 16.7 | 13.8 | 14.3 | 16.4 |
| Touchdowns | 8 | 14 | 15 | 22 | 17 | 19 | 18 | 19 | 14 | 20 | 20 | 11 | 24 |
| Interceptions | 30 | 10 | 31 | 15 | 19 | 22 | 23 | 22 | 30 | 16 | 21 | 20 | 15 |
| Percent Intercepted | 10.1 | 3.4 | 9.7 | 5.1 | 5.4 | 6.0 | 6.8 | 7.4 | 10.6 | 4.4 | 7.0 | 6.8 | 4.7 |
| **PUNTING:** | | | | | | | | | | | | | |
| Number | 54 | 72 | 46 | 50 | 69 | 66 | 50 | 66 | 48 | 54 | 63 | 62 | 50 |
| Average Distance | 46.4 | 41.3 | 45.5 | 42.1 | 39.0 | 39.4 | 43.8 | 40.8 | 43.6 | 43.4 | 44.3 | 41.2 | 39.5 |
| **PUNT RETURNS:** | | | | | | | | | | | | | |
| Number | 15 | 35 | 24 | 20 | 34 | 22 | 27 | 17 | 34 | 21 | 26 | 28 | 31 |
| Yards | 48 | 249 | 168 | 91 | 296 | 144 | 199 | 100 | 166 | 198 | 162 | 182 | 242 |
| Average Yards | 3.2 | 7.1 | 7.0 | 4.6 | 8.7 | 6.5 | 7.4 | 5.9 | 4.9 | 9.4 | 6.2 | 6.5 | 7.8 |
| Touchdowns | 0 | 1 | 0 | 0 | 0 | 0 | 0 | 0 | 0 | 0 | 0 | 0 | 0 |
| **KICKOFF RETURNS:** | | | | | | | | | | | | | |
| Number | 44 | 37 | 62 | 31 | 45 | 57 | 52 | 47 | 53 | 48 | 57 | 38 | 42 |
| Yards | 1253 | 1029 | 1177 | 803 | 979 | 1158 | 1083 | 995 | 1076 | 1078 | 1245 | 769 | 719 |
| Average Yards | 28.5 | 27.8 | 19.0 | 25.9 | 21.8 | 20.3 | 20.8 | 21.2 | 20.3 | 22.5 | 21.8 | 20.2 | 17.1 |
| Touchdowns | 1 | 1 | 0 | 1 | 0 | 0 | 0 | 0 | 0 | 0 | 0 | 0 | 0 |
| **INTERCEPTION RETURNS:** | | | | | | | | | | | | | |
| Number | 24 | 32 | 5 | 33 | 21 | 13 | 22 | 23 | 20 | 21 | 25 | 12 | 23 |
| Yards | 272 | 627 | 58 | 366 | 314 | 185 | 182 | 253 | 277 | 165 | 419 | 159 | 210 |
| Average Yards | 11.3 | 19.6 | 11.6 | 11.1 | 15.0 | 14.2 | 8.3 | 11.0 | 13.9 | 7.9 | 16.8 | 13.3 | 9.1 |
| Touchdowns | 1 | 4 | 1 | 2 | 2 | 0 | 0 | 2 | 1 | 0 | 0 | 0 | 1 |
| **PENALTIES:** | | | | | | | | | | | | | |
| Number | 59 | 75 | 48 | 72 | 60 | 61 | 59 | 55 | 54 | 58 | 52 | 64 | 68 |
| Yards | 538 | 704 | 526 | 671 | 637 | 636 | 517 | 532 | 597 | 565 | 500 | 580 | 654 |
| **FUMBLES:** | | | | | | | | | | | | | |
| Number | 20 | 13 | 27 | 21 | 19 | 23 | 29 | 28 | 31 | 25 | 35 | 15 | 31 |
| Number Lost | 9 | 9 | 14 | 11 | 11 | 15 | 13 | 12 | 15 | 13 | 23 | 8 | 19 |
| **POINTS:** | | | | | | | | | | | | | |
| Total | 234 | 299 | 217 | 369 | 212 | 209 | 297 | 261 | 246 | 275 | 230 | 205 | 309 |
| PAT Attempts | 27 | 38 | 26 | 45 | 28 | 25 | 35 | 32 | 27 | 33 | 30 | 25 | 34 |
| PAT Made | 27 | 37 | 25 | 44 | 27 | 24 | 34 | 31 | 24 | 33 | 29 | 23 | 34 |
| FG Attempts | 30 | 20 | 21 | 25 | 12 | 13 | 29 | 23 | 28 | 21 | 16 | 20 | 32 |
| FG Made | 15 | 8 | 12 | 17 | 5 | 9 | 17 | 12 | 16 | 14 | 7 | 10 | 21 |
| Percent FG Made | 50.0 | 40.0 | 57.1 | 68.0 | 41.7 | 69.2 | 58.6 | 52.2 | 57.1 | 66.7 | 43.8 | 50.0 | 65.6 |
| Safeties | 0 | 2 | 0 | 2 | 1 | 1 | 1 | 1 | 0 | 1 | 0 | 1 | 1 |

**1960 NFL CHAMPIONSHIP GAME**
**December 26, at Philadelphia**
**(Attendance 67,325)**

## Start with Hornung, End with Dean

The Green Bay Packers, a tough, young team built by coach Vince Lombardi, came to Franklin Field to face the Eagles, a veteran team centering around Norm Van Brocklin and Chuck Bednarik, for the NFL title. The Packers got the first break of the game by recovering an Eagle fumble on the Philadelphia 14-yard line on the first play from scrimmage, but four Green Bay running plays gained only nine yards. The Eagles took the ball on downs but fumbled it away three plays later on the 22-yard line. Again the Packers couldn't move the ball, and they had to settle for a Paul Hornung field goal. The quarter ended with the score 3-0, as both defenses played well against the enemy's strength. The Eagles shut off the Green Bay running game; the Packers stopped Van Brocklin's passes. The halftime score was Philadelphia 10, Green Bay 6, and neither team scored in the third quarter. Within two minutes of the fourth period, however, Green Bay capped an 80-yard drive with a Bart Starr-to-Max McGee touchdown pass to give the Packers a 13-10 lead. On the kickoff following the touchdown, Ted Dean brought the Eagles back into the game by returning the ball to the Green Bay 39. Seven plays later, Dean carried the ball over from the 5-yard line. The Packers drove downfield in the waning minutes, but time ran out with the ball on the Philadelphia 9-yard line and the score 17-13 in favor of the Eagles.

### SCORING

| | | | | | |
|---|---|---|---|---|---|
| PHILADELPHIA | 0 | 10 | 0 | 7–17 |
| GREEN BAY | 3 | 3 | 0 | 7–13 |

First Quarter

| | | |
|---|---|---|
| G. B. | Hornung, 20 yard field goal | 6:20 |

Second Quarter

| | | |
|---|---|---|
| G. B. | Hornung, 23 yard field goal | 1:44 |
| PHI. | McDonald, 35 yard pass from Van Brocklin<br>PAT – Walston (kick) | 8:08 |
| PHI. | Walston, 15 yard field goal | 11:48 |

Fourth Quarter

| | | |
|---|---|---|
| G. B. | McGee, 7 yard pass from Starr<br>PAT – Hornung (kick) | 1:53 |
| PHI. | Dean, 5 yard rush<br>PAT – Walston (kick) | 5:21 |

### TEAM STATISTICS

| PHI. | | G.B. |
|---|---|---|
| 13 | First Downs – Total | 22 |
| 5 | First Downs – Rushing | 14 |
| 6 | First Downs – Passing | 8 |
| 2 | First Downs – Penalty | 0 |
| 99 | Rushing Yardage | 223 |
| 20 | Pass Attempts | 35 |
| 9 | Pass Completions | 21 |
| 45.0 | Completion Percentage | 60.0 |
| 204 | Passing Yardage | 178 |
| 10.2 | Avg. Yards per Attempt | 5.1 |
| 22.7 | Avg. Yards per Completion | 8.5 |
| 7 | Yards Lost Tackled | 0 |
| 197 | Net Passing Yardage | 178 |
| 0 | Interceptions By | 1 |
| 0 | Interception Return Yardage | 0 |
| 3 | Fumbles – Number | 1 |
| 2 | Fumbles – Lost Ball | 1 |
| 0 | Penalties – Number | 4 |
| 0 | Yards Penalized | 27 |
| 0 | Missed Field Goals | 1 |

### INDIVIDUAL STATISTICS

| PHILADELPHIA | No. | Yds. | Avg. | GREEN BAY | No. | Yds. | Avg. |
|---|---|---|---|---|---|---|---|
| **PUNTING** | | | | | | | |
| Van Brocklin | 6 | | 39.5 | McGee | 5 | | 45.2 |
| **PUNT RETURNS** | | | | | | | |
| Dean | 1 | 10 | 10.0 | Wood | 2 | 11 | 5.5 |
| | | | | Carpenter | 2 | 7 | 3.5 |
| | | | | | 4 | 18 | 4.5 |
| **KICKOFF RETURNS** | | | | | | | |
| Dean | 1 | 58 | 58.0 | Symank | 2 | 49 | 24.5 |
| Brown | 1 | 20 | 20.0 | | | | |
| Lucas | 1 | 9 | 9.0 | | | | |
| Robb | 1 | 4 | 4.0 | | | | |
| | 4 | 91 | 22.8 | | | | |

### PHILADELPHIA EAGLES 10-2-0 Buck Shaw

| Scores of Each Game | | |
|---|---|---|
| 24 | CLEVELAND | 41 |
| 27 | Dallas | 25 |
| 31 | ST. LOUIS | 27 |
| 28 | DETROIT | 10 |
| 31 | Cleveland | 29 |
| 34 | PITTSBURGH | 7 |
| 19 | WASHINGTON | 13 |
| 17 | New York | 10 |
| 31 | NEW YORK | 23 |
| 20 | St. Louis | 6 |
| 21 | Pittsburgh | 27 |
| 38 | Washington | 28 |

| Use Name | Pos. | Hgt | Wgt | Age | Int | Pts |
|---|---|---|---|---|---|---|
| Jim McCusker | OT | 6'2" | 245 | 24 | | |
| J. D. Smith | OT | 6'5" | 250 | 24 | | 6 |
| Howard Keys | C-OT | 6'3" | 235 | 25 | | |
| John Wilcox | DE-OT | 6'5" | 230 | 22 | | |
| Stan Campbell | OG | 6' | 230 | 30 | | |
| Jerry Huth | OG | 6' | 228 | 27 | | |
| John Wittenborn (from SF) | OG | 6'2" | 230 | 24 | | |
| Bill Lapham | C | 6'3" | 250 | 26 | | |
| Marion Campbell | DE | 6'3" | 250 | 31 | | |
| Joe Robb | LB-DE | 6'3" | 225 | 23 | | |
| Gene Gossage | DT-DE | 6'3" | 236 | 25 | | |
| Riley Gunnels | DT | 6'3" | 240 | 23 | | |
| Jess Richardson | DT | 6'2" | 262 | 30 | | |
| Ed Khayat | DE-DT | 6'3" | 240 | 25 | | |
| Maxie Baughan | LB | 6'1" | 220 | 22 | 3 | |
| John Nocera | LB | 6'1" | 215 | 26 | | |
| Chuck Weber | LB | 6'1" | 235 | 31 | 6 | |
| Bob Pellegrini | OG-LB | 6'2" | 235 | 25 | | |
| Chuck Bednarik | C-LB | 6'3" | 235 | 35 | 2 | |
| Tom Brookshier | DB | 6' | 198 | 28 | 1 | |
| Don Burroughs | DB | 6'4" | 186 | 29 | 9 | |
| Jimmy Carr | DB | 6'1" | 198 | 27 | 2 | 6 |
| Bobby Freeman | DB | 6'1" | 200 | 27 | 4 | |
| Bobby Jackson | DB | 6'1" | 190 | 24 | | |
| Gene Johnson | DB | 6' | 190 | 25 | 3 | |
| Sonny Jurgensen | QB | 5'11" | 200 | 26 | | |
| Norm Van Brocklin | QB | 6'1" | 202 | 34 | | |
| Jerry Reichow | OE-QB | 6'2" | 220 | 25 | | |
| Billy Barnes | HB | 5'11" | 198 | 25 | | 36 |
| Timmy Brown | HB | 5'10" | 195 | 23 | | 24 |
| Theron Sapp | HB | 6'1" | 200 | 25 | | |
| Ted Dean | FB-HB | 6'2" | 210 | 22 | | 18 |
| Clarence Peaks | FB | 6'1" | 220 | 24 | | 18 |
| Tommy McDonald | FL | 5'10" | 182 | 26 | | 78 |
| Dick Lucas | OE | 6'2" | 210 | 26 | | |
| Pete Retzlaff | OE | 6'1" | 210 | 29 | | 30 |
| Bobby Walston | FL-OE | 6' | 190 | 31 | | 105 |

### CLEVELAND BROWNS 8-3-1 Paul Brown

| Scores of Each Game | | |
|---|---|---|
| 41 | Philadelphia | 24 |
| 28 | PITTSBURGH | 20 |
| 48 | Dallas | 7 |
| 29 | PHILADELPHIA | 31 |
| 31 | Washington | 10 |
| 13 | NEW YORK | 17 |
| 28 | ST. LOUIS | 27 |
| 10 | Pittsburgh | 14 |
| 17 | St. Louis | 17 |
| 27 | WASHINGTON | 16 |
| 42 | CHICAGO | 0 |
| 48 | New York | 34 |

| Use Name | Pos. | Hgt | Wgt | Age | Int | Pts |
|---|---|---|---|---|---|---|
| Bob Denton | OT | 6'4" | 240 | 26 | | |
| Mike McCormack | OT | 6'4" | 247 | 33 | | |
| Dick Schafrath | OT | 6'3" | 245 | 24 | | |
| Gene Selawski | OT | 6'4" | 252 | 24 | | |
| Gene Hickerson | OG | 6'3" | 248 | 25 | | |
| Jim Ray Smith | OG | 6'3" | 245 | 29 | | |
| John Wooten | OG | 6'2" | 248 | 25 | | |
| John Morrow | C | 6'3" | 240 | 27 | | |
| Jim Houston | DE | 6'2" | 230 | 23 | | |
| Jim Marshall | DE | 6'3" | 220 | 23 | | |
| Paul Wiggin | DE | 6'3" | 240 | 26 | 1 | 6 |
| Bob Gain | DT | 6'3" | 260 | 32 | 1 | 6 |
| Floyd Peters | DT | 6'4" | 250 | 25 | | |
| Jim Prestel | DT | 6'5" | 250 | 23 | | |
| Larry Stephens | DT | 6'4" | 248 | 22 | 1 | 6 |
| Vince Costello | LB | 6' | 225 | 28 | | |
| Galen Fiss | LB | 6' | 227 | 30 | 1 | |
| Walt Michaels | LB | 6' | 237 | 31 | | |
| Dave Lloyd | C-LB | 6'3" | 248 | 24 | | |
| Ross Fichtner | DB | 6' | 185 | 22 | | |
| Don Fleming | DB | 6' | 185 | 23 | 5 | |
| Bobby Franklin | DB | 5'11" | 180 | 24 | 8 | 12 |
| Rich Mostardi | DB | 5'11" | 188 | 22 | | |
| Bernie Parrish | DB | 5'11" | 195 | 25 | 6 | 6 |
| Jim Shofner | DB | 6'2" | 190 | 24 | 8 | |
| Len Dawson | QB | 6' | 195 | 26 | | |
| Milt Plum | QB | 6'1" | 205 | 26 | | 12 |
| Prentice Gautt | HB | 6' | 195 | 22 | | 6 |
| Bobby Mitchell | HB | 6' | 188 | 25 | | 72 |
| Jamie Caleb | FB-HB | 6'1" | 210 | 23 | | 6 |
| Jimmy Brown | FB | 6'2" | 228 | 24 | | 66 |
| Ray Renfro | FL | 6'1" | 192 | 29 | | 24 |
| A. D. Williams | OE-FL | 6'2" | 210 | 27 | | |
| Leon Clarke | OE | 6'4" | 234 | 27 | | 24 |
| Rich Kreitling | OE | 6'2" | 208 | 25 | | 18 |
| Fred Murphy | OE | 6'3" | 205 | 22 | | |
| Gern Nagler | OE | 6'2" | 190 | 27 | | 18 |
| Sam Baker | K | 6'2" | 217 | 28 | | 80 |

Lou Groza – Voluntarily Retired

### NEW YORK GIANTS 6-4-2 Jim Lee Howell

| Scores of Each Game | | |
|---|---|---|
| 21 | San Francisco | 19 |
| 35 | St. Louis | 14 |
| 19 | Pittsburgh | 17 |
| 24 | WASHINGTON | 24 |
| 13 | ST. LOUIS | 20 |
| 17 | Cleveland | 13 |
| 27 | PITTSBURGH | 24 |
| 10 | PHILADELPHIA | 17 |
| 23 | Philadelphia | 31 |
| 31 | DALLAS | 31 |
| 17 | Washington | 3 |
| 34 | CLEVELAND | 48 |

| Use Name | Pos. | Hgt | Wgt | Age | Int | Pts |
|---|---|---|---|---|---|---|
| Don Boll | OT | 6'2" | 270 | 33 | | |
| Rosey Brown | OT | 6'3" | 245 | 27 | | |
| Frank Youso | OT | 6'4" | 260 | 24 | | |
| Lou Cordileone | OG | 6' | 240 | 23 | | |
| Bill Crawford | OG | 6'1" | 235 | 23 | | |
| Darrell Dess | OG | 6' | 235 | 24 | | |
| Jack Stroud | OG | 6'1" | 235 | 31 | | |
| Ray Wietecha | C | 6'1" | 225 | 31 | | |
| Bob Schmidt | OT-OG-C | 6'4" | 245 | 24 | | |
| Jim Katcavage | DE | 6'3" | 230 | 25 | | |
| Andy Robustelli | DE | 6'1" | 230 | 34 | | |
| Tom Scott | LB-DE | 6'2" | 220 | 30 | 1 | 6 |
| Rosey Grier | DT | 6'5" | 285 | 27 | 2 | |
| Proverb Jacobs | DT | 6'4" | 255 | 25 | | |
| Dick Modzelewski | DT | 6' | 260 | 29 | | |
| Sam Huff | LB | 6'1" | 230 | 25 | 3 | |
| Jim Leo | LB | 6'1" | 215 | 22 | | |
| Cliff Livingston | LB | 6'3" | 215 | 30 | 1 | |
| Harland Svare | LB | 6' | 215 | 29 | 1 | |
| Lindon Crow | DB | 6'1" | 205 | 27 | 3 | 6 |
| Dick Lynch | DB | 6'1" | 200 | 24 | 3 | 6 |
| Dick Nolan | DB | 6'1" | 185 | 28 | 3 | |
| Jimmy Patton | DB | 6' | 180 | 28 | 6 | |
| Lee Riley | DB | 6'1" | 190 | 28 | 1 | |
| Bill Stits | DB | 6' | 195 | 29 | | |
| Chuck Conerly | QB | 6'1" | 185 | 36 | | |
| Lee Grosscup | QB | 6'1" | 185 | 23 | | |
| George Shaw | QB | 6'1" | 180 | 27 | | |
| Don Chandler | HB | 6'2" | 205 | 25 | | |
| Frank Gifford | HB | 6'1" | 200 | 30 | | 42 |
| Joe Morrison | HB | 6'1" | 195 | 22 | | 30 |
| Ed Sutton | HB | 6'1" | 207 | 25 | | |
| Alex Webster | HB | 6'3" | 220 | 29 | | |
| Mel Triplett | FB | 6'1" | 215 | 28 | | 36 |
| Phil King | HB-FB | 6'4" | 225 | 24 | | |
| Bill Kimber | OE | 6'2" | 190 | 24 | | |
| Kyle Rote | OE | 6' | 200 | 31 | | 60 |
| Bob Schnelker | OE | 6'3" | 215 | 30 | | 12 |
| Pat Summerall | OE | 6'4" | 235 | 30 | | 71 |
| Bob Simms | DE-LB-OE | 6'1" | 210 | 22 | | |

### ST. LOUIS CARDINALS 6-5-1 Pop Ivy

| Scores of Each Game | | |
|---|---|---|
| 43 | Los Angeles | 21 |
| 14 | NEW YORK | 35 |
| 27 | Philadelphia | 31 |
| 14 | Pittsburgh | 27 |
| 12 | DALLAS | 10 |
| 20 | New York | 13 |
| 44 | WASHINGTON | 7 |
| 27 | Cleveland | 28 |
| 26 | Washington | 14 |
| 17 | CLEVELAND | 17 |
| 6 | PHILADELPHIA | 20 |
| 38 | PITTSBURGH | 7 |

| Use Name | Pos. | Hgt | Wgt | Age | Int | Pts |
|---|---|---|---|---|---|---|
| Ed Cook | OT | 6'2" | 245 | 28 | | |
| Dale Memmelaar | OT | 6'2" | 265 | 23 | | |
| Ken Panfil | OT | 6'6" | 265 | 29 | | |
| Tom Day | OG-OT | 6'2" | 240 | 25 | | |
| Ken Gray | OG | 6'2" | 245 | 24 | | |
| Mike McGee | OG | 6'1" | 230 | 22 | | |
| Mike Rabold | OG | 6'2" | 235 | 23 | | |
| Don Gillis | C | 6'3" | 250 | 25 | | |
| Ernie Fritsch | LB-C | 6' | 230 | 23 | | |
| Luke Owens | DE | 6'2" | 255 | 27 | 2 | |
| Jerry Perry | DE | 6'4" | 240 | 29 | | 44 |
| Leo Sugar | DE | 6'1" | 220 | 31 | | |
| Ed Culpepper | DT | 6'1" | 255 | 26 | | |
| Frank Fuller | DT | 6'4" | 245 | 31 | 2 | |
| Don Owens (from PHI) | DT | 6'5" | 255 | 28 | | |
| Tom Redmond | DT | 6'5" | 250 | 23 | | |
| Ted Bates | LB | 6'3" | 220 | 23 | | |
| Bill Koman | LB | 6'2" | 230 | 26 | 1 | |
| Dale Meinert | LB | 6'2" | 218 | 27 | 3 | |
| John Tracey | LB | 6'3" | 228 | 26 | 1 | 2 |
| Charley Ellzey | C-LB | 6'3" | 245 | 22 | | |
| Joe Driskill | DB | 6'1" | 195 | 23 | | |
| Freddy Glick | DB | 6'1" | 185 | 23 | | |
| Jimmy Hill | DB | 6'2" | 190 | 31 | | |
| Billy Stacy | DB | 6'1" | 195 | 24 | 4 | 6 |
| Larry Wilson | DB | 6' | 187 | 22 | 2 | |
| Jerry Norton | DB | 5'11" | 195 | 30 | 10 | |
| Bobby Towns | HB-OE-DB | 6'1" | 180 | 22 | | |
| King Hill | QB | 6'3" | 207 | 24 | | 6 |
| George Izo | QB | 6'3" | 230 | 23 | | |
| John Roach | QB | 6'4" | 195 | 27 | | 6 |
| Joe Childress | HB | 6' | 200 | 26 | | 12 |
| Bobby Joe Conrad | HB | 6' | 195 | 25 | | 34 |
| John David Crow | HB | 6'2" | 215 | 25 | | 54 |
| Willie West | HB | 5'10" | 185 | 22 | | |
| Mal Hammack | FB | 6'2" | 205 | 27 | | 12 |
| Frank Mestnik | FB | 6'2" | 200 | 22 | | 18 |
| Hugh McInnis | OE | 6'3" | 215 | 22 | | |
| Sonny Randle | OE | 6'2" | 187 | 24 | | 90 |
| Perry Richards | OE | 6'2" | 205 | 26 | | |

### PITTSBURGH STEELERS 5-6-1 Buddy Parker

| Scores of Each Game | | |
|---|---|---|
| 35 | Dallas | 28 |
| 20 | Cleveland | 28 |
| 17 | NEW YORK | 19 |
| 27 | ST. LOUIS | 14 |
| 27 | Washington | 27 |
| 13 | GREEN BAY | 19 |
| 7 | Philadelphia | 34 |
| 24 | New York | 27 |
| 14 | CLEVELAND | 10 |
| 22 | WASHINGTON | 10 |
| 27 | PHILADELPHIA | 21 |
| 7 | St. Louis | 38 |

| Use Name | Pos. | Hgt | Wgt | Age | Int | Pts |
|---|---|---|---|---|---|---|
| Byron Beams | OT | 6'6" | 248 | 26 | | |
| John Kapele | OT | 6' | 240 | 23 | | |
| Frank Varrichione | OT | 6'1" | 230 | 28 | | |
| Dan James | C-OT | 6'4" | 275 | 23 | | |
| John Nisby | OG | 6'1" | 230 | 27 | | |
| Mike Sandusky | OG | 6' | 230 | 27 | | |
| Ron Stehouwer | OT-OG | 6'2" | 240 | 23 | | |
| Ed Beatty | C | 6'3" | 225 | 28 | | |
| Billy Ray Smith | DE | 6'4" | 230 | 25 | | |
| George Tarasovic | DE | 6'4" | 245 | 31 | 1 | |
| Ernie Stautner | DT-DE | 6'1" | 230 | 35 | | |
| Joe Krupa | DT | 6'2" | 225 | 27 | | |
| Joe Lewis | DT | 6'2" | 260 | 25 | | 6 |
| Ken Longenecker | DT | 6'4" | 285 | 22 | | |
| Will Renfro | DE-DT | 6'5" | 220 | 28 | | |
| Dick Campbell | LB | 6'1" | 225 | 24 | 1 | |
| Rudy Hayes | LB | 6' | 215 | 25 | | |
| Mike Henry | LB | 6'2" | 215 | 24 | | |
| John Reger | LB | 6' | 230 | 29 | 1 | |
| Dean Derby | DB | 6' | 185 | 26 | 3 | |
| Dick Moegle | DB | 6' | 195 | 26 | 6 | |
| Jack Morris (from LA) | DB | 6' | 190 | 28 | | |
| Bert Rechichar | DB | 6'1" | 210 | 30 | 1 | 15 |
| Scooter Scudero | DB | 5'10" | 174 | 30 | | |
| Don Sutherin | DB | 5'10" | 190 | 24 | 1 | |
| Fred Williamson | DB | 6'2" | 205 | 22 | | |
| Junior Wren | DB | 6' | 205 | 30 | 2 | |
| Rudy Bukich | QB | 6'1" | 200 | 29 | | |
| Bobby Layne | QB | 6'1" | 210 | 33 | | 48 |
| Rex Johnston | HB | 6'1" | 195 | 22 | | |
| Tom Tracy | FB-HB | 5'9" | 205 | 28 | | 63 |
| Tom Barnett | DB-HB | 5'11" | 190 | 23 | | |
| John Henry Johnson | FB | 6'2" | 215 | 30 | | 18 |
| Larry Krutko | FB | 6' | 225 | 25 | | |
| Charlie Scales | FB | 5'11" | 210 | 21 | | |
| Buddy Dial | FL | 6'1" | 195 | 23 | | 54 |
| Darrell Brewster | OE | 6'3" | 210 | 30 | | |
| Jack McClairen | OE | 6'4" | 215 | 29 | | |
| Preston Carpenter | HB-OE | 6'2" | 205 | 26 | | 12 |
| Jimmy Orr | FL-OE | 5'11" | 200 | 24 | | 24 |
| Bobby Joe Green | K | 5'11" | 175 | 22 | | |

Ron Hall – Military Service

### WASHINGTON REDSKINS 1-9-2 Mike Nixon

| Scores of Each Game | | |
|---|---|---|
| 0 | Baltimore | 20 |
| 26 | DALLAS | 14 |
| 24 | New York | 24 |
| 27 | PITTSBURGH | 27 |
| 10 | CLEVELAND | 31 |
| 7 | St. Louis | 44 |
| 13 | Philadelphia | 19 |
| 14 | ST. LOUIS | 26 |
| 10 | Pittsburgh | 22 |
| 16 | Cleveland | 27 |
| 3 | NEW YORK | 17 |
| 28 | PHILADELPHIA | 38 |

| Use Name | Pos. | Hgt | Wgt | Age | Int | Pts |
|---|---|---|---|---|---|---|
| Ray Lemek | OT | 6' | 240 | 26 | | |
| Don Lawrence | DT-OT | 6'1" | 245 | 23 | | |
| Don Stallings | DE-DT-OT | 6'4" | 250 | 21 | | |
| Fran O'Brien | OG | 6'1" | 240 | 25 | | |
| Vince Promuto | OG | 6'1" | 240 | 22 | | |
| Red Stephens | OG | 6' | 232 | 30 | | |
| Bob Whitlow | OG | 6'1" | 232 | 24 | | |
| Jim Schrader | C | 6'2" | 252 | 28 | | |
| Bob Khayat | OG-C | 6'2" | 230 | 22 | | 64 |
| John Paluck | DE | 6'2" | 235 | 27 | | |
| Art Gob (to LA-A) | DE | 6'4" | 230 | 23 | | |
| Andy Stynchula | C-DE | 6'3" | 255 | 21 | | |
| Ray Krouse | DT | 6'3" | 270 | 33 | | |
| Bob Toneff | DT | 6'3" | 265 | 30 | | |
| Rod Breedlove | LB | 6'2" | 220 | 22 | 3 | |
| Ralph Felton | LB | 5'11" | 210 | 28 | | |
| Dick Lasse | LB | 6'2" | 225 | 24 | 3 | |
| Bill Roehnelt | LB | 6'1" | 230 | 24 | | |
| Roy Wilkins | LB | 6'3" | 223 | 26 | | |
| Billy Brewer | DB | 6' | 190 | 25 | | |
| Jim Crotty | DB | 5'11" | 195 | 22 | 1 | |
| Ben Scotti | DB | 6'1" | 185 | 23 | 4 | |
| Jim Wulff | DB | 5'11" | 185 | 24 | | |
| Gary Glick | HB-DB | 6'2" | 200 | 29 | 3 | 6 |
| Pat Heenan | OE-DB | 6'1" | 190 | 22 | 1 | |
| Eagle Day | QB | 6' | 185 | 28 | | |
| Ralph Guglielmi | QB | 6'1" | 195 | 27 | | |
| M. C. Reynolds | QB | 6' | 195 | 25 | | |
| Dick Haley | HB | 5'10" | 195 | 23 | | |
| Ed Vereb | HB | 6' | 190 | 26 | | |
| Sam Horner | DB-HB | 6' | 195 | 22 | | |
| Dick James | DB-HB | 5'9" | 180 | 26 | | 36 |
| Jim Podoley | OE-HB | 6'2" | 205 | 27 | | 6 |
| Don Bosseler | FB | 6'1" | 212 | 24 | | 12 |
| Johnny Olszewski | FB | 5'11" | 202 | 29 | | 18 |
| Bill Anderson | OE | 6'3" | 210 | 24 | | 18 |
| Tom Osborne | OE | 6'3" | 190 | 23 | | |
| Joe Walton | OE | 5'11" | 205 | 25 | | 18 |

## PHILADELPHIA EAGLES

### RUSHING

| Last Name | No. | Yds | Avg | TD |
|---|---|---|---|---|
| Peaks | 86 | 465 | 5.4 | 3 |
| Barnes | 117 | 315 | 2.7 | 4 |
| Dean | 113 | 304 | 2.7 | 0 |
| Brown | 9 | 35 | 3.2 | 2 |
| Sapp | 9 | 20 | 2.2 | 0 |
| Jurgensen | 4 | 5 | 1.3 | 0 |
| Retzlaff | 2 | 3 | 1.5 | 0 |
| Van Brocklin | 11 | -13 | -1.2 | 0 |

### RECEIVING

| Last Name | No. | Yds | Avg | TD |
|---|---|---|---|---|
| Retzlaff | 46 | 826 | 18 | 5 |
| McDonald | 39 | 801 | 21 | 13 |
| Walston | 30 | 563 | 19 | 4 |
| Barnes | 19 | 132 | 7 | 2 |
| Dean | 15 | 218 | 15 | 3 |
| Peaks | 14 | 116 | 8 | 0 |
| Brown | 9 | 247 | 27 | 2 |
| Lucas | 3 | 34 | 11 | 0 |
| Sapp | 2 | 20 | 10 | 0 |

### PUNT RETURNS

| Last Name | No. | Yds | Avg | TD |
|---|---|---|---|---|
| Dean | 16 | 65 | 4 | 0 |
| Brown | 10 | 47 | 5 | 0 |
| Jackson | 1 | 5 | 5 | 0 |
| McDonald | 1 | 2 | 2 | 0 |

### KICKOFF RETURNS

| Last Name | No. | Yds | Avg | TD |
|---|---|---|---|---|
| Dean | 26 | 533 | 21 | 0 |
| Brown | 11 | 295 | 27 | 0 |
| McDonald | 2 | 45 | 23 | 0 |
| Robb | 4 | 44 | 11 | 0 |
| Reichow | 4 | 28 | 7 | 0 |
| Baughan | 2 | 18 | 9 | 0 |
| Carr | 1 | 5 | 5 | 0 |
| Lucas | 1 | 5 | 5 | 0 |

### PASSING – PUNTING – KICKING

**PASSING**

| Last Name | Att | Comp | % | Yds | Yd/Att | TD | Int–% | RK |
|---|---|---|---|---|---|---|---|---|
| Van Brocklin | 284 | 153 | 54 | 2471 | 8.7 | 24 | 17– 6 | 2 |
| Jurgensen | 44 | 24 | 55 | 486 | 11.0 | 5 | 1– 2 | |
| Barnes | 3 | 0 | 0 | 0 | 0.0 | 0 | 2– 67 | |

**PUNTING**

| Last Name | No | Avg |
|---|---|---|
| Van Brocklin | 60 | 43.1 |

**KICKING**

| Last Name | XP | Att | % | FG | Att | % |
|---|---|---|---|---|---|---|
| Walston | 39 | 40 | 98 | 14 | 20 | 70 |
| Wittenborn | 0 | 0 | 0 | 0 | 3 | 0 |

## CLEVELAND BROWNS

### RUSHING

| Last Name | No. | Yds | Avg | TD |
|---|---|---|---|---|
| Brown | 215 | 1257 | 5.8 | 9 |
| Mitchell | 111 | 506 | 4.6 | 5 |
| Gautt | 28 | 159 | 5.7 | 1 |
| Caleb | 8 | 60 | 7.5 | 1 |
| Dawson | 1 | 0 | 0.0 | 0 |
| Baker | 1 | -11 | -11.0 | 0 |
| Kreitling | 2 | -17 | -8.5 | 0 |
| Plum | 17 | -24 | -1.4 | 2 |

### RECEIVING

| Last Name | No. | Yds | Avg | TD |
|---|---|---|---|---|
| Mitchell | 45 | 612 | 14 | 6 |
| Nagler | 36 | 616 | 17 | 3 |
| Renfro | 24 | 378 | 16 | 4 |
| Brown | 19 | 204 | 11 | 2 |
| Kreitling | 16 | 316 | 20 | 3 |
| Clarke | 11 | 184 | 17 | 4 |
| Caleb | 5 | -18 | -4 | 0 |
| Murphy | 2 | 36 | 18 | 0 |
| Gautt | 1 | 10 | 10 | 0 |
| Williams | 1 | 5 | 5 | 0 |

### PUNT RETURNS

| Last Name | No. | Yds | Avg | TD |
|---|---|---|---|---|
| Shofner | 11 | 105 | 10 | 0 |
| Mitchell | 9 | 101 | 11 | 0 |
| Franklin | 1 | 2 | 2 | 0 |

### KICKOFF RETURNS

| Last Name | No. | Yds | Avg | TD |
|---|---|---|---|---|
| Mitchell | 17 | 432 | 25 | 1 |
| Brown | 14 | 300 | 21 | 0 |
| Caleb | 5 | 90 | 18 | 0 |
| Gautt | 3 | 47 | 16 | 0 |
| Franklin | 1 | 23 | 23 | 0 |
| Fleming | 1 | 8 | 8 | 0 |
| Parrish | 2 | 0 | 0 | 0 |
| Fichtner | 1 | 0 | 0 | 0 |
| Stephens | 1 | 0 | 0 | 0 |

### PASSING – PUNTING – KICKING

**PASSING**

| Last Name | Att | Comp | % | Yds | Yd/Att | TD | Int–% | RK |
|---|---|---|---|---|---|---|---|---|
| Plum | 250 | 151 | 60 | 2297 | 9.2 | 21 | 5– 2 | 1 |
| Dawson | 13 | 8 | 62 | 23 | 1.8 | 0 | 0– 0 | |
| Mitchell | 1 | 1 | 100 | 23 | 23.0 | 1 | 0– 0 | |

**PUNTING**

| Last Name | No | Avg |
|---|---|---|
| Baker | 55 | 42.0 |

**KICKING**

| Last Name | XP | Att | % | FG | Att | % |
|---|---|---|---|---|---|---|
| Baker | 44 | 46 | 96 | 12 | 20 | 60 |

## NEW YORK GIANTS

### RUSHING

| Last Name | No. | Yds | Avg | TD |
|---|---|---|---|---|
| Triplett | 124 | 573 | 4.6 | 4 |
| Morrison | 103 | 346 | 3.4 | 2 |
| Gifford | 77 | 232 | 3.0 | 4 |
| Sutton | 20 | 135 | 6.8 | 0 |
| King | 26 | 97 | 3.7 | 0 |
| Webster | 22 | 48 | 2.2 | 0 |
| Chandler | 2 | 19 | 9.5 | 0 |
| Conerly | 14 | 1 | 0.1 | 0 |
| Grosscup | 3 | 1 | 0.3 | 0 |
| Shaw | 15 | -12 | -0.8 | 0 |

### RECEIVING

| Last Name | No. | Yds | Avg | TD |
|---|---|---|---|---|
| Rote | 42 | 750 | 18 | 10 |
| Schnelker | 38 | 610 | 16 | 2 |
| Morrison | 29 | 367 | 13 | 3 |
| Gifford | 24 | 344 | 14 | 3 |
| Webster | 8 | 106 | 13 | 0 |
| Triplett | 5 | 48 | 10 | 2 |
| King | 3 | 6 | 2 | 0 |
| Kimber | 2 | 48 | 24 | 0 |
| Sutton | 2 | 30 | 15 | 0 |
| Simms | 1 | 58 | 58 | 0 |
| Summerall | 1 | 15 | 15 | 0 |
| Dess | 1 | 3 | 3 | 0 |

### PUNT RETURNS

| Last Name | No. | Yds | Avg | TD |
|---|---|---|---|---|
| Stits | 18 | 166 | 9 | 0 |
| Riley | 10 | 42 | 4 | 0 |
| Crow | 2 | 1 | 1 | 0 |
| Patton | 1 | 0 | 0 | 0 |

### KICKOFF RETURNS

| Last Name | No. | Yds | Avg | TD |
|---|---|---|---|---|
| Stits | 20 | 486 | 24 | 0 |
| Sutton | 2 | 223 | 19 | 0 |
| King | 2 | 73 | 37 | 0 |
| Riley | 3 | 67 | 22 | 0 |
| Triplett | 2 | 38 | 19 | 0 |
| Youso | 1 | 7 | 7 | 0 |
| Brown | 1 | 0 | 0 | 0 |

### PASSING – PUNTING – KICKING

**PASSING**

| Last Name | Att | Comp | % | Yds | Yd/Att | TD | Int–% | RK |
|---|---|---|---|---|---|---|---|---|
| Shaw | 155 | 76 | 49 | 1263 | 8.1 | 11 | 13– 8 | 9 |
| Conerly | 134 | 66 | 49 | 954 | 7.1 | 8 | 7– 5 | 7 |
| Grosscup | 25 | 11 | 44 | 144 | 5.8 | 1 | 5– 4 | |
| Gifford | 6 | 3 | 50 | 24 | 4.0 | 0 | 1– 17 | |
| Morrison | 1 | 0 | 0 | 0 | 0.0 | 0 | 1–100 | |
| Summerall | 1 | 0 | 0 | 0 | 0.0 | 0 | 0– 0 | |

**PUNTING**

| Last Name | No | Avg |
|---|---|---|
| Chandler | 31 | 40.5 |
| Conerly | 18 | 36.9 |

**KICKING**

| Last Name | XP | Att | % | FG | Att | % |
|---|---|---|---|---|---|---|
| Summerall | 32 | 32 | 100 | 13 | 26 | 50 |

## ST. LOUIS CARDINALS

### RUSHING

| Last Name | No. | Yds | Avg | TD |
|---|---|---|---|---|
| Crow | 183 | 1071 | 5.9 | 6 |
| Mestnick | 104 | 429 | 4.1 | 3 |
| Hammack | 96 | 347 | 3.6 | 2 |
| Childress | 34 | 240 | 7.5 | 0 |
| Conrad | 23 | 91 | 4.0 | 0 |
| Hill | 16 | 47 | 2.9 | 1 |
| Norton | 2 | 47 | 23.5 | 0 |
| West | 7 | 45 | 6.4 | 0 |
| Roach | 19 | 39 | 2.1 | 1 |

### RECEIVING

| Last Name | No. | Yds | Avg | TD |
|---|---|---|---|---|
| Randle | 62 | 893 | 14 | 15 |
| Crow | 25 | 462 | 18 | 3 |
| McInnis | 13 | 260 | 20 | 0 |
| Childress | 11 | 202 | 18 | 2 |
| Conrad | 7 | 103 | 15 | 0 |
| Hammack | 4 | 36 | 9 | 0 |
| Mestrick | 3 | 24 | 8 | 0 |
| Richards | 1 | 10 | 10 | 0 |

### PUNT RETURNS

| Last Name | No. | Yds | Avg | TD |
|---|---|---|---|---|
| Conrad | 8 | 86 | 11 | 0 |
| Stacy | 14 | 62 | 4 | 0 |
| West | 5 | 58 | 12 | 0 |
| Wilson | 3 | 26 | 9 | 0 |

### KICKOFF RETURNS

| Last Name | No. | Yds | Avg | TD |
|---|---|---|---|---|
| West | 13 | 370 | 28 | 0 |
| Conrad | 12 | 338 | 28 | 0 |
| Stacy | 6 | 146 | 24 | 0 |
| Wilson | 6 | 115 | 19 | 0 |
| Mestnick | 3 | 39 | 13 | 0 |
| Hammack | 2 | 23 | 12 | 0 |
| Memmelaar | 1 | 8 | 8 | 0 |
| Bates | 1 | 6 | 6 | 0 |
| Driskill | 1 | 0 | 0 | 0 |

### PASSING – PUNTING – KICKING

**PASSING**

| Last Name | Att | Comp | % | Yds | Yd/Att | TD | Int–% | RK |
|---|---|---|---|---|---|---|---|---|
| Roach | 188 | 87 | 46 | 1423 | 7.6 | 17 | 19– 10 | 13 |
| K. Hill | 55 | 20 | 36 | 205 | 3.7 | 1 | 5– 9 | |
| Izo | 24 | 10 | 42 | 115 | 4.8 | 0 | 0– 0 | |
| Crow | 18 | 9 | 50 | 247 | 13.7 | 2 | 1– 6 | |

**PUNTING**

| Last Name | No | Avg |
|---|---|---|
| Norton | 39 | 45.6 |
| Hill | 5 | 39.6 |

**KICKING**

| Last Name | XP | Att | % | FG | Att | % |
|---|---|---|---|---|---|---|
| Conrad | 28 | 29 | 97 | 2 | 5 | 40 |
| Perry | 5 | 5 | 100 | 13 | 20 | 65 |

## PITTSBURGH STEELERS

### RUSHING

| Last Name | No. | Yds | Avg | TD |
|---|---|---|---|---|
| Tracy | 192 | 680 | 3.5 | 5 |
| Johnson | 118 | 621 | 5.3 | 2 |
| Krutko | 17 | 99 | 5.8 | 0 |
| Scales | 26 | 81 | 3.1 | 0 |
| Orr | 8 | 57 | 7.1 | 0 |
| Carpenter | 17 | 36 | 2.1 | 0 |
| Barnett | 6 | 25 | 4.2 | 0 |
| Layne | 19 | 12 | 0.6 | 2 |
| Johnston | 4 | 12 | 3.0 | 0 |
| Dial | 1 | 8 | 8.0 | 0 |
| Bukich | 3 | -8 | -2.7 | 0 |

### RECEIVING

| Last Name | No. | Yds | Avg | TD |
|---|---|---|---|---|
| Dial | 40 | 972 | 24 | 9 |
| Orr | 29 | 541 | 19 | 4 |
| Carpenter | 29 | 495 | 17 | 2 |
| Tracy | 24 | 349 | 15 | 4 |
| Johnson | 12 | 112 | 9 | 1 |
| Brewster | 2 | 26 | 13 | 0 |
| McClairen | 1 | 17 | 17 | 0 |
| Krutko | 1 | 8 | 8 | 0 |
| Scales | 1 | -2 | -2 | 0 |
| Varrichione | 0 | -7 | 0 | 0 |

### PUNT RETURNS

| Last Name | No. | Yds | Avg | TD |
|---|---|---|---|---|
| Carpenter | 13 | 120 | 9 | 0 |
| Johnston | 12 | 45 | 4 | 0 |
| Moegle | 3 | 15 | 5 | 0 |
| Scudero | 2 | 3 | 2 | 0 |

### KICKOFF RETURNS

| Last Name | No. | Yds | Avg | TD |
|---|---|---|---|---|
| Johnston | 18 | 393 | 22 | 0 |
| Carpenter | 10 | 255 | 26 | 0 |
| Moegle | 7 | 174 | 25 | 0 |
| Scales | 5 | 100 | 20 | 0 |
| Tracy | 1 | 30 | 30 | 0 |
| Hayes | 1 | 11 | 11 | 0 |
| McClairen | 1 | 1 | 1 | 0 |
| Varrichione | 1 | 0 | 0 | 0 |

### PASSING – PUNTING – KICKING

**PASSING**

| Last Name | Att | Comp | % | Yds | Yd/Att | TD | Int–% | RK |
|---|---|---|---|---|---|---|---|---|
| Layne | 209 | 103 | 49 | 1814 | 8.7 | 13 | 17– 8 | 6 |
| Bukich | 51 | 25 | 49 | 358 | 7.0 | 2 | 3– 6 | |
| Tracy | 22 | 9 | 41 | 322 | 14.6 | 4 | 1– 5 | |
| Carpenter | 2 | 1 | 50 | 2 | 1.0 | 0 | 0– 0 | |
| Johnson | 1 | 1 | 100 | 15 | 15.0 | 1 | 0– 0 | |

**PUNTING**

| Last Name | No | Avg |
|---|---|---|
| Green | 64 | 44.2 |

**KICKING**

| Last Name | XP | Att | % | FG | Att | % |
|---|---|---|---|---|---|---|
| Layne | 21 | 22 | 95 | 5 | 6 | 83 |
| Rechichar | 6 | 6 | 100 | 3 | 7 | 43 |
| Tracy | 0 | 0 | 0 | 3 | 6 | 50 |

## WASHINGTON REDSKINS

### RUSHING

| Last Name | No. | Yds | Avg | TD |
|---|---|---|---|---|
| Bosseler | 109 | 428 | 3.9 | 2 |
| Guglielmi | 79 | 247 | 3.1 | 0 |
| Olszewski | 75 | 227 | 3.0 | 3 |
| James | 73 | 199 | 2.7 | 4 |
| Horner | 22 | 80 | 3.6 | 0 |
| Podoley | 29 | 52 | 1.8 | 0 |
| Vereb | 19 | 38 | 2.0 | 0 |
| Reynolds | 4 | 20 | 5.0 | 0 |
| Glick | 1 | 15 | 15.0 | 0 |
| Anderson | 1 | 6 | 6.0 | 0 |
| Day | 3 | 1 | 0.3 | 0 |

### RECEIVING

| Last Name | No. | Yds | Avg | TD |
|---|---|---|---|---|
| Anderson | 38 | 488 | 13 | 3 |
| Walton | 27 | 401 | 15 | 3 |
| Podoley | 17 | 244 | 14 | 1 |
| James | 16 | 243 | 15 | 2 |
| Bosseler | 13 | 86 | 7 | 0 |
| Olszewski | 10 | 62 | 6 | 0 |
| Vereb | 9 | 119 | 13 | 0 |
| Horner | 7 | 106 | 15 | 0 |
| Osborne | 7 | 46 | 7 | 0 |
| Haley | 3 | 21 | 7 | 0 |

### PUNT RETURNS

| Last Name | No. | Yds | Avg | TD |
|---|---|---|---|---|
| James | 7 | 46 | 7 | 0 |
| Horner | 3 | 16 | 5 | 0 |
| Podoley | 3 | 3 | 1 | 0 |
| Olszewski | 1 | 0 | 0 | 0 |
| Vereb | 1 | 0 | 0 | 0 |

### KICKOFF RETURNS

| Last Name | No. | Yds | Avg | TD |
|---|---|---|---|---|
| Horner | 24 | 511 | 21 | 0 |
| James | 19 | 458 | 24 | 0 |
| Olszewski | 5 | 119 | 24 | 0 |
| Vereb | 5 | 119 | 24 | 0 |
| Podoley | 4 | 87 | 22 | 0 |
| Wilkins | 2 | 24 | 12 | 0 |
| Stallings | 1 | 19 | 19 | 0 |
| O'Brien | 1 | 16 | 16 | 0 |
| Lawrence | 1 | 10 | 10 | 0 |

### PASSING – PUNTING – KICKING

**PASSING**

| Last Name | Att | Comp | % | Yds | Yd/Att | TD | Int–% | RK |
|---|---|---|---|---|---|---|---|---|
| Guglielmi | 223 | 125 | 56 | 1547 | 6.9 | 9 | 19– 9 | 9 |
| Reynolds | 30 | 13 | 44 | 154 | 5.1 | 0 | 3– 10 | |
| Day | 19 | 9 | 47 | 115 | 6.1 | 0 | 1– 5 | |
| James | 1 | 0 | 0 | 0 | 0.0 | 0 | 0– 0 | |
| Vereb | 1 | 0 | 0 | 0 | 0.0 | 0 | 0– 0 | |

**PUNTING**

| Last Name | No | Avg |
|---|---|---|
| Day | 59 | 42.0 |
| Horner | 1 | 48.0 |

**KICKING**

| Last Name | XP | Att | % | FG | Att | % |
|---|---|---|---|---|---|---|
| Khayat | 19 | 19 | 100 | 15 | 23 | 65 |

## GREEN BAY PACKERS 8-4-0 Vince Lombardi

| Scores of Each Game | | |
|---|---|---|
| 14 | CHICAGO | 17 |
| 28 | DETROIT | 9 |
| 35 | BALTIMORE | 21 |
| 41 | SAN FRANCISCO | 14 |
| 19 | Pittsburgh | 13 |
| 24 | Baltimore | 38 |
| 41 | DALLAS | 7 |
| 31 | LOS ANGELES | 33 |
| 10 | Detroit | 23 |
| 41 | Chicago | 13 |
| 13 | San Francisco | 0 |
| 35 | Los Angeles | 21 |

| Use Name | Pos. | Hgt | Wgt | Age | Int | Pts |
|---|---|---|---|---|---|---|
| Forrest Gregg | OT | 6'4" | 250 | 27 | | |
| Norm Masters | OT | 6'2" | 250 | 27 | | |
| Bob Skoronski | OT | 6'3" | 250 | 27 | | |
| Andy Cvercko | OG | 6' | 240 | 23 | | |
| Jerry Kramer | OG | 6'3" | 250 | 25 | | |
| Fuzzy Thurston | OG | 6'1" | 250 | 27 | | |
| Ken Iman | C | 6'1" | 230 | 21 | | |
| Jim Ringo | C | 6'1" | 235 | 29 | | |
| Willie Davis | DE | 6'3" | 240 | 27 | | 6 |
| Bill Quinlan | DE | 6'3" | 250 | 28 | | |
| Jim Temp | DE | 6'4" | 250 | 27 | | |
| Dave Hanner | DT | 6'2" | 260 | 31 | | |
| Henry Jordan | DT | 6'3" | 250 | 25 | | |
| Ken Beck | DE-DT | 6'2" | 250 | 25 | | |
| Johnny Miller | DE-DT | 6'5" | 260 | 26 | | |
| Tom Bettis | LB | 6'2" | 225 | 27 | | |
| Dan Currie | LB | 6'3" | 240 | 26 | 4 | |
| Bill Forester | LB | 6'3" | 240 | 29 | 2 | |
| Ray Nitschke | LB | 6'3" | 235 | 24 | 3 | 6 |
| Hank Gremminger | DB | 6'1" | 205 | 27 | 3 | |
| Dale Hackbart | DB | 6'3" | 200 | 24 | | |
| Dick Pesonen | DB | 6' | 190 | 22 | | |
| Johnny Symank | DB | 5'11" | 180 | 25 | 1 | |
| Em Tunnell | DB | 6'1" | 210 | 38 | 3 | |
| Jesse Whittenton | DB | 6' | 195 | 26 | 6 | |
| Willie Wood | DB | 5'10" | 185 | 24 | | |
| Lamar McHan | QB | 6'1" | 210 | 28 | | 6 |
| Bart Starr | QB | 6'1" | 200 | 27 | | |
| Paul Hornung | HB | 6'2" | 215 | 24 | | 176 |
| Tom Moore | HB | 6'2" | 215 | 22 | | 30 |
| Paul Winslow | HB | 5'11" | 200 | 22 | | 6 |
| Larry Hickman | FB | 6'2" | 230 | 24 | | |
| Jim Taylor | FB | 6' | 215 | 25 | | 66 |
| Boyd Dowler | FL | 6'5" | 220 | 23 | | 12 |
| Lew Carpenter | OE-FL | 6'1" | 215 | 28 | | |
| Gary Knafelc | OE | 6'4" | 220 | 28 | | |
| Ron Kramer | OE | 6'3" | 230 | 25 | | |
| Max McGee | OE | 6'3" | 205 | 28 | | 24 |
| Steve Meilinger | OE | 6'2" | 230 | 30 | | |

## DETROIT LIONS 7-5-0 George Wilson

| Scores of Each Game | | |
|---|---|---|
| 9 | Green Bay | 28 |
| 10 | SAN FRANCISCO | 14 |
| 10 | Philadelphia | 28 |
| 30 | BALTIMORE | 17 |
| 35 | Los Angeles | 48 |
| 24 | San Francisco | 0 |
| 12 | LOS ANGELES | 10 |
| 7 | Chicago | 28 |
| 23 | GREEN BAY | 10 |
| 20 | Baltimore | 15 |
| 23 | DALLAS | 14 |
| 36 | CHICAGO | 0 |

| Use Name | Pos. | Hgt | Wgt | Age | Int | Pts |
|---|---|---|---|---|---|---|
| Ollie Spencer | C-OT | 6'2" | 250 | 29 | | |
| John Gordy | OG-OT | 6'3" | 250 | 24 | | |
| Willie McClung | DT-OT | 6'2" | 260 | 31 | | |
| Grady Alderman | OG | 6'2" | 230 | 21 | | |
| Bob Grottkau | OG | 6'4" | 235 | 23 | | |
| Harley Sewell | OG | 6'1" | 230 | 29 | | |
| Bob Scholtz | C | 6'4" | 250 | 22 | | |
| Bill Glass | DE | 6'5" | 255 | 24 | | |
| Gil Mains | DE | 6'2" | 250 | 30 | | |
| Darris McCord | OT-DE | 6'4" | 250 | 27 | | |
| Sam Williams | LB-DE | 6'5" | 235 | 29 | | |
| Roger Brown | DT | 6'5" | 290 | 23 | | |
| Alex Karras | DT | 6'2" | 245 | 24 | | |
| Jim Weatherall | DT | 6'4" | 250 | 30 | | |
| Carl Brettschneider | LB | 6'1" | 225 | 28 | | |
| Jim Martin | LB | 6'2" | 230 | 36 | | 65 |
| Max Messner | LB | 6'3" | 225 | 22 | 1 | |
| Joe Schmidt | LB | 6'1" | 220 | 28 | 2 | 12 |
| Wayne Walker | LB | 6'2" | 225 | 23 | 1 | 2 |
| Night Train Lane | DB | 6'1" | 195 | 32 | 5 | 6 |
| Dick LeBeau | DB | 6'1" | 185 | 23 | 4 | |
| Gary Lowe | DB | 5'11" | 195 | 26 | 2 | |
| Bruce Maher | DB | 5'11" | 190 | 23 | 1 | 2 |
| Jim Steffen | DB | 6' | 195 | 23 | | |
| Dave Whitsell | DB | 6' | 190 | 24 | | |
| Yale Lary | DB | 6' | 190 | 29 | 3 | |
| Earl Morrall | QB | 6'1" | 206 | 26 | | 6 |
| Jim Ninowski | QB | 6'1" | 200 | 24 | | 30 |
| Warren Rabb | QB | 6'1" | 196 | 23 | | |
| Terry Barr | HB | 6' | 190 | 25 | | 12 |
| Dan Lewis | HB | 6'1" | 200 | 24 | | 12 |
| Ken Webb | FB-HB | 5'11" | 210 | 25 | | 12 |
| Nick Pietrosante | FB | 6'2" | 225 | 23 | | 48 |
| Hopalong Cassady | HB-FL | 5'10" | 185 | 26 | | 12 |
| Dave Middleton | OE-FL | 6'1" | 195 | 27 | | |
| Gail Cogdill | OE | 6'2" | 195 | 23 | | 6 |
| Glenn Davis | OE | 6' | 180 | 26 | | |
| Jim Gibbons | OE | 6'2" | 220 | 24 | | 12 |
| Steve Junker | OE | 6'3" | 220 | 25 | | |

## SAN FRANCISCO FORTY NINERS 7-5-0 Red Hickey

| Scores of Each Game | | |
|---|---|---|
| 19 | NEW YORK | 21 |
| 13 | LOS ANGELES | 9 |
| 14 | Detroit | 10 |
| 10 | Chicago | 27 |
| 14 | Green Bay | 41 |
| 25 | CHICAGO | 7 |
| 0 | DETROIT | 24 |
| 26 | Dallas | 14 |
| 30 | Baltimore | 22 |
| 23 | Los Angeles | 7 |
| 0 | GREEN BAY | 13 |
| 34 | BALTIMORE | 10 |

| Use Name | Pos. | Hgt | Wgt | Age | Int | Pts |
|---|---|---|---|---|---|---|
| Len Rohde | OT | 6'4" | 240 | 22 | | |
| Bob St. Clair | OT | 6'9" | 265 | 29 | | |
| John Thomas | OT | 6'4" | 246 | 25 | | |
| Bruce Bosley | OG | 6'2" | 240 | 26 | | |
| Ted Connolly | OG | 6'3" | 242 | 28 | | |
| Mike Magac | OG | 6'3" | 240 | 22 | | |
| Karl Rubke | C | 6'4" | 240 | 24 | | |
| Frank Morze | DT-C | 6'4" | 264 | 26 | | |
| Dan Colchico | DE | 6'4" | 236 | 23 | | |
| Ed Henke | DE | 6'3" | 227 | 32 | | |
| Charlie Krueger | DE | 6'4" | 245 | 24 | | 2 |
| Monte Clark | DT | 6'6" | 260 | 23 | | |
| Leo Nomellini | DT | 6'3" | 262 | 35 | | 2 |
| Henry Schmidt | DT | 6'4" | 260 | 23 | | |
| Bob Harrison | LB | 6'2" | 220 | 23 | 1 | |
| Matt Hazeltine | LB | 6'1" | 220 | 27 | | |
| Gorden Kelley | LB | 6'3" | 230 | 22 | 2 | |
| Clancy Osborne | LB | 6'3" | 218 | 25 | | |
| Jerry Wilson (from PHI) | LB | 6'2" | 235 | 23 | | |
| Dave Baker | DB | 6' | 193 | 23 | 10 | |
| Eddie Dove | DB | 6'2" | 180 | 23 | 3 | |
| Lenny Lyles | DB | 6'2" | 202 | 24 | | 6 |
| Jerry Mertens | DB | 6' | 183 | 24 | 2 | |
| Jimmy Ridlon | DB | 6'1" | 177 | 25 | | |
| Abe Woodson | HB-DB | 5'11" | 188 | 25 | 2 | |
| John Brodie | QB | 6'1" | 186 | 25 | | 6 |
| Y. A. Tittle | QB | 6' | 195 | 33 | | |
| Bob Waters | QB | 6'2" | 184 | 22 | | |
| Hugh McElhenny | HB | 6'1" | 198 | 31 | | 6 |
| Ray Norton | HB | 6'2" | 184 | 23 | | |
| J. D. Smith | FB-HB | 6'1" | 200 | 27 | | 36 |
| Joe Perry | FB | 6' | 206 | 33 | | 6 |
| C. R. Roberts | FB | 6'3" | 197 | 24 | | 12 |
| R. C. Owens | OE-FL | 6'3" | 190 | 25 | | 36 |
| Clyde Conner | OE | 6'2" | 190 | 27 | | 12 |
| Dee Mackey | OE | 6'5" | 236 | 24 | | |
| Monte Stickles | OE | 6'4" | 230 | 22 | | |
| Billy Wilson | FL-OE | 6'3" | 190 | 33 | | 6 |
| Tommy Davis | K | 6' | 212 | 25 | | 78 |

## BALTIMORE COLTS 6-6-0 Weeb Ewbank

| Scores of Each Game | | |
|---|---|---|
| 20 | WASHINGTON | 0 |
| 42 | CHICAGO | 7 |
| 21 | Green Bay | 35 |
| 31 | LOS ANGELES | 17 |
| 17 | DETROIT | 30 |
| 45 | Dallas | 7 |
| 38 | GREEN BAY | 24 |
| 24 | Chicago | 20 |
| 22 | SAN FRANCISCO | 30 |
| 15 | DETROIT | 20 |
| 3 | Los Angeles | 10 |
| 10 | San Francisco | 34 |

| Use Name | Pos. | Hgt | Wgt | Age | Int | Pts |
|---|---|---|---|---|---|---|
| Jim Parker | OT | 6'3" | 275 | 26 | | |
| Sherman Plunkett | OT | 6'4" | 270 | 26 | | |
| George Preas | OT | 6'2" | 255 | 28 | | |
| Lebron Shields | DE-OT | 6'4" | 240 | 23 | | 2 |
| Steve Myhra | OG | 6'1" | 240 | 26 | | 62 |
| Palmer Pyle | OG | 6'2" | 240 | 23 | | |
| Alex Sandusky | OG | 6'1" | 238 | 28 | | |
| Art Spinney | OG | 6' | 236 | 33 | | |
| Buzz Nutter | C | 6'4" | 240 | 29 | | |
| Ordell Braase | DE | 6'4" | 242 | 28 | | |
| Gino Marchetti | DE | 6'4" | 245 | 34 | | |
| Jim Colvin | OG-DE | 6'2" | 240 | 23 | | |
| Don Joyce | DT-DE | 6'3" | 250 | 30 | | |
| Art Donovan | DT | 6'2" | 270 | 35 | | |
| Big Daddy Lipscomb | DT | 6'6" | 288 | 28 | | 2 |
| Marv Matuszak | LB | 6'3" | 228 | 29 | | |
| Bill Pellington | LB | 6'2" | 238 | 31 | 1 | |
| Don Shinnick | LB | 6' | 235 | 25 | 5 | |
| Dick Szymanski | LB | 6'3" | 235 | 28 | 1 | |
| Zeke Smith | DE-LB | 6'2" | 230 | 24 | | |
| Bobby Boyd | DB | 5'10" | 192 | 22 | 7 | |
| Milt Davis | DB | 6'1" | 180 | 31 | 6 | |
| Andy Nelson | DB | 6'1" | 180 | 27 | 6 | |
| Jackie Simpson | DB | 5'10" | 185 | 26 | | |
| Johnny Sample | HB-DB | 6'1" | 203 | 23 | 4 | 6 |
| Carl Taseff | HB-DB | 5'11" | 194 | 31 | | |
| Ray Brown | QB | 6'2" | 195 | 24 | | |
| Johnny Unitas | QB | 6'1" | 194 | 27 | | |
| Alex Hawkins | HB | 6'1" | 190 | 23 | | 30 |
| Ed Kovac | HB | 6' | 197 | 22 | | |
| Lenny Moore | HB | 6'1" | 190 | 27 | | 78 |
| Mike Sommer | HB | 5'11" | 190 | 25 | | |
| Jim Welch | HB | 6' | 190 | 22 | | |
| Alan Ameche | FB | 6' | 220 | 27 | | 18 |
| Billy Pricer | FB | 5'10" | 210 | 25 | | 12 |
| Ray Berry | OE | 6'2" | 190 | 27 | | 60 |
| Jim Mutscheller | OE | 6'1" | 204 | 30 | | 12 |
| Art DeCarlo | DB-OE | 6'2" | 202 | 30 | | |
| Jerry Richardson | HB-OE | 6'3" | 185 | 24 | | 6 |

## CHICAGO BEARS 5-6-1 George Halas

| Scores of Each Game | | |
|---|---|---|
| 17 | Green Bay | 14 |
| 7 | Baltimore | 42 |
| 34 | LOS ANGELES | 27 |
| 27 | SAN FRANCISCO | 10 |
| 24 | Los Angeles | 24 |
| 7 | San Francisco | 25 |
| 20 | BALTIMORE | 24 |
| 28 | DETROIT | 7 |
| 17 | DALLAS | 7 |
| 13 | GREEN BAY | 41 |
| 0 | Cleveland | 42 |
| 0 | Detroit | 36 |

| Use Name | Pos. | Hgt | Wgt | Age | Int | Pts |
|---|---|---|---|---|---|---|
| Stan Fanning | OT | 6'6" | 252 | 22 | | |
| Bob Kilcullen | OT | 6'3" | 245 | 24 | | |
| Herm Lee | OT | 6'4" | 247 | 29 | | |
| Bob Wetoska | OT | 6'3" | 250 | 22 | | |
| Roger Davis | OG | 6'3" | 235 | 22 | | |
| Stan Jones | OG | 6'1" | 250 | 29 | | |
| Ted Karras | OG | 6'1" | 235 | 27 | | |
| Bob Konovsky | OG | 6'2" | 245 | 26 | | |
| John Mellekas | C | 6'3" | 255 | 27 | | |
| Doug Atkins | DE | 6'8" | 255 | 30 | | |
| Maury Youmans | OT-DE | 6'6" | 230 | 23 | | |
| Fred Williams | DT | 6'4" | 248 | 30 | | |
| Bill Bishop | OT-DT | 6'4" | 248 | 29 | | |
| Earl Leggett | DE-DT | 6'3" | 250 | 26 | 1 | |
| Joe Fortunato | LB | 6' | 225 | 30 | | |
| Bill George | LB | 6'2" | 235 | 29 | 1 | |
| Ken Kirk | LB | 6'2" | 230 | 22 | | |
| Larry Morris | LB | 6'2" | 230 | 25 | 1 | |
| Roger LeClerc | C-DT-LB | 6'3" | 235 | 22 | | |
| Erich Barnes | DB | 6'2" | 198 | 25 | | |
| J. C. Caroline | DB | 6'1" | 190 | 27 | 3 | 6 |
| Pete Manning | DB | 6'3" | 208 | 24 | | |
| Richie Petitbon | DB | 6'3" | 205 | 22 | 2 | |
| Justin Rowland | DB | 6'2" | 188 | 22 | | |
| Charlie Sumner | DB | 6'1" | 195 | 30 | | |
| Vic Zucco | DB | 6' | 187 | 25 | 2 | |
| Zeke Bratkowski | QB | 6'2" | 203 | 28 | | |
| Ed Brown | QB | 6'2" | 208 | 31 | | 12 |
| Charlie Bivins | HB | 6'2" | 212 | 21 | | |
| Willie Galimore | HB | 6'1" | 187 | 25 | | 6 |
| Johnny Morris | HB | 5'10" | 180 | 25 | | 36 |
| Glen Shaw | HB | 6'1" | 217 | 21 | | |
| John Adams | FB | 6'3" | 235 | 23 | | |
| Rick Casares | FB | 6'2" | 225 | 29 | | 30 |
| Merrill Douglas | FB | 6' | 204 | 24 | | |
| Angie Coia | OE | 6'2" | 211 | 22 | | 24 |
| Willard Dewveall | OE | 6'4" | 218 | 23 | | 30 |
| Jim Dooley | OE | 6'4" | 198 | 30 | | 6 |
| Bo Farrington | OE | 6'3" | 217 | 24 | | |
| Harlon Hill | OE | 6'3" | 200 | 28 | | |
| John Aveni | K | 6'3" | 210 | 25 | | 44 |

## LOS ANGELES RAMS 4-7-1 Bob Waterfield

| Scores of Each Game | | |
|---|---|---|
| 21 | ST. LOUIS | 43 |
| 9 | San Francisco | 13 |
| 27 | Chicago | 34 |
| 17 | Baltimore | 31 |
| 24 | CHICAGO | 24 |
| 48 | DETROIT | 35 |
| 38 | Dallas | 13 |
| 10 | Detroit | 12 |
| 33 | Green Bay | 31 |
| 7 | SAN FRANCISCO | 23 |
| 10 | BALTIMORE | 3 |
| 21 | GREEN BAY | 35 |

| Use Name | Pos. | Hgt | Wgt | Age | Int | Pts |
|---|---|---|---|---|---|---|
| Jim Boeke | OT | 6'5" | 230 | 21 | | |
| Charlie Bradshaw | OT | 6'6" | 255 | 24 | | |
| John Guzik | OG | 6'3" | 236 | 23 | | |
| Roy Hord | OG | 6'4" | 232 | 25 | | |
| Chuck Janerette | OG | 6'3" | 240 | 21 | | |
| Buck Lansford | OG | 6'2" | 232 | 27 | | |
| Art Hunter | C | 6'4" | 248 | 27 | | |
| Gene Brito | DE | 6'1" | 230 | 34 | | |
| Lamar Lundy | DE | 6'7" | 235 | 25 | 1 | 6 |
| Lou Michaels | DE | 6'2" | 248 | 24 | | 7 |
| John Baker | DT-DE | 6'6" | 290 | 25 | 1 | |
| John Lovetere | DT | 6'4" | 280 | 24 | | 6 |
| George Strugar | DT | 6'5" | 260 | 25 | | |
| John Kennerson | DE-DT | 6'3" | 255 | 21 | | |
| Bill Jobko | LB | 6'2" | 218 | 24 | 1 | |
| Bob Long | LB | 6'3" | 234 | 26 | 1 | |
| Jack Pardee | LB | 6'2" | 220 | 24 | 1 | |
| Les Richter | LB | 6'3" | 232 | 29 | 2 | 2 |
| Jerry Stalcup | OG-LB | 6' | 220 | 22 | 1 | |
| Charley Britt | DB | 6'2" | 180 | 22 | 5 | 6 |
| Don Ellersick | DB | 6'1" | 193 | 22 | 2 | |
| Carl Karilivacz | DB | 6' | 190 | 29 | | |
| Ed Meador | DB | 5'11" | 185 | 23 | 4 | 6 |
| Will Sherman | DB | 6'2" | 197 | 31 | 1 | |
| Vern Valdez | DB | 5'11" | 190 | 24 | 1 | |
| Buddy Humphrey | QB | 6'1" | 200 | 24 | | |
| Frank Ryan | QB | 6'3" | 195 | 4 | | 12 |
| Billy Wade | QB | 6'2" | 203 | 29 | | 12 |
| Jon Arnett | HB | 5'11" | 193 | 25 | | 24 |
| Dick Bass | HB | 5'10" | 190 | 23 | | |
| Tom Wilson | HB | 6' | 204 | 27 | | 12 |
| Clendon Thomas | DB-FL-HB | 6'2" | 190 | 23 | 1 | 12 |
| Joe Marconi | FB | 6'2" | 220 | 26 | | 18 |
| Ollie Matson | FL-FB | 6'2" | 210 | 30 | | 6 |
| Carroll Dale | OE | 6'1" | 194 | 22 | | 18 |
| Jim Phillips | OE | 6'1" | 200 | 23 | | 48 |
| Del Shofner | DB-OE | 6'3" | 192 | 24 | 1 | 6 |
| Danny Villanueva | K | 5'11" | 200 | 22 | | 64 |

## DALLAS COWBOYS 0-11-1 Tom Landry

| Scores of Each Game | | |
|---|---|---|
| 28 | PITTSBURGH | 35 |
| 25 | PHILADELPHIA | 27 |
| 14 | Washington | 26 |
| 7 | CLEVELAND | 48 |
| 10 | St. Louis | 12 |
| 7 | BALTIMDRE | 45 |
| 13 | LOS ANGELES | 38 |
| 7 | Green Bay | 41 |
| 14 | SAN FRANCISCO | 26 |
| 7 | Chicago | 17 |
| 31 | New York | 31 |
| 14 | Detroit | 23 |

| Use Name | Pos. | Hgt | Wgt | Age | Int | Pts |
|---|---|---|---|---|---|---|
| Byron Bradfute | OT | 6'3" | 243 | 22 | | |
| Paul Dickson | OT | 6'5" | 250 | 23 | | |
| Bob Fry | OT | 6'4" | 240 | 29 | | |
| Dick Klein | OT | 6'4" | 255 | 26 | | |
| Mike Falls | OG | 6'1" | 240 | 26 | | |
| Buzz Guy | OG | 6'3" | 247 | 25 | | |
| Duane Putnam | OG | 6' | 233 | 32 | | |
| Mike Connelly | C | 6'3" | 235 | 24 | | |
| John Houser | C | 6'3" | 238 | 24 | | |
| Nate Borden | DE | 6' | 240 | 28 | | |
| Gene Cronin | DE | 6'2" | 232 | 27 | 1 | |
| John Gonzaga | DE | 6'3" | 244 | 27 | | |
| Don Healy | DT | 6'3" | 264 | 24 | | |
| Bill Herchman | DT | 6'2" | 245 | 27 | | |
| Ed Husmann | DT | 6' | 238 | 29 | | |
| Tom Braatz | LB | 6'1" | 220 | 27 | 1 | |
| Wayne Hansen | LB | 6'2" | 228 | 32 | 2 | |
| Jack Patera | LB | 6'1" | 240 | 28 | 1 | |
| Jerry Tubbs | LB | 6'2" | 220 | 25 | 1 | |
| Bob Bercich | DB | 6'1" | 198 | 23 | 2 | |
| Don Bishop | DB | 6'2" | 204 | 25 | 3 | |
| Bill Butler | DB | 5'10" | 182 | 23 | 1 | |
| Fred Doelling | DB | 5'10" | 190 | 21 | | |
| Tom Franckhauser | DB | 6' | 196 | 23 | 3 | |
| Jim Mooty | DB | 5'11" | 177 | 22 | | |
| Gary Wisener | OE-DB | 6'1" | 206 | 22 | | |
| Ray Fisher – Injury | | | | | | |
| Chuck Howley – Injury | | | | | | |
| Don Heinrich | QB | 6' | 182 | 29 | | |
| Eddie LeBaron | QB | 5'9" | 166 | 30 | | 6 |
| Don Meredith | QB | 6'2" | 198 | 22 | | |
| L. G. Dupre | HB | 5'11" | 190 | 28 | | 30 |
| Don McIlhenny | HB | 6' | 204 | 25 | | 12 |
| Gene Babb | FB | 6'3" | 218 | 25 | | 6 |
| Mike Dowdle | FB | 6'3" | 210 | 22 | | |
| Walt Kowalczyk | FB | 6' | 205 | 25 | | 12 |
| Ray Mathews | FL | 6' | 200 | 31 | | |
| Dick Bielski | OE | 6'1" | 227 | 28 | | 6 |
| Frank Clarke | OE | 6' | 215 | 27 | | 18 |
| Jim Doran | OE | 6'2" | 211 | 32 | | 18 |
| Fred Dugan | OE | 6'3" | 200 | 26 | | 6 |
| Billy Howton | OE | 6'2" | 195 | 30 | | 24 |
| Woodley Lewis | OE | 6' | 195 | 35 | | |
| Dave Sherer | OE | 6'3" | 225 | 23 | | |
| Fred Cone | K | 5'11" | 198 | 34 | | 39 |

## GREEN BAY PACKERS

**RUSHING**

| Last Name | No. | Yds | Avg | TD |
|---|---|---|---|---|
| Taylor | 230 | 1101 | 4.8 | 11 |
| Hornung | 160 | 671 | 4.2 | 13 |
| Moore | 45 | 237 | 5.3 | 4 |
| McHan | 8 | 67 | 8.4 | 1 |
| Carpenter | 1 | 24 | 24.0 | 0 |
| Hickman | 7 | 22 | 3.1 | 0 |
| Starr | 7 | 12 | 1.7 | 0 |
| McGee | 2 | 11 | 5.5 | 0 |
| Dowler | 1 | 8 | 8.0 | 0 |
| Winslow | 2 | –3 | –1.5 | 0 |

**RECEIVING**

| Last Name | No. | Yds | Avg | TD |
|---|---|---|---|---|
| McGee | 38 | 787 | 21 | 4 |
| Dowler | 30 | 505 | 17 | 2 |
| Hornung | 28 | 257 | 9 | 2 |
| Taylor | 15 | 121 | 8 | 0 |
| Knafelc | 14 | 164 | 12 | 0 |
| Moore | 5 | 40 | 8 | 1 |
| R. Kramer | 4 | 55 | 14 | 0 |
| Meilinger | 2 | 43 | 22 | 0 |
| Carpenter | 1 | 21 | 21 | 0 |

**PUNT RETURNS**

| Last Name | No. | Yds | Avg | TD |
|---|---|---|---|---|
| Wood | 16 | 106 | 7 | 0 |
| Carpenter | 9 | 59 | 7 | 0 |
| Forester | 1 | 7 | 7 | 0 |

**KICKOFF RETURNS**

| Last Name | No. | Yds | Avg | TD |
|---|---|---|---|---|
| Moore | 12 | 397 | 33 | 0 |
| Carpenter | 12 | 249 | 21 | 0 |
| Symank | 4 | 103 | 26 | 0 |
| Hickman | 3 | 54 | 18 | 0 |
| Nitschke | 2 | 33 | 17 | 0 |
| Temp | 1 | 16 | 16 | 0 |
| Meilinger | 1 | 0 | 0 | 0 |

**PASSING – PUNTING – KICKING**

| PASSING | Att | Comp | % | Yds | Yd/Att | TD | Int–% | RK |
|---|---|---|---|---|---|---|---|---|
| Starr | 172 | 98 | 57 | 1358 | 7.9 | 4 | 8– 5 | 5 |
| McHan | 91 | 33 | 36 | 517 | 5.7 | 3 | 5– 5 | |
| Hornung | 16 | 6 | 38 | 118 | 7.4 | 2 | 0– 0 | |

| PUNTING | No | Avg |
|---|---|---|
| McGee | 31 | 41.6 |
| Dowler | 18 | 40.5 |

| KICKING | XP | Att | % | FG | Att | % |
|---|---|---|---|---|---|---|
| Hornung | 41 | 41 | 100 | 15 | 28 | 54 |

## DETROIT LIONS

**RUSHING**

| Last Name | No. | Yds | Avg | TD |
|---|---|---|---|---|
| Pietrosante | 161 | 872 | 5.4 | 8 |
| Lewis | 92 | 438 | 4.8 | 1 |
| Webb | 59 | 166 | 2.8 | 2 |
| Ninowski | 32 | 81 | 2.5 | 5 |
| Barr | 17 | 74 | 4.4 | 1 |
| Morrall | 10 | 37 | 3.7 | 1 |
| Cassady | 17 | 28 | 1.6 | 1 |
| Lary | 1 | 19 | 19.0 | 0 |
| Middleton | 3 | –1 | –0.3 | 0 |

**RECEIVING**

| Last Name | No. | Yds | Avg | TD |
|---|---|---|---|---|
| Gibbons | 51 | 604 | 12 | 2 |
| Cogdill | 43 | 642 | 15 | 1 |
| Cassady | 20 | 238 | 12 | 1 |
| Pietrosante | 13 | 129 | 10 | 0 |
| Lewis | 12 | 192 | 16 | 1 |
| Webb | 10 | 68 | 7 | 0 |
| Junker | 6 | 55 | 9 | 0 |
| Middleton | 5 | 51 | 10 | 0 |
| Barr | 5 | 26 | 5 | 1 |
| Davis | 1 | 17 | 17 | 0 |

**PUNT RETURNS**

| Last Name | No. | Yds | Avg | TD |
|---|---|---|---|---|
| Barr | 14 | 104 | 7 | 0 |
| Steffen | 14 | 83 | 6 | 0 |
| Cassady | 1 | 25 | 25 | 0 |
| Maher | 1 | 10 | 10 | 0 |
| Lary | 1 | 5 | 5 | 0 |

**KICKOFF RETURNS**

| Last Name | No. | Yds | Avg | TD |
|---|---|---|---|---|
| Steffen | 8 | 225 | 28 | 0 |
| Maher | 10 | 214 | 21 | 0 |
| Lewis | 10 | 202 | 20 | 0 |
| Cassady | 4 | 82 | 21 | 0 |
| Barr | 4 | 81 | 20 | 0 |
| Pietrosante | 2 | 58 | 29 | 0 |
| Webb | 3 | 38 | 13 | 0 |
| LeBeau | 2 | 16 | 8 | 0 |

**PASSING – PUNTING – KICKING**

| PASSING | Att | Comp | % | Yds | Yd/Att | TD | Int–% | RK |
|---|---|---|---|---|---|---|---|---|
| Ninowski | 283 | 134 | 47 | 1599 | 5.7 | 2 | 18– 6 | 17 |
| Morrall | 49 | 32 | 65 | 423 | 8.6 | 4 | 3– 6 | |
| Barr | 1 | 0 | 0 | 0 | 0.0 | 0 | 0– 0 | |

| PUNTING | No | Avg |
|---|---|---|
| Lary | 64 | 43.8 |

| KICKING | XP | Att | % | FG | Att | % |
|---|---|---|---|---|---|---|
| Martin | 26 | 28 | 93 | 13 | 24 | 54 |

## SAN FRANCISCO FORTY NINERS

**RUSHING**

| Last Name | No. | Yds | Avg | TD |
|---|---|---|---|---|
| Smith | 174 | 780 | 4.5 | 5 |
| McElhenny | 95 | 347 | 3.7 | 0 |
| Roberts | 73 | 213 | 2.9 | 2 |
| Brodie | 18 | 171 | 9.5 | 1 |
| Perry | 36 | 95 | 2.6 | 1 |
| Tittle | 10 | 61 | 6.1 | 0 |
| Waters | 1 | 8 | 8.0 | 0 |
| Woodson | 4 | 4 | 1.0 | 0 |
| Norton | 2 | 2 | 1.0 | 0 |

**RECEIVING**

| Last Name | No. | Yds | Avg | TD |
|---|---|---|---|---|
| Connor | 38 | 531 | 14 | 2 |
| Owens | 37 | 532 | 14 | 6 |
| Smith | 36 | 181 | 5 | 1 |
| Stickles | 22 | 252 | 11 | 0 |
| McElhenny | 14 | 114 | 8 | 1 |
| Mackey | 12 | 159 | 13 | 0 |
| Roberts | 9 | 49 | 5 | 0 |
| Wilson | 3 | 51 | 17 | 1 |
| Perry | 3 | –3 | –1 | 0 |

**PUNT RETURNS**

| Last Name | No. | Yds | Avg | TD |
|---|---|---|---|---|
| Woodson | 13 | 174 | 13 | 0 |
| Dove | 11 | 43 | 4 | 0 |

**KICKOFF RETURNS**

| Last Name | No. | Yds | Avg | TD |
|---|---|---|---|---|
| Lyles | 17 | 526 | 31 | 1 |
| Woodson | 17 | 498 | 29 | 0 |
| Colchico | 5 | 68 | 14 | 0 |
| Roberts | 3 | 60 | 20 | 0 |
| Clark | 1 | 15 | 15 | 0 |
| J. Wilson | 1 | 0 | 0 | 0 |

**PASSING – PUNTING – KICKING**

| PASSING | Att | Comp | % | Yds | Yd/Att | TD | Int–% | RK |
|---|---|---|---|---|---|---|---|---|
| Brodie | 207 | 103 | 50 | 1111 | 5.4 | 6 | 9– 4 | 12 |
| Tittle | 127 | 69 | 54 | 694 | 5.5 | 4 | 3– 2 | 8 |
| Waters | 2 | 2 | 100 | 61 | 30.5 | 1 | 0– 0 | |

| PUNTING | No | Avg |
|---|---|---|
| Davis | 62 | 44.1 |
| Baker | 3 | 47.7 |

| KICKING | XP | Att | % | FG | Att | % |
|---|---|---|---|---|---|---|
| Davis | 21 | 21 | 100 | 19 | 32 | 59 |

## BALTIMORE COLTS

**RUSHING**

| Last Name | No. | Yds | Avg | TD |
|---|---|---|---|---|
| Moore | 91 | 374 | 4.1 | 4 |
| Hawkins | 76 | 267 | 3.5 | 2 |
| Ameche | 80 | 263 | 3.3 | 3 |
| Unitas | 36 | 195 | 5.4 | 0 |
| Pricer | 46 | 131 | 2.8 | 1 |
| Brown | 2 | 25 | 12.5 | 0 |
| Welch | 5 | 23 | 4.6 | 0 |
| Sample | 1 | 7 | 7.0 | 0 |
| Taseff | 4 | 3 | 0.8 | 0 |
| Kovac | 4 | 1 | 0.3 | 0 |

**RECEIVING**

| Last Name | No. | Yds | Avg | TD |
|---|---|---|---|---|
| Berry | 74 | 1298 | 18 | 10 |
| Moore | 45 | 936 | 21 | 9 |
| Hawkins | 25 | 280 | 11 | 3 |
| Mutscheller | 18 | 271 | 15 | 2 |
| DeCarlo | 8 | 116 | 15 | 0 |
| Richardson | 8 | 90 | 11 | 1 |
| Pricer | 8 | 77 | 10 | 1 |
| Ameche | 7 | 56 | 8 | 0 |
| Kovac | 2 | 27 | 14 | 0 |
| Taseff | 1 | 13 | 13 | 0 |

**PUNT RETURNS**

| Last Name | No. | Yds | Avg | TD |
|---|---|---|---|---|
| Sample | 14 | 101 | 7 | 0 |
| Taseff | 6 | 25 | 4 | 0 |
| Nelson | 3 | 1 | 0 | 0 |

**KICKOFF RETURNS**

| Last Name | No. | Yds | Avg | TD |
|---|---|---|---|---|
| Sample | 18 | 519 | 29 | 1 |
| Taseff | 14 | 291 | 21 | 0 |
| Pricer | 6 | 88 | 15 | 0 |
| Welch | 4 | 80 | 20 | 0 |
| Moore | 1 | 23 | 23 | 0 |
| Pellington | 2 | 11 | 6 | 0 |
| Sommer | 1 | 10 | 10 | 0 |
| Kovac | 1 | 8 | 8 | 0 |

**PASSING – PUNTING – KICKING**

| PASSING | Att | Comp | % | Yds | Yd/Att | TD | Int–% | RK |
|---|---|---|---|---|---|---|---|---|
| Unitas | 378 | 190 | 50 | 3099 | 8.2 | 25 | 24– 6 | 3 |
| Brown | 13 | 6 | 46 | 65 | 5.0 | 1 | 0– 0 | |
| Moore | 1 | 0 | 0 | 0 | 0.0 | 0 | 0– 0 | |

| PUNTING | No | Avg |
|---|---|---|
| Brown | 52 | 38.5 |

| KICKING | XP | Att | % | FG | Att | % |
|---|---|---|---|---|---|---|
| Myhra | 35 | 37 | 95 | 9 | 19 | 47 |

## CHICAGO BEARS

**RUSHING**

| Last Name | No. | Yds | Avg | TD |
|---|---|---|---|---|
| Casares | 160 | 566 | 3.5 | 5 |
| J. Morris | 73 | 417 | 5.7 | 3 |
| Galimore | 74 | 368 | 5.0 | 1 |
| Adams | 23 | 114 | 5.0 | 0 |
| Brown | 19 | 89 | 4.7 | 2 |
| Douglas | 11 | 82 | 7.5 | 0 |
| Bratkowski | 8 | 20 | 2.5 | 0 |
| Farrington | 1 | –2 | –2.0 | 0 |
| Coia | 3 | –4 | –1.3 | 0 |
| Bivens | 1 | –11 | –11.0 | 0 |

**RECEIVING**

| Last Name | No. | Yds | Avg | TD |
|---|---|---|---|---|
| Dewveall | 43 | 804 | 19 | 5 |
| Dooley | 36 | 426 | 12 | 1 |
| Coia | 25 | 478 | 19 | 4 |
| J. Morris | 20 | 224 | 11 | 3 |
| Casares | 8 | 64 | 8 | 0 |
| Hill | 5 | 98 | 20 | 0 |
| Galimore | 3 | 35 | 12 | 0 |
| Douglas | 2 | 11 | 6 | 0 |
| Adams | 2 | –20 | –10 | 0 |
| Lee | 1 | 16 | 16 | 0 |
| Brown | 1 | –6 | 0 | 0 |

**PUNT RETURNS**

| Last Name | No. | Yds | Avg | TD |
|---|---|---|---|---|
| Zucco | 10 | 83 | 8 | 0 |
| J. Morris | 13 | 75 | 6 | 0 |
| Petitbon | 2 | 22 | 11 | 0 |
| Coia | 2 | 2 | 1 | 0 |

**KICKOFF RETURNS**

| Last Name | No. | Yds | Avg | TD |
|---|---|---|---|---|
| J. Morris | 19 | 384 | 20 | 0 |
| Bivens | 15 | 362 | 24 | 0 |
| Galimore | 12 | 292 | 24 | 0 |
| Zucco | 1 | 17 | 17 | 0 |

**PASSING – PUNTING – KICKING**

| PASSING | Att | Comp | % | Yds | Yd/Att | TD | Int–% | RK |
|---|---|---|---|---|---|---|---|---|
| Bratkowski | 175 | 87 | 50 | 1051 | 6.0 | 6 | 21– 12 | 16 |
| Brown | 149 | 59 | 40 | 1079 | 7.2 | 7 | 11– 7 | 14 |

| PUNTING | No | Avg |
|---|---|---|
| Brown | 56 | 39.8 |
| Bratkowski | 7 | 36.0 |
| Casares | 1 | 60.0 |

| KICKING | XP | Att | % | FG | Att | % |
|---|---|---|---|---|---|---|
| Aveni | 23 | 25 | 92 | 7 | 16 | 44 |

## LOS ANGELES RAMS

**RUSHING**

| Last Name | No. | Yds | Avg | TD |
|---|---|---|---|---|
| Arnett | 104 | 436 | 4.2 | 2 |
| Marconi | 42 | 240 | 5.7 | 3 |
| Wade | 26 | 171 | 6.6 | 2 |
| Matson | 61 | 170 | 2.9 | 1 |
| Bass | 31 | 153 | 4.9 | 0 |
| Wilson | 41 | 139 | 3.4 | 0 |
| Ryan | 19 | 85 | 4.5 | 1 |
| Thomas | 16 | 63 | 3.9 | 0 |
| Humphrey | 2 | 7 | 3.5 | 0 |
| Shofner | 1 | –15 | –15.0 | 0 |

**RECEIVING**

| Last Name | No. | Yds | Avg | TD |
|---|---|---|---|---|
| Phillips | 52 | 883 | 17 | 8 |
| Arnett | 29 | 226 | 8 | 2 |
| Dale | 19 | 336 | 18 | 3 |
| Thomas | 17 | 275 | 16 | 2 |
| Matson | 15 | 98 | 7 | 0 |
| Bass | 13 | 92 | 7 | 0 |
| Shofner | 12 | 122 | 10 | 1 |
| Wilson | 11 | 82 | 7 | 2 |
| Marconi | 9 | 32 | 4 | 0 |
| Ryan | 0 | 32 | 0 | 1 |
| Wade | 0 | 10 | 0 | 0 |

**PUNT RETURNS**

| Last Name | No. | Yds | Avg | TD |
|---|---|---|---|---|
| Bass | 11 | 62 | 6 | 0 |
| Arnett | 10 | 60 | 6 | 0 |
| Lovetere | 1 | 6 | 6 | 1 |
| Sherman | 1 | 1 | 1 | 0 |
| Matson | 1 | 0 | 0 | 0 |
| Meador | 1 | 0 | 0 | 0 |

**KICKOFF RETURNS**

| Last Name | No. | Yds | Avg | TD |
|---|---|---|---|---|
| Arnett | 17 | 416 | 24 | 0 |
| Bass | 11 | 246 | 22 | 0 |
| Matson | 9 | 216 | 24 | 0 |
| Wilson | 2 | 48 | 24 | 0 |
| Michaels | 1 | 15 | 15 | 0 |

**PASSING – PUNTING – KICKING**

| PASSING | Att | Comp | % | Yds | Yd/Att | TD | Int–% | RK |
|---|---|---|---|---|---|---|---|---|
| Wade | 182 | 106 | 58 | 1294 | 7.1 | 12 | 11– 6 | 4 |
| Ryan | 128 | 62 | 48 | 816 | 6.4 | 7 | 9– 7 | 14 |
| Humphrey | 24 | 9 | 38 | 78 | 3.3 | 0 | 2– 8 | |
| Arnett | 1 | 0 | 0 | 0 | 0.0 | 0 | 0– 0 | |

| PUNTING | No | Avg |
|---|---|---|
| Shofner | 54 | 42.6 |
| Marconi | 10 | 40.8 |

| KICKING | XP | Att | % | FG | Att | % |
|---|---|---|---|---|---|---|
| Villaneuva | 28 | 28 | 100 | 12 | 19 | 63 |
| Richter | 2 | 2 | 100 | 0 | 0 | 0 |
| Michaels | 1 | 1 | 100 | 2 | 3 | 67 |

## DALLAS COWBOYS

**RUSHING**

| Last Name | No. | Yds | Avg | TD |
|---|---|---|---|---|
| Dupre | 104 | 362 | 3.5 | 3 |
| McIlhenny | 96 | 321 | 3.3 | 1 |
| Kowalczyk | 50 | 156 | 3.1 | 1 |
| Babb | 39 | 115 | 2.9 | 0 |
| LeBaron | 17 | 94 | 5.5 | 1 |
| Meredith | 3 | 4 | 1.3 | 0 |
| Heinrich | 2 | 3 | 1.5 | 0 |
| Clarke | 1 | –6 | –6.0 | 0 |

**RECEIVING**

| Last Name | No. | Yds | Avg | TD |
|---|---|---|---|---|
| Doran | 31 | 554 | 18 | 3 |
| Dugan | 29 | 461 | 16 | 1 |
| Howton | 23 | 363 | 16 | 4 |
| Dupre | 21 | 216 | 10 | 2 |
| McIlhenny | 15 | 120 | 8 | 1 |
| Kowalczyk | 14 | 143 | 10 | 1 |
| Babb | 13 | 140 | 11 | 1 |
| Clarke | 9 | 290 | 32 | 3 |
| Bielski | 4 | 38 | 10 | 1 |
| Mathews | 3 | 44 | 15 | 0 |
| Lewis | 1 | 19 | 19 | 0 |

**PUNT RETURNS**

| Last Name | No. | Yds | Avg | TD |
|---|---|---|---|---|
| Butler | 13 | 131 | 10 | 0 |
| Mooty | 8 | 37 | 5 | 0 |
| Franckhauser | 2 | 7 | 4 | 0 |

**KICKOFF RETURNS**

| Last Name | No. | Yds | Avg | TD |
|---|---|---|---|---|
| Franckhauser | 26 | 526 | 20 | 0 |
| Butler | 20 | 399 | 20 | 0 |
| Mooty | 12 | 210 | 18 | 0 |
| Babb | 3 | 46 | 15 | 0 |
| Dupre | 2 | 44 | 22 | 0 |
| Dowdle | 2 | 22 | 11 | 0 |
| Putnam | 1 | 13 | 13 | 0 |
| Bielski | 1 | 4 | 4 | 0 |
| Kowalczyk | 1 | 0 | 0 | 0 |
| Sherer | 1 | 0 | 0 | 0 |

**PASSING – PUNTING – KICKING**

| PASSING | Att | Comp | % | Yds | Yd/Att | TD | Int–% | RK |
|---|---|---|---|---|---|---|---|---|
| LeBaron | 225 | 111 | 49 | 1736 | 7.7 | 12 | 25– 11 | 9 |
| Meredith | 68 | 29 | 43 | 281 | 4.1 | 2 | 5– 7 | |
| Heinrich | 61 | 23 | 38 | 371 | 6.1 | 3 | 3– 5 | |

| PUNTING | No | Avg |
|---|---|---|
| Sherer | 57 | 42.5 |
| LeBaron | 3 | 33.0 |

| KICKING | XP | Att | % | FG | Att | % |
|---|---|---|---|---|---|---|
| Cone | 21 | 23 | 91 | 6 | 13 | 46 |

# 1960 A.F.L. A New Competitor

Even before the first game was played the new American Football League was a flurry of activity. Commissioner Joe Foss, the former South Dakota governor chosen by the team owners to run the league, faced a major problem when the Minneapolis owners quit the circuit in January to accept an NFL team in 1961. This strategic move by the NFL shut the new circuit out of the Midwest and almost killed it in the cradle, but the upstarts did not give up. After several days of discussion the league owners turned down a bid from an Atlanta group and instead granted the eighth franchise to a syndicate from Oakland, California. The AFL finally had its full contingent of cities—Boston, New York, Buffalo, Houston, Dallas, Denver, Los Angeles, and Oakland. In New York, Dallas, and Los Angeles, the new league would be bucking NFL teams. Oakland in reality would have to compete with the NFL San Francisco '49ers. Buffalo and Boston were both graveyards for previous pro-football failures, while Denver and Houston were virgin territory.

Work went on during the summer, when players had to be signed. The AFL honored existing NFL contracts with players and lured away no players from the established league. The new teams picked up experience by signing NFL rejects and oldsters. Most of the AFL quarterbacks had NFL credits, such as George Blanda, Jack Kemp, Babe Parilli, Tom O'Connell, Al Dorow, and Cotton Davidson. Some players from the Canadian League seized upon the AFL as a chance to play again in the United States. Frank Tripuka, Dave Kocourek, Goose Gonsoulin, Butch Songin, Al Jamison, and Sherrill Headrick all had been playing north of the border before signing with the AFL. And a flock of unknown rookies and free agents were signing, hard-working if unspectacular football players with a desire to play football for a living. Such unheralded names as Charley Hennigan, Abner Haynes, Jim Otto, and Larry Grantham went unnoticed by pro scouts until turning up in AFL training camps.

But the most spectacular aspect of the player recruiting was the bidding war with NFL teams over well-known college players. The new league wanted to build its image by signing the cream of the graduating college class, and some clubs engaged in financial combat with an NFL team to woo an All-American collegian. Some young men found this courtship so intoxicating that they signed contracts with both contestants. A series of court battles ensued that gave the AFL such dual signers as Heisman Trophy winner Billy Cannon, Johnny Robinson, and Charlie Flowers.

Another item on the agenda was finding a place to play. New York and Oakland fared the worst in the stadium hunt, with New York having to settle for the grimy old Polo Grounds, while Oakland had to play its home games in San Francisco because there was no stadium in Oakland. Houston played its games in a high-school facility and Denver used a minor-league baseball field.

A fourteen-game schedule was adopted for the league, and the two-point conversion rule, where the team may run or pass for two points after a touchdown, was put into effect for all games. But the most important move by Commissioner Foss was the signing of a national television contract with the American Broadcasting System which provided a needed $150,000 to each team.

After all this, play was ready to begin. Although average attendance per game was only 16,000, the AFL would survive 1960 and be back for more.

## EASTERN DIVISION

**Houston Oilers**—The players came from all over, Billy Cannon, the Heisman Trophy halfback from Louisiana State, had signed a three-year contract for $100,000, one of the richest pacts in pro history. George Blanda had come out off a year's retirement after a ten-year career with the Chicago Bears. Charley Hennigan had been teaching high-school biology, and he taped his final paycheck from the school inside his helmet for inspiration in dull moments. Bill Groman was an unknown rookie from Heidelberg. Al Jamison came down from the Canadian League. Coach Lou Rymkus blended all the parts together into a high-scoring machine which took command in the Eastern Division right from the start. The Oilers at first relied on Blanda's long bombs to Groman and Hennigan, but Cannon recovered from a slow start to give the ground game some punch and the Oilers won the first AFL Eastern crown.

**New York Titans**—The drab old Polo Grounds, abandoned since 1957, was dusted off to serve as home for the Titans. While Titan games were played in virtual anonymity (with highly inflated announced attendance figures), the NFL Giants were playing to a packed house week after week within walking distance at Yankee Stadium. The Titans admittedly were no match for the Giants yet, but they did play interesting, wide-open football. Although fullback Bill Mathis showed promise as a runner after winning a job in mid-season, the attack lived on quarterback Al Dorow's scrambling runs and long passes to speedsters Art Powell and Don Maynard. The Titan defense was virtually nonexistent, although young Larry Grantham showed well as linebacker. The Titans won interesting games, as when they beat Denver 28-24 by blocking a punt with twenty seconds left in the game, and they lost interesting games, like a 50-43 shootout with the Chargers. But the death of guard Howard Glenn with a broken neck after the October 9 game with Houston and the dearth of paying fans cast a deep shadow over this debut season.

**Buffalo Bills**—The Bills were an early-AFL rarity, a team trying to live on its defense. They had two tough linemen in Lavern Torczon and Chuck McMurtry, a mobile, hard-hitting middle linebacker in Archie Matsos, and one of the league's better secondaries, headed by NFL veterans Richie McCabe and Jim Wagstaff. But the offense couldn't launch an effective passing attack, the staple of most AFL clubs this year. Tom O'Connell, the old Cleveland quarterback, could not hold the starting passer's job given to him at the outset of the season, and Penn State All-American Rickie Lucas flopped both at quarterback and halfback. Johnny Green, an unheralded rookie, eventually took charge of the offense, whose main weapons were runner Wray Carlton and flanker Elbert Dubenion. The high point of the year was a 32-3 upset of the Los Angeles Chargers, but the Buffalo attack stalled too often to do any better than third place in the East.

**Boston Patriots**—The AFL broke into the box scores in Boston on Friday night, September 9. A crowd of 21,597 fans turned out at Boston University Field to watch the first regular-season AFL game ever, between the Patriots and the Denver Broncos. The Patriots displayed their weak attack right from the start by losing 13-10 to the Broncos. Coach Lou Saban had little speed in an offense led by quarterback Butch Songin, a thirty-six-year-old veteran of the Canadian League who doubled as a local high-school coach, but the defense held together well around a nucleus of Bob Dee, Tom Addison, Fred Bruney, and Ross O'Hanley. With a 35-0 trouncing of the Chargers and a 42-14 beating of the Texans to their credit, the Patriots stayed at the break-even point until losing all four of their final games. In the season's finale, before a sell-out Boston crowd of 27,123, the Pats lost 37-21 to Houston. More importantly, coach Saban shifted Gino Cappelletti from defensive back to split end for this game and discovered Boston's top receiver for the next few years.

## WESTERN DIVISION

**Los Angeles Chargers**—The eeriest sight in pro football was the Los Angeles Chargers playing to vast stretches of empty seats in the huge Memorial Coliseum. But despite the sparse fan support, coach Sid Gillman, who had coached the Rams last season, built a high-scoring outfit which took the Western Division crown in this first AFL season. The Chargers dropped three of their first five contests before hitting their stride, losing only once in their last nine games. The offense led this second-half charge, scoring 41 or more points in each of the last four games. Although the Chargers had shelled out a lot of money for Mississippi fullback Charlie Flowers, the offensive stars were quarterback Jack Kemp, rejected by the Steelers, Giants, and '49ers in the NFL; halfback Paul Lowe, an unknown rookie from Oregon State; and tackle Ron Mix, a first-draft choice of the NFL Colts. Tragedy hit the club when end Ralph Anderson, the team's leading receiver, died of a diabetes attack in November. But in general the Chargers were an artistic if not a financial success.

**Dallas Texans**—The Texans had the league's best runner, best defense, and worst luck. Halfback Abner Haynes, a speedster from North Texas State, was the AFL's first running star, carrying the ball for 875 yards, catching passes out of the backfield, and running back kicks with an exciting flair. The defense posted three shutouts and allowed a grand total of seven points in its last three games, the stingiest unit in this offense-oriented season. End Mel Branch, tackle Paul Rochester, middle linebacker Sherrill Headrick, and backs Dave Webster and Johnny Bookman were the main pillars of coach Hank Stram's defense. Only a couple of heartbreaking losses kept the Texans from challenging for the Western crown, as they lost 21-20 to the Chargers, 37-35 to the Titans, and 20-19 to the Raiders. But after the season the Texans could look back on a 17-0 victory over the Chargers and a 24-0 victory over the Oilers, shutouts over both divisional champions.

**Oakland Raiders**—Because of the problem of getting a late start, due to Oakland replacing Minneapolis as the eighth club in the new circuit, businessman Chet Soda, who headed the group granted the Oakland franchise, did not have an easy time when it came to signing players. But coach Ernie Erdelatz weeded through the available talent and built a surprisingly respectable team. He found two quarterbacks in rookie Tom Flores and NFL veteran Babe Parilli and three hard-working runners in Tony Teresa, Billy Lott, and Jack Larscheid. From this quickly organized squad, two players would stick with the Raiders through the entire ten-year life of the AFL—center Jim Otto and guard Wayne Hawkins.

**Denver Broncos**—With Gene Mingo returning a punt 76 yards for a touchdown, the Broncos beat the Boston Patriots 13-10 in the first regular-season AFL game. But Denver's main offensive weapon didn't join the team until the third week of the season. End Lionel Taylor, a slow-footed but sure-handed receiver, practiced with the Broncos for four days before catching eleven passes against the Titans on September 25, and he went on to catch enough passes in twelve games to lead the league in receiving. The Broncos lived on the pass, with thirty-two-year-old Frank Tripuka throwing 478 passes all year, including fifty-two against the Oilers on November 6. The airborne Denver attack boasted the league's top point producer in halfback and kicker Gene Mingo, but the defense leaked profusely despite fine seasons by tackle Bud McFadin and safety Goose Gonsoulin. With opposing teams scoring freely, the Broncos went winless in their last eight games, salvaging only a 38-38 tie with Boston by coming back from a 38-7 deficit in the third quarter.

**FINAL TEAM STATISTICS**

### OFFENSE

| Statistic | BOSTON | BUFFALO | DALLAS | DENVER | HOUSTON | L.A. | NEW YORK | OAKLAND |
|---|---|---|---|---|---|---|---|---|
| **FIRST DOWNS:** | | | | | | | | |
| Total | 234 | 211 | 272 | 248 | 262 | 263 | 286 | 254 |
| by Rushing | 86 | 77 | 119 | 84 | 83 | 96 | 111 | 98 |
| by Passing | 126 | 109 | 136 | 141 | 153 | 141 | 152 | 138 |
| by Penalty | 22 | 25 | 17 | 23 | 26 | 26 | 23 | 18 |
| **RUSHING:** | | | | | | | | |
| Number | 401 | 462 | 483 | 440 | 474 | 437 | 485 | 475 |
| Yards | 1218 | 1211 | 1814 | 1195 | 1565 | 1536 | 1460 | 1785 |
| Average Yards | 3.0 | 2.6 | 3.8 | 2.7 | 3.3 | 3.5 | 3.0 | 3.7 |
| Touchdowns | 11 | 15 | 24 | 10 | 15 | 24 | 14 | 23 |
| **PASSING:** | | | | | | | | |
| Attempts | 475 | 447 | 435 | 508 | 456 | 441 | 474 | 463 |
| Completions | 223 | 184 | 209 | 259 | 218 | 229 | 236 | 235 |
| Completion Percentage | 46.9 | 41.2 | 48.0 | 51.0 | 47.8 | 51.9 | 49.8 | 50.8 |
| Yards | 2865 | 2689 | 2831 | 3247 | 3371 | 3177 | 3334 | 2923 |
| Average Yards per Attempt | 6.0 | 6.0 | 6.5 | 6.4 | 7.4 | 7.2 | 7.0 | 6.3 |
| Average Yards per Completion | 12.8 | 14.6 | 13.5 | 12.5 | 15.5 | 13.9 | 14.1 | 12.4 |
| Touchdowns | 25 | 19 | 16 | 24 | 31 | 21 | 32 | 18 |
| Interceptions | 23 | 29 | 19 | 35 | 28 | 29 | 28 | 28 |
| Percent Intercepted | 4.8 | 6.5 | 4.4 | 6.9 | 6.1 | 6.6 | 5.9 | 6.0 |
| **PUNTING:** | | | | | | | | |
| Number | 78 | 89 | 61 | 70 | 72 | 58 | 62 | 76 |
| Average Distance | 35.8 | 39.0 | 39.3 | 37.3 | 35.8 | 39.7 | 37.1 | 38.9 |
| **PUNT RETURNS:** | | | | | | | | |
| Number | 28 | 27 | 33 | 29 | 15 | 32 | 17 | 26 |
| Yards | 203 | 185 | 496 | 261 | 208 | 301 | 120 | 151 |
| Average Yards | 7.3 | 6.9 | 15.0 | 9.0 | 13.9 | 9.4 | 7.1 | 5.8 |
| Touchdowns | 0 | 0 | 1 | 1 | 0 | 1 | 1 | 0 |
| **KICKOFF RETURNS:** | | | | | | | | |
| Number | 60 | 47 | 40 | 67 | 48 | 58 | 62 | 63 |
| Yards | 1421 | 945 | 845 | 1547 | 1225 | 1213 | 1580 | 1504 |
| Average Yards | 23.7 | 20.1 | 21.1 | 23.1 | 25.5 | 20.9 | 25.5 | 23.9 |
| Touchdowns | 0 | 0 | 0 | 0 | 2 | 0 | 2 | 0 |
| **INTERCEPTION RETURNS:** | | | | | | | | |
| Number | 25 | 33 | 32 | 27 | 25 | 28 | 24 | 25 |
| Yards | 312 | 356 | 410 | 417 | 190 | 317 | 201 | 278 |
| Average Yards | 12.5 | 10.8 | 12.8 | 15.4 | 7.6 | 11.3 | 8.4 | 11.1 |
| Touchdowns | 0 | 4 | 4 | 2 | 0 | 2 | 1 | 1 |
| **PENALTIES:** | | | | | | | | |
| Number | 69 | 57 | 80 | 54 | 75 | 70 | 53 | 71 |
| Yards | 730.5 | 615 | 753 | 501 | 750 | 648 | 672 | 718 |
| **FUMBLES:** | | | | | | | | |
| Number | 36 | 30 | 30 | 32 | 36 | 31 | 36 | 41 |
| Number Lost | 22 | 15 | 18 | 17 | 17 | 16 | 20 | 18 |
| **POINTS:** | | | | | | | | |
| Total | 286 | 296 | 362 | 309 | 379 | 373 | 382 | 319 |
| PAT (Kick) Attempts | 32 | 34 | 44 | 36 | 47 | 47 | 50 | 39 |
| PAT (Kick) Made | 30 | 28 | 42 | 33 | 46 | 46 | 47 | 37 |
| PAT (Rush or Pass) Attempts | 5 | 3 | 2 | 1 | 0 | 0 | 1 | 4 |
| PAT (Rush or Pass) Made | 4 | 2 | 1 | 0 | 0 | 0 | 1 | 2 |
| FG Attempts | 23 | 26 | 34 | 28 | 34 | 24 | 21 | 25 |
| FG Made | 8 | 12 | 14 | 18 | 15 | 13 | 9 | 6 |
| Percent FG Made | 34.8 | 46.2 | 41.2 | 64.3 | 44.1 | 54.2 | 42.9 | 24.0 |
| Safeties | 1 | 0 | 0 | 0 | 0 | 0 | 0 | 1 |

### DEFENSE

| Statistic | BOSTON | BUFFALO | DALLAS | DENVER | HOUSTON | L.A. | NEW YORK | OAKLAND |
|---|---|---|---|---|---|---|---|---|
| **FIRST DOWNS:** | | | | | | | | |
| Total | 237 | 225 | 253 | 254 | 282 | 259 | 252 | 268 |
| by Rushing | 78 | 103 | 76 | 112 | 90 | 97 | 99 | 99 |
| by Passing | 135 | 109 | 148 | 123 | 164 | 138 | 133 | 146 |
| by Penalty | 24 | 13 | 29 | 19 | 28 | 24 | 20 | 23 |
| **RUSHING:** | | | | | | | | |
| Number | 477 | 474 | 422 | 541 | 438 | 414 | 449 | 442 |
| Yards | 1513 | 1393 | 980 | 2145 | 1027 | 1750 | 1378 | 1598 |
| Average Yards | 3.2 | 2.9 | 2.3 | 4.0 | 2.3 | 4.2 | 3.1 | 3.6 |
| Touchdowns | 21 | 15 | 14 | 19 | 6 | 24 | 20 | 17 |
| **PASSING:** | | | | | | | | |
| Attempts | 429 | 429 | 503 | 387 | 557 | 467 | 450 | 477 |
| Completions | 210 | 185 | 261 | 189 | 271 | 227 | 216 | 234 |
| Completion Percentage | 49.0 | 43.1 | 51.2 | 48.8 | 48.7 | 48.6 | 48.0 | 49.1 |
| Yards | 2958 | 2461 | 3002 | 2987 | 3874 | 2851 | 2919 | 3385 |
| Average Yards per Attempt | 6.9 | 5.7 | 6.0 | 7.7 | 7.0 | 6.1 | 6.5 | 7.1 |
| Average Yards per Completion | 14.1 | 13.3 | 11.5 | 15.8 | 14.3 | 12.6 | 13.5 | 14.5 |
| Touchdowns | 19 | 19 | 19 | 25 | 28 | 21 | 27 | 28 |
| Interceptions | 25 | 33 | 32 | 27 | 25 | 28 | 24 | 25 |
| Percent Intercepted | 5.8 | 7.7 | 6.4 | 7.0 | 4.5 | 6.0 | 5.3 | 5.2 |
| **PUNTING:** | | | | | | | | |
| Number | 74 | 77 | 78 | 67 | 68 | 62 | 65 | 75 |
| Average Distance | 37.2 | 37.6 | 37.5 | 39.0 | 37.1 | 40.2 | 37.0 | 37.5 |
| **PUNT RETURNS:** | | | | | | | | |
| Number | 21 | 33 | 27 | 20 | 28 | 17 | 31 | 30 |
| Yards | 361 | 232 | 157 | 149 | 258 | 197 | 342 | 229 |
| Average Yards | 17.2 | 7.0 | 5.8 | 7.5 | 9.2 | 11.6 | 11.0 | 7.6 |
| Touchdowns | 3 | 0 | 0 | 1 | 0 | 0 | 0 | 0 |
| **KICKOFF RETURNS:** | | | | | | | | |
| Number | 50 | 55 | 57 | 54 | 46 | 70 | 70 | 43 |
| Yards | 1123 | 1402 | 1347 | 1087 | 1096 | 1481 | 1785 | 959 |
| Average Yards | 22.5 | 25.5 | 23.6 | 20.1 | 23.8ᵃ | 21.2 | 25.5 | 22.3 |
| Touchdowns | 1 | 0 | 1 | 1 | 0 | 0 | 1 | 1 |
| **INTERCEPTION RETURNS:** | | | | | | | | |
| Number | 23 | 29 | 19 | 35 | 28 | 29 | 28 | 28 |
| Yards | 336 | 422 | 171 | 343 | 316 | 284 | 228 | 381 |
| Average Yards | 14.6 | 14.6 | 9.0 | 9.8 | 11.3 | 9.8 | 8.1 | 13.6 |
| Touchdowns | 3 | 2 | 0 | 3 | 2 | 1 | 0 | 3 |
| **PENALTIES:** | | | | | | | | |
| Number | 77 | 62 | 59 | 62 | 74 | 59 | 77 | 59 |
| Yards | 825 | 608.5 | 579 | 633 | 664 | 569 | 911 | 598 |
| **FUMBLES:** | | | | | | | | |
| Number | 41 | 27 | 34 | 26 | 42 | 39 | 27 | 36 |
| Number Lost | 20 | 16 | 16 | 17 | 26 | 17 | 16 | 15 |
| **POINTS:** | | | | | | | | |
| Total | 349 | 303 | 253 | 393 | 285 | 336 | 399 | 388 |
| PAT (Kick) Made | 43 | 37 | 31 | 48 | 33 | 40 | 51 | 46 |
| FG Attempts | 27 | 27 | 23 | 28 | 27 | 28 | 25 | 30 |
| FG Made | 10 | 14 | 4 | 17 | 12 | 14 | 10 | 14 |
| Percent FG Made | 37.0 | 51.9 | 17.4 | 60.7 | 44.4 | 50.0 | 40.0 | 46.7 |
| Safeties | 0 | 1 | 0 | 0 | 0 | 1 | 0 | 0 |

---

**1960 AFL CHAMPIONSHIP GAME**
January 1, at Houston
(Attendance 32,183)

## Age and Blanda and a Crown

The Oilers and Chargers met on New Year's Day to decide the first AFL championship. Both clubs had high scoring offenses, but the defensive units turned in surprisingly strong performances. The only scoring of the first quarter came on a pair of field goals by Ben Agajanian, Los Angeles' forty-one-year-old kicking specialist. George Blanda, the old man in the Houston lineup, put the Oilers ahead early in the second period with a 17-yard touchdown pass to fullback Dave Smith and the successful conversion. Blanda and Agajanian both added three-pointers late in the quarter to make the score 10-9 Houston at the half. The offenses moved better in the second half, with the Oilers relying on Blanda's passing and the Chargers on Paul Lowe's running. Houston upped its lead to eight points with a seven-yard Blanda-to-Bill Groman touchdown pass, but the Chargers came right back on a long drive culminating in Lowe's two-yard dash into the end zone. Leading 17-16 after three quarters, the Oilers broke open a long pass play, a very common occurrence in the early AFL. Billy Cannon came out of the backfield and took a George Blanda pass 88 yards to a touchdown, with the extra point running the score to 24-16. The Oilers led by eight points, but the Chargers could tie the game in one swoop with a touchdown and a two-point conversion. Twice the Chargers drove deep into Houston territory only to lose the ball on downs on the 35-yard line and on the 22-yard line. The final Los Angeles drive died with one minute left, turning the ball and the league championship over to the Oilers.

### SCORING

| | | | |
|---|---|---|---|
| HOUSTON | 0  10  7  7—24 | | |
| LOS ANGELES | 6  3  7  0—16 | | |

**First Quarter**
L.A.   Agajanian, 38 yard field goal   4:02
L.A.   Agajanian, 22 yard field goal   8:16

**Second Quarter**
Hous.   Smith, 17 yard pass from Blanda   3:51
　　　　PAT—Blanda (kick)
Hous.   Blanda, 18 yard field goal   8:45
L.A.   Agajanian, 27 yard field goal   14:55

**Third Quarter**
Hous.   Groman, 7 yard pass from Blanda
　　　　PAT—Blanda (kick)
L.A.   Lowe, 2 yard rush
　　　　PAT—Agajanian (kick)

**Fourth Quarter**
Hous.   Cannon, 88 yard pass from Blanda
　　　　PAT—Blanda (kick)

### TEAM STATISTICS

| HOUS. | | L.A. |
|---|---|---|
| 17 | First Downs—Total | 21 |
| 4 | First Downs—Rushing | 11 |
| 13 | First Downs—Passing | 9 |
| 0 | First Downs—Penalty | 1 |
| 0 | Fumbles—Number | 2 |
| 0 | Fumbles—Lost Ball | 0 |
| 4 | Penalties—Number | 3 |
| 54 | Yards Penalized | 15 |
| 0 | Giveaways | 2 |
| 2 | Takeaways | 0 |
| +2 | Difference | −2 |

### INDIVIDUAL STATISTICS

**RUSHING**

| HOUSTON | No. | Yds. | Avg. | LOS ANGELES | No. | Yds. | Avg. |
|---|---|---|---|---|---|---|---|
| Cannon | 18 | 50 | 2.8 | Lowe | 21 | 165 | 7.9 |
| Smith | 19 | 45 | 2.4 | Ferguson | 4 | 11 | 2.8 |
| Hall | 3 | 5 | 1.6 | Ford | 2 | −5 | −2.5 |
| | 40 | 100 | 2.5 | Kemp | 6 | −9 | −1.5 |
| | | | | | 33 | 162 | 4.9 |

**RECEIVING**

| HOUSTON | No. | Yds. | Avg. | LOS ANGELES | No. | Yds. | Avg. |
|---|---|---|---|---|---|---|---|
| Smith | 5 | 52 | 10.4 | Norton | 6 | 55 | 9.2 |
| Hennigan | 4 | 71 | 17.8 | Womble | 6 | 29 | 4.8 |
| Cannon | 3 | 128 | 42.7 | Kocourek | 3 | 57 | 19.0 |
| Groman | 3 | 37 | 12.3 | Lowe | 3 | 5 | 1.7 |
| Carson | 1 | 13 | 13.0 | Ferguson | 2 | 19 | 9.5 |
| | 16 | 301 | 18.8 | Flowers | 1 | 6 | 6.0 |
| | | | | | 21 | 171 | 8.1 |

**PUNTING**

| HOUSTON | No. | | Avg. | LOS ANGELES | No. | | Avg. |
|---|---|---|---|---|---|---|---|
| Milstead | 5 | | 34.0 | Laraba | 4 | | 41.0 |

**PUNT RETURNS**

| HOUSTON | No. | Yds. | Avg. | LOS ANGELES | No. | Yds. | Avg. |
|---|---|---|---|---|---|---|---|
| None | | | | Harris | 1 | 27 | 27.0 |
| | | | | Sears | 1 | 15 | 15.0 |
| | | | | | 2 | 42 | 21.0 |

**KICKOFF RETURNS**

| HOUSTON | No. | Yds. | Avg. | LOS ANGELES | No. | Yds. | Avg. |
|---|---|---|---|---|---|---|---|
| Cannon | 3 | 81 | 27.0 | Lowe | 4 | 101 | 25.3 |
| Hall | 2 | 47 | 23.5 | Ford | 1 | 22 | 22.0 |
| | 5 | 128 | 25.6 | | 5 | 123 | 24.6 |

**INTERCEPTION RETURNS**

| HOUSTON | No. | Yds. | Avg. | LOS ANGELES | | | |
|---|---|---|---|---|---|---|---|
| Gordon | 1 | 27 | 27.0 | None | | | |
| Dukes | 1 | 8 | 8.0 | | | | |
| | 2 | 35 | 17.5 | | | | |

**PASSING**

| HOUSTON | Att. | Comp. | Comp. Pct. | Yds. | Int. | Yds/ Att. | Yds/ Comp. |
|---|---|---|---|---|---|---|---|
| Blanda | 31 | 16 | 51.6 | 301 | 0 | 9.7 | 18.8 |
| Cannon | 1 | 0 | 0.0 | 0 | 0 | — | — |
| | 32 | 16 | 50.0 | 301 | 0 | 9.4 | 18.8 |

| LOS ANGELES | Att. | Comp. | Comp. Pct. | Yds. | Int. | Yds/ Att. | Yds/ Comp. |
|---|---|---|---|---|---|---|---|
| Kemp | 41 | 21 | 51.2 | 171 | 2 | 4.2 | 8.1 |

### HOUSTON OILERS 10-4-0 Lou Rymkus

**Scores of Each Game**

| | | |
|---|---|---|
| 37 | Oakland | 22 |
| 38 | LOS ANGELES | 28 |
| 13 | OAKLAND | 14 |
| 27 | NEW YORK | 21 |
| 20 | DALLAS | 10 |
| 42 | New York | 28 |
| 24 | Buffalo | 25 |
| 45 | Denver | 25 |
| 21 | Los Angeles | 24 |
| 20 | DENVER | 10 |
| 24 | Boston | 10 |
| 0 | Dallas | 24 |
| 31 | BUFFALO | 23 |
| 37 | BOSTON | 21 |

| Use Name | Pos. | Hgt | Wgt | Age | Int | Pts |
|---|---|---|---|---|---|---|
| Gary Greaves | OT | 6'3" | 235 | 24 | | |
| Al Jamison | OT | 6'5" | 240 | 23 | | |
| Rich Michael | OT | 6'3" | 230 | 21 | | |
| Fred Wallner | OG | 6'2" | 235 | 31 | | |
| Hogan Wharton | OG | 6'2" | 245 | 24 | | |
| Wahoo McDaniel | OG | 6' | 230 | 23 | | |
| Bob Talamini | OG | 6'1" | 230 | 21 | | |
| George Belotti | C | 6'4" | 255 | 25 | | |
| John Simerson | C | 6'3" | 255 | 25 | | |
| Dalva Allen | DE | 6'5" | 245 | 24 | 1 | |
| Don Floyd | DE | 6'4" | 230 | 22 | | |
| Dan Lanpheer | DE | 6'2" | 220 | 22 | | |
| Pete Davidson | DT | 6'5" | 255 | 26 | | |
| Jerry Helluin | DT | 6'2" | 260 | 30 | | |
| George Shirkey | DT | 6'4" | 260 | 23 | | |
| Orville Trask | DT | 6'4" | 260 | 25 | | |
| Mike Dukes | LB | 6'3" | 225 | 24 | 2 | |
| Dennit Morris | LB | 6'1" | 225 | 24 | 4 | |
| Phil Perlo | LB | 6' | 220 | 24 | | |
| Hugh Pitts | LB | 6'2" | 225 | 26 | | |
| Tony Banfield | DB | 6'1" | 185 | 21 | 3 | |
| Bobby Gordon | DB | 6' | 195 | 24 | 3 | |
| Mark Johnston | DB | 6' | 203 | 22 | 4 | |
| Charlie Kendall | DB | 6'2" | 185 | 25 | 2 | |
| Jim Norton | DB | 6'3" | 182 | 21 | 1 | |
| Julian Spence | DB | 5'11" | 170 | 31 | 4 | |
| George Blanda | QB | 6'1" | 210 | 32 | | 115 |
| Jacky Lee | QB | 6'1" | 185 | 21 | | |
| Charley Milstead | QB | 6'2" | 190 | 22 | | |
| Don Brown | HB | 6'1" | 205 | 23 | | |
| Billy Cannon | HB | 6'1" | 210 | 23 | | 42 |
| Ken Hall | HB | 6'1" | 200 | 24 | | 6 |
| Charley Tolar | HB | 5'7" | 195 | 22 | | 18 |
| Doug Cline | FB | 6'1" | 210 | 21 | | 12 |
| Dave Smith | FB | 6'1" | 205 | 23 | | 42 |
| Bob White | FB | 6'2" | 220 | 22 | | |
| Jack Atchason (from BOS) | OE | 6'4" | 215 | 23 | | 6 |
| Johnny Carson | OE | 6'3" | 205 | 30 | | 24 |
| Bill Groman | OE | 6' | 194 | 24 | | 72 |
| Charley Hennigan | OE | 6' | 190 | 24 | | 36 |
| John White | OE | 6'4" | 230 | 22 | | |
| Al Witcher | DE-OE | 6'1" | 200 | 23 | 1 | 6 |

### NEW YORK TITANS 7-7-0 Sammy Baugh

**Scores of Each Game**

| | | |
|---|---|---|
| 27 | BUFFALO | 3 |
| 24 | BOSTON | 28 |
| 28 | DENVER | 24 |
| 37 | Dallas | 35 |
| 21 | Houston | 27 |
| 17 | Buffalo | 13 |
| 28 | HOUSTON | 42 |
| 27 | OAKLAND | 28 |
| 7 | LOS ANGELES | 21 |
| 21 | Boston | 38 |
| 41 | DALLAS | 35 |
| 30 | Denver | 27 |
| 31 | Oakland | 28 |
| 43 | Los Angeles | 50 |

| Use Name | Pos. | Hgt | Wgt | Age | Int | Pts |
|---|---|---|---|---|---|---|
| Larry Baker | OT | 6'2" | 240 | 23 | | |
| Ernie Barnes | OT | 6'3" | 257 | 21 | | |
| Gene Cockrell | OT | 6'3" | 247 | 27 | | |
| Jack Klotz | OT | 6'5" | 260 | 26 | | |
| Dan Callahan | OG | 6' | 230 | 22 | | |
| Frank D'Agostino | OG | 6'1" | 245 | 26 | | |
| Howard Glenn (died Oct. 9) | OG | 6' | 235 | 25 | | |
| John McMullan | OG | 6' | 244 | 25 | | |
| Bob Mischak | OG | 6' | 238 | 27 | | |
| Mike Hudock | C | 6'2" | 245 | 25 | | |
| Ed Cooke | DE | 6'4" | 245 | 25 | | |
| Bob Reifsnyder | DE | 6'2" | 250 | 23 | | |
| Joe Ryan | DE | 6'2" | 235 | 26 | | |
| Nick Mumley | OT-DE | 6'6" | 245 | 24 | 1 | 6 |
| Dick Guesman | DT | 6'4" | 255 | 24 | | |
| Joe Katchik | DT | 6'9" | 290 | 26 | | |
| Tom Saidock | DT | 6'5" | 260 | 28 | | |
| Sid Youngelman | DT | 6'3" | 265 | 28 | | |
| Leon Dumbrowski | LB | 6' | 215 | 22 | | |
| Roger Ellis | LB | 6'3" | 233 | 22 | 1 | |
| Larry Grantham | LB | 6' | 195 | 21 | 5 | |
| Bob Marques | LB | 6' | 220 | 23 | | |
| Hall Whitley | LB | 6'2" | 225 | 25 | | |
| Eddie Bell | DB | 6'1" | 215 | 29 | 2 | |
| Charlie Dupre | DB | 6' | 195 | 24 | | |
| Dick Felt | DB | 6' | 185 | 22 | 5 | 12 |
| Fred Julian | DB | 5'9" | 185 | 22 | 6 | |
| Corky Tharp | DB | 5'10" | 180 | 27 | 2 | |
| Rick Sapienza | HB-DB | 5'11" | 185 | 24 | | |
| Al Dorow | QB | 6' | 195 | 30 | | 42 |
| Dick Jamieson | QB | 6'1" | 190 | 24 | | |
| Bob Scrabis | QB | 6'3" | 220 | 24 | | |
| Dewey Bohling | HB | 5'11" | 190 | 21 | | 36 |
| Leon Burton | HB | 5'9" | 172 | 25 | | 18 |
| Don Herndon | HB | 6' | 195 | 26 | | 6 |
| Bill Shockley | HB | 6' | 185 | 22 | | 86 |
| Pete Hart | FB | 5'9" | 190 | 22 | | |
| Bill Mathis | FB | 6'1" | 205 | 21 | | 12 |
| Joe Pagliei | FB | 6' | 220 | 26 | | 6 |
| Ken Campbell | OE | 6'1" | 213 | 21 | | |
| Don Maynard | OE | 6' | 185 | 24 | | 36 |
| Art Powell | OE | 6'3" | 210 | 23 | | 84 |
| Dave Ross | OE | 6'3" | 210 | 22 | | 6 |
| Thurlow Cooper | DE-OE | 6'4" | 228 | 27 | | 20 |

### BUFFALO BILLS 5-8-1 Buster Ramsey

**Scores of Each Game**

| | | |
|---|---|---|
| 3 | New York | 27 |
| 21 | DENVER | 27 |
| 13 | Boston | 0 |
| 10 | LOS ANGELES | 24 |
| 13 | NEW YORK | 17 |
| 38 | OAKLAND | 9 |
| 25 | HOUSTON | 24 |
| 28 | DALLAS | 45 |
| 7 | Oakland | 20 |
| 32 | Los Angeles | 3 |
| 38 | Denver | 38 |
| 38 | BOSTON | 14 |
| 23 | Houston | 31 |
| 7 | Dallas | 24 |

| Use Name | Pos. | Hgt | Wgt | Age | Int | Pts |
|---|---|---|---|---|---|---|
| Tony Discenzo (from BOS) | OT | 6'5" | 240 | 24 | | |
| Ed Meyer | OT | 6'2" | 240 | 23 | | |
| Harold Olson | OT | 6'3" | 266 | 21 | | |
| Bob Sedlock | OT | 6'4" | 295 | 23 | | |
| Phil Blazer | OG | 6'1" | 235 | 24 | | |
| Don Chelf | OG | 6'3" | 235 | 25 | | |
| Ed Muelhaupt | OG | 6'3" | 230 | 24 | | |
| Dan McGrew | C | 6'2" | 250 | 22 | | |
| Leroy Moore | DE | 6' | 230 | 24 | | |
| Charlie Rutkowski | DE | 6'3" | 248 | 22 | | |
| Lavern Torczon | DE | 6'2" | 240 | 24 | | |
| Mack Yoho | DE | 6'2" | 240 | 24 | 1 | 12 |
| Gene Grabosky | DT | 6'5" | 275 | 23 | | |
| Chuck McMurtry | DT | 6' | 310 | 22 | | |
| John Scott | DT | 6'4" | 260 | 24 | | |
| Jim Sorey | DT | 6'4" | 270 | 23 | | |
| Bernie Buzynski | LB | 6'3" | 228 | 22 | 1 | |
| Joe Hergert | LB | 6'1" | 217 | 24 | 1 | 12 |
| Jack Laraway | LB | 6'1" | 220 | 24 | | |
| Archie Matsos | LB | 6' | 220 | 25 | 8 | 6 |
| Sam Palumbo | LB | 6'2" | 230 | 29 | | |
| Dennis Remmert | LB | 6'3" | 215 | 21 | | |
| Joe Schaffer | LB | 6' | 210 | 22 | 1 | |
| Jack Johnson | DB | 6'3" | 195 | 26 | 2 | |
| Billy Kinard | DB | 6' | 185 | 26 | 4 | |
| Richie McCabe | DB | 6'1" | 185 | 26 | 4 | |
| Jim Wagstaff | DB | 6'2" | 190 | 24 | 6 | 6 |
| Billy Atkins | HB-DB | 6'1" | 195 | 25 | 5 | 45 |
| Bob Brodhead | QB | 6'2" | 207 | 23 | | 2 |
| Johnny Green | QB | 6'3" | 198 | 23 | | 12 |
| Tom O'Connell | QB | 5'11" | 190 | 28 | | 8 |
| Richie Lucas | HB-QB | 6' | 190 | 21 | | 48 |
| Elbert Dubenion | HB | 6' | 190 | 25 | | 48 |
| Willmer Fowler | HB | 5'11" | 185 | 23 | | 6 |
| Darrell Harper | HB | 6'1" | 195 | 21 | | |
| Joe Kulbacki | HB | 6' | 185 | 22 | | 6 |
| Harold Lewis | HB | 6' | 200 | 24 | | |
| Wray Carlton | FB | 6'2" | 210 | 22 | | 66 |
| Carl Smith | FB | 6' | 200 | 25 | | 6 |
| Bob Barrett | OE | 6'3" | 200 | 24 | | |
| Dick Brubaker | OE | 6' | 195 | 28 | | 6 |
| Dan Chamberlain | OE | 6'4" | 200 | 23 | | 24 |
| Monte Crockett | OE | 6'3" | 210 | 21 | | 6 |
| Al Hoisington (from OAK) | OE | 6'3" | 200 | 25 | | 12 |
| Tom Rychlec | OE | 6'3" | 220 | 26 | | |

### BOSTON PATRIOTS 5-9-0 Lou Saban

**Scores of Each Game**

| | | |
|---|---|---|
| 10 | DENVER | 13 |
| 28 | New York | 24 |
| 0 | BUFFALO | 13 |
| 35 | Los Angeles | 0 |
| 14 | Oakland | 27 |
| 24 | Denver | 31 |
| 16 | LOS ANGELES | 45 |
| 34 | OAKLAND | 28 |
| 38 | NEW YORK | 21 |
| 42 | DALLAS | 14 |
| 10 | HOUSTON | 24 |
| 14 | Buffalo | 38 |
| 0 | Dallas | 34 |
| 21 | Houston | 37 |

| Use Name | Pos. | Hgt | Wgt | Age | Int | Pts |
|---|---|---|---|---|---|---|
| Bob Cross | OT | 6'4" | 245 | 29 | | |
| Jerry DeLucca | OT | 6'3" | 250 | 24 | | |
| George McGee | OT | 6'2" | 255 | 24 | | |
| Abe Cohen | OG | 5'11" | 230 | 26 | | |
| Jack Davis | OG | 6' | 226 | 27 | | |
| Bob Lee | OG | 6'1" | 245 | 24 | | |
| Charlie Leo | OG | 6' | 233 | 25 | | |
| Walt Cudzik | C | 6'2" | 226 | 27 | | |
| Bill Danenhauer (from DEN) | DE | 6'4" | 245 | 25 | | |
| Bob Dee | DE | 6'3" | 234 | 27 | 1 | |
| Harry Jacobs | DE | 6'2" | 235 | 23 | 4 | |
| Don McComb | DE | 6'4" | 240 | 26 | | |
| Al Richardson | DE | 6'3" | 250 | 26 | | |
| Al Crow | DT | 6'6" | 260 | 27 | | |
| Art Hauser | DT | 6' | 243 | 29 | | |
| Jim Hunt | DT | 5'11" | 245 | 21 | | |
| Harry Jagielski | DT | 6' | 260 | 28 | | |
| Bob Yates | DT | 6'3" | 250 | 21 | | |
| Tom Addison | LB | 6'3" | 230 | 24 | | |
| Phil Bennett | LB | 6'3" | 225 | 24 | | |
| Bill Brown | LB | 6'1" | 230 | 23 | 1 | |
| Jack Rudolph | LB | 6'3" | 225 | 22 | 2 | |
| Tony Sardisco | LB | 6'2" | 225 | 27 | | |
| Fred Bruney | DB | 5'10" | 188 | 29 | 3 | |
| Ross O'Hanley | DB | 6' | 185 | 21 | 3 | |
| Chuck Shonta | DB | 6' | 190 | 22 | 2 | 6 |
| Bob Soltis | DB | 6'2" | 205 | 23 | 2 | |
| Clyde Washington | DB | 6' | 195 | 22 | 3 | |
| Gino Cappelletti | OE-DB | 6' | 190 | 26 | 4 | 60 |
| Tom Dimitroff | QB | 5'11" | 200 | 25 | | |
| Tom Greene | QB | 6'1" | 190 | 22 | | |
| Butch Songin | QB | 6'2" | 190 | 36 | | 12 |
| Harvey White | QB | 6'1" | 190 | 22 | | |
| Walter Beach | HB | 6' | 180 | 25 | | 6 |
| Ron Burton | HB | 5'10" | 190 | 23 | | 6 |
| Dick Christy | HB | 5'10" | 192 | 24 | | 36 |
| Jake Crouthamel | HB | 5'11" | 190 | 22 | | |
| Larry Garron | HB | 6' | 185 | 23 | | |
| Jerry Green | HB | 6' | 190 | 23 | | |
| Walt Livingston | HB | 6' | 185 | 25 | | 6 |
| Ger Schwedes | HB | 6'1" | 205 | 21 | | |
| Billy Wells | HB | 5'9" | 175 | 28 | | 6 |
| Jim Crawford | FB | 6'1" | 205 | 24 | | 14 |
| Bill Larson | FB | 5'10" | 190 | 21 | | |
| Alan Miller | FB | 6' | 195 | 22 | | 18 |
| Joe Biscaha | OE | 6'1" | 195 | 22 | | |
| Jim Colclough | OE | 6' | 185 | 24 | | 54 |
| Joe Johnson | OE | 6' | 185 | 30 | | 18 |
| Oscar Lofton | OE | 6'6" | 218 | 22 | | 24 |
| Mike Long | OE | 6' | 188 | 21 | | |
| Tom Stephens | OE | 6'1" | 190 | 24 | | 18 |

## HOUSTON OILERS

### RUSHING

| Last Name | No. | Yds | Avg | TD |
|---|---|---|---|---|
| Cannon | 152 | 644 | 4.2 | 1 |
| Smith | 154 | 643 | 4.2 | 5 |
| Tolar | 54 | 179 | 3.3 | 3 |
| Hall | 30 | 118 | 3.9 | 0 |
| Cline | 37 | 105 | 2.8 | 2 |
| Talamini | 0 | 14 | 0.0 | 0 |
| Milstead | 6 | −21 | −3.5 | 0 |
| Lee | 16 | −57 | −3.6 | 0 |
| Blanda | 25 | −60 | −2.4 | 4 |

### RECEIVING

| Last Name | No. | Yds | Avg | TD |
|---|---|---|---|---|
| Groman | 72 | 1473 | 20 | 12 |
| Carson | 45 | 604 | 13 | 4 |
| Hennigan | 44 | 722 | 16 | 6 |
| Smith | 22 | 216 | 10 | 2 |
| Cannon | 15 | 187 | 12 | 5 |
| Tolar | 7 | 71 | 10 | 0 |
| Atchason | 5 | 48 | 10 | 1 |
| Witcher | 4 | 34 | 9 | 1 |
| Cline | 4 | 15 | 4 | 0 |
| J. White | 1 | 18 | 18 | 0 |
| Norton | 1 | 5 | 5 | 0 |

### PUNT RETURNS

| Last Name | No. | Yds | Avg | TD |
|---|---|---|---|---|
| Cannon | 4 | 96 | 24 | 0 |
| Hall | 6 | 72 | 12 | 0 |
| Tolar | 5 | 40 | 8 | 0 |

### KICKOFF RETURNS

| Last Name | No. | Yds | Avg | TD |
|---|---|---|---|---|
| Hall | 19 | 594 | 31 | 1 |
| Cannon | 8 | 266 | 33 | 1 |
| Tolar | 13 | 249 | 19 | 0 |
| Dukes | 4 | 58 | 15 | 0 |
| Cline | 3 | 42 | 14 | 0 |
| Jamison | 1 | 5 | 5 | 0 |
| J. White | 0 | 11 | 11 | 0 |

### PASSING – PUNTING – KICKING Statistics

**PASSING**

| Last Name | Att | Comp | % | Yds | Yd/Att | TD | Int-% | RK |
|---|---|---|---|---|---|---|---|---|
| Blanda | 363 | 169 | 47 | 2413 | 6.6 | 24 | 26− 6 | 5 |
| Lee | 77 | 41 | 53 | 842 | 10.9 | 5 | 6− 8 | |
| Milstead | 7 | 4 | 57 | 43 | 6.1 | 0 | 0− 0 | |
| Smith | 5 | 3 | 60 | 70 | 14.0 | 1 | 0− 0 | |
| Cannon | 3 | 0 | 0 | 0 | 0.0 | 0 | 0− 0 | |
| Groman | 1 | 1 | 100 | 3 | 3.0 | 1 | 0− 0 | |

**PUNTING**

| Last Name | No | Avg |
|---|---|---|
| Milstead | 66 | 35.8 |
| Hall | 6 | 35.0 |

**KICKING**

| Last Name | XP | Att | % | FG | Att | % |
|---|---|---|---|---|---|---|
| Blanda | 46 | 47 | 98 | 15 | 34 | 44 |

## NEW YORK TITANS

### RUSHING

| Last Name | No. | Yds | Avg | TD |
|---|---|---|---|---|
| Bohling | 123 | 431 | 3.5 | 2 |
| Mathis | 92 | 307 | 3.3 | 2 |
| Dorow | 124 | 167 | 1.3 | 7 |
| Shockley | 37 | 156 | 4.2 | 0 |
| Burton | 16 | 119 | 7.4 | 1 |
| Hart | 25 | 113 | 4.5 | 0 |
| Pagliei | 17 | 69 | 4.1 | 1 |
| Jamieson | 8 | −61 | −7.6 | 0 |

### RECEIVING

| Last Name | No. | Yds | Avg | TD |
|---|---|---|---|---|
| Maynard | 72 | 1265 | 18 | 6 |
| Powell | 69 | 1167 | 17 | 14 |
| Bohling | 30 | 268 | 9 | 4 |
| Mathis | 18 | 103 | 6 | 0 |
| Ross | 10 | 122 | 12 | 1 |
| Cooper | 9 | 161 | 18 | 3 |
| Shockley | 8 | 69 | 9 | 2 |
| Herndon | 5 | 57 | 11 | 1 |
| Hart | 3 | 19 | 6 | 0 |
| Burton | 3 | 8 | 3 | 0 |
| Pagliei | 1 | 13 | 13 | 0 |
| Sapienza | 1 | 4 | 4 | 0 |
| Klotz | 0 | 5 | 0 | 0 |

### PUNT RETURNS

| Last Name | No. | Yds | Avg | TD |
|---|---|---|---|---|
| Burton | 12 | 93 | 8 | 0 |
| Donnahoo | 1 | 15 | 15 | 1 |
| Shockley | 3 | 12 | 4 | 0 |
| Tharp | 1 | 0 | 0 | 0 |

### KICKOFF RETURNS

| Last Name | No. | Yds | Avg | TD |
|---|---|---|---|---|
| Burton | 31 | 897 | 29 | 2 |
| Shockley | 17 | 411 | 24 | 0 |
| Herndon | 5 | 114 | 23 | 0 |
| Powell | 2 | 63 | 32 | 0 |
| Maynard | 3 | 59 | 20 | 0 |
| Baker | 1 | 18 | 18 | 0 |
| Reifsnyder | 1 | 16 | 16 | 0 |
| Klotz | 1 | 8 | 8 | 0 |
| Cooper | 1 | 0 | 0 | 0 |

### PASSING – PUNTING – KICKING

**PASSING**

| Last Name | Att | Comp | % | Yds | Yd/Att | TD | Int-% | RK |
|---|---|---|---|---|---|---|---|---|
| Dorow | 396 | 201 | 51 | 2748 | 6.9 | 26 | 26− 7 | 2 |
| Jamieson | 70 | 35 | 50 | 586 | 8.4 | 6 | 2− 3 | |
| Bohling | 5 | 0 | 0 | 0 | 0.0 | 0 | 0− 0 | |
| Scrabis | 3 | 0 | 0 | 0 | 0.0 | 0 | 0− 0 | |

**PUNTING**

| Last Name | No | Avg |
|---|---|---|
| Pagliei | 48 | 37.1 |
| Sapienza | 8 | 32.4 |
| Dorow | 6 | 44.0 |

**KICKING**

| Last Name | XP | Att | % | FG | Att | % |
|---|---|---|---|---|---|---|
| Shockley | 47 | 50 | 94 | 9 | 21 | 43 |

**2 POINT XP**
Cooper (1)

## BUFFALO BILLS

### RUSHING

| Last Name | No. | Yds | Avg | TD |
|---|---|---|---|---|
| Carlton | 137 | 533 | 3.9 | 7 |
| Fowler | 93 | 370 | 4.0 | 1 |
| Kulbacki | 41 | 108 | 2.6 | 1 |
| Dubenion | 16 | 94 | 5.9 | 1 |
| Lucas | 46 | 90 | 1.9 | 2 |
| Smith | 19 | 61 | 3.2 | 0 |
| Atkins | 2 | 47 | 23.5 | 0 |
| Brodhead | 21 | 45 | 2.1 | 0 |
| Harper | 1 | 3 | 3.0 | 0 |
| O'Connell | 22 | −24 | −1.0 | 0 |
| Green | 46 | −156 | −3.4 | 2 |

### RECEIVING

| Last Name | No. | Yds | Avg | TD |
|---|---|---|---|---|
| Rychlec | 45 | 590 | 13 | 0 |
| Dubenion | 42 | 752 | 18 | 7 |
| Carlton | 29 | 477 | 16 | 4 |
| Chamberlain | 17 | 279 | 16 | 4 |
| Crockett | 14 | 173 | 12 | 1 |
| Fowler | 10 | 99 | 10 | 0 |
| Hoisington | 8 | 141 | 18 | 2 |
| Smith | 7 | 127 | 18 | 1 |
| Brubaker | 7 | 75 | 11 | 1 |
| Lucas | 5 | 58 | 12 | 1 |
| Kulbacki | 2 | 9 | 5 | 0 |
| Green | 1 | 0 | 0 | 0 |

### PUNT RETURNS

| Last Name | No. | Yds | Avg | TD |
|---|---|---|---|---|
| Kulbacki | 12 | 100 | 8 | 0 |
| Kinard | 2 | 24 | 12 | 0 |
| Matsos | 1 | 20 | 20 | 0 |
| Dubenion | 2 | 6 | 3 | 0 |
| Crockett | 1 | 5 | 5 | 0 |
| Lucas | 4 | 3 | 1 | 0 |
| Lewis | 1 | 2 | 2 | 0 |

### KICKOFF RETURNS

| Last Name | No. | Yds | Avg | TD |
|---|---|---|---|---|
| Kulbacki | 13 | 226 | 17 | 0 |
| Fowler | 12 | 201 | 17 | 0 |
| Lewis | 4 | 97 | 24 | 0 |
| Smith | 2 | 72 | 36 | 0 |
| Dubenion | 4 | 68 | 17 | 0 |
| Kinard | 1 | 39 | 39 | 0 |
| Hoisington | 2 | 25 | 13 | 0 |
| Chamberlain | 1 | 24 | 24 | 0 |
| Rychlec | 1 | 3 | 3 | 0 |

### PASSING – PUNTING – KICKING

**PASSING**

| Last Name | Att | Comp | % | Yds | Yd/Att | TD | Int-% | RK |
|---|---|---|---|---|---|---|---|---|
| Green | 228 | 89 | 39 | 1267 | 5.6 | 10 | 10− 4 | 8 |
| O'Connell | 145 | 65 | 45 | 1033 | 7.1 | 7 | 13− 9 | 8 |
| Lucas | 49 | 23 | 47 | 314 | 6.4 | 2 | 3− 6 | |
| Brodhead | 25 | 7 | 28 | 75 | 3.0 | 0 | 3− 12 | |

**PUNTING**

| Last Name | No | Avg |
|---|---|---|
| Atkins | 89 | 39.0 |

**KICKING**

| Last Name | XP | Att | % | FG | Att | % |
|---|---|---|---|---|---|---|
| Atkins | 27 | 32 | 84 | 6 | 13 | 46 |
| Harper | 1 | 2 | 50 | 2 | 3 | 67 |
| Hergert | 0 | 0 | 0 | 2 | 4 | 50 |
| Yoho | 0 | 0 | 0 | 2 | 5 | 40 |
| O'Connell | 0 | 0 | 0 | 1 | 0 | |

**2 POINT XP**
Brodhead (1)
O'Connell (1)

## BOSTON PATRIOTS

### RUSHING

| Last Name | No. | Yds | Avg | TD |
|---|---|---|---|---|
| Miller | 101 | 416 | 4.2 | 1 |
| Christy | 78 | 363 | 4.7 | 4 |
| Burton | 66 | 280 | 4.3 | 1 |
| Crawford | 51 | 238 | 4.7 | 2 |
| Wells | 14 | 59 | 4.2 | 0 |
| Garron | 8 | 27 | 3.4 | 0 |
| Crouthamel | 4 | 16 | 4.0 | 0 |
| Livingston | 10 | 16 | 1.6 | 1 |
| Washington | 2 | 10 | 5.0 | 0 |
| White | 5 | 7 | 1.4 | 0 |
| Beach | 6 | −4 | −0.7 | 0 |
| Dimitroff | 2 | −10 | −5.0 | 0 |
| Greene | 16 | −27 | −1.7 | 0 |
| Songin | 36 | −140 | −3.9 | 2 |

### RECEIVING

| Last Name | No. | Yds | Avg | TD |
|---|---|---|---|---|
| Colclough | 49 | 666 | 14 | 9 |
| Miller | 29 | 284 | 10 | 2 |
| Christy | 26 | 268 | 10 | 2 |
| Stephens | 22 | 320 | 15 | 3 |
| Burton | 21 | 196 | 9 | 0 |
| Lofton | 19 | 360 | 19 | 4 |
| Wells | 14 | 206 | 15 | 1 |
| Johnson | 11 | 186 | 17 | 3 |
| Crawford | 10 | 92 | 9 | 0 |
| Beach | 9 | 132 | 15 | 1 |
| Green | 3 | 52 | 17 | 0 |
| White | 2 | 24 | 12 | 0 |
| Long | 2 | 10 | 5 | 0 |
| Cappelletti | 1 | 28 | 28 | 0 |
| Cudzik | 1 | 11 | 11 | 0 |
| Garron | 1 | 8 | 8 | 0 |
| Livingston | 1 | 0 | 0 | 0 |

### PUNT RETURNS

| Last Name | No. | Yds | Avg | TD |
|---|---|---|---|---|
| Christy | 8 | 73 | 9 | 0 |
| Wells | 12 | 66 | 6 | 0 |
| Bruney | 4 | 31 | 8 | 0 |
| Beach | 1 | 21 | 21 | 0 |
| Cohen | 1 | 9 | 9 | 0 |
| Cappelletti | 1 | 3 | 3 | 0 |
| Burton | 1 | 0 | 0 | 0 |

### KICKOFF RETURNS

| Last Name | No. | Yds | Avg | TD |
|---|---|---|---|---|
| Christy | 24 | 617 | 26 | 0 |
| Wells | 11 | 275 | 25 | 0 |
| Burton | 4 | 161 | 40 | 0 |
| Beach | 7 | 146 | 21 | 0 |
| Cappelletti | 4 | 100 | 25 | 0 |
| Bruney | 2 | 39 | 20 | 0 |
| Crouthamel | 2 | 27 | 14 | 0 |
| Garron | 1 | 21 | 21 | 0 |
| Hunt | 1 | 8 | 8 | 0 |
| Team | 1 | 8 | 8 | 0 |
| Greene | 1 | 3 | 3 | 0 |
| Livingston | 1 | 3 | 3 | 0 |

### PASSING – PUNTING – KICKING

**PASSING**

| Last Name | Att | Comp | % | Yds | Yd/Att | TD | Int-% | RK |
|---|---|---|---|---|---|---|---|---|
| Songin | 392 | 187 | 48 | 2476 | 6.3 | 22 | 15− 4 | 4 |
| Greene | 63 | 27 | 43 | 251 | 4.0 | 1 | 6− 10 | |
| Christy | 11 | 6 | 55 | 94 | 8.5 | 2 | 2− 18 | |
| White | 7 | 3 | 43 | 44 | 6.3 | 0 | 0− 0 | |
| Dimitroff | 2 | 0 | 0 | 0 | 0.0 | 0 | 0− 0 | |

**PUNTING**

| Last Name | No | Avg |
|---|---|---|
| Greene | 59 | 37.9 |
| Washington | 17 | 31.7 |

**KICKING**

| Last Name | XP | Att | % | FG | Att | % |
|---|---|---|---|---|---|---|
| Cappelletti | 30 | 32 | 94 | 8 | 21 | 38 |
| Crawford | 0 | 0 | 0 | 1 | 0 | |
| Cudzik | 0 | 0 | 0 | 1 | 0 | |

**2 POINT XP**
Cappelletti (3)
Crawford (1)

| Scores of Each Game | | Use Name | Pos. | Hgt | Wgt | Age | Int | Pts | Use Name | Pos. | Hgt | Wgt | Age | Int | Pts | Use Name | Pos. | Hgt | Wgt | Age | Int | Pts |
|---|---|---|---|---|---|---|---|---|---|---|---|---|---|---|---|---|---|---|---|---|---|---|

## LOS ANGELES CHARGERS 10-4-0 Sid Gillman

| | | | | | | | | | | | | | | | | | | | | | | |
|---|---|---|---|---|---|---|---|---|---|---|---|---|---|---|---|---|---|---|---|---|---|---|
| 21 | DALLAS | 20 | Dick Chorovich | OT | 6'4" | 260 | 27 | | | Al Bansavage | LB | 6'2" | 230 | 22 | | | Bobby Clatterbuck | QB | 6'3" | 196 | 28 | | |
| 28 | Houston | 38 | Sam DeLuca | OT | 6'2" | 245 | 24 | | | Hubert Bobo | LB | 6'1" | 214 | 25 | | | Jack Kemp | QB | 6'1" | 200 | 26 | | 48 |
| 0 | Dallas | 17 | Ron Mix | OT | 6'4" | 245 | 22 | | | Ron Botcham | LB | 6'1" | 238 | 25 | 2 | | Bob Laraba | LB-QB | 6'3" | 194 | 27 | 1 | |
| 24 | Buffalo | 10 | Ernie Wright | OT | 6'4" | 270 | 21 | | | Charlie Brueckman | LB | 6'2" | 225 | 24 | | | Fred Ford (from BUF) | HB | 5'8" | 180 | 22 | | 12 |
| 0 | BOSTON | 35 | Al Barry | OG | 6'2" | 235 | 29 | | | Emil Karas | LB | 6'3" | 225 | 26 | | | Paul Lowe | HB | 6' | 180 | 23 | | 66 |
| 23 | Denver | 19 | Fred Cole | OG | 5'11" | 226 | 23 | | | Rommie Loudd | LB | 6'3" | 226 | 26 | 3 | | Ron Waller | HB | 5'11" | 184 | 27 | | |
| 45 | Boston | 16 | Orlando Ferrante | OG | 6'3" | 225 | 22 | | | Bob Garner | DB | 5'10" | 190 | 25 | 2 | | Howie Ferguson | FB | 6'2" | 217 | 30 | | 36 |
| 21 | New York | 7 | Charlie Kempinski | OG | 6' | 235 | 21 | | | Dick Harris | DB | 5'11" | 174 | 23 | 5 | 6 | Charlie Flowers | FB | 6'1" | 207 | 23 | | 12 |
| 24 | HOUSTON | 21 | Don Rogers | C | 6'2" | 235 | 23 | | | Charley McNeil | DB | 5'11" | 178 | 24 | 3 | | Blanche Martin (from NY) | FB | 6' | 195 | 23 | | 6 |
| 3 | BUFFALO | 32 | Ben Donnell | DE | 6'5" | 248 | 23 | | | Doyle Nix | DB | 6'1" | 195 | 27 | 4 | 6 | Royce Womble | FL | 6' | 184 | 29 | | 24 |
| 52 | OAKLAND | 28 | Art Gob (from WAS-N) | DE | 6'4" | 230 | 23 | | | Jesse Thomas | DB | 5'10" | 180 | 31 | | | Ralph Anderson* | OE | 6'4" | 225 | 23 | | 30 |
| 41 | Oakland | 17 | Ron Nery | DE | 6'6" | 226 | 25 | | | Henry Wallace | DB | 6' | 195 | 22 | | | Howard Clark | OE | 6'2" | 204 | 25 | | |
| 41 | DENVER | 33 | Maury Schleicher | DE | 6'3" | 240 | 23 | 1 | | Bob Zeman | DB | 6'1" | 203 | 23 | 2 | | Dave Kocourek | OE | 6'5" | 225 | 23 | | 6 |
| 50 | NEW YORK | 43 | Paul Maguire | OE-DE | 6' | 210 | 22 | 3 | 6 | Jimmy Sears | HB-DB | 5'11" | 187 | 29 | 2 | | Trusse Norris | OE | 6'1" | 190 | 23 | | |
| | | | Gary Finneran | DT | 6'3" | 240 | 26 | | | | | | | | | | Don Norton | OE | 6'1" | 180 | 22 | | 30 |
| | | | John Kompara | DT | 6'2" | 245 | 23 | | | | | | | | | | Ben Agajanian | K | 6' | 220 | 41 | | 85 |
| | | | Volney Peters | DT | 6'4" | 240 | 31 | | | | | | | | | | | | | | | | |

* died Nov. 26 of diabetes

## DALLAS TEXANS 8-6-0 Hank Stram

| | | | | | | | | | | | | | | | | | | | | | | |
|---|---|---|---|---|---|---|---|---|---|---|---|---|---|---|---|---|---|---|---|---|---|---|
| 20 | Los Angeles | 21 | Jerry Cornelison | OT | 6'3" | 250 | 23 | | | Walt Corey | LB | 6' | 215 | 22 | 3 | | Cotton Davidson | QB | 6'1" | 180 | 28 | | 17 |
| 34 | Oakland | 16 | Charley Diamond | OT | 6'2" | 235 | 24 | | | Ted Greene | LB | 6'1" | 230 | 24 | | | Hunter Enis | QB | 6'2" | 190 | 23 | | 18 |
| 17 | LOS ANGELES | 0 | R. B. Nunnery | OT | 6'4" | 275 | 26 | | | Sherrill Headrick | LB | 6'2" | 215 | 23 | 2 | | Abner Haynes | HB | 6' | 185 | 22 | | 72 |
| 35 | NEW YORK | 37 | Jack Stone | OT | 6'2" | 245 | 23 | | | Bob Hudson (to DEN) | LB | 6'4" | 230 | 30 | 1 | | Curley Johnson | HB | 6'1" | 215 | 25 | | 14 |
| 19 | OAKLAND | 20 | Sid Fournet | OG | 6' | 235 | 27 | | | Smokey Stover | LB | 6' | 215 | 21 | 1 | | Johnny Robinson | HB | 6' | 195 | 21 | | 54 |
| 10 | Houston | 20 | Billy Krisher | OG | 6'1" | 235 | 24 | | | Johnny Bookman | DB | 5'11" | 185 | 25 | 4 | | Jim Swink | HB | 6'1" | 185 | 24 | | |
| 17 | Denver | 14 | Al Reynolds | OG | 6'3" | 225 | 22 | | | Don Flynn | DB | 6' | 205 | 25 | 3 | 6 | Bo Dickinson | FB | 6'2" | 220 | 25 | | 6 |
| 45 | Buffalo | 28 | Marvin Terrell | OG | 6'1" | 235 | 22 | | | Jimmy Harris | DB | 6'1" | 175 | 25 | 2 | | Jack Spikes | FB | 6'2" | 220 | 22 | | 103 |
| 34 | DENVER | 7 | Jim Barton | C | 6'5" | 250 | 25 | | | Charlie Jackson | DB | 5'11" | 180 | 24 | | | Ed Bernet | OE | 6'3" | 205 | 27 | | |
| 14 | Boston | 42 | Tom Dimmick | C | 6'6" | 255 | 29 | | | Dave Webster | DB | 6'4" | 215 | 22 | 6 | 18 | Max Boydston | OE | 6'2" | 215 | 27 | | 18 |
| 35 | New York | 41 | Mel Branch | DE | 6'2" | 220 | 23 | | | Duane Wood | DB | 6'1" | 180 | 24 | 4 | 6 | Bob Bryant | OE | 6'5" | 230 | 23 | | |
| 24 | HOUSTON | 0 | Dick Frey | DE | 6'2" | 230 | 29 | | | Carroll Zaruba | DB | 5'9" | 210 | 26 | | | Chris Burford | OE | 6'3" | 210 | 22 | | 30 |
| 34 | BOSTON | 0 | Paul Miller | DE | 6'2" | 235 | 28 | | | Clem Daniels | HB-DB | 6'1" | 220 | 23 | 3 | | | | | | | | |
| 24 | BUFFALO | 7 | Ray Collins | DT | 5'11" | 250 | 32 | | | | | | | | | | | | | | | | |
| | | | Rufus Granderson | DT | 6'5" | 277 | 23 | | | | | | | | | | | | | | | | |
| | | | Walter Napier | DT | 6'4" | 280 | 24 | | | | | | | | | | | | | | | | |
| | | | Paul Rochester | DT | 6'2" | 250 | 23 | | | | | | | | | | | | | | | | |

## OAKLAND RAIDERS 6-8-0 Eddie Erdalatz

| | | | | | | | | | | | | | | | | | | | | | | |
|---|---|---|---|---|---|---|---|---|---|---|---|---|---|---|---|---|---|---|---|---|---|---|
| 22 | HOUSTON | 37 | Don Churchwell | OT | 6'1" | 255 | 23 | | | Bob Dougherty | LB | 6'1" | 240 | 26 | | | Tom Flores | QB | 6'1" | 190 | 23 | | 18 |
| 16 | DALLAS | 34 | Bill Striegel (from BOS) | OT | 6'2" | 240 | 24 | | | Billy Locklin | LB | 6'2" | 225 | 22 | | | Paul Larson | QB | 5'11" | 180 | 28 | | |
| 14 | Houston | 13 | Dalton Truax | OT | 6'2" | 235 | 25 | | | Tom Louderback | LB | 6'2" | 235 | 26 | 2 | | Babe Parilli | QB | 6'1" | 190 | 30 | | 6 |
| 14 | Denver | 31 | Don Deskins | OG | 6'3" | 240 | 27 | | | Riley Morris | LB | 6'2" | 230 | 23 | | | Bob Keyes | HB | 5'10" | 183 | 24 | | |
| 20 | Dallas | 19 | John Dittrich | OG | 6'1" | 240 | 27 | | | Alex Bravo | DB | 6' | 190 | 28 | 4 | | Jack Larscheid | HB | 5'6" | 162 | 26 | | 12 |
| 27 | BOSTON | 14 | Wayne Hawkins | OG | 6' | 240 | 24 | | | Joe Cannavino | DB | 5'11" | 185 | 24 | 4 | | Nyle McFarlane | HB | 6'2" | 205 | 24 | | 12 |
| 9 | Buffalo | 38 | Don Manoukian | OG | 5'9" | 242 | 25 | | | Wayne Crow | DB | 6' | 205 | 22 | 4 | | Billy Reynolds | HB | 5'10" | 200 | 26 | | |
| 28 | New York | 27 | Ron Sabal | OG | 6'2" | 230 | 23 | | | L. C. Joyner | DB | 6'1" | 187 | 25 | | | Tony Teresa | HB | 5'9" | 185 | 26 | | 60 |
| 28 | Boston | 34 | Jim Otto | C | 6'2" | 227 | 22 | | | Eddie Macon | DB | 6' | 180 | 32 | 9 | 6 | Billy Lott | FB | 6' | 205 | 25 | | 38 |
| 20 | BUFFALO | 7 | Larry Barnes | DE | 6'1" | 230 | 27 | | 55 | John Harris | HB-DB | 6'1" | 195 | 27 | | | J. D. Smith | FB | 6' | 220 | 25 | | 50 |
| 28 | Los Angeles | 52 | Carmen Cavalli | DE | 6'4" | 240 | 25 | | | | | | | | | | Doug Asad | OE | 6'3" | 200 | 22 | | 6 |
| 17 | LOS ANGELES | 41 | George Fields | DE | 6'3" | 245 | 24 | 2 | | | | | | | | | Al Goldstein | OE | 6' | 204 | 24 | | 12 |
| 28 | NEW YORK | 31 | Charley Powell | DE | 6'2" | 227 | 28 | | | | | | | | | | Charley Hardy | OE | 6' | 183 | 26 | | 18 |
| 48 | DENVER | 10 | Ray Armstrong | DT | 6'1" | 235 | 22 | | | | | | | | | | Gene Prebola | OE | 6'3" | 215 | 22 | | 12 |
| | | | Joe Barbee | DT | 6'3" | 250 | 27 | | | | | | | | | | | | | | | | |
| | | | Paul Oglesby | DT | 6'4" | 235 | 20 | | | | | | | | | | | | | | | | |
| | | | Ron Warzeka | DT | 6'4" | 250 | 29 | | | | | | | | | | | | | | | | |

## DENVER BRONCOS 4-9-1 Frankie Filchock

| | | | | | | | | | | | | | | | | | | | | | | |
|---|---|---|---|---|---|---|---|---|---|---|---|---|---|---|---|---|---|---|---|---|---|---|
| 13 | Boston | 10 | Eldon Danenhauer | OT | 6'4" | 235 | 24 | | | Vaughan Alliston | LB | 6' | 218 | 26 | 1 | | Tom Dublinski | QB | 6'2" | 205 | 30 | | |
| 27 | Buffalo | 21 | Gordy Holz | OT | 6'4" | 270 | 26 | | | Hardy Brown | LB | 6' | 190 | 36 | | | George Herring | QB | 6'2" | 200 | 25 | | |
| 24 | New York | 28 | Willie Smith | OT | 6'2" | 255 | 22 | | | Al Day | LB | 6'2" | 216 | 22 | | | Frank Tripucka | QB | 6'2" | 205 | 32 | | |
| 31 | OAKLAND | 14 | Ken Adamson | OG | 6'2" | 215 | 21 | | | Pete Mangum | LB | 6' | 220 | 28 | | | Henry Bell | HB | 5'10" | 210 | 23 | | |
| 19 | LOS ANGELES | 23 | Jack Davis | OG | 6'2" | 235 | 25 | | | Frank Bernardi | DB | 5'9" | 185 | 27 | | | Al Carmichael | HB | 6'1" | 195 | 30 | | 42 |
| 31 | BOSTON | 24 | Carl Larpenter | OG | 6'4" | 235 | 23 | | | Dick Doyle | DB | 6' | 190 | 29 | 1 | | Gene Mingo | HB | 6'1" | 200 | 21 | | 123 |
| 14 | DALLAS | 17 | Dave Strickland | OG | 6' | 220 | 28 | | | Goose Gonsoulin | DB | 6'3" | 205 | 22 | 11 | | Bob Stransky | HB | 6'1" | 180 | 24 | | |
| 25 | HOUSTON | 45 | Frank Kuchta | C | 6'2" | 235 | 24 | | | John Pyeatt | DB | 6'3" | 204 | 26 | 4 | 6 | Ted Wegert (from NY-to BUF) | HB | 5'11" | 200 | 28 | | 12 |
| 7 | Dallas | 34 | Mike Nichols | C | 6'3" | 225 | 21 | | | Al Romine | DB | 6'2" | 195 | 27 | 3 | | Don Allen | FB | 6' | 200 | 23 | | 6 |
| 10 | Houston | 20 | Chuck Gavin | DE | 6'1" | 235 | 26 | | | Bob McNamara | HB-DB | 6' | 188 | 26 | 4 | 12 | J. W. Brodnax | FB | 6' | 208 | 23 | | 6 |
| 38 | BUFFALO | 38 | Bill Yelverton | DE | 6'4" | 220 | 26 | 1 | 6 | | | | | | | | Dave Rolle | FB | 6' | 215 | 22 | | 18 |
| 27 | NEW YORK | 30 | Joe Young | DE | 6'3" | 245 | 25 | | | | | | | | | | Don Carothers | OE | 6'5" | 225 | 24 | | |
| 33 | Los Angeles | 41 | John Hatley | DT | 6'3" | 260 | 29 | | | | | | | | | | Pat Epperson | OE | 6'3" | 225 | 24 | | |
| 10 | Oakland | 48 | Bud McFadin | DT | 6'3" | 260 | 32 | | | | | | | | | | Jim Greer | OE | 6'3" | 215 | 26 | | 6 |
| | | | Hal Smith (from BOS) | DT | 6'5" | 250 | 25 | | | | | | | | | | Bill Jessup | OE | 6'1" | 195 | 31 | | 6 |
| | | | Don King | OT-DT | 6'3" | 255 | 30 | 2 | | | | | | | | | Lionel Taylor | OE | 6'2" | 214 | 24 | | 72 |
| | | | | | | | | | | | | | | | | | Ken Carpenter | HB-OE | 6' | 212 | 34 | | 6 |

## LOS ANGELES CHARGERS

### RUSHING

| Last Name | No. | Yds | Avg | TD |
|---|---|---|---|---|
| Lowe | 136 | 855 | 6.3 | 9 |
| Ferguson | 126 | 438 | 3.5 | 4 |
| Ford | 38 | 194 | 5.1 | 2 |
| Flowers | 39 | 161 | 4.1 | 1 |
| Martin | 18 | 58 | 3.2 | 0 |
| Laraba | 4 | 7 | 1.8 | 0 |
| Waller | 9 | 5 | 0.6 | 0 |
| Norton | 1 | 2 | 2.0 | 0 |
| Clatterbuck | 6 | -6 | -1.0 | 0 |
| Kemp | 90 | -103 | -1.1 | 8 |

### RECEIVING

| Last Name | No. | Yds | Avg | TD |
|---|---|---|---|---|
| Anderson | 44 | 614 | 14 | 5 |
| Kocourek | 40 | 662 | 17 | 1 |
| Womble | 32 | 316 | 10 | 4 |
| Clark | 27 | 431 | 16 | 0 |
| Norton | 25 | 414 | 17 | 5 |
| Lowe | 23 | 377 | 16 | 2 |
| Ferguson | 21 | 168 | 8 | 2 |
| Flowers | 12 | 153 | 13 | 1 |
| Martin | 4 | 23 | 6 | 1 |
| Waller | 3 | 24 | 8 | 0 |
| Ford | 1 | 5 | 5 | 0 |

### PUNT RETURNS

| Last Name | No. | Yds | Avg | TD |
|---|---|---|---|---|
| Harris | 13 | 105 | 8 | 0 |
| Sears | 9 | 101 | 11 | 0 |
| Garner | 6 | 85 | 14 | 0 |
| Ford | 2 | 6 | 3 | 0 |
| Maguire | 1 | 4 | 4 | 1 |
| Lowe | 1 | 0 | 0 | 0 |

### KICKOFF RETURNS

| Last Name | No. | Yds | Avg | TD |
|---|---|---|---|---|
| Lowe | 28 | 611 | 22 | 0 |
| Ford | 18 | 400 | 22 | 0 |
| Sears | 8 | 155 | 19 | 0 |
| Norton | 8 | 153 | 19 | 0 |
| DeLuca | 1 | 0 | 0 | 0 |

### PASSING – PUNTING – KICKING

PASSING

| Last Name | Att | Comp | % | Yds | Yd/Att | TD | Int–% | RK |
|---|---|---|---|---|---|---|---|---|
| Kemp | 406 | 211 | 52 | 3018 | 7.4 | 20 | 25– 6 | 1 |
| Clatterbuck | 23 | 15 | 65 | 112 | 4.9 | 1 | 1– 4 | |
| Laraba | 7 | 2 | 29 | 23 | 3.3 | 0 | 2– 29 | |
| Lowe | 3 | 1 | 33 | 24 | 8.0 | 0 | 0– 0 | |
| Ford | 1 | 0 | 0 | 0 | 0.0 | 0 | 0– 0 | |
| Waller | 1 | 0 | 0 | 0 | 0.0 | 0 | 1–100 | |

PUNTING

| Last Name | No | Avg |
|---|---|---|
| Maguire | 43 | 40.5 |
| Laraba | 15 | 37.2 |

KICKING

| Last Name | XP | Att | % | FG | Att | % |
|---|---|---|---|---|---|---|
| Agajanian | 46 | 47 | 98 | 13 | 24 | 54 |

## DALLAS TEXANS

### RUSHING

| Last Name | No. | Yds | Avg | TD |
|---|---|---|---|---|
| Haynes | 156 | 875 | 5.6 | 9 |
| Robinson | 98 | 458 | 4.8 | 4 |
| Spikes | 115 | 457 | 4.0 | 5 |
| Dickinson | 35 | 143 | 4.1 | 1 |
| Johnson | 23 | 43 | 1.9 | 1 |
| Swink | 10 | 15 | 1.5 | 0 |
| Daniels | 1 | -2 | -2.0 | 0 |
| Enis | 12 | -12 | -1.0 | 3 |
| Davidson | 31 | -122 | -3.9 | 1 |

### RECEIVING

| Last Name | No. | Yds | Avg | TD |
|---|---|---|---|---|
| Haynes | 55 | 576 | 10 | 3 |
| Burford | 46 | 789 | 17 | 5 |
| Robinson | 41 | 611 | 15 | 4 |
| Boydston | 29 | 357 | 12 | 3 |
| Spikes | 11 | 158 | 14 | 0 |
| Johnson | 10 | 174 | 17 | 1 |
| Bryant | 5 | 43 | 9 | 0 |
| Bernet | 4 | 49 | 12 | 0 |
| Swink | 4 | 37 | 9 | 0 |
| Dickinson | 3 | 38 | 13 | 0 |
| Davidson | 1 | -1 | -1 | 0 |

### PUNT RETURNS

| Last Name | No. | Yds | Avg | TD |
|---|---|---|---|---|
| Haynes | 14 | 215 | 15 | 0 |
| Robinson | 14 | 207 | 15 | 1 |
| Daniels | 3 | 69 | 23 | 0 |
| Harris | 1 | 5 | 5 | 0 |
| Rochester | 1 | 0 | 0 | 0 |

### KICKOFF RETURNS

| Last Name | No. | Yds | Avg | TD |
|---|---|---|---|---|
| Haynes | 19 | 434 | 23 | 0 |
| Daniels | 9 | 162 | 18 | 0 |
| Harris | 5 | 117 | 23 | 0 |
| Robinson | 3 | 54 | 18 | 0 |
| Swink | 1 | 36 | 36 | 0 |
| Dickinson | 2 | 29 | 15 | 0 |
| Johnson | 1 | 13 | 13 | 0 |

### PASSING – PUNTING – KICKING

PASSING

| Last Name | Att | Comp | % | Yds | Yd/Att | TD | Int–% | RK |
|---|---|---|---|---|---|---|---|---|
| Davidson | 379 | 179 | 47 | 2474 | 6.5 | 15 | 16– 4 | 5 |
| Enis | 54 | 30 | 56 | 357 | 6.6 | 1 | 2– 4 | |
| Haynes | 1 | 0 | 0 | 0 | 0.0 | 0 | 0– 0 | |
| Robinson | 1 | 0 | 0 | 0 | 0.0 | 0 | 1–100 | |

PUNTING

| Last Name | No | Avg |
|---|---|---|
| Davidson | 58 | 39.4 |
| Johnson | 3 | 36.7 |

KICKING

| Last Name | XP | Att | % | FG | Att | % |
|---|---|---|---|---|---|---|
| Spikes | 34 | 36 | 94 | 13 | 31 | 42 |
| Davidson | 8 | 8 | 100 | 1 | 1 | 100 |
| Flynn | 0 | 0 | 0 | 0 | 1 | 0 |
| Johnson | 0 | 0 | 0 | 0 | 1 | 0 |

2 POINT XP
Johnson (1)

## OAKLAND RAIDERS

### RUSHING

| Last Name | No. | Yds | Avg | TD |
|---|---|---|---|---|
| Teresa | 139 | 608 | 4.4 | 6 |
| Lott | 99 | 520 | 5.3 | 5 |
| Larscheid | 94 | 397 | 4.2 | 1 |
| Smith | 63 | 214 | 3.4 | 6 |
| McFarlane | 4 | 52 | 13.0 | 0 |
| Parilli | 32 | 25 | 0.8 | 1 |
| Keyes | 1 | 7 | 7.0 | 0 |
| Reynolds | 1 | 6 | 6.0 | 0 |
| Goldstein | 3 | -2 | -0.7 | 0 |
| Flores | 39 | -42 | -1.1 | 3 |

### RECEIVING

| Last Name | No. | Yds | Avg | TD |
|---|---|---|---|---|
| Lott | 49 | 524 | 11 | 1 |
| Teresa | 35 | 393 | 11 | 4 |
| Prebola | 33 | 404 | 12 | 2 |
| Goldstein | 27 | 354 | 13 | 1 |
| Hardy | 24 | 423 | 18 | 3 |
| Larscheid | 22 | 187 | 9 | 1 |
| Smith | 17 | 194 | 11 | 1 |
| Asad | 14 | 197 | 14 | 1 |
| McFarlane | 5 | 89 | 18 | 2 |
| Reynolds | 3 | 43 | 14 | 0 |
| Keyes | 1 | 19 | 19 | 0 |
| Parilli | 1 | 0 | 0 | 0 |

### PUNT RETURNS

| Last Name | No. | Yds | Avg | TD |
|---|---|---|---|---|
| Larscheid | 12 | 106 | 9 | 0 |
| Reynolds | 7 | 24 | 3 | 0 |
| Teresa | 5 | 12 | 2 | 0 |
| Keyes | 1 | 5 | 5 | 0 |
| Cannavino | 1 | 4 | 4 | 0 |

### KICKOFF RETURNS

| Last Name | No. | Yds | Avg | TD |
|---|---|---|---|---|
| Larscheid | 30 | 852 | 28 | 0 |
| Smith | 14 | 373 | 27 | 1 |
| McFarlane | 5 | 71 | 14 | 0 |
| Asad | 3 | 66 | 22 | 0 |
| Teresa | 4 | 61 | 15 | 0 |
| Harris | 3 | 38 | 13 | 0 |
| Deskins | 1 | 15 | 15 | 0 |
| Morris | 1 | 3 | 3 | 0 |

### PASSING – PUNTING – KICKING

PASSING

| Last Name | Att | Comp | % | Yds | Yd/Att | TD | Int–% | RK |
|---|---|---|---|---|---|---|---|---|
| Flores | 252 | 136 | 54 | 1738 | 6.9 | 12 | 12– 5 | 2 |
| Parilli | 187 | 87 | 47 | 1003 | 5.4 | 5 | 11– 6 | 10 |
| Teresa | 18 | 9 | 50 | 111 | 6.2 | 1 | 3– 17 | |
| Larscheid | 6 | 3 | 50 | 71 | 11.8 | 0 | 2– 33 | |

PUNTING

| Last Name | No | Avg |
|---|---|---|
| Crow | 76 | 38.9 |

KICKING

| Last Name | XP | Att | % | FG | Att | % |
|---|---|---|---|---|---|---|
| Barnes | 37 | 39 | 95 | 6 | 25 | 24 |

2 POINT XP
Lott (1)
Smith (1)

## DENVER BRONCOS

### RUSHING

| Last Name | No. | Yds | Avg | TD |
|---|---|---|---|---|
| Rolle | 130 | 501 | 3.9 | 2 |
| Mingo | 83 | 323 | 3.9 | 4 |
| Bell | 43 | 238 | 5.5 | 0 |
| Carmichael | 41 | 211 | 5.1 | 2 |
| Wegert | 36 | 161 | 4.5 | 1 |
| Stransky | 28 | 78 | 2.8 | 0 |
| McNamara | 17 | 33 | 1.9 | 1 |
| Brodnax | 15 | 18 | 1.2 | 0 |
| Allen | 30 | 18 | 0.6 | 1 |
| Carpenter | 4 | 13 | 3.3 | 0 |
| Nichols | 0 | 3 | 0.0 | 0 |
| Taylor | 2 | -6 | -3.0 | 0 |
| Herring | 5 | -46 | -9.2 | 0 |
| Tripucka | 37 | -226 | -6.1 | 0 |

### RECEIVING

| Last Name | No. | Yds | Avg | TD |
|---|---|---|---|---|
| Taylor | 92 | 1235 | 13 | 12 |
| Carmichael | 32 | 616 | 19 | 5 |
| Carpenter | 29 | 350 | 12 | 1 |
| Greer | 22 | 284 | 13 | 1 |
| Rolle | 21 | 122 | 6 | 1 |
| Mingo | 19 | 156 | 8 | 1 |
| Epperson | 11 | 99 | 9 | 0 |
| Jessup | 9 | 120 | 13 | 1 |
| McNamara | 7 | 143 | 20 | 1 |
| Wegert | 5 | 68 | 14 | 1 |
| Brodnax | 5 | 39 | 8 | 1 |
| Allen | 5 | 34 | 7 | 0 |
| Stransky | 3 | 11 | 4 | 0 |
| Carothers | 2 | 25 | 13 | 0 |
| Bell | 2 | 13 | 7 | 0 |

### PUNT RETURNS

| Last Name | No. | Yds | Avg | TD |
|---|---|---|---|---|
| Carmichael | 15 | 101 | 7 | 0 |
| Mingo | 3 | 92 | 31 | 1 |
| McNamara | 11 | 68 | 6 | 0 |
| Wegert | 4 | 25 | 6 | 0 |

### KICKOFF RETURNS

| Last Name | No. | Yds | Avg | TD |
|---|---|---|---|---|
| Carmichael | 22 | 581 | 26 | 0 |
| Wegert | 10 | 252 | 25 | 0 |
| Mingo | 9 | 209 | 23 | 0 |
| McNamara | 9 | 192 | 21 | 0 |
| Stransky | 7 | 153 | 22 | 0 |
| Brodnax | 5 | 117 | 23 | 0 |
| Allen | 5 | 72 | 14 | 0 |
| Bell | 2 | 60 | 30 | 0 |
| W. Smith | 1 | 13 | 13 | 0 |
| Greer | 1 | 11 | 11 | 0 |
| Strickland | 1 | 9 | 9 | 0 |

### PASSING – PUNTING – KICKING

PASSING

| Last Name | Att | Comp | % | Yds | Yd/Att | TD | Int–% | RK |
|---|---|---|---|---|---|---|---|---|
| Tripucka | 478 | 248 | 52 | 3038 | 6.4 | 24 | 34– 7 | 7 |
| Herring | 22 | 9 | 41 | 137 | 6.2 | 0 | 1– 5 | |
| Mingo | 7 | 1 | 14 | 46 | 6.6 | 0 | 0– 0 | |
| Carmichael | 1 | 1 | 100 | 26 | 26.0 | 0 | 0– 0 | |

PUNTING

| Last Name | No | Avg |
|---|---|---|
| Herring | 70 | 37.3 |

KICKING

| Last Name | XP | Att | % | FG | Att | % |
|---|---|---|---|---|---|---|
| Mingo | 33 | 36 | 92 | 18 | 28 | 64 |

# 1961 N.F.L. Bypassing the Crisis

For some teams, the forward pass became less important than the weekend pass. President Kennedy's activation of reserve units because of the Berlin crisis drafted many players into active military duty, among them Paul Hornung, Bobby Mitchell, Ray Nitschke, Boyd Dowler, Dick Schafrath, Bob DeMarco, John Gordy, and John Paluck. Since all of the reservists were stationed within the continental United States, most of the affected players could get back to their teams on a weekend pass, then return to their military base on Monday morning. Commissioner Pete Rozelle also had contact with the federal government, but not as a soldier. He successfully persuaded Congress to pass a bill officially exempting the NFL's package TV deal with CBS from anti-trust legislation.

## EASTERN CONFERENCE

**New York Giants**—After the Giants lost to the Cards on opening day and looked sluggish in the first half against the Steelers, Giant coach Allie Sherman yanked quarterback Chuck Conerly and replaced him with newly acquired Y. A. Tittle. The bald-headed Tittle won the first-string job by pulling out a victory over the Steelers and flawlessly directed the New York attack through the season. With Del Shofner, Joe Walton, and Erich Barnes—all, like Tittle, acquired in off-season trades—blending in with the holdover Giant stars, New York climbed into a first-place tie with Philadelphia by beating the Eagles 38-21 in Yankee Stadium on November 12 and took sole possession of the top spot by knocking off the Eagles 28-24 in Philadelphia on December 10. Needing at least a tie to clinch the title, the Giants played Cleveland to a 7-7 deadlock to end the season.

**Philadelphia Eagles**—Starting with Timmy Brown's 105-yard kickoff return on the first play of the season, the Eagles displayed the league's most explosive offense. Sonny Jurgensen replaced the retired Norm Van Brocklin at quarterback and surpassed all expectations by throwing thirty-two touchdown passes in a superior air attack featuring receivers Tommy McDonald and Pete Retzlaff. But two flaws sabotaged the Eagles' title chances—a weak running game and a thin defensive secondary. Cornerback Tom Brookshier broke a leg in a 16-14 victory over the Bears, and the Giants exploited substitute Glen Amerson's inexperience the next week in a 38-21 New York win.

**Cleveland Browns**—Paul Brown may have been the coach of the 1950s, but a storm was gathering against him in the 1960s. Several Cleveland players, including Jimmy Brown, found the coach's stern way of dealing with his men increasingly hard to take, and quarterback Milt Plum was openly critical of Brown's system of sending every play in via alternating messenger guards. But despite the growing dissension and a disappointing defensive secondary, the Browns again were in the thick of the Eastern title chase. They trailed New York by only one game until a 37-21 Giant win on November 26 ended their hopes.

**St. Louis Cardinals**—Injuries crippled the Cardinal offense even before the season started. Halfback John David Crow broke an ankle, and quarterback Sam Etcheverry, debuting in the NFL after a great nine-year career in Canada, came up with a sore arm to put a dent in the running and passing attacks. Coach Pop Ivy kept his team together, throwing Prentice Gautt into Crow's spot and spelling Etcheverry with Ralph Guglielmi, and the Cards came up with upset wins over New York and Philadelphia. But more injuries, such as Ken Panfil's bad knee, dropped the club into the lower ranks in the East and prompted coach Ivy to resign with two games left.

**Pittsburgh Steelers**—Old age was catching up with the Steelers. Bobby Layne spent several weeks in drydock with a bad shoulder, ends Preston Carpenter and Bob Schnelker had lost their speed, and defensive linemen Ernie Stautner, Big Daddy Lipscomb, and Joe Krupa all were on the decline. With Layne out, Rudy Bukich, who had done more sitting than playing in his past six seasons, took over at quarterback and showed a good arm and no consistency. Only fullback John Henry Johnson, flanker Buddy Dial, defensive back Johnny Sample, and linebackers John Reger and Myron Pottios had top-notch seasons.

**Dallas Cowboys**—After going winless through their inaugural 1960 season, the Cowboys quickly picked up their first victory by beating Pittsburgh 27-24 on opening day. After four weeks, the Cowboys had also beaten Minnesota twice to climb to a 3-1 record before the league caught up with them. Two blue-chip rookies made the Cowboys a much improved team. Halfback Don Perkins, who missed the 1960 season with a broken foot, raced to 815 yards rushing with a fine showing late in the season. The defensive addition was Bob Lilly, a quick and strong defensive end who put heavy pressure on enemy passers. Veterans Eddie LeBaron and Billy Howton combined for many short pass completions, while Frank Clarke suddenly developed into a dangerous deep receiver.

**Washington Redskins**—Rookie head coach Bill McPeak and rookie quarterback Norm Snead both suffered through a frightening debut. McPeak found himself in charge of a club with no runners, no blockers, and a porous defensive secondary. Snead learned quickly how to throw under pressure, with his line giving him no protection from swarms of defenders clawing and thrashing him. After thirteen losses and heavy underdogs against the Dallas Cowboys, the Redskins won 34-24 to avert the stigma of a victoryless season.

## WESTERN CONFERENCE

**Green Bay Packers**—Coach Vince Lombardi had built his team around good blocking and good tackling. His offense had the league's best running attack, with two superb guards in Jerry Kramer and Fuzzy Thurston escorting runners Jim Taylor, Paul Hornung, and Tommy Moore around end in the famous Green Bay power sweep. Against the run the Packers defense was murder, with a quick forward wall of Bill Quinlan, Henry Jordan, Dave Hanner, and Willie Davis perfectly complemented by smart linebackers Bill Forester, Ray Nitschke, and Dan Currie. The Packers were a brutally physical team, with quarterback Bart Starr directing the violence with pinpoint passing and a knack for picking apart enemy defenses. After losing to the Lions on opening day, Green Bay won its next six games and had the Western title sewed up with two weeks left in the season.

**Detroit Lions**—Detroit fans found it hard to believe that the Lions were NFL powers. Five times the Lions lost at home, with a 49-0 pasting by the '49ers the ultimate humiliation. But the Lions saved their best for the road by going undefeated. Coach George Wilson had built a defense to match Green Bay's, a unit with size, speed, and experience in all sectors. No other team could match tackles Alex Karras and Roger Brown, Joe Schmidt had no peer as a middle linebacker, and Yale Lary and Night Train Lane had a world of savvy in the secondary.

**Baltimore Colts**—Johnny Unitas' passes still packed the Baltimore attack with explosives, but the Colt defense no longer could defuse enemy offenses. With Big Daddy Lipscomb and Johnny Sample traded to Pittsburgh and Art Donovan at the end of his career, opponents found it easier to move the ball against the Colts than it had been in the late 1950s. A slow start of two wins in the first five games made any title hopes seem very slim, and even a 45-21 mid-season ambush of the Packers couldn't halt the Colts' decline into mediocrity. But the colts still showcased several fine individual performances, such as the explosive running and receiving of Lenny Moore, the continued superb pass-catching of Ray Berry, and All-Pro seasons from Jim Parker and Gino Marchetti.

**Chicago Bears**—First place in the West rode on the November 12 meeting of the Bears and Packers in Wrigley Field. Green Bay's record was 6-2, coming off a 45-21 pasting by the Colts; the Bears' record was 5-3, fresh from a close 16-14 loss to the Eagles. Although the Packers had shut the Bears out 24-0 in an earlier meeting, Chicago fans whipped themselves into a fury over the game. They saw a good game, as the Packers ran out to a 28-7 lead and then barely held on for a 31-28 triumph. The Bears did not recapture first place, but they did refurbish their passing attack this year. The main addition was rookie Mike Ditka, the first tight end to win a national following for his devastating blocking and effective receiving.

**San Francisco '49ers**—The shotgun formation burned the league up for five weeks. Using this pass-oriented formation, the '49ers won four of their first five games, including triumphs of 35-3 over Washington, 49-0 over Detroit, and 35-0 over Los Angeles. Coach Red Hickey was alternating John Brodie, rookie Bill Kilmer, and Bobby Waters at the quarterback slot on alternate plays, loading the shotgun with quarterback plunges, halfback reverses, and a spate of passes. But the dream ended on October 22 in Chicago. Knowing that a center could not block well while looking between his legs to hike a ball back to a tailback, Bear defensive coach Clark Shaughnessy put middle linebacker Bill George right over the center and had him charge straight through to the quarterback on every play. By halftime, the Bears had demoralized the '49ers; by the final gun, the Bears had won 31-0. Thus exposed, the shotgun never again exploded.

**Los Angeles Rams**—The Rams had a lot of offensive talent for a sixth-place team. Jon Arnett and Dick Bass were top-notch runners, Ollie Matson a multitalented back, and both Jim Phillips and Carroll Dale fine receivers. There was no fuse at quarterback, however, to start the machine rolling, as neither Zeke Bratkowski nor Frank Ryan showed any consistency in running the attack. The porous offensive line helped neither passers nor runners, and outside of rookie end Deacon Jones, bright spots were scarce for the defensive unit.

**Minnesota Vikings**—The Vikings, this year's expansion team, quickly surpassed Dallas' 1960 record as a new team by beating the Chicago Bears 37-13 in their first league game. The three wins the Vikes captured for the season surprised most experts and made Norm Van Brocklin's coaching debut a success. Van Brocklin stepped right from the playing ranks as quarterback with the Eagles into the head coach's job at Minnesota, and his quarterback was one with a style most unlike his own. While Van Brocklin was a pocket passer whom only a tidal wave could force to run, rookie Fran Tarkenton became the talk of the league with his scrambling.

## FINAL STATISTICS

### OFFENSE

| | BALT. | CHI. | CLEVE. | DALLAS | DET. | G.BAY | L.A. | MINN. | N.Y. | PHIL. | PITT. | ST.L. | S.F. | WASH. |
|---|---|---|---|---|---|---|---|---|---|---|---|---|---|---|
| **FIRST DOWNS:** | | | | | | | | | | | | | | |
| Total | 274 | 239 | 246 | 239 | 233 | 274 | 236 | 236 | 275 | 252 | 239 | 202 | 258 | 193 |
| by Rushing | 124 | 103 | 116 | 100 | 96 | 142 | 109 | 104 | 99 | 78 | 102 | 83 | 116 | 55 |
| by Passing | 135 | 113 | 120 | 130 | 122 | 115 | 111 | 123 | 160 | 158 | 123 | 110 | 132 | 124 |
| by Penalty | 15 | 23 | 10 | 9 | 15 | 17 | 16 | 9 | 16 | 16 | 14 | 9 | 10 | 14 |
| **RUSHING:** | | | | | | | | | | | | | | |
| Number | 456 | 436 | 476 | 416 | 439 | 474 | 415 | 419 | 464 | 373 | 543 | 386 | 448 | 361 |
| Yards | 2119 | 1890 | 2163 | 1819 | 1868 | 2350 | 1958 | 1897 | 1857 | 1507 | 1761 | 1405 | 2100 | 1072 |
| Average Yards | 4.6 | 4.3 | 4.5 | 4.4 | 4.3 | 5.0 | 4.7 | 4.5 | 4.0 | 4.0 | 3.2 | 3.6 | 4.7 | 3.0 |
| Touchdowns | 17 | 16 | 15 | 6 | 16 | 27 | 17 | 14 | 13 | 10 | 10 | 8 | 27 | 9 |
| **PASSING:** | | | | | | | | | | | | | | |
| Attempts | 438 | 349 | 320 | 422 | 398 | 306 | 386 | 377 | 416 | 429 | 334 | 351 | 346 | 420 |
| Completions | 232 | 186 | 185 | 215 | 186 | 177 | 199 | 203 | 215 | 241 | 176 | 168 | 187 | 189 |
| Completion Pct. | 53.0 | 53.3 | 57.8 | 50.9 | 46.7 | 57.8 | 51.6 | 53.8 | 51.7 | 56.2 | 52.7 | 47.9 | 54.0 | 45.0 |
| Passing Yards (Gross) | 3018 | 3011 | 2538 | 2918 | 2830 | 2502 | 2709 | 2527 | 3035 | 3824 | 2622 | 2434 | 3057 | 2566 |
| Yards Lost Tackled | 215 | 339 | 164 | 257 | 286 | 138 | 372 | 538 | 295 | 219 | 290 | 461 | 253 | 391 |
| Net Yards | 2803 | 2672 | 2374 | 2661 | 2544 | 2364 | 2337 | 1989 | 2740 | 3605 | 2332 | 1973 | 2804 | 2175 |
| Yds. per Att (Gross) | 6.9 | 8.6 | 7.9 | 6.9 | 7.1 | 8.2 | 7.0 | 6.7 | 7.3 | 8.9 | 7.9 | 6.9 | 8.8 | 6.1 |
| Yds. per Comp (Gross) | 13.0 | 16.2 | 13.7 | 13.6 | 15.2 | 14.1 | 13.6 | 12.4 | 14.1 | 15.9 | 14.9 | 14.5 | 16.3 | 13.6 |
| Touchdowns | 17 | 26 | 20 | 23 | 14 | 18 | 13 | 22 | 27 | 34 | 23 | 21 | 15 | 12 |
| Interceptions | 29 | 24 | 13 | 27 | 27 | 16 | 21 | 22 | 23 | 26 | 34 | 23 | 19 | 28 |
| Pct. Intercepted | 6.6 | 6.9 | 4.1 | 6.4 | 6.8 | 5.2 | 5.4 | 5.8 | 5.5 | 6.1 | 10.2 | 6.6 | 5.5 | 6.7 |
| **PUNTING:** | | | | | | | | | | | | | | |
| Number | 42 | 60 | 53 | 61 | 56 | 51 | 64 | 63 | 68 | 55 | 73 | 85 | 59 | 70 |
| Average Distance | 43.0 | 41.7 | 43.3 | 36.7 | 47.6 | 43.0 | 40.1 | 39.0 | 43.9 | 43.7 | 47.0 | 44.7 | 44.6 | 38.1 |
| **PUNT RETURNS:** | | | | | | | | | | | | | | |
| Number | 33 | 27 | 28 | 23 | 38 | 20 | 14 | 23 | 42 | 34 | 40 | 26 | 24 | 28 |
| Yards | 269 | 170 | 283 | 103 | 357 | 355 | 184 | 309 | 289 | 353 | 447 | 236 | 232 | 197 |
| Average Yards | 8.2 | 6.3 | 10.1 | 4.5 | 9.4 | 17.8 | 13.1 | 13.4 | 6.9 | 10.4 | 11.2 | 9.1 | 9.7 | 7.0 |
| Touchdowns | 0 | 0 | 1 | 0 | 0 | 2 | 1 | 1 | 0 | 1 | 1 | 1 | 1 | 0 |
| **KICKOFF RETURNS:** | | | | | | | | | | | | | | |
| Number | 53 | 51 | 50 | 64 | 50 | 41 | 56 | 72 | 38 | 53 | 49 | 47 | 49 | 64 |
| Yards | 1182 | 1247 | 1115 | 1345 | 1097 | 1077 | 1463 | 1568 | 850 | 1313 | 1020 | 992 | 1302 | 1661 |
| Average Yards | 22.3 | 24.5 | 22.3 | 21.0 | 21.9 | 26.3 | 26.1 | 21.8 | 22.4 | 24.8 | 20.8 | 21.1 | 26.6 | 26.0 |
| Touchdowns | 0 | 0 | 1 | 0 | 1 | 0 | 1 | 0 | 0 | 1 | 0 | 0 | 1 | 0 |
| **INTERCEPTION RETURNS:** | | | | | | | | | | | | | | |
| Number | 16 | 24 | 20 | 25 | 29 | 29 | 23 | 22 | 33 | 17 | 25 | 24 | 19 | 26 |
| Yards | 123 | 371 | 160 | 374 | 312 | 446 | 277 | 356 | 526 | 239 | 498 | 459 | 322 | 325 |
| Average Yards | 7.7 | 15.5 | 8.0 | 15.0 | 10.8 | 15.4 | 12.0 | 16.2 | 15.9 | 14.1 | 19.9 | 19.1 | 16.9 | 12.5 |
| Touchdowns | 0 | 0 | 0 | 0 | 1 | 2 | 0 | 2 | 4 | 0 | 2 | 5 | 0 | 2 |
| **PENALTIES:** | | | | | | | | | | | | | | |
| Number | 69 | 81 | 47 | 47 | 69 | 66 | 63 | 36 | 59 | 42 | 52 | 57 | 65 | 70 |
| Yards | 589 | 719.5 | 455 | 427 | 678 | 647 | 599 | 375 | 629 | 500 | 486 | 535 | 635 | 651 |
| **FUMBLES:** | | | | | | | | | | | | | | |
| Number | 21 | 23 | 28 | 46 | 25 | 18 | 21 | 36 | 40 | 25 | 34 | 39 | 25 | 18 |
| Number Lost | 13 | 14 | 20 | 21 | 15 | 10 | 11 | 22 | 20 | 14 | 22 | 18 | 17 | 12 |
| **POINTS:** | | | | | | | | | | | | | | |
| Total | 302 | 326 | 319 | 236 | 270 | 391 | 263 | 285 | 368 | 361 | 295 | 279 | 346 | 174 |
| PAT Attempts | 34 | 42 | 39 | 29 | 32 | 49 | 32 | 37 | 46 | 46 | 36 | 37 | 44 | 23 |
| PAT Made | 33 | 41 | 37 | 29 | 31 | 49 | 32 | 36 | 46 | 43 | 34 | 34 | 44 | 21 |
| FG Attempts | 39 | 27 | 23 | 24 | 33 | 24 | 27 | 21 | 34 | 25 | 28 | 17 | 22 | 28 |
| FG Made | 21 | 11 | 16 | 11 | 15 | 16 | 13 | 9 | 14 | 14 | 15 | 7 | 12 | 5 |
| Percent FG Made | 53.8 | 40.7 | 69.6 | 45.8 | 45.5 | 66.7 | 48.1 | 42.9 | 41.2 | 56.0 | 53.6 | 41.2 | 54.5 | 17.9 |
| Safeties | 1 | 0 | 0 | 0 | 1 | 0 | 0 | 0 | 2 | 0 | 0 | 1 | 1 | 0 |

### DEFENSE

| | BALT. | CHI. | CLEVE. | DALLAS | DET. | G.BAY | L.A. | MINN. | N.Y. | PHIL. | PITT. | ST.L. | S.F. | WASH. |
|---|---|---|---|---|---|---|---|---|---|---|---|---|---|---|
| **FIRST DOWNS:** | | | | | | | | | | | | | | |
| Total | 232 | 223 | 243 | 254 | 222 | 245 | 279 | 291 | 212 | 267 | 218 | 215 | 234 | 261 |
| by Rushing | 108 | 80 | 87 | 122 | 89 | 110 | 136 | 147 | 86 | 116 | 71 | 91 | 90 | 94 |
| by Passing | 110 | 124 | 146 | 120 | 121 | 117 | 121 | 132 | 110 | 145 | 132 | 112 | 132 | 154 |
| by Penalty | 14 | 19 | 10 | 12 | 12 | 18 | 22 | 12 | 16 | 6 | 15 | 12 | 12 | 13 |
| **RUSHING:** | | | | | | | | | | | | | | |
| Number | 418 | 401 | 411 | 454 | 412 | 412 | 508 | 493 | 419 | 474 | 396 | 477 | 419 | 412 |
| Yards | 1869 | 1652 | 1605 | 2161 | 1520 | 1694 | 2440 | 2667 | 1761 | 2007 | 1463 | 1676 | 1701 | 1550 |
| Average Yards | 4.5 | 4.1 | 3.9 | 4.8 | 3.7 | 4.1 | 4.8 | 5.4 | 4.2 | 4.2 | 3.7 | 3.5 | 4.1 | 3.8 |
| Touchdowns | 17 | 10 | 16 | 20 | 14 | 12 | 26 | 29 | 6 | 12 | 11 | 9 | 13 | 10 |
| **PASSING:** | | | | | | | | | | | | | | |
| Attempts | 351 | 398 | 358 | 326 | 385 | 414 | 328 | 365 | 386 | 383 | 420 | 389 | 380 | 409 |
| Completions | 161 | 209 | 200 | 168 | 203 | 218 | 184 | 194 | 176 | 224 | 201 | 187 | 196 | 238 |
| Completion Pct. | 45.9 | 52.5 | 55.9 | 51.5 | 52.7 | 52.7 | 56.1 | 53.2 | 45.6 | 58.5 | 47.9 | 48.1 | 51.6 | 58.2 |
| Passing Yards (Gross) | 2320 | 3164 | 2831 | 2635 | 2744 | 2630 | 2642 | 3051 | 2600 | 3183 | 2780 | 2644 | 2874 | 3493 |
| Yards Lost Tackled | 407 | 367 | 305 | 204 | 326 | 273 | 269 | 125 | 399 | 263 | 334 | 334 | 394 | 218 |
| Net Yards | 1913 | 2797 | 2526 | 2431 | 2418 | 2357 | 2373 | 2926 | 2201 | 2920 | 2446 | 2310 | 2480 | 3275 |
| Yds. per Att (Gross) | 6.6 | 7.9 | 7.9 | 8.1 | 7.1 | 6.4 | 8.1 | 8.4 | 6.7 | 8.3 | 6.6 | 6.8 | 7.6 | 8.5 |
| Yds. per Comp (Gross) | 14.4 | 15.1 | 14.2 | 15.7 | 13.5 | 12.1 | 14.4 | 15.7 | 14.8 | 14.2 | 13.8 | 14.1 | 14.7 | 14.7 |
| Touchdowns | 18 | 27 | 16 | 21 | 11 | 13 | 19 | 21 | 21 | 23 | 22 | 18 | 18 | 37 |
| Interceptions | 16 | 24 | 20 | 25 | 29 | 29 | 23 | 22 | 33 | 17 | 25 | 24 | 19 | 26 |
| Pct. Intercepted | 4.6 | 6.0 | 5.6 | 7.7 | 7.5 | 7.0 | 7.0 | 6.0 | 8.5 | 4.4 | 6.0 | 6.2 | 5.0 | 6.4 |
| **PUNTING:** | | | | | | | | | | | | | | |
| Number | 64 | 66 | 54 | 43 | 67 | 49 | 51 | 46 | 83 | 64 | 86 | 67 | 62 | 58 |
| Average Distance | 41.4 | 42.7 | 42.9 | 45.5 | 43.0 | 37.8 | 43.3 | 41.4 | 42.4 | 41.8 | 43.8 | 42.0 | 44.0 | 44.2 |
| **PUNT RETURNS:** | | | | | | | | | | | | | | |
| Number | 18 | 24 | 27 | 17 | 21 | 25 | 36 | 23 | 32 | 30 | 32 | 53 | 32 | 30 |
| Yards | 248 | 302 | 213 | 193 | 273 | 313 | 384 | 138 | 247 | 235 | 251 | 438 | 269 | 280 |
| Average Yards | 13.8 | 12.6 | 7.9 | 11.4 | 13.0 | 12.5 | 10.7 | 6.0 | 7.7 | 7.8 | 7.8 | 8.3 | 8.4 | 9.3 |
| Touchdowns | 1 | 1 | 0 | 0 | 1 | 1 | 0 | 0 | 0 | 1 | 1 | 1 | 1 | 1 |
| **KICKOFF RETURNS:** | | | | | | | | | | | | | | |
| Number | 57 | 55 | 56 | 43 | 49 | 69 | 53 | 51 | 59 | 58 | 50 | 50 | 58 | 29 |
| Yards | 1552 | 1219 | 1465 | 978 | 1184 | 1597 | 1380 | 1148 | 1288 | 1224 | 1156 | 1007 | 1368 | 666 |
| Average Yards | 27.2 | 22.2 | 26.2 | 22.7 | 24.2 | 23.1 | 26.0 | 22.5 | 21.8 | 21.1 | 23.1 | 20.1 | 23.6 | 23.0 |
| Touchdowns | 0 | 1 | 1 | 0 | 2 | 0 | 0 | 0 | 0 | 1 | 0 | 0 | 0 | 0 |
| **INTERCEPTION RETURNS:** | | | | | | | | | | | | | | |
| Number | 29 | 24 | 13 | 27 | 27 | 16 | 21 | 22 | 23 | 26 | 34 | 23 | 19 | 28 |
| Yards | 406 | 346 | 302 | 589 | 314 | 238 | 280 | 219 | 246 | 294 | 510 | 318 | 249 | 477 |
| Average Yards | 14.0 | 14.4 | 23.2 | 21.8 | 11.6 | 14.9 | 13.3 | 10.0 | 10.7 | 11.3 | 15.0 | 13.8 | 13.1 | 17.0 |
| Touchdowns | 1 | 0 | 1 | 6 | 0 | 0 | 0 | 2 | 1 | 1 | 2 | 0 | 0 | 2 |
| **PENALTIES:** | | | | | | | | | | | | | | |
| Number | 66 | 86 | 38 | 38 | 39 | 52 | 75 | 65 | 67 | 62 | 57 | 59 | 56 | 63 |
| Yards | 547.5 | 860 | 367 | 362 | 381 | 609 | 662 | 638 | 677 | 684 | 533 | 546 | 456 | 603 |
| **FUMBLES:** | | | | | | | | | | | | | | |
| Number | 19 | 22 | 23 | 30 | 21 | 30 | 27 | 31 | 43 | 27 | 36 | 36 | 21 | 33 |
| Number Lost | 8 | 13 | 18 | 18 | 12 | 17 | 16 | 23 | 21 | 16 | 20 | 20 | 12 | 15 |
| **POINTS:** | | | | | | | | | | | | | | |
| Total | 307 | 302 | 270 | 380 | 258 | 223 | 333 | 407 | 220 | 297 | 287 | 267 | 272 | 392 |
| PAT Attempts | 37 | 39 | 34 | 49 | 28 | 26 | 45 | 52 | 29 | 38 | 37 | 30 | 32 | 50 |
| PAT Made | 37 | 36 | 33 | 44 | 28 | 26 | 45 | 50 | 29 | 36 | 35 | 30 | 32 | 49 |
| FG Attempts | 26 | 27 | 28 | 28 | 34 | 21 | 21 | 26 | 20 | 24 | 26 | 38 | 29 | 24 |
| FG Made | 16 | 10 | 11 | 14 | 20 | 13 | 6 | 15 | 5 | 11 | 10 | 19 | 16 | 13 |
| Percent FG Made | 61.5 | 37.0 | 39.3 | 50.0 | 58.8 | 61.9 | 28.6 | 57.7 | 25.0 | 45.8 | 38.5 | 50.0 | 55.2 | 54.2 |
| Safeties | 0 | 1 | 0 | 0 | 1 | 1 | 0 | 0 | 1 | 0 | 0 | 0 | 0 | 2 |

### SCORING

| | | | | |
|---|---|---|---|---|
| GREEN BAY | 0 | 24 | 10 | 3–37 |
| NEW YORK | 0 | 0 | 0 | 0– 0 |

Second Quarter

| | | |
|---|---|---|
| G.B. | Hornung, 6 yard rush<br>PAT – Hornung (kick) | 0:04 |
| G.B. | Dowler, 13 yard pass from Starr<br>PAT – Hornung (kick) | 4:19 |
| G.B. | R. Kramer, 14 yard pass from Starr<br>PAT – Hornung (kick) | 10:04 |
| G.B. | Hornung, 17 yard field goal | 15:00 |

Third Quarter

| | | |
|---|---|---|
| G.B. | Hornung, 22 yard field goal | 9:55 |
| G.B. | R. Kramer, 13 yard pass from Starr<br>PAT – Hornung (kick) | 12:12 |

Fourth Quarter

| | | |
|---|---|---|
| G.B. | Hornung, 19 yard field goal | 6:48 |

### TEAM STATISTICS

| G.B. | | N.Y. |
|---|---|---|
| 19 | First Downs – Total | 6 |
| 10 | First Downs – Rushing | 1 |
| 8 | First Downs – Passing | 4 |
| 1 | First Downs – Penalty | 1 |
| 1 | Fumbles – Number | 5 |
| 0 | Fumbles – Number Lost | 1 |
| 4 | Penalties – Number | 4 |
| 16 | Yards Penalized | 38 |
| 0 | Giveaways | 5 |
| 5 | Takeaways | 0 |
| +5 | Difference | –5 |

## 1961 NFL CHAMPIONSHIP GAME
December 31, at Green Bay
(Attendance 39,029)

## New York's Cold Reception

Although the Packers had won five Western titles before this year, this was the first NFL championship game ever staged in Green Bay. The sub-freezing Wisconsin weather suited the Packers fine as they easily rolled over the Giants. The first quarter was scoreless, but New York's Kyle Rote dropped a sure touchdown pass deep in Green Bay territory. The Giants blew another touchdown in the second quarter when halfback Bob Gaiters overthrew Rote in the end zone. The Packers, meanwhile, took a comfortable lead by scoring three touchdowns in the quarter. Paul Hornung, on leave from the Army, scored from the 6-yard line after an 80-yard Packer drive, Boyd Dowler scored on a Bart Starr pass after a Ray Nitschke interception, and a Starr-to-Ron Kramer touchdown pass followed another Packer interception. Hornung added all the extra points and a 17-yard field goal to run the halftime score to 24-0. With their running game ineffective, the Giants turned to the pass, but Green Bay's Jess Whittenton blanketed top receiver Del Shofner like a shadow. While their defense continued to thwart the Giants, the Packers added ten more points in the third quarter to put the game on ice. The Packers turned a fumbled punt by Joe Morrison into a Hornung field goal, and another sustained drive resulted in Ron Kramer's second touchdown catch. A fourth-quarter Hornung field goal made the final score 37-0 and gave Hornung a record 19 points for the championship game.

### INDIVIDUAL STATISTICS

| GREEN BAY | No | Yds | Avg. | NEW YORK | No | Yds | Avg. |
|---|---|---|---|---|---|---|---|
| **RUSHING** | | | | | | | |
| Hornung | 20 | 89 | 4.5 | Webster | 7 | 19 | 2.7 |
| Taylor | 14 | 69 | 4.9 | Wells | 3 | 9 | 3.0 |
| Moore | 6 | 25 | 4.2 | King | 2 | 5 | 2.5 |
| Roach | 1 | 0 | 0.0 | Gaiters | 1 | 2 | 2.0 |
| Pitts | 3 | –2 | –0.7 | Tittle | 1 | –4 | –4.0 |
| | 44 | 181 | 4.1 | | 14 | 31 | 2.2 |
| **RECEIVING** | | | | | | | |
| R. Kramer | 4 | 80 | 20.0 | Rote | 3 | 54 | 18.0 |
| Hornung | 3 | 47 | 15.7 | Shofner | 3 | 41 | 13.7 |
| Dowler | 3 | 37 | 12.3 | Webster | 3 | 5 | 1.7 |
| | 10 | 164 | 16.4 | Walton | 1 | 19 | 19.0 |
| | | | | | 10 | 119 | 11.9 |
| **PUNTING** | | | | | | | |
| Dowler | 5 | | 42.0 | Chandler | 5 | | 39.2 |
| **PUNT RETURNS** | | | | | | | |
| Wood | 1 | 4 | 4.0 | Morrison | 2 | 10 | 5.0 |
| **KICKOFF RETURNS** | | | | | | | |
| Nitschke | 1 | 18 | 18.0 | Wells | 5 | 98 | 19.6 |
| | | | | Gaiters | 1 | 21 | 21.0 |
| | | | | | 6 | 119 | 19.8 |
| **INTERCEPTION RETURNS** | | | | | | | |
| Adderley | 1 | 14 | 14.0 | None | | | |
| Gremminger | 1 | 13 | 13.0 | | | | |
| Nitschke | 1 | 9 | 9.0 | | | | |
| Whittenton | 1 | 0 | 0.0 | | | | |
| | 4 | 36 | 9.0 | | | | |

**PASSING**

| GREEN BAY | Att | Comp | Comp Pct. | Yds | Int | Yds/ Att. | Yds/ Comp | Yards Lost Tackled |
|---|---|---|---|---|---|---|---|---|
| Starr | 17 | 10 | 58.8 | 164 | 0 | 9.6 | 16.4 | 0 |
| Hornung | 2 | 0 | 0.0 | 0 | 0 | – | – | 0 |
| | 19 | 10 | 52.6 | 164 | 0 | 8.6 | 16.4 | 0 |
| **NEW YORK** | | | | | | | | |
| Tittle | 20 | 6 | 30.0 | 65 | 4 | 3.3 | 10.8 | 2–15 |
| Conerly | 8 | 4 | 50.0 | 54 | 0 | 6.8 | 13.5 | 1– 5 |
| Gaiters | 1 | 0 | 0.0 | 0 | 0 | – | – | 0 |
| | 29 | 10 | 34.5 | 119 | 4 | 4.1 | 11.9 | 3–20 |

### NEW YORK GIANTS 10-3-1 Allie Sherman

| Scores of Each Game | | |
|---|---|---|
| 10 | ST. LOUIS | 21 |
| 17 | Pittsburgh | 14 |
| 24 | Washington | 21 |
| 24 | St. Louis | 9 |
| 31 | Dallas | 10 |
| 24 | LOS ANGELES | 14 |
| 16 | DALLAS | 17 |
| 53 | WASHINGTON | 0 |
| 38 | PHILADELPHIA | 21 |
| 42 | PITTSBURGH | 21 |
| 37 | Cleveland | 21 |
| 17 | GREEN BAY | 20 |
| 28 | Philadelphia | 24 |
| 7 | CLEVELAND | 7 |

| Use Name | Pos. | Hgt | Wgt | Age | Int | Pts |
|---|---|---|---|---|---|---|
| Rosey Brown | OT | 6'3" | 255 | 28 | | |
| Chuck Janerette | OT | 6'3" | 250 | 22 | | |
| Darrell Dess | OG | 6' | 245 | 25 | | |
| Zeke Smith | OG | 6'2" | 235 | 25 | | |
| Jack Stroud | OG | 6'1" | 250 | 32 | | |
| Mickey Walker | OG | 6' | 230 | 21 | | |
| Ray Wietecha | C | 6'1" | 230 | 32 | | |
| Greg Larson | OT-C | 6'2" | 245 | 22 | | |
| Jim Katcavage | DE | 6'3" | 240 | 26 | | 2 |
| Andy Robustelli | DE | 6'1" | 235 | 35 | | |
| Rosey Grier | DT | 6'5" | 290 | 28 | | |
| Dick Modzelewski | DT | 6' | 260 | 30 | | 2 |
| Larry Hayes | LB | 6'3" | 230 | 26 | | 6 |
| Sam Huff | LB | 6'1" | 230 | 26 | 3 | 6 |
| Cliff Livingston | LB | 6'3" | 215 | 31 | 3 | |
| Tom Scott | LB | 6'2" | 220 | 31 | 1 | 6 |
| Bob Simms | LB | 6'1" | 230 | 23 | | |
| Gene Johnson (from MIN) | DB | 6' | 180 | 26 | | |
| Dick Lynch | DB | 6'1" | 205 | 25 | 9 | |
| Dick Nolan | DB | 6'1" | 185 | 29 | | |
| Jimmy Patton | DB | 6' | 185 | 27 | 8 | 6 |
| Bill Stits | DB | 6' | 195 | 30 | | |
| Erich Barnes | HB-DB | 6'2" | 198 | 26 | 7 | 18 |
| Allan Webb | HB-DB | 5'11" | 180 | 26 | | |
| Chuck Conerly | QB | 6'1" | 185 | 37 | | |
| Lee Grosscup | QB | 6'1" | 185 | 24 | | |
| Y. A. Tittle | QB | 6' | 195 | 34 | | 18 |
| Don Chandler | HB | 6'2" | 210 | 26 | | |
| Bob Gaiters | HB | 5'11" | 210 | 23 | | 42 |
| Phil King | HB | 6'4" | 225 | 25 | | |
| Joel Wells | HB | 6'1" | 198 | 20 | | 12 |
| Joe Morrison | DB-HB | 6'1" | 212 | 23 | 2 | 12 |
| Alex Webster | FB | 6'3" | 225 | 30 | | 30 |
| Pete Hall | OE | 6'2" | 200 | 23 | | |
| Kyle Rote | OE | 6' | 200 | 32 | | 42 |
| Del Shofner | OE | 6'3" | 185 | 25 | | 66 |
| Joe Walton | OE | 5'11" | 200 | 26 | | 12 |
| Pat Summerall | K | 6'4" | 235 | 31 | | 88 |

Frank Gifford – Voluntarily Retired

Jim Podoley – Injury

### PHILADELPHIA EAGLES 10-4-0 Nick Skorich

| Scores of Each Game | | |
|---|---|---|
| 27 | CLEVELAND | 20 |
| 14 | WASHINGTON | 7 |
| 27 | ST. LOUIS | 30 |
| 21 | PITTSBURGH | 16 |
| 20 | St. Louis | 7 |
| 43 | Dallas | 7 |
| 27 | Washington | 24 |
| 16 | CHICAGO | 14 |
| 21 | New York | 38 |
| 24 | Cleveland | 45 |
| 35 | DALLAS | 13 |
| 35 | Pittsburgh | 24 |
| 24 | NEW YORK | 28 |
| 27 | Detroit | 24 |

| Use Name | Pos. | Hgt | Wgt | Age | Int | Pts |
|---|---|---|---|---|---|---|
| Jim McCusker | OT | 6'2" | 245 | 25 | | |
| Don Oakes | OT | 6'3" | 245 | 23 | | |
| J. D. Smith | OT | 6'5" | 250 | 25 | | |
| Stan Campbell | OG | 6' | 230 | 31 | | |
| John Wittenborn | OG | 6'2" | 240 | 25 | | |
| Howard Keys | C | 6'3" | 240 | 26 | | |
| Gene Gossage | DE | 6'3" | 240 | 26 | | |
| Will Renfro | DE | 6'5" | 235 | 29 | | |
| Leo Sugar | DE | 6'1" | 230 | 32 | | |
| Marion Campbell | DT | 6'3" | 250 | 32 | | |
| Riley Gunnels | DT | 6'3" | 250 | 24 | | |
| Ed Khayat | DT | 6'3" | 248 | 26 | | |
| Jess Richardson | DT | 6'2" | 265 | 31 | | |
| Maxie Baughan | LB | 6'1" | 226 | 23 | 1 | |
| Chuck Bednarik | LB | 6'3" | 235 | 36 | 2 | |
| John Nocera | LB | 6'1" | 220 | 27 | | |
| Bob Pellegrini | LB | 6'2" | 225 | 26 | | |
| Chuck Weber | LB | 6'1" | 235 | 32 | 1 | |
| Glen Amerson | DB | 6'1" | 186 | 22 | | |
| Tom Brookshier | DB | 6' | 198 | 29 | 2 | |
| Don Burroughs | DB | 6'4" | 190 | 30 | 7 | |
| Jimmy Carr | DB | 6'1" | 210 | 28 | 2 | |
| Irv Cross | DB | 6'1" | 190 | 22 | 2 | |
| Bobby Freeman | DB | 6'1" | 200 | 28 | | |
| King Hill | QB | 6'3" | 213 | 25 | | |
| Sonny Jurgensen | QB | 5'11" | 200 | 27 | | |
| Billy Barnes | HB | 5'11" | 202 | 26 | | 24 |
| Timmy Brown | HB | 5'10" | 190 | 24 | | 30 |
| Ted Dean | HB | 6'2" | 210 | 23 | | 18 |
| Clarence Peaks | FB | 6'1" | 220 | 25 | | 30 |
| Theron Sapp | FB | 6'1" | 205 | 26 | | 6 |
| Tommy McDonald | FL | 5'10" | 172 | 27 | | 78 |
| Dick Lucas | OE | 6'2" | 216 | 27 | | 30 |
| Pete Retzlaff | OE | 6'1" | 212 | 30 | | 48 |
| John Tracey | OE | 6'3" | 225 | 28 | | |
| Bobby Walston | OE | 6' | 195 | 32 | | 97 |

### CLEVELAND BROWNS 8-5-1 Paul Brown

| Scores of Each Game | | |
|---|---|---|
| 20 | Philadelphia | 27 |
| 20 | ST. LOUIS | 17 |
| 25 | DALLAS | 7 |
| 31 | WASHINGTON | 7 |
| 17 | GREEN BAY | 49 |
| 30 | Pittsburgh | 28 |
| 21 | St. Louis | 10 |
| 13 | PITTSBURGH | 17 |
| 17 | Washington | 6 |
| 45 | PHILADELPHIA | 24 |
| 21 | NEW YORK | 37 |
| 38 | Dallas | 17 |
| 14 | Chicago | 17 |
| 7 | New York | 7 |

| Use Name | Pos. | Hgt | Wgt | Age | Int | Pts |
|---|---|---|---|---|---|---|
| Lou Groza | OT | 6'3" | 248 | 37 | | 85 |
| Errol Linden | OT | 6'5" | 260 | 23 | | |
| Mike McCormack | OT | 6'4" | 250 | 34 | | |
| Ed Nutting | OT | 6'4" | 246 | 22 | | |
| Dick Schafrath | OT | 6'3" | 255 | 25 | | |
| Duane Putnam | OG | 6' | 233 | 33 | | |
| Jim Ray Smith | OG | 6'3" | 245 | 30 | | |
| John Wooten | OG | 6'2" | 250 | 26 | | |
| John Morrow | C | 6'3" | 248 | 28 | | |
| Jim Houston | DE | 6'2" | 235 | 24 | | |
| Paul Wiggin | DE | 6'3" | 245 | 27 | | |
| Johnny Brewer | DE | 6'4" | 225 | 24 | | |
| Bob Gain | DT | 6'3" | 260 | 33 | | |
| Floyd Peters | DT | 6'4" | 255 | 26 | | |
| Larry Stephens | DT | 6'4" | 260 | 23 | | |
| Vince Costello | LB | 6' | 232 | 29 | | 6 |
| Galen Fiss | LB | 6' | 227 | 31 | 1 | |
| Walt Michaels | LB | 6' | 237 | 32 | 2 | |
| Dave Lloyd | C-LB | 6'3" | 248 | 25 | | |
| Ross Fichtner | DB | 6' | 185 | 23 | | |
| Don Fleming | DB | 6' | 188 | 24 | 3 | |
| Bernie Parrish | DB | 5'11" | 195 | 26 | 7 | 6 |
| Jim Shofner | DB | 6'2" | 190 | 25 | 5 | |
| Bobby Franklin | DB | 5'11" | 182 | 25 | 2 | 6 |
| Len Dawson | QB | 6' | 195 | 27 | | |
| Milt Plum | QB | 6'1" | 205 | 27 | | 6 |
| Bobby Mitchell | HB | 6' | 192 | 26 | | 60 |
| Tom Watkins | HB | 6'1" | 195 | 24 | | 6 |
| Jimmy Brown | FB | 6'2" | 228 | 25 | | 60 |
| Preston Powell | FB | 6'2" | 225 | 24 | | |
| Ray Renfro | FL | 6'1" | 192 | 30 | | 36 |
| Leon Clarke | OE | 6'4" | 235 | 28 | | 12 |
| Bob Crespino | OE | 6'4" | 217 | 23 | | 6 |
| Charley Ferguson | OE | 6'5" | 217 | 21 | | 6 |
| Rich Kreitling | OE | 6'2" | 208 | 26 | | 18 |
| Gern Nagler | OE | 6'2" | 190 | 28 | | 6 |
| Sam Baker | K | 6'2" | 217 | 29 | | |

Gene Hickerson – Broken Leg

### ST. LOUIS CARDINALS 7-7-0 Pop Ivy Chuck Drulis Ray Prochaska Ray Willsey

| Scores of Each Game | | |
|---|---|---|
| 21 | New York | 10 |
| 17 | Cleveland | 20 |
| 30 | Philadelphia | 27 |
| 9 | NEW YORK | 24 |
| 7 | PHILADELPHIA | 20 |
| 24 | Washington | 0 |
| 10 | CLEVELAND | 21 |
| 31 | Dallas | 17 |
| 14 | DETROIT | 45 |
| 0 | Baltimore | 16 |
| 27 | Pittsburgh | 30 |
| 38 | WASHINGTON | 24 |
| 31 | DALLAS | 13 |
| 20 | PITTSBURGH | 0 |

| Use Name | Pos. | Hgt | Wgt | Age | Int | Pts |
|---|---|---|---|---|---|---|
| Ed Cook | OT | 6'2" | 240 | 29 | | |
| Charley Granger (from DAL) | OT | 6'2" | 240 | 23 | | |
| Ernie McMillan | OT | 6'6" | 255 | 23 | | |
| Dale Memmelaar | OT | 6'2" | 245 | 24 | | |
| Ken Panfil | OT | 6'6" | 255 | 30 | | |
| Jerry Perry | OT | 6'4" | 240 | 30 | | 51 |
| Bob DeMarco | OG | 6'3" | 240 | 23 | | |
| Ken Gray | OG | 6'2" | 240 | 25 | | |
| Mike McGee | OG | 6'1" | 230 | 23 | | |
| Tom Redmond | OG | 6'5" | 240 | 24 | | |
| Charley Ellzey | C | 6'3" | 240 | 23 | | |
| Don Gillis | C | 6'3" | 250 | 26 | | |
| Bob Griffin (from DEN-A) | LB-C | 6'3" | 250 | 32 | | |
| Ed Henke | DE | 6'3" | 230 | 33 | | |
| Luke Owens | DE | 6'2" | 255 | 28 | | |
| Joe Robb | DE | 6'3" | 230 | 24 | 1 | |
| Frank Fuller | DT | 6'4" | 245 | 32 | | |
| Ron McDole | DT | 6'3" | 250 | 21 | | |
| Don Owens | DT | 6'5" | 255 | 29 | | |
| Ted Bates | LB | 6'3" | 220 | 24 | | |
| Bill Koman | LB | 6'2" | 230 | 27 | 1 | |
| Monte Lee | LB | 6'4" | 225 | 23 | 1 | |
| Dale Meinert | LB | 6'2" | 220 | 28 | 2 | |
| Joe Driskill | DB | 6'1" | 195 | 24 | | |
| Jimmy Hill | DB | 6'2" | 190 | 32 | 4 | 6 |
| Jerry Norton | DB | 5'11" | 195 | 31 | 7 | 12 |
| Willie West | DB | 5'10" | 185 | 23 | 1 | 6 |
| Larry Wilson | DB | 6' | 187 | 23 | 3 | 2 |
| Pat Fischer | HB-DB | 5'10" | 165 | 21 | | |
| Billy Stacy | HB-DB | 6'1" | 190 | 25 | 4 | 24 |
| Sam Etcheverry | QB | 5'11" | 190 | 31 | | |
| Ralph Guglielmi | QB | 6'1" | 195 | 28 | | 6 |
| Charley Johnson | QB | 6' | 190 | 24 | | |
| Bobby Joe Conrad | HB | 6' | 195 | 26 | | 22 |
| John David Crow | HB | 6'2" | 215 | 26 | | 24 |
| Prentice Gautt | HB | 6' | 200 | 23 | | 36 |
| Ken Hall (from HOU-A) | HB | 6'1" | 210 | 25 | | |
| Mal Hammack | FB | 6'2" | 205 | 28 | | 6 |
| Frank Mestnik | FB | 6'2" | 200 | 23 | | 12 |
| Taz Anderson | OE | 6'2" | 200 | 22 | | 18 |
| Dick Lage | OE | 6'4" | 228 | 21 | | |
| Hugh McInnis | OE | 6'3" | 220 | 23 | | |
| Sonny Randle | OE | 6'2" | 187 | 25 | | 54 |

Joe Childress – Injury

### PITTSBURGH STEELERS 6-8-0 Buddy Parker

| Scores of Each Game | | |
|---|---|---|
| 24 | Dallas | 27 |
| 14 | NEW YORK | 17 |
| 14 | Los Angeles | 24 |
| 16 | Philadelphia | 21 |
| 20 | WASHINGTON | 0 |
| 28 | CLEVELAND | 30 |
| 20 | SAN FRANCISCO | 10 |
| 17 | Cleveland | 13 |
| 37 | DALLAS | 7 |
| 21 | New York | 42 |
| 30 | ST. LOUIS | 27 |
| 24 | PHILADELPHIA | 35 |
| 30 | Washington | 14 |
| 0 | St. Louis | 20 |

| Use Name | Pos. | Hgt | Wgt | Age | Int | Pts |
|---|---|---|---|---|---|---|
| Charlie Bradshaw | OT | 6'6" | 255 | 25 | | |
| Dan James | OT | 6'4" | 280 | 24 | | |
| Dick Klein (to BOS-A) | OT | 6'4" | 255 | 27 | | |
| John Nisby | OG | 6'1" | 230 | 28 | | |
| Mike Sandusky | OG | 6' | 230 | 28 | | |
| Ron Stehouwer | OG | 6'2" | 230 | 24 | | |
| Buzz Nutter | C | 6'4" | 230 | 30 | | |
| George Demko | DE | 6'3" | 240 | 26 | | |
| John Kapele | DE | 6' | 240 | 24 | | |
| Lou Michaels | DE | 6'2" | 235 | 25 | 1 | 72 |
| Ernie Stautner | DT-DE | 6'1" | 230 | 36 | | |
| Joe Krupa | DT | 6'2" | 225 | 28 | | |
| Big Daddy Lipscomb | DT | 6'6" | 288 | 29 | | |
| Mike Henry | LB | 6'2" | 215 | 25 | 1 | |
| Myron Pottios | LB | 6'2" | 240 | 22 | 2 | |
| John Reger | LB | 6' | 230 | 30 | 1 | |
| Bob Schmitz | LB | 6'1" | 235 | 23 | | |
| Wilbert Scott | LB | 6' | 215 | 22 | | |
| George Tarasovic | LB | 6'4" | 245 | 32 | 1 | |
| Len Burnett | DB | 6'1" | 195 | 22 | | |
| Bill Butler | DB | 5'10" | 185 | 24 | 3 | 6 |
| Willie Daniel | DB | 5'11" | 185 | 23 | 3 | |
| Johnny Sample | DB | 6'1" | 200 | 24 | 8 | 12 |
| Jackie Simpson | DB | 5'10" | 185 | 27 | 2 | |
| Brady Keys | HB-DB | 6' | 185 | 25 | 2 | |
| Dick Haley (from MIN) | FL-DB | 5'10" | 195 | 24 | 1 | |
| Rudy Bukich | QB | 6'1" | 205 | 30 | | 12 |
| Bobby Layne | QB | 6'1" | 210 | 34 | | 5 |
| Terry Nofsinger | QB | 6'4" | 205 | 23 | | |
| Dick Hoak | HB | 5'11" | 190 | 22 | | |
| Jack Stanton | HB | 6'1" | 190 | 23 | | |
| Tom Tracy | HB | 5'9" | 205 | 29 | | 20 |
| John Henry Johnson | FB | 6'2" | 215 | 31 | | 42 |
| Charlie Scales | FB | 5'11" | 215 | 22 | | |
| Buddy Dial | FL | 6'1" | 195 | 24 | | 72 |
| Red Mack | HB-FL | 5'10" | 185 | 24 | | 12 |
| Preston Carpenter | OE | 6'2" | 190 | 27 | | 24 |
| Henry Clement | OE | 6'2" | 200 | 21 | | |
| Bob Coronado | OE | 6'1" | 195 | 25 | | |
| Steve Meilinger (to STL) | OE | 6'2" | 230 | 31 | | |
| Bob Schnelker (from MIN) | OE | 6'3" | 215 | 31 | | 24 |
| Bobby Joe Green | K | 5'11" | 175 | 23 | | |

## NEW YORK GIANTS

### Rushing

| Last Name | No. | Yds | Avg | TD |
|---|---|---|---|---|
| Webster | 196 | 928 | 4.7 | 2 |
| Gaiters | 116 | 460 | 4.0 | 6 |
| Wells | 65 | 216 | 3.3 | 1 |
| Tittle | 25 | 85 | 3.4 | 3 |
| Webb | 6 | 51 | 8.5 | 0 |
| Morrison | 33 | 48 | 1.5 | 1 |
| Chandler | 3 | 30 | 10.0 | 0 |
| Conerly | 13 | 16 | 1.2 | 0 |
| Grosscup | 2 | 10 | 5.0 | 0 |
| King | 4 | 7 | 1.8 | 0 |
| Shofner | 1 | 6 | 6.0 | 0 |

### Receiving

| Last Name | No. | Yds | Avg | TD |
|---|---|---|---|---|
| Shofner | 68 | 1125 | 17 | 11 |
| Rote | 53 | 805 | 15 | 7 |
| Walton | 36 | 544 | 15 | 2 |
| Webster | 26 | 313 | 12 | 3 |
| Morrison | 11 | 67 | 6 | 1 |
| Gaiters | 11 | 54 | 5 | 1 |
| Wells | 6 | 31 | 5 | 1 |
| Barnes | 2 | 74 | 37 | 1 |
| Hall | 2 | 22 | 11 | 0 |

### Punt Returns

| Last Name | No. | Yds | Avg | TD |
|---|---|---|---|---|
| Stits | 17 | 132 | 8 | 0 |
| Wells | 17 | 90 | 5 | 0 |
| Webb | 5 | 61 | 12 | 0 |
| Morrison | 3 | 6 | 2 | 0 |

### Kickoff Returns

| Last Name | No. | Yds | Avg | TD |
|---|---|---|---|---|
| Gaiters | 11 | 288 | 26 | 0 |
| Wells | 12 | 273 | 23 | 0 |
| Webb | 8 | 156 | 20 | 0 |
| Stits | 4 | 87 | 22 | 0 |
| Morrison | 2 | 32 | 16 | 0 |
| Simms | 1 | 14 | 14 | 0 |

### Passing – Punting – Kicking

**PASSING**

| Last Name | Att | Comp | % | Yds | Yd/Att | TD | Int– | % | RK |
|---|---|---|---|---|---|---|---|---|---|
| Tittle | 285 | 163 | 57 | 2272 | 8.0 | 17 | 12– | 4 | 3 |
| Conerly | 106 | 44 | 42 | 634 | 6.0 | 7 | 8– | 8 | |
| Grosscup | 22 | 5 | 23 | 87 | 4.0 | 1 | 3– | 14 | |
| Gaiters | 3 | 3 | 100 | 42 | 14.0 | 2 | 0– | 0 | |

**PUNTING**

| Last Name | No | Avg |
|---|---|---|
| Chandler | 68 | 43.9 |

**KICKING**

| Last Name | XP | Att | % | FG | Att | % |
|---|---|---|---|---|---|---|
| Summerall | 46 | 46 | 100 | 14 | 34 | 41 |

## PHILADELPHIA EAGLES

### Rushing

| Last Name | No. | Yds | Avg | TD |
|---|---|---|---|---|
| Peaks | 135 | 471 | 3.5 | 5 |
| Brown | 50 | 338 | 6.8 | 1 |
| Dean | 66 | 321 | 4.9 | 2 |
| Barnes | 92 | 309 | 3.4 | 1 |
| Jurgensen | 20 | 27 | 1.4 | 0 |
| Sapp | 7 | 24 | 3.4 | 1 |
| Hill | 2 | 9 | 4.5 | 0 |
| Retzlaff | 1 | 8 | 8.0 | 0 |

### Receiving

| Last Name | No. | Yds | Avg | TD |
|---|---|---|---|---|
| McDonald | 64 | 1144 | 18 | 13 |
| Retzlaff | 50 | 769 | 15 | 8 |
| Walston | 34 | 569 | 17 | 2 |
| Peaks | 32 | 472 | 15 | 0 |
| Dean | 21 | 335 | 16 | 1 |
| Barnes | 15 | 194 | 13 | 3 |
| Brown | 14 | 264 | 19 | 2 |
| Lucas | 8 | 67 | 8 | 5 |
| Sapp | 3 | 10 | 3 | 0 |

### Punt Returns

| Last Name | No. | Yds | Avg | TD |
|---|---|---|---|---|
| Dean | 18 | 140 | 8 | 0 |
| Brown | 8 | 125 | 16 | 1 |
| Cross | 7 | 77 | 11 | 0 |
| Baughan | 1 | 11 | 11 | 0 |

### Kickoff Returns

| Last Name | No. | Yds | Avg | TD |
|---|---|---|---|---|
| Brown | 29 | 811 | 28 | 1 |
| Dean | 21 | 462 | 22 | 0 |
| Peaks | 2 | 29 | 15 | 0 |
| Cross | 1 | 11 | 11 | 0 |

### Passing – Punting – Kicking

**PASSING**

| Last Name | Att | Comp | % | Yds | Yd/Att | TD | Int– | % | RK |
|---|---|---|---|---|---|---|---|---|---|
| Jurgensen | 416 | 235 | 56 | 3723 | 8.9 | 32 | 24– | 5 | 5 |
| Hill | 12 | 6 | 50 | 101 | 8.4 | 2 | 2– | 17 | |
| Peaks | 1 | 0 | 0 | 0 | 0.0 | 0 | 0– | 0 | |

**PUNTING**

| Last Name | No | Avg |
|---|---|---|
| Hill | 55 | 43.7 |

**KICKING**

| Last Name | XP | Att | % | FG | Att | % |
|---|---|---|---|---|---|---|
| Walston | 43 | 46 | 93 | 14 | 25 | 56 |

## CLEVELAND BROWNS

### Rushing

| Last Name | No. | Yds | Avg | TD |
|---|---|---|---|---|
| Brown | 305 | 1408 | 4.6 | 8 |
| Mitchell | 101 | 548 | 5.4 | 5 |
| Watkins | 43 | 209 | 4.9 | 0 |
| Franklin | 1 | 12 | 12.0 | 1 |
| Powell | 1 | 5 | 5.0 | 0 |
| Kreitling | 0 | 4 | 0.0 | 0 |
| McCormack | 0 | 4 | 0.0 | 0 |
| Dawson | 1 | –10 | –10.0 | 0 |
| Plum | 24 | –17 | –0.7 | 1 |

### Receiving

| Last Name | No. | Yds | Avg | TD |
|---|---|---|---|---|
| Renfro | 48 | 834 | 17 | 6 |
| Brown | 46 | 459 | 10 | 2 |
| Mitchell | 32 | 368 | 12 | 3 |
| Kreitling | 21 | 229 | 11 | 3 |
| Nagler | 19 | 241 | 13 | 1 |
| Clarke | 11 | 211 | 19 | 2 |
| Watkins | 4 | 66 | 17 | 1 |
| Ferguson | 2 | 68 | 34 | 1 |
| Crespino | 2 | 62 | 31 | 1 |

### Punt Returns

| Last Name | No. | Yds | Avg | TD |
|---|---|---|---|---|
| Mitchell | 14 | 164 | 12 | 1 |
| Shofner | 14 | 119 | 9 | 0 |

### Kickoff Returns

| Last Name | No. | Yds | Avg | TD |
|---|---|---|---|---|
| Mitchell | 16 | 428 | 27 | 1 |
| Powell | 16 | 321 | 20 | 0 |
| Watkins | 9 | 226 | 25 | 0 |
| Baker | 3 | 57 | 19 | 0 |
| Brown | 2 | 50 | 25 | 0 |
| Stephens | 1 | 15 | 15 | 0 |
| Fichtner | 1 | 11 | 11 | 0 |
| Linden | 1 | 5 | 5 | 0 |
| Brewer | 1 | 2 | 2 | 0 |

### Passing – Punting – Kicking

**PASSING**

| Last Name | Att | Comp | % | Yds | Yd/Att | TD | Int– | % | RK |
|---|---|---|---|---|---|---|---|---|---|
| Plum | 302 | 177 | 59 | 2416 | 8.0 | 18 | 10– | 3 | 1 |
| Dawson | 15 | 7 | 47 | 85 | 5.7 | 1 | 3– | 20 | |
| Brown | 3 | 1 | 33 | 37 | 12.3 | 1 | 0– | 0 | |

**PUNTING**

| Last Name | No | Avg |
|---|---|---|
| Baker | 53 | 43.3 |

**KICKING**

| Last Name | XP | Att | % | FG | Att | % |
|---|---|---|---|---|---|---|
| Groza | 37 | 38 | 97 | 16 | 23 | 70 |

## ST. LOUIS CARDINALS

### Rushing

| Last Name | No. | Yds | Avg | TD |
|---|---|---|---|---|
| Gautt | 129 | 523 | 4.1 | 3 |
| Mestnik | 95 | 334 | 3.5 | 1 |
| Crow | 48 | 192 | 4.0 | 1 |
| Guglielmi | 22 | 101 | 4.6 | 1 |
| Hammack | 18 | 79 | 4.4 | 1 |
| Etcheverry | 33 | 73 | 2.2 | 0 |
| Anderson | 15 | 39 | 2.6 | 1 |
| McInnis | 4 | 30 | 7.5 | 0 |
| Conrad | 20 | 22 | 1.1 | 0 |
| Norton | 1 | 15 | 15.0 | 0 |
| Johnson | 1 | –3 | –3.0 | 0 |

### Receiving

| Last Name | No. | Yds | Avg | TD |
|---|---|---|---|---|
| Randle | 44 | 591 | 13 | 9 |
| Conrad | 30 | 499 | 17 | 2 |
| Anderson | 22 | 399 | 18 | 2 |
| Crow | 20 | 306 | 15 | 3 |
| Stacy | 12 | 241 | 20 | 1 |
| Gautt | 12 | 132 | 11 | 3 |
| Mestnik | 12 | 29 | 2 | 1 |
| McInnis | 7 | 107 | 15 | 0 |
| Hammack | 5 | 70 | 14 | 0 |
| Hall | 3 | 38 | 13 | 0 |
| Fischer | 1 | 22 | 22 | 0 |

### Punt Returns

| Last Name | No. | Yds | Avg | TD |
|---|---|---|---|---|
| Conrad | 5 | 103 | 21 | 1 |
| West | 11 | 98 | 9 | 0 |
| Fischer | 4 | 18 | 5 | 0 |
| Stacy | 5 | 9 | 2 | 0 |
| Driskill | 1 | 8 | 8 | 0 |

### Kickoff Returns

| Last Name | No. | Yds | Avg | TD |
|---|---|---|---|---|
| Fischer | 17 | 426 | 25 | 0 |
| West | 16 | 340 | 21 | 0 |
| Wilson | 4 | 83 | 21 | 0 |
| Stacy | 3 | 60 | 20 | 0 |
| Conrad | 1 | 28 | 28 | 0 |
| Mestnik | 2 | 27 | 14 | 0 |
| Lee | 1 | 12 | 12 | 0 |
| Driskill | 2 | 8 | 4 | 0 |
| Hammack | 1 | 8 | 8 | 0 |

### Passing – Punting – Kicking

**PASSING**

| Last Name | Att | Comp | % | Yds | Yd/Att | TD | Int– | % | RK |
|---|---|---|---|---|---|---|---|---|---|
| Etcheverry | 196 | 96 | 49 | 1275 | 6.5 | 14 | 11– | 6 | 11 |
| Guglielmi | 116 | 56 | 48 | 927 | 8.0 | 5 | 8– | 7 | |
| Crow | 14 | 4 | 29 | 76 | 5.4 | 1 | 1– | 7 | |
| Johnson | 13 | 5 | 38 | 51 | 4.0 | 0 | 2– | 15 | |
| Gautt | 11 | 6 | 55 | 100 | 9.1 | 1 | 1– | 9 | |
| Conrad | 1 | 1 | 100 | 5 | 5.0 | 0 | 0– | 0 | |

**PUNTING**

| Last Name | No | Avg |
|---|---|---|
| Norton | 85 | 44.7 |

**KICKING**

| Last Name | XP | Att | % | FG | Att | % |
|---|---|---|---|---|---|---|
| Perry | 30 | 33 | 91 | 7 | 16 | 44 |
| Conrad | 4 | 4 | 100 | 0 | 1 | 0 |

## PITTSBURGH STEELERS

### Rushing

| Last Name | No. | Yds | Avg | TD |
|---|---|---|---|---|
| Johnson | 213 | 787 | 3.7 | 6 |
| Tracy | 147 | 402 | 2.7 | 2 |
| Hoak | 85 | 302 | 3.6 | 0 |
| Scales | 50 | 184 | 3.7 | 0 |
| Green | 2 | 37 | 18.5 | 0 |
| Keys | 6 | 14 | 2.3 | 0 |
| Layne | 8 | 11 | 1.4 | 0 |
| Carpenter | 7 | 9 | 1.3 | 0 |
| Meilinger | 1 | 6 | 6.0 | 0 |
| Dial | 3 | 6 | 2.0 | 0 |
| Nofsinger | 6 | 6 | 1.0 | 0 |
| Bukich | 14 | 4 | 0.3 | 2 |
| Coronado | 1 | –7 | –7.0 | 0 |

### Receiving

| Last Name | No. | Yds | Avg | TD |
|---|---|---|---|---|
| Dial | 53 | 1047 | 20 | 12 |
| Carpenter | 33 | 460 | 14 | 4 |
| Schnelker | 24 | 401 | 17 | 4 |
| Johnson | 24 | 262 | 11 | 1 |
| Tracy | 14 | 133 | 10 | 1 |
| Mack | 8 | 128 | 16 | 2 |
| Meilinger | 8 | 103 | 13 | 0 |
| Scales | 7 | 43 | 6 | 0 |
| Clement | 5 | 65 | 13 | 0 |
| Haley | 3 | 43 | 14 | 0 |
| Coronado | 3 | 32 | 11 | 0 |
| Hoak | 3 | 18 | 6 | 0 |

### Punt Returns

| Last Name | No. | Yds | Avg | TD |
|---|---|---|---|---|
| Sample | 26 | 283 | 11 | 1 |
| Keys | 9 | 135 | 15 | 0 |
| Carpenter | 3 | 18 | 6 | 0 |
| Butler | 2 | 11 | 6 | 0 |

### Kickoff Returns

| Last Name | No. | Yds | Avg | TD |
|---|---|---|---|---|
| Sample | 23 | 532 | 23 | 0 |
| Haley | 13 | 278 | 21 | 0 |
| Butler | 6 | 117 | 20 | 0 |
| Scales | 3 | 41 | 14 | 0 |
| Keys | 2 | 41 | 21 | 0 |
| Johnson | 1 | 11 | 11 | 0 |
| Schmitz | 1 | 0 | 0 | 0 |

### Passing – Punting – Kicking

**PASSING**

| Last Name | Att | Comp | % | Yds | Yd/Att | TD | Int– | % | RK |
|---|---|---|---|---|---|---|---|---|---|
| Bukich | 156 | 89 | 57 | 1253 | 8.0 | 11 | 16– | 10 | 9 |
| Layne | 149 | 75 | 50 | 1205 | 8.1 | 11 | 16– | 11 | 14 |
| Tracy | 12 | 4 | 33 | 73 | 6.1 | 0 | 0– | 0 | |
| Nofsinger | 11 | 7 | 64 | 78 | 7.1 | 0 | 0– | 0 | |
| Hoak | 3 | 1 | 33 | 13 | 4.3 | 1 | 1– | 33 | |
| Johnson | 2 | 0 | 0 | 0 | 0.0 | 0 | 1– | 50 | |
| Green | 1 | 0 | 0 | 0 | 0.0 | 0 | 0– | 0 | |

**PUNTING**

| Last Name | No | Avg |
|---|---|---|
| Green | 73 | 47.0 |

**KICKING**

| Last Name | XP | Att | % | FG | Att | % |
|---|---|---|---|---|---|---|
| Michaels | 27 | 29 | 93 | 15 | 26 | 58 |
| Layne | 5 | 5 | 100 | 0 | 0 | 0 |
| Tracy | 2 | 2 | 100 | 0 | 0 | 0 |
| Green | 0 | 0 | 0 | | 1 | 0 |

EASTERN CONFERENCE – Continued

**DALLAS COWBOYS** 4-9-1 Tom Landry

| Scores of Each Game | | |
|---|---|---|
| 27 | PITTSBURGH | 24 |
| 21 | MINNESOTA | 7 |
| 7 | Cleveland | 25 |
| 28 | Minnesota | 0 |
| 10 | NEW YORK | 31 |
| 7 | PHILADELPHIA | 43 |
| 17 | New York | 16 |
| 17 | ST. LOUIS | 31 |
| 7 | Pittsburgh | 37 |
| 28 | WASHINGTON | 28 |
| 13 | Philadelphia | 35 |
| 17 | CLEVELAND | 38 |
| 13 | St. Louis | 31 |
| 24 | Washington | 34 |

| Use Name | Pos. | Hgt | Wgt | Age | Int | Pts |
|---|---|---|---|---|---|---|
| Byron Bradfute | OT | 6'3" | 243 | 23 | | |
| Bob Fry | OT | 6'4" | 240 | 30 | | |
| Bob McCreary | OT | 6'5" | 256 | 22 | | |
| Andy Cvercko | OG | 6' | 240 | 24 | | |
| Mike Falls | OG | 6'1" | 240 | 27 | | |
| Bob Grottkau | OG | 6'4" | 230 | 24 | | |
| John Houser | OG | 6'3" | 242 | 25 | | |
| Mike Connelly | C | 6'3" | 235 | 25 | | |
| Nate Borden | DE | 6' | 240 | 29 | | |
| Bob Lilly | DE | 6'4" | 248 | 22 | | |
| Ken Frost | DT | 6'4" | 245 | 22 | 1 | |
| Don Healy | DT | 6'3" | 264 | 25 | 1 | |
| Bill Herchman | DT | 6'2" | 250 | 28 | | |
| Sonny Davis | LB | 6'2" | 220 | 22 | | |
| Mike Dowdle | LB | 6'3" | 210 | 23 | 1 | |
| Chuck Howley | LB | 6'3" | 230 | 25 | 1 | |
| Jack Patera | LB | 6'1" | 240 | 29 | | |
| Jerry Tubbs | LB | 6'2" | 220 | 26 | 3 | |
| Gene Babb | FB-LB | 6'3" | 218 | 26 | | |
| Bob Bercich | DB | 6'1" | 198 | 24 | 3 | |
| Don Bishop | DB | 6'2" | 204 | 26 | 8 | |
| Tom Franckhauser | DB | 6' | 196 | 24 | 1 | |
| Jimmy Harris | DB | 6'1" | 180 | 26 | 2 | |
| Warren Livingston | DB | 5'10" | 180 | 23 | 1 | |
| Dick Moegle | DB | 6' | 195 | 27 | 2 | |
| Buddy Humphrey | QB | 6'1" | 200 | 25 | | |
| Eddie LeBaron | QB | 5'9" | 160 | 31 | | |
| Don Meredith | QB | 6'2" | 198 | 23 | | 6 |
| L. G. Dupre | HB | 5'11" | 190 | 29 | | |
| Don Perkins | HB | 5'10" | 198 | 23 | | 30 |
| J. W. Lockett (from SF) | FB | 6'2" | 230 | 24 | | 18 |
| Amos Marsh | FB | 6'1" | 208 | 22 | | 18 |
| Merrill Douglas | HB-FB | 6' | 204 | 25 | | |
| Dick Bielski | OE | 6'1" | 227 | 29 | | 46 |
| Frank Clarke | OE | 6' | 215 | 28 | | 54 |
| Jim Doran | OE | 6'2" | 211 | 33 | | 12 |
| Billy Howton | OE | 6'2" | 185 | 31 | | 24 |
| Lee Murchison | OE | 6'3" | 205 | 23 | | |
| Glynn Gregory | DB-OE | 6'2" | 200 | 22 | 1 | |
| Allen Green | K | 6'2" | 215 | 23 | | 34 |

**WASHINGTON REDSKINS** 1-12-1 Bill McPeak

| Scores of Each Game | | |
|---|---|---|
| 3 | San Francisco | 35 |
| 7 | Philadelphia | 14 |
| 21 | NEW YORK | 24 |
| 7 | Cleveland | 31 |
| 0 | Pittsburgh | 20 |
| 0 | ST. LOUIS | 24 |
| 24 | PHILADELPHIA | 27 |
| 0 | New York | 53 |
| 6 | CLEVELAND | 17 |
| 28 | Dallas | 28 |
| 6 | BALTIMORE | 27 |
| 24 | St. Louis | 38 |
| 14 | PITTSBURGH | 30 |
| 34 | DALLAS | 24 |

| Use Name | Pos. | Hgt | Wgt | Age | Int | Pts |
|---|---|---|---|---|---|---|
| Ray Lemek | OT | 6' | 240 | 27 | | |
| Riley Mattson | OT | 6'4" | 248 | 22 | | |
| Fran O'Brien | OT | 6'1" | 250 | 26 | | |
| Bernie Darre | OG | 6'2" | 230 | 21 | | |
| Vince Promuto | OG | 6'1" | 243 | 23 | | |
| Ed Beatty (from PIT) | C | 6'3" | 237 | 29 | | |
| Fred Hageman | C | 6'4" | 244 | 23 | | |
| Jim Schrader | C | 6'2" | 252 | 29 | | |
| John Paluck | DE | 6'2" | 240 | 28 | 1 | |
| Andy Stynchula | DE | 6'3" | 250 | 22 | | |
| Gene Cronin | LB-DE | 6'2" | 228 | 28 | | |
| Don Lawrence | DT | 6'1" | 245 | 24 | | |
| Joe Rutgens | DT | 6'2" | 265 | 22 | | |
| Bob Toneff | DT | 6'3" | 270 | 31 | | |
| Rod Breedlove | LB | 6'2" | 225 | 23 | 2 | |
| Dick Lasse | LB | 6'2" | 225 | 25 | | |
| Doyle Schick | LB | 6'1" | 210 | 22 | | |
| Roy Wilkins | LB | 6'3" | 228 | 27 | | |
| Jim Crotty (to BUF-A) | DB | 5'11" | 190 | 23 | | |
| Dale Hackbart | DB | 6'3" | 210 | 25 | 6 | 12 |
| Jim Kerr | DB | 6' | 195 | 22 | 7 | |
| Joe Krakoski | DB | 6'2" | 200 | 24 | 4 | |
| Ben Scotti | DB | 6'1" | 186 | 24 | 1 | |
| Jim Steffen (from DET) | DB | 6' | 195 | 24 | 1 | |
| Jim Wulff | HB-DB | 5'11" | 184 | 25 | 3 | |
| George Izo | QB | 6'3" | 214 | 24 | | |
| Norm Snead | QB | 6'4" | 215 | 21 | | 18 |
| Lew Luce | HB | 6' | 187 | 23 | | |
| Mike Sommer (from BAL) | HB | 5'11" | 190 | 26 | | |
| Sam Horner | DB-HB | 6' | 198 | 23 | | 6 |
| Dick James | DB-HB | 5'9" | 175 | 27 | 1 | 30 |
| Don Bosseler | FB | 6'1" | 212 | 25 | | 18 |
| Jim Cunningham | FB | 5'11" | 220 | 22 | | 12 |
| Bill Anderson | OE | 6'3" | 214 | 25 | | |
| John Aveni | OE | 6'3" | 215 | 26 | | 42 |
| Fred Dugan | OE | 6'3" | 198 | 27 | | 24 |
| Steve Junker | OE | 6'3" | 217 | 26 | | |
| Tom Osborne | OE | 6'3" | 190 | 24 | | 12 |

WESTERN CONFERENCE

**GREEN BAY PACKERS** 11-3-0 Vince Lombardi

| Scores of Each Game | | |
|---|---|---|
| 13 | DETROIT | 17 |
| 30 | SAN FRANCISCO | 10 |
| 24 | CHICAGO | 0 |
| 45 | BALTIMORE | 7 |
| 49 | Cleveland | 17 |
| 33 | Minnesota | 7 |
| 28 | MINNESOTA | 10 |
| 21 | Baltimore | 45 |
| 31 | Chicago | 28 |
| 35 | LOS ANGELES | 17 |
| 17 | Detroit | 9 |
| 20 | NEW YORK | 17 |
| 21 | San Francisco | 22 |
| 24 | Los Angeles | 17 |

| Use Name | Pos. | Hgt | Wgt | Age | Int | Pts |
|---|---|---|---|---|---|---|
| Forrest Gregg | OT | 6'4" | 250 | 28 | | |
| Norm Masters | OT | 6'2" | 250 | 28 | | |
| Bob Skoronski | OT | 6'3" | 250 | 28 | | |
| Jerry Kramer | OG | 6'3" | 250 | 26 | | |
| Fuzzy Thurston | OG | 6'1" | 250 | 28 | | |
| Ken Iman | C | 6'1" | 230 | 22 | | |
| Jim Ringo | C | 6'1" | 235 | 30 | | |
| Ben Davidson | DE | 6'8" | 275 | 21 | | |
| Willie Davis | DE | 6'3" | 240 | 28 | | |
| Bill Quinlan | DE | 6'3" | 250 | 29 | | |
| Dave Hanner | DT | 6'2" | 260 | 32 | 1 | |
| Henry Jordan | DT | 6'3" | 250 | 26 | | |
| Ron Kostelnik | DT | 6'4" | 260 | 21 | | |
| Tom Bettis | LB | 6'2" | 225 | 28 | | |
| Dan Currie | LB | 6'3" | 240 | 27 | 3 | 6 |
| Bill Forester | LB | 6'3" | 240 | 30 | 2 | |
| Ray Nitschke | LB | 6'3" | 235 | 25 | 2 | |
| Nelson Toburen | LB | 6'3" | 235 | 22 | | |
| Herb Adderley | DB | 6'1" | 205 | 22 | 1 | |
| Hank Gremminger | DB | 6'1" | 205 | 28 | 5 | |
| Johnny Symank | DB | 5'11" | 180 | 26 | 5 | |
| Em Tunnell | DB | 6'1" | 210 | 39 | | |
| Jesse Whittenton | DB | 6' | 195 | 27 | 5 | 6 |
| Willie Wood | DB | 5'10" | 185 | 25 | 5 | 12 |
| John Roach | QB | 6'4" | 200 | 28 | | 6 |
| Bart Starr | QB | 6'1" | 200 | 28 | | 6 |
| Lew Carpenter | HB | 6'1" | 215 | 29 | | |
| Paul Hornung | HB | 6'2" | 215 | 25 | | 146 |
| Tom Moore | HB | 6'2" | 215 | 23 | | 12 |
| Elijah Pitts | HB | 6'1" | 200 | 22 | | 6 |
| Jim Taylor | FB | 6' | 215 | 26 | | 96 |
| Boyd Dowler | FL | 6'5" | 220 | 24 | | 18 |
| Lee Folkins | OE | 6'5" | 220 | 22 | | |
| Gary Knafelc | OE | 6'4" | 220 | 29 | | 24 |
| Ron Kramer | OE | 6'3" | 230 | 26 | | 24 |
| Max McGee | OE | 6'3" | 205 | 29 | | 42 |
| Ben Agajanian (from DAL-A) | K | 6' | 220 | 42 | | 11 |

**DETROIT LIONS** 8-5-1 George Wilson

| Scores of Each Game | | |
|---|---|---|
| 17 | Green Bay | 13 |
| 16 | Baltimore | 15 |
| 0 | SAN FRANCISCO | 49 |
| 17 | CHICAGO | 31 |
| 14 | LOS ANGELES | 13 |
| 14 | BALTIMORE | 17 |
| 28 | Los Angeles | 10 |
| 20 | San Francisco | 20 |
| 45 | St. Louis | 14 |
| 37 | Minnesota | 10 |
| 9 | GREEN BAY | 17 |
| 16 | Chicago | 15 |
| 13 | MINNESOTA | 7 |
| 24 | PHILADELPHIA | 27 |

| Use Name | Pos. | Hgt | Wgt | Age | Int | Pts |
|---|---|---|---|---|---|---|
| Dan LaRose | OT | 6'5" | 250 | 21 | | |
| Willie McClung | OT | 6'2" | 260 | 32 | | |
| Ollie Spencer | OG-OT | 6'2" | 250 | 30 | | |
| Harley Sewell | OG | 6'1" | 230 | 30 | | |
| Dick Mills | OG | 6'3" | 240 | 21 | | |
| John Gordy | OT-OG | 6'3" | 250 | 25 | | |
| Bob Scholtz | C | 6'4" | 250 | 23 | | |
| Bob Whitlow (from WAS) | OG-C | 6'1" | 236 | 25 | | |
| Bill Glass | DE | 6'5" | 255 | 25 | | |
| Darris McCord | DE | 6'4" | 250 | 28 | 1 | |
| Sam Williams | OE-DE | 6'5" | 235 | 30 | | |
| Roger Brown | DT | 6'5" | 300 | 24 | 1 | |
| John Gonzaga | DT | 6'3" | 250 | 28 | | |
| Alex Karras | DT | 6'2" | 245 | 25 | | |
| Gil Mains | DT | 6'2" | 250 | 31 | | |
| Paul Ward | DT | 6'3" | 247 | 24 | | |
| Carl Brettschneider | LB | 6'1" | 225 | 29 | | |
| Jim Martin | LB | 6'2" | 230 | 37 | | 70 |
| Max Messner | LB | 6'3" | 225 | 23 | | |
| Joe Schmidt | LB | 6'1" | 220 | 29 | 4 | 6 |
| Wayne Walker | LB | 6'2" | 225 | 24 | 2 | 6 |
| Night Train Lane | DB | 6'1" | 200 | 33 | 6 | |
| Dick LeBeau | DB | 6'1" | 185 | 24 | 3 | |
| Gary Lowe | DB | 5'11" | 195 | 27 | 5 | 2 |
| Bruce Maher | DB | 5'11" | 190 | 24 | 1 | |
| Yale Lary | DB | 6' | 190 | 30 | 6 | |
| Earl Morrall | QB | 6'1" | 206 | 27 | | |
| Jim Ninowski | QB | 6'1" | 200 | 25 | | 30 |
| Hopalong Cassady | HB | 5'10" | 185 | 27 | | 12 |
| Dan Lewis | HB | 6'1" | 200 | 25 | | 24 |
| Johnny Olszewski | FB | 5'11" | 202 | 30 | | |
| Nick Pietrosante | FB | 6'2" | 225 | 24 | | 30 |
| Ken Webb | FB | 5'11" | 205 | 26 | | 6 |
| Terry Barr | FL | 6' | 190 | 26 | | 36 |
| Pat Studstill | FL | 6'1" | 180 | 23 | | 6 |
| Gail Cogdill | OE | 6'2" | 195 | 24 | | 36 |
| Glenn Davis | OE | 6' | 180 | 27 | | |
| Jim Gibbons | OE | 6'2" | 220 | 25 | | 6 |

**BALTIMORE COLTS** 8-6-0 Weeb Ewbank

| Scores of Each Game | | |
|---|---|---|
| 27 | LOS ANGELES | 24 |
| 15 | DETROIT | 16 |
| 34 | MINNESOTA | 33 |
| 7 | Green Bay | 45 |
| 10 | Chicago | 24 |
| 17 | Detroit | 14 |
| 20 | CHICAGO | 21 |
| 45 | GREEN BAY | 21 |
| 20 | Minnesota | 28 |
| 16 | ST. LOUIS | 0 |
| 27 | Washington | 6 |
| 20 | SAN FRANCISCO | 17 |
| 17 | Los Angeles | 34 |
| 27 | San Francisco | 24 |

| Use Name | Pos. | Hgt | Wgt | Age | Int | Pts |
|---|---|---|---|---|---|---|
| Tom Gilburg | OT | 6'5" | 245 | 22 | | |
| Jim Parker | OT | 6'3" | 275 | 27 | | |
| George Preas | OT | 6'2" | 250 | 29 | | |
| Wiley Feagin | OG | 6'2" | 235 | 24 | | |
| Alex Sandusky | OG | 6'1" | 242 | 29 | | |
| Palmer Pyle | OG | 6'2" | 250 | 24 | | |
| Dick Szymanski | C | 6'3" | 235 | 28 | | |
| Ordell Braase | DE | 6'4" | 242 | 29 | | |
| Gino Marchetti | DE | 6'4" | 245 | 35 | | 2 |
| John Diehl | DT | 6'7" | 285 | 25 | | |
| Art Donovan | DT | 6'2" | 265 | 36 | | |
| Joe Lewis | DT | 6'2" | 250 | 26 | | |
| Jim Colvin | DE-DT | 6'2" | 250 | 24 | | |
| Billy Ray Smith | DE-DT | 6'4" | 235 | 26 | | |
| Marv Matuszak | LB | 6'3" | 230 | 32 | | |
| Bill Pellington | LB | 6'2" | 238 | 32 | 3 | |
| Don Shinnick | LB | 6' | 235 | 26 | 2 | |
| Steve Myhra | OG-LB | 6'1" | 240 | 27 | | 96 |
| Jackie Burkett | C-LB | 6'4" | 230 | 24 | 1 | |
| Bobby Boyd | DB | 5'10" | 190 | 23 | 2 | |
| Gary Glick (from WAS) | DB | 6'2" | 200 | 30 | 4 | |
| Bob Harrison | DB | 5'11" | 187 | 22 | 3 | |
| Lenny Lyles | DB | 6'2" | 202 | 25 | | |
| Andy Nelson | DB | 6'1" | 180 | 28 | | |
| Carl Taseff (to PHI) | DB | 5'11" | 194 | 32 | 1 | |
| Jim Welch | HB-DB | 6' | 190 | 23 | | 6 |
| Lamar McHan | QB | 6'1" | 205 | 29 | | |
| Johnny Unitas | QB | 6'1" | 194 | 28 | | 12 |
| Alex Hawkins | HB | 6'1" | 190 | 24 | | 30 |
| Jerry Hill | HB | 5'11" | 210 | 21 | | |
| Tom Matte | HB | 6' | 192 | 22 | | |
| Lenny Moore | HB | 6'1" | 190 | 28 | | 90 |
| Joe Perry | FB | 6' | 195 | 34 | | 24 |
| Mark Smolinski | FB | 6' | 222 | 22 | | 6 |
| Ray Berry | OE | 6'2" | 190 | 28 | | |
| Ken Gregory | OE | 6' | 190 | 24 | | |
| Aubrey Linne | OE | 6'7" | 235 | 22 | | |
| Dee Mackey | OE | 6'5" | 236 | 25 | | |
| Jim Mutscheller | OE | 6'1" | 205 | 31 | | 12 |
| Jimmy Orr | OE | 5'11" | 180 | 25 | | 24 |

## EASTERN CONFERENCE—Continued

### DALLAS COWBOYS

**RUSHING**

| Last Name | No. | Yds | Avg | TD |
|---|---|---|---|---|
| Perkins | 200 | 815 | 4.1 | 4 |
| Marsh | 84 | 379 | 4.5 | 1 |
| Lockett | 77 | 298 | 3.9 | 1 |
| Meredith | 22 | 176 | 8.0 | 1 |
| LeBaron | 20 | 72 | 3.6 | 0 |
| Dupre | 16 | 60 | 3.8 | 0 |
| Douglas | 5 | 24 | 4.8 | 0 |
| Howton | 1 | 9 | 9.0 | 0 |

**RECEIVING**

| Last Name | No. | Yds | Avg | TD |
|---|---|---|---|---|
| Howton | 56 | 785 | 14 | 4 |
| Clarke | 41 | 919 | 22 | 9 |
| Perkins | 32 | 298 | 9 | 1 |
| Bielski | 26 | 377 | 15 | 3 |
| Marsh | 21 | 189 | 9 | 2 |
| Lockett | 19 | 149 | 8 | 2 |
| Doran | 13 | 153 | 12 | 2 |
| Dupre | 6 | 49 | 8 | 0 |
| Gregory | 3 | 30 | 10 | 0 |
| Douglas | 1 | −2 | −2 | 0 |

**PUNT RETURNS**

| Last Name | No. | Yds | Avg | TD |
|---|---|---|---|---|
| Marsh | 14 | 71 | 5 | 0 |
| Livingston | 6 | 20 | 3 | 0 |
| Perkins | 1 | 8 | 8 | 0 |
| Dupre | 2 | 4 | 2 | 0 |

**KICKOFF RETURNS**

| Last Name | No. | Yds | Avg | TD |
|---|---|---|---|---|
| Marsh | 26 | 667 | 26 | 0 |
| Perkins | 22 | 443 | 20 | 0 |
| Dupre | 6 | 110 | 18 | 0 |
| Lockett | 5 | 61 | 12 | 0 |
| Babb | 2 | 34 | 17 | 0 |
| Dowdle | 2 | 33 | 17 | 0 |
| Douglas | 1 | 12 | 12 | 0 |
| Doran | 1 | 0 | 0 | 0 |

**PASSING**

| Last Name | Att | Comp | % | Yds | Yd/Att | TD | Int− | % | RK |
|---|---|---|---|---|---|---|---|---|---|
| LeBaron | 236 | 120 | 51 | 1741 | 7.4 | 14 | 16− | 7 | 12 |
| Meredith | 182 | 94 | 52 | 1161 | 6.4 | 9 | 11− | 6 | 15 |
| Humphrey | 2 | 1 | 50 | 16 | 8.0 | 0 | 0− | 0 | |
| Lockett | 2 | 0 | 0 | 0 | 0.0 | 0 | 0− | 0 | |

**PUNTING**

| Last Name | No | Avg |
|---|---|---|
| Green | 61 | 36.7 |

**KICKING**

| Last Name | XP | Att | % | FG | Att | % |
|---|---|---|---|---|---|---|
| Green | 19 | 19 | 100 | 5 | 15 | 33 |
| Bielski | 10 | 10 | 100 | 6 | 9 | 67 |

### WASHINGTON REDSKINS

**RUSHING**

| Last Name | No. | Yds | Avg | TD |
|---|---|---|---|---|
| James | 71 | 374 | 5.3 | 3 |
| Horner | 96 | 275 | 2.9 | 0 |
| Bosseler | 77 | 220 | 2.9 | 2 |
| Cunningham | 69 | 160 | 2.3 | 1 |
| Snead | 34 | 47 | 1.4 | 3 |
| Anderson | 3 | 5 | 1.7 | 0 |
| Luce | 3 | 1 | 0.3 | 0 |
| Sommer | 11 | 1 | 0.9 | 0 |
| Izo | 3 | −1 | −0.3 | 0 |

**RECEIVING**

| Last Name | No. | Yds | Avg | TD |
|---|---|---|---|---|
| Dugan | 53 | 817 | 15 | 4 |
| Anderson | 40 | 637 | 16 | 0 |
| Osborne | 22 | 297 | 14 | 2 |
| James | 20 | 298 | 15 | 2 |
| Bosseler | 16 | 94 | 6 | 1 |
| Cunningham | 12 | 90 | 8 | 1 |
| Horner | 10 | 113 | 11 | 1 |
| Junker | 9 | 130 | 14 | 0 |
| Aveni | 6 | 84 | 14 | 1 |
| Sommer | 1 | 31 | 31 | 0 |
| Wulff | 1 | 6 | 6 | 0 |

**PUNT RETURNS**

| Last Name | No. | Yds | Avg | TD |
|---|---|---|---|---|
| Steffen | 19 | 153 | 8 | 0 |
| James | 12 | 90 | 8 | 0 |
| Sommer | 2 | 26 | 13 | 0 |
| Kerr | 5 | 23 | 5 | 0 |
| Luce | 1 | 0 | 0 | 0 |

**KICKOFF RETURNS**

| Last Name | No. | Yds | Avg | TD |
|---|---|---|---|---|
| Steffen | 29 | 691 | 24 | 0 |
| James | 21 | 617 | 29 | 0 |
| Kerr | 14 | 385 | 28 | 0 |
| Sommer | 4 | 98 | 25 | 0 |
| Cunningham | 4 | 80 | 20 | 0 |
| Luce | 4 | 77 | 19 | 0 |
| Horner | 4 | 75 | 19 | 0 |
| Stynchula | 2 | 73 | 37 | 0 |
| Junker | 1 | 0 | 0 | 0 |

**PASSING**

| Last Name | Att | Comp | % | Yds | Yd/Att | TD | Int− | % | RK |
|---|---|---|---|---|---|---|---|---|---|
| Snead | 375 | 172 | 46 | 2337 | 6.2 | 11 | 22− | 6 | 16 |
| Izo | 40 | 16 | 40 | 214 | 5.4 | 1 | 6− | 15 | |
| James | 4 | 1 | 25 | 15 | 3.8 | 0 | 0− | 0 | |
| Aveni | 1 | 0 | 0 | 0 | 0.0 | 0 | 0− | 0 | |

**PUNTING**

| Last Name | No | Avg |
|---|---|---|
| Horner | 63 | 38.2 |
| James | 6 | 35.0 |
| Cunningham | 1 | 46.0 |

**KICKING**

| Last Name | XP | Att | % | FG | Att | % |
|---|---|---|---|---|---|---|
| Aveni | 21 | 23 | 91 | 5 | 28 | 18 |

## WESTERN CONFERENCE

### GREEN BAY PACKERS

**RUSHING**

| Last Name | No. | Yds | Avg | TD |
|---|---|---|---|---|
| Taylor | 243 | 1307 | 5.4 | 15 |
| Hornung | 127 | 597 | 4.7 | 8 |
| Moore | 61 | 302 | 5.0 | 1 |
| Pitts | 23 | 75 | 3.3 | 1 |
| Starr | 12 | 56 | 4.7 | 1 |
| R. Kramer | 5 | 13 | 2.6 | 0 |
| Carpenter | 1 | 5 | 5.0 | 0 |
| Roach | 2 | −5 | −2.5 | 1 |

**RECEIVING**

| Last Name | No. | Yds | Avg | TD |
|---|---|---|---|---|
| McGee | 51 | 883 | 17 | 7 |
| Dowler | 36 | 633 | 18 | 3 |
| R. Kramer | 35 | 559 | 16 | 4 |
| Taylor | 25 | 175 | 7 | 1 |
| Hornung | 15 | 145 | 10 | 2 |
| Moore | 8 | 41 | 5 | 1 |
| Knafelc | 3 | 32 | 11 | 0 |
| Carpenter | 3 | 29 | 10 | 0 |
| Pitts | 1 | 5 | 5 | 0 |

**PUNT RETURNS**

| Last Name | No. | Yds | Avg | TD |
|---|---|---|---|---|
| Wood | 14 | 225 | 16 | 2 |
| Carpenter | 6 | 130 | 22 | 0 |

**KICKOFF RETURNS**

| Last Name | No. | Yds | Avg | TD |
|---|---|---|---|---|
| Adderley | 18 | 478 | 27 | 0 |
| Moore | 15 | 409 | 27 | 0 |
| Symank | 4 | 121 | 30 | 0 |
| Forester | 3 | 55 | 18 | 0 |
| Pitts | 1 | 14 | 14 | 0 |

**PASSING**

| Last Name | Att | Comp | % | Yds | Yd/Att | TD | Int− | % | RK |
|---|---|---|---|---|---|---|---|---|---|
| Starr | 295 | 172 | 58 | 2418 | 8.2 | 16 | 16− | 5 | 3 |
| Hornung | 5 | 3 | 60 | 42 | 8.4 | 1 | 0− | 0 | |
| Roach | 4 | 0 | 0 | 0 | 0.0 | 0 | 0− | 0 | |
| Moore | 2 | 2 | 100 | 42 | 21.0 | 1 | 0− | 0 | |

**PUNTING**

| Last Name | No | Avg |
|---|---|---|
| Dowler | 38 | 44.1 |
| McGee | 13 | 40.0 |

**KICKING**

| Last Name | XP | Att | % | FG | Att | % |
|---|---|---|---|---|---|---|
| Hornung | 41 | 41 | 100 | 15 | 22 | 68 |
| Agajanian | 8 | 8 | 100 | 1 | 2 | 50 |

### DETROIT LIONS

**RUSHING**

| Last Name | No. | Yds | Avg | TD |
|---|---|---|---|---|
| Pietrosante | 201 | 841 | 4.2 | 5 |
| Lewis | 110 | 451 | 4.1 | 4 |
| Ninowski | 33 | 238 | 7.2 | 5 |
| Cassady | 31 | 131 | 4.2 | 1 |
| Olszewski | 30 | 109 | 3.6 | 0 |
| Morrall | 20 | 86 | 4.3 | 0 |
| Lary | 1 | 14 | 14.0 | 0 |
| Webb | 7 | 6 | 0.9 | 1 |
| Barr | 6 | −8 | −1.3 | 0 |

**RECEIVING**

| Last Name | No. | Yds | Avg | TD |
|---|---|---|---|---|
| Cogdill | 45 | 956 | 21 | 6 |
| Gibbons | 45 | 566 | 13 | 1 |
| Barr | 40 | 630 | 16 | 6 |
| Peitrosante | 26 | 315 | 12 | 0 |
| Davis | 9 | 115 | 13 | 0 |
| Lewis | 8 | 118 | 15 | 0 |
| Studstill | 5 | 54 | 11 | 0 |
| Cassady | 5 | 45 | 9 | 1 |
| Olszewski | 1 | 14 | 14 | 0 |
| Williams | 1 | 10 | 10 | 0 |
| Webb | 1 | 7 | 7 | 0 |

**PUNT RETURNS**

| Last Name | No. | Yds | Avg | TD |
|---|---|---|---|---|
| Cassady | 16 | 159 | 10 | 0 |
| Studstill | 8 | 75 | 9 | 0 |
| Gibbons | 1 | 14 | 14 | 0 |
| Lary | 1 | 8 | 8 | 0 |
| Lane | 1 | 6 | 6 | 0 |

**KICKOFF RETURNS**

| Last Name | No. | Yds | Avg | TD |
|---|---|---|---|---|
| Studstill | 16 | 448 | 28 | 1 |
| Cassady | 9 | 127 | 14 | 0 |
| Olszewski | 4 | 59 | 15 | 0 |
| Maher | 1 | 19 | 19 | 0 |
| Williams | 1 | 4 | 4 | 0 |
| Webb | 0 | 5 | 0 | 0 |

**PASSING**

| Last Name | Att | Comp | % | Yds | Yd/Att | TD | Int− | % | RK |
|---|---|---|---|---|---|---|---|---|---|
| Ninowski | 247 | 117 | 47 | 1921 | 7.8 | 7 | 18− | 7 | 17 |
| Morrall | 150 | 69 | 46 | 909 | 6.1 | 7 | 9− | 6 | 18 |
| Cassady | 1 | 0 | 0 | 0 | 0.0 | 0 | 0− | 0 | |

**PUNTING**

| Last Name | No | Avg |
|---|---|---|
| Lary | 52 | 48.4 |
| Morrall | 3 | 37.7 |
| Studstill | 1 | 32.0 |

**KICKING**

| Last Name | XP | Att | % | FG | Att | % |
|---|---|---|---|---|---|---|
| Martin | 25 | 26 | 96 | 15 | 30 | 50 |
| Walker | 6 | 6 | 100 | 0 | 3 | 0 |

### BALTIMORE COLTS

**RUSHING**

| Last Name | No. | Yds | Avg | TD |
|---|---|---|---|---|
| Perry | 168 | 675 | 4.0 | 3 |
| Moore | 92 | 648 | 7.0 | 7 |
| Hawkins | 86 | 379 | 4.4 | 4 |
| Unitas | 54 | 190 | 3.5 | 2 |
| Smolinski | 31 | 98 | 3.2 | 0 |
| Welch | 1 | 60 | 60.0 | 1 |
| Matte | 13 | 54 | 4.2 | 0 |
| Hill | 1 | 4 | 4.0 | 0 |
| McHan | 4 | 1 | 0.3 | 0 |

**RECEIVING**

| Last Name | No. | Yds | Avg | TD |
|---|---|---|---|---|
| Berry | 75 | 873 | 12 | 0 |
| Moore | 49 | 728 | 15 | 8 |
| Perry | 34 | 322 | 9 | 1 |
| Mutscheller | 20 | 370 | 19 | 2 |
| Hawkins | 20 | 158 | 8 | 1 |
| Orr | 18 | 357 | 20 | 4 |
| Smolinski | 9 | 100 | 11 | 0 |
| Mackey | 4 | 66 | 17 | 0 |
| Matte | 1 | 8 | 8 | 0 |
| Szymanski | 1 | 5 | 5 | 0 |

**PUNT RETURNS**

| Last Name | No. | Yds | Avg | TD |
|---|---|---|---|---|
| Boyd | 18 | 173 | 10 | 0 |
| Taseff | 5 | 39 | 8 | 0 |
| Hawkins | 4 | 20 | 5 | 0 |
| Nelson | 4 | 19 | 5 | 0 |
| Harrison | 1 | 16 | 16 | 0 |
| Smolinski | 1 | 2 | 2 | 0 |

**KICKOFF RETURNS**

| Last Name | No. | Yds | Avg | TD |
|---|---|---|---|---|
| Lyles | 28 | 672 | 24 | 0 |
| Harrison | 11 | 250 | 23 | 0 |
| Welch | 5 | 146 | 29 | 0 |
| Matte | 2 | 50 | 25 | 0 |
| Smolinski | 3 | 27 | 9 | 0 |
| Lewis | 1 | 14 | 14 | 0 |
| Matuszak | 1 | 14 | 14 | 0 |
| Mackey | 1 | 6 | 6 | 0 |
| Gregory | 1 | 3 | 3 | 0 |

**PASSING**

| Last Name | Att | Comp | % | Yds | Yd/Att | TD | Int− | % | RK |
|---|---|---|---|---|---|---|---|---|---|
| Unitas | 420 | 229 | 55 | 2990 | 7.1 | 16 | 24− | 6 | 8 |
| McHan | 15 | 3 | 20 | 28 | 1.9 | 1 | 4− | 27 | |
| Moore | 2 | 0 | 0 | 0 | 0.0 | 0 | 1− | 50 | |
| Boyd | 1 | 0 | 0 | 0 | 0.0 | 0 | 0− | 0 | |

**PUNTING**

| Last Name | No | Avg |
|---|---|---|
| Gilburg | 42 | 43.0 |

**KICKING**

| Last Name | XP | Att | % | FG | Att | % |
|---|---|---|---|---|---|---|
| Myhra | 33 | 34 | 97 | 21 | 39 | 54 |

**WESTERN CONFERENCE — Continued**

## CHICAGO BEARS 8-6-0 George Halas

Scores of Each Game:

| | | |
|---|---|---|
| 13 | Minnesota | 37 |
| 21 | Los Angeles | 17 |
| 0 | Green Bay | 24 |
| 31 | Detroit | 17 |
| 24 | BALTIMORE | 10 |
| 31 | SAN FRANCISCO | 0 |
| 21 | Baltimore | 20 |
| 14 | Philadelphia | 16 |
| 28 | GREEN BAY | 31 |
| 31 | San Francisco | 41 |
| 28 | LOS ANGELES | 24 |
| 15 | DETROIT | 16 |
| 17 | CLEVELAND | 14 |
| 52 | MINNESOTA | 35 |

| Use Name | Pos. | Hgt | Wgt | Age | Int | Pts |
|---|---|---|---|---|---|---|
| Art Anderson | OT | 6'3" | 244 | 24 | | |
| Herm Lee | OT | 6'4" | 247 | 30 | | |
| Stan Fanning | OT | 6'6" | 270 | 23 | | |
| Roger Davis | OG | 6'1" | 250 | 23 | | |
| Stan Jones | OG | 6'1" | 243 | 28 | | |
| Ted Karras | OG | 6'1" | 240 | 28 | | |
| Bob Wetoska | OG | 6'3" | 240 | 23 | | |
| Roger LeClerc | C | 6'3" | 235 | 23 | | 70 |
| Mike Pyle | C | 6'3" | 240 | 22 | | |
| Doug Atkins | DE | 6'8" | 255 | 31 | | |
| Bob Kilcullen | DE | 6'3" | 245 | 25 | | |
| Maury Youmans | DE | 6'6" | 260 | 24 | | |
| John Mellekas | DT | 6'3" | 255 | 28 | | |
| Fred Williams | DT | 6'4" | 248 | 31 | | |
| Joe Fortunato | LB | 6' | 225 | 31 | 3 | |
| Bill George | LB | 6'2" | 235 | 30 | 3 | |
| Larry Morris | LB | 6'2" | 230 | 26 | 1 | |
| Ken Kirk | C-LB | 6'2" | 230 | 23 | | |
| J.C. Caroline | DB | 6'1" | 190 | 28 | 3 | |
| Bobby Jackson | DB | 6'1" | 190 | 25 | | |
| Pete Manning | DB | 6'1" | 195 | 22 | | |
| Don Mullins | DB | 6'3" | 208 | 25 | | |
| Richie Petitbon | DB | 6'3" | 205 | 23 | 5 | |
| Rosey Taylor | DB | 5'11" | 186 | 22 | | |
| Dave Whitsell | DB | 6' | 190 | 25 | 6 | |
| Ed Brown | QB | 6'2" | 210 | 32 | | 4 |
| Dick Norman | QB | 6'3" | 210 | 23 | | |
| Billy Wade | QB | 6'2" | 210 | 30 | | 12 |
| Charlie Bivins | HB | 6'2" | 212 | 22 | | 6 |
| Willie Galimore | HB | 6'1" | 187 | 26 | | 42 |
| J.D. Smith | HB | 6' | 210 | 26 | | |
| John Adams | FB | 6'3" | 235 | 24 | | 6 |
| Bill Brown | FB | 5'11" | 218 | 23 | | |
| Rick Casares | FB | 6'2" | 225 | 30 | | 48 |
| Johnny Morris | FL | 5'10" | 180 | 26 | | 24 |
| Angie Coia | OE | 6'2" | 202 | 23 | | 18 |
| Mike Ditka | OE | 6'4" | 198 | 31 | | 72 |
| Jim Dooley | OE | 6'3" | 217 | 25 | | 24 |
| Bo Farrington | OE | 6'3" | 217 | 25 | | |
| Harlon Hill | DB-OE | 6'3" | 200 | 29 | 3 | |

Earl Leggett — Knee Injury

## SAN FRANCISCO FORTY NINERS 7-6-1 Red Hickey

Scores of Each Game:

| | | |
|---|---|---|
| 35 | WASHINGTON | 3 |
| 10 | Green Bay | 30 |
| 49 | Detroit | 0 |
| 35 | LOS ANGELES | 0 |
| 38 | Minnesota | 24 |
| 0 | Chicago | 31 |
| 10 | Pittsburgh | 20 |
| 20 | DETROIT | 20 |
| 7 | Los Angeles | 17 |
| 41 | CHICAGO | 31 |
| 38 | MINNESOTA | 28 |
| 17 | Baltimore | 20 |
| 22 | GREEN BAY | 21 |
| 24 | BALTIMORE | 27 |

| Use Name | Pos. | Hgt | Wgt | Age | Int | Pts |
|---|---|---|---|---|---|---|
| Len Rohde | OT | 6'4" | 240 | 23 | | |
| Bob St. Clair | OT | 6'9" | 265 | 30 | | |
| John Thomas | LB-OT | 6'4" | 246 | 26 | | |
| Bruce Bosley | OG | 6'2" | 240 | 27 | | |
| Ted Connolly | OG | 6'3" | 242 | 29 | | |
| Bill Lopasky | OG | 6'2" | 235 | 24 | | |
| Mike Magac | OG | 6'3" | 240 | 23 | | |
| Frank Morze | C | 6'4" | 264 | 27 | | |
| Dan Colchico | DE | 6'3" | 236 | 24 | | |
| Lou Cordileone | DE | 6' | 245 | 24 | | |
| Charlie Krueger | DE | 6'4" | 245 | 25 | 2 | |
| Roland Lakes | OT-DE | 6'4" | 247 | 21 | | |
| Monte Clark | DT | 6'6" | 260 | 24 | | |
| Leo Nomellini | DT | 6'3" | 262 | 36 | | |
| Bob Harrison | LB | 6'2" | 220 | 24 | 2 | |
| Matt Hazeltine | LB | 6'1" | 220 | 28 | 1 | |
| Carl Kammerer | LB | 6'3" | 237 | 24 | | |
| Gorden Kelley | LB | 6'3" | 230 | 23 | 1 | |
| Dave Baker | DB | 6' | 193 | 24 | 6 | |
| Eddie Dove | DB | 6'2" | 180 | 24 | 3 | |
| Jim Johnson | DB | 6'2" | 190 | 23 | 5 | |
| Jerry Mertens | DB | 6' | 183 | 25 | | |
| Jimmy Ridlon | DB | 6'1" | 177 | 26 | | |
| Abe Woodson | HB-DB | 5'11" | 188 | 26 | 1 | 12 |
| John Brodie | QB | 6'1" | 186 | 26 | | 12 |
| Billy Kilmer | QB | 6' | 190 | 21 | | 60 |
| Bob Waters | QB | 6'2" | 184 | 23 | | 18 |
| Don McIlhenny | HB | 6' | 185 | 26 | | |
| Dale Messer | HB | 5'10" | 175 | 24 | | |
| Ray Norton | HB | 6'2" | 184 | 24 | | |
| J.D. Smith | FB-HB | 6'1" | 200 | 28 | | 54 |
| Bill Cooper | FB | 6'1" | 215 | 22 | | 6 |
| C.R. Roberts | FB | 6'3" | 197 | 25 | | 6 |
| Bernie Casey | OE | 6'4" | 215 | 22 | | 6 |
| Clyde Conner | OE | 6'2" | 190 | 28 | | 6 |
| R.C. Owens | OE | 6'3" | 195 | 26 | | 36 |
| Monte Stickles | OE | 6'4" | 230 | 23 | | 30 |
| Aaron Thomas | OE | 6'3" | 208 | 23 | | 12 |
| Tommy Davis | K | 6' | 212 | 26 | | 80 |

## LOS ANGELES RAMS 4-10-0 Bob Waterfield

Scores of Each Game:

| | | |
|---|---|---|
| 24 | Baltimore | 27 |
| 17 | CHICAGO | 21 |
| 24 | PITTSBURGH | 14 |
| 0 | San Francisco | 35 |
| 13 | Detroit | 14 |
| 14 | New York | 24 |
| 10 | DETROIT | 28 |
| 31 | MINNESOTA | 17 |
| 17 | SAN FRANCISCO | 7 |
| 17 | Green Bay | 35 |
| 24 | Chicago | 28 |
| 21 | Minnesota | 42 |
| 34 | BALTIMORE | 17 |
| 17 | GREEN BAY | 24 |

| Use Name | Pos. | Hgt | Wgt | Age | Int | Pts |
|---|---|---|---|---|---|---|
| Jim Boeke | OT | 6'5" | 245 | 22 | | |
| Willie Hector | OT | 6'2" | 220 | 21 | | |
| Frank Varrichione | OT | 6'1" | 235 | 29 | | |
| Charley Cowan | OG | 6'4" | 250 | 23 | | |
| Roy Hord | OG | 6'4" | 250 | 23 | | |
| Joe Scibelli | OG | 6'1" | 250 | 22 | | |
| Bruce Tarbox | OG | 6'2" | 230 | 22 | | |
| Art Hunter | C | 6'4" | 248 | 28 | | |
| Deacon Jones | DE | 6'5" | 240 | 22 | | |
| Lamar Lundy | DE | 6'7" | 235 | 26 | | |
| John Baker | DT-DE | 6'6" | 290 | 26 | | |
| Urban Henry | DT | 6'4" | 265 | 26 | | |
| John Lovetere | DT | 6'4" | 280 | 24 | | |
| George Strugar | DT | 6'5" | 258 | 26 | 1 | |
| Bill Jobko | LB | 6'2" | 220 | 25 | 1 | |
| Bob Long | LB | 6'3" | 235 | 27 | 1 | |
| Marlin McKeever | LB | 6'1" | 230 | 21 | | |
| Jack Pardee | LB | 6'2" | 225 | 25 | 1 | |
| Les Richter | LB | 6'3" | 235 | 30 | 4 | |
| Charley Britt | DB | 6'2" | 185 | 23 | 5 | |
| Ross Coyle | DB | 6'1" | 200 | 28 | 6 | |
| Lindon Crow | DB | 6'1" | 200 | 28 | 6 | |
| Alvin Hall | DB | 6' | 193 | 28 | | |
| Elbert Kimbrough | DB | 5'11" | 195 | 22 | | |
| Ed Meador | DB | 5'11" | 185 | 24 | 1 | |
| Clendon Thomas | DB | 6'2" | 192 | 24 | 3 | |
| Zeke Bratkowski | QB | 6'2" | 203 | 29 | | 18 |
| Frank Ryan | QB | 6'3" | 200 | 25 | | |
| Jon Arnett | HB | 5'11" | 194 | 26 | | 30 |
| Pervis Atkins | HB | 6'1" | 195 | 25 | | |
| Ollie Matson | HB | 6'2" | 210 | 31 | | 30 |
| Tom Wilson | HB | 6' | 204 | 28 | | 6 |
| Dick Bass | FB | 5'10" | 200 | 24 | | 30 |
| Joe Marconi | FB | 6'2" | 225 | 27 | | 24 |
| Frank Williams | FB | 6'2" | 215 | 29 | | |
| Duane Allen | OE | 6'4" | 210 | 23 | | 12 |
| Carroll Dale | OE | 6'1" | 195 | 23 | | 12 |
| Jim Phillips | OE | 6'1" | 198 | 24 | | 30 |
| Danny Villanueva | K | 5'11" | 200 | 23 | | 71 |

Gene Brito — Illness

## MINNESOTA VIKINGS 3-11-0 Norm Van Brocklin

Scores of Each Game:

| | | |
|---|---|---|
| 37 | CHICAGO | 13 |
| 7 | Dallas | 21 |
| 33 | Baltimore | 34 |
| 0 | DALLAS | 28 |
| 24 | SAN FRANCISCO | 38 |
| 7 | GREEN BAY | 33 |
| 10 | Green Bay | 28 |
| 17 | Los Angeles | 31 |
| 28 | BALTIMORE | 20 |
| 10 | DETROIT | 37 |
| 28 | San Francisco | 38 |
| 42 | LOS ANGELES | 21 |
| 7 | Detroit | 13 |
| 35 | Chicago | 52 |

| Use Name | Pos. | Hgt | Wgt | Age | Int | Pts |
|---|---|---|---|---|---|---|
| Bob Denton | OT | 6'4" | 240 | 27 | | |
| Frank Youso | OT | 6'4" | 260 | 25 | | |
| Paul Dickson | DT-OT | 6'5" | 250 | 24 | | |
| Grady Alderman | OG | 6'2" | 235 | 22 | | |
| Jerry Huth | OG | 6' | 228 | 28 | | |
| Ken Petersen | OG | 6'2" | 235 | 22 | | |
| Mike Rabold | OG | 6'2" | 238 | 23 | | |
| Bill Lapham | C | 6'3" | 250 | 27 | | |
| Don Joyce | DE | 6'3" | 250 | 31 | | |
| Jim Leo | DE | 6'1" | 225 | 23 | | |
| Jim Marshall | DE | 6'3" | 230 | 23 | | |
| Lebron Shields | DE | 6'4" | 245 | 24 | | |
| Bill Bishop | DT | 6'4" | 248 | 30 | | |
| Ed Culpepper | DT | 6'1" | 255 | 27 | | |
| Jim Prestel | DT | 6'5" | 250 | 24 | | |
| Dick Grecni | LB | 6'1" | 230 | 23 | 1 | |
| Rip Hawkins | LB | 6'3" | 230 | 22 | 5 | |
| Clancy Osborne | LB | 6'3" | 217 | 26 | 4 | |
| Karl Rubke | C-LB | 6'4" | 240 | 25 | 1 | |
| Dean Derby (from PIT) | DB | 6' | 190 | 27 | 3 | |
| Jack Morris | DB | 6' | 190 | 29 | 2 | |
| Rich Mostardi | DB | 5'11" | 188 | 23 | 2 | |
| Dick Pesonen | DB | 6' | 190 | 23 | 1 | |
| Justin Rowland | DB | 6'2" | 188 | 23 | 1 | |
| Charlie Sumner | DB | 6'1" | 195 | 31 | 2 | |
| Will Sherman | HB-DB | 6'2" | 197 | 32 | | |
| George Shaw | QB | 6'1" | 180 | 28 | | |
| Fran Tarkenton | QB | 6'1" | 190 | 21 | | 30 |
| Jamie Caleb | HB | 6'1" | 210 | 24 | | |
| Billy Gault | HB | 6'1" | 185 | 24 | | |
| Tommy Mason | HB | 6' | 195 | 22 | | 18 |
| Hugh McElhenny | HB | 6'1" | 198 | 32 | | 42 |
| Ray Hayes | FB | 6'3" | 235 | 26 | | 12 |
| Doug Mayberry | FB | 6'1" | 225 | 24 | | |
| Mel Triplett | FB | 6'1" | 215 | 29 | | 6 |
| Dave Middleton | OE | 6'1" | 190 | 28 | | 12 |
| Fred Murphy | OE | 6'3" | 205 | 23 | | |
| Jerry Reichow | OE | 6'2" | 220 | 26 | | 66 |
| Gordon Smith | OE | 6'2" | 200 | 22 | | 24 |
| A.D. Williams | OE | 6'2" | 210 | 28 | | 6 |
| Mike Mercer | K | 6' | 220 | 25 | | 63 |

## WESTERN CONFERENCE – Continued

### CHICAGO BEARS

**RUSHING**

| Last Name | No. | Yds | Avg | TD |
|---|---|---|---|---|
| Galimore | 153 | 707 | 4.6 | 4 |
| Casares | 135 | 588 | 4.4 | 8 |
| Wade | 45 | 255 | 5.7 | 2 |
| Bivins | 43 | 188 | 4.4 | 1 |
| B. Brown | 22 | 81 | 3.7 | 0 |
| J. Morris | 8 | 49 | 6.1 | 0 |
| E. Brown | 13 | 18 | 1.4 | 0 |
| Smith | 3 | 6 | 2.0 | 0 |
| Adams | 14 | −2 | −0.1 | 1 |

**RECEIVING**

| Last Name | No. | Yds | Avg | TD |
|---|---|---|---|---|
| Ditka | 56 | 1076 | 19 | 12 |
| J. Morris | 36 | 548 | 15 | 4 |
| Galimore | 33 | 502 | 15 | 3 |
| Farrington | 21 | 349 | 17 | 4 |
| Coia | 12 | 249 | 21 | 3 |
| Casares | 8 | 69 | 9 | 0 |
| Dooley | 6 | 90 | 15 | 0 |
| Adams | 5 | 80 | 16 | 0 |
| Bivins | 4 | −9 | −2 | 0 |
| Hill | 3 | 51 | 17 | 0 |
| B. Brown | 2 | 6 | 3 | 0 |

**PUNT RETURNS**

| Last Name | No. | Yds | Avg | TD |
|---|---|---|---|---|
| J. Morris | 23 | 155 | 7 | 0 |
| Petitbon | 2 | 9 | 5 | 0 |
| Taylor | 1 | 4 | 4 | 0 |
| L. Morris | 1 | 2 | 2 | 0 |

**KICKOFF RETURNS**

| Last Name | No. | Yds | Avg | TD |
|---|---|---|---|---|
| Bivins | 25 | 668 | 27 | 0 |
| Taylor | 14 | 379 | 27 | 0 |
| Galimore | 5 | 82 | 16 | 0 |
| B. Brown | 4 | 54 | 14 | 0 |
| J. Morris | 2 | 46 | 23 | 0 |
| Smith | 1 | 18 | 18 | 0 |

**PASSING – PUNTING – KICKING**

PASSING

| Last Name | Att | Comp | % | Yds | Yd/Att | TD | Int− | % | RK |
|---|---|---|---|---|---|---|---|---|---|
| Wade | 250 | 139 | 56 | 2258 | 9.0 | 22 | 13− | 5 | 2 |
| E. Brown | 98 | 46 | 47 | 742 | 7.6 | 4 | 11− | 11 | |
| Adams | 1 | 1 | 100 | 11 | 11.0 | 0 | 0− | 0 | |

PUNTING

| Last Name | No | Avg |
|---|---|---|
| E. Brown | 58 | 42.2 |
| Adams | 2 | 28.0 |

KICKING

| Last Name | XP | Att | % | FG | Att | % |
|---|---|---|---|---|---|---|
| LeClerc | 40 | 41 | 98 | 10 | 24 | 42 |
| E. Brown | 1 | 1 | 100 | 1 | 2 | 50 |
| George | 0 | 0 | 0 | 0 | 1 | 0 |

### SAN FRANCISCO FORTY NINERS

**RUSHING**

| Last Name | No. | Yds | Avg | TD |
|---|---|---|---|---|
| Smith | 167 | 823 | 4.9 | 8 |
| Kilmer | 96 | 509 | 5.3 | 10 |
| Roberts | 63 | 338 | 5.4 | 1 |
| Waters | 47 | 233 | 5.0 | 3 |
| Brodie | 28 | 90 | 3.2 | 2 |
| McIlhenny | 10 | 34 | 3.4 | 0 |
| Woodson | 14 | 23 | 1.6 | 0 |
| Cooper | 8 | 17 | 2.1 | 1 |
| Messer | 3 | 13 | 4.3 | 0 |
| Norton | 2 | −2 | −1.0 | 0 |
| A. Thomas | 1 | −15 | −15.0 | 0 |
| Owens | 0 | 23 | 0.0 | 1 |

**RECEIVING**

| Last Name | No. | Yds | Avg | TD |
|---|---|---|---|---|
| Owens | 55 | 1032 | 19 | 5 |
| Stickles | 43 | 794 | 18 | 5 |
| Smith | 28 | 343 | 12 | 1 |
| A. Thomas | 15 | 301 | 20 | 2 |
| Conner | 11 | 177 | 16 | 1 |
| Casey | 10 | 185 | 19 | 1 |
| Roberts | 10 | 83 | 8 | 0 |
| Woodson | 8 | 74 | 9 | 0 |
| Messer | 3 | 33 | 11 | 0 |
| McIlhenny | 1 | 6 | 6 | 0 |

**PUNT RETURNS**

| Last Name | No. | Yds | Avg | TD |
|---|---|---|---|---|
| Woodson | 16 | 172 | 11 | 1 |
| Dove | 6 | 49 | 8 | 0 |
| Messer | 2 | 11 | 6 | 0 |

**KICKOFF RETURNS**

| Last Name | No. | Yds | Avg | TD |
|---|---|---|---|---|
| Woodson | 27 | 782 | 29 | 1 |
| McIlhenny | 6 | 189 | 32 | 0 |
| Smith | 7 | 158 | 23 | 0 |
| Norton | 1 | 60 | 60 | 0 |
| Cooper | 3 | 44 | 15 | 0 |
| Messer | 3 | 36 | 12 | 0 |
| Kammerer | 1 | 18 | 18 | 0 |

**PASSING – PUNTING – KICKING**

PASSING

| Last Name | Att | Comp | % | Yds | Yd/Att | TD | Int− | % | RK |
|---|---|---|---|---|---|---|---|---|---|
| Brodie | 283 | 155 | 55 | 2588 | 9.1 | 14 | 12− | 4 | 5 |
| Kilmer | 34 | 19 | 56 | 286 | 8.4 | 0 | 4− | 12 | |
| Waters | 28 | 13 | 46 | 183 | 6.5 | 1 | 2− | 7 | |
| Smith | 1 | 0 | 0 | 0 | 0.0 | 0 | 1− | 100 | |

PUNTING

| Last Name | No | Avg |
|---|---|---|
| Davis | 50 | 45.4 |
| Kilmer | 9 | 40.4 |

KICKING

| Last Name | XP | Att | % | FG | Att | % |
|---|---|---|---|---|---|---|
| Davis | 44 | 44 | 100 | 12 | 22 | 55 |

### LOS ANGELES RAMS

**RUSHING**

| Last Name | No. | Yds | Avg | TD |
|---|---|---|---|---|
| Arnett | 158 | 609 | 3.9 | 4 |
| Bass | 98 | 608 | 6.2 | 4 |
| Wilson | 44 | 220 | 5.0 | 1 |
| Matson | 24 | 181 | 7.5 | 2 |
| Marconi | 36 | 146 | 4.1 | 3 |
| Ryan | 38 | 139 | 3.7 | 0 |
| Bratkowski | 12 | 36 | 3.0 | 3 |
| Atkins | 5 | 19 | 3.8 | 0 |

**RECEIVING**

| Last Name | No. | Yds | Avg | TD |
|---|---|---|---|---|
| Phillips | 78 | 1092 | 14 | 5 |
| Dale | 35 | 561 | 16 | 2 |
| Matson | 29 | 537 | 19 | 3 |
| Arnett | 28 | 194 | 7 | 0 |
| Bass | 16 | 145 | 9 | 0 |
| Atkins | 5 | 67 | 13 | 0 |
| Marconi | 4 | 20 | 5 | 1 |
| Allen | 2 | 80 | 40 | 2 |
| Wilson | 1 | 12 | 12 | 0 |
| Scibelli | 1 | 1 | 1 | 0 |

**PUNT RETURNS**

| Last Name | No. | Yds | Avg | TD |
|---|---|---|---|---|
| Bass | 4 | 109 | 27 | 1 |
| Arnett | 10 | 75 | 8 | 0 |

**KICKOFF RETURNS**

| Last Name | No. | Yds | Avg | TD |
|---|---|---|---|---|
| Bass | 23 | 698 | 30 | 0 |
| Arnett | 25 | 653 | 26 | 1 |
| Atkins | 4 | 77 | 19 | 0 |
| Varrichione | 3 | 23 | 8 | 0 |
| Jones | 1 | 12 | 12 | 0 |

**PASSING – PUNTING – KICKING**

PASSING

| Last Name | Att | Comp | % | Yds | Yd/Att | TD | Int− | % | RK |
|---|---|---|---|---|---|---|---|---|---|
| Bratkowski | 230 | 124 | 54 | 1547 | 6.7 | 8 | 13− | 6 | 13 |
| Ryan | 142 | 72 | 51 | 1115 | 7.9 | 5 | 7− | 5 | 10 |
| Arnett | 13 | 3 | 23 | 47 | 3.6 | 0 | 1− | 8 | |
| Villanueva | 1 | 0 | 0 | 0 | 0.0 | 0 | 0− | 0 | |

PUNTING

| Last Name | No | Avg |
|---|---|---|
| Villanueva | 46 | 40.1 |
| Bratkowski | 12 | 38.2 |
| Marconi | 6 | 44.2 |

KICKING

| Last Name | XP | Att | % | FG | Att | % |
|---|---|---|---|---|---|---|
| Villanueva | 32 | 32 | 100 | 13 | 27 | 48 |

### MINNESOTA VIKINGS

**RUSHING**

| Last Name | No. | Yds | Avg | TD |
|---|---|---|---|---|
| McElhenny | 120 | 570 | 4.8 | 3 |
| Triplett | 80 | 407 | 5.1 | 4 |
| Hayes | 73 | 319 | 4.4 | 2 |
| Tarkenton | 56 | 308 | 5.5 | 5 |
| Mason | 60 | 226 | 3.8 | 3 |
| Mayberry | 13 | 40 | 3.1 | 0 |
| Shaw | 10 | 39 | 3.9 | 0 |
| Caleb | 3 | 11 | 3.7 | 0 |
| Reichow | 3 | 9 | 3.0 | 0 |
| Mercer | 1 | −32 | −32.0 | 0 |

**RECEIVING**

| Last Name | No. | Yds | Avg | TD |
|---|---|---|---|---|
| Reichow | 50 | 859 | 17 | 11 |
| McElhenny | 37 | 283 | 8 | 3 |
| Middleton | 30 | 444 | 15 | 2 |
| Mason | 20 | 122 | 6 | 0 |
| Hayes | 16 | 121 | 8 | 0 |
| Williams | 13 | 174 | 13 | 0 |
| Smith | 12 | 320 | 27 | 4 |
| Triplett | 10 | 41 | 4 | 0 |
| Sherman | 2 | 40 | 20 | 0 |
| Mayberry | 2 | 18 | 9 | 0 |
| Caleb | 2 | −8 | −4 | 0 |

**PUNT RETURNS**

| Last Name | No. | Yds | Avg | TD |
|---|---|---|---|---|
| McElhenny | 8 | 155 | 19 | 1 |
| Mason | 14 | 146 | 10 | 0 |
| Caleb | 1 | 8 | 8 | 0 |

**KICKOFF RETURNS**

| Last Name | No. | Yds | Avg | TD |
|---|---|---|---|---|
| Mason | 25 | 603 | 24 | 0 |
| Caleb | 22 | 504 | 23 | 0 |
| Rowland | 8 | 175 | 22 | 0 |
| Pesonen | 6 | 136 | 23 | 0 |
| McElhenny | 2 | 59 | 30 | 0 |
| Triplett | 3 | 41 | 14 | 0 |
| Gault | 2 | 41 | 21 | 0 |
| Leo | 3 | 9 | 3 | 0 |
| Hayes | 1 | 0 | 0 | 0 |

**PASSING – PUNTING – KICKING**

PASSING

| Last Name | Att | Comp | % | Yds | Yd/Att | TD | Int− | % | RK |
|---|---|---|---|---|---|---|---|---|---|
| Tarkenton | 280 | 157 | 56 | 1997 | 7.1 | 18 | 17− | 6 | 7 |
| Shaw | 91 | 46 | 51 | 530 | 5.8 | 4 | 4− | 4 | |
| Reichow | 3 | 0 | 0 | 0 | 0.0 | 0 | 1− | 33 | |
| Caleb | 1 | 0 | 0 | 0 | 0.0 | 0 | 0− | 0 | |
| Mason | 1 | 0 | 0 | 0 | 0.0 | 0 | 0− | 0 | |
| McElhenny | 1 | 0 | 0 | 0 | 0.0 | 0 | 0− | 0 | |

PUNTING

| Last Name | No | Avg |
|---|---|---|
| Mercer | 63 | 39.0 |

KICKING

| Last Name | XP | Att | % | FG | Att | % |
|---|---|---|---|---|---|---|
| Mercer | 36 | 37 | 97 | 9 | 21 | 43 |

# 1961 A.F.L. The Feuding Ends at the Altar

Commissioner Joe Foss had enough problems to keep him busy this year. His authority to govern the league was actually at stake in one incident. To get a jump on the NFL in signing rookies, the team owners conducted a secret draft of college seniors in November, with each club taking six name players. Foss, who set the date for the draft in December, was not informed of this draft, and when he found out about it he declared it invalid. A potential revolt of the owners narrowed down to a public feud between Foss and New York Titan owner Harry Wismer. The Titans had selected Syracuse runner Ernie Davis in the November draft that Foss nullified, and when Buffalo picked Davis in the official December draft Wismer let loose his full vocal fury on Foss. Despite Wismer's calls for Foss's ouster, the commissioner stayed in office, directed the official draft, and won a five-year renewal of his contract from the owners when the season ended. The most amazing development came in the spring of 1962 when Foss was Wismer's best man at his wedding.

Attendance around the league also troubled Foss. League attendance rose a slight amount, up to 17,000, and Houston, Buffalo, Boston, and San Diego showed increases in home attendance. In these cases, though, it was generally a case of going from horrible to merely bad. The AFL was providing exciting, wide-open games for television, but fans did not yet think it reasonable to pay to see these new teams play.

The anti-trust suit filed by the AFL against the NFL was still going through the judicial process, so the main confrontation between the two leagues was still taking place at the box office and in the signing of rookie players. The NFL was winning on all fronts in the attendance war, and the old league also grabbed off the lion's share of graduating seniors from the class of 1961. With the element of surprise gone, the AFL signed only a handful of name collegians, among them Ken Rice, Art Baker, E. J. Holub, and Earl Faison.

The league also signed a new player from a different route, one who had played out his option in the NFL. Willard Dewveall, an offensive end with the Chicago Bears, played through 1960 without signing a new contract and agreed to terms with the Houston Oilers for the 1961 season. Dewveall thus became the first player to jump to the AFL from the active ranks of the NFL.

While new players were coming into the league, some of the old ones were lost to the federal activation of Reserve units in response to the Berlin crisis. The activated players all were stationed in the continental United States, and most were able to make the league games on weekend passes. These weekday soldiers and weekend football warriors included Ron Mix, Larry Grantham, Ross O'Hanley, Proverb Jacobs, Richie Lucas, Bill Roehnelt, George McGee, Oscar Lofton, John Jelacik, and Herm Urenda.

A new city also joined the circuit as owner Barron Hilton picked up his Los Angeles Chargers and transplanted them in the virgin soil of San Diego. Attendance in San Diego topped that of Los Angeles, but the Chargers still lost money while winning on the field.

One innovation by the league this season was the scheduling of an All-Star Game after the season to showcase the league's talent. Although some NFL boosters snickered at the contest, it provided one more television date for the league to win new fans.

## EASTERN DIVISION

**Houston Oilers**—The Oilers were mired in last place with a 1-3-1 record when owner Bud Adams canned head coach Lou Rymkus and replaced him with assistant Wally Lemm. The club's fortunes immediately turned around, as the Oilers won all their remaining nine games with a blistering offensive blitzkrieg. Lemm gave the quarterback job back to George Blanda, whom Rymkus had benched in favor of Jacky Lee, and Blanda responded with a pro record of thirty-six touchdown passes, a pair of 400 passing-yards games, and reliable long-range place-kicking, including boots of 55 and 53 yards. Charley Hennigan and Bill Groman were Blanda's deep targets, while Billy Cannon and Charley Tolar punched out yardage on the ground at a steady clip. The Oilers took over first place by beating Boston 27-15 on November 12, and they kept on wining right to the end. Coach Lemm summed up his perfect relief job by saying, "I feel like someone who inherited a million dollars in tarnished silverware. All I did was polish it."

**Boston Patriots**—Like the Oilers, the Patriots profited from a mid-season switch in coaches. After Mike Holovak succeeded Lou Saban as head coach, the Patriots won seven of nine games to streak into first place, only to have the Oilers win nine out of nine over the same span to win the title. The Boston attack featured no stars but still was second in the league in points scored. Butch Songin and Babe Parilli, a pair of senior citizens, shared the quarterback job and found converted defensive back Gino Cappelletti their favorite receiver. Cappelletti's kicking, however, was the spearhead of the Boston attack and won him the AFL scoring title. The Pats lost only to Houston over the last eight games, but that one loss was enough to foil the late-season drive.

**New York Titans**—Owner Harry Wismer made news this year. He made news with his feud with coach Sammy Baugh. He made news by publicly calling for Commissioner Joe Foss's ouster and more news when they finally made up. And he made news by announcing that his losses for 1960 and 1961 totaled $1.2 million. Wismer made more news than his football team, which played its games in virtual privacy. Three wins in the first four games got the Titans out to an early lead in the East, but a rash of injuries plus hot streaks by Houston and Boston pushed New York back into third place. Although fullback Billy Mathis developed into a bruising runner, the Titans still relied on Al Dorow's passes to Don Maynard and Art Powell for most of the offense. But while the Titans moved well through the air, enemy passers found the New York secondary easy pickings in return.

**Buffalo Bills**—In a league not known for great quarterbacks, the Bills had the worst quarterback situation. Ex-Redskin M. C. Reynolds, sophomore Johnny Green, and ex-Lion Warren Raab were uniformly unimpressive, and the offense sputtered despite some fine rookies in the lineup. Fullback Art Baker contributed power running, end Glenn Bass injected speed into the attack after being cut by San Diego, and Al Bemiller, Billy Shaw, Stew Barber, and Ken Rice all won jobs in the offensive line. But without a competent quarterback, the Bills had to rely on the defense to stay competitive. Lavern Torczon, Chuck McMurtry, Archie Matsos, and Billy Atkins stood out as defenders, but the unbalanced team effort cost head coach Buster Ramsey his job at the end of the season.

## WESTERN DIVISION

**San Diego Chargers**—The Chargers celebrated their move to San Diego by winning their first eleven games to make a shambles out of the Western Division race. Head coach and general manager Sid Gillman built his defensive unit into the league's best with the addition of three excellent rookies. End Earl Faison put steady pressure on enemy passers, tackle Ernie Ladd contributed 315 pounds of muscle to the center of the line, and middle linebacker Chuck Allen, a lightly regarded twenty-eighth draft choice, was a sensation until breaking his ankle late in the year. With Dick Harris and Charley McNeil heading up a solid secondary, the San Diego defense had no weak spots. The offense held up its end of the bargain, with Jack Kemp, Paul Lowe, Dave Kocourek, and Ron Mix starring. But the team's real star was Gillman, one of the few AFL general managers who was successfully signing most of the rookies on his draft list.

**Dallas Texans**—The Texans matched the Chargers in signing blue-chip rookies but fell farther behind them in the standings. Professional debuts by Jim Tyrer, Jerry Mays, E. J. Holub, and Dave Grayson did not prevent a slump by the defense and the team's dropping below .500 for the season. After winning three of their first four games, the Texans went into a six-game losing streak that ended the Western Division race. The team's passing attack did not live up to expectations, as quarterback Cotton Davidson was very erratic, but the running corps of Abner Haynes, Jack Spikes, Frank Jackson, and Bo Dickinson led the league in rushing yardage. Both lines had weak links, though, and suffered periodic breakdowns, throwing a mid-season monkey wrench into high pre-season hopes.

**Denver Broncos**—Without a balanced offensive diet, the Broncos grew weaker as the season progressed. The Denver running attack was dead last in the league, with the offense totally dependent on the passing of Frank Tripuka and George Herring. The Broncos threw the ball so often that split end Lionel Taylor set a new professional record with 100 catches for the season, not bad for a man the Chicago Bears had cut two years ago. Taylor's strong suit was his glue-fingered hands, but his lack of speed was underlined by his scoring only four touchdowns on the 100 receptions. After seven games, the Broncos had a respectable 3-4 record, but by then enemy defenses had wised up to the Denver air show. The Broncos lost their last seven games, and coach Frankie Filchock lost his job in the process.

**Oakland Raiders**—When the Raiders lost their first game 55-0 to Houston and their second game 44-0 to San Diego, the tone for a disastrous season was set. Coach Ernie Erdelatz was fired after the two opening massacres, but replacement Marty Feldman couldn't do much better with this squad. The Raiders scored the fewest points in the league, allowed the most points, and attracted minuscule crowds to their home games on the foreign turf of San Francisco's Candlestick Park. Not all the Raider players were inept, only most of them. Center Jim Otto won praise as the league's best at his position, Fred Williamson played well at cornerback, and halfback Clem Daniels showed promise after being picked up as a free agent. But a pair of mid-season victories over Denver and Buffalo was the best the Raiders could do as they lost their last six games of the season.

**FINAL TEAM STATISTICS**

| | OFFENSE | | | | | | | | DEFENSE | | | | | | | |
|---|---|---|---|---|---|---|---|---|---|---|---|---|---|---|---|---|
| | BOSTON | BUFFALO | DALLAS | DENVER | HOUSTON | NEW YORK | OAKLAND | SAN DIEGO | BOSTON | BUFFALO | DALLAS | DENVER | HOUSTON | NEW YORK | OAKLAND | SAN DIEGO |
| **FIRST DOWNS:** | | | | | | | | | | | | | | | | |
| Total | 238 | 243 | 247 | 219 | 293 | 247 | 200 | 208 | 243 | 200 | 238 | 233 | 235 | 242 | 280 | 224 |
| by Rushing | 93 | 92 | 112 | 66 | 97 | 100 | 65 | 81 | 72 | 61 | 89 | 83 | 87 | 100 | 135 | 79 |
| by Passing | 120 | 128 | 122 | 127 | 182 | 126 | 116 | 110 | 151 | 124 | 129 | 127 | 126 | 121 | 129 | 124 |
| by Penalty | 25 | 23 | 13 | 26 | 14 | 21 | 19 | 17 | 20 | 15 | 20 | 23 | 22 | 21 | 16 | 21 |
| **RUSHING:** | | | | | | | | | | | | | | | | |
| Number | 389 | 438 | 439 | 333 | 452 | 426 | 350 | 391 | 350 | 349 | 410 | 435 | 365 | 414 | 494 | 401 |
| Yards | 1675 | 1606 | 2183 | 1091 | 1896 | 1678 | 1234 | 1466 | 1041 | 1377 | 1525 | 1633 | 1634 | 1880 | 2382 | 1357 |
| Average Yards | 4.3 | 3.7 | 5.0 | 3.3 | 4.2 | 3.9 | 3.5 | 3.7 | 3.0 | 3.9 | 3.7 | 3.8 | 4.5 | 4.5 | 4.8 | 3.4 |
| Touchdowns | 15 | 18 | 23 | 11 | 15 | 17 | 10 | 24 | 9 | 9 | 18 | 17 | 17 | 20 | 36 | 7 |
| **PASSING:** | | | | | | | | | | | | | | | | |
| Attempts | 420 | 439 | 399 | 568 | 498 | 460 | 423 | 423 | 479 | 430 | 439 | 433 | 493 | 462 | 409 | 485 |
| Completions | 206 | 194 | 177 | 265 | 254 | 204 | 209 | 190 | 241 | 206 | 219 | 194 | 212 | 211 | 192 | 224 |
| Completion Percentage | 49.0 | 44.2 | 44.4 | 46.7 | 51.0 | 44.3 | 49.4 | 44.9 | 50.3 | 47.9 | 49.9 | 44.8 | 43.0 | 45.7 | 46.9 | 46.2 |
| Passing Yards | 2795 | 2786 | 2815 | 3004 | 4568 | 2733 | 2514 | 3121 | 3490 | 3237 | 3077 | 3060 | 2750 | 3044 | 2942 | 2736 |
| Average Yards per Attempt | 6.7 | 6.3 | 7.1 | 5.3 | 9.2 | 5.9 | 5.9 | 7.4 | 7.3 | 7.5 | 7.0 | 7.1 | 5.6 | 6.6 | 7.2 | 5.6 |
| Average Yards per Completion | 13.6 | 14.4 | 15.9 | 11.3 | 18.0 | 13.4 | 12.0 | 16.4 | 14.5 | 15.7 | 14.1 | 15.8 | 13.0 | 14.4 | 15.3 | 12.2 |
| Times Tackled Attempting to Pass | 33 | 63 | 24 | 33 | 14 | 41 | 45 | 28 | 44 | 36 | 34 | 33 | 41 | 31 | 20 | 42 |
| Yards Lost Attempting to Pass | 256 | 442 | 239 | 284 | 176 | 346 | 463 | 274 | 408 | 350 | 300 | 275 | 359 | 247 | 168 | 373 |
| Net Yards | 2539 | 2344 | 2576 | 2720 | 4392 | 2387 | 2051 | 2847 | 3082 | 2887 | 2777 | 2785 | 2391 | 2797 | 2774 | 2363 |
| Touchdowns | 29 | 15 | 18 | 18 | 48 | 20 | 17 | 17 | 27 | 28 | 20 | 30 | 13 | 26 | 22 | 16 |
| Interceptions | 21 | 25 | 27 | 45 | 29 | 32 | 28 | 25 | 22 | 29 | 24 | 26 | 33 | 25 | 24 | 49 |
| Percent Intercepted | 5.0 | 5.7 | 6.8 | 7.9 | 5.8 | 7.0 | 6.6 | 5.9 | 4.6 | 6.7 | 5.7 | 6.0 | 6.7 | 5.4 | 5.6 | 10.1 |
| **PUNTING:** | | | | | | | | | | | | | | | | |
| Number | 62 | 85 | 62 | 80 | 56 | 74 | 75 | 63 | 71 | 75 | 63 | 77 | 81 | 70 | 50 | 70 |
| Average Distance | 38.8 | 44.5 | 39.9 | 39.4 | 39.1 | 41.8 | 39.0 | 41.5 | 40.7 | 38.7 | 41.7 | 40.8 | 40.7 | 42.4 | 40.4 | 40.1 |
| **PUNT RETURNS:** | | | | | | | | | | | | | | | | |
| Number | 35 | 19 | 26 | 33 | 19 | 26 | 15 | 29 | 15 | 45 | 20 | 26 | 20 | 20 | 34 | 22 |
| Yards | 288 | 187 | 219 | 369 | 118 | 463 | 117 | 458 | 245 | 291 | 216 | 368 | 271 | 284 | 352 | 192 |
| Average Yards | 8.2 | 9.8 | 8.4 | 11.2 | 6.2 | 17.8 | 7.8 | 15.8 | 16.3 | 6.5 | 10.8 | 14.2 | 13.6 | 14.2 | 10.4 | 8.7 |
| Touchdowns | 2 | 0 | 0 | 2 | 0 | 2 | 0 | 2 | 2 | 1 | 1 | 0 | 0 | 0 | 1 | 1 |
| **KICKOFF RETURNS:** | | | | | | | | | | | | | | | | |
| Number | 49 | 57 | 53 | 66 | 43 | 66 | 68 | 39 | 53 | 54 | 65 | 42 | 66 | 51 | 45 | 65 |
| Yards | 1136 | 1208 | 1465 | 1501 | 940 | 1213 | 1383 | 642 | 1255 | 1112 | 1249 | 720 | 1481 | 1084 | 1066 | 1521 |
| Average Yards | 23.2 | 21.2 | 27.6 | 22.7 | 21.9 | 18.4 | 20.3 | 16.5 | 23.7 | 20.6 | 19.2 | 17.1 | 22.4 | 21.3 | 23.7 | 23.4 |
| Touchdowns | 2 | 1 | 1 | 1 | 0 | 0 | 0 | 0 | 1 | 1 | 1 | 1 | 1 | 1 | 0 | 0 |
| **INTERCEPTION RETURNS:** | | | | | | | | | | | | | | | | |
| Number | 22 | 29 | 24 | 26 | 33 | 25 | 24 | 49 | 21 | 25 | 27 | 45 | 29 | 32 | 28 | 25 |
| Yards | 326 | 311 | 418 | 355 | 528 | 315 | 285 | 929 | 198 | 398 | 424 | 818 | 407 | 670 | 280 | 272 |
| Average Yards | 14.8 | 10.7 | 17.4 | 13.7 | 16.0 | 12.6 | 11.9 | 19.0 | 9.4 | 15.9 | 15.7 | 18.2 | 14.0 | 20.9 | 10.0 | 10.9 |
| Touchdowns | 2 | 1 | 3 | 0 | 0 | 1 | 2 | 9 | 1 | 4 | 1 | 5 | 2 | 5 | 1 | 1 |
| **PENALTIES:** | | | | | | | | | | | | | | | | |
| Number | 64 | 65 | 89 | 60 | 83 | 60 | 53 | 88 | 67 | 76 | 62 | 98 | 57 | 86 | 62 | 54 |
| Yards | 659 | 549 | 874.5 | 560 | 889 | 585 | 456 | 682.5 | 661.5 | 693 | 619 | 799 | 588 | 869.5 | 524 | 501 |
| **FUMBLES:** | | | | | | | | | | | | | | | | |
| Number | 24 | 32 | 32 | 40 | 21 | 32 | 28 | 32 | 36 | 20 | 31 | 25 | 31 | 36 | 29 | 33 |
| Number Lost | 9 | 17 | 18 | 23 | 10 | 20 | 16 | 19 | 20 | 15 | 18 | 14 | 31 | 21 | 12 | 17 |
| **POINTS:** | | | | | | | | | | | | | | | | |
| Total | 413 | 294 | 334 | 251 | 513 | 301 | 237 | 396 | 313 | 342 | 343 | 432 | 242 | 390 | 458 | 219 |
| PAT (kick) Attempts | 50 | 31 | 40 | 27 | 66 | 39 | 25 | 50 | 40 | 42 | 38 | 55 | 26 | 48 | 53 | 26 |
| PAT (kick) Made | 48 | 29 | 37 | 27 | 65 | 37 | 24 | 43 | 40 | 41 | 37 | 51 | 22 | 46 | 50 | 23 |
| PAT (Rush or Pass) Attempts | 2 | 7 | 4 | 5 | 0 | 1 | 4 | 2 | 1 | 1 | 6 | 1 | 7 | 2 | 6 | 1 |
| PAT (Rush or Pass) Made | 1 | 4 | 3 | 3 | 0 | 0 | 2 | 1 | 0 | 1 | 3 | 1 | 2 | 1 | 6 | 1 |
| FG Attempts | 32 | 26 | 24 | 25 | 26 | 23 | 26 | 27 | 23 | 28 | 31 | 26 | 24 | 27 | 5 | 23 |
| FG Made | 17 | 9 | 7 | 8 | 16 | 8 | 11 | 13 | 9 | 13 | 12 | 13 | 6 | 14 | 12 | 10 |
| Percent FG Made | 53.1 | 34.6 | 29.2 | 32.0 | 61.5 | 34.8 | 42.3 | 48.1 | 39.1 | 46.4 | 38.7 | 50.0 | 25.0 | 51.9 | 44.4 | 43.5 |
| Safeties | 0 | 1 | 0 | 1 | 0 | 0 | 1 | 0 | 0 | 1 | 0 | 1 | 0 | 1 | 1 | |

## SCORING

| | | | | | |
|---|---|---|---|---|---|
| SAN DIEGO | 0 | 0 | 0 | 3 – | 3 |
| HOUSTON | 0 | 3 | 7 | 0 – | 10 |

**Second Quarter**
Hous.   Blanda, 46 yard field goal    8:06

**Third Quarter**
Hous.   Cannon, 35 yard pass from Blanda    11:39
     PAT—Blanda (kick)

**Fourth Quarter**
S.D.   Blair, 12 yard field goal    0:39

## TEAM STATISTICS

| S.D. | | HOUS. |
|---|---|---|
| 15 | First Downs—Total | 18 |
| 6 | First Downs—Rushing | 6 |
| 8 | First Downs—Passing | 8 |
| 1 | First Downs—Penalty | 4 |
| 2 | Fumbles—Number | 5 |
| 2 | Fumbles—Number Lost | 1 |
| 10 | Penalties—Number | 5 |
| 106 | Yards Penalized | 68 |
| 6 | Giveaways | 7 |
| 7 | Takeaways | 6 |
| +1 | Difference | –1 |

**1961 AFL CHAMPIONSHIP GAME**
December 24, at San Diego
(Attendance 29,556)

## Oiling the Defense

For a second straight year, the defensive units excelled in the AFL championship game. The Chargers and Oilers, repeat winners of their divisional races, both found interceptions easy to come by, the Chargers picking off six passes and the Oilers four. Played on a sunny, 59-degree Christmas Eve, the game was a showcase for turnovers, with seven fumbles plus all the interceptions thwarting most offensive drives. Neither club generated much offense in the first half, with the only score coming on a 46-yard field goal by George Blanda late in the second quarter. The Oilers, who hadn't lost a game since Wally Lemm took over as head coach three months back, stubbornly defended their 3-0 lead throughout the third quarter and added to it late in the period. The Oilers had the ball on the San Diego 35-yard line with a third-and-five situation when a strong Charger pass rush forced Blanda out of his protective pocket. Rolling to his right, Blanda saw halfback Billy Cannon open down the middle and hit him with a pass on the 17-yard line. Cannon made a leaping catch, sidestepped a defender, and raced into the end zone. Blanda's extra point made the score 10-0 and put a heavy load of pressure on the San Diego offense. With Jack Kemp throwing freely, the Chargers broke the ice with a 12-yard George Blair field goal in the first minute of the fourth quarter, but a final San Diego bid fell short when Houston's Julian Spence picked off a Kemp pass on the Oiler 30-yard line with under two minutes left in the game.

## INDIVIDUAL STATISTICS

**RUSHING**

| SAN DIEGO | No. | Yds. | Avg. | HOUSTON | No. | Yds. | Avg. |
|---|---|---|---|---|---|---|---|
| Roberson | 8 | 37 | 4.6 | Tolar | 16 | 52 | 3.3 |
| Lowe | 5 | 30 | 6.0 | Cannon | 15 | 48 | 3.2 |
| Lincoln | 3 | 7 | 2.3 | Blanda | 2 | -4 | -2.0 |
| Kemp | 4 | 5 | 1.3 | | 33 | 96 | 2.9 |
| | 20 | 79 | 4.0 | | | | |

**RECEIVING**

| SAN DIEGO | No. | Yds. | Avg. | HOUSTON | No. | Yds. | Avg. |
|---|---|---|---|---|---|---|---|
| Kocourek | 7 | 123 | 17.6 | Cannon | 5 | 53 | 10.6 |
| D. Norton | 3 | 48 | 16.0 | Hennigan | 5 | 43 | 8.6 |
| Flowers | 2 | 17 | 8.5 | Groman | 3 | 32 | 10.7 |
| Roberson | 1 | 11 | 11.0 | Dewveall | 2 | 10 | 5.0 |
| Lowe | 1 | 10 | 10.0 | Tolar | 2 | 2 | 1.0 |
| Scarpitto | 1 | 9 | 9.0 | McLeod | 1 | 20 | 20.0 |
| Hayes | 1 | 5 | 5.0 | | 18 | 160 | 8.9 |
| Lincoln | 1 | 3 | 3.0 | | | | |
| | 17 | 226 | 13.3 | | | | |

**PUNTING**

| SAN DIEGO | No. | | Avg. | HOUSTON | No. | | Avg. |
|---|---|---|---|---|---|---|---|
| Maguire | 6 | | 33.3 | J. Norton | 4 | | 41.5 |

**PUNT RETURNS**

| SAN DIEGO | No. | Yds. | Avg. | HOUSTON | | | |
|---|---|---|---|---|---|---|---|
| Lincoln | 1 | 16 | 16.0 | None | | | |

**KICKOFF RETURNS**

| SAN DIEGO | No. | Yds. | Avg. | HOUSTON | | | |
|---|---|---|---|---|---|---|---|
| Lowe | 1 | 27 | 27.0 | None | | | |
| Roberson | 1 | 23 | 23.0 | | | | |
| | 2 | 50 | 25.0 | | | | |

**INTERCEPTION RETURNS**

| SAN DIEGO | No. | Yds. | Avg. | HOUSTON | No. | Yds. | Avg. |
|---|---|---|---|---|---|---|---|
| Whitehead | 2 | 45 | 15.0 | Cline | 1 | 7 | 7.0 |
| McNeil | 2 | 15 | 7.5 | Glick | 1 | 0 | 0.0 |
| Zeman | 2 | 0 | 0.0 | Johnston | 1 | 0 | 0.0 |
| | 6 | 60 | 10.0 | Spence | 1 | 0 | 0.0 |
| | | | | | 4 | 7 | 1.8 |

**PASSING**

| SAN DIEGO | Att. | Comp. | Comp. Pct. | Yds. | Int. | Yds/Att. | Yds/Comp. | Yards Lost Tackled |
|---|---|---|---|---|---|---|---|---|
| Kemp | 32 | 17 | 53.1 | 226 | 4 | 7.1 | 13.3 | 6-49 |
| **HOUSTON** | | | | | | | | |
| Blanda | 40 | 18 | 45.0 | 160 | 5 | 4.0 | 8.9 | 0 |
| Gorman | 1 | 0 | 0.0 | 0 | 0 | — | — | 0 |
| | 41 | 18 | 43.9 | 160 | 6 | 3.9 | 8.9 | 0 |

## HOUSTON OILERS 10-3-1 Lou Rymkus  Wally Lemm

| Scores of Each Game | | Use Name | Pos. | Hgt | Wgt | Age | Int | Pts |
|---|---|---|---|---|---|---|---|---|
| 55 | OAKLAND | 0 | Al Jamison | OT | 6'5" | 245 | 24 | | |
| 24 | San Diego | 34 | Bob Kelly | OT | 6'3" | 250 | 21 | | |
| 21 | Dallas | 26 | Rich Michael | OT | 6'3" | 230 | 22 | | |
| 12 | BUFFALO | 22 | Leo Reed (to DEN) | OG | 6'4" | 240 | 21 | | |
| 31 | Boston | 31 | Bob Talamini | OG | 6'1" | 230 | 22 | | |
| 38 | DALLAS | 7 | Hogan Wharton | OG | 6'2" | 245 | 25 | | |
| 28 | Buffalo | 16 | Bob Schmidt | C | 6'4" | 245 | 24 | | |
| 55 | Denver | 14 | Dalva Allen | DE | 6'5" | 245 | 25 | | |
| 27 | BOSTON | 15 | Don Floyd | DE | 6'4" | 225 | 23 | | |
| 49 | NEW YORK | 13 | Dick Frey | OG-DE | 6'2" | 235 | 30 | | |
| 45 | DENVER | 14 | Byron Beams | DT | 6' | 238 | 30 | | |
| 33 | SAN DIEGO | 13 | Ed Husmann | DT | 6'4" | 240 | 24 | | |
| 48 | New York | 21 | George Shirkey | DT | 6'4" | 260 | 26 | 1 | |
| 47 | Oakland | 16 | Orville Trask | | | | | | |

| Use Name | Pos. | Hgt | Wgt | Age | Int | Pts |
|---|---|---|---|---|---|---|
| Ron Botcham | LB | 6'1" | 230 | 26 | | |
| Doug Cline | LB | 6'2" | 220 | 22 | 1 | 12 |
| Mike Dukes | LB | 6'3" | 230 | 25 | 2 | |
| John Guzik | LB | 6'3" | 228 | 24 | | |
| Gene Jones | LB | 6' | 200 | 24 | | |
| Jack Laraway | LB | 6'1" | 215 | 25 | 1 | |
| Dennit Morris | LB | 6'1" | 225 | 25 | 1 | |
| Tony Banfield | DB | 6'1" | 185 | 22 | 8 | |
| Freddy Glick | DB | 6'1" | 190 | 24 | 4 | |
| Mark Johnston | DB | 6' | 200 | 23 | 3 | 6 |
| Charley Milstead | DB | 6'2" | 190 | 23 | 2 | 1 |
| Jim Norton | DB | 6'3" | 190 | 22 | 9 | |
| Gary Wisener | DB | 6'1" | 205 | 23 | | |
| Julian Spence | FL-DB | 5'11" | 158 | 32 | 1 | |

| Use Name | Pos. | Hgt | Wgt | Age | Int | Pts |
|---|---|---|---|---|---|---|
| George Blanda | QB | 6'1" | 210 | 33 | | 112 |
| Jacky Lee | QB | 6'1" | 185 | 22 | | |
| Billy Cannon | HB | 6'1" | 212 | 24 | | 90 |
| Ken Hall (to STL-N) | HB | 6'1" | 210 | 25 | | 6 |
| Claude King | HB | 5'11" | 185 | 22 | | 18 |
| Dave Smith | FB | 6'1" | 210 | 24 | | 18 |
| Charley Tolar | FB | 5'7" | 200 | 23 | | 30 |
| Charley Hennigan | FL | 6' | 185 | 25 | | 72 |
| Willard Dewveall | OE | 6'4" | 220 | 24 | | 18 |
| Bill Groman | OE | 6' | 195 | 25 | | 108 |
| Bob McLeod | OE | 6'5" | 225 | 22 | | 12 |
| John White | OE | 6'4" | 230 | 23 | | 6 |

## BOSTON PATRIOTS 9-4-1 Lou Saban  Mike Holovak

| Scores of Each Game | | Use Name | Pos. | Hgt | Wgt | Age | Int | Pts |
|---|---|---|---|---|---|---|---|---|
| 20 | NEW YORK | 21 | Jerry DeLucca | OT | 6'3" | 250 | 25 | | |
| 45 | DENVER | 17 | Milt Graham | OT | 6'6" | 235 | 27 | | |
| 23 | Buffalo | 21 | Dick Klein (from PIT-N) | OT | 6'4" | 255 | 27 | | |
| 30 | New York | 37 | Charley Long | OT | 6'3" | 240 | 23 | | |
| 27 | SAN DIEGO | 38 | John Simerson | OT | 6'3" | 255 | 26 | | |
| 31 | HOUSTON | 31 | Charlie Leo | OG | 6' | 240 | 26 | | |
| 52 | BUFFALO | 21 | Willis Perkins (from HOU) | OG | 6' | 240 | 24 | | |
| 18 | Dallas | 17 | Tony Sardisco | OG | 6'2" | 235 | 28 | | |
| 28 | DALLAS | 21 | Walt Cudzik | C | 6'2" | 235 | 28 | | |
| 15 | Houston | 27 | Bob Yates | C | 6'3" | 230 | 22 | | |
| 20 | OAKLAND | 17 | Bob Dee | DE | 6'3" | 240 | 28 | | |
| 28 | Denver | 24 | Larry Eisenhauer | DE | 6'5" | 235 | 21 | | |
| 35 | Oakland | 21 | Leroy Moore | DE | 6' | 232 | 25 | | |
| 41 | San Diego | 0 | Houston Antwine | DT | 6'2" | 250 | 22 | | |
| | | | Jim Hunt | DT | 5'11" | 245 | 22 | | |
| | | | Paul Lindquist | DT | 6'3" | 265 | 23 | | |

| Use Name | Pos. | Hgt | Wgt | Age | Int | Pts |
|---|---|---|---|---|---|---|
| Tom Addison | LB | 6'3" | 235 | 25 | 4 | |
| Harry Jacobs | LB | 6'2" | 235 | 24 | | |
| Rommie Loudd | LB | 6'3" | 230 | 27 | 1 | |
| Frank Robotti | LB | 6' | 220 | 22 | | |
| Walter Beach | DB | 6' | 185 | 26 | 1 | |
| Fred Bruney | DB | 5'10" | 190 | 30 | 2 | |
| Ron Hall | DB | 6' | 190 | 24 | 2 | |
| Ross O'Hanley | DB | 6' | 175 | 22 | | |
| Al Romine | DB | 6'2" | 195 | 28 | | |
| Chuck Shonta | DB | 6' | 190 | 23 | 1 | |
| Bob Soltis | DB | 6'2" | 190 | 23 | 2 | |
| Bobby Towns | DB | 6'1" | 180 | 23 | | |
| Don Webb | DB | 5'10" | 180 | 22 | 5 | 24 |
| Clyde Washington | HB-DB | 6' | 195 | 23 | 4 | |

Oscar Lofton — Military Service

| Use Name | Pos. | Hgt | Wgt | Age | Int | Pts |
|---|---|---|---|---|---|---|
| Babe Parilli | QB | 6'1" | 190 | 31 | | 32 |
| Butch Songin | QB | 6'2" | 205 | 37 | | 6 |
| Tom Yewcic | HB-QB | 5'11" | 185 | 29 | | 6 |
| Ron Burton | HB | 5'10" | 190 | 24 | | 18 |
| Larry Garron | HB | 6' | 200 | 24 | | 36 |
| Ray Ratkowski | HB | 6' | 195 | 21 | | |
| Ger Schwedes | HB | 6'1" | 205 | 22 | | |
| Jim Crawford | FB | 6'1" | 205 | 26 | | 66 |
| Billy Lott | FL | 6' | 190 | 27 | | 147 |
| Gino Cappelletti | OE | 6' | 185 | 25 | | 54 |
| Jim Colclough | OE | 6'2" | 190 | 25 | | 6 |
| Joe Johnson | OE | 6'2" | 190 | 25 | | |
| Bill Kimber | OE | 6'1" | 195 | 25 | | 18 |
| Tom Stephens | | | | | | |

George McGee — Military Service

## NEW YORK TITANS 7-7-0 Sammy Baugh

| Scores of Each Game | | Use Name | Pos. | Hgt | Wgt | Age | Int | Pts |
|---|---|---|---|---|---|---|---|---|
| 21 | Boston | 20 | Gene Cockrell | OT | 6'3" | 247 | 28 | | |
| 31 | Buffalo | 41 | Moses Gray | OT | 6'3" | 260 | 23 | | |
| 35 | DENVER | 28 | Jack Klotz | OT | 6'5" | 260 | 27 | | |
| 37 | BOSTON | 30 | Ed Walsh | OT | 6'4" | 243 | 25 | | |
| 10 | SAN DIEGO | 25 | Tom Budrewicz | OG | 6'2" | 245 | 24 | | |
| 10 | Denver | 27 | John McMullan | OG | 6' | 244 | 26 | | |
| 14 | Oakland | 6 | Bob Mischak | OG | 6' | 240 | 28 | | |
| 13 | San Diego | 48 | Bob O'Neil | OG | 6'1" | 238 | 28 | | |
| 23 | OAKLAND | 12 | Roger Ellis | C | 6'3" | 233 | 23 | | |
| 13 | Houston | 49 | Mike Hudock | C | 6'2" | 245 | 26 | | |
| 21 | BUFFALO | 14 | Ed Cooke | DE | 6'4" | 250 | 26 | 3 | |
| 28 | Dallas | 7 | Nick Mumley | DE | 6'6" | 255 | 25 | | |
| 21 | HOUSTON | 48 | Bob Reifsnyder | DE | 6'2" | 260 | 24 | | |
| 24 | Dallas | 35 | Dick Guesman | DT | 6'4" | 255 | 25 | 39 | |
| | | | Proverb Jacobs | DT | 6'4" | 255 | 26 | | |
| | | | Tom Saidock | DT | 6'5" | 260 | 29 | | |
| | | | Sid Youngelman | DE-DT | 6'3" | 265 | 29 | | |

| Use Name | Pos. | Hgt | Wgt | Age | Int | Pts |
|---|---|---|---|---|---|---|
| Hubert Bobo | LB | 6'1" | 218 | 26 | 4 | |
| Jerry Fields | LB | 6'2" | 222 | 22 | | |
| Jim Furey | LB | 6' | 228 | 27 | | |
| Larry Grantham | LB | 6' | 205 | 22 | 1 | |
| Johnny Bookman | DB | 5'11" | 185 | 26 | 6 | |
| Dick Felt | DB | 6' | 180 | 28 | 4 | 6 |
| Don Flynn (from DAL) | DB | 6' | 205 | 26 | 2 | |
| Paul Hynes (from DAL) | DB | 6'1" | 210 | 21 | | |
| Dainard Paulson | DB | 5'11" | 190 | 24 | 1 | |
| Bert Rechichar | DB | 6'1" | 210 | 31 | | |
| Lee Riley | DB | 6'1" | 190 | 29 | 4 | |
| Junior Wren | DB | 6' | 192 | 31 | 1 | |

| Use Name | Pos. | Hgt | Wgt | Age | Int | Pts |
|---|---|---|---|---|---|---|
| Don Allard | QB | 6' | 190 | 25 | | |
| Al Dorow | QB | 6' | 195 | 31 | | 24 |
| Dick Jamieson | QB | 6'1" | 192 | 25 | | |
| Bob Scrabis | QB | 6'3" | 225 | 25 | | 6 |
| Jim Apple | HB | 6' | 200 | 22 | | |
| Dick Christy | HB | 5'10" | 195 | 25 | | 30 |
| Bob Renn | HB | 6' | 180 | 27 | | 6 |
| Bill Shockley (to BUF) | HB | 6' | 185 | 23 | | 25 |
| Mel West (from BOS) | HB | 5'9" | 190 | 22 | | 18 |
| Bob Brooks | FB | 6' | 215 | 21 | | |
| Bill Mathis | FB | 6'1" | 220 | 24 | | 48 |
| Don Maynard | FL | 6' | 185 | 25 | | 48 |
| Thurlow Cooper | OE | 6'4" | 228 | 28 | | 24 |
| Curley Johnson | OE | 6' | 215 | 26 | | |
| Art Powell | OE | 6'3" | 212 | 24 | | 30 |

## BUFFALO BILLS 6-8-0 Buster Ramsey

| Scores of Each Game | | Use Name | Pos. | Hgt | Wgt | Age | Int | Pts |
|---|---|---|---|---|---|---|---|---|
| 10 | DENVER | 22 | Don Chelf | OT | 6'3" | 235 | 26 | | |
| 41 | NEW YORK | 31 | Harold Olson | OT | 6'3" | 260 | 22 | | |
| 21 | BOSTON | 23 | Ken Rice | OT | 6'2" | 250 | 21 | | |
| 11 | SAN DIEGO | 19 | John Dittrich | OG | 6'1" | 240 | 28 | | |
| 22 | Houston | 12 | Ed Muelhaupt | OG | 6'3" | 230 | 25 | 6 | |
| 27 | DALLAS | 24 | Billy Shaw | OG | 6'2" | 240 | 21 | | |
| 21 | Boston | 52 | Wayne Wolf | OG | 6'2" | 243 | 22 | | |
| 16 | HOUSTON | 28 | Al Bemiller | C | 6'3" | 225 | 22 | | |
| 22 | OAKLAND | 31 | Lavern Torczon | DE | 6'2" | 235 | 25 | | |
| 30 | Dallas | 20 | Mack Yoho | DE | 6'2" | 240 | 25 | 1 | |
| 23 | Denver | 10 | Tom Day | DE | 6'2" | 245 | 26 | | |
| 14 | New York | 21 | Chuck McMurtry | DT | 6' | 285 | 23 | | |
| 26 | Oakland | 21 | John Scott | DT | 6'4" | 260 | 25 | | |
| 10 | San Diego | 28 | Jim Sorey | DT | 6'4" | 280 | 24 | | |

| Use Name | Pos. | Hgt | Wgt | Age | Int | Pts |
|---|---|---|---|---|---|---|
| Stew Barber | OT-LB | 6'3" | 235 | 22 | 3 | 6 |
| Ralph Felton | LB | 5'11" | 210 | 29 | 2 | |
| Joe Hergert | LB | 6'1" | 215 | 25 | 1 | 18 |
| Cotton Letner | LB | 6'1" | 215 | 24 | | |
| Archie Matsos | LB | 6' | 215 | 26 | 2 | |
| Billy Atkins | DB | 6'1" | 195 | 26 | 10 | 41 |
| Jim Crotty (from WAS-N) | DB | 5'11" | 190 | 23 | 2 | |
| Jack Johnson (to DAL) | DB | 6'3" | 200 | 27 | | |
| Billy Majors | DB | 6' | 175 | 22 | | |
| Richie McCabe | DB | 6'1" | 187 | 27 | 1 | |
| Don McDonald | DB | 5'11" | 185 | 24 | | 6 |
| Vern Valdez | DB | 5'11" | 190 | 25 | 2 | |
| Jim Wagstaff | DB | 6'2" | 190 | 25 | 3 | |

| Use Name | Pos. | Hgt | Wgt | Age | Int | Pts |
|---|---|---|---|---|---|---|
| Johnny Green | QB | 6'3" | 198 | 24 | | 6 |
| Tom O'Connell | QB | 5'11" | 180 | 29 | | |
| Warren Rabb | QB | 6'1" | 204 | 24 | | 2 |
| M. C. Reynolds | QB | 6' | 195 | 26 | | 24 |
| Richie Lucas | DB-HB-QB | 6' | 190 | 22 | 2 | 12 |
| Dewey Bohling (from NY) | HB | 5'11" | 190 | 22 | | 18 |
| Fred Brown | HB | 5'11" | 187 | 21 | | 12 |
| Wray Carlton | HB | 6'2" | 210 | 23 | | 24 |
| Dan Chamberlain | HB | 6'4" | 200 | 24 | | |
| Elbert Dubenion | HB | 6' | 190 | 26 | | 48 |
| Willmer Fowler | HB | 5'11" | 185 | 24 | | |
| Art Baker | FB | 6' | 220 | 23 | | 18 |
| Glenn Bass | OE | 6'2" | 190 | 22 | | |
| Monte Crockett | OE | 6'3" | 210 | 22 | | |
| Perry Richards | OE | 6'2" | 205 | 27 | | 18 |
| Tom Rychlec | OE | 6'3" | 220 | 27 | | 12 |

## HOUSTON OILERS

### RUSHING

| Last Name | No. | Yds | Avg | TD |
|---|---|---|---|---|
| Cannon | 200 | 948 | 4.7 | 6 |
| Tolar | 157 | 577 | 3.7 | 4 |
| Smith | 60 | 258 | 4.3 | 2 |
| King | 12 | 50 | 4.2 | 2 |
| Lee | 8 | 36 | 4.5 | 0 |
| Hall | 7 | 13 | 1.9 | 0 |
| Blanda | 7 | 12 | 1.7 | 0 |
| Groman | 1 | 2 | 2.0 | 1 |

### RECEIVING

| Last Name | No. | Yds | Avg | TD |
|---|---|---|---|---|
| Hennigan | 82 | 1746 | 21 | 12 |
| Groman | 50 | 1175 | 24 | 17 |
| Cannon | 43 | 586 | 14 | 9 |
| Tolar | 24 | 219 | 9 | 1 |
| McLeod | 14 | 172 | 12 | 2 |
| White | 13 | 238 | 18 | 1 |
| Dewveall | 12 | 200 | 17 | 3 |
| Smith | 10 | 131 | 13 | 1 |
| King | 3 | 83 | 28 | 1 |
| Hall | 1 | 20 | 20 | 1 |
| Spence | 1 | 14 | 14 | 0 |
| Blanda | 1 | −16 | −16 | 0 |

### PUNT RETURNS

| Last Name | No. | Yds | Avg | TD |
|---|---|---|---|---|
| Cannon | 9 | 70 | 8 | 0 |
| King | 7 | 32 | 5 | 0 |
| Smith | 1 | 15 | 15 | 0 |
| Hall | 2 | 1 | 1 | 0 |

### KICKOFF RETURNS

| Last Name | No. | Yds | Avg | TD |
|---|---|---|---|---|
| Cannon | 18 | 439 | 24 | 0 |
| King | 8 | 190 | 24 | 0 |
| Hall | 6 | 140 | 23 | 0 |
| Dukes | 4 | 57 | 14 | 0 |
| Tolar | 2 | 42 | 21 | 0 |
| Cline | 1 | 24 | 24 | 0 |
| Laraway | 1 | 22 | 22 | 0 |
| McLeod | 1 | 13 | 13 | 0 |
| Wharton | 1 | 8 | 8 | 0 |
| Smith | 1 | 5 | 5 | 0 |

### PASSING – PUNTING – KICKING Statistics

**PASSING**

| Last Name | Att | Comp | % | Yds | Yd/Att | TD | Int–% | RK |
|---|---|---|---|---|---|---|---|---|
| Blanda | 362 | 187 | 52 | 3330 | 9.2 | 36 | 22– 6 | 1 |
| Lee | 127 | 66 | 52 | 1205 | 9.4 | 12 | 6– 5 | |
| Cannon | 5 | 0 | 0 | 0 | 0.0 | 0 | 1– 20 | |
| Smith | 2 | 1 | 50 | 33 | 16.5 | 0 | 0– 0 | |
| Groman | 1 | 0 | 0 | 0 | 0.0 | 0 | 0– 0 | |
| Tolar | 1 | 0 | 0 | 0 | 0.0 | 0 | 0– 0 | |

**PUNTING**

| | No | Avg |
|---|---|---|
| Norton | 48 | 40.7 |
| Hall | 8 | 29.8 |

**KICKING**

| | XP | Att | % | FG | Att | % |
|---|---|---|---|---|---|---|
| Blanda | 64 | 65 | 98 | 16 | 26 | 62 |
| Milstead | 1 | 1 | 100 | 0 | 0 | 0 |

## BOSTON PATRIOTS

### RUSHING

| Last Name | No. | Yds | Avg | TD |
|---|---|---|---|---|
| Lott | 100 | 461 | 4.7 | 5 |
| Garron | 69 | 389 | 5.6 | 2 |
| Burton | 82 | 260 | 3.2 | 2 |
| Parilli | 38 | 183 | 4.8 | 5 |
| Crawford | 41 | 148 | 3.6 | 0 |
| Yewcic | 11 | 51 | 4.6 | 1 |
| Songin | 8 | 39 | 4.9 | 0 |
| Colclough | 3 | 37 | 12.3 | 0 |
| Schwedes | 10 | 14 | 1.4 | 0 |
| Washington | 1 | 3 | 3.0 | 0 |

### RECEIVING

| Last Name | No. | Yds | Avg | TD |
|---|---|---|---|---|
| Cappelletti | 45 | 768 | 17 | 8 |
| Colclough | 42 | 757 | 18 | 9 |
| Lott | 32 | 333 | 10 | 6 |
| Garron | 24 | 341 | 14 | 3 |
| Stephens | 19 | 186 | 10 | 2 |
| Burton | 13 | 115 | 9 | 0 |
| Crawford | 9 | 85 | 9 | 0 |
| Johnson | 9 | 82 | 9 | 1 |
| Yewcic | 6 | 56 | 9 | 0 |
| Schwedes | 1 | 21 | 21 | 0 |
| Shonta | 1 | 9 | 9 | 0 |

### PUNT RETURNS

| Last Name | No. | Yds | Avg | TD |
|---|---|---|---|---|
| Burton | 8 | 128 | 16 | 0 |
| Bruney | 23 | 109 | 5 | 0 |
| Klein | 1 | 23 | 23 | 0 |
| Webb | 1 | 20 | 20 | 1 |
| Lott | 1 | 8 | 8 | 0 |
| Moore | 1 | 0 | 0 | 0 |

### KICKOFF RETURNS

| Last Name | No. | Yds | Avg | TD |
|---|---|---|---|---|
| Garron | 16 | 438 | 27 | 1 |
| Burton | 15 | 401 | 27 | 1 |
| Beach | 2 | 38 | 19 | 0 |
| Long | 4 | 24 | 6 | 0 |
| Webb | 1 | 21 | 21 | 0 |
| Ratkowski | 1 | 17 | 17 | 0 |
| Stephens | 1 | 6 | 6 | 0 |
| Schwedes | 1 | 0 | 0 | 0 |
| Cudzik | 1 | 0 | 0 | 0 |

### PASSING – PUNTING – KICKING Statistics

**PASSING**

| Last Name | Att | Comp | % | Yds | Yd/Att | TD | Int–% | RK |
|---|---|---|---|---|---|---|---|---|
| Songin | 212 | 98 | 46 | 1429 | 6.7 | 14 | 9– 4 | 3 |
| Parilli | 198 | 104 | 53 | 1314 | 6.7 | 13 | 9– 5 | 2 |
| Yewcic | 8 | 3 | 38 | 25 | 3.1 | 1 | 2– 25 | |
| Burton | 1 | 0 | 0 | 0 | 0.0 | 0 | 1–100 | |
| Cappelletti | 1 | 1 | 100 | 27 | 27.0 | 1 | 0– 0 | |

**PUNTING**

| | No | Avg |
|---|---|---|
| Yewcic | 62 | 38.8 |

**KICKING**

| | XP | Att | % | FG | Att | % |
|---|---|---|---|---|---|---|
| Cappelletti | 48 | 50 | 96 | 17 | 32 | 53 |

**2 POINT XP**
Parilli (1)

## NEW YORK TITANS

### RUSHING

| Last Name | No. | Yds | Avg | TD |
|---|---|---|---|---|
| Mathis | 202 | 846 | 4.2 | 7 |
| West | 72 | 322 | 4.5 | 3 |
| Dorow | 54 | 317 | 5.9 | 4 |
| Christy | 81 | 180 | 2.2 | 2 |
| Brooks | 15 | 55 | 3.7 | 0 |
| Renn | 1 | 14 | 14.0 | 0 |
| Shockley | 5 | 9 | 1.8 | 0 |
| Johnson | 1 | 3 | 3.0 | 0 |
| Apple | 7 | 2 | 0.3 | 0 |
| Scrabis | 1 | 1 | 1.0 | 0 |

### RECEIVING

| Last Name | No. | Yds | Avg | TD |
|---|---|---|---|---|
| Powell | 71 | 881 | 12 | 5 |
| Maynard | 43 | 629 | 15 | 8 |
| Christy | 29 | 521 | 18 | 1 |
| Renn | 18 | 268 | 15 | 1 |
| Cooper | 15 | 208 | 14 | 4 |
| West | 13 | 146 | 11 | 0 |
| Mathis | 12 | 42 | 4 | 1 |
| Shockley | 3 | 27 | 9 | 0 |
| Johnson | 1 | 32 | 32 | 0 |
| O'Neil | 1 | −13 | −13 | 0 |

### PUNT RETURNS

| Last Name | No. | Yds | Avg | TD |
|---|---|---|---|---|
| Christy | 18 | 383 | 21 | 2 |
| West | 2 | 51 | 26 | 0 |
| Apple | 2 | 12 | 6 | 0 |
| Maynard | 1 | 9 | 9 | 0 |
| Shockley | 2 | 6 | 3 | 0 |
| Cockrell | 1 | 2 | 2 | 0 |

### KICKOFF RETURNS

| Last Name | No. | Yds | Avg | TD |
|---|---|---|---|---|
| Christy | 15 | 360 | 24 | 0 |
| West | 13 | 306 | 24 | 0 |
| Shockley | 12 | 261 | 22 | 0 |
| Renn | 10 | 201 | 20 | 0 |
| Brooks | 8 | 111 | 14 | 0 |
| Johnson | 5 | 84 | 17 | 0 |
| Hynes | 2 | 45 | 23 | 0 |
| Saidock | 2 | 26 | 13 | 0 |
| Ellis | 3 | 25 | 8 | 0 |
| Fields | 1 | 19 | 19 | 0 |
| Apple | 1 | 16 | 16 | 0 |
| Walsh | 2 | 15 | 8 | 0 |
| Budrewicz | 1 | 0 | 0 | 0 |
| Cooper | 1 | 0 | 0 | 0 |

### PASSING – PUNTING – KICKING Statistics

**PASSING**

| Last Name | Att | Comp | % | Yds | Yd/Att | TD | Int–% | RK |
|---|---|---|---|---|---|---|---|---|
| Dorow | 438 | 197 | 45 | 2651 | 6.1 | 19 | 30– 7 | 7 |
| Scrabis | 21 | 7 | 33 | 82 | 3.9 | 1 | 2– 10 | |
| Christy | 1 | 0 | 0 | 0 | 0.0 | 0 | 0– 0 | |

**PUNTING**

| | No | Avg |
|---|---|---|
| Johnson | 66 | 42.7 |
| Wren | 8 | 33.9 |

**KICKING**

| | XP | Att | % | FG | Att | % |
|---|---|---|---|---|---|---|
| Guesman | 24 | 26 | 92 | 5 | 15 | 33 |
| Shockley | 13 | 13 | 100 | 4 | 9 | 44 |
| Cooper | 0 | 0 | 0 | 1 | 0 | 0 |

## BUFFALO BILLS

### RUSHING

| Last Name | No. | Yds | Avg | TD |
|---|---|---|---|---|
| Baker | 152 | 498 | 3.3 | 3 |
| Carlton | 101 | 311 | 3.1 | 4 |
| Brown | 53 | 192 | 3.6 | 1 |
| Dubenion | 17 | 173 | 10.2 | 2 |
| Bohling | 55 | 153 | 2.8 | 2 |
| Reynolds | 30 | 142 | 4.7 | 4 |
| Atkins | 2 | 87 | 43.5 | 1 |
| Rabb | 13 | 47 | 3.6 | 0 |
| Lucas | 10 | 15 | 1.5 | 0 |
| Green | 14 | 15 | 1.1 | 1 |
| Bass | 2 | 8 | 4.0 | 0 |
| Fowler | 1 | 2 | 2.0 | 0 |
| Rychlec | 1 | −18 | −18.0 | 0 |

### RECEIVING

| Last Name | No. | Yds | Avg | TD |
|---|---|---|---|---|
| Bass | 50 | 765 | 15 | 3 |
| Rychlec | 33 | 405 | 12 | 2 |
| Dubenion | 31 | 461 | 15 | 6 |
| Crockett | 20 | 325 | 16 | 0 |
| Richards | 19 | 285 | 15 | 3 |
| Carlton | 17 | 193 | 11 | 0 |
| Bohling | 13 | 217 | 17 | 1 |
| Baker | 6 | 73 | 12 | 0 |
| Lucas | 6 | 69 | 12 | 0 |
| Chamberlain | 1 | 16 | 16 | 0 |
| Brown | 1 | 11 | 11 | 0 |

### PUNT RETURNS

| Last Name | No. | Yds | Avg | TD |
|---|---|---|---|---|
| Bass | 8 | 75 | 9 | 0 |
| Wagstaff | 1 | 35 | 35 | 0 |
| Valdez | 1 | 30 | 30 | 0 |
| Atkins | 2 | 30 | 15 | 0 |
| Brown | 2 | 14 | 7 | 0 |
| Dubenion | 1 | 3 | 3 | 0 |
| Bohling | 4 | 0 | 0 | 0 |

### KICKOFF RETURNS

| Last Name | No. | Yds | Avg | TD |
|---|---|---|---|---|
| Dubenion | 16 | 329 | 21 | 0 |
| Baker | 12 | 281 | 23 | 0 |
| Bohling | 10 | 246 | 25 | 0 |
| Lucas | 7 | 126 | 18 | 0 |
| Brown | 2 | 105 | 53 | 1 |
| Carlton | 4 | 60 | 15 | 0 |
| Rice | 2 | 13 | 7 | 0 |
| Richards | 1 | 10 | 10 | 0 |
| Crockett | 1 | 0 | 0 | 0 |

### PASSING – PUNTING – KICKING Statistics

**PASSING**

| Last Name | Att | Comp | % | Yds | Yd/Att | TD | Int–% | RK |
|---|---|---|---|---|---|---|---|---|
| Reynolds | 181 | 83 | 46 | 1004 | 5.6 | 2 | 13– 7 | 9 |
| Green | 126 | 56 | 44 | 903 | 7.2 | 6 | 5– 4 | |
| Rabb | 74 | 34 | 46 | 586 | 7.9 | 5 | 2– 3 | |
| Lucas | 50 | 20 | 40 | 282 | 5.6 | 2 | 4– 8 | |
| O'Connell | 5 | 1 | 20 | 11 | 2.2 | 0 | 1– 20 | |
| Carlton | 2 | 0 | 0 | 0 | 0.0 | 0 | 0– 0 | |
| Bohling | 1 | 0 | 0 | 0 | 0.0 | 0 | 0– 0 | |

**PUNTING**

| | No | Avg |
|---|---|---|
| Atkins | 84 | 45.0 |

**KICKING**

| | XP | Att | % | FG | Att | % |
|---|---|---|---|---|---|---|
| Atkins | 29 | 31 | 94 | 2 | 6 | 33 |
| Hergert | 0 | 0 | 0 | 6 | 14 | 43 |
| Yoho | 0 | 0 | 0 | 4 | 0 | 0 |

**2 POINT XP**
Lucas (3)
Rabb (1)

## SAN DIEGO CHARGERS 12-2-0 Sid Gillman

**Scores of Each Game**

| | | |
|---|---|---|
| 26 | Dallas | 10 |
| 44 | OAKLAND | 0 |
| 34 | HOUSTON | 24 |
| 19 | Buffalo | 11 |
| 38 | Boston | 27 |
| 25 | New York | 10 |
| 41 | Oakland | 10 |
| 37 | DENVER | 0 |
| 48 | NEW YORK | 13 |
| 19 | Denver | 16 |
| 24 | DALLAS | 14 |
| 13 | Houston | 33 |
| 28 | BUFFALO | 10 |
| 0 | BOSTON | 41 |

| Use Name | Pos. | Hgt | Wgt | Age | Int | Pts |
|---|---|---|---|---|---|---|
| Sam DeLuca | OT | 6'2" | 245 | 25 | | |
| Ron Mix | OT | 6'4" | 245 | 23 | | |
| Sherman Plunkett | OT | 6'4" | 285 | 27 | | |
| Ernie Wright | OT | 6'4" | 270 | 20 | | |
| Ernie Barnes | OG | 6'3" | 260 | 22 | | |
| Orlando Ferrante | OG | 6' | 230 | 28 | | |
| Gene Selawski | OT-OG | 6'4" | 252 | 25 | | |
| Geroge Belotti (from HOU) | C | 6'4" | 250 | 26 | | |
| Don Rogers | C | 6'2" | 250 | 24 | | |
| Earl Faison | DE | 6'5" | 256 | 22 | | 2 |
| Ron Nery | DE | 6'6" | 230 | 26 | | |
| Bill Hudson | DT | 6'4" | 270 | 25 | 1 | 6 |
| Ernie Ladd | DT | 6'9" | 315 | 22 | | |
| Henry Schmidt | DT | 6'4" | 260 | 24 | | |
| Chuck Allen | LB | 6'1" | 218 | 21 | 5 | 6 |
| Emil Karas | LB | 6'3" | 230 | 27 | 3 | |
| Paul Maguire | LB | 6' | 215 | 23 | 1 | |
| Maury Schleicher | LB | 6'3" | 240 | 24 | | |
| Bob Laraba | HB-LB | 6'3" | 195 | 28 | 5 | 19 |
| George Blair | DB | 5'11" | 190 | 23 | 2 | 81 |
| Claude Gibson | DB | 6'1" | 190 | 22 | 5 | 2 |
| Dick Harris | DB | 5'11" | 175 | 24 | 7 | 18 |
| Charley McNeil | DB | 5'11" | 175 | 25 | 9 | 12 |
| Bud Whitehead | DB | 6' | 180 | 22 | 1 | |
| Bob Zeman | DB | 6'1" | 203 | 24 | 8 | 6 |
| Hunter Enis | QB | 6'2" | 190 | 24 | | 12 |
| Jack Kemp | QB | 6'1" | 200 | 27 | | 36 |
| Keith Lincoln | HB | 6'2" | 205 | 22 | | 18 |
| Paul Lowe | HB | 6' | 180 | 24 | | 54 |
| Bo Roberson | HB | 6'1" | 185 | 26 | | 18 |
| Charlie Flowers | FB | 6'1" | 220 | 24 | | 18 |
| Bob Scarpitto | FL | 5'11" | 185 | 22 | | 12 |
| Howard Clark | OE | 6'2" | 215 | 26 | | |
| Luther Hayes | OE | 6'4" | 200 | 22 | | 18 |
| Dave Kocourek | OE | 6'5" | 230 | 24 | | 24 |
| Don Norton | OE | 6'1" | 185 | 23 | | 36 |
| Jacque Mackinnon | OG-OE | 6'4" | 240 | 22 | | |

## DALLAS TEXANS 6-8-0 Hank Stram

**Scores of Each Game**

| | | |
|---|---|---|
| 10 | SAN DIEGO | 26 |
| 42 | Oakland | 35 |
| 26 | HOUSTON | 21 |
| 19 | Denver | 12 |
| 24 | Buffalo | 27 |
| 7 | Houston | 38 |
| 17 | BOSTON | 18 |
| 21 | Boston | 28 |
| 20 | BUFFALO | 30 |
| 14 | San Diego | 24 |
| 43 | OAKLAND | 11 |
| 7 | New York | 28 |
| 49 | DENVER | 21 |
| 35 | NEW YORK | 24 |

| Use Name | Pos. | Hgt | Wgt | Age | Int | Pts |
|---|---|---|---|---|---|---|
| Jerry Cornelison | OT | 6'3" | 250 | 24 | | |
| Charley Diamond | OT | 6'2" | 235 | 25 | | |
| Jim Tyrer | OT | 6'6" | 292 | 22 | | |
| John Cadwell | OG | 6'3" | 230 | 22 | | |
| Sid Fournet | OG | 6' | 240 | 28 | | |
| Billy Krisher | OG | 6'1" | 235 | 25 | | |
| Al Reynolds | OG | 6'3" | 235 | 23 | | |
| Marvin Terrell | OG | 6'1" | 235 | 23 | | |
| Jon Gilliam | C | 6'2" | 225 | 22 | | |
| Mel Branch | DE | 6'2" | 230 | 24 | | |
| Luther Jeralds | DE | 6'3" | 235 | 23 | | |
| Paul Miller | DE | 6'2" | 240 | 29 | | |
| Ray Collins | DT | 5'11" | 250 | 33 | | |
| Jerry Mays | DT | 6'4" | 245 | 21 | 1 | |
| Walter Napier | DT | 6'4" | 270 | 25 | | |
| Paul Rochester | DT | 6'2" | 250 | 24 | | |
| Ted Greene | LB | 6'1" | 230 | 27 | 1 | |
| Sherrill Headrick | LB | 6'2" | 215 | 24 | 2 | 12 |
| E. J. Holub | LB | 6'4" | 230 | 23 | 1 | |
| Smokey Stover | LB | 6' | 230 | 22 | 2 | |
| Dave Grayson | DB | 5'10" | 180 | 22 | 3 | 6 |
| Ed Kelley | DB | 6'2" | 195 | 26 | | |
| Doyle Nix | DB | 6'1" | 195 | 28 | 3 | |
| Dave Webster | DB | 6'4" | 220 | 23 | 5 | |
| Duane Wood | DB | 6'1" | 190 | 25 | 4 | |
| Cotton Davidson | QB | 6'1" | 185 | 28 | | 26 |
| Randy Duncan | QB | 6' | 185 | 23 | | |
| Tom Greene | QB | 6'1" | 190 | 23 | | |
| Abner Haynes | HB | 6' | 180 | 22 | | 78 |
| Frank Jackson | HB | 6'1" | 182 | 21 | | 30 |
| Johnny Robinson | HB | 6' | 195 | 22 | | 42 |
| Bo Dickenson | FB | 6'2" | 210 | 26 | | 34 |
| Billy Pricer | FB | 5'10" | 215 | 26 | | |
| Jack Spikes | FB | 6'2" | 225 | 23 | | 54 |
| Charley Barnes | OE | 6'5" | 230 | 24 | | |
| Max Boydston | OE | 6'2" | 210 | 28 | | 6 |
| Chris Burford | OE | 6'3" | 210 | 23 | | 30 |
| Tony Romeo | OE | 6'2" | 215 | 22 | | |
| Ben Agajanian (to GB-N) | K | 6' | 220 | 42 | | 16 |

## DENVER BRONCOS 3-11-0 Frankie Filchock

**Scores of Each Game**

| | | |
|---|---|---|
| 22 | Buffalo | 10 |
| 17 | Boston | 45 |
| 28 | New York | 35 |
| 19 | Oakland | 33 |
| 24 | DALLAS | 19 |
| 27 | OAKLAND | 24 |
| 27 | NEW YORK | 10 |
| 0 | San Diego | 37 |
| 14 | HOUSTON | 55 |
| 16 | SAN DIEGO | 19 |
| 10 | BUFFALO | 23 |
| 14 | Houston | 45 |
| 24 | BOSTON | 28 |
| 21 | Dallas | 49 |

| Use Name | Pos. | Hgt | Wgt | Age | Int | Pts |
|---|---|---|---|---|---|---|
| Eldon Danenhauer | OT | 6'4" | 235 | 25 | | |
| Jerry Sturm | FB-OT | 6'3" | 235 | 24 | | |
| Ken Adamson | OG | 6'2" | 225 | 22 | | |
| Buzz Guy (from HOU) | OG | 6'3" | 250 | 26 | | |
| Carl Larpenter | OG | 6'4" | 235 | 24 | | |
| Jim Barton | C | 6'5" | 250 | 26 | | |
| Mike Nichols | C | 6'3" | 225 | 22 | | |
| John Cash | DE | 6'3" | 230 | 25 | | |
| Chuck Gavin | DE | 6'1" | 240 | 27 | | 6 |
| Bob Konovsky | DE | 6'2" | 250 | 27 | | |
| Joe Young | DE | 6'3" | 245 | 26 | | |
| Art Hauser | DT | 6' | 240 | 30 | | |
| Gordy Holz | DT | 6'4" | 270 | 27 | | |
| Jack Mattox | DT | 6'4" | 240 | 22 | | |
| Bud McFadin | DT | 6'3" | 280 | 33 | | |
| Jim Eifrid | LB | 6'1" | 240 | 23 | | |
| Bob Griffin (to STL-N) | LB | 6'3" | 250 | 32 | | |
| Bob Hudson | LB | 6'4" | 235 | 31 | 3 | |
| Pat Lamberti (from NY) | LB | 6'2" | 225 | 23 | 1 | |
| Wahoo McDaniel | LB | 6' | 240 | 24 | | |
| Bill Roehnelt | LB | 6'1" | 225 | 25 | | |
| Jackie Simpson | LB | 6'3" | 230 | 25 | | |
| Jerry Stalcup | LB | 6' | 240 | 23 | | |
| Goose Gonsoulin | DB | 6'3" | 205 | 23 | 6 | |
| Jim McMillin | DB | 5'11" | 180 | 23 | 5 | |
| Bob McNamara | DB | 6' | 190 | 27 | 3 | |
| Phil Nugent | DB | 6'2" | 195 | 22 | 7 | |
| John Pyeatt | DB | 6'3" | 204 | 27 | | |
| Jimmy Sears | DB | 5'11" | 187 | 30 | | |
| Dan Smith | DB | 5'10" | 180 | 26 | | |
| George Herring | QB | 6'2" | 200 | 26 | | 12 |
| Frank Tripucka | QB | 6'3" | 205 | 33 | | |
| Buddy Allen | HB | 5'10" | 190 | 23 | | |
| Al Carmichael | HB | 6'1" | 195 | 31 | | |
| Dale Evans | HB | 6'3" | 210 | 22 | | |
| Al Frazier | HB | 5'11" | 180 | 26 | | 50 |
| Jack Hill | HB | 6'1" | 185 | 27 | | 31 |
| Gene Mingo | HB | 6' | 200 | 22 | | 32 |
| Donnie Stone | HB | 6'2" | 210 | 26 | | 48 |
| Jerry Traynham | HB | 5'10" | 190 | 22 | | |
| Dave Ames (from NY) | DB-HB | 6' | 185 | 24 | 1 | |
| Fred Bukaty | FB | 5'11" | 195 | 22 | | 32 |
| Jim Stinnette | LB-FB | 6'1" | 230 | 23 | 1 | 6 |
| Gene Prebola | OE | 6'3" | 215 | 23 | | 8 |
| Lionel Taylor | OE | 6'2" | 214 | 25 | | 24 |

## OAKLAND RAIDERS 2-12-0 Marty Feldman

**Scores of Each Game**

| | | |
|---|---|---|
| 0 | Houston | 55 |
| 0 | San Diego | 44 |
| 35 | DALLAS | 42 |
| 33 | DENVER | 19 |
| 24 | Denver | 27 |
| 10 | SAN DIEGO | 41 |
| 6 | NEW YORK | 14 |
| 31 | Buffalo | 22 |
| 12 | New York | 23 |
| 17 | Boston | 20 |
| 11 | Dallas | 43 |
| 21 | BUFFALO | 26 |
| 21 | BOSTON | 35 |
| 16 | HOUSTON | 47 |

| Use Name | Pos. | Hgt | Wgt | Age | Int | Pts |
|---|---|---|---|---|---|---|
| Jim Brewington | OT | 6'6" | 280 | 22 | | |
| Cliff Roberts | OT | 6'3" | 260 | 26 | | |
| Ron Sabal | OT | 6'2" | 245 | 24 | | |
| Jack Stone | OT | 6'2" | 245 | 24 | | |
| Wayne Hawkins | OG | 6' | 235 | 23 | | |
| Herb Roedel | OG | 6'3" | 230 | 22 | | |
| Willie Smith | OG | 6'2" | 255 | 23 | | |
| Jim Otto | C | 6'2" | 240 | 23 | | |
| Jon Jelacic | DE | 6'3" | 255 | 24 | | |
| Charley Powell | DE | 6'2" | 245 | 29 | | |
| George Fields | DT | 6'3" | 245 | 25 | | |
| Gary Finneran | DT | 6'3" | 240 | 27 | | |
| Harry Jagielski (from BOS) | DT | 6' | 260 | 29 | 1 | |
| Volney Peters | DT | 6'4" | 245 | 32 | | |
| Hal Smith | DT | 6'5" | 250 | 26 | | |
| Bob Voight | DT | 6'5" | 265 | 24 | | |
| Al Bansavage | LB | 6'2" | 220 | 23 | | |
| Bob Dougherty | LB | 6'2" | 240 | 27 | 2 | |
| Tom Louderback | LB | 6'2" | 235 | 27 | 1 | 6 |
| Riley Morris | LB | 6'2" | 230 | 24 | 3 | 6 |
| Alex Bravo | DB | 6' | 190 | 29 | 2 | |
| Joe Cannavino | DB | 5'11" | 185 | 25 | 5 | |
| Bob Garner | DB | 5'10" | 190 | 26 | 2 | |
| John Harris | DB | 6'1" | 195 | 28 | 3 | |
| Fred Williamson | DB | 6'2" | 205 | 23 | 5 | |
| Tom Flores | QB | 6'1" | 190 | 24 | | 6 |
| Nick Papac | QB | 5'11" | 190 | 26 | | 6 |
| Wayne Crow | HB | 6' | 205 | 23 | | 14 |
| Clem Daniels | HB | 6'1" | 220 | 24 | | 12 |
| George Fleming | HB | 5'11" | 188 | 22 | | 63 |
| Charley Fuller | HB | 5'11" | 176 | 22 | | 12 |
| Jack Larschied | HB | 5'6" | 162 | 27 | | |
| Jim Jones | FB | 6'1" | 212 | 25 | | |
| Walt Kowalczyk | FB | 6' | 216 | 26 | | |
| Alan Miller | FB | 6' | 197 | 23 | | 42 |
| Doug Asad | OE | 6'3" | 205 | 23 | | 12 |
| Jerry Burch | OE | 6'1" | 195 | 21 | | 6 |
| Bob Coolbaugh | OE | 6'3" | 200 | 21 | | 26 |
| Charley Hardy | OE | 6' | 185 | 27 | | 24 |

## SAN DIEGO CHARGERS

### RUSHING

| Last Name | No. | Yds | Avg | TD |
|---|---|---|---|---|
| Lowe | 175 | 767 | 4.4 | 9 |
| Roberson | 58 | 275 | 4.7 | 3 |
| Flowers | 51 | 177 | 3.5 | 3 |
| Lincoln | 41 | 150 | 3.7 | 0 |
| Kemp | 43 | 105 | 2.4 | 6 |
| Enis | 16 | 13 | 0.8 | 2 |
| Laraba | 5 | 5 | 1.0 | 1 |

### RECEIVING

| Last Name | No. | Yds | Avg | TD |
|---|---|---|---|---|
| Kocourek | 55 | 1055 | 19 | 4 |
| Norton | 47 | 816 | 17 | 6 |
| Lowe | 17 | 103 | 6 | 0 |
| Flowers | 16 | 175 | 11 | 0 |
| Hayes | 14 | 280 | 20 | 3 |
| Lincoln | 12 | 208 | 17 | 2 |
| Clark | 11 | 182 | 17 | 0 |
| Scarpitto | 9 | 163 | 18 | 2 |
| Roberson | 6 | 81 | 14 | 0 |
| MacKinnon | 3 | 58 | 19 | 0 |

### PUNT RETURNS

| Last Name | No. | Yds | Avg | TD |
|---|---|---|---|---|
| Gibson | 14 | 209 | 15 | 0 |
| Lincoln | 7 | 150 | 21 | 1 |
| Scarpitto | 4 | 47 | 12 | 0 |
| Zeman | 2 | 47 | 24 | 1 |
| Selawski | 1 | 5 | 5 | 0 |
| Lowe | 1 | 0 | 0 | 0 |

### KICKOFF RETURNS

| Last Name | No. | Yds | Avg | TD |
|---|---|---|---|---|
| Lowe | 10 | 240 | 24 | 0 |
| Roberson | 13 | 207 | 16 | 0 |
| Lincoln | 4 | 98 | 25 | 0 |
| Scarpitto | 3 | 50 | 17 | 0 |
| Schmidt | 1 | 22 | 22 | 0 |
| Gibson | 3 | 16 | 5 | 0 |
| Karas | 1 | 5 | 5 | 0 |
| Blair | 1 | 2 | 2 | 0 |
| Selawski | 1 | 1 | 1 | 0 |
| Mix | 1 | 0 | 0 | 0 |
| Ferrante | 1 | 0 | 0 | 0 |

### PASSING – PUNTING – KICKING Statistics

PASSING

| Last Name | Att | Comp | % | Yds | Yd/Att | TD | Int–% | RK |
|---|---|---|---|---|---|---|---|---|
| Kemp | 364 | 165 | 45 | 2686 | 7.4 | 15 | 22– 6 | 5 |
| Enis | 55 | 23 | 42 | 365 | 6.6 | 2 | 3– 5 | |
| Lowe | 4 | 2 | 50 | 70 | 17.5 | 0 | 0– 0 | |

PUNTING

| Last Name | No | Avg |
|---|---|---|
| Maguire | 62 | 42.2 |

KICKING

| Last Name | XP | Att | % | FG | Att | % |
|---|---|---|---|---|---|---|
| Blair | 42 | 47 | 89 | 13 | 27 | 48 |
| Laraba | 1 | 2 | 50 | 0 | 0 | 0 |
| Lincoln | 0 | 1 | 0 | 0 | 0 | 0 |

2 POINT XP
Gibson (1)

## DALLAS TEXANS

### RUSHING

| Last Name | No. | Yds | Avg | TD |
|---|---|---|---|---|
| Haynes | 179 | 841 | 4.7 | 9 |
| Jackson | 65 | 386 | 5.9 | 3 |
| Spikes | 39 | 334 | 8.6 | 5 |
| Dickinson | 71 | 263 | 3.7 | 3 |
| Robinson | 52 | 200 | 3.9 | 2 |
| Davidson | 21 | 123 | 5.9 | 1 |
| Duncan | 5 | 42 | 8.5 | 0 |
| Pricer | 5 | 13 | 2.6 | 0 |
| Gilliam | 1 | –6 | –6.0 | 0 |
| Burford | 1 | –13 | –13.0 | 0 |

### RECEIVING

| Last Name | No. | Yds | Avg | TD |
|---|---|---|---|---|
| Burford | 51 | 850 | 17 | 5 |
| Robinson | 35 | 601 | 17 | 5 |
| Haynes | 34 | 558 | 16 | 3 |
| Dickinson | 14 | 209 | 15 | 2 |
| Jackson | 13 | 171 | 13 | 2 |
| Boydston | 12 | 167 | 14 | 1 |
| Spikes | 8 | 136 | 17 | 0 |
| Romeo | 7 | 89 | 13 | 0 |
| Pricer | 2 | 21 | 11 | 0 |
| Barnes | 1 | 13 | 13 | 0 |

### PUNT RETURNS

| Last Name | No. | Yds | Avg | TD |
|---|---|---|---|---|
| Haynes | 19 | 196 | 10 | 0 |
| Mays | 1 | 12 | 12 | 0 |
| Headrick | 2 | 5 | 3 | 0 |
| Robinson | 2 | 4 | 2 | 0 |
| Jackson | 1 | 2 | 2 | 0 |
| Miller | 1 | 0 | 0 | 0 |

### KICKOFF RETURNS

| Last Name | No. | Yds | Avg | TD |
|---|---|---|---|---|
| Grayson | 16 | 453 | 28 | 0 |
| Jackson | 24 | 645 | 27 | 0 |
| Haynes | 8 | 270 | 34 | 1 |
| Gilliam | 1 | 23 | 23 | 0 |
| Pricer | 1 | 19 | 19 | 0 |
| Stover | 1 | 15 | 15 | 0 |
| Mays | 1 | 13 | 13 | 0 |

### PASSING – PUNTING – KICKING Statistics

PASSING

| Last Name | Att | Comp | % | Yds | Yd/Att | TD | Int–% | RK |
|---|---|---|---|---|---|---|---|---|
| Davidson | 330 | 151 | 46 | 2445 | 7.4 | 17 | 23– 7 | 5 |
| Duncan | 67 | 25 | 37 | 361 | 5.4 | 1 | 3– 4 | |
| Jackson | 2 | 1 | 50 | 9 | 4.5 | 0 | 1– 50 | |

PUNTING

| Last Name | No | Avg |
|---|---|---|
| Davidson | 61 | 40.6 |

KICKING

| Last Name | XP | Att | % | FG | Att | % |
|---|---|---|---|---|---|---|
| Davidson | 20 | 20 | 100 | 0 | 2 | 0 |
| Spikes | 10 | 13 | 77 | 4 | 13 | 31 |
| Agajanian | 7 | 7 | 100 | 3 | 9 | 33 |

2 POINT XP
Dickinson (2)
Spikes (1)

## DENVER BRONCOS

### RUSHING

| Last Name | No. | Yds | Avg | TD |
|---|---|---|---|---|
| Stone | 127 | 505 | 4.0 | 4 |
| Bukaty | 76 | 187 | 2.5 | 5 |
| Ames | 19 | 114 | 6.0 | 0 |
| Frazier | 23 | 110 | 4.8 | 0 |
| Herring | 15 | 74 | 4.9 | 2 |
| Mingo | 18 | 51 | 2.8 | 0 |
| Sturm | 8 | 31 | 3.9 | 0 |
| Carmichael | 15 | 24 | 1.6 | 0 |
| Traynham | 6 | 12 | 2.0 | 0 |
| Stinnette | 19 | 8 | 0.4 | 0 |
| Allen | 3 | –4 | –1.3 | 0 |
| Tripucka | 4 | –8 | –2.0 | 0 |

### RECEIVING

| Last Name | No. | Yds | Avg | TD |
|---|---|---|---|---|
| Taylor | 100 | 1176 | 13 | 4 |
| Frazier | 47 | 799 | 17 | 6 |
| Stone | 38 | 344 | 9 | 4 |
| Prebola | 29 | 349 | 12 | 1 |
| Bukaty | 14 | 94 | 7 | 0 |
| Stinnette | 11 | 58 | 5 | 1 |
| Mingo | 8 | 110 | 14 | 2 |
| Ames | 6 | 20 | 3 | 0 |
| Carmichael | 5 | 23 | 5 | 0 |
| Hill | 4 | 33 | 8 | 0 |
| Sturm | 2 | –1 | –1 | 0 |
| Traynham | 1 | –1 | –1 | 0 |

### PUNT RETURNS

| Last Name | No. | Yds | Avg | TD |
|---|---|---|---|---|
| Frazier | 18 | 231 | 13 | 1 |
| Carmichael | 7 | 58 | 8 | 0 |
| Gavin | 1 | 45 | 45 | 1 |
| McNamara | 4 | 17 | 4 | 0 |
| Ames | 2 | 17 | 9 | 0 |
| Mingo | 1 | 1 | 1 | 0 |

### KICKOFF RETURNS

| Last Name | No. | Yds | Avg | TD |
|---|---|---|---|---|
| Frazier | 18 | 504 | 28 | 1 |
| Carmichael | 16 | 310 | 19 | 0 |
| Ames | 12 | 240 | 20 | 0 |
| Stone | 9 | 215 | 24 | 0 |
| Mingo | 4 | 120 | 30 | 0 |
| Bukaty | 3 | 41 | 14 | 0 |
| Gonsoulin | 1 | 34 | 34 | 0 |
| Hill | 1 | 23 | 23 | 0 |
| Prebola | 1 | 8 | 8 | 0 |
| Stinnette | 1 | 6 | 6 | 0 |

### PASSING – PUNTING – KICKING Statistics

PASSING

| Last Name | Att | Comp | % | Yds | Yd/Att | TD | Int–% | RK |
|---|---|---|---|---|---|---|---|---|
| Tripucka | 344 | 167 | 49 | 1690 | 4.9 | 10 | 21– 6 | 8 |
| Herring | 211 | 93 | 44 | 1160 | 5.5 | 5 | 22– 10 | 10 |
| Mingo | 8 | 4 | 50 | 136 | 17.0 | 2 | 0– 0 | |
| Stone | 2 | 1 | 50 | 18 | 9.0 | 1 | 0– 0 | |
| Taylor | 2 | 0 | 0 | 0 | 0.0 | 0 | 1– 50 | |
| Frazier | 1 | 0 | 0 | 0 | 0.0 | 0 | 1– 100 | |

PUNTING

| Last Name | No | Avg |
|---|---|---|
| Herring | 80 | 39.4 |

KICKING

| Last Name | XP | Att | % | FG | Att | % |
|---|---|---|---|---|---|---|
| Hill | 16 | 16 | 100 | 5 | 15 | 33 |
| Mingo | 11 | 11 | 100 | 3 | 10 | 30 |

2 POINT XP
Bukaty (1)
Frazier (1)
Prebola (1)

## OAKLAND RAIDERS

### RUSHING

| Last Name | No. | Yds | Avg | TD |
|---|---|---|---|---|
| Crow | 119 | 490 | 4.1 | 2 |
| Miller | 85 | 255 | 3.0 | 3 |
| Daniels | 31 | 154 | 5.1 | 2 |
| Fuller | 38 | 134 | 3.5 | 0 |
| Fleming | 31 | 112 | 3.6 | 1 |
| Flores | 23 | 36 | 1.6 | 1 |
| Papac | 6 | 28 | 4.7 | 1 |
| Kowalczyk | 10 | 28 | 2.8 | 0 |
| Larschied | 6 | 3 | 0.5 | 0 |

### RECEIVING

| Last Name | No. | Yds | Avg | TD |
|---|---|---|---|---|
| Asad | 36 | 501 | 14 | 2 |
| Miller | 36 | 315 | 9 | 4 |
| Coolbaugh | 32 | 435 | 14 | 4 |
| Hardy | 24 | 337 | 14 | 4 |
| Crow | 23 | 196 | 9 | 0 |
| Burch | 18 | 235 | 13 | 1 |
| Daniels | 13 | 150 | 12 | 0 |
| Fuller | 12 | 277 | 23 | 2 |
| Fleming | 10 | 49 | 5 | 0 |
| Kowalczyk | 3 | 8 | 3 | 0 |
| Larschied | 2 | 11 | 6 | 0 |

### PUNT RETURNS

| Last Name | No. | Yds | Avg | TD |
|---|---|---|---|---|
| Fuller | 4 | 52 | 13 | 0 |
| Daniels | 5 | 34 | 7 | 0 |
| Fleming | 3 | 24 | 8 | 0 |
| Garner | 2 | 5 | 3 | 0 |
| H. Smith | 1 | 2 | 2 | 0 |

### KICKOFF RETURNS

| Last Name | No. | Yds | Avg | TD |
|---|---|---|---|---|
| Fleming | 29 | 588 | 20 | 0 |
| Daniels | 13 | 276 | 21 | 0 |
| Larschied | 9 | 254 | 28 | 0 |
| Fuller | 8 | 155 | 19 | 0 |
| Miller | 6 | 66 | 11 | 0 |
| Kowalczyk | 1 | 19 | 19 | 0 |
| Coolbaugh | 1 | 15 | 15 | 0 |
| Asad | 1 | 10 | 10 | 0 |

### PASSING – PUNTING – KICKING Statistics

PASSING

| Last Name | Att | Comp | % | Yds | Yd/Att | TD | Int–% | RK |
|---|---|---|---|---|---|---|---|---|
| Flores | 366 | 190 | 52 | 2176 | 6.0 | 15 | 19– 5 | 3 |
| Papac | 44 | 13 | 30 | 173 | 3.9 | 2 | 7– 16 | |
| Crow | 10 | 6 | 60 | 165 | 16.5 | 0 | 0– 0 | |
| Fleming | 1 | 0 | 0 | 0 | 0.0 | 0 | 1– 100 | |
| Fuller | 1 | 0 | 0 | 0 | 0.0 | 0 | 0– 0 | |
| Larschied | 1 | 0 | 0 | 0 | 0.0 | 0 | 1– 100 | |

PUNTING

| Last Name | No | Avg |
|---|---|---|
| Crow | 61 | 42.8 |
| Burch | 11 | 28.6 |

KICKING

| Last Name | XP | Att | % | FG | Att | % |
|---|---|---|---|---|---|---|
| Fleming | 24 | 25 | 96 | 11 | 26 | 42 |

2 POINT XP
Coolbaugh (1)
Crow (1)

# 1962 N.F.L. Millions from the Stay-at-Homes

It was a year of renewal, consolidation, innovation, and departures. Commissioner Pete Rozelle renewed the NFL's television contract with CBS at a new rate of $4.65 million per year, and the club owners rewarded Rozelle with a new five-year contract with a hefty raise. The consolidation took place in Los Angeles, where full control of the Rams was reacquired by Dan Reeves. After taking in Edwin Pauley and Fred Levy as partners, Reeves fell to feuding with his co-owners in recent years, so Rozelle arranged for the submission of secret bids for the controlling interest in the team, which Reeves won. Innovation brought the league a new rule against grabbing another player's face mask, ground-breaking for a Hall of Fame in Canton, Ohio, and a fabulously popular pre-season doubleheader in Cleveland. And leaving the NFL stage this year, by death, were Mrs. Violet Bidwill Wolfner and James Clark, owners of the Cardinals and Eagles, and, by pink slips, long-time coaches Paul Brown and Weeb Ewbank.

## EASTERN CONFERENCE

**New York Giants**—After fourteen years of professional football, thirty-five-year-old Y. A. Tittle became an overnight sensation as the Giant quarterback. Tittle set a new NFL record of thirty-three touchdown passes in a season, including seven in one game against the Redskins, but his style captivated New York fans more than his passing. He would retreat to his protective pocket and calmly survey the field, a thin, middle-aged man defying the behemoths rushing at him. He would back-pedal with tacklers closing in on him and flip an unexpected screen pass to Alex Webster behind a covey of blockers. Near the goal line he often ran the ball in on the bootleg play, outsprinting the deceived defenders on his aged legs. With a strong cast of players surrounding Tittle, the Giants got to the championship game by winning their last nine games.

**Pittsburgh Steelers**—Bobby Layne had reason to smile after his final NFL season. He wound up his career with 196 touchdown passes, surpassing Sammy Baugh's old mark of 186, and he led the Steelers to three straight wins at the end of the year to capture second place in the East. Other oldsters besides Layne turned in key performances, such as John Henry Johnson, Ernie Stautner, and Big Daddy Lipscomb. Holdover receiver Buddy Dial starred as a deep threat, and newcomer Lou Michaels excelled as a place-kicker. Perhaps the most important job was coach Buddy Parker's patch-up of the defense after injuries wiped out all his linebackers and personal differences elbowed Johnny Sample into disfavor.

**Cleveland Browns**—The Paul Brown era crashed to an end in a year of disappointment and tragedy. Brown had traded fleet Bobby Mitchell to Washington for the draft rights to Heisman Trophy winner Ernie Davis of Syracuse. Davis, a powerful halfback, was expected to team with Jimmy Brown in a strong running duo, but leukemia struck the rookie down before he ever played a professional game. With no good running halfbacks to divert the enemy's forces, fullback Brown for the first time ever failed to win the league rushing crown. After a lackluster campaign in which the Browns were never contenders, owner Art Modell shocked the football world by firing the most successful coach in pro-football history.

**Washington Redskins**—The Redskins fielded their first black players this year in Bobby Mitchell, John Nisby, Leroy Jackson, and Ron Hatcher, and the club's fortunes immediately rocketed upward. Mitchell, obtained from Cleveland for the draft rights to Ernie Davis, set the league on fire with his spectacular receiving from his new flanker position, and with quarterback Norm Snead getting good protection from the bolstered offensive line, an all-out passing attack brought the Skins four wins and two ties in their first six contests before their running game and loose pass defense caught up with them.

**Dallas Cowboys**—Coach Tom Landry had been a great defensive player, but his coaching genius was in a different direction. The Dallas offense was the second best in the league, trailing only the Packers in points scored, but the Dallas defense was the second worst in the league, with only Minnesota allowing more points. Landry got good mileage out of quarterbacks Eddie LeBaron and Don Meredith by shuffling them in and out of the lineup on every play. But once LeBaron was injured in mid-season and Meredith had to go it alone at quarterback, the attack slipped and the Cowboys dropped five of their last six matches.

**St. Louis Cardinals**—Although Wally Lemm turned out a losing squad in his first year on the job, he did uncover a fine young passer in Charley Johnson. After sitting on the bench last year and beginning this season as Sam Etcheverry's back-up, Johnson won the quarterback job four games into the season. During the remaining stretch he learned by experience and threw a lot of passes to his complementary receivers, speedster Sonny Randle and sure-handed Bobby Joe Conrad. But even with strong running from John David Crow, the attack never caught fire, due to a mediocre line.

**Philadelphia Eagles**—The fair Philadelphia defense had sufficed when the offense was churning out points at a furious pace, but injuries this year crippled the attack and sent the Eagles tumbling into last place. Quarterback Sonny Jurgensen, still bothered by a shoulder separation suffered in last season's Playoff Bowl, found himself throwing the ball to a bunch of strangers. Only Tommy McDonald stayed healthy among the receivers, as Pete Retzlaff, Bobby Walston, and Dick Lucas all broke arms and Hopalong Cassady broke a leg, while runner Ted Dean joined the parade with a broken foot.

## WESTERN CONFERENCE

**Green Bay Packers**—Even with Paul Hornung below par physically, the Packers overwhelmed the league with All-Pro performances. Fullback Jim Taylor, whose strong point was neither size nor speed but meanness, took the rushing title away from Jimmy Brown and also led the league in scoring with nineteen touchdowns. Bart Starr compiled the best passing record in the circuit, while Willie Wood intercepted the most aerials. The wire service All-Pro teams were overloaded with Packers as fullback Taylor, end Ron Kramer, offensive linemen Forrest Gregg, Jerry Kramer, Fuzzy Thurston, and Jim Ringo, defensive linemen Willie Davis and Henry Jordan, linebackers Bill Forester and Dan Currie, and cornerback Herb Adderley all won honors.

**Detroit Lions**—Eleven wins are usually good enough for a championship, but the Lions had to settle for second place in the West behind the stampeding Green Bay Packers. The Lions did expose Vince Lombardi's supermen as mere mortals, however, in their Thanksgiving Day meeting in Detroit. The unbeaten Packers that day ran up against a fired-up Detroit defense that turned in an almost perfect performance. Tackle Roger Brown constantly blasted into the Green Bay backfield, linebacker Joe Schmidt blitzed Packer quarterback Bart Starr into the ground, and the defensive unit kept the Packers scoreless until late in the 26-14 upset victory.

**Chicago Bears**—Like the Packers and Lions, the Bears had a tough defense at the core of the team. The front four and secondary were solid if not spectacular, but the linebacking corps of Joe Fortunato, Bill George, and Larry Morris ranked with the NFL's best. Offensively, coach George Halas had to scramble around for runners when injuries sidelined Rick Casares and Willie Galimore. Ex-Ram Joe Marconi did a yeoman's job at fullback, while freshman Ronnie Bull hustled enough to win Rookie of the Year honors. The air attack moved well on Billy Wade's passes to Mike Ditka and Johnny Morris, but the defense dominated the Bears, as a bruising 3-0 victory over the Lions to close the season underlined.

**Baltimore Colts**—The last few seasons had been lackluster, and a 7-7 record this season brought coach Weeb Ewbank's regime to an end. Quarterback Johnny Unitas still was the consummate passer and signal-caller, but his supporting cast was looking slightly worn. The running attack was weak, the offensive line was aging, and the place-kicking was unsure. Strong points included a competent defense and a pair of good receivers in Jimmy Orr and Ray Berry, but not enough to save coach Ewbank's job.

**San Francisco '49ers**—Before the season started, coach Red Hickey called this club the best football team he had ever coached. But once the schedule began, injuries turned the '49ers into a very ordinary team. Tackle Bob St. Clair, the team's best offensive lineman, went to the sidelines with an injured Achilles tendon, and halfback Billy Kilmer, an exciting runner, passer, and blocker, missed the final three games after breaking a leg in a car accident. The defense also slipped a notch, as too much youth subverted the secondary and too much age cut down on tackle Leo Nomellini's quickness.

**Minnesota Vikings**—The Vikings couldn't match the three wins of their first campaign, but coach Norm Van Brocklin was gathering good young players who would later make Minnesota a title contender. Free agent Mick Tingelhoff won the center's job, rookie linebacker Roy Winston showed promise, and cornerback Ed Sharockman had a good NFL debut after missing 1961 with a broken leg. Aside from these three freshmen, improvement came from youngsters already on the roster, such as quarterback Fran Tarkenton, halfback Tommy Mason, tackle Grady Alderman, defensive end Jim Marshall, and middle linebacker Rip Hawkins.

**Los Angeles Rams**—Dan Reeves bought out partners Edwin Pauley and Fred Levy, thus ending the front-office bickering that had plagued the team in recent years. But while the ownership picture cleared up, the squad on the field collapsed in a wreck. The Rams won only one game all season, with their offense the worst in the league. Head coach Bob Waterfield tired of all the losing and quit after eight games, leaving the battered team to assistant Harland Svare. But even this season, the worst in Ram history, turned up two bright spots in rookies Merlin Olsen and Roman Gabriel.

## FINAL TEAM STATISTICS

**OFFENSE**

| | BALT. | CHI. | CLEVE. | DALLAS | DET. | G.BAY | L.A. | MINN. | N.Y. | PHIL. | PITT. | ST.L. | S.F. | WASH. |
|---|---|---|---|---|---|---|---|---|---|---|---|---|---|---|
| **FIRST DOWNS:** | | | | | | | | | | | | | | |
| Total | 251 | 228 | 252 | 246 | 243 | 281 | 201 | 223 | 267 | 235 | 261 | 268 | 239 | 241 |
| by Rushing | 94 | 88 | 105 | 101 | 103 | 145 | 84 | 102 | 92 | 76 | 133 | 109 | 112 | 59 |
| by Passing | 145 | 128 | 133 | 136 | 124 | 120 | 107 | 107 | 150 | 146 | 112 | 138 | 112 | 156 |
| by Penalty | 12 | 12 | 14 | 9 | 16 | 16 | 10 | 14 | 25 | 13 | 16 | 21 | 15 | 26 |
| **RUSHING:** | | | | | | | | | | | | | | |
| Numbers | 448 | 386 | 414 | 434 | 489 | 518 | 376 | 426 | 430 | 324 | 572 | 416 | 460 | 371 |
| Yards | 1601 | 1489 | 1772 | 2040 | 1922 | 2460 | 1689 | 1864 | 1698 | 1155 | 2333 | 1698 | 1873 | 1088 |
| Average Yards | 3.6 | 3.9 | 4.3 | 4.7 | 3.9 | 4.7 | 4.5 | 4.4 | 3.9 | 3.6 | 4.1 | 4.1 | 4.1 | 2.9 |
| Touchdowns | 9 | 17 | 18 | 16 | 14 | 36 | 10 | 7 | 11 | 13 | 17 | 20 | 15 | 10 |
| **PASSING:** | | | | | | | | | | | | | | |
| Attempts | 423 | 430 | 370 | 380 | 379 | 311 | 372 | 348 | 411 | 428 | 319 | 434 | 323 | 428 |
| Completions | 237 | 229 | 200 | 200 | 211 | 187 | 189 | 170 | 215 | 228 | 160 | 220 | 185 | 223 |
| Completion Pct. | 56.0 | 53.3 | 54.1 | 52.6 | 55.7 | 60.1 | 50.8 | 48.9 | 52.3 | 53.3 | 50.2 | 50.7 | 57.3 | 52.1 |
| Passing Yardage | 3330 | 3286 | 2747 | 3115 | 2827 | 2621 | 2524 | 2699 | 3446 | 3632 | 2419 | 3388 | 2491 | 3532 |
| Avg. Yds per Att. | 7.9 | 7.6 | 7.4 | 8.2 | 7.5 | 8.4 | 6.8 | 7.8 | 8.4 | 8.5 | 7.6 | 7.8 | 7.7 | 8.3 |
| Avg. Yds per Comp. | 14.1 | 14.3 | 13.7 | 15.6 | 13.4 | 14.0 | 13.4 | 15.9 | 16.0 | 15.9 | 15.1 | 15.4 | 13.5 | 15.8 |
| Yards Lost Tackled | 265 | 226 | 213 | 243 | 246 | 290 | 348 | 483 | 139 | 247 | 350 | 288 | 423 | 309 |
| Net Yards | 3065 | 3060 | 2534 | 2872 | 2581 | 2331 | 2176 | 2216 | 3307 | 3385 | 2069 | 3100 | 2068 | 3223 |
| Touchdowns | 27 | 20 | 17 | 31 | 19 | 14 | 14 | 22 | 35 | 23 | 14 | 18 | 19 | 27 |
| Interceptions | 25 | 28 | 16 | 17 | 24 | 13 | 19 | 31 | 22 | 31 | 23 | 30 | 19 | 27 |
| Pct. Intercepted | 5.9 | 6.5 | 4.3 | 4.5 | 6.3 | 4.2 | 5.1 | 8.9 | 5.4 | 7.2 | 7.2 | 6.9 | 5.9 | 6.3 |
| **PUNTING:** | | | | | | | | | | | | | | |
| Number | 58 | 69 | 45 | 57 | 53 | 50 | 87 | 65 | 55 | 64 | 60 | 59 | 48 | 63 |
| Average Distance | 41.5 | 43.7 | 42.8 | 45.4 | 45.3 | 40.9 | 45.5 | 40.3 | 40.6 | 42.9 | 40.0 | 38.3 | 45.6 | 34.5 |
| **PUNT RETURNS:** | | | | | | | | | | | | | | |
| Number | 34 | 39 | 20 | 17 | 39 | 31 | 27 | 34 | 17 | 14 | 19 | 20 | 27 | 29 |
| Yards | 272 | 281 | 111 | 81 | 502 | 290 | 252 | 374 | 58 | 95 | 169 | 134 | 207 | 184 |
| Average Yards | 8.0 | 7.2 | 5.6 | 4.8 | 12.9 | 9.4 | 9.3 | 11.0 | 3.4 | 6.8 | 8.9 | 6.7 | 7.7 | 6.3 |
| Touchdowns | 0 | 1 | 0 | 0 | 0 | 0 | 0 | 0 | 0 | 0 | 0 | 0 | 1 | 0 |
| **KICKOFF RETURNS:** | | | | | | | | | | | | | | |
| Number | 55 | 53 | 46 | 59 | 46 | 30 | 60 | 67 | 54 | 61 | 62 | 64 | 62 | 61 |
| Yards | 1263 | 1129 | 983 | 1207 | 1124 | 716 | 1447 | 1522 | 1405 | 1385 | 1350 | 1495 | 1739 | 1720 |
| Average Yards | 23.0 | 21.3 | 21.4 | 20.5 | 24.4 | 23.9 | 24.1 | 22.7 | 26.0 | 22.7 | 21.8 | 23.4 | 28.0 | 28.2 |
| Touchdowns | 0 | 0 | 0 | 1 | 0 | 1 | 0 | 0 | 1 | 1 | 0 | 0 | 0 | 1 |
| **INTERCEPTION RETURNS:** | | | | | | | | | | | | | | |
| Number | 23 | 23 | 24 | 20 | 24 | 31 | 19 | 25 | 26 | 26 | 28 | 16 | 12 | 28 |
| Yards | 331 | 468 | 352 | 366 | 269 | 452 | 261 | 280 | 332 | 289 | 318 | 229 | 127 | 285 |
| Average Yards | 14.4 | 20.3 | 14.7 | 18.3 | 11.2 | 14.6 | 13.7 | 11.2 | 12.8 | 11.1 | 11.4 | 14.3 | 10.6 | 10.2 |
| Touchdowns | 0 | 2 | 0 | 1 | 2 | 1 | 2 | 1 | 0 | 0 | 2 | 1 | 0 | 0 |
| **PENALTIES:** | | | | | | | | | | | | | | |
| Number | 63 | 69 | 56 | 62 | 62 | 59 | 71 | 44 | 62 | 58 | 45 | 56 | 63 | 62 |
| Yards | 675 | 776 | 600 | 639 | 624 | 617 | 704 | 447 | 601 | 619 | 427 | 655 | 636 | 663 |
| **FUMBLES:** | | | | | | | | | | | | | | |
| Number | 26 | 29 | 24 | 32 | 26 | 29 | 26 | 37 | 24 | 25 | 24 | 36 | 24 | 31 |
| Number Lost | 19 | 16 | 17 | 19 | 18 | 15 | 16 | 23 | 14 | 13 | 13 | 21 | 14 | 17 |
| **POINTS:** | | | | | | | | | | | | | | |
| Total | 293 | 321 | 291 | 398 | 315 | 415 | 220 | 254 | 398 | 282 | 312 | 287 | 282 | 305 |
| PAT Attempts | 37 | 41 | 36 | 51 | 38 | 53 | 27 | 31 | 49 | 38 | 33 | 39 | 36 | 39 |
| PAT Made | 31 | 36 | 33 | 50 | 37 | 52 | 26 | 31 | 47 | 36 | 32 | 38 | 36 | 38 |
| FG Attempts | 28 | 27 | 31 | 27 | 34 | 21 | 20 | 25 | 28 | 19 | 42 | 14 | 23 | 25 |
| FG Made | 12 | 13 | 14 | 14 | 14 | 15 | 10 | 11 | 19 | 6 | 26 | 5 | 10 | 11 |
| Percent FG Made | 42.9 | 48.1 | 45.2 | 51.9 | 41.2 | 71.4 | 50.0 | 44.0 | 67.9 | 31.6 | 61.9 | 35.7 | 43.5 | 44.0 |
| Safeties | 2 | 0 | 0 | 0 | 4 | 0 | 1 | 2 | 0 | 0 | 2 | 0 | 0 | 0 |

**DEFENSE**

| | BALT. | CHI. | CLEVE. | DALLAS | DET. | G.BAY | L.A. | MINN. | N.Y. | PHIL. | PITT. | ST.L. | S.F. | WASH. |
|---|---|---|---|---|---|---|---|---|---|---|---|---|---|---|
| **FIRST DOWNS:** | | | | | | | | | | | | | | |
| Total | 226 | 228 | 263 | 274 | 180 | 191 | 256 | 266 | 256 | 275 | 250 | 251 | 240 | 280 |
| by Rushing | 91 | 108 | 122 | 93 | 62 | 88 | 119 | 119 | 100 | 128 | 78 | 93 | 107 | 95 |
| by Passing | 119 | 101 | 125 | 166 | 105 | 94 | 124 | 139 | 136 | 129 | 157 | 141 | 113 | 165 |
| by Penalty | 16 | 19 | 16 | 15 | 13 | 9 | 13 | 8 | 20 | 18 | 15 | 17 | 20 | 20 |
| **RUSHING:** | | | | | | | | | | | | | | |
| Numbers | 423 | 438 | 466 | 387 | 353 | 404 | 501 | 463 | 413 | 526 | 363 | 452 | 464 | 411 |
| Yards | 1504 | 2073 | 1940 | 1510 | 1231 | 1531 | 2092 | 1978 | 1677 | 2126 | 1419 | 1724 | 2241 | 1636 |
| Average Yards | 3.6 | 4.7 | 4.2 | 3.9 | 3.5 | 3.8 | 4.2 | 4.3 | 4.1 | 4.0 | 3.9 | 3.8 | 4.8 | 4.0 |
| Touchdowns | 17 | 17 | 17 | 17 | 6 | 4 | 14 | 20 | 13 | 23 | 13 | 18 | 22 | 12 |
| **PASSING:** | | | | | | | | | | | | | | |
| Attempts | 381 | 363 | 341 | 437 | 367 | 355 | 379 | 397 | 450 | 363 | 438 | 377 | 296 | 412 |
| Completions | 206 | 170 | 189 | 233 | 187 | 187 | 217 | 214 | 223 | 198 | 223 | 196 | 164 | 247 |
| Completion Pct. | 54.1 | 46.8 | 55.4 | 53.3 | 51.0 | 52.7 | 57.3 | 53.9 | 49.6 | 54.5 | 50.9 | 52.0 | 55.4 | 60.0 |
| Passing Yardage | 2975 | 2460 | 2277 | 3904 | 2441 | 2084 | 3144 | 3365 | 3238 | 3023 | 3490 | 3302 | 2494 | 3860 |
| Avg. Yds per Att. | 7.8 | 6.8 | 6.7 | 8.9 | 6.7 | 5.9 | 8.3 | 8.5 | 7.2 | 8.3 | 8.0 | 8.8 | 8.4 | 9.4 |
| Avg. Yds per Comp. | 14.4 | 14.5 | 12.0 | 16.8 | 13.1 | 11.1 | 14.5 | 15.7 | 14.5 | 15.3 | 15.7 | 16.8 | 15.2 | 15.6 |
| Yards Lost Tackled | 356 | 386 | 293 | 230 | 455 | 338 | 255 | 242 | 369 | 103 | 284 | 315 | 186 | 258 |
| Net Yards | 2619 | 2074 | 1984 | 3674 | 1986 | 1746 | 2889 | 3123 | 2869 | 2920 | 3206 | 2987 | 2308 | 3602 |
| Touchdowns | 19 | 14 | 15 | 33 | 11 | 10 | 25 | 29 | 21 | 16 | 34 | 21 | 17 | 35 |
| Interceptions | 23 | 23 | 24 | 20 | 24 | 31 | 19 | 25 | 26 | 26 | 28 | 16 | 12 | 28 |
| Pct. Intercepted | 6.0 | 6.3 | 7.0 | 4.6 | 6.5 | 8.7 | 5.0 | 6.3 | 5.8 | 7.2 | 6.4 | 4.2 | 4.1 | 6.8 |
| **PUNTING:** | | | | | | | | | | | | | | |
| Number | 67 | 71 | 56 | 63 | 70 | 58 | 56 | 52 | 65 | 42 | 62 | 61 | 61 | 49 |
| Average Distance | 42.7 | 41.8 | 40.6 | 40.6 | 44.1 | 43.2 | 45.5 | 43.3 | 38.8 | 38.2 | 40.7 | 40.6 | 44.6 | 42.4 |
| **PUNT RETURNS:** | | | | | | | | | | | | | | |
| Number | 23 | 32 | 15 | 28 | 31 | 20 | 55 | 32 | 24 | 24 | 18 | 26 | 32 | 7 |
| Yards | 182 | 308 | 121 | 190 | 326 | 183 | 567 | 261 | 138 | 174 | 119 | 122 | 285 | 34 |
| Average Yards | 7.9 | 9.6 | 8.1 | 6.8 | 10.5 | 9.2 | 10.3 | 8.2 | 5.8 | 7.3 | 6.6 | 4.7 | 8.9 | 4.9 |
| Touchdowns | 0 | 0 | 0 | 0 | 0 | 1 | 1 | 0 | 0 | 0 | 0 | 0 | 0 | 0 |
| **KICKOFF RETURNS:** | | | | | | | | | | | | | | |
| Number | 52 | 60 | 49 | 63 | 55 | 76 | 50 | 52 | 63 | 56 | 54 | 41 | 51 | 58 |
| Yards | 1433 | 1514 | 1098 | 1604 | 1379 | 1524 | 1211 | 1149 | 1700 | 1459 | 1151 | 870 | 1140 | 1253 |
| Average Yards | 27.6 | 25.2 | 22.4 | 25.5 | 25.1 | 20.1 | 24.2 | 22.1 | 27.0 | 26.1 | 21.3 | 21.2 | 22.4 | 21.6 |
| Touchdowns | 1 | 0 | 0 | 1 | 0 | 0 | 0 | 0 | 0 | 1 | 0 | 0 | 0 | 2 |
| **INTERCEPTION RETURNS:** | | | | | | | | | | | | | | |
| Number | 25 | 28 | 16 | 17 | 24 | 13 | 19 | 31 | 22 | 31 | 23 | 30 | 19 | 27 |
| Yards | 386 | 328 | 161 | 263 | 352 | 122 | 293 | 445 | 182 | 555 | 257 | 389 | 334 | 292 |
| Average Yards | 15.4 | 11.7 | 10.1 | 15.5 | 14.7 | 9.4 | 15.4 | 14.4 | 8.3 | 17.9 | 11.2 | 13.0 | 17.6 | 10.8 |
| Touchdowns | 0 | 1 | 0 | 1 | 0 | 1 | 2 | 1 | 0 | 2 | 0 | 1 | 3 | 0 |
| **PENALTIES:** | | | | | | | | | | | | | | |
| Number | 71 | 65 | 53 | 56 | 51 | 54 | 52 | 68 | 58 | 48 | 53 | 63 | 57 | 83 |
| Yards | 792 | 643 | 547 | 569 | 527 | 611 | 592 | 633 | 636 | 479 | 581 | 584 | 626 | 863 |
| **FUMBLES:** | | | | | | | | | | | | | | |
| Number | 32 | 37 | 23 | 33 | 34 | 28 | 30 | 30 | 30 | 22 | 21 | 23 | 22 | 28 |
| Number Lost | 19 | 24 | 13 | 16 | 23 | 19 | 18 | 18 | 13 | 13 | 10 | 15 | 14 | 20 |
| **POINTS:** | | | | | | | | | | | | | | |
| Total | 288 | 287 | 257 | 402 | 177 | 148 | 334 | 410 | 283 | 356 | 363 | 361 | 331 | 376 |
| PAT Attempts | 37 | 34 | 34 | 52 | 19 | 17 | 42 | 52 | 35 | 43 | 48 | 44 | 42 | 49 |
| PAT Made | 35 | 31 | 32 | 49 | 19 | 17 | 38 | 51 | 34 | 41 | 48 | 43 | 39 | 46 |
| FG Attempts | 22 | 31 | 14 | 25 | 25 | 22 | 33 | 30 | 27 | 37 | 19 | 33 | 20 | 26 |
| FG Made | 9 | 16 | 7 | 13 | 14 | 9 | 14 | 15 | 13 | 19 | 9 | 18 | 12 | 12 |
| Percent FG Made | 40.9 | 51.6 | 50.0 | 52.0 | 56.0 | 40.9 | 42.4 | 50.0 | 48.1 | 51.4 | 47.4 | 54.5 | 60.0 | 46.2 |
| Safeties | 2 | 2 | 0 | 1 | 1 | 1 | 1 | 1 | 0 | 0 | 0 | 0 | 2 | 0 |

**1962 NFL CHAMPIONSHIP GAME**
December 30, at New York
(Attendance 64,892)

## A Dismal Homecoming

A bone-chilling thirty-five-mile-per-hour wind lanced through Yankee Stadium, where the temperature was 20 degrees at game time and dropped steadily all afternoon. The Giants were out to avenge last year's loss to the Packers but fell short in a bitterly contested, hard-hitting ground game. The wind and cold made passing close to impossible, so the game was fought out primarily between the opposing lines and power runners. One particularly brutal pairing was Packer fullback Jim Taylor and Giant linebacker Sam Huff, the two of them butting heads constantly all game long. The Packers punched out yardage behind the crisp blocking of their offensive line and scored in the opening period on a 26-yard Jerry Kramer field goal. The Packers got a break in the second quarter when Dan Currie's hard tackle knocked the football loose from Phil King on the Giant 28-yard line. On the first play after the recovery, Paul Hornung passed 21 yards to Boyd Dowler on the halfback option, and Jim Taylor blasted through the line for the last seven yards on the next play. The Packers led 10-0 at halftime, but the Giants finally scored in the third period when Erich Barnes blocked Max McGee's punt and Jim Collier fell on it in the end zone for a touchdown. On the next series of downs, the Packers again punted, but New York's Sam Horner fumbled the ball and Green Bay recovered on the Giant 40-yard line. After that, the Packers never lost momentum, and two more Kramer field goals made the final score 16-7.

### TEAM STATISTICS

| N. Y. | | G. B. |
|---|---|---|
| 18 | First Downs – Total | 18 |
| 5 | First Downs – Rushing | 11 |
| 11 | First Downs – Passing | 6 |
| 2 | First Downs – Penalty | 1 |
| 7 | Punts – Number | 6 |
| 42.0 | Punts – Average Distance | 25.5 |
| 0 | Punt Return Yardage | 36 |
| 0 | Interception Returns – Number | 1 |
| 0 | Interception Return – Yards | 30 |
| 3 | Fumbles – Number | 2 |
| 2 | Fumbles – Number Lost | 0 |
| 4 | Penalties – Number | 5 |
| 62 | Yards – Penalized | 44 |
| 3 | Giveaways | 0 |
| 0 | Takeaways | 3 |
| –3 | Difference | +3 |

### SCORING

| | | | | |
|---|---|---|---|---|
| NEW YORK | 0 | 0 | 7 | 0– 7 |
| GREEN BAY | 3 | 7 | 3 | 3–16 |

First Quarter
G.B. J. Kramer, 26 yard field goal 7:11

Second Quarter
G.B. Taylor, 7 yard rush 12:21
PAT – J. Kramer (kick)

Third Quarter
N.Y. Collier, recovered blocked punt in the end zone. 7:26
PAT – Chandler (kick)
G.B. J. Kramer, 29 yard field goal 11:00

Fourth Quarter
G.B. J. Kramer, 30 yard field goal 13:10

### INDIVIDUAL STATISTICS

**RUSHING**

| NEW YORK | No | Yds | Avg. | GREEN BAY | No | Yds | Avg. |
|---|---|---|---|---|---|---|---|
| Webster | 15 | 56 | 3.7 | Taylor | 31 | 85 | 2.7 |
| King | 11 | 38 | 3.5 | Hornung | 8 | 35 | 4.4 |
| | 26 | 94 | 3.6 | Moore | 6 | 24 | 4.0 |
| | | | | Starr | 1 | 4 | 4.0 |
| | | | | | 46 | 148 | 3.2 |

**RECEIVING**

| NEW YORK | No | Yds | Avg. | GREEN BAY | No | Yds | Avg. |
|---|---|---|---|---|---|---|---|
| Walton | 5 | 75 | 15.0 | Dowler | 4 | 48 | 12.0 |
| Shofner | 5 | 69 | 13.8 | Taylor | 3 | 20 | 6.7 |
| Gifford | 4 | 34 | 8.5 | R. Kramer | 2 | 25 | 12.5 |
| King | 2 | 14 | 7.0 | McGee | 1 | 13 | 13.0 |
| Webster | 1 | 5 | 5.0 | | 10 | 106 | 10.6 |
| Morrison | 1 | 0 | 0.0 | | | | |
| | 18 | 197 | 10.9 | | | | |

**PASSING**

| | Att | Comp | Comp Pct. | Yds | Int | Yds/ Att. | Yds/ Comp |
|---|---|---|---|---|---|---|---|
| NEW YORK | | | | | | | |
| Tittle | 41 | 18 | 43.9 | 197 | 1 | 4.8 | 10.9 |
| GREEN BAY | | | | | | | |
| Starr | 21 | 9 | 42.9 | 85 | 0 | 4.0 | 9.4 |
| Hornung | 1 | 1 | 100.0 | 21 | 0 | 21.0 | 21.0 |
| | 22 | 10 | 45.5 | 106 | 0 | 4.8 | 10.6 |

**NEW YORK GIANTS 12-2-0 Allie Sherman**

| Scores of Each Game | | |
|---|---|---|
| 7 | Cleveland | 17 |
| 29 | Philadelphia | 13 |
| 31 | Pittsburgh | 27 |
| 31 | St. Louis | 14 |
| 17 | PITTSBURGH | 20 |
| 17 | DETROIT | 14 |
| 49 | WASHINGTON | 34 |
| 31 | ST. LOUIS | 28 |
| 41 | Dallas | 10 |
| 42 | Washington | 24 |
| 19 | PHILADELPHIA | 14 |
| 26 | Chicago | 24 |
| 17 | CLEVELAND | 13 |
| 41 | DALLAS | 31 |

| Use Name | Pos. | Hgt | Wgt | Age | Int | Pts |
|---|---|---|---|---|---|---|
| Rosey Brown | OT | 6'3" | 255 | 29 | | |
| Jack Stroud | OT | 6'1" | 250 | 33 | | |
| Reed Bohovich | OG-OT | 6'3" | 260 | 21 | | |
| Bookie Bolin | OG | 6'2" | 235 | 22 | | |
| Darrell Dess | OG | 6' | 245 | 26 | | |
| Greg Larson | C-OG | 6'2" | 245 | 23 | | |
| Ray Wietecha | C | 6'1" | 230 | 33 | | |
| Ken Byers | DE | 6'1" | 240 | 22 | | |
| Jim Katcavage | DE | 6'3" | 240 | 27 | 1 | |
| Andy Robustelli | DE | 6'1" | 235 | 36 | | |
| Rosey Grier | DT | 6'5" | 290 | 29 | | |
| Chuck Janerette | DT | 6'3" | 250 | 23 | | |
| Dick Modzelewski | DT | 6' | 260 | 31 | | |
| Sam Huff | LB | 6'1" | 230 | 27 | 1 | |
| Dick Lasse | LB | 6'2" | 225 | 26 | | |
| Tom Scott | LB | 6'2" | 220 | 32 | 1 | |
| Mickey Walker | LB | 6' | 230 | 22 | | |
| Bill Winter | LB | 6'3" | 220 | 22 | | |
| Erich Barnes | DB | 6'2" | 198 | 27 | 6 | |
| Sam Horner | DB | 6' | 198 | 24 | | |
| Dick Lynch | DB | 6'1" | 205 | 26 | 5 | 12 |
| Jimmy Patton | DB | 6' | 185 | 28 | 7 | |
| Dick Pesonen | DB | 6' | 190 | 24 | 2 | |
| Allan Webb | DB | 5'11" | 180 | 27 | 3 | |
| Ralph Gugliemi | QB | 6'1" | 195 | 29 | | |
| Y. A. Tittle | QB | 6' | 195 | 35 | | 12 |
| Johnny Counts | HB | 5'10" | 170 | 23 | | 6 |
| Paul Dudley | HB | 6' | 185 | 22 | | 6 |
| Phil King | HB | 6'4" | 225 | 26 | | 12 |
| Joe Morrison | DB-HB | 6'1" | 212 | 24 | | 18 |
| Alex Webster | FB | 6'3" | 225 | 31 | | 54 |
| Frank Gifford | FL | 6'1" | 190 | 32 | | 48 |
| Jim Collier | OE | 6'2" | 195 | 23 | | |
| Del Shofner | OE | 6'3" | 185 | 26 | | 72 |
| Aaron Thomas (from SF) | OE | 6'3" | 208 | 24 | | |
| Joe Walton | OE | 5'11" | 200 | 27 | | 54 |
| Don Chandler | K | 6'2" | 210 | 27 | | 104 |

**PITTSBURGH STEELERS 9-5-0 Buddy Parker**

| Scores of Each Game | | |
|---|---|---|
| 7 | Detroit | 45 |
| 30 | Dallas | 28 |
| 27 | NEW YORK | 31 |
| 13 | PHILADELPHIA | 7 |
| 20 | New York | 17 |
| 27 | DALLAS | 42 |
| 14 | CLEVELAND | 41 |
| 39 | MINNESOTA | 31 |
| 26 | St. Louis | 17 |
| 23 | WASHINGTON | 21 |
| 14 | Cleveland | 35 |
| 19 | ST. LOUIS | 7 |
| 26 | Philadelphia | 17 |
| 27 | Washington | 24 |

| Use Name | Pos. | Hgt | Wgt | Age | Int | Pts |
|---|---|---|---|---|---|---|
| Charlie Bradshaw | OT | 6'6" | 255 | 26 | | |
| Dan James | OT | 6'4" | 280 | 25 | | |
| Ray Lemek | OG | 6' | 240 | 28 | | |
| Mike Sandusky | OG | 6' | 230 | 29 | | |
| Ron Stehouwer | OG | 6'2" | 230 | 25 | | |
| Buzz Nutter | C | 6'4" | 230 | 31 | | |
| Lou Michaels | DE | 6'2" | 235 | 26 | | 110 |
| Ernie Stautner | DE | 6'1" | 230 | 37 | 1 | 2 |
| John Kenerson (to NY-A) | DT | 6'3" | 255 | 23 | | |
| Joe Krupa | DT | 6'2" | 225 | 29 | | |
| Big Daddy Lipscomb | DT | 6'6" | 288 | 30 | | |
| George Strugar (to NY-A) | DT | 6'5" | 258 | 27 | | |
| Lou Cordileone (from LA) | DE-DT | 6' | 245 | 25 | | |
| Myron Pottios - Broken Arm | | | | | | |
| Tom Bettis | LB | 6'2" | 225 | 29 | | |
| Rudy Hayes | LB | 6' | 215 | 27 | | |
| Ken Kirk | LB | 6'2" | 230 | 24 | | |
| John Reger | LB | 6' | 230 | 31 | 1 | |
| Bob Schmitz | LB | 6'1" | 235 | 25 | 3 | 6 |
| Bob Simms (from NY) | LB | 6'1" | 230 | 24 | | |
| George Tarasovic | LB | 6'4" | 245 | 33 | 4 | |
| Willie Daniel | DB | 5'11" | 185 | 24 | 5 | 6 |
| Glenn Glass | DB | 6' | 190 | 25 | | |
| Dick Haley | DB | 5'10" | 195 | 26 | 4 | |
| Brady Keys | DB | 6' | 185 | 26 | 3 | |
| Johnny Sample | DB | 6'1" | 200 | 25 | | |
| Jackie Simpson | DB | 5'10" | 185 | 28 | | |
| Clendon Thomas | DB | 6'2" | 192 | 25 | 7 | |
| Ed Brown | QB | 6'2" | 210 | 33 | | |
| Bobby Layne | QB | 6'1" | 210 | 35 | | 6 |
| Terry Nofsinger | QB | 6'4" | 205 | 24 | | |
| Gary Ballman | HB | 6' | 190 | 22 | | |
| Dick Hoak | HB | 5'11" | 190 | 23 | | 24 |
| Tom Tracy | HB | 5'9" | 205 | 30 | | |
| Joe Womack | HB | 5'9" | 210 | 25 | | 30 |
| Bob Ferguson | FB | 5'11" | 220 | 21 | | |
| John Henry Johnson | FB | 6'2" | 215 | 32 | | 54 |
| Buddy Dial | FL | 6'1" | 195 | 25 | | 36 |
| Red Mack | FL | 5'10" | 185 | 25 | | 12 |
| John Burrell | OE | 6'3" | 188 | 22 | | |
| Preston Carpenter | OE | 6'2" | 190 | 28 | | 24 |
| Harlon Hill (to DET) | OE | 6'3" | 200 | 30 | | |
| John Powers | OE | 6'2" | 215 | 21 | | |

**CLEVELAND BROWNS 7-6-1 Paul Brown**

| Scores of Each Game | | |
|---|---|---|
| 17 | NEW YORK | 7 |
| 16 | WASHINGTON | 17 |
| 7 | Philadelphia | 35 |
| 19 | DALLAS | 10 |
| 14 | BALTIMORE | 36 |
| 34 | St. Louis | 7 |
| 41 | Pittsburgh | 14 |
| 14 | PHILADELPHIA | 14 |
| 9 | Washington | 17 |
| 38 | ST. LOUIS | 14 |
| 35 | PITTSBURGH | 14 |
| 21 | Dallas | 45 |
| 13 | New York | 17 |
| 13 | San Francisco | 10 |

| Use Name | Pos. | Hgt | Wgt | Age | Int | Pts |
|---|---|---|---|---|---|---|
| John Brown | OT | 6'2" | 245 | 23 | | |
| Mike McCormack | OT | 6'4" | 250 | 35 | | |
| Dick Schafrath | OT | 6'3" | 255 | 26 | | |
| Gene Hickerson | OG | 6'3" | 248 | 27 | | |
| Jim Ray Smith | OG | 6'3" | 245 | 31 | | |
| John Wooten | OG | 6'2" | 250 | 27 | | |
| John Morrow | C | 6'3" | 248 | 29 | | |
| Frank Morze | C | 6'4" | 264 | 28 | | |
| Bill Glass | DE | 6'5" | 255 | 26 | | |
| Jim Houston | DE | 6'2" | 235 | 25 | | |
| Paul Wiggin | DE | 6'3" | 245 | 28 | | |
| Bob Gain | DT | 6'3" | 260 | 34 | | |
| Frank Parker | DT | 6'5" | 250 | 22 | | |
| Floyd Peters | DT | 6'4" | 255 | 27 | 1 | |
| Vince Costello | LB | 6' | 232 | 30 | 3 | 6 |
| Galen Fiss | LB | 6' | 227 | 32 | 4 | |
| Mike Lucci | LB | 6'2" | 220 | 22 | | |
| Sam Tidmore | LB | 6'1" | 220 | 23 | | |
| Ross Fichtner | DB | 6' | 185 | 24 | 7 | |
| Don Fleming | DB | 6' | 188 | 25 | 2 | |
| Bobby Franklin | DB | 5'11" | 182 | 26 | 1 | |
| Bernie Parrish | DB | 5'11" | 195 | 27 | 2 | |
| Jim Shofner | DB | 6'2" | 190 | 26 | 4 | |
| Jim Shorter | DB | 5'11" | 180 | 21 | | |
| John Furman | QB | 6'4" | 205 | 22 | | |
| Jim Ninowski | QB | 6'1" | 200 | 26 | | |
| Frank Ryan | QB | 6'3" | 200 | 26 | | 6 |
| Ernie Green | HB | 6'2" | 205 | 23 | | 6 |
| Charlie Scales | HB | 5'11" | 215 | 23 | | 18 |
| Tom Wilson | FB-HB | 6' | 204 | 29 | | 6 |
| Jimmy Brown | FB | 6'2" | 228 | 26 | | 108 |
| Ray Renfro | FL | 6'1" | 192 | 31 | | 24 |
| Johnny Brewer | OE | 6'4" | 225 | 25 | | 12 |
| Leon Clarke | OE | 6'4" | 235 | 29 | | |
| Gary Collins | OE | 6'4" | 208 | 21 | | 12 |
| Bob Crespino | OE | 6'4" | 217 | 24 | | |
| Rich Kreitling | OE | 6'2" | 208 | 27 | | 18 |
| Lou Groza | K | 6'3" | 248 | 38 | | 75 |

**WASHINGTON REDSKINS 5-7-2 Bill McPeak**

| Scores of Each Game | | |
|---|---|---|
| 35 | Dallas | 35 |
| 17 | Cleveland | 16 |
| 24 | ST. LOUIS | 14 |
| 20 | LOS ANGELES | 14 |
| 17 | St. Louis | 17 |
| 27 | Philadelphia | 21 |
| 34 | New York | 49 |
| 10 | DALLAS | 38 |
| 17 | CLEVELAND | 9 |
| 21 | Pittsburgh | 23 |
| 24 | NEW YORK | 42 |
| 14 | PHILADELPHIA | 37 |
| 21 | Baltimore | 34 |
| 24 | PITTSBURGH | 27 |

| Use Name | Pos. | Hgt | Wgt | Age | Int | Pts |
|---|---|---|---|---|---|---|
| Fran O'Brien | OT | 6'1" | 250 | 27 | | |
| Riley Mattson | OT | 6'4 | 248 | 23 | | |
| Bob Khayat | OG | 6'2 | 230 | 24 | | 71 |
| Charlie Moore | OG | 6'5" | 230 | 22 | | |
| John Nisby | OG | 6'1" | 247 | 29 | | |
| Vince Promuto | OG | 6'1" | 243 | 24 | | |
| Fred Hageman | C | 6'4" | 244 | 24 | | |
| Gene Cronin | DE | 6'2" | 228 | 29 | | |
| Ed Khayat | DE | 6'3" | 248 | 27 | | |
| John Paluck | DE | 6'2" | 240 | 29 | | |
| Andy Stynchula | DE | 6'3" | 257 | 23 | | |
| Ben Davidson | DT | 6'8" | 275 | 22 | | |
| Joe Rutgens | DT | 6'2" | 265 | 23 | | |
| Bob Toneff | DT | 6'3" | 275 | 32 | | |
| Rod Breedlove | LB | 6'2" | 225 | 24 | 3 | |
| Gorden Kelley | LB | 6'3 | 230 | 24 | 2 | |
| Al Miller | LB | 6' | 220 | 22 | | |
| Bob Pellegrini | LB | 6'2" | 225 | 27 | 4 | |
| Claude Crabb | DB | 6' | 190 | 22 | 6 | |
| Doug Elmore | DB | 6' | 188 | 22 | 2 | |
| Bobby Freeman | DB | 6'1" | 200 | 29 | 3 | |
| Dale Hackbart | DB | 6'3" | 210 | 26 | 3 | |
| Jim Kerr | DB | 6' | 195 | 23 | 1 | |
| Jim Steffen | DB | 6' | 195 | 25 | 4 | 6 |
| Ron Hatcher | FB-DB | 5'11" | 215 | 23 | | |
| Galen Hall | QB | 5'10" | 205 | 23 | 6 | |
| George Izo | QB | 6'3 | 214 | 25 | | |
| Norm Snead | QB | 6'4" | 215 | 22 | | 18 |
| Billy Barnes | HB | 5'11" | 202 | 27 | | 18 |
| Leroy Jackson | HB | 6' | 190 | 22 | | 6 |
| Dick James | HB | 5'9" | 175 | 28 | | 30 |
| Don Bosseler | FB | 6'1" | 212 | 26 | | 12 |
| Jim Cunningham | FB | 5'11" | 220 | 23 | | 12 |
| Bobby Mitchell | FL | 6' | 192 | 27 | | 72 |
| Bill Anderson | OE | 6'2" | 214 | 26 | | 12 |
| Fred Dugan | OE | 6'3" | 198 | 28 | | 30 |
| Steve Junker | OE | 6'3" | 217 | 27 | | 12 |
| Hugh Smith | OE | 6'4" | 215 | 24 | | |

**DALLAS COWBOYS 5-8-1 Tom Landry**

| Scores of Each Game | | |
|---|---|---|
| 35 | WASHINGTON | 35 |
| 28 | PITTSBURGH | 30 |
| 27 | Los Angeles | 17 |
| 10 | Cleveland | 19 |
| 41 | PHILADELPHIA | 19 |
| 42 | Pittsburgh | 27 |
| 24 | ST. LOUIS | 28 |
| 38 | Washington | 10 |
| 10 | NEW YORK | 41 |
| 33 | CHICAGO | 34 |
| 14 | Philadelphia | 28 |
| 45 | CLEVELAND | 21 |
| 20 | St. Louis | 52 |
| 31 | New York | 41 |

| Use Name | Pos. | Hgt | Wgt | Age | Int | Pts |
|---|---|---|---|---|---|---|
| Clyde Brock | OT | 6'5" | 268 | 22 | | |
| Monte Clark | OT | 6'6" | 260 | 25 | | |
| Bob Fry | OT | 6'4" | 240 | 31 | | |
| Dale Memmelaar | OT | 6'2" | 245 | 25 | | |
| Andy Cvercko | OG | 6' | 243 | 25 | | |
| Joe Bob Isbell | OG | 6'1" | 225 | 22 | | |
| Mike Connelly | C | 6'3" | 235 | 26 | | |
| Lynn Hoyem | C | 6'4" | 225 | 22 | | |
| George Andrie | DE | 6'7" | 247 | 22 | | |
| Bob Lilly | DE | 6'4" | 248 | 23 | | |
| Ken Frost | DT | 6'4" | 245 | 23 | | |
| John Meyers | DT | 6'6" | 267 | 22 | | |
| Guy Reese | DT | 6'5" | 238 | 22 | | |
| Mike Dowdle | LB | 6'3" | 210 | 24 | 1 | |
| Chuck Howley | LB | 6'3" | 230 | 26 | 2 | |
| Bob Lang | LB | 6'3" | 235 | 28 | | |
| Don Talbert | LB | 6'5" | 225 | 22 | | |
| Jerry Tubbs | LB | 6'2" | 220 | 27 | 4 | |
| Don Bishop | DB | 6'2" | 204 | 27 | 6 | 6 |
| Mike Gaechter | DB | 6' | 190 | 22 | 5 | 6 |
| Cornell Green | DB | 6'4" | 210 | 22 | | |
| Warren Livingston | DB | 5'10" | 180 | 24 | | |
| Dick Nolan | DB | 6'1" | 185 | 30 | | |
| Jerry Norton | DB | 5'11" | 195 | 32 | 2 | 6 |
| John Houser – Injury | | | | | | |
| Ed Nutting – Injury | | | | | | |
| Buddy Humphrey | QB | 6'1" | 200 | 26 | | |
| Eddie LeBaron | QB | 5'9" | 160 | 32 | | |
| Don Meredith | QB | 6'2" | 198 | 24 | | |
| Amos Bullocks | HB | 6'1" | 197 | 23 | | 18 |
| Don Perkins | HB | 5'10" | 198 | 24 | | 42 |
| J. W. Lockett | FB | 6'2" | 230 | 25 | | 18 |
| Amos Marsh | FB | 6'1" | 208 | 23 | | 54 |
| Frank Clarke | FL | 6' | 215 | 29 | | 84 |
| Donnie Davis | FL | 6'4" | 214 | 22 | | |
| Lee Folkins | OE | 6'5" | 220 | 23 | | 36 |
| Billy Howton | OE | 6'2" | 194 | 32 | | 36 |
| Pettis Norman | OE | 6'3" | 215 | 22 | | |
| Glynn Gregory | DB-OE | 6'2" | 200 | 23 | | |
| Sam Baker | K | 6'2" | 217 | 30 | | 92 |

## NEW YORK GIANTS

### RUSHING

| Last Name | No. | Yds | Avg | TD |
|---|---|---|---|---|
| Webster | 207 | 743 | 3.6 | 5 |
| King | 108 | 460 | 4.3 | 2 |
| Morrison | 35 | 146 | 4.2 | 1 |
| Tittle | 17 | 108 | 6.4 | 2 |
| Dudley | 27 | 100 | 3.7 | 0 |
| Counts | 14 | 55 | 3.9 | 0 |
| Guglielmi | 11 | 40 | 3.6 | 0 |
| Gifford | 2 | 18 | 9.0 | 1 |
| Shofner | 1 | 4 | 4.0 | 0 |
| Thomas | 1 | −9 | −9.0 | 0 |
| Chandler | 1 | −11 | −11.0 | 0 |

### RECEIVING

| Last Name | No. | Yds | Avg | TD |
|---|---|---|---|---|
| Shofner | 53 | 1133 | 21 | 12 |
| Webster | 47 | 477 | 10 | 4 |
| Gifford | 39 | 796 | 20 | 7 |
| Walton | 33 | 406 | 12 | 9 |
| King | 15 | 186 | 12 | 1 |
| Dudley | 9 | 112 | 12 | 1 |
| Morrison | 6 | 107 | 18 | 2 |
| Thomas | 4 | 80 | 20 | 0 |
| Counts | 4 | 62 | 16 | 0 |
| Collier | 1 | 27 | 27 | 0 |
| Robustelli | 1 | 26 | 26 | 0 |

### PUNT RETURNS

| Last Name | No. | Yds | Avg | TD |
|---|---|---|---|---|
| Counts | 8 | 33 | 4 | 0 |
| Morrison | 5 | 22 | 4 | 0 |
| Horner | 3 | 3 | 1 | 0 |
| Patton | 1 | 0 | 0 | 0 |

### KICKOFF RETURNS

| Last Name | No. | Yds | Avg | TD |
|---|---|---|---|---|
| Counts | 26 | 784 | 30 | 1 |
| Horner | 11 | 242 | 22 | 0 |
| Dudley | 8 | 229 | 29 | 0 |
| Morrison | 5 | 113 | 23 | 0 |
| King | 2 | 37 | 19 | 0 |
| Collier | 1 | 0 | 0 | 0 |
| Walker | 1 | 0 | 0 | 0 |

### PASSING – PUNTING – KICKING

| PASSING | Att | Comp | % | Yds | Yd/Att | TD | Int− | % | RK |
|---|---|---|---|---|---|---|---|---|---|
| Tittle | 375 | 200 | 53 | 3224 | 8.6 | 33 | 20− | 5 | 2 |
| Guglielmi | 31 | 14 | 45 | 210 | 6.8 | 2 | 1− | 3 | |
| Gifford | 2 | 1 | 50 | 12 | 6.0 | 0 | 0− | 0 | |
| Dudley | 1 | 0 | 0 | 0 | 0.0 | 0 | 1−100 | | |

| PUNTING | No | Avg |
|---|---|---|
| Chandler | 55 | 40.6 |

| KICKING | XP | Att | % | FG | Att | % |
|---|---|---|---|---|---|---|
| Chandler | 47 | 48 | 98 | 19 | 28 | 68 |

## PITTSBURGH STEELERS

### RUSHING

| Last Name | No. | Yds | Avg | TD |
|---|---|---|---|---|
| Johnson | 251 | 1141 | 4.5 | 7 |
| Womack | 128 | 468 | 3.7 | 5 |
| Hoak | 117 | 442 | 3.8 | 4 |
| Tracy | 20 | 116 | 5.8 | 0 |
| Hill | 7 | 72 | 10.3 | 0 |
| Burrell | 6 | 38 | 6.3 | 0 |
| Ferguson | 20 | 37 | 1.9 | 0 |
| Layne | 15 | 25 | 1.7 | 1 |
| Ballman | 3 | 7 | 2.3 | 0 |
| Mack | 2 | −2 | −1.0 | 0 |
| Carpenter | 1 | −3 | −3.0 | 0 |
| Brown | 2 | −8 | −4.0 | 0 |

### RECEIVING

| Last Name | No. | Yds | Avg | TD |
|---|---|---|---|---|
| Dial | 50 | 981 | 20 | 6 |
| Carpenter | 36 | 492 | 14 | 4 |
| Johnson | 32 | 226 | 7 | 2 |
| Hoak | 9 | 133 | 15 | 0 |
| Mack | 8 | 203 | 25 | 2 |
| Burrell | 8 | 193 | 24 | 0 |
| Hill | 7 | 101 | 14 | 0 |
| Womack | 6 | 57 | 10 | 0 |
| Tracy | 2 | 11 | 6 | 0 |
| Powers | 1 | 16 | 16 | 0 |
| Ferguson | 1 | 6 | 6 | 0 |

### PUNT RETURNS

| Last Name | No. | Yds | Avg | TD |
|---|---|---|---|---|
| Carpenter | 7 | 109 | 16 | 0 |
| Keys | 7 | 46 | 7 | 0 |
| Haley | 1 | 13 | 13 | 0 |
| Sample | 4 | 1 | 0 | 0 |

### KICKOFF RETURNS

| Last Name | No. | Yds | Avg | TD |
|---|---|---|---|---|
| Keys | 28 | 667 | 24 | 0 |
| Glass | 16 | 396 | 25 | 0 |
| Haley | 7 | 105 | 15 | 0 |
| Sample | 2 | 52 | 26 | 0 |
| Hoak | 2 | 40 | 20 | 0 |
| Ferguson | 2 | 30 | 15 | 0 |
| Carpenter | 1 | 29 | 29 | 0 |
| Womack | 1 | 16 | 16 | 0 |
| Michaels | 2 | 15 | 8 | 0 |
| Sandusky | 1 | 0 | 0 | 0 |

### PASSING – PUNTING – KICKING

| PASSING | Att | Comp | % | Yds | Yd/Att | TD | Int− | % | RK |
|---|---|---|---|---|---|---|---|---|---|
| Layne | 233 | 116 | 50 | 1686 | 7.2 | 9 | 17− | 7 | 15 |
| Brown | 84 | 43 | 51 | 726 | 8.6 | 5 | 6− | 7 | |
| Hoak | 1 | 0 | 0 | 0 | 0.0 | 0 | 0− | 0 | |
| Tracy | 1 | 1 | 100 | 7 | 7.0 | 0 | 0− | 0 | |

| PUNTING | No | Avg |
|---|---|---|
| Brown | 60 | 40.0 |

| KICKING | XP | Att | % | FG | Att | % |
|---|---|---|---|---|---|---|
| Michaels | 32 | 33 | 97 | 26 | 42 | 62 |

## CLEVELAND BROWNS

### RUSHING

| Last Name | No. | Yds | Avg | TD |
|---|---|---|---|---|
| Jimmy Brown | 230 | 996 | 4.3 | 13 |
| Ryan | 42 | 242 | 5.8 | 1 |
| Scales | 56 | 239 | 4.3 | 3 |
| Wilson | 46 | 141 | 3.1 | 1 |
| Green | 31 | 139 | 4.5 | 0 |
| Ninowski | 9 | 15 | 1.7 | 0 |

### RECEIVING

| Last Name | No. | Yds | Avg | TD |
|---|---|---|---|---|
| Jimmy Brown | 47 | 517 | 11 | 5 |
| Kreitling | 44 | 659 | 15 | 3 |
| Renfro | 31 | 638 | 21 | 4 |
| Brewer | 22 | 290 | 13 | 2 |
| Green | 17 | 194 | 11 | 1 |
| Collins | 11 | 153 | 14 | 2 |
| Clarke | 10 | 106 | 11 | 0 |
| Wilson | 8 | 110 | 14 | 0 |
| Scales | 8 | 67 | 8 | 0 |
| Crespino | 2 | 13 | 7 | 0 |

### PUNT RETURNS

| Last Name | No. | Yds | Avg | TD |
|---|---|---|---|---|
| Shofner | 8 | 33 | 4 | 0 |
| Green | 5 | 31 | 6 | 0 |

### KICKOFF RETURNS

| Last Name | No. | Yds | Avg | TD |
|---|---|---|---|---|
| Wilson | 11 | 307 | 28 | 0 |
| Green | 13 | 250 | 19 | 0 |
| Scales | 9 | 154 | 17 | 0 |
| Tidmore | 2 | 39 | 20 | 0 |
| Collins | 1 | 0 | 0 | 0 |

### PASSING – PUNTING – KICKING

| PASSING | Att | Comp | % | Yds | Yd/Att | TD | Int− | % | RK |
|---|---|---|---|---|---|---|---|---|---|
| Ryan | 194 | 112 | 58 | 1541 | 7.9 | 10 | 7− | 4 | 4 |
| Ninowski | 173 | 87 | 50 | 1178 | 6.8 | 7 | 8− | 5 | 14 |
| Jimmy Brown | 2 | 1 | 50 | 28 | 14.0 | 0 | 0− | 0 | |
| Scales | 1 | 0 | 0 | 0 | 0.0 | 0 | 1−100 | | |

| PUNTING | No | Avg |
|---|---|---|
| Collins | 45 | 42.8 |

| KICKING | XP | Att | % | FG | Att | % |
|---|---|---|---|---|---|---|
| Groza | 33 | 35 | 94 | 14 | 31 | 45 |

## WASHINGTON REDSKINS

### RUSHING

| Last Name | No. | Yds | Avg | TD |
|---|---|---|---|---|
| Barnes | 159 | 492 | 3.1 | 3 |
| Bosseler | 93 | 336 | 3.6 | 2 |
| Cunningham | 35 | 144 | 4.1 | 1 |
| Jackson | 49 | 112 | 2.3 | 0 |
| James | 9 | 13 | 1.4 | 0 |
| Snead | 20 | 10 | 0.5 | 3 |
| Mitchell | 1 | 5 | 5.0 | 0 |
| Hall | 2 | 2 | 1.0 | 1 |
| Izo | 1 | −3 | −3.0 | 0 |
| Dugan | 1 | −9 | −9.0 | 0 |
| Elmore | 1 | −14 | −14 | 0 |

### RECEIVING

| Last Name | No. | Yds | Avg | TD |
|---|---|---|---|---|
| Mitchell | 72 | 1384 | 19 | 11 |
| Dugan | 36 | 466 | 13 | 5 |
| Bosseler | 32 | 258 | 8 | 0 |
| Anderson | 23 | 386 | 17 | 2 |
| James | 19 | 373 | 20 | 5 |
| Barnes | 14 | 220 | 16 | 0 |
| Junker | 11 | 149 | 14 | 2 |
| Jackson | 10 | 253 | 25 | 1 |
| Cunningham | 6 | 43 | 7 | 1 |

### PUNT RETURNS

| Last Name | No. | Yds | Avg | TD |
|---|---|---|---|---|
| James | 19 | 145 | 8 | 0 |
| Steffen | 6 | 30 | 5 | 0 |
| Mitchell | 3 | 7 | 2 | 0 |
| Kerr | 1 | 2 | 2 | 0 |

### KICKOFF RETURNS

| Last Name | No. | Yds | Avg | TD |
|---|---|---|---|---|
| James | 32 | 889 | 28 | 0 |
| Mitchell | 12 | 398 | 33 | 1 |
| Jackson | 10 | 272 | 27 | 0 |
| Steffen | 4 | 107 | 27 | 0 |
| Cunningham | 2 | 54 | 27 | 0 |
| Miller | 1 | 0 | 0 | 0 |

### PASSING – PUNTING – KICKING

| PASSING | Att | Comp | % | Yds | Yd/Att | TD | Int− | % | RK |
|---|---|---|---|---|---|---|---|---|---|
| Snead | 354 | 184 | 52 | 2926 | 8.3 | 22 | 22− | 6 | 8 |
| Izo | 37 | 17 | 46 | 284 | 7.7 | 3 | 4− | 11 | |
| Hall | 32 | 19 | 59 | 274 | 8.6 | 2 | 1− | 3 | |
| Barnes | 4 | 3 | 75 | 48 | 12.0 | 0 | 0− | 0 | |
| Elmore | 1 | 0 | 0 | 0 | 0.0 | 0 | 0− | 0 | |

| PUNTING | No | Avg |
|---|---|---|
| Elmore | 54 | 34.4 |
| Anderson | 7 | 33.6 |
| Hackbart | 2 | 39.0 |

| KICKING | XP | Att | % | FG | Att | % |
|---|---|---|---|---|---|---|
| B. Khayat | 38 | 38 | 100 | 11 | 25 | 44 |

## DALLAS COWBOYS

### RUSHING

| Last Name | No. | Yds | Avg | TD |
|---|---|---|---|---|
| Perkins | 222 | 945 | 4.3 | 7 |
| Marsh | 144 | 802 | 5.6 | 6 |
| Bullocks | 33 | 196 | 5.9 | 2 |
| Meredith | 21 | 74 | 3.5 | 0 |
| Lockett | 8 | 24 | 3.0 | 1 |
| LeBaron | 6 | −1 | −0.2 | 0 |

### RECEIVING

| Last Name | No. | Yds | Avg | TD |
|---|---|---|---|---|
| Howton | 49 | 706 | 14 | 6 |
| Clarke | 47 | 1043 | 22 | 14 |
| Folkins | 39 | 536 | 14 | 6 |
| Marsh | 35 | 467 | 13 | 2 |
| Perkins | 13 | 104 | 8 | 0 |
| Lockett | 7 | 78 | 11 | 0 |
| Gregory | 3 | 70 | 23 | 0 |
| Bullocks | 3 | 46 | 15 | 1 |
| Norman | 2 | 34 | 17 | 0 |
| Davis | 2 | 31 | 16 | 0 |

### PUNT RETURNS

| Last Name | No. | Yds | Avg | TD |
|---|---|---|---|---|
| Lockett | 8 | 45 | 6 | 0 |
| Gaechter | 6 | 32 | 5 | 0 |
| Marsh | 3 | 4 | 1 | 0 |

### KICKOFF RETURNS

| Last Name | No. | Yds | Avg | TD |
|---|---|---|---|---|
| Marsh | 29 | 725 | 25 | 1 |
| Bullocks | 14 | 265 | 19 | 0 |
| Lockett | 6 | 130 | 22 | 0 |
| Davis | 4 | 66 | 17 | 0 |
| Gaechter | 1 | 16 | 16 | 0 |
| Norman | 2 | 5 | 3 | 0 |
| Cverko | 1 | 0 | 0 | 0 |
| Memmalaer | 1 | 0 | 0 | 0 |
| Talbert | 1 | 0 | 0 | 0 |

### PASSING – PUNTING – KICKING

| PASSING | Att | Comp | % | Yds | Yd/Att | TD | Int− | % | RK |
|---|---|---|---|---|---|---|---|---|---|
| Meredith | 212 | 105 | 50 | 1679 | 7.9 | 15 | 8− | 4 | 10 |
| LeBaron | 166 | 95 | 57 | 1436 | 8.7 | 16 | 9− | 5 | 3 |
| Baker | 1 | 0 | 0 | 0 | 0.0 | 0 | 0− | 0 | |
| Lockett | 1 | 0 | 0 | 0 | 0.0 | 0 | 0− | 0 | |

| PUNTING | No | Avg |
|---|---|---|
| Baker | 57 | 45.4 |

| KICKING | XP | Att | % | FG | Att | % |
|---|---|---|---|---|---|---|
| Baker | 50 | 51 | 98 | 14 | 27 | 52 |

| Scores of Each Game | | Use Name | Pos. | Hgt | Wgt | Age | Int | Pts |
|---|---|---|---|---|---|---|---|---|

## EASTERN CONFERENCE — Continued

### ST. LOUIS CARDINALS 4-9-1 Wally Lemm

**Scores of Each Game**

| | | | |
|---|---|---|---|
| 27 | Philadelphia | 21 | |
| 0 | Green Bay | 17 | |
| 14 | Washington | 24 | |
| 14 | NEW YORK | 31 | |
| 17 | WASHINGTON | 21 | |
| 7 | CLEVELAND | 34 | |
| 28 | Dallas | 24 | |
| 28 | New York | 31 | |
| 17 | PITTSBURGH | 26 | |
| 14 | Cleveland | 38 | |
| 17 | SAN FRANCISCO | 24 | |
| 7 | Pittsburgh | 19 | |
| 52 | DALLAS | 20 | |
| 45 | PHILADELPHIA | 35 | |

| Use Name | Pos. | Hgt | Wgt | Age | Int | Pts |
|---|---|---|---|---|---|---|
| Ed Cook | OT | 6'2" | 240 | 30 | | |
| Fate Echols | OT | 6'1" | 255 | 23 | | |
| Irv Goode | OT | 6'4" | 235 | 21 | | |
| Ernie McMillan | OT | 6'6" | 255 | 24 | | |
| Ken Panfil | OT | 6'6" | 255 | 31 | | |
| Ken Gray | OG | 6'2" | 240 | 26 | | |
| Mike McGee | OG | 6'1" | 230 | 24 | | |
| Jerry Perry | OG | 6'4" | 240 | 31 | | 53 |
| Tom Redmond | OG | 6'5" | 240 | 25 | | |
| Bob DeMarco | C | 6'3" | 240 | 24 | | |
| Ed Henke | DE | 6'3" | 230 | 34 | | |
| Luke Owens | DE | 6'2" | 255 | 29 | | |
| Joe Robb | DE | 6'3" | 230 | 25 | | |
| Frank Fuller | DT | 6'4" | 245 | 33 | | |
| George Hultz | DT | 6'4" | 250 | 23 | | |
| Don Owens | DT | 6'5" | 255 | 30 | | |
| Ted Bates | LB | 6'3" | 220 | 26 | | |
| Garland Boyette | LB | 6'1" | 225 | 22 | | |
| Bill Koman | LB | 6'2" | 230 | 28 | | |
| Dale Meinert | LB | 6'2" | 220 | 29 | 1 | |
| Marion Rushing | LB | 6'2" | 210 | 25 | | |
| Roland Jackson | FB-LB | 6' | 210 | 22 | | |
| Norm Beal | DB | 5'11" | 170 | 22 | | |
| Pat Fischer | DB | 5'10" | 165 | 22 | 3 | |
| Jimmy Hill | DB | 6'2" | 190 | 33 | 2 | |
| Billy Stacy | DB | 6'1" | 190 | 26 | 6 | |
| Larry Wilson | DB | 6' | 187 | 24 | 2 | 6 |
| Sam Etcheverry | QB | 5'11" | 190 | 32 | | |
| Charley Johnson | QB | 6' | 190 | 25 | | 18 |
| Joe Childress | HB | 6' | 200 | 28 | | 6 |
| John David Crow | HB | 6'2" | 215 | 27 | | 102 |
| Prentice Gautt | FB | 6' | 200 | 24 | | 12 |
| Bill Triplett | DB-HB | 6'2" | 212 | 23 | 1 | |
| Mal Hammack | FB | 6'2" | 205 | 29 | | 6 |
| Bobby Joe Conrad | FL | 6' | 195 | 27 | | 24 |
| Taz Anderson | OE | 6'2" | 200 | 23 | | 18 |
| Chuck Bryant | OE | 6'2" | 220 | 21 | | |
| Jack Elwell | OE | 6'3" | 200 | 22 | | |
| Hugh McInnis | OE | 6'3" | 220 | 24 | | |
| Sonny Randle | OE | 6'2" | 187 | 24 | | 42 |
| Jim Bakken | K | 6' | 200 | 21 | | |

Don Gillis — Injury
Monte Lee — Military Service

### PHILADELPHIA EAGLES 3-10-1 Nick Skorich

**Scores of Each Game**

| | | | |
|---|---|---|---|
| 21 | ST. LOUIS | 27 | |
| 13 | NEW YORK | 29 | |
| 35 | CLEVELAND | 7 | |
| 7 | Pittsburgh | 13 | |
| 19 | Dallas | 41 | |
| 21 | WASHINGTON | 27 | |
| 21 | Minnesota | 31 | |
| 14 | Cleveland | 14 | |
| 0 | GREEN BAY | 49 | |
| 14 | New York | 19 | |
| 28 | DALLAS | 14 | |
| 37 | Washington | 14 | |
| 37 | PITTSBURGH | 26 | |
| 35 | St. Louis | 45 | |

| Use Name | Pos. | Hgt | Wgt | Age | Int | Pts |
|---|---|---|---|---|---|---|
| Jim McCusker | OT | 6'2" | 245 | 26 | | |
| J. D. Smith | OT | 6'5" | 250 | 26 | | |
| Bob Butler | OG | 6'1" | 235 | 21 | | |
| Pete Case | OG | 6'3" | 230 | 21 | | |
| Roy Hord (from LA) | OG | 6'4" | 250 | 27 | | |
| John Wittenborn | OG | 6'2" | 240 | 26 | | 6 |
| Jim Schrader | C | 6'2" | 252 | 30 | | |
| Howard Keys | OT-OG-C | 6'3" | 240 | 27 | | |
| John Baker | DE | 6'6" | 290 | 27 | | |
| Bobby Richards | DE | 6'2" | 225 | 23 | | |
| Gene Gossage | OG-DE | 6'3" | 240 | 27 | | |
| Dick Stafford | DT-DE | 6'3" | 235 | 22 | | |
| Jim Beaver | DT | 6'1" | 235 | 23 | | |
| Riley Gunnels | DT | 6'3" | 250 | 25 | | |
| John Kapele (from PIT) | DT | 6' | 240 | 25 | | |
| Joe Lewis | DT | 6'2" | 250 | 27 | | |
| Dan Oakes | DT | 6'3" | 245 | 24 | | |
| Maxie Baughan | LB | 6'1" | 226 | 24 | 1 | |
| Chuck Bednarik | LB | 6'3" | 235 | 37 | | |
| Bob Harrison | LB | 6'2" | 220 | 25 | 2 | |
| John Nocera | LB | 6'1" | 220 | 28 | 1 | |
| Mike Woulfe | LB | 6'2" | 225 | 23 | | |
| Don Burroughs | DB | 6'4" | 190 | 31 | 7 | |
| Jimmy Carr | DB | 6'1" | 180 | 29 | 3 | |
| Irv Cross | DB | 6'1" | 190 | 23 | 5 | |
| Mike McClellan | DB | 6'1" | 185 | 23 | 3 | |
| Ben Scotti | DB | 6'1" | 186 | 25 | 4 | |
| King Hill | QB | 6'3" | 213 | 26 | | 6 |
| Sonny Jurgensen | QB | 5'11" | 200 | 28 | | 12 |
| Timmy Brown | HB | 5'10" | 190 | 25 | | 78 |
| Ted Dean | HB | 6'2" | 210 | 24 | | |
| Don Jonas | HB | 5'11" | 195 | 23 | | |
| Theron Sapp | HB | 6'1" | 205 | 27 | | 12 |
| Clarence Peaks | HB | 6'1" | 220 | 26 | | 18 |
| Merrill Douglas | HB-FB | 6' | 204 | 26 | | |
| Frank Budd | FL | 6' | 187 | 23 | | 6 |
| Hopalong Cassady (from CLE) | FL | 5'10" | 185 | 28 | | 12 |
| Tommy McDonald | FL | 5'10" | 172 | 28 | | 60 |
| Ken Gregory | OE | 6' | 190 | 25 | | |
| Dick Lucas | OE | 6'2" | 216 | 28 | | 6 |
| Pete Retzlaff | OE | 6'1" | 210 | 31 | | 18 |
| Ralph Smith | OE | 6'2" | 205 | 23 | | |
| Bobby Walston | OE | 6' | 195 | 33 | | 48 |

## WESTERN CONFERENCE

### GREEN BAY PACKERS 13-1-0 Vince Lombardi

**Scores of Each Game**

| | | | |
|---|---|---|---|
| 34 | MINNESOTA | 7 | |
| 17 | ST. LOUIS | 0 | |
| 49 | CHICAGO | 0 | |
| 9 | DETROIT | 7 | |
| 48 | Minnesota | 21 | |
| 31 | SAN FRANCISCO | 13 | |
| 17 | Baltimore | 6 | |
| 38 | Chicago | 7 | |
| 49 | Philadelphia | 0 | |
| 17 | BALTIMORE | 13 | |
| 14 | Detroit | 26 | |
| 41 | LOS ANGELES | 10 | |
| 31 | San Francisco | 21 | |
| 20 | Los Angeles | 17 | |

| Use Name | Pos. | Hgt | Wgt | Age | Int | Pts |
|---|---|---|---|---|---|---|
| Forrest Gregg | OT | 6'4" | 250 | 29 | | |
| Norm Masters | OT | 6'2" | 250 | 29 | | |
| Bob Skoronski | OT | 6'3" | 250 | 29 | | |
| Ed Blaine | OG | 6'2" | 240 | 22 | | |
| Jerry Kramer | OG | 6'3" | 250 | 27 | | 65 |
| Fuzzy Thurston | OG | 6'1" | 250 | 29 | | |
| Ken Iman | C | 6'1" | 230 | 23 | | |
| Jim Ringo | C | 6'1" | 235 | 31 | | |
| Willie Davis | DE | 6'3" | 240 | 29 | | 6 |
| Bill Quinlan | DE | 6'3" | 250 | 30 | 1 | |
| Ron Gassert | DT | 6'3" | 250 | 22 | | |
| Dave Hanner | DT | 6'2" | 260 | 33 | 1 | |
| Henry Jordan | DT | 6'3" | 250 | 27 | 1 | |
| Ron Kostelnik | DT | 6'4" | 260 | 22 | | |
| Dan Currie | LB | 6'3" | 240 | 28 | | |
| Bill Forester | LB | 6'3" | 240 | 31 | | |
| Ray Nitschke | LB | 6'3" | 235 | 26 | 4 | |
| Nelson Toburen | LB | 6'3" | 235 | 23 | | |
| Herb Adderley | DB | 6'1" | 205 | 23 | 7 | 12 |
| Hank Gremminger | DB | 6'1" | 205 | 29 | 5 | |
| Johnny Symank | DB | 5'11" | 180 | 27 | | |
| Jesse Whittenton | DB | 6' | 195 | 28 | 3 | |
| Howie Williams | DB | 6'2" | 190 | 25 | | |
| Willie Wood | DB | 5'10" | 185 | 26 | 9 | |
| John Roach | QB | 6'4" | 200 | 29 | | |
| Bart Starr | QB | 6'1" | 200 | 29 | | 6 |
| Paul Hornung | HB | 6'2" | 215 | 26 | | 74 |
| Tom Moore | HB | 6'2" | 215 | 24 | | 42 |
| Elijah Pitts | HB | 6'1" | 200 | 23 | | 12 |
| Earl Gros | FB | 6'3" | 220 | 21 | | 12 |
| Jim Taylor | FB | 6' | 215 | 30 | | 114 |
| Lew Carpenter | FL | 6'1" | 215 | 30 | | |
| Boyd Dowler | FL | 6'5" | 220 | 25 | | 12 |
| Gary Barnes | OE | 6'4" | 210 | 27 | | |
| Gary Knafelc | OE | 6'4" | 220 | 30 | | |
| Ron Kramer | OE | 6'3" | 230 | 27 | | 42 |
| Max McGee | OE | 6'3" | 205 | 30 | | 18 |

### DETROIT LIONS 11-3-0 George Wilson

**Scores of Each Game**

| | | | |
|---|---|---|---|
| 45 | PITTSBURGH | 7 | |
| 45 | SAN FRANCISCO | 24 | |
| 29 | Baltimore | 20 | |
| 7 | Green Bay | 9 | |
| 13 | LOS ANGELES | 10 | |
| 14 | New York | 17 | |
| 11 | CHICAGO | 3 | |
| 12 | Los Angeles | 3 | |
| 38 | San Francisco | 24 | |
| 21 | Minnesota | 6 | |
| 26 | GREEN BAY | 14 | |
| 21 | BALTIMORE | 14 | |
| 37 | MINNESOTA | 23 | |
| 0 | Chicago | 3 | |

| Use Name | Pos. | Hgt | Wgt | Age | Int | Pts |
|---|---|---|---|---|---|---|
| Dan LaRose | OT | 6'5" | 250 | 22 | | |
| John Lomakoski | OT | 6'4" | 250 | 21 | | |
| Dick Mills | OG | 6'3" | 240 | 22 | | |
| Harley Sewell | OG | 6'1" | 230 | 31 | | |
| John Gordy | OT-OG | 6'3" | 250 | 26 | | |
| Bob Whitlow | C | 6'1" | 236 | 26 | | |
| Bob Scholtz | OT-C | 6'4" | 250 | 24 | | |
| Darris McCord | DE | 6'4" | 250 | 29 | | 2 |
| Leo Sugar | DE | 6'1" | 230 | 33 | | |
| Sam Williams | DE | 6'5" | 235 | 31 | 1 | 12 |
| Roger Brown | DT | 6'5" | 300 | 25 | | 4 |
| Mike Bundra | DT | 6'3" | 250 | 23 | | |
| John Gonzaga | DT | 6'3" | 250 | 29 | | |
| Alex Karras | DT | 6'2" | 245 | 26 | 1 | 2 |
| Paul Ward | DT | 6'3" | 247 | 25 | | |
| Carl Brettschneider | LB | 6'1" | 225 | 30 | 2 | |
| Max Messner | LB | 6'3" | 225 | 24 | | |
| Joe Schmidt | LB | 6'2" | 220 | 30 | 1 | |
| Wayne Walker | LB | 6'2" | 225 | 25 | 1 | 64 |
| Dave Lloyd | C-LB | 6'3" | 248 | 26 | | |
| Night Train Lane | DB | 6'1" | 200 | 34 | 4 | |
| Dick LeBeau | DB | 6'1" | 185 | 25 | 4 | 12 |
| Gary Lowe | DB | 5'11" | 195 | 28 | 2 | |
| Yale Lary | DB | 6' | 190 | 31 | 8 | |
| Bruce Maher | HB-DB | 5'11" | 190 | 25 | | |
| Tom Hall | OE-DB | 6'1" | 195 | 21 | | |
| Earl Morrall | QB | 6'1" | 206 | 28 | | 6 |
| Milt Plum | QB | 6'1" | 205 | 28 | | 21 |
| Dick Compton | HB | 6'1" | 190 | 22 | | |
| Dan Lewis | HB | 6'1" | 200 | 26 | | 42 |
| Tom Watkins | HB | 6'1" | 195 | 25 | | 18 |
| Nick Pietrosante | FB | 6'2" | 225 | 24 | | |
| Ken Webb | FB | 5'11" | 205 | 27 | | 6 |
| Terry Barr | FL | 6' | 190 | 27 | | 18 |
| Pat Studstill | FL | 6'1" | 180 | 24 | | 24 |
| Gail Cogdill | OE | 6'2" | 195 | 25 | | 48 |
| Jim Gibbons | OE | 6'2" | 220 | 26 | | 12 |
| Larry Vargo | OE | 6'3" | 200 | 22 | | |

Jim Martin — Voluntarily Retired

### CHICAGO BEARS 9-5-0 George Halas

**Scores of Each Game**

| | | | |
|---|---|---|---|
| 30 | San Francisco | 14 | |
| 27 | Los Angeles | 23 | |
| 0 | Green Bay | 49 | |
| 13 | Minnesota | 0 | |
| 27 | SAN FRANCISCO | 34 | |
| 35 | BALTIMORE | 15 | |
| 3 | Detroit | 11 | |
| 7 | GREEN BAY | 38 | |
| 31 | MINNESOTA | 30 | |
| 34 | Dallas | 33 | |
| 57 | Baltimore | 0 | |
| 24 | NEW YORK | 26 | |
| 30 | LOS ANGELES | 14 | |
| 3 | DETROIT | 0 | |

| Use Name | Pos. | Hgt | Wgt | Age | Int | Pts |
|---|---|---|---|---|---|---|
| Art Anderson | OT | 6'3" | 244 | 25 | | |
| Jim Cadile | OT | 6'3" | 230 | 21 | | |
| Herm Lee | OT | 6'4" | 247 | 31 | | |
| Bob Wetoska | OT | 6'3" | 240 | 24 | | |
| Roger Davis | OG | 6'3" | 235 | 24 | | |
| Stan Jones | OG | 6'1" | 250 | 31 | | |
| Ted Karras | OG | 6'1" | 243 | 29 | | |
| Mike Pyle | C | 6'3" | 240 | 23 | | |
| Doug Atkins | DE | 6'8" | 255 | 32 | | |
| Ed O'Bradovich | DE | 6'3" | 255 | 22 | | |
| Maury Youmans | DE | 6'6" | 260 | 25 | | |
| Stan Fanning | DT | 6'6" | 270 | 24 | | |
| Bob Kilcullen | DT | 6'3" | 245 | 26 | | |
| Earl Leggett | DT | 6'3" | 250 | 28 | | |
| Fred Williams | DT | 6'4" | 248 | 32 | | |
| Joe Fortunato | LB | 6' | 225 | 32 | 3 | |
| Bill George | LB | 6'2" | 235 | 31 | 2 | |
| Roger LeClerc | LB | 6'3" | 235 | 24 | | 75 |
| Larry Morris | LB | 6'2" | 230 | 27 | 2 | |
| J. C. Caroline | DB | 6'1" | 190 | 29 | 2 | |
| Bennie McRae | DB | 6'1" | 180 | 21 | 1 | |
| Don Mullins | DB | 6'1" | 195 | 23 | | |
| Tommy Neck | DB | 5'11" | 190 | 23 | | |
| Richie Petitbon | DB | 6'3" | 205 | 24 | 6 | 6 |
| Rosey Taylor | DB | 5'11" | 186 | 23 | 2 | 12 |
| Dave Whitsell | DB | 6' | 190 | 26 | 5 | |
| Rudy Bukich | QB | 6'1" | 205 | 31 | | |
| Billy Wade | QB | 6'2" | 210 | 31 | | 30 |
| Charlie Bivins | HB | 6'2" | 212 | 23 | | 6 |
| Ronnie Bull | HB | 6' | 200 | 22 | | 6 |
| Willie Galimore | HB | 6'1" | 187 | 27 | | 12 |
| Billy Martin | HB | 5'11" | 197 | 24 | | 6 |
| Rick Casares | FB | 6'2" | 225 | 28 | | 18 |
| Joe Marconi | FB | 6'2" | 225 | 31 | | 36 |
| Johnny Morris | FL | 5'10" | 180 | 27 | | 30 |
| John Adams | OE | 6'3" | 235 | 25 | | 18 |
| Angie Coia | OE | 6'2" | 202 | 24 | | 24 |
| Mike Ditka | OE | 6'3" | 230 | 22 | | 36 |
| Jim Dooley | OE | 6'4" | 198 | 32 | | |
| Bo Farrington | OE | 6'3" | 217 | 26 | | 6 |
| Bobby Joe Green | K | 5'11" | 175 | 24 | | |

## EASTERN CONFERENCE—Continued

### ST. LOUIS CARDINALS

**RUSHING**

| Last Name | No. | Yds | Avg | TD |
|---|---|---|---|---|
| Crow | 192 | 751 | 3.9 | 14 |
| Gautt | 114 | 470 | 4.1 | 2 |
| Childress | 37 | 162 | 4.4 | 0 |
| Hammack | 38 | 160 | 4.2 | 1 |
| Johnson | 25 | 138 | 5.5 | 3 |
| Triplett | 2 | 12 | 6.0 | 0 |
| Etcheverry | 8 | 5 | 0.6 | 0 |

**RECEIVING**

| Last Name | No. | Yds | Avg | TD |
|---|---|---|---|---|
| Randle | 63 | 1158 | 18 | 7 |
| Conrad | 62 | 954 | 15 | 4 |
| Anderson | 35 | 555 | 15 | 3 |
| Crow | 23 | 246 | 11 | 3 |
| Gautt | 16 | 240 | 15 | 0 |
| Childress | 15 | 207 | 14 | 1 |
| Hammack | 4 | 27 | 7 | 0 |
| Elwell | 1 | 11 | 11 | 0 |
| McInnis | 1 | 10 | 10 | 0 |

**PUNT RETURNS**

| Last Name | No. | Yds | Avg | TD |
|---|---|---|---|---|
| Beal | 7 | 46 | 7 | 0 |
| Fischer | 4 | 37 | 9 | 0 |
| Stacy | 5 | 35 | 7 | 0 |
| Conrad | 2 | 10 | 5 | 0 |
| Crow | 2 | 6 | 3 | 0 |

**KICKOFF RETURNS**

| Last Name | No. | Yds | Avg | TD |
|---|---|---|---|---|
| Triplett | 24 | 608 | 25 | 0 |
| Beal | 16 | 394 | 25 | 0 |
| Fischer | 7 | 187 | 27 | 0 |
| Gautt | 6 | 124 | 21 | 0 |
| Stacy | 5 | 121 | 24 | 0 |
| Hammack | 2 | 36 | 18 | 0 |
| Childress | 3 | 19 | 6 | 0 |
| Anderson | 1 | 6 | 6 | 0 |

**PASSING – PUNTING – KICKING**

| PASSING | Att | Comp | % | Yds | Yd/Att | TD | Int– | % | RK |
|---|---|---|---|---|---|---|---|---|---|
| Johnson | 308 | 150 | 49 | 2440 | 7.9 | 16 | 20– | 7 | 13 |
| Etcheverry | 106 | 58 | 55 | 707 | 6.7 | 2 | 10– | 9 | |
| Crow | 20 | 12 | 60 | 241 | 12.1 | 0 | 0– | 0 | |

| PUNTING | No | Avg |
|---|---|---|
| Etcheverry | 59 | 38.3 |

| KICKING | XP | Att | % | FG | Att | % |
|---|---|---|---|---|---|---|
| Perry | 38 | 39 | 97 | 5 | 12 | 42 |
| Bakken | 0 | 0 | 0 | 0 | 1 | 0 |
| Conrad | 0 | 0 | 0 | 0 | 1 | 0 |

### PHILADELPHIA EAGLES

**RUSHING**

| Last Name | No. | Yds | Avg | TD |
|---|---|---|---|---|
| Brown | 137 | 545 | 4.0 | 5 |
| Peaks | 137 | 447 | 3.3 | 3 |
| Sapp | 23 | 53 | 2.3 | 2 |
| Jurgensen | 17 | 44 | 2.6 | 2 |
| Hill | 4 | 40 | 10.0 | 1 |
| Smith | 1 | 13 | 13.0 | 0 |
| Douglas | 4 | 7 | 1.8 | 0 |
| Cassady | 1 | 6 | 6.0 | 0 |

**RECEIVING**

| Last Name | No. | Yds | Avg | TD |
|---|---|---|---|---|
| McDonald | 58 | 1146 | 20 | 10 |
| Brown | 52 | 849 | 16 | 6 |
| Peaks | 39 | 347 | 9 | 0 |
| Retzlaff | 30 | 584 | 19 | 3 |
| Lucas | 19 | 236 | 12 | 1 |
| Cassady | 14 | 188 | 13 | 2 |
| Sapp | 6 | 80 | 13 | 0 |
| Budd | 5 | 130 | 26 | 1 |
| Walston | 4 | 43 | 11 | 0 |
| Smith | 1 | 29 | 29 | 0 |

**PUNT RETURNS**

| Last Name | No. | Yds | Avg | TD |
|---|---|---|---|---|
| Brown | 6 | 81 | 14 | 0 |
| Cassady | 8 | 49 | 6 | 0 |
| McDonald | 5 | 8 | 2 | 0 |
| Cross | 1 | 2 | 2 | 0 |
| Smith | 1 | 2 | 2 | 0 |

**KICKOFF RETURNS**

| Last Name | No. | Yds | Avg | TD |
|---|---|---|---|---|
| Brown | 30 | 831 | 28 | 1 |
| Cassady | 24 | 482 | 20 | 0 |
| Douglas | 6 | 136 | 23 | 0 |
| Dean | 4 | 83 | 21 | 0 |
| Cross | 2 | 72 | 36 | 0 |
| Baughan | 3 | 9 | 3 | 0 |
| Woulfe | 2 | 5 | 3 | 0 |

**PASSING – PUNTING – KICKING**

| PASSING | Att | Comp | % | Yds | Yd/Att | TD | Int– | % | RK |
|---|---|---|---|---|---|---|---|---|---|
| Jurgensen | 366 | 196 | 54 | 3261 | 8.9 | 22 | 26– | 7 | 5 |
| Hill | 61 | 31 | 51 | 361 | 5.9 | 0 | 5– | 8 | |
| McDonald | 1 | 1 | 100 | 10 | 10.0 | 1 | 0– | 0 | |

| PUNTING | No | Avg |
|---|---|---|
| Hill | 64 | 42.9 |

| KICKING | XP | Att | % | FG | Att | % |
|---|---|---|---|---|---|---|
| Walston | 36 | 38 | 95 | 4 | 15 | 27 |
| Wittenborn | 0 | 0 | 0 | 2 | 4 | 50 |

## WESTERN CONFERENCE

### GREEN BAY PACKERS

**RUSHING**

| Last Name | No. | Yds | Avg | TD |
|---|---|---|---|---|
| Taylor | 272 | 1474 | 5.4 | 19 |
| Moore | 112 | 377 | 3.4 | 7 |
| Hornung | 57 | 219 | 3.8 | 5 |
| Gros | 29 | 155 | 5.3 | 2 |
| Pitts | 22 | 110 | 5.0 | 2 |
| Starr | 21 | 72 | 3.4 | 1 |
| McGee | 3 | 52 | 17.3 | 0 |
| Roach | 1 | 5 | 5.0 | 0 |
| R. Kramer | 1 | –4 | –4.0 | 0 |

**RECEIVING**

| Last Name | No. | Yds | Avg | TD |
|---|---|---|---|---|
| McGee | 49 | 820 | 17 | 3 |
| Dowler | 49 | 724 | 15 | 2 |
| R. Kramer | 37 | 555 | 15 | 7 |
| Taylor | 22 | 106 | 5 | 0 |
| Moore | 11 | 100 | 9 | 0 |
| Hornung | 9 | 168 | 19 | 0 |
| Carpenter | 7 | 104 | 15 | 0 |
| Pitts | 3 | 44 | 15 | 0 |

**PUNT RETURNS**

| Last Name | No. | Yds | Avg | TD |
|---|---|---|---|---|
| Wood | 23 | 273 | 12 | 0 |
| Pitts | 7 | 17 | 2 | 0 |
| Kostelnik | 1 | 0 | 0 | 0 |

**KICKOFF RETURNS**

| Last Name | No. | Yds | Avg | TD |
|---|---|---|---|---|
| Adderley | 15 | 418 | 28 | 1 |
| Moore | 13 | 284 | 22 | 0 |
| Gros | 1 | 7 | 7 | 0 |
| Nitschke | 1 | 7 | 7 | 0 |

**PASSING – PUNTING – KICKING**

| PASSING | Att | Comp | % | Yds | Yd/Att | TD | Int– | % | RK |
|---|---|---|---|---|---|---|---|---|---|
| Starr | 285 | 178 | 62 | 2438 | 8.6 | 12 | 9– | 3 | 1 |
| Roach | 12 | 3 | 25 | 33 | 2.8 | 0 | 0– | 0 | |
| Hornung | 6 | 4 | 67 | 80 | 13.3 | 0 | 2– | 33 | |
| Moore | 5 | 2 | 40 | 70 | 14.0 | 2 | 1– | 20 | |
| Pitts | 2 | 0 | 0 | 0 | 0.0 | 0 | 0– | 0 | |
| McGee | 1 | 0 | 0 | 0 | 0.0 | 0 | 1– | 100 | |

| PUNTING | No | Avg |
|---|---|---|
| Dowler | 36 | 43.1 |
| McGee | 14 | 35.4 |

| KICKING | XP | Att | % | FG | Att | % |
|---|---|---|---|---|---|---|
| J. Kramer | 38 | 39 | 97 | 9 | 11 | 82 |
| Hornung | 14 | 14 | 100 | 6 | 10 | 60 |

### DETROIT LIONS

**RUSHING**

| Last Name | No. | Yds | Avg | TD |
|---|---|---|---|---|
| Lewis | 120 | 488 | 4.1 | 6 |
| Watkins | 113 | 485 | 4.3 | 3 |
| Pietrosante | 134 | 445 | 3.3 | 2 |
| Webb | 70 | 267 | 3.8 | 1 |
| Plum | 29 | 170 | 5.9 | 1 |
| Morrall | 17 | 65 | 3.8 | 1 |
| Maher | 3 | 8 | 2.7 | 0 |
| Compton | 1 | 3 | 3.0 | 0 |
| Cogdill | 1 | 2 | 2.0 | 0 |
| Studstill | 1 | –11 | –11.0 | 0 |

**RECEIVING**

| Last Name | No. | Yds | Avg | TD |
|---|---|---|---|---|
| Cogdill | 53 | 991 | 19 | 7 |
| Studstill | 36 | 479 | 13 | 4 |
| Gibbons | 33 | 318 | 10 | 2 |
| Pietrosante | 26 | 251 | 10 | 2 |
| Barr | 25 | 425 | 17 | 3 |
| Lewis | 16 | 158 | 10 | 1 |
| Watkins | 12 | 85 | 7 | 0 |
| Webb | 10 | 120 | 12 | 0 |

**PUNT RETURNS**

| Last Name | No. | Yds | Avg | TD |
|---|---|---|---|---|
| Studstill | 29 | 457 | 16 | 0 |
| Watkins | 8 | 42 | 5 | 0 |
| Maher | 2 | 3 | 2 | 0 |

**KICKOFF RETURNS**

| Last Name | No. | Yds | Avg | TD |
|---|---|---|---|---|
| Studstill | 20 | 511 | 26 | 0 |
| Watkins | 17 | 452 | 27 | 0 |
| Maher | 7 | 141 | 20 | 0 |
| Hall | 1 | 16 | 16 | 0 |
| Cogdill | 1 | 4 | 4 | 0 |

**PASSING – PUNTING – KICKING**

| PASSING | Att | Comp | % | Yds | Yd/Att | TD | Int– | % | RK |
|---|---|---|---|---|---|---|---|---|---|
| Plum | 325 | 179 | 55 | 2378 | 7.3 | 15 | 20– | 6 | 11 |
| Morrall | 52 | 32 | 62 | 449 | 8.6 | 4 | 4– | 8 | |
| Lary | 1 | 0 | 0 | 0 | 0.0 | 0 | 0– | 0 | |
| Lewis | 1 | 0 | 0 | 0 | 0.0 | 0 | 0– | 0 | |

| PUNTING | No | Avg |
|---|---|---|
| Lary | 52 | 45.3 |
| Morrall | 1 | 48.0 |

| KICKING | XP | Att | % | FG | Att | % |
|---|---|---|---|---|---|---|
| Walker | 37 | 37 | 100 | 9 | 22 | 41 |
| Plum | 0 | 0 | 0 | 5 | 12 | 42 |

### CHICAGO BEARS

**RUSHING**

| Last Name | No. | Yds | Avg | TD |
|---|---|---|---|---|
| Marconi | 89 | 406 | 4.6 | 5 |
| Bull | 113 | 363 | 3.2 | 1 |
| Casares | 75 | 255 | 3.4 | 2 |
| Galimore | 43 | 233 | 5.4 | 2 |
| Wade | 40 | 146 | 3.7 | 5 |
| Bivins | 14 | 44 | 3.1 | 0 |
| Martin | 9 | 28 | 3.1 | 1 |
| Anderson | 1 | 7 | 7.0 | 0 |
| J. Morris | 2 | 7 | 3.5 | 0 |

**RECEIVING**

| Last Name | No. | Yds | Avg | TD |
|---|---|---|---|---|
| Ditka | 58 | 904 | 16 | 5 |
| J. Morris | 58 | 889 | 15 | 5 |
| Bull | 31 | 331 | 11 | 0 |
| Marconi | 23 | 306 | 13 | 1 |
| Coia | 22 | 361 | 16 | 4 |
| Farrington | 13 | 197 | 15 | 1 |
| Casares | 10 | 71 | 7 | 1 |
| Adams | 5 | 111 | 22 | 3 |
| Galimore | 5 | 56 | 11 | 0 |
| Bivins | 3 | 52 | 17 | 0 |
| Martin | 1 | 8 | 8 | 0 |

**PUNT RETURNS**

| Last Name | No. | Yds | Avg | TD |
|---|---|---|---|---|
| J. Morris | 20 | 208 | 10 | 0 |
| Martin | 17 | 62 | 4 | 0 |
| Taylor | 2 | 11 | 6 | 1 |

**KICKOFF RETURNS**

| Last Name | No. | Yds | Avg | TD |
|---|---|---|---|---|
| Martin | 25 | 515 | 21 | 0 |
| Bivins | 12 | 243 | 20 | 0 |
| Bull | 9 | 235 | 26 | 0 |
| Taylor | 4 | 98 | 25 | 0 |
| Marconi | 2 | 30 | 15 | 0 |
| O'Bradovich | 1 | 8 | 8 | 0 |

**PASSING – PUNTING – KICKING**

| PASSING | Att | Comp | % | Yds | Yd/Att | TD | Int– | % | RK |
|---|---|---|---|---|---|---|---|---|---|
| Wade | 412 | 225 | 55 | 3172 | 7.7 | 18 | 24– | 6 | 9 |
| Bukich | 13 | 3 | 23 | 79 | 6.1 | 1 | 4– | 31 | |
| Bull | 3 | 0 | 0 | 0 | 0.0 | 0 | 0– | 0 | |
| Casares | 2 | 1 | 50 | 35 | 17.5 | 1 | 0– | 0 | |

| PUNTING | No | Avg |
|---|---|---|
| Green | 69 | 43.7 |

| KICKING | XP | Att | % | FG | Att | % |
|---|---|---|---|---|---|---|
| Leclerc | 36 | 40 | 90 | 13 | 27 | 48 |

| Scores of Each Game | | |
|---|---|---|

**WESTERN CONFERENCE — Continued**

## BALTIMORE COLTS 7-7-0 Weeb Ewbank

| Scores | | | Use Name | Pos. | Hgt | Wgt | Age | Int | Pts |
|---|---|---|---|---|---|---|---|---|---|
| 30 | LOS ANGELES | 27 | Tom Gilburg | OT | 6'5" | 245 | 23 | | |
| 34 | Minnesota | 7 | George Preas | OT | 6'2" | 250 | 30 | | |
| 20 | DETROIT | 29 | Dan Sullivan | OT | 6'3" | 250 | 23 | | |
| 13 | SAN FRANCISCO | 21 | Jim Parker | OG-OT | 6'3" | 275 | 28 | | |
| 36 | Cleveland | 14 | Wiley Feagin | OG | 6'2" | 235 | 25 | | |
| 15 | Chicago | 35 | Bill Kirchiro | OG | 6'1" | 235 | 21 | | |
| 6 | GREEN BAY | 17 | Palmer Pyle | OG | 6'2" | 250 | 25 | | |
| 22 | San Francisco | 3 | Alex Sandusky | OG | 6'1" | 242 | 30 | | |
| 14 | Los Angeles | 2 | Dick Szymanski | C | 6'3" | 235 | 30 | | |
| 13 | Green Bay | 17 | Ordell Braase | DE | 6'4" | 242 | 30 | | |
| 0 | CHICAGO | 57 | Gino Marchetti | DE | 6'4" | 245 | 36 | | |
| 14 | Detroit | 21 | Don Thompson | DE | 6'4" | 225 | 23 | | |
| 34 | WASHINGTON | 21 | Jim Colvin | DT | 6'2" | 250 | 25 | | |
| 42 | MINNESOTA | 17 | John Diehl | DT | 6'7" | 285 | 26 | | |
| | | | Billy Ray Smith | DT | 6'4" | 235 | 27 | | |

| Use Name | Pos. | Hgt | Wgt | Age | Int | Pts |
|---|---|---|---|---|---|---|
| Jackie Burkett | LB | 6'4" | 230 | 25 | 2 | |
| Bill Pellington | LB | 6'2" | 238 | 33 | 2 | |
| Bill Saul | LB | 6'4" | 225 | 21 | | 2 |
| Don Shinnick | LB | 6' | 235 | 27 | 5 | |
| Dave Yohn | LB | 6' | 220 | 24 | | |
| Wendell Harris | DB | 5'11" | 190 | 21 | 2 | 9 |
| Lenny Lyles | DB | 6'2" | 202 | 26 | | |
| Andy Nelson | DB | 6'1" | 180 | 29 | 4 | |
| Jim Welch | DB | 6' | 190 | 24 | 1 | |
| Bobby Boyd | HB-DB | 5'10" | 190 | 24 | 7 | |
| | | | | | | |
| Jerry Hill — Injury | | | | | | |

| Use Name | Pos. | Hgt | Wgt | Age | Int | Pts |
|---|---|---|---|---|---|---|
| Lamar McHan | QB | 6'1" | 205 | 30 | | |
| Johnny Unitas | QB | 6'1" | 194 | 29 | | |
| Bob Clemens | HB | 6'1" | 208 | 23 | | |
| Alex Hawkins | HB | 6'1" | 190 | 25 | | 24 |
| Tom Matte | HB | 6' | 192 | 23 | | 18 |
| Lenny Moore | HB | 6'1" | 190 | 29 | | 24 |
| Joe Perry | FB | 6' | 195 | 35 | | |
| Mark Smolinski | FB | 6' | 222 | 23 | | 12 |
| Jimmy Orr | FL | 5'11" | 180 | 26 | | 66 |
| Bake Turner | FL | 6' | 180 | 22 | | 6 |
| Ray Berry | OE | 6'2" | 190 | 29 | | 18 |
| Dick Bielski | OE | 6'1" | 227 | 30 | | 70 |
| Dee Mackey | OE | 6'5" | 236 | 26 | | 24 |
| R. C. Owens | OE | 6'3" | 195 | 27 | | 12 |

## SAN FRANCISCO FORTY NINERS 6-8-0 Red Hickey

| Scores | | | Use Name | Pos. | Hgt | Wgt | Age | Int | Pts |
|---|---|---|---|---|---|---|---|---|---|
| 14 | CHICAGO | 30 | Leon Donohue | OT | 6'4" | 245 | 23 | | |
| 24 | Detroit | 45 | Roland Lakes | OT | 6'4" | 247 | 22 | | |
| 21 | MINNESOTA | 7 | Bob St. Clair | OT | 6'9" | 265 | 31 | | |
| 21 | BALTIMORE | 13 | John Sutro | OT | 6'4" | 245 | 21 | | |
| 34 | Chicago | 27 | Bruce Bosley | OG | 6'2" | 240 | 28 | | |
| 13 | Green Bay | 31 | Ted Connolly | OG | 6'3" | 242 | 30 | | |
| 14 | LOS ANGELES | 28 | Mike Magac | OG | 6'3" | 240 | 24 | | |
| 3 | Baltimore | 22 | John Mellekas | C | 6'3" | 255 | 29 | | |
| 24 | DETROIT | 38 | Dan Colchico | DE | 6'3" | 240 | 25 | | |
| 35 | Los Angeles | 17 | Clark Miller | DE | 6'5" | 245 | 23 | | |
| 24 | St. Louis | 17 | Len Rohde | DE | 6'4" | 240 | 24 | | |
| 24 | Minnesota | 12 | Charlie Krueger | DT | 6'4" | 245 | 24 | | |
| 21 | GREEN BAY | 31 | Leo Nomellini | DT | 6'3" | 262 | 37 | | |
| 10 | CLEVELAND | 13 | | | | | | | |

| Use Name | Pos. | Hgt | Wgt | Age | Int | Pts |
|---|---|---|---|---|---|---|
| Matt Hazeltine | LB | 6'1" | 220 | 29 | 2 | |
| Carl Kammerer | LB | 6'3" | 237 | 25 | 1 | |
| Ed Pine | LB | 6'4" | 230 | 22 | 2 | |
| Karl Rubke | LB | 6'4" | 240 | 26 | | |
| John Thomas | LB | 6'4" | 246 | 27 | | |
| Eddie Dove | DB | 6'2" | 180 | 25 | 1 | |
| Elbert Kimbrough | DB | 5'11" | 195 | 23 | | |
| Jerry Mertens | DB | 6' | 183 | 26 | 2 | |
| Jimmy Ridlon | DB | 6'1" | 177 | 27 | 1 | |
| Abe Woodson | DB | 5'11" | 188 | 27 | 2 | 12 |
| | | | | | | |
| Dave Baker — Military Service | | | | | | |

| Use Name | Pos. | Hgt | Wgt | Age | Int | Pts |
|---|---|---|---|---|---|---|
| John Brodie | QB | 6'1" | 186 | 27 | | 24 |
| Bob Waters | QB | 6'2" | 184 | 24 | | |
| Billy Kilmer | HB-QB | 6' | 190 | 23 | | 36 |
| Bob Gaiters (from NY) | HB | 5'11" | 210 | 24 | | |
| J. D. Smith | FB-HB | 6'1" | 200 | 29 | | 42 |
| Dale Messer | DB-HB | 5'10" | 175 | 25 | 1 | |
| Bill Cooper | FB | 6'1" | 215 | 23 | | |
| C. R. Roberts | FB | 6'3" | 197 | 26 | | |
| Jim Vollenweider | FB | 6'1" | 210 | 22 | | |
| Lloyd Winston | FB | 6'2" | 215 | 22 | | |
| Bernie Casey | FL | 6'4" | 215 | 23 | | 36 |
| Jim Johnson | FL | 6'2" | 190 | 24 | | 24 |
| Kay McFarland | FL | 6'2" | 180 | 23 | | |
| Clyde Conner | OE | 6'2" | 190 | 29 | | 24 |
| Monte Stickles | OE | 6'4" | 230 | 24 | | 18 |
| Tommy Davis | K | 6' | 212 | 27 | | 66 |

## MINNESOTA VIKINGS 2-11-1 Norm Van Brocklin

| Scores | | | Use Name | Pos. | Hgt | Wgt | Age | Int | Pts |
|---|---|---|---|---|---|---|---|---|---|
| 7 | Green Bay | 34 | Grady Alderman | OT | 6'2" | 235 | 23 | | |
| 7 | BALTIMORE | 34 | Errol Linden | OT | 6'5" | 260 | 24 | | |
| 7 | San Francisco | 21 | Frank Youso | OT | 6'4" | 260 | 26 | | |
| 0 | CHICAGO | 13 | Larry Bowie | OG | 6'2" | 235 | 22 | | |
| 21 | GREEN BAY | 48 | Jerry Huth | OG | 6' | 228 | 29 | | |
| 38 | Los Angeles | 14 | Mike Rabold | OG | 6'2" | 238 | 24 | | |
| 31 | PHILADELPHIA | 21 | Mick Tingelhoff | C | 6'1" | 230 | 22 | | |
| 31 | Pittsburgh | 39 | Bob Denton | DE | 6'4" | 240 | 28 | | |
| 30 | Chicago | 31 | Jim Leo | DE | 6'1" | 225 | 24 | 2 | |
| 6 | DETROIT | 17 | Jim Marshall | DE | 6'3" | 230 | 24 | | |
| 24 | LOS ANGELES | 24 | Paul Dickson | DT | 6'5" | 250 | 25 | | |
| 12 | SAN FRANCISCO | 35 | Jim Prestel | DT | 6'5" | 250 | 25 | | |
| 23 | Detroit | 37 | | | | | | | |
| 17 | Baltimore | 42 | | | | | | | |

| Use Name | Pos. | Hgt | Wgt | Age | Int | Pts |
|---|---|---|---|---|---|---|
| Jim Christopherson | LB | 6' | 215 | 24 | 1 | 61 |
| Rip Hawkins | LB | 6'3" | 230 | 23 | 1 | 2 |
| Cliff Livingston | LB | 6'3" | 215 | 32 | | |
| Clancy Osborne | LB | 6'3" | 217 | 27 | | |
| Roy Winston | LB | 6' | 225 | 22 | | |
| Bill Butler | DB | 5'10" | 194 | 25 | 5 | 6 |
| Dean Derby | DB | 6' | 190 | 28 | 4 | |
| Tom Franckhauser | DB | 6' | 196 | 25 | 4 | |
| Chuck Lamson | DB | 6' | 185 | 23 | 1 | |
| Ed Sharockman | DB | 6' | 195 | 24 | 6 | 6 |
| Charlie Sumner | DB | 6'1" | 195 | 32 | 3 | |

| Use Name | Pos. | Hgt | Wgt | Age | Int | Pts |
|---|---|---|---|---|---|---|
| John McCormick | QB | 6'1" | 210 | 26 | | |
| Fran Tarkenton | QB | 6'1" | 190 | 22 | | 12 |
| Tommy Mason | HB | 6' | 195 | 23 | | 48 |
| Hugh McElhenny | HB | 6'1" | 198 | 33 | | |
| Bob Reed | HB | 5'11" | 187 | 22 | | 6 |
| Bill Brown | FB | 5'11" | 218 | 24 | | 6 |
| Doug Mayberry | FB | 6'1" | 225 | 25 | | 12 |
| Mel Triplett | FB | 6'1" | 215 | 30 | | 18 |
| Oscar Donahue | FL | 6'3" | 195 | 24 | | |
| Tom Adams | OE | 6'5" | 210 | 22 | | |
| Charley Ferguson | OE | 6'5" | 212 | 22 | | 36 |
| Jerry Reichow | OE | 6'2" | 220 | 27 | | 18 |
| Gordon Smith | OE | 6'2" | 200 | 23 | | |
| Steve Stonebreaker | OE | 6'3" | 220 | 24 | | 6 |
| Mike Mercer | K | 6' | 220 | 26 | | 3 |

## LOS ANGELES RAMS 1-12-1 Bob Waterfield Harland Svare

| Scores | | | Use Name | Pos. | Hgt | Wgt | Age | Int | Pts |
|---|---|---|---|---|---|---|---|---|---|
| 27 | Baltimore | 30 | Jim Boeke | OT | 6'5" | 245 | 23 | | |
| 23 | CHICAGO | 27 | Joe Carollo | OT | 6'2" | 258 | 22 | | |
| 17 | DALLAS | 27 | Frank Varrichione | OT | 6'1" | 235 | 30 | | |
| 14 | Washington | 20 | Charley Cowan | OG | 6'4" | 250 | 24 | | |
| 10 | Detroit | 13 | Duane Putnam | OG | 6' | 233 | 34 | | |
| 14 | MINNESOTA | 38 | Joe Scibelli | OG | 6'1" | 250 | 23 | | |
| 28 | San Francisco | 14 | Art Hunter | C | 6'4" | 248 | 29 | | |
| 3 | DETROIT | 12 | Deacon Jones | DE | 6'5" | 240 | 23 | | |
| 2 | BALTIMORE | 14 | Lamar Lundy | DE | 6'7" | 235 | 27 | | |
| 17 | SAN FRANCISCO | 24 | Larry Stephens | DE | 6'4" | 260 | 24 | | |
| 24 | Minnesota | 24 | John Lovetere | DT | 6'4" | 280 | 24 | | |
| 10 | Green Bay | 41 | Merlin Olsen | DT | 6'5" | 265 | 21 | 1 | 6 |
| 14 | Chicago | 30 | | | | | | | |
| 17 | GREEN BAY | 20 | | | | | | | |

| Use Name | Pos. | Hgt | Wgt | Age | Int | Pts |
|---|---|---|---|---|---|---|
| Mike Henry | LB | 6'2" | 215 | 26 | 1 | |
| Bill Jobko | LB | 6'2" | 220 | 26 | | |
| Marlin McKeever | LB | 6'1" | 230 | 22 | 2 | |
| Jack Pardee | LB | 6'2" | 225 | 26 | | 8 |
| Les Richter | LB | 6'3" | 235 | 31 | | |
| Larry Hayes | C-LB | 6'3" | 230 | 27 | | |
| Charley Britt | DB | 6'2" | 185 | 24 | 3 | |
| Lindon Crow | DB | 6'1" | 200 | 29 | 5 | 6 |
| Alvin Hall | DB | 6' | 193 | 29 | 1 | |
| Ed Meador | DB | 5'11" | 185 | 25 | 1 | |
| Carver Shannon | DB | 6'1" | 198 | 24 | 4 | |
| Bobby Smith | DB | 6' | 185 | 24 | 1 | |

| Use Name | Pos. | Hgt | Wgt | Age | Int | Pts |
|---|---|---|---|---|---|---|
| Zeke Bratkowski | QB | 6'2" | 203 | 30 | | |
| Roman Gabriel | QB | 6'4" | 220 | 22 | | |
| Ron Miller | QB | 6' | 190 | 23 | | |
| Jon Arnett | HB | 5'11" | 194 | 27 | | 12 |
| Dick Bass | FB-HB | 5'10" | 200 | 25 | | 48 |
| Ollie Matson | FB | 6'2" | 210 | 32 | | 6 |
| Art Perkins | FB | 6' | 220 | 22 | | 12 |
| Glen Shaw | FB | 6'1" | 217 | 23 | | |
| Pervis Atkins | HB-FL | 6'1" | 195 | 26 | | 6 |
| Duane Allen | OE | 6'4" | 210 | 24 | | 12 |
| Carroll Dale | OE | 6'1" | 195 | 24 | | 18 |
| Karl Finch | OE | 6'3" | 195 | 23 | | |
| Jim Phillips | OE | 6'1" | 198 | 25 | | 30 |
| Danny Villanueva | K | 5'11" | 200 | 24 | | 56 |

## WESTERN CONFERENCE—Continued

### BALTIMORE COLTS

**RUSHING**

| Last Name | No. | Yds | Avg | TD |
|---|---|---|---|---|
| Moore | 106 | 470 | 4.4 | 2 |
| Perry | 94 | 359 | 3.8 | 0 |
| Smolinski | 85 | 265 | 3.1 | 1 |
| Matte | 74 | 226 | 3.1 | 2 |
| Unitas | 50 | 137 | 2.7 | 0 |
| Hawkins | 29 | 87 | 3.0 | 4 |
| Turner | 1 | 17 | 17.0 | 0 |
| Orr | 1 | 14 | 14.0 | 0 |
| Boyd | 2 | 13 | 6.5 | 0 |
| Clemens | 2 | 9 | 4.5 | 0 |
| McHan | 4 | 4 | 1.0 | 0 |

**RECEIVING**

| Last Name | No. | Yds | Avg | TD |
|---|---|---|---|---|
| Orr | 55 | 974 | 18 | 11 |
| Berry | 51 | 687 | 13 | 3 |
| Mackey | 25 | 396 | 16 | 4 |
| Owens | 25 | 307 | 12 | 2 |
| Perry | 22 | 194 | 9 | 0 |
| Moore | 18 | 215 | 12 | 2 |
| Bielski | 15 | 200 | 13 | 2 |
| Smolinski | 13 | 128 | 10 | 1 |
| Matte | 8 | 81 | 10 | 1 |
| Hawkins | 4 | 37 | 9 | 0 |
| Turner | 1 | *111 | 111 | 1 |

*Includes lateral

**PUNT RETURNS**

| Last Name | No. | Yds | Avg | TD |
|---|---|---|---|---|
| Turner | 10 | 95 | 10 | 0 |
| Harris | 8 | 61 | 8 | 0 |
| Hawkins | 11 | 42 | 4 | 0 |
| Boyd | 3 | 23 | 8 | 0 |
| Nelson | 2 | 22 | 11 | 0 |
| Shinnick | 0 | 29 | 0 | 0 |

**KICKOFF RETURNS**

| Last Name | No. | Yds | Avg | TD |
|---|---|---|---|---|
| Matte | 27 | 613 | 23 | 0 |
| Turner | 20 | 504 | 25 | 0 |
| Harris | 3 | 86 | 29 | 0 |
| Hawkins | 2 | 35 | 18 | 0 |
| Smolinski | 2 | 20 | 10 | 0 |
| Diehl | 1 | 5 | 5 | 0 |

**PASSING — PUNTING — KICKING**

| PASSING | Att | Comp | % | Yds | Yd/Att | TD | Int— | % | RK |
|---|---|---|---|---|---|---|---|---|---|
| Unitas | 389 | 222 | 57 | 2967 | 7.6 | 23 | 23— | 6 | 7 |
| McHan | 20 | 10 | 50 | 278 | 13.9 | 3 | 2— | 10 | |
| Matte | 13 | 5 | 38 | 85 | 6.5 | 1 | 0— | 0 | |
| Hawkins | 1 | 0 | 0 | 0 | 0.0 | 0 | 0— | 0 | |

| PUNTING | No | Avg |
|---|---|---|
| Gilburg | 57 | 41.8 |
| McHan | 1 | 22.0 |

| KICKING | XP | Att | % | FG | Att | % |
|---|---|---|---|---|---|---|
| Bielski | 25 | 28 | 89 | 11 | 25 | 44 |
| Harris | 6 | 9 | 67 | 1 | 3 | 33 |

### SAN FRANCISCO FORTY NINERS

**RUSHING**

| Last Name | No. | Yds | Avg | TD |
|---|---|---|---|---|
| Smith | 258 | 907 | 3.5 | 6 |
| Kilmer | 93 | 478 | 5.1 | 5 |
| Brodie | 37 | 258 | 7.0 | 4 |
| Gaiters | 43 | 193 | 4.5 | 0 |
| Waters | 12 | 42 | 3.5 | 0 |
| Vollenweider | 11 | 37 | 3.4 | 0 |
| Roberts | 9 | 19 | 2.1 | 0 |
| Cooper | 2 | −2 | −1.0 | 0 |
| Winston | 1 | −15 | −15.0 | 0 |

**RECEIVING**

| Last Name | No. | Yds | Avg | TD |
|---|---|---|---|---|
| Casey | 53 | 819 | 15 | 6 |
| Johnson | 34 | 627 | 18 | 4 |
| Conner | 24 | 240 | 10 | 4 |
| Stickles | 22 | 366 | 17 | 3 |
| Smith | 21 | 197 | 9 | 1 |
| Kilmer | 16 | 152 | 10 | 1 |
| Gaiters | 5 | 47 | 9 | 0 |
| Vollenweider | 4 | 21 | 5 | 0 |
| Messer | 3 | 30 | 10 | 0 |
| McFarland | 3 | 24 | 8 | 0 |
| Roberts | 2 | 0 | 0 | 0 |
| Winston | 1 | 2 | 2 | 0 |

**PUNT RETURNS**

| Last Name | No. | Yds | Avg | TD |
|---|---|---|---|---|
| Woodson | 19 | 179 | 9 | 1 |
| Dove | 5 | 21 | 4 | 0 |
| Messer | 3 | 7 | 2 | 0 |

**KICKOFF RETURNS**

| Last Name | No. | Yds | Avg | TD |
|---|---|---|---|---|
| Woodson | 37 | 1157 | 31 | 0 |
| Gaiters | 11 | 273 | 25 | 0 |
| Vollenweider | 6 | 113 | 19 | 0 |
| Messer | 4 | 112 | 28 | 0 |
| Winston | 3 | 67 | 22 | 0 |
| Cooper | 1 | 17 | 17 | 0 |

**PASSING — PUNTING — KICKING**

| PASSING | Att | Comp | % | Yds | Yd/Att | TD | Int— | % | RK |
|---|---|---|---|---|---|---|---|---|---|
| Brodie | 304 | 175 | 58 | 2272 | 7.5 | 18 | 16— | 5 | 6 |
| Kilmer | 13 | 8 | 62 | 191 | 14.7 | 1 | 3— | 23 | |
| Waters | 6 | 2 | 33 | 28 | 4.7 | 0 | 0— | 0 | |
| Gaiters | 2 | 0 | 0 | 0 | 0.0 | 0 | 0— | 0 | |

| PUNTING | No | Avg |
|---|---|---|
| Davis | 48 | 45.6 |

| KICKING | XP | Att | % | FG | Att | % |
|---|---|---|---|---|---|---|
| Davis | 36 | 36 | 100 | 10 | 23 | 43 |

### MINNESOTA VIKINGS

**RUSHING**

| Last Name | No. | Yds | Avg | TD |
|---|---|---|---|---|
| Mason | 167 | 740 | 4.4 | 2 |
| Tarkenton | 41 | 361 | 8.8 | 2 |
| Mayberry | 74 | 274 | 3.7 | 1 |
| McElhenny | 50 | 200 | 4.0 | 0 |
| Triplett | 52 | 160 | 3.1 | 2 |
| Brown | 34 | 103 | 3.0 | 0 |
| Reed | 6 | 22 | 3.7 | 0 |
| McCormick | 2 | 4 | 2.0 | 0 |

**RECEIVING**

| Last Name | No. | Yds | Avg | TD |
|---|---|---|---|---|
| Reichow | 39 | 561 | 14 | 3 |
| Mason | 36 | 603 | 17 | 6 |
| Donahue | 16 | 285 | 18 | 1 |
| McElhenny | 16 | 191 | 12 | 0 |
| Ferguson | 14 | 364 | 26 | 6 |
| Stonebreaker | 12 | 227 | 19 | 1 |
| Mayberry | 11 | 100 | 9 | 1 |
| Brown | 10 | 124 | 12 | 1 |
| Smith | 7 | 138 | 20 | 1 |
| Reed | 4 | 37 | 9 | 1 |
| Adams | 3 | 51 | 17 | 0 |
| Triplett | 2 | 30 | 15 | 1 |
| Tarkenton | 0 | −12 | 0 | 0 |

**PUNT RETURNS**

| Last Name | No. | Yds | Avg | TD |
|---|---|---|---|---|
| Butler | 12 | 169 | 14 | 0 |
| Reed | 9 | 82 | 9 | 0 |
| Mason | 6 | 52 | 9 | 0 |
| McElhenny | 5 | 43 | 9 | 0 |
| Sharockman | 1 | 16 | 16 | 0 |
| Franckhauser | 1 | 12 | 12 | 0 |

**KICKOFF RETURNS**

| Last Name | No. | Yds | Avg | TD |
|---|---|---|---|---|
| Butler | 26 | 588 | 23 | 0 |
| Reed | 13 | 337 | 26 | 0 |
| Mason | 12 | 301 | 25 | 0 |
| McElhenny | 7 | 160 | 23 | 0 |
| Sharockman | 3 | 71 | 24 | 0 |
| Prestel | 2 | 29 | 15 | 0 |
| Denton | 1 | 17 | 17 | 0 |
| Stonebreaker | 1 | 12 | 12 | 0 |
| Bowie | 2 | 7 | 4 | 0 |

**PASSING — PUNTING — KICKING**

| PASSING | Att | Comp | % | Yds | Yd/Att | TD | Int— | % | RK |
|---|---|---|---|---|---|---|---|---|---|
| Tarkenton | 329 | 163 | 50 | 2595 | 7.9 | 22 | 25— | 8 | 12 |
| McCormick | 18 | 7 | 39 | 104 | 5.8 | 0 | 5— | 28 | |
| Mason | 1 | 0 | 0 | 0 | 0.0 | 0 | 1— | 100 | |

| PUNTING | No | Avg |
|---|---|---|
| McCormick | 46 | 39.0 |
| Mercer | 19 | 43.5 |

| KICKING | XP | Att | % | FG | Att | % |
|---|---|---|---|---|---|---|
| Christopherson | 28 | 28 | 100 | 11 | 20 | 55 |
| Mercer | 3 | 3 | 100 | 0 | 5 | 0 |

### LOS ANGELES RAMS

**RUSHING**

| Last Name | No. | Yds | Avg | TD |
|---|---|---|---|---|
| Bass | 196 | 1033 | 5.3 | 6 |
| Arnett | 76 | 238 | 3.1 | 2 |
| Perkins | 48 | 181 | 3.8 | 2 |
| Gabriel | 18 | 93 | 5.2 | 0 |
| Shaw | 18 | 76 | 4.2 | 0 |
| Miller | 3 | 27 | 9.0 | 0 |
| Atkins | 7 | 19 | 2.7 | 0 |
| Bratkowski | 7 | 14 | 2.0 | 0 |
| Richter | 0 | 8 | 0.00 | 0 |
| Matson | 3 | 0 | 0.00 | 0 |

**RECEIVING**

| Last Name | No. | Yds | Avg | TD |
|---|---|---|---|---|
| Phillips | 60 | 875 | 15 | 5 |
| Atkins | 35 | 393 | 11 | 1 |
| Bass | 30 | 262 | 9 | 2 |
| Dale | 29 | 584 | 20 | 3 |
| Perkins | 14 | 83 | 6 | 0 |
| Arnett | 12 | 137 | 11 | 0 |
| Allen | 3 | 90 | 30 | 2 |
| Shaw | 3 | 51 | 17 | 0 |
| Matson | 3 | 49 | 16 | 1 |

**PUNT RETURNS**

| Last Name | No. | Yds | Avg | TD |
|---|---|---|---|---|
| Atkins | 11 | 94 | 9 | 0 |
| Bass | 6 | 81 | 14 | 0 |
| Arnett | 5 | 49 | 10 | 0 |
| Hall | 4 | 21 | 5 | 0 |
| Smith | 1 | 7 | 7 | 0 |

**KICKOFF RETURNS**

| Last Name | No. | Yds | Avg | TD |
|---|---|---|---|---|
| Atkins | 28 | 676 | 24 | 0 |
| Bass | 19 | 446 | 23 | 0 |
| Hall | 8 | 178 | 22 | 0 |
| Arnett | 2 | 87 | 44 | 0 |
| Smith | 2 | 60 | 30 | 0 |
| Jones | 1 | 0 | 0 | 0 |

**PASSING — PUNTING — KICKING**

| PASSING | Att | Comp | % | Yds | Yd/Att | TD | Int— | % | RK |
|---|---|---|---|---|---|---|---|---|---|
| Bratkowski | 219 | 110 | 50 | 1541 | 7.0 | 9 | 16— | 7 | 16 |
| Gabriel | 101 | 57 | 56 | 670 | 6.6 | 3 | 2— | 2 | |
| Miller | 43 | 17 | 40 | 250 | 5.8 | 1 | 1— | 2 | |
| Arnett | 5 | 3 | 60 | 28 | 5.6 | 1 | 0— | 0 | |
| Bass | 3 | 1 | 33 | 22 | 7.3 | 0 | 0— | 0 | |
| Matson | 1 | 1 | 100 | 13 | 13.0 | 0 | 0— | 0 | |

| PUNTING | No | Avg |
|---|---|---|
| Villanueva | 87 | 45.5 |

| KICKING | XP | Att | % | FG | Att | % |
|---|---|---|---|---|---|---|
| Villanueva | 26 | 27 | 96 | 10 | 20 | 50 |

The near collapse of the New York franchise was the league's biggest headache this year. A sports truism says that no circuit can be big league without a healthy New York franchise, but the media there had practically ignored the Titans. Owner Harry Wismer's boisterous outbursts against Commissioner Joe Foss, head coach Sammy Baugh, and the NFL Giants had stripped the club of most of its dignity and left it a local joke in New York. The Titans became a ghost team, playing its games before empty stands in the shadows of the old, decrepit Polo Grounds. But Wismer's verbal antics paled in the face of his financial ills, and the joke almost turned into an obituary. Wismer had been losing money in a steady outflow since the league began, and the till finally ran dry in November. When the players' paychecks bounced, the word was out that Wismer was broke. To keep the Titans going, Commissioner Foss stepped in and ran the club with league funds, thus averting the embarrassment of the New York franchise folding in mid-season. While league intervention kept the ship from sinking this year, new skippers for the franchise would be needed for next year.

Dallas owner Lamar Hunt was far from broke, but the situation in that city was a failing one for the AFL. Hunt had been an original founder of the new league when his bid for an NFL franchise for Dallas was turned down in the late 1950s. Once it was certain that the AFL would get off the ground, the NFL had put an expansion team in Dallas. Fans flocked to see the NFL Cowboys play, while the AFL Texans starved in a land full of football fans. Even with the team on the road to a championship this season, attendance stayed low, so Hunt started shopping around for a new place to settle his team.

But attendance in general around the circuit took a sharp turn upward. The number of paid fans at league games increased 20 percent over last year, filling both the stands and the team's coffers very pleasantly. Seats with fans in them looked much better than empty bleachers on ABC's national broadcasts, which still provided the league with enough money to keep the circuit solvent.

A less favorable development was the decision against the anti-trust suit against the NFL. The United States District Court in Baltimore ruled against the suit, and the team owners voted to appeal the decision and keep the legal process moving.

But fans are concerned less with lawsuits, attendance figures, and league maneuvering than with the playing on the field. The Dallas Texans blossomed into the league's top team, a colorful bunch of youngsters who swept through the league behind Len Dawson, a cool quarterback with six years of non-activity in the NFL behind him. The Eastern Division race came down to a tight struggle between the Houston Oilers and the Boston Patriots that kept interest in the league alive through the end of the schedule. The clubs in New York, Oakland, and Denver faired very poorly and definitely needed help to become competitive in the near future, but the level of competition in general was markedly improved over the past. The crowning achievement of the season was the championship game between the Texans and Oilers, played before a full house in Houston. The game ran into the second overtime period before Dallas' Tommy Brooker won it on a field goal. The longest game ever played up until then, this match kept television viewers glued to their TV sets well into the evening, convincing some of them that perhaps the AFL had something going for itself.

## EASTERN DIVISION

**Houston Oilers**—When Oiler coach Wally Lemm resigned to head up the NFL St. Louis Cardinals, Houston owner Bud Adams replied by hiring deposed St. Louis coach Pop Ivy. Although Ivy was reputed to be an offensive genius, the Houston attack bogged down in the early part of the season. A bad back made Billy Cannon a shadow of his former self, quarterback George Blanda started serving up interceptions at a generous rate, and end Bill Groman suddenly wasn't getting open for passes any more. But like last year, the Oilers caught fire after a slow start. With squat Charley Tolar leading the way with his running, the Oilers won their last seven games, sweeping into first place by beating Boston on November 18 and winning every game the rest of the way.

**Boston Patriots**—Coach Mike Holovak's collection of unknown veterans and youngsters from local colleges battled Houston tooth and nail for the Eastern crown. The defense, led by Larry Eisenhauer, Houston Antwine, and rookie Nick Buoniconti, was more impressive as a unit than as individuals, while the offense scratched out points on Babe Parilli's passing, Ron Burton's running, and Gino Cappelletti's kicking. The Oilers recovered from a slow start to climb right behind the first-place Patriots, and the top spot rode on their November 18 meeting in Houston. Boston not only lost the game 21-17 and first place; they also lost quarterback Parilli with a broken collarbone. Reserve passer Tom Yewcic led the Pats to victories the rest of the way until stumbling 20-0 in the final game against Oakland and thus conceding the Eastern crown to Houston.

**Buffalo Bills**—The Bills had always had a tough defense, and now coach Lou Saban was building an offense that could score points. The main addition was fullback Cookie Gilchrist, a Canadian League veteran who turned out to be the best power runner in the league. Saban also picked up a fine quarterback when he claimed Jack Kemp off the San Diego waiver list. Kemp had a broken hand at the time, but Saban carried him on the roster until he healed in time to star in the last three games of the year. The defense also got an injection of new blood when rookies Tom Sestak, Mike Stratton, Ray Abruzzese, Booker Edgerson, and Carl Charon all won starting positions. The new players needed time to jell, as the Bills lost their first five games, but seven wins and a tie in the last nine games showed Buffalo fans and coach Saban that he had built a winner.

**New York Titans**—The front-office situation was so chaotic that the Titans were lucky to finish out the year. Owner Harry Wismer was broke by November, no longer able even to pay his players. With attendance microscopic, the team's image laughable, and the players clamoring for money, the league office stepped in and ran the team the rest of the year. The Titans stayed surprisingly competitive on the field through all the commotion. Coach Bulldog Turner discovered a good quarterback in ex-giant Lee Grosscup, and when injuries kayoed Grosscup, Turner came up with another passer in ex-Bill Johnny Green. Art Powell, Dick Christy, and Don Maynard were the principal targets for these passers, and with fullback Bill Mathis injured most of the season, the pass again was New York's sole offensive threat. Even with good seasons from Larry Grantham and Lee Riley, the defense leaked profusely and condemned the Titans to last place in the East.

## WESTERN DIVISION

**Dallas Texans**—Hank Stram had coached Len Dawson when both were at Purdue, and when the Cleveland Browns cut the quarterback before the season started, Stram immediately invited him to join the Texans. Dawson made up for the six years he sat on NFL benches by passing for twenty-nine touchdowns and leading the Texans to the AFL championship. Runners-up to San Diego the past two years, the Texans dethroned the Chargers by adding Dawson and key rookies Curtis McClinton, Fred Arbanas, Bobby Hunt, Bill Hull, Bill Miller, Bobby Ply, and Tommy Brooker. Stram got All-Pro performances from holdovers Abner Haynes, Chris Burford, Jim Tyrer, Mel Branch, Jerry Mays, E. J. Holub, and Sherrill Headrick, and the Texans swept to the Western crown while the stands stayed clean of paying customers.

**Denver Broncos**—The Broncos put all their chips on their passing attack and got away with it for two months. With ancient quarterback Frank Tripuka throwing bushels of passes to Lionel Taylor, Bo Dickinson, Gene Prebola, and Bob Scarpitto, the Broncos won seven of their first nine contests to contend for the Western title for the first time ever. But since Denver had no running game and a mediocre defense, the rest of the league wised up to its unbalanced attack over the second half of the season. The Broncos lost their last five games and wound up at a 7-7 mark, but the season was an exciting one for Denver fans and new coach Jack Faulkner. Three of the Broncos won individual league titles, Lionel Taylor in receiving, Gene Mingo in scoring and field goals, and Jim Fraser in punting.

**San Diego Chargers**—After two years as champs in the West, the Chargers suddenly had problems fielding a healthy team. Linebacker Bob Laraba was killed in an off-season car accident, and an amazing string of injuries left the Chargers an empty shell of their winning teams. Halfback Paul Lowe started the parade by breaking his arm in a pre-season game, and a string of teammates fell in line behind him. Rookie flanker Lance Alworth, linebacker Chuck Allen, defensive back Charley McNeil, and center Wayne Frazier all missed large portions of the schedule with various ailments, and a total of eleven starters were knocked out for seven or more games. To make this season a total loss, quarterback Jack Kemp broke his hand, and when coach Sid Gillman tried to slip him through on waivers to the reserve list, Buffalo claimed him for the $100 waiver price. With rookies and substitutes playing out the schedule, the Chargers lost eight of their last nine games to sink out of contention in the West.

**Oakland Raiders**—The Raiders were no great football team, as the six-game losing streak left over from last year testified, but the lung infection that sidelined quarterback Tom Flores for the season left the Raiders in desperate straits. They began the year with M. C. Reynolds and Don Heinrich, a pair of old NFL rejects, as passers, but coach Marty Feldman decided to go shopping for another quarterback after only one game. He bought Cotton Davidson from Dallas, and Davidson played out the Oakland schedule with a bad shoulder. The rest of the Raider squad contained little quality outside of Jim Otto, Clem Daniels, and Fred Williamson, and the team proceeded to lose its first thirteen games to run its losing streak to a record nineteen games. On the last day of the season they treated their fans in Frank Youell Field, their temporary home in Oakland, to a 20-0 victory over Boston, their first triumph in over a year.

## FINAL TEAM STATISTICS

### OFFENSE

| | BOSTON | BUFFALO | DALLAS | DENVER | HOUSTON | NEW YORK | OAKLAND | SAN DIEGO |
|---|---|---|---|---|---|---|---|---|
| **FIRST DOWNS:** | | | | | | | | |
| Total | 230 | 238 | 259 | 270 | 266 | 206 | 187 | 217 |
| by Rushing | 100 | 119 | 119 | 72 | 95 | 60 | 72 | 82 |
| by Passing | 114 | 96 | 125 | 177 | 157 | 131 | 100 | 113 |
| by Penalty | 16 | 23 | 15 | 21 | 14 | 15 | 15 | 22 |
| **RUSHING:** | | | | | | | | |
| Number | 432 | 501 | 479 | 322 | 457 | 317 | 367 | 410 |
| Yards | 1970 | 2480 | 2407 | 1298 | 1742 | 1213 | 1392 | 1647 |
| Average Yards | 4.6 | 5.0 | 5.0 | 4.0 | 3.8 | 3.8 | 3.8 | 4.0 |
| Touchdowns | 11 | 20 | 21 | 12 | 15 | 9 | 14 | 13 |
| **PASSING:** | | | | | | | | |
| Attempts | 382 | 351 | 322 | 559 | 475 | 505 | 446 | 416 |
| Completions | 195 | 150 | 195 | 292 | 227 | 242 | 175 | 168 |
| Completion Percentage | 51.0 | 42.7 | 60.6 | 52.2 | 47.8 | 47.9 | 39.2 | 40.4 |
| Passing Yards | 2930 | 2181 | 2824 | 3739 | 3323 | 3161 | 2671 | 2686 |
| Average Yards per Attempt | 7.7 | 6.2 | 8.8 | 6.7 | 7.0 | 6.3 | 6.0 | 6.5 |
| Average Yards per Completion | 15.0 | 14.5 | 14.5 | 12.8 | 14.6 | 13.1 | 15.3 | 16.0 |
| Times Tackled Attempting to Pass | 23 | 23 | 41 | 30 | 11 | 54 | 44 | 28 |
| Yards Lost Attempting to Pass | 164 | 197 | 369 | 335 | 94 | 419 | 376 | 252 |
| Net Yards | 2766 | 1984 | 2455 | 3404 | 3229 | 2742 | 2295 | 2434 |
| Touchdowns | 25 | 15 | 29 | 21 | 32 | 20 | 11 | 23 |
| Interceptions | 13 | 26 | 17 | 40 | 48 | 35 | 29 | 34 |
| Percent Intercepted | 3.4 | 7.4 | 5.3 | 7.2 | 10.1 | 6.9 | 6.5 | 8.2 |
| **PUNTING:** | | | | | | | | |
| Number | 69 | 76 | 54 | 60 | 56 | 78 | 83 | 79 |
| Average Distance | 38.5 | 38.8 | 35.8 | 42.9 | 41.0 | 41.0 | 37.4 | 41.6 |
| **PUNT RETURNS:** | | | | | | | | |
| Number | 26 | 28 | 27 | 19 | 28 | 25 | 34 | 29 |
| Yards | 138 | 196 | 236 | 128 | 314 | 308 | 257 | 278 |
| Average Yards | 5.3 | 7.0 | 8.7 | 6.7 | 11.2 | 12.3 | 7.6 | 9.6 |
| Touchdowns | 0 | 1 | 0 | 0 | 1 | 3 | 0 | 0 |
| **KICKOFF RETURNS:** | | | | | | | | |
| Number | 53 | 52 | 37 | 57 | 48 | 73 | 65 | 67 |
| Yards | 1200 | 1176 | 955 | 1210 | 1245 | 1579 | 1425 | 1585 |
| Average Yards | 22.6 | 22.6 | 25.8 | 21.2 | 25.9 | 21.6 | 21.9 | 23.7 |
| Touchdowns | 1 | 2 | 0 | 0 | 0 | 0 | 1 | 1 |
| **INTERCEPTION RETURNS:** | | | | | | | | |
| Number | 25 | 36 | 32 | 27 | 35 | 29 | 29 | 29 |
| Yards | 365 | 505 | 395 | 483 | 340 | 356 | 390 | 340 |
| Average Yards | 14.6 | 14.0 | 12.3 | 17.9 | 9.7 | 12.3 | 13.4 | 11.7 |
| Touchdowns | 3 | 3 | 0 | 4 | 2 | 1 | 1 | 1 |
| **PENALTIES:** | | | | | | | | |
| Number | 52 | 74 | 66 | 64 | 63 | 84 | 69 | 88 |
| Yards | 456 | 797 | 644 | 613 | 633 | 771 | 695 | 768 |
| **FUMBLES:** | | | | | | | | |
| Number | 37 | 27 | 26 | 28 | 17 | 35 | 31 | 24 |
| Number Lost | 20 | 12 | 14 | 14 | 9 | 20 | 20 | 14 |
| **POINTS:** | | | | | | | | |
| Total | 346 | 309 | 389 | 353 | 387 | 278 | 213 | 314 |
| PAT (kick) Attempts | 40 | 40 | 49 | 36 | 49 | 32 | 23 | 35 |
| PAT (kick) Made | 38 | 34 | 47 | 34 | 48 | 31 | 20 | 31 |
| PAT (Rush or Pass) Attempts | 1 | 1 | 1 | 3 | 1 | 2 | 4 | 3 |
| PAT (Rush or Pass) Made | 1 | 1 | 0 | 1 | 1 | 1 | 2 | 2 |
| FG Attempts | 37 | 23 | 27 | 39 | 26 | 27 | 27 | 20 |
| FG Made | 20 | 9 | 14 | 27 | 11 | 13 | 9 | 17 |
| Percent FG Made | 54.1 | 39.1 | 51.9 | 69.2 | 42.3 | 48.1 | 33.3 | 85.0 |
| Safeties | 0 | 0 | 0 | 2 | 1 | 0 | 0 | 0 |

### DEFENSE

| | BOSTON | BUFFALO | DALLAS | DENVER | HOUSTON | NEW YORK | OAKLAND | SAN DIEGO |
|---|---|---|---|---|---|---|---|---|
| **FIRST DOWNS:** | | | | | | | | |
| Total | 220 | 229 | 234 | 234 | 217 | 253 | 233 | 248 |
| by Rushing | 68 | 89 | 76 | 88 | 75 | 103 | 115 | 105 |
| by Passing | 136 | 129 | 143 | 131 | 126 | 122 | 106 | 120 |
| by Penalty | 16 | 11 | 20 | 15 | 16 | 28 | 12 | 23 |
| **RUSHING:** | | | | | | | | |
| Number | 393 | 373 | 351 | 439 | 362 | 453 | 477 | 437 |
| Yards | 1426 | 1687 | 1250 | 1868 | 1569 | 2049 | 2397 | 1903 |
| Average Yards | 3.6 | 4.5 | 3.6 | 4.3 | 4.3 | 4.5 | 5.0 | 4.4 |
| Touchdowns | 14 | 10 | 14 | 11 | 10 | 19 | 21 | 16 |
| **PASSING:** | | | | | | | | |
| Attempts | 450 | 440 | 467 | 423 | 486 | 417 | 371 | 402 |
| Completions | 216 | 215 | 239 | 202 | 213 | 194 | 169 | 196 |
| Completion Percentage | 48.0 | 48.9 | 51.2 | 47.8 | 43.8 | 46.5 | 45.6 | 48.8 |
| Passing Yards | 3435 | 2996 | 2953 | 2894 | 2865 | 2929 | 2517 | 2926 |
| Average Yards per Attempt | 7.6 | 6.8 | 6.3 | 6.8 | 5.9 | 7.0 | 6.8 | 7.3 |
| Average Yards per Completion | 15.9 | 13.9 | 12.4 | 14.3 | 13.5 | 15.1 | 14.9 | 14.9 |
| Times Tackled Attempting to Pass | 34 | 32 | 28 | 25 | 32 | 36 | 23 | 44 |
| Yards Lost Attempting to Pass | 327 | 254 | 252 | 224 | 304 | 323 | 211 | 311 |
| Net Yards | 3108 | 2742 | 2701 | 2670 | 2561 | 2606 | 2306 | 2615 |
| Touchdowns | 19 | 24 | 13 | 24 | 18 | 28 | 21 | 29 |
| Interceptions | 25 | 36 | 32 | 27 | 35 | 29 | 29 | 29 |
| Percent Intercepted | 5.6 | 8.2 | 6.9 | 6.4 | 7.2 | 7.0 | 7.8 | 7.2 |
| **PUNTING:** | | | | | | | | |
| Number | 79 | 70 | 63 | 66 | 72 | 70 | 67 | 68 |
| Average Distance | 38.5 | 38.1 | 41.2 | 41.5 | 38.9 | 37.9 | 40.9 | 40.7 |
| **PUNT RETURNS:** | | | | | | | | |
| Number | 11 | 33 | 26 | 27 | 28 | 31 | 34 | 26 |
| Yards | 54 | 202 | 219 | 245 | 259 | 295 | 352 | 229 |
| Average Yards | 4.9 | 6.1 | 8.4 | 9.1 | 9.3 | 9.5 | 10.4 | 8.8 |
| Touchdowns | 0 | 0 | 1 | 0 | 2 | 0 | 1 | 1 |
| **KICKOFF RETURNS:** | | | | | | | | |
| Number | 64 | 56 | 72 | 64 | 55 | 46 | 39 | 56 |
| Yards | 1697 | 1177 | 1559 | 1401 | 1155 | 1194 | 961 | 1231 |
| Average Yards | 26.5 | 21.0 | 21.7 | 21.9 | 21.0 | 26.0 | 24.6 | 22.0 |
| Touchdowns | 1 | 1 | 0 | 1 | 0 | 1 | 0 | 1 |
| **INTERCEPTION RETURNS:** | | | | | | | | |
| Number | 13 | 26 | 17 | 40 | 48 | 35 | 29 | 34 |
| Yards | 55 | 299 | 113 | 421 | 725 | 544 | 509 | 508 |
| Average Yards | 4.2 | 11.5 | 6.6 | 10.5 | 15.1 | 15.5 | 17.6 | 14.9 |
| Touchdowns | 1 | 0 | 0 | 5 | 2 | 3 | 3 | 1 |
| **PENALTIES:** | | | | | | | | |
| Number | 62 | 80 | 64 | 76 | 65 | 73 | 75 | 65 |
| Yards | 554 | 786 | 660 | 678 | 559 | 711 | 720 | 709 |
| **FUMBLES:** | | | | | | | | |
| Number | 26 | 26 | 29 | 34 | 25 | 30 | 25 | 30 |
| Number Lost | 10 | 14 | 16 | 19 | 17 | 16 | 18 | 13 |
| **POINTS:** | | | | | | | | |
| Total | 295 | 272 | 233 | 334 | 270 | 423 | 370 | 392 |
| PAT (kick) Attempts | 33 | 33 | 27 | 38 | 32 | 51 | 46 | 44 |
| PAT (kick) Made | 32 | 30 | 24 | 36 | 30 | 46 | 44 | 41 |
| PAT (Rush or Pass) Attempts | 3 | 2 | 2 | 3 | 1 | 1 | 0 | 4 |
| PAT (Rush or Pass) Made | 1 | 1 | 1 | 0 | 1 | 0 | 0 | 4 |
| FG Attempts | 26 | 20 | 28 | 27 | 31 | 31 | 32 | 31 |
| FG Made | 15 | 10 | 11 | 16 | 14 | 21 | 16 | 17 |
| Percent FG Made | 57.7 | 50.0 | 39.3 | 59.3 | 45.2 | 67.7 | 50.0 | 54.8 |
| Safeties | 0 | 0 | 0 | 0 | 0 | 0 | 1 | 2 |

### SCORING

```
HOUSTON   0   0   7  10   0   0—17
DALLAS    3  14   0   0   0   3—20
```

**First Quarter**
Dall.  Brooker, 16 yard field goal — 10:32

**Second Quarter**
Dall.  Haynes, 28 yard pass from Dawson — 0:27
       PAT—Brooker (kick)
Dall.  Haynes, 2 yard rush — 11:21
       PAT—Brooker (kick)

**Third Quarter**
Hous.  Dewveall, 15 yard pass from Blanda — 3:10
       PAT—Blanda (kick)

**Fourth Quarter**
Hous.  Blanda, 31 yard field goal — 3:53
Hous.  Tolar, 1 yard rush — 9:22
       PAT—Blanda (kick)

**Second Overtime (Sixth Quarter)**
Dall.  Brooker, 25 yard field goal — 2:54

### TEAM STATISTICS

| DALLAS | | HOU. |
|---|---|---|
| 19 | First Downs—Total | 21 |
| 10 | First Downs—Rushing | 6 |
| 5 | First Downs—Passing | 15 |
| 4 | First Downs—Penalty | 0 |
| 2 | Fumbles—Number | 0 |
| 1 | Fumbles—Number Lost | 0 |
| 6 | Penalties—Number | 6 |
| 42 | Yards Penalized | 50 |
| 1 | Giveaways | 5 |
| 5 | Takeaways | 1 |
| +4 | Difference | −4 |

## 1962 AFL CHAMPIONSHIP GAME
December 23, at Houston
(Attendance 37,981)

### The Longest Afternoon

Houston had won its third straight Eastern title, but the Dallas Texans, making their first title-game appearance, almost blew the Oilers off the field in the first half, running up a 17-0 score on two Abner Haynes touchdowns and a Tommy Brooker field goal. The Oilers came out for the second half in top gear, however, and quickly fought back into the game. George Blanda passed to Willard Dewveall for 15 yards and Houston's first points early in the third quarter. With their backs against the wall, the Oilers rallied to tie the score in the fourth period. Blanda kicked a 31-yard field goal early in the period, and Charley Tolar scored on a one-yard plunge with five minutes left in the game. Blanda's extra point tied the score at 17-17, and regulation time ran out without any further scoring. As the teams readied for overtime, the captains met at midfield for the coin toss for the next periods. Instructed to take advantage of the wind, Dallas' Abner Haynes blundered by electing to kick off, thus giving the Oilers the advantage of both receiving and having the wind at their backs. The Oilers couldn't score, however, and the Texans took the ball at mid-field near the end of the first overtime period on a Bill Hull interception. With Jack Spikes carrying and receiving the ball on key plays, the Texans moved down to the Houston 19-yard line. Tommy Brooker then booted a 25-yard field goal which ended Houston's championship reign and pro football's longest game.

### INDIVIDUAL STATISTICS

**RUSHING**

| HOUSTON | No. | Yds. | Avg. | | DALLAS | No. | Yds. | Avg. |
|---|---|---|---|---|---|---|---|---|
| Tolar | 17 | 58 | 3.4 | | Spikes | 11 | 77 | 7.0 |
| Cannon | 11 | 37 | 3.4 | | McClinton | 24 | 70 | 2.9 |
| Smith | 2 | 3 | 1.5 | | Dawson | 5 | 26 | 5.2 |
| | 30 | 98 | 3.3 | | Haynes | 14 | 26 | 1.9 |
| | | | | | | 54 | 199 | 3.7 |

**RECEIVING**

| HOUSTON | No. | Yds. | Avg. | | DALLAS | No. | Yds. | Avg. |
|---|---|---|---|---|---|---|---|---|
| Dewveall | 6 | 95 | 15.8 | | Haynes | 3 | 45 | 15.0 |
| Cannon | 6 | 54 | 9.0 | | Spikes | 2 | 24 | 12.0 |
| McLeod | 5 | 70 | 14.0 | | Arbanas | 2 | 21 | 10.5 |
| Hennigan | 3 | 37 | 11.3 | | McClinton | 1 | 4 | 4.0 |
| Tolar | 1 | 8 | 8.0 | | Bishop | 1 | −6 | −6.0 |
| Smith | 1 | 6 | 6.0 | | | 9 | 88 | 9.8 |
| Jamison | 1 | −9 | −9.0 | | | | | |
| | 23 | 261 | 11.3 | | | | | |

**PUNTING**

| HOUSTON | No. | Yds. | Avg. | | DALLAS | No. | Yds. | Avg. |
|---|---|---|---|---|---|---|---|---|
| Norton | 3 | | 39.3 | | Wilson | 6 | | 32.0 |
| | | | | | Saxton | 2 | | 29.0 |
| | | | | | | 8 | | 31.2 |

**PUNT RETURNS**

| HOUSTON | No. | Yds. | Avg. | | DALLAS | No. | Yds. | Avg. |
|---|---|---|---|---|---|---|---|---|
| Jancik | 1 | 0 | 0.0 | | Jackson | 1 | 0 | 0.0 |

**KICKOFF RETURNS**

| HOUSTON | No. | Yds. | Avg. | | DALLAS | No. | Yds. | Avg. |
|---|---|---|---|---|---|---|---|---|
| Jancik | 5 | 139 | 27.8 | | Grayson | 3 | 64 | 21.3 |
| | | | | | Haynes | 1 | 22 | 22.0 |
| | | | | | | 4 | 86 | 21.5 |

**INTERCEPTION RETURNS**

| HOUSTON | No. | Yds. | Avg. | | DALLAS | No. | Yds. | Avg. |
|---|---|---|---|---|---|---|---|---|
| None | | | | | Robinson | 2 | 50 | 25.0 |
| | | | | | Holub | 1 | 43 | 43.0 |
| | | | | | Hull | 1 | 23 | 23.0 |
| | | | | | Grayson | 1 | 20 | 20.0 |
| | | | | | | 5 | 136 | 27.2 |

**PASSING**

| HOUSTON | Att. | Comp. | Comp. Pct. | Yds. | Int. | Yds/ Att. | Yds/ Comp. | Yards Lost Tackled |
|---|---|---|---|---|---|---|---|---|
| Blanda | 46 | 23 | 50.0 | 261 | 5 | 5.7 | 11.3 | 0 |

| DALLAS | Att. | Comp. | Comp. Pct. | Yds. | Int. | Yds/ Att. | Yds/ Comp. | Yards Lost Tackled |
|---|---|---|---|---|---|---|---|---|
| Dawson | 14 | 9 | 64.3 | 88 | 0 | 6.3 | 9.8 | 6—50 |

## HOUSTON OILERS 11-3-0 Pop Ivy

| Scores of Each Game | | | Use Name | Pos. | Hgt | Wgt | Age | Int | Pts | Use Name | Pos. | Hgt | Wgt | Age | Int | Pts | Use Name | Pos. | Hgt | Wgt | Age | Int | Pts |
|---|---|---|---|---|---|---|---|---|---|---|---|---|---|---|---|---|---|---|---|---|---|---|---|
| 28 | Buffalo | 23 | Al Jamison | OT | 6'5" | 250 | 25 | | | Doug Cline | LB | 6'2" | 230 | 23 | 2 | | George Blanda | QB | 6'1" | 212 | 34 | | 81 |
| 21 | Boston | 34 | Rich Michael | OT | 6'3" | 242 | 23 | | | Mike Dukes | LB | 6'3" | 230 | 26 | 2 | | Jacky Lee | QB | 6'1" | 185 | 23 | | |
| 42 | San Diego | 17 | Walt Suggs | OT | 6'5" | 245 | 23 | | | Tom Goode | LB | 6'3" | 235 | 23 | | | Billy Cannon | HB | 6'1" | 215 | 25 | | 80 |
| 17 | BUFFALO | 14 | John Frongillo | OG | 6'3" | 250 | 22 | | | Larry Onesti | LB | 6' | 205 | 23 | | | Dave Smith | FB | 6'1" | 210 | 25 | | 18 |
| 56 | NEW YORK | 17 | Bob Talamini | OG | 6'1" | 255 | 23 | | | Gene Babb | FB-LB | 6'3" | 220 | 27 | 2 | 6 | Charley Tolar | HB-FB | 5'7" | 198 | 24 | | 48 |
| 10 | Denver | 20 | Bill Wegener | OG | 5'10" | 245 | 21 | | | Tony Banfield | DB | 6'1" | 185 | 23 | 6 | 6 | Charley Hennigan | FL | 6' | 187 | 26 | | 48 |
| 7 | DALLAS | 31 | Hogan Wharton | OG | 6'2" | 250 | 26 | | | Freddy Glick | DB | 6'1" | 190 | 25 | 3 | | Willard Dewveall | OE | 6'4" | 230 | 25 | | 30 |
| 14 | Dallas | 6 | Bob Schmidt | C | 6'4" | 250 | 26 | | | Bobby Jancik | DB | 5'11" | 178 | 22 | 2 | | Charley Frazier | OE | 6' | 160 | 23 | | 6 |
| 28 | Oakland | 20 | Gary Cutsinger | DE | 6'4" | 240 | 21 | 1 | | Mark Johnston | DB | 6'2" | 200 | 24 | 4 | | Bill Groman | OE | 6' | 200 | 26 | | 18 |
| 21 | BOSTON | 17 | Don Floyd | DE | 6'4" | 247 | 24 | 4 | 6 | Jim Norton | DB | 6'3" | 195 | 23 | 8 | | Bob McCleod | OE | 6'5" | 240 | 23 | | 36 |
| 33 | SAN DIEGO | 27 | Dan Lanphear | DE | 6'2" | 230 | 24 | | | Bob Suci | DB | 5'10" | 178 | 24 | 1 | | | | | | | | |
| 34 | DENVER | 17 | Ron McDole | DE | 6'3" | 255 | 23 | | | | | | | | | | | | | | | | |
| 32 | OAKLAND | 17 | Ed Culpepper | DT | 6'1" | 260 | 28 | | | | | | | | | | | | | | | | |
| 44 | New York | 10 | Bill Herchman | DT | 6'2" | 255 | 29 | | | | | | | | | | | | | | | | |
| | | | Ed Husmann | DT | 6' | 245 | 31 | | | | | | | | | | | | | | | | |
| | | | Bob Kelly | DT | 6'3" | 250 | 22 | | | | | | | | | | | | | | | | |
| | | | Bill Miller | DT | 6'4" | 270 | 24 | | | | | | | | | | | | | | | | |

## BOSTON PATRIOTS 9-4-1 Mike Holovak

| Scores of Each Game | | | Use Name | Pos. | Hgt | Wgt | Age | Int | Pts | Use Name | Pos. | Hgt | Wgt | Age | Int | Pts | Use Name | Pos. | Hgt | Wgt | Age | Int | Pts |
|---|---|---|---|---|---|---|---|---|---|---|---|---|---|---|---|---|---|---|---|---|---|---|---|
| 28 | Dallas | 42 | Milt Graham | OT | 6'6" | 235 | 28 | | | Tom Addison | LB | 6'3" | 230 | 26 | 5 | 6 | Don Allard | QB | 6' | 188 | 26 | | |
| 21 | HOUSTON | 21 | Dick Klein | OT | 6'4" | 254 | 28 | | | Nick Buoniconti | LB | 5'11" | 220 | 21 | 2 | | Babe Parilli | QB | 6'1" | 190 | 32 | | 12 |
| 41 | DENVER | 16 | Charley Long | OT | 6'3" | 230 | 24 | | | Harry Jacobs | LB | 6'2" | 235 | 25 | | | Tom Yewcic | QB | 5'11" | 185 | 30 | | 12 |
| 43 | New York | 14 | Charlie Leo | OG | 6' | 240 | 27 | | | Rommie Loudd | LB | 6'3" | 225 | 28 | | | Ron Burton | HB | 5'10" | 190 | 25 | | 42 |
| 7 | DALLAS | 27 | Billy Neighbors | OG | 5'11" | 240 | 22 | | | Jack Rudolph | LB | 6'3" | 230 | 24 | | | Jim Crawford | HB | 6'1" | 200 | 26 | | 26 |
| 24 | SAN DIEGO | 20 | Tony Sardisco | OG | 6'2" | 230 | 29 | | | Fred Bruney | DB | 5'10" | 190 | 31 | 3 | 6 | Claude King | HB | 5'11" | 195 | 23 | | 6 |
| 26 | OAKLAND | 16 | Walt Cudzik | C | 6'2" | 235 | 29 | | | Dick Felt | DB | 6' | 185 | 29 | 5 | | Larry Garron | FB | 6' | 215 | 25 | | 36 |
| 28 | Buffalo | 28 | Bob Yates | C | 6'3" | 230 | 23 | | | Ron Hall | DB | 6' | 190 | 25 | 3 | 6 | Billy Lott | FB | 6' | 205 | 27 | | |
| 33 | Denver | 29 | Bob Dee | DE | 6'3" | 240 | 29 | | | Ross O'Hanley | DB | 6' | 185 | 23 | 5 | | Gino Capelletti | FL | 6' | 190 | 28 | | 128 |
| 17 | Houston | 21 | Larry Eisenhauer | DE | 6'5" | 230 | 22 | | | Chuck Shonta | DB | 6' | 190 | 24 | 2 | | Jim Colclough | OE | 6' | 185 | 26 | | 60 |
| 21 | BUFFALO | 10 | Jim Hunt | DE | 5'11" | 245 | 23 | | | Don Webb | HB-DB | 5'10" | 200 | 23 | | | Tony Romeo | OE | 6'2" | 220 | 23 | | 6 |
| 24 | NEW YORK | 17 | Houston Antwine | DT | 6' | 250 | 23 | | | | | | | | | | Tom Stephens | OE | 6'1" | 220 | 26 | | |
| 20 | San Diego | 14 | Jess Richardson | DT | 6'2" | 265 | 32 | | | Oscar Lofton — Military Service | | | | | | | | | | | | | |
| 0 | Oakland | 20 | | | | | | | | George McGee — Military Service | | | | | | | | | | | | | |

## BUFFALO BILLS 7-6-1 Lou Saban

| Scores of Each Game | | | Use Name | Pos. | Hgt | Wgt | Age | Int | Pts | Use Name | Pos. | Hgt | Wgt | Age | Int | Pts | Use Name | Pos. | Hgt | Wgt | Age | Int | Pts |
|---|---|---|---|---|---|---|---|---|---|---|---|---|---|---|---|---|---|---|---|---|---|---|---|
| 23 | HOUSTON | 28 | Stew Barber | OT | 6'3" | 242 | 23 | | | Ralph Felton | LB | 5'11" | 210 | 30 | | | Al Dorow | QB | 6' | 195 | 32 | | |
| 20 | DENVER | 23 | Jerry DeLucca | OT | 6'3" | 250 | 26 | | | Tom Louderback | LB | 6'2" | 235 | 28 | | | Jack Kemp (from SD) | QB | 6'1" | 205 | 28 | | 12 |
| 6 | NEW YORK | 17 | Harold Olson | OT | 6'3" | 258 | 23 | | | Archie Matsos | LB | 6' | 220 | 27 | | | Warren Rabb | QB | 6'1" | 205 | 25 | | 20 |
| 21 | Dallas | 41 | Tom Day | OG | 6'2" | 245 | 27 | | | Marv Matuszak | LB | 6'3" | 230 | 31 | 6 | | Manch Wheeler | QB | 6' | 190 | 23 | | |
| 14 | Houston | 17 | George Flint | OG | 6'4" | 245 | 24 | | | Mike Stratton | LB | 6'3" | 225 | 20 | 6 | | Wayne Crow | HB | 6' | 205 | 24 | | 12 |
| 35 | SAN DIEGO | 10 | Billy Shaw | OG | 6'2" | 240 | 22 | | | John Tracey | OE-LB | 6'3" | 225 | 29 | | | Elbert Dubenion | HB | 6' | 197 | 27 | | 36 |
| 14 | OAKLAND | 6 | Al Bemiller | C | 6'3" | 238 | 23 | | | Ray Abruzzese | DB | 6'1" | 190 | 24 | 3 | | Carey Henley | HB | 5'10" | 200 | 23 | | |
| 45 | Denver | 38 | Frank Jackunas | C | 6'3" | 225 | 21 | | | Joe Cannavino | DB | 5'11" | 187 | 26 | 1 | | Art Baker | FB | 6' | 220 | 24 | | 6 |
| 28 | BOSTON | 28 | Leroy Moore (from BOS) | DE | 6' | 232 | 26 | 1 | 6 | Carl Charon | DB | 5'10" | 185 | 21 | 7 | 12 | Wray Carlton | HB-FB | 6'2" | 220 | 24 | | 12 |
| 40 | San Diego | 20 | Nate Borden | DE | 6' | 238 | 30 | | | Jim Crotty | DB | 5'11" | 190 | 24 | | | Cookie Gilchrist | FB | 6'3" | 246 | 27 | | 128 |
| 10 | Oakland | 6 | Mack Yoho | DT | 6'2" | 238 | 26 | | 23 | Booker Edgerson | DB | 5'10" | 178 | 23 | 6 | | Willie Jones | FB | 5'11" | 208 | 22 | | |
| 10 | Boston | 21 | Don Healy | DT | 6'3" | 264 | 26 | | | Carl Taseff | DB | 5'11" | 193 | 33 | 2 | | Glenn Bass | OE | 6'2" | 197 | 23 | | 24 |
| 23 | DALLAS | 14 | Tom Saidock | DT | 6'5" | 260 | 30 | | | Willie West | DB | 5'10" | 193 | 24 | 3 | | Monte Crockett | OE | 6'3" | 218 | 23 | | |
| 20 | New York | 3 | Tom Sestak | DT | 6'5" | 267 | 26 | 1 | 6 | John Yaccino | DB | 6' | 190 | 24 | | | Tom Rychlec | OE | 6'3" | 220 | 28 | | 6 |
| | | | Jim Sorey | DT | 6'4" | 285 | 25 | | | | | | | | | | Ernie Warlick | OE | 6'4" | 235 | 30 | | 12 |
| | | | Sid Youngelman | DT | 6'3" | 256 | 30 | | | Ken Rice — Knee Injury | | | | | | | | | | | | | |

## NEW YORK TITANS 5-9-0 Bulldog Turner

| Scores of Each Game | | | Use Name | Pos. | Hgt | Wgt | Age | Int | Pts | Use Name | Pos. | Hgt | Wgt | Age | Int | Pts | Use Name | Pos. | Hgt | Wgt | Age | Int | Pts |
|---|---|---|---|---|---|---|---|---|---|---|---|---|---|---|---|---|---|---|---|---|---|---|---|
| 28 | Oakland | 17 | Fran Morelli | OT | 6'2" | 258 | 23 | | | Hubert Bobo | LB | 6'1" | 220 | 27 | 1 | | Johnny Green | QB | 6'3" | 208 | 25 | | 18 |
| 14 | San Diego | 40 | Alex Kroll | C-OT | 6'3" | 230 | 24 | | | Ed Cooke | LB | 6'4" | 250 | 27 | 1 | 6 | Lee Grosscup | QB | 6'1" | 187 | 25 | | |
| 17 | Buffalo | 6 | Moses Gray | DT-OT | 6'3" | 260 | 24 | | | Roger Ellis | LB | 6'3" | 233 | 24 | | | Dean Look | QB | 5'11" | 185 | 25 | | |
| 10 | DENVER | 32 | Gene Cockrell | DE-OT | 6'3" | 247 | 29 | | | Jerry Fields | LB | 6'1" | 222 | 23 | | | Bob Scrabis | QB | 6'3" | 225 | 26 | | |
| 14 | BOSTON | 43 | Sid Fournet | OG | 6' | 240 | 29 | | | Larry Grantham | LB | 6' | 200 | 23 | 2 | 6 | Butch Songin | QB | 6'2" | 205 | 38 | | |
| 17 | Houston | 56 | Bob Mischak | OG | 6' | 240 | 29 | | | Billy Atkins | DB | 6'1" | 196 | 27 | 4 | | Harold Stephens | QB | 5'11" | 175 | 23 | | |
| 17 | Dallas | 20 | Mike Hudock | C | 6'2" | 245 | 27 | | | Wayne Fontes | DB | 6' | 190 | 22 | 4 | 6 | Dick Christy | HB | 5'10" | 192 | 26 | | 48 |
| 23 | SAN DIEGO | 3 | Karl Kaimer | DE | 6'3" | 230 | 23 | | | Paul Hynes | DB | 6'1" | 210 | 22 | 2 | | Curley Johnson | HB | 6' | 215 | 27 | | |
| 31 | OAKLAND | 21 | John Kenerson (from PIT-N) | DE | 6'3" | 255 | 29 | | | Dainard Paulson | DB | 5'11" | 190 | 25 | 3 | | Bill Shockley | HB | 6' | 185 | 24 | | 68 |
| 31 | DALLAS | 52 | Nick Mumley | DE | 6'6" | 255 | 26 | | | Lee Riley | DB | 6'1" | 195 | 30 | 11 | | Jim Tiller | HB | 5'9" | 165 | 23 | | |
| 46 | Denver | 45 | Lavern Torczon (from BUF) | DE | 6'2" | 235 | 26 | | | Ed Kovac | HB-DB | 6' | 200 | 24 | 1 | | Mel West | HB | 5'9" | 190 | 23 | | |
| 17 | Boston | 24 | Bob Watters | DE | 6'4" | 250 | 26 | | | | | | | | | | Charlie Flowers | FB | 6'1" | 217 | 25 | | |
| 3 | BUFFALO | 20 | Dick Guesman | DT | 6'4" | 255 | 26 | 2 | | | | | | | | | Bobby Fowler | FB | 5'11" | 212 | 26 | | |
| 10 | HOUSTON | 44 | Proverb Jacobs | DT | 6'4" | 260 | 27 | | | | | | | | | | Bill Mathis | FB | 6'1" | 220 | 23 | | 18 |
| | | | George Strugar (from PIT-N) | DT | 6'5" | 258 | 27 | | | | | | | | | | Don Maynard | FL | 6' | 185 | 26 | | 48 |
| | | | | | | | | | | | | | | | | | Thurlow Cooper | OE | 6'4" | 228 | 29 | | 8 |
| | | | | | | | | | | | | | | | | | Art Powell | OE | 6'3" | 212 | 25 | | 48 |
| | | | | | | | | | | | | | | | | | Perry Richards | OE | 6'2" | 205 | 28 | | |

## HOUSTON OILERS

### RUSHING

| Last Name | No. | Yds | Avg | TD |
|---|---|---|---|---|
| Tolar | 244 | 1012 | 4.1 | 7 |
| Cannon | 147 | 474 | 3.2 | 7 |
| Smith | 56 | 249 | 4.4 | 1 |
| Blanda | 3 | 6 | 2.0 | 0 |
| Lee | 4 | 1 | 0.3 | 0 |
| Babb | 3 | 0 | 0.0 | 0 |

### RECEIVING

| Last Name | No. | Yds | Avg | TD |
|---|---|---|---|---|
| Hennigan | 54 | 867 | 16 | 8 |
| McLeod | 33 | 578 | 18 | 6 |
| Dewveall | 33 | 576 | 17 | 5 |
| Cannon | 32 | 451 | 14 | 6 |
| Tolar | 30 | 251 | 8 | 1 |
| Groman | 21 | 328 | 16 | 3 |
| Smith | 17 | 117 | 7 | 2 |
| Frazier | 7 | 155 | 22 | 1 |

### PUNT RETURNS

| Last Name | No. | Yds | Avg | TD |
|---|---|---|---|---|
| Jancik | 14 | 164 | 12 | 0 |
| Glick | 12 | 79 | 7 | 0 |
| Banfield | 2 | 71 | 36 | 1 |

### KICKOFF RETURNS

| Last Name | No. | Yds | Avg | TD |
|---|---|---|---|---|
| Jancik | 24 | 726 | 30 | 0 |
| Cannon | 18 | 442 | 25 | 0 |
| Smith | 2 | 37 | 19 | 0 |
| Glick | 1 | 22 | 22 | 0 |
| Tolar | 2 | 18 | 9 | 0 |
| McLeod | 1 | 0 | 0 | 0 |

### PASSING – PUNTING – KICKING

PASSING

| Last Name | Att | Comp | % | Yds | Yd/Att | TD | Int–% | RK |
|---|---|---|---|---|---|---|---|---|
| Blanda | 418 | 197 | 47 | 2810 | 6.7 | 27 | 42– 10 | 5 |
| Lee | 50 | 26 | 52 | 433 | 8.7 | 4 | 5– 10 | |
| Cannon | 3 | 2 | 67 | 46 | 15.3 | 1 | 0– 0 | |
| Smith | 3 | 2 | 67 | 34 | 11.3 | 0 | 0– 0 | |
| Tolar | 1 | 0 | 0 | 0 | 0.0 | 0 | 1–100 | |

PUNTING

| Last Name | No | Avg |
|---|---|---|
| Norton | 55 | 41.7 |

KICKING

| Last Name | XP | Att | % | FG | Att | % |
|---|---|---|---|---|---|---|
| Blanda | 48 | 49 | 98 | 11 | 26 | 42 |

2 POINT XP
Cannon (1)

## BOSTON PATRIOTS

### RUSHING

| Last Name | No. | Yds | Avg | TD |
|---|---|---|---|---|
| Burton | 134 | 548 | 4.0 | 2 |
| Crawford | 139 | 459 | 3.3 | 2 |
| Garron | 67 | 392 | 5.8 | 2 |
| Yewcic | 33 | 215 | 6.5 | 2 |
| Parilli | 28 | 169 | 6.0 | 2 |
| King | 21 | 144 | 6.8 | 1 |
| Lott | 8 | 34 | 4.2 | 0 |
| Colclough | 1 | 14 | 14.0 | 0 |
| Cappelletti | 1 | –5 | –5.0 | 0 |

### RECEIVING

| Last Name | No. | Yds | Avg | TD |
|---|---|---|---|---|
| Colclough | 40 | 868 | 22 | 10 |
| Burton | 40 | 461 | 12 | 4 |
| Romeo | 34 | 608 | 18 | 1 |
| Cappelletti | 34 | 479 | 14 | 5 |
| Crawford | 22 | 224 | 10 | 2 |
| Garron | 18 | 236 | 7 | 3 |
| King | 5 | 42 | 8 | 0 |
| Webb | 1 | 11 | 11 | 0 |
| Lott | 1 | 1 | 1 | 0 |

### PUNT RETURNS

| Last Name | No. | Yds | Avg | TD |
|---|---|---|---|---|
| Burton | 21 | 122 | 6 | 0 |
| Bruney | 3 | 8 | 3 | 0 |
| Buoniconti | 1 | 8 | 8 | 0 |
| Hall | 1 | 0 | 0 | 0 |

### KICKOFF RETURNS

| Last Name | No. | Yds | Avg | TD |
|---|---|---|---|---|
| Garron | 24 | 686 | 29 | 0 |
| Burton | 13 | 238 | 18 | 0 |
| King | 9 | 177 | 20 | 0 |
| Stephens | 2 | 46 | 23 | 0 |
| Crawford | 2 | 24 | 12 | 0 |
| Loudd | 1 | 15 | 15 | 0 |
| Dee | 1 | 14 | 14 | 0 |
| Jacobs | 1 | 0 | 0 | 0 |

### PASSING – PUNTING – KICKING

PASSING

| Last Name | Att | Comp | % | Yds | Yd/Att | TD | Int–% | RK |
|---|---|---|---|---|---|---|---|---|
| Parilli | 253 | 140 | 55 | 1988 | 7.9 | 18 | 8– 3 | 2 |
| Yewcic | 126 | 54 | 43 | 903 | 7.2 | 7 | 5– 4 | |
| Garron | 3 | 1 | 33 | 39 | 13.0 | 0 | 0– 0 | |

PUNTING

| Last Name | No | Avg |
|---|---|---|
| Yewcic | 68 | 38.7 |

KICKING

| Last Name | XP | Att | % | FG | Att | % |
|---|---|---|---|---|---|---|
| Cappelletti | 38 | 40 | 95 | 20 | 37 | 54 |

2 POINT XP
Crawford (1)

## BUFFALO BILLS

### RUSHING

| Last Name | No. | Yds | Avg | TD |
|---|---|---|---|---|
| Gilchrist | 214 | 1096 | 5.1 | 13 |
| Crow | 110 | 589 | 5.4 | 1 |
| Carlton | 94 | 530 | 5.6 | 2 |
| Kemp | 20 | 84 | 4.2 | 2 |
| Rabb | 37 | 77 | 2.1 | 3 |
| Dorow | 15 | 57 | 3.8 | 0 |
| Dubenion | 7 | 40 | 5.7 | 0 |
| Jones | 4 | 17 | 4.2 | 0 |
| Baker | 2 | 9 | 4.5 | 0 |
| Wheeler | 3 | 7 | 2.3 | 0 |
| Henley | 3 | 2 | 0.6 | 0 |

### RECEIVING

| Last Name | No. | Yds | Avg | TD |
|---|---|---|---|---|
| Warlick | 35 | 482 | 14 | 2 |
| Dubenion | 33 | 571 | 17 | 5 |
| Bass | 32 | 555 | 17 | 4 |
| Gilchrist | 24 | 319 | 13 | 2 |
| Crow | 8 | 80 | 10 | 1 |
| Carlton | 7 | 54 | 8 | 0 |
| Rychlec | 6 | 66 | 11 | 1 |
| Baker | 3 | 12 | 4 | 0 |
| Tracey | 1 | 28 | 28 | 0 |
| Crockett | 1 | 14 | 14 | 0 |

### PUNT RETURNS

| Last Name | No. | Yds | Avg | TD |
|---|---|---|---|---|
| West | 14 | 112 | 8 | 0 |
| Rychlec | 1 | 24 | 24 | 0 |
| Taseff | 4 | 18 | 5 | 0 |
| Abruzzese | 3 | 17 | 6 | 0 |
| Moore | 2 | 12 | 6 | 0 |
| Sestak | 2 | 6 | 3 | 0 |
| Cannavino | 1 | 3 | 3 | 0 |
| Edgerson | 1 | 1 | 1 | 0 |
| Charon | 0 | 3 | 0 | 1 |

### KICKOFF RETURNS

| Last Name | No. | Yds | Avg | TD |
|---|---|---|---|---|
| Jones | 14 | 287 | 21 | 0 |
| Dubenion | 7 | 231 | 33 | 1 |
| Baker | 7 | 220 | 31 | 1 |
| Abruzzese | 10 | 194 | 19 | 0 |
| Gilchrist | 7 | 150 | 21 | 0 |
| Henley | 5 | 90 | 18 | 0 |
| Flint | 1 | 4 | 4 | 0 |
| DeLucca | 1 | 0 | 0 | 0 |

### PASSING – PUNTING – KICKING

PASSING

| Last Name | Att | Comp | % | Yds | Yd/Att | TD | Int–% | RK |
|---|---|---|---|---|---|---|---|---|
| Rabb | 177 | 67 | 38 | 1196 | 6.8 | 10 | 14– 8 | 6 |
| Kemp | 139 | 64 | 46 | 928 | 6.7 | 5 | 6– 4 | |
| Dorow | 75 | 30 | 40 | 333 | 4.4 | 2 | 7– 9 | |
| Crow | 4 | 2 | 50 | 16 | 4.0 | 0 | 1– 25 | |
| Taseff | 1 | 0 | 0 | 0 | 0.0 | 0 | 0– 0 | |

PUNTING

| Last Name | No | Avg |
|---|---|---|
| Crow | 75 | 39.0 |

KICKING

| Last Name | XP | Att | % | FG | Att | % |
|---|---|---|---|---|---|---|
| Yoho | 20 | 24 | 83 | 1 | 3 | 33 |
| Gilchrist | 14 | 16 | 88 | 8 | 20 | 40 |

2 POINT XP
Rabb (1)

## NEW YORK TITANS

### RUSHING

| Last Name | No. | Yds | Avg | TD |
|---|---|---|---|---|
| Christy | 114 | 535 | 4.6 | 3 |
| Mathis | 71 | 245 | 3.4 | 3 |
| Johnson | 26 | 114 | 4.3 | 0 |
| Flowers | 21 | 78 | 3.7 | 0 |
| Grosscup | 8 | 62 | 7.7 | 0 |
| Tiller | 31 | 43 | 1.3 | 0 |
| Green | 17 | 35 | 2.1 | 3 |
| Stephens | 6 | 33 | 5.5 | 0 |
| Fowler | 5 | 27 | 5.4 | 0 |
| West | 9 | 16 | 1.7 | 0 |
| Songin | 4 | 11 | 2.7 | 0 |
| Look | 2 | 9 | 4.5 | 0 |
| Kovac | 3 | 5 | 1.6 | 0 |

### RECEIVING

| Last Name | No. | Yds | Avg | TD |
|---|---|---|---|---|
| Powell | 64 | 1130 | 18 | 8 |
| Christy | 62 | 538 | 9 | 3 |
| Maynard | 56 | 1041 | 19 | 8 |
| Johnson | 14 | 62 | 4 | 0 |
| Tiller | 13 | 108 | 8 | 0 |
| Cooper | 12 | 122 | 10 | 1 |
| Flowers | 7 | 55 | 8 | 0 |
| Richards | 6 | 69 | 12 | 0 |
| Mathis | 6 | 32 | 5 | 0 |
| Kovac | 1 | 3 | 3 | 0 |
| West | 1 | 1 | 1 | 0 |

### PUNT RETURNS

| Last Name | No. | Yds | Avg | TD |
|---|---|---|---|---|
| Christy | 15 | 250 | 17 | 2 |
| Tiller | 9 | 47 | 5 | 0 |
| Cooke | 1 | 11 | 11 | 1 |

### KICKOFF RETURNS

| Last Name | No. | Yds | Avg | TD |
|---|---|---|---|---|
| Christy | 38 | 824 | 22 | 0 |
| Tiller | 22 | 462 | 21 | 0 |
| West | 3 | 131 | 44 | 0 |
| Shockley | 3 | 73 | 24 | 0 |
| Kovac | 4 | 72 | 18 | 0 |
| Johnson | 1 | 14 | 14 | 0 |
| Cooper | 1 | 3 | 3 | 0 |
| Fournet | 1 | 0 | 0 | 0 |

### PASSING – PUNTING – KICKING

PASSING

| Last Name | Att | Comp | % | Yds | Yd/Att | TD | Int–% | RK |
|---|---|---|---|---|---|---|---|---|
| Green | 258 | 128 | 50 | 1741 | 6.8 | 10 | 18– 7 | 4 |
| Grosscup | 126 | 57 | 45 | 855 | 6.8 | 8 | 8– 6 | |
| Songin | 90 | 42 | 47 | 442 | 4.9 | 2 | 7– 8 | |
| Stephens | 22 | 15 | 68 | 123 | 5.6 | 0 | 0– 0 | |
| Christy | 6 | 0 | 0 | 0 | 0.0 | 0 | 0– 0 | |
| Scrabis | 2 | 0 | 0 | 0 | 0.0 | 0 | 1– 50 | |
| Look | 1 | 0 | 0 | 0 | 0.0 | 0 | 1–100 | |

PUNTING

| Last Name | No | Avg |
|---|---|---|
| Johnson | 50 | 39.9 |
| Atkins | 21 | 46.1 |
| Green | 3 | 40.3 |
| Paulson | 3 | 37.7 |

KICKING

| Last Name | XP | Att | % | FG | Att | % |
|---|---|---|---|---|---|---|
| Shockley | 29 | 29 | 100 | 13 | 26 | 50 |
| Guesman | 2 | 3 | 67 | 1 | 0 | |

2 POINT XP
Cooper (1)

## DALLAS TEXANS 11-3-0 Hank Stram

### Scores of Each Game

| | | |
|---|---|---|
| 42 | BOSTON | 28 |
| 26 | Oakland | 16 |
| 41 | BUFFALO | 21 |
| 28 | San Diego | 32 |
| 27 | Boston | 7 |
| 20 | NEW YORK | 17 |
| 31 | Houston | 7 |
| 6 | HOUSTON | 14 |
| 52 | New York | 31 |
| 24 | Denver | 3 |
| 35 | OAKLAND | 7 |
| 14 | Buffalo | 23 |
| 17 | DENVER | 10 |
| 26 | SAN DIEGO | 17 |

| Use Name | Pos. | Hgt | Wgt | Age | Int | Pts |
|---|---|---|---|---|---|---|
| Jerry Cornelison | OT | 6'3" | 250 | 25 | | |
| Charley Diamond | OT | 6'2" | 262 | 26 | | |
| Jim Tyrer | OT | 6'6" | 290 | 23 | | |
| Carl Larpenter | OG-OT | 6'4" | 240 | 25 | | |
| Sonny Bishop | OG | 6'2" | 235 | 22 | | |
| Curt Merz | OG | 6'4" | 250 | 24 | | |
| Al Reynolds | OG | 6'3" | 235 | 24 | | |
| Marvin Terrell | OG | 6'1" | 235 | 24 | | |
| Jon Gilliam | C | 6'2" | 240 | 23 | | |
| Mel Branch | DE | 6'2" | 230 | 25 | | |
| Dick Davis | DE | 6'2" | 230 | 23 | | |
| Bill Hull | DE | 6'6" | 245 | 21 | | |
| Paul Rochester | DT | 6'2" | 260 | 25 | | |
| Jerry Mays | DE-DT | 6'4" | 247 | 22 | | |
| Walt Corey | LB | 6' | 220 | 24 | | |
| Ted Greene | LB | 6'1" | 230 | 28 | | |
| Sherrill Headrick | LB | 6'2" | 215 | 25 | 3 | |
| Smokey Stover | LB | 6' | 235 | 23 | | |
| E. J. Holub | C-LB | 6'4" | 225 | 24 | 2 | |
| Dave Grayson | DB | 5'10" | 180 | 23 | 4 | |
| Bobby Hunt | DB | 6'1" | 180 | 22 | 8 | |
| Ed Kelley | DB | 6'2" | 195 | 27 | | |
| Bobby Ply | DB | 6'1" | 190 | 21 | 7 | |
| Duane Wood | DB | 6'1" | 200 | 26 | 4 | |
| Johnny Robinson | HB-DB | 6' | 198 | 23 | 4 | |
| Len Dawson | QB | 6' | 190 | 28 | | 18 |
| Eddie Wilson | QB | 6' | 190 | 22 | | |
| Abner Haynes | HB | 6' | 190 | 24 | | 114 |
| Frank Jackson | HB | 6'1" | 182 | 22 | | 24 |
| Jimmy Saxton | HB | 5'11" | 173 | 21 | | |
| Curtis McClinton | FB | 6'3" | 232 | 23 | | 12 |
| Jack Spikes | FB | 6'2" | 220 | 24 | | 7 |
| Fred Arbanas | OE | 6'3" | 236 | 23 | | 36 |
| Tommy Brooker | OE | 6'2" | 225 | 22 | | 87 |
| Chris Burford | OE | 6'3" | 215 | 24 | | 72 |
| Bill Miller | OE | 6' | 190 | 20 | | |
| Tom Pennington | K | 6'2" | 210 | 22 | | 19 |

Dave Webster — Injury

## DENVER BRONCOS 7-7-0 Jack Faulkner

### Scores of Each Game

| | | |
|---|---|---|
| 30 | SAN DIEGO | 21 |
| 23 | Buffalo | 20 |
| 16 | Boston | 41 |
| 32 | New York | 10 |
| 44 | OAKLAND | 7 |
| 23 | Oakland | 6 |
| 20 | HOUSTON | 10 |
| 38 | BUFFALO | 45 |
| 23 | San Diego | 20 |
| 29 | BOSTON | 33 |
| 3 | DALLAS | 24 |
| 45 | NEW YORK | 46 |
| 17 | Houston | 34 |
| 10 | Dallas | 17 |

| Use Name | Pos. | Hgt | Wgt | Age | Int | Pts |
|---|---|---|---|---|---|---|
| Eldon Danenhauer | OT | 6'4" | 245 | 26 | | |
| Jim Perkins | OT | 6'5" | 250 | 23 | | |
| Jerry Sturm | OT | 6'3" | 245 | 25 | | |
| Ken Adamson | OG | 6'2" | 225 | 23 | | |
| John Denvir | OG | 6'4" | 245 | 24 | | |
| Bob McCullough | OG | 6'2" | 240 | 21 | | |
| Jim Barton | C | 6'5" | 250 | 27 | | |
| John Cash | DE | 6'3" | 240 | 26 | 1 | |
| Chuck Gavin | DE | 6'1" | 245 | 28 | 1 | |
| Larry Jordan | DE | 6'6" | 230 | 24 | | |
| Don Joyce | DE | 6'3" | 260 | 32 | | |
| Gordy Holz | DT | 6'4" | 260 | 28 | | |
| Ike Lassiter | DE-DT | 6'5" | 270 | 21 | | |
| Bud McFadin | DG | 6'3" | 270 | 34 | | 6 |
| Tom Erlandson | LB | 6'3" | 220 | 22 | 1 | |
| Jim Fraser | LB | 6'3" | 240 | 26 | 1 | 2 |
| Wahoo McDaniel | LB | 6' | 240 | 25 | 4 | |
| Bill Roehnelt | LB | 6'1" | 230 | 26 | | |
| Jerry Stalcup | LB | 6' | 230 | 24 | | |
| Goose Gonsoulin | DB | 6'3" | 210 | 24 | 7 | 6 |
| Chuck Marshall | DB | 6' | 180 | 23 | | |
| John McGeever | DB | 6'1" | 195 | 23 | 2 | 6 |
| Jim McMillin | DB | 5'11" | 190 | 24 | 4 | 12 |
| Tom Minter (to BUF) | DB | 5'10" | 178 | 22 | | |
| Justin Rowland | DB | 6'2" | 190 | 24 | | |
| Bob Zeman | DB | 6'1" | 203 | 25 | 6 | 6 |
| George Shaw | QB | 6'1" | 185 | 29 | | 6 |
| Frank Tripucka | QB | 6'2" | 208 | 34 | | 6 |
| Al Frazier | HB | 5'11" | 180 | 27 | | 18 |
| Gene Mingo | HB | 6'1" | 200 | 23 | | 137 |
| Donnie Stone | HB | 6'2" | 205 | 25 | | 30 |
| Jerry Tarr | HB | 6' | 190 | 22 | | 12 |
| Bo Dickinson | FB | 6'2" | 220 | 27 | | 24 |
| Johnny Olszewski | FB | 5'11" | 202 | 31 | | 6 |
| Jim Stinnette | FB | 6'1" | 230 | 24 | | 6 |
| Bob Scarpitto | FL | 5'11" | 195 | 23 | | 36 |
| Gene Prebola | OE | 6'3" | 225 | 24 | | 8 |
| Lionel Taylor | OE | 6'2" | 215 | 26 | | 24 |

## SAN DIEGO CHARGERS 4-10-0 Sid Gillman

### Scores of Each Game

| | | |
|---|---|---|
| 21 | Denver | 30 |
| 40 | NEW YORK | 14 |
| 17 | HOUSTON | 42 |
| 42 | Oakland | 33 |
| 32 | DALLAS | 28 |
| 10 | Buffalo | 35 |
| 20 | Boston | 24 |
| 3 | New York | 23 |
| 20 | DENVER | 23 |
| 20 | BUFFALO | 40 |
| 27 | Houston | 33 |
| 31 | OAKLAND | 21 |
| 14 | BOSTON | 20 |
| 17 | Dallas | 26 |

| Use Name | Pos. | Hgt | Wgt | Age | Int | Pts |
|---|---|---|---|---|---|---|
| Jack Klotz (from NY) | OT | 6'5" | 260 | 28 | | |
| Sherman Plunkett | OT | 6'4" | 297 | 28 | | |
| Ernie Wright | OT | 6'4" | 265 | 21 | | |
| Ron Mix | OG-OT | 6'4" | 245 | 24 | | |
| Ernie Barnes | OG | 6'3" | 247 | 23 | | |
| Pat Shea | OG | 6'1" | 230 | 23 | | |
| Dick Hudson | OT-OG | 6'4" | 260 | 22 | | |
| Sam Gruneisen | LB-OG | 6'1" | 232 | 21 | | |
| Don Rogers | OG-C | 6'2" | 250 | 25 | | |
| Wayne Frazier | LB-C | 6'2" | 235 | 22 | | |
| Earl Faison | DE | 6'5" | 256 | 23 | 1 | |
| Paul Miller | DE | 6'2" | 240 | 30 | | |
| Ron Nery | DE | 6'6" | 244 | 27 | | |
| Bill Hudson | DT | 6'4" | 277 | 26 | | |
| Ernie Ladd | DT | 6'9" | 317 | 23 | | |
| Henry Schmidt | DE-DT | 6'4" | 246 | 25 | | |
| Chuck Allen | LB | 6'1" | 220 | 22 | 1 | |
| Frank Buncom | LB | 6'1" | 225 | 22 | 4 | |
| Emil Karas | LB | 6'3" | 230 | 28 | 2 | |
| Paul Maguire | LB | 6' | 223 | 24 | 1 | |
| Bob Mitinger | LB | 6'2" | 222 | 22 | | |
| Maury Schleicher | LB | 6'3" | 240 | 25 | | |
| Bob Bethune | DB | 5'11" | 190 | 23 | 3 | |
| George Blair | DB | 5'11" | 197 | 24 | 2 | 82 |
| Claude Gibson | DB | 6'1" | 193 | 23 | 8 | 6 |
| Dick Harris | DB | 5'11" | 175 | 25 | 5 | |
| Charley McNeil | DB | 5'11" | 180 | 26 | 1 | |
| Bud Whitehead | DB | 6' | 180 | 23 | 1 | |
| John Hadl | QB | 6'2" | 205 | 22 | | 6 |
| Val Keckin | QB | 6'4" | 215 | 25 | | |
| Dick Wood (to DEN) | QB | 6'5" | 200 | 26 | | |
| Keith Lincoln | HB | 6'2" | 205 | 23 | | 24 |
| Bert Coan | HB | 6'4" | 215 | 22 | | |
| Fred Gillett | HB | 6'3" | 225 | 24 | | |
| Hez Braxton | FB | 6'2" | 227 | 26 | | 8 |
| Bobby Jackson | FB | 6'3" | 227 | 22 | | 42 |
| Jacque Mackinnon | FB | 6'4" | 240 | 23 | | 12 |
| Gerry McDougall | FB | 6'2" | 227 | 27 | | 18 |
| Lance Alworth | OE | 6' | 183 | 22 | | |
| Reg Carolan | OE | 6'6" | 225 | 22 | | 6 |
| Dave Kocourek | OE | 6'5" | 230 | 25 | | 26 |
| Don Norton | OE | 6'1" | 185 | 24 | | 42 |
| Jerry Robinson | OE | 5'11" | 190 | 23 | | 18 |

Bob Laraba — died Feb. 16, 1962 — auto accident
Sam DeLuca — Voluntarily Retired
Paul Lowe — Broken Arm

## OAKLAND RAIDERS 1-13-0 Marty Feldman  Red Conkright

### Scores of Each Game

| | | |
|---|---|---|
| 17 | NEW YORK | 28 |
| 16 | DALLAS | 26 |
| 33 | SAN DIEGO | 42 |
| 7 | Denver | 44 |
| 6 | DENVER | 23 |
| 6 | Buffalo | 14 |
| 16 | Boston | 26 |
| 21 | New York | 31 |
| 20 | HOUSTON | 28 |
| 6 | BUFFALO | 10 |
| 7 | Dallas | 35 |
| 21 | San Diego | 31 |
| 17 | Houston | 32 |
| 20 | BOSTON | 0 |

| Use Name | Pos. | Hgt | Wgt | Age | Int | Pts |
|---|---|---|---|---|---|---|
| Charley Brown | OT | 6'4" | 245 | 25 | | |
| Pete Nicklas | OT | 6'4" | 240 | 22 | | |
| Jim Norris | OT | 6'4" | 235 | 22 | | |
| Jack Stone | OT | 6'2" | 245 | 25 | | |
| Stan Campbell | OG | 6' | 230 | 32 | | |
| Dan Ficca | OG | 6'1" | 230 | 23 | | |
| Wayne Hawkins | OG | 6' | 235 | 24 | | |
| Jim Otto | C | 6'2" | 240 | 24 | | |
| Dalva Allen | DE | 6'5" | 245 | 26 | | |
| Dan Birdwell | DE | 6'4" | 232 | 21 | | |
| Jon Jelacic | DE | 6'3" | 255 | 25 | 1 | |
| Riley Morris | DE | 6'2" | 235 | 25 | | |
| Joe Novsek | DE | 6'4" | 237 | 22 | | |
| Chuck McMurtry | DT | 6' | 280 | 24 | | |
| George Shirkey | DT | 6'4" | 255 | 25 | | |
| Orville Trask | OT | 6'4" | 260 | 27 | | |
| Bob Dougherty | LB | 6' | 240 | 28 | | |
| Charley Rieves | LB | 5'11" | 215 | 23 | | |
| Jackie Simpson | DB | 6'1" | 225 | 26 | 3 | 15 |
| George Boynton | DB | 5'11" | 190 | 24 | | |
| Bob Garner | DB | 5'10" | 175 | 27 | 3 | |
| Mel Montalbo | DB | 6'1" | 190 | 23 | | |
| Tom Morrow | DB | 5'11" | 180 | 24 | 10 | |
| Rich Mostardi | DB | 5'11" | 188 | 24 | | |
| Henry Rivera | DB | 5'11" | 180 | 22 | | |
| Vern Valdez | DB | 5'11" | 190 | 26 | 4 | |
| Fred Williamson | DB | 6'2" | 208 | 24 | 8 | 6 |
| Cotton Davidson (from DAL) | QB | 6'1" | 187 | 29 | | 25 |
| Hunter Enis (from DEN) | QB | 6'2" | 195 | 25 | | |
| Chan Gallegos | QB | 5'9" | 175 | 22 | | |
| Don Heinrich | QB | 6' | 180 | 31 | | |
| M. C. Reynolds | QB | 6' | 195 | 27 | | |
| Dobie Craig | HB | 6'4" | 200 | 23 | | 24 |
| Clem Daniels | HB | 6'1" | 220 | 25 | | 48 |
| Charley Fuller | HB | 5'11" | 175 | 23 | | |
| Harold Lewis | HB | 6' | 204 | 26 | | |
| Bo Roberson | HB | 6'1" | 197 | 27 | | 44 |
| Gene White | HB | 6'1" | 197 | 22 | | 8 |
| Alan Miller | FB | 6' | 205 | 24 | | 6 |
| Willie Simpson | FB | 6' | 218 | 23 | | |
| Max Boydston | OE | 6'2" | 220 | 29 | | |
| Dick Dorsey | OE | 6'3" | 200 | 24 | | 12 |
| Charley Hardy | OE | 6' | 185 | 28 | | |
| Ben Agajanian | K | 6' | 220 | 43 | | 25 |

Tom Flores – Illness (tuberculosis)

## DALLAS TEXANS

### RUSHING

| Last Name | No. | Yds | Avg | TD |
|---|---|---|---|---|
| Haynes | 221 | 1049 | 4.7 | 13 |
| McClinton | 111 | 604 | 5.4 | 2 |
| Dawson | 38 | 252 | 6.6 | 0 |
| Jackson | 47 | 251 | 5.3 | 3 |
| Spikes | 57 | 232 | 4.0 | 0 |
| Burford | 1 | 13 | 13.0 | 0 |
| Wilson | 1 | 5 | 5.0 | 0 |
| Saxton | 3 | 1 | 0.3 | 0 |

### RECEIVING

| Last Name | No. | Yds | Avg | TD |
|---|---|---|---|---|
| Burford | 45 | 645 | 14 | 12 |
| Haynes | 39 | 573 | 15 | 6 |
| Arbanas | 29 | 469 | 16 | 6 |
| McClinton | 29 | 333 | 11 | 0 |
| Miller | 23 | 277 | 12 | 0 |
| Jackson | 10 | 177 | 18 | 1 |
| Spikes | 10 | 132 | 13 | 1 |
| Saxton | 5 | 64 | 13 | 0 |
| Brooker | 4 | 138 | 35 | 3 |
| Robinson | 1 | 16 | 16 | 0 |

### PUNT RETURNS

| Last Name | No. | Yds | Avg | TD |
|---|---|---|---|---|
| Haynes | 15 | 119 | 8 | 0 |
| Jackson | 11 | 117 | 11 | 0 |
| Grayson | 1 | 0 | 0 | 0 |

### KICKOFF RETURNS

| Last Name | No. | Yds | Avg | TD |
|---|---|---|---|---|
| Grayson | 18 | 535 | 30 | 0 |
| Jackson | 10 | 254 | 25 | 0 |
| Saxton | 4 | 77 | 19 | 0 |
| McClinton | 2 | 32 | 16 | 0 |
| Spikes | 2 | 30 | 15 | 0 |
| Haynes | 1 | 27 | 27 | 0 |

### PASSING – PUNTING – KICKING

**PASSING**

| Last Name | Att | Comp | % | Yds | Yd/Att | TD | Int-% | RK |
|---|---|---|---|---|---|---|---|---|
| Dawson | 310 | 189 | 61 | 2759 | 8.9 | 29 | 17- 5 | 1 |
| Wilson | 11 | 6 | 55 | 65 | 5.9 | 0 | 0- 0 | |
| Haynes | 1 | 0 | 0 | 0 | 0.0 | 0 | 0- 0 | |

**PUNTING**

| Last Name | No | Avg |
|---|---|---|
| Wilson | 47 | 35.8 |
| Saxton | 3 | 46.3 |

**KICKING**

| Last Name | XP | Att | % | FG | Att | % |
|---|---|---|---|---|---|---|
| Brooker | 33 | 33 | 100 | 12 | 22 | 55 |
| Pennington | 13 | 15 | 87 | 2 | 5 | 40 |
| Spikes | 1 | 1 | 100 | 0 | 0 | 0 |

## DENVER BRONCOS

### RUSHING

| Last Name | No. | Yds | Avg | TD |
|---|---|---|---|---|
| Stone | 94 | 360 | 3.8 | 3 |
| Mingo | 43 | 287 | 3.8 | 5 |
| Dickinson | 73 | 247 | 3.3 | 0 |
| Frazier | 39 | 168 | 4.2 | 2 |
| Olszewski | 33 | 114 | 3.4 | 0 |
| Stinnette | 21 | 87 | 4.1 | 1 |
| Taylor | 2 | 26 | 13.0 | 0 |
| Shaw | 4 | 10 | 2.5 | 1 |
| Tripucka | 2 | -1 | -0.5 | 1 |

### RECEIVING

| Last Name | No. | Yds | Avg | TD |
|---|---|---|---|---|
| Taylor | 77 | 908 | 12 | 4 |
| Dickinson | 60 | 554 | 9 | 4 |
| Prebola | 41 | 599 | 15 | 1 |
| Scarpitto | 35 | 667 | 19 | 6 |
| Stone | 20 | 223 | 11 | 0 |
| Mingo | 14 | 107 | 8 | 0 |
| Olszewski | 13 | 150 | 12 | 1 |
| Stinnette | 13 | 109 | 8 | 0 |
| Frazier | 11 | 211 | 19 | 1 |
| Tarr | 8 | 211 | 26 | 2 |

### PUNT RETURNS

| Last Name | No. | Yds | Avg | TD |
|---|---|---|---|---|
| Zeman | 5 | 59 | 12 | 0 |
| Mingo | 7 | 36 | 5 | 0 |
| Frazier | 5 | 32 | 6 | 0 |
| Minter | 2 | 1 | 1 | 0 |

### KICKOFF RETURNS

| Last Name | No. | Yds | Avg | TD |
|---|---|---|---|---|
| Frazier | 19 | 388 | 20 | 0 |
| Minter | 10 | 227 | 23 | 0 |
| Tarr | 8 | 217 | 27 | 0 |
| McGeever | 5 | 143 | 29 | 0 |
| Mingo | 6 | 99 | 17 | 0 |
| Olszewski | 3 | 66 | 22 | 0 |
| Stinnette | 2 | 27 | 14 | 0 |
| Dickinson | 2 | 26 | 13 | 0 |
| Danenhauer | 1 | 11 | 11 | 0 |
| McMillin | 1 | 6 | 6 | 0 |

### PASSING – PUNTING – KICKING

**PASSING**

| Last Name | Att | Comp | % | Yds | YdTAtt | TD | Int-% | RK |
|---|---|---|---|---|---|---|---|---|
| Tripucka | 440 | 240 | 55 | 2917 | 6.6 | 17 | 25- 6 | 3 |
| Shaw | 110 | 49 | 45 | 783 | 7.1 | 4 | 14- 13 | |
| Stone | 3 | 1 | 33 | 13 | 4.3 | 0 | 0- 0 | |
| Mingo | 2 | 1 | 50 | 18 | 9.0 | 0 | 1- 50 | |
| Taylor | 2 | 0 | 0 | 0 | 0.0 | 0 | 0- 0 | |

**PUNTING**

| Last Name | No | Avg |
|---|---|---|
| Fraser | 54 | 44.4 |
| McDaniel | 5 | 34.6 |

**KICKING**

| Last Name | XP | Att | % | FG | Att | % |
|---|---|---|---|---|---|---|
| Mingo | 32 | 34 | 94 | 27 | 39 | 69 |
| Fraser | 2 | 2 | 100 | 0 | 0 | 0 |

**2 POINT XP**
Prebola (1)

## SAN DIEGO CHARGERS

### RUSHING

| Last Name | No. | Yds | Avg | TD |
|---|---|---|---|---|
| Lincoln | 117 | 574 | 4.8 | 2 |
| Jackson | 106 | 411 | 3.8 | 5 |
| MacKinnon | 59 | 240 | 4.0 | 0 |
| McDougall | 43 | 197 | 4.5 | 3 |
| Hadl | 40 | 139 | 3.4 | 1 |
| Braxton | 17 | 35 | 2.1 | 1 |
| Alworth | 1 | 17 | 17.0 | 0 |
| Robinson | 2 | 10 | 5.0 | 0 |
| Coan | 12 | 10 | 0.8 | 0 |
| Gillett | 2 | 8 | 4.0 | 0 |
| Keckin | 1 | 3 | 3.0 | 0 |
| Wood | 1 | 0 | 0.0 | 0 |

### RECEIVING

| Last Name | No. | Yds | Avg | TD |
|---|---|---|---|---|
| Norton | 48 | 771 | 16 | 7 |
| Kocourek | 39 | 688 | 18 | 4 |
| Robinson | 21 | 391 | 19 | 3 |
| Lincoln | 16 | 214 | 13 | 1 |
| Jackson | 13 | 136 | 10 | 2 |
| Alworth | 10 | 226 | 23 | 3 |
| MacKinnon | 9 | 125 | 14 | 2 |
| McDougall | 4 | 27 | 7 | 0 |
| Braxton | 4 | 17 | 4 | 0 |
| Carolan | 3 | 39 | 13 | 1 |
| Coan | 1 | 52 | 52 | 0 |

### PUNT RETURNS

| Last Name | No. | Yds | Avg | TD |
|---|---|---|---|---|
| Harris | 7 | 95 | 14 | 0 |
| Lincoln | 11 | 94 | 9 | 0 |
| Gibson | 10 | 89 | 9 | 0 |
| Braxton | 1 | 0 | 0 | 0 |

### KICKOFF RETURNS

| Last Name | No. | Yds | Avg | TD |
|---|---|---|---|---|
| Robinson | 32 | 748 | 23 | 0 |
| Lincoln | 14 | 398 | 28 | 1 |
| Bethune | 12 | 251 | 21 | 0 |
| McDougall | 3 | 71 | 24 | 0 |
| Gibson | 2 | 55 | 28 | 0 |
| Coan | 2 | 31 | 16 | 0 |
| Jackson | 1 | 16 | 16 | 0 |
| Klotz | 1 | 15 | 15 | 0 |

### PASSING – PUNTING – KICKING

**PASSING**

| Last Name | Att | Comp | % | Yds | Yd/Att | TD | Int-% | RK |
|---|---|---|---|---|---|---|---|---|
| Hadl | 260 | 107 | 41 | 1632 | 6.3 | 15 | 24- 9 | 7 |
| Wood | 97 | 41 | 42 | 655 | 6.8 | 4 | 7- 7 | |
| Keckin | 9 | 5 | 56 | 64 | 7.1 | 0 | 1- 11 | |
| Lincoln | 5 | 2 | 40 | 43 | 8.6 | 2 | 0- 0 | |

**PUNTING**

| Last Name | No | Avg |
|---|---|---|
| Maguire | 79 | 41.6 |

**KICKING**

| Last Name | XP | Att | % | FG | Att | % |
|---|---|---|---|---|---|---|
| Blair | 31 | 35 | 89 | 17 | 20 | 85 |

**2 POINT XP**
Braxton (1)
Kocourek (1)

## OAKLAND RAIDERS

### RUSHING

| Last Name | No. | Yds | Avg | TD |
|---|---|---|---|---|
| Daniels | 161 | 766 | 4.7 | 7 |
| Roberson | 89 | 270 | 3.0 | 3 |
| Miller | 65 | 182 | 2.8 | 1 |
| Davidson | 25 | 54 | 2.1 | 3 |
| W. Simpson | 10 | 32 | 3.2 | 0 |
| Gallegos | 3 | 25 | 8.3 | 0 |
| Enis | 2 | 24 | 12.0 | 0 |
| Lewis | 9 | 18 | 2.0 | 0 |
| Reynolds | 1 | 9 | 9.0 | 0 |
| Craig | 1 | 8 | 8.0 | 0 |
| Heinrich | 1 | 4 | 4.0 | 0 |

### RECEIVING

| Last Name | No. | Yds | Avg | TD |
|---|---|---|---|---|
| Boydston | 30 | 374 | 12 | 0 |
| Roberson | 29 | 583 | 20 | 3 |
| Craig | 27 | 492 | 18 | 4 |
| Daniels | 24 | 318 | 13 | 1 |
| Dorsey | 21 | 344 | 16 | 2 |
| Miller | 20 | 259 | 13 | 0 |
| Lewis | 7 | 53 | 8 | 0 |
| White | 6 | 101 | 17 | 1 |
| Hardy | 6 | 80 | 13 | 0 |
| Fuller | 5 | 67 | 13 | 0 |

### PUNT RETURNS

| Last Name | No. | Yds | Avg | TD |
|---|---|---|---|---|
| Garner | 20 | 162 | 8 | 0 |
| Lewis | 9 | 65 | 7 | 0 |
| Valdez | 2 | 14 | 7 | 0 |
| Morrow | 2 | 13 | 7 | 0 |
| Williamson | 1 | 3 | 3 | 0 |

### KICKOFF RETURNS

| Last Name | No. | Yds | Avg | TD |
|---|---|---|---|---|
| Roberson | 27 | 748 | 28 | 1 |
| Daniels | 24 | 530 | 22 | 0 |
| Lewis | 3 | 65 | 22 | 0 |
| Miller | 6 | 45 | 8 | 0 |
| Dougherty | 1 | 20 | 20 | 0 |
| Garner | 1 | 8 | 8 | 0 |
| W. Simpson | 1 | 7 | 7 | 0 |
| Norris | 1 | 2 | 2 | 0 |
| Novsek | 1 | 0 | 0 | 0 |

### PASSING – PUNTING – KICKING

**PASSING**

| Last Name | Att | Comp | % | Yds | Yd/Att | TD | Int-% | RK |
|---|---|---|---|---|---|---|---|---|
| Davidson | 321 | 119 | 37 | 1977 | 6.2 | 7 | 23- 7 | 8 |
| Enis | 51 | 27 | 53 | 225 | 4.4 | 1 | 2- 2 | |
| Gallegos | 35 | 18 | 51 | 298 | 8.5 | 2 | 3- 9 | |
| Heinrich | 29 | 10 | 34 | 156 | 5.4 | 1 | 2- 7 | |
| Roberson | 6 | 0 | 0 | 0 | 0.0 | 0 | 0- 0 | |
| Reynolds | 5 | 2 | 40 | 23 | 4.6 | 0 | 0- 0 | |
| Daniels | 1 | 0 | 0 | 0 | 0.0 | 0 | 0- 0 | |

**PUNTING**

| Last Name | No | Avg |
|---|---|---|
| Morrow | 45 | 36.7 |
| Davidson | 40 | 39.2 |

**KICKING**

| Last Name | XP | Att | % | FG | Att | % |
|---|---|---|---|---|---|---|
| Agajanian | 10 | 11 | 91 | 5 | 14 | 36 |
| J. Simpson | 6 | 6 | 100 | 3 | 10 | 30 |
| Davidson | 4 | 5 | 80 | 1 | 2 | 50 |
| Birdwell | 0 | 0 | 0 | 0 | 0 | 0 |

**2 POINTS XP**
Roberson (1)
White (1)

# 1963 N.F.L. The Best Bet: No Bet

Commissioner Pete Rozelle dropped a bombshell when he announced that certain players had been betting on NFL games. Although none of the men had bet against their own teams, Rozelle decided that players must be above suspicion. Stars Paul Hornung of Green Bay and Alex Karras of Detroit were suspended indefinitely by Rozelle for placing a series of bets on league games, while five other members of the Detroit club were fined $2,000 apiece for betting on the championship game. Another touchy decision by Rozelle was to play the regular slate of games on November 24, a day of mourning for the assassinated President John F. Kennedy. Another tragedy was the death on May 10 of "Big Daddy" Lipscomb, one of the greatest defensive tackles of all time. He was found dead of an overdose of heroin, although many people believe that Lipscomb was drunk and was given the fatal dose after being knocked out in a robbery attempt. On the plus side, though, was the opening of the Hall of Fame in Canton, with seventeen charter members inducted.

## EASTERN CONFERENCE

**New York Giants**—Two losses in the first five games created doubts over the aging Giants, but the team looked pleasantly ripe rather than overage by the end of the season. Winning nine of their last ten games, the Giants captured the Eastern crown for the third straight time. The New York offense, relying heavily on Y. A. Tittle's passes to split end Del Shofner, included such aged stars as Tittle, Frank Gifford, Rosey Brown, and Jack Stroud, while the defense numbered gaffers like Andy Robustelli, Dick Modzelewski, and Tom Scott as starters. But the Giants were old pros, winning all the games they needed to win and keeping their mistakes to a minimum.

**Cleveland Browns**—With Blanton Collier now the head coach, fullback Jimmy Brown came to camp in a much better state of mind. Brown ran wild once the regular season began, carrying the ball like a workhorse without ever looking tired. After eight games he was already over 1,000 yards for the campaign, and by the end of the season he had set a new record of 1,863 yards. Brown's running kept the Browns in the Eastern race until the Lions knocked them out one week from the end of the season. But in falling short of the title, the Browns did uncover in Frank Ryan their best quarterback since Otto Graham.

**St. Louis Cardinals**—Young Charley Johnson's passing was the spectacular element in the Cardinal attack, but the running game showed the greatest versatility and depth. Both John David Crow and Prentice Gautt went out with injuries, leaving the Cards without their regular running backs. To replace the injured men, coach Wally Lemm shifted Bill Triplett from defensive back to offensive halfback, and he promoted veteran Joe Childress to a starter's position after several seasons of sitting on the bench. Both runners placed in the top ten in the NFL rushing statistics and provided a fine complement to Johnson's passes to Sonny Randle and Bobby Joe Conrad.

**Pittsburgh Steelers**—The Steelers had played three ties during the season, so that they could win the title with the best percentage although winning fewer games than the Giants. This constitutional crisis of sorts was averted when the Giants crushed Pittsburgh 33-17. Still, the Steelers surprised most observers by getting as far as they did, relying on players whose futures seemed behind them. The attack depended on power running from John Henry Johnson and Dick Hoak, while the defense was a hardnosed outfit that compensated well for the absence of Big Daddy Lipscomb, who died tragically before the season began.

**Dallas Cowboys**—Although considered an outside contender for the Eastern crown, the Cowboys never got off the ground after losing their first two games. But although the defense still needed major work and the offensive line needed some shoring up, the Cowboys were still adding good young players to their core. Two rookies made good impressions, Lee Roy Jordan at outside linebacker and Tony Liscio at offensive tackle. In addition, Don Meredith assumed full-time duties at quarterback while Bob Lilly blossomed into a great defensive lineman after being shifted from end to tackle.

**Washington Redskins**—The long suit in the Redskin attack was the passing game, headed up by young quarterback Norm Snead. Better at the long pass than the short pass, Snead operated a long-range attack with passes to Bobby Mitchell, Fred Dugan, Bill Anderson, and rookie Pat Richter. Mitchell remained the star of the team, the most dangerous receiver in the league after he caught the ball. The running backs were slow and brittle, however, and the defense needed patching up.

**Philadelphia Eagles**—Winless in their last nine games, the Eagles did not even have injuries as an excuse for their last-place finish. What they could blame was poor morale on a team with better talent than the record indicated. The problems began in training camp when both Sonny Jurgensen and King Hill walked out in a joint holdout for more money. Left without a quarterback, the Eagles gave in to their demands, only to have Jurgensen bothered by various injuries during the season. Coach Nick Skorich got no production out of his fullbacks, had problems in the offensive line, and lost several mediocre defensive linemen with leg problems.

## WESTERN CONFERENCE

**Chicago Bears**—A brutally effective defense brought coach George Halas his first championship in seventeen years. Assistant coach George Allen had installed a zone pass defense that made the Chicago unit the toughest in the league. Allowing only 10 points per game, the Bear defense grew famous around the league as it began to win games with minimal help from the offense. Doug Atkins, Ed O'Bradovich, Bill George, Joe Fortunato, Larry Morris, Richie Petitbon, and Rosey Taylor shone the brightest on defense, while the offense, led by Billy Wade, Johnny Morris, and Mike Ditka, was programmed to stick with safe running plays and short passes without any probability of interception.

**Green Bay Packers**—Paul Hornung was hardly missed, but the loss of quarterback Bart Starr for four games with a broken hand cost the Packers dearly. Tommy Moore and Elijah Pitts filled in admirably for Hornung at halfback, and guard Jerry Kramer handled the placekicking duties with style. An opening 10-3 loss to the Bears was written off as a fluke, but when Chicago kept winning, first place in the West was on the line in the November 17 rematch at Chicago. By that time, however, Starr was out of action, and Zeke Bratkowski was running the Packer attack. The Bears swept the Pack out of Wrigley Field in taking a 26-7 victory, thus ending Green Bay domination.

**Baltimore Colts**—New coach Don Shula's regime began with five losses in the first eight games, hardly a reason for enthusiasm, but a fine stretch run served notice that the Colts were still title contenders. Shula had Johnny Unitas, Jim Parker, Ray Berry, Gino Marchetti, and some other veterans of the 1958-59 championship squads, but he also started blending in new talent of his own. Jerry Hill was promoted to starting fullback, and Tom Matte took over at halfback when Lenny Moore missed most the campaign with an appendectomy and a head injury. Two future stars joined the offensive line when tight end John Mackey and tackle Bob Vogel, both rookies, won starting jobs in the forward wall, and two more freshmen, Fred Miller and Johnny Logan, made the defensive unit.

**Detroit Lions**—The suspension of Alex Karras by Commissioner Rozelle sorely hurt the defensive line, and injuries further ripped up the once impregnable Detroit defense. Three starting defensive backs went out of the lineup with injuries, Yale Lary and Night Train Lane with bad knees and Gary Lowe with a sheared tendon, and Darris McCord and Joe Schmidt stayed on the field even though below par physically. The offense received an unexpected boost when Earl Morrall developed into a first-class quarterback in beating Milt Plum out of the starting job. But the Detroit attack was not strong enough to carry the club, while the defense was no longer healthy enough to lead the way.

**Minnesota Vikings**—The three-year-old Vikings were quickly losing their image as an expansion club as the young men in the lineup began maturing and blending together. The Vikings won five games and tied one, with the tie coming against the bruising Chicago Bears in a key December contest. Two other games resulted in near misses for the Vikings. They had the Packers beat with under two minutes left in the game, but a ten-yard field goal was blocked by Green Bay's Herb Adderley to thwart Minnesota's bid. The Vikings also had the Colts licked until Johnny Unitas drove his team 88 yards in forty-five seconds to a winning touchdown.

**Los Angeles Rams**—When the Rams dropped their first five games, fans expected a repeat of last year's disastrous season. Starting in mid-season, however, the team put together an improved offense with a sturdy defense to win five of its last nine games. The offensive upswing came from the confident play of quarterback Roman Gabriel, the fine running and blocking of rookie fullback Ben Wilson, and an improved offensive line. The defensive front four of Deacon Jones, Lamar Lundy, Merlin Olsen, and Roosevelt Grier combined size and quickness, while linebacker Jack Pardee and cornerback Eddie Meador held the back lines of the defense together.

**San Francisco '49ers**—Abe Woodson brought three kickoffs back for touchdowns and caused so much commotion with his speed that opposing teams resorted to squib kickoffs late in the year. Woodson was the only offense the '49ers had, as the attack lost quarterback John Brodie with a broken arm, leaving the signal-calling up to journeyman Lamar McHan. The defense also suffered losses, as Charlie Krueger, Jerry Mertens, Walt Rock, and Floyd Dean all missed most of the season with knee injuries. When the team went completely flat, dissension spread through the club, and coach Red Hickey was fired in mid-season in favor of the younger Jack Christiansen.

## FINAL TEAM STATISTICS

### OFFENSE

| | BALT. | CHI. | CLEVE. | DALLAS | DET. | G.BAY | L.A. | MINN. | N.Y. | PHIL. | PITT. | ST.L. | S.F. | WASH. |
|---|---|---|---|---|---|---|---|---|---|---|---|---|---|---|
| **FIRST DOWNS:** | | | | | | | | | | | | | | |
| Total | 257 | 257 | 252 | 248 | 230 | 258 | 209 | 223 | 278 | 203 | 272 | 254 | 183 | 244 |
| by Rushing | 95 | 108 | 135 | 105 | 91 | 114 | 80 | 97 | 95 | 78 | 122 | 105 | 87 | 81 |
| by Passing | 149 | 117 | 100 | 132 | 124 | 126 | 117 | 112 | 164 | 114 | 129 | 134 | 87 | 140 |
| by Penalty | 13 | 32 | 17 | 11 | 15 | 18 | 12 | 14 | 19 | 11 | 21 | 15 | 9 | 23 |
| **RUSHING:** | | | | | | | | | | | | | | |
| Number | 396 | 487 | 460 | 420 | 415 | 504 | 405 | 445 | 453 | 376 | 578 | 423 | 406 | 344 |
| Yards | 1642 | 1679 | 2639 | 1795 | 1601 | 2248 | 1393 | 1842 | 1777 | 1438 | 2136 | 1839 | 1454 | 1289 |
| Average Yards | 4.1 | 3.4 | 5.7 | 4.3 | 3.9 | 4.5 | 3.4 | 4.1 | 3.9 | 3.8 | 3.7 | 4.3 | 3.6 | 3.7 |
| Touchdowns | 11 | 15 | 15 | 18 | 11 | 22 | 14 | 17 | 12 | 8 | 14 | 10 | 8 | 15 |
| **PASSING:** | | | | | | | | | | | | | | |
| Attempts | 433 | 404 | 322 | 375 | 406 | 345 | 384 | 355 | 426 | 380 | 368 | 438 | 349 | 430 |
| Completions | 248 | 221 | 164 | 200 | 202 | 179 | 186 | 197 | 243 | 193 | 170 | 228 | 156 | 204 |
| Completion Pct. | 57.3 | 54.7 | 50.9 | 53.3 | 49.8 | 51.9 | 48.4 | 55.5 | 57.0 | 50.8 | 46.2 | 52.1 | 44.7 | 47.4 |
| Passing Yards | 3605 | 2670 | 2449 | 2799 | 2997 | 2711 | 2558 | 2687 | 3558 | 2666 | 3028 | 3403 | 2090 | 3525 |
| Avg. Yds per Att. | 8.3 | 6.6 | 7.6 | 7.5 | 7.4 | 7.9 | 6.7 | 7.6 | 8.4 | 7.0 | 8.2 | 7.8 | 6.0 | 8.2 |
| Avg. Yds. per Comp. | 14.5 | 12.1 | 14.9 | 14.0 | 14.8 | 15.1 | 13.8 | 13.6 | 14.6 | 13.8 | 17.8 | 14.9 | 13.4 | 17.3 |
| Times Tackled | 44 | 20 | 25 | 43 | 33 | 20 | 59 | 51 | 35 | 27 | 30 | 40 | 35 | 43 |
| Yds. Lost Tackled | 309 | 177 | 232 | 331 | 274 | 178 | 481 | 518 | 311 | 252 | 251 | 372 | 263 | 391 |
| Net Yards | 3296 | 2493 | 2217 | 2468 | 2723 | 2533 | 2077 | 2169 | 3247 | 2414 | 2777 | 3031 | 1827 | 3134 |
| Touchdowns | 20 | 18 | 27 | 20 | 26 | 22 | 11 | 16 | 39 | 22 | 21 | 30 | 13 | 17 |
| Interceptions | 12 | 14 | 20 | 21 | 26 | 21 | 22 | 17 | 21 | 31 | 20 | 21 | 22 | 34 |
| Pct. Intercepted | 2.8 | 3.5 | 6.2 | 5.6 | 6.4 | 6.1 | 5.7 | 4.8 | 4.9 | 8.2 | 5.4 | 4.8 | 6.3 | 7.9 |
| **PUNTING:** | | | | | | | | | | | | | | |
| Number | 56 | 64 | 54 | 71 | 66 | 51 | 85 | 70 | 59 | 69 | 59 | 65 | 73 | 53 |
| Average Distance | 41.0 | 46.5 | 40.0 | 44.2 | 44.6 | 44.7 | 44.7 | 38.7 | 44.9 | 43.1 | 39.4 | 40.7 | 45.4 | 41.7 |
| **PUNT RETURNS:** | | | | | | | | | | | | | | |
| Number | 53 | 30 | 25 | 23 | 57 | 26 | 31 | 35 | 40 | 26 | 31 | 26 | 18 | 30 |
| Yards | 485 | 277 | 285 | 177 | 635 | 229 | 206 | 405 | 364 | 226 | 281 | 166 | 99 | 391 |
| Average Yards | 9.2 | 9.2 | 11.4 | 7.7 | 11.1 | 8.8 | 6.6 | 11.6 | 9.1 | 8.7 | 9.1 | 6.4 | 5.5 | 13.0 |
| Touchdowns | 0 | 0 | 0 | 0 | 1 | 0 | 0 | 1 | 0 | 0 | 0 | 0 | 0 | 0 |
| **KICKOFF RETURNS:** | | | | | | | | | | | | | | |
| Number | 52 | 26 | 50 | 48 | 45 | 46 | 70 | 69 | 46 | 61 | 49 | 52 | 62 | 64 |
| Yards | 1114 | 424 | 1099 | 1100 | 949 | 1122 | 1651 | 1556 | 1018 | 1527 | 1312 | 1070 | 1659 | 1718 |
| Average Yards | 21.4 | 16.3 | 22.0 | 22.9 | 21.1 | 24.4 | 23.6 | 22.6 | 22.1 | 25.0 | 26.8 | 20.6 | 26.8 | 26.8 |
| Touchdowns | 0 | 0 | 0 | 0 | 0 | 1 | 1 | 1 | 0 | 1 | 1 | 0 | 3 | 1 |
| **INTERCEPTION RETURNS:** | | | | | | | | | | | | | | |
| Number | 15 | 36 | 22 | 26 | 24 | 22 | 19 | 11 | 34 | 15 | 25 | 18 | 14 | 21 |
| Yards | 174 | 537 | 343 | 549 | 470 | 312 | 182 | 200 | 546 | 210 | 330 | 383 | 221 | 357 |
| Average Yards | 11.6 | 14.9 | 15.6 | 21.1 | 19.6 | 14.2 | 9.6 | 18.2 | 16.1 | 14.0 | 13.2 | 21.3 | 15.8 | 17.0 |
| Touchdowns | 2 | 4 | 1 | 0 | 3 | 0 | 0 | 2 | 5 | 1 | 1 | 2 | 0 | 2 |
| **PENALTIES:** | | | | | | | | | | | | | | |
| Number | 77 | 92 | 52 | 67 | 60 | 53 | 70 | 58 | 67 | 53 | 51 | 69 | 51 | 74 |
| Yards | 823 | 804 | 609 | 627 | 531 | 517 | 788 | 627 | 755 | 558 | 495 | 692 | 439 | 736 |
| **FUMBLES:** | | | | | | | | | | | | | | |
| Number | 35 | 16 | 25 | 29 | 26 | 30 | 30 | 45 | 28 | 30 | 25 | 29 | 25 | 32 |
| Number Lost | 25 | 11 | 17 | 15 | 14 | 20 | 17 | 18 | 13 | 16 | 13 | 18 | 8 | 19 |
| **POINTS:** | | | | | | | | | | | | | | |
| Total | 316 | 301 | 343 | 305 | 326 | 369 | 210 | 309 | 448 | 242 | 321 | 341 | 198 | 279 |
| PAT Attempts | 35 | 37 | 43 | 40 | 42 | 46 | 26 | 39 | 57 | 32 | 37 | 44 | 24 | 35 |
| PAT Made | 32 | 35 | 40 | 38 | 42 | 43 | 25 | 39 | 52 | 29 | 34 | 44 | 24 | 33 |
| FG Attempts | 39 | 33 | 23 | 20 | 26 | 34 | 17 | 24 | 29 | 15 | 41 | 21 | 31 | 26 |
| FG Made | 24 | 14 | 15 | 9 | 10 | 16 | 9 | 12 | 18 | 7 | 21 | 11 | 10 | 12 |
| Percent FG Made | 61.5 | 42.4 | 65.2 | 45.0 | 38.5 | 47.1 | 52.9 | 50.0 | 62.1 | 46.7 | 51.2 | 52.4 | 32.3 | 46.2 |
| Safeties | 1 | 1 | 0 | 0 | 1 | 1 | 1 | 0 | 0 | 0 | 1 | 0 | 0 | 0 |

### DEFENSE

| | BALT. | CHI. | CLEVE. | DALLAS | DET. | G.BAY | L.A. | MINN. | N.Y. | PHIL. | PITT. | ST.L. | S.F. | WASH. |
|---|---|---|---|---|---|---|---|---|---|---|---|---|---|---|
| **FIRST DOWNS:** | | | | | | | | | | | | | | |
| Total | 228 | 196 | 242 | 266 | 194 | 193 | 244 | 258 | 213 | 266 | 244 | 235 | 304 | 285 |
| by Rushing | 89 | 82 | 99 | 114 | 74 | 92 | 100 | 103 | 89 | 125 | 90 | 105 | 121 | 110 |
| by Passing | 118 | 96 | 129 | 139 | 109 | 87 | 126 | 143 | 106 | 131 | 132 | 107 | 168 | 154 |
| by Penalty | 21 | 18 | 14 | 13 | 11 | 14 | 18 | 12 | 18 | 10 | 22 | 23 | 15 | 21 |
| **RUSHING:** | | | | | | | | | | | | | | |
| Number | 434 | 412 | 423 | 455 | 405 | 428 | 431 | 410 | 411 | 466 | 419 | 461 | 488 | 469 |
| Yards | 1794 | 1442 | 1651 | 2094 | 1564 | 1586 | 1785 | 1733 | 1669 | 1985 | 1728 | 1802 | 2076 | 1863 |
| Average Yards | 4.1 | 3.5 | 3.9 | 4.6 | 3.9 | 3.7 | 4.1 | 4.2 | 4.1 | 4.3 | 4.1 | 3.9 | 4.3 | 4.0 |
| Touchdowns | 16 | 7 | 10 | 12 | 12 | 11 | 14 | 12 | 14 | 17 | 14 | 19 | 20 | 12 |
| **PASSING:** | | | | | | | | | | | | | | |
| Attempts | 348 | 353 | 408 | 403 | 378 | 378 | 379 | 404 | 368 | 375 | 384 | 370 | 450 | 417 |
| Completions | 181 | 164 | 208 | 202 | 183 | 180 | 208 | 233 | 176 | 211 | 191 | 180 | 244 | 230 |
| Completion Pct. | 52.0 | 46.5 | 51.0 | 50.1 | 48.4 | 47.6 | 54.9 | 57.7 | 47.8 | 56.3 | 49.7 | 48.6 | 54.2 | 55.2 |
| Passing Yards | 2589 | 2045 | 2718 | 3392 | 2597 | 2340 | 3025 | 3362 | 2588 | 3106 | 3400 | 2519 | 3581 | 3484 |
| Avg. Yds per Att. | 7.4 | 5.8 | 6.7 | 8.4 | 6.9 | 6.2 | 8.0 | 8.3 | 7.0 | 8.3 | 8.9 | 6.8 | 8.0 | 8.4 |
| Avg. Yds. per Comp. | 14.3 | 12.5 | 13.1 | 16.8 | 14.2 | 13.0 | 14.5 | 14.4 | 14.7 | 14.7 | 17.8 | 14.0 | 14.7 | 15.1 |
| Times Tackled | 45 | 36 | 29 | 20 | 45 | 39 | 27 | 45 | 57 | 29 | 34 | 41 | 25 | 33 |
| Yds. Lost Tackled | 347 | 311 | 243 | 161 | 400 | 327 | 272 | 364 | 499 | 270 | 299 | 367 | 210 | 270 |
| Net Yards | 2242 | 1734 | 2475 | 3231 | 2197 | 2013 | 2753 | 2998 | 2089 | 2836 | 3101 | 2152 | 3371 | 3214 |
| Touchdowns | 19 | 10 | 16 | 31 | 17 | 9 | 25 | 31 | 22 | 28 | 21 | 13 | 27 | 33 |
| Interceptions | 15 | 36 | 22 | 26 | 24 | 22 | 19 | 11 | 34 | 15 | 25 | 18 | 14 | 21 |
| Pct. Intercepted | 4.3 | 10.2 | 5.4 | 6.5 | 6.3 | 5.8 | 5.0 | 2.7 | 9.2 | 4.0 | 6.5 | 4.9 | 3.1 | 5.0 |
| **PUNTING:** | | | | | | | | | | | | | | |
| Number | 72 | 73 | 57 | 50 | 83 | 59 | 61 | 60 | 71 | 57 | 66 | 74 | 55 | 57 |
| Average Distance | 43.5 | 43.2 | 43.7 | 43.2 | 45.5 | 43.4 | 42.5 | 43.9 | 40.4 | 39.1 | 44.5 | 40.1 | 43.1 | 44.5 |
| **PUNT RETURNS:** | | | | | | | | | | | | | | |
| Number | 19 | 34 | 22 | 36 | 29 | 29 | 60 | 27 | 32 | 34 | 29 | 25 | 50 | 25 |
| Yards | 119 | 277 | 216 | 176 | 319 | 220 | 681 | 155 | 283 | 451 | 287 | 294 | 587 | 161 |
| Average Yards | 6.3 | 8.1 | 9.8 | 4.9 | 11.0 | 7.6 | 11.4 | 5.7 | 8.8 | 13.3 | 9.9 | 11.8 | 11.7 | 6.4 |
| Touchdowns | 0 | 0 | 0 | 0 | 0 | 0 | 0 | 0 | 0 | 0 | 0 | 0 | 2 | 0 |
| **KICKOFF RETURNS:** | | | | | | | | | | | | | | |
| Number | 66 | 52 | 58 | 47 | 56 | 69 | 44 | 48 | 69 | 31 | 53 | 51 | 37 | 59 |
| Yards | 1520 | 1261 | 1424 | 1125 | 1206 | 1331 | 1076 | 1342 | 1816 | 727 | 1133 | 1279 | 816 | 1263 |
| Average Yards | 23.0 | 24.3 | 24.6 | 23.9 | 21.5 | 19.3 | 24.5 | 28.0 | 26.3 | 23.5 | 21.4 | 25.1 | 22.1 | 21.4 |
| Touchdowns | 0 | 0 | 1 | 0 | 0 | 0 | 2 | 3 | 1 | 0 | 0 | 1 | 0 | 1 |
| **INTERCEPTION RETURNS:** | | | | | | | | | | | | | | |
| Number | 12 | 14 | 20 | 21 | 26 | 21 | 22 | 17 | 21 | 31 | 20 | 21 | 22 | 34 |
| Yards | 161 | 216 | 317 | 437 | 393 | 297 | 369 | 168 | 379 | 516 | 316 | 284 | 283 | 678 |
| Average Yards | 13.4 | 15.4 | 15.9 | 20.8 | 15.1 | 14.1 | 16.8 | 9.9 | 18.0 | 16.6 | 15.8 | 13.5 | 12.9 | 19.9 |
| Touchdowns | 1 | 1 | 1 | 5 | 3 | 1 | 2 | 2 | 1 | 1 | 1 | 0 | 1 | 3 |
| **PENALTIES:** | | | | | | | | | | | | | | |
| Number | 58 | 78 | 63 | 52 | 57 | 59 | 63 | 59 | 66 | 54 | 78 | 51 | 73 | 83 |
| Yards | 685 | 718 | 592 | 479 | 624 | 568 | 558 | 621 | 617 | 598 | 780 | 577 | 667 | 917 |
| **FUMBLES:** | | | | | | | | | | | | | | |
| Number | 32 | 36 | 13 | 23 | 24 | 31 | 25 | 50 | 38 | 23 | 31 | 32 | 27 | 20 |
| Number Lost | 17 | 18 | 10 | 11 | 11 | 21 | 13 | 31 | 16 | 15 | 19 | 19 | 13 | 10 |
| **POINTS:** | | | | | | | | | | | | | | |
| Total | 285 | 144 | 262 | 378 | 265 | 206 | 350 | 390 | 280 | 381 | 295 | 285 | 391 | 398 |
| PAT Attempts | 36 | 18 | 30 | 48 | 32 | 23 | 43 | 50 | 39 | 47 | 36 | 34 | 51 | 50 |
| PAT Made | 33 | 18 | 29 | 45 | 30 | 23 | 39 | 49 | 37 | 42 | 34 | 34 | 50 | 47 |
| FG Attempts | 27 | 17 | 35 | 33 | 24 | 33 | 35 | 22 | 14 | 31 | 22 | 26 | 27 | 33 |
| FG Made | 12 | 6 | 17 | 15 | 13 | 15 | 17 | 13 | 3 | 19 | 15 | 15 | 11 | 17 |
| Percent FG Made | 44.4 | 35.3 | 48.6 | 45.5 | 54.2 | 45.5 | 48.6 | 59.1 | 21.4 | 61.3 | 68.2 | 57.7 | 40.7 | 51.1 |
| Safeties | 0 | 0 | 1 | 0 | 2 | 0 | 1 | 1 | 0 | 0 | 0 | 0 | 1 | 0 |

## 1963 NFL CHAMPIONSHIP GAME

December 29, at Chicago
(Attendance 45,801)

## Shofner's Hands and Tittle's Knee

The Bears and Giants, long-time rivals in the NFL, met in the eight-degree cold of Wrigley Field to decide the league championship. The two clubs played with contrasting styles, as the Giants depended heavily on Y. A. Tittle's passes, while the Bears relied on a fierce defense to force the enemy into mistakes. The Bears, however, made the first mistake when quarterback Billy Wade fumbled the ball away on the New York 17-yard line. The Giants then marched 83 yards, with a Tittle-to-Gifford pass counting for six points. After Don Chandler added the extra point, neither team could move the ball until Chicago's Willie Galimore fumbled on his own 31. On the next play, Del Shofner got free in the end zone but had a perfect Tittle pass bounce off his frigid hands. The Bear defense then took matters into hand, as Larry Morris picked off a Tittle screen pass and ran the ball back to the New York 5. Two plays later, Wade's quarterback sneak tied the score. The Giants added three points on a Chandler field goal to make the halftime score 10-7, New York. Tittle had twisted his knee in the second quarter, and he had trouble planting his feet while throwing after that. Late in the third period Ed O'Bradovich intercepted another Tittle screen pass, bringing it back to the New York 14. Three plays later, Wade snuck across the goal line to put the Bears ahead for the first time in the game. Tittle kept throwing the ball through the fourth quarter, but the Chicago defense intercepted two passes and protected the 14-10 margin of victory.

### TEAM STATISTICS

| CHIC. | | N.Y. |
|---|---|---|
| 14 | First Downs – Total | 17 |
| 6 | First Downs – Rushing | 8 |
| 7 | First Downs – Passing | 9 |
| 1 | First Downs – Penalty | 0 |
| 7 | Punts – Number | 4 |
| 41.0 | Punts – Average Distance | 43.3 |
| 5 | Punt Return – Yards | 21 |
| 5 | Interception Returns – Number | 0 |
| 71 | Interception Return – Yards | 0 |
| 2 | Fumbles – Number | 2 |
| 2 | Fumbles – Lost Ball | 1 |
| 5 | Penalties -- Number | 3 |
| 35 | Yards Penalized | 25 |
| 2 | Giveaways | 6 |
| 6 | Takeaways | 2 |
| +4 | Difference | 4 |

### SCORING

| | | | | |
|---|---|---|---|---|
| CHICAGO | 7 | 0 | 7 | 0–14 |
| NEW YORK | 7 | 3 | 0 | 0–10 |

First Quarter
N.Y. Gifford, 14 yard pass from Tittle 7:22
PAT – Chandler (kick)
CHI. Wade, 2 yard rush 14:44
PAT – Jencks (kick)

Second Quarter
N.Y. Chandler, 13 yard field goal 5:11

Third Quarter
CHI. Wade, 1 yard rush 12:48
PAT – Jencks (kick)

### INDIVIDUAL STATISTICS

**RUSHING**

| CHICAGO | No | Yds | Avg. | NEW YORK | No | Yds | Avg. |
|---|---|---|---|---|---|---|---|
| Bull | 13 | 42 | 3.2 | Morrison | 18 | 61 | 3.4 |
| Wade | 8 | 34 | 4.5 | King | 9 | 39 | 4.3 |
| Galimore | 7 | 12 | 1.7 | McElhenny | 7 | 19 | 2.7 |
| Marconi | 3 | 5 | 1.7 | Webster | 3 | 7 | 2.3 |
| | 31 | 93 | 3.0 | Tittle | 1 | 2 | 2.0 |
| | | | | | 38 | 128 | 3.4 |

**RECEIVING**

| CHICAGO | No | Yds | Avg. | NEW YORK | No | Yds | Avg. |
|---|---|---|---|---|---|---|---|
| Marconi | 3 | 64 | 21.3 | Gifford | 3 | 45 | 15.0 |
| Ditka | 3 | 38 | 12.7 | Morrison | 3 | 18 | 6.0 |
| J. Morris | 2 | 19 | 9.5 | Thomas | 2 | 46 | 23.0 |
| Coia | 1 | 22 | 22.0 | McElhenny | 2 | 20 | 10.0 |
| Bull | 1 | −5 | −5.0 | Webster | 1 | 18 | 18.0 |
| | 10 | 138 | 13.8 | | 11 | 147 | 13.4 |

**PASSING**

| | Att | Comp | Comp Pct. | Yds | Int | Yds/ Att. | Yds/ Comp | Yards Lost Tackled |
|---|---|---|---|---|---|---|---|---|
| **CHICAGO** | | | | | | | | |
| Wade | 28 | 10 | 35.7 | 138 | 0 | 4.9 | 13.4 | 9 |
| **NEW YORK** | | | | | | | | |
| Tittle | 29 | 11 | 37.9 | 147 | 5 | 5.1 | 13.4 | 7 |
| Griffing | 1 | 0 | 0.0 | 0 | 0 | – | – | 0 |
| | 30 | 11 | 36.7 | 147 | 5 | 4.9 | 13.4 | 7 |

## NEW YORK GIANTS 11-3-0 Allie Sherman

**Scores of Each Game**

| | | |
|---|---|---|
| 37 | Baltimore | 28 |
| 0 | Pittsburgh | 31 |
| 37 | Philadelphia | 14 |
| 24 | Washington | 14 |
| 24 | CLEVELAND | 35 |
| 37 | DALLAS | 21 |
| 33 | Cleveland | 6 |
| 38 | St. Louis | 21 |
| 42 | PHILADELPHIA | 14 |
| 48 | SAN FRANCISCO | 14 |
| 17 | ST. LOUIS | 24 |
| 34 | Dallas | 27 |
| 44 | WASHINGTON | 14 |
| 33 | PITTSBURGH | 17 |

| Use Name | Pos. | Hgt | Wgt | Age | Int | Pts |
|---|---|---|---|---|---|---|
| Rosey Brown | OT | 6'3" | 255 | 30 | | |
| Lou Kirouac | OT | 6'3" | 230 | 23 | | |
| Jack Stroud | OT | 6'1" | 250 | 34 | | |
| Lane Howell | DT-OT | 6'5" | 255 | 22 | | |
| Bookie Bolin | OG | 6'2" | 235 | 23 | | |
| Darrell Dess | OG | 6' | 245 | 27 | | |
| Ken Byers | DE-OG | 6'1" | 240 | 24 | | |
| Greg Larson | C | 6'2" | 245 | 24 | | |
| Jim Katcavage | DE | 6'3" | 240 | 28 | | 6 |
| Andy Robustelli | DE | 6'1" | 235 | 37 | | |
| John Lovetere | DT | 6'4" | 283 | 27 | | |
| Dick Modzelewski | DT | 6' | 260 | 32 | | |
| Bob Taylor | DE-DT | 6'3" | 235 | 23 | | |
| Al Gursky | LB | 6'1" | 210 | 22 | | |
| Jerry Hillebrand | LB | 6'3" | 240 | 23 | 5 | 6 |
| Sam Huff | LB | 6'1" | 230 | 28 | 4 | 6 |
| Tom Scott | LB | 6'2" | 220 | 33 | | |
| Mickey Walker | LB | 6'2" | 230 | 23 | | |
| Bill Winter | LB | 6'3" | 220 | 23 | 1 | |
| Erich Barnes | DB | 6'2" | 198 | 28 | 3 | |
| Eddie Dove (from SF) | DB | 6'2" | 180 | 26 | 2 | |
| Dick Lynch | DB | 6'1" | 205 | 27 | 9 | 18 |
| Jimmy Patton | DB | 6' | 185 | 29 | 6 | |
| Dick Pesonen | DB | 6' | 190 | 25 | 1 | |
| Allan Webb | DB | 5'11" | 180 | 28 | 3 | |
| Louis Guy | FL-DB | 6' | 185 | 22 | | |
| Glynn Griffing | QB | 6'1" | 200 | 21 | | |
| Y. A. Tittle | QB | 6' | 195 | 36 | | 12 |
| Bob Anderson | HB | 6'2" | 210 | 26 | | |
| Johnny Counts | HB | 5'10" | 170 | 24 | | |
| Charlie Killett | HB | 6'1" | 205 | 22 | | |
| Phil King | HB | 6'4" | 225 | 27 | | 48 |
| Hugh McElhenny | HB | 6'1" | 190 | 34 | | 12 |
| Joe Morrison | FL-HB | 6'1" | 212 | 25 | | 60 |
| Alex Webster | FB | 6'3" | 225 | 32 | | 24 |
| Frank Gifford | FL | 6'1" | 190 | 33 | | 42 |
| Aaron Thomas | OE-FL | 6'3" | 208 | 25 | | 18 |
| Del Shofner | OE | 6'3" | 185 | 27 | | 54 |
| Joe Walton | OE | 5'11" | 200 | 28 | | 36 |
| Don Chandler | K | 6'2" | 210 | 28 | | 106 |

## CLEVELAND BROWNS 10-4-0 Blanton Collier

**Scores of Each Game**

| | | |
|---|---|---|
| 37 | WASHINGTON | 14 |
| 41 | Dallas | 24 |
| 20 | LOS ANGELES | 6 |
| 35 | PITTSBURGH | 23 |
| 35 | New York | 24 |
| 37 | PHILADELPHIA | 7 |
| 6 | NEW YORK | 33 |
| 23 | Philadelphia | 17 |
| 7 | Pittsburgh | 9 |
| 14 | St. Louis | 20 |
| 27 | DALLAS | 17 |
| 24 | St. Louis | 10 |
| 10 | Detroit | 38 |
| 27 | Washington | 20 |

| Use Name | Pos. | Hgt | Wgt | Age | Int | Pts |
|---|---|---|---|---|---|---|
| John Brown | OT | 6'2" | 248 | 24 | | |
| Monte Clark | OT | 6'6" | 265 | 26 | | |
| Jim McCusker | OT | 6'2" | 245 | 27 | | |
| Dick Schafrath | OT | 6'3" | 255 | 27 | | |
| Roger Shoals | OT | 6'4" | 255 | 24 | | |
| Ted Connolly | OG | 6'3" | 242 | 31 | | |
| Gene Hickerson | OG | 6'3" | 248 | 28 | | |
| John Wooten | OG | 6'2" | 250 | 28 | | |
| John Morrow | C | 6'3" | 248 | 30 | | |
| Frank Morze | C | 6'4" | 280 | 29 | | |
| Bill Glass | DE | 6'5" | 255 | 27 | | |
| Paul Wiggin | DE | 6'3" | 245 | 29 | 1 | |
| Bob Gain | DT | 6'3" | 260 | 35 | | |
| Jim Kanicki | DT | 6'4" | 270 | 21 | | |
| Frank Parker | DT | 6'5" | 255 | 23 | | |
| Vince Costello | LB | 6' | 228 | 31 | 7 | |
| Galen Fiss | LB | 6' | 227 | 33 | 2 | |
| Tom Goosby | LB | 6' | 235 | 24 | | |
| Jim Houston | LB | 6'2" | 240 | 26 | 1 | |
| Mike Lucci | LB | 6'2" | 223 | 23 | | |
| Stan Sczurek | LB | 5'11" | 225 | 24 | | |
| Sam Tidmore | LB | 6'1" | 225 | 24 | | |
| Walter Beach | DB | 6' | 185 | 28 | | |
| Larry Benz | DB | 5'11" | 185 | 22 | 7 | |
| Ross Fichtner | DB | 6' | 185 | 25 | 2 | 6 |
| Bernie Parrish | DB | 5'11" | 195 | 28 | | |
| Jim Shofner | DB | 6'2" | 192 | 27 | | |
| Jim Shorter | DB | 5'11" | 186 | 22 | | |
| Bobby Franklin | HB-DB | 5'11" | 182 | 27 | 2 | |
| Jim Ninowski | QB | 6'1" | 207 | 27 | | |
| Frank Ryan | QB | 6'3" | 200 | 27 | | 12 |
| Ernie Green | HB | 6'2" | 205 | 24 | | 18 |
| Charlie Scales | HB | 5'11" | 215 | 24 | | 6 |
| Ken Webb | HB | 5'11" | 205 | 28 | | |
| Jimmy Brown | FB | 6'2" | 228 | 27 | | 90 |
| Gary Collins | FL | 6'4" | 208 | 22 | | 78 |
| Ray Renfro | FL | 6'1" | 192 | 32 | | 6 |
| Johnny Brewer | OE | 6'4" | 235 | 26 | | |
| Bob Crespino | OE | 6'4" | 225 | 25 | | 6 |
| Tom Hutchinson | OE | 6'1" | 190 | 22 | | |
| Rich Kreitling | OE | 6'2" | 208 | 28 | | 36 |
| Lou Groza | K | 6'3" | 250 | 39 | | 85 |

Don Fleming – killed in construction accident, June 4, 1963

## ST. LOUIS CARDINALS 9-5-0 Wally Lemm

**Scores of Each Game**

| | | |
|---|---|---|
| 34 | Dallas | 7 |
| 28 | Philadelphia | 24 |
| 10 | Pittsburgh | 23 |
| 56 | Minnesota | 14 |
| 24 | PITTSBURGH | 23 |
| 7 | GREEN BAY | 30 |
| 21 | Washington | 7 |
| 21 | NEW YORK | 38 |
| 24 | WASHINGTON | 20 |
| 20 | Cleveland | 14 |
| 24 | New York | 17 |
| 10 | CLEVELAND | 24 |
| 38 | PHILADELPHIA | 14 |
| 24 | DALLAS | 28 |

| Use Name | Pos. | Hgt | Wgt | Age | Int | Pts |
|---|---|---|---|---|---|---|
| Irv Goode | OT | 6'4" | 245 | 22 | | |
| Ernie McMillan | OT | 6'6" | 255 | 25 | | |
| Bob Reynolds | OT | 6'6" | 256 | 22 | | |
| Ed Cook | OG-OT | 6'2" | 240 | 31 | | |
| Ken Gray | OG | 6'2" | 240 | 27 | | |
| John Houser | OG | 6'3" | 242 | 27 | | |
| Bob DeMarco | C | 6'3" | 240 | 25 | | |
| Don Brumm | DE | 6'3" | 225 | 20 | | |
| Ed Henke | DE | 6'3" | 230 | 35 | | |
| Tom Redmond | DE | 6'5" | 240 | 26 | | |
| Joe Robb | DE | 6'3" | 230 | 26 | | |
| Fate Echols | DT | 6'1" | 260 | 24 | | |
| Don Owens | DT | 6'5" | 255 | 31 | | |
| Luke Owens | DT | 6'2" | 255 | 30 | | |
| Sam Silas | DT | 6'4" | 250 | 20 | | |
| Garland Boyette | LB | 6'1" | 225 | 23 | | |
| Bill Koman | LB | 6'2" | 230 | 29 | | |
| Dave Meggyesy | LB | 6'1" | 215 | 21 | | |
| Dale Meinert | LB | 6'2" | 220 | 30 | | |
| Marion Rushing | LB | 6'2" | 210 | 26 | | |
| Larry Stallings | LB | 6'2" | 225 | 21 | | |
| Jimmy Burson | DB | 6' | 180 | 21 | | |
| Pat Fischer | DB | 5'10" | 165 | 23 | 8 | |
| Jimmy Hill | DB | 6'2" | 190 | 34 | 3 | 6 |
| Billy Stacy | DB | 6'1" | 190 | 27 | 1 | |
| Johnny Symank | DB | 5'11" | 180 | 28 | 1 | 6 |
| Jerry Stovall | DB | 6'2" | 195 | 21 | 1 | |
| Larry Wilson | DB | 6' | 185 | 25 | 4 | 12 |
| Buddy Humphrey | QB | 6'1" | 197 | 27 | | |
| Charley Johnson | QB | 6' | 190 | 26 | | 6 |
| John David Crow | HB | 6'2" | 215 | 28 | | |
| Bob Paremore | HB | 5'11" | 190 | 23 | | 12 |
| Bill Triplett | HB | 6'2" | 210 | 24 | | 48 |
| Joe Childress | FB-HB | 6' | 210 | 29 | | |
| Prentice Gautt | FB | 6' | 200 | 25 | | |
| Bill Thornton | FB | 6'1" | 205 | 23 | | 6 |
| Mal Hammack | OE-FB | 6'2" | 205 | 30 | | |
| Bobby Joe Conrad | FL | 6' | 195 | 28 | | 60 |
| Taz Anderson | OE | 6'2" | 200 | 24 | | |
| Billy Gambrell | OE | 5'10" | 175 | 21 | | |
| Sonny Randle | OE | 6'2" | 187 | 27 | | 72 |
| Jackie Smith | OE | 6'4" | 205 | 22 | | 12 |
| Jim Bakken | K | 6' | 200 | 22 | | 77 |

John Wittenborn – Injury

## PITTSBURGH STEELERS 7-4-3 Buddy Parker

**Scores of Each Game**

| | | |
|---|---|---|
| 21 | Philadelphia | 21 |
| 31 | NEW YORK | 0 |
| 23 | ST. LOUIS | 10 |
| 23 | Cleveland | 35 |
| 23 | St. Louis | 24 |
| 38 | WASHINGTON | 21 |
| 27 | DALLAS | 21 |
| 14 | Green Bay | 33 |
| 9 | CLEVELAND | 7 |
| 34 | Washington | 28 |
| 17 | CHICAGO | 17 |
| 20 | PHILADELPHIA | 17 |
| 24 | Dallas | 19 |
| 17 | New York | 33 |

| Use Name | Pos. | Hgt | Wgt | Age | Int | Pts |
|---|---|---|---|---|---|---|
| Art Anderson | OT | 6'3" | 244 | 26 | | |
| Charlie Bradshaw | OT | 6'6" | 255 | 27 | | |
| Dan James | OT | 6'4" | 260 | 26 | | |
| Ray Lemek | OG | 6' | 240 | 29 | | |
| Mike Sandusky | OG | 6' | 230 | 30 | | |
| Ron Stehouwer | OG | 6'2" | 230 | 26 | | |
| Buzz Nutter | C | 6'4" | 230 | 32 | | |
| John Baker | DE | 6'6" | 270 | 28 | | |
| Lou Michaels | DE | 6'2" | 235 | 27 | 1 | 95 |
| Ernie Stautner | DT-DE | 6'1" | 230 | 38 | | |
| Frank Atkinson | DT | 6'3" | 240 | 22 | | |
| Lou Cordileone | DT | 6' | 250 | 26 | | |
| Joe Krupa | DT | 6'2" | 235 | 30 | | |
| Myron Pottios | LB | 6'2" | 240 | 23 | 4 | |
| John Reger | LB | 6' | 230 | 32 | 1 | |
| Bob Rowley | LB | 6'2" | 225 | 21 | | |
| Andy Russell | LB | 6'3" | 210 | 21 | 3 | |
| Bob Schmitz | LB | 6'1" | 230 | 25 | | 2 |
| George Tarasovic (to PHI) | LB | 6'4" | 245 | 34 | | |
| Jim Bradshaw | DB | 6'1" | 190 | 24 | 1 | |
| Willie Daniel | DB | 5'11" | 185 | 25 | | |
| Glenn Glass | DB | 6' | 190 | 26 | 1 | |
| Dick Haley | DB | 5'10" | 190 | 27 | 6 | 6 |
| Brady Keys | DB | 6' | 185 | 27 | | |
| Clendon Thomas | DB | 6'2" | 195 | 26 | 8 | |
| Ed Brown | QB | 6'2" | 210 | 34 | | 12 |
| Bill Nelsen | QB | 6' | 195 | 22 | | |
| Terry Nofsinger | QB | 6'4" | 205 | 25 | | |
| Dick Hoak | HB | 5'11" | 190 | 24 | | 42 |
| Theron Sapp (from PHI) | HB | 6'1" | 200 | 28 | | 6 |
| Tom Tracy (to WAS) | HB | 5'9" | 205 | 31 | | 8 |
| Bob Ferguson (to MIN) | FB | 5'11" | 220 | 22 | | 6 |
| John Henry Johnson | FB | 6'2" | 215 | 33 | | 30 |
| Gary Ballman | FL | 6' | 195 | 23 | | 36 |
| Roy Curry | OE | 6'1" | 195 | 23 | | 6 |
| John Burrell | OE | 6'3" | 188 | 23 | | |
| Preston Carpenter | OE | 6'2" | 205 | 29 | | 6 |
| Buddy Dial | OE | 6'1" | 195 | 26 | | 54 |
| Red Mack | OE | 5'10" | 185 | 26 | | 18 |
| John Powers | OE | 6'2" | 210 | 22 | | |

Big Daddy Lipscomb – died May 10

## DALLAS COWBOYS 4-10-0 Tom Landry

**Scores of Each Game**

| | | |
|---|---|---|
| 7 | ST. LOUIS | 34 |
| 24 | CLEVELAND | 41 |
| 17 | Washington | 21 |
| 21 | Philadelphia | 24 |
| 17 | DETROIT | 14 |
| 21 | New York | 37 |
| 21 | Pittsburgh | 27 |
| 35 | WASHINGTON | 20 |
| 24 | San Francisco | 31 |
| 27 | PHILADELPHIA | 27 |
| 17 | Cleveland | 27 |
| 34 | NEW YORK | 34 |
| 19 | PITTSBURGH | 24 |
| 28 | St. Louis | 24 |

| Use Name | Pos. | Hgt | Wgt | Age | Int | Pts |
|---|---|---|---|---|---|---|
| Bob Fry | OT | 6'4" | 232 | 32 | | |
| Tony Liscio | OT | 6'5" | 240 | 23 | | |
| Ed Nutting | OT | 6'4" | 246 | 24 | | |
| Ray Schoenke | OT | 6'3" | 234 | 21 | | |
| Joe Bob Isbell | OG | 6'1" | 225 | 23 | | |
| Dale Memmelaar | OG | 6'2" | 245 | 26 | | |
| Lance Poimbeouf | OG | 6'3" | 225 | 23 | | |
| Jim Ray Smith | OT-OG | 6'3" | 245 | 32 | | |
| Mike Connelly | C | 6'3" | 242 | 27 | | |
| Lynn Hoyem | OG-C | 6'4" | 240 | 23 | | |
| George Andrie | DE | 6'7" | 248 | 23 | | |
| Larry Stephens | DE | 6'4" | 260 | 25 | | |
| Bob Lilly | DT-DE | 6'4" | 250 | 24 | | 6 |
| John Meyers | DT | 6'6" | 267 | 23 | | |
| Guy Reese | DT | 6'5" | 258 | 23 | | |
| Dave Edwards | LB | 6'3" | 215 | 24 | 1 | |
| Harold Hays | LB | 6'3" | 235 | 22 | | |
| Chuck Howley | LB | 6'3" | 223 | 27 | 2 | |
| Lee Roy Jordan | LB | 6'2" | 210 | 22 | 3 | |
| Jerry Tubbs | LB | 6'2" | 215 | 28 | 2 | |
| Don Bishop | DB | 6'2" | 210 | 28 | 5 | |
| Mike Gaechter | DB | 6' | 196 | 23 | 3 | |
| Cornell Green | DB | 6'4" | 216 | 23 | 7 | 6 |
| Warren Livingston | DB | 5'10" | 185 | 25 | 3 | |
| Jerry Overton | DB | 6'2" | 190 | 22 | | |
| Jimmy Ridlon | DB | 6'1" | 177 | 28 | | |
| Eddie LeBaron | QB | 5'9" | 170 | 33 | | |
| Don Meredith | QB | 6'2" | 200 | 25 | | 18 |
| Amos Bullocks | HB | 6'1" | 202 | 24 | | 12 |
| Wendell Hays | HB | 6'2" | 210 | 22 | | |
| Amos Marsh | HB | 6'1" | 223 | 24 | | 30 |
| Jim Stiger | HB | 5'11" | 190 | 22 | | 6 |
| Don Perkins | FB | 5'10" | 196 | 25 | | 42 |
| Frank Clarke | FL | 6' | 215 | 30 | | 60 |
| Gary Barnes | OE | 6'4" | 210 | 23 | | |
| Lee Folkins | OE | 6'5" | 220 | 24 | | 24 |
| Billy Howton | OE | 6'2" | 194 | 33 | | 18 |
| Pettis Norman | OE | 6'3" | 210 | 23 | | 18 |
| Sam Baker | K | 6'2" | 220 | 31 | | 65 |

Maury Youmans – Injury
Dan Talbert – Military Service

## NEW YORK GIANTS

### RUSHING
| Last Name | No. | Yds | Avg | TD |
|---|---|---|---|---|
| King | 161 | 613 | 3.8 | 3 |
| Morrison | 119 | 568 | 4.8 | 3 |
| Webster | 75 | 255 | 3.4 | 4 |
| McElhenny | 55 | 175 | 3.2 | 0 |
| Tittle | 18 | 99 | 5.5 | 2 |
| Killett | 11 | 36 | 3.3 | 0 |
| Griffing | 5 | 20 | 4.0 | 0 |
| Gifford | 4 | 10 | 2.5 | 0 |
| Chandler | 1 | 0 | 0.0 | 0 |
| Anderson | 1 | -2 | -2.0 | 0 |

### RECEIVING
| Last Name | No. | Yds | Avg | TD |
|---|---|---|---|---|
| Shofner | 64 | 1181 | 18 | 9 |
| Gifford | 42 | 657 | 16 | 7 |
| King | 32 | 377 | 12 | 5 |
| Morrison | 31 | 284 | 9 | 7 |
| Walton | 26 | 371 | 14 | 6 |
| Thomas | 22 | 469 | 21 | 3 |
| Webster | 15 | 128 | 9 | 0 |
| McElhenny | 11 | 91 | 8 | 2 |

### PUNT RETURNS
| Last Name | No. | Yds | Avg | TD |
|---|---|---|---|---|
| Dove | 17 | 198 | 12 | 0 |
| McElhenny | 13 | 74 | 6 | 0 |
| Pesonen | 7 | 47 | 7 | 0 |
| Webb | 3 | 45 | 15 | 0 |

### KICKOFF RETURNS
| Last Name | No. | Yds | Avg | TD |
|---|---|---|---|---|
| Killett | 14 | 332 | 24 | 0 |
| Pesonen | 8 | 197 | 25 | 0 |
| McElhenny | 6 | 136 | 23 | 0 |
| Counts | 5 | 107 | 21 | 0 |
| Morrison | 4 | 75 | 19 | 0 |
| Webb | 3 | 62 | 21 | 0 |
| Dove | 3 | 56 | 19 | 0 |
| Guy | 3 | 44 | 15 | 0 |
| Scott | 0 | 9 | 0 | 0 |

### PASSING — PUNTING — KICKING

PASSING
| Last Name | Att | Comp | % | Yds | Yd/Att | TD | Int- | % | RK |
|---|---|---|---|---|---|---|---|---|---|
| Tittle | 367 | 221 | 60 | 3145 | 8.6 | 36 | 14- | 4 | 1 |
| Griffing | 40 | 16 | 40 | 306 | 7.7 | 3 | 4- | 10 | |
| Morrison | 2 | 1 | 50 | 18 | 9.0 | 0 | 0- | 0 | |

PUNTING
| Last Name | No | Avg |
|---|---|---|
| Chandler | 59 | 44.9 |

KICKING
| Last Name | XP | Att | % | FG | Att | % |
|---|---|---|---|---|---|---|
| Chandler | 52 | 56 | 93 | 18 | 29 | 62 |

## CLEVELAND BROWNS

### RUSHING
| Last Name | No. | Yds | Avg | TD |
|---|---|---|---|---|
| Jim Brown | 291 | 1863 | 6.4 | 12 |
| Green | 87 | 526 | 6.0 | 0 |
| Ryan | 62 | 224 | 3.6 | 2 |
| Webb | 12 | 58 | 4.8 | 0 |
| Scales | 2 | -3 | -1.5 | 1 |
| Franklin | 1 | -10 | -10.0 | 0 |
| Ninowski | 5 | -19 | -3.8 | 0 |

### RECEIVING
| Last Name | No. | Yds | Avg | TD |
|---|---|---|---|---|
| Collins | 43 | 674 | 16 | 13 |
| Brewer | 29 | 454 | 16 | 0 |
| Green | 28 | 305 | 11 | 3 |
| Jim Brown | 24 | 268 | 11 | 3 |
| Kreitling | 22 | 386 | 18 | 6 |
| Hutchinson | 9 | 244 | 27 | 0 |
| Renfro | 4 | 82 | 21 | 1 |
| Crespino | 2 | 22 | 11 | 1 |
| Webb | 2 | 2 | 1 | 0 |
| Scales | 1 | 13 | 13 | 0 |
| Ryan | 0 | -1 | 0 | 0 |

### PUNT RETURNS
| Last Name | No. | Yds | Avg | TD |
|---|---|---|---|---|
| Shorter | 7 | 134 | 19 | 0 |
| Green | 6 | 79 | 13 | 0 |
| Shofner | 9 | 41 | 5 | 0 |
| Parrish | 3 | 31 | 10 | 0 |

### KICKOFF RETURNS
| Last Name | No. | Yds | Avg | TD |
|---|---|---|---|---|
| Scales | 16 | 432 | 27 | 0 |
| Green | 18 | 394 | 22 | 0 |
| Shorter | 9 | 219 | 24 | 0 |
| Franklin | 2 | 33 | 17 | 0 |
| Webb | 1 | 12 | 12 | 0 |
| Tidmore | 1 | 5 | 5 | 0 |
| Morrow | 1 | 4 | 4 | 0 |
| Benz | 1 | 0 | 0 | 0 |
| Shofner | 1 | 0 | 0 | 0 |

### PASSING — PUNTING — KICKING

PASSING
| Last Name | Att | Comp | % | Yds | Yd/Att | TD | Int- | % | RK |
|---|---|---|---|---|---|---|---|---|---|
| Ryan | 256 | 135 | 53 | 2026 | 7.9 | 25 | 13- | 5 | 4 |
| Ninowski | 61 | 29 | 48 | 423 | 6.9 | 2 | 6- | 10 | |
| Jim Brown | 4 | 0 | 0 | 0 | 0.0 | 0 | 0- | 0 | |
| Groza | 1 | 0 | 0 | 0 | 0.0 | 0 | 1- | 100 | |

PUNTING
| Last Name | No | Avg |
|---|---|---|
| Collins | 54 | 40.0 |

KICKING
| Last Name | XP | Att | % | FG | Att | % |
|---|---|---|---|---|---|---|
| Groza | 40 | 43 | 93 | 15 | 23 | 65 |

## ST. LOUIS CARDINALS

### RUSHING
| Last Name | No. | Yds | Avg | TD |
|---|---|---|---|---|
| Childress | 174 | 701 | 4.0 | 2 |
| Triplett | 134 | 652 | 4.9 | 5 |
| Johnson | 41 | 143 | 3.5 | 1 |
| Thornton | 19 | 111 | 5.8 | 1 |
| Paremore | 36 | 107 | 3.0 | 0 |
| Wilson | 2 | 38 | 19.0 | 0 |
| Crow | 9 | 34 | 3.8 | 0 |
| Stovall | 1 | 32 | 32.0 | 0 |
| Hammack | 3 | 16 | 5.3 | 0 |
| Gautt | 3 | 5 | 1.7 | 0 |
| Conrad | 1 | 0 | 0.0 | 0 |

### RECEIVING
| Last Name | No. | Yds | Avg | TD |
|---|---|---|---|---|
| Conrad | 73 | 967 | 13 | 10 |
| Randle | 51 | 1014 | 20 | 12 |
| Triplett | 31 | 396 | 13 | 3 |
| Smith | 28 | 445 | 16 | 2 |
| Childress | 25 | 354 | 14 | 2 |
| Paremore | 6 | 89 | 15 | 1 |
| Anderson | 5 | 47 | 9 | 0 |
| Thornton | 4 | 10 | 3 | 0 |
| Gambrell | 3 | 63 | 21 | 0 |
| Hammack | 1 | 15 | 15 | 0 |
| Gautt | 1 | 3 | 3 | 0 |

### PUNT RETURNS
| Last Name | No. | Yds | Avg | TD |
|---|---|---|---|---|
| Gambrell | 11 | 111 | 10 | 0 |
| Fischer | 9 | 25 | 3 | 0 |
| Paremore | 4 | 23 | 6 | 0 |
| Stacy | 1 | 6 | 6 | 0 |
| Conrad | 1 | 1 | 1 | 0 |

### KICKOFF RETURNS
| Last Name | No. | Yds | Avg | TD |
|---|---|---|---|---|
| Stovall | 15 | 419 | 28 | 0 |
| Paremore | 12 | 292 | 24 | 0 |
| Triplett | 14 | 229 | 16 | 0 |
| Thornton | 4 | 70 | 18 | 0 |
| Hammack | 4 | 60 | 15 | 0 |
| Goode | 1 | 0 | 0 | 0 |
| Gray | 1 | 0 | 0 | 0 |
| Redmond | 1 | 0 | 0 | 0 |

### PASSING — PUNTING — KICKING

PASSING
| Last Name | Att | Comp | % | Yds | Yd/Att | TD | Int- | % | RK |
|---|---|---|---|---|---|---|---|---|---|
| Johnson | 423 | 222 | 52 | 3280 | 7.8 | 28 | 21- | 5 | 5 |
| Humphrey | 11 | 4 | 36 | 96 | 8.7 | 1 | 0- | 0 | |
| Crow | 3 | 2 | 67 | 27 | 9.0 | 1 | 0- | 0 | |
| Gautt | 1 | 0 | 0 | 0 | 0.0 | 0 | 0- | 0 | |

PUNTING
| Last Name | No | Avg |
|---|---|---|
| Stovall | 65 | 40.7 |

KICKING
| Last Name | XP | Att | % | FG | Att | % |
|---|---|---|---|---|---|---|
| Bakken | 44 | 44 | 100 | 11 | 21 | 52 |

## PITTSBURGH STEELERS

### RUSHING
| Last Name | No. | Yds | Avg | TD |
|---|---|---|---|---|
| Johnson | 186 | 773 | 4.2 | 4 |
| Hoak | 216 | 679 | 3.1 | 6 |
| Sapp | 104 | 452 | 4.3 | 1 |
| Ferguson | 46 | 172 | 3.7 | 1 |
| Tracy | 29 | 61 | 2.1 | 1 |
| Ballman | 8 | 59 | 7.4 | 0 |
| Brown | 15 | 20 | 1.3 | 2 |
| Mack | 2 | 1 | 0.5 | 0 |
| Carpenter | 1 | -3 | -3.0 | 0 |
| Nelsen | 1 | -6 | -6.0 | 0 |

### RECEIVING
| Last Name | No. | Yds | Avg | TD |
|---|---|---|---|---|
| Dial | 60 | 1295 | 22 | 9 |
| Ballman | 26 | 492 | 19 | 5 |
| Mack | 25 | 618 | 25 | 3 |
| Johnson | 21 | 145 | 7 | 1 |
| Carpenter | 17 | 233 | 14 | 1 |
| Hoak | 11 | 118 | 11 | 1 |
| Tracy | 7 | 112 | 16 | 0 |
| Sapp | 4 | 36 | 9 | 0 |
| Ferguson | 3 | 7 | 2 | 0 |
| Burrell | 2 | 27 | 14 | 0 |
| Curry | 1 | 31 | 31 | 1 |

### PUNT RETURNS
| Last Name | No. | Yds | Avg | TD |
|---|---|---|---|---|
| Keys | 13 | 198 | 15 | 0 |
| Haley | 12 | 59 | 5 | 0 |
| Thomas | 6 | 24 | 4 | 0 |

### KICKOFF RETURNS
| Last Name | No. | Yds | Avg | TD |
|---|---|---|---|---|
| Ballman | 22 | 698 | 32 | 1 |
| Thomas | 12 | 286 | 24 | 0 |
| Keys | 9 | 219 | 24 | 0 |
| Sapp | 5 | 58 | 12 | 0 |
| Glass | 2 | 46 | 23 | 0 |
| Curry | 1 | 27 | 27 | 0 |
| Cordileone | 1 | 18 | 18 | 0 |

### PASSING — PUNTING — KICKING

PASSING
| Last Name | Att | Comp | % | Yds | Yd/Att | TD | Int- | % | RK |
|---|---|---|---|---|---|---|---|---|---|
| Brown | 362 | 168 | 46 | 2982 | 8.2 | 21 | 20- | 6 | 9 |
| Tracy | 4 | 1 | 25 | 23 | 5.8 | 0 | 0- | 0 | |
| Nofsinger | 3 | 2 | 67 | 46 | 15.3 | 0 | 0- | 0 | |
| Nelsen | 2 | 0 | 0 | 0 | 0.0 | 0 | 0- | 0 | |

PUNTING
| Last Name | No | Avg |
|---|---|---|
| Brown | 57 | 39.6 |
| J. Bradshaw | 2 | 35.0 |

KICKING
| Last Name | XP | Att | % | FG | Att | % |
|---|---|---|---|---|---|---|
| Michaels | 32 | 35 | 91 | 21 | 41 | 51 |
| Tracy | 2 | 2 | 100 | 0 | 0 | 0 |

## DALLAS COWBOYS

### RUSHING
| Last Name | No. | Yds | Avg | TD |
|---|---|---|---|---|
| Perkins | 149 | 614 | 4.1 | 7 |
| Marsh | 99 | 483 | 4.9 | 5 |
| Bullocks | 96 | 341 | 3.6 | 2 |
| Meredith | 41 | 185 | 4.5 | 3 |
| Stiger | 31 | 140 | 4.5 | 1 |
| Baker | 1 | 15 | 15.0 | 0 |
| Clarke | 1 | 12 | 12.0 | 0 |
| LeBaron | 2 | 5 | 2.5 | 0 |

### RECEIVING
| Last Name | No. | Yds | Avg | TD |
|---|---|---|---|---|
| Clarke | 43 | 833 | 19 | 10 |
| Howton | 33 | 514 | 16 | 3 |
| Folkins | 31 | 407 | 13 | 4 |
| Marsh | 26 | 224 | 9 | 0 |
| Norman | 18 | 341 | 19 | 3 |
| Barnes | 15 | 195 | 13 | 0 |
| Perkins | 14 | 84 | 6 | 0 |
| Stiger | 13 | 131 | 10 | 0 |
| Bullocks | 7 | 70 | 10 | 0 |

### PUNT RETURNS
| Last Name | No. | Yds | Avg | TD |
|---|---|---|---|---|
| Stiger | 14 | 141 | 10 | 0 |
| Overton | 5 | 32 | 6 | 0 |
| Gaechter | 2 | 2 | 1 | 0 |
| Howley | 1 | 2 | 2 | 0 |
| Norman | 1 | 0 | 0 | 0 |

### KICKOFF RETURNS
| Last Name | No. | Yds | Avg | TD |
|---|---|---|---|---|
| Bullocks | 19 | 453 | 24 | 0 |
| Stiger | 18 | 432 | 24 | 0 |
| Marsh | 9 | 167 | 19 | 0 |
| Hays | 2 | 48 | 24 | 0 |

### PASSING — PUNTING — KICKING

PASSING
| Last Name | Att | Comp | % | Yds | Yd/Att | TD | Int- | % | RK |
|---|---|---|---|---|---|---|---|---|---|
| Meredith | 310 | 167 | 54 | 2381 | 7.7 | 17 | 18- | 6 | 10 |
| LeBaron | 65 | 33 | 51 | 418 | 6.4 | 3 | 3- | 5 | |

PUNTING
| Last Name | No | Avg |
|---|---|---|
| Baker | 71 | 44.2 |

KICKING
| Last Name | XP | Att | % | FG | Att | % |
|---|---|---|---|---|---|---|
| Baker | 38 | 38 | 100 | 9 | 20 | 45 |

## EASTERN CONFERENCE – Continued

### WASHINGTON REDSKINS 3-11-0 Bill McPeak

| Scores of Each Game | | | Use Name | Pos. | Hgt | Wgt | Age | Int | Pts |
|---|---|---|---|---|---|---|---|---|---|
| 14 | Cleveland | 37 | Fran O'Brien | OT | 6'1" | 260 | 28 | | |
| 37 | Los Angeles | 14 | Riley Mattson | OT | 6'4" | 257 | 24 | | |
| 21 | DALLAS | 17 | Andy Cvercko (from CLE) | OG | 6' | 243 | 26 | | |
| 14 | NEW YORK | 24 | Wiley Feagin | OG | 6'2" | 235 | 26 | | |
| 24 | PHILADELPHIA | 37 | John Nisby | OG | 6'1" | 247 | 30 | | |
| 27 | Pittsburgh | 38 | Vince Promuto | OG | 6'1" | 240 | 25 | | |
| 7 | ST. LOUIS | 21 | Fred Hageman | C | 6'4" | 242 | 25 | | |
| 20 | Dallas | 35 | John Paluck | DE | 6'2" | 252 | 30 | 1 | |
| 20 | St. Louis | 24 | Ron Snidow | DE | 6'4" | 245 | 21 | | |
| 28 | PITTSBURGH | 34 | Andy Stynchula | DE | 6'3" | 257 | 24 | | |
| 13 | Philadelphia | 10 | Ben Davidson | DT | 6'8" | 275 | 23 | | |
| 20 | BALTIMORE | 36 | Ed Khayat | DT | 6'3" | 245 | 28 | | |
| 14 | New York | 44 | Joe Rutgens | DT | 6'2" | 265 | 24 | | |
| 20 | CLEVELAND | 27 | Bob Toneff | DT | 6'3" | 275 | 33 | | |

| Use Name | Pos. | Hgt | Wgt | Age | Int | Pts |
|---|---|---|---|---|---|---|
| Rod Breedlove | LB | 6'2" | 227 | 25 | 1 | |
| Harry Butsko | LB | 6'3" | 220 | 22 | | |
| Carl Kammerer | LB | 6'3" | 237 | 26 | 2 | |
| Gorden Kelley | LB | 6'3" | 230 | 25 | | |
| Al Miller | LB | 6' | 228 | 23 | | |
| Bob Pellegrini | LB | 6'2" | 235 | 28 | 2 | |
| Claude Crabb | DB | 6' | 197 | 23 | 3 | 6 |
| Dale Hackbart | DB | 6'3" | 208 | 27 | 1 | |
| Ted Rzempoluch | DB | 6'1" | 195 | 22 | | |
| Johnny Sample | DB | 6'1" | 200 | 26 | 1 | |
| Lonnie Sanders | DB | 6'3" | 200 | 21 | 3 | |
| Jim Steffen | DB | 6' | 200 | 26 | 5 | 6 |

| Use Name | Pos. | Hgt | Wgt | Age | Int | Pts |
|---|---|---|---|---|---|---|
| George Izo | QB | 6'3" | 214 | 26 | | |
| Norm Snead | QB | 6'4" | 215 | 23 | | 12 |
| Billy Barnes | HB | 5'11" | 195 | 28 | | 36 |
| Leroy Jackson | HB | 6' | 190 | 23 | | |
| Dick James | DB-HB | 5'9" | 180 | 29 | 2 | 36 |
| Don Bosseler | FB | 6'1" | 212 | 27 | | 12 |
| Jim Cunningham | FB | 5'11" | 224 | 24 | | 6 |
| Dave Francis | FB | 6'1" | 210 | 22 | | |
| Frank Budd | FL | 5'10" | 187 | 24 | | |
| Bobby Mitchell | FL | 6' | 195 | 28 | | 48 |
| Bill Anderson | OE | 6'3" | 215 | 27 | | 6 |
| Jim Collier | OE | 6'2" | 195 | 24 | | |
| Fred Dugan | OE | 6'3" | 194 | 29 | | 18 |
| Pat Richter | OE | 6'5" | 230 | 22 | | 18 |
| Bob Khayat | K | 6'2" | 230 | 25 | | 69 |

### PHILADELPHIA EAGLES 2-10-2 Nick Skorich

| Scores of Each Game | | | Use Name | Pos. | Hgt | Wgt | Age | Int | Pts |
|---|---|---|---|---|---|---|---|---|---|
| 21 | PITTSBURGH | 21 | Dave Graham | OT | 6'3" | 240 | 24 | | |
| 24 | ST. LOUIS | 28 | J. D. Smith | OT | 6'5" | 250 | 27 | | |
| 14 | NEW YORK | 37 | Howard Keys | OG-C-OT | 6'3" | 240 | 28 | | |
| 24 | DALLAS | 21 | Ed Blaine | OG | 6'2" | 240 | 23 | | |
| 37 | Washington | 24 | Bill Byrne | OG | 6' | 240 | 22 | | |
| 7 | Cleveland | 37 | Pete Case | OG | 6'3" | 237 | 22 | | |
| 7 | Chicago | 16 | Jim Skaggs | OG | 6'2" | 230 | 23 | | |
| 17 | CLEVELAND | 23 | Jim Schrader | C | 6'2" | 250 | 31 | | |
| 14 | New York | 42 | Jerry Mazzanti | DE | 6'3" | 240 | 23 | | |
| 20 | Dallas | 27 | Bill Quinlan | DE | 6'3" | 250 | 31 | | |
| 10 | WASHINGTON | 13 | Bobby Richards | DE | 6'2" | 240 | 24 | | |
| 20 | Pittsburgh | 20 | Dick Stafford | DE | 6'4" | 270 | 23 | | |
| 14 | St. Louis | 38 | Frank Fuller | DT | 6'4" | 250 | 34 | | |
| 13 | MINNESOTA | 34 | Riley Gunnels | DT | 6'3" | 250 | 26 | | |
| | | | Ray Mansfield | DT | 6'3" | 250 | 22 | | |
| | | | John Mellekas | DT | 6'3" | 255 | 30 | | |

| Use Name | Pos. | Hgt | Wgt | Age | Int | Pts |
|---|---|---|---|---|---|---|
| Maxie Baughan | LB | 6'1" | 226 | 25 | 1 | |
| Lee Roy Caffey | LB | 6'3" | 230 | 23 | 1 | 6 |
| Bob Harrison | LB | 6'2" | 220 | 26 | | |
| Ralph Heck | LB | 6'2" | 220 | 22 | | |
| Dave Lloyd | LB | 6'3" | 248 | 27 | 3 | |
| Don Burroughs | DB | 6'4" | 190 | 32 | 4 | |
| Jimmy Carr | DB | 6'1" | 205 | 30 | 1 | |
| Irv Cross | DB | 6'1" | 192 | 24 | 2 | |
| Mike McClellan | DB | 6'1" | 185 | 24 | 1 | |
| Nate Ramsey | DB | 6'1" | 195 | 22 | 1 | |
| Ben Scotti | DB | 6'1" | 186 | 26 | 1 | |

Mike Woulfe – Injury
Gene Gossage – Canadian Football League

| Use Name | Pos. | Hgt | Wgt | Age | Int | Pts |
|---|---|---|---|---|---|---|
| Ralph Guglielmi (from NY) | QB | 6'1" | 195 | 30 | | |
| King Hill | QB | 6'3" | 213 | 27 | | |
| Sonny Jurgensen | QB | 5'11" | 200 | 29 | | 6 |
| Timmy Brown | HB | 5'10" | 190 | 26 | | 66 |
| Paul Dudley | HB | 6' | 185 | 23 | | |
| Tom Woodeshick | HB | 6' | 210 | 21 | | |
| Ted Dean | FB-HB | 6'2" | 210 | 25 | | |
| Clarence Peaks | FB | 6'1" | 220 | 27 | | 12 |
| Ron Goodwin | FL | 6' | 170 | 21 | | 24 |
| Tommy McDonald | FL | 5'10" | 172 | 29 | | 48 |
| Gary Henson | OE | 6'3" | 200 | 23 | | |
| Dick Lucas | OE | 6'2" | 215 | 29 | | |
| Pete Retzlaff | OE | 6'1" | 210 | 32 | | 24 |
| Ralph Smith | OE | 6'2" | 203 | 24 | | 6 |
| Mike Clark | K | 6'1" | 200 | 22 | | 50 |

## WESTERN CONFERENCE

### CHICAGO BEARS 11-1-2 George Halas

| Scores of Each Game | | | Use Name | Pos. | Hgt | Wgt | Age | Int | Pts |
|---|---|---|---|---|---|---|---|---|---|
| 10 | Green Bay | 3 | Steve Barnett | OT | 6'1" | 255 | 22 | | |
| 28 | Minnesota | 7 | Herm Lee | OT | 6'4" | 247 | 32 | | |
| 37 | Detroit | 21 | Bob Wetoska | OT | 6'3" | 240 | 25 | | |
| 10 | BALTIMORE | 3 | Jim Cadile | OG | 6'3" | 230 | 22 | | |
| 52 | Los Angeles | 14 | Roger Davis | OG | 6'3" | 235 | 25 | | |
| 14 | San Francisco | 20 | Ted Karras | OG | 6'1" | 243 | 30 | | |
| 16 | PHILADELPHIA | 7 | Mike Pyle | C | 6'3" | 245 | 24 | | |
| 17 | Baltimore | 7 | Doug Atkins | DE | 6'8" | 255 | 33 | 1 | 2 |
| 6 | LOS ANGELES | 0 | Bob Kilcullen | DE | 6'3" | 245 | 27 | | |
| 26 | GREEN BAY | 7 | Ed O'Bradovich | DE | 6'3" | 255 | 23 | | |
| 17 | Pittsburgh | 17 | John Johnson | DT | 6'5" | 260 | 22 | | |
| 17 | MINNESOTA | 17 | Stan Jones | DT | 6'1" | 250 | 32 | | |
| 27 | SAN FRANCISCO | 7 | Earl Leggett | DT | 6'3" | 250 | 29 | | |
| 24 | DETROIT | 14 | Fred Williams | DT | 6'4" | 248 | 33 | | |

| Use Name | Pos. | Hgt | Wgt | Age | Int | Pts |
|---|---|---|---|---|---|---|
| Tom Bettis | LB | 6'2" | 235 | 30 | | |
| Joe Fortunato | LB | 6' | 225 | 33 | 2 | |
| Bill George | LB | 6'2" | 235 | 32 | 1 | |
| Roger LeClerc | LB | 6'3" | 235 | 25 | 1 | 39 |
| Larry Morris | LB | 6'2" | 230 | 28 | | |
| J. C. Caroline | DB | 6'1" | 190 | 30 | 1 | |
| Larry Glueck | DB | 6' | 190 | 21 | 1 | |
| Bennie McRae | DB | 6'1" | 180 | 22 | 6 | 6 |
| Richie Petitbon | DB | 6'3" | 205 | 25 | 8 | 6 |
| Rosey Taylor | DB | 5'11" | 186 | 24 | 9 | 6 |
| Dave Whitsell | DB | 6' | 190 | 27 | 6 | 6 |

| Use Name | Pos. | Hgt | Wgt | Age | Int | Pts |
|---|---|---|---|---|---|---|
| Rudy Bukich | QB | 6'1" | 205 | 32 | | 6 |
| Billy Wade | QB | 6'2" | 205 | 32 | | 36 |
| Charlie Bivins | HB | 6'2" | 212 | 24 | | |
| Ronnie Bull | HB | 6' | 200 | 23 | | 18 |
| Willie Galimore | HB | 6'1" | 187 | 28 | | 30 |
| Billy Martin | HB | 5'11" | 196 | 25 | | |
| Rick Casares | FB | 6'2" | 225 | 32 | | 6 |
| Joe Marconi | FB | 6'2" | 225 | 29 | | 24 |
| Johnny Morris | FL | 5'10" | 180 | 28 | | 12 |
| Angie Coia | OE | 6'2" | 202 | 25 | | 6 |
| Mike Ditka | OE | 6'3" | 230 | 23 | | 48 |
| Bo Farrington | OE | 6'3" | 217 | 27 | | 12 |
| Bob Jencks | OE | 6'5" | 227 | 22 | | 38 |
| Bobby Joe Green | K | 5'11" | 175 | 25 | | |

### GREEN BAY PACKERS 11-2-1 Vince Lombardi

| Scores of Each Game | | | Use Name | Pos. | Hgt | Wgt | Age | Int | Pts |
|---|---|---|---|---|---|---|---|---|---|
| 3 | CHICAGO | 10 | Forrest Gregg | OT | 6'4" | 250 | 30 | | |
| 31 | DETROIT | 10 | Norm Masters | OT | 6'2" | 250 | 30 | | |
| 31 | BALTIMORE | 20 | Bob Skoronski | C-OT | 6'3" | 250 | 30 | | |
| 42 | LOS ANGELES | 10 | Dan Grimm | OG | 6'3" | 240 | 22 | | |
| 37 | Minnesota | 28 | Jerry Kramer | OG | 6'3" | 255 | 28 | | 91 |
| 30 | St. Louis | 7 | Fuzzy Thurston | OG | 6'1" | 250 | 30 | | |
| 34 | Baltimore | 20 | Ken Iman | C | 6'1" | 230 | 24 | | |
| 33 | PITTSBURGH | 14 | Jim Ringo | C | 6'1" | 235 | 32 | | |
| 28 | MINNESOTA | 7 | Lionel Aldridge | DE | 6'4" | 240 | 21 | | |
| 7 | Chicago | 26 | Willie Davis | DE | 6'3" | 240 | 30 | | 2 |
| 28 | SAN FRANCISCO | 10 | Urban Henry | DT-DE | 6'4" | 265 | 28 | | |
| 13 | Detroit | 13 | Dave Hanner | DT | 6'2" | 260 | 34 | 1 | |
| 31 | Los Angeles | 14 | Ron Kostelnik | DT | 6'4" | 260 | 23 | | |
| 21 | San Francisco | 17 | Henry Jordan | DE-DT | 6'3" | 250 | 28 | | |

| Use Name | Pos. | Hgt | Wgt | Age | Int | Pts |
|---|---|---|---|---|---|---|
| Dan Currie | LB | 6'3" | 240 | 29 | 1 | |
| Bill Forester | LB | 6'3" | 240 | 32 | 1 | |
| Ed Holler | LB | 6'2" | 230 | 23 | | |
| Ray Nitschke | LB | 6'3" | 235 | 27 | 2 | |
| Dave Robinson | LB | 6'3" | 240 | 22 | | |
| Herb Adderley | DB | 6'1" | 205 | 24 | 5 | 6 |
| Hank Gremminger | DB | 6'1" | 205 | 30 | 3 | 6 |
| Jerry Norton | DB | 5'11" | 195 | 33 | | |
| Jesse Whittenton | DB | 6' | 195 | 29 | 4 | |
| Willie Wood | DB | 5'10" | 190 | 27 | 5 | |

Paul Hornung – Suspended by commissioner

| Use Name | Pos. | Hgt | Wgt | Age | Int | Pts |
|---|---|---|---|---|---|---|
| John Roach | QB | 6'4" | 200 | 30 | | |
| Bart Starr | QB | 6'1" | 200 | 30 | | |
| Lew Carpenter | HB | 6'1" | 215 | 31 | | |
| Tom Moore | HB | 6'2" | 215 | 25 | | 48 |
| Elijah Pitts | HB | 6'1" | 200 | 24 | | 36 |
| Earl Gros | FB | 6'3" | 230 | 22 | | 12 |
| Frank Mestnik | FB | 6'2" | 220 | 25 | | |
| Jim Taylor | FB | 6' | 215 | 28 | | 60 |
| Boyd Dowler | FL | 6'5" | 225 | 26 | | 36 |
| Bob Jeter | FL | 6'1" | 190 | 25 | | |
| Jan Barrett (to OAK-A) | OE | 6'3" | 230 | 23 | | |
| Marv Fleming | OE | 6'4" | 225 | 21 | | 12 |
| Ron Kramer | OE | 6'3" | 240 | 28 | | 24 |
| Max McGee | OE | 6'3" | 205 | 31 | | 36 |

### BALTIMORE COLTS 8-6-0 Don Shula

| Scores of Each Game | | | Use Name | Pos. | Hgt | Wgt | Age | Int | Pts |
|---|---|---|---|---|---|---|---|---|---|
| 28 | NEW YORK | 37 | Tom Gilburg | OT | 6'5" | 245 | 24 | | |
| 20 | San Francisco | 14 | George Preas | OT | 6'2" | 250 | 31 | | |
| 20 | Green Bay | 31 | Bob Vogel | OT | 6'5" | 232 | 21 | | |
| 3 | Chicago | 10 | Dan Sullivan | OG-OT | 6'3" | 250 | 24 | | |
| 20 | SAN FRANCISCO | 3 | Jim Parker | OG | 6'3" | 275 | 29 | | |
| 25 | Detroit | 21 | Palmer Pyle | OG | 6'2" | 250 | 26 | | |
| 20 | GREEN BAY | 34 | Alex Sandusky | OG | 6'1" | 242 | 31 | | |
| 7 | CHICAGO | 17 | Dick Szymanski | C | 6'3" | 235 | 31 | | |
| 24 | DETROIT | 21 | Ordell Braase | DE | 6'4" | 242 | 31 | | |
| 37 | Minnesota | 34 | Gino Marchetti | DE | 6'4" | 245 | 37 | | 6 |
| 16 | Los Angeles | 17 | Don Thompson | DE | 6'4" | 225 | 24 | | |
| 36 | Washington | 20 | Jim Colvin | DT | 6'2" | 255 | 26 | | 2 |
| 41 | MINNESOTA | 10 | John Diehl | DT | 6'7" | 285 | 27 | | |
| 19 | LOS ANGELES | 16 | Fred Miller | DT | 6'3" | 240 | 22 | | |

| Use Name | Pos. | Hgt | Wgt | Age | Int | Pts |
|---|---|---|---|---|---|---|
| Jackie Burkett | LB | 6'4" | 230 | 26 | | |
| Jim Maples | LB | 6'4" | 225 | 22 | | |
| Bill Pellington | LB | 6'2" | 238 | 34 | | |
| Bill Saul | LB | 6'4" | 225 | 22 | | |
| Don Shinnick | LB | 6' | 235 | 28 | 2 | |
| Bobby Boyd | DB | 5'10" | 190 | 25 | 3 | 6 |
| Wendell Harris | DB | 5'11" | 190 | 22 | | |
| Jerry Logan | DB | 6'1" | 185 | 22 | 1 | |
| Lenny Lyles | DB | 6'2" | 202 | 27 | 2 | 6 |
| Andy Nelson | DB | 6'1" | 180 | 30 | 3 | 6 |
| Jim Welch | DB | 6' | 190 | 25 | 4 | |

Billy Ray Smith – Injury

| Use Name | Pos. | Hgt | Wgt | Age | Int | Pts |
|---|---|---|---|---|---|---|
| Gary Cuozzo | QB | 6'1" | 190 | 22 | | |
| Johnny Unitas | QB | 6'1" | 194 | 30 | | |
| Tom Matte | HB | 6' | 195 | 24 | | 30 |
| Lenny Moore | HB | 6'1" | 190 | 30 | | 24 |
| Alex Hawkins | OE-HB | 6'1" | 190 | 26 | | |
| Nate Craddock | FB | 6' | 220 | 20 | | |
| Jerry Hill | FB | 5'11" | 210 | 23 | | 36 |
| J. W. Lockett | FB | 6'2" | 230 | 26 | | 6 |
| Jimmy Orr | FL | 5'11" | 175 | 27 | | 30 |
| Willie Richardson | FL | 6'2" | 198 | 23 | | |
| Ray Berry | OE | 6'2" | 190 | 30 | | 18 |
| Dick Bielski | OE | 6'1" | 225 | 31 | | |
| John Mackey | OE | 6'3" | 220 | 21 | | 42 |
| R. C. Owens | OE | 6'3" | 195 | 28 | | |
| Butch Wilson | OE | 6'2" | 210 | 21 | | |
| Jim Martin | K | 6'2" | 230 | 39 | | 104 |

## WASHINGTON REDSKINS

### EASTERN CONFERENCE—Continued

**RUSHING**

| Last Name | No. | Yds | Avg | TD |
|---|---|---|---|---|
| James | 105 | 384 | 3.7 | 4 |
| Barnes | 93 | 374 | 4.0 | 5 |
| Bosseler | 79 | 290 | 3.7 | 2 |
| Snead | 23 | 100 | 4.3 | 2 |
| Cunningham | 16 | 33 | 2.1 | 1 |
| Jackson | 3 | 30 | 10.0 | 0 |
| Mitchell | 3 | 24 | 8.0 | 0 |
| Izo | 3 | 4 | 1.3 | 0 |

**RECEIVING**

| Last Name | No. | Yds | Avg | TD |
|---|---|---|---|---|
| Mitchell | 69 | 1436 | 21 | 7 |
| Richter | 27 | 383 | 14 | 3 |
| Bosseler | 25 | 289 | 12 | 0 |
| Dugan | 20 | 288 | 14 | 3 |
| James | 15 | 302 | 20 | 2 |
| Barnes | 15 | 256 | 17 | 1 |
| Anderson | 14 | 288 | 21 | 1 |
| Cunningham | 8 | 86 | 11 | 0 |
| Budd | 5 | 106 | 21 | 0 |

**PUNT RETURNS**

| Last Name | No. | Yds | Avg | TD |
|---|---|---|---|---|
| James | 16 | 214 | 13 | 0 |
| Steffen | 5 | 83 | 17 | 0 |
| Mitchell | 6 | 49 | 8 | 0 |
| Sample | 2 | 45 | 23 | 0 |
| Barnes | 1 | 0 | 0 | 0 |

**KICKOFF RETURNS**

| Last Name | No. | Yds | Avg | TD |
|---|---|---|---|---|
| James | 30 | 830 | 28 | 0 |
| Mitchell | 9 | 343 | 38 | 1 |
| Budd | 10 | 252 | 25 | 0 |
| Jackson | 5 | 113 | 23 | 0 |
| Cunningham | 6 | 96 | 16 | 0 |
| Steffen | 3 | 84 | 28 | 0 |
| Snidow | 1 | 0 | 0 | |

**PASSING — PUNTING — KICKING**

| PASSING | Att | Comp | % | Yds | Yd/Att | TD | Int— | % | RK |
|---|---|---|---|---|---|---|---|---|---|
| Snead | 363 | 175 | 48 | 3043 | 8.4 | 13 | 27— | 7 | 11 |
| Izo | 58 | 25 | 43 | 378 | 6.5 | 3 | 6— | 10 | |
| Barnes | 4 | 3 | 75 | 81 | 20.3 | 1 | 0— | 0 | |
| Anderson | 1 | 0 | 0 | 0 | 0.0 | 0 | 1—100 | | |
| James | 1 | 0 | 0 | 0 | 0.0 | 0 | 0— | 0 | |

| PUNTING | No | Avg |
|---|---|---|
| Richter | 53 | 41.7 |

| KICKING | XP | Att | % | FG | Att | % |
|---|---|---|---|---|---|---|
| B. Khayat | 33 | 35 | 94 | 12 | 26 | 46 |

## PHILADELPHIA EAGLES

**RUSHING**

| Last Name | No. | Yds | Avg | TD |
|---|---|---|---|---|
| Brown | 192 | 841 | 4.4 | 6 |
| Dean | 79 | 268 | 3.4 | 0 |
| Peaks | 64 | 212 | 3.3 | 1 |
| Jurgensen | 13 | 38 | 2.9 | 1 |
| Guglielmi | 4 | 23 | 5.8 | 0 |
| Dudley | 11 | 21 | 1.9 | 0 |
| Woodeshick | 5 | 18 | 3.6 | 0 |
| Hill | 3 | -1 | -0.3 | 0 |

**RECEIVING**

| Last Name | No. | Yds | Avg | TD |
|---|---|---|---|---|
| Retzlaff | 57 | 895 | 16 | 4 |
| McDonald | 41 | 731 | 18 | 8 |
| Brown | 36 | 487 | 14 | 4 |
| Peaks | 22 | 167 | 8 | 1 |
| Goodwin | 15 | 215 | 14 | 4 |
| Dean | 14 | 108 | 8 | 0 |
| R. Smith | 5 | 63 | 13 | 1 |
| Dudley | 1 | 8 | 8 | 0 |
| Woodeshick | 1 | -3 | -3 | 0 |

**PUNT RETURNS**

| Last Name | No. | Yds | Avg | TD |
|---|---|---|---|---|
| Brown | 16 | 152 | 10 | 0 |
| Dean | 10 | 74 | 7 | 0 |

**KICKOFF RETURNS**

| Last Name | No. | Yds | Avg | TD |
|---|---|---|---|---|
| Brown | 33 | 945 | 29 | 1 |
| Dean | 16 | 425 | 27 | 0 |
| Woodeshick | 3 | 72 | 24 | 0 |
| Henson | 3 | 21 | 7 | 0 |
| R. Smith | 2 | 18 | 9 | 0 |
| Caffey | 1 | 6 | 6 | 0 |

**PASSING — PUNTING — KICKING**

| PASSING | Att | Comp | % | Yds | Yd/Att | TD | Int— | % | RK |
|---|---|---|---|---|---|---|---|---|---|
| Hill | 186 | 91 | 49 | 1213 | 6.5 | 10 | 17— | 9 | 14 |
| Jurgensen | 184 | 99 | 54 | 1413 | 7.7 | 11 | 13— | 7 | 12 |
| Guglielmi | 24 | 7 | 29 | 118 | 4.9 | 0 | 3— | 13 | |
| Brown | 3 | 1 | 33 | 11 | 3.7 | 1 | 1— | 33 | |

| PUNTING | No | Avg |
|---|---|---|
| Hill | 69 | 43.1 |

| KICKING | XP | Att | % | FG | Att | % |
|---|---|---|---|---|---|---|
| Clark | 29 | 32 | 91 | 7 | 15 | 47 |

## WESTERN CONFERENCE

## CHICAGO BEARS

**RUSHING**

| Last Name | No. | Yds | Avg | TD |
|---|---|---|---|---|
| Marconi | 118 | 446 | 3.8 | 2 |
| Bull | 117 | 404 | 3.5 | 1 |
| Galimore | 85 | 321 | 3.8 | 5 |
| Casares | 65 | 277 | 4.3 | 0 |
| Wade | 45 | 132 | 2.9 | 6 |
| Bivins | 44 | 104 | 2.4 | 0 |
| J. Morris | 1 | 10 | 10.0 | 0 |
| Coia | 2 | 2 | 1.0 | 0 |
| Bukich | 7 | 1 | 0.1 | 1 |
| Whitsell | 1 | -8 | -8.0 | 0 |
| Green | 2 | -10 | -5.0 | 0 |

**RECEIVING**

| Last Name | No. | Yds | Avg | TD |
|---|---|---|---|---|
| Ditka | 59 | 794 | 13 | 8 |
| J. Morris | 47 | 705 | 15 | 2 |
| Marconi | 28 | 335 | 12 | 2 |
| Farrington | 21 | 335 | 16 | 2 |
| Bull | 19 | 132 | 7 | 2 |
| Casares | 19 | 94 | 5 | 1 |
| Galimore | 13 | 131 | 10 | 0 |
| Coia | 11 | 116 | 11 | 1 |
| Bivins | 3 | 22 | 7 | 0 |
| Jencks | 1 | 6 | 6 | 0 |

**PUNT RETURNS**

| Last Name | No. | Yds | Avg | TD |
|---|---|---|---|---|
| J. Morris | 16 | 164 | 10 | 0 |
| Martin | 2 | 62 | 31 | 0 |
| Taylor | 12 | 51 | 4 | 0 |

**KICKOFF RETURNS**

| Last Name | No. | Yds | Avg | TD |
|---|---|---|---|---|
| Taylor | 6 | 118 | 20 | 0 |
| Bull | 7 | 105 | 15 | 0 |
| Martin | 4 | 99 | 25 | 0 |
| Bivins | 2 | 40 | 20 | 0 |
| Galimore | 1 | 19 | 19 | 0 |
| Casares | 2 | 18 | 9 | 0 |
| Marconi | 2 | 15 | 8 | 0 |
| Johnson | 1 | 10 | 10 | 0 |
| Pyle | 1 | 0 | 0 | 0 |

**PASSING — PUNTING — KICKING**

| PASSING | Att | Comp | % | Yds | Yd/Att | TD | Int— | % | RK |
|---|---|---|---|---|---|---|---|---|---|
| Wade | 356 | 192 | 54 | 2301 | 6.5 | 15 | 12— | 3 | 8 |
| Bukich | 43 | 29 | 67 | 369 | 8.6 | 3 | 2— | 5 | |
| Bull | 3 | 0 | 0 | 0 | 0.0 | 0 | 0— | 0 | |
| Green | 1 | 0 | 0 | 0 | 0.0 | 0 | 0— | 0 | |
| LeClerc | 1 | 0 | 0 | 0 | 0.0 | 0 | 0— | 0 | |

| PUNTING | No | Avg |
|---|---|---|
| Green | 64 | 46.5 |

| KICKING | XP | Att | % | FG | Att | % |
|---|---|---|---|---|---|---|
| Jencks | 35 | 37 | 95 | 1 | 10 | 10 |
| LeClerc | 0 | 0 | 0 | 13 | 23 | 57 |

## GREEN BAY PACKERS

**RUSHING**

| Last Name | No. | Yds | Avg | TD |
|---|---|---|---|---|
| Taylor | 248 | 1018 | 4.1 | 9 |
| Moore | 132 | 658 | 5.0 | 6 |
| Pitts | 54 | 212 | 3.9 | 5 |
| Gros | 48 | 203 | 4.2 | 2 |
| Starr | 13 | 116 | 8.9 | 0 |
| Roach | 3 | 31 | 10.3 | 0 |
| Carpenter | 2 | 8 | 4.0 | 0 |
| Mestnik | 1 | 4 | 4.0 | 0 |
| Norton | 2 | 0 | 0.0 | 0 |

**RECEIVING**

| Last Name | No. | Yds | Avg | TD |
|---|---|---|---|---|
| Dowler | 53 | 901 | 17 | 6 |
| McGee | 39 | 749 | 19 | 6 |
| R. Kramer | 32 | 537 | 17 | 4 |
| Moore | 23 | 237 | 10 | 2 |
| Taylor | 13 | 68 | 5 | 1 |
| Pitts | 9 | 54 | 6 | 1 |
| Fleming | 7 | 132 | 19 | 2 |
| Gros | 1 | 19 | 19 | 0 |
| Carpenter | 1 | 12 | 12 | 0 |
| Jeter | 1 | 2 | 2 | 0 |

**PUNT RETURNS**

| Last Name | No. | Yds | Avg | TD |
|---|---|---|---|---|
| Wood | 19 | 169 | 9 | 0 |
| Pitts | 7 | 60 | 9 | 0 |

**KICKOFF RETURNS**

| Last Name | No. | Yds | Avg | TD |
|---|---|---|---|---|
| Adderley | 20 | 597 | 30 | 1 |
| Gros | 17 | 430 | 25 | 0 |
| Carpenter | 5 | 75 | 15 | 0 |
| Wood | 1 | 20 | 20 | 0 |
| Fleming | 1 | 0 | 0 | 0 |
| J. Kramer | 1 | 0 | 0 | 0 |
| Mestnik | 1 | 0 | 0 | 0 |

**PASSING — PUNTING — KICKING**

| PASSING | Att | Comp | % | Yds | Yd/Att | TD | Int— | % | RK |
|---|---|---|---|---|---|---|---|---|---|
| Starr | 244 | 132 | 54 | 1855 | 7.6 | 15 | 10— | 4 | 7 |
| Roach | 84 | 38 | 45 | 620 | 7.4 | 4 | 8— | 10 | |
| Moore | 4 | 3 | 75 | 99 | 24.8 | 1 | 0— | 0 | |
| Pitts | 2 | 2 | 100 | 41 | 20.5 | 1 | 0— | 0 | |

| PUNTING | No | Avg |
|---|---|---|
| Norton | 51 | 44.7 |

| KICKING | XP | Att | % | FG | Att | % |
|---|---|---|---|---|---|---|
| J. Kramer | 43 | 46 | 93 | 16 | 34 | 47 |

## BALTIMORE COLTS

**RUSHING**

| Last Name | No. | Yds | Avg | TD |
|---|---|---|---|---|
| Matte | 133 | 541 | 4.1 | 4 |
| Hill | 100 | 440 | 4.4 | 5 |
| Lockett | 81 | 273 | 3.4 | 0 |
| Unitas | 47 | 224 | 4.8 | 0 |
| Moore | 27 | 136 | 5.0 | 2 |
| Cuozzo | 3 | 26 | 8.7 | 0 |
| Mackey | 1 | 3 | 3.0 | 0 |
| Craddock | 1 | 1 | 1.0 | 0 |
| Hawkins | 3 | -2 | -0.7 | 0 |

**RECEIVING**

| Last Name | No. | Yds | Avg | TD |
|---|---|---|---|---|
| Matte | 48 | 466 | 10 | 1 |
| Berry | 44 | 703 | 16 | 3 |
| Orr | 41 | 708 | 17 | 5 |
| Mackey | 35 | 726 | 21 | 7 |
| Hill | 22 | 304 | 14 | 1 |
| Moore | 21 | 288 | 14 | 2 |
| Richardson | 17 | 204 | 12 | 0 |
| Lockett | 16 | 158 | 10 | 1 |
| Hawkins | 3 | 41 | 14 | 0 |
| Owens | 1 | 7 | 7 | 0 |

**PUNT RETURNS**

| Last Name | No. | Yds | Avg | TD |
|---|---|---|---|---|
| Logan | 28 | 279 | 10 | 0 |
| Hawkins | 17 | 156 | 9 | 0 |
| Richardson | 5 | 43 | 9 | 0 |
| Moore | 2 | 7 | 4 | 0 |
| Hill | 1 | 0 | 0 | 0 |

**KICKOFF RETURNS**

| Last Name | No. | Yds | Avg | TD |
|---|---|---|---|---|
| Matte | 16 | 331 | 21 | 0 |
| Mackey | 9 | 271 | 30 | 0 |
| Harris | 8 | 198 | 25 | 0 |
| Logan | 8 | 170 | 21 | 0 |
| Lockett | 3 | 52 | 17 | 0 |
| Hill | 2 | 32 | 16 | 0 |
| Gilburg | 3 | 29 | 10 | 0 |
| Richardson | 1 | 16 | 16 | 0 |
| Parker | 1 | 15 | 15 | 0 |
| Bielski | 1 | 0 | 0 | 0 |

**PASSING — PUNTING — KICKING**

| PASSING | Att | Comp | % | Yds | Yd/Att | TD | Int— | % | RK |
|---|---|---|---|---|---|---|---|---|---|
| Unitas | 410 | 237 | 58 | 3481 | 8.5 | 20 | 12— | 3 | 2 |
| Cuozzo | 17 | 10 | 59 | 104 | 6.1 | 0 | 0— | 0 | |
| Matte | 5 | 1 | 20 | 20 | 4.0 | 0 | 0— | 0 | |

| PUNTING | No | Avg |
|---|---|---|
| Gilburg | 52 | 41.8 |
| Logan | 4 | 30.3 |

| KICKING | XP | Att | % | FG | Att | % |
|---|---|---|---|---|---|---|
| Martin | 32 | 35 | 91 | 24 | 39 | 62 |

**WESTERN CONFERENCE — Continued**

## DETROIT LIONS 5-8-1 George Wilson

**Scores of Each Game**

| | | |
|---|---|---|
| 23 | Los Angeles | 2 |
| 10 | Green Bay | 31 |
| 21 | CHICAGO | 37 |
| 26 | SAN FRANCISCO | 3 |
| 14 | Dallas | 17 |
| 21 | BALTIMORE | 25 |
| 28 | MINNESOTA | 10 |
| 45 | San Francisco | 7 |
| 21 | Baltimore | 24 |
| 21 | LOS ANGELES | 28 |
| 31 | Minnesota | 34 |
| 13 | GREEN BAY | 13 |
| 38 | CLEVELAND | 10 |
| 14 | Chicago | 24 |

| Use Name | Pos. | Hgt | Wgt | Age | Int | Pts |
|---|---|---|---|---|---|---|
| Daryl Sanders | OT | 6'5" | 240 | 21 | | |
| Lucien Reeberg | OT | 6'4" | 308 | 22 | | |
| Dan LaRose | OG-OT | 6'5" | 250 | 23 | | |
| John Gordy | OG | 6'3" | 250 | 27 | | |
| John Gonzaga | OT-OG | 6'3" | 250 | 30 | | |
| Bob Whitlow | C | 6'1" | 236 | 27 | | |
| Bob Scholtz | OT-C | 6'4" | 250 | 25 | | |
| Darris McCord | DE | 6'4" | 250 | 30 | 1 | 6 |
| Sam Williams | DE | 6'5" | 235 | 32 | | |
| Jim Simon | LB-DE | 6'5" | 225 | 22 | | |
| Roger Brown | DT | 6'5" | 300 | 26 | 1 | |
| Mike Bundra | DT | 6'3" | 260 | 24 | | |
| Floyd Peters | DT | 6'4" | 255 | 28 | | |

Alex Karras — Suspended by commissioner

| Use Name | Pos. | Hgt | Wgt | Age | Int | Pts |
|---|---|---|---|---|---|---|
| Carl Brettschneider | LB | 6'1" | 225 | 31 | | |
| Ernie Clark | LB | 6'1" | 220 | 25 | | |
| Dennis Gaubetz | LB | 6'2" | 205 | 22 | 1 | |
| Monte Lee | LB | 6'4" | 220 | 25 | | |
| Max Messner | LB | 6'3" | 225 | 25 | | |
| Joe Schmidt | LB | 6'1" | 220 | 31 | | |
| Wayne Walker | LB | 6'2" | 225 | 26 | 1 | 56 |
| Larry Vargo | OE-LB | 6'3" | 215 | 23 | 1 | 6 |
| Night Train Lane | DB | 6'1" | 200 | 35 | 5 | |
| Dick LeBeau | DB | 6'1" | 185 | 26 | 5 | 6 |
| Gary Lowe | DB | 5'11" | 195 | 29 | 2 | |
| Bruce Maher | DB | 5'11" | 190 | 26 | 1 | 2 |
| Dick Compton | HB-DB | 6'1" | 195 | 23 | 1 | |
| Yale Lary | DB | 6' | 190 | 32 | 2 | 6 |
| Tom Hall | OE-DB | 6'1" | 195 | 22 | 3 | 6 |

| Use Name | Pos. | Hgt | Wgt | Age | Int | Pts |
|---|---|---|---|---|---|---|
| Earl Morrall | QB | 6'1" | 206 | 29 | | 6 |
| Milt Plum | QB | 6'1" | 205 | 29 | | 16 |
| Hopalong Cassady | HB | 5'10" | 185 | 29 | | |
| Larry Ferguson | HB | 5'10" | 185 | 22 | | |
| Dan Lewis | HB | 6'1" | 200 | 27 | | 12 |
| Tom Watkins | HB | 6'1" | 195 | 26 | | 24 |
| Nick Pietrosante | FB | 6'2" | 225 | 26 | | 30 |
| Nick Ryder | FB | 6' | 205 | 22 | | 6 |
| Ollie Matson | HB-FB | 6'2" | 210 | 33 | | |
| Terry Barr | FL | 6' | 190 | 28 | | 78 |
| Gail Cogdill | OE | 6'2" | 195 | 26 | | 60 |
| Jim Gibbons | OE | 6'2" | 220 | 27 | | 6 |
| Al Greer | OE | 6'4" | 190 | 24 | | |

Pat Studstill — Injury

## MINNESOTA VIKINGS 5-8-1 Norm Van Brocklin

**Scores of Each Game**

| | | |
|---|---|---|
| 24 | San Francisco | 20 |
| 7 | CHICAGO | 28 |
| 45 | SAN FRANCISCO | 14 |
| 14 | ST. LOUIS | 56 |
| 28 | GREEN BAY | 37 |
| 24 | Los Angeles | 27 |
| 10 | Detroit | 28 |
| 21 | LOS ANGELES | 13 |
| 7 | Green Bay | 28 |
| 34 | BALTIMORE | 37 |
| 34 | DETROIT | 31 |
| 17 | Chicago | 17 |
| 10 | Baltimore | 41 |
| 34 | Philadelphia | 13 |

| Use Name | Pos. | Hgt | Wgt | Age | Int | Pts |
|---|---|---|---|---|---|---|
| Grady Alderman | OT | 6'2" | 245 | 24 | | |
| Errol Linden | OT | 6'5" | 260 | 25 | | |
| Jim Battle | OG | 6'1" | 240 | 25 | | |
| Larry Bowie | OG | 6'2" | 245 | 23 | | |
| Jerry Huth | OG | 6' | 228 | 30 | | |
| Dave O'Brien | OG | 6'3" | 235 | 23 | | |
| Mick Tingelhoff | C | 6'1" | 235 | 23 | | |
| Bob Denton | DE | 6'4" | 240 | 29 | | |
| Don Hultz | DE | 6'3" | 220 | 22 | 1 | 6 |
| Jim Marshall | DE | 6'3" | 235 | 25 | | 6 |
| Paul Dickson | DT | 6'5" | 255 | 26 | | |
| Jim Prestel | DT | 6'5" | 260 | 26 | | |
| Pat Russ | DT | 6'4" | 255 | 23 | | |

| Use Name | Pos. | Hgt | Wgt | Age | Int | Pts |
|---|---|---|---|---|---|---|
| John Campbell | LB | 6'3" | 215 | 24 | | |
| Rip Hawkins | LB | 6'3" | 230 | 24 | 1 | |
| Bill Jobko | LB | 6'2" | 220 | 27 | | |
| Steve Stonebreaker | LB | 6'3" | 220 | 25 | | |
| Roy Winston | LB | 6'1" | 225 | 23 | 1 | 6 |
| Lee Calland | DB | 6' | 190 | 22 | | |
| Terry Dillon | DB | 6' | 193 | 22 | | |
| Tom Franckhauser | DB | 6' | 196 | 26 | 2 | |
| Karl Kassulke | DB | 6' | 193 | 21 | | |
| Terry Kosens | DB | 6'3" | 195 | 21 | | |
| Chuck Lamson | DB | 6' | 185 | 24 | 1 | |
| Ed Sharockman | DB | 6' | 200 | 23 | 5 | 6 |

| Use Name | Pos. | Hgt | Wgt | Age | Int | Pts |
|---|---|---|---|---|---|---|
| Fran Tarkenton | QB | 6'1" | 190 | 23 | | 6 |
| Ron Vander Kelen | QB | 6'1" | 185 | 23 | | |
| Bill Butler | HB | 5'10" | 194 | 26 | | 6 |
| Tommy Mason | HB | 6' | 196 | 24 | | 54 |
| Bob Reed | HB | 5'11" | 187 | 23 | | |
| Tom Wilson | HB | 6' | 204 | 30 | | 24 |
| Bill Brown | FB | 5'11" | 218 | 25 | | 48 |
| Jim Boylan | FL | 6'1" | 185 | 24 | | 6 |
| Leon Clarke | FL | 6'4" | 235 | 30 | | |
| Ray Poage | FL | 6'4" | 203 | 22 | | 12 |
| Paul Flatley | OE | 6'1" | 187 | 22 | | 24 |
| Jerry Reichow | OE | 6'2" | 220 | 28 | | 18 |
| Gordon Smith | OE | 6'2" | 215 | 24 | | 12 |
| Fred Cox | K | 5'10" | 205 | 24 | | 75 |

## LOS ANGELES RAMS 5-9-0 Harland Svare

**Scores of Each Game**

| | | |
|---|---|---|
| 2 | DETROIT | 23 |
| 14 | WASHINGTON | 37 |
| 6 | Cleveland | 20 |
| 10 | Green Bay | 42 |
| 14 | CHICAGO | 52 |
| 27 | MINNESOTA | 24 |
| 28 | SAN FRANCISCO | 21 |
| 13 | Minnesota | 21 |
| 0 | Chicago | 6 |
| 28 | Detroit | 21 |
| 17 | BALTIMORE | 16 |
| 21 | San Francisco | 21 |
| 14 | GREEN BAY | 31 |
| 16 | Baltimore | 19 |

| Use Name | Pos. | Hgt | Wgt | Age | Int | Pts |
|---|---|---|---|---|---|---|
| Jim Baeke | OT | 6'5" | 245 | 24 | | |
| Joe Carollo | OT | 6'2" | 260 | 23 | | |
| Frank Varrichione | OT | 6'1" | 237 | 31 | | |
| Don Chuy | OG | 6'1" | 255 | 22 | | |
| Charley Cowan | OG | 6'4" | 255 | 25 | | |
| Joe Scibelli | OG | 6'1" | 250 | 24 | | |
| Harley Sewell | OG | 6'1" | 230 | 32 | | |
| Larry Hayes | C | 6'3" | 230 | 28 | | |
| Art Hunter | C | 6'4" | 248 | 30 | | |
| Stan Fanning | DE | 6'6" | 270 | 25 | | |
| Deacon Jones | DE | 6'5" | 250 | 24 | 1 | |
| Lamar Lundy | DE | 6'7" | 235 | 28 | | |
| Rosey Grier | DT | 6'5" | 290 | 30 | | |
| Merlin Olsen | DT | 6'5" | 265 | 22 | | |

| Use Name | Pos. | Hgt | Wgt | Age | Int | Pts |
|---|---|---|---|---|---|---|
| Mike Henry | LB | 6'2" | 220 | 27 | 5 | |
| Cliff Livingston | LB | 6'3" | 215 | 33 | 1 | |
| Jack Pardee | LB | 6'2" | 225 | 27 | 2 | |
| Bill Swain | LB | 6'2" | 228 | 22 | | |
| Ken Kirk | C-LB | 6'2" | 225 | 25 | | |
| Charley Britt | DB | 6'2" | 185 | 25 | 1 | |
| Lindon Crow | DB | 6' | 200 | 30 | 2 | |
| John Griffin | DB | 6'1" | 190 | 23 | | |
| Alvin Hall | DB | 6' | 198 | 30 | | |
| Bobby Smith | DB | 6' | 190 | 25 | 2 | |
| Nat Whitmyer | DB | 6' | 183 | 22 | 1 | |
| Ed Meador | DB | 5'11" | 193 | 26 | 6 | |
| Carver Shannon | HB-DB | 6'1" | 198 | 25 | | 6 |

| Use Name | Pos. | Hgt | Wgt | Age | Int | Pts |
|---|---|---|---|---|---|---|
| Terry Baker | QB | 6'3" | 195 | 22 | | |
| Zeke Bratkowski (to GB) | QB | 6'2" | 203 | 31 | | |
| Roman Gabriel | QB | 6'4" | 255 | 23 | | 18 |
| Jon Arnett | HB | 5'11" | 194 | 28 | | 12 |
| Pervis Atkins | HB | 6'1" | 195 | 27 | | 6 |
| Dick Bass | HB | 5'10" | 200 | 26 | | 30 |
| Art Perkins | FB | 6' | 225 | 23 | | 24 |
| Ben Wilson | FB | 6' | 225 | 23 | | 12 |
| Jim Phillips | FL | 6'1" | 198 | 26 | | |
| John Adams | OE | 6'3" | 235 | 26 | | |
| Duane Allen | OE | 6'4" | 225 | 25 | | |
| Carroll Dale | OE | 6'1" | 195 | 25 | | 42 |
| Marlin McKeever | OE | 6'1" | 235 | 23 | | |
| Danny Villanueva | K | 5'11" | 200 | 25 | | 52 |

## SAN FRANCISCO FORTY NINERS 2-12-0 Red Hickey Jack Christiansen

**Scores of Each Game**

| | | |
|---|---|---|
| 20 | MINNESOTA | 24 |
| 14 | BALTIMORE | 20 |
| 14 | Minnesota | 45 |
| 3 | Detroit | 26 |
| 3 | Baltimore | 20 |
| 20 | CHICAGO | 14 |
| 21 | Los Angeles | 28 |
| 7 | DETROIT | 45 |
| 31 | DALLAS | 24 |
| 10 | New York | 48 |
| 14 | Green Bay | 28 |
| 17 | LOS ANGELES | 21 |
| 7 | Chicago | 27 |
| 17 | GREEN BAY | 21 |

| Use Name | Pos. | Hgt | Wgt | Age | Int | Pts |
|---|---|---|---|---|---|---|
| Clyde Brock (from DAL) | OT | 6'5" | 268 | 23 | | |
| Len Rohde | OT | 6'4" | 240 | 25 | | |
| Bob St. Clair | OT | 6'5" | 265 | 32 | | |
| Leon Donahue | OG | 6'4" | 245 | 24 | | |
| Mike Magac | OG | 6'3" | 240 | 25 | | |
| John Thomas | OG | 6'4" | 246 | 28 | | |
| Bruce Bosley | OG-C | 6'2" | 240 | 29 | | |
| Karl Rubke | DE-C | 6'4" | 240 | 27 | | |
| Clark Miller | DE | 6'5" | 245 | 24 | | |
| Dan Colchico | DE | 6'4" | 236 | 26 | | |
| Roland Lakes | DT-DE | 6'4" | 273 | 23 | | |
| Charlie Krueger | DT | 6'4" | 245 | 27 | | |
| Leo Nomellini | DT | 6'3" | 262 | 38 | | |
| Walt Rock | DT | 6'5" | 240 | 22 | | |
| Chuck Sieminski | DT | 6'4" | 245 | 23 | | |
| Roy Williams | DT | 6'7" | 265 | 25 | | |

| Use Name | Pos. | Hgt | Wgt | Age | Int | Pts |
|---|---|---|---|---|---|---|
| Bill Cooper | LB | 6'1" | 215 | 24 | | |
| Mike Dowdle | LB | 6'3" | 237 | 25 | 2 | |
| Matt Hazeltine | LB | 6'1" | 220 | 30 | | |
| Ed Pine | LB | 6'4" | 230 | 23 | 1 | |
| Kermit Alexander | DB | 5'11" | 186 | 22 | 5 | |
| Elbert Kimbrough | DB | 5'11" | 190 | 24 | 1 | |
| Howie Williams (from GB) | DB | 6'2" | 190 | 26 | | |
| Abe Woodson | DB | 5'11" | 188 | 28 | 3 | 18 |
| Jim Johnson | FL-HB | 6'2" | 190 | 25 | 2 | |

Billy Kilmer — Broken Leg
Jerry Mertens — Knee Injury
Dave Baker — Military Service

| Use Name | Pos. | Hgt | Wgt | Age | Int | Pts |
|---|---|---|---|---|---|---|
| John Brodie | QB | 6'1" | 186 | 28 | | |
| Lamar McHan (from BAL) | QB | 6'1" | 205 | 31 | | |
| Bob Waters | QB | 6'2" | 184 | 25 | | |
| Don Lisbon | HB | 6' | 190 | 22 | | 12 |
| Dale Messer | HB | 5'10" | 175 | 26 | | |
| Jim Vollenweider | HB | 6'1" | 210 | 23 | | 12 |
| Mike Lind | FB | 6'2" | 215 | 23 | | |
| Joe Perry | FB | 6' | 200 | 36 | | |
| J. D. Smith | FB | 6'1" | 200 | 30 | | 36 |
| Lloyd Winston | FB | 6'2" | 215 | 23 | | 6 |
| Bernie Casey | FL | 6'4" | 215 | 24 | | 42 |
| Kay McFarland | FL | 6'2" | 180 | 24 | | 6 |
| Clyde Conner | OE | 6'2" | 190 | 30 | | |
| Gary Knafelc | OE | 6'4" | 220 | 31 | | 12 |
| Monte Stickles | OE | 6'4" | 230 | 25 | | |
| Tommy Davis | K | 6' | 212 | 28 | | 54 |

## WESTERN CONFERENCE—Continued

### DETROIT LIONS

**RUSHING**

| Last Name | No. | Yds | Avg | TD |
|---|---|---|---|---|
| Lewis | 133 | 528 | 4.0 | 2 |
| Watkins | 97 | 423 | 4.4 | 2 |
| Pietrosante | 112 | 418 | 3.7 | 5 |
| Morrall | 26 | 105 | 4.0 | 1 |
| Lary | 1 | 26 | 26.0 | 0 |
| Plum | 9 | 26 | 2.9 | 0 |
| Ryder | 10 | 23 | 2.3 | 1 |
| Ferguson | 13 | 23 | 1.8 | 0 |
| Matson | 13 | 20 | 1.5 | 0 |
| Barr | 1 | 9 | 9.0 | 0 |

**RECEIVING**

| Last Name | No. | Yds | Avg | TD |
|---|---|---|---|---|
| Barr | 66 | 1086 | 16 | 13 |
| Cogdill | 48 | 945 | 20 | 10 |
| Gibbons | 32 | 412 | 13 | 1 |
| Pietrosante | 16 | 173 | 11 | 0 |
| Watkins | 16 | 168 | 11 | 1 |
| Lewis | 15 | 115 | 8 | 0 |
| Hall | 3 | 29 | 10 | 1 |
| Compton | 2 | 41 | 21 | 0 |
| Matson | 2 | 20 | 10 | 0 |
| Ferguson | 2 | 8 | 4 | 0 |

**PUNT RETURNS**

| Last Name | No. | Yds | Avg | TD |
|---|---|---|---|---|
| Watkins | 32 | 399 | 12 | 1 |
| Ferguson | 11 | 108 | 10 | 0 |
| Hall | 10 | 107 | 11 | 0 |
| Compton | 2 | 11 | 6 | 0 |
| Cassady | 1 | 7 | 7 | 0 |
| Maher | 1 | 3 | 3 | 0 |

**KICKOFF RETURNS**

| Last Name | No. | Yds | Avg | TD |
|---|---|---|---|---|
| Watkins | 21 | 447 | 21 | 0 |
| Ferguson | 9 | 231 | 26 | 0 |
| Hall | 6 | 143 | 24 | 0 |
| Matson | 3 | 61 | 20 | 0 |
| Ryder | 3 | 33 | 11 | 0 |
| Clark | 1 | 13 | 13 | 0 |
| Compton | 1 | 13 | 13 | 0 |
| Vargo | 1 | 8 | 8 | 0 |

**PASSING – PUNTING – KICKING** Statistics

PASSING
| Last Name | Att | Comp | % | Yds | Yd/Att | TD | Int– | % | RK |
|---|---|---|---|---|---|---|---|---|---|
| Morrall | 328 | 174 | 53 | 2621 | 8.0 | 24 | 14– | 4 | 3 |
| Plum | 77 | 27 | 35 | 339 | 4.4 | 2 | 12– | 16 | |
| Pietrosante | 1 | 1 | 100 | 37 | 37.0 | 0 | 0– | 0 | |

PUNTING
| Last Name | No | Avg |
|---|---|---|
| Lary | 35 | 48.9 |
| Morrall | 29 | 39.4 |
| Compton | 2 | 42.5 |

KICKING
| Last Name | XP | Att | % | FG | Att | % |
|---|---|---|---|---|---|---|
| Walker | 29 | 29 | 100 | 9 | 22 | 41 |
| Plum | 13 | 13 | 100 | 1 | 4 | 25 |

### MINNESOTA VIKINGS

**RUSHING**

| Last Name | No. | Yds | Avg | TD |
|---|---|---|---|---|
| Mason | 166 | 763 | 4.6 | 7 |
| Brown | 128 | 445 | 3.5 | 5 |
| Wilson | 73 | 282 | 3.9 | 4 |
| Tarkenton | 28 | 162 | 5.8 | 1 |
| Reed | 21 | 88 | 4.2 | 0 |
| Vander Kelen | 8 | 65 | 8.1 | 0 |
| Butler | 17 | 48 | 2.8 | 0 |
| Reichow | 1 | –12 | –12.0 | 0 |

**RECEIVING**

| Last Name | No. | Yds | Avg | TD |
|---|---|---|---|---|
| Flatley | 51 | 867 | 17 | 4 |
| Mason | 40 | 365 | 9 | 2 |
| Reichow | 35 | 479 | 14 | 3 |
| Brown | 17 | 109 | 6 | 2 |
| Poage | 15 | 354 | 24 | 2 |
| Reed | 13 | 137 | 11 | 0 |
| Wilson | 7 | 48 | 7 | 0 |
| Smith | 6 | 177 | 30 | 2 |
| Boylan | 6 | 78 | 13 | 1 |
| Butler | 4 | 39 | 10 | 0 |
| Clarke | 3 | 34 | 11 | 0 |

**PUNT RETURNS**

| Last Name | No. | Yds | Avg | TD |
|---|---|---|---|---|
| Butler | 21 | 220 | 10 | 0 |
| Reed | 9 | 91 | 10 | 0 |
| Mason | 4 | 63 | 16 | 0 |
| Kassulke | 1 | 31 | 31 | 0 |

**KICKOFF RETURNS**

| Last Name | No. | Yds | Avg | TD |
|---|---|---|---|---|
| Butler | 33 | 713 | 22 | 0 |
| Reed | 13 | 367 | 28 | 0 |
| Sharockman | 7 | 139 | 20 | 0 |
| Brown | 3 | 105 | 35 | 1 |
| Franckhauser | 4 | 94 | 24 | 0 |
| Mason | 3 | 61 | 20 | 0 |
| Calland | 2 | 45 | 23 | 0 |
| Smith | 2 | 24 | 12 | 0 |
| Campbell | 1 | 8 | 8 | 0 |
| Bowie | 1 | 0 | 0 | 0 |

**PASSING – PUNTING – KICKING**

PASSING
| Last Name | Att | Comp | % | Yds | Yd/Att | TD | Int– | % | RK |
|---|---|---|---|---|---|---|---|---|---|
| Tarkenton | 297 | 170 | 57 | 2311 | 7.8 | 15 | 15– | 5 | 6 |
| Vander Kelen | 58 | 27 | 47 | 376 | 6.5 | 1 | 2– | 3 | |

PUNTING
| Last Name | No | Avg |
|---|---|---|
| Cox | 70 | 38.7 |

KICKING
| Last Name | XP | Att | % | FG | Att | % |
|---|---|---|---|---|---|---|
| Cox | 39 | 39 | 100 | 12 | 24 | 50 |

### LOS ANGELES RAMS

**RUSHING**

| Last Name | No. | Yds | Avg | TD |
|---|---|---|---|---|
| Bass | 143 | 520 | 3.6 | 5 |
| Wilson | 109 | 394 | 3.6 | 1 |
| Arnett | 58 | 208 | 3.6 | 1 |
| Gabriel | 39 | 132 | 3.4 | 3 |
| Perkins | 37 | 70 | 1.9 | 4 |
| Baker | 9 | 46 | 5.1 | 0 |
| Dale | 1 | 12 | 12.0 | 0 |
| Atkins | 5 | 11 | 2.2 | 0 |
| Meador | 1 | 1 | 1.0 | 0 |
| Bratkowski | 4 | –3 | –0.8 | 0 |

**RECEIVING**

| Last Name | No. | Yds | Avg | TD |
|---|---|---|---|---|
| Phillips | 54 | 793 | 15 | 1 |
| Dale | 34 | 638 | 19 | 7 |
| Bass | 30 | 348 | 12 | 0 |
| Arnett | 15 | 119 | 8 | 1 |
| Atkins | 14 | 174 | 12 | 1 |
| McKeever | 11 | 152 | 14 | 0 |
| Wilson | 9 | 173 | 19 | 1 |
| Adams | 9 | 93 | 10 | 0 |
| Perkins | 8 | 61 | 8 | 0 |
| Shannon | 2 | 7 | 4 | 0 |

**PUNT RETURNS**

| Last Name | No. | Yds | Avg | TD |
|---|---|---|---|---|
| Shannon | 15 | 132 | 9 | 0 |
| Atkins | 12 | 36 | 3 | 0 |
| Smith | 2 | 20 | 10 | 0 |
| Bass | 1 | 11 | 11 | 0 |
| Arnett | 1 | 7 | 7 | 0 |

**KICKOFF RETURNS**

| Last Name | No. | Yds | Avg | TD |
|---|---|---|---|---|
| Shannon | 28 | 823 | 29 | 1 |
| Atkins | 19 | 429 | 23 | 0 |
| Arnett | 12 | 279 | 23 | 0 |
| Whitmyer | 3 | 80 | 27 | 0 |
| Wilson | 1 | 17 | 17 | 0 |
| Perkins | 1 | 15 | 15 | 0 |
| McKeever | 2 | 8 | 4 | 0 |
| Cowan | 2 | 0 | 0 | 0 |
| Hall | 1 | 0 | 0 | 0 |
| Olsen | 1 | 0 | 0 | 0 |

**PASSING – PUNTING – KICKING**

PASSING
| Last Name | Att | Comp | % | Yds | Yd/Att | TD | Int– | % | RK |
|---|---|---|---|---|---|---|---|---|---|
| Gabriel | 281 | 130 | 46 | 1947 | 6.9 | 8 | 11– | 4 | 13 |
| Bratkowski | 93 | 49 | 53 | 567 | 6.1 | 4 | 9– | 10 | |
| Baker | 19 | 11 | 58 | 140 | 7.4 | 0 | 4– | 21 | |
| Arnett | 1 | 0 | 0 | 0 | 0.0 | 0 | 1– | 100 | |
| Bass | 1 | 0 | 0 | 0 | 0.0 | 0 | 0– | 0 | |

PUNTING
| Last Name | No | Avg |
|---|---|---|
| Villanueva | 81 | 45.4 |
| Adams | 4 | 30.3 |

KICKING
| Last Name | XP | Att | % | FG | Att | % |
|---|---|---|---|---|---|---|
| Villanueva | 25 | 26 | 96 | 9 | 17 | 53 |

### SAN FRANCISCO FORTY NINERS

**RUSHING**

| Last Name | No. | Yds | Avg | TD |
|---|---|---|---|---|
| Smith | 162 | 560 | 3.5 | 5 |
| Lisbon | 109 | 399 | 3.7 | 4 |
| Winston | 27 | 127 | 4.7 | 1 |
| Vollenweider | 47 | 124 | 2.6 | 2 |
| Perry | 24 | 98 | 4.1 | 0 |
| Brodie | 7 | 63 | 9.0 | 0 |
| McHan | 17 | 59 | 3.5 | 0 |
| Lind | 8 | 26 | 3.3 | 0 |
| Waters | 5 | –2 | –0.4 | 0 |

**RECEIVING**

| Last Name | No. | Yds | Avg | TD |
|---|---|---|---|---|
| Casey | 47 | 762 | 16 | 7 |
| Lisbon | 21 | 259 | 12 | 2 |
| Knafelc | 18 | 221 | 12 | 2 |
| Smith | 17 | 196 | 12 | 1 |
| Conner | 16 | 247 | 15 | 0 |
| Stickles | 11 | 152 | 14 | 0 |
| McFarland | 11 | 126 | 11 | 1 |
| Johnson | 6 | 63 | 11 | 0 |
| Perry | 4 | 12 | 3 | 0 |
| Lind | 2 | 13 | 7 | 0 |
| Winston | 2 | 13 | 7 | 0 |
| Vollenweider | 1 | 26 | 26 | 0 |

**PUNT RETURNS**

| Last Name | No. | Yds | Avg | TD |
|---|---|---|---|---|
| Woodson | 13 | 95 | 7 | 0 |
| Messer | 5 | 4 | 1 | 0 |

**KICKOFF RETURNS**

| Last Name | No. | Yds | Avg | TD |
|---|---|---|---|---|
| Woodson | 29 | 935 | 32 | 3 |
| Alexander | 24 | 638 | 27 | 0 |
| Vollenweider | 4 | 75 | 19 | 0 |
| Cooper | 2 | 8 | 4 | 0 |
| St. Clair | 2 | 3 | 2 | 0 |
| Stickles | 1 | 0 | 0 | 0 |

**PASSING – PUNTING – KICKING**

PASSING
| Last Name | Att | Comp | % | Yds | Yd/Att | TD | Int– | % | RK |
|---|---|---|---|---|---|---|---|---|---|
| McHan | 196 | 83 | 42 | 1243 | 6.3 | 8 | 11– | 6 | 15 |
| Waters | 88 | 42 | 48 | 435 | 4.9 | 1 | 6– | 7 | |
| Brodie | 61 | 30 | 49 | 367 | 6.0 | 3 | 4– | 7 | |
| Lisbon | 2 | 1 | 50 | 45 | 22.5 | 1 | 0– | 0 | |
| Davis | 1 | 0 | 0 | 0 | 0.0 | 0 | 0– | 0 | |
| Perry | 1 | 0 | 0 | 0 | 0.0 | 0 | 0– | 0 | |
| Vollenweider | 1 | 0 | 0 | 0 | 0.0 | 0 | 1– | 100 | |

PUNTING
| Last Name | No | Avg |
|---|---|---|
| Davis | 73 | 45.4 |

KICKING
| Last Name | XP | Att | % | FG | Att | % |
|---|---|---|---|---|---|---|
| Davis | 24 | 24 | 100 | 10 | 31 | 32 |

# 1963 A.F.L. Approaching Pay Dirt

Three AFL franchises found secure footing this season after three years of tenuous existence. The Dallas Texans, the 1962 league champions, defended their title as the Kansas City Chiefs, as owner Lamar Hunt tired of losing money and playing second banana to the Cowboys in Dallas. With an attractive young team, the Chiefs sold 15,000 season tickets and made money in their first season in the Midwest. On the East Coast, the New York Titans became the New York Jets and left behind the laughable image of the Harry Wismer years. New owner Sonny Werblin and new coach Weeb Ewbank could not immediately produce a winning club, but they did give the AFL a major-league operation in New York. On the West Coast, young Al Davis took charge of the Oakland Raiders and built them from doormats into an exciting club that barely missed a divisional crown. All three of these clubs enjoyed big increases in attendance, and each of them would use their new revenues to sign top rookies for next year—a cycle that could only lead upward for the league.

## EASTERN DIVISION

**Boston Patriots**—When the television coverage of the Eastern Division playoff between the Patriots and Bills began, viewers saw not players warming up but bulldozers scraping Buffalo's War Memorial Stadium clear of snow. The Patriots had made it to this frigid showdown with a solid defense, a scrappy offense, and a clutch field-goal kicker in Gino Cappelletti. Larry Eisenhauer, Houston Antwine, and Tom Addison steadied the defense, while middle linebacker Nick Buoniconti added the spice with his frequent blitzes. Don Webb, the team's best defensive back, sat out the whole season on the disabled list, but his platoon covered for him better than the offense covered for Ron Burton. With Burton sidelined for the entire schedule with a bad back, the Patriot attack lost most of its speed. But the collapse of the Oilers, the reorganization of the Jets, and the poor start by the Bills kept the Patriots in the divisional race all season. The Patriots and Bills finished in a tie for first place, and in the winter cold of Buffalo the Patriots' old pros won the title 26-8.

**Buffalo Bills**—Favored by many experts to win the Eastern Division, the Bills fell flat on their face in September. Their first four games netted them three losses and a tie, dropping them into last place before they finally jelled in the month of October. Showing an ability to win close games, the Bills then took seven of their last ten games to catch Boston in a tie for the Eastern title. Quarterback Jack Kemp hit Elbert Dubenion and Bill Miller with pinpoint passes, while Cookie Gilchrist carried the running chores without much help from the halfbacks. The two leading halfbacks were knocked out with hurts, Wray Carolton with a groin injury and Roger Kochman with a leg injury that ended his career after only eight professional games. Gilchrist kept plowing ahead despite little injuries, and he set a new record of 243 yards rushing in one game, on December 8 against New York. The defense was strong up front but vulnerable in the backfield.

**Houston Oilers**—After three years atop the Eastern Division, the Oilers learned the hard reality of how the other half lives by falling to third place. The defending champs lost their last four straight and five of their last six games, looking more often like a routed army than like a respected football team. Injuries took a hand in the collapse, as a bad back forced tackle Al Jamison into retirement, a pulled thigh muscle kept halfback Billy Cannon on the bench most of the season, and a broken jaw sidelined defensive end Don Floyd for half the schedule. Without Jamison and Cannon, the Houston pass blocking was atrocious, subjecting thirty-six-year-old George Blanda to a rush unfit for a man his age. Cannon's absence also put the whole rushing load on fullback Charley Tolar, who got little help from rookie halfback Bill Tobin. The defense put up no pass rush without Floyd, leaving enemy passers free to spot their receivers in leisure. With all their wounded, the Oilers still managed to stay in the Eastern race until the Patriots demolished them 45-3 on November 1.

**New York Jets**—New general manager and head coach Weeb Ewbank completely overhauled the team, shuffling players in and out of the pre-season training camp in a steady flow. Looking to shore up the barren New York roster, Ewbank signed free agents cut loose by NFL teams. He especially pounced on players cut from his old Baltimore team, picking up from this source Dee Mackey, Mark Smolinski, Bake Turner, Dave Yohn, and rookies Winston Hill and Bill Baird. For a quarterback, Ewbank discovered Dick Wood, a strong-armed young passer cut loose most recently by the Denver Broncos. Although Wood could throw perfect long passes, his bad knees made him totally immobile, so Ewbank tailored his blocking solely to protect his passer. Billy Mathis and Mark Smolinski won starting backfield jobs on their ability to block, and the offensive line, led by 297-pound Sherman Plunkett, shielded Wood from most enemy interference.

## WESTERN DIVISION

**San Diego Chargers**—In winning their third Western title in four years, the Chargers fielded a backfield as exciting as any in pro football. They had a good veteran quarterback in Tobin Rote, back in the United States after three seasons in the Canadian League, and a good young quarterback in John Hadl. For runners they had Paul Lowe and Keith Lincoln, both quick, slashing runners who could get through the smallest openings in the line. The flanker was Lance Alworth, who came back from an injury-plagued rookie season to tantalize crowds with his leaping grabs and streaking deep patterns. With these talents operating behind a solid line, the San Diego offense put more points on the board than any other attack in the league, but coach Sid Gillman's riches did not end there. The defense also was both colorful and efficient, with Earl Faison, Ernie Ladd, Chuck Allen, and Dick Harris the stars of the unit. Avoiding the string of injuries that ruined the past season, the Chargers found their greatest challenge for the divisional crown not from the defending champion Kansas City team but instead from the surprising Oakland Raiders. Twice the Raiders beat the Chargers, pulling within one game of the top with a 41-27 victory with two weeks left in the season, but the Chargers won both their remaining contests to salt away the championship.

**Oakland Raiders**—Leaving a comfortable assistantship in San Diego to take over as head coach in Oakland, Al Davis blended holdovers from the disastrous 1962 season with free agents cut loose by other clubs and came up with an exciting team. Davis signed split end Art Powell, who had played out his option in New York, got Tom Flores back from illness, and coaxed several useful players away from other teams at a minimal cost. The offense relied on the passing of quarterbacks Flores and Cotton Davidson to receivers Powell and Bo Roberson and on the running of Clem Daniels to pile up points. Daniels combined speed and power to set a new AFL rushing record with 1,099 yards, and he was also a dangerous deep pass receiving threat coming out of the backfield. The defense had few recognizable names, but terrorized opponents with a dazzling array of blitzes. End Dalva Allen and rookie tackle Dave Costa anchored the forward wall, ex-Bill Archie Matsos starred at middle linebacker, and holdover backs Fred Williamson and Tom Morrow prospered in Davis' new setup. After starting out the season with two wins, the Raiders lost four straight games to Eastern opponents, but then the miracle began. Oakland started winning and never stopped, taking their last eight contests to finish one game behind the Chargers.

**Kansas City Chiefs**—A fatal injury to rookie Stone Johnson in a pre-season game started the Chiefs' season on a foreboding note and dampened the club's enthusiasm. After beating Denver 59-7 to open the season, the Chiefs then won only once in their next ten games. The defense, bolstered by rookies Buck Buchanan and Bobby Bell, stayed tough, but a breakdown in blocking short-circuited the offense. Enemy defenses constantly rushed quarterback Len Dawson with blitzes that his blockers could not pick up, and backs Curtis McClinton and Abner Haynes both fell off from their 1963 performances. Haynes, the AFL's first star, slipped so much that he was restricted to returning kicks for a time. The mid-season drought ended any hopes of repeating as Western champions, and the Chiefs hit the bottom when the New York Jets shut them out 17-0 in a November meeting in New York. After that point, however, the Chiefs put the abundant talent on their roster to full use as they won their last three games.

**Denver Broncos**—When the Broncos at last uncovered a major-league runner, their passing attack fell apart. The Broncos had always lived and died on the passing of Frank Tripuka, relying on the air game to overcome the lack of any ground attack. Rookie fullback Billy Joe gave the club its first running threat, someone who could break tackles and pick up vital first-down yardage, but Tripuka's arm was no longer up to the weekly strain. After two games, both of which the Broncos lost, Tripuka quit, leaving rookie Mickey Slaughter the only quarterback on the roster. Coach Jack Faulkner then signed ex-Viking John McCormick, and after only four days of practice with the team McCormick led the Broncs to a 14-0 victory over Boston. Next came a 50-34 ambushing of the San Diego Chargers, in which McCormick directed the Denver offense with the precision of a surgeon. With better days obviously on the way, the Broncos suffered a loss from which they never recovered when the Houston Oilers tore up McCormick's knee on the way to a 33-24 victory.

## FINAL TEAM STATISTICS
Note: Only offensive totals are available

| | BOSTON | BUFFALO | DENVER | HOUSTON | KANSAS CITY | NEW YORK | OAKLAND | SAN DIEGO |
|---|---|---|---|---|---|---|---|---|
| **FIRST DOWNS:** | | | | | | | | |
| by Rushing | 100 | 107 | 84 | 68 | 94 | 52 | 85 | 112 |
| by Passing | 107 | 147 | 133 | 169 | 141 | 121 | 142 | 124 |
| **RUSHING:** | | | | | | | | |
| Number | 437 | 455 | 384 | 341 | 400 | 306 | 359 | 395 |
| Yards | 1618 | 1838 | 1508 | 1209 | 1697 | 969 | 1595 | 2201 |
| Average Yards | 3.7 | 4.0 | 3.9 | 3.5 | 4.2 | 3.2 | 4.4 | 5.6 |
| Touchdowns | 17 | 21 | 10 | 11 | 12 | 8 | 11 | 20 |
| **PASSING:** | | | | | | | | |
| Attempts | 410 | 457 | 453 | 501 | 439 | 480 | 442 | 357 |
| Completions | 184 | 227 | 217 | 261 | 231 | 209 | 191 | 202 |
| Percentage | 44.9 | 49.7 | 47.9 | 52.1 | 52.6 | 43.5 | 43.2 | 56.6 |
| Net Yards | 2547 | 3057 | 2487 | 3210 | 2651 | 2530 | 2926 | 2950 |
| Touchdowns | 17 | 16 | 23 | 26 | 30 | 21 | 31 | 28 |
| Interceptions | 29 | 24 | 28 | 33 | 22 | 29 | 24 | 24 |
| Percent Intercepted | 7.1 | 5.3 | 6.2 | 6.6 | 5.0 | 6.0 | 5.4 | 6.7 |
| **PUNTING:** | | | | | | | | |
| Number | 75 | 62 | 81 | 65 | 62 | 72 | 76 | 61 |
| Average Distance | 38.4 | 40.2 | 44.3 | 42.9 | 43.1 | 42.1 | 39.5 | 37.9 |
| **PUNT RETURNS:** | | | | | | | | |
| Number | 40 | 37 | 30 | 36 | 26 | 17 | 36 | 22 |
| Yards | 373 | 316 | 387 | 339 | 259 | 202 | 395 | 261 |
| Average Yards | 9.3 | 8.5 | 12.9 | 9.4 | 10.0 | 11.9 | 11.0 | 11.9 |
| Touchdowns | 0 | 0 | 0 | 0 | 0 | 1 | 2 | 0 |
| **KICKOFF RETURNS:** | | | | | | | | |
| Number | 52 | 52 | 78 | 69 | 47 | 74 | 53 | 52 |
| Yards | 1109 | 1133 | 1801 | 1821 | 1172 | 1463 | 1008 | 1168 |
| Average Yards | 21.3 | 21.8 | 23.1 | 26.4 | 24.9 | 19.8 | 19.0 | 22.5 |
| Touchdowns | 0 | 0 | 1 | 0 | 1 | 0 | 0 | 0 |
| **INTERCEPTION RETURNS:** | | | | | | | | |
| Number | 30 | 22 | 15 | 36 | 26 | 21 | 35 | 29 |
| Yards | 662 | 156 | 170 | 453 | 450 | 284 | 389 | 316 |
| Average Yards | 22.1 | 7.1 | 11.3 | 12.6 | 17.3 | 13.5 | 11.1 | 10.9 |
| Touchdowns | 3 | 1 | 1 | 2 | 1 | 0 | 2 | 1 |
| **POINTS:** | | | | | | | | |
| Total | 327 | 304 | 301 | 302 | 347 | 249 | 363 | 399 |
| PAT (kick) Attempts | 36 | 37 | 35 | 39 | 44 | 30 | 47 | 48 |
| PAT (kick) Made | 35 | 32 | 35 | 39 | 43 | 30 | 47 | 44 |
| PAT (2–pt) Attempts | 1 | 2 | 1 | 0 | 1 | 2 | 1 | 2 |
| PAT (2–pt) Made | 0 | 2 | 1 | 0 | 1 | 0 | 0 | 2 |
| FG Attempts | 38 | 23 | 29 | 22 | 28 | 24 | 19 | 27 |
| FG Made | 22 | 10 | 16 | 9 | 8 | 9 | 8 | 17 |
| Percent FG Made | 57.9 | 43.5 | 55.2 | 40.9 | 28.6 | 37.5 | 42.1 | 63.0 |
| Safeties | 2 | 0 | 0 | 0 | 0 | 0 | 2 | 0 |

## 1963 AFL CHAMPIONSHIP GAME
January 5, at San Diego
(Attendance 30,127)

### Boston's Buttery Defense

In the fourth AFL championship game, San Diego's famous offense made mincemeat out of Boston's heralded defense. On the second play from scrimmage of the game, Keith Lincoln took a handoff and burst through the middle of the Boston defense for a 56-yard gain; Tobin Rote's quarterback sneak seven plays later gave San Diego a quick 7-0 lead. As soon as the Chargers got the ball back, Lincoln headed around end for a 67-yard touchdown run, making the score 14-0. The Patriots came back with a quick touchdown, but a 58-yard touchdown run by Paul Lowe, the third long run of the first quarter for the Chargers, made the score 21-7. George Blair and Gino Cappelletti exchanged field goals early in the second quarter, but Don Norton scored on a 14-yard pass play to give the Chargers a 31-10 lead at halftime. The Patriot attack got nowhere in the second half, as the San Diego line rushed quarterback Babe Parilli ferociously every time he dropped back to pass. The Chargers, however, kept adding points against the Boston defense. Lance Alworth, the Chargers' chief pass receiver, scored in the third period on a 48-yard pass from Rote, and Lincoln added his third touchdown on a 25-yard pass from reserve quarterback John Hadl in the fourth quarter. Hadl then scored on a one-yard plunge with less than two minutes remaining in the game, and George Blair's kick made the final score a lopsided 51-10. Although not even close, the game helped the AFL by showcasing an exciting offensive team in the Chargers, a direct contrast with the defense-oriented NFL champions, the Chicago Bears.

### SCORING

| | | | | |
|---|---|---|---|---|
| SAN DIEGO | 21 | 10 | 7 | 13–51 |
| BOSTON | 7 | 3 | 0 | 0–10 |

**First Quarter**
S.D.   Rote, 2 yard rush
       PAT—Blair (kick)
S.D.   Lincoln, 67 yard rush
       PAT—Blair (kick)
Bos.   Garron, 7 yard rush
       PAT—Cappelletti (kick)
S.D.   Lowe, 58 yard rush
       PAT—Blair (kick)

**Second Quarter**
S.D.   Blair, 11 yard field goal
Bos.   Cappelletti, 15 yard field goal
S.D.   Norton, 14 yard pass from Rote
       PAT—Blair (kick)

**Third Quarter**
S.D.   Alworth, 48 yard pass from Rote
       PAT—Blair (kick)

**Fourth Quarter**
S.D.   Lincoln, 25 yard pass from Hadl
       PAT—Pass (No Good)
S.D.   Hadl, 1 yard rush
       PAT—Blair (kick)

### TEAM STATISTICS

| S.D. | | BOS. |
|---|---|---|
| 21 | First Downs—Total | 14 |
| 11 | First Downs—Rushing | 6 |
| 9 | First Downs—Passing | 8 |
| 1 | First Downs—Penalty | 0 |
| 1 | Fumbles—Number | 1 |
| 1 | Fumbles—Lost Ball | 0 |
| 6 | Penalties—Number | 1 |
| 30 | Yards Penalized | 18 |
| 1 | Giveaways | 2 |
| 2 | Takeaways | 1 |
| +1 | Difference | −1 |

### INDIVIDUAL STATISTICS

**RUSHING**

| SAN DIEGO | No | Yds | Avg. | BOSTON | No | Yds | Avg. |
|---|---|---|---|---|---|---|---|
| Lincoln | 13 | 206 | 15.8 | Crump | 7 | 18 | 2.6 |
| Lowe | 12 | 94 | 7.8 | Garron | 3 | 15 | 5.0 |
| Rote | 4 | 15 | 3.8 | Lott | 3 | 15 | 5.0 |
| McDougall | 1 | 2 | 2.0 | Yewcic | 1 | 14 | 14.0 |
| Hadl | 1 | 1 | 1.0 | Parilli | 1 | 10 | 10.0 |
| Jackson | 1 | 0 | 0.0 | Burton | 1 | 3 | 3.0 |
| | 32 | 318 | 9.9 | | 16 | 75 | 4.7 |

**RECEIVING**

| SAN DIEGO | No | Yds | Avg. | BOSTON | No | Yds | Avg. |
|---|---|---|---|---|---|---|---|
| Lincoln | 7 | 123 | 17.6 | Burton | 4 | 12 | 3.0 |
| Alworth | 4 | 77 | 19.3 | Colclough | 3 | 26 | 8.7 |
| MacKinnon | 2 | 52 | 26.0 | Cappelletti | 2 | 72 | 36.0 |
| Norton | 2 | 44 | 22.0 | Graham | 2 | 68 | 34.0 |
| Kocourek | 1 | 5 | 5.0 | Crump | 2 | 28 | 14.0 |
| McDougall | 1 | 4 | 4.0 | Lott | 2 | 16 | 8.0 |
| | 17 | 305 | 17.9 | Garron | 2 | 6 | 3.0 |
| | | | | | 17 | 228 | 13.4 |

**PUNTING**

| SAN DIEGO | No | Yds | Avg. | BOSTON | No | Yds | Avg. |
|---|---|---|---|---|---|---|---|
| Maguire | 2 | | 43.5 | Yewcic | 7 | | 46.9 |

**KICKOFF RETURNS**

| SAN DIEGO | No | Yds | Avg. | BOSTON | No | Yds | Avg. |
|---|---|---|---|---|---|---|---|
| Alworth | 2 | 47 | 23.5 | Crump | 2 | 31 | 15.5 |
| Lowe | 1 | 23 | 23.0 | Burton | 2 | 27 | 13.5 |
| | 3 | 70 | 23.3 | Garron | 2 | 22 | 11.0 |
| | | | | Suci | 1 | 18 | 18.0 |
| | | | | Romeo | 1 | 9 | 9.0 |
| | | | | Yates | 1 | 5 | 5.0 |
| | | | | | 9 | 112 | 12.4 |

**INTERCEPTION RETURNS**

| SAN DIEGO | No | Yds | Avg. | BOSTON |
|---|---|---|---|---|
| Maguire | 1 | 10 | 10.0 | None |
| Mitinger | 1 | 5 | 5.0 | |
| | 2 | 15 | 7.5 | |

**PASSING**

| SAN DIEGO | Att. | Comp. | Comp. Pct. | Yds. | Int. | Yds/ Att. | Yds/ Comp. |
|---|---|---|---|---|---|---|---|
| Rote | 15 | 10 | 66.7 | 173 | 0 | 11.5 | 17.3 |
| Hadl | 10 | 6 | 60.0 | 112 | 0 | 11.2 | 18.7 |
| Lincoln | 1 | 1 | 100.0 | 20 | 0 | 20.0 | 20.0 |
| | 26 | 17 | 65.4 | 305 | 0 | 11.7 | 17.9 |
| **BOSTON** | | | | | | | |
| Parilli | 29 | 14 | 48.3 | 189 | 1 | 6.5 | 13.5 |
| Yewcic | 8 | 3 | 37.5 | 39 | 1 | 4.9 | 13.0 |
| | 37 | 17 | 45.9 | 228 | 2 | 6.2 | 13.4 |

| Scores of Each Game | | Use Name | Pos. | Hgt | Wgt | Age | Int | Pts |
|---|---|---|---|---|---|---|---|---|

**BOSTON PATRIOTS 7-6-1 Mike Holovak**

| | | | Use Name | Pos. | Hgt | Wgt | Age | Int | Pts |
|---|---|---|---|---|---|---|---|---|---|
| 38 | NEW YORK | 14 | Don Oakes | OT | 6'3" | 255 | 25 | | |
| 13 | San Diego | 17 | Bob Yates | OT | 6'3" | 230 | 24 | | |
| 20 | Oakland | 14 | Charley Long | OG | 6'3" | 250 | 25 | | |
| 10 | Denver | 14 | Billy Neighbors | OG | 5'11" | 240, | 23 | | |
| 24 | New York | 31 | Dave Watson | OG | 6'1" | 220 | 22 | | |
| 20 | OAKLAND | 14 | Walt Cudzik | C | 6'2" | 235 | 30 | | |
| 40 | DENVER | 21 | Bob Dee | DE | 6'3" | 240 | 30 | | |
| 21 | Buffalo | 28 | Larry Eisenhauer | DE | 6'5" | 245 | 23 | 1 | |
| 45 | HOUSTON | 3 | Jim Hunt | DE | 5'11" | 245 | 24 | 1 | 6 |
| 6 | SAN DIEGO | 7 | Houston Antwine | DT | 6' | 250 | 24 | | |
| 24 | KANSAS CITY | 24 | Jerry DeLucca (from BUF) | DT | 6'3" | 250 | 27 | | |
| 17 | BUFFALO | 7 | Milt Graham | DT | 6'6" | 235 | 29 | | |
| 46 | Houston | 28 | Bill Hudson | DT | 6'4" | 255 | 27 | | |
| 3 | Kansas City | 35 | Jess Richardson | DT | 6'2" | 265 | 33 | | |
| | **EAST Playoff** | | | | | | | | |
| 26 | Buffalo | 8 | | | | | | | |

| Use Name | Pos. | Hgt | Wgt | Age | Int | Pts |
|---|---|---|---|---|---|---|
| Tom Addison | LB | 6'3" | 230 | 27 | 4 | |
| Nick Buoniconti | LB | 5'11" | 220 | 22 | 3 | |
| Don McKinnon | LB | 6'3" | 215 | 21 | | |
| Jack Rudolph | LB | 6'3" | 230 | 25 | | |
| Dick Felt | DB | 6' | 185 | 30 | 3 | |
| Ron Hall | DB | 6' | 190 | 26 | 3 | |
| Ross O'Hanley | DB | 6' | 185 | 24 | 3 | |
| Chuck Shonta | DB | 6' | 200 | 25 | 3 | |
| Bob Suci | DB | 5'10" | 185 | 25 | 8 | 12 |
| Tom Stephens | OE-DB | 6'1" | 215 | 27 | 1 | |
| | | | | | | |
| Don Webb — Injury | | | | | | |

| Use Name | Pos. | Hgt | Wgt | Age | Int | Pts |
|---|---|---|---|---|---|---|
| Babe Parilli | QB | 6'1" | 190 | 33 | | 30 |
| Tom Yewcic | QB | 5'11" | 185 | 31 | | 6 |
| *Ron Burton | HB | 5'10" | 190 | 26 | | |
| Jim Crawford | HB | 6'1" | 200 | 27 | | 6 |
| Tom Neumann | HB | 5'11" | 205 | 22 | | 6 |
| Harry Crump | FB | 6' | 205 | 22 | | 30 |
| Larry Garron | FB | 6' | 215 | 26 | | 24 |
| Billy Lott | FB | 6' | 205 | 28 | | 24 |
| Jim Colclough | FL | 6' | 185 | 27 | | 18 |
| Gino Cappelletti | OE | 6' | 190 | 29 | | 113 |
| Art Graham | OE | 6'1" | 205 | 22 | | 30 |
| Tony Romeo | OE | 6'2" | 220 | 24 | | 18 |
| | | | | | | |
| *Played only in playoffs | | | | | | |

**BUFFALO BILLS 7-6-1 Lou Saban**

| | | | Use Name | Pos. | Hgt | Wgt | Age | Int | Pts |
|---|---|---|---|---|---|---|---|---|---|
| 10 | San Diego | 14 | Stew Barber | OT | 6'3" | 250 | 24 | | |
| 17 | Oakland | 35 | Dave Behrman | OT | 6'5" | 260 | 21 | | |
| 27 | KANSAS CITY | 27 | Ken Rice | OG-OT | 6'2" | 250 | 23 | | |
| 20 | HOUSTON | 31 | Tom Day | OG | 6'2" | 250 | 28 | | |
| 12 | OAKLAND | 0 | George Flint | OG | 6'4" | 246 | 25 | | |
| 35 | Kansas City | 26 | Dick Hudson | OG | 6'4" | 264 | 23 | | |
| 14 | Houston | 28 | Charlie Leo | OG | 6' | 240 | 28 | | |
| 28 | BOSTON | 21 | Billy Shaw | OG | 6'3" | 250 | 23 | | |
| 30 | Denver | 28 | Al Bemiller | C | 6'3" | 235 | 24 | | |
| 27 | DENVER | 17 | Ron McDole | DE | 6'3" | 250 | 23 | | |
| 13 | SAN DIEGO | 23 | Leroy Moore | DE | 6' | 232 | 27 | | |
| 7 | Boston | 17 | Mack Yoho | DE | 6'2" | 238 | 27 | 62 | |
| 45 | NEW YORK | 14 | Jim Dunaway | DT | 6'4" | 270 | 21 | | |
| 19 | New York | 10 | Tom Sestak | DT | 6'5" | 270 | 27 | | |
| | **EAST Playoff** | | Sid Youngelman | DT | 6'3" | 260 | 31 | | |
| 8 | BOSTON | 26 | | | | | | | |

| Use Name | Pos. | Hgt | Wgt | Age | Int | Pts |
|---|---|---|---|---|---|---|
| Harry Jacobs | LB | 6'2" | 230 | 26 | 1 | |
| Marv Matuszak | LB | 6'3" | 230 | 32 | | |
| Herb Paterra | LB | 6'1" | 222 | 22 | | |
| Mike Stratton | LB | 6'3" | 230 | 21 | 3 | 6 |
| John Tracey | LB | 6'3" | 225 | 30 | 5 | 2 |
| Ray Abruzzese | DB | 6'1" | 194 | 25 | 3 | |
| Carl Charon | DB | 5'10" | 194 | 22 | | 6 |
| Booker Edgerson | DB | 5'10" | 177 | 24 | 1 | |
| Henry Rivera | DB | 5'11" | 180 | 23 | | |
| Gene Sykes | DB | 6'1" | 200 | 22 | | |
| Willie West | DB | 5'10" | 193 | 25 | 5 | |
| George Saimes | HB-DB | 5'10" | 192 | 21 | 4 | |

| Use Name | Pos. | Hgt | Wgt | Age | Int | Pts |
|---|---|---|---|---|---|---|
| Jack Kemp | QB | 6'1" | 200 | 29 | | 48 |
| Daryle Lamonica | QB | 6'2" | 216 | 22 | | 2 |
| Glenn Bass | HB | 6'2" | 195 | 24 | | 6 |
| Hez Braxton | HB | 6'2" | 227 | 27 | | |
| Fred Brown | HB | 5'11" | 190 | 23 | | 6 |
| Wray Carlton | HB | 6'2" | 220 | 25 | | |
| Wayne Crow | HB | 6' | 205 | 25 | | |
| Roger Kochman | HB | 6'2" | 205 | 21 | | 6 |
| Ed Rutkowski | HB | 6'1" | 200 | 22 | | 6 |
| Cookie Gilchrist | FB | 6'3" | 250 | 28 | | 84 |
| Jesse Murdock (from OAK) | FB | 6'2" | 203 | 24 | | |
| Elbert Dubenion | FL | 6' | 188 | 28 | | 24 |
| Charley Ferguson | OE | 6'5" | 215 | 23 | | 18 |
| Bill Miller | OE | 6' | 200 | 21 | | 18 |
| Ernie Warlick | OE | 6'4" | 232 | 31 | | 6 |

**HOUSTON OILERS 6-8-0 Pop Ivy**

| | | | Use Name | Pos. | Hgt | Wgt | Age | Int | Pts |
|---|---|---|---|---|---|---|---|---|---|
| 13 | OAKLAND | 24 | Bob Kelly | OT | 6'3" | 260 | 23 | | |
| 20 | DENVER | 14 | Rich Michael | OT | 6'3" | 238 | 24 | | |
| 17 | New York | 24 | Walt Suggs | OT | 6'5" | 255 | 24 | | |
| 31 | Buffalo | 20 | Bob Talamini | OG | 6'1" | 250 | 24 | | |
| 7 | Kansas City | 28 | Bill Wegener | OG | 5'10" | 245 | 22 | | |
| 33 | Denver | 24 | Hogan Wharton | OG | 6'2" | 250 | 27 | | |
| 28 | BUFFALO | 14 | John Frongillo | C | 6'3" | 255 | 23 | | |
| 28 | KANSAS CITY | 7 | Bob Schmidt | C | 6'4" | 250 | 27 | | |
| 3 | Boston | 45 | Gary Cutsinger | DE | 6'4" | 245 | 24 | | |
| 31 | NEW YORK | 27 | Don Floyd | DE | 6'4" | 245 | .25 | | |
| 0 | San Diego | 27 | Willis Perkins | DE | 6' | 245 | 26 | | |
| 28 | BOSTON | 46 | Ed Culpepper | DT | 6'1" | 260 | 29 | | |
| 14 | SAN DIEGO | 20 | Ed Husmann | DT | 6' | 245 | 32 | | |
| 49 | Oakland | 52 | Dudley Meredith | DT | 6'4" | 275 | 28 | | |

| Use Name | Pos. | Hgt | Wgt | Age | Int | Pts |
|---|---|---|---|---|---|---|
| Johnny Baker | LB | 6'3" | 220 | 22 | | |
| Danny Brabham | LB | 6'4" | 235 | 22 | 1 | |
| Doug Cline | LB | 6'2" | 227 | 24 | 3 | |
| Mike Dukes | LB | 6'3" | 230 | 27 | 1 | |
| Tom Goode | LB | 6'3" | 235 | 24 | | |
| Larry Onesti | LB | 6' | 195 | 24 | | |
| Gene Babb | FB-LB | 6'3" | 220 | 28 | 2 | |
| Tony Banfield | DB | 6'1" | 185 | 24 | 7 | |
| Freddy Glick | DB | 6'1" | 190 | 26 | 12 | 6 |
| Bobby Jancik | DB | 5'11" | 178 | 23 | 3 | |
| Mark Johnston | DB | 6' | 200 | 25 | 1 | 6 |
| Jim Norton | DB | 6'3" | 190 | 24 | 6 | |

| Use Name | Pos. | Hgt | Wgt | Age | Int | Pts |
|---|---|---|---|---|---|---|
| George Blanda | QB | 6'1" | 215 | 35 | | 64 |
| Jacky Lee | QB | 6'1" | 187 | 24 | | |
| Bobby Brezina | HB | 6' | 200 | 21 | | |
| Billy Cannon | HB | 6'1" | 210 | 26 | | |
| Bill Tobin | HB | 5'11" | 210 | 21 | | 32 |
| Dave Smith | FB | 6'1" | 210 | 26 | | 30 |
| Charley Tolar | FB | 5'7" | 200 | 25 | | 18 |
| Charley Hennigan | FL | 6' | 187 | 27 | | 60 |
| Randy Kerbow | FL | 6'1" | 190 | 21 | | |
| Willard Dewveall | OE | 6'4" | 225 | 26 | | 42 |
| Charley Frazier | OE | 6' | 162 | 24 | | 6 |
| Bob McLeod | OE | 6'5" | 230 | 24 | | 30 |

**NEW YORK JETS 5-8-1 Weeb Ewbank**

| | | | Use Name | Pos. | Hgt | Wgt | Age | Int | Pts |
|---|---|---|---|---|---|---|---|---|---|
| 14 | Boston | 38 | Winston Hill | OT | 6'4" | 275 | 21 | | |
| 24 | HOUSTON | 17 | Jack Klotz | OT | 6'5" | 250 | 29 | | |
| 10 | OAKLAND | 7 | Sherman Plunkett | OT | 6'4" | 297 | 29 | | |
| 31 | BOSTON | 24 | Bob Butler | OG | 6'1" | 230 | 22 | | |
| 20 | San Diego | 24 | Dan Ficca | OG | 6'1" | 245 | 24 | | |
| 26 | Oakland | 49 | Sid Fournet | OG | 6' | 240 | 30 | | |
| 35 | DENVER | 35 | Roy Hord | OG | 6'4" | 245 | 28 | | |
| 7 | SAN DIEGO | 53 | Pete Perreault | OG | 6'3" | 245 | 24 | | |
| 27 | Houston | 31 | Mike Hudock | C | 6'2" | 245 | 28 | | |
| 14 | Denver | 9 | Lavern Torczon | DE | 6'2" | 238 | 27 | 1 | |
| 17 | KANSAS CITY | 0 | Bob Watters | DE | 6'4" | 245 | 28 | | |
| 14 | Buffalo | 45 | Ed Cooke | LB-DE | 6'4" | 250 | 28 | | |
| 10 | BUFFALO | 19 | Dick Guesman | DT | 6'4" | 255 | 27 | 57 | |
| 0 | Kansas City | 48 | Chuck Janerette | DT | 6'3" | 250 | 24 | 1 | |
| | | | Bob McAdams | DT | 6'3" | 250 | 23 | | |
| | | | George Strugar | DT | 6'5" | 260 | 28 | | |

| Use Name | Pos. | Hgt | Wgt | Age | Int | Pts |
|---|---|---|---|---|---|---|
| Ted Bates | LB | 6'3" | 220 | 26 | | |
| Roger Ellis | LB | 6'4" | 233 | 25 | | |
| Larry Grantham | LB | 6' | 200 | 24 | 3 | 6 |
| Walt Michaels | LB | 6' | 240 | 34 | | |
| Jim Price | LB | 6'2" | 225 | 22 | 1 | |
| Dave Yohn | LB | 6' | 225 | 25 | | |
| Billy Atkins (to BUF) | DB | 6'1" | 196 | 28 | | |
| Bill Baird | DB | 5'10" | 182 | 24 | 6 | 6 |
| Dainard Paulson | DB | 5'11" | 190 | 26 | 6 | |
| Marsh Starks | DB | 6' | 190 | 24 | | 6 |
| Tony Stricker | DB | 6' | 185 | 22 | 1 | |
| Clyde Washington | DB | 6' | 206 | 25 | 2 | |
| Dave West | DB | 6'3" | 190 | 25 | | |
| Bill Wood | DB | 5'11" | 190 | 24 | | |

| Use Name | Pos. | Hgt | Wgt | Age | Int | Pts |
|---|---|---|---|---|---|---|
| Ed Chlebek | QB | 5'11" | 175 | 22 | | |
| Johnny Green | QB | 6'3" | 208 | 26 | | |
| Galen Hall | QB | 5'10" | 205 | 23 | | 6 |
| Dick Wood | QB | 6'5" | 205 | 27 | | 6 |
| Dick Christy | HB | 5'10" | 195 | 27 | | 6 |
| Bill Mathis | HB | 6'1" | 220 | 24 | | 12 |
| Bill Perkins | HB | 6'2" | 225 | 22 | | |
| Curley Johnson | FB | 6' | 210 | 28 | | |
| Mark Smolinski | FB | 6' | 222 | 24 | | 30 |
| Don Maynard | FL | 6' | 185 | 27 | | 54 |
| Ken Gregory | OE | 6' | 190 | 26 | | |
| Gene Heeter | OE | 6'4" | 235 | 22 | | 6 |
| Dee Mackey | OE | 6'5" | 236 | 27 | | 18 |
| Bake Turner | OE | 6' | 180 | 23 | | 36 |

## BOSTON PATRIOTS

### RUSHING
| Last Name | No. | Yds | Avg | TD |
|---|---|---|---|---|
| Garron | 179 | 750 | 4.1 | 2 |
| Crawford | 71 | 233 | 3.3 | 1 |
| Yewcic | 22 | 161 | 7.3 | 1 |
| Neumann | 44 | 148 | 3.4 | 0 |
| Parilli | 36 | 126 | 3.5 | 5 |
| Crump | 49 | 120 | 2.5 | 5 |
| Lott | 35 | 78 | 2.2 | 3 |
| Cappelletti | 1 | 2 | 2.0 | 0 |

### RECEIVING
| Last Name | No. | Yds | Avg | TD |
|---|---|---|---|---|
| Colclough | 42 | 693 | 17 | 3 |
| Cappelletti | 34 | 493 | 15 | 2 |
| Romeo | 31 | 438 | 14 | 3 |
| Garron | 26 | 418 | 16 | 2 |
| A. Graham | 21 | 550 | 26 | 5 |
| Crawford | 10 | 84 | 8 | 0 |
| Neumann | 10 | 48 | 5 | 1 |
| Lott | 3 | 61 | 20 | 1 |
| Crump | 3 | 19 | 6 | 0 |

### PUNT RETURNS
| Last Name | No. | Yds | Avg | TD |
|---|---|---|---|---|
| Suci | 25 | 233 | 9 | 0 |
| Stephens | 14 | 117 | 8 | 0 |
| Garron | 1 | 23 | 23 | 0 |

### KICKOFF RETURNS
| Last Name | No. | Yds | Avg | TD |
|---|---|---|---|---|
| Garron | 28 | 693 | 25 | 0 |
| Suci | 17 | 360 | 21 | 0 |
| Crump | 3 | 33 | 11 | 0 |
| Romeo | 1 | 9 | 9 | 0 |
| Watson | 1 | 9 | 9 | 0 |
| Yates | 2 | 5 | 3 | 0 |

### PASSING – PUNTING – KICKING

**PASSING**
| Last Name | Att | Comp | % | Yds | Yd/Att | TD | Int–% | RK |
|---|---|---|---|---|---|---|---|---|
| Parilli | 337 | 153 | 45 | 2345 | 7.0 | 13 | 24– 7 | 9 |
| Yewcic | 70 | 29 | 41 | 444 | 6.3 | 4 | 5– 7 | |
| Crawford | 2 | 2 | 100 | 27 | 13.5 | 0 | 0– 0 | |
| Garron | 1 | 0 | 0 | 0 | 0.0 | 0 | 0– 0 | |

**PUNTING**
| Last Name | No | Avg |
|---|---|---|
| Yewcic | 73 | 39.4 |

**KICKING**
| Last Name | XP | Att | % | FG | Att | % |
|---|---|---|---|---|---|---|
| Cappelletti | 35 | 36 | 97 | 22 | 38 | 58 |

## BUFFALO BILLS

### RUSHING
| Last Name | No. | Yds | Avg | TD |
|---|---|---|---|---|
| Gilchrist | 232 | 979 | 4.2 | 12 |
| Kochman | 47 | 232 | 4.9 | 0 |
| Kemp | 52 | 226 | 4.3 | 8 |
| Rutowski | 48 | 144 | 3.0 | 0 |
| Carlton | 29 | 125 | 4.3 | 0 |
| Bass | 14 | 59 | 4.2 | 0 |
| Saimes | 12 | 41 | 3.4 | 0 |
| Brown | 6 | 18 | 3.0 | 1 |
| Lamonica | 9 | 8 | 0.9 | 0 |
| Crow | 6 | 6 | 1.0 | 0 |

### RECEIVING
| Last Name | No. | Yds | Avg | TD |
|---|---|---|---|---|
| Miller | 69 | 860 | 12 | 3 |
| Dubenion | 54 | 970 | 18 | 4 |
| Warlick | 24 | 479 | 20 | 1 |
| Gilchrist | 24 | 211 | 9 | 2 |
| Rutkowski | 19 | 264 | 14 | 1 |
| Ferguson | 9 | 181 | 20 | 3 |
| Bass | 9 | 153 | 17 | 1 |
| Saimes | 6 | 12 | 2 | 0 |
| Crow | 5 | 69 | 14 | 0 |
| Kochman | 4 | 148 | 37 | 1 |
| Brown | 2 | 7 | 4 | 0 |
| Stratton | 1 | 19 | 19 | 0 |
| Carlton | 1 | 9 | 9 | 0 |

### PUNT RETURNS
| Last Name | No. | Yds | Avg | TD |
|---|---|---|---|---|
| Abruzzese | 17 | 152 | 9 | 0 |
| West | 11 | 86 | 8 | 0 |
| Rutkowski | 8 | 67 | 8 | 0 |
| Kochman | 1 | 11 | 11 | 0 |

### KICKOFF RETURNS
| Last Name | No. | Yds | Avg | TD |
|---|---|---|---|---|
| Rutkowski | 13 | 396 | 30 | 0 |
| Dubenion | 13 | 333 | 26 | 0 |
| Saimes | 7 | 140 | 20 | 0 |
| Abruzzese | 6 | 118 | 20 | 0 |
| West | 6 | 56 | 9 | 0 |
| Brown | 2 | 40 | 20 | 0 |
| Tracey | 1 | 21 | 21 | 0 |
| Rivera | 1 | 20 | 20 | 0 |
| Murdock | 1 | 17 | 17 | 0 |
| Barber | 1 | 9 | 9 | 0 |
| Paterra | 1 | 0 | 0 | 0 |
| Matuszak | 1 | 17 | 17 | 0 |

### PASSING – PUNTING – KICKING

**PASSING**
| Last Name | Att | Comp | % | Yds | Yd/Att | TD | Int–% | RK |
|---|---|---|---|---|---|---|---|---|
| Kemp | 384 | 193 | 50 | 2910 | 7.6 | 13 | 20– 5 | 4 |
| Lamonica | 71 | 33 | 46 | 437 | 6.1 | 3 | 4– 6 | |
| Gilchrist | 1 | 1 | 100 | 35 | 35.0 | 0 | 0– 0 | |
| Rutkowski | 1 | 0 | 0 | 0 | 0.0 | 0 | 0– 0 | |

**PUNTING**
| Last Name | No | Avg |
|---|---|---|
| Lamonica | 51 | 40.6 |
| Crow | 10 | 42.4 |

**KICKING**
| Last Name | XP | Att | % | FG | Att | % |
|---|---|---|---|---|---|---|
| Yoho | 32 | 37 | 86 | 10 | 23 | 43 |

**2 POINT XP**
Lamonica
Tracey

## HOUSTON OILERS

### RUSHING
| Last Name | No. | Yds | Avg | TD |
|---|---|---|---|---|
| Tolar | 194 | 659 | 3.4 | 3 |
| Tobin | 75 | 270 | 3.6 | 4 |
| Smith | 50 | 202 | 4.0 | 3 |
| Cannon | 13 | 45 | 3.4 | 0 |
| Norton | 1 | 15 | 15.0 | 0 |
| Lee | 2 | 9 | 4.5 | 0 |
| Babb | 1 | 7 | 7.0 | 0 |
| Blanda | 4 | 1 | 0.2 | 0 |

### RECEIVING
| Last Name | No. | Yds | Avg | TD |
|---|---|---|---|---|
| Hennigan | 61 | 1051 | 17 | 10 |
| Dewveall | 58 | 752 | 13 | 7 |
| Tolar | 41 | 275 | 7 | 0 |
| McLeod | 33 | 530 | 16 | 5 |
| Smith | 24 | 270 | 11 | 2 |
| Frazier | 16 | 269 | 17 | 1 |
| Tobin | 13 | 272 | 13 | 1 |
| Kerbow | 5 | 61 | 12 | 0 |
| Cannon | 5 | 39 | 8 | 0 |

### PUNT RETURNS
| Last Name | No. | Yds | Avg | TD |
|---|---|---|---|---|
| Glick | 19 | 171 | 9 | 0 |
| Jancik | 13 | 145 | 11 | 0 |
| Norton | 4 | 23 | 6 | 0 |

### KICKOFF RETURNS
| Last Name | No. | Yds | Avg | TD |
|---|---|---|---|---|
| Jancik | 45 | 1317 | 29 | 0 |
| Glick | 20 | 451 | 23 | 0 |
| Cannon | 2 | 39 | 20 | 0 |
| Tobin | 1 | 10 | 10 | 0 |
| Tolar | 1 | 4 | 4 | 0 |

### PASSING – PUNTING – KICKING

**PASSING**
| Last Name | Att | Comp | % | Yds | Yd/Att | TD | Int–% | RK |
|---|---|---|---|---|---|---|---|---|
| Blanda | 423 | 224 | 53 | 3003 | 7.0 | 24 | 25– 6 | 4 |
| Lee | 75 | 37 | 49 | 475 | 6.3 | 2 | 8–11 | |
| Smith | 2 | 0 | 0 | 0 | 0.0 | 0 | 0– 0 | |
| Cannon | 1 | 0 | 0 | 0 | 0.0 | 0 | 0– 0 | |

**PUNTING**
| Last Name | No | Avg |
|---|---|---|
| Norton | 65 | 42.9 |

**KICKING**
| Last Name | XP | Att | % | FG | Att | % |
|---|---|---|---|---|---|---|
| Blanda | 39 | 39 | 100 | 9 | 22 | 41 |

**2 POINT XP**
Tobin

## NEW YORK JETS

### RUSHING
| Last Name | No. | Yds | Avg | TD |
|---|---|---|---|---|
| Smolinski | 150 | 561 | 3.7 | 4 |
| Mathis | 107 | 268 | 2.5 | 1 |
| Christy | 26 | 88 | 3.4 | 1 |
| Hall | 9 | 24 | 2.7 | 1 |
| D. Wood | 7 | 17 | 2.4 | 1 |
| Perkins | 3 | 8 | 2.6 | 0 |
| Maynard | 2 | 6 | 3.0 | 0 |
| Johnson | 2 | 6 | 3.0 | 0 |

### RECEIVING
| Last Name | No. | Yds | Avg | TD |
|---|---|---|---|---|
| Turner | 71 | 1007 | 14 | 6 |
| Maynard | 38 | 780 | 21 | 9 |
| Smolinski | 34 | 278 | 8 | 1 |
| Mackey | 23 | 263 | 11 | 3 |
| Mathis | 18 | 177 | 10 | 1 |
| Gregory | 9 | 90 | 10 | 0 |
| Heeter | 8 | 160 | 20 | 1 |
| Christy | 8 | 73 | 9 | 0 |

### PUNT RETURNS
| Last Name | No. | Yds | Avg | TD |
|---|---|---|---|---|
| Baird | 4 | 143 | 36 | 1 |
| Christy | 9 | 46 | 5 | 0 |
| Starks | 3 | 7 | 2 | 0 |
| Maynard | 1 | 6 | 6 | 0 |

### KICKOFF RETURNS
| Last Name | No. | Yds | Avg | TD |
|---|---|---|---|---|
| Christy | 24 | 585 | 24 | 0 |
| Starks | 19 | 336 | 18 | 0 |
| Turner | 14 | 299 | 21 | 0 |
| Stricker | 4 | 90 | 23 | 0 |
| Johnson | 6 | 77 | 13 | 0 |
| Perkins | 4 | 55 | 14 | 0 |
| Mathis | 1 | 11 | 11 | 0 |
| Smolinski | 1 | 10 | 10 | 0 |
| Mackey | 1 | 0 | 0 | 0 |

### PASSING – PUNTING – KICKING

**PASSING**
| Last Name | Att | Comp | % | Yds | Yd/Att | TD | Int–% | RK |
|---|---|---|---|---|---|---|---|---|
| D. Wood | 351 | 160 | 46 | 2202 | 6.3 | 18 | 18– 5 | 6 |
| Hall | 118 | 45 | 38 | 611 | 5.2 | 3 | 9– 8 | |
| Green | 6 | 2 | 33 | 10 | 1.7 | 0 | 1–17 | |
| Chlebek | 4 | 2 | 50 | 5 | 1.3 | 0 | 0– 0 | |
| Mathis | 1 | 0 | 0 | 0 | 0.0 | 0 | 1–100 | |

**PUNTING**
| Last Name | No | Avg |
|---|---|---|
| Johnson | 71 | 42.6 |

**KICKING**
| Last Name | XP | Att | % | FG | Att | % |
|---|---|---|---|---|---|---|
| Guesman | 30 | 30 | 100 | 9 | 24 | 31 |

| Scores of Each Game | | Use Name | Pos. | Hgt | Wgt | Age | Int | Pts | Use Name | Pos. | Hgt | Wgt | Age | Int | Pts | Use Name | Pos. | Hgt | Wgt | Age | Int | Pts |
|---|---|---|---|---|---|---|---|---|---|---|---|---|---|---|---|---|---|---|---|---|---|---|

## SAN DIEGO CHARGERS 11-3-0  Sid Gillman

| Score | Opp | Opp Score | Use Name | Pos. | Hgt | Wgt | Age | Int | Pts | Use Name | Pos. | Hgt | Wgt | Age | Int | Pts | Use Name | Pos. | Hgt | Wgt | Age | Int | Pts |
|---|---|---|---|---|---|---|---|---|---|---|---|---|---|---|---|---|---|---|---|---|---|---|---|
| 14 | BUFFALO | 10 | Ron Mix | OT | 6'4" | 250 | 25 | | | Chuck Allen | LB | 6'1" | 225 | 23 | 5 | 6 | John Hadl | QB | 6'2" | 205 | 23 | | |
| 17 | BOSTON | 13 | Ernie Park | OT | 6'3" | 240 | 21 | | | Frank Buncom | LB | 6'1" | 235 | 23 | | | Tobin Rote | QB | 6'3" | 220 | 35 | | 12 |
| 24 | KANSAS CITY | 10 | Ernie Wright | OT | 6'4" | 265 | 22 | | | Emil Karas | LB | 6'3" | 235 | 29 | 2 | | Paul Lowe | HB | 6' | 205 | 26 | | 60 |
| 34 | Denver | 50 | Sam DeLuca | OG | 6'2" | 242 | 27 | | | Bobby Lane | LB | 6'2" | 222 | 23 | | | Bobby Jackson | FB | 6'3" | 238 | 23 | | 24 |
| 24 | NEW YORK | 20 | Sam Gruneisen | OG | 6'1" | 252 | 22 | | | Paul Maguire | LB | 6' | 225 | 25 | 4 | | Keith Lincoln | FB | 6'2" | 212 | 24 | | 48 |
| 38 | Kansas City | 17 | Pat Shea | OG | 6'1" | 243 | 24 | | | Bob Mitinger | LB | 6'2" | 235 | 23 | 3 | | Gerry McDougall | FB | 6'2" | 225 | 28 | | 6 |
| 33 | OAKLAND | 34 | Walt Sweeney | OG | 6'3" | 240 | 22 | | | George Blair | DB | 5'11" | 195 | 25 | 1 | 95 | Lance Alworth | FL | 6' | 185 | 23 | | 66 |
| 53 | New York | 7 | Don Rogers | C | 6'2" | 245 | 26 | | | Gary Glick | DB | 6'2" | 200 | 32 | 1 | | Reg Carolan | OE | 6'6" | 235 | 23 | | |
| 7 | Boston | 6 | Earl Faison | DE | 6'5" | 262 | 24 | | 2 | Dick Harris | DB | 5'11" | 187 | 26 | 8 | 6 | Dave Kocourek | OE | 6'5" | 245 | 26 | | 32 |
| 23 | Buffalo | 13 | Bob Petrich | DE | 6'4" | 252 | 22 | | | Charley McNeil | DB | 5'11" | 180 | 27 | 4 | | Jacque MacKinnon | OE | 6'4" | 250 | 24 | | 24 |
| 27 | HOUSTON | 0 | George Gross | DT | 6'3" | 260 | 22 | | | Dick Westmoreland | DB | 6'1" | 180 | 22 | | | Don Norton | OE | 6'1" | 195 | 25 | | 6 |
| 27 | Oakland | 41 | Ernie Ladd | DT | 6'9" | 321 | 24 | | | Bud Whitehead | DB | 6' | 185 | 24 | 1 | | Jerry Robinson | OE | 5'11" | 190 | 24 | | 12 |
| 20 | Houston | 14 | Henry Schmidt | DT | 6'4" | 254 | 26 | | | Keith Kinderman | FB-DB | 6' | 208 | 23 | | | | | | | | | |
| 58 | DENVER | 20 | | | | | | | | | | | | | | | | | | | | | |

## OAKLAND RAIDERS 10-4-0  Al Davis

| Score | Opp | Opp Score | Use Name | Pos. | Hgt | Wgt | Age | Int | Pts | Use Name | Pos. | Hgt | Wgt | Age | Int | Pts | Use Name | Pos. | Hgt | Wgt | Age | Int | Pts |
|---|---|---|---|---|---|---|---|---|---|---|---|---|---|---|---|---|---|---|---|---|---|---|---|
| 24 | Houston | 13 | Proverb Jacobs | OT | 6'4" | 260 | 28 | | | Bob Dougherty | LB | 6' | 240 | 29 | | | Cotton Davidson | QB | 6'1" | 180 | 30 | | 24 |
| 35 | BUFFALO | 17 | Dick Klein | OT | 6'4" | 255 | 29 | | | Archie Matsos | LB | 6' | 212 | 28 | 4 | | Tom Flores | QB | 6'1" | 196 | 26 | | |
| 14 | BOSTON | 20 | Frank Youso | OT | 6'4" | 255 | 27 | | | Clancy Osborne | LB | 6'3" | 218 | 28 | 2 | | Clem Daniels | HB | 6'1" | 220 | 26 | | 48 |
| 7 | New York | 10 | Sonny Bishop | OG | 6'2" | 240 | 23 | | | Charley Rieves | LB | 5'11" | 218 | 24 | | | Mike Somner | HB | 5'11" | 192 | 28 | | |
| 0 | Buffalo | 12 | Wayne Hawkins | OG | 6' | 240 | 25 | | | Jackie Simpson | LB | 6'1" | 225 | 27 | 2 | | Doug Mayberry | FB | 6'1" | 220 | 26 | | |
| 14 | Boston | 20 | Ollie Spencer | OG | 6'2" | 240 | 32 | | | Claude Gibson | DB | 6'1" | 190 | 24 | 3 | 12 | Alan Miller | FB | 6' | 205 | 25 | | 30 |
| 49 | NEW YORK | 26 | Bob Mischak | OE-OG | 6' | 240 | 30 | | | Joe Krakoski | DB | 6'2" | 195 | 26 | 4 | | Glen Shaw | FB | 6'1" | 225 | 24 | | 12 |
| 34 | San Diego | 33 | Jim Otto | C | 6'2" | 240 | 25 | | | Jim McMillin | DB | 5'11" | 190 | 25 | 4 | 6 | Bo Roberson | HB-FL | 6'1" | 197 | 28 | | 18 |
| 10 | KANSAS CITY | 7 | Dalva Allen | DE | 6'5" | 262 | 30 | | | Tom Morrow | DB | 5'11" | 187 | 25 | 9 | | Jan Barrett (from GB-N) | OE | 6'3" | 230 | 23 | | |
| 22 | Kansas City | 7 | Dan Birdwell | DE | 6'4" | 240 | 22 | | | Warren Powers | DB | 6' | 188 | 22 | | | Dobie Craig | OE | 6'4" | 200 | 24 | | 12 |
| 26 | Denver | 10 | Jon Jelacic | DE | 6'3" | 255 | 26 | 1 | 12 | Fred Williamson | DB | 6'2" | 215 | 25 | 6 | | Ken Herock | OE | 6'3" | 230 | 22 | | 18 |
| 41 | SAN DIEGO | 27 | Dave Costa | DT | 6'3" | 245 | 21 | | | Herm Urenda | OE-DB | 5'11" | 170 | 23 | | | Art Powell | OE | 6'3" | 212 | 26 | | 96 |
| 35 | DENVER | 31 | Chuck McMurtry | DT | 6' | 270 | 25 | | | | | | | | | | Mike Mercer | K | 6' | 200 | 27 | | 71 |
| 52 | HOUSTON | 49 | Jim Norris | DT | 6'4" | 235 | 23 | | | | | | | | | | | | | | | | |

## KANSAS CITY CHIEFS 5-7-2  Hank Stram

| Score | Opp | Opp Score | Use Name | Pos. | Hgt | Wgt | Age | Int | Pts | Use Name | Pos. | Hgt | Wgt | Age | Int | Pts | Use Name | Pos. | Hgt | Wgt | Age | Int | Pts |
|---|---|---|---|---|---|---|---|---|---|---|---|---|---|---|---|---|---|---|---|---|---|---|---|
| 59 | Denver | 7 | Charley Diamond | OT | 6'2" | 262 | 27 | | | Bobby Bell | LB | 6'4" | 228 | 23 | 1 | | Len Dawson | QB | 6' | 190 | 29 | | 12 |
| 27 | Buffalo | 27 | Dave Hill | OT | 6'5" | 255 | 22 | | | Walt Corey | LB | 6' | 220 | 25 | | | Eddie Wilson | QB | 6' | 190 | 23 | | |
| 10 | San Diego | 24 | Jim Tyrer | OT | 6'6" | 290 | 24 | | | Sherrill Headrick | LB | 6'2" | 215 | 26 | 2 | 6 | Bert Coan | HB | 6'4" | 220 | 23 | | |
| 28 | HOUSTON | 7 | Denny Biodrowski | OG | 6'1" | 255 | 23 | | | Smokey Stover | LB | 6' | 235 | 24 | | | Abner Haynes | HB | 6' | 190 | 25 | | 36 |
| 26 | BUFFALO | 35 | Ed Budde | OG | 6'5" | 260 | 22 | | | E. J. Holub | C-LB | 6'4" | 225 | 25 | 5 | | Jerrel Wilson | LB-HB | 6'4" | 225 | 21 | | |
| 17 | SAN DIEGO | 38 | Bill Diamond | OG | 6' | 240 | 23 | | | Dave Grayson | DB | 5'10" | 184 | 24 | 5 | 6 | Curtis McClinton | FB | 6'3" | 232 | 24 | | 36 |
| 7 | Houston | 28 | Al Reynolds | OG | 6'3" | 235 | 25 | | | Bobby Hunt | DB | 6'1" | 180 | 23 | 6 | | Jack Spikes | FB | 6'2" | 225 | 24 | | 47 |
| 7 | Oakland | 10 | Marvin Terrell | OG | 6'1" | 240 | 25 | | | Bobby Ply | DB | 6'1" | 190 | 22 | | | Frank Jackson | FL | 6'1" | 190 | 23 | | 54 |
| 7 | OAKLAND | 22 | Jon Gilliam | C | 6'2" | 240 | 24 | | | Johnny Robinson | DB | 6' | 195 | 24 | 3 | | Fred Arbanas | OE | 6'3" | 240 | 24 | | 36 |
| 24 | Boston | 24 | Mel Branch | DE | 6'2" | 230 | 26 | | | Charley Warner | DB | 5'11" | 180 | 23 | 1 | | Tommy Brooker | OE | 6'2" | 230 | 23 | | 38 |
| 0 | New York | 17 | Jerry Mays | DE | 6'4" | 240 | 24 | | 6 | Duane Wood | DB | 6'1" | 200 | 27 | 3 | 6 | Chris Burford | OE | 6'3" | 210 | 25 | | 56 |
| 24 | Boston | 24 | Curt Merz | OG-DE | 6'4" | 250 | 25 | | | | | | | | | | Dick Johnson | OE | 6'4" | 220 | 24 | | 6 |
| 52 | DENVER | 21 | Buck Buchanan | DT | 6'7" | 276 | 23 | | | | | | | | | | | | | | | | |
| 35 | BOSTON | 3 | Curt Farrier | DT | 6'6" | 270 | 22 | | | | | | | | | | | | | | | | |
| 48 | NEW YORK | 0 | Paul Rochester (to NY) | DT | 6'2" | 260 | 26 | | | | | | | | | | | | | | | | |

## DENVER BRONCOS 2-11-1  Jack Faulkner

| Score | Opp | Opp Score | Use Name | Pos. | Hgt | Wgt | Age | Int | Pts | Use Name | Pos. | Hgt | Wgt | Age | Int | Pts | Use Name | Pos. | Hgt | Wgt | Age | Int | Pts |
|---|---|---|---|---|---|---|---|---|---|---|---|---|---|---|---|---|---|---|---|---|---|---|---|
| 7 | KANSAS CITY | 59 | Eldon Danenhauer | OT | 6'4" | 245 | 27 | | | Tom Erlandson | LB | 6'3" | 235 | 23 | | | Don Breaux | QB | 6'1" | 205 | 23 | | |
| 14 | Houston | 20 | Harold Olson | OT | 6'3" | 255 | 24 | | | Jim Fraser | LB | 6'3" | 236 | 27 | | | John McCormick | QB | 6'1" | 210 | 26 | | |
| 14 | BOSTON | 10 | Jim Perkins | OT | 6'5" | 250 | 24 | | | Jerry Hopkins | LB | 6'2" | 235 | 22 | 1 | | Mickey Slaughter | QB | 6' | 190 | 21 | | 6 |
| 50 | SAN DIEGO | 34 | Ernie Barnes | OG | 6'3" | 243 | 24 | | | Wahoo McDaniel | LB | 6' | 238 | 26 | 2 | | Frank Tripucka | QB | 6'2" | 208 | 35 | | |
| 24 | HOUSTON | 33 | Bob McCullough | OG | 6'2" | 245 | 22 | | | John Nocera | LB | 6'1" | 230 | 29 | | | Hewritt Dixon | HB | 6'2" | 215 | 23 | | 12 |
| 21 | Boston | 40 | Tom Nomina | OG | 6'5" | 270 | 21 | | | Leon Simmons | LB | 6' | 225 | 24 | | | Bob Gaiters | HB | 5'11" | 210 | 25 | | 6 |
| 35 | New York | 35 | Frank Jackunas | C | 6'1" | 225 | 22 | | | Willie Brown | DB | 6'1" | 190 | 22 | 1 | | Gene Mingo | HB | 6'1" | 200 | 24 | | 83 |
| 28 | BUFFALO | 30 | Jerry Sturm | C | 6'3" | 245 | 26 | | | Goose Gonsoulin | DB | 6'3" | 210 | 25 | 6 | 6 | Donnie Stone | HB | 6'2" | 205 | 26 | | 24 |
| 17 | Buffalo | 27 | Chuck Gavin | DE | 6'1" | 250 | 29 | | | Tom Janik | DB | 6'3" | 200 | 22 | 2 | | Clarence Walker | HB | 6'1" | 205 | 24 | | |
| 9 | NEW YORK | 14 | Ray Jacobs | DE | 6'3" | 275 | 23 | | | John McGeever | DB | 6'1" | 195 | 24 | | | Charley Mitchell | DB-HB | 5'11" | 185 | 23 | 1 | 6 |
| 10 | OAKLAND | 26 | Ike Lassiter | DE | 6'5" | 270 | 22 | | | John Sklopan | DB | 5'11" | 190 | 22 | | | Bo Dickinson (to HOU) | FB | 6'2" | 220 | 28 | | 6 |
| 21 | Kansas City | 52 | Ron Nery (to HOU) | DE | 6'6" | 244 | 28 | | | Bruce Starling | DB | 6'1" | 186 | 21 | | | Billy Joe | FB | 6'2" | 250 | 22 | | 30 |
| 31 | Oakland | 35 | Gordy Holz | DT | 6'4" | 260 | 29 | 1 | | Bob Zeman | DB | 6'1" | 203 | 26 | 1 | | Don Coffey | FL | 6'3" | 190 | 23 | | |
| 20 | San Diego | 58 | Bud McFadin | DT | 6'3" | 280 | 35 | | 6 | | | | | | | | Al Frazier | FL | 5'11" | 180 | 28 | | |
| | | | Anton Peters | DT | 6'3" | 250 | 21 | | | | | | | | | | Bill Groman | FL | 6' | 190 | 27 | | 18 |
| | | | | | | | | | | | | | | | | | Bob Scarpitto | FL | 5'11" | 196 | 24 | | 30 |
| | | | | | | | | | | | | | | | | | Gene Prebola | OE | 6'3" | 225 | 25 | | 14 |
| | | | | | | | | | | | | | | | | | Tom Rychlec | OE | 6'3" | 225 | 29 | | |
| | | | | | | | | | | | | | | | | | Lionel Taylor | OE | 6'2" | 215 | 27 | | 60 |

## SAN DIEGO CHARGERS

### RUSHING

| Last Name | No. | Yds | Avg | TD |
|---|---|---|---|---|
| Lowe | 177 | 1010 | 5.7 | 8 |
| Lincoln | 128 | 826 | 6.5 | 5 |
| McDougall | 38 | 199 | 5.2 | 1 |
| Jackson | 18 | 64 | 3.6 | 4 |
| Rote | 24 | 62 | 2.6 | 2 |
| Hadl | 8 | 26 | 3.3 | 0 |
| Alworth | 2 | 14 | 7.0 | 0 |

### RECEIVING

| Last Name | No. | Yds | Avg | TD |
|---|---|---|---|---|
| Alworth | 61 | 1205 | 20 | 11 |
| Lowe | 26 | 191 | 7 | 2 |
| Lincoln | 24 | 325 | 14 | 3 |
| Kocourek | 23 | 359 | 16 | 5 |
| Norton | 21 | 281 | 13 | 1 |
| Robinson | 18 | 315 | 18 | 1 |
| MacKinnon | 11 | 262 | 24 | 4 |
| McDougall | 10 | 115 | 12 | 0 |
| Jackson | 8 | 85 | 11 | 0 |

### PUNT RETURNS

| Last Name | No. | Yds | Avg | TD |
|---|---|---|---|---|
| Alworth | 11 | 120 | 11 | 0 |
| Lincoln | 7 | 98 | 14 | 0 |
| Harris | 4 | 43 | 11 | 0 |

### KICKOFF RETURNS

| Last Name | No. | Yds | Avg | TD |
|---|---|---|---|---|
| Lincoln | 17 | 439 | 26 | 0 |
| Alworth | 10 | 216 | 22 | 0 |
| Westmoreland | 10 | 204 | 20 | 0 |
| Lowe | 5 | 132 | 26 | 0 |
| McDougall | 3 | 77 | 26 | 0 |
| Harris | 2 | 34 | 17 | 0 |
| Robinson | 2 | 27 | 14 | 0 |
| Sweeney | 1 | 18 | 18 | 0 |
| Jackson | 1 | 16 | 16 | 0 |
| Maguire | 1 | 5 | 5 | 0 |

### PASSING – PUNTING – KICKING

| PASSING | Att | Comp | % | Yds | Yd/Att | TD | Int-% | | RK |
|---|---|---|---|---|---|---|---|---|---|
| Rote | 286 | 170 | 59 | 2510 | 8.7 | 20 | 17- | 6 | 1 |
| Hadl | 64 | 28 | 44 | 502 | 7.8 | 6 | 6- | 9 | |
| Lowe | 4 | 2 | 50 | 100 | 25.0 | 1 | 1- | 25 | |
| Lincoln | 1 | 0 | 0 | 0 | 0.0 | 0 | 0- | 0 | |
| McDougall | 1 | 1 | 100 | 11 | 11.0 | 1 | 0- | 0 | |
| Norton | 1 | 1 | 100 | 15 | 15.0 | 0 | 0- | 0 | |

| PUNTING | No | Avg |
|---|---|---|
| Maguire | 58 | 38.6 |
| Hadl | 2 | 37.5 |

| KICKING | XP | Att | % | FG | Att | % |
|---|---|---|---|---|---|---|
| Blair | 44 | 48 | 92 | 17 | 27 | 63 |

2 POINT XP
Faison
Kocourek

## OAKLAND RAIDERS

### RUSHING

| Last Name | No. | Yds | Avg | TD |
|---|---|---|---|---|
| Daniels | 214 | 1099 | 5.1 | 3 |
| Miller | 62 | 270 | 4.4 | 3 |
| Davidson | 26 | 115 | 4.4 | 4 |
| Roberson | 19 | 47 | 2.2 | 0 |
| Shaw | 20 | 46 | 2.3 | 1 |
| Sommer | 5 | 21 | 4.2 | 0 |
| Flores | 11 | 2 | 0.2 | 0 |
| Mercer | 1 | -5 | -5.0 | 0 |

### RECEIVING

| Last Name | No. | Yds | Avg | TD |
|---|---|---|---|---|
| Powell | 73 | 1304 | 18 | 16 |
| Miller | 34 | 404 | 12 | 2 |
| Daniels | 30 | 685 | 23 | 1 |
| Roberson | 25 | 407 | 16 | 3 |
| Herock | 15 | 269 | 18 | 2 |
| Craig | 7 | 205 | 29 | 2 |
| Shaw | 2 | 64 | 32 | 1 |
| Mischak | 2 | 25 | 13 | 0 |
| Sommer | 1 | 24 | 24 | 0 |
| Barrett | 1 | 9 | 9 | 0 |

### PUNT RETURNS

| Last Name | No. | Yds | Avg | TD |
|---|---|---|---|---|
| Gibson | 26 | 307 | 12 | 2 |
| Sommer | 4 | 44 | 11 | 0 |
| Roberson | 2 | 34 | 17 | 0 |
| Krakoski | 4 | 10 | 3 | 0 |

### KICKOFF RETURNS

| Last Name | No. | Yds | Avg | TD |
|---|---|---|---|---|
| Roberson | 38 | 809 | 21 | 0 |
| Sommer | 5 | 102 | 20 | 0 |
| McMillin | 1 | 23 | 23 | 0 |
| Shaw | 2 | 19 | 10 | 0 |
| Simpson | 1 | 11 | 11 | 0 |
| Gibson | 2 | 10 | 5 | 0 |
| Klein | 1 | 7 | 7 | 0 |
| Birdwell | 1 | 7 | 7 | 0 |
| Herock | 1 | 3 | 3 | 0 |

### PASSING – PUNTING – KICKING

| PASSING | Att | Comp | % | Yds | Yd/Att | TD | Int-% | | RK |
|---|---|---|---|---|---|---|---|---|---|
| Flores | 247 | 113 | 46 | 2101 | 8.5 | 20 | 13- | 5 | 3 |
| Davidson | 194 | 77 | 40 | 1276 | 6.5 | 11 | 10- | 5 | 8 |
| Daniels | 1 | 1 | 100 | 10 | 10.0 | 0 | 0- | 0 | |

| PUNTING | No | Avg |
|---|---|---|
| Mercer | 75 | 40.0 |

| KICKING | XP | Att | % | FG | Att | % |
|---|---|---|---|---|---|---|
| Mercer | 47 | 47 | 100 | 8 | 19 | 42 |

## KANSAS CITY CHIEFS

### RUSHING

| Last Name | No. | Yds | Avg | TD |
|---|---|---|---|---|
| McClinton | 142 | 568 | 4.0 | 3 |
| Haynes | 99 | 352 | 3.9 | 3 |
| Dawson | 37 | 272 | 7.4 | 2 |
| Spikes | 84 | 257 | 3.1 | 2 |
| Coan | 17 | 100 | 5.9 | 0 |
| Jackson | 3 | 52 | 17.3 | 1 |
| E. Wilson | 8 | 45 | 5.6 | 0 |
| J. Wilson | 9 | 41 | 4.6 | 0 |
| Burford | 1 | 10 | 10.0 | 0 |

### RECEIVING

| Last Name | No. | Yds | Avg | TD |
|---|---|---|---|---|
| Burford | 68 | 824 | 12 | 9 |
| Jackson | 50 | 785 | 16 | 8 |
| Arbanas | 34 | 373 | 11 | 6 |
| Haynes | 33 | 470 | 14 | 2 |
| McClinton | 27 | 301 | 11 | 3 |
| Spikes | 11 | 125 | 11 | 1 |
| Coan | 2 | 35 | 18 | 0 |
| Brooker | 2 | 32 | 16 | 0 |
| J. Wilson | 2 | 21 | 11 | 0 |
| Johnson | 2 | 17 | 9 | 1 |

### PUNT RETURNS

| Last Name | No. | Yds | Avg | TD |
|---|---|---|---|---|
| Jackson | 11 | 95 | 9 | 0 |
| Haynes | 6 | 57 | 10 | 0 |
| Grayson | 3 | 39 | 20 | 0 |
| Warner | 4 | 25 | 6 | 0 |
| Wood | 1 | 18 | 18 | 0 |
| Robinson | 1 | 16 | 16 | 0 |
| Headrick | 1 | 9 | 9 | 0 |

### KICKOFF RETURNS

| Last Name | No. | Yds | Avg | TD |
|---|---|---|---|---|
| Grayson | 20 | 570 | 29 | 1 |
| Haynes | 12 | 317 | 26 | 0 |
| Warner | 9 | 215 | 24 | 0 |
| Jackson | 1 | 20 | 20 | 0 |
| J. Wilson | 1 | 20 | 20 | 0 |
| Stover | 2 | 18 | 9 | 0 |
| Spikes | 2 | 12 | 6 | 0 |

### PASSING – PUNTING – KICKING

| PASSING | Att | Comp | % | Yds | Yd/Att | TD | Int-% | | RK |
|---|---|---|---|---|---|---|---|---|---|
| Dawson | 352 | 190 | 54 | 2389 | 6.7 | 26 | 19- | 5 | 2 |
| E. Wilson | 82 | 39 | 48 | 537 | 6.5 | 3 | 2- | 2 | |
| Haynes | 2 | 1 | 50 | 24 | 12.0 | 0 | 0- | 0 | |
| McClinton | 2 | 1 | 50 | 33 | 16.5 | 1 | 0- | 0 | |
| Spikes | 1 | 0 | 0 | 0 | 0.0 | 0 | 1-100 | | |

| PUNTING | No | Avg |
|---|---|---|
| J. Wilson | 60 | 43.8 |
| E. Wilson | 1 | 43.0 |

| KICKING | XP | Att | % | FG | Att | % |
|---|---|---|---|---|---|---|
| Spikes | 23 | 24 | 96 | 2 | 13 | 15 |
| Brooker | 20 | 20 | 100 | 6 | 15 | 40 |

2 POINT XP
Burford

## DENVER BRONCOS

### RUSHING

| Last Name | No. | Yds | Avg | TD |
|---|---|---|---|---|
| Joe | 154 | 649 | 4.2 | 4 |
| Stone | 96 | 382 | 3.9 | 3 |
| Slaughter | 32 | 124 | 3.9 | 1 |
| Dixon | 23 | 105 | 4.5 | 2 |
| Mingo | 24 | 90 | 3.7 | 0 |
| Breaux | 10 | 51 | 5.1 | 0 |
| Mitchell | 23 | 45 | 2.0 | 0 |
| Dickinson | 6 | 32 | 5.3 | 0 |
| Gaiters | 9 | 20 | 2.2 | 0 |
| Walker | 2 | 14 | 7.0 | 0 |
| Barnes | 0 | 2 | 0.0 | 0 |
| McCormick | 3 | -5 | -1.7 | 0 |

### RECEIVING

| Last Name | No. | Yds | Avg | TD |
|---|---|---|---|---|
| Taylor | 78 | 1101 | 14 | 10 |
| Prebola | 30 | 471 | 16 | 2 |
| Groman | 27 | 437 | 16 | 3 |
| Stone | 22 | 208 | 9 | 1 |
| Scarpitto | 21 | 463 | 22 | 5 |
| Joe | 15 | 90 | 6 | 1 |
| Dixon | 10 | 130 | 13 | 0 |
| Mitchell | 8 | 71 | 9 | 0 |
| Dickinson | 6 | 57 | 10 | 0 |
| Mingo | 3 | 11 | 4 | 0 |
| Gaiters | 1 | 74 | 74 | 1 |
| Rychlec | 1 | 9 | 9 | 0 |

### PUNT RETURNS

| Last Name | No. | Yds | Avg | TD |
|---|---|---|---|---|
| Mitchell | 12 | 141 | 12 | 0 |
| Mingo | 7 | 85 | 12 | 0 |
| Dixon | 3 | 58 | 19 | 0 |
| Frazier | 3 | 42 | 14 | 0 |
| Zeman | 2 | 32 | 16 | 0 |
| Brown | 3 | 29 | 10 | 0 |

### KICKOFF RETURNS

| Last Name | No. | Yds | Avg | TD |
|---|---|---|---|---|
| Mitchell | 37 | 954 | 26 | 1 |
| Gaiters | 11 | 225 | 20 | 0 |
| Dixon | 9 | 195 | 22 | 0 |
| Frazier | 7 | 185 | 24 | 0 |
| Mingo | 7 | 151 | 22 | 0 |
| Brown | 3 | 70 | 23 | 0 |
| Scarpitto | 1 | 8 | 8 | 0 |
| Olson | 2 | 0 | 0 | 0 |
| Fraser | 1 | 0 | 0 | 0 |
| Groman | 0 | 9 | 0 | 0 |
| Gonsoulin | 0 | 4 | 0 | 0 |

### PASSING – PUNTING – KICKING

| PASSING | Att | Comp | % | Yds | Yd/Att | TD | Int-% | | RK |
|---|---|---|---|---|---|---|---|---|---|
| Slaughter | 223 | 112 | 50 | 1689 | 7.5 | 12 | 14- | 6 | 7 |
| Breaux | 138 | 70 | 51 | 935 | 6.7 | 7 | 6- | 4 | |
| McCormick | 72 | 28 | 39 | 417 | 5.7 | 4 | 3- | 4 | |
| Tripucka | 15 | 7 | 47 | 31 | 2.1 | 0 | 5- | 33 | |
| Stone | 3 | 0 | 0 | 0 | 0.0 | 0 | 0- | 0 | |
| Mingo | 1 | 0 | | 0 | 0.0 | 0 | 0- | 0 | |
| Taylor | 1 | 0 | 0 | 0 | 0.0 | 0 | 0- | 0 | |

| PUNTING | No | Avg |
|---|---|---|
| Fraser | 78 | 46.1 |

| KICKING | XP | Att | % | FG | Att | % |
|---|---|---|---|---|---|---|
| Mingo | 35 | 35 | 100 | 16 | 29 | 55 |

2 POINT XP
Prebola

# 1964 N.F.L.  A  Blue-Chip  Business

The war between the leagues was going nicely for the NFL, as all but two NFL teams made a profit during 1964. Only St. Louis and Dallas lost money, and neither had the excuse of direct AFL competition. Franchises now were blue-chip investments, with price tags well into the millions of dollars. Two of the franchises changed hands this year: William Clay Ford purchased the Detroit Lions and Jerry Wolman headed a syndicate that bought the Philadelphia Eagles. The leagues were still at war, but the NFL owners worried very little at this point.

## EASTERN CONFERENCE

**Cleveland Browns**—The Browns added a little variety to their attack to win their first conference title since 1957. Jimmy Brown still was the ultimate runner, but he got some help in the ball-carrying department from halfback Ernie Green. For the first time in years the Browns also launched a dangerous passing game, with Gary Collins and rookie Paul Warfield providing quarterback Frank Ryan with two fine receivers. Led by tackle Dick Schafrath, the offensive line both cleared paths for the runners and protected quarterback Ryan with equal expertise. The defense had problems defending against the pass, but ex-Giant Dick Modzelewski made the line very tough against the run.

**St. Louis Cardinals**—Coach Wally Lemm put together a marvelously balanced team, only to have it fall apart on three embarrassing occasions. In a four-week span in mid-season, the Cards lost 47-27 to Baltimore, dropped a 31-13 decision to Dallas, and were beaten 34-17 by the collapsing New York Giants. But before and after this cold spell, the Cardinals showed a versatile offense and spirited defense. Quarterback Charley Johnson had a propensity for throwing interceptions, but he usually made up for his errant tosses with long gainers. The strong offensive line cleared the way for runners John David Crow, Joe Childress, and Willie Crenshaw, while the defense combined a small but quick line with steady linebackers and an aggressive secondary featuring Pat Fischer and Larry Wilson.

**Washington Redskins**—Quarterback Sonny Jurgensen, obtained in a trade with the Eagles, had few peers as a passer, and receivers Bobby Mitchell, Angelo Coia, and Preston Carpenter gave him an abundance of open receivers. Rookie halfback Charley Taylor injected speed into the running attack. But the Washington offense also had a big hole at fullback and a spotty front line of blockers, making it difficult for Jurgensen, Taylor, and Mitchell to shine their brightest. Even with a defense bolstered by ex-Giant Sam Huff and rookie Paul Krause, the Redskins lost their first four games with poor offensive performances. But after rookies Len Hauss and George Seals were thrust into the offensive line, the Skins revived and won six of their next eight games.

**Philadelphia Eagles**—Joe Kuharich signed a fifteen-year contract as coach and general manager and immediately dived into the trading market to rebuild the Eagles. In a blinding series of deals, he obtained Norm Snead from Washington, Earl Gros and Jim Ringo from Green Bay, Ollie Matson and Floyd Peters from Detroit, Sam Baker from Dallas, and Ray Poage and Don Hultz from Minnesota. Add three good rookies in Bob Brown, Mike Morgan, and Joe Scarpati, and solid holdovers like Pete Retzlaff, Maxie Baughan, Don Burroughs, and Irv Cross, and the Eagles had the makings of a good football team.

**Dallas Cowboys**—Even after the Cowboys obtained star wide receivers Tommy McDonald and Buddy Dial, the offense had problems scoring points. One cause of the trouble was Don Meredith's leg injury, which had him hobbling through a sub-par season, and another was the erratic kicking of rookie Dick Van Raaphorst. Given the field-goal kicking job after Sam Baker was dealt to Philadelphia, Van Raaphorst cost the Cowboys several games by blowing easy kicks. Although Don Perkins and Frank Clarke kept up their good work, the Dallas offense fell off from its 1963 performance. The defense, however, suddenly blended together into a strong unit.

**Pittsburgh Steelers**—Coach Buddy Parker had an intricate plan to improve the Steelers this year. He drafted University of Pittsburgh star Paul Martha as a flanker, and then traded incumbent flanker Buddy Dial to Dallas for the draft rights to All-American defensive lineman Scott Appleton from the University of Texas. The whole maneuver failed miserably when Appleton signed with the AFL Houston Oilers, and Martha was a king-sized bust as a pass receiver. Rookies Ben McGee and Chuck Hinton took up the slack in the defensive line, but no one could fill Dial's vacated receiver spot opposite Gary Ballman.

**New York Giants**—The New York dynasty crashed heavily to pieces this season. Coach Allie Sherman had traded off Sam Huff and Dick Modzelewski during the off season, hoping to fill their spots with younger men, but none of the replacements came close to the steadiness of the two departed defenders. To add to Sherman's headaches, veterans Y. A. Tittle, Alex Webster, Frank Gifford, Del Shofner, Jack Stroud, and Andy Robustelli all showed signs of advanced old age.

## WESTERN CONFERENCE

**Baltimore Colts**—Coach Don Shula had tried to trade Lenny Moore all summer but had found no takers. Moore had lost his halfback job to Tom Matte and was coming off two injury-plagued seasons which cut his market value down to nothing. Once the regular season started, though, Moore won back his job and set a new NFL record with twenty touchdowns. Moore, Tony Lorick, and Jerry Hill provided tough running, and the Baltimore passing attack was even more effective than usual. The defense responded to the offensive improvement by playing better than anyone could expect, with veterans Gino Marchetti, Bill Pellington, and Bob Boyd the core around which a group of average defenders clustered into a solid unit. With a proper mixture of veterans and youngsters, the Colts captured the conference crown.

**Green Bay Packers**—Paul Hornung rejoined the Packers after his year's suspension but left his kicking eye behind. The Pack lost three games because of easy kicks Hornung missed, such as the 21-20 loss to the Colts in which Hornung missed an extra point. Outside of this one serious flaw, the Packers still were a solid, precise football team. Bart Starr and Jim Taylor starred in the backfield, and the offensive line graded out well despite the trading of Jim Ringo to Philadelphia and the loss of Jerry Kramer to stomach surgery. No one moved the ball easily against the Green Bay defense, which boasted of four All-Pros in Willie Davis, Henry Jordan, Ray Nitschke, and Willie Wood.

**Minnesota Vikings**—With three straight wins to end the year, the Vikings jumped up into a second-place tie in the West with the Packers. The Vikings had caught up with Green Bay after only four years in existence, and the main stepladder to progress was the Minnesota offense. At quarterback the Vikings had Fran Tarkenton, the original and best scrambler in the league. The halfback was Tommy Mason, the team's breakaway threat, and the fullback was Bill Brown, a squat young man equally adept at running, receiving, and blocking. The offensive line was not spectacular but good enough to allow the backs to star, while the Minnesota defense was making slower but sure progress.

**Detroit Lions**—Age was cutting heavily into the vaunted Detroit defense. Night Train Lane was thirty-six and bothered by a bad knee, Yale Lary was thirty-three, Joe Schmidt was thirty-two with a bad shoulder, and Sam Williams was thirty-three. When all these veterans could play at top form, the Lion defense still was one of the league's best, but the days where one or more of them had to sit the game out were growing more frequent. The offense was still a rather plodding unit, with flanker Terry Barr the only speedster on the attack. With neither Milt Plum nor Earl Morrall able to take over at quarterback, the offense was far from ready to pick up the slack left by the aging defense.

**Los Angeles Rams**—Despite a late-season slump which saw them go winless in their last five games, the Rams developed two solid lines this year. The offensive line of Joe Wendryhoski, Joe Scibelli, Don Chuy, Joe Carollo, and Frank Varricheone was quietly efficient, while the defensive front four of Deacon Jones, Merlin Olsen, Roosevelt Grier, and Lamar Lundy won attention for their speed and violence. The backfields were less settled, as two rookies started in the defensive secondary and three freshman won jobs in the offensive backfield. Bucky Pope surprised everyone with his deep pass receiving as a flanker, and Les Josephson filled in well for the sore-kneed Dick Bass. Rookie Bill Munson won the quarterback job, giving the Rams a second good young quarterback to go along with Roman Gabriel.

**Chicago Bears**—The Chicago offense had been nothing to write home about last year, but when injuries cut the marvelous defense down to life size, the Bears plummeted into the depths of the Western Conference. When the Bears lost three of their first four games, one of them to the Colts by 52-0, hopes for a repeat championship fluttered away. To get some additional punch from the offense, which had been crippled by the pre-season deaths of Willie Galimore and Bo Farrington in an auto accident, coach George Halas used strong-armed Rudy Bukich more often at quarterback and geared his attack around passes to Johnny Morris and Mike Ditka. Although the passes were successful often enough to place Morris and Ditka one-two in the league receiving statistics and to give Morris a new NFL season's record of ninety-three receptions, the Bear season was a huge disappointment.

**San Francisco '49ers**—When all their running backs were knocked out with injuries, the '49ers couldn't find enough offensive dynamite in the rest of the lineup to ignite the attack. Although Bernie Casey, Monte Stickles, and rookie Dave Parks were a fine trio of receivers, quarterback John Brodie was not a great enough passer to overcome the lack of any ground attack. The defense gave up no easy yardage, with Charlie Krueger, Clark Miller, Matt Hazeltine, rookie Dave Wilcox, and converted flanker Jim Johnson the main ribs of the unit.

## FINAL TEAM STATISTICS

### OFFENSE

| | BALT. | CHI. | CLEVE. | DALLAS | DET. | G.BAY | L.A. | MINN. | N.Y. | PHIL. | PITT. | ST.L. | S.F. | WASH. |
|---|---|---|---|---|---|---|---|---|---|---|---|---|---|---|
| **FIRST DOWNS:** | | | | | | | | | | | | | | |
| Total | 245 | 248 | 255 | 230 | 221 | 250 | 208 | 258 | 240 | 243 | 233 | 275 | 233 | 193 |
| by Rushing | 100 | 83 | 119 | 89 | 87 | 133 | 78 | 124 | 81 | 100 | 110 | 95 | 76 | 70 |
| by Passing | 129 | 141 | 118 | 119 | 115 | 106 | 104 | 115 | 140 | 126 | 105 | 152 | 136 | 116 |
| by Penalty | 16 | 24 | 18 | 22 | 19 | 11 | 26 | 19 | 19 | 17 | 18 | 28 | 21 | 7 |
| **RUSHING:** | | | | | | | | | | | | | | |
| Number | 456 | 356 | 435 | 421 | 412 | 495 | 400 | 519 | 435 | 430 | 516 | 456 | 383 | 366 |
| Yards | 2007 | 1166 | 2163 | 1691 | 1414 | 2276 | 1629 | 2183 | 1404 | 1922 | 2102 | 1770 | 1332 | 1237 |
| Average Yards | 4.4 | 3.3 | 5.0 | 4.0 | 3.4 | 4.6 | 4.1 | 4.2 | 3.2 | 4.5 | 4.1 | 3.9 | 3.5 | 3.4 |
| Touchdowns | 29 | 5 | 14 | 15 | 7 | 23 | 11 | 14 | 12 | 16 | 14 | 12 | 11 | 11 |
| **PASSING:** | | | | | | | | | | | | | | |
| Attempts | 345 | 494 | 344 | 404 | 386 | 321 | 368 | 326 | 431 | 397 | 323 | 422 | 461 | 415 |
| Completions | 176 | 282 | 181 | 192 | 206 | 186 | 173 | 179 | 217 | 199 | 141 | 223 | 225 | 214 |
| Completion Pct. | 51.0 | 57.1 | 52.6 | 47.5 | 53.4 | 57.9 | 47.0 | 54.9 | 50.3 | 50.1 | 43.7 | 52.8 | 48.8 | 51.6 |
| Passing Yards | 3045 | 3056 | 2542 | 2516 | 2890 | 2474 | 2769 | 2614 | 2848 | 2746 | 2308 | 3045 | 2990 | 3071 |
| Avg. Yds per Att. | 8.8 | 6.2 | 7.4 | 6.2 | 7.5 | 7.7 | 7.5 | 8.0 | 6.6 | 6.9 | 7.2 | 7.2 | 6.5 | 7.4 |
| Avg. Yds per Comp. | 17.3 | 10.8 | 14.0 | 13.1 | 14.0 | 13.3 | 16.0 | 14.6 | 13.1 | 13.8 | 16.4 | 13.7 | 13.3 | 14.4 |
| Times Tackled | 39 | 30 | 28 | 68 | 37 | 47 | 65 | 48 | 45 | 35 | 51 | 37 | 27 | 44 |
| Yards Lost Tackled | 273 | 215 | 219 | 503 | 332 | 369 | 490 | 491 | 373 | 268 | 450 | 298 | 249 | 350 |
| Net Yards | 2772 | 2841 | 2323 | 2013 | 2558 | 2105 | 2279 | 2123 | 2475 | 2478 | 1858 | 2747 | 2741 | 2721 |
| Touchdowns | 22 | 25 | 28 | 10 | 23 | 16 | 18 | 23 | 16 | 19 | 14 | 21 | 18 | 25 |
| Interceptions | 9 | 21 | 19 | 24 | 21 | 6 | 20 | 12 | 26 | 18 | 24 | 24 | 22 | 16 |
| Pct. Intercepted | 2.6 | 4.3 | 5.5 | 5.9 | 5.4 | 1.9 | 5.4 | 3.7 | 6.0 | 4.5 | 7.4 | 5.7 | 4.8 | 3.9 |
| **PUNTING:** | | | | | | | | | | | | | | |
| Number | 59 | 71 | 49 | 78 | 68 | 56 | 82 | 72 | 74 | 73 | 62 | 56 | 79 | 91 |
| Average Distance | 41.8 | 44.5 | 41.9 | 38.9 | 45.7 | 42.2 | 44.1 | 46.4 | 45.4 | 41.7 | 43.2 | 40.9 | 45.6 | 41.2 |
| **PUNT RETURNS:** | | | | | | | | | | | | | | |
| Number | 48 | 30 | 20 | 40 | 35 | 34 | 34 | 35 | 28 | 28 | 30 | 24 | 43 | 32 |
| Yards | 453 | 219 | 303 | 459 | 411 | 443 | 181 | 306 | 193 | 201 | 238 | 251 | 322 | 230 |
| Average Yards | 9.4 | 7.3 | 15.2 | 11.5 | 11.7 | 13.0 | 5.3 | 8.7 | 6.9 | 7.2 | 7.9 | 10.5 | 7.5 | 7.2 |
| Touchdowns | 0 | 0 | 1 | 1 | 2 | 1 | 0 | 0 | 0 | 0 | 0 | 1 | 1 | 0 |
| **KICKOFF RETURNS:** | | | | | | | | | | | | | | |
| Number | 39 | 58 | 57 | 46 | 57 | 45 | 56 | 53 | 67 | 59 | 56 | 63 | 57 | 52 |
| Yards | 926 | 1314 | 1323 | 1102 | 1327 | 1160 | 1258 | 1130 | 1688 | 1365 | 1356 | 1424 | 1393 | 1097 |
| Average Yards | 23.7 | 22.7 | 23.2 | 24.0 | 23.3 | 25.8 | 22.5 | 21.3 | 25.2 | 23.1 | 24.2 | 22.6 | 24.4 | 21.1 |
| Touchdowns | 0 | 1 | 0 | 0 | 0 | 0 | 0 | 0 | 1 | 0 | 0 | 0 | 0 | 0 |
| **INTERCEPTION RETURNS:** | | | | | | | | | | | | | | |
| Number | 23 | 10 | 19 | 18 | 22 | 16 | 17 | 19 | 15 | 17 | 12 | 25 | 15 | 34 |
| Yards | 366 | 258 | 444 | 316 | 267 | 263 | 487 | 224 | 179 | 272 | 96 | 388 | 155 | 317 |
| Average Yards | 15.9 | 25.8 | 23.4 | 17.6 | 12.1 | 16.4 | 28.6 | 11.8 | 11.9 | 16.0 | 8.0 | 15.5 | 10.3 | 9.3 |
| Touchdowns | 1 | 0 | 3 | 2 | 0 | 1 | 3 | 4 | 1 | 2 | 1 | 5 | 0 | 3 |
| **PENALTIES:** | | | | | | | | | | | | | | |
| Number | 74 | 96 | 60 | 97 | 75 | 50 | 76 | 71 | 65 | 42 | 59 | 64 | 79 | 87 |
| Yards | 785 | 817 | 611 | 952 | 674 | 576 | 803 | 787 | 532 | 450 | 615 | 579 | 741 | 825 |
| **FUMBLES:** | | | | | | | | | | | | | | |
| Number | 31 | 19 | 15 | 38 | 23 | 25 | 40 | 37 | 44 | 33 | 28 | 29 | 42 | 27 |
| Number Lost | 10 | 12 | 7 | 19 | 13 | 17 | 19 | 18 | 23 | 22 | 17 | 16 | 24 | 17 |
| **POINTS:** | | | | | | | | | | | | | | |
| Total | 428 | 260 | 415 | 250 | 280 | 342 | 283 | 355 | 241 | 312 | 253 | 357 | 236 | 307 |
| PAT Attempts | 54 | 32 | 50 | 30 | 34 | 44 | 33 | 42 | 30 | 38 | 31 | 40 | 30 | 39 |
| PAT Made | 53 | 29 | 49 | 28 | 32 | 42 | 31 | 40 | 28 | 36 | 28 | 40 | 30 | 35 |
| FG Attempts | 35 | 23 | 33 | 29 | 25 | 39 | 24 | 33 | 20 | 26 | 25 | 38 | 25 | 28 |
| FG Made | 17 | 13 | 22 | 14 | 14 | 12 | 18 | 21 | 9 | 16 | 13 | 25 | 8 | 12 |
| Pct. FG Made | 48.6 | 56.5 | 66.7 | 48.3 | 56.0 | 30.8 | 75.0 | 63.6 | 45.0 | 61.5 | 52.0 | 65.8 | 32.0 | 42.9 |
| Safeties | 0 | 0 | 0 | 0 | 1 | 0 | 0 | 0 | 0 | 0 | 0 | 1 | 1 | 1 |

### DEFENSE

| | BALT. | CHI. | CLEVE. | DALLAS | DET. | G.BAY | L.A. | MINN. | N.Y. | PHIL. | PITT. | ST.L. | S.F. | WASH. |
|---|---|---|---|---|---|---|---|---|---|---|---|---|---|---|
| **FIRST DOWNS:** | | | | | | | | | | | | | | |
| Total | 242 | 248 | 275 | 211 | 241 | 197 | 235 | 216 | 247 | 234 | 253 | 235 | 255 | 243 |
| by Rushing | 93 | 99 | 119 | 71 | 92 | 95 | 92 | 94 | 101 | 93 | 109 | 96 | 90 | 101 |
| by Passing | 121 | 121 | 137 | 121 | 128 | 91 | 131 | 105 | 127 | 128 | 121 | 128 | 138 | 125 |
| by Penalty | 28 | 28 | 19 | 19 | 21 | 11 | 12 | 17 | 19 | 13 | 23 | 11 | 27 | 17 |
| **RUSHING:** | | | | | | | | | | | | | | |
| Number | 422 | 436 | 465 | 439 | 429 | 417 | 419 | 389 | 468 | 445 | 454 | 414 | 443 | 440 |
| Yards | 1798 | 1863 | 2012 | 1504 | 1638 | 1532 | 1501 | 1616 | 1919 | 1746 | 1994 | 1800 | 1560 | 1813 |
| Average Yards | 4.3 | 4.3 | 4.3 | 3.4 | 3.8 | 3.7 | 3.6 | 4.2 | 4.1 | 3.9 | 4.4 | 4.0 | 3.5 | 4.1 |
| Touchdowns | 13 | 19 | 18 | 6 | 10 | 15 | 14 | 10 | 15 | 15 | 15 | 13 | 11 | 20 |
| **PASSING:** | | | | | | | | | | | | | | |
| Attempts | 385 | 366 | 401 | 377 | 406 | 318 | 435 | 375 | 361 | 406 | 378 | 389 | 434 | 406 |
| Completions | 217 | 188 | 230 | 172 | 226 | 173 | 213 | 182 | 188 | 202 | 185 | 193 | 232 | 193 |
| Completion Pct. | 56.4 | 51.4 | 57.4 | 45.6 | 55.7 | 54.4 | 49.0 | 48.5 | 52.1 | 49.8 | 48.9 | 49.6 | 53.5 | 47.5 |
| Passing Yards | 2621 | 2897 | 2932 | 2571 | 2906 | 1980 | 3094 | 2993 | 2799 | 2950 | 2582 | 2848 | 3141 | 2600 |
| Avg. Yds per Att. | 6.8 | 7.9 | 7.3 | 6.8 | 7.2 | 6.2 | 7.1 | 8.0 | 7.8 | 7.3 | 6.8 | 7.3 | 7.2 | 6.4 |
| Avg. Yds per Comp. | 12.1 | 15.4 | 12.7 | 14.9 | 12.9 | 11.4 | 14.5 | 16.4 | 14.9 | 14.6 | 14.0 | 14.8 | 13.5 | 13.5 |
| Times Tackled | 57 | 30 | 28 | 45 | 50 | 45 | 49 | 36 | 44 | 47 | 42 | 42 | 43 | 43 |
| Yards Lost Tackled | 489 | 275 | 222 | 325 | 482 | 333 | 400 | 269 | 355 | 379 | 345 | 356 | 297 | 353 |
| Net Yards | 2132 | 2622 | 2710 | 2246 | 2424 | 1647 | 2694 | 2724 | 2444 | 2571 | 2237 | 2492 | 2844 | 2247 |
| Touchdowns | 14 | 27 | 18 | 22 | 14 | 11 | 27 | 23 | 28 | 18 | 16 | 21 | 23 | 16 |
| Interceptions | 23 | 10 | 19 | 18 | 22 | 16 | 17 | 19 | 15 | 17 | 12 | 25 | 15 | 34 |
| Pct. Intercepted | 6.0 | 2.7 | 4.7 | 4.8 | 5.4 | 5.0 | 3.9 | 5.1 | 4.2 | 4.2 | 3.2 | 6.4 | 3.5 | 8.4 |
| **PUNTING:** | | | | | | | | | | | | | | |
| Number | 73 | 62 | 57 | 80 | 66 | 72 | 73 | 71 | 59 | 80 | 67 | 67 | 76 | 67 |
| Average Distance | 44.0 | 46.6 | 39.7 | 43.5 | 44.0 | 43.5 | 45.1 | 43.8 | 42.2 | 40.5 | 39.5 | 43.5 | 45.8 | 42.1 |
| **PUNT RETURNS:** | | | | | | | | | | | | | | |
| Number | 25 | 35 | 20 | 19 | 33 | 31 | 43 | 30 | 40 | 35 | 24 | 26 | 50 | 50 |
| Yards | 175 | 436 | 183 | 52 | 243 | 397 | 360 | 247 | 559 | 333 | 172 | 151 | 540 | 362 |
| Average Yards | 7.0 | 12.5 | 15.3 | 2.7 | 7.4 | 12.8 | 8.4 | 8.2 | 14.0 | 9.5 | 7.2 | 5.8 | 10.8 | 7.2 |
| Touchdowns | 1 | 0 | 0 | 0 | 0 | 2 | 0 | 0 | 2 | 0 | 0 | 0 | 2 | 0 |
| **KICKOFF RETURNS:** | | | | | | | | | | | | | | |
| Number | 70 | 47 | 75 | 50 | 48 | 60 | 58 | 57 | 45 | 55 | 40 | 63 | 37 | 60 |
| Yards | 1490 | 1183 | 1517 | 1090 | 1052 | 1320 | 1544 | 1324 | 990 | 1319 | 989 | 1663 | 883 | 1499 |
| Average Yards | 21.3 | 25.2 | 20.2 | 21.8 | 21.9 | 22.0 | 26.6 | 23.2 | 22.0 | 24.0 | 24.7 | 26.4 | 23.9 | 25.0 |
| Touchdowns | 0 | 0 | 0 | 0 | 0 | 0 | 0 | 2 | 0 | 0 | 0 | 0 | 0 | 0 |
| **INTERCEPTION RETURNS:** | | | | | | | | | | | | | | |
| Number | 9 | 21 | 19 | 24 | 21 | 6 | 20 | 12 | 26 | 18 | 24 | 24 | 22 | 16 |
| Yards | 119 | 260 | 154 | 370 | 247 | 58 | 452 | 149 | 332 | 273 | 465 | 302 | 530 | 321 |
| Average Yards | 13.2 | 12.4 | 8.1 | 15.4 | 11.8 | 9.7 | 22.6 | 10.6 | 12.8 | 15.2 | 19.4 | 12.6 | 24.1 | 20.1 |
| Touchdowns | 0 | 1 | 0 | 4 | 3 | 0 | 2 | 0 | 2 | 3 | 6 | 0 | 2 | 3 |
| **PENALTIES:** | | | | | | | | | | | | | | |
| Number | 59 | 84 | 64 | 75 | 83 | 56 | 70 | 70 | 75 | 71 | 81 | 71 | 76 | 60 |
| Yards | 641 | 743 | 643 | 781 | 805 | 521 | 675 | 708 | 674 | 748 | 706 | 695 | 783 | 624 |
| **FUMBLES:** | | | | | | | | | | | | | | |
| Number | 28 | 32 | 30 | 26 | 29 | 34 | 28 | 32 | 42 | 27 | 24 | 24 | 33 | 42 |
| Number Lost | 18 | 20 | 21 | 20 | 8 | 25 | 13 | 16 | 18 | 12 | 14 | 14 | 14 | 21 |
| **POINTS:** | | | | | | | | | | | | | | |
| Total | 225 | 379 | 293 | 289 | 260 | 245 | 339 | 296 | 399 | 313 | 315 | 331 | 330 | 305 |
| PAT Attempts | 28 | 47 | 36 | 34 | 29 | 30 | 44 | 36 | 49 | 40 | 39 | 36 | 40 | 39 |
| PAT Made | 27 | 46 | 32 | 32 | 29 | 29 | 42 | 33 | 46 | 40 | 36 | 34 | 39 | 36 |
| FG Attempts | 24 | 26 | 23 | 29 | 38 | 23 | 27 | 28 | 39 | 26 | 25 | 34 | 34 | 27 |
| FG Made | 10 | 17 | 15 | 17 | 19 | 12 | 11 | 13 | 19 | 11 | 15 | 27 | 17 | 11 |
| Pct. FG Made | 41.7 | 65.4 | 65.2 | 58.6 | 50.0 | 52.2 | 40.7 | 46.4 | 48.7 | 42.3 | 60.0 | 79.4 | 50.0 | 40.7 |
| Safeties | 0 | 0 | 0 | 1 | 0 | 0 | 0 | 1 | 1 | 0 | 0 | 0 | 0 | 1 |

## 1964 NFL CHAMPIONSHIP GAME

December 27, at Cleveland
(Attendance 79,544)

## Whitewashing the Aerialists

The Colts came into the game as heavy favorites, but the Cleveland defense effectively shut off the famous Baltimore passing attack as the Browns themselves made several big plays through the air. Neither club scored in the first half, as quarterbacks Johnny Unitas and Frank Ryan both used conservative plays to feel out the enemy. Early in the third quarter, however, a 29-yard punt by Baltimore's Tom Gilburg gave the Browns good field position and led to Lou Groza's 43-yard field goal, which finally broke the scoreless deadlock. As soon as the Browns got the ball back, they sprang Jimmy Brown loose on a pitchout good for 46 yards; in short order, Ryan hit Gary Collins with an 18-yard scoring pass. Then, just before the end of the quarter, Ryan stunned the Colts by throwing a 42-yard bomb to Collins, which, along with the extra point, ran the score up to 17-0. The Colts, in a state of shock over this sudden Cleveland outburst, tried to fight their way back into the game but could make no headway against the charged-up Brown defense. The Browns added a nine-yard Groza field goal early in the final period to run their lead to 20-0, and Ryan threw a 51-yard scoring pass to Gary Collins, the third touchdown of the afternoon for the tall flanker, to make the final score a decisive 27-0 to give Cleveland their first championship since 1955.

### TEAM STATISTICS

| CLEVE. | | BALT. |
|---|---|---|
| 20 | First Downs – Total | 11 |
| 8 | First Downs – Rushing | 5 |
| 9 | First Downs – Passing | 4 |
| 3 | First Downs – Penalty | 2 |
| 3 | Punts – Number | 4 |
| 44.0 | Punts – Average Distance | 33.8 |
| 1 | Punt Returns – Number | 2 |
| 13 | Punt Returns – Yards | 18 |
| 2 | Interception Returns – Number | 1 |
| 10 | Interception Returns – Yards | 14 |
| 0 | Fumbles – Number | 2 |
| 0 | Fumbles – Lost Ball | 2 |
| 7 | Penalties – Number | 5 |
| 59 | Yards Penalized | 48 |
| 1 | Giveaways | 4 |
| 4 | Takeaways | 1 |
| +3 | Difference | −3 |

### SCORING

| | | | | |
|---|---|---|---|---|
| CLEVELAND | 0 | 0 | 17 | 10–27 |
| BALTIMORE | 0 | 0 | 0 | 0– 0 |

Third Quarter
- Cle. Groza, 43 yard field goal
- Cle. Collins, 18 yard pass from Ryan; PAT – Groza (kick)
- Cle. Collins, 42 yard pass from Ryan; PAT – Groza (kick)

Fourth Quarter
- Cle. Groza, 9 yard field goal
- Cle. Collins, 51 yard pass from Ryan; PAT – Groza (kick)

### INDIVIDUAL STATISTICS

**RUSHING**

| CLEVELAND | No | Yds | Avg. | BALTIMORE | No | Yds | Avg. |
|---|---|---|---|---|---|---|---|
| Brown | 27 | 114 | 4.2 | Moore | 9 | 40 | 4.4 |
| Green | 10 | 29 | 2.9 | Hill | 9 | 31 | 3.4 |
| Ryan | 3 | 2 | 0.7 | Unitas | 6 | 30 | 5.0 |
| Warfield | 1 | −3 | −3.0 | Boyd | 1 | −9 | −9.0 |
| | 41 | 142 | 3.5 | | 25 | 92 | 3.7 |

**RECEIVING**

| CLEVELAND | No | Yds | Avg. | BALTIMORE | No | Yds | Avg. |
|---|---|---|---|---|---|---|---|
| Collins | 5 | 130 | 26.0 | Berry | 3 | 38 | 12.7 |
| Brown | 3 | 37 | 12.3 | Lorick | 3 | 18 | 6.0 |
| Brewer | 2 | 26 | 13.0 | Orr | 2 | 31 | 15.5 |
| Warfield | 1 | 13 | 13.0 | Moore | 2 | 4 | 2.0 |
| | 11 | 206 | 18.7 | Mackey | 1 | 2 | 2.0 |
| | | | | Hill | 1 | 2 | 2.0 |
| | | | | | 12 | 95 | 7.9 |

**PASSING**

| | Att | Comp | Comp Pct. | Yds | Int | Yds/ Att. | Yds/ Comp | Yards Lost Tackled |
|---|---|---|---|---|---|---|---|---|
| **CLEVELAND** | | | | | | | | |
| Ryan | 18 | 11 | 61.6 | 206 | 1 | 11.4 | 18.7 | 9 |
| **BALTIMORE** | | | | | | | | |
| Unitas | 20 | 12 | 60.0 | 95 | 2 | 4.8 | 7.9 | 6 |

## CLEVELAND BROWNS 10-3-1 Blanton Collier

| Scores of Each Game | | |
|---|---|---|
| 27 | Washington | 13 |
| 33 | ST. LOUIS | 33 |
| 28 | Philadelphia | 20 |
| 27 | DALLAS | 6 |
| 7 | PITTSBURGH | 23 |
| 20 | Dallas | 16 |
| 42 | NEW YORK | 20 |
| 30 | Pittsburgh | 17 |
| 34 | WASHINGTON | 24 |
| 37 | DETROIT | 21 |
| 21 | Green Bay | 28 |
| 38 | PHILADELPHIA | 24 |
| 19 | St. Louis | 28 |
| 52 | New York | 20 |

| Use Name | Pos. | Hgt | Wgt | Age | Int | Pts |
|---|---|---|---|---|---|---|
| John Brown | OT | 6'2" | 248 | 25 | | |
| Monte Clark | OT | 6'6" | 265 | 27 | | |
| Dick Schafrath | OT | 6'3" | 255 | 28 | | |
| Roger Shoals | OG-OT | 6'4" | 255 | 25 | | 6 |
| Gene Hickerson | OG | 6'3" | 248 | 29 | | |
| Dale Memmelaar | OG | 6'2" | 248 | 27 | | |
| John Wooten | OG | 6'2" | 250 | 29 | | |
| John Morrow | C | 6'3" | 248 | 31 | | |
| Bill Glass | DE | 6'5" | 255 | 28 | | |
| Paul Wiggin | DE | 6'3" | 245 | 30 | | 6 |
| Sid Williams | DE | 6'2" | 235 | 22 | | 6 |
| Mike Bundra (from MIN) | DT | 6'3" | 260 | 25 | | |
| Bob Gain | DT | 6'3" | 260 | 36 | | |
| Jim Kanicki | DT | 6'4" | 270 | 22 | | |
| Dick Modzelewski | DT | 6' | 260 | 33 | | |
| Frank Parker | DT | 6'5" | 255 | 24 | | |

| Use Name | Pos. | Hgt | Wgt | Age | Int | Pts |
|---|---|---|---|---|---|---|
| Ed Bettridge | LB | 6'1" | 235 | 24 | | |
| Vince Costello | LB | 6' | 228 | 32 | 2 | |
| Galen Fiss | LB | 6' | 227 | 34 | 1 | |
| Jim Houston | LB | 6'2" | 240 | 27 | 2 | 6 |
| Mike Lucci | LB | 6'2" | 233 | 24 | | |
| Stan Sczurek | LB | 5'11" | 230 | 25 | | |
| Walter Beach | DB | 6' | 185 | 29 | 4 | 6 |
| Larry Benz | DB | 5'11" | 185 | 23 | 4 | |
| Lowell Caylor | DB | 6'3" | 205 | 23 | | |
| Ross Fichtner | DB | 6' | 185 | 26 | 2 | |
| Bobby Franklin | DB | 5'11" | 182 | 28 | | |
| Bernie Parrish | DB | 5'11" | 195 | 29 | 4 | 6 |
| Dave Raimey | DB | 5'10" | 195 | 23 | | |

| Use Name | Pos. | Hgt | Wgt | Age | Int | Pts |
|---|---|---|---|---|---|---|
| Jim Ninowski | QB | 6'1" | 207 | 28 | | |
| Frank Ryan | QB | 6'3" | 200 | 28 | | 6 |
| Ernie Green | HB | 6'2" | 205 | 25 | | 60 |
| Leroy Kelly | HB | 6' | 195 | 22 | | 6 |
| Jimmy Brown | FB | 6'2" | 228 | 28 | | 54 |
| Charlie Scales | FB | 5'11" | 215 | 25 | | 6 |
| Gary Collins | FL | 6'4" | 208 | 23 | | 48 |
| Clifton McNeil | FL | 6'2" | 185 | 24 | | 6 |
| Walter Roberts | FL | 5'10" | 175 | 22 | | 6 |
| Johnny Brewer | OE | 6'4" | 235 | 27 | | 18 |
| Tom Hutchinson | OE | 6'1" | 190 | 23 | | |
| Paul Warfield | OE | 6' | 188 | 21 | | 54 |
| Lou Groza | K | 6'3" | 250 | 40 | | 115 |

## ST. LOUIS CARDINALS 9-3-2 Wally Lemm

| Scores of Each Game | | |
|---|---|---|
| 16 | Dallas | 6 |
| 33 | Cleveland | 33 |
| 23 | San Francisco | 13 |
| 23 | Washington | 17 |
| 27 | Baltimore | 47 |
| 38 | WASHINGTON | 24 |
| 13 | DALLAS | 31 |
| 17 | New York | 34 |
| 34 | PITTSBURGH | 30 |
| 10 | NEW YORK | 10 |
| 38 | Philadelphia | 13 |
| 21 | Pittsburgh | 20 |
| 28 | CLEVELAND | 19 |
| 36 | PHILADELPHIA | 34 |

| Use Name | Pos. | Hgt | Wgt | Age | Int | Pts |
|---|---|---|---|---|---|---|
| Ernie McMillan | OT | 6'6" | 255 | 26 | | |
| Bob Reynolds | OT | 6'6" | 265 | 23 | | |
| Ed Cook | OG-OT | 6'2" | 250 | 32 | | |
| Irv Goode | OG | 6'4" | 250 | 23 | | |
| Ken Gray | OG | 6'2" | 250 | 28 | | |
| Rick Sortun | OG | 6'2" | 225 | 21 | | |
| Herschel Turner | OT-OG | 6'3" | 230 | 22 | | |
| Bob DeMarco | C | 6'3" | 240 | 26 | | |
| Don Brumm | DE | 6'3" | 245 | 21 | | |
| Tom Redmond | DE | 6'5" | 240 | 27 | | |
| Joe Robb | DE | 6'3" | 245 | 27 | | |
| Chuck Walker | DE | 6'2" | 235 | 23 | | |
| Ken Kortas | DT | 6'2" | 290 | 22 | | |
| Luke Owens | DT | 6'2" | 260 | 31 | | |
| Sam Silas | DT | 6'4" | 250 | 21 | | |

| Use Name | Pos. | Hgt | Wgt | Age | Int | Pts |
|---|---|---|---|---|---|---|
| Bill Koman | LB | 6'2" | 230 | 30 | 2 | |
| Dave Meggyesy | LB | 6'1" | 220 | 22 | | |
| Dale Meinert | LB | 6'2" | 220 | 31 | 2 | 6 |
| Marion Rushing | LB | 5'2" | 230 | 27 | | 2 |
| Larry Stallings | LB | 6'2" | 230 | 22 | 2 | |
| Monk Bailey | DB | 6' | 175 | 26 | | |
| Jimmy Burson | DB | 6' | 180 | 22 | 3 | 6 |
| Pat Fischer | DB | 5'10" | 180 | 24 | 10 | 18 |
| Jimmy Hill | DB | 6'2" | 195 | 35 | | |
| Jerry Stovall | DB | 6'2" | 205 | 22 | 3 | 6 |
| Larry Wilson | DB | 6' | 190 | 26 | 3 | 6 |

Bill Triplett – Illness

| Use Name | Pos. | Hgt | Wgt | Age | Int | Pts |
|---|---|---|---|---|---|---|
| Buddy Humphrey | QB | 6'1" | 200 | 28 | | |
| Charley Johnson | QB | 6' | 190 | 27 | | 12 |
| Joe Childress | HB | 6' | 210 | 30 | | 12 |
| Bob Paremore | HB | 5'11" | 190 | 24 | | |
| John David Crow | FB-HB | 6'2" | 220 | 29 | | 48 |
| Willie Crenshaw | FB | 6'2" | 215 | 23 | | 6 |
| Prentice Gautt | FB | 6' | 205 | 26 | | 12 |
| Bill Thornton | FB | 6'1" | 220 | 24 | | 6 |
| Bobby Joe Conrad | FL | 6' | 195 | 29 | | 36 |
| Taz Anderson | OE | 6'2" | 215 | 25 | | |
| Billy Gambrell | OE | 5'10" | 175 | 22 | | 12 |
| Sonny Randle | OE | 6'2" | 190 | 28 | | 30 |
| Jackie Smith | OE | 6'4" | 210 | 23 | | 24 |
| Mal Hammack | LB-OE | 6'2" | 210 | 31 | | |
| Jim Bakken | K | 6' | 200 | 23 | | 115 |

## PHILADELPHIA EAGLES 6-8-0 Joe Kuharich

| Scores of Each Game | | |
|---|---|---|
| 38 | NEW YORK | 7 |
| 24 | SAN FRANCISCO | 28 |
| 20 | CLEVELAND | 28 |
| 21 | PITTSBURGH | 7 |
| 20 | Washington | 35 |
| 23 | New York | 17 |
| 34 | Pittsburgh | 10 |
| 10 | WASHINGTON | 21 |
| 10 | Los Angeles | 20 |
| 17 | Dallas | 14 |
| 13 | ST. LOUIS | 38 |
| 24 | Cleveland | 38 |
| 24 | DALLAS | 14 |
| 34 | St. Louis | 36 |

| Use Name | Pos. | Hgt | Wgt | Age | Int | Pts |
|---|---|---|---|---|---|---|
| Bob Brown | OT | 6'4" | 280 | 21 | | |
| Dave Graham | OT | 6'3" | 250 | 25 | | |
| Jim Skaggs | OT | 6'2" | 230 | 24 | | |
| Ed Blaine | OG | 6'2" | 240 | 24 | | |
| Pete Case | OG | 6'3" | 243 | 23 | | |
| Lynn Hoyem | C | 6'4" | 240 | 24 | | |
| Jim Ringo | C | 6'1" | 230 | 33 | | |
| Jim Schrader | C | 6'2" | 250 | 32 | | |
| Riley Gunnels | DE | 6'3" | 253 | 27 | | |
| Don Hultz | DE | 6'3" | 235 | 23 | | |
| Bobby Richards | DE | 6'2" | 245 | 25 | | |
| George Tarasovic | DE | 6'4" | 245 | 35 | | |
| Don Thompson | DE | 6'4" | 240 | 25 | | |
| Ed Khayat | DT | 6'3" | 245 | 29 | | |
| John Meyers | DT | 6'6" | 267 | 24 | | |
| Floyd Peters | DT | 6'4" | 255 | 29 | | |

| Use Name | Pos. | Hgt | Wgt | Age | Int | Pts |
|---|---|---|---|---|---|---|
| Maxie Baughan | LB | 6'1" | 230 | 26 | | |
| Ralph Heck | LB | 6'2" | 224 | 23 | | |
| Dave Lloyd | LB | 6'3" | 248 | 28 | 3 | |
| Mike Morgan | LB | 6'4" | 232 | 22 | | 6 |
| Don Burroughs | DB | 6'4" | 187 | 33 | 2 | |
| Irv Cross | DB | 6'1" | 195 | 25 | 3 | 6 |
| Glenn Glass | DB | 6' | 190 | 27 | 1 | |
| Nate Ramsey | DB | 6'1" | 200 | 23 | 5 | |
| Joe Scarpati | DB | 5'10" | 185 | 22 | 3 | 6 |
| Claude Crabb | FL-DB | 6' | 197 | 24 | | |

Jerry Mazzanti – Military Service
Mike McClellan – Military Service
Fate Echols – Canadian Football League

| Use Name | Pos. | Hgt | Wgt | Age | Int | Pts |
|---|---|---|---|---|---|---|
| Jack Concannon | QB | 6'3" | 195 | 21 | | 6 |
| King Hill | QB | 6'3" | 213 | 28 | | |
| Norm Snead | QB | 6'4" | 215 | 24 | | 12 |
| Timmy Brown | HB | 5'10" | 200 | 27 | | 60 |
| Roger Gill | HB | 6'1" | 200 | 23 | | |
| Ollie Matson | HB | 6'2" | 210 | 34 | | 30 |
| Earl Gros | FB | 6'3" | 230 | 23 | | 12 |
| Izzy Lang | FB | 6'1" | 230 | 21 | | |
| Tom Woodeshick | FB | 6' | 205 | 22 | | 12 |
| Red Mack | FL | 5'10" | 185 | 27 | | 6 |
| Ron Goodwin | OE-FL | 6' | 184 | 22 | | 18 |
| Ray Poage | OE | 6'4" | 203 | 23 | | 6 |
| Pete Retzlaff | OE | 6'1" | 214 | 33 | | 48 |
| Ralph Smith | DB-OE | 6'2" | 213 | 25 | | |
| Sam Baker | K | 6'2" | 220 | 32 | | 84 |

## WASHINGTON REDSKINS 6-8-0 Bill McPeak

| Scores of Each Game | | |
|---|---|---|
| 13 | CLEVELAND | 27 |
| 18 | Dallas | 24 |
| 10 | New York | 13 |
| 17 | ST. LOUIS | 23 |
| 35 | PHILADELPHIA | 20 |
| 24 | St. Louis | 38 |
| 27 | CHICAGO | 20 |
| 21 | Philadelphia | 10 |
| 24 | Cleveland | 34 |
| 30 | Pittsburgh | 0 |
| 28 | DALLAS | 16 |
| 36 | NEW YORK | 21 |
| 7 | PITTSBURGH | 14 |
| 17 | Baltimore | 45 |

| Use Name | Pos. | Hgt | Wgt | Age | Int | Pts |
|---|---|---|---|---|---|---|
| Steve Barnett | OT | 6'1" | 255 | 23 | | |
| Riley Mattson | OT | 6'4" | 254 | 25 | | |
| Fran O'Brien | OT | 6'1" | 255 | 29 | | |
| John Nisby | OG | 6'1" | 238 | 31 | | |
| Vince Promuto | OG | 6'1" | 245 | 26 | | |
| George Seals | OG | 6'2" | 250 | 21 | | |
| Fred Hageman | C | 6'4" | 242 | 26 | | |
| Len Hauss | C | 6'2" | 220 | 22 | | |
| Carl Kammerer | DE | 6'3" | 237 | 27 | | |
| John Paluck | DE | 6'2" | 245 | 32 | | 2 |
| Ron Snidow | DE | 6'4" | 250 | 22 | | |
| Joe Rutgens | DT | 6'2" | 255 | 25 | | |
| Bob Toneff | DT | 6'3" | 257 | 34 | | |
| Fred Williams | DT | 6'4" | 248 | 34 | | |

| Use Name | Pos. | Hgt | Wgt | Age | Int | Pts |
|---|---|---|---|---|---|---|
| Rod Breedlove | LB | 6'2" | 227 | 26 | | |
| Jimmy Carr | LB | 6'1" | 210 | 31 | 2 | |
| Sam Huff | LB | 6'1" | 230 | 29 | 4 | |
| Bob Pellegrini | LB | 6'2" | 237 | 29 | | |
| John Reger | LB | 6' | 230 | 33 | 3 | 6 |
| Paul Krause | DB | 6'3" | 198 | 22 | 12 | 6 |
| Johnny Sample | DB | 6'1" | 200 | 27 | 4 | 6 |
| Lonnie Sanders | DB | 6'3" | 210 | 22 | 2 | |
| Jim Shorter | DB | 5'11" | 186 | 23 | 1 | |
| Jim Steffen | DB | 6' | 196 | 27 | 4 | |
| Tom Walters | DB | 6'2" | 195 | 22 | 2 | |

| Use Name | Pos. | Hgt | Wgt | Age | Int | Pts |
|---|---|---|---|---|---|---|
| George Izo | QB | 6'3" | 218 | 27 | | |
| Sonny Jurgensen | QB | 5'11" | 200 | 30 | | 18 |
| Dick Shiner | QB | 6' | 190 | 22 | | |
| Pervis Atkins | HB | 6'1" | 217 | 28 | | 6 |
| Charley Taylor | HB | 6'3" | 215 | 23 | | 60 |
| Tom Tracy | HB | 5'9" | 205 | 32 | | 6 |
| Don Bosseler | FB | 6'1" | 214 | 28 | | |
| J.W. Lockett | FB | 6'2" | 226 | 27 | | 18 |
| Ozzie Clay | FL | 6' | 190 | 22 | | |
| Joe Hernandez | FL | 6'2" | 180 | 24 | | |
| Bobby Mitchell | FL | 6' | 196 | 29 | | 60 |
| Preston Carpenter | OE | 6'2" | 190 | 30 | | 18 |
| Angie Coia | OE | 6'2" | 202 | 26 | | 30 |
| Pat Richter | OE | 6'5" | 230 | 23 | | |
| Jim Martin | K | 6'2" | 238 | 40 | | 71 |

## DALLAS COWBOYS 5-8-1 Tom Landry

| Scores of Each Game | | |
|---|---|---|
| 6 | ST. LOUIS | 16 |
| 24 | WASHINGTON | 18 |
| 17 | Pittsburgh | 23 |
| 6 | Cleveland | 27 |
| 13 | NEW YORK | 13 |
| 16 | CLEVELAND | 20 |
| 31 | St. Louis | 13 |
| 24 | Chicago | 10 |
| 31 | New York | 21 |
| 14 | PHILADELPHIA | 17 |
| 16 | Washington | 28 |
| 21 | GREEN BAY | 45 |
| 14 | Philadelphia | 24 |
| 17 | PITTSBURGH | 14 |

| Use Name | Pos. | Hgt | Wgt | Age | Int | Pts |
|---|---|---|---|---|---|---|
| Jim Boeke | OT | 6'5" | 255 | 25 | | |
| Bill Frank | OT | 6'5" | 255 | 26 | | |
| Bob Fry | OT | 6'4" | 238 | 33 | | |
| Tony Liscio | OT | 6'5" | 240 | 24 | | |
| Ray Schoenke | OT | 6'3" | 234 | 22 | | |
| Jim Ray Smith | OG-OT | 6'3" | 245 | 33 | | |
| Joe Bob Isbell | OG | 6'1" | 250 | 24 | | |
| Jake Kupp | OG | 6'3" | 215 | 22 | | |
| Mike Connelly | C | 6'3" | 242 | 28 | | |
| Dave Manders | C | 6'2" | 240 | 22 | | |
| George Andrie | DE | 6'7" | 264 | 24 | | |
| Larry Stephens | DE | 6'4" | 260 | 26 | | |
| Maury Youmans | DE | 6'6" | 260 | 27 | | |
| Jim Colvin | DT | 6'2" | 253 | 27 | | |
| Bob Lilly | DT | 6'4" | 250 | 25 | | |

| Use Name | Pos. | Hgt | Wgt | Age | Int | Pts |
|---|---|---|---|---|---|---|
| Dave Edwards | LB | 6'3" | 213 | 25 | 1 | |
| Harold Hays | LB | 6'3" | 235 | 23 | | |
| Chuck Howley | LB | 6'3" | 223 | 28 | 2 | |
| Lee Roy Jordon | LB | 6'2" | 215 | 23 | 1 | |
| Jerry Tubbs | LB | 6'2" | 215 | 29 | 2 | |
| Don Bishop | DB | 6'2" | 215 | 29 | | |
| Mike Gaechter | DB | 6' | 196 | 24 | | |
| Cornell Green | DB | 6'4" | 220 | 24 | | |
| Warren Livingston | DB | 5'10" | 185 | 26 | 1 | 6 |
| Mel Renfro | DB | 6' | 190 | 22 | 7 | 12 |
| Jimmy Ridlon | DB | 6'1" | 180 | 29 | 4 | 12 |

Jerry Overton – Off-season accident
Don Talbert – Military Service

| Use Name | Pos. | Hgt | Wgt | Age | Int | Pts |
|---|---|---|---|---|---|---|
| Billy Lothridge | QB | 6'1" | 185 | 20 | | 6 |
| Don Meredith | QB | 6'2" | 205 | 26 | | 24 |
| John Roach | QB | 6'4" | 200 | 31 | | |
| Amos Bullocks | HB | 6'1" | 202 | 25 | | |
| Perry Lee Dunn | HB | 6'2" | 200 | 21 | | 6 |
| Amos Marsh | HB | 6'1" | 225 | 25 | | 12 |
| Jim Stiger | FB-HB | 5'11" | 190 | 23 | | 12 |
| Don Perkins | FB | 5'10" | 196 | 26 | | 36 |
| Frank Clarke | FL | 6' | 215 | 31 | | 30 |
| Buddy Dial | FL | 6'1" | 195 | 27 | | |
| Tommy McDonald | FL | 5'10" | 172 | 30 | | 12 |
| Lee Folkins | OE | 6'5" | 220 | 25 | | |
| Pete Gent | OE | 6'4" | 215 | 21 | | |
| Pettis Norman | OE | 6'3" | 223 | 24 | | 12 |
| Dick Van Raaphorst | K | 5'11" | 215 | 21 | | 70 |

## CLEVELAND BROWNS

### RUSHING

| Last Name | No. | Yds | Avg | TD |
|---|---|---|---|---|
| Jimmy Brown | 280 | 1446 | 5.2 | 7 |
| Green | 109 | 491 | 4.5 | 6 |
| Ryan | 37 | 217 | 5.9 | 1 |
| Kelly | 6 | 12 | 2.0 | 0 |
| Scales | 2 | 5 | 2.5 | 0 |
| Ninowski | 1 | −8 | −8.0 | 0 |

### RECEIVING

| Last Name | No. | Yds | Avg | TD |
|---|---|---|---|---|
| Warfield | 52 | 920 | 18 | 9 |
| Jimmy Brown | 36 | 340 | 9 | 2 |
| Collins | 35 | 544 | 16 | 8 |
| Brewer | 25 | 338 | 14 | 3 |
| Green | 25 | 283 | 11 | 4 |
| McNeil | 4 | 69 | 17 | 1 |
| Hutchinson | 3 | 24 | 8 | 0 |
| Roberts | 1 | 24 | 24 | 1 |

### PUNT RETURNS

| Last Name | No. | Yds | Avg | TD |
|---|---|---|---|---|
| Kelly | 9 | 171 | 19 | 1 |
| Roberts | 10 | 132 | 13 | 0 |
| Williams | 1 | 0 | 0 | 0 |

### KICKOFF RETURNS

| Last Name | No. | Yds | Avg | TD |
|---|---|---|---|---|
| Roberts | 24 | 661 | 28 | 0 |
| Kelly | 24 | 582 | 24 | 0 |
| Scales | 5 | 75 | 15 | 0 |
| Warfield | 1 | 4 | 4 | 0 |
| Franklin | 1 | 1 | 1 | 0 |
| Clark | 1 | 0 | 0 | 0 |
| Williams | 1 | 0 | 0 | 0 |

### PASSING – PUNTING – KICKING

| PASSING | Att | Comp | % | Yds | Yd/Att | TD | Int– | % | RK |
|---|---|---|---|---|---|---|---|---|---|
| Ryan | 334 | 174 | 52 | 2404 | 7.2 | 25 | 19– | 6 | 6 |
| Ninowski | 9 | 6 | 67 | 125 | 13.9 | 2 | 0– | 0 | |
| Jimmy Brown | 1 | 1 | 100 | 13 | 13.0 | 0 | 0– | 0 | |

| PUNTING | No | Avg |
|---|---|---|
| Collins | 48 | 42.0 |
| Franklin | 1 | 36.0 |

| KICKING | XP | Att | % | FG | Att | % |
|---|---|---|---|---|---|---|
| Groza | 49 | 50 | 98 | 22 | 33 | 67 |

## ST. LOUIS CARDINALS

### RUSHING

| Last Name | No. | Yds | Avg | TD |
|---|---|---|---|---|
| Crow | 163 | 554 | 3.4 | 7 |
| Childress | 102 | 413 | 4.0 | 0 |
| Crenshaw | 60 | 297 | 5.0 | 1 |
| Thornton | 39 | 236 | 6.1 | 1 |
| Gautt | 59 | 191 | 3.2 | 1 |
| Johnson | 31 | 93 | 3.0 | 2 |
| Wilson | 2 | −14 | −7.0 | 0 |

### RECEIVING

| Last Name | No. | Yds | Avg | TD |
|---|---|---|---|---|
| Conrad | 61 | 780 | 13 | 6 |
| Smith | 47 | 657 | 14 | 4 |
| Randle | 25 | 517 | 21 | 5 |
| Gambrell | 24 | 398 | 17 | 2 |
| Crow | 23 | 257 | 11 | 1 |
| Childress | 12 | 203 | 17 | 2 |
| Gautt | 9 | 72 | 8 | 1 |
| Crenshaw | 8 | 58 | 7 | 0 |
| Anderson | 7 | 60 | 9 | 0 |
| Thornton | 7 | 43 | 6 | 0 |

### PUNT RETURNS

| Last Name | No. | Yds | Avg | TD |
|---|---|---|---|---|
| Gambrell | 12 | 126 | 11 | 0 |
| Bruson | 12 | 125 | 10 | 1 |

### KICKOFF RETURNS

| Last Name | No. | Yds | Avg | TD |
|---|---|---|---|---|
| Stovall | 24 | 566 | 24 | 0 |
| Crenshaw | 13 | 340 | 26 | 0 |
| Paremore | 9 | 192 | 21 | 0 |
| Gautt | 5 | 104 | 21 | 0 |
| Gambrell | 4 | 92 | 23 | 0 |
| Hammack | 2 | 61 | 31 | 0 |
| Burson | 2 | 38 | 19 | 0 |
| Conrad | 1 | 26 | 26 | 0 |
| Thornton | 1 | 5 | 5 | 0 |
| Gray | 2 | 0 | 0 | 0 |

### PASSING – PUNTING – KICKING

| PASSING | Att | Comp | % | Yds | Yd/Att | TD | Int– | % | RK |
|---|---|---|---|---|---|---|---|---|---|
| Johnson | 420 | 223 | 53 | 3045 | 7.3 | 21 | 24– | 6 | 7 |
| Crow | 1 | 0 | 0 | 0 | 0 | 0 | 0– | 0 | |
| Humphrey | 1 | 0 | 0 | 0 | 0.0 | 0. | 0– | 0 | |

| PUNTING | No | Avg |
|---|---|---|
| Smith | 41 | 40.4 |
| Stovall | 15 | 42.1 |

| KICKING | XP | Att | % | FG | Att | % |
|---|---|---|---|---|---|---|
| Bakken | 40 | 40 | 100 | 25 | 38 | 66 |

## PHILADELPHIA EAGLES

### RUSHING

| Last Name | No. | Yds | Avg | TD |
|---|---|---|---|---|
| Gros | 154 | 748 | 4.9 | 2 |
| Matson | 96 | 404 | 4.2 | 4 |
| T. Brown | 90 | 356 | 4.0 | 5 |
| Woodeshick | 37 | 180 | 4.9 | 2 |
| Concannon | 16 | 134 | 8.4 | 1 |
| Snead | 16 | 59 | 3.7 | 2 |
| Lang | 12 | 37 | 3.1 | 0 |
| Hill | 8 | 27 | 3.4 | 0 |
| Goodwin | 1 | −23 | −23.0 | 0 |

### RECEIVING

| Last Name | No. | Yds | Avg | TD |
|---|---|---|---|---|
| Retzlaff | 51 | 855 | 17 | 8 |
| Poage | 37 | 479 | 13 | 1 |
| Gros | 29 | 234 | 8 | 0 |
| Goodwin | 23 | 335 | 15 | 3 |
| Matson | 17 | 242 | 14 | 1 |
| T. Brown | 15 | 244 | 16 | 5 |
| Mack | 8 | 169 | 21 | 1 |
| Lang | 6 | 69 | 12 | 0 |
| Gill | 4 | 58 | 15 | 0 |
| Smith | 4 | 35 | 9 | 0 |
| Woodeshick | 4 | 12 | 3 | 0 |
| Crabb | 1 | 14 | 14 | 0 |

### PUNT RETURNS

| Last Name | No. | Yds | Avg | TD |
|---|---|---|---|---|
| T. Brown | 10 | 96 | 10 | 0 |
| Gill | 6 | 61 | 10 | 0 |
| Lang | 6 | 26 | 4 | 0 |
| Matson | 2 | 10 | 5 | 0 |
| Scarpati | 1 | 6 | 6 | 0 |
| Hultz | 1 | 2 | 2 | 0 |
| Glass | 1 | 0 | 0 | 0 |
| Mack | 1 | 0 | 0 | 0 |

### KICKOFF RETURNS

| Last Name | No. | Yds | Avg | TD |
|---|---|---|---|---|
| T. Brown | 30 | 692 | 23 | 0 |
| Lang | 13 | 352 | 27 | 0 |
| Gill | 7 | 167 | 24 | 0 |
| Matson | 3 | 104 | 35 | 0 |
| Gros | 2 | 38 | 19 | 0 |
| Glass | 1 | 12 | 12 | 0 |
| Morgan | 2 | 0 | 0 | 0 |
| Thompson | 1 | 0 | 0 | 0 |

### PASSING – PUNTING – KICKING

| PASSING | Att | Comp | % | Yds | Yd/Att | TD | Int– | % | RK |
|---|---|---|---|---|---|---|---|---|---|
| Snead | 283 | 138 | 49 | 1906 | 6.7 | 14 | 12– | 4 | 11 |
| Hill | 88 | 49 | 56 | 641 | 7.3 | 3 | 4– | 5 | |
| Concannon | 23 | 12 | 52 | 199 | 8.7 | 2 | 1– | 4 | |
| T. Brown | 2 | 0 | 0 | 0 | 0.0 | 0 | 1– | 50 | |
| Gros | 1 | 0 | 0 | 0 | 0.0 | 0 | 0– | 0 | |

| PUNTING | No | Avg |
|---|---|---|
| Baker | 49 | 42.3 |
| Hill | 24 | 40.3 |

| KICKING | XP | Att | % | FG | Att | % |
|---|---|---|---|---|---|---|
| Baker | 36 | 37 | 97 | 16 | 26 | 62 |

## WASHINGTON REDSKINS

### RUSHING

| Last Name | No. | Yds | Avg | TD |
|---|---|---|---|---|
| Taylor | 199 | 755 | 3.8 | 5 |
| Lockett | 63 | 175 | 2.8 | 1 |
| Atkins | 25 | 98 | 3.9 | 1 |
| Tracy | 24 | 67 | 2.8 | 1 |
| Jurgensen | 27 | 57 | 2.1 | 3 |
| Bosseler | 22 | 46 | 2.1 | 0 |
| Mitchell | 2 | 33 | 16.5 | 0 |
| Shiner | 2 | 8 | 4.0 | 0 |
| Carpenter | 1 | 7 | 7.0 | 0 |
| Richter | 1 | −9 | −9.0 | 0 |

### RECEIVING

| Last Name | No. | Yds | Avg | TD |
|---|---|---|---|---|
| Mitchell | 60 | 904 | 15 | 10 |
| Taylor | 53 | 814 | 15 | 5 |
| Carpenter | 31 | 466 | 15 | 3 |
| Coia | 29 | 500 | 17 | 5 |
| Lockett | 20 | 204 | 10 | 2 |
| Atkins | 8 | 35 | 4 | 0 |
| Bosseler | 6 | 56 | 9 | 0 |
| Richter | 4 | 49 | 12 | 0 |
| Tracy | 2 | 25 | 13 | 0 |
| Hernandez | 1 | 18 | 18 | 0 |

### PUNT RETURNS

| Last Name | No. | Yds | Avg | TD |
|---|---|---|---|---|
| Atkins | 13 | 138 | 11 | 0 |
| Hernandez | 5 | 49 | 10 | 0 |
| Shorter | 6 | 19 | 3 | 0 |
| Carpenter | 2 | 19 | 10 | 0 |
| Clay | 4 | 5 | 1 | 0 |
| Carr | 1 | 0 | 0 | 0 |
| Kammerer | 1 | 0 | 0 | 0 |

### KICKOFF RETURNS

| Last Name | No. | Yds | Avg | TD |
|---|---|---|---|---|
| Clay | 19 | 482 | 25 | 0 |
| Atkins | 14 | 319 | 23 | 0 |
| Shorter | 5 | 81 | 16 | 0 |
| Lockett | 3 | 72 | 24 | 0 |
| Mitchell | 3 | 58 | 19 | 0 |
| Mattson | 3 | 30 | 10 | 0 |
| Taylor | 1 | 20 | 20 | 0 |
| Hernandez | 1 | 19 | 19 | 0 |
| Snidow | 1 | 16 | 16 | 0 |
| Carr | 1 | 0 | 0 | 0 |
| Pellegrini | 1 | 0 | 0 | 0 |

### PASSING – PUNTING – KICKING

| PASSING | Att | Comp | % | Yds | Yd/Att | TD | Int– | % | RK |
|---|---|---|---|---|---|---|---|---|---|
| Jurgensen | 385 | 207 | 54 | 2934 | 7.6 | 24 | 13– | 3 | 3 |
| Izo | 18 | 5 | 28 | 83 | 4.6 | 1 | 2– | 11 | |
| Taylor | 10 | 2 | 20 | 54 | 5.4 | 0 | 1– | 10 | |
| Carpenter | 1 | 0 | 0 | 0 | 0.0 | 0 | 0– | 5 | |
| Shiner | 1 | 0 | 0 | 0 | 0.0 | 0 | 0– | 0 | |

| PUNTING | No | Avg |
|---|---|---|
| Richter | 91 | 41.2 |

| KICKING | XP | Att | % | FG | Att | % |
|---|---|---|---|---|---|---|
| Martin | 35 | 39 | 90 | 12 | 28 | 43 |

## DALLAS COWBOYS

### RUSHING

| Last Name | No. | Yds | Avg | TD |
|---|---|---|---|---|
| Perkins | 174 | 768 | 4.4 | 6 |
| Marsh | 100 | 401 | 4.0 | 2 |
| Stiger | 68 | 280 | 4.1 | 1 |
| Dunn | 26 | 103 | 4.0 | 1 |
| Meredith | 32 | 81 | 2.5 | 4 |
| Clarke | 10 | 46 | 4.6 | 0 |
| Roach | 8 | 9 | 1.1 | 0 |
| Folkins | 1 | 9 | 9.0 | 0 |
| Lothridge | 2 | −6 | −3.0 | 1 |

### RECEIVING

| Last Name | No. | Yds | Avg | TD |
|---|---|---|---|---|
| Clarke | 65 | 973 | 15 | 5 |
| McDonald | 46 | 612 | 13 | 2 |
| Norman | 24 | 311 | 13 | 2 |
| Perkins | 15 | 155 | 10 | 0 |
| Marsh | 15 | 131 | 9 | 0 |
| Dial | 11 | 178 | 16 | 0 |
| Stiger | 9 | 85 | 9 | 1 |
| Folkins | 5 | 41 | 8 | 0 |
| Dunn | 2 | 30 | 15 | 0 |

### PUNT RETURNS

| Last Name | No. | Yds | Avg | TD |
|---|---|---|---|---|
| Renfro | 32 | 418 | 13 | 1 |
| Gaechter | 5 | 24 | 5 | 0 |
| McDonald | 2 | 17 | 9 | 0 |
| Stiger | 1 | 0 | 0 | 0 |

### KICKOFF RETURNS

| Last Name | No. | Yds | Avg | TD |
|---|---|---|---|---|
| Renfro | 40 | 1017 | 25 | 0 |
| Dunn | 2 | 333 | 17 | 0 |
| Gaechter | 1 | 31 | 31 | 0 |
| Bullocks | 1 | 19 | 19 | 0 |
| Marsh | 1 | 2 | 2 | 0 |
| Folkins | 1 | 0 | 0 | 0 |

### PASSING – PUNTING – KICKING

| PASSING | Att | Comp | % | Yds | Yd/Att | TD | Int– | % | RK |
|---|---|---|---|---|---|---|---|---|---|
| Meredith | 323 | 158 | 49 | 2143 | 6.6 | 9 | 16– | 5 | 15 |
| Roach | 68 | 32 | 47 | 349 | 5.1 | 1 | 6– | 9 | |
| Lothridge | 9 | 2 | 22 | 24 | 2.7 | 0 | 2– | 22 | |
| Dunn | 2 | 0 | 0 | 0 | 0.0 | 0 | 0– | 0 | |
| Clarke | 1 | 0 | 0 | 0 | 0.0 | 0 | 0– | 0 | |
| Stiger | 1 | 0 | 0 | 0 | 0.0 | 0 | 0– | 0 | |

| PUNTING | No | Avg |
|---|---|---|
| Lothridge | 62 | 40.3 |
| Folkins | 15 | 33.1 |
| Howley | 1 | 37.0 |

| KICKING | XP | Att | % | FG | Att | % |
|---|---|---|---|---|---|---|
| Van Raaphorst | 28 | 29 | 97 | 14 | 29 | 48 |

**EASTERN CONFERENCE – Continued**

## PITTSBURGH STEELERS 5-9-0 Buddy Parker

| Scores of Each Game | | |
|---|---|---|
| 14 | LOS ANGELES | 26 |
| 27 | NEW YORK | 24 |
| 23 | DALLAS | 17 |
| 7 | Philadelphia | 21 |
| 23 | Cleveland | 7 |
| 10 | Minnesota | 30 |
| 10 | PHILADELPHIA | 34 |
| 17 | CLEVELAND | 30 |
| 30 | St. Louis | 34 |
| 0 | WASHINGTON | 30 |
| 44 | New York | 17 |
| 20 | ST. LOUIS | 21 |
| 14 | Washington | 7 |
| 14 | Dallas | 17 |

| Use Name | Pos. | Hgt | Wgt | Age | Int | Pts |
|---|---|---|---|---|---|---|
| Charlie Bradshaw | OT | 6'6" | 255 | 28 | | |
| Dan James | OT | 6'4" | 250 | 27 | | |
| Ray Lemek | OG | 6' | 240 | 30 | | |
| Mike Sandusky | OG | 6' | 230 | 31 | | |
| Ron Stehouwer | OG | 6'2" | 230 | 27 | | |
| Buzz Nutter | C | 6'4" | 230 | 33 | | |
| John Baker | DE | 6'6" | 270 | 29 | | |
| Dan LaRose | DE | 6'5" | 250 | 24 | | |
| Ben McGee | DE | 6'2" | 250 | 22 | | |
| Urban Henry | DT | 6'4" | 265 | 29 | | |
| Chuck Hinton | DT | 6'5" | 235 | 25 | 1 | 6 |
| Joe Krupa | DT | 6'2" | 235 | 31 | | |
| Ray Mansfield | DT | 6'3" | 255 | 23 | | |
| Bob Harrison | LB | 6'2" | 225 | 27 | | |
| Max Messner (from NY) | LB | 6'3" | 225 | 26 | | |
| Myron Pottios | LB | 6'2" | 240 | 24 | 1 | |
| Bill Saul | LB | 6'4" | 225 | 23 | 1 | |
| Bob Schmitz | LB | 6'1" | 230 | 26 | | |
| Bob Soleau | LB | 6'2" | 235 | 23 | | |
| Ed Holler | LB | 6'2" | 235 | 24 | 1 | |
| Jim Bradshaw | DB | 6'1" | 190 | 25 | 1 | 12 |
| Willie Daniel | DB | 5'11" | 185 | 26 | 2 | |
| Dick Haley | DB | 5'10" | 190 | 28 | 2 | |
| Brady Keys | DB | 6' | 190 | 28 | 2 | |
| Bob Sherman | DB | 6'2" | 195 | 22 | | |
| Ed Brown | QB | 6'2" | 210 | 35 | | 12 |
| Bill Nelsen | QB | 6' | 195 | 23 | | |
| Terry Nofsinger | QB | 6'4" | 205 | 26 | | |
| Tom Wade | QB | 6'2" | 195 | 22 | | |
| Dick Hoak | HB | 5'11" | 190 | 25 | | 30 |
| Phil King | HB | 6'4" | 218 | 28 | | 12 |
| Theron Sapp | HB | 6'1" | 200 | 29 | | |
| Marv Woodson | HB | 6' | 195 | 21 | | |
| John Henry Johnson | FB | 6'2" | 215 | 34 | | 48 |
| Clarence Peaks | FB | 6'1" | 212 | 28 | | 12 |
| Gary Ballman | OE-FL | 6' | 195 | 24 | | 42 |
| Paul Martha | OE-FL | 6' | 185 | 21 | | |
| John Burrell | OE | 6'3" | 190 | 24 | | |
| Jim Kelly | OE | 6'2" | 215 | 22 | | 6 |
| Chuck Logan | OE | 6'4" | 210 | 21 | | |
| John Powers | OE | 6'2" | 210 | 23 | | |
| Clendon Thomas | DB-OE | 6'2" | 195 | 27 | 1 | 6 |
| Mike Clark | K | 6'1" | 200 | 23 | | 67 |

Andy Russell – Military Service

## NEW YORK GIANTS 2-10-2 Allie Sherman

| Scores of Each Game | | |
|---|---|---|
| 7 | Philadelphia | 38 |
| 24 | Pittsburgh | 27 |
| 13 | WASHINGTON | 10 |
| 3 | Detroit | 26 |
| 13 | Dallas | 13 |
| 17 | PHILADELPHIA | 23 |
| 20 | Cleveland | 42 |
| 34 | ST. LOUIS | 17 |
| 21 | DALLAS | 31 |
| 10 | St. Louis | 10 |
| 17 | PITTSBURGH | 44 |
| 21 | Washington | 36 |
| 21 | MINNESOTA | 30 |
| 20 | CLEVELAND | 52 |

| Use Name | Pos. | Hgt | Wgt | Age | Int | Pts |
|---|---|---|---|---|---|---|
| Roger Anderson | OT | 6'5" | 255 | 21 | | |
| Rosey Brown | OT | 6'3" | 255 | 31 | | |
| Lane Howell | OT | 6'5" | 255 | 23 | | |
| Frank Lasky | OT | 6'2" | 265 | 22 | | |
| Jack Stroud | OT | 6'1" | 250 | 35 | | |
| Bookie Bolin | OG | 6'2" | 240 | 24 | | |
| Ken Byers (to MIN) | OG | 6'1" | 240 | 24 | | |
| Darrell Dess | OG | 6' | 245 | 28 | | |
| Mickey Walker | C-OG | 6' | 235 | 24 | | |
| Greg Larson | C | 6'2" | 250 | 25 | | |
| Jim Katcavage | DE | 6'3" | 240 | 29 | | |
| Andy Robustelli | DE | 6'1" | 235 | 38 | | |
| Andy Stynchula | DT | 6'3" | 250 | 25 | | 1 |
| Bob Taylor | DE | 6'3" | 240 | 24 | | |
| John Contoulis | DT | 6'4" | 260 | 23 | | |
| John Lovetere | DT | 6'4" | 285 | 28 | | |
| Jim Moran | DT | 6'5" | 255 | 21 | | |
| Tom Costello | LB | 6'3" | 220 | 23 | | |
| Jerry Hillebrand | LB | 6'3" | 240 | 24 | 1 | |
| Tom Scott | LB | 6'2" | 220 | 34 | 2 | |
| Lou Slaby | LB | 6'3" | 235 | 22 | 2 | |
| Bill Winter | LB | 6'3" | 220 | 24 | | |
| Erich Barnes | DB | 6'2" | 198 | 29 | 2 | 12 |
| Dick Lynch | DB | 6'1" | 205 | 28 | 4 | |
| Andy Nelson | DB | 6'1" | 180 | 31 | 1 | |
| Jimmy Patton | DB | 6' | 185 | 30 | 2 | |
| Dick Pesonen | DB | 6' | 190 | 26 | | |
| Allan Webb | DB | 5'11" | 180 | 29 | 1 | |
| Henry Schictle | QB | 6'2" | 190 | 21 | | |
| Y.A. Tittle | QB | 6' | 195 | 37 | | 6 |
| Gary Wood | QB | 5'11" | 188 | 21 | | 18 |
| Dick James | DB-HB | 5'9" | 182 | 30 | | 24 |
| Steve Thurlow | HB | 6'3" | 210 | 21 | | 6 |
| Clarence Childs | HB | 6' | 180 | 25 | | 6 |
| Alex Webster | FB | 6'3" | 220 | 33 | | 18 |
| Ernie Wheelwright | FB | 6'3" | 220 | 27 | | 18 |
| Frank Gifford | FL | 6'1" | 190 | 34 | | 24 |
| Homer Jones | FL | 6'2" | 205 | 23 | | |
| R. C. Owens | FL | 6'3" | 195 | 29 | | |
| Joe Morrison | HB-FL-OE | 6'1" | 212 | 26 | | 18 |
| Bob Crespino | OE | 6'4" | 225 | 26 | | |
| Del Shofner | OE | 6'3" | 185 | 28 | | |
| Aaron Thomas | FL-OE | 6'3" | 210 | 26 | | 36 |
| Don Chandler | K | 6'2" | 210 | 29 | | 54 |

Joe Walton – Injury

**WESTERN CONFERENCE**

## BALTIMORE COLTS 12-2-0 Don Shula

| Scores of Each Game | | |
|---|---|---|
| 24 | Minnesota | 34 |
| 21 | Green Bay | 20 |
| 52 | CHICAGO | 0 |
| 35 | LOS ANGELES | 20 |
| 47 | ST. LOUIS | 27 |
| 24 | GREEN BAY | 21 |
| 34 | Detroit | 0 |
| 37 | SAN FRANCISCO | 7 |
| 40 | Chicago | 24 |
| 17 | MINNESOTA | 14 |
| 24 | Los Angeles | 7 |
| 14 | San Francisco | 3 |
| 14 | DETROIT | 31 |
| 45 | WASHINGTON | 17 |

| Use Name | Pos. | Hgt | Wgt | Age | Int | Pts |
|---|---|---|---|---|---|---|
| George Preas | OT | 6'2" | 250 | 32 | | |
| Tom Gilburg | OT | 6'5" | 245 | 25 | | |
| Lou Kirouac | OT | 6'3" | 240 | 24 | | |
| Bob Vogel | OT | 6'5" | 250 | 22 | | |
| Jim Parker | OG | 6'3" | 275 | 30 | | |
| Alex Sandusky | OG | 6'1" | 242 | 32 | | |
| Dan Sullivan | OT-OG | 6'3" | 250 | 25 | | |
| Dick Szymanski | C | 6'3" | 235 | 32 | | |
| Ordell Braase | DE | 6'4" | 242 | 32 | | |
| Gino Marchetti | DE | 6'4" | 245 | 38 | | |
| Lou Michaels | DE | 6'2" | 235 | 28 | | 104 |
| John Diehl | DT | 6'7" | 275 | 28 | | |
| Fred Miller | DT | 6'3" | 245 | 23 | | |
| Guy Reese | DT | 6'5" | 258 | 24 | | |
| Billy Ray Smith | DT | 6'4" | 240 | 29 | | |
| Jackie Burkett | LB | 6'4" | 228 | 27 | | |
| Ted Davis | LB | 6'1" | 225 | 22 | | |
| Bill Pellington | LB | 6'2" | 238 | 35 | 2 | |
| Don Shinnick | LB | 6' | 235 | 29 | 3 | |
| Steve Stonebreaker | LB | 6'3" | 220 | 26 | | 6 |
| Wendell Harris | DB | 5'11" | 190 | 23 | 1 | |
| Alvin Haymond | DB | 6' | 190 | 25 | | |
| Jerry Logan | DB | 6'1" | 185 | 23 | 6 | 6 |
| Lenny Lyles | DB | 6'2" | 202 | 28 | 2 | |
| Jim Welch | DB | 6' | 190 | 26 | | |
| Bobby Boyd | HB-DB | 5'10" | 190 | 26 | 9 | |
| Gary Cuozzo | QB | 6'1" | 195 | 23 | | |
| Johnny Unitas | QB | 6'1" | 194 | 31 | | 12 |
| Tom Matte | HB | 6' | 205 | 25 | | 6 |
| Lenny Moore | HB | 6'1" | 190 | 31 | | 120 |
| Jerry Hill | FB | 5'11" | 210 | 24 | | 36 |
| Joe Don Looney | FB | 6'1" | 230 | 21 | | 12 |
| Tony Lorick | FB | 6'1" | 203 | 22 | | 24 |
| Jimmy Orr | FL | 5'11" | 175 | 28 | | 36 |
| Willie Richardson | FL | 6'2" | 198 | 24 | | |
| Ray Berry | OE | 6'2" | 187 | 31 | | 36 |
| Alex Hawkins | OE | 6'1" | 190 | 27 | | 6 |
| John Mackey | OE | 6'3" | 217 | 22 | | 12 |
| Neal Petties | OE | 6'2" | 198 | 23 | | 6 |
| Butch Wilson | OE | 6'2" | 218 | 22 | | 6 |

## GREEN BAY PACKERS 8-5-1 Vince Lombardi

| Scores of Each Game | | |
|---|---|---|
| 23 | CHICAGO | 12 |
| 20 | BALTIMORE | 21 |
| 14 | Detroit | 10 |
| 23 | MINNESOTA | 24 |
| 24 | SAN FRANCISCO | 14 |
| 21 | Baltimore | 24 |
| 17 | LOS ANGELES | 27 |
| 42 | Minnesota | 13 |
| 30 | DETROIT | 7 |
| 14 | San Francisco | 24 |
| 28 | CLEVELAND | 21 |
| 45 | Dallas | 21 |
| 17 | Chicago | 3 |
| 24 | Los Angeles | 24 |

| Use Name | Pos. | Hgt | Wgt | Age | Int | Pts |
|---|---|---|---|---|---|---|
| Forrest Gregg | OT | 6'4" | 250 | 31 | | |
| Steve Wright | OT | 6'6" | 250 | 22 | | |
| Norm Masters | OT | 6'2" | 250 | 31 | | |
| Bob Skoronski | C-OT | 6'3" | 250 | 31 | | |
| Dan Grimm | OG | 6'3" | 245 | 23 | | |
| Fuzzy Thurston | OG | 6'1" | 245 | 31 | | |
| Jerry Kramer | OG | 6'3" | 245 | 29 | | |
| John McDowell | OT-OG | 6'3" | 260 | 21 | | |
| Ken Bowman | C | 6'3" | 230 | 21 | | |
| Lionel Aldridge | DE | 6'4" | 245 | 22 | | 6 |
| Willie Davis | DE | 6'3" | 245 | 31 | | |
| Lloyd Voss | DE | 6'4" | 245 | 22 | | |
| Dave Hanner | DT | 6'2" | 260 | 35 | | |
| Henry Jordan | DT | 6'3" | 250 | 29 | | 6 |
| Ron Kostelnik | DT | 6'4" | 260 | 24 | | |
| Gene Breen | LB | 6'2" | 225 | 23 | | |
| Lee Roy Caffey | LB | 6'3" | 240 | 24 | 1 | |
| Dan Currie | LB | 6'3" | 240 | 30 | 2 | |
| Ray Nitschke | LB | 6'3" | 240 | 28 | 2 | |
| Dave Robinson | LB | 6'3" | 245 | 23 | | |
| Tommy Crutcher | FB-LB | 6'3" | 220 | 22 | | |
| Herb Adderley | DB | 6'1" | 210 | 25 | 4 | |
| Tom Brown | DB | 6'1" | 190 | 23 | 1 | |
| Hank Gremminger | DB | 6'1" | 200 | 31 | 1 | |
| Doug Hart | DB | 6' | 190 | 25 | 1 | |
| Jerry Norton | DB | 5'11" | 195 | 34 | | |
| Jesse Whittenton | DB | 6' | 195 | 30 | 1 | |
| Willie Wood | DB | 5'10" | 190 | 28 | 3 | 7 |
| Zeke Bratkowski | QB | 6'2" | 200 | 32 | | |
| Dennis Claridge | QB | 6'3" | 225 | 22 | | |
| Bart Starr | QB | 6'1" | 200 | 31 | | 18 |
| Paul Hornung | HB | 6'2" | 215 | 27 | | 107 |
| Tom Moore | HB | 6'2" | 210 | 26 | | 24 |
| Elijah Pitts | HB | 6'1" | 205 | 25 | | 12 |
| Jim Taylor | FB | 6' | 215 | 29 | | 90 |
| Boyd Dowler | FL | 6'5" | 225 | 27 | | 30 |
| Bob Long | FL | 6'3" | 190 | 23 | | |
| Bob Jeter | OE-FL | 6'1" | 205 | 26 | | |
| Marv Fleming | OE | 6'4" | 230 | 22 | | |
| Ron Kramer | OE | 6'3" | 240 | 29 | | |
| Max McGee | OE | 6'3" | 205 | 32 | | 42 |

Ken Iman – Broken Hand

## MINNESOTA VIKINGS 8-5-1 Norm Van Brocklin

| Scores of Each Game | | |
|---|---|---|
| 34 | BALTIMORE | 24 |
| 28 | CHICAGO | 34 |
| 13 | Los Angeles | 22 |
| 24 | Green Bay | 23 |
| 20 | DETROIT | 24 |
| 30 | PITTSBURGH | 10 |
| 27 | San Francisco | 22 |
| 13 | GREEN BAY | 42 |
| 24 | SAN FRANCISCO | 7 |
| 14 | Baltimore | 17 |
| 23 | Detroit | 23 |
| 34 | LOS ANGELES | 13 |
| 30 | New York | 21 |
| 41 | Chicago | 14 |

| Use Name | Pos. | Hgt | Wgt | Age | Int | Pts |
|---|---|---|---|---|---|---|
| Grady Alderman | OT | 6'2" | 245 | 25 | | |
| Errol Linden | OT | 6'5" | 260 | 26 | | |
| Larry Bowie | OG | 6'2" | 245 | 24 | | |
| Palmer Pyle | OG | 6'2" | 250 | 27 | | |
| Milt Sunde | OG | 6'2" | 222 | 21 | | |
| Mick Tingelhoff | C | 6'1" | 235 | 24 | | |
| Bob Denton | DE | 6'4" | 244 | 30 | | |
| Carl Eller | DE | 6'6" | 247 | 22 | | 6 |
| Jim Marshall | DE | 6'3" | 235 | 26 | | |
| Howard Simpson | DE | 6'5" | 230 | 21 | | |
| Paul Dickson | DT | 6'5" | 255 | 27 | | |
| Dave O'Brien | DT | 6'3" | 247 | 23 | | |
| Jim Prestel | DT | 6'5" | 275 | 27 | 1 | 6 |
| John Campbell | LB | 6'3" | 215 | 25 | | |
| Rip Hawkins | LB | 6'3" | 230 | 25 | 2 | 12 |
| Bill Jobko | LB | 6'2" | 225 | 28 | | |
| John Kirby | LB | 6'3" | 222 | 22 | | |
| Bill Swain | LB | 6'2" | 228 | 23 | | |
| Roy Winston | LB | 6'1" | 230 | 24 | 3 | |
| Lee Calland | DB | 6' | 190 | 23 | | |
| Karl Kassulke | DB | 6' | 193 | 22 | 3 | |
| George Rose | DB | 5'11" | 190 | 21 | 6 | 6 |
| Ed Sharockman | DB | 6' | 200 | 24 | 1 | |
| Bill Butler | HB-DB | 5'10" | 200 | 27 | 2 | |
| Larry Vargo | OE-DB | 6'3" | 215 | 24 | 1 | |
| Fran Tarkenton | QB | 6'1" | 190 | 24 | | 12 |
| Ron Vander Kelen | QB | 6'1" | 185 | 24 | | |
| Ted Dean | HB | 6'2" | 213 | 26 | | |
| Tommy Mason | HB | 6' | 196 | 25 | | 30 |
| Tom Michel | HB | 6' | 210 | 23 | | |
| Bill Brown | FB | 5'11" | 220 | 26 | | 96 |
| Darrell Lester | FB | 6'2" | 225 | 23 | | |
| Bill McWatters | FB | 6' | 225 | 22 | | 6 |
| Tom Hall | FL | 6'1" | 195 | 23 | | 12 |
| Hal Bedsole | OE | 6'4" | 230 | 22 | | 30 |
| Paul Flatley | OE | 6'1" | 187 | 23 | | 18 |
| Bob Lacey | OE | 6'3" | 205 | 22 | | |
| Jerry Reichow | OE | 6'2" | 220 | 29 | | 12 |
| Gordon Smith | OE | 6'2" | 220 | 25 | | 6 |
| Fred Cox | K | 5'10" | 200 | 25 | | 103 |
| Bobby Walden | K | 6' | 195 | 26 | | |

Chuck Lamson – Injury
Terry Dillon – Accidentally Drowned in May

## EASTERN CONFERENCE—Continued

### PITTSBURGH STEELERS

**RUSHING**

| Last Name | No. | Yds | Avg | TD |
|---|---|---|---|---|
| Johnson | 235 | 1048 | 4.5 | 7 |
| Peaks | 118 | 503 | 4.3 | 2 |
| Hoak | 84 | 258 | 3.1 | 2 |
| Brown | 26 | 110 | 4.2 | 2 |
| King | 26 | 71 | 2.7 | 1 |
| Ballman | 11 | 43 | 3.9 | 0 |
| Nelsen | 3 | 17 | 5.7 | 0 |
| Sapp | 4 | 15 | 3.8 | 0 |
| Martha | 4 | 12 | 3.0 | 0 |
| Powers | 2 | 10 | 5.0 | 0 |
| Holler | 1 | 8 | 8.0 | 0 |
| Thomas | 2 | 7 | 3.5 | 0 |

**RECEIVING**

| Last Name | No. | Yds | Avg | TD |
|---|---|---|---|---|
| Ballman | 47 | 935 | 20 | 7 |
| Thomas | 17 | 334 | 20 | 1 |
| Johnson | 17 | 69 | 4 | 1 |
| Hoak | 12 | 137 | 11 | 3 |
| Peaks | 12 | 113 | 9 | 0 |
| Kelly | 10 | 186 | 19 | 1 |
| Powers | 8 | 193 | 24 | 0 |
| Martha | 6 | 145 | 24 | 0 |
| Burrell | 6 | 113 | 19 | 0 |
| King | 4 | 32 | 8 | 1 |
| Sapp | 1 | 44 | 44 | 0 |
| Logan | 1 | 7 | 7 | 0 |

**PUNT RETURNS**

| Last Name | No. | Yds | Avg | TD |
|---|---|---|---|---|
| Keys | 14 | 172 | 12 | 0 |
| Martha | 13 | 64 | 5 | 0 |
| J. Bradshaw | 1 | 2 | 2 | 0 |
| Baker | 1 | 0 | 0 | 0 |
| Woodson | 1 | 0 | 0 | 0 |

**KICKOFF RETURNS**

| Last Name | No. | Yds | Avg | TD |
|---|---|---|---|---|
| Ballman | 14 | 386 | 28 | 0 |
| Peaks | 12 | 326 | 27 | 0 |
| Woodson | 5 | 178 | 36 | 0 |
| Thomas | 7 | 171 | 24 | 0 |
| Keys | 7 | 168 | 24 | 0 |
| Sapp | 4 | 43 | 11 | 0 |
| King | 2 | 27 | 14 | 0 |
| Martha | 1 | 26 | 26 | 0 |
| Lemek | 1 | 19 | 19 | 0 |
| Kelly | 1 | 12 | 12 | 0 |
| Burrell | 2 | 0 | 0 | 0 |

**PASSING**

| Last Name | Att | Comp | % | Yds | Yd/Att | TD | Int– | % | RK |
|---|---|---|---|---|---|---|---|---|---|
| Brown | 272 | 121 | 44 | 1990 | 7.3 | 12 | 19– | 7 | 14 |
| Nelsen | 42 | 16 | 38 | 276 | 6.6 | 2 | 3– | 7 | |
| Nofsinger | 4 | 3 | 75 | 35 | 8.8 | 0 | 1– | 25 | |
| Wade | 3 | 1 | 33 | 7 | 2.3 | 0 | 0– | 0 | |
| Ballman | 1 | 0 | 0 | 0 | 0.0 | 0 | 1– | 100 | |
| Hoak | 1 | 0 | 0 | 0 | 0.0 | 0 | 0– | 0 | |

**PUNTING**

| Last Name | No | Avg |
|---|---|---|
| Brown | 31 | 43.4 |
| Holler | 31 | 43.0 |

**KICKING**

| Last Name | XP | Att | % | FG | Att | % |
|---|---|---|---|---|---|---|
| Clark | 28 | 31 | 90 | 13 | 25 | 52 |

### NEW YORK GIANTS

**RUSHING**

| Last Name | No. | Yds | Avg | TD |
|---|---|---|---|---|
| Wheelwright | 100 | 402 | 4.0 | 0 |
| Webster | 76 | 210 | 2.8 | 3 |
| Thurlow | 64 | 210 | 3.3 | 0 |
| James | 55 | 189 | 3.4 | 3 |
| Wood | 39 | 158 | 4.1 | 3 |
| Morrison | 45 | 138 | 3.1 | 1 |
| Childs | 40 | 102 | 2.6 | 0 |
| Gifford | 1 | 2 | 2.0 | 1 |
| Tittle | 15 | -7 | -0.5 | 1 |

**RECEIVING**

| Last Name | No. | Yds | Avg | TD |
|---|---|---|---|---|
| Thomas | 43 | 624 | 15 | 6 |
| Morrison | 40 | 505 | 13 | 2 |
| Gifford | 29 | 429 | 15 | 3 |
| Shofner | 22 | 323 | 15 | 0 |
| Webster | 19 | 199 | 10 | 0 |
| Wheelwright | 14 | 204 | 15 | 3 |
| Crespino | 12 | 165 | 14 | 0 |
| James | 12 | 101 | 8 | 1 |
| Childs | 11 | 97 | 9 | 0 |
| Thurlow | 7 | 74 | 11 | 1 |
| Jones | 4 | 82 | 21 | 0 |
| Owens | 4 | 45 | 11 | 0 |

**PUNT RETURNS**

| Last Name | No. | Yds | Avg | TD |
|---|---|---|---|---|
| James | 21 | 153 | 7 | 0 |
| Childs | 6 | 40 | 7 | 0 |
| Barnes | 1 | 0 | 0 | 0 |

**KICKOFF RETURNS**

| Last Name | No. | Yds | Avg | TD |
|---|---|---|---|---|
| Childs | 34 | 987 | 29 | 1 |
| James | 23 | 515 | 22 | 0 |
| Jones | 6 | 111 | 19 | 0 |
| Morrison | 4 | 75 | 19 | 0 |

**PASSING**

| Last Name | Att | Comp | % | Yds | Yd/Att | TD | Int– | % | RK |
|---|---|---|---|---|---|---|---|---|---|
| Tittle | 281 | 147 | 52 | 1798 | 6.4 | 10 | 22– | 8 | 16 |
| Wood | 143 | 66 | 46 | 952 | 6.7 | 6 | 3– | 2 | 13 |
| Thurlow | 5 | 3 | 60 | 65 | 13.0 | 0 | 0– | 0 | |
| Gifford | 1 | 1 | 100 | 33 | 33.0 | 0 | 0– | 0 | |
| James | 1 | 0 | 0 | 0 | 0.0 | 0 | 1– | 100 | |

**PUNTING**

| Last Name | No | Avg |
|---|---|---|
| Chandler | 73 | 45.6 |
| James | 1 | 35.0 |

**KICKING**

| Last Name | XP | Att | % | FG | Att | % |
|---|---|---|---|---|---|---|
| Chandler | 27 | 29 | 93 | 9 | 20 | 45 |
| Stynchula | 1 | 1 | 100 | 0 | 0 | 0 |

## WESTERN CONFERENCE

### BALTIMORE COLTS

**RUSHING**

| Last Name | No. | Yds | Avg | TD |
|---|---|---|---|---|
| Moore | 157 | 584 | 3.7 | 16 |
| Lorick | 100 | 513 | 5.1 | 4 |
| Hill | 88 | 384 | 4.4 | 5 |
| Matte | 42 | 215 | 5.1 | 1 |
| Unitas | 37 | 162 | 4.4 | 2 |
| Looney | 23 | 127 | 5.5 | 1 |
| Boyd | 1 | 25 | 25.0 | 0 |
| Mackey | 1 | -1 | -1.0 | 0 |
| Cuozzo | 7 | -2 | -0.3 | 0 |

**RECEIVING**

| Last Name | No. | Yds | Avg | TD |
|---|---|---|---|---|
| Berry | 43 | 663 | 15 | 6 |
| Orr | 40 | 867 | 22 | 6 |
| Mackey | 22 | 406 | 18 | 2 |
| Moore | 21 | 472 | 22 | 3 |
| Hill | 14 | 113 | 8 | 1 |
| Lorick | 11 | 164 | 15 | 0 |
| Matte | 10 | 169 | 17 | 0 |
| Wilson | 7 | 86 | 12 | 1 |
| Richardson | 3 | 42 | 14 | 0 |
| Hawkins | 2 | 42 | 21 | 1 |
| Petties | 2 | 20 | 10 | 1 |
| Looney | 1 | 1 | 1 | 1 |

**PUNT RETURNS**

| Last Name | No. | Yds | Avg | TD |
|---|---|---|---|---|
| Harris | 17 | 214 | 13 | 0 |
| Hawkins | 16 | 122 | 8 | 0 |
| Logan | 13 | 111 | 9 | 0 |
| Haymond | 1 | 6 | 6 | 0 |
| Davis | 1 | 0 | 0 | 0 |

**KICKOFF RETURNS**

| Last Name | No. | Yds | Avg | TD |
|---|---|---|---|---|
| Lorick | 13 | 385 | 30 | 0 |
| Looney | 14 | 345 | 25 | 0 |
| Hill | 4 | 85 | 21 | 0 |
| Matte | 3 | 71 | 24 | 0 |
| Gilburg | 1 | 19 | 19 | 0 |
| Davis | 1 | 12 | 12 | 0 |
| Petties | 1 | 9 | 9 | 0 |
| Boyd | 1 | 0 | 0 | 0 |
| Haymond | 1 | 0 | 0 | 0 |

**PASSING**

| Last Name | Att | Comp | % | Yds | Yd/Att | TD | Int– | % | RK |
|---|---|---|---|---|---|---|---|---|---|
| Unitas | 305 | 158 | 52 | 2824 | 9.3 | 19 | 6– | 2 | 4 |
| Cuozzo | 36 | 15 | 42 | 163 | 4.5 | 2 | 3– | 8 | |
| Matte | 4 | 3 | 75 | 58 | 14.5 | 1 | 0– | 0 | |

**PUNTING**

| Last Name | No | Avg |
|---|---|---|
| Looney | 32 | 42.4 |
| Gilburg | 27 | 41.0 |

**KICKING**

| Last Name | XP | Att | % | FG | Att | % |
|---|---|---|---|---|---|---|
| Michaels | 53 | 54 | 98 | 17 | 35 | 49 |

### GREEN BAY PACKERS

**RUSHING**

| Last Name | No. | Yds | Avg | TD |
|---|---|---|---|---|
| Taylor | 235 | 1169 | 5.0 | 12 |
| Hornung | 103 | 415 | 4.0 | 5 |
| Moore | 102 | 371 | 3.6 | 2 |
| Starr | 24 | 165 | 6.9 | 3 |
| Pitts | 27 | 127 | 4.7 | 1 |
| Norton | 1 | 24 | 24.0 | 0 |
| Crutcher | 1 | 5 | 5.0 | 0 |
| Bratkowski | 2 | 0 | 0.0 | 0 |

**RECEIVING**

| Last Name | No. | Yds | Avg | TD |
|---|---|---|---|---|
| Dowler | 45 | 623 | 14 | 5 |
| Taylor | 38 | 354 | 9 | 3 |
| R. Kramer | 34 | 551 | 16 | 0 |
| McGee | 31 | 592 | 19 | 6 |
| Moore | 17 | 140 | 8 | 2 |
| Hornung | 9 | 98 | 11 | 0 |
| Pitts | 6 | 38 | 6 | 0 |
| Fleming | 4 | 36 | 9 | 0 |
| Jeter | 1 | 23 | 23 | 0 |
| Long | 1 | 19 | 19 | 0 |

**PUNT RETURNS**

| Last Name | No. | Yds | Avg | TD |
|---|---|---|---|---|
| Wood | 19 | 252 | 13 | 0 |
| Pitts | 15 | 191 | 13 | 1 |

**KICKOFF RETURNS**

| Last Name | No. | Yds | Avg | TD |
|---|---|---|---|---|
| Adderly | 19 | 508 | 27 | 0 |
| Moore | 16 | 431 | 27 | 0 |
| Brown | 7 | 167 | 24 | 0 |
| Crutcher | 2 | 54 | 27 | 0 |
| Caffey | 1 | 0 | 0 | 0 |

**PASSING**

| Last Name | Att | Comp | % | Yds | Yd/Att | TD | Int– | % | RK |
|---|---|---|---|---|---|---|---|---|---|
| Starr | 272 | 163 | 60 | 2144 | 7.9 | 15 | 4– | 1 | 1 |
| Bratkowski | 36 | 19 | 53 | 277 | 7.7 | 1 | 1– | 3 | |
| Hornung | 10 | 3 | 30 | 25 | 2.5 | 0 | 1– | 10 | |
| Moore | 3 | 1 | 33 | 28 | 9.3 | 0 | 0– | 0 | |

**PUNTING**

| Last Name | No | Avg |
|---|---|---|
| Norton | 56 | 42.2 |

**KICKING**

| Last Name | XP | Att | % | FG | Att | % |
|---|---|---|---|---|---|---|
| Hornung | 41 | 43 | 95 | 12 | 38 | 32 |
| Wood | 1 | 1 | 100 | 0 | 1 | 0 |

### MINNESOTA VIKINGS

**RUSHING**

| Last Name | No. | Yds | Avg | TD |
|---|---|---|---|---|
| Brown | 226 | 866 | 3.8 | 7 |
| Mason | 169 | 691 | 4.1 | 4 |
| Tarkenton | 50 | 330 | 6.6 | 2 |
| Michel | 39 | 129 | 3.3 | 0 |
| McWatters | 14 | 60 | 4.3 | 1 |
| Dean | 5 | 30 | 6.0 | 0 |
| Lester | 4 | 18 | 4.5 | 0 |
| Walden | 1 | 18 | 18.0 | 0 |
| Butler | 5 | 11 | 2.2 | 0 |
| Vander Kelen | 1 | 10 | 10.0 | 0 |
| Smith | 1 | 2 | 2.0 | 0 |
| Hall | 4 | -4 | -1.0 | 0 |
| Alderman | 0 | 22 | 0.0 | 0 |

**RECEIVING**

| Last Name | No. | Yds | Avg | TD |
|---|---|---|---|---|
| Brown | 48 | 703 | 15 | 9 |
| Flatley | 28 | 450 | 16 | 3 |
| Mason | 26 | 239 | 9 | 1 |
| Hall | 23 | 325 | 14 | 2 |
| Reichow | 20 | 284 | 14 | 2 |
| Bedsole | 18 | 295 | 16 | 5 |
| Smith | 10 | 211 | 21 | 1 |
| McWatters | 2 | -1 | -1 | 0 |
| Butler | 1 | 58 | 58 | 0 |
| Dean | 1 | 23 | 23 | 0 |
| Michel | 1 | 14 | 14 | 0 |
| Vargo | 1 | 13 | 13 | 0 |

**PUNT RETURNS**

| Last Name | No. | Yds | Avg | TD |
|---|---|---|---|---|
| Butler | 22 | 156 | 7 | 0 |
| Mason | 10 | 150 | 15 | 0 |
| Dean | 2 | 0 | 0 | 0 |
| Kassulke | 1 | 0 | 0 | 0 |

**KICKOFF RETURNS**

| Last Name | No. | Yds | Avg | TD |
|---|---|---|---|---|
| Butler | 26 | 597 | 23 | 0 |
| Michel | 8 | 192 | 24 | 0 |
| Rose | 8 | 180 | 23 | 0 |
| Brown | 5 | 68 | 14 | 0 |
| Dean | 3 | 50 | 17 | 0 |
| Mason | 2 | 36 | 18 | 0 |
| McWatters | 1 | 7 | 7 | 0 |

**PASSING**

| Last Name | Att | Comp | % | Yds | Yd/Att | TD | Int– | % | RK |
|---|---|---|---|---|---|---|---|---|---|
| Tarkenton | 306 | 171 | 56 | 2506 | 8.2 | 22 | 11– | 4 | 2 |
| Vander Kelen | 19 | 7 | 37 | 78 | 4.1 | 0 | 1– | 5 | |
| Mason | 1 | 1 | 100 | 30 | 30.0 | 1 | 0– | 0 | |

**PUNTING**

| Last Name | No | Avg |
|---|---|---|
| Walden | 72 | 46.4 |

**KICKING**

| Last Name | XP | Att | % | FG | Att | % |
|---|---|---|---|---|---|---|
| Cox | 40 | 42 | 95 | 21 | 33 | 64 |

**WESTERN CONFERENCE—Continued**

## DETROIT LIONS 7-5-2 George Wilson

| Scores of Each Game | | | Use Name | Pos. | Hgt | Wgt | Age | Int | Pts |
|---|---|---|---|---|---|---|---|---|---|
| 26 | San Francisco | 17 | Daryl Sanders | OT | 6'5" | 250 | 22 | | |
| 17 | Los Angeles | 17 | J. D. Smith | OT | 6'5" | 250 | 28 | | |
| 10 | GREEN BAY | 14 | John Gonzaga | OG-OT | 6'3" | 250 | 31 | | |
| 26 | NEW YORK | 3 | John Gordy | OG | 6'3" | 250 | 28 | | |
| 24 | Minnesota | 20 | Jim Simon | OG | 6'5" | 235 | 23 | | |
| 10 | Chicago | 0 | Wally Hilgenberg | LB-OG | 6'3" | 225 | 21 | | |
| 0 | BALTIMORE | 34 | Bob Whitlow | C | 6'1" | 236 | 28 | | |
| 37 | LOS ANGELES | 17 | Bob Schlotz | OT-C | 6'4" | 250 | 26 | | |
| 7 | Green Bay | 30 | Darris McCord | DE | 6'4" | 250 | 31 | | |
| 21 | Cleveland | 37 | Bill Quinlan | DE | 6'3" | 240 | 32 | 1 | |
| 23 | MINNESOTA | 23 | Sam Williams | DE | 6'5" | 235 | 33 | | 6 |
| 24 | CHICAGO | 27 | Roger Brown | DT | 6'5" | 300 | 27 | | |
| 31 | Baltimore | 14 | Alex Karras | DT | 6'2" | 245 | 28 | 2 | |
| 24 | SAN FRANCISCO | 7 | Roger LaLonde | DT | 6'3" | 255 | 22 | | |

| Use Name | Pos. | Hgt | Wgt | Age | Int | Pts |
|---|---|---|---|---|---|---|
| Ernie Clark | LB | 6'1" | 220 | 26 | | |
| Dennis Gaubatz | LB | 6'2" | 220 | 23 | 1 | 2 |
| Monte Lee | LB | 6'4" | 220 | 26 | | |
| Joe Schmidt | LB | 6'1" | 220 | 32 | | |
| Wayne Walker | LB | 6'2" | 225 | 27 | 1 | 74 |
| Night Train Lane | DB | 6'2" | 200 | 36 | 1 | |
| Dick LeBeau | DB | 6'1" | 185 | 27 | 5 | |
| Bruce Maher | DB | 5'11" | 190 | 27 | 2 | |
| Wayne Rasmussen | DB | 6'2" | 180 | 22 | | |
| Bobby Thompson | DB | 5'10" | 175 | 24 | 3 | |
| Dick Compton | HB-DB | 6'1" | 195 | 24 | | |
| Yale Lary | DB | 6' | 190 | 33 | 6 | |
| Gary Lowe | HB-DB | 5'11" | 195 | 30 | | |

Lucian Reeberg—Died Jan. 31, 1964 of Uremia

| Use Name | Pos. | Hgt | Wgt | Age | Int | Pts |
|---|---|---|---|---|---|---|
| Sonny Gibbs | QB | 6'7" | 230 | 23 | | |
| Earl Morrall | QB | 6'1" | 206 | 30 | | |
| Milt Plum | QB | 6'1" | 205 | 30 | | 6 |
| Dan Lewis | HB | 6'1" | 200 | 28 | | 12 |
| Hugh McElhenny | HB | 6'1" | 190 | 35 | | |
| Tom Watkins | HB | 6'1" | 195 | 27 | | 24 |
| Pat Batten | FB | 6'2" | 225 | 22 | | |
| Nick Pietrosante | FB | 6'2" | 225 | 27 | | 24 |
| Nick Ryder | FB | 6' | 210 | 23 | | 6 |
| Terry Barr | FL | 6' | 190 | 29 | | 54 |
| Pat Studstill | FL | 6'1" | 175 | 26 | | 6 |
| Gail Cogdill | OE | 6'2" | 195 | 27 | | 18 |
| Jim Gibbons | OE | 6'2" | 220 | 26 | | 48 |
| Hugh McInnis | OE | 6'3" | 220 | 26 | | |
| Warren Wells | OE | 6'1" | 195 | 21 | | |

## LOS ANGELES RAMS 5-7-2 Harland Svare

| Scores of Each Game | | | Use Name | Pos. | Hgt | Wgt | Age | Int | Pts |
|---|---|---|---|---|---|---|---|---|---|
| 26 | Pittsburgh | 14 | Joe Carollo | OT | 6'2" | 262 | 24 | | |
| 17 | DETROIT | 17 | Frank Varrichione | OT | 6'1" | 237 | 32 | | |
| 22 | MINNESOTA | 13 | Charley Cowan | OG-OT | 6'4" | 267 | 26 | | |
| 20 | Baltimore | 35 | Don Chuy | OG | 6'1" | 255 | 23 | | |
| 17 | Chicago | 38 | Roger Davis | OG | 6'3" | 235 | 26 | | |
| 42 | SAN FRANCISCO | 14 | Joe Scibelli | OG | 6'1" | 260 | 25 | | |
| 7 | Green Bay | 17 | Fred Whittingham | OG | 6'1" | 240 | 25 | | |
| 17 | Detroit | 37 | Art Hunter | C | 6'4" | 248 | 31 | | |
| 20 | PHILADELPHIA | 10 | Joe Wendryhoski | C | 6'2" | 245 | 25 | | |
| 24 | CHICAGO | 34 | Deacon Jones | DE | 6'3" | 267 | 25 | | |
| 7 | BALTIMORE | 24 | Lamar Lundy | DE | 6'7" | 250 | 29 | 1 | 6 |
| 13 | Minnesota | 34 | Rosey Grier | DT | 6'5" | 290 | 31 | | |
| 7 | San Francisco | 28 | Gary Larsen | DT | 6'5" | 245 | 24 | | |
| 24 | GREEN BAY | 24 | Merlin Olsen | DT | 6'5" | 275 | 23 | | |

| Use Name | Pos. | Hgt | Wgt | Age | Int | Pts |
|---|---|---|---|---|---|---|
| Marv Harris | LB | 6'1" | 225 | 22 | | |
| Mike Henry | LB | 6'2" | 227 | 28 | | |
| Cliff Livingston | LB | 6'3" | 215 | 34 | | |
| Jack Pardee | LB | 6'2" | 230 | 28 | 1 | |
| Andy Von Sonn | LB | 6'2" | 223 | 23 | | |
| Frank Budka | DB | 6' | 195 | 22 | 2 | |
| Lindon Crow | DB | 6' | 200 | 31 | 1 | |
| Aaron Martin | DB | 6' | 185 | 23 | 2 | 6 |
| Ed Meador | DB | 5'11" | 198 | 27 | 3 | |
| Jerry Richardson | DB | 6'3" | 190 | 21 | 5 | |
| Bobby Smith | DB | 6' | 197 | 26 | 2 | 12 |

| Use Name | Pos. | Hgt | Wgt | Age | Int | Pts |
|---|---|---|---|---|---|---|
| Roman Gabriel | QB | 6'4" | 220 | 24 | | 6 |
| Bill Munson | QB | 6'2" | 187 | 22 | | |
| Terry Baker | HB | 6'3" | 200 | 23 | | |
| Carver Shannon | HB | 6'1" | 206 | 26 | | |
| Ben Wilson | HB | 6' | 225 | 24 | | 36 |
| Dick Bass | FB | 5'10" | 200 | 27 | | 12 |
| Les Josephson | FB | 6' | 210 | 22 | | 24 |
| Willie Brown | FL | 6' | 186 | 21 | | |
| Jim Phillips | FL | 6'1" | 195 | 27 | | 12 |
| Duane Allen | OE | 6'4" | 225 | 26 | | 6 |
| Carroll Dale | OE | 6'1" | 195 | 26 | | 12 |
| Marlin McKeever | OE | 6'1" | 235 | 24 | | 6 |
| Bucky Pope | FL | 6'5" | 195 | 21 | | 60 |
| Billy Truax | OE | 6'5" | 240 | 21 | | |
| Bruce Gossett | K | 6'2" | 225 | 21 | | 85 |
| Danny Villanueva | K | 5'11" | 213 | 26 | | |

## CHICAGO BEARS 5-9-0 George Halas

| Scores of Each Game | | | Use Name | Pos. | Hgt | Wgt | Age | Int | Pts |
|---|---|---|---|---|---|---|---|---|---|
| 12 | Green Bay | 23 | George Burman | OT | 6'3" | 240 | 21 | | |
| 34 | Minnesota | 28 | Herm Lee | OT | 6'4" | 247 | 33 | | |
| 0 | Baltimore | 52 | Bob Wetoska | OT | 6'3" | 240 | 26 | | |
| 21 | San Francisco | 31 | Jim Cadile | OG | 6'3" | 240 | 23 | | |
| 38 | LOS ANGELES | 17 | Dick Evey | OG | 6'2" | 225 | 23 | | |
| 0 | DETROIT | 10 | Ted Karras | OG | 6'1" | 243 | 31 | | |
| 20 | Washington | 27 | Mike Rabold | OG | 6'2" | 238 | 26 | | |
| 10 | DALLAS | 24 | Mike Pyle | C | 6'3" | 245 | 25 | | |
| 24 | BALTIMORE | 40 | Doug Atkins | DE | 6'8" | 255 | 34 | | |
| 34 | Los Angeles | 24 | Bob Kilcullen | DE | 6'3" | 245 | 28 | | |
| 23 | SAN FRANCISCO | 21 | Ed O'Bradovich | DE | 6'3" | 255 | 24 | | |
| 27 | Detroit | 24 | John Johnson | DT | 6'5" | 260 | 23 | | |
| 3 | GREEN BAY | 17 | Stan Jones | DT | 6'1" | 250 | 33 | | |
| 14 | MINNESOTA | 41 | Earl Leggett | DT | 6'3" | 250 | 30 | | |

| Use Name | Pos. | Hgt | Wgt | Age | Int | Pts |
|---|---|---|---|---|---|---|
| Joe Fortunato | LB | 6' | 225 | 34 | | |
| Bill George | LB | 6'2" | 235 | 33 | 2 | |
| Roger LeClerc | LB | 6'3" | 235 | 26 | | 30 |
| Larry Morris | LB | 6'2" | 230 | 29 | | |
| Jim Purnell | LB | 6'2" | 205 | 22 | | |
| Mike Reilly | LB | 6'2" | 210 | 21 | | |
| J. C. Caroline | DB | 6'1" | 190 | 31 | 4 | |
| Larry Glueck | DB | 6' | 190 | 22 | | |
| Bennie McRae | DB | 6'1" | 180 | 23 | 2 | |
| Richie Petitbon | DB | 6'3" | 205 | 26 | | |
| John Sisk | DB | 6'3" | 195 | 22 | | |
| Rosey Taylor | DB | 5'11" | 186 | 25 | 2 | |
| Dave Whitsell | HB-DB | 6' | 190 | 28 | 2 | |

Bo Farrington / Willie Galimore } Died in auto accident during training camp, July 26, 1964

| Use Name | Pos. | Hgt | Wgt | Age | Int | Pts |
|---|---|---|---|---|---|---|
| Rudy Bukich | QB | 6'1" | 205 | 33 | | |
| Larry Rakestraw | QB | 6'2" | 195 | 22 | | |
| Billy Wade | QB | 6'2" | 205 | 33 | | 6 |
| Jon Arnett | HB | 5'11" | 203 | 29 | | 18 |
| Charlie Bivins | HB | 6'2" | 212 | 25 | | 6 |
| Ronnie Bull | HB | 6' | 200 | 24 | | 6 |
| Andy Livingston | HB | 6' | 234 | 19 | | 6 |
| Billy Martin | HB | 5'11" | 196 | 26 | | |
| Rick Casares | FB | 6'2" | 225 | 33 | | 12 |
| Joe Marconi | FB | 6'2" | 225 | 30 | | 30 |
| Johnny Morris | FL | 5'10" | 180 | 29 | | 60 |
| Gary Barnes | OE-FL | 6'4" | 210 | 24 | | |
| Mike Ditka | OE | 6'3" | 230 | 24 | | 36 |
| Bob Jencks | OE | 6'5" | 227 | 23 | | 38 |
| Rich Kreitling | OE | 6'2" | 208 | 29 | | 12 |
| Bill Martin | OE | 6'4" | 240 | 21 | | |
| Bobby Joe Green | K | 5'11" | 175 | 26 | | |

## SAN FRANCISCO FORTY NINERS 4-10-0 Jack Christiansen

| Scores of Each Game | | | Use Name | Pos. | Hgt | Wgt | Age | Int | Pts |
|---|---|---|---|---|---|---|---|---|---|
| 17 | DETROIT | 26 | Walt Rock | OT | 6'5" | 245 | 23 | | |
| 28 | Philadelphia | 24 | Len Rohde | OT | 6'4" | 240 | 26 | | |
| 13 | ST. LOUIS | 23 | Leon Donahue | OG | 6'4" | 245 | 25 | | |
| 31 | CHICAGO | 21 | Mike Magac | OG | 6'3" | 240 | 26 | | |
| 14 | Green Bay | 24 | Howard Mudd | OG | 6'3" | 240 | 22 | | |
| 14 | Los Angeles | 42 | John Thomas | OG | 6'4" | 246 | 29 | | |
| 22 | MINNESOTA | 27 | Bruce Bosley | C | 6'2" | 240 | 30 | | |
| 7 | Baltimore | 37 | Frank Morze | C | 6'2" | 180 | 26 | | |
| 7 | Minnesota | 24 | Dan Colchico | DE | 6'4" | 245 | 27 | | |
| 24 | GREEN BAY | 14 | Clark Miller | DE | 6'5" | 245 | 25 | | |
| 21 | Chicago | 23 | Karl Rubke | DE | 6'4" | 240 | 28 | | |
| 3 | BALTIMORE | 14 | Charlie Krueger | DT | 6'4" | 250 | 28 | | |
| 28 | LOS ANGELES | 7 | Roland Lakes | DT | 6'4" | 263 | 24 | | |
| 7 | Detroit | 24 | Chuck Sieminski | DT | 6'4" | 255 | 24 | | |

| Use Name | Pos. | Hgt | Wgt | Age | Int | Pts |
|---|---|---|---|---|---|---|
| Bill Cooper | LB | 6'1" | 215 | 25 | | |
| Floyd Dean | LB | 6'4" | 245 | 24 | | |
| Mike Dowdle | LB | 6'3" | 230 | 26 | 1 | |
| Matt Hazeltine | LB | 6'1" | 230 | 31 | 1 | |
| Ed Pine | LB | 6'4" | 235 | 24 | | |
| Dave Wilcox | LB | 6'3" | 230 | 21 | 1 | |
| Kermit Alexander | DB | 5'11" | 186 | 23 | 5 | 6 |
| Charley Britt (from MIN) | DB | 6'2" | 180 | 26 | | |
| Jim Johnson | DB | 6'2" | 190 | 26 | 3 | |
| Elbert Kimbrough | DB | 5'11" | 190 | 25 | 2 | |
| Jerry Mertens | DB | 6' | 185 | 28 | | |
| Ben Scotti | DB | 6'1" | 181 | 27 | | |
| Abe Woodson | DB | 5'11" | 188 | 29 | 2 | |

Bob St. Clair — Heel Injury

| Use Name | Pos. | Hgt | Wgt | Age | Int | Pts |
|---|---|---|---|---|---|---|
| John Brodie | QB | 6'1" | 200 | 29 | | 12 |
| George Mira | QB | 5'11" | 183 | 22 | | |
| Billy Kilmer | HB-QB | 6' | 190 | 24 | | |
| Rudy Johnson | HB | 5'1" | 190 | 22 | | 6 |
| Dave Kopay | HB | 6'2" | 206 | 22 | | 12 |
| Don Lisbon | HB | 6' | 197 | 23 | | 6 |
| Gary Lewis | FB | 6'3" | 215 | 22 | | 6 |
| Mike Lind | FB | 6'2" | 215 | 24 | | 42 |
| J. D. Smith | FB | 6'1" | 210 | 31 | | |
| Bernie Casey | FL | 6'4" | 215 | 26 | | 24 |
| Dale Messer | FL | 5'10" | 175 | 27 | | |
| Kay McFarland | OE | 6'2" | 180 | 25 | | |
| Dave Parks | OE | 6'2" | 195 | 22 | | 48 |
| Bob Poole | OE | 6'4" | 216 | 22 | | |
| Monte Stickles | OE | 6'4" | 230 | 26 | | 18 |
| Tommy Davis | K | 6' | 212 | 29 | | 54 |

## WESTERN CONFERENCE—Continued

### DETROIT LIONS

**RUSHING**

| Last Name | No. | Yds | Avg | TD |
|---|---|---|---|---|
| Pietrosante | 147 | 536 | 3.6 | 4 |
| Lewis | 122 | 463 | 3.8 | 1 |
| Watkins | 80 | 218 | 2.7 | 1 |
| Morrall | 10 | 70 | 7.0 | 0 |
| McElhenny | 22 | 48 | 2.2 | 0 |
| Barr | 2 | 31 | 15.5 | 0 |
| Plum | 12 | 28 | 2.3 | 1 |
| Lary | 2 | 11 | 5.5 | 0 |
| Ryder | 11 | 11 | 1.0 | 0 |
| Compton | 3 | 2 | 0.7 | 0 |
| Cogdill | 1 | −4 | −4.0 | 0 |

**RECEIVING**

| Last Name | No. | Yds | Avg | TD |
|---|---|---|---|---|
| Barr | 57 | 1030 | 18 | 9 |
| Cogdill | 45 | 665 | 15 | 2 |
| Gibbons | 45 | 605 | 13 | 8 |
| Pietrosante | 19 | 152 | 8 | 0 |
| Lewis | 11 | 129 | 12 | 1 |
| Watkins | 10 | 125 | 13 | 1 |
| Studstill | 7 | 102 | 15 | 1 |
| McElhenny | 5 | 16 | 3 | 0 |
| Ryder | 4 | 30 | 8 | 1 |
| Wells | 2 | 21 | 11 | 0 |
| McInnis | 1 | 15 | 15 | 0 |

**PUNT RETURNS**

| Last Name | No. | Yds | Avg | TD |
|---|---|---|---|---|
| Watkins | 16 | 238 | 15 | 2 |
| Studstill | 17 | 137 | 8 | 0 |
| Thompson | 1 | 27 | 27 | 0 |
| McElhenny | 1 | 0 | 0 | 0 |
| Maher | 0 | 9 | 0 | 0 |

**KICKOFF RETURNS**

| Last Name | No. | Yds | Avg | TD |
|---|---|---|---|---|
| Studstill | 29 | 708 | 24 | 0 |
| Watkins | 16 | 368 | 23 | 0 |
| McElhenny | 3 | 72 | 24 | 0 |
| Ryder | 2 | 37 | 19 | 0 |
| Clark | 2 | 29 | 15 | 0 |
| Lee | 1 | 25 | 25 | 0 |
| Thompson | 1 | 24 | 24 | 0 |
| Rasmussen | 1 | 20 | 20 | 0 |
| Hilgenberg | 1 | 2 | 2 | 0 |
| Simon | 1 | 0 | 0 | 0 |
| Compton | 0 | 42 | 0 | 0 |

**PASSING — PUNTING — KICKING**

PASSING

| Last Name | Att | Comp | % | Yds | Yd/Att | TD | Int− | % | RK |
|---|---|---|---|---|---|---|---|---|---|
| Plum | 287 | 154 | 54 | 2241 | 7.8 | 18 | 15− | 5 | 5 |
| Morrall | 91 | 50 | 55 | 588 | 6.5 | 4 | 3− | 3 | |
| Gibbs | 3 | 1 | 33 | 3 | 1.0 | 0 | 1− | 33 | |
| Barr | 1 | 0 | 0 | 0 | 0.0 | 0 | 0− | 0 | |
| Lewis | 1 | 0 | 0 | 0 | 0.0 | 0 | 0− | 0 | |
| Lowe | 1 | 0 | 0 | 0 | 0.0 | 0 | 1−100 | | |
| Pietrosante | 1 | 0 | 0 | 0 | 0.0 | 0 | 1−100 | | |
| Watkins | 1 | 1 | 100 | 58 | 58.0 | 1 | 0− | 0 | |

PUNTING

| Last Name | No | Avg |
|---|---|---|
| Lary | 67 | 46.3 |
| Morrall | 1 | 8.0 |

KICKING

| Last Name | XP | Att | % | FG | Att | % |
|---|---|---|---|---|---|---|
| Walker | 32 | 34 | 94 | 14 | 25 | 56 |

### LOS ANGELES RAMS

**RUSHING**

| Last Name | No. | Yds | Avg | TD |
|---|---|---|---|---|
| Wilson | 159 | 553 | 3.5 | 5 |
| Josephson | 96 | 451 | 4.7 | 3 |
| Bass | 72 | 342 | 4.8 | 2 |
| Munson | 19 | 150 | 7.9 | 0 |
| Baker | 24 | 82 | 3.4 | 0 |
| Shannon | 17 | 35 | 2.1 | 0 |
| Pope | 2 | 11 | 5.5 | 0 |
| Gabriel | 11 | 5 | 0.5 | 1 |

**RECEIVING**

| Last Name | No. | Yds | Avg | TD |
|---|---|---|---|---|
| McKeever | 41 | 582 | 14 | 1 |
| Dale | 32 | 544 | 17 | 2 |
| Pope | 25 | 786 | 31 | 10 |
| Josephson | 21 | 269 | 13 | 1 |
| Phillips | 17 | 245 | 14 | 2 |
| Wilson | 15 | 116 | 8 | 1 |
| Bass | 9 | 83 | 9 | 0 |
| Baker | 8 | 92 | 12 | 0 |
| Allen | 2 | 29 | 15 | 1 |
| Shannon | 2 | 4 | 2 | 0 |
| Brown | 1 | 19 | 19 | 0 |

**PUNT RETURNS**

| Last Name | No. | Yds | Avg | TD |
|---|---|---|---|---|
| Shannon | 15 | 81 | 5 | 0 |
| Smith | 12 | 68 | 6 | 0 |
| Brown | 4 | 23 | 6 | 0 |
| Meador | 2 | 9 | 5 | 0 |
| Bass | 1 | 0 | 0 | 0 |

**KICKOFF RETURNS**

| Last Name | No. | Yds | Avg | TD |
|---|---|---|---|---|
| Smith | 20 | 489 | 24 | 0 |
| Shannon | 18 | 442 | 25 | 0 |
| Meador | 6 | 148 | 25 | 0 |
| Brown | 6 | 122 | 20 | 0 |
| Bass | 1 | 25 | 25 | 0 |
| Martin | 2 | 18 | 9 | 0 |
| Larsen | 2 | 14 | 7 | 0 |
| Harris | 1 | 0 | 0 | 0 |

**PASSING — PUNTING — KICKING**

PASSING

| Last Name | Att | Comp | % | Yds | Yd/Att | TD | Int− | % | RK |
|---|---|---|---|---|---|---|---|---|---|
| Munson | 223 | 108 | 48 | 1533 | 6.9 | 9 | 15− | 7 | 17 |
| Gabriel | 143 | 65 | 45 | 1236 | 8.6 | 9 | 5− | 3 | 9 |
| Baker | 1 | 0 | 0 | 0 | 0.0 | 0 | 0− | 0 | |
| Meador | 1 | 0 | 0 | 0 | 0.0 | 0 | 0− | 0 | |

PUNTING

| Last Name | No | Avg |
|---|---|---|
| Villanueva | 82 | 44.1 |

KICKING

| Last Name | XP | Att | % | FG | Att | % |
|---|---|---|---|---|---|---|
| Gossett | 31 | 33 | 94 | 18 | 24 | 75 |

### CHICAGO BEARS

**RUSHING**

| Last Name | No. | Yds | Avg | TD |
|---|---|---|---|---|
| Arnett | 119 | 400 | 3.4 | 1 |
| Bull | 86 | 320 | 3.7 | 1 |
| Casares | 35 | 123 | 3.5 | 0 |
| Marconi | 46 | 98 | 2.1 | 2 |
| Wade | 24 | 96 | 4.0 | 1 |
| Bivins | 29 | 92 | 3.2 | 0 |
| Bukich | 12 | 28 | 2.3 | 0 |
| Whitsell | 1 | 14 | 14.0 | 0 |
| Green | 2 | −2 | −1.0 | 0 |
| Livingston | 2 | −3 | −1.5 | 0 |

**RECEIVING**

| Last Name | No. | Yds | Avg | TD |
|---|---|---|---|---|
| J. Morris | 93 | 1200 | 13 | 10 |
| Ditka | 75 | 897 | 12 | 5 |
| Arnett | 25 | 223 | 9 | 2 |
| Kreitling | 20 | 185 | 9 | 2 |
| Marconi | 20 | 181 | 9 | 3 |
| Bull | 15 | 35 | 2 | 0 |
| Casares | 14 | 113 | 8 | 2 |
| Bivins | 11 | 59 | 5 | 1 |
| Barnes | 4 | 61 | 15 | 0 |
| Bill Martin | 3 | 93 | 31 | 0 |
| Billy Martin | 1 | 9 | 9 | 0 |
| Livingston | 1 | 0 | 0 | 0 |

**PUNT RETURNS**

| Last Name | No. | Yds | Avg | TD |
|---|---|---|---|---|
| Arnett | 19 | 188 | 10 | 0 |
| Billy Martin | 11 | 31 | 3 | 0 |

**KICKOFF RETURNS**

| Last Name | No. | Yds | Avg | TD |
|---|---|---|---|---|
| Billy Martin | 24 | 534 | 22 | 0 |
| Arnett | 15 | 331 | 22 | 0 |
| Bivins | 8 | 218 | 27 | 0 |
| Livingston | 6 | 167 | 28 | 1 |
| Bull | 2 | 44 | 22 | 0 |
| Marconi | 2 | 12 | 6 | 0 |
| Purnell | 1 | 8 | 8 | 0 |

**PASSING — PUNTING — KICKING**

PASSING

| Last Name | Att | Comp | % | Yds | Yd/Att | TD | Int− | % | RK |
|---|---|---|---|---|---|---|---|---|---|
| Wade | 327 | 182 | 56 | 1944 | 5.9 | 13 | 14− | 4 | 10 |
| Bukich | 160 | 99 | 62 | 1099 | 6.8 | 12 | 7− | 4 | 8 |
| Arnett | 4 | 0 | 0 | 0 | 0.0 | 0 | 0− | 0 | |
| Bull | 3 | 1 | 33 | 13 | 4.3 | 0 | 0− | 0 | |

PUNTING

| Last Name | No | Avg |
|---|---|---|
| Green | 71 | 44.5 |

KICKING

| Last Name | XP | Att | % | FG | Att | % |
|---|---|---|---|---|---|---|
| Jencks | 29 | 32 | 91 | 3 | 7 | 43 |
| LeClerc | 0 | 0 | 0 | 10 | 16 | 63 |

### SAN FRANCISCO FORTY NINERS

**RUSHING**

| Last Name | No. | Yds | Avg | TD |
|---|---|---|---|---|
| Kopay | 75 | 271 | 3.6 | 0 |
| Lind | 100 | 256 | 2.6 | 7 |
| Mira | 18 | 177 | 9.8 | 0 |
| Lisbon | 55 | 162 | 2.9 | 0 |
| Brodie | 27 | 135 | 5.0 | 2 |
| Lewis | 43 | 115 | 2.7 | 1 |
| Kilmer | 36 | 113 | 3.1 | 0 |
| Smith | 13 | 55 | 4.2 | 0 |
| R. Johnson | 16 | 48 | 3.0 | 1 |

**RECEIVING**

| Last Name | No. | Yds | Avg | TD |
|---|---|---|---|---|
| Casey | 58 | 808 | 14 | 4 |
| Stickles | 40 | 685 | 17 | 3 |
| Parks | 36 | 703 | 20 | 8 |
| Lind | 25 | 178 | 7 | 0 |
| Kopay | 20 | 135 | 7 | 2 |
| Lisbon | 13 | 104 | 8 | 1 |
| Kilmer | 11 | 136 | 12 | 0 |
| Lewis | 7 | 73 | 10 | 0 |
| McFarland | 5 | 67 | 13 | 0 |
| R. Johnson | 5 | 21 | 4 | 0 |
| Messer | 4 | 72 | 18 | 0 |
| Poole | 1 | 8 | 8 | 0 |

**PUNT RETURNS**

| Last Name | No. | Yds | Avg | TD |
|---|---|---|---|---|
| Alexander | 21 | 189 | 9 | 1 |
| Woodson | 22 | 133 | 6 | 0 |

**KICKOFF RETURNS**

| Last Name | No. | Yds | Avg | TD |
|---|---|---|---|---|
| Woodson | 32 | 880 | 28 | 0 |
| Alexander | 20 | 483 | 24 | 0 |
| Kopay | 2 | 30 | 15 | 0 |
| Lewis | 1 | 0 | 0 | 0 |
| Pine | 1 | 0 | 0 | 0 |
| Thomas | 1 | 0 | 0 | 0 |

**PASSING — PUNTING — KICKING**

PASSING

| Last Name | Att | Comp | % | Yds | Yd/Att | TD | Int− | % | RK |
|---|---|---|---|---|---|---|---|---|---|
| Brodie | 392 | 193 | 49 | 2498 | 6.4 | 14 | 16− | 4 | 12 |
| Mira | 53 | 23 | 43 | 331 | 6.3 | 2 | 5− | 9 | |
| Kilmer | 14 | 8 | 57 | 92 | 6.6 | 1 | 1− | 7 | |
| Kopay | 1 | 0 | 0 | 0 | 0.0 | 0 | 0− | 0 | |
| Lind | 1 | 1 | 100 | 69 | 69.0 | 1 | 0− | 0 | |

PUNTING

| Last Name | No | Avg |
|---|---|---|
| Davis | 79 | 45.6 |

KICKING

| Last Name | XP | Att | % | FG | Att | % |
|---|---|---|---|---|---|---|
| Davis | 30 | 30 | 100 | 8 | 25 | 32 |

# 1964 A.F.L. TV and New York, An Unbeatable Combination

"People have now stopped asking me if we are going to make it," said Commissioner Joe Foss after signing a new television contract with the National Broadcasting Company. Starting in 1965, NBC would handle the national TV coverage of AFL games and pay the league $36 million for five seasons from 1965 to 1969. With all clubs sharing equally in the television pot, Foss no longer had any worries about any teams going bankrupt. He also had no worries over job security, as the team owners extended him a new three-year contract with a sizable raise in salary.

One of the most gratifying developments for Foss was the sudden popularity of the New York Jets. Only two years before they were the bankrupt Titans, playing in an ancient ball park and living off league funds. Now they played in the new Shea Stadium, set a single-game attendance record three times during this season, and had solid ownership led by Sonny Werblin. With the New York team healthy and strong, the whole league found new respect coming from the East Coast media.

## EASTERN DIVISION

**Buffalo Bills**—The heart of the Bills, the AFL's first great ball-control team, was a powerful fullback and a bruising defensive line. Cookie Gilchrist as usual took care of the heavy-duty running chores, leading the league in rushing despite the lack of an accomplished running mate at halfback. The Bills passed the ball less frequently than the other AFL clubs, as Jack Kemp ran the offense quite conservatively. But when the attack bogged down, coach Lou Saban could send young Daryle Lamonica in at quarterback. A second-year pro with a liking for the long pass, Lamonica relieved Kemp in several games and pulled out victories with deep bombs to Elbert Dubenion and Glenn Bass. Supporting the offense was a strong line featuring Billy Shaw and Stew Barber. The defensive unit also boasted of a strong line, as Ron McDole, Jim Dunaway, Tom Sestak, and Tom Day jelled into the league's best front four, and a tight group of linebackers and backs played well enough behind this line to make the Buffalo defense the stingiest in allowing points. The Bills won games by outplaying opponents in the line, by blocking and tackling better, and if the offense ever needed a three-point boost, coach Saban unveiled pro football's first soccer-style place-kicker in Pete Gogolak, a Hungarian refugee who kicked the ball sideways accurately enough to score 102 points. With a full pantry of hard-nosed ball players, the Bills swept their first nine games and put down a late Boston challenge to win the Eastern crown.

**Boston Patriots**—Closing with a rush, the Patriots just missed repeating as Eastern champion. Starting with a November 6 win over Houston, they won five straight games to pull within a half game of the first-place Bills before their season-closing showdown on December 20. The Pats had won last year's playoff game in frigid Buffalo, but the Bills turned the tables this year by winning this key game 24-14 in a snowstorm in Boston. The Patriots got as far as they did with little help from rookies, as coach Mike Holovak continued to depend on his shopworn veterans. Thirty-three-year-old Babe Parilli won his first All-Pro honors by passing for thirty-one touchdowns, while slow-footed Gino Cappelletti caught seven TD passes and scored a league-leading 155 points on his receiving and kicking. The defense was still the Patriots' long suit, bailing the team out in victories of 17-14 over Oakland and 12-7 over Denver. The front four of Larry Eisenhauer, Bob Dee, Houston Antwine, and Jim Hunt stood firm against enemy runners, while linebacker Nick Buoniconti blitzed opposing quarterbacks to distraction. But time was growing short for the Patriots, who would soon have to replace such oldsters as Parilli, Cappelletti, and Dee.

**New York Jets**—With their move into spanking new Shea Stadium, the Jets immediately became the attendance sensation of the league. Their first game in the new park drew an AFL record crowd of 45,665, the second game attracted 47,746, and the November 8 match with Buffalo brought out 60,300 fans. Several factors contributed to the Jets' sudden popularity, such as the new stadium, the scarcity of available tickets for Giant games, the scheduling of games on Saturday nights, and a close identification with the colorful baseball Mets. The fans who did come out saw a team rapidly improving with good young talent. This year's rich rookie class included Matt Snell, a talented all-around fullback; Gerry Philbin and Bert Wilder, a pair of strong defensive ends; Ralph Baker, who won a starting linebacker spot; John Schmitt and Dave Herman, two reserve offensive linemen who would star in later years; and place-kicker Jim Turner. Another newcomer won a large following, as middle linebacker Wahoo McDaniel became a folk hero with New York fans with his violent tackles. Holdovers such as Larry Grantham, Bill Mathis, Don Maynard, Bake Turner, Winston Hill, and Dainard Paulson formed the nucleus of a good club, but any championships would have to wait until a top quarterback was acquired.

**Houston Oilers**—Hopes that 1963 was just an isolated bad year for the Oilers faded as they lost nine straight games in the center of the schedule. Sammy Baugh was this year's head coach, with Pop

Ivy disposed of for not winning a championship last season, and Baugh would get the ax after this losing campaign. The Oiler roster carried heavy doses of both rookies and aging veterans. Of the several freshmen to make the squad, Sid Blanks, Scott Appleton, Pete Jacquess, W. K. Hicks, Benny Nelson, and Willie Frazier saw considerable action. At the other end of the spectrum, thirty-six-year-old George Blanda, thirty-six-year-old Bud McFadin, and thirty-four-year-old Ed Hussman held down starting posts in the Houston lineup. In between the two extremes of age came players in their prime—Charley Hennigan, Freddy Glick, Bob Talamini, and Doug Cline. Hennigan, who was Blanda's favorite pass receiver, hauled in 101 passes to set a new professional record. But not enough Oiler players were at the peak of their powers, and the team hung all its hopes on this year's youngsters improving in the near future.

## WESTERN DIVISION

**San Diego Chargers**—Tobin Rote's old arm had few passes left in it, so John Hadl assumed the bulk of the quarterbacking duties and took the Chargers back to the championship game. The road was a little rockier this year, though. After beating Houston to open the season, the Chargers lost to Boston and Buffalo and just managed a tie with New York. With none of the Western teams very hot in the early going, San Diego then rocketed out to a comfortable lead by winning their next six games. Even a late-season slump, in which they lost three of their last four games, could not bring the Chargers back to the pack. But despite their streaky play, the Chargers boasted of one of the deepest squads in the league. They had good runners in Keith Lincoln and Paul Lowe, pro football's most exciting receiver in Lance Alworth, fine offensive linemen in Ron Mix and Walt Sweeney, and good defenders in Earl Faison, Ernie Ladd, Chuck Allen, Frank Buncom, and Dick Westmoreland. The only thing missing from the San Diego arsenal was a consistent field-goal kicker. The Chargers tried Keith Lincoln, Herb Travenio, Ben Agajanian, and George Blair at the spot during the season. But that lack was not enough to keep the Chargers away from their fourth Western crown in five years.

**Kansas City Chiefs**—On paper, the Chiefs looked unbeatable; on the field, the Chiefs were a .500 club. They looked like the best team in the league when they beat the Chargers 49-6 and dismantled the Jets 24-7, but they looked like scrubs while losing 33-27 to the lowly Broncos. No one could figure out how a team with good offensive and defensive units could lose seven games, but the Chiefs complicated coach Hank Stram's life by doing that. Len Dawson sparked the attack with thirty touchdown passes despite a trio of slow receivers, while the Kansas City running corps was brimming with talent. Abner Haynes was less consistent but still dangerous at halfback, rookie Mack Lee Hill bulled his way into the starting lineup, and Curtis McClinton, Jack Spikes, and Bert Coan provided unheard-of depth. The defense was one of the league's best, with two superb linemen in Jerry Mays and Buck Buchanan, a trio of fine linebackers in E. J. Holub, Sherrill Headrick, and Bobby Bell, and top backs in Dave Grayson, Duane Wood, Bobby Hunt, and Johnny Robinson. But the Chiefs found ways to lose that defied the heavy weight of their roster.

**Oakland Raiders**—The miraculous finish of 1963 wore off as the Raiders lost their first five games, but Al Davis' men came back in the second half of the schedule to prove that they were indeed a solid football team. The final five games brought four wins and a tie to Oakland, and among the defeated teams were San Diego and Buffalo, the teams headed for the championship game. The Raiders no longer had the element of surprise on their side, as the rest of the league had seen their blitzes last year and no longer took them lightly, but they resorted to a more settled style of play with fine results in the back stretch. Clem Daniels got off to a slow start, but the powerful halfback recovered to star during the Raiders' late drive. Helping Daniels with strong blocking was Billy Cannon, obtained from Houston to fill the gap at fullback. The defense was strengthened by the addition of end Ben Davidson, a huge lineman cut by the NFL Washington Redskins, and rookie linebacker Dan Conners—and despite the disappointing third-place finish, coach Davis was happy about adding new talent to his future champions.

**Denver Broncos**—Coach Jack Faulkner resorted to lend lease to get himself a quarterback, sending defensive tackle Bud McFadin to Houston in exchange for quarterback Jacky Lee, who was to return to Houston after two seasons. The deal won press space but few ball games, as Lee was a distinct disappointment in leading the attack. The offensive line was a shambles, however, and few passers could have accomplished much behind it. The poor blocking wasted some good offensive talent, such as split end Lionel Taylor, tight end Hewritt Dixon, halfback Charley Mitchell, and fullback Billy Joe. The defense was easy to march through but did cause enemy quarterbacks some pain with a late-season blitzing campaign; the best performances were turned in by Ray Jacobs, Jerry Hopkins, Willie Brown, and Goose Gonsoulin. The Broncos went into the season with no title hopes, but when they were massacred in the first four games, coach Faulkner got the ax and assistant Mac Speedie took over as head man.

**FINAL TEAM STATISTICS**

### OFFENSE

| | BOSTON | BUFFALO | DENVER | HOUSTON | K. CITY | NEW YORK | OAKLAND | SAN DIEGO |
|---|---|---|---|---|---|---|---|---|
| **FIRST DOWNS:** | | | | | | | | |
| Total | 226 | 255 | 207 | **284** | 250 | 209 | 270 | 254 |
| by Rushing | 66 | **114** | 78 | 80 | 90 | 79 | 63 | 85 |
| by Passing | 144 | 130 | 116 | **186** | 148 | 108 | **186** | 156 |
| by Penalty | 16 | 11 | 13 | 18 | 12 | **22** | 21 | 13 |
| **RUSHING:** | | | | | | | | |
| Number | 381 | **492** | 391 | 327 | 415 | 384 | 331 | 392 |
| Yards | 1361 | **2040** | 1311 | 1347 | 1825 | 1457 | 1480 | 1522 |
| Average Yards | 3.6 | 4.1 | 3.4 | 4.1 | 4.4 | 3.8 | **4.5** | 3.9 |
| Touchdowns | 9 | **25** | 10 | 14 | 14 | 11 | 9 | 14 |
| **PASSING:** | | | | | | | | |
| Attempts | 476 | 397 | 456 | **592** | 412 | 451 | 521 | 445 |
| Completions | 229 | 174 | 230 | **299** | 228 | 201 | 253 | 224 |
| Completion Percentage | 48.1 | 43.8 | 50.4 | 50.5 | **55.3** | 44.6 | 48.6 | 50.3 |
| Passing Yardage | 3467 | 3422 | 2541 | 3734 | 3321 | 2694 | **3886** | 3363 |
| Average Yards per Attempt | 7.3 | **8.6** | 5.6 | 6.3 | 8.1 | 6.0 | 7.5 | 7.6 |
| Average Yards per Completion | 15.1 | **19.7** | 11.0 | 12.5 | 14.6 | 13.4 | 15.4 | 15.0 |
| Times Tackled Attempting to Pass | 29 | 35 | 61 | 23 | 44 | 27 | 56 | **22** |
| Yards Lost Attempting to Pass | 301 | 256 | 520 | **207** | 446 | 262 | 464 | 221 |
| Net Yards | 3166 | 3166 | 2021 | **3527** | 2875 | 2432 | 3422 | 3142 |
| Touchdowns | 31 | 19 | 14 | 19 | **32** | 19 | 28 | 28 |
| Interceptions | 27 | 34 | 32 | 29 | **21** | 33 | 33 | 30 |
| Percent Intercepted | 5.7 | 8.6 | 7.0 | **4.9** | 5.1 | 7.3 | 6.3 | 6.7 |
| **PUNTING:** | | | | | | | | |
| Number | 78 | 65 | **83** | 55 | 79 | 79 | 59 | 63 |
| Average Distance | 38.0 | 42.7 | **43.4** | 41.2 | 42.5 | 41.3 | 41.5 | 39.3 |
| **PUNT RETURNS:** | | | | | | | | |
| Number | 38 | **46** | 25 | 19 | 40 | 38 | 33 | 34 |
| Yards | 276 | 421 | 259 | 252 | 400 | 283 | **447** | 283 |
| Average Yards | 7.3 | 9.2 | 10.4 | 13.3 | 10.0 | 7.4 | **13.5** | 8.3 |
| Touchdowns | 0 | **1** | **1** | **1** | 0 | 0 | 0 | 0 |
| **KICKOFF RETURNS:** | | | | | | | | |
| Number | 58 | 48 | **76** | 66 | 57 | 54 | 61 | 53 |
| Yards | 1167 | 1018 | **1758** | 1559 | 1261 | 1088 | 1525 | 1288 |
| Average Yards | 20.1 | 21.2 | 23.1 | 23.6 | 22.1 | 20.1 | **25.0** | 24.3 |
| Touchdowns | 0 | 0 | 0 | 0 | 0 | 0 | 0 | 0 |
| **INTERCEPTION RETURNS:** | | | | | | | | |
| Number | 31 | 28 | 32 | 30 | 28 | **34** | 26 | 30 |
| Yards | 427 | 470 | 459 | 437 | 408 | 477 | 430 | **487** |
| Average Yards | 13.8 | **16.8** | 14.3 | 14.6 | 14.6 | 14.0 | 16.5 | 16.2 |
| Touchdowns | 1 | 2 | 1 | 3 | 1 | 1 | **4** | 2 |
| **PENALTIES:** | | | | | Not Available | | | |
| Number | | | | | | | | |
| Yards | | | | | | | | |
| **FUMBLES:** | | | | | | | | |
| Number | 23 | 32 | 27 | 24 | 36 | **15** | 30 | 30 |
| Number Lost | 12 | 18 | 8 | 15 | 20 | **7** | 18 | 16 |
| **POINTS:** | | | | | | | | |
| Total | 365 | **400** | 240 | 310 | 366 | 278 | 303 | 341 |
| PAT (kick) Attempts | 36 | **46** | 25 | 38 | **46** | 33 | 34 | 43 |
| PAT (kick) Made | 36 | 45 | 22 | 37 | **46** | 33 | 34 | 39 |
| PAT (Rush or Pass) Attempts | 5 | 2 | 3 | 1 | 3 | 1 | 2 | 1 |
| PAT (Rush or Pass) Made | 3 | 2 | **3** | 0 | 1 | 0 | 1 | 1 |
| FG Attempts | **39** | 29 | 34 | 29 | 17 | 27 | 24 | 26 |
| FG Made | **25** | 19 | 14 | 13 | 8 | 13 | 15 | 12 |
| Percent FG Made | 64.1 | **65.5** | 41.2 | 44.8 | 47.1 | 48.1 | 62.5 | 46.2 |
| Safeties | 1 | **3** | 0 | 0 | 1 | 1 | 0 | 0 |

### DEFENSE

| | BOSTON | BUFFALO | DENVER | HOUSTON | K. CITY | NEW YORK | OAKLAND | SAN DIEGO |
|---|---|---|---|---|---|---|---|---|
| **FIRST DOWNS:** | | | | | | | | |
| Total | 243 | **206** | 271 | 276 | 211 | 245 | 255 | 248 |
| by Rushing | 63 | **48** | 100 | 103 | 77 | 79 | 103 | 82 |
| by Passing | 165 | 145 | 148 | 159 | **124** | 152 | 134 | 147 |
| by Penalty | 15 | 13 | 23 | 14 | **10** | 14 | 18 | 19 |
| **RUSHING:** | | | | | | | | |
| Number | 356 | **300** | 424 | 438 | 390 | 410 | 396 | 399 |
| Yards | 1143 | **913** | 2064 | 1961 | 1315 | 1675 | 1750 | 1522 |
| Average Yards | 3.2 | **3.0** | 4.9 | 4.5 | 3.4 | 4.1 | 4.4 | 3.8 |
| Touchdowns | 10 | **4** | 21 | 18 | 9 | 14 | 20 | 10 |
| **PASSING:** | | | | | | | | |
| Attempts | 530 | 517 | 440 | **433** | 440 | 473 | **433** | 484 |
| Completions | 261 | 241 | 215 | 229 | 218 | 228 | **206** | 240 |
| Completion Percentage | 49.2 | **46.6** | 48.9 | 52.9 | 49.5 | 48.2 | 47.6 | 49.6 |
| Passing Yardage | 3645 | 3361 | 3353 | 3469 | **2910** | 3472 | 3292 | 2926 |
| Average Yards per Attempt | 6.9 | 6.5 | 7.6 | 8.0 | 6.6 | 7.3 | 7.6 | **6.0** |
| Average Yards per Completion | 14.0 | 13.9 | 15.6 | 15.1 | 13.3 | 15.2 | 16.0 | **12.2** |
| Times Tackled Attempting to Pass | 47 | **50** | 44 | 25 | 28 | 28 | 37 | 38 |
| Yards Lost Attempting to Pass | 428 | 396 | **447** | 189 | 279 | 231 | 299 | 408 |
| Net Yards | 3217 | 2965 | 2906 | 3280 | 2631 | 3241 | 2993 | **2518** |
| Touchdowns | 23 | 24 | 29 | 24 | 25 | 22 | **21** | 22 |
| Interceptions | 31 | 28 | 32 | 30 | 28 | **34** | 26 | 30 |
| Percent Intercepted | 5.8 | 5.4 | **7.3** | 6.9 | 6.4 | 7.2 | 6.0 | 6.2 |
| **PUNTING:** | | | | | | | | |
| Number | 82 | **87** | 59 | 56 | 78 | 71 | 66 | 62 |
| Average Distance | 41.5 | 41.9 | 41.4 | **39.1** | 40.7 | 40.5 | 41.7 | 41.3 |
| **PUNT RETURNS:** | | | | | | | | |
| Number | **24** | **24** | 40 | 33 | 36 | 43 | 41 | 32 |
| Yards | 185 | 250 | 526 | 295 | 251 | 426 | 272 | 416 |
| Average Yards | 7.7 | 10.4 | 13.2 | 8.9 | 7.0 | 9.9 | **6.6** | 13.0 |
| Touchdowns | 0 | 0 | 1 | 0 | 0 | 1 | 0 | 1 |
| **KICKOFF RETURNS:** | | | | | | | | |
| Number | 70 | 59 | **44** | 53 | 64 | 53 | 64 | 66 |
| Yards | 1637 | 1385 | 1166 | **978** | 1459 | 1236 | 1239 | 1564 |
| Average Yards | 23.4 | 23.5 | 26.5 | **18.5** | 22.8 | 23.3 | 19.4 | 23.7 |
| Touchdowns | 1 | 0 | 0 | 0 | 0 | 0 | 0 | 0 |
| **INTERCEPTION RETURNS:** | | | | | | | | |
| Number | 27 | 34 | 32 | 29 | **21** | 33 | 33 | 30 |
| Yards | 485 | 406 | 441 | 496 | **228** | 448 | 713 | 378 |
| Average Yards | 18.0 | 11.9 | 13.8 | 17.1 | **10.9** | 13.6 | 21.6 | 12.6 |
| Touchdowns | 1 | 0 | 1 | 3 | **3** | 1 | 4 | 1 |
| **PENALTIES:** | | | | | Not Available | | | |
| Number | | | | | | | | |
| Yards | | | | | | | | |
| **FUMBLES:** | | | | | | | | |
| Number | 33 | 24 | **40** | 21 | 29 | 19 | 19 | 32 |
| Number Lost | 17 | 15 | **21** | 8 | 18 | 10 | 10 | 15 |
| **POINTS:** | | | | | | | | |
| Total | 297 | **242** | 438 | 355 | 306 | 315 | 350 | 300 |
| PAT (kick) Attempts | 33 | **23** | 52 | 43 | 36 | 38 | 43 | 33 |
| PAT (kick) Made | 32 | **22** | 52 | 41 | 34 | 36 | 43 | 32 |
| PAT (Rush or Pass) Attempts | 3 | 5 | **0** | 2 | 2 | 1 | 2 | 3 |
| PAT (Rush or Pass) Made | 2 | 2 | **0** | 1 | 1 | 0 | 1 | 3 |
| FG Attempts | 27 | 27 | 25 | 30 | **20** | 27 | 34 | 32 |
| FG Made | 15 | 14 | 22 | 14 | 14 | 15 | **11** | 14 |
| Percent FG Made | 50.0 | 51.9 | 88.0 | 46.7 | 70.0 | 55.6 | **32.3** | 43.8 |
| Safeties | **0** | **0** | 4 | **0** | **0** | **0** | 1 | 2 |

---

**1964 AFL CHAMPIONSHIP GAME**
December 26, at Buffalo
(Attendance 40,242)

## No Instant Replay

The San Diego Chargers started fast in defending their AFL title, but the sturdy Buffalo defense caught up and turned the game around before the first half ended. The first time the Chargers got their hands on the ball they drove 80 yards in four plays: Keith Lincoln, the star of last year's championship game, ran 38 yards on one play, and Tobin Rote found Dave Kocourek with a pass good for 26 yards and the first touchdown of the game. Lincoln's extra point made the score 7-0, and some fans expected the Chargers to turn the game into a rout as they had the year before. On the Chargers' next drive, however, the Bills made the key play of the game. When Lincoln caught a short pass in the flat, Buffalo linebacker Mike Stratton leveled him with a crunching tackle that knocked the ball loose and broke one of Lincoln's ribs. With their star back out of action, the Chargers never again could move the ball against the Buffalo defense. Pete Gogolak scored the Bills' first three points on a 12-yard field goal, and 10 second-quarter points gave Buffalo a 13-7 lead at halftime. The third period was scoreless, but the differences in the teams showed through clearly. The San Diego running attack missed the injured Lincoln dearly, while Cookie Gilchrist blasted into the Chargers' line with jackhammer force and regularity. While the San Diego attack withered in the face of the Buffalo pass rush, the Bills added a final touchdown when a Jack Kemp-to-Glenn Bass pass covering 48 yards brought the ball down to the one-yard line before Kemp went over for the 20-7 victory and Buffalo's first major-league sports championship.

### SCORING

| | | | | | |
|---|---|---|---|---|---|
| BUFFALO | 3 | 10 | 0 | 7 | 20 |
| SAN DIEGO | 7 | 0 | 0 | 0 | 7 |

First Quarter
S.D. Kocourek, 26 yard pass from Rote
    PAT—Lincoln (kick)
BUF. Gogolak, 12 yard field goal

Second Quarter
BUF. Carlton, 4 yard rush
    PAT—Gogolak (kick)
BUF. Gogolak, 17 yard field goal

Fourth Quarter
BUF. Kemp, 1 yard rush
    PAT—Gogolak (kick)

### TEAM STATISTICS

| BUFF. | | S.D. |
|---|---|---|
| 21 | First Downs—Total | 15 |
| 12 | First Downs—Rushing | 7 |
| 8 | First Downs—Passing | 7 |
| 1 | First Downs—Penalty | 1 |
| 0 | Fumbles—Number | 1 |
| 0 | Fumbles—Number Lost | 0 |
| 3 | Penalties—Number | 3 |
| 45 | Yards Penalized | 20 |
| 0 | Missed Field Goals | 0 |

### INDIVIDUAL STATISTICS

**BUFFALO**

| | No | Yds | Avg. |
|---|---|---|---|
| **RUSHING** | | | |
| Gilchrist | 16 | 122 | 7.6 |
| Carlton | 18 | 70 | 3.9 |
| Kemp | 5 | 16 | 3.2 |
| Dubenion | 1 | 9 | 9.0 |
| Lamonica | 1 | 2 | 2.0 |
| | 41 | 219 | 5.3 |
| **RECEIVING** | | | |
| Dubenion | 3 | 36 | 12.0 |
| Bass | 2 | 70 | 35.0 |
| Warlick | 2 | 41 | 20.5 |
| Gilchrist | 2 | 22 | 11.0 |
| Ross | 1 | -1 | -1.0 |
| | 10 | 168 | 16.8 |
| **PUNTING** | | | |
| Maguire | 5 | | 46.8 |
| **PUNT RETURNS** | | | |
| Clarke | 1 | 6 | 6.0 |
| **KICKOFF RETURNS** | | | |
| Rutkowski | 1 | 27 | 27.0 |
| Warner | 1 | 17 | 17.0 |
| | 2 | 44 | 22.0 |
| **INTERCEPTION RETURNS** | | | |
| Warner | 1 | 8 | 8.0 |
| Byrd | 1 | 0 | 0.0 |
| Stratton | 1 | 0 | 0.0 |
| | 3 | 8 | 2.7 |

**SAN DIEGO**

| | No | Yds | Avg. |
|---|---|---|---|
| **RUSHING** | | | |
| Lincoln | 3 | 47 | 15.7 |
| Lowe | 7 | 34 | 4.9 |
| MacKinnon | 1 | 17 | 17.0 |
| Kinderman | 4 | 14 | 3.5 |
| Hadl | 1 | 13 | 13.0 |
| Rote | 1 | 6 | 6.0 |
| Norton | 1 | -7 | -7.0 |
| | 18 | 124 | 6.9 |
| **RECEIVING** | | | |
| Kinderman | 4 | 52 | 13.0 |
| MacKinnon | 3 | 12 | 4.0 |
| Kocourek | 2 | 52 | 26.0 |
| Lowe | 2 | 9 | 4.5 |
| Norton | 1 | 13 | 13.0 |
| Lincoln | 1 | 11 | 11.0 |
| | 13 | 149 | 11.5 |
| **PUNTING** | | | |
| Hadl | 5 | | 36.4 |
| **PUNT RETURNS** | | | |
| Robinson | 1 | 30 | 30.0 |
| Duncan | 1 | 28 | 28.0 |
| | 2 | 58 | 29.0 |
| **KICKOFF RETURNS** | | | |
| Duncan | 3 | 147 | 49.0 |
| Warren | 1 | 28 | 28.0 |
| | 4 | 175 | 43.8 |
| **INTERCEPTION RETURNS** | | | |
| None | | | |

**PASSING**

| | Att. | Comp. | Comp. Pct. | Yds. | Int. | Yds/Att. | Yds/Comp. |
|---|---|---|---|---|---|---|---|
| BUFFALO | | | | | | | |
| Kemp | 20 | 10 | 50.0 | 168 | 0 | 8.4 | 16.8 |
| SAN DIEGO | | | | | | | |
| Rote | 26 | 10 | 38.5 | 118 | 2 | 4.5 | 11.8 |
| Hadl | 10 | 3 | 30.0 | 31 | 1 | 3.1 | 10.3 |
| | 36 | 13 | 36.1 | 149 | 3 | 4.1 | 11.5 |

## BUFFALO BILLS 12-2-0 Lou Saban

| Scores of Each Game | | | Use Name | Pos. | Hgt | Wgt | Age | Int | Pts |
|---|---|---|---|---|---|---|---|---|---|
| 34 | KANSAS CITY | 17 | Stew Barber | OT | 6'3" | 250 | 25 | | |
| 30 | DENVER | 13 | Dick Hudson | OT | 6'4" | 272 | 24 | | |
| 30 | SAN DIEGO | 3 | Joe O'Donnell | OT | 6'2" | 246 | 22 | | |
| 23 | OAKLAND | 20 | Al Bemiller | OG | 6'3" | 260 | 25 | | |
| 48 | Houston | 17 | George Flint | OG | 6'4" | 244 | 26 | | |
| 35 | Kansas City | 22 | Billy Shaw | OG | 6'3" | 248 | 24 | | |
| 34 | NEW YORK | 24 | Walt Cudzik | C | 6'2" | 240 | 31 | | |
| 24 | HOUSTON | 10 | Tom Day | DE | 6'2" | 250 | 29 | | |
| 20 | New York | 7 | Ron McDole | DE | 6'3" | 264 | 24 | 1 | |
| 28 | BOSTON | 36 | Jim Dunaway | DT | 6'4" | 276 | 22 | | |
| 27 | San Diego | 24 | Tom Keating | DT | 6'3" | 242 | 21 | | |
| 13 | Oakland | 16 | Dudley Meredith | DT | 6'4" | 275 | 29 | | |
| 30 | Denver | 19 | Tom Sestak | DT | 6'5" | 270 | 28 | 1 | 6 |
| 24 | Boston | 14 | | | | | | | |

| Use Name | Pos. | Hgt | Wgt | Age | Int | Pts |
|---|---|---|---|---|---|---|
| Harry Jacobs | LB | 6'2" | 225 | 27 | 2 | |
| Paul Maguire | LB | 6' | 220 | 26 | | |
| Mike Stratton | LB | 6'3" | 240 | 22 | 1 | |
| John Tracey | LB | 6'3" | 225 | 31 | 3 | |
| Ray Abbruzzese | DB | 6'1" | 194 | 26 | | |
| Butch Byrd | DB | 6' | 211 | 22 | 7 | 6 |
| Hagood Clarke | DB | 6' | 188 | 22 | | 6 |
| Ollie Dobbins | DB | 5'11" | 185 | 22 | | |
| Booker Edgerson | DB | 5'10" | 180 | 25 | 4 | |
| George Saimes | DB | 5'10" | 195 | 22 | 6 | |
| Gene Sykes | DB | 6'1" | 195 | 23 | 2 | |
| Charley Ferguson — Injury | | | | | | |

| Use Name | Pos. | Hgt | Wgt | Age | Int | Pts |
|---|---|---|---|---|---|---|
| Jack Kemp | QB | 6'1" | 200 | 30 | | 30 |
| Daryle Lamonica | QB | 6'2" | 215 | 23 | | 40 |
| Joe Auer | HB | 6'1" | 205 | 22 | | 18 |
| Wray Carlton | HB | 6'2" | 216 | 26 | | 6 |
| Bobby Smith | HB | 6' | 203 | 22 | | 24 |
| Cookie Gilchrist | FB | 6'3" | 250 | 29 | | 36 |
| Willie Ross | FB | 5'10" | 200 | 23 | | 6 |
| Elbert Dubenion | FL | 6' | 187 | 29 | | 60 |
| Ed Rutkowski | FL | 6'1" | 208 | 23 | | 6 |
| Glenn Bass | OE | 6'2" | 206 | 25 | | 42 |
| Bill Groman | OE | 6' | 195 | 28 | | 6 |
| Ernie Warlick | OE | 6'4" | 235 | 32 | | |
| Pete Gogolak | K | 6'2" | 200 | 22 | | 102 |

## BOSTON PATRIOTS 10-3-1 Mike Holovak

| Scores of Each Game | | | Use Name | Pos. | Hgt | Wgt | Age | Int | Pts |
|---|---|---|---|---|---|---|---|---|---|
| 17 | Oakland | 14 | Don Oakes | OT | 6'3" | 255 | 26 | | |
| 33 | San Diego | 28 | Bob Schmidt | OT | 6'4" | 250 | 28 | | |
| 26 | NEW YORK | 10 | Bob Yates | OT | 6'3" | 230 | 25 | | |
| 39 | Denver | 10 | Charley Long | OG | 6'3" | 250 | 26 | | |
| 17 | SAN DIEGO | 26 | Billy Neighbors | OG | 5'11" | 240 | 24 | | |
| 43 | OAKLAND | 43 | Dave Watson | OG | 6'1" | 230 | 23 | | |
| 24 | KANSAS CITY | 7 | Jon Morris | C | 6'4" | 240 | 22 | | |
| 14 | New York | 35 | Bob Dee | DE | 6'3" | 240 | 31 | | |
| 25 | HOUSTON | 24 | Larry Eisenhauer | DE | 6'5" | 250 | 24 | | |
| 36 | Buffalo | 28 | Jim Hunt | DE-DT | 5'11" | 245 | 25 | | |
| 12 | DENVER | 7 | Len St. Jean | DE | 6'1" | 240 | 22 | | |
| 34 | Houston | 17 | Houston Antwine | DT | 6' | 270 | 25 | | |
| 31 | Kansas City | 24 | Jerry DeLucca | DT | 6'3" | 250 | 28 | | |
| 14 | BUFFALO | 24 | Jess Richardson | DT | 6'2" | 265 | 34 | | |

| Use Name | Pos. | Hgt | Wgt | Age | Int | Pts |
|---|---|---|---|---|---|---|
| Tom Addison | LB | 6'3" | 230 | 28 | 2 | |
| Nick Buoniconti | LB | 5'11" | 220 | 23 | 5 | |
| Mike Dukes | LB | 6'3" | 235 | 28 | 1 | |
| Lonnie Farmer | LB | 6' | 220 | 23 | | |
| Jack Rudolph | LB | 6'3" | 230 | 26 | | |
| Don McKinnon | C-LB | 6'3" | 230 | 22 | | |
| Dave Cloutier | DB | 6' | 195 | 25 | | |
| Dick Felt | DB | 6' | 185 | 31 | 2 | |
| Ron Hall | DB | 6' | 190 | 27 | 11 | |
| Ross O'Hanley | DB | 6' | 185 | 25 | 3 | 6 |
| Chuck Shonta | DB | 6' | 200 | 26 | 1 | |
| Don Webb | DB | 5'10" | 200 | 25 | 6 | |
| Tom Stephens | OE-DB | 6'1" | 215 | 28 | | |

| Use Name | Pos. | Hgt | Wgt | Age | Int | Pts |
|---|---|---|---|---|---|---|
| Babe Parilli | QB | 6'1" | 190 | 34 | | 12 |
| Tom Yewcic | QB | 5'11" | 185 | 32 | | |
| Ron Burton | HB | 5'10" | 190 | 27 | | 30 |
| J. D. Garrett | HB | 5'11" | 195 | 22 | | 12 |
| Jim Crawford | FB | 6'1" | 205 | 28 | | |
| Larry Garron | FB | 6' | 195 | 27 | | 54 |
| Jim Colclough | FL | 6' | 185 | 28 | | 34 |
| Al Snyder | FL | 6' | 195 | 22 | | |
| Gino Cappelletti | OE | 6' | 190 | 30 | | 155 |
| Art Graham | OE | 6'1" | 205 | 23 | | 36 |
| Tony Romeo | OE | 6'2" | 230 | 25 | | 24 |

## NEW YORK JETS 5-8-1 Weeb Ewbank

| Scores of Each Game | | | Use Name | Pos. | Hgt | Wgt | Age | Int | Pts |
|---|---|---|---|---|---|---|---|---|---|
| 30 | DENVER | 6 | Winston Hill | OT | 6'4" | 275 | 22 | | |
| 10 | Boston | 26 | Jim McCusker | OT | 6'2" | 250 | 28 | | |
| 17 | SAN DIEGO | 17 | Sherman Plunkett | OT | 6'4" | 295 | 30 | | |
| 35 | OAKLAND | 13 | Sam DeLuca | OG | 6'2" | 250 | 30 | | |
| 24 | HOUSTON | 21 | Dan Ficca | OG | 6'1" | 250 | 25 | | |
| 24 | Buffalo | 34 | Dave Herman | OG | 6'2" | 255 | 22 | | |
| 35 | BOSTON | 14 | Pete Perreault | OG | 6'3" | 245 | 25 | | |
| 7 | BUFFALO | 20 | Mike Hudock | C | 6'2" | 245 | 29 | | |
| 16 | Denver | 20 | John Schmitt | C | 6'4" | 265 | 21 | | |
| 26 | Oakland | 35 | Gerry Philbin | DE | 6'2" | 245 | 23 | | |
| 27 | KANSAS CITY | 14 | Lavern Torczon | DE | 6'2" | 250 | 28 | 1 | 6 |
| 3 | San Diego | 38 | Bob Watters | DE | 6'4" | 245 | 28 | | |
| 17 | Houston | 33 | Bert Wilder | DE | 6'3" | 245 | 24 | | |
| 7 | Kansas City | 24 | Gordy Holz | DT | 6'4" | 260 | 30 | | |
| | | | Bob McAdams | DT | 6'3" | 250 | 24 | | |
| | | | Paul Rochester | DT | 6'2" | 250 | 27 | | |

| Use Name | Pos. | Hgt | Wgt | Age | Int | Pts |
|---|---|---|---|---|---|---|
| Ralph Baker | LB | 6'3" | 235 | 22 | 2 | |
| Ed Cummings | LB | 6'2" | 232 | 23 | 1 | |
| Larry Grantham | LB | 6' | 206 | 25 | 2 | |
| Wahoo McDaniel | LB | 6' | 240 | 27 | 3 | 6 |
| Bob Rowley | LB | 6'2" | 225 | 22 | | |
| Mark Johnston (from OAK) | DB | 6' | 200 | 26 | 1 | |
| Bill Pashe | DB | 5'11" | 185 | 23 | | |
| Dainard Paulson | DB | 5'11" | 190 | 27 | 12 | 6 |
| Bill Rademacher | DB | 6'1" | 190 | 22 | 1 | |
| Marsh Starks | DB | 6' | 190 | 25 | 1 | |
| Vince Turner | DB | 5'11" | 190 | 21 | 1 | |
| Clyde Washington | DB | 6' | 206 | 26 | | |
| Bill Baird | HB-DB | 5'10" | 180 | 25 | 8 | 6 |

| Use Name | Pos. | Hgt | Wgt | Age | Int | Pts |
|---|---|---|---|---|---|---|
| Mike Taliaferro | QB | 6'2" | 210 | 22 | | |
| Dick Wood | QB | 6'5" | 205 | 28 | | 6 |
| Pete Liske | DB-QB | 6'2" | 195 | 23 | | |
| Curley Johnson | HB | 6' | 215 | 29 | | |
| Bill Mathis | HB | 6'2" | 220 | 25 | | 24 |
| Mark Smolinski | FB | 6' | 215 | 25 | | 6 |
| Matt Snell | FB | 6'2" | 220 | 22 | | 36 |
| Jim Evans | FL | 6'1" | 190 | 24 | | |
| Al Lawson | FL | 5'11" | 190 | 22 | | |
| Don Maynard | FL | 6' | 185 | 28 | | 48 |
| Gene Heeter | OE | 6'4" | 235 | 23 | | 6 |
| Dee Mackey | OE | 6'5" | 225 | 28 | | |
| Bake Turner | OE | 6' | 185 | 24 | | 54 |
| Jim Turner | K | 6'2" | 205 | 23 | | 72 |

## HOUSTON OILERS 4-10-0 Sammy Baugh

| Scores of Each Game | | | Use Name | Pos. | Hgt | Wgt | Age | Int | Pts |
|---|---|---|---|---|---|---|---|---|---|
| 21 | San Diego | 27 | Staley Faulkner | OT | 6'3" | 245 | 23 | | |
| 42 | OAKLAND | 28 | Jerry Fowler | OT | 6'3" | 255 | 23 | | |
| 38 | Denver | 17 | Bob Kelly | OT | 6'3" | 260 | 24 | | |
| 7 | Kansas City | 28 | Jack Klotz | OT | 6'5" | 250 | 30 | | |
| 17 | BUFFALO | 48 | Walt Suggs | OT | 6'5" | 260 | 25 | | |
| 21 | New York | 24 | Sonny Bishop | OG | 6'2" | 245 | 24 | | |
| 17 | SAN DIEGO | 20 | John Frongillo | OG | 6'3" | 250 | 24 | | |
| 10 | Buffalo | 24 | Bob Talamini | OG | 6'1" | 255 | 25 | | |
| 24 | Boston | 25 | John Wittenborn | OG | 6'2" | 240 | 28 | | |
| 10 | Oakland | 20 | Tom Goode | C | 6'3" | 250 | 25 | | |
| 19 | KANSAS CITY | 28 | Gary Cutsinger | DE | 6'4" | 245 | 23 | | |
| 17 | BOSTON | 34 | Don Floyd | DE | 6'4" | 247 | 26 | | 6 |
| 33 | NEW YORK | 17 | Scott Appleton | DT | 6'3" | 250 | 22 | 2 | |
| 34 | DENVER | 15 | Ed Husmann | DT | 6' | 245 | 34 | | |
| | | | Bud McFadin | DT | 6'3" | 270 | 36 | | |

| Use Name | Pos. | Hgt | Wgt | Age | Int | Pts |
|---|---|---|---|---|---|---|
| Danny Brabham | LB | 6'4" | 240 | 23 | | |
| Doug Cline | LB | 6'2" | 230 | 25 | | |
| Sammy Odom | LB | 6'2" | 235 | 22 | 2 | |
| Larry Onesti | LB | 6' | 200 | 25 | | |
| Charley Rieves | LB | 5'11" | 218 | 25 | 1 | |
| Johnny Baker | OE-LB | 6'3" | 225 | 23 | 1 | 6 |
| Freddy Glick | DB | 6'1" | 190 | 27 | 5 | |
| W. K. Hicks | DB | 6'1" | 185 | 21 | 5 | |
| Pete Jaquess | DB | 6' | 180 | 22 | 8 | 6 |
| Benny Nelson | DB | 6' | 185 | 22 | 1 | 6 |
| Jim Norton | DB | 6' | 190 | 25 | 2 | |
| Bobby Jancik | FL-DB | 5'11" | 178 | 24 | 3 | 6 |
| Rich Michael — Injury | | | | | | |

| Use Name | Pos. | Hgt | Wgt | Age | Int | Pts |
|---|---|---|---|---|---|---|
| George Blanda | QB | 6'1" | 215 | 36 | | 76 |
| Don Trull | QB | 6'1" | 180 | 22 | | |
| Sid Blanks | HB | 6' | 198 | 23 | | 42 |
| Ode Burrell | HB | 6' | 185 | 24 | | 6 |
| Dalton Hoffman | FB | 6'1" | 207 | 22 | | 6 |
| Dave Smith | FB | 6'1" | 210 | 27 | | |
| Charley Tolar | FB | 5'7" | 200 | 26 | | 24 |
| Charley Hennigan | FL | 6' | 187 | 28 | | 48 |
| Dobie Craig | OE | 6'4" | 200 | 25 | | 6 |
| Willard Dewveall | OE | 6'4" | 230 | 27 | | 24 |
| Charley Frazier | OE | 6' | 175 | 25 | | 12 |
| Willie Frazier | OE | 6'4" | 225 | 21 | | 6 |
| Bob McLeod | OE | 6'5" | 230 | 25 | | 12 |

## BUFFALO BILLS

### Rushing

| Last Name | No. | Yds | Avg | TD |
|---|---|---|---|---|
| Gilchrist | 230 | 981 | 4.3 | 6 |
| Smith | 62 | 306 | 4.9 | 4 |
| Lamonica | 55 | 289 | 5.3 | 6 |
| Auer | 63 | 191 | 3.0 | 2 |
| Kemp | 37 | 124 | 3.4 | 5 |
| Carlton | 39 | 114 | 2.9 | 1 |
| Dubenion | 1 | 20 | 20.0 | 0 |
| Ross | 4 | 14 | 3.5 | 1 |
| Hudson | 1 | 1 | 1.0 | 0 |

### Receiving

| Last Name | No. | Yds | Avg | TD |
|---|---|---|---|---|
| Bass | 43 | 897 | 21 | 7 |
| Dubenion | 42 | 1139 | 27 | 10 |
| Gilchrist | 30 | 345 | 12 | 0 |
| Warlick | 23 | 478 | 21 | 0 |
| Rutkowski | 13 | 234 | 18 | 1 |
| Auer | 11 | 166 | 15 | 0 |
| Smith | 6 | 72 | 12 | 0 |
| Groman | 4 | 68 | 17 | 1 |
| Carlton | 2 | 23 | 12 | 0 |

### Punt Returns

| Last Name | No. | Yds | Avg | TD |
|---|---|---|---|---|
| Clarke | 33 | 317 | 10 | 1 |
| Rutkowski | 8 | 45 | 6 | 0 |
| Byrd | 2 | 4 | 2 | 0 |

### Kickoff Returns

| Last Name | No. | Yds | Avg | TD |
|---|---|---|---|---|
| Rutkowski | 21 | 498 | 24 | 0 |
| Clarke | 16 | 330 | 21 | 0 |
| Smith | 3 | 68 | 23 | 0 |
| Barber | 2 | 0 | 0 | 0 |
| Maguire | 1 | 0 | 0 | 0 |
| Auer | 0 | 1 | 0 | 0 |

### Passing – Punting – Kicking

PASSING

| Last Name | Att | Comp | % | Yds | Yd/Att | TD | Int | % | RK |
|---|---|---|---|---|---|---|---|---|---|
| Kemp | 269 | 119 | 44 | 2285 | 8.5 | 13 | 26- | 10 | 6 |
| Lamonica | 128 | 55 | 43 | 1137 | 8.9 | 6 | 8- | 6 | |

PUNTING

| Last Name | No | Avg |
|---|---|---|
| Maguire | 65 | 42.7 |

KICKING

| Last Name | XP | Att | % | FG | Att | % |
|---|---|---|---|---|---|---|
| Gogolak | 45 | 46 | 98 | 19 | 29 | 66 |

2 POINT XP
Lamonica (2)

## BOSTON PATRIOTS

### Rushing

| Last Name | No. | Yds | Avg | TD |
|---|---|---|---|---|
| Garron | 183 | 585 | 3.2 | 2 |
| Burton | 102 | 340 | 3.3 | 3 |
| Garrett | 56 | 259 | 4.6 | 2 |
| Parilli | 34 | 168 | 4.9 | 2 |
| Cappelletti | 1 | 7 | 7.0 | 0 |
| Yewcic | 5 | 2 | 0.4 | 0 |

### Receiving

| Last Name | No. | Yds | Avg | TD |
|---|---|---|---|---|
| Cappelletti | 49 | 865 | 18 | 7 |
| Graham | 45 | 720 | 16 | 6 |
| Garron | 40 | 350 | 9 | 7 |
| Colclough | 32 | 657 | 21 | 5 |
| Burton | 27 | 306 | 11 | 2 |
| Romeo | 26 | 445 | 17 | 4 |
| Garrett | 8 | 101 | 13 | 0 |
| Snyder | 1 | 12 | 12 | 0 |
| Crawford | 1 | 11 | 11 | 0 |

### Punt Returns

| Last Name | No. | Yds | Avg | TD |
|---|---|---|---|---|
| Cloutier | 20 | 136 | 7 | 0 |
| Burton | 11 | 78 | 7 | 0 |
| Stephens | 5 | 34 | 7 | 0 |
| Garrett | 2 | 28 | 14 | 0 |

### Kickoff Returns

| Last Name | No. | Yds | Avg | TD |
|---|---|---|---|---|
| Garrett | 32 | 749 | 23 | 0 |
| Garron | 10 | 198 | 20 | 0 |
| Burton | 7 | 131 | 19 | 0 |
| Cloutier | 1 | 46 | 46 | 0 |
| Dukes | 2 | 33 | 17 | 0 |
| Stephens | 2 | 5 | 3 | 0 |
| Romeo | 1 | 5 | 5 | 0 |
| Oakes | 1 | 0 | 0 | 0 |
| Watson | 1 | 0 | 0 | 0 |
| Yates | 1 | 0 | 0 | 0 |

### Passing – Punting – Kicking

PASSING

| Last Name | Att | Comp | % | Yds | Yd/Att | TD | Int | % | RK |
|---|---|---|---|---|---|---|---|---|---|
| Parilli | 473 | 228 | 48 | 3465 | 7.3 | 31 | 27- | 6 | 3 |
| Garron | 2 | 0 | 0 | 0.0 | 0 | 0- | 0 | | |
| Yewcic | 1 | 1 | 100 | 2 | 2.0 | 0 | 0- | 0 | |

PUNTING

| Last Name | No | Avg |
|---|---|---|
| Yewcic | 72 | 38.7 |
| Parilli | 5 | 36.0 |

KICKING

| Last Name | XP | Att | % | FG | Att | % |
|---|---|---|---|---|---|---|
| Cappelletti | 36 | 36 | 100 | 25 | 39 | 64 |

2 POINT XP
Cappelletti
Colclough (2)

## NEW YORK JETS

### Rushing

| Last Name | No. | Yds | Avg | TD |
|---|---|---|---|---|
| Snell | 215 | 948 | 4.4 | 5 |
| Mathis | 105 | 305 | 2.9 | 4 |
| Smolinski | 34 | 117 | 3.4 | 1 |
| Taliaferro | 9 | 45 | 5.0 | 0 |
| Johnson | 6 | 22 | 3.7 | 0 |
| Baird | 1 | 8 | 8.0 | 0 |
| Wood | 9 | 6 | 0.7 | 1 |
| Maynard | 3 | 3 | 1.0 | 0 |
| J. Turner | 1 | 3 | 3.0 | 0 |
| Liske | 1 | 0 | 0.0 | 0 |

### Receiving

| Last Name | No. | Yds | Avg | TD |
|---|---|---|---|---|
| B. Turner | 58 | 974 | 17 | 9 |
| Snell | 56 | 393 | 7 | 1 |
| Maynard | 46 | 847 | 18 | 8 |
| Mackey | 14 | 213 | 15 | 0 |
| Heeter | 13 | 153 | 12 | 1 |
| Evans | 7 | 56 | 8 | 0 |
| Mathis | 4 | 39 | 10 | 0 |
| Smolinski | 3 | 19 | 6 | 0 |

### Punt Returns

| Last Name | No. | Yds | Avg | TD |
|---|---|---|---|---|
| Baird | 18 | 170 | 9 | 0 |
| Starks | 5 | 36 | 7 | 0 |
| Paulson | 8 | 34 | 4 | 0 |
| Pashe | 4 | 28 | 7 | 0 |
| Rademacher | 1 | 3 | 3 | 0 |
| V. Turner | 2 | 2 | 1 | 0 |
| Rowley | 0 | 10 | 0 | 0 |

### Kickoff Returns

| Last Name | No. | Yds | Avg | TD |
|---|---|---|---|---|
| Evans | 13 | 259 | 20 | 0 |
| Baird | 11 | 240 | 22 | 0 |
| Starks | 7 | 183 | 26 | 0 |
| Snell | 7 | 158 | 23 | 0 |
| Johnson | 4 | 62 | 16 | 0 |
| V. Turner | 1 | 25 | 25 | 0 |
| Smolinski | 2 | 19 | 10 | 0 |
| Heeter | 1 | 0 | 0 | 0 |
| Mathis | 1 | 0 | 0 | 0 |
| McCusker | 1 | 0 | 0 | 0 |
| Perreault | 1 | 0 | 0 | 0 |

### Passing – Punting – Kicking

PASSING

| Last Name | Att | Comp | % | Yds | Yd/Att | TD | Int | % | RK |
|---|---|---|---|---|---|---|---|---|---|
| Wood | 358 | 169 | 47 | 2298 | 6.4 | 17 | 25- | 7 | 6 |
| Taliaferro | 73 | 23 | 32 | 341 | 4.7 | 2 | 5- | 7 | |
| Liske | 18 | 9 | 50 | 55 | 3.1 | 0 | 2- | 11 | |
| Johnson | 1 | 0 | 0 | 0.0 | 0 | 0- | 0 | | |
| Snell | 1 | 0 | 0 | 0.0 | 0 | 1- | 100 | | |

PUNTING

| Last Name | No | Avg |
|---|---|---|
| Johnson | 77 | 42.4 |

KICKING

| Last Name | XP | Att | % | FG | Att | % |
|---|---|---|---|---|---|---|
| J. Turner | 33 | 33 | 100 | 13 | 27 | 48 |

## HOUSTON OILERS

### Rushing

| Last Name | No. | Yds | Avg | TD |
|---|---|---|---|---|
| Blanks | 145 | 756 | 5.2 | 6 |
| Tolar | 139 | 515 | 3.7 | 4 |
| Trull | 12 | 42 | 3.5 | 0 |
| Smith | 8 | 16 | 2.0 | 0 |
| Burrell | 8 | 10 | 1.3 | 0 |
| Hoffman | 2 | 3 | 1.5 | 1 |
| Blanda | 4 | -2 | -0.5 | 0 |
| C. Frazier | 1 | -4 | -4.0 | 0 |

### Receiving

| Last Name | No. | Yds | Avg | TD |
|---|---|---|---|---|
| Hennigan | 101 | 1546 | 15 | 8 |
| Blanks | 56 | 497 | 9 | 1 |
| Dewveall | 38 | 552 | 15 | 4 |
| Tolar | 35 | 244 | 7 | 0 |
| C. Frazier | 31 | 423 | 14 | 2 |
| W. Frazier | 9 | 208 | 23 | 1 |
| McLeod | 8 | 81 | 10 | 2 |
| Smith | 7 | 38 | 5 | 0 |
| Burrell | 5 | 73 | 15 | 0 |
| Craig | 4 | 46 | 12 | 1 |
| Baker | 2 | 18 | 9 | 0 |
| Jancik | 1 | 14 | 14 | 0 |
| Hoffman | 1 | 1 | 1 | 0 |
| Bishop | 1 | 0 | 0 | 0 |
| Blanda | 0 | -7 | 0 | 0 |

### Punt Returns

| Last Name | No. | Yds | Avg | TD |
|---|---|---|---|---|
| Jancik | 12 | 220 | 18 | 1 |
| Glick | 6 | 32 | 5 | 0 |
| Burrell | 1 | 0 | 0 | 0 |

### Kickoff Returns

| Last Name | No. | Yds | Avg | TD |
|---|---|---|---|---|
| Jancik | 21 | 488 | 23 | 0 |
| Burrell | 17 | 449 | 26 | 1 |
| Nelson | 13 | 304 | 23 | 0 |
| Blanks | 9 | 207 | 23 | 0 |
| Hoffman | 2 | 52 | 26 | 0 |
| Glick | 1 | 27 | 27 | 0 |
| W. Frazier | 1 | 0 | 0 | 0 |

### Passing – Punting – Kicking

PASSING

| Last Name | Att | Comp | % | Yds | Yd/Att | TD | Int | % | RK |
|---|---|---|---|---|---|---|---|---|---|
| Blanda | 505 | 262 | 52 | 3287 | 6.5 | 17 | 27- | 5 | 3 |
| Trull | 86 | 36 | 42 | 439 | 5.1 | 1 | 2- | 2 | |
| Blanks | 1 | 1 | 100 | 8 | 8.0 | 0 | 0- | 0 | |

PUNTING

| Last Name | No | Avg |
|---|---|---|
| Norton | 53 | 42.8 |

KICKING

| Last Name | XP | Att | % | FG | Att | % |
|---|---|---|---|---|---|---|
| Blanda | 37 | 38 | 97 | 13 | 29 | 45 |

## SAN DIEGO CHARGERS 8-5-1 Sid Gillman

| Scores of Each Game | | |
|---|---|---|
| 27 | HOUSTON | 21 |
| 28 | BOSTON | 33 |
| 3 | Buffalo | 30 |
| 17 | New York | 17 |
| 26 | Boston | 17 |
| 42 | DENVER | 14 |
| 20 | Houston | 17 |
| 31 | OAKLAND | 17 |
| 31 | Denver | 20 |
| 28 | Kansas City | 14 |
| 24 | BUFFALO | 27 |
| 38 | NEW YORK | 3 |
| 6 | KANSAS CITY | 49 |
| 20 | Oakland | 21 |

| Use Name | Pos. | Hgt | Wgt | Age | Int | Pts |
|---|---|---|---|---|---|---|
| Gary Kirner | OT | 6'3" | 245 | 22 | | |
| Ron Mix | OT | 6'4" | 250 | 26 | | |
| Ernie Park | OT | 6'3" | 253 | 22 | | |
| Ernie Wright | OT | 6'4" | 265 | 24 | | |
| Sam Gruneisen | OG | 6'1" | 255 | 23 | | |
| Lloyd McCoy | OG | 6'1" | 245 | 22 | | |
| Pat Shea | OG | 6'1" | 245 | 25 | | |
| Walt Sweeney | OG | 6'3" | 255 | 23 | | |
| Don Rogers | C | 6'2" | 245 | 27 | | |
| Earl Faison | DE | 6'5" | 270 | 25 | 1 | 6 |
| Bob Mitinger | DE | 6'2" | 245 | 24 | | |
| Bob Petrich | DE | 6'4" | 257 | 23 | 1 | |
| George Gross | DT | 6'3" | 270 | 23 | | |
| Ernie Ladd | DT | 6'9" | 295 | 25 | | |
| Fred Moore | DT | 6'3" | 255 | 24 | | |
| Henry Schmidt | DT | 6'4" | 270 | 27 | 1 | 6 |

| Use Name | Pos. | Hgt | Wgt | Age | Int | Pts |
|---|---|---|---|---|---|---|
| Chuck Allen | LB | 6'1" | 225 | 24 | 4 | |
| Frank Buncom | LB | 6'1" | 235 | 24 | 1 | |
| Ron Carpenter | LB | 6'2" | 230 | 23 | 1 | |
| Bob Horton | LB | 6'2" | 230 | 21 | | |
| Emil Karas | LB | 6'3" | 235 | 30 | | |
| Bobby Lane | LB | 6'2" | 222 | 24 | | |
| George Blair | DB | 5'11" | 195 | 26 | | 14 |
| Speedy Duncan | DB | 5'10" | 180 | 21 | 1 | |
| Kenny Graham | DB | 6' | 200 | 22 | 4 | |
| Dick Harris | DB | 5'11" | 187 | 27 | 3 | |
| Charley McNeil | DB | 5'11" | 180 | 28 | 2 | |
| Jimmy Warren | DB | 5'11" | 185 | 25 | 2 | |
| Dick Westmoreland | DB | 6'1" | 190 | 23 | 6 | |
| Bud Whitehead | FL-DB | 6' | 185 | 25 | 3 | |

| Use Name | Pos. | Hgt | Wgt | Age | Int | Pts |
|---|---|---|---|---|---|---|
| John Hadl | QB | 6'2" | 210 | 24 | | 6 |
| Tobin Rote | QB | 6'3" | 220 | 36 | | |
| Paul Lowe | HB | 6' | 205 | 27 | | 30 |
| Mario Mendez | HB | 5'11" | 200 | 22 | | |
| Keith Kinderman | FB | 6' | 215 | 24 | | |
| Keith Lincoln | FB | 6'2" | 213 | 25 | | 67 |
| Gerry McDougall | FB | 6'2" | 225 | 29 | | 14 |
| Lance Alworth | FL | 6' | 185 | 24 | | 90 |
| Dave Kocourek | OE | 6'5" | 245 | 27 | | 30 |
| Don Norton | OE | 6'1" | 195 | 26 | | 36 |
| Jerry Robinson | OE | 5'11" | 200 | 25 | | |
| Jacque MacKinnon | FB-OE | 6'4" | 250 | 25 | | 12 |
| Ben Agajanian | K | 6' | 225 | 45 | | 14 |
| Herb Travenio | K | 6' | 218 | 33 | | 16 |

## KANSAS CITY CHIEFS 7-7-0 Hank Stram

| Scores of Each Game | | |
|---|---|---|
| 17 | Buffalo | 34 |
| 21 | Oakland | 9 |
| 28 | HOUSTON | 7 |
| 27 | Denver | 33 |
| 22 | BUFFALO | 35 |
| 7 | Boston | 24 |
| 49 | DENVER | 39 |
| 42 | OAKLAND | 7 |
| 14 | SAN DIEGO | 28 |
| 28 | Houston | 19 |
| 14 | New York | 27 |
| 24 | BOSTON | 31 |
| 49 | San Diego | 6 |
| 24 | NEW YORK | 7 |

| Use Name | Pos. | Hgt | Wgt | Age | Int | Pts |
|---|---|---|---|---|---|---|
| Jerry Cornelison | OT | 6'3" | 250 | 27 | | |
| Dave Hill | OT | 6'5" | 260 | 23 | | |
| Jim Tyrer | OT | 6'6" | 292 | 25 | | |
| Denny Biodrowski | OG | 6'1" | 255 | 24 | | |
| Ed Budd | OG | 6'5" | 260 | 23 | | |
| Curt Merz | OG | 6'4" | 250 | 26 | | |
| Al Reynolds | OG | 6'3" | 235 | 26 | | |
| Jon Gilliam | C | 6'2" | 240 | 25 | | |
| Mel Branch | DE | 6'2" | 230 | 27 | | |
| Ed Lothamer | DE | 6'5" | 240 | 21 | | |
| Jerry Mays | DT-DE | 6'4" | 250 | 24 | | |
| Buck Buchanan | DT | 6'7" | 280 | 24 | | |
| Curt Farrier | DT | 6'6" | 245 | 23 | | |
| John Maczuzak | DT | 6'5" | 250 | 21 | | |
| Hatch Rosdahl (from BUF) | DT | 6'5" | 250 | 21 | | |

| Use Name | Pos. | Hgt | Wgt | Age | Int | Pts |
|---|---|---|---|---|---|---|
| Walt Corey | LB | 6' | 242 | 26 | 1 | |
| Sherrill Headrick | LB | 6'2" | 215 | 27 | 1 | |
| E. J. Holub | LB | 6'4" | 225 | 26 | | |
| Smokey Stover | LB | 6' | 232 | 25 | 2 | |
| Bobby Bell | DE-LB | 6'4" | 228 | 24 | 1 | 6 |
| Dave Grayson | DB | 5'10" | 184 | 25 | 7 | |
| Bobby Hunt | DB | 6'1" | 190 | 24 | 7 | 6 |
| Willie Mitchell | DB | 6'1" | 190 | 23 | 1 | |
| Bobby Ply | DB | 6'1" | 190 | 23 | 1 | |
| Johnny Robinson | DB | 6' | 195 | 25 | 2 | |
| Charley Warner (to BUF) | DB | 5'11" | 180 | 24 | 1 | |
| Duane Wood | DB | 6'1" | 200 | 28 | 5 | |

| Use Name | Pos. | Hgt | Wgt | Age | Int | Pts |
|---|---|---|---|---|---|---|
| Pete Beathard | QB | 6'2" | 205 | 22 | | |
| Len Dawson | QB | 6' | 190 | 30 | | 12 |
| Eddie Wilson | QB | 6' | 190 | 24 | | 6 |
| Bert Coan | HB | 6'4" | 220 | 24 | | 12 |
| Abner Haynes | HB | 6' | 190 | 26 | | 48 |
| Jerrel Wilson | HB | 6'4" | 225 | 22 | | |
| Mack Lee Hill | FB | 5'11" | 225 | 24 | | 36 |
| Curtis McClinton | FB | 6'3" | 232 | 25 | | 20 |
| Jack Spikes (to SD) | FB | 6'2" | 220 | 26 | | |
| Frank Jackson | FL | 6'1" | 190 | 24 | | 54 |
| Fred Arbanas | OE | 6'3" | 240 | 25 | | 24 |
| Tommy Brooker | OE | 6'2" | 230 | 24 | | 70 |
| Chris Burford | OE | 6'3" | 210 | 26 | | 42 |
| Reg Carolan | OE | 6'6" | 232 | 24 | | 6 |

## OAKLAND RAIDERS 5-7-2 Al Davis

| Scores of Each Game | | |
|---|---|---|
| 14 | BOSTON | 17 |
| 28 | Houston | 42 |
| 9 | KANSAS CITY | 21 |
| 20 | Buffalo | 23 |
| 13 | New York | 35 |
| 43 | Boston | 43 |
| 40 | DENVER | 7 |
| 17 | San Diego | 31 |
| 7 | Kansas City | 42 |
| 20 | HOUSTON | 10 |
| 35 | NEW YORK | 26 |
| 20 | Denver | 20 |
| 16 | BUFFALO | 13 |
| 21 | SAN DIEGO | 20 |

| Use Name | Pos. | Hgt | Wgt | Age | Int | Pts |
|---|---|---|---|---|---|---|
| Proverb Jacobs | OT | 6'4" | 260 | 29 | | |
| Dick Klein | OT | 6'4" | 250 | 30 | | |
| Ken Rice | OT | 6'2" | 240 | 24 | | |
| Frank Youso | OT | 6'4" | 250 | 28 | | |
| Wayne Hawkins | OG | 6' | 240 | 26 | | |
| Bob Mischak | OG | 6' | 230 | 31 | | |
| Jim Otto | C | 6'2" | 240 | 26 | | |
| Dalva Allen | DE | 6'5" | 245 | 28 | | |
| Ben Davidson | DE | 6'8" | 265 | 24 | | |
| Jon Jelacic | DE | 6'3" | 255 | 27 | | |
| Dan Birdwell | DT | 6'4" | 250 | 23 | 2 | |
| Doug Brown | DT | 6'4" | 250 | 24 | | |
| Dave Costa | DT | 6'2" | 250 | 22 | | |
| Rex Mirich | DT | 6'4" | 250 | 23 | | |
| Jim Norris | DT | 6'4" | 235 | 24 | 2 | |

| Use Name | Pos. | Hgt | Wgt | Age | Int | Pts |
|---|---|---|---|---|---|---|
| Bill Budness | LB | 6'1" | 215 | 21 | 2 | |
| Dan Conners | LB | 6'1" | 230 | 22 | | |
| Archie Matsos | LB | 6' | 212 | 29 | 2 | |
| Clancy Osborne | LB | 6'3" | 220 | 29 | | |
| Jackie Simpson | LB | 6'1" | 225 | 28 | | |
| J. R. Williamson | LB | 6'2" | 220 | 22 | | |
| Claude Gibson | DB | 6'1" | 190 | 25 | 2 | |
| Louis Guy | DB | 6' | 190 | 23 | | |
| Joe Krakoski | DB | 6'2" | 195 | 27 | | |
| Tom Morrow | DB | 5'11" | 187 | 26 | 4 | |
| Warren Powers | DB | 6' | 185 | 23 | 5 | |
| Howie Williams | DB | 6'2" | 185 | 27 | 1 | |
| Fred Williamson | DB | 6'2" | 215 | 26 | 6 | |
| | | | | | | |
| Alan Miller — Injury | | | | | | |

| Use Name | Pos. | Hgt | Wgt | Age | Int | Pts |
|---|---|---|---|---|---|---|
| Cotton Davidson | QB | 6'1" | 180 | 32 | | 12 |
| Tom Flores | QB | 6'1" | 190 | 27 | | |
| Billy Cannon | FB-HB | 6'1" | 225 | 27 | | 48 |
| Clem Daniels | HB | 6'1" | 220 | 27 | | 48 |
| Bo Dickinson | FB | 6'2" | 220 | 29 | | |
| Bobby Jackson (from HOU) | FB | 6'3" | 225 | 24 | | 18 |
| Glen Shaw | FB | 6'1" | 225 | 25 | | 12 |
| Bo Roberson | FL | 6'1" | 190 | 29 | | 6 |
| Jan Barrett | OE | 6'3" | 222 | 24 | | 12 |
| Fred Gillett | OE | 6'2" | 220 | 26 | | |
| Ken Herock | OE | 6'2" | 230 | 23 | | 12 |
| Bill Miller | OE | 6' | 190 | 22 | | |
| Art Powell | OE | 6'3" | 212 | 27 | | 66 |
| Mike Mercer | K | 6' | 200 | 28 | | 79 |

## DENVER BRONCOS 2-11-1 Jack Faulkner  Mac Speedie

| Scores of Each Game | | |
|---|---|---|
| 6 | New York | 30 |
| 13 | Buffalo | 30 |
| 17 | HOUSTON | 38 |
| 10 | BOSTON | 39 |
| 33 | KANSAS CITY | 27 |
| 14 | San Diego | 42 |
| 7 | Oakland | 40 |
| 39 | Kansas City | 49 |
| 20 | SAN DIEGO | 31 |
| 20 | NEW YORK | 16 |
| 7 | Boston | 12 |
| 20 | OAKLAND | 20 |
| 19 | BUFFALO | 30 |
| 15 | Houston | 34 |

| Use Name | Pos. | Hgt | Wgt | Age | Int | Pts |
|---|---|---|---|---|---|---|
| Eldon Danenhauer | OT | 6'4" | 245 | 28 | | |
| Harold Olson | OT | 6'3" | 255 | 25 | | |
| Jim Perkins | OT | 6'5" | 250 | 25 | | |
| Ernie Barnes | OG | 6'3" | 243 | 25 | | |
| Bob McCullough | OG | 6'2" | 245 | 23 | | |
| Tom Nomina | OG | 6'5" | 270 | 22 | | |
| Don Shackleford | OG | 6'4" | 255 | 21 | | |
| Jerry Sturm | C-OG | 6'3" | 260 | 27 | | |
| Ray Kubala | C | 6'4" | 245 | 22 | | |
| Ed Cooke | DE | 6'4" | 250 | 29 | 6 | |
| Stan Fanning (from HOU) | DE | 6'6" | 270 | 26 | | |
| Ike Lassiter | DE | 6'5" | 270 | 23 | | |
| Leroy Moore | DE | 6' | 230 | 28 | 1 | |
| Dick Guesman | DT | 6'4" | 255 | 28 | | 31 |
| Ray Jacobs | DT | 6'3" | 265 | 24 | | |
| Chuck Janerette | DT | 6'3" | 265 | 25 | | |

| Use Name | Pos. | Hgt | Wgt | Age | Int | Pts |
|---|---|---|---|---|---|---|
| Tom Erlandson | LB | 6'3" | 235 | 24 | | |
| Jim Fraser | LB | 6'3" | 236 | 28 | 1 | |
| Jerry Hopkins | LB | 6'2" | 235 | 23 | 2 | |
| Larry Jordan | LB | 6'6" | 230 | 26 | | |
| Marv Matuszak | LB | 6'3" | 240 | 33 | 2 | |
| Jim Price | LB | 6'2" | 230 | 23 | | |
| Billy Atkins | DB | 6'1" | 195 | 29 | | |
| Norm Bass | DB | 6'3" | 210 | 25 | | |
| Willie Brown | DB | 6'1" | 190 | 23 | 9 | |
| Goose Gonsoulin | DB | 6'3" | 210 | 26 | 7 | |
| John Griffin | DB | 6'1" | 190 | 24 | | |
| Tom Janik | DB | 6'3" | 200 | 23 | 6 | |
| John McGeever | DB | 6'1" | 195 | 25 | 6 | |
| Jim McMillin (from OAK) | DB | 5'11" | 195 | 26 | 1 | 6 |
| Willie West (to NY) | DB | 5'10" | 193 | 26 | 2 | |
| Jim Wright | DB | 5'11" | 190 | 25 | 1 | |

| Use Name | Pos. | Hgt | Wgt | Age | Int | Pts |
|---|---|---|---|---|---|---|
| Jacky Lee | QB | 6'1" | 187 | 25 | | 18 |
| Mickey Slaughter | QB | 6' | 190 | 22 | | 2 |
| Gene Mingo (to OAK) | HB | 6'1" | 190 | 25 | | 39 |
| Charley Mitchell | HB | 5'11" | 185 | 24 | | 36 |
| Billy Joe | FB | 6'2" | 250 | 23 | | 14 |
| Donnie Stone | FB | 6'2" | 205 | 27 | | |
| Al Denson | FL | 6'2" | 208 | 22 | | 8 |
| Bob Scarpitto | FL | 5'11" | 196 | 25 | | 24 |
| Odell Barry | OE | 5'10" | 180 | 22 | | 6 |
| Matt Snorton | OE | 6'5" | 250 | 21 | | |
| Lionel Taylor | OE | 6'2" | 215 | 28 | | 42 |
| Hewritt Dixon | HB-OE | 6'2" | 217 | 24 | | 6 |
| | | | | | | |
| John McCormick — Knee Injury | | | | | | |
| Bob Zeman — Injury | | | | | | |

## SAN DIEGO CHARGERS

### RUSHING

| Last Name | No. | Yds | Avg | TD |
|---|---|---|---|---|
| Lincoln | 155 | 632 | 4.1 | 4 |
| Lowe | 130 | 496 | 3.8 | 3 |
| MacKinnon | 24 | 124 | 5.2 | 2 |
| Kinderman | 24 | 111 | 4.6 | 0 |
| McDougall | 23 | 73 | 3.2 | 2 |
| Hadl | 20 | 70 | 3.5 | 1 |
| Alworth | 3 | 60 | 20.0 | 2 |
| Robinson | 1 | 10 | 10.0 | 0 |
| Rote | 10 | -12 | -1.2 | 0 |

### RECEIVING

| Last Name | No. | Yds | Avg | TD |
|---|---|---|---|---|
| Alworth | 61 | 1235 | 20 | 13 |
| Norton | 49 | 669 | 14 | 6 |
| Lincoln | 34 | 302 | 9 | 2 |
| Kocourek | 33 | 593 | 18 | 5 |
| Lowe | 14 | 182 | 13 | 2 |
| MacKinnon | 10 | 177 | 18 | 0 |
| Robinson | 10 | 93 | 9 | 0 |
| McDougall | 8 | 106 | 13 | 0 |
| Kinderman | 3 | 21 | 7 | 0 |
| Whitehead | 1 | -4 | -4 | 0 |
| Rote | 1 | -11 | -11 | 0 |

### PUNT RETURNS

| Last Name | No. | Yds | Avg | TD |
|---|---|---|---|---|
| Alworth | 18 | 189 | 11 | 0 |
| Robinson | 7 | 41 | 6 | 0 |
| Graham | 2 | 24 | 12 | 0 |
| Duncan | 4 | 19 | 5 | 0 |
| Westmoreland | 2 | 10 | 5 | 0 |
| Warren | 1 | 0 | 0 | 0 |

### KICKOFF RETURNS

| Last Name | No. | Yds | Avg | TD |
|---|---|---|---|---|
| Westmoreland | 18 | 360 | 20 | 0 |
| Warren | 13 | 353 | 27 | 0 |
| Duncan | 9 | 318 | 35 | 0 |
| Graham | 7 | 172 | 25 | 0 |
| Robinson | 3 | 70 | 23 | 0 |
| Carpenter | 1 | 15 | 15 | 0 |
| Norton | 1 | 0 | 0 | 0 |
| Wright | 1 | 0 | 0 | 0 |

### PASSING – PUNTING – KICKING

**PASSING**

| Last Name | Att | Comp | % | Yds | Yd/Att | TD | Int-% | RK |
|---|---|---|---|---|---|---|---|---|
| Hadl | 274 | 147 | 54 | 2157 | 7.9 | 18 | 15- 6 | 2 |
| Rote | 163 | 74 | 45 | 1156 | 7.1 | 9 | 15- 9 | 11 |
| Lincoln | 4 | 2 | 50 | 61 | 15.3 | 1 | 0- 0 | |
| Lowe | 2 | 0 | 0 | 0 | 0.0 | 0 | 0- 0 | |
| Alworth | 1 | 1 | 100 | -11 | -11.0 | 0 | 0- 0 | |
| Kinderman | 1 | 0 | 0 | 0 | 0.0 | 0 | 0- 0 | |

**PUNTING**

| Last Name | No | Avg |
|---|---|---|
| Hadl | 62 | 39.5 |
| Whitehead | 1 | 30.0 |

**KICKING**

| Last Name | XP | Att | % | FG | Att | % |
|---|---|---|---|---|---|---|
| Lincoln | 16 | 17 | 94 | 5 | 12 | 42 |
| Travenio | 10 | 12 | 83 | 2 | 5 | 40 |
| Agajanian | 8 | 8 | 100 | 2 | 4 | 50 |
| Blair | 5 | 6 | 83 | 3 | 5 | 60 |

**2 POINT XP**
McDougall

## KANSAS CITY CHIEFS

### RUSHING

| Last Name | No. | Yds | Avg | TD |
|---|---|---|---|---|
| Haynes | 139 | 697 | 5.0 | 4 |
| M. Hill | 105 | 576 | 5.5 | 4 |
| McClinton | 73 | 252 | 3.5 | 1 |
| Spikes | 34 | 112 | 3.3 | 0 |
| Dawson | 40 | 89 | 2.2 | 0 |
| Coan | 11 | 56 | 5.1 | 2 |
| Beathard | 4 | 43 | 10.8 | 0 |
| E. Wilson | 6 | 5 | 0.8 | 1 |
| Jackson | 2 | 5 | 2.5 | 0 |
| J. Wilson | 1 | -10 | -10.0 | 0 |

### RECEIVING

| Last Name | No. | Yds | Avg | TD |
|---|---|---|---|---|
| Jackson | 62 | 943 | 15 | 9 |
| Burford | 51 | 675 | 13 | 7 |
| Haynes | 38 | 562 | 15 | 3 |
| Arbanas | 34 | 686 | 20 | 8 |
| M. Hill | 19 | 144 | 8 | 2 |
| McClinton | 13 | 221 | 17 | 2 |
| Spikes | 5 | 17 | 3 | 0 |
| Carolan | 3 | 54 | 18 | 1 |
| Coan | 2 | 8 | 4 | 0 |
| J. Wilson | 1 | 11 | 11 | 0 |

### PUNT RETURNS

| Last Name | No. | Yds | Avg | TD |
|---|---|---|---|---|
| Warner | 12 | 165 | 14 | 0 |
| Mitchell | 18 | 160 | 9 | 0 |
| Jackson | 11 | 103 | 9 | 0 |
| Robinson | 1 | 16 | 16 | 0 |
| Haynes | 1 | 11 | 11 | 0 |

### KICKOFF RETURNS

| Last Name | No. | Yds | Avg | TD |
|---|---|---|---|---|
| Grayson | 30 | 679 | 23 | 0 |
| Warner | 12 | 301 | 25 | 0 |
| Haynes | 12 | 278 | 23 | 0 |
| Coan | 5 | 124 | 25 | 0 |
| Lothamer | 1 | 0 | 0 | 0 |
| Rosdahl | 1 | 0 | 0 | 0 |
| Stover | 1 | 0 | 0 | 0 |

### PASSING – PUNTING – KICKING

**PASSING**

| Last Name | Att | Comp | % | Yds | Yd/Att | TD | Int-% | RK |
|---|---|---|---|---|---|---|---|---|
| Dawson | 354 | 199 | 56 | 2879 | 8.1 | 30 | 18- 5 | 1 |
| E. Wilson | 47 | 25 | 53 | 392 | 8.3 | 1 | 1- 2 | |
| Beathard | 9 | 4 | 44 | 50 | 5.6 | 1 | 2- 22 | |
| Haynes | 1 | 0 | 0 | 0 | 0.0 | 0 | 0- 0 | |
| Spikes | 1 | 0 | 0 | 0 | 0.0 | 0 | 0- 0 | |

**PUNTING**

| Last Name | No | Avg |
|---|---|---|
| J. Wilson | 78 | 42.6 |
| E. Wilson | 1 | 32.0 |

**KICKING**

| Last Name | XP | Att | % | FG | Att | % |
|---|---|---|---|---|---|---|
| Brooker | 46 | 46 | 100 | 8 | 17 | 47 |

**2 POINT XP**
McClinton

## OAKLAND RAIDERS

### RUSHING

| Last Name | No. | Yds | Avg | TD |
|---|---|---|---|---|
| Daniels | 173 | 824 | 4.8 | 2 |
| Cannon | 89 | 338 | 3.8 | 3 |
| C. Davidson | 29 | 167 | 5.8 | 2 |
| Jackson | 23 | 64 | 2.8 | 3 |
| Flores | 11 | 64 | 5.8 | 0 |
| Shaw | 9 | 26 | 2.9 | 2 |
| Dickinson | 4 | 8 | 2.0 | 0 |
| Roberson | 1 | -4 | -4.0 | 0 |
| Youso | 0 | 4 | 0.0 | 0 |

### RECEIVING

| Last Name | No. | Yds | Avg | TD |
|---|---|---|---|---|
| Powell | 76 | 1361 | 18 | 11 |
| Roberson | 44 | 624 | 14 | 1 |
| Daniels | 42 | 696 | 17 | 6 |
| Cannon | 37 | 454 | 12 | 5 |
| Herock | 23 | 360 | 16 | 2 |
| Barrett | 12 | 212 | 18 | 2 |
| Jackson | 10 | 81 | 8 | 0 |
| Shaw | 3 | 31 | 10 | 0 |
| Dickinson | 3 | 28 | 9 | 0 |
| Miller | 2 | 29 | 15 | 0 |

### PUNT RETURNS

| Last Name | No. | Yds | Avg | TD |
|---|---|---|---|---|
| Gibson | 29 | 419 | 14 | 0 |
| Roberson | 1 | 20 | 20 | 0 |
| Krakoski | 1 | 8 | 8 | 0 |
| Morrow | 1 | 0 | 0 | 0 |

### KICKOFF RETURNS

| Last Name | No. | Yds | Avg | TD |
|---|---|---|---|---|
| Roberson | 36 | 975 | 27 | 0 |
| Cannon | 21 | 518 | 25 | 0 |
| Jackson | 2 | 32 | 16 | 0 |
| Daniels | 1 | 32 | 32 | 0 |
| Conners | 1 | 0 | 0 | 0 |
| Dickinson | 1 | 0 | 0 | 0 |
| Klein | 1 | 0 | 0 | 0 |

### PASSING – PUNTING – KICKING

**PASSING**

| Last Name | Att | Comp | % | Yds | Yd/Att | TD | Int-% | RK |
|---|---|---|---|---|---|---|---|---|
| C. Davidson | 320 | 155 | 48 | 2497 | 7.8 | 21 | 19- 6 | 5 |
| Flores | 200 | 98 | 49 | 1389 | 7.0 | 7 | 14- 7 | 6 |
| Daniels | 1 | 0 | 0 | 0 | 0.0 | 0 | 0- 0 | |

**PUNTING**

| Last Name | No | Avg |
|---|---|---|
| Mercer | 58 | 42.1 |

**KICKING**

| Last Name | XP | Att | % | FG | Att | % |
|---|---|---|---|---|---|---|
| Mercer | 34 | 34 | 100 | 15 | 24 | 63 |

## DENVER BRONCOS

### RUSHING

| Last Name | No. | Yds | Avg | TD |
|---|---|---|---|---|
| Mitchell | 177 | 590 | 3.3 | 5 |
| Joe | 112 | 415 | 3.7 | 2 |
| Lee | 42 | 163 | 3.9 | 3 |
| Slaughter | 20 | 54 | 2.7 | 0 |
| Stone | 12 | 26 | 2.2 | 0 |
| Mingo | 6 | 26 | 4.3 | 0 |
| Dixon | 18 | 25 | 1.4 | 0 |
| Barry | 3 | 7 | 2.3 | 0 |
| Scarpitto | 1 | 5 | 5.0 | 0 |

### RECEIVING

| Last Name | No. | Yds | Avg | TD |
|---|---|---|---|---|
| Taylor | 76 | 873 | 11 | 7 |
| Dixon | 38 | 585 | 15 | 1 |
| Scarpitto | 35 | 375 | 11 | 4 |
| Mitchell | 33 | 225 | 7 | 0 |
| Denson | 25 | 383 | 15 | 1 |
| Joe | 12 | 16 | 1 | 0 |
| Stone | 4 | 38 | 10 | 0 |
| Barry | 4 | 31 | 8 | 0 |
| Mingo | 4 | 25 | 6 | 1 |

### PUNT RETURNS

| Last Name | No. | Yds | Avg | TD |
|---|---|---|---|---|
| Barry | 16 | 149 | 9 | 1 |
| Mitchell | 9 | 110 | 12 | 0 |

### KICKOFF RETURNS

| Last Name | No. | Yds | Avg | TD |
|---|---|---|---|---|
| Barry | 47 | 1245 | 27 | 0 |
| Mitchell | 10 | 221 | 22 | 0 |
| Mingo | 8 | 163 | 20 | 0 |
| West | 5 | 142 | 28 | 0 |
| Dixon | 6 | 89 | 15 | 0 |
| Olson | 2 | 27 | 14 | 0 |
| Shackleford | 1 | 13 | 13 | 0 |
| Jordan | 1 | 0 | 0 | 0 |
| Sturm | 1 | 0 | 0 | 0 |

### PASSING – PUNTING – KICKING

**PASSING**

| Last Name | Att | Comp | % | Yds | Yd/Att | TD | Int-% | RK |
|---|---|---|---|---|---|---|---|---|
| Lee | 265 | 133 | 50 | 1611 | 6.1 | 11 | 20- 8 | 10 |
| Slaughter | 189 | 97 | 51 | 930 | 4.9 | 3 | 11- 6 | 9 |
| Mitchell | 1 | 0 | 0 | 0 | 0.0 | 0 | 0- 0 | |
| Taylor | 1 | 0 | 0 | 0 | 0.0 | 0 | 1-100 | |

**PUNTING**

| Last Name | No | Avg |
|---|---|---|
| Fraser | 72 | 44.7 |
| Janik | 10 | 37.4 |

**KICKING**

| Last Name | XP | Att | % | FG | Att | % |
|---|---|---|---|---|---|---|
| Guesman | 13 | 15 | 87 | 6 | 22 | 27 |
| Mingo | 9 | 10 | 90 | 8 | 12 | 67 |

**2 POINT XP**
Denson
Joe
Slaughter

# 1965 N.F.L. Passing Pioneers and Hello, Dixie

The league lost two long-standing members when Curly Lambeau and Jack Mara died in June. Lambeau had founded the Green Bay Packers in 1919 and coached them through 1949, molding them into NFL powers until a postwar slump set in. Mara had for years run the New York Giants, founded by his father Tim Mara, and his death put his younger brother Wellington at the head of the New York organization. But life went on as usual in the league, with a hot Western Division race, new stars in Gale Sayers, Bob Hayes, and Dick Butkus, and the usual assortment of injuries, errors, and great plays. To spread the riches around—and also rake in some more money—the league voted to expand into Atlanta starting in 1966, reaching into the Deep South for the first time.

## EASTERN CONFERENCE

**Cleveland Browns**—Even with Paul Warfield sidelined for most of the year by a shoulder injury and the defense saddled with the weight of advancing years, the Browns still ran away with the Eastern crown. Coach Blanton Collier had some of the finest offensive assets in the division, including a solid line, a reliable flanker in Gary Collins, a steady quarterback in Frank Ryan, and the incomparable Jimmy Brown at fullback, and the patchwork defense held up well enough to win eleven games. The Browns counted their riches even in the specialists' department, with forty-one-year-old Lou Groza an accurate place-kicker, Leroy Kelly a good punt returner, Walter Roberts a dangerous kickoff returner, and Gary Collins a fine punter in addition to his pass-catching chores.

**Dallas Cowboys**—The Cowboys failed to break the .500 barrier, but they did uncover one of the league's most exciting performers in rookie end Bob Hayes. A world-record-holding sprinter, Hayes terrorized defensive backs with his pure speed, streaking away from them with no possibility of being caught from behind once in the clear. While Hayes scored thirteen touchdowns, tackle Ralph Neely went unnoticed by all but the coaches with a fine rookie season. Coach Tom Landry added several other freshmen who would contribute to the strong Dallas teams of the next few years in Dan Reeves, Jethro Pugh, Craig Morton, and Obert Logan.

**New York Giants**—After losing all five of their pre-season games, the Giants obtained quarterback Earl Morrall from Detroit and finished in a surprising tie for second place in the East. Morrall gave the team a steady hand at the head of the offense and threw for twenty-two touchdowns. Joining Morrall in the backfield was a collection of young runners known collectively in the press as the Baby Bulls. Tucker Frederickson, Steve Thurlow, Ernie Koy, and Chuck Mercein all ground out hard overland yardage despite a lack of speed, and split end Homer Jones gave the Giants all the speed they needed in a pass receiver. Even with only a faint knowledge of pass patterns, Jones picked up over 700 yards as a receiver on only twenty-six catches after breaking into the starting lineup in mid-season.

**Washington Redskins**—The Redskins lost their first five games with a poor offensive show that improved only a little over the season. The Washington running attack was the league's worst, as there still was no full-time fullback, and halfback Charley Taylor came nowhere near duplicating his fine rookie season. The passing offense also slumped, as Bobby Mitchell alone among the receivers consistently got open for Sonny Jurgensen's passes. The Washington defense was a competent unit but was hurt when cornerback Johnny Sample was suspended late in the season for insubordination.

**Philadelphia Eagles**—Joe Kuharich had traded the Eagles into respectability last year, but progress came more slowly this season. The big trouble spot was the defensive line, which put no pressure at all on enemy passers. The Eagles resorted to frequent blitzing to compensate for the weak line, but this just made them vulnerable to quick passes. The offense was sound throughout, starting with the Bob Brown-led line. Timmy Brown starred at halfback, using his quickness to best advantage on runs and passes, Earl Gros complemented Brown with his power at fullback, and Norm Snead showed progress at quarterback.

**St. Louis Cardinals**—Tied with the Browns for first place in the East on October 17, the Cards swan-dived out of contention by losing eight of the next nine games and their last six contests straight. Injuries to Charley Johnson, Larry Wilson, and Jerry Stovall contributed to the collapse, and the trading of John David Crow to San Francisco hurt the club more than had been expected. Crow had been a clutch runner, the man to give the ball in when vital yardage was needed, and his departure left the Cards without a leader in the backfield.

**Pittsburgh Steelers**—Head coach Buddy Parker quit two weeks before the season opener, saying, "I can't win with this bunch of stiffs." On that pleasant note, assistant Mike Nixon took over as head man for a brutal 2-12 season. Nixon benched veteran quarterback Ed Brown and replaced him with Bill Nelsen, who played most of the season on a bad knee, which made him a sitting duck for enemy pass-rushers. The running attack lost its best man when John Henry Johnson was sidelined by a bad knee, and the receiving corps was so thin that the starting split end, Clendon Thomas, was a converted defensive back. When Parker had quit as coach of the Detroit Lions before the 1957 season, the Lions went on to win the championship. This time, Parker knew what he was doing.

## WESTERN CONFERENCE

**Green Bay Packers**—The return of guard Jerry Kramer from stomach surgery, the purchase of kicker Don Chandler from New York, and the development of Marv Fleming, Doug Hart, and Tom Brown into starters plastered over the few cracks in the Packers' solid front. After battling the Colts all season for the Western Conference lead, the Packers blew a chance to clinch the championship by managing only a tie with San Francisco in the final regular-season game. Baltimore and Green Bay finished with identical 10-3-1 records and squared off in a playoff game for the Western crown. The Colts came into the playoff game with no experienced quarterback, but their fired-up defense knocked the ball loose from Bill Anderson on the first play from scrimmage, and Don Shinnick ran the fumble 25 yards for a Baltimore touchdown. Quarterback Bart Starr was shaken up on the play and missed most of the game, but the Packers fought back against the spirited Colts to tie the score at 10-10 with a Chandler field goal late in the game. For the second time in history, a pro-football game went into overtime, and another Chandler field goal, which the Colts and many observers claimed went wide, gave the Packers the victory after 13:39 of overtime play.

**Baltimore Colts**—Driving along to a repeat Western championship, the Colts suddenly lost both their quarterbacks, with Johnny Unitas ripping up a knee in the twelfth game and Gary Cuozzo dislocating a shoulder one week later. Coach Don Shula put halfback Tom Matte into the signal caller's spot, equipping him with a wrist band with some basic plays written on it. Relying on roll-out passes, quarterback keepers, pitchouts, and a fanatical defense, the Colts beat the Rams 20-17 in their final game to get into a Western Conference playoff with the Packers.

**Chicago Bears**—One of the Bears' three first-round draft picks, defensive end Steve DeLong got away to the AFL, but George Halas opened his wallet wide to sign the other two. Halfback Gale Sayers and linebacker Dick Butkus immediately rewarded Halas' genorosity with All-Pro rookie seasons. Sayers burst on the national consciousness like a comet, slamming through holes at top speed and eluding defensive backs by outdodging and outrunning them. Starring as a kick returner and pass receiver as well as a runner, Sayers scored a record twenty-two touchdowns in the season. While Sayers souped up the Bear offense, Butkus helped return the defense to a high peak with his ferocity at middle linebacker.

**San Francisco '49ers**—With John Brodie suddenly putting all his talent together in a marvelous season, the '49er offense suddenly blossomed into the league's most explosive. Wide receivers Bernie Casey and Dave Parks gave Brodie two fine targets to hit, and the offensive line gave him good protection against enemy pass rushes. The running game improved immensely over last year with the addition of two new hard-chargers, rookie fullback Ken Willand and ex-Cardinal halfback John David Crow. The defense, however, was as undistinguished as the attack was dynamic.

**Minnesota Vikings**— The Viking offense still put on a good show, but the defense failed to show the expected progress, seven times getting burned for 35 or more points. This so frustrated head coach Norm Van Brocklin that he resigned in mid-season, only to be talked out of it after a couple of days by the front office. One of Van Brocklin's biggest problems was a growing tension between himself and quarterback Fran Tarkenton. The coach kept trying to make a strict pocket passer out of Tarkenton, while the quarterback stuck to his free-wheeling, scrambling style.

**Detroit Lions**—Owner William Clay Ford started the year by firing all of head coach George Wilson's assistants, a warning to Wilson to win or face the same fate. Wilson throught it over for a couple of days and handed in his resignation. Harry Gilmer took over as head man and ran into a flood of injuries that weighted the club down in sixth place. One of Gilmer's first decisions was to rely on one quarterback, so he kept Milt Plum and traded Earl Morrall to New York. The only problem was, Plum had a poor year, while Morrall rejuvenated the Giants with his fine passing. With the offense erratic, the Detroit defense no longer was strong enough to carry the team.

**Los Angeles Rams**—The front four of Deacon Jones, Merlin Olsen, Rosie Grier, and Lamar Lundy became the league's most famous defensive line and often carried the rest of the Los Angeles defense, which was ladened with as many as five rookie starters at one point. The running attack was weak, but the blocking and receiving gave quarterbacks Bill Munson and Roman Gabriel something to work with. Munson started the first ten games and led the club to only one win despite frequent flashes of talent, and Gabriel headed the attack for the final four games after Munson hurt a knee.

## FINAL TEAM STATISTICS

### OFFENSE

| | BALT. | CHI. | CLEVE. | DALLAS | DET. | G.BAY | L.A. | MINN. | N.Y. | PHIL. | PITT. | ST.L. | S.F. | WASH. |
|---|---|---|---|---|---|---|---|---|---|---|---|---|---|---|
| **FIRST DOWNS:** | | | | | | | | | | | | | | |
| Total | 266 | 257 | 257 | 211 | 204 | 201 | 251 | 277 | 230 | 267 | 194 | 251 | **292** | 210 |
| by Rushing | 94 | 132 | **133** | 87 | 93 | 85 | 76 | 130 | 91 | 94 | 71 | 90 | 97 | 69 |
| by Passing | 144 | 110 | 97 | 108 | 93 | 103 | 153 | 126 | 112 | 149 | 104 | 143 | **172** | 125 |
| by Penalty | **28** | 15 | 27 | 16 | 18 | 13 | 22 | 21 | 27 | 24 | 19 | 18 | 23 | 16 |
| **RUSHING:** | | | | | | | | | | | | | | |
| Number | 445 | 479 | 476 | 416 | 453 | 432 | 378 | **505** | 423 | 404 | 407 | 431 | 428 | 354 |
| Yards | 1593 | 2131 | **2331** | 1608 | 1469 | 1488 | 1464 | 2278 | 1651 | 1824 | 1378 | 1619 | 1783 | 1037 |
| Average Yards | 3.6 | 4.4 | **4.9** | 3.9 | 3.2 | 3.4 | 3.9 | 4.5 | 3.9 | 4.5 | 3.4 | 3.8 | 4.2 | 2.9 |
| Touchdowns | 13 | **27** | 19 | 8 | 16 | 14 | 8 | 19 | 12 | 21 | 10 | 10 | 13 | 7 |
| **PASSING:** | | | | | | | | | | | | | | |
| Attempts | 399 | 361 | 329 | 362 | 374 | 306 | 445 | 372 | 342 | 434 | 354 | 448 | **454** | 427 |
| Completions | 222 | 201 | 160 | 168 | 170 | 166 | 230 | 189 | 171 | 223 | 161 | 221 | **272** | 220 |
| Completion Pct. | 55.6 | 55.7 | 48.6 | 46.4 | 45.5 | 54.2 | 51.7 | 50.8 | 50.0 | 51.4 | 45.5 | 49.3 | **59.9** | 51.5 |
| Passing Yards | 3330 | 3020 | 2339 | 2756 | 2083 | 2508 | 3059 | 2861 | 2685 | 3442 | 2503 | 3222 | **3633** | 2908 |
| Avg. Yds per Att. | 8.3 | **8.4** | 7.1 | 7.6 | 5.6 | 8.2 | 6.9 | 7.7 | 7.9 | 7.9 | 7.1 | 7.2 | 8.0 | 6.8 |
| Avg. Yds per Comp. | 15.0 | 15.0 | 14.6 | **16.4** | 12.3 | 15.1 | 13.3 | 15.1 | 15.7 | 15.4 | 15.5 | 14.6 | 13.4 | 13.2 |
| Tackled Att. to Pass | 43 | 30 | 31 | 55 | 26 | 43 | 45 | 35 | 31 | 33 | 62 | 30 | **19** | 39 |
| Yards Lost Tackled | 325 | 254 | 272 | 369 | 249 | 395 | 344 | 315 | 255 | 254 | 527 | 279 | **146** | 337 |
| Net Yards | 3005 | 2766 | 2067 | 2387 | 1834 | 2113 | 2715 | 2546 | 2430 | 3188 | 1976 | 2943 | **3487** | 2571 |
| Touchdowns | 31 | 22 | 23 | 25 | 14 | 19 | 22 | 21 | 23 | 22 | 10 | 20 | **35** | 20 |
| Interceptions | 17 | **12** | 16 | 18 | 26 | 14 | 19 | **12** | 16 | 26 | 35 | 25 | 21 | 20 |
| Pct. Intercepted | 4.3 | 3.3 | 4.9 | 5.0 | 7.0 | 4.6 | 4.3 | **3.2** | 4.7 | 6.0 | 9.9 | 5.6 | 4.6 | 4.7 |
| **PUNTS:** | | | | | | | | | | | | | | |
| Number | 56 | 58 | 69 | 73 | **78** | 74 | 66 | 51 | 61 | 56 | **78** | 67 | 54 | 70 |
| Average Distance | 39.6 | 42.7 | 45.7 | 41.3 | 42.8 | 42.9 | 39.7 | 42.1 | 41.6 | 42.2 | 45.1 | 40.4 | **45.8** | 42.1 |
| **PUNT RETURNS:** | | | | | | | | | | | | | | |
| Number | **45** | 29 | 36 | 39 | 34 | 22 | 32 | 22 | 24 | 21 | 33 | 23 | 38 | 39 |
| Yards | 421 | 289 | **427** | 312 | 358 | 65 | 225 | 115 | 35 | 183 | 259 | 27 | 283 | 415 |
| Average Yards | 9.4 | 10.0 | **11.9** | 8.0 | 10.5 | 3.0 | 7.0 | 5.2 | 1.5 | 8.7 | 7.8 | 1.2 | 7.4 | 10.6 |
| Touchdowns | 0 | 1 | **2** | 0 | 0 | 0 | 0 | 1 | 0 | 1 | 0 | 0 | 0 | 1 |
| **KICKOFF RETURNS:** | | | | | | | | | | | | | | |
| Number | 52 | 45 | 53 | 44 | 52 | 50 | 53 | **67** | 60 | 60 | 61 | 55 | 59 | 49 |
| Yards | 1242 | 1146 | 1209 | 1166 | 1416 | 1040 | 1351 | **1524** | 1303 | 1438 | 1238 | 1287 | 1276 | 1011 |
| Average Yards | 23.9 | 25.5 | 22.8 | 26.5 | **27.2** | 20.8 | 25.5 | 22.7 | 21.7 | 24.0 | 20.3 | 23.4 | 21.6 | 20.6 |
| Touchdowns | 0 | **1** | 0 | **1** | 0 | 0 | 0 | **1** | 0 | 0 | 0 | 0 | 0 | 0 |
| **INTERCEPTION RETURNS:** | | | | | | | | | | | | | | |
| Number | 22 | 20 | 24 | 18 | 26 | **27** | 11 | 19 | 16 | 25 | 12 | 17 | 13 | **27** |
| Yards | 318 | 307 | 349 | 198 | 343 | **561** | 224 | 286 | 249 | 313 | 282 | 328 | 97 | 535 |
| Average Yards | 14.5 | 15.4 | 14.5 | 11.0 | 13.2 | 20.8 | 20.4 | 15.1 | 15.6 | 12.5 | **23.5** | 19.3 | 7.5 | 19.8 |
| Touchdowns | **4** | 2 | 1 | 2 | 3 | **4** | 1 | 2 | 1 | 3 | 2 | 1 | 0 | 2 |
| **PENALTIES:** | | | | | | | | | | | | | | |
| Number | 69 | **96** | 84 | 68 | 77 | 48 | 61 | 76 | 61 | 61 | 40 | 45 | 79 | 81 |
| Yards | 616 | 826 | **976** | 710 | 767 | 529 | 560 | 771 | 618 | 686 | 326 | 458 | 785 | 692 |
| **FUMBLES:** | | | | | | | | | | | | | | |
| Number | 31 | 33 | 20 | 31 | 27 | 18 | 40 | 41 | 31 | 21 | 42 | **15** | 33 | 41 |
| Number Lost | 19 | 16 | 9 | 17 | 15 | 12 | 22 | 25 | 14 | 10 | 22 | **7** | 19 | 21 |
| **POINTS:** | | | | | | | | | | | | | | |
| Total | 389 | 409 | 363 | 325 | 257 | 316 | 269 | 383 | 270 | 363 | 202 | 296 | **421** | 257 |
| PAT Attempts | 48 | **54** | 45 | 40 | 33 | 38 | 32 | 44 | 37 | 48 | 25 | 33 | 53 | 33 |
| PAT Made | 48 | **52** | 45 | 37 | 33 | 37 | 30 | 44 | 34 | 45 | 19 | 33 | **52** | 29 |
| FG Attempts | 28 | 26 | 25 | 27 | 22 | 26 | 26 | **35** | 25 | 25 | 19 | 31 | 27 | 22 |
| FG Made | 17 | 11 | 16 | 16 | 8 | 17 | 15 | **23** | 4 | 10 | 11 | 21 | 17 | 10 |
| Percent FG Made | 60.7 | 42.3 | 64.0 | 59.3 | 36.4 | 65.4 | 57.7 | 65.7 | 16.0 | 40.0 | 57.9 | **67.7** | 63.0 | 45.5 |
| Safeties | 1 | 0 | 0 | 0 | 1 | 0 | 1 | **3** | 1 | 0 | 0 | 1 | 0 | 0 |

### DEFENSE

| | BALT. | CHI. | CLEVE. | DALLAS | DET. | G.BAY | L.A. | MINN. | N.Y. | PHIL. | PITT. | ST.L. | S.F. | WASH. |
|---|---|---|---|---|---|---|---|---|---|---|---|---|---|---|
| **FIRST DOWNS:** | | | | | | | | | | | | | | |
| Total | 233 | 244 | 265 | 240 | 210 | 240 | **208** | 242 | 266 | 243 | 243 | 238 | 259 | 237 |
| by Rushing | **78** | 87 | 104 | 80 | 84 | 115 | 82 | 99 | 108 | 100 | 122 | 89 | 94 | 100 |
| by Passing | 131 | 136 | 135 | 138 | 104 | 111 | 113 | 120 | 140 | 129 | 109 | 133 | 139 | **101** |
| by Penalty | 24 | 21 | 26 | 22 | 22 | 14 | 13 | 23 | 18 | 14 | **12** | 16 | 26 | 36 |
| **RUSHING:** | | | | | | | | | | | | | | |
| Number | 410 | **400** | 412 | 422 | 409 | 480 | 417 | 408 | 447 | 419 | 483 | 433 | 405 | 486 |
| Yards | 1483 | 1530 | 1866 | 1444 | 1460 | 1988 | **1409** | 1755 | 1956 | 1582 | 2080 | 1813 | 1535 | 1753 |
| Average Yards | 3.6 | 3.8 | 4.5 | 3.4 | 3.6 | 4.1 | **3.4** | 4.3 | 4.4 | 3.8 | 4.3 | 4.2 | 3.8 | 3.6 |
| Touchdowns | 11 | 11 | 11 | 13 | **9** | 10 | 16 | 17 | 20 | 11 | 19 | 11 | 20 | 18 |
| **PASSING:** | | | | | | | | | | | | | | |
| Attempts | 400 | 444 | 419 | 426 | 344 | 383 | 349 | 357 | 393 | 393 | 353 | 380 | 448 | **318** |
| Completions | 213 | 217 | 204 | 205 | 190 | 187 | 205 | 187 | 208 | 215 | 173 | 184 | 225 | **161** |
| Completion Pct. | 53.3 | 48.9 | 48.7 | **48.1** | 55.2 | 48.8 | 58.7 | 52.4 | 52.9 | 54.7 | 49.0 | 48.4 | 50.2 | 50.6 |
| Passing Yards | 2903 | 3086 | 3153 | 3063 | 2508 | **2316** | 2884 | 2692 | 3251 | 3123 | 2703 | 2826 | 3302 | 2539 |
| Avg. Yds per Att. | 7.3 | 7.0 | 7.5 | 7.2 | 7.3 | **6.0** | 8.3 | 7.5 | 8.3 | 7.9 | 7.7 | 7.4 | 7.4 | 8.0 |
| Avg. Yds per Comp. | 13.6 | 14.2 | 15.5 | 14.9 | 13.2 | **12.4** | 14.1 | 14.4 | 15.6 | 14.5 | 15.6 | 15.4 | 14.7 | 15.8 |
| Tackled Att. to Pass | 39 | 40 | 38 | 39 | **49** | 44 | 32 | 23 | 39 | 37 | 33 | 39 | 25 | 45 |
| Yards Lost Tackled | 341 | 348 | 307 | 315 | 411 | 335 | 270 | 199 | 294 | 287 | 253 | 342 | 197 | **422** |
| Net Yards | 2562 | 2738 | 2846 | 2748 | 2097 | **1981** | 2614 | 2493 | 2957 | 2836 | 2450 | 2484 | 3105 | 2117 |
| Touchdowns | 22 | 18 | 31 | 17 | 21 | **11** | 22 | 31 | 18 | 28 | 25 | 24 | 24 | 15 |
| Interceptions | 22 | 20 | 24 | 18 | 26 | **27** | 11 | 19 | 16 | 25 | 12 | 17 | 13 | **27** |
| Pct. Intercepted | 5.5 | 4.5 | 5.7 | 4.2 | 7.6 | 7.0 | 3.2 | 5.3 | 4.1 | 6.4 | 3.4 | 4.5 | 2.9 | **8.5** |
| **PUNTS:** | | | | | | | | | | | | | | |
| Number | 71 | 65 | 69 | 71 | 74 | 60 | 66 | 64 | 45 | 54 | **76** | 65 | 62 | 69 |
| Average Distance | 43.9 | 42.3 | 41.1 | 42.9 | 42.9 | 42.1 | 45.4 | **38.4** | 42.7 | 41.8 | 42.2 | 43.3 | 41.9 | 43.4 |
| **PUNT RETURNS:** | | | | | | | | | | | | | | |
| Number | 26 | **22** | 36 | 26 | 39 | 36 | 25 | 29 | **22** | 37 | 44 | 32 | 33 | 30 |
| Yards | 198 | **123** | 259 | 139 | 318 | 290 | 176 | 261 | 137 | 263 | 437 | 267 | 408 | 138 |
| Average Yards | 7.6 | 5.6 | 7.2 | 5.3 | 8.2 | 8.1 | 7.0 | 9.0 | 6.2 | 7.1 | 9.9 | 8.3 | 12.4 | **4.6** |
| Touchdowns | **0** | **0** | **0** | 1 | 1 | **0** | 1 | **0** | **0** | **0** | 2 | **0** | 1 | **0** |
| **KICKOFF RETURNS:** | | | | | | | | | | | | | | |
| Number | 63 | 72 | 58 | 63 | 43 | 52 | 54 | 62 | 54 | 58 | **30** | 50 | 59 | 42 |
| Yards | 1346 | 1583 | 1334 | 1229 | 858 | 1216 | 1364 | 1557 | 1175 | 1531 | **684** | 1228 | 1566 | 976 |
| Average Yards | 21.4 | 22.0 | 23.0 | **19.5** | 20.0 | 23.4 | 25.3 | 25.1 | 21.8 | 26.4 | 22.8 | 24.6 | 26.5 | 23.2 |
| Touchdowns | 1 | **0** | **0** | **0** | **0** | **0** | **0** | 1 | **0** | **0** | **0** | **0** | 1 | **0** |
| **INTERCEPTION RETURNS:** | | | | | | | | | | | | | | |
| Number | 17 | **12** | 16 | 18 | 26 | 14 | 19 | **12** | 16 | 26 | 35 | 25 | 21 | 20 |
| Yards | 341 | 219 | 275 | 268 | 515 | 209 | **156** | 215 | 182 | 476 | 646 | 465 | 232 | 191 |
| Average Yards | 20.1 | 18.3 | 17.2 | 14.9 | 19.8 | 14.9 | **8.2** | 17.9 | 11.4 | 18.3 | 18.5 | 18.6 | 11.0 | 9.6 |
| Touchdowns | 1 | 3 | 1 | **0** | 2 | 1 | **0** | 1 | 1 | 6 | 6 | 1 | 3 | 2 |
| **PENALTIES:** | | | | | | | | | | | | | | |
| Number | 80 | 68 | 62 | 50 | 61 | 67 | 70 | 66 | **83** | 66 | 58 | 70 | 71 | 74 |
| Yards | 786 | 611 | 586 | 483 | 637 | 677 | 566 | 643 | **848** | 653 | 615 | 750 | 727 | 738 |
| **FUMBLES:** | | | | | | | | | | | | | | |
| Number | 33 | 33 | 13 | **37** | 33 | **37** | 27 | 25 | 32 | 32 | 28 | 29 | 34 | 31 |
| Number Lost | 14 | **24** | 8 | 20 | 20 | 23 | 15 | 11 | 20 | 11 | 15 | 15 | 17 | 15 |
| **POINTS:** | | | | | | | | | | | | | | |
| Total | 284 | 275 | 325 | 280 | 295 | **224** | 328 | 403 | 338 | 359 | 397 | 309 | 402 | 301 |
| PAT Attempts | 35 | 33 | 43 | 33 | 36 | **22** | 40 | 53 | 41 | 47 | 53 | 37 | 52 | 38 |
| PAT Made | 35 | 30 | 40 | 29 | 36 | **22** | 40 | 52 | 40 | 44 | 49 | 36 | 48 | 37 |
| FG Attempts | 23 | 24 | **18** | 30 | 22 | 33 | 32 | 20 | 29 | 26 | 26 | 32 | 27 | 22 |
| FG Made | 13 | 15 | **9** | 17 | 13 | 22 | 16 | 11 | 16 | 11 | 10 | 17 | 14 | 12 |
| Percent FG Made | 56.5 | 62.5 | 50.0 | 56.7 | 59.1 | 66.7 | 50.0 | 55.0 | 55.2 | 42.3 | **38.5** | 53.1 | 51.9 | 54.5 |
| Safeties | **0** | 1 | **0** | 1 | 2 | 2 | **0** | **0** | 2 | **0** | **0** | **0** | **0** | **0** |

### 1965 NFL CHAMPIONSHIP GAME

January 2, at Green Bay
(Attendance 50,777)

## Bulldozing the Defense

After two years as Western Division runners-up, the Green Bay Packers returned to the NFL championship game they had won in 1961 and 1962. The Cleveland Browns, the defending NFL champions, came into Lambeau Field to furnish the opposition. The playing field was muddy and footing uncertain, making straight-ahead running plays the best bets of the afternoon. The Packer defense gave Green Bay a decisive edge by dogging Cleveland fullback Jimmy Brown all afternoon, while Packer runners Jim Taylor and Paul Hornung followed strong blocking to eat up yardage on the ground. Packer quarterback Bart Starr crossed up the Browns on the first series of downs by throwing the ball; he hit Carroll Dale with a long pass that gave the Packers a quick 7-0 lead. The Browns retaliated by moving steadily downfield and scoring on a Frank Ryan-to-Gary Collins pass. The extra point went awry, however, and the Packers still led 7-6. A Lou Groza field goal gave the Browns a 9-7 lead at the end of the first quarter, and three second-period field goals, one by Groza and two by Green Bay's Don Chandler, made the halftime score 13-12 in favor of the Packers. Coach Vince Lombardi stressed ball control to his players, and the Packer offense came out for the second half ready to grind out difficult yardage. Using off-tackle blasts and power sweeps with Taylor and Hornung carrying the ball, the Packers drove 90 yards on 11 plays in the third quarter, eating up seven minutes of the clock while putting seven more points on the scoreboard. Whenever the Browns got the ball in the second half, they couldn't move against the Green Bay defense; whenever the Packers had the ball, they would hold onto it for several precious minutes before giving it up. In all, the Green Bay offensive line contributed the most to the Packer victory by constantly knocking the Cleveland defenders back to make room for Taylor and Hornung in the 20-12 victory.

### SCORING

| | | | | | |
|---|---|---|---|---|---|
| **GREEN BAY** | **7** | **6** | **7** | **3** | **–23** |
| **CLEVELAND** | **9** | **3** | **0** | **0** | **–12** |

First Quarter
- G.B. Dale, 47 yard pass from Starr
  - PAT – Chandler (kick)
- Cle. Collins, 17 yard pass from Ryan
  - PAT – No Good
- Cle. Groza, 24 yard field goal

Second Quarter
- G.B. Chandler, 15 yard field goal
- G.B Chandler, 23 yard field goal
- Cle. Groza, 28 yard field goal

Third Quarter
- G.B. Hornung, 13 yard rush
  - PAT – Chandler (kick)

Fourth Quarter
- G.B. Chandler, 29 yard field goal

### TEAM STATISTICS

| G.B. | | CLEVE. |
|---|---|---|
| 21 | First Downs – Total | 8 |
| 10 | First Downs – Rushing | 2 |
| 9 | First Downs – Passing | 5 |
| 2 | First Downs – Penalty | 1 |
| 3 | Punts – Number | 4 |
| 38.3 | Punts – Average Distance | 46.0 |
| 2 | Punt Returns – Number | 1 |
| –10 | Punt Returns – Yards | 11 |
| 2 | Interception Returns – Number | 1 |
| 15 | Interception Returns – Yards | 0 |
| 0 | Fumbles – Number | 0 |
| 3 | Penalties – Number | 2 |
| 35 | Yards Penalized | 20 |
| 1 | Giveaways | 2 |
| 2 | Takeaways | 1 |
| +1 | Difference | –1 |

### INDIVIDUAL STATISTICS

**RUSHING**

| GREEN BAY | No. | Yds. | Avg. | CLEVELAND | No. | Yds. | Avg. |
|---|---|---|---|---|---|---|---|
| Hornung | 18 | 105 | 5.8 | Brown | 12 | 50 | 4.2 |
| Taylor | 27 | 96 | 3.6 | Ryan | 3 | 9 | 3.0 |
| Moore | 2 | 3 | 1.5 | Green | 3 | 5 | 1.7 |
| | 47 | 204 | 4.3 | | 18 | 64 | 3.6 |

**RECEIVING**

| GREEN BAY | No. | Yds. | Avg. | CLEVELAND | No. | Yds. | Avg. |
|---|---|---|---|---|---|---|---|
| Dowler | 5 | 59 | 11.8 | Brown | 3 | 44 | 14.7 |
| Dale | 2 | 60 | 30.0 | Collins | 3 | 41 | 13.7 |
| Taylor | 2 | 20 | 10.0 | Warfield | 2 | 30 | 15.0 |
| Hornung | 1 | 8 | 8.0 | | 8 | 115 | 14.4 |
| | 10 | 147 | 14.7 | | | | |

**PASSING**

| | Att | Comp | Comp Pct. | Yds | Int | Yds/ Att. | Yds/ Comp | Yards Lost Tackled |
|---|---|---|---|---|---|---|---|---|
| **GREEN BAY** | | | | | | | | |
| Starr | 18 | 10 | 55.6 | 147 | 1 | 8.2 | 14.7 | |
| Hornung | 1 | 0 | 0.0 | 0 | 0 | – | – | |
| | 19 | 10 | 52.6 | 147 | 1 | 7.7 | 14.7 | 19 |
| **CLEVELAND** | | | | | | | | |
| Ryan | 18 | 8 | 44.4 | 115 | 2 | 6.4 | 14.4 | 18 |

## CLEVELAND BROWNS 11-3-0 Blanton Collier

| Scores of Each Game | | |
|---|---|---|
| 17 | Washington | 7 |
| 13 | ST. LOUIS | 49 |
| 35 | Philadelphia | 17 |
| 24 | PITTSBURGH | 19 |
| 23 | DALLAS | 17 |
| 38 | New York | 14 |
| 17 | MINNESOTA | 27 |
| 38 | PHILADELPHIA | 34 |
| 34 | NEW YORK | 21 |
| 24 | Dallas | 17 |
| 42 | Pittsburgh | 21 |
| 24 | WASHINGTON | 16 |
| 7 | Los Angeles | 42 |
| 27 | St. Louis | 24 |

| Use Name | Pos. | Hgt | Wgt | Age | Int | Pts |
|---|---|---|---|---|---|---|
| John Brown | OT | 6'2" | 248 | 26 | | |
| Monte Clark | OT | 6'6" | 265 | 28 | | |
| Dick Schafrath | OT | 6'3" | 255 | 29 | | |
| Gene Hickerson | OG | 6'3" | 248 | 30 | | |
| Dale Memmelaar | OG | 6'2" | 248 | 28 | | |
| John Wooten | OG | 6'2" | 250 | 30 | | |
| John Morrow | C | 6'3" | 248 | 32 | | |
| Jim Garcia | DE | 6'4" | 240 | 21 | | |
| Bill Glass | DE | 6'5" | 255 | 29 | 1 | |
| Paul Wiggin | DE | 6'3" | 245 | 31 | | |
| Walter Johnson | DT | 6'3" | 265 | 22 | | |
| Jim Kanicki | DT | 6'4" | 270 | 23 | | |
| Dick Modzelewski | DT | 6' | 260 | 34 | | |
| Vince Costello | LB | 6' | 228 | 33 | 3 | |
| Galen Fiss | LB | 6' | 227 | 35 | 1 | |
| Jim Houston | LB | 6'2" | 240 | 28 | 2 | |
| Dale Lindsey | LB | 6'3" | 220 | 22 | 1 | |
| Stan Sczurek | LB | 5'11" | 230 | 26 | 1 | |
| Sid Williams | LB | 6'2" | 235 | 23 | 1 | |
| Erich Barnes | DB | 6'2" | 198 | 30 | 1 | |
| Walter Beach | DB | 6' | 185 | 30 | | |
| Larry Benz | DB | 5'11" | 185 | 24 | 5 | |
| Ross Fichtner | DB | 6' | 185 | 27 | 4 | 6 |
| Bobby Franklin | DB | 5'11" | 182 | 29 | | |
| Mike Howell | DB | 6'1" | 187 | 22 | | |
| Bernie Parrish | DB | 5'11" | 195 | 30 | 4 | |
| Jim Ninowski | QB | 6'1" | 207 | 29 | | |
| Frank Ryan | QB | 6'3" | 200 | 29 | | |
| Ernie Green | HB | 6'2" | 205 | 26 | | 24 |
| Leroy Kelly | HB | 6' | 195 | 23 | | 12 |
| Jimmy Brown | FB | 6'2" | 228 | 29 | | 126 |
| Jamie Caleb | FB | 6'1" | 210 | 28 | | |
| Charlie Scales | FB | 5'11" | 215 | 26 | | |
| Gary Collins | FL | 6'4" | 208 | 24 | | 60 |
| Clifton McNeil | FL | 6'2" | 185 | 25 | | |
| Johnny Brewer | TE | 6'4" | 235 | 28 | | 6 |
| Ralph Smith | TE | 6'2" | 215 | 26 | | |
| Tom Hutchinson | OE | 6'1" | 190 | 24 | | 12 |
| Walter Roberts | OE | 5'10" | 175 | 23 | | 24 |
| Paul Warfield | OE | 6' | 188 | 22 | | |
| Lou Groza | K | 6'3" | 250 | 41 | | 93 |

Frank Parker – Operation

## DALLAS COWBOYS 7-7-0 Tom Landry

| Scores of Each Game | | |
|---|---|---|
| 31 | NEW YORK | 2 |
| 27 | WASHINGTON | 7 |
| 13 | St. Louis | 20 |
| 24 | PHILADELPHIA | 35 |
| 17 | Cleveland | 23 |
| 3 | Green Bay | 13 |
| 13 | Pittsburgh | 22 |
| 39 | SAN FRANCISCO | 31 |
| 24 | PITTSBURGH | 17 |
| 17 | CLEVELAND | 24 |
| 31 | Washington | 34 |
| 21 | Philadelphia | 19 |
| 27 | ST. LOUIS | 13 |
| 38 | New York | 20 |

| Use Name | Pos. | Hgt | Wgt | Age | Int | Pts |
|---|---|---|---|---|---|---|
| Jim Boeke | OT | 6'5" | 255 | 26 | | |
| Ralph Neely | OT | 6'5" | 257 | 21 | | |
| Don Talbert | OT | 6'5" | 240 | 25 | | |
| Mike Connelly | OG | 6'3" | 248 | 29 | | |
| Leon Donahue (from SF) | OG | 6'4" | 245 | 26 | | |
| Mitch Johnson | OG | 6'4" | 245 | 23 | | |
| Jake Kupp | OG | 6'3" | 233 | 23 | | |
| Dave Manders | C | 6'2" | 240 | 23 | | |
| George Andrie | DE | 6'7" | 255 | 25 | | 6 |
| Garry Porterfield | DE | 6'3" | 223 | 22 | | |
| Jethro Pugh | DE | 6'6" | 255 | 21 | | |
| Maury Youmans | DE | 6'6" | 253 | 28 | | |
| Larry Stephens | DT-DE | 6'4" | 250 | 27 | | |
| Jim Colvin | DT | 6'2" | 255 | 28 | | |
| John Diehl (to OAK-A) | DT | 6'7" | 250 | 29 | | |
| Bob Lilly | DT | 6'4" | 255 | 26 | 1 | 6 |
| Dave Edwards | LB | 6'3" | 226 | 26 | 2 | |
| Harold Hays | LB | 6'3" | 223 | 24 | | |
| Chuck Howley | LB | 6'3" | 223 | 29 | | |
| Lee Roy Jordan | LB | 6'2" | 216 | 24 | | |
| Jerry Tubbs | LB | 6'2" | 222 | 30 | 2 | |
| Russell Wayt | LB | 6'4" | 235 | 22 | | |
| Don Bishop | DB | 6'2" | 216 | 30 | | |
| Mike Gaechter | DB | 6' | 190 | 25 | 2 | 6 |
| Cornell Green | DB | 6'4" | 215 | 25 | 3 | 6 |
| Warren Livingston | DB | 5'10" | 190 | 27 | 3 | |
| Obert Logan | DB | 5'10" | 180 | 23 | 3 | 6 |
| Mel Renfro | HB-DB | 6' | 195 | 23 | 2 | 12 |
| Don Meredith | QB | 6'2" | 206 | 27 | | 6 |
| Craig Morton | QB | 6'4" | 216 | 22 | | |
| Jerry Rhome | QB | 6' | 180 | 23 | | |
| Perry Lee Dunn | HB | 6'2" | 200 | 22 | | 18 |
| Dan Reeves | HB | 6'1" | 203 | 21 | | 18 |
| Don Perkins | FB | 5'10" | 206 | 27 | | |
| J. D. Smith | FB | 6'1" | 210 | 32 | | 18 |
| A. D. Whitfield | FB | 5'10" | 200 | 21 | | |
| Buddy Dial | FL | 6'1" | 195 | 28 | | 6 |
| Pete Gent | FL | 6'4" | 210 | 22 | | 12 |
| Pettis Norman | TE | 6'3" | 223 | 25 | | 18 |
| Frank Clarke | OE | 6' | 210 | 32 | | 24 |
| Bob Hayes | OE | 6' | 190 | 22 | | 78 |
| Colin Ridgway | K | 6'5" | 211 | 26 | | |
| Danny Villanueva | K | 5'11" | 200 | 27 | | 85 |

Joe Bob Isbell – Injury
Tony Liscio – Injury

## NEW YORK GIANTS 7-7-0 Allie Sherman

| Scores of Each Game | | |
|---|---|---|
| 2 | Dallas | 31 |
| 16 | Philadelphia | 14 |
| 23 | Pittsburgh | 13 |
| 14 | Minnesota | 40 |
| 35 | PHILADELPHIA | 27 |
| 14 | CLEVELAND | 38 |
| 14 | ST. LOUIS | 10 |
| 7 | WASHINGTON | 23 |
| 21 | Cleveland | 34 |
| 28 | St. Louis | 15 |
| 14 | CHICAGO | 35 |
| 35 | PITTSBURGH | 10 |
| 27 | Washington | 10 |
| 20 | DALLAS | 38 |

| Use Name | Pos. | Hgt | Wgt | Age | Int | Pts |
|---|---|---|---|---|---|---|
| Rosey Brown | OT | 6'3" | 255 | 32 | | |
| Frank Lasky | OT | 6'2" | 265 | 23 | | |
| John McDowell | OT | 6'3" | 260 | 22 | | |
| Bookie Bolin | OG | 6'2" | 240 | 25 | | |
| Pete Case | OG | 6'3" | 243 | 24 | | |
| Roger Davis | OG | 6'3" | 240 | 27 | | |
| Mickey Walker | OG | 6' | 235 | 25 | | |
| Greg Larson | C | 6'2" | 250 | 26 | | |
| Bob Scholtz | C | 6'4" | 250 | 27 | | |
| Glen Condren | DE | 6'2" | 225 | 23 | | |
| Rosey Davis | DE | 6'5" | 260 | 23 | | |
| Jim Katcavage | DE | 6'3" | 240 | 30 | | 2 |
| Andy Stynchula | DE | 6'3" | 250 | 26 | | 21 |
| Roger Anderson | DT | 6'5" | 265 | 22 | | |
| Mike Bundra | DT | 6'3" | 260 | 26 | | |
| Roger LaLonde | DT | 6'3" | 255 | 23 | | |
| John Lovetere | DT | 6'4" | 285 | 29 | | |
| Dave O'Brien | DT | 6'3" | 247 | 24 | | |
| Jim Carroll | LB | 6'1" | 225 | 22 | 1 | |
| Tom Costello | LB | 6'3" | 220 | 24 | | |
| Jerry Hillebrand | LB | 6'3" | 240 | 25 | 2 | 6 |
| Bill Swain | LB | 6'2" | 228 | 24 | | |
| Olen Underwood | LB | 6'1" | 210 | 23 | 1 | |
| Lou Slaby | DT-LB | 6'3" | 235 | 23 | | |
| Henry Carr | DB | 6'3" | 205 | 22 | 2 | |
| Clarence Childs | DB | 6' | 180 | 26 | | |
| Spider Lockhart | DB | 6'2" | 185 | 22 | 4 | |
| Dick Lynch | DB | 6'1" | 198 | 29 | 4 | 6 |
| Jimmy Patton | DB | 6' | 185 | 31 | 1 | |
| Allan Webb | DB | 5'11" | 180 | 30 | | |
| Willie Williams | DB | 6' | 190 | 22 | 1 | |
| Earl Morrall | QB | 6'1" | 206 | 31 | | |
| Bob Timberlake | QB | 6'4" | 220 | 22 | | 24 |
| Gary Wood | QB | 5'11" | 188 | 22 | | 1 |
| Tucker Frederickson | FB-HB | 6'3" | 220 | 22 | | 36 |
| Ernie Koy | HB | 6'2" | 225 | 22 | | |
| Smith Reed | HB | 6' | 215 | 23 | | |
| Steve Thurlow | HB | 6'3" | 216 | 22 | | 30 |
| Chuck Mercein | FB | 6'3" | 230 | 22 | | 12 |
| Ernie Wheelwright | FB | 6'3" | 240 | 28 | | |
| Bob Crespino | TE | 6'4" | 225 | 27 | | 24 |
| Aaron Thomas | FL-TE | 6'3" | 210 | 27 | | 30 |
| Homer Jones | FL | 6'2" | 205 | 24 | | 36 |
| Joe Morrison | FL | 6'1" | 212 | 27 | | 30 |
| Bob Lacey | OE | 6'3" | 205 | 23 | | |
| Del Shofner | OE | 6'3" | 185 | 29 | | 12 |

Jim Moran – Broken Leg

## WASHINGTON REDSKINS 6-8-0 Bill McPeak

| Scores of Each Game | | |
|---|---|---|
| 7 | CLEVELAND | 17 |
| 7 | Dallas | 27 |
| 10 | Detroit | 14 |
| 16 | ST. LOUIS | 37 |
| 7 | BALTIMORE | 38 |
| 24 | St. Louis | 20 |
| 23 | PHILADELPHIA | 21 |
| 23 | New York | 7 |
| 14 | Philadelphia | 21 |
| 31 | Pittsburgh | 3 |
| 34 | DALLAS | 31 |
| 16 | Cleveland | 24 |
| 10 | NEW YORK | 27 |
| 35 | PITTSBURGH | 14 |

| Use Name | Pos. | Hgt | Wgt | Age | Int | Pts |
|---|---|---|---|---|---|---|
| Fran O'Brien | OT | 6'1" | 255 | 30 | | |
| Jim Snowden | DE-OT | 6'3" | 255 | 23 | | |
| Don Croftcheck | OG | 6'1" | 230 | 22 | | |
| Darrell Dess | OG | 6' | 245 | 29 | | |
| Vince Promuto | OG | 6'1" | 245 | 27 | | |
| Robert Reed | OG | 6'1" | 250 | 22 | | |
| Dave Crossan | C | 6'3" | 245 | 25 | | |
| Len Hauss | C | 6'2" | 235 | 23 | | |
| Carl Kammerer | DE | 6'3" | 243 | 28 | | |
| John Paluck | DE | 6'2" | 245 | 32 | | |
| Bill Quinlan | DE | 6'3" | 250 | 33 | | |
| Ron Snidow | DE | 6'4" | 250 | 23 | 1 | |
| Joe Rutgens | DT | 6'2" | 255 | 26 | | |
| Fred Williams | DT | 6'4" | 256 | 35 | | |
| Willie Adams | LB | 6'2" | 235 | 23 | | |
| Jimmy Carr | LB | 6'1" | 225 | 32 | | |
| Chris Hanburger | LB | 6'2" | 218 | 24 | 1 | |
| Sam Huff | LB | 6'1" | 230 | 30 | 2 | |
| Bob Pellegrini | LB | 6'2" | 242 | 30 | | 6 |
| John Reger | LB | 6' | 220 | 34 | | |
| Rickie Harris | DB | 6' | 182 | 22 | 1 | 12 |
| Johnny Sample | DB | 6'1" | 205 | 28 | 6 | |
| Lonnie Sanders | DB | 6'3" | 207 | 23 | 4 | |
| Jim Shorter | DB | 5'11" | 185 | 24 | 2 | 6 |
| Jim Steffen | DB | 6' | 196 | 28 | 3 | |
| Tom Walters | DB | 6'2" | 195 | 23 | 1 | 6 |
| Paul Krause | FL-DB | 6'3" | 195 | 23 | 6 | 6 |
| Sonny Jurgensen | QB | 5'11" | 205 | 31 | | 12 |
| Dick Shiner | QB | 6' | 197 | 23 | | |
| Pervis Atkins (to OAK-A) | HB | 6'1" | 210 | 29 | | |
| George Hughley | HB | 6'2" | 223 | 26 | | 6 |
| Dan Lewis | HB | 6'1" | 200 | 29 | | 24 |
| Charley Taylor | HB | 6'3" | 210 | 24 | | 36 |
| Bob Briggs | FB | 6'1" | 228 | 22 | | |
| Rick Casares | FB | 6'2" | 225 | 34 | | |
| Bobby Mitchell | FL | 6' | 196 | 30 | | 36 |
| Bill Hunter | DB-FL | 6'1" | 185 | 22 | | 6 |
| Fred Mazurek | DB-FL | 5'11" | 192 | 22 | | |
| Jerry Smith | TE | 6'2" | 208 | 22 | | 12 |
| Preston Carpenter | OE | 6'2" | 208 | 31 | | |
| Angie Coia | OE | 6'2" | 196 | 27 | | 18 |
| Bob Jencks | OE | 6'5" | 227 | 24 | | 59 |
| Pat Richter | OE | 6'5" | 230 | 24 | | 12 |
| John Seedborg | K | 6' | 227 | 22 | | |

## PHILADELPHIA EAGLES 5-9-0 Joe Kuharich

| Scores of Each Game | | |
|---|---|---|
| 34 | ST. LOUIS | 27 |
| 14 | NEW YORK | 16 |
| 17 | CLEVELAND | 35 |
| 35 | Dallas | 24 |
| 27 | New York | 35 |
| 14 | PITTSBURGH | 20 |
| 21 | Washington | 23 |
| 34 | Cleveland | 38 |
| 21 | WASHINGTON | 14 |
| 24 | Baltimore | 34 |
| 28 | St. Louis | 24 |
| 19 | DALLAS | 21 |
| 47 | Pittsburgh | 13 |
| 28 | DETROIT | 35 |

| Use Name | Pos. | Hgt | Wgt | Age | Int | Pts |
|---|---|---|---|---|---|---|
| Bob Brown | OT | 6'4" | 276 | 22 | | |
| Dave Graham | OT | 6'3" | 250 | 26 | | |
| Lane Howell | OT | 6'5" | 255 | 24 | | |
| Ed Blaine | OG | 6'2" | 240 | 25 | | |
| Jim Skaggs | OT-OG | 6'2" | 250 | 25 | | |
| Lynn Hoyem | C-OG | 6'4" | 253 | 25 | | |
| Dave Recher | C | 6'1" | 240 | 22 | | |
| Jim Ringo | C | 6'1" | 230 | 34 | | |
| Bobby Richards | DE | 6'2" | 245 | 26 | | |
| George Tarasovic | DE | 6'4" | 248 | 36 | 1 | 12 |
| Don Hultz | LB-DE | 6'3" | 235 | 24 | 1 | |
| Ed Khayat | DT | 6'3" | 250 | 30 | | |
| John Meyers | DT | 6'6" | 276 | 25 | 2 | |
| Floyd Peters | DT | 6'4" | 255 | 30 | | |
| Erwin Will | DT | 6'5" | 270 | 22 | | |
| Maxie Baughan | LB | 6'1" | 227 | 27 | 1 | 6 |
| Ralph Heck | LB | 6'2" | 230 | 24 | | |
| Dave Lloyd | LB | 6'3" | 248 | 29 | 2 | 10 |
| Mike Morgan | LB | 6'4" | 242 | 23 | 1 | |
| Harold Wells | LB | 6'2" | 223 | 26 | | |
| Irv Cross | DB | 6'1" | 190 | 26 | 3 | |
| Al Nelson | DB | 5'11" | 180 | 21 | 2 | |
| Jim Nettles | DB | 5'9" | 175 | 23 | 3 | 6 |
| Nate Ramsey | DB | 6'1" | 200 | 24 | 6 | |
| Bob Shann | DB | 6'1" | 187 | 22 | | 6 |
| Joe Scarpati | HB-DB | 5'10" | 185 | 23 | 3 | |
| Claude Crabb | FL-DB | 6' | 190 | 25 | | |
| Jack Concannon | QB | 6'3" | 195 | 22 | | |
| King Hill | QB | 6'3" | 213 | 29 | | 12 |
| Norm Snead | QB | 6'4" | 205 | 25 | | 18 |
| Timmy Brown | HB | 5'10" | 198 | 28 | | 54 |
| Ollie Matson | HB | 6'2" | 210 | 35 | | 18 |
| Earl Gros | FB | 6'3" | 220 | 24 | | 54 |
| Izzy Lang | FB | 6'1" | 230 | 22 | | 6 |
| Tom Woodeshick | FB | 6' | 220 | 23 | | |
| Glenn Glass | FL | 6' | 203 | 28 | | |
| Ron Goodwin | OE-FL | 6' | 180 | 23 | | 6 |
| Roger Gill | TE | 6'1" | 200 | 24 | | |
| Bill Cronin | TE | 6'4" | 220 | 22 | | |
| Jim Kelly | TE | 6'2" | 215 | 23 | | |
| Pete Retzlaff | TE | 6'1" | 214 | 34 | | 60 |
| Fred Hill | OE | 6'2" | 215 | 22 | | |
| Ray Poage | OE | 6'4" | 200 | 24 | | 30 |
| Sam Baker | K | 6'2" | 218 | 33 | | 65 |

Jerry Mazzanti – Military Service
Mike McClellan – Military Service

## CLEVELAND BROWNS

### Rushing

| Last Name | No. | Yds | Avg | TD |
|---|---|---|---|---|
| Jimmy Brown | 289 | 1544 | 5.3 | 17 |
| Green | 111 | 436 | 3.9 | 2 |
| Kelly | 37 | 139 | 3.8 | 0 |
| Ryan | 19 | 72 | 3.8 | 0 |
| Scales | 11 | 59 | 5.4 | 0 |
| Ninowski | 4 | 46 | 11.5 | 0 |
| Roberts | 3 | 30 | 10.0 | 0 |
| Collins | 1 | 16 | 16.0 | 0 |
| Franklin | 1 | −11 | −11.0 | 0 |

### Receiving

| Last Name | No. | Yds | Avg | TD |
|---|---|---|---|---|
| Collins | 50 | 884 | 18 | 10 |
| Jimmy Brown | 34 | 328 | 10 | 4 |
| Green | 25 | 298 | 12 | 2 |
| Roberts | 16 | 314 | 20 | 4 |
| Brewer | 13 | 174 | 13 | 1 |
| Kelly | 9 | 122 | 14 | 0 |
| Hutchinson | 6 | 113 | 19 | 2 |
| McNeil | 3 | 69 | 23 | 0 |
| Warfield | 3 | 30 | 10 | 0 |
| Scales | 1 | 7 | 7 | 0 |

### Punt Returns

| Last Name | No. | Yds | Avg | TD |
|---|---|---|---|---|
| Kelly | 17 | 265 | 16 | 2 |
| Roberts | 18 | 162 | 9 | 0 |
| Scales | 1 | 0 | 0 | 0 |

### Kickoff Returns

| Last Name | No. | Yds | Avg | TD |
|---|---|---|---|---|
| Kelly | 24 | 621 | 26 | 0 |
| Roberts | 18 | 493 | 27 | 0 |
| Scales | 4 | 88 | 22 | 0 |
| Green | 1 | 4 | 4 | 0 |
| Howell | 2 | 3 | 2 | 0 |
| Hutchinson | 2 | 0 | 0 | 0 |
| Franklin | 1 | 0 | 0 | 0 |
| Lindsey | 1 | 0 | 0 | 0 |

### Passing

| Last Name | Att | Comp | % | Yds | Yd/Att | TD | Int−% | RK |
|---|---|---|---|---|---|---|---|---|
| Ryan | 243 | 119 | 49 | 1751 | 7.2 | 18 | 13− 5 | 12 |
| Ninowski | 83 | 40 | 48 | 549 | 6.6 | 4 | 3− 4 | |
| Jimmy Brown | 2 | 1 | 50 | 39 | 19.5 | 1 | 0− 0 | |
| Groza | 1 | 0 | 0 | 0 | 0.0 | 0 | 0− 0 | |

### Punting

| Last Name | No | Avg |
|---|---|---|
| Collins | 65 | 46.7 |
| Franklin | 4 | 29.5 |

### Kicking

| Last Name | XP | Att | % | FG | Att | % |
|---|---|---|---|---|---|---|
| Groza | 45 | 45 | 100 | 16 | 25 | 64 |

## DALLAS COWBOYS

### Rushing

| Last Name | No. | Yds | Avg | TD |
|---|---|---|---|---|
| Perkins | 177 | 690 | 3.9 | 0 |
| Smith | 86 | 295 | 3.4 | 2 |
| Meredith | 35 | 247 | 7.1 | 1 |
| Dunn | 54 | 171 | 3.2 | 2 |
| Reeves | 33 | 102 | 3.1 | 2 |
| Clarke | 8 | 58 | 7.3 | 0 |
| Rhome | 4 | 11 | 2.8 | 0 |
| Whitfield | 1 | 0 | 0.0 | 0 |
| Hayes | 4 | −8 | −2.0 | 1 |
| Morton | 3 | −8 | −2.7 | 0 |

### Receiving

| Last Name | No. | Yds | Avg | TD |
|---|---|---|---|---|
| Hayes | 46 | 1003 | 22 | 12 |
| Clarke | 41 | 682 | 17 | 4 |
| Dial | 17 | 283 | 17 | 1 |
| Gent | 16 | 233 | 15 | 2 |
| Perkins | 14 | 142 | 10 | 0 |
| Norman | 11 | 110 | 10 | 3 |
| Reeves | 9 | 210 | 23 | 1 |
| Dunn | 8 | 74 | 9 | 1 |
| Smith | 5 | 10 | 2 | 1 |

### Punt Returns

| Last Name | No. | Yds | Avg | TD |
|---|---|---|---|---|
| Hayes | 12 | 153 | 13 | 0 |
| Renfro | 24 | 145 | 6 | 0 |

### Kickoff Returns

| Last Name | No. | Yds | Avg | TD |
|---|---|---|---|---|
| Renfro | 21 | 630 | 30 | 1 |
| Hayes | 17 | 450 | 26 | 0 |
| Reeves | 2 | 45 | 23 | 0 |
| Neely | 2 | 13 | 7 | 0 |

### Passing

| Last Name | Att | Comp | % | Yds | Yd/Att | TD | Int−% | RK |
|---|---|---|---|---|---|---|---|---|
| Meredith | 305 | 141 | 46 | 2415 | 7.9 | 22 | 13− 4 | 8 |
| Morton | 34 | 17 | 50 | 173 | 5.1 | 2 | 4− 12 | |
| Rhome | 21 | 9 | 43 | 157 | 7.5 | 1 | 1− 5 | |
| Reeves | 2 | 1 | 50 | 11 | 5.5 | 0 | 0− 0 | |

### Punting

| Last Name | No | Avg |
|---|---|---|
| Villanueva | 60 | 41.8 |
| Ridgway | 13 | 39.2 |

### Kicking

| Last Name | XP | Att | % | FG | Att | % |
|---|---|---|---|---|---|---|
| Villanueva | 37 | 38 | 97 | 16 | 27 | 59 |

## NEW YORK GIANTS

### Rushing

| Last Name | No. | Yds | Avg | TD |
|---|---|---|---|---|
| Frederickson | 195 | 659 | 3.4 | 5 |
| Thurlow | 106 | 440 | 4.2 | 4 |
| Koy | 35 | 174 | 5.0 | 0 |
| Wheelwright | 24 | 96 | 4.0 | 0 |
| Reed | 19 | 70 | 3.7 | 0 |
| Wood | 5 | 68 | 13.6 | 0 |
| Mercein | 18 | 55 | 3.1 | 2 |
| Morrall | 17 | 52 | 3.1 | 0 |
| Morrison | 3 | 20 | 6.7 | 1 |
| Jones | 1 | 17 | 17.0 | 0 |

### Receiving

| Last Name | No. | Yds | Avg | TD |
|---|---|---|---|---|
| Morrison | 41 | 574 | 14 | 4 |
| Thomas | 27 | 631 | 23 | 5 |
| Jones | 26 | 709 | 27 | 6 |
| Frederickson | 24 | 177 | 7 | 1 |
| Shofner | 22 | 388 | 18 | 2 |
| Thurlow | 9 | 54 | 6 | 1 |
| Crespino | 7 | 57 | 8 | 4 |
| Reed | 6 | 42 | 7 | 0 |
| Koy | 4 | 22 | 6 | 0 |
| Mercein | 3 | 14 | 5 | 0 |
| Wheelwright | 2 | 17 | 9 | 0 |

### Punt Returns

| Last Name | No. | Yds | Avg | TD |
|---|---|---|---|---|
| Williams | 18 | 28 | 2 | 0 |
| Carr | 4 | 13 | 3 | 0 |
| Lockhart | 2 | −6 | −3 | 0 |

### Kickoff Returns

| Last Name | No. | Yds | Avg | TD |
|---|---|---|---|---|
| Childs | 29 | 718 | 25 | 0 |
| Koy | 21 | 401 | 19 | 0 |
| Williams | 5 | 113 | 23 | 0 |
| Webb | 2 | 48 | 24 | 0 |
| Thurlow | 1 | 19 | 19 | 0 |
| Mercein | 1 | 4 | 4 | 0 |
| Brown | 1 | 0 | 0 | 0 |

### Passing

| Last Name | Att | Comp | % | Yds | Yd/Att | TD | Int−% | RK |
|---|---|---|---|---|---|---|---|---|
| Morrall | 302 | 155 | 51 | 2446 | 8.1 | 22 | 12− 5 | |
| Wood | 36 | 15 | 42 | 190 | 5.3 | 1 | 2− 6 | |
| Koy | 2 | 0 | 0 | 0 | 0.0 | 0 | 1− 50 | |
| Frederickson | 1 | 0 | 0 | 0 | 0.0 | 0 | 1−100 | |
| Thurlow | 1 | 1 | 100 | 49 | 49.0 | 0 | 0− 0 | |

### Punting

| Last Name | No | Avg |
|---|---|---|
| Koy | 55 | 41.2 |
| Lockhart | 6 | 44.5 |

### Kicking

| Last Name | XP | Att | % | FG | Att | % |
|---|---|---|---|---|---|---|
| Timberlake | 21 | 22 | 95 | 1 | 15 | 7 |
| Stynchula | 12 | 13 | 92 | 3 | 7 | 43 |
| Wood | 1 | 1 | 100 | 0 | 0 | 0 |
| Hillebrand | 0 | 0 | 0 | 0 | 1 | 0 |
| Mercein | 0 | 0 | 0 | 0 | 2 | 0 |

## WASHINGTON REDSKINS

### Rushing

| Last Name | No. | Yds | Avg | TD |
|---|---|---|---|---|
| Taylor | 145 | 402 | 2.8 | 3 |
| Lewis | 117 | 343 | 2.9 | 2 |
| Hughley | 37 | 175 | 4.7 | 0 |
| Atkins | 18 | 44 | 2.4 | 0 |
| Shiner | 12 | 35 | 2.9 | 0 |
| Jurgensen | 17 | 23 | 1.4 | 2 |
| Briggs | 6 | 10 | 1.7 | 0 |
| Casares | 2 | 5 | 2.5 | 0 |

### Receiving

| Last Name | No. | Yds | Avg | TD |
|---|---|---|---|---|
| Mitchell | 60 | 867 | 14 | 6 |
| Taylor | 40 | 577 | 14 | 3 |
| Lewis | 25 | 276 | 11 | 2 |
| Carpenter | 23 | 298 | 13 | 0 |
| Smith | 19 | 257 | 14 | 2 |
| Coia | 18 | 240 | 13 | 3 |
| Richter | 16 | 189 | 12 | 2 |
| Hughley | 9 | 93 | 10 | 1 |
| Briggs | 3 | 40 | 13 | 0 |
| Jencks | 2 | 20 | 10 | 0 |
| Krause | 2 | 17 | 9 | 0 |
| Hunter | 1 | 29 | 29 | 1 |
| Casares | 1 | 5 | 5 | 0 |
| Atkins | 1 | 0 | 0 | 0 |

### Punt Returns

| Last Name | No. | Yds | Avg | TD |
|---|---|---|---|---|
| Harris | 31 | 377 | 12 | 1 |
| Mitchell | 1 | 15 | 15 | 0 |
| Hughley | 2 | 12 | 6 | 0 |
| Atkins | 3 | 11 | 4 | 0 |
| Mazurek | 1 | 0 | 0 | 0 |
| Pellegrini | 1 | 0 | 0 | 0 |

### Kickoff Returns

| Last Name | No. | Yds | Avg | TD |
|---|---|---|---|---|
| Hunter | 18 | 432 | 24 | 0 |
| Hughley | 13 | 295 | 23 | 0 |
| Mitchell | 5 | 106 | 21 | 0 |
| Harris | 5 | 96 | 19 | 0 |
| Walters | 2 | 30 | 15 | 0 |
| Atkins | 1 | 15 | 15 | 0 |
| Taylor | 1 | 15 | 15 | 0 |
| Kammerer | 1 | 14 | 14 | 0 |
| Briggs | 2 | 8 | 4 | 0 |
| Hanburger | 1 | 0 | 0 | 0 |

### Passing

| Last Name | Att | Comp | % | Yds | Yd/Att | TD | Int−% | RK |
|---|---|---|---|---|---|---|---|---|
| Jurgensen | 356 | 190 | 53 | 2367 | 6.7 | 15 | 16− 5 | 10 |
| Shiner | 65 | 28 | 43 | 470 | 7.2 | 3 | 4− 6 | |
| Taylor | 4 | 1 | 25 | 45 | 11.3 | 1 | 0− 0 | |
| Lewis | 2 | 1 | 50 | 26 | 13.0 | 1 | 0− 0 | |

### Punting

| Last Name | No | Avg |
|---|---|---|
| Richter | 54 | 43.8 |
| Snidow | 9 | 37.3 |
| Seedburg | 7 | 35.3 |

### Kicking

| Last Name | XP | Att | % | FG | Att | % |
|---|---|---|---|---|---|---|
| Jencks | 29 | 33 | 88 | 10 | 22 | 46 |

## PHILADELPHIA EAGLES

### Rushing

| Last Name | No. | Yds | Avg | TD |
|---|---|---|---|---|
| T. Brown | 158 | 861 | 5.4 | 6 |
| Gros | 145 | 479 | 3.3 | 7 |
| Woodeshick | 28 | 145 | 5.2 | 0 |
| Concannon | 9 | 104 | 11.6 | 0 |
| Matson | 22 | 103 | 4.7 | 2 |
| Snead | 24 | 81 | 3.4 | 3 |
| Lang | 10 | 25 | 2.5 | 1 |
| K. Hill | 7 | 20 | 2.9 | 2 |
| Scarpati | 1 | 6 | 6.0 | 0 |

### Receiving

| Last Name | No. | Yds | Avg | TD |
|---|---|---|---|---|
| Retzlaff | 66 | 1190 | 18 | 10 |
| T. Brown | 50 | 682 | 14 | 3 |
| Poage | 31 | 612 | 20 | 5 |
| Gros | 29 | 271 | 9 | 2 |
| Goodwin | 18 | 252 | 14 | 1 |
| Glass | 15 | 201 | 13 | 0 |
| Woodeshick | 6 | 86 | 14 | 0 |
| Crabb | 2 | 41 | 21 | 0 |
| Lang | 2 | 30 | 15 | 0 |
| Matson | 2 | 29 | 15 | 1 |
| Gill | 1 | 27 | 27 | 0 |
| F. Hill | 1 | 21 | 21 | 0 |

### Punt Returns

| Last Name | No. | Yds | Avg | TD |
|---|---|---|---|---|
| Cross | 14 | 79 | 6 | 0 |
| Shann | 1 | 63 | 63 | 1 |
| Gill | 2 | 28 | 14 | 0 |
| T. Brown | 4 | 13 | 3 | 0 |

### Kickoff Returns

| Last Name | No. | Yds | Avg | TD |
|---|---|---|---|---|
| Nelson | 26 | 683 | 26 | 0 |
| Cross | 25 | 662 | 26 | 0 |
| T. Brown | 3 | 46 | 15 | 0 |
| Lang | 3 | 36 | 12 | 0 |
| Wells | 1 | 8 | 8 | 0 |
| Morgan | 1 | 3 | 3 | 0 |
| Gill | 1 | 0 | 0 | 0 |

### Passing

| Last Name | Att | Comp | % | Yds | Yd/Att | TD | Int−% | RK |
|---|---|---|---|---|---|---|---|---|
| Snead | 288 | 150 | 52 | 2346 | 8.2 | 15 | 13− 5 | 7 |
| K. Hill | 113 | 60 | 53 | 857 | 7.6 | 5 | 10− 9 | |
| Concannon | 29 | 12 | 41 | 176 | 6.1 | 1 | 3− 10 | |
| Gros | 2 | 1 | 50 | 63 | 31.5 | 1 | 0− 0 | |
| T. Brown | 1 | 0 | 0 | 0 | 0.0 | 0 | 0− 0 | |
| Poage | 1 | 0 | 0 | 0 | 0.0 | 0 | 0− 0 | |

### Punting

| Last Name | No | Avg |
|---|---|---|
| Baker | 37 | 41.9 |
| K. Hill | 19 | 42.8 |

### Kicking

| Last Name | XP | Att | % | FG | Att | % |
|---|---|---|---|---|---|---|
| Baker | 38 | 40 | 95 | 9 | 23 | 39 |
| Lloyd | 7 | 7 | 100 | 1 | 2 | 50 |

**EASTERN CONFERENCE – Continued**

**ST. LOUIS CARDINALS 5-9-0 Wally Lemm**

| Scores of Each Game | | |
|---|---|---|
| 27 | Philadelphia | 34 |
| 49 | Cleveland | 13 |
| 20 | DALLAS | 13 |
| 37 | Washington | 16 |
| 20 | Pittsburgh | 7 |
| 20 | WASHINGTON | 24 |
| 10 | New York | 14 |
| 21 | PITTSBURGH | 17 |
| 13 | Chicago | 34 |
| 15 | NEW YORK | 28 |
| 24 | PHILADELPHIA | 28 |
| 3 | LOS ANGELES | 27 |
| 13 | Dallas | 27 |
| 24 | CLEVELAND | 27 |

| Use Name | Pos. | Hgt | Wgt | Age | Int | Pts |
|---|---|---|---|---|---|---|
| Ernie McMillan | OT | 6'6" | 260 | 27 | | |
| Bob Reynolds | OT | 6'6" | 265 | 24 | | |
| Ed Cook | OG-OT | 6'2" | 250 | 33 | | |
| Irv Goode | OG | 6'4" | 250 | 24 | | |
| Ken Gray | OG | 6'2" | 250 | 29 | | |
| Rick Sortun | OG | 6'2" | 235 | 22 | | |
| Herschel Turner | OT-OG | 6'3" | 230 | 23 | | |
| Mike Alford | C | 6'3" | 230 | 22 | | |
| Bob DeMarco | C | 6'3" | 240 | 27 | | |
| Don Brumm | DE | 6'3" | 245 | 22 | | 6 |
| Mike Melinkovich | DE | 6'4" | 240 | 23 | | |
| Tom Redmond | DE | 6'5" | 250 | 28 | | |
| Joe Robb | DE | 6'3" | 245 | 28 | | |
| Ed McQuarters | DT | 6'1" | 250 | 22 | | |
| Luke Owens | DT | 6'2" | 255 | 32 | | |
| Sam Silas | DT | 6'4" | 250 | 22 | | |
| Chuck Walker | DT | 6'2" | 245 | 24 | | |
| Bill Koman | LB | 6'2" | 230 | 31 | 1 | |
| Dave Meggyesy | LB | 6'1" | 220 | 23 | | |
| Dale Meinert | LB | 6'2" | 220 | 32 | | |
| Marion Rushing | LB | 6'2" | 230 | 28 | | |
| Dave Simmons | LB | 6'4" | 245 | 22 | | |
| Larry Stallings | LB | 6'2" | 230 | 23 | | 6 |
| Monk Bailey | DB | 6' | 180 | 27 | | |
| Jimmy Burson | DB | 6' | 180 | 23 | 5 | |
| Pat Fischer | DB | 5'10" | 170 | 25 | 3 | |
| Carl Silvestri | DB | 6' | 195 | 22 | | |
| Jerry Stovall | DB | 6'2" | 205 | 23 | 2 | |
| Larry Wilson | DB | 6' | 190 | 27 | 6 | 6 |
| Abe Woodson | DB | 5'11" | 190 | 30 | | |
| Buddy Humphrey | QB | 6'1" | 200 | 29 | | |
| Charley Johnson | QB | 6' | 190 | 28 | | 6 |
| Terry Nofsinger | QB | 6'4" | 215 | 27 | | 6 |
| Prentice Gautt | HB | 6' | 210 | 27 | | 12 |
| Bill Triplett | HB | 6'2" | 210 | 26 | | 42 |
| Joe Childress | FB | 6' | 210 | 31 | | |
| Willie Crenshaw | FB | 6'2" | 230 | 24 | | 6 |
| Bill Thornton | FB | 6'1" | 215 | 25 | | |
| Bobby Joe Conrad | FL | 6' | 195 | 30 | | 30 |
| Mal Hammack | TE | 6'2" | 210 | 32 | | |
| Chuck Logan | TE | 6'4" | 210 | 22 | | |
| Jackie Smith | TE | 6'4" | 215 | 24 | | 12 |
| Billy Gambrell | OE | 5'10" | 175 | 23 | | 12 |
| Ray Ogden | OE | 6'5" | 225 | 22 | | |
| Sonny Randle | OE | 6'2" | 190 | 29 | | 54 |
| Jim Bakken | K | 6' | 200 | 24 | | 96 |

**PITTSBURGH STEELERS 2-12-0 Mike Nixon**

| Scores of Each Game | | |
|---|---|---|
| 9 | GREEN BAY | 41 |
| 17 | San Francisco | 27 |
| 13 | NEW YORK | 23 |
| 19 | Cleveland | 24 |
| 7 | ST. LOUIS | 20 |
| 20 | Philadelphia | 14 |
| 22 | DALLAS | 13 |
| 17 | St. Louis | 21 |
| 17 | Dallas | 24 |
| 3 | WASHINGTON | 31 |
| 21 | CLEVELAND | 42 |
| 10 | New York | 35 |
| 13 | PHILADELPHIA | 47 |
| 14 | Washington | 35 |

| Use Name | Pos. | Hgt | Wgt | Age | Int | Pts |
|---|---|---|---|---|---|---|
| Charlie Bradshaw | OT | 6'6" | 260 | 29 | | |
| Dan James | OT | 6'4" | 250 | 28 | | |
| Bob Nichols | OT | 6'3" | 250 | 22 | | |
| Ray Lemek | OG | 6' | 240 | 31 | | |
| Mike Magac | OG | 6'3" | 240 | 27 | | |
| Mike Sandusky | OG | 6' | 235 | 32 | | |
| Ed Adamchik (from NY) | C | 6'2" | 235 | 23 | | |
| Ken Henson | C | 6'6" | 260 | 22 | | |
| Art Hunter | C | 6'4" | 247 | 32 | | |
| John Baker | DE | 6'6" | 270 | 30 | | |
| Ben McGee | DE | 6'2" | 225 | 23 | | |
| Fran Mallick | DT-DE | 6'3" | 245 | 24 | | |
| Riley Gunnels | DT | 6'3" | 253 | 28 | | |
| Chuck Hinton | DT | 6'5" | 260 | 26 | | |
| Ken Kortas | DT | 6'2" | 280 | 23 | | |
| Ray Mansfield | DT | 6'3" | 250 | 24 | | |
| Rod Breedlove | LB | 6'2" | 227 | 27 | | |
| Gene Breen | LB | 6'2" | 230 | 24 | | |
| John Campbell | LB | 6'3" | 225 | 26 | | 6 |
| Max Messner | LB | 6'3" | 225 | 27 | 1 | |
| Ed Pine | LB | 6'4" | 235 | 25 | | |
| Myron Pottios | LB | 6'2" | 240 | 25 | | |
| Bob Schmitz | LB | 6'1" | 240 | 27 | | |
| Jim Bradshaw | DB | 6'1" | 205 | 26 | 5 | 6 |
| Willie Daniel | DB | 5'11" | 185 | 27 | 1 | 6 |
| Bob Hohn | DB | 6' | 190 | 24 | | |
| Brady Keys | DB | 6' | 198 | 29 | 1 | |
| Bob Sherman | DB | 6'2" | 195 | 23 | 1 | |
| Marv Woodson | DB | 6' | 195 | 22 | 3 | 6 |
| Ed Brown (to BAL) | QB | 6'2" | 220 | 36 | | |
| Bill Nelsen | QB | 6' | 195 | 24 | | 6 |
| Tom Wade | QB | 6'2" | 195 | 23 | | |
| Cannonball Butler | HB | 5'10" | 195 | 22 | | 6 |
| Dick Hoak | HB | 5'11" | 190 | 26 | | 36 |
| John Henry Johnson | FB | 6'2" | 205 | 35 | | |
| Mike Lind | FB | 6'2" | 225 | 25 | | 12 |
| Clarence Peaks | FB | 6'1" | 215 | 29 | | |
| Theron Sapp | FB | 6'1" | 210 | 30 | | |
| Red Mack | FL | 5'10" | 185 | 28 | | |
| Paul Martha | HB-FL | 6' | 185 | 22 | | |
| Gary Ballman | OE-FL | 6' | 200 | 25 | | 48 |
| John Hilton | TE | 6'5" | 220 | 23 | | |
| John Powers | LB-TE | 6'2" | 210 | 24 | | |
| Duane Allen (to BAL) | OE | 6'4" | 225 | 27 | | |
| Lee Folkins | TE | 6'5" | 215 | 26 | | 6 |
| Roy Jefferson | OE | 6'2" | 195 | 21 | | 6 |
| Jerry Simmons | OE | 6'1" | 190 | 22 | | |
| Clendon Thomas | DB-OE | 6'2" | 205 | 28 | | 6 |
| Mike Clark | K | 6'1" | 205 | 24 | | 52 |
| Frank Lambert | K | 6'3" | 200 | 22 | | |

Andy Russell – Military Service

**WESTERN CONFERENCE**

**GREEN BAY PACKERS 10-3-1 Vince Lombardi**

| Scores of Each Game | | |
|---|---|---|
| 41 | Pittsburgh | 9 |
| 20 | BALTIMORE | 17 |
| 23 | CHICAGO | 14 |
| 27 | SAN FRANCISCO | 10 |
| 31 | Detroit | 21 |
| 13 | DALLAS | 3 |
| 10 | Chicago | 31 |
| 7 | DETROIT | 12 |
| 6 | LOS ANGELES | 3 |
| 38 | Minnesota | 13 |
| 10 | Los Angeles | 21 |
| 24 | MINNESOTA | 19 |
| 42 | Baltimore | 27 |
| 24 | San Francisco | 24 |
| | **Playoff** | |
| 13 | BALTIMORE | 10 |

| Use Name | Pos. | Hgt | Wgt | Age | Int | Pts |
|---|---|---|---|---|---|---|
| Steve Wright | OT | 6'6" | 250 | 23 | | |
| Bob Skoronski | OT | 6'3" | 250 | 32 | | |
| Forrest Gregg | OG-OT | 6'4" | 250 | 32 | | |
| Dan Grimm | OG | 6'3" | 245 | 24 | | |
| Jerry Kramer | OG | 6'3" | 245 | 30 | | |
| Fuzzy Thurston | OG | 6'1" | 245 | 32 | | |
| Ken Bowman | C | 6'3" | 230 | 22 | | |
| Bill Curry | C | 6'2" | 235 | 22 | | |
| Lionel Aldridge | DE | 6'4" | 245 | 23 | | |
| Willie Davis | DE | 6'3" | 245 | 32 | 1 | |
| Lloyd Voss | DE | 6'4" | 260 | 23 | | |
| Henry Jordan | DT | 6'3" | 250 | 30 | | |
| Ron Kostelnik | DT | 6'4" | 260 | 25 | | |
| Bud Marshall | DT | 6'5" | 270 | 23 | | |
| Lee Roy Caffey | LB | 6'3" | 250 | 25 | 1 | 6 |
| Tommy Crutcher | LB | 6'3" | 230 | 23 | 1 | |
| Ray Nitschke | LB | 6'3" | 240 | 29 | 1 | |
| Dave Robinson | LB | 6'3" | 245 | 24 | 3 | |
| Herb Adderley | DB | 6'1" | 210 | 26 | 6 | 18 |
| Tom Brown | DB | 6'1" | 190 | 24 | 3 | |
| Hank Gremminger | DB | 6'1" | 200 | 32 | | |
| Doug Hart | DB | 6' | 190 | 26 | 4 | 6 |
| Bob Jeter | DB | 6'1" | 205 | 27 | 1 | |
| Willie Wood | DB | 5'10" | 190 | 29 | 6 | |
| Zeke Bratkowski | QB | 6'2" | 200 | 33 | | |
| Dennis Claridge | QB | 6'3" | 225 | 23 | | |
| Bart Starr | QB | 6'1" | 200 | 32 | | 6 |
| Junior Coffey | HB | 6'1" | 210 | 23 | | |
| Paul Hornung | HB | 6'2" | 215 | 28 | | 48 |
| Allen Jacobs | FB | 6'1" | 215 | 24 | | |
| Tom Moore | HB | 6'2" | 210 | 27 | | 6 |
| Elijah Pitts | HB | 6'1" | 205 | 26 | | 30 |
| Jim Taylor | FB | 6' | 215 | 30 | | 24 |
| Carroll Dale | FL | 6'1" | 200 | 27 | | 12 |
| Bob Long | FL | 6'3" | 190 | 24 | | 24 |
| Bill Anderson | TE | 6'3" | 215 | 29 | | 6 |
| Marv Fleming | TE | 6'4" | 235 | 23 | | 12 |
| Boyd Dowler | OE | 6'5" | 225 | 28 | | 24 |
| Max McGee | OE | 6'3" | 205 | 33 | | 6 |
| Don Chandler | K | 6'2" | 210 | 30 | | 88 |

**BALTIMORE COLTS 10-3-1 Don Shula**

| Scores of Each Game | | |
|---|---|---|
| 35 | MINNESOTA | 16 |
| 17 | Green Bay | 20 |
| 27 | SAN FRANCISCO | 24 |
| 31 | DETROIT | 7 |
| 38 | Washington | 7 |
| 35 | LOS ANGELES | 20 |
| 34 | San Francisco | 28 |
| 26 | Chicago | 21 |
| 41 | Minnesota | 21 |
| 34 | PHILADELPHIA | 24 |
| 24 | Detroit | 24 |
| 0 | CHICAGO | 13 |
| 27 | GREEN BAY | 42 |
| 20 | Los Angeles | 17 |
| | **Playoff** | |
| 10 | Green Bay | 13 |

| Use Name | Pos. | Hgt | Wgt | Age | Int | Pts |
|---|---|---|---|---|---|---|
| Tom Gilburg | OT | 6'5" | 245 | 26 | | |
| George Preas | OT | 6'2" | 250 | 33 | | |
| Bob Vogel | OT | 6'5" | 250 | 23 | | |
| Jim Parker | OG | 6'3" | 275 | 31 | | |
| Alex Sandusky | OG | 6'1" | 242 | 33 | | |
| Dan Sullivan | OG | 6'3" | 250 | 26 | | |
| Buzz Nutter | C | 6'4" | 240 | 34 | | |
| Dick Szymanski | C | 6'3" | 235 | 33 | | |
| Ordell Braase | DE | 6'4" | 242 | 33 | | |
| Roy Hilton | DE | 6'6" | 225 | 20 | | |
| Lou Michaels | DE | 6'2" | 240 | 29 | | 101 |
| Fred Miller | DT | 6'3" | 245 | 24 | | |
| Guy Reese | DT | 6'5" | 260 | 25 | | |
| Billy Ray Smith | DT | 6'4" | 240 | 30 | 1 | |
| Glenn Ressler | C-DT | 6'3" | 235 | 21 | | |
| Jackie Burkett | LB | 6'4" | 228 | 28 | | |
| Ted Davis | LB | 6'1" | 225 | 23 | | |
| Dennis Gaubatz | LB | 6'2" | 220 | 24 | 1 | |
| Monte Lee | LB | 6'4" | 220 | 27 | | |
| Don Shinnick | LB | 6' | 235 | 30 | 1 | |
| Steve Stonebreaker | LB | 6'3" | 222 | 27 | 1 | |
| Mike Curtis | FB-LB | 6'2" | 225 | 22 | | |
| Bobby Boyd | DB | 5'10" | 190 | 27 | 9 | 6 |
| Wendell Harris | DB | 5'11" | 185 | 24 | 3 | |
| Alvin Haymond | DB | 6' | 190 | 23 | 3 | 6 |
| Jerry Logan | DB | 6'1" | 185 | 24 | 2 | 12 |
| Lenny Lyles | DB | 6'2" | 202 | 29 | 1 | |
| Jim Welch | DB | 6' | 190 | 27 | | |
| Gary Cuozzo | QB | 6'1" | 195 | 24 | | |
| Johnny Unitas | QB | 6'1" | 194 | 32 | | 6 |
| Lenny Moore | HB | 6'1" | 190 | 32 | | 48 |
| Tom Matte | QB-HB | 6' | 205 | 26 | | 6 |
| Jerry Hill | FB | 5'11" | 210 | 25 | | 30 |
| Tony Lorick | FB | 6'1" | 215 | 23 | | 18 |
| Jimmy Orr | FL | 5'11" | 175 | 29 | | 60 |
| Willie Richardson | FL | 6'2" | 198 | 25 | | 6 |
| John Mackey | TE | 6'3" | 217 | 23 | | 42 |
| Butch Wilson | TE | 6'2" | 218 | 23 | | |
| Ray Berry | OE | 6'2" | 187 | 32 | | 42 |
| Alex Hawkins | FL-OE | 6'1" | 186 | 28 | | 6 |
| Neal Petties | FL-OE | 6'2" | 198 | 24 | | |

Lou Kirouac – Injury

Gino Marchetti – Voluntarily Retired

**CHICAGO BEARS 9-5-0 George Halas**

| Scores of Each Game | | |
|---|---|---|
| 24 | San Francisco | 52 |
| 28 | Los Angeles | 30 |
| 14 | Green Bay | 23 |
| 31 | LOS ANGELES | 6 |
| 45 | Minnesota | 37 |
| 38 | DETROIT | 10 |
| 31 | GREEN BAY | 10 |
| 21 | BALTIMORE | 26 |
| 34 | ST. LOUIS | 13 |
| 17 | Detroit | 10 |
| 35 | New York | 14 |
| 13 | Baltimore | 0 |
| 61 | SAN FRANCISCO | 20 |
| 17 | MINNESOTA | 24 |

| Use Name | Pos. | Hgt | Wgt | Age | Int | Pts |
|---|---|---|---|---|---|---|
| Herm Lee | OT | 6'4" | 247 | 34 | | |
| Dick Leeuwenberg | OT | 6'5" | 242 | 21 | | |
| Bob Wetoska | OT | 6'3" | 240 | 27 | | |
| Jim Cadile | OG | 6'3" | 240 | 24 | | |
| Mike Rabold | OG | 6'2" | 238 | 27 | | |
| George Seals | DT-OG | 6'2" | 260 | 22 | | |
| Mike Pyle | C | 6'3" | 250 | 26 | | |
| Doug Atkins | DE | 6'8" | 255 | 35 | 1 | |
| Dick Evey | DE | 6'2" | 225 | 24 | 1 | |
| Bob Kilcullen | DE | 6'3" | 245 | 29 | | |
| Ed O'Bradovich | DE | 6'3" | 255 | 25 | | |
| John Johnson | DT | 6'5" | 260 | 24 | | |
| Stan Jones | DT | 6'1" | 250 | 34 | | |
| Earl Leggett | DT | 6'3" | 265 | 31 | | |
| Dennis Murphy | DT | 6'1" | 250 | 21 | | |
| Dick Butkus | LB | 6'3" | 240 | 21 | 5 | |
| Joe Fortunato | LB | 6' | 225 | 35 | 2 | |
| Bill George | LB | 6'2" | 235 | 34 | | |
| Roger LeClerc | LB | 6'3" | 235 | 27 | | 85 |
| Larry Morris | LB | 6'2" | 230 | 30 | | |
| Jim Purnell | LB | 6'2" | 205 | 23 | | |
| Mike Reilly | LB | 6'2" | 238 | 22 | | |
| J. C. Caroline | DB | 6'1" | 190 | 32 | | |
| Larry Glueck | DB | 6' | 190 | 23 | | |
| Bennie McRae | DB | 6'1" | 180 | 24 | 4 | 6 |
| Richie Petitbon | DB | 6'3" | 205 | 27 | 2 | |
| Ron Smith | DB | 6'1" | 185 | 22 | | |
| Rosey Taylor | DB | 5'11" | 186 | 26 | 1 | 6 |
| Dave Whitsell | DB | 6' | 190 | 29 | 4 | 6 |
| Rudy Bukich | QB | 6'1" | 205 | 34 | | 18 |
| Billy Wade | QB | 6'2" | 205 | 34 | | |
| Jon Arnett | HB | 5'11" | 203 | 30 | | 30 |
| Charlie Bivins | HB | 6'2" | 212 | 26 | | 12 |
| Ronnie Bull | HB | 6' | 200 | 25 | | 24 |
| Gale Sayers | HB | 6' | 198 | 22 | | 132 |
| Ralph Kurek | FB | 6'2" | 210 | 22 | | |
| Andy Livingston | FB | 6' | 234 | 20 | | 12 |
| Joe Marconi | FB | 6'2" | 225 | 31 | | |
| Johnny Morris | FL | 5'10" | 180 | 30 | | 24 |
| Mike Ditka | TE | 6'3" | 230 | 25 | | 12 |
| Billy Martin | TE | 6'4" | 240 | 22 | | |
| Dick Gordon | OE | 5'11" | 190 | 20 | | 18 |
| Jim Jones | OE | 6'2" | 187 | 21 | | 24 |
| Bobby Joe Green | K | 5'11" | 175 | 27 | | |

Riley Mattson – Injury
Palmer Pyle – Injury

## EASTERN CONFERENCE – Continued

### ST. LOUIS CARDINALS

**RUSHING**

| Last Name | No. | Yds | Avg | TD |
|---|---|---|---|---|
| Triplett | 174 | 617 | 3.5 | 6 |
| Crenshaw | 127 | 437 | 3.4 | 0 |
| Thornton | 31 | 188 | 6.1 | 0 |
| Gautt | 44 | 175 | 4.0 | 2 |
| Childress | 19 | 94 | 4.9 | 0 |
| Johnson | 25 | 60 | 2.4 | 1 |
| Bakken | 1 | 28 | 28.0 | 0 |
| Gambrell | 4 | 15 | 3.8 | 0 |
| Humphrey | 2 | 4 | 2.0 | 0 |
| Nofsinger | 4 | 1 | 0.3 | 1 |

**RECEIVING**

| Last Name | No. | Yds | Avg | TD |
|---|---|---|---|---|
| Conrad | 58 | 909 | 16 | 5 |
| Randle | 51 | 845 | 17 | 9 |
| Smith | 41 | 648 | 16 | 2 |
| Triplett | 26 | 256 | 10 | 1 |
| Crenshaw | 23 | 232 | 10 | 1 |
| Gambrell | 9 | 171 | 19 | 2 |
| Gautt | 9 | 128 | 14 | 0 |
| Childress | 3 | 27 | 9 | 0 |
| Thornton | 1 | 6 | 6 | 0 |

**PUNT RETURNS**

| Last Name | No. | Yds | Avg | TD |
|---|---|---|---|---|
| Silvestri | 3 | 21 | 7 | 0 |
| Woodson | 18 | 7 | 0 | 0 |
| Burson | 1 | 0 | 0 | 0 |
| Gambrell | 1 | -1 | -1 | 0 |

**KICKOFF RETURNS**

| Last Name | No. | Yds | Avg | TD |
|---|---|---|---|---|
| Woodson | 27 | 665 | 25 | 0 |
| Gambrell | 9 | 216 | 24 | 0 |
| Stovall | 7 | 198 | 28 | 0 |
| Silvestri | 4 | 96 | 24 | 0 |
| Ogden | 2 | 55 | 28 | 0 |
| Hammack | 3 | 34 | 11 | 0 |
| Crenshaw | 2 | 23 | 12 | 0 |
| Koman | 1 | 0 | 0 | 0 |

**PASSING – PUNTING – KICKING**

| PASSING | Att | Comp | % | Yds | Yd/Att | TD | Int-% | RK |
|---|---|---|---|---|---|---|---|---|
| Johnson | 322 | 155 | 48 | 2439 | 7.6 | 18 | 15- 5 | 11 |
| Humphrey | 105 | 58 | 55 | 736 | 7.0 | 1 | 9- 9 | |
| Nofsinger | 20 | 8 | 40 | 47 | 2.4 | 1 | 1- 5 | |
| Gautt | 1 | 0 | 0 | 0 | 0.0 | 0 | 0- 0 | |

| PUNTING | No | Avg |
|---|---|---|
| Smith | 39 | 39.3 |
| Bakken | 26 | 42.2 |
| Stovall | 2 | 40.0 |

| KICKING | XP | Att | % | FG | Att | % |
|---|---|---|---|---|---|---|
| Bakken | 33 | 33 | 100 | 21 | 31 | 68 |

### PITTSBURGH STEELERS

**RUSHING**

| Last Name | No. | Yds | Avg | TD |
|---|---|---|---|---|
| Hoak | 131 | 426 | 3.3 | 5 |
| Lind | 111 | 375 | 3.4 | 1 |
| Peaks | 47 | 230 | 4.9 | 0 |
| Butler | 46 | 108 | 2.3 | 0 |
| Nelsen | 26 | 84 | 3.2 | 1 |
| Sapp | 14 | 54 | 3.9 | 0 |
| Ballman | 17 | 46 | 2.7 | 3 |
| Wade | 8 | 43 | 5.4 | 0 |
| Johnson | 3 | 11 | 3.7 | 0 |
| Martha | 2 | 3 | 1.5 | 0 |
| Jefferson | 1 | -1 | -1.0 | 0 |
| Brown | 2 | -3 | -1.5 | 0 |

**RECEIVING**

| Last Name | No. | Yds | Avg | TD |
|---|---|---|---|---|
| Ballman | 40 | 859 | 21 | 5 |
| Thomas | 25 | 431 | 17 | 1 |
| Lind | 25 | 236 | 9 | 1 |
| Hoak | 19 | 228 | 12 | 1 |
| Jefferson | 13 | 287 | 22 | 1 |
| Martha | 11 | 171 | 16 | 0 |
| Butler | 9 | 117 | 13 | 1 |
| Folkins | 5 | 58 | 12 | 0 |
| Hilton | 4 | 32 | 8 | 0 |
| Mack | 3 | 41 | 14 | 0 |
| Peaks | 3 | 22 | 7 | 0 |
| Simmons | 2 | 16 | 8 | 0 |
| Sapp | 1 | 10 | 10 | 0 |
| Nelsen | 1 | -5 | -5 | 0 |

**PUNT RETURNS**

| Last Name | No. | Yds | Avg | TD |
|---|---|---|---|---|
| Jefferson | 13 | 100 | 8 | 0 |
| Keys | 10 | 77 | 8 | 0 |
| J. Bradshaw | 5 | 73 | 15 | 0 |
| Thomas | 5 | 9 | 2 | 0 |

**KICKOFF RETURNS**

| Last Name | No. | Yds | Avg | TD |
|---|---|---|---|---|
| Butler | 25 | 509 | 20 | 0 |
| Peaks | 20 | 429 | 21 | 0 |
| Ballman | 8 | 150 | 19 | 0 |
| Sapp | 5 | 77 | 15 | 0 |
| Woodson | 2 | 45 | 23 | 0 |
| Simmons | 1 | 28 | 28 | 0 |

**PASSING – PUNTING – KICKING**

| PASSING | Att | Comp | % | Yds | Yd/Att | TD | Int-% | RK |
|---|---|---|---|---|---|---|---|---|
| Nelsen | 270 | 121 | 45 | 1917 | 7.1 | 8 | 17- 6 | 15 |
| Wade | 66 | 33 | 50 | 463 | 7.0 | 2 | 13- 20 | |
| Brown | 23 | 10 | 44 | 204 | 8.9 | 1 | 5- 22 | |

| PUNTING | No | Avg |
|---|---|---|
| Lambert | 78 | 45.1 |
| Brown | 2 | 40.0 |

| KICKING | XP | Att | % | FG | Att | % |
|---|---|---|---|---|---|---|
| Clark | 19 | 24 | 79 | 11 | 19 | 58 |

## WESTERN CONFERENCE

### GREEN BAY PACKERS

**RUSHING**

| Last Name | No. | Yds | Avg | TD |
|---|---|---|---|---|
| Taylor | 207 | 734 | 3.5 | 4 |
| Hornung | 89 | 299 | 3.4 | 5 |
| Starr | 18 | 169 | 9.4 | 1 |
| Moore | 51 | 124 | 2.4 | 0 |
| Pitts | 54 | 122 | 2.3 | 4 |
| Chandler | 1 | 27 | 27.0 | 0 |
| Coffey | 3 | 12 | 4.0 | 0 |
| Jacobs | 3 | 5 | 1.7 | 0 |
| Bratkowski | 4 | -1 | -0.3 | 0 |
| Claridge | 2 | -3 | -1.5 | 0 |

**RECEIVING**

| Last Name | No. | Yds | Avg | TD |
|---|---|---|---|---|
| Dowler | 44 | 610 | 14 | 4 |
| Dale | 20 | 382 | 19 | 2 |
| Taylor | 20 | 207 | 10 | 0 |
| Hornung | 19 | 336 | 18 | 3 |
| Fleming | 14 | 141 | 10 | 2 |
| Long | 13 | 304 | 23 | 4 |
| Pitts | 11 | 182 | 17 | 1 |
| McGee | 10 | 154 | 15 | 1 |
| Anderson | 8 | 105 | 13 | 1 |
| Moore | 7 | 87 | 12 | 1 |

**PUNT RETURNS**

| Last Name | No. | Yds | Avg | TD |
|---|---|---|---|---|
| Wood | 13 | 38 | 3 | 0 |
| Pitts | 8 | 27 | 3 | 0 |
| Adderley | 1 | 0 | 0 | 0 |

**KICKOFF RETURNS**

| Last Name | No. | Yds | Avg | TD |
|---|---|---|---|---|
| Pitts | 20 | 396 | 20 | 0 |
| Moore | 15 | 361 | 24 | 0 |
| Adderley | 10 | 221 | 22 | 0 |
| Crutcher | 3 | 53 | 18 | 0 |
| Coffey | 1 | 9 | 9 | 0 |
| Grimm | 1 | 0 | 0 | 0 |

**PASSING – PUNTING – KICKING**

| PASSING | Att | Comp | % | Yds | Yd/Att | TD | Int-% | RK |
|---|---|---|---|---|---|---|---|---|
| Starr | 251 | 140 | 56 | 2055 | 8.2 | 16 | 9- 4 | 4 |
| Bratkowski | 48 | 21 | 44 | 348 | 7.3 | 3 | 4- 8 | |
| Moore | 2 | 2 | 100 | 22 | 11.0 | 0 | 0- 0 | |
| Hornung | 2 | 1 | 50 | 19 | 9.5 | 0 | 1- 50 | |
| Pitts | 2 | 1 | 50 | 51 | 25.5 | 0 | 0- 0 | |
| Claridge | 1 | 1 | 100 | 13 | 13.0 | 0 | 0- 0 | |

| PUNTING | No | Avg |
|---|---|---|
| Chandler | 74 | 42.9 |

| KICKING | XP | Att | % | FG | Att | % |
|---|---|---|---|---|---|---|
| Chandler | 37 | 38 | 97 | 17 | 26 | 65 |

### BALTIMORE COLTS

**RUSHING**

| Last Name | No. | Yds | Avg | TD |
|---|---|---|---|---|
| Hill | 147 | 516 | 3.5 | 5 |
| Moore | 133 | 464 | 3.5 | 5 |
| Lorick | 63 | 296 | 4.7 | 1 |
| Matte | 69 | 235 | 3.4 | 1 |
| Unitas | 17 | 68 | 4.0 | 1 |
| Cuozzo | 6 | 8 | 1.3 | 0 |
| Mackey | 1 | 7 | 7.0 | 0 |
| Curtis | 6 | 1 | 0.2 | 0 |

**RECEIVING**

| Last Name | No. | Yds | Avg | TD |
|---|---|---|---|---|
| Berry | 58 | 739 | 13 | 7 |
| Orr | 45 | 847 | 19 | 10 |
| Mackey | 40 | 814 | 20 | 7 |
| Moore | 27 | 414 | 15 | 3 |
| Hill | 20 | 112 | 6 | 0 |
| Lorick | 15 | 184 | 12 | 2 |
| Matte | 12 | 131 | 11 | 0 |
| Hawkins | 2 | 32 | 16 | 1 |
| Wilson | 1 | 38 | 38 | 0 |
| Richardson | 1 | 14 | 14 | 1 |
| Curtis | 1 | 5 | 5 | 0 |

**PUNT RETURNS**

| Last Name | No. | Yds | Avg | TD |
|---|---|---|---|---|
| Haymond | 41 | 403 | 10 | 0 |
| Hawkins | 4 | 18 | 5 | 0 |

**KICKOFF RETURNS**

| Last Name | No. | Yds | Avg | TD |
|---|---|---|---|---|
| Haymond | 20 | 614 | 31 | 0 |
| Lorick | 9 | 211 | 23 | 0 |
| Matte | 8 | 211 | 26 | 0 |
| Curtis | 2 | 10 | 5 | 0 |
| Hill | 1 | 3 | 3 | 0 |
| Hawkins | 2 | 0 | 0 | 0 |

**PASSING – PUNTING – KICKING**

| PASSING | Att | Comp | % | Yds | Yd/Att | TD | Int-% | RK |
|---|---|---|---|---|---|---|---|---|
| Unitas | 282 | 164 | 58 | 2530 | 9.0 | 23 | 12- 4 | 2 |
| Cuozzo | 105 | 54 | 51 | 700 | 6.7 | 7 | 4- 4 | |
| Matte | 7 | 1 | 14 | 19 | 2.7 | 0 | 1- 14 | |

| PUNTING | No | Avg |
|---|---|---|
| Gilburg | 54 | 39.6 |

| KICKING | XP | Att | % | FG | Att | % |
|---|---|---|---|---|---|---|
| Michaels | 48 | 48 | 100 | 17 | 28 | 61 |

### CHICAGO BEARS

**RUSHING**

| Last Name | No. | Yds | Avg | TD |
|---|---|---|---|---|
| Sayers | 166 | 867 | 5.2 | 14 |
| Bull | 91 | 417 | 4.6 | 3 |
| Livingston | 63 | 363 | 5.8 | 2 |
| Arnett | 102 | 363 | 3.6 | 5 |
| Marconi | 19 | 47 | 2.5 | 0 |
| Bukich | 28 | 33 | 1.2 | 3 |
| Wade | 5 | 18 | 3.6 | 0 |
| J. Jones | 2 | 13 | 6.5 | 0 |
| Gordon | 2 | 10 | 5.0 | 0 |
| Kurek | 1 | 0 | 0.0 | 0 |

**RECEIVING**

| Last Name | No. | Yds | Avg | TD |
|---|---|---|---|---|
| J. Morris | 53 | 846 | 16 | 4 |
| Ditka | 36 | 454 | 13 | 2 |
| Sayers | 29 | 507 | 17 | 6 |
| J. Jones | 21 | 350 | 17 | 4 |
| Bull | 16 | 186 | 12 | 1 |
| Gordon | 13 | 279 | 21 | 3 |
| Livingston | 12 | 134 | 11 | 0 |
| Arnett | 12 | 114 | 10 | 0 |
| Bivins | 4 | 108 | 27 | 2 |
| Marconi | 4 | 43 | 11 | 0 |
| Martin | 1 | -1 | -1 | 0 |

**PUNT RETURNS**

| Last Name | No. | Yds | Avg | TD |
|---|---|---|---|---|
| Sayers | 16 | 238 | 15 | 1 |
| Arnett | 11 | 52 | 5 | 0 |
| Smith | 1 | 2 | 2 | 0 |
| Gordon | 1 | -3 | -3 | 0 |

**KICKOFF RETURNS**

| Last Name | No. | Yds | Avg | TD |
|---|---|---|---|---|
| Sayers | 21 | 660 | 31 | 1 |
| Gordon | 14 | 242 | 17 | 0 |
| Arnett | 5 | 150 | 30 | 0 |
| Livingston | 2 | 66 | 33 | 0 |
| Smith | 1 | 17 | 17 | 0 |
| Kurek | 1 | 11 | 11 | 0 |
| LeClerc | 1 | 0 | 0 | 0 |

**PASSING – PUNTING – KICKING**

| PASSING | Att | Comp | % | Yds | Yd/Att | TD | Int-% | RK |
|---|---|---|---|---|---|---|---|---|
| Bukich | 312 | 176 | 56 | 2641 | 8.5 | 20 | 9- 3 | 1 |
| Wade | 41 | 20 | 49 | 204 | 5.0 | 0 | 2- 5 | |
| Bull | 3 | 2 | 67 | 63 | 21.0 | 0 | 0- 0 | |
| Sayers | 3 | 2 | 67 | 53 | 17.7 | 1 | 1- 33 | |
| Arnett | 2 | 1 | 50 | 59 | 29.5 | 1 | 0- 0 | |

| PUNTING | No | Avg |
|---|---|---|
| Green | 58 | 42.7 |

| KICKING | XP | Att | % | FG | Att | % |
|---|---|---|---|---|---|---|
| LeClerc | 52 | 52 | 100 | 11 | 26 | 42 |

WESTERN CONFERENCE – Continued

## SAN FRANCISCO FORTY NINERS 7-6-1 Jack Christiansen

| Scores of Each Game | | |
|---|---|---|
| 52 | CHICAGO | 24 |
| 27 | PITTSBURGH | 17 |
| 24 | Baltimore | 27 |
| 10 | Green Bay | 27 |
| 45 | Los Angeles | 21 |
| 41 | MINNESOTA | 42 |
| 28 | BALTIMORE | 34 |
| 31 | Dallas | 39 |
| 27 | Detroit | 21 |
| 30 | LOS ANGELES | 27 |
| 45 | Minnesota | 24 |
| 17 | DETROIT | 14 |
| 20 | Chicago | 61 |
| 24 | GREEN BAY | 24 |

| Use Name | Pos. | Hgt | Wgt | Age | Int | Pts |
|---|---|---|---|---|---|---|
| Jim Norton | OT | 6'4" | 255 | 22 | | |
| Walt Rock | OT | 6'5" | 245 | 24 | | |
| Len Rohde | OT | 6'4" | 245 | 27 | | |
| Howard Mudd | OG | 6'3" | 240 | 23 | | |
| John Thomas | OG | 6'4" | 246 | 30 | | |
| Jim Wilson | OG | 6'3" | 255 | 24 | | |
| Bruce Bosley | C | 6'2" | 240 | 31 | | |
| Joe Cerne | C | 6'2" | 235 | 22 | | |
| Dan Colchico | DE | 6'4" | 245 | 28 | | |
| Dan LaRose | DE | 6'5" | 250 | 25 | | |
| Clark Miller | DE | 6'5" | 245 | 26 | | 6 |
| Karl Rubke | DE | 6'4" | 240 | 29 | | |
| Charlie Krueger | DT | 6'4" | 254 | 29 | | 6 |
| Roland Lakes | DT | 6'4" | 263 | 25 | | |
| Chuck Sieminski | DT | 6'4" | 265 | 25 | | |

| Use Name | Pos. | Hgt | Wgt | Age | Int | Pts |
|---|---|---|---|---|---|---|
| Ed Beard | LB | 6'2" | 245 | 25 | | |
| Jack Chapple | LB | 6'2" | 227 | 22 | | 6 |
| Floyd Dean | LB | 6'4" | 245 | 25 | | |
| Mike Dowdle | LB | 6'3" | 235 | 27 | | |
| Bob Harrison | LB | 6'2" | 225 | 28 | | |
| Matt Hazeltine | LB | 6'1" | 230 | 32 | 1 | |
| Dave Wilcox | LB | 6'3" | 230 | 22 | 1 | 6 |
| Kermit Alexander | DB | 5'11" | 186 | 24 | 3 | |
| George Donnelly | DB | 6'3" | 205 | 22 | | |
| Jim Johnson | DB | 6'2" | 190 | 27 | 6 | |
| Elbert Kimbrough | DB | 5'11" | 190 | 26 | 2 | |
| Jerry Mertens | DB | 6' | 185 | 29 | | |
| Wayne Swinford | DB | 6' | 190 | 22 | | |

| Use Name | Pos. | Hgt | Wgt | Age | Int | Pts |
|---|---|---|---|---|---|---|
| John Brodie | QB | 6'1" | 200 | 30 | | 6 |
| George Mira | QB | 5'11" | 190 | 23 | | |
| John David Crow | HB | 6'2" | 215 | 30 | | 54 |
| Rudy Johnson | HB | 5'11" | 190 | 23 | | |
| Dave Kopay | HB | 6'2" | 217 | 23 | | 24 |
| Gary Lewis | FB | 6'3" | 230 | 23 | | 18 |
| Ken Willard | FB | 6'2" | 230 | 22 | | 54 |
| Bernie Casey | FL | 6'4" | 215 | 26 | | 48 |
| Dale Messer | FL | 5'10" | 175 | 28 | | |
| Bob Poole | TE | 6'4" | 216 | 23 | | |
| Monte Stickles | TE | 6'4" | 230 | 27 | | 6 |
| Vern Burke | OE | 6'4" | 200 | 24 | | 6 |
| Kay McFarland | OE | 6'2" | 180 | 26 | | 6 |
| Dave Parks | OE | 6'2" | 195 | 23 | | 72 |
| Tommy Davis | K | 6' | 212 | 30 | | 103 |

## MINNESOTA VIKINGS 7-7-0 Norm Van Brocklin

| Scores of Each Game | | |
|---|---|---|
| 16 | Baltimore | 35 |
| 29 | DETROIT | 31 |
| 38 | Los Angeles | 35 |
| 40 | NEW YORK | 14 |
| 37 | CHICAGO | 45 |
| 42 | San Francisco | 41 |
| 27 | Cleveland | 17 |
| 24 | LOS ANGELES | 13 |
| 21 | BALTIMORE | 41 |
| 13 | GREEN BAY | 38 |
| 24 | SAN FRANCISCO | 45 |
| 19 | Green Bay | 24 |
| 29 | Detroit | 7 |
| 24 | Chicago | 17 |

| Use Name | Pos. | Hgt | Wgt | Age | Int | Pts |
|---|---|---|---|---|---|---|
| Grady Alderman | OT | 6'2" | 240 | 26 | | |
| Errol Linden | OT | 6'5" | 260 | 27 | | |
| Archie Sutton | OT | 6'4" | 262 | 22 | | |
| Larry Bowie | OG | 6'2" | 250 | 25 | | |
| Ken Byers | OG | 6'1" | 240 | 25 | | |
| Milt Sunde | C-OG | 6'2" | 234 | 22 | | |
| Mick Tingelhoff | C | 6'1" | 237 | 25 | | |
| Carl Eller | DE | 6'6" | 255 | 23 | 2 | |
| Jim Marshall | DE | 6'3" | 235 | 27 | | |
| Paul Dickson | DT | 6'5" | 255 | 28 | | |
| Gary Larsen | DT | 6'5" | 250 | 25 | | |
| Jim Prestel | DT | 6'5" | 275 | 28 | 2 | |

| Use Name | Pos. | Hgt | Wgt | Age | Int | Pts |
|---|---|---|---|---|---|---|
| Rip Hawkins | LB | 6'3" | 235 | 26 | 3 | 6 |
| Bill Jobko | LB | 6'2" | 235 | 29 | | |
| John Kirby | LB | 6'3" | 222 | 23 | | |
| Lonnie Warwick | LB | 6'3" | 225 | 23 | | 6 |
| Roy Winston | LB | 6'1" | 230 | 25 | | |
| Gary Hill | DB | 6' | 190 | 24 | | |
| Lee Calland | DB | 6' | 200 | 21 | | |
| Jeff Jordan | DB | 6'4" | 190 | 21 | 4 | |
| Karl Kassulke | DB | 6' | 193 | 23 | 2 | |
| Earsell Mackbee | DB | 6'1" | 195 | 24 | | |
| George Rose | DB | 5'11" | 190 | 22 | 1 | |
| Ed Sharockman | DB | 6' | 200 | 25 | 6 | 6 |
| Larry Vargo | DB | 6'3" | 215 | 25 | 3 | |

| Use Name | Pos. | Hgt | Wgt | Age | Int | Pts |
|---|---|---|---|---|---|---|
| Bob Berry | QB | 5'11" | 190 | 23 | | |
| Fran Tarkenton | QB | 6'1" | 190 | 25 | | 6 |
| Ron Vander Kelen | QB | 6'1" | 185 | 25 | | |
| Billy Barnes | HB | 5'11" | 202 | 30 | | |
| Dick James | HB | 5'9" | 185 | 31 | | |
| Phil King | HB | 6'4" | 220 | 29 | | 6 |
| Tommy Mason | HB | 6' | 196 | 26 | | 66 |
| Dave Osborn | HB | 6' | 205 | 22 | | 12 |
| Jim Young | HB | 6' | 205 | 22 | | |
| Bill Brown | FB | 6' | 228 | 23 | | 42 |
| Jim Phillips | FL | 6'1" | 195 | 28 | | 6 |
| Lance Rentzel | HB-FL | 6'2" | 210 | 21 | | 6 |
| Tom Hall | OE-FL | 6'1" | 195 | 24 | | 12 |
| Hal Bedsole | TE | 6'4" | 230 | 23 | | 18 |
| Paul Flatley | OE | 6'1" | 187 | 24 | | 42 |
| Gordon Smith | OE | 6'2" | 220 | 26 | | 30 |
| Fred Cox | K | 5'10" | 200 | 26 | | 113 |
| Bobby Walden | K | 6' | 195 | 27 | | |

## DETROIT LIONS 6-7-1 Harry Gilmer

| Scores of Each Game | | |
|---|---|---|
| 20 | LOS ANGELES | 0 |
| 31 | Minnesota | 29 |
| 14 | WASHINGTON | 10 |
| 7 | Baltimore | 31 |
| 21 | GREEN BAY | 31 |
| 10 | Chicago | 38 |
| 31 | Los Angeles | 7 |
| 12 | Green Bay | 7 |
| 21 | SAN FRANCISCO | 27 |
| 10 | CHICAGO | 17 |
| 24 | BALTIMORE | 24 |
| 14 | San Francisco | 17 |
| 7 | MINNESOTA | 29 |
| 35 | Philadelphia | 28 |

| Use Name | Pos. | Hgt | Wgt | Age | Int | Pts |
|---|---|---|---|---|---|---|
| Daryl Sanders | OT | 6'5" | 250 | 23 | | |
| Roger Shoals | OT | 6'4" | 255 | 26 | | |
| John Gonzaga | OG-OT | 6'3" | 250 | 32 | | |
| John Gordy | OG | 6'3" | 250 | 29 | | |
| Ted Karras | OG | 6'1" | 243 | 32 | | |
| Jim Simon | OG | 6'5" | 235 | 24 | | |
| Ed Flanagan | C | 6'3" | 250 | 21 | | |
| Bob Whitlow | C | 6'1" | 236 | 29 | | |
| Larry Hand | DE | 6'4" | 245 | 25 | | |
| Darris McCord | DE | 6'4" | 250 | 32 | | |
| Sam Williams | DE | 6'5" | 235 | 34 | | |
| Roger Brown | DT | 6'5" | 300 | 28 | 2 | |
| Alex Karras | DT | 6'2" | 245 | 29 | | |
| Jerry Rush | DT | 6'4" | 255 | 33 | | |

| Use Name | Pos. | Hgt | Wgt | Age | Int | Pts |
|---|---|---|---|---|---|---|
| Ernie Clark | LB | 6'1" | 220 | 27 | 1 | |
| Wally Hilgenburg | LB | 6'3" | 225 | 22 | | |
| Mike Lucci | LB | 6'2" | 223 | 25 | | |
| Joe Schmidt | LB | 6'1" | 220 | 33 | 4 | |
| Wayne Walker | LB | 6'2" | 225 | 28 | 2 | 57 |
| Jimmy Hill | DB | 6'2" | 195 | 36 | 1 | |
| Jim Kearney | DB | 6'2" | 200 | 22 | | |
| Night Train Lane | DB | 6'1" | 200 | 37 | | |
| Dick LeBeau | DB | 6'1" | 185 | 28 | 7 | 6 |
| Bruce Maher | DB | 5'11" | 190 | 28 | 4 | |
| Wayne Rasmussen | DB | 6'2" | 180 | 23 | 5 | 12 |
| Bobby Thompson | DB | 5'10" | 175 | 25 | 2 | |
| Tom Vaughn | DB | 5'11" | 195 | 22 | | |

J. D. Smith – Injury
Warren Wells – Military Service

| Use Name | Pos. | Hgt | Wgt | Age | Int | Pts |
|---|---|---|---|---|---|---|
| George Izo | QB | 6'3" | 218 | 28 | | |
| Tom Myers | QB | 6' | 188 | 21 | | |
| Milt Plum | QB | 6'1" | 205 | 31 | | 18 |
| Bobby Felts (from BAL) | HB | 6'2" | 205 | 22 | | |
| Joe Don Looney | HB | 6'1" | 230 | 22 | | 36 |
| Amos Marsh | HB | 6'2" | 220 | 26 | | 48 |
| Tom Watkins | HB | 6'1" | 195 | 28 | | |
| Tom Nowatzke | FB | 6'3" | 228 | 22 | | 12 |
| Nick Pietrosante | FB | 6'2" | 225 | 28 | | 6 |
| Terry Barr | FL | 6' | 190 | 30 | | 18 |
| Pat Studstill | FL | 6'1" | 175 | 27 | | 18 |
| Jim Gibbons | TE | 6'2" | 220 | 29 | | 12 |
| Ron Kramer | TE | 6'3" | 240 | 30 | | 6 |
| Gail Cogdill | OE | 6'2" | 195 | 24 | | |
| John Henderson | OE | 6'3" | 190 | 22 | | 6 |

## LOS ANGELES RAMS 4-10-0 Harland Svare

| Scores of Each Game | | |
|---|---|---|
| 0 | Detroit | 20 |
| 30 | CHICAGO | 28 |
| 35 | MINNESOTA | 38 |
| 6 | Chicago | 31 |
| 21 | SAN FRANCISCO | 45 |
| 20 | Baltimore | 35 |
| 7 | DETROIT | 31 |
| 13 | Minnesota | 24 |
| 3 | Green Bay | 6 |
| 27 | San Francisco | 30 |
| 21 | GREEN BAY | 10 |
| 27 | St. Louis | 3 |
| 42 | CLEVELAND | 7 |
| 17 | BALTIMORE | 20 |

| Use Name | Pos. | Hgt | Wgt | Age | Int | Pts |
|---|---|---|---|---|---|---|
| Joe Carollo | OT | 6'2" | 263 | 25 | | |
| Charley Cowan | OT | 6'4" | 275 | 27 | | |
| Roger Pillath | OT | 6'4" | 255 | 23 | | |
| Frank Varrichione | OT | 6'1" | 237 | 33 | | |
| Don Chuy | OG | 6'1" | 256 | 24 | | |
| Joe Scibelli | OG | 6'1" | 264 | 26 | | |
| Joe Wendryhoski | C-OG | 6'2" | 245 | 26 | | |
| Ken Iman | C | 6'1" | 235 | 26 | | |
| Frank Marchlewski | C | 6'2" | 226 | 21 | | |
| Deacon Jones | DE | 6'5" | 260 | 26 | | 2 |
| Lamar Lundy | DE | 6'7" | 260 | 30 | | |
| Tim Powell | DE | 6'4" | 248 | 21 | | |
| Rosey Grier | DT | 6'5" | 290 | 32 | | |
| Frank Molden | DT | 6'5" | 285 | 23 | 1 | 6 |
| Merlin Olsen | DT | 6'5" | 276 | 24 | | |

| Use Name | Pos. | Hgt | Wgt | Age | Int | Pts |
|---|---|---|---|---|---|---|
| Fred Brown | LB | 6'5" | 223 | 22 | | |
| Mack Byrd | LB | 6' | 215 | 22 | | |
| Dan Currie | LB | 6'3" | 240 | 31 | | |
| Tony Guillory | LB | 6'4" | 220 | 22 | | |
| Cliff Livingston | LB | 6'3" | 212 | 35 | 1 | |
| Mike Strofolino (to BAL) | LB | 6'2" | 240 | 21 | | |
| Doug Woodlief | LB | 6'3" | 235 | 21 | | |
| Chuck Lamson | DB | 6' | 190 | 26 | 2 | |
| Aaron Martin | DB | 6' | 185 | 24 | 2 | 6 |
| Dan McIlhany | DB | 6'1" | 195 | 22 | 2 | |
| Jerry Richardson | DB | 6'3" | 190 | 22 | 1 | |
| Bobby Smith (to DET) | DB | 6' | 197 | 27 | | |
| Ed Meador | DB | 5'11" | 203 | 28 | 2 | 6 |
| Clancy Williams | HB-DB | 6'2" | 198 | 22 | | |

Bucky Pope – Knee Injury
Jack Pardee – Voluntarily Retired

| Use Name | Pos. | Hgt | Wgt | Age | Int | Pts |
|---|---|---|---|---|---|---|
| Roman Gabriel | QB | 6'4" | 225 | 25 | | 12 |
| Bill Munson | QB | 6'2" | 197 | 23 | | 6 |
| Ron Smith | QB | 6'5" | 220 | 23 | | |
| Terry Baker | HB | 6'3" | 200 | 24 | | 18 |
| Les Josephson | HB | 6' | 210 | 23 | | |
| Willie Brown | FL-HB | 6' | 185 | 22 | | 6 |
| Dick Bass | FB | 5'10" | 198 | 28 | | 24 |
| Jim Stiger (from DAL) | FB | 5'11" | 214 | 24 | | |
| Ben Wilson | FB | 6' | 225 | 25 | | 6 |
| Tommy McDonald | FL | 5'10" | 175 | 31 | | 54 |
| Marlin McKeever | TE | 6'1" | 227 | 25 | | 24 |
| Billy Truax | TE | 6'5" | 240 | 22 | | 6 |
| Steve Heckard | OE | 6'1" | 195 | 22 | | |
| Jack Snow | OE | 6'2" | 210 | 22 | | 16 |
| Jon Kilgore | K | 6'1" | 200 | 21 | | |
| Bruce Gossett | K | 6'2" | 230 | 22 | | 75 |
| Billy Lothridge | K | 6'1" | 194 | 21 | | |

**WESTERN CONFERENCE – Continued**

## SAN FRANCISCO FORTY NINERS

### Rushing

| Last Name | No. | Yds | Avg | TD |
|---|---|---|---|---|
| Willard | 189 | 778 | 4.1 | 5 |
| Crow | 132 | 514 | 3.9 | 2 |
| Lewis | 52 | 256 | 4.9 | 3 |
| Kopay | 28 | 81 | 2.9 | 2 |
| Mira | 5 | 64 | 12.8 | 0 |
| Brodie | 15 | 60 | 4.0 | 1 |
| Davis | 1 | 21 | 21.0 | 0 |
| R. Johnson | 6 | 9 | 1.5 | 0 |

### Receiving

| Last Name | No. | Yds | Avg | TD |
|---|---|---|---|---|
| Parks | 80 | 1344 | 17 | 12 |
| Casey | 59 | 765 | 13 | 8 |
| Stickles | 35 | 343 | 10 | 1 |
| Willard | 32 | 253 | 8 | 4 |
| Crow | 28 | 493 | 18 | 7 |
| Kopay | 11 | 147 | 13 | 1 |
| Lewis | 10 | 25 | 3 | 0 |
| McFarland | 8 | 106 | 13 | 1 |
| R. Johnson | 3 | 49 | 16 | 0 |
| Messer | 2 | 41 | 21 | 0 |
| Burke | 2 | 38 | 19 | 1 |
| Poole | 2 | 29 | 15 | 0 |

### Punt Returns

| Last Name | No. | Yds | Avg | TD |
|---|---|---|---|---|
| Alexander | 35 | 262 | 7 | 0 |
| Swinford | 2 | 18 | 9 | 0 |
| Lewis | 1 | 3 | 3 | 0 |

### Kickoff Returns

| Last Name | No. | Yds | Avg | TD |
|---|---|---|---|---|
| Alexander | 32 | 741 | 23 | 0 |
| Lewis | 15 | 355 | 24 | 0 |
| R. Johnson | 4 | 71 | 18 | 0 |
| Swinford | 4 | 61 | 15 | 0 |
| Messer | 1 | 27 | 27 | 0 |
| Kopay | 1 | 21 | 21 | 0 |
| Cerne | 1 | 0 | 0 | 0 |
| Rubke | 1 | 0 | 0 | 0 |

### Passing

| Last Name | Att | Comp | % | Yds | Yd/Att | TD | Int–% | RK |
|---|---|---|---|---|---|---|---|---|
| Brodie | 391 | 242 | 62 | 3112 | 8.0 | 30 | 16– 4 | 3 |
| Mira | 58 | 28 | 48 | 460 | 7.9 | 4 | 3– 5 | |
| Crow | 4 | 2 | 50 | 61 | 15.3 | 1 | 1– 25 | |
| Willard | 1 | 0 | 0 | 0 | 0.0 | 0 | 1–100 | |

### Punting

| Last Name | No | Avg |
|---|---|---|
| Davis | 54 | 45.8 |

### Kicking

| Last Name | XP | Att | % | FG | Att | % |
|---|---|---|---|---|---|---|
| Davis | 52 | 53 | 98 | 17 | 27 | 63 |

## MINNESOTA VIKINGS

### Rushing

| Last Name | No. | Yds | Avg | TD |
|---|---|---|---|---|
| Brown | 160 | 699 | 4.4 | 6 |
| Mason | 141 | 597 | 4.2 | 10 |
| Tarkenton | 56 | 356 | 6.4 | 1 |
| King | 72 | 356 | 4.9 | 3 |
| Barnes | 48 | 148 | 3.1 | 0 |
| Osborn | 20 | 106 | 5.3 | 2 |
| Vander Kelen | 4 | 13 | 3.3 | 0 |
| Young | 3 | 4 | 1.3 | 0 |
| Rentzel | 1 | −1 | −1.0 | 0 |

### Receiving

| Last Name | No. | Yds | Avg | TD |
|---|---|---|---|---|
| Flatley | 50 | 896 | 18 | 7 |
| Brown | 41 | 503 | 12 | 1 |
| Smith | 22 | 431 | 20 | 5 |
| Mason | 22 | 321 | 15 | 1 |
| Hall | 15 | 287 | 19 | 2 |
| Phillips | 15 | 185 | 12 | 1 |
| King | 12 | 96 | 8 | 1 |
| Bedsole | 8 | 123 | 15 | 3 |
| Barnes | 3 | 15 | 5 | 0 |
| Osborn | 1 | 4 | 4 | 0 |

### Punt Returns

| Last Name | No. | Yds | Avg | TD |
|---|---|---|---|---|
| Mason | 9 | 63 | 7 | 0 |
| Hall | 3 | 21 | 7 | 0 |
| Warwick | 1 | 10 | 10 | 1 |
| Rentzel | 4 | 9 | 2 | 0 |
| Young | 4 | 7 | 2 | 0 |
| James | 1 | 5 | 5 | 0 |

### Kickoff Returns

| Last Name | No. | Yds | Avg | TD |
|---|---|---|---|---|
| Rentzel | 23 | 602 | 26 | 1 |
| Osborn | 18 | 422 | 23 | 0 |
| James | 11 | 212 | 19 | 0 |
| Hall | 4 | 93 | 23 | 0 |
| Young | 4 | 78 | 20 | 0 |
| Mason | 3 | 66 | 22 | 0 |
| Barnes | 3 | 37 | 12 | 0 |
| King | 1 | 14 | 14 | 0 |

### Passing

| Last Name | Att | Comp | % | Yds | Yd/Att | TD | Int–% | RK |
|---|---|---|---|---|---|---|---|---|
| Tarkenton | 329 | 171 | 52 | 2609 | 7.9 | 19 | 11– 3 | 6 |
| Vander Kelen | 40 | 18 | 45 | 252 | 6.3 | 2 | 0– 0 | |
| Berry | 2 | 0 | 0 | 0 | 0.0 | 0 | 0– 0 | |
| Mason | 1 | 0 | 0 | 0 | 0.0 | 0 | 1–100 | |

### Punting

| Last Name | No | Avg |
|---|---|---|
| Walden | 51 | 42.1 |

### Kicking

| Last Name | XP | Att | % | FG | Att | % |
|---|---|---|---|---|---|---|
| Cox | 44 | 44 | 100 | 23 | 35 | 66 |

## DETROIT LIONS

### Rushing

| Last Name | No. | Yds | Avg | TD |
|---|---|---|---|---|
| Marsh | 131 | 495 | 3.8 | 6 |
| Pietrosante | 107 | 374 | 3.5 | 1 |
| Looney | 114 | 356 | 3.1 | 5 |
| Watkins | 29 | 95 | 3.3 | 0 |
| Nowatzke | 27 | 73 | 2.7 | 1 |
| Felts | 22 | 58 | 2.6 | 0 |
| Plum | 21 | 37 | 1.8 | 3 |
| Sanders | 1 | 2 | 2.0 | 0 |
| Studstill | 1 | −4 | −4.0 | 0 |
| Izo | 1 | −5 | −5.0 | 0 |
| Barr | 1 | −12 | −12.0 | 0 |

### Receiving

| Last Name | No. | Yds | Avg | TD |
|---|---|---|---|---|
| Studstill | 28 | 389 | 14 | 3 |
| Barr | 24 | 433 | 18 | 3 |
| Cogdill | 20 | 247 | 12 | 0 |
| Kramer | 18 | 206 | 11 | 1 |
| Pietrosante | 18 | 163 | 9 | 0 |
| Marsh | 17 | 159 | 9 | 2 |
| Gibbons | 12 | 111 | 9 | 2 |
| Looney | 12 | 109 | 9 | 1 |
| Henderson | 8 | 140 | 18 | 1 |
| Watkins | 5 | 53 | 11 | 0 |
| Nowatzke | 5 | 45 | 9 | 1 |
| Felts | 3 | 28 | 9 | 0 |

### Punt Returns

| Last Name | No. | Yds | Avg | TD |
|---|---|---|---|---|
| Watkins | 23 | 234 | 10 | 0 |
| Vaughn | 2 | 50 | 25 | 0 |
| Studstill | 5 | 47 | 9 | 0 |
| Felts | 3 | 27 | 9 | 0 |

### Kickoff Returns

| Last Name | No. | Yds | Avg | TD |
|---|---|---|---|---|
| Watkins | 17 | 584 | 34 | 0 |
| Felts | 18 | 422 | 23 | 0 |
| Vaughn | 13 | 316 | 24 | 0 |
| Studstill | 10 | 257 | 26 | 0 |
| Nowatzke | 2 | 12 | 6 | 0 |
| Lucci | 1 | 0 | 0 | 0 |

### Passing

| Last Name | Att | Comp | % | Yds | Yd/Att | TD | Int–% | RK |
|---|---|---|---|---|---|---|---|---|
| Plum | 308 | 143 | 46 | 1710 | 5.6 | 12 | 19– 6 | 14 |
| Izo | 59 | 24 | 41 | 357 | 6.1 | 2 | 6– 10 | |
| Myers | 5 | 3 | 60 | 16 | 3.2 | 0 | 1– 20 | |
| Felts | 1 | 0 | 0 | 0 | 0.0 | 0 | 0– 0 | |
| Marsh | 1 | 0 | 0 | 0 | 0.0 | 0 | 0– 0 | |

### Punting

| Last Name | No | Avg |
|---|---|---|
| Studstill | 78 | 42.8 |

### Kicking

| Last Name | XP | Att | % | FG | Att | % |
|---|---|---|---|---|---|---|
| Walker | 33 | 33 | 100 | 8 | 22 | 36 |

## LOS ANGELES RAMS

### Rushing

| Last Name | No. | Yds | Avg | TD |
|---|---|---|---|---|
| Bass | 121 | 549 | 4.5 | 2 |
| Josephson | 71 | 225 | 3.2 | 0 |
| Wilson | 60 | 189 | 3.2 | 1 |
| Munson | 26 | 157 | 6.0 | 1 |
| W. Brown | 44 | 133 | 3.0 | 0 |
| Baker | 25 | 82 | 3.3 | 1 |
| Gabriel | 23 | 79 | 3.4 | 2 |
| Stiger | 14 | 62 | 4.4 | 0 |
| Meador | 2 | 35 | 17.5 | 1 |
| Williams | 3 | 3 | 1.0 | 0 |

### Receiving

| Last Name | No. | Yds | Avg | TD |
|---|---|---|---|---|
| McDonald | 67 | 1036 | 15 | 9 |
| McKeever | 44 | 542 | 12 | 4 |
| Snow | 38 | 559 | 15 | 3 |
| Baker | 22 | 210 | 10 | 2 |
| Bass | 21 | 230 | 11 | 2 |
| Josephson | 18 | 169 | 9 | 0 |
| Wilson | 9 | 110 | 12 | 0 |
| Truax | 6 | 108 | 18 | 1 |
| W. Brown | 4 | 91 | 23 | 1 |
| Stiger | 1 | 9 | 9 | 0 |
| Heckard | 1 | 4 | 4 | 0 |

### Punt Returns

| Last Name | No. | Yds | Avg | TD |
|---|---|---|---|---|
| Stiger | 16 | 120 | 8 | 0 |
| W. Brown | 9 | 63 | 7 | 0 |
| B. Smith | 10 | 56 | 6 | 0 |
| Bass | 1 | 0 | 0 | 0 |

### Kickoff Returns

| Last Name | No. | Yds | Avg | TD |
|---|---|---|---|---|
| W. Brown | 24 | 615 | 26 | 0 |
| B. Smith | 18 | 475 | 26 | 0 |
| Williams | 9 | 213 | 24 | 0 |
| Wilson | 3 | 66 | 22 | 0 |
| Stiger | 2 | 28 | 14 | 0 |

### Passing

| Last Name | Att | Comp | % | Yds | Yd/Att | TD | Int–% | RK |
|---|---|---|---|---|---|---|---|---|
| Munson | 267 | 144 | 54 | 1701 | 6.4 | 10 | 14– 5 | 13 |
| Gabriel | 173 | 83 | 48 | 1321 | 7.6 | 5 | 5– 3 | 9 |
| Josephson | 2 | 1 | 50 | 15 | 7.5 | 1 | 0– 0 | |
| Baker | 1 | 1 | 100 | 14 | 14.0 | 0 | 0– 0 | |
| Meador | 1 | 0 | 0 | 0 | 0.0 | 0 | 0– 0 | |
| Wilson | 1 | 1 | 100 | 8 | 8.0 | 0 | 0– 0 | |

### Punting

| Last Name | No | Avg |
|---|---|---|
| Lothridge | 42 | 38.5 |
| Kilgore | 24 | 41.6 |

### Kicking

| Last Name | XP | Att | % | FG | Att | % |
|---|---|---|---|---|---|---|
| Gossett | 30 | 32 | 94 | 15 | 26 | 58 |

# 1965 A.F.L. Sonny and Joe and John

After years in show business, New York Jet owner Sonny Werblin was a firm believer in the star system, of the gate pull of a big-name star. Werblin set out with checkbook in hand and bagged two of college football's biggest names, Alabama's Joe Namath and Notre Dame's John Huarte, with astronomical contracts that dwarfed the pacts of even the biggest veteran stars. Some people talked about the two fine young quarterbacks Werblin had signed, some talked about the misplaced values of a society that rewarded football players with small fortunes while grossly underpaying schoolteachers, but the important thing was that they talked. They talked about Joe Namath, they talked about the New York Jets, and they talked about the AFL. They stopped talking about whether the AFL would survive; they talked more now of when the leagues would be on a par.

When the league schedule started, a lot of those talking people came out to the games. Opening day in Houston saw a crowd of 52,680 turn out to see the lowly Oilers beat the Jets, with Joe Namath glued to the bench all afternoon. One week later, 53,658 fans filled Shea Stadium in New York to welcome Namath to the big city. Namath's development into a fine passer by mid-season furthered his publicity value and made Werblin's move look like a stroke of genius.

The league was feeling confident enough to vote for expansion in 1966, setting up a new team in Miami, which had flopped as a pro-football town in 1946 but was now a fast-growing metropolis. Only a few years ago, the league had been more worried about franchises folding than in creating new outposts for the AFL.

## EASTERN DIVISION

**Buffalo Bills**—The trade of Cookie Gilchrist to Denver took most of the punch out of the running game, and injuries to Elbert Dubenion and Glenn Bass robbed the team of its starting wide receivers, but the Bills coasted to another Eastern title on a stone-wall defense and Pete Gogolak's strong right leg. Anonymous people manned the defense, but although Ron McDole, Tom Day, Tom Sestak, Jim Dunaway, Mike Stratton, Harry Jacobs, John Tracey, Butch Byrd, Hagood Clarke, George Saimes, and Charley Warner were short on reputation as individuals, respect for them as a unit was universal. The offense began with a strong line but lacked the backs and ends to take full advantage of the blocking. Gilchrist had been dealt off because of recurring feuds with coach Lou Saban, but replacement Billy Joe was no match for Cookie as a runner, receiver, or blocker. The other runners—Wray Carlton, Bobby Smith, and Donnie Stone—were pedestrian pluggers. With Dubenion and Bass sidelined, journeymen Bo Roberson and Charley Ferguson filled the wide receiver spots, but quarterback Jack Kemp orchestrated this collection of odds and ends into a steady unit which headed for their third straight championship game in Lou Saban's last year before returning to college coaching.

**New York Jets**—Owner Sonny Werblin set the football world on its ear by signing the two most glamorous rookie quarterbacks to expensive contracts, Joe Namath to a $400,000 pact and Heisman Trophy winner John Huarte to a $200,000 pact. Huarte missed training camp because of the College All-Star Game and spent the year on the taxi squad, but Namath made a big splash right from the start. After sitting out the first few games, Namath took over the quarterback job and showed a quick release that triggered a strong passing arm. In addition, his sudden affluence and swinging bachelor's lifestyle made the newspapers constantly about him and proved to be a bonanza of publicity for the Jets and the AFL. But if Namath and Huarte attracted all the attention, other rookies made the Jets a stronger club down the second half of the season. George Sauer, playing tight end out of necessity, middle linebacker Al Atkinson, defensive end Verlon Biggs, defensive tackle Jim Harris, and defensive backs Jim Hudson and Cornell Gordon all put in solid freshman years for the improved New Yorkers who won five of their last eight games.

**Boston Patriots**—Head coach Mike Holovak had never paid much attention to pre-season games, expecting his team to start playing for real once the starting bell rang. The Patriots lost all five of their exhibition games this year, but then kept losing right into October. Winless in the first seven games, the Pats made a comeback in the second half of the schedule, but their horrid start killed any chances of challenging Buffalo for first place. Holovak had never gone all out to sign prestigious college seniors, relying instead on veterans and rookies from small and local schools, and now this policy was showing up in the deterioration of the team. The defense, long the club's strong point, began to creak with age, while the offense suffered because of Babe Parilli's off season. The thirty-four-year-old Parilli gave up twenty-six interceptions, a sign that his arm was losing its old zip. The Pats did sign two big-name rookie runners, Jim Nance and Joe Bellino, but neither had a good freshman season. Nance played overweight all year, while Bellino, making his pro debut after three years in the Navy, did not have the size to be a consistent ground-gainer.

**Houston Oilers**—With the exception of W. K. Hicks, the Oilers were using the same men in the defensive secondary that staffed the championship Houston teams in the early years of the AFL. Enemy passers burned the Oiler secondary for twenty-seven touchdown passes, a sign of the improvement in AFL play and of the lack of foresight in the Houston management. With the worst defense in the league, head coach Hugh Taylor was fortunate to pick up four wins in his year at the helm. The offense was in no shape to carry the team, as it had weaknesses in all sectors. The offensive line needed help, and the receiving fell off because of Charley Hennigan's bad knee. Halfback Sid Blanks missed the season with a knee injury, and fullback Charley Tolar had slowed up considerably, throwing the brunt of the running chores on 185-pound Ode Burrell. At quarterback, thirty-seven-year-old George Blanda was plagued with a flood of interceptions, but young Don Trull still saw little action. But even with all their problems, the Oilers did put together some good games, like a 19-17 upset of Buffalo and a 31-10 pasting of Boston.

## WESTERN DIVISION

**San Diego Chargers**—Although the San Diego defense ranked with Buffalo's at the top of the league, the offense still won most of the headlines for the Chargers. The versatile attack boasted of stars in all quarters. Linemen Ron Mix and Walt Sweeney were among the AFL's best, and flanker Lance Alworth gained a phenomenal 1,602 yards with a variety of leaping, diving, and streaking catches which netted him fourteen touchdowns. Quarterback John Hadl developed into a top-flight pro as a passer and play-caller. Halfback Paul Lowe hustled his way to a new league rushing record of 1,121 yards, and Keith Lincoln combined with rookie Gene Foster to provide punch at the fullback slot. But the San Diego defense bailed out the offense on its rare off days, as in a 13-13 tie with Boston and a 10-10 tie with the Chiefs. Earl Faison and Ernie Ladd still stacked up runners and passers, but both star linemen expressed dissatisfaction with the organization and were playing out their option. Fitting right in with the veterans were several newcomers to the unit, rookies Rick Redman, Steve DeLong, Dick Degan, and Speedy Duncan—enough to give the Chargers their fifth Western crown in six years.

**Oakland Raiders**—Head coach and general manager Al Davis kept building the Raiders with top rookie talent. This year's batch of Oakland freshmen included wide receiver Fred Biletnikoff, cornerback Kent McCloughan, linebacker Gus Otto, and offensive tackles Bob Svihus and Harry Schuh. The Raiders now had sufficient depth to compensate for injuries, as Tom Flores and Dick Wood handled the quarterbacking in fine fashion with Cotton Davidson out for most of the year with an injury. The offense, with Clem Daniels and Art Powell the main guns, performed quite well, and the defense had two solid rookie starters in Otto and McCloughan and an All-Pro cornerback in Dave Grayson. An inability to beat San Diego and Buffalo killed the Oakland title chances, as the Raiders dropped all four of their contests with the divisional champions-to-be.

**Kansas City Chiefs**—With one of the deepest rosters in pro football, the Chiefs seemed to be playing in the shadow of an evil star. Since the team moved to Kansas City in 1963, serious injury or death struck four Chief players. Stone Johnson suffered a fatal neck injury in a 1963 pre-season game, Ed Budde almost died from a blow on the head when attacked on the street in 1964, Fred Arbanas lost most of the vision in his left eye from an off-the-field altercation, and fullback Mack Lee Hill died on the operating table of complications following knee surgery midway through this season. On the field, the Chiefs had a habit of winning some games in impressive fashion, then going flat and losing to a weaker team. The Kansas City offense still was a top-flight unit, with the receiving strengthened by rookie Otis Taylor and the running game weakened by the trade of Abner Haynes and the tragic death of Hill. The defense had no problems with men like Jerry Mays, Buck Buchanan, E. J. Holub, Sherrill Headrick, Bobby Bell, Fred Williamson, and Johnny Robinson in the lineup.

**Denver Broncos**—For the first time in their history, the Broncos relied on the running game as their main offensive threat. Trades brought fullback Cookie Gilchrist and halfback Abner Haynes, both legendary AFL runners, to Denver during the summer, and while Gilchrist still bulled over tackles at peak form, Haynes lost his starting job to rookie Wendell Hayes. At any rate, the depth in the running-back slots kept the attack alive despite severe uncertainty at quarterback. Coach Mac Speedie used John McCormick, Mickey Slaughter, and Jacky Lee in the passer's spot and was satisfied with none of them. Lionel Taylor got open for enough passes from the three quarterbacks to lead the league in receiving, his fifth pass-catching title in the AFL's six years of play, but none of the other receivers on the team made much of a dent on enemy defenses.

**FINAL TEAM STATISTICS**

## OFFENSE

| Category | BOSTON | BUFFALO | DENVER | HOUSTON | K. CITY | NEW YORK | OAKLAND | SAN DIEGO |
|---|---|---|---|---|---|---|---|---|
| **FIRST DOWNS:** | | | | | | | | |
| Total | 214 | 206 | 255 | 227 | 232 | 213 | 225 | 268 |
| by Rushing | 55 | 69 | 111 | 63 | 101 | 77 | 72 | 127 |
| by Passing | 130 | 119 | 117 | 140 | 121 | 121 | 134 | 127 |
| by Penalty | 29 | 18 | 27 | 24 | 10 | 15 | 19 | 14 |
| **RUSHING:** | | | | | | | | |
| Number | 373 | 392 | 453 | 324 | 418 | 367 | 390 | 486 |
| Yards | 1117 | 1288 | 1829 | 1175 | 1752 | 1476 | 1538 | 1998 |
| Average Yards | 3.0 | 3.3 | 4.0 | 3.6 | 4.2 | 4.0 | 3.9 | 4.1 |
| Touchdowns | 8 | 16 | 14 | 8 | 15 | 11 | 8 | 13 |
| **PASSING:** | | | | | | | | |
| Attempts | 473 | 461 | 482 | 550 | 395 | 459 | 431 | 401 |
| Completions | 193 | 208 | 222 | 224 | 199 | 209 | 195 | 203 |
| Completion Percentage | 40.8 | 45.1 | 46.1 | 40.7 | 50.4 | 45.5 | 45.2 | 50.6 |
| Passing Yards | 2854 | 2744 | 2848 | 3070 | 2894 | 2751 | 2713 | 3379 |
| Average Yards Per Attempt | 6.0 | 6.0 | 5.9 | 5.6 | 7.3 | 6.0 | 6.3 | 8.4 |
| Average Yards Per Completion | 14.8 | 13.2 | 12.8 | 13.7 | 14.5 | 13.2 | 13.9 | 16.6 |
| Times Tackled Attempting to Pass | 37 | 29 | 24 | 31 | 37 | 17 | 33 | 27 |
| Yards Lost Attempting to Pass | 347 | 283 | 208 | 257 | 351 | 162 | 253 | 276 |
| Net Yards | 2507 | 2461 | 2640 | 2813 | 2543 | 2589 | 2460 | 3103 |
| Touchdowns | 19 | 13 | 18 | 25 | 22 | 21 | 22 | 23 |
| Interceptions | 29 | 24 | 30 | 35 | 20 | 22 | 17 | 26 |
| Percent Intercepted | 6.1 | 5.2 | 6.2 | 6.4 | 5.1 | 4.8 | 3.9 | 6.5 |
| **PUNTING:** | | | | | | | | |
| Number | 82 | 80 | 68 | 85 | 72 | 72 | 75 | 70 |
| Average Distance | 40.1 | 43.0 | 42.3 | 43.7 | 44.6 | 45.3 | 41.1 | 40.0 |
| **PUNT RETURNS:** | | | | | | | | |
| Number | 27 | 36 | 37 | 28 | 38 | 29 | 34 | 38 |
| Yards | 152 | 389 | 355 | 189 | 419 | 166 | 365 | 508 |
| Average Yards | 5.6 | 10.8 | 9.6 | 6.8 | 11.0 | 5.7 | 10.7 | 13.4 |
| Touchdowns | 0 | 0 | 1 | 0 | 1 | 0 | 1 | 2 |
| **KICKOFF RETURNS:** | | | | | | | | |
| Number | 60 | 45 | 71 | 77 | 48 | 54 | 46 | 50 |
| Yards | 1191 | 1022 | 1731 | 1669 | 1080 | 1107 | 990 | 1028 |
| Average Yards | 19.9 | 22.7 | 24.4 | 21.7 | 22.5 | 20.5 | 21.5 | 20.6 |
| Touchdowns | 0 | 2 | 1 | 0 | 0 | 0 | 0 | 0 |
| **INTERCEPTION RETURNS:** | | | | | | | | |
| Number | 21 | 32 | 25 | 27 | 20 | 26 | 24 | 28 |
| Yards | 233 | 393 | 465 | 416 | 342 | 235 | 482 | 377 |
| Average Yards | 11.1 | 12.3 | 18.6 | 15.4 | 17.1 | 9.0 | 20.1 | 13.5 |
| Touchdowns | 0 | 1 | 3 | 0 | 2 | 0 | 4 | 3 |
| **PENALTIES:** | | | | | | | | |
| Number | 58 | 78 | 69 | 76 | 70 | 58 | 69 | 84 |
| Yards | 537 | 685 | 750 | 856 | 744 | 684 | 661 | 929 |
| **FUMBLES:** | | | | | | | | |
| Number | 24 | 28 | 29 | 23 | 34 | 27 | 17 | 22 |
| Number Lost | 12 | 14 | 16 | 11 | 20 | 18 | 9 | 13 |
| **POINTS:** | | | | | | | | |
| Total | 244 | 313 | 303 | 298 | 322 | 285 | 298 | 340 |
| PAT (Kick) Attempts | 27 | 31 | 32 | 34 | 37 | 31 | 35 | 40 |
| PAT (Kick) Made | 27 | 31 | 32 | 34 | 37 | 31 | 35 | 40 |
| PAT (Rush or Pass) Attempts | 0 | 2 | 6 | 3 | 3 | 1 | 0 | 1 |
| PAT (Rush or Pass) Made | 0 | 0 | 2 | 2 | 3 | 1 | 0 | 0 |
| FG Attempts | 27 | 46 | 29 | 23 | 30 | 34 | 34 | 30 |
| FG Made | 17 | 28 | 13 | 12 | 13 | 20 | 17 | 18 |
| Percent FG Made | 63.0 | 60.9 | 44.8 | 52.2 | 43.3 | 58.8 | 50.0 | 60.0 |
| Safeties | 2 | 0 | 1 | 0 | 0 | 1 | 0 | 0 |

## DEFENSE

| Category | BOSTON | BUFFALO | DENVER | HOUSTON | K. CITY | NEW YORK | OAKLAND | SAN DIEGO |
|---|---|---|---|---|---|---|---|---|
| **FIRST DOWNS:** | | | | | | | | |
| Total | 232 | 226 | 244 | 271 | 207 | 235 | 235 | 190 |
| by Rushing | 92 | 65 | 87 | 132 | 69 | 85 | 90 | 55 |
| by Passing | 127 | 141 | 138 | 111 | 113 | 136 | 125 | 118 |
| by Penalty | 13 | 20 | 19 | 28 | 25 | 14 | 20 | 17 |
| **RUSHING:** | | | | | | | | |
| Number | 425 | 360 | 384 | 508 | 381 | 432 | 407 | 306 |
| Yards | 1531 | 1114 | 1337 | 2683 | 1376 | 1551 | 1487 | 1094 |
| Average Yards | 3.6 | 3.1 | 3.5 | 5.3 | 3.6 | 3.6 | 3.7 | 3.6 |
| Touchdowns | 10 | 5 | 24 | 17 | 12 | 10 | 10 | 7 |
| **PASSING:** | | | | | | | | |
| Attempts | 431 | 502 | 440 | 416 | 451 | 472 | 466 | 474 |
| Completions | 206 | 227 | 202 | 177 | 216 | 220 | 199 | 206 |
| Completion Percentage | 47.8 | 45.2 | 45.9 | 42.5 | 47.9 | 46.6 | 42.7 | 43.5 |
| Passing Yards | 2891 | 3416 | 3265 | 2643 | 2711 | 2900 | 2947 | 2480 |
| Average Yards Per Attempt | 6.7 | 6.8 | 7.4 | 6.4 | 6.0 | 6.1 | 6.3 | 5.2 |
| Average Yards Per Completion | 14.0 | 15.0 | 16.2 | 14.9 | 12.6 | 13.2 | 14.8 | 12.0 |
| Times Tackled Attempting to Pass | 30 | 28 | 26 | 22 | 39 | 22 | 30 | 38 |
| Yards Lost Attempting to Pass | 291 | 246 | 305 | 173 | 326 | 238 | 246 | 312 |
| Net Yards | 2600 | 3170 | 2960 | 2470 | 2385 | 2662 | 2701 | 2168 |
| Touchdowns | 17 | 19 | 23 | 27 | 18 | 22 | 20 | 17 |
| Interceptions | 21 | 32 | 25 | 27 | 20 | 26 | 24 | 28 |
| Percent Intercepted | 4.9 | 6.4 | 5.7 | 6.5 | 4.4 | 5.5 | 5.2 | 5.9 |
| **PUNTING:** | | | | | | | | |
| Number | 78 | 76 | 73 | 59 | 83 | 78 | 77 | 80 |
| Average Distance | 42.1 | 40.2 | 45.9 | 42.5 | 44.1 | 39.8 | 42.1 | 43.4 |
| **PUNT RETURNS:** | | | | | | | | |
| Number | 33 | 30 | 26 | 48 | 29 | 40 | 34 | 27 |
| Yards | 232 | 222 | 343 | 494 | 401 | 352 | 257 | 242 |
| Average Yards | 7.0 | 7.4 | 13.2 | 10.3 | 13.8 | 8.8 | 7.6 | 9.0 |
| Touchdowns | 0 | 0 | 1 | 2 | 2 | 0 | 0 | 0 |
| **KICKOFF RETURNS:** | | | | | | | | |
| Number | 41 | 60 | 58 | 48 | 56 | 60 | 62 | 66 |
| Yards | 946 | 1449 | 1197 | 995 | 1173 | 1421 | 1227 | 1410 |
| Average Yards | 23.1 | 24.2 | 20.6 | 20.7 | 20.9 | 23.7 | 19.8 | 21.4 |
| Touchdowns | 1 | 0 | 0 | 0 | 0 | 0 | 0 | 0 |
| **INTERCEPTION RETURNS:** | | | | | | | | |
| Number | 29 | 24 | 30 | 35 | 20 | 22 | 17 | 26 |
| Yards | 365 | 467 | 426 | 471 | 238 | 339 | 186 | 451 |
| Average Yards | 12.6 | 19.5 | 14.2 | 13.5 | 11.9 | 15.4 | 10.9 | 17.3 |
| Touchdowns | 4 | 1 | 2 | 3 | 0 | 2 | 0 | 1 |
| **PENALTIES:** | | | | | | | | |
| Number | 72 | 69 | 86 | 67 | 60 | 77 | 77 | 62 |
| Yards | 658 | 832 | 836 | 701 | 623 | 865 | 666 | 665 |
| **FUMBLES:** | | | | | | | | |
| Number | 17 | 33 | 27 | 31 | 24 | 25 | 23 | 24 |
| Number Lost | 9 | 25 | 14 | 13 | 13 | 14 | 14 | 13 |
| **POINTS:** | | | | | | | | |
| Total | 302 | 226 | 392 | 429 | 285 | 303 | 239 | 227 |
| PAT (Kick) Attempts | 28 | 21 | 50 | 48 | 33 | 33 | 29 | 25 |
| PAT (Kick) Made | 28 | 21 | 50 | 48 | 33 | 33 | 29 | 25 |
| PAT (Rush or Pass) Attempts | 6 | 4 | 0 | 2 | 1 | 2 | 1 | 0 |
| PAT (Rush or Pass) Made | 2 | 4 | 0 | 2 | 0 | 0 | 0 | 0 |
| FG Attempts | 40 | 30 | 24 | 43 | 28 | 34 | 20 | 34 |
| FG Made | 22 | 15 | 14 | 25 | 16 | 20 | 10 | 16 |
| Percent FG Made | 55.0 | 50.0 | 58.3 | 58.1 | 57.1 | 58.8 | 50.0 | 47.1 |
| Safeties | 0 | 1 | 0 | 1 | 0 | 0 | 0 | 2 |

## 1965 AFL CHAMPIONSHIP GAME

December 26, at San Diego
(Attendance 30,361)

### Stubbornly Brilliant

The San Diego weather was mild compared with last year's chill in Buffalo, but the Bills' defense played the same hard-hitting game and again would up as victors. Buffalo's strong front four and tight pass defense completely handcuffed the favored Chargers, as they never could get past the Buffalo 24-yard line. Through the first quarter and the first ten minutes of the second quarter, both defenses kept the scoreboard empty, but the Bills scored on a Jack Kemp-to-Ernie Warlick pass with five minutes left before intermission. The Chargers then punted the ball back to the Bills, and Butch Byrd returned the kick 74 yards down the sideline for another Buffalo score. The two quick touchdowns gave the Bills a 14-0 lead to take into the clubhouse at halftime, while the Chargers had to ponder on the goose egg on their side of the scoreboard. Going back to last year's championship game, the Chargers now were scoreless in their last five quarters against the Buffalo defense. The second half proved no more pleasant for the Chargers, as John Hadl, Keith Lincoln, Paul Lowe, and Lance Alworth could not get the ball across the Buffalo goal line. Jack Kemp, meanwhile, guided the Bills' offense steadily against the stubborn San Diego defense. Pete Gogolak booted a pair of field goals in the third quarter to give the Bills some breathing room, and his 32-yarder in the fourth quarter ran the final score to 23-0. Quarterback Kemp, a former Charger, won the game MVP award for his surgical precision in running the attack.

### SCORING

| | | | | | |
|---|---|---|---|---|---|
| SAN DIEGO | 0 | 0 | 0 | 0 — | 0 |
| BUFFALO | 0 | 14 | 6 | 3 — | 23 |

Second Quarter
Buf.　Warlick, 18 yard pass from Kemp
　　　PAT—Gogolak (kick)
Buf.　Byrd, 74 yard punt return
　　　PAT—Gogolak (kick)
Third Quarter
Buf.　Gogolak, 11 yard field goal
Buf.　Gogolak, 39 yard field goal
Fourth Quarter
Buf.　Gogolak, 32 yard field goal

### TEAM STATISTICS

| S.D. | | BUF. |
|---|---|---|
| 12 | First Downs—Total | 23 |
| 5 | First Downs—Rushing | 13 |
| 7 | First Downs—Passing | 9 |
| 0 | First Downs—Penalty | 1 |
| 7 | Punts—Number | 4 |
| 40.7 | Punts—Average Distance | 46.3 |
| 3 | Penalties—Number | 2 |
| 41 | Yards—Penalized | 21 |
| 2 | Missed Field Goals | 2 |

### INDIVIDUAL STATISTICS

**SAN DIEGO** / **BUFFALO**

#### RUSHING

| SAN DIEGO | No. | Yds. | Avg. | BUFFALO | No. | Yds. | Avg. |
|---|---|---|---|---|---|---|---|
| Lowe | 12 | 57 | 4.8 | Carlton | 16 | 63 | 3.9 |
| Hadl | 8 | 24 | 3.0 | Joe | 16 | 35 | 2.2 |
| Lincoln | 4 | 16 | 4.0 | Stone | 3 | 5 | 1.7 |
| Foster | 2 | 9 | 4.5 | Smith | 1 | 5 | 5.0 |
| Breaux | 1 | -2 | -2.0 | | 36 | 108 | 3.0 |
| | 27 | 104 | 3.9 | | | | |

#### RECEIVING

| SAN DIEGO | No. | Yds. | Avg. | BUFFALO | No. | Yds. | Avg. |
|---|---|---|---|---|---|---|---|
| Alworth | 4 | 82 | 20.5 | Roberson | 3 | 88 | 29.3 |
| Lowe | 3 | 3 | 1.0 | Warlick | 3 | 35 | 11.7 |
| Norton | 1 | 35 | 35.0 | Costa | 2 | 32 | 16.0 |
| Farr | 1 | 24 | 24.0 | Tracy | 1 | 12 | 12.0 |
| MacKinnon | 1 | 10 | 10.0 | | 9 | 167 | 18.6 |
| Lincoln | 1 | 7 | 7.0 | | | | |
| Kocourek | 1 | 3 | 3.0 | | | | |
| | 12 | 164 | 13.7 | | | | |

#### PUNT RETURNS

| SAN DIEGO | No. | Yds. | Avg. | BUFFALO | No. | Yds. | Avg. |
|---|---|---|---|---|---|---|---|
| Duncan | 1 | 12 | 12.0 | Byrd | 3 | 87 | 29.0 |

#### KICKOFF RETURNS

| SAN DIEGO | No. | Yds. | Avg. | BUFFALO | No. | Yds. | Avg. |
|---|---|---|---|---|---|---|---|
| Duncan | 2 | 62 | 31.0 | Warner | 1 | 17 | 17.0 |
| Farr | 1 | 35 | 35.0 | | | | |
| | 3 | 97 | 32.3 | | | | |

#### INTERCEPTION RETURNS

| SAN DIEGO | No. | Yds. | Avg. | BUFFALO | No. | Yds. | Avg. |
|---|---|---|---|---|---|---|---|
| Warren | 1 | 0 | 0.0 | Byrd | 1 | 24 | 24.0 |
| | | | | Jacobs | 1 | 12 | 12.0 |
| | | | | | 2 | 36 | 18.0 |

#### PASSING

| SAN DIEGO | Att. | Comp. | Comp. Pct. | Yds. | Int. | Yds/Att. | Yds/Comp. | Yards Lost Tackled |
|---|---|---|---|---|---|---|---|---|
| Hadl | 23 | 11 | 47.8 | 140 | 1 | 6.1 | 12.7 | |
| Breaux | 2 | 1 | 50.0 | 24 | 0 | 12.0 | 24.0 | |
| | 25 | 12 | 48.0 | 164 | 2 | 6.6 | 13.7 | 45 |
| **BUFFALO** | | | | | | | | |
| Kemp | 19 | 8 | 42.1 | 155 | 1 | 8.2 | 19.4 | |
| Lamonica | 1 | 1 | 100.0 | 12 | 0 | 12.0 | 12.0 | |
| | 20 | 9 | 45.0 | 167 | 1 | 8.4 | 18.6 | 15 |

## BUFFALO BILLS 10-3-1 Lou Saban

**Scores of Each Game**

| | | |
|---|---|---|
| 24 | BOSTON | 7 |
| 30 | Denver | 15 |
| 33 | NEW YORK | 21 |
| 17 | OAKLAND | 12 |
| 3 | SAN DIEGO | 34 |
| 23 | Kansas City | 7 |
| 31 | DENVER | 13 |
| 17 | HOUSTON | 19 |
| 23 | Boston | 7 |
| 17 | Oakland | 14 |
| 20 | San Diego | 20 |
| 29 | Houston | 18 |
| 34 | KANSAS CITY | 25 |
| 12 | New York | 14 |

| Use Name | Pos. | Hgt | Wgt | Age | Int | Pts |
|---|---|---|---|---|---|---|
| Stew Barber | OT | 6'3" | 250 | 26 | | |
| Dick Hudson | OT | 6'4" | 272 | 25 | | |
| Joe O'Donnell | OT | 6'2" | 246 | 23 | | |
| Al Bemiller | OG | 6'3" | 260 | 26 | | |
| George Flint | OG | 6'4" | 244 | 27 | | |
| Billy Shaw | OG | 6'3" | 248 | 25 | | |
| Dave Behrman | C | 6'5" | 260 | 23 | | |
| Tom Day | DE | 6'2" | 250 | 30 | 1 | |
| Ron McDole | DE | 6'3" | 264 | 25 | 1 | |
| Jim Dunaway | DT | 6'4" | 276 | 23 | | |
| Tom Keating | DT | 6'3" | 242 | 22 | | |
| Dudley Meredith | DT | 6'4" | 275 | 30 | | |
| Henry Schmidt | DT | 6'4" | 270 | 28 | | |
| Tom Sestak | OT-DT | 6'5" | 270 | 29 | | |

| Use Name | Pos. | Hgt | Wgt | Age | Int | Pts |
|---|---|---|---|---|---|---|
| Harry Jacobs | LB | 6'2" | 225 | 28 | 1 | |
| Bill Laskey | LB | 6'2" | 250 | 22 | | |
| Paul Maguire | LB | 6' | 220 | 27 | | |
| Marty Schottenheimer | LB | 6'3" | 225 | 22 | | |
| Mike Stratton | OE-LB | 6'3" | 240 | 23 | 2 | |
| John Tracey | OE-LB | 6'3" | 225 | 32 | 1 | |
| Butch Byrd | DB | 6' | 211 | 23 | 5 | |
| Hagood Clarke | DB | 6' | 188 | 23 | 7 | |
| Booker Edgerson | DB | 5'10" | 180 | 26 | 5 | |
| Tom Janik | DB | 6'3" | 200 | 24 | | |
| George Saimes | DB | 5'10" | 195 | 23 | 4 | 6 |
| Gene Sykes | DB | 6'1" | 195 | 24 | | |
| Charley Warner | HB-DB | 5'11" | 180 | 25 | 5 | 24 |

| Use Name | Pos. | Hgt | Wgt | Age | Int | Pts |
|---|---|---|---|---|---|---|
| Jack Kemp | QB | 6'1" | 200 | 31 | | 24 |
| Daryle Lamonica | QB | 6'2" | 215 | 24 | | 6 |
| Joe Auer | HB | 6'1" | 205 | 23 | | |
| Wray Carlton | HB | 6'2" | 216 | 27 | | 42 |
| Bobby Smith | HB | 6' | 203 | 24 | | 6 |
| Billy Joe | FB | 6'2" | 250 | 24 | | 36 |
| Donnie Stone | FB | 6'2" | 205 | 28 | | |
| Elbert Dubenion | FL | 6' | 187 | 30 | | 6 |
| Floyd Hudlow | FL | 5'11" | 185 | 21 | | |
| Bo Roberson (from OAK) | FL | 6'1" | 190 | 30 | | 18 |
| Ed Rutkowski | FL | 6'1" | 208 | 24 | | 6 |
| Glenn Bass | OE | 6'2" | 206 | 26 | | 6 |
| Paul Costa | OE | 6'4" | 240 | 23 | | |
| Charley Ferguson | OE | 6'5" | 215 | 25 | | 12 |
| Bill Groman | OE | 6' | 195 | 29 | | |
| Pete Mills | OE | 5'11" | 180 | 22 | | |
| Ernie Warlick | OE | 6'4" | 235 | 33 | | 6 |
| Pete Gogolak | K | 6'2" | 200 | 23 | | 115 |

## NEW YORK JETS 5-8-1 Weeb Ewbank

**Scores of Each Game**

| | | |
|---|---|---|
| 21 | Houston | 27 |
| 10 | KANSAS CITY | 14 |
| 21 | Buffalo | 33 |
| 13 | Denver | 16 |
| 24 | OAKLAND | 24 |
| 9 | SAN DIEGO | 34 |
| 45 | DENVER | 10 |
| 13 | Kansas City | 10 |
| 30 | Boston | 20 |
| 41 | HOUSTON | 14 |
| 23 | BOSTON | 27 |
| 7 | San Diego | 38 |
| 14 | Oakland | 24 |
| 14 | BUFFALO | 12 |

| Use Name | Pos. | Hgt | Wgt | Age | Int | Pts |
|---|---|---|---|---|---|---|
| Nick DeFelice | OT | 6'3" | 250 | 25 | | |
| Winston Hill | OT | 6'4" | 275 | 23 | | |
| Sherman Plunkett | OT | 6'4" | 295 | 31 | | |
| Sam DeLuca | OG | 6'2" | 250 | 29 | | |
| Dan Ficca | OG | 6'1" | 250 | 26 | | |
| Dave Herman | OG | 6'2" | 255 | 23 | | |
| Pete Perreault | OG | 6'2" | 245 | 26 | | |
| Mike Hudock | C | 6'2" | 245 | 30 | | |
| John Schmitt | C | 6'4" | 265 | 22 | | |
| Gerry Philbin | DE | 6'2" | 245 | 24 | | |
| Lavern Torczon | DE | 6'2" | 250 | 29 | | |
| Bert Wilder | DE | 6'3" | 245 | 25 | | |
| Verlon Biggs | DT-DE | 6'4" | 250 | 22 | 1 | |
| Jim Harris | DT | 6'4" | 265 | 21 | | |
| Paul Rochester | DT | 6'2" | 250 | 28 | | |
| Arnie Simkus | DT | 6'4" | 240 | 22 | | |

| Use Name | Pos. | Hgt | Wgt | Age | Int | Pts |
|---|---|---|---|---|---|---|
| Al Atkinson | LB | 6'1" | 225 | 22 | 1 | |
| Ralph Baker | LB | 6'3" | 235 | 23 | 2 | |
| Larry Grantham | LB | 6' | 212 | 28 | 1 | |
| Wahoo McDaniel | LB | 6' | 240 | 28 | 1 | |
| Jim O'Mahoney | LB | 6'1" | 233 | 24 | | |
| Ray Abbruzzese | DB | 6'1" | 200 | 27 | 2 | |
| Bill Baird | DB | 5'10" | 180 | 26 | 3 | |
| Cornell Gordon | DB | 6' | 185 | 24 | 2 | |
| Dainard Paulson | DB | 5'11" | 190 | 28 | 7 | |
| Bill Rademacher | DB | 6'1" | 190 | 23 | | |
| Clyde Washington | DB | 6' | 206 | 27 | | |
| Willie West | DB | 5'10" | 185 | 27 | 6 | |
| Jim Hudson | HB-DB | 6'2" | 210 | 22 | | |

| Use Name | Pos. | Hgt | Wgt | Age | Int | Pts |
|---|---|---|---|---|---|---|
| Joe Namath | QB | 6'2" | 194 | 22 | | |
| Mike Taliaferro | QB | 6'2" | 210 | 23 | | |
| Charley Browning | HB | 6' | 220 | 22 | | |
| Kern Carson (from SD) | HB | 6' | 202 | 23 | | 12 |
| Cosmo Iacavazzi | HB | 5'11" | 200 | 22 | | |
| Curley Johnson | HB | 6' | 215 | 30 | | 6 |
| Bill Mathis | HB | 6'1" | 220 | 26 | | 36 |
| Bob Schweickert | HB | 6'1" | 195 | 22 | | |
| Mark Smolinski | FB | 6' | 215 | 26 | | |
| Matt Snell | FB | 6'2" | 220 | 23 | | 24 |
| Jim Evans | FL | 6'1" | 190 | 25 | | |
| Don Maynard | FL | 6' | 185 | 29 | | 84 |
| Gene Heeter | OE | 6'4" | 235 | 24 | | |
| Dee Mackey | OE | 6'5" | 225 | 29 | | 8 |
| Jerry Robinson | OE | 5'11" | 200 | 26 | | |
| George Sauer | OE | 6'1" | 206 | 21 | | 12 |
| Bake Turner | OE | 6' | 185 | 25 | | 12 |
| Jim Turner | K | 6'2" | 205 | 24 | | 91 |

## BOSTON PATRIOTS 4-8-2 Mike Holovak

**Scores of Each Game**

| | | |
|---|---|---|
| 7 | Buffalo | 24 |
| 10 | Houston | 31 |
| 10 | DENVER | 27 |
| 17 | Kansas City | 27 |
| 10 | OAKLAND | 24 |
| 13 | SAN DIEGO | 13 |
| 21 | Oakland | 30 |
| 22 | San Diego | 6 |
| 7 | BUFFALO | 23 |
| 20 | NEW YORK | 30 |
| 10 | KANSAS CITY | 10 |
| 27 | New York | 23 |
| 28 | Denver | 20 |
| 42 | HOUSTON | 14 |

| Use Name | Pos. | Hgt | Wgt | Age | Int | Pts |
|---|---|---|---|---|---|---|
| Tom Neville | OT | 6'4" | 230 | 22 | | |
| Don Oakes | OT | 6'3" | 255 | 27 | | |
| Bob Schmidt | OT | 6'4" | 255 | 27 | | |
| Bob Yates | OT | 6'3" | 230 | 26 | | |
| Justin Canale | OG | 6'2" | 230 | 21 | | |
| Charley Long | OG | 6'3" | 250 | 27 | | |
| Billy Neighbors | OG | 5'11" | 240 | 25 | | |
| Jon Morris | C | 6'4" | 240 | 22 | | |
| Bob Dee | DE | 6'3" | 240 | 32 | | |
| Larry Eisenhauer | DE | 6'5" | 250 | 25 | | |
| Jim Hunt | DE | 5'11" | 245 | 26 | | |
| Len St. Jean | DE | 6'1" | 240 | 23 | | |
| Bill Dawson | OE-DE | 6'3" | 240 | 21 | | |
| Houston Antwine | DT | 6' | 270 | 26 | 1 | |
| George Pyne | DT | 6'4" | 285 | 22 | | |

| Use Name | Pos. | Hgt | Wgt | Age | Int | Pts |
|---|---|---|---|---|---|---|
| Tom Addison | LB | 6'3" | 230 | 29 | 1 | |
| Nick Buoniconti | LB | 5'11" | 220 | 24 | 3 | |
| Mike Dukes (to NY) | LB | 6'2" | 235 | 29 | 1 | |
| Lonnie Farmer | LB | 6' | 220 | 24 | 1 | |
| Ed Meixler | LB | 6'3" | 245 | 22 | | |
| Jack Rudolph | LB | 6'3" | 230 | 27 | | |
| Jay Cunningham | DB | 5'10" | 185 | 22 | 2 | |
| Dick Felt | DB | 6' | 185 | 32 | | |
| White Graves | DB | 6' | 185 | 24 | | |
| Ron Hall | DB | 6' | 190 | 28 | 3 | |
| Tom Hennessey | DB | 6' | 180 | 25 | 2 | |
| Ross O'Hanley | DB | 6' | 185 | 26 | 1 | |
| Chuck Shonta | DB | 6' | 200 | 27 | 2 | |
| Don Webb | DB | 5'10" | 200 | 26 | 2 | |

| Use Name | Pos. | Hgt | Wgt | Age | Int | Pts |
|---|---|---|---|---|---|---|
| Babe Parilli | QB | 6'1" | 190 | 35 | | |
| Eddie Wilson | QB | 6' | 190 | 25 | | |
| Tom Yewcic | QB | 5'11" | 185 | 33 | | |
| Joe Bellino | HB | 5'9" | 187 | 27 | | |
| Ron Burton | HB | 5'10" | 190 | 28 | | 18 |
| J. D. Garrett | HB | 5'11" | 195 | 23 | | 18 |
| Larry Garron | FB | 6' | 195 | 28 | | 12 |
| Jim Nance | FB | 6'1" | 250 | 22 | | 30 |
| Jim Colclough | FL | 6' | 185 | 29 | | 18 |
| Ellis Johnson | HB-FL | 6'2" | 190 | 21 | | |
| Gino Cappelletti | OE | 6' | 190 | 31 | | 132 |
| Art Graham | OE | 6'1" | 205 | 24 | | |
| Tony Romeo | OE | 6'2" | 230 | 26 | | 12 |
| Jim Whalen | OE | 6'2" | 210 | 21 | | |

## HOUSTON OILERS 4-10-0 Hugh Taylor

**Scores of Each Game**

| | | |
|---|---|---|
| 27 | NEW YORK | 21 |
| 31 | BOSTON | 10 |
| 17 | Oakland | 21 |
| 14 | San Diego | 31 |
| 17 | Denver | 28 |
| 38 | KANSAS CITY | 36 |
| 19 | Buffalo | 17 |
| 21 | OAKLAND | 33 |
| 21 | DENVER | 31 |
| 14 | New York | 41 |
| 21 | Kansas City | 52 |
| 18 | BUFFALO | 29 |
| 26 | SAN DIEGO | 37 |
| 14 | Boston | 42 |

| Use Name | Pos. | Hgt | Wgt | Age | Int | Pts |
|---|---|---|---|---|---|---|
| Norm Evans | OT | 6'5" | 235 | 22 | | |
| Rich Michael | OT | 6'3" | 245 | 26 | | |
| Walt Suggs | OT | 6'5" | 260 | 26 | | |
| Maxie Williams | OT | 6'4" | 242 | 25 | | |
| Sonny Bishop | OG | 6'2" | 245 | 25 | | |
| John Frongillo | OG | 6'3" | 250 | 25 | | |
| Bob Talamini | OG | 6'1" | 255 | 26 | | |
| John Wittenborn | OG | 6'2" | 240 | 29 | | |
| Wayne Frazier | C | 6'2" | 245 | 26 | | |
| Tom Goode | C | 6'3" | 250 | 26 | | |
| Gary Cutsinger | DE | 6'4" | 245 | 24 | 1 | |
| Bob Evans | DE | 6'3" | 250 | 23 | | 6 |
| Don Floyd | DE | 6'4" | 247 | 27 | | |
| George Kinney | DE | 6'4" | 250 | 22 | | |
| Ray Straham | DE | 6'6" | 250 | 24 | | |
| Scott Appleton | DT | 6'3" | 250 | 23 | | |
| Jim Hayes | DT | 6'4" | 265 | 24 | | |
| Ed Husmann | DT | 6' | 245 | 34 | | |
| Bud McFadin | DT | 6'3" | 270 | 37 | | |

| Use Name | Pos. | Hgt | Wgt | Age | Int | Pts |
|---|---|---|---|---|---|---|
| Johnny Baker | LB | 6'3" | 225 | 24 | | |
| Danny Brabham | LB | 6'4" | 240 | 24 | | |
| Doug Cline | LB | 6'2" | 230 | 26 | | |
| Bobby Maples | LB | 6'3" | 230 | 22 | 1 | |
| Larry Onesti | LB | 6' | 200 | 26 | | 6 |
| Charley Rieves | LB | 5'11" | 218 | 26 | | |
| Tony Banfield | DB | 6'1" | 185 | 26 | 3 | |
| Freddy Glick | DB | 6'1" | 190 | 28 | 2 | |
| W. K. Hicks | DB | 6'1" | 185 | 22 | 9 | |
| Bobby Jancik | DB | 5'11" | 178 | 25 | 4 | |
| Pete Jaquess | DB | 6' | 180 | 23 | | |
| Jim Norton | DB | 6'3" | 190 | 26 | 7 | |

Sid Blanks — Knee Injury

| Use Name | Pos. | Hgt | Wgt | Age | Int | Pts |
|---|---|---|---|---|---|---|
| George Blanda | QB | 6'1" | 215 | 37 | | 61 |
| Don Trull | QB | 6'1" | 180 | 23 | | 12 |
| Ode Burrell | HB | 6' | 185 | 25 | | 46 |
| B. W. Cheeks | HB | 6'1" | 230 | 23 | | |
| Dalton Hoffman | FB | 6' | 207 | 23 | | |
| Harry Hooligan | FB | 6'2" | 225 | 27 | | |
| Bobby Jackson | FB | 6'3" | 238 | 25 | | 12 |
| Keith Kinderman | FB | 6' | 215 | 25 | | |
| Jack Spikes | FB | 6'2" | 220 | 27 | | 27 |
| Charley Tolar | HB | 5'7" | 200 | 27 | | |
| Charley Hennigan | FL | 6'1" | 187 | 29 | | 24 |
| Sammy Weir | FL | 5'9" | 170 | 23 | | |
| Dick Compton | OE | 6'1" | 195 | 25 | | 12 |
| Charley Frazier | OE | 6' | 175 | 26 | | 36 |
| Willie Frazier | OE | 6'4" | 225 | 22 | | 48 |
| Bob McLeod | OE | 6'5" | 230 | 26 | | 6 |

## BUFFALO BILLS

### RUSHING

| Last Name | No. | Yds | Avg | TD |
|---|---|---|---|---|
| Carlton | 156 | 592 | 3.8 | 6 |
| Joe | 123 | 377 | 3.1 | 4 |
| Smith | 43 | 137 | 3.2 | 1 |
| Stone | 19 | 61 | 3.2 | 0 |
| Kemp | 36 | 49 | 1.4 | 4 |
| Lamonica | 10 | 30 | 3.0 | 1 |
| Maguire | 1 | 21 | 21.0 | 0 |
| Auer | 3 | 19 | 6.3 | 0 |
| Warner | 1 | 2 | 2.0 | 0 |
| Roberson | 1 | −4 | −4.0 | 0 |

### RECEIVING

| Last Name | No. | Yds | Avg | TD |
|---|---|---|---|---|
| Roberson | 46 | 703 | 15 | 3 |
| Joe | 27 | 271 | 10 | 2 |
| Carlton | 24 | 196 | 8 | 1 |
| Costa | 21 | 401 | 19 | 0 |
| Ferguson | 21 | 262 | 12 | 2 |
| Bass | 18 | 299 | 17 | 1 |
| Dubenion | 18 | 281 | 16 | 1 |
| Rutkowski | 18 | 247 | 14 | 1 |
| Smith | 12 | 116 | 10 | 0 |
| Warlick | 8 | 112 | 14 | 1 |
| Stone | 6 | 29 | 5 | 0 |
| Mills | 1 | 43 | 43 | 0 |
| Warner | 1 | 11 | 11 | 1 |
| Tracey | 1 | 2 | 2 | 0 |
| Kemp | 1 | −9 | −9 | 0 |

### PUNT RETURNS

| Last Name | No. | Yds | Avg | TD |
|---|---|---|---|---|
| Byrd | 22 | 220 | 10 | 0 |
| Rutkowski | 11 | 127 | 12 | 0 |
| Warner | 1 | 16 | 16 | 0 |
| Clarke | 1 | 13 | 13 | 0 |
| Hudlow | 1 | 12 | 12 | 0 |
| Saimes | 0 | 1 | 0 | 0 |

### KICKOFF RETURNS

| Last Name | No. | Yds | Avg | TD |
|---|---|---|---|---|
| Warner | 32 | 825 | 26 | 2 |
| Roberson | 16 | 318 | 20 | 0 |
| Rutkowski | 5 | 97 | 19 | 0 |
| Hudlow | 2 | 36 | 18 | 0 |
| Maguire | 1 | 5 | 5 | 0 |
| Dunaway | 1 | 0 | 0 | 0 |

### PASSING – PUNTING – KICKING

| PASSING | Att | Comp | % | Yds | Yd/Att | TD | Int−% | RK |
|---|---|---|---|---|---|---|---|---|
| Kemp | 391 | 179 | 46 | 2368 | 6.1 | 10 | 18− 5 | 6 |
| Lamonica | 70 | 29 | 41 | 376 | 5.4 | 3 | 6− 9 | |

| PUNTING | No | Avg |
|---|---|---|
| Maguire | 80 | 43.0 |

| KICKING | XP | Att | % | FG | Att | % |
|---|---|---|---|---|---|---|
| Gogolak | 31 | 31 | 100 | 28 | 46 | 61 |

## NEW YORK JETS

### RUSHING

| Last Name | No. | Yds | Avg | TD |
|---|---|---|---|---|
| Snell | 169 | 763 | 4.5 | 4 |
| Mathis | 147 | 604 | 4.1 | 5 |
| Smolinski | 24 | 59 | 2.5 | 0 |
| Carson | 7 | 25 | 3.6 | 2 |
| Namath | 8 | 19 | 2.4 | 0 |
| McDaniel | 1 | 13 | 13.0 | 0 |
| Taliaferro | 7 | 4 | 0.6 | 0 |
| Johnson | 2 | 3 | 1.5 | 0 |
| Maynard | 1 | 2 | 2.0 | 0 |

### RECEIVING

| Last Name | No. | Yds | Avg | TD |
|---|---|---|---|---|
| Maynard | 68 | 1218 | 18 | 14 |
| Snell | 38 | 264 | 7 | 0 |
| B. Turner | 31 | 402 | 13 | 2 |
| Sauer | 29 | 301 | 10 | 2 |
| Mathis | 17 | 242 | 14 | 1 |
| Mackey | 16 | 255 | 16 | 1 |
| Smolinski | 6 | 25 | 4 | 0 |
| Evans | 2 | 24 | 12 | 0 |
| Heeter | 1 | 14 | 14 | 0 |
| Johnson | 1 | 6 | 6 | 1 |

### PUNT RETURNS

| Last Name | No. | Yds | Avg | TD |
|---|---|---|---|---|
| Baird | 14 | 88 | 6 | 0 |
| Robinson | 3 | 36 | 12 | 0 |
| West | 10 | 34 | 3 | 0 |
| Carson | 1 | 7 | 7 | 0 |
| B. Turner | 1 | 1 | 1 | 0 |

### KICKOFF RETURNS

| Last Name | No. | Yds | Avg | TD |
|---|---|---|---|---|
| B. Turner | 18 | 402 | 22 | 0 |
| Carson | 17 | 355 | 21 | 0 |
| Robinson | 7 | 164 | 23 | 0 |
| Smolinski | 6 | 98 | 16 | 0 |
| Baird | 2 | 50 | 25 | 0 |
| Browning | 1 | 31 | 31 | 0 |
| Sauer | 1 | 20 | 20 | 0 |
| Abruzzese | 1 | 16 | 16 | 0 |
| O'Mahoney | 1 | 15 | 15 | 0 |
| DeFelice | 1 | 0 | 0 | 0 |
| Hudson | 1 | 0 | 0 | 0 |
| Paulson | 1 | 0 | 0 | 0 |

### PASSING – PUNTING – KICKING

| PASSING | Att | Comp | % | Yds | Yd/Att | TD | Int−% | RK |
|---|---|---|---|---|---|---|---|---|
| Namath | 340 | 164 | 48 | 2220 | 6.5 | 18 | 15− 4 | 3 |
| Taliaferro | 119 | 45 | 38 | 531 | 4.5 | 3 | 7− 6 | |

| PUNTING | No | Avg |
|---|---|---|
| Johnson | 72 | 45.3 |

| KICKING | XP | Att | % | FG | Att | % |
|---|---|---|---|---|---|---|
| J. Turner | 31 | 31 | 100 | 20 | 34 | 59 |

**2 POINT XP**
Mackey

## BOSTON PATRIOTS

### RUSHING

| Last Name | No. | Yds | Avg | TD |
|---|---|---|---|---|
| Nance | 111 | 321 | 2.9 | 5 |
| Garron | 74 | 259 | 3.5 | 1 |
| Parilli | 50 | 200 | 4.0 | 0 |
| Garrett | 42 | 147 | 3.5 | 1 |
| Burton | 45 | 108 | 2.4 | 1 |
| Bellino | 24 | 49 | 2.0 | 0 |
| Johnson | 19 | 29 | 1.5 | 0 |
| Wilson | 8 | 4 | 0.5 | 0 |

### RECEIVING

| Last Name | No. | Yds | Avg | TD |
|---|---|---|---|---|
| Colclough | 40 | 677 | 17 | 3 |
| Cappelletti | 37 | 680 | 18 | 9 |
| Graham | 25 | 316 | 13 | 0 |
| Whalen | 22 | 381 | 17 | 0 |
| Garron | 15 | 222 | 15 | 1 |
| Romeo | 15 | 203 | 14 | 2 |
| Nance | 12 | 83 | 7 | 0 |
| Burton | 10 | 127 | 13 | 2 |
| Garrett | 7 | 49 | 7 | 2 |
| Bellino | 5 | 74 | 15 | 0 |
| Johnson | 4 | 29 | 7 | 0 |
| Yewcic | 1 | 13 | 13 | 0 |

### PUNT RETURNS

| Last Name | No. | Yds | Avg | TD |
|---|---|---|---|---|
| Burton | 15 | 61 | 4 | 0 |
| Cunningham | 5 | 35 | 7 | 0 |
| Hennessey | 5 | 21 | 4 | 0 |
| Garrett | 1 | 19 | 19 | 0 |
| Nance | 1 | 16 | 16 | 0 |

### KICKOFF RETURNS

| Last Name | No. | Yds | Avg | TD |
|---|---|---|---|---|
| Cunningham | 17 | 374 | 22 | 0 |
| Garrett | 12 | 232 | 19 | 0 |
| Burton | 7 | 188 | 27 | 0 |
| Garron | 5 | 141 | 28 | 0 |
| Bellino | 7 | 138 | 20 | 0 |
| Dukes | 3 | 45 | 15 | 0 |
| Nance | 3 | 40 | 13 | 0 |
| Johnson | 2 | 29 | 15 | 0 |
| Rudolph | 1 | 4 | 4 | 0 |
| Canale | 2 | 0 | 0 | 0 |
| Pyne | 1 | 0 | 0 | 0 |

### PASSING – PUNTING – KICKING

| PASSING | Att | Comp | % | Yds | Yd/Att | TD | Int−% | RK |
|---|---|---|---|---|---|---|---|---|
| Parilli | 426 | 173 | 41 | 2597 | 6.1 | 18 | 26− 6 | 7 |
| Wilson | 46 | 20 | 44 | 257 | 5.6 | 1 | 3− 7 | |
| Yewcic | 1 | 0 | 0 | 0 | 0.0 | 0 | 0− 0 | |

| PUNTING | No | Avg |
|---|---|---|
| Yewcic | 74 | 41.8 |
| E. Wilson | 5 | 38.8 |

| KICKING | XP | Att | % | FG | Att | % |
|---|---|---|---|---|---|---|
| Cappelletti | 27 | 27 | 100 | 17 | 27 | 63 |

## HOUSTON OILERS

### RUSHING

| Last Name | No. | Yds | Avg | TD |
|---|---|---|---|---|
| Burrell | 130 | 528 | 4.1 | 3 |
| Tolar | 73 | 230 | 3.2 | 0 |
| Spikes | 47 | 173 | 3.7 | 3 |
| Trull | 29 | 145 | 5.0 | 2 |
| Jackson | 37 | 85 | 2.3 | 2 |
| Hoffman | 1 | 11 | 11.0 | 0 |
| C. Frazier | 1 | 10 | 10.0 | 0 |
| Compton | 1 | 2 | 2.0 | 0 |
| Blanda | 4 | −6 | −1.5 | 0 |

### RECEIVING

| Last Name | No. | Yds | Avg | TD |
|---|---|---|---|---|
| Burrell | 55 | 650 | 12 | 4 |
| Hennigan | 41 | 578 | 14 | 4 |
| C. Frazier | 38 | 717 | 19 | 6 |
| Wil. Frazier | 37 | 521 | 14 | 8 |
| Tolar | 25 | 138 | 6 | 0 |
| McLeod | 15 | 226 | 15 | 1 |
| Spikes | 8 | 57 | 7 | 0 |
| Compton | 3 | 140 | 47 | 2 |
| Jackson | 1 | 31 | 31 | 0 |
| Weir | 1 | 12 | 12 | 0 |

### PUNT RETURNS

| Last Name | No. | Yds | Avg | TD |
|---|---|---|---|---|
| Jancik | 12 | 85 | 7 | 0 |
| Glick | 7 | 44 | 6 | 0 |
| Burrell | 3 | 39 | 13 | 0 |
| Jaquess | 4 | 17 | 4 | 0 |
| Hicks | 1 | 4 | 4 | 0 |
| Weir | 1 | 0 | 0 | 0 |

### KICKOFF RETURNS

| Last Name | No. | Yds | Avg | TD |
|---|---|---|---|---|
| Jancik | 18 | 430 | 24 | 0 |
| Jaquess | 13 | 280 | 22 | 0 |
| Weir | 10 | 215 | 22 | 0 |
| Burrell | 8 | 202 | 25 | 0 |
| Hicks | 7 | 181 | 26 | 0 |
| Glick | 4 | 84 | 21 | 0 |
| Kinderman | 4 | 72 | 18 | 0 |
| Compton | 4 | 68 | 17 | 0 |
| Spikes | 4 | 41 | 10 | 0 |
| Jackson | 2 | 39 | 20 | 0 |
| Williams | 1 | 23 | 23 | 0 |
| Cheeks | 1 | 19 | 19 | 0 |
| Maples | 1 | 15 | 15 | 0 |

### PASSING – PUNTING – KICKING

| PASSING | Att | Comp | % | Yds | Yd/Att | TD | Int−% | RK |
|---|---|---|---|---|---|---|---|---|
| Blanda | 442 | 186 | 42 | 2542 | 5.8 | 20 | 30− 7 | 8 |
| Trull | 107 | 38 | 36 | 528 | 4.9 | 5 | 5− 5 | |
| Tolar | 1 | 0 | 0 | 0 | 0.0 | 0 | 0− 0 | |

| PUNTING | No | Avg |
|---|---|---|
| Norton | 84 | 44.2 |

| KICKING | XP | Att | % | FG | Att | % |
|---|---|---|---|---|---|---|
| Blanda | 28 | 28 | 100 | 11 | 21 | 52 |
| Spikes | 6 | 6 | 100 | 1 | 2 | 50 |

**2 POINT XP**
Burrell (2)

## SAN DIEGO CHARGERS 9-2-3  Sid Gillman

| Scores of Each Game | | Use Name | Pos. | Hgt | Wgt | Age | Int | Pts |
|---|---|---|---|---|---|---|---|---|
| 34 | DENVER | 31 | Gary Kirner | OT | 6'3" | 245 | 23 | | |
| 17 | Oakland | 6 | Ron Mix | OT | 6'4" | 250 | 27 | | |
| 10 | KANSAS CITY | 10 | Ernie Park | OT | 6'3" | 253 | 25 | | |
| 31 | HOUSTON | 14 | Ernie Wright | OT | 6'4" | 265 | 26 | | |
| 34 | Buffalo | 3 | John Farris | OG | 6'4" | 245 | 24 | | |
| 13 | Boston | 13 | Ed Mitchell | OG | 6'2" | 265 | 23 | | |
| 34 | New York | 9 | Pat Shea | OG | 6'1" | 245 | 26 | | |
| 6 | BOSTON | 22 | Walt Sweeney | OG | 6'3" | 255 | 24 | | |
| 35 | Denver | 21 | Sam Gruneisen | C | 6'1" | 255 | 24 | | |
| 7 | Kansas City | 31 | Steve DeLong | DE | 6'3" | 245 | 22 | | |
| 20 | BUFFALO | 20 | Earl Faison | DE | 6'5" | 270 | 26 | 1 | 6 |
| 38 | NEW YORK | 7 | Howard Kindig | DE | 6'6" | 250 | 24 | | |
| 37 | Houston | 26 | Bob Petrich | DE | 6'4" | 257 | 24 | | |
| 24 | OAKLAND | 14 | George Gross | DT | 6'3" | 270 | 24 | | |
| | | | Ernie Ladd | DT | 6'9" | 295 | 26 | | |
| | | | Fred Moore | DT | 6'3" | 255 | 25 | | |

| Use Name | Pos. | Hgt | Wgt | Age | Int | Pts |
|---|---|---|---|---|---|---|
| Chuck Allen | LB | 6'1" | 225 | 25 | 1 | |
| Frank Buncom | LB | 6'1" | 235 | 25 | | |
| Ron Carpenter | LB | 6'2" | 230 | 24 | | |
| Dick Degen | LB | 6'1" | 225 | 23 | 2 | |
| Bob Horton | LB | 6'2" | 230 | 22 | | |
| Rick Redman | LB | 5'11" | 220 | 22 | 1 | |
| Speedy Duncan | DB | 5'10" | 180 | 22 | 4 | 12 |
| Kenny Graham | DB | 6' | 200 | 23 | 5 | 6 |
| Dick Harris | DB | 6'1" | 187 | 28 | 1 | |
| Jack Jacobson | DB | 6'2" | 200 | 24 | | |
| Jimmy Warren | DB | 5'11" | 185 | 26 | 5 | |
| Dick Westmoreland | DB | 6'1" | 190 | 24 | 1 | |
| Bud Whitehead | DB | 6' | 185 | 26 | 7 | 6 |
| Bob Zeman | DB | 6'1" | 195 | 28 | | |

| Use Name | Pos. | Hgt | Wgt | Age | Int | Pts |
|---|---|---|---|---|---|---|
| Don Breaux | QB | 6'1" | 200 | 25 | | |
| John Hadl | QB | 6'2" | 210 | 25 | | 6 |
| Steve Tensi | QB | 6'5" | 207 | 22 | | |
| Gene Foster | FB-HB | 5'11" | 200 | 22 | | 12 |
| Paul Lowe | HB | 6' | 205 | 28 | | 48 |
| Jim Allison | FB | 6' | 225 | 22 | | |
| Keith Lincoln | FB | 6'2" | 212 | 26 | | 42 |
| Lance Alworth | FL | 6' | 185 | 25 | | 84 |
| Sammy Taylor | FL | 6' | 190 | 25 | | |
| Dave Kocourek | OE | 6'5" | 245 | 28 | | 12 |
| Jacque MacKinnon | OE | 6'4" | 250 | 26 | | |
| Don Norton | OE | 6'1" | 195 | 27 | | 12 |
| Herb Travenio | K | 6' | 218 | 34 | | 94 |

## OAKLAND RAIDERS 8-5-1  Al Davis

| Scores of Each Game | | Use Name | Pos. | Hgt | Wgt | Age | Int | Pts |
|---|---|---|---|---|---|---|---|---|
| 37 | KANSAS CITY | 10 | Harry Schuh | OG-OT | 6'2" | 260 | 22 | | |
| 6 | SAN DIEGO | 17 | Bob Svihus | OT | 6'4" | 245 | 22 | | |
| 21 | HOUSTON | 17 | Frank Youso | OT | 6'4" | 250 | 29 | | |
| 12 | Buffalo | 17 | Rich Zecher | OT | 6'2" | 250 | 27 | | |
| 24 | Boston | 10 | Wayne Hawkins | OG | 6' | 240 | 27 | | |
| 24 | New York | 24 | Marv Marinovich | OG | 6'3" | 250 | 26 | | |
| 30 | BOSTON | 21 | Bob Mischak | OG | 6' | 230 | 32 | | |
| 7 | Kansas City | 14 | Ken Rice | OG | 6'2" | 240 | 25 | | |
| 33 | Houston | 21 | Jim Otto | C | 6'2" | 240 | 27 | | |
| 14 | BUFFALO | 17 | Ben Davidson | DE | 6'8" | 265 | 25 | | |
| 28 | Denver | 20 | Ike Lassiter | DE | 6'5" | 270 | 24 | | |
| 24 | DENVER | 13 | Carleton Oats | DE | 6'2" | 235 | 22 | | |
| 24 | NEW YORK | 14 | Dan Birdwell | DT | 6'4" | 250 | 24 | | |
| 14 | San Diego | 24 | Dave Costa | DT | 6'2" | 250 | 23 | | |
| | | | John Diehl (from DAL-N) | DT | 6'7" | 250 | 29 | | |
| | | | Rex Mirich | DT | 6'4" | 250 | 24 | | |

| Use Name | Pos. | Hgt | Wgt | Age | Int | Pts |
|---|---|---|---|---|---|---|
| Bill Budness | LB | 6'1" | 215 | 22 | 1 | |
| Dan Conners | LB | 6'2" | 230 | 23 | | |
| Dick Herman | LB | 6'2" | 215 | 22 | | |
| Archie Matsos | LB | 6' | 212 | 30 | 3 | |
| Gus Otto | LB | 6'2" | 220 | 22 | 3 | 12 |
| J. R. Williamson | LB | 6'2" | 220 | 23 | | |
| Dave Grayson | DB | 5'10" | 185 | 26 | 3 | 12 |
| Claude Gibson | DB | 6'1" | 190 | 26 | 4 | 6 |
| Joe Krakoski | DB | 6'2" | 195 | 28 | | |
| Kent McCloughan | DB | 6'1" | 190 | 22 | 3 | |
| Warren Powers | DB | 6' | 185 | 24 | 5 | |
| Howie Williams | DB | 6'2" | 185 | 28 | 2 | |

| Use Name | Pos. | Hgt | Wgt | Age | Int | Pts |
|---|---|---|---|---|---|---|
| Cotton Davidson | QB | 6'1" | 180 | 33 | | |
| Tom Flores | QB | 6'1" | 190 | 28 | | |
| Dick Wood | QB | 6'5" | 200 | 29 | | 6 |
| Clem Daniels | HB | 6'1" | 220 | 28 | | 72 |
| Gene Mingo | HB | 6'1" | 190 | 26 | | 24 |
| Larry Todd | HB | 6'1" | 185 | 22 | | |
| Roger Hagberg | FB | 6'2" | 220 | 26 | | 6 |
| Alan Miller | FB | 6' | 210 | 27 | | 24 |
| Fred Biletnikoff | FL | 6'1" | 190 | 22 | | |
| Pervis Atkins (from WAS-N) | OE | 6'1" | 195 | 29 | | |
| Billy Cannon | OE | 6'1" | 225 | 28 | | |
| Ken Herock | OE | 6'2" | 230 | 24 | | |
| Art Powell | OE | 6'3" | 212 | 28 | | 72 |
| Mike Mercer | K | 6' | 200 | 29 | | 62 |

## KANSAS CITY CHIEFS 7-5-2  Hank Stram

| Scores of Each Game | | Use Name | Pos. | Hgt | Wgt | Age | Int | Pts |
|---|---|---|---|---|---|---|---|---|
| 10 | Oakland | 37 | Jerry Cornelison | OT | 6'3" | 250 | 28 | | |
| 14 | New York | 10 | Dave Hill | OT | 6'5" | 260 | 24 | | |
| 10 | San Diego | 10 | Jim Tyrer | OT | 6'6" | 292 | 26 | | |
| 27 | BOSTON | 17 | Denny Biodrowski | OG | 6'1" | 255 | 25 | | |
| 31 | Denver | 23 | Ed Budde | OG | 6'5" | 260 | 24 | | |
| 7 | BUFFALO | 23 | Curt Merz | OG | 6'4" | 250 | 27 | | |
| 36 | Houston | 38 | Al Reynolds | OG | 6'3" | 235 | 27 | | |
| 14 | OAKLAND | 7 | Jon Gilliam | C | 6'2" | 240 | 26 | | |
| 10 | NEW YORK | 13 | Mel Branch | DE | 6'2" | 230 | 28 | | |
| 31 | SAN DIEGO | 7 | Chuck Hurston | DE | 6'6" | 227 | 22 | | |
| 10 | Boston | 10 | Ed Lothamer | DE | 6'5" | 245 | 22 | | |
| 52 | HOUSTON | 21 | Buck Buchanan | DT | 6'7" | 280 | 25 | | |
| 25 | Buffalo | 34 | Al Dotson | DT | 6'5" | 255 | 22 | | |
| 45 | DENVER | 35 | Curt Farrier | DT | 6'6" | 245 | 24 | | |
| | | | Jerry Mays | DT | 6'4" | 250 | 25 | | |
| | | | Hatch Rosdahl | DT | 6'5" | 250 | 22 | | |

| Use Name | Pos. | Hgt | Wgt | Age | Int | Pts |
|---|---|---|---|---|---|---|
| Ronnie Caveness | LB | 6'1" | 215 | 22 | | |
| Walt Corey | LB | 6' | 242 | 27 | | |
| Jim Fraser | LB | 6'3" | 236 | 29 | | |
| Sherrill Headrick | LB | 6'2" | 215 | 28 | 1 | |
| E. J. Holub | LB | 6'4" | 225 | 27 | 1 | |
| Smokey Stover | LB | 6' | 232 | 26 | | |
| Bobby Bell | DE-LB | 6'4" | 228 | 25 | 4 | 6 |
| Bobby Hunt | DB | 6'1" | 190 | 25 | 1 | |
| Willie Mitchell | DB | 6'1" | 185 | 23 | 2 | 12 |
| Bobby Ply | DB | 6'1" | 190 | 24 | | |
| Johnny Robinson | DB | 6' | 195 | 26 | 5 | |
| Fred Williamson | DB | 6'2" | 215 | 27 | 6 | |

| Use Name | Pos. | Hgt | Wgt | Age | Int | Pts |
|---|---|---|---|---|---|---|
| Pete Beathard | QB | 6'2" | 205 | 23 | | 26 |
| Len Dawson | QB | 6' | 190 | 31 | | 12 |
| Soloman Brannan | HB | 6'1" | 188 | 23 | | |
| Bert Coan | HB | 6'4" | 220 | 25 | | 18 |
| *Mack Lee Hill | HB | 5'11" | 225 | 25 | | 18 |
| Jerrel Wilson | HB | 6'4" | 225 | 23 | | 2 |
| Curtis McClinton | FB | 6'3" | 232 | 26 | | 54 |
| Frank Jackson | FL | 6'1" | 190 | 25 | | 6 |
| Frank Pitts | FL | 6'2" | 190 | 21 | | |
| Fred Arbanas | OE | 6'3" | 240 | 26 | | 24 |
| Tommy Brooker | OE | 6'2" | 230 | 25 | | 76 |
| Chris Burford | OE | 6'3" | 210 | 27 | | 36 |
| Reg Carolan | OE | 6'6" | 232 | 25 | | 2 |
| Otis Taylor | OE | 6'2" | 215 | 22 | | 30 |

*Died Dec. 14, 1965 after knee surgery

## DENVER BRONCOS 4-10-0  Mac Speedie

| Scores of Each Game | | Use Name | Pos. | Hgt | Wgt | Age | Int | Pts |
|---|---|---|---|---|---|---|---|---|
| 31 | San Diego | 34 | Lee Bernet | OT | 6'2" | 245 | 21 | | |
| 15 | BUFFALO | 30 | Bob Breitenstein | OT | 6'3" | 250 | 22 | | |
| 27 | Boston | 10 | Eldon Danenhauer | OT | 6'4" | 245 | 29 | | |
| 16 | NEW YORK | 13 | Jon Hohman | OG | 6'1" | 240 | 22 | | |
| 23 | KANSAS CITY | 31 | Bob McCullough | OG | 6'2" | 245 | 24 | | |
| 28 | HOUSTON | 17 | Tom Nomina | OG | 6'5" | 270 | 23 | | |
| 13 | Buffalo | 31 | Charlie Parker | OG | 6'1" | 245 | 23 | | |
| 10 | New York | 45 | Jerry Sturm | OG | 6'3" | 260 | 28 | | |
| 21 | SAN DIEGO | 35 | Ray Kubala | C | 6'4" | 245 | 23 | | |
| 31 | Houston | 21 | Ed Cooke | DE | 6'4" | 250 | 30 | 3 | |
| 20 | OAKLAND | 28 | Leroy Moore | DE | 6' | 230 | 29 | | |
| 13 | Oakland | 24 | Ray Jacobs | DT | 6'3" | 265 | 25 | | |
| 20 | BOSTON | 28 | Chuck Janerette | DT | 6'3" | 265 | 26 | 1 | |
| 35 | Kansas City | 45 | Max Leetzow | DT | 6'4" | 240 | 22 | | |
| | | | Jim Thompson | DT | 6'3" | 255 | 24 | | |

| Use Name | Pos. | Hgt | Wgt | Age | Int | Pts |
|---|---|---|---|---|---|---|
| John Bramlett | LB | 6'2" | 210 | 24 | 1 | 12 |
| Ed Cummings | LB | 6'2" | 228 | 24 | | |
| Tom Erlandson | LB | 6'3" | 235 | 25 | 1 | |
| Jerry Hopkins | LB | 6'2" | 235 | 24 | 1 | |
| Gene Jeter | LB | 6'3" | 230 | 23 | | |
| Jim Thibert | LB | 6'3" | 230 | 25 | | |
| Willie Brown | DB | 6'1" | 190 | 24 | 2 | |
| Gerry Bussell | DB | 6' | 185 | 22 | | |
| Miller Farr (to SD) | DB | 6'1" | 188 | 22 | 2 | |
| Goose Gonsoulin | DB | 6'3" | 210 | 27 | 6 | 2 |
| John Griffin | DB | 6'1" | 190 | 25 | 4 | 12 |
| Gary Kroner | DB | 6'1" | 200 | 24 | | 71 |
| John McGeever | DB | 5'11" | 195 | 26 | 1 | |
| Jim McMillin | DB | 5'11" | 195 | 27 | | |
| Nemiah Wilson | DB | 6' | 180 | 22 | 3 | 6 |

| Use Name | Pos. | Hgt | Wgt | Age | Int | Pts |
|---|---|---|---|---|---|---|
| Jacky Lee | QB | 6'1" | 187 | 26 | | |
| John McCormick | QB | 6'1" | 210 | 28 | | |
| Mickey Slaughter | QB | 6' | 190 | 23 | | |
| Paul Carmichael | HB | 6'4" | 200 | 20 | | |
| Wendell Hayes | HB | 6'2" | 195 | 24 | | 44 |
| Abner Haynes | HB | 6' | 190 | 27 | | 36 |
| Charley Mitchell | HB | 5'11" | 185 | 25 | | |
| Cookie Gilchrist | FB | 6'3" | 250 | 30 | | 42 |
| Darrell Lester | FB | 6'2" | 225 | 24 | | |
| Al Denson | FL | 6'2" | 208 | 23 | | |
| Bob Scarpitto | FL | 5'11" | 196 | 26 | | 30 |
| Hewritt Dixon | OE | 6'2" | 217 | 25 | | 12 |
| Odell Barry | OE | 5'10" | 180 | 23 | | |
| Lionel Taylor | OE | 6'2" | 215 | 29 | | 36 |

## SAN DIEGO CHARGERS

### RUSHING

| Last Name | No. | Yds | Avg | TD |
|---|---|---|---|---|
| Lowe | 222 | 1121 | 5.1 | 7 |
| Foster | 121 | 469 | 3.9 | 2 |
| Lincoln | 74 | 302 | 4.1 | 3 |
| Allison | 29 | 100 | 3.5 | 0 |
| Hadl | 28 | 91 | 3.3 | 1 |
| MacKinnon | 3 | 17 | 5.7 | 0 |
| Breaux | 1 | −1 | −1.0 | 0 |
| Shea | 1 | −5 | −5.0 | 0 |
| Norton | 1 | −5 | −5.0 | 0 |
| Alworth | 3 | −12 | −4.0 | 0 |
| Sweeney | 0 | 8 | 0.0 | 0 |

### RECEIVING

| Last Name | No. | Yds | Avg | TD |
|---|---|---|---|---|
| Alworth | 69 | 1602 | 23 | 14 |
| Norton | 34 | 485 | 14 | 2 |
| Kocourek | 28 | 363 | 13 | 2 |
| Lincoln | 23 | 376 | 16 | 4 |
| Foster | 17 | 199 | 12 | 0 |
| Lowe | 17 | 126 | 7 | 1 |
| Allison | 8 | 109 | 13 | 0 |
| Mackinnon | 6 | 106 | 18 | 0 |
| Taylor | 1 | 13 | 13 | 0 |

### PUNT RETURNS

| Last Name | No. | Yds | Avg | TD |
|---|---|---|---|---|
| Duncan | 30 | 464 | 15 | 2 |
| Graham | 5 | 36 | 7 | 0 |
| Harris | 3 | 8 | 3 | 0 |

### KICKOFF RETURNS

| Last Name | No. | Yds | Avg | TD |
|---|---|---|---|---|
| Duncan | 26 | 612 | 24 | 0 |
| Foster | 5 | 108 | 22 | 0 |
| Allison | 4 | 80 | 20 | 0 |
| Lincoln | 2 | 46 | 23 | 0 |
| Harris | 1 | 15 | 15 | 0 |
| Kirner | 1 | 0 | 0 | 0 |
| Mackinnon | 1 | 0 | 0 | 0 |

### PASSING — PUNTING — KICKING

| Last Name | Att | Comp | % | Yds | Yd/Att | TD | Int−% | RK |
|---|---|---|---|---|---|---|---|---|
| PASSING | | | | | | | | |
| Hadl | 348 | 174 | 50 | 2798 | 8.0 | 20 | 21− 6 | 2 |
| Breaux | 43 | 22 | 51 | 404 | 9.4 | 2 | 4− 9 | |
| Lowe | 4 | 3 | 75 | 81 | 20.3 | 0 | 0− 0 | |
| Foster | 3 | 2 | 67 | 31 | 10.3 | 0 | 0− 0 | |
| Lincoln | 3 | 2 | 67 | 65 | 21.7 | 1 | 1− 33 | |

| PUNTING | No | Avg |
|---|---|---|
| Hadl | 38 | 40.7 |
| Redman | 29 | 39.5 |
| Allison | 2 | 36.0 |
| Whitehead | 1 | 40.0 |

| KICKING | XP | Att | % | FG | Att | % |
|---|---|---|---|---|---|---|
| Travenio | 40 | 40 | 100 | 18 | 30 | 60 |

## OAKLAND RAIDERS

### RUSHING

| Last Name | No. | Yds | Avg | TD |
|---|---|---|---|---|
| Daniels | 219 | 884 | 4.0 | 5 |
| Miller | 73 | 272 | 3.7 | 1 |
| Todd | 32 | 142 | 3.3 | 2 |
| Hagberg | 48 | 171 | 3.6 | 1 |
| Flores | 11 | 32 | 2.9 | 0 |
| Wood | 4 | 16 | 4.0 | 1 |
| Mercer | 1 | −1 | −1.0 | 0 |

### RECEIVING

| Last Name | No. | Yds | Avg | TD |
|---|---|---|---|---|
| Powell | 52 | 800 | 15 | 12 |
| Daniels | 36 | 568 | 16 | 7 |
| Biletnikoff | 24 | 331 | 14 | 0 |
| Miller | 21 | 208 | 10 | 3 |
| Herock | 18 | 221 | 12 | 0 |
| Hagberg | 12 | 121 | 10 | 0 |
| Todd | 8 | 106 | 13 | 0 |
| Cannon | 7 | 127 | 18 | 0 |
| Atkins | 1 | 6 | 6 | 0 |
| Mingo | 1 | 5 | 5 | 0 |

### PUNT RETURNS

| Last Name | No. | Yds | Avg | TD |
|---|---|---|---|---|
| Gibson | 31 | 357 | 12 | 1 |
| Krakoski | 2 | 5 | 3 | 0 |
| Hagberg | 1 | 3 | 3 | 0 |

### KICKOFF RETURNS

| Last Name | No. | Yds | Avg | TD |
|---|---|---|---|---|
| Todd | 20 | 461 | 23 | 0 |
| Gibson | 9 | 186 | 21 | 0 |
| Hagberg | 3 | 50 | 17 | 0 |
| Grayson | 1 | 34 | 34 | 0 |
| Herman | 1 | 0 | 0 | 0 |

### PASSING — PUNTING — KICKING

| Last Name | Att | Comp | % | Yds | Yd/Att | TD | Int−% | RK |
|---|---|---|---|---|---|---|---|---|
| PASSING | | | | | | | | |
| Flores | 269 | 122 | 45 | 1593 | 5.9 | 14 | 11− 4 | 5 |
| Wood | 157 | 69 | 44 | 1003 | 6.4 | 8 | 6− 4 | 4 |
| Daniels | 2 | 2 | 100 | 95 | 47.5 | 0 | 0− 0 | |
| C. Davidson | 1 | 1 | 100 | 8 | 8.0 | 0 | 0− 0 | |
| Mercer | 1 | 1 | 100 | 14 | 14.0 | 0 | 0− 0 | |
| Todd | 1 | 0 | 0 | 0 | 0.0 | 0 | 0− 0 | |

| PUNTING | No | Avg |
|---|---|---|
| Mercer | 75 | 41.1 |

| KICKING | XP | Att | % | FG | Att | % |
|---|---|---|---|---|---|---|
| Mercer | 35 | 35 | 100 | 9 | 15 | 60 |
| Mingo | 0 | 0 | 0 | 8 | 19 | 42 |

## KANSAS CITY CHIEFS

### RUSHING

| Last Name | No. | Yds | Avg | TD |
|---|---|---|---|---|
| McClinton | 175 | 661 | 3.8 | 6 |
| M. Hill | 125 | 627 | 5.0 | 2 |
| Dawson | 43 | 142 | 3.3 | 0 |
| Beathard | 25 | 138 | 5.5 | 4 |
| Coan | 45 | 137 | 3.0 | 1 |
| Jackson | 1 | 26 | 26.0 | 0 |
| Taylor | 2 | 17 | 8.5 | 0 |
| Wilson | 2 | 4 | 2.0 | 0 |

### RECEIVING

| Last Name | No. | Yds | Avg | TD |
|---|---|---|---|---|
| Burford | 47 | 575 | 12 | 6 |
| McClinton | 37 | 590 | 16 | 3 |
| Jackson | 28 | 440 | 16 | 1 |
| Taylor | 26 | 446 | 17 | 5 |
| Arbanas | 24 | 418 | 17 | 4 |
| M. Hill | 21 | 264 | 13 | 1 |
| Coan | 9 | 85 | 9 | 2 |
| Carolan | 6 | 65 | 11 | 0 |
| Pitts | 1 | 11 | 11 | 0 |

### PUNT RETURNS

| Last Name | No. | Yds | Avg | TD |
|---|---|---|---|---|
| Mitchell | 19 | 242 | 13 | 1 |
| Jackson | 13 | 163 | 13 | 0 |
| Brannan | 5 | 10 | 2 | 0 |
| Pitts | 1 | 4 | 4 | 0 |

### KICKOFF RETURNS

| Last Name | No. | Yds | Avg | TD |
|---|---|---|---|---|
| Coan | 19 | 479 | 25 | 0 |
| Jackson | 9 | 260 | 29 | 0 |
| Brannan | 9 | 226 | 25 | 0 |
| Pitts | 5 | 100 | 20 | 0 |
| Stover | 3 | 72 | 0 | 0 |
| Fraser | 1 | 5 | 5 | 0 |
| Mays | 2 | 3 | 2 | 0 |

### PASSING — PUNTING — KICKING

| Last Name | Att | Comp | % | Yds | Yd/Att | TD | Int−% | RK |
|---|---|---|---|---|---|---|---|---|
| PASSING | | | | | | | | |
| Dawson | 305 | 163 | 53 | 2262 | 7.4 | 21 | 14− 5 | 1 |
| Beathard | 89 | 36 | 41 | 632 | 7.1 | 1 | 6− 7 | |
| McClinton | 1 | 0 | 0 | 0 | 0.0 | 0 | 0− 0 | |

| PUNTING | No | Avg |
|---|---|---|
| Wilson | 68 | 46.1 |
| Fraser | 3 | 27.0 |

| KICKING | XP | Att | % | FG | Att | % |
|---|---|---|---|---|---|---|
| Brooker | 37 | 37 | 100 | 13 | 30 | 43 |

**2 POINT XP**
Beathard
Carolan
Wilson

## DENVER BRONCOS

### RUSHING

| Last Name | No. | Yds | Avg | TD |
|---|---|---|---|---|
| Gilchrist | 252 | 954 | 3.8 | 6 |
| Hayes | 130 | 526 | 4.1 | 5 |
| Haynes | 41 | 166 | 4.1 | 3 |
| Scarpitto | 4 | 94 | 23.5 | 0 |
| Slaughter | 20 | 75 | 3.8 | 0 |
| Barry | 2 | 19 | 9.5 | 0 |
| Lee | 2 | 1 | 0.5 | 0 |
| McCormick | 1 | −2 | −2.0 | 0 |
| Denson | 1 | −4 | −4.0 | 0 |

### RECEIVING

| Last Name | No. | Yds | Avg | TD |
|---|---|---|---|---|
| Taylor | 85 | 1131 | 13 | 6 |
| Scarpitto | 32 | 585 | 18 | 5 |
| Haynes | 26 | 216 | 8 | 2 |
| Dixon | 25 | 354 | 14 | 2 |
| Hayes | 24 | 294 | 12 | 2 |
| Gilchrist | 18 | 154 | 9 | 1 |
| Denson | 9 | 102 | 11 | 0 |
| Barry | 2 | 11 | 6 | 0 |
| McCullough | 1 | 1 | 1 | 0 |

### PUNT RETURNS

| Last Name | No. | Yds | Avg | TD |
|---|---|---|---|---|
| Barry | 21 | 210 | 10 | 0 |
| Haynes | 14 | 121 | 9 | 1 |
| Bussell | 2 | 24 | 12 | 0 |

### KICKOFF RETURNS

| Last Name | No. | Yds | Avg | TD |
|---|---|---|---|---|
| Haynes | 34 | 901 | 27 | 0 |
| Barry | 26 | 611 | 24 | 0 |
| Farr | 7 | 123 | 18 | 0 |
| Bussell | 5 | 103 | 21 | 0 |
| Hayes | 4 | 93 | 23 | 0 |
| Carmichael | 1 | 15 | 15 | 0 |
| Dixon | 1 | 8 | 8 | 0 |

### PASSING — PUNTING — KICKING

| Last Name | Att | Comp | % | Yds | Yd/Att | TD | Int−% | RK |
|---|---|---|---|---|---|---|---|---|
| PASSING | | | | | | | | |
| McCormick | 253 | 103 | 41 | 1292 | 5.1 | 7 | 14− 6 | 10 |
| Slaughter | 147 | 75 | 51 | 864 | 5.9 | 6 | 12− 8 | 9 |
| Lee | 80 | 44 | 55 | 692 | 8.7 | 5 | 3− 4 | |
| Hayes | 1 | 0 | 0 | 0 | 0.0 | 0 | 1−100 | |
| Haynes | 1 | 0 | 0 | 0 | 0.0 | 0 | 0− 0 | |

| PUNTING | No | Avg |
|---|---|---|
| Scarpitto | 67 | 42.3 |
| McCormick | 1 | 45.0 |

| KICKING | XP | Att | % | FG | Att | % |
|---|---|---|---|---|---|---|
| Kroner | 32 | 32 | 100 | 13 | 29 | 45 |

**2 POINT XP**
Gunsoulin
Hayes

The war between the two leagues was getting very expensive. To sign heralded rookies Donny Anderson, Jim Grabowski, and Tommy Nobis, NFL clubs had to give each of them contracts more lucrative than that given to Joe Namath by the AFL Jets last year. But after the New York Giants signed kicker Pete Gogolak away from the AFL Buffalo Bills, the heat of battle became unbearable. Considering the signing of Gogolak as a direct slap, the AFL owners went all out to pirate away established NFL stars. With John Brodie, Roman Gabriel, and Mike Ditka on the verge of jumping and other NFL stars thinking it over, the established league sat down with the upstarts to discuss terms of peace. In June, officials of both leagues announced a merger that would change the organizational set-up of pro football. With Pete Rozelle as Commissioner over both leagues, the NFL and AFL would conduct a common draft of college players starting next year and would finish this season with the first Super Bowl between the two league champions.

## EASTERN CONFERENCE

**Dallas Cowboys**—With Don Meredith at quarterback, the Dallas offense was the league's most versatile and explosive. Bob Hayes used his sprinter's speed to gain 1,232 yards on passes, while Dan Reeves succeeded at halfback despite his slowness afoot. Signed two years ago as a free agent, Reeves hustled his way to sixteen touchdowns, eight each by running and receiving, and was a threat to throw the option pass on sweeps. Ralph Neely led the blocking in a strong offensive line. The defense, loaded with quality players, led the league in sacking enemy quarterbacks and gave up yardage with extreme reluctance. Coach Tom Landry had been collecting talent for years and now all the pieces had fit together.

**Cleveland Browns**—Jimmy Brown had retired to become an actor, but no one could blame replacement Leroy Kelly for Cleveland's slip to second place. Kelly had distinguished himself for two years as a kick returner, and when he was thrust into Brown's vacant shoes at fullback, he surprised the league by rushing for 1,141 yards, second only to Gale Sayers in the NFL. Kelly relied more on speed than did Brown, leaving the power running to Ernie Green. Paul Warfield returned from last year's shoulder injury to join Gary Collins in the wide receiving duo, and Frank Ryan found his targets often enough to throw for twenty-nine touchdowns. The Browns' fatal flaw this season was a slow start in which they lost two of their first three games.

**Philadelphia Eagles**—Despite a weak passing attack, the Eagles reached third place with their best record in five years. Behind a good offensive line, the running corps of Timmy Brown, Earl Gros, Tom Woodeshick, and Izzy Lang ate up large chunks of yardage, and Brown also doubled as the team's top kickoff returner, bringing two kickoffs back for touchdowns in one game against the Cowboys. The lack of quality receivers and Norm Snead's poor season hurt the attack, but the defense showed enough strength to carry the team.

**St. Louis Cardinals**—The Cards had a new coach in Charley Winner but the same old problem with injuries. Battling with Dallas for first place in the East, the Cards lost quarterback Charley Johnson with a knee injury and they scored only fifty-two points in their last five games, losing four of them, to fall to fourth place. Injuries also stripped end Sonny Randle, offensive linemen Bob DeMarco, Ken Gray, and Irv Goode, and cornerback Pat Fischer from the active rolls for varying lengths of time.

**Washington Redskins**—The Redskins brought former Cleveland great Otto Graham back to pro football as head coach, and Graham as expected put the emphasis in the Washington attack on the pass. The air game worked fine, with Sonny Jurgensen doing the pitching and Charley Taylor, converted from halfback to end in mid-season, Bobby Mitchell, and Jerry Smith doing most of the catching. Even without a legitimate running attack, the Redskins could put points on the scoreboard. But the defense needed time to jell, with seven new faces in the starting lineup.

**Pittsburgh Steelers**—Coach Bill Austin took the Steelers to five wins despite some severe problems on offense. The line blocked poorly, rookie Willie Asbury was the only effective runner, and the quarterback situation was unstable. Bill Nelsen hurt his knee in the second game of the year, and Ron Smith, let go by the Packers, filled in at quarterback for most of the season. The defense carried the club through the body of the schedule, but Nelsen returned to action for the last three games and beat New York 47-28 and Atlanta 57-33 to end the year.

**Atlanta Falcons**—The Falcons lost their first nine NFL games but came back to win three of their last five contests to escape the cellar in their first season in the league. Junior Coffey, obtained from Green Bay in the expansion draft, developed into a fine runner, but most of the impressive performances were turned in by rookies such as linebacker Tommy Nobis, quarterback Randy Johnson, and defensive backs Bob Riggle, Nick Rassas, and Ken Reaves.

**New York Giants**—With Tucker Frederickson out all year with a bad knee, Earl Morrall sidelined for the last half of the schedule with a broken wrist, and the defense a horrendous hodgepodge of journeymen and youth, the Giants suffered through the worst season in their history. They beat the Redskins 13-10 in mid-October for their only win of the year, and the rematch in late November resulted in a 72-41 embarrassment.

## WESTERN CONFERENCE

**Green Bay Packers**—The Packers shelled out about $1,000,000 to sign All-American runners Donny Anderson and Jim Grabowski, but Vince Lombardi kept his Green Bay machine running with old pros and a few key replacement parts. With Paul Hornung bothered by a neck injury, Elijah Pitts did most of the playing at halfback, while ex-Ram Carroll Dale slipped past Max McGee into the starting lineup as a wide receiver. On defense, quick Bob Jeter switched from offensive end to capture a cornerback slot. The heart of the Packers, however, was still the troop of seasoned veterans who had grown used to the taste of winning, and that was good enough to bring the Packers home first in the West.

**Baltimore Colts**—The Colts lost the opening game of the season to the Packers and struggled futilely to catch up the rest of the year. With a veteran team that was approaching old age all at once, the Colts had solid units both on defense and offense. The defensive line relied on quickness and got some size late in the year when Gino Marchetti came out of retirement; the linebacking was strengthened by the conversion of Mike Curtis from fullback to a corner linebacker; and Bobby Boyd, Lenny Lyles, Alvin Haymond, Jerry Logan, and Jim Welch blanketed enemy pass receivers from their deep spots. The offense moved on the arm of Johnny Unitas, but the Colts lost twice to the Packers and had to settle for second place behind them.

**Los Angeles Rams**—The Rams had to go to court to get George Allen to be their head coach, but the results proved well worth the trouble. Allen rebuilt the Los Angeles defense into one of the league's best. He inherited a great front four in Deacon Jones, Lamar Lundy, Merlin Olsen, and Rosie Grier, but he completely overhauled the linebacking. He talked Jack Pardee out of retirement, signed Bill George as a free agent after the Bears cut him, and traded for Maxie Baughan from the Eagles and Myron Pottios from the Steelers. To tighten up the secondary, he brought in Irv Cross from Philadelphia. Although the offense lacked flair, the improved defense carried the club to its first winning season since 1958.

**San Francisco '49ers**—With the Houston Oilers trying to lure him into the AFL, John Brodie bargained himself into a multiyear contract worth over $900,000. With his financial future secure, Brodie did nothing to show that he could lead a team to a championship. With a good line, punishing runners in Ken Willard and John David Crow, and fine wide receivers like Bernie Casey and Dave Parks, the San Francisco attack ran in spurts, running up big scores against Detroit, Chicago, and Atlanta and losing 28-3 to Minnesota and 34-3 to Los Angeles.

**Chicago Bears**—With George Halas taking George Allen into court to keep him from resigning as an assistant coach, with Doug Atkins and Mike Ditka openly critical of Halas, with Rudy Bukich suffering through a miserable campaign, and with Johnny Morris sidelined with a bad knee, Bear fans found Gale Sayers' superb season a pleasant diversion from the Bears' problems. Sayers improved on his rookie season by leading the NFL in rushing, catching thirty-four passes and breaking off two touchdowns in pacing the league in kickoff returning. Adding together his rushing, receiving, and returning totals, Sayers gained 2,440 yards, a new record.

**Detroit Lions**—Problems at quarterback made the Detroit offense a plodding affair. Milt Plum began the year as signal-caller but was out of service with a mid-season injury. Karl Sweetan, who had spent last season with the semi-pro Pontiac Arrows, stepped in and did a creditable job as a passer but could not ignite the attack into steady fireworks. On one play, however, Sweetan got the offense moving, passing to Pat Studstill for a 99-yard touchdown against the Colts on October 16. Studstill was one of the league's sensations, developing into a dangerous pass receiver despite his small size and very ordinary speed. Another player to attract attention was Garo Yepremian, a soccer-style place-kicker from Cyprus who was signed in mid-season and booted a record six field goals against the Vikings on November 13.

**Minnesota Vikings**—Expecting to move up into championship status for the last few seasons, the Vikings simply were not improving with their current team. The defense was not getting much better, halfback Tommy Mason was spending more time hurt than healthy, and quarterback Fran Tarkenton was hardly on speaking terms with coach Norm Van Brocklin. Once in a while the potential would show through in big victories such as the 20-17 triumph over Green Bay, but this promising team kept losing without much promise of winning.

## FINAL TEAM STATISTICS

### DEFENSE

| | ATL. | BALT. | CHI. | CLEV. | DALL. | DET. | G.B. | L.A. | MINN. | N.Y. | PHIL. | PITT. | ST.L. | S.F. | WASH. |
|---|---|---|---|---|---|---|---|---|---|---|---|---|---|---|---|
| **FIRST DOWNS:** Total | 295 | 245 | 239 | 255 | 221 | 240 | 211 | 196 | 213 | 273 | 249 | 238 | 209 | 238 | 261 |
| by Rushing | 126 | 94 | 116 | 113 | 64 | 109 | 106 | 64 | 85 | 122 | 139 | 107 | 68 | 88 | 106 |
| by Passing | 151 | 134 | 116 | 124 | 140 | 108 | 106 | 114 | 116 | 137 | 139 | 105 | 109 | 126 | 134 |
| by Penalty | 18 | 17 | 21 | 18 | 17 | 23 | 15 | 18 | 12 | 14 | 20 | 26 | 32 | 24 | 21 |
| **RUSHING:** Number | 472 | 460 | 466 | 450 | 356 | 479 | 446 | 401 | 412 | 480 | 390 | 468 | 377 | 414 | 438 |
| Yards | 2172 | 1733 | 1604 | 1894 | 1176 | 2006 | 1644 | 1302 | 1686 | 2053 | 1693 | 1786 | 1192 | 1629 | 1831 |
| Average Yards | 4.6 | 3.8 | 3.4 | 4.2 | 3.3 | 4.2 | 3.7 | 3.2 | 4.1 | 4.3 | 4.3 | 3.8 | 3.2 | 3.9 | 4.2 |
| Touchdowns | 20 | 7 | 13 | 16 | 11 | 16 | 9 | 10 | 15 | 23 | 13 | 11 | 11 | 15 | 19 |
| **PASSING:** Attempts | 396 | 425 | 406 | 406 | 457 | 363 | 390 | 406 | 391 | 357 | 446 | 397 | 443 | 414 | 411 |
| Completions | 227 | 240 | 202 | 221 | 212 | 210 | 202 | 190 | 206 | 194 | 226 | 192 | 197 | 206 | 224 |
| Completion Percentage | 57.3 | 56.5 | 49.8 | 54.4 | 46.4 | 57.9 | 51.8 | 46.8 | 52.7 | 54.3 | 50.7 | 48.4 | 44.5 | 49.8 | 54.5 |
| Passing Yards | 3376 | 2759 | 2600 | 2650 | 2802 | 2702 | 2316 | 2830 | 2426 | 3086 | 2964 | 2849 | 2733 | 2895 | 3237 |
| Average Yards per Attempt | 8.5 | 6.5 | 6.4 | 6.5 | 6.5 | 7.4 | 11.5 | 6.9 | 6.2 | 8.6 | 6.6 | 7.2 | 6.2 | 7.0 | 7.9 |
| Average Yards per Completion | 14.9 | 11.5 | 12.9 | 12.0 | 13.2 | 12.9 | 11.5 | 14.9 | 11.8 | 15.9 | 13.1 | 14.8 | 13.9 | 14.1 | 14.5 |
| Times Tackled Attempting to Pass | 34 | 30 | 46 | 35 | 60 | 34 | 30 | 45 | 25 | 26 | 31 | 42 | 52 | 47 | 47 |
| Yards Lost Tackled Attempting to Pass | 276 | 401 | 250 | 278 | 420 | 294 | 171 | 361 | 190 | 194 | 300 | 242 | 433 | 345 | 376 |
| Net Yards | 3100 | 2358 | 2367 | 2372 | 2382 | 2408 | 1959 | 2469 | 2236 | 2892 | 2677 | 2607 | 2300 | 2550 | 2861 |
| Touchdowns | 26 | 19 | 23 | 14 | 17 | 23 | 7 | 26 | 14 | 17 | 23 | 27 | 21 | 18 | 23 |
| Interceptions | 19 | 22 | 18 | 30 | 17 | 15 | 28 | 26 | 17 | 23 | 20 | 24 | 21 | 23 | 23 |
| Percent Intercepted | 4.8 | 5.2 | 4.4 | 7.4 | 3.7 | 6.6 | 7.2 | 6.4 | 3.6 | 4.6 | 4.5 | 6.0 | 4.7 | 5.6 | 5.6 |
| **PUNTS:** Number | 38 | 38 | 71 | 56 | 79 | 71 | 69 | 73 | 72 | 58 | 60 | 64 | 85 | 76 | 61 |
| Average Distance | 38.6 | 40.6 | 42.4 | 39.7 | 42.4 | 41.1 | 41.3 | 43.8 | 40.6 | 39.8 | 39.9 | 37.8 | 40.7 | 41.2 | 38.4 |
| **PUNT RETURNS:** Number | 35 | 30 | 46 | 23 | 26 | 27 | 30 | 49 | 28 | 28 | 31 | 42 | 50 | 59 | 40 |
| Yards | 197 | 130 | 250 | 111 | 108 | 98 | 171 | 269 | 250 | 218 | 300 | 242 | 159 | 368 | 248 |
| Average Yards | 5.6 | 4.3 | 5.4 | 4.8 | 4.2 | 3.6 | 5.7 | 5.5 | 8.9 | 8.1 | 9.7 | 5.8 | 6.4 | 11.2 | 6.2 |
| Touchdowns | 0 | 0 | 0 | 0 | 0 | 0 | 0 | 0 | 0 | 0 | 0 | 0 | 0 | 0 | 0 |
| **KICKOFF RETURNS:** Number | 44 | 63 | 49 | 68 | 78 | 45 | 52 | 58 | 50 | 49 | 65 | 63 | 50 | 59 | 70 |
| Yards | 962 | 1320 | 1055 | 1501 | 1699 | 1004 | 1213 | 1329 | 1203 | 1085 | 1330 | 1485 | 1021 | 1343 | 1488 |
| Average | 21.9 | 21.0 | 21.5 | 22.1 | 21.8 | 22.3 | 24.1 | 22.9 | 24.1 | 22.1 | 20.5 | 23.6 | 20.4 | 22.8 | 21.3 |
| Touchdowns | 0 | 0 | 0 | 0 | 0 | 0 | 0 | 0 | 0 | 0 | 0 | 0 | 0 | 0 | 0 |
| **INTERCEPTION RETURNS:** Number | 27 | 27 | 23 | 15 | 14 | 28 | 5 | 17 | 22 | 31 | 22 | 22 | 19 | 26 | 20 |
| Yards | 385 | 438 | 426 | 68 | 274 | 409 | 75 | 338 | 337 | 465 | 380 | 319 | 236 | 334 | 251 |
| Average Yards | 14.3 | 16.2 | 18.5 | 4.5 | 19.6 | 14.7 | 15.0 | 19.9 | 15.3 | 15.0 | 17.3 | 14.5 | 12.4 | 12.8 | 12.6 |
| Touchdowns | 3 | 3 | 3 | 0 | 0 | 3 | 0 | 0 | 0 | 4 | 0 | 0 | 0 | 0 | 0 |
| **PENALTIES:** Number | 66 | 69 | 71 | 61 | 63 | 61 | 67 | 76 | 67 | 83 | 63 | 82 | 83 | 91 | 62 |
| Yards | 588 | 704 | 636 | 563 | 778 | 564 | 745 | 704 | 667 | 788 | 703 | 835 | 761 | 938 | 626 |
| **FUMBLES:** Number | 24 | 25 | 35 | 24 | 23 | 19 | 26 | 37 | 24 | 19 | 30 | 37 | 20 | 22 | 36 |
| Number Lost | 13 | 18 | 23 | 19 | 10 | 11 | 14 | 20 | 8 | 14 | 15 | 20 | 10 | 11 | 20 |
| **POINTS:** Total | 437 | 226 | 272 | 259 | 239 | 317 | 163 | 212 | 304 | 501 | 340 | 347 | 265 | 325 | 355 |
| PAT Attempts | 52 | 25 | 32 | 28 | 29 | 38 | 16 | 26 | 33 | 66 | 40 | 42 | 28 | 40 | 40 |
| PAT Made | 48 | 25 | 29 | 28 | 29 | 38 | 16 | 26 | 32 | 64 | 40 | 38 | 28 | 37 | 40 |
| FG Attempts | 41 | 33 | 29 | 19 | 31 | 31 | 27 | 19 | 41 | 32 | 20 | 38 | 41 | 38 | 31 |
| FG Made | 25 | 17 | 19 | 12 | 12 | 17 | 15 | 10 | 24 | 13 | 13 | 24 | 23 | 16 | 21 |
| Percent FG Made | 61.0 | 51.5 | 41.4 | 67.9 | 38.7 | 54.8 | 55.6 | 45.5 | 58.5 | 56.5 | 66.7 | 57.6 | 56.1 | 51.6 | 67.7 |
| Safeties | 0 | 0 | 0 | 0 | 0 | 0 | 0 | 0 | 0 | 0 | 0 | 0 | 0 | 0 | 0 |

### OFFENSE

| | ATL. | BALT. | CHI. | CLEV. | DALL. | DET. | G.B. | L.A. | MINN. | N.Y. | PHIL. | PITT. | ST.L. | S.F. | WASH. |
|---|---|---|---|---|---|---|---|---|---|---|---|---|---|---|---|
| **FIRST DOWNS:** Total | 211 | 237 | 196 | 278 | 287 | 216 | 231 | 255 | 279 | 236 | 231 | 207 | 212 | 282 | 225 |
| by Rushing | 85 | 82 | 96 | 117 | 124 | 73 | 98 | 103 | 126 | 80 | 112 | 65 | 88 | 101 | 78 |
| by Passing | 104 | 142 | 85 | 142 | 139 | 126 | 115 | 133 | 132 | 129 | 104 | 117 | 108 | 153 | 130 |
| by Penalty | 22 | 13 | 15 | 19 | 24 | 17 | 18 | 19 | 21 | 27 | 15 | 25 | 16 | 28 | 17 |
| **RUSHING:** Number | 405 | 418 | 463 | 415 | 471 | 394 | 475 | 448 | 551 | 380 | 478 | 375 | 458 | 422 | 356 |
| Yards | 1519 | 1556 | 1927 | 2166 | 2122 | 1429 | 1673 | 1742 | 2091 | 1457 | 1859 | 1092 | 1601 | 1790 | 1377 |
| Average Yards | 3.8 | 3.7 | 4.1 | 5.2 | 4.5 | 3.6 | 3.5 | 3.9 | 3.8 | 3.8 | 3.9 | 2.9 | 3.5 | 4.2 | 3.9 |
| Touchdowns | 11 | 7 | 12 | 26 | 24 | 13 | 18 | 12 | 15 | 7 | 13 | 11 | 10 | 12 | 9 |
| **PASSING:** Attempts | 381 | 401 | 338 | 402 | 413 | 456 | 318 | 450 | 417 | 424 | 378 | 401 | 386 | 500 | 443 |
| Completions | 175 | 221 | 159 | 212 | 214 | 239 | 193 | 249 | 216 | 208 | 179 | 188 | 180 | 261 | 255 |
| Completion Percentage | 45.9 | 55.1 | 47.0 | 52.7 | 51.8 | 52.4 | 60.7 | 55.3 | 51.8 | 49.1 | 47.4 | 46.9 | 46.6 | 52.2 | 57.6 |
| Passing Yards | 2362 | 2930 | 2016 | 3142 | 3331 | 2424 | 2831 | 2891 | 2932 | 2999 | 2159 | 2887 | 2292 | 3239 | 3230 |
| Average Yards per Attempt | 6.2 | 7.9 | 5.0 | 7.8 | 8.1 | 5.0 | 8.9 | 6.4 | 7.0 | 7.1 | 5.7 | 7.2 | 5.9 | 6.5 | 7.3 |
| Average Yards per Completion | 13.5 | 14.4 | 12.7 | 14.8 | 15.6 | 11.5 | 14.7 | 11.6 | 13.6 | 14.4 | 12.7 | 15.3 | 12.7 | 12.4 | 12.7 |
| Times Tackled Attempting to Pass | 38 | 34 | 29 | 29 | 42 | 31 | 31 | 54 | 31 | 62 | 31 | 66 | 43 | 47 | 27 |
| Yards Lost Tackled Attempting to Pass | 345 | 244 | 239 | 237 | 308 | 328 | 229 | 351 | 384 | 524 | 259 | 523 | 316 | 247 | 216 |
| Net Yards | 2017 | 2686 | 1772 | 2905 | 3023 | 2424 | 2602 | 2540 | 2548 | 2475 | 1900 | 2364 | 1940 | 2992 | 3014 |
| Touchdowns | 14 | 17 | 23 | 30 | 24 | 28 | 14 | 17 | 22 | 31 | 22 | 18 | 13 | 26 | 20 |
| Interceptions | 27 | 18 | 23 | 15 | 14 | 18 | 5 | 17 | 18 | 22 | 22 | 22 | 19 | 26 | 20 |
| Percent Intercepted | 7.1 | 6.7 | 6.8 | 3.7 | 3.4 | 6.1 | 1.6 | 3.8 | 5.3 | 7.3 | 5.8 | 5.5 | 4.9 | 5.2 | 4.5 |
| **PUNTS:** Number | 73 | 49 | 80 | 57 | 65 | 72 | 62 | 71 | 60 | 53 | 65 | 78 | 81 | 70 | 68 |
| Average Distance | 40.7 | 45.6 | 42.0 | 39.0 | 39.2 | 41.1 | 41.0 | 42.8 | 41.1 | 38.9 | 39.8 | 42.1 | 35.6 | 40.6 | 42.4 |
| **PUNT RETURNS:** Number | 18 | 45 | 25 | 24 | 41 | 38 | 37 | 45 | 31 | 22 | 31 | 21 | 40 | 45 | 29 |
| Yards | 100 | 357 | 97 | 146 | 258 | 396 | 215 | 341 | 129 | 120 | 162 | 43 | 316 | 238 | 201 |
| Average Yards | 5.6 | 7.9 | 3.9 | 6.1 | 6.3 | 10.4 | 5.8 | 7.6 | 4.2 | 5.5 | 5.2 | 2.0 | 7.9 | 5.3 | 6.9 |
| Touchdowns | 1 | 0 | 0 | 0 | 0 | 1 | 1 | 0 | 0 | 0 | 0 | 0 | 0 | 1 | 1 |
| **KICKOFF RETURNS:** Number | 82 | 51 | 48 | 54 | 44 | 58 | 42 | 42 | 52 | 80 | 64 | 64 | 57 | 56 | 69 |
| Yards | 1737 | 1094 | 1341 | 1111 | 1006 | 1316 | 903 | 1015 | 987 | 1616 | 1419 | 1384 | 1348 | 1326 | 1435 |
| Average | 21.2 | 21.5 | 27.9 | 20.6 | 22.9 | 22.7 | 21.5 | 24.2 | 19.0 | 20.2 | 22.2 | 21.6 | 23.6 | 23.7 | 20.8 |
| Touchdowns | 1 | 0 | 1 | 0 | 0 | 0 | 0 | 0 | 0 | 0 | 0 | 0 | 0 | 0 | 0 |
| **INTERCEPTION RETURNS:** Number | 19 | 22 | 15 | 30 | 17 | 24 | 28 | 26 | 14 | 17 | 20 | 24 | 19 | 18 | 23 |
| Yards | 177 | 267 | 155 | 408 | 303 | 366 | 547 | 362 | 230 | 217 | 345 | 280 | 330 | 379 | 369 |
| Average | 9.3 | 12.1 | 10.3 | 13.6 | 17.8 | 15.3 | 19.5 | 13.9 | 16.4 | 12.8 | 17.3 | 11.7 | 15.7 | 21.1 | 16.0 |
| Touchdowns | 0 | 0 | 0 | 1 | 1 | 0 | 6 | 4 | 0 | 0 | 0 | 0 | 1 | 0 | 1 |
| **PENALTIES:** Number | 79 | 64 | 80 | 69 | 83 | 82 | 57 | 72 | 67 | 57 | 63 | 75 | 67 | 86 | 64 |
| Yards | 753 | 617 | 714 | 747 | 824 | 931 | 544 | 651 | 787 | 602 | 666 | 768 | 586 | 819 | 591 |
| **FUMBLES:** Number | 30 | 19 | 26 | 23 | 23 | 33 | 23 | 25 | 33 | 29 | 32 | 34 | 26 | 26 | 27 |
| Number Lost | 19 | 12 | 12 | 10 | 10 | 17 | 19 | 14 | 14 | 13 | 17 | 17 | 18 | 12 | 15 |
| **POINTS:** Total | 204 | 314 | 234 | 403 | 445 | 206 | 335 | 289 | 292 | 263 | 326 | 316 | 264 | 320 | 351 |
| PAT Attempts | 26 | 36 | 26 | 54 | 56 | 23 | 43 | 29 | 34 | 31 | 39 | 36 | 28 | 39 | 41 |
| PAT Made | 21 | 36 | 24 | 52 | 56 | 23 | 41 | 29 | 34 | 31 | 38 | 35 | 27 | 38 | 39 |
| FG Attempts | 29 | 32 | 33 | 23 | 31 | 30 | 28 | 49 | 33 | 18 | 25 | 32 | 40 | 33 | 34 |
| FG Made | 9 | 21 | 18 | 19 | 17 | 15 | 28 | 28 | 18 | 16 | 18 | 20 | 23 | 16 | 22 |
| Percent FG Made | 47.4 | 53.8 | 60.0 | 39.1 | 54.8 | 50.0 | 42.9 | 57.1 | 54.5 | 57.1 | 72.0 | 65.6 | 57.5 | 51.6 | 64.7 |
| Safeties | 1 | 0 | 1 | 1 | 0 | 1 | 1 | 1 | 1 | 0 | 1 | 0 | 0 | 1 | 1 |

---

## Super-bound

A trip to the first Super Bowl awaited the winner of this NFL championship game, which featured the Packers and the Cowboys. The Packers took an early lead on a Bart Starr-to-Elijah Pitts touchdown pass and immediately added on another touchdown when Mel Renfro fumbled the kickoff and Jim Grabowski ran the recovery in from 17 yards out. The Cowboys, one of pro football's exciting young teams, came right back with two touchdowns to tie the score, 14-14, at the end of one quarter. The Packers scored in the second period on a long Bart Starr-to-Carroll Dale pass, while the Cowboys answered only with a Danny Villanueva field goal. Another Villanueva three-pointer lowered the Packer lead to 21-20 in the third quarter, but touchdown passes to Boyd Dowler and Max McGee ran the score to 34-20 and seemingly put the game on ice. The Cowboys fought back, however, scoring on a long pass from Don Meredith to Frank Clarke. In the final minutes, Dallas drove for the winning touchdown, only to fall short when Meredith's fourth-down pass was intercepted in the end zone by Tom Brown.

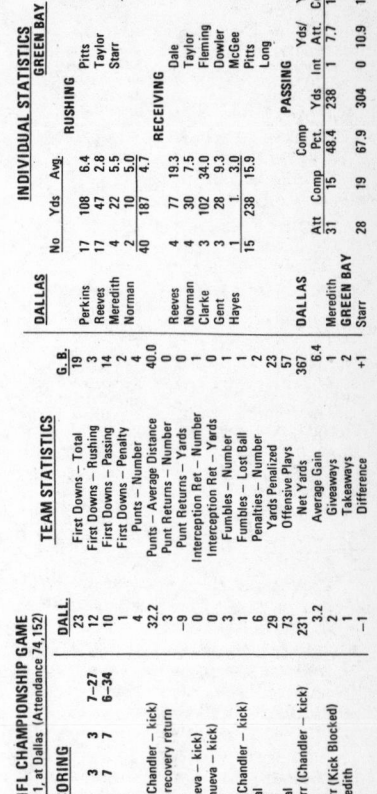

### INDIVIDUAL STATISTICS

**GREEN BAY**

RUSHING

| | No | Yds | Avg. |
|---|---|---|---|
| Pitts | 12 | 66 | 5.5 |
| Taylor | 10 | 37 | 3.7 |
| Starr | 2 | -1 | -0.5 |
| | 24 | 102 | 4.3 |

RECEIVING

| | No | Yds | Avg. |
|---|---|---|---|
| Dale | 5 | 128 | 25.6 |
| Taylor | 5 | 23 | 4.6 |
| Fleming | 3 | 50 | 16.7 |
| Dowler | 3 | 49 | 16.3 |
| McGee | 1 | 17 | 17.0 |
| Pitts | 1 | 9 | 9.0 |
| | 19 | 304 | 16.0 |

**DALLAS**

RUSHING

| | No | Yds | Avg. |
|---|---|---|---|
| Perkins | 17 | 108 | 6.4 |
| Reeves | 17 | 47 | 2.8 |
| Meredith | 4 | 22 | 5.5 |
| Norman | 2 | 10 | 5.0 |
| | 40 | 187 | 4.7 |

RECEIVING

| | No | Yds | Avg. |
|---|---|---|---|
| Reeves | 4 | 77 | 19.3 |
| Norman | 4 | 30 | 7.5 |
| Clarke | 3 | 102 | 34.0 |
| Gent | 3 | 28 | 9.3 |
| Hayes | 1 | 1 | 3.0 |
| | 15 | 238 | 15.9 |

PASSING

| | Att | Comp | Pct. Comp | Yds | Int | Yds/ Comp | Yds Lost Tackled |
|---|---|---|---|---|---|---|---|
| **DALLAS** | | | | | | | |
| Meredith | 31 | 15 | 48.4 | 238 | 1 | 15.9 | 2-7 |
| **GREEN BAY** | | | | | | | |
| Starr | 28 | 19 | 67.9 | 304 | 1 | 16.0 | 5-39 |

### TEAM STATISTICS

| | G.B. | DALL. |
|---|---|---|
| First Downs — Total | 19 | 23 |
| First Downs — Rushing | 4 | 12 |
| First Downs — Passing | 14 | 10 |
| Punts — Number | 4 | 4 |
| Punts — Average Distance | 40.0 | 32.2 |
| Punt Returns — Number | 0 | 3 |
| Punt Returns — Number | 0 | 0 |
| Interception Ret — Number | 3 | 3 |
| Interception Ret — Yards | 14 | 6 |
| Fumbles — Number | 4 | 29 |
| Fumbles — Lost Ball | 2 | 73 |
| Yards Penalized | 57 | 231 |
| Offensive Plays | | |
| Net Yards | | |
| Average Gain | 6.4 | 3.2 |
| Takeaways | 1 | 2 |
| Giveaways | 2 | 1 |
| Difference | +1 | -1 |

### 1966 NFL CHAMPIONSHIP GAME
January 1, at Dallas (Attendance 74,152)

SCORING

| | | | | | |
|---|---|---|---|---|---|
| DALLAS | 14 | 3 | 3 | 7 | — 27 |
| GREEN BAY | 14 | 7 | 0 | 13 | — 34 |

**First Quarter**
GB Pitts, 17 yd pass by Starr (Chandler – kick)
GB Grabowski, 18 yd Fumble recovery return (Chandler – kick)
DA Reeves, 3 yd rush (Villanueva – kick)
DA Perkins, 23 yd rush (Villanueva – kick)

**Second Quarter**
GB Dale, 51 yd pass by Starr (Chandler – kick)
DA Villanueva, 11 yd field goal

**Third Quarter**
DA Villanueva, 32 yd field goal

**Fourth Quarter**
GB Dowler, 16 yd pass by Starr (Chandler – kick)
GB McGee, 28 yd pass by Starr (Kick Blocked)
DA Clarke, 68 yd pass by Meredith (Villanueva – kick)

## DALLAS COWBOYS 10-3-1 Tom Landry

| Scores of Each Game | | |
|---|---|---|
| 52 | NEW YORK | 7 |
| 28 | MINNESOTA | 17 |
| 47 | Atlanta | 14 |
| 56 | PHILADELPHIA | 7 |
| 10 | St. Louis | 10 |
| 21 | Clevleand | 30 |
| 52 | PITTSBURGH | 21 |
| 23 | Philadelphia | 24 |
| 31 | Washington | 30 |
| 20 | Pittsburgh | 7 |
| 26 | CLEVELAND | 14 |
| 31 | ST. LOUIS | 17 |
| 31 | WASHINGTON | 34 |
| 17 | New York | 7 |

| Use Name | Pos. | Hgt | Wgt | Age | Int | Pts |
|---|---|---|---|---|---|---|
| Jim Boeke | OT | 6'5" | 255 | 27 | | |
| Ralph Neely | OT | 6'5" | 257 | 22 | | |
| Tony Liscio | OG-OT | 6'5" | 255 | 26 | | |
| Leon Donahue | OG | 6'4" | 245 | 27 | | |
| John Niland | OG | 6'4" | 250 | 22 | | |
| Mike Connelly | OT-OG | 6'3" | 248 | 30 | | |
| Dave Manders | C | 6'2" | 240 | 24 | | |
| Malcolm Walker | OT-C | 6'4" | 245 | 23 | | |
| George Andrie | DE | 6'7" | 255 | 26 | 1 | 6 |
| Larry Stephens | DE | 6'4" | 250 | 28 | | |
| Jethro Pugh | DT-DE | 6'6" | 250 | 22 | | |
| John Wilbur | DT-DE | 6'3" | 250 | 23 | | |
| Jim Colvin | DT | 6'2" | 255 | 29 | | |
| Bob Lilly | DT | 6'4" | 255 | 27 | | |
| Bill Sandeman | DT | 6'6" | 250 | 23 | | |
| Willie Townes | DE-DT | 6'5" | 265 | 23 | | 2 |
| Dave Edwards | LB | 6'3" | 226 | 27 | 1 | |
| Harold Hays | LB | 6'3" | 223 | 25 | | |
| Chuck Howley | LB | 6'3" | 223 | 30 | | 6 |
| Lee Roy Jordan | LB | 6'2" | 216 | 25 | 1 | 6 |
| Jerry Tubbs | LB | 6'2" | 222 | 31 | 1 | |
| Dick Daniels | DB | 5'9" | 180 | 20 | | |
| Mike Gaechter | DB | 6' | 190 | 26 | 3 | |
| Cornell Green | DB | 6'4" | 215 | 26 | 4 | 6 |
| Mike Johnson | DB | 5'10" | 186 | 22 | | |
| Warren Livingston | DB | 5'10" | 190 | 28 | 2 | |
| Obert Logan | DB | 5'10" | 180 | 24 | 2 | |
| Mel Renfro | HB-DB | 6' | 195 | 24 | 2 | 6 |
| Jim Steffen – Injury | | | | | | |
| Don Meredith | QB | 6'2" | 206 | 28 | | 30 |
| Craig Morton | QB | 6'4" | 216 | 23 | | |
| Jerry Rhome | QB | 6' | 187 | 24 | | |
| Dan Reeves | HB | 6'1" | 203 | 22 | | 96 |
| Les Shy | HB | 6'1" | 210 | 22 | | 6 |
| Walt Garrison | FB-HB | 6' | 200 | 22 | | 6 |
| Don Perkins | FB | 5'10" | 206 | 28 | | 48 |
| J. D. Smith | FB | 6'1" | 210 | 33 | | 6 |
| Buddy Dial | FL | 6'1" | 195 | 29 | | 6 |
| Pete Gent | FL | 6'4" | 210 | 23 | | 6 |
| Frank Clarke | TE | 6' | 210 | 33 | | 24 |
| Pettis Norman | TE | 6'3" | 223 | 26 | | |
| Bob Hayes | OE | 6' | 190 | 23 | | 78 |
| Danny Villanueva | K | 5'11" | 200 | 28 | | 107 |

## PHILADELPHIA EAGLES 9-5-0 Joe Kuharich

| Scores of Each Game | | |
|---|---|---|
| 13 | St. Louis | 16 |
| 23 | ATLANTA | 10 |
| 35 | NEW YORK | 17 |
| 10 | ST. LOUIS | 41 |
| 7 | Dallas | 56 |
| 31 | Pittsburgh | 14 |
| 31 | New York | 3 |
| 13 | WASHINGTON | 27 |
| 24 | DALLAS | 23 |
| 7 | Cleveland | 27 |
| 35 | San Francisco | 34 |
| 27 | PITTSBURGH | 23 |
| 33 | CLEVELAND | 21 |
| 37 | Washington | 28 |

| Use Name | Pos. | Hgt | Wgt | Age | Int | Pts |
|---|---|---|---|---|---|---|
| Bob Brown | OT | 6'4" | 276 | 23 | | |
| Dave Graham | OT | 6'3" | 250 | 27 | | |
| Lane Howell | OT | 6'5" | 270 | 25 | | |
| Ray Rissmiller | OT | 6'4" | 250 | 24 | | |
| Ed Blaine | OG | 6'2" | 240 | 26 | | |
| Jim Skaggs | OG | 6'2" | 250 | 26 | | |
| Bruce Van Dyke | OG | 6'2" | 235 | 22 | | |
| Lynn Hoyem | C-OG | 6'4" | 253 | 26 | | |
| Dave Recher | C | 6'1" | 245 | 23 | | |
| Jim Ringo | C | 6'1" | 230 | 35 | | |
| Randy Beisler | DE | 6'4" | 245 | 21 | | |
| Don Hultz | DE | 6'3" | 235 | 25 | | |
| Gary Pettigrew | DE | 6'4" | 245 | 21 | | |
| Dave Cahill | DT | 6'3" | 238 | 24 | | |
| John Meyers | DT | 6'6" | 276 | 26 | | |
| Floyd Peters | DT | 6'4" | 255 | 31 | | |
| Ike Kelley | LB | 5'11" | 225 | 22 | | |
| Dave Lloyd | LB | 6'3" | 248 | 30 | 3 | |
| Mike Morgan | LB | 6'4" | 242 | 24 | 1 | |
| Arunas Vasys | LB | 6'2" | 225 | 23 | | |
| Harold Wells | LB | 6'2" | 220 | 27 | 1 | 6 |
| Fred Whittingham | LB | 6'1" | 240 | 27 | 1 | |
| Aaron Martin | DB | 6' | 185 | 25 | 1 | 6 |
| Ron Medved | DB | 6'1" | 210 | 22 | | |
| Al Nelson | DB | 5'11" | 186 | 22 | 1 | 6 |
| Jim Nettles | DB | 5'9" | 180 | 24 | 3 | 6 |
| Nate Ramsey | DB | 6'1" | 200 | 25 | 1 | |
| Joe Scarpati | DB | 5'10" | 185 | 24 | 8 | |
| Fred Brown – Knee Injury | | | | | | |
| Frank Molden – Knee Injury | | | | | | |
| Ray Poage – Knee Injury | | | | | | |
| Bob Shann – Injury | | | | | | |
| Jack Concannon | QB | 6'3" | 195 | 23 | | 12 |
| King Hill | QB | 6'3" | 213 | 30 | | |
| Norm Snead | QB | 6'4" | 205 | 26 | | 6 |
| Timmy Brown | HB | 5'10" | 198 | 29 | | 48 |
| Ollie Matson | HB | 6'2" | 210 | 36 | | 12 |
| Earl Gros | FB | 6'3" | 220 | 25 | | 54 |
| Izzy Lang | FB | 6'1" | 230 | 23 | | 6 |
| Tom Woodeshick | HB-FB | 6' | 220 | 24 | | 30 |
| Willie Brown | FL | 6' | 185 | 23 | | |
| T.J. Jackson | FL | 6' | 180 | 23 | | |
| Ron Goodwin | OE-FL | 6' | 180 | 24 | | 6 |
| Pete Retzlaff | TE | 6'1" | 214 | 35 | | 36 |
| Dave Lince | TE | 6'6" | 250 | 22 | | |
| Fred Hill | OE | 6'2" | 215 | 23 | | |
| Ben Hawkins | FL-OE | 6' | 180 | 22 | | |
| Sam Baker | K | 6'2" | 218 | 34 | | 92 |

## CLEVELAND BROWNS 9-5-0 Blanton Collier

| Scores of Each Game | | |
|---|---|---|
| 38 | Washington | 14 |
| 20 | GREEN BAY | 21 |
| 28 | ST. LOUIS | 34 |
| 28 | New York | 7 |
| 41 | PITTSBURGH | 10 |
| 30 | DALLAS | 21 |
| 49 | Atlanta | 17 |
| 6 | Pittsburgh | 16 |
| 27 | PHILADELPHIA | 7 |
| 14 | WASHINGTON | 3 |
| 14 | Dallas | 26 |
| 49 | NEW YORK | 40 |
| 21 | Philadelphia | 33 |
| 38 | St. Louis | 10 |

| Use Name | Pos. | Hgt | Wgt | Age | Int | Pts |
|---|---|---|---|---|---|---|
| Jim Battle | OT | 6'4" | 235 | 25 | | |
| John Brown | OT | 6'2" | 248 | 27 | | |
| Monte Clark | OT | 6'6" | 265 | 29 | | |
| Dick Schafrath | OT | 6'3" | 255 | 30 | | |
| Gene Hickerson | OG | 6'3" | 248 | 31 | | |
| Joe Bob Isbell | OG | 6'1" | 250 | 26 | | |
| John Wooten | OG | 6'2" | 250 | 31 | | |
| Fred Hoaglin | C | 6'4" | 240 | 22 | | |
| John Morrow | C | 6'3" | 248 | 33 | | |
| Bill Glass | DE | 6'5" | 255 | 30 | | 6 |
| Paul Wiggin | DE | 6'3" | 245 | 32 | 1 | |
| Walter Johnson | DT | 6'3" | 265 | 23 | | |
| Jim Kanicki | DT | 6'4" | 270 | 24 | | |
| Dick Modzelewski | DT | 6' | 260 | 35 | | |
| Frank Parker | DT | 6'5" | 270 | 26 | | |
| Johnny Brewer | LB | 6'4" | 235 | 29 | 1 | |
| Vince Costello | LB | 6' | 228 | 34 | 1 | |
| Galen Fiss | LB | 6' | 227 | 36 | | |
| Dale Lindsey | LB | 6'3" | 220 | 23 | | |
| Sid Williams | LB | 6'2" | 235 | 24 | | |
| Jim Houston | TE-LB | 6'2" | 240 | 29 | 2 | 7 |
| Erich Barnes | DB | 6'2" | 198 | 31 | 4 | |
| Walter Beach | DB | 6' | 185 | 31 | 1 | |
| Ross Fichtner | DB | 6' | 185 | 28 | 8 | 6 |
| Bobby Franklin | DB | 5'11" | 182 | 30 | | |
| Mike Howell | DB | 6'1" | 187 | 23 | 8 | |
| Ernie Kellerman | DB | 6' | 183 | 22 | 3 | |
| Bernie Parrish (to HOU-A) | DB | 5'11" | 195 | 31 | 1 | |
| Gary Lane | QB | 6'1" | 210 | 23 | | |
| Jim Ninowski | QB | 6'1" | 207 | 30 | | |
| Frank Ryan | QB | 6'3" | 200 | 30 | | |
| Leroy Kelly | HB | 6' | 195 | 24 | | 96 |
| Randy Schultz | FB-HB | 5'11" | 210 | 22 | | |
| Ernie Green | FB | 6'2" | 205 | 27 | | 54 |
| Charlie Harraway | FB | 6'2" | 230 | 21 | | |
| Nick Pietrosante | FB | 6'2" | 225 | 29 | | |
| Gary Collins | FL | 6'4" | 208 | 25 | | 72 |
| Clifton McNeil | FL | 6'2" | 185 | 26 | | 12 |
| Milt Morin | TE | 6'4" | 250 | 24 | | 18 |
| Ralph Smith | TE | 6'2" | 215 | 27 | | 18 |
| Paul Warfield | OE | 6' | 188 | 23 | | 36 |
| Walter Roberts | FL-OE | 5'10" | 163 | 24 | | |
| Lou Groza | K | 6'3" | 250 | 42 | | 78 |

## ST. LOUIS CARDINALS 8-5-1 Charley Winner

| Scores of Each Game | | |
|---|---|---|
| 16 | PHILADELPHIA | 13 |
| 23 | WASHINGTON | 7 |
| 34 | Cleveland | 28 |
| 41 | Philadelphia | 10 |
| 24 | NEW YORK | 19 |
| 10 | DALLAS | 10 |
| 20 | Washington | 26 |
| 24 | CHICAGO | 17 |
| 20 | New York | 17 |
| 9 | Pittsburgh | 30 |
| 6 | PITTSBURGH | 3 |
| 17 | Dallas | 31 |
| 10 | Atlanta | 16 |
| 10 | CLEVELAND | 38 |

| Use Name | Pos. | Hgt | Wgt | Age | Int | Pts |
|---|---|---|---|---|---|---|
| John McDowell | OT | 6'3" | 260 | 23 | | |
| Ernie McMillan | OT | 6'6" | 260 | 28 | | |
| Bob Reynolds | OT | 6'6" | 265 | 25 | | |
| Dave O'Brien | OG-OT | 6'3" | 247 | 25 | | |
| Ken Gray | OG | 6'2" | 250 | 30 | | |
| Frank Roy | OG | 6'2" | 230 | 23 | | |
| Rick Sortun | OG | 6'2" | 235 | 23 | | |
| Irv Goode | C-OG | 6'4" | 250 | 25 | | |
| Bob DeMarco | C | 6'3" | 240 | 28 | | |
| Dick Kasperek | C | 6'3" | 225 | 22 | | |
| Don Brumm | DE | 6'3" | 245 | 23 | | |
| Mike Melinkovich | DE | 6'4" | 245 | 24 | | |
| Joe Robb | DE | 6'3" | 245 | 29 | | |
| Dave Long | DT-DE | 6'4" | 235 | 21 | | |
| Sam Silas | DT | 6'4" | 250 | 23 | | |
| Chuck Walker | DT | 6'2" | 245 | 25 | | |
| Fred Heron | DE-DT | 6'4" | 250 | 21 | | |
| Bill Koman | LB | 6'2" | 230 | 32 | | |
| Dave Meggyesy | LB | 6'1" | 220 | 24 | | |
| Dale Meinert | LB | 6'2" | 220 | 33 | | |
| Dave Simmons | LB | 6'4" | 245 | 23 | | |
| Larry Stallings | LB | 6'2" | 230 | 24 | 1 | |
| Mike Strofolino | LB | 6'2" | 230 | 22 | | |
| Jimmy Burson | DB | 6' | 180 | 24 | 2 | |
| Pat Fischer | DB | 5'10" | 170 | 26 | 1 | |
| Jim Heidel | DB | 6'1" | 185 | 22 | | |
| Jerry Stovall | DB | 6'2" | 205 | 24 | 3 | 6 |
| Bobby Williams | DB | 6'1" | 185 | 24 | | |
| Larry Wilson | DB | 6' | 190 | 28 | 10 | 12 |
| Abe Woodson | DB | 5'11" | 190 | 31 | 4 | |
| Bill Thornton – Injury | | | | | | |
| Jim Hart | QB | 6'2" | 195 | 22 | | |
| Charley Johnson | QB | 6' | 190 | 29 | | 12 |
| Terry Nofsinger | QB | 6'4" | 215 | 28 | | 12 |
| Charlie Bryant | HB | 6'1" | 207 | 25 | | |
| Roy Shivers | HB | 6' | 200 | 24 | | 6 |
| Bill Triplett | HB | 6'2" | 210 | 27 | | |
| Johnny Roland | FB-HB | 6'2" | 207 | 23 | | 36 |
| Willie Crenshaw | FB | 6'2" | 230 | 25 | | |
| Prentice Gautt | HB-FB | 6' | 210 | 28 | | 12 |
| Bobby Joe Conrad | FL | 6' | 195 | 31 | | 12 |
| Mal Hammack | TE | 6'2" | 210 | 33 | | |
| Ray Ogden | TE | 6'5" | 225 | 23 | | |
| Jackie Smith | TE | 6'4" | 215 | 25 | | 18 |
| Sonny Randle | OE | 6'2" | 190 | 30 | | 12 |
| Billy Gambrell | FL-OE | 5'10" | 175 | 24 | | 30 |
| Jim Bakken | K | 6' | 200 | 25 | | 96 |

## WASHINGTON REDSKINS 7-7-0 Otto Graham

| Scores of Each Game | | |
|---|---|---|
| 14 | CLEVELAND | 38 |
| 7 | St. Louis | 23 |
| 33 | Pittsburgh | 27 |
| 24 | PITTSBURGH | 10 |
| 33 | ATLANTA | 20 |
| 10 | New York | 13 |
| 26 | ST. LOUIS | 20 |
| 27 | Philadelphia | 13 |
| 10 | Blatimore | 37 |
| 30 | DALLAS | 31 |
| 3 | Cleveland | 14 |
| 72 | NEW YORK | 41 |
| 34 | Dallas | 31 |
| 28 | PHILADELPHIA | 37 |

| Use Name | Pos. | Hgt | Wgt | Age | Int | Pts |
|---|---|---|---|---|---|---|
| Mitch Johnson | OT | 6'4" | 245 | 24 | | |
| John Kelly | OT | 6'3" | 256 | 22 | | |
| Jim Snowden | OT | 6'3" | 255 | 24 | | |
| Tom Goosby | OG | 6' | 235 | 27 | | |
| Jake Kupp | OG | 6'3" | 233 | 24 | | |
| Vince Promuto | OG | 6'1" | 245 | 28 | | |
| Ray Schoenke | OG | 6'3" | 234 | 24 | | |
| Don Croftcheck | LB-OG | 6'1" | 230 | 23 | | |
| Dave Crossan | C | 6'3" | 245 | 26 | | |
| Len Hauss | C | 6'2" | 235 | 24 | | |
| Willie Adams | DE | 6'2" | 235 | 24 | | |
| Bill Briggs | DE | 6'3" | 250 | 22 | | |
| Carl Kammerer | DE | 6'3" | 243 | 29 | | |
| Ron Snidow | DE | 6'4" | 250 | 24 | | |
| Walt Barnes | DT | 6'3" | 250 | 22 | | |
| Stan Jones | DT | 6'1" | 250 | 35 | | |
| Joe Rutgens | DT | 6'2" | 255 | 27 | | |
| Jim Carroll (from NY) | LB | 6'1" | 230 | 23 | 1 | |
| Chris Hanburger | LB | 6'2" | 218 | 25 | 1 | |
| Sam Huff | LB | 6'1" | 230 | 31 | 1 | |
| Steve Jackson | LB | 6'1" | 225 | 23 | 1 | |
| John Reger | LB | 6' | 220 | 35 | 3 | 6 |
| Billy Clay | DB | 6'1" | 192 | 22 | 1 | |
| Rickie Harris | DB | 6' | 182 | 23 | 1 | 6 |
| Paul Krause | DB | 6'3" | 195 | 24 | 2 | |
| Brig Owens | DB | 5'11" | 190 | 23 | 7 | 12 |
| Lonnie Sanders | DB | 6'3" | 207 | 24 | | |
| Jim Shorter | DB | 5'11" | 185 | 25 | 5 | |
| Tom Walters | DB | 6'2" | 195 | 24 | | |
| John Seedborg – Military Service | | | | | | |
| Sonny Jurgensen | QB | 5'11" | 205 | 32 | | |
| Dick Shiner | QB | 6' | 197 | 24 | | |
| Ron Rector (to ATL) | HB | 6' | 200 | 22 | | |
| Steve Thurlow (from NY) | HB | 6'3" | 216 | 23 | | |
| Tom Barrington | FB-HB | 6'1" | 218 | 22 | | |
| Joe Kantor | FB | 6'1" | 217 | 23 | | |
| A. D. Whitfield | FB | 5'10" | 200 | 22 | | 18 |
| Joe Don Looney (fron DET) | HB-FB | 6'1" | 230 | 23 | | 24 |
| John Burrell | FL | 6'3" | 195 | 26 | | |
| Fred Mazurek | FL | 5'11" | 192 | 23 | | |
| Bobby Mitchell | FL | 6' | 196 | 31 | | 60 |
| Jim Avery | TE | 6'2" | 235 | 22 | | |
| Pat Richter | TE | 6'5" | 230 | 25 | | |
| Jerry Smith | TE | 6'2" | 208 | 23 | | 36 |
| Pat Hodgson | OE | 6'2" | 190 | 22 | | |
| Charley Taylor | HB-OE | 6'3" | 210 | 25 | | 90 |
| Charlie Gogolak | K | 5'10" | 165 | 21 | | 105 |

## DALLAS COWBOYS

### RUSHING
| Last Name | No. | Yds | Avg | TD |
|---|---|---|---|---|
| Reeves | 175 | 757 | 4.3 | 8 |
| Perkins | 186 | 726 | 3.9 | 8 |
| Meredith | 38 | 242 | 6.4 | 5 |
| Shy | 17 | 118 | 6.9 | 1 |
| Garrison | 16 | 62 | 3.9 | 1 |
| Renfro | 8 | 52 | 6.5 | 0 |
| Morton | 7 | 50 | 7.1 | 0 |
| Clarke | 8 | 49 | 6.1 | 0 |
| Rhome | 7 | 37 | 5.3 | 0 |
| Villanueva | 1 | 23 | 23.0 | 0 |
| Smith | 7 | 7 | 1.0 | 1 |
| Hayes | 1 | -1 | -1.0 | 0 |

### RECEIVING
| Last Name | No. | Yds | Avg | TD |
|---|---|---|---|---|
| Hayes | 64 | 1232 | 19 | 13 |
| Reeves | 41 | 557 | 14 | 8 |
| Gent | 27 | 474 | 18 | 1 |
| Clarke | 26 | 355 | 14 | 4 |
| Perkins | 23 | 231 | 10 | 0 |
| Dial | 14 | 252 | 18 | 1 |
| Norman | 12 | 144 | 12 | 0 |
| Renfro | 4 | 65 | 16 | 0 |
| Garrison | 2 | 18 | 9 | 0 |
| Smith | 1 | 3 | 3 | 0 |

### PUNT RETURNS
| Last Name | No. | Yds | Avg | TD |
|---|---|---|---|---|
| Renfro | 21 | 123 | 6 | 0 |
| Hayes | 17 | 106 | 6 | 0 |
| Howley | 1 | 30 | 30 | 0 |
| Reeves | 2 | -1 | -1 | 0 |

### KICKOFF RETURNS
| Last Name | No. | Yds | Avg | TD |
|---|---|---|---|---|
| Renfro | 19 | 487 | 26 | 1 |
| Garrison | 20 | 445 | 22 | 0 |
| Reeves | 3 | 56 | 19 | 0 |
| Neely | 2 | 18 | 9 | 0 |

### PASSING – PUNTING – KICKING

PASSING
| Last Name | Att | Comp | % | Yds | Yd/Att | TD | Int-% | RK |
|---|---|---|---|---|---|---|---|---|
| Meredith | 344 | 177 | 51 | 2805 | 8.2 | 24 | 12- 3 | 4 |
| Rhome | 36 | 21 | 58 | 253 | 7.0 | 1 | 0- 1 | 3 |
| Morton | 27 | 13 | 48 | 225 | 8.3 | 3 | 1- 4 | |
| Reeves | 6 | 3 | 50 | 48 | 8.0 | 0 | 0- 0 | |

PUNTING
| Last Name | No | Avg |
|---|---|---|
| Villanueva | 65 | 39.2 |

KICKING
| Last Name | XP | Att | % | FG | Att | % |
|---|---|---|---|---|---|---|
| Villanueva | 56 | 56 | 100 | 17 | 31 | 55 |

## PHILADELPHIA EAGLES

### RUSHING
| Last Name | No. | Yds | Avg | TD |
|---|---|---|---|---|
| T. Brown | 161 | 548 | 3.4 | 3 |
| Gros | 102 | 396 | 3.9 | 7 |
| Woodeshick | 85 | 330 | 3.9 | 4 |
| Lang | 52 | 239 | 4.6 | 1 |
| Concannon | 25 | 195 | 7.8 | 2 |
| Matson | 29 | 101 | 3.5 | 1 |
| Snead | 15 | 32 | 2.1 | 1 |
| Baker | 1 | 15 | 15.0 | 0 |
| F. Hill | 1 | 5 | 5.0 | 0 |
| K. Hill | 7 | -2 | -0.3 | 0 |

### RECEIVING
| Last Name | No. | Yds | Avg | TD |
|---|---|---|---|---|
| Retzlaff | 40 | 653 | 16 | 6 |
| T. Brown | 33 | 371 | 11 | 3 |
| F. Hill | 29 | 304 | 10 | 0 |
| Gros | 18 | 214 | 12 | 2 |
| Goodwin | 16 | 212 | 13 | 1 |
| Hawkins | 14 | 143 | 10 | 0 |
| Lang | 12 | 107 | 9 | 0 |
| Woodeshick | 10 | 118 | 12 | 1 |
| Matson | 6 | 30 | 5 | 1 |
| Concannon | 1 | 7 | 7 | 0 |

### PUNT RETURNS
| Last Name | No. | Yds | Avg | TD |
|---|---|---|---|---|
| Martin | 11 | 118 | 11 | 1 |
| Hawkins | 9 | 47 | 5 | 0 |
| Concannon | 2 | 3 | 2 | 0 |
| Nelson | 1 | 3 | 3 | 0 |
| T. Brown | 1 | 0 | 0 | 0 |
| W. Brown | 5 | -1 | 0 | 0 |
| Scarpati | 2 | -8 | -4 | 0 |

### KICKOFF RETURNS
| Last Name | No. | Yds | Avg | TD |
|---|---|---|---|---|
| T. Brown | 20 | 562 | 28 | 2 |
| Matson | 26 | 544 | 21 | 0 |
| Martin | 4 | 132 | 33 | 0 |
| W. Brown | 4 | 58 | 15 | 0 |
| Nelson | 2 | 34 | 17 | 0 |
| Whittingham | 2 | 33 | 17 | 0 |
| Beisler | 1 | 17 | 17 | 0 |
| Jackson | 1 | 16 | 16 | 0 |
| Lince | 1 | 13 | 13 | 0 |
| Medved | 2 | 10 | 5 | 0 |
| Hawkins | 1 | 0 | 0 | 0 |

PASSING
| Last Name | Att | Comp | % | Yds | Yd/Att | TD | Int-% | RK |
|---|---|---|---|---|---|---|---|---|
| Snead | 226 | 103 | 46 | 1275 | 5.6 | 8 | 11- 5 | 16 |
| K. Hill | 97 | 53 | 55 | 571 | 5.9 | 5 | 7- 7 | |
| Concannon | 51 | 21 | 41 | 262 | 5.1 | 1 | 4- 8 | |
| Lang | 3 | 2 | 67 | 51 | 17.0 | 0 | 0- 0 | |
| Gros | 1 | 0 | 0 | 0 | 0 | 0 | 0- 0 | |

PUNTING
| Last Name | No | Avg |
|---|---|---|
| Baker | 42 | 41.1 |
| K. Hill | 23 | 37.5 |

KICKING
| Last Name | XP | Att | % | FG | Att | % |
|---|---|---|---|---|---|---|
| Baker | 38 | 39 | 97 | 18 | 25 | 72 |

## CLEVELAND BROWNS

### RUSHING
| Last Name | No. | Yds | Avg | TD |
|---|---|---|---|---|
| Kelly | 209 | 1141 | 5.5 | 15 |
| Green | 144 | 750 | 5.2 | 3 |
| Ryan | 36 | 156 | 4.3 | 0 |
| Harraway | 7 | 40 | 5.7 | 0 |
| Collins | 2 | 38 | 19.0 | 0 |
| Schultz | 7 | 32 | 4.6 | 0 |
| Pietrosante | 7 | 20 | 2.9 | 0 |
| Ninowski | 3 | -11 | -3.7 | 0 |

### RECEIVING
| Last Name | No. | Yds | Avg | TD |
|---|---|---|---|---|
| Collins | 56 | 946 | 17 | 12 |
| Green | 45 | 445 | 10 | 6 |
| Warfield | 36 | 741 | 21 | 5 |
| Kelly | 32 | 366 | 11 | 1 |
| Morin | 23 | 333 | 14 | 3 |
| Smith | 13 | 183 | 14 | 3 |
| McNeil | 2 | 94 | 47 | 2 |
| Roberts | 2 | 19 | 10 | 0 |
| Pietrosante | 1 | 12 | 12 | 0 |
| Houston | 1 | 10 | 10 | 1 |
| Costello | 1 | -7 | -7 | 0 |

### PUNT RETURNS
| Last Name | No. | Yds | Avg | TD |
|---|---|---|---|---|
| Kelly | 13 | 104 | 8 | 0 |
| Roberts | 11 | 42 | 4 | 0 |

### KICKOFF RETURNS
| Last Name | No. | Yds | Avg | TD |
|---|---|---|---|---|
| Roberts | 20 | 454 | 23 | 0 |
| Kelly | 19 | 403 | 21 | 0 |
| Harraway | 9 | 193 | 21 | 0 |
| Schultz | 3 | 52 | 17 | 0 |
| Pietrosante | 2 | 9 | 5 | 0 |
| Smith | 1 | 0 | 0 | 0 |

PASSING
| Last Name | Att | Comp | % | Yds | Yd/Att | TD | Int-% | RK |
|---|---|---|---|---|---|---|---|---|
| Ryan | 382 | 200 | 52 | 2974 | 7.8 | 29 | 14- 4 | 3 |
| Ninowski | 18 | 11 | 61 | 175 | 9.7 | 4 | 1- 6 | |
| Groza | 1 | 1 | 100 | -7 | -7.0 | 0 | 0- 0 | |
| Kelly | 1 | 0 | 0 | 0 | 0 | 0 | 0- 0 | |

PUNTING
| Last Name | No | Avg |
|---|---|---|
| Collins | 57 | 39.0 |

KICKING
| Last Name | XP | Att | % | FG | Att | % |
|---|---|---|---|---|---|---|
| Groza | 51 | 52 | 98 | 9 | 23 | 39 |
| Houston | 1 | 1 | 100 | 0 | 0 | 0 |

## ST. LOUIS CARDINALS

### RUSHING
| Last Name | No. | Yds | Avg | TD |
|---|---|---|---|---|
| Roland | 192 | 695 | 3.6 | 5 |
| Gautt | 110 | 370 | 3.4 | 1 |
| Crenshaw | 94 | 360 | 3.8 | 0 |
| Johnson | 20 | 39 | 2.0 | 2 |
| Bryant | 5 | 31 | 6.2 | 0 |
| Gambrell | 3 | 26 | 8.7 | 0 |
| Nofsinger | 18 | 25 | 1.4 | 2 |
| Triplett | 13 | 25 | 1.9 | 0 |
| Stovall | 1 | 17 | 17.0 | 0 |
| Smith | 1 | 8 | 8.0 | 0 |
| Shivers | 1 | 5 | 5.0 | 0 |

### RECEIVING
| Last Name | No. | Yds | Avg | TD |
|---|---|---|---|---|
| Smith | 45 | 810 | 18 | 3 |
| Conrad | 34 | 388 | 11 | 2 |
| Gambrell | 24 | 409 | 17 | 5 |
| Roland | 21 | 213 | 10 | 0 |
| Randle | 17 | 218 | 13 | 2 |
| Gautt | 16 | 114 | 7 | 1 |
| Crenshaw | 15 | 46 | 3 | 0 |
| Shivers | 5 | 81 | 16 | 0 |
| Triplett | 2 | 6 | 3 | 0 |
| Sortun | 1 | 7 | 7 | 0 |

### PUNT RETURNS
| Last Name | No. | Yds | Avg | TD |
|---|---|---|---|---|
| Roland | 20 | 221 | 11 | 1 |
| Shivers | 16 | 49 | 3 | 0 |
| Gambrell | 4 | 46 | 12 | 0 |

### KICKOFF RETURNS
| Last Name | No. | Yds | Avg | TD |
|---|---|---|---|---|
| Shivers | 27 | 762 | 28 | 1 |
| Roland | 15 | 347 | 23 | 0 |
| Williams | 7 | 132 | 19 | 0 |
| Bryant | 2 | 70 | 35 | 0 |
| Gambrell | 1 | 16 | 16 | 0 |
| Roy | 2 | 10 | 5 | 0 |
| Long | 1 | 9 | 9 | 0 |
| Melinkovich | 1 | 2 | 2 | 0 |
| Ogden | 1 | 0 | 0 | 0 |

PASSING
| Last Name | Att | Comp | % | Yds | Yd/Att | TD | Int-% | RK |
|---|---|---|---|---|---|---|---|---|
| Johnson | 205 | 103 | 50 | 1334 | 6.5 | 10 | 11- 5 | 9 |
| Nofsinger | 162 | 68 | 42 | 799 | 4.9 | 2 | 8- 5 | 18 |
| Hart | 11 | 4 | 36 | 29 | 2.6 | 0 | 0- 0 | |
| Roland | 8 | 5 | 63 | 130 | 16.3 | 1 | 0- 0 | |

PUNTING
| Last Name | No | Avg |
|---|---|---|
| Smith | 47 | 37.9 |
| Bakken | 29 | 33.1 |
| Stovall | 5 | 27.8 |

KICKING
| Last Name | XP | Att | % | FG | Att | % |
|---|---|---|---|---|---|---|
| Bakken | 27 | 28 | 96 | 23 | 40 | 58 |

## WASHINGTON REDSKINS

### RUSHING
| Last Name | No. | Yds | Avg | TD |
|---|---|---|---|---|
| Whitfield | 93 | 472 | 5.1 | 2 |
| Taylor | 87 | 262 | 3.0 | 3 |
| Thurlow | 80 | 260 | 3.3 | 0 |
| Looney | 63 | 220 | 3.5 | 4 |
| Mitchell | 13 | 141 | 10.8 | 1 |
| Rector | 9 | 40 | 4.4 | 0 |
| Barrington | 10 | 37 | 3.7 | 0 |
| Jurgensen | 12 | 14 | 1.2 | 0 |
| Shiner | 1 | 10 | 10.0 | 0 |
| Kantor | 1 | 2 | 2.0 | 0 |

### RECEIVING
| Last Name | No. | Yds | Avg | TD |
|---|---|---|---|---|
| Taylor | 72 | 1119 | 16 | 12 |
| Mitchell | 58 | 905 | 16 | 9 |
| Smith | 54 | 686 | 13 | 6 |
| Thurlow | 23 | 165 | 7 | 0 |
| Whitfield | 18 | 101 | 6 | 1 |
| Looney | 12 | 49 | 4 | 0 |
| Richter | 7 | 100 | 14 | 0 |
| Kupp | 4 | 28 | 7 | 0 |
| Mazurek | 2 | 28 | 14 | 0 |
| Barrington | 2 | 23 | 12 | 0 |
| Rector | 2 | 9 | 5 | 0 |
| Burrell | 1 | 9 | 9 | 0 |
| Johnson | 1 | 1 | 1 | 0 |

### PUNT RETURNS
| Last Name | No. | Yds | Avg | TD |
|---|---|---|---|---|
| Harris | 18 | 108 | 6 | 1 |
| Taylor | 5 | 63 | 13 | 0 |
| Mitchell | 4 | 21 | 5 | 0 |
| Mazurek | 2 | 9 | 5 | 0 |

### KICKOFF RETURNS
| Last Name | No. | Yds | Avg | TD |
|---|---|---|---|---|
| Mazurek | 21 | 505 | 24 | 0 |
| Harris | 20 | 405 | 20 | 0 |
| Looney | 13 | 265 | 20 | 0 |
| Taylor | 3 | 98 | 33 | 0 |
| Rector | 3 | 65 | 22 | 0 |
| Barrington | 2 | 39 | 20 | 0 |
| Croftcheck | 2 | 36 | 18 | 0 |
| Kantor | 2 | 35 | 18 | 0 |
| Jackson | 2 | 26 | 13 | 0 |
| Johnson | 2 | 22 | 11 | 0 |
| Barnes | 1 | 14 | 14 | 0 |
| Goosby | 1 | 0 | 0 | 0 |

PASSING
| Last Name | Att | Comp | % | Yds | Yd/Att | TD | Int-% | RK |
|---|---|---|---|---|---|---|---|---|
| Jurgensen | 436 | 254 | 58 | 3209 | 7.4 | 28 | 19- 4 | 2 |
| Shiner | 5 | 0 | 0 | 0 | 0.0 | 0 | 1- 20 | |
| Barrington | 1 | 0 | 0 | 0 | 0.0 | 0 | 0- 0 | |
| Mitchell | 1 | 1 | 100 | 21 | 21.0 | 0 | 0- 0 | |

PUNTING
| Last Name | No | Avg |
|---|---|---|
| Richter | 68 | 42.4 |

KICKING
| Last Name | XP | Att | % | FG | Att | % |
|---|---|---|---|---|---|---|
| Gogolak | 39 | 41 | 95 | 22 | 34 | 65 |

EASTERN CONFERENCE – Continued

**PITTSBURGH STEELERS 5-8-1 Bill Austin**

| Scores of Each Game | | |
|---|---|---|
| 34 | NEW YORK | 34 |
| 17 | DETROIT | 3 |
| 27 | WASHINGTON | 33 |
| 10 | Washington | 24 |
| 10 | Cleveland | 41 |
| 14 | PHILADELPHIA | 31 |
| 21 | Dallas | 52 |
| 16 | CLEVELAND | 6 |
| 20 | ST. LOUIS | 9 |
| 7 | DALLAS | 20 |
| 3 | St. Louis | 6 |
| 23 | Philadelphia | 27 |
| 47 | New York | 28 |
| 57 | Atlanta | 33 |

| Use Name | Pos. | Hgt | Wgt | Age | Int | Pts |
|---|---|---|---|---|---|---|
| Charlie Bradshaw | OT | 6'6" | 260 | 30 | | |
| Dan James | OT | 6'4" | 250 | 29 | | |
| Fran O'Brien (from WAS) | OT | 6'1" | 255 | 30 | | |
| Roger Pillath | OT | 6'4" | 242 | 24 | | |
| Larry Gagner | OG | 6'3" | 240 | 22 | | |
| Mike Magac | OG | 6'3" | 240 | 28 | | |
| Eli Strand | OG | 6'2" | 250 | 23 | | |
| Ralph Wenzel | OG | 6'3" | 240 | 23 | | |
| Pat Killorin | C | 6'2" | 220 | 22 | | |
| Ray Mansfield | C | 6'3" | 250 | 25 | | |
| John Baker | DE | 6'6" | 270 | 31 | | |
| Ben McGee | DE | 6'2" | 225 | 24 | | |
| Tim Powell | DE | 6'4" | 248 | 22 | | |
| Riley Gunnels | DT | 6'3" | 253 | 29 | 1 | |
| Chuck Hinton | DT | 6'5" | 260 | 27 | | |
| Ken Kortas | DT | 6'5" | 280 | 24 | | |
| Lloyd Voss | DT | 6'4" | 260 | 24 | | |
| Rod Breedlove | LB | 6'2" | 227 | 28 | 2 | |
| Gene Breen | LB | 6'2" | 230 | 25 | | |
| John Campbell | LB | 6'3" | 225 | 27 | 2 | |
| Andy Russell | LB | 6'3" | 215 | 24 | | 7 |
| Bill Saul | LB | 6'4" | 225 | 25 | 2 | |
| Bob Schmitz (to MIN) | LB | 6'1" | 240 | 28 | | |
| Jim Bradshaw | DB | 6'1" | 205 | 27 | 4 | 6 |
| Willie Daniel | DB | 5'11" | 185 | 28 | | |
| Bob Hohn | DB | 6' | 190 | 25 | | |
| Brady Keys | DB | 6' | 198 | 30 | 4 | |
| Paul Martha | DB | 6' | 185 | 23 | 3 | |
| Clendon Thomas | DB | 6'2" | 205 | 29 | 2 | 6 |
| Marv Woodson | DB | 6' | 195 | 23 | 4 | 6 |
| George Izo | QB | 6'3" | 218 | 29 | | |
| Ron Meyer | QB | 6'4" | 205 | 22 | | |
| Bill Nelsen | QB | 6' | 195 | 25 | | |
| Ron Smith | QB | 6'5" | 220 | 24 | | |
| Amos Bullocks | HB | 6'1" | 202 | 27 | | 12 |
| Cannonball Butler | HB | 5'10" | 185 | 23 | | 24 |
| Dick Hoak | HB | 5'11" | 190 | 27 | | 6 |
| Bobby Smith | HB | 6' | 203 | 24 | | |
| Dick Leftridge | FB | 6'2" | 240 | 21 | | 12 |
| Mike Lind | FB | 6'2" | 225 | 26 | | |
| Willie Asbury | FB | 6'1" | 230 | 23 | | 54 |
| Roy Jefferson | FL | 6'2" | 195 | 22 | | 24 |
| John Hilton | TE | 6'5" | 220 | 24 | | 24 |
| Tony Jeter | TE | 6'3" | 220 | 22 | | |
| Steve Smith | TE | 6'5" | 240 | 22 | | |
| Jerry Simmons | OE | 6'1" | 190 | 23 | | 6 |
| J. R. Wilburn | OE | 6'2" | 190 | 23 | | |
| Gary Ballman | FL-OE | 6' | 200 | 26 | | 30 |
| Mike Clark | K | 6'1" | 205 | 25 | | 97 |
| Frank Lambert | K | 6'3" | 200 | 23 | | |

Theron Sapp – Injury

**ATLANTA FALCONS 3-11-0 Norb Hecker**

| Scores of Each Game | | |
|---|---|---|
| 14 | LOS ANGELES | 19 |
| 10 | Philadelphia | 23 |
| 10 | Detroit | 28 |
| 14 | DALLAS | 47 |
| 20 | Washington | 33 |
| 7 | SAN FRANCISCO | 44 |
| 3 | Green Bay | 56 |
| 17 | CLEVELAND | 49 |
| 7 | BALTIMORE | 19 |
| 27 | New York | 16 |
| 6 | Chicago | 23 |
| 20 | Minnesota | 13 |
| 16 | ST. LOUIS | 10 |
| 33 | PITTSBURGH | 57 |

| Use Name | Pos. | Hgt | Wgt | Age | Int | Pts |
|---|---|---|---|---|---|---|
| Rich Koeper | OT | 6'4" | 245 | 23 | | |
| Errol Linden | OT | 6'5" | 260 | 28 | | |
| Jim Simon | OT | 6'5" | 235 | 25 | | |
| Don Talbert | OT | 6'5" | 240 | 26 | | |
| Lou Kirouac | OG | 6'3" | 240 | 25 | | 46 |
| Ed Cook | OG | 6'2" | 250 | 34 | | |
| Dan Grimm | OG | 6'3" | 245 | 25 | | |
| Frank Marchlewski | C | 6'2" | 238 | 22 | | |
| Bob Whitlow | C | 6'1" | 236 | 30 | | |
| Bobby Richards | DE | 6'2" | 247 | 27 | | |
| Sam Williams | DE | 6'5" | 235 | 35 | | |
| Karl Rubke | DE | 6'4" | 244 | 30 | | |
| Jerry Jones | DT-DE | 6'3" | 277 | 22 | | |
| Bud Marshall (from WAS) | DT | 6'5" | 270 | 24 | | |
| Guy Reese | DT | 6'5" | 260 | 26 | | |
| Chuck Sieminski | DT | 6'4" | 265 | 26 | | |
| Joe Szczercko | DT | 6' | 245 | 24 | | |
| Ralph Heck | LB | 6'2" | 230 | 25 | | |
| Bill Jobko | LB | 6'2" | 235 | 30 | 2 | |
| Larry Morris | LB | 6'2" | 230 | 31 | | |
| Tommy Nobis | LB | 6'2" | 230 | 22 | | |
| Marion Rushing | LB | 6'2" | 230 | 29 | 3 | |
| Lee Calland | DB | 6' | 190 | 25 | 3 | |
| Nick Rassas | DB | 6' | 190 | 22 | | |
| Ken Reaves | DB | 6'3" | 200 | 21 | 1 | |
| Jerry Richardson | DB | 6'3" | 190 | 23 | 5 | |
| Bob Riggle | DB | 6'1" | 200 | 22 | 3 | 6 |
| Carl Silvestri | DB | 6' | 195 | 23 | | |
| Tommy Tolleson | DB | 6' | 185 | 23 | | |
| Ron Smith | HB-DB | 6'1" | 180 | 23 | 2 | |
| Dennis Claridge | QB | 6'3" | 225 | 24 | | |
| Randy Johnson | QB | 6'3" | 195 | 22 | | 24 |
| Steve Sloan | QB | 6'1" | 185 | 22 | | |
| Junior Coffey | HB | 6'1" | 210 | 24 | | 30 |
| Perry Lee Dunn | HB | 6'2" | 200 | 23 | | |
| Rudy Johnson | HB | 5'11" | 190 | 24 | | |
| Preston Ridlehuber | HB | 6'2" | 215 | 22 | | 12 |
| Jimmy Sidle | TE-HB | 6'2" | 215 | 23 | | |
| Charlie Scales | FB | 5'11" | 215 | 27 | | |
| Ernie Wheelwright | FB | 6'3" | 240 | 29 | | 36 |
| Bill Wolski | FB | 5'11" | 203 | 22 | | |
| Glenn Glass (to DEN-A) | FL | 6' | 203 | 29 | | |
| Bob Sherlag | FL | 6' | 197 | 23 | | 6 |
| Gary Barnes | OE-FL | 6'4" | 210 | 26 | | 6 |
| Alex Hawkins | OE-FL | 6'1" | 186 | 29 | | 12 |
| Taz Anderson | TE | 6'2" | 215 | 27 | | 18 |
| Billy Martin | TE | 6'4" | 240 | 23 | | |
| Hugh McInnis | TE | 6'3" | 220 | 28 | | |
| Vern Burke | OE | 6'4" | 202 | 25 | | 6 |
| Angie Coia | OE | 6'2" | 196 | 28 | | |
| Tom Hutchinson | OE | 6'1" | 190 | 25 | | |
| Billy Lothridge | K | 6'1" | 194 | 22 | | |
| Wade Traynham | K | 6'2" | 218 | 24 | | 2 |

**NEW YORK GIANTS 1-12-1 Allie Sherman**

| Scores of Each Game | | |
|---|---|---|
| 34 | Pittsburgh | 34 |
| 7 | Dallas | 52 |
| 17 | Philadelphia | 35 |
| 7 | CLEVELAND | 28 |
| 19 | St. Louis | 24 |
| 13 | WASHINGTON | 10 |
| 3 | PHILADELPHIA | 31 |
| 17 | ST. LOUIS | 20 |
| 14 | Los Angeles | 55 |
| 16 | ATLANTA | 27 |
| 41 | Washington | 72 |
| 40 | Cleveland | 49 |
| 28 | PITTSBURGH | 47 |
| 7 | DALLAS | 17 |

| Use Name | Pos. | Hgt | Wgt | Age | Int | Pts |
|---|---|---|---|---|---|---|
| Roger Davis | OT | 6'3" | 240 | 28 | | |
| Francis Peay | OT | 6'5" | 250 | 22 | | |
| Willie Young | OT | 6' | 247 | 23 | | |
| Bob Scholtz | C-OT | 6'4" | 250 | 28 | | |
| Bookie Bolin | OG | 6'2" | 240 | 26 | | |
| Pete Case | OG | 6'3" | 245 | 25 | | |
| Darrell Dess (from WAS) | OG | 6' | 245 | 30 | | |
| Charlie Harper | OG | 6'2" | 248 | 22 | | |
| Greg Larson | C | 6'2" | 250 | 27 | | |
| Joe Wellborn | C | 6'2" | 215 | 20 | | |
| Glen Condren | DE | 6'2" | 250 | 24 | | |
| Rosey Davis | DE | 6'5" | 260 | 24 | | |
| Jim Garcia | DE | 6'4" | 250 | 22 | | |
| Jim Katcavage | DE | 6'3" | 240 | 31 | | |
| Bill Matan | DE | 6'4" | 240 | 22 | | |
| Don Davis | DT | 6'6" | 260 | 22 | | |
| Jim Moran | DT | 6'5" | 270 | 23 | | |
| Jim Prestel | DT | 6'5" | 275 | 29 | | |
| Mike Ciccolella | LB | 6'1" | 235 | 22 | | |
| Jerry Hillebrand | LB | 6'3" | 240 | 26 | 1 | 6 |
| Stan Sczurek | LB | 5'11" | 230 | 27 | | |
| Jeff Smith | LB | 6' | 237 | 22 | 1 | |
| Larry Vargo | LB | 6'3" | 215 | 26 | 1 | |
| Henry Carr | DB | 6'3" | 195 | 23 | 4 | 6 |
| Clarence Childs | DB | 6' | 180 | 27 | 2 | 6 |
| Phil Harris | DB | 6' | 195 | 21 | | |
| Wendell Harris | DB | 5'11" | 185 | 25 | 1 | 6 |
| Spider Lockhart | DB | 6'2" | 175 | 23 | 6 | |
| Dick Lynch | DB | 6'1" | 198 | 30 | | |
| Jimmy Patton | DB | 6' | 185 | 32 | 1 | |
| Tom Kennedy | QB | 6'1" | 200 | 27 | | |
| Earl Morrall | QB | 6'1" | 206 | 32 | | |
| Gary Wood | QB | 5'11" | 188 | 23 | | 18 |
| Steve Bowman | HB | 6' | 195 | 21 | | |
| Allen Jacobs | FB | 6'1" | 215 | 25 | | 6 |
| Dan Lewis | HB | 6'1" | 200 | 30 | | 6 |
| Smith Reed | HB | 6' | 215 | 24 | | |
| Ernie Koy | FB-HB | 6'2" | 230 | 23 | | |
| Chuck Mercein | FB | 6'3" | 230 | 23 | | |
| Pep Menefee | FL | 6'1" | 198 | 24 | | |
| Joe Morrison | HB-FB-FL | 6'1" | 212 | 28 | | 48 |
| Bob Crespino | TE | 6'4" | 225 | 28 | | 12 |
| Aaron Thomas | TE | 6'3" | 210 | 28 | | 24 |
| Freeman White | LB-TE | 6'5" | 225 | 22 | | |
| Del Shofner | OE | 6'3" | 185 | 30 | | |
| Homer Jones | FL-OE | 6'2" | 205 | 25 | | 48 |
| Pete Gogolak | K | 6'2" | 200 | 24 | | 77 |

Tucker Frederickson – Knee Injury
Bill Swain – Knee Injury

WESTERN CONFERENCE

**GREEN BAY PACKERS 12-2-0 Vince Lombardi**

| Scores of Each Game | | |
|---|---|---|
| 24 | BALTIMORE | 3 |
| 21 | Cleveland | 20 |
| 24 | LOS ANGELES | 13 |
| 23 | DETROIT | 14 |
| 20 | San Francisco | 21 |
| 17 | Chicago | 0 |
| 56 | ATLANTA | 3 |
| 31 | Detroit | 7 |
| 17 | MINNESOTA | 20 |
| 13 | CHICAGO | 6 |
| 28 | Minnesota | 16 |
| 20 | SAN FRANCISCO | 7 |
| 14 | Baltimore | 10 |
| 27 | Los Angeles | 23 |

| Use Name | Pos. | Hgt | Wgt | Age | Int | Pts |
|---|---|---|---|---|---|---|
| Bob Skoronski | OT | 6'3" | 250 | 33 | | |
| Steve Wright | OT | 6'6" | 250 | 24 | | |
| Forrest Gregg | OG-OT | 6'4" | 250 | 33 | | |
| Gale Gillingham | OG | 6'3" | 250 | 22 | | |
| Jerry Kramer | OG | 6'3" | 245 | 31 | | |
| Fuzzy Thurston | OG | 6'1" | 245 | 33 | | |
| Ken Bowman | C | 6'3" | 230 | 23 | | |
| Bill Curry | C | 6'2" | 235 | 23 | | |
| Lionel Aldridge | DE | 6'4" | 245 | 24 | | |
| Bob Brown | DE | 6'5" | 270 | 26 | | |
| Willie Davis | DE | 6'3" | 245 | 33 | | |
| Henry Jordan | DT | 6'3" | 250 | 31 | | |
| Ron Kostelnik | DT | 6'4" | 260 | 26 | | |
| Jim Weatherwax | DT | 6'7" | 275 | 23 | | |
| Lee Roy Caffey | LB | 6'3" | 250 | 26 | 3 | 6 |
| Tommy Crutcher | LB | 6'3" | 230 | 24 | 1 | |
| Ray Nitschke | LB | 6'3" | 240 | 30 | 2 | |
| Dave Robinson | LB | 6'3" | 245 | 25 | 5 | |
| Phil Vandersea | LB | 6'3" | 225 | 23 | | |
| Herb Adderley | DB | 6'1" | 210 | 27 | 4 | 6 |
| Tom Brown | DB | 6'1" | 190 | 25 | 4 | |
| Doug Hart | DB | 6' | 190 | 27 | 1 | 6 |
| Dave Hathcock | DB | 6' | 190 | 23 | | |
| Bob Jeter | DB | 6'1" | 205 | 28 | 5 | 12 |
| Willie Wood | DB | 5'10" | 190 | 30 | 3 | 6 |
| Zeke Bratkowski | QB | 6'2" | 200 | 34 | | |
| Bart Starr | QB | 6'1" | 200 | 33 | | 12 |
| Donny Anderson | HB | 6'3" | 220 | 23 | | 18 |
| Paul Hornung | HB | 6'2" | 215 | 29 | | 30 |
| Elijah Pitts | HB | 6'1" | 205 | 27 | | 60 |
| Jim Grabowski | FB | 6'2" | 225 | 22 | | 6 |
| Jim Taylor | FB | 6' | 215 | 31 | | 36 |
| Carroll Dale | FL | 6'1" | 200 | 28 | | 42 |
| Bob Long | FL | 6'3" | 190 | 25 | | |
| Red Mack (from ATL) | FL | 5'10" | 185 | 29 | | |
| Bill Anderson | TE | 6'3" | 216 | 30 | | |
| Allen Brown | TE | 6'5" | 240 | 23 | | |
| Marv Fleming | TE | 6'4" | 235 | 24 | | 12 |
| Boyd Dowler | OE | 6'5" | 225 | 29 | | |
| Max McGee | OE | 6'3" | 205 | 34 | | 6 |
| Don Chandler | K | 6'2" | 210 | 31 | | 77 |

**BALTIMORE COLTS 9-5-0 Don Shula**

| Scores of Each Game | | |
|---|---|---|
| 3 | Green Bay | 24 |
| 38 | Minnesota | 23 |
| 36 | SAN FRANCISCO | 14 |
| 17 | Chicago | 27 |
| 45 | DETROIT | 14 |
| 20 | MINNESOTA | 17 |
| 17 | Los Angeles | 3 |
| 37 | WASHINGTON | 10 |
| 19 | Atlanta | 7 |
| 14 | Detroit | 20 |
| 7 | LOS ANGELES | 23 |
| 21 | CHICAGO | 16 |
| 10 | GREEN BAY | 14 |
| 30 | San Francisco | 14 |

| Use Name | Pos. | Hgt | Wgt | Age | Int | Pts |
|---|---|---|---|---|---|---|
| Sam Ball | OT | 6'4" | 240 | 22 | | |
| Jim Parker | OT | 6'3" | 275 | 32 | | |
| Bob Vogel | OT | 6'5" | 250 | 24 | | |
| Glenn Ressler | C-OT | 6'3" | 235 | 22 | | |
| Dale Memmelaar | OG | 6'2" | 248 | 29 | | |
| Alex Sandusky | OG | 6'1" | 242 | 34 | | |
| Dan Sullivan | OG | 6'3" | 250 | 27 | | |
| Dick Szymanski | C | 6'3" | 235 | 34 | | |
| Ordell Braase | DE | 6'4" | 242 | 34 | | |
| Roy Hilton | DE | 6'6" | 240 | 21 | | |
| Gino Marchetti | DE | 6'4" | 245 | 40 | | |
| Lou Michaels | DE | 6'2" | 250 | 30 | | 98 |
| Fred Miller | DT | 6'3" | 245 | 25 | | |
| Billy Ray Smith | DT | 6'4" | 250 | 31 | | |
| Andy Stynchula | DE-DT | 6'3" | 250 | 27 | | |
| Barry Brown | LB | 6'3" | 230 | 23 | 1 | |
| Jackie Burkett | LB | 6'4" | 228 | 29 | | |
| Mike Curtis | LB | 6'2" | 232 | 23 | | 6 |
| Ted Davis | LB | 6'1" | 232 | 24 | 1 | |
| Dennis Gaubatz | LB | 6'2" | 232 | 25 | 2 | |
| Don Shinnick | LB | 6' | 228 | 31 | 3 | |
| Steve Stonebreaker | LB | 6'3" | 228 | 28 | 1 | |
| Tom Bleick | DB | 6'2" | 200 | 23 | | |
| Bobby Boyd | DB | 5'10" | 190 | 28 | 6 | 6 |
| George Harold | DB | 6'3" | 205 | 24 | | |
| Alvin Haymond | DB | 6' | 190 | 24 | 4 | 6 |
| Jerry Logan | DB | 6'1" | 185 | 25 | 3 | |
| Lenny Lyles | DB | 6'2" | 202 | 30 | 1 | |
| Jim Welch | DB | 6' | 190 | 28 | | |
| Gary Cuozzo | QB | 6'1" | 195 | 25 | | |
| Johnny Unitas | QB | 6'1" | 194 | 33 | | 6 |
| Jerry Allen | HB | 6'1" | 205 | 25 | | |
| Tom Matte | HB | 6' | 205 | 27 | | 18 |
| Lenny Moore | FL-HB | 6'1" | 190 | 33 | | 18 |
| Bob Baldwin | FB-HB | 6'1" | 225 | 23 | | |
| Jerry Hill | FB | 5'11" | 210 | 26 | | |
| Tony Lorick | FB | 6'1" | 215 | 24 | | 18 |
| Jimmy Orr | FL | 5'11" | 185 | 30 | | 18 |
| Willie Richardson | FL | 6'2" | 198 | 26 | | 12 |
| John Mackey | TE | 6'3" | 217 | 24 | | 54 |
| Butch Wilson | TE | 6'2" | 228 | 24 | | 12 |
| Ray Berry | OE | 6'2" | 187 | 33 | | 42 |
| Neal Petties | OE | 6'2" | 198 | 25 | | |
| David Lee | K | 6'4" | 215 | 22 | | |

| RUSHING | | | | | RECEIVING | | | | | PUNT RETURNS | | | | | KICKOFF RETURNS | | | | | PASSING – PUNTING – KICKING | |
|---|---|---|---|---|---|---|---|---|---|---|---|---|---|---|---|---|---|---|---|---|---|
| Last Name | No. | Yds | Avg | TD | Last Name | No. | Yds | Avg | TD | Last Name | No. | Yds | Avg | TD | Last Name | No. | Yds | Avg | TD | Last Name | Statistics |

## EASTERN CONFERENCE—Continued

### PITTSBURGH STEELERS

**Rushing**

| Last Name | No. | Yds | Avg | TD |
|---|---|---|---|---|
| Asbury | 169 | 544 | 3.2 | 7 |
| Hoak | 81 | 212 | 2.6 | 1 |
| Butler | 46 | 114 | 2.5 | 2 |
| B. Smith | 24 | 93 | 3.9 | 0 |
| Bullocks | 29 | 83 | 2.9 | 1 |
| Jefferson | 2 | 36 | 18.0 | 0 |
| Nelsen | 6 | 18 | 3.0 | 0 |
| Leftridge | 8 | 17 | 2.1 | 2 |
| Lind | 3 | 4 | 1.3 | 0 |
| Meyer | 1 | -2 | -2.0 | 0 |
| R. Smith | 4 | -9 | -2.3 | 0 |
| Izo | 2 | -18 | -9.0 | 0 |

**Receiving**

| Last Name | No. | Yds | Avg | TD |
|---|---|---|---|---|
| Hilton | 46 | 603 | 13 | 4 |
| Ballman | 41 | 663 | 16 | 5 |
| Jefferson | 32 | 772 | 24 | 4 |
| Hoak | 23 | 239 | 10 | 0 |
| Asbury | 19 | 228 | 12 | 2 |
| Wilburn | 7 | 103 | 15 | 0 |
| Simmons | 6 | 68 | 11 | 1 |
| Bullocks | 5 | 64 | 13 | 1 |
| Butler | 4 | 93 | 23 | 1 |
| B. Smith | 3 | 26 | 9 | 0 |
| Jeter | 2 | 18 | 9 | 0 |

**Punt Returns**

| Last Name | No. | Yds | Avg | TD |
|---|---|---|---|---|
| Jefferson | 12 | 29 | 2 | 0 |
| Keys | 5 | 11 | 2 | 0 |
| J. Bradshaw | 2 | 3 | 2 | 0 |
| Simmons | 2 | 0 | 0 | 0 |

**Kickoff Returns**

| Last Name | No. | Yds | Avg | TD |
|---|---|---|---|---|
| Ballman | 20 | 477 | 24 | 0 |
| Butler | 17 | 454 | 27 | 1 |
| Simmons | 10 | 196 | 20 | 0 |
| Woodson | 6 | 113 | 19 | 0 |
| Martha | 2 | 39 | 20 | 0 |
| Saul | 2 | 35 | 18 | 0 |
| Keys | 1 | 18 | 18 | 0 |
| Campbell | 1 | 15 | 15 | 0 |
| Lind | 1 | 15 | 15 | 0 |
| Russell | 2 | 12 | 6 | 0 |
| Leftridge | 1 | 10 | 10 | 0 |
| Hilton | 1 | 0 | 0 | 0 |

**PASSING**

| Last Name | Att | Comp | % | Yds | Yd/Att | TD | Int–% | | RK |
|---|---|---|---|---|---|---|---|---|---|
| R. Smith | 181 | 79 | 44 | 1249 | 6.9 | 8 | 12– | 7 | 12 |
| Nelsen | 112 | 63 | 56 | 1122 | 10.0 | 7 | 1– | 1 | |
| Izo | 81 | 35 | 43 | 360 | 4.4 | 2 | 8– | 10 | |
| Meyer | 19 | 7 | 37 | 59 | 3.1 | 0 | 1– | 5 | |
| Hoak | 6 | 4 | 67 | 87 | 14.5 | 1 | 0– | 0 | |
| Asbury | 1 | 0 | 0 | 0 | 0.0 | 0 | 0– | 0 | |
| Bullocks | 1 | 0 | 0 | 0 | 0.0 | 0 | 0– | 0 | |

**PUNTING**

| Last Name | No | Avg |
|---|---|---|
| Lambert | 78 | 42.1 |

**KICKING**

| Last Name | XP | Att | % | FG | Att | % |
|---|---|---|---|---|---|---|
| Clark | 34 | 34 | 100 | 21 | 32 | 66 |
| Russell | 1 | 1 | 100 | 0 | 0 | 0 |

### ATLANTA FALCONS

**Rushing**

| Last Name | No. | Yds | Avg | TD |
|---|---|---|---|---|
| Coffey | 199 | 722 | 3.6 | 4 |
| Wheelwright | 121 | 458 | 3.8 | 3 |
| Ran. Johnson | 35 | 142 | 4.1 | 4 |
| Dunn | 22 | 52 | 2.4 | 0 |
| Scales | 10 | 38 | 3.8 | 0 |
| Ridlehuber | 4 | 23 | 5.8 | 0 |
| Lothridge | 1 | 22 | 22.0 | 0 |
| Claridge | 5 | 15 | 3.0 | 0 |
| Sidle | 1 | 12 | 12.0 | 0 |
| Rud. Johnson | 3 | 3 | 1.0 | 0 |

**Receiving**

| Last Name | No. | Yds | Avg | TD |
|---|---|---|---|---|
| Hawkins | 44 | 661 | 15 | 2 |
| Martin | 29 | 330 | 11 | 0 |
| Burke | 28 | 348 | 12 | 1 |
| Coffey | 15 | 182 | 12 | 1 |
| Wheelwright | 15 | 137 | 9 | 3 |
| Barnes | 12 | 173 | 14 | 1 |
| Anderson | 10 | 195 | 20 | 3 |
| Dunn | 5 | 45 | 9 | 0 |
| Coia | 4 | 93 | 23 | 0 |
| Ridlehuber | 4 | 84 | 21 | 2 |
| Sherlag | 4 | 53 | 13 | 1 |
| Scales | 3 | 16 | 5 | 0 |
| Hutchinson | 1 | 28 | 28 | 0 |
| Sidle | 1 | 16 | 16 | 0 |
| Marchlewski | 0 | 1 | 0 | 0 |

**Punt Returns**

| Last Name | No. | Yds | Avg | TD |
|---|---|---|---|---|
| Smith | 11 | 80 | 7 | 0 |
| Rassas | 4 | 10 | 3 | 0 |
| Sherlag | 2 | 8 | 4 | 0 |
| Reaves | 1 | 2 | 2 | 0 |

**Kickoff Returns**

| Last Name | No. | Yds | Avg | TD |
|---|---|---|---|---|
| Smith | 43 | 1013 | 24 | 0 |
| Rassas | 8 | 203 | 25 | 0 |
| Sidle | 6 | 117 | 20 | 0 |
| Scales | 5 | 101 | 20 | 0 |
| Reaves | 4 | 85 | 21 | 0 |
| Rushing | 2 | 52 | 26 | 0 |
| Morris | 5 | 50 | 10 | 0 |
| Dunn | 2 | 36 | 18 | 0 |
| Hawkins | 1 | 30 | 30 | 0 |
| Wolski | 1 | 21 | 21 | 0 |
| Coffey | 1 | 18 | 18 | 0 |
| Glass | 1 | 11 | 11 | 0 |
| Heck | 1 | 0 | 0 | 0 |
| Martin | 1 | 0 | 0 | 0 |
| Sherlag | 1 | 0 | 0 | 0 |

**PASSING**

| Last Name | Att | Comp | % | Yds | Yd/Att | TD | Int–% | | RK |
|---|---|---|---|---|---|---|---|---|---|
| Ran. Johnson | 295 | 129 | 44 | 1795 | 6.1 | 12 | 21– | 7 | 17 |
| Claridge | 70 | 40 | 57 | 471 | 6.7 | 2 | 2– | 3 | |
| Sloan | 13 | 6 | 46 | 96 | 7.4 | 0 | 2– | 15 | |
| Dunn | 2 | 0 | 0 | 0 | 0.0 | 0 | 2–100 | | |
| Lothridge | 1 | 0 | 0 | 0 | 0.0 | 0 | 0– | 0 | |

**PUNTING**

| Last Name | No | Avg |
|---|---|---|
| Lothridge | 73 | 40.7 |

**KICKING**

| Last Name | XP | Att | % | FG | Att | % |
|---|---|---|---|---|---|---|
| Kirouac | 19 | 24 | 79 | 9 | 18 | 50 |
| Traynham | 2 | 2 | 100 | 0 | 1 | 0 |

### NEW YORK GIANTS

**Rushing**

| Last Name | No. | Yds | Avg | TD |
|---|---|---|---|---|
| Mercein | 94 | 327 | 3.5 | 0 |
| Morrison | 67 | 275 | 4.1 | 2 |
| Jacobs | 77 | 273 | 3.5 | 1 |
| Wood | 28 | 196 | 7.0 | 3 |
| Lewis | 32 | 164 | 5.1 | 1 |
| Koy | 66 | 146 | 2.2 | 0 |
| Jones | 5 | 43 | 8.6 | 0 |
| Kennedy | 5 | 16 | 3.2 | 0 |
| Morrall | 5 | 12 | 2.4 | 0 |
| Larson | 0 | -2 | 0.0 | 0 |

**Receiving**

| Last Name | No. | Yds | Avg | TD |
|---|---|---|---|---|
| Jones | 48 | 1044 | 22 | 8 |
| Morrison | 46 | 724 | 16 | 6 |
| Thomas | 43 | 683 | 16 | 4 |
| Mercein | 27 | 152 | 6 | 0 |
| Crespino | 16 | 167 | 10 | 2 |
| Jacobs | 10 | 69 | 7 | 0 |
| Koy | 8 | 43 | 5 | 0 |
| Lewis | 6 | 87 | 15 | 0 |
| Shofner | 3 | 19 | 6 | 0 |
| Menefee | 1 | 11 | 11 | 0 |

**Punt Returns**

| Last Name | No. | Yds | Avg | TD |
|---|---|---|---|---|
| Lockhart | 17 | 113 | 7 | 0 |
| P. Harris | 5 | 7 | 1 | 0 |

**Kickoff Returns**

| Last Name | No. | Yds | Avg | TD |
|---|---|---|---|---|
| Childs | 34 | 855 | 25 | 1 |
| P. Harris | 22 | 480 | 22 | 0 |
| Lewis | 13 | 214 | 16 | 0 |
| Koy | 3 | 20 | 7 | 0 |
| Jacobs | 2 | 18 | 9 | 0 |
| White | 2 | 14 | 7 | 0 |
| W. Harris | 1 | 9 | 9 | 0 |
| Young | 2 | 6 | 3 | 0 |
| Rog. Davis | 1 | 0 | 0 | 0 |

**PASSING**

| Last Name | Att | Comp | % | Yds | Yd/Att | TD | Int–% | | RK |
|---|---|---|---|---|---|---|---|---|---|
| Wood | 170 | 81 | 48 | 1142 | 6.7 | 6 | 13– | 8 | 15 |
| Morrall | 151 | 71 | 47 | 1105 | 7.3 | 7 | 12– | 8 | 14 |
| Kennedy | 100 | 55 | 55 | 748 | 7.5 | 7 | 6– | 6 | |
| Koy | 2 | 0 | 0 | 0 | 0.0 | 0 | 0– | 0 | |
| Lewis | 1 | 1 | 100 | 4 | 4.0 | 0 | 0– | 0 | |

**PUNTING**

| Last Name | No | Avg |
|---|---|---|
| Koy | 49 | 39.4 |
| Lockhart | 4 | 32.8 |

**KICKING**

| Last Name | XP | Att | % | FG | Att | % |
|---|---|---|---|---|---|---|
| Gogolak | 29 | 31 | 94 | 16 | 28 | 57 |

## WESTERN CONFERENCE

### GREEN BAY PACKERS

**Rushing**

| Last Name | No. | Yds | Avg | TD |
|---|---|---|---|---|
| Taylor | 204 | 705 | 3.5 | 4 |
| Pitts | 115 | 393 | 3.4 | 7 |
| Hornung | 76 | 200 | 2.6 | 2 |
| Grabowski | 29 | 127 | 4.4 | 1 |
| Starr | 21 | 104 | 5.0 | 2 |
| D. Anderson | 25 | 104 | 4.2 | 2 |
| Chandler | 1 | 33 | 33.0 | 0 |
| Bratkowski | 4 | 7 | 1.8 | 0 |

**Receiving**

| Last Name | No. | Yds | Avg | TD |
|---|---|---|---|---|
| Taylor | 41 | 331 | 8 | 2 |
| Dale | 37 | 876 | 24 | 7 |
| Fleming | 31 | 361 | 12 | 3 |
| Dowler | 29 | 392 | 14 | 0 |
| Pitts | 26 | 460 | 18 | 3 |
| Hornung | 14 | 192 | 14 | 3 |
| McGee | 4 | 91 | 23 | 1 |
| Grabowski | 4 | 13 | 3 | 0 |
| Long | 3 | 68 | 23 | 0 |
| D. Anderson | 2 | 33 | 17 | 0 |
| B. Anderson | 2 | 14 | 7 | 0 |

**Punt Returns**

| Last Name | No. | Yds | Avg | TD |
|---|---|---|---|---|
| D. Anderson | 6 | 124 | 21 | 1 |
| Wood | 22 | 82 | 4 | 0 |
| Pitts | 7 | 9 | 1 | 0 |
| T. Brown | 2 | 0 | 0 | 0 |

**Kickoff Returns**

| Last Name | No. | Yds | Avg | TD |
|---|---|---|---|---|
| D. Anderson | 23 | 533 | 23 | 0 |
| Adderley | 14 | 320 | 23 | 0 |
| Vandersea | 3 | 50 | 17 | 0 |
| Pitts | 1 | 0 | 0 | 0 |
| Wood | 1 | 0 | 0 | 0 |

**PASSING**

| Last Name | Att | Comp | % | Yds | Yd/Att | TD | Int–% | | RK |
|---|---|---|---|---|---|---|---|---|---|
| Starr | 251 | 156 | 62 | 2257 | 9.0 | 14 | 3– | 1 | 1 |
| Bratkowski | 64 | 36 | 56 | 569 | 8.9 | 4 | 2– | 3 | |
| Pitts | 2 | 0 | 0 | 0 | 0.0 | 0 | 0– | 0 | |
| Hornung | 1 | 1 | 100 | 5 | 5.0 | 0 | 0– | 0 | |

**PUNTING**

| Last Name | No | Avg |
|---|---|---|
| Chandler | 60 | 40.9 |
| D. Anderson | 2 | 44.5 |

**KICKING**

| Last Name | XP | Att | % | FG | Att | % |
|---|---|---|---|---|---|---|
| Chandler | 41 | 43 | 95 | 12 | 28 | 43 |

### BALTIMORE COLTS

**Rushing**

| Last Name | No. | Yds | Avg | TD |
|---|---|---|---|---|
| Lorick | 143 | 524 | 3.7 | 3 |
| Hill | 104 | 395 | 3.8 | 0 |
| Matte | 86 | 381 | 4.4 | 0 |
| Moore | 63 | 209 | 3.3 | 3 |
| Unitas | 20 | 44 | 2.2 | 1 |
| Cuozzo | 1 | 9 | 9.0 | 0 |
| Mackey | 1 | -6 | -6.0 | 0 |

**Receiving**

| Last Name | No. | Yds | Avg | TD |
|---|---|---|---|---|
| Berry | 56 | 786 | 14 | 7 |
| Mackey | 50 | 829 | 17 | 9 |
| Orr | 37 | 618 | 17 | 3 |
| Matte | 23 | 307 | 13 | 3 |
| Moore | 21 | 260 | 12 | 0 |
| Richardson | 14 | 246 | 18 | 2 |
| Lorick | 12 | 81 | 7 | 0 |
| Hill | 5 | 18 | 4 | 0 |
| Wilson | 3 | 27 | 9 | 2 |

**Punt Returns**

| Last Name | No. | Yds | Avg | TD |
|---|---|---|---|---|
| Haymond | 40 | 347 | 9 | 0 |
| Davis | 2 | 7 | 4 | 0 |
| Logan | 1 | 3 | 3 | 0 |
| Allen | 1 | 0 | 0 | 0 |
| Matte | 1 | 0 | 0 | 0 |

**Kickoff Returns**

| Last Name | No. | Yds | Avg | TD |
|---|---|---|---|---|
| Moore | 18 | 453 | 25 | 0 |
| Haymond | 10 | 223 | 22 | 0 |
| Lorick | 10 | 214 | 21 | 0 |
| Curtis | 3 | 64 | 21 | 0 |
| Matte | 3 | 55 | 18 | 0 |
| Allen | 3 | 53 | 18 | 0 |
| Baldwin | 2 | 18 | 9 | 0 |
| Brown | 2 | 14 | 7 | 0 |

**PASSING**

| Last Name | Att | Comp | % | Yds | Yd/Att | TD | Int–% | | RK |
|---|---|---|---|---|---|---|---|---|---|
| Unitas | 348 | 195 | 56 | 2748 | 7.9 | 22 | 24– | 7 | 5 |
| Cuozzo | 50 | 26 | 52 | 424 | 8.5 | 4 | 2– | 4 | |
| Matte | 3 | 0 | 0 | 0 | 0.0 | 0 | 1– | 33 | |

**PUNTING**

| Last Name | No | Avg |
|---|---|---|
| Lee | 49 | 45.6 |

**KICKING**

| Last Name | XP | Att | % | FG | Att | % |
|---|---|---|---|---|---|---|
| Michaels | 35 | 36 | 97 | 21 | 39 | 54 |

**WESTERN CONFERENCE – Continued**

## LOS ANGELES RAMS 8-6-0 George Allen

| Score | Opponent | Opp. |
|---|---|---|
| 19 | Atlanta | 14 |
| 31 | CHICAGO | 17 |
| 13 | Green Bay | 24 |
| 34 | SAN FRANCISCO | 3 |
| 14 | Detroit | 7 |
| 7 | Minnesota | 35 |
| 10 | Chicago | 17 |
| 3 | BALTIMORE | 17 |
| 13 | San Francisco | 21 |
| 55 | NEW YORK | 14 |
| 21 | MINNESOTA | 6 |
| 23 | Baltimore | 7 |
| 23 | DETROIT | 3 |
| 23 | GREEN BAY | 27 |

| Use Name | Pos. | Hgt | Wgt | Age | Int | Pts |
|---|---|---|---|---|---|---|
| Joe Carollo | OT | 6'2" | 263 | 26 | | |
| Charley Cowan | OT | 6'4" | 275 | 28 | | |
| Bob Nichols | OT | 6'3" | 250 | 23 | | |
| Don Chuy | OG | 6'1" | 256 | 25 | | |
| Ted Karras | OG | 6'1" | 243 | 33 | | |
| Joe Scibelli | OG | 6'1" | 264 | 27 | | |
| Tom Mack | OG | 6'3" | 245 | 22 | | |
| Ken Iman | C | 6'1" | 235 | 27 | | |
| Joe Wendryhoski | C | 6'2" | 245 | 27 | | |
| Bruce Anderson | DE | 6'4" | 230 | 22 | | |
| Deacon Jones | DE | 6'5" | 260 | 27 | 1 | |
| Lamar Lundy | DE | 6'7" | 260 | 31 | 1 | 6 |
| Rosey Grier | DT | 6'5" | 290 | 33 | | 2 |
| Earl Leggett | DT | 6'3" | 265 | 32 | | |
| Merlin Olsen | DT | 6'5" | 276 | 25 | | |
| Maxie Baughan | LB | 6'1" | 227 | 28 | 2 | |
| Dan Currie | LB | 6'3" | 240 | 32 | | |
| Bill George | LB | 6'2" | 235 | 35 | | |
| Jack Pardee | LB | 6'2" | 230 | 30 | 2 | |
| Myron Pottios | LB | 6'2" | 240 | 26 | | |
| Doug Woodlief | LB | 6'3" | 235 | 22 | | |
| Irv Cross | DB | 6'1" | 190 | 27 | 1 | 6 |
| Hank Gremminger | DB | 6'1" | 200 | 33 | 1 | |
| Chuck Lamson | DB | 6' | 190 | 27 | 5 | 6 |
| Clancy Williams | DB | 6'2" | 198 | 23 | 8 | 6 |
| George Youngblood | DB | 6'3" | 200 | 21 | | |
| Ed Meador | DB | 5'11" | 203 | 29 | 5 | |
| Claude Crabb | FL-DB | 6' | 190 | 26 | | |
| Tony Guillory – Injury | | | | | | |
| Roman Gabriel | QB | 6'4" | 225 | 26 | | 18 |
| Bill Munson | QB | 6'2" | 197 | 24 | | |
| Tom Moore | HB | 6'2" | 210 | 28 | | 24 |
| Les Josephson | HB | 6' | 210 | 24 | | 6 |
| Jim Stiger | FB-HB | 5'11" | 214 | 25 | | 6 |
| Dick Bass | FB | 5'10" | 198 | 29 | | 48 |
| Henry Dyer | FB | 6'2" | 225 | 21 | | |
| Tommy McDonald | FL | 5'10" | 175 | 32 | | 12 |
| Marlin McKeever | TE | 6'1" | 227 | 26 | | 6 |
| Dave Pivec | TE | 6'3" | 240 | 22 | | |
| Billy Truax | TE | 6'5" | 240 | 23 | | 6 |
| Steve Heckard | OE | 6'1" | 195 | 23 | | |
| Bucky Pope | FL-OE | 6'5" | 195 | 23 | | 6 |
| Jack Snow | OE | 6'2" | 212 | 23 | | 18 |
| Bruce Gossett | K | 6'2" | 230 | 23 | | 113 |
| Jon Kilgore | K | 6'1" | 200 | 22 | | |

## SAN FRANCISCO FORTY NINERS 6-6-2 Jack Christiansen

| Score | Opponent | Opp. |
|---|---|---|
| 20 | MINNESOTA | 20 |
| 14 | Baltimore | 36 |
| 3 | Los Angeles | 34 |
| 21 | GREEN BAY | 20 |
| 44 | Atlanta | 7 |
| 27 | DETROIT | 24 |
| 3 | Minnesota | 28 |
| 21 | LOS ANGELES | 13 |
| 30 | Chicago | 30 |
| 34 | PHILADELPHIA | 35 |
| 41 | Detroit | 14 |
| 7 | Green Bay | 20 |
| 41 | CHICAGO | 14 |
| 14 | BALTIMORE | 30 |

| Use Name | Pos. | Hgt | Wgt | Age | Int | Pts |
|---|---|---|---|---|---|---|
| Dave McCormick | OT | 6'6" | 250 | 23 | | |
| Walt Rock | OT | 6'5" | 257 | 25 | | |
| Len Rohde | OT | 6'4" | 255 | 28 | | |
| Howard Mudd | OG | 6'3" | 263 | 24 | | |
| John Thomas | OG | 6'4" | 250 | 31 | | |
| Jim Wilson | OG | 6'3" | 255 | 25 | | |
| Bruce Bosley | C | 6'2" | 246 | 32 | | |
| Joe Cerne | C | 6'2" | 235 | 23 | | |
| Stan Hindman | DE | 6'3" | 232 | 22 | | |
| Clark Miller | DE | 6'5" | 245 | 27 | | |
| Jim Norton | DT-DE | 6'4" | 255 | 23 | | |
| Charlie Johnson | DT | 6'2" | 266 | 22 | | |
| Charlie Krueger | DT | 6'4" | 267 | 30 | | |
| Roland Lakes | DT | 6'4" | 285 | 26 | | |
| Ed Beard | LB | 6'2" | 225 | 26 | | |
| Mike Dowdle | LB | 6'3" | 248 | 28 | 1 | 6 |
| Bob Harrison | LB | 6'2" | 225 | 29 | | |
| Matt Hazeltine | LB | 6'1" | 230 | 33 | 1 | 6 |
| Dave Wilcox | LB | 6'3" | 234 | 23 | | |
| Kermit Alexander | DB | 5'11" | 186 | 25 | 4 | 12 |
| George Donnelly | DB | 6'3" | 205 | 23 | 2 | |
| Jim Johnson | DB | 6'2" | 187 | 28 | 4 | 6 |
| Elbert Kimbrough | DB | 5'11" | 196 | 27 | 3 | |
| Mel Phillips | DB | 6' | 188 | 24 | | |
| Al Randolph | DB | 6'2" | 190 | 22 | 3 | 6 |
| John Brodie | QB | 6'1" | 210 | 31 | | 18 |
| Billy Kilmer | QB | 6' | 204 | 26 | | |
| George Mira | QB | 5'11" | 192 | 24 | | |
| John David Crow | HB | 6'2" | 224 | 31 | | 24 |
| Bob Daugherty | HB | 6'2" | 205 | 24 | | |
| Jim Jackson | HB | 6' | 180 | 22 | | 6 |
| Dave Kopay | HB | 6'2" | 225 | 24 | | 12 |
| Gary Lewis | FB | 6'3" | 230 | 24 | | 18 |
| Ken Willard | FB | 6'2" | 230 | 23 | | 42 |
| Bernie Casey | FL | 6'4" | 210 | 27 | | 6 |
| Kay McFarland | FL | 6'2" | 186 | 27 | | 6 |
| Dick Witcher | FL | 6'3" | 210 | 21 | | 6 |
| Kent Kramer | TE | 6'5" | 230 | 22 | | 18 |
| Monte Stickles | TE | 6'4" | 235 | 28 | | 12 |
| Dave Parks | OE | 6'2" | 207 | 24 | | 30 |
| Wayne Swinford | OE | 6' | 200 | 23 | | |
| Tommy Davis | K | 6' | 220 | 31 | | 86 |

## CHICAGO BEARS 5-7-2 George Halas

| Score | Opponent | Opp. |
|---|---|---|
| 3 | Detroit | 14 |
| 17 | Los Angeles | 31 |
| 13 | Minnesota | 10 |
| 27 | BALTIMORE | 17 |
| 0 | GREEN BAY | 17 |
| 17 | LOS ANGELES | 10 |
| 17 | St. Louis | 24 |
| 10 | DETROIT | 10 |
| 30 | SAN FRANCISCO | 30 |
| 6 | Green Bay | 13 |
| 23 | ATLANTA | 6 |
| 16 | Baltimore | 21 |
| 14 | San Francisco | 41 |
| 41 | MINNESOTA | 28 |

| Use Name | Pos. | Hgt | Wgt | Age | Int | Pts |
|---|---|---|---|---|---|---|
| Herm Lee | OT | 6'4" | 247 | 35 | | |
| Riley Mattson | OT | 6'4" | 255 | 27 | | |
| Bob Wetoska | OT | 6'3" | 240 | 28 | | |
| Jim Cadile | OG | 6'3" | 240 | 25 | | |
| Mike Rabold | OG | 6'2" | 238 | 28 | | |
| George Seals | OT-OG | 6'2" | 260 | 23 | | |
| Roger LeClerc | C | 6'3" | 235 | 28 | | 78 |
| Mike Pyle | C | 6'3" | 250 | 27 | | |
| Doug Atkins | DE | 6'8" | 255 | 36 | 1 | |
| Ed O'Bradovich | DE | 6'3" | 255 | 26 | | 6 |
| Brian Schweda | DE | 6'3" | 240 | 23 | | |
| Frank Cornish | DT | 6'6" | 285 | 22 | | |
| Dick Evey | DT | 6'2" | 225 | 25 | | |
| John Johnson | DT | 6'5" | 260 | 25 | | |
| Bob Kilcullen | DT | 6'3" | 245 | 30 | | |
| Doug Buffone | LB | 6'1" | 218 | 22 | | |
| Dick Butkus | LB | 6'3" | 245 | 22 | 1 | |
| Joe Fortunato | LB | 6' | 225 | 36 | 1 | 6 |
| Jim Purnell | LB | 6'2" | 225 | 24 | | |
| Mike Reilly | LB | 6'2" | 238 | 23 | | |
| Charlie Brown | DB | 6'1" | 193 | 23 | | |
| Curtis Gentry | DB | 6' | 187 | 25 | 1 | |
| Benny McRae | DB | 6'1" | 180 | 25 | 3 | |
| Richie Petitbon | DB | 6'3" | 205 | 28 | 4 | |
| Rosey Taylor | DB | 5'11" | 186 | 27 | 1 | |
| Dave Whitsell | DB | 6' | 190 | 30 | 3 | |
| Andy Livingston - Knee Injury | | | | | | |
| Rudy Bukich | QB | 6'1" | 205 | 35 | | 12 |
| Larry Rakestraw | QB | 6'2" | 195 | 24 | | |
| Billy Wade | QB | 6'2" | 205 | 35 | | |
| Jon Arnett | HB | 5'11" | 203 | 31 | | 6 |
| Gale Sayers | HB | 6' | 198 | 23 | | 72 |
| Brian Piccolo | FB-HB | 6' | 205 | 22 | | |
| Ralph Kurek | FB | 6'2" | 210 | 23 | | 6 |
| Joe Marconi | FB | 6'2" | 225 | 32 | | |
| Ronnie Bull | HB-FB | 6' | 200 | 26 | | |
| Johnny Morris | FL | 5'10" | 180 | 31 | | |
| Duane Allen | TE | 6'4" | 225 | 28 | | |
| Charlie Bivins | TE | 6'2" | 212 | 27 | | |
| Mike Ditka | TE | 6'3" | 230 | 26 | | 12 |
| Dick Gordon | OE | 5'11" | 190 | 21 | | 6 |
| Jim Jones | OE | 6'2" | 187 | 22 | | 30 |
| Bobby Joe Green | K | 5'11" | 175 | 28 | | |

## DETROIT LIONS 4-9-1 Harry Gilmer

| Score | Opponent | Opp. |
|---|---|---|
| 14 | CHICAGO | 3 |
| 3 | Pittsburgh | 17 |
| 28 | ATLANTA | 10 |
| 14 | Green Bay | 23 |
| 7 | LOS ANGELES | 14 |
| 14 | Baltimore | 45 |
| 24 | San Francisco | 27 |
| 7 | GREEN BAY | 31 |
| 10 | Chicago | 10 |
| 32 | Minnesota | 31 |
| 20 | BALTIMORE | 14 |
| 14 | SAN FRANCISCO | 41 |
| 3 | Los Angeles | 23 |
| 16 | MINNESOTA | 28 |

| Use Name | Pos. | Hgt | Wgt | Age | Int | Pts |
|---|---|---|---|---|---|---|
| Daryl Sanders | OT | 6'5" | 250 | 24 | | |
| Roger Shoals | OT | 6'4" | 255 | 27 | | |
| J. D. Smith | OT | 6'5" | 250 | 30 | | |
| John Gordy | OG | 6'3" | 250 | 30 | | |
| Bob Kowalkowski | OG | 6'3" | 245 | 22 | | |
| Doug Van Horn | OG | 6'2" | 245 | 22 | | |
| Mike Alford | C | 6'3" | 235 | 23 | | |
| Ed Flanagan | C | 6'3" | 250 | 22 | | |
| Larry Hand | DE | 6'4" | 245 | 26 | | |
| Jerry Mazzanti | DE | 6'3" | 240 | 26 | | |
| Darris McCord | DE | 6'4" | 250 | 33 | | |
| Roger Brown | DT | 6'5" | 300 | 29 | | |
| Alex Karras | DT | 6'2" | 245 | 30 | | |
| Jerry Rush | DT | 6'4" | 270 | 24 | | |
| Ernie Clark | LB | 6'1" | 220 | 28 | 1 | |
| Bill Cody | LB | 6'1" | 220 | 22 | | |
| Wally Hilgenberg | LB | 6'3" | 225 | 23 | | |
| Mike Lucci | LB | 6'2" | 223 | 26 | 5 | 6 |
| Lou Slaby | LB | 6'3" | 235 | 24 | | |
| Wayne Walker | LB | 6'2" | 225 | 29 | 1 | 17 |
| Jim Kearney | DB | 6'2" | 200 | 23 | | |
| Dick LeBeau | DB | 6'1" | 185 | 29 | 4 | |
| Bruce Maher | DB | 5'11" | 190 | 29 | 5 | |
| Wayne Rasmussen | DB | 6'2" | 180 | 24 | 3 | |
| Bobby Smith | DB | 6' | 197 | 28 | | |
| Bobby Thompson | DB | 5'10" | 175 | 26 | 4 | |
| Tom Vaughn | DB | 5'11" | 195 | 23 | 1 | |
| Tom Watkins – Operation | | | | | | |
| Warren Wells – Military Service | | | | | | |
| Tom Myers | QB | 6' | 188 | 22 | | |
| Milt Plum | QB | 6'1" | 205 | 32 | | 1 |
| Karl Sweetan | QB | 6'1" | 210 | 23 | | 6 |
| Bobby Felts | HB | 6'2" | 202 | 23 | | 12 |
| Amos Marsh | HB | 6'1" | 220 | 27 | | 18 |
| Bruce McLenna | HB | 6'3" | 225 | 24 | | |
| Jim Todd | HB | 5'11" | 195 | 23 | | |
| Tom Nowatzke | FB | 6'3" | 233 | 23 | | 42 |
| Pat Studstill | FL | 6'1" | 175 | 28 | | 30 |
| Willie Walker | FL | 6'3" | 200 | 23 | | |
| Johnnie Robinson | DB-FL | 6'3" | 205 | 21 | | 6 |
| Jim Gibbons | TE | 6'2" | 220 | 30 | | 6 |
| Ron Kramer | TE | 6'3" | 240 | 31 | | |
| Gail Cogdill | OE | 6'2" | 195 | 29 | | 6 |
| Bill Malinchak | OE | 6'1" | 190 | 22 | | |
| John Henderson | FL-OE | 6'3" | 190 | 23 | | |
| Garo Yepremian | K | 5'8" | 160 | 22 | | 50 |

## MINNESOTA VIKINGS 4-9-1 Norm Van Brocklin

| Score | Opponent | Opp. |
|---|---|---|
| 20 | San Francisco | 20 |
| 23 | BALTIMORE | 38 |
| 17 | Dallas | 28 |
| 10 | CHICAGO | 13 |
| 35 | LOS ANGELES | 7 |
| 17 | Baltimore | 20 |
| 28 | SAN FRANCISCO | 3 |
| 20 | Green Bay | 17 |
| 31 | DETROIT | 32 |
| 6 | Los Angeles | 21 |
| 16 | GREEN BAY | 28 |
| 13 | ATLANTA | 20 |
| 28 | Detroit | 16 |
| 28 | Chicago | 41 |

| Use Name | Pos. | Hgt | Wgt | Age | Int | Pts |
|---|---|---|---|---|---|---|
| Doug Davis | OT | 6'4" | 240 | 22 | | |
| Chuck Arrobio | OT | 6'4" | 250 | 22 | | |
| Grady Alderman | OT | 6'2" | 240 | 27 | | |
| Archie Sutton | OT | 6'4" | 262 | 23 | | |
| Larry Bowie | OG | 6'2" | 250 | 26 | | |
| Milt Sunde | OG | 6'2" | 234 | 23 | | |
| Jim Vellone | OG | 6'2" | 255 | 22 | | |
| Mick Tinglehoff | C | 6'1" | 237 | 26 | | |
| Carl Eller | DE | 6'6" | 255 | 24 | | |
| Jim Marshall | DE | 6'3" | 235 | 28 | | |
| Paul Dickson | DT | 6'5" | 255 | 29 | | |
| Gary Larsen | DT | 6'5" | 250 | 26 | | |
| Jerry Shay | DT | 6'3" | 240 | 22 | | |
| Mike Tilleman | DT | 6'5" | 260 | 22 | | |
| Don Hansen | LB | 6'3" | 226 | 22 | | |
| John Kirby | LB | 6'3" | 222 | 24 | | |
| Dave Tobey | LB | 6'3" | 230 | 23 | | |
| Lonnie Warwick | LB | 6'3" | 225 | 24 | 2 | |
| Roy Winston | LB | 6'1" | 230 | 26 | | |
| Mike Fitzgerald | DB | 5'10" | 180 | 25 | 1 | |
| Dale Hackbart | DB | 6'3" | 210 | 30 | 5 | 6 |
| Jeff Jordan | DB | 6'4" | 190 | 22 | | |
| Karl Kassulke | DB | 6' | 193 | 24 | 2 | |
| Earsell Mackbee | DB | 6'1" | 195 | 25 | 2 | |
| George Rose | DB | 5'11" | 190 | 23 | 1 | |
| Ed Sharockman | DB | 6' | 200 | 26 | 1 | |
| Ken Byers – Injury | | | | | | |
| Bob Berry | QB | 5'11" | 190 | 24 | | |
| Fran Tarkenton | QB | 6'1" | 190 | 26 | | 24 |
| Ron Vander Kelen | QB | 6'1" | 185 | 26 | | |
| Billy Barnes | HB | 5'11" | 202 | 31 | | 6 |
| Jim Lindsey | HB | 6'2" | 200 | 21 | | 18 |
| Tommy Mason | HB | 6' | 196 | 27 | | 18 |
| Dave Osborn | HB | 6' | 205 | 23 | | 18 |
| Jeff Williams | HB | 6'1" | 210 | 22 | | |
| Jim Young | HB | 6' | 205 | 23 | | |
| Bill Brown | FB | 5'11" | 230 | 28 | | 36 |
| Phil King | HB-FB | 6'4" | 220 | 30 | | 6 |
| Jim Phillips | FL | 6'1" | 195 | 29 | | 18 |
| Lance Rentzel | OE-FL | 6'2" | 210 | 22 | | |
| Hal Bedsole | TE | 6'4" | 230 | 24 | | |
| Preston Carpenter (from WAS) | TE | 6'2" | 208 | 32 | | 24 |
| John Powers | TE | 6'2" | 210 | 25 | | |
| Paul Flatley | OE | 6'1" | 187 | 25 | | 18 |
| Tom Hall | FL-OE | 6'1" | 195 | 25 | | 12 |
| Fred Cox | K | 5'10" | 200 | 27 | | 88 |
| Bobby Walden | K | 6' | 195 | 28 | | |

## WESTERN CONFERENCE – Continued

### LOS ANGELES RAMS

**RUSHING**

| Last Name | No. | Yds | Avg | TD |
|---|---|---|---|---|
| Bass | 248 | 1090 | 4.4 | 8 |
| Moore | 104 | 272 | 2.6 | 1 |
| Gabriel | 52 | 176 | 3.4 | 3 |
| Josephson | 14 | 97 | 6.9 | 0 |
| Stiger | 24 | 95 | 4.0 | 0 |
| Meador | 1 | 7 | 7.0 | 0 |
| Munson | 4 | 3 | 0.8 | 0 |
| Iman | 1 | 2 | 2.0 | 0 |

**RECEIVING**

| Last Name | No. | Yds | Avg | TD |
|---|---|---|---|---|
| Moore | 60 | 433 | 7 | 3 |
| McDonald | 55 | 714 | 13 | 2 |
| Snow | 34 | 634 | 19 | 3 |
| Bass | 31 | 274 | 9 | 0 |
| Truax | 29 | 314 | 11 | 0 |
| McKeever | 23 | 277 | 12 | 1 |
| Stiger | 8 | 72 | 9 | 1 |
| Heckard | 5 | 102 | 20 | 0 |
| Josephson | 2 | 10 | 5 | 1 |
| Crabb | 1 | 47 | 47 | 0 |
| Pope | 1 | 14 | 14 | 1 |

**PUNT RETURNS**

| Last Name | No. | Yds | Avg | TD |
|---|---|---|---|---|
| Stiger | 33 | 259 | 8 | 0 |
| Cross | 12 | 82 | 7 | 0 |

**KICKOFF RETURNS**

| Last Name | No. | Yds | Avg | TD |
|---|---|---|---|---|
| Williams | 15 | 420 | 28 | 0 |
| Cross | 12 | 348 | 29 | 0 |
| Stiger | 7 | 150 | 21 | 0 |
| Dyer | 5 | 61 | 12 | 0 |
| Currie | 1 | 25 | 25 | 0 |
| McKeever | 1 | 8 | 8 | 0 |
| Lamson | 1 | 3 | 3 | 0 |

**PASSING**

| Last Name | Att | Comp | % | Yds | Yd/Att | TD | Int-% | RK |
|---|---|---|---|---|---|---|---|---|
| Gabriel | 397 | 217 | 55 | 2540 | 6.4 | 10 | 16– 4 | 7 |
| Munson | 50 | 30 | 60 | 284 | 5.7 | 2 | 1– 2 | |
| Kilgore | 1 | 1 | 100 | 47 | 47.0 | 0 | 0– 0 | |
| Meador | 1 | 0 | 0 | 0 | 0.0 | 0 | 0– 0 | |
| Moore | 1 | 1 | 100 | 20 | 20.0 | 0 | 0– 0 | |

**PUNTING**

| Last Name | No | Avg |
|---|---|---|
| Kilgore | 71 | 42.8 |

**KICKING**

| Last Name | XP | Att | % | FG | Att | % |
|---|---|---|---|---|---|---|
| Gossett | 29 | 29 | 100 | 28 | 49 | 57 |

### SAN FRANCISCO FORTY NINERS

**RUSHING**

| Last Name | No. | Yds | Avg | TD |
|---|---|---|---|---|
| Willard | 191 | 763 | 4.0 | 5 |
| Crow | 121 | 477 | 3.9 | 1 |
| Kopay | 47 | 204 | 4.3 | 1 |
| Lewis | 36 | 130 | 3.6 | 2 |
| Mira | 10 | 103 | 10.3 | 0 |
| Davis | 3 | 43 | 14.3 | 0 |
| Casey | 1 | 23 | 23.0 | 0 |
| Kilmer | 3 | 23 | 7.7 | 0 |
| Brodie | 5 | 18 | 3.6 | 3 |
| Jackson | 4 | 7 | 1.8 | 0 |
| Parks | 1 | –1 | –1.0 | 0 |

**RECEIVING**

| Last Name | No. | Yds | Avg | TD |
|---|---|---|---|---|
| Parks | 66 | 974 | 15 | 5 |
| Casey | 50 | 669 | 13 | 1 |
| Willard | 42 | 351 | 8 | 2 |
| Crow | 30 | 341 | 11 | 3 |
| Stickles | 27 | 315 | 12 | 2 |
| McFarland | 13 | 219 | 17 | 1 |
| Witcher | 10 | 115 | 12 | 1 |
| Kopay | 10 | 67 | 7 | 1 |
| Lewis | 7 | 44 | 6 | 1 |
| Kramer | 5 | 81 | 16 | 3 |
| Jackson | 1 | 63 | 63 | 1 |

**PUNT RETURNS**

| Last Name | No. | Yds | Avg | TD |
|---|---|---|---|---|
| Alexander | 30 | 198 | 7 | 1 |
| Kopay | 4 | 28 | 7 | 0 |
| Swinford | 8 | 12 | 2 | 0 |
| Jackson | 2 | 0 | 0 | 0 |
| Donnelly | 1 | 0 | 0 | 0 |

**KICKOFF RETURNS**

| Last Name | No. | Yds | Avg | TD |
|---|---|---|---|---|
| Alexander | 37 | 984 | 27 | 0 |
| Jackson | 8 | 162 | 20 | 0 |
| Swinford | 4 | 73 | 18 | 0 |
| Lewis | 3 | 65 | 22 | 0 |
| Kopay | 2 | 20 | 10 | 0 |
| Phillips | 1 | 20 | 20 | 0 |
| Hindman | 1 | 2 | 2 | 0 |

**PASSING**

| Last Name | Att | Comp | % | Yds | Yd/Att | TD | Int-% | RK |
|---|---|---|---|---|---|---|---|---|
| Brodie | 427 | 232 | 54 | 2810 | 6.6 | 16 | 22– 5 | 8 |
| Mira | 53 | 22 | 42 | 284 | 5.4 | 5 | 2– 4 | |
| Kilmer | 16 | 5 | 31 | 84 | 5.3 | 0 | 1– 6 | |
| Crow | 4 | 2 | 50 | 61 | 15.3 | 0 | 1– 25 | |

**PUNTING**

| Last Name | No | Avg |
|---|---|---|
| Davis | 63 | 41.4 |
| Kilmer | 7 | 33.4 |

**KICKING**

| Last Name | XP | Att | % | FG | Att | % |
|---|---|---|---|---|---|---|
| Davis | 38 | 39 | 97 | 16 | 31 | 52 |

### CHICAGO BEARS

**RUSHING**

| Last Name | No. | Yds | Avg | TD |
|---|---|---|---|---|
| Sayers | 229 | 1231 | 5.4 | 8 |
| Bull | 100 | 318 | 3.2 | 0 |
| Kurek | 52 | 179 | 3.4 | 1 |
| Arnett | 55 | 178 | 3.2 | 1 |
| Bukich | 18 | 14 | 0.8 | 2 |
| Piccolo | 3 | 12 | 4.0 | 0 |
| Marconi | 3 | 5 | 1.7 | 0 |
| Gordon | 1 | 2 | 2.0 | 0 |
| Rakestraw | 1 | –5 | –5.0 | 0 |
| Jones | 1 | –7 | –7.0 | 0 |

**RECEIVING**

| Last Name | No. | Yds | Avg | TD |
|---|---|---|---|---|
| Sayers | 34 | 447 | 13 | 2 |
| Ditka | 32 | 378 | 12 | 2 |
| Jones | 28 | 504 | 18 | 5 |
| Bull | 20 | 174 | 9 | 0 |
| Gordon | 15 | 210 | 14 | 1 |
| Kurek | 10 | 178 | 18 | 0 |
| Arnett | 10 | 42 | 4 | 0 |
| Morris | 5 | 49 | 10 | 0 |
| Allen | 3 | 28 | 9 | 0 |
| Bivins | 2 | 6 | 3 | 0 |

**PUNT RETURNS**

| Last Name | No. | Yds | Avg | TD |
|---|---|---|---|---|
| Arnett | 15 | 58 | 4 | 0 |
| Sayers | 6 | 44 | 7 | 0 |
| Gordon | 4 | –5 | –1 | 0 |

**KICKOFF RETURNS**

| Last Name | No. | Yds | Avg | TD |
|---|---|---|---|---|
| Sayers | 23 | 718 | 31 | 2 |
| Gordon | 19 | 521 | 27 | 0 |
| Arnett | 2 | 39 | 20 | 0 |
| Butkus | 3 | 32 | 11 | 0 |
| Taylor | 1 | 3 | 3 | 0 |
| Brown | 0 | 28 | 0 | 0 |

**PASSING**

| Last Name | Att | Comp | % | Yds | Yd/Att | TD | Int-% | RK |
|---|---|---|---|---|---|---|---|---|
| Bukich | 309 | 147 | 48 | 1858 | 6.0 | 10 | 21– 7 | 13 |
| Wade | 21 | 9 | 43 | 79 | 3.8 | 0 | 1– 5 | |
| Sayers | 6 | 2 | 33 | 58 | 9.7 | 0 | 1– 17 | |
| Arnett | 1 | 0 | 0 | 0 | 0.0 | 0 | 0– 0 | |
| Bull | 1 | 1 | 100 | 21 | 21.0 | 0 | 0– 0 | |

**PUNTING**

| Last Name | No | Avg |
|---|---|---|
| Green | 80 | 42.0 |

**KICKING**

| Last Name | XP | Att | % | FG | Att | % |
|---|---|---|---|---|---|---|
| Leclerc | 24 | 25 | 96 | 18 | 30 | 60 |

### DETROIT LIONS

**RUSHING**

| Last Name | No. | Yds | Avg | TD |
|---|---|---|---|---|
| Nowatzke | 151 | 512 | 3.4 | 6 |
| Marsh | 134 | 433 | 3.2 | 3 |
| Sweetan | 34 | 219 | 6.4 | 1 |
| Felts | 34 | 83 | 2.4 | 2 |
| Plum | 12 | 59 | 4.9 | 0 |
| McLenna | 16 | 51 | 3.2 | 0 |
| Studstill | 2 | 20 | 10.0 | 0 |
| Todd | 2 | 6 | 3.0 | 0 |
| Wil. Walker | 1 | 4 | 4.0 | 0 |

**RECEIVING**

| Last Name | No. | Yds | Avg | TD |
|---|---|---|---|---|
| Studstill | 67 | 1266 | 19 | 5 |
| Nowatzke | 54 | 316 | 6 | 1 |
| Cogdill | 47 | 411 | 9 | 1 |
| Kramer | 37 | 432 | 12 | 0 |
| Marsh | 12 | 111 | 9 | 0 |
| Henderson | 6 | 121 | 20 | 0 |
| Malinchak | 5 | 34 | 7 | 0 |
| McLenna | 3 | 13 | 4 | 0 |
| Felts | 2 | 1 | 1 | 0 |
| Wil. Walker | 1 | 21 | 21 | 0 |
| Gibbons | 1 | 2 | 2 | 1 |

**PUNT RETURNS**

| Last Name | No. | Yds | Avg | TD |
|---|---|---|---|---|
| Robinson | 13 | 185 | 14 | 1 |
| Vaughn | 18 | 179 | 10 | 0 |
| Felts | 2 | 20 | 10 | 0 |
| Todd | 5 | 12 | 2 | 0 |

**KICKOFF RETURNS**

| Last Name | No. | Yds | Avg | TD |
|---|---|---|---|---|
| Vaughn | 23 | 595 | 26 | 0 |
| Felts | 20 | 392 | 20 | 0 |
| Robinson | 6 | 127 | 21 | 0 |
| Todd | 3 | 105 | 35 | 0 |
| Slaby | 1 | 14 | 14 | 0 |
| Mazzanti | 1 | 8 | 8 | 0 |
| Alford | 1 | 0 | 0 | 0 |

**PASSING**

| Last Name | Att | Comp | % | Yds | Yd/Att | TD | Int-% | RK |
|---|---|---|---|---|---|---|---|---|
| Sweetan | 309 | 157 | 51 | 1809 | 5.9 | 4 | 14– 5 | 11 |
| Plum | 146 | 82 | 56 | 943 | 6.5 | 4 | 13– 9 | 10 |
| Myers | 1 | 0 | 0 | 0 | 0.0 | 0 | 1–100 | |

**PUNTING**

| Last Name | No | Avg |
|---|---|---|
| Studstill | 72 | 41.1 |

**KICKING**

| Last Name | XP | Att | % | FG | Att | % |
|---|---|---|---|---|---|---|
| Yepremian | 11 | 11 | 100 | 13 | 22 | 59 |
| Way. Walker | 11 | 11 | 100 | 2 | 8 | 25 |
| Plum | 1 | 1 | 100 | 0 | 0 | 0 |

### MINNESOTA VIKINGS

**RUSHING**

| Last Name | No. | Yds | Avg | TD |
|---|---|---|---|---|
| Brown | 251 | 829 | 3.3 | 6 |
| Tarkenton | 62 | 376 | 6.1 | 4 |
| Osborn | 87 | 344 | 4.0 | 1 |
| Mason | 58 | 235 | 4.1 | 2 |
| Lindsey | 57 | 146 | 2.6 | 1 |
| Walden | 5 | 82 | 16.4 | 0 |
| King | 17 | 40 | 2.4 | 0 |
| Vender Kelen | 4 | 19 | 4.8 | 0 |
| Barnes | 5 | 16 | 3.2 | 1 |
| Berry | 3 | 12 | 4.0 | 0 |
| Williams | 1 | 2 | 2.0 | 0 |
| Carpenter | 1 | –10 | –10.0 | 0 |

**RECEIVING**

| Last Name | No. | Yds | Avg | TD |
|---|---|---|---|---|
| Flatley | 50 | 777 | 16 | 3 |
| Brown | 37 | 359 | 10 | 0 |
| Phillips | 32 | 554 | 17 | 3 |
| Carpenter | 30 | 518 | 17 | 4 |
| Hall | 23 | 271 | 12 | 2 |
| Lindsey | 20 | 250 | 13 | 2 |
| Osborn | 15 | 141 | 9 | 2 |
| Mason | 7 | 39 | 6 | 1 |
| King | 2 | 24 | 12 | 1 |
| Rentzel | 2 | 10 | 5 | 0 |
| Barnes | 1 | 20 | 20 | 0 |

**PUNT RETURNS**

| Last Name | No. | Yds | Avg | TD |
|---|---|---|---|---|
| Sharockman | 9 | 95 | 11 | 0 |
| Rentzel | 11 | 16 | 1 | 0 |
| Hall | 3 | 9 | 3 | 0 |
| Young | 2 | 7 | 4 | 0 |
| Lindsey | 2 | 4 | 2 | 0 |
| Williams | 4 | –2 | –1 | 0 |

**KICKOFF RETURNS**

| Last Name | No. | Yds | Avg | TD |
|---|---|---|---|---|
| Fitzgerald | 14 | 301 | 22 | 0 |
| Rentzel | 9 | 181 | 20 | 0 |
| Hall | 7 | 141 | 20 | 0 |
| Young | 5 | 105 | 21 | 0 |
| Lindsey | 4 | 79 | 20 | 0 |
| King | 6 | 78 | 13 | 0 |
| Williams | 3 | 61 | 20 | 0 |
| Rose | 1 | 20 | 20 | 0 |
| Osborn | 1 | 19 | 19 | 0 |
| Winston | 1 | 2 | 2 | 0 |
| Sunde | 1 | 0 | 0 | 0 |

**PASSING**

| Last Name | Att | Comp | % | Yds | Yd/Att | TD | Int-% | RK |
|---|---|---|---|---|---|---|---|---|
| Tarkenton | 358 | 192 | 54 | 2561 | 7.2 | 17 | 16– 4 | 6 |
| Berry | 37 | 13 | 35 | 215 | 5.8 | 1 | 5– 14 | |
| Vander Kelen | 20 | 10 | 50 | 147 | 7.4 | 0 | 1– 5 | |
| Brown | 1 | 0 | 0 | 0 | 0.0 | 0 | 0– 0 | |
| King | 1 | 1 | 100 | 9 | 9.0 | 0 | 0– 0 | |

**PUNTING**

| Last Name | No | Avg |
|---|---|---|
| Walden | 60 | 41.1 |

**KICKING**

| Last Name | XP | Att | % | FG | Att | % |
|---|---|---|---|---|---|---|
| Cox | 34 | 34 | 100 | 18 | 33 | 55 |

# 1966 A.F.L. Peace and the Super Bowl

After the New York Giants signed kicker Pete Gogolak away from the Buffalo Bills, the AFL owners decided to declare full-scale war against the NFL. Al Davis, the energetic young leader of the Oakland franchise, was put in charge of the war effort as Commissioner of the League, replacing Joe Foss in April, and an all-out effort was launched to steal star NFL players. Quarterbacks were special targets, with John Brodie and Roman Gabriel considered likely candidates to jump. With the bidding war for graduating collegians already costing clubs heavily, financial competition for established players would make bankruptcy a possibility for some teams. The two leagues sat down to put an end to the suicidal war, and the merger agreement was unveiled in June. Pete Rozelle became Commissioner over both leagues, the AFL agreed to pay reparations to the NFL teams, and a championship game—soon dubbed the Super Bowl—was arranged for the two league champions. By 1970, the AFL would be absorbed into the NFL, with all franchises to remain intact in their present locations. With peace at hand, Al Davis left the AFL office to return to Oakland as managing partner, just in time to preside over the opening of the new Oakland-Alameda County Coliseum. Milt Woodard took over as league president and would guide the league well up until its absorption into the NFL in 1970.

## EASTERN DIVISION

**Buffalo Bills**—Head coach Lou Saban was looking for new challenges after winning two straight AFL championships, so he resigned to become top man at the University of Maryland. Assistant Coach Joe Collier took over the top spot and kept the Bills exactly as Saban had molded them, a tough defensive team with a ball-control offense. With a bad knee bothering Tom Sestak, Jim Dunaway and Ron McDole provided leadership in the defensive line, while the tight linebacking crew of Mike Stratton, Harry Jacobs, and John Tracey held the defense together. In the secondary, Butch Byrd, George Saimes, Hagood Clarke, and Tom Janik strangled enemy passing attacks. The Buffalo offense got help from rookies Bobby Burnett and Bobby Crockett. Burnett joined with Wray Carlton in providing the running necessary for the methodical Buffalo attack, while Crockett won the starting split-end job. The team surpassed last year's squad on paper, but lost twice to Boston during the season and headed into the final weekend a half game behind the Patriots. The Jets did their part by beating the Pats 38-28, and the Bills capitalized by defeating Denver to take their third straight Eastern title.

**Boston Patriots**—Jim Nance cut down on his weight and set the league on fire with his rushing in his second pro year. Using pure power plus surprising speed, Nance pounded away at defenses in work-horse fashion, gaining an AFL record 1,458 yards and eleven touchdowns for his troubles. Quarterback Babe Parilli used Nance to set up his passes, and receivers Art Graham, Gino Cappelletti, and Jim Whalen gave him targets to hit when not handing off to Nance. Parilli ran the attack so well that John Huarte, the Heisman Trophy winner obtained from the New York Jets, rarely took his warm-up wraps off. The Boston defense stuck to the same lines as in recent years, with a strong front four, a lot of blitzing from middle linebacker Nick Buoniconti, and a lukewarm secondary. With Cappelletti in top form as a place-kicker, the Pats had a final ace whenever their offense stalled in enemy territory. Coach Mike Holovak prepared his team well for the schedule, and the team twice beat the Bills during the year to take a slight lead into the final game of the year against New York, but dropped a 38-28 decision as Parilli passed for 379 yards.

**New York Jets**—With a wealth of young offensive talent, the Jets made an early run at the Eastern title with four straight wins to open the season. Joe Namath, Matt Snell, George Sauer, Emerson Boozer, Pete Lammons, Winston Hill, Dave Herman, and John Schmitt were all twenty-five years old or less, and veterans like Billy Mathis, Sherman Plunkett, Don Maynard, and Sam DeLuca added stability to this dynamic attack. The defense contained players of widely varied talents. Verlon Biggs, Gerry Philbin, and Al Atkinson were good young talents, but only Larry Grantham had a good season among the veterans. After the good start, several factors caught up with the Jets and dragged them back into third place. The defense had problems stopping enemy passers, Namath had problems with interceptions, and the Jets had problems winning away from Shea Stadium, beating only weak Denver and Miami teams on the road.

**Houston Oilers**—After losing his job with the St. Louis Cardinals, Wally Lemm returned to the Oilers as head coach for the second time. In his previous term in Texas he had taken the Oilers to a divisional crown in 1961 after being promoted to the top spot in mid-season. This year he went along mostly with the same veterans who had won for him five years ago, but the results were different, only three wins and a tie for fourth place with the fledgling Dolphins. George Blanda, Charley Hennigan, Rich Michael, Don Floyd, Freddy Glick, Bob McLeod, Jim Norton, and Bob Talamini started this year after starting for Lemm in his first regime. Veteran NFL players such as John Henry Johnson and Bernie Parrish further added to the age on the team but contributed little on the field. After opening the

season with a 45-7 win over Denver and a 31-0 thumping of Oakland, the Oilers lost most of their games the rest of the way.

**Miami Dolphins**—The Dolphins had problems at almost every position in their first year, but nowhere more than at quarterback. Of the two passers taken in the expansion draft, Eddie Wilson hurt a knee in training camp and missed the season, while Dick Wood had very little left in his arm. Rookie Rick Norton went out with a fractured jaw in mid-season, leaving coach George Wilson with George Wilson, Jr., his son, as the starting quarterback. Not one to be accused of nepotism, coach Wilson promoted John Stofa from the North American Football League for the last few games, and Stofa came through with four touchdown passes in the season-ending victory over Houston. Stocked mostly with over-the-hill veterans, the Dolphins got their existence off to an auspicious start when Joe Auer returned the opening kickoff of their first game all the way for a touchdown.

## WESTERN DIVISION

**Kansas City Chiefs**—The first AFL Super Bowl representatives swept through their schedule with a powerful offense and well-coordinated defense. The Chiefs had shelled out a lot of money to halfback Mike Garrett in a pre-merger signing, and the short halfback gave the Chiefs a dangerous breakaway runner in the backfield. Curtis McClinton and Bert Coan also pitched in with hard work as ball carriers, making it hard for defenses to watch for Len Dawson passes. Chris Burford continued to run his precise patterns from the split end position, and Otis Taylor provided a deep threat at flanker with a fine sophomore season. Jim Tyrer and Ed Budde starred in the offensive line, but their comrades there showed considerably less consistency. The attack got by on the brilliance of the backs and ends, but the defense got by with a few stars and some mediocre talents.

**Oakland Raiders**—During Al Davis' two-month term as AFL Commissioner, the Raiders hired Johnny Rauch as their new head coach, and when Davis returned to Oakland as managing partner, some observers expected a conflict between the two men. Davis and Rauch got along well, but the Raiders finished in second place for the third time in four years. The Raiders won four of six meetings with Western opponents but lost three times to Eastern teams to kill their title chances. Despite top performances from Clem Daniels and Art Powell, the attack was a mediocre unit, but the defense played consistently well with flashes of brilliance. Tom Keating, obtained from the Buffalo Bills, used his extraordinary quickness to put a strong rush on enemy passers, and defensive ends Ben Davidson and Ike Lassiter added size to the line. The linebacking showed improvement as the young starters gained experience. The secondary was perhaps the league's best, with Dave Grayson, Kent McCloughan, and Rodger Bird each an individual star. Still, the Raiders needed a little more experience on defense and a little more punch on offense.

**San Diego Chargers**—The Chargers underwent a lot of changes this year, including a drop out of first place. The team's ownership changed hands in August when Barron Hilton sold the club to a group headed by Eugene Klein and Sam Schulman, and head coach Sid Gillman also sent a group of veteran players into exile. Salary disputes sent defensive linemen Ernie Ladd to Houston and Earl Faison to Miami, and the expansion draft to stock the Dolphins siphoned off defensive backs Jim Warren and Dick Westmoreland. A broken ankle sidelined middle linebacker Chuck Allen for most of the campaign, making the defense a patchwork quilt. Two veterans on offense, halfback Paul Lowe and tackle Ron Mix, suffered through off seasons, but a strong passing attack kept the Chargers rolling. Rookie Gary Garrison joined flanker Lance Alworth in a devastating receiving combo, giving quarterback John Hadl many opportunities to throw the ball. Even with all their problems, the Chargers kept the winning habit by taking their first four games, but once enemy offenses learned they could run on the San Diego line, the Chargers limped home to third place.

**Denver Broncos**—The Broncos scored the fewest points of any team in pro football, with problems in all sectors of the offense. Quarterbacks came and went on the Denver roster all season. John McCormick started for most of the campaign but showed very little; Mickey Slaughter, an occasional starter for the last three years, rarely got off the bench; veteran Tobin Rote came out of retirement, threw eight passes, and went right back into retirement; and rookies Max Chaboian and Scotty Glacken got late-season starting shots. With the revolving door at quarterback, end Lionel Taylor's catches fell off to thirty-five, his lowest since the AFL began. The running corps was hurt by the absence of Cookie Gilchrist, who held out into the season and was dealt to Miami, and Eldon Danehauer's injury took the best blocker out of the line. The best offense on the Broncos this year came from the kick returners, as Goldie Sellers and Nemiah Wilson scored three times on kickoff returns and Abner Haynes had the second highest average in the league for punt returns. The defense changed personnel less often than the offense but got little better results. The whole situation prompted head coach Mac Speedie to quit after two games, and assistant Ray Malavasi guided the team the rest of the way.

**FINAL TEAM STATISTICS**

OFFENSE / DEFENSE

| | BOSTON (O) | BUFFALO (O) | DENVER (O) | HOUSTON (O) | K.CITY (O) | MIAMI (O) | NEW YORK (O) | OAKLAND (O) | SAN DIEGO (O) | BOSTON (D) | BUFFALO (D) | DENVER (D) | HOUSTON (D) | K.CITY (D) | MIAMI (D) | NEW YORK (D) | OAKLAND (D) | SAN DIEGO (D) |
|---|---|---|---|---|---|---|---|---|---|---|---|---|---|---|---|---|---|---|
| **FIRST DOWNS:** | | | | | | | | | | | | | | | | | | |
| Total | 243 | 255 | 171 | 246 | 266 | 200 | 254 | 226 | 230 | 243 | 192 | 251 | 244 | 222 | 237 | 231 | 211 | 260 |
| by Rushing | 100 | 110 | 61 | 76 | 106 | 75 | 81 | 70 | 77 | 68 | 49 | 101 | 88 | 75 | 83 | 81 | 84 | 127 |
| by Passing | 121 | 126 | 95 | 144 | 140 | 103 | 145 | 144 | 137 | 153 | 131 | 122 | 131 | 125 | 140 | 131 | 106 | 116 |
| by Penalty | 22 | 19 | 15 | 26 | 20 | 22 | 28 | 12 | 16 | 22 | 12 | 28 | 25 | 22 | 14 | 19 | 21 | 17 |
| **RUSHING:** | | | | | | | | | | | | | | | | | | |
| Number | 471 | 455 | 376 | 413 | 439 | 394 | 376 | 363 | 361 | 369 | 344 | 441 | 422 | 353 | 416 | 388 | 418 | 497 |
| Yards | 1963 | 1892 | 1173 | 1515 | 2274 | 1410 | 1442 | 1427 | 1537 | 1135 | 1051 | 2029 | 1833 | 1356 | 1510 | 1524 | 1792 | 2403 |
| Average Yards | 4.2 | 4.2 | 3.1 | 3.7 | 5.2 | 3.6 | 3.8 | 3.9 | 4.3 | 3.1 | 3.1 | 4.6 | 4.3 | 3.8 | 3.6 | 3.9 | 4.3 | 4.8 |
| Touchdowns | 17 | 19 | 6 | 11 | 19 | 5 | 15 | 13 | 9 | 7 | 6 | 17 | 10 | 10 | 15 | 14 | 16 | 19 |
| **PASSING:** | | | | | | | | | | | | | | | | | | |
| Attempts | 393 | 473 | 402 | 485 | 377 | 454 | 514 | 450 | 434 | 509 | 466 | 396 | 438 | 494 | 425 | 467 | 405 | 382 |
| Completions | 186 | 199 | 166 | 226 | 199 | 179 | 251 | 212 | 224 | 247 | 205 | 192 | 209 | 226 | 198 | 212 | 183 | 170 |
| Completion Percentage | 47.3 | 42.1 | 41.3 | 46.6 | 52.8 | 39.4 | 48.8 | 47.1 | 51.6 | 48.5 | 44.0 | 48.5 | 47.7 | 45.8 | 46.6 | 45.4 | 45.2 | 44.5 |
| Passing Yards | 2784 | 3000 | 2351 | 3168 | 3123 | 2374 | 3556 | 3425 | 3347 | 3565 | 3307 | 2819 | 3390 | 2876 | 3281 | 3064 | 2440 | 2386 |
| Avg. Yards per Attempt | 7.1 | 6.3 | 5.8 | 6.5 | 8.3 | 5.2 | 6.9 | 7.6 | 7.7 | 7.0 | 7.1 | 7.1 | 7.7 | 5.8 | 7.7 | 6.6 | 6.0 | 6.2 |
| Avg. Yards per Completion | 15.0 | 15.1 | 14.2 | 14.0 | 15.7 | 13.3 | 14.2 | 16.2 | 14.9 | 14.4 | 16.1 | 14.7 | 16.2 | 12.7 | 16.6 | 14.5 | 13.3 | 14.0 |
| Times Tackled Att. to Pass | 25 | 16 | 37 | 28 | 30 | 36 | 9 | 34 | 32 | 22 | 32 | 33 | 21 | 26 | 16 | 35 | 36 | 26 |
| Yards Lost Tackled | 211 | 144 | 356 | 271 | 283 | 326 | 92 | 281 | 331 | 209 | 249 | 304 | 228 | 262 | 180 | 310 | 322 | 231 |
| Net Yards | 2573 | 2856 | 1995 | 2897 | 2840 | 2048 | 3464 | 3144 | 3016 | 3356 | 3058 | 2515 | 3162 | 2614 | 3101 | 2754 | 2118 | 2155 |
| Touchdowns | 20 | 15 | 12 | 29 | 31 | 16 | 21 | 26 | 29 | 26 | 22 | 26 | 35 | 18 | 25 | 19 | 15 | 13 |
| Interceptions | 21 | 21 | 30 | 28 | 15 | 32 | 29 | 26 | 15 | 22 | 29 | 13 | 18 | 33 | 31 | 21 | 23 | 27 |
| Percent Intercepted | 5.3 | 4.4 | 7.5 | 5.8 | 4.0 | 7.0 | 5.6 | 5.8 | 3.5 | 4.3 | 6.2 | 3.3 | 4.1 | 6.7 | 7.3 | 4.5 | 5.7 | 7.1 |
| **PUNTING:** | | | | | | | | | | | | | | | | | | |
| Number | 76 | 69 | 77 | 69 | 62 | 82 | 62 | 74 | 66 | 86 | 84 | 60 | 68 | 69 | 64 | 81 | 73 | 52 |
| Average Distance | 36.5 | 41.2 | 45.2 | 42.2 | 43.8 | 39.4 | 42.5 | 41.6 | 37.0 | 38.5 | 39.6 | 42.7 | 40.0 | 41.3 | 43.9 | 40.4 | 41.3 | 43.0 |
| **PUNT RETURNS:** | | | | | | | | | | | | | | | | | | |
| Number | 24 | 43 | 26 | 23 | 31 | 21 | 36 | 41 | 21 | 20 | 20 | 38 | 37 | 36 | 40 | 24 | 35 | 16 |
| Yards | 143 | 411 | 235 | 159 | 276 | 204 | 260 | 367 | 257 | 127 | 301 | 296 | 269 | 359 | 412 | 121 | 343 | 84 |
| Average Yards | 6.0 | 9.6 | 9.0 | 6.9 | 8.9 | 9.7 | 7.2 | 9.0 | 12.2 | 6.4 | 15.1 | 7.8 | 7.3 | 10.0 | 10.3 | 5.0 | 9.8 | 5.3 |
| Touchdowns | 0 | 2 | 0 | 0 | 2 | 0 | 0 | 0 | 1 | 1 | 2 | 0 | 0 | 1 | 1 | 0 | 1 | 0 |
| **KICKOFF RETURNS:** | | | | | | | | | | | | | | | | | | |
| Number | 54 | 51 | 58 | 64 | 54 | 65 | 62 | 60 | 55 | 46 | 65 | 43 | 60 | 84 | 46 | 57 | 56 | 66 |
| Yards | 1145 | 1064 | 1558 | 1514 | 1148 | 1507 | 1300 | 1191 | 1282 | 988 | 1329 | 1000 | 1385 | 2045 | 939 | 1368 | 1268 | 1387 |
| Average Yards | 21.2 | 20.9 | 26.9 | 23.7 | 21.3 | 23.2 | 21.0 | 19.9 | 23.3 | 21.5 | 20.4 | 23.3 | 23.1 | 24.3 | 20.4 | 24.0 | 22.6 | 21.0 |
| Touchdowns | 0 | 1 | 3 | 0 | 0 | 1 | 1 | 0 | 0 | 0 | 0 | 2 | 1 | 1 | 1 | 1 | 1 | 0 |
| **INTERCEPTION RETURNS:** | | | | | | | | | | | | | | | | | | |
| Number | 22 | 29 | 13 | 18 | 33 | 31 | 21 | 23 | 27 | 21 | 21 | 30 | 28 | 15 | 32 | 29 | 26 | 15 |
| Yards | 348 | 472 | 109 | 259 | 408 | 522 | 218 | 380 | 359 | 204 | 303 | 545 | 448 | 225 | 370 | 297 | 405 | 278 |
| Average Yards | 15.8 | 16.3 | 8.4 | 14.4 | 12.4 | 16.8 | 10.4 | 16.5 | 13.3 | 9.7 | 14.4 | 18.2 | 16.0 | 15.0 | 11.6 | 10.2 | 15.6 | 18.5 |
| Touchdowns | 0 | 4 | 0 | 0 | 4 | 4 | 1 | 0 | 0 | 2 | 1 | 2 | 3 | 2 | 1 | 2 | 0 | 0 |
| **PENALTIES:** | | | | | | | | | | | | | | | | | | |
| Number | 64 | 62 | 66 | 71 | 61 | 73 | 64 | 80 | 68 | 76 | 55 | 75 | 69 | 56 | 79 | 85 | 54 | 60 |
| Yards | 601 | 637 | 771 | 682 | 680 | 660 | 682 | 752 | 667 | 757 | 546 | 576 | 725 | 592 | 852 | 883 | 614 | 527 |
| **FUMBLES:** | | | | | | | | | | | | | | | | | | |
| Number | 25 | 27 | 36 | 19 | 21 | 29 | 19 | 22 | 17 | 30 | 19 | 35 | 25 | 21 | 25 | 15 | 28 | 17 |
| Number Lost | 13 | 15 | 17 | 12 | 16 | 10 | 9 | 12 | 7 | 15 | 9 | 18 | 13 | 8 | 15 | 8 | 17 | 8 |
| **POINTS:** | | | | | | | | | | | | | | | | | | |
| Total | 315 | 358 | 196 | 335 | 448 | 213 | 322 | 315 | 335 | 283 | 255 | 381 | 396 | 276 | 362 | 312 | 288 | 284 |
| PAT (kick) Attempts | 36 | 42 | 20 | 40 | 52 | 23 | 35 | 40 | 40 | 36 | 28 | 46 | 49 | 28 | 42 | 36 | 31 | 32 |
| PAT (kick) Made | 35 | 41 | 20 | 39 | 48 | 23 | 34 | 39 | 39 | 34 | 28 | 46 | 49 | 28 | 38 | 34 | 30 | 31 |
| PAT (Rush or Pass) Attempts | 2 | 1 | 2 | 1 | 3 | 3 | 3 | 0 | 1 | 0 | 3 | 1 | 1 | 4 | 2 | 1 | 3 | 1 |
| PAT (Rush or Pass) Made | 2 | 0 | 1 | 0 | 2 | 2 | 2 | 0 | 0 | 0 | 1 | 1 | 1 | 1 | 1 | 1 | 2 | 1 |
| FG Attempts | 32 | 38 | 25 | 30 | 28 | 22 | 35 | 30 | 31 | 26 | 22 | 40 | 30 | 28 | 36 | 28 | 30 | 31 |
| FG Made | 16 | 19 | 14 | 16 | 22 | 10 | 18 | 12 | 16 | 11 | 13 | 17 | 15 | 18 | 18 | 18 | 16 | 17 |
| Percent FG Made | 50.0 | 50.0 | 56.0 | 53.3 | 78.6 | 45.5 | 51.4 | 40.0 | 51.6 | 42.3 | 59.1 | 42.5 | 50.0 | 64.3 | 50.0 | 64.3 | 53.3 | 54.8 |
| Safeties | 0 | 1 | 0 | 1 | 2 | 2 | 1 | 0 | 1 | 0 | 0 | 0 | 0 | 0 | 0 | 0 | 1 | 1 |

---

**1966 AFL
CHAMPIONSHIP GAME**
January 1, at Buffalo
(Attendance 42,080)

## Super Reps

This year's AFL title was the most desirable in the league's short history, for this year's champion would get the chance to play the NFL champion in the first Super Bowl. The Buffalo Bills had won the last two AFL titles, but the Kansas City Chiefs solved the tough Buffalo defense and scored a decisive 31-7 victory. Len Dawson passed the Chiefs into a quick 7-0 lead with a 29-yard pass to Fred Arbanas early in the game. The Bills came back to tie the score on a surprise long pass to Elbert Dubenion from Jack Kemp, but the Chiefs moved ahead 14-7 with a second-quarter touchdown pass from Dawson to Otis Taylor. Toward the end of the first half Buffalo appeared on the verge of tying the game, but a key interception spelled disaster for the Bills. With Buffalo driving and but ten yards from a touchdown, Kemp's pass was intercepted in the end zone by Johnny Robinson, who ran the ball back 72 yards to set up a 32-yard field goal by Mike Mercer and run the score to 17-7 at halftime. The third quarter passed without any scoring, and the Chiefs put the game out of reach with a pair of fourth-quarter touchdowns. Mike Garrett, the star rookie halfback, scored from the one-yard line and the 18-yard line on running plays. The Bills remained scoreless and as a result of the Kansas City defense outshining the more famous Buffalo unit, the front four completely stifling the Bills' running game and putting a strong rush on Kemp when he dropped back to pass, the Chiefs became the AFL's first Super Bowl representatives.

### SCORING

| | | | | | |
|---|---|---|---|---|---|
| **BUFFALO** | 7 | 0 | 0 | 0— | 7 |
| **KANSAS CITY** | 7 | 10 | 0 | 14— | 31 |

First Quarter
K.C.   Arbanas, 29 yard pass from Dawson
     PAT — Mercer (kick)
BUFF.   Dubenion, 69 yard pass from Kemp
     PAT — Lusteg (kick)

Second Quarter
K.C.   Taylor, 29 yard pass from Dawson
     PAT — Mercer (kick)
K.C.   Mercer, 32 yard Field goal

Fourth Quarter
K.C.   Garrett, 1 yard rush
     PAT — Mercer (kick)
K.C.   Garrett, 18 yard rush
     PAT — Mercer (kick)

### TEAM STATISTICS

| BUFF. | | K.C. |
|---|---|---|
| 9 | First Downs — Total | 14 |
| 2 | First Downs — Rushing | 6 |
| 7 | First Downs — Passing | 8 |
| 0 | First Downs — Penalty | 0 |
| 8 | Punts — Number | 6 |
| 39.3 | Punts — Average Distance | 42.3 |
| 3 | Penalties — Number | 4 |
| 23 | Yards Penalized | 40 |
| 0 | Missed Field Goals | 1 |

### INDIVIDUAL STATISTICS

**RUSHING**

| BUFFALO | No | Yds | Avg. | | KANSAS CITY | No | Yds | Avg. |
|---|---|---|---|---|---|---|---|---|
| Carlton | 9 | 31 | 3.4 | | Garrett | 13 | 39 | 3.0 |
| Burnett | 3 | 6 | 2.0 | | McClinton | 11 | 38 | 3.5 |
| Kemp | 1 | 3 | 3.0 | | Dawson | 5 | 28 | 5.6 |
| | 13 | 40 | 3.1 | | Coan | 2 | 6 | 3.0 |
| | | | | | Eu. Thomas | 2 | 2 | 1.0 |
| | | | | | | 33 | 113 | 3.4 |

**RECEIVING**

| BUFFALO | No | Yds | Avg. | | KANSAS CITY | No | Yds | Avg. |
|---|---|---|---|---|---|---|---|---|
| Burnett | 6 | 127 | 21.2 | | Taylor | 5 | 78 | 15.6 |
| Dubenion | 2 | 79 | 39.5 | | Burford | 4 | 76 | 19.0 |
| Bass | 2 | 26 | 13.0 | | Garrett | 4 | 16 | 4.0 |
| Crockett | 1 | 16 | 16.0 | | Arbanas | 2 | 44 | 22.0 |
| Carlton | 1 | 5 | 5.0 | | McClinton | 1 | 13 | 13.0 |
| | 12 | 253 | 21.1 | | | 16 | 227 | 14.2 |

**PUNT RETURNS**

| BUFFALO | No | Yds | Avg. | | KANSAS CITY | No | Yds | Avg. |
|---|---|---|---|---|---|---|---|---|
| Byrd | 3 | 0 | 0.0 | | Garrett | 3 | 37 | 12.3 |
| Rutkowski | 2 | 16 | 8.0 | | | | | |
| | 5 | 16 | 3.2 | | | | | |

**KICKOFF RETURNS**

| BUFFALO | No | Yds | Avg. | | KANSAS CITY | No | Yds | Avg. |
|---|---|---|---|---|---|---|---|---|
| Warner | 5 | 91 | 18.2 | | Coan | 1 | 35 | 35.0 |
| Meredith | 1 | 8 | 8.0 | | Garrett | 1 | 3 | 3.0 |
| | 6 | 99 | 16.5 | | | 2 | 38 | 19.0 |

**INTERCEPTION RETURNS**

| BUFFALO | No | Yds | Avg. | | KANSAS CITY | No | Yds | Avg. |
|---|---|---|---|---|---|---|---|---|
| None | | | | | Robinson | 1 | 72 | 72.0 |
| | | | | | Em. Thomas | 1 | 26 | 26.0 |
| | | | | | | 2 | 98 | 49.0 |

**PASSING**

| BUFFALO | Att | Comp | Comp Pct. | Yds | Int | Yds/ Att | Yds/ Comp | Yards Tackled |
|---|---|---|---|---|---|---|---|---|
| Kemp | 27 | 12 | 44.4 | 253 | 2 | 9.4 | 21.1 | 38 |
| **KANSAS CITY** | | | | | | | | |
| Dawson | 24 | 16 | 66.7 | 227 | 0 | 9.5 | 14.2 | 63 |

### BUFFALO BILLS 9-4-1 Joe Collier

| Scores of Each Game | | |
|---|---|---|
| 7 | San Diego | 27 |
| 20 | KANSAS CITY | 42 |
| 58 | MIAMI | 24 |
| 27 | HOUSTON | 20 |
| 29 | Kansas City | 14 |
| 10 | BOSTON | 20 |
| 17 | SAN DIEGO | 17 |
| 33 | New York | 23 |
| 29 | Miami | 0 |
| 14 | NEW YORK | 3 |
| 42 | Houston | 20 |
| 31 | Oakland | 10 |
| 3 | Boston | 14 |
| 38 | DENVER | 21 |

| Use Name | Pos. | Hgt | Wgt | Age | Int | Pts |
|---|---|---|---|---|---|---|
| Stew Barber | OT | 6'3" | 250 | 27 | | |
| Wayne DeSutter | OT | 6'4" | 250 | 22 | | |
| Dick Hudson | OT | 6'4" | 265 | 26 | | |
| Joe O'Donnell | OG | 6'2" | 252 | 24 | | |
| Remi Prudhomme | OG | 6'4" | 240 | 24 | | |
| Billy Shaw | OG | 6'3" | 260 | 26 | | |
| Bob Schmidt | OT-C | 6'4" | 250 | 30 | | |
| Al Bemiller | OG-C | 6'3" | 240 | 27 | | |
| Tom Day | DE | 6'2" | 250 | 31 | | |
| Ron McDole | DE | 6'3" | 275 | 26 | 1 | |
| Dave Costa | DT | 6'2" | 250 | 24 | | |
| Jim Dunaway | DT | 6'4" | 280 | 24 | | 6 |
| Dudley Meredith | DT | 6'4" | 285 | 31 | | |
| Tom Sestak | DT | 6'5" | 270 | 30 | | |
| Paul Guidry | LB | 6'3" | 225 | 22 | | |
| Harry Jacobs | LB | 6'2" | 226 | 29 | 2 | |
| Paul Maguire | LB | 6' | 228 | 28 | | |
| Marty Schottenheimer | LB | 6'3" | 225 | 23 | 1 | |
| Mike Stratton | LB | 6'3" | 235 | 24 | 3 | 6 |
| John Tracey | LB | 6'3" | 228 | 33 | 1 | |
| Butch Byrd | DB | 6' | 211 | 24 | 6 | 12 |
| Hagood Clarke | DB | 6' | 203 | 24 | 5 | 6 |
| Booker Edgerson | DB | 5'10" | 188 | 27 | | |
| Tom Janik | DB | 6'3" | 200 | 25 | 8 | 12 |
| Charlie King | DB | 6' | 185 | 23 | 1 | |
| George Saimes | DB | 5'10" | 185 | 24 | 1 | |
| Charley Warner | DB | 5'11" | 170 | 26 | | 6 |
| Jack Kemp | QB | 6'1" | 200 | 32 | | 30 |
| Daryle Lamonica | QB | 6'2" | 218 | 25 | | 6 |
| Bobby Burnett | HB | 6'2" | 208 | 23 | | 48 |
| Allen Smith | HB | 6' | 200 | 23 | | |
| Wray Carlton | FB | 6'2" | 230 | 28 | | 36 |
| Doug Goodwin | FB | 6'2" | 228 | 24 | | |
| Jack Spikes | FB | 6'2" | 220 | 28 | | 24 |
| Elbert Dubenion | FL | 6' | 190 | 31 | | 12 |
| Paul Costa | TE | 6'4" | 255 | 24 | | 18 |
| Glenn Bass | OE | 6'2" | 206 | 27 | | |
| Bobby Crockett | OE | 6' | 195 | 23 | | 18 |
| Charley Ferguson | OE | 6'5" | 224 | 26 | | 6 |
| Pete Mills | OE | 5'11" | 180 | 23 | | |
| Ed Rutkowski | OE | 6'1" | 208 | 25 | | 12 |
| Booth Lusteg | K | 5'11" | 190 | 25 | | 98 |

### BOSTON PATRIOTS 8-4-2 Mike Holovak

| Scores of Each Game | | |
|---|---|---|
| 0 | San Diego | 24 |
| 24 | Denver | 10 |
| 24 | KANSAS CITY | 43 |
| 24 | NEW YORK | 24 |
| 20 | Buffalo | 10 |
| 35 | SAN DIEGO | 17 |
| 24 | OAKLAND | 21 |
| 10 | DENVER | 17 |
| 27 | HOUSTON | 21 |
| 27 | Kansas City | 27 |
| 20 | Miami | 14 |
| 14 | BUFFALO | 3 |
| 38 | Houston | 14 |
| 28 | New York | 38 |

| Use Name | Pos. | Hgt | Wgt | Age | Int | Pts |
|---|---|---|---|---|---|---|
| Tom Neville | OT | 6'4" | 230 | 23 | | |
| Don Oakes | OT | 6'3" | 255 | 28 | | |
| Karl Singer | OT | 6'3" | 245 | 22 | | |
| Justin Canale | OG | 6'2" | 230 | 22 | | |
| Charley Long | OG | 6'3" | 250 | 28 | | |
| Len St. Jean | OG | 6'1" | 240 | 24 | | |
| Joe Avezzano | C | 6'2" | 235 | 22 | | |
| Jon Morris | C | 6'4" | 240 | 23 | | |
| Jim Boudreaux | DE | 6'4" | 245 | 21 | | |
| Bob Dee | DE | 6'3" | 240 | 33 | | |
| Larry Eisenhauer | DE | 6'5" | 250 | 26 | | |
| Houstine Antwine | DT | 6' | 270 | 27 | | |
| Jim Hunt | DT | 5'11" | 245 | 27 | | 6 |
| Ed Khayat | DT | 6'3" | 250 | 31 | | |
| John Mangum | DT | 6'3" | 275 | 22 | | |
| Tom Addison | LB | 6'3" | 230 | 30 | | |
| Nick Buoniconti | LB | 5'11" | 220 | 25 | 4 | |
| Lonnie Farmer | LB | 6' | 220 | 25 | | |
| Jim Fraser | LB | 6'3" | 235 | 30 | 1 | |
| Doug Satcher | LB | 6' | 222 | 21 | | |
| Jay Cunningham | DB | 5'10" | 180 | 23 | | |
| Dick Felt | DB | 6' | 185 | 33 | 2 | |
| White Graves | DB | 6' | 185 | 23 | 1 | |
| Ron Hall | DB | 6' | 190 | 29 | 6 | |
| Tom Hennessey | DB | 6' | 185 | 26 | 6 | |
| Billy Johnson | DB | 5'11" | 180 | 23 | | |
| Vic Purvis | DB | 5'11" | 200 | 22 | | |
| Chuck Shonta | DB | 6' | 200 | 28 | 1 | |
| Don Webb | DB | 5'10" | 200 | 27 | 1 | |
| John Huarte | QB | 6' | 190 | 22 | | |
| Babe Parilli | QB | 6'1" | 190 | 36 | | 6 |
| Tom Yewcic | QB | 5'11" | 185 | 34 | | |
| J. D. Garrett | HB | 5'11" | 195 | 24 | | |
| Larry Garron | HB | 6' | 195 | 29 | | 54 |
| Bob Cappadonna | FB | 6'1" | 230 | 22 | | 8 |
| Jim Nance | FB | 6'1" | 235 | 23 | | 66 |
| Joe Bellino | FL | 5'9" | 185 | 28 | | 6 |
| Gino Cappelletti | FL | 6' | 190 | 32 | | 119 |
| Tony Romeo | TE | 6'2" | 230 | 27 | | 2 |
| Jim Whalen | TE | 6'2" | 210 | 22 | | 24 |
| Jim Colclough | OE | 6' | 185 | 30 | | |
| Art Graham | OE | 6'1" | 205 | 25 | | 24 |
| Ellis Johnson | OE | 6'2" | 190 | 22 | | |

### NEW YORK JETS 6-6-2 Weeb Ewbank

| Scores of Each Game | | |
|---|---|---|
| 19 | Miami | 14 |
| 52 | HOUSTON | 13 |
| 16 | Denver | 7 |
| 24 | Boston | 24 |
| 17 | SAN DIEGO | 16 |
| 0 | Houston | 24 |
| 21 | OAKLAND | 24 |
| 23 | BUFFALO | 33 |
| 3 | Buffalo | 14 |
| 30 | MIAMI | 13 |
| 24 | KANSAS CITY | 32 |
| 28 | Oakland | 28 |
| 27 | San Diego | 42 |
| 38 | BOSTON | 28 |

| Use Name | Pos. | Hgt | Wgt | Age | Int | Pts |
|---|---|---|---|---|---|---|
| Nick DeFelice | OT | 6'3" | 250 | 26 | | |
| Mitch Dudek | OT | 6'4" | 245 | 22 | | |
| Winston Hill | OT | 6'4" | 274 | 24 | | |
| Sherman Plunkett | OT | 6'4" | 300 | 32 | | |
| Steve Chomyszak | C-OT | 6'5" | 265 | 21 | | |
| Sam DeLuca | OG | 6'2" | 250 | 30 | | |
| Dan Ficca | OG | 6'1" | 245 | 27 | | |
| Dave Herman | OG | 6'2" | 255 | 24 | | |
| Pete Perreault | OG | 6'3" | 245 | 27 | | |
| John Schmitt | C | 6'4" | 265 | 23 | | |
| Jim Waskiewicz | C | 6'4" | 227 | 22 | | |
| Verlon Biggs | DE | 6'4" | 253 | 23 | | |
| Gerry Philbin | DE | 6'2" | 245 | 25 | | |
| Bill Yearby | DE | 6'3" | 235 | 22 | | |
| Bert Wilder | DT-DE | 6'3" | 245 | 26 | | |
| Bob Werl | OG-DE | 6'3" | 240 | 23 | | |
| Jim Harris | DT | 6'4" | 280 | 22 | | |
| Paul Rochester | DT | 6'2" | 250 | 29 | | |
| Henry Schmidt | DT | 6'4" | 255 | 29 | | |
| Al Atkinson | LB | 6'1" | 230 | 23 | 4 | |
| Ralph Baker | LB | 6'3" | 228 | 24 | | |
| Paul Crane | LB | 6'2" | 205 | 22 | | |
| Larry Grantham | LB | 6' | 206 | 27 | 1 | |
| Jim O'Mahoney | LB | 6'1" | 228 | 25 | | |
| Ray Abruzzese | DB | 6'1" | 194 | 28 | 2 | |
| Bill Baird | DB | 5'10" | 180 | 27 | 5 | 6 |
| Cornell Gordon | DB | 6' | 185 | 25 | | |
| Jim Gray | DB | 6' | 180 | 24 | | |
| Pat Gucciardo | DB | 5'11" | 185 | 22 | | |
| Sherman Lewis | DB | 5'10" | 180 | 24 | | |
| Dainard Paulson | DB | 5'11" | 190 | 29 | | |
| Johnny Sample | DB | 6'1" | 205 | 29 | 6 | |
| Jim Hudson | DB | 6'2" | 210 | 23 | 3 | |
| Dee Mackey – Injury | | | | | | |
| Joe Namath | QB | 6'2" | 190 | 23 | | 12 |
| Mike Taliaferro | QB | 6'2" | 205 | 24 | | 2 |
| Emerson Boozer | HB | 5'11" | 215 | 23 | | 36 |
| Earl Christy | HB | 5'11" | 190 | 23 | | |
| Bill Mathis | HB | 6'1" | 220 | 27 | | 18 |
| Allen Smith | HB | 5'11" | 195 | 22 | | |
| Mark Smolinski | FB | 6' | 215 | 27 | | 18 |
| Matt Snell | FB | 6'2" | 220 | 24 | | 48 |
| Don Maynard | FL | 6' | 180 | 30 | | 30 |
| Sammy Weir | FL | 5'9" | 170 | 24 | | |
| Pete Lammons | TE | 6'3" | 235 | 22 | | 24 |
| Bill Rademacher | OE | 6'1" | 190 | 24 | | |
| George Sauer | OE | 6'1" | 206 | 22 | | 32 |
| Bake Turner | OE | 6' | 180 | 26 | | |
| Curley Johnson | K | 6' | 215 | 31 | | 6 |
| Jim Turner | K | 6'2" | 205 | 25 | | 88 |

### HOUSTON OILERS 3-11-0 Wally Lemm

| Scores of Each Game | | |
|---|---|---|
| 45 | DENVER | 7 |
| 31 | OAKLAND | 0 |
| 13 | New York | 52 |
| 20 | Buffalo | 27 |
| 38 | Denver | 40 |
| 24 | NEW YORK | 0 |
| 13 | MIAMI | 20 |
| 23 | Kansas City | 48 |
| 23 | Oakland | 38 |
| 21 | Boston | 27 |
| 20 | BUFFALO | 42 |
| 22 | SAN DIEGO | 28 |
| 14 | BOSTON | 38 |
| 28 | Miami | 29 |

| Use Name | Pos. | Hgt | Wgt | Age | Int | Pts |
|---|---|---|---|---|---|---|
| George Allen | OT | 6'7" | 270 | 22 | | |
| Glen Ray Hines | OT | 6'5" | 255 | 22 | | |
| Rich Michael | OT | 6'3" | 242 | 27 | | |
| Walt Suggs | OT | 6'5" | 245 | 27 | | |
| Sonny Bishop | OG | 6'2" | 245 | 26 | | |
| Bob Talamini | OG | 6'1" | 255 | 27 | | |
| John Wittenborn | OG | 6'2" | 240 | 30 | | |
| John Frongillo | C | 6'3" | 255 | 26 | | |
| Gary Cutsinger | DE | 6'4" | 245 | 25 | | |
| Don Floyd | DE | 6'4" | 250 | 28 | | |
| Ed Scrutchins | DE | 6'3" | 260 | 25 | | |
| Scott Appleton | DT | 6'3" | 255 | 24 | | |
| Jim Hayes | DT | 6'4" | 260 | 25 | | |
| Pat Holmes | DT | 6'5" | 270 | 26 | | |
| Ernie Ladd | DT | 6'9" | 295 | 27 | | |
| George Rice | OG-DT | 6'3" | 267 | 22 | | |
| Johnny Baker | LB | 6'3" | 238 | 25 | 1 | |
| Garland Boyette | LB | 6'1" | 238 | 26 | | |
| Danny Brabham | LB | 6'4" | 233 | 25 | | |
| John Carrell | LB | 6'3" | 227 | 23 | | |
| Ronnie Caveness | LB | 6'1" | 225 | 23 | 1 | |
| Doug Cline (to SD) | LB | 6'2" | 230 | 27 | 1 | 6 |
| Bobby Maples | LB | 6'3" | 245 | 23 | | |
| John Meyer | LB | 6'1" | 225 | 24 | | |
| Olen Underwood | LB | 6'1" | 230 | 24 | | |
| Freddy Glick | DB | 6'1" | 190 | 29 | 4 | |
| W. K. Hicks | DB | 6'1" | 185 | 23 | 3 | |
| Bobby Jancik | DB | 5'11" | 178 | 26 | 2 | |
| Jim Norton | DB | 6'3" | 190 | 27 | 4 | |
| Bernie Parrish | DB | 5'11" | 195 | 31 | 2 | |
| Mickey Sutton | DB | 6' | 190 | 23 | | |
| Allen Trammell | DB | 6' | 190 | 24 | | |
| Theo Viltz | DB | 6'2" | 190 | 23 | | |
| George Blanda | QB | 6'1" | 220 | 38 | | 87 |
| Buddy Humphrey | QB | 6'1" | 200 | 30 | | |
| Jacky Lee | QB | 6'1" | 190 | 27 | | |
| Don Trull | QB | 6'1" | 190 | 24 | | 42 |
| Sid Blanks | HB | 6' | 205 | 25 | | 12 |
| Ode Burrell | HB | 6' | 185 | 26 | | 30 |
| Hoyle Granger | FB-HB | 6'1" | 225 | 22 | | 12 |
| John Henry Johnson | FB | 6'2" | 225 | 36 | | 18 |
| Donnie Stone | FB | 6'2" | 225 | 29 | | |
| Charley Tolar | FB | 5'7" | 200 | 28 | | |
| Larry Elkins | FL | 6'1" | 190 | 23 | | 18 |
| Charley Hennigan | FL | 6' | 187 | 30 | | 18 |
| Bob McLeod | TE | 6'5" | 230 | 27 | | 18 |
| Bob Poole | TE | 6'4" | 215 | 24 | | |
| Charley Frazier | OE | 6' | 175 | 27 | | 72 |

### MIAMI DOLPHINS 3-11-0 George Wilson

| Scores of Each Game | | |
|---|---|---|
| 14 | OAKLAND | 23 |
| 14 | NEW YORK | 19 |
| 24 | Buffalo | 58 |
| 10 | San Diego | 44 |
| 10 | Oakland | 21 |
| 24 | DENVER | 7 |
| 20 | Houston | 13 |
| 0 | BUFFALO | 29 |
| 16 | Kansas City | 34 |
| 13 | New York | 30 |
| 14 | BOSTON | 20 |
| 7 | Denver | 17 |
| 18 | KANSAS CITY | 19 |
| 29 | HOUSTON | 28 |

| Use Name | Pos. | Hgt | Wgt | Age | Int | Pts |
|---|---|---|---|---|---|---|
| Norm Evans | OT | 6'5" | 235 | 23 | | |
| Ernie Park | OT | 6'3" | 253 | 24 | | |
| Maxie Williams | OT | 6'4" | 240 | 26 | | |
| Billy Neighbors | OG | 5'11" | 245 | 26 | | |
| Ken Rice | OG | 6'2" | 240 | 26 | | |
| Jim Higgins | OT-OG | 6'1" | 250 | 24 | | |
| Tom Goode | C | 6'3" | 240 | 27 | | |
| Mike Hudock | C | 6'2" | 245 | 31 | | |
| Mel Branch | DE | 6'2" | 230 | 29 | | |
| Whit Canale | DE | 6'3" | 245 | 24 | | |
| Ed Cooke | DE | 6'4" | 250 | 31 | | |
| Earl Faison (from SD) | DE | 6'5" | 265 | 27 | 1 | |
| John Holmes | DE | 6'2" | 248 | 22 | | |
| Lavern Torczon | DE | 6'2" | 250 | 30 | | |
| Al Dotson | DT | 6'4" | 255 | 23 | | |
| Tom Nomina | DT | 6'5" | 270 | 24 | | |
| Rich Zecher | DT | 6'2" | 240 | 23 | | |
| Bob Bruggers | LB | 6'1" | 225 | 22 | | |
| Frank Emanuel | LB | 6'3" | 225 | 23 | 1 | |
| Tom Erlandson | LB | 6'3" | 235 | 26 | 3 | 6 |
| Wahoo McDaniel | LB | 6' | 230 | 29 | 2 | |
| Jack Rudolph | LB | 6'3" | 225 | 28 | 1 | |
| Jack Thornton | LB | 6'1" | 230 | 21 | | |
| Pete Jaquess | DB | 6' | 185 | 24 | 3 | 6 |
| John McGeever | DB | 6'1" | 195 | 27 | 2 | |
| Bob Neff | DB | 6'1" | 185 | 22 | 1 | |
| Bob Petrella | DB | 6' | 185 | 21 | | |
| Hal Wantland | DB | 6' | 195 | 22 | | |
| Jimmy Warren | DB | 5'11" | 185 | 27 | 5 | 6 |
| Willie West | DB | 5'10" | 187 | 28 | 8 | |
| Dick Westmoreland | DB | 6'1" | 195 | 25 | 4 | 6 |
| Ross O'Hanley – Injury | | | | | | |
| Eddie Wilson – Knee Injury | | | | | | |
| Rick Norton | QB | 6'1" | 198 | 22 | | |
| John Stofa | QB | 6'3" | 210 | 24 | | |
| George Wilson | QB | 6'1" | 190 | 23 | | 2 |
| Dick Wood | QB | 6'5" | 200 | 30 | | 6 |
| Joe Auer | HB | 6'1" | 200 | 24 | | 54 |
| Bill Hunter | HB | 6'1" | 180 | 23 | | |
| Gene Mingo | HB | 6'1" | 190 | 27 | | 53 |
| Sam Price | FB-HB | 5'11" | 215 | 22 | | |
| Rick Casares | FB | 6'2" | 233 | 35 | | 6 |
| George Chesser | FB | 6'2" | 225 | 23 | | |
| Cookie Gilchrist | FB | 6'3" | 250 | 31 | | 6 |
| Billy Joe | FB | 6'2" | 236 | 25 | | 8 |
| Frank Jackson | FL | 6'1" | 190 | 26 | | 12 |
| Bo Roberson | FL | 6'1" | 190 | 31 | | 12 |
| John Roderick | FL | 6'1" | 180 | 22 | | 6 |
| Bill Cronin | TE | 6'4" | 230 | 23 | | 6 |
| Dave Kocourek | TE | 6'5" | 240 | 29 | | 12 |
| Wes Mathews | OE | 5'10" | 180 | 22 | | |
| Stan Mitchell | OE | 6'2" | 220 | 22 | | |
| Doug Moreau | OE | 6'2" | 193 | 21 | | |
| Karl Noonan | OE | 6'3" | 185 | 22 | | 6 |
| Howard Twilley | OE | 5'10" | 180 | 22 | | |

## BUFFALO BILLS

### Rushing

| Last Name | No. | Yds | Avg | TD |
|---|---|---|---|---|
| Burnett | 187 | 766 | 4.1 | 4 |
| Carlton | 156 | 696 | 4.5 | 6 |
| Smith | 31 | 148 | 4.8 | 0 |
| Kemp | 40 | 130 | 3.3 | 5 |
| Spikes | 28 | 119 | 4.3 | 3 |
| Dubenion | 3 | 16 | 5.3 | 0 |
| Rutkowski | 1 | 10 | 10.0 | 0 |
| Lamonica | 9 | 6 | 0.7 | 1 |
| P. Costa | 0 | 1 | 0.0 | 0 |

### Receiving

| Last Name | No. | Yds | Avg | TD |
|---|---|---|---|---|
| Dubenion | 50 | 747 | 15 | 2 |
| Burnett | 34 | 419 | 12 | 4 |
| Crockett | 31 | 533 | 17 | 3 |
| P. Costa | 27 | 400 | 15 | 3 |
| Carlton | 21 | 280 | 13 | 0 |
| Ferguson | 16 | 293 | 18 | 1 |
| Bass | 10 | 130 | 13 | 0 |
| Rutkowski | 6 | 150 | 25 | 1 |
| Spikes | 2 | 45 | 23 | 1 |
| O'Donnell | 1 | 2 | 2 | 0 |
| Smith | 1 | 1 | 1 | 0 |

### Punt Returns

| Last Name | No. | Yds | Avg | TD |
|---|---|---|---|---|
| Rutkowski | 18 | 209 | 12 | 1 |
| Byrd | 23 | 186 | 8 | 1 |
| Clarke | 2 | 12 | 6 | 0 |
| Stratton | 0 | 4 | 0 | 0 |

### Kickoff Returns

| Last Name | No. | Yds | Avg | TD |
|---|---|---|---|---|
| Warner | 33 | 846 | 26 | 1 |
| Rutkowski | 6 | 121 | 20 | 0 |
| Mills | 4 | 76 | 19 | 0 |
| Prudhomme | 1 | 16 | 16 | 0 |
| Schmidt | 1 | 2 | 2 | 0 |
| DeSutter | 2 | 0 | 0 | 0 |
| Ferguson | 2 | 0 | 0 | 0 |
| D. Costa | 1 | 0 | 0 | 0 |
| Maguire | 1 | 0 | 0 | 0 |
| O'Donnell | 0 | 3 | 0 | 0 |

### Passing – Punting – Kicking

| PASSING | Att | Comp | % | Yds | Yd/Att | TD | Int-% | RK |
|---|---|---|---|---|---|---|---|---|
| Kemp | 389 | 166 | 43 | 2451 | 6.3 | 11 | 16— 4 | 7 |
| Lamonica | 84 | 33 | 39 | 549 | 6.5 | 4 | 5— | 6 |

| PUNTING | No | Avg |
|---|---|---|
| Maguire | 69 | 41.2 |

| KICKING | XP | Att | % | FG | Att | % |
|---|---|---|---|---|---|---|
| Lusteg | 41 | 42 | 98 | 19 | 38 | 50 |

## BOSTON PATRIOTS

### Rushing

| Last Name | No. | Yds | Avg | TD |
|---|---|---|---|---|
| Nance | 299 | 1458 | 4.9 | 11 |
| Garron | 101 | 319 | 3.2 | 4 |
| Cappadonna | 22 | 88 | 4.0 | 1 |
| Parilli | 28 | 42 | 1.5 | 1 |
| Huarte | 7 | 40 | 5.7 | 0 |
| Garrett | 13 | 21 | 1.6 | 0 |
| Yewcic | 1 | −5 | −5.0 | 0 |

### Receiving

| Last Name | No. | Yds | Avg | TD |
|---|---|---|---|---|
| Graham | 51 | 673 | 13 | 4 |
| Cappelletti | 43 | 676 | 16 | 6 |
| Garron | 30 | 416 | 14 | 5 |
| Whalen | 29 | 502 | 17 | 4 |
| Colclough | 16 | 284 | 18 | 0 |
| Nance | 8 | 103 | 13 | 0 |
| Bellino | 6 | 77 | 13 | 1 |
| Romeo | 2 | 46 | 23 | 0 |
| Garrett | 1 | 7 | 7 | 0 |

### Punt Returns

| Last Name | No. | Yds | Avg | TD |
|---|---|---|---|---|
| Purvis | 5 | 43 | 9 | 0 |
| Hennessey | 7 | 39 | 6 | 0 |
| B. Johnson | 7 | 37 | 5 | 0 |
| Bellino | 4 | 19 | 5 | 0 |
| Graves | 1 | 5 | 5 | 0 |

### Kickoff Returns

| Last Name | No. | Yds | Avg | TD |
|---|---|---|---|---|
| Bellino | 18 | 410 | 23 | 0 |
| Cunningham | 17 | 371 | 22 | 0 |
| Purvis | 8 | 185 | 23 | 0 |
| Garron | 2 | 49 | 25 | 0 |
| Cappadonna | 3 | 46 | 15 | 0 |
| E. Johnson | 2 | 45 | 23 | 0 |
| Singer | 1 | 27 | 27 | 0 |
| Mangum | 1 | 8 | 8 | 0 |
| Colclough | 1 | 2 | 2 | 0 |
| B. Johnson | 1 | 2 | 2 | 0 |

### Passing – Punting – Kicking

| PASSING | Att | Comp | % | Yds | Yd/Att | TD | Int-% | RK |
|---|---|---|---|---|---|---|---|---|
| Parilli | 382 | 181 | 47 | 2721 | 7.1 | 20 | 20— 5 | 6 |
| Huarte | 11 | 5 | 46 | 63 | 5.7 | 0 | 1— | 9 |

| PUNTING | No | Avg |
|---|---|---|
| Fraser | 53 | |
| Yewcic | 20 | 36.6 |

| KICKING | XP | Att | % | FG | Att | % |
|---|---|---|---|---|---|---|
| Cappelletti | 35 | 36 | 97 | 16 | 32 | 50 |

2 POINT XP
Cappadonna
Romeo

## NEW YORK JETS

### Rushing

| Last Name | No. | Yds | Avg | TD |
|---|---|---|---|---|
| Snell | 178 | 644 | 3.6 | 4 |
| Boozer | 97 | 455 | 4.7 | 5 |
| Mathis | 72 | 208 | 2.9 | 2 |
| Smolinski | 21 | 69 | 3.3 | 2 |
| Namath | 6 | 42 | 7.0 | 2 |
| Johnson | 2 | 24 | 12.0 | 0 |

### Receiving

| Last Name | No. | Yds | Avg | TD |
|---|---|---|---|---|
| Sauer | 63 | 1079 | 17 | 5 |
| Maynard | 48 | 840 | 18 | 5 |
| Snell | 48 | 346 | 7 | 4 |
| Lammons | 31 | 565 | 14 | 4 |
| Mathis | 22 | 379 | 17 | 1 |
| Smolinski | 11 | 74 | 7 | 1 |
| Boozer | 8 | 133 | 17 | 0 |
| B. Turner | 7 | 115 | 16 | 0 |
| Johnson | 1 | 18 | 18 | 1 |
| Weir | 1 | 4 | 4 | 0 |
| Rademacher | 1 | 3 | 3 | 0 |

### Punt Returns

| Last Name | No. | Yds | Avg | TD |
|---|---|---|---|---|
| Lewis | 7 | 76 | 11 | 0 |
| B. Turner | 10 | 60 | 6 | 0 |
| Weir | 8 | 48 | 6 | 0 |
| Baird | 5 | 35 | 7 | 0 |
| Christy | 5 | 23 | 5 | 0 |
| Hudson | 1 | 18 | 18 | 0 |

### Kickoff Returns

| Last Name | No. | Yds | Avg | TD |
|---|---|---|---|---|
| Boozer | 26 | 659 | 25 | 1 |
| Christy | 10 | 203 | 20 | 0 |
| Weir | 6 | 121 | 20 | 0 |
| Lewis | 5 | 121 | 24 | 0 |
| Gray | 5 | 77 | 15 | 0 |
| Smolinski | 6 | 59 | 10 | 0 |
| B. Turner | 2 | 50 | 25 | 0 |
| Wilder | 1 | 6 | 6 | 0 |
| Johnson | 1 | 4 | 4 | 0 |

### Passing – Punting – Kicking

| PASSING | Att | Comp | % | Yds | Yd/Att | TD | Int-% | RK |
|---|---|---|---|---|---|---|---|---|
| Namath | 471 | 232 | 49 | 3379 | 7.2 | 19 | 27— 6 | 4 |
| Taliaferro | 41 | 19 | 46 | 177 | 4.3 | 2 | 2— | 5 |
| Hudson | 1 | 0 | 0 | 0 | 0.0 | 0 | 0— | 0 |
| Snell | 1 | 0 | 0 | 0 | 0.0 | 0 | 0— | 0 |

| PUNTING | No | Avg |
|---|---|---|
| Johnson | 62 | 42.5 |

| KICKING | XP | Att | % | FG | Att | % |
|---|---|---|---|---|---|---|
| J. Turner | 34 | 35 | 97 | 18 | 35 | 51 |

2 POINT XP
Sauer
Taliaferro

## HOUSTON OILERS

### Rushing

| Last Name | No. | Yds | Avg | TD |
|---|---|---|---|---|
| Burrell | 122 | 406 | 3.3 | 0 |
| Granger | 56 | 388 | 6.9 | 1 |
| Blanks | 71 | 235 | 3.3 | 0 |
| Johnson | 70 | 226 | 3.2 | 3 |
| Trull | 38 | 139 | 3.7 | 7 |
| Tolar | 46 | 105 | 2.3 | 0 |
| Stone | 6 | 18 | 3.0 | 0 |
| Blanda | 3 | 1 | 0.3 | 0 |
| Lee | 1 | −3 | −3.0 | 0 |

### Receiving

| Last Name | No. | Yds | Avg | TD |
|---|---|---|---|---|
| Frazier | 57 | 1129 | 20 | 12 |
| Burrell | 33 | 400 | 12 | 5 |
| Hennigan | 27 | 313 | 12 | 3 |
| McLeod | 23 | 339 | 15 | 3 |
| Elkins | 21 | 283 | 13 | 3 |
| Blanks | 19 | 234 | 12 | 2 |
| Tolar | 13 | 68 | 5 | 0 |
| Poole | 12 | 131 | 11 | 0 |
| Granger | 12 | 104 | 9 | 1 |
| Johnson | 8 | 150 | 19 | 0 |
| Stone | 1 | 17 | 17 | 0 |

### Punt Returns

| Last Name | No. | Yds | Avg | TD |
|---|---|---|---|---|
| Burrell | 8 | 78 | 10 | 0 |
| Jancik | 10 | 62 | 6 | 0 |
| Trammell | 5 | 19 | 4 | 0 |

### Kickoff Returns

| Last Name | No. | Yds | Avg | TD |
|---|---|---|---|---|
| Jancik | 34 | 875 | 26 | 0 |
| Blanks | 21 | 487 | 23 | 0 |
| Trammell | 3 | 63 | 21 | 0 |
| Boyette | 3 | 42 | 14 | 0 |
| Hayes | 2 | 31 | 16 | 0 |
| Burrell | 1 | 16 | 16 | 0 |

### Passing – Punting – Kicking

| PASSING | Att | Comp | % | Yds | Yd/Att | TD | Int-% | RK |
|---|---|---|---|---|---|---|---|---|
| Blanda | 271 | 122 | 45 | 1764 | 6.5 | 17 | 21— 8 | 9 |
| Trull | 172 | 84 | 49 | 1200 | 7.0 | 10 | 5— 3 | 4 |
| Humphrey | 32 | 15 | 47 | 168 | 5.3 | 2 | 1— 3 | |
| Lee | 8 | 4 | 50 | 27 | 3.4 | 0 | 1— | 13 |
| Burrell | 1 | 1 | 100 | 9 | 9.0 | 0 | 0— | 0 |
| Tolar | 1 | 0 | 0 | 0 | 0.0 | 0 | 0— | 0 |

| PUNTING | No | Avg |
|---|---|---|
| Norton | 69 | 42.2 |

| KICKING | XP | Att | % | FG | Att | % |
|---|---|---|---|---|---|---|
| Blanda | 39 | 40 | 98 | 16 | 30 | 53 |

## MIAMI DOLPHINS

### Rushing

| Last Name | No. | Yds | Avg | TD |
|---|---|---|---|---|
| Auer | 121 | 416 | 3.4 | 4 |
| Gilchrist | 72 | 262 | 3.6 | 0 |
| Joe | 71 | 232 | 3.3 | 2 |
| Wilson | 27 | 137 | 5.1 | 0 |
| Casares | 43 | 135 | 3.1 | 0 |
| Price | 31 | 107 | 3.5 | 0 |
| Chesser | 16 | 74 | 4.6 | 0 |
| Jackson | 2 | 22 | 11.0 | 0 |
| Stofa | 3 | 17 | 5.7 | 0 |
| Wood | 5 | 6 | 1.2 | 1 |
| Norton | 3 | 2 | 0.7 | 0 |

### Receiving

| Last Name | No. | Yds | Avg | TD |
|---|---|---|---|---|
| Kocourek | 27 | 320 | 12 | 2 |
| Roberson | 26 | 519 | 20 | 2 |
| Auer | 22 | 263 | 12 | 2 |
| Noonan | 17 | 224 | 13 | 1 |
| Jackson | 16 | 317 | 20 | 2 |
| Joe | 13 | 116 | 9 | 1 |
| Gilchrist | 13 | 110 | 8 | 1 |
| Roderick | 11 | 156 | 14 | 1 |
| Twilley | 10 | 128 | 13 | 0 |
| Casares | 8 | 45 | 6 | 1 |
| Cronin | 7 | 83 | 12 | 1 |
| Mingo | 3 | 40 | 13 | 0 |
| Moreau | 2 | 15 | 8 | 0 |
| Price | 2 | 14 | 7 | 0 |
| Matthews | 1 | 20 | 20 | 0 |
| Chesser | 1 | 4 | 4 | 0 |

### Punt Returns

| Last Name | No. | Yds | Avg | TD |
|---|---|---|---|---|
| Auer | 5 | 99 | 20 | 0 |
| Neff | 10 | 60 | 6 | 0 |
| Matthews | 4 | 38 | 10 | 0 |
| Jackson | 2 | 7 | 4 | 0 |

### Kickoff Returns

| Last Name | No. | Yds | Avg | TD |
|---|---|---|---|---|
| Auer | 28 | 698 | 25 | 1 |
| Neff | 15 | 376 | 25 | 0 |
| Matthews | 5 | 109 | 22 | 0 |
| Jackson | 4 | 105 | 26 | 0 |
| Hunter | 5 | 84 | 17 | 0 |
| Jaquess | 5 | 77 | 15 | 0 |
| Roderick | 1 | 17 | 17 | 0 |
| Branch | 1 | 15 | 15 | 0 |
| Bruggers | 1 | 3 | 3 | 0 |
| Noonan | 0 | 23 | 0 | 0 |

### Passing – Punting – Kicking

| PASSING | Att | Comp | % | Yds | Yd/Att | TD | Int-% | RK |
|---|---|---|---|---|---|---|---|---|
| Wood | 230 | 83 | 36 | 993 | 4.3 | 4 | 14— 6 | 10 |
| Wilson | 112 | 46 | 41 | 764 | 6.8 | 5 | 10— | 9 |
| Stofa | 57 | 29 | 51 | 425 | 7.5 | 4 | 2— | 8 |
| Norton | 55 | 21 | 38 | 192 | 3.5 | 3 | 6— | 11 |

| PUNTING | No | Avg |
|---|---|---|
| Wilson | 42 | 42.1 |
| McDaniel | 32 | 38.2 |
| Chesser | 7 | 33.3 |

| KICKING | XP | Att | % | FG | Att | % |
|---|---|---|---|---|---|---|
| Mingo | 23 | 23 | 100 | 10 | 22 | 46 |

2 POINT XP
Joe
Wilson

## KANSAS CITY CHIEFS 11-2-1 Hank Stram

**Scores of Each Game**

| | | |
|---|---|---|
| 42 | Buffalo | 20 |
| 32 | Oakland | 10 |
| 43 | Boston | 24 |
| 14 | BUFFALO | 29 |
| 37 | DENVER | 10 |
| 13 | OAKLAND | 34 |
| 56 | Denver | 10 |
| 48 | HOUSTON | 23 |
| 24 | SAN DIEGO | 14 |
| 34 | MIAMI | 16 |
| 27 | BOSTON | 27 |
| 32 | New York | 24 |
| 19 | Miami | 18 |
| 27 | San Diego | 17 |

| Use Name | Pos. | Hgt | Wgt | Age | Int | Pts |
|---|---|---|---|---|---|---|
| Tony DiMidio | OT | 6'3" | 250 | 24 | | |
| Dave Hill | OT | 6'5" | 254 | 25 | | |
| Jim Tyrer | OT | 6'6" | 292 | 27 | | |
| Denny Biodrowski | OG | 6'1" | 255 | 26 | | |
| Ed Budde | OG | 6'5" | 260 | 25 | | |
| Curt Merz | OG | 6'4" | 267 | 28 | | |
| Al Reynolds | OG | 6'3" | 250 | 28 | | |
| Hatch Rosdahl | OG | 6'5" | 250 | 23 | | |
| Wayne Frazier | C | 6'2" | 245 | 26 | | |
| Jon Gilliam | C | 6'2" | 240 | 27 | | |
| Aaron Brown | DE | 6'5" | 250 | 22 | | |
| Chuck Hurston | DE | 6'6" | 230 | 23 | | |
| Jerry Mays | DE | 6'4" | 252 | 26 | | |
| Buck Buchanan | DT | 6'7" | 287 | 26 | | |
| Ed Lothamer | DT | 6'5" | 270 | 23 | | |
| Andy Rice | DT | 6'3" | 266 | 24 | | |

| Use Name | Pos. | Hgt | Wgt | Age | Int | Pts |
|---|---|---|---|---|---|---|
| Bud Abell | LB | 6'3" | 220 | 25 | | |
| Bobby Bell | LB | 6'4" | 228 | 26 | 2 | 6 |
| Walt Corey | LB | 6' | 233 | 28 | | |
| Sherrill Headrick | LB | 6'2" | 240 | 29 | 2 | |
| E. J. Holub | LB | 6'4" | 236 | 28 | | |
| Smokey Stover | LB | 6' | 227 | 27 | 1 | |
| Solomon Brannan | DB | 6'1" | 188 | 24 | | |
| Jimmy Hill | DB | 6'2" | 198 | 37 | | |
| Bobby Hunt | DB | 6'1" | 193 | 26 | 10 | |
| Willie Mitchell | DB | 6'1" | 185 | 24 | 3 | 6 |
| Bobby Ply | DB | 6'1" | 190 | 25 | 1 | |
| Johnny Robinson | DB | 6' | 205 | 27 | 10 | 6 |
| Fletcher Smith | DB | 6'2" | 188 | 22 | 2 | |
| Emmitt Thomas | DB | 6'2" | 190 | 23 | | |
| Fred Williamson | DB | 6'2" | 210 | 28 | 4 | |

| Use Name | Pos. | Hgt | Wgt | Age | Int | Pts |
|---|---|---|---|---|---|---|
| Pete Beathard | QB | 6'2" | 210 | 24 | | 6 |
| Len Dawson | QB | 6' | 190 | 32 | | |
| Bert Coan | HB | 6'4" | 220 | 26 | | 54 |
| Mike Garrett | HB | 5'9" | 195 | 22 | | 48 |
| Gene Thomas | HB | 6'4" | 210 | 23 | | 6 |
| Curtis McClinton | FB | 6'3" | 227 | 28 | | 54 |
| Jerrel Wilson | FB | 6'4" | 222 | 24 | | 2 |
| Otis Taylor | FL | 6'2" | 211 | 23 | | 48 |
| Fred Arbanas | TE | 6'3" | 240 | 27 | | 26 |
| Chris Burford | OE | 6'3" | 210 | 28 | | 48 |
| Reg Carolan | OE | 6'6" | 238 | 26 | | 18 |
| Frank Pitts | OE | 6'2" | 190 | 22 | | 6 |
| Tommy Brooker | K | 6'2" | 235 | 26 | | 19 |
| Mike Mercer (from OAK) | K | 6' | 210 | 30 | | 98 |

Curt Farrier — Injury

## OAKLAND RAIDERS 8-5-1 Johnny Rauch

| | | |
|---|---|---|
| 23 | Miami | 14 |
| 0 | Houston | 31 |
| 10 | KANSAS CITY | 32 |
| 20 | SAN DIEGO | 29 |
| 21 | MIAMI | 10 |
| 34 | Kansas City | 13 |
| 24 | New York | 21 |
| 21 | Boston | 24 |
| 38 | HOUSTON | 23 |
| 41 | San Diego | 19 |
| 17 | Denver | 3 |
| 10 | BUFFALO | 31 |
| 28 | NEW YORK | 28 |
| 28 | DENVER | 10 |

| Use Name | Pos. | Hgt | Wgt | Age | Int | Pts |
|---|---|---|---|---|---|---|
| Jim Harvey | OT | 6'5" | 245 | 23 | | |
| Harry Schuh | OT | 6'2" | 260 | 23 | | |
| Bob Svihus | OT | 6'4" | 255 | 23 | | |
| Wayne Hawkins | OG | 6' | 240 | 28 | | |
| Palmer Pyle | OG | 6'2" | 245 | 29 | | |
| Dick Tyson | OG | 6'2" | 245 | 22 | | |
| Jim Otto | C | 6'2" | 240 | 28 | | |
| Ben Davidson | DE | 6'8" | 265 | 26 | | |
| Greg Kent | DE | 6'6" | 275 | 23 | | |
| Ike Lassiter | DE | 6'5" | 270 | 25 | 1 | |
| Carleton Oats | DT-DE | 6'2" | 235 | 23 | | |
| Dan Birdwell | DT | 6'4" | 250 | 25 | 1 | |
| Dave Daniels | DT | 6'3" | 245 | 25 | | |
| Tom Keating | DT | 6'3" | 247 | 23 | | |
| Rex Mirich | DT | 6'4" | 250 | 25 | | |

| Use Name | Pos. | Hgt | Wgt | Age | Int | Pts |
|---|---|---|---|---|---|---|
| Bill Budness | LB | 6'1" | 215 | 23 | | |
| Dan Conners | LB | 6'1" | 240 | 24 | 2 | 6 |
| Rich Jackson | LB | 6'2" | 230 | 25 | | |
| Bill Laskey | LB | 6'2" | 240 | 23 | | |
| Gus Otto | LB | 6'2" | 220 | 23 | | |
| Ray Schmautz | LB | 6'1" | 225 | 23 | | |
| J. R. Williamson | LB | 6'2" | 220 | 24 | | |
| Rodger Bird | DB | 5'11" | 195 | 23 | 4 | |
| Dave Grayson | DB | 5'10" | 185 | 27 | 3 | |
| Joe Krakoski | DB | 6'2" | 195 | 29 | | |
| Kent McCloughan | DB | 6'1" | 190 | 23 | 4 | |
| Warren Powers | DB | 6' | 190 | 25 | 5 | |
| Howie Williams | DB | 6'2" | 187 | 29 | 3 | |
| Willie Williams | DB | 6' | 190 | 23 | | |

George Flint — Injury

| Use Name | Pos. | Hgt | Wgt | Age | Int | Pts |
|---|---|---|---|---|---|---|
| Cotton Davidson | QB | 6'1" | 180 | 34 | | |
| Tom Flores | QB | 6'1" | 190 | 29 | | 6 |
| Charlie Green | QB | 6' | 190 | 23 | | |
| Pervis Atkins | HB | 6'1" | 195 | 30 | | |
| Pete Banaszak | HB | 5'11" | 200 | 22 | | |
| Clem Daniels | HB | 6'1" | 218 | 29 | | 60 |
| Roger Hagberg | FB | 6'1" | 215 | 27 | | 6 |
| Hewritt Dixon | HB-FB | 6'2" | 225 | 26 | | 54 |
| Fred Biletnikoff | FL | 6'1" | 190 | 23 | | 18 |
| Billy Cannon | TE | 6'1" | 215 | 29 | | 12 |
| Tom Mitchell | TE | 6'2" | 235 | 22 | | 6 |
| Bill Miller | OE | 6' | 190 | 24 | | |
| Art Powell | OE | 6'3" | 212 | 29 | | 66 |
| Larry Todd | OE | 6'1" | 185 | 23 | | 6 |
| Mike Eischeid | K | 6' | 190 | 25 | | 70 |

## SAN DIEGO CHARGERS 7-6-1 Sid Gillman

| | | |
|---|---|---|
| 27 | BUFFALO | 7 |
| 24 | BOSTON | 0 |
| 29 | Oakland | 20 |
| 44 | MIAMI | 10 |
| 16 | New York | 17 |
| 17 | Buffalo | 17 |
| 17 | Boston | 35 |
| 24 | DENVER | 17 |
| 14 | Kansas City | 24 |
| 19 | OAKLAND | 41 |
| 17 | Denver | 20 |
| 28 | Houston | 22 |
| 42 | NEW YORK | 27 |
| 17 | KANSAS CITY | 27 |

| Use Name | Pos. | Hgt | Wgt | Age | Int | Pts |
|---|---|---|---|---|---|---|
| Gary Kirner | OT | 6'3" | 248 | 24 | | |
| Ron Mix | OT | 6'4" | 250 | 28 | | |
| Terry Owens | OT | 6'6" | 240 | 22 | | |
| Ernie Wright | OT | 6'4" | 265 | 26 | | |
| Don Estes | OG | 6'2" | 250 | 23 | | |
| John Farris | OG | 6'4" | 245 | 25 | | |
| Ed Mitchell | OG | 6'2" | 280 | 24 | | |
| Walt Sweeney | OG | 6'3" | 250 | 25 | | |
| Sam Gruneisen | C | 6'1" | 240 | 25 | | |
| Paul Latzke | C | 6'4" | 245 | 24 | | |
| Jim Griffin | DE | 6'3" | 255 | 24 | | |
| Howard Kindig | DE | 6'6" | 255 | 25 | 1 | |
| Fred Moore | DE | 6'3" | 255 | 26 | | |
| Bob Petrich | DE | 6'4" | 250 | 25 | | |
| Houston Ridge | DE | 6'4" | 232 | 22 | | |
| Steve DeLong | DT | 6'3" | 252 | 23 | | |
| George Gross | DT | 6'3" | 258 | 25 | | |
| Larry Martin | DT | 6'2" | 270 | 24 | | |

| Use Name | Pos. | Hgt | Wgt | Age | Int | Pts |
|---|---|---|---|---|---|---|
| Chuck Allen | LB | 6'1" | 225 | 26 | 1 | |
| Frank Buncom | LB | 6'1" | 240 | 26 | | |
| Dick Degen | LB | 6'1" | 220 | 24 | 1 | |
| Tom Good | LB | 6' | 230 | 22 | | |
| Emil Karas | LB | 6'3" | 230 | 32 | | |
| Mike London | LB | 6'2" | 230 | 21 | | |
| John Milks | LB | 6' | 222 | 22 | 1 | |
| Bob Mitinger | LB | 6'2" | 230 | 26 | | |
| Rick Redman | LB | 5'11" | 225 | 23 | 2 | 6 |
| Joe Beauchamp | DB | 6' | 185 | 22 | 2 | |
| Speedy Duncan | DB | 5'10" | 175 | 23 | 7 | 6 |
| Miller Farr | DB | 6'1" | 192 | 23 | 3 | |
| Kenny Graham | DB | 6' | 195 | 24 | 5 | 6 |
| Dave Plump | DB | 6'1" | 195 | 23 | | |
| Jim Tolbert | DB | 6'3" | 207 | 22 | 1 | |
| Bud Whitehead | DB | 6' | 185 | 27 | 2 | |
| Nat Whitmyer | DB | 6' | 180 | 25 | | |
| Bob Zeman | DB | 6'1" | 205 | 29 | | |

| Use Name | Pos. | Hgt | Wgt | Age | Int | Pts |
|---|---|---|---|---|---|---|
| John Hadl | QB | 6'2" | 215 | 26 | | 12 |
| Dan Henning | QB | 6' | 195 | 24 | | |
| Steve Tensi | QB | 6'5" | 215 | 23 | | |
| Paul Lowe | HB | 6' | 205 | 29 | | 18 |
| Gene Foster | FB-HB | 5'11" | 212 | 23 | | 18 |
| Jim Allison | FB | 6' | 220 | 23 | | 12 |
| Keith Lincoln | FB | 6'2" | 215 | 27 | | 18 |
| John Travis | FB | 6'1" | 216 | 23 | | |
| Lance Alworth | FL | 6' | 180 | 26 | | 78 |
| Willie Frazier | TE | 6'4" | 235 | 23 | | 12 |
| Jacque MacKinnon | TE | 6'4" | 250 | 27 | | 36 |
| Gary Garrison | OE | 6'1" | 190 | 23 | | 24 |
| Don Norton | OE | 6'1" | 195 | 28 | | |
| Dick Van Raaphorst | K | 5'11" | 215 | 23 | | 87 |

Pat Shea — Injury

## DENVER BRONCOS 4-10-0 Mac Speedie  Ray Malavasi

| | | |
|---|---|---|
| 7 | Houston | 45 |
| 10 | BOSTON | 24 |
| 7 | NEW YORK | 16 |
| 40 | HOUSTON | 38 |
| 10 | Kansas City | 37 |
| 7 | Miami | 24 |
| 10 | KANSAS CITY | 56 |
| 17 | Boston | 24 |
| 17 | San Diego | 24 |
| 3 | OAKLAND | 17 |
| 20 | SAN DIEGO | 17 |
| 17 | MIAMI | 7 |
| 10 | Oakland | 28 |
| 21 | Buffalo | 38 |

| Use Name | Pos. | Hgt | Wgt | Age | Int | Pts |
|---|---|---|---|---|---|---|
| Lee Bernet | OT | 6'2" | 245 | 22 | | |
| Bob Breitenstein | OT | 6'3" | 270 | 23 | | |
| Sam Brunelli | OG | 6'1" | 240 | 23 | | |
| John Gonzaga | OG | 6'3" | 250 | 33 | | |
| Jon Hohman | OG | 6'1" | 245 | 23 | | |
| Bill Keating | OG | 6'2" | 236 | 21 | | |
| Pat Matson | OG | 6'1" | 250 | 22 | | |
| Jerry Sturm | OG | 6'3" | 260 | 29 | | |
| Larry Kaminski | C | 6'2" | 240 | 21 | | |
| Ray Kubala | C | 6'4" | 245 | 24 | | |
| Marvin Davis | DE | 6'4" | 252 | 22 | | |
| Dan LaRose | DE | 6'5" | 250 | 26 | | |
| Max Leetzow | DE | 6'4" | 240 | 23 | | |
| George Tarasovic | DE | 6'4" | 250 | 37 | | |
| Larry Cox | DT | 6'2" | 250 | 22 | | |
| Jerry Inman | DT | 6'3" | 255 | 26 | | |
| Ray Jacobs | DT | 6'3" | 275 | 26 | | |
| Bob Young | DT | 6'2" | 275 | 23 | | |

| Use Name | Pos. | Hgt | Wgt | Age | Int | Pts |
|---|---|---|---|---|---|---|
| John Bramlett | LB | 6'2" | 220 | 25 | 1 | 6 |
| Don Gulseth | LB | 6'1" | 240 | 24 | | |
| Jerry Hopkins | LB | 6'2" | 235 | 25 | 2 | |
| Gene Jeter | LB | 6'3" | 230 | 24 | | |
| Archie Matsos (to SD) | LB | 6' | 212 | 31 | 3 | |
| Ron Sbranti | LB | 6'2" | 230 | 21 | | |
| Willie Brown | DB | 6'1" | 190 | 25 | 3 | |
| Billy Fletcher | DB | 5'10" | 190 | 22 | | |
| Goose Gonsoulin | DB | 6'3" | 210 | 28 | | |
| John Griffin | DB | 6'1" | 190 | 26 | | |
| Bob Richardson | DB | 6'1" | 180 | 22 | | |
| Lew Scott | DB | 5'10" | 173 | 23 | | |
| Goldie Sellers | DB | 6'2" | 198 | 24 | 3 | 12 |
| Nemiah Wilson | DB | 6' | 165 | 23 | 1 | 6 |
| Lonnie Wright | DB | 6'2" | 205 | 22 | 1 | |
| Eric Crabtree | OE-DB | 5'11" | 190 | 21 | | |

Eldon Danenhauer — Injury

| Use Name | Pos. | Hgt | Wgt | Age | Int | Pts |
|---|---|---|---|---|---|---|
| Max Choboian | QB | 6'4" | 205 | 24 | | 12 |
| Scotty Glacken | QB | 6' | 190 | 21 | | |
| John McCormick | QB | 6'1" | 190 | 29 | | |
| Tobin Rote | QB | 6'3" | 220 | 38 | | |
| Mickey Slaughter | QB | 6' | 190 | 25 | | |
| Abner Haynes | HB | 6' | 190 | 28 | | 18 |
| Charley Mitchell | HB | 5'11" | 185 | 26 | | 12 |
| Mike Kellogg | FB | 6' | 220 | 23 | | |
| Darrell Lester | FB | 6'2" | 220 | 25 | | 6 |
| Wendell Hayes | HB-FB | 6'2" | 195 | 25 | | 6 |
| Bob Scarpitto | FL | 5'11" | 196 | 27 | | 32 |
| Al Denson | TE | 6'2" | 208 | 24 | | 18 |
| Max Wettstein | TE | 6'3" | 217 | 22 | | |
| Jason Franci | OE | 6'1" | 210 | 22 | | |
| Glenn Glass | OE | 6' | 203 | 29 | | |
| Lionel Taylor | OE | 6'2" | 215 | 30 | | 6 |
| Gary Kroner | K | 6'1" | 200 | 25 | | 62 |

## KANSAS CITY CHIEFS

### RUSHING

| Last Name | No. | Yds | Avg | TD |
|---|---|---|---|---|
| Garrett | 147 | 801 | 5.5 | 6 |
| McClinton | 140 | 540 | 3.9 | 4 |
| Coan | 96 | 521 | 5.4 | 7 |
| Dawson | 24 | 167 | 7.0 | 0 |
| Beathard | 20 | 152 | 7.6 | 1 |
| G. Thomas | 7 | 53 | 7.6 | 1 |
| Taylor | 2 | 33 | 16.5 | 0 |
| Wilson | 3 | 7 | 2.3 | 0 |

### RECEIVING

| Last Name | No. | Yds | Avg | TD |
|---|---|---|---|---|
| Taylor | 58 | 1297 | 22 | 8 |
| Burford | 58 | 758 | 13 | 8 |
| Arbanas | 22 | 305 | 14 | 4 |
| McClinton | 19 | 285 | 15 | 5 |
| Coan | 18 | 131 | 7 | 2 |
| Garrett | 15 | 175 | 12 | 1 |
| Carolan | 7 | 154 | 22 | 3 |
| Pitts | 1 | 11 | 11 | 0 |
| Wilson | 1 | 7 | 7 | 0 |

### PUNT RETURNS

| Last Name | No. | Yds | Avg | TD |
|---|---|---|---|---|
| Garrett | 17 | 139 | 8 | 1 |
| E. Thomas | 9 | 56 | 6 | 0 |
| Brown | 1 | 43 | 43 | 0 |
| Pitts | 1 | 21 | 21 | 1 |
| Williamson | 1 | 10 | 10 | 0 |
| Mitchell | 1 | 7 | 7 | 0 |
| Ply | 1 | 0 | 0 | 0 |

### KICKOFF RETURNS

| Last Name | No. | Yds | Avg | TD |
|---|---|---|---|---|
| E. Thomas | 29 | 673 | 23 | 0 |
| Garrett | 14 | 323 | 23 | 0 |
| G. Thomas | 3 | 62 | 21 | 0 |
| Brannan | 1 | 24 | 24 | 0 |
| Coan | 1 | 22 | 22 | 0 |
| Brown | 1 | 6 | 6 | 0 |
| Stover | 3 | 0 | 0 | 0 |
| Taylor | 2 | 0 | 0 | 0 |
| Pitts | 0 | 38 | 0 | 0 |

### PASSING – PUNTING – KICKING

**PASSING**

| Last Name | Att | Comp | % | Yds | Yd/Att | TD | Int–% | RK |
|---|---|---|---|---|---|---|---|---|
| Dawson | 284 | 159 | 56 | 2527 | 8.9 | 26 | 10— 4 | 1 |
| Beathard | 90 | 39 | 43 | 578 | 6.4 | 4 | 4— 4 | |
| Coan | 1 | 1 | 100 | 18 | 18.0 | 1 | 0— 0 | |
| Garrett | 1 | 0 | 0 | 0 | 0.0 | 0 | 0— 0 | |
| Taylor | 1 | 0 | 0 | 0 | 0.0 | 0 | 1—100 | |

**PUNTING**

| Last Name | No | Avg |
|---|---|---|
| Wilson | 61 | 44.5 |
| Mercer | 9 | 41.4 |

**KICKING**

| Last Name | XP | Att | % | FG | Att | % |
|---|---|---|---|---|---|---|
| Mercer | 35 | 38 | 92 | 21 | 30 | 70 |
| Brooker | 13 | 13 | 100 | 2 | 2 | 100 |
| Smith | 2 | 4 | 50 | 0 | 0 | 0 |

**2 POINT XP**
Arbanas
Wilson

## OAKLAND RAIDERS

### RUSHING

| Last Name | No. | Yds | Avg | TD |
|---|---|---|---|---|
| C. Daniels | 204 | 801 | 3.9 | 7 |
| Hagberg | 62 | 282 | 4.6 | 0 |
| Dixon | 68 | 277 | 3.7 | 1 |
| Flores | 5 | 50 | 10.0 | 1 |
| Banaszak | 4 | 18 | 4.5 | 0 |
| Atkins | 14 | 10 | 0.7 | 0 |
| C. Davidson | 6 | −11 | −1.8 | 0 |

### RECEIVING

| Last Name | No. | Yds | Avg | TD |
|---|---|---|---|---|
| Powell | 53 | 1026 | 19 | 11 |
| C. Daniels | 40 | 652 | 16 | 3 |
| Dixon | 29 | 345 | 12 | 1 |
| Mitchell | 23 | 301 | 13 | 1 |
| Hagberg | 21 | 248 | 12 | 1 |
| Biletnikoff | 17 | 272 | 16 | 3 |
| Cannon | 14 | 436 | 31 | 2 |
| Todd | 14 | 134 | 10 | 1 |
| Banaszak | 1 | 11 | 11 | 0 |

### PUNT RETURNS

| Last Name | No. | Yds | Avg | TD |
|---|---|---|---|---|
| Bird | 37 | 323 | 9 | 0 |
| Krakoski | 2 | 19 | 10 | 0 |
| Atkins | 1 | 13 | 13 | 0 |
| Cannon | 1 | 12 | 12 | 0 |

### KICKOFF RETURNS

| Last Name | No. | Yds | Avg | TD |
|---|---|---|---|---|
| Atkins | 29 | 608 | 21 | 0 |
| Bird | 19 | 390 | 21 | 0 |
| Grayson | 6 | 128 | 21 | 0 |
| W. Williams | 2 | 52 | 26 | 0 |
| Hagberg | 1 | 13 | 13 | 0 |
| Mirich | 2 | 0 | 0 | 0 |
| Powers | 1 | 0 | 0 | 0 |

### PASSING – PUNTING – KICKING

**PASSING**

| Last Name | Att | Comp | % | Yds | Yd/Att | TD | Int–% | RK |
|---|---|---|---|---|---|---|---|---|
| Flores | 306 | 151 | 49 | 2638 | 8.6 | 24 | 14— 5 | 3 |
| C. Davidson | 139 | 59 | 42 | 770 | 5.5 | 2 | 11— 8 | |
| C. Daniels | 3 | 0 | 0 | 0 | 0.0 | 0 | 1— 33 | |
| Green | 2 | 2 | 100 | 17 | 8.5 | 0 | 0— 0 | |

**PUNTING**

| Last Name | No | Avg |
|---|---|---|
| Eischeid | 64 | 42.3 |

**KICKING**

| Last Name | XP | Att | % | FG | Att | % |
|---|---|---|---|---|---|---|
| Eischeid | 37 | 37 | 100 | 11 | 26 | 42 |

## SAN DIEGO CHARGERS

### RUSHING

| Last Name | No. | Yds | Avg | TD |
|---|---|---|---|---|
| Lowe | 146 | 643 | 4.4 | 3 |
| Foster | 81 | 352 | 4.4 | 1 |
| Lincoln | 58 | 214 | 3.7 | 1 |
| Allison | 31 | 213 | 6.9 | 2 |
| Hadl | 38 | 95 | 2.5 | 2 |
| Redman | 2 | 14 | 7.0 | 0 |
| Alworth | 3 | 10 | 3.3 | 0 |
| Tensi | 1 | −1 | −1.0 | 0 |
| Garrison | 1 | −3 | −3.0 | 0 |

### RECEIVING

| Last Name | No. | Yds | Avg | TD |
|---|---|---|---|---|
| Alworth | 73 | 1383 | 19 | 13 |
| Garrison | 46 | 642 | 14 | 4 |
| MacKinnon | 26 | 477 | 18 | 6 |
| Foster | 26 | 260 | 10 | 2 |
| Lincoln | 14 | 264 | 19 | 2 |
| Allison | 12 | 99 | 8 | 0 |
| Lowe | 12 | 41 | 3 | 0 |
| Frazier | 9 | 144 | 16 | 2 |
| Norton | 4 | 50 | 13 | 0 |
| Hadl | 2 | −13 | −7 | 0 |

### PUNT RETURNS

| Last Name | No. | Yds | Avg | TD |
|---|---|---|---|---|
| Duncan | 18 | 238 | 13 | 1 |
| Graham | 2 | 15 | 8 | 0 |
| Plump | 1 | 4 | 4 | 0 |

### KICKOFF RETURNS

| Last Name | No. | Yds | Avg | TD |
|---|---|---|---|---|
| Duncan | 25 | 642 | 26 | 0 |
| Plump | 15 | 345 | 23 | 0 |
| Lowe | 7 | 167 | 24 | 0 |
| Beauchamp | 4 | 64 | 16 | 0 |
| Farr | 2 | 54 | 27 | 0 |
| Whitmyer | 1 | 10 | 10 | 0 |
| Gruneisen | 1 | 0 | 0 | 0 |

### PASSING – PUNTING – KICKING

**PASSING**

| Last Name | Att | Comp | % | Yds | Yd/Att | TD | Int–% | RK |
|---|---|---|---|---|---|---|---|---|
| Hadl | 375 | 200 | 53 | 2846 | 7.6 | 23 | 14— 4 | 2 |
| Tensi | 52 | 21 | 40 | 405 | 7.8 | 5 | 1— 2 | |
| Lincoln | 4 | 2 | 50 | 71 | 17.8 | 1 | 0— 0 | |
| Lowe | 3 | 1 | 33 | 25 | 8.3 | 0 | 0— 0 | |

**PUNTING**

| Last Name | No | Avg |
|---|---|---|
| Redman | 66 | 37.0 |

**KICKING**

| Last Name | XP | Att | % | FG | Att | % |
|---|---|---|---|---|---|---|
| Van Raaphorst | 29 | 40 | 98 | 16 | 31 | 52 |

## DENVER BRONCOS

### RUSHING

| Last Name | No. | Yds | Avg | TD |
|---|---|---|---|---|
| Hayes | 105 | 417 | 4.0 | 1 |
| Haynes | 129 | 304 | 2.4 | 2 |
| Mitchell | 70 | 199 | 2.8 | 0 |
| Scarpitto | 4 | 110 | 27.5 | 1 |
| Lester | 34 | 84 | 2.5 | 0 |
| Choboian | 21 | 45 | 2.1 | 2 |
| Slaughter | 1 | 10 | 10.0 | 0 |
| Kellogg | 6 | 3 | 0.5 | 0 |
| McCormick | 4 | 2 | 0.5 | 0 |
| Glacken | 2 | −1 | −0.5 | 0 |

### RECEIVING

| Last Name | No. | Yds | Avg | TD |
|---|---|---|---|---|
| Haynes | 46 | 480 | 10 | 1 |
| Denson | 36 | 725 | 20 | 3 |
| Taylor | 35 | 448 | 13 | 1 |
| Scarpitto | 21 | 335 | 16 | 4 |
| Mitchell | 14 | 239 | 17 | 2 |
| Hayes | 8 | 49 | 6 | 0 |
| Lester | 2 | 26 | 13 | 1 |
| Crabtree | 1 | 38 | 38 | 0 |
| Franci | 1 | 8 | 8 | 0 |
| Kellogg | 1 | 5 | 5 | 0 |
| Wright | 1 | −2 | −2 | 0 |

### PUNT RETURNS

| Last Name | No. | Yds | Avg | TD |
|---|---|---|---|---|
| Haynes | 10 | 119 | 12 | 0 |
| Scott | 7 | 56 | 8 | 0 |
| Sellers | 6 | 49 | 8 | 0 |
| Wilson | 2 | 10 | 5 | 0 |
| Lester | 1 | 1 | 1 | 0 |

### KICKOFF RETURNS

| Last Name | No. | Yds | Avg | TD |
|---|---|---|---|---|
| Sellers | 19 | 541 | 28 | 2 |
| Wilson | 10 | 309 | 31 | 1 |
| Scott | 9 | 282 | 31 | 0 |
| Haynes | 9 | 229 | 25 | 0 |
| Crabtree | 5 | 129 | 26 | 0 |
| Mitchell | 3 | 55 | 18 | 0 |
| Lester | 1 | 11 | 11 | 0 |
| Sturm | 1 | 2 | 2 | 0 |
| Inman | 1 | 0 | 0 | 0 |

### PASSING – PUNTING – KICKING

**PASSING**

| Last Name | Att | Comp | % | Yds | Yd/Att | TD | Int–% | RK |
|---|---|---|---|---|---|---|---|---|
| McCormick | 193 | 68 | 35 | 993 | 5.1 | 6 | 15— 8 | 11 |
| Choboian | 163 | 82 | 50 | 1110 | 6.8 | 4 | 12— 7 | 8 |
| Slaughter | 25 | 7 | 28 | 124 | 5.0 | 1 | 0— 0 | |
| Glacken | 11 | 6 | 55 | 84 | 7.6 | 1 | 0— 0 | |
| Rote | 8 | 3 | 38 | 40 | 5.0 | 0 | 1— 13 | |
| Haynes | 2 | 0 | 0 | 0 | 0.0 | 0 | 2—100 | |

**PUNTING**

| Last Name | No | Avg |
|---|---|---|
| Scarpitto | 76 | 45.8 |

**KICKING**

| Last Name | XP | Att | % | FG | Att | % |
|---|---|---|---|---|---|---|
| Kroner | 20 | 20 | 100 | 14 | 25 | 56 |

**2 POINT XP**
Scarpitto

# Super Bowl I

January 15, at Los Angeles

(Attendance 61,946)

# Thirty Minutes of Equality

It seemed somehow unreal. The Green Bay Packers and the Kansas City Chiefs had always been parts of different universes in the world of sports. But here they were, the champions of the NFL and the AFL, meeting on the field in a confrontation many thought was years away.

Until recently, the NFL had not even recognized that the AFL was there. The established league considered the newer league an inferior and annoying upstart, worthy only of contempt when it first began. But while AFL scores were never posted in NFL stadia, NFL owners felt the AFL's presence directly when the new league began signing a fair share of top players and driving player salaries up in general. Despite the icy external show, fans knew that the NFL people wanted nothing better than the death of the AFL.

The AFL people, however, had never denied the NFL's existence; in fact, they used the older league as an open measure of their own league. NFL games were reported right along with AFL games on the scoreboard, as if both belonged on an equal footing, and AFL clubs were measured by the hypothetical situation of how they would do against a good NFL team. Ultimate success for the AFL would be standing shoulder to shoulder with the NFL.

The war between the leagues had been fought in courtrooms and the press, with subpoenas and checkbooks. The NFL looked down on the new league with utter disdain at first, but as the rich men who owned AFL clubs bid up player salaries and threatened to lure away established NFL stars, the officials of the older league decided to swallow some pride and look for a way to end the war between the circuits.

Negotiations in the spring brought about a peace agreement between the leagues that changed the structure of pro football as it had been in the 1960s. The NFL and AFL agreed to end their financial war by holding a common draft of college seniors and respecting each other's player contracts, and although the AFL clubs had to pay reparations, the clubs of both leagues now were coequal members of a joint structure. By the end of the decade, the AFL would be absorbed completely into an expanded NFL.

But the biggest dividend for the football fan was the establishment of an NFL-AFL championship game between the two league champions. Unofficially dubbed "The Super Bowl" by the media, this game would bring together the top teams in two leagues which had never played each other. This year's game would be unprecedented.

Older fans, of course, remembered the startling entry of the Cleveland Browns into the NFL in 1950. The Browns had completely dominated the AAFC during its four-year existence, but many fans and reporters looked on that circuit as an inferior league. The Browns relished the chance to prove that *they* were not inferior, and they decisively defeated the defending champion Philadelphia Eagles in their first confrontation with NFL competition. The Browns went on to take the league title in that first season, and some fans liked the chances of the AFL team in the Super Bowl because of the Browns' example.

Emerging as the AFL champion and Super Bowl representative were the Kansas City Chiefs, a team which had played three years in Dallas before moving to Missouri. Owned by Lamar Hunt and coached from the beginning by Hank Stram, the Chiefs had compiled an 11-2-1 record during the season and dissected a strong Buffalo team in the AFL championship game. Len Dawson, who had been waived out of the NFL after five years of bench-sitting, had found himself as a quarterback in the AFL, excelling both as a passer and a play-caller. Otis Taylor, Mike Garrett, Ed Budde, Jim Tyrer, and Buck Buchanan were all talented young pros who obviously could make most teams in the NFL. For the rest of the Kansas City offense and most of the defense, a lingering doubt remained. How well would these men, all solid AFL players, make out against the best the NFL could offer?

That best, for the fourth time in the last six years, was the Green Bay Packers, that hard-hitting precision machine hand-built by coach Vince Lombardi. Although the parts were aging, Lombardi's machine

still was a multifaceted wonder. His offensive line was quietly but constantly effective in moving people aside, and the running backs were the hard-nosed types who thrived on power sweeps and off-tackle smashes. At the heart of the attack was quarterback Bart Starr, a marvelous football tactician with a penchant for throwing very few interceptions. The Packer defense had set standards for all pro-football teams. Green Bay's mobile front four, big yet fast linebackers, and ball-hawking man-to-man pass defenders had written the book on modern defense. Presiding over it all and adding the special edge was coach Lombardi, the inspirational leader, the tough disciplinarian, the devout Catholic and family man, and a football theorist who set a tone for pro football which still is strong. Lombardi believed that the team that blocks and tackles best wins, and he drilled his teams to block crisply, to tackle hard, and to win.

So, on a warm January day in Los Angeles, the champions of two different leagues who played the same game but had never met came together on the same field. At first it was strange to see these two teams at the same time, but the fans and teams themselves soon settled into a very important football game for a lot of money plus the title of champion of all professional football.

The Chiefs fought the Packers to a standstill for most of the first period, but Green Bay got onto the scoreboard with a 37-yard pass from Bart Starr to Max McGee. Filling in for the injured Boyd Dowler, the thirty-four-year-old McGee would haul in seven passes today; eased out of the starting lineup this past season, he had caught only three passes during the regular campaign.

The Packers, however, were giving the Chiefs their first taste of what NFL teams had had to put up with for years. The only AFL fullback who had ever run with the ferocity of Jim Taylor was Cookie Gilchrist, who now was past his prime. The AFL had never produced as violent and perceptive a middle linebacker as Ray Nitschke, or as devastating a pair of corner linebackers as Dave Robinson and Lee Roy Caffey. The first quarter ended with the score only 7-0, but the Packers seemed to be on the verge of blowing the game wide open.

Far from folding, however, the Chiefs played their best football of the afternoon in the second period. Dawson's passes seemingly were finding gaps in the Packers' pass defense. Throwing both to his ends and backs, Dawson methodically moved the Chiefs downfield until they had the ball on the Green Bay seven-yard line. A short pass to fullback Curtis McClinton carried the ball into the end zone and marked the first time an AFL team had scored on an NFL team; some experts had freely predicted a Green Bay shutout in this contest. Seconds after the touchdown, Mike Mercer's extra-point kick knotted the score at 7-7.

With all expectations of an easy rout laid to rest, the Packers went to work on the next series of downs. Mixing passes and running plays, Starr drove the Packers deep into Kansas City territory, keying on several weak points he had discovered in the Chiefs' defense. He found that the Packers could run at end Chuck Hurston and tackle Andy Rice and throw against Sherrill Headrick, Fred Williamson, and Willie Mitchell; these men had held up against AFL competition but seemed out of their depth against the Packers. Green Bay especially enjoyed throwing against Williamson, since he had bragged that his hammer tackle, which was really only a forearm smash, would wreak havoc with the Packers. In the second half, Williamson himself would be carried from the field unconscious, the victim of a Green Bay "hammer tackle" of sorts.

Moving fairly easy through the Chiefs, the Packers scored their second touchdown on a 14-yard run by Jim Taylor, who simply ran over several Chiefs on the way to the end zone. Don Chandler's kick made the score 14-7, but the Chiefs were not yet ready to give up. Dawson responded with his own passing attack, and a 31-yard Mercer field goal cut the Green Bay lead to 14-10 at halftime.

The Chiefs had stayed surprisingly close to the Packers in the first half, and a good final thirty minutes of play could have brought them an upset victory. Beginning the second half with high hopes, the Chiefs

114

quickly met with a misfortune which let all the air out of them. Dawson dropped back to pass but was surrounded by a strong Green Bay pass rush; instead of eating the ball and taking the loss, he heaved the ball downfield. Willie Wood of the Packers picked it off and brought it back all the way to the Kansas City five-yard line. Elijah Pitts carried it over from there, and the game was never the same afterward. The Packers oozed confidence the rest of the afternoon, while the Chiefs simply looked outmanned.

Dawson found it much harder to move the ball in the second half, and the Chiefs never threatened to score in the final two periods. The Packers, meanwhile, took firm control of the game with good blocking and tackling. Max McGee's second touchdown catch of the day built the Packer lead up to 28-10 after three quarters, and Elijah Pitts' second touchdown run made the final score 35-10.

The Chiefs came away beaten but not disgraced. Although the Green Bay steamroller eventually ground them down, the Chiefs never gave up, and their first-half showing proved that an AFL club could hold its own with a top NFL club—at least for thirty minutes. Coach Stram did learn from the game which of his players could be exploited by a strong club, and he was making plans to replace certain men before a week had passed after the game.

For Vince Lombardi and the Packers, the victory added one more trophy to their collection. Green Bay had won several NFL titles in the 1960s, and now they had won the Super Bowl, a distinct product of this decade.

Some people claimed that Super Bowl I proved the inferiority of the AFL. Probably closer to the truth was the statement that the Chiefs were not inferior to the NFL, only to the Green Bay Packers.

---

| KANSAS CITY | | GREEN BAY |
|---|---|---|
| | OFFENSE | |
| Burford | LE | Dale |
| Tyrer | LT | Skoronski |
| Budde | LG | Thurston |
| Frazier | C | Curry |
| Merz | RG | Kramer |
| Hill | RT | Gregg |
| Arbanas | RE | Fleming |
| Dawson | QB | Starr |
| O. Taylor | FL | Dowler |
| Garrett | HB | E. Pitts |
| McClinton | FB | J. Taylor |
| | DEFENSE | |
| Mays | LE | Davis |
| Rice | LT | Kostelnik |
| Buchanan | RT | Jordan |
| Hurston | RE | Aldridge |
| Bell | LLB | D. Robinson |
| Headrick | MLB | Nitschke |
| Holub | RLB | Coffey |
| Williamson | LCB | Adderley |
| Mitchell | RCB | Jeter |
| Hunt | LS | T. Brown |
| J. Robinson | RS | Wood |

**SUBSTITUTES**

**KANSAS CITY**

Offense

| | |
|---|---|
| Beathard | Gilliam |
| Biodrowski | F. Pitts |
| Carolan | Reynolds |
| Coan | G. Thomas |
| DiMidio | |

Defense

| | |
|---|---|
| Abell | Smith |
| A. Brown | Stover |
| Corey | E. Thomas |
| Ply | |

Kickers

| | |
|---|---|
| Mercer | Wilson |

**GREEN BAY**

Offense

| | |
|---|---|
| B. Anderson | Long |
| D. Anderson | Mack |
| Bowman | McGee |
| Bratkowski | Vandersea |
| Gillingham | Wright |
| Grabowski | |

Defense

| | |
|---|---|
| B. Brown | Heathcock |
| Crutcher | Weatherwax |
| Hart | |

Kicker

| | |
|---|---|
| Chandler | |

---

## SCORING

| | | | | |
|---|---|---|---|---|
| KANSAS CITY | 0 | 10 | 0 | 0—10 |
| GREEN BAY | 7 | 7 | 14 | 7—35 |

First Quarter
G.B. McGee, 37 yard pass from Starr
PAT — Chandler (kick)

Second Quarter
K.C. McClinton, 17 yard pass from Dawson PAT — Mercer (kick)
G.B. Taylor, 14 yard rush PAT — Chandler (kick)
K.C. Mercer, 31 yard field goal

Third Quarter
G.B. Pitts, 5 yard rush PAT — Chandler (kick)
G.B. McGee, 13 yard pass from Starr PAT — Chandler (kick)

Fourth Quarter
G.B. Pitts, 1 yard rush PAT — Chandler (kick)

---

## TEAM STATISTICS

| K.C. | | G.B. |
|---|---|---|
| 17 | First Downs — Total | 21 |
| 4 | First Downs — Rushing | 10 |
| 12 | First Downs — Passing | 11 |
| 1 | First Downs — Penalty | 0 |
| 1 | Fumbles — Number | 1 |
| 0 | Fumbles — Lost Ball | 0 |
| 4 | Penalties — Number | 4 |
| 26 | Yards Penalized | 40 |
| 64 | Total Offensive Plays | 64 |
| 239 | Total Net Yards | 358 |
| 3.7 | Average Gain | 5.6 |
| 1 | Missed Field Goals | 0 |
| 1 | Giveaways | 1 |
| 1 | Takeaways | 1 |
| 0 | Difference | 0 |

* includes Punts

---

## INDIVIDUAL STATISTICS

| KANSAS CITY | | | | GREEN BAY | | | |
|---|---|---|---|---|---|---|---|
| | No | Yds | Avg. | | No | Yds | Avg. |
| **RUSHING** | | | | | | | |
| Dawson | 3 | 24 | 8.0 | Taylor | 16 | 53 | 3.3 |
| Garrett | 6 | 17 | 2.8 | Pitts | 11 | 45 | 4.1 |
| McClinton | 6 | 16 | 2.7 | D. Anderson | 4 | 30 | 7.5 |
| Beathard | 1 | 14 | 14.0 | Grabowski | 2 | 2 | 1.0 |
| Coan | 3 | 1 | 0.3 | | 33 | 130 | 3.9 |
| | 19 | 72 | 3.8 | | | | |
| **RECEIVING** | | | | | | | |
| Burford | 4 | 67 | 16.8 | McGee | 7 | 138 | 19.7 |
| Taylor | 4 | 57 | 14.3 | Dale | 4 | 59 | 14.8 |
| Garrett | 3 | 28 | 9.3 | Pitts | 2 | 32 | 16.0 |
| McClinton | 2 | 34 | 17.0 | Fleming | 2 | 22 | 11.0 |
| Arbanas | 2 | 30 | 15.0 | Taylor | 1 | —1 | —1.0 |
| Carolan | 1 | 7 | 7.0 | | 16 | 250 | 15.6 |
| Coan | 1 | 5 | 5.0 | | | | |
| | 17 | 228 | 13.4 | | | | |
| **PUNTING** | | | | | | | |
| Wilson | 7 | | 45.3 | Chandler | 3 | | 43.3 |
| | | | | D. Anderson | 1 | | 43.0 |
| | | | | | 4 | | 43.3 |
| **PUNT RETURNS** | | | | | | | |
| Garrett | 2 | 17 | 9.5 | D. Anderson | 3 | 25 | 8.3 |
| E. Thomas | 1 | 2 | 2.0 | Wood | 1 | —2 | —2.0 |
| | 3 | 19 | 6.3 | | 4 | 23 | 5.8 |
| **KICKOFF RETURNS** | | | | | | | |
| Coan | 4 | 87 | 21.8 | Adderley | 2 | 40 | 20.0 |
| Garrett | 2 | 43 | 21.5 | D. Anderson | 1 | 25 | 25.0 |
| | 6 | 130 | 21.7 | | 3 | 65 | 21.7 |
| **INTERCEPTION RETURNS** | | | | | | | |
| Mitchell | 1 | 0 | 0.0 | Wood | 1 | 50 | 50.0 |

**PASSING**

| KANSAS CITY | Att | Comp | Comp Pct. | Yds | Int | Yds/ Att. | Yds/ Comp | Yards Lost Tackled |
|---|---|---|---|---|---|---|---|---|
| Dawson | 27 | 16 | 59.3 | 211 | 1 | 7.8 | 13.2 | 43 |
| Beathard | 5 | 1 | 20.0 | 17 | 0 | 3.4 | 17.0 | 18 |
| | 32 | 17 | 53.1 | 228 | 1 | 7.1 | 13.4 | 6—61 |
| **GREEN BAY** | | | | | | | | |
| Starr | 23 | 16 | 69.6 | 250 | 1 | 10.9 | 15.6 | 3—22 |
| Bratkowski | 1 | 0 | 0.0 | 0 | 0 | — | — | 0 |
| | 24 | 16 | 66.7 | 250 | 1 | 10.4 | 15.6 | 3—22 |

# 1967 N.F.L.   Four Crowns and Then Some

With expansion to New Orleans bringing league membership to sixteen clubs, the NFL revamped its post-season playoff system by dividing the Eastern and Western conferences into four four-team divisions. The champions of the Coastal and Central divisions would meet for the Western crown, and the champions of the Capitol and Century divisions would meet for the Eastern crown; the winners of these matches then would clash for the NFL championship. This new arrangement expanded post-season title play to three weeks, with conference championships, the league championship, and the Super Bowl.

## EASTERN CONFERENCE — CAPITOL DIVISION

**Dallas Cowboys**—Injuries to Don Meredith, Dan Reeves, and Dave Manders slowed the offense up, but the Cowboys still had more than enough power to take the Capitol Division crown. The Cowboys had depth few teams could match, so that coach Tom Landry could find adequate replacements for his wounded troops. When quarterback Meredith missed three games, young Craig Morton filled in well, and Mike Connelly took over for Manders at center. The Dallas defense kept its fine edge, with Bob Lilly, Chuck Howley, and Cornell Green winning All-Pro honors.

**Philadelphia Eagles**—A disappointing season had fans calling for coach Joe Kuharich's ouster at the end of the year. The Eagles hoped to challenge the Cowboys after obtaining receivers Gary Ballman and Mike Ditka, but with their rash of injuries the Eagles were lucky to hold onto second place. Timmy Brown, Bob Brown, Lane Howell, Al Nelson, Ditka, and Ballman all missed stretches of the schedule. Despite poor protection, quarterback Norm Snead had a good year, with flanker Ben Hawkins his chief pass receiver. The Eagle defense, however, could be blamed more on a lack of talent in the line than on injuries.

**Washington Redskins**—Three Redskin receivers finished in the top four in the receiving statistics, and Sonny Jurgensen won the league passing title, yet the Skins finished in third place in the Capitol Division. The running and kicking games gave the passing attack little support, so opposing defenses knew the Redskins would come out throwing. Coach Otto Graham thought he had found a good fullback in first-draft choice Ray McDonald, but the big freshman was a big disappointment.

**New Orleans Saints**—Coach Tom Fears stocked his team liberally with veterans, with Billy Kilmer, Jim Taylor, Ray Poage, Dough Atkins, Earl Leggett, Lou Cordileone, Jackie Burkett, and Dave Whitsell all key men. The Saints did uncover two good rookies in Dan Abramowicz, a slow-footed receiver with good moves, and defensive tackle Dave Rowe, but the team relied mostly on oldsters whose best days were behind them.

## CENTURY DIVISION

**Cleveland Browns**—A bad arm troubled quarterback Frank Ryan, defensive ends Paul Wiggin and Bill Glass slumped off in their early thirties, Erich Barnes was slowing up at cornerback, and forty-three-year-old Lou Groza was not getting the old zip into his kicks. The Browns still had top performers in Leroy Kelly, Paul Warfield, Gary Collins, Dick Schafrath, Gene Hickerson, Jim Houston and other veterans at their peak, and with the other clubs in the Century Division experiencing problems, the Browns coasted to the title without much of a challenge.

**New York Giants**—The Giants sent a bundle of draft choices to Minnesota for quarterback Fran Tarkenton, and the scrambling quarterback immediately injected an element of excitement back into the team. Tarkenton found a kindred spirit in split end Homer Jones, a fast receiver who ran around until he got open rather than execute precise pass patterns; Tarkenton found Jones in the open often enough for Jones to gain 1,209 yards and score thirteen touchdowns.

**St. Louis Cardinals**—The Cards had some of the league's best talent, a flashy blitzing defense, and a top place-kicker in Jim Bakken, but head coach Charlie Winner had his hands full of problems this season. Before the regular season even started, quarterback Charley Johnson was drafted into the Army, leaving inexperienced Jim Hart at the throttle; the youngster showed a strong arm and a tendency to throw interceptions. By the end of the year, racial tension burst into the open, with black players claiming that not enough of them were used on defense.

**Pittsburgh Steelers**—Bill Nelsen's bad knees again forced the Steelers to field a substitute quarterback for part of the season, and this year's emergency passer was Kent Nix, former Green Bay taxi-squader. The

Pittsburgh offense frightened few opponents, but the defense was a solid, hard-working unit that kept the Steelers in most of their games. The club won only four games, but their losses included a 27-24 decision to New York and a 15-10 defeat by Washington.

## WESTERN CONFERENCE — CENTRAL DIVISION

**Green Bay Packers**—Coach Vince Lombardi thought he was well covered at running back despite the departure of both Jim Taylor and Paul Hornung from the roster, but injuries sent him scurrying in all directions for healthy ball-carriers. Elijah Pitts and Jim Grabowski missed the late-season games with physical ills, leaving Lombardi with only Donny Anderson from the regular runners. To flesh out the backfield, Lombardi picked up journeymen Ben Wilson and Chuck Mercein and started playing rookie Travis Williams at halfback. Williams was the talk of the league with his blistering kickoff returning, and now he combined with the other substitute Packer ball-carriers in a backfield that didn't look good but punched out the necessary yardage to win.

**Chicago Bears**—The Bear defense regularly held opponents under 20 points, but the offense rarely capitalized on this during the first half of the schedule. Over the last seven games, however, the offense generated enough points to win five and tie one. Gale Sayers shone as usual throughout the year, but other players helped him move the ball down the stretch. Jack Concannon, the scrambling quarterback obtained from Philadelphia for Mike Ditka, settled comfortably into the Chicago system after October, hustling Brian Piccolo provided a running threat besides Sayers, and Dick Gordon developed into a dangerous receiver. After this flourishing finish, seventy-three-year-old George Halas called it quits as a coach.

**Detroit Lions**—The team had problems in the passing and kicking departments, but two gilt-edge rookies entertained fans all season. Halfback Mel Farr ran for 860 yards to give the Lions their first running threat in years. In the defensive secondary, rookie Lem Barney covered the league's best receivers without giving anything away, and once he got his hands on an errant enemy pass he threatened to sprint away to a touchdown.

**Minnesota Vikings**—Gone were coach Norm Van Brocklin, Fran Tarkenton, and Tommy Mason, and coming down from Canada were new head coach Bud Grant and quarterback Joe Kapp. The trade of Tarkenton to New York gave the Vikings some extra high draft choices, so their rookie class was a rich one, including Alan Page, Gene Washington, Clint Jones, John Beasley, and Bob Grim.

## COASTAL DIVISION

**Los Angeles Rams**—Myron Pottios took over for the retired Bill George at middle linebacker, and big Roger Brown was purchased from Detroit to replace the injured Rosie Grier, but the defense continued to play with an almost perfect teamwork. Quarterback Roman Gabriel ran a ball-control offense that scored enough points to win eleven games and lose only one during the season. The Baltimore Colts stayed right with the Rams in the standings, but Los Angeles took the Coastal title by outscoring Baltimore in their two meetings.

**Baltimore Colts**—Even while replacing some old veterans, the Colts still swept to a 11-1-2 record. Receivers Ray Berry and Jimmy Orr went out with injuries, and subs Willie Richardson and Alex Hawkins filled in in fine fashion. Offensive tackle Jim Parker retired in mid-season with physical ills, and Sam Ball effectively plugged the hole in the line. Two rookies, huge tackle Bubba Smith and safety Rick Volk, saved a lot of action on defense. But Johnny Unitas and the tough Colt defense kept the Colts strong during all the changes.

**San Francisco '49ers**—Quarterback John Brodie was inconsistent, split end Dave Parks was hurt, and the team lost three of four games with the Rams and Colts. The defense developed into a solid unit, with a strong pass rush, a top linebacker in Dave Wilcox, and two good cornerbacks in Jim Johnson and Kermit Alexander, but the offense lacked the firepower to move the club above the .500 mark.

**Atlanta Falcons**—The rookie crop brought little help, leaving the Falcons with the same top men as last year. Tommy Nobis, Randy Johnson, and Junior Coffey continued the strong play of their rookie seasons, but coach Norb Hecker could augment his squad only with castoffs from other clubs as defensive tackle Jim Norton, split end Jerry Simmons, and veteran flanker Tommy McDonald helped out among the bargain acquisitions.

## FINAL TEAM STATISTICS

### OFFENSE

| | ATL. | BALT. | CHI. | CLEV. | DALL. | DET. | G.B. | L.A. | MINN. | N.O. | N.Y. | PHIL. | PITT. | ST.L. | S.F. | WASH. |
|---|---|---|---|---|---|---|---|---|---|---|---|---|---|---|---|---|
| **FIRST DOWNS:** | | | | | | | | | | | | | | | | |
| Total | 180 | 289 | 175 | 238 | 261 | 215 | 243 | 262 | 199 | 220 | 274 | 239 | 252 | 248 | 242 | 280 |
| by Rushing | 68 | 105 | 98 | 119 | 109 | 104 | 115 | 106 | 91 | 67 | 115 | 69 | 83 | 97 | 101 | 82 |
| by Passing | 95 | 159 | 62 | 102 | 141 | 92 | 112 | 133 | 85 | 135 | 135 | 146 | 145 | 131 | 121 | 177 |
| by Penalty | 17 | 25 | 15 | 17 | 11 | 19 | 16 | 23 | 23 | 18 | 24 | 24 | 24 | 20 | 20 | 21 |
| **RUSHING:** | | | | | | | | | | | | | | | | |
| Number | 344 | 443 | 489 | 444 | 477 | 473 | 474 | 490 | 454 | 334 | 436 | 328 | 431 | 472 | 434 | 345 |
| Yards | 1303 | 1645 | 1852 | 2139 | 1900 | 1907 | 1915 | 1906 | 1811 | 1192 | 1864 | 1250 | 1397 | 1839 | 1764 | 1247 |
| Average Yards | 3.8 | 3.7 | 3.8 | 4.8 | 4.0 | 4.0 | 4.0 | 3.9 | 4.0 | 3.6 | 4.3 | 3.8 | 3.2 | 3.9 | 4.1 | 3.6 |
| Touchdowns | 6 | 21 | 12 | 15 | 13 | 14 | 18 | 16 | 10 | 9 | 16 | 12 | 13 | 15 | 16 | 13 |
| **PASSING:** | | | | | | | | | | | | | | | | |
| Attempts | 370 | 457 | 268 | 333 | 417 | 351 | 331 | 390 | 336 | 478 | 406 | 445 | 442 | 431 | 469 | 527 |
| Completions | 179 | 265 | 131 | 160 | 210 | 160 | 182 | 206 | 150 | 237 | 221 | 244 | 214 | 204 | 228 | 301 |
| Completion Percentage | 48.4 | 58.0 | 48.9 | 48.0 | 50.4 | 45.6 | 55.0 | 52.8 | 44.6 | 49.6 | 54.4 | 54.8 | 48.4 | 47.3 | 48.6 | 57.1 |
| Passing Yards | 2144 | 3561 | 1673 | 2314 | 3093 | 1826 | 2758 | 2947 | 1951 | 2989 | 3382 | 3463 | 2781 | 3170 | 2862 | 3887 |
| Average Yards per Attempt (Gross) | 5.8 | 7.8 | 6.2 | 6.9 | 7.4 | 5.2 | 8.3 | 7.6 | 5.8 | 6.3 | 8.3 | 7.8 | 6.3 | 7.4 | 6.1 | 7.4 |
| Average Yards per Completion (Gross) | 12.0 | 13.4 | 12.8 | 14.5 | 14.7 | 11.4 | 15.2 | 14.3 | 13.0 | 12.6 | 15.3 | 14.2 | 13.0 | 15.5 | 12.6 | 12.9 |
| Times Tackled Attempting to Pass | 49 | 25 | 27 | 44 | 42 | 24 | 41 | 25 | 35 | 52 | 37 | 49 | 30 | 24 | 26 | 19 |
| Yards Lost Tackled Attempting to Pass | 434 | 198 | 232 | 372 | 294 | 195 | 394 | 213 | 284 | 391 | 342 | 369 | 270 | 229 | 208 | 157 |
| Net Yards | 1710 | 3363 | 1441 | 1942 | 2799 | 1631 | 2364 | 2734 | 1667 | 2598 | 3040 | 3094 | 2511 | 2941 | 2654 | 3730 |
| Touchdowns | 13 | 22 | 9 | 22 | 28 | 14 | 15 | 28 | 11 | 13 | 33 | 30 | 19 | 20 | 16 | 31 |
| Interceptions | 25 | 17 | 18 | 18 | 28 | 19 | 27 | 16 | 24 | 23 | 20 | 24 | 29 | 35 | 26 | 17 |
| Percent Intercepted | 6.8 | 3.7 | 6.7 | 5.4 | 6.7 | 5.4 | 8.2 | 4.1 | 7.1 | 4.8 | 4.9 | 5.4 | 6.6 | 8.1 | 5.5 | 3.2 |
| **PUNTS:** | | | | | | | | | | | | | | | | |
| Number | 87 | 49 | 79 | 67 | 67 | 83 | 66 | 68 | 75 | 74 | 55 | 61 | 72 | 62 | 73 | 72 |
| Average Distance | 43.7 | 42.3 | 42.9 | 37.1 | 40.4 | 40.5 | 36.5 | 42.2 | 410 | 42.9 | 36.0 | 38.3 | 38.1 | 40.8 | 37.6 | 41.3 |
| **PUNT RETURNS:** | | | | | | | | | | | | | | | | |
| Number | 25 | 42 | 22 | 35 | 33 | 34 | 39 | 50 | 35 | 23 | 22 | 29 | 30 | 34 | 35 | 34 |
| Yards | 94 | 323 | 194 | 357 | 320 | 97 | 157 | 328 | 107 | 79 | 102 | 158 | 143 | 198 | 314 | 203 |
| Average Yards | 3.8 | 7.7 | 8.8 | 10.2 | 9.7 | 2.9 | 4.0 | 6.6 | 3.1 | 3.4 | 4.6 | 5.4 | 4.8 | 5.8 | 9.0 | 6.0 |
| Touchdowns | 0 | 1 | 1 | 1 | 1 | 0 | 0 | 0 | 0 | 0 | 0 | 0 | 0 | 0 | 0 | 0 |
| **KICKOFF RETURNS:** | | | | | | | | | | | | | | | | |
| Number | 69 | 42 | 47 | 55 | 48 | 50 | 46 | 43 | 53 | 72 | 69 | 62 | 58 | 66 | 56 | 61 |
| Yards | 1471 | 988 | 1157 | 1396 | 1014 | 1145 | 1241 | 1033 | 1215 | 1739 | 1363 | 1246 | 1221 | 1372 | 1326 | 1330 |
| Average Yards | 21.3 | 23.5 | 24.6 | 25.4 | 21.1 | 22.9 | 27.0 | 24.0 | 22.9 | 24.2 | 19.8 | 20.1 | 21.1 | 20.8 | 23.7 | 21.8 |
| Touchdowns | 1 | 0 | 3 | 1 | 0 | 0 | 4 | 0 | 1 | 2 | 0 | 0 | 0 | 0 | 0 | 1 |
| **INTERCEPTION RETURNS:** | | | | | | | | | | | | | | | | |
| Number | 17 | 32 | 28 | 22 | 29 | 23 | 26 | 32 | 16 | 22 | 17 | 21 | 26 | 19 | 16 | 20 |
| Yards | 343 | 453 | 334 | 375 | 331 | 343 | 284 | 476 | 316 | 333 | 209 | 274 | 264 | 205 | 198 | 183 |
| Average Yards | 20.2 | 14.2 | 11.9 | 17.0 | 11.4 | 14.9 | 10.9 | 14.9 | 19.8 | 15.1 | 12.3 | 13.0 | 10.2 | 10.8 | 12.4 | 9.2 |
| Touchdowns | 2 | 3 | 2 | 3 | 3 | 6 | 2 | 4 | 2 | 2 | 0 | 2 | 1 | 1 | 0 | 1 |
| **PENALTIES:** | | | | | | | | | | | | | | | | |
| Number | 88 | 52 | 98 | 72 | 81 | 65 | 48 | 85 | 100 | 76 | 80 | 77 | 68 | 65 | 89 | 67 |
| Yards | 866 | 458 | 953 | 773 | 785 | 712 | 531 | 854 | 1075 | 785 | 842 | 830 | 759 | 720 | 931 | 588 |
| **FUMBLES:** | | | | | | | | | | | | | | | | |
| Number | 20 | 13 | 25 | 24 | 26 | 32 | 19 | 32 | 23 | 21 | 21 | 22 | 33 | 23 | 20 | 26 |
| Number Lost | 14 | 8 | 14 | 17 | 14 | 21 | 10 | 13 | 13 | 14 | 10 | 16 | 16 | 11 | 10 | 14 |
| **POINTS:** | | | | | | | | | | | | | | | | |
| Total | 175 | 394 | 239 | 334 | 342 | 260 | 332 | 398 | 233 | 233 | 369 | 351 | 281 | 333 | 273 | 347 |
| PAT Attempts | 22 | 48 | 29 | 43 | 45 | 34 | 39 | 48 | 26 | 27 | 49 | 45 | 35 | 36 | 33 | 47 |
| PAT Made | 22 | 46 | 26 | 43 | 41 | 33 | 39 | 48 | 26 | 27 | 45 | 45 | 35 | 36 | 33 | 42 |
| FG Attempts | 18 | 37 | 26 | 23 | 23 | 21 | 29 | 43 | 33 | 32 | 21 | 19 | 22 | 39 | 33 | 26 |
| FG Made | 7 | 20 | 13 | 11 | 9 | 7 | 19 | 20 | 17 | 14 | 10 | 12 | 12 | 27 | 14 | 7 |
| Percent FG Made | 38.9 | 54.1 | 50.0 | 47.8 | 39.1 | 33.3 | 65.5 | 46.5 | 51.5 | 43.8 | 47.6 | 63.2 | 54.5 | 69.2 | 42.4 | 26.9 |
| Safeties | 0 | 0 | 0 | 0 | 2 | 1 | 1 | 1 | 0 | 1 | 0 | 0 | 0 | 0 | 0 | 1 |

### DEFENSE

| | ATL. | BALT. | CHI. | CLEV. | DALL. | DET. | G.B. | L.A. | MINN. | N.O. | N.Y. | PHIL. | PITT. | ST.L. | S.F. | WASH. |
|---|---|---|---|---|---|---|---|---|---|---|---|---|---|---|---|---|
| **FIRST DOWNS:** | | | | | | | | | | | | | | | | |
| Total | 294 | 208 | 215 | 281 | 236 | 205 | 183 | 200 | 217 | 276 | 261 | 286 | 228 | 216 | 237 | 274 |
| by Rushing | 124 | 78 | 91 | 115 | 64 | 98 | 98 | 75 | 105 | 114 | 113 | 105 | 80 | 79 | 92 | 98 |
| by Passing | 152 | 116 | 98 | 153 | 145 | 85 | 78 | 104 | 90 | 138 | 125 | 161 | 128 | 117 | 128 | 153 |
| by Penalty | 18 | 14 | 26 | 13 | 27 | 22 | 7 | 21 | 22 | 24 | 23 | 20 | 20 | 20 | 17 | 23 |
| **RUSHING:** | | | | | | | | | | | | | | | | |
| Number | 504 | 387 | 419 | 459 | 339 | 471 | 443 | 361 | 500 | 469 | 416 | 434 | 418 | 410 | 407 | 431 |
| Yards | 2139 | 1411 | 1531 | 1767 | 1081 | 1795 | 1923 | 1119 | 2104 | 2092 | 1799 | 1741 | 1377 | 1502 | 1698 | 1852 |
| Average Yards | 4.2 | 3.6 | 3.7 | 3.8 | 3.2 | 3.8 | 4.3 | 3.1 | 4.2 | 4.5 | 4.3 | 4.0 | 3.3 | 3.7 | 4.2 | 4.3 |
| Touchdowns | 18 | 5 | 11 | 15 | 11 | 15 | 7 | 6 | 12 | 22 | 20 | 16 | 12 | 13 | 17 | 19 |
| **PASSING:** | | | | | | | | | | | | | | | | |
| Attempts | 421 | 395 | 384 | 454 | 482 | 312 | 337 | 445 | 314 | 410 | 389 | 480 | 397 | 360 | 403 | 468 |
| Completions | 238 | 221 | 164 | 250 | 260 | 143 | 155 | 212 | 149 | 207 | 195 | 255 | 201 | 169 | 212 | 261 |
| Completion Percentage | 56.5 | 55.9 | 42.7 | 55.1 | 53.9 | 45.8 | 46.0 | 47.6 | 47.5 | 50.5 | 50.1 | 53.1 | 50.6 | 46.9 | 52.6 | 55.8 |
| Passing Yards | 3588 | 2678 | 2146 | 3231 | 3167 | 2089 | 1644 | 2694 | 2071 | 3035 | 2731 | 3382 | 2854 | 3023 | 2755 | 3713 |
| Average Yards per Attempt (Gross) | 8.5 | 6.8 | 5.6 | 7.1 | 6.6 | 6.7 | 4.9 | 6.1 | 6.6 | 7.4 | 7.0 | 7.0 | 7.2 | 8.4 | 6.8 | 7.9 |
| Average Yards per Completion (Gross) | 15.1 | 12.1 | 13.1 | 12.9 | 12.2 | 14.6 | 10.6 | 12.7 | 13.9 | 14.7 | 14.0 | 13.3 | 14.2 | 17.9 | 13.0 | 14.2 |
| Times Tackled Attempting to Pass | 21 | 36 | 30 | 41 | 45 | 39 | 29 | 43 | 36 | 23 | 31 | 23 | 29 | 37 | 48 | 38 |
| Yards Lost Tackled Attempting to Pass | 196 | 246 | 271 | 332 | 377 | 356 | 267 | 287 | 319 | 199 | 246 | 151 | 276 | 340 | 409 | 310 |
| Net Yards | 3392 | 2432 | 1875 | 2899 | 2790 | 1733 | 1377 | 2407 | 1752 | 2836 | 2485 | 3231 | 2578 | 2683 | 2346 | 3403 |
| Touchdowns | 31 | 13 | 14 | 19 | 21 | 11 | 13 | 14 | 17 | 25 | 25 | 29 | 22 | 26 | 19 | 25 |
| Interceptions | 17 | 32 | 28 | 22 | 29 | 23 | 26 | 32 | 16 | 22 | 17 | 21 | 26 | 19 | 16 | 20 |
| Percent Intercepted | 4.0 | 8.1 | 7.3 | 4.8 | 6.0 | 7.4 | 7.7 | 7.2 | 5.1 | 5.4 | 4.4 | 4.4 | 6.5 | 5.3 | 4.0 | 4.3 |
| **PUNTS:** | | | | | | | | | | | | | | | | |
| Number | 49 | 69 | 77 | 62 | 72 | 79 | 75 | 86 | 79 | 63 | 56 | 50 | 70 | 81 | 70 | 72 |
| Average Distance | 39.9 | 39.4 | 41.3 | 39.9 | 42.5 | 39.3 | 41.6 | 40.8 | 38.9 | 39.9 | 39.7 | 38.8 | 38.9 | 39.0 | 43.8 | 40.1 |
| **PUNT RETURNS:** | | | | | | | | | | | | | | | | |
| Number | 54 | 21 | 41 | 29 | 37 | 38 | 13 | 33 | 39 | 35 | 21 | 33 | 39 | 24 | 29 | 36 |
| Yards | 408 | 144 | 168 | 70 | 266 | 323 | 22 | 240 | 163 | 261 | 214 | 130 | 277 | 79 | 175 | 234 |
| Average Yards | 7.6 | 6.9 | 4.1 | 2.4 | 7.2 | 8.5 | 1.7 | 7.3 | 4.2 | 7.5 | 10.2 | 3.9 | 7.1 | 3.3 | 6.0 | 6.5 |
| Touchdowns | 0 | 0 | 0 | 0 | 0 | 1 | 0 | 0 | 0 | 0 | 0 | 0 | 1 | 1 | 1 | 0 |
| **KICKOFF RETURNS:** | | | | | | | | | | | | | | | | |
| Number | 38 | 65 | 52 | 59 | 59 | 43 | 59 | 66 | 48 | 51 | 69 | 59 | 56 | 65 | 54 | 54 |
| Yards | 889 | 1483 | 1064 | 1288 | 1350 | 959 | 1276 | 1414 | 1076 | 1166 | 1511 | 1466 | 1300 | 1481 | 1311 | 1223 |
| Average Yards | 23.4 | 22.8 | 20.5 | 21.8 | 22.9 | 22.3 | 21.6 | 21.4 | 22.4 | 22.9 | 21.9 | 24.8 | 23.2 | 22.8 | 24.3 | 22.6 |
| Touchdowns | 0 | 1 | 0 | 2 | 0 | 1 | 0 | 2 | 0 | 0 | 1 | 2 | 1 | 1 | 1 | 1 |
| **INTERCEPTION RETURNS:** | | | | | | | | | | | | | | | | |
| Number | 25 | 17 | 18 | 18 | 28 | 19 | 27 | 16 | 24 | 23 | 20 | 24 | 29 | 35 | 26 | 17 |
| Yards | 326 | 272 | 246 | 290 | 353 | 235 | 370 | 186 | 315 | 303 | 216 | 429 | 368 | 469 | 292 | 251 |
| Average Yards | 13.0 | 16.0 | 13.7 | 16.1 | 12.6 | 12.4 | 13.7 | 11.6 | 13.1 | 13.2 | 10.8 | 17.9 | 12.7 | 13.4 | 11.2 | 14.8 |
| Touchdowns | 4 | 2 | 1 | 1 | 3 | 2 | 3 | 0 | 4 | 0 | 1 | 3 | 1 | 5 | 3 | 1 |
| **PENALTIES:** | | | | | | | | | | | | | | | | |
| Number | 87 | 82 | 82 | 57 | 64 | 73 | 55 | 91 | 90 | 83 | 68 | 67 | 73 | 89 | 64 | 86 |
| Yards | 853 | 927 | 782 | 655 | 717 | 822 | 482 | 912 | 906 | 824 | 774 | 715 | 833 | 782 | 596 | 882 |
| **FUMBLES:** | | | | | | | | | | | | | | | | |
| Number | 26 | 17 | 23 | 28 | 27 | 13 | 23 | 18 | 38 | 21 | 28 | 28 | 26 | 19 | 24 | 21 |
| Number Lost | 10 | 8 | 16 | 14 | 19 | 10 | 14 | 13 | 19 | 10 | 15. | 14 | 13 | 13 | 13 | 14 |
| **POINTS:** | | | | | | | | | | | | | | | | |
| Total | 422 | 198 | 218 | 297 | 268 | 259 | 209 | 196 | 294 | 379 | 379 | 409 | 320 | 356 | 337 | 353 |
| PAT Attempts | 53 | 21 | 27 | 37 | 35 | 32 | 24 | 23 | 34 | 48 | 48 | 52 | 39 | 46 | 41 | 46 |
| PAT Made | 52 | 21 | 26 | 36 | 34 | 31 | 23 | 22 | 34 | 46 | 47 | 52 | 36 | 42 | 40 | 45 |
| FG Attempts | 39 | 28 | 26 | 25 | 23 | 29 | 28 | 26 | 31 | 29 | 21 | 32 | 30 | 19 | 35 | 24 |
| FG Made | 16 | 17 | 10 | 13 | 8 | 12 | 14 | 12 | 18 | 15 | .14 | 15 | 16 | 12 | 17 | 10 |
| Percent FG Made | 41.0 | 60.7 | 38.5 | 52.0 | 34.8 | 41.4 | 50.0 | 46.2 | 58.1 | 51.7 | 66.7 | 46.9 | 53.3 | 63.2 | 48.6 | 41.7 |
| Safeties | 2 | 0 | 0 | 0 | 0 | 0 | 0 | 0 | 1 | 0 | 1 | 0 | 1 | 1 | 0 | 1 |

## CONFERENCE PLAYOFFS

December 23, at Milwaukee (Attendance 49,861)

., Milwaukee (Attendance 49,861)

### SCORING

| | | | | |
|---|---|---|---|---|
| GREEN BAY | 0 | 14 | 7 | 7–28 |
| LOS ANGELES | 7 | 0 | 0 | 0– 7 |

First Quarter
L.A. Casey, 28 yard pass from Gabriel
PAT–Gossett (kick)

Second Quarter
G.B. Williams, 46 yard rush
PAT–Chandler (kick)
G.B. Dale, 18 yard pass from Starr
PAT–Chandler (kick)

Third Quarter
G.B. Mercein, 6 yard rush
PAT–Chandler (kick)

Fourth Quarter
G.B. Williams, 2 yard rush
PAT–Chandler (kick)

### TEAM STATISTICS

| G.B. | | L.A. |
|---|---|---|
| 20 | First Downs–Total | 12 |
| 11 | First Downs–Rushing | 2 |
| 8 | First Downs–Passing | 9 |
| 1 | First Downs–Penalty | 1 |
| 1 | Times Tackled Passing | 5 |
| 11 | Yards Lost–Tackled | 44 |
| 3 | Fumbles–Number | 0 |
| 3 | Fumbles–Lost Ball | 0 |
| 7 | Penalties–Number | 3 |
| 44 | Yards Penalized | 25 |
| 5 | Punts–Number | 6 |
| 32.6 | Punts–Average Distance | 39.3 |
| 3 | Punt Returns–Number | 1 |
| 44 | Punt Returns–Yards | 0 |
| 2 | Kickoff Returns–Number | 4 |
| 19 | Kickoff Returns–Yards | 80 |
| 1 | Interception Returns–Number | 1 |
| 20 | Interception Returns–Yards | 24 |
| 4 | Giveaways | 1 |
| 1 | Takeaways | 4 |
| –3 | Difference | +3 |

### INDIVIDUAL STATISTICS

| GREEN BAY | No | Yds | Avg. | LOS ANGELES | No | Yds | Avg. |
|---|---|---|---|---|---|---|---|
| **RUSHING** | | | | | | | |
| Williams | 18 | 88 | 4.9 | Bass | 14 | 40 | 2.9 |
| Anderson | 12 | 52 | 4.3 | Jo'phson | 9 | 16 | 1.8 |
| Mercein | 12 | 13 | 1.1 | Gabriel | 3 | 6 | 2.0 |
| Starr | 2 | 8 | 4.0 | Mason | 2 | 13 | 6.5 |
| Wilson | 1 | 2 | 2.0 | | 28 | 75 | 2.7 |
| | 45 | 163 | 3.6 | | | | |
| **RECEIVING** | | | | | | | |
| Dale | 6 | 109 | 18.2 | Casey | 5 | 82 | 16.4 |
| Dowler | 3 | 35 | 11.7 | Traux | 2 | 45 | 22.5 |
| Fleming | 3 | 30 | 10.0 | Jo'phson | 2 | 30 | 15.0 |
| Anderson | 2 | 30 | 15.0 | Snow | 1 | 17 | 17.0 |
| Mercein | 2 | 10 | 5.0 | Pope | 1 | 12 | 12.0 |
| Williams | 1 | 8 | 8.0 | | 11 | 186 | 16.9 |
| | 17 | 222 | 13.1 | | | | |

**PASSING**

| G.B. | Att. | Cmp. | Comp. Pct. | Yds. | Int. | Yds/ Att. | Yds/ Comp. |
|---|---|---|---|---|---|---|---|
| Starr | 23 | 17 | 73.9 | 222 | 1 | 9.7 | 13.1 |
| **L.A.** | | | | | | | |
| Gabriel | 31 | 11 | 35.5 | 186 | 1 | 6.0 | 16.9 |

| | | | | |
|---|---|---|---|---|
| DALLAS | 14 | 10 | 21 | 7–52 |
| CLEVELAND | 0 | 7 | 0 | 7–14 |

First Quarter
Dal. Baynham, 3 yard pass from Meredith
PAT–Villanueva (kick)
Dal. Perkins, 4 yard rush
PAT–Villanueva (kick)

Second Quarter
Dal. Hayes, 86 yard pass from Meredith
PAT–Villanueva (kick)
Dal. Villanueva, 10 yard field goal
Cle. Morin, 13 yard pass from Ryan
PAT–Groza (kick)

Third Quarter
Dal. Baynham, 1 yard rush
PAT–Villanueva (kick)
Dal. Perkins, 1 yard rush
PAT–Villanueva (kick)
Dal. Green, 60 yard interception return
PAT–Villanueva (kick)

Fourth Quarter
Dal. Baynham, 1 yard rush
PAT–Villanueva (kick)
Cle. Warfield, 75 yard pass from Ryan
PAT–Groza (kick)

December 24, at Dallas (Attendance 70,786)

### TEAM STATISTICS

| DAL. | | CLE. |
|---|---|---|
| 22 | First Downs–Total | 15 |
| 13 | First Downs–Rushing | 4 |
| 7 | First Downs–Passing | 10 |
| 2 | First Downs–Penalty | 1 |
| 1 | Times Tackled Passing | 5 |
| 2 | Yards Lost Tackled | 31 |
| 2 | Fumbles–Number | 0 |
| 1 | Fumbles–Lost Ball | 0 |
| 2 | Penalties–Number | 2 |
| 10 | Yards Penalized | 18 |
| 2 | Punts–Number | 7 |
| 44.5 | Punts–Average Distance | 39.8 |
| 4 | Punt Returns–Number | 2 |
| 155 | Punt Returns–Yards | 11 |
| 1 | Kickoff Returns–Number | 7 |
| 4 | Kickoff Returns–Yards | 112 |
| 1 | Interception Returns–Number | 1 |
| 60 | Interception Returns–Yards | 0 |
| 2 | Giveaways | 1 |
| 1 | Takeaways | 2 |
| –1 | Difference | +1 |

### INDIVIDUAL STATISTICS

| DALLAS | No | Yds | Avg. | CLEVELAND | No | Yds | Avg. |
|---|---|---|---|---|---|---|---|
| **RUSHING** | | | | | | | |
| Perkins | 18 | 74 | 4.1 | Kelly | 15 | 96 | 6.4 |
| Baynham | 13 | 50 | 3.8 | Green | 10 | 49 | 4.9 |
| Garrison | 9 | 33 | 3.6 | Ryan | 2 | 14 | 7.0 |
| Clarke | 1 | 8 | 8.0 | | 27 | 159 | 5.9 |
| Reeves | 3 | 7 | 2.3 | | | | |
| Meredith | 2 | 6 | 3.0 | | | | |
| | 46 | 178 | 3.9 | | | | |
| **RECEIVING** | | | | | | | |
| Hayes | 5 | 144 | 28.8 | Kelly | 4 | 39 | 9.8 |
| Rentzel | 3 | 65 | 21.7 | Warf'ld | 3 | 99 | 33.9 |
| Reeves | 1 | 9 | 9.0 | Morin | 3 | 35 | 11.7 |
| Perkins | 1 | 4 | 4.0 | Green | 3 | 18 | 6.0 |
| Baynham | 1 | 3 | 3.0 | Collins | 1 | 3 | 3.0 |
| | 11 | 225 | 20.5 | | 14 | 194 | 13.9 |

**PASSING**

| DALL. | Att | Cmp | Pct | Yds | Int | Yd/A | Yd/C |
|---|---|---|---|---|---|---|---|
| Meredith | 12 | 10 | 83.3 | 212 | 0 | 17.7 | 21.2 |
| Morton | 3 | 1 | 33.3 | 13 | 1 | 4.3 | 13.0 |
| | 15 | 11 | 73.3 | 225 | 1 | 15.0 | 20.5 |
| **CLEVE.** | | | | | | | |
| Ryan | 30 | 14 | 46.7 | 194 | 1 | 6.5 | 13.9 |

| Scores of Each Game | | Use Name | Pos. | Hgt | Wgt | Age | Int | Pts |
|---|---|---|---|---|---|---|---|---|

## CAPITOL DIVISION

### DALLAS COWBOYS 9-5-0 Tom Landry

| Scores of Each Game | | |
|---|---|---|
| 21 | Cleveland | 14 |
| 38 | NEW YORK | 24 |
| 13 | LOS ANGELES | 35 |
| 17 | Washington | 14 |
| 14 | NEW ORLEANS | 10 |
| 24 | Pittsburgh | 21 |
| 14 | Philadelphia | 21 |
| 37 | ATLANTA | 7 |
| 27 | New Orleans | 10 |
| 20 | WASHINGTON | 27 |
| 46 | ST. LOUIS | 21 |
| 17 | Baltimore | 23 |
| 38 | PHILADELPHIA | 17 |
| 16 | San Francisco | 24 |

| Use Name | Pos. | Hgt | Wgt | Age | Int | Pts |
|---|---|---|---|---|---|---|
| Jim Boeke | OT | 6'5" | 260 | 28 | | |
| Ralph Neely | OT | 6'5" | 265 | 23 | | |
| Tony Liscio | OT | 6'5" | 255 | 27 | | |
| Leon Donahue | OG | 6'4" | 245 | 28 | | |
| John Niland | OG | 6'4" | 245 | 23 | | |
| John Wilbur | OG | 6'3" | 240 | 24 | | |
| Mike Connelly | C | 6'3" | 248 | 31 | | |
| Malcolm Walker | OT-C | 6'4" | 250 | 24 | | |
| George Andrie | DE | 6'7" | 250 | 27 | | |
| Larry Stephens | DE | 6'4" | 250 | 29 | | |
| Willie Townes | DE | 6'5" | 260 | 24 | | |
| Ron East | DT | 6'4" | 242 | 24 | | |
| Bob Lilly | DT | 6'4" | 260 | 28 | | |
| Jethro Pugh | DT | 6'6" | 260 | 23 | | 2 |
| Dave Edwards | LB | 6'3" | 228 | 28 | 3 | 6 |
| Harold Hays | LB | 6'3" | 225 | 26 | | |
| Chuck Howley | LB | 6'3" | 225 | 31 | 1 | 6 |
| Lee Roy Jordan | LB | 6'2" | 225 | 26 | 3 | 8 |
| Phil Clark | DB | 6'2" | 207 | 22 | 1 | |
| Dick Daniels | DB | 5'9" | 180 | 21 | | |
| Mike Gaechter | DB | 6' | 190 | 27 | 2 | |
| Cornell Green | DB | 6'4" | 208 | 27 | 7 | |
| Mike Johnson | DB | 5'10" | 184 | 23 | 5 | |
| Mel Renfro | DB | 6' | 190 | 25 | 7 | |
| Buddy Dial — Injury | | | | | | |
| Dave Manders — Injury | | | | | | |
| Don Meredith | QB | 6'2" | 205 | 29 | | |
| Craig Morton | QB | 6'4" | 216 | 24 | | |
| Jerry Rhome | QB | 6' | 185 | 25 | | |
| Craig Baynham | HB | 6'1" | 200 | 23 | | 6 |
| Dan Reeves | HB | 6'1" | 200 | 23 | | 66 |
| Les Shy | HB | 6'1" | 200 | 23 | | |
| Don Perkins | FB | 5'10" | 200 | 29 | | 36 |
| Walt Garrison | HB-FB | 6' | 205 | 23 | | |
| Pete Gent | FL | 6'4" | 205 | 24 | | 6 |
| Lance Rentzel | OE-FL | 6'2" | 200 | 23 | | 48 |
| Frank Clarke | TE | 6' | 210 | 34 | | 12 |
| Pettis Norman | TE | 6'3" | 225 | 27 | | 12 |
| Rayfield Wright | TE | 6'7" | 235 | 22 | | |
| Bob Hayes | OE | 6' | 185 | 24 | | 66 |
| Sims Stokes | OE | 6'1" | 198 | 23 | | |
| Harold Deters | K | 6' | 200 | 23 | | 12 |
| Danny Villanueva | K | 5'11" | 200 | 29 | | 56 |

### PHILADELPHIA EAGLES 6-7-1 Joe Kuharich

| Scores of Each Game | | |
|---|---|---|
| 35 | WASHINGTON | 24 |
| 6 | BALTIMORE | 38 |
| 34 | PITTSBURGH | 24 |
| 38 | Atlanta | 7 |
| 27 | SAN FRANCISCO | 28 |
| 14 | St. Louis | 48 |
| 21 | DALLAS | 14 |
| 24 | New Orleans | 31 |
| 17 | Los Angeles | 33 |
| 48 | NEW ORLEANS | 21 |
| 7 | New York | 44 |
| 35 | Washington | 35 |
| 17 | Dallas | 38 |
| 28 | CLEVELAND | 24 |

| Use Name | Pos. | Hgt | Wgt | Age | Int | Pts |
|---|---|---|---|---|---|---|
| Bob Brown | OT | 6'4" | 295 | 24 | | |
| Lane Howell | OT | 6'5" | 272 | 26 | | |
| Randy Beisler | DE-OT | 6'4" | 245 | 22 | | |
| Dick Hart | OG | 6'2" | 250 | 24 | | |
| Jim Skaggs | OG | 6'2" | 252 | 27 | | |
| Bill Stetz | OG | 6'3" | 250 | 23 | | |
| Gordon Wright | OG | 6'3" | 245 | 23 | | |
| Lynn Hoyem | C-OG | 6'4" | 253 | 27 | | |
| Dave Recher | C | 6'1" | 246 | 24 | | |
| Jim Ringo | C | 6'1" | 230 | 36 | | |
| Don Hultz | DE | 6'3" | 242 | 26 | 1 | 6 |
| Gary Pettigrew | DE | 6'4" | 245 | 22 | | |
| Mel Tom | DE | 6'4" | 243 | 26 | | |
| Dean Wink | DE | 6'4" | 246 | 22 | | |
| John Meyers | DT | 6'6" | 276 | 24 | | |
| Floyd Peters | DT | 6'4" | 255 | 32 | 1 | |
| Fred Brown | LB | 6'5" | 232 | 24 | 2 | |
| Ike Kelley | LB | 5'11" | 225 | 23 | 1 | |
| Dave Lloyd | LB | 6'3" | 248 | 31 | 1 | |
| Mike Morgan | LB | 6'4" | 242 | 25 | 1 | |
| Arunas Vasys | LB | 6'2" | 235 | 24 | | |
| Harold Wells | LB | 6'2" | 220 | 28 | 1 | |
| Jim Gray | DB | 6' | 182 | 25 | | |
| Aaron Martin | DB | 6' | 190 | 26 | 2 | |
| Ron Medved | DB | 6'1" | 210 | 23 | 2 | |
| Jim Nettles | DB | 5'9" | 177 | 25 | 4 | 6 |
| Al Nelson | DB | 5'11" | 186 | 23 | | |
| Nate Ramsey | DB | 6'1" | 200 | 26 | | |
| Taft Reed | DB | 6'2" | 200 | 25 | | |
| Joe Scarpati | DB | 5'10" | 185 | 25 | 4 | 6 |
| Bob Shann | DB | 6'1" | 190 | 24 | 1 | |
| Dave Graham — Injury | | | | | | |
| Frank Molden — Knee Injury | | | | | | |
| Benjy Dial | QB | 6'1" | 185 | 24 | | |
| King Hill | QB | 6'3" | 216 | 31 | | |
| Norm Snead | QB | 6'4" | 215 | 27 | | 12 |
| Timmy Brown | HB | 5'10" | 198 | 30 | | 12 |
| Harry Jones | HB | 6'2" | 205 | 22 | | |
| Harry Wilson | HB | 5'11" | 204 | 22 | | |
| Izzy Lang | FB | 6'1" | 232 | 24 | | 30 |
| Tom Woodeshick | HB-FB | 6' | 220 | 25 | | 60 |
| Chuck Hughes | FL | 5'11" | 172 | 24 | | |
| Ron Goodwin | OE-FL | 6' | 180 | 25 | | |
| Ben Hawkins | OE-FL | 6' | 180 | 23 | | 60 |
| Mike Ditka | TE | 6'3" | 235 | 27 | | 12 |
| Pete Emelianchik | TE | 6'2" | 220 | 24 | | |
| Jim Kelly | TE | 6'2" | 218 | 25 | | 24 |
| Dave Lince | TE | 6'6" | 265 | 23 | | |
| Fred Hill | OE | 6'2" | 215 | 24 | | |
| Gary Ballman | FL-OE | 6' | 205 | 27 | | 42 |
| Sam Baker | K | 6'2" | 218 | 35 | | 81 |

### WASHINGTON REDSKINS 5-6-3 Otto Graham

| Scores of Each Game | | |
|---|---|---|
| 24 | Philadelphia | 35 |
| 30 | New Orleans | 10 |
| 38 | NEW YORK | 34 |
| 14 | DALLAS | 17 |
| 20 | Atlanta | 20 |
| 28 | Los Angeles | 28 |
| 13 | BALTIMORE | 17 |
| 21 | ST. LOUIS | 27 |
| 31 | SAN FRANCISCO | 28 |
| 27 | Dallas | 20 |
| 37 | Cleveland | 42 |
| 35 | PHILADELPHIA | 35 |
| 15 | Pittsburgh | 10 |
| 14 | NEW ORLEANS | 30 |

| Use Name | Pos. | Hgt | Wgt | Age | Int | Pts |
|---|---|---|---|---|---|---|
| Mitch Johnson | OT | 6'4" | 250 | 25 | | |
| John Kelly | OT | 6'3" | 250 | 23 | | |
| Jim Snowden | OT | 6'3" | 255 | 25 | | |
| Don Bandy | OG | 6'3" | 250 | 22 | | |
| Vince Promuto | OG | 6'1" | 245 | 29 | | |
| Ray Schoenke | OG | 6'3" | 250 | 25 | | |
| Dave Crossan | C | 6'3" | 245 | 27 | | |
| Len Hauss | C | 6'2" | 235 | 25 | | |
| Heath Wingate | C | 6'2" | 240 | 25 | | |
| Bill Briggs | DE | 6'3" | 250 | 23 | | |
| Carl Kammerer | DE | 6'3" | 243 | 25 | | |
| Ron Snidow | DE | 6'4" | 250 | 25 | | |
| Walt Barnes | DT | 6'3" | 250 | 23 | | |
| Spain Musgrave | DT | 6'4" | 275 | 22 | | |
| Jim Prestel | DT | 6'5" | 275 | 30 | | |
| Joe Rutgens | DT | 6'2" | 255 | 28 | | |
| Ed Breding | LB | 6'4" | 235 | 22 | | 2 |
| Jim Carroll | LB | 6'1" | 230 | 24 | 1 | |
| Chris Hanburger | LB | 6'2" | 218 | 26 | | |
| Larry Hendershot | LB | 6'3" | 240 | 22 | | |
| Sam Huff | LB | 6'1" | 230 | 32 | 2 | |
| Steve Jackson | LB | 6'1" | 225 | 24 | | |
| Sid Williams | LB | 6'2" | 235 | 25 | | |
| Rickie Harris | DB | 6' | 182 | 24 | 1 | |
| Paul Krause | DB | 6'3" | 195 | 25 | 8 | |
| Brig Owens | DB | 5'11" | 190 | 24 | 1 | 8 |
| Lonnie Sanders | DB | 6'3" | 207 | 25 | | |
| Jim Shorter | DB | 5'11" | 185 | 26 | 4 | |
| Tom Walters | DB | 6'2" | 195 | 25 | | |
| Dick Smith | OE-DB | 6' | 205 | 23 | 3 | |
| Sonny Jurgensen | QB | 5'11" | 203 | 33 | | 12 |
| Jim Ninowski | QB | 6'1" | 207 | 31 | | |
| Jerry Allen | HB | 6'1" | 205 | 26 | | 24 |
| Pete Larson | HB | 6'1" | 200 | 23 | | 6 |
| Steve Thurlow | HB | 6'3" | 222 | 24 | | |
| Joe Don Looney | FB-HB | 6'1" | 230 | 24 | | 6 |
| Ray McDonald | FB | 6'4" | 248 | 23 | | 24 |
| A. D. Whitfield | FB | 5'10" | 200 | 23 | | 18 |
| John Burrell | FL | 6'3" | 195 | 27 | | |
| T. J. Jackson | DB-FL | 6' | 180 | 24 | | |
| John Love | DB-FL | 5'11" | 185 | 22 | | 34 |
| Bobby Mitchell | HB-FL | 6' | 196 | 32 | | 42 |
| Pat Richter | TE | 6'5" | 230 | 26 | | |
| Jerry Smith | TE | 6'2" | 208 | 24 | | 72 |
| Charley Taylor | OE | 6'3" | 210 | 26 | | 54 |
| Bruce Alford | K | 6' | 185 | 22 | | 6 |
| Charlie Gogolak | K | 5'10" | 165 | 22 | | 6 |
| Gene Mingo (from MIA-A) | K | 6'1" | 190 | 28 | | 32 |

### NEW ORLEANS 3-11-0 Tom Fears

| Scores of Each Game | | |
|---|---|---|
| 13 | LOS ANGELES | 27 |
| 10 | WASHINGTON | 30 |
| 7 | CLEVELAND | 42 |
| 21 | New York | 27 |
| 10 | Dallas | 14 |
| 13 | San Francisco | 27 |
| 10 | PITTSBURGH | 14 |
| 31 | PHILADELPHIA | 24 |
| 10 | DALLAS | 27 |
| 21 | Philadelphia | 48 |
| 27 | ATLANTA | 24 |
| 20 | St. Louis | 31 |
| 10 | Baltimore | 30 |
| 30 | Washington | 14 |

| Use Name | Pos. | Hgt | Wgt | Age | Int | Pts |
|---|---|---|---|---|---|---|
| Dick Anderson | OT | 6'5" | 245 | 22 | | 2 |
| George Harvey | OT | 6'4" | 245 | 21 | | |
| Jerry Jones | OT | 6'3" | 270 | 23 | | |
| Dave McCormick | OT | 6'6" | 250 | 24 | | |
| Ray Rissmiller | OT | 6'4" | 250 | 25 | | |
| Jerry Sturm | OT | 6'3" | 260 | 30 | | |
| Roy Schmidt | OG | 6'3" | 250 | 25 | | |
| Eli Strand | OG | 6'2" | 250 | 24 | | |
| Del Williams | OG | 6'2" | 245 | 21 | | |
| Joe Wendryhoski | C | 6'2" | 245 | 28 | | |
| Doug Atkins | DE | 6'8" | 270 | 37 | | |
| Jim Garcia | DE | 6'4" | 250 | 24 | | |
| Brian Schweda | DE | 6'3" | 240 | 24 | | |
| Lou Cordileone | DT | 6' | 250 | 30 | | |
| Earl Leggett | DT | 6'3" | 265 | 33 | | |
| Dave Rowe | DT | 6'6" | 265 | 22 | | |
| Mike Tilleman | DT | 6'5" | 260 | 23 | | |
| Jackie Burkett | LB | 6'4" | 228 | 30 | 3 | |
| Bill Cody | LB | 6'1" | 220 | 23 | | |
| Ted Davis | LB | 6'1" | 232 | 25 | | |
| Les Kelley | LB | 6'3" | 233 | 22 | | |
| Dave Simmons | LB | 6'4" | 245 | 24 | 1 | |
| Steve Stonebreaker | LB | 6'3" | 228 | 29 | | |
| Phil Vandersea | LB | 6'3" | 225 | 24 | | |
| Fred Whittingham | LB | 6'1" | 240 | 28 | 1 | |
| Bo Burris | DB | 6'3" | 195 | 22 | | |
| Bruce Cortez | DB | 6' | 175 | 21 | | |
| John Douglas | DB | 6'1" | 195 | 22 | 1 | |
| Ben Hart | DB | 6'2" | 205 | 21 | 1 | |
| Jim Heidel | DB | 6'1" | 185 | 23 | 1 | |
| Obert Logan | DB | 5'10" | 180 | 25 | 3 | |
| George Rose | DB | 5'11" | 190 | 24 | 1 | |
| Dave Whitsell | DB | 6' | 190 | 31 | 10 | 12 |
| Gary Cuozzo | QB | 6'1" | 195 | 26 | | 6 |
| Billy Kilmer | QB | 6' | 204 | 27 | | 6 |
| Gary Wood | QB | 5'11" | 188 | 24 | | |
| Tom Barrington | HB | 6'1" | 213 | 23 | | |
| Charlie Brown | HB | 5'10" | 187 | 21 | | 12 |
| John Gilliam | HB | 6'1" | 190 | 22 | | 12 |
| Jimmy Jordan | HB | 6'1" | 200 | 23 | | |
| Don McCall | HB | 5'11" | 195 | 22 | | 12 |
| Randy Schultz | FB-HB | 5'11" | 210 | 23 | | 12 |
| Jim Taylor | FB | 6' | 215 | 32 | | 12 |
| Ernie Wheelwright (from ATL) | FB | 6'3" | 236 | 30 | | 6 |
| Elijah Nevett | FL | 6' | 185 | 23 | | |
| Walter Roberts | FL | 5'10" | 163 | 25 | | 30 |
| Tom Hall | OE-FL | 6'1" | 195 | 26 | | |
| Vern Burke | TE | 6'4" | 202 | 26 | | |
| Jim Hester | TE | 6'4" | 225 | 22 | | |
| Kent Kramer | TE | 6'5" | 235 | 23 | | 12 |
| Dan Abramowicz | OE | 6'1" | 197 | 22 | | 36 |
| Ray Poage | OE | 6'4" | 205 | 26 | | |
| Charlie Durkee | K | 5'11" | 165 | 23 | | 69 |
| Tom McNeill | K | 6'1" | 195 | 25 | | |

## CAPITOL DIVISION

### DALLAS COWBOYS

**RUSHING**

| Last Name | No. | Yds | Avg | TD |
|---|---|---|---|---|
| Perkins | 201 | 823 | 4.1 | 6 |
| Reeves | 173 | 603 | 3.5 | 5 |
| Garrison | 24 | 146 | 6.1 | 0 |
| Norman | 9 | 91 | 10.1 | 0 |
| Meredith | 28 | 84 | 3.0 | 0 |
| Clarke | 4 | 72 | 18.0 | 0 |
| Shy | 17 | 59 | 3.5 | 0 |
| Morton | 15 | 42 | 2.8 | 0 |
| Baynham | 3 | 6 | 2.0 | 1 |
| Rhome | 2 | −11 | −5.5 | 0 |
| Villanueva | 1 | −15 | −15.0 | 0 |

**RECEIVING**

| Last Name | No. | Yds | Avg | TD |
|---|---|---|---|---|
| Rentzel | 58 | 996 | 17 | 8 |
| Hayes | 49 | 998 | 20 | 10 |
| Reeves | 39 | 490 | 13 | 6 |
| Norman | 20 | 220 | 11 | 2 |
| Perkins | 18 | 116 | 6 | 0 |
| Clarke | 9 | 119 | 13 | 1 |
| Gent | 9 | 88 | 10 | 1 |
| Shy | 3 | 36 | 12 | 0 |
| Baynham | 3 | 13 | 4 | 0 |
| Garrison | 2 | 17 | 9 | 0 |

**PUNT RETURNS**

| Last Name | No. | Yds | Avg | TD |
|---|---|---|---|---|
| Hayes | 24 | 276 | 12 | 1 |
| Rentzel | 6 | 45 | 18 | 0 |
| Renfro | 3 | −1 | 0 | 0 |

**KICKOFF RETURNS**

| Last Name | No. | Yds | Avg | TD |
|---|---|---|---|---|
| Garrison | 20 | 366 | 18 | 0 |
| Baynham | 12 | 331 | 28 | 0 |
| Renfro | 5 | 112 | 22 | 0 |
| Shy | 5 | 96 | 19 | 0 |
| Stokes | 4 | 92 | 23 | 0 |
| Hayes | 1 | 17 | 17 | 0 |
| East | 1 | 0 | 0 | 0 |

**PASSING – PUNTING – KICKING Statistics**

PASSING

| Last Name | Att | Comp | % | Yds | Yd/Att | TD | Int–% | RK |
|---|---|---|---|---|---|---|---|---|
| Meredith | 255 | 128 | 50 | 1834 | 7.2 | 16 | 6 | 8 |
| Morton | 137 | 69 | 50 | 978 | 7.1 | 10 | 7 | |
| Rhome | 18 | 9 | 50 | 86 | 4.8 | 0 | 1–6 | |
| Reeves | 7 | 4 | 57 | 195 | 27.9 | 2 | 1–14 | |

PUNTING

| Last Name | No | Avg |
|---|---|---|
| Villanueva | 67 | 40.4 |

KICKING

| Last Name | XP | Att | % | FG | Att | % |
|---|---|---|---|---|---|---|
| Villanueva | 32 | 34 | 94 | 8 | 19 | 42 |
| Deters | 9 | 10 | 90 | 1 | 4 | 25 |

### PHILADELPHIA EAGLES

**RUSHING**

| Last Name | No. | Yds | Avg | TD |
|---|---|---|---|---|
| Woodeshick | 155 | 670 | 4.3 | 6 |
| Lang | 101 | 336 | 3.4 | 3 |
| T. Brown | 53 | 179 | 3.4 | 1 |
| Snead | 9 | 30 | 3.3 | 2 |
| Jones | 8 | 17 | 2.1 | 0 |
| Ballman | 1 | 17 | 17.0 | 1 |
| Goodwin | 1 | 1 | 1.0 | 0 |

**RECEIVING**

| Last Name | No. | Yds | Avg | TD |
|---|---|---|---|---|
| Hawkins | 59 | 1265 | 21 | 10 |
| Ballman | 36 | 524 | 15 | 6 |
| Woodeshick | 34 | 391 | 12 | 4 |
| Ditka | 26 | 274 | 11 | 2 |
| Lang | 26 | 201 | 8 | 3 |
| T. Brown | 22 | 202 | 9 | 1 |
| Kelly | 21 | 345 | 16 | 4 |
| F. Hill | 9 | 144 | 16 | 0 |
| Goodwin | 6 | 65 | 11 | 0 |
| Jones | 3 | 32 | 11 | 0 |
| Wilson | 2 | 20 | 10 | 0 |

**PUNT RETURNS**

| Last Name | No. | Yds | Avg | TD |
|---|---|---|---|---|
| Martin | 20 | 128 | 6 | 0 |
| Shann | 3 | 17 | 6 | 0 |
| Hughes | 3 | 11 | 4 | 0 |
| Scarpati | 1 | 2 | 2 | 0 |
| Lince | 1 | 0 | 0 | 0 |
| Reed | 1 | 0 | 0 | 0 |

**KICKOFF RETURNS**

| Last Name | No. | Yds | Avg | TD |
|---|---|---|---|---|
| T. Brown | 13 | 301 | 23 | 0 |
| Hawkins | 10 | 250 | 25 | 0 |
| Wilson | 7 | 150 | 21 | 0 |
| Hughes | 7 | 126 | 18 | 0 |
| Shann | 6 | 133 | 22 | 0 |
| Reed | 5 | 111 | 22 | 0 |
| Lince | 3 | 46 | 15 | 0 |
| Ballman | 2 | 43 | 22 | 0 |
| Jones | 2 | 32 | 16 | 0 |
| Gray | 1 | 30 | 30 | 0 |
| F. Brown | 1 | 17 | 17 | 0 |
| Medved | 1 | 7 | 7 | 0 |
| Beisler | 1 | 0 | 0 | 0 |
| Kelley | 1 | 0 | 0 | 0 |
| Ramsey | 1 | 0 | 0 | 0 |
| Vasys | 1 | 0 | 0 | 0 |

**PASSING – PUNTING – KICKING Statistics**

PASSING

| Last Name | Att | Comp | % | Yds | Yd/Att | TD | Int–% | RK |
|---|---|---|---|---|---|---|---|---|
| Snead | 434 | 240 | 55 | 3399 | 7.8 | 29 | 24–6 | 5 |
| K. Hill | 7 | 2 | 29 | 33 | 4.7 | 1 | 0–0 | |
| Dial | 3 | 1 | 33 | 5 | 1.7 | 0 | 0–0 | |
| Lang | 1 | 1 | 100 | 26 | 26.0 | 0 | 0–0 | |

PUNTING

| Last Name | No | Avg |
|---|---|---|
| Baker | 61 | 38.3 |

KICKING

| Last Name | XP | Att | % | FG | Att | % |
|---|---|---|---|---|---|---|
| Baker | 45 | 45 | 100 | 12 | 19 | 63 |

### WASHINGTON REDSKINS

**RUSHING**

| Last Name | No. | Yds | Avg | TD |
|---|---|---|---|---|
| Whitfield | 91 | 384 | 4.2 | 1 |
| Allen | 77 | 262 | 3.4 | 3 |
| McDonald | 52 | 223 | 4.3 | 4 |
| Mitchell | 61 | 189 | 3.1 | 1 |
| Larson | 25 | 84 | 3.4 | 1 |
| Jurgensen | 15 | 46 | 3.1 | 2 |
| Thurlow | 13 | 33 | 2.5 | 0 |
| Looney | 11 | 26 | 2.4 | 1 |

**RECEIVING**

| Last Name | No. | Yds | Avg | TD |
|---|---|---|---|---|
| Taylor | 70 | 990 | 14 | 9 |
| J. Smith | 67 | 849 | 13 | 12 |
| Mitchell | 60 | 866 | 14 | 6 |
| Whitfield | 36 | 494 | 14 | 2 |
| Love | 17 | 248 | 15 | 1 |
| Allen | 11 | 101 | 9 | 1 |
| Thurlow | 10 | 95 | 10 | 0 |
| McDonald | 10 | 60 | 6 | 0 |
| Burrell | 9 | 95 | 11 | 0 |
| Larson | 8 | 45 | 6 | 0 |
| Richter | 1 | 31 | 31 | 0 |
| Looney | 1 | 12 | 12 | 0 |
| Hanburger | 1 | 1 | 1 | 0 |

**PUNT RETURNS**

| Last Name | No. | Yds | Avg | TD |
|---|---|---|---|---|
| Harris | 23 | 208 | 9 | 0 |
| Love | 11 | −5 | −1 | 0 |

**KICKOFF RETURNS**

| Last Name | No. | Yds | Avg | TD |
|---|---|---|---|---|
| Harris | 25 | 580 | 23 | 0 |
| Love | 17 | 422 | 25 | 1 |
| T. Jackson | 7 | 131 | 19 | 0 |
| D. Smith | 4 | 120 | 30 | 0 |
| Looney | 2 | 42 | 21 | 0 |
| Kelly | 2 | 19 | 10 | 0 |
| Allen | 1 | 13 | 13 | 0 |
| Burrell | 1 | 2 | 2 | 0 |
| Briggs | 1 | 1 | 1 | 0 |
| McDonald | 1 | 0 | 0 | 0 |

**PASSING – PUNTING – KICKING Statistics**

PASSING

| Last Name | Att | Comp | % | Yds | Yd/Att | TD | Int–% | RK |
|---|---|---|---|---|---|---|---|---|
| Jurgenson | 508 | 288 | 57 | 3747 | 7.4 | 31 | 16–3 | 1 |
| Ninowski | 18 | 12 | 67 | 123 | 6.8 | 0 | 1–6 | |
| Mitchell | 1 | 1 | 100 | 17 | 17.0 | 0 | 0–0 | |

PUNTING

| Last Name | No | Avg |
|---|---|---|
| Richter | 72 | 41.3 |

KICKING

| Last Name | XP | Att | % | FG | Att | % |
|---|---|---|---|---|---|---|
| Mingo | 20 | 22 | 91 | 4 | 10 | 40 |
| Love | 10 | 11 | 91 | 2 | 7 | 29 |
| Alford | 3 | 4 | 75 | 0 | 2 | 0 |
| Gogolak | 3 | 3 | 100 | 1 | 4 | 25 |
| Owens | 2 | 3 | 67 | 0 | 2 | 0 |

### NEW ORLEANS SAINTS

**RUSHING**

| Last Name | No. | Yds | Avg | TD |
|---|---|---|---|---|
| Taylor | 130 | 390 | 3.0 | 2 |
| Wheelwright | 80 | 241 | 3.0 | 1 |
| Kilmer | 20 | 142 | 7.1 | 0 |
| Barrington | 34 | 121 | 3.6 | 0 |
| Schultz | 32 | 117 | 3.7 | 2 |
| McCall | 21 | 86 | 4.1 | 1 |
| Cuozzo | 19 | 43 | 2.3 | 1 |
| Gilliam | 7 | 41 | 5.9 | 0 |
| McNeill | 4 | 38 | 9.5 | 0 |
| Brown | 8 | 16 | 2.0 | 2 |

**RECEIVING**

| Last Name | No. | Yds | Avg | TD |
|---|---|---|---|---|
| Abramowicz | 50 | 721 | 14 | 6 |
| Taylor | 38 | 251 | 7 | 0 |
| Poage | 24 | 380 | 16 | 0 |
| Gilliam | 22 | 264 | 12 | 1 |
| Kramer | 20 | 207 | 10 | 2 |
| Hall | 19 | 249 | 13 | 0 |
| Roberts | 17 | 384 | 23 | 3 |
| Schultz | 14 | 186 | 13 | 0 |
| Wheelwright | 13 | 107 | 8 | 0 |
| Burke | 8 | 84 | 11 | 0 |
| McCall | 4 | 75 | 19 | 1 |
| Barrington | 4 | 50 | 13 | 0 |
| Brown | 3 | 23 | 8 | 0 |
| Hester | 2 | 10 | 5 | 0 |

**PUNT RETURNS**

| Last Name | No. | Yds | Avg | TD |
|---|---|---|---|---|
| Roberts | 11 | 50 | 5 | 0 |
| Douglas | 2 | 15 | 8 | 0 |
| Gilliam | 7 | 13 | 2 | 0 |
| Brown | 3 | 1 | 0 | 0 |

**KICKOFF RETURNS**

| Last Name | No. | Yds | Avg | TD |
|---|---|---|---|---|
| Roberts | 28 | 737 | 26 | 1 |
| Gilliam | 16 | 481 | 30 | 1 |
| McCall | 7 | 198 | 28 | 0 |
| Barrington | 7 | 113 | 16 | 0 |
| Brown | 5 | 103 | 21 | 0 |
| Jordan | 3 | 56 | 19 | 0 |
| Rose | 1 | 21 | 21 | 0 |
| Douglas | 1 | 17 | 17 | 0 |
| Vandersea | 1 | 13 | 13 | 0 |
| Logan | 1 | 0 | 0 | 0 |
| Nevett | 1 | 0 | 0 | 0 |
| Sturm | 1 | 0 | 0 | 0 |

**PASSING – PUNTING – KICKING Statistics**

PASSING

| Last Name | Att | Comp | % | Yds | Yd/Att | TD | Int–% | RK |
|---|---|---|---|---|---|---|---|---|
| Cuozzo | 260 | 134 | 52 | 1562 | 6.0 | 7 | 12–5 | 9 |
| Kilmer | 204 | 97 | 48 | 1341 | 6.6 | 6 | 11–5 | 15 |
| Wood | 11 | 5 | 46 | 62 | 5.6 | 0 | 0–0 | |
| Barrington | 2 | 0 | 0 | 0 | 0.0 | 0 | 0–0 | |
| McNeill | 1 | 1 | 100 | 24 | 24.0 | 0 | 0–0 | |

PUNTING

| Last Name | No | Avg |
|---|---|---|
| McNeill | 74 | 42.9 |

KICKING

| Last Name | XP | Att | % | FG | Att | % |
|---|---|---|---|---|---|---|
| Durkee | 27 | 27 | 100 | 14 | 32 | 44 |

## CENTURY DIVISION

### CLEVELAND BROWNS 9-5-0  Blanton Collier

**Scores of Each Game**

| | | |
|---|---|---|
| 14 | DALLAS | 21 |
| 14 | Detroit | 31 |
| 42 | New Orleans | 7 |
| 21 | PITTSBURGH | 10 |
| 20 | ST. LOUIS | 16 |
| 24 | CHICAGO | 0 |
| 34 | New York | 38 |
| 34 | Pittsburgh | 14 |
| 7 | Green Bay | 55 |
| 14 | MINNESOTA | 10 |
| 42 | WASHINGTON | 37 |
| 24 | NEW YORK | 14 |
| 20 | St. Louis | 16 |
| 24 | Philadelphia | 28 |

| Use Name | Pos. | Hgt | Wgt | Age | Int | Pts |
|---|---|---|---|---|---|---|
| Monte Clark | OT | 6'6" | 255 | 30 | | |
| John Demarie | OT | 6'3" | 250 | 22 | | |
| Dick Schafrath | OT | 6'3" | 255 | 31 | | |
| Jim Copeland | OG | 6'3" | 230 | 22 | | |
| Gene Hickerson | OG | 6'3" | 248 | 32 | | |
| Joe Taffoni | OG | 6'3" | 245 | 22 | | |
| John Wooten | OG | 6'2" | 250 | 32 | | |
| Fred Hoaglin | C | 6'4" | 240 | 23 | | |
| Bill Glass | DE | 6'5" | 255 | 31 | 1 | |
| Jack Gregory | DE | 6'6" | 245 | 22 | | |
| Paul Wiggin | DE | 6'3" | 245 | 33 | | |
| Walter Johnson | DT | 6'3" | 270 | 24 | | |
| Jim Kanicki | DT | 6'4" | 270 | 25 | | |
| Frank Parker | DT | 6'5" | 270 | 27 | | |
| Billy Andrews | LB | 6' | 225 | 22 | | |
| Johnny Brewer | LB | 6'4" | 235 | 30 | 2 | 6 |
| Jim Houston | LB | 6'2" | 245 | 30 | 3 | 12 |
| Dale Lindsey | LB | 6'3" | 225 | 24 | 1 | |
| Bob Matheson | LB | 6'4" | 240 | 22 | 1 | |
| Erich Barnes | DB | 6'2" | 198 | 32 | 4 | |
| Ben Davis | DB | 5'11" | 185 | 21 | 1 | 6 |
| Ross Fichtner | DB | 6' | 185 | 29 | 4 | |
| Mike Howell | DB | 6'1" | 187 | 24 | 3 | |
| Ernie Kellerman | DB | 6' | 183 | 23 | 1 | |
| Carl Ward | DB | 5'9" | 180 | 23 | 1 | 6 |
| George Youngblood (to NO) | DB | 6'3" | 205 | 22 | | |
| Gary Lane | QB | 6'1" | 210 | 24 | | |
| Frank Ryan | QB | 6'3" | 200 | 31 | | |
| Dick Shiner | QB | 6' | 197 | 25 | | |
| Leroy Kelly | HB | 6' | 200 | 25 | | 78 |
| Larry Conjar | FB | 6' | 215 | 21 | | |
| Ernie Green | FB | 6'2" | 205 | 28 | | 36 |
| Charlie Harraway | FB | 6'2" | 230 | 22 | | |
| Nick Pietrosante | FB | 6'2" | 225 | 30 | | |
| Eppie Barney | FL | 6' | 198 | 23 | | |
| Gary Collins | FL | 6'4" | 215 | 26 | | 42 |
| Ron Green | FL | 6'1" | 200 | 23 | | |
| Clifton McNeil | FL | 6'2" | 185 | 27 | | 12 |
| Ron Duncan | TE | 6'6" | 255 | 24 | | |
| Milt Morin | TE | 6'4" | 250 | 25 | | |
| Ralph Smith | TE | 6'2" | 220 | 28 | | 12 |
| Paul Warfield | OE | 6' | 188 | 24 | | 48 |
| Lou Groza | K | 6'3" | 250 | 43 | | 76 |

### NEW YORK GIANTS 7-7-0  Allie Sherman

| | | |
|---|---|---|
| 37 | St. Louis | 20 |
| 24 | Dallas | 38 |
| 34 | Washington | 38 |
| 27 | NEW ORLEANS | 21 |
| 27 | Pittsburgh | 24 |
| 21 | GREEN BAY | 48 |
| 38 | CLEVELAND | 34 |
| 24 | Minnesota | 27 |
| 7 | Chicago | 34 |
| 28 | PITTSBURGH | 20 |
| 44 | PHILADELPHIA | 7 |
| 14 | Cleveland | 24 |
| 7 | DETROIT | 30 |
| 37 | ST. LOUIS | 14 |

| Use Name | Pos. | Hgt | Wgt | Age | Int | Pts |
|---|---|---|---|---|---|---|
| Francis Peay | OT | 6'5" | 250 | 23 | | |
| Willie Young | OT | 6' | 250 | 24 | | |
| Bookie Bolin | OG | 6'2" | 240 | 27 | | |
| Pete Case | OG | 6'3" | 255 | 26 | | |
| Darrell Dess | OG | 6' | 245 | 31 | 6 | |
| Andy Gross | OG | 6' | 230 | 21 | | |
| Charlie Harper | OG | 6'2" | 250 | 23 | | |
| Chuck Hinton | C | 6'2" | 235 | 24 | | |
| Greg Larson | C | 6'2" | 250 | 28 | | |
| Glen Condren | DE | 6'5" | 250 | 25 | | |
| Rosey Davis | DE | 6'5" | 260 | 25 | | |
| Jim Katcavage | DE | 6'3" | 240 | 32 | | |
| Randy Staten | DE | 6'1" | 225 | 23 | | |
| Bruce Anderson | DT | 6'4" | 250 | 23 | | |
| Roger Anderson | DT | 6'5" | 265 | 24 | | |
| Jim Colvin | DT | 6'2" | 245 | 30 | | |
| Bob Lurtsema | DT | 6'6" | 250 | 25 | | |
| Jim Moran | DT | 6'5" | 275 | 24 | | |
| Ken Avery | LB | 6'1" | 220 | 23 | | |
| Mike Ciccolella | LB | 6'1" | 235 | 23 | | |
| Vince Costello | LB | 6' | 228 | 35 | 4 | |
| Dick Kotite | LB | 6'2" | 230 | 26 | 1 | |
| Bill Swain | LB | 6'2" | 230 | 26 | 1 | |
| Ed Weisacosky | LB | 6' | 236 | 23 | | |
| Freeman White | DB-LB | 6'5" | 225 | 23 | 2 | |
| Henry Carr | DB | 6'3" | 195 | 24 | 1 | |
| Clarence Childs | DB | 6' | 180 | 28 | | |
| Wendell Harris | DB | 5'11" | 185 | 26 | 1 | 2 |
| Dave Hathcock | DB | 6' | 195 | 24 | | |
| Spider Lockhart | DB | 6'2" | 175 | 24 | 5 | |
| Bobby Post | DB | 6'1" | 195 | 22 | | |
| Willie Williams | DB | 6' | 190 | 24 | 1 | |
| Scott Eaton | DB | 6'3" | 195 | 23 | 2 | |
| Earl Morrall | QB | 6'1" | 206 | 33 | | 6 |
| Fran Tarkenton | QB | 6'1" | 190 | 27 | | 12 |
| Allen Jacobs | HB | 6'1" | 215 | 26 | | |
| Randy Minniear | HB | 6' | 200 | 23 | | 12 |
| Bill Triplett | HB | 6'2" | 210 | 28 | | 12 |
| Ernie Koy | FB-HB | 6'2" | 230 | 24 | | 30 |
| Tucker Frederickson | FB | 6'3" | 230 | 24 | | 12 |
| Joe Morrison | HB-FB-FL | 6'1" | 212 | 29 | | 54 |
| Bob Crespino | TE | 6'4" | 225 | 29 | | 6 |
| Aaron Thomas | TE | 6'3" | 210 | 29 | | 54 |
| Del Shofner | OE | 6'3" | 190 | 31 | | 6 |
| Homer Jones | FL-OE | 6'2" | 215 | 26 | | 84 |
| Pete Gogolak | K | 6'2" | 200 | 25 | | 46 |
| Les Murdock | K | 6'3" | 245 | 23 | | 25 |

Don Davis — Injury  
Tom Kennedy — Injury

Jeff Smith — Knee Injury  
Larry Vargo — Knee Injury  
Smith Reed — Military Service

### ST. LOUIS CARDINALS 6-7-1  Charlie Winner

| | | |
|---|---|---|
| 20 | NEW YORK | 37 |
| 28 | Pittsburgh | 14 |
| 38 | DETROIT | 28 |
| 34 | Minnesota | 24 |
| 16 | Cleveland | 20 |
| 48 | PHILADELPHIA | 14 |
| 23 | GREEN BAY | 31 |
| 27 | Washington | 21 |
| 14 | PITTSBURGH | 14 |
| 3 | Chicago | 30 |
| 21 | Dallas | 46 |
| 31 | NEW ORLEANS | 20 |
| 16 | CLEVELAND | 20 |
| 14 | New York | 37 |

| Use Name | Pos. | Hgt | Wgt | Age | Int | Pts |
|---|---|---|---|---|---|---|
| Ernie McMillan | OT | 6'6" | 260 | 29 | | |
| Bob Reynolds | OT | 6'6" | 265 | 26 | | |
| Clyde Williams | OT | 6'2" | 255 | 27 | | |
| Dave O'Brien | OG-OT | 6'3" | 245 | 26 | | |
| Ken Gray | OG | 6'3" | 250 | 31 | | |
| Ed Marcontell (to HOU-A) | OG | 6' | 260 | 23 | | |
| Rick Sortun | OG | 6'2" | 235 | 24 | | |
| Irv Goode | C-OG | 6'4" | 250 | 26 | | |
| Bob DeMarco | C | 6'3" | 240 | 29 | | |
| Dick Kasperek | C | 6'3" | 225 | 23 | | |
| Don Brumm | DE | 6'3" | 245 | 24 | | |
| Joe Robb | DE | 6'3" | 245 | 30 | | |
| Bob Rowe | DE | 6'4" | 255 | 22 | | |
| Dave Long | DT-DE | 6'4" | 235 | 22 | | |
| Sam Silas | DT | 6'4" | 250 | 24 | | |
| Chuck Walker | DT | 6'2" | 245 | 26 | | |
| Fred Heron | DE-DT | 6'4" | 250 | 22 | | |
| Jerry Hillebrand | LB | 6'3" | 240 | 27 | | |
| Bill Koman | LB | 6'2" | 230 | 33 | | |
| Dave Meggyesy | LB | 6'1" | 220 | 25 | | |
| Dale Meinert | LB | 6'2" | 220 | 34 | 1 | |
| Larry Stallings | LB | 6'2" | 230 | 25 | | |
| Mike Strofolino | LB | 6'2" | 230 | 23 | | |
| Mike Barnes | DB | 6'3" | 205 | 22 | | |
| Jimmy Burson | DB | 6' | 180 | 25 | 2 | |
| Pat Fischer | DB | 5'10" | 170 | 27 | 4 | 6 |
| Chuck Latourette | DB | 6' | 190 | 22 | | |
| Phil Spiller | DB | 6' | 195 | 22 | 2 | |
| Jerry Stovall | DB | 6'2" | 205 | 25 | 4 | |
| Bobby Williams | DB | 6'1" | 185 | 25 | 2 | |
| Larry Wilson | DB | 6' | 190 | 29 | 4 | |
| Jim Hart | QB | 6'2" | 195 | 23 | | 18 |
| Charley Johnson | QB | 6' | 190 | 30 | | |
| Charlie Bryant | HB | 6'1" | 207 | 26 | | |
| Roy Shivers | HB | 6' | 200 | 25 | | 6 |
| Johnny Roland | FB-HB | 6'2" | 207 | 24 | | 66 |
| Willie Crenshaw | FB | 6'2" | 230 | 26 | | |
| Bill Thornton | FB | 6'1" | 215 | 27 | | |
| Prentice Gautt | HB-FB | 6' | 210 | 29 | | 12 |
| Bobby Joe Conrad | FL | 6' | 195 | 32 | | 12 |
| Dave Williams | FL | 6'2" | 205 | 22 | | 30 |
| Chuck Logan | TE | 6'4" | 220 | 24 | | |
| Jackie Smith | TE | 6'4" | 215 | 26 | | 54 |
| Ted Wheeler | TE | 6'2" | 230 | 21 | | |
| Billy Gambrell | FL-OE | 5'10" | 175 | 25 | | 12 |
| Jim Bakken | K | 6' | 200 | 26 | | 117 |

### PITTSBURGH STEELERS 4-9-1  Bill Austin

| | | |
|---|---|---|
| 41 | CHICAGO | 13 |
| 14 | ST. LOUIS | 28 |
| 24 | Philadelphia | 34 |
| 10 | Cleveland | 21 |
| 24 | NEW YORK | 27 |
| 21 | DALLAS | 24 |
| 14 | New Orleans | 10 |
| 14 | CLEVELAND | 34 |
| 14 | St. Louis | 14 |
| 20 | New York | 28 |
| 27 | MINNESOTA | 41 |
| 24 | Detroit | 14 |
| 10 | WASHINGTON | 15 |
| 24 | Green Bay | 17 |

| Use Name | Pos. | Hgt | Wgt | Age | Int | Pts |
|---|---|---|---|---|---|---|
| John Brown | OT | 6'2" | 248 | 28 | | |
| Mike Haggerty | OT | 6'4" | 230 | 21 | | |
| Fran O'Brien | OT | 6'1" | 265 | 31 | | |
| Larry Gagner | OG | 6'3" | 240 | 23 | | |
| Bruce Van Dyke | OG | 6'2" | 235 | 23 | | |
| Ralph Wenzel | OG | 6'3" | 240 | 24 | | |
| Sam Davis | OT-OG | 6'1" | 245 | 23 | | |
| Ray Mansfield | C | 6'3" | 250 | 26 | | |
| John Baker | DE | 6'6" | 270 | 32 | 1 | |
| Jerry Mazzanti | DE | 6'3" | 240 | 27 | | |
| Ben McGee | DE | 6'2" | 260 | 25 | 1 | 6 |
| Lloyd Voss | DE | 6'4" | 260 | 25 | 1 | |
| Dick Arndt | DT | 6'5" | 265 | 23 | | |
| Chuck Hinton | DT | 6'5" | 260 | 28 | 6 | |
| Ken Kortas | DT | 6'2" | 280 | 25 | 6 | |
| Rod Breedlove | LB | 6'2" | 225 | 29 | | |
| John Campbell | LB | 6'3" | 225 | 28 | 2 | |
| Ray May | LB | 6'1" | 230 | 22 | | |
| Andy Russell | LB | 6'3" | 215 | 25 | 3 | |
| Bill Saul | LB | 6'4" | 225 | 26 | 1 | |
| Jim Bradshaw | DB | 6'1" | 205 | 28 | | |
| John Foruria | DB | 6'2" | 205 | 22 | | |
| Bob Hohn | DB | 6' | 185 | 26 | 2 | |
| Paul Martha | DB | 6' | 185 | 24 | 4 | |
| Bobby Morgan | DB | 6' | 205 | 27 | | |
| Clendon Thomas | DB | 6'2" | 200 | 30 | 2 | |
| Marv Woodson | DB | 6' | 195 | 24 | 7 | |
| Rich Bader | QB | 6'1" | 190 | 24 | | |
| Bill Nelsen | QB | 6' | 195 | 26 | | |
| Kent Nix | QB | 6'1" | 195 | 23 | | 12 |
| Charlie Bivins (to BUF-A) | HB | 6'2" | 212 | 28 | | 6 |
| Cannonball Butler | HB | 5'10" | 185 | 24 | | |
| Dick Hoak | HB | 5'11" | 190 | 28 | | 12 |
| Don Shy | HB | 6'1" | 215 | 21 | | 30 |
| Willie Asbury | FB | 6'1" | 230 | 24 | | 24 |
| Earl Gros | FB | 6'3" | 230 | 26 | | 6 |
| Roy Jefferson | FL | 6'2" | 195 | 23 | | 24 |
| Jerry Marion | FL | 5'10" | 175 | 22 | | |
| Chet Anderson | TE | 6'3" | 245 | 22 | | 12 |
| John Hilton | TE | 6'5" | 220 | 25 | | 30 |
| Dick Compton | OE | 6'1" | 195 | 27 | | 6 |
| Marshall Cropper | OE | 6'3" | 210 | 23 | | |
| J. R. Wilburn | OE | 6'2" | 190 | 24 | | 30 |
| Mike Clark | K | 6'1" | 200 | 26 | | 71 |
| Jim Elliott | K | 5'11" | 184 | 24 | | |

Wally Hilgenburg — Injury

## CENTURY DIVISION

### CLEVELAND BROWNS

**RUSHING**

| Last Name | No. | Yds | Avg | TD |
|---|---|---|---|---|
| Kelly | 235 | 1205 | 5.1 | 11 |
| E. Green | 145 | 710 | 4.9 | 4 |
| Conjar | 20 | 78 | 3.9 | 0 |
| Pietrosante | 10 | 73 | 7.3 | 0 |
| Ryan | 22 | 57 | 2.6 | 0 |
| Lane | 2 | 21 | 10.5 | 0 |
| Warfield | 2 | 10 | 5.0 | 0 |
| Collins | 1 | 6 | 6.0 | 0 |
| Shiner | 2 | −7 | −3.5 | 0 |
| Harraway | 5 | −14 | −2.8 | 0 |

**RECEIVING**

| Last Name | No. | Yds | Avg | TD |
|---|---|---|---|---|
| E. Green | 39 | 369 | 9 | 2 |
| Warfield | 32 | 702 | 22 | 8 |
| Collins | 32 | 500 | 16 | 7 |
| Kelly | 20 | 282 | 14 | 2 |
| Smith | 14 | 211 | 15 | 1 |
| Morin | 7 | 90 | 13 | 0 |
| Conjar | 6 | 68 | 11 | 0 |
| Pietrosante | 6 | 56 | 9 | 0 |
| McNeil | 3 | 33 | 11 | 2 |
| Barney | 1 | 3 | 3 | 0 |

**PUNT RETURNS**

| Last Name | No. | Yds | Avg | TD |
|---|---|---|---|---|
| Davis | 18 | 229 | 13 | 1 |
| Ward | 6 | 62 | 10 | 0 |
| Kelly | 9 | 59 | 7 | 0 |
| Harraway | 1 | 7 | 7 | 0 |
| Youngblood | 1 | 0 | 0 | 0 |

**KICKOFF RETURNS**

| Last Name | No. | Yds | Avg | TD |
|---|---|---|---|---|
| Davis | 27 | 708 | 26 | 0 |
| Ward | 22 | 546 | 25 | 1 |
| Kelly | 5 | 131 | 26 | 0 |
| Barney | 1 | 11 | 11 | 0 |

**PASSING – PUNTING – KICKING**

| PASSING | Att | Comp | % | Yds | Yd/Att | TD | Int–% | RK |
|---|---|---|---|---|---|---|---|---|
| Ryan | 280 | 136 | 49 | 2026 | 7.2 | 20 | 16– 6 | 7 |
| Lane | 43 | 21 | 49 | 254 | 5.9 | 2 | 1– 2 | |
| Shiner | 9 | 3 | 33 | 34 | 3.8 | 0 | 1–11 | |
| Kelly | 1 | 0 | 0 | 0 | 0.0 | 0 | 0– 0 | |

| PUNTING | No | Avg | | | | | | |
|---|---|---|---|---|---|---|---|---|
| Collins | 57 | 36.5 | | | | | | |
| Kelly | 10 | 40.7 | | | | | | |

| KICKING | XP | Att | % | FG | Att | % |
|---|---|---|---|---|---|---|
| Groza | 43 | 43 | 100 | 11 | 23 | 48 |

### NEW YORK GIANTS

**RUSHING**

| Last Name | No. | Yds | Avg | TD |
|---|---|---|---|---|
| Koy | 146 | 704 | 4.8 | 4 |
| Frederickson | 97 | 311 | 3.2 | 2 |
| Tarkenton | 44 | 306 | 7.0 | 2 |
| Triplett | 58 | 171 | 2.9 | 2 |
| Morrison | 36 | 161 | 4.5 | 2 |
| Minniear | 35 | 98 | 2.8 | 1 |
| Jones | 5 | 60 | 12.0 | 1 |
| Jacobs | 11 | 23 | 2.1 | 0 |
| Morrall | 4 | 11 | 2.8 | 1 |
| Case | 0 | 16 | 0.0 | 0 |
| Young | 0 | 2 | 0.0 | 0 |
| Dess | 0 | 1 | 0.0 | 1 |

**RECEIVING**

| Last Name | No. | Yds | Avg | TD |
|---|---|---|---|---|
| Thomas | 51 | 877 | 17 | 9 |
| Jones | 49 | 1209 | 25 | 13 |
| Morrison | 37 | 524 | 14 | 7 |
| Koy | 32 | 212 | 7 | 1 |
| Frederickson | 19 | 153 | 8 | 0 |
| Crespino | 10 | 125 | 13 | 1 |
| Minniear | 8 | 49 | 6 | 1 |
| Shofner | 7 | 146 | 21 | 1 |
| Triplett | 7 | 69 | 10 | 0 |
| Eaton | 1 | 18 | 18 | 0 |

**PUNT RETURNS**

| Last Name | No. | Yds | Avg | TD |
|---|---|---|---|---|
| Lockhart | 7 | 54 | 8 | 0 |
| Williams | 6 | 28 | 5 | 0 |
| Minniear | 4 | 13 | 3 | 0 |
| Hathcock | 3 | 7 | 2 | 0 |
| Harris | 2 | 0 | 0 | 0 |

**KICKOFF RETURNS**

| Last Name | No. | Yds | Avg | TD |
|---|---|---|---|---|
| Childs | 29 | 603 | 21 | 0 |
| Hathcock | 14 | 315 | 23 | 0 |
| Triplett | 7 | 139 | 20 | 0 |
| Minniear | 6 | 98 | 16 | 0 |
| Jones | 2 | 38 | 19 | 0 |
| Frederickson | 1 | 19 | 19 | 0 |
| Koy | 1 | 18 | 18 | 0 |
| Crespino | 1 | 7 | 7 | 0 |
| Lurtsema | 1 | 7 | 7 | 0 |
| Post | 1 | 0 | 0 | 0 |

**PASSING – PUNTING – KICKING**

| PASSING | Att | Comp | % | Yds | Yd/Att | TD | Int–% | RK |
|---|---|---|---|---|---|---|---|---|
| Tarkenton | 377 | 204 | 54 | 3088 | 8.2 | 29 | 19– 5 | 3 |
| Morrall | 24 | 13 | 54 | 181 | 7.5 | 3 | 1– 4 | |
| Koy | 4 | 3 | 75 | 101 | 25.3 | 1 | 0– 0 | |
| Morrison | 1 | 1 | 100 | 12 | 12.0 | 0 | 0– 0 | |

| PUNTING | No | Avg | | | | | | |
|---|---|---|---|---|---|---|---|---|
| Koy | 40 | 37.7 | | | | | | |
| Morrall | 15 | 31.5 | | | | | | |

| KICKING | XP | Att | % | FG | Att | % |
|---|---|---|---|---|---|---|
| Gogolak | 28 | 29 | 97 | 6 | 10 | 60 |
| Murdock | 13 | 15 | 87 | 4 | 9 | 44 |
| Harris | 2 | 2 | 100 | 0 | 1 | 0 |

### ST. LOUIS CARDINALS

**RUSHING**

| Last Name | No. | Yds | Avg | TD |
|---|---|---|---|---|
| Roland | 234 | 876 | 3.7 | 10 |
| Gautt | 142 | 573 | 4.0 | 1 |
| Crenshaw | 44 | 149 | 3.4 | 0 |
| Smith | 9 | 86 | 9.6 | 0 |
| Shivers | 20 | 64 | 3.2 | 1 |
| Hart | 13 | 36 | 2.8 | 3 |
| Latourette | 2 | 23 | 11.5 | 0 |
| Bryant | 3 | 16 | 5.3 | 0 |
| Thornton | 4 | 9 | 2.3 | 0 |
| D. Williams | 1 | 7 | 7.0 | 0 |

**RECEIVING**

| Last Name | No. | Yds | Avg | TD |
|---|---|---|---|---|
| Smith | 56 | 1205 | 22 | 9 |
| Conrad | 47 | 637 | 14 | 2 |
| D. Williams | 28 | 405 | 14 | 5 |
| Gambrell | 28 | 398 | 14 | 2 |
| Roland | 20 | 269 | 13 | 1 |
| Gautt | 15 | 202 | 13 | 1 |
| Crenshaw | 6 | 30 | 5 | 0 |
| Shivers | 3 | 15 | 5 | 0 |
| Thornton | 1 | 9 | 9 | 0 |

**PUNT RETURNS**

| Last Name | No. | Yds | Avg | TD |
|---|---|---|---|---|
| Spiller | 15 | 124 | 8 | 0 |
| Shivers | 9 | 36 | 4 | 0 |
| Latourette | 6 | 21 | 4 | 0 |
| Roland | 3 | 17 | 6 | 0 |
| C. Williams | 1 | 0 | 0 | 0 |

**KICKOFF RETURNS**

| Last Name | No. | Yds | Avg | TD |
|---|---|---|---|---|
| B. Williams | 24 | 583 | 24 | 0 |
| Bryant | 14 | 324 | 23 | 0 |
| Spiller | 10 | 219 | 22 | 0 |
| Shivers | 9 | 160 | 18 | 0 |
| Stallings | 2 | 39 | 20 | 0 |
| Roland | 2 | 33 | 17 | 0 |
| Crenshaw | 2 | 14 | 7 | 0 |
| Barnes | 1 | 0 | 0 | 0 |
| Fischer | 1 | 0 | 0 | 0 |
| Sortun | 1 | 0 | 0 | 0 |

**PASSING – PUNTING – KICKING**

| PASSING | Att | Comp | % | Yds | Yd/Att | TD | Int–% | RK |
|---|---|---|---|---|---|---|---|---|
| Hart | 397 | 192 | 48 | 3008 | 7.6 | 19 | 30– 8 | 10 |
| Johnson | 29 | 12 | 41 | 162 | 5.6 | 1 | 3– 10 | |
| Roland | 4 | 0 | 0 | 0 | 0.0 | 0 | 1– 25 | |
| Smith | 1 | 0 | 0 | 0 | 0.0 | 0 | 1–100 | |

| PUNTING | No | Avg | | | | | | |
|---|---|---|---|---|---|---|---|---|
| Latourette | 62 | 40.8 | | | | | | |

| KICKING | XP | Att | % | FG | Att | % |
|---|---|---|---|---|---|---|
| Bakken | 36 | 36 | 100 | 27 | 39 | 69 |

### PITTSBURGH STEELERS

**RUSHING**

| Last Name | No. | Yds | Avg | TD |
|---|---|---|---|---|
| Shy | 99 | 341 | 3.4 | 4 |
| Asbury | 80 | 315 | 3.9 | 4 |
| Butler | 90 | 293 | 3.3 | 0 |
| Gros | 72 | 252 | 3.5 | 1 |
| Hoak | 52 | 142 | 2.7 | 1 |
| Nix | 15 | 45 | 3.0 | 2 |
| Bivins | 7 | 23 | 3.3 | 1 |
| Hilton | 1 | 15 | 15.0 | 0 |
| Compton | 1 | 1 | 1.0 | 0 |
| Jefferson | 5 | −11 | −2.2 | 0 |
| Nelsen | 9 | −19 | −2.1 | 0 |

**RECEIVING**

| Last Name | No. | Yds | Avg | TD |
|---|---|---|---|---|
| Wilburn | 51 | 767 | 15 | 5 |
| Compton | 42 | 507 | 12 | 1 |
| Jefferson | 29 | 459 | 16 | 4 |
| Hilton | 26 | 343 | 13 | 5 |
| Gros | 19 | 175 | 9 | 0 |
| Hoak | 17 | 111 | 7 | 1 |
| Shy | 12 | 152 | 13 | 1 |
| Anderson | 8 | 141 | 18 | 2 |
| Butler | 4 | 23 | 6 | 0 |
| Asbury | 3 | 52 | 17 | 0 |
| Bivins | 1 | 24 | 24 | 0 |
| Marion | 1 | 16 | 16 | 0 |
| Cropper | 1 | 11 | 11 | 0 |

**PUNT RETURNS**

| Last Name | No. | Yds | Avg | TD |
|---|---|---|---|---|
| Bradshaw | 16 | 97 | 6 | 0 |
| Thomas | 9 | 34 | 4 | 0 |
| Jefferson | 1 | 10 | 10 | 0 |
| Marion | 1 | 2 | 2 | 0 |
| Shy | 1 | −5 | −5 | 0 |

**KICKOFF RETURNS**

| Last Name | No. | Yds | Avg | TD |
|---|---|---|---|---|
| Shy | 21 | 473 | 23 | 0 |
| Martha | 18 | 403 | 22 | 0 |
| Butler | 10 | 223 | 22 | 0 |
| Russell | 6 | 97 | 16 | 0 |
| Campbell | 1 | 25 | 25 | 0 |
| Hilton | 1 | 0 | 0 | 0 |
| May | 1 | 0 | 0 | 0 |

**PASSING – PUNTING – KICKING**

| PASSING | Att | Comp | % | Yds | Yd/Att | TD | Int–% | RK |
|---|---|---|---|---|---|---|---|---|
| Nix | 268 | 136 | 51 | 1587 | 5.9 | 19 | 19– 7 | 13 |
| Nelsen | 165 | 74 | 45 | 1125 | 6.8 | 10 | 9– 5 | 12 |
| Hoak | 8 | 4 | 50 | 69 | 8.6 | 1 | 1–13 | |
| Clark | 1 | 0 | 0 | 0 | 0.0 | 0 | 0– 0 | |

| PUNTING | No | Avg | | | | | | |
|---|---|---|---|---|---|---|---|---|
| Elliott | 72 | 38.1 | | | | | | |

| KICKING | XP | Att | % | FG | Att | % |
|---|---|---|---|---|---|---|
| Clark | 35 | 35 | 100 | 12 | 22 | 55 |

## CENTRAL DIVISION

### GREEN BAY PACKERS 9-4-1 Vince Lombardi

| Scores of Each Game | | |
|---|---|---|
| 17 | DETROIT | 17 |
| 13 | CHICAGO | 10 |
| 23 | ATLANTA | 0 |
| 27 | Detroit | 17 |
| 7 | MINNESOTA | 10 |
| 48 | New York | 21 |
| 31 | St. Louis | 23 |
| 10 | Baltimore | 13 |
| 55 | CLEVELAND | 7 |
| 13 | SAN FRANCISCO | 0 |
| 17 | Chicago | 13 |
| 30 | Minnesota | 27 |
| 24 | Los Angeles | 27 |
| 17 | PITTSBURGH | 24 |

| Use Name | Pos. | Hgt | Wgt | Age | Int | Pts |
|---|---|---|---|---|---|---|
| Forest Gregg | OT | 6'4" | 250 | 34 | | |
| Bob Skoronski | OT | 6'3" | 245 | 34 | | |
| Steve Wright | OT | 6'6" | 250 | 25 | | |
| Gale Gillingham | OG | 6'3" | 255 | 23 | | |
| Jerry Kramer | OG | 6'3" | 245 | 32 | | |
| Fuzzy Thurston | OG | 6'1" | 245 | 34 | | |
| Ken Bowman | C | 6'3" | 230 | 24 | | |
| Bob Hyland | OG-C | 6'5" | 250 | 22 | | |
| Lionel Aldridge | DE | 6'4" | 245 | 25 | | |
| Bob Brown | DE | 6'5" | 260 | 27 | | |
| Willie Davis | DE | 6'3" | 245 | 34 | | 2 |
| Henry Jordan | DT | 6'3" | 250 | 32 | | |
| Ron Kostelnik | DT | 6'4" | 260 | 27 | | |
| Jim Weatherwax | DT | 6'7" | 260 | 24 | | |

| Use Name | Pos. | Hgt | Wgt | Age | Int | Pts |
|---|---|---|---|---|---|---|
| Lee Roy Caffey | LB | 6'3" | 250 | 27 | 2 | |
| Tommy Crutcher | LB | 6'3" | 230 | 25 | | |
| Jim Flanigan | LB | 6'3" | 230 | 22 | | |
| Ray Nitschke | LB | 6'3" | 240 | 31 | 3 | 6 |
| Dave Robinson | LB | 6'3" | 240 | 26 | 4 | |
| Herb Adderley | DB | 6'1" | 200 | 28 | 4 | 6 |
| Tom Brown | DB | 6'1" | 190 | 26 | 1 | |
| Doug Hart | DB | 6' | 190 | 28 | | |
| Bob Jeter | DB | 6'1" | 205 | 29 | 8 | |
| John Rowser | DB | 6'1" | 180 | 23 | | |
| Willie Wood | DB | 5'10" | 190 | 31 | 4 | |

| Use Name | Pos. | Hgt | Wgt | Age | Int | Pts |
|---|---|---|---|---|---|---|
| Zeke Bratkowski | QB | 6'2" | 210 | 35 | | |
| Don Horn | QB | 6'2" | 195 | 22 | | |
| Bart Starr | QB | 6'1" | 190 | 34 | | |
| Donny Anderson | HB | 6'3" | 210 | 24 | | 54 |
| Elijah Pitts | HB | 6'1" | 205 | 28 | | 36 |
| Travis Williams | HB | 6'1" | 210 | 21 | | 36 |
| Jim Grabowski | FB | 6'2" | 220 | 23 | | 18 |
| Chuck Mercein (from NY) | FB | 6'3" | 230 | 24 | | 8 |
| Ben Wilson | FB | 6' | 225 | 27 | | 12 |
| Carroll Dale | FL | 6'2" | 200 | 29 | | 30 |
| Bob Long | FL | 6'3" | 205 | 26 | | |
| Claudis James | HB-FL | 6'2" | 190 | 23 | | |
| Allen Brown | TE | 6'5" | 235 | 24 | | |
| Dick Capp | TE | 6'3" | 235 | 23 | | |
| Marv Fleming | TE | 6'4" | 235 | 25 | | 6 |
| Boyd Dowler | OE | 6'5" | 225 | 30 | | 24 |
| Max McGee | OE | 6'3" | 210 | 35 | | |
| Don Chandler | K | 6'2" | 210 | 32 | | 96 |

### CHICAGO BEARS 7-6-1 George Halas

| Scores of Each Game | | |
|---|---|---|
| 13 | Pittsburgh | 41 |
| 10 | Green Bay | 13 |
| 17 | Minnesota | 7 |
| 3 | BALTIMORE | 24 |
| 14 | DETROIT | 3 |
| 0 | Cleveland | 24 |
| 17 | LOS ANGELES | 28 |
| 27 | Detroit | 13 |
| 34 | NEW YORK | 7 |
| 30 | ST. LOUIS | 3 |
| 13 | GREEN BAY | 17 |
| 28 | San Francisco | 14 |
| 10 | MINNESOTA | 10 |
| 23 | Atlanta | 14 |

| Use Name | Pos. | Hgt | Wgt | Age | Int | Pts |
|---|---|---|---|---|---|---|
| Randy Jackson | OT | 6'5" | 245 | 23 | | |
| Dan James | OT | 6'4" | 250 | 30 | | |
| Bob Pickens | OT | 6'4" | 258 | 24 | | |
| George Seals | OT | 6'2" | 260 | 24 | | |
| Bob Wetoska | OG | 6'3" | 240 | 29 | | |
| Jim Cadile | OG | 6'3" | 240 | 26 | | |
| Don Croftcheck | OG | 6'1" | 230 | 24 | | |
| Doug Kriewald | OG | 6'4" | 245 | 23 | | |
| Mike Rabold | OG | 6'2" | 250 | 29 | | |
| Mike Pyle | C | 6'3" | 250 | 28 | | |
| Marty Amsler | DE | 6'5" | 260 | 24 | 1 | |
| Ed O'Bradovich | DE | 6'3" | 255 | 27 | | |
| Loyd Phillips | DE | 6'3" | 230 | 22 | | |
| Frank Cornish | DT | 6'6" | 270 | 23 | 2 | |
| Dick Evey | DT | 6'2" | 245 | 26 | | |
| John Johnson | DT | 6'5" | 260 | 26 | | |
| Frank McRae | DT | 6'7" | 270 | 23 | | |

| Use Name | Pos. | Hgt | Wgt | Age | Int | Pts |
|---|---|---|---|---|---|---|
| Doug Buffone | LB | 6'1" | 230 | 23 | 3 | 6 |
| Dick Butkus | LB | 6'3" | 245 | 23 | 1 | |
| Rudy Kuechenberg | LB | 6'2" | 215 | 24 | | |
| Jim Purnell | LB | 6'2" | 238 | 25 | | |
| Mike Reilly | LB | 6'2" | 230 | 24 | | |
| Charlie Brown | DB | 6'1" | 193 | 24 | 1 | |
| Al Dodd | DB | 6' | 180 | 22 | | |
| Curtis Gentry | DB | 6' | 185 | 26 | 4 | |
| Bennie McRae | DB | 6'1" | 180 | 26 | 5 | 12 |
| Richie Petitbon | DB | 6'3" | 205 | 29 | 5 | |
| Joe Taylor | DB | 6'2" | 195 | 26 | 1 | |
| Rosey Taylor | DB | 5'11" | 186 | 28 | 5 | 6 |

| Use Name | Pos. | Hgt | Wgt | Age | Int | Pts |
|---|---|---|---|---|---|---|
| Rudy Bukich | QB | 6'1" | 205 | 36 | | |
| Jack Concannon | QB | 6'3" | 205 | 24 | | 18 |
| Larry Rakestraw | QB | 6'2" | 195 | 25 | | 12 |
| Gale Sayers | HB | 6' | 198 | 24 | | 72 |
| Ronnie Bull | FB-HB | 6' | 200 | 27 | | 6 |
| Ralph Kurek | FB | 6'2" | 210 | 24 | | |
| Andy Livingston | FB | 6' | 234 | 22 | | |
| Brian Piccolo | HB-FB | 6' | 205 | 23 | | |
| Johnny Morris | FL | 5'10" | 180 | 32 | | 6 |
| Duane Allen | TE | 6'2" | 230 | 23 | | |
| Austin Denney | TE | 6'2" | 230 | 23 | | |
| Terry Stoepel | TE | 6'4" | 235 | 22 | | |
| Dick Gordon | OE | 5'11" | 190 | 22 | | 30 |
| Bob Jones | OE | 6'4" | 195 | 22 | | 6 |
| Jim Jones | OE | 6'2" | 187 | 23 | | |
| Bobby Joe Green | K | 5'11" | 175 | 29 | | |
| Mac Percival | K | 6'4" | 217 | 27 | | 65 |

### DETROIT LIONS 5-7-2 Joe Schmidt

| Scores of Each Game | | |
|---|---|---|
| 17 | Green Bay | 17 |
| 31 | CLEVELAND | 14 |
| 28 | St. Louis | 38 |
| 17 | GREEN BAY | 27 |
| 3 | Chicago | 14 |
| 24 | ATLANTA | 3 |
| 45 | San Francisco | 3 |
| 13 | CHICAGO | 27 |
| 10 | Minnesota | 10 |
| 7 | Baltimore | 41 |
| 7 | LOS ANGELES | 31 |
| 14 | PITTSBURGH | 24 |
| 30 | New York | 7 |
| 14 | MINNESOTA | 3 |

| Use Name | Pos. | Hgt | Wgt | Age | Int | Pts |
|---|---|---|---|---|---|---|
| Charlie Bradshaw | OT | 6'6" | 260 | 31 | | |
| Bill Cottrell | OT | 6'3" | 265 | 22 | | |
| Roger Shoals | OT | 6'4" | 255 | 28 | | |
| Randy Winkler | OT | 6'5" | 260 | 24 | | |
| Frank Gallagher | OG | 6'2" | 240 | 24 | | |
| John Gordy | OG | 6'3" | 250 | 31 | | |
| Bob Kowalkowski | OG | 6'3" | 245 | 23 | | |
| Chuck Walton | OG | 6'3" | 250 | 26 | | |
| Ed Flanagan | C | 6'3" | 250 | 23 | | |
| Larry Hand | DE | 6'4" | 245 | 27 | 2 | 12 |
| Lew Kamanu | DE | 6'4" | 245 | 23 | | |
| John McCambridge | DE | 6'4" | 245 | 21 | | |
| Darris McCord | DE | 6'4" | 250 | 34 | 1 | |
| Mike Melinkovich | DE | 6'4" | 245 | 25 | | |
| Alex Karras | DT | 6'2" | 245 | 31 | | |
| Denis Moore | DT | 6'5" | 230 | 23 | | |
| Jerry Rush | DT | 6'4" | 270 | 25 | | |

| Use Name | Pos. | Hgt | Wgt | Age | Int | Pts |
|---|---|---|---|---|---|---|
| Ernie Clark | LB | 6'1" | 220 | 29 | 1 | |
| Ron Goovert | LB | 5'11" | 225 | 23 | | |
| Mike Lucci | LB | 6'2" | 230 | 27 | 2 | 6 |
| Paul Naumoff | LB | 6'1" | 210 | 22 | | |
| Wayne Walker | LB | 6'2" | 225 | 30 | | 26 |
| Lem Barney | DB | 6' | 202 | 21 | 10 | 18 |
| Mike Bass | DB | 6' | 190 | 22 | | |
| Dick LeBeau | DB | 6'1" | 185 | 30 | 4 | |
| Bruce Maher | DB | 5'11" | 190 | 30 | 2 | 2 |
| Wayne Rasmussen | DB | 6'2" | 180 | 25 | | |
| Bobby Thompson | DB | 5'10" | 175 | 27 | | |
| Tom Vaughn | DB | 5'11" | 195 | 24 | 1 | |
| Mike Weger | DB | 6'2" | 195 | 21 | | |
| | | | | | | |
| Johnnie Robinson — Injury | | | | | | |

| Use Name | Pos. | Hgt | Wgt | Age | Int | Pts |
|---|---|---|---|---|---|---|
| Milt Plum | QB | 6'1" | 205 | 33 | | |
| Karl Sweetan | QB | 6'1" | 200 | 24 | | 6 |
| Mel Farr | HB | 6'2" | 208 | 22 | | 36 |
| Bobby Felts | HB | 6'2" | 202 | 24 | | |
| Tom Watkins | HB | 6'1" | 195 | 30 | | 30 |
| Amos Marsh | FB | 6'1" | 220 | 28 | | 18 |
| Tom Nowatzke | FB | 6'3" | 222 | 24 | | 36 |
| Pat Studstill | FL | 6'1" | 175 | 29 | | 12 |
| John Henderson | OE-FL | 6'3" | 190 | 24 | | |
| Jim Gibbons | TE | 6'2" | 220 | 31 | | |
| Ron Kramer | TE | 6'3" | 240 | 32 | | |
| Jerry Zawadzkas | TE | 6'4" | 220 | 20 | | |
| Gail Cogdill | OE | 6'2" | 195 | 30 | | 6 |
| Bill Malinchak | OE | 6'1" | 190 | 23 | | 24 |
| Garo Yepremian | K | 5'8" | 160 | 23 | | 28 |

### MINNESOTA VIKINGS 3-8-3 Bud Grant

| Scores of Each Game | | |
|---|---|---|
| 21 | SAN FRANCISCO | 27 |
| 3 | Los Angeles | 39 |
| 7 | CHICAGO | 17 |
| 24 | ST. LOUIS | 34 |
| 10 | Green Bay | 7 |
| 20 | BALTIMORE | 20 |
| 20 | Atlanta | 21 |
| 27 | NEW YORK | 24 |
| 10 | DETROIT | 10 |
| 10 | Cleveland | 14 |
| 41 | Pittsburgh | 27 |
| 27 | GREEN BAY | 30 |
| 10 | Chicago | 10 |
| 3 | Detroit | 14 |

| Use Name | Pos. | Hgt | Wgt | Age | Int | Pts |
|---|---|---|---|---|---|---|
| Grady Alderman | OT | 6'2" | 240 | 28 | | |
| Bob Breitenstein (from DEN) | OT | 6'3" | 267 | 24 | | |
| Doug Davis | OT | 6'4" | 250 | 23 | | |
| Archie Sutton | OT | 6'4" | 265 | 24 | | |
| Larry Bowie | OG | 6'2" | 255 | 27 | | |
| John Pentecost | OG | 6'2" | 250 | 24 | | |
| Milt Sunde | OG | 6'2" | 250 | 24 | | |
| Jim Vellone | OT-OG | 6'2" | 255 | 23 | | |
| Mick Tingelhoff | C | 6'1" | 237 | 27 | | |
| Carl Eller | DE | 6'6" | 265 | 25 | | |
| Jim Marshall | DE | 6'3" | 235 | 29 | | |
| Archie Simkus | DE | 6'4" | 250 | 24 | | |
| Paul Dickson | DT | 6'5" | 255 | 30 | | |
| Gary Larsen | DT | 6'5" | 255 | 27 | | |
| Alan Page | DT | 6'5" | 255 | 22 | | |
| Jerry Shay | DT | 6'3" | 245 | 23 | | |

| Use Name | Pos. | Hgt | Wgt | Age | Int | Pts |
|---|---|---|---|---|---|---|
| Paul Faust | LB | 6' | 220 | 23 | | |
| Don Hansen | LB | 6'3" | 228 | 23 | | |
| Jim Hargrove | LB | 6'3" | 230 | 22 | 1 | 6 |
| John Kirby | LB | 6'3" | 235 | 25 | | |
| Dave Tobey | LB | 6'3" | 230 | 24 | | |
| Lonnie Warwick | LB | 6'3" | 235 | 25 | 2 | |
| Roy Winston | LB | 6'1" | 230 | 27 | | |
| Al Coleman | DB | 6'1" | 195 | 22 | | |
| Mike Fitzgerald (to NY-ATL) | DB | 5'10" | 180 | 26 | | |
| Dale Hackbart | DB | 6'3" | 210 | 31 | 2 | 6 |
| Jeff Jordan | DB | 6'4" | 190 | 23 | | |
| Karl Kassulke | DB | 6' | 195 | 25 | 2 | |
| Brady Keys (from PIT) | DB | 6' | 185 | 31 | 3 | |
| Earsell Mackbee | DB | 6'1" | 195 | 26 | 5 | 12 |
| Ed Sharockman | DB | 6' | 200 | 27 | 3 | |

| Use Name | Pos. | Hgt | Wgt | Age | Int | Pts |
|---|---|---|---|---|---|---|
| Bob Berry | QB | 5'11" | 190 | 25 | | |
| Joe Kapp | QB | 6'2" | 212 | 29 | | 12 |
| Ron Vander Kelen | QB | 6'1" | 190 | 27 | | 6 |
| Earl Denny | HB | 6'1" | 200 | 22 | | |
| Clint Jones | HB | 6' | 206 | 22 | | 6 |
| Jim Lindsey | HB | 6'2" | 200 | 22 | | |
| Dave Osborn | HB | 6' | 205 | 24 | | 18 |
| Pete Tatman | HB | 6'1" | 220 | 22 | | |
| Bill Brown | FB | 5'11" | 230 | 29 | | 30 |
| Jim Phillips | FL | 6'1" | 195 | 30 | | 18 |
| Bob Grim | DB-FL | 6' | 197 | 22 | | 6 |
| John Beasley | TE | 6'3" | 228 | 22 | | 24 |
| Marlin McKeever | TE | 6'1" | 235 | 27 | | |
| Paul Flatley | OE | 6'1" | 187 | 26 | | |
| Gene Washington | OE | 6'3" | 216 | 23 | | 12 |
| Fred Cox | K | 5'10" | 200 | 28 | | 77 |
| Bobby Walden | K | 6' | 190 | 29 | | |

## CENTRAL DIVISION

### GREEN BAY PACKERS

**RUSHING**

| Last Name | No. | Yds | Avg | TD |
|---|---|---|---|---|
| Grabowski | 120 | 466 | 3.9 | 2 |
| Wilson | 103 | 453 | 4.4 | 2 |
| Anderson | 97 | 402 | 4.1 | 6 |
| Pitts | 77 | 247 | 3.2 | 6 |
| Williams | 35 | 188 | 5.4 | 1 |
| Starr | 21 | 90 | 4.3 | 0 |
| Mercein | 14 | 46 | 4.0 | 1 |
| Dale | 1 | 9 | 9.0 | 0 |
| Bratkowski | 5 | 6 | 1.2 | 0 |
| Horn | 1 | −2 | −2.0 | 0 |

**RECEIVING**

| Last Name | No. | Yds | Avg | TD |
|---|---|---|---|---|
| Dowler | 54 | 836 | 15 | 4 |
| Dale | 35 | 738 | 21 | 5 |
| Anderson | 22 | 331 | 15 | 3 |
| Pitts | 15 | 210 | 14 | 0 |
| Wilson | 14 | 88 | 6 | 0 |
| Grabowski | 12 | 171 | 14 | 1 |
| Fleming | 10 | 126 | 13 | 1 |
| Long | 8 | 96 | 12 | 0 |
| Williams | 5 | 80 | 16 | 1 |
| A. Brown | 3 | 43 | 14 | 0 |
| McGee | 3 | 33 | 11 | 0 |
| Mercein | 1 | 6 | 6 | 0 |

**PUNT RETURNS**

| Last Name | No. | Yds | Avg | TD |
|---|---|---|---|---|
| Anderson | 9 | 98 | 11 | 0 |
| T. Brown | 9 | 40 | 4 | 0 |
| Pitts | 9 | 16 | 2 | 0 |
| Wood | 12 | 3 | 0 | |

**KICKOFF RETURNS**

| Last Name | No. | Yds | Avg | TD |
|---|---|---|---|---|
| Williams | 18 | 739 | 41 | 4 |
| Anderson | 11 | 226 | 21 | 0 |
| Adderley | 10 | 207 | 21 | 0 |
| Crutcher | 3 | 48 | 16 | 0 |
| A. Brown | 1 | 13 | 13 | 0 |
| Hart | 1 | 8 | 8 | 0 |
| Robinson | 1 | 0 | 0 | 0 |
| Wood | 1 | 0 | 0 | 0 |

**PASSING – PUNTING – KICKING**

PASSING

| Last Name | Att | Comp | % | Yds | Yd/Att | TD | Int–% | RK |
|---|---|---|---|---|---|---|---|---|
| Starr | 210 | 115 | 55 | 1823 | 8.7 | 9 | 17–8 | 6 |
| Bratkowski | 94 | 53 | 56 | 724 | 7.7 | 5 | 9–10 | |
| Horn | 24 | 12 | 50 | 171 | 7.1 | 1 | 1–4 | |
| Anderson | 2 | 1 | 50 | 19 | 9.5 | 0 | 0–0 | |
| Pitts | 1 | 1 | 100 | 21 | 21.0 | 0 | 0–0 | |

PUNTING

| Last Name | No | Avg |
|---|---|---|
| Anderson | 65 | 36.6 |
| Chandler | 1 | 31.0 |

KICKING

| Last Name | XP | Att | % | FG | Att | % |
|---|---|---|---|---|---|---|
| Chandler | 39 | 39 | 100 | 19 | 29 | 66 |
| Mercein | 2 | 3 | 67 | 0 | 1 | 0 |

### CHICAGO BEARS

**RUSHING**

| Last Name | No. | Yds | Avg | TD |
|---|---|---|---|---|
| Sayers | 186 | 880 | 4.7 | 7 |
| Piccolo | 87 | 317 | 3.6 | 0 |
| Concannon | 67 | 279 | 4.2 | 3 |
| Bull | 61 | 176 | 2.9 | 0 |
| Kurek | 37 | 112 | 3.0 | 0 |
| Rakestraw | 11 | 42 | 3.8 | 2 |
| Livingston | 28 | 41 | 1.5 | 0 |
| J. Jones | 4 | 19 | 4.8 | 0 |
| Morris | 1 | 6 | 6.0 | 0 |
| Gordon | 3 | −7 | −2.3 | 0 |
| Bukich | 4 | −13 | −3.3 | 0 |

**RECEIVING**

| Last Name | No. | Yds | Avg | TD |
|---|---|---|---|---|
| Gordon | 31 | 534 | 17 | 5 |
| Morris | 20 | 231 | 12 | 1 |
| Bull | 18 | 250 | 14 | 1 |
| Sayers | 16 | 126 | 8 | 1 |
| Piccolo | 13 | 103 | 8 | 0 |
| Denny | 12 | 113 | 9 | 0 |
| J. Jones | 7 | 138 | 20 | 0 |
| Livingston | 5 | 62 | 12 | 0 |
| Kurek | 5 | 30 | 6 | 0 |
| B. Jones | 3 | 80 | 27 | 1 |
| Stoepel | 1 | 6 | 6 | 0 |

**PUNT RETURNS**

| Last Name | No. | Yds | Avg | TD |
|---|---|---|---|---|
| Gordon | 12 | 82 | 7 | 0 |
| Sayers | 3 | 80 | 27 | 1 |
| Morris | 4 | 24 | 6 | 0 |
| Dodd | 3 | 8 | 3 | 0 |

**KICKOFF RETURNS**

| Last Name | No. | Yds | Avg | TD |
|---|---|---|---|---|
| Sayers | 16 | 603 | 38 | 3 |
| Gordon | 16 | 397 | 25 | 0 |
| Kurek | 5 | 81 | 16 | 0 |
| Dodd | 3 | 34 | 11 | 0 |
| Brown | 2 | 34 | 17 | 0 |
| J. Taylor | 1 | 8 | 8 | 0 |
| Jackson | 1 | 0 | 0 | 0 |
| Kriewald | 1 | 0 | 0 | 0 |
| Kuechenberg | 1 | 0 | 0 | 0 |
| Stoepel | 1 | 0 | 0 | 0 |

**PASSING – PUNTING – KICKING**

PASSING

| Last Name | Att | Comp | % | Yds | Yd/Att | TD | Int–% | RK |
|---|---|---|---|---|---|---|---|---|
| Concannon | 186 | 92 | 49 | 1260 | 6.8 | 6 | 14–8 | 17 |
| Rakestraw | 44 | 21 | 48 | 228 | 5.2 | 2 | 2–5 | |
| Bukich | 33 | 18 | 55 | 185 | 5.6 | 0 | 2–6 | |
| Sayers | 5 | 0 | 0 | 0 | 0.0 | 0 | 0–0 | |

PUNTING

| Last Name | No | Avg |
|---|---|---|
| Green | 79 | 42.9 |

KICKING

| Last Name | XP | Att | % | FG | Att | % |
|---|---|---|---|---|---|---|
| Percival | 26 | 29 | 90 | 13 | 26 | 50 |

### DETROIT LIONS

**RUSHING**

| Last Name | No. | Yds | Avg | TD |
|---|---|---|---|---|
| Farr | 206 | 860 | 4.2 | 3 |
| Watkins | 106 | 361 | 3.4 | 4 |
| Nowatzke | 70 | 288 | 4.1 | 4 |
| Marsh | 58 | 229 | 3.9 | 2 |
| Sweetan | 17 | 93 | 5.5 | 1 |
| Felts | 10 | 66 | 6.6 | 0 |
| Plum | 6 | 5 | 0.8 | 0 |
| Flanagan | 0 | 5 | 0.0 | 0 |

**RECEIVING**

| Last Name | No. | Yds | Avg | TD |
|---|---|---|---|---|
| Farr | 39 | 317 | 8 | 3 |
| Malinchak | 26 | 397 | 15 | 4 |
| Cogdill | 21 | 322 | 15 | 0 |
| Nowatzke | 21 | 145 | 7 | 2 |
| Henderson | 13 | 144 | 11 | 0 |
| Studstill | 10 | 162 | 16 | 2 |
| Gibbons | 10 | 107 | 11 | 0 |
| Watkins | 8 | 93 | 12 | 1 |
| Marsh | 7 | 103 | 15 | 1 |
| Kramer | 4 | 40 | 10 | 0 |
| Walton | 1 | −4 | −4 | 0 |

**PUNT RETURNS**

| Last Name | No. | Yds | Avg | TD |
|---|---|---|---|---|
| Watkins | 15 | 57 | 4 | 0 |
| Thompson | 9 | 20 | 2 | 0 |
| Barney | 4 | 14 | 4 | 0 |
| Vaughn | 4 | 7 | 2 | 0 |
| Weger | 1 | 0 | 0 | 0 |
| Felts | 1 | −1 | −1 | 0 |

**KICKOFF RETURNS**

| Last Name | No. | Yds | Avg | TD |
|---|---|---|---|---|
| Vaughn | 16 | 446 | 28 | 0 |
| Watkins | 20 | 411 | 21 | 0 |
| Thompson | 4 | 134 | 34 | 0 |
| Barney | 5 | 87 | 17 | 0 |
| Goovert | 2 | 40 | 20 | 0 |
| Weger | 2 | 27 | 14 | 0 |
| Zawadzkas | 1 | 0 | 0 | 0 |

**PASSING – PUNTING – KICKING**

PASSING

| Last Name | Att | Comp | % | Yds | Yd/Att | TD | Int–% | RK |
|---|---|---|---|---|---|---|---|---|
| Sweetan | 177 | 74 | 42 | 901 | 5.1 | 10 | 11–6 | 18 |
| Plum | 172 | 86 | 50 | 925 | 5.4 | 4 | 8–5 | 14 |
| Farr | 2 | 0 | 0 | 0 | 0.0 | 0 | 0–0 | |

PUNTING

| Last Name | No | Avg |
|---|---|---|
| Barney | 47 | 37.4 |
| Studstill | 36 | 44.5 |

KICKING

| Last Name | XP | Att | % | FG | Att | % |
|---|---|---|---|---|---|---|
| Yepremian | 22 | 23 | 96 | 2 | 6 | 33 |
| Walker | 11 | 11 | 100 | 1 | 5 | 33 |

### MINNESOTA VIKINGS

**RUSHING**

| Last Name | No. | Yds | Avg | TD |
|---|---|---|---|---|
| Osborn | 215 | 972 | 4.5 | 2 |
| Brown | 185 | 610 | 3.3 | 5 |
| Kapp | 27 | 167 | 6.2 | 2 |
| Jones | 13 | 23 | 1.8 | 0 |
| Grim | 1 | 20 | 20.0 | 0 |
| Lindsey | 4 | 10 | 2.5 | 0 |
| Vander Kelen | 9 | 9 | 1.0 | 1 |

**RECEIVING**

| Last Name | No. | Yds | Avg | TD |
|---|---|---|---|---|
| Osborn | 34 | 272 | 8 | 1 |
| Flatley | 23 | 232 | 10 | 0 |
| Brown | 22 | 263 | 12 | 0 |
| Phillips | 21 | 352 | 17 | 3 |
| McKeever | 14 | 184 | 13 | 0 |
| Washington | 13 | 384 | 30 | 2 |
| Beasley | 13 | 120 | 9 | 4 |
| Grim | 6 | 108 | 18 | 1 |
| Lindsey | 4 | 36 | 9 | 0 |

**PUNT RETURNS**

| Last Name | No. | Yds | Avg | TD |
|---|---|---|---|---|
| Grim | 25 | 101 | 4 | 0 |
| Keys | 7 | 7 | 1 | 0 |
| Fitzgerald | 2 | 4 | 2 | 0 |
| Sharockman | 4 | 0 | 0 | 0 |

**KICKOFF RETURNS**

| Last Name | No. | Yds | Avg | TD |
|---|---|---|---|---|
| Jones | 25 | 597 | 24 | 1 |
| Grim | 22 | 493 | 22 | 0 |
| Fitzgerald | 12 | 240 | 20 | 0 |
| Lindsey | 3 | 71 | 24 | 0 |
| Sharockman | 1 | 22 | 22 | 0 |
| Denny | 1 | 18 | 18 | 0 |
| Tatman | 1 | 14 | 14 | 0 |

**PASSING – PUNTING – KICKING**

PASSING

| Last Name | Att | Comp | % | Yds | Yd/Att | TD | Int–% | RK |
|---|---|---|---|---|---|---|---|---|
| Kapp | 214 | 102 | 48 | 1386 | 6.5 | 8 | 17–8 | 19 |
| Vander Kelen | 115 | 45 | 39 | 522 | 4.5 | 3 | 7–6 | |
| Berry | 7 | 3 | 43 | 43 | 6.1 | 0 | 0–0 | |

PUNTING

| Last Name | No | Avg |
|---|---|---|
| Walden | 75 | 41.6 |

KICKING

| Last Name | XP | Att | % | FG | Att | % |
|---|---|---|---|---|---|---|
| Cox | 26 | 26 | 100 | 17 | 33 | 52 |

| Scores of Each Game | | | Use Name | Pos. | Hgt | Wgt | Age | Int | Pts |

## COASTAL DIVISION

### LOS ANGELES RAMS 11-1-2 George Allen

| | Score | | Use Name | Pos. | Hgt | Wgt | Age | Int | Pts |
|---|---|---|---|---|---|---|---|---|---|
| 27 | New Orleans | 13 | Joe Carollo | OT | 6'2" | 258 | 27 | | |
| 39 | MINNESOTA | 3 | Charley Cowan | OT | 6'4" | 265 | 29 | | |
| 35 | Dallas | 13 | Bob Nichols | OT | 6'3" | 250 | 24 | | |
| 24 | SAN FRANCISCO | 27 | Don Chuy | OG | 6'1" | 255 | 26 | | |
| 24 | Baltimore | 24 | Tom Mack | OG | 6'3" | 245 | 23 | | |
| 28 | WASHINGTON | 28 | Joe Scibelli | OG | 6'1" | 255 | 28 | | |
| 28 | Chicago | 17 | Ken Iman | C | 6'1" | 240 | 28 | | |
| 17 | San Francisco | 7 | George Burman | OG-C | 6'3" | 255 | 24 | | |
| 33 | PHILADELPHIA | 17 | Deacon Jones | DE | 6'5" | 260 | 28 | | 2 |
| 31 | Atlanta | 3 | Lamar Lundy | DE | 6'7" | 260 | 32 | | |
| 31 | Detroit | 7 | Gregg Schumacher | DE | 6'2" | 240 | 25 | | |
| 20 | ATLANTA | 3 | Roger Brown | DT | 6'5" | 300 | 30 | | |
| 27 | GREEN BAY | 24 | Merlin Olsen | DT | 6'5" | 276 | 26 | | |
| 34 | BALTIMORE | 10 | Diron Talbert | DE-DT | 6'3" | 238 | 23 | | |
| | | | Dave Cahill | DE-DT | 6'3" | 238 | 25 | | |

| Use Name | Pos. | Hgt | Wgt | Age | Int | Pts |
|---|---|---|---|---|---|---|
| Maxie Baughan | LB | 6'1" | 230 | 29 | 4 | |
| Gene Breen | LB | 6'2" | 230 | 26 | | |
| Tony Guillory | LB | 6'4" | 236 | 24 | | |
| Jack Pardee | LB | 6'2" | 230 | 31 | 6 | 12 |
| Myron Pottios | LB | 6'2" | 240 | 27 | 1 | |
| Doug Woodlief | LB | 6'3" | 230 | 23 | 2 | |
| Claude Crabb | DB | 6'1" | 192 | 27 | 1 | |
| Irv Cross | DB | 6'1" | 195 | 28 | 2 | |
| Willie Daniel | DB | 5'11" | 190 | 29 | 2 | |
| Chuck Lamson | DB | 6' | 195 | 28 | 2 | |
| Ed Meador | DB | 5'11" | 200 | 30 | 8 | 12 |
| Clancy Williams | DB | 6'2" | 198 | 24 | 4 | |
| Kelton Winston | DB | 6' | 195 | 26 | | |

Hal Bedsole — Injury
Henry Dyer — Injury
Rosey Grier — Injury

| Use Name | Pos. | Hgt | Wgt | Age | Int | Pts |
|---|---|---|---|---|---|---|
| Roman Gabriel | QB | 6'4" | 230 | 27 | | 36 |
| Bill Munson | QB | 6'2" | 200 | 25 | | |
| Willie Ellison | HB | 6'1" | 207 | 22 | | |
| Les Josephson | HB | 6' | 220 | 25 | | 48 |
| Tommy Mason | HB | 6' | 190 | 28 | | |
| Dick Bass | FB | 5'10" | 195 | 30 | | 42 |
| Jim Stiger | FB | 5'11" | 214 | 26 | | |
| Bernie Casey | FL | 6'4" | 210 | 28 | | 48 |
| Billy Truax | TE | 6'5" | 235 | 24 | | 24 |
| Dave Pivec | LB-TE | 6'3" | 240 | 23 | | 6 |
| Bucky Pope | OE | 6'5" | 205 | 24 | | 12 |
| Jack Snow | OE | 6'2" | 195 | 24 | | 48 |
| Wendell Tucker | OE | 5'10" | 185 | 23 | | |
| Bruce Gossett | K | 6'2" | 230 | 24 | | 108 |
| Jon Kilgore | K | 6'1" | 205 | 23 | | |

### BALTIMORE COLTS 11-1-2 Don Shula

| | Score | | Use Name | Pos. | Hgt | Wgt | Age | Int | Pts |
|---|---|---|---|---|---|---|---|---|---|
| 38 | ATLANTA | 31 | Sam Ball | OT | 6'4" | 240 | 23 | | |
| 38 | Philadelphia | 6 | Jim Parker | OT | 6'3" | 275 | 33 | | |
| 41 | SAN FRANCISCO | 7 | Bob Vogel | OT | 6'5" | 250 | 25 | | |
| 24 | Chicago | 3 | Norman Davis | OG | 6'3" | 250 | 22 | | |
| 24 | LOS ANGELES | 24 | Dale Memmelaar | OG | 6'2" | 246 | 30 | | |
| 20 | Minnesota | 20 | Glenn Ressler | OG | 6'3" | 250 | 23 | | |
| 17 | Washington | 13 | Dan Sullivan | OG | 6'3" | 250 | 28 | | |
| 13 | GREEN BAY | 10 | Dick Szymanski | C | 6'3" | 235 | 35 | | |
| 49 | Atlanta | 7 | Bill Curry | LB-C | 6'2" | 235 | 24 | | |
| 41 | DETROIT | 7 | Ordell Braase | DE | 6'4" | 245 | 35 | | 6 |
| 26 | San Francisco | 9 | Roy Hilton | DE | 6'6" | 240 | 24 | | |
| 23 | DALLAS | 17 | Lou Michaels | DE | 6'2" | 250 | 31 | | 106 |
| 30 | NEW ORLEANS | 10 | Bubba Smith | DE | 6'7" | 295 | 22 | | |
| 10 | Los Angeles | 34 | Fred Miller | DT | 6'3" | 250 | 26 | | |
| | | | Billy Ray Smith | DT | 6'4" | 250 | 32 | | |
| | | | Andy Stynchula | DE-DT | 6'3" | 250 | 28 | | |

| Use Name | Pos. | Hgt | Wgt | Age | Int | Pts |
|---|---|---|---|---|---|---|
| Barry Brown | LB | 6'3" | 235 | 24 | | |
| Mike Curtis | LB | 6'2" | 232 | 24 | 1 | |
| Dennis Gaubatz | LB | 6'2" | 232 | 26 | 2 | |
| Ron Porter | LB | 6'3" | 232 | 22 | 1 | |
| Don Shinnick | LB | 6' | 228 | 32 | 3 | |
| Bobby Boyd | DB | 5'10" | 192 | 29 | 6 | 6 |
| George Harold | DB | 6'3" | 194 | 25 | | |
| Alvin Haymond | DB | 6' | 194 | 25 | 2 | |
| Jerry Logan | DB | 6'1" | 190 | 26 | 4 | 6 |
| Lenny Lyles | DB | 6'2" | 204 | 31 | 5 | 6 |
| Preston Pearson | DB | 6'1" | 190 | 22 | | |
| Charlie Stukes | DB | 6'3" | 212 | 23 | 2 | |
| Rick Volk | DB | 6'3" | 195 | 22 | 6 | 6 |
| Jim Welch | HB-DB | 6' | 196 | 29 | | |

| Use Name | Pos. | Hgt | Wgt | Age | Int | Pts |
|---|---|---|---|---|---|---|
| Johnny Unitas | QB | 6'1" | 196 | 34 | | |
| Jim Ward | QB | 6'2" | 195 | 23 | | |
| Tom Matte | HB | 6' | 214 | 28 | | 72 |
| Lenny Moore | HB | 6'1" | 198 | 34 | | 24 |
| Jerry Hill | FB | 5'11" | 215 | 27 | | 12 |
| Tony Lorick | FB | 6'1" | 217 | 25 | | 36 |
| Don Alley | FL | 6'2" | 200 | 21 | | |
| Jimmy Orr | FL | 5'11" | 185 | 31 | | 6 |
| Willie Richardson | FL | 6'2" | 198 | 27 | | 48 |
| John Mackey | TE | 6'3" | 224 | 25 | | 18 |
| Butch Wilson | TE | 6'2" | 228 | 25 | | |
| Ray Berry | OE | 6'2" | 190 | 34 | | 6 |
| Ray Perkins | OE | 6' | 183 | 25 | | 12 |
| Alex Hawkins (from ATL) | FL-OE | 6'1" | 186 | 30 | | 24 |
| David Lee | K | 6'4" | 215 | 23 | | |

### SAN FRANCISCO FORTY-NINERS 7-7-0 Jack Christiansen

| | Score | | Use Name | Pos. | Hgt | Wgt | Age | Int | Pts |
|---|---|---|---|---|---|---|---|---|---|
| 27 | Minnesota | 21 | Dave Hettema | OT | 6'4" | 247 | 25 | | |
| 38 | ATLANTA | 7 | Walt Rock | OT | 6'5" | 255 | 26 | | |
| 7 | Baltimore | 41 | Len Rohde | OT | 6'4" | 250 | 29 | | |
| 27 | Los Angeles | 24 | Elmer Collett | OG | 6'4" | 230 | 22 | | |
| 28 | Philadelphia | 27 | Howard Mudd | OG | 6'3" | 254 | 25 | | |
| 27 | NEW ORLEANS | 13 | Don Parker | OG | 6'3" | 235 | 22 | | |
| 3 | DETROIT | 45 | John Thomas | OG | 6'4" | 250 | 32 | | |
| 7 | LOS ANGELES | 17 | Bruce Bosley | C | 6'2" | 244 | 33 | | |
| 28 | Washington | 31 | Joe Cerne | C | 6'2" | 240 | 24 | | |
| 0 | Green Bay | 13 | Stan Hindman | DE | 6'3" | 232 | 23 | | |
| 9 | BALTIMORE | 26 | Tom Holzer | DE | 6'4" | 250 | 22 | | |
| 14 | CHICAGO | 28 | Walter Johnson | DE | 6'4" | 225 | 23 | | |
| 34 | Atlanta | 28 | Clark Miller | DE | 6'5" | 247 | 28 | | 1 |
| 24 | DALLAS | 16 | Charlie Johnson | DT | 6'2" | 265 | 23 | | |
| | | | Charlie Krueger | DT | 6'4" | 260 | 31 | | |
| | | | Roland Lakes | DT | 6'4" | 280 | 27 | | |

| Use Name | Pos. | Hgt | Wgt | Age | Int | Pts |
|---|---|---|---|---|---|---|
| Ed Beard | LB | 6'2" | 226 | 27 | | |
| Bob Harrison | LB | 6'2" | 228 | 30 | | |
| Matt Hazeltine | LB | 6'1" | 230 | 34 | | |
| Frank Nunley | LB | 6'2" | 220 | 21 | 1 | |
| Dave Wilcox | LB | 6'3" | 234 | 24 | 2 | |
| Kermit Alexander | DB | 5'11" | 180 | 26 | 5 | |
| George Donnelly | DB | 6'3" | 210 | 24 | | |
| Goose Gonsoulin | DB | 6'3" | 210 | 29 | 3 | |
| Jim Jackson | DB | 6' | 193 | 23 | 1 | |
| Jim Johnson | DB | 6'2" | 187 | 29 | 2 | |
| Mel Phillips | DB | 6' | 192 | 25 | 1 | |
| Al Randolph | DB | 6'2" | 192 | 23 | | |
| Wayne Trimble | DB | 6'3" | 203 | 21 | | |

Kay McFarland — Injury

| Use Name | Pos. | Hgt | Wgt | Age | Int | Pts |
|---|---|---|---|---|---|---|
| John Brodie | QB | 6'1" | 210 | 32 | | 6 |
| George Mira | QB | 5'11" | 190 | 25 | | |
| Steve Spurrier | QB | 6'2" | 203 | 22 | | |
| John David Crow | HB | 6'2" | 224 | 32 | | 30 |
| Doug Cunningham | HB | 5'11" | 185 | 21 | | 12 |
| Dave Kopay | HB | 6'2" | 218 | 25 | | |
| Bill Tucker | FB-HB | 6'2" | 222 | 23 | | |
| Gary Lewis | FB | 6'3" | 230 | 25 | | 42 |
| Ken Willard | FB | 6'2" | 230 | 24 | | 36 |
| Chip Myers | FL | 6'4" | 185 | 22 | | |
| Wayne Swinford | FL | 6' | 192 | 24 | | |
| Dick Witcher | TE-FL | 6'3" | 204 | 22 | | 18 |
| Dave Olerich | TE | 6'1" | 220 | 22 | | |
| Monte Stickles | TE | 6'4" | 235 | 29 | | |
| Bob Windsor | TE | 6'4" | 223 | 24 | | 18 |
| Dave Parks | OE | 6'2" | 207 | 25 | | 12 |
| Sonny Randle | OE | 6'2" | 190 | 31 | | 24 |
| Tommy Davis | K | 6' | 220 | 32 | | 75 |

### ATLANTA FALCONS 1-12-1 Norb Hecker

| | Score | | Use Name | Pos. | Hgt | Wgt | Age | Int | Pts |
|---|---|---|---|---|---|---|---|---|---|
| 31 | Baltimore | 38 | Errol Linden | OT | 6'5" | 260 | 29 | | |
| 7 | San Francisco | 38 | Bill Sandeman (from NO) | OT | 6'6" | 250 | 24 | | |
| 0 | Green Bay | 38 | Don Talbert | OT | 6'5" | 255 | 27 | | |
| 7 | PHILADELPHIA | 38 | Jim Simon | OG-OT | 6'5" | 240 | 26 | | |
| 20 | WASHINGTON | 20 | Ed Cook | OG | 6'2" | 250 | 35 | | |
| 3 | Detroit | 24 | Dan Grimm | OG | 6'3" | 245 | 26 | | |
| 21 | MINNESOTA | 20 | Tom Harmon | OG | 6'4" | 238 | 25 | | |
| 7 | Dallas | 37 | Lou Kirouac | OG | 6'3" | 240 | 26 | | |
| 7 | BALTIMORE | 49 | Jake Kupp (to NO) | OG | 6'3" | 233 | 25 | | |
| 3 | LOS ANGELES | 31 | Jim Wilson | OG | 6'3" | 258 | 26 | | |
| 24 | New Orleans | 27 | Frank Marchlewski | C | 6'2" | 238 | 23 | | |
| 3 | Los Angeles | 20 | Karl Rubke | DT-C | 6'4" | 244 | 31 | | |
| 28 | SAN FRANCISCO | 34 | Bob Hughes | DE | 6'4" | 255 | 22 | | |
| 14 | CHICAGO | 23 | Bobby Richards | DE | 6'2" | 245 | 28 | | |
| | | | Sam Williams | DE | 6'5" | 245 | 36 | | |
| | | | Bo Wood | DE | 6'3" | 225 | 21 | | |
| | | | Jim Norton | DT | 6'4" | 254 | 24 | | 1 |
| | | | Chuck Sieminski | DT | 6'4" | 270 | 27 | | |
| | | | Joe Szczecko | DT | 6' | 245 | 25 | | |

| Use Name | Pos. | Hgt | Wgt | Age | Int | Pts |
|---|---|---|---|---|---|---|
| Dick Absher (from WAS) | LB | 6'4" | 227 | 23 | | 4 |
| Andy Bowling | LB | 6'3" | 235 | 22 | | |
| Ralph Heck | LB | 6'2" | 230 | 26 | | |
| Tommy Nobis | LB | 6'2" | 235 | 23 | 3 | 6 |
| Marion Rushing | LB | 6'2" | 230 | 30 | 1 | |
| Bob Sanders | LB | 6'3" | 235 | 24 | | |
| Tom Bleick | DB | 6'2" | 200 | 24 | | |
| Lee Calland | DB | 6' | 190 | 26 | 3 | 6 |
| Floyd Hudlow | DB | 5'11" | 195 | 23 | 2 | |
| Nick Rassas | DB | 6' | 190 | 23 | | |
| Ken Reaves | DB | 6'3" | 205 | 22 | 7 | |
| Jerry Richardson | DB | 6'3" | 190 | 24 | | |
| Bob Riggle | DB | 6'1" | 200 | 23 | | |

| Use Name | Pos. | Hgt | Wgt | Age | Int | Pts |
|---|---|---|---|---|---|---|
| Randy Johnson | QB | 6'3" | 196 | 23 | | 6 |
| Terry Nofsinger | QB | 6'4" | 215 | 29 | | |
| Steve Sloan | QB | 6' | 185 | 23 | | |
| Perry Lee Dunn | HB | 6'2" | 215 | 24 | | |
| Tom Moore | HB | 6'2" | 210 | 29 | | |
| Ron Rector | HB | 6' | 200 | 23 | | |
| Junior Coffey | FB | 6'1" | 210 | 25 | | 30 |
| Jim Mankins | FB | 6'1" | 235 | 23 | | |
| Tommy McDonald | FL | 5'10" | 175 | 33 | | 24 |
| Ron Smith | DB-FL | 6'1" | 192 | 24 | | 6 |
| Taz Anderson | TE | 6'2" | 228 | 26 | | 6 |
| Billy Martin | TE | 6'4" | 235 | 24 | | 18 |
| Ray Ogden (from NO) | OE | 6'5" | 225 | 24 | | 6 |
| Gary Barnes | OE | 6'4" | 210 | 27 | | 6 |
| Jerry Simmons (from NO) | OE | 6'1" | 190 | 24 | | 12 |
| Billy Lothridge | K | 6'1" | 195 | 23 | | |
| Wade Traynham | K | 6'2" | 218 | 25 | | 43 |

## COASTAL DIVISION

### LOS ANGELES RAMS

| RUSHING Last Name | No. | Yds | Avg | TD |
|---|---|---|---|---|
| Josephson | 178 | 800 | 4.5 | 4 |
| Bass | 187 | 627 | 3.4 | 6 |
| Mason | 63 | 213 | 3.4 | 2 |
| Gabriel | 43 | 198 | 4.6 | 6 |
| Ellison | 14 | 84 | 6.0 | 0 |
| Stiger | 3 | 6 | 2.0 | 0 |
| Munson | 2 | −22 | −11.0 | 0 |

| RECEIVING Last Name | No. | Yds | Avg | TD |
|---|---|---|---|---|
| Casey | 53 | 871 | 16 | 8 |
| Truax | 37 | 487 | 13 | 4 |
| Josephson | 37 | 400 | 11 | 4 |
| Snow | 28 | 735 | 26 | 8 |
| Bass | 27 | 212 | 8 | 1 |
| Mason | 13 | 70 | 5 | 0 |
| Pope | 8 | 152 | 19 | 2 |
| Pivec | 2 | 2 | 1 | 1 |
| Ellison | 1 | 18 | 18 | 0 |

| PUNT RETURNS Last Name | No. | Yds | Avg | TD |
|---|---|---|---|---|
| Cross | 17 | 136 | 8 | 0 |
| Meador | 21 | 131 | 6 | 0 |
| Tucker | 6 | 40 | 7 | 0 |
| Winston | 1 | 12 | 12 | 0 |
| Stiger | 4 | 9 | 2 | 0 |
| Crabb | 1 | 0 | 0 | 0 |

| KICKOFF RETURNS Last Name | No. | Yds | Avg | TD |
|---|---|---|---|---|
| Ellison | 13 | 340 | 26 | 0 |
| Tucker | 11 | 242 | 22 | 0 |
| Williams | 7 | 161 | 23 | 0 |
| Cross | 4 | 134 | 34 | 0 |
| Josephson | 5 | 91 | 18 | 0 |
| Winston | 3 | 65 | 22 | 0 |

PASSING – PUNTING – KICKING

| PASSING Last Name | Att | Comp | % | Yds | Yd/Att | TD | Int−% | RK |
|---|---|---|---|---|---|---|---|---|
| Gabriel | 371 | 196 | 53 | 2779 | 7.5 | 25 | 13− 4 | 4 |
| Munson | 10 | 5 | 50 | 38 | 3.8 | 1 | 2−20 | |
| Josephson | 5 | 2 | 40 | 47 | 9.4 | 0 | 1−20 | |
| Mason | 3 | 2 | 67 | 65 | 21.7 | 1 | 0− 0 | |
| Meador | 1 | 1 | 100 | 18 | 18.0 | 1 | 0− 0 | |

| PUNTING | No | Avg |
|---|---|---|
| Kilgore | 68 | 42.2 |

| KICKING | XP | Att | % | FG | Att | % |
|---|---|---|---|---|---|---|
| Gossett | 48 | 48 | 100 | 20 | 43 | 47 |

### BALTIMORE COLTS

| RUSHING Last Name | No. | Yds | Avg | TD |
|---|---|---|---|---|
| Matte | 147 | 636 | 4.3 | 9 |
| Lorick | 133 | 436 | 3.3 | 6 |
| Hill | 90 | 311 | 3.5 | 2 |
| Moore | 42 | 132 | 3.1 | 4 |
| Unitas | 22 | 89 | 4.0 | 0 |
| Ward | 5 | 23 | 4.6 | 0 |
| Hawkins | 2 | 12 | 6.0 | 0 |
| Welch | 2 | 6 | 3.0 | 0 |

| RECEIVING Last Name | No. | Yds | Avg | TD |
|---|---|---|---|---|
| Richardson | 63 | 860 | 14 | 8 |
| Mackey | 55 | 686 | 12 | 3 |
| Matte | 35 | 496 | 14 | 3 |
| Hawkins | 27 | 469 | 17 | 4 |
| Lorick | 22 | 189 | 9 | 0 |
| Hill | 19 | 156 | 8 | 0 |
| Perkins | 16 | 302 | 19 | 2 |
| Moore | 13 | 153 | 12 | 0 |
| Berry | 11 | 167 | 15 | 1 |
| Orr | 3 | 72 | 24 | 1 |
| Alley | 1 | 11 | 11 | 0 |

| PUNT RETURNS Last Name | No. | Yds | Avg | TD |
|---|---|---|---|---|
| Haymond | 26 | 155 | 6 | 0 |
| Volk | 11 | 88 | 8 | 0 |
| Logan | 5 | 80 | 16 | 1 |

| KICKOFF RETURNS Last Name | No. | Yds | Avg | TD |
|---|---|---|---|---|
| Moore | 16 | 392 | 25 | 0 |
| Haymond | 13 | 326 | 25 | 0 |
| Lorick | 8 | 212 | 27 | 0 |
| Stukes | 1 | 19 | 19 | 0 |
| Logan | 2 | 17 | 9 | 0 |
| Matte | 1 | 14 | 14 | 0 |
| Davis | 1 | 8 | 8 | 0 |

| PASSING Last Name | Att | Comp | % | Yds | Yd/Att | TD | Int−% | RK |
|---|---|---|---|---|---|---|---|---|
| Unitas | 436 | 255 | 58 | 3428 | 7.9 | 20 | 16− 4 | 2 |
| Ward | 16 | 9 | 56 | 115 | 7.2 | 2 | 1− 6 | |
| Matte | 5 | 1 | 20 | 18 | 3.6 | 0 | 0− 0 | |

| PUNTING | No | Avg |
|---|---|---|
| Lee | 49 | 42.3 |

| KICKING | XP | Att | % | FG | Att | % |
|---|---|---|---|---|---|---|
| Michaels | 46 | 48 | 96 | 20 | 37 | 54 |

### SAN FRANCISCO FORTY NINERS

| RUSHING Last Name | No. | Yds | Avg | TD |
|---|---|---|---|---|
| Willard | 169 | 510 | 3.0 | 5 |
| Crow | 113 | 479 | 4.2 | 2 |
| Lewis | 67 | 342 | 5.1 | 6 |
| Cunningham | 43 | 212 | 4.9 | 2 |
| Brodie | 20 | 147 | 7.4 | 1 |
| Mira | 7 | 23 | 3.3 | 0 |
| Kopay | 6 | 21 | 3.5 | 0 |
| Spurrier | 5 | 18 | 3.6 | 0 |
| Windsor | 1 | 7 | 7.0 | 0 |
| Tucker | 3 | 5 | 1.7 | 0 |

| RECEIVING Last Name | No. | Yds | Avg | TD |
|---|---|---|---|---|
| Witcher | 46 | 705 | 15 | 3 |
| Randle | 33 | 502 | 15 | 4 |
| Crow | 31 | 373 | 12 | 3 |
| Parks | 26 | 313 | 12 | 2 |
| Willard | 23 | 242 | 11 | 1 |
| Windsor | 21 | 254 | 12 | 2 |
| Lewis | 21 | 218 | 10 | 1 |
| Cunningham | 13 | 121 | 9 | 0 |
| Stickles | 7 | 86 | 12 | 0 |
| Tucker | 2 | 22 | 11 | 0 |
| Myers | 2 | 13 | 7 | 0 |
| Kopay | 2 | 11 | 6 | 0 |
| Olerich | 1 | 2 | 2 | 0 |

| PUNT RETURNS Last Name | No. | Yds | Avg | TD |
|---|---|---|---|---|
| Cunningham | 27 | 249 | 9 | 0 |
| Alexander | 6 | 64 | 11 | 0 |
| Tucker | 1 | 1 | 1 | 0 |
| Gonsoulin | 1 | 0 | 0 | 0 |

| KICKOFF RETURNS Last Name | No. | Yds | Avg | TD |
|---|---|---|---|---|
| Cunningham | 31 | 826 | 27 | 0 |
| Tucker | 9 | 199 | 22 | 0 |
| Lewis | 9 | 190 | 21 | 0 |
| Swinford | 2 | 51 | 26 | 0 |
| Kopay | 1 | 21 | 21 | 0 |
| Windsor | 1 | 21 | 21 | 0 |
| Alexander | 1 | 18 | 18 | 0 |
| Nunley | 2 | 0 | 0 | 0 |

| PASSING Last Name | Att | Comp | % | Yds | Yd/Att | TD | Int−% | RK |
|---|---|---|---|---|---|---|---|---|
| Brodie | 349 | 168 | 48 | 2013 | 5.8 | 11 | 16− 5 | 11 |
| Mira | 65 | 35 | 54 | 592 | 9.1 | 5 | 3− 5 | |
| Spurrier | 50 | 23 | 46 | 211 | 4.2 | 0 | 7−14 | |
| Crow | 5 | 2 | 40 | 46 | 9.2 | 0 | 0− 0 | |

| PUNTING | No | Avg |
|---|---|---|
| Spurrier | 73 | 37.6 |

| KICKING | XP | Att | % | FG | Att | % |
|---|---|---|---|---|---|---|
| Davis | 33 | 33 | 100 | 14 | 33 | 42 |

### ATLANTA FALCONS

| RUSHING Last Name | No. | Yds | Avg | TD |
|---|---|---|---|---|
| Coffey | 180 | 722 | 4.0 | 4 |
| Johnson | 24 | 144 | 6.0 | 1 |
| Rector | 24 | 127 | 5.3 | 0 |
| Moore | 53 | 104 | 2.0 | 0 |
| Dunn | 27 | 63 | 2.3 | 0 |
| Smith | 8 | 42 | 5.3 | 0 |
| Nofsinger | 3 | 33 | 11.0 | 0 |
| Lothridge | 1 | 16 | 16.0 | 0 |
| Mankins | 2 | 7 | 3.5 | 0 |
| Sloan | 1 | 2 | 2.0 | 0 |

| RECEIVING Last Name | No. | Yds | Avg | TD |
|---|---|---|---|---|
| McDonald | 33 | 436 | 13 | 4 |
| Coffey | 30 | 196 | 7 | 1 |
| Simmons | 23 | 312 | 14 | 2 |
| Ogden | 20 | 327 | 16 | 1 |
| Martin | 15 | 182 | 12 | 3 |
| Dunn | 13 | 111 | 9 | 0 |
| Smith | 11 | 227 | 21 | 0 |
| Barnes | 10 | 154 | 15 | 1 |
| Moore | 10 | 74 | 7 | 0 |
| Anderson | 8 | 99 | 12 | 1 |
| Rector | 4 | 13 | 3 | 0 |
| Mankins | 1 | 11 | 11 | 0 |

| PUNT RETURNS Last Name | No. | Yds | Avg | TD |
|---|---|---|---|---|
| Smith | 20 | 92 | 5 | 0 |
| Hudlow | 1 | 2 | 2 | 0 |
| Simmons | 3 | 0 | 0 | 0 |

| KICKOFF RETURNS Last Name | No. | Yds | Avg | TD |
|---|---|---|---|---|
| Smith | 39 | 976 | 25 | 1 |
| Dunn | 7 | 128 | 18 | 0 |
| Hudlow | 2 | 56 | 28 | 0 |
| Rassas | 2 | 51 | 26 | 0 |
| Ogden | 3 | 41 | 14 | 0 |
| Simmons | 2 | 38 | 19 | 0 |
| Linden | 3 | 37 | 12 | 0 |
| Mankins | 1 | 12 | 12 | 0 |
| Wood | 1 | 9 | 9 | 0 |
| Talbert | 1 | 2 | 2 | 0 |
| Martin | 1 | 0 | 0 | 0 |
| Sandeman | 1 | 0 | 0 | 0 |

| PASSING Last Name | Att | Comp | % | Yds | Yd/Att | TD | Int−% | RK |
|---|---|---|---|---|---|---|---|---|
| Johnson | 288 | 142 | 49 | 1620 | 5.6 | 10 | 21− 7 | 16 |
| Nofsinger | 60 | 30 | 50 | 352 | 5.9 | 1 | 2− 3 | |
| Sloan | 18 | 4 | 22 | 38 | 2.1 | 0 | 2−11 | |
| Dunn | 2 | 1 | 50 | 32 | 16.0 | 1 | 0− 0 | |
| Moore | 2 | 2 | 100 | 102 | 51.0 | 1 | 0− 0 | |

| PUNTING | No | Avg |
|---|---|---|
| Lothridge | 87 | 43.7 |

| KICKING | XP | Att | % | FG | Att | % |
|---|---|---|---|---|---|---|
| Traynham | 22 | 22 | 100 | 7 | 18 | 39 |
| Absher | 4 | 4 | 100 | 0 | 1 | 0 |

# 1967 A.F.L.  Coming Up to Equal Footing

The AFL wasn't ready yet to win a Super Bowl, but the clubs in the newer league won some respect with their showing in interleague pre-season games. The games were far more competitive than had been expected, and the AFL drew first blood when the Denver Broncos beat the Detroit Lions 13-7 in the first interleague contest. The two leagues battled on even lines through the late-summer games, but the AFL administered the worst beating when the Chiefs, still smarting from their Super Bowl loss to Green Bay, crushed the Chicago Bears 66-27. The pre-season series seemed to prove that AFL teams could play on a par with average NFL teams but that time was needed to catch up with NFL powers like the Packers.

Time was on the AFL's side, however, as the common draft assured a steady flow of young talent into the league. Teams like Boston and Denver, which had never done well in signing its draft choices, now had an easier time coming to terms with graduating collegiate talent. The AFL teams also were moving into better stadia, with the San Diego Chargers this year setting up shop in a new municipal stadium.

## EASTERN DIVISION

**Houston Oilers—**A 3-11 team only a year ago, the Oilers used a fine rookie class and a revitalized defense to capture their first divisional crown since 1962. Every adjustment head coach Wally Lemm made in the defense worked out splendidly; he moved veterans around and inserted rookies with the touch of a chess grandmaster. Pat Holmes, a disappointment last year as a tackle, caught fire as an end. Second-year man George Rice took over a tackle spot and drew compliments around the league. Rookie linebacker George Webster combined size, speed, and sound football sense in an All-Pro freshman season, and his linebacking mates were Garland Boyette and Olen Underwood. W. K. Hicks and Jim Norton held onto their secondary posts, but joining them were newcomers Miller Farr, a quick cornerback picked up in a trade from San Diego, and rookie strong safety Ken Houston. This rebuilt unit allowed only eighteen touchdowns all year. The leading lights of the offense were fullback Hoyle Granger, quarterback Pete Beathard, who was picked up in mid-season from Kansas City, and star guard Bob Talamini.

**New York Jets—**As usual, the Jets looked like a sure title winner until December, and then, as usual, they fell apart. Ending November with a 7-2-1 record and a one-game lead over the coming Houston Oilers, the Jets started December by losing to Denver, Kansas City, and Oakland. They straightened out in time to beat San Diego in the season's finale, but by then the Oilers had locked up first place. The Jet pass defense contributed heavily to this year's late slump, as the line failed to rush enemy passers consistently and the secondary was not airtight. The Jets also had offensive problems, although Joe Namath and receivers George Sauer and Don Maynard bombed enemy defenses regularly. Fullback Matt Snell, the team's workhorse, ripped up a knee in the opening game and didn't return to action until mid-November; by then, halfback Emerson Boozer had gone out with an injured knee of his own.

**Buffalo Bills—**The Buffalo defensive unit stayed strong despite the loss of middle linebacker Harry Jacobs for the last seven games with a broken elbow, but the offense, never too robust to begin with, broke down completely under a rash of knee injuries. Bobby Crockett, last year's rookie receiving threat, sat out the entire year with a bad knee, while running back Bobby Burnett, veteran guard Billy Shaw, and split end Art Powell missed at least half the schedule with their knee injuries. Quarterback Jack Kemp's bad season further hurt the attack, and only newcomer Keith Lincoln, picked up in a swap with San Diego, kept the offense alive with his running and receiving. With all the injuries, the Bills scored more than 20 points in only three games all year—not nearly enough for a fourth straight championship.

**Miami Dolphins—**By mid-season rookie Bob Griese had taken over as the starting quarterback. Showing a strong arm and unshakable poise, Griese hooked up with rookie split end Jack Clancy in an effective passing combination. Outside of these two rookies, however, the Miami offense gave fans little to cheer about. Halfback Abner Haynes was long past his prime and was shipped out to New York before the year ended. The line had huge gaps, and flanker Howard Twilley had neither size nor speed. The defense, though not one of the league's best, did field several representative ball players.

**Boston Patriots—**Jim Nance still dominated the team with his powerful ball-carrying, but the supporting cast on the Patriots slipped, and they fell to last place in the East. With no speed at halfback or in the receivers, and with Babe Parilli showing advanced symptoms of old age, defenses waited for Nance's smashes into the line, yet the big fullback from Syracuse still bowled over the expectant defenders for 1,216 yards.

## WESTERN DIVISION

**Oakland Raiders—**In a daring trade, the Raiders sent quarterback Tom Flores and split end Art Powell, both established starters, to Buffalo for quarterback Daryle Lamonica and Glenn Bass. Bass didn't make the team, but Lamonica developed into a fine long passer. End Bill Miller came from Buffalo at little cost and gave Lamonica a steady target. Willie Brown came over from Denver and beat All-Pro Dave Grayson out of a cornerback position. Thirty-nine-year-old George Blanda signed aboard after being released by Houston; the old-timer backed up Lamonica and led the league in scoring with his steady place-kicking. The rookie crop turned up guard Gene Upshaw, who immediately ranked among the league's best offensive linemen, and linebacker Duane Benson, who played on the special teams with zeal. Of course, the Raiders already had some top-notch players, with Billy Cannon, Jim Otto, Ben Davidson, Tom Keating, and Kent McCloughan winning All-League honors among the returning veterans. The Raiders' depth showed when halfback Clem Daniels broke his ankle late in the year and Pete Banaszak filled in with no noticeable drop in quality. Thus, the Raiders easily swept the Western Division title.

**Kansas City Chiefs—**AFL clubs learned well the lesson taught by the Green Bay Packers in the first Super Bowl. The Packers had singled out certain weak links in the Kansas City defense and ruthlessly exploited them, and now the AFL clubs found success in directing their attacks right at the same people. Enemy offenses singled out for special treatment, linebackers Chuck Hurston and Sherrill Headrick and cornerbacks Fred Williamson and Willie Mitchell, and by the time coach Hank Stram could readjust his defense the Chiefs had lost all four of their meetings with Oakland and San Diego and all chances for a repeat title in the West. But Stram did substitute some young talent into the lineup, and after Bud Abell, Emmitt Thomas, Fletcher Smith, and rookies Jim Lynch and Willie Lanier got their bearings, the Kansas City linebacking and secondary were a lot tougher. Aside from closing out the season with three straight wins, the high point of the year was the unveiling of two spectacular special team rookies: Norwegian place-kicker Jan Stenerud, and kick returner Noland Smith.

**San Diego Chargers—**The Chargers got off to a fast start and had high hopes of regaining the Western Division title, only to lose their last four games and slip back into a third-place finish. Coach Sid Gillman's biggest headache was his defense, which disintegrated down the stretch. Despite high-priced talents like Scott Appleton and Steve DeLong, the line put practically no pressure at all on enemy passers, and, given time, opposing quarterbacks found the San Diego secondary easy to pick apart. The offense kept the title drive alive until late in the season and kept the fans filing into the new San Diego Stadium. Enemy defenses had to worry first about flanker Lance Alworth, pro football's premier deep pass receiver, but if they paid too much attention to him, quarterback John Hadl simply threw to ends Gary Garrison and Willie Frazier, both fine pass catchers in their own right. The line was one of the best in pro football, especially at protecting the passer, and the San Diego running attack got a quick shot of energy in the form of Dickie Post and Brad Hubbert, a pair of rookie backs.

**Denver Broncos—**Lou Saban returned to pro football as head coach and general manager of the Broncos and immediately ripped the club apart to get a fresh start in building a winner. At times during the season Saban was starting fifteen rookies on the two platoons, a sign of his willingness to go with youth now to build a winner later. The team's biggest problems came in pass defense, where a rookie-laden secondary and linebacking corps could not handle good air attacks. The defensive line showed more stability as veteran Dave Costa, obtained from Buffalo for a draft pick, starred at a tackle post and youngsters Rich Jackson and Pete Duranko showed promise at the ends. Saban rebuilt the offense into a creditable unit, although the line was manned by and large with inexperienced or mediocre players. Saban got himself a quarterback by trading two first-round draft choices to San Diego for Steve Tensi, a promising young passer who learned as he played in Denver. Two fine wide receivers surfaced in Al Denson, last year's tight end, and Eric Crabtree, one of last year's bench warmers, while the running game improved immensely with the arrival of rookie halfback Floyd Little.

## FINAL TEAM STATISTICS

| OFFENSE | | | | | | | | | | DEFENSE | | | | | | | | |
|---|---|---|---|---|---|---|---|---|---|---|---|---|---|---|---|---|---|---|
| BOSTON | BUFFALO | DENVER | HOUSTON | K.CITY | MIAMI | NEW YORK | OAKLAND | SAN DIEGO | | BOSTON | BUFFALO | DENVER | HOUSTON | K.CITY | MIAMI | NEW YORK | OAKLAND | SAN DIEGO |
| | | | | | | | | | **FIRST DOWNS:** | | | | | | | | | |
| 219 | 203 | 172 | 207 | 251 | 212 | **282** | 250 | 259 | Total | 219 | 201 | 276 | 233 | 221 | 269 | 203 | **182** | 251 |
| 80 | 65 | 65 | 111 | **116** | 65 | 82 | 79 | 88 | by Rushing | 61 | 73 | 115 | 86 | 73 | 115 | 80 | **60** | 88 |
| 120 | 119 | 91 | 86 | 117 | 123 | **180** | 154 | 150 | by Passing | 138 | 106 | 143 | 126 | 132 | 133 | 111 | **103** | 148 |
| 19 | 19 | 16 | 10 | 18 | **24** | 20 | 17 | 21 | by Penalty | 20 | 22 | 18 | 21 | 16 | 21 | **12** | 19 | 15 |
| | | | | | | | | | **RUSHING** | | | | | | | | | |
| 391 | 371 | 420 | **476** | 462 | 326 | 389 | 458 | 417 | Number | 417 | 437 | 444 | 424 | **343** | 466 | 386 | 352 | 441 |
| 1604 | 1271 | 1265 | **2122** | 2018 | 1323 | 1307 | 1928 | 1715 | Yards | 1350 | 1622 | 2076 | 1637 | 1408 | 2145 | 1633 | **1129** | 1553 |
| 4.1 | 3.4 | 3.0 | **4.5** | 4.4 | 4.1 | 3.4 | 4.2 | 4.1 | Average Yards | 3.2 | 3.7 | 4.7 | 3.9 | 4.1 | 4.6 | 4.2 | **3.2** | 3.5 |
| 10 | 9 | 10 | 12 | 18 | 10 | 17 | **19** | 14 | Touchdowns | 12 | 11 | 21 | **7** | 10 | 18 | 14 | 9 | 17 |
| | | | | | | | | | **PASSING:** | | | | | | | | | |
| 434 | 434 | 374 | 332 | 382 | 480 | **515** | 464 | 463 | Attempts | 423 | 377 | 459 | 461 | 462 | **349** | 424 | 459 | 464 |
| 191 | 183 | 150 | 143 | 213 | 229 | 271 | 236 | 230 | Completions | 211 | **162** | 214 | 228 | 229 | 188 | 195 | 189 | 230 |
| 44.0 | 42.2 | 40.1 | 43.1 | **55.8** | 47.7 | 52.6 | 50.9 | 49.7 | Completion Percentage | 49.9 | 43.0 | 46.6 | 49.5 | 49.6 | 53.9 | 46.0 | **41.2** | 49.6 |
| 2784 | 2763 | 2190 | 1532 | 2773 | 2741 | **4128** | 3541 | 3517 | Passing Yards | 3123 | **2191** | 3289 | 2619 | 2890 | 3082 | 2489 | 2831 | 3455 |
| 6.4 | 6.4 | 5.9 | 4.6 | 7.3 | 5.7 | **8.0** | 7.6 | 7.6 | Avg. Yards per Attempt | 7.4 | 5.8 | 7.2 | **5.7** | 6.3 | 8.8 | 5.9 | 6.2 | 7.5 |
| 14.6 | 15.1 | 14.6 | 10.7 | 13.0 | 12.0 | 15.2 | 15.0 | **15.3** | Avg. Yards per Completion | 14.8 | 13.5 | 15.4 | **11.5** | 12.6 | 16.4 | 12.8 | 15.0 | 15.0 |
| 45 | 45 | 58 | 20 | 32 | 41 | 28 | 40 | 11 | Time Tackled Att. to Pass | 31 | 43 | 18 | 25 | 38 | 28 | 39 | **67** | 31 |
| 361 | 446 | 508 | 151 | 301 | 405 | 283 | 353 | 107 | Yards Lost Tackled | 267 | 366 | 164 | 201 | 354 | 247 | 347 | **666** | 303 |
| 2423 | 2317 | 1682 | 1381 | 2472 | 2336 | **3845** | 3188 | 3410 | Net Yards | 2856 | **1825** | 3125 | 2418 | 2536 | 2835 | 2142 | 2165 | 3152 |
| 20 | 14 | 17 | 11 | 26 | 16 | 27 | **33** | 26 | Touchdowns | 28 | 17 | 27 | **10** | 13 | 31 | 20 | 18 | 26 |
| 32 | 34 | 18 | 20 | 19 | 28 | 29 | 23 | 24 | Interceptions | 17 | 27 | 28 | 26 | **31** | 28 | 27 | 30 | 13 |
| 7.4 | 7.8 | **4.8** | 6.0 | 5.0 | 5.8 | 5.6 | 5.0 | 5.2 | Percent Intercepted | 4.0 | 7.2 | 6.1 | 5.6 | 6.7 | **8.0** | 6.4 | 6.5 | 2.8 |
| | | | | | | | | | **PUNTS:** | | | | | | | | | |
| 65 | 77 | **105** | 71 | 61 | 70 | 65 | 76 | 63 | Number | 73 | 74 | 65 | 63 | 64 | 52 | 79 | **111** | 72 |
| 40.5 | 43.1 | **44.9** | 42.6 | 41.3 | 41.6 | 42.1 | 44.3 | 37.5 | Average Distance | 41.9 | 41.0 | 41.5 | 41.0 | 43.0 | 41.1 | 43.2 | 41.9 | 45.2 |
| | | | | | | | | | **PUNT RETURNS:** | | | | | | | | | |
| 43 | 47 | 26 | 20 | 33 | 25 | 48 | **51** | 39 | Number | 31 | 33 | 61 | 41 | 31 | 41 | 36 | 37 | **21** |
| 412 | 199 | 351 | 255 | 245 | 128 | 326 | **642** | 480 | Yards | 252 | 301 | 718 | 383 | 331 | 268 | 311 | 250 | **224** |
| 9.6 | 4.2 | **13.5** | 12.8 | 7.4 | 5.1 | 6.8 | 12.6 | 12.3 | Average Yards | 8.1 | 9.1 | 11.8 | 9.3 | 10.7 | **6.5** | 8.6 | 6.8 | 10.7 |
| 0 | 0 | **1** | 0 | 0 | 0 | 0 | 0 | 0 | Touchdowns | 0 | 0 | 0 | 0 | 0 | 0 | 1 | 0 | 0 |
| | | | | | | | | | **KICKOFF RETURNS:** | | | | | | | | | |
| **73** | 51 | 60 | 44 | 53 | 67 | 57 | 45 | 54 | Number | 45 | 56 | **42** | 51 | 55 | 46 | 64 | 82 | 63 |
| 1436 | 1113 | **1518** | 1020 | 1245 | 1443 | 1144 | 962 | 1239 | Yards | **946** | 1292 | 1046 | 950 | 1207 | 1079 | 1387 | 1707 | 1506 |
| 19.7 | 21.8 | **25.3** | 23.2 | 23.5 | 21.5 | 20.1 | 21.4 | 22.9 | Average Yards | 21.0 | 23.1 | 24.9 | **18.6** | 21.9 | 23.5 | 21.7 | 20.8 | 23.9 |
| 0 | 0 | 0 | **1** | **1** | 0 | 0 | 0 | 0 | Touchdowns | 0 | 0 | 1 | 0 | 1 | 0 | 0 | 0 | 0 |
| | | | | | | | | | **INTERCEPTION RETURNS:** | | | | | | | | | |
| 17 | 27 | 28 | 26 | **31** | 28 | 27 | 30 | 13 | Number | 32 | 34 | 18 | 20 | 19 | 28 | 29 | 23 | 24 |
| 257 | 401 | 413 | **676** | 578 | 402 | 322 | 404 | 274 | Yards | 640 | 554 | 262 | **156** | 471 | 395 | 711 | 209 | 329 |
| 15.1 | 14.9 | 14.8 | **26.0** | 18.6 | 14.4 | 11.9 | 13.5 | 21.1 | Average Yards | 20.0 | 16.3 | 14.6 | **7.8** | 24.8 | 14.1 | 24.5 | 9.1 | 13.7 |
| 2 | 3 | 3 | **6** | 4 | 1 | 1 | 4 | 2 | Touchdowns | 7 | 2 | 2 | 1 | 5 | 3 | 5 | **0** | 1 |
| | | | | | | | | | **PENALTIES:** | | | | | | | | | |
| 59 | **74** | 48 | 61 | 68 | 53 | 64 | 71 | 72 | Number | 70 | 51 | 58 | 59 | **76** | 59 | 67 | 69 | 61 |
| 520 | **828** | 512 | 698 | 680 | 490 | 691 | 768 | 817 | Yards | 722 | 507 | 628 | 614 | **757** | 691 | 717 | 702 | 666 |
| | | | | | | | | | **FUMBLES:** | | | | | | | | | |
| 37 | 32 | 30 | 17 | 28 | 36 | **15** | 19 | 18 | Number | 26 | 26 | 23 | 29 | **34** | 19 | 24 | 29 | 22 |
| 22 | 13 | 12 | **7** | 8 | 16 | 8 | 13 | 10 | Number Lost | 17 | 9 | 13 | 13 | **18** | 8 | 6 | 15 | 10 |
| | | | | | | | | | **POINTS:** | | | | | | | | | |
| 280 | 237 | 256 | 258 | 408 | 219 | 371 | **468** | 360 | Total | 389 | 285 | 409 | **199** | 254 | 407 | 329 | 233 | 352 |
| 31 | 26 | 30 | 30 | 45 | 28 | 40 | **57** | 45 | PAT (kick) Attempts | 46 | 33 | 50 | 14 | 28 | 50 | 40 | 27 | 44 |
| 30 | 25 | 28 | 30 | 45 | 27 | 36 | **56** | 45 | PAT (kick) Made | 44 | 32 | 48 | 14 | 28 | 47 | 39 | 26 | 44 |
| 2 | 1 | 1 | 1 | 4 | 0 | **6** | 1 | 0 | PAT (2 Point) Attempts | 2 | 0 | 2 | 4 | 2 | 3 | 1 | 2 | 0 |
| 0 | 1 | 1 | 0 | 2 | 0 | **4** | 1 | 0 | PAT (2 Point) Made | 0 | 0 | 2 | 3 | 1 | 0 | 1 | 2 | 0 |
| 31 | 27 | 28 | 28 | **36** | 18 | 32 | 30 | 30 | FG Attempts | 31 | 38 | 31 | 42 | 25 | 26 | 26 | 14 | 27 |
| 16 | 16 | 12 | 14 | **21** | 8 | 17 | 20 | 15 | FG Made | 19 | 17 | 15 | 23 | 14 | 14 | 14 | 9 | 14 |
| 51.6 | 59.3 | 42.9 | 50.0 | 58.3 | 44.4 | 53.1 | **66.7** | 50.0 | Percent | 61.3 | **44.7** | 48.4 | 54.8 | 56.0 | 53.8 | 53.8 | 64.3 | 51.9 |
| **2** | 0 | **2** | 0 | 1 | 0 | 0 | 1 | 0 | Safeties | 0 | 2 | 0 | 1 | 1 | 0 | 0 | 0 | 1 |

## HOUSTON OILERS 9-4-1 Wally Lemm

| Scores of Each Game | | |
|---|---|---|
| 20 | KANSAS CITY | 25 |
| 20 | Buffalo | 3 |
| 3 | San Diego | 13 |
| 10 | DENVER | 6 |
| 28 | New York | 28 |
| 24 | Kansas City | 19 |
| 10 | BUFFALO | 3 |
| 7 | Boston | 18 |
| 20 | Denver | 18 |
| 27 | BOSTON | 6 |
| 17 | MIAMI | 14 |
| 7 | OAKLAND | 19 |
| 24 | SAN DIEGO | 17 |
| 41 | Miami | 10 |

| Use Name | Pos. | Hgt | Wgt | Age | Int | Pts |
|---|---|---|---|---|---|---|
| Glen Ray Hines | OT | 6'5" | 270 | 23 | | |
| Walt Suggs | OT | 6'5" | 265 | 28 | | |
| Sonny Bishop | OG | 6'2" | 245 | 27 | | |
| Ed Marcontell (from StL-N) | OG | 6' | 260 | 23 | | |
| Tom Regner | OG | 6'1" | 255 | 23 | | |
| Bob Talamini | OG | 6'1" | 255 | 28 | | |
| Bobby Maples | C | 6'3" | 245 | 24 | | |
| Don Floyd | DE | 6'4" | 245 | 29 | | |
| Pat Holmes | DE | 6'5" | 260 | 27 | | |
| Willie Jones | DE | 6'2" | 260 | 25 | | |
| Carel Stith | DE | 6'5" | 270 | 22 | | |
| Bud Marshall | DT | 6'5" | 270 | 25 | | |
| Willie Parker | DT | 6'2" | 270 | 22 | | |
| Andy Rice (from KC) | DT | 6'3" | 266 | 25 | | |
| George Rice | DT | 6'3" | 260 | 23 | | |

| Use Name | Pos. | Hgt | Wgt | Age | Int | Pts |
|---|---|---|---|---|---|---|
| Pete Barnes | LB | 6'3" | 245 | 22 | | |
| Garland Boyette | LB | 6'1" | 240 | 27 | | |
| Danny Brabham | LB | 6'4" | 233 | 26 | | |
| Ronnie Caveness | LB | 6'1" | 225 | 24 | | |
| Olen Underwood | LB | 6'1" | 230 | 25 | 1 | |
| George Webster | LB | 6'4" | 223 | 21 | 1 | |
| Larry Carwell | DB | 6'1" | 187 | 23 | | |
| Miller Farr | DB | 6'1" | 188 | 24 | 10 | 18 |
| W. K. Hicks | DB | 6'1" | 190 | 24 | 3 | |
| Ken Houston | DB | 6'3" | 190 | 22 | 4 | 18 |
| Bobby Jancik | DB | 5'11" | 178 | 27 | 1 | |
| Pete Johns | DB | 6'3" | 188 | 22 | | |
| Zeke Moore | DB | 6'2" | 190 | 23 | | 6 |
| Jim Norton | DB | 6'3" | 180 | 28 | 6 | 6 |

Gary Cutsinger – Back Injury

| Use Name | Pos. | Hgt | Wgt | Age | Int | Pts |
|---|---|---|---|---|---|---|
| Billy Anderson | QB | 6'1" | 195 | 26 | | |
| Pete Beathard (from KC) | QB | 6'2" | 210 | 25 | | 6 |
| Bob Davis | QB | 6'3" | 202 | 21 | | |
| Jacky Lee (to KC) | QB | 6'1" | 188 | 28 | | |
| Sid Blanks | HB | 6' | 208 | 26 | | 12 |
| Woody Campbell | HB | 5'11" | 205 | 22 | | 36 |
| Hoyle Granger | FB | 6'1" | 225 | 23 | | 54 |
| Roy Hopkins | FB | 6'1" | 227 | 22 | | |
| Glenn Bass | FL | 6'2" | 206 | 28 | | 6 |
| Ode Burrell | FL | 6' | 195 | 27 | | |
| Larry Elkins | FL | 6'1" | 195 | 24 | | |
| Bob Poole | TE | 6'4" | 215 | 25 | | |
| Alvin Reed | TE | 6'5" | 228 | 23 | | 6 |
| Charley Frazier | OE | 6' | 188 | 28 | | 6 |
| Lionel Taylor | OE | 6'2" | 215 | 31 | | 6 |
| John Wittenborn | K | 6'2" | 240 | 31 | | 72 |

## NEW YORK JETS 8-5-1 Weeb Ewbank

| Scores of Each Game | | |
|---|---|---|
| 17 | Buffalo | 20 |
| 38 | Denver | 24 |
| 29 | MIAMI | 7 |
| 27 | OAKLAND | 14 |
| 28 | HOUSTON | 28 |
| 33 | Miami | 14 |
| 30 | BOSTON | 23 |
| 18 | Kansas City | 42 |
| 20 | BUFFALO | 10 |
| 29 | Boston | 24 |
| 24 | DENVER | 33 |
| 7 | KANSAS CITY | 21 |
| 29 | Oakland | 38 |
| 42 | San Diego | 31 |

| Use Name | Pos. | Hgt | Wgt | Age | Int | Pts |
|---|---|---|---|---|---|---|
| Winston Hill | OT | 6'4" | 275 | 25 | | |
| Sherman Plunkett | OT | 6'4" | 330 | 33 | | |
| Jim Harris | OT | 6'4" | 280 | 23 | | |
| Paul Seiler | OG-OT | 6'4" | 255 | 21 | | |
| Dave Herman | OG | 6'2" | 255 | 25 | | |
| Pete Perreault | OG | 6'3" | 245 | 28 | | |
| Randy Rasmussen | OG | 6'2" | 255 | 22 | | |
| Jeff Richardson | OG | 6'3" | 250 | 22 | | |
| John Matlock | C | 6'4" | 246 | 22 | | |
| John Schmitt | C | 6'4" | 245 | 24 | | |
| Verlon Biggs | DE | 6'4" | 260 | 24 | | |
| Gerry Philbin | DE | 6'2" | 248 | 26 | | |
| Bert Wilder | DT-DE | 6'3" | 245 | 27 | | |
| Dennis Randall | DT | 6'6" | 245 | 21 | | |
| Paul Rochester | DT | 6'2" | 255 | 30 | | |
| John Elliott | LB-DE-DT | 6'4" | 245 | 22 | | |

| Use Name | Pos. | Hgt | Wgt | Age | Int | Pts |
|---|---|---|---|---|---|---|
| Al Atkinson | LB | 6'1" | 228 | 24 | 5 | |
| Ralph Baker | LB | 6'3" | 228 | 25 | 1 | |
| Paul Crane | LB | 6'2" | 205 | 23 | | |
| Larry Grantham | LB | 6' | 206 | 28 | 5 | |
| Carl McAdams | LB | 6'3" | 240 | 23 | | |
| Jim Waskiewicz | OT-LB | 6'4" | 235 | 23 | | |
| Bill Baird | DB | 5'10" | 180 | 28 | 3 | |
| Randy Beverly | DB | 5'11" | 185 | 23 | 4 | |
| Solomon Brannan | DB | 6'1" | 185 | 25 | | |
| Cornell Gordon | DB | 6' | 187 | 26 | 1 | |
| Jim Hudson | DB | 6'2" | 210 | 24 | 4 | |
| Henry King | DB | 6'4" | 205 | 22 | | |
| Sherman Lewis | DB | 5'10" | 180 | 25 | | |
| Bill Rademacher | DB | 6'1" | 190 | 25 | | |
| Johnny Sample | DB | 6'1" | 208 | 30 | 4 | 6 |

| Use Name | Pos. | Hgt | Wgt | Age | Int | Pts |
|---|---|---|---|---|---|---|
| Joe Namath | QB | 6'2" | 195 | 24 | | 6 |
| Mike Taliaferro | QB | 6'2" | 205 | 25 | | |
| Jim Turner | QB | 6'2" | 205 | 26 | | 87 |
| Emerson Boozer | HB | 5'11" | 207 | 24 | | 78 |
| Earl Christy | HB | 5'11" | 195 | 24 | | |
| Bill Mathis | HB | 6'1" | 220 | 28 | | 46 |
| Billy Joe | FB | 6'2" | 236 | 26 | | 12 |
| Mark Smolinski | FB | 6' | 215 | 28 | | 24 |
| Matt Snell | FB | 6'2" | 220 | 25 | | |
| Don Maynard | FL | 6' | 180 | 31 | | 62 |
| Bob Schweickert | FL | 6'1" | 190 | 24 | | |
| Curley Johnson | TE | 6' | 215 | 32 | | |
| Pete Lammons | TE | 6'3" | 228 | 23 | | 12 |
| George Sauer | OE | 6'1" | 195 | 23 | | 38 |
| Bake Turner | OE | 6' | 180 | 27 | | |

## BUFFALO BILLS 4-10-0 Joe Collier

| Scores of Each Game | | |
|---|---|---|
| 20 | NEW YORK | 17 |
| 3 | HOUSTON | 20 |
| 0 | BOSTON | 23 |
| 17 | SAN DIEGO | 37 |
| 17 | Denver | 16 |
| 20 | OAKLAND | 24 |
| 3 | Houston | 10 |
| 35 | MIAMI | 13 |
| 10 | New York | 20 |
| 20 | DENVER | 21 |
| 14 | Miami | 17 |
| 13 | Kansas City | 23 |
| 44 | Boston | 16 |
| 21 | Oakland | 28 |

| Use Name | Pos. | Hgt | Wgt | Age | Int | Pts |
|---|---|---|---|---|---|---|
| Stew Barber | OT | 6'3" | 252 | 28 | | |
| Dick Cunningham | OT | 6'2" | 242 | 22 | | |
| Dick Hudson | OT | 6'4" | 265 | 27 | | |
| Gary Bugenhagen | OG | 6'2" | 248 | 22 | | |
| Joe O'Donnell | OG | 6'2" | 252 | 25 | | |
| Billy Shaw | OG | 6'3" | 258 | 27 | | |
| Al Bemiller | C | 6'3" | 246 | 28 | | |
| Bob Schmidt | C | 6'4" | 250 | 31 | | |
| Ron McDole | DE | 6'4" | 270 | 27 | 1 | |
| Bob Petrich | DE | 6'4" | 250 | 26 | | |
| Remi Prudhomme | DE | 6'4" | 263 | 25 | | |
| Jim Dunaway | DT | 6'4" | 280 | 25 | 1 | |
| Dudley Meredith | DT | 6'4" | 285 | 32 | 1 | |
| Tom Sestak | DT | 6'5" | 260 | 31 | | 6 |

Bobby Crockett – Knee Injury

| Use Name | Pos. | Hgt | Wgt | Age | Int | Pts |
|---|---|---|---|---|---|---|
| Paul Guidry | LB | 6'3" | 234 | 23 | | |
| Harry Jacobs | LB | 6'2" | 244 | 30 | | |
| Jim LeMoine | LB | 6'2" | 245 | 22 | | |
| Paul Maguire | LB | 6' | 230 | 29 | | |
| Marty Schottenheimer | LB | 6'3" | 225 | 24 | 3 | 6 |
| Mike Stratton | LB | 6'3" | 244 | 25 | 1 | |
| John Tracey | TE-LB | 6'3" | 228 | 34 | 1 | |
| Butch Byrd | DB | 6' | 208 | 25 | 5 | |
| Hagood Clarke | DB | 6' | 195 | 25 | | |
| Booker Edgerson | DB | 5'10" | 183 | 28 | 2 | |
| Tom Janik | DB | 6'3" | 190 | 26 | 10 | 12 |
| Charlie King | DB | 6' | 185 | 24 | | |
| John Pitts | DB | 6'4" | 218 | 22 | | |
| George Saimes | DB | 5'10" | 188 | 25 | 2 | |

Charley Ferguson – Injury
George Flint – Injury

| Use Name | Pos. | Hgt | Wgt | Age | Int | Pts |
|---|---|---|---|---|---|---|
| Tom Flores | QB | 6'1" | 200 | 30 | | |
| Jack Kemp | QB | 6'1" | 204 | 33 | | 14 |
| Teddy Bailey | HB | 6' | 220 | 23 | | |
| Charlie Bivins (from PIT-N) | HB | 6'2" | 212 | 28 | | |
| Bobby Burnett | HB | 6'2" | 208 | 24 | | |
| Gene Donaldson | HB | 6'2" | 225 | 25 | | |
| Allen Smith | HB | 6' | 200 | 24 | | |
| Keith Lincoln | FB-HB | 6'2" | 216 | 28 | | 54 |
| Jack Spikes | FB | 6'2" | 220 | 29 | | |
| Wray Carlton | HB-FB | 6'2" | 224 | 29 | | 18 |
| Elbert Dubenion | FL | 6' | 187 | 32 | | |
| Tony King | FL | 6'1" | 194 | 23 | | |
| Monte Ledbetter (from HOU) | FL | 6'2" | 185 | 24 | | 12 |
| Ed Rutkowski | FL | 6'1" | 198 | 26 | | |
| Paul Costa | TE | 6'4" | 246 | 25 | | 12 |
| Bill Masters | TE | 6'5" | 235 | 23 | | 12 |
| Art Powell | OE | 6'3" | 214 | 30 | | 24 |
| Mike Mercer | K | 6' | 217 | 31 | | 73 |

## MIAMI DOLPHINS 4-10-0 George Wilson

| Scores of Each Game | | |
|---|---|---|
| 35 | DENVER | 21 |
| 0 | KANSAS CITY | 24 |
| 7 | New York | 29 |
| 0 | Kansas City | 41 |
| 10 | Boston | 41 |
| 14 | NEW YORK | 33 |
| 13 | Buffalo | 35 |
| 0 | San Diego | 24 |
| 17 | Oakland | 31 |
| 17 | BUFFALO | 14 |
| 14 | Houston | 17 |
| 41 | SAN DIEGO | 24 |
| 41 | BOSTON | 32 |
| 10 | HOUSTON | 41 |

| Use Name | Pos. | Hgt | Wgt | Age | Int | Pts |
|---|---|---|---|---|---|---|
| Norm Evans | OT | 6'5" | 250 | 24 | | |
| Jack Pyburn | OT | 6'6" | 240 | 22 | | |
| Charlie Fowler | OG-OT | 6'2" | 260 | 23 | | |
| Billy Neighbors | OG | 5'11" | 250 | 27 | | |
| Ken Rice | OG | 6'2" | 240 | 27 | | |
| Freddie Woodson | OG | 6'2" | 250 | 23 | | |
| Maxie Williams | OT-OG | 6'4" | 250 | 27 | | |
| Tom Goode | C | 6'3" | 245 | 28 | | |
| Mel Branch | DE | 6'2" | 235 | 30 | | |
| Ed Cooke | DE | 6'4" | 250 | 32 | | |
| Jim Riley | DE | 6'4" | 240 | 22 | | |
| Claude Brownlee | DT | 6'4" | 265 | 23 | | |
| Ray Jacobs | DT | 6'3" | 285 | 27 | | |
| Tom Nomina | DT | 6'5" | 260 | 25 | | |
| John Richardson | DT | 6'2" | 250 | 22 | | |
| Rich Zecher (to BUF) | DT | 6'2" | 240 | 24 | | |

| Use Name | Pos. | Hgt | Wgt | Age | Int | Pts |
|---|---|---|---|---|---|---|
| John Bramlett | LB | 6'2" | 220 | 26 | 4 | |
| Bob Bruggers | LB | 6'1" | 225 | 23 | 1 | |
| Frank Emanuel | LB | 6'3" | 225 | 24 | 1 | |
| Tom Erlandson | LB | 6'3" | 220 | 27 | 1 | |
| Jerry Hopkins | LB | 6'2" | 235 | 26 | | |
| Wahoo McDaniel | LB | 6' | 230 | 30 | 1 | |
| Pete Jaquess (to DEN) | DB | 6' | 184 | 25 | | |
| Mack Lamb | DB | 6'1" | 188 | 23 | | |
| Bob Neff | DB | 6' | 180 | 23 | 1 | |
| Bob Petrella | DB | 6' | 185 | 22 | 3 | |
| Jimmy Warren | DB | 5'11" | 175 | 28 | 4 | 6 |
| Willie West | DB | 5'10" | 187 | 29 | 1 | |
| Dick Westmoreland | DB | 6'1" | 190 | 26 | 10 | 6 |
| Tom Beier | FL-DB | 5'11" | 198 | 22 | 1 | |

| Use Name | Pos. | Hgt | Wgt | Age | Int | Pts |
|---|---|---|---|---|---|---|
| Bob Griese | QB | 6'1" | 190 | 22 | | 6 |
| Rick Norton | QB | 6'1" | 190 | 23 | | |
| Archie Roberts | QB | 6' | 193 | 24 | | |
| John Stofa | QB | 6'3" | 210 | 25 | | 6 |
| Joe Auer | HB | 6'1" | 205 | 25 | | 18 |
| Jack Harper | HB | 5'11" | 190 | 22 | | 24 |
| Abner Haynes (to NY) | HB | 6' | 190 | 29 | | 12 |
| Larry Seiple | HB | 6' | 200 | 22 | | |
| George Chesser | FB | 6'2" | 220 | 24 | | |
| Stan Mitchell | FB | 6'2" | 220 | 23 | | 24 |
| Sam Price | HB-FB | 5'11" | 215 | 23 | | 12 |
| Jack Clancy | FL | 6'1" | 195 | 23 | | 12 |
| Frank Jackson | FL | 6'1" | 185 | 27 | | 6 |
| John Roderick | FL | 6'1" | 180 | 23 | | |
| Preston Carpenter | TE | 6'2" | 208 | 33 | | |
| Doug Moreau | TE | 6'2" | 205 | 22 | | 18 |
| Karl Noonan | OE | 6'3" | 190 | 23 | | 6 |
| Howard Twilley | OE | 5'10" | 180 | 23 | | 12 |
| Booth Lusteg | K | 5'11" | 190 | 26 | | 39 |
| Gene Mingo (to WAS-N) | K | 6'1" | 190 | 28 | | 12 |

## BOSTON PATRIOTS 3-10-1 Mike Holovak

| Scores of Each Game | | |
|---|---|---|
| 21 | Denver | 26 |
| 14 | San Diego | 28 |
| 7 | Oakland | 35 |
| 23 | Buffalo | 0 |
| 31 | SAN DIEGO | 31 |
| 41 | MIAMI | 10 |
| 14 | OAKLAND | 48 |
| 23 | New York | 30 |
| 18 | HOUSTON | 7 |
| 10 | KANSAS CITY | 33 |
| 24 | NEW YORK | 29 |
| 6 | Houston | 27 |
| 16 | BUFFALO | 44 |
| 32 | Miami | 41 |

| Use Name | Pos. | Hgt | Wgt | Age | Int | Pts |
|---|---|---|---|---|---|---|
| Jim Boudreaux | OT | 6'4" | 245 | 22 | | |
| Tom Neville | OT | 6'4" | 255 | 24 | | |
| Don Oakes | OT | 6'3" | 255 | 29 | | |
| Karl Singer | OT | 6'3" | 250 | 23 | | |
| Justin Canale | OG | 6'2" | 250 | 23 | | 1 |
| Charley Long | OG | 6'3" | 250 | 29 | | |
| Len St. Jean | OG | 6'1" | 240 | 25 | | |
| Jon Morris | C | 6'4" | 240 | 24 | | |
| Bob Dee | DE | 6'3" | 250 | 34 | | |
| Larry Eisenhauer | DE | 6'5" | 255 | 27 | | |
| Tom Fussell | DE | 6'3" | 245 | 21 | | |
| Houston Antwine | DT | 6' | 270 | 28 | | |
| Jim Hunt | DT | 5'11" | 255 | 28 | | 2 |
| John Mangum | DT | 6'3" | 270 | 23 | | |
| Mel Witt | DT | 6'3" | 265 | 21 | | |
| Ed Toner | LB-DT | 6'3" | 250 | 22 | | |

| Use Name | Pos. | Hgt | Wgt | Age | Int | Pts |
|---|---|---|---|---|---|---|
| Tom Addison | LB | 6'3" | 230 | 31 | | |
| Nick Buoniconti | LB | 5'11" | 220 | 26 | 4 | 2 |
| Ray Ilg | LB | 6'1" | 220 | 21 | | |
| Ed Philpott | LB | 6'3" | 240 | 21 | | |
| Doug Satcher | LB | 6' | 220 | 22 | | |
| John Charles | DB | 6'1" | 200 | 23 | 1 | 6 |
| Jay Cunningham | DB | 5'10" | 180 | 24 | 1 | 6 |
| White Graves | DB | 6' | 185 | 24 | | |
| Ron Hall | DB | 6' | 190 | 30 | 1 | |
| Billy Johnson | DB | 5'11" | 175 | 24 | | |
| Leroy Mitchell | DB | 6'2" | 200 | 22 | 3 | |
| Vic Purvis | DB | 5'11" | 200 | 23 | | |
| Chuck Shonta | DB | 6' | 200 | 29 | 3 | |
| Don Webb | DB | 5'10" | 200 | 28 | 4 | |

| Use Name | Pos. | Hgt | Wgt | Age | Int | Pts |
|---|---|---|---|---|---|---|
| John Huarte | QB | 6' | 190 | 23 | | |
| Babe Parilli | QB | 6'1" | 190 | 37 | | |
| Don Trull (from HOU) | QB | 6'1" | 190 | 25 | | 18 |
| Joe Bellino | HB | 5'9" | 185 | 29 | | |
| J. D. Garrett | HB | 5'11" | 195 | 25 | | 6 |
| Larry Garron | HB | 6' | 195 | 30 | | 30 |
| Bobby Leo | HB | 5'10" | 180 | 22 | | 6 |
| Jim Nance | FB | 6'1" | 240 | 24 | | 48 |
| Bob Cappadona | FB | 6'1" | 230 | 23 | | 6 |
| Gino Cappelletti | FL | 6' | 190 | 33 | | 95 |
| Bobby Nichols | TE | 6'2" | 220 | 23 | | |
| Tony Romeo | TE | 6'2" | 230 | 28 | | |
| Jim Whalen | TE | 6'2" | 210 | 23 | | 30 |
| Jim Colclough | OE | 6' | 185 | 31 | | |
| Art Graham | OE | 6'1" | 205 | 26 | | 24 |
| Terry Swanson | K | 6' | 210 | 22 | | |

## HOUSTON OILERS

### RUSHING

| Last Name | No. | Yds | Avg | TD |
|---|---|---|---|---|
| Granger | 236 | 1194 | 5.1 | 6 |
| Campbell | 110 | 511 | 4.6 | 4 |
| Blanks | 66 | 206 | 3.1 | 1 |
| Beathard | 32 | 133 | 4.2 | 1 |
| Hopkins | 13 | 42 | 3.2 | 0 |
| Davis | 5 | 32 | 6.4 | 0 |
| Elkins | 2 | 19 | 9.5 | 0 |
| Lee | 6 | -3 | -0.5 | 0 |
| Burrell | 3 | -3 | -1.0 | 0 |
| Norton | 1 | -7 | -7.0 | 0 |

### RECEIVING

| Last Name | No. | Yds | Avg | TD |
|---|---|---|---|---|
| Granger | 31 | 300 | 10 | 3 |
| Frazier | 23 | 253 | 11 | 1 |
| Taylor | 18 | 233 | 13 | 1 |
| Campbell | 17 | 136 | 8 | 2 |
| Burrell | 12 | 193 | 16 | 0 |
| Reed | 11 | 144 | 13 | 1 |
| Blanks | 11 | 93 | 8 | 1 |
| Bass | 5 | 42 | 8 | 1 |
| Poole | 4 | 55 | 14 | 0 |
| Elkins | 3 | 32 | 11 | 0 |
| Hopkins | 3 | 9 | 3 | 0 |
| Lee | 1 | -1 | -1 | 0 |

### PUNT RETURNS

| Last Name | No. | Yds | Avg | TD |
|---|---|---|---|---|
| Carwell | 9 | 154 | 17 | 0 |
| Moore | 5 | 82 | 16 | 0 |
| Jancik | 6 | 19 | 3 | 0 |

### KICKOFF RETURNS

| Last Name | No. | Yds | Avg | TD |
|---|---|---|---|---|
| Moore | 14 | 405 | 29 | 1 |
| Jancik | 16 | 349 | 22 | 0 |
| Carwell | 8 | 164 | 21 | 0 |
| Houston | 2 | 40 | 20 | 0 |
| Hopkins | 1 | 26 | 26 | 0 |
| Campbell | 1 | 19 | 19 | 0 |
| Farr | 1 | 17 | 17 | 0 |
| Reed | 1 | 0 | 0 | 0 |

### PASSING — PUNTING — KICKING Statistics

**PASSING**

| Last Name | Att | Comp | % | Yds | Yd/Att | TD | Int-% | RK |
|---|---|---|---|---|---|---|---|---|
| Beathard | 231 | 94 | 41 | 1114 | 4.8 | 9 | 14-6 | 9 |
| Lee | 91 | 42 | 46 | 414 | 4.6 | 3 | 6-7 | |
| Davis | 19 | 9 | 47 | 71 | 3.7 | 0 | 2-11 | |
| Campbell | 1 | 0 | 0 | 0 | 0.0 | 0 | 0-0 | |

**PUNTING**

| Last Name | No | Avg |
|---|---|---|
| Norton | 71 | 42.6 |

**KICKING**

| Last Name | XP | Att | % | FG | Att | % |
|---|---|---|---|---|---|---|
| Wittenborn | 30 | 30 | 100 | 14 | 28 | 50 |

## NEW YORK JETS

### RUSHING

| Last Name | No. | Yds | Avg | TD |
|---|---|---|---|---|
| Boozer | 119 | 442 | 3.7 | 10 |
| Mathis | 78 | 243 | 3.1 | 4 |
| Snell | 61 | 207 | 3.4 | 0 |
| Joe | 37 | 154 | 4.2 | 2 |
| Smolinski | 64 | 139 | 2.2 | 1 |
| Taliaferro | 2 | 20 | 10.0 | 0 |
| Maynard | 4 | 18 | 4.5 | 0 |
| Namath | 6 | 14 | 2.3 | 0 |
| Schweickert | 1 | 1 | 1.0 | 0 |
| Sauer | 1 | -3 | -3.0 | 0 |

### RECEIVING

| Last Name | No. | Yds | Avg | TD |
|---|---|---|---|---|
| Sauer | 75 | 1189 | 16 | 6 |
| Maynard | 71 | 1434 | 20 | 10 |
| Lammons | 45 | 515 | 11 | 2 |
| Mathis | 25 | 429 | 17 | 3 |
| Smolinski | 21 | 177 | 8 | 3 |
| Boozer | 12 | 205 | 17 | 3 |
| Snell | 11 | 54 | 5 | 0 |
| Joe | 8 | 85 | 11 | 0 |
| B. Turner | 3 | 40 | 13 | 0 |

### PUNT RETURNS

| Last Name | No. | Yds | Avg | TD |
|---|---|---|---|---|
| Baird | 25 | 219 | 9 | 0 |
| Christy | 16 | 83 | 5 | 0 |
| Lewis | 7 | 24 | 3 | 0 |

### KICKOFF RETURNS

| Last Name | No. | Yds | Avg | TD |
|---|---|---|---|---|
| Christy | 23 | 521 | 23 | 0 |
| Boozer | 11 | 213 | 19 | 0 |
| Brannan | 9 | 204 | 23 | 0 |
| B. Turner | 4 | 40 | 10 | 0 |
| Lewis | 1 | 22 | 22 | 0 |
| McAdams | 1 | 16 | 16 | 0 |
| Smolinski | 1 | 3 | 3 | 0 |
| Waskiewicz | 2 | 0 | 0 | 0 |
| Wilder | 1 | 0 | 0 | 0 |

**PASSING**

| Last Name | Att | Comp | % | Yds | Yd/Att | TD | Int-% | RK |
|---|---|---|---|---|---|---|---|---|
| Namath | 491 | 258 | 53 | 4007 | 8.2 | 26 | 28-6 | 3 |
| Taliaferro | 20 | 11 | 55 | 96 | 4.8 | 1 | 1-5 | |
| J. Turner | 4 | 2 | 50 | 25 | 6.3 | 0 | 0-0 | |

**PUNTING**

| Last Name | No | Avg |
|---|---|---|
| Johnson | 65 | 42.1 |

**KICKING**

| Last Name | XP | Att | % | FG | Att | % |
|---|---|---|---|---|---|---|
| J. Turner | 36 | 39 | 92 | 17 | 32 | 53 |

**2 POINT XP**
Mathis (2)
Maynard
Sauer

## BUFFALO BILLS

### RUSHING

| Last Name | No. | Yds | Avg | TD |
|---|---|---|---|---|
| Lincoln | 159 | 601 | 3.8 | 4 |
| Carlton | 107 | 467 | 4.4 | 3 |
| Burnett | 45 | 96 | 2.1 | 0 |
| Bivins | 15 | 58 | 3.9 | 0 |
| Kemp | 36 | 58 | 1.6 | 2 |
| Spikes | 4 | 9 | 2.3 | 0 |
| Donaldson | 3 | -1 | -0.3 | 0 |
| Dubenion | 2 | -17 | -8.5 | 0 |

### RECEIVING

| Last Name | No. | Yds | Avg | TD |
|---|---|---|---|---|
| Lincoln | 41 | 558 | 14 | 5 |
| Costa | 39 | 726 | 19 | 2 |
| Dubenion | 25 | 384 | 15 | 0 |
| Powell | 20 | 346 | 17 | 4 |
| Masters | 20 | 274 | 14 | 2 |
| Ledbetter | 13 | 204 | 16 | 2 |
| Burnett | 11 | 114 | 10 | 0 |
| Carlton | 9 | 97 | 11 | 0 |
| Rutkowski | 6 | 59 | 10 | 0 |
| Donaldson | 1 | 20 | 20 | 0 |
| Tracey | 1 | 15 | 15 | 0 |
| Spikes | 1 | 9 | 9 | 0 |

### PUNT RETURNS

| Last Name | No. | Yds | Avg | TD |
|---|---|---|---|---|
| Byrd | 30 | 142 | 5 | 0 |
| Rutkowski | 15 | 43 | 3 | 0 |
| C. King | 1 | 12 | 12 | 0 |
| Edgerson | 1 | 2 | 2 | 0 |

### KICKOFF RETURNS

| Last Name | No. | Yds | Avg | TD |
|---|---|---|---|---|
| Bivins | 16 | 380 | 24 | 0 |
| Smith | 16 | 346 | 22 | 0 |
| C. King | 12 | 316 | 26 | 0 |
| Rutkowski | 3 | 71 | 24 | 0 |
| Meredith | 3 | 0 | 0 | 0 |
| Guidry | 1 | 0 | 0 | 0 |

**PASSING**

| Last Name | Att | Comp | % | Yds | Yd/Att | TD | Int-% | RK |
|---|---|---|---|---|---|---|---|---|
| Kemp | 369 | 161 | 44 | 2503 | 6.8 | 14 | 26-7 | 8 |
| Flores | 64 | 22 | 34 | 260 | 4.1 | 0 | 8-13 | |
| Rutkowski | 1 | 0 | 0 | 0 | 0.0 | 0 | 0-0 | |

**PUNTING**

| Last Name | No | Avg |
|---|---|---|
| Maguire | 77 | 43.1 |

**KICKING**

| Last Name | XP | Att | % | FG | Att | % |
|---|---|---|---|---|---|---|
| Mercer | 25 | 25 | 100 | 16 | 27 | 59 |

**2 POINT XP**
Kemp

## MIAMI DOLPHINS

### RUSHING

| Last Name | No. | Yds | Avg | TD |
|---|---|---|---|---|
| Haynes | 72 | 346 | 4.8 | 2 |
| Mitchell | 83 | 269 | 3.2 | 3 |
| Harper | 41 | 197 | 4.8 | 1 |
| Price | 46 | 179 | 3.9 | 1 |
| Griese | 37 | 157 | 4.2 | 1 |
| Auer | 44 | 128 | 2.9 | 1 |
| Seiple | 3 | 58 | 19.3 | 0 |
| Jackson | 1 | 48 | 48.0 | 0 |
| Norton | 7 | 14 | 2.0 | 0 |
| Chesser | 2 | 3 | 1.5 | 0 |
| Stofa | 2 | 2 | 1.0 | 1 |
| Moreau | 1 | -2 | -2.0 | 0 |
| Clancy | 3 | -4 | -1.3 | 0 |

### RECEIVING

| Last Name | No. | Yds | Avg | TD |
|---|---|---|---|---|
| Clancy | 67 | 868 | 13 | 2 |
| Moreau | 34 | 410 | 12 | 3 |
| Twilley | 24 | 314 | 13 | 2 |
| Auer | 18 | 218 | 12 | 2 |
| Mitchell | 18 | 133 | 7 | 1 |
| Haynes | 16 | 100 | 6 | 0 |
| Noonan | 12 | 141 | 12 | 1 |
| Harper | 11 | 212 | 19 | 3 |
| Carpenter | 10 | 127 | 13 | 0 |
| Jackson | 9 | 122 | 14 | 1 |
| Price | 8 | 56 | 7 | 1 |
| Seiple | 1 | 21 | 21 | 0 |
| Beier | 1 | 19 | 19 | 0 |

### PUNT RETURNS

| Last Name | No. | Yds | Avg | TD |
|---|---|---|---|---|
| Auer | 9 | 42 | 5 | 0 |
| Haynes | 6 | 37 | 6 | 0 |
| Neff | 6 | 34 | 6 | 0 |
| Harper | 4 | 15 | 4 | 0 |

### KICKOFF RETURNS

| Last Name | No. | Yds | Avg | TD |
|---|---|---|---|---|
| Haynes | 26 | 569 | 22 | 0 |
| Auer | 21 | 441 | 21 | 0 |
| Neff | 15 | 351 | 23 | 0 |
| Carpenter | 3 | 87 | 29 | 0 |
| Roderick | 4 | 63 | 16 | 0 |
| Mitchell | 2 | 57 | 29 | 0 |

**PASSING**

| Last Name | Att | Comp | % | Yds | Yd/Att | TD | Int-% | RK |
|---|---|---|---|---|---|---|---|---|
| Griese | 331 | 166 | 50 | 2005 | 6.1 | 15 | 18-5 | 5 |
| Norton | 133 | 53 | 40 | 596 | 4.5 | 1 | 9-7 | |
| Roberts | 10 | 5 | 50 | 11 | 1.1 | 0 | 1-10 | |
| Seiple | 2 | 2 | 100 | 61 | 30.5 | 0 | 0-0 | |
| Stofa | 2 | 2 | 100 | 51 | 25.5 | 0 | 0-0 | |
| Clancy | 1 | 1 | 100 | 17 | 17.0 | 0 | 0-0 | |
| Lusteg | 1 | 0 | 0 | 0 | 0.0 | 0 | 0-0 | |

**PUNTING**

| Last Name | No | Avg |
|---|---|---|
| Seiple | 70 | 41.6 |

**KICKING**

| Last Name | XP | Att | % | FG | Att | % |
|---|---|---|---|---|---|---|
| Lusteg | 18 | 18 | 100 | 7 | 12 | 58 |
| Mingo | 9 | 9 | 100 | 1 | 6 | 17 |

## BOSTON PATRIOTS

### RUSHING

| Last Name | No. | Yds | Avg | TD |
|---|---|---|---|---|
| Nance | 269 | 1216 | 4.5 | 7 |
| Garron | 46 | 163 | 3.5 | 0 |
| Cappadona | 28 | 100 | 3.6 | 0 |
| Parilli | 14 | 61 | 4.4 | 0 |
| Trull | 22 | 30 | 1.4 | 3 |
| Bellino | 6 | 15 | 2.5 | 0 |
| Garrett | 5 | 7 | 1.4 | 0 |
| Leo | 1 | 7 | 7.0 | 0 |
| Huarte | 2 | 5 | 2.5 | 0 |
| Graham | 1 | -5 | -5.0 | 0 |

### RECEIVING

| Last Name | No. | Yds | Avg | TD |
|---|---|---|---|---|
| Graham | 41 | 606 | 15 | 4 |
| Whalen | 39 | 651 | 17 | 5 |
| Cappelletti | 35 | 397 | 11 | 3 |
| Garron | 30 | 507 | 17 | 5 |
| Nance | 22 | 196 | 9 | 1 |
| Colclough | 14 | 263 | 19 | 0 |
| Cappadona | 6 | 104 | 17 | 1 |
| Leo | 1 | 25 | 25 | 1 |
| Nichols | 1 | 19 | 19 | 0 |
| Garrett | 1 | 12 | 12 | 0 |
| Romeo | 1 | 4 | 4 | 0 |

### PUNT RETURNS

| Last Name | No. | Yds | Avg | TD |
|---|---|---|---|---|
| Bellino | 15 | 129 | 9 | 0 |
| Johnson | 6 | 124 | 21 | 0 |
| Cunningham | 17 | 105 | 6 | 0 |
| Leo | 5 | 54 | 11 | 0 |

### KICKOFF RETURNS

| Last Name | No. | Yds | Avg | TD |
|---|---|---|---|---|
| Cunningham | 30 | 627 | 21 | 0 |
| Bellino | 18 | 357 | 20 | 0 |
| Leo | 11 | 232 | 21 | 0 |
| Garrett | 4 | 73 | 18 | 0 |
| Garron | 3 | 73 | 24 | 0 |
| Singer | 2 | 29 | 15 | 0 |
| Cappadona | 3 | 26 | 9 | 0 |
| Ilg | 1 | 10 | 10 | 0 |
| Johnson | 1 | 9 | 9 | 0 |

**PASSING**

| Last Name | Att | Comp | % | Yds | Yd/Att | TD | Int-% | RK |
|---|---|---|---|---|---|---|---|---|
| Parilli | 344 | 161 | 47 | 2317 | 6.7 | 19 | 24-7 | 6 |
| Trull | 92 | 31 | 34 | 480 | 5.2 | 1 | 7-8 | |
| Huarte | 9 | 3 | 33 | 25 | 2.8 | 0 | 1-11 | |

**PUNTING**

| Last Name | No | Avg |
|---|---|---|
| Swanson | 65 | 40.5 |

**KICKING**

| Last Name | XP | Att | % | FG | Att | % |
|---|---|---|---|---|---|---|
| Cappelletti | 29 | 30 | 97 | 16 | 31 | 52 |
| Canale | 1 | 1 | 100 | 0 | 0 | |

## OAKLAND RAIDERS 13-1-0 Johnny Rauch

### Scores of Each Game

| |  | |
|---|---|---|
| 51 | DENVER | 0 |
| 35 | BOSTON | 7 |
| 23 | KANSAS CITY | 21 |
| 14 | New York | 27 |
| 24 | Buffalo | 20 |
| 48 | Boston | 14 |
| 51 | SAN DIEGO | 10 |
| 21 | Denver | 17 |
| 31 | MIAMI | 17 |
| 44 | Kansas City | 22 |
| 41 | San Diego | 21 |
| 19 | Houston | 7 |
| 38 | NEW YORK | 29 |
| 28 | BUFFALO | 21 |

| Use Name | Pos. | Hgt | Wgt | Age | Int | Pts |
|---|---|---|---|---|---|---|
| Harry Schuh | OT | 6'2" | 260 | 24 | | |
| Bob Svihus | OT | 6'4" | 245 | 24 | | |
| Dan Archer | OG-OT | 6'5" | 245 | 22 | | |
| Jim Harvey | OG | 6'5" | 245 | 24 | | |
| Wayne Hawkins | OG | 6' | 240 | 29 | | |
| Bob Kruse | OG | 6'2" | 250 | 25 | | |
| Gene Upshaw | OT-OG | 6'5" | 255 | 22 | | |
| Jim Otto | C | 6'2" | 240 | 29 | | |
| Ben Davidson | DE | 6'8" | 265 | 27 | | |
| Ike Lassiter | DE | 6'5" | 270 | 26 | | |
| Carleton Oats | DE | 6'2" | 235 | 24 | | 6 |
| Dan Birdwell | DT | 6'4" | 250 | 26 | 1 | 2 |
| Tom Keating | DT | 6'3" | 247 | 24 | | |
| Richard Sligh | DT | 7' | 300 | 22 | | |

| Use Name | Pos. | Hgt | Wgt | Age | Int | Pts |
|---|---|---|---|---|---|---|
| Duane Benson | LB | 6'2" | 215 | 22 | | |
| Bill Budness | LB | 6'1" | 215 | 24 | | |
| Dan Conners | LB | 6'1" | 230 | 25 | 3 | 12 |
| Bill Fairband | LB | 6'3" | 228 | 21 | | |
| Bill Laskey | LB | 6'2" | 235 | 24 | | |
| Gus Otto | LB | 6'2" | 220 | 24 | 1 | |
| J. R. Williamson | LB | 6'2" | 220 | 25 | 2 | |
| Rodger Bird | DB | 5'11" | 195 | 24 | | |
| Willie Brown | DB | 6'1" | 190 | 26 | 7 | 6 |
| Dave Grayson | DB | 5'10" | 185 | 28 | 4 | |
| Kent McCloughan | DB | 6'1" | 190 | 24 | 2 | |
| Warren Powers | DB | 6' | 190 | 26 | 6 | 12 |
| Howie Williams | DB | 6'2" | 186 | 30 | 4 | |

Charley Warner — Injury

| Use Name | Pos. | Hgt | Wgt | Age | Int | Pts |
|---|---|---|---|---|---|---|
| George Blanda | QB | 6'1" | 215 | 39 | | 116 |
| Daryle Lamonica | QB | 6'2" | 215 | 26 | | 24 |
| Pete Banaszak | HB | 5'11" | 200 | 23 | | 12 |
| Estes Banks | HB | 6'1" | 200 | 22 | | |
| Clem Daniels | HB | 6'1" | 218 | 30 | | 36 |
| Larry Todd | HB | 6'1" | 185 | 24 | | 12 |
| Roger Hagberg | FB | 6'2" | 215 | 28 | | 18 |
| Hewritt Dixon | HB-FB | 6'2" | 220 | 27 | | 42 |
| Fred Biletnikoff | FL | 6'1" | 190 | 24 | | 30 |
| Rod Sherman | FL | 6' | 190 | 22 | | 6 |
| Billy Cannon | TE | 6'1" | 215 | 30 | | 60 |
| Dave Kocourek | TE | 6'5" | 240 | 30 | | 2 |
| Ken Herock | OE | 6'2" | 230 | 26 | | |
| Bill Miller | OE | 6' | 190 | 25 | | 36 |
| Warren Wells | OE | 6'1" | 190 | 24 | | 36 |
| Mike Eischeid | K | 6' | 190 | 26 | | |

## KANSAS CITY CHIEFS 9-5-0 Hank Stram

### Scores of Each Game

| |  | |
|---|---|---|
| 25 | Houston | 20 |
| 24 | Miami | 0 |
| 21 | Oakland | 23 |
| 41 | MIAMI | 0 |
| 31 | San Diego | 45 |
| 19 | HOUSTON | 24 |
| 52 | DENVER | 9 |
| 42 | NEW YORK | 18 |
| 33 | Boston | 10 |
| 16 | SAN DIEGO | 17 |
| 22 | OAKLAND | 44 |
| 23 | BUFFALO | 13 |
| 21 | New York | 7 |
| 38 | Denver | 24 |

| Use Name | Pos. | Hgt | Wgt | Age | Int | Pts |
|---|---|---|---|---|---|---|
| Dave Hill | OT | 6'5" | 260 | 26 | | |
| Bob Kelly | OT | 6'3" | 265 | 27 | | |
| Jim Tyrer | OT | 6'6" | 292 | 28 | | |
| Tony DiMidio | C-OT | 6'3" | 250 | 25 | | |
| Denny Biodrowski | OG | 6'1" | 255 | 27 | | |
| Ed Budde | OG | 6'5" | 260 | 26 | | |
| Curt Merz | OG | 6'4" | 267 | 29 | | |
| Al Reynolds | OG | 6'3" | 250 | 29 | | |
| Wayne Frazier (to BUF) | C | 6'2" | 245 | 27 | | |
| Jon Gilliam | C | 6'2" | 240 | 28 | | |
| Mike Hudock | C | 6'2" | 245 | 32 | | |
| Jerry Mays | DE | 6'4" | 252 | 27 | | |
| Gene Trosch | DT-DE | 6'7" | 277 | 22 | | |
| Buck Buchanan | DT | 6'7" | 287 | 27 | | |
| Ernie Ladd (from HOU) | DT | 6'9" | 292 | 28 | | |
| Ed Lothamer | DE-DT | 6'5" | 260 | 24 | | |

| Use Name | Pos. | Hgt | Wgt | Age | Int | Pts |
|---|---|---|---|---|---|---|
| Bud Abell | LB | 6'3" | 220 | 26 | | |
| Bobby Bell | LB | 6'4" | 228 | 27 | 4 | 6 |
| Sherrill Headrick | LB | 6'2" | 240 | 30 | 1 | |
| Chuck Hurston | LB | 6'6" | 240 | 24 | | |
| Willie Lanier | LB | 6'1" | 245 | 22 | | |
| Jim Lynch | LB | 6'1" | 235 | 22 | 1 | |
| E. J. Holub | C-LB | 6'4" | 236 | 29 | | |
| Bobby Hunt | DB | 6'1" | 193 | 27 | 5 | |
| Jim Kearney | DB | 6'2" | 206 | 24 | | |
| Sam Longmire | DB | 6'3" | 195 | 24 | | |
| Willie Mitchell | DB | 6'1" | 185 | 25 | 4 | 6 |
| Johnny Robinson | DB | 6' | 205 | 28 | 5 | |
| Fletcher Smith | DB | 6'2" | 188 | 23 | 6 | |
| Emmitt Thomas | DB | 6'2" | 192 | 24 | 4 | 6 |
| Fred Williamson | DB | 6'2" | 210 | 29 | 1 | 6 |

Aaron Brown — Thigh Injury

| Use Name | Pos. | Hgt | Wgt | Age | Int | Pts |
|---|---|---|---|---|---|---|
| Len Dawson | QB | 6' | 190 | 33 | | |
| Bert Coan | HB | 6'4" | 220 | 27 | | 24 |
| Mike Garrett | HB | 5'9" | 200 | 23 | | 60 |
| Gene Thomas | HB | 6'1" | 210 | 24 | | 18 |
| Curtis McClinton | FB | 6'3" | 227 | 29 | | 20 |
| Jerrel Wilson | FB | 6'4" | 222 | 25 | | |
| Gloster Richardson | FL | 6' | 200 | 24 | | 12 |
| Noland Smith | FL | 5'6" | 154 | 23 | | 6 |
| Otis Taylor | FL | 6'2" | 215 | 24 | | 72 |
| Fred Arbanas | TE | 6'3" | 240 | 28 | | 30 |
| Reg Carolan | TE | 6'6" | 240 | 27 | | 2 |
| Chris Burford | OE | 6'3" | 210 | 29 | | 18 |
| Frank Pitts | OE | 6'2" | 200 | 23 | | 12 |
| Jan Stenerud | K | 6'2" | 187 | 24 | | 108 |
| Wayne Walker | K | 6'2" | 215 | 22 | | |

## SAN DIEGO CHARGERS 8-5-1 Sid Gillman

### Scores of Each Game

| |  | |
|---|---|---|
| 28 | BOSTON | 14 |
| 13 | HOUSTON | 3 |
| 37 | Buffalo | 17 |
| 31 | Boston | 31 |
| 45 | KANSAS CITY | 31 |
| 38 | Denver | 21 |
| 10 | Oakland | 51 |
| 24 | MIAMI | 0 |
| 17 | Kansas City | 16 |
| 24 | DENVER | 20 |
| 21 | OAKLAND | 41 |
| 24 | Miami | 41 |
| 17 | Houston | 24 |
| 31 | NEW YORK | 42 |

| Use Name | Pos. | Hgt | Wgt | Age | Int | Pts |
|---|---|---|---|---|---|---|
| Harold Akin | OT | 6'5" | 262 | 22 | | |
| Gary Kirner | OT | 6'3" | 248 | 25 | | |
| Ron Mix | OT | 6'4" | 250 | 29 | | |
| Terry Owens | OT | 6'6" | 240 | 23 | | |
| Ernie Wright | OT | 6'4" | 265 | 27 | | |
| Ed Mitchell | OG | 6'2" | 280 | 25 | | |
| Walt Sweeney | OG | 6'3" | 255 | 26 | | |
| Larry Little | DT-OG | 6'1" | 265 | 21 | | |
| Sam Gruneisen | C | 6'1" | 240 | 26 | | |
| Paul Latzke | C | 6'4" | 240 | 25 | | |
| Tom Day | DE | 6'2" | 262 | 32 | | |
| Jim Griffin | DE | 6'3" | 255 | 25 | | |
| Howard Kindig (to BUF) | DE | 6'6" | 255 | 26 | | |
| Scott Appleton | DT | 6'3" | 256 | 25 | | 6 |
| Ron Billingsley | DT | 6'8" | 265 | 22 | | |
| Steve DeLong | DT | 6'3" | 252 | 24 | | |
| George Gross | DT | 6'3" | 258 | 26 | | |
| Houston Ridge | DT | 6'4" | 235 | 23 | | |

| Use Name | Pos. | Hgt | Wgt | Age | Int | Pts |
|---|---|---|---|---|---|---|
| Chuck Allen | LB | 6'1" | 225 | 27 | 2 | |
| Johnny Baker | LB | 6'3" | 238 | 26 | | |
| Frank Buncom | LB | 6'1" | 240 | 27 | | |
| Bernie Erickson | LB | 6'2" | 238 | 22 | 1 | |
| Ron McCall | LB | 6'2" | 245 | 22 | | |
| Bob Print | LB | 6' | 220 | 23 | | |
| Rick Redman | LB | 5'11" | 225 | 24 | 2 | |
| Jeff Staggs | LB | 6'2" | 248 | 23 | | |
| Joe Beauchamp | DB | 6' | 185 | 23 | 3 | |
| Speedy Duncan | DB | 5'10" | 175 | 24 | 2 | 18 |
| Kenny Graham | DB | 6' | 195 | 25 | 2 | 6 |
| Bob Howard | DB | 6'1" | 190 | 22 | | |
| Frank Marsh | DB | 6'2" | 205 | 26 | | |
| Jim Tolbert | DB | 6'3" | 207 | 23 | 1 | |
| Bud Whitehead | HB-DB | 6' | 185 | 28 | | |

Nat Whitmyer — Injury

| Use Name | Pos. | Hgt | Wgt | Age | Int | Pts |
|---|---|---|---|---|---|---|
| John Hadl | QB | 6'2" | 215 | 27 | | 18 |
| Kay Stephenson | QB | 6'1" | 205 | 22 | | |
| Gene Foster | HB | 5'11" | 212 | 24 | | |
| Paul Lowe | HB | 6' | 205 | 30 | | 6 |
| Dickie Post | HB | 5'9" | 190 | 21 | | 48 |
| Jim Allison | FB | 6' | 220 | 24 | | |
| Brad Hubbert | FB | 6'1" | 227 | 26 | | 24 |
| Russ Smith | HB-FB | 6'1" | 225 | 23 | | 6 |
| Lance Alworth | FL | 6' | 180 | 27 | | 54 |
| Willie Frazier | TE | 6'4" | 225 | 24 | | 60 |
| Jacque MacKinnon | TE | 6'4" | 250 | 28 | | 12 |
| Ollie Cordill | OE | 6'2" | 180 | 24 | | |
| Gary Garrison | OE | 6'1" | 195 | 23 | | 12 |
| Steve Newell | OE | 6'1" | 186 | 22 | | |
| Dick Van Raaphorst | K | 5'11" | 215 | 24 | | 90 |

## DENVER BRONCOS 3-11-0 Lou Saban

### Scores of Each Game

| |  | |
|---|---|---|
| 26 | BOSTON | 21 |
| 0 | Oakland | 51 |
| 21 | Miami | 35 |
| 24 | NEW YORK | 38 |
| 6 | Houston | 10 |
| 16 | BUFFALO | 17 |
| 21 | SAN DIEGO | 38 |
| 9 | Kansas City | 52 |
| 17 | OAKLAND | 21 |
| 18 | HOUSTON | 20 |
| 21 | Buffalo | 20 |
| 20 | San Diego | 24 |
| 33 | New York | 24 |
| 24 | KANSAS CITY | 38 |

| Use Name | Pos. | Hgt | Wgt | Age | Int | Pts |
|---|---|---|---|---|---|---|
| Dave Behrman | OT | 6'5" | 260 | 25 | | |
| Bob Breitenstein (to MIN-N) | OT | 6'3" | 267 | 24 | | |
| Sam Brunelli | OT | 6'1" | 255 | 24 | | |
| Tom Cichowski | OT | 6'4" | 250 | 22 | | |
| Mike Current (from MIA) | OT | 6'4" | 250 | 21 | | |
| Pat Matson | OG | 6'1" | 250 | 23 | | |
| Ernie Park | OG | 6'3" | 240 | 25 | | |
| Don Smith | OG | 6'4" | 240 | 24 | | |
| Dick Tyson | OG | 6'2" | 245 | 24 | | |
| Bob Young | OG | 6'2" | 260 | 24 | | |
| George Goeddeke | C-OG | 6'3" | 240 | 22 | | |
| Larry Kaminski | C | 6'2" | 240 | 22 | | |
| Ray Kubala | C | 6'4" | 245 | 25 | | |
| Roger LeClerc | C | 6'3" | 245 | 29 | 5 | |
| Pete Duranko | DE | 6'2" | 240 | 23 | | |
| Rich Jackson | DE | 6'2" | 255 | 26 | 2 | |
| Rex Mirich | DE | 6'4" | 250 | 26 | | |
| Dave Costa | DT | 6'2" | 250 | 25 | | |
| Larry Cox | DT | 6'2" | 250 | 23 | | |
| Jerry Inman | DT | 6'3" | 255 | 27 | | |
| Bill Keating (to MIA) | DT | 6'2" | 236 | 22 | | |

| Use Name | Pos. | Hgt | Wgt | Age | Int | Pts |
|---|---|---|---|---|---|---|
| Lou Andrus | LB | 6'6" | 255 | 24 | | |
| Carl Cunningham | LB | 6'3" | 240 | 23 | 1 | |
| John Huard | LB | 6' | 220 | 23 | 2 | |
| Gene Jeter | LB | 6'3" | 230 | 25 | | |
| Chip Myrtle | LB | 6'2" | 215 | 22 | 1 | |
| Frank Richter | LB | 6'3" | 230 | 22 | 2 | |
| Henry Sorrell | LB | 6'1" | 215 | 23 | | |
| Jack Lentz | DB | 6' | 195 | 22 | 4 | |
| Bobby Ply (from KC-BUF) | Db | 6'1" | 190 | 26 | | |
| Errol Prisby | DB | 5'10" | 184 | 24 | | |
| Goldie Sellers | DB | 6'2" | 198 | 25 | 7 | 6 |
| Jim Summers | DB | 5'10" | 175 | 21 | | |
| Gene Sykes | DB | 6'1" | 195 | 26 | 2 | |
| Nemiah Wilson | DB | 6' | 165 | 24 | 4 | 12 |
| Lonnie Wright | DB | 6'2" | 205 | 23 | 4 | |
| Tom Cassese | HB-DB | 6'1" | 197 | 21 | 1 | |

Max Leetzow — Injury

| Use Name | Pos. | Hgt | Wgt | Age | Int | Pts |
|---|---|---|---|---|---|---|
| Scotty Glacken | QB | 6' | 190 | 22 | | |
| Jim LeClair | QB | 6'1" | 208 | 23 | | 6 |
| Steve Tensi | QB | 6'5" | 215 | 24 | | |
| Floyd Little | HB | 5'10" | 195 | 25 | | 12 |
| Fran Lynch | HB | 6'1" | 210 | 21 | | |
| Charley Mitchell | HB | 5'11" | 185 | 27 | | |
| Cookie Gilchrist | FB | 6'3" | 250 | 32 | | |
| Wendell Hayes | FB | 6'2" | 220 | 26 | | 26 |
| Bo Hickey | FB | 5'11" | 225 | 21 | | 2 |
| Mike Kellogg | FB | 6' | 220 | 24 | | |
| Al Denson | FL | 6'2" | 208 | 25 | | 66 |
| Bob Scarpitto | FL | 5'11" | 196 | 28 | | |
| Tom Beer | TE | 6'2" | 235 | 22 | | |
| Andre White | TE | 6'5" | 225 | 22 | | 2 |
| Eric Crabtree | OE | 5'11" | 182 | 22 | | 30 |
| Neal Sweeney | OE | 6'2" | 170 | 24 | | |
| Rick Duncan | K | 6' | 208 | 26 | | 9 |
| Dick Humphreys | K | 6'1" | 240 | 27 | | 39 |
| Gary Kroner | K | 6'1" | 200 | 26 | | 11 |

## RUSHING

### OAKLAND RAIDERS

| Last Name | No. | Yds | Avg | TD |
|---|---|---|---|---|
| Daniels | 130 | 575 | 4.4 | 4 |
| Dixon | 153 | 559 | 3.7 | 5 |
| Banaszak | 68 | 376 | 5.5 | 1 |
| Hagberg | 44 | 146 | 3.3 | 2 |
| Todd | 29 | 116 | 4.0 | 2 |
| Lamonica | 22 | 110 | 5.0 | 4 |
| Banks | 10 | 26 | 2.6 | 0 |
| Sherman | 1 | 13 | 13.0 | 1 |
| Wells | 1 | 7 | 7.0 | 0 |

### KANSAS CITY CHIEFS

| Last Name | No. | Yds | Avg | TD |
|---|---|---|---|---|
| Garrett | 236 | 1087 | 4.6 | 9 |
| McClinton | 97 | 392 | 4.0 | 2 |
| Coan | 63 | 275 | 4.4 | 4 |
| G. Thomas | 35 | 133 | 3.8 | 1 |
| Dawson | 20 | 68 | 3.4 | 0 |
| Taylor | 5 | 29 | 5.8 | 0 |
| Pitts | 3 | 19 | 6.3 | 1 |
| Wilson | 1 | 10 | 10.0 | 0 |
| N. Smith | 1 | 8 | 8.0 | 0 |

### SAN DIEGO CHARGERS

| Last Name | No. | Yds | Avg | TD |
|---|---|---|---|---|
| Post | 161 | 663 | 4.1 | 7 |
| Hubbert | 116 | 643 | 5.5 | 2 |
| Smith | 22 | 115 | 5.2 | 1 |
| Hadl | 37 | 107 | 2.9 | 3 |
| Foster | 38 | 78 | 2.1 | 0 |
| Lowe | 28 | 71 | 2.5 | 1 |
| Allison | 10 | 34 | 3.4 | 0 |
| Stephenson | 2 | 11 | 5.5 | 0 |
| Alworth | 1 | 5 | 5.0 | 0 |
| Garrison | 1 | 1 | 1.0 | 0 |
| Redman | 1 | −13 | −13.0 | 0 |

### DENVER BRONCOS

| Last Name | No. | Yds | Avg | TD |
|---|---|---|---|---|
| Little | 130 | 381 | 2.9 | 1 |
| Mitchell | 82 | 308 | 3.8 | 0 |
| Hickey | 73 | 263 | 3.6 | 4 |
| Hayes | 85 | 255 | 3.0 | 4 |
| Gilchrist | 10 | 21 | 2.1 | 0 |
| Glacken | 1 | 10 | 10.0 | 0 |
| Lynch | 2 | 7 | 3.5 | 0 |
| LeClair | 8 | 6 | 0.8 | 1 |
| Cassese | 1 | 5 | 5.0 | 0 |
| Scarpitto | 1 | 5 | 5.0 | 0 |
| Tensi | 24 | 4 | 0.2 | 0 |
| Crabtree | 2 | 2 | 1.0 | 0 |
| Denson | 1 | −2 | −2.0 | 0 |

## RECEIVING

### OAKLAND RAIDERS

| Last Name | No. | Yds | Avg | TD |
|---|---|---|---|---|
| Dixon | 59 | 563 | 10 | 2 |
| Biletnikoff | 40 | 876 | 22 | 5 |
| Miller | 38 | 537 | 14 | 6 |
| Cannon | 32 | 629 | 20 | 10 |
| Daniels | 16 | 222 | 14 | 2 |
| Banaszak | 16 | 192 | 12 | 1 |
| Wells | 13 | 302 | 23 | 6 |
| Hagberg | 11 | 114 | 10 | 1 |
| Sherman | 5 | 61 | 12 | 0 |
| Todd | 4 | 42 | 11 | 0 |
| Kocourek | 1 | 4 | 4 | 0 |
| Herock | 1 | −1 | −1 | 0 |

### KANSAS CITY CHIEFS

| Last Name | No. | Yds | Avg | TD |
|---|---|---|---|---|
| Taylor | 59 | 958 | 16 | 11 |
| Garrett | 46 | 261 | 6 | 1 |
| McClinton | 26 | 219 | 8 | 1 |
| Burford | 25 | 389 | 16 | 3 |
| Arbanas | 20 | 295 | 15 | 5 |
| G. Thomas | 13 | 99 | 8 | 2 |
| Richardson | 12 | 312 | 26 | 2 |
| Coan | 5 | 41 | 8 | 0 |
| Pitts | 4 | 131 | 33 | 1 |
| Carolan | 2 | 26 | 13 | 0 |
| N. Smith | 1 | 42 | 42 | 0 |

### SAN DIEGO CHARGERS

| Last Name | No. | Yds | Avg | TD |
|---|---|---|---|---|
| Frazier | 57 | 922 | 16 | 10 |
| Alworth | 52 | 1010 | 19 | 9 |
| Garrison | 44 | 772 | 18 | 2 |
| Post | 32 | 278 | 9 | 1 |
| Hubbert | 19 | 214 | 11 | 2 |
| Foster | 9 | 46 | 5 | 0 |
| Mackinnon | 7 | 176 | 25 | 2 |
| Newell | 7 | 68 | 10 | 0 |
| Lowe | 2 | 25 | 13 | 0 |
| Smith | 1 | 6 | 6 | 0 |

### DENVER BRONCOS

| Last Name | No. | Yds | Avg | TD |
|---|---|---|---|---|
| Denson | 46 | 899 | 20 | 11 |
| Crabtree | 46 | 716 | 16 | 5 |
| Hayes | 13 | 125 | 10 | 0 |
| Beer | 11 | 155 | 14 | 0 |
| Hickey | 7 | 36 | 5 | 1 |
| Mitchell | 7 | 15 | 2 | 0 |
| Little | 7 | 11 | 2 | 0 |
| Sweeney | 6 | 136 | 23 | 0 |
| White | 5 | 87 | 17 | 0 |
| Scarpitto | 1 | 14 | 14 | 0 |
| Gilchrist | 1 | −4 | −4 | 0 |

## PUNT RETURNS

### OAKLAND RAIDERS

| Last Name | No. | Yds | Avg | TD |
|---|---|---|---|---|
| Bird | 46 | 612 | 13 | 0 |
| Powers | 2 | 19 | 10 | 0 |
| Grayson | 3 | 11 | 4 | 0 |

### KANSAS CITY CHIEFS

| Last Name | No. | Yds | Avg | TD |
|---|---|---|---|---|
| N. Smith | 26 | 212 | 8 | 0 |
| Garrett | 4 | 22 | 6 | 0 |
| E. Thomas | 2 | 8 | 4 | 0 |
| Robinson | 1 | 3 | 3 | 0 |

### SAN DIEGO CHARGERS

| Last Name | No. | Yds | Avg | TD |
|---|---|---|---|---|
| Duncan | 36 | 434 | 12 | 0 |
| Graham | 3 | 46 | 15 | 0 |

### DENVER BRONCOS

| Last Name | No. | Yds | Avg | TD |
|---|---|---|---|---|
| Little | 16 | 270 | 17 | 1 |
| Sellers | 4 | 24 | 6 | 0 |
| Crabtree | 2 | 24 | 12 | 0 |
| Huard | 1 | 19 | 19 | 0 |
| Cassese | 3 | 14 | 5 | 0 |

## KICKOFF RETURNS

### OAKLAND RAIDERS

| Last Name | No. | Yds | Avg | TD |
|---|---|---|---|---|
| Grayson | 19 | 405 | 21 | 0 |
| Sherman | 12 | 279 | 23 | 0 |
| Bird | 6 | 143 | 24 | 0 |
| Todd | 5 | 123 | 25 | 0 |
| Hagberg | 2 | 12 | 6 | 0 |
| Benson | 1 | 0 | 0 | 0 |

### KANSAS CITY CHIEFS

| Last Name | No. | Yds | Avg | TD |
|---|---|---|---|---|
| N. Smith | 41 | 1148 | 28 | 1 |
| G. Thomas | 6 | 56 | 9 | 0 |
| Coan | 1 | 29 | 29 | 0 |
| Carolan | 1 | 2 | 2 | 0 |
| Lanier | 1 | 1 | 1 | 0 |
| Buchanan | 1 | 0 | 0 | 0 |
| Hill | 1 | 0 | 0 | 0 |
| Lothamer | 1 | 0 | 0 | 0 |
| Pitts | 0 | 9 | 0 | 0 |

### SAN DIEGO CHARGERS

| Last Name | No. | Yds | Avg | TD |
|---|---|---|---|---|
| Tolbert | 18 | 441 | 25 | 0 |
| Post | 15 | 371 | 25 | 0 |
| Duncan | 9 | 231 | 26 | 0 |
| Lowe | 8 | 145 | 18 | 0 |
| Smith | 3 | 51 | 17 | 0 |
| Erickson | 1 | 0 | 0 | 0 |

### DENVER BRONCOS

| Last Name | No. | Yds | Avg | TD |
|---|---|---|---|---|
| Little | 35 | 942 | 27 | 0 |
| Mitchell | 8 | 164 | 21 | 0 |
| Sellers | 6 | 120 | 20 | 0 |
| Wilson | 4 | 106 | 27 | 0 |
| Hayes | 3 | 104 | 35 | 0 |
| Lynch | 1 | 27 | 27 | 0 |
| Crabtree | 1 | 26 | 26 | 0 |
| Cassese | 1 | 19 | 19 | 0 |
| Beer | 1 | 10 | 10 | 0 |

## PASSING – PUNTING – KICKING

### OAKLAND RAIDERS

**PASSING**

| Last Name | Att | Comp | % | Yds | Yd/Att | TD | Int–% | RK |
|---|---|---|---|---|---|---|---|---|
| Lamonica | 425 | 220 | 52 | 3228 | 7.6 | 30 | 20– 5 | 1 |
| Blanda | 38 | 15 | 39 | 285 | 7.5 | 3 | 3– 8 | |
| Daniels | 1 | 1 | 100 | 28 | 28.0 | 0 | 0– 0 | |

**PUNTING**

| Last Name | No | Avg |
|---|---|---|
| Eischeid | 76 | 44.3 |

**KICKING**

| Last Name | XP | Att | % | FG | Att | % |
|---|---|---|---|---|---|---|
| Blanda | 56 | 57 | 98 | 20 | 30 | 67 |

**2 POINT XP**

Kocourek

### KANSAS CITY CHIEFS

**PASSING**

| Last Name | Att | Comp | % | Yds | Yd/Att | TD | Int–% | RK |
|---|---|---|---|---|---|---|---|---|
| Dawson | 357 | 206 | 58 | 2651 | 7.4 | 24 | 17– 5 | 2 |
| Garrett | 4 | 1 | 25 | 17 | 4.3 | 1 | 0– 0 | |

**PUNTING**

| Last Name | No | Avg |
|---|---|---|
| Wilson | 41 | 42.4 |
| Walker | 19 | 38.7 |
| Carolan | 1 | 42.0 |

**KICKING**

| Last Name | XP | Att | % | FG | Att | % |
|---|---|---|---|---|---|---|
| Stenerud | 45 | 45 | 100 | 21 | 36 | 58 |

**2 POINT XP**

Carolan
McClinton

### SAN DIEGO CHARGERS

**PASSING**

| Last Name | Att | Comp | % | Yds | Yd/Att | TD | Int–% | RK |
|---|---|---|---|---|---|---|---|---|
| Hadl | 427 | 217 | 51 | 3365 | 7.9 | 24 | 22– 5 | 4 |
| Stephenson | 26 | 11 | 42 | 117 | 4.5 | 2 | 2– 8 | |
| Post | 6 | 1 | 17 | 9 | 1.5 | 0 | 0– 0 | |
| Alworth | 1 | 0 | 0 | 0 | 0.0 | 0 | 0– 0 | |
| Foster | 1 | 0 | 0 | 0 | 0.0 | 0 | 0– 0 | |
| Lowe | 1 | 1 | 100 | 26 | 26.0 | 0 | 0– 0 | |
| Whitehead | 1 | 0 | 0 | 0 | 0.0 | 0 | 0– 0 | |

**PUNTING**

| Last Name | No | Avg |
|---|---|---|
| Redman | 58 | 37.0 |
| Cordill | 3 | 48.3 |
| Hadl | 2 | 35.0 |

**KICKING**

| Last Name | XP | Att | % | FG | Att | % |
|---|---|---|---|---|---|---|
| Van Raaphorst | 45 | 45 | 100 | 15 | 30 | 50 |

### DENVER BRONCOS

**PASSING**

| Last Name | Att | Comp | % | Yds | Yd/Att | TD | Int–% | RK |
|---|---|---|---|---|---|---|---|---|
| Tensi | 325 | 131 | 40 | 1915 | 5.9 | 16 | 17– 5 | 7 |
| LeClair | 45 | 19 | 42 | 275 | 6.1 | 1 | 1– 2 | |
| Glacken | 4 | 0 | 0 | 0 | 0.0 | 0 | 0– 0 | |

**PUNTING**

| Last Name | No | Avg |
|---|---|---|
| Scarpitto | 105 | 44.9 |

**KICKING**

| Last Name | XP | Att | % | FG | Att | % |
|---|---|---|---|---|---|---|
| Humphreys | 18 | 19 | 95 | 7 | 15 | 47 |
| Kroner | 5 | 6 | 83 | 2 | 2 | 100 |
| Duncan | 3 | 3 | 100 | 2 | 5 | 40 |
| LeClerc | 2 | 2 | 100 | 1 | 6 | 17 |

**2 POINT XP**

Hayes

# 1967 Championship Games

## Green Bay's Golden Gamble

Last year's game between the Packers and Cowboys had been an NFL classic, but their rematch this season ranked among the most memorable football games of all time. Both clubs had won conference playoffs to get this far, with Green Bay beating the Rams 28-7 and Dallas clobbering the Browns 52-14, and they clashed for the NFL title in a titanic struggle under nightmarish conditions.

At game time the temperature in Green Bay was 13 degrees below zero, and a fifteen-mile-per-hour wind made it almost unbearable for player and spectator alike. Somewhat better acclimated to the cold than the Cowboys, the Packers mounted a 14-0 lead by early in the second quarter. The Dallas defense, however, took matters into its own hands. Willie Townes hit Starr attempting to pass, and when the ball squirted loose George Andrie picked it up and ran it into the end zone. When Willie Wood fumbled a punt a short time later, the Cowboys added a field goal to cut the score to 14-10 at halftime.

In the fourth period, the Cowboys went ahead on the first play when halfback Dan Reeves surprised the Packer secondary by throwing a long option pass to Lance Rentzel. With their backs to the wall, the Pack still trailed 17-14 when they took over the ball on their own 31-yard line with 4:50 left in the game. Mixing running plays and passes to his backs, Starr moved the Packers quickly downfield until they had a first down on the Dallas one-yard line with under a minute left on the clock. Twice Donny Anderson tried to run it in, twice he failed, and twice Starr called time out. With no time outs remaining and twenty seconds on the clock, the Packers snubbed a field-goal try and put all their chips on one last running play. At the snap, guard Jerry Kramer pushed Jethro Pugh out of the way, and Starr plunged through the gap for the winning touchdown.

### SCORING

|  | | | | |
|---|---|---|---|---|
| GREEN BAY | 7 | 7 | 0 | 7—21 |
| DALLAS | 0 | 10 | 0 | 7—17 |

**First Quarter**
G.B. Dowler, 8 yard pass from Starr
    PAT — Chandler (kick)

**Second Quarter**
G.B. Dowler, 43 yard pass from Starr
    PAT — Chandler (kick)
Dal. Andrie, 7 yard fumble return (by Starr)
    PAT — Villanueva (kick)
Dal. Villanueva, 21 yard field goal

**Fourth Quarter**
Dal. Rentzel, 50 yard pass from Reeves
    PAT — Villanueva (kick)
G.B. Starr, 1 yard rush
    PAT — Chandler (kick)

### TEAM STATISTICS

| G. B. | | DAL. |
|---|---|---|
| 18 | First Downs — Total | 11 |
| 5 | First Downs — Rushing | 4 |
| 10 | First Downs — Passing | 6 |
| 3 | First Downs — Penalty | 1 |
| 1 | Interception Returns — Number | 0 |
| 15 | Interception Returns — Yards | 0 |
| 3 | Fumbles — Number | 3 |
| 2 | Fumbles — Lost Ball | 1 |
| 2 | Penalties — Number | 7 |
| 10 | Yards Penalized | 58 |
| 2 | Giveaways | 2 |
| 2 | Takeaways | 2 |
| 0 | Difference | 0 |

### INDIVIDUAL STATISTICS

#### RUSHING

| GREEN BAY | No | Yds | Avg. | DALLAS | No | Yds | Avg. |
|---|---|---|---|---|---|---|---|
| Anderson | 18 | 35 | 1.9 | Perkins | 17 | 51 | 3.0 |
| Mercein | 6 | 20 | 3.3 | Reeves | 13 | 42 | 3.2 |
| Williams | 4 | 13 | 3.3 | Meredith | 1 | 9 | 9.0 |
| Wilson | 3 | 11 | 3.7 | Baynham | 1 | −2 | −2.0 |
| Starr | 1 | 1 | 1.0 | Clarke | 1 | −8 | −8.0 |
|  | 32 | 80 | 2.5 |  | 33 | 92 | 2.8 |

#### RECEIVING

| | No | Yds | Avg. | | No | Yds | Avg. |
|---|---|---|---|---|---|---|---|
| Dowler | 4 | 77 | 19.3 | Hayes | 3 | 16 | 5.3 |
| Anderson | 4 | 44 | 11.0 | Reeves | 3 | 11 | 3.7 |
| Dale | 3 | 44 | 14.7 | Rentzel | 2 | 61 | 30.5 |
| Mercein | 2 | 22 | 11.0 | Clarke | 2 | 24 | 12.0 |
| Williams | 1 | 4 | 4.0 | Baynham | 1 | −3 | −3.0 |
|  | 14 | 191 | 13.6 |  | 11 | 109 | 9.9 |

#### PUNTING

| | No | | Avg. | | No | | Avg. |
|---|---|---|---|---|---|---|---|
| Anderson | 8 |  | 29.0 | Villanueva | 8 |  | 39.1 |

#### PUNT RETURNS

| | No | Yds | Avg. | | | | |
|---|---|---|---|---|---|---|---|
| Wood | 4 | 21 | 5.3 | None |  |  |  |
| Brown | 1 | −2 | −2.0 |  |  |  |  |
|  | 5 | 19 | 3.8 |  |  |  |  |

#### KICKOFF RETURNS

| | No | Yds | Avg. | | No | Yds | Avg. |
|---|---|---|---|---|---|---|---|
| Caffey | 1 | 7 | 7.0 | Stevens | 2 | 15 | 7.5 |
| Crutcher | 1 | 3 | 3.0 | Stokes | 1 | 28 | 28.0 |
| Weatherwax | 1 | 0 | 0.0 |  | 3 | 43 | 14.3 |
|  | 3 | 10 | 3.3 |  |  |  |  |

#### PASSING

| GREEN BAY | Att | Comp | Comp Pct. | Yds | Int | Yds/ Att. | Yds/ Comp | Yards Lost Tackled |
|---|---|---|---|---|---|---|---|---|
| Starr | 24 | 14 | 58.3 | 191 | 0 | 8.0 | 13.6 | 8—76 |
| **DALLAS** | | | | | | | | |
| Meredith | 25 | 10 | 40.0 | 59 | 1 | 2.4 | 5.9 | 1— 9 |
| Reeves | 1 | 1 | 100.0 | 50 | 0 | 50.0 | 50.0 | 0— 0 |
|  | 26 | 11 | 42.3 | 109 | 1 | 4.2 | 9.9 | 1— 9 |

---

## Lamonica's Field-Goal Touchdown

The Oilers had won the Eastern Division title because of their strong defense, but the Raiders had no problems moving the ball in this championship game. With guard Gene Upshaw leading a fired-up Oakland offensive line, the Raiders attacked the Oilers on the ground, with Hewritt Dixon and Pete Banaszak steadily eating up the yardage all afternoon. George Blanda, whom the Oilers had put on waivers before the season, opened the scoring with a 37-yard field goal, and a 69-yard touchdown run around left end by Dixon gave Oakland more momentum. With eighteen seconds left in the half, the Raiders lined up for a close field-goal attempt, only to have holder Daryle Lamonica jump up and throw a touchdown pass to tight end Dave Kocourek.

Trailing 17-0 and getting nowhere against the Oakland defense, the Oilers needed some fireworks at the start of the second half to get back into the game. Instead, Zeke Moore fumbled the kickoff and gave the ball back to the Raiders deep in Houston territory. The Raiders needed seven plays to reach the end zone, with Lamonica sneaking over from the 1 for the score.

Once the score reached 24-0, all the steam leaked out of the Oilers. Fullback Hoyle Granger, the key to the Houston ground attack, never got untracked all day, and quarterback Pete Beathard had no success passing against the swarming Oakland secondary.

After three periods, the score had risen to 27-0, but the Oilers finally got on the scoreboard with a touchdown pass from Beathard to Charley Frazier plus John Whittenborn's extra point. That was the only Houston score of the day, however, and before the final gun sounded, the Raiders added ten points on a Blanda field goal and a scoring pass from Lamonica to Bill Miller. The 40-7 victory put the Raiders into the Super Bowl, but an Achilles tendon injury suffered by defensive tackle Tom Keating would hobble him for that upcoming match.

### SCORING

|  | | | | |
|---|---|---|---|---|
| OAKLAND | 3 | 14 | 10 | 13—40 |
| HOUSTON | 0 | 0 | 0 | 7— 7 |

**First Quarter**
Oak. Blanda, 37 yard field goal

**Second Quarter**
Oak. Dixon, 69 yard rush
    PAT — Blanda (kick)
Oak. Kocourek, 17 yard pass from Lamonica
    PAT — Blanda (kick)

**Third Quarter**
Oak. Lamonica, 1 yard rush
    PAT — Blanda (kick)
Oak. Blanda, 40 yard field goal

**Fourth Quarter**
Oak. Blanda, 42 yard field goal
Hous. Frazier, 5 yard pass from Beathard
    PAT — Wittenborn (kick)
Oak. Blanda, 36 yard field goal
Oak. Miller, 12 yard pass from Lamonica
    PAT — Blanda (kick)

### TEAM STATISTICS

| OAK. | | HOUS. |
|---|---|---|
| 18 | First Downs — Total | 11 |
| 11 | First Downs — Rushing | 4 |
| 6 | First Downs — Passing | 6 |
| 1 | First Downs — Penalty | 1 |
| 0 | Fumbles — Number | 4 |
| 0 | Fumbles — Lost Ball | 2 |
| 4 | Penalties — Number | 7 |
| 69 | Yards Penalized | 45 |
| 2 | Missed Field Goals | 0 |
| 0 | Giveaways | 3 |
| 3 | Takeaways | 0 |
| +3 | Difference | −3 |

### INDIVIDUAL STATISTICS

#### RUSHING

| OAKLAND | No | Yds | Avg. | HOUSTON | No | Yds | Avg. |
|---|---|---|---|---|---|---|---|
| Dixon | 21 | 144 | 6.9 | Granger | 14 | 19 | 1.4 |
| Banaszak | 15 | 116 | 7.7 | Campbell | 6 | 15 | 2.5 |
| Lamonica | 5 | 22 | 4.4 | Blanks | 1 | 6 | 6.0 |
| Hagberg | 2 | −1 | −0.5 | Beathard | 1 | −2 | −2.0 |
| Todd | 4 | −8 | −2.0 |  | 22 | 38 | 1.7 |
| Biletnikoff | 1 | −10 | −10.0 |  |  |  |  |
|  | 48 | 263 | 5.5 |  |  |  |  |

#### RECEIVING

| | No | Yds | Avg. | | No | Yds | Avg. |
|---|---|---|---|---|---|---|---|
| Miller | 3 | 32 | 10.7 | Frazier | 7 | 81 | 11.6 |
| Cannon | 2 | 31 | 15.5 | Reed | 4 | 60 | 15.0 |
| Biletnikoff | 2 | 19 | 9.5 | Campbell | 2 | 5 | 2.5 |
| Kocourek | 1 | 17 | 17.0 | Taylor | 1 | 6 | 6.0 |
| Dixon | 1 | 8 | 8.0 | Granger | 1 | −10 | −10.0 |
| Banaszak | 1 | 4 | 4.0 |  | 15 | 142 | 9.5 |
|  | 10 | 111 | 11.1 |  |  |  |  |

#### PUNTING

| | No | | Avg. | | No | | Avg. |
|---|---|---|---|---|---|---|---|
| Eischeid | 4 |  | 44.3 | Norton | 11 |  | 38.5 |

#### PUNT RETURNS

| | No | Yds | Avg. | | | | |
|---|---|---|---|---|---|---|---|
| Bird | 5 | 49 | 9.8 | None |  |  |  |
| Sherman | 1 | −2 | −2.0 |  |  |  |  |
|  | 6 | 47 | 7.8 |  |  |  |  |

#### KICKOFF RETURNS

| | No | Yds | Avg. | | No | Yds | Avg. |
|---|---|---|---|---|---|---|---|
| Grayson | 1 | 47 | 47.0 | Jancik | 4 | 100 | 25.0 |
| Todd | 1 | 32 | 32.0 | Moore | 3 | 87 | 29.0 |
|  | 2 | 79 | 39.5 | Burrell | 1 | 28 | 28.0 |
|  |  |  |  | Suggs | 1 | 0 | 0.0 |
|  |  |  |  |  | 9 | 215 | 23.9 |

#### INTERCEPTION RETURNS

| | No | Yds | Avg. | | | | |
|---|---|---|---|---|---|---|---|
| Brown | 1 | 2 | 2.0 | None |  |  |  |

#### PASSING

| OAKLAND | Att | Comp | Comp Pct. | Yds | Int | Yds/ Att. | Yds/ Comp | Yards Lost Tackled |
|---|---|---|---|---|---|---|---|---|
| Lamonica | 24 | 10 | 41.7 | 111 | 0 | 4.6 | 11.1 |  |
| Blanda | 2 | 0 | 0.0 | 0 | 0 | 0 | 0 |  |
|  | 26 | 10 | 38.5 | 111 | 0 | 4.3 | 11.1 | 10 |
| **HOUSTON** | | | | | | | | |
| Beathard | 35 | 15 | 40.5 | 142 | 1 | 4.1 | 9.5 | 34 |

# The Errors of Youth

The Packers might naturally have suffered a mental letdown after their cliff-hanging NFL championship match with the Dallas Cowboys, but the knowledge that this was Vince Lombardi's last game as head coach gave the team all the incentive it needed against the AFL champion Oakland Raiders. In his nine seasons at Green Bay, Lombardi had turned the Packers from chronic losers to perennial champions, and his players were determined that he go out a winner.

The Oakland Raiders, on the other hand, had just won their first AFL crown by severely thrashing the Houston Oilers in the championship game. Like the Kansas City Chiefs last year, the Raiders had several players obviously good enough for any league, but other Oakland players would have to prove themselves against the Packers. They did, but what hurt the Raiders this day were mistakes, the sort of errors that plague young teams in any league.

The first quarter went fairly evenly, with the only scoring coming on Don Chandler's 39-yard field goal. Another Chandler three-pointer upped the score to 6-0 in the second quarter, and then the Raiders made their first costly mistake. The Packers had the ball on their own 38-yard line when Bart Starr dropped back to pass. Someone in the Raider secondary missed his assignment and left Boyd Dowler all alone downfield; Starr hit him with a perfect pass, which he carried to the end zone. With the extra point making the score 13-0, the Raiders seemed close to early death in this contest.

Daryle Lamonica revived his team's failing spirits, however, by driving the Raiders downfield and hitting Bill Miller with a 23-yard touchdown pass. The Oakland defense then stopped the Packer offense, but Rodger Bird, normally a sure-handed punt returner, called for a fair catch and fumbled the ball. The Packers recovered near mid-field and converted the break into another Chandler field goal and a 16-7 halftime lead.

Using their ball-control offense, the Packers nursed their lead through the second half and built it up to 33-14 on a Donny Anderson touchdown, a Chandler field goal, and Herb Adderley's return of an interception for a touchdown. Lamonica threw another touchdown pass to Miller in the fourth quarter, but that only made the final score a clear-cut 33-14. Vince Lombardi, retiring to the front office, was going out a winner.

## GREEN BAY — OAKLAND

### OFFENSE

| GREEN BAY | | OAKLAND |
|---|---|---|
| Dowler | LE | Miller |
| Skoronski | LT | Svihus |
| Gillingham | LG | Upshaw |
| Bowman | C | J. Otto |
| Kramer | RG | Hawkins |
| Gregg | RT | Schuh |
| Fleming | RE | Cannon |
| Starr | QB | Lamonica |
| Dale | FL | Biletnikoff |
| Anderson | HB | Banaszak |
| Wilson | FB | Dixon |

### DEFENSE

| GREEN BAY | | OAKLAND |
|---|---|---|
| Davis | LE | Lassiter |
| Kostelnik | LT | Birdwell |
| Jordan | RT | Keating |
| Aldridge | RE | Davidson |
| Robinson | LLB | Laskey |
| Nitschke | MLB | Connors |
| Caffey | RLB | G. Otto |
| Adderley | LCB | McCloughan |
| Jeter | RCB | W. Brown |
| T. Brown | LS | Powers |
| Wood | RS | H. Williams |

### SUBSTITUTES

**GREEN BAY**

Offense

| | |
|---|---|
| Bratkowski | McGee |
| Capp | Mercein |
| Hyland | Thurston |
| Long | T. Williams |

Defense

| | |
|---|---|
| B. Brown | Hart |
| Crutcher | Rowser |
| Flanigan | Weatherwax |

Kicker

Chandler

**OAKLAND**

Offense

| | |
|---|---|
| Archer | Kocourek |
| Hagberg | Kruse |
| Harvey | Todd |
| Herock | Wells |

Defense

| | |
|---|---|
| Bird | Oates |
| Benson | Sligh |
| Budness | Williamson |
| Grayson | |

Kickers

| | |
|---|---|
| Blanda | Eischeid |

## SCORING

| | | | | |
|---|---|---|---|---|
| GREEN BAY | 3 | 13 | 10 | 7—33 |
| OAKLAND | 0 | 7 | 0 | 7—14 |

**First Quarter**

G.B. Chandler, 39 yard field goal

**Second Quarter**

G.B. Chandler, 20 yard field goal
G.B. Dowler, 62 yard pass from Starr PAT — Chandler (kick)
Oak. Miller, 23 yard pass from Lamonica PAT — Blanda (kick)
G.B. Chandler, 43 yard field goal

**Third Quarter**

G.B. Anderson, 2 yard rush PAT — Chandler (kick)
G.B. Chandler, 31 yard field goal

**Fourth Quarter**

G.B. Adderley, 60 yard interception return PAT — Chandler (kick)
Oak. Miller, 23 yard pass from Lamonica PAT — Blanda (kick)

## TEAM STATISTICS

| G.B. | | OAK. |
|---|---|---|
| 19 | First Downs — Total | 16 |
| 11 | First Downs — Rushing | 5 |
| 7 | First Downs — Passing | 10 |
| 1 | First Downs — Penalties | 1 |
| 0 | Fumbles — Number | 3 |
| 0 | Fumbles — Lost Ball | 2 |
| 1 | Penalties — Number | 4 |
| 12 | Yards Penalized | 31 |
| 69 | Total Offensive Plays | 57 |
| 322 | Total Net Yards | 293 |
| 4.7 | Average Gain | 5.1 |
| 0 | Missed Field Goals | 1 |
| 0 | Giveaways | 3 |
| 3 | Takeaways | 0 |
| +3 | Difference | −3 |

## INDIVIDUAL STATISTICS

### RUSHING

| GREEN BAY | No | Yds | Avg. | OAKLAND | No | Yds | Avg. |
|---|---|---|---|---|---|---|---|
| Wilson | 17 | 62 | 3.6 | Dixon | 12 | 54 | 4.5 |
| Anderson | 14 | 48 | 3.4 | Todd | 2 | 37 | 18.5 |
| Williams | 8 | 36 | 4.5 | Banaszak | 6 | 16 | 2.7 |
| Starr | 1 | 14 | 14.0 | | 20 | 107 | 5.4 |
| Mercein | 1 | 0 | 0.0 | | | | |
| | 41 | 160 | 3.9 | | | | |

### RECEIVING

| GREEN BAY | No | Yds | Avg. | OAKLAND | No | Yds | Avg. |
|---|---|---|---|---|---|---|---|
| Dale | 4 | 43 | 10.8 | Miller | 5 | 84 | 16.8 |
| Fleming | 4 | 35 | 8.8 | Banaszak | 4 | 69 | 17.3 |
| Dowler | 2 | 71 | 35.5 | Cannon | 2 | 25 | 12.5 |
| Anderson | 2 | 18 | 9.0 | Biletnikoff | 2 | 10 | 5.0 |
| McGee | 1 | 35 | 35.0 | Wells | 1 | 17 | 17.0 |
| | 13 | 202 | 15.5 | Dixon | 1 | 3 | 3.0 |
| | | | | | 15 | 208 | 13.9 |

### PUNTING

| GREEN BAY | No | | Avg. | OAKLAND | No | | Avg. |
|---|---|---|---|---|---|---|---|
| Anderson | 6 | | 39.0 | Eischeid | 6 | | 44.0 |

### PUNT RETURNS

| GREEN BAY | No | Yds | Avg. | OAKLAND | No | Yds | Avg. |
|---|---|---|---|---|---|---|---|
| Wood | 5 | 35 | 7.0 | Bird | 2 | 12 | 6.0 |

### KICKOFF RETURNS

| GREEN BAY | No | Yds | Avg. | OAKLAND | No | Yds | Avg. |
|---|---|---|---|---|---|---|---|
| Adderley | 1 | 24 | 14.0 | Todd | 3 | 63 | 21.0 |
| Williams | 1 | 18 | 18.0 | Grayson | 2 | 61 | 30.5 |
| Crutcher | 1 | 7 | 7.0 | Hawkins | 1 | 3 | 3.0 |
| | 3 | 49 | 16.3 | Kocourek | 1 | 0 | 0.0 |
| | | | | | 7 | 127 | 18.1 |

### INTERCEPTION RETURNS

| GREEN BAY | No | Yds | Avg. | OAKLAND | | | |
|---|---|---|---|---|---|---|---|
| Adderley | 1 | 60 | 60.0 | None | | | |

### PASSING

| GREEN BAY | Att | Comp | Comp Pct. | Yds | Int | Yds/ Att. | Yds/ Comp | Yards Lost Tackled |
|---|---|---|---|---|---|---|---|---|
| Starr | 24 | 13 | 54.2 | 202 | 0 | 8.4 | 15.5 | 4—30 |

| OAKLAND | Att | Comp | Comp Pct. | Yds | Int | Yds/ Att. | Yds/ Comp | Yards Lost Tackled |
|---|---|---|---|---|---|---|---|---|
| Lamonica | 34 | 15 | 44.1 | 208 | 1 | 6.1 | 13.9 | 3—22 |

# 1968 N.F.L. Eleven Missing Monuments

A lot of familiar faces were missing from NFL playing fields this season. Retired from active duty were Ray Berry, Jim Parker, Lenny Moore, Lou Groza, Sam Huff, Del Shofner, Jim Ringo, Jim Taylor, and Don Chandler, all of them top-notch performers in the league since the 1950s. Berry left with a record 631 lifetime receptions, Groza with records of twenty-one active professional seasons and 1,608 points scored, and Ringo left with an appearance record streak of 182 consecutive games, a streak still running at his retirement. Also tucked away in front-office positions out of the public's eye were George Halas and Vince Lombardi, two of the most famous coaches in pro-football history. Age prompted Halas to leave the sidelines, while Lombardi quit because he had accomplished everything in his nine years as Packer head coach.

## EASTERN CONFERENCE — CAPITOL DIVISION

**Dallas Cowboys**—Depth was the key to the Cowboys' continued stay atop the Capitol Division. When quarterback Don Meredith needed a rest, young Craig Morton filled in and kept the offense rolling smoothly. When halfback Dan Reeves hurt his knee in the season's fourth game, substitute runners Craig Baynham and Walt Garrison filled the breach. Other top reserves on this team were Malcolm Walker, Rayfield Wright, Larry Cole, and Blaine Nye, each of whom could have started on most NFL teams.

**New York Giants**—The aerial circus of Fran Tarkenton to Homer Jones kept the attack alive, but the rest of the team needed shoring up. The running backs were slow, the defensive line couldn't mount an effective pass rush, and the linebacking was inexperienced and easily fooled. They did beat Dallas, but that was more a fluke than a true reading of the team.

**Washington Redskins**—Combined with the retirement of Sam Huff, a pair of decisions that backfired helped bring Otto Graham's pro coaching career to an end. Graham sent a first-draft pick to Los Angeles for rookie quarterback Gary Beban, last year's Heisman Trophy winner at UCLA. After signing with the Redskins for a lucrative salary, Beban flopped in training camp as a quarterback, spent most of the year on the taxi squad, and flopped late in the season as a running back. Another Graham move that didn't work out was the trading of safety Paul Krause to Minnesota.

**Philadelphia Eagles**—Norm Snead broke his leg in the first pre-season game, the Eagles lost their first eleven regular season games, owner Jerry Wolman went bankrupt, and coach Joe Kuharich heard hometown crowds screaming for his head. The Eagles ended their losing streak by beating Detroit 12-0 on four Sam Baker field goals, and a second win one week later gave the club some dignity but removed all chances of landing O. J. Simpson next year. At the end of the year, Leonard Tose bought the team from Wolman and canned Kuharich, fifteen-year contract and all.

## CENTURY DIVISION

**Cleveland Browns**—When the Browns dropped two of their first three games with a meager offensive output, coach Blanton Collier benched quarterback Frank Ryan in favor of ex-Steeler Bill Nelsen. Playing behind the solid Cleveland line, Nelsen stayed healthy all season and put some life in the Browns' attack. With Nelsen, Leroy Kelly, and Paul Warfield leading the way, the Browns began an eight-game winning streak on October 20 by beating the undefeated Colts. The streak came to an end only on the final Sunday of the season, when a meaningless loss to St. Louis tightened the final standings.

**St. Louis Cardinals**—The Cards beat the Browns twice, but Cleveland finished ahead by half a game. With a strong, balanced squad, the Cards had severe problems with Western opponents, losing to the Rams, Colts, and 49ers and just barely beating the Falcons 17-12. Despite the near miss at the title, several developments pleased coach Charley Winner. Quarterback Jim Hart improved considerably in his second year at the helm, cutting his interceptions from 30 down to 18. The defense replaced retired linebackers Dale Meinert and Bill Koman without a hitch, and rookie Chuck Latourette put on a good show as a kick returner, punter and sometimes defensive back.

**New Orleans Saints**—Although the Saints won four games, their move up to third place was due more to the Steelers' deterioration than to their own improvement. Coach Tom Fears improved his offense by signing end Dave Parks after he played out his option at San Francisco. He had to pay a steep price, however, when Commissioner Pete Rozelle deemed rookie tackle Kevin Hardy and next year's number-one draft pick as San Francisco's just renumeration.

**Pittsburgh Steelers**—The Steelers combined a poor offense with a limp defense in an irresistible combination for defeat, and head coach Bill Austin found himself discharged after the debacle ended. Dick Hoak and Roy Jefferson turned in good offensive performances, but they were hardly noticeable admidst the mediocrity.

## WESTERN CONFERENCE — CENTRAL DIVISION

**Minnesota Vikings**—The Vikings won the Central Division title with a defense as rugged as the Minnesota weather in December. The front line of Carl Eller, Jim Marshall, Alan Page, and Gary Larsen now ranked with Los Angeles' Fearsome Foursome as the top defensive lines in the league, and the linebacking and secondary were without weakness. The acquisition of safety Paul Krause from the Redskins was the knot that tied the Vikings' pass defense together. Although the offense ranked fourteenth in the league in total yardage and dead last in passing, quarterback Joe Kapp won as many headlines as the defensive people with his intense competitiveness and wobbling passes which often hit their mark in clutch situations.

**Chicago Bears**—Head coach Jim Dooley lost his first two games and then beat the Vikings at a terrible cost. In that game, Jack Concannon went out with a fractured collarbone and Rudy Bukich with a shoulder separation. After third-stringer Larry Rakestraw failed to move the team, Dooley gave rookie Virgil Carter a shot at quarterback. Carter drove the Bears to four straight wins before more injuries ended the team's title hopes. In the victory over San Francisco, a tackle by Kermit Alexander ripped ligaments and cartilage in Gale Sayers' right knee. One week later, a broken ankle ended Carter's fine rookie season.

**Green Bay Packers**—Vince Lombardi had quit as head coach, confining himself to the general manager's desk, and the Packers, under Phil Bengston, dropped to a 6-7-1 mark. Age was catching up on the players of the championship teams of the early 1960s, and replacements were not turning up. A bad arm kept quarterback Bart Starr out of action for almost half the season, and Don Chandler retired, leaving the Packers with no reliable place-kicker.

**Detroit Lions**—Last year's top newcomers had been Mel Farr and Lem Barney; this year's pair were wide receiver Earl McCullough and tight end Charlie Sanders. These two rookies joined with newcomers Bill Munson and Billy Gambrell to make the Detroit passing game a genuine threat to enemy defenses. Injuries plagued the running corps, however, and the reconstructed Lions needed more time together to play as a team.

## COASTAL DIVISION

**Baltimore Colts**—A few weeks before their season's opener, the Colts had a solid team everywhere but at quarterback. Johnny Unitas was bothered by a bad elbow, so coach Don Shula sent a fourth-round draft pick and reserve end Butch Wilson to New York for journeyman quarterback Earl Morrall. Shula expected Morrall to fill in while Unitas recuperated, but while Unitas sat out most of the season, Morrall used his pinpoint passing and poised signal calling to lead the Colts to a 13-1 season. Morrall's job was made easier by the running of Tom Matte, the blocking and receiving of John Mackey, and the line play of Bob Vogel, while the defense made life miserable for heralded enemy quarterbacks.

**Los Angeles Rams**—Despite a string of injuries, the Rams fought their way to a 10-3-1 record. But after the season ended, owner Dan Reeves fired George Allen. Personality differences and Allen's practice of trading off draft picks for older pros convinced Reeves that he'd be better off with a different coach, but the Ram players immediately raised an outcry in favor of their deposed coach. The protests had some effect, because when Reeves held a press conference to name the new coach, he announced the return of Allen.

**San Francisco '49ers**—New head coach Dick Nolan took over a talent squad in his first head assignment, but he couldn't get his team past the Colts and Rams in the Coastal Division. With three losses and a tie against these two rivals, the '49ers had the misfortune of playing in pro football's strongest division. The '49ers did well against the rest of the league, with a steady attack their chief weapon. Bolstered by Nolan's confidence in him, quarterback John Brodie took firm charge of the offense, finding ex-Brown Clifton McNeil a most congenial pass receiver.

**Atlanta Falcons**—When the Falcons lost their first three games of the season, coach Norb Hecker was canned and ex-Viking head man Norm Van Brocklin given the job, and he tore the club apart in search of a winning combination. After a 30-7 loss to Cleveland, he put five starting players on waivers. He gave a starting safetyman's job to Billy Lothridge, a punting specialist with only one kidney. He dropped promising Randy Johnson from the starting lineup and promoted Bob Berry, whom he had coached in Minnesota to starting quarterback.

## DEFENSE

Team columns: ATL. | BALT. | CHI. | CLEV. | DALL. | DET. | G.B. | L.A. | MINN. | N.O. | N.Y. | PHIL. | PITT. | ST.L. | S.F. | WASH.

## FINAL TEAM STATISTICS

**FIRST DOWNS:**
- Total
- by Rushing
- by Passing
- by Penalty

**RUSHING:**
- Number
- Yards
- Average Yards
- Touchdowns

**PASSING:**
- Attempts
- Completions
- Completion Percentage
- Passing Yards
- Average Yards per Attempt
- Average Yards per Completion
- Times Tackled Attempting to Pass
- Yards Lost Tackled Attempting to Pass
- Net Yards
- Touchdowns
- Interceptions
- Percent Intercepted

**PUNTS:**
- Number
- Average Distance

**PUNT RETURNS:**
- Number
- Yards
- Average Yards
- Touchdowns

**KICKOFF RETURNS:**
- Number
- Yards
- Average Yards
- Touchdowns

**INTERCEPTION RETURNS:**
- Number
- Yards
- Average Yards
- Touchdowns

**PENALTIES:**
- Number
- Yards

**FUMBLES:**
- Number
- Number Lost

**POINTS:**
- Total
- PAT Attempts
- PAT Made
- FG Attempts
- FG Made
- Percent FG Made
- Safeties

## OFFENSE

Team columns: ATL. | BALT. | CHI. | CLEV. | DALL. | DET. | G.B. | L.A. | MINN. | N.O. | N.Y. | PHIL. | PITT. | ST.L. | S.F. | WASH.

---

## CONFERENCE PLAYOFFS

### WESTERN——December 22, at Baltimore (Attendance 60,238)

**TEAM STATISTICS**

| TEAM STATISTICS | MIN. | BAL. |
|---|---|---|
| First Downs — Total | 4 | 15 |
| First Downs — Rushing | 2 | 2 |
| First Downs — Passing | 1 | 12 |
| First Downs — Penalty | 1 | 4 |
| Times Tackled Passing | 3 | 35 |
| Yards Lost — Passing | 21 |  |
| Fumbles — Number | 4 | 2 |
| Fumbles — Lost Ball | 4 | 38 |
| Penalties — Number | 30 | 5 |
| Yards Penalized | 6 | 40.4 |
| Punts — Average Distance | 39.6 | 11 |
| Punt Returns — Number | 7 | 54 |
| Punt Returns — Yards | 5 | 44 |
| Kickoff Returns — Number | 113 | 2 |
| Interception Returns — Number |  |  |
| Interception Returns — Yards | 21 |  |

**INDIVIDUAL STATISTICS**

**MINNESOTA**

| RUSHING | No | Yds | Avg |
|---|---|---|---|
| Kapp | 10 | 52 | 5.2 |
| Brown | 10 | 30 | 3.0 |
| Osborn | 5 | 4 | 0.8 |
| Jones | 1 | -1 | -1.0 |
| Lindsey | 1 | 3 | 3.0 |

| RECEIVING | No | Yds | Avg |
|---|---|---|---|
| Brown | 8 | 83 | 10.3 |
| Wash'ton | 2 | 95 | 19.0 |
| Beasley | 5 | 36 | 3.0 |
| Henderson | 5 | 33 | 6.6 |
| Jones | 5 | 45 | 9.0 |
| Lindsey | 1 | 1 | 1.0 |
| Martin | 1 | 23 | 23.3 |

| PASSING | Att | Cmp | Int | Yds | Yd/A | Yd/C |
|---|---|---|---|---|---|---|
| Morrall | 22 | 13 | 280 |  | 12.7 | 21.5 |
| Kapp | 44 | 26 | 287 | 2 | 6.5 | 11.0 |

**BALTIMORE**

| RECEIVING | No | Yds | Avg |
|---|---|---|---|
| Matte | 14 | 31 |  |
| J. Hill | 8 | 10 |  |
| Mackey | 4 | 9 |  |
| Pearson | 27 | 50 |  |
| Rich'son | 6 | 148 | 24.7 |
| Mackey | 2 | 92 | 46.0 |
| Orr | 2 | 36 | 18.0 |
| Mitchell | 1 | 3 | 3.0 |
| Pearson | 12 | 180 | 23.3 |

---

### SCORING

**BALTIMORE** 0 7 14 3—24
**MINNESOTA** 0 0 0 14—14

**Second Quarter**
Bal. Mitchell, 3 yd pass from Morrall
  PAT — Michaels (kick)

**Third Quarter**
Bal. Mackey, 49 yard pass from Morrall
Bal. Curtis, 60 yard fumble return
  PAT — Michaels (kick)

**Fourth Quarter**
Min. Martin, 1 yard pass from Kapp
Bal. Michaels, 33 yard field goal
Min. Brown, 7 yard pass from Kapp
  PAT — Cox (kick)

---

### EASTERN——December 21, at Cleveland (Attendance 81,497)

**TEAM STATISTICS**

| TEAM STATISTICS | CLE. | DAL. |
|---|---|---|
| First Downs — Total | 12 | 13 |
| First Downs — Rushing | 4 | 5 |
| First Downs — Passing | 8 | 8 |
| First Downs — Penalty |  | 2 |
| Times Tackled Passing | 1 | 25 |
| Yards Lost — Tackled | 5 |  |
| Fumbles — Number | 6 | 4 |
| Fumbles — Lost Ball | 40 | 5 |
| Penalties — Number | 7 | 41.0 |
| Yards Penalized | 36.1 | 5 |
| Punts — Average Distance | 3 |  |
| Punt Returns — Number | 6 | 72 |
| Punt Returns — Yards | 67 | 6 |
| Kickoff Returns — Number | 52 | 4 |
| Interception Returns — Number | 2 | 4 |
| Interception Returns — Yards | 2 | -2 |
| Giveaways |  |  |
| Takeaways | +2 |  |

**INDIVIDUAL STATISTICS**

**DALLAS**

| RUSHING | No | Yds | Avg |
|---|---|---|---|
| Perkins | 14 | 51 | 3.6 |
| Morton | 2 | 14 | 7.0 |
| Baynham | 10 | 7 | 0.7 |
| Garrison | 1 | 6 | 6.0 |
| Meredith | 1 | 3 | 5.0 |
| Shy | 1 | 3 | 1.5 |

| RECEIVING | No | Yds | Avg |
|---|---|---|---|
| Hayes | 4 | 86 | 21.5 |
| Rentzel | 4 | 47 | 11.8 |
| Garrison | 2 | 46 | 23.0 |
| Baynham | 2 | 26 | 13.0 |
| Norman | 1 | -2 | -2.0 |

| PASSING | Att | Cmp | Pct. | Yds | Int | Yd/A | Yd/C |
|---|---|---|---|---|---|---|---|
| Meredith | 25 | 13 | 52.0 | 203 | 3 | 8.1 | 15.6 |
| Morton | 23 | 8 | 39.1 | 163 | 1 | 7.1 | 18.1 |
| Norman | 9 | 3 | 33.3 | 42 | 4 | 4.7 | 14.0 |
| | 32 | 12 | 37.5 | 205 | 4 | 6.4 | 17.1 |

**CLEVELAND**

| RUSHING | No | Yds | Avg |
|---|---|---|---|
| Kelly | 20 | 87 | 4.4 |
| Harraway | 5 | 12 | 2.4 |
| E. Green | 5 | 5 | 1.7 |
| Nelsen | 2 | -2 | -1.0 |

| RECEIVING | No | Yds | Avg |
|---|---|---|---|
| Warfield | 4 | 86 | 21.5 |
| Morin | 4 | 47 | 11.8 |
| Kelly | 2 | 46 | 23.0 |
| Collins | 2 | 26 | 13.0 |
| Harraway | 1 | -2 | -2.0 |

| PASSING | Att | Cmp | Pct. | Yds | Int | Yd/A | Yd/C |
|---|---|---|---|---|---|---|---|
| Nelsen | 25 | 13 | 52.0 | 203 | 1 | 8.1 | 15.6 |
| Morton | 23 | 8 | 39.1 | 163 |  | 7.1 | 18.1 |

### SCORING

**CLEVELAND** 3 7 14 7—31
**DALLAS** 7 7 3 7—20

**First Quarter**
Cle. Cockroft, 38 yard field goal
Dal. Howley, 44 yard fumble return
  PAT — Clark (kick)

**Second Quarter**
Dal. Clark, 16 yard field goal
Cle. Kelly, 46 yard pass from Nelsen
  PAT — Cockroft (kick)

**Third Quarter**
Cle. Lindsey, 27 yd interception return
Cle. Kelly, 35 yard run
  PAT — Cockroft (kick)
Dal. Clark, 47 yard field goal

**Fourth Quarter**
Cle. E. Green, 2 yard rush
  PAT — Cockroft (kick)
Dal. Garrison, 2 yard pass from Morton
  PAT — Clark (kick)

| | Scores of Each Game | | Use Name | Pos. | Hgt | Wgt | Age | Int | Pts |
|---|---|---|---|---|---|---|---|---|---|

**CAPITOL DIVISION**

## DALLAS COWBOYS 12-2-0 Tom Landry

Scores of Each Game:

| | | |
|---|---|---|
| 59 | DETROIT | 13 |
| 28 | CLEVELAND | 7 |
| 45 | Philadelphia | 13 |
| 27 | St. Louis | 10 |
| 34 | PHILADELPHIA | 14 |
| 20 | Minnesota | 7 |
| 17 | GREEN BAY | 28 |
| 17 | New Orleans | 3 |
| 21 | NEW YORK | 27 |
| 44 | Washington | 24 |
| 34 | Chicago | 3 |
| 29 | WASHINGTON | 20 |
| 28 | PITTSBURGH | 7 |
| 28 | New York | 10 |

| Use Name | Pos. | Hgt | Wgt | Age | Int | Pts |
|---|---|---|---|---|---|---|
| Tony Liscio | OT | 6'5" | 255 | 28 | | |
| Ralph Neely | OT | 6'5" | 265 | 24 | | |
| Rayfield Wright | TE-OT | 6'7" | 243 | 23 | | 6 |
| John Niland | OG | 6'4" | 245 | 24 | | |
| Blaine Nye | OG | 6'4" | 255 | 22 | | |
| John Wilbur | OG | 6'3" | 240 | 25 | | |
| Dave Manders | C | 6'2" | 250 | 26 | | |
| Malcolm Walker | OT-C | 6'4" | 250 | 25 | | |
| George Andrie | DE | 6'7" | 250 | 28 | | |
| Larry Cole | DE | 6'4" | 230 | 21 | 1 | 12 |
| Willie Townes | DE | 6'5" | 260 | 25 | | 6 |
| Andy Stynchula | DT-DE | 6'3" | 250 | 29 | | |
| Ron East | DT | 6'4" | 242 | 25 | | |
| Bob Lilly | DT | 6'4" | 260 | 29 | | |
| Jethro Pugh | DT | 6'6" | 260 | 24 | | 2 |
| Jackie Burkett | LB | 6'4" | 228 | 31 | | |
| Dave Edwards | LB | 6'3" | 228 | 29 | | |
| Chuck Howley | LB | 6'3" | 225 | 32 | 6 | 6 |
| Lee Roy Jordan | LB | 6'2" | 225 | 27 | 3 | |
| D. D. Lewis | LB | 6'2" | 210 | 22 | | |
| Dave Simmons | LB | 6'4" | 245 | 25 | 1 | |
| Phil Clark | DB | 6'2" | 210 | 23 | | |
| Dick Daniels | DB | 5'9" | 180 | 22 | 2 | |
| Mike Gaechter | DB | 6' | 190 | 28 | 3 | |
| Cornell Green | DB | 6'4" | 208 | 28 | 4 | 6 |
| Mike Johnson | DB | 5'10" | 184 | 24 | 3 | |
| Mel Renfro | DB | 6' | 190 | 26 | 3 | |
| Don Meredith | QB | 6'2" | 205 | 30 | | 6 |
| Craig Morton | QB | 6'4" | 216 | 25 | | 12 |
| Craig Baynham | HB | 6'1" | 206 | 24 | | 48 |
| Dan Reeves | HB | 6'1" | 200 | 24 | | 30 |
| Les Shy | HB | 6'1" | 200 | 24 | | 6 |
| Walt Garrison | FB | 6' | 205 | 24 | | 30 |
| Don Perkins | FB | 5'10" | 200 | 30 | | 36 |
| Bob Hayes | WR | 6' | 185 | 25 | | 72 |
| Dennis Homan | WR | 6'1" | 180 | 22 | | 6 |
| Dave McDaniels | WR | 6'4" | 200 | 23 | | |
| Sonny Randle (from SF) | WR | 6'2" | 190 | 32 | | 6 |
| Lance Rentzel | WR | 6'2" | 200 | 24 | | 36 |
| Pete Gent | TE | 6'4" | 205 | 25 | | |
| Pettis Norman | TE | 6'3" | 225 | 28 | | 6 |
| Mike Clark | K | 6'1" | 200 | 27 | | 105 |
| Ron Widby | K | 6'4" | 210 | 23 | | |

Buddy Dial — Injury
Leon Donohue — Injury

## NEW YORK GIANTS 7-7-0 Allie Sherman

Scores of Each Game:

| | | |
|---|---|---|
| 34 | Pittsburgh | 20 |
| 34 | Philadelphia | 25 |
| 48 | WASHINGTON | 21 |
| 33 | NEW ORLEANS | 21 |
| 21 | Atlanta | 24 |
| 10 | SAN FRANCISCO | 26 |
| 13 | Washington | 10 |
| 0 | BALTIMORE | 26 |
| 27 | Dallas | 21 |
| 7 | PHILADELPHIA | 6 |
| 21 | Los Angeles | 24 |
| 10 | Cleveland | 45 |
| 21 | ST. LOUIS | 28 |
| 10 | DALLAS | 28 |

| Use Name | Pos. | Hgt | Wgt | Age | Int | Pts |
|---|---|---|---|---|---|---|
| Rich Buzin | OT | 6'4" | 250 | 22 | | |
| Charlie Harper | OT | 6'2" | 250 | 24 | | |
| Steve Wright | OT | 6'6" | 250 | 26 | | |
| Willie Young | OT | 6' | 250 | 25 | | |
| Pete Case | OG | 6'3" | 245 | 27 | | |
| Darrell Dess | OG | 6' | 245 | 32 | | |
| Andy Gross | OG | 6' | 230 | 22 | | |
| Doug Van Horn | OG | 6'2" | 245 | 24 | | |
| Chuck Hinton | C | 6'2" | 235 | 25 | | |
| Greg Larson | C | 6'2" | 250 | 28 | | |
| Bruce Anderson | DE | 6'4" | 250 | 24 | | |
| McKinley Boston | DE | 6'2" | 245 | 22 | | |
| Jim Katcavage | DE | 6'3" | 240 | 33 | | |
| Roger Anderson | DT | 6'5" | 265 | 25 | 1 | |
| Bob Lurtsema | DT | 6'6" | 250 | 26 | 1 | |
| Sam Silas | DT | 6'4" | 250 | 25 | | |
| Ken Avery | LB | 6'1" | 220 | 24 | | |
| Barry Brown | LB | 6'3" | 235 | 25 | | |
| Mike Ciccolella | LB | 6'1" | 235 | 24 | 1 | |
| Vince Costello | LB | 6' | 228 | 36 | | |
| Tommy Crutcher | LB | 6'3" | 230 | 26 | | |
| Henry Davis | LB | 6'3" | 235 | 25 | | |
| Scott Eaton | DB | 6'3" | 195 | 24 | 4 | |
| Jim Holifield | DB | 6'2" | 195 | 22 | | |
| Spider Lockhart | DB | 6'2" | 175 | 25 | 8 | 12 |
| Bruce Maher | DB | 5'11" | 190 | 31 | 1 | |
| Willie Williams | DB | 6' | 190 | 25 | 10 | |
| Freeman White | TE-DB | 6'5" | 225 | 24 | | |
| Gary Lane | QB | 6'1" | 210 | 25 | | |
| Fran Tarkenton | QB | 6'1" | 190 | 28 | | 18 |
| Gary Wood | QB | 5'11" | 188 | 25 | | |
| Ronnie Blye | HB | 5'11" | 185 | 24 | | 6 |
| Bobby Duhon | HB | 6' | 190 | 21 | | 24 |
| Randy Minniear | HB | 6' | 200 | 24 | | 12 |
| Ernie Koy | FB-HB | 6'2" | 230 | 25 | | 24 |
| Tucker Frederickson | FB | 6'3" | 230 | 25 | | 18 |
| Homer Jones | WR | 6'2" | 220 | 27 | | 42 |
| Joe Koontz | WR | 6'1" | 192 | 23 | | |
| Joe Morrison | WR | 6'1" | 212 | 30 | | 36 |
| Bob Crespino | TE-WR | 6'4" | 225 | 30 | | |
| Butch Wilson | TE | 6'2" | 228 | 26 | | |
| Aaron Thomas | WR-TE | 6'3" | 210 | 30 | | 24 |
| Pete Gogolak | K | 6'2" | 185 | 26 | | 78 |

Smith Reed — Military Service

## WASHINGTON REDSKINS 5-9-0 Otto Graham

Scores of Each Game:

| | | |
|---|---|---|
| 38 | Chicago | 28 |
| 17 | New Orleans | 37 |
| 21 | New York | 48 |
| 17 | PHILADELPHIA | 14 |
| 16 | PITTSBURGH | 13 |
| 14 | St. Louis | 41 |
| 10 | NEW YORK | 13 |
| 14 | Minnesota | 27 |
| 16 | Philadelphia | 10 |
| 24 | DALLAS | 44 |
| 7 | GREEN BAY | 27 |
| 20 | Dallas | 29 |
| 21 | CLEVELAND | 24 |
| 14 | DETROIT | 3 |

| Use Name | Pos. | Hgt | Wgt | Age | Int | Pts |
|---|---|---|---|---|---|---|
| Walt Rock | OT | 6'5" | 255 | 27 | | |
| Jim Snowden | OT | 6'3" | 255 | 26 | | |
| Fred Washington | OT | 6'5" | 268 | 23 | | |
| Ray Schoenke | OG-OT | 6'3" | 250 | 26 | | |
| Don Bandy | OG | 6'3" | 250 | 23 | | |
| Willie Banks | OG | 6'2" | 237 | 22 | | |
| Vince Promuto | OG | 6'1" | 245 | 30 | | |
| John Wooten | OG | 6'2" | 250 | 33 | | |
| Dave Crossan | C | 6'3" | 245 | 28 | | |
| Len Hauss | C | 6'2" | 235 | 26 | | |
| Carl Kammerer | DE | 6'3" | 243 | 31 | | |
| Spain Musgrove | DT-DE | 6'4" | 275 | 23 | | |
| Walt Barnes | DT | 6'3" | 250 | 24 | | |
| Frank Bosch | DT | 6'4" | 246 | 22 | | |
| Dennis Crane | DT | 6'6" | 260 | 23 | | |
| Joe Rutgens | DT | 6'2" | 255 | 29 | | |
| Ed Breding | LB | 6'4" | 235 | 23 | | |
| Jim Carroll | LB | 6'1" | 230 | 25 | | |
| Chris Hanburger | LB | 6'2" | 218 | 27 | 2 | 6 |
| Mike Morgan | LB | 6'4" | 242 | 26 | 2 | |
| Tom Roussel | LB | 6'3" | 235 | 23 | | |
| Pat Fischer | DB | 5'10" | 170 | 28 | 2 | |
| George Harold | DB | 6'3" | 194 | 26 | | |
| Rickie Harris | DB | 6' | 182 | 25 | 2 | |
| Aaron Martin | DB | 6' | 190 | 27 | 4 | |
| Brig Owens | DB | 5'11" | 190 | 25 | 8 | |
| Jim Smith | DB | 6'3" | 195 | 21 | | 6 |
| Dick Smith | HB-DB | 6' | 205 | 24 | 1 | |
| Sonny Jurgensen | QB | 5'11" | 203 | 34 | | 6 |
| Jim Ninowski | QB | 6'1" | 207 | 32 | | |
| Harry Theofiledes | QB | 5'11" | 180 | 24 | | |
| Gary Beban | HB-QB | 6'1" | 195 | 22 | | |
| Jerry Allen | HB | 6'1" | 205 | 27 | | 30 |
| Bob Brunet | HB | 6'1" | 205 | 22 | | 6 |
| Pete Larson | HB | 6'1" | 200 | 24 | | 12 |
| Ray McDonald | FB | 6'4" | 248 | 24 | | |
| Steve Thurlow | FB | 6'3" | 222 | 25 | | |
| A. D. Whitfield | FB | 5'10" | 200 | 24 | | |
| Charley Taylor | WR | 6'3" | 210 | 27 | | 30 |
| Bobby Mitchell | WR | 6' | 196 | 33 | | |
| Jerry Smith | TE-WR | 6'2" | 208 | 25 | | 36 |
| Ken Barefoot | TE | 6'5" | 228 | 27 | | |
| Marlin McKeever | TE | 6'1" | 235 | 28 | | |
| Pat Richter | TE | 6'5" | 230 | 27 | | 54 |
| Mike Bragg | K | 5'11" | 186 | 21 | | |
| Charlie Gogolak | K | 5'10" | 165 | 23 | | 57 |

John Love — Military Service
Sam Huff — Voluntarily Retired
Joe Don Looney — Military Service

## PHILADELPHIA EAGLES 2-12-0 Joe Kuharich

Scores of Each Game:

| | | |
|---|---|---|
| 13 | Green Bay | 30 |
| 25 | NEW YORK | 34 |
| 13 | DALLAS | 45 |
| 14 | Washington | 17 |
| 14 | Dallas | 34 |
| 16 | CHICAGO | 29 |
| 3 | Pittsburgh | 6 |
| 17 | ST. LOUIS | 45 |
| 10 | WASHINGTON | 16 |
| 6 | New York | 7 |
| 13 | Cleveland | 47 |
| 12 | Detroit | 0 |
| 29 | NEW ORLEANS | 17 |
| 17 | MINNESOTA | 24 |

| Use Name | Pos. | Hgt | Wgt | Age | Int | Pts |
|---|---|---|---|---|---|---|
| Bob Brown | OT | 6'4" | 295 | 25 | | |
| Dave Graham | OT | 6'3" | 250 | 29 | | |
| Lane Howell | OT | 6'5" | 272 | 27 | | |
| Mike Dirks | OG | 6'2" | 250 | 22 | | |
| Dick Hart | OG | 6'2" | 250 | 25 | | |
| Mark Nordquist | OG | 6'4" | 235 | 22 | | |
| Gene Ceppetelli | C | 6'2" | 247 | 26 | | |
| Mike Evans | C | 6'5" | 250 | 21 | | |
| Dave Recher | C | 6'1" | 246 | 25 | | |
| Don Hultz | DE | 6'3" | 242 | 27 | | |
| Gary Pettigrew | DE | 6'4" | 245 | 23 | | |
| Tim Rossovich | DE | 6'4" | 245 | 22 | | |
| Mel Tom | DE | 6'4" | 248 | 27 | | |
| Frank Molden | DT | 6'5" | 280 | 26 | | |
| Floyd Peters | DT | 6'2" | 255 | 33 | 1 | |
| Dean Wink | DT | 6'4" | 246 | 23 | | |
| Randy Beisler | DE-DT | 6'4" | 245 | 23 | 1 | |
| Fred Brown | LB | 6'5" | 232 | 25 | | |
| Wayne Colman | LB | 6'1" | 230 | 22 | | |
| Dave Lloyd | LB | 6'3" | 248 | 32 | | |
| Arunas Vasys | LB | 6'2" | 235 | 25 | | |
| Harold Wells | LB | 6'2" | 220 | 29 | 2 | |
| Adrian Young | DB | 6'1" | 225 | 22 | | |
| Alvin Haymond | DB | 6' | 194 | 26 | 1 | 12 |
| John Mallory | DB | 6' | 180 | 22 | | 6 |
| Ron Medved | DB | 6'1" | 210 | 24 | 1 | |
| Al Nelson | DB | 5'11" | 186 | 24 | 3 | |
| Jim Nettles | DB | 5'9" | 177 | 26 | | |
| Nate Ramsey | DB | 6'1" | 200 | 27 | 2 | |
| Joe Scarpati | HB-DB | 5'10" | 185 | 26 | 2 | |
| John Huarte | QB | 6' | 190 | 24 | | |
| Norm Snead | QB | 6'4" | 215 | 28 | | |
| Izzy Lang | HB | 6'1" | 232 | 25 | | 6 |
| Harry Jones | HB | 6'2" | 205 | 23 | | |
| Cyril Pinder | HB | 6'2" | 222 | 21 | | |
| Larry Conjar | FB | 6' | 214 | 22 | | 2 |
| Tom Woodeshick | FB | 6' | 220 | 26 | | 18 |
| Gary Ballman | WR | 6' | 205 | 28 | | 24 |
| Ron Goodwin | WR | 6' | 180 | 26 | | |
| Ben Hawkins | WR | 6' | 180 | 24 | | 30 |
| Chuck Hughes | WR | 5'11" | 170 | 25 | | |
| Mike Ditka | TE | 6'3" | 235 | 28 | | 12 |
| Fred Hill | TE | 6'2" | 215 | 25 | | 18 |
| Sam Baker | K | 6'2" | 218 | 36 | | 74 |
| Rick Duncan | K | 6' | 208 | 27 | | |

Ike Kelley — Knee Injury
Jim Skaggs — Knee Injury
Harry Wilson — Injury

## CAPITOL DIVISION

### DALLAS COWBOYS

**RUSHING**

| Last Name | No. | Yds | Avg | TD |
|---|---|---|---|---|
| Perkins | 191 | 836 | 4.4 | 4 |
| Baynham | 103 | 438 | 4.3 | 5 |
| Garrison | 45 | 271 | 6.0 | 5 |
| Shy | 64 | 179 | 2.8 | 1 |
| Reeves | 40 | 178 | 4.5 | 4 |
| Meredith | 22 | 123 | 5.6 | 1 |
| Norman | 4 | 51 | 12.8 | 0 |
| Morton | 4 | 28 | 7.0 | 2 |
| Hayes | 4 | 2 | 0.5 | 0 |
| Gent | 2 | −5 | −2.5 | 0 |
| Wright | 1 | −10 | −10.0 | 0 |

**RECEIVING**

| Last Name | No. | Yds | Avg | TD |
|---|---|---|---|---|
| Rentzel | 54 | 1009 | 19 | 6 |
| Hayes | 53 | 909 | 17 | 10 |
| Baynham | 29 | 380 | 13 | 3 |
| Norman | 18 | 204 | 11 | 1 |
| Perkins | 17 | 180 | 11 | 2 |
| Gent | 16 | 194 | 12 | 0 |
| Shy | 10 | 105 | 11 | 0 |
| Garrison | 7 | 111 | 16 | 0 |
| Reeves | 7 | 84 | 12 | 1 |
| Homan | 4 | 92 | 23 | 1 |
| Randle | 4 | 56 | 14 | 1 |
| Wright | 1 | 15 | 15 | 1 |

**PUNT RETURNS**

| Last Name | No. | Yds | Avg | TD |
|---|---|---|---|---|
| Hayes | 15 | 312 | 21 | 2 |
| Rentzel | 14 | 93 | 7 | 0 |
| Homan | 1 | 0 | 0 | 0 |

**KICKOFF RETURNS**

| Last Name | No. | Yds | Avg | TD |
|---|---|---|---|---|
| Baynham | 23 | 590 | 26 | 0 |
| Daniels | 9 | 193 | 21 | 0 |
| Homan | 2 | 21 | 11 | 0 |
| Hayes | 1 | 20 | 20 | 0 |
| Neely | 3 | 17 | 6 | 0 |
| Norman | 1 | 0 | 0 | 0 |

**PASSING – PUNTING – KICKING**

PASSING

| Last Name | Att | Comp | % | Yds | Yd/Att | TD | Int− | % | RK |
|---|---|---|---|---|---|---|---|---|---|
| Meredith | 309 | 171 | 55 | 2500 | 8.1 | 21 | 12− | 4 | 2 |
| Morton | 85 | 44 | 52 | 752 | 8.9 | 4 | 6− | 7 | |
| Reeves | 4 | 2 | 50 | 43 | 10.8 | 0 | 0− | 0 | |
| Baynham | 1 | 0 | 0 | 0 | 0.0 | 0 | 0− | 0 | |

PUNTING

| Last Name | No | Avg |
|---|---|---|
| Widby | 59 | 40.9 |

KICKING

| Last Name | XP | Att | % | FG | Att | % |
|---|---|---|---|---|---|---|
| M. Clark | 54 | 54 | 100 | 17 | 29 | 59 |

### NEW YORK GIANTS

**RUSHING**

| Last Name | No. | Yds | Avg | TD |
|---|---|---|---|---|
| Frederickson | 142 | 486 | 3.4 | 1 |
| Koy | 89 | 394 | 4.4 | 3 |
| Duhon | 101 | 362 | 3.6 | 3 |
| Tarkenton | 57 | 301 | 5.3 | 3 |
| Blye | 53 | 243 | 4.6 | 1 |
| Minniear | 14 | 38 | 2.7 | 0 |
| Morrison | 9 | 28 | 3.1 | 0 |
| Jones | 3 | 18 | 6.0 | 0 |
| Thomas | 2 | 14 | 7.0 | 0 |
| Wood | 2 | 0 | 0.0 | 0 |
| Young | 2 | −2 | −1.0 | 0 |

**RECEIVING**

| Last Name | No. | Yds | Avg | TD |
|---|---|---|---|---|
| Jones | 45 | 1057 | 23 | 7 |
| Morrison | 37 | 425 | 11 | 6 |
| Duhon | 37 | 373 | 10 | 1 |
| Thomas | 29 | 449 | 15 | 4 |
| Koy | 12 | 59 | 5 | 1 |
| Blye | 10 | 91 | 9 | 0 |
| Frederickson | 10 | 64 | 6 | 2 |
| Crespino | 7 | 130 | 19 | 0 |
| Wilson | 4 | 34 | 9 | 0 |
| Minniear | 4 | 32 | 8 | 0 |
| Larson | 0 | 1 | 0 | |

**PUNT RETURNS**

| Last Name | No. | Yds | Avg | TD |
|---|---|---|---|---|
| Lockhart | 13 | 69 | 5 | 0 |
| Duhon | 7 | 32 | 5 | 0 |

**KICKOFF RETURNS**

| Last Name | No. | Yds | Avg | TD |
|---|---|---|---|---|
| Blye | 35 | 734 | 21 | 0 |
| Duhon | 13 | 214 | 16 | 0 |
| Holifield | 7 | 111 | 16 | 0 |
| Frederickson | 2 | 13 | 7 | 0 |
| Koontz | 1 | 13 | 13 | 0 |
| Hinton | 1 | 12 | 12 | 0 |
| Lurtsema | 1 | 11 | 11 | 0 |
| Eaton | 1 | 2 | 2 | 0 |
| Williams | 1 | 0 | 0 | 0 |

**PASSING – PUNTING – KICKING**

PASSING

| Last Name | Att | Comp | % | Yds | Yd/Att | TD | Int− | % | RK |
|---|---|---|---|---|---|---|---|---|---|
| Tarkenton | 337 | 182 | 54 | 2555 | 7.6 | 21 | 12− | 4 | 5 |
| Wood | 24 | 9 | 38 | 123 | 5.1 | 0 | 5− | 21 | |
| Koy | 3 | 2 | 67 | 13 | 4.3 | 0 | 0− | 0 | |
| Duhon | 2 | 2 | 100 | 24 | 12.0 | 0 | 0− | 0 | |

PUNTING

| Last Name | No | Avg |
|---|---|---|
| Koy | 44 | 37.5 |
| Williams | 10 | 29.1 |
| Lockhart | 3 | 36.7 |

KICKING

| Last Name | XP | Att | % | FG | Att | % |
|---|---|---|---|---|---|---|
| Gogolak | 36 | 36 | 100 | 14 | 24 | 58 |

### WASHINGTON REDSKINS

**RUSHING**

| Last Name | No. | Yds | Avg | TD |
|---|---|---|---|---|
| Allen | 123 | 399 | 3.2 | 4 |
| Brunet | 71 | 227 | 3.2 | 0 |
| Thurlow | 51 | 184 | 3.6 | 0 |
| Larson | 44 | 132 | 3.0 | 1 |
| Whitfield | 37 | 125 | 3.4 | 0 |
| Mitchell | 10 | 46 | 4.6 | 0 |
| Jurgensen | 8 | 21 | 2.6 | 1 |
| Beban | 5 | 18 | 3.6 | 0 |
| Ninowski | 2 | 13 | 6.5 | 0 |
| D. Smith | 3 | 5 | 1.7 | 0 |
| Theofiledes | 3 | 0 | 0.0 | 0 |
| Taylor | 2 | −3 | −1.5 | 0 |
| Bragg | 1 | −3 | −3.0 | 0 |

**RECEIVING**

| Last Name | No. | Yds | Avg | TD |
|---|---|---|---|---|
| Taylor | 48 | 650 | 14 | 5 |
| Jerry Smith | 45 | 626 | 14 | 6 |
| Richter | 42 | 533 | 13 | 9 |
| Allen | 21 | 294 | 14 | 1 |
| Brunet | 18 | 160 | 9 | 1 |
| Mitchell | 14 | 130 | 9 | 0 |
| Whitfield | 13 | 107 | 8 | 0 |
| Thurlow | 12 | 151 | 13 | 0 |
| Larson | 12 | 146 | 12 | 1 |
| D. Smith | 1 | 15 | 15 | 0 |
| Beban | 1 | 12 | 12 | 0 |

**PUNT RETURNS**

| Last Name | No. | Yds | Avg | TD |
|---|---|---|---|---|
| Harris | 19 | 144 | 8 | 0 |
| Jim Smith | 6 | 38 | 6 | 0 |
| Martin | 2 | 12 | 6 | 0 |
| Mitchell | 1 | 0 | 0 | 0 |
| Owens | 1 | 0 | 0 | 0 |

**KICKOFF RETURNS**

| Last Name | No. | Yds | Avg | TD |
|---|---|---|---|---|
| Harris | 23 | 579 | 25 | 0 |
| Mitchell | 11 | 235 | 21 | 0 |
| D. Smith | 10 | 228 | 23 | 0 |
| Larson | 6 | 151 | 25 | 0 |
| Martin | 7 | 146 | 21 | 0 |
| Jim Smith | 3 | 61 | 20 | 0 |
| Rock | 2 | 10 | 5 | 0 |
| Barnes | 1 | 0 | 0 | 0 |
| McKeever | 1 | 0 | 0 | 0 |

**PASSING – PUNTING – KICKING**

PASSING

| Last Name | Att | Comp | % | Yds | Yd/Att | TD | Int− | % | RK |
|---|---|---|---|---|---|---|---|---|---|
| Jurgensen | 292 | 167 | 57 | 1980 | 6.8 | 17 | 11− | 4 | 8 |
| Ninowski | 95 | 49 | 52 | 633 | 6.7 | 4 | 6− | 6 | |
| Theofiledes | 20 | 11 | 55 | 211 | 10.6 | 2 | 1− | 5 | |
| Beban | 1 | 0 | 0 | 0 | 0.0 | 0 | 0− | 0 | |

PUNTING

| Last Name | No | Avg |
|---|---|---|
| Bragg | 76 | 43.3 |

KICKING

| Last Name | XP | Att | % | FG | Att | % |
|---|---|---|---|---|---|---|
| Gogolak | 30 | 31 | 97 | 9 | 19 | 47 |

### PHILADELPHIA EAGLES

**RUSHING**

| Last Name | No. | Yds | Avg | TD |
|---|---|---|---|---|
| Woodeshick | 217 | 947 | 4.4 | 3 |
| Lang | 69 | 235 | 3.4 | 0 |
| Pinder | 40 | 117 | 2.9 | 0 |
| Ballman | 1 | 30 | 30.0 | 0 |
| Snead | 9 | 27 | 3.0 | 0 |
| Jones | 22 | 24 | 1.1 | 0 |
| Conjar | 8 | 21 | 2.6 | 0 |
| Huarte | 2 | 9 | 4.5 | 0 |

**RECEIVING**

| Last Name | No. | Yds | Avg | TD |
|---|---|---|---|---|
| Hawkins | 42 | 707 | 17 | 5 |
| Woodeshick | 36 | 328 | 9 | 0 |
| F. Hill | 30 | 370 | 12 | 3 |
| Ballman | 30 | 341 | 11 | 4 |
| Lang | 17 | 147 | 9 | 0 |
| Pinder | 16 | 166 | 10 | 0 |
| Ditka | 13 | 111 | 9 | 2 |
| Jones | 5 | 87 | 17 | 0 |
| Hughes | 3 | 39 | 13 | 0 |
| Mallory | 1 | 58 | 58 | 1 |
| Baker | 1 | 3 | 3 | 0 |

**PUNT RETURNS**

| Last Name | No. | Yds | Avg | TD |
|---|---|---|---|---|
| Haymond | 15 | 201 | 13 | 1 |
| Mallory | 4 | 46 | 12 | 0 |
| Scarpati | 5 | 17 | 3 | 0 |

**KICKOFF RETURNS**

| Last Name | No. | Yds | Avg | TD |
|---|---|---|---|---|
| Haymond | 28 | 677 | 24 | 1 |
| Nelson | 11 | 308 | 28 | 0 |
| Hawkins | 12 | 254 | 21 | 0 |
| Mallory | 6 | 94 | 16 | 0 |
| Rossovich | 2 | 20 | 10 | 0 |
| Jones | 1 | 18 | 18 | 0 |
| Graham | 1 | 8 | 8 | 0 |

**PASSING – PUNTING – KICKING**

PASSING

| Last Name | Att | Comp | % | Yds | Yd/Att | TD | Int− | % | RK |
|---|---|---|---|---|---|---|---|---|---|
| Snead | 291 | 152 | 52 | 1655 | 5.7 | 11 | 21− | 7 | 15 |
| Huarte | 15 | 7 | 47 | 110 | 7.3 | 1 | 2− | 13 | |
| Scarpati | 2 | 1 | 50 | 3 | 1.5 | 0 | 0− | 0 | |
| Baker | 1 | 1 | 100 | 58 | 58.0 | 1 | 0− | 0 | |

PUNTING

| Last Name | No | Avg |
|---|---|---|
| Baker | 55 | 40.9 |
| Duncan | 5 | 45.6 |

KICKING

| Last Name | XP | Att | % | FG | Att | % |
|---|---|---|---|---|---|---|
| Baker | 17 | 21 | 81 | 19 | 30 | 63 |

## CENTURY DIVISION

### CLEVELAND BROWNS 10-4-0 Blanton Collier

| Scores of Each Game | | |
|---|---|---|
| 24 | New Orleans | 10 |
| 7 | Dallas | 28 |
| 6 | LOS ANGELES | 24 |
| 31 | PITTSBURGH | 24 |
| 21 | ST. LOUIS | 27 |
| 30 | Baltimore | 20 |
| 30 | ATLANTA | 7 |
| 33 | San Francisco | 21 |
| 35 | NEW ORLEANS | 17 |
| 45 | Pittsburgh | 24 |
| 47 | PHILADELPHIA | 13 |
| 45 | NEW YORK | 10 |
| 24 | Washington | 21 |
| 16 | St. Louis | 27 |

| Use Name | Pos. | Hgt | Wgt | Age | Int | Pts |
|---|---|---|---|---|---|---|
| Monte Clark | OT | 6'6" | 255 | 31 | | |
| Dick Schafrath | OT | 6'3" | 255 | 32 | | |
| Joe Taffoni | OT | 6'3" | 250 | 23 | | |
| Jim Copeland | OG | 6'2" | 245 | 23 | | |
| John Demarie | OG | 6'3" | 255 | 23 | | |
| Gene Hickerson | OG | 6'3" | 248 | 33 | | |
| Fred Hoaglin | C | 6'4" | 240 | 24 | | |
| Bob Whitlow | C | 6'1" | 236 | 32 | | |
| Bill Glass | DE | 6'5" | 255 | 32 | 2 | 6 |
| Jack Gregory | DE | 6'6" | 250 | 23 | | |
| Ron Snidow | DE | 6'4" | 250 | 26 | | |
| Marv Upshaw | DE | 6'3" | 245 | 21 | | |
| Walter Johnson | DT | 6'3" | 270 | 25 | | |
| Jim Kanicki | DT | 6'4" | 270 | 26 | | |
| Bill Sabatino | DT | 6'3" | 245 | 23 | | |

| Use Name | Pos. | Hgt | Wgt | Age | Int | Pts |
|---|---|---|---|---|---|---|
| Billy Andrews | LB | 6' | 225 | 23 | | |
| John Garlington | LB | 6'1" | 225 | 22 | 1 | |
| Jim Houston | LB | 6'2" | 245 | 31 | 3 | |
| Dale Lindsey | LB | 6'3" | 225 | 25 | 1 | |
| Bob Matheson | LB | 6'4" | 240 | 23 | 2 | |
| Wayne Meylan | LB | 6'1" | 240 | 22 | | |
| Erich Barnes | DB | 6'2" | 198 | 33 | 3 | 6 |
| Ben Davis | DB | 5'11" | 185 | 22 | 8 | |
| Mike Howell | DB | 6'1" | 187 | 25 | 6 | |
| Nate James | DB | 6'1" | 195 | 23 | | |
| Ernie Kellerman | DB | 6' | 183 | 24 | 6 | |
| Alvin Mitchell | DB | 6'3" | 195 | 24 | | |
| Carl Ward | DB | 5'9" | 180 | 24 | | |

| Use Name | Pos. | Hgt | Wgt | Age | Int | Pts |
|---|---|---|---|---|---|---|
| Bill Nelsen | QB | 6' | 195 | 27 | | 6 |
| Frank Ryan | QB | 6'3" | 200 | 32 | | |
| Leroy Kelly | HB | 6' | 200 | 26 | | 120 |
| Reece Morrison | HB | 6' | 205 | 22 | | 12 |
| Ernie Green | FB | 6'2" | 205 | 29 | | 12 |
| Charlie Harraway | FB | 6'2" | 230 | 23 | | 6 |
| Charlie Leigh | FB | 5'11" | 205 | 22 | | 6 |
| Eppie Barney | WR | 6' | 204 | 24 | | 12 |
| Gary Collins | WR | 6'4" | 215 | 27 | | |
| Ron Green | WR | 6'1" | 200 | 24 | | |
| Tommy McDonald | WR | 5'10" | 175 | 34 | | 6 |
| Paul Warfield | WR | 6' | 188 | 25 | | 72 |
| Milt Morin | TE | 6'4" | 250 | 26 | | 30 |
| Ralph Smith | TE | 6'2" | 220 | 29 | | |
| Don Cockroft | K | 6'1" | 185 | 23 | | 100 |

### ST. LOUIS CARDINALS 9-4-1 Charlie Winner

| Scores of Each Game | | |
|---|---|---|
| 13 | LOS ANGELES | 24 |
| 17 | San Francisco | 35 |
| 21 | New Orleans | 20 |
| 10 | DALLAS | 27 |
| 27 | Cleveland | 21 |
| 41 | WASHINGTON | 14 |
| 31 | NEW ORLEANS | 17 |
| 45 | Philadelphia | 17 |
| 28 | PITTSBURGH | 28 |
| 0 | Baltimore | 27 |
| 17 | ATLANTA | 12 |
| 20 | Pittsburgh | 10 |
| 28 | New York | 21 |
| 27 | CLEVELAND | 16 |

| Use Name | Pos. | Hgt | Wgt | Age | Int | Pts |
|---|---|---|---|---|---|---|
| Bob Duncum | OT | 6'3" | 250 | 24 | | |
| Ernie McMillan | OT | 6'6" | 260 | 30 | | |
| Bob Reynolds | OT | 6'6" | 265 | 27 | | |
| Clyde Williams | OG-OT | 6'2" | 255 | 28 | | |
| Ken Gray | OG | 6'2" | 250 | 32 | | |
| Rick Sortun | OG | 6'2" | 235 | 25 | | |
| Ted Wheeler | OG | 6'3" | 245 | 22 | | |
| Irv Goode | C-OG | 6'4" | 250 | 27 | | |
| Bob DeMarco | C | 6'3" | 240 | 30 | | |
| Dick Kasperek | C | 6'3" | 225 | 24 | | |
| Don Brumm | DE | 6'3" | 245 | 25 | | 6 |
| Dave Long | DE | 6'4" | 235 | 23 | | |
| Chuck Walker | DE | 6'2" | 245 | 27 | | |
| Fred Heron | DT | 6'4" | 250 | 23 | | |
| Bob Rowe | DT | 6'4" | 260 | 23 | | |
| Joe Schmiesing | DE-DT | 6'4" | 243 | 23 | | |

| Use Name | Pos. | Hgt | Wgt | Age | Int | Pts |
|---|---|---|---|---|---|---|
| Ernie Clark | LB | 6'1" | 230 | 30 | 1 | |
| Dave Meggyesy | LB | 6'1" | 220 | 26 | | |
| Jamie Rivers | LB | 6'2" | 235 | 22 | 2 | |
| Rocky Rosema | LB | 6'2" | 220 | 22 | | |
| Larry Stallings | LB | 6'2" | 230 | 26 | | |
| Mike Strofolino | LB | 6'2" | 230 | 24 | | |
| Bob Atkins | DB | 6'3" | 212 | 22 | 2 | |
| Mike Barnes | DB | 6' | 185 | 32 | 1 | |
| Brady Keys | DB | 6' | 190 | 23 | | 6 |
| Chuck Latourette | DB | 6'3" | 207 | 26 | 3 | |
| Lonnie Sanders | DB | 6'3" | 207 | 26 | 3 | |
| Mac Sauls | DB | 6' | 185 | 23 | | |
| Jerry Stovall | DB | 6'2" | 205 | 26 | | |
| Larry Wilson | DB | 6' | 190 | 30 | 4 | |

| Use Name | Pos. | Hgt | Wgt | Age | Int | Pts |
|---|---|---|---|---|---|---|
| Jim Hart | QB | 6'2" | 195 | 24 | | 36 |
| Charley Johnson | QB | 6' | 190 | 31 | | |
| MacArthur Lane | HB | 6' | 220 | 26 | | |
| Johnny Roland | HB | 6'2" | 207 | 25 | | 12 |
| Roy Shivers | HB | 6' | 200 | 26 | | 42 |
| Willie Crenshaw | FB | 6'2" | 230 | 27 | | 42 |
| Cid Edwards | FB | 6'2" | 230 | 24 | | 6 |
| Bobby Joe Conrad | WR | 6' | 195 | 33 | | 24 |
| Jerry Daanen | WR | 6' | 190 | 23 | | |
| Freddie Hyatt | WR | 6'3" | 212 | 22 | | |
| Bob Lee | WR | 6'3" | 200 | 23 | | |
| Dave Williams | WR | 6'2" | 205 | 23 | | 36 |
| Chuck Logan | TE | 6'4" | 220 | 25 | | |
| Jackie Smith | TE | 6'4" | 215 | 27 | | 30 |
| Jim Bakken | K | 6' | 200 | 27 | | 85 |

### NEW ORLEANS SAINTS 4-9-1 Tom Fears

| Scores of Each Game | | |
|---|---|---|
| 10 | CLEVELAND | 24 |
| 37 | WASHINGTON | 17 |
| 20 | ST. LOUIS | 21 |
| 21 | New York | 38 |
| 20 | MINNESOTA | 17 |
| 16 | Pittsburgh | 12 |
| 17 | St. Louis | 31 |
| 3 | DALLAS | 17 |
| 17 | Cleveland | 35 |
| 7 | Green Bay | 29 |
| 20 | Detroit | 20 |
| 17 | CHICAGO | 23 |
| 17 | Philadelphia | 29 |
| 24 | PITTSBURGH | 14 |

| Use Name | Pos. | Hgt | Wgt | Age | Int | Pts |
|---|---|---|---|---|---|---|
| Jim Boeke | OT | 6'5" | 260 | 29 | | |
| Jerry Jones | OT | 6'3" | 265 | 24 | | |
| Dave McCormick | OT | 6'6" | 250 | 25 | | |
| Jerry Sturm | OT | 6'3" | 260 | 31 | | |
| Jake Kupp | OG | 6'3" | 233 | 26 | | |
| Ross Gwinn | OG | 6'3" | 273 | 24 | | |
| Roy Schmidt | OG | 6'3" | 250 | 26 | | |
| Del Williams | OG | 6'2" | 245 | 22 | | |
| Joe Wendryhoski | C | 6'2" | 245 | 29 | | |
| Doug Atkins | DE | 6'8" | 270 | 38 | | |
| Brian Schweda | DE | 6'3" | 240 | 25 | | |
| Tom Carr | DT | 6'3" | 267 | 26 | | |
| Lou Cordileone | DT | 6' | 250 | 31 | 1 | |
| Earl Leggett | DT | 6'3" | 265 | 34 | | |
| Dave Rowe | DT | 6'6" | 265 | 23 | | |
| Mike Tilleman | DE-DT | 6'5" | 280 | 24 | | |

| Use Name | Pos. | Hgt | Wgt | Age | Int | Pts |
|---|---|---|---|---|---|---|
| Johnny Brewer | LB | 6'4" | 235 | 31 | | |
| Bill Cody | LB | 6'1" | 220 | 24 | | |
| Ted Davis | LB | 6'1" | 232 | 26 | | |
| Jim Ferguson | LB | 6'4" | 240 | 25 | | |
| Les Kelley | LB | 6'3" | 233 | 23 | 1 | |
| Steve Stonebreaker | LB | 6'3" | 225 | 30 | | |
| Fred Whittingham | LB | 6'1" | 240 | 29 | 1 | |
| Bo Burris | DB | 6'3" | 195 | 23 | 3 | 6 |
| John Douglas | DB | 6'1" | 195 | 23 | | |
| Ross Fichtner | DB | 6' | 195 | 30 | | |
| Gene Howard | DB | 6' | 190 | 21 | 3 | |
| Elbert Kimbrough | DB | 5'11" | 197 | 29 | 1 | |
| Elijah Nevett | DB | 6' | 185 | 24 | | |
| Dave Whitsell | DB | 6' | 190 | 32 | 6 | 6 |
| George Youngblood | DB | 6'3" | 205 | 23 | | |

| Use Name | Pos. | Hgt | Wgt | Age | Int | Pts |
|---|---|---|---|---|---|---|
| Billy Kilmer | QB | 6' | 204 | 28 | | 12 |
| Ronnie South | QB | 6'1" | 195 | 23 | | |
| Karl Sweetan | QB | 6'1" | 200 | 25 | | |
| Charlie Brown | HB | 5'11" | 187 | 22 | | 6 |
| Don McCall | HB | 5'11" | 195 | 23 | | 36 |
| Tom Barrington | FB-HB | 6'1" | 213 | 24 | | 6 |
| Tony Baker | FB | 5'11" | 230 | 23 | | |
| Tony Lorick | FB | 6'1" | 217 | 26 | | 18 |
| Ernie Wheelwright | FB | 6'3" | 236 | 31 | | 6 |
| Randy Schultz | HB-FB | 5'11" | 210 | 24 | | |
| Dan Abramowicz | WR | 6'1" | 195 | 23 | | 42 |
| John Gilliam | WR | 6'1" | 190 | 23 | | |
| Dave Parks | WR | 6'2" | 203 | 26 | | |
| Dave Szymakowski | WR | 6'2" | 198 | 22 | | |
| Jim Hester | TE | 6'4" | 225 | 23 | | 12 |
| Ray Poage | TE | 6'4" | 205 | 27 | | |
| Monte Stickles | TE | 6'4" | 235 | 30 | | 12 |
| Charlie Durkee | K | 5'11" | 165 | 24 | | 84 |
| Jim Fraser | K | 6'3" | 235 | 32 | | |
| Tom McNeill | K | 6'1" | 195 | 26 | | |

### PITTSBURGH STEELERS 2-11-1 Bill Austin

| Scores of Each Game | | |
|---|---|---|
| 20 | NEW YORK | 34 |
| 10 | Los Angeles | 45 |
| 7 | BALTIMORE | 41 |
| 24 | Cleveland | 31 |
| 13 | Washington | 16 |
| 12 | NEW ORLEANS | 16 |
| 6 | PHILADELPHIA | 3 |
| 41 | Atlanta | 21 |
| 28 | St. Louis | 28 |
| 24 | CLEVELAND | 45 |
| 28 | SAN FRANCISCO | 45 |
| 10 | ST. LOUIS | 20 |
| 7 | Dallas | 28 |
| 14 | New Orleans | 24 |

| Use Name | Pos. | Hgt | Wgt | Age | Int | Pts |
|---|---|---|---|---|---|---|
| John Brown | OT | 6'2" | 248 | 29 | | |
| Mike Haggerty | OT | 6'4" | 230 | 22 | | |
| Fran O'Brien | OT | 6'1" | 265 | 32 | | |
| Ernie Ruple | OT | 6'4" | 256 | 22 | | |
| Mike Taylor | OT | 6'4" | 247 | 23 | | |
| Sam Davis | OG | 6'1" | 245 | 24 | | |
| Larry Gagner | OG | 6'3" | 240 | 24 | | |
| Bruce Van Dyke | OG | 6'2" | 235 | 24 | | |
| Ralph Wenzel | OG | 6'3" | 240 | 25 | | |
| Mike Connelly | C | 6'3" | 248 | 32 | | |
| Ray Mansfield | C | 6'3" | 250 | 27 | | |
| Ben McGee | DE | 6'2" | 260 | 26 | | |
| Lloyd Voss | DE | 6'4" | 260 | 26 | | |
| Dick Arndt | DT | 6'5" | 265 | 24 | | |
| Chuck Hinton | DT | 6'5" | 260 | 29 | | |
| Ken Kortas | DT | 6'2" | 280 | 24 | | |
| Frank Parker | DT | 6'5" | 270 | 28 | | |

| Use Name | Pos. | Hgt | Wgt | Age | Int | Pts |
|---|---|---|---|---|---|---|
| John Campbell | LB | 6'3" | 225 | 29 | 1 | |
| Dick Capp | LB | 6'3" | 235 | 24 | | |
| John Foruria | LB | 6'2" | 205 | 23 | | |
| Jerry Hillebrand | LB | 6'3" | 240 | 28 | 2 | |
| Ray May | LB | 6'1" | 230 | 23 | 3 | 6 |
| Andy Russell | LB | 6'2" | 215 | 26 | 2 | |
| Bill Saul | LB | 6'4" | 225 | 27 | | |
| Lou Harris | DB | 6' | 180 | 22 | | |
| Bob Hohn | DB | 6' | 185 | 27 | | |
| Paul Martha | DB | 6' | 185 | 25 | 3 | 6 |
| Clendon Thomas | DB | 6'2" | 200 | 31 | 3 | |
| Bob Wade | DB | 6'2" | 200 | 23 | | |
| Marv Woodson | DB | 6' | 195 | 25 | 3 | |

| Use Name | Pos. | Hgt | Wgt | Age | Int | Pts |
|---|---|---|---|---|---|---|
| Kent Nix | QB | 6'1" | 195 | 24 | | |
| Dick Shiner | QB | 6' | 197 | 26 | | |
| Rocky Bleier | HB | 5'11" | 190 | 22 | | |
| Dick Hoak | HB | 6'1" | 190 | 29 | | 24 |
| Don Shy | HB | 6'1" | 210 | 22 | | 6 |
| Tom Watkins | HB | 5'11" | 195 | 31 | | |
| Willie Asbury | FB | 6'1" | 230 | 25 | | |
| Earl Gros | FB | 6'3" | 230 | 27 | | 36 |
| Dick Compton | WR | 6'1" | 200 | 28 | | |
| Marshall Cropper | WR | 6'3" | 210 | 24 | | |
| Ken Hebert | WR | 6' | 200 | 23 | | |
| Roy Jefferson | WR | 6'2" | 195 | 24 | | 72 |
| J. R. Wilburn | WR | 6'2" | 190 | 25 | | 18 |
| Jon Henderson | DB-WR | 6' | 195 | 23 | | |
| John Hilton | TE | 6'5" | 220 | 26 | | 6 |
| Tony Jeter | TE | 6'3" | 223 | 21 | | |
| Dick Kotite | TE | 6'3" | 235 | 25 | | 12 |
| Booth Lusteg | K | 5'11" | 190 | 27 | | 50 |
| Bill Shockley | K | 6' | 185 | 30 | | 2 |
| Bobby Walden | K | 6' | 190 | 30 | | |

## CENTURY DIVISION

### CLEVELAND BROWNS

RUSHING

| Last Name | No. | Yds | Avg | TD |
|---|---|---|---|---|
| Kelly | 248 | 1239 | 5.0 | 16 |
| Harraway | 91 | 334 | 3.7 | 0 |
| E. Green | 41 | 152 | 3.7 | 0 |
| Leigh | 23 | 144 | 6.3 | 1 |
| Ryan | 11 | 64 | 5.8 | 0 |
| Morrison | 18 | 39 | 2.2 | 1 |
| Nelsen | 13 | 30 | 2.3 | 1 |
| Smith | 1 | 13 | 13.0 | 0 |
| Morin | 1 | 8 | 8.0 | 0 |
| Barney | 0 | 8 | 0.0 | 1 |

RECEIVING

| Last Name | No. | Yds | Avg | TD |
|---|---|---|---|---|
| Warfield | 50 | 1067 | 21 | 12 |
| Morin | 43 | 792 | 18 | 5 |
| Kelly | 22 | 297 | 14 | 4 |
| Barney | 18 | 189 | 11 | 1 |
| E. Green | 16 | 142 | 9 | 2 |
| Harraway | 12 | 162 | 14 | 1 |
| Collins | 9 | 230 | 26 | 0 |
| McDonald | 7 | 113 | 16 | 1 |
| Leigh | 3 | -4 | -1 | 0 |
| Morrison | 2 | 40 | 20 | 1 |
| Smith | 2 | 11 | 6 | 0 |

PUNT RETURNS

| Last Name | No. | Yds | Avg | TD |
|---|---|---|---|---|
| Leigh | 14 | 76 | 5 | 0 |
| Davis | 9 | 11 | 1 | 0 |
| Kelly | 1 | 9 | 9 | 0 |

KICKOFF RETURNS

| Last Name | No. | Yds | Avg | TD |
|---|---|---|---|---|
| Leigh | 14 | 322 | 23 | 0 |
| Ward | 13 | 236 | 18 | 0 |
| James | 8 | 166 | 21 | 0 |
| Davis | 8 | 152 | 19 | 0 |
| Morrison | 4 | 85 | 21 | 0 |
| Kelly | 1 | 10 | 10 | 0 |
| Smith | 1 | 3 | 3 | 0 |
| Andrews | 1 | 0 | 0 | 0 |
| Barnes | 1 | 0 | 0 | 0 |
| Copeland | 1 | 0 | 0 | 0 |
| Houston | 1 | 0 | 0 | 0 |
| Howell | 1 | 0 | 0 | 0 |

PASSING – PUNTING – KICKING

| PASSING | Att | Comp | % | Yds | Yd/Att | TD | Int- | % | RK |
|---|---|---|---|---|---|---|---|---|---|
| Nelsen | 293 | 152 | 52 | 2366 | 8.1 | 19 | 10- | 3 | 6 |
| Ryan | 66 | 31 | 47 | 639 | 9.7 | 7 | 6- | 9 | |
| Kelly | 4 | 1 | 25 | 34 | 8.5 | 1 | 0- | 0 | |

| PUNTING | No | Avg |
|---|---|---|
| Cockroft | 61 | 37.7 |
| Collins | 2 | 26.0 |

| KICKING | XP | Att | % | FG | Att | % |
|---|---|---|---|---|---|---|
| Cockroft | 46 | 48 | 96 | 18 | 24 | 75 |

### ST. LOUIS CARDINALS

RUSHING

| Last Name | No. | Yds | Avg | TD |
|---|---|---|---|---|
| Crenshaw | 203 | 813 | 4.0 | 6 |
| Roland | 121 | 455 | 3.8 | 2 |
| Edwards | 31 | 214 | 6.9 | 1 |
| Shivers | 44 | 184 | 4.2 | 4 |
| Smith | 12 | 163 | 13.6 | 3 |
| Lane | 23 | 74 | 3.2 | 0 |
| D. Williams | 3 | 47 | 15.7 | 0 |
| Hart | 19 | 20 | 1.1 | 6 |
| Latourette | 1 | 15 | 15.0 | 0 |
| Wilson | 1 | 12 | 12.0 | 0 |
| Johnson | 5 | -1 | -0.2 | 0 |

RECEIVING

| Last Name | No. | Yds | Avg | TD |
|---|---|---|---|---|
| Smith | 49 | 789 | 16 | 2 |
| D. Williams | 43 | 682 | 16 | 6 |
| Conrad | 32 | 449 | 14 | 4 |
| Crenshaw | 23 | 232 | 10 | 1 |
| Shivers | 9 | 103 | 11 | 3 |
| Roland | 8 | 97 | 12 | 0 |
| Daanen | 4 | 35 | 9 | 0 |
| Edwards | 1 | 2 | 2 | 0 |

PUNT RETURNS

| Last Name | No. | Yds | Avg | TD |
|---|---|---|---|---|
| Latourette | 28 | 345 | 12 | 1 |
| Roland | 3 | 11 | 4 | 0 |

KICKOFF RETURNS

| Last Name | No. | Yds | Avg | TD |
|---|---|---|---|---|
| Latourette | 46 | 1237 | 27 | 0 |
| Crenshaw | 6 | 104 | 17 | 0 |
| Roland | 3 | 63 | 21 | 0 |
| Long | 1 | 0 | 0 | 0 |

PASSING – PUNTING – KICKING

| PASSING | Att | Comp | % | Yds | Yd/Att | TD | Int- | % | RK |
|---|---|---|---|---|---|---|---|---|---|
| Hart | 316 | 140 | 44 | 2059 | 6.5 | 15 | 18- | 6 | 14 |
| Johnson | 67 | 29 | 43 | 330 | 4.9 | 1 | 1- | 1 | |
| Latourette | 1 | 0 | 0 | | 0.0 | 0 | 0- | 0 | |
| Roland | 1 | 0 | 0 | 0 | 0.0 | 0 | 1- | 100 | |

| PUNTING | No | Avg |
|---|---|---|
| Latourette | 65 | 41.6 |

| KICKING | XP | Att | % | FG | Att | % |
|---|---|---|---|---|---|---|
| Bakken | 40 | 40 | 100 | 15 | 24 | 63 |

### NEW ORLEANS SAINTS

RUSHING

| Last Name | No. | Yds | Avg | TD |
|---|---|---|---|---|
| McCall | 155 | 637 | 4.1 | 4 |
| Lorick | 104 | 344 | 3.3 | 0 |
| Schultz | 43 | 152 | 3.5 | 0 |
| Barrington | 45 | 111 | 2.5 | 0 |
| Wheelwright | 21 | 99 | 4.7 | 1 |
| Kilmer | 21 | 97 | 4.6 | 2 |
| Gilliam | 2 | 36 | 18.0 | 0 |
| Abramowicz | 2 | 27 | 13.5 | 0 |
| Poage | 1 | 22 | 22.0 | 0 |
| South | 4 | 5 | 1.3 | 0 |
| Baker | 4 | 2 | 0.5 | 0 |
| McNeill | 2 | 1 | 0.5 | 0 |
| Whitsell | 1 | -1 | -1.0 | 0 |
| Sweetan | 4 | -5 | -1.3 | 0 |

RECEIVING

| Last Name | No. | Yds | Avg | TD |
|---|---|---|---|---|
| Abramowicz | 54 | 890 | 16 | 7 |
| Lorick | 26 | 272 | 10 | 3 |
| McCall | 26 | 270 | 10 | 2 |
| Parks | 25 | 258 | 10 | 0 |
| Gilliam | 24 | 284 | 11 | 0 |
| Hester | 17 | 300 | 18 | 2 |
| Stickles | 15 | 206 | 14 | 2 |
| Schultz | 12 | 34 | 3 | 0 |
| Barrington | 9 | 33 | 4 | 1 |
| Poage | 1 | 11 | 11 | 0 |
| Wheelwright | 1 | -9 | -9 | 0 |

PUNT RETURNS

| Last Name | No. | Yds | Avg | TD |
|---|---|---|---|---|
| Gilliam | 15 | 60 | 4 | 0 |
| Brown | 8 | 60 | 8 | 1 |
| Howard | 8 | 42 | 5 | 0 |
| Nevett | 3 | -9 | -3 | 0 |

KICKOFF RETURNS

| Last Name | No. | Yds | Avg | TD |
|---|---|---|---|---|
| Howard | 23 | 533 | 23 | 0 |
| Gilliam | 15 | 328 | 22 | 0 |
| Brown | 8 | 137 | 17 | 0 |
| Nevett | 2 | 94 | 47 | 0 |
| Stonebreaker | 1 | 22 | 22 | 0 |
| Kelley | 1 | 20 | 20 | 0 |
| Douglas | 1 | 10 | 10 | 0 |
| Jones | 1 | 5 | 5 | 0 |
| Whitsell | 1 | 0 | 0 | 0 |

PASSING – PUNTING – KICKING

| PASSING | Att | Comp | % | Yds | Yd/Att | TD | Int- | % | RK |
|---|---|---|---|---|---|---|---|---|---|
| Kilmer | 315 | 167 | 53 | 2060 | 6.5 | 15 | 17- | 5 | 10 |
| Sweetan | 78 | 27 | 35 | 318 | 4.1 | 1 | 9- | 12 | |
| South | 38 | 14 | 37 | 129 | 3.4 | 1 | 3- | 8 | |
| Barrington | 6 | 2 | 33 | 42 | 7.0 | 0 | 0- | 0 | |
| McCall | 1 | 0 | 0 | | 0.0 | 0 | 0- | 0 | |
| Parks | 1 | 0 | 0 | | 0.0 | 0 | 0- | 0 | |

| PUNTING | No | Avg |
|---|---|---|
| McNeill | 49 | 41.0 |
| South | 14 | 27.6 |
| Fraser | 11 | 35.5 |
| Lorick | 1 | 36.0 |

| KICKING | XP | Att | % | FG | Att | % |
|---|---|---|---|---|---|---|
| Durkee | 27 | 27 | 100 | 19 | 37 | 51 |

### PITTSBURGH STEELERS

RUSHING

| Last Name | No. | Yds | Avg | TD |
|---|---|---|---|---|
| Hoak | 175 | 858 | 4.9 | 3 |
| Gros | 151 | 579 | 3.8 | 3 |
| Shy | 35 | 106 | 3.0 | 1 |
| Jefferson | 6 | 57 | 9.5 | 0 |
| Shiner | 14 | 53 | 3.8 | 0 |
| Bleier | 6 | 39 | 6.5 | 0 |
| Nix | 6 | 15 | 2.5 | 0 |
| Asbury | 4 | 9 | 2.3 | 0 |
| Walden | 2 | 5 | 2.5 | 0 |

RECEIVING

| Last Name | No. | Yds | Avg | TD |
|---|---|---|---|---|
| Jefferson | 58 | 1074 | 19 | 11 |
| Wilburn | 39 | 514 | 13 | 3 |
| Hoak | 28 | 253 | 9 | 1 |
| Gros | 27 | 211 | 8 | 3 |
| Hilton | 20 | 285 | 14 | 1 |
| Shy | 13 | 106 | 8 | 0 |
| Kotite | 6 | 65 | 11 | 2 |
| Compton | 5 | 45 | 9 | 1 |
| Cropper | 4 | 54 | 14 | 0 |
| Bleier | 3 | 68 | 23 | 0 |
| Asbury | 3 | 27 | 9 | 0 |
| Henderson | 3 | 26 | 9 | 0 |
| Hillebrand | 1 | 27 | 27 | 0 |
| Jeter | 1 | 9 | 9 | 0 |

PUNT RETURNS

| Last Name | No. | Yds | Avg | TD |
|---|---|---|---|---|
| Jefferson | 28 | 274 | 10 | 1 |
| Harris | 6 | 21 | 4 | 0 |
| Bleier | 2 | 13 | 7 | 0 |
| Watkins | 2 | 0 | 0 | 0 |

KICKOFF RETURNS

| Last Name | No. | Yds | Avg | TD |
|---|---|---|---|---|
| Shy | 28 | 682 | 24 | 0 |
| Henderson | 29 | 589 | 20 | 0 |
| Bleier | 6 | 119 | 20 | 0 |
| Cropper | 3 | 53 | 8 | 0 |
| Watkins | 1 | 22 | 22 | 0 |
| Harris | 1 | 19 | 19 | 0 |
| Hilton | 1 | 9 | 9 | 0 |
| Taylor | 1 | 9 | 9 | 0 |

PASSING – PUNTING – KICKING

| PASSING | Att | Comp | % | Yds | Yd/Att | TD | Int- | % | RK |
|---|---|---|---|---|---|---|---|---|---|
| Shiner | 304 | 148 | 49 | 1856 | 6.1 | 18 | 17- | 6 | 12 |
| Nix | 130 | 56 | 43 | 720 | 5.5 | 4 | 8- | 6 | |
| Hoak | 16 | 7 | 44 | 188 | 11.8 | 0 | 1- | 6 | |
| Walden | 1 | 0 | 0 | | 0.0 | 0 | 0- | 0 | |

| PUNTING | No | Avg |
|---|---|---|
| Walden | 68 | 40.4 |

| KICKING | XP | Att | % | FG | Att | % |
|---|---|---|---|---|---|---|
| Lusteg | 26 | 29 | 90 | 8 | 20 | 40 |
| Shockley | 2 | 3 | 67 | 0 | 1 | 0 |

## CENTRAL DIVISION

### MINNESOTA VIKINGS 8-6-0 Bud Grant

| Scores of Each Game | |
|---|---|
| 47 | ATLANTA 7 |
| 26 | Green Bay 13 |
| 17 | CHICAGO 27 |
| 24 | DETROIT 10 |
| 17 | New Orleans 20 |
| 7 | DALLAS 20 |
| 24 | Chicago 26 |
| 27 | WASHINGTON 14 |
| 14 | GREEN BAY 10 |
| 13 | Detroit 6 |
| 9 | Baltimore 21 |
| 3 | LOS ANGELES 31 |
| 30 | San Francisco 20 |
| 24 | Philadelphia 17 |

| Use Name | Pos. | Hgt | Wgt | Age | Int | Pts |
|---|---|---|---|---|---|---|
| Grady Alderman | OT | 6'2" | 240 | 29 | | |
| Doug Davis | OT | 6'4" | 250 | 24 | | |
| Ron Yary | OT | 6'6" | 265 | 22 | | |
| Bookie Bolin | OG | 6'2" | 240 | 28 | | |
| Larry Bowie | OG | 6'2" | 255 | 28 | | |
| Milt Sunde | OG | 6'2" | 250 | 25 | | |
| Jim Vellone | OG | 6'2" | 255 | 24 | | |
| Mick Tingelhoff | C | 6'1" | 237 | 28 | | |
| Carl Eller | DE | 6'6" | 265 | 26 | | |
| Jim Marshall | DE | 6'3" | 235 | 30 | 2 | |
| Steve Smith | DE | 6'5" | 240 | 24 | | |
| Paul Dickson | DT | 6'5" | 255 | 31 | | |
| Gary Larsen | DT | 6'5" | 255 | 28 | | |
| Alan Page | DT | 6'5" | 265 | 23 | | |
| Jim Hargrove | LB | 6'3" | 230 | 22 | | |
| Wally Hilgenberg | LB | 6'3" | 225 | 25 | | |
| John Kirby | LB | 6'3" | 235 | 26 | | |
| Mike McGill | LB | 6'2" | 237 | 21 | | |
| Lonnie Warwick | LB | 6'3" | 235 | 26 | | |
| Roy Winston | LB | 6'1" | 230 | 28 | | |
| Bobby Bryant | DB | 6' | 175 | 24 | 2 | 6 |
| Dale Hackbart | DB | 6'3" | 210 | 32 | | |
| Karl Kassulke | DB | 6' | 195 | 26 | 1 | |
| Paul Krause | DB | 6'3" | 195 | 26 | 7 | |
| Earsell Mackbee | DB | 6'1" | 195 | 27 | 2 | |
| Ed Sharockman | DB | 6' | 200 | 28 | 4 | |
| Charlie West | DB | 6'1" | 190 | 22 | | 6 |
| Gary Cuozzo | QB | 6'1" | 198 | 27 | | |
| King Hill (from PHI) | QB | 6'3" | 216 | 32 | | |
| Joe Kapp | QB | 6'2" | 212 | 30 | | 18 |
| Earl Denny | HB | 6'1" | 200 | 23 | | |
| Clint Jones | HB | 6' | 206 | 23 | | 6 |
| Dave Osborn | HB | 6' | 205 | 25 | | |
| Jim Lindsey | FB-HB | 6'2" | 200 | 23 | | 24 |
| Bill Brown | FB | 5'11" | 230 | 30 | | 84 |
| Oscar Reed | HB-FB | 5'11" | 220 | 24 | | |
| Bob Goodridge | WR | 6'2" | 202 | 22 | | |
| Bob Grim | WR | 6' | 197 | 23 | | |
| Tom Hall | WR | 6'1" | 195 | 27 | | 6 |
| John Henderson | WR | 6'3" | 190 | 25 | | |
| Art Powell | WR | 6'3" | 214 | 31 | | |
| Gene Washington | WR | 6'3" | 218 | 24 | | 36 |
| John Beasley | TE | 6'3" | 228 | 23 | | |
| Billy Martin | TE | 6'4" | 235 | 25 | | 6 |
| Fred Cox | K | 5'10" | 200 | 29 | | 88 |

Don Hansen — Knee Injury

### CHICAGO BEARS 7-7-0 Jim Dooley

| Scores of Each Game | |
|---|---|
| 28 | WASHINGTON 38 |
| 0 | Detroit 42 |
| 27 | Minnesota 17 |
| 7 | Baltimore 28 |
| 10 | DETROIT 28 |
| 29 | Philadelphia 16 |
| 26 | MINNESOTA 24 |
| 13 | Green Bay 10 |
| 27 | SAN FRANCISCO 19 |
| 13 | ATLANTA 16 |
| 3 | DALLAS 34 |
| 23 | New Orleans 17 |
| 17 | Los Angeles 16 |
| 27 | GREEN BAY 28 |

| Use Name | Pos. | Hgt | Wgt | Age | Int | Pts |
|---|---|---|---|---|---|---|
| Randy Jackson | OT | 6'5" | 245 | 24 | | |
| Wayne Mass | OT | 6'4" | 245 | 22 | | |
| Bob Pickens | OT | 6'4" | 258 | 25 | | |
| Bob Wetoska | C-OT | 6'3" | 240 | 30 | | |
| Jim Cadile | OG | 6'3" | 240 | 27 | | |
| Doug Kriewald | OG | 6'4" | 245 | 23 | | |
| George Seals | OG | 6'2" | 260 | 25 | | |
| Mike Pyle | C | 6'3" | 250 | 29 | | |
| Ed O'Bradovich | DE | 6'3" | 255 | 28 | | |
| Loyd Phillips | DE | 6'3" | 240 | 23 | 2 | |
| Willie Holman | DT-DE | 6'4" | 250 | 23 | | |
| Frank Cornish | DT | 6'6" | 285 | 24 | | |
| Dick Evey | DT | 6'2" | 245 | 27 | 1 | |
| John Johnson | DT | 6'5" | 260 | 27 | | |
| Doug Buffone | LB | 6'1" | 230 | 24 | 1 | |
| Dick Butkus | LB | 6'3" | 245 | 24 | 3 | |
| Rudy Kuechenberg | LB | 6'2" | 215 | 25 | | |
| Dan Pride | LB | 6'3" | 225 | 26 | | |
| Jim Purnell | LB | 6'2" | 238 | 26 | | |
| Mike Reilly | LB | 6'2" | 230 | 25 | | |
| Clarence Childs | DB | 6' | 180 | 29 | | |
| Curtis Gentry | DB | 6' | 185 | 27 | 1 | |
| Major Hazelton | DB | 6'1" | 185 | 23 | | |
| Bennie McRae | DB | 6' | 180 | 27 | 4 | |
| Richie Petitbon | DB | 6'3" | 205 | 30 | 2 | |
| Joe Taylor | DB | 6'2" | 200 | 27 | 1 | |
| Rosey Taylor | DB | 5'11" | 186 | 29 | 3 | 6 |
| Rudy Bukich | QB | 6'1" | 205 | 37 | | |
| Virgil Carter | QB | 6'1" | 185 | 22 | | 24 |
| Jack Concannon | QB | 6'3" | 205 | 25 | | 12 |
| Larry Rakestraw | QB | 6'2" | 195 | 26 | | |
| Garry Lyle | HB | 6'2" | 198 | 22 | | |
| Gale Sayers | HB | 6'1" | 205 | 25 | | 12 |
| Brian Piccolo | HB | 6' | 205 | 24 | | 12 |
| Ralph Kurek | FB | 6'2" | 210 | 25 | | 6 |
| Andy Livingston | FB | 6' | 234 | 23 | | |
| Ronnie Bull | HB-FB | 6' | 200 | 28 | | 18 |
| Mike Hull | TE-FB | 6'3" | 220 | 23 | | |
| Dick Gordon | WR | 5'11" | 190 | 23 | | 24 |
| Bob Jones | WR | 6'4" | 196 | 23 | | |
| Cecil Turner | WR | 5'10" | 170 | 24 | | 12 |
| Bob Wallace | WR | 6'3" | 211 | 22 | | 12 |
| Austin Denney | TE | 6'2" | 230 | 24 | | 12 |
| Emilio Vallez | TE | 6'3" | 220 | 23 | | |
| Bobby Joe Green | K | 5'11" | 175 | 30 | | |
| Jon Kilgore | K | 6'1" | 205 | 24 | | |
| Mac Percival | K | 6'4" | 217 | 28 | | 100 |

Marty Amster — Injury
Terry Stoepel — Military Service

### GREEN BAY PACKERS 6-7-1 Phil Bengtson

| Scores of Each Game | |
|---|---|
| 30 | PHILADELPHIA 13 |
| 13 | MINNESOTA 26 |
| 17 | DETROIT 23 |
| 38 | Atlanta 7 |
| 14 | LOS ANGELES 16 |
| 14 | Detroit 14 |
| 28 | Dallas 17 |
| 10 | CHICAGO 13 |
| 10 | Minnesota 14 |
| 29 | NEW ORLEANS 7 |
| 27 | Washington 7 |
| 20 | San Francisco 27 |
| 3 | BALTIMORE 16 |
| 28 | Chicago 27 |

| Use Name | Pos. | Hgt | Wgt | Age | Int | Pts |
|---|---|---|---|---|---|---|
| Forrest Gregg | OT | 6'4" | 250 | 35 | | |
| Dick Himes | OT | 6'4" | 244 | 22 | | |
| Francis Peay | OT | 6'5" | 250 | 24 | | |
| Bob Skoronski | OT | 6'3" | 245 | 35 | | |
| Gale Gillingham | OG | 6'3" | 255 | 24 | | |
| Jerry Kramer | OG | 6'3" | 245 | 33 | | 21 |
| Bill Lueck | OG | 6'3" | 235 | 22 | | |
| Ken Bowman | C | 6'3" | 230 | 25 | | |
| Bob Hyland | OG-C | 6'5" | 250 | 23 | | |
| Lionel Aldridge | DE | 6'4" | 245 | 26 | | |
| Leo Carroll | DE | 6'7" | 250 | 24 | | |
| Willie Davis | DE | 6'3" | 245 | 35 | | |
| Francis Winkler | DE | 6'3" | 230 | 21 | | |
| Leon Crenshaw | DT | 6'6" | 280 | 25 | | |
| Henry Jordan | DT | 6'3" | 250 | 33 | | |
| Ron Kostelnik | DT | 6'4" | 260 | 28 | | |
| Bob Brown | DE-DT | 6'5" | 260 | 28 | | |
| Lee Roy Caffey | LB | 6'3" | 250 | 28 | | |
| Fred Carr | LB | 6'5" | 238 | 22 | | |
| Jim Flanigan | LB | 6'3" | 240 | 23 | | |
| Ray Nitschke | LB | 6'3" | 240 | 32 | 2 | |
| Dave Robinson | LB | 6'3" | 240 | 27 | 2 | |
| Phil Vandersea | TE-LB | 6'3" | 225 | 25 | | |
| Herb Adderley | DB | 6'1" | 200 | 29 | 3 | |
| Tom Brown | DB | 6'1" | 190 | 27 | 4 | 12 |
| Doug Hart | DB | 6'1" | 190 | 29 | 1 | |
| Bob Jeter | DB | 6'1" | 205 | 30 | 3 | |
| John Rowser | DB | 6'1" | 180 | 24 | | |
| Gordon Rule | DB | 6'2" | 180 | 22 | | |
| Willie Wood | DB | 5'10" | 190 | 32 | 2 | |
| Zeke Bratkowski | QB | 6'2" | 210 | 36 | | |
| Don Horn | QB | 6'2" | 195 | 23 | | |
| Bart Starr | QB | 6'1" | 190 | 34 | | 6 |
| Bill Stevens | QB | 6'3" | 195 | 23 | | |
| Donny Anderson | HB | 6'3" | 210 | 25 | | 36 |
| Elijah Pitts | HB | 6'1" | 205 | 29 | | 12 |
| Travis Williams | HB | 6'1" | 210 | 22 | | |
| Jim Grabowski | FB | 6'2" | 220 | 24 | | 24 |
| Chuck Mercein | FB | 6'3" | 230 | 25 | | 19 |
| Carroll Dale | WR | 6'1" | 200 | 30 | | 48 |
| Boyd Dowler | WR | 6'5" | 225 | 31 | | 36 |
| Claudis James | WR | 6'2" | 190 | 24 | | 12 |
| Bucky Pope | WR | 6'5" | 200 | 25 | | |
| Marv Fleming | TE | 6'4" | 235 | 26 | | 18 |
| Errol Mann | K | 6' | 203 | 27 | | 4 |
| Mike Mercer (from BUF-A) | K | 6' | 217 | 32 | | 33 |

Jim Weatherwax — Knee Injury
Ben Wilson — Knee Injury

### DETROIT LIONS 4-8-2 Joe Schmidt

| Scores of Each Game | |
|---|---|
| 13 | Dallas 59 |
| 42 | CHICAGO 0 |
| 23 | Green Bay 17 |
| 10 | Minnesota 24 |
| 28 | Chicago 10 |
| 14 | GREEN BAY 14 |
| 7 | SAN FRANCISCO 14 |
| 7 | Los Angeles 10 |
| 10 | BALTIMORE 27 |
| 6 | MINNESOTA 13 |
| 20 | NEW ORLEANS 20 |
| 0 | PHILADELPHIA 12 |
| 24 | Atlanta 7 |
| 3 | Washington 14 |

| Use Name | Pos. | Hgt | Wgt | Age | Int | Pts |
|---|---|---|---|---|---|---|
| Charlie Bradshaw | OT | 6'6" | 260 | 32 | | |
| Bill Cottrell | OT | 6'3" | 250 | 23 | | |
| Rocky Freitas | OT | 6'6" | 258 | 22 | | |
| Greg Kent | OT | 6'6" | 265 | 25 | | |
| Roger Shoals | OT | 6'4" | 255 | 29 | | |
| Frank Gallagher | OG | 6'2" | 240 | 25 | | |
| Bob Kowalkowski | OG | 6'3" | 245 | 24 | | |
| Chuck Walton | OG | 6'3" | 250 | 24 | | |
| Ed Flanagan | C | 6'3" | 250 | 24 | | |
| John Baker | DE | 6'6" | 270 | 33 | | |
| Larry Hand | DE | 6'4" | 245 | 24 | | |
| Lew Kamanu | DE | 6'4" | 245 | 24 | | |
| Joe Robb | DE | 6'3" | 245 | 31 | | |
| Alex Karras | DT | 6'2" | 255 | 32 | | |
| Denis Moore | DT | 6'5" | 255 | 25 | | |
| Jerry Rush | DT | 6'4" | 260 | 26 | | |
| Chuck Sieminski | DT | 6'4" | 270 | 28 | | |
| Mike Lucci | LB | 6'2" | 230 | 28 | 1 | |
| Ed Mooney | LB | 6'2" | 238 | 23 | | |
| Paul Naumoff | LB | 6'1" | 225 | 23 | 1 | |
| Bill Swain | LB | 6'2" | 230 | 27 | 1 | 6 |
| Wayne Walker | LB | 6'2" | 225 | 31 | 1 | 24 |
| Lem Barney | DB | 6' | 185 | 22 | 7 | 12 |
| Dick LeBeau | DB | 6'1" | 185 | 31 | 5 | |
| Wayne Rasmussen | DB | 6'1" | 175 | 26 | | |
| Bobby Rasmussen | DB | 5'10" | 185 | 28 | | |
| Tom Vaughn | DB | 5'11" | 190 | 25 | 3 | |
| Mike Weger | DB | 6'2" | 185 | 22 | 5 | |
| Jim Welch | HB-DB | 6' | 196 | 30 | | |
| Greg Landry | QB | 6'4" | 205 | 21 | | 6 |
| Bill Munson | QB | 6'2" | 200 | 26 | | 6 |
| Mike Campbell | HB | 5'11" | 200 | 23 | | |
| Nick Eddy | HB | 6'1" | 205 | 24 | | |
| Mel Farr | HB | 6'2" | 205 | 23 | | 42 |
| Dave Kopay | FB-HB | 6'2" | 225 | 26 | | |
| Tom Nowatzke | FB | 6'3" | 230 | 25 | | 6 |
| Bill Triplett | HB-FB | 6'2" | 210 | 29 | | |
| Billy Gambrell | WR | 5'10" | 175 | 26 | | 42 |
| Bill Malinchak | WR | 6'1" | 200 | 24 | | |
| Earl McCullouch | WR | 5'11" | 172 | 22 | | 30 |
| Phil Odle | WR | 5'11" | 187 | 25 | | |
| Jim Gibbons | TE | 6'2" | 230 | 32 | | |
| Charlie Sanders | TE | 6'4" | 215 | 22 | | 6 |
| Jerry DePoyster | K | 6'1" | 200 | 22 | | 27 |

## CENTRAL DIVISION

### MINNESOTA VIKINGS

**RUSHING**

| Last Name | No. | Yds | Avg | TD |
|---|---|---|---|---|
| Brown | 222 | 805 | 3.6 | 11 |
| Jones | 128 | 536 | 4.2 | 1 |
| Kapp | 50 | 269 | 5.4 | 3 |
| Lindsey | 53 | 152 | 2.9 | 4 |
| Osborn | 42 | 140 | 3.3 | 0 |
| Denny | 2 | 9 | 4.5 | 0 |
| Reed | 2 | 6 | 3.0 | 0 |
| Cuozzo | 1 | 4 | 4.0 | 0 |
| Hill | 1 | 1 | 1.0 | 0 |

**RECEIVING**

| Last Name | No. | Yds | Avg | TD |
|---|---|---|---|---|
| Washington | 46 | 756 | 16 | 6 |
| Brown | 31 | 329 | 11 | 3 |
| Beasley | 23 | 289 | 13 | 0 |
| Hall | 19 | 268 | 14 | 1 |
| Lindsey | 15 | 148 | 10 | 0 |
| Martin | 10 | 101 | 10 | 1 |
| Henderson | 4 | 42 | 11 | 0 |
| Jones | 4 | 26 | 7 | 0 |
| Powell | 1 | 31 | 31 | 0 |
| Goodridge | 1 | 5 | 5 | 0 |

**PUNT RETURNS**

| Last Name | No. | Yds | Avg | TD |
|---|---|---|---|---|
| West | 20 | 201 | 10 | 1 |
| Bryant | 10 | 49 | 5 | 0 |

**KICKOFF RETURNS**

| Last Name | No. | Yds | Avg | TD |
|---|---|---|---|---|
| West | 22 | 576 | 26 | 0 |
| Bryant | 19 | 373 | 20 | 0 |
| Jones | 4 | 60 | 15 | 0 |
| Denny | 3 | 19 | 6 | 0 |
| Sharockman | 1 | 14 | 14 | 0 |
| Lindsey | 1 | 7 | 7 | 0 |
| Alderman | 1 | 0 | 0 | 0 |
| Martin | 1 | 0 | 0 | 0 |

**PASSING - PUNTING - KICKING**

PASSING

| Last Name | Att | Comp | % | Yds | Yd/Att | TD | Int– | % | RK |
|---|---|---|---|---|---|---|---|---|---|
| Kapp | 248 | 129 | 52 | 1695 | 6.8 | 10 | 17– | 7 | 13 |
| Hill | 71 | 33 | 47 | 531 | 7.5 | 3 | 6– | 8 | |
| Cuozzo | 33 | 24 | 73 | 297 | 9.0 | 1 | 0– | 0 | |
| Brown | 1 | 1 | 100 | 3 | 3.0 | 0 | 0– | 0 | |

PUNTING

| Last Name | No | Avg |
|---|---|---|
| Hill | 33 | 41.0 |
| Martin | 28 | 37.4 |

KICKING

| Last Name | XP | Att | % | FG | Att | % |
|---|---|---|---|---|---|---|
| Cox | 31 | 32 | 97 | 19 | 29 | 66 |

### CHICAGO BEARS

**RUSHING**

| Last Name | No. | Yds | Avg | TD |
|---|---|---|---|---|
| Sayers | 138 | 856 | 6.2 | 2 |
| Bull | 107 | 472 | 4.4 | 3 |
| Piccolo | 123 | 450 | 3.7 | 2 |
| Carter | 48 | 265 | 5.5 | 4 |
| Concannon | 28 | 104 | 3.7 | 2 |
| Kurek | 17 | 95 | 5.6 | 1 |
| Wallace | 3 | 29 | 9.7 | 0 |
| Lyle | 4 | 28 | 7.0 | 0 |
| Livingston | 7 | 25 | 3.6 | 0 |
| Hull | 12 | 22 | 1.8 | 0 |
| Turner | 2 | 16 | 8.0 | 0 |
| Rakestraw | 9 | 12 | 1.3 | 0 |
| Green | 1 | 4 | 4.0 | 0 |
| Denney | 1 | -1 | -1.0 | 0 |

**RECEIVING**

| Last Name | No. | Yds | Avg | TD |
|---|---|---|---|---|
| Gordon | 29 | 477 | 16 | 4 |
| Piccolo | 28 | 291 | 10 | 0 |
| Denney | 23 | 247 | 11 | 2 |
| Wallace | 19 | 281 | 15 | 2 |
| Bull | 17 | 145 | 9 | 0 |
| Sayers | 15 | 117 | 8 | 0 |
| Turner | 14 | 208 | 15 | 2 |
| Lyle | 5 | 32 | 6 | 0 |
| Kurek | 4 | 50 | 13 | 0 |
| Hull | 4 | 20 | 5 | 0 |

**PUNT RETURNS**

| Last Name | No. | Yds | Avg | TD |
|---|---|---|---|---|
| Sayers | 2 | 29 | 15 | 0 |
| Wallace | 6 | 27 | 5 | 0 |
| Turner | 9 | 19 | 2 | 0 |
| Gordon | 1 | 5 | 5 | 0 |
| Hazelton | 1 | 1 | 1 | 0 |

**KICKOFF RETURNS**

| Last Name | No. | Yds | Avg | TD |
|---|---|---|---|---|
| Sayers | 17 | 461 | 27 | 0 |
| Turner | 20 | 363 | 18 | 0 |
| Childs | 8 | 291 | 36 | 0 |
| Gordon | 3 | 97 | 32 | 0 |
| Wallace | 3 | 80 | 27 | 0 |
| Kurek | 4 | 48 | 12 | 0 |
| Butkus | 2 | 30 | 15 | 0 |
| Kuechenburg | 1 | 0 | 0 | 0 |

**PASSING - PUNTING - KICKING**

PASSING

| Last Name | Att | Comp | % | Yds | Yd/Att | TD | Int– | % | RK |
|---|---|---|---|---|---|---|---|---|---|
| Concannon | 143 | 71 | 50 | 715 | 5.0 | 5 | 9– | 6 | 16 |
| Carter | 122 | 55 | 45 | 769 | 6.3 | 4 | 5– | 4 | |
| Rakestraw | 67 | 30 | 45 | 361 | 5.4 | 1 | 7– | 10 | |
| Bukich | 7 | 2 | 29 | 23 | 3.3 | 0 | 0– | 0 | |
| Sayers | 2 | 0 | 0 | 0 | 0.0 | 0 | 0– | 0 | |
| Bull | 1 | 0 | 0 | 0 | 0.0 | 0 | 0– | 0 | |
| Kilgore | 1 | 0 | 0 | 0 | 0.0 | 0 | 0– | 0 | |

PUNTING

| Last Name | No | Avg |
|---|---|---|
| Kilgore | 35 | 35.2 |
| Green | 27 | 42.3 |
| Lyle | 4 | 33.5 |

KICKING

| Last Name | XP | Att | % | FG | Att | % |
|---|---|---|---|---|---|---|
| Percival | 25 | 25 | 100 | 25 | 36 | 69 |

### GREEN BAY PACKERS

**RUSHING**

| Last Name | No. | Yds | Avg | TD |
|---|---|---|---|---|
| Anderson | 170 | 761 | 4.5 | 5 |
| Grabowski | 135 | 518 | 3.8 | 3 |
| Pitts | 72 | 264 | 3.7 | 2 |
| Williams | 33 | 63 | 1.9 | 0 |
| Starr | 11 | 62 | 5.6 | 1 |
| Mercein | 17 | 49 | 2.9 | 1 |
| Bratkowski | 8 | 24 | 3.0 | 0 |
| James | 1 | 15 | 15.0 | 0 |
| Horn | 3 | -7 | -2.3 | 0 |

**RECEIVING**

| Last Name | No. | Yds | Avg | TD |
|---|---|---|---|---|
| Dowler | 45 | 668 | 15 | 6 |
| Dale | 42 | 818 | 19 | 8 |
| Anderson | 25 | 333 | 13 | 1 |
| Fleming | 25 | 278 | 11 | 3 |
| Grabowski | 18 | 210 | 12 | 0 |
| Pitts | 17 | 142 | 8 | 0 |
| James | 8 | 148 | 19 | 2 |
| Williams | 5 | 48 | 10 | 0 |
| Mercein | 3 | 6 | 2 | 0 |

**PUNT RETURNS**

| Last Name | No. | Yds | Avg | TD |
|---|---|---|---|---|
| Wood | 26 | 126 | 5 | 0 |
| T. Brown | 16 | 111 | 7 | 1 |
| Pitts | 1 | 1 | 1 | 0 |

**KICKOFF RETURNS**

| Last Name | No. | Yds | Avg | TD |
|---|---|---|---|---|
| Williams | 28 | 599 | 21 | 0 |
| Adderley | 14 | 331 | 24 | 0 |
| Pitts | 2 | 40 | 20 | 0 |
| Robinson | 2 | 29 | 15 | 0 |
| Vandersea | 1 | 8 | 8 | 0 |
| Winkler | 1 | 0 | 0 | 0 |

**PASSING - PUNTING - KICKING**

PASSING

| Last Name | Att | Comp | % | Yds | Yd/Att | TD | Int– | % | RK |
|---|---|---|---|---|---|---|---|---|---|
| Starr | 171 | 109 | 64 | 1617 | 9.5 | 15 | 8– | 5 | 4 |
| Bratkowski | 126 | 68 | 54 | 835 | 6.6 | 3 | 7– | 6 | |
| Horn | 16 | 10 | 63 | 187 | 11.7 | 2 | 0– | 0 | |
| Anderson | 3 | 1 | 33 | 12 | 4.0 | 1 | 0– | 0 | |
| Stevens | 2 | 0 | 0 | 0 | 0.0 | 0 | 0– | 0 | |

PUNTING

| Last Name | No | Avg |
|---|---|---|
| Anderson | 59 | 40.0 |

KICKING

| Last Name | XP | Att | % | FG | Att | % |
|---|---|---|---|---|---|---|
| Mercer | 12 | 14 | 86 | 7 | 12 | 58 |
| Kramer | 9 | 9 | 100 | 4 | 9 | 44 |
| Mercein | 7 | 7 | 100 | 2 | 5 | 40 |
| Mann | 4 | 4 | 100 | 0 | 3 | 0 |

### DETROIT LIONS

**RUSHING**

| Last Name | No. | Yds | Avg | TD |
|---|---|---|---|---|
| Farr | 128 | 597 | 4.7 | 3 |
| Triplett | 120 | 384 | 3.2 | 0 |
| Kopay | 53 | 207 | 3.9 | 0 |
| Eddy | 48 | 176 | 3.7 | 0 |
| Nowatzke | 36 | 116 | 3.2 | 1 |
| Munson | 25 | 109 | 4.4 | 1 |
| Landry | 7 | 39 | 5.6 | 1 |
| Campbell | 7 | 24 | 3.4 | 0 |
| DePoyster | 1 | 20 | 20.0 | 0 |
| Welch | 3 | 14 | 4.7 | 0 |
| McCullouch | 3 | 13 | 4.3 | 0 |
| Sanders | 2 | 3 | 1.5 | 0 |

**RECEIVING**

| Last Name | No. | Yds | Avg | TD |
|---|---|---|---|---|
| McCullouch | 40 | 680 | 17 | 5 |
| Sanders | 40 | 533 | 13 | 1 |
| Gambrell | 28 | 492 | 18 | 7 |
| Triplett | 28 | 135 | 5 | 0 |
| Farr | 24 | 375 | 16 | 4 |
| Kopay | 18 | 130 | 7 | 0 |
| Eddy | 8 | 91 | 11 | 0 |
| Odle | 6 | 71 | 12 | 0 |
| Nowatzke | 4 | 6 | 2 | 0 |
| Gibbons | 2 | 38 | 19 | 0 |
| Campbell | 2 | 15 | 8 | 0 |
| Malinchak | 1 | 41 | 41 | 0 |

**PUNT RETURNS**

| Last Name | No. | Yds | Avg | TD |
|---|---|---|---|---|
| Barney | 13 | 79 | 6 | 0 |
| Eddy | 4 | 10 | 3 | 0 |
| Vaughn | 2 | 0 | 0 | 0 |

**KICKOFF RETURNS**

| Last Name | No. | Yds | Avg | TD |
|---|---|---|---|---|
| Barney | 25 | 670 | 27 | 1 |
| Thompson | 17 | 363 | 21 | 0 |
| Vaughn | 5 | 128 | 26 | 0 |
| Nowatzke | 3 | 34 | 11 | 0 |
| Kopay | 2 | 29 | 15 | 0 |
| Gambrell | 1 | 12 | 12 | 0 |
| Mooney | 1 | 11 | 11 | 0 |

**PASSING - PUNTING - KICKING**

PASSING

| Last Name | Att | Comp | % | Yds | Yd/Att | TD | Int– | % | RK |
|---|---|---|---|---|---|---|---|---|---|
| Munson | 329 | 181 | 55 | 2311 | 7.0 | 15 | 8– | 2 | 7 |
| Landry | 48 | 23 | 48 | 338 | 7.0 | 2 | 7– | 15 | |

PUNTING

| Last Name | No | Avg |
|---|---|---|
| DePoyster | 71 | 40.4 |

KICKING

| Last Name | XP | Att | % | FG | Att | % |
|---|---|---|---|---|---|---|
| DePoyster | 18 | 20 | 90 | 3 | 15 | 20 |
| Walker | 6 | 6 | 100 | 6 | 14 | 43 |

## COASTAL DIVISION

### BALTIMORE COLTS 13-1-0 Don Shula

**Scores of Each Game**

| | | |
|---|---|---|
| 27 | SAN FRANCISCO | 10 |
| 28 | Atlanta | 20 |
| 41 | Pittsburgh | 7 |
| 28 | CHICAGO | 7 |
| 42 | San Francisco | 14 |
| 20 | CLEVELAND | 30 |
| 27 | LOS ANGELES | 10 |
| 26 | New York | 0 |
| 27 | Detroit | 10 |
| 27 | ST. LOUIS | 0 |
| 21 | MINNESOTA | 9 |
| 44 | ATLANTA | 0 |
| 16 | Green Bay | 3 |
| 28 | Los Angeles | 24 |

| Use Name | Pos. | Hgt | Wgt | Age | Int | Pts |
|---|---|---|---|---|---|---|
| Sam Ball | OT | 6'4" | 240 | 24 | | |
| Bob Vogel | OT | 6'5" | 250 | 26 | | |
| Cornelius Johnson | OG | 6'2" | 245 | 25 | | |
| Glen Ressler | OG | 6'3" | 250 | 24 | | |
| Dan Sullivan | OG | 6'3" | 250 | 29 | | |
| Bill Curry | C | 6'2" | 235 | 25 | | |
| Dick Szymanski | C | 6'3" | 235 | 36 | | |
| Ordell Braase | DE | 6'4" | 245 | 36 | | |
| Roy Hilton | DE | 6'6" | 240 | 23 | 1 | 6 |
| Lou Michaels | DE | 6'2" | 250 | 32 | | 102 |
| John Williams | DE | 6'3" | 256 | 22 | | |
| Fred Miller | DT | 6'3" | 250 | 27 | | |
| Billy Ray Smith | DT | 6'4" | 250 | 33 | | |
| Bubba Smith | DE-DT | 6'7" | 295 | 23 | | |
| Mike Curtis | LB | 6'2" | 232 | 25 | 2 | 6 |
| Dennis Gaubatz | LB | 6'2" | 232 | 27 | 2 | |
| Bob Grant | LB | 6'2" | 225 | 21 | | |
| Ron Porter | LB | 6'3" | 232 | 23 | | |
| Don Shinnick | LB | 6' | 228 | 33 | 1 | |
| Sid Williams | LB | 6'2" | 235 | 26 | | |
| Ocie Austin | DB | 6'3" | 200 | 21 | | |
| Bobby Boyd | DB | 5'10" | 192 | 30 | 8 | 6 |
| Jerry Logan | DB | 6'1" | 190 | 27 | 3 | |
| Lenny Lyles | DB | 6'2" | 204 | 32 | 5 | |
| Charlie Stukes | DB | 6'3" | 212 | 24 | 1 | 6 |
| Rick Volk | DB | 6'3" | 195 | 23 | 6 | |
| Earl Morrall | QB | 6'1" | 206 | 34 | | 6 |
| Johnny Unitas | QB | 6'1" | 196 | 35 | | |
| Jim Ward | QB | 6'2" | 195 | 24 | | |
| Timmy Brown | HB | 5'10" | 198 | 31 | | 12 |
| Tom Matte | HB | 6' | 214 | 29 | | 60 |
| Preston Pearson | HB | 6'1" | 190 | 23 | | 24 |
| Terry Cole | FB | 6'1" | 220 | 23 | | 18 |
| Jerry Hill | FB | 5'11" | 215 | 28 | | 12 |
| Gail Cogdill (from DET) | WR | 6'2" | 195 | 31 | | |
| Alex Hawkins | WR | 6'1" | 186 | 31 | | |
| Jimmy Orr | WR | 5'11" | 185 | 32 | | 36 |
| Ray Perkins | WR | 6' | 183 | 26 | | 6 |
| Willie Richardson | WR | 6'2" | 198 | 28 | | 48 |
| John Mackey | TE | 6'2" | 224 | 26 | | 30 |
| Tom Mitchell | TE | 6'2" | 215 | 24 | | 24 |
| David Lee | K | 6'4" | 215 | 24 | | |

### LOS ANGELES RAMS 10-3-1 George Allen

| | | |
|---|---|---|
| 24 | St. Louis | 13 |
| 45 | PITTSBURGH | 10 |
| 24 | Cleveland | 6 |
| 24 | SAN FRANCISCO | 10 |
| 16 | Green Bay | 14 |
| 27 | ATLANTA | 14 |
| 10 | Baltimore | 27 |
| 10 | DETROIT | 7 |
| 17 | Atlanta | 10 |
| 20 | San Francisco | 20 |
| 24 | NEW YORK | 21 |
| 31 | Minnesota | 3 |
| 16 | CHICAGO | 17 |
| 24 | BALTIMORE | 28 |

| Use Name | Pos. | Hgt | Wgt | Age | Int | Pts |
|---|---|---|---|---|---|---|
| Joe Carollo | OT | 6'2" | 258 | 28 | | |
| Charley Cowan | OT | 6'4" | 265 | 30 | | |
| Jim Wilson | OT | 6'3" | 258 | 27 | | |
| Don Chuy | OG | 6'1" | 255 | 27 | | |
| Tom Mack | OG | 6'3" | 250 | 24 | | |
| Joe Scibelli | OG | 6'1" | 255 | 29 | | |
| George Burman | C-OG | 6'3" | 255 | 25 | | |
| Ken Iman | C | 6'1" | 240 | 29 | | |
| Frank Marchlewski (from ATL) | C | 6'2" | 238 | 24 | | |
| Deacon Jones | DE | 6'5" | 260 | 29 | | |
| Lamar Lundy | DE | 6'7" | 260 | 33 | | |
| Gregg Schumacher | DE | 6'2" | 240 | 26 | | |
| Coy Bacon | DT | 6'4" | 270 | 26 | | |
| Roger Brown | DT | 6'5" | 300 | 31 | | |
| Merlin Olsen | DT | 6'5" | 276 | 27 | | |
| Diron Talbert | DT | 6'5" | 238 | 24 | | |
| Maxie Baughan | LB | 6'1" | 230 | 30 | 4 | |
| Gene Breen | LB | 6'2" | 230 | 27 | | |
| Tony Guillory | LB | 6'4" | 236 | 25 | | |
| Dean Halverson | LB | 6'2" | 220 | 22 | | |
| Jack Pardee | LB | 6'2" | 230 | 32 | 2 | 12 |
| Myron Pottios | LB | 6'2" | 235 | 28 | | |
| Doug Woodlief | LB | 6'3" | 230 | 24 | | |
| Claude Crabb | DB | 6' | 192 | 28 | | |
| Irv Cross | DB | 6'1" | 195 | 29 | 3 | |
| Willie Daniel | DB | 5'11" | 190 | 30 | | |
| Ed Meador | DB | 5'11" | 200 | 31 | 6 | |
| Ron Smith | DB | 6'1" | 192 | 25 | 3 | 6 |
| Clancy Williams | DB | 6'2" | 203 | 25 | 7 | |
| Kelton Winston | DB | 6' | 195 | 27 | | |

Dave Cahill — Knee Injury
Chuck Lamson — Injury
Les Josephson — Foot Injury

| Use Name | Pos. | Hgt | Wgt | Age | Int | Pts |
|---|---|---|---|---|---|---|
| Roman Gabriel | QB | 6'4" | 230 | 28 | | 24 |
| Milt Plum | QB | 6'1" | 205 | 34 | | |
| Mike Dennis | HB | 6'1" | 207 | 24 | | |
| Willie Ellison | HB | 6'1" | 207 | 23 | | 42 |
| Vilnis Ezerins | FB-HB | 6'1" | 217 | 23 | | |
| Tommy Mason | FB-HB | 6' | 200 | 29 | | 18 |
| Dick Bass | FB | 5'10" | 195 | 31 | | 18 |
| Henry Dyer | FB | 6'2" | 235 | 23 | | 6 |
| Bernie Casey | WR | 6'4" | 212 | 29 | | 30 |
| Harold Jackson | WR | 5'10" | 175 | 22 | | |
| Jack Snow | WR | 6'2" | 195 | 25 | | 18 |
| Pat Studstill | WR | 6'1" | 175 | 30 | | 6 |
| Wendell Tucker | WR | 5'10" | 185 | 24 | | 24 |
| Dave Pivic | TE | 6'3" | 240 | 24 | | 2 |
| Billy Truax | TE | 6'5" | 235 | 25 | | 18 |
| Bruce Gossett | K | 6'2" | 230 | 25 | | 88 |

### SAN FRANCISCO FORTY NINERS 7-6-1 Dick Nolan

| | | |
|---|---|---|
| 10 | Baltimore | 27 |
| 35 | ST. LOUIS | 17 |
| 28 | ATLANTA | 13 |
| 10 | Los Angeles | 24 |
| 14 | BALTIMORE | 42 |
| 26 | New York | 10 |
| 14 | Detroit | 7 |
| 21 | CLEVELAND | 33 |
| 19 | Chicago | 27 |
| 20 | LOS ANGELES | 20 |
| 45 | Pittsburgh | 28 |
| 27 | GREEN BAY | 20 |
| 20 | MINNESOTA | 3 |
| 14 | Atlanta | 12 |

| Use Name | Pos. | Hgt | Wgt | Age | Int | Pts |
|---|---|---|---|---|---|---|
| Cas Banaszek | OT | 6'3" | 235 | 22 | | |
| Forrest Blue | OT | 6'5" | 248 | 22 | | |
| Lance Olssen | OT | 6'5" | 257 | 21 | | |
| Len Rohde | OT | 6'4" | 250 | 30 | | |
| Elmer Collett | OG | 6'4" | 244 | 23 | | |
| Howard Mudd | OG | 6'3" | 254 | 26 | | |
| Woody Peoples | OG | 6'2" | 247 | 25 | | |
| Bruce Bosley | C | 6'2" | 244 | 34 | | |
| Bill Belk | DE | 6'3" | 242 | 22 | 1 | 6 |
| Stan Hindman | DE | 6'3" | 232 | 24 | 1 | 6 |
| Clark Miller | DE | 6'5" | 247 | 29 | | |
| Charlie Johnson | DT | 6'2" | 265 | 24 | | |
| Charlie Krueger | DT | 6'4" | 260 | 32 | | |
| Roland Lakes | DT | 6'4" | 280 | 28 | | |
| Kevin Hardy | DE-DT | 6'5" | 287 | 23 | | |

George Donnelly — Injury

| Use Name | Pos. | Hgt | Wgt | Age | Int | Pts |
|---|---|---|---|---|---|---|
| Ed Beard | LB | 6'2" | 226 | 28 | 2 | |
| Tommy Hart | LB | 6'3" | 212 | 23 | | |
| Harold Hays | LB | 6'3" | 225 | 27 | | |
| Matt Hazeltine | LB | 6'1" | 230 | 35 | | |
| Frank Nunley | LB | 6'2" | 230 | 22 | | |
| Dave Wilcox | LB | 6'3" | 234 | 25 | | |
| Kermit Alexander | DB | 5'11" | 180 | 27 | 9 | 6 |
| Johnny Fuller | DB | 6' | 175 | 22 | 2 | |
| Jim Johnson | DB | 6'2" | 187 | 30 | 1 | |
| Mel Phillips | DB | 6' | 192 | 26 | | |
| Al Randolph | DB | 6'2" | 192 | 24 | 4 | |
| John Woitt | DB | 5'11" | 174 | 22 | | |

Tom Holzer — Injury
George Rose — Injury
Don Parker — Knee Injury
John Thomas — Knee Injury
Dave Hettema — Military Service

| Use Name | Pos. | Hgt | Wgt | Age | Int | Pts |
|---|---|---|---|---|---|---|
| John Brodie | QB | 6'1" | 210 | 33 | | |
| George Mira | QB | 5'11" | 190 | 26 | | |
| Steve Spurrier | QB | 6'2" | 203 | 23 | | |
| Doug Cunningham | HB | 5'11" | 193 | 22 | | |
| Clem Daniels | HB | 6'1" | 218 | 31 | | |
| Gary Lewis | HB | 6'3" | 230 | 26 | | 24 |
| Ken Willard | FB | 6'2" | 230 | 25 | | 42 |
| Bill Tucker | TE-FB | 6'2" | 220 | 24 | | 42 |
| Kay McFarland | WR | 6'2" | 186 | 29 | | 6 |
| Clifton McNeil | WR | 6'2" | 185 | 28 | | 42 |
| Dick Witcher | WR | 6'3" | 204 | 23 | | 12 |
| Dave Olerich | TE | 6'1" | 220 | 23 | | |
| Bob Windsor | TE | 6'4" | 224 | 25 | | 12 |
| John David Crow | HB-TE | 6'2" | 224 | 33 | | 30 |
| Tommy Davis | K | 6' | 220 | 33 | | 53 |
| Dennis Patera | K | 6' | 225 | 22 | | 16 |

### ATLANTA FALCONS 2-12-0 Norb Hecker  Norm Van Brocklin

| | | |
|---|---|---|
| 7 | Minnesota | 47 |
| 20 | BALTIMORE | 28 |
| 13 | San Francisco | 28 |
| 7 | GREEN BAY | 38 |
| 24 | NEW YORK | 21 |
| 27 | Los Angeles | 27 |
| 7 | Cleveland | 30 |
| 21 | PITTSBURGH | 41 |
| 10 | LOS ANGELES | 17 |
| 16 | Chicago | 13 |
| 12 | St. Louis | 17 |
| 0 | Baltimore | 44 |
| 7 | DETROIT | 24 |
| 12 | SAN FRANCISCO | 14 |

| Use Name | Pos. | Hgt | Wgt | Age | Int | Pts |
|---|---|---|---|---|---|---|
| Errol Linden | OT | 6'5" | 260 | 30 | | |
| Bill Sandeman | OT | 6'6" | 250 | 25 | | |
| Don Talbert | OT | 6'5" | 255 | 28 | | |
| Steve Duich | OG | 6'3" | 248 | 22 | | |
| Dan Grimm | OG | 6'3" | 245 | 27 | | |
| Jim Simon | OG | 6'5" | 240 | 27 | | |
| Randy Winkler | OT-OG | 6'5" | 255 | 25 | | |
| Joe Cerne | C | 6'2" | 240 | 25 | | |
| Phil Sobocinski | C | 6'3" | 235 | 22 | | |
| Rick Cash | DE | 6'5" | 260 | 23 | | |
| Claude Humphrey | DE | 6'5" | 255 | 24 | | |
| Jim Garcia | DT-DE | 6'4" | 250 | 24 | | |
| Carlton Dabney | DT | 6'5" | 250 | 21 | 1 | |
| Jim Norton (to PHI) | DT | 6'4" | 254 | 25 | | |
| Jerry Shay | DT | 6'5" | 245 | 24 | | |
| Art Strahan | DT | 6'5" | 266 | 25 | | |
| Joe Szczecko | DT | 6' | 245 | 26 | | |

Junior Coffey — Knee Injury

| Use Name | Pos. | Hgt | Wgt | Age | Int | Pts |
|---|---|---|---|---|---|---|
| Dick Absher | LB | 6'4" | 227 | 24 | | |
| Ron Acks | LB | 6'2" | 225 | 23 | | |
| Grady Allen | LB | 6'3" | 215 | 22 | | |
| Greg Brezina | LB | 6'2" | 220 | 22 | | |
| Ralph Heck | LB | 6'2" | 230 | 27 | 1 | |
| Tommy Nobis | LB | 6'2" | 235 | 24 | 1 | |
| Marion Rushing (to HOU-A) | LB | 6'2" | 230 | 31 | | |
| Jimmy Burson | DB | 6' | 185 | 26 | 4 | 6 |
| Lee Calland | DB | 6' | 190 | 27 | 2 | |
| Ollie Cordill | DB | 6'2" | 180 | 25 | | |
| Mike Freeman | DB | 5'11" | 190 | 24 | | |
| Floyd Hudlow | DB | 5'11" | 195 | 24 | | |
| Billy Lothridge | DB | 6'1" | 195 | 24 | 3 | |
| Nick Rassas | DB | 6' | 190 | 24 | 1 | |
| Ken Reaves | DB | 6'3" | 205 | 23 | 1 | 6 |
| Phil Spiller (to CIN-A) | DB | 6' | 195 | 23 | | |
| Larry Suchy | DB | 5'11" | 180 | 22 | | |

Bob Sanders — Injury

| Use Name | Pos. | Hgt | Wgt | Age | Int | Pts |
|---|---|---|---|---|---|---|
| Bob Berry | QB | 5'11" | 190 | 26 | | 12 |
| Randy Johnson | QB | 6'3" | 196 | 24 | | 6 |
| Bruce Lemmerman | QB | 6'1" | 196 | 22 | | |
| Joe Auer | HB | 6'1" | 205 | 26 | | |
| Charlie Bryant | HB | 6'1" | 207 | 27 | | |
| Cannonball Butler | HB | 5'10" | 185 | 25 | | 12 |
| Perry Lee Dunn | HB | 6'2" | 215 | 25 | | 18 |
| Billy Harris | HB | 6' | 195 | 22 | | 6 |
| Dwight Lee (from SF) | HB | 6'2" | 198 | 22 | | |
| Doug Goodwin | FB | 6'2" | 228 | 26 | | |
| Brendan McCarthy (to DEN-A) | FB | 6'3" | 220 | 23 | | 6 |
| Harmon Wages | HB-FB | 6'2" | 210 | 22 | | 6 |
| Dave Dunaway (from GB) | WR | 6'2" | 205 | 23 | | |
| Rick Eber | WR | 6' | 173 | 23 | | |
| Paul Flatley | WR | 6'1" | 187 | 27 | | |
| Bob Long | WR | 6'3" | 205 | 27 | | 24 |
| Jerry Simmons | WR | 6'1" | 190 | 25 | | |
| John Wright | WR | 6' | 195 | 22 | | |
| Mike Donohoe | TE | 6'3" | 227 | 23 | | 6 |
| Ray Ogden | TE | 6'5" | 225 | 25 | | 12 |
| Bob Etter | K | 5'11" | 152 | 23 | | 50 |

## COASTAL DIVISION

### BALTIMORE COLTS

#### RUSHING

| Last Name | No. | Yds | Avg | TD |
|---|---|---|---|---|
| Matte | 183 | 662 | 3.6 | 9 |
| Cole | 104 | 418 | 4.0 | 3 |
| Hill | 91 | 360 | 4.0 | 1 |
| Brown | 39 | 159 | 4.1 | 2 |
| MacKey | 10 | 103 | 10.3 | 0 |
| Pearson | 19 | 78 | 4.1 | 0 |
| Morrall | 11 | 18 | 1.6 | 1 |
| Lee | 3 | 12 | 4.0 | 0 |
| Unitas | 3 | -1 | -0.3 | 0 |

#### RECEIVING

| Last Name | No. | Yds | Avg | TD |
|---|---|---|---|---|
| Mackey | 45 | 644 | 14 | 5 |
| Richardson | 37 | 698 | 19 | 8 |
| Orr | 29 | 743 | 26 | 6 |
| Matte | 25 | 275 | 11 | 1 |
| Hill | 18 | 161 | 9 | 1 |
| Perkins | 15 | 227 | 15 | 1 |
| Cole | 13 | 75 | 6 | 0 |
| Mitchell | 6 | 117 | 20 | 4 |
| Brown | 4 | 53 | 13 | 0 |
| Cogdill | 3 | 42 | 14 | 0 |
| Pearson | 2 | 70 | 35 | 2 |
| Hawkins | 2 | 31 | 16 | 0 |

#### PUNT RETURNS

| Last Name | No. | Yds | Avg | TD |
|---|---|---|---|---|
| Volk | 25 | 198 | 8 | 2 |
| Brown | 16 | 125 | 8 | 0 |
| Logan | 1 | 27 | 27 | 0 |

#### KICKOFF RETURNS

| Last Name | No. | Yds | Avg | TD |
|---|---|---|---|---|
| Pearson | 15 | 527 | 35 | 2 |
| Brown | 15 | 298 | 20 | 0 |
| Cole | 5 | 123 | 25 | 0 |
| Matte | 1 | 22 | 22 | 0 |
| Porter | 1 | 19 | 19 | 0 |
| Logan | 1 | 14 | 14 | 0 |

#### PASSING – PUNTING – KICKING

| PASSING | Att | Comp | % | Yds | Yd/Att | TD | Int– | % | RK |
|---|---|---|---|---|---|---|---|---|---|
| Morrall | 317 | 182 | 57 | 2909 | 9.2 | 26 | 17– | 5 | 1 |
| Unitas | 32 | 11 | 34 | 139 | 4.3 | 2 | 4 | 13 | |
| Ward | 9 | 3 | 33 | 46 | 5.1 | 0 | 1– | 11 | |
| Matte | 1 | 0 | 0 | 0 | 0.0 | 0 | 0– | 0 | |

| PUNTING | No | Avg |
|---|---|---|
| Lee | 49 | 39.5 |

| KICKING | XP | Att | % | FG | Att | % |
|---|---|---|---|---|---|---|
| Michaels | 48 | 50 | 96 | 18 | 28 | 64 |

### LOS ANGELES RAMS

#### RUSHING

| Last Name | No. | Yds | Avg | TD |
|---|---|---|---|---|
| Ellison | 151 | 616 | 4.1 | 5 |
| Bass | 121 | 494 | 4.1 | 1 |
| Mason | 108 | 395 | 3.7 | 3 |
| Gabriel | 34 | 139 | 4.1 | 4 |
| Dennis | 29 | 136 | 4.7 | 0 |
| Dyer | 55 | 136 | 2.5 | 1 |
| Meador | 1 | 11 | 11.0 | 0 |
| Plum | 2 | 3 | 1.5 | 0 |
| Ezerins | 2 | 2 | 1.0 | 0 |

#### RECEIVING

| Last Name | No. | Yds | Avg | TD |
|---|---|---|---|---|
| Truax | 35 | 417 | 12 | 3 |
| Casey | 29 | 565 | 19 | 5 |
| Snow | 29 | 500 | 17 | 3 |
| Bass | 27 | 195 | 7 | 2 |
| Ellison | 20 | 248 | 12 | 2 |
| Mason | 15 | 144 | 10 | 0 |
| Dennis | 8 | 53 | 7 | 0 |
| Dyer | 8 | 37 | 5 | 0 |
| Tucker | 7 | 124 | 18 | 4 |
| Studstill | 7 | 108 | 15 | 1 |
| Pivec | 3 | 27 | 9 | 0 |
| Gabriel | 1 | -5 | -5 | 0 |

#### PUNT RETURNS

| Last Name | No. | Yds | Avg | TD |
|---|---|---|---|---|
| Smith | 27 | 171 | 6 | 0 |
| Meador | 17 | 136 | 8 | 0 |

#### KICKOFF RETURNS

| Last Name | No. | Yds | Avg | TD |
|---|---|---|---|---|
| Smith | 26 | 718 | 28 | 1 |
| Ellison | 12 | 268 | 22 | 0 |
| Meador | 1 | 20 | 20 | 0 |
| Williams | 1 | 16 | 16 | 0 |
| Dennis | 2 | 2 | 1 | 0 |
| Pivec | 2 | 0 | 0 | 0 |
| Ezerins | 1 | 0 | 0 | 0 |

#### PASSING – PUNTING – KICKING

| PASSING | Att | Comp | % | Yds | Yd/Att | TD | Int– | % | RK |
|---|---|---|---|---|---|---|---|---|---|
| Gabriel | 366 | 184 | 50 | 2364 | 6.5 | 19 | 16– | 4 | 9 |
| Plum | 12 | 5 | 42 | 49 | 4.1 | 1 | 1– | 8 | |
| Dennis | 2 | 0 | 0 | 0 | 0.0 | 0 | 0– | 0 | |
| Mason | 2 | 0 | 0 | 0 | 0.0 | 0 | 0– | 0 | |
| Ellison | 1 | 0 | 0 | 0 | 0.0 | 0 | 0– | 0 | |
| Studstill | 1 | 0 | 0 | 0 | 0.0 | 0 | 0– | 0 | |

| PUNTING | No | Avg |
|---|---|---|
| Studstill | 81 | 39.6 |

| KICKING | XP | Att | % | FG | Att | % |
|---|---|---|---|---|---|---|
| Gossett | 37 | 37 | 100 | 17 | 31 | 55 |

### SAN FRANCISCO FORTY NINERS

#### RUSHING

| Last Name | No. | Yds | Avg | TD |
|---|---|---|---|---|
| Willard | 227 | 967 | 4.3 | 7 |
| Lewis | 141 | 573 | 4.1 | 1 |
| Tucker | 30 | 135 | 4.5 | 3 |
| Brodie | 18 | 71 | 3.9 | 0 |
| Daniels | 12 | 37 | 3.1 | 0 |
| Cunningham | 6 | 7 | 1.2 | 0 |
| Mira | 1 | 5 | 5.0 | 0 |
| Crow | 4 | 4 | 1.0 | 0 |
| McNeil | 1 | -1 | -1.0 | 0 |
| Spurrier | 1 | -15 | -15.0 | 0 |

#### RECEIVING

| Last Name | No. | Yds | Avg | TD |
|---|---|---|---|---|
| McNeil | 71 | 994 | 14 | 7 |
| Witcher | 39 | 531 | 14 | 1 |
| Willard | 36 | 232 | 6 | 0 |
| Crow | 31 | 531 | 17 | 5 |
| Lewis | 27 | 244 | 9 | 3 |
| Tucker | 15 | 197 | 13 | 4 |
| Windsor | 8 | 146 | 18 | 2 |
| McFarland | 5 | 140 | 28 | 1 |
| Cunningham | 2 | 25 | 13 | 0 |
| Daniels | 2 | 23 | 12 | 0 |

#### PUNT RETURNS

| Last Name | No. | Yds | Avg | TD |
|---|---|---|---|---|
| Alexander | 24 | 87 | 4 | 0 |
| Fuller | 12 | 33 | 3 | 0 |

#### KICKOFF RETURNS

| Last Name | No. | Yds | Avg | TD |
|---|---|---|---|---|
| Alexander | 20 | 360 | 18 | 0 |
| Cunningham | 14 | 286 | 20 | 0 |
| Daniels | 10 | 206 | 21 | 0 |
| Tucker | 5 | 103 | 21 | 0 |
| Fuller | 1 | 23 | 23 | 0 |
| Hays | 2 | 21 | 11 | 0 |
| Banaszek | 1 | 15 | 15 | 0 |
| Olerich | 1 | 4 | 4 | 0 |
| Hart | 1 | 3 | 3 | 0 |
| Nunley | 2 | 0 | 0 | 0 |
| Peoples | 1 | 0 | 0 | 0 |

#### PASSING – PUNTING – KICKING

| PASSING | Att | Comp | % | Yds | Yd/Att | TD | Int– | % | RK |
|---|---|---|---|---|---|---|---|---|---|
| Brodie | 404 | 234 | 58 | 3020 | 7.5 | 22 | 21– | 5 | 3 |
| Mira | 11 | 4 | 36 | 44 | 4.0 | 1 | 1– | 9 | |
| McNeil | 2 | 1 | 50 | 43 | 21.5 | 1 | 1– | 50 | |

| PUNTING | No | Avg |
|---|---|---|
| Spurrier | 68 | 39.0 |

| KICKING | XP | Att | % | FG | Att | % |
|---|---|---|---|---|---|---|
| Davis | 26 | 26 | 100 | 9 | 16 | 56 |
| Patera | 10 | 12 | 83 | 2 | 8 | 25 |

### ATLANTA FALCONS

#### RUSHING

| Last Name | No. | Yds | Avg | TD |
|---|---|---|---|---|
| Butler | 94 | 365 | 3.9 | 2 |
| Dunn | 72 | 219 | 3.0 | 3 |
| Wages | 59 | 211 | 3.6 | 0 |
| Harris | 53 | 144 | 2.7 | 0 |
| Berry | 26 | 139 | 5.3 | 2 |
| Johnson | 11 | 97 | 8.8 | 1 |
| McCarthy | 31 | 86 | 2.8 | 1 |
| Bryant | 9 | 29 | 3.2 | 0 |
| Auer | 3 | 19 | 6.3 | 0 |
| Ogden | 1 | 12 | 12.0 | 0 |
| Lee | 6 | 7 | 1.2 | 0 |
| Lemmerman | 1 | 0 | 0.0 | 0 |
| Simmons | 1 | -6 | -6.0 | 0 |
| Lothridge | 1 | -16 | -16.0 | 0 |

#### RECEIVING

| Last Name | No. | Yds | Avg | TD |
|---|---|---|---|---|
| Simmons | 28 | 479 | 17 | 0 |
| Ogden | 25 | 452 | 18 | 2 |
| Long | 22 | 484 | 22 | 4 |
| Flatley | 20 | 305 | 15 | 0 |
| Wages | 16 | 121 | 8 | 1 |
| Butler | 15 | 127 | 8 | 0 |
| McCarthy | 13 | 119 | 9 | 0 |
| Dunn | 9 | 118 | 13 | 0 |
| Donohoe | 6 | 52 | 9 | 1 |
| Harris | 3 | 118 | 39 | 1 |
| Bryant | 1 | 11 | 11 | 0 |

#### PUNT RETURNS

| Last Name | No. | Yds | Avg | TD |
|---|---|---|---|---|
| Burson | 11 | 56 | 5 | 0 |
| Rassas | 4 | 10 | 3 | 0 |
| Spiller | 1 | 0 | 0 | 0 |

#### KICKOFF RETURNS

| Last Name | No. | Yds | Avg | TD |
|---|---|---|---|---|
| Butler | 37 | 799 | 22 | 0 |
| Rassas | 10 | 180 | 18 | 0 |
| Bryant | 5 | 112 | 22 | 0 |
| Lee | 3 | 63 | 21 | 0 |
| Auer | 2 | 31 | 16 | 0 |
| Talbert | 3 | 30 | 10 | 0 |
| Wages | 1 | 23 | 23 | 0 |
| Donohoe | 1 | 22 | 22 | 0 |
| Szczecko | 3 | 18 | 6 | 0 |
| Spiller | 1 | 18 | 18 | 0 |
| Harris | 1 | 16 | 16 | 0 |
| Grimm | 1 | 4 | 4 | 0 |
| Allen | 1 | 0 | 0 | 0 |
| Cerne | 1 | 0 | 0 | 0 |

#### PASSING – PUNTING – KICKING

| PASSING | Att | Comp | % | Yds | Yd/Att | TD | Int– | % | RK |
|---|---|---|---|---|---|---|---|---|---|
| Johnson | 156 | 73 | 47 | 892 | 5.7 | 2 | 10– | 6 | 17 |
| Berry | 153 | 81 | 53 | 1433 | 9.4 | 7 | 13– | 8 | 11 |
| Lemmerman | 15 | 3 | 20 | 40 | 2.7 | 0 | 1– | 7 | |
| Wages | 2 | 1 | 50 | 21 | 10.5 | 0 | 0– | 0 | |

| PUNTING | No | Avg |
|---|---|---|
| Lothridge | 75 | 44.3 |

| KICKING | XP | Att | % | FG | Att | % |
|---|---|---|---|---|---|---|
| Etter | 17 | 19 | 89 | 11 | 21 | 52 |

# 1968 A.F.L. The Jets, Heidi, and Howls

Heidi, the Swiss mountain girl from the storybooks, had football fans flooding telephone lines with cries of protest on November 17. With the Jets beating Oakland 32-29 with two minutes left in the game, NBC television was faced with a dilemma; it could either continue coverage of the football game to its conclusion or it could broadcast a special dramatization of "Heidi" at its scheduled hour and leave the football game before time ran out. NBC opted for "Heidi," and football fans poured calls of protest into the television station for taking the game off the air. To add fuel to the fire, the Raiders scored two touchdowns in those last minutes to take the game 43-32. NBC tried to make amends by showing films of the final two minutes of action on the late news shows, and the network promised never again to get burned with such a decision.

## EASTERN DIVISION

**New York Jets**—There was no December collapse for the Jets this year, as they won their last three games from Miami, Cincinnati, and Miami, both easy marks. In first place heading into the final month, the Jets this year held onto the top spot right to the end. The New York offense was too much for the rest of the Eastern Division, with Joe Namath riding herd on one of pro football's most explosive attacks. Continuing to hit George Sauer and Don Maynard with bullet passes at regular intervals, Namath also blossomed into a top diagnostician, deftly sending runners Matt Snell and Emerson Boozer into the line at the right time more often than not. Much had been expected of the New York offense, and it delivered in style; but the New York defense, consistently downgraded by opponents and the press, hung together in a unit which jumped on every enemy mistake. Even place-kicker Jim Turner, aided by new holder Babe Parilli, had a good year. With the Eastern title in their pockets, the Jets headed for a post-season date with destiny.

**Houston Oilers**—The Oilers caught lightning in a bottle in their surprise 1967 Eastern title, but they dropped this year to a 7-7 mark more typical of a young club still in the midst of rebuilding. Paced by two of the league's top defensive players in George Webster and Miller Farr, the Oilers still surrendered points grudgingly, but the Houston attack frightened few opponents. Fullback Hoyle Granger ran well behind a strong line, but neither he nor Woody Campbell had game-breaking speed. The receiving was strengthened by rookies Mac Haik and Jim Beirne and the development of Alvin Reed into a top tight end, but quarterback problems made the Oiler passing game extremely erratic. Pete Beathard displayed a strong arm and periods of inaccuracy before an appendectomy shelved him late in the year, and Don Trull, picked up after the Patriots cut him, was not a permanent answer.

**Miami Dolphins**—Fullback Larry Csonka needed time to get used to pro football but showed unmistakable power as a runner. Catching on more quickly was halfback Jim Kiick, a fifth-round draft pick who was a reliable runner and receiver. The defense was shored up by freshmen Manny Fernandez and Dick Anderson; Fernandez, signed as a free agent, provided the team's only pass-rushing, while safetyman Anderson had a flair for both tackling and intercepting. Another rookie, tackle Doug Crusan, won a starting job in the offensive line. Of course, some of the veterans also turned in good performances, with quarterback Bob Griese leading the way. The second-year passer had a good season despite poor protection and the loss of Jack Clancy, his favorite receiver, to knee surgery. Split end Karl Noonan, a slow but meticulous receiver, filled in for Clancy and hauled in fifty-eight passes.

**Boston Patriots**—Coach Mike Holovak made a break with the past by trading veteran quarterback Babe Parilli to New York for young Mike Taliaferro, but the Boston attack suffered for the change. Taliaferro could not ignite the offense and lost his job to rookie Tom Sherman. Other veteran Patriot players endured poor seasons. A bad ankle robbed Jim Nance of much of his effectiveness, and bad knees put defensive end Larry Eisenhauer and middle linebacker Nick Buoniconti out of action for several games. Coach Holovak got good work from cornerback Leroy Mitchell, tight end Jim Whalen, center Jon Morris, and defensive tackle Houston Antwine, but the Patriots needed a complete overhauling.

**Buffalo Bills**—The Bills' quarterback ills started when veterans Jack Kemp and Tom Flores were both injured before the regular season began. Coach Joel Collier started the year with rookie Dan Darragh as the signal-caller, but with the offensive line thinned out by injuries and age, Darragh soon was racked up enough by enemy defenses that his knee gave out. Next on the firing line was Kay Stephenson,

a young man picked up from San Diego, and he lasted a couple of games before going out with a broken collarbone. Ed Rutkowski, a veteran utility man who had last played quarterback at Notre Dame six years ago, then stepped in and stayed healthy while guiding the Bills to the end of the season. The team scored the least points in the league but did have the satisfaction of beating the Jets 37-35 for their only victory of the season. The Bills had been a championship team only two years before, so coach Collier paid with his head two games into the campaign.

## WESTERN DIVISION

**Oakland Raiders**—The Raiders were hit with a long string of injuries, yet still charged to a 12-2 record and a tie for the Western title. Defensive tackle Tom Keating missed the entire season with an Achilles-tendon injury suffered in last year's AFL championship game, but Carleton Oats filled in competently and Dan Birdwell compensated with his best year ever. When linebacker Bill Laskey also hurt his Achilles tendon, rookie Chip Oliver stepped into the starting lineup with a fine performance. When a knee injury shelved cornerback Kent McCloughan in mid-season, the Raiders had an exciting substitute in rookie Butch Atkinson. The offense avoided injuries but found two new starters in wide receiver Warren Wells and halfback Charlie Smith. With the title on the line, Daryle Lamonica threw five touchdown passes to win the playoff game 41-6.

**Kansas City Chiefs**—The Chiefs came back from last year's poor season to tie for first place in the West with a 12-2 record. The Kansas City defense allowed the fewest points in the league, with top players in all departments. Jerry Mays and Buck Buchanan starred in the line, the linebacking trio of Bobby Bell, Willie Lanier, and Jim Lynch was tops in the league, and safety Johnny Robinson steadied a secondary with several new starters. The offense matched the defense in efficiency, although an injury to Otis Taylor put more emphasis on a ball-control attack. Rookie fullback Robert Holmes, an unknown fourteenth-round draft pick, surprised everyone with his dogged ball-carrying, while veterans Mike Garrett and Curtis McClinton were bothered by injuries.

**San Diego Chargers**—The Chargers made the Western pennant race a three-way affair until dropping three of their last four games. Before home-town audiences, the Chargers lost 37-15 to New York, 40-3 to Kansas City, and 34-27 to Oakland, shooting all their title hopes to pieces. The Chargers had to be ranked among the league powers, but they could not beat the other top teams like the Jets, Chiefs, and Raiders. The biggest problem for coach Sid Gillman was his defense. The front four of Steve DeLong, Scott Appleton, Russ Washington, and Houston Ridge had good college press clippings but rarely got to the enemy passer, the linebacking was no better than adequate, and the secondary was solid only at Kenny Graham's strong safety spot. The San Diego attack as always found ways to put points on the scoreboard regularly. Quarterback John Hadl, operating behind an excellent offensive line, kept receivers Lance Alworth and Gary Garrison busy catching passes, and although fullback Brad Hubbert missed most of the season with a knee injury, halfback Dickie Post kept up the fine running of his rookie year.

**Denver Broncos**—The Broncos embarrassed themselves by losing 24-10 to the new Cincinnati Bengals on opening day, but they jelled into a respectable team after losing their first three games. In a five-week stretch from October 6 to November 3, Denver beat the Bengals, Jets, Dolphins, and Patriots while losing only to the Chargers. The key to this hot streak was the heavy pressure put on opposing passers by the Bronco defensive line, with end Rich Jackson developing into an All-Pro performer and tackle Dave Costa providing steady play against the run. The linebacking and secondary still was in a state of flux, but the strong pressure exerted by the line prevented passers from exploiting these weak spots. The Denver attack moved the ball well until quarterback Steve Tensi and split end Al Denson both went out in mid-season with broken collarbones, but rookie Marlin Briscoe, the first black ever to play regularly at T-formation quarterback in the pro ranks, kept the club interesting to the end with his scrambling and clutch passing.

**Cincinnati Bengals**—Paul Brown had built the Cleveland Browns into a powerhouse by signing poised players returning from World War II, but he set a different course for the new Cincinnati Bengals. Brown threw his lineup open to rookies and young players who had not fit in elsewhere. With so many inexperienced players in the lineup, most clubs would have suffered through a dismal season of hard learning, but Brown drilled his young Bengals so that they learned and played competitive football right from the start.

## FINAL TEAM STATISTICS

### OFFENSE

| | BOSTON | BUFFALO | CIN. | DENVER | HOUSTON | K.C. | MIAMI | N.Y. | OAKLAND | S.D. |
|---|---|---|---|---|---|---|---|---|---|---|
| **FIRST DOWNS:** | | | | | | | | | | |
| Total | 181 | 159 | 171 | 217 | 240 | 223 | 247 | 249 | 287 | 270 |
| by Rushing | 69 | 71 | 85 | 75 | 99 | 123 | 78 | 80 | 97 | 93 |
| by Passing | 94 | 72 | 73 | 124 | 128 | 89 | 144 | 144 | 162 | 164 |
| by Penalty | 18 | 16 | 13 | 18 | 13 | 11 | 25 | 25 | 28 | 13 |
| **RUSHING:** | | | | | | | | | | |
| Number | 421 | 400 | 421 | 411 | 462 | 537 | 417 | 467 | 471 | 428 |
| Yards | 1362 | 1527 | 1807 | 1614 | 1804 | 2227 | 1704 | 2168 | 1608 | 1765 |
| Average Yards | 3.1 | 3.8 | 4.3 | 3.9 | 3.9 | 4.1 | 4.1 | 3.4 | 4.6 | 4.1 |
| Touchdowns | 8 | 9 | 14 | 11 | 16 | 16 | 12 | 22 | 16 | 12 |
| **PASSING:** | | | | | | | | | | |
| Attempts | 409 | 405 | 313 | 427 | 414 | 270 | 423 | 436 | 468 | 472 |
| Completions | 160 | 168 | 167 | 179 | 191 | 156 | 216 | 217 | 237 | 225 |
| Completion Percentage | 39.1 | 41.5 | 53.4 | 41.9 | 46.1 | 57.8 | 51.1 | 49.8 | 50.6 | 47.7 |
| Passing Yards | 2121 | 1714 | 1896 | 2826 | 2864 | 2492 | 2843 | 3574 | 3771 | 3813 |
| Average Yards per Att. | 5.2 | 4.2 | 6.1 | 6.6 | 6.9 | 9.2 | 6.7 | 8.1 | 8.1 | 8.1 |
| Average Yards per Comp. | 13.3 | 10.2 | 11.4 | 15.8 | 15.0 | 16.0 | 13.2 | 16.5 | 15.9 | 16.9 |
| Tackled Att. to pass | 38 | 39 | 38 | 51 | 29 | 24 | 52 | 18 | 29 | 18 |
| Yards Lost Tackled | 356 | 371 | 277 | 469 | 316 | 216 | 441 | 135 | 243 | 190 |
| Net Yards | 1765 | 1343 | 1619 | 2357 | 2548 | 2276 | 2402 | 3439 | 3528 | 3623 |
| Touchdowns | 16 | 7 | 8 | 20 | 17 | 20 | 21 | 20 | 31 | 29 |
| Interceptions | 33 | 28 | 11 | 27 | 25 | 11 | 22 | 19 | 18 | 33 |
| Percent Intercepted | 8.1 | 6.9 | 3.5 | 6.3 | 6.0 | 4.1 | 5.2 | 4.4 | 3.8 | 7.0 |
| **PUNTS:** | | | | | | | | | | |
| Number | 96 | 100 | 84 | 96 | 73 | 65 | 75 | 68 | 64 | 56 |
| Average Distance | 39.9 | 41.8 | 40.9 | 42.7 | 41.2 | 45.3 | 40.6 | 43.8 | 43.6 | 40.7 |
| **PUNT RETURNS:** | | | | | | | | | | |
| Number | 37 | 44 | 30 | 38 | 52 | 31 | 28 | 36 | 55 | 39 |
| Yards | 197 | 301 | 196 | 332 | 443 | 450 | 205 | 286 | 666 | 292 |
| Average Yards | 5.3 | 6.8 | 6.5 | 8.7 | 8.5 | 14.5 | 7.3 | 7.9 | 12.1 | 7.5 |
| Touchdowns | 0 | 1 | 0 | 1 | 0 | 2 | 0 | 0 | 2 | 1 |
| **KICKOFF RETURNS:** | | | | | | | | | | |
| Number | 71 | 69 | 54 | 60 | 53 | 38 | 50 | 46 | 49 | 51 |
| Yards | 1442 | 1537 | 1068 | 1361 | 1235 | 736 | 1134 | 995 | 1092 | 1065 |
| Average Yards | 20.3 | 22.3 | 19.8 | 22.7 | 23.3 | 19.9 | 22.7 | 21.6 | 22.3 | 20.9 |
| Touchdowns | 0 | 1 | 0 | 0 | 0 | 0 | 0 | 0 | 0 | 0 |
| **INTERCEPTION RETURNS:** | | | | | | | | | | |
| Number | 23 | 22 | 10 | 20 | 20 | 37 | 22 | 28 | 25 | 20 |
| Yards | 220 | 475 | 144 | 165 | 396 | 469 | 386 | 456 | 424 | 275 |
| Average Yards | 9.6 | 21.6 | 14.4 | 8.3 | 19.8 | 12.7 | 17.5 | 16.3 | 17.0 | 13.8 |
| Touchdowns | 1 | 4 | 2 | 0 | 5 | 2 | 1 | 2 | 4 | 2 |
| **PENALTIES:** | | | | | | | | | | |
| Number | 67 | 67 | 55 | 73 | 61 | 66 | 48 | 76 | 81 | 72 |
| Yards | 682 | 687 | 586 | 772 | 644 | 650 | 485 | 742 | 958 | 654 |
| **FUMBLES:** | | | | | | | | | | |
| Number | 28 | 23 | 27 | 28 | 28 | 26 | 17 | 19 | 34 | 20 |
| Number Lost | 20 | 14 | 10 | 13 | 13 | 16 | 8 | 9 | 21 | 12 |
| **POINTS:** | | | | | | | | | | |
| Total | 229 | 199 | 215 | 255 | 303 | 371 | 276 | 419 | 453 | 382 |
| PAT (kick) Attempts | 26 | 19 | 24 | 32 | 38 | 40 | 36 | 43 | 54 | 43 |
| PAT (kick) Made | 26 | 19 | 24 | 31 | 37 | 39 | 36 | 43 | 54 | 40 |
| PAT (2-Point) Attempts | 0 | 3 | 1 | 0 | 0 | 0 | 0 | 2 | 1 | 2 |
| PAT (2-Point) Made | 0 | 2 | 0 | 0 | 0 | 0 | 0 | 1 | 1 | 2 |
| FG Attempts | 27 | 28 | 27 | 23 | 29 | 40 | 19 | 46 | 34 | 32 |
| FG Made | 15 | 14 | 13 | 10 | 12 | 30 | 8 | 34 | 21 | 22 |
| Percent FG Made | 55.6 | 50.0 | 48.1 | 43.5 | 41.4 | 75.0 | 42.1 | 73.9 | 61.8 | 68.8 |
| Safeties | 1 | 1 | 1 | 1 | 1 | 1 | 0 | 1 | 2 | 1 |

### DEFENSE

| | BOSTON | BUFFALO | CIN. | DENVER | HOUSTON | K.C. | MIAMI | N.Y. | OAKLAND | S.D. |
|---|---|---|---|---|---|---|---|---|---|---|
| **FIRST DOWNS:** | | | | | | | | | | |
| Total | 237 | 210 | 275 | 251 | 198 | 215 | 240 | 178 | 215 | 225 |
| by Rushing | 86 | 85 | 116 | 94 | 89 | 52 | 116 | 59 | 83 | 90 |
| by Passing | 123 | 103 | 140 | 145 | 96 | 140 | 112 | 104 | 113 | 118 |
| by Penalty | 28 | 22 | 19 | 12 | 13 | 23 | 12 | 15 | 19 | 17 |
| **RUSHING:** | | | | | | | | | | |
| Number | 479 | 505 | 473 | 457 | 462 | 365 | 445 | 368 | 442 | 439 |
| Yards | 1825 | 2021 | 2097 | 1861 | 1704 | 1266 | 2172 | 1195 | 1804 | 1641 |
| Average Yards | 3.8 | 4.0 | 4.4 | 4.1 | 3.7 | 3.5 | 4.9 | 3.2 | 4.1 | 3.7 |
| Touchdowns | 22 | 15 | 13 | 20 | 9 | 4 | 19 | 9 | 12 | 13 |
| **PASSING:** | | | | | | | | | | |
| Attempts | 416 | 340 | 411 | 429 | 359 | 461 | 342 | 403 | 446 | 430 |
| Completions | 200 | 143 | 212 | 217 | 158 | 214 | 179 | 187 | 189 | 217 |
| Completion Percentage | 48.1 | 42.1 | 51.6 | 50.6 | 44.0 | 46.4 | 52.3 | 46.4 | 42.4 | 50.5 |
| Passing Yards | 2826 | 2477 | 2903 | 3419 | 2003 | 3262 | 2904 | 2567 | 2657 | 2896 |
| Average Yards per Att. | 6.8 | 7.3 | 7.1 | 8.0 | 5.6 | 7.1 | 8.5 | 6.4 | 6.0 | 6.7 |
| Average Yards per Comp. | 14.1 | 17.3 | 13.7 | 15.8 | 12.7 | 15.2 | 16.2 | 13.7 | 14.1 | 13.3 |
| Tackled Att. to pass | 27 | 31 | 32 | 31 | 33 | 45 | 21 | 43 | 49 | 24 |
| Yards Lost Tackled | 236 | 273 | 283 | 256 | 332 | 439 | 192 | 399 | 400 | 204 |
| Net Yards | 2590 | 2204 | 2620 | 3163 | 1671 | 2823 | 2712 | 2168 | 2257 | 2692 |
| Touchdowns | 20 | 19 | 25 | 25 | 13 | 14 | 23 | 17 | 13 | 20 |
| Interceptions | 23 | 22 | 10 | 20 | 20 | 37 | 22 | 28 | 25 | 20 |
| Percent Intercepted | 5.5 | 6.5 | 2.4 | 4.7 | 5.6 | 8.0 | 6.4 | 6.9 | 5.6 | 4.7 |
| **PUNTS:** | | | | | | | | | | |
| Number | 81 | 75 | 63 | 76 | 88 | 73 | 55 | 98 | 94 | 74 |
| Average Distance | 40.5 | 39.7 | 44.2 | 43.0 | 44.1 | 42.8 | 43.4 | 38.4 | 42.3 | 42.3 |
| **PUNT RETURNS:** | | | | | | | | | | |
| Number | 59 | 45 | 41 | 46 | 40 | 31 | 28 | 39 | 40 | 21 |
| Yards | 502 | 521 | 252 | 282 | 379 | 220 | 250 | 531 | 211 | 220 |
| Average Yards | 8.5 | 11.6 | 6.1 | 6.1 | 9.5 | 7.1 | 8.9 | 13.6 | 5.3 | 10.5 |
| Touchdowns | 1 | 1 | 0 | 0 | 1 | 0 | 0 | 3 | 0 | 1 |
| **KICKOFF RETURNS:** | | | | | | | | | | |
| Number | 40 | 49 | 40 | 29 | 58 | 54 | 54 | 82 | 75 | 60 |
| Yards | 901 | 1062 | 977 | 704 | 1302 | 1044 | 1108 | 1664 | 1652 | 1251 |
| Average Yards | 22.5 | 21.7 | 24.4 | 24.3 | 22.4 | 19.3 | 20.5 | 20.3 | 22.0 | 20.9 |
| Touchdowns | 0 | 0 | 0 | 1 | 0 | 0 | 0 | 0 | 0 | 0 |
| **INTERCEPTION RETURNS:** | | | | | | | | | | |
| Number | 33 | 28 | 11 | 27 | 25 | 11 | 22 | 19 | 18 | 33 |
| Yards | 510 | 472 | 79 | 328 | 326 | 119 | 432 | 455 | 155 | 534 |
| Average Yards | 15.5 | 16.9 | 7.2 | 12.1 | 13.0 | 10.8 | 19.6 | 23.9 | 8.6 | 16.2 |
| Touchdowns | 3 | 6 | 0 | 3 | 2 | 0 | 3 | 4 | 0 | 2 |
| **PENALTIES:** | | | | | | | | | | |
| Number | 70 | 66 | 62 | 64 | 54 | 62 | 70 | 65 | 90 | 63 |
| Yards | 874 | 540 | 632 | 750 | 526 | 564 | 655 | 695 | 932 | 692 |
| **FUMBLES:** | | | | | | | | | | |
| Number | 37 | 24 | 19 | 24 | 17 | 22 | 28 | 29 | 24 | 26 |
| Number Lost | 17 | 13 | 9 | 12 | 10 | 12 | 18 | 15 | 15 | 15 |
| **POINTS:** | | | | | | | | | | |
| Total | 406 | 367 | 329 | 404 | 248 | 170 | 355 | 280 | 233 | 310 |
| PAT (kick) Attempts | 49 | 41 | 39 | 47 | 25 | 18 | 44 | 34 | 23 | 35 |
| PAT (kick) Made | 49 | 40 | 37 | 47 | 25 | 18 | 43 | 33 | 22 | 35 |
| PAT (2-Point) Attempts | 0 | 0 | 0 | 1 | 0 | 0 | 1 | 2 | 3 | 1 |
| PAT (2-Point) Made | 0 | 0 | 0 | 1 | 0 | 0 | 1 | 2 | 1 | 0 |
| FG Attempts | 31 | 48 | 35 | 34 | 30 | 27 | 24 | 17 | 28 | 31 |
| FG Made | 21 | 27 | 18 | 21 | 21 | 14 | 12 | 9 | 17 | 19 |
| Percent FG Made | 67.7 | 56.3 | 51.4 | 61.8 | 70.0 | 51.9 | 50.0 | 52.9 | 60.7 | 61.3 |
| Safeties | 0 | 0 | 0 | 1 | 0 | 1 | 0 | 0 | 1 | 1 |

## WESTERN DIVISION PLAYOFF
December 22 at Oakland
(Attendance 53,605)

### SCORING

| | | | | | |
|---|---|---|---|---|---|
| OAKLAND | 21 | 7 | 0 | 13—41 |
| KANSAS CITY | 0 | 6 | 0 | 0— 6 |

**First Quarter**
Oak.   Biletnikoff, 24 yard pass from Lamonica
     PAT—Blanda (kick)
Oak.   Wells, 23 yard pass from Lamonica
     PAT—Blanda (kick)
Oak.   Biletnikoff, 44 yard pass from Lamonica
     PAT—Blanda (kick)

**Second Quarter**
K.C.   Stenerud, 10 yard field goal
K.C.   Stenerud, 8 yard field goal
Oak.   Biletnikoff, 54 yard pass from Lamonica
     PAT—Blanda (kick)

**Fourth Quarter**
Oak.   Wells, 35 yard pass from Lamonica
     PAT—Blanda (kick)
Oak.   Blanda, 41 yard field goal
Oak.   Blanda, 40 yard field goal

### TEAM STATISTICS

| | OAK. | | K.C. |
|---|---|---|---|
| First Downs—Total | 22 | | 13 |
| First Downs—Rushing | 7 | | 3 |
| First Downs—Passing | 14 | | 9 |
| First Downs—Penalty | 1 | | 1 |
| Fumbles—Number | 2 | | 2 |
| Fumbles—Lost Ball | 0 | | 0 |
| Penalties—Number | 1 | | 2 |
| Yards Penalized | 2 | | 20 |
| Missed Field Goals | 0 | | 1 |
| Offensive Plays—Total | 70 | | 61 |
| Net Yards | 454 | | 312 |
| Average Gain | 6.5 | | 5.1 |
| Giveaways | 0 | | 4 |
| Takeaways | 4 | | 0 |
| Difference | +4 | | −4 |

### INDIVIDUAL STATISTICS

#### RUSHING

| OAKLAND | No. | Yds. | Avg. | KANSAS CITY | No. | Yds. | Avg. |
|---|---|---|---|---|---|---|---|
| Smith | 13 | 74 | 5.7 | Holmes | 13 | 46 | 3.5 |
| Banaszak | 3 | 19 | 6.3 | Hayes | 3 | 10 | 3.3 |
| Dixon | 10 | 13 | 1.3 | Dawson | 2 | 9 | 4.5 |
| Hagberg | 4 | 12 | 3.0 | Garrett | 6 | 5 | 0.8 |
| | 30 | 118 | 3.9 | | 24 | 70 | 2.9 |

#### RECEIVING

| OAKLAND | No. | Yds. | Avg. | KANSAS CITY | No. | Yds. | Avg. |
|---|---|---|---|---|---|---|---|
| Biletnikoff | 7 | 180 | 25.7 | Pitts | 5 | 56 | 11.2 |
| Smith | 5 | 52 | 10.4 | Taylor | 4 | 117 | 29.3 |
| Wells | 4 | 93 | 23.3 | Garrett | 4 | 31 | 7.8 |
| Cannon | 2 | 15 | 7.5 | Richardson | 3 | 57 | 19.0 |
| Dixon | 1 | 7 | 7.0 | Holmes | 1 | −8 | −8.0 |
| | 19 | 347 | 18.3 | | 17 | 253 | 14.9 |

#### PUNTING

| OAKLAND | No. | Yds. | Avg. | KANSAS CITY | No. | Yds. | Avg. |
|---|---|---|---|---|---|---|---|
| Eischeid | 5 | | 45.4 | Wilson | 6 | | 50.3 |

#### PUNT RETURNS

| OAKLAND | No. | Yds. | Avg. | KANSAS CITY | No. | Yds. | Avg. |
|---|---|---|---|---|---|---|---|
| Bird | 3 | 29 | 9.7 | Smith | 2 | −9 | −4.5 |

#### KICKOFF RETURNS

| OAKLAND | No. | Yds. | Avg. | KANSAS CITY | No. | Yds. | Avg. |
|---|---|---|---|---|---|---|---|
| Atkinson | 1 | 34 | 34.0 | Smith | 5 | 73 | 14.6 |
| | | | | Mitchell | 2 | 46 | 23.0 |
| | | | | Lanier | 1 | 0 | 0.0 |
| | | | | | 8 | 119 | 14.9 |

#### INTERCEPTION RETURNS

| OAKLAND | No. | Yds. | Avg. | KANSAS CITY | | | |
|---|---|---|---|---|---|---|---|
| Wilson | 1 | 14 | 14.0 | None | | | |
| Hopkins | 1 | 7 | 7.0 | | | | |
| Connors | 1 | 5 | 5.0 | | | | |
| Brown | 1 | 0 | 0.0 | | | | |
| | 4 | 26 | 6.5 | | | | |

#### PASSING

| OAKLAND | Att. | Comp. | Comp. Pct. | Yds. | Int. | Yds/ Att. | Yds/ Comp. | Yards Lost Tackled |
|---|---|---|---|---|---|---|---|---|
| Lamonica | 39 | 19 | 48.7 | 347 | 0 | 8.9 | 18.3 | 1-11 |
| **KANSAS CITY** | | | | | | | | |
| Dawson | 36 | 17 | 47.2 | 253 | 4 | 7.0 | 14.9 | 1-11 |

**NEW YORK JETS** 11-3-0 Weeb Ewbank

| Scores of Each Game | | |
|---|---|---|
| 20 | Kansas City | 19 |
| 47 | Boston | 31 |
| 35 | Buffalo | 37 |
| 23 | SAN DIEGO | 20 |
| 13 | DENVER | 21 |
| 20 | Houston | 14 |
| 48 | BOSTON | 14 |
| 25 | BUFFALO | 21 |
| 26 | HOUSTON | 7 |
| 32 | Oakland | 43 |
| 37 | San Diego | 15 |
| 35 | MIAMI | 17 |
| 27 | CINCINNATI | 14 |
| 31 | Miami | 7 |

| Use Name | Pos. | Hgt | Wgt | Age | Int | Pts |
|---|---|---|---|---|---|---|
| Winston Hill | OT | 6'4" | 280 | 26 | | |
| Sam Walton | OT | 6'5" | 270 | 25 | | |
| Jeff Richardson | C-OT | 6'3" | 250 | 23 | | |
| Randy Rasmussen | OG | 6'2" | 255 | 23 | | |
| Bob Talamini | OG | 6'1" | 255 | 29 | | |
| Dave Herman | OT-OG | 6'2" | 255 | 26 | | |
| John Schmitt | C | 6'4" | 245 | 25 | | |
| Paul Crane | LB-C | 6'2" | 205 | 24 | | 2 |
| Verlon Biggs | DE | 6'4" | 270 | 25 | | |
| Gerry Philbin | DE | 6'2" | 245 | 27 | | |
| Steve Thompson | DE | 6'5" | 245 | 23 | | |
| John Elliott | DT | 6'4" | 245 | 23 | | |
| Ray Hayes | DT | 6'5" | 245 | 21 | | |
| Karl Henke | DT | 6'4" | 245 | 23 | | |
| Paul Rochester | DT | 6'2" | 255 | 31 | | |
| Carl McAdams | DE-DT | 6'3" | 240 | 24 | | |
| Al Atkinson | LB | 6'1" | 230 | 25 | 2 | |
| Ralph Baker | LB | 6'3" | 235 | 26 | 3 | |
| Larry Grantham | LB | 6' | 210 | 29 | | |
| Mike Stromberg | LB | 6'2" | 235 | 23 | | |
| Bill Baird | DB | 5'10" | 180 | 29 | 4 | |
| Randy Beverly | DB | 5'11" | 185 | 24 | 4 | 6 |
| Earl Christy | DB | 5'11" | 195 | 25 | 1 | |
| Mike D'Amato | DB | 6'2" | 204 | 25 | | |
| John Dockery | DB | 6' | 186 | 23 | | |
| Cornell Gordon | DB | 6' | 187 | 27 | 2 | |
| Jim Hudson | DB | 6'2" | 210 | 25 | 5 | |
| Jim Richards | DB | 6'1" | 180 | 21 | | |
| Johnny Sample | DB | 6'1" | 208 | 31 | 7 | 6 |
| Paul Seiler – Military Service | | | | | | |
| Joe Namath | QB | 6'2" | 195 | 25 | | 12 |
| Babe Parilli | QB | 6'1" | 190 | 38 | | 6 |
| Jim Turner | QB | 6'2" | 205 | 27 | | 145 |
| Emerson Boozer | HB | 5'11" | 204 | 25 | | 30 |
| Bill Mathis | HB | 6'1" | 220 | 29 | | 38 |
| Billy Joe | FB | 6'2" | 236 | 27 | | 18 |
| Matt Snell | FB | 6'2" | 220 | 26 | | 42 |
| Lee White | FB | 6'4" | 240 | 22 | | |
| Mark Smolinski | TE-FB | 6' | 215 | 29 | | 6 |
| Don Maynard | WR | 6' | 180 | 32 | | 60 |
| Harvey Nairn | WR | 6'1" | 178 | 22 | | |
| Bill Rademacher | WR | 6'1" | 190 | 26 | | |
| George Sauer | WR | 6'1" | 195 | 24 | | 18 |
| Bake Turner | WR | 6' | 180 | 28 | | 12 |
| Curley Johnson | TE | 6' | 215 | 33 | | |
| Pete Lammons | TE | 6'3" | 228 | 24 | | 18 |

**HOUSTON OILERS** 7-7-0 Wally Lemm

| Scores of Each Game | | |
|---|---|---|
| 21 | KANSAS CITY | 26 |
| 24 | Miami | 10 |
| 14 | San Diego | 30 |
| 15 | OAKLAND | 24 |
| 7 | MIAMI | 24 |
| 16 | Boston | 0 |
| 14 | NEW YORK | 20 |
| 30 | Buffalo | 7 |
| 27 | Cincinnati | 17 |
| 7 | New York | 26 |
| 38 | DENVER | 17 |
| 10 | Kansas City | 24 |
| 35 | BUFFALO | 6 |
| 45 | BOSTON | 17 |

| Use Name | Pos. | Hgt | Wgt | Age | Int | Pts |
|---|---|---|---|---|---|---|
| Glen Ray Hines | OT | 6'5" | 265 | 24 | | |
| Bob Robertson | OT | 6'4" | 246 | 21 | | |
| Walt Suggs | OT | 6'5" | 265 | 29 | | |
| Sonny Bishop | OG | 6'2" | 245 | 28 | | |
| Tom Regner | OG | 6'1" | 255 | 24 | | |
| Dick Swatland | OG | 6'3" | 245 | 22 | | |
| Bobby Maples | C | 6'3" | 245 | 25 | | |
| Steve Quinn | C | 6'1" | 225 | 22 | | |
| Elvin Bethea | DE | 6'3" | 250 | 22 | | |
| Gary Cutsinger | DE | 6'4" | 245 | 27 | | |
| Pat Holmes | DE | 6'5" | 250 | 28 | | |
| Bud Marshall | DT | 6'5" | 275 | 26 | | |
| Dudley Meredith (from BUF) | DT | 6'4" | 285 | 33 | | |
| Willie Parker | DT | 6'2" | 265 | 23 | | |
| George Rice | DT | 6'3" | 260 | 24 | | |
| Carel Stith | DT | 6'5" | 265 | 23 | | |
| Tom Domres | DE-DT | 6'3" | 255 | 21 | | |
| Pete Barnes | LB | 6'3" | 245 | 23 | | |
| Garland Boyette | LB | 6'1" | 245 | 28 | 1 | |
| Ronnie Caveness | LB | 6'1" | 225 | 25 | | |
| Marion Rushing (from ATL-N) | LB | 6'2" | 230 | 31 | | |
| Rich Stotter | LB | 6' | 225 | 23 | | |
| Olen Underwood | LB | 6'1" | 230 | 26 | 1 | 2 |
| George Webster | LB | 6'4" | 223 | 22 | 1 | |
| Larry Carwell | DB | 6'1" | 190 | 24 | 4 | 6 |
| Miller Farr | DB | 6'1" | 190 | 25 | 3 | 12 |
| W. K. Hicks | DB | 6'1" | 195 | 25 | 3 | |
| Ken Houston | DB | 6'3" | 192 | 23 | 5 | 12 |
| Pete Johns | DB | 6'3" | 190 | 23 | | |
| Zeke Moore | DB | 6'2" | 198 | 24 | | |
| Jim Norton | DB | 6'3" | 180 | 29 | 2 | |
| Bob Smith | DB | 6' | 180 | 23 | | |
| Pete Beathard | QB | 6'2" | 207 | 26 | | 12 |
| Bob Davis | QB | 6'3" | 208 | 22 | | 6 |
| Don Trull | QB | 6'1" | 196 | 26 | | |
| Sid Blanks | HB | 6' | 210 | 27 | | |
| Ode Burrell | HB | 6' | 192 | 28 | | |
| Woody Campbell | HB | 5'11" | 202 | 23 | | 36 |
| Hoyle Granger | FB | 6'1" | 225 | 24 | | 42 |
| Roy Hopkins | FB | 6'1" | 225 | 23 | | |
| Glenn Bass | WR | 6'2" | 210 | 29 | | |
| Jim Beirne | WR | 6'2" | 196 | 21 | | 24 |
| Charley Frazier | WR | 6' | 184 | 29 | | |
| Mac Haik | WR | 6'1" | 196 | 22 | | 48 |
| Lionel Taylor | WR | 6'2" | 215 | 32 | | |
| Jim LeMoine | TE | 6'2" | 245 | 23 | | |
| Alvin Reed | TE | 6'5" | 230 | 24 | | 30 |
| Wayne Walker | K | 6'2" | 215 | 23 | | 50 |
| John Wittenborn | K | 6'2" | 240 | 32 | | 23 |

**MIAMI DOLPHINS** 5-8-1 George Wilson

| Scores of Each Game | | |
|---|---|---|
| 10 | HOUSTON | 24 |
| 21 | OAKLAND | 47 |
| 3 | KANSAS CITY | 48 |
| 24 | Houston | 7 |
| 14 | BUFFALO | 14 |
| 24 | Cincinnati | 22 |
| 14 | Denver | 21 |
| 28 | San Diego | 34 |
| 21 | Buffalo | 17 |
| 21 | CINCINNATI | 38 |
| 34 | Boston | 10 |
| 17 | New York | 35 |
| 38 | BOSTON | 7 |
| 7 | NEW YORK | 31 |

| Use Name | Pos. | Hgt | Wgt | Age | Int | Pts |
|---|---|---|---|---|---|---|
| Doug Crusan | OT | 6'5" | 255 | 22 | | |
| Norm Evans | OT | 6'5" | 250 | 25 | | |
| Jack Pyburn | OT | 6'6" | 250 | 23 | | |
| Charlie Fowler | OG | 6'2" | 260 | 24 | | |
| Billy Neighbors | OG | 5'11" | 250 | 28 | | |
| Maxie Williams | OG | 6'4" | 250 | 28 | | |
| Freddie Woodson | DE-OG | 6'2" | 255 | 24 | | |
| Tom Goode | C | 6'3" | 250 | 29 | | |
| Mel Branch | DE | 6'2" | 235 | 31 | | |
| Manny Fernandez | DE | 6'2" | 250 | 22 | | |
| Bob Joswick | DE | 6'5" | 250 | 22 | | |
| Jim Riley | DE | 6'4" | 255 | 23 | | |
| Ray Jacobs | DT | 6'3" | 285 | 28 | | |
| Tom Nomina | DT | 6'5" | 260 | 26 | | |
| John Richardson | DT | 6'2" | 260 | 23 | | |
| Jim Urbanek | DT | 6'4" | 270 | 23 | | |
| Rudy Barber | LB | 6'1" | 255 | 23 | | |
| John Bramlett | LB | 6'2" | 210 | 27 | 2 | |
| Bob Bruggers (to SD) | LB | 6'1" | 230 | 24 | | |
| Randy Edmunds | LB | 6'2" | 220 | 22 | 1 | |
| Frank Emanuel | LB | 6'3" | 225 | 25 | 2 | 6 |
| Jimmy Keyes | LB | 6'2" | 225 | 24 | | 51 |
| Wahoo McDaniel | LB | 6' | 230 | 31 | | |
| Ed Weisacosky | LB | 6' | 230 | 24 | | |
| Dick Anderson | DB | 6'2" | 205 | 22 | 8 | 6 |
| Mack Lamb | DB | 6'1" | 188 | 24 | 1 | |
| Bob Neff | DB | 6' | 180 | 24 | | |
| Bob Petrella | DB | 6' | 185 | 23 | 1 | |
| Jimmy Warren | DB | 5'11" | 175 | 29 | 2 | |
| Dick Washington | DB | 6'1" | 205 | 23 | | |
| Willie West | DB | 5'10" | 187 | 30 | 4 | 6 |
| Dick Westmoreland | DB | 6'1" | 195 | 27 | 1 | |
| Jack Clancy – Knee Injury | | | | | | |
| Bob Griese | QB | 6'1" | 190 | 23 | | 6 |
| Kim Hammond | QB | 6'1" | 192 | 23 | | |
| Rick Norton | QB | 6'1" | 190 | 24 | | |
| Jack Harper | HB | 5'11" | 190 | 23 | | |
| Jim Kiick | HB | 5'11" | 215 | 22 | | 24 |
| Sam Price | HB | 5'11" | 215 | 24 | | |
| Gary Tucker | HB | 5'11" | 195 | 23 | | |
| Larry Seiple | TE-HB | 6' | 213 | 23 | | 6 |
| Larry Csonka | FB | 6'3" | 240 | 21 | | 42 |
| Stan Mitchell | HB-FB | 6'2" | 225 | 24 | | 24 |
| Bill Darnall | WR | 6'2" | 197 | 24 | | |
| Gene Milton | WR | 5'10" | 170 | 23 | | 6 |
| Karl Noonan | WR | 6'3" | 190 | 24 | | 66 |
| Howard Twilley | WR | 5'10" | 180 | 24 | | 6 |
| Jim Cox | TE | 6'2" | 227 | 24 | | |
| Doug Moreau | TE | 6'2" | 215 | 23 | | 27 |

**BOSTON PATRIOTS** 4-10-0 Mike Holovak

| Scores of Each Game | | |
|---|---|---|
| 16 | Buffalo | 7 |
| 31 | NEW YORK | 47 |
| 20 | Denver | 17 |
| 10 | Oakland | 41 |
| 0 | HOUSTON | 16 |
| 23 | BUFFALO | 6 |
| 14 | New York | 48 |
| 14 | DENVER | 35 |
| 17 | SAN DIEGO | 27 |
| 17 | Kansas City | 31 |
| 10 | MIAMI | 34 |
| 33 | CINCINNATI | 14 |
| 7 | Miami | 38 |
| 17 | Houston | 45 |

| Use Name | Pos. | Hgt | Wgt | Age | Int | Pts |
|---|---|---|---|---|---|---|
| Jim Boudreaux | OT | 6'4" | 245 | 23 | | |
| Paul Feldhausen | OT | 6'6" | 270 | 22 | | |
| Tom Funchess | OT | 6'5" | 260 | 23 | | |
| Tom Neville | OT | 6'4" | 255 | 25 | | |
| Don Oakes | OT | 6'3" | 255 | 30 | | |
| Karl Singer | OT | 6'3" | 255 | 24 | | |
| Justin Canale | OG | 6'2" | 250 | 24 | | |
| Charley Long | OG | 6'3" | 250 | 30 | | |
| Len St. Jean | OG | 6'1" | 245 | 26 | | |
| Jon Morris | C | 6'4" | 240 | 25 | | |
| J. R. Williamson | LB-C | 6'2" | 220 | 26 | | |
| Dennis Byrd | DE | 6'4" | 260 | 21 | | |
| Larry Eisenhauer | DE | 6'5" | 255 | 28 | | |
| Mel Witt | DE | 6'3" | 265 | 22 | 1 | 6 |
| Houston Antwine | DT | 6' | 270 | 29 | | |
| Whit Canale | DT | 6'3" | 245 | 26 | | |
| Jim Hunt | DT | 5'11" | 255 | 29 | | |
| Ed Toner | DT | 6'3" | 250 | 23 | | |
| Nick Buoniconti | LB | 5'11" | 220 | 27 | 3 | |
| Jim Cheyunski | LB | 6'2" | 225 | 22 | 1 | |
| Ray Ilg | LB | 6'1" | 220 | 22 | | |
| Ed Koontz | LB | 6'2" | 230 | 21 | | |
| Ed Philpott | LB | 6'3" | 240 | 22 | 4 | 6 |
| Doug Satcher | LB | 6' | 220 | 23 | 1 | 2 |
| John Charles | DB | 6'1" | 200 | 24 | | |
| Billy Johnson | DB | 5'11" | 180 | 25 | 2 | |
| Daryle Johnson | DB | 5'11" | 190 | 22 | 1 | |
| Art McMahon | DB | 5'11" | 185 | 22 | 2 | |
| Leroy Mitchell | DB | 6'2" | 190 | 23 | 7 | |
| Willie Porter | DB | 5'11" | 195 | 22 | | |
| Don Webb | DB | 5'10" | 195 | 29 | | |
| King Corcoran | QB | 6' | 200 | 26 | | |
| Tom Sherman | QB | 6' | 190 | 22 | | |
| Mike Taliaferro | QB | 6'2" | 205 | 26 | | |
| Larry Garron | HB | 6' | 195 | 31 | | 6 |
| Gene Thomas (to OAK) | HB | 6'1" | 210 | 25 | | 12 |
| R. C. Gamble | FB-HB | 6'3" | 220 | 21 | | 12 |
| Preston Johnson | FB | 6'2" | 230 | 23 | | |
| Jim Nance | FB | 6'1" | 240 | 25 | | 24 |
| Gino Cappelletti | WR | 6' | 190 | 34 | | 83 |
| Jim Colclough | WR | 6' | 185 | 32 | | |
| Art Graham | WR | 6'1" | 205 | 27 | | 6 |
| Bobby Leo | WR | 5'10" | 180 | 23 | | |
| Aaron Marsh | WR | 6'1" | 190 | 23 | | 24 |
| Bill Murphy | WR | 6'1" | 185 | 21 | | |
| Bob Scarpitto | WR | 5'11" | 190 | 29 | | 6 |
| Bobby Nichols | TE | 6'2" | 220 | 24 | | |
| Jim Whalen | TE | 6'2" | 210 | 24 | | 42 |
| Terry Swanson | K | 6' | 210 | 23 | | |

**BUFFALO BILLS** 1-12-1 Joe Collier

| Scores of Each Game | | |
|---|---|---|
| 7 | BOSTON | 16 |
| 6 | OAKLAND | 48 |
| 23 | Cincinnati | 34 |
| 37 | NEW YORK | 35 |
| 7 | KANSAS CITY | 18 |
| 14 | Miami | 14 |
| 6 | Boston | 23 |
| 7 | HOUSTON | 30 |
| 21 | New York | 25 |
| 17 | MIAMI | 21 |
| 6 | SAN DIEGO | 21 |
| 32 | Denver | 34 |
| 10 | Oakland | 13 |
| 6 | Houston | 35 |

| Use Name | Pos. | Hgt | Wgt | Age | Int | Pts |
|---|---|---|---|---|---|---|
| Stew Barber | OT | 6'3" | 248 | 29 | | |
| Dick Cunningham | OT | 6'2" | 244 | 23 | | |
| Ray Rissmiller | OT | 6'4" | 250 | 26 | | |
| Mike McBath | DE-OT | 6'4" | 248 | 22 | | |
| George Flint | OG | 6'4" | 240 | 30 | | |
| Bob Kalsu | OG | 6'3" | 235 | 23 | | |
| Billy Shaw | OG | 6'3" | 252 | 28 | | |
| Al Bemiller | C | 6'3" | 243 | 29 | | |
| Jack Frantz | C | 6'3" | 230 | 21 | | |
| Tom Day | DE | 6'2" | 265 | 33 | | |
| Ron McDole | DE | 6'3" | 270 | 28 | 2 | |
| Howard Kindig | C-DE | 6'6" | 264 | 27 | | |
| Jim Dunaway | DT | 6'4" | 282 | 26 | | |
| Tom Sestak | DT | 6'5" | 262 | 32 | | |
| Bob Tatarek | DT | 6'4" | 255 | 22 | | |
| Edgar Chandler | LB | 6'3" | 222 | 22 | | |
| Paul Guidry | LB | 6'3" | 228 | 24 | 1 | |
| Harry Jacobs | LB | 6'2" | 226 | 31 | | |
| Paul Maguire | LB | 6' | 228 | 30 | | |
| Marty Schottenheimer | LB | 6'3" | 224 | 25 | 1 | |
| Mike Stratton | LB | 6'3" | 230 | 26 | 1 | |
| Butch Byrd | DB | 6' | 196 | 26 | 6 | 6 |
| Hagood Clarke | DB | 6' | 192 | 26 | | 6 |
| Booker Edgerson | DB | 5'10" | 183 | 29 | 4 | 12 |
| Tom Janik | DB | 6'3" | 195 | 27 | 3 | 6 |
| Jerry Lawson | DB | 5'11" | 192 | 23 | | |
| John Pitts | DB | 6'4" | 215 | 23 | 2 | |
| George Saimes | DB | 5'10" | 185 | 26 | 2 | |
| Charlie Brown | HB-DB | 6'1" | 195 | 25 | | |
| Jack Kemp – Knee Injury | | | | | | |
| Joe O'Donnell – Knee Injury | | | | | | |
| Charley Ferguson – Injury | | | | | | |
| Dan Darragh | QB | 6'3" | 196 | 21 | | |
| Tom Flores | QB | 6'1" | 202 | 31 | | |
| Benny Russell | QB | 6'1" | 190 | 24 | | |
| Kay Stephenson | QB | 6'1" | 210 | 23 | | |
| Ed Rutkowski | WR-QB | 6'1" | 200 | 27 | | 6 |
| Max Anderson | HB | 5'8" | 180 | 23 | | 18 |
| Gary McDermott | HB | 6'1" | 211 | 22 | | 26 |
| Charley Mitchell | HB | 5'11" | 185 | 28 | | |
| Ben Gregory | FB-HB | 6'3" | 220 | 21 | | 6 |
| Bob Cappadonna | FB | 6'1" | 230 | 24 | | 20 |
| Wayne Patrick | FB | 6'2" | 225 | 22 | | |
| Keith Lincoln (to SD) | HB-FB | 6'2" | 216 | 29 | | |
| Bobby Crockett | WR | 6' | 200 | 25 | | |
| Elbert Dubenion | WR | 6' | 187 | 33 | | |
| Monte Ledbetter | WR | 6'2" | 185 | 25 | | 6 |
| Haven Moses | WR | 6'3" | 200 | 22 | | 12 |
| Richard Trapp | WR | 6'1" | 174 | 21 | | |
| Bill Masters | TE | 6'5" | 225 | 24 | | |
| Paul Costa | OT-TE | 6'4" | 248 | 26 | | 12 |
| Bruce Alford | K | 6' | 185 | 23 | | 57 |
| Mike Mercer (to GB-N) | K | 6' | 217 | 32 | | 4 |

## NEW YORK JETS

### RUSHING

| Last Name | No. | Yds | Avg | TD |
|---|---|---|---|---|
| Snell | 179 | 747 | 4.2 | 6 |
| Boozer | 143 | 441 | 3.1 | 5 |
| Mathis | 74 | 208 | 2.8 | 5 |
| Joe | 42 | 186 | 4.4 | 3 |
| Sauer | 2 | 21 | 10.5 | 0 |
| Smolinski | 12 | 15 | 1.3 | 0 |
| Namath | 5 | 11 | 2.2 | 2 |
| Parilli | 7 | -2 | -0.3 | 1 |
| Johnson | 2 | -6 | -3.0 | 0 |
| Rademacher | 1 | -13 | -13.0 | 0 |

### RECEIVING

| Last Name | No. | Yds | Avg | TD |
|---|---|---|---|---|
| Sauer | 66 | 1141 | 17 | 3 |
| Maynard | 57 | 1297 | 23 | 10 |
| Lammons | 32 | 400 | 13 | 3 |
| Snell | 16 | 105 | 7 | 1 |
| Boozer | 12 | 101 | 8 | 0 |
| B. Turner | 10 | 241 | 24 | 2 |
| Mathis | 9 | 149 | 17 | 1 |
| Smolinski | 6 | 40 | 7 | 0 |
| Johnson | 5 | 78 | 16 | 0 |
| Joe | 2 | 11 | 6 | 0 |
| Rademacher | 2 | 11 | 6 | 0 |

### PUNT RETURNS

| Last Name | No. | Yds | Avg | TD |
|---|---|---|---|---|
| Christy | 13 | 116 | 9 | 0 |
| Baird | 18 | 111 | 6 | 0 |
| Richards | 4 | 57 | 14 | 0 |
| Philbin | 1 | 2 | 2 | 0 |

### KICKOFF RETURNS

| Last Name | No. | Yds | Avg | TD |
|---|---|---|---|---|
| Christy | 25 | 599 | 24 | 0 |
| B. Turner | 14 | 319 | 23 | 0 |
| D'Amato | 1 | 32 | 32 | 0 |
| Snell | 3 | 28 | 9 | 0 |
| Smolinski | 1 | 17 | 17 | 0 |
| Rademacher | 1 | 0 | 0 | 0 |

### PASSING – PUNTING – KICKING

**PASSING**

| Last Name | Att | Comp | % | Yds | Yd/Att | TD | Int-% | | RK |
|---|---|---|---|---|---|---|---|---|---|
| Namath | 380 | 187 | 49 | 3147 | 8.3 | 15 | 17- | 4 | 3 |
| Parilli | 55 | 29 | 53 | 401 | 7.3 | 5 | 2- | 4 | |
| Snell | 1 | 1 | 100 | 26 | 26.0 | 0 | 0- | 0 | |

**PUNTING**

| Last Name | No | Avg |
|---|---|---|
| Johnson | 68 | 43.8 |

**KICKING**

| Last Name | XP | Att | % | FG | Att | % |
|---|---|---|---|---|---|---|
| J. Turner | 43 | 43 | 100 | 34 | 46 | 74 |

**2 POINT XP**
Mathis

## HOUSTON OILERS

### RUSHING

| Last Name | No. | Yds | Avg | TD |
|---|---|---|---|---|
| Granger | 202 | 848 | 4.2 | 7 |
| Campbell | 115 | 436 | 3.8 | 6 |
| Blanks | 63 | 169 | 2.7 | 0 |
| Hopkins | 31 | 104 | 3.4 | 0 |
| Davis | 15 | 91 | 6.1 | 1 |
| Beathard | 18 | 79 | 4.4 | 2 |
| Trull | 14 | 47 | 3.4 | 0 |
| Norton | 1 | 20 | 20.0 | 0 |
| Haik | 2 | 7 | 3.5 | 0 |
| Beirne | 1 | 3 | 3.0 | 0 |

### RECEIVING

| Last Name | No. | Yds | Avg | TD |
|---|---|---|---|---|
| Reed | 46 | 747 | 16 | 5 |
| Haik | 32 | 584 | 18 | 8 |
| Beirne | 31 | 474 | 15 | 4 |
| Granger | 26 | 361 | 14 | 0 |
| Campbell | 21 | 234 | 11 | 0 |
| Blanks | 13 | 184 | 14 | 0 |
| Frazier | 9 | 123 | 14 | 0 |
| Taylor | 6 | 90 | 15 | 0 |
| Hopkins | 4 | 40 | 10 | 0 |
| Burrell | 2 | 35 | 18 | 0 |
| Wittenborn | 1 | -8 | -8 | 0 |

### PUNT RETURNS

| Last Name | No. | Yds | Avg | TD |
|---|---|---|---|---|
| Carwell | 27 | 227 | 8 | 0 |
| Blanks | 22 | 179 | 8 | 0 |
| Burrell | 2 | 26 | 13 | 0 |
| Moore | 1 | 11 | 11 | 0 |

### KICKOFF RETURNS

| Last Name | No. | Yds | Avg | TD |
|---|---|---|---|---|
| Moore | 32 | 787 | 25 | 0 |
| Carwell | 15 | 335 | 22 | 0 |
| Burrell | 2 | 70 | 35 | 0 |
| Hopkins | 1 | 21 | 21 | 0 |
| Houston | 1 | 13 | 13 | 0 |
| Robertson | 2 | 9 | 5 | 0 |

### PASSING – PUNTING – KICKING

**PASSING**

| Last Name | Att | Comp | % | Yds | Yd/Att | TD | Int-% | | RK |
|---|---|---|---|---|---|---|---|---|---|
| Beathard | 223 | 105 | 47 | 1559 | 7.0 | 7 | 16- | 7 | 8 |
| Trull | 105 | 53 | 50 | 864 | 8.2 | 10 | 3- | 3 | |
| Davis | 86 | 33 | 38 | 441 | 5.1 | 0 | 6- | 7 | |

**PUNTING**

| Last Name | No | Avg |
|---|---|---|
| Norton | 73 | 41.2 |

**KICKING**

| Last Name | XP | Att | % | FG | Att | % |
|---|---|---|---|---|---|---|
| Walker | 26 | 26 | 100 | 8 | 16 | 50 |
| Wittenborn | 11 | 11 | 100 | 4 | 13 | 31 |

## MIAMI DOLPHINS

### RUSHING

| Last Name | No. | Yds | Avg | TD |
|---|---|---|---|---|
| Kiick | 165 | 621 | 3.8 | 4 |
| Csonka | 138 | 540 | 3.9 | 6 |
| Griese | 42 | 230 | 5.5 | 1 |
| Mitchell | 54 | 176 | 3.3 | 1 |
| Milton | 2 | 46 | 23.0 | 0 |
| Seiple | 5 | 42 | 8.4 | 0 |
| Price | 5 | 27 | 5.4 | 0 |
| Tucker | 4 | 13 | 3.3 | 0 |
| Norton | 1 | 9 | 9.0 | 0 |
| Hammond | 1 | 0 | 0.0 | 0 |

### RECEIVING

| Last Name | No. | Yds | Avg | TD |
|---|---|---|---|---|
| Noonan | 58 | 760 | 13 | 11 |
| Kiick | 44 | 422 | 10 | 0 |
| Twilley | 39 | 604 | 15 | 1 |
| Moreau | 27 | 365 | 14 | 3 |
| Cox | 11 | 147 | 13 | 0 |
| Csonka | 11 | 118 | 11 | 1 |
| Milton | 9 | 143 | 16 | 1 |
| Mitchell | 8 | 190 | 24 | 3 |
| Seiple | 7 | 69 | 10 | 1 |
| Darnall | 2 | 25 | 13 | 0 |

### PUNT RETURNS

| Last Name | No. | Yds | Avg | TD |
|---|---|---|---|---|
| Neff | 8 | 71 | 9 | 0 |
| Milton | 6 | 55 | 9 | 0 |
| Tucker | 5 | 40 | 8 | 0 |
| Anderson | 5 | 18 | 4 | 0 |
| Washington | 1 | 15 | 15 | 0 |
| Harper | 1 | 7 | 7 | 0 |
| Warren | 2 | -1 | -1 | 0 |

### KICKOFF RETURNS

| Last Name | No. | Yds | Avg | TD |
|---|---|---|---|---|
| Milton | 18 | 408 | 23 | 0 |
| Warren | 10 | 227 | 23 | 0 |
| Neff | 5 | 190 | 38 | 0 |
| Anderson | 6 | 106 | 18 | 0 |
| Tucker | 3 | 54 | 18 | 0 |
| Kiick | 1 | 28 | 28 | 0 |
| Price | 1 | 22 | 22 | 0 |
| Harper | 1 | 18 | 18 | 0 |
| Urbanek | 2 | 15 | 8 | 0 |
| Richardson | 1 | 1 | 1 | 0 |
| Woodson | 1 | 0 | 0 | 0 |
| Cox | 0 | 41 | 0 | 0 |

### PASSING – PUNTING – KICKING

**PASSING**

| Last Name | Att | Comp | % | Yds | Yd/Att | TD | Int-% | | RK |
|---|---|---|---|---|---|---|---|---|---|
| Griese | 355 | 186 | 52 | 2473 | 7.0 | 21 | 16- | 5 | 4 |
| Norton | 41 | 17 | 41 | 254 | 6.2 | 0 | 4- | 10 | |
| Hammond | 26 | 13 | 50 | 116 | 4.5 | 0 | 2- | 8 | |
| Kiick | 1 | 0 | 0 | 0 | 0.0 | 0 | 0- | 0 | |

**PUNTING**

| Last Name | No | Avg |
|---|---|---|
| Seiple | 75 | 40.6 |

**KICKING**

| Last Name | XP | Att | % | FG | Att | % |
|---|---|---|---|---|---|---|
| Keyes | 30 | 30 | 100 | 7 | 16 | 44 |
| Moreau | 6 | 6 | 100 | 1 | 3 | 33 |

## BOSTON PATRIOTS

### RUSHING

| Last Name | No. | Yds | Avg | TD |
|---|---|---|---|---|
| Nance | 177 | 593 | 3.4 | 4 |
| Gamble | 78 | 311 | 4.0 | 1 |
| Thomas | 88 | 215 | 2.4 | 2 |
| Garron | 36 | 97 | 2.7 | 1 |
| Sherman | 25 | 80 | 3.2 | 0 |
| Taliaferro | 8 | 51 | 6.4 | 0 |
| Marsh | 4 | 8 | 2.0 | 0 |
| P. Johnson | 2 | 6 | 3.0 | 0 |
| Cappelletti | 1 | 2 | 2.0 | 0 |
| Whalen | 1 | 0 | 0.0 | 0 |
| Corcoran | 1 | -1 | -1.0 | 0 |

### RECEIVING

| Last Name | No. | Yds | Avg | TD |
|---|---|---|---|---|
| Whalen | 47 | 718 | 15 | 7 |
| Marsh | 19 | 331 | 17 | 4 |
| Murphy | 18 | 268 | 15 | 0 |
| Graham | 16 | 242 | 15 | 1 |
| Nance | 14 | 51 | 4 | 0 |
| Cappelletti | 13 | 182 | 14 | 2 |
| Gamble | 11 | 55 | 5 | 1 |
| Thomas | 10 | 85 | 9 | 0 |
| Colclough | 8 | 136 | 17 | 0 |
| Scarpitto | 2 | 49 | 25 | 1 |
| Garron | 1 | 4 | 4 | 0 |
| J. Canale | 1 | 0 | 0 | 0 |

### PUNT RETURNS

| Last Name | No. | Yds | Avg | TD |
|---|---|---|---|---|
| Porter | 22 | 135 | 6 | 0 |
| B. Johnson | 10 | 34 | 3 | 0 |
| Leo | 2 | 12 | 6 | 0 |
| Graham | 2 | 11 | 6 | 0 |
| D. Johnson | 1 | 5 | 5 | 0 |

### KICKOFF RETURNS

| Last Name | No. | Yds | Avg | TD |
|---|---|---|---|---|
| Porter | 36 | 812 | 23 | 0 |
| B. Johnson | 22 | 442 | 20 | 0 |
| Marsh | 4 | 74 | 19 | 0 |
| D. Johnson | 3 | 63 | 21 | 0 |
| Thomas | 1 | 22 | 22 | 0 |
| Long | 2 | 20 | 10 | 0 |
| Graham | 1 | 9 | 9 | 0 |
| Cheyunski | 1 | 0 | 0 | 0 |
| Gamble | 1 | 0 | 0 | 0 |

### PASSING – PUNTING – KICKING

**PASSING**

| Last Name | Att | Comp | % | Yds | Yd/Att | TD | Int-% | | RK |
|---|---|---|---|---|---|---|---|---|---|
| Sherman | 226 | 90 | 40 | 1199 | 5.3 | 12 | 16- | 7 | 9 |
| Taliaferro | 176 | 67 | 38 | 889 | 5.1 | 4 | 15- | 9 | 11 |
| Corcoran | 7 | 3 | 43 | 33 | 4.7 | 0 | 2- | 29 | |

**PUNTING**

| Last Name | No | Avg |
|---|---|---|
| Swanson | 62 | 39.5 |
| Scarpitto | 34 | 40.6 |

**KICKING**

| Last Name | XP | Att | % | FG | Att | % |
|---|---|---|---|---|---|---|
| Cappelletti | 26 | 26 | 100 | 15 | 27 | 56 |

## BUFFALO BILLS

### RUSHING

| Last Name | No. | Yds | Avg | TD |
|---|---|---|---|---|
| Anderson | 147 | 525 | 3.6 | 2 |
| Gregory | 52 | 283 | 5.4 | 1 |
| Cappadona | 73 | 272 | 3.7 | 1 |
| McDermott | 47 | 102 | 2.2 | 3 |
| Rutkowski | 20 | 96 | 4.8 | 1 |
| Lincoln | 26 | 84 | 3.2 | 0 |
| Masters | 6 | 70 | 11.7 | 0 |
| Brown | 3 | 39 | 13.0 | 0 |
| Stephenson | 4 | 30 | 7.5 | 0 |
| Costa | 2 | 11 | 5.5 | 1 |
| Darragh | 13 | 11 | 0.8 | 0 |
| Maguire | 1 | 6 | 6.0 | 0 |
| Patrick | 1 | 2 | 2.0 | 0 |
| Moses | 5 | -4 | -0.8 | 0 |

### RECEIVING

| Last Name | No. | Yds | Avg | TD |
|---|---|---|---|---|
| Moses | 42 | 633 | 15 | 2 |
| Trapp | 24 | 235 | 10 | 0 |
| Anderson | 22 | 140 | 6 | 0 |
| McDermott | 20 | 115 | 6 | 1 |
| Cappadona | 18 | 92 | 5 | 2 |
| Costa | 15 | 172 | 11 | 1 |
| Masters | 8 | 101 | 13 | 0 |
| Crockett | 6 | 76 | 13 | 0 |
| Gregory | 5 | 21 | 4 | 0 |
| Ledbetter | 4 | 94 | 24 | 1 |
| Rutkowski | 1 | 27 | 27 | 0 |
| Patrick | 1 | 5 | 5 | 0 |
| Lincoln | 1 | 3 | 3 | 0 |
| Bemiller | 1 | 0 | 0 | 0 |

### PUNT RETURNS

| Last Name | No. | Yds | Avg | TD |
|---|---|---|---|---|
| Clarke | 29 | 241 | 8 | 1 |
| Trapp | 5 | 26 | 5 | 0 |
| Rutkowski | 8 | 23 | 3 | 0 |
| Byrd | 2 | 11 | 6 | 0 |

### KICKOFF RETURNS

| Last Name | No. | Yds | Avg | TD |
|---|---|---|---|---|
| Anderson | 39 | 971 | 25 | 1 |
| Brown | 12 | 274 | 23 | 0 |
| Mitchell | 5 | 98 | 20 | 0 |
| Rutkowski | 5 | 87 | 17 | 0 |
| Costa | 5 | 68 | 14 | 0 |
| Lincoln | 2 | 37 | 19 | 0 |
| McDermott | 1 | 16 | 16 | 0 |
| Maguire | 1 | 5 | 5 | 0 |
| Barber | 1 | 0 | 0 | 0 |
| Ledbetter | 0 | 18 | 0 | 0 |

### PASSING – PUNTING – KICKING

**PASSING**

| Last Name | Att | Comp | % | Yds | Yd/Att | TD | Int-% | | RK |
|---|---|---|---|---|---|---|---|---|---|
| Darragh | 215 | 92 | 43 | 917 | 4.3 | 3 | 14- | 7 | 10 |
| Rutkowski | 100 | 41 | 41 | 380 | 3.8 | 0 | 6- | 6 | |
| Stephenson | 79 | 29 | 37 | 364 | 4.6 | 4 | 7- | 9 | |
| Flores | 5 | 3 | 60 | 15 | 3.0 | 0 | 1- | 20 | |
| McDermott | 3 | 2 | 67 | 35 | 11.7 | 0 | 0- | 0 | |
| Russell | 2 | 1 | 50 | 3 | 1.5 | 0 | 0- | 0 | |
| Anderson | 1 | 0 | 0 | 0 | 0.0 | 0 | 0- | 0 | |

**PUNTING**

| Last Name | No | Avg |
|---|---|---|
| Maguire | 100 | 41.8 |

**KICKING**

| Last Name | XP | Att | % | FG | Att | % |
|---|---|---|---|---|---|---|
| Alford | 15 | 15 | 100 | 14 | 24 | 58 |
| Mercer | 4 | 4 | 100 | 0 | 4 | 0 |

**2 POINT XP**
Cappadona
McDermott

## OAKLAND RAIDERS 12-2-0 Johnny Rauch

| Scores of Each Game | | |
|---|---|---|
| 48 | Buffalo | 6 |
| 47 | Miami | 21 |
| 24 | Houston | 15 |
| 41 | BOSTON | 10 |
| 14 | SAN DIEGO | 23 |
| 10 | Kansas City | 24 |
| 31 | CINCINNATI | 10 |
| 38 | KANSAS CITY | 21 |
| 43 | Denver | 7 |
| 43 | NEW YORK | 32 |
| 34 | Cincinnati | 0 |
| 13 | BUFFALO | 10 |
| 33 | DENVER | 27 |
| 34 | San Diego | 27 |
| | Playoff | |
| 41 | KANSAS CITY | 6 |

| Use Name | Pos. | Hgt | Wgt | Age | Int | Pts |
|---|---|---|---|---|---|---|
| Harry Schuh | OT | 6'2" | 260 | 25 | | |
| Art Shell | OT | 6'5" | 255 | 21 | | |
| Bob Svihus | OT | 6'4" | 245 | 25 | | |
| Jim Harvey | OG-OT | 6'5" | 245 | 25 | | |
| Wayne Hawkins | OG | 6' | 240 | 30 | | |
| Bob Kruse | OG | 6'2" | 250 | 26 | | |
| Gene Upshaw | OG | 6'5" | 255 | 23 | | |
| Jim Otto | C | 6'2" | 248 | 30 | | |
| Ben Davidson | DE | 6'8" | 275 | 28 | | |
| Ike Lassiter | DE | 6'5" | 270 | 27 | | |
| Carleton Oats | DE | 6'2" | 260 | 25 | | |
| Dan Birdwell | DT | 6'4" | 250 | 27 | | |
| Al Dotson | DT | 6'4" | 260 | 25 | | |
| Karl Rubke | C-DT | 6'4" | 234 | 32 | | |

Tom Keating – Foot Injury
Bill Laskey – Foot Injury

| Use Name | Pos. | Hgt | Wgt | Age | Int | Pts |
|---|---|---|---|---|---|---|
| Duane Benson | LB | 6'2" | 215 | 23 | | |
| Bill Budness | LB | 6'1" | 215 | 25 | | |
| Dan Conners | LB | 6'1" | 230 | 26 | 2 | |
| Bill Fairband | LB | 6'3" | 228 | 22 | | |
| Jerry Hopkins | LB | 6'2" | 238 | 27 | | |
| Dave Ogas | LB | 6'3" | 240 | 22 | | |
| Chip Oliver | LB | 6'2" | 220 | 22 | | |
| Gus Otto | LB | 6'2" | 220 | 25 | | |
| Butch Atkinson | DB | 6' | 180 | 21 | 4 | 18 |
| Rodger Bird | DB | 5'11" | 195 | 25 | 3 | 6 |
| Willie Brown | DB | 6'1" | 190 | 27 | 2 | 6 |
| Dave Grayson | DB | 5'10" | 185 | 29 | 10 | 6 |
| Kent McCloughan | DB | 6'1" | 190 | 25 | 1 | |
| Warren Powers | DB | 6' | 190 | 27 | 1 | |
| Howie Williams | DB | 6'2" | 190 | 31 | 2 | |
| Nemiah Wilson | DB | 6' | 165 | 25 | | |

| Use Name | Pos. | Hgt | Wgt | Age | Int | Pts |
|---|---|---|---|---|---|---|
| George Blanda | QB | 6'1" | 215 | 40 | | 117 |
| Cotton Davidson | QB | 6'1" | 180 | 36 | | |
| Daryle Lamonica | QB | 6'2" | 215 | 27 | | 6 |
| Pete Banaszak | HB | 5'11" | 200 | 24 | | 30 |
| Preston Ridlehuber | HB | 6'2" | 215 | 24 | | 6 |
| Charlie Smith | HB | 6'1" | 205 | 22 | | 42 |
| Larry Todd | HB | 6'1" | 185 | 25 | | 12 |
| Hewritt Dixon | FB | 6'2" | 230 | 28 | | 26 |
| Roger Hagberg | FB | 6'2" | 215 | 29 | | 12 |
| Fred Biletnikoff | WR | 6'1" | 190 | 25 | | 42 |
| Eldridge Dickey | WR | 6'2" | 198 | 22 | | |
| John Eason | WR | 6'2" | 220 | 23 | | |
| Bill Miller | WR | 6' | 190 | 26 | | 6 |
| John Roderick | WR | 6'1" | 180 | 24 | | |
| Warren Wells | WR | 6'1" | 190 | 25 | | 72 |
| Billy Cannon | TE | 6'1" | 215 | 31 | | 36 |
| Dave Kocourek | TE | 6'5" | 235 | 31 | | 6 |
| Mike Eischeid | K | 6' | 190 | 27 | | |

## KANSAS CITY CHIEFS 12-2-0 Hank Stram

| Scores of Each Game | | |
|---|---|---|
| 26 | Houston | 21 |
| 19 | NEW YORK | 20 |
| 34 | DENVER | 2 |
| 48 | Miami | 3 |
| 18 | Buffalo | 7 |
| 13 | CINCINNATI | 3 |
| 24 | OAKLAND | 10 |
| 27 | SAN DIEGO | 20 |
| 21 | Oakland | 38 |
| 16 | Cincinnati | 9 |
| 31 | BOSTON | 17 |
| 24 | HOUSTON | 10 |
| 40 | San Diego | 3 |
| 30 | Denver | 7 |
| | Playoff | |
| 6 | Oakland | 41 |

| Use Name | Pos. | Hgt | Wgt | Age | Int | Pts |
|---|---|---|---|---|---|---|
| Dave Hill | OT | 6'5" | 260 | 27 | | |
| Jim Tyrer | OT | 6'6" | 275 | 29 | | |
| Ed Budde | OG | 6'5" | 260 | 27 | | |
| George Daney | OG | 6'3" | 240 | 32 | | |
| Curt Merz | OG | 6'4" | 267 | 30 | | |
| Mo Moorman | OG | 6'5" | 252 | 24 | | |
| E. J. Holub | C | 6'4" | 236 | 30 | | |
| Aaron Brown | DE | 6'5" | 265 | 24 | | |
| Jerry Mays | DE | 6'4" | 252 | 28 | | |
| Remi Prudhomme | DT-DE | 6'4" | 250 | 26 | | |
| Buck Buchanan | DT | 6'7" | 287 | 28 | 1 | 2 |
| Ernie Ladd | DT | 6'9" | 290 | 29 | 1 | |
| Ed Lothamer | DT | 6'5" | 270 | 25 | | |
| Curley Culp | OG-DT | 6'1" | 265 | 22 | | |

| Use Name | Pos. | Hgt | Wgt | Age | Int | Pts |
|---|---|---|---|---|---|---|
| Bud Abell | LB | 6'3" | 220 | 27 | 2 | |
| Bobby Bell | LB | 6'4" | 228 | 28 | 5 | |
| Chuck Hurston | LB | 6'6" | 240 | 25 | | |
| Willie Lanier | LB | 6'1" | 245 | 23 | 4 | 6 |
| Jim Lynch | LB | 6'1" | 235 | 23 | 3 | 6 |
| Dave Martin | LB | 6' | 215 | 21 | | |
| Caesar Belser | DB | 6' | 212 | 23 | | |
| Jim Kearney | DB | 6'2" | 206 | 25 | 3 | |
| Willie Mitchell | DB | 6'1" | 185 | 26 | 5 | |
| Johnny Robinson | DB | 6' | 205 | 29 | 6 | |
| Goldie Sellers | DB | 6'2" | 198 | 26 | 3 | 6 |
| Emmitt Thomas | DB | 6'2" | 192 | 25 | 4 | |

Gene Trosch – Injury

| Use Name | Pos. | Hgt | Wgt | Age | Int | Pts |
|---|---|---|---|---|---|---|
| Len Dawson | QB | 6' | 190 | 34 | | |
| Jacky Lee | QB | 6'1" | 185 | 29 | | |
| Mike Livingston | QB | 6'3" | 205 | 22 | | |
| Bert Coan | HB | 6'4" | 220 | 28 | | 6 |
| Mike Garrett | HB | 5'9" | 200 | 24 | | 36 |
| Paul Lowe (from SD) | HB | 6' | 205 | 31 | | |
| Wendell Hayes | FB-HB | 6'2" | 220 | 27 | | 30 |
| Robert Holmes | FB | 5'9" | 220 | 22 | | 42 |
| Curtis McClinton | FB | 6'3" | 227 | 30 | | |
| Jack Gehrke | WR | 6' | 178 | 22 | | |
| Sam Longmire | WR | 6'3" | 195 | 25 | | |
| Frank Pitts | WR | 6'2" | 200 | 24 | | 36 |
| Gloster Richardson | WR | 6' | 200 | 25 | | 36 |
| Noland Smith | WR | 5'6" | 154 | 24 | | 6 |
| Otis Taylor | WR | 6'2" | 215 | 25 | | 30 |
| Fred Arbanas | TE | 6'3" | 240 | 29 | | |
| Reg Carolan | TE | 6'6" | 240 | 28 | | |
| Jan Stenerud | K | 6'2" | 187 | 25 | | 129 |
| Jerrel Wilson | K | 6'4" | 222 | 26 | | |

## SAN DIEGO CHARGERS 9-5-0 Sid Gillman

| Scores of Each Game | | |
|---|---|---|
| 29 | CINCINNATI | 13 |
| 30 | HOUSTON | 14 |
| 31 | Cincinnati | 10 |
| 20 | New York | 23 |
| 23 | Oakland | 14 |
| 55 | DENVER | 24 |
| 20 | Kansas City | 27 |
| 34 | MIAMI | 28 |
| 27 | Boston | 17 |
| 21 | Buffalo | 6 |
| 15 | NEW YORK | 37 |
| 47 | Denver | 23 |
| 3 | KANSAS CITY | 40 |
| 27 | OAKLAND | 34 |

| Use Name | Pos. | Hgt | Wgt | Age | Int | Pts |
|---|---|---|---|---|---|---|
| Harold Akin | OT | 6'5" | 260 | 23 | | |
| Ron Mix | OT | 6'4" | 250 | 30 | | |
| Terry Owens | OT | 6'6" | 270 | 24 | | |
| Bob Wells | OT | 6'4" | 270 | 23 | | |
| Gary Kirner | OG | 6'3" | 255 | 26 | | |
| Larry Little | OG | 6'1" | 270 | 22 | | |
| Jim Schmedding | OG | 6'2" | 250 | 22 | | |
| Walt Sweeney | OG | 6'3" | 260 | 27 | | |
| Sam Gruneisen | C | 6'1" | 250 | 27 | | |
| Paul Latzke | C | 6'4" | 240 | 26 | | |
| Bill Lenkaitis | C | 6'3" | 250 | 22 | | |
| Marty Baccaglio (to CIN) | DE | 6'3" | 245 | 23 | | |
| Steve DeLong | DE | 6'3" | 252 | 25 | | |
| Houston Ridge | DE | 6'4" | 245 | 24 | | |
| Ron Billingsley | DT-DE | 6'8" | 265 | 23 | | |
| Scott Appleton | DT | 6'3" | 260 | 26 | | |
| Bob Briggs | DT | 6'4" | 270 | 23 | | |
| Russ Washington | DT | 6'6" | 290 | 21 | | |

| Use Name | Pos. | Hgt | Wgt | Age | Int | Pts |
|---|---|---|---|---|---|---|
| Chuck Allen | LB | 6'1" | 225 | 28 | 1 | |
| Bernie Erickson (to CIN) | LB | 6'2" | 240 | 23 | | |
| Tom Erlandson | LB | 6'3" | 220 | 28 | 2 | |
| Jim Fetherston | LB | 6'2" | 225 | 23 | 1 | |
| Curtis Jones | LB | 6'2" | 245 | 25 | | |
| Ron McCall | LB | 6'2" | 245 | 23 | | |
| Bob Mitinger | LB | 6'2" | 230 | 28 | | |
| Bob Print | LB | 6' | 220 | 24 | | |
| Rick Redman | LB | 5'11" | 225 | 25 | | |
| Jeff Staggs | LB | 6'2" | 240 | 24 | 2 | |
| Joe Beauchamp | DB | 6' | 185 | 24 | 5 | 12 |
| Speedy Duncan | DB | 5'10" | 175 | 25 | 1 | 6 |
| Dick Farley | DB | 6' | 185 | 22 | | |
| Kenny Graham | DB | 6' | 205 | 26 | 5 | |
| Bob Howard | DB | 6'1" | 190 | 23 | 1 | |
| Dick Speights | DB | 5'11" | 175 | 22 | | |
| Jim Tolbert | DB | 6'3" | 207 | 24 | 2 | |
| Bud Whitehead | DB | 6' | 185 | 29 | | |
| Ken Dyer | WR-DB | 6'3" | 185 | 22 | | 6 |

| Use Name | Pos. | Hgt | Wgt | Age | Int | Pts |
|---|---|---|---|---|---|---|
| Jon Brittenum | QB | 6' | 185 | 24 | | |
| John Hadl | QB | 6'2" | 215 | 28 | | 12 |
| Dickie Post | HB | 5'9" | 190 | 22 | | 18 |
| Russ Smith | HB | 6'1" | 209 | 24 | | 24 |
| Jim Allison | FB | 6' | 215 | 25 | | |
| Gene Foster | FB | 5'11" | 220 | 25 | | 6 |
| Brad Hubbert | FB | 6'1" | 227 | 27 | | 12 |
| Gerry McDougall | FB | 6'2" | 225 | 33 | | |
| Lance Alworth | WR | 6' | 180 | 28 | | 62 |
| Lane Fenner | WR | 6'5" | 210 | 23 | | |
| Gary Garrison | WR | 6'1" | 195 | 24 | | 60 |
| Phil Tuckett | WR | 6' | 180 | 23 | | |
| Willie Frazier | TE | 6'4" | 235 | 25 | | 18 |
| Jacque MacKinnon | TE | 6'4" | 240 | 29 | | 38 |
| Andre White (from CIN) | TE | 6'5" | 225 | 23 | | |
| Dennis Partee | K | 6'2" | 208 | 22 | | 106 |

## DENVER BRONCOS 5-9-0 Lou Saban

| Scores of Each Game | | |
|---|---|---|
| 10 | Cincinnati | 24 |
| 2 | Kansas City | 34 |
| 17 | BOSTON | 20 |
| 10 | CINCINNATI | 7 |
| 21 | New York | 13 |
| 24 | San Diego | 55 |
| 21 | MIAMI | 14 |
| 35 | Boston | 14 |
| 7 | OAKLAND | 43 |
| 17 | Houston | 38 |
| 34 | BUFFALO | 32 |
| 23 | SAN DIEGO | 47 |
| 27 | Oakland | 33 |
| 7 | KANSAS CITY | 30 |

| Use Name | Pos. | Hgt | Wgt | Age | Int | Pts |
|---|---|---|---|---|---|---|
| Sam Brunelli | OT | 6'1" | 270 | 25 | | |
| Tom Cichowski | OT | 6'4" | 250 | 23 | | |
| Mike Current | OT | 6'4" | 260 | 22 | | |
| Wallace Dickey | OT | 6'3" | 260 | 27 | | |
| George Gaiser | OT | 6'4" | 255 | 23 | | |
| George Goeddeke | OG | 6'3" | 245 | 23 | | |
| Buzz Highsmith | OG | 6'4" | 230 | 25 | | |
| Bob Vaughn | OG | 6'4" | 240 | 23 | | |
| Bob Young | OG | 6'2" | 260 | 25 | | |
| Jay Bachman | C | 6'3" | 250 | 22 | | |
| Larry Kaminski | C | 6'2" | 245 | 23 | | |
| Pete Duranko | DE | 6'2" | 252 | 24 | | |
| Rich Jackson | DE | 6'2" | 255 | 27 | | |
| Paul Smith | DE | 6'3" | 245 | 23 | | |
| Dave Costa | DT | 6'2" | 265 | 26 | | |
| Larry Cox | DT | 6'2" | 250 | 24 | | |
| Jerry Inman | DT | 6'3" | 255 | 28 | | |
| Rex Mirich | DT | 6'4" | 250 | 27 | | |

| Use Name | Pos. | Hgt | Wgt | Age | Int | Pts |
|---|---|---|---|---|---|---|
| Carl Cunningham | LB | 6'3" | 240 | 24 | 1 | |
| Fred Forsberg | LB | 6'1" | 235 | 24 | 1 | |
| John Huard | LB | 6' | 220 | 24 | 2 | |
| Gordon Lambert | LB | 6'5" | 245 | 23 | | |
| Frank Richter | LB | 6'3" | 230 | 23 | | |
| Dave Tobey | LB | 6'3" | 230 | 25 | | |
| Chip Myrtle | TE-LB | 6'2" | 225 | 23 | | 2 |
| Drake Garrett | DB | 5'9" | 183 | 23 | 2 | |
| Charlie Greer | DB | 6' | 205 | 22 | 4 | |
| Gus Holloman | DB | 6'3" | 195 | 22 | 1 | |
| Pete Jaquess | DB | 6' | 182 | 26 | 5 | |
| Jack Lentz | DB | 6' | 195 | 23 | 1 | |
| Hal Lewis | DB | 6'2" | 188 | 25 | | |
| Tommy Luke | DB | 6' | 190 | 26 | | |
| Alex Moore | DB | 6' | 195 | 23 | | |
| Tom Oberg | DB | 6' | 185 | 23 | 3 | |
| Jesse Stokes | DB | 6' | 190 | 24 | | |

| Use Name | Pos. | Hgt | Wgt | Age | Int | Pts |
|---|---|---|---|---|---|---|
| Marlin Briscoe | QB | 5'10" | 177 | 22 | | 18 |
| Joe DiVito | QB | 6'2" | 205 | 22 | | |
| Jim LeClair | QB | 6'1" | 208 | 24 | | |
| John McCormick | QB | 6'1" | 190 | 31 | | |
| Steve Tensi | QB | 6'5" | 215 | 25 | | |
| Terry Erwin | HB | 6' | 190 | 21 | | |
| Hub Lindsey | HB | 5'11" | 196 | 22 | | |
| Floyd Little | HB | 5'10" | 195 | 26 | | 30 |
| Fran Lynch | HB | 6'1" | 194 | 22 | | 24 |
| Garrett Ford | FB | 6'2" | 230 | 22 | | 6 |
| Brendan McCarthy (from ATL-N) | FB | 6'3" | 220 | 23 | | 12 |
| Eric Crabtree | WR | 5'11" | 182 | 23 | | 30 |
| Al Denson | WR | 6'2" | 208 | 26 | | 30 |
| Mike Haffner | WR | 6'2" | 205 | 26 | | 6 |
| Jim Jones | WR | 6'2" | 195 | 24 | | 12 |
| Bobby Moten | WR | 6'4" | 212 | 25 | | |
| Bill Van Heusen | WR | 6'1" | 200 | 22 | | 18 |
| Tom Beer | TE | 6'4" | 230 | 23 | | 6 |
| Dave Washington | TE | 6'4" | 228 | 27 | | |
| Bobby Howfield | K | 5'9" | 180 | 31 | | 57 |
| Bob Humphreys | K | 6'1" | 240 | 28 | | 4 |

## CINCINNATI BENGALS 3-11-0 Paul Brown

| Scores of Each Game | | |
|---|---|---|
| 13 | San Diego | 29 |
| 24 | DENVER | 10 |
| 34 | BUFFALO | 23 |
| 10 | SAN DIEGO | 31 |
| 7 | Denver | 10 |
| 3 | Kansas City | 13 |
| 22 | MIAMI | 24 |
| 10 | Oakland | 31 |
| 17 | HOUSTON | 27 |
| 9 | KANSAS CITY | 16 |
| 38 | Miami | 21 |
| 0 | OAKLAND | 34 |
| 14 | Boston | 33 |
| 14 | New York | 27 |

| Use Name | Pos. | Hgt | Wgt | Age | Int | Pts |
|---|---|---|---|---|---|---|
| Howard Fest | OT | 6'6" | 265 | 22 | | |
| Bob Kelly | OT | 6'3" | 270 | 28 | | |
| Ernie Wright | OT | 6'4" | 270 | 28 | | |
| Dan Archer | OG-OT | 6'5" | 245 | 23 | | |
| Pat Matson | OG | 6'1" | 245 | 24 | | |
| Dave Middendorf | OG | 6'3" | 260 | 22 | | |
| Pete Perreault | OG | 6'3" | 248 | 29 | | |
| Bob Johnson | C | 6'5" | 260 | 22 | | |
| John Matlock | OT-C | 6'4" | 255 | 23 | | |
| Jim Griffin | DE | 6'3" | 265 | 26 | | 6 |
| Harry Gunner | DE | 6'6" | 250 | 23 | 1 | 2 |
| Willie Jones | DE | 6'2" | 260 | 26 | | |
| Dennis Randall | DE | 6'6" | 240 | 22 | | |
| Steve Chomyszak | DT | 6'5" | 280 | 23 | | |
| Bill Kindricks | DT | 6'3" | 268 | 22 | | |
| Andy Rice | DT | 6'3" | 268 | 26 | | |
| Bill Staley | DT | 6'3" | 250 | 21 | | |

| Use Name | Pos. | Hgt | Wgt | Age | Int | Pts |
|---|---|---|---|---|---|---|
| Al Beauchamp | LB | 6'2" | 236 | 24 | 2 | 6 |
| Danny Brabham | LB | 6'4" | 233 | 27 | | |
| Frank Buncom | LB | 6'1" | 245 | 28 | | |
| Paul Elzey | LB | 6'3" | 235 | 22 | | |
| Sherrill Headrick | LB | 6'2" | 240 | 31 | 1 | |
| Mike Hibler | LB | 6'1" | 235 | 22 | | |
| Wayne McClure | LB | 6'1" | 225 | 22 | | |
| John Neidert (to NY) | LB | 6'2" | 230 | 22 | | |
| Curt Frazier | DB | 5'11" | 193 | 23 | | |
| White Graves | DB | 6' | 185 | 25 | | |
| Rex Keeling | DB | 6'3" | 220 | 24 | | |
| Charlie King | DB | 6' | 184 | 25 | 1 | 6 |
| Bill Scott | DB | 6' | 188 | 24 | | |
| Fletcher Smith | DB | 6'2" | 178 | 24 | 1 | |
| Phil Spiller (from ATL-N) | DB | 6' | 195 | 23 | | |
| Bobby Hunt | HB-DB | 6'1" | 190 | 28 | 1 | 6 |
| Jess Phillips | HB-DB | 6'1" | 205 | 21 | 3 | |

| Use Name | Pos. | Hgt | Wgt | Age | Int | Pts |
|---|---|---|---|---|---|---|
| John Stofa | QB | 6'3" | 210 | 26 | | |
| Dewey Warren | QB | 6' | 205 | 23 | | |
| Sam Wyche | QB | 6'4" | 210 | 23 | | |
| Essex Johnson | HB | 5'9" | 190 | 21 | | 18 |
| Paul Robinson | HB | 6' | 200 | 23 | | 54 |
| Ted Washington | HB | 5'11" | 210 | 22 | | |
| Estes Banks | FB | 6'1" | 220 | 23 | | 6 |
| Ron Lamb (from DEN) | FB | 6'2" | 225 | 24 | | |
| Tom Smiley | FB | 6'1" | 235 | 24 | | 6 |
| Saint Saffold | WR | 6'4" | 202 | 24 | | |
| Rod Sherman | WR | 6' | 190 | 23 | | 10 |
| Monk Williams | WR | 5'7" | 155 | 23 | | |
| Warren McVea | HB-WR | 5'10" | 182 | 22 | | 18 |
| Ken Herock | TE | 6'2" | 230 | 27 | | |
| Bill Peterson | TE | 6'3" | 230 | 23 | | |
| Bob Trumpy | WR-TE | 6'6" | 220 | 23 | | 18 |
| Dale Livingston | K | 6' | 210 | 23 | | 59 |

## OAKLAND RAIDERS

### RUSHING

| Last Name | No. | Yds | Avg | TD |
|---|---|---|---|---|
| Dixon | 206 | 865 | 4.2 | 2 |
| Smith | 95 | 504 | 3.6 | 5 |
| Banaszak | 91 | 362 | 4.0 | 4 |
| Hagberg | 39 | 164 | 4.2 | 1 |
| Lamonica | 19 | 98 | 5.2 | 1 |
| Todd | 13 | 89 | 6.8 | 2 |
| Eischeid | 2 | 41 | 20.5 | 0 |
| Wells | 2 | 38 | 19.0 | 1 |
| Ridlehuber | 4 | 7 | 1.8 | 0 |

### RECEIVING

| Last Name | No. | Yds | Avg | TD |
|---|---|---|---|---|
| Biletnikoff | 61 | 1037 | 17 | 6 |
| Wells | 53 | 1137 | 21 | 11 |
| Dixon | 38 | 360 | 9 | 2 |
| Cannon | 23 | 360 | 16 | 6 |
| Smith | 22 | 321 | 15 | 2 |
| Banaszak | 15 | 182 | 12 | 1 |
| Miller | 9 | 176 | 20 | 1 |
| Hagberg | 8 | 78 | 10 | 1 |
| Todd | 4 | 40 | 10 | 0 |
| Kocourek | 3 | 46 | 15 | 1 |
| Dickey | 1 | 34 | 34 | 0 |

### PUNT RETURNS

| Last Name | No. | Yds | Avg | TD |
|---|---|---|---|---|
| Atkinson | 36 | 490 | 14 | 2 |
| Bird | 11 | 128 | 12 | 0 |
| Dickey | 6 | 48 | 8 | 0 |
| Shell | 1 | 0 | 0 | 0 |
| Wilson | 1 | 0 | 0 | 0 |

### KICKOFF RETURNS

| Last Name | No. | Yds | Avg | TD |
|---|---|---|---|---|
| Atkinson | 32 | 802 | 25 | 0 |
| Smith | 8 | 167 | 21 | 0 |
| Wilson | 4 | 84 | 21 | 0 |
| Hagberg | 1 | 21 | 21 | 0 |
| Dickey | 1 | 17 | 17 | 0 |
| Kruse | 1 | 1 | 1 | 0 |
| Hopkins | 1 | 0 | 0 | 0 |
| G. Otto | 1 | 0 | 0 | 0 |

### PASSING — PUNTING — KICKING

PASSING

| Last Name | Att | Comp | % | Yds | Yd/Att | TD | Int-% | RK |
|---|---|---|---|---|---|---|---|---|
| Lamonica | 416 | 206 | 50 | 3245 | 7.8 | 25 | 15— 4 | 2 |
| Blanda | 49 | 30 | 61 | 522 | 10.7 | 6 | 2— 4 | |
| C. Davidson | 2 | 1 | 50 | 4 | 2.0 | 0 | 0— 0 | |
| Banaszak | 1 | 0 | 0 | 0 | 0.0 | 0 | 1—100 | |

PUNTING

| Last Name | No | Avg |
|---|---|---|
| Eischeid | 64 | 43.6 |

KICKING

| Last Name | XP | Att | % | FG | Att | % |
|---|---|---|---|---|---|---|
| Blanda | 54 | 54 | 100 | 21 | 34 | 62 |

2 POINT XP
Dixon

## KANSAS CITY CHIEFS

### RUSHING

| Last Name | No. | Yds | Avg | TD |
|---|---|---|---|---|
| Holmes | 174 | 866 | 5.0 | 7 |
| Garrett | 164 | 564 | 3.4 | 3 |
| Hayes | 85 | 340 | 4.0 | 4 |
| Coan | 40 | 160 | 4.0 | 1 |
| McClinton | 24 | 107 | 4.5 | 0 |
| Pitts | 11 | 107 | 9.7 | 0 |
| Taylor | 5 | 41 | 8.2 | 1 |
| Dawson | 20 | 40 | 2.0 | 0 |
| Arbanas | 3 | 14 | 4.7 | 0 |
| Livingston | 2 | 2 | 1.0 | 0 |
| Wilson | 5 | 1 | 0.2 | 0 |
| Lowe | 2 | −1 | −0.5 | 0 |
| Smith | 2 | −2 | −1.0 | 0 |
| Richardson | 1 | −3 | −3.0 | 0 |

### RECEIVING

| Last Name | No. | Yds | Avg | TD |
|---|---|---|---|---|
| Garrett | 33 | 359 | 11 | 3 |
| Pitts | 30 | 655 | 22 | 6 |
| Richardson | 22 | 494 | 22 | 6 |
| Taylor | 20 | 420 | 21 | 4 |
| Holmes | 19 | 201 | 11 | 0 |
| Hayes | 12 | 108 | 9 | 1 |
| Arbanas | 11 | 189 | 17 | 0 |
| McClinton | 3 | −4 | −1 | 0 |
| Carolan | 2 | 26 | 13 | 0 |
| Coan | 2 | 15 | 8 | 0 |
| Smith | 1 | 15 | 15 | 0 |
| Wilson | 1 | 14 | 14 | 0 |

### PUNT RETURNS

| Last Name | No. | Yds | Avg | TD |
|---|---|---|---|---|
| Smith | 18 | 270 | 15 | 1 |
| Sellers | 7 | 129 | 18 | 1 |
| Robinson | 2 | 26 | 13 | 0 |
| Mitchell | 1 | 21 | 21 | 0 |
| Garrett | 2 | 4 | 2 | 0 |
| Belser | 1 | 0 | 0 | 0 |

### KICKOFF RETURNS

| Last Name | No. | Yds | Avg | TD |
|---|---|---|---|---|
| Smith | 23 | 549 | 24 | 0 |
| Coan | 5 | 100 | 20 | 0 |
| Sellers | 2 | 40 | 20 | 0 |
| Belser | 4 | 38 | 10 | 0 |
| Kearney | 1 | 9 | 9 | 0 |
| Abell | 1 | 0 | 0 | 0 |
| Daney | 1 | 0 | 0 | 0 |
| Prudhomme | 1 | 0 | 0 | 0 |

### PASSING — PUNTING — KICKING

PASSING

| Last Name | Att | Comp | % | Yds | Yd/Att | TD | Int-% | RK |
|---|---|---|---|---|---|---|---|---|
| Dawson | 224 | 131 | 59 | 2109 | 9.4 | 17 | 9— 4 | 1 |
| Lee | 45 | 25 | 56 | 383 | 8.5 | 3 | 1— 2 | |
| Garrett | 1 | 0 | 0 | 0 | 0.0 | 0 | 1—100 | |

PUNTING

| Last Name | No | Avg |
|---|---|---|
| Wilson | 63 | 45.1 |
| Carolan | 2 | 50.5 |

KICKING

| Last Name | XP | Att | % | FG | Att | % |
|---|---|---|---|---|---|---|
| Stenerud | 39 | 40 | 98 | 30 | 40 | 75 |

## SAN DIEGO CHARGERS

### RUSHING

| Last Name | No. | Yds | Avg | TD |
|---|---|---|---|---|
| Post | 151 | 758 | 5.0 | 3 |
| Smith | 88 | 426 | 4.8 | 4 |
| Foster | 109 | 394 | 3.6 | 1 |
| Hubbert | 28 | 119 | 4.3 | 2 |
| Allison | 23 | 31 | 1.3 | 0 |
| Alworth | 3 | 18 | 6.0 | 0 |
| Hadl | 23 | 14 | 0.6 | 2 |
| Brittenum | 2 | −4 | −2.0 | 0 |

### RECEIVING

| Last Name | No. | Yds | Avg | TD |
|---|---|---|---|---|
| Alworth | 68 | 1312 | 19 | 10 |
| Garrison | 52 | 1103 | 21 | 10 |
| MacKinnon | 33 | 646 | 20 | 6 |
| Foster | 23 | 224 | 10 | 0 |
| Post | 18 | 165 | 9 | 0 |
| Frazier | 16 | 237 | 15 | 3 |
| Smith | 7 | 71 | 10 | 0 |
| Hubbert | 5 | 11 | 2 | 0 |
| Allison | 2 | 22 | 11 | 0 |
| White | 2 | 18 | 9 | 0 |
| Dyer | 1 | 22 | 22 | 0 |

### PUNT RETURNS

| Last Name | No. | Yds | Avg | TD |
|---|---|---|---|---|
| Duncan | 18 | 206 | 11 | 1 |
| Graham | 13 | 61 | 5 | 0 |
| Smith | 8 | 25 | 3 | 0 |

### KICKOFF RETURNS

| Last Name | No. | Yds | Avg | TD |
|---|---|---|---|---|
| Duncan | 25 | 586 | 23 | 0 |
| Post | 10 | 199 | 20 | 0 |
| Allison | 7 | 121 | 17 | 0 |
| Whitehead | 2 | 81 | 41 | 0 |
| Speights | 1 | 21 | 21 | 0 |
| Smith | 1 | 20 | 20 | 0 |
| Baccaglio | 2 | 0 | 0 | 0 |
| Latzke | 1 | 0 | 0 | 0 |

### PASSING — PUNTING — KICKING

PASSING

| Last Name | Att | Comp | % | Yds | Yd/Att | TD | Int-% | RK |
|---|---|---|---|---|---|---|---|---|
| Hadl | 440 | 208 | 47 | 3473 | 7.9 | 27 | 32— 7 | 5 |
| Brittenum | 17 | 9 | 53 | 125 | 7.4 | 1 | 1— 6 | |
| Foster | 7 | 6 | 86 | 169 | 24.1 | 0 | 0— 0 | |
| Post | 4 | 1 | 25 | 23 | 5.8 | 0 | 0— 0 | |
| Smith | 3 | 0 | 0 | 0 | | 1 | 0— 0 | |
| Allison | 1 | 1 | 100 | 23 | 23.0 | 1 | 0— 0 | |

PUNTING

| Last Name | No | Avg |
|---|---|---|
| Partee | 56 | 40.7 |

KICKING

| Last Name | XP | Att | % | FG | Att | % |
|---|---|---|---|---|---|---|
| Partee | 40 | 43 | 93 | 22 | 32 | 69 |

2 POINT XP
Alworth
MacKinnon

## DENVER BRONCOS

### RUSHING

| Last Name | No. | Yds | Avg | TD |
|---|---|---|---|---|
| Little | 158 | 584 | 3.7 | 3 |
| Briscoe | 41 | 308 | 7.5 | 3 |
| Lynch | 66 | 221 | 3.3 | 4 |
| Ford | 41 | 186 | 4.5 | 1 |
| McCarthy | 28 | 89 | 3.2 | 0 |
| Erwin | 24 | 76 | 3.2 | 0 |
| LeClair | 12 | 40 | 3.3 | 0 |
| Moore | 4 | 22 | 5.5 | 0 |
| Lindsey | 4 | 17 | 4.3 | 0 |
| Van Heusen | 1 | 6 | 6.0 | 0 |
| Tensi | 6 | 2 | 0.3 | 0 |
| Haffner | 2 | 2 | 1.0 | 0 |
| DiVito | 1 | −1 | −1.0 | 0 |
| Jones | 1 | −1 | −1.0 | 0 |

### RECEIVING

| Last Name | No. | Yds | Avg | TD |
|---|---|---|---|---|
| Crabtree | 35 | 601 | 17 | 5 |
| Denson | 34 | 586 | 17 | 5 |
| Beer | 20 | 276 | 14 | 1 |
| Van Heusen | 19 | 353 | 19 | 3 |
| Little | 19 | 331 | 17 | 1 |
| Jones | 13 | 190 | 15 | 2 |
| Haffner | 12 | 232 | 19 | 1 |
| McCarthy | 7 | 69 | 10 | 2 |
| Ford | 6 | 40 | 7 | 0 |
| Lynch | 4 | 52 | 13 | 0 |
| Moore | 3 | 35 | 12 | 0 |
| Erwin | 2 | 21 | 11 | 0 |
| Myrtle | 1 | 18 | 18 | 0 |
| Washington | 1 | 12 | 12 | 0 |

### PUNT RETURNS

| Last Name | No. | Yds | Avg | TD |
|---|---|---|---|---|
| Little | 24 | 261 | 11 | 1 |
| Greer | 9 | 53 | 6 | 0 |
| Luke | 3 | 13 | 4 | 0 |
| Jaquess | 2 | 5 | 3 | 0 |

### KICKOFF RETURNS

| Last Name | No. | Yds | Avg | TD |
|---|---|---|---|---|
| Little | 26 | 649 | 25 | 0 |
| Holloman | 7 | 194 | 28 | 0 |
| Stokes | 5 | 106 | 21 | 0 |
| Garrett | 3 | 77 | 26 | 0 |
| Moore | 4 | 74 | 19 | 0 |
| Lindsey | 3 | 72 | 24 | 0 |
| Erwin | 3 | 55 | 18 | 0 |
| Greer | 2 | 41 | 21 | 0 |
| Luke | 2 | 34 | 17 | 0 |
| Crabtree | 1 | 30 | 30 | 0 |
| Forsberg | 2 | 16 | 8 | 0 |
| Dickey | 1 | 13 | 13 | 0 |
| Jaquess | 1 | 0 | 0 | 0 |

### PASSING — PUNTING — KICKING

PASSING

| Last Name | Att | Comp | % | Yds | Yd/Att | TD | Int-% | RK |
|---|---|---|---|---|---|---|---|---|
| Briscoe | 224 | 93 | 42 | 1589 | 7.1 | 14 | 13— 6 | 7 |
| Tensi | 119 | 48 | 40 | 709 | 6.0 | 5 | 8— 7 | |
| LeClair | 54 | 27 | 50 | 401 | 7.4 | 1 | 5— 9 | |
| McCormick | 19 | 8 | 42 | 89 | 4.7 | 0 | 1— 5 | |
| DiVito | 6 | 1 | 17 | 16 | 2.7 | 0 | 0— 0 | |
| Little | 2 | 0 | 0 | 0 | 0.0 | 0 | 0— 0 | |
| Lynch | 2 | 1 | 50 | 4 | 2.0 | 0 | 0— 0 | |
| Haffner | 1 | 1 | 100 | 18 | 18.0 | 0 | 0— 0 | |

PUNTING

| Last Name | No | Avg |
|---|---|---|
| Van Heusen | 88 | 43.8 |
| DiVito | 8 | 30.3 |

KICKING

| Last Name | XP | Att | % | FG | Att | % |
|---|---|---|---|---|---|---|
| Howfield | 30 | 30 | 100 | 9 | 18 | 50 |
| Humphreys | 1 | 1 | 100 | 1 | 5 | 20 |

## CINCINNATI BENGALS

### RUSHING

| Last Name | No. | Yds | Avg | TD |
|---|---|---|---|---|
| Robinson | 238 | 1023 | 4.3 | 8 |
| E. Johnson | 26 | 178 | 6.8 | 3 |
| Smiley | 63 | 146 | 2.3 | 1 |
| McVea | 9 | 133 | 14.8 | 1 |
| Banks | 34 | 131 | 3.9 | 0 |
| Lamp | 39 | 107 | 2.7 | 0 |
| Wyche | 12 | 74 | 6.2 | 0 |
| Saffold | 1 | 21 | 21.0 | 0 |
| Warren | 4 | 17 | 4.3 | 0 |
| Livingston | 1 | 11 | 11.0 | 0 |
| Keeling | 1 | 10 | 10.0 | 0 |
| Phillips | 1 | 7 | 7.0 | 0 |
| Hunt | 1 | 5 | 5.0 | 0 |
| Washington | 1 | 4 | 4.0 | 0 |
| Sherman | 1 | 3 | 3.0 | 0 |
| Stofa | 10 | 1 | 0.1 | 0 |
| Trumpy | 1 | −1 | −1.0 | 0 |

### RECEIVING

| Last Name | No. | Yds | Avg | TD |
|---|---|---|---|---|
| Trumpy | 37 | 639 | 17 | 3 |
| Sherman | 31 | 374 | 12 | 1 |
| Robinson | 24 | 128 | 5 | 1 |
| McVea | 21 | 264 | 13 | 2 |
| Smiley | 19 | 86 | 5 | 0 |
| Saffold | 16 | 172 | 11 | 0 |
| Lamb | 7 | 87 | 12 | 0 |
| Herock | 6 | 75 | 13 | 0 |
| Banks | 4 | 15 | 4 | 1 |
| E. Johnson | 1 | 33 | 33 | 0 |
| Peterson | 1 | 10 | 10 | 0 |
| Wyche | 1 | 5 | 5 | 0 |

### PUNT RETURNS

| Last Name | No. | Yds | Avg | TD |
|---|---|---|---|---|
| E. Johnson | 22 | 111 | 5 | 0 |
| Spiller | 2 | 51 | 26 | 0 |
| Phillips | 2 | 16 | 8 | 0 |
| Williams | 2 | 14 | 7 | 0 |
| King | 1 | 3 | 3 | 0 |
| Robinson | 1 | 1 | 1 | 0 |

### KICKOFF RETURNS

| Last Name | No. | Yds | Avg | TD |
|---|---|---|---|---|
| McVea | 14 | 310 | 22 | 0 |
| E. Johnson | 14 | 266 | 19 | 0 |
| Banks | 6 | 106 | 18 | 0 |
| Williams | 5 | 112 | 22 | 0 |
| Spiller | 5 | 91 | 18 | 0 |
| Peterson | 3 | 80 | 27 | 0 |
| Robinson | 3 | 58 | 19 | 0 |
| Lamb | 1 | 24 | 24 | 0 |
| Phillips | 1 | 23 | 23 | 0 |
| McClure | 1 | 11 | 11 | 0 |
| Randall | 1 | 11 | 11 | 0 |
| Neidert | 1 | 0 | 0 | 0 |
| Saffold | 1 | 0 | 0 | 0 |

### PASSING — PUNTING — KICKING

PASSING

| Last Name | Att | Comp | % | Yds | Yd/Att | TD | Int-% | RK |
|---|---|---|---|---|---|---|---|---|
| Stofa | 177 | 85 | 48 | 896 | 5.1 | 5 | 5— 3 | 6 |
| Warren | 80 | 47 | 59 | 506 | 6.3 | 1 | 4— 5 | |
| Wyche | 55 | 35 | 64 | 494 | 9.0 | 2 | 2— 4 | |
| Keeling | 1 | 0 | 0 | 0 | 0.0 | 0 | 0— 0 | |

PUNTING

| Last Name | No | Avg |
|---|---|---|
| Livingston | 70 | 43.4 |
| Smith | 8 | 28.8 |
| Keeling | 6 | 28.3 |

KICKING

| Last Name | XP | Att | % | FG | Att | % |
|---|---|---|---|---|---|---|
| Livingston | 20 | 20 | 100 | 13 | 26 | 50 |
| Sherman | 4 | 4 | 100 | 0 | 1 | 0 |

# 1968 Championship Games

## NFL CHAMPIONSHIP GAME
December 29, at Cleveland
(Attendance 80,628)

### Evening a Past Account

The conference playoffs had produced one expected result and one upset. The Baltimore Colts beat the Minnesota Vikings 24-14 as they had been picked to do, but the Cleveland Browns had surprised the Dallas Cowboys by knocking them off 31-20 in Don Meredith's playing farewell.

The Colts and Browns had met for the NFL title four years ago, with the Browns stunning Baltimore with a 27-0 upset. The Colts again were favored this year, but their stifling defense smothered the Cleveland attack and evened the score from 1964.

The Browns had the first scoring opportunity of the game when Don Cockroft attempted a 41-yard field goal, but Bubba Smith blocked the kick. With Bill Nelsen rushed incessantly and Leroy Kelly hounded every time he touched the ball, the Browns rarely crossed into Baltimore territory all afternoon.

The first period ended without a score, but a Lou Michaels field goal gave Baltimore a 3-0 lead early in the second period. With the Colt blockers beating the Cleveland front four regularly, the Colts put together a sixty-yard, ten-play drive which ended in Tom Matte's plunge into the end zone. When the Browns tried to come back with a pass, Mike Curtis intercepted and gave the ball to his offense on the Cleveland 33. Matte ran for twelve yards on the first play, then Jerry Hill carried for nine, and Matte finally covered the last twelve yards with a dodging run through the Cleveland secondary. The halftime score was 17-0, and the Browns looked like a beaten team.

The Colts stuck to the ground in the second half, eating up yardage and time with Matte and Hill running the ball. A time-consuming drive led to Matte's third touchdown of the day in the third quarter, and ten more points in the final period ran the final score up to 34-0. After this one-sided affair ended a quick survey of the press box uncovered not one writer who gave the New York Jets a chance against the Colts in the Super Bowl.

### SCORING

| | | | |
|---|---|---|---|
| CLEVELAND | 0 | 0 | 0–0 |
| BALTIMORE | 0 | 17 | 7 | 10–34 |

Second Quarter
Bal.   Michaels, 28 yard field goal
Bal.   Matte, 1 yard rush
      PAT—Michaels (kick)
Bal.   Matte, 12 yard rush
      PAT—Michaels (kick)

Third Quarter
Bal.   Matte, 2 yard rush
      PAT—Michaels (kick)

Fourth Quarter
Bal.   Michaels, 10 yard field goal
Bal.   Brown, 4 yard run
      PAT—Michaels (Kick)

### TEAM STATISTICS

| CLE. | | BAL. |
|---|---|---|
| 12 | First Downs—Total | 22 |
| 2 | First Downs—Rushing | 13 |
| 8 | First Downs—Passing | 8 |
| 2 | First Downs—Penalty | 1 |
| 2 | Fumbles—Number | 2 |
| 1 | Fumbles—Lost Ball | 1 |
| 7 | Penalties—Number | 3 |
| 54 | Yards Penalized | 15 |
| 2 | Missed Field Goals | 0 |
| 3 | Giveaways | 2 |
| 2 | Takeaways | 3 |
| –1 | Difference | +1 |

### INDIVIDUAL STATISTICS

| CLEVELAND | No | Yds | Avg. | BALTIMORE | No | Yds | Avg. |
|---|---|---|---|---|---|---|---|
| **RUSHING** | | | | | | | |
| Kelly | 13 | 28 | 2.2 | Matte | 17 | 88 | 5.2 |
| Harraway | 6 | 26 | 4.3 | Hill | 11 | 60 | 5.5 |
| Green | 1 | 2 | 2.0 | Brown | 5 | 18 | 3.6 |
| | 20 | 56 | 2.8 | Cole | 3 | 14 | 4.7 |
| | | | | Mackey | 2 | 4 | 2.0 |
| | | | | Morrall | 1 | 0 | 0.0 |
| | | | | | 39 | 184 | 4.7 |
| **RECEIVING** | | | | | | | |
| Harraway | 4 | 40 | 10.0 | Richardson | 3 | 78 | 26.0 |
| Morin | 3 | 41 | 13.7 | Mackey | 2 | 34 | 17.0 |
| Kelly | 3 | 27 | 9.0 | Orr | 2 | 33 | 16.5 |
| Warfield | 2 | 30 | 15.0 | Matte | 2 | 15 | 7.5 |
| Collins | 1 | 13 | 13.0 | Mitchell | 1 | 7 | 7.0 |
| | 13 | 151 | 11.6 | Cole | 1 | 2 | 2.0 |
| | | | | | 11 | 169 | 15.4 |
| **PUNTING** | | | | | | | |
| Cockroft | 5 | | 33.4 | Lee | 2 | | 37.0 |
| **PUNT RETURNS** | | | | | | | |
| Davis | 1 | 4 | 4.0 | Brown | 1 | 0 | 0.0 |
| **KICKOFF RETURNS** | | | | | | | |
| Morrison | 3 | 51 | 19.0 | Pearson | 1 | 21 | 21.0 |
| Davis | 3 | 40 | 13.3 | | | | |
| | 6 | 91 | 15.2 | | | | |
| **INTERCEPTION RETURNS** | | | | | | | |
| Davis | 1 | 0 | 0.0 | Volk | 1 | 26 | 26.0 |
| | | | | Curtis | 1 | 0 | 0.0 |
| | | | | | 2 | 26 | 13.0 |

| CLEVELAND | Att. | Comp. | Comp. Pct. | Yds. | Int. | Yds/ Att. | Yds/ Comp. | Yards Lost Tackled |
|---|---|---|---|---|---|---|---|---|
| **PASSING** | | | | | | | | |
| Nelsen | 26 | 11 | 42.3 | 132 | 2 | 5.1 | 12.0 | |
| Ryan | 6 | 2 | 33.3 | 19 | 0 | 3.3 | 8.5 | |
| | 32 | 13 | 40.6 | 151 | 2 | 4.7 | 11.6 | 4–34 |
| **BALTIMORE** | | | | | | | | |
| Morrall | 25 | 11 | 44.4 | 169 | 1 | 6.8 | 15.4 | 0–0 |

---

## AFL CHAMPIONSHIP GAME
December 29, at New York
(Attendance 62,627)

### Down and Up, but Never Sideways

After beating the Chiefs in a Western Division playoff, the Oakland Raiders came to New York to face the brash, young New York Jets for the AFL title. Joe Namath came out throwing, and after only 3:39 of the opening period, the Jets had scored on a Namath-to-Don Maynard pass. Jim Turner later added a field goal to give the Jets a 10-0 lead after one quarter. Oakland wide receiver Fred Biletnikoff started getting open in the second quarter, however, and Daryle Lamonica hit him with a touchdown pass early in the period. Before the half ended, Jim Turner and George Blanda each kicked a three-pointer to make the score 13-10 in favor of the Jets.

Early in the second half, Lamonica's long bombs to Biletnikoff and Warren Wells gave the Raiders a first down on the New York 6-yard line. Three plays moved the ball only to the 1-yard line, so Blanda kicked a short field goal to knot the score at 13-13.

Late in the third period it was New York's turn to move. Namath mixed his plays well in driving the Jets 80 yards to a touchdown, with the final 20 yards coming on a pass to tight end Pete Lammons. Turner's kick made the count 20-13 with one period left.

The Raiders struck deep into New York territory early in the quarter, but had to settle for another Blanda field goal. Trailing 20-16, the Raiders turned the game around when George Atkinson picked off a Namath pass and returned it 32 yards to the New York 5. Pete Banaszak scored on the next play to put the Raiders ahead for the first time. Less than a minute later, a 52-yard pass play from Namath to Maynard brought the Jets into striking range of the Oakland end zone, and another pass to Maynard took the ball across the goal line and put New York on top 27-23. The Raiders drove right back into New York territory, but the Jets got the ball by recovering a loose lateral pass which the Raiders thought was an incomplete forward pass. After that, the Jets just hung on for their Super Bowl destiny.

### SCORING

| | | | | |
|---|---|---|---|---|
| NEW YORK | 10 | 3 | 7 | 7–27 |
| OAKLAND | 0 | 10 | 3 | 10–23 |

First Quarter
N.Y.   Maynard, 14 yard pass from Namath
      PAT—J. Turner (kick)
N.Y.   J. Turner, 33 yard field goal

Second Quarter
Oak.   Biletnikoff, 29 yard pass from Lamonica
      PAT—Blanda (kick)
N.Y.   J. Turner, 36 yard field goal
Oak.   Blanda, 26 yard field goal

Third Quarter
Oak.   Blanda, 9 yard field goal
N.Y.   Lammons, 20 yard pass from Namath
      PAT—J. Turner (kick)

Fourth Quarter
Oak.   Blanda, 20 yard field goal
Oak.   Banaszak, 4 yard rush
      PAT—Blanda (kick)
N.Y.   Maynard, 6 yard pass from Namath
      PAT—J. Turner (kick)

### TEAM STATISTICS

| N.Y. | | OAK. |
|---|---|---|
| 25 | First Downs—Total | 18 |
| 9 | First Downs—Rushing | 3 |
| 15 | First Downs—Passing | 14 |
| 1 | First Downs—Penalty | 1 |
| 1 | Fumbles—Number | 2 |
| 1 | Fumbles—Lost Ball | 0 |
| 4 | Penalties—Number | 2 |
| 26 | Yards Penalized | 23 |
| 1 | Missed Field Goals | 1 |
| 2 | Giveaways | 0 |
| 0 | Takeaways | 2 |
| –2 | Difference | +2 |

### INDIVIDUAL STATISTICS

| NEW YORK | No | Yds | Avg. | OAKLAND | No | Yds | Avg. |
|---|---|---|---|---|---|---|---|
| **RUSHING** | | | | | | | |
| Snell | 19 | 71 | 3.7 | Dixon | 8 | 42 | 5.3 |
| Boozer | 11 | 51 | 4.6 | Banaszak | 3 | 6 | 2.0 |
| Namath | 1 | 14 | 14.0 | Lamonica | 3 | 1 | 0.3 |
| Mathis | 3 | 8 | 2.7 | Smith | 5 | 1 | 0.2 |
| | 34 | 144 | 4.2 | | 19 | 50 | 2.6 |
| **RECEIVING** | | | | | | | |
| Sauer | 7 | 70 | 10.0 | Biletnikoff | 7 | 190 | 11.2 |
| Maynard | 6 | 118 | 19.7 | Dixon | 5 | 48 | 9.6 |
| Lammons | 4 | 52 | 13.0 | Cannon | 4 | 69 | 17.3 |
| Snell | 1 | 15 | 15.0 | Wells | 3 | 83 | 27.7 |
| Boozer | 1 | 11 | 11.0 | Banaszak | 1 | 11 | 11.0 |
| | 19 | 266 | 14.0 | | 20 | 401 | 20.1 |
| **PUNTING** | | | | | | | |
| Johnson | 10 | | 41.5 | Eischeid | 7 | | 42.7 |
| **PUNT RETURNS** | | | | | | | |
| Baird | 2 | 8 | 4.0 | Atkinson | 2 | 11 | 5.5 |
| Christy | 1 | 0 | 0.0 | Bird | 2 | 6 | 3.0 |
| | 3 | 8 | 2.7 | | 4 | 17 | 4.3 |
| **KICKOFF RETURNS** | | | | | | | |
| Christy | 3 | 86 | 28.7 | Atkinson | 4 | 112 | 28.0 |
| B. Turner | 1 | 24 | 24.0 | Smith | 1 | 17 | 17.0 |
| | 4 | 110 | 27.5 | | 5 | 129 | 25.8 |
| **INTERCEPTION RETURNS** | | | | | | | |
| None | | | | Atkinson | 1 | 32 | 32.0 |

| NEW YORK | Att. | Comp. | Comp. Pct. | Yds. | Int. | Yds/ Att. | Yds/ Comp. | Yards Lost Tackled |
|---|---|---|---|---|---|---|---|---|
| **PASSING** | | | | | | | | |
| Namath | 49 | 19 | 38.8 | 266 | 1 | 5.4 | 14.0 | 10 |
| **OAKLAND** | | | | | | | | |
| Lamonica | 47 | 20 | 42.6 | 401 | 0 | 8.5 | 20.1 | 8 |

150

# The Ironclad Guarantee

When Joe Namath, three days before the game, said, "I think we'll win it; in fact, I'll guarantee it," people snickered. The New York Jets were close to three-touchdown underdogs against the Baltimore Colts, and everyone expected to see the Colts, an establishment NFL team, clobber the long-haired Jets and shut the mouth of their free-spirit quarterback. Coached by Don Shula, the Colts had a feared defense that mixed zone pass coverage and frequent blitzes and a poised offense led by quarterback Earl Morrall, who had substituted spectacularly during the season for the sore-armed Johnny Unitas.

On offense, the Colts did everything in the first half except score. They drove to the New York 20-yard line only to lose the ball on an interception. They recovered a fumble on the New York 12 only to have Lou Michaels miss a close-range field goal. They sprang Tom Matte loose on a 58-yard run only to suffer another interception to kill the drive. The play that typified the Colts' frustration the best came in the second quarter. On a razzle-dazzle play, Earl Morrall handed the ball off, got it back on a lateral, and looked downfield for a receiver. He never noticed Jimmy Orr free in the end zone, so alone that he was jumping up and down and waving his arms to get attention. Morrall instead threw the ball down the middle right into the arms of New York's Jim Hudson.

The Jets, meanwhile, unexpectedly used the off-tackle smash as their main offensive weapon. With Winston Hill leading the way, fullback Matt Snell repeatedly picked up five and six yards through the right side of the Colt line. Whenever the Colts threw their blitz at Namath, he somehow smelled it out and beat it by shooting a quick pass to George Sauer. Mixing his plays well, Namath led the Jets on an 80-yard drive in twelve plays, with Snell carrying the ball into the end zone from the four-yard line. At halftime, the Jets were ahead 7-0.

The script stayed the same in the second half. The Jets ground out the yardage slowly, scoring on three Jim Turner field goals, while Morrall could not get the Colts on the scoreboard. Johnny Unitas, sore arm and all, took over at quarterback in the final period, and although he drove the Colts to a touchdown, it was too little too late. The Jets had won the Super Bowl 16-7; the AFL had finally triumphed.

| NEW YORK JETS | | BALTIMORE |
|---|---|---|
| **OFFENSE** | | |
| Sauer | LE | Orr |
| W. Hill | LT | Vogel |
| Talamini | LG | Ressler |
| Schmitt | C | Curry |
| Rasmussen | RG | Sullivan |
| Herman | RT | Ball |
| Lammons | TE | Mackey |
| Namath | QB | Morrall |
| Maynard | FL | W. Richardson |
| Boozer | RB | Matte |
| Snell | RB | J. Hill |
| **DEFENSE** | | |
| Philbin | LE | B. Smith |
| Rochester | LT | B. R. Smith |
| Elliot | RT | Miller |
| Biggs | RE | Braase |
| Baker | LLB | Curtis |
| Atkinson | MLB | Gaubatz |
| Grantham | RLB | Shinnick |
| Sample | LHB | Boyd |
| Beverly | RHB | Lyles |
| Hudson | LS | Logan |
| Baird | FS | Volk |

**SUBSTITUTES**

**NEW YORK**

*Offense*

| | |
|---|---|
| Crane | J. Richardson |
| Mathis | Smolinski |
| Parilli | B. Turner |
| Rademacher | Walton |

*Defense*

| | |
|---|---|
| Christy | McAdams |
| D'Amato | Neidert |
| Dockery | Richards |
| Gordon | Thompson |

*Kickers*

| | |
|---|---|
| Johnson | J. Turner |

**BALTIMORE**

*Offense*

| | |
|---|---|
| Brown | Pearson |
| Cole | Perkins |
| Hawkins | Szymanski |
| Johnson | Unitas |
| Mitchell | J. Williams |

*Defense*

| | |
|---|---|
| Austin | Porter |
| Hilton | Stukes |
| Michaels | S. Williams |

*Kicker*

Lee

## SCORING

| | |  |  |
|---|---|---|---|
| NEW YORK JETS | 0 7 6 3—16 | | |
| BALTIMORE | 0 0 0 7— 7 | | |

**Second Quarter**

| | | |
|---|---|---|
| N.Y. Snell, 4 yard rush | | 5:57 |
| PAT — Turner (kick) | | |

**Third Quarter**

| | | |
|---|---|---|
| N.Y. Turner, 32 yd field goal | | 4:52 |
| N.Y. Turner, 30 yd field goal | | 11:02 |

**Fourth Quarter**

| | | |
|---|---|---|
| N.Y. Turner, 9 yard field goal | | 1:34 |
| Balt. Hill, 1 yard rush | | 11:41 |
| PAT — Michaels (kick) | | |

## TEAM STATISTICS

| N.Y. | | BALT. |
|---|---|---|
| 21 | First Downs — Total | 18 |
| 10 | First Downs — Rushing | 7 |
| 10 | First Downs — Passing | 9 |
| 1 | First Downs — Penalty | 2 |
| 1 | Fumbles — Number | 1 |
| 1 | Fumbles — Lost Ball | 1 |
| 5 | Penalties — Number | 3 |
| 28 | Yards Penalized | 23 |
| 74 | Total Offensive Plays | 64 |
| 337 | Total Net Yards | 324 |
| 4.6 | Average Gain | 5.1 |
| 2 | Field Goals Missed | 2 |
| 1 | Giveaways | 5 |
| 5 | Takeaways | 1 |
| +4 | Difference | −4 |

## INDIVIDUAL STATISTICS

| NEW YORK JETS | No | Yds | Avg. | BALTIMORE | No | Yds | Avg. |
|---|---|---|---|---|---|---|---|
| **RUSHING** | | | | | | | |
| Snell | 30 | 121 | 4.0 | Matte | 11 | 116 | 10.5 |
| Boozer | 10 | 19 | 1.9 | Hill | 9 | 29 | 3.2 |
| Mathis | 3 | 2 | 0.7 | Unitas | 1 | 0 | 0.0 |
| | 43 | 142 | 3.3 | Morrall | 2 | −2 | −1.0 |
| | | | | | 23 | 143 | 6.2 |
| **RECEIVING** | | | | | | | |
| Sauer | 8 | 133 | 16.6 | Richardson | 6 | 58 | 9.7 |
| Snell | 4 | 40 | 10.0 | Orr | 3 | 42 | 14.0 |
| Mathis | 3 | 20 | 6.7 | Mackey | 3 | 35 | 11.7 |
| Lammons | 2 | 13 | 6.5 | Matte | 2 | 30 | 15.0 |
| | 17 | 206 | 12.1 | Hill | 2 | 1 | 0.5 |
| | | | | Mitchell | 1 | 15 | 15.0 |
| | | | | | 17 | 181 | 10.6 |
| **PUNTING** | | | | | | | |
| Johnson | 4 | | 38.8 | Lee | 3 | | 44.3 |
| **PUNT RETURNS** | | | | | | | |
| Baird | 1 | 0 | 0.0 | Brown | 4 | 34 | 8.5 |
| **KICKOFF RETURNS** | | | | | | | |
| Christy | 1 | 25 | 25.0 | Pearson | 2 | 59 | 29.5 |
| | | | | Brown | 2 | 45 | 22.5 |
| | | | | | 4 | 104 | 26.0 |
| **INTERCEPTION RETURNS** | | | | | | | |
| Beverly | 2 | 0 | 0.0 | None | | | |
| Hudson | 1 | 9 | 9.0 | | | | |
| Sample | 1 | 0 | 0.0 | | | | |
| | 4 | 9 | 2.3 | | | | |

| NEW YORK | Att | Comp | Comp Pct. | Yds | Int | Yds/ Att. | Yds/ Comp | Yards Lost Tackled |
|---|---|---|---|---|---|---|---|---|
| **PASSING** | | | | | | | | |
| Namath | 28 | 17 | 60.7 | 206 | 0 | 7.4 | 12.1 | 2—11 |
| Parilli | 1 | 0 | 0.0 | 0 | 0 | — | — | 0 |
| | 29 | 17 | 58.6 | 206 | 0 | 7.1 | 12.1 | 2—11 |
| **BALTIMORE** | | | | | | | | |
| Morrall | 17 | 6 | 35.3 | 71 | 3 | 4.2 | 11.8 | 0 |
| Unitas | 24 | 11 | 45.8 | 110 | 1 | 4.6 | 10.0 | 0 |
| | 41 | 17 | 41.5 | 181 | 4 | 4.4 | 10.6 | 0 |

# 1969 N.F.L. Equalizing the Competition

It took a thirty-five-hour, forty-five minute meeting to do it, but the NFL came up with a blueprint for next year's merger of the two leagues. Commissioner Pete Rozelle announced on May 17 that both leagues would be part of the NFL next year and that the Baltimore Colts, Cleveland Browns, and Pittsburgh Steelers had agreed to join the present ten AFL clubs in the American Conference, while the thirteen remaining old-line NFL clubs would form the National Conference. Each conference would be parted into Eastern, Central, and Western divisions, and interconference play would begin in the regular season. In other words, this would be the last year in which the NFL and AFL would be separate, distinctive entries.

## EASTERN CONFERENCE—CAPITAL DIVISION

**Dallas Cowboys—** Don Meredith and Don Perkins both retired this year, but the Cowboys came up with an entire new backfield and kept on winning without a hitch. Craig Morton moved up into the starting quarterback spot, Walt Garrison, a rodeo cowboy in the summer, took over at fullback, and rookie Calvin Hill, a product of the Ivy League, led the league in rushing all season only to lose the title when sidelined with an injury for the final game of the year. All the other parts of the Cowboy machine were in fine order. Bob Hayes and Lance Rentzel provided speed at wide receiver, the offensive line was both strong and deep, and the defense pressured quarterbacks unmercifully whenever they attempted to pass.

**Washington Redskins—**In search of new challenges, Vince Lombardi packed his bags and moved to Washington as the head coach and general manager of the Redskins. The results were immediate, as the Skins had their first winning season since 1955. Lombardi had a good passing attack left over from the previous regime, and he constructed a solid running game with rookie halfback Larry Brown and ex-Brown fullback Charlie Harraway. On defense, Lombardi concentrated on the pass defense, rigging up a tight secondary of Pat Fischer, Mike Bass, Brig Owens, and Rickie Harris.

**New Orleans Saints—**Billy Kilmer was no glamorous quarterback, but he was a fine leader who moved the team well. The strength of the attack was the stable of receivers; Dan Abramowicz, Al Dodd, and Dave Parks had few peers as a group. Coach Tom Fears added a running game to the offense by coming up with Andy Livingston and Tony Baker as his new running backs. Livingston came over from the Bears, and Baker came off of last year's taxi squad; both ran with power and speed. The defense was a trouble area, although tackles Dave Rowe and Mike Tilleman played well.

**Philadelphia Eagles—**The Eagles began a rebuilding program under the new leadership of general manager Pete Retzlaff and head coach Jerry Williams this year. The team still finished in last place, but emphasis was placed on developing young players for the future. Williams gave plenty of playing time to rookies Leroy Keyes, Ernie Calloway, and Bill Bradley, and young veterans like Ben Hawkins, Harold Jackson, Mike Evans, Gary Pettigrew, and Tim Rossovich all were handed full-time starting jobs.

## CENTURY DIVISION

**Cleveland Browns—**The Browns were loaded with offensive talent, such as quarterback Bill Nelsen, runner Leroy Kelly, receivers Gary Collins, Paul Warfield, and Milt Morin, and blockers Dick Schafrath and Gene Hickerson. The defense, however, featured several young Turks amidst some overage and mediocre players. Jack Gregory developed into a strong pass-rusher toward the end of the season, rookie Walt Sumner filled in well for the injured Ben Davis at cornerback, and Ernie Kellerman kept up his good work at strong safety, but problems arose at middle linebacker, where Dale Lindsey was barely adequate, and cornerback, where thirty-four-year-old Erich Barnes was playing on borrowed time.

**New York Giants—**When the Giants lost all their pre-season games, owner Wellington Mara canned coach Allie Sherman, long-term contract and all, and elevated assistant Alex Webster. The Giants responded by beating the Vikings. Things leveled off after that, with the Giants winning some and losing some as befits a mediocre team. One of the biggest enigmas of the year was Homer Jones, who found his way into the end zone only once all year.

**St. Louis Cardinals—**Injuries to Jerry Stovall, Bob Atkins, and Jamie Rivers made the Cards vulnerable to the pass; the New Orleans Saints exploited this weakness to win a 52-41 decision. The offense could produce points in a hurry, with a good line, good receivers in John Gilliam, Dave Williams, and Jackie Smith and powerful runners in Cid Edwards and Johnny Roland. Charley Johnson and Jim Hart split the quarterbacking chores, but neither could provide leadership.

**Pittsburgh Steelers—**New head coach Chuck Noll won only one game all year but still felt that progress was made in several areas. The defensive line was upgraded by ferocious rookie tackle Joe Greene, the secondary found a hard-hitting safety in Chuck Beatty, and the offensive line improved with the development of young veterans Larry Gagner, Bruce Van Dyke, and Ray Mansfield. Noll also got good seasons out of veterans Roy Jefferson, Ben McGee, and Andy Russell but was disappointed by a poor rookie season for Terry Hanratty.

## WESTERN CONFERENCE — CENTRAL DIVISION

**Minnesota Vikings—**Although the heart of the Vikings was their defense, the biggest star on the team was a quarterback who had problems passing. Joe Kapp, whose passes wobbled ominously but often found the mark, set the tone of the Vikings with actions, such as his scrambling runs which included hurdling over defenders and bulling through tacklers. The Viking attack was unrelenting but unspectacular, leading the league in points scored primarily because the defense kept giving it the ball.

**Detroit Lions—**Just as when he had played, coach Joe Schmidt's Lions relied on the defense to carry the club. The front four was anchored by Alex Karras, the linebacking trio of Paul Naumoff, Mike Lucci, and Wayne Walker combined mobility and strength, and cornerbacks Lem Barney and Dick LeBeau made passing a difficult task for enemy quarterbacks. The Lion quarterback situation was unsettled, however, as Bill Munson and Greg Landry split the job with indifferent results, and injuries to Mel Farr and Nick Eddy hurt the running game.

**Green Bay Packers—**The Packers remained a tough team despite several problems. Bart Starr missed the last four games with a shoulder injury, Jerry Kramer and Bob Skoronski retired, and age was creeping up on the defensive line. The most damaging deficiency, however, was the lack of a reliable place-kicker. Coach Phil Bengtson started the year with Mike Mercer, who hit on only five of seventeen field-goal attempts, and then switched to Booth Lusteg, whose one-for-five record was no improvement.

**Chicago Bears—**Gale Sayers recaptured his old form after a hesitant start and rocketed to the NFL rushing crown. Outside of that, the Bears endured a campaign of unbroken gloom. The team lost its first seven games, beat the just as miserable Pittsburgh Steelers, then went on to lose their last six games. Coach Jim Dooley juggled his quarterbacks to get some life into the passing attack, but all he got for his troubles were some unhappy passers. Jack Concannon started the year at the controls, but when he couldn't move the team, Dooley put rookie Bobby Douglass into the lineup.

## COASTAL DIVISION

**Los Angeles Rams—**Old pros like Deacon Jones, Merlin Olsen, Jack Pardee, Maxie Baughan, Clancy Williams, and Eddie Meador made few errors on defense, the hallmark of a George Allen team, and the Roman Gabriel-led offense rarely turned the ball over without holding onto it for a stretch. Operating behind a superb line of Bob Brown, Charlie Cowan, Tom Mack, Joe Scibelli, and Ken Iman, Gabriel ground out yardage with handoffs to rookie Larry Smith, Les Josephson, and Tommy Mason and with quick passes to Jack Snow, Wendell Tucker, and Billy Truax. The Rams' ball-control tactics worked so well that they won their first eleven games.

**Baltimore Colts—**The ill omen of their Super Bowl defeat followed the Colts through this season. Ordell Braase, Don Shinnick, and Bobby Boyd retired after the loss to the Jets, and Jerry Hill, Terry Cole, Willie Richardson, John Mackey, Lou Michaels, Dennis Gaubatz, and Lenny Lyles suffered through sub-par seasons. Thus, one year after winning the NFL championship, the Colts had a completely different look. Ted Hendricks, Roy Hilton, Bob Grant, Charlie Stukes, and Tommy Maxwell were new starters on defense, with Mike Curtis having to learn the middle linebacker spot. Johnny Unitas reclaimed the quarterback position but showed little fire.

**Atlanta Falcons—**Coach Norm Van Brocklin fielded two strong defensive ends in Claude Humphrey and John Zook, a top cornerback in Ken Reaves, a good tight end in Jim Mitchell, and a potential All-Pro tackle in George Kunz. One of Van Brocklin's biggest problems, however, was that his offensive line, with four rookie starters, could not pass-block.

**San Francisco '49ers—**Injuries cut down Kevin Hardy, John Brodie, Stan Hindman, Ed Beard, and Johnny Fuller, retirement erased Matt Hazeltine, and the '49ers fell back into the basement in the Coastal Division. Coach Dick Nolan had veteran talent in such as Ken Willard, Elmer Collett, Charlie Krueger, Dave Wilcox, Jim Johnson, and mid-season pickup Rosey Taylor, and he had rookie talent in Gene Washington, Skip Vanderbundt, Ted Kwalick, and Earl Edwards, but the '49ers persisted as one of pro football's top enigmas.

## FINAL TEAM STATISTICS — OFFENSE

| | ATL. | BALT. | CHI. | CLEV. | DALL. | DET. | G.B. | L.A. | MINN. | N.O. | N.Y. | PHIL. | PITT. | ST.L. | S.F. | WASH. |
|---|---|---|---|---|---|---|---|---|---|---|---|---|---|---|---|---|
| **FIRST DOWNS:** Total | 209 | 255 | 237 | 250 | 275 | 198 | 242 | 209 | 239 | 282 | 235 | 231 | 210 | 224 | 253 | 256 |
| by Rushing | 97 | 99 | 120 | 97 | 133 | 83 | 95 | 75 | 102 | 93 | 91 | 83 | 81 | 83 | 84 | 84 |
| by Passing | 89 | 140 | 97 | 138 | 125 | 93 | 122 | 114 | 117 | 158 | 133 | 132 | 115 | 125 | 153 | 149 |
| by Penalty | 23 | 16 | 20 | 15 | 17 | 22 | 25 | 20 | 20 | 31 | 11 | 16 | 14 | 16 | 16 | 23 |
| **RUSHING:** Number | 455 | 417 | 462 | 447 | 532 | 474 | 432 | 382 | 489 | 399 | 397 | 395 | 400 | 382 | 391 | 377 |
| Yards | 2058 | 1490 | 2078 | 1788 | 2276 | 1755 | 1692 | 1413 | 1850 | 1705 | 1593 | 1563 | 1542 | 1446 | 1536 | 1532 |
| Average Yards | 4.5 | 3.5 | 4.5 | 4.0 | 4.3 | 3.7 | 3.9 | 3.7 | 3.8 | 4.3 | 4.0 | 4.0 | 3.8 | 3.9 | 3.9 | 4.1 |
| Touchdowns | 9 | 16 | 14 | 17 | 17 | 11 | 11 | 11 | 15 | 12 | 11 | 10 | 8 | 17 | 13 | 11 |
| **PASSING:** Attempts | 282 | 384 | 378 | 355 | 355 | 329 | 416 | 346 | 453 | 435 | 458 | 391 | 430 | 496 | 444 |
| Completions | 149 | 225 | 199 | 189 | 165 | 182 | 222 | 176 | 245 | 234 | 216 | 176 | 216 | 278 | 275 |
| Completion Percentage | 52.8 | 50.3 | 52.6 | 53.2 | 50.2 | 53.4 | 54.1 | 50.9 | 53.8 | 47.2 | 50.2 | 56.0 | 61.9 |
| Passing Yards | 2230 | 3143 | 2830 | 2929 | 1958 | 2678 | 2498 | 2974 | 3076 | 3022 | 2940 | 3379 | 3106 |

| | MINN. | L.A. | G.B. | DET. | CLEV. | DALL. | CHI. | BALT. | ATL. | N.O. | N.Y. | PHIL. | PITT. | ST.L. | S.F. | WASH. |
|---|---|---|---|---|---|---|---|---|---|---|---|---|---|---|---|---|

---

## FINAL TEAM STATISTICS — DEFENSE

| | ATL. | BALT. | CHI. | CLEV. | DALL. | DET. | G.B. | L.A. | MINN. | N.O. | N.Y. | PHIL. | PITT. | ST.L. | S.F. | WASH. |
|---|---|---|---|---|---|---|---|---|---|---|---|---|---|---|---|---|
| **FIRST DOWNS:** Total | 254 | 256 | 208 | 257 | 203 | 182 | 224 | 242 | 158 | 242 | 243 | 268 | 260 | 289 | 242 | 277 |
| by Rushing | 120 | 70 | 89 | 120 | 52 | 64 | 103 | 84 | 55 | 88 | 120 | 111 | 101 | 83 | 91 | 149 |
| by Passing | 120 | 164 | 98 | 121 | 141 | 101 | 107 | 125 | 88 | 131 | 103 | 136 | 142 | 185 | 128 | 110 |
| by Penalty | 14 | 22 | 21 | 16 | 10 | 17 | 14 | 33 | 15 | 23 | 20 | 17 | 17 | 21 | 23 | 18 |

---

## CONFERENCE PLAYOFFS

### SCORING

```
MINNESOTA       7   0   7   9-23
LOS ANGELES     7  10   0   3-20
```

First Quarter
LA  Klein, 3 yard pass from Gabriel
    PAT—Gossett (kick)
Mn. Osborn, 1 yard rush
    PAT—Cox (kick)

Second Quarter
LA  Gossett, 20 yard field goal
LA  Truax, 2 yard pass from Gabriel
    PAT—Gossett (kick)

Third Quarter
Mn. Osborn, 1 yard rush
    PAT—Cox (kick)

Fourth Quarter
LA  Gossett, 27 yard field goal
Mn. Kapp, 2 yard rush
    PAT—Cox (kick)
Mn. Eller, Safety-tackled Gabriel in
    end zone.

### TEAM STATISTICS

| | MINN. | L.A. |
|---|---|---|
| First Downs—Total | 18 | 19 |
| First Downs—Rushing | 7 | 10 |
| First Downs—Passing | 10 | 9 |
| First Downs—Penalty | 1 | 0 |
| Times Tackled Passing | 2 | 0 |
| Yards Lost—Tackled | 18 | 21 |
| Fumbles—Number | 3 | 0 |
| Fumbles—Lost Ball | 1 | 0 |
| Penalties—Number | 4 | 0 |
| Punts—Number | 36 | 37 |
| Punts—Average Distance | 39.3 | 36.3 |
| Punt Returns—Number | 3 | 8 |
| Punt Returns—Yards | | |
| Kickoff Returns—Number | 6 | 1 |
| Interception Returns—Number | 0 | 2 |
| Interception Returns—Yards | 0 | 69 |
| Missed Field Goals | 1 | 2 |
| Giveaways | 3 | 1 |
| Takeaways | 1 | 3 |
| Difference | -2 | +2 |

### INDIVIDUAL STATISTICS

**MINNESOTA**

RUSHING
| | No | Yds | Avg. |
|---|---|---|---|
| Kapp | 11 | 60 | 5.5 |
| Osborn | 4 | 26 | 6.5 |
| Brown | 4 | 22 | 5.5 |
| Reed | 10 | 16 | 1.6 |
| | 29 | 126 | 4.2 |

RECEIVING
| | No | Yds | Avg. |
|---|---|---|---|
| Washington | 4 | 90 | 22.5 |
| Henderson | 4 | 68 | 17.0 |
| Brown | 2 | 20 | 10.0 |
| Reed | 2 | 18 | 9.0 |

PASSING
| | Att. | Cmp. | Pct. | Yds. | Int. | Yd/A | Yd/C |
|---|---|---|---|---|---|---|---|
| MINN. Kapp | 19 | 12 | 63.2 | 196 | 2 | 10.3 | 16.3 |

**LOS ANGELES**

RUSHING
| | No | Yds | Avg. |
|---|---|---|---|
| Smith | 7 | 42 | 6.0 |
| Gabriel | 13 | 30 | 2.3 |
| Ellison | 8 | 22 | 2.8 |
| Mason | 1 | 3 | 3.3 |
| | 29 | 97 | |

RECEIVING
| | No | Yds | Avg. |
|---|---|---|---|
| Josephson | 4 | | |
| Smith | 6 | | |
| Tucker | 2 | | |
| Klein | 2 | 196 | 16.3 |

PASSING
| | Att. | Cmp. | Pct. | Yds. | Int. | Yd/A | Yd/C |
|---|---|---|---|---|---|---|---|
| L.A. Gabriel | 32 | 22 | 62.5 | 150 | 1 | 4.7 | 6.8 |

---

## December 28, at Dallas (Attendance 69,321)

### SCORING

```
DALLAS       0   0   0   7-14
CLEVELAND    7  10   7  14-38
```

First Quarter
Cle. Scott, 2 yard rush
     PAT—Cockroft (kick)

Second Quarter
Cle. Morin, 6 yard pass from Nelsen
     PAT—Cockroft (kick)
Cle. Cockroft, 29 field goal

Third Quarter
Cle. Scott, 2 yard rush
     PAT—Cockroft (kick)

Fourth Quarter
Cle. Morton, 2 yard rush
     PAT—Clark (kick)
Cle. Sumner, 88 yard interception
     return   PAT—Cockroft (kick)
Dal. Rentzel, 5 yard pass from Staubach
     PAT—Clark (kick)

### TEAM STATISTICS

| | DAL. | CLE. |
|---|---|---|
| First Downs—Total | 17 | 22 |
| First Downs—Rushing | 6 | 7 |
| First Downs—Passing | 9 | 7 |
| First Downs—Penalty | 2 | 1 |
| Times Tackled Passing | 6 | 7 |
| Yards Lost—Tackled | 19 | 7 |
| Fumbles—Number | 1 | 0 |
| Fumbles—Lost Ball | 0 | 6 |
| Penalties—Number | 8 | 50 |
| Yards Penalized | 51 | 1 |
| Punts—Number | 5 | 4 |
| Punts—Average Distance | 36.2 | 34.0 |
| Punt Returns—Number | 5 | 1 |
| Punt Returns—Yards | 106 | 123 |
| Kickoff Returns—Number | 0 | 1 |
| Interception Returns—Number | 0 | 3 |
| Interception Returns—Yards | 0 | 56 |
| Giveaways | 3 | |
| Difference | -3 | +3 |

### INDIVIDUAL

**DALLAS**

RUSHING
| | No | Yds | Avg. |
|---|---|---|---|
| Garrison | 9 | 49 | 5.4 |
| Staubach | 3 | 22 | 7.3 |
| Hill | 4 | 12 | 3.0 |
| Shy | 2 | 0 | 0.0 |
| | 25 | 100 | |

RECEIVING
| | No | Yds | Avg. |
|---|---|---|---|
| Hayes | 4 | 44 | 11.0 |
| Rentzel | 3 | 41 | 13.7 |
| Garrison | 2 | 15 | 7.5 |
| Hill | 2 | 26 | 13.0 |
| Reeves | 1 | 3 | 3.0 |

PASSING
| | Att. | Cmp. | Pct. | Yds. | Int. | Yd/A | Yd/C |
|---|---|---|---|---|---|---|---|
| DALLAS Morton | 24 | 8 | 33.3 | 92 | 2 | 3.8 | 11.5 |
| Staubach | 5 | 4 | 80.0 | 44 | 0 | 8.8 | 11.0 |
| CLEVE. Nelsen | 27 | 18 | 66.7 | 35 | 0 | | 17.5 |
| Rhome | 2 | 2 | 100.0 | 254 | 0 | 69.0 | 12.7 |

**CLEVELAND**

RUSHING
| | No | Yds | Avg. |
|---|---|---|---|
| Kelly | 19 | 66 | 3.5 |
| Scott | 11 | 33 | 3.0 |
| Cockroft | 2 | -5 | -2.5 |
| Johnson | 35 | 97 | 2.8 |

RECEIVING
| | No | Yds | Avg. |
|---|---|---|---|
| Warfield | 8 | 99 | 11.4 |
| Morin | 4 | 52 | 13.0 |
| Collins | 2 | 19 | 9.5 |
| Kelly | 2 | 10 | 5.0 |
| Morrison | 1 | 18 | 18.0 |
| Jones | 1 | 17 | 17.0 |
| | 20 | 254 | 12.7 |

| Scores of Each Game | Use Name | Pos. | Hgt | Wgt | Age | Int | Pts |
|---|---|---|---|---|---|---|---|

## CAPITOL DIVISION

### DALLAS COWBOYS 11-2-1 Tom Landry

| Scores | | | Use Name | Pos. | Hgt | Wgt | Age | Int | Pts |
|---|---|---|---|---|---|---|---|---|---|
| 24 | ST. LOUIS | 3 | Tony Liscio | OT | 6'5" | 255 | 29 | | |
| 21 | New Orleans | 17 | Ralph Neely | OT | 6'5" | 265 | 25 | | |
| 38 | Philadelphia | 7 | Rayfield Wright | TE-OT | 6'7" | 250 | 24 | | |
| 24 | Atlanta | 17 | John Niland | OG | 6'4" | 245 | 25 | | |
| 49 | PHILADELPHIA | 14 | Blaine Nye | OG | 6'4" | 250 | 23 | | |
| 25 | NEW YORK | 3 | John Wilbur | OG | 6'3" | 240 | 26 | | |
| 10 | Cleveland | 42 | Dave Manders | C | 6'2" | 250 | 27 | | |
| 33 | NEW ORLEANS | 17 | Malcolm Walker | C | 6'4" | 250 | 26 | | |
| 41 | Washington | 28 | George Andrie | DE | 6'7" | 250 | 29 | | 2 |
| 23 | Los Angeles | 24 | Larry Cole | DE | 6'4" | 255 | 22 | 1 | 6 |
| 24 | SAN FRANCISCO | 24 | Halvor Hagen | OT-DE | 6'5" | 250 | 24 | | |
| 10 | Pittsburgh | 7 | Ron East | DT | 6'4" | 242 | 26 | | |
| 27 | BALTIMORE | 10 | Bob Lilly | DT | 6'4" | 260 | 30 | | 6 |
| 20 | WASHINGTON | 10 | Jethro Pugh | DT | 6'6" | 260 | 25 | | |

| Use Name | Pos. | Hgt | Wgt | Age | Int | Pts |
|---|---|---|---|---|---|---|
| Jackie Burkett | LB | 6'4" | 228 | 32 | | |
| Dave Edwards | LB | 6'3" | 228 | 30 | 1 | |
| Chuck Howley | LB | 6'3" | 225 | 33 | 2 | |
| Lee Roy Jordan | LB | 6'2" | 220 | 28 | 2 | |
| Tom Stincic | LB | 6'2" | 226 | 22 | | |
| Fred Whittingham | LB | 6'1" | 240 | 30 | | |
| Otto Brown | DB | 6'1" | 188 | 22 | 1 | |
| Phil Clark | DB | 6'2" | 210 | 24 | 2 | |
| Mike Gaechter | DB | 6' | 190 | 29 | 3 | |
| Cornell Green | DB | 6'4" | 208 | 29 | 2 | |
| Mike Johnson | DB | 5'10" | 184 | 25 | | |
| Mel Renfro | DB | 6' | 190 | 27 | 10 | |

D. D. Lewis — Military Service
Willie Townes — Injury

| Use Name | Pos. | Hgt | Wgt | Age | Int | Pts |
|---|---|---|---|---|---|---|
| Bob Belden | QB | 6'2" | 210 | 22 | | |
| Craig Morton | QB | 6'4" | 214 | 26 | | 6 |
| Roger Staubach | QB | 6'2" | 195 | 27 | | 6 |
| Craig Baynham | HB | 6'1" | 206 | 25 | | |
| Calvin Hill | HB | 6'3" | 230 | 22 | | 48 |
| Les Shy | HB | 6'1" | 200 | 25 | | 12 |
| Dan Reeves | FB-HB | 6'1" | 200 | 25 | | 30 |
| Walt Garrison | FB | 6' | 205 | 25 | | 12 |
| Claxton Welch | HB-FB | 5'11" | 200 | 22 | | |
| Bobby Joe Conrad | WR | 6' | 195 | 34 | | |
| Richmond Flowers | WR | 6' | 183 | 22 | | |
| Bob Hayes | WR | 5'11" | 185 | 26 | | 24 |
| Dennis Homan | WR | 6'1" | 180 | 23 | | |
| Lance Rentzel | WR | 6'2" | 202 | 25 | | 78 |
| Mike Ditka | TE | 6'3" | 225 | 29 | | 18 |
| Pettis Norman | TE | 6'3" | 220 | 29 | | 18 |
| Mike Clark | K | 6'1" | 205 | 28 | | 103 |
| Ron Widby | K | 6'4" | 210 | 24 | | |

### WASHINGTON REDSKINS 7-5-2 Vince Lombardi

| Scores | | | Use Name | Pos. | Hgt | Wgt | Age | Int | Pts |
|---|---|---|---|---|---|---|---|---|---|
| 26 | New Orleans | 20 | Walt Rock | OT | 6'5" | 255 | 28 | | |
| 23 | Cleveland | 27 | Jim Snowden | OT | 6'3" | 255 | 27 | | |
| 17 | San Francisco | 17 | Ray Schoenke | C-OT | 6'3" | 250 | 27 | | |
| 33 | ST. LOUIS | 17 | Willie Banks | OG | 6'2" | 237 | 23 | | |
| 20 | NEW YORK | 14 | Steve Duich | OG | 6'3" | 248 | 23 | | |
| 14 | Pittsburgh | 7 | Vince Promuto | OG | 6'1" | 245 | 31 | | |
| 17 | Baltimore | 41 | Dave Crossan | C | 6'3" | 245 | 29 | | |
| 28 | PHILADELPHIA | 28 | Len Hauss | C | 6'2" | 235 | 27 | | |
| 28 | DALLAS | 41 | Leo Carroll | DE | 6'7" | 250 | 25 | | |
| 27 | ATLANTA | 20 | John Hoffman | DE | 6'7" | 260 | 26 | | 6 |
| 13 | LOS ANGELES | 24 | Carl Kammerer | DE | 6'3" | 243 | 32 | | |
| 34 | Philadelphia | 29 | Clark Miller | DE | 6'5" | 246 | 30 | | |
| 17 | NEW ORLEANS | 14 | Frank Bosch | DT | 6'4" | 246 | 23 | | |
| 10 | Dallas | 20 | Dennis Crane | DT | 6'6" | 260 | 24 | | |
| | | | Spain Musgrave | DT | 6'4" | 275 | 24 | | |
| | | | Jim Norton | DT | 6'4" | 254 | 26 | | |
| | | | Joe Rutgens | DT | 6'2" | 255 | 30 | | |

| Use Name | Pos. | Hgt | Wgt | Age | Int | Pts |
|---|---|---|---|---|---|---|
| Chris Hanburger | LB | 6'2" | 218 | 28 | | 6 |
| Sam Huff | LB | 6'1" | 230 | 34 | 3 | 6 |
| Marlin McKeever | LB | 6'1" | 235 | 29 | 2 | |
| Harold McLinton | LB | 6'2" | 235 | 22 | | |
| Tom Roussel | LB | 6'3" | 235 | 22 | | |
| John Didion | C-LB | 6'4" | 245 | 21 | | |
| Mike Bass | DB | 6' | 190 | 24 | 3 | |
| Tom Brown | DB | 6'1" | 195 | 28 | | |
| Pat Fischer | DB | 5'10" | 170 | 29 | 2 | |
| Rickie Harris | DB | 6' | 182 | 26 | 4 | 6 |
| Brig Owens | DB | 5'11" | 190 | 26 | 3 | |
| Ted Vactor | DB | 6' | 185 | 25 | | |
| Bob Wade | DB | 6'2" | 200 | 24 | | |

| Use Name | Pos. | Hgt | Wgt | Age | Int | Pts |
|---|---|---|---|---|---|---|
| Sonny Jurgensen | QB | 5'11" | 203 | 35 | | 6 |
| Frank Ryan | QB | 6'3" | 207 | 33 | | |
| Jerry Allen | HB | 6'1" | 200 | 28 | | |
| Larry Brown | HB | 5'11" | 195 | 21 | | 24 |
| Dave Kopay | FB-HB | 6'2" | 225 | 27 | | |
| Henry Dyer | FB | 6'2" | 230 | 24 | | 6 |
| Charlie Harraway | FB | 6'3" | 220 | 26 | | 54 |
| Chuck Mercein | FB | 6'3" | 232 | 26 | | |
| Gary Beban | WR | 6'1" | 195 | 23 | | |
| Bob Long | WR | 6'3" | 205 | 28 | | 6 |
| Walter Roberts | WR | 5'10" | 163 | 27 | | |
| Charley Taylor | WR | 6'3" | 210 | 28 | | 48 |
| Pat Richter | TE | 6'5" | 230 | 28 | | |
| Jerry Smith | TE | 6'2" | 208 | 26 | | 54 |
| Mike Bragg | K | 5'11" | 186 | 22 | | |
| Curt Knight | K | 6'1" | 190 | 26 | | 83 |

### NEW ORLEANS SAINTS 5-9-0 Tom Fears

| Scores | | | Use Name | Pos. | Hgt | Wgt | Age | Int | Pts |
|---|---|---|---|---|---|---|---|---|---|
| 20 | WASHINGTON | 26 | Jerry Jones | OT | 6'3" | 265 | 25 | | |
| 17 | DALLAS | 21 | Errol Linden | OT | 6'5" | 250 | 31 | | |
| 17 | Los Angeles | 36 | Don Talbert | OT | 6'5" | 255 | 29 | | |
| 17 | CLEVELAND | 27 | Norman Davis | OG | 6'3" | 245 | 24 | | |
| 10 | BALTIMORE | 30 | Jake Kupp | OG | 6'3" | 246 | 27 | | |
| 10 | Philadelphia | 13 | John Shinners | OG | 6'2" | 254 | 22 | | |
| 51 | St. Louis | 42 | Del Williams | OG | 6'2" | 245 | 23 | | |
| 17 | Dallas | 33 | Jerry Sturm | C | 6'3" | 265 | 32 | | |
| 25 | New York | 24 | Doug Atkins | DE | 6'8" | 275 | 39 | | |
| 43 | SAN FRANCISCO | 38 | Dan Colchico | DE | 6'4" | 245 | 32 | | |
| 26 | PHILADELPHIA | 17 | Dave Long | DE | 6'4" | 245 | 24 | | |
| 17 | Atlanta | 45 | Richard Neal | DE | 6'3" | 254 | 21 | | |
| 14 | Washington | 17 | Mike Rengel | DT | 6'5" | 260 | 22 | | |
| 27 | PITTSBURGH | 24 | Dave Rowe | DT | 6'6" | 280 | 24 | | |
| | | | Mike Tilleman | DT | 6'5" | 280 | 25 | | |

| Use Name | Pos. | Hgt | Wgt | Age | Int | Pts |
|---|---|---|---|---|---|---|
| Dick Absher | LB | 6'4" | 227 | 25 | 1 | |
| Johnny Brewer | LB | 6'4" | 235 | 32 | | |
| Bill Cody | LB | 6'1" | 227 | 25 | | |
| Ted Davis | LB | 6'1" | 232 | 27 | | |
| Les Kelley | LB | 6'1" | 232 | 27 | | |
| Mike Morgan | LB | 6'4" | 242 | 27 | | |
| Bill Saul | LB | 6'4" | 225 | 28 | | |
| Bo Burris | DB | 6'3" | 195 | 24 | 1 | |
| Ollie Cordill | DB | 6'2" | 180 | 26 | | |
| Gene Howard | DB | 6' | 190 | 22 | 2 | |
| Elijah Nevett | DB | 6' | 185 | 25 | 3 | |
| Steve Preece | DB | 6'1" | 195 | 22 | 1 | 6 |
| Bobby Thompson | DB | 5'10" | 188 | 29 | 1 | |
| Carl Ward | DB | 5'9" | 180 | 25 | | |
| Dave Whitsell | DB | 6' | 185 | 33 | 3 | |

Lou Cordileone — Knee Injury

| Use Name | Pos. | Hgt | Wgt | Age | Int | Pts |
|---|---|---|---|---|---|---|
| Edd Hargett | QB | 5'11" | 186 | 22 | | |
| Billy Kilmer | QB | 6' | 204 | 29 | | |
| Jim Ninowski | QB | 6'1" | 207 | 33 | | |
| Joe Don Looney | HB | 6'1" | 230 | 26 | | |
| Don Shy | HB | 6'1" | 205 | 23 | | 12 |
| Tony Baker | FB-HB | 5'11" | 230 | 24 | | 12 |
| Tom Barrington | FB-HB | 6'1" | 213 | 25 | | 6 |
| Andy Livingston | FB | 6' | 234 | 24 | | 48 |
| Tony Lorick | FB | 6'1" | 217 | 27 | | |
| Ernie Wheelwright | FB | 6'3" | 236 | 32 | | 30 |
| Dan Abramowicz | WR | 6'1" | 195 | 24 | | 42 |
| Al Dodd | WR | 6' | 180 | 24 | | 6 |
| Dave Parks | TE-WR | 6'2" | 203 | 27 | | 18 |
| Jim Hester | TE | 6'4" | 250 | 24 | | 6 |
| Ray Poage | TE | 6'4" | 215 | 28 | | 24 |
| Tom Dempsey | K | 6'1" | 264 | 28 | | 99 |
| Tom McNeill | K | 6'1" | 195 | 27 | | |

### PHILADELPHIA EAGLES 4-9-1 Jerry Williams

| Scores | | | Use Name | Pos. | Hgt | Wgt | Age | Int | Pts |
|---|---|---|---|---|---|---|---|---|---|
| 20 | CLEVELAND | 27 | Joe Carollo | OT | 6'2" | 258 | 29 | | |
| 41 | PITTSBURGH | 27 | Dave Graham | OT | 6'3" | 250 | 30 | | |
| 7 | DALLAS | 38 | Lane Howell | OT | 6'5" | 272 | 28 | | |
| 20 | Baltimore | 24 | Don Chuy | OG | 6'1" | 255 | 28 | | |
| 14 | Dallas | 49 | Dick Hart | OG | 6'2" | 255 | 26 | | |
| 13 | NEW ORLEANS | 10 | Jim Skaggs | OG | 6'2" | 252 | 29 | | |
| 23 | New York | 20 | Mark Nordquist | C-OG | 6'4" | 242 | 23 | | |
| 28 | Washington | 28 | Gene Ceppetelli (to NY) | C | 6'2" | 247 | 27 | | |
| 17 | LOS ANGELES | 23 | Mike Evans | C | 6'5" | 250 | 22 | | |
| 34 | St. Louis | 30 | Don Hultz | DE | 6'3" | 242 | 28 | | |
| 17 | New Orleans | 26 | Tim Rossovich | DE | 6'4" | 260 | 23 | | |
| 29 | WASHINGTON | 34 | Mel Tom | DE | 6'4" | 250 | 23 | | 2 |
| 3 | ATLANTA | 27 | Ernie Calloway | DT | 6'6" | 240 | 21 | | |
| 13 | San Francisco | 14 | Mike Dirks | DT | 6'2" | 246 | 23 | | |
| | | | Floyd Peters | DT | 6'4" | 255 | 34 | | |
| | | | Gary Pettigrew | DE-DT | 6'4" | 255 | 24 | | |

| Use Name | Pos. | Hgt | Wgt | Age | Int | Pts |
|---|---|---|---|---|---|---|
| Wayne Colman (to NO) | LB | 6'1" | 230 | 23 | 1 | |
| Tony Guillory | LB | 6'4" | 235 | 26 | | |
| Bill Hobbs | LB | 6' | 213 | 23 | | |
| Jay Johnson | LB | 6'3" | 230 | 23 | | |
| Ike Kelley | LB | 5'11" | 222 | 25 | | |
| Dave Lloyd | LB | 6'3" | 248 | 33 | 2 | |
| Ron Porter (from BAL) | LB | 6'3" | 232 | 24 | | |
| Adrian Young | LB | 6'1" | 225 | 23 | 1 | |
| Bill Bradley | DB | 5'11" | 190 | 22 | 1 | 6 |
| Irv Cross | DB | 6'1" | 195 | 30 | 1 | |
| Ron Medved | DB | 6'1" | 195 | 25 | | |
| Al Nelson | DB | 5'11" | 186 | 25 | 3 | |
| Nate Ramsey | DB | 6'1" | 200 | 28 | 2 | 6 |
| Jimmy Raye | DB | 6' | 185 | 23 | | |
| Joe Scarpati | DB | 5'10" | 185 | 27 | 4 | 6 |

| Use Name | Pos. | Hgt | Wgt | Age | Int | Pts |
|---|---|---|---|---|---|---|
| George Mira | QB | 5'11" | 190 | 27 | | |
| Norm Snead | QB | 6'4" | 215 | 29 | | 12 |
| Ronnie Blye | HB | 5'11" | 185 | 25 | | |
| Harry Jones | HB | 6'2" | 205 | 24 | | |
| Leroy Keyes | HB | 6'3" | 208 | 22 | | 18 |
| Harry Wilson | HB | 5'11" | 204 | 24 | | |
| Cyril Pinder | FB-HB | 6'2" | 222 | 22 | | 6 |
| Tom Woodeschick | FB | 6' | 225 | 27 | | 24 |
| Gary Ballman | WR | 6' | 205 | 29 | | 12 |
| Ben Hawkins | WR | 6' | 180 | 25 | | 48 |
| Chuck Hughes | WR | 5'11" | 175 | 26 | | |
| Harold Jackson | WR | 5'10" | 175 | 23 | | 54 |
| Kent Lawrence | WR | 5'11" | 175 | 22 | | |
| Fred Brown | TE | 6'5" | 237 | 26 | | |
| Fred Hill | TE | 6'2" | 215 | 26 | | 6 |
| Sam Baker | K | 6'2" | 218 | 37 | | 79 |

## CAPITOL DIVISION

### DALLAS COWBOYS

**RUSHING**

| Last Name | No. | Yds | Avg | TD |
|---|---|---|---|---|
| Hill | 204 | 942 | 4.6 | 8 |
| Garrison | 176 | 818 | 4.6 | 2 |
| Reeves | 59 | 173 | 2.9 | 4 |
| Shy | 42 | 154 | 3.7 | 1 |
| Morton | 16 | 62 | 3.9 | 1 |
| Staubach | 15 | 60 | 4.0 | 1 |
| Welch | 6 | 21 | 3.5 | 0 |
| Norman | 5 | 20 | 4.0 | 0 |
| Hayes | 4 | 17 | 4.3 | 0 |
| Rentzel | 2 | 11 | 5.5 | 0 |
| Baynham | 3 | −2 | −0.7 | 0 |

**RECEIVING**

| Last Name | No. | Yds | Avg | TD |
|---|---|---|---|---|
| Rentzel | 43 | 960 | 22 | 12 |
| Hayes | 40 | 746 | 19 | 4 |
| Hill | 20 | 232 | 12 | 0 |
| Reeves | 18 | 187 | 10 | 0 |
| Ditka | 17 | 268 | 16 | 3 |
| Norman | 13 | 238 | 18 | 3 |
| Garrison | 13 | 131 | 10 | 0 |
| Homan | 12 | 240 | 20 | 0 |
| Shy | 8 | 124 | 16 | 1 |
| Conrad | 4 | 74 | 19 | 0 |
| Wright | 1 | 12 | 12 | 0 |

**PUNT RETURNS**

| Last Name | No. | Yds | Avg | TD |
|---|---|---|---|---|
| Hayes | 18 | 179 | 10 | 0 |
| Renfro | 15 | 80 | 5 | 0 |
| Rentzel | 4 | 14 | 4 | 0 |
| Johnson | 1 | 0 | 0 | 0 |

**KICKOFF RETURNS**

| Last Name | No. | Yds | Avg | TD |
|---|---|---|---|---|
| Flowers | 11 | 238 | 22 | 0 |
| Hill | 4 | 125 | 31 | 0 |
| Baynham | 6 | 114 | 19 | 0 |
| Welch | 5 | 112 | 22 | 0 |
| Hayes | 3 | 80 | 27 | 0 |
| Shy | 3 | 47 | 16 | 0 |
| Garrison | 1 | 2 | 2 | 0 |
| Green | 2 | 0 | 0 | 0 |
| Johnson | 1 | 0 | 0 | 0 |

**PASSING**

| Last Name | Att | Comp | % | Yds | Yd/Att | TD | Int− | % | RK |
|---|---|---|---|---|---|---|---|---|---|
| Morton | 302 | 162 | 54 | 2619 | 8.7 | 21 | 15− | 5 | 5 |
| Staubach | 47 | 23 | 49 | 421 | 9.0 | 1 | 2− | 4 | |
| Hill | 3 | 3 | 100 | 137 | 45.7 | 2 | 0− | 0 | |
| Reeves | 3 | 1 | 33 | 35 | 11.7 | 0 | 1− | 33 | |

**PUNTING**

| Last Name | No | Avg |
|---|---|---|
| Widby | 63 | 43.3 |

**KICKING**

| Last Name | XP | Att | % | FG | Att | % |
|---|---|---|---|---|---|---|
| M. Clark | 43 | 44 | 98 | 20 | 36 | 56 |

### WASHINGTON REDSKINS

**RUSHING**

| Last Name | No. | Yds | Avg | TD |
|---|---|---|---|---|
| L. Brown | 202 | 888 | 4.4 | 4 |
| Harraway | 141 | 428 | 3.0 | 6 |
| Jurgensen | 17 | 156 | 9.2 | 1 |
| Taylor | 3 | 24 | 8.0 | 0 |
| Dyer | 6 | 18 | 3.0 | 0 |
| Smith | 3 | 8 | 2.7 | 0 |
| Kopay | 3 | 4 | 1.3 | 0 |
| Allen | 1 | 3 | 3.0 | 0 |
| Bragg | 1 | 3 | 3.0 | 0 |

**RECEIVING**

| Last Name | No. | Yds | Avg | TD |
|---|---|---|---|---|
| Taylor | 71 | 883 | 12 | 8 |
| Harraway | 55 | 489 | 9 | 3 |
| Smith | 54 | 682 | 13 | 9 |
| Long | 48 | 533 | 11 | 1 |
| L. Brown | 34 | 302 | 9 | 0 |
| Kopay | 6 | 60 | 10 | 0 |
| Roberts | 4 | 66 | 17 | 0 |
| Dyer | 2 | 86 | 43 | 1 |
| Allen | 1 | 5 | 5 | 0 |

**PUNT RETURNS**

| Last Name | No. | Yds | Avg | TD |
|---|---|---|---|---|
| Harris | 14 | 158 | 11 | 1 |
| Roberts | 12 | 32 | 3 | 0 |

**KICKOFF RETURNS**

| Last Name | No. | Yds | Avg | TD |
|---|---|---|---|---|
| Harris | 19 | 458 | 24 | 0 |
| Roberts | 17 | 383 | 23 | 0 |
| Dyer | 11 | 207 | 19 | 0 |
| Kopay | 9 | 187 | 21 | 0 |
| McKeever | 2 | 31 | 16 | 0 |
| Snowden | 2 | 2 | 2 | 0 |
| Richter | 1 | 0 | 0 | 0 |

**PASSING**

| Last Name | Att | Comp | % | Yds | Yd/Att | TD | Int− | % | RK |
|---|---|---|---|---|---|---|---|---|---|
| Jurgensen | 442 | 274 | 62 | 3102 | 7.0 | 22 | 15− | 3 | 1 |
| Ryan | 1 | 1 | 100 | 4 | 4.0 | 0 | 0− | 0 | |
| Knight | 1 | 0 | 0 | 0 | 0.0 | 0 | 1− | 100 | |

**PUNTING**

| Last Name | No | Avg |
|---|---|---|
| Bragg | 70 | 42.2 |

**KICKING**

| Last Name | XP | Att | % | FG | Att | % |
|---|---|---|---|---|---|---|
| Knight | 35 | 36 | 97 | 16 | 27 | 59 |

### NEW ORLEANS SAINTS

**RUSHING**

| Last Name | No. | Yds | Avg | TD |
|---|---|---|---|---|
| Livingston | 181 | 761 | 4.2 | 5 |
| Baker | 134 | 642 | 4.8 | 1 |
| Wheelwright | 25 | 85 | 3.4 | 4 |
| Shy | 21 | 75 | 3.6 | 1 |
| Abramowicz | 3 | 61 | 20.3 | 0 |
| Barrington | 7 | 33 | 4.7 | 1 |
| Kilmer | 11 | 18 | 1.6 | 0 |
| Hargett | 5 | 15 | 3.0 | 0 |
| Dodd | 3 | 12 | 4.0 | 0 |
| Lorick | 5 | 11 | 2.2 | 0 |
| Poage | 1 | −3 | −3.0 | 0 |
| Looney | 3 | −5 | −1.7 | 0 |

**RECEIVING**

| Last Name | No. | Yds | Avg | TD |
|---|---|---|---|---|
| Abramowicz | 73 | 1015 | 14 | 7 |
| Dodd | 37 | 600 | 16 | 1 |
| Baker | 34 | 352 | 10 | 1 |
| Parks | 31 | 439 | 14 | 3 |
| Livingston | 28 | 278 | 10 | 3 |
| Poage | 18 | 236 | 13 | 4 |
| Shy | 9 | 141 | 16 | 1 |
| Wheelwright | 8 | 68 | 9 | 1 |
| Barrington | 4 | 42 | 11 | 0 |
| Hester | 3 | 44 | 15 | 1 |

**PUNT RETURNS**

| Last Name | No. | Yds | Avg | TD |
|---|---|---|---|---|
| Dodd | 15 | 106 | 7 | 0 |
| Howard | 9 | 73 | 8 | 0 |
| Thompson | 4 | 25 | 6 | 0 |
| Barrington | 1 | 8 | 8 | 0 |
| Ward | 1 | 5 | 5 | 0 |

**KICKOFF RETURNS**

| Last Name | No. | Yds | Avg | TD |
|---|---|---|---|---|
| Shy | 16 | 447 | 28 | 0 |
| Barrington | 17 | 394 | 23 | 0 |
| Howard | 9 | 227 | 25 | 0 |
| Dodd | 8 | 171 | 21 | 0 |
| Thompson | 5 | 101 | 20 | 0 |
| Ward | 3 | 58 | 19 | 0 |
| Nevett | 2 | 53 | 27 | 0 |
| Hester | 1 | 4 | 4 | 0 |
| Preece | 1 | 0 | 0 | 0 |

**PASSING**

| Last Name | Att | Comp | % | Yds | Yd/Att | TD | Int− | % | RK |
|---|---|---|---|---|---|---|---|---|---|
| Kilmer | 360 | 193 | 54 | 2532 | 7.0 | 20 | 17− | 5 | 8 |
| Hargett | 52 | 31 | 60 | 403 | 7.8 | 0 | 0− | 0 | |
| Ninowski | 34 | 17 | 50 | 227 | 6.7 | 1 | 2− | 6 | |
| Livingston | 4 | 3 | 75 | 38 | 9.5 | 1 | 1− | 25 | |
| Barrington | 2 | 1 | 50 | 15 | 7.5 | 0 | 0− | 0 | |
| Looney | 1 | 0 | 0 | 0 | 0.0 | 0 | 0− | 0 | |

**PUNTING**

| Last Name | No | Avg |
|---|---|---|
| Cordill | 42 | 40.9 |
| McNeill | 7 | 44.6 |

**KICKING**

| Last Name | XP | Att | % | FG | Att | % |
|---|---|---|---|---|---|---|
| Dempsey | 33 | 35 | 94 | 22 | 41 | 54 |

### PHILADELPHIA EAGLES

**RUSHING**

| Last Name | No. | Yds | Avg | TD |
|---|---|---|---|---|
| Woodeshick | 186 | 831 | 4.5 | 4 |
| Keyes | 121 | 361 | 3.0 | 3 |
| Pinder | 60 | 309 | 5.2 | 1 |
| Blye | 8 | 25 | 3.1 | 0 |
| Mira | 3 | 16 | 5.3 | 0 |
| Jackson | 2 | 10 | 5.0 | 0 |
| Wilson | 4 | 7 | 1.8 | 0 |
| Bradley | 1 | 5 | 5.0 | 0 |
| Snead | 8 | 2 | 0.3 | 2 |
| Jones | 1 | 0 | 0.0 | 0 |
| Hawkins | 1 | −3 | −3.0 | 0 |

**RECEIVING**

| Last Name | No. | Yds | Avg | TD |
|---|---|---|---|---|
| Jackson | 65 | 1116 | 17 | 9 |
| Hawkins | 43 | 761 | 18 | 8 |
| Ballman | 31 | 492 | 16 | 2 |
| Keyes | 29 | 276 | 10 | 0 |
| Woodeshick | 22 | 177 | 8 | 0 |
| Pinder | 12 | 77 | 6 | 0 |
| Hill | 6 | 64 | 11 | 1 |
| Hughes | 3 | 29 | 10 | 0 |
| Blye | 2 | −6 | −3 | 0 |
| Brown | 1 | 20 | 20 | 0 |
| Lawrence | 1 | 10 | 10 | 0 |
| Wilson | 1 | 6 | 6 | 0 |

**PUNT RETURNS**

| Last Name | No. | Yds | Avg | TD |
|---|---|---|---|---|
| Bradley | 28 | 181 | 6 | 0 |
| Lawrence | 2 | 26 | 13 | 0 |
| Scarpati | 4 | 6 | 2 | 0 |
| Hawkins | 1 | 6 | 6 | 0 |
| Hughes | 1 | 0 | 0 | 0 |

**KICKOFF RETURNS**

| Last Name | No. | Yds | Avg | TD |
|---|---|---|---|---|
| Bradley | 21 | 467 | 22 | 0 |
| Blye | 19 | 370 | 19 | 0 |
| Keyes | 9 | 200 | 22 | 0 |
| Lawrence | 5 | 97 | 19 | 0 |
| Nelson | 3 | 63 | 21 | 0 |
| Pinder | 4 | 56 | 14 | 0 |
| Graham | 2 | 5 | 3 | 0 |

**PASSING**

| Last Name | Att | Comp | % | Yds | Yd/Att | TD | Int− | % | RK |
|---|---|---|---|---|---|---|---|---|---|
| Snead | 379 | 190 | 50 | 2768 | 7.3 | 19 | 23− | 6 | 12 |
| Mira | 76 | 25 | 33 | 240 | 3.2 | 1 | 5− | 7 | |
| Keyes | 2 | .1 | 50 | 14 | 7.0 | 0 | 0− | 0 | |
| Bradley | 1 | 0 | 0 | 0 | 0.0 | 0 | 0− | 0 | |

**PUNTING**

| Last Name | No | Avg |
|---|---|---|
| Bradley | 74 | 39.8 |

**KICKING**

| Last Name | XP | Att | % | FG | Att | % |
|---|---|---|---|---|---|---|
| Baker | 31 | 31 | 100 | 16 | 30 | 53 |

## CENTURY DIVISION

### CLEVELAND BROWNS 10-3-1 Blanton Collier

| Scores of Each Game | |
|---|---|
| 27 | Philadelphia 20 |
| 27 | WASHINGTON 23 |
| 21 | DETROIT 28 |
| 27 | New Orleans 17 |
| 42 | PITTSBURGH 31 |
| 21 | ST. LOUIS 21 |
| 42 | DALLAS 10 |
| 3 | Minnesota 51 |
| 24 | Pittsburgh 3 |
| 28 | NEW YORK 17 |
| 28 | Chicago 24 |
| 20 | GREEN BAY 7 |
| 27 | St. Louis 21 |
| 14 | New York 27 |

| Use Name | Pos. | Hgt | Wgt | Age | Int | Pts |
|---|---|---|---|---|---|---|
| Monte Clark | OT | 6'6" | 250 | 32 | | |
| Bob Oliver | OT | 6'3" | 240 | 22 | | |
| Dick Schafrath | OT | 6'3" | 248 | 33 | | |
| Joe Taffoni | OT | 6'3" | 250 | 24 | | |
| Jim Copeland | OG | 6'2" | 245 | 24 | | |
| John Demarie | OG | 6'3" | 255 | 24 | | |
| Gene Hickerson | OG | 6'3" | 248 | 34 | | |
| Chuck Reynolds | OG | 6'2" | 240 | 22 | | |
| Fred Hoaglin | C | 6'4" | 250 | 25 | | |
| Jack Gregory | DE | 6'6" | 250 | 24 | 1 | |
| Ron Snidow | DE | 6'4" | 250 | 27 | | |
| Marv Upshaw | DT-DE | 6'3" | 245 | 22 | 1 | |
| Walter Johnson | DT | 6'3" | 275 | 26 | | 6 |
| Jim Kanicki | DT | 6'4" | 270 | 27 | | |
| Joe Righetti | DT | 6'3" | 253 | 21 | | |
| Al Jenkins | DE-DT | 6'2" | 255 | 23 | | |

| Use Name | Pos. | Hgt | Wgt | Age | Int | Pts |
|---|---|---|---|---|---|---|
| Billy Andrews | LB | 6' | 225 | 24 | | |
| John Garlington | LB | 6'1" | 225 | 23 | 2 | |
| Jim Houston | LB | 6'2" | 240 | 32 | | |
| Dale Lindsey | LB | 6'3" | 225 | 26 | 1 | |
| Bob Matheson | LB | 6'4" | 240 | 24 | | |
| Wayne Meylan | LB | 6'1" | 235 | 23 | | |
| Erich Barnes | DB | 6'2" | 212 | 34 | 1 | 6 |
| Dean Brown | DB | 5'10" | 170 | 21 | | |
| Mike Howell | DB | 6'1" | 190 | 26 | 6 | |
| Ernie Kellerman | DB | 6' | 185 | 25 | 3 | 6 |
| Alvin Mitchell | DB | 6'3" | 195 | 25 | | |
| Freddie Summers | DB | 6'1" | 180 | 22 | | |
| Walt Sumner | DB | 6'1" | 180 | 22 | 4 | 6 |

Ben Davis — Knee Injury

| Use Name | Pos. | Hgt | Wgt | Age | Int | Pts |
|---|---|---|---|---|---|---|
| Bill Nelsen | QB | 6' | 195 | 28 | | |
| Jerry Rhome | QB | 6' | 185 | 27 | | |
| Ron Johnson | HB | 6'1" | 205 | 21 | | 42 |
| Reece Morrison | HB | 6' | 205 | 23 | | 6 |
| Bo Scott | FB | 6'3" | 210 | 26 | | |
| Charlie Leigh | FB | 5'11" | 205 | 23 | | |
| Leroy Kelly | HB-FB | 6' | 200 | 27 | | 60 |
| Gary Collins | WR | 6'4" | 220 | 28 | | 66 |
| Fair Hooker | WR | 6'1" | 193 | 22 | | |
| Dave Jones | WR | 6'2" | 185 | 22 | | |
| Paul Warfield | WR | 6' | 188 | 26 | | 60 |
| Chip Glass | TE | 6'4" | 236 | 22 | | -12 |
| Milt Morin | TE | 6'4" | 250 | 27 | | |
| Don Cockroft | K | 6'1" | 185 | 24 | | 81 |

### NEW YORK GIANTS 6-8-0 Allie Sherman

| Scores of Each Game | |
|---|---|
| 24 | MINNESOTA 23 |
| 0 | Detroit 24 |
| 28 | CHICAGO 24 |
| 10 | PITTSBURGH 7 |
| 14 | Washington 20 |
| 3 | Dallas 25 |
| 20 | PHILADELPHIA 23 |
| 17 | St. Louis 42 |
| 24 | NEW ORLEANS 25 |
| 17 | Cleveland 28 |
| 10 | Green Bay 20 |
| 49 | ST. LOUIS 6 |
| 21 | Pittsburgh 17 |
| 27 | CLEVELAND 14 |

| Use Name | Pos. | Hgt | Wgt | Age | Int | Pts |
|---|---|---|---|---|---|---|
| Rich Buzin | OT | 6'4" | 250 | 23 | | |
| Steve Wright | OT | 6'6" | 250 | 27 | | |
| Willie Young | OT | 6' | 265 | 26 | | |
| Pete Case | OG | 6'2" | 245 | 28 | | |
| Darrell Dess | OG | 6' | 245 | 33 | | |
| Doug Van Horn | OG | 6'2" | 245 | 25 | | |
| Charlie Harper | OT-OG | 6'2" | 250 | 25 | | |
| Chuck Hinton | C | 6'2" | 235 | 26 | | |
| Greg Larson | C | 6'2" | 250 | 30 | | |
| Bruce Anderson | DE | 6'4" | 250 | 25 | | |
| Fred Dryer | DE | 6'6" | 235 | 23 | | |
| John Johnson | DT | 6'5" | 260 | 28 | | |
| Tim McCann | DT | 6'5" | 265 | 22 | | |
| Frank Molden | DT | 6'5" | 280 | 27 | | |
| Frank Parker | DT | 6'5" | 270 | 29 | | |
| Joe Szczecko | DT | 6' | 245 | 27 | | |
| Bob Lurtsema | DE-DT | 6'6" | 250 | 27 | | |

| Use Name | Pos. | Hgt | Wgt | Age | Int | Pts |
|---|---|---|---|---|---|---|
| McKinley Boston | LB | 6'2" | 245 | 23 | | |
| Tommy Crutcher | LB | 6'3" | 230 | 27 | 1 | |
| Henry Davis | LB | 6'3" | 235 | 26 | | |
| Ralph Heck | LB | 6'2" | 230 | 28 | 2 | |
| Ray Hickl | LB | 6'2" | 210 | 22 | | |
| John Kirby (from MIN) | LB | 6'3" | 235 | 27 | | |
| Harold Wells | LB | 6'2" | 220 | 30 | | |
| Al Brenner | DB | 6'1" | 185 | 22 | | |
| Scott Eaton | DB | 6'3" | 195 | 25 | 2 | 6 |
| Jim Holifield | DB | 6'2" | 195 | 23 | 1 | |
| Spider Lockhart | DB | 6'2" | 175 | 26 | 2 | |
| Tom Longo | DB | 6'1" | 198 | 25 | 2 | |
| Bruce Maher | DB | 5'11" | 185 | 32 | 5 | |
| Willie Williams | DB | 6' | 190 | 26 | 4 | |

Bobby Duhon — Injury

| Use Name | Pos. | Hgt | Wgt | Age | Int | Pts |
|---|---|---|---|---|---|---|
| Milt Plum | QB | 6'1" | 205 | 35 | | |
| Frank Tarkenton | QB | 6'1" | 190 | 29 | | |
| Gary Wood | QB | 5'11" | 188 | 26 | | |
| John Fuqua | HB | 5'11" | 200 | 22 | | |
| Randy Minniear | HB | 6' | 210 | 25 | | 6 |
| Ernie Koy | FB-HB | 6'2" | 230 | 26 | | 36 |
| Joe Morrison | WR-HB | 6'1" | 212 | 31 | | 66 |
| Junior Coffey (from ATL) | FB | 6'1" | 210 | 27 | | |
| Tucker Frederickson | FB | 6'3" | 220 | 26 | | 6 |
| Dave Dunaway | WR | 6'2" | 205 | 24 | | |
| Don Herrmann | WR | 6'2" | 195 | 22 | | 30 |
| Rich Houston | WR | 6'2" | 197 | 23 | | |
| Homer Jones | WR | 6'2" | 215 | 28 | | 6 |
| Dick Kotite | TE | 6'3" | 235 | 26 | | 6 |
| Freeman White | TE | 6'5" | 225 | 25 | | 6 |
| Butch Wilson | TE | 6'2" | 228 | 27 | | |
| Aaron Thomas | WR-TE | 6'3" | 210 | 31 | | 18 |
| Pete Gogolak | K | 6'2" | 185 | 27 | | 66 |
| Curley Johnson | K | 6' | 215 | 34 | | |

### ST. LOUIS CARDINALS 4-9-1 Charlie Winner

| Scores of Each Game | |
|---|---|
| 3 | Dallas 24 |
| 20 | CHICAGO 17 |
| 27 | Pittsburgh 14 |
| 17 | Washington 33 |
| 10 | MINNESOTA 27 |
| 21 | Cleveland 21 |
| 42 | NEW ORLEANS 51 |
| 42 | NEW YORK 17 |
| 0 | Detroit 20 |
| 30 | PHILADELPHIA 34 |
| 47 | PITTSBURGH 10 |
| 6 | New York 49 |
| 21 | CLEVELAND 27 |
| 28 | Green Bay 45 |

| Use Name | Pos. | Hgt | Wgt | Age | Int | Pts |
|---|---|---|---|---|---|---|
| Vern Emerson | OT | 6'5" | 260 | 23 | | |
| Ernie McMillan | OT | 6'6" | 260 | 31 | | |
| Bob Reynolds | OT | 6'6" | 265 | 28 | | |
| Clyde Williams | OT | 6'2" | 250 | 29 | | |
| Irv Goode | OG | 6'4" | 250 | 28 | | |
| Ken Gray | OG | 6'2" | 250 | 33 | | |
| Rick Sortun | OG | 6'2" | 240 | 26 | | |
| Bob DeMarco | C | 6'3" | 245 | 31 | | |
| Wayne Mulligan | C | 6'2" | 245 | 22 | | |
| Don Brumm | DE | 6'3" | 245 | 26 | | |
| Rolf Krueger | DE | 6'4" | 245 | 22 | | |
| Cal Snowden | DE | 6'4" | 235 | 22 | | |
| Chuck Walker | DE | 6'2" | 250 | 28 | | |
| Fred Heron | DT | 6'4" | 255 | 24 | | |
| Bob Rowe | DT | 6'4" | 255 | 24 | 2 | 6 |
| Joe Schmiesing | DT | 6'4" | 245 | 24 | | |

| Use Name | Pos. | Hgt | Wgt | Age | Int | Pts |
|---|---|---|---|---|---|---|
| Chip Healy | LB | 6'3" | 230 | 22 | | |
| Dave Meggyesy | LB | 6'1" | 230 | 27 | | |
| Dave Olerich | LB | 6'1" | 220 | 24 | | |
| Jamie Rivers | LB | 6'2" | 235 | 23 | | |
| Rocky Rosema | LB | 6'2" | 230 | 23 | 1 | |
| Larry Stallings | LB | 6'2" | 230 | 27 | | 6 |
| Bob Atkins | DB | 6'3" | 212 | 23 | 3 | |
| Lonnie Sanders | DB | 6'2" | 205 | 27 | | |
| Mac Sauls | DB | 6' | 185 | 24 | | |
| Jerry Stovall | DB | 6'2" | 195 | 27 | 1 | |
| Roger Wehrli | DB | 6'1" | 185 | 21 | 3 | |
| Larry Wilson | DB | 6' | 190 | 31 | 2 | 6 |
| Mike Wilson | DB | 5'11" | 185 | 22 | | |
| Terry Brown | WR-DB | 6'1" | 205 | 22 | 1 | |

| Use Name | Pos. | Hgt | Wgt | Age | Int | Pts |
|---|---|---|---|---|---|---|
| Jim Hart | QB | 6'2" | 205 | 25 | | 12 |
| King Hill | QB | 6'3" | 216 | 33 | | |
| Charley Johnson | QB | 6' | 190 | 32 | | 6 |
| MacArthur Lane | HB | 6' | 220 | 27 | | 6 |
| Johnny Roland | HB | 6'2" | 215 | 26 | | 36 |
| Roy Shivers | HB | 6' | 200 | 24 | | 18 |
| Willie Crenshaw | FB | 6'2" | 230 | 28 | | 18 |
| Cid Edwards | FB | 6'2" | 230 | 25 | | 18 |
| Jerry Daanen | WR | 6' | 190 | 24 | | |
| John Gilliam | WR | 6'1" | 190 | 24 | | 60 |
| Freddie Hyatt | WR | 6'3" | 212 | 23 | | |
| Dave Williams | WR | 6'2" | 205 | 24 | | 42 |
| Bob Brown | TE | 6'3" | 225 | 26 | | 6 |
| Jackie Smith | TE | 6'4" | 230 | 28 | | 6 |
| Jim Bakken | K | 6' | 200 | 28 | | 74 |

### PITTSBURGH STEELERS 1-13-0 Chuck Noll

| Scores of Each Game | |
|---|---|
| 16 | DETROIT 13 |
| 27 | Philadelphia 41 |
| 14 | ST. LOUIS 27 |
| 7 | New York 10 |
| 31 | Cleveland 42 |
| 7 | WASHINGTON 14 |
| 34 | GREEN BAY 38 |
| 7 | Chicago 38 |
| 3 | CLEVELAND 24 |
| 14 | Minnesota 52 |
| 10 | St. Louis 47 |
| 7 | DALLAS 10 |
| 17 | NEW YORK 21 |
| 24 | New Orleans 27 |

| Use Name | Pos. | Hgt | Wgt | Age | Int | Pts |
|---|---|---|---|---|---|---|
| John Brown | OT | 6'2" | 255 | 30 | | |
| Mike Haggerty | OT | 6'4" | 240 | 23 | | |
| Mike Taylor (to NO) | OT | 6'4" | 245 | 24 | | |
| Sam Davis | OG | 6'1" | 245 | 25 | | |
| Larry Gagner | OG | 6'3" | 240 | 25 | | |
| Bruce Van Dyke | OG | 6'2" | 246 | 25 | | |
| Ralph Wenzel | OG | 6'3" | 236 | 26 | | |
| Jon Kolb | C | 6'2" | 220 | 22 | | |
| Ray Mansfield | C | 6'3" | 240 | 28 | | |
| L. C. Greenwood | DE | 6'5" | 240 | 22 | | |
| Ben McGee | DE | 6'2" | 250 | 27 | | |
| Lloyd Voss | DE | 6'4" | 256 | 27 | | |
| Dick Arndt | DT | 6'5" | 265 | 25 | | |
| Joe Greene | DT | 6'4" | 270 | 22 | | |
| Chuck Hinton | DT | 6'5" | 258 | 30 | 1 | |
| Clarence Washington | DT | 6'5" | 265 | 22 | | |

| Use Name | Pos. | Hgt | Wgt | Age | Int | Pts |
|---|---|---|---|---|---|---|
| John Campbell (to BAL) | LB | 6'3" | 225 | 30 | | |
| Doug Fisher | LB | 6'1" | 225 | 22 | | |
| Jerry Hillebrand | LB | 6'3" | 240 | 29 | 1 | |
| Ray May | LB | 6'1" | 230 | 24 | 2 | |
| Andy Russell | LB | 6'3" | 225 | 27 | 2 | |
| Brian Stenger | LB | 6'4" | 220 | 22 | 3 | |
| Sid Williams | LB | 6'2" | 235 | 27 | | |
| Chuck Beatty | DB | 6'2" | 207 | 23 | | |
| Lee Calland (from CHI) | DB | 6' | 190 | 28 | 2 | |
| Bob Hohn | DB | 6' | 185 | 28 | 5 | |
| Paul Martha | DB | 6'1" | 187 | 26 | 5 | |
| Clancy Oliver | DB | 6'1" | 180 | 21 | | |
| Jim Shorter | DB | 5'11" | 180 | 28 | 3 | |
| Marv Woodson (to NO) | DB | 6' | 195 | 26 | 1 | |

Rocky Bleier — Military Service

| Use Name | Pos. | Hgt | Wgt | Age | Int | Pts |
|---|---|---|---|---|---|---|
| Terry Hanratty | QB | 6'1" | 200 | 21 | | |
| Kent Nix | QB | 6'1" | 195 | 25 | | |
| Dick Shiner | QB | 6'2" | 197 | 27 | | 6 |
| Bob Campbell | HB | 6' | 195 | 22 | | |
| Dick Hoak | HB | 5'11" | 195 | 30 | | 18 |
| Don McCall | HB | 5'11" | 195 | 24 | | 6 |
| Warren Bankston | FB | 6'4" | 226 | 22 | | |
| Earl Gros | FB | 6'3" | 220 | 28 | | 42 |
| Don Alley | WR | 6'2" | 200 | 23 | | |
| Marshall Cropper | WR | 6' | 195 | 24 | | 18 |
| Jon Henderson | WR | 6'2" | 190 | 25 | | |
| Roy Jefferson | WR | 6'2" | 190 | 25 | | 54 |
| J. R. Wilburn | WR | 6'2" | 190 | 26 | | |
| Erwin Williams | WR | 6'5" | 215 | 22 | | 6 |
| Bob Adams | TE | 6'2" | 225 | 23 | | |
| John Hilton | TE | 6'5" | 222 | 27 | | |
| Gene Mingo | K | 6'1" | 216 | 30 | | 62 |
| Bobby Walden | K | 6' | 190 | 30 | | |

## CENTURY DIVISION

### CLEVELAND BROWNS

**RUSHING**

| Last Name | No. | Yds | Avg | TD |
|---|---|---|---|---|
| Kelly | 196 | 817 | 4.2 | 9 |
| R. Johnson | 137 | 471 | 3.4 | 7 |
| Morrison | 60 | 301 | 5.0 | 1 |
| Scott | 44 | 157 | 3.6 | 0 |
| Morin | 2 | 30 | 15.0 | 0 |
| Warfield | 2 | 23 | 11.5 | 0 |
| Rhome | 1 | 0 | 0.0 | 0 |
| Nelsen | 5 | −11 | −2.2 | 0 |

**RECEIVING**

| Last Name | No. | Yds | Avg | TD |
|---|---|---|---|---|
| Collins | 54 | 786 | 15 | 11 |
| Warfield | 42 | 886 | 21 | 10 |
| Morin | 37 | 495 | 13 | 0 |
| R. Johnson | 24 | 164 | 7 | 0 |
| Kelly | 20 | 267 | 13 | 1 |
| Morrison | 6 | 71 | 12 | 0 |
| Scott | 6 | 25 | 4 | 0 |
| Glass | 4 | 91 | 23 | 2 |
| Jones | 2 | 33 | 17 | 0 |
| Hooker | 2 | 21 | 11 | 0 |
| Leigh | 2 | −9 | −5 | 0 |

**PUNT RETURNS**

| Last Name | No. | Yds | Avg | TD |
|---|---|---|---|---|
| Sumner | 9 | 88 | 10 | 0 |
| Morrison | 11 | 49 | 4 | 0 |
| Kelly | 7 | 28 | 4 | 0 |
| Leigh | 5 | 18 | 4 | 0 |

**KICKOFF RETURNS**

| Last Name | No. | Yds | Avg | TD |
|---|---|---|---|---|
| Scott | 25 | 722 | 29 | 0 |
| Morrison | 9 | 155 | 17 | 0 |
| Brown | 2 | 45 | 23 | 0 |
| R. Johnson | 1 | 31 | 31 | 0 |
| Kelly | 2 | 26 | 13 | 0 |
| Leigh | 2 | 6 | 3 | 0 |
| Howell | 1 | 0 | 0 | 0 |
| Jenkins | 1 | 0 | 0 | 0 |
| Kanicki | 1 | 0 | 0 | 0 |
| Mathesen | 1 | 0 | 0 | 0 |
| Mitchell | 1 | 0 | 0 | 0 |

**PASSING**

| Last Name | Att | Comp | % | Yds | Yd/Att | TD | Int− | % | RK |
|---|---|---|---|---|---|---|---|---|---|
| Nelson | 352 | 190 | 54 | 2743 | 7.8 | 23 | 19− | 5 | 6 |
| Rhome | 19 | 7 | 37 | 35 | 1.8 | 0 | 2− | 11 | |
| Kelly | 5 | 1 | 20 | 36 | 7.2 | 1 | 0− | 0 | |
| Morrison | 1 | 1 | 100 | 16 | 16.0 | 0 | 0− | 0 | |
| R. Johnson | 1 | 0 | 0 | 0 | 0.0 | 0 | 0− | 0 | |

**PUNTING**

| Last Name | No | Avg |
|---|---|---|
| Cockroft | 57 | 37.5 |
| Collins | 3 | 37.3 |

**KICKING**

| Last Name | XP | Att | % | FG | Att | % |
|---|---|---|---|---|---|---|
| Cockroft | 45 | 45 | 100 | 12 | 23 | 52 |

### NEW YORK GIANTS

**RUSHING**

| Last Name | No. | Yds | Avg | TD |
|---|---|---|---|---|
| Coffey | 131 | 511 | 3.9 | 2 |
| Morrison | 107 | 387 | 3.6 | 4 |
| Koy | 76 | 300 | 3.9 | 2 |
| Tarkenton | 37 | 172 | 4.6 | 0 |
| Minniear | 35 | 141 | 4.0 | 1 |
| Frederickson | 33 | 136 | 4.1 | 0 |
| Fuqua | 20 | 89 | 4.5 | 0 |
| Houston | 1 | 11 | 11.0 | 0 |
| Jones | 3 | 8 | 2.7 | 0 |
| Dunaway | 1 | 4 | 4.0 | 0 |
| Wood | 1 | 3 | 3.0 | 0 |
| Plum | 1 | −1 | −1.0 | 0 |

**RECEIVING**

| Last Name | No. | Yds | Avg | TD |
|---|---|---|---|---|
| Morrison | 44 | 647 | 15 | 7 |
| Jones | 42 | 744 | 18 | 1 |
| Herrmann | 33 | 423 | 13 | 5 |
| White | 29 | 315 | 11 | 0 |
| Thomas | 22 | 348 | 16 | 3 |
| Koy | 19 | 152 | 8 | 4 |
| Frederickson | 14 | 95 | 7 | 1 |
| Coffey | 14 | 89 | 6 | 3 |
| Wilson | 10 | 132 | 13 | 0 |
| Minniear | 6 | 68 | 11 | 0 |
| Fuqua | 3 | 11 | 4 | 0 |
| Houston | 2 | 69 | 35 | 0 |
| Dunaway | 2 | 37 | 19 | 0 |
| Young | 1 | 8 | 8 | 0 |
| Kotite | 1 | 2 | 2 | 1 |

**PUNT RETURNS**

| Last Name | No. | Yds | Avg | TD |
|---|---|---|---|---|
| Lockhart | 10 | 29 | 3 | 0 |
| Minniear | 3 | 15 | 5 | 0 |
| Brenner | 2 | 6 | 3 | 0 |

**KICKOFF RETURNS**

| Last Name | No. | Yds | Avg | TD |
|---|---|---|---|---|
| Fuqua | 20 | 399 | 20 | 0 |
| Houston | 12 | 252 | 21 | 0 |
| Holifield | 8 | 156 | 20 | 0 |
| Williams | 6 | 96 | 16 | 0 |
| Minniear | 5 | 83 | 17 | 0 |
| Brenner | 2 | 39 | 20 | 0 |
| Longo | 2 | 31 | 16 | 0 |
| Lockhart | 1 | 19 | 19 | 0 |

**PASSING**

| Last Name | Att | Comp | % | Yds | Yd/Att | TD | Int− | % | RK |
|---|---|---|---|---|---|---|---|---|---|
| Tarkenton | 409 | 220 | 54 | 2918 | 7.1 | 23 | 8− | 2 | 3 |
| Wood | 16 | 10 | 63 | 106 | 6.6 | 1 | 0− | 0 | |
| Plum | 9 | 3 | 33 | 37 | 4.1 | 0 | 0− | 0 | |
| Koy | 1 | 1 | 100 | 15 | 15.0 | 0 | 0− | 0 | |

**PUNTING**

| Last Name | No | Avg |
|---|---|---|
| Koy | 26 | 35.9 |
| C. Johnson | 22 | 37.4 |
| Dunaway | 13 | 38.2 |
| Gogolak | 12 | 40.9 |

**KICKING**

| Last Name | XP | Att | % | FG | Att | % |
|---|---|---|---|---|---|---|
| Gogolak | 33 | 33 | 100 | 11 | 21 | 52 |

### ST. LOUIS CARDINALS

**RUSHING**

| Last Name | No. | Yds | Avg | TD |
|---|---|---|---|---|
| Edwards | 107 | 504 | 4.7 | 3 |
| Roland | 138 | 498 | 3.6 | 5 |
| Crenshaw | 55 | 172 | 3.1 | 3 |
| Shivers | 27 | 115 | 4.3 | 2 |
| Lane | 25 | 93 | 3.7 | 1 |
| Johnson | 17 | 51 | 3.0 | 1 |
| Hart | 7 | 16 | 2.3 | 2 |
| D. Williams | 1 | 1 | 1.0 | 0 |
| Smith | 4 | 0 | 0.0 | 0 |
| Gilliam | 1 | −4 | −4.0 | 0 |

**RECEIVING**

| Last Name | No. | Yds | Avg | TD |
|---|---|---|---|---|
| D. Williams | 56 | 702 | 13 | 7 |
| Gilliam | 52 | 997 | 19 | 9 |
| Smith | 43 | 561 | 13 | 1 |
| Edwards | 23 | 309 | 13 | 0 |
| Roland | 12 | 136 | 11 | 1 |
| Crenshaw | 11 | 94 | 9 | 0 |
| Lane | 9 | 61 | 7 | 0 |
| Shivers | 7 | 61 | 9 | 1 |
| Daanen | 2 | 12 | 6 | 0 |
| T. Brown | 1 | 7 | 7 | 0 |

**PUNT RETURNS**

| Last Name | No. | Yds | Avg | TD |
|---|---|---|---|---|
| Wehrli | 13 | 65 | 5 | 0 |
| Roland | 10 | 53 | 5 | 0 |
| Shivers | 9 | 44 | 5 | 0 |
| T. Brown | 6 | 39 | 7 | 0 |

**KICKOFF RETURNS**

| Last Name | No. | Yds | Avg | TD |
|---|---|---|---|---|
| Lane | 20 | 523 | 26 | 0 |
| Gilliam | 11 | 339 | 31 | 1 |
| T. Brown | 15 | 320 | 21 | 0 |
| Shivers | 10 | 205 | 21 | 0 |
| M. Wilson | 4 | 66 | 17 | 0 |
| Crenshaw | 4 | 34 | 9 | 0 |
| Wehrli | 1 | 18 | 18 | 0 |
| Olerich | 2 | 2 | 1 | 0 |
| C. Williams | 1 | 0 | 0 | 0 |

**PASSING**

| Last Name | Att | Comp | % | Yds | Yd/Att | TD | Int− | % | RK |
|---|---|---|---|---|---|---|---|---|---|
| Johnson | 260 | 131 | 50 | 1847 | 7.1 | 13 | 13− | 5 | 13 |
| Hart | 169 | 84 | 50 | 1086 | 6.4 | 6 | 12− | 7 | 18 |
| Hill | 1 | 1 | 100 | 7 | 7.0 | 0 | 0− | 0 | |

**PUNTING**

| Last Name | No | Avg |
|---|---|---|
| Hill | 73 | 37.6 |

**KICKING**

| Last Name | XP | Att | % | FG | Att | % |
|---|---|---|---|---|---|---|
| Bakken | 38 | 40 | 95 | 12 | 24 | 50 |

### PITTSBURGH STEELERS

**RUSHING**

| Last Name | No. | Yds | Avg | TD |
|---|---|---|---|---|
| Hoak | 151 | 531 | 3.5 | 2 |
| Gros | 116 | 343 | 3.0 | 4 |
| Bankston | 62 | 259 | 4.2 | 1 |
| Hanratty | 10 | 106 | 10.6 | 0 |
| McCall | 30 | 98 | 3.3 | 0 |
| Nix | 10 | 70 | 7.0 | 0 |
| Shiner | 14 | 55 | 3.9 | 1 |
| Jefferson | 4 | 46 | 11.5 | 0 |
| Wilburn | 2 | 29 | 14.5 | 0 |
| B. Campbell | 1 | 5 | 5.0 | 0 |

**RECEIVING**

| Last Name | No. | Yds | Avg | TD |
|---|---|---|---|---|
| Jefferson | 67 | 1079 | 16 | 9 |
| Wilburn | 20 | 373 | 19 | 0 |
| Hoak | 20 | 190 | 10 | 1 |
| Gros | 17 | 131 | 8 | 3 |
| Hilton | 12 | 231 | 19 | 0 |
| Henderson | 12 | 188 | 16 | 3 |
| Cropper | 9 | 116 | 13 | 0 |
| Adams | 6 | 80 | 13 | 0 |
| Bankston | 6 | 6 | 1 | 0 |
| E. Williams | 3 | 14 | 5 | 1 |
| McCall | 2 | 2 | 1 | 0 |
| B. Campbell | 1 | 32 | 32 | 0 |
| Alley | 1 | 16 | 16 | 0 |

**PUNT RETURNS**

| Last Name | No. | Yds | Avg | TD |
|---|---|---|---|---|
| B. Campbell | 28 | 133 | 5 | 0 |
| Jefferson | 4 | 23 | 6 | 0 |
| Hoak | 1 | 9 | 9 | 0 |
| Martha | 3 | 0 | 0 | 0 |
| Davis | 1 | 0 | 0 | 0 |

**KICKOFF RETURNS**

| Last Name | No. | Yds | Avg | TD |
|---|---|---|---|---|
| McCall | 21 | 532 | 25 | 1 |
| B. Campbell | 26 | 522 | 20 | 0 |
| Bankston | 4 | 89 | 22 | 0 |
| Jefferson | 4 | 80 | 20 | 0 |
| Woodson | 1 | 18 | 18 | 0 |
| Davis | 3 | 0 | 0 | 0 |
| Kolb | 1 | 0 | 0 | 0 |

**PASSING**

| Last Name | Att | Comp | % | Yds | Yd/Att | TF | Int− | % | RK |
|---|---|---|---|---|---|---|---|---|---|
| Shiner | 209 | 97 | 46 | 1422 | 6.8 | 7 | 10− | 5 | 15 |
| Hanratty | 126 | 52 | 41 | 716 | 5.7 | 8 | 13− | 10 | |
| Nix | 53 | 25 | 47 | 290 | 5.5 | 2 | 6− | 11 | |
| Hoak | 3 | 2 | 67 | 30 | 10.0 | 0 | 0− | 0 | |

**PUNTING**

| Last Name | No | Avg |
|---|---|---|
| Walden | 77 | 42.3 |

**KICKING**

| Last Name | XP | Att | % | FG | Att | % |
|---|---|---|---|---|---|---|
| Mingo | 26 | 26 | 100 | 12 | 26 | 46 |

## CENTRAL DIVISION

### MINNESOTA VIKINGS 12-2-0 Bud Grant

**Scores of Each Game**

| | | |
|---|---|---|
| 23 | New York | 24 |
| 52 | BALTIMORE | 14 |
| 19 | GREEN BAY | 7 |
| 31 | Chicago | 0 |
| 27 | St. Louis | 10 |
| 24 | DETROIT | 10 |
| 31 | CHICAGO | 14 |
| 51 | CLEVELAND | 3 |
| 9 | Green Bay | 7 |
| 52 | PITTSBURGH | 14 |
| 27 | Detroit | 0 |
| 20 | Los Angeles | 13 |
| 10 | SAN FRANCISCO | |
| 3 | Atlanta | 10 |

| Use Name | Pos. | Hgt | Wgt | Age | Int | Pts |
|---|---|---|---|---|---|---|
| Grady Alderman | OT | 6'2" | 242 | 30 | | |
| Doug Davis | OT | 6'4" | 255 | 25 | | |
| Ron Yary | OT | 6'6" | 265 | 23 | | |
| Bookie Bolin | OG | 6'2" | 250 | 29 | | |
| Milt Sunde | OG | 6'2" | 250 | 26 | | |
| Jim Vellone | OG | 6'2" | 255 | 25 | | |
| Ed White | OG | 6'2" | 252 | 22 | | |
| Mick Tingelhoff | C | 6'1" | 237 | 29 | | |
| Carl Eller | DE | 6'6" | 265 | 27 | | |
| Jim Marshall | DE | 6'3" | 260 | 31 | 1 | |
| Steve Smith | DE | 6'5" | 240 | 25 | | |
| Paul Dickson | DT | 6'5" | 257 | 32 | | |
| Gary Larsen | DT | 6'5" | 260 | 29 | | |
| Alan Page | DT | 6'5" | 260 | 24 | | 6 |
| Jim Hargrove | LB | 6'3" | 232 | 24 | | |
| Wally Hilgenberg | LB | 6'3" | 235 | 26 | | |
| Mike McGill | LB | 6'2" | 237 | 22 | | |
| Mike Reilly | LB | 6'2" | 235 | 26 | | 6 |
| Lonnie Warwick | LB | 6'3" | 237 | 27 | 4 | |
| Roy Winston | LB | 6'1" | 230 | 29 | 3 | |
| Bobby Bryant | DB | 6' | 175 | 25 | 8 | |
| Karl Kassulke | DB | 6' | 195 | 27 | 2 | |
| Paul Krause | DB | 6'3" | 195 | 27 | 5 | 6 |
| Earsell Mackbee | DB | 6'1" | 195 | 28 | 6 | |
| Ed Sharockman | DB | 6' | 200 | 29 | 1 | |
| Charlie West | DB | 6'1" | 190 | 23 | | |
| Dale Hackbart | LB-DB | 6'3" | 214 | 33 | | |
| Gary Cuozzo | QB | 6'1" | 195 | 28 | | |
| Joe Kapp | QB | 6'2" | 215 | 31 | | |
| Bob Lee | QB | 6'2" | 195 | 23 | | |
| Billy Harris | HB | 6' | | | | |
| Clint Jones | HB | 6' | 206 | 24 | | 18 |
| Dave Osborn | HB | 6' | 205 | 26 | | 48 |
| Bill Brown | FB | 5'11" | 230 | 31 | | 18 |
| Jim Lindsey | HB-FB | 6'2" | 212 | 24 | | 12 |
| Oscar Reed | HB-FB | 5'11" | 222 | 25 | | 18 |
| Bob Grim | WR | 6' | 197 | 24 | | 6 |
| Tom Hall | WR | 6'1" | 195 | 28 | | |
| John Henderson | WR | 6'3" | 190 | 26 | | 30 |
| Gene Washington | WR | 6'3" | 218 | 25 | | 54 |
| John Beasley | TE | 6'3" | 230 | 24 | | 30 |
| Kent Kramer | TE | 6'5" | 235 | 25 | | 6 |
| Fred Cox | K | 5'10" | 200 | 30 | | 121 |

### DETROIT LIONS 9-4-1 Joe Schmidt

**Scores of Each Game**

| | | |
|---|---|---|
| 13 | Pittsburgh | 16 |
| 24 | NEW YORK | 0 |
| 28 | Cleveland | 21 |
| 17 | GREEN BAY | 28 |
| 13 | CHICAGO | 7 |
| 10 | Minnesota | 24 |
| 26 | San Francisco | 14 |
| 27 | ATLANTA | 21 |
| 20 | ST. LOUIS | 0 |
| 16 | Green Bay | 10 |
| 0 | MINNESOTA | 27 |
| 17 | Baltimore | 17 |
| 28 | LOS ANGELES | 0 |
| 20 | Chicago | 3 |

| Use Name | Pos. | Hgt | Wgt | Age | Int | Pts |
|---|---|---|---|---|---|---|
| Rocky Freitas | OT | 6'6" | 260 | 23 | | |
| Roger Shoals | OT | 6'4" | 255 | 30 | | |
| Jim Yarbrough | OT | 6'6" | 250 | 22 | | |
| Frank Gallagher | OG | 6'2" | 240 | 26 | | |
| Bob Kowalkowski | OG | 6'3" | 245 | 25 | | |
| Rocky Rasley | OG | 6'3" | 248 | 22 | | |
| Chuck Walton | OG | 6'3" | 250 | 28 | | |
| Ed Flanagan | C | 6'3" | 250 | 25 | | |
| Bill Cottrell | OG-C | 6'3" | 250 | 24 | | |
| Larry Hand | DE | 6'4" | 245 | 29 | | |
| Joe Robb | DE | 6'3" | 245 | 32 | | |
| Denis Moore | DT-DE | 6'5" | 255 | 25 | | |
| Alex Karras | DT | 6'2" | 255 | 33 | 1 | |
| Jerry Rush | DT | 6'4" | 260 | 27 | | |
| Dan Goich | DE-DT | 6'4" | 265 | 25 | | |
| Mike Lucci | LB | 6'2" | 230 | 29 | | |
| Ed Mooney | LB | 6'2" | 240 | 24 | | |
| Paul Naumoff | LB | 6'1" | 225 | 24 | | |
| Tom Nowatzke | LB | 6'3" | 230 | 26 | | |
| Bill Swain | LB | 6'2" | 230 | 28 | | |
| Wayne Walker | LB | 6'2" | 225 | 32 | 1 | |
| Lem Barney | DB | 6' | 185 | 23 | 8 | 6 |
| Dick LeBeau | DB | 6'1" | 185 | 32 | 6 | |
| Wayne Rasmussen | DB | 6'2" | 175 | 27 | | |
| Tom Vaughn | DB | 5'11" | 190 | 26 | 2 | |
| Mike Weger | DB | 6'2" | 185 | 23 | 3 | |
| Bobby Williams | DB | 6'1" | 205 | 27 | | |
| Greg Barton | QB | 6'2" | 195 | 23 | | |
| Greg Landry | QB | 6'4" | 205 | 22 | | 6 |
| Bill Munson | QB | 6'2" | 200 | 27 | | |
| Nick Eddy | HB | 6'1" | 205 | 25 | | 18 |
| Mel Farr | HB | 6'2" | 205 | 24 | | 24 |
| Altie Taylor | HB | 5'10" | 196 | 21 | | |
| Bill Triplett | FB | 6'2" | 210 | 30 | | 24 |
| Larry Watkins | FB | 6'2" | 215 | 22 | | |
| Bill Malinchak | WR | 6'1" | 200 | 25 | | |
| Earl McCullouch | WR | 5'11" | 180 | 23 | | 30 |
| Phil Odle | WR | 5'11" | 190 | 26 | | |
| Larry Walton | WR | 5'11" | 180 | 22 | | |
| John Wright | WR | 6' | 197 | 23 | | 18 |
| Craig Cotton | TE | 6'4" | 222 | 22 | | |
| Charlie Sanders | TE | 6'4" | 215 | 23 | | 18 |
| Rick Duncan | K | 6' | 208 | 28 | | |
| Errol Mann | K | 6' | 200 | 28 | | 101 |

### GREEN BAY PACKERS 8-6-0 Phil Bengtson

**Scores of Each Game**

| | | |
|---|---|---|
| 17 | CHICAGO | 0 |
| 14 | SAN FRANCISCO | 7 |
| 7 | Minnesota | 19 |
| 28 | Detroit | 17 |
| 21 | Los Angeles | 34 |
| 28 | ATLANTA | 10 |
| 38 | Pittsburgh | 34 |
| 6 | Baltimore | 14 |
| 7 | MINNESOTA | 9 |
| 10 | DETROIT | 16 |
| 20 | NEW YORK | 10 |
| 7 | Cleveland | 20 |
| 21 | Chicago | 3 |
| 45 | ST. LOUIS | 28 |

| Use Name | Pos. | Hgt | Wgt | Age | Int | Pts |
|---|---|---|---|---|---|---|
| Forrest Gregg | OT | 6'4" | 250 | 36 | | |
| Bill Hayhoe | OT | 6'8" | 258 | 22 | | |
| Dick Himes | OT | 6'4" | 244 | 23 | | |
| Francis Peay | OT | 6'5" | 250 | 25 | | |
| Dave Bradley | OG | 6'4" | 245 | 22 | | |
| Gale Gillingham | OG | 6'3" | 255 | 25 | | |
| Bill Lueck | OG | 6'3" | 235 | 23 | | |
| Ken Bowman | C | 6'3" | 230 | 26 | | |
| Bob Hyland | OG-C | 6'5" | 250 | 24 | | |
| Lionel Aldridge | DE | 6'4" | 245 | 27 | | |
| Willie Davis | DE | 6'3" | 245 | 36 | 1 | |
| Phil Vandersea | DE | 6'3" | 235 | 26 | | |
| Francis Winkler | DE | 6'3" | 230 | 22 | | |
| Bob Brown | DT | 6'5" | 260 | 29 | | |
| Henry Jordan | DT | 6'3" | 250 | 34 | | |
| Rich Moore | DT | 6'6" | 285 | 22 | | |
| Jim Weatherwax | DT | 6'7" | 260 | 21 | | |
| Lee Roy Caffey | LB | 6'3" | 250 | 29 | 2 | |
| Fred Carr | LB | 6'5" | 238 | 23 | | |
| Jim Flanigan | LB | 6'3" | 240 | 24 | | |
| Ray Nitschke | LB | 6'3" | 235 | 33 | 2 | |
| Dave Robinson | LB | 6'3" | 240 | 28 | | |
| Herb Adderley | DB | 6'1" | 200 | 30 | 5 | 6 |
| Doug Hart | DB | 6' | 190 | 30 | 3 | 6 |
| Bob Jeter | DB | 6'1" | 205 | 31 | 3 | |
| John Rowser | DB | 6'1" | 180 | 25 | | |
| Gordon Rule | DB | 6'2" | 180 | 23 | | |
| Willie Wood | DB | 5'10" | 190 | 33 | 3 | |
| Don Horn | QB | 6'2" | 195 | 24 | | 6 |
| Bart Starr | QB | 6'1" | 190 | 36 | | |
| Bill Stevens | QB | 6'3" | 195 | 24 | | |
| Donny Anderson | HB | 6'3" | 210 | 26 | | 12 |
| Elijah Pitts | HB | 6'1" | 205 | 30 | | |
| Travis Williams | HB | 6'1" | 210 | 23 | | 54 |
| Jim Grabowski | FB | 6'2" | 220 | 25 | | 12 |
| Perry Williams | FB | 6'2" | 220 | 22 | | |
| Dave Hampton | HB-FB | 6' | 210 | 22 | | 42 |
| Carroll Dale | WR | 6'1" | 200 | 31 | | 36 |
| Boyd Dowler | WR | 6'5" | 225 | 32 | | 24 |
| John Spilis | WR | 6'3" | 205 | 21 | | |
| Marv Fleming | TE | 6'4" | 235 | 27 | | 12 |
| Ron Jones | TE | 6'3" | 220 | 22 | | |
| Booth Lusteg | K | 5'11" | 190 | 28 | | 15 |
| Mike Mercer | K | 6' | 217 | 33 | | 38 |

Zeke Bratkowski — Voluntarily Retired

### CHICAGO BEARS 1-13-0 Jim Dooley

**Scores of Each Game**

| | | |
|---|---|---|
| 0 | Green Bay | 17 |
| 17 | St. Louis | 20 |
| 24 | New York | 28 |
| 0 | MINNESOTA | 31 |
| 7 | Detroit | 13 |
| 7 | LOS ANGELES | 9 |
| 14 | Minnesota | 31 |
| 38 | PITTSBURGH | 7 |
| 31 | Atlanta | 48 |
| 21 | BALTIMORE | 24 |
| 24 | CLEVELAND | 28 |
| 21 | San Francisco | 42 |
| 3 | GREEN BAY | 21 |
| 3 | DETROIT | 20 |

| Use Name | Pos. | Hgt | Wgt | Age | Int | Pts |
|---|---|---|---|---|---|---|
| Randy Jackson | OT | 6'5" | 245 | 25 | | |
| Wayne Mass | OT | 6'4" | 245 | 23 | | |
| Rufus Mayes | OT | 6'5" | 255 | 21 | | |
| Bob Pickens | OT | 6'4" | 258 | 26 | | |
| Bob Wetoska | C-OT | 6'3" | 240 | 31 | | |
| Jim Cadile | OG | 6'3" | 240 | 24 | | |
| Howard Mudd (from SF) | OG | 6'3" | 252 | 27 | | |
| George Seals | OG | 6'2" | 260 | 26 | | |
| Jim Ferguson (from ATL) | C | 6'4" | 240 | 26 | | |
| Mike Pyle | C | 6'3" | 250 | 30 | | |
| Marty Amsler | DE | 6'5" | 255 | 26 | | |
| Dave Hale | DE | 6'7" | 230 | 22 | | |
| Willie Holman | DE | 6'4" | 250 | 24 | | |
| Ed O'Bradovich | DE | 6'3" | 255 | 29 | 2 | |
| Loyd Phillips | DE | 6'3" | 240 | 24 | | |
| Frank Cornish | DT | 6'6" | 300 | 25 | | |
| Dick Evey | DT | 6'2" | 245 | 28 | 2 | |
| Ken Kortas | DT | 6'2" | 280 | 27 | | |
| Doug Buffone | LB | 6'1" | 230 | 25 | 2 | |
| Dick Butkus | LB | 6'3" | 245 | 25 | 2 | 2 |
| Tim Casey (to DEN-A) | LB | 6'1" | 225 | 25 | | |
| Rudy Kuechenberg | LB | 6'2" | 215 | 26 | | |
| Dave Martin | LB | 6'1" | 225 | 22 | | |
| Dan Pride | LB | 6'3" | 225 | 27 | 1 | |
| Dick Daniels | DB | 5'9" | 180 | 23 | 3 | |
| Major Hazelton | DB | 6'1" | 185 | 24 | | |
| Bennie McRae | DB | 6'1" | 180 | 28 | 1 | |
| Joe Taylor | DB | 6'2" | 200 | 28 | 3 | |
| George Youngblood | DB | 6'3" | 205 | 24 | 3 | 6 |
| Garry Lyle | HB-DB | 6'2" | 198 | 23 | 1 | |
| Virgil Carter | QB | 6'1" | 185 | 23 | | |
| Jack Concannon | QB | 6'3" | 205 | 26 | | 6 |
| Bobby Douglass | QB | 6'3" | 215 | 22 | | 12 |
| Gale Sayers | HB | 6' | 198 | 26 | | 48 |
| Brian Piccolo | FB-HB | 6' | 205 | 25 | | 18 |
| Ronnie Bull | FB | 6' | 200 | 29 | | |
| Mike Hull | FB | 6'3" | 220 | 24 | | 6 |
| Ralph Kurek | FB | 6'2" | 210 | 26 | | |
| Ross Montgomery | FB | 6'3" | 220 | 22 | | |
| Ron Copeland | WR | 6'4" | 196 | 22 | | |
| Dick Gordon | WR | 5'11" | 190 | 24 | | 24 |
| Bob Jones | WR | 6'4" | 196 | 24 | | |
| Jerry Simmons (from ATL) | WR | 6'1" | 190 | 26 | | |
| Cecil Turner | WR | 5'10" | 170 | 25 | | |
| Bob Wallace | TE | 6'3" | 211 | 23 | | 30 |
| Austin Denney | TE | 6'2" | 230 | 25 | | |
| Emilio Vallez | TE | 6'2" | 210 | 23 | | |
| Ray Odgen | WR-TE | 6'5" | 225 | 26 | | |
| Bobby Joe Green | K | 5'11" | 175 | 31 | | |
| Mac Percival | K | 6'4" | 220 | 29 | | 50 |

Terry Stoepel — Military Service

## CENTRAL DIVISION

### MINNESOTA VIKINGS

**RUSHING**

| Last Name | No. | Yds | Avg | TD |
|---|---|---|---|---|
| Osborn | 186 | 643 | 3.5 | 7 |
| Brown | 126 | 430 | 3.4 | 3 |
| Reed | 83 | 393 | 4.7 | 1 |
| Jones | 54 | 241 | 4.5 | 3 |
| Kapp | 22 | 104 | 4.7 | 0 |
| Lindsey | 6 | 21 | 3.5 | 1 |
| Harris | 6 | 13 | 2.2 | 0 |
| Lee | 3 | 9 | 3.0 | 0 |
| Cuozzo | 3 | −4 | −1.3 | 0 |

**RECEIVING**

| Last Name | No. | Yds | Avg | TD |
|---|---|---|---|---|
| Washington | 39 | 821 | 21 | 9 |
| Henderson | 34 | 553 | 16 | 5 |
| Beasley | 33 | 361 | 11 | 4 |
| Osborn | 22 | 236 | 11 | 1 |
| Brown | 21 | 183 | 9 | 0 |
| Grim | 10 | 155 | 16 | 1 |
| Reed | 7 | 59 | 8 | 2 |
| Jones | 3 | 23 | 8 | 0 |
| Lindsey | 2 | 45 | 23 | 1 |
| Kramer | 2 | 37 | 19 | 1 |
| Harris | 2 | 13 | 7 | 0 |
| Hall | 1 | 12 | 12 | 0 |

**PUNT RETURNS**

| Last Name | No. | Yds | Avg | TD |
|---|---|---|---|---|
| West | 39 | 245 | 6 | 0 |
| Grim | 4 | 12 | 3 | 0 |
| Bryant | 2 | 9 | 5 | 0 |

**KICKOFF RETURNS**

| Last Name | No. | Yds | Avg | TD |
|---|---|---|---|---|
| Jones | 17 | 444 | 26 | 0 |
| West | 9 | 240 | 27 | 0 |
| Reed | 1 | 38 | 38 | 0 |
| Lindsey | 2 | 26 | 13 | 0 |
| Harris | 1 | 23 | 23 | 0 |
| Smith | 1 | 3 | 3 | 0 |
| Alderman | 1 | 0 | 0 | 0 |
| Sunde | 1 | 0 | 0 | 0 |

**PASSING – PUNTING – KICKING**

PASSING

| Last Name | Att | Comp | % | Yds | Yd/Att | TD | Int− | % | RK |
|---|---|---|---|---|---|---|---|---|---|
| Kapp | 237 | 120 | 51 | 1726 | 7.3 | 19 | 13− | 5 | 10 |
| Cuozzo | 98 | 49 | 50 | 693 | 7.1 | 4 | 5− | 5 | |
| Lee | 11 | 7 | 64 | 79 | 7.2 | 1 | 0− | 0 | |

PUNTING

| Last Name | No | Avg |
|---|---|---|
| Lee | 67 | 40.0 |

KICKING

| Last Name | XP | Att | % | FG | Att | % |
|---|---|---|---|---|---|---|
| Cox | 43 | 43 | 100 | 26 | 37 | 70 |

### DETROIT LIONS

**RUSHING**

| Last Name | No. | Yds | Avg | TD |
|---|---|---|---|---|
| Triplett | 111 | 377 | 3.4 | 3 |
| Taylor | 118 | 348 | 2.9 | 4 |
| Eddy | 78 | 272 | 3.5 | 2 |
| Farr | 58 | 245 | 4.2 | 4 |
| Landry | 33 | 243 | 7.4 | 1 |
| Watkins | 62 | 201 | 3.2 | 1 |
| Barney | 3 | 36 | 12.0 | 0 |
| Munson | 7 | 31 | 4.4 | 0 |
| L. Walton | 2 | 6 | 3.0 | 0 |
| McCullouch | 1 | 4 | 4.0 | 0 |
| Sanders | 1 | −8 | −8.0 | 0 |

**RECEIVING**

| Last Name | No. | Yds | Avg | TD |
|---|---|---|---|---|
| Sanders | 42 | 656 | 16 | 3 |
| McCullouch | 33 | 529 | 16 | 5 |
| Triplett | 13 | 141 | 11 | 0 |
| Farr | 13 | 94 | 7 | 0 |
| Watkins | 13 | 87 | 7 | 0 |
| Taylor | 13 | 86 | 7 | 0 |
| Wright | 12 | 130 | 11 | 2 |
| L. Walton | 12 | 109 | 9 | 0 |
| Eddy | 10 | 78 | 8 | 1 |
| Malinchak | 2 | 24 | 12 | 0 |
| Odle | 2 | 24 | 12 | 0 |

**PUNT RETURNS**

| Last Name | No. | Yds | Avg | TD |
|---|---|---|---|---|
| Barney | 9 | 191 | 21 | 1 |
| L. Walton | 9 | 24 | 3 | 0 |
| Vaughn | 2 | 10 | 5 | 0 |
| Eddy | 1 | 5 | 5 | 0 |

**KICKOFF RETURNS**

| Last Name | No. | Yds | Avg | TD |
|---|---|---|---|---|
| Williams | 17 | 563 | 33 | 1 |
| L. Walton | 12 | 230 | 19 | 0 |
| Barney | 7 | 154 | 22 | 0 |
| Vaughn | 2 | 44 | 22 | 0 |
| Nowatzke | 1 | 14 | 14 | 0 |
| Mooney | 2 | 12 | 6 | 0 |
| Yarbrough | 1 | 0 | 0 | 0 |

**PASSING – PUNTING – KICKING**

PASSING

| Last Name | Att | Comp | % | Yds | Yd/Att | TD | Int− | % | RK |
|---|---|---|---|---|---|---|---|---|---|
| Munson | 166 | 84 | 51 | 1062 | 6.4 | 7 | 8− | 5 | 14 |
| Landry | 160 | 80 | 50 | 853 | 5.3 | 4 | 10− | 6 | 20 |
| Barton | 1 | 0 | 0 | 0 | 0.0 | 0 | 0− | 0 | |
| Farr | 1 | 0 | 0 | 0 | 0.0 | 0 | 0− | 0 | |
| L. Walton | 1 | 1 | 100 | 43 | 43.0 | 1 | 0− | 0 | |

PUNTING

| Last Name | No | Avg |
|---|---|---|
| Barney | 66 | 34.1 |
| Malinchak | 5 | 36.8 |
| Duncan | 3 | 25.7 |

KICKING

| Last Name | XP | Att | % | FG | Att | % |
|---|---|---|---|---|---|---|
| Mann | 26 | 26 | 100 | 25 | 37 | 68 |

### GREEN BAY PACKERS

**RUSHING**

| Last Name | No. | Yds | Avg | TD |
|---|---|---|---|---|
| T. Williams | 129 | 536 | 4.2 | 4 |
| Hampton | 80 | 365 | 4.6 | 4 |
| Anderson | 87 | 288 | 3.3 | 1 |
| Grabowski | 73 | 261 | 3.6 | 1 |
| Pitts | 35 | 134 | 3.8 | 0 |
| Starr | 7 | 60 | 8.6 | 0 |
| P. Williams | 18 | 55 | 3.1 | 0 |
| Horn | 3 | −7 | −2.3 | 1 |

**RECEIVING**

| Last Name | No. | Yds | Avg | TD |
|---|---|---|---|---|
| Dale | 45 | 879 | 20 | 6 |
| Dowler | 31 | 477 | 15 | 4 |
| T. Williams | 27 | 275 | 10 | 3 |
| Fleming | 18 | 226 | 13 | 2 |
| Hampton | 15 | 216 | 14 | 2 |
| Anderson | 14 | 308 | 22 | 1 |
| Grabowski | 12 | 98 | 8 | 1 |
| Pitts | 9 | 47 | 5 | 1 |
| Spilis | 7 | 89 | 13 | 0 |
| P. Williams | 4 | 63 | 16 | 0 |

**PUNT RETURNS**

| Last Name | No. | Yds | Avg | TD |
|---|---|---|---|---|
| T. Williams | 8 | 189 | 24 | 1 |
| Pitts | 16 | 60 | 4 | 0 |
| Wood | 8 | 38 | 5 | 0 |

**KICKOFF RETURNS**

| Last Name | No. | Yds | Avg | TD |
|---|---|---|---|---|
| Hampton | 22 | 582 | 26 | 1 |
| T. Williams | 21 | 517 | 25 | 1 |
| Robinson | 3 | 31 | 10 | 0 |
| Pitts | 1 | 22 | 22 | 0 |
| Gillingham | 1 | 13 | 13 | 0 |
| Hyland | 1 | 0 | 0 | 0 |
| P. Williams | 1 | 0 | 0 | 0 |

**PASSING – PUNTING – KICKING**

PASSING

| Last Name | Att | Comp | % | Yds | Yd/Att | TD | Int− | % | RK |
|---|---|---|---|---|---|---|---|---|---|
| Horn | 168 | 89 | 53 | 1505 | 9.0 | 11 | 11− | 7 | 11 |
| Starr | 148 | 92 | 62 | 1161 | 7.8 | 9 | 6− | 4 | 2 |
| Stevens | 3 | 1 | 33 | 12 | 4.0 | 0 | 0− | 0 | |

PUNTING

| Last Name | No | Avg |
|---|---|---|
| Anderson | 58 | 40.2 |
| Dowler | 1 | 34.0 |

KICKING

| Last Name | XP | Att | % | FG | Att | % |
|---|---|---|---|---|---|---|
| Mercer | 23 | 23 | 100 | 5 | 17 | 29 |
| Lusteg | 12 | 12 | 100 | 1 | 5 | 20 |

### CHICAGO BEARS

**RUSHING**

| Last Name | No. | Yds | Avg | TD |
|---|---|---|---|---|
| Sayers | 236 | 1032 | 4.4 | 8 |
| Douglass | 51 | 408 | 8.0 | 2 |
| Bull | 44 | 187 | 4.3 | 0 |
| Piccolo | 45 | 148 | 3.3 | 2 |
| Hull | 29 | 81 | 2.8 | 1 |
| Concannon | 22 | 62 | 2.8 | 1 |
| Montgomery | 15 | 52 | 3.5 | 0 |
| Gordon | 2 | 28 | 14.0 | 0 |
| Kurek | 8 | 24 | 3.0 | 0 |
| Carter | 4 | 19 | 4.8 | 0 |
| Green | 1 | 17 | 17.0 | 0 |
| Wallace | 4 | 16 | 4.0 | 0 |
| Denney | 1 | 4 | 4.0 | 0 |

**RECEIVING**

| Last Name | No. | Yds | Avg | TD |
|---|---|---|---|---|
| Wallace | 47 | 553 | 12 | 5 |
| Gordon | 36 | 414 | 12 | 4 |
| Denney | 22 | 203 | 9 | 1 |
| Piccolo | 17 | 143 | 8 | 1 |
| Sayers | 17 | 116 | 7 | 0 |
| Simmons | 14 | 182 | 13 | 0 |
| Bull | 14 | 91 | 7 | 0 |
| Hull | 12 | 63 | 5 | 0 |
| Ogden | 7 | 100 | 14 | 0 |
| Kurek | 4 | 30 | 8 | 0 |
| Montgomery | 2 | 8 | 4 | 0 |
| Turner | 1 | 19 | 19 | 0 |
| Lyle | 1 | 11 | 11 | 0 |

**PUNT RETURNS**

| Last Name | No. | Yds | Avg | TD |
|---|---|---|---|---|
| Lyle | 12 | 78 | 7 | 0 |
| Piccolo | 9 | 43 | 5 | 0 |
| Turner | 8 | 32 | 4 | 0 |
| Gordon | 1 | 11 | 11 | 0 |

**KICKOFF RETURNS**

| Last Name | No. | Yds | Avg | TD |
|---|---|---|---|---|
| Sayers | 14 | 339 | 24 | 0 |
| Turner | 10 | 326 | 33 | 0 |
| Lyle | 11 | 248 | 23 | 0 |
| Gordon | 6 | 105 | 18 | 0 |
| Kurek | 4 | 66 | 17 | 0 |
| Butkus | 3 | 28 | 9 | 0 |
| Seals | 2 | 20 | 10 | 0 |
| Holman | 1 | 0 | 0 | 0 |
| Kuechenberg | 1 | 0 | 0 | 0 |

**PASSING – PUNTING – KICKING**

PASSING

| Last Name | Att | Comp | % | Yds | Yd/Att | TD | Int− | % | RK |
|---|---|---|---|---|---|---|---|---|---|
| Concannon | 160 | 87 | 54 | 783 | 4.9 | 4 | 8− | 5 | 16 |
| Douglass | 148 | 68 | 46 | 773 | 5.2 | 5 | 8− | 5 | 19 |
| Carter | 71 | 36 | 51 | 343 | 4.8 | 2 | 5− | 7 | |
| Green | 2 | 2 | 100 | 30 | 15.0 | 0 | 0− | 0 | |
| Sayers | 2 | 0 | 0 | 0 | 0.0 | 0 | 0− | 0 | |
| Bull | 1 | 0 | 0 | 0 | 0.0 | 0 | 0− | 0 | |

PUNTING

| Last Name | No | Avg |
|---|---|---|
| Green | 76 | 39.0 |

KICKING

| Last Name | XP | Att | % | FG | Att | % |
|---|---|---|---|---|---|---|
| Percival | 26 | 26 | 100 | 8 | 21 | 38 |

## COASTAL DIVISION

### LOS ANGELES RAMS 11-3-0 George Allen

Scores of Each Game:

| | | |
|---|---|---|
| 27 | Baltimore | 20 |
| 17 | ATLANTA | 7 |
| 36 | NEW ORLEANS | 17 |
| 27 | San Francisco | 21 |
| 34 | GREEN BAY | 21 |
| 9 | Chicago | 7 |
| 38 | Atlanta | 6 |
| 41 | SAN FRANCISCO | 30 |
| 23 | Philadelphia | 17 |
| 24 | DALLAS | 23 |
| 24 | Washington | 13 |
| 13 | MINNESOTA | 20 |
| 0 | Detroit | 28 |
| 7 | BALTIMORE | 13 |

| Use Name | Pos. | Hgt | Wgt | Age | Int | Pts |
|---|---|---|---|---|---|---|
| Bob Brown | OT | 6'4" | 275 | 26 | | |
| Charley Cowan | OT | 6'4" | 265 | 31 | | |
| Mitch Johnson | OT | 6'4" | 250 | 27 | | |
| Mike LaHood | OG | 6'3" | 248 | 24 | | |
| Tom Mack | OG | 6'3" | 250 | 25 | | |
| Joe Scibelli | OG | 6'1" | 255 | 30 | | |
| George Burman | C-OG | 6'3" | 255 | 26 | | |
| Ken Iman | C | 6'1" | 240 | 30 | | |
| Frank Marchlewski | C | 6'2" | 240 | 25 | | |
| Rick Cash | DE | 6'5" | 260 | 24 | | |
| Deacon Jones | DE | 6'5" | 250 | 30 | | |
| Lamar Lundy | DE | 6'7" | 250 | 34 | | |
| Diron Talbert | DE | 6'5" | 245 | 25 | | |
| Coy Bacon | DT | 6'4" | 270 | 27 | | |
| Roger Brown | DT | 6'5" | 285 | 32 | | |
| Merlin Olsen | DT | 6'5" | 270 | 28 | | |
| Maxie Baughan | LB | 6'1" | 230 | 31 | | |
| Jack Pardee | LB | 6'2" | 225 | 33 | 1 | |
| John Pergine | LB | 6'1" | 225 | 22 | | |
| Myron Pottios | LB | 6'2" | 232 | 29 | 1 | |
| Jim Purnell | LB | 6'2" | 238 | 27 | | |
| Doug Woodlief | LB | 6'3" | 225 | 25 | 4 | |
| Willie Daniel | DB | 5'11" | 190 | 31 | 1 | |
| Alvin Haymond | DB | 6' | 194 | 27 | | |
| Ed Meador | DB | 5'11" | 190 | 32 | 5 | 12 |
| Jim Nettles | DB | 5'9" | 177 | 27 | 2 | |
| Richie Petitbon | DB | 6'3" | 208 | 31 | 5 | |
| Nate Shaw | DB | 6'2" | 205 | 24 | | |
| Ron Smith | DB | 6'1" | 192 | 26 | 3 | 6 |
| Clancy Williams | DB | 6'2" | 194 | 26 | 4 | |
| Roman Gabriel | QB | 6'4" | 220 | 29 | | 30 |
| Karl Sweetan | QB | 6'1" | 200 | 26 | | |
| Mike Dennis | HB | 6'1" | 207 | 25 | | |
| Willie Ellison | HB | 6'1" | 200 | 24 | | 12 |
| Larry Smith | HB | 6'3" | 220 | 21 | | 18 |
| Dick Bass | FB | 5'10" | 195 | 32 | | |
| Les Josephson | FB | 6' | 207 | 26 | | 12 |
| Izzy Lang | FB | 6'1" | 232 | 26 | | |
| Tommy Mason | HB-FB | 6' | 195 | 30 | | 12 |
| David Ray | WR | 6' | 195 | 24 | | |
| Jack Snow | WR | 6'2" | 190 | 26 | | 36 |
| Pat Studstill | WR | 6'1" | 175 | 31 | | |
| Wendell Tucker | WR | 5'10" | 185 | 25 | | 42 |
| Pat Curran | TE | 6'3" | 238 | 23 | | |
| Bob Klein | TE | 6'5" | 235 | 22 | | 6 |
| Billy Truax | TE | 6'5" | 235 | 26 | | 30 |
| Bruce Gossett | K | 6'2" | 230 | 26 | | 102 |

Jim Wilson — Injury

### BALTIMORE COLTS 8-5-1 Don Shula

Scores of Each Game:

| | | |
|---|---|---|
| 20 | LOS ANGELES | 27 |
| 14 | Minnesota | 52 |
| 21 | Atlanta | 14 |
| 24 | PHILADELPHIA | 20 |
| 30 | New Orleans | 10 |
| 21 | SAN FRANCISCO | 24 |
| 41 | WASHINGTON | 17 |
| 14 | GREEN BAY | 6 |
| 17 | San Francisco | 20 |
| 24 | Chicago | 21 |
| 13 | ATLANTA | 6 |
| 17 | DETROIT | 17 |
| 10 | Dallas | 27 |
| 13 | Los Angeles | 7 |

| Use Name | Pos. | Hgt | Wgt | Age | Int | Pts |
|---|---|---|---|---|---|---|
| Sam Ball | OT | 6'4" | 240 | 25 | | |
| Bob Vogel | OT | 6'5" | 250 | 27 | | |
| Dan Grimm (to WAS) | OG | 6'3" | 245 | 28 | | |
| Cornelius Johnson | OG | 6'2" | 245 | 26 | | |
| Glenn Ressler | OG | 6'3" | 250 | 25 | | |
| Dan Sullivan | OG | 6'3" | 250 | 30 | | |
| John Williams | OG | 6'3" | 256 | 23 | | |
| Bill Curry | C | 6'2" | 235 | 26 | | |
| Carl Mauck | C | 6'3" | 240 | 22 | | |
| Roy Hilton | DE | 6'6" | 240 | 24 | | |
| Lou Michaels | DE | 6'2" | 250 | 33 | | 75 |
| Bubba Smith | DE | 6'7" | 295 | 24 | | |
| Ron Kostelnik | DT | 6'4" | 260 | 29 | | |
| Fred Miller | DT | 6'3" | 250 | 28 | | |
| Billy Ray Smith | DT | 6'4" | 250 | 34 | | |
| Mike Curtis | LB | 6'2" | 232 | 26 | | |
| Dennis Gaubatz | LB | 6'2" | 232 | 28 | 1 | |
| Bob Grant | LB | 6'2" | 225 | 23 | 3 | |
| Ted Hendricks | LB | 6'7" | 215 | 21 | | |
| Butch Riley | LB | 6'2" | 220 | 22 | | |
| Don Shinnick | LB | 6' | 228 | 34 | | |
| Ocie Austin | DB | 6'3" | 200 | 22 | 2 | |
| Jim Duncan | DB | 6'2" | 200 | 23 | | 6 |
| Jerry Logan | DB | 6'1" | 190 | 28 | 1 | |
| Lenny Lyles | DB | 6'2" | 204 | 33 | | |
| Tommy Maxwell | DB | 6'2" | 195 | 22 | 3 | |
| Charlie Stukes | DB | 6'3" | 212 | 25 | 1 | |
| Rick Volk | DB | 6'3" | 195 | 24 | 4 | |
| Earl Morrall | QB | 6'1" | 206 | 35 | | |
| Johnny Unitas | QB | 6'1" | 196 | 36 | | |
| Tom Matte | HB | 6' | 214 | 30 | | 78 |
| Preston Pearson | HB | 6'1" | 190 | 24 | | |
| Terry Cole | FB | 6'1" | 220 | 24 | | 18 |
| Larry Conjar | FB | 6' | 214 | 23 | | |
| Perry Lee Dunn | FB | 6'2" | 215 | 26 | | |
| Jerry Hill | FB | 5'11" | 215 | 29 | | 12 |
| Eddie Hinton | WR | 6' | 200 | 22 | | |
| Jimmy Orr | WR | 5'11" | 185 | 33 | | 12 |
| Ray Perkins | WR | 6' | 183 | 27 | | 18 |
| Willie Richardson | WR | 6'2" | 198 | 29 | | 18 |
| Sam Havrilak | DB-WR | 6'2" | 195 | 21 | | 6 |
| John Mackey | TE | 6'3" | 224 | 27 | | 12 |
| Tom Mitchell | TE | 6'2" | 215 | 25 | | 18 |
| Roland Moss | TE | 6'3" | 215 | 22 | | |
| David Lee | K | 6'4" | 230 | 25 | | |

### ATLANTA FALCONS 6-8-0 Norm Van Brocklin

Scores of Each Game:

| | | |
|---|---|---|
| 24 | SAN FRANCISCO | 12 |
| 7 | Los Angeles | 17 |
| 14 | BALTIMORE | 21 |
| 17 | DALLAS | 24 |
| 21 | San Francsico | 7 |
| 10 | Green Bay | 28 |
| 6 | LOS ANGELES | 38 |
| 21 | Detroit | 27 |
| 48 | CHICAGO | 31 |
| 20 | Washington | 27 |
| 6 | Baltimore | 13 |
| 45 | NEW ORLEANS | 17 |
| 27 | Philadelphia | 3 |
| 10 | MINNESOTA | 3 |

| Use Name | Pos. | Hgt | Wgt | Age | Int | Pts |
|---|---|---|---|---|---|---|
| Bob Kelly | OT | 6'3" | 270 | 29 | | |
| George Kunz | OT | 6'5" | 245 | 22 | | |
| Bill Sandeman | OT | 6'6" | 250 | 26 | | |
| Bob Breitenstein | OG-OT | 6'3" | 267 | 26 | | |
| Dick Enderle | OG | 6'1" | 247 | 21 | | |
| Mal Snider | OG | 6'4" | 235 | 22 | | 6 |
| Roy Schmidt | OT-OG | 6'3" | 250 | 27 | | |
| Bruce Bosley | C | 6'2" | 244 | 35 | | |
| Jim Waskiewicz | C | 6'4" | 240 | 25 | | |
| Bob Hughes | DE | 6'4" | 250 | 24 | | |
| Claude Humphrey | DE | 6'5" | 255 | 25 | | 6 |
| John Zook | DE | 6'5" | 240 | 21 | 2 | |
| Dave Cahill | DT | 6'3" | 245 | 27 | | |
| Glen Condren | DT | 6'2" | 250 | 23 | | |
| Bill Sabatino | DT | 6'3" | 245 | 24 | | |
| Jerry Shay | DT | 6'3" | 245 | 25 | | |
| Ron Acks | LB | 6'2" | 225 | 24 | | 6 |
| Grady Allen | LB | 6'3" | 225 | 23 | 1 | |
| Greg Brezina | LB | 6'2" | 220 | 23 | 1 | |
| Ted Cottrell | LB | 6'1" | 232 | 22 | | |
| Fritz Greenlee | LB | 6'2" | 230 | 25 | | |
| Don Hansen | LB | 6'3" | 228 | 25 | 2 | |
| Tommy Nobis | LB | 6'2" | 235 | 25 | 1 | |
| Jeff Van Note | LB | 6'2" | 230 | 23 | | |
| Mike Freeman | DB | 5'11" | 190 | 25 | | |
| Al Lavan | DB | 6' | 194 | 22 | 2 | |
| John Mallory | DB | 6' | 190 | 23 | 1 | |
| Ken Reaves | DB | 6'3" | 205 | 24 | 5 | |
| Rudy Redmond | DB | 6' | 185 | 22 | 5 | |
| Jim Weatherford | DB | 5'10" | 180 | 23 | 1 | 6 |
| Nate Wright (to STL) | DB | 5'11" | 180 | 21 | 2 | |
| Bob Berry | QB | 5'11 | 190 | 27 | | |
| Randy Johnson | QB | 6'3" | 196 | 25 | | 6 |
| Bruce Lemmerman | QB | 6'1" | 196 | 23 | | 6 |
| Cannonball Butler | HB | 5'10" | 185 | 26 | | 30 |
| Gary McDermott | HB | 6'1" | 211 | 23 | | |
| Jeff Stanciel | HB | 6' | 192 | 22 | | |
| Paul Gipson | FB-HB | 6' | 205 | 23 | | 6 |
| Harmon Wages | FB | 6'1" | 210 | 23 | | 18 |
| Charlie Bryant | HB-FB | 6'1" | 207 | 28 | | |
| Gail Cogdill | WR | 6'2" | 200 | 32 | | 30 |
| Paul Flatley | WR | 6'1" | 187 | 28 | | 36 |
| Bob Lee | WR | 6'3" | 200 | 24 | | |
| Monte Ledbetter (From BUF-A) | WR | 6'2" | 185 | 26 | | |
| Tom McCauley | WR | 6'3" | 184 | 22 | | |
| Jim Mitchell | TE | 6'2" | 224 | 21 | | 24 |
| Ralph Smith | TE | 6'2" | 220 | 30 | | |
| Bob Etter | K | 5'11" | 152 | 24 | | 78 |
| Billy Lothridge | K | 6'1" | 190 | 25 | | |

Randy Winkler — Military Service

### SAN FRANCISCO FORTY NINERS 4-8-2 Dick Nolan

Scores of Each Game:

| | | |
|---|---|---|
| 12 | Atlanta | 24 |
| 7 | Green Bay | 14 |
| 17 | WASHINGTON | 17 |
| 21 | LOS ANGELES | 27 |
| 7 | ATLANTA | 21 |
| 24 | Baltimore | 21 |
| 14 | DETROIT | 26 |
| 30 | Los Angeles | 41 |
| 20 | BALTIMORE | 17 |
| 38 | New Orleans | 43 |
| 24 | Dallas | 24 |
| 42 | CHICAGO | 21 |
| 7 | Minnesota | 10 |
| 14 | PHILADELPHIA | 13 |

| Use Name | Pos. | Hgt | Wgt | Age | Int | Pts |
|---|---|---|---|---|---|---|
| Cas Banaszek | OT | 6'3" | 240 | 23 | | |
| Lance Olssen | OT | 6'5" | 267 | 22 | | |
| Len Rohde | OT | 6'4" | 250 | 31 | | |
| Elmer Collett | OG | 6'4" | 244 | 24 | | |
| Woody Peoples | OG | 6'2" | 247 | 26 | | |
| Randy Beisler | OT-OG | 6'4" | 255 | 24 | | |
| Forrest Blue | C | 6'5" | 248 | 23 | | |
| Bill Belk | DE | 6'3" | 242 | 23 | | |
| Tommy Hart | DE | 6'3" | 235 | 24 | | |
| Stan Hindman | DE | 6'3" | 237 | 25 | | |
| Earl Edwards | DT-DE | 6'6" | 276 | 24 | | |
| Charlie Krueger | DT | 6'4" | 270 | 33 | 1 | |
| Roland Lakes | DT | 6'4" | 265 | 29 | | 6 |
| Sam Silas | DE-DT | 6'4" | 255 | 26 | | |
| Ed Beard | LB | 6'2" | 220 | 29 | | |
| Harold Hays | LB | 6'3" | 225 | 28 | | |
| Frank Nunley | LB | 6'2" | 230 | 23 | 1 | |
| Jim Sniadecki | LB | 6'2" | 220 | 22 | | |
| Skip Vanderbundt | LB | 6'3" | 240 | 22 | | |
| Dave Wilcox | LB | 6'3" | 237 | 26 | 2 | |
| Kermit Alexander | DB | 5'11" | 186 | 28 | 5 | |
| Johnny Fuller | DB | 6' | 175 | 23 | 1 | |
| Jim Johnson | DB | 6'2" | 187 | 31 | 5 | |
| Mel Phillips | DB | 6' | 192 | 27 | | |
| Al Randolph | DB | 6'2" | 204 | 25 | 2 | |
| Rosey Taylor (from CHI) | DB | 5'11" | 186 | 30 | 2 | |
| John Woitt | DB | 5'11" | 170 | 23 | 1 | 6 |
| John Brodie | QB | 6'1" | 204 | 34 | | |
| Steve Spurrier | QB | 6'2" | 203 | 24 | | |
| Doug Cunningham | HB | 5'11" | 190 | 23 | | 18 |
| Gene Moore | HB | 6' | 208 | 22 | | |
| Noland Smith (From KC-A) | HB | 5'6" | 156 | 25 | | |
| Jimmy Thomas | HB | 6'1" | 216 | 22 | | 36 |
| Gary Lewis | FB-HB | 6'3" | 230 | 27 | | |
| Ken Willard | FB | 6'2" | 225 | 26 | | 60 |
| Bill Tucker | FB | 6'2" | 226 | 25 | | 24 |
| Lee Johnson | WR | 6'1" | 204 | 24 | | |
| Clifton McNeil | WR | 6'2" | 185 | 29 | | 18 |
| Gene Washington | WR | 6'1" | 186 | 22 | | 18 |
| Dick Witcher | WR | 6'3" | 204 | 24 | | 18 |
| Bill Wondolowski | WR | 5'10" | 168 | 22 | | |
| Ted Kwalick | TE | 6'4" | 230 | 22 | | 6 |
| Bob Windsor | TE | 6'4" | 230 | 26 | | 12 |
| Tommy Davis | K | 6' | 225 | 34 | | 22 |
| Momcilo Gavric | K | 5'10" | 167 | 31 | | 31 |
| Jon Kilgore | K | 6'1" | 205 | 25 | | |

Kevin Hardy — Knee Injury
Dave Hettema — Military Service
Matt Hazeltine — Voluntary Retirement

## COASTAL DIVISION

### LOS ANGELES RAMS

**RUSHING**

| Last Name | No. | Yds | Avg | TD |
|---|---|---|---|---|
| L. Smith | 166 | 599 | 3.6 | 1 |
| Josephson | 124 | 461 | 3.7 | 0 |
| Gabriel | 35 | 156 | 4.5 | 5 |
| Mason | 33 | 135 | 4.1 | 1 |
| Ellison | 20 | 56 | 2.8 | 1 |
| Meador | 1 | 5 | 5.0 | 0 |
| Bass | 1 | 1 | 1.0 | 0 |
| Lang | 1 | 1 | 1.0 | 0 |
| Sweetan | 1 | -1 | -1.0 | 0 |

**RECEIVING**

| Last Name | No. | Yds | Avg | TD |
|---|---|---|---|---|
| Snow | 49 | 734 | 15 | 6 |
| L. Smith | 46 | 300 | 7 | 2 |
| Tucker | 38 | 629 | 17 | 7 |
| Truax | 37 | 431 | 12 | 5 |
| Josephson | 32 | 295 | 9 | 2 |
| Mason | 11 | 185 | 17 | 1 |
| Ellison | 4 | 31 | 8 | 1 |
| Studstill | 3 | 28 | 9 | 0 |
| Klein | 2 | 17 | 9 | 1 |

**PUNT RETURNS**

| Last Name | No. | Yds | Avg | TD |
|---|---|---|---|---|
| Haymond | 33 | 435 | 13 | 0 |
| R. Smith | 23 | 122 | 5 | 0 |
| Pergine | 1 | 0 | 0 | 0 |
| Meador | 1 | -1 | -1 | 0 |

**KICKOFF RETURNS**

| Last Name | No. | Yds | Avg | TD |
|---|---|---|---|---|
| R. Smith | 27 | 585 | 22 | 0 |
| Haymond | 16 | 375 | 23 | 0 |
| Lang | 4 | 70 | 18 | 0 |
| Ellison | 2 | 38 | 19 | 0 |
| Curran | 2 | 28 | 14 | 0 |
| Burman | 1 | 11 | 11 | 0 |
| Klein | 1 | 0 | 0 | 0 |

**PASSING – PUNTING – KICKING**

**PASSING**

| Last Name | Att | Comp | % | Yds | Yd/Att | TD | Int– | % | RK |
|---|---|---|---|---|---|---|---|---|---|
| Gabriel | 399 | 217 | 54 | 2549 | 6.4 | 24 | 7– | 2 | 4 |
| Sweetan | 13 | 5 | 38 | 101 | 7.8 | 1 | 0– | 0 | |
| Ellison | 2 | 0 | 0 | 0 | 0.0 | 0 | 0– | 0 | |
| Meador | 1 | 0 | 0 | 0 | 0.0 | 0 | 0– | 0 | |
| L. Smith | 1 | 0 | 0 | 0 | 0.0 | 0 | 0– | 0 | |

**PUNTING**

| Last Name | No | Avg |
|---|---|---|
| Studstill | 80 | 40.7 |

**KICKING**

| Last Name | XP | Att | % | FG | Att | % |
|---|---|---|---|---|---|---|
| Gossett | 36 | 36 | 100 | 22 | 34 | 65 |

### BALTIMORE COLTS

**RUSHING**

| Last Name | No. | Yds | Avg | TD |
|---|---|---|---|---|
| Matte | 235 | 909 | 3.9 | 11 |
| Cole | 73 | 204 | 2.8 | 2 |
| Hill | 49 | 143 | 2.9 | 2 |
| Pearson | 24 | 81 | 3.4 | 0 |
| Havrilak | 5 | 49 | 9.8 | 1 |
| Dunn | 13 | 45 | 3.5 | 0 |
| Perkins | 3 | 36 | 12.0 | 0 |
| Unitas | 11 | 23 | 2.1 | 0 |
| Mackey | 2 | 3 | 1.5 | 0 |
| Conjar | 1 | 0 | 0.0 | 0 |
| Hinton | 1 | -3 | -3.0 | 0 |

**RECEIVING**

| Last Name | No. | Yds | Avg | TD |
|---|---|---|---|---|
| Richardson | 43 | 646 | 15 | 3 |
| Matte | 43 | 513 | 12 | 2 |
| Mackey | 34 | 443 | 13 | 2 |
| Perkins | 28 | 391 | 14 | 3 |
| Orr | 25 | 474 | 19 | 2 |
| Hinton | 13 | 269 | 21 | 1 |
| Hill | 11 | 44 | 4 | 0 |
| Mitchell | 9 | 199 | 22 | 3 |
| Cole | 9 | 65 | 7 | 1 |
| Dunn | 5 | 30 | 6 | 0 |
| Pearson | 4 | 64 | 16 | 0 |
| Havrilak | 1 | 5 | 5 | 0 |

**PUNT RETURNS**

| Last Name | No. | Yds | Avg | TD |
|---|---|---|---|---|
| Volk | 10 | 58 | 6 | 0 |
| Havrilak | 13 | 56 | 4 | 0 |
| Logan | 8 | 41 | 5 | 0 |
| Pearson | 6 | 37 | 6 | 0 |

**KICKOFF RETURNS**

| Last Name | No. | Yds | Avg | TD |
|---|---|---|---|---|
| Pearson | 31 | 706 | 23 | 0 |
| Duncan | 19 | 560 | 29 | 1 |
| Hinton | 1 | 24 | 24 | 0 |

**PASSING**

| Last Name | Att | Comp | % | Yds | Yd/Att | TD | Int– | % | RK |
|---|---|---|---|---|---|---|---|---|---|
| Unitas | 327 | 178 | 54 | 2342 | 7.2 | 12 | 20– | 6 | 9 |
| Morrall | 99 | 46 | 46 | 755 | 7.6 | 5 | 7– | 7 | |
| Matte | 3 | 1 | 33 | 46 | 15.3 | 0 | 0– | 0 | |

**PUNTING**

| Last Name | No | Avg |
|---|---|---|
| Lee | 57 | 45.3 |

**KICKING**

| Last Name | XP | Att | % | FG | Att | % |
|---|---|---|---|---|---|---|
| Michaels | 33 | 34 | 97 | 14 | 31 | 45 |

### ATLANTA FALCONS

**RUSHING**

| Last Name | No. | Yds | Avg | TD |
|---|---|---|---|---|
| Butler | 163 | 655 | 4.0 | 3 |
| Wages | 72 | 375 | 5.2 | 2 |
| Gipson | 62 | 303 | 4.9 | 1 |
| Bryant | 50 | 246 | 4.9 | 0 |
| Mitchell | 5 | 77 | 15.4 | 0 |
| Berry | 20 | 68 | 3.4 | 0 |
| Lemmerman | 10 | 57 | 5.7 | 1 |
| Johnson | 11 | 55 | 5.0 | 1 |
| McCauley | 2 | 49 | 24.5 | 0 |
| McDermott | 7 | 6 | 0.9 | 0 |
| Stanceil | 4 | -1 | -0.3 | 0 |

**RECEIVING**

| Last Name | No. | Yds | Avg | TD |
|---|---|---|---|---|
| Flatley | 45 | 834 | 19 | 6 |
| Cogdill | 24 | 374 | 16 | 5 |
| Mitchell | 22 | 339 | 15 | 4 |
| Wages | 22 | 228 | 10 | 1 |
| Butler | 17 | 297 | 17 | 2 |
| Gipson | 4 | 33 | 8 | 0 |
| Smith | 2 | 17 | 9 | 0 |
| Bryant | 2 | 15 | 8 | 0 |
| Ledbetter | 1 | 16 | 16 | 0 |
| Brezina | 1 | 9 | 9 | 0 |

**PUNT RETURNS**

| Last Name | No. | Yds | Avg | TD |
|---|---|---|---|---|
| Mallory | 13 | 42 | 3 | 0 |
| Freeman | 4 | 30 | 8 | 0 |
| Wright | 4 | 21 | 5 | 0 |
| Cahill | 1 | 0 | 0 | 0 |
| McCauley | 4 | -11 | -3 | 0 |

**KICKOFF RETURNS**

| Last Name | No. | Yds | Avg | TD |
|---|---|---|---|---|
| Bryant | 21 | 407 | 19 | 0 |
| Butler | 13 | 405 | 31 | 0 |
| Gipson | 9 | 145 | 16 | 0 |
| Wages | 6 | 76 | 13 | 0 |
| Snider | 1 | 48 | 48 | 1 |
| Kunz | 1 | 13 | 13 | 0 |
| Stanceil | 1 | 10 | 10 | 0 |

**PASSING**

| Last Name | Att | Comp | % | Yds | Yd/Att | TD | Int– | % | RK |
|---|---|---|---|---|---|---|---|---|---|
| Berry | 124 | 71 | 57 | 1087 | 8.8 | 10 | 2– | 2 | |
| Johnson | 93 | 51 | 55 | 788 | 8.5 | 8 | 5– | 5 | |
| Lemmerman | 62 | 25 | 40 | 330 | 5.3 | 1 | 4– | 6 | |
| Gipson | 1 | 0 | 0 | 0 | 0.0 | 0 | 1–100 | | |
| Lothridge | 1 | 1 | 100 | 9 | 9.0 | 0 | 0– | 0 | |
| Wages | 1 | 1 | 100 | 16 | 16.0 | 1 | 0– | 0 | |

**PUNTING**

| Last Name | No | Avg |
|---|---|---|
| Lothridge | 69 | 41.2 |

**KICKING**

| Last Name | XP | Att | % | FG | Att | % |
|---|---|---|---|---|---|---|
| Etter | 33 | 33 | 100 | 15 | 30 | 50 |

### SAN FRANCISCO FORTY NINERS

**RUSHING**

| Last Name | No. | Yds | Avg | TD |
|---|---|---|---|---|
| Willard | 171 | 557 | 3.3 | 7 |
| Cunningham | 147 | 541 | 3.7 | 3 |
| Thomas | 23 | 190 | 8.3 | 1 |
| Tucker | 20 | 72 | 3.6 | 2 |
| Brodie | 11 | 62 | 5.6 | 0 |
| Spurrier | 5 | 49 | 9.8 | 0 |
| Windsor | 5 | 39 | 7.8 | 0 |
| Davis | 2 | 21 | 10.5 | 0 |
| Lewis | 4 | 5 | 1.3 | 0 |
| Moore | 2 | 4 | 2.0 | 0 |
| Washington | 1 | -4 | -4.0 | 0 |

**RECEIVING**

| Last Name | No. | Yds | Avg | TD |
|---|---|---|---|---|
| Washington | 51 | 711 | 14 | 3 |
| Cunningham | 51 | 484 | 9 | 0 |
| Windsor | 49 | 597 | 12 | 2 |
| Willard | 36 | 326 | 9 | 3 |
| Witcher | 33 | 435 | 13 | 3 |
| Thomas | 18 | 364 | 20 | 5 |
| McNeil | 17 | 255 | 15 | 3 |
| Tucker | 14 | 104 | 7 | 2 |
| L. Johnson | 4 | 42 | 11 | 0 |
| Kwalick | 2 | 32 | 16 | 1 |
| Moore | 2 | 28 | 14 | 0 |
| Edwards | 1 | 1 | 1 | 0 |

**PUNT RETURNS**

| Last Name | No. | Yds | Avg | TD |
|---|---|---|---|---|
| Smith | 10 | 46 | 5 | 0 |
| Cunningham | 3 | 23 | 8 | 0 |
| Fuller | 5 | 12 | 2 | 0 |
| Alexander | 4 | -18 | -5 | 0 |

**KICKOFF RETURNS**

| Last Name | No. | Yds | Avg | TD |
|---|---|---|---|---|
| Smith | 14 | 315 | 23 | 0 |
| Cunningham | 9 | 207 | 23 | 0 |
| Fuller | 8 | 155 | 19 | 0 |
| Lewis | 5 | 155 | 31 | 0 |
| Alexander | 3 | 47 | 16 | 0 |
| Taylor | 1 | 16 | 16 | 0 |
| Wilcox | 1 | 10 | 10 | 0 |
| Edwards | 3 | 3 | 1 | 0 |
| Kwalick | 1 | 0 | 0 | 0 |
| Sniadecki | 1 | 0 | 0 | 0 |
| Tucker | 1 | 0 | 0 | 0 |

**PASSING**

| Last Name | Att | Comp | % | Yds | Yd/Att | TD | Int– | % | RK |
|---|---|---|---|---|---|---|---|---|---|
| Brodie | 347 | 194 | 56 | 2405 | 6.9 | 16 | 15– | 4 | 7 |
| Spurrier | 146 | 81 | 55 | 926 | 6.3 | 5 | 11– | 8 | 17 |
| Cunningham | 3 | 3 | 100 | 48 | 16.0 | 1 | 0– | 0 | |

**PUNTING**

| Last Name | No | Avg |
|---|---|---|
| Kilgore | 36 | 40.3 |
| Davis | 23 | 41.5 |
| Spurrier | 12 | 39.0 |

**KICKING**

| Last Name | XP | Att | % | FG | Att | % |
|---|---|---|---|---|---|---|
| Gavric | 22 | 24 | 92 | 3 | 11 | 27 |
| Davis | 13 | 13 | 100 | 3 | 10 | 30 |

# 1969 A.F.L. Losing One Status to Gain Another

With the announcement of the realignment of pro football for 1970, the AFL learned that this was its last season in existence. None of the league officials grieved very heavily, since all ten clubs would be part of the NFL's American Conference next year, but some fans and players openly mourned the passing of the AFL as a separate organization. With two distinct leagues, the Super Bowl had much of the flavor of baseball's World Series, but some people expected the excitement to pale with the amalgamation into one league.

Twenty players from the premier season of 1960 still were active in 1969. George Blanda, Billy Cannon, Gino Cappelletti, Tom Flores, Larry Grantham, Wayne Hawkins, Jim Hunt, Harry Jacobs, Jack Kemp, Jacky Lee, Paul Lowe, Paul Maguire, Billy Mathis, Don Maynard, Ron Mix, Jim Otto, Babe Parilli, Johnny Robinson, Paul Rochester, and Ernie Wright all followed different paths into the new league, and each of them stuck around for ten years to watch the AFL progress from an inferior product in fancy settings to a top-notch league on a par with the long-established NFL.

The AFL went out not with a whisper but with the trumpets of victory. The Kansas City Chiefs, who won the league championship in a new playoff setup which pitted first- and second-place finishers in the opposite divisions against each other in an opening round before the championship game, won a final triumph for the AFL by beating the Minnesota Vikings 23-7 in the Super Bowl.

## EASTERN DIVISION

**New York Jets**—The Jets coasted to another divisional title, beating every Eastern opponent they met during the season. Their four losses to Western teams, however, pointed out weak spots in the defending champions' club. The New York secondary folded against a good passing attack. Last year's starting cornerbacks, Johnny Sample and Randy Beverly, both fell out of favor with coach Weeb Ewbank, and the younger replacements couldn't handle top-notch receivers. A strong pass rush and good linebacking compensated for the leaky secondary to some extent, with Gerry Philbin, John Elliott, and Larry Grantham key men in the front lines. The Jet offense still put a lot of points on the scoreboard, with Joe Namath, Matt Snell, Emerson Boozer, Don Maynard, George Sauer, and Pete Lammons moving the ball against the best of defenses.

**Houston Oilers**—The Houston defense played so well that the team won half its games with little help from the offense. Elvin Bethea, George Webster, Miller Farr, and Ken Houston all ranked with the AFL's top defenders, and Zeke Moore, Garland Boyette, and W. K. Hicks were quality players who stood up to any attack in the league. Not even the absence of Leroy Mitchell, the fine cornerback obtained from Boston who suffered a broken neck in training camp, seriously hurt the Oilers' defense. The offense, however, creaked and groaned with pain in several spots. Hoyle Granger and Roy Hopkins, the starting runners, both were fullback types, strong on straight-ahead plays but not fast enough to make outside plays work. Pete Beathard compounded the unit's problems by failing to ignite an effective passing attack; after leading the club to a divisional crown in 1967, the twenty-seven-year-old passer had made little progress since.

**Boston Patriots**—New head coach Clive Rush found instant unpopularity with the fans and press when the Patriots lost their first seven games of the season, but his charges found themselves and won four of their next five matches. They shut out Houston 24-0, beat Cincinnati, Buffalo, and Miami, and lost to Miami 17-16 when Rush elected to gamble for a two-point conversion which failed. The Boston defense, stripped of stars Nick Buoniconti and Leroy Mitchell in off-season trades, had no charismatic players or exciting standouts, but the unit grew tighter with each game. The offense got a boost from rookies Carl Garrett, Ron Sellers, and Mike Montler and veterans Mike Taliaferro and Jim Nance, both rebounding from off-seasons.

**Buffalo Bills**—Head coach Johnny Rauch quit the Oakland Raiders to come to Buffalo, and he lost more games in this one year than he had in three years in Oakland. But the big story of the season was the arrival of O. J. Simpson. The Heisman Trophy winner from USC had openly expressed reluctance about playing in Buffalo, but once he signed with the Bills, he gave the team a much-needed running threat in the backfield. Simpson gained 697 yards rushing despite playing behind a porous line and under a head coach who built his offense around passing.

**Miami Dolphins**—The Dolphins slipped back into last place in the East, and head coach George Wilson paid for it with his job. Wilson, however, left behind a solid core of quality players for the next regime. Guard Larry Little and linebacker Nick Buoniconti had joined the team this year in trades which cost Miami very little, and rookies Lloyd

Mumford, Bill Stanfill, and Mercury Morris further swelled the ranks of top players on the team. Already on the Miami scene were Bob Griese, Larry Csonka, Jim Kiick, Manny Fernandez, and Howard Twilley—enough talent to change Miami's future fortunes.

## WESTERN DIVISION

**Oakland Raiders**—Throwing for thirty-four touchdowns, Lamonica won the league MVP award for the second time in the past three seasons. On the other end of Lamonica's passes were two complementary wide receivers, Warren Wells, whose strong point was speed, and Fred Biletnikoff, who relied on good moves and sure hands to make fifty-four catches. With the running attack a secondary feature, the offensive line spent most of its time expertly shielding Lamonica from enemy rushers. On defense, the Raiders got better the farther back you went. The line was adequate; Tom Keating recovered from his Achilles tendon injury, but Dan Birdwell missed most of the season with a bad knee. The linebacking corps of Dan Conners, Gus Otto, and Chip Oliver used the excellent mobility to fine advantage, and the secondary of Willie Brown, Nemiah Wilson, Dave Grayson, and George Atkinson had few peers in the pro ranks. With new coach John Madden blending all the pieces together into a harmonious whole, the Raiders edged the Chiefs out for first place in the West by beating them twice during the season.

**Kansas City Chiefs**—While the Raiders moved the ball primarily on passes, the Chiefs stuck to the ground on offense. Quarterbacks Len Dawson and Mike Livingston had a deep contingent of running backs to call on; Mike Garrett and Warren McVea provided speed from the halfback slot, and Robert Holmes and Wendell Hayes gave the Chiefs power at fullback. These four handled the running chores so well that coach Hank Stram moved Curtis McClinton to tight end and used rookie Ed Podolak exclusively as a kick returner. The Chiefs reversed Oakland's strategy and used the pass only to loosen enemy defenses for the run. The Kansas City defensive unit was brimming with talented players. Jerry Mays and Buck Buchanan had long starred in the line, and Aaron Brown and Curley Culp had fit in since the championship season of 1966. The linebacking trio of Bobby Bell, Willie Lanier, and Jim Lynch had everything. The secondary of Emmitt Thomas, rookie Jim Marsalis, Johnny Robinson, and Jim Kearney left few enemy receivers unattended.

**San Diego Chargers**—Five games from the end of the season, a bad case of ulcers forced Sid Gillman to give up the coaching reign and concentrate on his general manager's duties. Of course, the Chargers' 4-5-0 record at the time may have contributed to Gillman's decision and to his ulcers. Assistant Charlie Waller moved up to head coach, and after the Chargers lost their first game for him, the team won its last four outings. The talent on the roster was deep enough to make winning an expected event, not just a late-season occurrence. Halfback Dickie Post, receivers Lance Alworth and Gary Garrison, and guard Walt Sweeney all stood out for excellence, but the Chargers were let down by John Hadl's poor season and Ron Mix's injury-plagued campaign. The defense got good years out of Steve DeLong, Pete Barnes, Rick Redman, Jim Hill, Bob Howard, and Kenny Graham, but the rest of the unit needed patching up.

**Denver Broncos**—The Broncos began the season with impressive victories over the Patriots and Jets, but injuries took most of the steam out of the offense by mid-season. Quarterback Steve Tensi was bothered by a bad knee, receivers Mike Haffner and Bill Van Heusen missed the last month of the season with injured knees, and runner Floyd Little missed five games with shoulder and knee problems. Little's absence particularly hurt the team, as he had developed into a top runner before getting hurt. Inexperience rather than injuries troubled the defense, but this young unit came up with occasional sterling performances like a 13-0 shutout of the Chargers. The strength of the defense lay up front, where Rich Jackson and Dave Costa were two of the league's top linemen. The linebackers and deep backs all were young players, with speedy rookie cornerback Bill Thompson one of the most exciting newcomers in the AFL.

**Cincinnati Bengals**—Paul Brown's youth parade brought Greg Cook, Speedy Thomas, Horst Muhlmann, Bill Bergey, Royce Berry, and Ken Riley to Cincinnati as freshman starters this year, with Cook an immediate sensation at quarterback. After starring in the College All-Star game, the blond, handsome Cook reported to the Bengal's training camp and took right over as the offensive leader. On opening day, he threw two touchdown passes in leading the team to a victory over Miami. One week later, he threw three scoring passes and ran for another six points in engineering an upset over San Diego, and he helped beat the Chiefs in their third game. Cook then sat out a month of action with a sore passing arm, but he returned to beat Oakland.

## FINAL TEAM STATISTICS

### OFFENSE

| | BOSTON | BUFFALO | CIN. | DENVER | HOUSTON | K.C. | MIAMI | NEW YORK | OAKLAND | S.D. |
|---|---|---|---|---|---|---|---|---|---|---|
| **FIRST DOWNS:** | | | | | | | | | | |
| Total | 166 | 224 | 172 | 243 | 256 | 258 | 224 | 252 | 261 | 275 |
| by Rushing | 64 | 83 | 66 | 87 | 95 | 129 | 73 | 98 | 84 | 119 |
| by Passing | 87 | 122 | 95 | 130 | 146 | 125 | 131 | 130 | 153 | 131 |
| by Penalty | 15 | 19 | 11 | 26 | 15 | 4 | 20 | 24 | 24 | 25 |
| **RUSHING:** | | | | | | | | | | |
| Number | 367 | 384 | 363 | 394 | 440 | 522 | 401 | 469 | 459 | 455 |
| Yards | 1489 | 1522 | 1523 | 1637 | 1706 | 2220 | 1513 | 1782 | 1765 | 1985 |
| Average Yards | 4.1 | 4.0 | 4.2 | 4.2 | 3.9 | 4.3 | 3.8 | 3.8 | 3.8 | 4.4 |
| Touchdowns | 11 | 7 | 10 | 12 | 12 | 19 | 12 | 14 | 4 | 18 |
| **PASSING:** | | | | | | | | | | |
| Attempts | 338 | 442 | 308 | 403 | 489 | 351 | 424 | 394 | 439 | 444 |
| Completions | 162 | 215 | 163 | 192 | 239 | 196 | 201 | 203 | 227 | 208 |
| Completion Percentage | 47.9 | 48.6 | 52.9 | 47.6 | 48.9 | 55.8 | 47.4 | 51.5 | 51.7 | 46.8 |
| Passing Yards | 2191 | 2716 | 2720 | 2835 | 3147 | 2638 | 2558 | 2939 | 3375 | 2927 |
| Average Yards per Att. | 6.5 | 6.1 | 8.8 | 7.0 | 6.4 | 7.5 | 6.0 | 7.5 | 7.7 | 6.6 |
| Average Yards per Comp. | 13.5 | 12.6 | 16.7 | 14.8 | 13.2 | 13.5 | 12.7 | 14.5 | 14.9 | 14.1 |
| Tackled Att. to Pass | 24 | 42 | 57 | 44 | 36 | 26 | 53 | 16 | 12 | 33 |
| Yards Lost Tackled | 261 | 371 | 375 | 311 | 322 | 251 | 481 | 138 | 104 | 301 |
| Net Yards | 1930 | 2345 | 2345 | 2524 | 2825 | 2387 | 2077 | 2801 | 3271 | 2626 |
| Touchdowns | 19 | 17 | 22 | 23 | 15 | 16 | 12 | 21 | 36 | 13 |
| Interceptions | 18 | 30 | 15 | 23 | 31 | 20 | 29 | 20 | 26 | 21 |
| Percent Intercepted | 5.3 | 6.8 | 4.9 | 5.7 | 6.3 | 5.7 | 6.8 | 5.1 | 5.9 | 4.7 |
| **PUNTS:** | | | | | | | | | | |
| Number | 70 | 78 | 85 | 72 | 70 | 68 | 85 | 56 | 69 | 71 |
| Average Distance | 41.5 | 44.5 | 38.8 | 40.1 | 38.9 | 44.4 | 40.6 | 44.3 | 42.7 | 44.6 |
| **PUNT RETURNS:** | | | | | | | | | | |
| Number | 23 | 31 | 23 | 37 | 43 | 32 | 45 | 39 | 39 | 31 |
| Yards | 212 | 187 | 135 | 450 | 391 | 251 | 266 | 256 | 225 | 300 |
| Average Yards | 9.2 | 6.0 | 5.9 | 12.2 | 9.1 | 7.8 | 5.9 | 6.6 | 5.8 | 9.7 |
| Touchdowns | 0 | 0 | 0 | 0 | 0 | 0 | 0 | 0 | 0 | 0 |
| **KICKOFF RETURNS:** | | | | | | | | | | |
| Number | 54 | 62 | 55 | 56 | 49 | 41 | 60 | 46 | 42 | 39 |
| Yards | 1247 | 1475 | 1165 | 1323 | 1141 | 1090 | 1383 | 985 | 996 | 842 |
| Average Yards | 23.1 | 23.8 | 21.2 | 23.6 | 23.3 | 26.6 | 23.1 | 21.4 | 23.7 | 21.6 |
| Touchdowns | 0 | 0 | 0 | 0 | 0 | 1 | 1 | 0 | 0 | 0 |
| **INTERCEPTION RETURNS:** | | | | | | | | | | |
| Number | 20 | 19 | 21 | 14 | 23 | 32 | 18 | 29 | 26 | 31 |
| Yards | 326 | 251 | 362 | 228 | 335 | 595 | 317 | 348 | 484 | 444 |
| Average Yards | 16.3 | 13.2 | 17.2 | 16.3 | 14.6 | 18.6 | 17.6 | 12.0 | 18.6 | 14.3 |
| Touchdowns | 1 | 1 | 1 | 2 | 2 | 2 | 2 | 1 | 4 | 3 |
| **PENALTIES:** | | | | | | | | | | |
| Number | 77 | 67 | 50 | 80 | 70 | 62 | 53 | 61 | 100 | 63 |
| Yards | 837 | 632 | 556 | 753 | 730 | 757 | 631 | 725 | 1274 | 731 |
| **FUMBLES:** | | | | | | | | | | |
| Number | 15 | 35 | 30 | 15 | 24 | 34 | 27 | 19 | 17 | 27 |
| Number Lost | 10 | 21 | 23 | 8 | 17 | 19 | 13 | 13 | 7 | 13 |
| **POINTS:** | | | | | | | | | | |
| Total | 266 | 230 | 280 | 297 | 278 | 359 | 233 | 353 | 377 | 288 |
| PAT (kick) Attempts | 29 | 24 | 33 | 37 | 29 | 38 | 27 | 33 | 45 | 34 |
| PAT (kick) Made | 26 | 23 | 32 | 36 | 29 | 38 | 26 | 33 | 45 | 33 |
| PAT (2–Point) Attempts | 3 | 2 | 0 | 0 | 2 | 2 | 1 | 4 | 0 | 1 |
| PAT (2–Point) Made | 1 | 0 | 0 | 0 | 2 | 0 | 0 | 1 | 0 | 0 |
| FG Attempts | 34 | 26 | 24 | 29 | 40 | 35 | 22 | 47 | 37 | 28 |
| FG Made | 14 | 17 | 16 | 13 | 19 | 27 | 13 | 32 | 20 | 15 |
| Percent FG Made | 41.2 | 65.4 | 66.7 | 44.8 | 47.5 | 77.1 | 59.1 | 68.1 | 54.1 | 53.6 |
| Safeties | 2 | 0 | 1 | 0 | 1 | 0 | 0 | 0 | 1 | 0 |

### DEFENSE

| | BOSTON | BUFFALO | CIN. | DENVER | HOUSTON | K.C. | MIAMI | NEW YORK | OAKLAND | S.D. |
|---|---|---|---|---|---|---|---|---|---|---|
| **FIRST DOWNS:** | | | | | | | | | | |
| Total | 278 | 236 | 278 | 276 | 183 | 181 | 206 | 229 | 232 | 232 |
| by Rushing | 142 | 106 | 135 | 95 | 77 | 53 | 66 | 63 | 90 | 71 |
| by Passing | 115 | 118 | 130 | 151 | 93 | 111 | 126 | 151 | 107 | 148 |
| by Penalty | 21 | 12 | 13 | 30 | 13 | 17 | 14 | 15 | 35 | 13 |
| **RUSHING:** | | | | | | | | | | |
| Number | 528 | 454 | 523 | 436 | 430 | 314 | 422 | 343 | 438 | 366 |
| Yards | 2359 | 1858 | 2651 | 1709 | 1556 | 1091 | 1489 | 1326 | 1661 | 1442 |
| Average Yards | 4.5 | 4.1 | 5.1 | 3.9 | 3.6 | 3.5 | 3.5 | 3.9 | 3.8 | 3.9 |
| Touchdowns | 18 | 17 | 13 | 15 | 10 | 6 | 9 | 7 | 13 | 11 |
| **PASSING:** | | | | | | | | | | |
| Attempts | 348 | 368 | 396 | 437 | 371 | 426 | 404 | 437 | 422 | 423 |
| Completions | 203 | 175 | 205 | 223 | 167 | 200 | 196 | 232 | 164 | 241 |
| Completion Percentage | 58.3 | 47.6 | 51.8 | 51.0 | 45.0 | 46.9 | 48.5 | 53.1 | 38.9 | 57.0 |
| Passing Yards | 2610 | 2772 | 2866 | 3295 | 2495 | 2491 | 2845 | 3086 | 2511 | 3075 |
| Average Yards per Att. | 7.5 | 7.5 | 7.2 | 7.5 | 6.7 | 5.8 | 7.0 | 7.1 | 6.0 | 7.3 |
| Average Yards per Comp. | 12.9 | 15.8 | 14.0 | 14.8 | 14.9 | 12.5 | 14.5 | 13.3 | 15.3 | 12.8 |
| Tackled Att. to Pass | 22 | 31 | 16 | 45 | 32 | 48 | 25 | 42 | 47 | 35 |
| Yards Lost Tackled | 159 | 296 | 180 | 363 | 278 | 419 | 208 | 330 | 402 | 280 |
| Net Yards | 2451 | 2476 | 2686 | 2932 | 2217 | 2072 | 2637 | 2756 | 2109 | 2795 |
| Touchdowns | 18 | 21 | 24 | 19 | 18 | 10 | 25 | 22 | 15 | 22 |
| Interceptions | 20 | 19 | 21 | 14 | 23 | 32 | 18 | 29 | 26 | 31 |
| Percent Intercepted | 5.7 | 5.2 | 5.3 | 3.2 | 6.2 | 7.5 | 4.5 | 6.6 | 6.2 | 7.3 |
| **PUNTS:** | | | | | | | | | | |
| Number | 55 | 62 | 55 | 71 | 85 | 84 | 80 | 69 | 87 | 76 |
| Average Distance | 38.6 | 42.7 | 41.4 | 43.1 | 43.1 | 43.0 | 44.1 | 39.8 | 41.8 | 40.3 |
| **PUNT RETURNS:** | | | | | | | | | | |
| Number | 19 | 45 | 39 | 35 | 37 | 43 | 30 | 28 | 37 | 30 |
| Yards | 114 | 466 | 297 | 246 | 196 | 502 | 130 | 280 | 151 | 291 |
| Average Yards | 6.0 | 10.4 | 7.6 | 7.0 | 5.3 | 11.7 | 4.3 | 10.0 | 4.1 | 9.7 |
| Touchdowns | 0 | 0 | 0 | 0 | 0 | 0 | 0 | 0 | 0 | 0 |
| **KICKOFF RETURNS:** | | | | | | | | | | |
| Number | 56 | 55 | 39 | 21 | 38 | 59 | 47 | 72 | 64 | 53 |
| Yards | 1068 | 1322 | 1065 | 471 | 792 | 1431 | 1073 | 1669 | 1518 | 1238 |
| Average Yards | 19.1 | 24.0 | 27.3 | 22.4 | 20.8 | 24.3 | 22.8 | 23.2 | 23.7 | 23.4 |
| Touchdowns | 0 | 0 | 1 | 1 | 0 | 0 | 0 | 0 | 0 | 0 |
| **INTERCEPTION RETURNS:** | | | | | | | | | | |
| Number | 18 | 30 | 15 | 23 | 31 | 20 | 29 | 20 | 26 | 21 |
| Yards | 225 | 449 | 239 | 421 | 441 | 325 | 596 | 380 | 349 | 265 |
| Average Yards | 12.5 | 15.0 | 15.9 | 18.3 | 14.2 | 16.3 | 20.6 | 19.0 | 13.4 | 12.6 |
| Touchdowns | 1 | 2 | 0 | 4 | 3 | 3 | 3 | 2 | 1 | 0 |
| **PENALTIES:** | | | | | | | | | | |
| Number | 69 | 71 | 72 | 84 | 61 | 39 | 66 | 69 | 81 | 71 |
| Yards | 810 | 719 | 824 | 901 | 592 | 443 | 840 | 788 | 918 | 791 |
| **FUMBLES:** | | | | | | | | | | |
| Number | 33 | 25 | 19 | 24 | 27 | 25 | 27 | 25 | 25 | 13 |
| Number Lost | 14 | 18 | 15 | 14 | 17 | 15 | 13 | 16 | 16 | 6 |
| **POINTS:** | | | | | | | | | | |
| Total | 316 | 359 | 367 | 344 | 279 | 177 | 332 | 269 | 242 | 276 |
| PAT (kick) Attempts | 38 | 40 | 42 | 38 | 33 | 17 | 33 | 28 | 27 | 33 |
| PAT (kick) Made | 37 | 39 | 41 | 38 | 33 | 16 | 32 | 28 | 26 | 31 |
| PAT (2–Point) Attempts | 0 | 0 | 0 | 2 | 0 | 2 | 4 | 4 | 2 | 1 |
| PAT (2–Point) Made | 0 | 0 | 0 | 0 | 0 | 0 | 1 | 2 | 0 | 1 |
| FG Attempts | 28 | 41 | 46 | 32 | 30 | 27 | 36 | 27 | 30 | 25 |
| FG Made | 17 | 26 | 24 | 22 | 16 | 15 | 24 | 15 | 14 | 13 |
| Percent FG Made | 60.7 | 63.4 | 52.2 | 68.8 | 53.3 | 55.6 | 66.7 | 55.6 | 46.7 | 52.0 |
| Safeties | 0 | 1 | 1 | 0 | 0 | 1 | 2 | 0 | 0 | 0 |

## INTER–DIVISIONAL PLAYOFFS

### December 20, at New York (Attendance 62,977)

#### SCORING

| | | | | | |
|---|---|---|---|---|---|
| NEW YORK | 3 | 0 | 0 | 3 | – 6 |
| KANSAS CITY | 0 | 3 | 3 | 7 | –13 |

First Quarter
N.Y. J. Turner, 27 yard field goal

Second Quarter
K.C. Stenerud, 23 yard field goal

Third Quarter
K.C. Stenerud, 25 yard field goal

Fourth Quarter
N.Y. J. Turner, 7 yard field goal
K.C. Richardson, 19 yard pass from Dawson PAT–Stenerud (kick)

#### TEAM STATISTICS

| N.Y. | | K.C. |
|---|---|---|
| 19 | First Downs–Total | 14 |
| 5 | First Downs–Rushing | 3 |
| 11 | First Downs–Passing | 9 |
| 3 | First Downs–Penalty | 2 |
| 1 | Fumbles–Number | 0 |
| 1 | Fumbles–Lost Ball | 0 |
| 3 | Penalties–Number | 5 |
| 15 | Yards Penalized | 63 |
| 0 | Missed Field Goals | 3 |
| 64 | Offensive Plays–Total | 59 |
| 235 | Net Yards | 276 |
| 3.7 | Average Gain | 4.7 |
| 4 | Giveaways | 0 |
| 0 | Takeaways | 4 |
| –4 | Difference | +4 |

#### INDIVIDUAL STATISTICS

| NEW YORK | No | Yds | Avg. | KANSAS CITY | No | Yds | Avg. |
|---|---|---|---|---|---|---|---|
| **RUSHING** | | | | | | | |
| Snell | 12 | 61 | 5.1 | Garrett | 18 | 67 | 3.7 |
| Boozer | 3 | 14 | 4.7 | Hayes | 10 | 32 | 3.2 |
| Mathis | 6 | 11 | 1.8 | Holmes | 1 | 0 | 0.0 |
| Namath | 1 | 1 | 1.0 | McVea | 1 | 0 | 0.0 |
| | 22 | 87 | 4.0 | | 30 | 99 | 3.3 |
| **RECEIVING** | | | | | | | |
| Sauer | 5 | 61 | 12.2 | Hayes | 5 | 46 | 9.2 |
| Lammons | 3 | 37 | 12.3 | Taylor | 2 | 74 | 37.0 |
| B. Turner | 2 | 25 | 12.5 | Arbanas | 2 | 39 | 19.5 |
| Maynard | 1 | 18 | 18.0 | Holmes | 1 | 29 | 29.0 |
| Boozer | 1 | 10 | 10.0 | Richardson | 1 | 19 | 19.0 |
| Snell | 1 | 9 | 9.0 | Pitts | 1 | –6 | –6.0 |
| Mathis | 1 | 4 | 4.0 | | 12 | 201 | 16.8 |
| | 14 | 164 | 11.7 | | | | |
| **PUNTING** | | | | | | | |
| O'Neal | 5 | | 37.2 | Wilson | 6 | | 33.5 |
| **PUNT RETURNS** | | | | | | | |
| Battle | 2 | 10 | 5.0 | Garrett | 1 | 10 | 10.0 |
| | | | | Mitchell | 1 | 4 | 4.0 |
| | | | | | 2 | 14 | 7.0 |
| **KICKOFF RETURNS** | | | | | | | |
| Battle | 3 | 64 | 21.3 | Holmes | 2 | 33 | 16.5 |
| Nock | 1 | 33 | 33.0 | Hayes | 1 | 31 | 31.0 |
| | 4 | 97 | 24.3 | | 3 | 64 | 21.3 |
| **INTERCEPTION RETURNS** | | | | | | | |
| None | | | | Marsalis | 2 | 42 | 21.0 |
| | | | | Thomas | 1 | 0 | 0.0 |
| | | | | | 3 | 42 | 14.0 |

**PASSING**

| | Att. | Comp. | Comp. Pct. | Yds. | Int. | Yds/ Att. | Yds/ Comp. | Yds Lost Tkld. |
|---|---|---|---|---|---|---|---|---|
| **NEW YORK** | | | | | | | | |
| Namath | 40 | 14 | 35.0 | 164 | 3 | 4.1 | 11.7 | 2–16 |
| **KANSAS CITY** | | | | | | | | |
| Dawson | 27 | 12 | 44.4 | 201 | 0 | 7.4 | 16.8 | 2–24 |

### December 21, at Oakland (Attendance 53,539)

#### SCORING

| | | | | | |
|---|---|---|---|---|---|
| OAKLAND | 28 | 7 | 14 | 7 | –56 |
| HOUSTON | 0 | 0 | 0 | 7 | – 7 |

First Quarter
Oak. Biletnikoff, 13 yard pass from Lamonica PAT–Blanda (kick)
Oak. Atkinson, 57 yard interception return PAT–Blanda (kick)
Oak. Sherman, 24 yard pass from Lamonica PAT–Blanda (kick)
Oak. Biletnikoff, 31 yard pass from Lamonica PAT–Blanda (kick)

Second Quarter
Oak. Smith, 60 yard pass from Lamonica PAT–Blanda (kick)

Third Quarter
Oak. Sherman, 23 yard pass from Lamonica PAT–Blanda (kick)
Oak. Gannon, 3 yard pass from Lamonica PAT–Blanda (kick)

Fourth Quarter
Hou. Reed, 8 yard pass from Beathard PAT–Gerela (kick)
Oak. Hubbard, 4 yard rush PAT–Blanda (kick)

#### TEAM STATISTICS

| OAK. | | HOUS. |
|---|---|---|
| 17 | First Downs–Total | 14 |
| 5 | First Downs–Rushing | 1 |
| 11 | First Downs–Passing | 10 |
| 1 | First Downs–Penalty | 3 |
| 3 | Fumbles–Number | 3 |
| 1 | Fumbles–Lost Ball | 2 |
| 7 | Penalties–Number | 3 |
| 63 | Yards Penalized | 48 |
| 0 | Missed Field Goals | 0 |
| 60 | Offensive Plays–Total | 71 |
| 412 | Net Yards | 197 |
| 6.9 | Average Gain | 2.8 |
| 4 | Giveaways | 5 |
| 5 | Takeaways | 4 |
| +1 | Difference | –1 |

#### INDIVIDUAL STATISTICS

| OAKLAND | No | Yds | Avg. | HOUSTON | No | Yds | Avg. |
|---|---|---|---|---|---|---|---|
| **RUSHING** | | | | | | | |
| Dixon | 13 | 48 | 3.7 | Granger | 14 | 29 | 2.1 |
| Todd | 8 | 31 | 3.9 | LeVias | 1 | 4 | 4.0 |
| Hubbard | 6 | 19 | 3.2 | Campbell | 1 | 0 | 0.0 |
| Hagberg | 2 | 9 | 4.5 | Beathard | 3 | –5 | –1.7 |
| Smith | 8 | 3 | 0.4 | | 19 | 28 | 1.5 |
| | 37 | 110 | 3.0 | | | | |
| **RECEIVING** | | | | | | | |
| Smith | 4 | 103 | 25.8 | Reed | 7 | 81 | 11.6 |
| Sherman | 4 | 60 | 15.0 | Beirne | 5 | 48 | 9.6 |
| Biletnikoff | 3 | 70 | 23.3 | Granger | 3 | 31 | 10.3 |
| Todd | 1 | 40 | 40.0 | Haik | 2 | 42 | 21.0 |
| Hubbard | 1 | 33 | 33.0 | LeVias | 1 | 7 | 7.0 |
| Cannon | 1 | 3 | 3.0 | | 18 | 209 | 11.6 |
| | 14 | 309 | 22.1 | | | | |
| **PUNTING** | | | | | | | |
| Eischeid | 5 | | 42.0 | Burrell | 11 | | 41.4 |
| **PUNT RETURNS** | | | | | | | |
| Atkinson | 2 | 19 | 9.5 | LeVias | 2 | 4 | 2.0 |
| Sherman | 1 | 8 | 8.0 | | | | |
| | 3 | 27 | 9.0 | | | | |
| **KICKOFF RETURNS** | | | | | | | |
| Atkinson | 1 | 38 | 38.0 | LeVias | 4 | 69 | 17.3 |
| Sherman | 1 | 26 | 26.0 | Burrell | 3 | 61 | 20.3 |
| | 2 | 64 | 32.0 | | 7 | 130 | 18.6 |
| **INTERCEPTION RETURNS** | | | | | | | |
| Atkinson | 1 | 57 | 57.0 | Farr | 1 | 0 | 0.0 |
| Brown | 1 | 15 | 15.0 | Moore | 1 | 0 | 0.0 |
| Wilson | 1 | 0 | 0.0 | Peacock | 1 | 0 | 0.0 |
| | 3 | 72 | 24.0 | | 3 | 0 | 0.0 |

**PASSING**

| | Att. | Cmp. | Comp. Pct. | Yds. | Int. | Yds/ Att. | Yds/ Comp. | Lost Tkld. |
|---|---|---|---|---|---|---|---|---|
| **OAKLAND** | | | | | | | | |
| Lamonica | 17 | 13 | 76.5 | 276 | 1 | 16.2 | 21.2 | |
| Blanda | 5 | 1 | 20.0 | 33 | 2 | 6.6 | 33.0 | |
| | 22 | 14 | 63.6 | 309 | 3 | 14.0 | 22.1 | 1– 7 |
| **HOUSTON** | | | | | | | | |
| Beathard | 46 | 18 | 39.1 | 209 | 3 | 4.5 | 11.6 | 6–40 |

## NEW YORK JETS 10-4-0 Weeb Ewbank

| Scores of Each Game | | |
|---|---|---|
| 33 | Buffalo | 19 |
| 19 | Denver | 21 |
| 27 | San Diego | 34 |
| 23 | Boston | 14 |
| 21 | Cincinnati | 7 |
| 26 | HOUSTON | 17 |
| 23 | BOSTON | 17 |
| 34 | MIAMI | 31 |
| 16 | BUFFALO | 6 |
| 16 | KANSAS CITY | 34 |
| 40 | CINCINNATI | 7 |
| 14 | OAKLAND | 27 |
| 34 | Houston | 26 |
| 27 | Miami | 9 |

| Use Name | Pos. | Hgt | Wgt | Age | Int | Pts |
|---|---|---|---|---|---|---|
| Winston Hill | OT | 6'4" | 280 | 27 | | |
| Sam Walton | OT | 6'5" | 270 | 26 | | |
| Roger Finnie | OT | 6'3" | 245 | 23 | | |
| Paul Seiler | C-OT | 6'4" | 255 | 23 | | |
| Dave Herman | OG | 6'2" | 255 | 27 | | |
| Pete Perreault | OG | 6'3" | 248 | 30 | | |
| Randy Rasmussen | OG | 6'2" | 255 | 24 | | |
| Gordon Wright | OG | 6'3" | 245 | 25 | | |
| John Schmitt | C | 6'4" | 245 | 26 | | |
| Paul Crane | LB-C | 6'2" | 205 | 25 | 3 | 12 |
| Verlon Biggs | DE | 6'4" | 270 | 26 | | |
| Jimmie Jones | DE | 6'3" | 215 | 22 | | |
| Gerry Philbin | DE | 6'2" | 245 | 28 | 1 | |
| John Elliott | DT | 6'4" | 245 | 24 | | |
| Carl McAdams | DT | 6'3" | 240 | 25 | | |
| Paul Rochester | DT | 6'2" | 255 | 32 | | |
| Steve Thompson | DT | 6'5" | 245 | 24 | | |
| Al Atkinson | LB | 6'1" | 230 | 26 | 2 | |
| Ralph Baker | LB | 6'3" | 235 | 27 | 1 | |
| Jim Carroll | LB | 6'1" | 230 | 26 | | |
| Larry Grantham | LB | 6' | 210 | 30 | | |
| John Neidert | LB | 6'2" | 230 | 23 | | |
| Bill Baird | DB | 5'10" | 180 | 30 | 5 | |
| Mike Battle | DB | 6'1" | 175 | 23 | 1 | |
| Randy Beverly | DB | 5'11" | 185 | 25 | 2 | |
| John Dockery | DB | 6' | 186 | 24 | 5 | |
| Cornell Gordon | DB | 6' | 187 | 28 | 4 | |
| Jim Hudson | DB | 6'2" | 210 | 26 | 2 | |
| Cecil Leonard | DB | 5'11" | 170 | 23 | | |
| Jim Richards | DB | 6'1" | 180 | 22 | 3 | |
| Harvey Nairn – Military Service | | | | | | |
| Joe Namath | QB | 6'2" | 195 | 26 | | 12 |
| Babe Parilli | QB | 6'1" | 190 | 39 | | |
| Jim Turner | QB | 6'2" | 205 | 28 | | 129 |
| Al Woodall | QB | 6'5" | 210 | 23 | | |
| Emerson Boozer | HB | 5'11" | 204 | 26 | | 24 |
| Bill Mathis | HB | 6'1" | 220 | 30 | | 30 |
| George Nock | HB | 5'10" | 200 | 23 | | |
| Matt Snell | FB | 6'2" | 220 | 27 | | 30 |
| Lee White | FB | 6'4" | 240 | 23 | | |
| Don Maynard | WR | 6' | 180 | 33 | | 38 |
| Steve O'Neal | WR | 6'3" | 185 | 23 | | |
| George Sauer | WR | 6'1" | 195 | 25 | | 48 |
| Bake Turner | WR | 6' | 180 | 29 | | 18 |
| Pete Lammons | TE | 6'3" | 228 | 25 | | 12 |
| Wayne Stewart | TE | 6'7" | 202 | 22 | | |

## HOUSTON OILERS 6-6-2 Wally Lemm

| Scores of Each Game | | |
|---|---|---|
| 17 | Oakland | 21 |
| 17 | Buffalo | 3 |
| 22 | MIAMI | 10 |
| 28 | BUFFALO | 14 |
| 0 | Kansas City | 24 |
| 17 | New York | 26 |
| 24 | DENVER | 21 |
| 0 | Boston | 24 |
| 31 | CINCINNATI | 31 |
| 20 | Denver | 20 |
| 32 | Miami | 7 |
| 17 | SAN DIEGO | 21 |
| 26 | NEW YORK | 34 |
| 27 | BOSTON | 23 |

| Use Name | Pos. | Hgt | Wgt | Age | Int | Pts |
|---|---|---|---|---|---|---|
| Elbert Drungo | OT | 6'5" | 250 | 26 | | |
| Glen Ray Hines | OT | 6'5" | 265 | 25 | | |
| Walt Suggs | OT | 6'5" | 260 | 30 | | |
| Sonny Bishop | OG | 6'2" | 245 | 29 | | |
| Jim LeMoine | OG | 6'2" | 245 | 24 | | |
| Tom Regner | OG | 6'1" | 255 | 25 | | |
| Hank Autry | C | 6'3" | 230 | 22 | | |
| Bobby Maples | C | 6'3" | 245 | 26 | | |
| Elvin Bethea | DE | 6'3" | 250 | 23 | | 2 |
| Pat Holmes | DE | 6'5" | 250 | 29 | | |
| Glenn Woods | DE | 6'4" | 250 | 23 | | |
| Ben Mayes | DT-DE | 6'5" | 265 | 24 | | |
| Tom Domres | DT | 6'3" | 255 | 22 | | 6 |
| Willie Parker | DT | 6'2" | 265 | 24 | | |
| George Rice | DT | 6'3" | 260 | 25 | | |
| Carel Stith | DT | 6'5" | 265 | 24 | | |
| Garland Boyette | LB | 6'1" | 245 | 29 | | |
| Ron Pritchard | LB | 6'1" | 222 | 22 | | |
| Olen Underwood | LB | 6'1" | 230 | 27 | 1 | |
| Loyd Wainscott | LB | 6'1" | 235 | 22 | | |
| Ed Watson | LB | 6'2" | 222 | 24 | | |
| George Webster | LB | 6'4" | 223 | 23 | 2 | |
| John Douglas | DB | 6'1" | 195 | 24 | | |
| Miller Farr | DB | 6'1" | 190 | 26 | 6 | |
| W. K. Hicks | DB | 6'1" | 195 | 26 | 4 | |
| Ken Houston | DB | 6'3" | 192 | 24 | 4 | 6 |
| Zeke Moore | DB | 6'2" | 198 | 25 | 4 | 6 |
| Johnny Peacock | DB | 6'2" | 205 | 22 | 2 | 6 |
| Leroy Mitchell – Broken Neck | | | | | | |
| Pete Beathard | QB | 6'2" | 207 | 27 | | 12 |
| Bob Davis | QB | 6'3" | 208 | 23 | | |
| Don Trull | QB | 6'1" | 196 | 27 | | 12 |
| Ode Burrell | HB | 6' | 192 | 29 | | |
| Woody Campbell | HB | 5'11" | 202 | 24 | | 6 |
| Mike Richardson | HB | 5'11" | 185 | 22 | | 2 |
| Hoyle Granger | FB-HB | 6'1" | 225 | 25 | | 24 |
| Roy Hopkins | FB | 6'1" | 225 | 24 | | 30 |
| Rich Johnson | HB-FB | 6'1" | 210 | 22 | | 6 |
| Jim Beirne | WR | 6'2" | 196 | 22 | | 26 |
| Mac Haik | WR | 6'1" | 196 | 23 | | 6 |
| Charlie Joiner | WR | 5'11" | 185 | 21 | | |
| Jerry LeVias | WR | 5'10" | 175 | 22 | | 30 |
| Paul Zaeske | WR | 6'2" | 200 | 23 | | |
| Ed Carrington | TE | 6'4" | 225 | 25 | | |
| Alvin Reed | TE | 6'5" | 230 | 25 | | 12 |
| Roy Gerela | K | 5'10" | 185 | 21 | | 86 |

## BOSTON PATRIOTS 4-10-0 Clive Rush

| Scores of Each Game | | |
|---|---|---|
| 7 | Denver | 35 |
| 0 | KANSAS CITY | 31 |
| 23 | OAKLAND | 38 |
| 14 | NEW YORK | 23 |
| 16 | Buffalo | 23 |
| 10 | SAN DIEGO | 13 |
| 17 | New York | 23 |
| 24 | HOUSTON | 0 |
| 16 | MIAMI | 17 |
| 25 | Cincinnati | 14 |
| 35 | BUFFALO | 21 |
| 38 | Miami | 23 |
| 18 | San Diego | 28 |
| 23 | Houston | 27 |

| Use Name | Pos. | Hgt | Wgt | Age | Int | Pts |
|---|---|---|---|---|---|---|
| Tom Funchess | OT | 6'5" | 260 | 24 | | |
| Ezell Jones | OT | 6'4" | 255 | 22 | | 2 |
| Tom Neville | OT | 6'4" | 255 | 26 | | |
| Charley Long | OG | 6'3" | 250 | 31 | | |
| Len St. Jean | OG | 6'1" | 245 | 27 | | |
| Mike Montler | C-OG | 6'4" | 270 | 25 | | |
| Jon Morris | C | 6'4" | 240 | 26 | | |
| J. R. Williamson | LB-C | 6'2" | 220 | 27 | | |
| Ron Berger | DE | 6'8" | 275 | 25 | | |
| Johnny Cagle | DE | 6'3" | 260 | 22 | | |
| Larry Eisenhauer | DE | 6'5" | 255 | 29 | | |
| Mel Witt | DE | 6'3" | 265 | 23 | | |
| Karl Henke | DT-DE | 6'4" | 245 | 24 | | |
| Houston Antwine | DT | 6' | 270 | 30 | | |
| Jim Hunt | DT | 5'11" | 255 | 30 | | |
| Ray Jacobs | DT | 6'3" | 285 | 29 | | |
| Ed Toner | DT | 6'3" | 250 | 24 | | |
| John Bramlett | LB | 6'2" | 210 | 28 | 1 | |
| Jim Cheyunski | LB | 6'2" | 220 | 23 | 1 | |
| Ed Philpott | LB | 6'3" | 240 | 23 | 4 | |
| Marty Schottenheimer | LB | 6'3" | 224 | 26 | 1 | |
| Larry Carwell | DB | 6'1" | 190 | 25 | 4 | |
| John Charles | DB | 6'1" | 200 | 25 | 4 | 6 |
| Tom Janik | DB | 6'3" | 195 | 28 | 1 | |
| Daryle Johnson | DB | 5'11" | 190 | 23 | 2 | 8 |
| Art McMahon | DB | 5'11" | 185 | 23 | | |
| John Outlaw | DB | 5'10" | 180 | 24 | | |
| Clarence Scott | DB | 6'2" | 205 | 25 | | |
| Don Webb | DB | 5'10" | 195 | 30 | 2 | |
| Kim Hammond | QB | 6'1" | 192 | 24 | | 2 |
| Mike Taliaferro | QB | 6'2" | 205 | 27 | | |
| Teddy Bailey | HB | 6' | 200 | 25 | | |
| Sid Blanks | HB | 6' | 210 | 28 | | |
| Carl Garrett | HB | 5'11" | 210 | 22 | | 42 |
| Bob Gladieux | HB | 5'11" | 190 | 22 | | |
| Jim Nance | FB | 6'1" | 240 | 26 | | 36 |
| R. C. Gamble | HB-FB | 6'3" | 220 | 22 | | |
| Gino Cappelletti | WR | 6' | 190 | 35 | | 68 |
| Charley Frazier | WR | 6' | 184 | 30 | | 42 |
| Aaron Marsh | WR | 6'1" | 190 | 24 | | |
| Bill Rademacher | WR | 6'1" | 190 | 27 | | 18 |
| Tom Richardson | WR | 6'2" | 195 | 24 | | |
| Ron Sellers | WR | 6'4" | 198 | 22 | | 36 |
| Ken Herock | TE | 6'2" | 230 | 28 | | |
| Jim Whalen | TE | 6'2" | 210 | 25 | | 6 |
| Barry Brown | LB-TE | 6'3" | 220 | 26 | | |

## BUFFALO BILLS 4-10-0 Johnny Rauch

| Scores of Each Game | | |
|---|---|---|
| 19 | NEW YORK | 33 |
| 3 | HOUSTON | 17 |
| 41 | DENVER | 28 |
| 14 | Houston | 28 |
| 23 | BOSTON | 16 |
| 21 | Oakland | 50 |
| 6 | Miami | 24 |
| 7 | KANSAS CITY | 29 |
| 6 | New York | 16 |
| 28 | MIAMI | 3 |
| 21 | Boston | 35 |
| 16 | CINCINNATI | 13 |
| 19 | Kansas City | 22 |
| 6 | San Diego | 45 |

| Use Name | Pos. | Hgt | Wgt | Age | Int | Pts |
|---|---|---|---|---|---|---|
| Stew Barber | OT | 6'3" | 248 | 30 | | |
| Paul Costa | OT | 6'4" | 248 | 27 | | |
| Howard Kindig | OT | 6'6" | 264 | 28 | | |
| Mike Richey | OT | 6'5" | 250 | 22 | | |
| George Flint | OG | 6'4" | 240 | 31 | | |
| Billy Shaw | OG | 6'3" | 252 | 29 | | |
| Angelo Loukas | OG | 6'3" | 250 | 22 | | |
| Joe O'Donnell | OG | 6'2" | 252 | 26 | | |
| Al Bemiller | C | 6'3" | 243 | 30 | | |
| Mike McBath | DE | 6'4" | 248 | 23 | | |
| Ron McDole | DE | 6'3" | 270 | 29 | | |
| Julian Nunamaker | DE | 6'3" | 250 | 23 | | |
| Chuck DeVleigher | DT | 6'4" | 265 | 22 | | |
| Jim Dunaway | DT | 6'4" | 282 | 27 | | |
| Waddey Harvey | DT | 6'4" | 270 | 22 | | |
| Bob Kruse | DT | 6'2" | 250 | 27 | | |
| Bob Tatarek | DT | 6'4" | 255 | 23 | | |
| Edgar Chandler | LB | 6'3" | 222 | 23 | | |
| Jerald Collins | LB | 6'1" | 220 | 22 | | |
| Paul Guidry | LB | 6'3" | 228 | 25 | 2 | |
| Harry Jacobs | LB | 6'2" | 226 | 32 | 2 | |
| Paul Maguire | LB | 6' | 228 | 31 | | |
| Dave Ogas | LB | 6'3" | 240 | 23 | | |
| Mike Stratton | LB | 6'3" | 230 | 27 | | |
| Butch Byrd | DB | 6' | 196 | 27 | 7 | 6 |
| Hilton Crawford | DB | 6' | 198 | 24 | | |
| Booker Edgerson | DB | 5'10" | 183 | 30 | 1 | 6 |
| John Pitts | DB | 6'4" | 215 | 24 | 2 | |
| Pete Richardson | DB | 6'1" | 205 | 22 | 2 | |
| George Saimes | DB | 5'10" | 185 | 27 | 3 | |
| Robert James | WR-DB | 6'1" | 177 | 22 | | |
| Bob Kalsu – Military Service | | | | | | |
| Dan Darragh | QB | 6'3" | 196 | 22 | | |
| James Harris | QB | 6'3" | 215 | 22 | | |
| Jack Kemp | QB | 6'1" | 204 | 35 | | |
| Tom Sherman (from BOS) | QB | 6' | 190 | 23 | | |
| Max Anderson | HB | 5'8" | 180 | 24 | | 6 |
| Preston Ridlehuber | HB | 6'2" | 215 | 25 | | |
| O. J. Simpson | HB | 6'2" | 204 | 22 | | 30 |
| Bill Enyart | FB | 6'4" | 236 | 22 | | 18 |
| Wayne Patrick | FB | 6'2" | 225 | 23 | | 18 |
| Marlin Briscoe | WR | 5'10" | 177 | 23 | | 30 |
| Bobby Crockett | WR | 6' | 200 | 26 | | |
| Monte Ledbetter (to ATL-N) | WR | 6'2" | 185 | 26 | | |
| Haven Moses | WR | 6'3" | 200 | 23 | | 30 |
| Roy Reeves | WR | 5'11" | 182 | 23 | | |
| Bubba Thornton | WR | 6' | 175 | 22 | | |
| Charley Ferguson | TE | 6'5" | 224 | 29 | | |
| Willie Grate | TE | 6'4" | 225 | 23 | | 6 |
| Bill Masters | TE | 6'5" | 225 | 25 | | 6 |
| Bruce Alford | K | 6' | 185 | 24 | | 74 |

## MIAMI DOLPHINS 3-10-1 George Wilson

| Scores of Each Game | | |
|---|---|---|
| 21 | Cincinnati | 27 |
| 17 | Oakland | 20 |
| 10 | Houston | 22 |
| 20 | OAKLAND | 20 |
| 14 | SAN DIEGO | 21 |
| 10 | Kansas City | 17 |
| 24 | BUFFALO | 6 |
| 31 | New York | 34 |
| 17 | Boston | 16 |
| 3 | Buffalo | 28 |
| 7 | HOUSTON | 32 |
| 23 | BOSTON | 38 |
| 27 | DENVER | 24 |
| 9 | NEW YORK | 27 |

| Use Name | Pos. | Hgt | Wgt | Age | Int | Pts |
|---|---|---|---|---|---|---|
| John Boynton | OT | 6'4" | 255 | 23 | | |
| Doug Crusan | OT | 6'5" | 255 | 23 | | |
| Norm Evans | OT | 6'5" | 250 | 26 | | |
| Billy Neighbors | OG | 5'11" | 250 | 29 | | |
| Maxie Williams | OG | 6'4" | 250 | 29 | | |
| Larry Little | OT-OG | 6'1" | 270 | 23 | | |
| Tom Goode | C | 6'3" | 250 | 30 | | |
| Jeff Richardson | OT-C | 6'3" | 250 | 24 | | |
| Norm McBride | DE | 6'3" | 235 | 22 | | |
| Jim Riley | DE | 6'4" | 255 | 24 | | |
| Bill Stanfill | DE | 6'5" | 250 | 22 | 2 | 12 |
| Bob Joswick | DT-DE | 6'5" | 250 | 23 | | |
| Manny Fernandez | DT | 6'2" | 250 | 23 | | |
| Bob Heinz | DT | 6'6" | 265 | 22 | | |
| John Richardson | DT | 6'2" | 260 | 24 | | |
| Freddie Woodson | OG-DT | 6'2" | 255 | 25 | | |
| Nick Buoniconti | LB | 5'11" | 220 | 28 | 3 | |
| Randy Edmunds | LB | 6'2" | 220 | 23 | | |
| Frank Emanuel | LB | 6'3" | 225 | 26 | | |
| Jimmy Keyes | LB | 6'2" | 225 | 25 | | |
| Dale McCullers | LB | 6'1" | 215 | 21 | | |
| Jesse Powell | LB | 6'1" | 212 | 22 | | |
| Ed Weisacosky | LB | 6' | 230 | 25 | 3 | |
| Dick Anderson | DB | 6'2" | 205 | 23 | 3 | |
| Tom Beier | DB | 5'11" | 198 | 24 | 1 | |
| Garry Grady | DB | 5'11" | 180 | 22 | | |
| Lloyd Mumphord | DB | 5'11" | 180 | 22 | 5 | |
| Willie Pearson | DB | 6' | 190 | 22 | | |
| Bob Petrella | DB | 6' | 185 | 24 | 1 | |
| Jimmy Warren | DB | 5'11" | 175 | 30 | | |
| Dick Westmoreland | DB | 6'1" | 195 | 28 | | |
| Bob Griese | QB | 6'1" | 190 | 24 | | |
| Rick Norton | QB | 6'1" | 190 | 25 | | |
| John Stofa (From CIN) | QB | 6'3" | 210 | 27 | | |
| Jim Kiick | HB | 5'11" | 215 | 23 | | 60 |
| Mercury Morris | HB | 5'10" | 185 | 22 | | 12 |
| Barry Pryor | HB | 6' | 215 | 23 | | |
| Larry Csonka | FB | 6'3" | 240 | 22 | | 18 |
| Stan Mitchell | FB | 6'2" | 225 | 25 | | |
| Jack Clancy | WR | 6'1" | 195 | 25 | | 6 |
| Bill Darnall | WR | 6'2" | 197 | 25 | | |
| Jimmy Hines | WR | 6' | 175 | 22 | | |
| Gene Milton | WR | 5'10" | 170 | 24 | | 6 |
| Karl Noonan | WR | 6'3" | 190 | 25 | | 18 |
| Howard Twilley | WR | 5'10" | 180 | 25 | | 6 |
| Tommy Boutwell | QB-WR | 6'2" | 205 | 22 | | |
| Jim Mertens | TE | 6'3" | 235 | 22 | | |
| Doug Moreau | TE | 6'2" | 215 | 24 | | |
| Larry Seiple | TE | 6' | 213 | 24 | | 30 |
| Karl Kremser | K | 6' | 180 | 24 | | 65 |

## NEW YORK JETS

### RUSHING

| Last Name | No. | Yds | Avg | TD |
|---|---|---|---|---|
| Snell | 191 | 695 | 3.6 | 4 |
| Boozer | 130 | 604 | 4.6 | 4 |
| Mathis | 96 | 355 | 3.7 | 4 |
| White | 28 | 88 | 3.1 | 0 |
| Namath | 11 | 33 | 3.0 | 2 |
| Woodall | 4 | 13 | 3.3 | 0 |
| Sauer | 1 | 5 | 5.0 | 0 |
| Perilli | 3 | 4 | 1.3 | 0 |
| B. Turner | 1 | −4 | −4.0 | 0 |
| Nock | 3 | −5 | −1.7 | 0 |
| Maynard | 1 | −6 | −6.0 | 0 |

### RECEIVING

| Last Name | No. | Yds | Avg | TD |
|---|---|---|---|---|
| Maynard | 47 | 938 | 20 | 6 |
| Sauer | 45 | 745 | 17 | 8 |
| Lammons | 33 | 400 | 12 | 2 |
| Snell | 22 | 187 | 9 | 1 |
| Boozer | 20 | 222 | 11 | 0 |
| Mathis | 18 | 183 | 10 | 1 |
| B. Turner | 11 | 221 | 20 | 3 |
| Stewart | 5 | 39 | 8 | 0 |
| Dockery | 1 | 6 | 6 | 0 |
| White | 1 | −2 | −2 | 0 |

### PUNT RETURNS

| Last Name | No. | Yds | Avg | TD |
|---|---|---|---|---|
| Battle | 34 | 235 | 7 | 0 |
| Baird | 4 | 21 | 5 | 0 |
| Leonard | 1 | 0 | 0 | 0 |

### KICKOFF RETURNS

| Last Name | No. | Yds | Avg | TD |
|---|---|---|---|---|
| Battle | 31 | 750 | 24 | 0 |
| Leonard | 7 | 120 | 17 | 0 |
| B. Turner | 3 | 74 | 25 | 0 |
| Richards | 2 | 36 | 18 | 0 |
| White | 1 | 5 | 5 | 0 |
| Carroll | 1 | 0 | 0 | 0 |
| Sauer | 1 | 0 | 0 | 0 |

### PASSING — PUNTING — KICKING Statistics

| PASSING | Att | Comp | % | Yds | Yd/Att | TD | Int− | % | RK |
|---|---|---|---|---|---|---|---|---|---|
| Namath | 361 | 185 | 51 | 2734 | 7.6 | 19 | 17− | 5 | 2 |
| Parilli | 24 | 14 | 58 | 138 | 5.8 | 2 | 1− | 4 | |
| Woodall | 9 | 4 | 44 | 67 | 7.4 | 0 | 2− | 22 | |

| PUNTING | No | Avg |
|---|---|---|
| O'Neal | 54 | 44.3 |
| B. Turner | 2 | 44.5 |

| KICKING | XP | Att | % | FG | Att | % |
|---|---|---|---|---|---|---|
| J. Turner | 33 | 33 | 100 | 32 | 47 | 68 |

2 POINT XP
Maynard

## HOUSTON OILERS

### RUSHING

| Last Name | No. | Yds | Avg | TD |
|---|---|---|---|---|
| Granger | 186 | 740 | 4.0 | 3 |
| Hopkins | 131 | 473 | 3.6 | 4 |
| Burrell | 41 | 147 | 3.6 | 0 |
| Campbell | 28 | 98 | 3.5 | 1 |
| Beathard | 19 | 89 | 4.7 | 2 |
| Richardson | 5 | 51 | 10.2 | 0 |
| Johnson | 11 | 42 | 3.8 | 0 |
| Trull | 8 | 25 | 3.1 | 2 |
| Haik | 2 | 21 | 10.5 | 0 |
| LeVias | 6 | 18 | 3.0 | 0 |
| Davis | 3 | 2 | 0.7 | 0 |

### RECEIVING

| Last Name | No. | Yds | Avg | TD |
|---|---|---|---|---|
| Reed | 51 | 664 | 13 | 2 |
| LeVias | 42 | 696 | 17 | 5 |
| Beirne | 42 | 540 | 13 | 4 |
| Hopkins | 29 | 338 | 12 | 1 |
| Haik | 27 | 375 | 14 | 1 |
| Granger | 27 | 330 | 12 | 1 |
| Campbell | 7 | 82 | 12 | 0 |
| Joiner | 7 | 77 | 11 | 0 |
| Burrell | 5 | 28 | 6 | 0 |
| Johnson | 2 | 17 | 9 | 1 |

### PUNT RETURNS

| Last Name | No. | Yds | Avg | TD |
|---|---|---|---|---|
| LeVias | 35 | 292 | 8 | 0 |
| Richardson | 7 | 93 | 13 | 0 |
| Burrell | 1 | 6 | 6 | 0 |

### KICKOFF RETURNS

| Last Name | No. | Yds | Avg | TD |
|---|---|---|---|---|
| LeVias | 38 | 940 | 25 | 0 |
| Burrell | 5 | 101 | 20 | 0 |
| Joiner | 3 | 73 | 24 | 0 |
| Reed | 3 | 0 | 0 | 0 |
| Houston | 0 | 27 | 0 | 0 |

### PASSING — PUNTING — KICKING

| PASSING | Att | Comp | % | Yds | Yd/Att | TD | Int− | % | RK |
|---|---|---|---|---|---|---|---|---|---|
| Beathard | 370 | 180 | 49 | 2455 | 6.6 | 10 | 21− | 6 | 8 |
| Trull | 75 | 34 | 45 | 469 | 6.3 | 3 | 6− | 8 | |
| Davis | 42 | 25 | 60 | 223 | 5.3 | 2 | 4− | 10 | |
| LeVias | 2 | 0 | 0 | 0 | 0.0 | 0 | 0− | 0 | |

| PUNTING | No | Avg |
|---|---|---|
| Gerela | 41 | 40.4 |
| Burrell | 29 | 36.8 |

| KICKING | XP | Att | % | FG | Att | % |
|---|---|---|---|---|---|---|
| Gerela | 29 | 29 | 100 | 19 | 40 | 48 |

2 POINT XP
Beirne
Richardson

## BOSTON PATRIOTS

### RUSHING

| Last Name | No. | Yds | Avg | TD |
|---|---|---|---|---|
| Nance | 193 | 750 | 3.9 | 6 |
| Garrett | 137 | 691 | 5.0 | 5 |
| Gamble | 16 | 35 | 2.2 | 0 |
| Blanks | 7 | 30 | 4.3 | 0 |
| Frazier | 2 | −1 | −0.5 | 0 |
| Taliaferro | 12 | −16 | −1.3 | 0 |

### RECEIVING

| Last Name | No. | Yds | Avg | TD |
|---|---|---|---|---|
| Garrett | 29 | 267 | 9 | 2 |
| Nance | 29 | 168 | 6 | 0 |
| Sellers | 27 | 705 | 26 | 6 |
| Frazier | 19 | 306 | 16 | 7 |
| Rademacher | 17 | 217 | 13 | 3 |
| Whalen | 16 | 235 | 15 | 1 |
| Marsh | 8 | 108 | 14 | 0 |
| Gamble | 7 | 74 | 11 | 0 |
| Brown | 6 | 69 | 12 | 0 |
| Blanks | 2 | 16 | 8 | 0 |
| Cappelletti | 1 | 21 | 21 | 0 |
| Richardson | 1 | 5 | 5 | 0 |

### PUNT RETURNS

| Last Name | No. | Yds | Avg | TD |
|---|---|---|---|---|
| Garrett | 12 | 159 | 13 | 0 |
| Carwell | 5 | 43 | 9 | 0 |
| Blanks | 5 | 10 | 2 | 0 |
| Janik | 1 | 0 | 0 | 0 |

### KICKOFF RETURNS

| Last Name | No. | Yds | Avg | TD |
|---|---|---|---|---|
| Garrett | 28 | 792 | 28 | 0 |
| Marsh | 6 | 136 | 23 | 0 |
| Blanks | 6 | 131 | 22 | 0 |
| Gladieux | 4 | 61 | 15 | 0 |
| Scott | 6 | 43 | 7 | 0 |
| Carwell | 1 | 28 | 28 | 0 |
| Gamble | 1 | 23 | 23 | 0 |
| Berger | 1 | 20 | 20 | 0 |
| Schott'nhmer | 1 | 13 | 13 | 0 |

### PASSING — PUNTING — KICKING

| PASSING | Att | Comp | % | Yds | Yd/Att | TD | Int− | % | RK |
|---|---|---|---|---|---|---|---|---|---|
| Taliaferro | 331 | 160 | 48 | 2160 | 6.5 | 19 | 18− | 5 | 11 |
| Hammond | 6 | 2 | 33 | 31 | 5.2 | 0 | 0− | 0 | |
| Garrett | 1 | 0 | 0 | 0 | 0.0 | 0 | 0− | 0 | |

| PUNTING | No | Avg |
|---|---|---|
| Janik | 70 | 41.5 |

| KICKING | XP | Att | % | FG | Att | % |
|---|---|---|---|---|---|---|
| Cappelletti | 26 | 27 | 96 | 14 | 34 | 41 |

2 POINT XP
Hammond

## BUFFALO BILLS

### RUSHING

| Last Name | No. | Yds | Avg | TD |
|---|---|---|---|---|
| Simpson | 181 | 697 | 3.9 | 2 |
| Patrick | 83 | 361 | 4.3 | 3 |
| Enyart | 47 | 191 | 4.1 | 1 |
| Kemp | 37 | 124 | 3.4 | 0 |
| Anderson | 13 | 74 | 5.7 | 1 |
| Ridlehuber | 4 | 25 | 6.3 | 0 |
| Harris | 10 | 25 | 2.5 | 0 |
| Sherman | 2 | 14 | 7.0 | 0 |
| Darragh | 6 | 14 | 2.3 | 0 |
| Masters | 1 | −3 | −3.0 | 0 |

### RECEIVING

| Last Name | No. | Yds | Avg | TD |
|---|---|---|---|---|
| Moses | 39 | 752 | 19 | 5 |
| Patrick | 35 | 229 | 7 | 0 |
| Masters | 33 | 387 | 12 | 1 |
| Briscoe | 32 | 532 | 17 | 5 |
| Simpson | 30 | 343 | 11 | 3 |
| Enyart | 19 | 186 | 10 | 2 |
| Thornton | 14 | 134 | 10 | 0 |
| Anderson | 7 | 65 | 9 | 0 |
| Crockett | 4 | 50 | 13 | 0 |
| Grate | 1 | 19 | 19 | 1 |
| James | 1 | 19 | 19 | 0 |

### PUNT RETURNS

| Last Name | No. | Yds | Avg | TD |
|---|---|---|---|---|
| Anderson | 19 | 142 | 7 | 0 |
| Byrd | 7 | 37 | 5 | 0 |
| Reeves | 2 | 3 | 2 | 0 |
| Ridlehuber | 1 | 3 | 3 | 0 |
| James | 1 | 2 | 2 | 0 |
| Richardson | 1 | 0 | 0 | 0 |

### KICKOFF RETURNS

| Last Name | No. | Yds | Avg | TD |
|---|---|---|---|---|
| Thornton | 30 | 749 | 25 | 0 |
| Simpson | 21 | 529 | 25 | 0 |
| Anderson | 4 | 86 | 22 | 0 |
| Crawford | 3 | 74 | 25 | 0 |
| Collins | 2 | 14 | 7 | 0 |
| Enyart | 1 | 12 | 12 | 0 |
| Harvey | 1 | 11 | 11 | 0 |

### PASSING — PUNTING — KICKING

| PASSING | Att | Comp | % | Yds | Yd/Att | TD | Int− | RK |
|---|---|---|---|---|---|---|---|---|
| Kemp | 344 | 170 | 49 | 1981 | 5.8 | 13 | 22− | 9 |
| Darragh | 52 | 24 | 46 | 365 | 7.0 | 1 | 6− | 12 |
| Harris | 36 | 15 | 42 | 270 | 7.5 | 1 | 1− | 3 |
| Sherman | 2 | 2 | 100 | 20 | 10.0 | 1 | 0− | 0 |
| Briscoe | 1 | 0 | 0 | 0 | 0.0 | 0 | 1− | 100 |
| Maguire | 1 | 1 | 100 | 19 | 19.0 | 0 | 0− | 0 |
| Ridlehuber | 1 | 1 | 100 | 45 | 45.0 | 1 | 0− | 0 |

| PUNTING | No | Avg |
|---|---|---|
| Maguire | 78 | 44.5 |

| KICKING | XP | Att | % | FG | Att | % |
|---|---|---|---|---|---|---|
| Alford | 23 | 24 | 96 | 17 | 26 | 65 |

## MIAMI DOLPHINS

### RUSHING

| Last Name | No. | Yds | Avg | TD |
|---|---|---|---|---|
| Kiick | 180 | 575 | 3.2 | 9 |
| Csonka | 131 | 566 | 4.3 | 2 |
| Morris | 23 | 110 | 4.8 | 1 |
| Griese | 21 | 102 | 4.9 | 0 |
| Mitchell | 28 | 80 | 2.9 | 0 |
| Milton | 7 | 62 | 8.9 | 0 |
| Norton | 8 | 16 | 2.0 | 0 |
| Hines | 1 | 7 | 7.0 | 0 |
| Seiple | 1 | 6 | 6.0 | 0 |
| Noonan | 1 | −11 | −11.0 | 0 |

### RECEIVING

| Last Name | No. | Yds | Avg | TD |
|---|---|---|---|---|
| Seiple | 41 | 577 | 14 | 5 |
| Kiick | 29 | 443 | 15 | 1 |
| Noonan | 29 | 307 | 11 | 3 |
| Clancy | 21 | 289 | 14 | 1 |
| Csonka | 21 | 183 | 9 | 1 |
| Milton | 12 | 179 | 15 | 0 |
| Twilley | 10 | 158 | 16 | 1 |
| Mitchell | 10 | 125 | 13 | 0 |
| Moreau | 10 | 136 | 14 | 0 |
| Morris | 6 | 65 | 11 | 0 |
| Boutwell | 4 | 29 | 7 | 0 |
| Mertens | 2 | 26 | 13 | 0 |
| Hines | 2 | 23 | 12 | 0 |
| Pryor | 2 | −3 | −2 | 0 |
| Darnall | 1 | 13 | 13 | 0 |
| Anderson | 1 | 8 | 8 | 0 |

### PUNT RETURNS

| Last Name | No. | Yds | Avg | TD |
|---|---|---|---|---|
| Morris | 25 | 172 | 7 | 0 |
| Anderson | 12 | 82 | 7 | 0 |
| Beier | 5 | 8 | 2 | 0 |
| Milton | 1 | 4 | 4 | 0 |
| McCullers | 1 | 0 | 0 | 0 |
| Twilley | 1 | 0 | 0 | 0 |

### KICKOFF RETURNS

| Last Name | No. | Yds | Avg | TD |
|---|---|---|---|---|
| Morris | 43 | 1136 | 26 | 1 |
| Milton | 8 | 166 | 21 | 0 |
| Beier | 4 | 58 | 15 | 0 |
| Hines | 1 | 22 | 22 | 0 |
| Mertens | 2 | 1 | 1 | 0 |
| Mumphord | 1 | 0 | 0 | 0 |
| Warren | 1 | 0 | 0 | 0 |

### PASSING — PUNTING — KICKING

| PASSING | Att | Comp | % | Yds | Yd/Att | TD | Int− | % | RK |
|---|---|---|---|---|---|---|---|---|---|
| Griese | 252 | 121 | 48 | 1695 | 6.7 | 10 | 16− | 6 | 10 |
| Norton | 148 | 65 | 44 | 709 | 4.8 | 2 | 11− | 7 | 12 |
| Stofa | 23 | 14 | 61 | 146 | 6.4 | 0 | 2− | 9 | |
| Seiple | 1 | 1 | 100 | 8 | 8.0 | 0 | 0− | 0 | |

| PUNTING | No | Avg |
|---|---|---|
| Seiple | 80 | 40.8 |
| Anderson | 5 | 37.6 |

| KICKING | XP | Att | % | FG | Att | % |
|---|---|---|---|---|---|---|
| Kremser | 26 | 27 | 96 | 13 | 22 | 59 |

## OAKLAND RAIDERS 12-1-1 John Madden

| Scores of Each Game | | |
|---|---|---|
| 21 | HOUSTON | 17 |
| 20 | MIAMI | 17 |
| 38 | Boston | 23 |
| 20 | Miami | 20 |
| 24 | Denver | 14 |
| 50 | BUFFALO | 21 |
| 24 | San Diego | 12 |
| 17 | Cincinnati | 31 |
| 41 | DENVER | 10 |
| 21 | SAN DIEGO | 16 |
| 27 | Kansas City | 24 |
| 27 | New York | 14 |
| 37 | CINCINNATI | 17 |
| 10 | KANSAS CITY | 6 |

| Use Name | Pos. | Hgt | Wgt | Age | Int | Pts |
|---|---|---|---|---|---|---|
| Harry Schuh | OT | 6'2" | 260 | 26 | | |
| Art Shell | OT | 6'5" | 255 | 22 | | |
| Bob Svihus | OT | 6'4" | 245 | 26 | | |
| George Buehler | OG | 6'2" | 260 | 22 | | |
| Jim Harvey | OG | 6'5" | 245 | 26 | | |
| Wayne Hawkins | OG | 6' | 240 | 31 | | |
| Gene Upshaw | OG | 6'5" | 255 | 24 | | |
| Jim Otto | C | 6'2" | 248 | 31 | | |
| Ben Davidson | DE | 6'8" | 275 | 29 | | |
| Ike Lassiter | DE | 6'5" | 270 | 28 | | |
| Carleton Oats | DT-DE | 6'2" | 260 | 26 | | |
| Dan Birdwell | DT | 6'4" | 250 | 28 | | |
| Al Dotson | DT | 6'4" | 260 | 26 | | 2 |
| Tom Keating | DT | 6'3" | 247 | 26 | | |
| Art Thoms | DT | 6'5" | 250 | 22 | | |
| Duane Benson | LB | 6'2" | 215 | 24 | | |
| Bill Budness | LB | 6'1" | 215 | 26 | | |
| Dan Conners | LB | 6'1 | 230 | 27 | 1 | 12 |
| Bill Laskey | LB | 6'2" | 235 | 26 | 3 | |
| Chip Oliver | LB | 6'2" | 220 | 23 | 1 | 6 |
| Gus Otto | LB | 6'2" | 220 | 26 | 2 | |
| Jackie Allen | DB | 6'1" | 187 | 21 | | |
| Butch Atkinson | DB | 6' | 180 | 22 | 2 | 6 |
| Willie Brown | DB | 6'1" | 190 | 28 | 5 | |
| Dave Grayson | DB | 5'10" | 185 | 30 | 8 | 6 |
| Kent McCloughan | DB | 6'1" | 190 | 26 | | |
| Howie Williams | DB | 6'2" | 190 | 32 | 2 | |
| Nemiah Wilson | DB | 6' | 165 | 26 | 2 | |
| George Blanda | QB | 6'1" | 215 | 41 | | 105 |
| Daryle Lamonica | QB | 6'2" | 215 | 28 | | 6 |
| Charlie Smith | HB | 6'1" | 205 | 23 | | 24 |
| Larry Todd | HB | 6'1" | 185 | 26 | | 12 |
| Pete Banaszak | FB-HB | 5'11" | 200 | 25 | | 18 |
| Hewritt Dixon | FB | 6'2" | 230 | 29 | | 6 |
| Marv Hubbard | FB | 6'1" | 215 | 23 | | |
| Fred Biletnikoff | WR | 6'1" | 190 | 26 | | 72 |
| Drew Buie | WR | 6'2" | 178 | 22 | | |
| Rod Sherman | WR | 6' | 190 | 24 | | |
| Warren Wells | WR | 6'1" | 190 | 26 | | 84 |
| Billy Cannon | TE | 6'1" | 215 | 32 | | 12 |
| Lloyd Edwards | TE | 6'3" | 248 | 22 | | |
| Roger Hagberg | TE | 6'2" | 215 | 30 | | 6 |
| Mike Eischeid | K | 6' | 190 | 28 | | |

## KANSAS CITY CHIEFS 11-3-0 Hank Stram

| Scores of Each Game | | |
|---|---|---|
| 27 | San Diego | 9 |
| 31 | Boston | 0 |
| 19 | Cincinnati | 24 |
| 26 | Denver | 13 |
| 24 | HOUSTON | 0 |
| 17 | MIAMI | 10 |
| 42 | CINCINNATI | 22 |
| 29 | Buffalo | 7 |
| 27 | SAN DIEGO | 3 |
| 34 | New York | 16 |
| 24 | OAKLAND | 27 |
| 31 | DENVER | 17 |
| 22 | BUFFALO | 19 |
| 6 | Oakland | 10 |

| Use Name | Pos. | Hgt | Wgt | Age | Int | Pts |
|---|---|---|---|---|---|---|
| Dave Hill | OT | 6'5" | 260 | 28 | | |
| Jim Tyrer | OT | 6'6" | 275 | 30 | | |
| Ed Budde | OG | 6'5" | 260 | 28 | | |
| George Daney | OG | 6'3" | 240 | 22 | | 6 |
| Mo Moorman | OG | 6'5" | 252 | 25 | | |
| E. J. Holub | C | 6'4" | 236 | 31 | | |
| Remi Prudhomme | C | 6'4" | 250 | 27 | | |
| Aaron Brown | DE | 6'5" | 265 | 25 | | |
| Jerry Mays | DE | 6'4" | 252 | 29 | | |
| Gene Trosch | DE | 6'7" | 277 | 24 | | |
| Buck Buchanan | DT | 6'7" | 287 | 29 | | |
| Curley Culp | DT | 6'1" | 265 | 23 | | |
| Ed Lothamer | DT | 6'5" | 270 | 26 | | |
| Bobby Bell | LB | 6'4" | 228 | 29 | | 6 |
| Chuck Hurston | LB | 6'6" | 240 | 26 | | |
| Willie Lanier | LB | 6'1" | 245 | 24 | 4 | |
| Jim Lynch | LB | 6'1" | 235 | 24 | 3 | |
| Bob Stein | LB | 6'2" | 235 | 21 | | |
| Caesar Belser | DB | 6' | 212 | 24 | | |
| Jim Kearney | DB | 6'2" | 206 | 26 | 5 | 6 |
| Jim Marsalis | DB | 5'11" | 194 | 23 | 2 | |
| Willie Mitchell | DB | 6'1" | 185 | 27 | 1 | |
| Johnny Robinson | DB | 6' | 205 | 30 | 8 | |
| Goldie Sellers | DB | 6'2" | 198 | 27 | | 6 |
| Emmitt Thomas | DB | 6'2" | 192 | 26 | 9 | 6 |
| Len Dawson | QB | 6' | 190 | 35 | | |
| Tom Flores (from BUF) | QB | 6'1" | 202 | 32 | | |
| Jacky Lee | QB | 6'1" | 185 | 30 | | |
| Mike Livingston | QB | 6'3" | 205 | 23 | | |
| Mike Garrett | HB | 5'9" | 200 | 25 | | 48 |
| Paul Lowe | HB | 6' | 205 | 32 | | |
| Warren McVea | HB | 5'10" | 182 | 23 | | 42 |
| Ed Podolak | HB | 6'1" | 204 | 22 | | |
| Noland Smith (to SF-N) | HB | 5'6" | 156 | 25 | | |
| Wendell Hayes | FB | 6'2" | 220 | 28 | | 24 |
| Robert Holmes | FB | 5'9" | 220 | 23 | | 30 |
| Frank Pitts | WR | 6'2" | 200 | 25 | | 12 |
| Gloster Richardson | WR | 6' | 200 | 26 | | 12 |
| Otis Taylor | WR | 6'2" | 215 | 26 | | 42 |
| Mickey McCarty | TE | 6'5" | 255 | 22 | | |
| Curtis McClinton | TE | 6'3" | 227 | 31 | | |
| Morris Stroud | TE | 6'10" | 235 | 23 | | |
| Fred Arbanas | OT-TE | 6'3" | 240 | 30 | | |
| Jan Stenerud | K | 6'2" | 187 | 26 | | 119 |
| Jerrel Wilson | K | 6'4" | 222 | 27 | | |

## SAN DIEGO CHARGERS 8-6-0 Sid Gillman Charlie Waller

| Scores of Each Game | | |
|---|---|---|
| 9 | KANSAS CITY | 27 |
| 20 | Cincinnati | 34 |
| 34 | NEW YORK | 27 |
| 21 | CINCINNATI | 14 |
| 21 | Miami | 14 |
| 13 | Boston | 10 |
| 12 | OAKLAND | 24 |
| 0 | Denver | 13 |
| 3 | Kansas City | 27 |
| 16 | Oakland | 21 |
| 45 | DENVER | 24 |
| 21 | Houston | 17 |
| 28 | BOSTON | 18 |
| 45 | BUFFALO | 6 |

| Use Name | Pos. | Hgt | Wgt | Age | Int | Pts |
|---|---|---|---|---|---|---|
| Gene Ferguson | OT | 6'7" | 306 | 21 | | 6 |
| Ron Mix | OT | 6'4" | 250 | 31 | | |
| Terry Owens | OT | 6'6" | 270 | 25 | | |
| Bob Wells | OT | 6'4" | 270 | 24 | | |
| Gary Kirner | OG | 6'3" | 255 | 27 | | |
| Jim Schmedding | OG | 6'2" | 250 | 23 | | |
| Walt Sweeney | OG | 6'3" | 260 | 28 | | |
| Sam Gruneisen | C | 6'1" | 250 | 28 | | |
| Bill Lenkaitis | OG-C | 6'3" | 250 | 23 | | |
| Ron Billingsley | DE | 6'8" | 265 | 24 | | |
| Steve DeLong | DE | 6'3" | 252 | 26 | | |
| Houston Ridge | DE | 6'4" | 245 | 25 | | |
| Bob Briggs | DT | 6'4" | 270 | 24 | | |
| LevertCarr | DT | 6'5" | 250 | 25 | | |
| Dan Sartin | DT | 6'1" | 245 | 23 | | |
| Russ Washington | DT | 6'6" | 290 | 22 | | |
| Chuck Allen | LB | 6'1" | 225 | 29 | | |
| Pete Barnes | LB | 6'3" | 245 | 24 | 5 | |
| Bob Bruggers | LB | 6'1" | 230 | 25 | 1 | |
| Jim Campbell | LB | 6'3" | 218 | 23 | 1 | |
| Jim Fetherston | LB | 6'2" | 225 | 24 | | |
| Rick Redman | LB | 5'11" | 225 | 26 | 1 | |
| Jeff Staggs | LB | 6'2" | 240 | 25 | | |
| Joe Beauchamp | DB | 6' | 185 | 25 | | |
| Speedy Duncan | DB | 5'10" | 175 | 26 | 6 | 6 |
| Dick Farley | DB | 6' | 185 | 23 | | |
| Kenny Graham | DB | 6' | 205 | 27 | 4 | 12 |
| Jim Hill | DB | 6'2" | 192 | 22 | 7 | |
| Bob Howard | DB | 6'1" | 190 | 24 | 6 | |
| Gene Huey | DB | 5'11" | 190 | 22 | | |
| Larry Rentz | DB | 6'1" | 170 | 22 | | |
| Jim Tolbert | DB | 6'3" | 207 | 25 | | |
| Marty Domres | QB | 6'3" | 212 | 22 | | 24 |
| John Hadl | QB | 6'2" | 215 | 29 | | 12 |
| Dickie Post | HB | 5'9" | 190 | 23 | | 36 |
| Ron Sayers | HB | 6'1" | 202 | 22 | | |
| Russ Smith | FB-HB | 6'1" | 209 | 25 | | 12 |
| Gene Foster | FB | 5'11" | 220 | 26 | | 6 |
| Brad Hubbert | FB | 6'1" | 227 | 28 | | 24 |
| Lance Alworth | WR | 6' | 180 | 29 | | 24 |
| Rick Eber | WR | 6' | 185 | 24 | | 6 |
| Gary Garrison | WR | 6'1" | 195 | 25 | | 42 |
| Richard Trapp | WR | 6'1" | 174 | 22 | | |
| Willie Frazier | TE | 6'4" | 235 | 26 | | |
| Jacque MacKinnon | TE | 6'4" | 240 | 30 | | |
| Jeff Queen | TE | 6'1" | 230 | 23 | | |
| Dennis Partee | K | 6'2" | 208 | 23 | | 78 |

## DENVER BRONCOS 5-8-1 Lou Saban

| Scores of Each Game | | |
|---|---|---|
| 35 | BOSTON | 7 |
| 21 | NEW YORK | 19 |
| 28 | Buffalo | 41 |
| 13 | KANSAS CITY | 26 |
| 14 | OAKLAND | 24 |
| 30 | Cincinnati | 23 |
| 21 | Houston | 24 |
| 13 | SAN DIEGO | 0 |
| 10 | Oakland | 41 |
| 20 | HOUSTON | 20 |
| 24 | San Diego | 45 |
| 17 | Kansas City | 31 |
| 24 | Miami | 27 |
| 27 | CINCINNATI | 16 |

| Use Name | Pos. | Hgt | Wgt | Age | Int | Pts |
|---|---|---|---|---|---|---|
| Sam Brunelli | OT | 6'1" | 270 | 26 | | |
| Mike Current | OT | 6'4" | 260 | 23 | | |
| Wallace Dickey | OT | 6'3" | 260 | 28 | | |
| George Goeddeke | OG | 6'3" | 253 | 24 | | |
| Buzz Highsmith | OG | 6'4" | 230 | 26 | | |
| Mike Schnitker | OG | 6'3" | 235 | 22 | | |
| Bob Young | OG | 6'2" | 260 | 26 | | |
| Jay Bachman | C | 6'3" | 250 | 23 | | |
| Larry Kaminski | C | 6'2" | 245 | 24 | | |
| Walt Barnes | DE | 6'3" | 250 | 25 | | |
| Pete Duranko | DE | 6'2" | 252 | 25 | | |
| Rich Jackson | DE | 6'2" | 255 | 28 | | |
| Dave Costa | DT | 6'2" | 265 | 27 | | |
| Jerry Inman | DT | 6'3" | 255 | 29 | | |
| Rex Mirich | DT | 6'4" | 250 | 28 | | |
| Paul Smith | DT | 6'3" | 245 | 24 | | |
| Tim Casey (from CHI-N) | LB | 6'1" | 225 | 25 | | |
| Gary Crane | LB | 6'4" | 230 | 22 | | |
| Ken Criter | LB | 5'11" | 223 | 22 | | |
| Carl Cunningham | LB | 6'3" | 240 | 25 | 2 | |
| John Huard | LB | 6' | 220 | 25 | 2 | |
| Gordon Lambert | LB | 6'5" | 245 | 24 | | |
| Chip Myrtle | LB | 6'2" | 225 | 24 | | |
| Frank Richter | LB | 6'3" | 230 | 24 | | |
| Phil Brady | DB | 6'2" | 211 | 26 | | |
| George Burrell | DB | 5'10" | 180 | 21 | 2 | 6 |
| Grady Cavness | DB | 5'11" | 187 | 22 | 2 | |
| Charlie Greer | DB | 6' | 205 | 23 | 2 | |
| Gus Holloman | DB | 6'3" | 195 | 23 | 1 | |
| Pete Jaquess | DB | 6' | 182 | 27 | | |
| Tom Oberg | DB | 6' | 185 | 24 | | |
| Jimmy Smith | DB | 6'3" | 190 | 24 | | |
| Bill Thompson | DB | 6'1" | 200 | 22 | 3 | 6 |
| Ted Alfen | HB-DB | 6' | 195 | 22 | | |
| Pete Liske | QB | 6'2" | 185 | 28 | | |
| Al Pastrana | QB | 6'1" | 190 | 24 | | |
| Steve Tensi | QB | 6'5" | 215 | 26 | | |
| Bobby Burnett | HB | 6'2" | 208 | 26 | | |
| Floyd Little | HB | 5'10" | 195 | 27 | | 42 |
| Frank Quayle | HB | 5'10" | 195 | 22 | | |
| Wandy Williams | HB | 6'1" | 193 | 23 | | 6 |
| Henry Jones | FB | 6'2" | 235 | 23 | | |
| Brendan McCarthy | FB | 6'3" | 220 | 24 | | |
| Tom Smiley | FB | 6'1" | 235 | 25 | | 24 |
| Fran Lynch | HB-FB | 6'1" | 194 | 23 | | 12 |
| Al Denson | WR | 6'2" | 208 | 27 | | 60 |
| John Embree | WR | 6'4" | 207 | 25 | | 30 |
| Mike Haffner | WR | 6'2" | 205 | 27 | | 30 |
| Bill Van Heusen | WR | 6'1" | 200 | 23 | | |
| Tom Beer | TE | 6'4" | 230 | 24 | | |
| Tom Buckman | TE | 6'4" | 230 | 22 | | 6 |
| Dave Pivec | TE | 6'3" | 240 | 25 | | |
| Bobby Howfield | K | 5'9" | 180 | 32 | | 75 |

## CINCINNATI BENGALS 4-9-1 Paul Brown

| Scores of Each Game | | |
|---|---|---|
| 27 | MIAMI | 21 |
| 34 | SAN DIEGO | 20 |
| 24 | KANSAS CITY | 19 |
| 14 | San Diego | 21 |
| 7 | NEW YORK | 21 |
| 23 | DENVER | 30 |
| 22 | Kansas City | 42 |
| 31 | OAKLAND | 17 |
| 31 | Houston | 31 |
| 14 | BOSTON | 25 |
| 7 | New York | 40 |
| 13 | Buffalo | 16 |
| 17 | Oakland | 37 |
| 16 | Denver | 27 |

| Use Name | Pos. | Hgt | Wgt | Age | Int | Pts |
|---|---|---|---|---|---|---|
| Howard Fest | OT | 6'6" | 265 | 23 | | |
| Frank Peters | OT | 6'4" | 250 | 21 | | |
| Ernie Wright | OT | 6'4" | 270 | 29 | | |
| Ernie Park | OG-OT | 6'3" | 240 | 27 | | |
| Justin Canale | OG | 6'2" | 250 | 25 | | |
| Guy Dennis | OG | 6'2" | 255 | 22 | | |
| Pat Matson | OG | 6'1" | 245 | 25 | | |
| Dave Middendorf | OG | 6'3" | 260 | 23 | | |
| Mike Wilson | OG | 6'1" | 240 | 21 | | |
| Bob Johnson | C | 6'5" | 260 | 23 | | |
| Marty Baccaglio | DE | 6'3" | 245 | 24 | | |
| Royce Berry | DE | 6'3" | 242 | 23 | | |
| Harry Gunner | DE | 6'6" | 250 | 24 | 1 | 6 |
| Steve Chomyszak | DT | 6'5" | 280 | 24 | | |
| Andy Rice | DT | 6'3" | 268 | 27 | | |
| Bill Staley | DT | 6'3" | 250 | 22 | | |
| Ken Avery | LB | 6'1" | 225 | 25 | | |
| Al Beauchamp | LB | 6'2" | 236 | 25 | 1 | |
| Bill Bergey | LB | 6'2" | 240 | 24 | 2 | |
| Tim Buchanan | LB | 6' | 233 | 23 | | |
| Ed Harmon | LB | 6'4" | 230 | 22 | | |
| Bill Peterson | LB | 6'3" | 230 | 24 | 4 | |
| Al Coleman | DB | 6'1" | 183 | 24 | | |
| Ken Dyer | DB | 6'3" | 185 | 23 | | |
| John Guillory | DB | 5'10" | 190 | 24 | 1 | |
| Bobby Hunt | DB | 6'1" | 190 | 29 | 4 | |
| Charlie King | DB | 6' | 184 | 26 | | |
| Ken Riley | DB | 6' | 182 | 22 | 4 | |
| Fletcher Smith | DB | 6'2" | 178 | 25 | 4 | |
| Jim Williams | DB | 6'1" | 190 | 23 | | |
| Greg Cook | QB | 6'3" | 212 | 22 | | 6 |
| Sam Wyche | QB | 6'4" | 210 | 24 | | 6 |
| Essex Johnson | HB | 5'9" | 190 | 22 | | |
| Paul Robinson | HB | 6' | 200 | 24 | | 24 |
| Ron Lamb | FB | 6'2" | 225 | 25 | | |
| Clem Turner | FB | 6'1" | 245 | 24 | | |
| Jess Phillips | HB-FB | 6'1" | 205 | 22 | | 18 |
| Eric Crabtree | WR | 5'11" | 182 | 24 | | 42 |
| Jack Gehrke | WR | 6' | 178 | 23 | | |
| Chip Myers | WR | 6'4" | 200 | 24 | | 12 |
| Tommie Smith | WR | 6'4" | 190 | 25 | | |
| Speedy Thomas | WR | 6'1" | 175 | 22 | | 24 |
| Bruce Coslet | TE | 6'3" | 225 | 23 | | 6 |
| Bob Trumpy | WR-TE | 6'6" | 220 | 24 | | 54 |
| Dale Livingston | K | 6' | 210 | 24 | | |
| Horst Muhlnan | K | 6'1" | 210 | 29 | | 80 |
| Terry Swanson | K | 6' | 210 | 24 | | |

Frank Buncom –Died Sept. 14, 1969 from pulmonary embolism

## OAKLAND RAIDERS

### RUSHING

| Last Name | No. | Yds | Avg | TD |
|---|---|---|---|---|
| Smith | 177 | 600 | 3.4 | 2 |
| Dixon | 107 | 398 | 3.7 | 0 |
| Banaszak | 88 | 377 | 4.3 | 0 |
| Todd | 47 | 198 | 4.2 | 1 |
| Hubbard | 21 | 119 | 5.7 | 0 |
| Lamonica | 13 | 36 | 2.8 | 1 |
| Wells | 3 | 24 | 8.0 | 0 |
| Eischeid | 1 | 10 | 10.0 | 0 |
| Hagberg | 1 | 3 | 3.0 | 0 |
| Blanda | 1 | 0 | 0.0 | 0 |

### RECEIVING

| Last Name | No. | Yds | Avg | TD |
|---|---|---|---|---|
| Biletnikoff | 54 | 837 | 15 | 12 |
| Wells | 47 | 1260 | 27 | 14 |
| Dixon | 33 | 275 | 8 | 1 |
| Smith | 30 | 322 | 11 | 2 |
| Cannon | 21 | 262 | 12 | 2 |
| Banaszak | 17 | 119 | 7 | 3 |
| Todd | 16 | 149 | 9 | 1 |
| Hagberg | 6 | 84 | 14 | 1 |
| Hubbard | 2 | 30 | 15 | 0 |
| Buie | 1 | 37 | 37 | 0 |

### PUNT RETURNS

| Last Name | No. | Yds | Avg | TD |
|---|---|---|---|---|
| Atkinson | 25 | 153 | 6 | 0 |
| Sherman | 9 | 46 | 5 | 0 |
| Grayson | 4 | 28 | 7 | 0 |
| Allen | 1 | -2 | -2 | 0 |

### KICKOFF RETURNS

| Last Name | No. | Yds | Avg | TD |
|---|---|---|---|---|
| Atkinson | 16 | 382 | 24 | 0 |
| Sherman | 12 | 300 | 25 | 0 |
| Smith | 10 | 247 | 25 | 0 |
| Allen | 3 | 67 | 22 | 0 |
| Benson | 1 | 0 | 0 | 0 |

### PASSING – PUNTING – KICKING

| PASSING | Att | Comp | % | Yds | Yd/Att | TD | Int— | % | RK |
|---|---|---|---|---|---|---|---|---|---|
| Lamonica | 426 | 221 | 52 | 3302 | 7.8 | 34 | 25— | 6 | 3 |
| Blanda | 13 | 6 | 46 | 73 | 5.6 | 2 | 1— | 8 | |

| PUNTING | No | Avg |
|---|---|---|
| Eischeid | 69 | 42.7 |

| KICKING | XP | Att | % | FG | Att | % |
|---|---|---|---|---|---|---|
| Blanda | 45 | 45 | 100 | 20 | 37 | 54 |

## KANSAS CITY CHIEFS

### RUSHING

| Last Name | No. | Yds | Avg | TD |
|---|---|---|---|---|
| Garrett | 168 | 732 | 4.4 | 6 |
| Holmes | 150 | 612 | 4.1 | 2 |
| McVea | 106 | 500 | 4.7 | 7 |
| Hayes | 62 | 208 | 3.4 | 4 |
| Livingston | 15 | 102 | 6.8 | 0 |
| Lowe | 10 | 33 | 3.3 | 0 |
| Pitts | 5 | 28 | 5.6 | 0 |
| Dawson | 1 | 3 | 3.0 | 0 |
| Lee | 1 | 3 | 3.0 | 0 |
| Arbanas | 1 | 1 | 1.0 | 0 |
| Flores | 1 | 0 | 0.0 | 0 |
| Taylor | 2 | -2 | -1.0 | 0 |

### RECEIVING

| Last Name | No. | Yds | Avg | TD |
|---|---|---|---|---|
| Garrett | 43 | 432 | 10 | 2 |
| Taylor | 41 | 696 | 17 | 7 |
| Pitts | 31 | 470 | 15 | 2 |
| Holmes | 26 | 266 | 10 | 3 |
| Richardson | 23 | 381 | 17 | 2 |
| Arbanas | 16 | 258 | 16 | 0 |
| Hayes | 9 | 64 | 7 | 0 |
| McVea | 7 | 71 | 10 | 0 |

### PUNT RETURNS

| Last Name | No. | Yds | Avg | TD |
|---|---|---|---|---|
| Smith | 9 | 107 | 12 | 0 |
| Mitchell | 13 | 101 | 8 | 0 |
| Garrett | 8 | 28 | 4 | 0 |
| Sellers | 2 | 15 | 8 | 0 |

### KICKOFF RETURNS

| Last Name | No. | Yds | Avg | TD |
|---|---|---|---|---|
| McVea | 13 | 318 | 24 | 0 |
| Mitchell | 7 | 178 | 25 | 0 |
| Podolak | 7 | 165 | 24 | 0 |
| Smith | 4 | 125 | 31 | 0 |
| Lowe | 5 | 116 | 23 | 0 |
| Hayes | 2 | 81 | 41 | 0 |
| Holmes | 2 | 54 | 27 | 0 |
| Bell | 1 | 53 | 53 | 1 |

### PASSING – PUNTING – KICKING

| PASSING | Att | Comp | % | Yds | Yd/Att | TD | Int— | % | RK |
|---|---|---|---|---|---|---|---|---|---|
| Dawson | 166 | 98 | 59 | 1323 | 8.0 | 9 | 13— | 8 | 6 |
| Livingston | 161 | 84 | 52 | 1123 | 7.0 | 4 | 6— | 4 | 4 |
| Lee | 20 | 12 | 60 | 109 | 5.5 | 1 | 1— | 5 | |
| Flores | 6 | 3 | 50 | 49 | 8.2 | 1 | 0— | 0 | |
| McVea | 3 | 1 | 33 | 50 | 16.7 | 1 | 0— | 0 | |

| PUNTING | No | Avg |
|---|---|---|
| Wilson | 68 | 44.4 |

| KICKING | XP | Att | % | FG | Att | % |
|---|---|---|---|---|---|---|
| Stenerud | 38 | 38 | 100 | 27 | 35 | 77 |

## SAN DIEGO CHARGERS

### RUSHING

| Last Name | No. | Yds | Avg | TD |
|---|---|---|---|---|
| Post | 182 | 873 | 4.8 | 6 |
| Hubbert | 94 | 333 | 3.5 | 4 |
| Foster | 64 | 236 | 3.7 | 0 |
| Smith | 51 | 211 | 4.1 | 2 |
| Domres | 19 | 145 | 7.6 | 4 |
| Hadl | 26 | 109 | 4.2 | 2 |
| Sayers | 14 | 53 | 3.8 | 0 |
| Alworth | 5 | 25 | 5.0 | 0 |

### RECEIVING

| Last Name | No. | Yds | Avg | TD |
|---|---|---|---|---|
| Alworth | 64 | 1003 | 16 | 4 |
| Garrison | 40 | 804 | 20 | 7 |
| Post | 24 | 235 | 10 | 0 |
| Frazier | 17 | 205 | 12 | 0 |
| Foster | 14 | 83 | 6 | 1 |
| Hubbert | 11 | 43 | 4 | 0 |
| Queen | 10 | 148 | 15 | 0 |
| Smith | 10 | 144 | 14 | 0 |
| Eber | 9 | 141 | 16 | 1 |
| MacKinnon | 7 | 82 | 12 | 0 |
| Trapp | 2 | 39 | 20 | 0 |

### PUNT RETURNS

| Last Name | No. | Yds | Avg | TD |
|---|---|---|---|---|
| Duncan | 27 | 280 | 10 | 0 |
| Graham | 3 | 15 | 5 | 0 |
| Smith | 1 | 5 | 5 | 0 |

### KICKOFF RETURNS

| Last Name | No. | Yds | Avg | TD |
|---|---|---|---|---|
| Duncan | 21 | 587 | 28 | 0 |
| Smith | 6 | 138 | 23 | 0 |
| Post | 4 | 74 | 19 | 0 |
| Sayers | 2 | 42 | 21 | 0 |
| Foster | 1 | 1 | 1 | 0 |
| Fetherston | 3 | 0 | 0 | 0 |
| Briggs | 1 | 0 | 0 | 0 |
| Huey | 1 | 0 | 0 | 0 |

### PASSING – PUNTING – KICKING

| PASSING | Att | Comp | % | Yds | Yd/Att | TD | Int— | % | RK |
|---|---|---|---|---|---|---|---|---|---|
| Hadl | 324 | 158 | 49 | 2253 | 7.0 | 10 | 11— | 3 | 5 |
| Domres | 112 | 47 | 42 | 631 | 5.6 | 2 | 10— | 0 | |
| Foster | 5 | 2 | 40 | 39 | 7.8 | 1 | 0— | 0 | |
| Post | 2 | 1 | 50 | 4 | 2.0 | 0 | 0— | 0 | |
| Hubbert | 1 | 0 | 0 | 0 | 0.0 | 0 | 0— | 0 | |

| PUNTING | No | Avg |
|---|---|---|
| Partee | 71 | 44.6 |

| KICKING | XP | Att | % | FG | Att | % |
|---|---|---|---|---|---|---|
| Partee | 33 | 33 | 100 | 15 | 28 | 54 |

## DENVER BRONCOS

### RUSHING

| Last Name | No. | Yds | Avg | TD |
|---|---|---|---|---|
| Little | 146 | 729 | 5.0 | 6 |
| Lynch | 96 | 407 | 4.2 | 2 |
| Quayle | 57 | 183 | 3.2 | 0 |
| Smiley | 56 | 166 | 3.0 | 3 |
| Tensi | 12 | 63 | 5.3 | 0 |
| Liske | 10 | 50 | 5.0 | 0 |
| Williams | 10 | 18 | 1.8 | 1 |
| Denson | 1 | 9 | 9.0 | 0 |
| Burnett | 5 | 9 | 1.8 | 0 |
| Jones | 1 | 3 | 3.0 | 0 |

### RECEIVING

| Last Name | No. | Yds | Avg | TD |
|---|---|---|---|---|
| Denson | 53 | 809 | 15 | 10 |
| Haffner | 35 | 563 | 16 | 5 |
| Embree | 29 | 469 | 16 | 5 |
| Little | 19 | 218 | 11 | 1 |
| Quayle | 11 | 167 | 15 | 0 |
| Beer | 9 | 200 | 22 | 0 |
| Pivic | 9 | 117 | 13 | 0 |
| Lynch | 9 | 86 | 10 | 0 |
| Williams | 5 | 56 | 11 | 0 |
| Smiley | 5 | 23 | 5 | 1 |
| Buckman | 4 | 48 | 12 | 1 |
| Van Heusen | 3 | 64 | 21 | 0 |
| Pastrana | 1 | 15 | 15 | 0 |

### PUNT RETURNS

| Last Name | No. | Yds | Avg | TD |
|---|---|---|---|---|
| Thompson | 25 | 288 | 12 | 0 |
| Little | 6 | 70 | 12 | 0 |
| Burrell | 5 | 56 | 11 | 0 |
| Greer | 1 | 36 | 36 | 0 |

### KICKOFF RETURNS

| Last Name | No. | Yds | Avg | TD |
|---|---|---|---|---|
| Williams | 23 | 574 | 25 | 0 |
| Thompson | 18 | 513 | 29 | 0 |
| Burrell | 6 | 108 | 18 | 0 |
| Little | 3 | 81 | 27 | 0 |
| Criter | 3 | 31 | 10 | 0 |
| Barnes | 1 | 16 | 16 | 0 |
| Hollomon | 1 | 0 | 0 | 0 |
| Myrtle | 1 | 0 | 0 | 0 |

### PASSING – PUNTING – KICKING

| PASSING | Att | Comp | % | Yds | Yd/Att | TD | Int— | % | RK |
|---|---|---|---|---|---|---|---|---|---|
| Tensi | 286 | 131 | 46 | 1990 | 7.0 | 14 | 12— | 4 | 7 |
| Liske | 115 | 61 | 53 | 845 | 7.4 | 9 | 11— | 10 | |
| Little | 2 | 0 | 0 | 0 | 0.0 | 0 | 0— | 0 | |

| PUNTING | No | Avg |
|---|---|---|
| Holloman | 47 | 39.7 |
| Van Heusen | 25 | 40.8 |

| KICKING | XP | Att | % | FG | Att | % |
|---|---|---|---|---|---|---|
| Howfield | 36 | 37 | 97 | 13 | 29 | 45 |

## CINCINNATI BENGALS

### RUSHING

| Last Name | No. | Yds | Avg | TD |
|---|---|---|---|---|
| Phillips | 118 | 578 | 4.9 | 3 |
| Robinson | 160 | 489 | 3.1 | 4 |
| Cook | 25 | 148 | 5.9 | 1 |
| Wyche | 12 | 107 | 8.9 | 1 |
| Turner | 23 | 105 | 4.6 | 0 |
| E. Johnson | 15 | 54 | 3.6 | 0 |
| Livingston | 1 | 18 | 18.0 | 0 |
| Thomas | 4 | 16 | 4.0 | 1 |
| Lamb | 5 | 8 | 1.6 | 0 |

### RECEIVING

| Last Name | No. | Yds | Avg | TD |
|---|---|---|---|---|
| Crabtree | 40 | 855 | 21 | 7 |
| Trumpy | 37 | 835 | 23 | 9 |
| Thomas | 33 | 481 | 15 | 3 |
| Robinson | 20 | 104 | 5 | 0 |
| Phillips | 13 | 128 | 10 | 0 |
| Myers | 10 | 205 | 21 | 2 |
| Turner | 5 | 14 | 3 | 0 |
| Riley | 2 | 15 | 8 | 0 |
| T. Smith | 1 | 41 | 41 | 0 |
| Coslet | 1 | 39 | 39 | 1 |
| E. Johnson | 1 | 3 | 3 | 0 |

### PUNT RETURNS

| Last Name | No. | Yds | Avg | TD |
|---|---|---|---|---|
| E. Johnson | 17 | 85 | 5 | 0 |
| Thomas | 4 | 15 | 4 | 0 |
| Coleman | 1 | 0 | 0 | 0 |
| Guillory | 1 | 0 | 0 | 0 |
| King | 0 | 35 | 0 | 0 |

### KICKOFF RETURNS

| Last Name | No. | Yds | Avg | TD |
|---|---|---|---|---|
| E. Johnson | 16 | 362 | 23 | 0 |
| Riley | 14 | 334 | 24 | 0 |
| Guillory | 8 | 170 | 21 | 0 |
| Robinson | 5 | 168 | 34 | 0 |
| Lamb | 5 | 64 | 13 | 0 |
| Phillips | 3 | 52 | 17 | 0 |
| Turner | 3 | 15 | 15 | 0 |
| Gunner | 1 | 0 | 0 | 0 |

### PASSING – PUNTING – KICKING

| PASSING | Att | Comp | % | Yds | Yd/Att | TD | Int— | % | RK |
|---|---|---|---|---|---|---|---|---|---|
| Cook | 197 | 106 | 54 | 1854 | 9.4 | 15 | 11— | 6 | 1 |
| Wyche | 108 | 54 | 50 | 838 | 7.8 | 7 | 4— | 4 | |
| Livingston | 2 | 2 | 100 | 15 | 7.5 | 0 | 0— | 0 | |
| Gehrke | 1 | 1 | 100 | 13 | 13.0 | 0 | 0— | 0 | |

| PUNTING | No | Avg |
|---|---|---|
| Livingston | 70 | 39.6 |
| Swanson | 12 | 38.3 |
| Muhlmann | 2 | 19.0 |
| Lamb | 1 | 29.0 |

| KICKING | XP | Att | % | FG | Att | % |
|---|---|---|---|---|---|---|
| Muhlmann | 32 | 33 | 97 | 16 | 24 | 67 |

## 1969 NFL CHAMPIONSHIP GAME
January 4, 1970 at Minnesota
(Attendance 46,503)

### SCORING

| MINNESOTA | 14 | 10 | 3 | 0—27 |
|---|---|---|---|---|
| CLEVELAND | 0 | 0 | 0 | 7—7 |

**First Quarter**
Min.   Kapp, 7 yard rush   3:48
     PAT—Cox (kick)
Min.   Washington, 75 yard pass from Kapp   7:07
     PAT—Cox (kick)
**Second Quarter**
Min.   Cox, 30 yard field goal   1:07
Min.   Osborn, 20 yard rush   10:15
     PAT—Cox (kick)
**Third Quarter**
Min.   Cox, 32 yard field goal   11:18
**Fourth Quarter**
Cle.   Collins, 3 yard pass from Nelsen   1:24
     PAT—Cockroft (kick)

### TEAM STATISTICS

| MINN. | | CLEVE. |
|---|---|---|
| 18 | First Downs—Total | 14 |
| 13 | First Downs—Rushing | 4 |
| 5 | First Downs—Passing | 10 |
| 0 | First Downs—Penalty | 0 |
| 0 | Fumbles—Number | 2 |
| 0 | Fumbles—Lost Ball | 1 |
| 3 | Penalties—Number | 1 |
| 33 | Yards Penalized | 5 |
| 0 | Giveaways | 3 |
| 3 | Takeaways | 0 |
| +3 | Difference | −3 |

### Viking Heat

The Browns had beaten the Cowboys 38-14 in the first round of the playoffs with a tight pass defense and sharp passing by Bill Nelsen, and they hoped to pull another upset over the Vikings in the NFL title match. The Vikings had crushed the Browns 51-3 in a regular-season meeting and had disposed of the powerful Los Angeles Rams 23-20 with a fourth-quarter rally in last week's opening playoff game, and their superb defense made them favorites for this game.

Conditions for the game were typical of Minnesota in January. Snow ringed the field, and 8-degree temperature chilled the spectators through their layers of clothing. The Browns suffered from the cold, resorting to heaters and special footgear to combat it, but the Vikings used no heaters at all. Coach Bud Grant said, "we generate our own heat."

On the first series of the game, the Browns showed their discomfort in this weather. Cornerback Walt Sumner slipped and fell while covering Viking receiver Gene Washington, and Joe Kapp hit his man with a pass good for 33 yards down to the Cleveland 24-yard line. The Vikings moved down to the 7-yard line, and Kapp scored on a play characteristic of his rough style. He bumped into fullback Bill Brown in his backfield, then stormed straight ahead and broke several tackles on his way to the end zone. Several minutes later, Cleveland cornerback Erich Barnes lost his footing and fell while covering Washington, and Kapp whipped a pass which the end carried 75 yards for a second Minnesota touchdown. Trailing 14-0 and fully aware that the Minnesota defense allowed its opponents an average of only ten points a game, the Browns looked like a beaten team before the first quarter had ended. With the Viking defense keeping the Cleveland attack bottled up all afternoon, Minnesota won the game 27-7 and the NFL championship in the team's ninth year of operation.

### INDIVIDUAL STATISTICS

#### RUSHING

| MINNESOTA | No | Yds | Avg. | CLEVELAND | No | Yds | Avg. |
|---|---|---|---|---|---|---|---|
| Osborn | 18 | 108 | 6.0 | Kelly | 15 | 80 | 5.3 |
| Kapp | 8 | 57 | 7.1 | Scott | 6 | 17 | 2.8 |
| Brown | 12 | 43 | 3.6 | | 21 | 97 | 4.6 |
| Reed | 5 | 7 | 1.4 | | | | |
| Jones | 2 | 7 | 3.5 | | | | |
| | 45 | 222 | 4.9 | | | | |

#### RECEIVING

| MINNESOTA | No | Yds | Avg. | CLEVELAND | No | Yds | Avg. |
|---|---|---|---|---|---|---|---|
| Washington | 3 | 120 | 40.0 | Scott | 5 | 56 | 11.2 |
| Henderson | 2 | 17 | 8.5 | Collins | 5 | 43 | 8.6 |
| Brown | 1 | 20 | 20.0 | Warfield | 4 | 47 | 11.8 |
| Beasley | 1 | 12 | 12.0 | Kelly | 2 | 17 | 8.5 |
| | 7 | 169 | 24.1 | Morin | 1 | 18 | 18.0 |
| | | | | | 17 | 181 | 10.6 |

#### PUNTING

| | No | Yds | Avg. | | No | Yds | Avg. |
|---|---|---|---|---|---|---|---|
| Lee | 3 | | 41.0 | Cockroft | 3 | | 33.0 |

#### PUNT RETURNS

| | No | Yds | Avg. | | No | Yds | Avg. |
|---|---|---|---|---|---|---|---|
| West | 1 | 1 | 1.0 | Kelly | 2 | 10 | 5.0 |
| | | | | Morrison | 1 | 11 | 11.0 |
| | | | | | 3 | 21 | 7.0 |

#### KICKOFF RETURNS

| | No | Yds | Avg. | | No | Yds | Avg. |
|---|---|---|---|---|---|---|---|
| West | 1 | 22 | 22.0 | Scott | 4 | 60 | 15.0 |
| Jones | 1 | 20 | 20.0 | Morrison | 1 | 23 | 23.0 |
| | 2 | 42 | 21.0 | | 5 | 83 | 16.6 |

#### INTERCEPTION RETURNS

| | No | Yds | Avg. | | |
|---|---|---|---|---|---|
| Hilgenberg | 1 | 0 | 0.0 | None | |
| Krause | 1 | 0 | 0.0 | | |
| | 2 | 0 | 0.0 | | |

#### PASSING

| MINNESOTA | Att. | Comp. | Comp. Pct. | Yds. | Int. | Yds/ Att. | Yds/ Comp. | Yards Lost Tackled |
|---|---|---|---|---|---|---|---|---|
| Kapp | 13 | 7 | 53.8 | 169 | 0 | 13.0 | 24.1 | 1— 8 |
| **CLEVELAND** | | | | | | | | |
| Nelsen | 33 | 17 | 51.5 | 181 | 2 | 5.5 | 10.6 | 2—10 |

---

## 1969 AFL CHAMPIONSHIP GAME
January 4, 1970 at Oakland
(Attendance 53,564)

### SCORING

| OAKLAND | 7 | 0 | 0 | 0—7 |
|---|---|---|---|---|
| KANSAS CITY | 0 | 7 | 7 | 3—17 |

**First Quarter**
Oak.   Smith, 3 yard rush   14:14
     PAT—Blanda (kick)
**Second Quarter**
K.C.   Hayes, 1 yard rush   13:10
     PAT—Stenerud (kick)
**Third Quarter**
K.C.   Holmes, 5 yard rush   11:17
     PAT—Stenerud (kick)
**Fourth Quarter**
K.C.   Stenerud, 22 yard field goal   10:12

### TEAM STATISTICS

| OAK. | | K.C. |
|---|---|---|
| 18 | First Downs—Total | 13 |
| 6 | First Downs—Rushing | 5 |
| 10 | First Downs—Passing | 6 |
| 2 | First Downs—Penalty | 2 |
| 1 | Fumbles—Number | 5 |
| 0 | Fumbles—Lost Ball | 4 |
| 5 | Penalties—Number | 5 |
| 45 | Yards Penalized | 43 |
| 4 | Giveaways | 4 |
| 4 | Takeaways | 4 |
| 0 | Difference | 0 |

### Finishing First When It Counts

The AFL installed a new playoff system for its final season, pitting the first-place finishers against the runners-up in the opposite division, with the winners playing for the league crown. The result was that two Western clubs met in the title game, as the first-place Raiders clobbered Houston 56-7 while the second-place Chiefs upset the New York Jets 13-6.

While the Raiders took a 7-0 lead on Charlie Smith's touchdown late in the first period, Kansas City passer Len Dawson found the Oakland defense hard to crack, as he missed on seven straight passes. Late in the second quarter, however, he hit Frank Pitts with a 41-yard bomb which brought the ball to the Oakland 1-yard line. From there, Wendell Hayes smashed over, and the Chiefs took a 7-7 tie into the locker room at halftime.

Early in the second half, Lamonica hurt his passing hand against the helmet of Aaron Brown and could not grip the ball properly the rest of the game. George Blanda relieved Lamonica at quarterback but had no miracles up his sleeve today. In addition to missing three field-goal attempts, he could not stand up under the Kansas City pass rush and saw one of his passes intercepted in the end zone. After intercepting Blanda's pass, Emmitt Thomas had run it out to the 6-yard line. Dawson then moved his team downfield through the air. Otis Taylor and Robert Holmes caught passes for long gains, and a pass interference penalty on the Raiders gave the Chiefs a first down on the Oakland 7. Holmes carried the ball three straight times to reach the end zone and put the Chiefs ahead 14-7.

Sore hand and all, Lamonica returned to the lineup in the final period, but three of his crippled passes were picked off by the Chiefs, who won the game 17-7 and headed off to the Super Bowl despite finishing second behind the Raiders in the regular season.

### INDIVIDUAL STATISTICS

#### RUSHING

| OAKLAND | No | Yds | Avg. | KANSAS CITY | No | Yds | Avg. |
|---|---|---|---|---|---|---|---|
| Dixon | 12 | 36 | 3.0 | Hayes | 8 | 35 | 4.4 |
| Smith | 12 | 31 | 2.6 | Garrett | 7 | 19 | 2.7 |
| Banaszak | 2 | 8 | 4.0 | Holmes | 18 | 14 | 0.8 |
| Todd | 2 | 4 | 2.0 | McVea | 3 | 13 | 4.3 |
| | 28 | 79 | 2.8 | Dawson | 3 | 5 | 1.7 |
| | | | | | 39 | 86 | 2.2 |

#### RECEIVING

| OAKLAND | No | Yds | Avg. | KANSAS CITY | No | Yds | Avg. |
|---|---|---|---|---|---|---|---|
| Smith | 8 | 86 | 10.8 | Taylor | 3 | 62 | 20.7 |
| Sherman | 3 | 45 | 15.0 | Holmes | 2 | 16 | 8.0 |
| Cannon | 2 | 22 | 11.0 | Pitts | 1 | 41 | 41.0 |
| Banaszak | 2 | 13 | 6.5 | Arbanas | 1 | 10 | 10.0 |
| Wells | 1 | 24 | 24.0 | | 7 | 129 | 18.4 |
| Dixon | 1 | 1 | 1.0 | | | | |
| | 17 | 191 | 11.2 | | | | |

#### PUNTING

| | No | Yds | Avg. | | No | Yds | Avg. |
|---|---|---|---|---|---|---|---|
| Eischeid | 6 | | 48.5 | Wilson | 8 | | 42.9 |

#### PUNT RETURNS

| | No | Yds | Avg. | | No | Yds | Avg. |
|---|---|---|---|---|---|---|---|
| Atkinson | 2 | −1 | −0.5 | Garrett | 4 | 9 | 2.3 |

#### KICKOFF RETURNS

| | No | Yds | Avg. | | No | Yds | Avg. |
|---|---|---|---|---|---|---|---|
| Atkinson | 3 | 95 | 31.7 | Holmes | 1 | 26 | 26.0 |
| Sherman | 1 | 17 | 17.0 | Hill | 1 | 0 | 0.0 |
| | 4 | 112 | 28.0 | Hayes | Lat | 17 | — |
| | | | | | 2 | 43 | 21.5 |

#### INTERCEPTION RETURNS

| | | | | | No | Yds | Avg. |
|---|---|---|---|---|---|---|---|
| None | | | | Thomas | 2 | 69 | 34.5 |
| | | | | Marsalis | 1 | 23 | 23.0 |
| | | | | Kearney | 1 | 17 | 17.0 |
| | | | | | 4 | 109 | 27.3 |

#### PASSING

| OAKLAND | Att. | Comp. | Comp. Pct. | Yds. | Int. | Yds/ Att. | Yds/ Comp. | Yards Lost Tackled |
|---|---|---|---|---|---|---|---|---|
| Lamonica | 39 | 15 | 38.5 | 167 | 3 | 4.3 | 11.1 | |
| Blanda | 6 | 2 | 33.3 | 24 | 1 | 4.0 | 12.0 | |
| | 45 | 17 | 37.8 | 191 | 4 | 4.2 | 11.2 | 4—37 |
| **KANSAS CITY** | | | | | | | | |
| Dawson | 17 | 7 | 41.2 | 129 | 0 | 7.6 | 18.4 | 1— 8 |

## An Upsetting Farewell

All of the Kansas City Chiefs wore a patch on their jerseys saying "AFL-10." This referred to the ten-year existence of the AFL, which would fade into oblivion after this game and the AFL All-Star Game a week later. As things turned out, the Chiefs took the AFL out in style by handily beating the NFL champion Minnesota Vikings.

It didn't figure. The Vikings had bullied their way through the NFL with a frightening defense, led by the front four of Jim Marshall, Carl Eller, Alan Page, and Gary Larsen and a ball-control attack paced by tough quarterback Joe Kapp. Odds-makers branded the Vikings as two-touchdown favorites to return the Super Bowl title to the NFL after a year in the possession of the AFL New York Jets.

The Chiefs had been to the Super Bowl before, however, and knew how to prepare better for the fanfare. While the Vikings were awed by the hubbub in New Orleans during the week before the game, the Chiefs seriously set about to avenge their loss to Green Bay in Super Bowl I.

The "I" formation that Kansas City used, concealing the position of their backs until the last moment before the play, gave the Minnesota defense some problems right from the start. The Chiefs assigned two men each to block Marshall and Eller, and this move gave the Kansas City backs room to run. Quarterback Len Dawson also found the Viking zone pass coverage less difficult than had been imagined, and he would complete twelve of seventeen passes through the afternoon.

The Kansas City defensive linemen, meanwhile, were putting hot pressure on Joe Kapp, forcing him to hurry his passes. While the defense harassed Kapp in the first period, Jan Stenerud booted a 48 yard field goal to put the Chiefs ahead 3-0.

The second quarter went no better for the Viking attack as the Chiefs scored 13 points to break the game open. Stenerud kicked another field goal, Mike Garrett scored a touchdown after the Vikings had fumbled deep in their own territory, and Stenerud's third field goal made the score 16-0 at halftime.

The Vikings came out for the second half ready to climb back into the game, and Kapp immediately led them on a 69-yard drive that led to the Vikings' first touchdown. But the Vikes could not score again, and Otis Taylor's brilliant 46-yard run with a short pass made the final score only a little worse, 23-7, in favor of the Chiefs and, for the final time, the AFL.

| KANSAS CITY | | MINNESOTA |
|---|---|---|
| **OFFENSE** | | |
| Pitts | WR | Washington |
| Tyrer | LT | Alderman |
| Budde | LG | Vellone |
| Holub | C | Tingelhoff |
| Moorman | RG | Sunde |
| Hill | RT | Yary |
| Arbanas | TE | Beasley |
| Taylor | WR | Henderson |
| Dawson | QB | Kapp |
| Garrett | RB | Osborn |
| Holmes | RB | B. Brown |
| **DEFENSE** | | |
| Mays | LE | Eller |
| Culp | LT | Larsen |
| Buchanan | RT | Page |
| A. Brown | RE | Marshall |
| Bell | LLB | Winston |
| Lanier | MLB | Warwick |
| Lynch | RLB | Hilgenberg |
| Marsalis | LCB | Mackbee |
| Thomas | RCB | Sharockman |
| Kearney | LS | Kassulke |
| Robinson | RS | Krause |

**SUBSTITUTES**

**KANSAS CITY**
*Offense*
| Daney | McVea |
|---|---|
| Hayes | Podolak |
| Livingston | Prudhomme |
| McClinton | Richardson |

*Defense*
| Belser | Sellers |
|---|---|
| Hurston | Stein |
| Lothamer | Trosch |
| Mitchell | |

*Kickers*
| Stenerud | Wilson |
|---|---|

**MINNESOTA**
*Offense*
| Cuozzo | Lee |
|---|---|
| Grim | Lindsey |
| Harris | Reed |
| Jones | Smith |
| Kramer | White |

*Defense*
| Dickson | McGill |
|---|---|
| Hackbart | West |
| Hargrove | |

*Kicker*
| | Cox |
|---|---|

### SCORING

| KANSAS CITY | 3 | 13 | 7 | 0—23 |
|---|---|---|---|---|
| MINNESOTA | 0 | 0 | 7 | 0— 7 |

**First Quarter**
K.C.   Stenerud, 48 yard field goal

**Second Quarter**
K.C.   Stenerud, 32 yard field goal
K.C.   Stenerud, 25 yard field goal
K.C.   Garrett, 5 yard rush
       PAT — Stenerud (kick)

**Third Quarter**
Minn.  Osborn, 4 yard rush
       PAT — Cox (kick)
K.C.   Taylor, 46 yard pass from Dawson
       PAT — Stenerud (kick)

### TEAM STATISTICS

| K.C. | | MINN. |
|---|---|---|
| 18 | First Downs — Total | 13 |
| 8 | First Downs — Rushing | 2 |
| 7 | First Downs — Passing | 10 |
| 3 | First Downs — Penalty | 1 |
| 0 | Fumbles — Number | 3 |
| 0 | Fumbles — Lost Ball | 2 |
| 4 | Penalties — Number | 6 |
| 47 | Yards Penalized | 67 |
| 62 | Total Offensive Plays | 50 |
| 273 | Total Net Yards | 239 |
| 4.4 | Average Gain | 4.8 |
| 0 | Missed Field Goals | 1 |
| 1 | Giveaways | 5 |
| 5 | Takeaways | 1 |
| +4 | Difference | —4 |

### INDIVIDUAL STATISTICS

| KANSAS CITY | No | Yds | Avg. | MINNESOTA | No | Yds | Avg. |
|---|---|---|---|---|---|---|---|
| **RUSHING** | | | | | | | |
| Garrett | 11 | 39 | 3.5 | Brown | 6 | 26 | 4.3 |
| Pitts | 3 | 37 | 12.3 | Reed | 4 | 17 | 4.3 |
| Hayes | 8 | 31 | 3.9 | Osborn | 7 | 15 | 2.1 |
| McVea | 12 | 26 | 2.2 | Kapp | 2 | 9 | 4.5 |
| Dawson | 3 | 11 | 3.7 | | 19 | 67 | 3.5 |
| Holmes | 5 | 7 | 1.4 | | | | |
| | 42 | 151 | 3.6 | | | | |
| **RECEIVING** | | | | | | | |
| Taylor | 6 | 81 | 13.5 | Henderson | 7 | 111 | 15.9 |
| Pitts | 3 | 33 | 11.0 | Brown | 3 | 11 | 3.7 |
| Garrett | 2 | 25 | 12.5 | Beasley | 2 | 41 | 20.5 |
| Hayes | 1 | 3 | 3.0 | Reed | 2 | 16 | 8.0 |
| | 12 | 142 | 11.8 | Osborn | 2 | 11 | 5.5 |
| | | | | Washington | 1 | 9 | 9.0 |
| | | | | | 17 | 199 | 11.7 |
| **PUNTING** | | | | | | | |
| Wilson | 4 | | 48.5 | Lee | 3 | | 37.0 |
| **PUNT RETURNS** | | | | | | | |
| Garrett | 1 | 0 | 0.0 | West | 2 | 18 | 9.0 |
| **KICKOFF RETURNS** | | | | | | | |
| Hayes | 2 | 36 | 18.0 | West | 3 | 46 | 15.3 |
| | | | | Jones | 1 | 33 | 33.0 |
| | | | | | 4 | 79 | 19.8 |
| **INTERCEPTION RETURNS** | | | | | | | |
| Lanier | 1 | 9 | 9.0 | Krause | 1 | 0 | 0.0 |
| Robinson | 1 | 9 | 9.0 | | | | |
| Thomas | 1 | 6 | 6.0 | | | | |
| | 3 | 24 | 8.0 | | | | |

### PASSING

| KANSAS CITY | Att | Comp | Comp Pct. | Yds | Int | Yds/ Att. | Yds/ Comp | Yards Lost Tackled |
|---|---|---|---|---|---|---|---|---|
| Dawson | 17 | 12 | 70.6 | 142 | 1 | 8.4 | 11.8 | 3—20 |

| MINNESOTA | Att | Comp | Comp Pct. | Yds | Int | Yds/ Att. | Yds/ Comp | Yards Lost Tackled |
|---|---|---|---|---|---|---|---|---|
| Kapp | 25 | 16 | 64.0 | 183 | 2 | 7.3 | 11.4 | |
| Cuozzo | 3 | 1 | 33.3 | 16 | 1 | 5.3 | 16.0 | |
| | 28 | 17 | 60.7 | 199 | 3 | 7.1 | 11.7 | 3—27 |

| Use Name (Nickname) - Positions | Team by Year | See Section | Hgt. | Wgt. | College | Int | Pts |
|---|---|---|---|---|---|---|---|
| Abell, Bud LB | 66-68KC-A | | 6'3" | 220 | Missouri | 2 | |
| Abruzzese, Ray DB | 62-64BufA 65-66NY-A | | 6'1" | 194 | Alabama | 10 | |
| Absher, Dick LB | 67Was 67-68Atl 69-71NO 72Phi | | 6'4" | 231 | Maryland | 3 | 4 |
| Adamchik, Ed C | 65NYG 65Pit | | 6'2" | 235 | Pittsburgh | | |
| Adams, John FB-OE | 59-62ChiB 63LA | 2 | 6'3" | 235 | Los Angeles State | | 24 |
| Adams, Tom OE | 62Min | | 6'5" | 210 | Minnesota-Duluth | | |
| Adams, Willie LB-DE | 65-66Was | | 6'2" | 235 | New Mexico State | | |
| Adamson, Ken OG | 60-62DenA | | 6'2" | 222 | Notre Dame | | |
| Adderley, Herb DB | 61-69GB 70-72Dal | 3 | 6'1" | 204 | Michigan State | 48 | 54 |
| Addison, Tommy LB | 60-67BosA | | 6'3" | 231 | South Carolina | 16 | 6 |
| Akin, Howard OT | 67-68SD-A | | 6'5" | 261 | Oklahoma State | | |
| Alderman, Grady OT-OG | 60Det 61-74Min | | 6'2" | 242 | Detroit | | |
| Aldridge, Lionel DE | 63-71GB 72-73SD | | 6'4" | 245 | Utah State | | 6 |
| Alexander, Kermit DB | 63-69SF 70-71LA 72-73Phi | 3 | 5'11" | 185 | U.C.L.A. | 43 | 36 |
| Alfen, Ted HB | 69DenA | | 6' | 195 | Springfield | | |
| Alford, Bruce K | 67Was 68-69BufA | 5 | 6' | 185 | Texas Christian | | 134 |
| Alford, Mike C | 65StL 66Det | | 6'3" | 233 | Auburn | | |
| Allard, Don QB | 61NY-A 61BosA | | 6' | 189 | Boston College | | |
| Allen, Buddy HB | 61DenA | | 5'10" | 190 | Utah State | | |
| Allen, Chuck LB | 61-69SD-A 70-71Pit 72Phi | | 6'1" | 224 | Washington | 28 | 12 |
| Allen, Dalva DE | 60-61HouA 62-64OakA | | 6'5" | 240 | Houston | 1 | |
| Allen, Don FB | 60DenA | 2 | 6' | 200 | Texas | | 6 |
| Allen, Duane OE-TE | 61-64LA 65Pit 65Bal 66-67ChiB | 2 | 6'4" | 221 | Mt. San Antonio J.C. Santa Ana J.C. | | 30 |
| Allen, George OT | 66HouA | | 6'7" | 270 | West Texas State | | |
| Allen, Jerry HB | 66Bal 67-69Was | 2 | 6'1" | 204 | Nebraska-Omaha | | 54 |
| Alley, Don WR-FL | 67Bal 69Pit | | 6'2" | 200 | Adams State | | |
| Allison, Jim FB | 65-68SD-A | 2 | 6' | 220 | San Diego State | | 12 |
| Alliston, Vaughan LB | 60DenA | | 6' | 218 | Mississippi | 1 | |
| Alworth, Lance (Bambi) FL-WR-OE | 62-69SD-A 70SD 71-72Dal | 23 | 6' | 182 | Arkansas | | 524 |
| Amerson, Glen DB | 61Phi | | 6'1" | 186 | Texas Tech | | |
| Ames, Dave HB-DB | 61NY-A 61DenA | | 6' | 185 | Richmond | 1 | |
| Amsler, Marty DE | 67ChiB 68JJ 69ChiB 70GB | | 6'5" | 257 | Indiana, Evansville | 1 | |
| Anderson, Art OT | 61-62ChiB 63Pit | | 6'3" | 244 | Idaho | | |
| Anderson, Bill OE-TE | 58-63Was 65-66GB | 2 | 6'3" | 211 | Tennessee | | 90 |
| Anderson, Billy QB | 67HouA | | 6'1" | 195 | Tulsa | | |
| Anderson, Bob HB | 63NYG | | 6'2" | 210 | Army | | |
| Anderson, Bruce DE-DT | 66LA 67-69NYG 70Was | | 6'4" | 246 | Willamette | | |
| Anderson, Chet TE | 67Pit | | 6'3" | 245 | Minnesota | | 12 |
| Anderson, Dick OT | 67NO | | 6'5" | 245 | Ohio State | | 2 |
| Anderson, Max HB | 68-69BufA 70KJ 71Buf | 23 | 5'8" | 180 | Arizona State | | 24 |
| Anderson, Ralph OE | 58ChiB 60LA-A died Nov. 26, 1960 — diabetes | 2 | 6'4" | 223 | Los Angeles State | | 36 |
| Anderson, Roger DT-OT | 64-65NYG 66CFL 67-68NYG | | 6'5" | 263 | Virginia Union | 1 | |
| Anderson, Taz OE-TE | 61-64StL 66-67Atl | 2 | 6'2" | 208 | Georgia Tech | | 60 |
| Andrie, George DE | 62-72Dal | | 6'7" | 252 | Marquette | 1 | 14 |
| Andrus, Lou LB | 67DenA | | 6'6" | 255 | Brigham Young | | |
| Antwine, Houston DT | 61-69BosA 70Bos 71NE 72Phi | | 6' | 265 | Southern Illinois | 1 | |
| Apple, Jim HB | 61NY-A | | 6' | 200 | Upsala | | |
| Appleton, Scott DT | 64-66HouA 67-68SD-A | | 6'3" | 254 | Texas | 2 | 6 |
| Arbanas, Fred TE-OE | 62DalA 63-69KC-A 70KC | 2 | 6'3" | 240 | Michigan State | | 206 |
| Archer, Dan OG-OT | 67OakA 68CinA | | 6'5" | 245 | Oregon | | |
| Armstrong, Ray DE | 60OakA | | 6'1" | 235 | Texas Christian | | |
| Arndt, Dick DT | 67-70Pit | | 6'5" | 265 | Stanford, Idaho | | |
| Arnett, Jon HB-FL-OE | 57-63LA 64-66ChiB | 123 | 5'11" | 197 | Southern Calif. | | 234 |
| Arrobio, Chuck OT | 66Min | | 6'4" | 250 | Southern Calif. | | |
| Asad, Doug DE | 60-61OakA | 2 | 6'3" | 203 | Northwestern | | 18 |
| Asbury, Willie FB | 66-68Pit | 2 | 6'1" | 230 | Kent State | | 78 |
| Atchason, Jack OE | 60BosA 60HouA | | 6'4" | 215 | Western Illinois | | 6 |
| Atkins, Billy DB-HB | 58-59SF 60-61BufA 62-63NY-A 63BufA 64DenA | 45 | 6'1" | 196 | Auburn | 20 | 86 |
| Atkins, Doug DE | 53-54Cle 55-66ChiB 67-69No | | 6'8" | 257 | Tennessee | 3 | 2 |
| Atkins, Pervis HB-FDL-OE | 61-63LA 64-65Was 65-66OakA | 23 | 6'1" | 200 | San Fran. State, New Mexico State | | 18 |
| Atkinson, Frank DT | 63Pit | | 6'3" | 240 | Stanford | | |
| Auer, Joe HB | 64-65BufA 66-67MiaA 68Atl | 23 | 6'1" | 204 | Miami (Fla.), Georgia Tech | | |
| Autry, Hank C | 69HouA 70Hou | | 6'3" | 233 | Southern Miss. | | |
| Aveni, John OE-K | 59-60ChiB 61Was | 5 | 6'3" | 212 | Indiana | | 144 |
| Avery, Jim TE | 66Was | | 6'2" | 235 | Northern Illinois | | |
| Avezzano, Joe C | 66BosA | | 6'2" | 235 | Florida State | | |
| Babb, Gene FB-LB | 57-58SF 60-61Dal 62-63HouA | 2 | 6'3" | 216 | Austin | 4 | 30 |
| Baccaglio, Marty DE | 68SD-A 68-69CinA 70Cin | | 6'3" | 245 | San Jose State | | |
| Bachman, Jay C | 68-69DenA 70-71Den | | 6'3" | 250 | Cincinnati | | |
| Badar, Rich QB | 67Pit | | 6'1" | 190 | Indiana | | |
| Bailey, Monk DB | 64-65StL | | 6' | 178 | Utah | | |
| Bailey, Teddy HB | 67BufA 69BosA | | 6' | 210 | Cincinnati | | |
| Baird, Bill DB-HB | 63-69NY-A | 3 | 5'10" | 180 | San Fran. State | 34 | 18 |
| Baker, Art FB | 61-62BufA | 2 | 6' | 220 | Syracuse | | 24 |
| Baker, Dave DB | 59-61SF 62-63MS | | 6' | 192 | Oklahoma | 21 | |
| Baker, John DE-DT-OT | 58-61LA 62Phi 63-67Pit 68Det | | 6'6" | 279 | N. Car. Central | 2 | |
| Baker, Johnny LB-DE | 63-66HouA 67SD-A | | 6'3" | 229 | Mississippi State | 2 | 6 |
| Baker, Larry OT | 60NY-A | | 6'2" | 240 | Bowling Green | | |
| Baker, Ralph LB | 64-69NY-A 70-74NYJ | | 6'3" | 232 | Penn State | 19 | 13 |
| Baker, Sam FB-K | 53Was 54-55MS 56-59Was 60-61Cle 62-63Dal 64-69Phi | 2 45 | 6'2" | 217 | Oregon State | | 977 |
| Baker, Terry HB-QB | 63-65LA | 2 | 6'3" | 198 | Oregon State | | 18 |
| Bakken, Jim K | 62-78StL | 45 | 6' | 199 | Wisconsin | | 1380 |
| Baldwin, Bob HB-FB | 66Bal | | 6'1" | 225 | Clemson | | |
| Ball, Sam OT | 66-70Bal | | 6'4" | 240 | Kentucky | | |
| Ballman, Gary WR-FL-OE-TE-HB | 62-66Pit 67-72Phi 72NYG 73Min | 23 | 6' | 203 | Michigan State | | 252 |
| Bandy, Don OG | 67-68Was | | 6'3" | 250 | Tulsa | | |
| Banfield, Tony DB | 60-63,65HouA | | 6'1" | 185 | Oklahoma State | 27 | 6 |
| Banks, Estes FB-HB | 67OakA 68CinA | 2 | 6'1" | 210 | Colorado | | |
| Bansavage, Al LB | 60LA-A 61OakA | | 6'2" | 225 | The Citadel, Southern Calif. | | |
| Barbee, Joe DT | 60OakA | | 6'3" | 250 | Kent State | | |
| Barber, Rudy LB | 68MiaA | | 6'1" | 255 | Bethune-Cookman | | |
| Barber, Stew OT-LB | 61-69BufA | | 6'3" | 247 | Penn State | 3 | 6 |
| Barefoot, Ken TE | 68Was | | 6'5" | 228 | Virginia Tech | | 6 |
| Barnes, Billy HB | 57-61Phi 62-63Was 65-66Min | 12 | 5'11" | 201 | Wake Forest | | 228 |
| Barnes, Charlie OE | 61DalA | | 6'5" | 230 | Northeast La. | | |
| Barnes, Erich DB | 58-60ChiB 61-64NYG 65-71Cle | | 6'2" | 201 | Purdue | 45 | 60 |
| Barnes, Ernie OG-OT | 60NY-A 61-62SD-A 63-64DenA | | 6'3" | 250 | N. Car. Central | | |
| Barnes, Gary OE-FL | 62GB 63Dal 64ChiB 66-67Atl | 2 | 6'4" | 210 | Clemson | | 12 |
| Barnes, Mike DB | 67-68StL | | 6'3" | 205 | Texas-Arlington | | |
| Barnes, Walt DE-DT | 66-68Was 69DenA 70-71Den 72JJ | | 6'3" | 250 | Nebraska | | |
| Barnett, Steve OT | 63ChiB 64Was | | 6'1" | 255 | Oregon | | |
| Barney, Eppie WR-FL | 67-68Cle | 2 | 6' | 201 | Iowa State | | 12 |
| Barr, Terry FL-DB-HB | 57-65Det | 23 | 6' | 189 | Michigan | 5 | 228 |
| Barrett, Bob OE | 60BufA | | 6'3" | 200 | Baldwin-Wallace | | |
| Barrett, Jan OE | 63GB 63-64OakA | 2 | 6'3" | 226 | Fresno State | | 12 |
| Barrington, Tom HB-FB | 66Was 67-70NO | 23 | 6'1" | 214 | Ohio State | | 24 |
| Barry, Odell OE | 64-65DenA | 3 | 5'10" | 180 | Findley | | 6 |
| Barton, Greg QB | 69Det 71-72CFL 74WFL | | 6'2" | 195 | Tulsa | | |
| Barton, Jim C | 60DalA 61-62DenA | | 6'5" | 250 | Marshall | | |
| Bass, Dick FB-HB | 60-69LA | 23 | 5'10" | 197 | U. of Pacific | | 252 |
| Bass, Glenn OE-HB-FL-WR | 61-66BufA 67-68HouA | 2 | 6'2" | 202 | East Carolina | | 102 |
| Bass, Norm DB | 64DenA 61-63 played major league baseball | | 6'3" | 210 | U. of Pacific | | |
| Bates, Ted LB | 59ChiC 60-62StL 63NY-A | | 6'3" | 219 | Oregon State | | |
| Batten, Pat FB | 64Det | | 6'2" | 225 | Hardin-Simmons | | |
| Battle, Jim OG | 63Min | | 6'1" | 240 | Southern Illinois | | |
| Battle, Jim OT | 66Cle | | 6'4" | 235 | Southern U. | | |
| Battle, Mike DB | 69NY-A 70NYJ | 3 | 6'1" | 175 | Southern Calif. | 1 | |
| Baughan, Maxie LB | 60-65Phi 66-70LA | | 6'1" | 227 | Georgia Tech | 18 | 6 |
| Baynham, Craig HB | 67-69Dal 70ChiB 71JJ 72StL | 23 | 6'1" | 204 | Georgia Tech | | 54 |
| Beach, Walter DB | 60-61BosA 63-66Cle | | 6' | 184 | Central Michigan | 6 | 12 |
| Beal, Norm DB | 62StL | | 5'11" | 170 | Missouri | | |
| Beans, Byron OT-DT | 59-60Pit 61HouA | | 6'6" | 249 | Notre Dame | | |
| Bears, Ed LB | 65-72SF | | 6'2" | 225 | Tennessee | 3 | |
| Beathard, Pete QB | 64-67KC-A 67-69HouA 70-71StL 72LA 73KC 74-75WFL 75Oak | 12 | 6'2" | 205 | Southern Calif. | | 68 |
| Beaver, Jim DT | 62Phi | | 6'1" | 235 | Florida | | |
| Beban, Gary QB-HB-WR | 68-69Was | | 6'1" | 195 | U.C.L.A. | | |
| Bedsole, Hal TE-OE | 64-66Min 67JJ | 2 | 6'4" | 230 | Southern Calif. | | 48 |
| Beer, Tom TE-OG | 67-69DenA 70Bos 71-72NE | 2 | 6'4" | 232 | Detroit, Houston | | 24 |
| Behrman, Dave OT-C | 63,65BufA 67DenA | | 6'5" | 260 | Michigan State | | |
| Beier, Tom DB-FL | 67,69MiaA | | 5'11" | 198 | Detroit, Miami (Fla.) | 2 | |
| Belden, Bob QB | 69-70Dal | | 6'2" | 208 | Notre Dame | | |
| Bell, Bobby LB | 63-69KC-A 70-74KC | | 6'4" | 228 | Minnesota | 26 | 54 |
| Bell, Henry HB | 60DenA | 2 | 5'10" | 210 | none | | |
| Bellino, Joe HB-FL | 65-67BosA | 23 | 5'9" | 186 | Navy | | |
| Belotti, George C | 60-61HouA 61SD-A | | 6'4" | 253 | Southern Calif. | | |
| Bemiller, Al C-OG | 61-69BufA | | 6'3" | 243 | Syracuse | | |
| Bengston, Phil | HC68-70GB | | | | Minnesota | | |
| Bennett, Phil LB | 60BosA | | 6'3" | 225 | Miami (Fla.) | | |
| Benz, Larry DB | 63-65Cle | | 5'11" | 185 | Northwestern | 16 | |
| Bercich, Bob DB | 60-61Dal | | 6'1" | 198 | Michigan State | 5 | |
| Bernet, Lee OT | 65-66DenA | | 6'2" | 245 | Wisconsin | | |
| Berry, Ray OE | 55-67Bal HC84-89NE (known as Raymond as head coach) | 2 | 6'2" | 189 | S.M.U. | | 408 |
| Bethune, Bob DB | 62SD-A | | 5'11" | 190 | Mississippi State | 3 | |
| Bettridge, Ed LB | 64Cle | | 6'1" | 235 | Bowling Green | | |
| Beverly, Randy DB | 67-69NY-A 70Bos 71NE | | 5'11" | 189 | Colorado State | 12 | 6 |
| Biodrowski, Denny OG | 63-67KC-A | | 6'1" | 255 | Memphis State | | |
| Bird, Rodger DB | 66-68OakA | 3 | 5'11" | 195 | Kentucky | 7 | 6 |
| Birdwell, Dan DT-DE | 62-69OakA | | 6'4" | 247 | Houston | 4 | 2 |
| Bishop, Don DB-FL-HB | 58-59Pit 59ChiB 60-65Dal | | 6'2" | 209 | Los Angeles City C. | 22 | 6 |
| Bishop, Sonny OG | 62DalA 63OakA 64-69HouA | | 6'2" | 243 | Fresno State | | |
| Bivins, Charlie HB-TE | 60-66ChiB 67Pit 67BufA | 23 | 6'2" | 212 | Morris Brown | | 36 |
| Blaine, Ed OG | 62GB 63-66Phi | | 6'2" | 240 | Missouri | | |
| Blair, George DB-K | 61-64SD-A | 5 | 5'11" | 194 | Mississippi | 5 | 272 |
| Blanda, George QB-DB-LB-K | 49-58ChiB 60-66HouA 67-69OakA 70-75Oak | 12 5 | 6'1" | 210 | Kentucky | 1 | 2002 |
| Blanks, Sid HB | 64HouA 65KJ 66-68HouA 69BosA 70Bos | 23 | 6' | 206 | Texas A&I | | 66 |
| Blazer, Phil OG | 60BufA | | 6'1" | 235 | North Carolina | | |
| Bleick, Tom DB | 66Bal 67Atl | | 6'2" | 200 | Georgia Tech | | |
| Blye (born Bliey), Ronnie HB | 68NYG 69Phi | 23 | 5'11" | 185 | Notre Dame, Florida A&M | | 6 |
| Bobo, Hubert LB | 60LA-A 61-62NY-A | | 6'1" | 217 | Ohio State | | 5 |
| Boeke, Jim OT | 60-63LA 64-67Dal 68NO | | 6'5" | 250 | Heidelberg | | |
| Bohling, Dewey HB | 60-61NY-A 61BufA | 2 | 5'11" | 190 | Hardin-Simmons | | 54 |
| Bohovich, Reed OG-OT | 62NYG | | 6'3" | 260 | Lehigh | | |
| Bolin, Bookie OG | 62-67NYG 68-69Min | | 6'2" | 240 | Mississippi | | |
| Bookman, Johnny DB | 57NYG 60DalA 61NY-A | | 5'11" | 182 | Miami (Fla.) | 13 | 6 |
| Bosch, Frank DT | 68-70Was | | 6'4" | 246 | Colorado | | |
| Bosley, Bruce OG-C-DE | 56-68SF 69Atl | | 6'2" | 240 | West Virginia | | |
| Bosseler, Don FB | 57-64Was | 2 | 6'1" | 212 | Miami (Fla.) | | 138 |
| Boston, McKinley DE-LB | 68-69NYG | | 6'2" | 245 | Minnesota | | |
| Botchan, Ron LB | 60LA-A 61HouA | | 6'1" | 234 | Occidental | 2 | |
| Boudreaux, Jim OT-DE | 66-68BosA | | 6'4" | 245 | Louisiana Tech | | |
| Boutwell, Tommy WR-QB | 69MiaA | | 6'2" | 205 | Southern Miss. | | |
| Bowie, Larry OG | 62-68Min | | 6'2" | 247 | Purdue | | |
| Bowling, Andy LB | 67Atl | | 6'3" | 235 | Virginia Tech | | |
| Bowman, Ken C | 64-73GB 74XJ | | 6'3" | 230 | Wisconsin | | |
| Bowman, Steve HB | 66NYG | | 6' | 195 | Alabama | | |
| Boyd, Bobby DB-HB | 60-68Bal | | 5'10" | 190 | Oklahoma | 57 | 30 |
| Boyette, Garland LB | 62-63StL 66-69HouA 70-72Hou | | 6'1" | 237 | Grambling | 2 | 6 |
| Boylan, Jim FL | 63Min | | 6'1" | 185 | Washington State | | 6 |
| Boynton, George DB | 62OakA | | 5'11" | 190 | East Texas State | | |
| Boynton, John OT | 69MiaA | | 6'4" | 255 | Tennessee | | |
| Braase, Ordell DE | 57-68Bal | | 6'4" | 240 | South Dakota | | |
| Brabham, Danny LB | 63-67HouA 68CinA | | 6'4" | 236 | Arkansas | | |
| Bradfute, Byron OT | 60-61Dal | | 6'3" | 243 | Southern Miss. | | |
| Bradshaw, Charlie OT | 58-60LA 61-66Pit 67-68Det | | 6'6" | 255 | Baylor | | |
| Bradshaw, Jim DB | 63-67Pit | | 6'1" | 199 | Tenn.-Chatanooga | 11 | 24 |
| Brady, Phil DB | 69DenA | | 6'2" | 211 | Brigham Young | | |
| Bramlett, John LB | 65-66DenA 67-68MiaA 69BosA 70Bos 71Atl | | 6'2" | 216 | Memphis State | 10 | 18 |
| Branch, Mel DE | 60-62DalA 63-65KC-A 66-68MiaA | | 6'2" | 231 | Louisiana State | | |
| Brannen, Solomon DB-HB | 65-66KC-A 67NY-A | | 6'1" | 188 | Morris Brown | | |
| Bratkowski, Zeke QB | 54ChiB 55-56MS 57-60ChiB 61-63LA 64-68GB 70VR 71GB | 12 4 | 6'4" | 204 | Georgia | | 30 |
| Bravo, Alex DB | 57-58LA 60-61OakA | | 6' | 190 | Cal. Poly-Pomona | 6 | |
| Braxton, Hez FB-HB | 62SD-A 63BufA | | 6'2" | 227 | Virginia Union | | 8 |
| Breaux, Don QB | 63DenA 65SD-A | 1 | 6'1" | 203 | McNeese State | | |
| Breding, Ed LB | 67-68Was | | 6'4" | 235 | Texas A&M | | 2 |
| Breedlove, Rod LB | 65-67Pit | | 6'2" | 225 | Maryland | 11 | |
| Breen, Gene LB | 64GB 65-66Pit 67-68LA | | 6'2" | 229 | Virginia Tech | | |

| Use Name (Nickname) - Positions | Team by Year | See Section | Hgt. | Wgt. | College | Int | Pts |
|---|---|---|---|---|---|---|---|
| Breitenstein, Bob OT-OG | 65-67DenA 67Min 69-70Atl | | 6'3" | 264 | Tulsa | | |
| Brenner, Al DB | 69-70NYG | | 6'1" | 200 | Michigan State | | |
| Brewer, Billy DB | 60Was | | 6' | 190 | Mississippi | | |
| Brewer, Johnny LB-OE-TE-DE | 61-67Cle 68-70NO | 2 | 6'4" | 233 | Mississippi | 3 | 42 |
| Brewington, Jim OT | 61OakA | | 6'6" | 280 | N. Car. Central | | |
| Brezina, Bobby HB | 63HouA | | 6' | 200 | Houston | | |
| Briggs, Bill DE | 66-67Was | | 6'3" | 250 | Iowa | | |
| Briggs, Bob FB | 65Was | | 6'1" | 228 | Central St.-Okla. | | |
| Britt, Charley DB | 60-63LA 64Min 64SF | | 6'2" | 183 | Georgia | 14 | 6 |
| Brittenum, Jon QB | 68SD-A | | 6' | 185 | Arkansas | | |
| Brock, Clyde OT | 62-63Dal 63SF | | 6'5" | 268 | Utah State | | |
| Brodhead, Bob QB | 60BufA | 1 | 6'2" | 207 | Duke | | 2 |
| Brodie, John QB | 57-73SF | 12 | 6'1" | 198 | Stanford | | 132 |
| Brodnax, J.W. FB | 60DenA | | 6' | 208 | Louisiana State | | 6 |
| Brooker, Tommy OE-K | 62DalA 63-66KC-A | 5 | 6'2" | 230 | Alabama | | 290 |
| Brooks, Bob FB | 61NY-A | | 6' | 215 | Ohio U. | | |
| Brown, Allen TE | 66-67GB | | 6'5" | 238 | Mississippi | | |
| Brown, Barry LB-TE | 66-67Bal 68NYG 69BosA 70Bos | 2 | 6'3" | 228 | Florida | 1 | |
| Brown, Bill LB | 60BosA | | 6'1" | 230 | Syracuse | 1 | |
| Brown, Bill FB | 61ChiB 62-74Min | 2 | 5'11" | 225 | Illinois | | 456 |
| Brown, Bob OT | 64-68Phi 69-70LA 71-73Oak | | 6'4" | 284 | Nebraska | | |
| Brown, Charley OT | 62OakA | | 6'4" | 245 | Houston | | |
| Brown, Charlie DB-HB | 66-67ChiB 68BufA | | 6'1" | 194 | Syracuse | 1 | |
| Brown, Charlie HB | 67-68NO | | 5'10" | 187 | Missouri | | 18 |
| Brown, Don HB | 60HouA | | 6'1" | 205 | Houston | | |
| Brown, Doug DT | 64OakA | | 6'4" | 250 | Fresno State | | |
| Brown, Fred HB | 61,63BufA | 2 | 5'11" | 189 | Georgia | | 18 |
| Brown, Fred LB-TE | 65LA 66KJ 67-69Phi | | 6'5" | 231 | Miami (Fla.) | 2 | |
| Brown, Jimmy FB | 57-65Cle | 23 | 6'2" | 228 | Syracuse | | 756 |
| Brown, John OT | 62-66Cle 67-71Pit 72JJ | | 6'2" | 250 | Syracuse | | |
| Brown, Roger DT | 60-66Det 67-69LA | | 6'5" | 298 | Md. Eastern Shore | 2 | 6 |
| Brown, Timmy HB | 59GB 60-67Phi 68Bal | 23 | 5'10" | 195 | Ball State | | 384 |
| Brown, Tom DB | 64-68GB 69Was 63 played major league baseball | 3 | 6'1" | 191 | Maryland | 13 | 12 |
| Brown, Willie FL-HB | 64-65LA 66Phi | | 6' | 185 | Southern Calif. | | |
| Brown, Willie DB | 63-66DenA 67-69OakA 70-78Oak | | 6'1" | 195 | Grambling | 54 | 12 |
| Browning, Charlie HB | 65NY-A | | 6' | 220 | Washington | | |
| Brownlee, Claude DT | 67MiaA | | 6'4" | 265 | Benedict | | |
| Bruggers, Bob LB | 66-68MiaA 68-69SD-A 70-71SD | | 6'1" | 226 | Minnesota | 2 | |
| Brumm, Don DE | 63-69StL 70-71Phi 72StL | | 6'3" | 243 | Purdue | | |
| Brunelli, Sam OT-OG | 66-69DenA 70-71Den 72JJ | | 6'1" | 263 | Colorado State | | |
| Bryant, Bob OE | 60DalA | | 6'5" | 230 | Texas | | |
| Bryant, Charlie HB-FB | 66-67StL 68-69Atl | 23 | 6'1" | 207 | Allen | | |
| Bryant, Chuck OE | 62StL | | 6'2" | 220 | Ohio State | | |
| Buchanan, Buck DT | 63-69KC-A 70-75KC | | 6'7" | 279 | Grambling | 3 | 2 |
| Buchanan, Tim LB | 69CinA | | 6' | 233 | Arizona State, Hawaii | | |
| Buckman, Tom TE | 69DenA 71JJ | | 6'4" | 230 | Texas A&M | | 6 |
| Budd, Frank FL | 62Phi 63Was | 2 | 5'10" | 187 | Villanova | | 6 |
| Budde, Ed OG | 63-69KC-A 70-76KC | | 6'5" | 261 | Michigan State | | |
| Budka, Frank DB | 64LA | | 6' | 195 | Notre Dame | 2 | |
| Budness, Bill LB | 62-69OakA 70Oak | | 6'1" | 215 | Boston U. | 3 | |
| Budrewicz, Tom OG | 61NY-A | | 6'2" | 245 | Brown | | |
| Bugenhagen, Gary OG-OT | 67BufA 70Bos | | 6'2" | 249 | Syracuse | | |
| Bukaty, Fred FB | 61DenA | 2 | 5'11" | 195 | Kansas | | 32 |
| Bukich, Rudy QB | 53LA 54-55MS 56LA 57-58Was 58-59ChiB 60-61Pit 62-68ChiB | 12 | 6'1" | 202 | Iowa, Southern Calif. | | 54 |
| Bull, Ronnie HB-FB | 62-70ChiB 91Phi | 2 | 6' | 200 | Baylor | | 84 |
| Bullocks, Amos HB | 62-64Dal 66Pit | 23 | 6'1" | 201 | Southern Illinois | | 42 |
| Buncom, Frank LB | 62-67SD-A 68CinA died Sept. 14, 1969 — pulmonary embolism | | 6'1" | 236 | Southern Calif. | 5 | |
| Bundra, Mike DT | 62-63Det 64Min 64Cle 65Bal | | 6'3" | 258 | Southern Calif. | | |
| Buoniconti, Nick LB | 62-68BosA 69MiaA 70-74Mia 75BG 76Mia | | 5'11" | 220 | Notre Dame | 32 | 8 |
| Burch, Jerry OE | 61OakA | 2 | 6'1" | 195 | Georgia Tech | | 6 |
| Burford, Chris OE | 60-62DalA 63-67KC-A | 2 | 6'3" | 211 | Stanford | | 332 |
| Burke, Vern OE-TE | 65SF 66Atl 67NO | 2 | 6'4" | 201 | Oregon State | | 12 |
| Burkett, Jackie LB-C | 61-66Bal 67NO 68-69Dal 70NO | | 6'4" | 229 | Auburn | 10 | |
| Burman, George C-OG-OT | 64ChiB 67-70LA 71-72Was | | 6'3" | 253 | Northwestern | | |
| Burnett, Bobby HB | 66-67BufA 68JJ 69DenA | 2 | 6'2" | 208 | Arkansas | | 48 |
| Burnett, Len DB | 61Pit | | 6'1" | 195 | Oregon | | |
| Burrell, George DB | 69DenA | | 5'10" | 180 | Pennsylvania | 2 | 6 |
| Burrell, John OE-FL | 62-64Pit 66-67Was | 2 | 6'3" | 191 | Rice | | |
| Burrell, Ode HB-FL | 64-69HouA | 234 | 6' | 189 | Mississippi State | | 82 |
| Burris, Bo DB | 67-69NO | | 6'3" | 190 | Houston | 4 | 6 |
| Burroughs, Don DB | 55-59LA 60-64Phi | | 6'4" | 185 | Colorado State | 50 | |
| Burson, Jimmy DB | 63-67StL 68Atl | | 6' | 181 | Auburn | 16 | 12 |
| Burton, Leon HB | 69NY-A | 3 | 5'9" | 172 | Arizona State | | 18 |
| Burton, Ron HB | 60-65BosA | 23 | 5'10" | 190 | Northwestern | | 114 |
| Bussell, Jerry DB | 65DenA | | 6' | 185 | Georgia Tech | | |
| Butkus, Dick LB | 65-73ChiB | | 6'3" | 244 | Illinois | 22 | 10 |
| Butler, Bill DB-HB | 59GB 60Dal 61Pit 62-64Min | 23 | 5'10" | 189 | Tenn.-Chatanooga | 11 | 24 |
| Butler, Bob OG | 62Phi 63NY-A | | 6'1" | 233 | Kentucky | | |
| Butler, Cannonball HB | 65-67Pit 68-71Atl 72StL 73JJ | 23 | 5'10" | 191 | Edward Waters | | 102 |
| Butsko, Harry LB | 63Was | | 6'3" | 220 | Maryland | | |
| Buzyniski, Bernie LB | 60BufA | | 6'3" | 228 | Holy Cross | 1 | |
| Byers, Ken OG-DE | 62-63NYG 64-65Min 66JJ | | 6'1" | 240 | Cincinnati | | |
| Byrd, Butch DB | 63-69BufA 70Buf 71Den | 3 | 6' | 203 | Boston U. | 40 | 36 |
| Byrd, Dennis DE | 68BosA | | 6'4" | 260 | N. Carolina State | | |
| Byrd, Mack LB | 65LA | | 6' | 215 | Southern Calif. | | |
| Byrne, Bill OG | 63Phi | | 6' | 240 | Boston College | | |
| Cadile, Jim OG-OT | 62-72ChiB | | 6'3" | 239 | San Jose State | | |
| Cadwell, John OG | 61DalA | | 6'3" | 240 | Oregon State | | |
| Caffey, Lee Roy LB | 63Phi 64-69GB 70ChiB 71Dal 72SD | | 6'3" | 247 | Texas A&M | 11 | 18 |
| Cagle, Johnny DE | 69BosA | | 6'3" | 260 | Clemson | | |
| Cahill, Dave DT-DE | 66Phi 67LA 68KJ 69Atl | | 6'3" | 240 | Arizona State | | |
| Caleb, Jamie HB-FB | 60Cle 61Min 62CFL 65Cle | 3 | 6'1" | 210 | Grambling | | 6 |
| Callahan, Dan OG | 60NY-A | | 6' | 230 | Wooster | | |
| Calland, Lee DB | 63-65Min 66-68Atl 69ChiB 69-72Pit | | 6' | 190 | Louisville | 19 | 6 |
| Campbell, Bob HB | 69Pit | 3 | 6' | 195 | Penn State | | |
| Campbell, Jim LB | 69SD-A | | 6'3" | 218 | West Texas State | 1 | |
| Campbell, John LB | 63-64Min 65-69Pit 69Bal | | 6'3" | 222 | Minnesota | 5 | 6 |
| Campbell, Ken OE | 60NY-A | | 6'1" | 213 | West Chester | | |
| Campbell, Mike HB | 68Det | | 5'11" | 200 | Lenoir Ryhne | | |

| Use Name (Nickname) - Positions | Team by Year | See Section | Hgt. | Wgt. | College | Int | Pts |
|---|---|---|---|---|---|---|---|
| Campbell, Woody HB | 67-69HouA 70-71Hou | 2 | 5'11" | 205 | Northwestern | | 90 |
| Canale, Justin OG | 65-68BosA 69CinA | | 6'2" | 242 | Mississippi State | | 1 |
| Canale, Whit DE-DT | 66MiaA 68BosA | | 6'3" | 245 | Tennessee | | |
| Cannavino, Joe DB | 60-61OakA 62BufA | | 5'11" | 186 | Ohio State | 10 | |
| Cannon, Billy TE-HB-FB-OE | 60-63HouA 64-69OakA 70KC | 23 | 6'1" | 216 | Louisiana State | | 392 |
| Capp, Dick LB-TE | 67GB 68Pit | | 6'3" | 235 | Boston College | | |
| Cappadonna, Bob FB | 66-67BosA 68BufA | 2 | 6'1" | 230 | Notre Dame, Northwestern | | 34 |
| Cappelletti, Gino FL-WR-OE-DB | 60-69BosA 70Bos | 2 5 | 6' | 190 | Minnesota | 4 | 1130 |
| Carlton, Wray HB-FB | 60-67BufA | 2 | 6'2" | 218 | Duke | | 204 |
| Carmichael, Paul HB | 65DenA | | 6' | 200 | El Camino J.C. | | |
| Carolan, Reg OE-TE | 62-63SD-A 64-68KC-A | 2 | 6'6" | 235 | Idaho | | 34 |
| Caroline, J.C. DB-HB | 56-65ChiB | 2 | 6'1" | 190 | Illinois | 24 | 36 |
| Carollo, Joe OT | 62-68LA 69-70Phi 71LA 72-73Cle | | 6'2" | 262 | Notre Dame | | |
| Carothers, Don OE | 60DenA | | 6'5" | 225 | Bradley | | |
| Carpenter, Preston OE-TE-HB | 56-59Cle 60-63Pit | 23 | 6'2" | 197 | Arkansas | | 144 |
| Carpenter, Ron LB | 64-64SD-A | | 6'2" | 230 | Texas A&M | 1 | |
| Carr, Henry DB | 65-67NYG | | 6'3" | 198 | Arizona State | 7 | 6 |
| Carr, Jimmy DB-LB-HB | 55,57ChiC 59-63Phi 64-65Was | 2 | 6'1" | 206 | Charleston | 15 | 6 |
| Carr, Tom DT | 68NO | | 6'3" | 267 | Morgan State | | |
| Carrell, John LB | 66HouA | | 6'3" | 227 | Texas Tech | | |
| Carrington, Ed TE | 69HouA | | 6'4" | 225 | Virginia | | |
| Carroll, Jim LB | 65-66NYG 66-68Was 69NY-A | | 6'1" | 229 | Notre Dame | 3 | |
| Carroll, Leo DE | 67KJ 68GB 69-70Was 71JJ | | 6'7" | 250 | Tulsa, San Diego State | | |
| Carson, Kern HB | 65SD-A 65NY-A | | 6' | 202 | San Diego State | | 12 |
| Carwell, Larry DB | 67-68HouA 69BosA 70Bos 71-72NE | 3 | 6'1" | 191 | Iowa State | 14 | 18 |
| Casares, Rick FB | 55-65ChiB 65Was 66MiaA | 2 | 6'2" | 226 | Florida | | 360 |
| Case, Pete OG | 62-64Phi 65-70NYG | | 6'3" | 242 | Georgia | | |
| Casey, Bernie FL-WR-OE | 61-66SF 67-68LA | 2 | 6'4" | 213 | Bowling Green | | 240 |
| Casey, Tim LB | 69ChiB 69DenA | | 6'1" | 225 | Oregon | | |
| Cash, John DE | 61-62DenA | | 6'3" | 235 | Allen | 1 | |
| Cassese, Tom DB-HB | 67DenA | | 6'1" | 197 | C.W. Post | 1 | |
| Cavalli, Carmen DE | 60OakA | | 6'4" | 245 | Richmond | | |
| Caveness, Ronnie LB | 65KC-A 66-68HouA | | 6'1" | 223 | Arkansas | 1 | |
| Cavness, Grady DB | 69DenA 70Atl | | 5'11" | 190 | Texas-El Paso | 2 | |
| Caylor, Lowell DB | 64Cle | | 6'3" | 205 | Miami-Ohio | | |
| Ceppetelli, Gene C | 68-69Phi 69NYG | | 6'2" | 247 | Villanova | | |
| Cerne, Joe C | 65-67SF 68Atl | | 6'2" | 238 | Northwestern | | |
| Chamberlain, Dan OE-HB | 60-61BufA | 2 | 6'4" | 200 | Sacramento State | | 24 |
| Chandler, Don HB-K | 56-64NYG 65-67GB | 45 | 6'2" | 208 | Florida | | 530 |
| Chapple, Jack LB | 65SF | | 6'2" | 227 | Stanford | | 6 |
| Charon, Carl DB | 62-63BufA | | 5'10" | 190 | Michigan State | 7 | 18 |
| Cheeks, B.W. HB | 65HouA | | 6'1" | 230 | Texas Southern | | |
| Chelf, Don OG-OT | 60-61BufA | | 6'3" | 235 | Iowa | | |
| Chesser, George FB | 66-67MiaA | | 6'2" | 223 | Mississippi, Delta State | | |
| Childress, Joe HB-FB | 56-59ChiC 60StL 61JJ 62-65StL | 2 | 6' | 202 | Auburn | | 96 |
| Childs, Clarence DB-HB | 64-67NYG 68ChiB | 23 | 6' | 180 | Florida A&M | 2 | 12 |
| Chlebek, Ed QB | 63NY-A | | 5'11" | 175 | Western Michigan | | |
| Choboian, Max QB | 66DenA | 1 | 6'4" | 205 | Oregon, Northridge State | | 12 |
| Christopherson, Jim LB | 62Min | 5 | 6' | 215 | Concordia (Minn.) | 1 | 61 |
| Christy, Dick HB | 58Pit 60BosA 61-63NY-A | 23 | 5'10" | 191 | N. Carolina State | | 120 |
| Christy, Earl HB-DB | 66-68NY-A | 3 | 5'11" | 193 | Md. Eastern Shore | 1 | 1 |
| Chuy, Don OG | 63-68LA 69Phi | | 6'1" | 255 | Clemson | | |
| Ciccolella, Mike LB | 66-68NYG | | 6'1" | 235 | Dayton | 1 | |
| Cichowski, Tom OT | 67-68DenA | | 6'4" | 250 | Maryland | | |
| Clancy, Jack WR-FL | 67MiaA 68KJ 69MiaA 70GB | 2 | 6'1" | 195 | Michigan | | 30 |
| Claridge, Dennis QB | 64-65GB 66Atl | 1 | 6'3" | 225 | Nebraska | | |
| Clark, Ernie LB | 63-67Det 68StL | | 6'1" | 222 | Michigan State | 4 | |
| Clark, Howard DE | 60LA-A 61SD-A | 2 | 6'2" | 210 | Tenn.-Chattanooga | | |
| Clark, Mike K | 63Phi 64-67Pit 68-71Dal 72JJ 73Dal | 5 | 6'1" | 203 | Texas A&M | | 724 |
| Clark, Monte OT-DT-DE | 59-61SF 62Dal 63-69Cle | | 6'6" | 260 | Southern Calif. | | |
| Clark, Phil DB | 67-69Dal 70ChiB 71NE | | 6'2" | 209 | Northwestern | 4 | |
| Clarke, Frank OE-FL-TE | 57-59Cle 60-67Dal | 2 | 6' | 211 | Colorado | | 306 |
| Clarke, Hagood DB | 64-68BufA | 3 | 6' | 193 | Florida | 12 | 18 |
| Clay, Billy DB | 66Was | | 6'1" | 192 | Mississippi | 1 | |
| Clay, Ozzie FL | 64Was | | 6' | 190 | Iowa State | | |
| Clemens, Bob HB | 62Bal | | 6'1" | 208 | Pittsburgh | | |
| Clement, Henry OE | 61Pit 62JJ | | 6'2" | 200 | North Carolina | | |
| Cline, Doug LB-FB | 60-66HouA 66SD-A | 2 | 6'2" | 225 | Clemson | 7 | 30 |
| Cloutier, Dave DB | 64BosA | | 6' | 195 | Maine | | |
| Coan, Bert HB | 62SD-A 63-68KC-A | 23 | 6'4" | 219 | Texas Christian, Kansas | | 114 |
| Cockrell, Gene (Bud) OT-DE | 60-62NY-A | | 6'3" | 247 | Oklahoma, Hardin-Simmons | | |
| Cody, Bill LB | 66Det 67-70NO 72Phi | | 6'1" | 225 | Auburn | | |
| Coffey, Don FL | 63DenA | | 6'3" | 190 | Memphis State | | |
| Coffey, Junior FB-HB | 65GB 66-67Atl 68KJ 69Atl 69NYG 70KJ 71NYG | 2 | 6'1" | 211 | Washington | | 90 |
| Cogdill, Gail OE-WR | 60-68Det 68Bal 69-70Atl | 2 | 6'2" | 195 | Washington State | | 216 |
| Cohen, Abe OG | 60BosA | | 5'11" | 230 | Tenn.-Chattanooga | | |
| Coia, Angelo OE | 60-63ChiB 64-65Was 66Atl | 2 | 6'2" | 202 | Southern Calif. | | 120 |
| Colchico, Dan DE | 60-65SF 69NO | | 6'4" | 240 | San Jose State | | |
| Colclough, Jim OE-FL-WR | 60-68BosA | 2 | 6' | 185 | Boston College | | 238 |
| Cole, Fred OG | 60LA-A | | 5'11" | 226 | Maryland | | |
| Cole, Terry FB | 68-69Bal 70Pit 71Mia | 2 | 6'1" | 220 | Indiana | | 36 |
| Collier, Blanton | HC63-70Cle | | | | Georgetown (Ky.) | | |
| Collier, Jim OE | 62NYG 63Was | | 6'2" | 195 | Arkansas | | |
| Collier, Joel | HC66-68BufA | | | | Northwestern | | |
| Collins, Gary FL-WR-OE | 62-71Cle | 2 4 | 6'4" | 211 | Maryland | | 420 |
| Colvin, Jim DT-DE-OG | 60-63Bal 64-66Dal 67NYG | | 6'2" | 250 | Houston | | 2 |
| Compton, Dick OE-DB-HB-WR | 62-64Det 65HouA 67-68Pit | 2 | 6'1" | 195 | McMurry | 1 | 24 |
| Concannon, Jack QB | 64-66Phi 67-71ChiB 75GB 75Det | 12 | 6'3" | 201 | Boston College | | 72 |
| Condren, Glen DT-DE | 65-67NYG 69-72Atl | | 6'2" | 246 | Oklahoma | | |
| Conjar, Larry FB | 65Cle 68Phi 69-70Bal | 2 | 6' | 214 | Washington State Notre Dame | | 2 |
| Connelly, Mike C-OG-OT | 60-67Dal 68Pit | | 6'3" | 242 | Utah State | | |
| Conners, Dan LB | 64-69OakA 70-74Oak | | 6'1" | 231 | Miami (Fla.) | 15 | 30 |
| Conrad, Bobby Joe FL-HB-WR-DB | 58-59ChiC 60-68StL 69Det | 23 5 | 6' | 194 | Texas A&M | 4 | 389 |
| Contoulis, John DT | 64NYG | | 6'4" | 260 | Connecticut | | |
| Cook, Ed OT-OG | 58-59ChiC 60-65StL 66-67Atl | | 6'" | 245 | Notre Dame | | |
| Cook, Greg QB | 69CinA 70-72SJ 73Cin | 12 | 6'3" | 214 | Cincinnati | | 6 |
| Cooke, Ed DE-LB | 58ChiB 58Phi 60-63NY-A 64-65DenA 66-67MiaA | | 6'4" | 248 | Maryland | 7 | 12 |
| Coolbaugh, Bob OE | 61OakA | 2 | 6'3" | 200 | Richmond | | 26 |
| Cooper, Bill FB-LB | 61-64SF | | 6'1" | 215 | Muskingum | | 6 |

| Use Name (Nickname) - Positions | Team by Year | See Section | Hgt. | Wgt. | College | Int | Pts |
|---|---|---|---|---|---|---|---|
| Cooper, Thurlow OE-DE | 60-62NY-A | 2 | 6'4" | 228 | Maine | | 52 |
| Copeland, Ron WR | 69ChiB | | 6'4" | 196 | U.C.L.A. | | |
| Corcoran, King QB | 68BosA | | 6' | 200 | Maryland | | |
| Cordileone, Lou DT-DE-OG | 60NYG 61SF 62LA 62-63Pit 67-68NO 69KJ | | 6' | 247 | Clemson | 1 | |
| Cordill, Ollie DB-OE | 67SD-A 68Atl 69NO | 4 | 6'2" | 180 | Memphis State | | |
| Corey, Walt LB | 60,62DalA 63-66KC-A | | 6' | 229 | Miami (Fla.) | 4 | |
| Cornelison, Jerry OT | 60-62DalA 64-65KC-A | | 6'3" | 250 | S.M.U. | | |
| Cornish, Frank DT | 66-70ChiB 70-71Mia 72Buf | | 6'6" | 285 | Grambling | 2 | |
| Coronado, Bob OE | 61Pit | | 6'1" | 195 | U. of Pacific | | |
| Cortez, Bruce DB | 67NO | | 6' | 175 | Parsons | | |
| Costa, Dave DT-DE | 63-65OakA 66BufA 67-69DenA 70-71Den 72-73SD 74Buf | | 6'2" | 257 | Utah | | 2 |
| Costa, Paul OT-TE-OE | 65-69BufA 70-72Buf | 2 | 6'4" | 252 | Notre Dame | | 42 |
| Costello, Tom LB | 64-65NYG | | 6'3" | 220 | Dayton | | |
| Costello, Vince LB | 57-66Cle 67-68NYG | | 6' | 228 | Ohio U. | 22 | 12 |
| Cottrell, Bill OT-C-OG | 67-70Det 71JJ 72Den | | 6'3" | 255 | Delaware Valley | | |
| Cottrell, Ted LB | 69-70Atl | | 6'1" | 233 | Delaware Valley | | |
| Counts, Johnny HB | 62-63NYG | 3 | 5'10" | 170 | Illinois | | 6 |
| Cowan, Charley OT-OG | 61-75LA | | 6'4" | 264 | N. Mex. Highlands | | |
| Cox, Jim TE | 68MiaA | 2 | 6'2" | 227 | Miami (Fla.) | | |
| Cox, Larry DT | 66-68DenA | | 6'2" | 250 | Abilene Christian | | |
| Coyle, Russ DB | 61LA | | 6'2" | 195 | Oklahoma | | |
| Crabb, Claude DB-FL | 62-63Was 64-65Phi 66-68LA | | 6' | 193 | Colorado | 10 | 6 |
| Crabtree, Eric WR-OE-DB | 66-68DenA 69CinA 70-71Cin 71NE | 2 | 5'11" | 184 | Pittsburgh | | 132 |
| Craddock, Nate FB | 63Bal | | 6' | 220 | Parsons | | |
| Craig, Dobie OE-HB | 62-63OakA 64HouA | 2 | 6'4" | 200 | Baylor, Howard Payne | | 42 |
| Crane, Dennis DT-OT | 68-69Was 70NYG | | 6'6" | 260 | Southern Calif. | | |
| Crane, Gary LB | 69DenA | | 6'4" | 230 | Arkansas State | | |
| Crane, Paul LB-C | 66-69NY-A 70-72NYJ | | 6'2" | 208 | Alabama | 5 | 14 |
| Crawford, Bill OG | 60NYG | | 6'1" | 235 | British Columbia | | |
| Crawford, Hilton DB | 69BufA | | 6' | 192 | Grambling | | |
| Crawford, Jim FB-HB | 60-64BosA | 2 | 6'1" | 203 | Wyoming | | 46 |
| Crenshaw, Leon DT | 68GB | | 6'6" | 280 | Tuskegee | | |
| Crenshaw, Willie FB | 64-69StL 70Den | 23 | 6'2" | 228 | Kansas State | | 108 |
| Crespino, Bob OE-TE-WR | 61-64Cle 64-68NYG | 2 | 6'4" | 223 | Mississippi | | 54 |
| Crockett, Bobby WR-OE | 66BufA 67KJ 68-69BufA | 2 | 6' | 198 | Arkansas | | 18 |
| Crockett, Monte OE | 60-62BufA | 2 | 6'3" | 213 | N. Mex. Highlands | | 6 |
| Croftcheck, Don OG-LB | 65-66Was 67ChiB | | 6'1" | 230 | Indiana | | |
| Cronin, Bill TE | 65Phi 66MiaA | | 6'4" | 225 | Boston College | | 6 |
| Cropper, Marshall WR-OE | 67-69Pit | 2 | 6'3" | 207 | Md. Eastern Shore | | |
| Cross, Irv DB | 61-65Phi 66-68LA 69Phi | 3 | 6'1" | 192 | Northwestern | 22 | 12 |
| Crossan, Dave C | 65-69Was | | 6'3" | 245 | Maryland | | |
| Crotty, Jim DB | 60-61Was 61-62BufA | | 5'11" | 192 | Notre Dame | 3 | |
| Crouthamel, Jake HB | 60BosA | | 5'11" | 195 | Dartmouth | | |
| Crow, Al DT | 60BosA | | 6'6" | 260 | William & Mary | | |
| Crow, John David HB-FB-TE | 58-59ChiC 60-64StL 65-68SF | 12 | 6'2" | 218 | Texas A&M | | 444 |
| Crow, Wayne HB-DB | 60-61OakA 62-63BufA | 2 4 | 6' | 205 | California | 4 | 26 |
| Crump, Harry FB | 63BosA | 2 | 6' | 205 | Boston College | | 30 |
| Crutcher, Tommy LB-FB | 64-67GB 68-69NYG 70KJ 71-72GB | | 6'3" | 229 | Texas Christian | 3 | |
| Cudzik, Walt C-LB | 54Was 60-63BosA 64BufA | | 6'2" | 231 | Purdue | | |
| Culpepper, Ed DT | 58-59ChiC 60StL 61Min 62-63HouA | | 6'1" | 255 | Alabama | | |
| Cummings, Ed LB | 64NY-A 65DenA | | 6'2" | 230 | Stanford | 1 | |
| Cunningham, Carl LB | 67-69DenA 70Den 71NO | | 6'3" | 240 | Houston | 4 | |
| Cunningham, Jay DB | 65-67BosA | 3 | 5'10" | 180 | Bowling Green | 3 | 6 |
| Cunningham, Jim FB | 61-63Was | 2 | 5'11" | 221 | Pittsburgh | | 30 |
| Cuozzo, Gary QB | 63-66Bal 67NO 68-71Min 72StL | 12 | 6'1" | 195 | Virginia | | 6 |
| Currie, Dan LB | 58-64GB 65-66LA | | 6'3" | 239 | Michigan State | 11 | 6 |
| Curry, Bill C-LB | 65-66GB 67-72Bal 73Hou 74LA | | 6'2" | 235 | Georgia Tech | | |
| Curry, Roy FL | 63Pit | | 6'1" | 195 | Jackson State | | 6 |
| Cutsinger, Gary DE | 62-66HouA 67XJ 68HouA | | 6'4" | 244 | Oklahoma State | | |
| Cvercko, Andy OG | 60GB 61-62Dal 63Cle 63Was | | 6' | 242 | Northwestern | | |
| Daanen, Jerry WR | 68-70StL | | 6' | 190 | Miami (Fla.) | | |
| Dabney, Carlton DT | 68Atl 69-70XJ | | 6'5" | 250 | Morgan State | 1 | |
| Dale, Carroll OE-FL | 60-64LA 65-72GB 73Min | 2 | 6'1" | 198 | Virginia Tech | | 312 |
| D'Amato, Mike DB | 68NY-A | | 6'2" | 204 | Hofstra | | |
| Danenhauer, Bill DE | 60DenA 60BosA | | 6'4" | 245 | Emporia State | | |
| Danenhauer, Eldon OT | 60-65DenA 66KJ | | 6'4" | 242 | Pittsburgh State | | |
| Daniel, Willie DB | 61-66Pit 67-69LA | | 5'11" | 187 | Mississippi State | 14 | 12 |
| Daniels, Clem HB-DB | 60DalA 61-67Oak 68SF | 23 | 6'1" | 219 | Prairie View | 3 | 324 |
| Daniels, Dave DT | 66OakA | | 6'3" | 245 | Florida A&M | | |
| Daniels, Dick DB | 68-69Dal 69-70ChiB 71JJ | | 5'9" | 180 | Pacific (Ore.) | 7 | |
| Darnell, Bill WR | 68-69MiaA 70JJ | | 6'2" | 197 | North Carolina | | |
| Darragh, Dan QB | 68-69BufA 70Buf | 1 | 6'3" | 196 | William & Mary | | |
| Darre, Bernie OG | 61Was | | 6'2" | 230 | Tulane | | |
| Daugherty, Bob HB | 66SF | | 6'2" | 205 | Tulsa | | |
| Davidson, Ben DE-DT | 61GB 62-63Was 64-69OakA 70-71Oak 72FJ | | 6'8" | 272 | Washington | | |
| Davidson, Cotton QB | 54Bal 55-56MS 57Bal 58CFL 60-62DalA 62-66OakA 67JJ 68OakA | 12 45 | 6'1" | 182 | Baylor | | 104 |
| Davidson, Pete DT | 60HouA | | 6'5" | 255 | The Citadel | | |
| Davis, Al | HC63-65OakA | | | | Wittenberg, Syracuse | | |
| Davis, Dick DE | 62DalA | | 6'2" | 230 | Kansas | | |
| Davis, Don DT | 66NYG 67JJ | | 6'6" | 260 | Los Angeles State | | |
| Davis, Donnie FL-TE | 62Dal 70Hou | | 6'4" | 220 | Southern U. | | |
| Davis, Doug OT | 66-72Min | | 6'4" | 250 | Kentucky | | |
| Davis, Glenn OE | 60-61Det | 2 | 6' | 180 | Ohio State | | |
| Davis, Jack OG | 60BosA | | 6' | 226 | Maryland | | |
| Davis, Jack OG | 60DenA | | 6'2" | 235 | Arizona | | |
| Davis, Marvin DE | 66DenA | | 6'4" | 252 | Wichita State | | |
| Davis, Norman OG | 67Bal 69NO 70Phi | | 6'3" | 247 | Grambling | | |
| Davis, Roger OG-OT | 60-63ChiB 64LA 65-66NYG | | 6'3" | 236 | Syracuse | | |
| Davis, Rosey DE | 65-67NYG | | 6'5" | 260 | Tennessee State | | |
| Davis, Sonny LB | 61Dal | | 6'2" | 220 | Baylor | | |
| Davis, Ted LB | 64-66Bal 67-69NO 70Mia | | 6'1" | 230 | Georgia Tech | 2 | |
| Davis, Tommy K | 59-69SF | 45 | 6' | 215 | Louisiana State | | 738 |
| Davis, Willie DE-OT | 58-59Cle 60-69GB | | 6'3" | 243 | Grambling | 2 | 16 |
| Dawson, Bill DE-OE | 65BosA | | 6'3" | 240 | Florida State | | |
| Dawson, Len QB | 57-59Pit 60-61Cle 62DalA 63-69KC-A 70-75KC | 12 | 6' | 190 | Purdue | | 54 |
| Day, Al LB | 60DenA | | 6'2" | 216 | Eastern Michigan | | |
| Day, Eagle QB | 59-60Was | 1 4 | 6' | 183 | Mississippi | | |

| Use Name (Nickname) - Positions | Team by Year | See Section | Hgt. | Wgt. | College | Int | Pts |
|---|---|---|---|---|---|---|---|
| Day, Tom DE-OG-DT-OT | 60StL 61-66BufA 67SD-A 68BufA | | 6'2" | 252 | N. Carolina A&T | 1 | |
| Dean, Floyd LB | 64-65SF | | 6'4" | 245 | Florida | | |
| Dean, Ted HB-FB | 60-63Phi 64Min | 23 | 6'2" | 211 | Wichita State | | 36 |
| Dee, Bob DE-DT | 57-58Was 60-67BosA | | 6'3" | 248 | Holy Cross | 1 | |
| DeFelice, Mick OT | 65-66NY-A | | 6'3" | 250 | Southern Conn. St. | | |
| Degen, Dick LB | 65-66SD-A | | 6'1" | 223 | Long Beach State | 3 | |
| DeLong, Steve DT-DE | 65-69SD-A 70-72SD 72ChiB | | 6'3" | 251 | Tennessee | 1 | |
| DeLucca, Sam OG-OT | 60LA-A 61SD-A 62VR 63SD-A 64-66NY-A | | 6'2" | 247 | South Carolina | | |
| DeLuca, Jerry OT-DT | 59Phi 60-61BosA 62-63BufA 63-64BosA | | 6'3" | 249 | Middle Tenn. St. | | |
| DeMarco, Bob C-OG | 61-69StL 70-71Mia 72-74Cle 75LA | | 6'3" | 243 | Indiana, Dayton | | |
| Demko, George DE | 61Pit | | 6'3" | 240 | Appalachian State | | |
| Denney, Austin TE | 67-69ChiB 70-71Buf | 2 | 6'2" | 230 | Tennessee | | 18 |
| Dennis, Mike HB | 68-69LA | 2 | 6'1" | 207 | Mississippi | | |
| Denny, Earl HB | 67-68Min | | 6'1" | 200 | Missouri | | |
| Denson, Al WR-FL-TE | 64-69DenA 70Den 71Min | 2 | 6'2" | 208 | Florida A&M | | 194 |
| Denton, Bob DE-OT | 60Cle 61-64Min | | 6'4" | 241 | U. of Pacific | | |
| Denvir, John OG | 62DenA | | 6'4" | 245 | Colorado | | |
| Deskins, Don OG | 60OakA | | 6'3" | 240 | Michigan | | |
| Dess, Darrell OG-OT | 58Pit 59-64NYG 65-66Was 66-69NYG | | 6' | 243 | N. Carolina State | | 6 |
| DeSutter, Wayne OT | 66BufA | | 6'4" | 250 | Illinois, Western Illinois | | |
| Deters, Harold K | 67Dal | 5 | 6' | 200 | N. Carolina State | | 12 |
| DeVleigher, Chuck DT | 69BufA | | 6'4" | 265 | Memphis State | | |
| Dewveall, Willard OE | 59-60ChiB 61-64HouA | 2 | 6'4" | 224 | S.M.U. | | 162 |
| Dial, Benjy QB | 67Phi | | 6'1" | 185 | East. New Mexico | | |
| Dial, Buddy FL-OE | 59-63Pit 64-66Dal 67-68JJ | 2 | 6'1" | 194 | Rice | | 284 |
| Diamond, Bill OG | 63KC-A | | 6' | 240 | Miami (Fla.) | | |
| Diamond, Charley OT | 60-62DalA 63KC-A | | 6'2" | 249 | Miami (Fla.) | | |
| Dickey, Eldridge WR | 68OakA 71Oak | | 6'2" | 198 | Tennessee State | | 6 |
| Dickey, Wallace OT | 68-69DenA | | 6'3" | 260 | SW Texas State | | |
| Dickinson, Bo FB | 60-61DalA 62-63DenA 63HouA 64OakA | 2 | 6'2" | 218 | Southern Miss. | | 70 |
| Dickson, Paul DT-OT | 59LA 60Dal 61-70Min 71StL | | 6'5" | 252 | Baylor | | |
| Diehl, John DT | 61-64Bal 65Dal 65OakA | | 6'7" | 276 | Virginia | | |
| Dillon, Terry DB | 63Min | | 6' | 193 | Montana | | |
| died May, 1964 — accidental drowning | | | | | | | |
| DiMidio, Tony OT-C | 66-67KC-A | | 6'3" | 250 | West Chester | | |
| Dimitroff, Tom QB | 60BosA | | 5'11" | 200 | Miami-Ohio | | |
| Dirks, Mike DT-OG | 68-71Phi | | 6'2" | 247 | Wyoming | | 6 |
| Discenzo, Tony OT | 60BosA 60BufA | | 6'5" | 240 | Michigan State | | |
| Ditka, Mike TE | 61-66Chi 67-68Phi 69-72Dal HC83-92Chi | 2 | 6'3" | 229 | Pittsburgh | | 270 |
| DiVito, Joe QB | 68DenA | | 6'2" | 205 | Boston College | | |
| Dixon, Hewritt FB-HB-OE | 63-65DenA 66-60OakA 70Oak 71JJ | 2 | 6'2" | 223 | Florida A&M | | 170 |
| Dobbins, Ollie DB | 64BufA | | 5'11" | 185 | Morgan State | | |
| Doelling, Fred DB | 60Dal | | 5'10" | 190 | Pennsylvania | | |
| Dombrowski, Leon LB | 60NY-A | | 6' | 215 | Delaware | | |
| Donahue, Oscar FL | 62Min | 2 | 6'3" | 195 | San Jose State | | |
| Donaldson, Gene FB | 67BufA | | 6'2" | 225 | Purdue | | |
| Donnahoo, Roger DB | 60NY-A | | 6' | 185 | Michigan State | 5 | 12 |
| Donnell, Ben DE | 60LA-A | | 6'5" | 248 | Vanderbilt | | |
| Donnelly, George DB | 65-67SF | | 6'3" | 207 | Illinois | 2 | |
| Donohue, Leon OG-OT | 62-65SF 65-67Dal 68JJ | | 6'4" | 245 | San Jose State | | |
| Dorsey, Dick OE | 62OakA | 2 | 6'3" | 200 | Southern Calif., Oklahoma | | 12 |
| Dotson, Al DT | 65KC-A 66MiaA 68-69OakA 70Oak | | 6'4" | 258 | Grambling | | 2 |
| Dougherty, Bob LB | 57LA 58Pit 60-63OakA | | 6' | 238 | Cincinnati, Kentucky | 3 | |
| Douglas, John DB | 67-68NO 69HouA 70JJ | | 6'1" | 195 | Texas Southern | 1 | |
| Douglas, Merrill FB-HB | 58-60ChiB 61Dal 62Phi | 2 | 6' | 204 | Utah | | 12 |
| Dove, Eddie DB | 59-63SF 63NYG | 3 | 6'2" | 181 | Colorado | 10 | |
| Dowdle, Mike LB-FB | 60-62Dal 63-66SF | | 6'3" | 226 | Texas | 6 | 6 |
| Dowler, Boyd FL-OE-WR | 59-69GB 70VR 71Was | 2 4 | 6'5" | 224 | Colorado | | 240 |
| Driskill, Joe DB | 60-61StL | | 6'1" | 195 | Northeast La. | | |
| Dubenion, Elbert FL-HB-WR | 60-68BufA | 23 | 6' | 189 | Bluffton | | 234 |
| Dudek, Mitch OT | 66NY-A | | 6'4" | 245 | Xavier-Ohio | | |
| Dudley, Paul HB | 62NYG 63Phi | 2 | 6' | 185 | Arkansas | | 6 |
| Dugan, Fred OE | 58-59SF 60Dal 61-63Was | 2 | 6'3" | 187 | Dayton | | 78 |
| Duich, Steve OG | 68Atl 69Was | | 6'3" | 248 | San Diego State | | |
| Dukes, Mike LB | 60-63HouA 64-65BosA 65NY-A | | 6'3" | 231 | Clemson | 9 | |
| Dunaway, Dave WR | 68GB 68Atl 69NYG | | 6'2" | 205 | Duke | | |
| Dunaway, Jim DT | 63-69BufA 70-71Buf 72Mia 73JJ | | 6'4" | 278 | Mississippi | 1 | 6 |
| Duncan, Randy QB | 61DalA | 1 | 6' | 185 | Iowa | | |
| Duncan, Rick K | 67DenA 68Phi 69Det | | 6' | 208 | Eastern Montana | | 9 |
| Duncan, Ron TE | 67Cle | | 6'6" | 255 | Wittenberg | | |
| Duncan, Speedy DB | 64-69SD-A 70SD 71-74Was | 3 | 5'10" | 177 | Jackson State | 24 | 54 |
| Duncom, Bob OT | 68StL | | 6'3" | 250 | West Texas State | | |
| Dunn, Perry Lee HB-FB | 64-65Dal 66-68Atl 69Bal | 2 | 6'2" | 208 | Mississippi | | 42 |
| Dupre, Charlie DB | 60NY-A | | 6'1" | 195 | Baylor | | |
| Durkee, Charlie (Mickey) K | 67-68,71-72NO | 5 | 5'11" | 165 | Oklahoma State | | 243 |
| Dyer, Henry FB | 66LA 67JJ 68LA 69-70Was | 2 | 6'2" | 230 | Grambling | | 12 |
| Dyer, Ken DB-WR | 68SD-A 69CinA 70-71Cin | | 6'3" | 187 | Arizona State | 3 | 6 |
| Eason, John WR | 68OakA | | 6'2" | 220 | Florida A&M | | |
| Eaton, Scott DB | 67-71NYG 72JJ | | 6'3" | 199 | Oregon State | 11 | 6 |
| Eber, Rick WR | 68Atl 69SD-A 70SD 71JJ | 2 | 6' | 181 | Tulsa | | 6 |
| Echols, Fate OT-DT | 62-63StL 64CFL | | 6'1" | 258 | Northwestern | | |
| Eddy, Nick HB | 68-70Det 71KJ 72Det | 2 | 6'1" | 207 | Notre Dame | | |
| Edgerson, Booker DB | 62-69BufA 70Den | | 5'10" | 182 | Western Illinois | 23 | 2 |
| Edmunds, Randy LB | 68-69MiaA 71NE 72Bal | | 6'2" | 223 | Georgia Tech | 1 | |
| Edwards, Dave LB | 63-75Dal | | 6'3" | 224 | Auburn | 13 | 6 |
| Edwards, Lloyd TE | 60OakA | | 6'3" | 248 | San Diego State | | |
| Eifrid, Jim LB | 61DenA | | 6' | 240 | Colorado State | | |
| Eisenhauer, Larry DE | 61-69BosA | | 6'5" | 247 | Boston College | 1 | |
| Elkins, Larry FL | 66-67HouA | 2 | 6'1" | 193 | Baylor | | 18 |
| Ellersick, Don DB | 60LA | | 6'1" | 193 | Washington State | 2 | |
| Elliott, Jim K | 67Pit | 4 | 5'11" | 184 | Presbyterian | | |
| Ellis, Roger LB-C | 60-63NY-A | | 6'3" | 233 | Maine | 1 | |
| Ellzey, Charley C-LB | 60-61StL | | 6'3" | 234 | Southern Miss. | | |
| Elmore, Doug DB | 62Was | 4 | 6' | 188 | Mississippi | | |
| Elwell, Jack OE | 62StL | | 6'3" | 200 | Purdue | | |
| Elzey, Paul LB | 68CinA | | 6'3" | 235 | Toledo | | |
| Emanuel, Frank LB | 66-69MiaA 70NO | | 6'3" | 225 | Tennessee | 4 | 6 |
| Embree, John WR | 69DenA 70Den 71JJ | 2 | 6'4" | 201 | Compton J.C. | | 30 |

| Use Name (Nickname) - Positions | Team by Year | See Section | Hgt. | Wgt. | College | Int | Pts |
|---|---|---|---|---|---|---|---|
| Emelianchik, Pete TE | 67Phi | | 6'2" | 220 | Richmond | | |
| Enis, Hunter QB | 60DalA 61SD-A 62DenA 62OakA | 12 | 6'2" | 192 | Texas Christian | | 30 |
| Epperson, Pat OE | 60DenA | 2 | 6'3" | 225 | Adams State | | |
| Erdelatz, Eddie | HC60OakA | | | | St. Mary's | | |
| Erickson, Bernie LB | 67-68SD-A 68CinA | | 6'2" | 239 | Abilene Christian | 1 | |
| Erlandson, Tom LB | 62-65DenA 66-67MiaA 68SD-A | | 6'3" | 229 | Washington State | 8 | 6 |
| Erwin, Terry HB | 68DenA | | 6' | 190 | Boston College | | |
| Estes, Don OG | 66SD-A | | 6'2" | 250 | Louisiana State | | |
| Etcheverry, Sam QB | 61-62StL | 12 4 | 5'11" | 190 | Denver | | |
| Etter, Bob K | 68-69Atl | 5 | 5'11" | 152 | Georgia | | 128 |
| Evans, Bob DE | 65HouA | | 6'3" | 250 | Texas A&M | | |
| Evans, Dale HB | 61DenA | | 6'3" | 210 | Kansas State | | |
| Evans, Jim FL | 64-65NY-A | | 6'1" | 190 | Texas-El Paso | | |
| Evey, Dick DT-DE-OG | 64-69ChiB 70LA 71Det | | 6'2" | 238 | Tennessee | 2 | |
| Ewbank, Weeb | HC54-62Bal HC63-69NY-A HC70-73NYJ | | | | Miami-Ohio | | |
| Ezerins, Vilnis HB-FB | 68LA | | 6'1" | 217 | Wis.-Whitewater | | |
| Fairband, Bill LB | 67-68OakA | | 6'3" | 228 | Colorado | | |
| Faison, Earl DE | 61-66SD-A 66MiaA | | 6'5" | 263 | Indiana | 6 | 14 |
| Falls, Mike OG | 60-61Dal | | 6'1" | 240 | Minnesota | | |
| Fanning, Stan OT-DE-DT | 60-62ChiB 63LA 64HouA | | 6'6" | 267 | Idaho | | |
| | 64DenA | | | | | | |
| Farley, Dick DB | 68-69SD-A | | 6' | 185 | Boston U. | | |
| Farmer, Lonnie LB | 64-66BosA | | 6' | 220 | Tenn.-Chattanooga | 1 | |
| Farr, Miller DB | 65DenA 65-66SD-A 67-69HouA | | 6'1" | 190 | Wichita State | 35 | 36 |
| | 70-72StL 73Det | | | | | | |
| Farrier, Curt DT | 63-65KC-A 66JJ | | 6'6" | 263 | Montana State | | |
| Farrington, Bo OE | 60-63ChiB | 2 | 6'3" | 217 | Prairie View | | 42 |
| killed in auto accident at 1964 training camp | | | | | | | |
| Farris, John OG | 65-66SD-A | | 6'4" | 245 | San Diego State | | |
| Faulkner, Jack | HC62-64DenA | | | | Miami-Ohio | | |
| Faulkner, Staley OT | 64HouA | | 6'3" | 245 | Texas | | |
| Faust, Paul LB | 67Min | | 6' | 220 | Minnesota | | |
| Feagin, Wiley OG | 61-62Bal 63Was | | 6'2" | 236 | Houston | | |
| Feldhausen, Paul OT | 68BosA | | 6'6" | 270 | Northland | | |
| Feldman, Marty | HC61-62OakA | | | | Oregon, Stanford | | |
| Felt, Dick DB | 60-61NY-A 62-66BosA | | 6' | 184 | Brigham Young | 18 | 6 |
| Felts, Bobby HB | 65Bal 65-67Det | 23 | 6'2" | 203 | Florida A&M | | 12 |
| Fenner, Lane WR | 68SD-A | | 6'5" | 210 | Florida State | | |
| Ferguson, Bob FB | 62-63Pit 63Min | 2 | 5'11" | 220 | Ohio State | | 6 |
| Ferguson, Charley OE-TE | 61Cle 62Min 63BufA | 2 | 6'5" | 218 | Tennessee State | | 78 |
| | 64JJ 65-66BufA 67-68JJ 69BufA | | | | | | |
| Ferguson, Jim C-LB | 68NO 69Atl 69ChiB 71JJ | | 6'4" | 240 | Southern Calif. | | |
| Ferguson, Larry HB | 63Det | | 5'10" | 185 | Iowa | | |
| Ferrante, Orlando OG | 60LA-A 61SD-A | | 6' | 230 | Southern Calif. | | |
| Fetherston, Jim LB | 68-69SD-A | | 6'2" | 225 | California | 1 | |
| Ficca, Dan OG | 62OakA 63-66NY-A | | 6'1" | 244 | Southern Calif. | | |
| Fichtner, Ross DB | 60-67Cle 68NO | | 6' | 186 | Purdue | 27 | 18 |
| Fields, George DE-DT | 60-61OakA | | 6'3" | 245 | Bakersfield State | 2 | |
| Fields, Jerry LB | 61-62NY-A | | 6'1" | 222 | Ohio State | | |
| Finch, Karl OE | 62LA | | 6'3" | 195 | Iowa, | | |
| | | | | | Cal. Poly-Pomona | | |
| Finneran, Gary DT | 60LA-A | | 6'3" | 240 | Southern Calif. | | |
| Fischer, Pat (Mouse) DB-HB | 61-67StL 68-77Was | 3 | 5'10" | 170 | Nebraska | 56 | 30 |
| Fisher, Doug LB | 69-70Pit | | 6'1" | 225 | San Diego State | | |
| Fiss, Galen LB | 56-66Cle | | 6' | 226 | Kansas | 13 | |
| Fitzgerald, Mike DB | 66-67Min 67NYG 67Atl | 3 | 5'10" | 180 | Iowa State | 1 | |
| Flanigan, Jim LB | 67-70GB 71NO | | 6'3" | 238 | Pittsburgh | 1 | |
| Flatley, Paul OE-WR | 63-67Min 68-70Atl | 2 | 6'1" | 187 | Northwestern | | 144 |
| Fleming, Don DB | 60-62Cle | | 6' | 187 | Florida | 10 | |
| died June 4, 1963 — construction accident | | | | | | | |
| Fleming, George HB | 61OakA | 23 5 | 5'11" | 188 | Washington | | 63 |
| Fleming, Marv TE-OE | 63-69GB 70-74Mia | 2 | 6'4" | 233 | Utah | | 96 |
| Fletcher, Billy DB | 66DenA | | 5'10" | 190 | Memphis State | | |
| Flint, George OG | 62-65BufA 66JJ 67-69BufA | | 6'4" | 243 | Arizona State | | |
| Flores, Tom QB | 60-61OakA 62IL 63-66OakA 67-69BufA | 12 | 6'1" | 194 | U. of Pacific | | 30 |
| | 69KC-A HC79-81Oak HC82-87Raid HC92-94Sea | | | | | | |
| Flowers, Charlie FB | 60LA-A 61SD-A 62NY-A | 2 | 6'1" | 215 | Mississippi | | 30 |
| Floyd, Don DE | 60-67HouA | | 6'4" | 242 | Texas Christian | 4 | 12 |
| Flynn, Don LB | 60-61DalA 61NY-A | | 6' | 205 | Houston | 5 | 6 |
| Folkins, Lee TE-DE | 61GB 62-64Dal 65Pit | 2 | 6'5" | 219 | Washington | | 66 |
| Fontes, Wayne DB | 62NY-A HC88-95Det | | 6' | 190 | Michigan State | 4 | 6 |
| Ford, Fred HB | 60BufA 60LA-A | 2 | 5'8" | 180 | Cal. Poly-Pomona | | 12 |
| Ford, Garrett FB | 68DenA | 2 | 6'2" | 230 | West Virginia | | 6 |
| Fortunato, Joe LB-FB | 55-66ChiB | | 6' | 225 | Mississippi State | 16 | 18 |
| Foruria, John DB-HB | 67-68Pit | | 6'2" | 205 | Idaho | | |
| Foster, Gene FB-HB | 65-69SD-A 70SD | 2 | 5'11" | 214 | Arizona State | | 46 |
| Fournet, Sid OG-LB-DE | 55-56LA 57Pit | | 6' | 235 | Louisiana State | 1 | |
| | 60-61DalA 62-63NY-A | | | | | | |
| Fowler, Bobby FB | 62NY-A | | 5'11" | 212 | Martin C.C. | | |
| Fowler, Charlie OG-OT | 67-68MiaA | | 6'2" | 260 | Houston | | |
| Fowler, Jerry OT | 64HouA | | 6'3" | 255 | Northwestern La. | | |
| Fowler, Wilmer HB | 60-61BufA | 2 | 5'11" | 185 | Northwestern | | 6 |
| Franci, Jason OE | 66DenA | | 6'1" | 210 | Cal.-Santa Barbara | | |
| Francis, Dave FB | 63Was | | 6'1" | 210 | Ohio State | | |
| Franckhauser, Tom DB | 59LA 60-61Dal 62-63Min | 3 | 6' | 195 | Purdue | 13 | |
| Frank, Bill OT | 64Dal | | 6'5" | 255 | Colorado | | |
| Franklin, Bobby DB-HB | 60-66Cle | | 5'11" | 182 | Mississippi | 13 | 18 |
| Frantz, Jack C | 68BufA | | 6'3" | 230 | California | | |
| Fraser, Jim LB-K | 62-64DenA 65KC-A 66BosA 68NO | 4 | 6'3" | 236 | Wisconsin | 3 | 2 |
| Frazier, Al HB-FL | 61-63DenA | 23 | 5'11" | 180 | Florida A&M | | 68 |
| Frazier, Charley OE-WR | 62-68HouA 69BosA 70Bos | 2 | 6' | 177 | Texas Southern | | 180 |
| Frazier, Curt DB | 68CinA | | 5'11" | 183 | Fresno State | | |
| Frazier, Wayne C-LB | 62SD-A 65HouA | | 6'2" | 243 | Auburn | | |
| | 66-67KC-A 67BufA | | | | | | |
| Frazier, Willie TE-OE | 64-66HouA 66-69SD-A 70SD | 2 | 6'4" | 235 | Ark.-Pine Bluff | | 222 |
| | 71Hou 71-72KC 74-75WFL 75Hou 76KJ | | | | | | |
| Frederickson, Tucker FB-HB | 65NYG 66KJ 67-71NYG | 2 | 6'3" | 233 | Auburn | | 102 |
| Freeman, Bobby DB-HB | 57-58Cle 59GB 60-61Phi 62Was | | 6'1" | 202 | Auburn | 15 | |
| Feeman, Mike DB | 68-70Atl | | 5'11" | 187 | Fresno State | 1 | |
| Frey, Dick DE-OG | 60DalA 61HouA | | 6'2" | 233 | Texas A&M | | |
| Fritsch, Ernie C-LB | 60StL | | 6' | 230 | Detroit | | |
| Frongillo, John OG-C | 62-66HouA | | 6''' | 252 | Baylor | | |
| Frost, Ken OT | 61-62Dal | | 6'4" | 245 | Tennessee | 1 | |
| Fuller, Charley HB | 61-62OakA | 2 | 5'11" | 176 | San Fran. State | | 12 |
| Furey, Jim LB | 60NY-A | | 6' | 228 | Kansas State | | |
| Furman, John QB | 62Cle | | 6'4" | 205 | Texas-El Paso | | |
| Fussell, Tom DE | 67BosA | | 6'3" | 245 | Louisiana State | | |

| Use Name (Nickname) - Positions | Team by Year | See Section | Hgt. | Wgt. | College | Int | Pts |
|---|---|---|---|---|---|---|---|
| Gabriel, Roman QB | 62-72LA 73-77Phi | 12 | 6'4" | 225 | N. Carolina State | | 180 |
| Gaechter, Mike DB | 62-69Dal | | 6' | 192 | Oregon | 21 | 12 |
| Gagner, Larry OG | 66-69Pit 70JJ 72KC | | 6'3" | 246 | Florida | | |
| Gaiser, George OT | 68DenA | | 6'4" | 255 | S.M.U. | | |
| Gaiters, Bob HB | 61-62NYG 62SF 63DenA | 23 | 5'11" | 210 | New Mexico State | | 48 |
| Galimore, Willie HB | 57-63ChiB | 23 | 6'1" | 187 | Florida A&M | | 222 |
| Killed in auto accident at 1964 training camp | | | | | | | |
| Gamble, R.C. HB-FB | 68-69BosA | 2 | 6'3" | 220 | S. Carolina State | | 12 |
| Gambrell, Billy OE-FL-WR | 63-67StL 68Det | 23 | 5'10" | 175 | South Carolina | | 105 |
| Garcia, Jim DE-DT | 65Cle 66NYG 67NO 68Atl | | 6'4" | 248 | Purdue | | |
| Garner, Bob DB | 60LA-A 61-62OakA | 3 | 5'10" | 185 | Fresno State | 7 | |
| Garrett, Drake QB | 68DenA 70Den | | 5'9" | 183 | Michigan State | 2 | |
| Garrett, J.D. HB | 64-67DenA | 23 | 5'11" | 195 | Grambling | | 36 |
| Garrett, Mike HB | 66-69KC-A 70KC 70-73SD | 23 | 5'9" | 199 | Southern Calif. | | 294 |
| Garron, Larry HB-FB | 60-68BosA | 23 | 6' | 199 | Western Illinois | | 252 |
| Gassert, Ron DT | 62GB | | 6'3" | 250 | Virginia | | |
| Gaubatz, Dennis LB | 63-64Det 65-69Bal | | 6'2" | 225 | Louisiana State | 10 | 2 |
| Gautt, Billy LB | 61Min | | 6'1" | 185 | Texas Christian | | |
| Gautt, Prentice HB-FB-LB | 60Cle 61-67StL | 2 | 6' | 204 | Oklahoma | | 102 |
| Gavin, Chuck DE | 60-63DenA | | 6'1" | 243 | Tennessee State | 1 | 6 |
| Gavric, Momcilo K | 69SF | 5 | 5'10" | 167 | Belgrade (Serbia) | | 31 |
| Gehrke, Jack WR | 68KC-A 69CinA 71Den 72JJ | 2 | 6' | 178 | Utah | | |
| Gent, Pete FL-TE-OE | 64-68Dal | 2 | 6'4" | 209 | Michigan State | | 24 |
| Gentry, Curtis DB | 66-68ChiB | | 6' | 186 | Md. Eastern Shore | 6 | |
| Gibbons, Jim OE-TE | 58-68Det | 2 | 6'2" | 220 | Iowa | | 120 |
| Gibbs, Sonny QB | 64Det | | 6'7" | 230 | Texas Christian | | |
| Gibson, Claude DB | 61-62SD-A 63-65OakA | 3 | 6'1" | 191 | N. Carolina State | 22 | 26 |
| Gilburg, Tom OT-K | 61-65Bal | 4 | 6'5" | 245 | Syracuse | | |
| Gilchrist, Cookie FB | 62-64BufA 65DenA | 2 5 | 6'3" | 249 | none | | 296 |
| | 66MiaA 67DenA | | | | | | |
| Gill, Roger HB-TE | 64-65Phi | | 6'1" | 200 | Texas Tech | | |
| Gillett, Fred HB-OE | 62SD-A 64OakA | | 6'3" | 228 | Los Angeles State | | |
| Gilliam, Jon C | 61-62DalA 63-67KC-A | | 6'2" | 238 | East Texas State | | |
| Gillis, Don C | 58-59ChiC 60-61StL 62JJ | | 6'3" | 245 | Rice | | |
| Gillman, Sid | HC55-59LA HC60LA-A HC61-69SD-A | | | | Ohio State | | |
| | HC71SD HC73-74Hou | | | | | | |
| Glacken, Scott QB | 66-67DenA | | 6' | 190 | Duke | | |
| Glass, Bill DE-C-OT | 58-61Det 62-68Cle | | 6'5" | 252 | Baylor | 4 | 12 |
| Glass, Glenn DB-FL-OE | 62-63Pit 64-65Phi | 2 | 6' | 197 | Tennessee | 2 | |
| | 66Atl 66DenA | | | | | | |
| Glenn, Howard OG | 60NY-A | | 6' | 235 | Linfield | | |
| Died Oct. 9, 1960 — Broken neck | | | | | | | |
| Glick, Freddie DB | 59ChiC 60StL 61-66HouA | 3 | 6'1" | 189 | Colorado State | 31 | 6 |
| Glueck, Larry DB | 63-65ChiB | | 6' | 190 | Villanova | 1 | |
| Gogolak, Charlie K | 66-68Was 70Bos 71-72NE | 5 | 5'10" | 168 | Princeton | | 270 |
| Gogolak, Pete K | 64-65BufA 66-74NYG | 5 | 6'2" | 193 | Cornell | | 863 |
| Goldstein, Al OE | 60OakA | 2 | 6' | 204 | North Carolina | | 12 |
| Gonsoulin, Goose DB | 60-66DenA 67SF | | 6'3" | 209 | Baylor | 46 | 14 |
| Gonzaga, John OT-OG-DT-DE | 56-59SF 60Dal | | 6'3" | 247 | none | | |
| | 61-65Det 66DenA | | | | | | |
| Good, Tom LB | 66SD-A | | 6' | 230 | Marshall | | |
| Goode, Irv OG-OT-C | 62-68StL | | 6'4" | 247 | Kentucky | | |
| Goode, Tom C-LB | 62-65HouA 66-69MiaA 70Bal | | 6'3" | 244 | Mississippi State | | |
| Goodridge, Bob WR | 68Min | | 6'2" | 202 | Vanderbilt | | |
| Goodwin, Doug FB | 66BufA 68Atl | | 6'2" | 228 | Md. Eastern Shore | | |
| Goodwin, Ron OE-FL-WR | 63-68Phi | 2 | 6' | 180 | Baylor | | 54 |
| Goosby, Tom OG-LB | 63Cle 66Was | | 6' | 235 | Baldwin-Wallace | | |
| Goovert, Ron LB | 67Det | | 5'11" | 225 | Michigan State | | |
| Gordon, Cornell DB | 65-69NY-A 70-72Den | | 6' | 187 | N. Carolina A&T | 14 | |
| Gordy, John OG-OT | 57Det 58VR 59-67Det | | 6'3" | 248 | Tennessee | | |
| Gossage, Gene DE-OG-DT | 60-62Phi 63CFL | | 6'3" | 239 | Northwestern | | |
| Gossett, Bruce K | 64-69LA 70-74SF | 5 | 6'2" | 229 | Clarion, Duquesne, | | 1031 |
| | | | | | Richmond | | |
| Grabosky, Gene DT | 60BufA | | 6'5" | 275 | Syracuse | | |
| Grabowski, Jim FB | 66-70GB 71ChiB | 2 | 6'2" | 221 | Illinois | | 66 |
| Grady, Garry DB | 69MiaA | | 5'11" | 180 | Eastern Michigan | | |
| Graham, Art OE-WR | 63-68BosA | 2 | 6'1" | 205 | Boston College | | 120 |
| Graham, Dave OT | 63-66Phi 67JJ 68-69Phi 70JJ | | 6'3" | 248 | Virginia | | |
| Graham, Kenny DB | 64-69SD-A 70Cin 70Pit | 3 | 6' | 201 | Washington State | 28 | 30 |
| Graham, Milt OT-DT | 61-63BosA | | 6'6" | 235 | Colgate | | |
| Granderson, Rufus DT | 60DalA | | 6'5" | 277 | Prairie View | | |
| Granger, Charley OT | 61Dal 61StL | | 6'2" | 240 | Southern U. | | |
| Granger, Hoyle FB-HB | 66-69HouA 70Hou 71NO 72Hou | 2 | 6'1" | 225 | Mississippi State | | 144 |
| Grantham, Larry LB | 60-69NY-A 70-73NYJ | | 6' | 204 | Mississippi | 24 | 18 |
| Grate, Willie TE | 69BufA 70Buf | | 6'4" | 225 | S. Carolina State | | 18 |
| Graves, White DB | 65-67BosA 68CinA | | 6' | 185 | Louisiana State | 3 | |
| Gray, Jim DB | 66NY-A 67Phi | | 6' | 181 | Toledo | | |
| Gray, Ken OG-LB | 58-59ChiC 60-69StL 70Hou | | 6'2" | 245 | Howard Payne | | |
| Gray, Moses OT-DT | 61-62NY-A | | 6'3" | 260 | Indiana | | |
| Grayson, Dave DB | 61-62DalA 63-64KC-A | 3 | 5'10" | 184 | Oregon | 48 | 36 |
| | 65-69OakA 70Oak | | | | | | |
| Greaves, Gary OT | 60HouA | | 6'3" | 235 | Miami (Fla.) | | |
| Grecni, Dick LB | 61Min | | 6'1" | 230 | Ohio U. | 1 | |
| Green, Allen K | 61Dal | 45 | 6'2" | 215 | Mississippi | | 34 |
| Green, Bobby Joe K | 60-61Pit 62-73ChiB | 4 | 5'11" | 175 | Florida | | |
| Green, Charlie QB | 66OakA | | 6' | 190 | Wittenberg | | |
| Green, Cornell DB | 62-74Dal | | 6'4" | 211 | Utah State | 34 | 24 |
| Green, Ernie HB-FB | 62-68Cle | 23 | 6'2" | 205 | Louisville | | 210 |
| Green, Jerry HB | 60BosA | | 6' | 190 | Georgia Tech | | |
| Green, Johnny QB | 60-61BufA 62-63NY-A | 12 | 6'3" | 203 | Tenn.-Chattanooga | | 36 |
| Green, Ron FL-WR | 67-68Cle | | 6'1" | 200 | North Dakota | | |
| Greene, Ted LB | 60-62DalA | | 6'1" | 230 | Tampa | 4 | |
| Greene, Tom QB | 60BosA 61DalA | 12 4 | 6'1" | 190 | Holy Cross | | |
| Greenlee, Fritz LB | 69SF | | 6'2" | 230 | Arizona State | | |
| Greer, Al OE | 63Det | | 6'4" | 190 | Jackson State | | |
| Greer, Jim OE | 60DenA | | 6'3" | 215 | Elizabeth City St. | | |
| Gregg, Forrest OT-OG-DT | 56GB 57MS 58-70GB 71Dal | | 6'4" | 249 | S.M.U. | | |
| | HC75-77Cle HC80-83Cin HC84-87GB | | | | | | |
| Gregory, Ben HB-FB | 68BufA | 2 | 6'3" | 220 | Nebraska | | |
| Gregory, Glynn OE-DB | 61-62Dal | | 6'2" | 200 | S.M.U. | 1 | |
| Gregory, Ken OE | 61Bal 62Phi 63NY-A | | 6' | 190 | Whittier | | |
| Gremminger, Hank DB | 56-65GB 66LA | | 6'1" | 201 | Baylor | 29 | 6 |
| Grier, Rosey DT-DE | 55-56NYG 57MS 58-62NYG | | 6'5" | 284 | Penn State | | 4 |
| | 63-66LA 67JJ | | | | | | |
| Griffin, Jim DE | 66-67SD-A 68CinA | | 6'3" | 258 | Grambling | | 6 |
| Griffin, John DB | 63LA 64-66DenA | | 6'1" | 190 | Memphis State | 4 | 12 |
| Griffing, Glynn QB | 63NYG | 1 | 6'1" | 200 | Mississippi | | |
| Grimm, Dan OG | 63-65GB 66-68Atl 69Bal 69Was | | 6'3" | 244 | Colorado | | |

| Use Name (Nickname) - Positions | Team by Year | See Section | Hgt. | Wgt. | College | Int | Pts |
|---|---|---|---|---|---|---|---|
| Groman, Bill OE-FL | 60-62HouA 63DenA 64-65BufA | 2 | 6' | 195 | Heidelberg | | 22 |
| Gros, Earl FB | 62-63GB 64-66Phi 67-69Pit 70NO | 2 | 6'3" | 224 | Louisiana State | | 228 |
| Gross, Andy OG | 67-68NYG | | 6' | 230 | Auburn | | |
| Gross, George DT | 63-67SD-A | | 6'3" | 263 | Auburn | | |
| Grosscup, Lee QB | 60-61NYG 62NY-A | 1 | 6'1" | 186 | Washington, Utah | | |
| Grottkau, Bob OG | 59-60Det 61Dal | | 6'4" | 228 | Oregon | | |
| Gruneisen, Sam C-OG-LB | 62-69SD-A 70-72SD 73Hou | | 6'1" | 248 | Villanova | | |
| Gucciardo, Pat DB | 66NY-A | | 5'11" | 185 | Kent State | | |
| Guesman, Dick DT | 62-63NY-A 64DenA | 5 | 6'4" | 255 | West Virginia | | 129 |
| Guiglielmi, Ralph QB | 55Was 56-57MS 58-60Was 61StL 62-63NYG 63Phi | 12 | 6'1" | 196 | Notre Dame | | 12 |
| Guidry, Paul LB | 66-69BufA 70-72Buf 73Hou | | 6'3" | 229 | Louisiana State, McNeese State | 5 | |
| Guillory, John DB | 69CinA 70Cin | | 5'10" | 190 | Stanford | 1 | |
| Guillory, Tony LB | 65LA 66KJ 67-68LA 69Phi | | 6'4" | 232 | Nebraska, Lamar | | |
| Gulseth, Don LB | 66DenA | | 6'1" | 240 | North Dakota | | |
| Gunnels, Riley DT-DE | 60-64Phi 65-66Pit | | 6'3" | 250 | Georgia | | |
| Gunner, Harry DE | 68-69CinA 70ChiB | | 6'6" | 250 | Oregon State | 2 | 8 |
| Gursky, Al LB | 63NYG | | 6'1" | 210 | Penn State | | |
| Guy, Louis DB-FL | 63NYG 64OakA | | 6' | 188 | Mississippi | | |
| Guzik, John LB-OG | 59-60LA 61HouA | | 6'3" | 231 | Pittsburgh | | |
| Gwinn, Ross OG | 68NO | | 6'3" | 273 | Northwestern La. | | |
| Hackbart, Dale DB | 60GB 61-63Was 64-65CFL 66-70Min 71-72StL 73Den | | 6'3" | 210 | Wisconsin | 19 | 24 |
| Hadl, John QB | 62-69SD-A 70-72SD 73-74LA 74-75GB 76-77Hou | 12 4 | 6'2" | 213 | Kansas | | 96 |
| Haffner, Mike WR | 68-69DenA 70Den 71Cin | 2 | 6'2" | 205 | U.C.L.A. | | 42 |
| Hagberg, Roger FB-TE | 65-69OakA | 2 | 6'2" | 216 | Minnesota | | 48 |
| Hageman, Fred C | 61-64Was | | 6'4" | 243 | Kansas | | |
| Haggerty, Mike OT | 67-70Pit 71NE 72Det | | 6'4" | 239 | Miami (Fla.) | | |
| Haik, Mac WR | 68-69HouA 70-71Hou | 2 | 6'1" | 196 | Mississippi | | 54 |
| Hale, Dave DT-DE | 67-71ChiB 72JJ 73ChiB | | 6'7" | 251 | Ottawa (Kan.) | | |
| Haley, Dick DB-HB-FL-OE | 59-60Was 61Min 61-64Pit | 3 | 5'10" | 193 | Pittsburgh | 14 | 12 |
| Hall, Alvin DB | 61-63LA | | 6' | 195 | none | 1 | |
| Hall, Galen QB | 62Was 63NY-A | 1 | 5'10" | 200 | Penn State | | 12 |
| Hall, Ken HB | 59ChiC 60-61HouA 61StL | 23 | 6'1" | 205 | Texas A&M | | 24 |
| Hall, Pete OE | 61NYG | | 6'2" | 200 | Marquette | | |
| Hall, Ron DB | 59Pit 60MS 61-67BosA | | 6' | 190 | Missouri Valley | 30 | 6 |
| Hall, Tom FL-OE-WR-DB | 62-63Det 64-66Min 67NO 68-69Min | 2 | 6'1" | 195 | Minnesota | 3 | 48 |
| Hammack, Mal FB-OE-TE-LB | 55ChiB 56MS 57-58ChiB 60-66StL | 2 | 6'2" | 205 | Florida | | 48 |
| Hammond, Kim QB | 68MiaA 69BosA | 1 | 6'1" | 192 | Florida State | | 2 |
| Hardy, Charley OE | 60-62OakA | 2 | 6' | 184 | San Jose State | | 42 |
| Harmon, Ed LB | 69CinA | | 6'4" | 230 | Louisville | | |
| Harmon, Tom OG | 67Atl | | 6'4" | 238 | Gustavus Adolphus | | |
| Harold, George DB | 66-67Bal 68Was | | 6'3" | 198 | Allen | | |
| Harper, Charlie OG-OT-DT | 66-72NYG | | 6'2" | 250 | Oklahoma State | | |
| Harper, Darrell HB | 60BufA | | 6'1" | 195 | Michigan | | 7 |
| Harper, Jack HB | 67-68MiaA | 2 | 5'11" | 190 | Florida | | 24 |
| Harris, Billy HB | 68Atl 69Min 70JJ 71NO | 2 | 6' | 196 | Colorado | | 6 |
| Harris, Dick DB | 60LA-A 61-65SD-A | 3 | 6' | 185 | McNeese State | 12 | |
| Harris, Jim DT | 65-67NY-A | | 6'4" | 275 | Utah State | | |
| Harris, John DB-HB | 60-61OakA | | 6'1" | 195 | Santa Monica J.C. | 3 | |
| Harris, Lou DB | 68Pit | | 6' | 180 | Kent State | | |
| Harris, Marv LB | 64LA | | 6'1" | 225 | Stanford | | |
| Harris, Phil DB | 66NYG | | 6' | 195 | Texas | | |
| Harris, Rickie DB | 65-70Was 71-72NE | 3 | 6' | 182 | Arizona | 15 | 24 |
| Harris, Wendell DB | 62-65Bal 66-67NYG | 3 5 | 5'11" | 188 | Louisiana State | 8 | 17 |
| Harrison, Bob LB | 59-61SF 62-63Phi 64Pit 65-67SF | | 6'2" | 223 | Oklahoma | 5 | |
| Harrison, Bob LB | 61Bal | | 5'11" | 187 | Ohio U. | 3 | |
| Hart, Ben DB | 67NO | | 6'2" | 205 | Oklahoma | 1 | |
| Hart, Dick OG | 67-70Phi 71JJ 72Buf | | 6'2" | 250 | none | | |
| Hart, Doug DB | 64-71GB | | 6' | 190 | Texas-Arlington | 15 | 32 |
| Hart, Pete FB | 60NY-A | 2 | 5'9" | 190 | Hardin-Simmons | | |
| Harvey, George OT | 67NO | | 6'4" | 245 | Kansas | | |
| Harvey, Jim OG-OT | 66-69OakA 70-71Oak | | 6'5" | 247 | Mississippi | | |
| Harvey, Waddey DT | 69BufA 70Buf | | 6'4" | 276 | Virginia Tech | | |
| Hatcher, Ron DB-FB | 62Was | | 5'11" | 215 | Michigan State | | |
| Hathcock, Dave DB | 66GB 67NYG | | 6' | 193 | Memphis State | | |
| Hawkins, Alex HB-OE-FL-WR | 59-65Bal 66-67Atl 67-68Bal | 23 | 6'1" | 188 | South Carolina | | 132 |
| Hawkins, Ben WR-FL-OE | 66-73Phi 74Cle | 2 | 6' | 180 | Arizona State | | 198 |
| Hawkins, Rip LB | 61-65Min | | 6'3" | 231 | North Carolina | 12 | 20 |
| Hawkins, Wayne OG | 60-69OakA | | 6' | 240 | U. of Pacific | | |
| Hayes, Jim DT | 65-66HouA | | 6'4" | 263 | Jackson State | | |
| Hayes, Larry C-LB | 61NYG 62-63LA | | 6'3" | 230 | Vanderbilt | | 6 |
| Hayes, Luther DE | 61SD-A | 2 | 6'4" | 200 | Southern Calif. | | 18 |
| Hayes, Ray FB | 61Min | 2 | 6'3" | 235 | Md.-Eastern Shore, Central St.-Okla. | | 12 |
| Hayes, Ray DT | 68NY-A | | 6'5" | 248 | Toledo | | |
| Hayes, Rudy LB | 59-60,62Pit | | 6' | 217 | Clemson | | |
| Hayes, Wendell FB-HB | 63Dal 65-67DenA 68-69KC-A 70-74KC | 2 | 6'2" | 215 | Humboldt State | | 214 |
| Haymond, Alvin DB | 64-67Bal 68Phi 69-71LA 72Was 73Hou | 3 | 6' | 193 | Southern U. | 10 | 30 |
| Haynes, Abner HB | 60-62DalA 63-64KC-A 65-66DenA 67MiaA 67NY-A | 23 | 6' | 188 | North Texas | | 414 |
| Hays, Harold LB | 63-67Dal 68-69SF | | 6'3" | 227 | Southern Miss. | | |
| Hazeltine, Matt LB | 55-68SF 69VR 70NYG | | 6'1" | 220 | California | 13 | 18 |
| Hazelton, Major DB | 68-69ChiB 70NO | | 6'1" | 185 | Florida A&M | | |
| Headrick, Sherrill LB | 60-62DalA 63-67KC-A 68CinA | | 6'2" | 223 | Texas Christian | 15 | 18 |
| Healy, Chip LB | 69-70StL | | 6'3" | 233 | Vanderbilt | | |
| Healy, Don DT-OG | 58-59ChiB 60-61Dal 62BufA | | 6'3" | 259 | Maryland | 1 | |
| Hebert, Ken WR | 68Pit | | 6' | 200 | Houston | | |
| Heck, Ralph LB | 63-65Phi 66-68Atl 69-71NYG | | 6'2" | 228 | Colorado | 5 | 6 |
| Heckard, Steve OE | 65-66LA | | 6'1" | 195 | Southern Calif., Davidson | | |
| Hector, Willie OT | 61LA | | 6'2" | 220 | U. of Pacific | | |
| Heenan, Pat DB-OE | 60Was | | 6'1" | 190 | Notre Dame | 1 | |
| Heeter, Gene OE | 63-65NY-A | 2 | 6'4" | 235 | West Virginia | | 12 |
| Heidel, Jim DB | 66StL 67NO | | 6'1" | 185 | Mississippi | 1 | |
| Hendershot, Larry LB | 67Was | | 6'3" | 240 | Arizona State | | |
| Henderson, John WR-OE-FL | 65-67Det 68-72Min | 2 | 6'3" | 191 | Michigan | | 60 |
| Henderson, John WR-DB | 68-69Pit 70Was | 23 | 6' | 198 | Colorado State | | 36 |
| Henke, Karl DT-DE | 68NY-A 69BosA | | 6'4" | 245 | Tulsa | | |
| Henley, Carey HB | 62BufA | | 5'10" | 200 | Tenn.-Chattanooga | | |
| Hennessey, Tom DB | 65-66BosA | | 6' | 183 | Holy Cross | 8 | |
| Hennigan, Charley FL-OE | 60-66HouA | 2 | 6' | 187 | Louisiana State, Northwestern La. | | 306 |
| Henning, Dan QB | 66SD-A HC83-86Atl HC89-91SD | | 6' | 195 | William & Mary | | |

| Use Name (Nickname) - Positions | Team by Year | See Section | Hgt. | Wgt. | College | Int | Pts |
|---|---|---|---|---|---|---|---|
| Henry, Mike LB | 59-61Pit 62-64LA | | 6'2" | 220 | Southern Calif. | | |
| Henry, Urban DT-DE | 61LA 63GB 64Pit | | 6'4" | 265 | Georgia Tech | | |
| Henson, Gary DE | 63Phi | | 6'3" | 200 | Colorado | | |
| Henson, Ken C | 65Pit | | 6'6" | 260 | Texas Christian | | |
| Hergert, Joe LB | 60-61BufA | 5 | 6'1" | 216 | Florida | 2 | 30 |
| Herman, Dave OG-OT | 64-69NY-A 70-73NYJ | | 6'2" | 255 | Michigan State | | |
| Herman, Dick LB | 65OakA | | 6'2" | 215 | Florida State | | |
| Hernandez, Joe FL | 64Was | | 6'2" | 180 | Arizona | | |
| Herndon, Don HB | 60NY-A | | 6' | 195 | Tampa | | 6 |
| Herock, Ken OE-TE | 63-65,67OakA 68CinA 69BosA | 2 | 6'2" | 230 | West Virginia | | 30 |
| Heron, Fred DT-DE | 66-72StL | | 6'4" | 255 | San Jose State | | |
| Herring, George QB | 60-61DenA | 1 4 | 6'2" | 200 | Southern Miss. | | 12 |
| Hester, Jim TE | 67-69NO 70ChiB | | 6'4" | 238 | North Dakota | | 18 |
| Hettema, Dave OT | 67SF 68-69MS 70Atl | | 6'4" | 249 | New Mexico | | |
| Hibler, Mike LB | 68CinA | | 6'1" | 235 | Stanford | | |
| Hickerson, Gene OG | 58-60Cle 61BL 62-73Cle | | 6'3" | 248 | Mississippi | | |
| Hickey, Bo FB | 67DenA | 2 | 5'11" | 225 | Maryland | | 30 |
| Hickl, Ray LB | 69-70NYG | | 6'2" | 215 | Texas A&I | | |
| Hickman, Larry FB | 59ChiC 60GB | | 6'2" | 227 | Baylor | | |
| Hicks, W.K. DB | 64-69HouA 70-72NYJ | | 6'1" | 191 | Texas Southern | 40 | |
| Higgins, Jim OG | 66MiaA | | 6'1" | 250 | Xavier-Ohio | | |
| Highsmith, Buzz OG-OT-C | 68-69DenA 72Hou | | 6'4" | 238 | Florida A&M | | |
| Hill, Dave OT | 63-69KC-A 70-74KC | | 6'5" | 259 | Auburn | | |
| Hill, Fred TE-OE-WR | 65-71Phi | 2 | 6'2" | 215 | Southern Calif. | | 30 |
| Hill, Gary DB | 65Min | | 6' | 200 | Southern Calif. | | |
| Hill, Jack HB | 61DenA | 5 | 6'1" | 185 | Utah State | | 31 |
| Hill, Jerry FB-HB | 61Bal 62JJ 63-70Bal | 2 | 5'11" | 212 | Wyoming | | 150 |
| Hill, Jimmy DB | 55-57ChiC 58AJ 59ChiC 60-64StL 65Det 66KC-A | | 6'2" | 192 | Sam Houston St. | 20 | 18 |
| Hill, King QB | 58-59ChiC 60StL 61-68Phi 68Min 69StL | 12 4 | 6'3" | 212 | Rice | | 54 |
| Hill, Mack Lee HB-FB | 64-65KC-A | 2 | 5'11" | 225 | Southern U. | | 54 |
| Died Dec. 14, 1965 after knee surgery | | | | | | | |
| Hill, Winston OT | 63-69NY-A 70-76NYJ 77LA | | 6'4" | 278 | Texas Southern | | |
| Hillebrand, Jerry LB | 63-66NYG 67StL 68-70Pit | | 6'3" | 240 | Colorado | 14 | 18 |
| Hilton, John TE | 65-69Pit 70GB 71Min 72-73Det 74WFL | 2 | 6'5" | 222 | Richmond | | 96 |
| Hindman, Stan DE-DT | 66-71,74SF | | 6'3" | 236 | Mississippi | 1 | 6 |
| Hines, Glen Ray OT | 66-69HouA 71-72NO 73Pit | | 6'5" | 264 | Arkansas | | |
| Hines, Jimmy WR | 69MiaA | | 6' | 175 | Texas Southern | | |
| Hinton, Chuck DT | 64-71Pit 71NYJ 72Bal | | 6'5" | 257 | N. Car. Central | 2 | 12 |
| Hinton, Chuck C | 67-69NYG | | 6'2" | 235 | Mississippi | | |
| Hoak, Dick HB | 61-70Pit | 12 | 5'11" | 191 | Penn State | | 198 |
| Hodgson, Pat OE | 66Was | | 6'2" | 190 | Georgia | | |
| Hoffman, Dalton FB | 64-65HouA | | 6' | 207 | Baylor | | 6 |
| Hohman, John OG | 65-66DenA | | 61" | 243 | Wisconsin | | |
| Hohn, Bob DB | 65-69Pit | | 6' | 187 | Nebraska | 7 | |
| Hoisington, Al OE | 60OakA 60BufA | | 6'3" | 200 | Pasadena City C. | | 12 |
| Holifield, Jim DB | 68-69NYG | | 6'3" | 195 | Jackson State | 1 | |
| Holler, Ed LB | 63GB 64Pit | 4 | 6'2" | 233 | South Carolina | 1 | |
| Holmes, John DE | 66MiaA | | 6'2" | 248 | Florida A&M | | |
| Holmes, Pat DE-DT | 66-69HouA 70-72Hou 73KC | | 6'5" | 254 | Texas Tech | 1 | |
| Holub, E.J. LB-C | 61-62DalA 63-69KC-A 70KC | | 6'4" | 231 | Texas Tech | 9 | |
| Holz, Gordy DT-OT | 60-63DenA 64NY-A | | 6'4" | 260 | Minnesota | 1 | |
| Holzer, Tom DE | 67SF 68JJ | | 6'4" | 250 | Louisville | | |
| Hooligan, Harry FB | 65HouA | | 6'2" | 225 | Bishop | | |
| Hopkins, Jerry LB | 63-66DenA 67MiaA 68OakA | | 6'2" | 236 | Texas A&M | 6 | |
| Hopkins, Roy FB | 67-69HouA 70Hou 71JJ | 2 | 6'1" | 233 | Texas Southern | | 48 |
| Hord, Roy OG | 60-62LA 62Phi 63NY-A | | 6'4" | 244 | Duke | | |
| Horner, Sam HB-DB | 60-61Was 62NYG | 234 | 6' | 197 | V.M.I. | | 6 |
| Hornung, Paul (The Golden Boy) HB-FB | 57-62GB 63SL 64-6GB | 12 5 | 6'2" | 215 | Notre Dame | | 760 |
| Horton, Bob LB | 64-65SD-A | | 6'2" | 230 | Boston U. | | |
| Houser, John OG-C | 57-59LA 60-61Dal 62JJ 63StL | | 6'3" | 239 | Redlands | | |
| Houston, Jim LB-DE-TE | 60-72Cle | | 6'2" | 239 | Ohio State | 14 | 25 |
| Howell, Lane OT-DT | 63-64NYG 65-69Phi | | 6'5" | 264 | Grambling | | |
| Howell, Mike DB | 65-72Cle 72Mia | | 6'1" | 189 | Grambling | 27 | |
| Howley, Chuck LB | 58-59ChiB 60JJ 61-73Dal | | 6'3" | 228 | West Virginia | 25 | |
| Hoyem, Lynn C-OG | 62-63Dal 64-67Phi | | 6'4" | 244 | Long Beach State | | |
| Huard, John LB | 67-69DenA 70-71JJ | | 6' | 220 | Maine | 6 | |
| Huarte, John QB | 66-67BosA 68Phi 70-71KC 72ChiB | 1 | 6' | 188 | Notre Dame | | |
| Hubbert, Brad FB | 67-69SD-A 70SD | 2 | 61" | 230 | Arizona | | 66 |
| Hudlow, Floyd DB-FL | 65BufA 67-68Atl | | 5'11" | 192 | Arizona | 2 | |
| Hudock, Mike C | 60-65NY-A 66MiaA 67KC-A | | 6'1" | 245 | Miami (Fla.) | | |
| Hudson, Bill DT | 61-62SD-A 63BosA | | 6'4" | 267 | Clemson | 1 | 6 |
| Hudson, Dick OT-OG | 62SD-A 63-67BufA | | 6'4" | 266 | Memphis State | | |
| Hudson, Jim DB | 65-69NY-A 70NYJ | | 6'2" | 210 | Texas | 14 | |
| Huey, Gene DB | 69SD-A | | 5'11" | 190 | Wyoming | | |
| Huff, Sam LB | 56-63NYG 64-67Was 68VR 69Was | | 6'1" | 230 | West Virginia | 30 | 30 |
| Hughes, Bob DE | 67,69Atl | | 6'4" | 253 | Jackson State | | |
| Hughes, Chuck WR | 67-69Phi 70-71Det | 2 | 5'11" | 173 | Texas-El Paso | | |
| Died Oct. 24, 1971 — heart attack | | | | | | | |
| Hughley, George HB | 65Was | 2 | 6'2" | 223 | Central St.-Okla. | | 6 |
| Hull, Bill DE | 62DalA | | 6'6" | 245 | Wake Forest | | |
| Hultz, Don DE-DT-LB | 63Min 64-73Phi 74ChiB | | 6'3" | 238 | Southern Miss. | 4 | 12 |
| Hultz, George DT | 62StL | | 6'4" | 250 | Southern Miss. | | |
| Humphrey, Buddy QB | 59-60LA 61-62Dal 63-65StL 66HouA | 1 | 6'1" | 198 | Baylor | | |
| Humphreys, Bob K | 67-68DenA | 5 | 6'1" | 240 | Wichita State | | 43 |
| Hunt, Bobby DB-HB | 62DalA 63-67KC-A 68-69CinA | | 6'1" | 188 | Auburn | 42 | 12 |
| Hunt, Jim (Earthquake) DT-DE | 60-69BosA 70Bos | | 5'11" | 249 | Prairie View | 1 | 14 |
| Hunter, Art C-OT-DT-DE | 54GB 55MS 56-59Cle 60-64LA 65Pit | | 6'4" | 243 | Notre Dame | | |
| Hunter, Bill FL-HB-DB | 65Was 66MiaA | | 6'1" | 183 | Syracuse | | 6 |
| Hurston, Chuck LB-DE | 65-69KC-A 70KC 71Buf | | 6'6" | 237 | Auburn | | |
| Husmann, Ed DT-OG-LB-DE | 53ChiC 54-55MS 56-59ChiC 60Dal 61-65HouA | | 6' | 235 | Nebraska | | |
| Hutchinson, Tom OE | 66Atl | 2 | 6'1" | 190 | Kentucky | | 12 |
| Huth, Jerry OG | 56NYG 57-58MS 59-60Phi 61-63Min | | 6' | 226 | Wake Forest | | 6 |
| Hynes, Paul DB | 61DalA 61-62NY-A | | 6'1" | 210 | Louisiana Tech | 2 | |
| Iacovazzi, Cosmo HB | 65NY-A | | 5'11" | 200 | Princeton | | |
| Ilg, Ray LB | 67-68BosA | | 6'1" | 220 | Colgate | | |
| Iman, Ken C | 60-63GB 64BH 65-74LA | | 6'1" | 236 | SE Missouri St. | | |
| Inman, Jerry DT | 66-69DenA 70-71Den 72JJ 73Den | | 6'3" | 255 | Oregon | | |
| Isbell, Joe Bob OG | 62-64Dal 65JJ 66Cle | | 6'1" | 238 | Houston | | |
| Izo, George QB | 60StL 61-64Was 65Det 66Pit | 1 | 6'3" | 218 | Notre Dame | | |

| Use Name (Nickname) - Positions | Team by Year | See Section | Hgt. | Wgt. | College | Int | Pts |
|---|---|---|---|---|---|---|---|
| Jackson, Bobby DB | 60Phi 61ChiB | | 6'1" | 190 | Alabama | | |
| Jackson, Bobby FB | 62-63SD-A 64HouA 64OakA 65HouA | 2 | 6'3" | 232 | New Mexico State | | 96 |
| Jackson, Frank FL-HB | 61-62DalA 63-65KC-A 66-67MiaA | 23 | 6'1" | 187 | S.M.U. | | 186 |
| Jackson, Jim DB-HB | 66-67SF | | 6' | 187 | Western Illinois | 1 | 6 |
| Jackson, Leroy HB | 62-63Was | 2 | 6' | 190 | Western Illinois | | 6 |
| Jackson, Rich DE-LB | 66OakA 67-69DenA 70-72Den 72Cle | | 6'2" | 252 | Southern U. | | 2 |
| Jackson, Roland FB-LB | 62StL | | 6' | 210 | Rice | | |
| Jackson, Steve LB | 66-67Was | | 6'1" | 225 | Texas-Arlington | 1 | |
| Jackson, T.J. FL-DB | 66Phi 67Was | | 6' | 180 | Illinois | | |
| Jackunas, Frank C | 62BufA 63DenA | | 6'3" | 225 | Detroit | | |
| Jacobs, Allen FB-HB | 65GB 66-67NYG | 2 | 6'1" | 215 | Utah | | 6 |
| Jacobs, Harry LB-DE | 60-62BosA 63-69BufA 72NO | | 6'2" | 228 | Bradley | 12 | |
| Jacobs, Proverb DT-OT | 58Phi 61NYG 61-62NY-A 63-64OakA | | 6'4" | 258 | California | | |
| Jacobs, Ray DT-DE | 63-66DenA 67-68MiaA 69BosA | | 6'3" | 276 | Howard Payne | | |
| Jacobson, Jack DB | 65SD-A | | 6'2" | 200 | Oklahoma State | | |
| Jagielski, Harry DT-OT | 56ChiC 56Was 60-61BosA 61OakA | | 6' | 257 | Indiana | 1 | |
| James, Claudis WR-HB-FL | 67-68GB | | 6'2" | 190 | Jackson State | | |
| James, Dan OT-C | 60-66Pit 67ChiB | | 6'4" | 262 | Ohio State | | |
| James, Dick HB-DB | 56-63Was 64NYG 65Min | 23 | 5'9" | 179 | Oregon | 12 | 204 |
| James, Nate DB | 68Cle | | 6'1" | 195 | Florida A&M | | |
| Jamison, Al OT | 60-62HouA | | 6'5" | 245 | Colgate | | |
| Jamieson, Dick QB | 60-61NY-A | 1 | 6'1" | 191 | Bradley | | |
| Jancik, Bobby DB-FL | 62-67HouA | 3 | 5'11" | 178 | Lamar | 15 | 6 |
| Janerette, Chuck DT-OT-OG | 60LA 61-62NYG 63NY-A 64-65SDenA | | 6'3" | 253 | Penn State | 2 | |
| Janik, Tom DB | 63-64DenA 65-68BufA 69BosA 70Bos 71NE | 4 | 6'3" | 198 | Texas A&M, Texas A&I | 25 | 36 |
| Jaquess, Pete DB | 64-65HouA 66-67MiaA 67-69DenA 70Den | | 6' | 182 | East. New Mexico | 16 | 12 |
| Jelacic, Jon DE-OG | 58NYG 61-64OakA | | 6'3" | 250 | Minnesota | 2 | 12 |
| Jencks, Bob OE-K | 63-64ChiB 65Was | 5 | 6'5" | 227 | Miami-Ohio | | 135 |
| Jeralds, Luther DE | 61DalA | | 6'3" | 235 | N. Car. Central | | |
| Jeter, Bob DB-FL-OE | 63-70GB 71-73ChiB | | 6'1" | 203 | Iowa | 26 | 12 |
| Jeter, Gene LB | 65-67DenA | | 6'3" | 230 | Ark.-Pine Bluff | | |
| Jeter, Tony TE | 66,68Pit | | 6'3" | 222 | Nebraska | | |
| Jobko, Bill LB | 58-62LA 63-65Min 66Atl | | 6'2" | 224 | Ohio State | 5 | |
| Joe, Billy FB | 63-64DenA 65BufA 66MiaA 67-68NY-A | 2 | 6'2" | 243 | Villanova | | 118 |
| Johns, Pete DB | 67-68HouA | | 6'3" | 189 | Tulane | | |
| Johnson, Billy DB | 66-68BosA | | 5'11" | 178 | Nebraska | 2 | |
| Johnson, Charley QB | 61-69StL 70-71Hou 72-75Den | 12 | 6' | 191 | New Mexico State | | 60 |
| Johnson, Charlie DT | 66-68SF | | 6'2" | 265 | Louisville | | |
| Johnson, Curley HB-TE-OE-FB-K | 60DalA 61-68NY-A 69NYG | 2 4 | 6' | 215 | Houston | | 26 |
| Johnson, Daryl DB | 68-69BosA 70Bos | | 5'11" | 190 | Morgan State | 5 | 8 |
| Johnson, Dick OE | 63KC-A | | 6'4" | 220 | Minnesota | | 6 |
| Johnson, Ellis HB-FL-OE | 65-66BosA | | 6'2" | 190 | Southeastern La. | | |
| Johnson, Gene DB | 59-60Phi 61Min 61NYG | | 6' | 187 | Cincinnati | 4 | |
| Johnson, Jay LB | 69-70Phi | | 6'3" | 230 | East Texas State | | |
| Johnson, Jimmy DB-FL | 61-76SF | 2 | 6'2" | 188 | U.C.L.A. | 47 | 38 |
| Johnson, John DT | 63-68ChiB 69NYG | | 6'5" | 260 | Indiana | | |
| Johnson, John Henry FB-HB-DB | 54-56SF 57-59Det 60-65Pit 66HouA | 2 | 6'2" | 210 | St. Mary's, Arizona State | | 330 |
| Johnson, Lee WR | 69-70SF | | 6'1" | 204 | Tennessee State | | |
| Johnson, Mike DB | 66-69Dal | | 5'10" | 185 | Kansas | 8 | |
| Johnson, Mitch OT-OG | 65Dal 66-67Was 69-70LA 71Cle 72Was | | 6'4" | 249 | Los Angeles State, U.C.L.A. | | |
| Johnson, Preston FB | 68BosA | | 6'2" | 230 | Florida A&M | | |
| Johnson, Rich HB-FB | 69HouA | | 6'1" | 210 | Illinois | | 6 |
| Johnson, Rudy HB | 64-65SF 66Atl | 2 | 5'11" | 190 | Nebraska | | 6 |
| Johnson, Walter DE | 67SF | | 6'4" | 225 | Tuskegee | | |
| Johnston, Mark DB | 60-63HouA 64OakA 64NY-A | | 6' | 201 | Northwestern | 13 | 12 |
| Johnston, Rex HB | 60Pit | | 6'1" | 195 | Southern Calif. | | |
| 1964 played major league baseball | | | | | | | |
| Jonas, Don HB | 62Phi | | 5'11" | 195 | Penn State | | |
| Jones, Bob WR-OE | 67-69ChiB | | 6'1" | 194 | San Diego State | | |
| Jones, Curtis LB | 68SD-A | | 6'2" | 245 | Missouri | | |
| Jones, Deacon DE | 61-71LA 72-73SD 74Was | | 6'5" | 254 | S. Carolina State, Miss. Valley State | 2 | 3 |
| Jones, Ezell OT | 69BosA 70Bos | | 6'4" | 255 | Minnesota | | |
| Jones, Gene LB | 61HouA | | 6' | 200 | Rice | | |
| Jones, Harry HB | 67-70Phi 71JJ | 2 | 6'2" | 205 | Arkansas | | |
| Jones, Henry FB | 69DenA | | 6'2" | 235 | Grambling | | |
| Jones, Homer WR-FL-OE | 64-69NYG 70Cle | 23 | 6'2" | 211 | Texas Southern | | 228 |
| Jones, Jerry OT-DT-DE | 66Atl 67-69NO | | 6'3" | 269 | Bowling Green | | |
| Jones, Jimmie OE-WR | 65-67ChiB 68DenA | 2 | 6'2" | 189 | Wisconsin | | 66 |
| Jones, Ron TE | 69GB | | 6'3" | 220 | Texas-El Paso | | |
| Jones, Stan OG-DT-OT | 54-65ChiB 66Was | | 6'1" | 252 | Maryland | | |
| Jones, Willie FB | 62BufA | | 5'11" | 208 | Purdue | | |
| Jones, Willie DT-DE | 67HouA 68CinA 70-71Cin | | 6'2" | 260 | Kansas State | | |
| Jordan, Henry DT-DE | 57-58Cle 59-69GB | | 6'3" | 249 | Virginia | | |
| Jordan, Jeff DB | 65-67Min | | 6'4" | 190 | Tulsa | | |
| Jordan, Jimmy HB | 67NO | | 6'1" | 200 | Florida | | |
| Jordan, Larry LB-DE | 62,64DenA | | 6'6" | 230 | Youngstown State | | |
| Jordan, Lee Roy LB | 63-76Dal | | 6'2" | 219 | Alabama | 32 | 20 |
| Josephson, Les FB-HB | 64-67LA 68FJ 69-74LA | 2 | 6' | 209 | Augustana (S.D.) | | 168 |
| Joswick, Bob DE-DT | 68-69MiaA | | 6'5" | 250 | Tulsa | | |
| Joyner, L.C. DB | 60OakA | | 6'1" | 197 | None | | |
| Julian, Fred DB | 60NY-A | | 5'9" | 185 | Michigan | 6 | |
| Junker, Steve OE | 57Det 58KJ 59-60Det 61-62Was | 2 | 6'3" | 217 | Xavier-Ohio | | 36 |
| Jurgensen, Sonny QB | 57-63Phi 64-74Was | 12 | 5'11" | 202 | Duke | | 90 |
| Kaimer, Karl DE | 62NY-A | | 6'3" | 230 | Boston U. | | |
| Kalsu, Bob OG | 68BufA 69MS | | 6'3" | 235 | Oklahoma | | |
| 1970 — Killed in action in Vietnam | | | | | | | |
| Kamanu, Lew DE | 67-68Det | | 6'4" | 245 | Weber State | | |
| Kammerer, Carl DE-LB | 61-62SF 63-69Was | | 6'3" | 240 | San Fran. State, U. of Pacific | 3 | |
| Kanicki, Jim DT | 63-69Cle 70-71NYG 72KJ | | 6'4" | 270 | Michigan State | | |
| Kantor, Joe FB | 66Was | | 6'1" | 217 | Notre Dame | | |
| Kapele, John DE-OT-DT | 60-62Pit 62Phi | | 6' | 240 | Utah, Brigham Young | | |
| Kapp, Joe QB | 67-69Min 70Bos 71HO | 12 | 6'2" | 214 | California | | 30 |
| Karas, Emil LB-DE | 59Was 60LA-A 61-64,66SD-A | | 6'3" | 230 | Dayton | 8 | |
| Karras, Alex DT | 58-62Det 63SL 64-70Det | | 6'2" | 248 | Iowa | 4 | 2 |

| Use Name (Nickname) - Positions | Team by Year | See Section | Hgt. | Wgt. | College | Int | Pts |
|---|---|---|---|---|---|---|---|
| Karras, Ted OG-OT-LB | 58-59Pit 60-64ChiB 65Det 66LA | | 6'1" | 240 | Indiana | | |
| Kasperak, Dick C | 66-68StL | | 6'3" | 225 | Iowa State | | |
| Kassulke, Karl DB | 63-72Min | | 6' | 194 | Drake | 19 | |
| 1973 — paralyzed in motorcycle accident | | | | | | | |
| Katcavage, Jim DE-DT | 56-68NYG | | 6'3" | 237 | Dayton | 1 | 12 |
| Katcik, Joe DT | 60NY-A | | 6'9" | 290 | Notre Dame | | |
| Keating, Bill OG-OT | 66-67DenA 67MiaA | | 6'2" | 236 | Michigan | | |
| Keckin, Val QB | 62SD-A | | 6'4" | 215 | Southern Miss. | | |
| Keating, Rex DB | 68CinA | | 6'3" | 220 | Samford | | |
| Kellerman, Ernie DB | 66-Cle 72Cin 73Buf | | 6' | 184 | Miami-Ohio | 19 | 6 |
| Kelley, Ed DB | 61-62DalA | | 6'2" | 195 | Texas | | |
| Kelley, Gorden LB | 60-61SF 62-63Was | | 6'3" | 230 | Georgia | 5 | |
| Kelley, Ike LB | 66-67Phi 68KJ 69-71Phi 72JJ | | 5'11" | 224 | Ohio State | 1 | |
| Kelley, Les LB | 67-69NO | | 6'3" | 233 | Alabama | 1 | |
| Kellogg, Mike FB | 66-67DenA | | 6' | 220 | Santa Clara | | |
| Kelly, Bob OT-DT | 61-64HouA 67KC-A 68CinA 69Atl | | 6'3" | 261 | New Mexico State | | |
| Kelly, Jim TE-OE | 64Pit, 65,67Phi | 2 | 6'2" | 216 | Notre Dame | | 30 |
| Kelly, Leroy HB-FB | 64-73Cle | 23 | 6' | 199 | Morgan State | | 540 |
| Kemp, Jack QB | 57Pit 58CFL 60LA-A 61-62SD-A 62-67BufA 68KJ 69BufA | 12 | 6'1" | 201 | Occidental | | 242 |
| Kempinski, Charlie OG | 60LA-A | | 6' | 235 | Mississippi | | |
| Kendall, Charlie DB | 60HouA | | 6'2" | 185 | U.C.L.A. | 2 | |
| Kenerson, John DE-OT | 60LA 62Pit 62NY-A | | 6'3" | 255 | Kentucky State | | |
| Kennedy, Tom QB | 66NYG 67JJ | 1 | 6'1" | 200 | Los Angeles State | | |
| Kent, Greg OT-DE | 66OakA 67CFL 68Det | | 6'6" | 270 | Wisconsin, Utah | | |
| Kerbow, Randy FL | 63HouA | | 6'1" | 190 | Rice | | |
| Kerr, Jim DB | 61-62Was | | 6' | 195 | Penn State | 8 | |
| Keyes, Bob HB | 60OakA | | 5'10" | 183 | San Diego State | | |
| Keyes, Jimmy LB | 68-69MiaA | 5 | 6'2" | 225 | Mississippi | | 51 |
| Keys, Brady DB-HB | 61-67Pit 67Min 68StL | 3 | 6' | 189 | Colorado State | 16 | |
| Keys, Howard (Sonny) C-OT-OG | 60-63Phi | | 6'3" | 239 | Oklahoma State | | |
| Khayat, Bob OG-C-K | 60,62-63Was | 5 | 6'2" | 230 | Mississippi | | 204 |
| Khayat, Ed DT-DE-OT | 57Was 58-61Phi 62-63Was 64-65Phi 66BosA HC71-72Phi | | 6'3" | 240 | Millsaps, Tulane | 1 | |
| Kilcullen, Bob DE-OT-DT | 57-58ChiB 59MS 60-66ChiB | | 6'3" | 245 | Texas Tech | | |
| Kilgore, Jon K | 65-67LA 68ChiB 69SF | 4 | 6'1" | 203 | Auburn | | |
| Killett, Charlie HB | 63NYG | | 6'1" | 205 | Memphis State | | |
| Killorin, Pat C | 66Pit | | 6'2" | 220 | Syracuse | | |
| Kimber, Bill OE | 59-60NYG 61BosA | | 6'2" | 192 | Florida State | | |
| Kimbrough, Elbert DB | 61LA 62-66SF 68NO | | 5'11" | 193 | Northwestern | 9 | |
| Kinderman, Keith FB-DB | 63-64SD-A 65HouA | | 6' | 213 | Florida State | | |
| Kindig, Howard DE-OT-C | 65-66SD 67-69BufA 70-71Buf 72Mia 73JJ 74NYJ | | 6'6" | 260 | Los Angeles State | 1 | |
| Kindricks, Bill OT | 68CinA | | 6'3" | 268 | Alabama A&M | | |
| King, Charlie DB | 66-67BufA 68-69CinA | | 6' | 185 | Purdue | 2 | 6 |
| King, Claude HB | 61HouA 62BosA | 2 | 5'11" | 190 | Houston | | 24 |
| King, Henry DB | 67NY-A | | 6'4" | 205 | Utah State | | |
| King, Phil (Chief) HB-FB | 58-63NYG 64Pit 65-66Min | 23 | 6'4" | 223 | Vanderbilt | | 96 |
| King, Tony FL | 67BufA | | 6'1" | 194 | Findlay | | |
| Kinney, George DE | 65HouA | | 6'4" | 250 | Wiley | | |
| Kirby, John LB | 64-69Min 69-70NYG | | 6'3" | 229 | Nebraska | | |
| Kirchiro, Bill OG | 62Bal | | 6'1" | 235 | Maryland | | |
| Kirk, Ken LB-C | 60-61ChiB 62Pit 63LA | | 6'2" | 229 | Mississippi | | |
| Kirner, Gary OT-OG | 64-69SD-A | | 6'3" | 249 | Southern Calif. | | |
| Kirouac, Lou OG-OT | 63NYG 64Bal 65JJ 66-67Atl | 5 | 6'3" | 238 | Boston College | | 46 |
| Klein, Dick OT | 58-59ChiB 60Dal 61Pit 61-62BosA 63-64OakA | | 6'4" | 254 | Georgia, Iowa | | |
| Klotz, Jack OT | 60-62NY-A 62SD-A 63NY-A 64HouA | | 6'5" | 256 | Widener | | |
| Kochman, Roger HB | 63BufA | 2 | 6'2" | 205 | Penn State | | |
| Kocourek, Dave OE-TE | 60LA-A 61-65SD-A 66MiaA 67-68OakA | 2 | 6'5" | 237 | Wisconsin | | 150 |
| Koeper, Rich OT | 66Atl | | 6'4" | 245 | Oregon State | | |
| Koman, Bill LB | 56Bal 57-58Phi 59ChiC 60-67StL | | 6'2" | 229 | North Carolina | 7 | |
| Kompara, John DT | 60LA-A | | 6'2" | 245 | South Carolina | | |
| Koontz, Ed LB | 68BosA | | 6'2" | 230 | Catawba | | |
| Koontz, Joe WR | 68NYG | | 6'1" | 192 | San Fran. State | | |
| Kopay, Dave HB-FB | 64-67SF 68Det 69-70Was 72NO 72GB | 2 | 6'2" | 220 | Washington | | 48 |
| Kortas, Ken DT | 64StL 65-68Pit 69ChiB | | 6'2" | 282 | Louisville | | 6 |
| Kosens, Terry DB | 63Min | | 6'3" | 195 | Hofstra | | |
| Kostelnik, Ron DT | 61-68GB 69Bal | | 6'4" | 260 | Cincinnati | | |
| Kotite, Rich TE-LB | 67NYG 68Pit 69,71-72NYG HC 91-94Phi HC 95NYJ | 2 | 6'3" | 233 | Miami (Fla.), Wagner | | 30 |
| Kovac, Ed HB-DB | 60Bal 62NY-A | | 6' | 199 | Cincinnati | 1 | |
| Kowalczyk, Walt FB-DB | 58-59Phi 60Dal 61OakA | 2 | 6' | 208 | Michigan State | 1 | 18 |
| Koy, Ernie HB-FB | 65-70NYG | 234 | 6'2" | 228 | Texas | | 90 |
| Krakoski, Joe DB | 61Was 63-66OakA | | 6'2" | 196 | Illinois | 8 | |
| Kramer, Jerry OG | 58-68GB | 5 | 6'3" | 246 | Idaho | | 177 |
| Kramer, Ron OE-TE | 57GB 58MS 59-64GB 65-67Det | 2 | 6'3" | 234 | Michigan | | 96 |
| Kreitling, Rich OE | 59-63Cle 64ChiB | 2 | 6'2" | 208 | Auburn, Illinois | | 102 |
| Kremser, Karl K | 69MiaA 70Mia | 5 | 6' | 178 | Army, Tennessee | | 67 |
| Kriewald, Doug OG | 67-68ChiB | | 6'4" | 245 | West Texas State | | |
| Krisher, Billy OG | 58Pit 60-61DalA | | 6'1" | 233 | Oklahoma | | |
| Kroll, Alex C-OT | 62NY-A | | 6'3" | 230 | Rutgers | | |
| Kroner, Gary DB-K | 65-67DenA | 5 | 6'1" | 200 | Wisconsin | | 144 |
| Krueger, Charlie DT-DE | 59-73SF | | 6'4" | 256 | Texas A&M | 1 | 12 |
| Krupa, Joe DT | 56-64Pit | | 6'2" | 232 | Purdue | | |
| Kruse, Bob OG-OT | 67-68OakA 69BufA | | 6'2" | 250 | Colorado State, Wayne State-Neb. | | |
| Kubala, Ray C | 64-67DenA | | 6'4" | 245 | Texas A&M | | |
| Kuechenberg, Rudy LB | 67-69ChiB 70GB 71Atl | | 6'2" | 215 | Indiana | | |
| Kulbacki, Joe HB | 60BufA | 2 | 6' | 185 | Purdue | | 6 |
| Kurek, Ralph FB | 65-70ChiB | 2 | 6'2" | 210 | Wisconsin | | 12 |
| Lacey, Bob OE | 64Min 65NYG | | 6'3" | 205 | North Carolina | | |
| Ladd, Ernie DT | 61-65SD-A 66-67HouA 67-68KC-A | | 6'9" | 302 | Grambling | 1 | |
| Lage, Dick OE | 61StL | | 6'4" | 222 | Lenoir Ryhne | | |
| Lakes, Roland DT-OT-OE | 61-70SF 71NYG | | 6'4" | 267 | Wichita State | | 6 |
| LaLonde, Roger DT | 64Det 65NYG | | 6'3" | 255 | Muskingum | | |
| Lamb, Mack DB | 67-68MiaA | | 6'1" | 188 | Tennessee State | 1 | |
| Lambert, Frank K | 65-66Pit | 4 | 6'3" | 200 | Mississippi | | |
| Lambert, Gordon (Pig) LB | 68-69DenA | | 6'5" | 245 | West Virginia, Tennessee-Martin | | |
| Lamberti, Pat LB | 61NY-A 61DenA | | 6'2" | 225 | Richmond | 1 | |
| Lammons, Pete TE | 67-60NY-A 70-71NYJ 72GB | 2 | 6'3" | 229 | Texas | | 84 |
| Lamonica, Daryle QB | 63-66BufA 67-69OakA 70-74Oak | 12 4 | 6'2" | 215 | Notre Dame | | 90 |
| Lamson, Chuck DB | 62-63Min 64JJ 65-67LA 68JJ | | 6' | 189 | Iowa State, Wyoming | 11 | 6 |
| Lane, Bobby LB | 63-64SD-A | | 6'2" | 222 | Baylor | | |
| Lane, Gary QB | 66-67Cle 68NYG | 1 | 6'1" | 210 | Missouri | | |

| Use Name (Nickname) - Positions | Team by Year | See Section | Hgt. | Wgt. | College | Int | Pts |
|---|---|---|---|---|---|---|---|
| Lang, Izzy FB-HB | 64-68Phi 69LA | 2 | 6'1" | 231 | Tennessee State | | 48 |
| Lanphear, Dan DE | 60,62HouA | | 6'2" | 225 | Wisconsin | | |
| Lapham, Bill C | 60Phi 61Min | | 6'3" | 250 | Drake, Iowa | | |
| Laraba, Bob LB-QB-HB | 60LA-A 61SD-A | | 6'3" | 195 | Texas-El Paso | 6 | 19 |
| Died Feb. 16, 1962 — auto accident | | | | | | | |
| Laraway, Jack LB | 60BufA 61HouA | | 6'1" | 218 | Purdue | 1 | |
| LaRose, Dan DE-OT-OG | 61-63Det 64Pit 65SF 66DenA | | 6'5" | 250 | Missouri | | |
| Larpenter, Carl OG-OT | 61-62DenA 62DalA | | 6'4" | 237 | Texas | | |
| Larscheid, Jack HB | 60-61OakA | 23 | 5'6" | 162 | U. of Pacific | | 12 |
| Larsen, Gary DT | 64LA 65-74Min | | 6'5" | 256 | Concordia (Minn.) | | |
| Larson, Bill FB | 60BosA | | 5'10" | 190 | Illinois Wesleyan | | |
| Larson, Greg C-OG-OT | 61-73NYG | | 6'2" | 249 | Minnesota | | |
| Larson, Pete HB | 67-68Was | 2 | 6'1" | 200 | Cornell | | 18 |
| Lasky, Frank OT | 64-65NYG | | 6'2" | 265 | Florida | | |
| Lasse, Dick LB | 58-59Pit 60-61Was 62NYG | | 6'2" | 222 | Syracuse | 3 | |
| Lassiter, Ike DE-DT | 62-64DenA 65-69OakA 70Bos 71NE | | 6'5" | 270 | St. Augustine | 1 | |
| Latourette, Chuck DB-WR | 67-68,70-71StL | 34 | 6' | 190 | Rice | | 12 |
| Latzke, Paul C | 66-68SD-A | | 6'4" | 242 | U. of Pacific | | |
| Lavan, Al DB | 69-70Atl | | 6'1" | 194 | Colorado State | 5 | |
| Lawrence, Don DT-OG-OT | 59-61Was | | 6'1" | 245 | Notre Dame | | |
| Lawrence, Kent WR | 69Phi 70Atl | | 5'11" | 175 | Georgia | | |
| Lawson, Al FL | 64NY-A | | 5'11" | 190 | Delaware State | | |
| Lawson, Jerry DB | 68BufA | | 5'11" | 192 | Utah | | |
| LeBeau, Dick DB | 59-72Det | | 6'1" | 185 | Ohio State | 62 | 14 |
| LeClair, Jim QB | 67-68DenA | 1 | 6'1" | 208 | C.W. Post | | 6 |
| LeClerc, Roger LB-C-DT | 60-66ChiB 67DenA | 5 | 6'3" | 236 | Trinity (Conn.) | | 382 |
| Ledbetter, Monte WR-FL | 67HouA 67-69BufA 69Atl | 2 | 6'2" | 185 | Northwestern La. | | 18 |
| Lee, Bob OG | 60BosA | | 6'1" | 245 | Missouri | | |
| Lee, Bob WR | 68StL 69Atl | | 6'3" | 200 | Minnesota | | |
| Lee, Dwight HB | 68SF 68Atl | | 6'2" | 198 | Michigan State | | |
| Lee, Herman OT-OG | 57Pit 58-66ChiB | | 6'4" | 244 | Florida A&M | | |
| Lee, Jacky QB | 60-63HouA 64-65DenA 66-67HouA | 12 | 6'1" | 186 | Cincinnati | | 18 |
| | 67-69KC-A | | | | | | |
| Lee, Monte LB | 61StL 62MS 63-64Det 65Bal | | 6'4" | 221 | Texas | 1 | |
| Leetzow, Max DE-DT | 65-66DenA 67JJ | | 6'4" | 240 | Idaho | | |
| Leeuwenberg, Dick OT | 65ChiB | | 6'5" | 242 | Stanford | | |
| Leftridge, Dick FB | 66Pit | | 6'2" | 240 | West Virginia | | |
| Leggett, Earl DT-DE | 57-60ChiB 61KJ 62-65ChiB | | 6'3" | 254 | Louisiana State | 1 | 2 |
| Lemek, Ray OT-OG | 57-61Was 62-65Pit | | 6' | 238 | Notre Dame | | |
| Lemm, Wally | HC61HouA HC62-65StL | | | | Carroll (Wis.) | | |
| | HC66-69HouA HC70Hou | | | | | | |
| Lemmerman, Bruce QB | 68-69Atl | 1 | 6'1" | 196 | Northridge State | | |
| LeMoine, Jim OG-LB-TE | 67BufA 68-69HouA | | 6'2" | 245 | Utah State | | |
| Lentz, Jack DB | 67-68DenA | | 6' | 195 | Holy Cross | 5 | |
| Leo, Bobby HB-WR | 67-68BosA | | 5'10" | 180 | Harvard | | 6 |
| Leo, Charlie /G | 60-62BosA 63BufA | | 6' | 238 | Indiana | | |
| Leo, Jim DE-LB | 60NYG 61-62Min | | 6'1" | 222 | Cincinnati | | |
| Lester, Darrell FB | 64Min 65-66DenA | 2 | 6'2" | 223 | McNeese State | | 6 |
| Letner, Cotton LB | 61BufA | | 6'1" | 215 | Tennessee | | |
| Lewis, Dan HB | 58-64Det 65Was 66NYG | 23 | 6'1" | 199 | Wisconson | | 144 |
| Lewis, Gary FB-HB | 64-69SF 70NO | 23 | 6'3" | 228 | Washington State, | | 108 |
| | | | | | Arizona State | | |
| Lewis, Hal DB | 68DenA | | 6'2" | 188 | Arizona State | | |
| Lewis, Harold HB-DB | 59Bal 60BufA 62OakA | | 6' | 200 | Houston | | |
| Lewis, Joe DT | 58-60Pit 61Bal 62Phi | | 6'2" | 256 | Compton C.C. | 1 | 6 |
| Lewis, Sherman DB | 66-67NY-A | | 5'10" | 180 | Michigan State | | |
| Lilly, Bob DT-DE | 61-74Dal | | 6'4" | 256 | Texas Christian | 1 | 24 |
| Lince, Dave TE | 66-67Phi | | 6'6" | 258 | North Dakota | | |
| Lincoln, Keith HB-FB | 61-66SD-A 67-68BufA 68SD-A | 23 5 | 6'2" | 212 | Washington State | | 271 |
| Lind, Mike FB | 63-64SF 65-66Pit | 2 | 6'2" | 220 | Notre Dame | | 54 |
| Linden, Errol OT | 61Cle 62-65Min 66-68Atl 69-70NO | | 6'5" | 258 | Houston | | |
| Lindquist, Paul DT | 61BosA | | 6'3" | 265 | New Hampshire | | |
| Lindsey, Dale LB | 65-72Cle 73NO | | 6'3" | 224 | Kentucky, | 8 | 6 |
| | | | | | Western Kentucky | | |
| Lindsey, Hub HB | 68DenA | | 5'11" | 196 | Wyoming | | |
| Lindsey, Jim HB-FB | 66-72Min | 2 | 6'2" | 206 | Arkansas | | 66 |
| Linne, Aubrey OE | 61Bal | | 6'7" | 235 | Texas Christian | | |
| Lisbon, Don HB | 63-64SF | 2 | 6' | 194 | Bowling Green | | 18 |
| Liscio, Tony OT-OG | 63-64Dal 65JJ 66-71Dal | | 6'5" | 251 | Tulsa | | |
| Liske, Pete QB | 64NY-A 65-68CFL 69DenA 70Den 71-72Phi | 12 | 6'2" | 199 | Penn State | | 12 |
| Livingston, Andy FB-HB | 64-65ChiB 66KJ | 2 | 6' | 234 | Phoenix Coll. | | 66 |
| | 67-68ChiB 69-70NO | | | | | | |
| Livingston, Cliff LB-DE | 54-61NYG 62Min 63-65LA | | 6'3" | 212 | U.C.L.A. | 8 | 6 |
| Livingston, Dale K | 68-69CinA 70GB | 45 | 6' | 210 | Eastern Michigan, | | 123 |
| | | | | | Western Michigan | | |
| Livingston, Walt HB | 60BosA | | 6' | 185 | Heidelberg | | |
| Livingston, Warren DB | 61-66Dal | | 5'10" | 185 | Arizona | 10 | 6 |
| Lloyd, Dave LB-C | 59-61Cle 62Det 63-70Phi | | 6'3" | 247 | Texas Tech, | 14 | 10 |
| | | | | | Georgia | | |
| Lockett, J.W. FB | 61SF 61-62Dal 63Bal 64Was | 2 | 6'2" | 229 | Central St.-Ohio | | 60 |
| Locklin, Billy LB | 60OakA | | 6'2" | 225 | New Mexico State | | |
| Lofton, Oscar OE | 60BosA 61-62MS | 2 | 6'6" | 218 | Southeastern La. | | 24 |
| Logan, Chuck TE-OE | 64Pit 65,67-68StL | | 6'4" | 215 | Northwestern | | |
| Logan, Jerry DB | 63-72Bal | 3 | 6'1" | 188 | West Texas State | 34 | 36 |
| Logan, Obert DB | 65-66Dal 67NO | | 5'10" | 180 | Trinity (Texas) | 8 | 6 |
| Lomakoski, John OT | 62Det | | 6'4" | 250 | Western Michigan | | |
| Lombardi, Vince | HC59-67GB HC69Was | | | | Fordham | | |
| Died Sept. 3, 1970 — Cancer | | | | | | | |
| London, Mike LB | 66SD-A | | 6'2" | 230 | Wisconsin | | |
| Long, Bob FL-WR | 64-67GB 68Atl 69Was 70LA | 2 | 6'3" | 199 | Wichita State | | 60 |
| Long, Charley OG-OT | 61-69BosA | | 6'3" | 247 | Tenn.-Chattanooga | | |
| Long, Dave DE-DT | 66-68StL 69-72NO | | 6'4" | 241 | Iowa | | |
| Long, Mike OE | 60BosA | | 6' | 188 | Brandeis | | |
| Longenecker, Ken DT | 60Pit | | 6'4" | 285 | Lebanon Valley | | |
| Longmire, Sam DB-WR | 67-68KC-A | | 6'3" | 195 | Purdue | | |
| Look, Dean QB | 62NY-A | | 5'11" | 185 | Michigan State | | |
| 1961 — Played major league baseball | | | | | | | |
| Looney, Joe Don FB-HB | 64Bal 65-66Det 66-67Was | 234 | 6'1" | 230 | Texas, | | 78 |
| | 68MS 69NO | | | | Texas Christian, | | |
| | | | | | Oklahoma | | |
| Lopasky, Bill OG | 61SF | | 6'2" | 235 | West Virginia | | |
| Lorick, Tony FB | 64-67Bal 68-69NO | 23 | 6'1" | 214 | Arizona State | | 114 |
| Lothamer, Ed DT-DE | 64-69KC-A 71-72KC | | 6'5" | 261 | Michigan State | | . |
| Lothridge, Billy QB-DB-K | 64Dal 65LA 66-71Atl 72Mia | 4 | 6'1" | 194 | Georgia Tech | 3 | 6 |
| Lott, Billy FB-HB-DB | 58NYG 60OakA 61-63BosA | 2 | 6' | 203 | Mississippi | | 128 |
| Loudd, Rommie LB | 60LA-A 61-62BosA | | 6'3" | 227 | U.C.L.A. | 4 | |
| Louderback, Tom LB-C-OG | 58-59Phi 60-61OakA 62BufA | | 6'2" | 235 | San Jose State | 3 | 6 |
| Loukas, Angelo OG-OT | 69BufA 70Bos | | 6'3" | 250 | Northwestern | | |
| Love, John FL-WR-DB | 67Was 68MS 72LA | 23 5 | 5'11" | 185 | North Texas | | 40 |
| Lovetere, John DT | 59-62LA 63-65NYG | | 6'4" | 280 | Compton C.C. | | 6 |
| Lowe, Gary DB-HB | 56-57Was 57-64Det | | 5'11" | 196 | Michigan State | 20 | 2 |
| Lowe, Paul HB | 60LA-A 61SD-A 62BA 63-67SD-A | 23 | 6' | 200 | Oregon State | | 282 |
| | 68-69KC-A | | | | | | |
| Lucas, Dick OE | 58Pit 60-63Pit | 2 | 6'2" | 213 | Boston College | | 36 |
| Lucas, Richie QB-HB-DB | 60-61BufA | 12 | 6' | 190 | Penn State | 2 | 30 |
| Lucci, Mike LB | 62-64Cle 65-73Det | | 6'2" | 230 | Pittsburgh, | 21 | 24 |
| | | | | | Tennessee | | |
| Luce, Lew HB | 61Was | | 6' | 187 | Penn State | | |
| Luke, Tommy DB | 68DenA | | 6' | 190 | Mississippi | | |
| Lundy, Lamar DE-OE | 57-69LA | 2 | 6'7" | 245 | Purdue | 3 | 54 |
| Lusteg, Booth K | 66BufA 67MiaA 68Pit 69GB | 5 | 5'11" | 190 | None | | 202 |
| Lyles, Lenny DB-HB | 58Bal 59-60SF 61-69Bal | 23 | 6'2" | 202 | Louisville | 16 | 48 |
| Lynch, Dick DB | 58Was 59-66NYG | | 6'1" | 202 | Notre Dame | 37 | 42 |
| Mack, Red FL-OE-HB | 61-63Pit 64Phi | 2 | 5'10" | 185 | Notre Dame | | 48 |
| | 65Pit 66Atl 66GB | | | | | | |
| Mackbee, Earsell DB | 65-69Min | | 6'1" | 195 | Utah State | 15 | 12 |
| Mackey, Dee OE | 60SF 61-62Bal 63-66NY-A | 2 | 6'5" | 232 | East Texas State | | 50 |
| Mackey, John TE-OE | 63-71Bal 72SD | 2 | 6'3" | 222 | Syracuse | | 228 |
| MacKinnon, Jacque TE-DE-FB-OG | 61-69SD-A 70Oak | 2 | 6'4" | 245 | Colgate | | 134 |
| Maczuzak, John DT | 64KC-A | | 6'5" | 250 | Pittsburgh | | |
| Magac, Mike OG | 60-64SF 65-66Pit | | 6'3" | 240 | Missouri | | |
| Maguire, Paul LB-DE-OE-K | 60LA-A 61-63SD-A | 4 | 6' | 224 | The Citadel | 9 | 6 |
| | 64-69BufA 70Buf | | | | | | |
| Maher, Bruce DB-HB | 60-67Det 68-69NYG | | 5'11" | 190 | Detroit | 22 | 6 |
| Majors, Billy DB | 61BufA | | 6' | 175 | Tennessee | | |
| Mallick, Fran DE-DT | 65Pit | | 6'3" | 245 | none | | |
| Mallory, John DB | 68Phi 69-71Atl | 3 | 6' | 188 | West Virginia | 2 | 24 |
| Mangum, John DT | 66-67BosA | | 6'3" | 273 | Southern Miss. | | |
| Mankins, Jim FB | 67Atl | | 6'1" | 235 | Florida State | | |
| Manning, Pete DB | 60-61ChiB | | 6'3" | 208 | Wake Forest | | |
| Manoukian, Don OG | 60OakA | | 5'9" | 242 | Stanford | | |
| Maples, Jim (Butch) LB | 63Bal | | 6'4" | 225 | Baylor | | |
| Marchiewski, Frank C | 65LA 66-68Atl 68-69LA 70Buf | | 6'2" | 237 | Minnesota | | |
| Marconi, Joe FB-HB | 56-61LA 62-66ChiB | 2 | 6'2" | 225 | West Virginia | | 234 |
| Marcontell, Ed OG | 67StL 67HouA | | 6' | 220 | Lamar | | |
| Marinovich, Marv OG | 65OakA | | 6'3" | 250 | Southern Calif. | | |
| Marion, Jerry FL | 67Pit | | 5'10" | 175 | Wyoming | | |
| Marques, Bob LB | 60NY-A | | 6' | 220 | Boston U. | | |
| Marsh, Aaron WR | 68-69BosA | 2 | 6' | 190 | Eastern Kentucky | | 24 |
| Marsh, Amos HB-FB | 61-64Dal 65-67Det | 23 | 6' | 218 | Oregon State | | 198 |
| Marsh, Frank DB | 67SD-A | | 6'2" | 205 | Oregon State | | |
| Marshall, Bud DT | 65GB 66Was 66Atl 67-68HouA | | 6'5" | 271 | Baylor, | | |
| | | | | | S.F. Austin State | | |
| Marshall, Chuck DB | 62DenA | | 6' | 180 | Oregon State | | |
| Marshall, Jim DE | 60Cle 61-79Min | | 6'3" | 239 | Ohio State | 1 | 8 |
| Martha, Paul DB-FL-OE-HB | 64-69Pit 70Den | 2 | 6' | 186 | Pittsburgh | 21 | 6 |
| Martin, Aaron DB | 64-65LA 66-67Phi 68Was | 3 | 6' | 187 | N. Car. Central | | |
| Martin, Billy TE-OE | 64-65ChiB | 2 4 | 6'4" | 238 | Georgia Tech | | 24 |
| | 66-67Atl 68Min | | | | | | |
| Martin, Billy HB | 62-64ChiB | 3 | 5'11" | 196 | Minnesota | | 6 |
| Martin, Blanche FB | 60NY-A 60LA-A | | 6' | 195 | Michigan State | | 6 |
| Martin, Dave LB | 68KC-A 69ChiB | | 6' | 220 | Notre Dame | | |
| Martin, Larry DT | 68SD-A | | 6'2" | 270 | San Diego State | | |
| Mason, Tommy HB-FB | 61-66Min 67-70LA 71Was 72JJ | 23 | 6' | 195 | Tulane | | 270 |
| Masters, Norm OT | 57-64GB | | 6'2" | 249 | Michigan State | | |
| Matan, Bill DE | 66NYG | | 6'4" | 240 | Kansas State | | |
| Mathis, Bill HB-FB | 60-69NY-A | 2 | 6'1" | 219 | Clemson | | 282 |
| Matsos, Archie LB | 60-62BufA 63-65OakA | | 6' | 215 | Michigan State | 22 | 6 |
| | 66DenA 66SD-A | | | | | | |
| Matte, Tom HB-QB | 61-72Bal | 123 | 6' | 207 | Ohio State | | 342 |
| Matthews, Wes OE | 66MiaA | | 5'10" | 180 | Northwestern Okla | | |
| Mattox, Jack DT | 61DenA | | 6'4" | 240 | Fresno State | | |
| Mattson, Riley OT | 61-64Was 65JJ 66ChiB | | 6'4" | 252 | Oregon | | |
| Mayberry, Doug FB | 61-62Min 63OakA | 2 | 6'1" | 223 | California, | | 12 |
| | | | | | Utah State | | |
| Mayes, Ben DE-DT | 69HouA | | 6'5" | 265 | Duke | | |
| Maynard, Don FL-WR-OE-HB | 58NYG 60-69NY-A | 23 | 6' | 180 | Rice, | | 532 |
| | 70-72NYJ 73StL | | | | Texas-El Paso | | |
| Mays, Jerry DE-DT | 61-62DalA 63-69KC-A 70KC | | 6'4" | 250 | S.M.U. | 1 | 6 |
| Mazurek, Fred FL-DB | 65-66Was | | 5'11" | 192 | Catholic, | | |
| | | | | | Pittsburgh | | |
| Mazzanti, Jerry DE | 63Phi 64-65MS 66Det 67Pit | | 6'3" | 240 | Arkansas | | |
| McAdams, Bob DT | 63-64NY-A | | 6'3" | 250 | N. Car. Central | | |
| McAdams, Carl LB-DT-DE | 67-69NY-A | | 6'3" | 240 | Oklahoma | | |
| McBride, Norm DE | 69MiaA 70Mia | | 6'3" | 240 | Utah | | |
| McCall, Don HB | 67-68NO 69Pit 70NO | 23 | 5'11" | 195 | Southern Calif. | | 60 |
| McCall, Ron LB | 67-68SD-A | | 6'2" | 245 | Weber State | | |
| McCambridge, John DE | 67Det | | 6'4" | 245 | Northwestern | | |
| McCann, Tim DT | 69NYG | | 6'5" | 265 | Princeton | | |
| McCarthy, Brandan FB | 68Atl 68-69SD-A | 2 | 6'3" | 220 | Boston College | | 18 |
| McCarty, Mickey TE | 69KC-A | | 6'5" | 255 | Texas Christian | | |
| McClellan, Mike DB | 62-63Phi 64-65MS | | 6'1" | 185 | Oklahoma | 4 | |
| McClinton, Curtis FB-TE | 62DalA 63-69KC-A | 2 | 6'3" | 230 | Kansas | | 196 |
| McCloughan, Kent DB | 65-69OakA 70Oak | | 6'1" | 190 | Nebraska | 15 | |
| McClure, Wayne LB | 68CinA 70Cin | | 6'1" | 225 | Mississippi | | |
| McComb, Don DE | 60BosA | | 6'4" | 240 | Villanova | | |
| McCord, Darris DE-DT-OT | 55-67Det | | 6'4" | 247 | Tennessee | 3 | 8 |
| McCormick, Dave OT | 66SF 67-68NO | | 6'6" | 250 | Louisiana State | | |
| McCormick, John QB | 62Min 63DenA 64KJ | 1 4 | 6'1" | 201 | Massachusetts | | |
| McCoy, Lloyd OG | 64SD-A | | 6'1" | 245 | San Diego State | | |
| McCreary, Bob OT | 61Bal | | 6'5" | 256 | Wake Forest | | |
| McCullers, Dale LB | 69MiaA | | 6'1" | 215 | Florida State | | |
| McCullough, Bob OG | 62-65DenA | | 6'5" | 244 | Colorado | | |
| McCusker, Jim OT | 58ChiC 59-62Phi 63Cle 64NY-A | | 6'2" | 246 | Pittsburgh | | |
| McDaniel, Wahoo LB-OG | 60HouA 61-63DenA | 4 | 6' | 235 | Oklahoma | 13 | 6 |
| | 64-65NY-A 66-68MiaA | | | | | | |
| McDaniels, Dave WR | 68Dal | | 6'4" | 200 | Miss. Valley State | | |
| McDermott, Gary HB | 68BufA 69Atl | 2 | 6'1" | 211 | Tulsa | 26 | |
| McDole, Ron DE-DT | 61StL 62HouA 63-69BufA | | 6'3" | 266 | Nebraska | 11 | 14 |
| | 70Buf 71-77Was | | | | | | |
| McDonald, Don DB | 61BufA | | 5'11" | 185 | Houston | | |
| McDonald, Ray FB | 67-68Was | 2 | 6'4" | 248 | Idaho | | 24 |
| McDonald, Tommy FL-HB-WR | 57-63Phi 64Dal 65-66LA | 23 | 5'10" | 176 | Oklahoma | | 510 |
| McDougall, Gerry FB | 62-64,68SD-A | 2 | 6'2" | 225 | U.C.L.A. | | 38 |
| McDowell, John OT-OG | 64GB 65NYG 66StL | | 6'3" | 260 | St. John's-Minn. | | |
| McFadin, Bud DT-DG-OG-LB | 52-56LA 60-63DenA | | 6'3" | 260 | Texas | 1 | 24 |
| | 64-65HouA | | | | | | |

| Use Name (Nickname) - Positions | Team by Year | See Section | Hgt. | Wgt. | College | Int | Pts |
|---|---|---|---|---|---|---|---|
| McFarland, Kay FL-OE-WR | 62-66SF 67JJ 68SF | 2 | 6'2" | 182 | Colorado State | | 24 |
| McFarlane, Nyle HB | 60OakA | | 6'2" | 205 | Brigham Young | | 12 |
| McGee, Ben DE-DT | 64-72Pit | | 6'2" | 255 | Jackson State | 1 | 6 |
| McGee, George OT | 60BosA 61-62MS | | 6'2" | 259 | Southern U. | | |
| McGee, Max OE | 54GB 55-56MS 57-67GB | 2 4 | 6'3" | 205 | Tulane | | 306 |
| McGee, Mike OG | 60-62StL | | 6'1" | 230 | Duke | | |
| McGeever, John DB | 62-65DenA 66MiaA | | 6'1" | 195 | Auburn | 11 | 6 |
| McGrew, Dan C | 60BufA | | 6'2" | 250 | Purdue | | |
| McIlhany, Danny DB | 65LA | | 6'1" | 195 | Texas A&M | 2 | |
| McInnis, Hugh OE-TE | 60-62StL 64Det 66Atl | 2 | 6'3" | 219 | Southern Miss. | | |
| McKeever, Marlin LB-TE-OE | 61-66LA 67Min 68-70Was 71-72LA 73Phi | 2 | 6'1" | 233 | Southern Calif. | 9 | 36 |
| McKinnon, Don LB-C | 63-64BosA | | 6'3" | 223 | Dartmouth | | |
| McLenna, Bruce HB | 66Det | | 6'3" | 225 | Michigan, Hillsdale | | |
| McLeod, Bob OE-TE | 61-66HouA | 2 | 6'5" | 231 | Abilene Christian | | 114 |
| McMahon, Art DB | 68-69BosA 70Bos 72NE | | 5'11" | 188 | N. Carolina State | 3 | |
| McMillan, Ernie OT | 61-74StL 75GB | | 6'6" | 258 | Illinois | | |
| McMillin, Jim DB | 61-62DenA 63-64OakA 64-65DenA | | 5'11" | 190 | Colorado State | 14 | 24 |
| McMullan, John OG | 60-61NY-A | | 6' | 244 | Notre Dame | | |
| McMurtry, Chuck DT | 60-61BufA 62-63OakA | | 6' | 286 | Whittier | | |
| McNamara, Bob DB-HB | 60-61DenA | | 6' | 189 | Minnesota | 7 | 12 |
| McNeil, Charlie DB | 60LA-A 61-64SD-A | | 5'11" | 179 | Compton C.C. | 19 | 12 |
| McNeil, Clifton WR-FL | 64-67Cle 68-69SF 70-71NYG 71-72Was 73Hou | 2 | 6'2" | 186 | Grambling | | 138 |
| McQuarters, Ed DT | 65StL | | 6'1" | 250 | Oklahoma | | |
| McRae, Bennie DB | 62-70ChiB 71NYG | | 6'1" | 180 | Michigan | 27 | 24 |
| McRae, Frank DT | 67ChiB | | 6'7" | 270 | Tennessee State | | |
| McWatters, Bill FB | 64Min | | 6' | 225 | North Texas | | |
| Meador, Ed DB | 59-70LA | 3 | 5'11" | 193 | Arkansas Tech | 46 | 36 |
| Medved, Ron DB | 66-70Phi | | 6'1" | 205 | Washington | 3 | |
| Meggyesy, Dave LB | 63-69StL | | 6'1" | 221 | Syracuse | | |
| Meinert, Dale LB-OG-OT | 58-59ChiC 60-67StL | | 6'2" | 219 | Oklahoma State | 9 | 6 |
| Meixler, Ed LB | 65BosA | | 6'3" | 245 | Boston U. | | |
| Melinkovich, Mike DE | 65-66StL 67Det | | 6'4" | 243 | Washington | | |
| Mellekas, John C-DT-OT | 56ChiB 57MS 58-61ChiB 62SF 63Phi | | 6'3" | 255 | Arizona | | |
| Memmelaar, Dale OG-OT | 59ChiC 60-61StL 62-63Dal 64-65Cle 66-67Dal | | 6'2" | 247 | Wyoming | | |
| Mendez, Mario HB | 64SD-A | | 5'11" | 200 | San Diego State | | |
| Menefee, Pep FL | 66NYG | | 6'1" | 198 | New Mexico State | | |
| Mercein, Chuck FB | 65-67NYG 67-68GB 69Was 70NYJ | 2 5 | 6'3" | 227 | Yale | | 45 |
| Mercer, Mike K | 61-62Min 63-66OakA 66KC-A 67-68BufA 68-69GB 70SD | 45 | 6' | 208 | Minnesota, Florida State, Hardin-Simmons, Arizona State | | 594 |
| Meredith, Don (Dandy Don) QB | 60-68Dal | 12 | 6'2" | 202 | S.M.U. | | |
| Meredith, Dudley DT | 63HouA 64-68BufA 68HouA | | 6'4" | 280 | Florida, Northwestern, Lamar | 1 | |
| Mertens, Jerry DB | 58-62SF 63KJ 64-65SF | | 6' | 184 | Drake | 8 | 6 |
| Mertens, Jim TE | 69MiaA | | 6'3" | 235 | Fairmont State | | |
| Merz, Curt OG-DE | 62DalA 63-68KC-A | | 6'4" | 257 | Iowa | | |
| Messer, Dale HB-FL-DB | 61-65SF | 2 | 5'10" | 175 | Fresno State | 1 | |
| Messner, Max LB | 60-63Det 64NYG 64-65Pit | | 6'3" | 225 | Cincinnati | 2 | |
| Mestnik, Frank FB | 60-61StL 63GB | 2 | 6'2" | 200 | Marquette | | 30 |
| Meyer, Ed OT | 60BufA | | 6'2" | 240 | West Texas State | | |
| Meyer, John LB | 66HouA | | 6'1" | 225 | Notre Dame | | |
| Meyer, Ron QB | 66Pit | | 6'4" | 205 | S. Dakota State | | |
| Meyers, John DT | 62-63Dal 64-67Pit | | 6'6" | 272 | Washington | 2 | |
| Meylan, Wayne LB | 68-69Cle 70Min | | 6'1" | 237 | Nebraska | | |
| Michael, Rich OT | 60-63HouA 64JJ 65-66HouA | | 6'3" | 238 | Ohio State | | |
| Michaels, Lou DE-K | 58-60LA 61-63Pit 64-69Bal 71GB | 5 | 6'2" | 243 | Kentucky | | 955 |
| Michel, Tom HB | 64Min | 2 | 6' | 210 | East Carolina | | |
| Middendorf, Dave OG | 68-69CinA 70NYJ | | 6'3" | 260 | Washington State | | |
| Milks, John LB | 66SD-A | | 6' | 222 | San Diego State | 1 | |
| Miller, Al LB | 62-63Was | | 6' | 224 | Ohio U. | | |
| Miller, Alan FB | 60BosA 61-63OakA 64JJ 65OakA | 2 | 6' | 202 | Boston College | | 120 |
| Miller, Bill DT | 62HouA | | 6'4" | 270 | N. Mex. Highlands | | |
| Miller, Bill OE-WR | 62DalA 63BufA 64,66-68OakA | 2 | 6' | 192 | Miami (Fla.) | | 60 |
| Miller, Clark DE | 62-68SF 69Was 70LA | | 6'5" | 246 | Utah State | 1 | 6 |
| Miller, Fred DT | 63-72Bal | | 6'3" | 248 | Louisiana State | | |
| Miller, Ron QB | 62LA | 1 | 6' | 190 | Wisconsin | | |
| Mills, Dick OG | 61-62Det | | 6'3" | 240 | Pittsburgh | | |
| Mills, Pete OE | 65-66BufA | | 5'11" | 180 | Wichita State | | |
| Milstead, Charlie QB-DB | 60-61HouA | 4 | 6'2" | 190 | Texas A&M | 2 | 1 |
| Milton, Gene WR | 68-69MiaA | 23 | 5'10" | 170 | Florida A&M | | 12 |
| Mingo, Gene HB-K | 60-63DenA 64-65OakA 66-67MiaA 67Was 69-70Pit | 23 5 | 6'1" | 199 | None | | 629 |
| Minniear, Randy HB | 67-69NYG 70Cle | 2 | 6' | 205 | Purdue | | 36 |
| Minter, Tom DB | 62DenA 62BufA | | 5'10" | 178 | Baylor | | |
| Mira, George QB | 64-68SF 69Phi 71Mia | 12 | 5'11" | 190 | Miami (Fla.) | | |
| Mirich, Rex DT-DE | 64-66OakA 67-69DenA 70Bos | | 6'4" | 251 | Arizona State | | |
| Mischak, Bob OG | 58NYG 60-62NY-A 63-65OakA | | 6' | 237 | Army | | |
| Mitchell, Alvin DB-WR | 68-69Cle 70Den | | 6'3" | 195 | Morgan State | | |
| Mitchell, Bobby FL-HB-WR | 58-61Cle 62-68Was | 23 | 6' | 192 | Illinois | | 546 |
| Mitchell, Charley HB-DB | 63-67DenA 68BufA | 23 | 5'11" | 185 | Washington | 1 | 54 |
| Mitchell, Ed OG | 65-67SD-A | | 6'2" | 275 | Southern U. | | |
| Mitchell, Stan FB-HB-OE | 66-69MiaA 70Mia 71JJ | 2 | 6'2" | 220 | Tennessee | | 54 |
| Mitchell, Willie DB | 64-69KC-A 70KC | 3 | 6'1" | 185 | Tennessee State | 16 | 24 |
| Mitinger, Bob LB-DE | 62-64,66,68SD-A | | 6'2" | 232 | Penn State | 3 | |
| Mix, Ron OT-OG | 60LA-A 61-69SD-A 70VR 71Oak | | 6'4" | 249 | Southern Calif. | | |
| Molden, Frank DT | 65LA 66-67KJ 68Phi 69NYG | | 6'5" | 282 | Jackson State | 1 | 6 |
| Montalbo, Mel DB | 62OakA | | 6'1" | 190 | Utah State | | |
| Moore, Alex DB | 68DenA | | 6' | 195 | Norfolk State | | |
| Moore, Charlie OG | 62Was | | 6'5" | 230 | Arkansas | | |
| Moore, Denis DT-DE | 67-69Det | | 6'5" | 247 | Southern Calif. | | |
| Moore, Fred DT-DE | 64-66SD-A | | 6'4" | 260 | Memphis State | 1 | |
| Moore, Gene HB | 69SF | | 6' | 208 | Occidental | | |
| Moore, Lenny HB-FL | 56-67Bal | 23 | 6'1" | 191 | Penn State | | 678 |
| Moore, Leroy DE | 60BufA 61-62BosA 62-63BufA 64-65DenA | | 6' | 231 | Ft. Valley State | 2 | 6 |
| Moore, Rich DT | 69-70GB | | 6'6" | 285 | Villanova | | |
| Moore, Tom HB | 60-65GB 66LA 67Atl | 23 | 6'2" | 213 | Vanderbilt | | 186 |
| Mooty, Jim DB | 60Dal | | 5'11" | 177 | Arkansas | | |
| Moran, Jim DT | 64NYG 65BL 66-67NYG | | 6'5" | 260 | Idaho | | |
| Moreau, Doug TE-OE | 66-69MiaA | 2 | 6'2" | 207 | Louisiana State | | 45 |
| Morelli, Fran OT | 62NY-A | | 6'2" | 258 | Colgate | | |
| Morgan, Bobby DB | 67Pit | | 6' | 205 | New Mexico | | |

| Use Name (Nickname) - Positions | Team by Year | See Section | Hgt. | Wgt. | College | Int | Pts |
|---|---|---|---|---|---|---|---|
| Morgan, Mike LB | 64-67Phi 68Was 69-70NO 71JJ | | 6'4" | 241 | Louisiana State | 6 | 12 |
| Morrall, Earl QB | 56SF 57-58Pit 58-64Det 65-67NYG 68-71Bal 72-76Mia | 12 4 | 6'1" | 205 | Michigan State | | 48 |
| Morris, Dennit LB | 58SF 60-61HouA | | 6'1" | 228 | Oklahoma | 5 | |
| Morris, Johnny FL-HB | 58-67ChiB | 23 | 5'10" | 180 | Cal.-Santa Barbara | | 222 |
| Morris, Larry LB-HB | 55-57LA 59-64ChiB 66Atl | 2 | 6'2" | 226 | Georgia Tech | 6 | 12 |
| Morris, Riley LB-DE | 60-62OakA | | 6'2" | 230 | Florida A&M | 3 | 6 |
| Morrison, Joe HB-FL-WR-FB-DB-OE | 59-72NYG | 23 | 6'1" | 210 | Cincinnati | | 390 |
| Morrow, John C-OG-DE | 56LA 57MS 58-59LA 60-66Cle | | 6'3" | 244 | Michigan | | |
| Morrow, Tommy DB | 62-64OakA | 4 | 5'11" | 185 | Southern Miss. | 23 | |
| Morze, Frank C-DT | 57-61SF 62-63Cle 64SF | | 6'4" | 272 | Boston College | | |
| Mostardo, Rich DB | 60Cle 61Min 62OakA | | 5'11" | 188 | Charleston, Kent State | 2 | |
| Moten, Bobby WR | 68DenA | | 6'4" | 212 | Bishop | | |
| Mudd, Howard OG | 64-69SF 69-70ChiB | | 6'3" | 251 | Michigan State, Hillsdale | | |
| Muelhaupt, Ed (Chuck) OG | 60-61BufA | | 6'3" | 230 | Iowa State | | |
| Mullins, Don DB | 61-62ChiB | | 6'1" | 195 | Houston | | |
| Mumley, Nick DE-OT | 60-62NY-A | | 6'6" | 252 | Purdue | 1 | 6 |
| Murchison, Lee OE | 61Dal | | 6'3" | 205 | U. of Pacific | | |
| Murdock, Jesse HB-FB | 63OakA 63BufA | | 6'2" | 203 | Calif. Western | | |
| Murdock, Les K | 67NYG | 5 | 6'3" | 245 | Florida State | | 25 |
| Murphy, Bill WR | 68BosA | 2 | 6'1" | 185 | Cornell | | |
| Murphy, Dennis DT | 65ChiB | | 6'1" | 250 | Florida | | |
| Murphy, Fred OE | 60Cle 61Min | | 6'3" | 205 | Georgia Tech | | |
| Musgrove, Spain DT-DE | 67-69Was 70Hou | | 6'4" | 275 | Utah State | | |
| Myers, Tom QB | 65-66Det | | 6' | 188 | Northwestern | | |
| Nairn, Harvey WR | 68NY-A 69MS | | 6'1" | 178 | Southern U. | | |
| Nance, Jim FB | 65-69BosA 70Bos 71NE 73NYJ | 2 | 6'1" | 241 | Syracuse | | 276 |
| Napier, Walter DT | 60-61DalA | | 6'4" | 275 | Paul Quinn | | |
| Neck, Tommy DB | 62ChiB | | 5'11" | 190 | Louisiana State | | |
| Neff, Bob DB | 66-68MiaA | 3 | 6' | 182 | S.F. Austin State | 2 | |
| Neidert, John (J.T.) LB | 68CinA 68-69NY-A 70ChiB | | 6'2" | 230 | Louisville | | |
| Neighbors, Billy OG | 62-65BosA 66-69MiaA | | 5'11" | 244 | Alabama | | |
| Nelson, Bill QB | 63-67Pit 68-72Cle | 12 | 6' | 195 | Southern Calif. | | 12 |
| Nelson, Al DB | 65-73Phi | 3 | 5'11" | 185 | Cincinnati | 13 | 18 |
| Nelson, Andy (Bones) DB | 57-63Bal 64NYG | | 6'1" | 180 | Memphis State | 33 | 18 |
| Nelson, Benny DB | 64HouA | | 6' | 185 | Alabama | 1 | 6 |
| Nery, Ron DE | 60LA-A 61SD-A 63DenA 63HouA | | 6'6" | 236 | Kansas State | | |
| Nettles, Jim DB | 65-68Phi 69-72LA | | 5'9" | 177 | Wisconsin | 26 | 24 |
| Neumann, Tom HB | 63BosA | 2 | 5'11" | 205 | Wisconsin, Northern Michigan | | 6 |
| Nevett, Elijah DB-FL | 67-70NO | | 6' | 185 | Clark Atlanta | 6 | |
| Newell, Steve OE | 67SD-A | | 6'1" | 186 | Long Beach State | | |
| Nichols, Bob OT | 65Pit 66-67LA | | 6'3" | 250 | Stanford | | |
| Nichols, Bobby TE | 66-67BosA | | 6'2" | 220 | Boston U. | | |
| Nichols, Mike C | 60-61DenA | | 6'3" | 225 | Ark.-Monticello | | |
| Nicklas, Pete OT | 62OakA | | 6'4" | 240 | Baylor | | |
| Ninowski, Jim QB | 58-59Cle 60-61Det 62-66Cle 67-68Was 69NO | 12 | 6'1" | 206 | Michigan State | | 60 |
| Nisby, John (Jack) OG | 57-61Pit 62-64Was | | 6'1" | 235 | U. of Pacific | | |
| Nitschke, Ray LB | 58-72GB | | 6'3" | 235 | Illinois | 25 | 12 |
| Nocera, John LB | 59-62Phi 63DenA | | 6'1" | 220 | Iowa | 1 | |
| Nofsinger, Terry QB | 61-64Pit 65-66StL 67Atl | 12 | 6'4" | 209 | Utah | | 18 |
| Nomina, Tom DT-OG | 63-65DenA 66-68MiaA | | 6'5" | 267 | Miami-Ohio | | |
| Noonan, Karl WR-OE | 66-69MiaA 70-71Mia 72KJ | 2 | 6'3" | 193 | Iowa | | 102 |
| Norman, Dick QB | 61ChiB | | 6'3" | 210 | Stanford | | |
| Norman, Pettis TE-OE | 62-70Dal 71-73SD | 2 | 6'3" | 220 | Johnson C. Smith | | 90 |
| Norris, Jim DT-OT | 62-64OakA | | 6'4" | 235 | Houston | 2 | |
| Norris, Trusse OE | 60LA-A | | 6'1" | 190 | U.C.L.A. | | |
| Norton, Don OE | 60LA-A 61-66SD-A | 2 | 6'1" | 190 | Iowa | | 162 |
| Norton, Jim DB | 60-68HouA | 4 | 6'3" | 187 | Idaho | 45 | |
| Norton, Jim DT-OT-OE | 65-66SF 67-68Atl 68Phi 69Was 70NYG | | 6'4" | 254 | Washington | 1 | |
| Norton, Ray HB | 60-61SF | | 6'2" | 184 | San Jose State | | |
| Norton, Rick QB | 66-69MiaA 70GB | 1 | 6'1" | 192 | Kentucky | | |
| Novsek, Joe DE | 62OakA | | 6'4" | 237 | Tulsa | | |
| Nowatzke, Tom FB-LB | 65-69Det 70-72Bal | 2 | 6'3" | 229 | Indiana | 1 | 102 |
| Nugent, Phil DB | 61DenA | | 6'2" | 195 | Tulane | 7 | |
| Nunnery, R.B. OT | 60DalA | | 6'4" | 275 | Louisiana State | | |
| Nutting, Ed OT | 61Cle 62JJ 63Dal | | 6'4" | 246 | Georgia Tech | | |
| Oakes, Don OT-DT | 61-62Phi 63-68BosA | | 6'3" | 253 | Virginia Tech | | |
| Oats, Carleton DE-DT | 65-69OakA 70-72Oak 73GB | | 6'2" | 252 | Florida A&M | | 6 |
| Oberg, Tom DB | 68-69DenA | | 6' | 185 | Oregon State, Portland State | 3 | |
| O'Bradovich, Ed DE | 62-71ChiB | | 6'3" | 255 | Illinois | | 8 |
| O'Brien, Dave DT-OT-OG | 63-64Min 65NYG 66-67StL | | 6'3" | 244 | Boston College | | |
| O'Brien, Fran OT-OG-DE | 59Cle 60-66Was 66-68Pit | | 6'1" | 253 | Michigan State | | |
| Odle, Phil WR | 68-70Det | | 5'11" | 191 | Brigham Young | | |
| Odom, Sammy LB | 64HouA | | 6'2" | 235 | Northwestern La. | 2 | |
| O'Donnell, Joe OG-OT | 64-67BufA 68KJ 69BufA 70-71Buf | | 6'2" | 253 | Michigan | | |
| Ogas, Dave LB | 68OakA 69BufA | | 6'3" | 240 | San Diego State | | |
| Ogden, Ray TE-WR-OE | 65-66StL 67NO 67-68Atl 69-71ChiB | 2 | 6'5" | 225 | Alabama | | 24 |
| Oglesby, Paul DT | 60OakA | | 6'4" | 235 | U.C.L.A. | | |
| O'Hanley, Ross DB | 60-65BosA 66JJ | | 6' | 183 | Boston College | 15 | 6 |
| Oliver, Bob OT | 69Cle | | 6'3" | 240 | Abilene Christian | | |
| Oliver, Chip LB | 68-69OakA | | 6'2" | 220 | Southern Calif. | 1 | 6 |
| Oliver, Clancy DB | 69-70Pit | | 6'1" | 180 | San Diego State | | |
| Olsen, Merlin DT | 62-76LA | | 6'5" | 270 | Utah State | 1 | 6 |
| Olson, Harold OT | 60-62BufA 63-64DenA | | 6'3" | 259 | Clemson | | |
| Olssen, Lance OT | 68-69SF | | 6'5" | 262 | Purdue | | |
| O'Mahoney, Jim LB | 65-66NY-A | | 6'1" | 231 | Miami (Fla.) | | |
| Onesti, Larry LB | 62-65HouA | | 6' | 200 | Northwestern | | 6 |
| Orr, Jimmy FL-OE-WR | 58-60Pit 61-70Bal | 2 4 | 5'11" | 185 | Clemson, Georgia | | 396 |
| Osborne, Clancy LB | 59-60SF 61-62Min 63-64OakA | | 6'3" | 218 | Arizona State | 6 | |
| Osborne, Tom OE | 60-61Was | 2 | 6'3" | 190 | Hastings | | 12 |
| Otto, Gus LB | 65-69OakA 70-73Oak | | 6'2" | 220 | Missouri | 6 | 12 |
| Otto, Jim C | 60-69OakA 70-74Oak | | 6'2" | 244 | Miami (Fla.) | | |
| Overton, Jerry DB | 63Dal | | 6'2" | 190 | Utah | | |
| Injured in accident before 1964 season | | | | | | | |
| Owens, Don DT-OT | 57Was 58-60Phi 60-63StL | | 6'5" | 255 | Southern Miss. | | 6 |
| Owens, Luke DE-DT-OT | 57Bal 58-59ChiC 60-65StL | | 6'2" | 254 | Kent State | | 2 |
| Owens, R.C. (Alley Oop) OE-FL | 57-61SF 62-63Bal 64NYG | 2 | 6'3" | 197 | Coll. of Idaho | | 138 |
| Pagliei, Joe FB | 59Phi 60NY-A | 4 | 6' | 220 | Clemson | | 6 |
| Paluck, John DE-DT | 56Was 57-58MS 59-65Was | | 6'2" | 241 | Pittsburgh | 2 | 8 |
| Papac, Nick QB | 61OakA | 1 | 5'11" | 190 | Fresno State | | 6 |

| Use Name (Nickname) - Positions | Team by Year | See Section | Hgt. | Wgt. | College | Int | Pts |
|---|---|---|---|---|---|---|---|
| Pardee, Jack LB | 57-64LA 65VR 66-70LA 71-72Was HC75-77Chi HC78-80Was HC90-94Hou | | 6'2" | 224 | Texas A&M | 22 | 38 |
| Paremore, Bob HB | 63-64StL | 2 | 5'11" | 190 | Florida A&M | | 12 |
| Parilli, Babe QB | 52-53GB 54-55MS 56Cle 57-58GB 59CFL 60OakA 61-67BosA 68-69NY-A | 12 | 6'1" | 190 | Kentucky | | 146 |
| Park, Ernie OT-OG | 63-65SD-A 66MiaA 67DenA 69CinA | | 6'3" | 247 | McMurry | | |
| Parker, Charlie OG | 65DenA | | 6'1" | 245 | Southern Miss. | | |
| Parker, Don OG | 67SF 68KJ | | 6'3" | 235 | Virginia | | |
| Parker, Frank DT | 62-64Cle 65IL 66-67Cle 68Pit 69NYG | | 6'5" | 263 | Oklahoma State | | |
| Parker, Jim OT-OG | 57-67Bal | | 6'3" | 273 | Ohio State | | |
| Parker, Willie DT | 68-69HouA 70Hou | | 6'2" | 266 | Ark.-Pine Bluff | | |
| Parks, Dave OE-TE-WR | 64-67SF 68-7NO 73Hou | 2 | 6'2" | 202 | Texas Tech | | 264 |
| Parrish, Bernie DB | 59-66Cle 66HouA | | 5'11" | 194 | Florida | 31 | 24 |
| Pashe, Bill DB | 64NY-A | | 5'11" | 185 | George Washington | | |
| Patera, Dennis K | 68SF | 5 | 6' | 225 | Brigham Young | | 16 |
| Patera, Herb LB | 63BufA | | 6'1" | 222 | Michigan State | | |
| Patton, Jimmy DB | 55-66NYG | 3 | 6' | 183 | Mississippi | 52 | 24 |
| Paulson, Dainard DB | 61-66NY-A | | 5'11" | 190 | Oregon State | 29 | 6 |
| Peacock, Johnny DB | 69HouA 70Hou | | 6'2" | 203 | Houston | 5 | 12 |
| Peaks, Clarence FB | 57-63Phi 64-65Pit | 23 | 6'1" | 218 | Michigan State | | 144 |
| Pearson, Willie DB | 69MiaA | | 6' | 190 | N. Carolina A&T | | |
| Pellegrini, Bob LB-OG | 56,58-61Phi 62-65Was | | 6'2" | 233 | Maryland | 13 | 6 |
| Pennington, Tom K | 62DalA | 5 | 6'2" | 210 | Georgia | | 19 |
| Pentecost, John OG | 67Min | | 6'2" | 250 | U.C.L.A. | | |
| Perkins, Art FB | 62-63LA | 2 | 6' | 223 | North Texas | | 36 |
| Perkins, Bill HB | 63NY-A | | 6'2" | 225 | Iowa | | |
| Perkins, Don FB-HB | 61-68Dal | 2 | 5'10" | 200 | New Mexico | | 270 |
| Perkins, Jim OT | 62-64DenA | | 6'5" | 250 | Colorado | | |
| Perkins, Ray WR-OE | 67-71Bal HC79-8NYG HC87-90TB | 2 | 6' | 183 | Alabama | | 66 |
| Perkins, Willie OG-DE | 61HouA 61BosA 63HouA | | 6' | 250 | Texas Southern | | |
| Perio, Phil LB | 60HouA | | 6' | 220 | Maryland | | |
| Perreault, Pete OG-OT | 63-67NY-A 68CinA 69BY-A 70NYJ 71Min | | 6'3" | 246 | Boston U. | | |
| Pesonen, Dick DB | 60GB 61Min 62-64NYG | | 6' | 190 | Minnesota, Minnesota-Duluth | 4 | |
| Peters, Anton DT | 63DenA | | 6'3" | 250 | Florida | | |
| Peters, Floyd DT | 59-62Cle 63Det 64-69Phi 70Was | | 6'4" | 254 | San Fran. State | 3 | |
| Peters, Frank OT | 69CinA | | 6'4" | 250 | Ohio U. | | |
| Peterson, Ken OG | 61Min | | 6'2" | 235 | Utah | | |
| Petitbon, Richie DB | 59-68ChiB 69-70LA 71-73Was HC93Was | | 6'3" | 206 | Tulane | 48 | 18 |
| Petrella, Bob DB | 66-69MiaA 70-71Mia | | 6' | 186 | Tennessee | 5 | |
| Petrich, Bob DE | 63-66SD-A 67BufA | | 6'4" | 253 | West Texas State | 1 | |
| Petties, Neal OE-FL | 64-66Bal | | 6'2" | 198 | San Diego State | | 6 |
| Philbin, Gerry DE | 64-69NY-A 70-72NYJ 73Phi 74WFL | | 6'2" | 245 | Buffalo | 1 | |
| Phillips, Jim (Red) OE-FL | 58-64LA 65-67Min | 2 | 6'1" | 197 | Auburn | | 04 |
| Phillips, Lloyd DE | 67-69ChiB | | 6'3" | 237 | Arkansas | 3 | |
| Philpott, Ed LB | 67-69BosA 70Bos 71NE | | 6'3" | 240 | Miami-Ohio | 9 | 6 |
| Piccolo, Brian HB-FB | 66-69ChiB Died June 16, 1970 — Cancer | 2 | 6' | 205 | Wake Forest | | 30 |
| Pickens, Bob OT | 67-69ChiB | | 6'4" | 258 | Wisconsin, Nebraska | | |
| Pietrosante, Nick FB | 59-65Det 66-67Cle | 2 | 6'2" | 225 | Notre Dame | | 180 |
| Pillath, Roger OT | 65LA 66Pit | | 6'4" | 249 | Wisconsin | | |
| Pine, Ed LB | 62-64SF 65Pit | | 6'4" | 233 | Utah | 3 | |
| Pitts, Elijah HB | 61-69GB 70LA 70NO 71GB | 23 | 6'1" | 204 | Philander Smith | | 210 |
| Pivec, Dave TE-LB | 66-68LA 69DenA | 2 | 6'3" | 240 | Notre Dame | | 8 |
| Plum, Milt QB | 57-61Cle 62-67Det 68LA 69NYG | 12 5 | 6'1" | 205 | Penn State | | 112 |
| Plump, Dave DB | 66SD-A | | 6'1" | 195 | Fresno State | | |
| Plunkett, Sherman (Tank) OT | 58-60Bal 61-62SD-A 63-67NY-A | | 6'4" | 290 | Md. Eastern Shore | | |
| Ply, Bobby DB | 62DalA 63-67KC-A 67BufA 67DenA | | 6'1" | 190 | Baylor | 9 | |
| Poage, Ray TE-OE-FL | 63Min 64-65Phi 66KJ 67-70NO 71Atl | 2 | 6'4" | 208 | Texas | | 78 |
| Poimbeouf, Lance OG | 63Dal | | 6'3" | 225 | Southwestern La. | | |
| Poole, Bob TE-OE-FL | 64-65SF 66-67HouA | 2 | 6'4" | 216 | Clemson | | |
| Pope, Bucky OE-WR | 64LA 65KJ 66-67LA 68GB | 2 | 6'5" | 199 | Duke, Catawba | | 78 |
| Porter, Willie DB | 68BosA | 3 | 5'11" | 195 | Texas Southern | | |
| Porterfield, Garry DE | 65Dal | | 6'3" | 223 | Tulsa | | |
| Post, Bobby DB | 67NYG | | 6'1" | 195 | Kings Point | | |
| Post, Dickie HB | 67-69SD-A 70SD 71Den 71Hou | 23 | 5'9" | 190 | Houston | | 114 |
| Pottios, Myron LB | 61Pit 62BA 63-65Pit 66-70LA 71-73Was | | 6'2" | 236 | Notre Dame | 12 | |
| Powell, Art OE-DB-WR | 59Phi 60-62NY-A 63-66OakA 67BufA 68Min | 2 | 6'3" | 211 | San Jose State | 3 | 492 |
| Powell, Preston FB | 61Cle | | 6'2" | 225 | Grambling | | |
| Powell, Tim DE | 65LA 66Pit | | 6'4" | 248 | Northwestern | | |
| Powers, John OE-TE-LB | 62-65Pit 66Min | | 6'2" | 211 | Campion, Notre Dame | | |
| Powers, Warren DB | 63-68OakA | | 6' | 188 | Nebraska | 22 | 12 |
| Preas, George OT-OG-LB | 55-65Bal | | 6'2" | 244 | Virginia Tech | | |
| Prebola, Gene OE | 60OakA 61-6DenA | 2 | 6'3" | 220 | Boston U. | | 42 |
| Prestel, Jim DT | 60Cle 61-66Min 66NYG 67Was | | 6'5" | 264 | Idaho | 1 | 8 |
| Price, Jim LB | 63NY-A 64DenA | | 6'2" | 228 | Auburn | 1 | |
| Price, Sam HB-FB | 66-68MiaA | 2 | 5'11" | 215 | Illinois | | 12 |
| Pride, Dan LB | 68-69ChiB | | 6'3" | 225 | Tennessee State, Jackson State | 1 | |
| Print, Bob LB | 67-68SD-A | | 6' | 220 | Dayton | | |
| Prisby, Errol DB | 67DenA | | 5'10" | 184 | Cincinnati | | |
| Promuto, Vince OG | 60-70Was | | 6'1" | 244 | Holy Cross | | |
| Prudhomme, Remi C-OG-DE-DT | 66-67BufA 68-69KC-A 70JJ 71-72NO 72Buf | | 6'4" | 251 | Louisiana State | | |
| Pryor, Barry HB | 69MiaA 70Mia | | 6'1" | 215 | Boston U. | | |
| Purnell, Jim LB | 64-68ChiB 69-72GB | | 6'2" | 229 | Wisconsin | 3 | |
| Purvis, Vic DB | 66-67BosA | | 5'11" | 200 | Southern Miss. | | |
| Pyburn, Jack OT | 67-68MiaA | | 6'6" | 245 | Texas A&M | | |
| Pyeatt, Johnny DB | 60-61DenA | | 6'3" | 204 | None | 4 | 6 |
| Pyle, Mike C | 61-69ChiB | | 6'3" | 247 | Yale | | |
| Pyle, Palmer OG | 60-63Bal 64Min 65JJ 66OakA | | 6'2" | 248 | Michigan State | | |
| Pyne, George DT | 65BosA | | 6'4" | 285 | Olivet | | |
| Quayle, Frank HB | 69DenA | 2 | 5'10" | 195 | Virginia | | |
| Quinlan, Bill DE | 57-58Cle 59-62GB 63Phi | | 6'3" | 248 | Michigan State | 3 | |
| Quinn, Steve C | 68HouA | | 6'1" | 225 | Notre Dame | | |
| Rabb, Warren QB | 60Det 61-62BufA | 12 | 6'1" | 202 | Louisiana State | | 22 |
| Rabold, Mike OG | 59Det 60StL 61-62Min 63-67ChiB | | 6'2" | 239 | Indiana | | |
| Rademacher, Bill WR-DB-OE | 64-68NY-A 69BosA 70Bos | 2 | 6'1" | 190 | Northern Michigan | 1 | 18 |
| Raimey, Dave DB | 64Cle | | 5'10" | 195 | Michigan | | |
| Rakestraw, larry QB | 64,66-68ChiB | 1 | 6'2" | 195 | Georgia | | 12 |
| Ramsey, Nate DB | 63-72Phi 73NO | | 6'1" | 200 | Indiana | 21 | 6 |
| Randall, Dennis DE-DT | 67NY-A 68CinA | | 6'6" | 243 | Oklahoma State | | |

| Use Name (Nickname) - Positions | Team by Year | See Section | Hgt. | Wgt. | College | Int | Pts |
|---|---|---|---|---|---|---|---|
| Randall, Sonny OE-WR | 59ChiC 60-66StL 67-68SF 68Dal | 2 | 6'2" | 189 | Virginia | | 390 |
| Rasmussen, Wayne DB | 64-72Det 73JJ | | 6'2" | 179 | S. Dakota State | 16 | 12 |
| Rassas, Nick DB | 66-68Atl | | 6' | 190 | Notre Dame | 1 | |
| Ratkowski, Ray HB | 61BosA | | 6' | 195 | Notre Dame | | |
| Raye, Jimmy DB | 69Phi | | 6' | 185 | Michigan State | | |
| Recher, Dave C | 65-68Phi | | 6'1" | 244 | Iowa | | |
| Rector, Ron HB | 66Was 66-67Atl | 2 | 6' | 200 | Northwestern | | |
| Redman, Rick LB | 65-69SD-A 70-73SD | 4 | 5'11" | 225 | Washington | 9 | 6 |
| Redmond, Tom DE-OG-OT | 60-65StL | | 6'5" | 243 | Vanderbilt | | |
| Reeberg, Lucien OT | 63Det Died Jan. 31, 1964 — Uremia | | 6'4" | 308 | Hampton U. | | |
| Reed, Bob HB | 62-63Min | 23 | 5'11" | 187 | U. of Pacific | | 6 |
| Reed, Leo OG-OT | 61HouA 61DenA | | 6'4" | 240 | Colorado State | | |
| Reed, Robert OG | 65Was | | 6'1" | 250 | Tennessee State | | |
| Reed, Smith HB | 65-66NYG 67-68MS | | 6' | 215 | Alcorn State | | |
| Reed, Taft DB | 67Phi | | 6'2" | 200 | Jackson State | | |
| Reese, Guy DT | 62-63Dal 64-65Bal 66Atl | | 6'5" | 255 | S.M.U. | | |
| Reeves, Dan HB-FB | 65-72Dal HC81-92Den HC93-95NYG | 12 | 6'1" | 201 | South Carolina | | 253 |
| Reeves, Roy WR | 69BufA | | 5'11" | 182 | South Carolina | | |
| Reger, John LB-OG | 55-63Pit 64-66Was | | 6' | 225 | Pittsburgh | 15 | 18 |
| Regner, Tom OG | 67-69HouA 70-72Hou | | 6'1" | 255 | Notre Dame | | |
| Reichow, Jerry OE-QB | 56-57Det 58KJ 59Det 60Phi 61-64Min | 12 | 6'2" | 217 | Iowa | | 144 |
| Reifsnyder, Bob DE | 60-61NY-A | | 6'2" | 255 | Navy | | |
| Reilly, Mike LB | 64-68ChiB 69Min | | 6'2" | 230 | Iowa | | 6 |
| Remmert, Dennis LB | 60BufA | | 6'3" | 215 | Iowa State | | |
| Rengel, Mike DT | 69NO 70JJ | | 6'5" | 260 | Air Force, Minnesota, Hawaii | | |
| Renn, Bob HB | 61NY-A | 2 | 6' | 180 | Florida State | | 6 |
| Rentz, Larry DB | 69SD-A | | 6'1" | 170 | Florida | | |
| Rentzel, Lance WR-FL-OE-HB | 65-66Min 67-70Dal 71-72LA 73SL 74LA | 23 | 6'2" | 203 | Oklahoma | | 248 |
| Retzlaff, Pete OE-TE-FL | 56-66Phi | 2 | 6'1" | 211 | S. Dakota State | | 282 |
| Reynolds, Al OG | 60-62DalA 63-67KC-A | | 6'3" | 238 | Tarkio | | |
| Reynolds, Bob OT | 63-71StL 72-73NE 73StL | | 6'6" | 264 | Bowling Green | | |
| Reynolds, Chuck C-OG | 69-70Cle | | 6'2" | 240 | Texas Christian, Tulsa | | 2 |
| Reynolds, M.C. (Chief) QB | 58-59ChiC 60Was 61BufA 62OakA | 12 | 6' | 193 | Louisiana State | | 24 |
| Rhome, Jerry QB | 65-67Dal 69Cle 70Hou 71LA | 12 | 6' | 186 | S.M.U., Tulsa | | 6 |
| Rice, George DT-OG | 66-69HouA | | 6'3" | 262 | Louisiana State | | |
| Rice, Ken OG-OT | 61BufA 62KJ 63BufA 64-65OakA 66-67MiaA | | 6'2" | 243 | Auburn | | |
| Richards, Bobby DE | 62-65Phi 66-67Atl | | 6'2" | 241 | Louisiana State | | |
| Richards, Jim DB | 68-69NY-A 70-71MS | | 6'1" | 180 | Virginia Tech | 3 | |
| Richards, Perry OE | 57Pit 58Det 59ChiC 60StL 61BufA 62NY-A | 2 | 6'2" | 205 | Detroit | | 24 |
| Richardson, Al DE | 60BosA | | 6'3" | 250 | Grambling | | |
| Richardson, Bob (Red) DB | 66DenA | | 6'1" | 180 | U.C.L.A. | | |
| Richardson, Jeff OT-C-OG | 67-68NY-A 69MiaA | | 6'3" | 253 | Michigan State | | |
| Richardson, Jerry (The Razor) FL-OE-HB | 59-60Bal | 2 | 6'3" | 185 | Wofford | | 24 |
| Richardson, Jerry DB | 64-65LA 66-67Atl | | 6'3" | 190 | West Texas State | 11 | |
| Richardson, Tom WR | 69BosA 70Bos | | 6'2" | 195 | Jackson State | | |
| Richardson, Willie FL-WR | 63-69Bal 70Mia 71Bal | 2 | 6'2" | 198 | Jackson State | | 150 |
| Richey, Mike OT | 69BufA 70NO | | 6'5" | 257 | North Carolina | | |
| Richter, Frank LB | 67-69DenA | | 6'3" | 230 | Georgia | 2 | |
| Richter, Pat OE-TE-K | 63-70Was | 2 4 | 6'5" | 230 | Wisconsin | | 84 |
| Ridge, Houston DE-DT | 66-69SD-A 70JJ | | 6'4" | 239 | San Diego State | | |
| Ridgeway, Colin K | 65Dal | | 6'5" | 211 | Lamar | | |
| Ridlehuber, Preston HB | 66Atl 68OakA 69BufA | | 6'2" | 215 | Georgia | | 18 |
| Ridlon, Jim DB | 57-62SF 63-64Dal | | 6'1" | 181 | Syracuse | 9 | 12 |
| Rieves, Charlie LB | 62-63OakA 64-65HouA | | 5'11" | 217 | Houston | 1 | |
| Riggle, Bob DB | 66-67Atl 68JJ | | 6'1" | 200 | Penn State | 3 | 6 |
| Righetti, Joe DT | 69-70Cle | | 6'3" | 253 | Waynesburg | | |
| Riley, Butch LB | 69Bal | | 6'2" | 220 | Texas A&I | | |
| Riley, Jim DE | 67-69MiaA 70-71Mia 72KJ | | 6'4" | 252 | Oklahoma | | |
| Ringo, Jim C | 53-63GB 64-67Phi HC76-77Buf | | 6'1" | 232 | Syracuse | | |
| Rissmiller, Ray OT | 66Phi 67NO 68BufA | | 6'4" | 250 | Georgia | | |
| Rivera, Hank DB | 62OakA 63BufA | | 5'11" | 180 | Oregon State | | |
| Roach, John QB-DB | 56ChiC 57-58MS 59ChiC 60StL 61-63GB 64Dal | 12 | 6'4" | 197 | S.M.U. | | 12 |
| Robb, Joe DE-LB | 59-60Phi 61-67StL 68-71Det | | 6'3" | 238 | Texas Christian | 1 | |
| Roberson, Bo FL-HB | 61SD-A 62-65OakA 65BufA 66MiaA | 23 | 6'1" | 192 | Cornell | | 116 |
| Roberts, Archie QB | 67MiaA | | 6'1" | 193 | Columbia | | |
| Roberts, Cliff OT | 61OakA | | 6'3" | 260 | Illinois | | |
| Roberts, C.R. FB | 59-62SF | 2 | 6'3" | 202 | Southern Calif. | | 24 |
| Roberts, Walter (The Flea) FL-WR-OE | 64-66Cle 67NO 69-70Was | 23 | 5'10" | 167 | San Jose State | | 66 |
| Robertson, Bob OT | 68HouA | | 6'4" | 246 | Illinois | | |
| Robinson, Dave LB | 63-72GB 73-74Was | | 6'3" | 243 | Penn State | 27 | 6 |
| Robinson, Jerry OE | 62-64SD-A 65NY-A | 23 | 5'11" | 195 | Grambling | | 30 |
| Robinson, Johnnie DB-FL | 66Det 67JJ | | 6'3" | 205 | Tennessee State | | 6 |
| Robinson, Johnny DB-HB | 60-62DalA 63-69KC-A 70-71KC | 2 | 6' | 200 | Louisiana State | 57 | 108 |
| Robotti, Frank LB | 61BosA | | 6' | 220 | Boston College | 2 | |
| Rochester, Paul DT | 60-62DalA 63KC-A 63-69NY-A | | 6'2" | 254 | Michigan State | | |
| Rock, Walt OT-DT | 63-67SF 68-73Was | | 6'5" | 252 | Maryland | | |
| Roderick, John FL-WR | 66-67MiaA 68OakA | 2 | 6'1" | 180 | S.M.U. | | 6 |
| Roedel, Herb (Clem) OG | 61OakA | | 6'3" | 230 | Marquette | | |
| Roehnelt, Bill LB | 58-59ChiB 60Was 61-62DenA | | 6'1" | 227 | Bradley | | |
| Rogers, Don C-OG | 60LA-A 61-64SD-A | | 6'2" | 245 | South Carolina | | |
| Rohde, Len OT-DE | 60-74SF | | 6'4" | 246 | Utah State | | |
| Roland, Johnny HB-FB | 66-72StL 73NYG | 23 | 6'2" | 213 | Missouri | | 216 |
| Rolle, Dave FB | 60DenA | 2 | 6' | 215 | Oklahoma | | 18 |
| Romeo, Tony OE-TE | 61DalA 62-67BosA | 2 | 6'2" | 225 | Florida State | | 62 |
| Rosdahl, Hatch DT-OG-DE | 64BufA 64-66KC-A | | 6'5" | 250 | Penn State | | |
| Rose, George DB | 64-66Min 67NO 68JJ | | 5'11" | 190 | Auburn | 9 | 6 |
| Rosema, Rocky LB | 68-71StL | | 6'2" | 228 | Michigan | 1 | |
| Ross, Dave OE | 60NY-A | 2 | 6'3" | 210 | Los Angeles State | | 6 |
| Ross, Willie FB | 64BufA | | 5'10" | 200 | Nebraska | | 6 |
| Rowland, Justin DB | 60ChiB 61Min 62DenA | | 6'2" | 189 | Texas Christian | 1 | |
| Rowley, Bob LB | 63Pit 64NY-A | | 6'2" | 225 | Virginia | | |
| Roy, Frank OG | 66StL | | 6'2" | 230 | Utah | | |
| Rubke, Karl LB-DE-C-DT | 57-60SF 61Min 62-65SF 66-67Atl 68OakA | | 6'4" | 240 | Southern Calif. | 2 | |
| Rudolph, Jack LB | 60,62-65BosA 66MiaA | | 6'3" | 228 | Georgia Tech | 3 | |
| Rule, Gordon DB | 68-69GB | | 6'2" | 180 | Dartmouth | | |
| Ruple, Ernie DT | 68Pit | | 6'4" | 256 | Arkansas | | |
| Rush, Jerry DT | 65-71Det | | 6'4" | 264 | Michigan State | | |
| Rushing, Marion LB | 59ChiC 60-61MS 62-65StL 66-68Atl 68HouA | | 6'2" | 223 | Southern Illinois | 4 | 2 |

| Use Name (Nickname) - Positions | Team by Year | See Section | Hgt. | Wgt. | College | Int | Pts |
|---|---|---|---|---|---|---|---|
| Russ, Pat DT | 63Min | | 6'4" | 255 | Purdue | | |
| Russell, Benny QB | 68BufA | | 6'1" | 190 | Louisville | | |
| Rutgens, Joe DT | 61-69Was | | 6'2" | 258 | Illinois | | |
| Rutkowski, Charlie DE | 60BufA | | 6'3" | 248 | Ripon | | |
| Rutkowski, Ed FL-HB-OE-QB-WR | 63-68BufA | 123 | 6'1" | 204 | Notre Dame | | 36 |
| Ryan, Frank QB | 58-61LA 62-68Cle 69-70Was | 12 | 6'3" | 199 | Rice | | 42 |
| Ryan, Joe DE | 60NY-A | | 6'2" | 235 | Villanova | | |
| Rychiec, Tom OE | 58Det 60-62BufA 63DenA | 2 | 6'3" | 220 | American Inter. | | 18 |
| Ryder, Nick FB | 63-64Det | | 6' | 208 | Miami (Fla.) | | 12 |
| Rzempoluch, Ted DB | 63Was | | 6'1" | 195 | Virginia | | |
| Sabal, Ron OT-OG | 60-61OakA | | 6'2" | 238 | Purdue | | |
| Sabatino, Bill DT | 68Cle 69Atl | | 6'3" | 245 | Colorado | | |
| Saffold, Saint WR | 68CinA | 2 | 6'4" | 202 | San Jose State | | |
| Saidock, Tom DT | 58Phi 59JJ 60-61NY-A 62BufA | | 6'5" | 261 | Michigan State | | |
| Saimes, George DB-HB | 63-69BufA 70-72Den | | 5'10" | 188 | Michigan State | 22 | 6 |
| St. Jean, Len OG-DE | 64-69BosA 70Bos 71-73NE | | 6'1" | 244 | Northern Michigan | | |
| Sample, Johnny DB-HB | 58-60Bal 61-62Pit 63-65Was 66-68NY-A | 3 | 6'1" | 203 | Md. Eastern Shore | 41 | 36 |
| Sandeman, Bill OT-DT | 66Dal 67NO 67-73Atl | | 6'6" | 254 | U. of Pacific | | |
| Sanders, Bob LB | 67Atl 68JJ | | 6'3" | 235 | North Texas | | |
| Sanders, Daryl OT | 63-66Det | | 6'5" | 248 | Ohio State | | |
| Sanders, Lonnie DB | 63-67Was 68-69StL | | 6'3" | 206 | Michigan State | 12 | |
| Sandusky, Alex OG | 54-66Bal | | 6'1" | 235 | Clarion | | |
| Sandusky, Mike OG | 57-65Phi | | 6' | 231 | Maryland | | |
| Sapienza, Rick DB-HB | 60NY-A | | 5'11" | 185 | Villanova | | |
| Sapp, Theron HB-FB | 59-63Phi 63-65Pit 66JJ | 2 | 6'1" | 203 | Georgia | | 30 |
| Sardisco, Tony OG-LB | 56Was 56SF 60-62BosA | | 6'2" | 226 | Tulane | | |
| Sartin, Dan DT | 69SD-A | | 6'1" | 245 | Mississippi | | |
| Satcher, Doug LB | 66-68BosA | | 6' | 221 | Southern Miss. | 1 | 2 |
| Sauer, George WR-OE | 65-69NY-A 70NYJ | 2 | 6'1" | 199 | Texas | | 172 |
| Saul, Bill LB | 62-63Bal 64,66-68Pit 69NO 70Det | | 6'4" | 225 | Penn State | 4 | 2 |
| Sauls, Mac DB | 68-69Atl | | 6' | 185 | SW Texas State | | |
| Saxton, Jimmy HB | 62DalA | | 5'11" | 173 | Texas | | |
| Sayers, Gale HB | 65-71ChiB | 23 | 6' | 199 | Kansas | | 336 |
| Sayers, Ron HB | 69SD-A | | 6'1" | 202 | Nebraska-Omaha | | |
| Sbranti, Ron LB | 66DenA | | 6'2" | 230 | Utah State | | |
| Scales, Charlie FB-HB | 60-61Pit 62-65Cle 66Atl | 23 | 5'11" | 214 | Indiana | | |
| Scarpati, Joe DB-HB | 64-69Phi 70NO 71JJ | | 5'10" | 185 | N. Carolina State | 25 | 18 |
| Scarpitto, Bob FL-WR | 61SD-A 62-67DenA 68BosA | 2 4 | 5'11" | 194 | Notre Dame | | 170 |
| Schaffer, Joe LB | 60BufA | | 6' | 210 | Tennessee | | |
| Schafrath, Dick OT-OG-DE | 57-71Cle | | 6'3" | 253 | Ohio State | | |
| Schick, Doyle LB | 61Was | | 6'1" | 210 | Kansas | | |
| Schictle, Henry QB | 64NYG | | 6'2" | 190 | Wichita State | | |
| Schleicher, Maury LB-DE | 59ChiC 60LA-A 61-62SD-A | | 6'3" | 238 | Penn State | 1 | |
| Schmautz, Ray LB | 66OakA | | 6'1" | 225 | San Diego State | | |
| Schmedding, Jim OG | 68-69SD-A 70SD | | 6'2" | 250 | Weber State | | |
| Schmidt, Bob C-OT-OG | 59-60NYG 61-63HouA 64-65BosA 66-67BufA | | 6'4" | 248 | Minnesota | | |
| Schmidt, Henry (Hank) DT-DE | 59-60SF 61-64SD-A 65BufA 66NY-A | | 6'4" | 258 | Southern Calif., Trinity (Texas) | 1 | 6 |
| Schmidt, Roy OG-OT | 67-68NO 69Atl 70Was 71Min | | 6'3" | 250 | Long Beach State | | |
| Schmitt, John C | 64-69NY-A 70-73NYJ 74GB | | 6'4" | 253 | Hofstra | | |
| Schmitz, Bob LB | 61-66Pit 66Min | | 6'1" | 235 | Wisconsin, Montana State | 3 | 8 |
| Schoenke, Ray OG-OT-C | 6t3-64Dal 66-75Was | | 6'3" | 246 | S.M.U. | | |
| Scholtz, Bob C-OG | 60-64Det 65-66NYG | | 6'4" | 250 | Notre Dame | | |
| Schottenheimer, Marty LB | 65-68BufA 69BosA 70Bos HC84-88Cle HC89-95KC | | 6'3" | 225 | Pittsburgh | 6 | 6 |
| Schuh, Harry OT-OG | 65-69OakA 70Oak 71-73LA 74GB | | 6'2" | 260 | Memphis State | | |
| Schultz, Randy HB-FB | 66Cle 67-68NO | 2 | 5'11" | 210 | Iowa State | | 12 |
| Schumacher, Gregg DE | 67-68LA | | 6'2" | 240 | Illinois | | |
| Schweda, Brian DE | 66ChiB 67-68NO | | 6'3' | 240 | Kansas | | |
| Schwedes, Ger HB | 60-61BosA | | 6'1" | 205 | Syracuse | | |
| Schweickert, Bob HB-FL | 65,67NY-A | | 6'1" | 193 | Virginia Tech | | |
| Scibelli, Joe OG | 61-75LA | | 6'1" | 256 | Notre Dame, American Inter. | | |
| Scott, Bill DB | 68DenA | | 6' | 188 | Idaho | | |
| Scott, Jack DT | 60-61BufA | | 6'4" | 260 | Ohio State | | |
| Scott, Lew DB | 66DenA | | 5'10" | 173 | Oregon State | | |
| Scott, Wilbert LB | 61Pit | | 6' | 215 | Indiana | | |
| Scotti, Ben DB | 59-61Was 62-63Phi 64SF | | 6'1" | 185 | Maryland | 10 | |
| Scrabis, Bob QB | 60-62NY-A | 1 | 6'3" | 223 | Penn State | | 6 |
| Scrutchins, Ed DE | 66HouA | | 6'3" | 260 | Toledo | | |
| Sczurek, Stan LB | 63-65Cle 66NYG | | 5'11" | 229 | Purdue | 1 | |
| Seals, George DT-OG-OT | 64Was 65-71ChiB 72-73KC | | 6'2" | 259 | Missouri | 1 | 6 |
| Sedlock, Bob OT | 60BufA | | 6'4" | 295 | Georgia | | |
| Seedborg, John K | 65Was 66MS | | 6' | 227 | Arizona State | | |
| Selawski, Gene OT-OG | 59LA 60Cle 61SD-A | | 6'4" | 252 | Purdue | | |
| Sellers, Goldie DB | 66-67SD-A 68-69KC-A 70LJ | 3 | 6'2" | 198 | Grambling | 13 | 30 |
| Sestak, Tom DT-OT | 62-68BufA | | 6'5" | 267 | Texas A&M, Baylor, McNeese State | 2 | 18 |
| Shackleford, Don OG | 64DenA | | 6'4" | 255 | U.of Pacific | | |
| Shann, Bob DB | 65Phi 66JJ 67Phi | | 6'1" | 189 | Boston College | 1 | 6 |
| Shannon, Carver DB-HB | 62-64LA | 3 | 6'1" | 201 | Southern Illinois | 4 | 6 |
| Sharockman, Ed DB | 62-72Min | | 6' | 200 | Pittsburgh | 40 | 36 |
| Shaw, Billy OG | 61-69BufA | | 6'3" | 250 | Georgia Tech | | |
| Shaw, Glenn FB-HB | 60ChiB 62LA 63-64OakA | 2 | 6'1" | 221 | Kentucky | | 24 |
| Shaw, Nate LB | 69-70LA | | 6'2" | 205 | Southern Calif. | | |
| Shay, Jerry DT | 66-67Min 68-69Atl 70-71NYG | | 6'3" | 244 | Purdue | | |
| Shea, Pat OG | 62-65SD-A | | 6'1" | 241 | Southern Calif. | | |
| Sherer, Dave OE | 59Bal 60Dal | 4 | 6'3" | 218 | S.M.U. | | |
| Sherlag, Bob FL | 66Atl | | 6' | 197 | Memphis State | | 6 |
| Sherman, Bob DB | 64-65Atl | | 6'2" | 195 | Iowa | 1 | |
| Sherman, Tom QB | 68-69BosA 69BufA | 12 | 6' | 190 | Penn State | | |
| Shields, Lebron DE-OT | 60Bal 61Min | | 6'4" | 243 | Tennessee | | 2 |
| Shiner, Dick QB | 64-66Was 67Cle 68-69Pit 70NYG 71,73Atl 73-74NE | 12 | 6' | 197 | Maryland | | 12 |
| Shinnick, Don LB | 57-69Bal | | 6' | 232 | U.C.L.A. | 37 | |
| Shirkey, George DT | 60-61HouA 62OakA | | 6'4" | 252 | Austin | | |
| Shivers, Roy HB | 66-72StL | 23 | 6' | 200 | Utah State | | 90 |
| Shoals, Roger OT-OG | 63-64Cle 65-70Det 71Den | | 6'4" | 256 | Maryland | | 6 |
| Shockley, Bill HB-K | 60-61NY-A 61BufA 62NY-A 68Pit | 23 5 | 6' | 185 | West Chester | | 181 |
| Shofner, Del OE-DB | 57-60LA 61-67NYG | 2 4 | 6'3" | 186 | Baylor | 3 | 306 |
| Shofner, Jim DB | 58-63Cle HC90Cle | 3 | 6'2" | 191 | Texas Christian | 20 | |
| Shonta, Chuck DB | 60-67BosA | | 6' | 196 | Eastern Michigan | 15 | 6 |
| Shorter, Jim DB | 62-63Cle 64-67Was 69Pit | | 5'11" | 184 | Detroit | 15 | 6 |

| Use Name (Nickname) - Positions | Team by Year | See Section | Hgt. | Wgt. | College | Int | Pts |
|---|---|---|---|---|---|---|---|
| Shy, Les HB | 68-69Dal 70NYG | 23 | 6'1" | 202 | Long Beach State | | 24 |
| Sidle, Jimmy TE-HB | 66Atl | | 6'2" | 215 | Auburn | | |
| Sieminski, Chuck DT | 63-65SF 66-67Atl 68Det | | 6'4" | 262 | Penn State | | |
| Silas, Sam DT-DE | 63-67StL 68NYG 69-70SF | | 6'4" | 251 | Southern Illinois | | |
| Silvestri, Carl DB | 65StL 66Atl | | 6' | 195 | Wisconsin | | |
| Simkus, Arnie DT-DE | 65NY-A 67Min | | 6'4" | 245 | Michigan | | |
| Simmons, Dave LB | 65-67StL 67NO 68Dal | | 6'4" | 245 | Georgia Tech | 2 | |
| Simmons, Jerry WR-OE | 65-67Pit 67NO 67-69Atl 69ChiB 71-74Den | 2 | 6'1" | 190 | Bethune-Cookman | | 54 |
| Simmons, Leon LB | 63DenA | | 6' | 225 | Grambling | | |
| Simms, Bob LB-OE-DE | 60-61NYG 62Pit | | 6'1" | 223 | Rutgers | | |
| Simon, Jim OG-OT-DE-LB | 63-65Det 66-68Atl | | 6'5" | 235 | Miami (Fla.) | | |
| Simpson, Howard DE | 64Min | | 6'5" | 230 | Auburn | | |
| Simpson, Jackie DB | 58-60Bal 61-62Pit | | 5'10" | 183 | Florida | 2 | |
| Simpson, Jackie LB | 61DenA 62-64OakA | 5 | 6'1" | 226 | Mississippi | 5 | 15 |
| Simpson, Willie FB | 62OakA | | 6' | 218 | San Fran. State | | |
| Singer, Karl OT | 66-68BosA | | 6'3" | 250 | Purdue | | |
| Sisk, John DB | 64ChiB | | 6'3" | 195 | Miami (Fla.) | | |
| Skaggs, Jim OG-OT | 63-67Phi 68KJ 69-72Phi | | 6'2" | 246 | Washington | | |
| Sklopan, John DB | 63DenA | | 5'11" | 190 | Southern Miss. | | |
| Skoronski, Bob OT-C | 56Gb 57-58MS 59-69GB | | 6'3" | 249 | Indiana | | |
| Slaby, Lou LB-DT | 64-65NYG 66Det | | 6'3" | 235 | Pittsburgh | | |
| Slaughter, Mickey QB | 63-66DenA | 12 | 6' | 190 | Louisiana Tech | | 8 |
| Sligh, Richard DT | 67OakA | | 7' | 300 | N. Carolina Central | | |
| Sloan, Steve QB | 66-67Atl | 1 | 6' | 185 | Alabama | | |
| Smiley, Tom FB | 68CinA 69DenA 70Hou | 2 | 6'1' | 235 | Arizona, Lamar | | 30 |
| Smith, Allen HB | 66NY-A | | 5'11" | 195 | Findlay | | |
| Smith, Allen HB | 66-67BufA | 2 | 6' | 200 | Ft. Valley State | | |
| Smith, Billy Ray DT-DE | 57LA 58-60Pit 61-62Bal 63JJ 64-70Bal | | 6'4" | 240 | Auburn, Arkansas | | |
| Smith, Bob DB | 68HouA | | 6' | 180 | Miami-Ohio | | |
| Smith, Bobby DB | 62-65LA 65-66Det | 3 | 6' | 193 | U.C.L.A. | 5 | 12 |
| Smith, Bobby HB | 64-65BufA 66Pit | 2 | 6' | 203 | North Texas | | 30 |
| Smith, Carl FB | 60BufA | | 6' | 200 | Tennessee | | 6 |
| Smith, Dan DB | 61DenA | | 5'10" | 180 | Northeastern Okla. | | |
| Smith, Dave FB | 60-64HouA | | 6'1" | 209 | Ripon | | 108 |
| Smith, Dick DB-HB-OE | 67-68Was | | 6' | 205 | Northwestern | 4 | |
| Smith, Don OG | 67DenA | | 6'4" | 240 | Florida A&M | | |
| Smith, Fletcher DB | 66-67KC-A 68-69CinA 70-71Cin | | 6'2" | 182 | Tennessee State | 15 | 2 |
| Smith, Gordon OE | 61-65Min | 2 | 6'2" | 211 | Arizona State, Missouri | | 78 |
| Smith, Hal DT | 60BosA 60DenA 61OakA | | 6'5" | 250 | U.C.L.A. | | |
| Smith, Hugh OE | 62Was | | 6'4" | 215 | Kansas | | |
| Smith, Jackie TE-OE | 63-77StL 78Dal | 2 4 | 6'4" | 225 | Northwestern La. | | 258 |
| Smith, J.D. FB-HB-DB | 56ChiB 56-64SF 65-66Dal | 2 | 6'1" | 205 | N. Carolina A&T | 2 | 276 |
| Smith, J.D. OT | 59-63Phi 64Det 65JJ 66Det | | 6'5" | 250 | Rice | | 6 |
| Smith, J.D. (Jet Stream) FB-HB | 60OakA 61ChiB | 2 | 6' | 215 | Compton C.C. | | |
| Smith, Jeff LB | 66NYG 67KJ | | 6' | 237 | Southern Calif. | 1 | |
| Smith, Jim DB | 68Was | | 6'3" | 195 | Oregon | | 6 |
| Smith, Jimmy DB | 69DenA | | 6'3" | 190 | Utah State | | |
| Smith, Jim Ray OG-OT-DE | 56-62Cle 63-64Dal | | 6'3" | 241 | Baylor | | |
| Smith, Noland (Super Gnat) WR-FL-HB | 67-69KC-A 69SF | 3 | 5'6" | 155 | Tennessee State | | 12 |
| Smith, Ralph (Catfish) TE-OE-DB | 62-64Phi 65-68Cle 69Atl | 2 | 6'2" | 214 | Mississippi | | 36 |
| Smith, Ron QB | 65LA 66Pit | 1 | 6'5" | 220 | Richmond | | |
| Smith, Russ HB-FB | 67-69SD-A 70SD | 2 | 6'1" | 214 | Miami (Fla.) | | 60 |
| Smith, Tommie WR | 69CinA | | 6'4" | 190 | San Jose State | | |
| Smith, Willie OG-OT | 60DenA 61OakA | | 6'2" | 255 | Michigan | | |
| Smith, Zeke OG-DE-LB | 60Bal 61NYG | | 6'2" | 233 | Auburn | | |
| Smolinski, Mark FB-TE | 61-62Bal 63-68NY-A | 2 | 6' | 218 | Wyoming | | 102 |
| Snead, Norm QB | 61-63Was 64-70Phi 71Min 72-74NYG 74-75SF 76NYG | 12 | 6'4" | 215 | Wake Forest | | 138 |
| Snell, Matt FB | 64-69NY-A 70-72NYJ | 2 | 6'2" | 220 | Ohio State | | 186 |
| Snidow, Ron DE-DT | 63-67Was 68-72Cle | | 6'4" | 249 | Oregon | 1 | 2 |
| Snorton, Matt DE | 64DenA | | 6'5" | 250 | Michigan State | | |
| Snowden, Jim OT-DE | 65-71Was 72JJ | | 6'3" | 255 | Notre Dame | | |
| Snyder, Al FL | 64BosA | | 6' | 195 | Holy Cross | | |
| Sobocinski, Phil C | 68Atl | | 6'3" | 235 | Wisconsin | | |
| Soleau, Bob LB | 64Pit | | 6'2" | 235 | William & Mary | | |
| Soltis, Bob DB | 60-61BosA | | 6'2" | 205 | Minnesota | 2 | |
| Sommer, Mike HB-DB | 58-59Was 59-61Bal 61Was 63OakA | 2 | 5'11" | 190 | George Washington | | 12 |
| Songin, Butch QB | 60-61BosA 62NY-A | 12 | 6'2" | 200 | Boston College | | 18 |
| Sorey, Jim (Bull) DT | 60-62BufA | | 6'4" | 278 | Texas Southern | | |
| Sorrell, Henry LB | 67DenA | | 6'1" | 215 | Tenn.-Chattanooga | | |
| Sortun, Rick OG | 64-69StL | | 6'2" | 234 | Washington | | |
| South, Ronnie QB | 68NO | 1 | 6'1" | 195 | Arkansas | | |
| Speights, Dick DB | 68SD-A | | 5'11" | 175 | Wyoming | | |
| Spence, Julian (Sus) DB-FL | 56ChiC 57SF 60-61HouA | | 5'11" | 170 | Sam Houston St. | 6 | |
| Spikes, Jack FB | 60-62DalA 63-64KC-A 64SD-A 65HouA 66-67BufA | 2 5 | 6'2" | 221 | Texas Christian | | 262 |
| Spiller, Phil DB | 67StL 68Atl 68CinA | | 6' | 195 | Los Angeles State | 2 | |
| Stacy, Billy DB-HB | 59ChiC 60-63StL | 23 | 6'1" | 191 | Mississippi State | 20 | 42 |
| Stafford, Dick DE-DT | 62-63Phi | | 6'4" | 253 | Texas Tech | | |
| Stalcup, Jerry LB-OG | 60LA 61-62DenA | | 6' | 230 | Wisconsin | 1 | |
| Stallings, Don DT-DE-OT | 60Was | | 6'4" | 250 | North Carolina | | |
| Stallings, Larry LB | 63-76StL | | 6'2" | 230 | Georgia Tech | 9 | 18 |
| Stanciel, Jeff HB | 69Atl | | 6' | 192 | Miss. Valley St. | | |
| Stanton, Jack HB | 61Pit | | 6'1" | 190 | N. Carolina State | | |
| Starks, Marsh DB | 63-64NY-A | 3 | 6' | 190 | Illinois | 1 | 6 |
| Starling, Bruce DB | 63DenA | | 6'1" | 186 | Florida | | |
| Starr, Bart QB | 56-71GB HC75-83GB | 12 | 6'1" | 197 | Alabama | | 90 |
| Staten, Randy DE | 67NYG | | 6'1" | 225 | Minnesota | | |
| Steffen, Jim DB | 59-61Det 61-65Was 68GJ | 3 | 6' | 196 | Occidental, U.C.L.A. | 17 | 12 |
| Stehouwer, Ron OG-OT | 60-64Pit | | 6'2" | 232 | Colorado State | | |
| Stephens, Harold QB | 62NY-A | | 5'11" | 175 | Hardin-Simmons | | |
| Stephens, Larry DE-DT | 60-61Cle 62LA 63-67Dal | | 6'4" | 245 | Texas | 1 | 6 |
| Stephens, Tom DE-DB | 60-64BosA | 2 | 6'1" | 207 | Syracuse | 1 | 36 |
| Stephenson, Kay QB | 67SD-A 68BufA HC83-85Buf | 1 | 6'1" | 208 | Florida | | |
| Stetz, Bill OG | 67Phi | | 6'3" | 250 | Boston College | | |
| Stevens, Bill QB | 68-69GB | | 6'3" | 195 | Texas-El Paso | | |
| Stickles, Monte OE-TE | 60-67SF 68NO | 2 | 6'4" | 232 | Notre Dame | | 96 |
| Stiger, Jim HB-FB | 63-65Dal 65-67LA | 23 | 5'11" | 204 | Washington | | 24 |
| Stinnette, Jim FB-LB | 61-62DenA | 2 | 6'1" | 230 | Oregon State | 1 | 12 |
| Stith, Carel DT-DE | 67-69HouA | | 6'5" | 267 | Nebraska | | |

| Use Name (Nickname) - Positions | Team by Year | See Section | Hgt. | Wgt. | College | Int | Pts |
|---|---|---|---|---|---|---|---|
| Stoepel, Terry TE | 67ChiB 68-69MS 70Hou | | 6'4" | 235 | Tulsa | | |
| Stofa, John QB | 66-67MiaA 68-69CinA 69MiaA 70Mia | 1 | 6'3" | 210 | Buffalo State | | 6 |
| Stokes, Jesse DB | 68DenA | | 6' | 190 | Corpus Christi | | |
| Stokes, Sims OE | 67Dal | | 6'1" | 198 | Kansas, Northern Arizona | | |
| Stone, Donnie HB-FB | 61-64DenA 65BufA 66HouA | 2 | 6'2" | 205 | Arkansas | | 102 |
| Stone, Jack OT | 60DalA 61-62OakA | | 6'2" | 245 | Oregon | | |
| Stonebreaker, Steve LB-OE | 62-63Min 64-66Bal 67-68NO | 2 | 6'3" | 223 | Detroit | 2 | 12 |
| Stotter, Rich LB | 68HouA | | 6' | 225 | Houston | | |
| Stovell, Jerry DB | 63-71StL | 34 | 6'2" | 201 | Louisiana State | 18 | 12 |
| Stover, Smokey LB | 60-62DalA 63-66KC-A | | 6' | 229 | Northeast La. | 6 | |
| Strahan, Art DT | 68Atl | | 6'5" | 266 | Texas Southern | | |
| Strahan, Ray DE | 65HouA | | 6'6" | 250 | Texas Southern | | |
| Stram, Hank | HC60-62DalA HC63-69KC-A HC70-74KC HC76-77NO | | | | Purdue | | |
| Strand, Eli (Deacon) OG | 66Pit 67NO | | 6'2" | 250 | Iowa State | | |
| Stransky, Bob HB | 60DenA | 2 | 6'1" | 180 | Colorado | | |
| Stratton, Mike LB | 62-69BufA 70-72Buf 73SD | | 6'3" | 236 | Tennessee | 21 | 12 |
| Stricker, Tony DB | 63NY-A | | 6' | 185 | Colorado | 1 | |
| Strickland, Dave OG | 60DenA | | 6' | 220 | Memphis State | | |
| Strofolino, Mike LB | 65LA 65Bal 66-68StL | | 6'2" | 223 | Villanova | | |
| Stromberg, Mike LB | 68NY-A | | 6'2" | 235 | Temple | | |
| Strugar, George DT | 57-61LA 62Pit 62-63NY-A | | 6'5" | 259 | Washington | 1 | |
| Studstill, Pat FL-WR | 61-62Det 63BL 64-67Det 68-71LA 72NE | 234 | 6'1" | 176 | Houston | | 114 |
| Sturm, Jerry C-OT-OG-FB | 61-66Den 67-70NO 71Hou 72Phi | | 6'3" | 257 | Illinois | | |
| Stynchula, Andy DE-DT-C | 60-63Was 64-65NYG 66-67Bal 68Dal | 5 | 6'3" | 252 | Penn State | | 22 |
| Suchy, Larry DB | 68Atl | | 5'11" | 180 | Mississippi Coll. | | |
| Suci, Bob DB | 62HouA 63BosA | 3 | 5'10" | 182 | Michigan State | 9 | 12 |
| Suggs, Walt OT-C | 62-69HouA 70-71Hou | | 6'5" | 257 | Mississippi State | | |
| Sullivan, Dan OG-OT | 62-72Bal | | 6'3" | 250 | Boston College | | |
| Summers, Jim DB | 67DenA | | 5'10" | 175 | Michigan State | | |
| Sunde, Milt OG-C | 64-74Min | | 6'2" | 245 | Minnesota | | |
| Sutro, John OT | 62SF | | 6'4" | 245 | San Jose State | | |
| Sutton, Archie OT | 65-67Min | | 6'4" | 263 | Illinois | | |
| Sutton, Mickey DB | 66HouA | | 6' | 190 | Auburn | | |
| Svihus, Bob OT-OG | 65-69OakA 70Oak 71-73NYJ | | 6'4" | 245 | Southern Calif. | | |
| Swain, Bill LB | 63LA 64Min 65NYG 66KJ 67NYG 68-69Det | | 6'2" | 229 | Oregon | 2 | 6 |
| Swanson, Terry K | 67-68BosA 69CinA | 4 | 6' | 210 | Massachusetts | | |
| Swetland, Dick OG | 68HouA | | 6'3" | 245 | Notre Dame | | |
| Sweeney, Neal OE | 67DenA | | 6'2" | 170 | Tulsa | | |
| Sweeney, Walt OG | 63-69BosA 70-73SD 74-75Was 76KJ | | 6'3" | 256 | Syracuse | | |
| Sweetan, Karl QB | 66-67Det 68NO 69-70LA | 12 | 6'1" | 203 | Texas A&M, Wake Forest | | 12 |
| Swinford, Wayne DB-OE-FL | 65-67SF | | 6' | 194 | Georgia | | |
| Swink, Jim HB | 60DalA | | 6'1" | 185 | Texas Christian | | |
| Sykes, Gene DB | 63-65BufA 67DenA | | 6'1" | 196 | Louisiana State | 4 | |
| Symank, Johnny DB | 57-62GB 63StL | | 5'11" | 180 | Florida | 19 | 6 |
| Szczecko, Joe DT | 66-68Atl 69NYG | | 6' | 245 | Northwestern | | |
| Szymakowski, Dave WR | 68NO | | 6'2" | 198 | West Texas State | | |
| Szymanski, Dick C-LB | 55Bal 56MS 57-68Bal | | 6'3" | 233 | Notre Dame | 6 | 6 |
| Talamini, Bob OG | 60-67HouA 68NY-A | | 6'1" | 249 | Kentucky | | |
| Talbert, Don OT-LB | 62Dal 63-64MS 65Dal 66-68Atl 69-70NO 71Dal | | 6'5" | 248 | Texas | | |
| Taliaferro, Mike QB | 64-67NY-A 68-69BosA 70Bos 71NE 72Buf | 12 | 6'2" | 206 | Illinois | | 2 |
| Tarasovic, George DE-LB-C | 52-53Pit 54-55MS 56-63Pit 63-65Phi 66DenA | | 6'4" | 245 | Louisiana State | 7 | 18 |
| Tarbox, Bruce OG | 61LA | | 6'2" | 230 | Syracuse | | |
| Tarkenton, Fran QB | 61-66Min 67-71NYG 72-78Min | 12 | 6'1" | 190 | Georgia | | 192 |
| Tarr, Jerry HB | 62DenA | | 6' | 190 | Oregon | | 12 |
| Tatman, Pete HB | 67Min | | 6'1" | 220 | Nebraska | | |
| Taylor, Bob DE-DT | 63-64NYG | | 6'3" | 238 | Md. Eastern Shore | | |
| Taylor, Jim FB | 59-66GB 67NO | 2 | 6' | 214 | Louisiana State | | 558 |
| Taylor, Lionel OE-WR-FL | 59ChiB 60-66DenA 67-68HouA | 2 | 6'2" | 215 | N. Mex. Highlands | | 270 |
| Taylor, Roosevelt DB | 61-69ChiB 69-71SF 72Was 73JJ | 3 | 5'11" | 186 | Grambling | 32 | 36 |
| Taylor, Sammy FL | 65SD-A | | 6' | 190 | Grambling | | |
| Tensi, Steve QB | 65-66SD-A 67-69DenA 70Den | 12 | 6'5" | 213 | Florida State | | |
| Teresa, Tony HB | 58SF 60OakA | 2 | 5'9" | 188 | San Jose State | | 60 |
| Terrell, Marvin OG | 60-62DalA 63KC-A | | 6'1" | 236 | Mississippi | | |
| Tharp, Corky DB | 60NY-A | | 5'10" | 180 | Alabama | 2 | |
| Theofiledes, Harry QB | 68Was | | 5'10" | 180 | Waynesburg | | |
| Thibert, Jim LB | 65DenA | | 6'3" | 230 | Toledo | | |
| Thomas, Aaron TE-OE-FL-WR | 61-62SF 62-70NYG | 2 | 6'3" | 209 | Oregon State | | 222 |
| Thomas, Clendon DB-OE-FL-HB | 58-61LA 62-68Pit | 2 | 6'2" | 196 | Oklahoma | 27 | 30 |
| Thomas, Gene HB | 66-67KC-A 68BosA 68OakA | 2 | 6'1" | 210 | Florida A&M | | 36 |
| Thomas, John OG-OT-LB | 58-67SF 68JJ | | 6'4" | 246 | U. of Pacific | | |
| Thompson, Bobby DB | 64-68Det 69NO | 3 | 5'10" | 179 | Arizona | 10 | |
| Thompson, Don DE | 62-63Bal 64Phi | | 6'4" | 230 | Richmond | | |
| Thompson, Jim DT | 65DenA | | 6'3" | 255 | Southern Illinois | | |
| Thornton, Bill FB | 63-65StL 66JJ 67StL | 2 | 6'1" | 214 | Nebraska | | 12 |
| Thornton, Bubba WR | 69BufA | 23 | 6' | 175 | Texas Christian | | |
| Thornton, Jack LB | 66MiaA | | 6'1" | 230 | Auburn | | |
| Thurlow, Steve HB-FB | 64-66NYG 66-68Was | 2 | 6'3" | 217 | Stanford | | 36 |
| Thurston, Fuzzy OG | 58Bal 59-67GB | | 6'1" | 247 | Valparaiso | | |
| Tidmore, Sam LB | 62-63Cle | | 6'1" | 223 | Ohio State | | |
| Tiller, Jim HB | 62NY-A | 2 | 5'9" | 165 | Purdue | | |
| Timberlake, Bob QB | 65NYG | 5 | 6'4" | 220 | Michigan | | 24 |
| Tingelhoff, Mick C | 62-78Min | | 6'1" | 237 | Nebraska | | |
| Tobey, Dave LB | 66-67Min 68DenA | | 6'3" | 230 | Oregon | | |
| Tobin, Bill HB | 63HouA | 2 | 5'11" | 210 | Missouri | | 32 |
| Toburen, Nelson LB | 61-62GB | | 6'3" | 235 | Wichita State | | |
| Todd, Jim HB | 66Det | | 5'11" | 195 | Ball State | | |
| Todd, Larry HB | 65-69OakA 70Oak | 23 | 6'1" | 185 | Arizona State | | 42 |
| Tolar, Charley FB-HB | 60-66HouA | 2 | 5'7" | 199 | Louisiana State, Northwestern La. | | 138 |
| Tolleson, Tommy DB | 66Atl | | 6' | 185 | Alabama | | |
| Toner, Ed DT-LB | 67-69BosA 70JJ | | 6'3" | 250 | Massachusetts | | |
| Torczon, LaVerne DE | 60-62BufA 62-65NY-A 66MiaA | | 6'2" | 243 | Nebraska | 2 | 6 |
| Townes, Willie DE-DT | 66-68Dal 69JJ 70NO | | 6'5" | 263 | Tulsa | | 8 |
| Towns, Bobby DB-DE-HB | 60StL 61BosA | | 6'1" | 180 | Georgia | | |
| Tracey, John (Jack) LB-OE-TE | 59ChiC 60StL 61Phi 62-67BufA | 2 | 6'3" | 225 | Texas A&M | 12 | 4 |
| Tracy, Tom (Tom the Bomb) HB-FB | 56-57Det 58-63Pit 63-64Was | 12 | 5'9" | 205 | Tennessee | | 199 |

| Use Name (Nickname) - Positions | Team by Year | See Section | Hgt. | Wgt. | College | Int | Pts |
|---|---|---|---|---|---|---|---|
| Trammell, Allen DB | 66HouA | | 6' | 190 | Florida | | |
| Trapp, Richard WR | 68BufA 69SD-A | 2 | 6'1" | 174 | Florida | | |
| Trask, Orville DT | 60-61HouA 62OakA | | 6'4" | 260 | Rice | 1 | |
| Travenio, Herb K | 64-65SD-A | 5 | 6' | 218 | none | | 110 |
| Travis, John FB | 66SD-A | | 6'1" | 216 | San Jose State | | |
| Traynham, Jerry HB | 61DenA | | 5'10" | 190 | Southern Calif. | | |
| Traynham, Wade K | 66-67Atl | 5 | 6'2" | 218 | Frederick | | 45 |
| Trimble, Wayne DB | 67SF | | 6'3" | 203 | Alabama | | |
| Triplett, Bill HB-FB-DB | 62-63StL 64IL 65-66StL 67NYG 68-72Det | 23 | 6'2" | 212 | Miami-Ohio | 1 | 132 |
| Tripucka, Frank QB | 49Det 50-52ChiC 52Dal 53-59CFL 60-63DenA | 12 4 | 6'2" | 192 | Notre Dame | | 36 |
| Trosch, Gene DE-DT | 67KC-A 68JJ 69KC-A 70LJ | | 6'7" | 277 | Miami (Fla.) | | |
| Truax, Billy TE-OE | 64-70LA 71-73Dal | 2 | 6'5" | 238 | Louisiana State | | 108 |
| Truax, Dalton OT | 60OakA | | 6'2" | 235 | Tulane | | |
| Trull, Don QB | 64-67HouA 67BosA 68-69HouA | 12 | 6'1" | 189 | Baylor | | 84 |
| Tubbs, Jerry LB-C | 57-58ChiC 58-59SF 60-66Dal | | 6'2" | 221 | Oklahoma | 17 | |
| Tucker, Bill FB-HB-TE | 67-70SF 71ChiB | 23 | 6'2" | 221 | Tennessee State | | 78 |
| Tucker, Gary HB | 68MiaA | | 5'11" | 195 | Vanderbilt, Tenn.-Chattanooga | | |
| Tucker, Wendell WR-OE | 67-70LA | 2 | 5'10" | 185 | S. Carolina State | | |
| Tuckett, Phil WR | 68SD-A | | 6' | 180 | Weber State | | |
| Turner, Bake OE-WR-FL | 62Bal 63-69NY-A 70Bos | 23 | 6' | 180 | Texas Tech | | 150 |
| Turner, Herschel OG-OT | 64-65StL | | 6'3" | 230 | Kentucky | | |
| Turner, Vince DB | 64NY-A | | 5'11" | 190 | Missouri | 1 | |
| Tyrer, Jim OT | 61-62DalA 63-69KC-A 70-73KC 74Was | | 6'6" | 283 | Ohio State | | |
| Tyson, Dick OG | 66OakA 67DenA | | 6'2" | 245 | Tulsa | | |
| Underwood, Olen LB | 65NYG 66-69HouA 70Hou 71Den | | 6'1" | 224 | Texas | 5 | 2 |
| Unitas, Johnny QB | 56-72Bal 73SD | 12 | 6'1" | 194 | Louisville | | 78 |
| Urbanek, Jim DT | 68MiaA | | 6'4" | 270 | Mississippi | | |
| Urenda, Herm DB-OE | 63OakA | | 5'11" | 170 | U. of Pacific | | |
| Valdez, Vern DB | 60LA 61BufA 62OakA | | 5'11" | 190 | Cal. Poly.-Pomona Cal.-San Diego | | |
| Vallez, Emilio TE | 68-69ChiB | | 6'2" | 210 | New Mexico | | |
| VanderKelen, Ron QB | 63-67Min | 12 | 6'1" | 186 | Wisconsin | | 6 |
| Vandersea, Phil LB-DE-TE | 66GB 67NO 68-69GB | | 6'3" | 228 | Massachusetts | | |
| Van Raaphorst, Dick K | 64Dal 66-67SD-A | 5 | 5'11" | 215 | Ohio State | | 247 |
| Vargo, Larry DB-OE-LB | 62-63Det 64-65Min 66NYG 67KJ | | 6'3" | 212 | Detroit | 6 | 6 |
| Varrichione, Frank OT | 55-60Pit 61-65LA | | 6'1" | 234 | Notre Dame | | |
| Vasys, Arunas HB | 66-68Phi | | 6'2" | 232 | Notre Dame | | |
| Vaughn, Bob OG | 68DenA | | 6'4" | 240 | Mississippi | | |
| Vaughn, Tom DB | 65-71Det | 3 | 5'11" | 192 | Iowa State | 9 | |
| Vellone, Jim OG-OT | 66-70Min 71IL | | 6'2" | 255 | Southern Calif. | | |
| Vereb, Ed HB | 60Was | | 6' | 190 | Maryland | | |
| Villanueva, Danny K | 60-64LA 65-67Dal | 45 | 5'11' | 202 | New Mexico State | | 491 |
| Viltz, Theo DB | 66HouA | | 6'2" | 190 | Southern Calif. | | |
| Vogel, Bob OT | 63-72Bal | | 6'5" | 248 | Ohio State | | |
| Voight, Bob DT | 61OakA | | 6'5" | 265 | Los Angeles State | | |
| Vollenweider, Jim HB-FB | 62-63SF | 2 | 6'1" | 210 | Miami (Fla.) | | 12 |
| Von Sonn, Andy LB | 64LA | | 6'2" | 231 | U.C.L.A. | | |
| Voss, Lloyd DE-DT-OT | 64-65GB 66-71Pit 72Den | | 6'4" | 256 | Nebraska | 1 | |
| Wade, Bill QB | 54-60LA 61-66ChiB | 12 | 6'2" | 204 | Vanderbilt | | 144 |
| Wade, Bob DB | 68Pit 69Was 70Den | | 6'2" | 200 | Morgan State | 1 | |
| Wade. Tom QB | 64-65Pit | 1 | 6'2" | 195 | Texas | | |
| Wagstaff, Jim DB | 59ChiC 60-61BufA | | 6'2" | 192 | Idaho State | 9 | 6 |
| Wainscott, Lloyd DB | 69HouA 70Hou | | 6'1" | 235 | Texas | | |
| Walker, Clarence HB | 63DenA | | 6'1" | 205 | Southern Illinois | | |
| Walker, Malcolm C-OT | 66-69Dal 70GB | | 6'4" | 249 | Rice | | |
| Walker, Mickey OG-LB-C | 61-65NYG | | 6'2" | 232 | Michigan State | | |
| Walker, Wayne LB-K | 58-72Det | 5 | 6'2" | 225 | Idaho | 14 | 345 |
| Walker, Wayne K | 67KC-A 68HouA | 5 | 6'2" | 215 | Northwestern La. | | 50 |
| Walker, Willie FL | 66Det | | 6'3" | 200 | Tennessee State | | |
| Wallace, Henry DB | 60LA-A | | 6' | 195 | U. of Pacific | | |
| Waller, Charlie | HC69SD-A HC70SD | | | | Georgia | | |
| Walsh, Ed OT | 61NY-A | | 6'4" | 243 | Widener | | |
| Walters, Tom DB | 64-67Was | | 6'2" | 195 | Southern Miss. | 3 | 6 |
| Walton, Joe OE-DE | 57-60Was 61-63NYG 64XJ HC83-89NYJ | 2 | 5'11" | 202 | Pittsburgh | 1 | 168 |
| Walton, Sam OT | 68-69NY-A 71Hou | | 6'5" | 270 | East Texas State | | |
| Wantland, Hal DB | 66MiaA | | 6' | 195 | Tennessee | | |
| Ward, Carl DB | 67-68Cle 69NO | 3 | 5'9" | 180 | Michigan | 1 | 6 |
| Ward, Jim QB | 67-68Bal 71Phi 72JJ | 1 | 6'2" | 197 | Gettysburg | | |
| Ward, Paul DT | 61-62Det | | 6'3" | 247 | Whitworth | | |
| Warlick, Ernie DE | 62-65BufA | 2 | 6'4" | 234 | N. Car. Central | | 24 |
| Warner, Charley DB-HB | 63-64KC-A 64-66BufA 67JJ | 3 | 5'11" | 178 | Prairie View | 7 | 30 |
| Warren, Dewey QB | 68CinA | 1 | 6' | 205 | Tennessee | | |
| Warren, Jimmy DB | 64-65SD-A 66-69MiaA 70-74,77Oak | 3 | 5'11" | 178 | Illinois | 25 | 24 |
| Warwick, Lonnie DB | 65-72Min 73-74Atl 75WFL | | 6'3" | 235 | Tennessee Tech | 12 | 6 |
| Warzeka, Ron DT | 60OakA | | 6'4" | 250 | Montana State | | |
| Washington, Clarence DT | 69-70Pit 71JJ | | 6'3" | 265 | Ark.-Pine Bluff | | |
| Washington, Clyde DB-HB | 60-61BosA 63-65NY-A | | 6' | 202 | Purdue | 9 | |
| Washington, Dave TE | 68DenA | | 6'4" | 228 | Southern Calif. | | |
| Washington, Dick DB | 68MiaA | | 6'1" | 205 | Bethune-Cookman | | |
| Washington, Fred OT | 68Was | | 6'5" | 268 | North Texas | | |
| Washington, Teddy HB | 68CinA | | 5'11" | 210 | Colorado, San Diego State | | |
| Waskiewicz, Jim C-OT-LB | 66-67NY-A 69Atl | | 6'4" | 237 | Wichita State | | |
| Waters, Bob QB | 60-63SF | 12 | 6'2" | 184 | Presbyterian | | 18 |
| Watkins, Tom HB | 61Cle 62-65Det 66JJ 67Det 68Pit | 23 | 6'1" | 195 | Iowa State | | 102 |
| Watson, Dave OG | 63-64BosA | | 6'1" | 225 | Georgia Tech | | |
| Watson, Ed LB | 69HouA | | 6'2" | 222 | Grambling | | |
| Watters, Bob DE | 62-64NY-A | | 6'4" | 247 | Lincoln (Mo.) | | |
| Wayt, Russell LB | 65Dal | | 6'4" | 235 | Rice | | |
| Weatherford, Jim DB | 69Atl | | 5'10" | 180 | Tennessee | 1 | 6 |
| Weatherwax, Jim DT | 66-67GB 68KJ 69GB | | 6'7" | 265 | West Texas State, Los Angeles State | | |
| Webb, Allan DB-HB | 61-65NYG | | 5'11" | 180 | Arnold | 7 | |
| Webb, Don HB-DB | 61-62BosA 63JJ 64-69BosA 70Bos 71NE | | 5'10" | 196 | Iowa State | 21 | 24 |
| Webb, Ken HB-FB | 58-62Det 63Cle | 23 | 5'11" | 207 | Presbyterian | | 54 |
| Webster, Dave DB | 60-61DalA 62JJ | | 6'4" | 218 | Prairie View | 11 | 18 |
| Wegener, Bucky OG | 62-63HouA | | 5'10" | 245 | Missouri | | |
| Weir, Sammy FL | 65HouA 66NY-A | | 5'9" | 170 | Arkansas State | | |
| Weisacosky, Ed LB | 67NYG 68-69MiaA 70Mia 71-72NE | | 6' | 228 | Miami (Fla.) | 3 | |

| Use Name (Nickname) - Positions | Team by Year | See Section | Hgt. | Wgt. | College | Int | Pts |
|---|---|---|---|---|---|---|---|
| Welch, Jim DB-HB | 60-67Bal 68Det | | 6' | 191 | S.M.U. | 5 | 6 |
| Wellborn, Joe C | 66NYG | | 6'2" | 215 | Texas A&M | | |
| Wells, Bob OT | 68-69SD-A | | 6'4" | 273 | Johnson C. Smith | | |
| Wells, Harold LB | 65-68Phi | | 6'2" | 221 | Purdue | 4 | 6 |
| Wells, Joel HB | 61NYG | 2 | 6'1" | 198 | Clemson | | 12 |
| Wells, Warren WR-OE | 64Det 65-66MS 67-69OakA 70Oak | 2 | 6'1" | 191 | Texas Southern | | 258 |
| 1971 — Declared ineligible to play pro football | | | | | | | |
| Wendryhoski, Joe C-OG | 64-66LA 67-68NO | | 6'2" | 245 | Illinois | | |
| Wenzel, Ralph OG | 66-70Pit 72-73SD | | 6'3" | 244 | San Diego State | | |
| Werl, Bob OG-DE | 66NY-A | | 6'3" | 240 | Miami (Fla.) | | |
| West, Dave DB | 63NY-A | | 6'3" | 190 | Central St.-Ohio | | |
| West, Mel HB | 61BosA 61-62NY-A | 2 | 5'9" | 190 | Missouri | | 18 |
| West, Willie DB-HB | 60-61StL 62-63BufA 64DenA 64-65NY-A 66-68MiaA | 3 | 5'10" | 188 | Oregon | 30 | 12 |
| Westmoreland, Dick DB | 63-65SD-A 66-69MiaA | 3 | 6'1" | 191 | N. Carolina A&T | 22 | 12 |
| Wetoska, Bob OT-OG-C | 60-69ChiB | | 6'3" | 241 | Notre Dame | | |
| Wettstein, Max TE | 66DenA | | 6'3" | 217 | Florida State | | |
| Whalen, Jim TE-OE | 65-69BosA 70-71Den 71Phi | 2 | 6'2" | 210 | Boston College | | 120 |
| Wharton, Hogan OG | 60-63HouA | | 6'2" | 248 | Houston | | |
| Wheeler, Manuch QB | 62BufA | | 6' | 190 | Maine | | |
| Wheeler, Ted OG-TE | 67-68StL 70ChiB | | 6'3" | 240 | West Texas State | | |
| Wheelwright, Ernie FB | 64-65NYG 66-67Atl 67-70NO | 2 | 6'3" | 235 | Southern Illinois | | 96 |
| White, Andre TE | 67DenA 68CinA 68SD-A | | 6'5" | 225 | Florida A&M | | 2 |
| White, Bob FB | 60HouA | | 6'2" | 220 | Ohio State | | |
| White, Freeman TE-DB-LB | 66-69NYG | 2 | 6'5" | 225 | Nebraska | 2 | 6 |
| White, Gene HB | 62OakA | | 6'1" | 197 | Florida A&M | | 8 |
| White, Harvey QB | 60BosA | | 6'1" | 190 | Clemson | | |
| White, John OE | 60-61HouA | | 6'4" | 230 | Texas Southern | | 6 |
| Whitehead, Bud DB-FL-HB | 61-68SD-A | | 6' | 184 | Florida State | 15 | 6 |
| Whitfield, A.D. HB | 65Dal 66-68Was | 2 | 5'10" | 200 | North Texas | | 36 |
| Whitley, Hall LB | 60NY-A | | 6'2" | 225 | Texas A&I | | |
| Whitlow, Bob C-OG | 60-61Was 61-65Det 66Atl 68Cle | | 6'1" | 236 | Indiana, Arizona | | |
| Whitmyer, Nat TE | 63LA 66SD-A 67JJ | | 6' | 182 | Washington | 1 | |
| Whitsell, Dave DB-HB | 58-60Det 61-66ChiB 67-69NO | | 6' | 189 | Indiana | 46 | 30 |
| Whitten, Jess DB | 56-57LA 58-64GB | | 6' | 193 | Texas-El Paso | 24 | 12 |
| Whittingham, Fred LB-OG | 64LA 66Phi 67-68NO 69Dal 70Bos 71Phi | | 6'1" | 240 | Brigham Young, Cal. Poly.-S.L.O. | 3 | |
| Wiggin, Paul DE | 57-67Cle HC75-77KC | | 6'3" | 242 | Stanford | 3 | 12 |
| Wilbur, John OG-DE-OT | 66-69Dal 70LA 71-73Was | | 6'3" | 245 | Stanford | | |
| Wilburn, J.R. WR-OE | 66-70Pit | 2 | 6'2" | 190 | South Carolina | | 48 |
| Wilcox, Dave LB | 64-74SF | | 6'3" | 235 | Oregon | 14 | 12 |
| Wilcox, John OT-DE | 60Phi | | 6'5" | 230 | Oregon | | |
| Wilder, Bert DE-DT | 64-67NY-A | | 6'3" | 245 | N. Carolina State | | |
| Will, Erwin DT | 65Phi | | 6'5" | 270 | Dayton | | |
| Willard, Ken FB | 65-73SF 74StL | 2 | 6'2" | 225 | North Carolina | | 372 |
| Williams, A.D. OE-FL | 59GB 60Cle 61Min | 2 | 6'2" | 210 | U. of Pacific | | |
| Williams, Bobby DB | 66-67StL 69-71Det | 3 | 6'1" | 195 | Central Okla. | 3 | 12 |
| Williams, Clancy DB-HB | 65-72LA | 3 | 6'2" | 197 | Washington State | 28 | 12 |
| Williams, Clyde OT-OG | 67-71StL | | 6'2" | 252 | Southern U. | | |
| Williams, Erwin WR | 69Pit | | 6'5" | 215 | Md. Eastern Shore | | 6 |
| Williams, Frank FB | 61LA | | 6'2" | 215 | Pepperdine | | |
| Williams, Howie DB | 62-63GB 63SF 64-69OakA | | 6'2" | 188 | Howard | 14 | |
| Williams, Jeff HB | 66Min | | 6'1" | 210 | Oklahoma State | | |
| Williams, Jim DB | 69CinA | | 6'1" | 190 | Alcorn State | | |
| Williams, Maxie OG-OT | 65HouA 66-69MiaA 70Mia | | 6'4" | 247 | Southeastern La. | | |
| Williams, Monk WR | 68CinA | | 5'7" | 155 | Ark.-Pine Bluff | | |
| Williams, Roy OT | 63SF | | 6'5" | 265 | U. of Pacific | | |
| Williams, Sam DE-OE-LB | 59LA 60-65Det 66-67Atl | | 6'5" | 235 | Michigan State | 1 | 20 |
| Williams, Sid LB-DE | 64-66Cle 67Was 68Bal 69Pit | | 6'2" | 235 | Southern U. | 1 | 6 |
| Williams, Travis (Roadrunner) HB | 67-70GB 71LA 72KJ | 23 | 6'1" | 210 | Arizona State | | 108 |
| Williams, Wendy HB | 69DenA 70Den | | 6' | 192 | Kansas, Hofstra | | 6 |
| Williams, Willie DB | 65NYG 66OakA 67-73NYG | | 6' | 190 | Grambling | 35 | |
| Williamson, Fred (The Hammer) DB | 60Pit 61-64OakA 65-67KC-A | | 6'2" | 210 | Northwestern | 36 | 12 |
| Williamson, J.R. LB-C | 64-67OakA 68-69BosA 70Bos 71JJ | | 6'2" | 220 | Louisiana Tech | 3 | |
| Willsey, Ray | HC61StL | | | | California | | |
| Wilson, Ben FB-HB | 63-65LA 67GB 68KJ | 2 | 6' | 225 | Southern Calif. | | 66 |
| Wilson, Butch TE-OE | 63-67Bal 68-69NYG | | 6'2" | 223 | Alabama | | 18 |
| Wilson, Eddie QB | 62DalA 63-64KC-A 65BosA 66KJ | 1 4 | 6' | 190 | Arizona | | 6 |

| Use Name (Nickname) - Positions | Team by Year | See Section | Hgt. | Wgt. | College | Int | Pts |
|---|---|---|---|---|---|---|---|
| Wilson, George QB | 66MiaA | 12 4 | 6'1" | 190 | Xavier-Ohio | | 2 |
| Wilson, Harry HB | 67Phi 68JJ 69Phi | | 5'11" | 204 | Nebraska | | |
| Wilson, Jerrel HB-FB-LB-K | 63-69KC-A 70-77KC 78NE | 4 | 6'4" | 222 | Southern Miss. | 4 | 4 |
| Wilson, Jim OG-OT | 65-66SF 67Atl 68LA 69-71JJ | | 6'3" | 257 | Georgia | | |
| Wilson, Larry DB | 60-72StL HC79StL | | 6' | 190 | Utah | 52 | 50 |
| Wilson, Mike DB | 69StL | | 5'11" | 185 | Western Illinois | | |
| Wingate, Heath C | 67Was | | 6'2" | 240 | Bowling Green | | |
| Wink, Dean DE-DT | 67-68Phi | | 6'4" | 246 | Yankton | | |
| Winkler, Francis DE | 68-69GB | | 6'3" | 230 | Memphis State | | |
| Winkler, Randy OG-OT | 67Det 68Atl 69-70MS 71GB | | 6'5" | 258 | Tarleton State | | |
| Winner, Charley | HC66-70StL HC74-75NYJ | | | | SE Missouri St., Washington-St.L. | | |
| Winslow, Paul HB | 60GB | | 5'11" | 200 | N. Car. Central | | 6 |
| Winslow, Kelton DB | 67-68LA | | 6' | 195 | Wiley | | |
| Winston, Floyd FB | 62-63SF | 2 | 6'2" | 215 | Southern Calif. | | 6 |
| Winston, Roy LB | 62-76Min | | 6'1" | 226 | Louisiana State | 12 | 20 |
| Winter, Bill LB | 62-64NYG | | 6'4" | 220 | St. Olaf | | |
| Wisener, Gary DB-OE | 60Dal 61HouA | | 6'1" | 206 | Baylor | | |
| Witcher, Al OE-DE | 60HouA | | 6'1" | 200 | Baylor | 1 | 8 |
| Witcher, Dick WR-TE-FL | 66-73SF | 2 | 6'3" | 205 | U.C.L.A. | | 90 |
| Witt, Mel DE-DT | 67-69BosA 70Bos | | 6'3" | 261 | Texas-Arlington | 1 | 6 |
| Wittenborn, John OG-K | 58-60SF 60-62Phi 63JJ | 5 | 6'2" | 238 | SE Missouri St. | | 101 |
| Woitt, John DB | 68-69SF | | 5'11" | 172 | Mississippi State | 1 | 6 |
| Wolff, Wayne OG | 61BufA | | 6'2" | 243 | Wake Forest | | |
| Wolski, Bill FB | 66Atl | | 5'11" | 203 | Notre Dame | | |
| Womack, Joe HB | 62Pit | 2 | 5'9" | 210 | Los Angeles State | | 30 |
| Wondolowski, Bill WR | 69SF | | 5'10" | 168 | Eastern Montana | | |
| Wood, Bill DB | 63NY-A | | 5'11" | 190 | West Va. Wesleyan | | |
| Wood, Bo DE | 67Atl | | 6'3" | 225 | North Carolina | | |
| Wood, Dick QB | 62SD-A 62DenA 63-64NY-A 65OakA 66MiaA | 12 | 6'5" | 202 | Auburn | | 24 |
| Wood, Duane DB | 62-63SF | | 6'1" | 196 | Oklahoma State | 20 | 12 |
| Wood, Gary QB | 64-66NYG 67NO 68-69NYG | 12 | 5'11" | 188 | Cornell | | 37 |
| Wood, Willie DB | 60-71GB | 3 | 5'10" | 189 | Southern Calif. | 48 | 25 |
| Woodeshick, Tom FB-HB | 63-71Phi 72StL | 2 | 6'1" | 219 | West Virginia | | 162 |
| Woodlief, Doug LB | 65-69LA 70JJ | | 6'3" | 231 | Memphis State | 6 | |
| Woods, Glenn DE | 69HouA | | 6'4" | 250 | Prairie View | | |
| Woodson, Abe DB-HB | 58-64SF 65-66StL | 3 | 5'11" | 188 | Illinois | 19 | 48 |
| Woodson, Freddie OG-DE-DT | 67-69MiaA | | 6'2" | 253 | Florida A&M | | |
| Woodson, Marv DB-HB | 64-69Pit 69NO | | 6' | 195 | Indiana | 18 | 12 |
| Woulfe, Mike LB | 62Phi 63JJ | | 6'2" | 225 | Colorado | | |
| Wright, Ernie OT | 60LA-A 61-67SD-A 68-69CinA 70-71Cin 72SD | | 6'4" | 268 | Ohio State | | |
| Wright, Gordon OG | 67Phi 69NY-A | | 6'3" | 245 | Delaware State | | |
| Wright, Jim DB | 64DenA | | 5'11" | 190 | Memphis State | 1 | |
| Wright, John WR | 68Atl 69Det 70JJ | 2 | 6' | 196 | Illinois | | 18 |
| Wright, Lonnie DB | 66-67DenA | | 6'2" | 205 | Colorado State | 5 | |
| 1967-72 — played in A.B.A. | | | | | | | |
| Wright, Steve OT-DE | 64-67GB 68-69NYG 70Was 71ChiB 72StL | | 6'6" | 250 | Alabama | | |
| Wulff, Jim DB | 60-61Was | | 6'1" | 185 | Michigan State | 3 | |
| Yaccino, John DB | 62BufA | | 6' | 190 | Pittsburgh | | |
| Yates, Bob OT-C-DT | 60-65BosA | | 6'3" | 233 | Syracuse | | |
| Yearby, Bill DE | 66NY-A | | 6'3" | 235 | Michigan | | |
| Yelverton, Bill DE | 60DenA | | 6'4" | 220 | Mississippi | 1 | 6 |
| Yewcic, Tom QB-HB | 61-66BosA | 12 4 | 5'11" | 185 | Michigan State | | 24 |
| 1957 — played major league baseball | | | | | | | |
| Yohn, Dave LB | 62Bal 63NY-A | | 6' | 223 | Gettysburg | | |
| Yoho, Mack DE | 60-63BufA | 5 | 6'2" | 239 | Miami-Ohio | 2 | 97 |
| Youmans, Maury DE-DT | 60-62ChiB 63JJ 64-65Dal | | 6'6" | 253 | Syracuse | | |
| Young, Jim HB | 65-66Min | | 6' | 205 | Queens (Ont.) | | |
| Young, Joe DE | 60-61DenA | | 6'3" | 245 | Marquette, Arizona | | |
| Youngblood, George DB | 66LA 67Cle 67-68NO 69ChiB 69-65OakA | | 6'3" | 204 | Los Angeles State | 3 | 6 |
| Youso, Frank OT | 58-69NYG 61-62Min 63-65OakA | | 6'4" | 257 | Minnesota | | |
| Zaeske, Paul WR | 69HouA 70Hou | | 6'2" | 200 | North Park | | |
| Zaruba, Carroll DB | 60DalA | | 5'9" | 210 | Nebraska | | |
| Zawadzkas, Jerry TE | 67Det | | 6'4" | 220 | Columbia | | |
| Zecher, Rich DT-OT | 65OakA 66-67MiaA 67BufA | | 6'2" | 240 | Utah State | | |
| Zeman, Bob DB | 60LA-A 61SD-A 62-63DenA 64JJ 65-66SD-A | | 6'1" | 202 | Wisconsin | 17 | 12 |

Lifetime Statistics - 1960-1969 Players Section 1 - **PASSING**
(All men with 25 or more passing attempts)

| Name | Years | Att. | Comp. | Comp. Pct. | Yards | Yds./ Att. | TD | Int. | Pct. Int. |
|---|---|---|---|---|---|---|---|---|---|
| Jon Arnett | 57-66 | 33 | 8 | 24.2 | 147 | 4.5 | 2 | 2 | 6.1 |
| Billy Barnes | 57-63,65-66 | 25 | 10 | 40.0 | 233 | 9.3 | 4 | 4 | 16.0 |
| Pete Beathard | 64-73,75 | 1282 | 575 | 44.9 | 8176 | 6.4 | 43 | 84 | 6.6 |
| George Blanda | 49-58,60-74 | 4007 | 1911 | 47.7 | 26920 | 6.7 | 236 | 277 | 6.9 |
| Zeke Bratkowski | 54,57-68,71 | 1484 | 762 | 51.3 | 10345 | 7.0 | 65 | 122 | 8.2 |
| Don Breaux | 63,65 | 181 | 92 | 50.8 | 1339 | 7.4 | 9 | 10 | 5.5 |
| Bob Brodhead | 60 | 25 | 7 | 28.0 | 75 | 3.0 | 0 | 3 | 12.0 |
| John Brodie | 57-73 | 4491 | 2469 | 55.0 | 31548 | 7.0 | 214 | 224 | 5.0 |
| Rudy Bukich | 53,56-68 | 1190 | 626 | 52.6 | 8433 | 7.1 | 61 | 74 | 6.2 |
| Max Chaboian | 66 | 163 | 82 | 50.3 | 1110 | 6.8 | 4 | 12 | 7.4 |
| Dennis Claridge | 64-66 | 71 | 41 | 57.7 | 484 | 6.8 | 2 | 2 | 2.8 |
| Jack Concannon | 64-71,74-75 | 1110 | 560 | 50.5 | 6270 | 5.6 | 36 | 63 | 5.7 |
| Greg Cook | 69,73 | 200 | 107 | 53.5 | 1865 | 9.3 | 15 | 11 | 5.5 |
| John David Crow | 58-68 | 70 | 33 | 47.1 | 759 | 10.8 | 5 | 5 | 7.1 |
| Garry Cuozzo | 63-72 | 1182 | 584 | 49.4 | 7402 | 6.3 | 43 | 55 | 4.7 |
| Dan Darragh | 68-70 | 296 | 127 | 42.9 | 1352 | 4.6 | 4 | 22 | 7.4 |
| Cotton Davidson | 54,57,60-66,68 | 1752 | 770 | 43.9 | 11760 | 6.7 | 73 | 108 | 6.2 |
| Len Dawson | 57-75 | 3741 | 2136 | 57.1 | 28711 | 7.7 | 239 | 183 | 4.9 |
| Eagle Day | 59-60 | 32 | 15 | 46.9 | 194 | 6.1 | 0 | 2 | 6.2 |
| Randy Duncan | 61 | 67 | 25 | 37.3 | 361 | 5.4 | 1 | 3 | 4.5 |
| Hunter Enis | 60-62 | 160 | 80 | 50.0 | 947 | 5.9 | 4 | 6 | 3.7 |
| Sam Etcheverry | 61-62 | 302 | 154 | 51.0 | 1982 | 6.6 | 16 | 21 | 7.0 |
| Tom Flores | 60-61,63-69 | 1715 | 838 | 48.9 | 11959 | 7.0 | 93 | 92 | 5.4 |
| Roman Gabriel | 62-77 | 4498 | 2366 | 52.6 | 29444 | 6.5 | 201 | 149 | 3.3 |
| Chan Gallegos | 62 | 35 | 18 | 51.4 | 298 | 8.5 | 2 | 3 | 8.6 |
| Johnny Green | 60-63 | 618 | 275 | 44.5 | 3921 | 6.3 | 26 | 34 | 5.5 |
| Tom Greene | 60-61 | 63 | 27 | 42.9 | 251 | 4.0 | 1 | 6 | 9.5 |
| Glynn Griffing | 63 | 40 | 16 | 40.0 | 306 | 7.7 | 3 | 4 | 10.0 |
| Lee Grosscup | 60-62 | 173 | 73 | 42.2 | 1086 | 6.3 | 10 | 12 | 6.9 |
| Ralph Gugliemi | 55,58-63 | 626 | 292 | 46.6 | 4119 | 6.6 | 24 | 52 | 8.3 |
| John Hadl | 62-77 | 4637 | 2363 | 50.4 | 33503 | 7.1 | 244 | 268 | 5.7 |
| Galen Hall | 62-63 | 150 | 64 | 42.7 | 885 | 5.9 | 5 | 10 | 6.7 |
| Kim Hammond | 68-69 | 32 | 15 | 46.9 | 147 | 4.6 | 0 | 2 | 6.3 |
| George Herring | 60-61 | 233 | 102 | 43.8 | 1297 | 5.6 | 5 | 23 | 9.9 |
| King Hill | 58-69 | 881 | 429 | 48.7 | 5553 | 6.3 | 37 | 71 | 8.1 |
| Dick Hoak | 61-70 | 40 | 20 | 50.0 | 427 | 10.7 | 4 | 3 | 7.5 |
| Paul Hornung | 57-62,64-66 | 55 | 24 | 43.6 | 383 | 7.0 | 5 | 4 | 7.3 |
| John Huarte | 66-68,70-72 | 48 | 19 | 39.6 | 230 | 4.8 | 1 | 5 | 10.4 |
| Buddy Humphrey | 59-66 | 175 | 87 | 49.7 | 1094 | 6.3 | 4 | 12 | 6.9 |
| George Izo | 60-66 | 317 | 132 | 41.6 | 1791 | 5.6 | 12 | 32 | 10.1 |
| Dick Jamieson | 60-61 | 70 | 35 | 50.0 | 586 | 8.4 | 6 | 2 | 2.9 |
| Charley Johnson | 61-75 | 3392 | 1737 | 51.2 | 24410 | 7.2 | 170 | 181 | 5.3 |
| Sonny Jurgensen | 57-74 | 4262 | 2433 | 57.1 | 32224 | 7.6 | 255 | 189 | 4.4 |
| Joe Kapp | 67-70 | 918 | 449 | 48.9 | 5911 | 6.4 | 40 | 64 | 7.0 |
| Jack Kemp | 57,60-67,69 | 3073 | 1436 | 46.7 | 21218 | 6.9 | 114 | 183 | 6.0 |
| Tom Kennedy | 66 | 100 | 55 | 55.0 | 748 | 7.5 | 7 | 6 | 6.0 |
| Daryle Lamonica | 63-74 | 2601 | 1288 | 49.5 | 19154 | 7.4 | 164 | 138 | 5.3 |
| Gary Lane | 66-68 | 43 | 21 | 48.8 | 254 | 5.9 | 2 | 1 | 2.3 |
| Jim LeClair | 67-68 | 99 | 46 | 46.5 | 676 | 6.8 | 2 | 6 | 6.1 |
| Jacky Lee | 60-69 | 838 | 430 | 51.3 | 6191 | 7.4 | 46 | 57 | 6.8 |
| Bruce Lemmerman | 68-69 | 77 | 28 | 36.4 | 370 | 4.8 | 1 | 5 | 6.5 |
| Pete Liske | 64,69-72 | 778 | 396 | 50.9 | 5170 | 6.6 | 30 | 46 | 5.9 |
| Richie Lucas | 60-61 | 99 | 43 | 43.4 | 596 | 6.0 | 4 | 7 | 7.1 |
| Tom Matte | 61-72 | 42 | 12 | 28.6 | 246 | 5.9 | 2 | 2 | 4.8 |
| John McCormick | 62-63,65-66,68 | 555 | 214 | 38.6 | 2895 | 5.2 | 17 | 38 | 6.8 |
| Don Meredith | 60-68 | 2308 | 1170 | 50.7 | 17199 | 7.5 | 135 | 111 | 4.8 |
| Ron Miller | 62 | 43 | 17 | 39.5 | 250 | 5.8 | 1 | 1 | 2.3 |
| George Mira | 64-69,71 | 346 | 148 | 42.8 | 2109 | 6.1 | 19 | 20 | 5.8 |
| Earl Morrall | 56-76 | 2689 | 1379 | 51.3 | 20809 | 7.7 | 161 | 148 | 5.5 |
| Bill Nelsen | 63-72 | 1905 | 963 | 50.6 | 14165 | 7.4 | 98 | 101 | 5.3 |
| Jim Ninowski | 58-69 | 1048 | 513 | 49.0 | 7133 | 6.8 | 34 | 67 | 6.4 |
| Terry Nofsinger | 61-67 | 260 | 118 | 45.4 | 1357 | 5.2 | 4 | 12 | 4.6 |
| Rick Norton | 66-70 | 382 | 159 | 41.6 | 1815 | 4.8 | 7 | 30 | 7.9 |
| Nick Papac | 61 | 44 | 13 | 29.5 | 173 | 3.9 | 2 | 7 | 15.8 |
| Babe Parilli | 52-53,56-58,60-69 | 3330 | 1552 | 46.6 | 22681 | 6.8 | 178 | 220 | 6.6 |
| Milt Plum | 57-69 | 2419 | 1306 | 54.0 | 17536 | 7.2 | 122 | 127 | 5.3 |
| Warren Rabb | 60-62 | 251 | 101 | 40.2 | 1782 | 7.1 | 15 | 16 | 6.4 |
| Larry Rakestraw | 64,66-68 | 111 | 51 | 45.9 | 589 | 5.3 | 4 | 9 | 8.1 |
| Dan Reeves | 65-72 | 32 | 14 | 43.8 | 370 | 11.6 | 2 | 4 | 12.5 |
| Jerry Reichow | 56-57,59-64 | 38 | 12 | 31.6 | 187 | 4.9 | 0 | 4 | 10.5 |
| M. C. Reynolds | 58-62 | 450 | 222 | 49.3 | 2932 | 6.5 | 17 | 28 | 6.2 |
| Jerry Rhome | 65-67,69-71 | 280 | 139 | 49.6 | 1628 | 5.8 | 7 | 14 | 5.0 |
| Johnny Roach | 56,59-64 | 413 | 182 | 44.1 | 2765 | 6.7 | 24 | 37 | 9.0 |
| Ed Rutkowski | 63-68 | 102 | 41 | 40.2 | 380 | 3.7 | 0 | 6 | 5.9 |
| Frank Ryan | 58-70 | 2133 | 1090 | 51.1 | 16042 | 7.5 | 149 | 111 | 5.2 |
| Bob Scrabis | 60-62 | 26 | 7 | 26.9 | 82 | 3.2 | 1 | 3 | 11.5 |
| Tom Sherman | 68-69 | 228 | 92 | 40.4 | 1219 | 5.3 | 16 | 16 | 7.0 |
| Dick Shiner | 64-71,73-74 | 736 | 354 | 48.1 | 4801 | 6.5 | 36 | 43 | 5.8 |
| Mickey Slaughter | 63-66 | 584 | 291 | 49.8 | 3607 | 6.3 | 22 | 37 | 6.3 |
| Steve Sloan | 66-67 | 31 | 10 | 32.3 | 134 | 4.3 | 0 | 4 | 12.9 |
| Ron Smith | 65-66 | 181 | 79 | 43.6 | 1249 | 6.9 | 8 | 12 | 6.6 |
| Norm Snead | 61-76 | 4353 | 2276 | 52.2 | 30797 | 7.1 | 196 | 257 | 5.9 |
| Butch Songin | 60-62 | 694 | 327 | 47.1 | 4347 | 6.3 | 38 | 31 | 4.5 |
| Ronnie South | 68 | 38 | 14 | 36.8 | 129 | 3.4 | 1 | 3 | 7.9 |
| Bart Starr | 56-71 | 3149 | 1808 | 57.4 | 24718 | 7.8 | 152 | 138 | 4.4 |
| Kay Stephenson | 67-68 | 105 | 40 | 38.1 | 481 | 4.6 | 6 | 9 | 8.6 |
| John Stofa | 66-70 | 312 | 146 | 46.8 | 1758 | 5.6 | 12 | 11 | 3.5 |
| Karl Sweetan | 66-70 | 590 | 269 | 45.6 | 3210 | 5.4 | 17 | 34 | 5.8 |
| Mike Taliaferro | 64-72 | 966 | 419 | 43.4 | 5241 | 5.4 | 36 | 63 | 6.5 |
| Fran Tarkenton | 61-78 | 6467 | 3686 | 57.0 | 47003 | 7.3 | 342 | 266 | 4.1 |
| Steve Tensi | 65-70 | 862 | 369 | 42.8 | 5558 | 6.4 | 43 | 46 | 5.3 |
| Tom Tracy | 56-64 | 67 | 24 | 35.8 | 854 | 12.7 | 6 | 5 | 7.5 |
| Frank Tripucka | 49-52,60-63 | 1745 | 879 | 50.4 | 10282 | 5.9 | 59 | 124 | 7.1 |
| Don Trull | 64-69 | 617 | 276 | 44.7 | 3980 | 6.5 | 30 | 28 | 4.5 |
| Johnny Unitas | 56-73 | 5186 | 2830 | 54.6 | 40239 | 7.8 | 290 | 253 | 4.9 |
| Ron Vander Kelen | 63-67 | 252 | 107 | 42.5 | 1375 | 5.5 | 6 | 11 | 4.4 |
| Billy Wade | 54-66 | 2523 | 1370 | 54.3 | 18530 | 7.3 | 124 | 134 | 5.3 |
| Tom Wade | 64-65 | 69 | 34 | 49.3 | 470 | 6.8 | 2 | 13 | 18.8 |
| Jim Ward | 67-68,71 | 26 | 13 | 50.0 | 165 | 6.3 | 2 | 2 | 7.7 |
| Dewey Warren | 68 | 80 | 47 | 58.8 | 506 | 6.3 | 1 | 4 | 5.0 |
| Bob Waters | 60-63 | 124 | 59 | 47.6 | 707 | 5.7 | 3 | 8 | 6.5 |
| Eddie Wilson | 62-65 | 186 | 90 | 48.4 | 1251 | 6.7 | 5 | 6 | 3.2 |
| George Wilson | 66 | 112 | 46 | 41.1 | 764 | 6.8 | 5 | 10 | 8.9 |
| Dick Wood | 62-66 | 1193 | 522 | 43.8 | 7151 | 6.0 | 51 | 70 | 5.9 |
| Gary Wood | 64-69 | 400 | 186 | 46.5 | 2575 | 6.4 | 14 | 23 | 5.7 |
| Tom Yewcic | 61-66 | 206 | 87 | 42.2 | 1374 | 6.7 | 12 | 12 | 5.8 |

Lifetime Statistics - 1960-1969 Players Section 2 - **RUSHING and RECEIVING**
(All men with 25 or more rushing attempts or 10 or more receptions)

| | | RUSHING | | | | RECEIVING | | | |
|---|---|---|---|---|---|---|---|---|---|
| Name | Years | Att. | Yards | Avg. | TD | Rec. | Yards | Avg. | TD |
| John Adams | 59-63 | 41 | 99 | 2.4 | 1 | 21 | 264 | 12.6 | 3 |
| Don Allen | 60 | 30 | 18 | 0.6 | 1 | 5 | 34 | 6.8 | 0 |
| Duane Allen | 61-67 | | | | | 10 | 227 | 22.7 | 5 |
| Jerry Allen | 66-69 | 201 | 664 | 3.3 | 7 | 33 | 400 | 12.1 | 2 |
| Jim Allison | 65-68 | 93 | 378 | 4.1 | 2 | 22 | 230 | 10.5 | 0 |
| Lance Alworth | 62-72 | 24 | 129 | 5.4 | 2 | 542 | 10267 | 18.9 | 85 |
| Bill Anderson | 58-63,65-66 | 4 | 11 | 2.8 | 0 | 168 | 3048 | 18.1 | 15 |
| Max Anderson | 68-69,71 | 160 | 599 | 3.7 | 3 | 29 | 205 | 7.1 | 0 |
| Ralph Anderson | 58,60 | | | | | 55 | 791 | 14.4 | 6 |
| Taz Anderson | 61-64,66-67 | | | | | 87 | 1335 | 15.3 | 9 |
| Fred Arbanas | 62-70 | 4 | 15 | 3.8 | 0 | 218 | 3101 | 14.2 | 34 |
| Jon Arnett | 57-66 | 964 | 3833 | 4.0 | 26 | 222 | 2290 | 10.3 | 10 |
| Doug Asad | 60-61 | | | | | 50 | 698 | 14.0 | 3 |
| Willie Asbury | 66-68 | 253 | 868 | 3.4 | 11 | 25 | 307 | 12.2 | 2 |
| Pervis Atkins | 61-66 | 74 | 201 | 2.7 | 1 | 64 | 675 | 10.5 | 2 |
| Joe Auer | 64-68 | 234 | 773 | 3.3 | 7 | 51 | 647 | 12.7 | 6 |
| Gene Babb | 57-58,60-63 | 152 | 461 | 3.0 | 3 | 33 | 281 | 8.5 | 1 |
| Art Baker | 61-62 | 154 | 507 | 3.3 | 3 | 9 | 85 | 9.4 | 0 |
| Sam Baker | 53,56-69 | 49 | 234 | 4.8 | 2 | 7 | 59 | 8.4 | 0 |
| Terry Baker | 63-65 | 58 | 210 | 3.6 | 1 | 30 | 302 | 10.1 | 2 |
| Gary Ballman | 62-73 | 41 | 202 | 4.9 | 4 | 323 | 5366 | 16.6 | 37 |
| Estes Banks | 67-68 | 44 | 157 | 3.6 | 0 | 4 | 15 | 3.8 | 1 |
| Billy Barnes | 57-63,65-66 | 994 | 3421 | 3.4 | 29 | 153 | 1786 | 11.7 | 9 |
| Gary Barnes | 62-64,66-67 | | | | | 41 | 583 | 14.2 | 2 |
| Eppie Barney | 67-68 | 0 | 8 | – | 1 | 19 | 192 | 10.1 | 1 |
| Terry Barr | 57-65 | 32 | 151 | 4.7 | 2 | 227 | 3810 | 16.8 | 35 |
| Jan Barrett | 63-64 | | | | | 13 | 221 | 17.0 | 2 |
| Tom Barrrington | 66-70 | 168 | 530 | 3.2 | 3 | 41 | 278 | 6.8 | 1 |
| Dick Bass | 60-69 | 1218 | 5417 | 4.4 | 34 | 204 | 1841 | 9.0 | 7 |
| Glenn Bass | 60-68 | 16 | 67 | 4.2 | 0 | 167 | 2841 | 17.0 | 17 |
| Craig Baynham | 67-70,72 | 152 | 553 | 3.6 | 6 | 45 | 466 | 10.4 | 3 |
| Pete Beathard | 64-73,75 | 131 | 680 | 5.2 | 11 | | | | |
| Hal Bedsole | 64-66 | | | | | 26 | 418 | 16.1 | 8 |
| Harry Bell | 60 | 42 | 238 | 5.5 | 0 | 2 | 13 | 6.5 | 0 |
| Joe Bellino | 65-67 | 30 | 64 | 2.1 | 0 | 11 | 153 | 13.9 | 1 |
| Ray Berry | 55-67 | | | | | 631 | 9275 | 14.7 | 68 |
| Charles Bivins | 60-67 | 153 | 498 | 3.3 | 3 | 28 | 262 | 9.4 | 3 |
| George Blanda | 49-58,60-75 | 144 | 268 | 1.9 | 9 | 1 | -16 | -16.0 | 0 |
| Sid Blanks | 64-70 | 365 | 1440 | 3.9 | 7 | 106 | 1073 | 10.1 | 4 |
| Ronnie Blye | 68-69 | 61 | 268 | 4.4 | 1 | 12 | 85 | 7.1 | 0 |
| Dewey Bohling | 60-61 | 178 | 584 | 3.3 | 4 | 43 | 485 | 11.3 | 5 |
| Don Bosseler | 57-64 | 775 | 3112 | 4.0 | 22 | 136 | 1083 | 8.0 | 1 |
| Zeke Bratkowski | 54,57-68,71 | 92 | 308 | 3.3 | 5 | | | | |
| Johnny Brewer | 61-70 | | | | | 89 | 1256 | 14.1 | 6 |
| John Brodie | 57-73 | 235 | 1167 | 5.0 | 22 | | | | |
| Barry Brown | 66-70 | | | | | 21 | 214 | 10.2 | 0 |
| Bill Brown | 61-74 | 1649 | 5838 | 3.5 | 52 | 286 | 3183 | 11.1 | 23 |
| Fred Brown | 61,63 | 59 | 210 | 3.6 | 2 | 3 | 18 | 6.0 | 0 |
| Jimmy Brown | 57-65 | 2359 | 12312 | 5.2 | 106 | 262 | 2499 | 9.5 | 20 |
| Timmy Brown | 59-68 | 889 | 3862 | 4.3 | 31 | 235 | 3399 | 14.5 | 26 |
| Willie Brown | 64-66 | 44 | 133 | 3.0 | 0 | 5 | 110 | 22.0 | 1 |
| Charlie Bryant | 66-69 | 67 | 322 | 4.8 | 0 | 3 | 26 | 8.7 | 0 |
| Frank Budd | 62-63 | | | | | 10 | 236 | 23.6 | 1 |
| Fred Bukaty | 61 | 76 | 187 | 2.5 | 5 | 15 | 94 | 6.7 | 0 |
| Rudy Bukich | 53,56-68 | 112 | 109 | 1.0 | 9 | | | | |
| Ronnie Bull | 62-71 | 881 | 3222 | 3.7 | 9 | 172 | 1479 | 8.6 | 5 |
| Amos Bullocks | 62-64,66 | 158 | 620 | 3.9 | 5 | 15 | 180 | 12.0 | 2 |
| Jerry Burch | 61 | | | | | 18 | 235 | 13.1 | 1 |
| Chris Burford | 60-67 | 3 | 10 | 3.3 | 0 | 391 | 5505 | 14.1 | 55 |
| Vern Burke | 65-67 | | | | | 38 | 470 | 12.4 | 2 |

Lifetime Statistics - 1960-1969 Players Section 2 - **RUSHING AND RECEIVING** (continued)
(All men with 25 or more rushing attempts or 10 or more receptions)

| Name | Years | RUSHING Att. | Yards | Avg. | TD | RECEIVING Rec. | Yards | Avg. | TD |
|---|---|---|---|---|---|---|---|---|---|
| Bobby Burnett | 66-67,69 | 237 | 871 | 3.7 | 4 | 45 | 533 | 11.8 | 4 |
| John Burrell | 62-64,66-67 | 6 | 38 | 6.3 | 0 | 26 | 437 | 16.8 | 0 |
| Ode Burrell | 64-69 | 304 | 1088 | 3.6 | 3 | 112 | 1379 | 12.3 | 9 |
| Ron Burton | 60-65 | 429 | 1536 | 3.6 | 9 | 111 | 1205 | 10.9 | 8 |
| Bill Butler | 59-64 | 29 | 108 | 3.7 | 0 | 6 | 95 | 15.8 | 0 |
| Cannonball Butler | 65-72 | 797 | 2768 | 3.5 | 9 | 89 | 959 | 10.8 | 7 |
| Woody Campbell | 67-71 | 408 | 1493 | 3.7 | 13 | 80 | 709 | 8.9 | 2 |
| Billy Cannon | 60-70 | 602 | 2455 | 4.1 | 17 | 236 | 3656 | 15.5 | 47 |
| Bob Cappadonna | 66-68 | 123 | 460 | 3.7 | 2 | 24 | 196 | 8.2 | 3 |
| Gino Cappelletti | 60-70 | 4 | 6 | 1.5 | 0 | 292 | 4589 | 15.7 | 42 |
| Wray Carlton | 60-67 | 819 | 3368 | 4.1 | 29 | 110 | 1329 | 12.1 | 5 |
| Reg Carolan | 62-68 | | | | | 23 | 364 | 15.8 | 5 |
| J.C. Caroline | 56-65 | 68 | 263 | 3.9 | 2 | 6 | 111 | 18.5 | 1 |
| Preston Carpenter | 56-67 | 223 | 884 | 4.0 | 1 | 305 | 4457 | 14.6 | 23 |
| Jimmy Carr | 55,57,59-65 | 30 | 115 | 3.8 | 0 | 9 | 157 | 17.4 | 0 |
| Rick Casares | 55-66 | 1431 | 5797 | 4.1 | 49 | 191 | 1588 | 8.3 | 11 |
| Bernie Casey | 61-68 | 1 | 23 | 23.0 | 0 | 359 | 5444 | 15.2 | 40 |
| Dan Chamberlain | 60-61 | | | | | 18 | 295 | 16.4 | 4 |
| Joe Childress | 56-60,62-65 | 530 | 2210 | 4.2 | 3 | 121 | 1700 | 14.0 | 13 |
| Clarence Childs | 64-68 | 40 | 102 | 2.6 | 0 | 11 | 97 | 8.8 | 0 |
| Dick Christy | 58,60-63 | 337 | 1267 | 3.8 | 10 | 132 | 1473 | 11.2 | 6 |
| Jack Clancy | 67,69-70 | 3 | -4 | -1.3 | 0 | 104 | 1401 | 13.5 | 5 |
| Howard Clark | 60-61 | | | | | 38 | 613 | 16.1 | 0 |
| Franke Clarke | 57-67 | 32 | 231 | 7.2 | 1 | 291 | 5426 | 18.6 | 50 |
| Doug Cline | 60-66 | 37 | 105 | 2.8 | 2 | 4 | 15 | 3.8 | 0 |
| Bert Coan | 62-68 | 284 | 1259 | 4.4 | 15 | 39 | 367 | 9.4 | 4 |
| Junior Coffey | 65-67,69,71 | 535 | 2037 | 3.8 | 10 | 64 | 487 | 7.6 | 5 |
| Gail Cogdill | 60-70 | 2 | -2 | -1.0 | 0 | 356 | 5696 | 16.0 | 34 |
| Angie Coia | 60-66 | 5 | -2 | -0.4 | 0 | 121 | 2037 | 16.8 | 20 |
| Jim Colclough | 60-68 | 4 | 51 | 12.8 | 0 | 283 | 5001 | 17.7 | 39 |
| Terry Cole | 68-71 | 189 | 641 | 3.4 | 5 | 25 | 171 | 6.8 | 1 |
| Gary Collins | 62-71 | 8 | 60 | 15.0 | 0 | 331 | 5299 | 16.0 | 70 |
| Dick Compton | 62-65,67-68 | 6 | 8 | 1.3 | 0 | 52 | 733 | 14.1 | 14 |
| Jack Concannon | 64-71,74-75 | 217 | 1026 | 4.7 | 12 | | | | |
| Larry Conjar | 67-70 | 30 | 102 | 3.4 | 0 | 6 | 68 | 11.3 | 0 |
| Bobby Joe Conrad | 58-69 | 118 | 441 | 3.7 | 2 | 422 | 5902 | 14.0 | 38 |
| Greg Cook | 69,73 | 25 | 148 | 5.9 | 1 | | | | |
| Bob Coolbaugh | 61 | | | | | 32 | 435 | 13.6 | 4 |
| Thurlow Cooper | 60-62 | | | | | 36 | 491 | 13.6 | 8 |
| Paul Costa | 65-72 | 2 | 12 | 6.0 | 1 | 102 | 1699 | 16.7 | 6 |
| Jim Cox | 68 | | | | | 11 | 147 | 13.4 | 0 |
| Eric Crabtree | 66-71 | 8 | 37 | 4.6 | 0 | 164 | 2663 | 16.2 | 22 |
| Dobie Craig | 62-64 | 1 | 8 | 8.0 | 0 | 38 | 743 | 19.6 | 7 |
| Jim Crawford | 60-64 | 302 | 1078 | 3.6 | 5 | 52 | 496 | 9.5 | 2 |
| Willie Crenshaw | 64-70 | 652 | 2428 | 3.7 | 15 | 104 | 797 | 7.7 | 3 |
| Bob Crespino | 61-68 | | | | | 58 | 741 | 12.8 | 9 |
| Bobby Crockett | 66,68-69 | | | | | 41 | 659 | 16.1 | 3 |
| Monte Crockett | 60-62 | | | | | 35 | 512 | 14.6 | 1 |
| Marshall Cropper | 67-69 | | | | | 14 | 181 | 12.9 | 0 |
| John David Crow | 58-68 | 1157 | 4963 | 4.3 | 38 | 258 | 3699 | 14.3 | 35 |
| Wayne Crow | 60-63 | 235 | 1085 | 4.6 | 3 | 36 | 345 | 9.6 | 1 |
| Harry Crump | 63 | 49 | 120 | 2.5 | 5 | 3 | 19 | 6.3 | 0 |
| Jim Cunningham | 61-63 | 120 | 337 | 2.8 | 3 | 26 | 219 | 8.4 | 2 |
| Gary Cuozzo | 63-72 | 16 | 176 | 2.3 | 1 | | | | |
| Carroll Dale | 60-73 | 4 | 30 | 7.5 | 0 | 438 | 8277 | 18.9 | 52 |
| Clem Daniels | 60-68 | 1146 | 5138 | 4.5 | 30 | 203 | 3314 | 16.3 | 24 |
| Cotton Davidson | 54,57,60-66,68 | 149 | 357 | 2.4 | 11 | | | | |
| Glenn Davis | 60-61 | | | | | 10 | 132 | 13.2 | 0 |
| Len Dawson | 57-75 | 294 | 1293 | 4.4 | 9 | | | | |
| Ted Dean | 60-64 | 263 | 923 | 3.5 | 2 | 51 | 684 | 13.4 | 4 |
| Austin Denney | 67-71 | 2 | 3 | 1.5 | 0 | 71 | 764 | 10.8 | 3 |
| Mike Dennis | 68-69 | 29 | 136 | 4.7 | 0 | 8 | 53 | 6.6 | 0 |
| Al Denson | 64-71 | 4 | 3 | 0.8 | 0 | 260 | 4275 | 16.4 | 32 |
| Willard Dewveall | 59-64 | | | | | 204 | 3304 | 16.2 | 27 |
| Buddy Dial | 59-66 | 4 | 14 | 3.5 | 0 | 261 | 5436 | 20.8 | 44 |
| Bo Dickinson | 60-64 | 189 | 693 | 3.7 | 4 | 86 | 886 | 10.3 | 6 |
| Mike Ditka | 61-72 | 2 | 2 | 1.0 | 0 | 427 | 5812 | 13.6 | 43 |
| Hewitt Dixon | 63-70 | 772 | 3090 | 4.0 | 15 | 263 | [illegible] | 10.7 | 13 |
| Oscar Donahue | 62 | | | | | 16 | 285 | 17.8 | 1 |
| Mike Dorsey | 62 | | | | | 21 | 344 | 16.4 | 2 |
| Merrill Douglas | 58-62 | 54 | 213 | 3.9 | 2 | 4 | 26 | 6.5 | 0 |
| Boyd Dowler | 59-69,71 | 2 | 28 | 14.0 | 0 | 474 | 7270 | 15.3 | 40 |
| Elbert Dubenion | 60-68 | 46 | 326 | 7.1 | 3 | [illegible] | [illegible] | [illegible] | 35 |
| Paul Dudley | 62-63 | 38 | 121 | 3.2 | 0 | 10 | 120 | 12.0 | 1 |
| Fred Dugan | 58-63 | 1 | -9 | -9 | 0 | 153 | 2226 | 14.5 | 13 |
| Perry Lee Dunn | 64-69 | 214 | 653 | 3.1 | 6 | 42 | 408 | 9.7 | 1 |
| Henry Dyer | 66,68-70 | 82 | 256 | 3.1 | 1 | 14 | 160 | 11.4 | 1 |
| Rick Eder | 68-70 | | | | | 11 | 184 | 16.7 | 1 |
| Nick Eddy | 68-70,72 | 152 | 523 | 3.4 | 3 | 24 | 237 | 9.9 | 2 |
| Larry Elkins | 66-67 | 2 | 19 | 9.5 | 0 | 24 | 315 | 13.1 | 3 |
| John Embree | 69-70 | | | | | 33 | 519 | 15.7 | 5 |
| Hunter Enis | 60-62 | 30 | 25 | 0.8 | 5 | | | | |
| Pat Epperson | 60 | | | | | 11 | 99 | 9.0 | 0 |
| Sam Etcheverry | 61-62 | 41 | 78 | 1.9 | 0 | | | | |
| Bo Farrington | 60-63 | 1 | -2 | -2.0 | 0 | 55 | 881 | 16.0 | 7 |
| Bobby Felts | 65-67 | 66 | 207 | 3.1 | 2 | 5 | 29 | 5.8 | 0 |
| Bob Ferguson | 62-63 | 66 | 209 | 3.2 | 1 | 4 | 13 | 3.3 | 0 |
| Charley Ferguson | 61-63,65-66,68-69 | | | | | 62 | 1168 | 18.8 | 13 |
| Paul Flatley | 63-70 | | | | | 306 | 4905 | 16.0 | 24 |
| George Fleming | 61 | 31 | 112 | 3.6 | 1 | 10 | 49 | 4.9 | 0 |
| Marv Fleming | 63-74 | | | | | 157 | 1823 | 11.6 | 16 |
| Tom Flores | 60-61,63-69 | 101 | 142 | 1.4 | 5 | | | | |
| Charlie Flowers | 60-62 | 111 | 416 | 3.7 | 4 | 35 | 383 | 10.9 | 1 |
| Lee Folkins | 61-65 | 1 | 9 | 9.0 | 0 | 80 | 1042 | 13.0 | 10 |
| Fred Ford | 60 | 38 | 194 | 5.1 | 2 | 1 | 5 | 5.0 | 0 |

| Name | Years | RUSHING Att. | Yards | Avg. | TD | RECEIVING Rec. | Yards | Avg. | TD |
|---|---|---|---|---|---|---|---|---|---|
| Garrett Ford | 68 | 41 | 186 | 4.5 | 1 | 6 | 40 | 6.7 | 0 |
| Gene Foster | 65-70 | 445 | 1613 | 3.6 | 4 | 99 | 904 | 9.1 | 3 |
| Willmer Fowler | 60-61 | 94 | 372 | 4.0 | 1 | 10 | 99 | 9.9 | 0 |
| Al Frazier | 61-63 | 62 | 278 | 4.5 | 2 | 58 | 1010 | 17.4 | 7 |
| Charley Frazier | 62-70 | 4 | 5 | 1.3 | 0 | 209 | 3461 | 16.6 | 30 |
| Willie Frazier | 64-72,75 | 6 | 118 | 19.7 | 1 | 207 | 3069 | 14.8 | 35 |
| Tucker Frederickson | 65,67-71 | 651 | 2209 | 3.4 | 9 | 128 | 1011 | 7.9 | 8 |
| Charley Fuller | 61-62 | 38 | 134 | 3.5 | 0 | 17 | 344 | 20.2 | 2 |
| Roman Gabriel | 62-77 | 354 | 1302 | 3.7 | 30 | 1 | -5 | -5.0 | 0 |
| Bob Gaiters | 61-63 | 168 | 673 | 4.0 | 6 | 17 | 175 | 10.3 | 2 |
| Willie Galimore | 57-63 | 670 | 2985 | 4.5 | 26 | 87 | 1201 | 13.8 | 10 |
| R.C. Gamble | 68-69 | 94 | 346 | 3.7 | 1 | 18 | 129 | 7.2 | 1 |
| Billy Gambrell | 63-68 | 7 | 41 | 5.9 | 0 | 116 | 1931 | 16.6 | 18 |
| J.D. Garrett | 64-67 | 116 | 434 | 3.7 | 3 | 17 | 169 | 9.9 | 2 |
| Mike Garrett | 66-73 | 1308 | 5481 | 4.2 | 35 | 238 | 2010 | 8.4 | 13 |
| Larry Garron | 60-68 | 763 | 2981 | 3.9 | 14 | 185 | 2502 | 13.5 | 26 |
| Prentice Gault | 60-67 | 629 | 2466 | 3.9 | 11 | 79 | 901 | 11.4 | 6 |
| Jack Gehrke | 68-69,71-72 | 1 | 2 | 2.0 | 0 | 14 | 254 | 18.1 | 0 |
| Pete Gent | 64-68 | 2 | -5 | -2.5 | 0 | 68 | 989 | 14.5 | 4 |
| Jim Gibbons | 58-68 | | | | | 287 | 3561 | 12.4 | 20 |
| Cookie Gilchrist | 62-67 | 1010 | 4293 | 4.3 | 37 | 110 | 1135 | 10.3 | 6 |
| Glenn Glass | 62-66 | | | | | 15 | 201 | 13.4 | 0 |
| Al Goldstein | 60 | 3 | -2 | -0.7 | 1 | 27 | 354 | 13.1 | 1 |
| Ron Goodwin | 63-68 | 2 | -22 | -11.0 | 0 | 78 | 1079 | 13.8 | 9 |
| Jim Grabowski | 66-71 | 475 | 1731 | 3.6 | 8 | 82 | 675 | 8.2 | 3 |
| Art Graham | 63-68 | 1 | -5 | -5.0 | 0 | 199 | 3107 | 15.6 | 20 |
| Hoyle Granger | 66-72 | 805 | 3653 | 4.5 | 19 | 134 | 1339 | 10.0 | 5 |
| Ernie Green | 62-68 | 668 | 3204 | 4.8 | 15 | 195 | 2036 | 10.4 | 20 |
| Johnny Green | 60-63 | 77 | -106 | -1.4 | 6 | 1 | 0 | 0.0 | 0 |
| Tom Greene | 60-61 | 16 | -27 | -1.7 | 0 | | | | |
| Jim Greer | 60 | | | | | 22 | 284 | 12.9 | 1 |
| Ben Gregory | 68 | 52 | 283 | 5.4 | 1 | 5 | 21 | 4.2 | 0 |
| Bill Groman | 60-65 | 1 | 2 | 2.0 | 1 | 174 | 3481 | 20.0 | 36 |
| Earl Gros | 62-70 | 821 | 3157 | 3.8 | 28 | 142 | 1255 | 8.8 | 10 |
| Ralph Guglielmi | 55,58-63 | 177 | 633 | 3.6 | 2 | | | | |
| John Hadl | 62-77 | 351 | 1112 | 3.2 | 16 | 3 | -9 | -3.0 | 0 |
| Mike Haffner | 68-71 | 3 | 3 | 1.0 | 0 | 59 | 991 | 16.8 | 7 |
| Roger Hagberg | 65-69 | 194 | 766 | 3.9 | 4 | 58 | 645 | 11.1 | 4 |
| Mac Haik | 67-71 | 4 | 28 | 7.0 | 0 | 76 | 1149 | 15.1 | 9 |
| Ken Hall | 59-61 | 51 | 212 | 4.2 | 0 | 8 | 118 | 14.8 | 2 |
| Tom Hall | 62-69 | 4 | -4 | -1.0 | 0 | 103 | 1441 | 14.0 | 8 |
| Mal Hammack | 55,57-66 | 320 | 1278 | 4.0 | 7 | 27 | 255 | 9.4 | 0 |
| Charley Hardy | 60-62 | | | | | 54 | 840 | 15.6 | 7 |
| Jack Harper | 67-68 | 41 | 197 | 4.8 | 1 | 11 | 212 | 19.3 | 3 |
| Billy Harris | 68-69,71 | 60 | 158 | 2.6 | 0 | 5 | 131 | 26.2 | 1 |
| Pete Hart | 60 | 25 | 113 | 4.5 | 0 | 3 | 19 | 6.3 | 0 |
| Alex Hawkins | 59-68 | 208 | 787 | 3.8 | 10 | 129 | 1751 | 13.6 | 12 |
| Ben Hawkins | 66-73 | 10 | 8 | 0.8 | 0 | 261 | 4764 | 18.3 | 32 |
| Luther Hayes | 61 | | | | | 14 | 280 | 20.0 | 3 |
| Ray Hayes | 61 | 73 | 319 | 4.4 | 2 | 16 | 121 | 8.1 | 0 |
| Wendell Hayes | 63,65-74 | 988 | 3758 | 3.8 | 28 | 161 | 1461 | 9.1 | 7 |
| Abner Haynes | 60-67 | 1036 | 4630 | 4.5 | 46 | 287 | 3535 | 12.3 | 20 |
| Gene Heeter | 63-65 | | | | | 22 | 327 | 14.9 | 2 |
| John Henderson | 65-72 | | | | | 108 | 1735 | 16.1 | 10 |
| Jon Henderson | 68-70 | | | | | 28 | 390 | 13.9 | 6 |
| Charley Hennigan | 60-66 | | | | | 410 | 6823 | 16.6 | 51 |
| Ken Herock | 63-69 | | | | | 63 | 924 | 14.7 | 4 |
| Bo Hickey | 67 | 73 | 263 | 3.6 | 4 | 7 | 36 | 5.1 | 1 |
| Fred Hill | 65-71 | 1 | 5 | 5.0 | 0 | 85 | 1005 | 11.8 | 5 |
| Jerry Hill | 61,63-70 | 606 | 2668 | 4.4 | 22 | 117 | 970 | 8.3 | 3 |
| King Hill | 58-69 | 88 | 306 | 3.5 | 9 | | | | |
| Mack Lee Hill | 64-65 | 230 | 1203 | 5.2 | 6 | 40 | 408 | 10.2 | 3 |
| John Hilton | 65-73 | 1 | 15 | 15.0 | 0 | 144 | 2047 | 14.2 | 16 |
| Dick Hoak | 61-70 | 1132 | 3965 | 3.5 | 25 | 146 | 1452 | 9.9 | 8 |
| Roy Hopkins | 67-70 | 232 | 826 | 3.6 | 7 | 50 | 529 | 10.6 | 1 |
| Sam Horner | 60-62 | 118 | 355 | 3.0 | 0 | 17 | 219 | 12.9 | 1 |
| Paul Hornung | 57-62,64-66 | 893 | 3711 | 4.2 | 50 | 130 | 1480 | 11.4 | 12 |
| Brad Hubbert | 67-70 | 287 | 1270 | 4.4 | 9 | 42 | 312 | 7.4 | 2 |
| Chuck Hughes | 67-71 | | | | | 15 | 262 | 17.5 | 0 |
| George Hughley | 65 | 37 | 175 | 4.7 | 0 | 9 | 93 | 10.3 | 1 |
| Tom Hutchinson | 63-66 | | | | | 19 | 409 | 21.5 | 2 |
| Bobby Jackson | 62-65 | 184 | 624 | 3.4 | 14 | 32 | 333 | 10.4 | 2 |
| Frank Jackson | 61-67 | 121 | 790 | 6.5 | 7 | 188 | 2955 | 15.7 | 24 |
| Leroy Jackson | 62-63 | 52 | 142 | 2.7 | 0 | 10 | 253 | 25.3 | 0 |
| Allen Jacobs | 65-67 | 91 | 301 | 3.3 | 1 | 10 | 69 | 6.9 | 0 |
| Dick James | 56-65 | 502 | 1930 | 3.8 | 19 | 104 | 1669 | 16.0 | 15 |
| Billy Joe | 63-68 | 539 | 2013 | 3.7 | 15 | 77 | 589 | 7.6 | 4 |
| Charley Johnson | 61-75 | 196 | 539 | 2.8 | 10 | | | | |
| Curley Johnson | 60-69 | 64 | 209 | 3.3 | 1 | 32 | 370 | 11.6 | 3 |
| Jim Johnson | 61-75 | | | | | 40 | 690 | 17.3 | 4 |
| John Henry Johnson | 54-66 | 1571 | 6803 | 4.3 | 48 | 186 | 1478 | 7.9 | 7 |
| Rudy Johnson | 64-66 | 25 | 60 | 2.4 | 1 | 8 | 70 | 8.8 | 0 |
| Harry Jones | 67-70 | 44 | 85 | 1.9 | 0 | 9 | 131 | 14.6 | 0 |
| Homer Jones | 64-70 | 17 | 146 | 8.6 | 1 | 224 | 4986 | 22.3 | 36 |
| Jim Jones | 65-68 | 8 | 24 | 3.0 | 0 | 69 | 1182 | 17.1 | 11 |
| Les Josephson | 64-67,69-74 | 797 | 3407 | 4.3 | 17 | 194 | 1970 | 10.2 | 11 |
| Steve Junker | 57,59-62 | | | | | 48 | 639 | 13.3 | 6 |
| Sonny Jurgensen | 57-74 | 181 | 493 | 2.7 | 15 | 1 | -3 | -3.0 | 0 |
| Joe Kapp | 67-70 | 119 | 611 | 5.1 | 5 | | | | |
| Jim Kelly | 64-65,67 | | | | | 31 | 531 | 17.1 | 5 |
| Leroy Kelly | 64-73 | 1727 | 7274 | 4.2 | 74 | 190 | 2281 | 12.0 | 13 |
| Jack Kemp | 57,60-67,69 | 394 | 796 | 2.0 | 40 | | | | |
| Claude King | 61-62 | 33 | 194 | 5.9 | 3 | 8 | 125 | 15.6 | 1 |
| Phil King | 58-66 | 569 | 2192 | 3.9 | 7 | 86 | 951 | 11.1 | 9 |

184

Lifetime Statistics - 1960-1969 Players Section 2 - RUSHING AND RECEIVING (continued)
(All men with 25 or more rushing attempts or 10 or more receptions)

| | | RUSHING | | | | RECEIVING | | | |
|---|---|---|---|---|---|---|---|---|---|
| Name | Years | Att. | Yards | Avg. | TD | Rec. | Yards | Avg. | TD |
| Roger Kochman | 63 | 47 | 232 | 4.9 | 0 | 4 | 148 | 37.0 | 1 |
| Dave Kocourek | 60-68 | | | | | 249 | 4090 | 16.4 | 24 |
| Dave Kopay | 64-72 | 235 | 876 | 3.7 | 3 | 77 | 593 | 7.7 | 4 |
| Dick Kotite | 67-69,71-72 | | | | | 17 | 213 | 12.5 | 5 |
| Walt Kowalczyk | 58-61 | 103 | 264 | 2.6 | 2 | 34 | 256 | 7.5 | 1 |
| Ernie Koy | 65-70 | 414 | 1723 | 4.2 | 9 | 76 | 498 | 6.6 | 6 |
| Ron Kramer | 57,59-67 | 6 | 9 | 1.5 | 0 | 229 | 3272 | 14.3 | 16 |
| Rich Kreitling | 59-64 | 2 | −13 | −6.5 | 0 | 123 | 1775 | 14.4 | 17 |
| Joe Kulbacki | 60 | 41 | 108 | 2.6 | 1 | 2 | 9 | 4.5 | 0 |
| Ralph Kurek | 65-70 | 121 | 434 | 3.6 | 2 | 26 | 299 | 11.5 | 0 |
| Pete Lammons | 66-72 | 0 | 3 | – | 0 | 185 | 2364 | 12.8 | 14 |
| Daryle Lamonica | 63-74 | 166 | 640 | 3.9 | 14 | | | | |
| Izzy Lang | 64-69 | 245 | 873 | 3.6 | 4 | 63 | 554 | 8.8 | 4 |
| Jack Larscheid | 60-61 | 100 | 400 | 4.0 | 1 | 24 | 198 | 8.3 | 1 |
| Pete Larson | 67-68 | | | | | 20 | 191 | 9.6 | 1 |
| Monte Ledbetter | 67-69 | | | | | 18 | 314 | 17.4 | 3 |
| Jacky Lee | 60-69 | 82 | 150 | 1.8 | 3 | 1 | −1 | −1.0 | 0 |
| Darrell Lester | 64-66 | 38 | 102 | 2.7 | 0 | 2 | 26 | 13.0 | 1 |
| Dan Lewis | 58-66 | 800 | 3205 | 4.0 | 19 | 99 | 1162 | 11.7 | 5 |
| Gary Lewis | 64-70 | 343 | 1421 | 4.1 | 13 | 72 | 604 | 8.4 | 5 |
| Keith Lincoln | 61-68 | 758 | 3383 | 4.5 | 19 | 165 | 2250 | 13.6 | 19 |
| Mike Lind | 63-66 | 222 | 661 | 3.0 | 8 | 52 | 427 | 8.2 | 1 |
| Jim Lindsey | 66-72 | 178 | 566 | 3.2 | 6 | 56 | 632 | 11.3 | -4 |
| Don Lisbon | 63-64 | 164 | 561 | 3.4 | 0 | 34 | 363 | 10.7 | 3 |
| Pete Liske | 64,69-72 | 38 | 141 | 3.7 | 2 | | | | |
| Andy Livingston | 64-65,67-70 | 291 | 1216 | 4.2 | 7 | 46 | 474 | 10.3 | 3 |
| J.W. Lockett | 61-64 | 229 | 170 | 3.4 | 3 | 62 | 589 | 9.5 | 7 |
| Oscar Lofton | 60 | | | | | 19 | 360 | 18.9 | 4 |
| Bob Long | 64-70 | | | | | 98 | 1539 | 15.7 | 10 |
| Joe Don Looney | 64-67,69 | 214 | 724 | 3.4 | 11 | 26 | 171 | 6.6 | 2 |
| Tony Lorick | 64-69 | 548 | 2124 | 3.9 | 14 | 86 | 890 | 10.3 | 5 |
| Billy Lott | 58,60-63 | 246 | 1123 | 4.6 | 13 | 85 | 919 | 10.8 | 8 |
| John Love | 67,72 | | | | | 18 | 267 | 14.8 | 2 |
| Paul Lowe | 60-61,63-69 | 1026 | 4995 | 4.9 | 40 | 111 | 1045 | 9.4 | 7 |
| Dick Lucas | 58,60-63 | | | | | 34 | 384 | 11.3 | 6 |
| Richie Lucas | 60-61 | 56 | 105 | 1.9 | 2 | 11 | 127 | 11.5 | 1 |
| Lamar Lundy | 57-69 | | | | | 35 | 584 | 16.7 | 6 |
| Lenny Lyles | 58-69 | 35 | 69 | 2.0 | 2 | 8 | 57 | 7.1 | 1 |
| Red Mack | 61-66 | 4 | −1 | −0.3 | 0 | 52 | 1159 | 22.3 | 8 |
| Dee Mackey | 60-65 | | | | | 94 | 1352 | 14.4 | 8 |
| John Mackey | 63-72 | 19 | 127 | 6.7 | 0 | 331 | 5236 | 15.8 | 38 |
| Jacques MacKinnon | 61-70 | 86 | 377 | 4.4 | 2 | 112 | 2109 | 18.8 | 20 |
| Joe Marconi | 56-66 | 673 | 2771 | 4.1 | 30 | 136 | 1326 | 9.8 | 9 |
| Aaron Marsh | 68-69 | 4 | 8 | 2.0 | 0 | 27 | 439 | 16.3 | 4 |
| Amos Marsh | 61-67 | 750 | 3222 | 4.3 | 25 | 133 | 1384 | 10.4 | 7 |
| Paul Martha | 64-70 | 6 | 15 | 2.5 | 0 | 17 | 316 | 18.6 | 0 |
| Billy Martin | 64-68 | | | | | 58 | 705 | 12.2 | 4 |
| Tommy Mason | 61-71 | 1040 | 4203 | 4.0 | 32 | 214 | 2324 | 10.9 | 13 |
| Bill Mathis | 60-69 | 1044 | 3589 | 3.4 | 37 | 149 | 1775 | 11.9 | 9 |
| Tom Matte | 61-72 | 1200 | 4646 | 3.9 | 45 | 249 | 2869 | 11.5 | 12 |
| Doug Mayberry | 61-63 | 87 | 314 | 3.6 | 1 | 13 | 118 | 9.1 | 1 |
| Don Maynard | 58,60-73 | 24 | 70 | 2.9 | 0 | 633 | 11834 | 18.7 | 88 |
| Don McCall | 67-70 | 229 | 884 | 3.9 | 6 | 37 | 390 | 10.5 | 3 |
| Brendan McCarthy | 68-69 | 59 | 175 | 3.0 | 1 | 20 | 184 | 9.2 | 2 |
| Curtis McClinton | 62-69 | 762 | 3124 | 4.1 | 18 | 154 | 1945 | 12.6 | 14 |
| Gary McDermott | 68-69 | 54 | 108 | 2.0 | 3 | 20 | 115 | 5.8 | 1 |
| Roy McDonald | 67-68 | 52 | 223 | 4.3 | 4 | 10 | 60 | 6.0 | 0 |
| Tommy McDonald | 57-68 | 17 | 22 | 1.3 | 0 | 495 | 8410 | 17.0 | 84 |
| Gerry McDougall | 62-64,68 | 104 | 469 | 4.5 | 6 | 22 | 248 | 11.3 | 0 |
| Kay McFarland | 62-66,68 | | | | | 45 | 682 | 15.2 | 4 |
| Max McGee | 54,57-67 | 12 | 121 | 10.1 | 0 | 345 | 6346 | 18.4 | 50 |
| Hugh McInnis | 60-62,64,66 | 4 | 30 | 7.5 | 0 | 22 | 392 | 17.8 | 0 |
| Marlin McKeever | 61-73 | | | | | 133 | 1737 | 13.1 | 6 |
| Bob McLeod | 61-66 | | | | | 126 | 1926 | 15.3 | 19 |
| Clifton McNeil | 64-73 | 5 | 6 | 1.2 | 0 | 181 | 2734 | 15.1 | 22 |
| Chuck Mercein | 65-70 | 163 | 531 | 3.3 | 4 | 37 | 205 | 5.5 | 1 |
| Don Meredith | 60-68 | 242 | 1216 | 5.0 | 15 | | | | |
| Dale Messer | 61-65 | | | | | 12 | 176 | 14.7 | 0 |
| Frank Mestnik | 60-61,63 | 200 | 767 | 3.8 | 4 | 15 | 53 | 3.5 | 1 |
| Tom Michel | 64 | 39 | 129 | 3.3 | 0 | 1 | 14 | 14.0 | 0 |
| Alan Miller | 60-63,65 | 386 | 1395 | 3.6 | 9 | 130 | 1470 | 11.3 | 11 |
| Bill Miller | 62-64,66-68 | | | | | 141 | 1879 | 13.3 | 10 |
| Gene Milton | 68-69 | 9 | 108 | 12.0 | 0 | 21 | 322 | 15.3 | 1 |
| Gene Mingo | 60-70 | 185 | 777 | 4.2 | 8 | 52 | 454 | 8.7 | 4 |
| Randy Minniear | 67-70 | 96 | 316 | 3.3 | 5 | 19 | 148 | 7.8 | 1 |
| George Mira | 60-64,71 | 50 | 379 | 7.6 | 0 | | | | |
| Bobby Mitchell | 58-68 | 513 | 2735 | 5.3 | 18 | 521 | 7954 | 15.3 | 65 |
| Charley Mitchell | 63-68 | 352 | 1142 | 3.2 | 5 | 62 | 650 | 8.9 | 3 |
| Stan Mitchell | 60-70 | 173 | 548 | 3.2 | 4 | 42 | 533 | 12.7 | 5 |
| Lenny Moore | 56-67 | 1069 | 5174 | 4.8 | 63 | 363 | 6039 | 16.6 | 48 |
| Tom Moore | 60-67 | 660 | 2445 | 3.7 | 21 | 141 | 1152 | 8.2 | 10 |
| Doug Moreau | 66-69 | 1 | −2 | −2.0 | 0 | 73 | 926 | 12.7 | 6 |
| Earl Morrall | 56-75 | 235 | 878 | 3.7 | 8 | | | | |
| Johnny Morris | 58-67 | 224 | 1040 | 4.6 | 5 | 356 | 5059 | 14.2 | 31 |
| Larry Morris | 55-57,59-66 | 40 | 148 | 3.7 | 1 | | | | |
| Joe Morrison | 59-72 | 677 | 2474 | 3.7 | 18 | 395 | 4993 | 12.6 | 47 |
| Bill Murphy | 68 | | | | | 18 | 268 | 14.9 | 0 |
| Jim Nance | 65-71,73 | 1341 | 5401 | 4.0 | 45 | 133 | 870 | 6.5 | 1 |
| Bill Nelsen | 63-72 | 84 | 89 | 1.1 | 2 | 1 | −5 | −5.0 | 0 |
| Tom Neumann | 63 | 44 | 148 | 3.4 | 0 | 10 | 48 | 4.8 | 0 |
| Jim Ninowski | 58-69 | 92 | 367 | 4.0 | 10 | | | | |
| Terry Nofsinger | 61-67 | 31 | 65 | 2.1 | 3 | | | | |
| Karl Noonan | 66-71 | 2 | −20 | −10.0 | 0 | 136 | 1798 | 13.2 | 17 |
| Pettis Norman | 62-73 | 23 | 198 | 8.6 | 0 | 183 | 2492 | 13.6 | 15 |
| Don Norton | 60-66 | 2 | −3 | −1.5 | 0 | 228 | 3486 | 15.3 | 27 |
| Tom Nowatzke | 65-72 | 361 | 1249 | 3.5 | 13 | 100 | 605 | 6.1 | 4 |
| Ray Ogden | 65-73 | 1 | 12 | 12.0 | 0 | 53 | 885 | 16.7 | 4 |
| Jimmy Orr | 58-70 | 15 | 122 | 8.1 | 0 | 400 | 7914 | 19.8 | 66 |
| Tom Osborne | 60-61 | | | | | 29 | 343 | 11.8 | 2 |
| R.C. Owens | 57-64 | 1 | 23 | 23.0 | 1 | 206 | 3285 | 15.9 | 22 |
| Bob Paremore | 63-64 | 36 | 107 | 3.0 | 0 | 6 | 89 | 14.8 | 1 |
| Babe Parilli | 52-53,56-58,60-69 | 394 | 1416 | 3.6 | 24 | | | | |
| Dave Parks | 64-73 | 4 | −10 | −2.5 | 0 | 360 | 5619 | 15.6 | 44 |
| Clarence Peaks | 57-65 | 951 | 3660 | 3.8 | 21 | 190 | 1793 | 9.4 | 3 |
| Art Perkins | 62-63 | 85 | 251 | 3.0 | 6 | 22 | 144 | 6.5 | 0 |
| Don Perkins | 61-68 | 1500 | 6217 | 4.1 | 42 | 146 | 1310 | 9.0 | 3 |
| Ray Perkins | 67-71 | 10 | 77 | 7.7 | 0 | 93 | 1538 | 16.5 | 11 |
| Jim Phillips | 58-67 | | | | | 401 | 6044 | 15.1 | 34 |
| Brian Piccolo | 66-69 | 258 | 927 | 3.6 | 4 | 58 | 537 | 9.3 | 1 |
| Nick Pietrosante | 59-67 | 955 | 4026 | 4.2 | 28 | 131 | 1391 | 10.6 | 2 |
| Elijah Pitts | 61-71 | 514 | 1788 | 3.5 | 28 | 104 | 1265 | 12.0 | 6 |
| Dave Pivec | 66-69 | | | | | 14 | 146 | 10.4 | 1 |
| Milt Plum | 57-69 | 217 | 531 | 2.4 | 13 | 1 | 20 | 20.0 | 0 |
| Ray Poage | 63-65,67-71 | 3 | 32 | 10.7 | 0 | 145 | 2309 | 15.9 | 13 |
| Bob Poole | 64-67 | | | | | 19 | 223 | 11.7 | 0 |
| Bucky Pope | 64,66-68 | 2 | 11 | 5.5 | 0 | 34 | 952 | 28.0 | 13 |
| Dickie Post | 67-71 | 608 | 2605 | 4.3 | 17 | 96 | 903 | 9.4 | 2 |
| Art Powell | 59-68 | | | | | 479 | 8046 | 16.8 | 81 |
| Gene Prebola | 60-63 | | | | | 133 | 1823 | 13.7 | 6 |
| Sam Price | 66-68 | 82 | 213 | 3.8 | 1 | 10 | 70 | 7.0 | 1 |
| Frank Quayle | 69 | 57 | 183 | 3.2 | 0 | 11 | 167 | 15.2 | 0 |
| Warren Rabb | 60-62 | 50 | 124 | 2.5 | 3 | | | | |
| Bill Rademacher | 64-70 | 1 | −13 | −13.0 | 0 | 24 | 282 | 11.8 | 3 |
| Sonny Randle | 59-68 | | | | | 365 | 5996 | 16.4 | 65 |
| Ron Rector | 66-67 | 33 | 167 | 5.1 | 0 | 6 | 22 | 3.7 | 0 |
| Bob Reed | 62-63 | 27 | 110 | 4.1 | 0 | 17 | 174 | 10.2 | 1 |
| Dan Reeves | 65-72 | 535 | 1990 | 3.7 | 25 | 129 | 1693 | 13.1 | 17 |
| Jerry Reichow | 56-57,59-64 | 20 | 105 | 5.3 | 0 | 172 | 2579 | 15.0 | 24 |
| Bob Renn | 61 | 1 | 14 | 14.0 | 0 | 18 | 268 | 14.9 | 1 |
| Lance Rentzel | 65-72,74 | 26 | 196 | 7.5 | 2 | 268 | 4826 | 18.0 | 38 |
| Pete Retzlaff | 56-66 | 6 | −4 | −0.7 | 0 | 452 | 7412 | 16.4 | 47 |
| M.C. Reynolds | 58-62 | 88 | 419 | 4.8 | 4 | | | | |
| Jerry Rhome | 65-67,69-71 | 26 | 91 | 3.5 | 1 | | | | |
| Perry Richards | 57-62 | | | | | 39 | 558 | 14.3 | 4 |
| Jerry Richardson | 59-60 | | | | | 15 | 171 | 11.4 | 4 |
| Willie Richardson | 63-71 | 2 | 27 | 13.5 | 0 | 195 | 2950 | 15.1 | 25 |
| Pat Richter | 63-70 | 1 | −9 | −9.0 | 0 | 99 | 1315 | 13.3 | 14 |
| Johnny Roach | 56,59-64 | 42 | 99 | 2.4 | 2 | | | | |
| Bo Roberson | 61-66 | 168 | 584 | 3.5 | 6 | 176 | 2917 | 16.6 | 12 |
| C.R. Roberts | 59-62 | 155 | 637 | 4.1 | 4 | 21 | 132 | 6.3 | 0 |
| Walter Roberts | 64-67,69-70 | 5 | 45 | 9.0 | 0 | 67 | 1218 | 18.2 | 9 |
| Jerry Robinson | 62-65 | 3 | 20 | 6.7 | 0 | 49 | 799 | 16.3 | 4 |
| Johnny Robinson | 60-71 | 150 | 658 | 4.4 | 6 | 77 | 1228 | 15.9 | 9 |
| John Roderick | 66-68 | | | | | 11 | 156 | 14.2 | 1 |
| Johnny Roland | 66-74 | 1015 | 3750 | 3.7 | 28 | 153 | 1430 | 9.3 | 6 |
| Dave Rolle | 60 | 130 | 501 | 3.9 | 2 | 21 | 122 | 5.8 | 1 |
| Tony Romeo | 61-67 | | | | | 116 | 1833 | 15.8 | 10 |
| Dave Ross | 60 | | | | | 10 | 122 | 12.2 | 1 |
| Ed Rutkowski | 63-68 | 69 | 250 | 3.6 | 1 | 63 | 981 | 15.6 | 4 |
| Frank Ryan | 58-70 | 310 | 1358 | 4.4 | 6 | 0 | 31 | – | 1 |
| Tom Rychlec | 58,60-63 | 1 | −18 | −18.0 | 0 | 87 | 1091 | 12.5 | 3 |
| Saint Saffold | 68 | 1 | 21 | 21.0 | 0 | 16 | 172 | 10.8 | 0 |
| Theron Sapp | 59-65 | 202 | 763 | 3.8 | 5 | 23 | 247 | 10.7 | 0 |
| George Sauer | 65-70 | 4 | 23 | 5.8 | 0 | 309 | 4965 | 16.1 | 28 |
| Gale Sayers | 65-71 | 991 | 4956 | 5.0 | 39 | 112 | 1307 | 11.7 | 9 |
| Charlie Scales | 60-66 | 157 | 603 | 3.8 | 4 | 21 | 144 | 6.9 | 0 |
| Bob Scarpitto | 61-68 | 10 | 214 | 21.4 | 1 | 156 | 2651 | 17.0 | 27 |
| Randy Schultz | 66-68 | 82 | 301 | 3.7 | 2 | 26 | 220 | 8.5 | 0 |
| Glen Shaw | 60,62-64 | 47 | 148 | 3.1 | 3 | 8 | 146 | 18.3 | 1 |
| Tom Sherman | 68-69 | 27 | 94 | 3.5 | 0 | | | | |
| Dick Shiner | 64-71,73-74 | 58 | 161 | 2.8 | 2 | | | | |
| Roy Shivers | 66-72 | 176 | 680 | 3.9 | 10 | 38 | 400 | 10.5 | 4 |
| Bill Shockley | 60-62,68 | 42 | 165 | 3.9 | 0 | 31 | 96 | 8.7 | 2 |
| Del Shofner | 57-67 | 4 | 1 | 0.3 | 0 | 349 | 6470 | 18.5 | 51 |
| Les Shy | 66-70 | 144 | 523 | 3.6 | 3 | 23 | 273 | 11.9 | 1 |
| Jerry Simmons | 65-69,71-74 | 3 | −3 | −1.0 | 0 | 138 | 2105 | 15.3 | 9 |
| Mickey Slaughter | 63-66 | 73 | 263 | 3.6 | 1 | | | | |
| Tom Smiley | 68-70 | 120 | 312 | 2.6 | 4 | 24 | 109 | 4.5 | 1 |
| Allen Smith | 66-67 | 31 | 148 | 4.8 | 0 | 1 | 1 | 1.0 | 0 |
| Bobby Smith | 64-66 | 129 | 536 | 4.2 | 5 | 21 | 214 | 10.2 | 0 |
| Dave Smith | 60-64 | 328 | 1368 | 4.2 | 11 | 80 | 772 | 9.7 | 7 |
| Gordon Smith | 61-65 | 1 | 2 | 2.0 | 0 | 57 | 1277 | 22.4 | 13 |
| Jackie Smith | 63-78 | 38 | 327 | 8.6 | 3 | 480 | 7918 | 16.5 | 40 |
| J.D. Smith | 56-66 | 1100 | 4672 | 4.2 | 40 | 127 | 1122 | 8.8 | 6 |
| J.D. Smith | 60-61 | 66 | 220 | 3.3 | 6 | 17 | 194 | 11.4 | 1 |
| Ralph Smith | 62-69 | 2 | 26 | 13.0 | 0 | 41 | 549 | 13.4 | 5 |
| Russ Smith | 67-70 | 213 | 915 | 4.3 | 10 | 23 | 265 | 11.5 | 0 |
| Mark Smolinski | 61-68 | 421 | 1323 | 3.1 | 9 | 103 | 841 | 8.2 | 7 |
| Norm Snead | 61-75 | 209 | 522 | 2.5 | 23 | | | | |
| Matt Snell | 64-72 | 1057 | 4285 | 4.1 | 24 | 193 | 1375 | 7.1 | 7 |
| Mike Sommer | 58-61,63 | 78 | 253 | 3.2 | 2 | 9 | 166 | 18.4 | 0 |
| Butch Songin | 60-62 | 48 | −90 | −1.9 | 2 | | | | |
| Jack Spikes | 60-67 | 408 | 1693 | 4.1 | 18 | 56 | 679 | 12.1 | 3 |
| Billy Stacy | 59-63 | | | | | 12 | 241 | 20.1 | 1 |
| Bart Starr | 56-71 | 247 | 1308 | 5.3 | 15 | | | | |
| Tom Stephens | 60-64 | | | | | 41 | 506 | 12.3 | 5 |
| Monte Stickles | 60-68 | | | | | 222 | 3199 | 14.4 | 16 |
| Jim Stiger | 63-67 | 140 | 583 | 4.2 | 2 | 31 | 297 | 9.6 | 2 |
| Jim Stinnette | 61-62 | 40 | 95 | 2.4 | 1 | 24 | 167 | 7.0 | 1 |
| Donnie Stone | 61-66 | 354 | 1352 | 3.8 | 10 | 91 | 859 | 9.4 | 7 |
| Steve Stonebraker | 62-68 | | | | | 12 | 227 | 18.9 | 1 |

Lifetime Statistics · 1960-1969 Players     Section 2 - RUSHING and RECEIVING (continued)
(All men with 25 or more rushing attempts or 10 or more receptions)

| Name | Years | RUSHING Att. | Yards | Avg. | TD | RECEIVING Rec. | Yards | Avg. | TD |
|---|---|---|---|---|---|---|---|---|---|
| Bob Stransky | 60 | 28 | 78 | 2.8 | 0 | 3 | 11 | 3.7 | 0 |
| Pat Studstill | 61-62,64-72 | 6 | 39 | 6.5 | 0 | 181 | 2840 | 15.7 | 18 |
| Kark Sweetan | 66-70 | 56 | 307 | 5.5 | 2 | | | | |
| Mike Taliaferro | 64-72 | 46 | 134 | 2.9 | 0 | | | | |
| Fran Tarkenton | 61-78 | 675 | 3674 | 5.4 | 32 | 0 | -12 | -- | 0 |
| Jim Taylor | 58-67 | 1941 | 8597 | 4.4 | 83 | 225 | 1756 | 7.8 | 10 |
| Lionel Taylor | 59-68 | 4 | 20 | 5.0 | 0 | 567 | 7195 | 12.7 | 45 |
| Steve Tensi | 65-70 | 47 | 82 | 1.7 | 0 | | | | |
| Tony Teresa | 58,60 | 139 | 608 | 4.4 | 6 | 35 | 393 | 11.2 | 4 |
| Aaron Thomas | 61-70 | 4 | -10 | -2.5 | 0 | 262 | 4554 | 17.4 | 37 |
| Clendon Thomas | 58-68 | 18 | 70 | 3.9 | 0 | 60 | 1046 | 17.4 | 4 |
| Gene Thomas | 66-68 | 130 | 401 | 3.1 | 4 | 23 | 184 | 8.0 | 2 |
| Bill Thornton | 63-65,67 | 93 | 544 | 5.8 | 2 | 13 | 68 | 5.2 | 0 |
| Bubba Thornton | 69 | | | | | 14 | 134 | 9.6 | 0 |
| Steve Thurlow | 64-68 | 314 | 1127 | 3.6 | 4 | 61 | 539 | 8.8 | 2 |
| Jim Tiller | 62 | 31 | 43 | 1.3 | 0 | 13 | 108 | 8.3 | 0 |
| Bill Tobin | 63 | 75 | 270 | 3.6 | 4 | 13 | 172 | 13.2 | 1 |
| Larry Todd | 65-70 | 138 | 625 | 4.5 | 5 | 51 | 522 | 10.2 | 2 |
| Charley Tolar | 60-66 | 907 | 3277 | 3.6 | 21 | 175 | 1266 | 7.2 | 2 |
| John Tracey | 59-67 | | | | | 20 | 303 | 15.2 | 0 |
| Tom Tracy | 56-64 | 808 | 2912 | 3.6 | 17 | 113 | 1468 | 13.0 | 14 |
| Richard Trapp | 68-69 | | | | | 26 | 274 | 10.5 | 0 |
| Bill Triplett | 62-63,65-72 | 681 | 2446 | 3.6 | 17 | 113 | 1055 | 9.3 | 5 |
| Frank Tripucka | 49-52,60-63 | 70 | -125 | -1.8 | 6 | | | | |
| Billy Truax | 64-73 | | | | | 199 | 2458 | 12.4 | 17 |
| Don Trull | 64-69 | 123 | 428 | 3.5 | 14 | | | | |
| Bill Tucker | 67-71 | 127 | 431 | 3.4 | 6 | 59 | 496 | 8.4 | 7 |
| Wendell Tucker | 67-70 | | | | | 57 | 983 | 17.2 | 11 |
| Bake Turner | 62-70 | 2 | 13 | 6.5 | 0 | 220 | 3539 | 16.1 | 25 |
| Johnny Unitas | 56-73 | 450 | 1777 | 3.9 | 13 | 1 | 1 | 1.0 | 0 |
| Ron Vander Kelen | 63-67 | 26 | 116 | 4.5 | 1 | | | | |

| Name | Years | RUSHING Att. | Yards | Avg. | TD | RECEIVING Rec. | Yards | Avg. | TD |
|---|---|---|---|---|---|---|---|---|---|
| Jim Vollenweider | 62-63 | 58 | 161 | 2.8 | 2 | 5 | 47 | 9.4 | 0 |
| Billy Wade | 54-66 | 318 | 1334 | 4.2 | 24 | 0 | 10 | -- | 0 |
| Joe Walton | 57-63 | | | | | 178 | 2628 | 14.8 | 28 |
| Ernie Warlick | 62-65 | | | | | 90 | 1551 | 17.2 | 4 |
| Bob Waters | 60-63 | 65 | 281 | 4.3 | 3 | | | | |
| Tom Watkins | 61-65,67-68 | 468 | 1791 | 3.8 | 10 | 55 | 590 | 10.7 | 4 |
| Ken Webb | 58-63 | 264 | 891 | 3.4 | 8 | 46 | 483 | 10.5 | 1 |
| Joel Wells | 61 | 65 | 216 | 3.3 | 1 | 6 | 31 | 5.2 | 1 |
| Warren Wells | 64,67-70 | 9 | 103 | 11.4 | 1 | 158 | 3655 | 23.1 | 42 |
| Mel West | 61-62 | 81 | 338 | 4.2 | 3 | 14 | 147 | 10.5 | 0 |
| Jim Whalen | 65-71 | 1 | 0 | 0.0 | 0 | 197 | 3155 | 16.0 | 20 |
| Ernie Wheelwright | 64-70 | 387 | 1426 | 3.7 | 9 | 54 | 531 | 9.8 | 7 |
| Freeman White | 66-69 | | | | | 29 | 315 | 10.9 | 1 |
| John White | 60-61 | | | | | 14 | 256 | 18.3 | 1 |
| A. D. Whitfield | 65-68 | 222 | 981 | 4.4 | 3 | 67 | 702 | 10.5 | 3 |
| J. R. Wilburn | 66-70 | 7 | 54 | 7.7 | 0 | 123 | 1834 | 14.9 | 8 |
| Ken Willard | 65-74 | 1622 | 6105 | 3.8 | 45 | 277 | 2184 | 7.9 | 17 |
| A. D. Williams | 59-61 | | | | | 15 | 190 | 12.7 | 1 |
| Travis Williams | 67-71 | 289 | 1166 | 4.0 | 6 | 52 | 598 | 11.5 | 5 |
| Ben Wilson | 63-65,67 | 431 | 1589 | 3.7 | 9 | 47 | 487 | 10.4 | 2 |
| Butch Wilson | 63-69 | | | | | 25 | 317 | 12.7 | 3 |
| George Wilson | 66 | 27 | 137 | 5.1 | 0 | | | | |
| Lloyd Winston | 62-63 | 28 | 112 | 4.0 | 1 | 3 | 15 | 5.0 | 0 |
| Dick Witcher | 66-73 | | | | | 172 | 2359 | 13.7 | 14 |
| Joe Womack | 62 | 128 | 468 | 3.7 | 5 | 6 | 57 | 9.5 | 0 |
| Dick Wood | 62-66 | 26 | 45 | 1.7 | 4 | | | | |
| Gary Wood | 64-69 | 75 | 419 | 5.6 | 6 | | | | |
| Tom Woodeshick | 63-72 | 836 | 3577 | 4.3 | 21 | 126 | 1175 | 9.3 | 6 |
| John Wright | 68-69 | | | | | 12 | 130 | 10.8 | 2 |
| Tom Yewcic | 61-66 | 72 | 424 | 5.9 | 4 | 7 | 69 | 9.9 | 0 |

Lifetime Statistics - 1960-1969 Players     Section 3 - PUNT RETURNS and KICKOFF RETURNS
(All men with 25 or more Punt Returns or 25 or more Kickoff Returns)

| Name | Year | PUNT RETURNS No. | Yards | Avg. | TD | KICKOFF RETURNS No. | Yards | Avg. | TD |
|---|---|---|---|---|---|---|---|---|---|
| Herb Adderley | 61-72 | 1 | 0 | 0.0 | 0 | 120 | 3080 | 25.7 | 2 |
| Kermit Alexander | 63-73 | 133 | 835 | 6.3 | 2 | 153 | 3586 | 23.4 | 0 |
| Lance Alworth | 62-72 | 29 | 309 | 10.7 | 0 | 10 | 216 | 21.6 | 0 |
| Max Anderson | 68-69,71 | 19 | 142 | 7.5 | 0 | 43 | 1057 | 24.6 | 1 |
| Jon Arnett | 57-66 | 120 | 981 | 8.2 | 1 | 126 | 3100 | 24.7 | 2 |
| Pervis Atkins | 61-66 | 40 | 292 | 7.3 | 0 | 95 | 2124 | 22.4 | 0 |
| Joe Auer | 64-68 | 14 | 141 | 10.1 | 0 | 51 | 1171 | 23.0 | 1 |
| Bill Baird | 63-69 | 88 | 787 | 8.9 | 1 | 13 | 290 | 22.3 | 0 |
| Gary Ballman | 62-73 | | | | | 66 | 1754 | 26.6 | 1 |
| Terry Barr | 57-65 | 50 | 262 | 5.2 | 0 | 26 | 655 | 25.2 | 1 |
| Tom Barrington | 66-70 | 1 | 8 | 8.0 | 0 | 32 | 675 | 21.1 | 0 |
| Odell Barry | 64-65 | 37 | 359 | 9.7 | 1 | 73 | 1856 | 25.4 | 0 |
| Dick Bass | 60-69 | 24 | 263 | 11.0 | 1 | 54 | 1415 | 26.2 | 0 |
| Mike Battle | 69-70 | 53 | 352 | 6.6 | 0 | 71 | 1641 | 23.1 | 0 |
| Craig Baynham | 67-70,72 | | | | | 41 | 1035 | 25.2 | 0 |
| Joe Bellino | 65-67 | 19 | 148 | 7.8 | 0 | 43 | 905 | 21.0 | 0 |
| Roger Bird | 66-68 | 94 | 283 | 5.4 | 0 | 25 | 533 | 21.3 | 0 |
| Charlie Bivins | 60-67 | | | | | 78 | 1911 | 24.5 | 0 |
| Sid Blanks | 64-70 | 36 | 272 | 7.6 | 0 | 43 | 977 | 22.7 | 0 |
| Ronnie Blye | 68-69 | | | | | 54 | 1104 | 20.4 | 0 |
| Jimmie Brown | 57-65 | | | | | 29 | 648 | 22.3 | 0 |
| Timmy Brown | 59-68 | 71 | 639 | 9.0 | 1 | 184 | 4781 | 26.0 | 5 |
| Tom Brown | 64-69 | 27 | 151 | 5.6 | 1 | 7 | 167 | 23.9 | 0 |
| Willie Brown | 64-66 | 18 | 85 | 4.7 | 0 | 34 | 795 | 23.4 | 0 |
| Charlie Bryant | 66-69 | | | | | 42 | 913 | 21.7 | 0 |
| Amos Bullocks | 62-64,66 | | | | | 34 | 737 | 21.7 | 0 |
| Ode Burrell | 64-69 | 15 | 149 | 9.9 | 0 | 33 | 838 | 25.4 | 1 |
| Leon Burton | 60 | 12 | 93 | 7.8 | 0 | 31 | 897 | 28.9 | 2 |
| Ron Burton | 60-65 | 56 | 389 | 6.9 | 0 | 46 | 1119 | 24.3 | 1 |
| Bill Butler | 59-64 | 88 | 850 | 9.7 | 2 | 132 | 2886 | 21.9 | 0 |
| Cannonball Butler | 65-72 | | | | | 133 | 2931 | 22.0 | 1 |
| Butch Byrd | 64-71 | | | | | 86 | 600 | 7.0 | 1 |
| Jamie Caleb | 60-61,65 | 1 | 8 | 8.0 | 0 | 27 | 594 | 22.0 | 0 |
| Bob Campbell | 69 | 28 | 133 | 4.8 | 0 | 26 | 522 | 20.1 | 0 |
| Billy Cannon | 60-70 | 14 | 178 | 12.7 | 0 | 67 | 1704 | 25.4 | 1 |
| Preston Carpenter | 56-67 | 26 | 284 | 10.9 | 0 | 29 | 752 | 25.9 | 0 |
| Larry Carwell | 67-72 | 49 | 474 | 9.7 | 0 | 25 | 557 | 22.3 | 0 |
| Clarence Childs | 64-68 | 6 | 40 | 6.7 | 0 | 134 | 3454 | 25.8 | 2 |
| Dick Christy | 58,60-65 | 67 | 905 | 13.5 | 4 | 117 | 2770 | 23.7 | 0 |
| Earl Christy | 66-68 | 34 | 222 | 6.5 | 0 | 58 | 1323 | 22.8 | 0 |
| Hagood Clarke | 64-68 | 65 | 583 | 9.0 | 2 | 16 | 330 | 20.6 | 0 |
| Bert Coan | 62-68 | | | | | 33 | 785 | 23.9 | 0 |
| Bobby Joe Conrad | 58-69 | 51 | 462 | 9.1 | 2 | 33 | 813 | 24.6 | 0 |
| Johnny Counts | 62-63 | 8 | 33 | 4.1 | 0 | 31 | 891 | 28.7 | 1 |
| Willie Crenshaw | 64-70 | | | | | 27 | 515 | 19.1 | 0 |
| Irv Cross | 61-69 | 51 | 376 | 7.4 | 0 | 44 | 1227 | 27.9 | 0 |
| Jay Cunningham | 65-67 | 22 | 140 | 6.4 | 0 | 64 | 1372 | 21.4 | 0 |
| Clem Daniels | 60-68 | 8 | 103 | 12.9 | 0 | 57 | 1206 | 21.2 | 0 |
| Ted Dean | 60-64 | 46 | 279 | 6.1 | 0 | 70 | 1553 | 22.2 | 0 |
| Eddie Dove | 59-63 | 61 | 437 | 7.2 | 0 | 3 | 56 | 18.7 | 0 |
| Elbert Dubenion | 60-68 | 3 | 9 | 3.0 | 0 | 40 | 961 | 24.0 | 1 |
| Speedy Duncan | 64-74 | 202 | 2201 | 10.9 | 4 | 180 | 4539 | 25.2 | 0 |
| Bobby Felts | 65-67 | 6 | 46 | 7.7 | 0 | 38 | 814 | 21.4 | 0 |
| Pat Fischer | 61-77 | 17 | 80 | 4.7 | 0 | 26 | 613 | 24.5 | 0 |
| Mike Fitzgerald | 66-67 | 2 | 4 | 2.0 | 0 | 26 | 541 | 20.8 | 0 |

| Name | Years | PUNT RETURNS No. | Yards | Avg. | TD | KICKOFF RETURNS No. | Yards | Avg. | TD |
|---|---|---|---|---|---|---|---|---|---|
| George Fleming | 61 | 3 | 24 | 8.0 | 0 | 60 | 1634 | 27.2 | 0 |
| Tom Frankhauser | 59-63 | 3 | 19 | 6.3 | 0 | 30 | 620 | 20.7 | 0 |
| Al Frazier | 61-63 | 26 | 305 | 11.7 | 1 | 44 | 1077 | 24.5 | 1 |
| Bob Gaiters | 61-63 | | | | | 33 | 786 | 23.8 | 0 |
| Willie Galimore | 57-63 | | | | | 43 | 1100 | 25.6 | 1 |
| Billy Gambrell | 63-68 | 28 | 282 | 10.1 | 0 | 15 | 336 | 22.4 | 0 |
| Bob Garner | 60-63 | 28 | 252 | 9.0 | 0 | 1 | 8 | 8.0 | 0 |
| J. D. Garrett | 64-67 | 3 | 47 | 15.7 | 0 | 48 | 1054 | 22.0 | 0 |
| Mike Garrett | 66-73 | 39 | 235 | 6.0 | 0 | 14 | 323 | 23.1 | 0 |
| Larry Garron | 60-68 | 1 | 23 | 23.0 | 0 | 89 | 2299 | 25.8 | 2 |
| Claude Gibson | 61-65 | 110 | 1381 | 12.6 | 3 | 17 | 268 | 15.8 | 0 |
| Freddie Glick | 59-66 | 44 | 326 | 7.4 | 0 | 26 | 584 | 22.5 | 0 |
| Kenny Graham | 64-70 | 29 | 238 | 8.2 | 0 | 7 | 172 | 24.6 | 0 |
| Dave Grayson | 61-70 | 10 | 78 | 7.8 | 0 | 110 | 2804 | 25.5 | 1 |
| Ernie Green | 62-68 | 11 | 110 | 10.0 | 0 | 32 | 648 | 20.3 | 0 |
| Dick Haley | 59-64 | 20 | 87 | 4.4 | 0 | 37 | 729 | 19.7 | 0 |
| Ken Hall | 59-61 | 11 | 164 | 14.9 | 1 | 31 | 833 | 26.9 | 1 |
| Dick Harris | 60-65 | 27 | 251 | 9.3 | 0 | 3 | 49 | 16.3 | 0 |
| Rickie Harris | 65-72 | 128 | 1029 | 8.0 | 3 | 102 | 2326 | 22.8 | 0 |
| Wendell Harris | 62-68 | 27 | 275 | 10.2 | 0 | 12 | 293 | 24.4 | 0 |
| Alex Hawkins | 59-68 | 52 | 358 | 6.9 | 0 | 6 | 86 | 14.3 | 0 |
| Alvin Haymond | 64-73 | 253 | 2148 | 8.5 | 1 | 170 | 4438 | 26.1 | 2 |
| Abner Haynes | 60-67 | 85 | 875 | 10.3 | 1 | 121 | 3025 | 25.0 | 1 |
| Jon Henderson | 68-70 | | | | | 30 | 589 | 19.6 | 0 |
| Sam Horner | 60-62 | 6 | 19 | 3.2 | 0 | 39 | 828 | 21.2 | 0 |
| Frank Jackson | 61-67 | 49 | 487 | 9.9 | 0 | 48 | 1284 | 26.8 | 0 |
| Dick James | 56-65 | 120 | 952 | 7.9 | 0 | 189 | 4676 | 24.7 | 0 |
| Bobby Jancik | 62-67 | 67 | 695 | 10.4 | 1 | 158 | 4185 | 26.5 | 0 |
| Homer Jones | 64-70 | | | | | 37 | 888 | 24.0 | 1 |
| Leroy Kelly | 64-73 | 94 | 990 | 10.5 | 1 | 76 | 1784 | 23.5 | 0 |
| Brady Keys | 61-68 | 65 | 646 | 9.9 | 0 | 47 | 1113 | 23.7 | 0 |
| Phil King | 58-66 | | | | | 30 | 592 | 19.7 | 0 |
| Ernie Koy | 65-70 | | | | | 25 | 439 | 17.6 | 0 |
| Jack Larscheid | 60-61 | 12 | 106 | 8.8 | 0 | 39 | 1106 | 28.4 | 0 |
| Chuck Latourette | 67-68,70-71 | 64 | 537 | 8.4 | 1 | 59 | 1491 | 25.3 | 0 |
| Dan Lewis | 58-66 | | | | | 30 | 535 | 17.8 | 0 |
| Gary Lewis | 64-70 | 1 | 3 | 3.0 | 0 | 32 | 784 | 24.5 | 0 |
| Keith Lincoln | 61-68 | 25 | 342 | 13.7 | 1 | 39 | 1018 | 26.1 | 1 |
| Jerry Logan | 63-72 | 62 | 577 | 9.3 | 1 | 12 | 217 | 18.1 | 0 |
| Joe Don Looney | 64-67,69 | | | | | 29 | 652 | 22.5 | 0 |
| Tony Lorick | 64-69 | | | | | 40 | 1022 | 25.6 | 0 |
| John Love | 67,72 | 21 | 34 | 1.6 | 0 | 25 | 589 | 23.6 | 0 |
| Paul Lowe | 60-61,63-69 | 2 | 0 | 0.0 | 0 | 63 | 1411 | 22.4 | 0 |
| Lenny Lyles | 58-69 | | | | | 81 | 2161 | 26.7 | 3 |
| John Mallory | 68-71 | 39 | 294 | 7.5 | 1 | 6 | 94 | 15.7 | 0 |
| Amos Marsh | 61-67 | 17 | 75 | 4.4 | 0 | 65 | 1561 | 24.0 | 1 |
| Aaron Martin | 64-68 | 33 | 258 | 7.8 | 1 | 13 | 296 | 22.8 | 0 |
| Billy Martin | 62-64 | 30 | 155 | 5.2 | 0 | 53 | 1148 | 21.7 | 0 |
| Tommy Mason | 61-71 | 46 | 483 | 10.5 | 0 | 45 | 1067 | 23.7 | 0 |
| Tom Matte | 61-72 | 1 | 0 | 0.0 | 0 | 62 | 1367 | 22.0 | 0 |
| Don Maynard | 58,60-73 | 26 | 132 | 5.1 | 0 | 14 | 343 | 24.5 | 0 |
| Don McCall | 67-70 | | | | | 29 | 756 | 26.1 | 1 |
| Tommy McDonald | 57-68 | 73 | 404 | 5.5 | 1 | 51 | 1055 | 20.7 | 0 |
| Ed Meador | 59-70 | 43 | 275 | 6.4 | 0 | 7 | 168 | 24.0 | 0 |
| Gene Milton | 68-69 | 7 | 59 | 8.4 | 0 | 26 | 574 | 22.1 | 0 |

Lifetime Statistics – 1960-1969 Players    Section 3 – PUNT RETURNS and KICKOFF RETURNS (continued)
(All men with 25 or more Punt Returns or 25 or more Kickoff Returns)

| Name | Years | PUNT RETURNS | | | | KICKOFF RETURNS | | | |
|---|---|---|---|---|---|---|---|---|---|
| | | No. | Yards | Avg. | TD | No. | Yards | Avg. | TD |
| Gene Mingo | 60-70 | 18 | 214 | 11.9 | 1 | 34 | 742 | 21.8 | 0 |
| Bobby Mitchell | 58-68 | 69 | 699 | 10.1 | 3 | 102 | 2690 | 26.4 | 5 |
| Charley Mitchell | 63-68 | 21 | 251 | 12.0 | 0 | 63 | 1492 | 23.7 | 1 |
| Willie Mitchell | 64-70 | 56 | 564 | 10.1 | 1 | 7 | 178 | 25.4 | 0 |
| Lenny Moore | 56-67 | 14 | 56 | 4.0 | 0 | 49 | 1180 | 24.1 | 1 |
| Tom Moore | 60-67 | | | | | 71 | 1882 | 26.5 | 0 |
| Johnny Morris | 58-67 | 104 | 893 | 8.6 | 1 | 54 | 1267 | 23.5 | 0 |
| Joe Morrison | 59-72 | 23 | 79 | 3.4 | 0 | 30 | 640 | 21.3 | 0 |
| Bob Neff | 66-68 | 24 | 165 | 6.9 | 0 | 35 | 917 | 26.2 | 0 |
| Al Nelson | 65-73 | 1 | 3 | 3.0 | 0 | 101 | 2625 | 26.0 | 0 |
| Jimmy Patton | 55-66 | 27 | 143 | 5.3 | 1 | 28 | 735 | 26.3 | 1 |
| Clarence Peaks | 57-65 | | | | | 39 | 882 | 22.6 | 0 |
| Elijah Pitts | 61-71 | 75 | 394 | 5.3 | 1 | 28 | 535 | 19.1 | 0 |
| Willie Porter | 68 | 22 | 135 | 6.1 | 0 | 36 | 812 | 22.6 | 0 |
| Dickie Post | 67-71 | | | | | 34 | 760 | 22.4 | 0 |
| Bob Reed | 62-63 | 18 | 173 | 9.6 | 0 | 26 | 704 | 27.1 | 0 |
| Lance Rentzel | 65-72,74 | 48 | 217 | 4.5 | 0 | 32 | 783 | 24.5 | 1 |
| Bo Roberson | 61-66 | 3 | 54 | 18.0 | 0 | 130 | 3057 | 23.5 | 1 |
| Walter Roberts | 64-67,69-70 | 72 | 446 | 6.2 | 0 | 107 | 2728 | 25.5 | 1 |
| Jerry Robinson | 62-65 | 10 | 77 | 7.7 | 0 | 44 | 1009 | 22.9 | 0 |
| Johnny Roland | 66-73 | 49 | 452 | 9.2 | 2 | 25 | 507 | 20.3 | 0 |
| Ed Rutkowski | 63-68 | 68 | 514 | 7.6 | 1 | 53 | 1270 | 24.0 | 0 |
| Johnny Sample | 58-68 | 68 | 559 | 8.2 | 1 | 60 | 1560 | 26.0 | 1 |
| Gale Sayers | 65-71 | 27 | 391 | 14.5 | 2 | 91 | 2781 | 30.6 | 6 |
| Charlie Scales | 60-66 | 1 | 0 | 0.0 | 0 | 46 | 991 | 21.5 | 0 |
| Goldie Sellers | 66-69 | 19 | 217 | 11.4 | 1 | 27 | 701 | 26.0 | 2 |
| Carver Shannon | 62-64 | 30 | 213 | 7.1 | 0 | 46 | 1265 | 27.5 | 1 |
| Roy Shivers | 66-72 | 34 | 129 | 3.8 | 0 | 48 | 1162 | 24.2 | 1 |
| Bill Shockley | 60-62,68 | 5 | 18 | 3.6 | 0 | 32 | 745 | 23.3 | 0 |
| Jim Shofner | 58-63 | 46 | 308 | 6.7 | 0 | 1 | 0 | 0.0 | 0 |
| Les Shy | 66-70 | | | | | 29 | 687 | 23.7 | 0 |
| Bobby Smith | 62-66 | 25 | 151 | 6.0 | 0 | 40 | 1024 | 25.6 | 0 |
| Noland Smith | 67-69 | 63 | 635 | 10.1 | 1 | 82 | 2137 | 26.1 | 1 |
| Billy Stacy | 59-63 | 54 | 393 | 7.3 | 2 | 26 | 607 | 23.3 | 0 |
| Marsh Starks | 63-64 | 8 | 43 | 5.4 | 0 | 26 | 519 | 20.0 | 0 |
| Jim Steffen | 59-66 | 47 | 349 | 7.4 | 0 | 44 | 1107 | 25.2 | 0 |
| Jim Stiger | 63-67 | 68 | 529 | 7.8 | 0 | 27 | 610 | 22.6 | 0 |
| Jerry Stovall | 63-71 | | | | | 46 | 1183 | 25.7 | 0 |
| Pat Studstill | 61-62,64-72 | 59 | 716 | 12.1 | 0 | 75 | 1924 | 25.7 | 1 |
| Bob Suci | 62-63 | 25 | 233 | 9.3 | 0 | 17 | 360 | 21.2 | 0 |
| Rosey Taylor | 61-72 | 15 | 66 | 4.4 | 1 | 26 | 614 | 23.6 | 0 |
| Bobby Thompson | 64-69 | 14 | 72 | 5.1 | 0 | 27 | 622 | 23.0 | 0 |
| Bubba Thornton | 69 | | | | | 30 | 749 | 25.0 | 0 |
| Larry Todd | 65-70 | | | | | 25 | 584 | 23.3 | 0 |
| Bill Triplett | 62-63,65-72 | | | | | 49 | 1058 | 21.6 | 0 |
| Bill Tucker | 67-71 | 1 | 1 | 1.0 | 0 | 40 | 879 | 22.0 | 0 |
| Bake Turner | 62-70 | 21 | 156 | 7.4 | 0 | 75 | 1688 | 22.5 | 0 |
| Tom Vaughn | 65-71 | 33 | 298 | 9.0 | 0 | 62 | 1595 | 25.7 | 0 |
| Carl Ward | 67-69 | 7 | 67 | 9.6 | 0 | 38 | 840 | 22.1 | 1 |
| Charley Warner | 63-66 | 17 | 206 | 12.1 | 0 | 86 | 2187 | 25.4 | 3 |
| Jimmy Warren | 64-74,77 | 4 | -1 | -0.3 | 0 | 30 | 684 | 22.8 | 0 |
| Tom Watkins | 61-65,67-68 | 96 | 970 | 10.1 | 3 | 101 | 2510 | 24.9 | 0 |
| Ken Webb | 58-63 | | | | | 27 | 561 | 20.8 | 0 |
| Willie West | 60-68 | 51 | 388 | 7.6 | 0 | 40 | 908 | 22.7 | 0 |
| Dick Westmoreland | 63-69 | 2 | 10 | 5.0 | 0 | 28 | 564 | 20.1 | 0 |
| Bobby Williams | 66-67,69-71 | | | | | 77 | 1934 | 25.1 | 2 |
| Clancy Williams | 65-72 | | | | | 32 | 810 | 25.3 | 0 |
| Travis Williams | 67-71 | 13 | 213 | 16.4 | 1 | 102 | 2801 | 27.5 | 6 |
| Willie Wood | 60-71 | 187 | 1391 | 7.4 | 2 | 3 | 20 | 6.7 | 0 |
| Abe Woodson | 58-66 | 123 | 956 | 7.8 | 2 | 193 | 5538 | 28.7 | 5 |

Lifetime Statistics – 1960-1969 Players    Section 4 – PUNTING
(All men with 25 or more Punts)

| Name | Years | No. | Avg. |
|---|---|---|---|
| Billy Atkins | 58-64 | 219 | 42.0 |
| Sam Baker | 53,56-69 | 701 | 42.7 |
| Jim Bakken | 62-77 | 61 | 37.5 |
| Zeke Bratkowski | 54,57-68,71 | 90 | 38.7 |
| Ode Burrell | 64-69 | 29 | 36.8 |
| Don Chandler | 56-67 | 660 | 43.5 |
| Gary Collins | 62-71 | 336 | 41.0 |
| Ollie Cordill | 67-69 | 45 | 41.4 |
| Wayne Crow | 60-63 | 222 | 40.2 |
| Cotton Davidson | 54,57,60-66,68 | 278 | 38.4 |
| Tommy Davis | 56-69 | 511 | 44.7 |
| Eagle Day | 59-60 | 59 | 42.0 |
| Boyd Dowler | 59-69,71 | 93 | 42.9 |
| Jim Elliott | 67 | 72 | 38.1 |
| Doug Elmore | 62 | 54 | 34.4 |
| Sam Etcheverry | 61-62 | 59 | 38.3 |
| Jim Fraser | 62-66,68 | 271 | 43.3 |
| Tom Gilburg | 61-65 | 232 | 41.4 |
| Allen Green | 61 | 61 | 36.7 |
| Bobby Joe Green | 60-73 | 970 | 42.6 |
| Tom Greene | 60-61 | 59 | 37.9 |
| John Hadl | 62-77 | 105 | 39.7 |
| George Herring | 60-61 | 150 | 38.4 |
| King Hill | 58-69 | 368 | 41.3 |
| Ed Holler | 63-64 | 31 | 43.0 |
| Sam Horner | 60-62 | 64 | 38.4 |
| Tom Janik | 63-71 | 253 | 39.1 |
| Curley Johnson | 60-69 | 556 | 42.5 |
| John Kilgore | 65-69 | 234 | 41.0 |
| Ernie Koy | 65-70 | 225 | 38.5 |
| Frank Lambert | 65-66 | 156 | 43.6 |
| Daryle Lamonica | 63-74 | 51 | 40.6 |
| Chuck Latourette | 67-68,70-71 | 248 | 40.5 |
| Dale Livingston | 68-70 | 146 | 41.1 |
| Joe Don Looney | 64-67,69 | 32 | 42.4 |
| Billy Lothridge | 64-72 | 532 | 41.0 |
| Paul Maguire | 60-70 | 794 | 41.7 |
| Billy Martin | 64-68 | 28 | 37.4 |
| John McCormick | 62-63,65-66,68 | 47 | 39.1 |
| Wahoo McDaniel | 60-68 | 37 | 37.7 |
| Max McGee | 54,57-67 | 256 | 41.6 |
| Mike Mercer | 61-70 | 307 | 40.6 |
| Charley Milstead | 60-61 | 66 | 35.8 |
| Earl Morrall | 56-76 | 106 | 37.7 |
| Tom Morrow | 62-64 | 45 | 36.7 |
| Jim Norton | 60-68 | 518 | 42.4 |
| Jimmy Orr | 58-70 | 59 | 39.4 |
| Joe Paglieri | 59-60 | 49 | 37.3 |
| Rick Redman | 65-73 | 153 | 37.5 |
| Pat Richter | 63-70 | 338 | 42.0 |
| Bob Scarpito | 61-68 | 282 | 44.0 |
| Dave Sherer | 59-60 | 102 | 42.2 |
| Del Shofner | 57-67 | 153 | 42.0 |
| Jackie Smith | 63-77 | 86 | 38.5 |
| Jerry Stovall | 63-71 | 87 | 40.2 |
| Pat Studstill | 61-62,64-72 | 560 | 40.7 |
| Terry Swanson | 67-69 | 139 | 39.8 |
| Frank Tripucka | 49-52,60-63 | 93 | 38.8 |
| Danny Villanueva | 60-67 | 488 | 42.7 |
| Eddie Wilson | 62-65 | 54 | 36.1 |
| George Wilson | 66 | 42 | 42.1 |
| Jerrel Wilson | 63-78 | 1069 | 43.2 |
| Tom Yewcic | 61-66 | 369 | 39.4 |

Lifetime Statistics – 1960-1969 Players    Section 5 – KICKING
(All men with 10 or more PAT or Field Goal attempts)

| Name | Years | PAT | PAT Att. | PAT Pct. | FG | FG Att. | FG Pct. |
|---|---|---|---|---|---|---|---|
| Bruce Alford | 67-69 | 41 | 43 | 95 | 31 | 52 | 60 |
| Billy Atkins | 58-64 | 56 | 63 | 89 | 8 | 19 | 42 |
| John Aveni | 59-61 | 72 | 80 | 90 | 22 | 63 | 35 |
| Sam Baker | 53,56-69 | 428 | 444 | 96 | 179 | 316 | 57 |
| Jim Bakken | 62-78 | 534 | 553 | 97 | 282 | 447 | 63 |
| George Blair | 61-64 | 122 | 136 | 90 | 50 | 79 | 63 |
| George Blanda | 49-58,60-75 | 941 | 957 | 98 | 335 | 638 | 53 |
| Tommy Brooker | 62-66 | 149 | 149 | 100 | 41 | 86 | 48 |
| Gino Cappelletti | 60-70 | 342 | 353 | 97 | 176 | 333 | 53 |
| Don Chandler | 56-67 | 248 | 258 | 96 | 94 | 161 | 58 |
| Jim Christopherson | 62 | 28 | 28 | 100 | 11 | 20 | 55 |
| Mike Clark | 63-71,73 | 325 | 338 | 96 | 133 | 232 | 57 |
| Bobby Joe Conrad | 58-69 | 95 | 99 | 96 | 14 | 33 | 42 |
| Cotton Davidson | 54,57,60-66,68 | 32 | 33 | 97 | 2 | 5 | 40 |
| Tommy Davis | 59-69 | 348 | 350 | 99 | 130 | 276 | 47 |
| Harold Deters | 67 | 9 | 10 | 90 | 1 | 4 | 25 |
| Charlie Durkee | 67-68,71-72 | 87 | 88 | 99 | 52 | 101 | 51 |
| Bob Etter | 68-69 | 50 | 52 | 96 | 26 | 51 | 51 |
| George Fleming | 61 | 24 | 25 | 96 | 11 | 26 | 42 |
| Momcilo Gavric | 69 | 22 | 24 | 92 | 3 | 11 | 27 |
| Cookie Gilchrist | 62-67 | 14 | 16 | 88 | 8 | 20 | 40 |
| Charlie Gogolak | 66-68,70-72 | 114 | 117 | 97 | 52 | 93 | 56 |
| Pete Gogolak | 64-74 | 344 | 354 | 97 | 173 | 294 | 59 |
| Bruce Gossett | 64-74 | 374 | 383 | 98 | 219 | 360 | 61 |
| Allen Green | 61 | 19 | 19 | 100 | 5 | 15 | 33 |
| Dick Guesman | 60-64 | 69 | 74 | 93 | 20 | 62 | 32 |
| Wendell Harris | 60-67 | 8 | 11 | 73 | 1 | 4 | 25 |
| Joe Hergert | 60-61 | | | | 8 | 18 | 44 |
| Jack Hill | 61 | 16 | 16 | 100 | 5 | 15 | 23 |
| Paul Hornung | 57-62,64-66 | 190 | 194 | 98 | 66 | 140 | 47 |
| Bob Humphreys | 67-68 | 19 | 20 | 95 | 8 | 20 | 40 |
| Bob Jencks | 63-65 | 93 | 102 | 91 | 14 | 39 | 36 |
| Jimmy Keyes | 68-69 | 30 | 30 | 100 | 7 | 16 | 44 |
| Bob Khayat | 60,62-63 | 90 | 92 | 98 | 38 | 74 | 51 |
| Lou Kirouac | 63-64,66-67 | 19 | 24 | 79 | 9 | 18 | 50 |
| Jerry Kramer | 58-68 | 90 | 94 | 96 | 29 | 54 | 54 |
| Karl Kremser | 69-70 | 28 | 29 | 97 | 13 | 23 | 57 |
| Gary Kroner | 65-67 | 57 | 58 | 98 | 29 | 56 | 52 |
| Roger LeClerc | 60-67 | 154 | 160 | 96 | 76 | 152 | 50 |
| Keith Lincoln | 61-68 | 16 | 18 | 89 | 5 | 12 | 42 |
| Dale Livingston | 68-70 | 39 | 41 | 95 | 28 | 54 | 52 |
| John Love | 67,72 | 10 | 11 | 91 | 2 | 7 | 29 |
| Booth Lusteg | 66-69 | 97 | 101 | 96 | 35 | 75 | 47 |
| Chuck Mercein | 65-70 | 9 | 10 | 90 | 2 | 8 | 25 |
| Mike Mercer | 61-70 | 288 | 295 | 98 | 102 | 193 | 53 |
| Lou Michaels | 58-69,71 | 386 | 402 | 96 | 187 | 341 | 55 |
| Gene Mingo | 60-70 | 215 | 223 | 96 | 112 | 219 | 51 |
| Les Murdock | 67 | 13 | 15 | 87 | 4 | 9 | 44 |
| Dennis Patera | 68 | 10 | 12 | 83 | 2 | 8 | 25 |
| Tom Pennington | 62 | 13 | 15 | 87 | 2 | 5 | 40 |
| Milt Plum | 57-69 | 16 | 16 | 100 | 6 | 16 | 38 |
| Bill Shockley | 60-62,68 | 91 | 95 | 96 | 26 | 57 | 46 |
| Jackie Simpson | 61-64 | 6 | 6 | 100 | 3 | 10 | 30 |
| Jack Spikes | 60-67 | 74 | 80 | 93 | 20 | 59 | 34 |
| Andy Stynchula | 60-68 | 13 | 14 | 93 | 3 | 7 | 43 |
| Bob Timberlake | 65 | 21 | 22 | 95 | 1 | 15 | 7 |
| Herb Travenio | 64-65 | 50 | 52 | 96 | 20 | 35 | 57 |
| Wade Traynham | 66-67 | 24 | 24 | 100 | 7 | 19 | 37 |
| Dick Van Raaphorst | 64,66-67 | 112 | 114 | 98 | 45 | 90 | 50 |
| Danny Villanueva | 60-67 | 236 | 241 | 98 | 85 | 160 | 53 |
| Wayne Walker | 67-68 | 26 | 26 | 100 | 8 | 16 | 50 |
| Wayne Walker | 58-72 | 172 | 175 | 98 | 53 | 131 | 40 |
| John Wittenborn | 58-62,64-68 | 41 | 41 | 100 | 20 | 45 | 44 |
| Mack Yoho | 60-63 | 52 | 61 | 85 | 13 | 35 | 40 |

# 1970-1979
# BIG DOLLARS — BIG PROBLEMS

On February 1, 1970 they made it official. As agreed upon three years and eight months before, the National and American Football Leagues entered into marriage. Their courtship was rocky to the very end. As late as January, the important matter of the older NFL's divisional realignment remained unsettled. But by March 16, the biggest problem faced by a "competition committee" of Tex Schramm, Vince Lombardi, Paul Brown and Al Davis upon convening in Honolulu was whether or not to allow the AFL's two-point option for touchdowns. After deciding to stick to the NFL's single-point rule, all that was left for the committee to take care of were minor matter regarding things such as putting players' names on jerseys and the type of football that would be used.

The two leagues officially became the American and National Football Conference of the National Football League, with Kansas City Chiefs owner Lamar Hunt and Chicago Bears owner George Halas selected as their respective figurehead presidents. In their first draft under one roof in February, the first player chosen was Terry Bradshaw, a strong-armed signal caller from Louisiana Tech, by Pittsburgh. Bradshaw went on to live up to his high rating and was only one of the many wise draft selections that enabled the Steelers to become an AFC powerhouse after years of mediocrity in the old NFL.

## Dynasties and Diversity

In September 1970, just a few weeks before the regular season began, Vince Lombardi, the dominant force in the '60's as head coach of the mighty Green Bay Packers, died of stomach cancer. His influence lived on, however, as bone-crunching defenses and conservative but powerful running attacks were what most head coaches felt that they needed to win games. In the very first interconference struggle on the first week of the '70 season, Bud Grant's Minnesota Vikings avenged their previous season's Super Bowl loss to Hank Stram's Kansas City Chiefs, defeating them 27-10 with a heavy dependence on ball control and an opportunistic defense. Grant said, "We proved that the defense of the 1960's can beat the offense of the '70's." Further proof was provided by Don Shula's Miami Dolphins, a team that went on to become the '70's first true dynasty, with three successive Super Bowl trips beginning in 1971.

After losing 24-3 to the Dallas Cowboys and Duane Thomas in Super Bowl VI, the stage was set for professional football's most impressive team performance, a perfect 17-0 season in '72. Behind the unspectacular but effective running of Larry Csonka, Jim Kiick and Mercury Morris, the smooth, calculated quarterbacking of Bob Griese and Earl Morrall and a defense that had "no names" but plenty of quickness and savvy, the Dolphins wrote 1972's biggest and most colorful story. Miami's 14-7 win over Washington in Super Bowl VII left them 17-0, including playoffs, the first NFL team to ever accomplish such a feat. In '73 the Dolphins finally lost (in their second game) but remained the league's best through their 24-7 rout of Minnesota in Super Bowl VIII.

Other NFL coaches quickly copied Shula's recipe, devising complicated defenses and run-oriented offenses. High scoring, pass-laden games, the kind that epitomized the AFL in its early days, became rare. Field position, zone defenses and cautious play selection that guaranteed a minimum of turnovers tended to eliminate some of the game's most exciting elements.

The Pittsburgh Steelers, the decade's second dynasty, won four Super Bowls in six years with an offense that depended on the running of Franco Harris and Rocky Bleier, spiced with occasional long passes from Bradshaw to Lynn Swann and John Stallworth. The strength of the team was its' impregnable defense, led by Mean Joe Greene, Jack Lambert, Jack Ham, L.C. Greenwood, and Mel Blount.

Two other teams of the decade could be considered near-dynasties for their consistent fine play: the Dallas Cowboys and the Oakland Raiders. Although both boasted sometimes spectacular offenses, their victories were rooted in crunching defensive work.

## New Rules

In general, rule changes during the decade were aimed at encouraging more offense and scoring. Before the 1972 season began, a rule changed that was designed to open the passing game by moving the hashmarks closer to the middle of the field, but it actually resulted in much greater success for "outside" running attacks. For Miami, this allowed the speedy Morris to provide a perfect complement to Csonka's inside strength. By season's end, both players were 1,000-yard runners, and the Dolphins had a new NFL rushing record with 2,960 yards. In '73, O. J. Simpson became the first player to rush for over 2,000 yards in a season.

The powers of the league realized there was nothing overly exciting about games like the '73 Super Bowl in which Miami lulled the Vikings — and numerous fans everywhere — to sleep. The recognized enough staleness in their product to warrant some more changes before the '74 season began. Pressure produced by the formation of the World Football League that same year further necessitated a new look. At a meeting in New York, NFL owners laid down the following rule changes:

■ Overtime. In an effort to do away with ties, a 15-minute, sudden-death extra period was introduced for preseason and regular-season games. If a score remained even at the completion of the extra period, the game would then be declared a tie.

■ Kicking. The goalposts were moved back 10 yards for the goal line to the end line to do away with an over-reliance on easy field goals. In addition, kickoffs were moved back five yards to the 35-yard line, and missed field goals would be returned to the line of scrimmage or the 20-yard line, whichever was further from the goal line. This meant the punter would become more important, with his placement and coffin-corner kicking ability outweighing the distance that he kicked he the ball. Finally, players on a team kicking a field goal or punting could not cross the line of scrimmage until the ball was kicked. This meant a punter's "hang time" would also become significant.

■ Passing. Roll-blocking and the cutting down of wide receivers

was eliminated to take away what had become a distinct advantage for defenses. Also, downfield defenders were allowed to make contact only once with potential receivers, and wide receivers blocking back toward the ball three yards from the line of scrimmage could not block below the waist.

■ Penalties. Infractions for offensive holding, illegal use of hands and tripping were reduced for 15 to 10 yards when they occurred in the area of the line of scrimmage to three yards beyond it.

In 1978, the NFL went to a 16-game schedule and added a second wild-card team to its playoffs, both moves calculated to increase revenue. To open up the passing game and make the product more appealing, defensive backs were further limited in their aggressive bumping tactics against receivers, and the head slap by defensive linemen was made illegal in 1977 and the following year offensive blocking rules were liberalized to allow greater use of the hands. By extending the season and handle new advantages to the passing attack, the rulemakers made the 300-yard game and the 3,000 yard season commonplace for the NFL throwers.

## A Rival League

In 1974, the NFL faced a new rival, the World Football League. The WFL opened on July 10 with 12 franchises, six of them in cities already occupied by NFL teams. It planned a 20-week regular season of what was being billed as wide-open football with 10 "revolutionary" rule changes (kickoffs from the 30-yard line to insure more runbacks, goal posts moved back to the back of the end zone, missed field goals returned to the line of scrimmage except when attempted inside the 20-yard line, an optional two-point conversion attempt, receivers needing just one foot in bounds for a completion, a fifth quarter split into two 7 1/2-minute segments to break ties, a restriction on fair catches of punts, motion permitted by an offensive back toward the line of scrimmage before the snapping of the ball, hashmarks moved in toward the center of the field, and the return of any incomplete pass into the end zone on fourth down to the previous line of scrimmage instead of being automatically returned to the 20-yard line).

The commissioner of the WFL was Gary L. Davidson, an attorney who founded the World Hockey Association. He resigned in '73 as president of the WHA to devote his full time and energy to the organization of the WFL. The 12 initial franchises were the Birmingham Americans, Chicago Fire, Detroit Wheels, the Hawaiians, Houston Texans, Jacksonville Sharks, Memphis Southmen, Southern California Sun and Florida Blazers. Games were scheduled primarily on Wednesdays and Thursdays, and a TV package with the independent TVS network was hoped to net in excess of $1 million for the clubs, with weekly telecasts aired live on Thursday nights on more than 135 stations across the country.

But what really made the NFL and sports fans take notice was the shocking announcement in the spring of '74 that Miami's Csonka, Kiick and wide receiver Paul Warfield planned to leave the team they helped make a dynasty after fulfilling the final year of their Dolphin contracts and jump to the WFL Toronto franchise (that was switched to Memphis before the season began to avoid conflict with the Canadian Football League). The combined offer to the trio from Toronto millionaire owner John Bassett came to $3.5 million.

But the WFL would have to depend on lesser-known players for the most part in its first year. On July 24, the Birmingham Americans pleased a legitimately large home-town crowd with a 58-33 victory over Memphis. NFL reject quarterbacks George Mira (Birmingham) and John Huarte (Memphis) engaged in the kind of barnburning passing battle that any football fan could savor. But in Philadelphia, doctored attendance figures gave the league its first real dose of adverse publicity. It was reported in mid-August that the Bell's actual paid attendance at its first home game was only 13,800 — a far cry from the 55,534 figure it threw out for public consumption. After the announced attendance of 64,719 for its second home game turned out to be a paltry 6,200 paid, Bells president John B. Kelly Jr., abruptly resigned from his post. It quickly become apparent that most of the league's teams were desperately under-capitalized. Franchises began moving or folding on a near-weekly basis. In early November, an emergency session was called in Chicago that ended with Davidson resigning as commissioner. Facing over-all debts reported as high as $20 million in its first season, the WFL no longer posed a serious threat to the NFL.

Under the direction of Chris Hemmeter, the original owner of the Hawaiian franchise, the league attempted to play the '75 season under a clever reorganizational plan built around shared profits. But even with the "Hemmeter Plan," a new $12 million deficit was incurred by the time the season was 10 weeks old, and in late October 1975, the league officially went under.

## TV Calls the Tune

Enhancing the merger of the two leagues in 1970 was a splendid wedding present from ABC-TV. For slightly more than $8 million each season, ABC agreed to telecast 13 prime-time games on Monday nights. The risk of professional football over-exposing itself the way boxing did was offset by an overall TV bill to the three major networks that came to about $150 million, including the three-year Monday night package. Divided out, it meant that each of the 26 NFL teams would receive approximately $1.7 million in 1970 — $500,000 more than what each NFL team got on 1969 and $800,00 more than each of the eight AFL franchises received.

Meanwhile, the NFL's viewing audience was multiplying rapidly every week. Before the '73 season began, Congress lifted the TV blackout on home games sold out 72 hours in advance, thanks mainly to the efforts of Massachusets Senator Torbert MacDonald. Rozelle, who claimed only seven NFL teams were assured of weekly sellouts, gloomily predicted disaster. But the Capital Hill politicians, at a time when Watergate was tarnishing their image, were anxious to provide a popular victory for fans. But the real victors were the TV people. Future TV contracts, not ticket-buying customers, would provide the game's main meal ticket. The number of "no shows" at games became a meaningful statistic, but the game didn't suffer so badly at the gate as to argue for a return of the blackout.

By 1978, industry sources called the NFL's contract the largest television package ever. In January of that year, a Louis Harris Sports survey found that 70 percent of the nation's sports fans said they followed football, compared to 54 percent who followed baseball. There seemed to be no limit.

## Trouble With the Troops

With once undreamed-of money pouring in from TV, the players quite naturally expected to join in the benefits. Before the merger season of 1970 even got underway, NFL players rallied together in early July and displayed surprisingly strong union strength by threatening to sit out the season unless management could settle a list of grievances, the biggest of which had to do with their pension

fund. Peace was assured in August, as the players received a pension fund increase of roughly $11 million, and although neither side was entirely satisfied with the settlement, a contract agreement that extended to the 1974 season enabled the emphasis in the decade's first three yards to be placed mainly in the game itself.

But, in 1974 it was time to negotiate a new contract with the NFL Players' Association. Renewed strike threats and legal hassles began early in 1974 and continued right up to the night of February 16, 1977, when NFLPA executive director Ed Garvey and Sargent Karch, management's main negotiator, finally reached a new contract agreement.

The three-year negotiation period was marked by preseason strikes in 1974 and '75 and by bitterness over the Rozelle Rule. That rule provided that the commissioner would decide the type of compensation a team would receive after losing a free agent. Such strong power in Rozelle's hands discouraged teams for signing free agents, fearing that the commissioner would set a stiff price that would wipe out any benefit. Negotiations made progress after a federal court found that the Rozelle Rule was illegal under antitrust laws. The agreement, which was struck in 1977, created a new free-agent system in which the losing team would receive draft choices from the signing team, with the player's salary determining the exact package. Although less restrictive than the Rozelle Rule, this new system still kept players shackled to one club, as teams were reluctant to give up key draft picks. The contract also preserve the college draft and increased some financial benefits for the players, while limiting some of the commissioner's lesser powers.

# N.F.C. 1970 The Monday-Night Circus

The TV gridiron fan found a new addiction this season: Monday-night football. The American Broadcasting Company telecast a game every Monday night of the season, with Howard Cosell, Don Meredith and Keith Jackson the men behind the mikes. For the first time ever, the game itself became secondary to the show put on by the announcers in the press box. Cosell, the verbose ex-labor lawyer who had built a reputation by being highly critical of almost everything, commented on each game in highly dramatic tones, while ex-Dallas Cowboy quarterback Don Meredith, dubbed "Dandy Don" by Cosell, mixed his analysis with homespun country witticisms. The interplay between these two, sometimes veering off into mutual needling, delighted some and drove others to turn the sound off on their sets. Jackson, the member of the trio who concentrated on reporting the game, was rewarded after the season by being dropped from the series.

## EASTERN DIVISION

**Dallas Cowboys**—The Cowboys had so much talent, some coaches would have been delighted to trade their starters for the Dallas second-stringers. With two good running backs already in the fold in Calvin Hill and Walt Garrison, the Cowboys this year added rookie Duane Thomas, an uncommunicative man who did his talking by running over people while carrying a football. Herb Adderley was obtained from Green Bay to further strengthen the secondary, and when Lance Rentzel sat out the last weeks of the season with personal problems, rookie Reggie Rucker filled in capably. Although the offensive line had always been strong, Dave Manders, Blaine Nye, and Rayfield Wright all rose up from the second string to win starting jobs. Even at quarterback, coach Tom Landry had his pick of a good pocket passer in Craig Morton or a top roll-out passer in Roger Staubach.

**New York Giants**—Quarterback Fran Tarkenton ran the attack with imagination, Ron Johnson developed into a superb runner and receiver after coming over from Cleveland, Tucker Frederickson shook the injury hex for this year, Clifton McNeil grabbed Tarkenton's passes, and the offensive line matured into a sturdy unit. The defense was less impressive, but aces Fred Dryer, Jim Files, and Spider Lockhart held the platoon together. After beating St. Louis one week from the end, the Giants held a share of first place with Dallas heading into their final game before losing 31-3 to the Rams.

**St. Louis Cardinals**—The Cards sailed into December with an 8-2-1 record and first place in the East was theirs for the taking. Twice during the year the Cards had beaten the Cowboys, laying a 38-0 drubbing on them in their meeting in Dallas. MacArthur Lane, Ernie McMillan, Larry Stallings, Roger Wehrli, and Larry Wilson all turned in All-Pro performances, while a host of other Cards all enjoyed good seasons. But just when the team seemed about to capture its first title since moving to St. Louis in 1960, the roof caved in. First the Detroit Lions beat them, then the New York Giants clubbed them 34-17 to knock them out of first place. Then, with the title a fleeting dream, the Cards dropped their finale 28-27 to the Redskins.

**Washington Redskins**—When training camp opened, head coach Vince Lombardi wasn't there; he was in the hospital, terminally ill with cancer. Assistant Bill Austin took over as head man until Lombardi got out of the hospital, but the all-time great coach died on September 3, two weeks before the start of the regular season. Austin guided the club through the season, but the team never really recovered from Lombardi's death. The only bright spot of the year was the development of runner Larry Brown into a star. Using his blockers well and fighting for every yard, Brown became the first Redskin to rush 1,000 yards.

**Philadelphia Eagles**—A flabby defense and an injury to fullback Tom Woodeshick shackled the Eagles into last place in the Eastern Division, but the team did have talent in several areas. The trio of Gary Ballman, Harold Jackson, and Ben Hawkins provided top-notch receiving, and Cyril Pinder ran well at halfback. The linebacking corps had three solid players in Adrian Young, Tim Rossovich, and Ron Porter; Rossovich had other skills in addition to his talents on the field. The curly-haired, mustachioed Rossovich would occasionally do unusual things, such as walking into a party with his hair on fire.

## CENTRAL DIVISION

**Minnesota Vikings**—The Vikings still had that marvelous defense, but they lacked that extra inspirational spark when quarterback Joe Kapp sat out the early games over a salary dispute and then was sold to Boston. Carl Eller, Alan Page, Paul Krause, and the other members of the defense smothered enough enemy offenses to win twelve games, while the offense operated just enough under Gary Cuozzo to make it back to first place this year. Place kicker Fred Cox could be counted on to make good on three-pointers within the

40-yard line to bail out the offense. But although Cuozzo passed the ball better than Kapp, the fanatical leadership Kapp provided was missing.

**Detroit Lions**—Even without a clear-cut starter at quarterback, the Lion attack still blossomed into a steady point-producing outfit. Bill Munson and Greg Landry split the passer's spot, although Landry played more as the season went on, and both found good runners in Mel Farr and Altie Taylor and good receivers in Earl McCullough, Larry Walton, and Charlie Sanders. The line gave both quarterbacks good protection and figured highly in the offense's performance. On defense, the linebacking and secondary corps were full with top players, with Dick LeBeau and Paul Naumoff of All-Pro quality, but the front four needed some new blood, as Alex Karras no longer was rushing quarterbacks as he once had.

**Chicago Bears**—Gale Sayers, the once incomparable runner, hurt his knee and went out of action early in the season for surgery. Brian Piccolo fell fatally ill with cancer. Quarterback Bobby Douglass threw four touchdown passes in his first starting assignment of the year, but broke his wrist late in the game and missed the rest of the year. Pre-season trades for Elijah Pitts, Lee Roy Caffey, and Craig Baynham didn't work out. But the Bears did win six games, and did uncover an exciting player in little Cecil Turner, who returned four kickoffs all the way to tie the NFL record.

**Green Bay Packers**—The Packers kept dropping veterans of the Lombardi years and suffered through another losing season. Willie Davis, Henry Jordan, and Boyd Dowler all retired, Elijah Pitts, Lee Roy Caffey, and Bob Hyland were dealt to Chicago, and Herb Adderley and Marv Fleming went to Dallas and Miami in trades. Of those staying on the scene, a sore arm hampered quarterback Bart Starr, a torn Achilles tendon sidelined linebacker Dave Robinson, and age started catching up on middle linebacker Ray Nitschke.

## WESTERN DIVISION

**San Francisco '49ers**—After years of near misses and disappointing finishes, the '49ers finally put everything together and won the Western crown. The offense, always respected, blossomed into one of pro football's best with fine seasons from John Brodie, Gene Washington, Forrest Blue, and Cas Banaszek. The entire front line had a good year, allowing Brodie to be dropped only eight times all season. The defense, however, surprised most experts by turning in a superb performance. Coach Dick Nolan rotated the front four spots and thus kept fresh men in the game at all times. Dave Wilcox starred at linebacker, and the secondary of Jim Johnson, rookie Bruce Taylor, Rosey Taylor, and Al Randolph discouraged enemy passers. The acquisition of place kicker Bruce Gossett from Los Angeles nicely rounded out the picture.

**Los Angeles Rams**—Coach George Allen kept adding veterans to the squad, this year bringing in Kermit Alexander, but the Rams fell just short of the Western title. The defense as usual made life difficult for enemy offenses, and the Los Angeles attack again moved slowly but surely under the direction of Roman Gabriel. The rise of the '49ers gave the Rams competition for the divisional crown, however, and a 28-23 loss to Detroit on the final Monday-night game of the year knocked the Rams out of first place for good. The team recovered to beat New York to end the season, but that was to be George Allen's last game with the Rams. Owner Dan Reeves, already dying with cancer, fired Allen after the season despite his 49-17-4 record.

**Atlanta Falcons**—After improving for several seasons, the Falcons fell back for the first time under coach Norm Van Brocklin's regime. One weight on the team's progress was a remarkably unexciting offense, with an unsettled quarterback situation, no speed in the running back and receiving spots, and chaos in the front line. The defense had three star players in end Claude Humphrey, middle linebacker Tommy Nobis, and cornerback Ken Reaves, but most of the other positions lacked a quality occupant.

**New Orleans Saints**—The Saints' roster was like a revolving door, with players joining and leaving the squad in steady flows all season. Head coach Tom Fears was one of the mid-season departures, with J. D. Roberts promoted from a minor-league team to take charge of the Saints. The Saints had a few good players who put out consistently good performances, but they were almost buried amidst the chaos and mediocrity which ruined the season for the team. Flanker Dan Abramowicz and defensive tackle Dave Rowe played well, but the hero of the club was place kicker Tom Dempsey, a man born without a right hand and without toes on his right foot. Using a special kicking shoe, Dempsey was an erratic kicker but made the record books by booting a 63-yard three-pointer to beat the Detroit Lions.

## FINAL TEAM STATISTICS

### OFFENSE

| | ATL. | CHI. | DALL. | DET. | G.B. | L.A. | MINN. | N.O. | N.Y.G. | PHIL. | ST.L. | S.F. | WASH. |
|---|---|---|---|---|---|---|---|---|---|---|---|---|---|
| **FIRST DOWNS:** | | | | | | | | | | | | | |
| Total | 199 | 179 | 229 | 243 | 194 | 224 | 225 | 183 | **257** | 229 | 226 | 237 | 249 |
| by Rushing | 76 | 55 | 119 | 113 | 69 | 93 | 98 | 55 | 94 | 81 | 110 | 86 | **122** |
| by Passing | 110 | 104 | 95 | 107 | 110 | 120 | 111 | 112 | **150** | 126 | 104 | 125 | 100 |
| by Penalty | 13 | 20 | 15 | 23 | 15 | 11 | 16 | 16 | 13 | 22 | 12 | 26 | **27** |
| **RUSHING:** | | | | | | | | | | | | | |
| Number | 431 | 353 | **522** | 514 | 453 | 430 | 508 | 371 | 465 | 450 | 429 | 471 | 444 |
| Yards | 1600 | 1092 | **2300** | 2127 | 1595 | 1763 | 1634 | 1215 | 1799 | 1539 | 1998 | 1580 | 2021 |
| Average Yards | 3.7 | 3.1 | 4.4 | 4.1 | 3.5 | 4.1 | 3.2 | 3.3 | 3.9 | 3.4 | **4.7** | 3.4 | 4.6 |
| Touchdowns | 4 | 3 | 16 | 16 | 8 | 12 | 16 | 4 | 11 | 11 | **18** | 13 | 11 |
| **PASSING:** | | | | | | | | | | | | | |
| Attempts | 342 | 422 | 297 | 294 | 351 | **426** | 344 | 415 | 403 | 410 | 390 | 383 | 342 |
| Completions | 197 | 210 | 149 | 167 | 177 | 218 | 173 | 213 | **230** | 218 | 178 | 226 | 203 |
| Completion Percentage | 57.6 | 49.8 | 50.2 | 56.8 | 50.4 | 51.2 | 50.3 | 51.3 | 57.1 | 53.2 | 45.6 | 59.0 | **59.4** |
| Passing Yards | 2262 | 2431 | 2445 | 2121 | 2196 | 2658 | 2378 | 2690 | 2892 | 2651 | 2689 | **2990** | 2357 |
| Avg. Yards per Attempt | 6.6 | 5.8 | **8.2** | 7.2 | 6.3 | 6.2 | 6.9 | 6.5 | 7.2 | 6.5 | 6.9 | 7.8 | 6.9 |
| Avg. Yards per Complet. | 11.5 | 11.6 | **16.4** | 12.7 | 12.4 | 12.2 | 13.7 | 12.6 | 12.6 | 12.2 | 15.1 | 13.2 | 11.6 |
| Times Tackled Passing | 53 | 33 | 39 | 36 | 43 | 23 | 29 | 28 | 37 | 23 | 26 | **8** | 29 |
| Yards Lost Tackled | 431 | 258 | 296 | 264 | 382 | 150 | 197 | 232 | 258 | 200 | 216 | **67** | 249 |
| Net Yards | 1831 | 2173 | 2149 | 1857 | 1814 | 2508 | 2181 | 2458 | 2634 | 2451 | 2473 | **2923** | 2108 |
| Touchdowns | 18 | 21 | 18 | 19 | 11 | 17 | 12 | 11 | 19 | 16 | 16 | **25** | 23 |
| Interceptions | 21 | 22 | 16 | 12 | 24 | 13 | 15 | 22 | 12 | 23 | 19 | **10** | **10** |
| Percent Intercepted | 6.1 | 5.2 | 5.4 | 4.1 | 6.8 | 3.1 | 4.4 | 5.3 | 3.0 | 5.6 | 4.9 | **2.6** | 2.9 |
| **PUNTS:** | | | | | | | | | | | | | |
| Number | 76 | 84 | 69 | 62 | **87** | 67 | 61 | 77 | 54 | 71 | 65 | 75 | 61 |
| Average Distance | 38.7 | 40.8 | 41.3 | 40.0 | 40.2 | 39.1 | 37.9 | **42.5** | 38.3 | 36.6 | 40.9 | 38.4 | 40.9 |
| **PUNT RETURNS:** | | | | | | | | | | | | | |
| Number | 34 | 57 | 32 | 34 | 25 | **62** | 35 | 29 | 29 | 32 | 41 | 48 | 27 |
| Yards | 356 | 246 | 237 | 306 | 98 | 418 | 216 | 214 | 193 | 100 | 315 | **550** | 45 |
| Average Yards | 10.5 | 4.3 | 7.4 | 9.0 | 3.9 | 6.7 | 6.2 | 7.4 | 6.7 | 3.1 | 7.7 | **11.5** | 1.7 |
| Touchdowns | **2** | 0 | 0 | 1 | 0 | 0 | 0 | 0 | 1 | 0 | 1 | 0 | 0 |
| **KICKOFF RETURNS:** | | | | | | | | | | | | | |
| Number | 47 | 56 | 37 | 43 | **63** | 47 | 36 | 53 | 52 | 59 | 47 | 49 | 61 |
| Yards | 916 | **1472** | 888 | 959 | 1422 | 1236 | 842 | 1044 | 1157 | 1252 | 926 | 967 | 1223 |
| Average Yards | 19.5 | 26.3 | 24.0 | 22.3 | 22.6 | **26.3** | 23.4 | 19.7 | 22.3 | 21.2 | 19.7 | 19.7 | 20.0 |
| Touchdowns | 0 | **4** | 1 | 1 | 2 | 1 | 0 | 0 | 0 | 0 | 0 | 0 | 0 |
| **INTERCEPTION RETURNS:** | | | | | | | | | | | | | |
| Number | 19 | 17 | 24 | **28** | 20 | 19 | **28** | 22 | 17 | 10 | 21 | 22 | 15 |
| Yards | 191 | 129 | 307 | **417** | 398 | 280 | 412 | 260 | 223 | 102 | 255 | 308 | 240 |
| Average Yards | 10.1 | 7.6 | 12.8 | 14.9 | **19.9** | 14.7 | 14.7 | 11.8 | 13.1 | 10.2 | 12.1 | 14.0 | 16.0 |
| Touchdowns | 0 | 0 | 0 | **4** | 1 | 2 | 2 | 0 | 0 | 0 | 2 | 2 | 0 |
| **PENALTIES:** | | | | | | | | | | | | | |
| Number | 76 | **94** | 87 | 58 | 76 | 88 | 60 | 91 | 71 | 73 | 84 | 88 | 65 |
| Yards | 807 | 853 | 934 | 659 | 691 | 959 | 631 | **1029** | 641 | 799 | 896 | 997 | 613 |
| **FUMBLES:** | | | | | | | | | | | | | |
| Number | **24** | 29 | 29 | 26 | 34 | 27 | 25 | 27 | 29 | 26 | **24** | **24** | 26 |
| Number Lost | 17 | 13 | **12** | 15 | 17 | 17 | 16 | 18 | 14 | 16 | 14 | 15 | 14 |
| **POINTS:** | | | | | | | | | | | | | |
| Total | 206 | 256 | 299 | 347 | 196 | 325 | 335 | 172 | 301 | 241 | 325 | **352** | 297 |
| PAT Attempts | 26 | 28 | 35 | **41** | 22 | 34 | 35 | 17 | 32 | 29 | 38 | **41** | 34 |
| PAT Made | 23 | 28 | 35 | **41** | 19 | 34 | 35 | 16 | 32 | 25 | 37 | 39 | 33 |
| FG Attempts | 25 | 34 | 27 | 29 | 28 | 45 | **46** | 34 | 41 | 25 | 32 | 31 | 27 |
| FG Made | 9 | 20 | 18 | 20 | 15 | 29 | **30** | 18 | 25 | 14 | 20 | 21 | 20 |
| Percent FG Made | 36.0 | 58.8 | 66.7 | 69.0 | 53.6 | 64.4 | 65.2 | 52.9 | 61.0 | 56.0 | 62.5 | 67.7 | **74.1** |
| Safeties | 0 | 0 | 0 | 0 | 0 | 0 | 0 | 0 | 1 | 0 | 0 | **2** | 0 |

### DEFENSE

| | ATL. | CHI. | DALL. | DET. | G.B. | L.A. | MINN. | N.O. | N.Y.G. | PHIL. | ST.L. | S.F. | WASH. |
|---|---|---|---|---|---|---|---|---|---|---|---|---|---|
| **FIRST DOWNS:** | | | | | | | | | | | | | |
| Total | 211 | 234 | 205 | 186 | 202 | 195 | **168** | 263 | 223 | 213 | 242 | 213 | 266 |
| by Rushing | 93 | 83 | 87 | **61** | 88 | 64 | 68 | 100 | 98 | 102 | 96 | 81 | 125 |
| by Passing | 98 | 133 | 105 | 112 | 102 | 113 | **89** | 150 | 110 | 95 | 116 | 110 | 125 |
| by Penalty | 20 | 18 | 13 | 13 | 12 | 18 | **11** | 13 | 15 | 16 | 30 | 22 | 16 |
| **RUSHING:** | | | | | | | | | | | | | |
| Number | 479 | 459 | 415 | **362** | 453 | 395 | 398 | 469 | 419 | 457 | 472 | 425 | 468 |
| Yards | 1722 | 1471 | 1656 | **1152** | 1829 | 1359 | 1365 | 1891 | 1692 | 2064 | 1762 | 1799 | 2068 |
| Average Yards | 3.6 | 3.2 | 4.0 | **3.2** | 4.0 | 3.4 | 3.4 | 4.0 | 4.0 | 4.5 | 3.7 | 4.2 | 4.4 |
| Touchdowns | 14 | 11 | 10 | 7 | 14 | 6 | **4** | 15 | 11 | 16 | 10 | 12 | 19 |
| **PASSING:** | | | | | | | | | | | | | |
| Attempts | 348 | 394 | 399 | 371 | 369 | 378 | 367 | 430 | 364 | **313** | 382 | 384 | 374 |
| Completions | 191 | 233 | 193 | 194 | 177 | 196 | 195 | 238 | 186 | **161** | 183 | 185 | 205 |
| Completion Percentage | 54.9 | 59.1 | 48.4 | 52.3 | 48.0 | 51.9 | 53.1 | 55.3 | 51.1 | 51.4 | **47.9** | 48.2 | 54.8 |
| Passing Yards | 2397 | 2925 | 2226 | 2491 | 2496 | 2615 | **1798** | 3197 | 2650 | 2176 | 2416 | 2434 | 2434 |
| Avg. Yards per Attempt | 6.9 | 7.4 | 5.6 | 6.7 | 6.8 | 6.9 | **4.9** | 7.4 | 7.3 | 7.0 | 6.3 | 6.3 | 6.5 |
| Avg. Yards per Complet. | 12.5 | 12.6 | 11.5 | 12.8 | 14.1 | 13.3 | **9.2** | 13.4 | 14.2 | 13.5 | 13.2 | 13.2 | 11.9 |
| Times Tackled Passing | 30 | 42 | 41 | 23 | 32 | **53** | 49 | 17 | 35 | 34 | 40 | 30 | 24 |
| Yards Lost Tackled | 243 | 329 | 313 | 195 | 270 | **426** | 360 | 136 | 279 | 287 | 309 | 261 | 169 |
| Net Yards | 2154 | 2596 | 1913 | 2296 | 2226 | 2189 | **1438** | 3061 | 2371 | 1889 | 2107 | 2173 | 2265 |
| Touchdowns | 11 | 18 | 10 | 14 | 13 | 15 | **6** | 19 | 19 | 16 | 16 | 19 | 14 |
| Interceptions | 19 | 17 | 24 | **28** | 20 | 19 | **28** | 22 | 17 | 10 | 21 | 22 | 15 |
| Percent Intercepted | 5.5 | 4.3 | 6.0 | 7.5 | 5.4 | 5.0 | **7.6** | 5.1 | 4.7 | 3.2 | 5.5 | 5.7 | 4.0 |
| **PUNTS:** | | | | | | | | | | | | | |
| Number | 60 | 87 | 74 | 70 | 71 | **88** | 84 | 56 | 62 | 62 | 80 | 82 | 56 |
| Average Distance | 41.2 | 37.6 | 41.1 | 39.1 | 40.1 | 37.8 | **37.5** | 40.4 | 39.7 | 39.1 | 40.0 | 40.4 | 39.3 |
| **PUNT RETURNS:** | | | | | | | | | | | | | |
| Number | 40 | 40 | 38 | 29 | 40 | 32 | 38 | 41 | **21** | 22 | 26 | 38 | 35 |
| Yards | 267 | 268 | 281 | 113 | 338 | 181 | 322 | 434 | **61** | 163 | 90 | 180 | 259 |
| Average Yards | 6.7 | 6.7 | 7.4 | 3.9 | 8.5 | 5.7 | 8.5 | 10.6 | **2.9** | 7.4 | 3.5 | 4.7 | 7.4 |
| Touchdowns | **0** | **0** | 1 | **0** | **0** | **0** | 1 | 1 | **0** | 1 | **0** | **0** | **0** |
| **KICKOFF RETURNS:** | | | | | | | | | | | | | |
| Number | 41 | 47 | 60 | 67 | 36 | **71** | 69 | 35 | 57 | 50 | 54 | 58 | 49 |
| Yards | 983 | 935 | 1142 | 1427 | 888 | 1278 | 1514 | **735** | 1359 | 1030 | 1262 | 1362 | 1181 |
| Average Yards | 24.0 | 19.9 | 19.0 | 21.3 | 24.7 | **18.0** | 21.9 | 21.0 | 23.8 | 20.6 | 23.4 | 23.5 | 24.1 |
| Touchdowns | 1 | **0** | **0** | **0** | **0** | **0** | 3 | **0** | 1 | 1 | 1 | **0** | 1 |
| **INTERCEPTION RETURNS:** | | | | | | | | | | | | | |
| Number | 21 | 22 | 16 | 12 | 24 | 13 | 15 | 22 | 12 | 23 | 19 | **10** | **10** |
| Yards | 283 | 251 | 259 | 174 | 421 | **92** | 175 | 256 | 172 | 461 | 276 | 95 | 181 |
| Average Yards | 13.5 | 11.4 | 16.2 | 14.5 | 17.5 | **7.1** | 11.7 | 11.6 | 14.3 | 20.0 | 14.5 | 9.5 | 18.1 |
| Touchdowns | 1 | 1 | 1 | 1 | 3 | **0** | **0** | 1 | **0** | 2 | **0** | **0** | 1 |
| **PENALTIES:** | | | | | | | | | | | | | |
| Number | **93** | 76 | 70 | 90 | 63 | 77 | 58 | 79 | 71 | 90 | 68 | 87 | 87 |
| Yards | 897 | 826 | 732 | 805 | 686 | 825 | 586 | 875 | 675 | **991** | 659 | 965 | 930 |
| **FUMBLES:** | | | | | | | | | | | | | |
| Number | 22 | 27 | 25 | 30 | 29 | 28 | 27 | 26 | 31 | 25 | 20 | **35** | 22 |
| Number Lost | 16 | 14 | 15 | 16 | 17 | 16 | 16 | 16 | 13 | 18 | 14 | **20** | 13 |
| **POINTS:** | | | | | | | | | | | | | |
| Total | 261 | 261 | 221 | 202 | 293 | 202 | **143** | 347 | 270 | 332 | 228 | 267 | 314 |
| PAT Attempts | 29 | 31 | 24 | 22 | 30 | 22 | **14** | 40 | 32 | 36 | 27 | 32 | 37 |
| PAT Made | 27 | 27 | 24 | 22 | 29 | 22 | **14** | 38 | 30 | 35 | 27 | 30 | 36 |
| FG Attempts | 40 | 29 | 26 | 26 | 42 | 25 | 27 | 34 | 29 | 39 | 26 | **24** | 26 |
| FG Made | 20 | 16 | 17 | 16 | 28 | 16 | 15 | 23 | 16 | 27 | **13** | 15 | 18 |
| Percent FG Made | **50.0** | 55.2 | 65.4 | 61.5 | 66.7 | 64.0 | 55.6 | 67.6 | 55.2 | 69.2 | **50.0** | 62.5 | 69.2 |
| Safeties | 0 | 0 | 1 | 0 | 0 | 0 | 0 | 0 | 0 | 0 | 0 | 0 | 1 |

## CONFERENCE PLAYOFFS

December 26, at Dallas
(Attendance 69,613)

### SCORING

| | | | | |
|---|---|---|---|---|
| **DALLAS** | 3 | 0 | 0 | 2–5 |
| **DETROIT** | 0 | 0 | 0 | 0–0 |

First Quarter
Dal. Clark, 26 yard field goal

Fourth Quarter
Dal. Andrie, Safety-tackled Landry

### TEAM STATISTICS

| DALLAS | | DETR. |
|---|---|---|
| 19 | First Downs–Total | 7 |
| 11 | First Downs–Rushing | 2 |
| 8 | First Downs–Passing | 5 |
| 0 | First Downs–Penalty | 0 |
| 0 | Fumbles–Number | 3 |
| 0 | Fumbles–Lost Ball | 2 |
| 6 | Penalties–Number | 0 |
| 47 | Yards Penalized | 0 |
| 0 | Missed Field Goals | 0 |
| 69 | Offensive Plays–Total | 50 |
| 231 | Net Yards | 156 |
| 3.3 | Average Gain | 3.1 |
| 1 | Giveaways | 3 |
| 3 | Takeaways | 1 |
| +2 | Difference | –2 |

### INDIVIDUAL STATISTICS

| DALLAS | No. | Yds. | Avg. | DETROIT | No. | Yds. | Avg. |
|---|---|---|---|---|---|---|---|
| **RUSHING** | | | | | | | |
| Thomas | 30 | 135 | 4.5 | Farr | 12 | 31 | 2.6 |
| Garrison | 17 | 72 | 4.2 | Taylor | 9 | 16 | 1.8 |
| Morton | 3 | 2 | 0.7 | Landry | 3 | 15 | 5.0 |
| | 50 | 209 | 4.2 | Owens | 2 | 9 | 4.5 |
| | | | | Walton | 1 | 5 | 5.0 |
| | | | | | 27 | 76 | 2.8 |
| **RECEIVING** | | | | | | | |
| Garrison | 2 | 8 | 4.0 | Walton | 3 | 39 | 13.0 |
| Hayes | 1 | 20 | 20.0 | Taylor | 2 | 7 | 3.5 |
| Norman | 1 | 10 | 10.0 | McCullough | 1 | 39 | 39.0 |
| | 4 | 38 | 9.5 | Owens | 1 | 7 | 7.0 |
| | | | | | 7 | 92 | 13.1 |
| **PUNTING** | | | | | | | |
| Widby | 8 | | 44.7 | Weaver | 8 | | 48.8 |
| **PUNT RETURNS** | | | | | | | |
| Renfro | 4 | 23 | 5.8 | Barney | 5 | 20 | 4.0 |
| | | | | Vaughan | 1 | 1 | 1.0 |
| | | | | | 6 | 21 | 3.5 |
| **KICKOFF RETURNS** | | | | | | | |
| Hayes | 1 | 16 | 16.0 | Williams | 1 | 24 | 24.0 |
| Waters | 1 | 9 | 9.0 | Maxwell | 1 | 13 | 13.0 |
| | 2 | 25 | 12.5 | | 2 | 37 | 18.5 |
| **INTERCEPTION RETURNS** | | | | | | | |
| Renfro | 1 | 13 | 13.0 | Weger | 1 | 31 | 31.0 |

**PASSING**

| DALLAS | Att. | Comp. | Comp. Pct. | Yds. | Int. | Yds/ Att. | Yds/ Comp. | Yds Lost Tkld. |
|---|---|---|---|---|---|---|---|---|
| Morton | 18 | 4 | 22.2 | 38 | 1 | 2.1 | 9.5 | 1–16 |
| **DETROIT** | | | | | | | | |
| Landry | 12 | 5 | 41.7 | 48 | 0 | 4.0 | 9.6 | |
| Munson | 8 | 2 | 25.0 | 44 | 1 | 5.5 | 22.0 | |
| | 20 | 7 | 35.0 | 92 | 1 | 4.8 | 13.1 | 3–12 |

December 27, at Bloomington
(Attendance 45,103)

### SCORING

| | | | | |
|---|---|---|---|---|
| **MINNESOTA** | 7 | 0 | 0 | 7–14 |
| **SAN FRANCISCO** | 7 | 3 | 0 | 7–17 |

First Quarter
Min. Krause, 22 yard fumble return
PAT–Cox (kick)
S.F. Witcher, 24 yard pass from Brodie
PAT–Gossett (kick)

Second Quarter
S.F. Gossett, 40 yard field goal

Fourth Quarter
S.F. Brodie, 1 yard rush
PAT–Gossett (kick)
Min. Washington, 24 yard pass from Cuozzo
PAT–Cox (kick)

### TEAM STATISTICS

| MINN. | | S.F. |
|---|---|---|
| 14 | First Downs–Total | 14 |
| 7 | First Downs–Rushing | 5 |
| 6 | First Downs–Passing | 8 |
| 1 | First Downs–Penalty | 1 |
| 3 | Fumbles–Number | 5 |
| 2 | Fumbles–Lost Ball | 3 |
| 1 | Penalties–Number | 3 |
| 5 | Yards Penalized | 37 |
| 2 | Missed Field Goals | 1 |
| 60 | Offensive Plays–Total | 71 |
| 241 | Net Yards | 289 |
| 4.1 | Average Gain | 4.1 |
| 4 | Giveaways | 3 |
| 3 | Takeaways | 4 |
| –1 | Difference | +1 |

### INDIVIDUAL STATISTICS

| MINNESOTA | No. | Yds. | Avg. | SAN FRANCISCO | No | Yds | Avg. |
|---|---|---|---|---|---|---|---|
| **RUSHING** | | | | | | | |
| Jones | 15 | 60 | 4.0 | Willard | 27 | 85 | 3.1 |
| Osborn | 12 | 41 | 3.4 | Tucker | 7 | 5 | 0.7 |
| Cuozzo | 1 | 11 | 11.0 | Brodie | 2 | 3 | 1.5 |
| Brown | 2 | 5 | 2.5 | Kwalick | 1 | 2 | 2.0 |
| | 30 | 117 | 3.9 | Cunningham | 1 | 0 | 0.0 |
| | | | | | 38 | 95 | 2.5 |
| **RECEIVING** | | | | | | | |
| Henderson | 5 | 80 | 16.0 | Tucker | 6 | 48 | 8.0 |
| Grim | 2 | 37 | 18.5 | Witcher | 4 | 45 | 11.3 |
| Washington | 1 | 24 | 24.0 | Kwalick | 3 | 45 | 15.0 |
| Jones | 1 | 5 | 5.0 | Washington | 2 | 45 | 22.5 |
| | 9 | 146 | 16.2 | Willard | 1 | 18 | 18.0 |
| | | | | | 16 | 201 | 12.6 |
| **PUNTING** | | | | | | | |
| McNeill | 7 | | 39.4 | Spurrier | 8 | | 33.8 |
| **PUNT RETURNS** | | | | | | | |
| None | | | | B. Taylor | 5 | 69 | 13.8 |
| **KICKOFF RETURNS** | | | | | | | |
| Jones | 3 | 49 | 16.3 | Beard | 1 | 17 | 17.0 |
| Brown | 1 | 23 | 23.0 | Tucker | 1 | 13 | 13.0 |
| | 4 | 72 | 18.0 | Hoskins | 1 | 0 | 0.0 |
| | | | | | 3 | 30 | 10.0 |
| **INTERCEPTION RETURNS** | | | | | | | |
| None | | | | Sniadecki | 1 | 5 | 5.0 |
| | | | | B. Taylor | 1 | 0 | 0.0 |
| | | | | | 2 | 5 | 2.5 |

**PASSING**

| MINNESOTA | Att. | Comp. | Comp. Pct. | Yds. | Int. | Yds/ Att. | Yds/ Comp. | Yds Lost Tkld. |
|---|---|---|---|---|---|---|---|---|
| Cuozzo | 27 | 9 | 33.3 | 146 | 2 | 5.4 | 16.2 | 3–22 |
| **SAN FRANCISCO** | | | | | | | | |
| Brodie | 32 | 16 | 50.0 | 201 | 0 | 6.3 | 12.6 | 1– 8 |

# 1970 N.F.C. — Eastern Division

## DALLAS COWBOYS 10-4-0 Tom Landry

| Scores of Each Game | | |
|---|---|---|
| 17 | Philadelphia | 7 |
| 28 | N. Y. GIANTS | 10 |
| 7 | St. Louis | 20 |
| 13 | ATLANTA | 0 |
| 13 | Minnesota | 54 |
| 27 | Kansas City | 16 |
| 21 | PHILADELPHIA | 17 |
| 20 | N. Y. Giants | 23 |
| 0 | ST. LOUIS | 38 |
| 45 | Washington | 21 |
| 16 | GREEN BAY | 3 |
| 34 | WASHINGTON | 0 |
| 6 | Cleveland | 2 |
| 52 | HOUSTON | 10 |

| Use Name | Pos. | Hgt | Wgt | Age | Int | Pts |
|---|---|---|---|---|---|---|
| Bob Asher | OT | 6'5" | 250 | 22 | | |
| Tony Liscio | OT | 6'5" | 255 | 30 | | |
| Ralph Neely | OT | 6'5" | 265 | 26 | | |
| Rayfield Wright | OT | 6'7" | 255 | 25 | | |
| John Niland | OG | 6'4" | 245 | 26 | | |
| Blaine Nye | OG | 6'4" | 250 | 24 | | |
| Halvor Hagen | C-OG | 6'5" | 253 | 23 | | |
| Dave Manders | C | 6'2" | 250 | 28 | | |
| George Andrie | DE | 6'7" | 250 | 30 | | |
| Larry Cole | DE | 6'4" | 255 | 23 | | |
| Pat Toomay | DE | 6'5" | 244 | 25 | | |
| Ron East | DT | 6'4" | 242 | 27 | | |
| Bob Lilly | DT | 6'4" | 260 | 31 | | |
| Jethro Pugh | DT | 6'6" | 260 | 26 | 1 | |
| Dave Edwards | LB | 6'3" | 225 | 31 | 2 | |
| Chuck Howley | LB | 6'3" | 225 | 34 | 2 | |
| Lee Roy Jordan | LB | 6'2" | 220 | 29 | 1 | |
| Steve Kiner | LB | 6' | 218 | 23 | 1 | |
| D. D. Lewis | LB | 6'2" | 225 | 24 | | |
| Tom Stincic | LB | 6'2" | 230 | 23 | 1 | |
| Herb Adderley | DB | 6'1" | 200 | 31 | 3 | |
| Richmond Flowers | DB | 6' | 180 | 23 | | |
| Cornell Green | DB | 6'4" | 208 | 30 | 1 | |
| Cliff Harris | DB | 6' | 184 | 21 | 2 | |
| Mel Renfro | DB | 6' | 190 | 28 | 4 | |
| Mark Washington | DB | 5'10" | 188 | 22 | 1 | 6 |
| Charlie Waters | DB | 6'1" | 193 | 21 | 5 | |
| Bob Belden | QB | 6'2" | 205 | 23 | | |
| Craig Morton | QB | 6'4" | 214 | 27 | | |
| Roger Staubach | QB | 6'2" | 197 | 28 | | |
| Dan Reeves | HB | 6'1" | 200 | 26 | | 12 |
| Claxton Welch | HB | 5'11" | 203 | 23 | | 6 |
| Calvin Hill | FB-HB | 6'3" | 227 | 23 | | 24 |
| Duane Thomas | FB-HB | 6'1" | 220 | 23 | | 30 |
| Walt Garrison | FB | 6' | 205 | 26 | | 30 |
| Margene Atkins | WR | 5'10" | 183 | 23 | | |
| Bob Hayes | WR | 6' | 185 | 27 | | 66 |
| Dennis Homan | WR | 6'1" | 180 | 24 | | |
| Lance Rentzel | WR | 6'2" | 202 | 26 | | 30 |
| Reggie Rucker | WR | 6'2" | 190 | 22 | | 6 |
| Mike Ditka | TE | 6'3" | 225 | 30 | | |
| Pettis Norman | TE | 6'3" | 220 | 30 | | |
| Mike Clark | K | 6'1" | 205 | 29 | | 89 |
| Ron Widby | K | 6'4" | 210 | 25 | | |

## NEW YORK GIANTS 9-5-0 Alex Webster

| Scores of Each Game | | |
|---|---|---|
| 16 | CHICAGO | 24 |
| 10 | Dallas | 28 |
| 10 | New Orleans | 14 |
| 30 | PHILADELPHIA | 23 |
| 16 | Boston | 0 |
| 35 | ST. LOUIS | 17 |
| 22 | N. Y. Jets | 10 |
| 23 | DALLAS | 20 |
| 35 | WASHINGTON | 33 |
| 20 | Philadelphia | 23 |
| 27 | Washington | 24 |
| 20 | BUFFALO | 6 |
| 34 | St. Louis | 17 |
| 3 | LOS ANGELES | 31 |

| Use Name | Pos. | Hgt | Wgt | Age | Int | Pts |
|---|---|---|---|---|---|---|
| Rich Buzin | OT | 6'4" | 250 | 24 | | |
| Dennis Crane | OT | 6'6" | 260 | 25 | | |
| Willie Young | OT | 6' | 265 | 27 | | |
| Charlie Harper | OG-OT | 6'2" | 250 | 26 | | |
| Willie Banks | OG | 6'2" | 237 | 24 | | |
| Pete Case | OG | 6'3" | 245 | 29 | | |
| Doug Van Horn | OG | 6'2" | 245 | 26 | | |
| Len Johnson | C-OG | 6'2" | 250 | 24 | | |
| Pat Hughes | C | 6'2" | 240 | 23 | | |
| Greg Larson | C | 6'2" | 250 | 31 | | |
| John Baker | DE | 6'5" | 260 | 28 | | |
| Fred Dryer | DE | 6'6" | 240 | 24 | | |
| Bob Lurtsema | DE | 6'6" | 250 | 28 | | |
| Jim Kanicki | DT | 6'4" | 270 | 28 | | |
| Jim Norton | DT | 6'4" | 254 | 27 | | |
| Jerry Shay | DT | 6'3" | 245 | 26 | | |
| John Douglas | LB | 6'2" | 225 | 25 | | |
| Jim Files | LB | 6'4" | 240 | 22 | 1 | 2 |
| Matt Hazeltine | LB | 6'1" | 225 | 37 | 1 | |
| Ralph Heck | LB | 6'2" | 230 | 29 | 1 | |
| Ray Hickl | LB | 6'2" | 220 | 23 | | |
| John Kirby | LB | 6'3" | 232 | 28 | | |
| Al Brenner | DB | 6'1" | 200 | 22 | | |
| Otto Brown | DB | 6'1" | 188 | 23 | | |
| Scott Eaton | DB | 6'3" | 205 | 26 | 2 | |
| Joe Green | DB | 5'11" | 195 | 23 | | |
| Spider Lockhart | DB | 6'2" | 175 | 27 | 4 | |
| Tom Longo | DB | 6'1" | 200 | 26 | 2 | |
| Kenny Parker | DB | 6'1" | 190 | 24 | | |
| Willie Williams | DB | 6' | 190 | 27 | 6 | |
| Dick Shiner | QB | 6' | 197 | 28 | | |
| Fran Tarkenton | QB | 6'1" | 190 | 30 | | 12 |
| Bobby Duhon | HB | 6' | 195 | 23 | | 6 |
| Ron Johnson | HB | 6'1" | 205 | 22 | | 72 |
| Les Shy | HB | 6'1" | 200 | 26 | | |
| Joe Morrison | FB-WR-HB | 6'1" | 212 | 32 | | |
| Tucker Frederickson | FB | 6'3" | 220 | 27 | | 24 |
| Ernie Koy | HB-FB | 6'2" | 225 | 27 | | |
| Don Herrmann | WR | 6'2" | 195 | 23 | | 12 |
| Rich Houston | WR | 6'2" | 197 | 24 | | |
| Clifton McNeil | WR | 6'2" | 187 | 30 | | 30 |
| Bob Tucker | TE | 6'3" | 230 | 25 | | 30 |
| Aaron Thomas | WR-TE | 6'3" | 210 | 32 | | 6 |
| Pete Gogolak | K | 6'2" | 190 | 28 | | 107 |
| Bill Johnson | K | 6'2" | 208 | 26 | | |

Junior Coffey – Knee Injury
Tommy Crutcher – Knee Injury

## ST. LOUIS CARDINALS 8-5-1 Charlie Winner

| Scores of Each Game | | |
|---|---|---|
| 13 | Los Angeles | 34 |
| 27 | WASHINGTON | 17 |
| 20 | DALLAS | 7 |
| 24 | NEW ORLEANS | 17 |
| 35 | Philadelphia | 20 |
| 17 | N. Y. Giants | 35 |
| 44 | HOUSTON | 0 |
| 31 | BOSTON | 0 |
| 38 | Dallas | 0 |
| 6 | Kansas City | 6 |
| 23 | PHILADELPHIA | 14 |
| 3 | Detroit | 16 |
| 17 | N. Y. GIANTS | 34 |
| 27 | Washington | 28 |

| Use Name | Pos. | Hgt | Wgt | Age | Int | Pts |
|---|---|---|---|---|---|---|
| Vern Emerson | OT | 6'5" | 260 | 24 | | |
| Ernie McMillan | OT | 6'6" | 255 | 32 | | |
| Bob Reynolds | OT | 6'6" | 265 | 29 | | |
| Clyde Williams | OG-OT | 6'2" | 250 | 30 | | |
| Irv Goode | OG | 6'4" | 255 | 29 | | |
| Chuck Hutchison | OG | 6'3" | 240 | 21 | | |
| Mike LaHood | OG | 6'3" | 250 | 25 | | |
| Wayne Mulligan | C | 6'2" | 245 | 23 | | |
| Rolf Krueger | DE | 6'4" | 250 | 23 | | |
| Cal Snowden | DE | 6'4" | 250 | 23 | | |
| Chuck Walker | DE | 6'2" | 250 | 29 | | |
| Joe Schmiesing | DT-DE | 6'4" | 250 | 25 | | |
| Fred Heron | DT | 6'4" | 260 | 25 | | |
| Bob Rowe | DT | 6'4" | 255 | 25 | | |
| Mike Siwok | DT | 6'3" | 260 | 22 | | |
| Chip Healy | LB | 6'3" | 235 | 23 | | |
| Dave Olerich | LB | 6'1" | 225 | 25 | | |
| Don Parish | LB | 6'1" | 220 | 22 | 1 | 6 |
| Jamie Rivers | LB | 6'2" | 235 | 24 | | |
| Rocky Romesa | LB | 6'2" | 230 | 24 | | |
| Larry Stallings | LB | 6'2" | 230 | 28 | 1 | |
| Terry Brown | DB | 6'1" | 210 | 23 | | |
| Miller Farr | DB | 6'1" | 190 | 27 | 5 | 6 |
| Chuck Latourette | DB | 6' | 190 | 25 | | 6 |
| Tony Plummer | DB | 5'11" | 190 | 23 | | |
| Jerry Stovall | DB | 6'2" | 195 | 28 | 2 | |
| Roger Wehrli | DB | 6'1" | 195 | 22 | 6 | |
| Larry Wilson | DB | 6' | 195 | 32 | 5 | |
| Nate Wright | DB | 5'11" | 180 | 22 | 1 | |
| Pete Beathard | QB | 6'2" | 210 | 28 | | |
| Jim Hart | QB | 6'2" | 205 | 26 | | |
| Charlie Pittman | HB | 6'1" | 200 | 22 | | |
| Roy Shivers | HB | 6' | 200 | 28 | | 12 |
| Paul White | HB | 6' | 200 | 22 | | |
| MacArthur Lane | FB-HB | 6' | 220 | 28 | | 78 |
| Cid Edwards | FB | 6'2" | 230 | 26 | | 12 |
| Johnny Roland | HB-FB | 6'2" | 215 | 27 | | 30 |
| Jerry Daanen | WR | 6' | 190 | 25 | | |
| John Gilliam | WR | 6'1" | 195 | 25 | | 36 |
| Freddie Hyatt | WR | 6'3" | 210 | 24 | | |
| Dave Williams | WR | 6'2" | 210 | 25 | | 18 |
| Bob Brown | TE | 6'3" | 225 | 27 | | |
| Jim McFarland | TE | 6'5" | 225 | 22 | | |
| Jackie Smith | TE | 6'4" | 235 | 29 | | 24 |
| Jim Bakken | K | 6' | 195 | 29 | | 97 |

## WASHINGTON REDSKINS 6-8-0 Bill Austin

| Scores of Each Game | | |
|---|---|---|
| 17 | San Francisco | 26 |
| 17 | St. Louis | 27 |
| 33 | Philadelphia | 21 |
| 31 | DETROIT | 10 |
| 20 | Oakland | 34 |
| 20 | CINCINNATI | 0 |
| 19 | Denver | 3 |
| 10 | MINNESOTA | 19 |
| 33 | N. Y. Giants | 35 |
| 21 | DALLAS | 45 |
| 24 | N. Y. GIANTS | 27 |
| 0 | Dallas | 34 |
| 24 | PHILADELPHIA | 6 |
| 28 | ST. LOUIS | 27 |

| Use Name | Pos. | Hgt | Wgt | Age | Int | Pts |
|---|---|---|---|---|---|---|
| Walt Rock | OT | 6'5" | 255 | 29 | | |
| Jim Snowden | OT | 6'3" | 255 | 28 | | |
| Steve Wright | OT | 6'6" | 250 | 28 | | |
| Paul Laaveg | OG | 6'4" | 245 | 21 | | |
| Vince Promuto | OG | 6'1" | 245 | 32 | | |
| Roy Schmidt | OG | 6'3" | 250 | 28 | | |
| Ray Schoenke | OG | 6'3" | 250 | 28 | | |
| Gene Hamlin | C | 6'3" | 245 | 24 | | |
| Len Hauss | C | 6'2" | 235 | 28 | | |
| Bruce Anderson | DE | 6'4" | 250 | 26 | | |
| Bill Brundige | DE | 6'5" | 270 | 21 | | |
| Leo Carroll | DE | 6'7" | 250 | 26 | | |
| Terry Hermeling | DE | 6'5" | 255 | 24 | | |
| John Hoffman | DE | 6'7" | 260 | 27 | | |
| Frank Bosch | DT | 6'4" | 246 | 24 | | |
| Floyd Peters | DT | 6'4" | 255 | 35 | | |
| Manny Sistrunk | DT | 6'5" | 265 | 23 | | |
| Chris Hanburger | LB | 6'2" | 218 | 29 | 1 | |
| Marlin McKeever | LB | 6'1" | 235 | 30 | | |
| Harold McLinton | LB | 6'2" | 235 | 23 | | |
| Tom Roussel | LB | 6'3" | 235 | 25 | | |
| Rusty Tillman | LB | 6'2" | 230 | 24 | | |
| John Didion | C-LB | 6'4" | 245 | 22 | | |
| Mike Bass | DB | 6' | 190 | 25 | 4 | |
| Pat Fischer | DB | 5'10" | 170 | 30 | 2 | |
| Jim Harris | DB | 5'11" | 173 | 24 | | |
| Rickie Harris | DB | 6' | 182 | 27 | 3 | |
| Jon Jaqua | DB | 6' | 190 | 22 | 1 | |
| Brig Owens | DB | 5'11" | 190 | 27 | 4 | |
| Ted Vactor | DB | 6' | 185 | 26 | | |
| Sonny Jurgensen | QB | 5'11" | 203 | 36 | | 6 |
| Frank Ryan | QB | 6'3" | 207 | 34 | | |
| Larry Brown | HB | 5'11" | 195 | 22 | | 42 |
| Bob Brunet | HB | 6'1" | 205 | 24 | | |
| Danny Pierce | FB-HB | 6'3" | 216 | 22 | | |
| Henry Dyer | FB | 6'2" | 230 | 25 | | |
| Charlie Harraway | FB | 6'2" | 215 | 25 | | 30 |
| Dave Kopay | HB-FB | 6'2" | 225 | 28 | | |
| Jon Henderson | WR | 6' | 200 | 25 | | 18 |
| Bill Malinchak | WR | 6'1" | 200 | 26 | | |
| Walter Roberts | WR | 5'10" | 163 | 28 | | 6 |
| Charley Taylor | WR | 6'3" | 210 | 29 | | 48 |
| Mack Alston | TE | 6'2" | 230 | 23 | | |
| Pat Richter | TE | 6'5" | 230 | 29 | | |
| Jerry Smith | TE | 6'2" | 208 | 27 | | 54 |
| Mike Bragg | K | 5'11" | 186 | 23 | | |
| Curt Knight | K | 6'1" | 190 | 27 | | 93 |

## PHILADELPHIA EAGLES 3-10-1 Jerry Williams

| Scores of Each Game | | |
|---|---|---|
| 7 | DALLAS | 17 |
| 16 | Chicago | 20 |
| 21 | WASHINGTON | 33 |
| 23 | N. Y. Giants | 30 |
| 20 | ST. LOUIS | 35 |
| 17 | Green Bay | 30 |
| 17 | Dallas | 21 |
| 24 | MIAMI | 17 |
| 13 | ATLANTA | 13 |
| 23 | N. Y. GIANTS | 20 |
| 14 | St. Louis | 23 |
| 10 | Baltimore | 29 |
| 6 | Washington | 24 |
| 30 | PITTSBURGH | 20 |

| Use Name | Pos. | Hgt | Wgt | Age | Int | Pts |
|---|---|---|---|---|---|---|
| Joe Carollo | OT | 6'2" | 265 | 30 | | |
| Wade Key | OT | 6'4" | 245 | 23 | | |
| Dick Stevens | OT | 6'4" | 240 | 22 | | |
| Norman Davis | OG | 6'3" | 245 | 25 | | |
| Dick Hart | OG | 6'2" | 250 | 27 | | |
| Jim Skaggs | OG | 6'2" | 250 | 30 | | |
| Mark Nordquist | C-OG | 6'4" | 246 | 24 | | |
| Mike Evans | C | 6'5" | 250 | 23 | | |
| Calvin Hunt | C | 6'3" | 243 | 22 | | |
| Don Brumm | DE | 6'3" | 245 | 27 | | |
| Ernie Calloway | DE | 6'6" | 240 | 22 | | |
| Mel Tom | DE | 6'4" | 250 | 29 | | |
| Mike Dirks | DT | 6'2" | 246 | 24 | | 6 |
| Gary Pettigrew | DT | 6'4" | 255 | 25 | | |
| Don Hultz | DE-DT | 6'3" | 240 | 29 | | |
| Carl Gersbach | LB | 6'1" | 230 | 23 | | |
| Bill Hobbs | LB | 6' | 220 | 24 | | |
| Jay Johnson | LB | 6'3" | 230 | 24 | | |
| Ike Kelley | LB | 5'11" | 224 | 26 | | |
| Dave Lloyd | LB | 6'3" | 248 | 34 | | |
| Ron Porter | LB | 6'3" | 232 | 25 | | |
| Tim Rossovich | LB | 6'4" | 250 | 24 | | |
| Adrian Young | LB | 6'1" | 232 | 24 | 2 | |
| Bill Bradley | DB | 5'11" | 190 | 23 | | |
| Richard Harvey | DB | 6'2" | 190 | 24 | | |
| Ed Hayes | DB | 6'1" | 185 | 24 | 1 | |
| Ray Jones | DB | 6' | 187 | 22 | 2 | |
| Ron Medved | DB | 6'1" | 200 | 26 | | |
| Al Nelson | DB | 5'11" | 186 | 26 | 2 | |
| Steve Preece | DB | 6'1" | 195 | 23 | 2 | 6 |
| Nate Ramsey | DB | 6'1" | 200 | 29 | 1 | |
| Jim Throner | DB | 6'2" | 194 | 21 | | |
| Rick Arrington | QB | 6'2" | 185 | 23 | | 6 |
| Norm Snead | QB | 6'4" | 215 | 30 | | 18 |
| Harry Jones | HB | 6'2" | 205 | 25 | | |
| Leroy Keyes | HB | 6'3" | 208 | 23 | | |
| Cyril Pinder | HB | 6'2" | 222 | 23 | | 12 |
| Larry Watkins | FB-HB | 6'2" | 215 | 23 | | 6 |
| Lee Bougess | FB | 6'2" | 210 | 22 | | 24 |
| Tom Woodeshick | FB | 6' | 222 | 28 | | 12 |
| Ben Hawkins | WR | 6' | 180 | 26 | | 24 |
| Harold Jackson | WR | 5'10" | 175 | 24 | | 30 |
| Billy Walik | WR | 5'11" | 180 | 22 | | |
| Steve Zabel | TE | 6'4" | 235 | 22 | | 6 |
| Gary Ballman | WR-TE | 6' | 205 | 30 | | 18 |
| Fred Hill | WR-TE | 6'2" | 215 | 27 | | 6 |
| Mark Moseley | K | 5'11" | 182 | 22 | | 67 |

Dave Graham – Injury

## DALLAS COWBOYS

### RUSHING

| Last Name | No. | Yds | Avg | TD |
|---|---|---|---|---|
| Thomas | 151 | 803 | 5.3 | 5 |
| Hill | 153 | 577 | 3.8 | 4 |
| Garrison | 126 | 507 | 4.0 | 3 |
| Staubach | 27 | 221 | 8.2 | 0 |
| Reeves | 35 | 84 | 2.4 | 2 |
| Morton | 16 | 37 | 2.3 | 0 |
| Hayes | 4 | 34 | 8.5 | 1 |
| Norman | 2 | 16 | 8.0 | 0 |
| Welch | 5 | 13 | 2.6 | 1 |
| Rentzel | 1 | 11 | 11.0 | 0 |
| Homan | 2 | -3 | -1.5 | 0 |

### RECEIVING

| Last Name | No. | Yds | Avg | TD |
|---|---|---|---|---|
| Hayes | 34 | 889 | 26 | 10 |
| Rentzel | 28 | 556 | 20 | 5 |
| Garrison | 21 | 205 | 10 | 2 |
| Hill | 13 | 95 | 7 | 0 |
| Reeves | 12 | 140 | 12 | 0 |
| Thomas | 10 | 73 | 7 | 0 |
| Rucker | 9 | 200 | 22 | 1 |
| Ditka | 8 | 98 | 12 | 0 |
| Homan | 7 | 105 | 15 | 0 |
| Norman | 6 | 70 | 12 | 0 |
| Kiner | 1 | 14 | 14 | 0 |

### PUNT RETURNS

| Last Name | No. | Yds | Avg | TD |
|---|---|---|---|---|
| Hayes | 15 | 116 | 8 | 0 |
| Renfro | 13 | 77 | 6 | 0 |
| Adkins | 4 | 44 | 11 | 0 |

### KICKOFF RETURNS

| Last Name | No. | Yds | Avg | TD |
|---|---|---|---|---|
| Thomas | 19 | 416 | 22 | 0 |
| Washington | 5 | 242 | 48 | 1 |
| Adkins | 7 | 149 | 21 | 0 |
| Kiner | 3 | 50 | 17 | 0 |
| Harris | 1 | 22 | 22 | 0 |
| Waters | 1 | 6 | 6 | 0 |
| Flowers | 1 | 3 | 3 | 0 |

### PASSING — PUNTING — KICKING

| PASSING | Att | Comp | % | Yds | Yd/Att | TD | Int- | % | RK |
|---|---|---|---|---|---|---|---|---|---|
| Morton | 207 | 102 | 49 | 1819 | 8.8 | 15 | 7- | 3 | 5 |
| Staubach | 82 | 44 | 54 | 542 | 6.6 | 2 | 8- | 10 | |
| Hill | 4 | 1 | 25 | 12 | 3.0 | 0 | 0- | 0 | |
| Reeves | 3 | 1 | 33 | 14 | 4.7 | 0 | 1- | 33 | |
| Rentzel | 1 | 1 | 100 | 58 | 58.0 | 1 | 0- | 0 | |

| PUNTING | No | Avg |
|---|---|---|
| Widby | 69 | 41.3 |

| KICKING | XP | Att | % | FG | Att | % |
|---|---|---|---|---|---|---|
| Clark | 35 | 35 | 100 | 18 | 27 | 67 |

## NEW YORK GIANTS

### RUSHING

| Last Name | No. | Yds | Avg | TD |
|---|---|---|---|---|
| R. Johnson | 263 | 1027 | 3.9 | 8 |
| Frederickson | 120 | 375 | 3.1 | 1 |
| Tarkenton | 43 | 236 | 5.5 | 2 |
| Duhon | 18 | 111 | 6.2 | 0 |
| Morrison | 11 | 25 | 2.3 | 0 |
| Shy | 4 | 13 | 3.3 | 0 |
| McNeil | 4 | 7 | 1.8 | 0 |
| Koy | 2 | 5 | 2.5 | 0 |

### RECEIVING

| Last Name | No. | Yds | Avg | TD |
|---|---|---|---|---|
| McNeil | 50 | 764 | 15 | 4 |
| R. Johnson | 48 | 487 | 10 | 4 |
| Tucker | 40 | 571 | 14 | 5 |
| Frederickson | 40 | 408 | 10 | 3 |
| Herrmann | 24 | 290 | 12 | 2 |
| Morrison | 11 | 136 | 12 | 0 |
| Thomas | 6 | 92 | 15 | 1 |
| Houston | 4 | 68 | 17 | 0 |
| Duhon | 4 | 58 | 15 | 0 |
| Shy | 2 | 8 | 4 | 0 |
| Koy | 1 | 10 | 10 | 0 |

### PUNT RETURNS

| Last Name | No. | Yds | Avg | TD |
|---|---|---|---|---|
| Duhon | 19 | 157 | 8 | 1 |
| Lockhart | 9 | 31 | 3 | 0 |
| Brenner | 1 | 5 | 5 | 0 |

### KICKOFF RETURNS

| Last Name | No. | Yds | Avg | TD |
|---|---|---|---|---|
| Shy | 21 | 544 | 26 | 0 |
| Duhon | 14 | 255 | 18 | 0 |
| Houston | 8 | 173 | 22 | 0 |
| R. Johnson | 5 | 140 | 28 | 0 |
| Green | 2 | 26 | 13 | 0 |
| Douglas | 1 | 16 | 16 | 0 |
| Hughes | 1 | 3 | 3 | 0 |

### PASSING — PUNTING — KICKING

| PASSING | Att | Comp | % | Yds | Yd/Att | TD | Int- | % | RK |
|---|---|---|---|---|---|---|---|---|---|
| Tarkenton | 389 | 219 | 56 | 2777 | 7.1 | 19 | 12- | 3 | 3 |
| Shiner | 12 | 9 | 75 | 87 | 7.3 | 0 | 0- | 0 | |
| Duhon | 2 | 2 | 100 | 28 | 14.0 | 0 | 0- | 0 | |

| PUNTING | No | Avg |
|---|---|---|
| B. Johnson | 43 | 39.5 |
| Koy | 11 | 33.5 |

| KICKING | XP | Att | % | FG | Att | % |
|---|---|---|---|---|---|---|
| Gogalak | 32 | 32 | 100 | 25 | 41 | 61 |

## ST. LOUIS CARDINALS

### RUSHING

| Last Name | No. | Yds | Avg | TD |
|---|---|---|---|---|
| Lane | 206 | 977 | 4.7 | 11 |
| Roland | 94 | 392 | 4.2 | 3 |
| Edwards | 70 | 350 | 5.0 | 1 |
| Shivers | 24 | 98 | 4.1 | 2 |
| Gilliam | 5 | 68 | 13.6 | 1 |
| Smith | 5 | 43 | 8.6 | 0 |
| Latourette | 2 | 38 | 19.0 | 0 |
| Hart | 18 | 18 | 1.0 | 0 |
| B. Brown | 1 | 8 | 8.0 | 0 |
| Pittman | 2 | 4 | 2.0 | 0 |
| Beathard | 2 | 2 | 1.0 | 0 |

### RECEIVING

| Last Name | No. | Yds | Avg | TD |
|---|---|---|---|---|
| Gilliam | 45 | 952 | 21 | 5 |
| Smith | 37 | 687 | 19 | 4 |
| Lane | 32 | 365 | 11 | 2 |
| D. Williams | 23 | 364 | 16 | 3 |
| Edwards | 19 | 150 | 8 | 1 |
| Roland | 17 | 96 | 6 | 1 |
| Shivers | 3 | 44 | 15 | 0 |
| Daanen | 2 | 31 | 16 | 0 |

### PUNT RETURNS

| Last Name | No. | Yds | Avg | TD |
|---|---|---|---|---|
| Latourette | 30 | 171 | 6 | 0 |
| Roland | 10 | 140 | 14 | 1 |
| Wehrli | 1 | 4 | 4 | 0 |

### KICKOFF RETURNS

| Last Name | No. | Yds | Avg | TD |
|---|---|---|---|---|
| Latourette | 13 | 254 | 20 | 0 |
| Pittman | 10 | 237 | 24 | 0 |
| Wright | 8 | 156 | 20 | 0 |
| Gilliam | 5 | 107 | 21 | 0 |
| White | 3 | 65 | 22 | 0 |
| Roland | 3 | 40 | 13 | 0 |
| Shivers | 2 | 35 | 18 | 0 |
| T. Brown | 2 | 32 | 16 | 0 |
| Wilson | 1 | 0 | 0 | 0 |

### PASSING — PUNTING — KICKING

| PASSING | Att | Comp | % | Yds | Yd/Att | TD | Int- | % | RK |
|---|---|---|---|---|---|---|---|---|---|
| Hart | 373 | 171 | 46 | 2575 | 6.9 | 14 | 18- | 5 | 9 |
| Beathard | 17 | 7 | 41 | 114 | 6.7 | 2 | 1- | 6 | |

| PUNTING | No | Avg |
|---|---|---|
| Latourette | 65 | 40.9 |

| KICKING | XP | Att | % | FG | Att | % |
|---|---|---|---|---|---|---|
| Bakken | 37 | 38 | 97 | 20 | 32 | 63 |

## WASHINGTON REDSKINS

### RUSHING

| Last Name | No. | Yds | Avg | TD |
|---|---|---|---|---|
| Brown | 237 | 1125 | 4.7 | 5 |
| Harraway | 146 | 577 | 4.0 | 5 |
| Dyer | 21 | 102 | 4.9 | 0 |
| Kopay | 13 | 49 | 3.8 | 0 |
| Jurgensen | 6 | 39 | 6.5 | 1 |
| Brunet | 9 | 37 | 4.1 | 0 |
| Smith | 2 | 29 | 14.5 | 0 |
| Bragg | 2 | 25 | 12.5 | 0 |
| Taylor | 1 | 17 | 17.0 | 0 |
| Roberts | 2 | 15 | 7.5 | 0 |
| Pierce | 5 | 6 | 1.2 | 0 |

### RECEIVING

| Last Name | No. | Yds | Avg | TD |
|---|---|---|---|---|
| Smith | 43 | 575 | 13 | 9 |
| Taylor | 42 | 593 | 14 | 8 |
| Brown | 37 | 341 | 9 | 2 |
| Roberts | 27 | 411 | 15 | 1 |
| Harraway | 24 | 136 | 6 | 0 |
| Henderson | 13 | 176 | 14 | 3 |
| Kopay | 7 | 24 | 3 | 0 |
| Dyer | 4 | 37 | 9 | 0 |
| Brunet | 3 | 28 | 9 | 0 |
| Richter | 2 | 30 | 15 | 0 |
| Pierce | 1 | 6 | 6 | 0 |

### PUNT RETURNS

| Last Name | No. | Yds | Avg | TD |
|---|---|---|---|---|
| Roberts | 10 | 28 | 3 | 0 |
| R. Harris | 14 | 10 | 1 | 0 |
| Vactor | 2 | 7 | 4 | 0 |
| Kopay | 1 | 0 | 0 | 0 |

### KICKOFF RETURNS

| Last Name | No. | Yds | Avg | TD |
|---|---|---|---|---|
| Vactor | 28 | 700 | 25 | 0 |
| R. Harris | 10 | 208 | 21 | 0 |
| J. Harris | 9 | 172 | 19 | 0 |
| Dyer | 5 | 78 | 16 | 0 |
| Hanburger | 2 | 33 | 17 | 0 |
| McKeever | 1 | 21 | 21 | 0 |
| Tillman | 1 | 10 | 10 | 0 |
| Brundige | 1 | 1 | 1 | 0 |
| Richter | 2 | 0 | 0 | 0 |
| Bass | 1 | 0 | 0 | 0 |
| Henderson | 1 | 0 | 0 | 0 |

### PASSING — PUNTING — KICKING

| PASSING | Att | Comp | % | Yds | Yd/Att | TD | Int- | % | RK |
|---|---|---|---|---|---|---|---|---|---|
| Jurgensen | 337 | 202 | 60 | 2354 | 7.0 | 23 | 10- | 3 | 2 |
| Ryan | 4 | 1 | 25 | 3 | 0.8 | 0 | 0- | 0 | |
| Bragg | 1 | 0 | 0 | 0 | 0.0 | 0 | 0- | 0 | |

| PUNTING | No | Avg |
|---|---|---|
| Bragg | 61 | 40.9 |

| KICKING | XP | Att | % | FG | Att | % |
|---|---|---|---|---|---|---|
| Knight | 33 | 34 | 97 | 20 | 27 | 74 |

## PHILADELPHIA EAGLES

### RUSHING

| Last Name | No. | Yds | Avg | TD |
|---|---|---|---|---|
| Pinder | 166 | 657 | 4.0 | 2 |
| Bouggess | 159 | 401 | 2.5 | 2 |
| Woodeshick | 52 | 254 | 4.9 | 2 |
| Watkins | 32 | 96 | 3.0 | 1 |
| H. Jones | 13 | 44 | 3.4 | 0 |
| Snead | 18 | 35 | 1.9 | 3 |
| Arrington | 4 | 33 | 8.3 | 1 |
| Bradley | 1 | 14 | 14.0 | 0 |
| Keyes | 2 | 7 | 3.5 | 0 |
| Hawkins | 2 | 3 | 1.5 | 0 |
| Jackson | 1 | -5 | -5.0 | 0 |

### RECEIVING

| Last Name | No. | Yds | Avg | TD |
|---|---|---|---|---|
| Bouggess | 50 | 401 | 8 | 2 |
| Ballman | 47 | 601 | 13 | 3 |
| Jackson | 41 | 613 | 15 | 5 |
| Hawkins | 30 | 612 | 20 | 4 |
| Pinder | 28 | 249 | 9 | 0 |
| Zabel | 8 | 119 | 15 | 1 |
| Woodeshick | 6 | 28 | 5 | 0 |
| Hill | 3 | 10 | 3 | 1 |
| Watkins | 3 | 6 | 2 | 0 |
| H. Jones | 1 | 12 | 12 | 0 |
| Walik | 1 | 0 | 0 | 0 |

### PUNT RETURNS

| Last Name | No. | Yds | Avg | TD |
|---|---|---|---|---|
| Walik | 20 | 78 | 4 | 0 |
| Hawkins | 10 | 16 | 2 | 0 |
| Hayes | 2 | 6 | 3 | 0 |

### KICKOFF RETURNS

| Last Name | No. | Yds | Avg | TD |
|---|---|---|---|---|
| Walik | 32 | 805 | 25 | 0 |
| Nelson | 10 | 187 | 19 | 0 |
| Hayes | 6 | 107 | 18 | 0 |
| R. Jones | 6 | 97 | 16 | 0 |
| H. Jones | 2 | 23 | 12 | 0 |
| Rossovich | 1 | 22 | 22 | 0 |
| Pettigrew | 1 | 11 | 11 | 0 |
| Hawkins | 1 | 0 | 0 | 0 |

### PASSING — PUNTING — KICKING

| PASSING | Att | Comp | % | Yds | Yd/Att | TD | Int- | % | RK |
|---|---|---|---|---|---|---|---|---|---|
| Snead | 335 | 181 | 54 | 2323 | 6.9 | 15 | 20- | 6 | 7 |
| Arrington | 73 | 37 | 51 | 328 | 4.5 | 1 | 3- | 4 | |
| Ballman | 1 | 0 | 0 | 0 | 0.0 | 0 | 0- | 0 | |
| Bouggess | 1 | 0 | 0 | 0 | 0.0 | 0 | 0- | 0 | |

| PUNTING | No | Avg |
|---|---|---|
| Bradley | 61 | 36.8 |
| Moseley | 10 | 35.0 |

| KICKING | XP | Att | % | FG | Att | % |
|---|---|---|---|---|---|---|
| Moseley | 25 | 28 | 89 | 14 | 25 | 56 |

## MINNESOTA VIKINGS 12-2-0  Bud Grant

| Scores of Each Game | | | Use Name | Pos. | Hgt | Wgt | Age | Int | Pts |
|---|---|---|---|---|---|---|---|---|---|
| 27 | KANSAS CITY | 10 | Grady Alderman | OT | 6'2" | 245 | 31 | | |
| 26 | NEW ORLEANS | 0 | Doug Davis | OT | 6'4" | 255 | 26 | | |
| 10 | Green Bay | 13 | Steve Smith | OT | 6'5" | 250 | 26 | | |
| 24 | Chicago | 0 | Ron Yary | OT | 6'6" | 255 | 24 | | |
| 54 | DALLAS | 13 | Milt Sunde | OG | 6'2" | 250 | 27 | | |
| 13 | LOS ANGELES | 3 | Jim Vellone | OG | 6'2" | 255 | 26 | | |
| 30 | Detroit | 17 | Ed White | OG | 6'2" | 260 | 23 | | |
| 19 | Washington | 10 | Mick Tingelhoff | C | 6'1" | 237 | 30 | | |
| 24 | DETROIT | 20 | Carl Eller | DE | 6'6" | 250 | 28 | | |
| 10 | GREEN BAY | 3 | Jim Marshall | DE | 6'3" | 248 | 32 | | |
| 10 | N. Y. Jets | 20 | John Ward | DE | 6'4" | 260 | 22 | | |
| 16 | CHICAGO | 13 | Paul Dickson | DT | 6'5" | 250 | 33 | | |
| 35 | Boston | 14 | Gary Larsen | DT | 6'5" | 260 | 30 | | |
| 37 | Atlanta | 7 | Alan Page | DT | 6'5" | 245 | 25 | 1 | 6 |

| Use Name | Pos. | Hgt | Wgt | Age | Int | Pts |
|---|---|---|---|---|---|---|
| Jim Hargrove | LB | 6'3" | 235 | 25 | | |
| Wally Hilgenberg | LB | 6'3" | 230 | 27 | 2 | |
| Mike McGill | LB | 6'2" | 235 | 23 | | 6 |
| Wayne Meylan | LB | 6'1" | 235 | 24 | | |
| Lonnie Warwick | LB | 6'3" | 237 | 28 | 3 | |
| Roy Winston | LB | 6'1" | 228 | 30 | 1 | 6 |
| Bobby Bryant | DB | 6' | 170 | 26 | 3 | 6 |
| John Charles | DB | 6'1" | 200 | 26 | 1 | |
| Dale Hackbart | DB | 6'3" | 205 | 34 | | |
| Karl Kassulke | DB | 6' | 195 | 28 | 3 | |
| Paul Krause | DB | 6'3" | 188 | 28 | 6 | |
| Ted Provost | DB | 6'2" | 195 | 22 | | |
| Ed Sharockman | DB | 6' | 200 | 30 | 7 | 18 |
| Charlie West | DB | 6'1" | 190 | 24 | 1 | |

Billy Harris — Injury

| Use Name | Pos. | Hgt | Wgt | Age | Int | Pts |
|---|---|---|---|---|---|---|
| Bill Cappleman | QB | 6'3" | 210 | 23 | | |
| Gary Cuozzo | QB | 6'1" | 195 | 29 | | |
| Bob Lee | QB | 6'2" | 195 | 24 | | 6 |
| Clint Jones | HB | 6' | 206 | 25 | | 54 |
| Dave Osborn | HB | 6' | 205 | 27 | | 36 |
| Bill Brown | FB | 5'11" | 230 | 32 | | 12 |
| Jim Lindsey | HB-FB | 6'2" | 210 | 25 | | 6 |
| Oscar Reed | HB-FB | 5'11" | 222 | 26 | | 6 |
| Bob Grim | WR | 6' | 200 | 25 | | |
| John Henderson | WR | 6'3" | 190 | 27 | | 12 |
| Gene Washington | WR | 6'3" | 208 | 26 | | 24 |
| John Beasley | TE | 6'3" | 233 | 25 | | 12 |
| Kent Kramer | TE | 6'5" | 235 | 26 | | |
| Stu Voigt | TE | 6'1" | 220 | 22 | | |
| Fred Cox | K | 5'10" | 200 | 31 | | 125 |
| Tom McNeill | K | 6'1" | 195 | 28 | | |

## DETROIT LIONS 10-4-0  Joe Schmidt

| Scores of Each Game | | | Use Name | Pos. | Hgt | Wgt | Age | Int | Pts |
|---|---|---|---|---|---|---|---|---|---|
| 40 | Green Bay | 0 | Rocky Freitas | OT | 6'6" | 280 | 24 | | |
| 38 | CINCINNATI | 3 | Roger Shoals | OT | 6'4" | 260 | 31 | | |
| 28 | CHICAGO | 14 | Jim Yarbrough | OT | 6'6" | 250 | 23 | | |
| 10 | Washington | 31 | Frank Gallagher | OG | 6'2" | 245 | 27 | | |
| 41 | Cleveland | 24 | Bob Kowalkowski | OG | 6'3" | 240 | 26 | | |
| 16 | Chicago | 10 | Rocky Rasley | OG | 6'3" | 250 | 23 | | |
| 17 | MINNESOTA | 30 | Chuck Walton | OG | 6'3" | 255 | 29 | | |
| 17 | New Orleans | 19 | Bill Cottrell | C | 6'3" | 255 | 25 | | |
| 20 | Minnesota | 24 | Ed Flanagan | C | 6'3" | 245 | 26 | | |
| 28 | SAN FRANCISCO | 7 | Larry Hand | DE | 6'4" | 250 | 30 | 1 | 6 |
| 28 | OAKLAND | 14 | Jim Mitchell | DE | 6'3" | 245 | 21 | | |
| 16 | ST. LOUIS | 3 | Joe Robb | DE | 6'3" | 245 | 33 | | |
| 28 | Los Angeles | 23 | Dan Goich | DT | 6'4" | 265 | 26 | | |
| 20 | GREEN BAY | 0 | Dave Haverdick | DT | 6'4" | 245 | 22 | | |
| | | | Alex Karras | DT | 6'2" | 245 | 34 | | |
| | | | Jerry Rush | DT | 6'4" | 265 | 28 | | |

| Use Name | Pos. | Hgt | Wgt | Age | Int | Pts |
|---|---|---|---|---|---|---|
| Mike Lucci | LB | 6'2" | 230 | 30 | 2 | |
| Ed Mooney | LB | 6'2" | 225 | 25 | | |
| Paul Naumoff | LB | 6'1" | 215 | 25 | | |
| Bill Saul | LB | 6'4" | 225 | 29 | | |
| Wayne Walker | LB | 6'2" | 228 | 33 | | |
| Lem Barney | DB | 6' | 188 | 24 | 7 | 18 |
| Dick LeBeau | DB | 6'1" | 185 | 33 | 9 | |
| Wayne Rasmussen | DB | 6'2" | 180 | 28 | 2 | |
| Tom Vaughn | DB | 5'11" | 190 | 27 | 1 | |
| Mike Weger | DB | 6'2" | 200 | 24 | 5 | 6 |
| Bobby Williams | DB | 6'1" | 200 | 28 | 1 | 6 |

| Use Name | Pos. | Hgt | Wgt | Age | Int | Pts |
|---|---|---|---|---|---|---|
| Greg Landry | QB | 6'4" | 205 | 23 | | 6 |
| Bill Munson | QB | 6'2" | 210 | 28 | | |
| Nick Eddy | HB | 6'1" | 207 | 26 | | 6 |
| Altie Taylor | HB | 5'10" | 196 | 22 | | 24 |
| Mel Farr | FB-HB | 6'2" | 210 | 25 | | 66 |
| Steve Owens | FB | 6'2" | 220 | 22 | | 12 |
| Bill Triplett | FB | 6'2" | 215 | 31 | | 6 |
| Bruce Maxwell | HB-FB | 6'1" | 220 | 23 | | |
| Charlie Brown | WR | 6'2" | 195 | 21 | | |
| Chuck Hughes | WR | 5'11" | 175 | 27 | | |
| Earl McCullouch | WR | 5'11" | 175 | 24 | | 24 |
| Phil Odle | WR | 5'11" | 195 | 27 | | |
| Larry Walton | WR | 5'11" | 180 | 23 | | 30 |
| John Wright | WR | 6' | 197 | 23 | | |
| Craig Cotton | TE | 6'4" | 222 | 23 | | |
| Charlie Sanders | TE | 6'4" | 235 | 24 | | 36 |
| Errol Mann | K | 6' | 200 | 29 | | 101 |
| Herman Weaver | K | 6'4" | 210 | 21 | | |

## CHICAGO BEARS 6-8-0  Jim Dooley

| Scores of Each Game | | | Use Name | Pos. | Hgt | Wgt | Age | Int | Pts |
|---|---|---|---|---|---|---|---|---|---|
| 24 | N. Y. Giants | 16 | Jeff Curchin | OT | 6'6" | 265 | 22 | | |
| 20 | PHILADELPHIA | 16 | Randy Jackson | OT | 6'5" | 245 | 26 | | |
| 14 | Detroit | 28 | Wayne Mass | OT | 6'4" | 240 | 24 | | |
| 0 | MINNESOTA | 24 | Jim Cadile | OG | 6'3" | 240 | 29 | | |
| 7 | SAN DIEGO | 20 | Glenn Holloway | OG | 6'3" | 245 | 21 | | |
| 10 | DETROIT | 16 | Howard Mudd | OG | 6'3" | 252 | 28 | | |
| 23 | Atlanta | 14 | Ted Wheeler | OG | 6'3" | 245 | 24 | | |
| 16 | SAN FRANCISCO | 37 | Bob Hyland | C | 6'5" | 250 | 25 | | |
| 19 | Green Bay | 20 | Harry Gunner | DE | 6'6" | 250 | 25 | | |
| 31 | BUFFALO | 13 | Ed O'Bradovich | DE | 6'3" | 255 | 26 | | |
| 20 | Baltimore | 21 | Willie Holman | DT-DE | 6'4" | 250 | 25 | | |
| 13 | Minnesota | 16 | Dave Hale | DT | 6'7" | 260 | 23 | | |
| 35 | GREEN BAY | 17 | George Seals | DT | 6'2" | 260 | 27 | 1 | |
| 24 | New Orleans | 3 | Bill Staley | DT | 6'3" | 248 | 23 | | |

| Use Name | Pos. | Hgt | Wgt | Age | Int | Pts |
|---|---|---|---|---|---|---|
| Ross Brupbacher | LB | 6'3" | 215 | 22 | 2 | |
| Doug Buffone | LB | 6'1" | 225 | 26 | 4 | |
| Dick Butkus | LB | 6'3" | 245 | 26 | 3 | |
| Lee Roy Caffey | LB | 6'3" | 250 | 30 | | |
| Jimmy Gunn | LB | 6'1" | 220 | 21 | | |
| John Neidert | LB | 6'2" | 230 | 24 | | |
| Phil Clark | DB | 6'2" | 208 | 25 | 1 | |
| Dick Daniels | DB | 5'9" | 180 | 24 | 2 | |
| Butch Davis | DB | 5'11" | 183 | 22 | 1 | |
| Bennie McRae | DB | 6'1" | 180 | 29 | 1 | |
| Ron Smith | DB | 6'1" | 192 | 27 | | |
| Joe Taylor | DB | 6'2" | 200 | 29 | 2 | |
| Garry Lyle | HB-DB | 6'2" | 198 | 24 | | |

Brian Piccolo — Died 6-16-70 — cancer

| Use Name | Pos. | Hgt | Wgt | Age | Int | Pts |
|---|---|---|---|---|---|---|
| Jack Concannon | QB | 6'3" | 205 | 27 | | 12 |
| Bobby Douglass | QB | 6'3" | 215 | 23 | | |
| Kent Nix | QB | 6'1" | 195 | 26 | | |
| Craig Baynham | HB | 6'1" | 203 | 26 | | |
| Gale Sayers | HB | 6' | 198 | 27 | | |
| Don Shy (from NO) | FB-HB | 6'1" | 205 | 24 | | 6 |
| Ronnie Bull | FB | 6'3" | 220 | 25 | | |
| Mike Hull | FB | 6'2" | 210 | 25 | | |
| Ralph Kurek | FB | 6'3" | 220 | 27 | | |
| Ross Montgomery | WR | 5'11" | 170 | 22 | | |
| Linzy Cole | WR | 6'4" | 210 | 22 | | 12 |
| George Farmer | WR | 5'11" | 190 | 25 | | 78 |
| Dick Gordon | WR | 6'4" | 210 | 23 | | 24 |
| Jim Seymour | WR | 5'10" | 176 | 26 | | 24 |
| Cecil Turner | TE | 6'4" | 250 | 25 | | |
| Jim Hester | TE | 6'5" | 225 | 27 | | 6 |
| Ray Ogden | TE | 6'3" | 211 | 24 | | |
| Bob Wallace | C-TE | 6'3" | 238 | 25 | | 6 |
| Rich Coady | K | 5'11" | 175 | 32 | | |
| Bobby Joe Green | K | 6'4" | 220 | 30 | | 88 |
| Mac Percival | | | | | | |

## GREEN BAY PACKERS 6-8-0  Phil Bengtson

| Scores of Each Game | | | Use Name | Pos. | Hgt | Wgt | Age | Int | Pts |
|---|---|---|---|---|---|---|---|---|---|
| 0 | DETROIT | 40 | Forrest Gregg | OT | 6'4" | 250 | 37 | | |
| 27 | ATLANTA | 24 | Bill Hayhoe | OT | 6'8" | 258 | 23 | | |
| 13 | MINNESOTA | 10 | Dick Himes | OT | 6'4" | 244 | 24 | | |
| 22 | San Diego | 20 | Francis Peay | OT | 6'5" | 250 | 26 | | |
| 21 | LOS ANGELES | 31 | Dave Bradley | OG | 6'4" | 245 | 23 | | |
| 30 | PHILADELPHIA | 17 | Gale Gillingham | OG | 6'3" | 255 | 26 | | |
| 10 | San Francisco | 26 | Bill Lueck | OG | 6'3" | 235 | 24 | | |
| 10 | BALTIMORE | 13 | Ken Bowman | C | 6'3" | 230 | 27 | | |
| 20 | CHICAGO | 19 | Malcolm Walker | OT-C | 6'4" | 250 | 27 | | |
| 3 | Minnesota | 10 | Lionel Aldridge | DE | 6'4" | 245 | 28 | | |
| 3 | Dallas | 16 | Marty Amsler | DE | 6'5" | 255 | 27 | | |
| 20 | Pittsburgh | 12 | Bob Brown | DE | 6'5" | 260 | 30 | | |
| 17 | Chicago | 35 | Clarence Williams | DE | 6'5" | 255 | 23 | | |
| 0 | Detroit | 20 | Kevin Hardy | DT | 6'5" | 260 | 25 | | |
| | | | Mike McCoy | DT | 6'5" | 284 | 21 | | |
| | | | Rich Moore | DT | 6'6" | 285 | 23 | | |

| Use Name | Pos. | Hgt | Wgt | Age | Int | Pts |
|---|---|---|---|---|---|---|
| Fred Carr | LB | 6'5" | 238 | 24 | 2 | |
| Jim Carter | LB | 6'3" | 235 | 21 | | |
| Jim Flanigan | LB | 6'3" | 240 | 25 | | |
| Rudy Kuechenberg | LB | 6'2" | 215 | 27 | | |
| Ray Nitschke | LB | 6'3" | 240 | 29 | 2 | |
| Dave Robinson | LB | 6'3" | 235 | 34 | | |
| Cleo Walker | C-LB | 6'3" | 220 | 22 | | |
| Ken Ellis | DB | 5'10" | 190 | 22 | 3 | |
| Lee Harden | DB | 6' | 190 | 31 | 3 | 6 |
| Doug Hart | DB | 6' | 190 | 31 | 3 | 6 |
| Ervin Hunt | DB | 6'2" | 190 | 23 | | |
| Bob Jeter | DB | 6'1" | 205 | 32 | 3 | |
| Al Matthews | DB | 5'11" | 190 | 22 | | |
| Willie Wood | DB | 5'10" | 190 | 34 | 7 | |

Zeke Bratkowski — Voluntarily Retired
Boyd Dowler — Voluntarily Retired

| Use Name | Pos. | Hgt | Wgt | Age | Int | Pts |
|---|---|---|---|---|---|---|
| Don Horn | QB | 6'2" | 195 | 25 | | |
| Rick Norton | QB | 6'1" | 190 | 26 | | |
| Frank Patrick | QB | 6'7" | 225 | 23 | | |
| Bart Starr | QB | 6'1" | 190 | 37 | | 6 |
| Donny Anderson | HB | 6'3" | 210 | 27 | | 30 |
| Larry Krause | HB | 6' | 208 | 22 | | 6 |
| Travis Williams | HB | 6'1" | 210 | 24 | | 12 |
| Jim Grabowski | FB | 6'2" | 220 | 26 | | 6 |
| Perry Williams | FB | 6'2" | 220 | 23 | | |
| Dave Hampton | HB-FB | 6' | 210 | 23 | | 6 |
| Mike Carter | WR | 6'1" | 210 | 22 | | |
| Jack Clancy | WR | 6'1" | 195 | 26 | | 12 |
| Carroll Dale | WR | 6'1" | 200 | 32 | | 12 |
| John Spilis | WR | 6'3" | 205 | 22 | | |
| John Hilton | TE | 6'5" | 225 | 28 | | 12 |
| Rich McGeorge | TE | 6'4" | 235 | 21 | | 6 |
| Dale Livingston | K | 6' | 210 | 25 | | 64 |

## MINNESOTA VIKINGS

### RUSHING
| Last Name | No. | Yds | Avg | TD |
|---|---|---|---|---|
| Osborn | 207 | 681 | 3.3 | 5 |
| Jones | 120 | 369 | 3.1 | 9 |
| Brown | 101 | 324 | 3.2 | 0 |
| Reed | 42 | 132 | 3.1 | 1 |
| Cuozzo | 17 | 61 | 3.6 | 0 |
| Lindsey | 11 | 47 | 4.3 | 0 |
| Lee | 10 | 20 | 2.0 | 1 |

### RECEIVING
| Last Name | No. | Yds | Avg | TD |
|---|---|---|---|---|
| Washington | 44 | 702 | 16 | 4 |
| Henderson | 31 | 527 | 17 | 2 |
| Grim | 23 | 287 | 12 | 0 |
| Osborn | 23 | 202 | 9 | 1 |
| Beasley | 17 | 237 | 14 | 2 |
| Brown | 15 | 149 | 10 | 2 |
| Jones | 9 | 117 | 13 | 0 |
| Reed | 6 | 53 | 9 | 0 |
| Lindsey | 4 | 94 | 24 | 1 |
| Kramer | 1 | 10 | 10 | 0 |

### PUNT RETURNS
| Last Name | No. | Yds | Avg | TD |
|---|---|---|---|---|
| West | 29 | 169 | 6 | 0 |
| Grim | 5 | 46 | 9 | 0 |
| Dickson | 1 | 1 | 1 | 0 |

### KICKOFF RETURNS
| Last Name | No. | Yds | Avg | TD |
|---|---|---|---|---|
| Jones | 19 | 452 | 24 | 0 |
| West | 11 | 319 | 29 | 0 |
| Reed | 5 | 71 | 14 | 0 |
| Smith | 1 | 0 | 0 | 0 |

### PASSING – PUNTING – KICKING
**PASSING**
| Last Name | Att | Comp | % | Yds | Yd/Att | TD | Int– | % | RK |
|---|---|---|---|---|---|---|---|---|---|
| Cuozzo | 257 | 128 | 50 | 1720 | 6.7 | 7 | 10– | 4 | 9 |
| Lee | 79 | 40 | 51 | 610 | 7.7 | 5 | 5– | 6 | |
| Cappleman | 7 | 4 | 57 | 49 | 7.0 | 0 | 0– | 0 | |
| Cox | 1 | 1 | 100 | -1 | -1.0 | 0 | 0– | 0 | |

**PUNTING**
| Last Name | No | Avg |
|---|---|---|
| McNeill | 61 | 37.9 |

**KICKING**
| Last Name | XP | Att | % | FG | Att | % |
|---|---|---|---|---|---|---|
| Cox | 35 | 35 | 100 | 30 | 46 | 65 |

## DETROIT LIONS

### RUSHING
| Last Name | No. | Yds | Avg | TD |
|---|---|---|---|---|
| Farr | 166 | 717 | 4.3 | 9 |
| Taylor | 198 | 666 | 3.4 | 2 |
| Landry | 35 | 350 | 10.0 | 1 |
| Triplett | 48 | 156 | 3.3 | 1 |
| Owens | 36 | 122 | 3.4 | 2 |
| Eddy | 18 | 47 | 2.6 | 1 |
| Munson | 9 | 33 | 3.7 | 0 |
| L. Walton | 2 | 20 | 10.0 | 0 |
| Maxwell | 1 | 9 | 9.0 | 0 |
| McCullouch | 1 | 7 | 7.0 | 0 |

### RECEIVING
| Last Name | No. | Yds | Avg | TD |
|---|---|---|---|---|
| Sanders | 40 | 544 | 14 | 6 |
| L. Walton | 30 | 532 | 18 | 5 |
| Farr | 29 | 213 | 7 | 2 |
| Taylor | 27 | 261 | 10 | 2 |
| McCullouch | 15 | 278 | 19 | 4 |
| Hughes | 8 | 162 | 20 | 0 |
| Triplett | 6 | 52 | 9 | 0 |
| Eddy | 4 | 22 | 6 | 0 |
| Owens | 4 | 21 | 5 | 0 |
| Brown | 2 | 38 | 19 | 0 |
| Cotton | 1 | 6 | 6 | 0 |
| Freitas | 1 | -8 | -8 | 0 |

### PUNT RETURNS
| Last Name | No. | Yds | Avg | TD |
|---|---|---|---|---|
| Barney | 25 | 259 | 10 | 1 |
| Eddy | 4 | 25 | 6 | 0 |
| Vaughn | 3 | 22 | 7 | 0 |
| L. Walton | 2 | 0 | 0 | 0 |

### KICKOFF RETURNS
| Last Name | No. | Yds | Avg | TD |
|---|---|---|---|---|
| Williams | 25 | 544 | 22 | 1 |
| Eddy | 7 | 168 | 24 | 0 |
| Barney | 2 | 96 | 48 | 0 |
| Vaughn | 3 | 66 | 22 | 0 |
| Owens | 1 | 26 | 26 | 0 |
| L. Walton | 1 | 21 | 21 | 0 |
| Maxwell | 1 | 20 | 20 | 0 |
| Mooney | 1 | 12 | 12 | 0 |
| Naumoff | 2 | 6 | 3 | 0 |

### PASSING – PUNTING – KICKING
**PASSING**
| Last Name | Att | Comp | % | Yds | Yd/Att | TD | Int– | % | RK |
|---|---|---|---|---|---|---|---|---|---|
| Munson | 158 | 84 | 53 | 1049 | 6.6 | 10 | 7– | 4 | 8 |
| Landry | 136 | 83 | 61 | 1072 | 7.9 | 9 | 5– | 4 | |

**PUNTING**
| Last Name | No | Avg |
|---|---|---|
| Weaver | 62 | 40.0 |

**KICKING**
| Last Name | XP | Att | % | FG | Att | % |
|---|---|---|---|---|---|---|
| Mann | 41 | 41 | 100 | 20 | 29 | 69 |

## CHICAGO BEARS

### RUSHING
| Last Name | No. | Yds | Avg | TD |
|---|---|---|---|---|
| Montgomery | 62 | 229 | 3.7 | 0 |
| Shy | 79 | 227 | 2.9 | 1 |
| Bull | 68 | 214 | 3.1 | 0 |
| Concannon | 42 | 136 | 3.2 | 2 |
| Hull | 32 | 99 | 3.1 | 0 |
| Baynham | 26 | 68 | 2.6 | 0 |
| Sayers | 23 | 52 | 2.3 | 0 |
| Kurek | 6 | 24 | 4.0 | 0 |
| Douglass | 7 | 22 | 3.1 | 0 |
| Gordon | 4 | 17 | 4.3 | 0 |
| Green | 1 | 7 | 7.0 | 0 |
| Turner | 3 | -3 | -1.0 | 0 |

### RECEIVING
| Last Name | No. | Yds | Avg | TD |
|---|---|---|---|---|
| Gordon | 71 | 1026 | 14 | 13 |
| Farmer | 31 | 496 | 16 | 2 |
| Wallace | 15 | 160 | 11 | 0 |
| Montgomery | 14 | 75 | 5 | 0 |
| Bull | 13 | 60 | 5 | 0 |
| Hull | 13 | 44 | 3 | 0 |
| Baynham | 12 | 43 | 4 | 0 |
| Shy | 10 | 149 | 15 | 0 |
| Hester | 7 | 54 | 8 | 0 |
| Seymour | 6 | 145 | 24 | 4 |
| Coady | 6 | 44 | 7 | 1 |
| Cole | 3 | 47 | 16 | 0 |
| Kurek | 3 | 11 | 4 | 0 |
| Turner | 2 | 53 | 27 | 0 |
| Percival | 1 | 19 | 19 | 0 |
| Ogden | 1 | 6 | 6 | 1 |
| Lyle | 1 | 5 | 5 | 0 |
| Sayers | 1 | -6 | -6 | 0 |

### PUNT RETURNS
| Last Name | No. | Yds | Avg | TD |
|---|---|---|---|---|
| Smith | 33 | 126 | 4 | 0 |
| Cole | 14 | 83 | 6 | 0 |
| Lyle | 9 | 37 | 4 | 0 |
| Turner | 1 | 0 | 0 | 0 |

### KICKOFF RETURNS
| Last Name | No. | Yds | Avg | TD |
|---|---|---|---|---|
| Turner | 23 | 752 | 33 | 4 |
| Smith | 28 | 651 | 23 | 0 |
| Montgomery | 4 | 69 | 17 | 0 |
| Butkus | 1 | 0 | 0 | 0 |

### PASSING – PUNTING – KICKING
**PASSING**
| Last Name | Att | Comp | % | Yds | Yd/Att | TD | Int– | % | RK |
|---|---|---|---|---|---|---|---|---|---|
| Concannon | 385 | 194 | 50 | 2130 | 5.5 | 16 | 18– | 5 | 9 |
| Douglass | 30 | 12 | 40 | 218 | 7.3 | 4 | 3– | 10 | |
| Bull | 4 | 2 | 50 | 46 | 11.5 | 1 | 1– | 25 | |
| Green | 2 | 2 | 100 | 37 | 18.5 | 0 | 0– | 0 | |
| Nix | 1 | 0 | 0 | 0 | 0.0 | 0 | 0– | 0 | |

**PUNTING**
| Last Name | No | Avg |
|---|---|---|
| Green | 83 | 40.9 |
| Lyle | 1 | 29.0 |

**KICKING**
| Last Name | XP | Att | % | FG | Att | % |
|---|---|---|---|---|---|---|
| Percival | 28 | 28 | 100 | 20 | 34 | 59 |

## GREEN BAY PACKERS

### RUSHING
| Last Name | No. | Yds | Avg | TD |
|---|---|---|---|---|
| Anderson | 222 | 853 | 3.8 | 5 |
| T. Williams | 74 | 276 | 3.7 | 1 |
| Grabowski | 67 | 210 | 3.1 | 1 |
| Hampton | 48 | 115 | 2.4 | 0 |
| Starr | 12 | 62 | 5.2 | 1 |
| P. Williams | 17 | 44 | 2.6 | 0 |
| Krause | 2 | 13 | 6.5 | 0 |
| Dale | 2 | 9 | 4.5 | 0 |
| Patrick | 2 | 5 | 2.5 | 0 |
| Horn | 5 | 4 | 0.8 | 0 |
| McGeorge | 1 | 3 | 3.0 | 0 |
| Livingston | 1 | 1 | 1.0 | 0 |

### RECEIVING
| Last Name | No. | Yds | Avg | TD |
|---|---|---|---|---|
| Dale | 49 | 814 | 17 | 2 |
| Anderson | 36 | 414 | 12 | 0 |
| Hilton | 25 | 350 | 14 | 4 |
| Grabowski | 19 | 83 | 4 | 0 |
| Clancy | 16 | 244 | 15 | 2 |
| T. Williams | 12 | 127 | 11 | 1 |
| Hampton | 7 | 23 | 3 | 0 |
| Spilis | 6 | 76 | 13 | 0 |
| P. Williams | 3 | 11 | 4 | 0 |
| McGeorge | 2 | 32 | 16 | 2 |
| Krause | 2 | 22 | 11 | 0 |

### PUNT RETURNS
| Last Name | No. | Yds | Avg | TD |
|---|---|---|---|---|
| Wood | 11 | 58 | 5 | 0 |
| Ellis | 7 | 27 | 4 | 0 |
| T. Williams | 4 | 20 | 5 | 0 |
| C. Williams | 1 | 0 | 0 | 0 |
| Harden | 2 | -7 | -4 | 0 |

### KICKOFF RETURNS
| Last Name | No. | Yds | Avg | TD |
|---|---|---|---|---|
| Krause | 18 | 513 | 29 | 1 |
| Ellis | 22 | 451 | 21 | 0 |
| T. Williams | 10 | 203 | 20 | 0 |
| Hampton | 6 | 188 | 31 | 1 |
| McCoy | 3 | 22 | 7 | 0 |
| Gregg | 2 | 21 | 11 | 0 |
| P. Williams | 1 | 20 | 20 | 0 |
| Himes | 1 | 4 | 4 | 0 |

### PASSING – PUNTING – KICKING
**PASSING**
| Last Name | Att | Comp | % | Yds | Yd/Att | TD | Int– | % | RK |
|---|---|---|---|---|---|---|---|---|---|
| Starr | 255 | 140 | 55 | 1645 | 6.5 | 3 | 13– | 5 | 1 |
| Horn | 76 | 28 | 37 | 428 | 5.6 | 2 | 10– | 13 | |
| Patrick | 14 | 6 | 43 | 59 | 4.2 | 0 | 1– | 7 | |
| Norton | 5 | 3 | 60 | 64 | 12.8 | 0 | 0– | 0 | |
| Anderson | 1 | 0 | 0 | 0 | 0.0 | 0 | 0– | 0 | |

**PUNTING**
| Last Name | No | Avg |
|---|---|---|
| Anderson | 81 | 40.8 |
| Livingston | 6 | 33.2 |

**KICKING**
| Last Name | XP | Att | % | FG | Att | % |
|---|---|---|---|---|---|---|
| Livingston | 19 | 21 | 90 | 15 | 28 | 54 |

## SAN FRANCISCO FORTY NINERS 10-3-1 Dick Nolan

### Scores of Each Game

| | | | |
|---|---|---|---|
| 26 | WASHINGTON | 17 | |
| 34 | CLEVELAND | 31 | |
| 20 | Atlanta | 21 | |
| 20 | Los Angeles | 6 | |
| 20 | NEW ORLEANS | 20 | |
| 19 | DENVER | 14 | |
| 26 | GREEN BAY | 10 | |
| 37 | Chicago | 16 | |
| 30 | Houston | 20 | |
| 7 | Detroit | 28 | |
| 13 | LOS ANGELES | 30 | |
| 24 | ATLANTA | 20 | |
| 38 | New Orleans | 27 | |
| 38 | Oakland | 7 | |

| Use Name | Pos. | Hgt | Wgt | Age | Int | Pts |
|---|---|---|---|---|---|---|
| Cas Banaszek | OT | 6'3" | 250 | 24 | | |
| Len Rohde | OT | 6'4" | 250 | 32 | | |
| Randy Beisler | OG-OT | 6'4" | 255 | 25 | | |
| Elmer Collett | OG | 6'4" | 240 | 25 | | |
| Bob Hoskins | OG | 6'2" | 235 | 24 | | |
| Woody Peoples | OG | 6'2" | 247 | 27 | | |
| Forrest Blue | C | 6'5" | 260 | 24 | | |
| Bill Belk | DE | 6'3" | 254 | 24 | | |
| Cedrick Hardman | DE | 6'3" | 255 | 21 | | |
| Tommy Hart | DE | 6'3" | 250 | 25 | | 1 |
| Stan Hindman | DE | 6'3" | 235 | 26 | | |
| Earl Edwards | DT | 6'6" | 265 | 24 | | |
| Charlie Krueger | DT | 6'4" | 270 | 34 | | |
| Roland Lakes | DT | 6'4" | 268 | 30 | | |
| Sam Silas | DE-DT | 6'4" | 255 | 27 | | |

| Use Name | Pos. | Hgt | Wgt | Age | Int | Pts |
|---|---|---|---|---|---|---|
| Ed Beard | LB | 6'2" | 220 | 30 | | |
| Carter Campbell | LB | 6'3" | 214 | 22 | | |
| Frank Nunley | LB | 6'2" | 220 | 24 | 3 | |
| Jim Sniadecki | LB | 6'2" | 220 | 23 | | |
| Skip Vanderbundt | LB | 6'3" | 234 | 23 | 3 | |
| Dave Wilcox | LB | 6'3" | 237 | 27 | 2 | |
| Johnny Fuller | DB | 6' | 175 | 24 | 1 | |
| Jim Johnson | DB | 6'2" | 184 | 32 | 2 | 8 |
| Mel Phillips | DB | 6' | 192 | 28 | 3 | 6 |
| Al Randolph | DB | 6'2" | 200 | 26 | 1 | 2 |
| Mike Simpson | DB | 5'11" | 175 | 23 | | |
| Bruce Taylor | DB | 6' | 180 | 22 | 3 | 6 |
| Rosey Taylor | DB | 5'11" | 186 | 31 | 3 | |

| Use Name | Pos. | Hgt | Wgt | Age | Int | Pts |
|---|---|---|---|---|---|---|
| John Brodie | QB | 6'1" | 203 | 35 | | 12 |
| Steve Spurrier | QB | 6'2" | 203 | 25 | | |
| Doug Cunningham | HB | 5'11" | 190 | 24 | | 18 |
| John Isenbarger | HB | 6'3" | 205 | 22 | | 6 |
| Jim Strong | HB | 6'1" | 204 | 23 | | |
| Jimmy Thomas | WR-HB | 6'1" | 216 | 23 | | 18 |
| Ken Willard | FB | 6'2" | 225 | 27 | | 60 |
| Bill Tucker | HB-FB | 6'2" | 216 | 26 | | 12 |
| Lee Johnson | WR | 6'1" | 204 | 25 | | |
| Preston Riley | WR | 6' | 180 | 22 | | |
| Gene Washington | WR | 6'1" | 186 | 23 | | 72 |
| Dick Witcher | WR | 6'3" | 204 | 25 | | 12 |
| Ted Kwalick | TE | 6'4" | 230 | 23 | | 6 |
| Bob Windsor | TE | 6'4" | 230 | 27 | | 12 |
| Bruce Gossett | K | 6'2" | 225 | 27 | | 102 |

## LOS ANGELES RAMS 9-4-1 George Allen

| | | | |
|---|---|---|---|
| 34 | ST. LOUIS | 13 | |
| 19 | Buffalo | 0 | |
| 37 | SAN DIEGO | 10 | |
| 6 | SAN FRANCISCO | 20 | |
| 31 | Green Bay | 21 | |
| 3 | Minnesota | 13 | |
| 30 | New Orleans | 17 | |
| 20 | ATLANTA | 10 | |
| 20 | N.Y. JETS | 31 | |
| 17 | Atlanta | 7 | |
| 30 | San Francisco | 13 | |
| 34 | NEW ORLEANS | 16 | |
| 23 | DETROIT | 28 | |
| 31 | N.Y. Giants | 3 | |

| Use Name | Pos. | Hgt | Wgt | Age | Int | Pts |
|---|---|---|---|---|---|---|
| Bob Brown | OT | 6'4" | 290 | 27 | | |
| Charley Cowan | OT | 6'4" | 265 | 32 | | |
| Mitch Johnson | OT | 6'4" | 260 | 28 | | |
| Tom Mack | OG | 6'3" | 250 | 26 | | |
| Joe Scibelli | OG | 6'1" | 255 | 31 | | |
| John Wilbur | OG | 6'3" | 240 | 27 | | |
| Ken Iman | C | 6'1" | 240 | 31 | | |
| George Burman | OG-C | 6'3" | 255 | 27 | | |
| Coy Bacon | DE | 6'4" | 270 | 28 | | 6 |
| Rick Cash | DE | 6'5" | 250 | 24 | | |
| Deacon Jones | DE | 6'5" | 250 | 31 | | |
| Clark Miller | DE | 6'5" | 246 | 31 | | |
| Dick Evey | DT | 6'2" | 245 | 29 | | |
| Merlin Olsen | DT | 6'5" | 270 | 29 | | |
| Diron Talbert | DT | 6'5" | 255 | 26 | | |

| Use Name | Pos. | Hgt | Wgt | Age | Int | Pts |
|---|---|---|---|---|---|---|
| Maxie Baughan | LB | 6'1" | 230 | 32 | 1 | |
| Jack Pardee | LB | 6'2" | 225 | 34 | 1 | |
| John Pergine | LB | 6'1" | 225 | 23 | | |
| Myron Pottios | LB | 6'2" | 232 | 30 | 2 | |
| Jim Purnell | LB | 6'2" | 238 | 28 | | |
| Jack Reynolds | LB | 6'1" | 232 | 22 | | |
| Rich Saul | LB | 6'3" | 235 | 22 | | |
| Kermit Alexander | DB | 5'11" | 186 | 29 | 4 | 6 |
| Alvin Haymond | DB | 6' | 194 | 28 | | 6 |
| Ed Meador | DB | 5'11" | 190 | 33 | 2 | |
| Jim Nettles | DB | 5'9" | 177 | 28 | 3 | |
| Richie Petitbon | DB | 6'3" | 208 | 32 | 1 | |
| Nate Shaw | DB | 6'2" | 205 | 25 | | |
| Clancy Williams | DB | 6'2" | 194 | 27 | 5 | 6 |

Doug Woodlief — Injury
Jim Wilson — Injury

| Use Name | Pos. | Hgt | Wgt | Age | Int | Pts |
|---|---|---|---|---|---|---|
| Roman Gabriel | QB | 6'4" | 220 | 30 | | 6 |
| Karl Sweetan | QB | 6'1" | 205 | 27 | | |
| Willie Ellison | HB | 6'1" | 200 | 25 | | 42 |
| Larry Smith | HB | 6'3" | 220 | 22 | | 12 |
| Tommy Mason | FB-HB | 6' | 195 | 31 | | 6 |
| Pat Curran | FB | 6'3" | 238 | 24 | | 6 |
| Les Josephson | HB-FB | 6'1" | 215 | 25 | | 30 |
| Jeff Jordan | WR | 6'3" | 205 | 29 | | |
| Bob Long | WR | 6' | 195 | 25 | | 6 |
| David Ray | WR | 6'2" | 197 | 27 | | 121 |
| Jack Snow | WR | 6'1" | 175 | 32 | | 12 |
| Pat Studstill | WR | 5'10" | 185 | 26 | | |
| Wendell Tucker | WR | 6'3" | 210 | 22 | | |
| Donnie Williams | WR | | | | | |
| Bob Klein | TE | 6'5" | 235 | 23 | | |
| Billy Truax | TE | 6'5" | 235 | 27 | | 18 |

## ATLANTA FALCONS 4-8-2 Norm Van Brocklin

| | | | |
|---|---|---|---|
| 14 | New Orleans | 3 | |
| 24 | Green Bay | 27 | |
| 21 | SAN FRANCISCO | 20 | |
| 0 | Dallas | 13 | |
| 10 | Denver | 24 | |
| 32 | NEW ORLEANS | 14 | |
| 14 | CHICAGO | 23 | |
| 10 | Los Angeles | 20 | |
| 13 | Philadelphia | 13 | |
| 7 | LOS ANGELES | 17 | |
| 7 | MIAMI | 20 | |
| 20 | San Francisco | 24 | |
| 27 | PITTSBURGH | 16 | |
| 7 | MINNESOTA | 37 | |

| Use Name | Pos. | Hgt | Wgt | Age | Int | Pts |
|---|---|---|---|---|---|---|
| Dave Hettema | OT | 6'4" | 250 | 28 | | |
| George Kunz | OT | 6'5" | 245 | 23 | | |
| Bill Sandeman | OT | 6'6" | 260 | 27 | | |
| Mal Snider | OT | 6'4" | 250 | 23 | | |
| Dick Enderle | OG | 6'1" | 258 | 22 | | |
| Andy Maurer | OG | 6'3" | 257 | 21 | | |
| Gary Roberts | OG | 6'2" | 242 | 23 | | |
| Bob Breitenstein | OT-OG | 6'3" | 267 | 27 | | |
| John Matlock | C | 6'4" | 250 | 24 | | |
| Jeff Van Note | C | 6'2" | 244 | 24 | | |
| Claude Humphrey | DE | 6'5" | 244 | 26 | 1 | |
| Randy Marshall | DE | 6'5" | 237 | 23 | | 6 |
| John Zook | DE | 6'5" | 240 | 22 | 1 | |
| Glen Condren | DT | 6'2" | 247 | 28 | | |
| Greg Lens | DT | 6'5" | 260 | 25 | | |
| Jim Sullivan | DE-DT | 6'4" | 240 | 26 | | |

Greg Brezina — Injury

| Use Name | Pos. | Hgt | Wgt | Age | Int | Pts |
|---|---|---|---|---|---|---|
| Ron Acks | LB | 6'2" | 225 | 25 | | |
| Grady Allen | LB | 6'3" | 230 | 24 | 1 | |
| Ted Cottrell | LB | 6'1" | 233 | 23 | | |
| Dean Halverson | LB | 6'2" | 220 | 24 | | |
| Don Hansen | LB | 6'3" | 220 | 24 | | |
| Tommy Nobis | LB | 6'2" | 237 | 26 | 2 | |
| John Small | LB | 6'5" | 254 | 23 | | |
| Grady Cavness | DB | 5'11" | 192 | 23 | | |
| Mike Freeman | DB | 5'11" | 180 | 26 | 1 | |
| Al Lavan | DB | 6'1" | 194 | 23 | 3 | |
| John Mallory | DB | 6' | 198 | 24 | 1 | 12 |
| Tom McCauley | DB | 6'3" | 184 | 21 | 1 | 6 |
| Ken Reaves | DB | 6'3" | 202 | 25 | 6 | |
| Rudy Redmond | DB | 6' | 190 | 23 | 1 | |

Carlton Dabney — Back Injury
Randy Winkler — Military Service

| Use Name | Pos. | Hgt | Wgt | Age | Int | Pts |
|---|---|---|---|---|---|---|
| Bob Berry | QB | 5'11" | 190 | 28 | | |
| Randy Johnson | QB | 6'3" | 210 | 26 | | |
| Cannonball Butler | HB | 5'10" | 195 | 27 | | 6 |
| Sonny Campbell | HB | 5'11" | 192 | 22 | | 12 |
| Paul Gipson | FB-HB | 6' | 205 | 24 | | 18 |
| Harmon Wages | FB | 6'1" | 215 | 24 | | 18 |
| Art Malone | HB-FB | 5'11" | 209 | 22 | | 6 |
| Mike Brunson | WR | 6'1" | 187 | 23 | | |
| Gail Cogdill | WR | 6'2" | 200 | 33 | | 6 |
| Paul Flatley | WR | 6'1" | 190 | 29 | | 6 |
| Kent Lawrence | WR | 5'11" | 175 | 23 | | |
| Todd Snyder | WR | 6'2" | 184 | 21 | | 12 |
| Mike Donohoe | TE | 6'3" | 227 | 25 | | 6 |
| Jim Mitchell | TE | 6'2" | 235 | 22 | | 42 |
| Billy Lothridge | K | 6'1" | 190 | 26 | | |
| Kenny Vinyard | K | 5'10" | 190 | 23 | | 50 |

## NEW ORLEANS SAINTS 2-11-1 Tom Fears J. D. Roberts

| | | | |
|---|---|---|---|
| 3 | ATLANTA | 14 | |
| 0 | Minnesota | 26 | |
| 14 | N.Y. GIANTS | 10 | |
| 17 | St. Louis | 24 | |
| 20 | San Francisco | 20 | |
| 14 | Atlanta | 32 | |
| 17 | LOS ANGELES | 30 | |
| 19 | DETROIT | 17 | |
| 10 | Miami | 21 | |
| 6 | DENVER | 31 | |
| 6 | Cincinnati | 26 | |
| 16 | Los Angeles | 34 | |
| 27 | SAN FRANCISCO | 38 | |
| 3 | CHICAGO | 24 | |

| Use Name | Pos. | Hgt | Wgt | Age | Int | Pts |
|---|---|---|---|---|---|---|
| Errol Linden | OT | 6'5" | 250 | 32 | | |
| Mike Richey | OT | 6'5" | 263 | 23 | | |
| Don Talbert | OT | 6'5" | 255 | 30 | | |
| Mike Taylor | OT | 6'4" | 245 | 25 | | |
| Jake Kupp | OG | 6'3" | 248 | 28 | | |
| John Shinners | OG | 6'2" | 254 | 23 | | |
| Doug Sutherland | OG | 6'3" | 250 | 22 | | |
| Jerry Sturm | C-OT-OG | 6'3" | 265 | 33 | | |
| Del Williams | C | 6'2" | 240 | 24 | | |
| Larry Estes | DE | 6'6" | 260 | 23 | | |
| Dave Long | DE | 6'4" | 245 | 25 | | |
| Richard Neal | DE | 6'3" | 254 | 22 | | |
| Willie Townes | DT-DE | 6'5" | 265 | 27 | | |
| Dave Rowe | DT | 6'6" | 280 | 25 | | |
| Clovis Swinney | DT | 6'5" | 240 | 25 | | |
| Mike Tilleman | DT | 6'5" | 280 | 26 | | |

| Use Name | Pos. | Hgt | Wgt | Age | Int | Pts |
|---|---|---|---|---|---|---|
| Dick Absher | LB | 6'4" | 235 | 26 | | |
| Johnny Brewer | LB | 6'4" | 235 | 33 | | |
| Jackie Burkett | LB | 6'4" | 228 | 33 | 4 | |
| Bill Cody | LB | 6'1" | 230 | 26 | | |
| Wayne Colman | LB | 6'1" | 230 | 24 | | |
| Frank Emanuel | LB | 6'3" | 225 | 27 | | |
| Hap Farber (from MIN) | LB | 6'1" | 220 | 22 | | |
| Harry Jacobs | LB | 6'2" | 226 | 33 | | |
| Mike Morgan | LB | 6'4" | 242 | 28 | 1 | 6 |
| Major Hazelton | DB | 6'1" | 185 | 25 | | |
| Hugo Hollas | DB | 6'1" | 190 | 25 | 5 | |
| Gene Howard | DB | 6' | 190 | 23 | | |
| Delles Howell | DB | 6'3" | 195 | 23 | 3 | |
| Dicky Lyons | DB | 6' | 190 | 23 | 1 | |
| Elijah Nevett | DB | 6' | 185 | 26 | 3 | |
| Joe Scarpati | DB | 5'10" | 185 | 28 | 1 | |
| Doug Wyatt | DB | 6'1" | 195 | 23 | 4 | |

Mike Rengel — Injury

| Use Name | Pos. | Hgt | Wgt | Age | Int | Pts |
|---|---|---|---|---|---|---|
| Edd Hargett | QB | 5'11" | 185 | 23 | | |
| Billy Kilmer | QB | 6' | 204 | 30 | | |
| Steve Ramsey | QB | 6'2" | 210 | 22 | | |
| Bill Dusenbery | HB | 6'2" | 198 | 21 | | |
| Don McCall | HB | 5'11" | 195 | 25 | | 6 |
| Vic Nyvall | HB | 5'10" | 185 | 22 | | |
| Elijah Pitts (from LA) | HB | 6'1" | 205 | 31 | | |
| Tony Baker | FB-HB | 5'11" | 225 | 25 | | 6 |
| Tom Barrington | FB-HB | 6'1" | 213 | 26 | | 12 |
| Dick Davis (from DEN) | FB-HB | 5'11" | 215 | 23 | | |
| Earl Gros | FB | 6'3" | 220 | 29 | | |
| Andy Livingston | FB | 6' | 235 | 25 | | |
| Jim Otis | FB | 6' | 220 | 23 | | |
| Ernie Wheelwright | FB | 6'3" | 235 | 33 | | |
| Gary Lewis | HB-FB | 6'3" | 230 | 28 | | |
| Dan Abramowicz | WR | 6'1" | 195 | 25 | | 30 |
| Ken Burrough | WR | 6'4" | 212 | 22 | | 12 |
| Al Dodd | WR | 6' | 180 | 25 | | 12 |
| Bob Shaw | WR | 6' | 194 | 21 | | |
| Dave Parks | TE | 6'2" | 203 | 28 | | 12 |
| Ray Poage | TE | 6'4" | 215 | 29 | | |
| Tom Dempsey | K | 6'1" | 264 | 29 | | 70 |
| Julian Fagan | K | 6'3" | 205 | 22 | | |

## SAN FRANCISCO FORTY NINERS

### RUSHING

| Last Name | No. | Yds | Avg | TD |
|---|---|---|---|---|
| Willard | 236 | 789 | 3.3 | 7 |
| Cunningham | 128 | 443 | 3.5 | 3 |
| Tucker | 42 | 137 | 3.3 | 1 |
| Thomas | 31 | 89 | 2.9 | 0 |
| Kwalick | 3 | 65 | 21.7 | 0 |
| Isenbarger | 18 | 43 | 2.4 | 0 |
| Brodie | 9 | 29 | 3.2 | 2 |
| Strong | 2 | 3 | 1.5 | 0 |
| Spurrier | 2 | −18 | −9.0 | 0 |

### RECEIVING

| Last Name | No. | Yds | Avg | TD |
|---|---|---|---|---|
| Washington | 53 | 1100 | 21 | 12 |
| Cunningham | 35 | 209 | 6 | 0 |
| Windsor | 31 | 363 | 12 | 2 |
| Willard | 31 | 259 | 8 | 3 |
| Witcher | 22 | 288 | 13 | 2 |
| Tucker | 17 | 108 | 6 | 1 |
| Thomas | 12 | 221 | 18 | 3 |
| Kwalick | 10 | 148 | 15 | 1 |
| Isenbarger | 8 | 158 | 20 | 1 |
| Riley | 7 | 136 | 19 | 0 |

### PUNT RETURNS

| Last Name | No. | Yds | Avg | TD |
|---|---|---|---|---|
| B. Taylor | 43 | 516 | 12 | 0 |
| Fuller | 4 | 29 | 7 | 0 |
| Riley | 1 | 5 | 5 | 0 |

### KICKOFF RETURNS

| Last Name | No. | Yds | Avg | TD |
|---|---|---|---|---|
| Tucker | 25 | 577 | 23 | 0 |
| B. Taylor | 12 | 190 | 16 | 0 |
| Thomas | 6 | 177 | 30 | 0 |
| Beard | 2 | 8 | 4 | 0 |
| Fuller | 1 | 8 | 8 | 0 |
| Belk | 1 | 7 | 7 | 0 |
| Riley | 1 | 0 | 0 | 0 |
| Windsor | 1 | 0 | 0 | 0 |

### PASSING – PUNTING – KICKING

PASSING

| Last Name | Att | Comp | % | Yds | Yd/Att | TD | Int– | % | RK |
|---|---|---|---|---|---|---|---|---|---|
| Brodie | 378 | 223 | 59 | 2941 | 7.8 | 24 | 10– | 3 | 1 |
| Spurrier | 4 | 3 | 75 | 49 | 12.3 | 1 | 0– | 0 | |
| Isenbarger | 1 | 0 | 0 | 0 | 0.0 | 0 | 0– | 0 | |

PUNTING

| Last Name | No | Avg |
|---|---|---|
| Spurrier | 75 | 38.4 |

KICKING

| Last Name | XP | Att | % | FG | Att | % |
|---|---|---|---|---|---|---|
| Gossett | 39 | 41 | 95 | 21 | 31 | 68 |

## LOS ANGELES RAMS

### RUSHING

| Last Name | No. | Yds | Avg | TD |
|---|---|---|---|---|
| Josephson | 150 | 640 | 4.3 | 5 |
| Ellison | 90 | 381 | 4.2 | 5 |
| Smith | 77 | 338 | 4.4 | 1 |
| Mason | 44 | 123 | 2.8 | 0 |
| Gabriel | 28 | 104 | 3.7 | 1 |
| Curran | 25 | 92 | 3.7 | 0 |
| Jordan | 10 | 50 | 5.0 | 0 |
| Studstill | 1 | 23 | 23.0 | 0 |
| Petitbon | 1 | 3 | 3.0 | 0 |
| Johnson | 1 | 1 | 1.0 | 0 |

### RECEIVING

| Last Name | No. | Yds | Avg | TD |
|---|---|---|---|---|
| Snow | 51 | 859 | 17 | 7 |
| Josephson | 44 | 427 | 10 | 0 |
| Truax | 36 | 420 | 12 | 3 |
| Smith | 24 | 164 | 7 | 1 |
| Studstill | 18 | 252 | 14 | 0 |
| Tucker | 12 | 230 | 19 | 0 |
| Mason | 12 | 127 | 11 | 1 |
| Ellison | 10 | 84 | 8 | 2 |
| Long | 3 | 35 | 12 | 1 |
| Curran | 3 | 25 | 8 | 0 |
| Klein | 2 | 20 | 10 | 0 |
| Ray | 1 | 11 | 11 | 0 |
| D. Williams | 1 | 9 | 9 | 0 |
| Jordan | 1 | −5 | −5 | 0 |

### PUNT RETURNS

| Last Name | No. | Yds | Avg | TD |
|---|---|---|---|---|
| Haymond | 53 | 376 | 7 | 0 |
| Alexander | 7 | 38 | 5 | 0 |
| Nettles | 2 | 4 | 2 | 0 |

### KICKOFF RETURNS

| Last Name | No. | Yds | Avg | TD |
|---|---|---|---|---|
| Haymond | 35 | 1022 | 29 | 1 |
| Alexander | 7 | 126 | 18 | 0 |
| Curran | 3 | 51 | 17 | 0 |
| Ellison | 1 | 20 | 20 | 0 |
| Johnson | 1 | 17 | 17 | 0 |

### PASSING – PUNTING – KICKING

PASSING

| Last Name | Att | Comp | % | Yds | Yd/Att | TD | Int– | % | RK |
|---|---|---|---|---|---|---|---|---|---|
| Gabriel | 407 | 211 | 52 | 2552 | 6.3 | 16 | 12– | 3 | 6 |
| Sweetan | 13 | 6 | 46 | 81 | 6.2 | 1 | 0– | 0 | |
| Curran | 2 | 0 | 0 | 0 | 0.0 | 0 | 1– | 50 | |
| Smith | 2 | 0 | 0 | 0 | 0.0 | 0 | 0– | 0 | |
| Josephson | 1 | 1 | 100 | 25 | 25.0 | 0 | 0– | 0 | |
| Studstill | 1 | 0 | 0 | 0 | 0.0 | 0 | 0– | 0 | |

PUNTING

| Last Name | No | Avg |
|---|---|---|
| Studstill | 67 | 39.1 |

KICKING

| Last Name | XP | Att | % | FG | Att | % |
|---|---|---|---|---|---|---|
| Ray | 34 | 34 | 100 | 29 | 45 | 64 |

## ATLANTA FALCONS

### RUSHING

| Last Name | No. | Yds | Avg | TD |
|---|---|---|---|---|
| Butler | 166 | 636 | 3.8 | 0 |
| Wages | 119 | 422 | 3.5 | 1 |
| Gipson | 52 | 177 | 3.4 | 0 |
| Malone | 40 | 136 | 3.4 | 0 |
| Campbell | 28 | 116 | 4.1 | 2 |
| Berry | 13 | 60 | 4.6 | 0 |
| Mitchell | 5 | 23 | 4.6 | 1 |
| Johnson | 7 | 21 | 3.0 | 0 |
| Brunson | 1 | 9 | 9.0 | 0 |

### RECEIVING

| Last Name | No. | Yds | Avg | TD |
|---|---|---|---|---|
| Mitchell | 44 | 650 | 15 | 6 |
| Flatley | 39 | 544 | 14 | 1 |
| Wages | 26 | 153 | 6 | 2 |
| Butler | 24 | 151 | 6 | 1 |
| Snyder | 23 | 311 | 14 | 2 |
| Gipson | 16 | 186 | 12 | 3 |
| Malone | 9 | 38 | 4 | 1 |
| Cogdill | 7 | 101 | 14 | 1 |
| Campbell | 7 | 92 | 13 | 0 |
| Donohoe | 2 | 36 | 18 | 1 |

### PUNT RETURNS

| Last Name | No. | Yds | Avg | TD |
|---|---|---|---|---|
| Mallory | 17 | 203 | 12 | 1 |
| McCauley | 14 | 138 | 10 | 1 |
| Freeman | 3 | 15 | 5 | 0 |

### KICKOFF RETURNS

| Last Name | No. | Yds | Avg | TD |
|---|---|---|---|---|
| Butler | 14 | 284 | 20 | 0 |
| Campbell | 10 | 230 | 23 | 0 |
| Gipson | 8 | 189 | 24 | 0 |
| Malone | 5 | 66 | 13 | 0 |
| Cavness | 3 | 61 | 20 | 0 |
| Brunson | 4 | 54 | 14 | 0 |
| Wages | 1 | 22 | 22 | 0 |
| Lavan | 1 | 10 | 10 | 0 |
| Freeman | 1 | 0 | 0 | 0 |

### PASSING – PUNTING – KICKING

PASSING

| Last Name | Att | Comp | % | Yds | Yd/Att | TD | Int– | % | RK |
|---|---|---|---|---|---|---|---|---|---|
| Berry | 269 | 156 | 58 | 1806 | 6.7 | 16 | 13– | 5 | 4 |
| Johnson | 72 | 40 | 56 | 443 | 6.2 | 2 | 8– | 11 | |
| Wages | 1 | 1 | 100 | 13 | 13.0 | 0 | 0– | 0 | |

PUNTING

| Last Name | No | Avg |
|---|---|---|
| Lothridge | 76 | 38.7 |

KICKING

| Last Name | XP | Att | % | FG | Att | % |
|---|---|---|---|---|---|---|
| Vinyard | 23 | 26 | 88 | 9 | 25 | 36 |

## NEW ORLEANS SAINTS

### RUSHING

| Last Name | No. | Yds | Avg | TD |
|---|---|---|---|---|
| Baker | 82 | 337 | 4.1 | 1 |
| Barrington | 72 | 228 | 3.2 | 2 |
| Otis | 71 | 211 | 3.0 | 0 |
| Pitts | 35 | 104 | 3.0 | 0 |
| Davis | 27 | 94 | 3.5 | 0 |
| McCall | 23 | 63 | 2.7 | 1 |
| Wheelwright | 16 | 45 | 2.8 | 0 |
| Kilmer | 12 | 42 | 3.5 | 0 |
| Dodd | 5 | 31 | 6.2 | 0 |
| Livingston | 10 | 29 | 2.9 | 0 |
| Poage | 1 | 13 | 13.0 | 0 |
| Abramowicz | 1 | 7 | 7.0 | 0 |
| Hargett | 4 | 7 | 1.8 | 0 |
| Dusenbery | 4 | 6 | 1.5 | 0 |
| Nyvall | 5 | 6 | 1.2 | 0 |
| Burrough | 1 | 4 | 4.0 | 0 |
| Gros | 4 | 2 | 0.5 | 0 |
| Fagan | 1 | −6 | −6.0 | 0 |

### RECEIVING

| Last Name | No. | Yds | Avg | TD |
|---|---|---|---|---|
| Abramowicz | 55 | 906 | 16 | 5 |
| Dodd | 28 | 484 | 17 | 1 |
| Parks | 26 | 447 | 17 | 2 |
| Barrington | 22 | 130 | 6 | 0 |
| Otis | 20 | 124 | 6 | 0 |
| Poage | 15 | 166 | 11 | 1 |
| Burrough | 13 | 196 | 15 | 2 |
| Baker | 12 | 47 | 4 | 0 |
| Pitts | 7 | 63 | 9 | 0 |
| McCall | 5 | 43 | 9 | 0 |
| Davis | 4 | 29 | 7 | 0 |
| Gros | 2 | 0 | 0 | 0 |
| Nyvall | 2 | −1 | −1 | 0 |
| Shaw | 1 | 49 | 49 | 0 |
| Wheelwright | 1 | 7 | 7 | 0 |

### PUNT RETURNS

| Last Name | No. | Yds | Avg | TD |
|---|---|---|---|---|
| Dodd | 14 | 129 | 9 | 0 |
| Lyons | 5 | 34 | 7 | 0 |
| Hollas | 4 | 22 | 6 | 0 |
| Wyatt | 1 | 15 | 15 | 0 |
| Howard | 5 | 14 | 3 | 0 |

### KICKOFF RETURNS

| Last Name | No. | Yds | Avg | TD |
|---|---|---|---|---|
| Dodd | 15 | 319 | 21 | 0 |
| Burrough | 15 | 298 | 20 | 0 |
| Dusenbery | 10 | 183 | 18 | 0 |
| Barrington | 6 | 129 | 22 | 0 |
| McCall | 1 | 26 | 26 | 0 |
| Otis | 2 | 22 | 11 | 0 |
| Pitts | 1 | 22 | 22 | 0 |
| Lyons | 1 | 20 | 20 | 0 |
| Lewis | 1 | 19 | 19 | 0 |
| Poage | 1 | 6 | 6 | 0 |

### PASSING – PUNTING – KICKING

PASSING

| Last Name | Att | Comp | % | Yds | Yd/Att | TD | Int– | % | RK |
|---|---|---|---|---|---|---|---|---|---|
| Kilmer | 237 | 135 | 57 | 1557 | 6.6 | 6 | 17– | 7 | 12 |
| Hargett | 175 | 78 | 45 | 1133 | 6.5 | 5 | 5– | 3 | 12 |
| Ramsey | 2 | 0 | 0 | 0 | 0.0 | 0 | 0– | 0 | |
| Dodd | 1 | 0 | 0 | 0 | 0.0 | 0 | 0– | 0 | |

PUNTING

| Last Name | No | Avg |
|---|---|---|
| Fagan | 77 | 42.5 |

KICKING

| Last Name | XP | Att | % | FG | Att | % |
|---|---|---|---|---|---|---|
| Dempsey | 16 | 17 | 94 | 18 | 34 | 53 |

# 1970 A.F.C. New League, Old Faces

In their first season in the NFL, the old AFL clubs found things rougher than they expected. In interconference games, the NFC came out on top in two thirds of them. An AFC team did win the Super Bowl, but that was the Baltimore Colts, an old-line NFL club which had moved over to the AFC this season along with Cleveland and Pittsburgh. Nevertheless, the ten clubs which had made up the AFL placed a good share of players on all All-Pro teams, and the two expansion teams which came out of the AFL gave good reason for the former members to be proud. The Miami Dolphins and Cincinnati Bengals, both created in the mid 1960s, each made the playoffs. The Atlanta Falcons and New Orleans Saints, NFL expansion teams from the same period, came nowhere near matching the record of these two.

## EASTERN DIVISION

**Baltimore Colts**—Soft-Spoken Don McCafferty took over as head coach after Don Shula quit to go to Miami, and the Colts rewarded him with a championship in his first season on the job. The Baltimore offense scored the most points in the conference, yet went through some mid-season changes. John Williams moved into the starting lineup at guard after an embarrassing 44-24 loss to Kansas City, hustling Tom Nowatzke filled in as running back when injuries kayoed Tom Matte, and oldsters Johnny Unitas and Earl Morrall occasionally relieved each other at quarterback. The defense, however, was a picture of stability, with stars Bubba Smith, Mike Curtis, Ted Hendricks, Rick Volk, and Jerry Logan leading a quick and mobile unit.

**Miami Dolphins**—The Dolphins had to pay highly to get Don Shula, including a first-draft choice which went to Baltimore as compensation, but the results proved the new coach's worth. Under Shula's direction, Bob Griese matured as a quarterback, Larry Csonka, Jim Kiick, and Mercury Morris developed into top runners, and the offensive line meshed into a fine unit, with Larry Little blossoming into a star. On defense, however, Shula did his best job, turning an indifferent unit into the conference's best. Five rookies started on defense, Mike Kolen, Doug Swift, Tim Foley, Curtis Johnson, and Jake Scott. The veteran pillars on the platoon were Manny Fernandez, Nick Buoniconti, and Dick Anderson.

**New York Jets**—Injuries destroyed the Jets' chances of defending their divisional title. Joe Namath's broken wrist robbed the offense of its leader, and a torn Achilles tendon took fullback Matt Snell out of the lineup just when he was running better than at any time in his career. Emerson Boozer, Don Maynard, and Roger Finnie also missed a lot of time in sick bay, forcing wholesale replacements on the offensive unit. Although Al Woodall, George Nock, and Rich Caster were capable substitutes, they could not replace the firepower lost in Namath, Snell, and Maynard. Injuries also hurt the defense, with Steve Thompson and Jim Hudson the major casualties, but that unit held together well and kept the Jets respectable in their worst moments.

**Buffalo Bills**—Rookie Dennis Shaw won the starting quarterback job and showed the potential to become a fine passer, while receiver Marlin Briscoe caught enough Shaw passes to lead the league in receiving. On the defensive unit, Al Cowlings, Edgar Chandler, and Bobby James showed talent and enthusiasm to make up for their inexperience. Unfortunate events of the year included O. J. Simpson's knee injury which sidelined him for the second half of the season, Mike Stratton's Achilles tendon injury, and Wayne Patrick's separated shoulder.

**Boston Patriots**—The Patriots shelled out a bundle to pick up quarterback Joe Kapp from Minnesota in mid-season, but Kapp was out of shape and unfamiliar with the Boston system; the result was a season in which he threw three touchdown passes and seventeen interceptions. Kapp's poor season fit in well with the entire situation on the Patriots. Running backs Jim Nance and Carl Garrett seemed apathetic at times, Gino Cappelletti continued to regress as a place kicker, the offensive line never lived up to its potential, and the defense lost Jim Cheyunski and rookie Phil Olsen to injuries. By mid-season, John Mazur had replaced Clive Rush as head coach.

## CENTRAL DIVISION

**Cincinnati Bengals**—Even with quarterback Greg Cook out of action with a bad shoulder, the Bengals still stormed into the playoffs and delighted coach 'Paul Brown by beating the Browns out for first place in the Central Division. The Cincinnati defense had been strengthened by rookies Mike Reid, Ron Carpenter, and Lemar Parrish, but the offense started out slowly under new quarterback Virgil Carter. After

losing six of their first seven games, the Bengals suddenly jelled; they beat Buffalo, Cleveland, Pittsburgh, and their other four remaining opponents to streak past the rival Browns from upstate. Starring along the way were runners Jess Phillips and Paul Robinson, receiver Chip Myers, center Bob Johnson, kicker Horst Muhlmann, linebacker Bill Bergey, and rookies Reid, Carpenter, and Parrish.

**Cleveland Browns**—Aside from Leroy Kelly's bad season and a chaotic linebacking situation, two off-season trades contributed the most to Cleveland's slump this year. With Bill Nelsen's bad knees making him a constant question mark, the Browns traded star receiver Paul Warfield to Miami for their first-draft pick, which Cleveland used to take Purdue quarterback Mike Phipps. Then the Browns shipped Ron Johnson, Jim Kanicki, and Wayne Meylan to New York for receiver Homer Jones. While Warfield and Johnson starred in their new surroundings, Phipps showed that he needed plenty more seasoning and Jones failed to even win a starting job.

**Pittsburgh Steelers**—Even with Terry Bradshaw not delivering as expected, the Steelers did make a mid-season run at the Central Division crown before slumping off into five losses in their last six games. The big improvement in the Steelers came on defense, where Mean Joe Greene and Andy Russell stood out on a unit with eleven solid starters. Less impressive was the offense, where coach Chuck Noll fielded a complete new set of runners and receivers to go with his rookie quarterback.

**Houston Oilers**—Coach Wally Lemm announced before the season that this was his final year with the Oilers, but his team gave him very little in the way of a going-away gift, as they dropped into last place in the AFC Central Division. Injuries hurt the team, as quarterback Charley Johnson, newly acquired from St. Louis, linebacker George Webster, guard Tom Regner, and fullback Hoyle Granger all suffered disabling wounds. But even without the injuries, the Oilers had too few good players to challenge seriously for the title in their weak division.

## WESTERN DIVISION

**Oakland Raiders**—Old George Blanda, playing his twenty-first season of pro football, made a specialty out of pulling games out of the fire at the last second as he saved five games in a row with late heroics. He filled in for the injured Daryle Lamonica and threw a pair of touchdown passes to beat Pittsburgh 31-14, he kicked a 48-yard field goal with three seconds left to tie Kansas City 17-17, he kicked a 52-yarder to beat Cleveland 23-20 in the last three seconds, he came off the bench to drive the Raiders to the winning touchdown in a 24-19 victory over Denver, and he kicked a field goal with four seconds left to beat San Diego 20-17—all of which helped Oakland to take first place in the West.

**Kansas City Chiefs**—The spark which had moved the club last year was missing, especially on offense; the Kansas City attack virtually ignored long-gaining plays and confined itself to short passes and inside running plays. The overconservative offense wasted the talents of Otis Taylor, who scored only three touchdowns all year, and Ed Podolak, who scored only four times after breaking into the starting lineup. Coach Hank Stram made only two substitutions in last year's lineup, replacing Mike Garrett at halfback with Podolak and promoting Jack Rudnay to starting center over sore-kneed E. J. Holub.

**San Diego Chargers**—With a flabby pass rush and a secondary that picked off only five enemy passes all year, the defense gave head coach Charlie Walker his biggest headache in his first full season on the job. The front four contained heralded ex-collegians in Steve DeLong, Ron Billingsley, and Gene Ferguson, but the best work came from unknown rookie Joe Owens. While Pete Barnes and Bob Babich solidified the linebacking, the secondary of Bob Howard, Joe Beauchamp, Jim Hill, and Jim Tolbert was remarkably undistinguished. Injuries to Dickie Post and Brad Hubbert hurt the running attack, but a strong passing game kept the offense in business.

**Denver Broncos**—The Broncos charged out of the starting gate with a 4-1 record, but problems at quarterback eventually caught up with the team. Steve Tensi missed most of the campaign with injuries and Pete Liske played quarterback most of the way. Although Liske had leadership ability and skill at reading defenses, the ex-Canadian League star did not have a strong enough arm to hold the job. By the end of the year, coach Lou Saban was playing rookie Al Pastrana at the spot with dismal results. The high point of the season for Saban was the development of Floyd Little into an All-Pro workhorse runner and the good showing of rookie Bobby Anderson.

## FINAL TEAM STATISTICS

### OFFENSE

| | BALT. | BOS. | BUFF. | CIN. | CLEV. | DENV. | HOUS. | K.C. | MIAMI | N.Y.J. | OAK. | PITT. | S.D. |
|---|---|---|---|---|---|---|---|---|---|---|---|---|---|
| FIRST DOWNS: | | | | | | | | | | | | | |
| Total | 242 | 184 | 203 | 210 | 239 | 217 | 232 | 183 | 228 | 230 | 270 | 206 | 231 |
| by Rushing | 70 | 63 | 71 | 100 | 87 | 84 | 88 | 83 | 106 | 90 | 107 | 84 | 83 |
| by Passing | 148 | 98 | 120 | 97 | 134 | 112 | 126 | 86 | 100 | 122 | 139 | 97 | 119 |
| by Penalty | 24 | 23 | 12 | 13 | 18 | 21 | 18 | 14 | 22 | 18 | 24 | 25 | 29 |
| RUSHING: | | | | | | | | | | | | | |
| Number | 411 | 334 | 367 | 461 | 462 | 436 | 419 | 448 | 492 | 463 | 471 | 432 | 395 |
| Yards | 1336 | 1040 | 1465 | 2057 | 1579 | 1802 | 1556 | 1858 | 2082 | 1653 | 1964 | 1715 | 1450 |
| Average Yards | 3.3 | 3.1 | 4.0 | 4.5 | 3.4 | 4.1 | 3.7 | 4.1 | 4.2 | 3.6 | 4.2 | 4.0 | 3.7 |
| Touchdowns | 9 | 11 | 8 | 16 | 14 | 17 | 10 | 11 | 14 | 11 | 7 | 13 | 9 |
| PASSING: | | | | | | | | | | | | | |
| Attempts | 416 | 392 | 402 | 339 | 392 | 403 | 470 | 289 | 299 | 386 | 418 | 384 | 387 |
| Completions | 219 | 176 | 213 | 172 | 190 | 183 | 238 | 154 | 159 | 193 | 210 | 150 | 192 |
| Completion Percentage | 52.6 | 44.9 | 53.0 | 50.7 | 48.5 | 45.4 | 50.6 | 53.3 | 53.2 | 50.0 | 50.2 | 39.1 | 49.6 |
| Passing Yards | 3087 | 1975 | 2916 | 2097 | 2752 | 2358 | 2768 | 2038 | 2284 | 2592 | 3029 | 2312 | 2936 |
| Avg. Yards per Attempt | 7.4 | 5.0 | 7.3 | 6.2 | 7.0 | 5.9 | 5.9 | 7.1 | 7.6 | 6.7 | 7.2 | 6.0 | 7.6 |
| Avg. Yards per Complet. | 14.1 | 11.2 | 13.7 | 12.2 | 14.5 | 12.9 | 11.6 | 13.2 | 14.4 | 13.4 | 14.4 | 15.4 | 15.3 |
| Times Tackled Passing | 33 | 42 | 53 | 31 | 16 | 44 | 33 | 38 | 36 | 35 | 19 | 28 | 57 |
| Yards Lost Tackled | 289 | 389 | 486 | 227 | 170 | 333 | 262 | 319 | 327 | 285 | 164 | 275 | 433 |
| Net Yards | 2798 | 1586 | 2430 | 1870 | 2582 | 2025 | 2506 | 1719 | 1957 | 2307 | 2865 | 2037 | 2503 |
| Touchdowns | 23 | 7 | 13 | 12 | 17 | 11 | 12 | 13 | 15 | 14 | 28 | 12 | 24 |
| Interceptions | 22 | 28 | 26 | 11 | 24 | 28 | 23 | 16 | 19 | 22 | 21 | 32 | 19 |
| Percent Intercepted | 5.3 | 7.1 | 6.5 | 3.2 | 6.1 | 6.9 | 4.9 | 5.5 | 6.4 | 5.7 | 5.0 | 8.3 | 4.9 |
| PUNTS: | | | | | | | | | | | | | |
| Number | 63 | 86 | 83 | 79 | 71 | 87 | 84 | 76 | 58 | 73 | 79 | 78 | 74 |
| Average Distance | 44.7 | 39.1 | 38.9 | 46.2 | 42.6 | 42.9 | 42.4 | 44.9 | 41.2 | 40.1 | 39.5 | 44.2 | 42.8 |
| PUNT RETURNS: | | | | | | | | | | | | | |
| Number | 36 | 32 | 45 | 37 | 34 | 63 | 41 | 31 | 30 | 26 | 37 | 51 | 31 |
| Yards | 351 | 305 | 298 | 327 | 236 | 556 | 257 | 371 | 295 | 150 | 308 | 281 | 173 |
| Average Yards | 9.8 | 9.5 | 6.6 | 8.8 | 6.9 | 8.8 | 6.3 | 12.0 | 9.8 | 5.8 | 8.3 | 5.5 | 5.6 |
| Touchdowns | 1 | 0 | 0 | 1 | 0 | 0 | 0 | 0 | 1 | 0 | 1 | 0 | 0 |
| KICKOFF RETURNS: | | | | | | | | | | | | | |
| Number | 45 | 62 | 62 | 39 | 44 | 49 | 55 | 44 | 48 | 56 | 44 | 40 | 42 |
| Yards | 1161 | 1275 | 1244 | 1002 | 1001 | 1114 | 1168 | 997 | 1036 | 1106 | 1017 | 997 | 813 |
| Average Yards | 25.8 | 20.6 | 20.1 | 25.7 | 22.8 | 22.7 | 21.2 | 22.7 | 21.6 | 19.8 | 23.1 | 24.9 | 19.4 |
| Touchdowns | 1 | 0 | 2 | 1 | 1 | 0 | 0 | 0 | 1 | 0 | 0 | 0 | 0 |
| INTERCEPTION RETURNS: | | | | | | | | | | | | | |
| Number | 25 | 8 | 11 | 23 | 19 | 16 | 18 | 31 | 23 | 23 | 19 | 23 | 9 |
| Yards | 408 | 184 | 179 | 180 | 324 | 220 | 242 | 395 | 414 | 281 | 112 | 266 | 90 |
| Average Yards | 16.3 | 23.0 | 16.3 | 7.8 | 17.1 | 13.8 | 13.4 | 12.7 | 18.0 | 12.2 | 5.9 | 11.6 | 10.0 |
| Touchdowns | 3 | 0 | 2 | 0 | 3 | 0 | 0 | 1 | 1 | 2 | 0 | 1 | 0 |
| PENALTIES: | | | | | | | | | | | | | |
| Number | 71 | 88 | 99 | 71 | 65 | 94 | 78 | 83 | 77 | 88 | 92 | 82 | 79 |
| Yards | 708 | 849 | 1108 | 831 | 634 | 887 | 833 | 888 | 834 | 1022 | 1021 | 835 | 852 |
| FUMBLES: | | | | | | | | | | | | | |
| Number | 25 | 18 | 37 | 22 | 24 | 23 | 26 | 26 | 24 | 20 | 21 | 30 | 19 |
| Number Lost | 14 | 13 | 26 | 12 | 14 | 13 | 15 | 15 | 11 | 11 | 9 | 16 | 6 |
| POINTS: | | | | | | | | | | | | | |
| Total | 321 | 149 | 204 | 312 | 286 | 253 | 217 | 272 | 297 | 255 | 300 | 210 | 282 |
| PAT Attempts | 38 | 18 | 25 | 34 | 35 | 28 | 23 | 26 | 33 | 28 | 36 | 26 | 35 |
| PAT Made | 36 | 17 | 24 | 33 | 34 | 27 | 23 | 26 | 33 | 28 | 36 | 24 | 34 |
| FG Attempts | 34 | 22 | 19 | 37 | 22 | 32 | 32 | 42 | 30 | 35 | 29 | 28 | 19 |
| FG Made | 19 | 8 | 10 | 25 | 12 | 18 | 18 | 30 | 22 | 19 | 16 | 10 | 12 |
| Percent FG Made | 55.9 | 36.4 | 52.6 | 67.6 | 54.5 | 56.3 | 56.3 | 71.4 | 73.3 | 54.3 | 55.2 | 35.7 | 63.2 |
| Safeties | 0 | 0 | 0 | 0 | 3 | 2 | 1 | 0 | 0 | 1 | 0 | 0 | 1 |

### DEFENSE

| | BALT. | BOS. | BUFF. | CIN. | CLEVE | DENV. | HOUS. | K.C. | MIAMI | N.Y.J. | OAK. | PITT. | S.D. |
|---|---|---|---|---|---|---|---|---|---|---|---|---|---|
| FIRST DOWNS: | | | | | | | | | | | | | |
| Total | 214 | 242 | 213 | 236 | 236 | 199 | 227 | 226 | 226 | 216 | 223 | 225 | 245 |
| by Rushing | 79 | 115 | 87 | 87 | 104 | 67 | 85 | 83 | 82 | 65 | 90 | 91 | 106 |
| by Passing | 120 | 105 | 103 | 131 | 120 | 118 | 115 | 111 | 128 | 122 | 104 | 120 | 117 |
| by Penalty | 15 | 22 | 23 | 18 | 12 | 14 | 27 | 32 | 16 | 29 | 29 | 14 | 22 |
| RUSHING: | | | | | | | | | | | | | |
| Number | 390 | 503 | 484 | 418 | 451 | 409 | 466 | 418 | 387 | 408 | 460 | 487 | 480 |
| Yards | 1439 | 2074 | 1718 | 1543 | 2006 | 1351 | 1793 | 1657 | 1453 | 1283 | 2027 | 1679 | 1967 |
| Average Yards | 3.7 | 4.1 | 3.5 | 3.7 | 4.4 | 3.3 | 3.8 | 4.0 | 3.8 | 3.1 | 4.4 | 3.4 | 4.1 |
| Touchdowns | 6 | 20 | 16 | 11 | 10 | 7 | 16 | 10 | 8 | 7 | 10 | 8 | 15 |
| PASSING: | | | | | | | | | | | | | |
| Attempts | 452 | 334 | 338 | 428 | 357 | 379 | 344 | 408 | 403 | 383 | 339 | 393 | 365 |
| Completions | 238 | 177 | 157 | 209 | 186 | 191 | 164 | 195 | 234 | 165 | 157 | 191 | 207 |
| Completion Percentage | 52.7 | 53.0 | 46.4 | 48.8 | 52.1 | 50.4 | 47.7 | 47.8 | 58.1 | 43.1 | 46.3 | 48.6 | 56.7 |
| Passing Yards | 2780 | 2430 | 2334 | 2885 | 2528 | 2810 | 2851 | 2280 | 2708 | 2680 | 2386 | 2555 | 2422 |
| Avg. Yards per Attempt | 6.2 | 7.3 | 6.9 | 6.7 | 7.1 | 7.4 | 8.3 | 5.6 | 6.7 | 7.0 | 7.0 | 6.5 | 6.6 |
| Avg. Yards per Complet. | 11.7 | 13.7 | 14.9 | 13.8 | 13.6 | 14.7 | 17.4 | 11.7 | 11.6 | 16.2 | 15.2 | 13.4 | 11.7 |
| Times Tackled Passing | 41 | 28 | 31 | 28 | 34 | 50 | 30 | 35 | 18 | 35 | 39 | 26 | 27 |
| Yards Lost Tackled | 374 | 243 | 246 | 250 | 290 | 456 | 246 | 270 | 157 | 308 | 297 | 238 | 207 |
| Net Yards | 2406 | 2187 | 2088 | 2635 | 2238 | 2354 | 2605 | 2010 | 2551 | 2372 | 2089 | 2317 | 2215 |
| Touchdowns | 16 | 19 | 15 | 18 | 16 | 20 | 25 | 15 | 17 | 20 | 22 | 21 | 13 |
| Interceptions | 25 | 8 | 11 | 23 | 19 | 16 | 18 | 31 | 23 | 23 | 19 | 23 | 9 |
| Percent Intercepted | 5.5 | 2.4 | 3.3 | 5.4 | 5.3 | 4.2 | 5.2 | 7.6 | 5.7 | 6.0 | 5.6 | 5.9 | 2.5 |
| PUNTS: | | | | | | | | | | | | | |
| Number | 78 | 63 | 76 | 80 | 66 | 89 | 77 | 79 | 63 | 68 | 80 | 85 | 64 |
| Average Distance | 38.4 | 43.8 | 44.0 | 43.8 | 42.4 | 44.9 | 44.4 | 43.4 | 41.7 | 38.9 | 41.6 | 41.9 | 44.1 |
| PUNT RETURNS: | | | | | | | | | | | | | |
| Number | 38 | 42 | 42 | 48 | 23 | 56 | 52 | 51 | 20 | 42 | 40 | 51 | 34 |
| Yards | 365 | 303 | 291 | 392 | 83 | 416 | 441 | 414 | 241 | 380 | 303 | 304 | 312 |
| Average Yards | 9.6 | 7.2 | 6.9 | 8.2 | 3.6 | 7.4 | 8.5 | 8.1 | 12.1 | 9.0 | 7.6 | 6.0 | 9.2 |
| Touchdowns | 1 | 1 | 2 | 2 | 0 | 0 | 0 | 0 | 1 | 1 | 0 | 1 | 0 |
| KICKOFF RETURNS: | | | | | | | | | | | | | |
| Number | 58 | 41 | 46 | 33 | 39 | 24 | 32 | 45 | 55 | 58 | 54 | 49 | 52 |
| Yards | 1237 | 841 | 1112 | 774 | 956 | 544 | 741 | 1128 | 1142 | 1210 | 1233 | 1068 | 1153 |
| Average Yards | 21.3 | 20.5 | 24.2 | 23.5 | 24.5 | 22.7 | 23.2 | 25.1 | 20.8 | 20.9 | 22.8 | 21.8 | 22.2 |
| Touchdowns | 0 | 2 | 1 | 0 | 0 | 0 | 0 | 0 | 1 | 2 | 0 | 1 | 0 |
| INTERCEPTION RETURNS: | | | | | | | | | | | | | |
| Number | 22 | 28 | 26 | 11 | 24 | 28 | 23 | 16 | 19 | 22 | 21 | 32 | 19 |
| Yards | 283 | 302 | 334 | 150 | 399 | 213 | 334 | 195 | 258 | 397 | 303 | 318 | 235 |
| Average Yards | 12.9 | 10.8 | 12.8 | 13.6 | 16.6 | 7.6 | 14.5 | 12.2 | 13.6 | 18.0 | 14.4 | 9.9 | 12.4 |
| Touchdowns | 1 | 2 | 0 | 0 | 4 | 0 | 2 | 0 | 1 | 3 | 1 | 1 | 0 |
| PENALTIES: | | | | | | | | | | | | | |
| Number | 101 | 101 | 73 | 81 | 88 | 82 | 76 | 77 | 68 | 70 | 87 | 76 | 89 |
| Yards | 1032 | 1096 | 814 | 784 | 871 | 817 | 833 | 817 | 704 | 655 | 1148 | 790 | 998 |
| FUMBLES: | | | | | | | | | | | | | |
| Number | 14 | 33 | 23 | 28 | 28 | 35 | 22 | 22 | 24 | 22 | 17 | 29 | 21 |
| Number Lost | 9 | 17 | 15 | 16 | 12 | 16 | 8 | 12 | 15 | 11 | 8 | 15 | 15 |
| POINTS: | | | | | | | | | | | | | |
| Total | 234 | 361 | 337 | 255 | 265 | 264 | 352 | 244 | 228 | 286 | 293 | 272 | 278 |
| PAT Attempts | 25 | 44 | 35 | 31 | 32 | 28 | 44 | 26 | 28 | 33 | 33 | 32 | 30 |
| PAT Made | 25 | 44 | 35 | 31 | 31 | 27 | 44 | 25 | 27 | 32 | 32 | 29 | 29 |
| FG Attempts | 37 | 28 | 46 | 24 | 26 | 36 | 30 | 28 | 22 | 32 | 31 | 32 | 40 |
| FG Made | 19 | 17 | 30 | 12 | 14 | 23 | 14 | 21 | 11 | 18 | 21 | 15 | 23 |
| Percent FG Made | 51.4 | 60.7 | 65.2 | 50.0 | 53.8 | 63.9 | 46.7 | 75.0 | 50.0 | 56.3 | 67.7 | 46.9 | 57.5 |
| Safeties | 1 | 1 | 1 | 1 | 0 | 0 | 1 | 0 | 0 | 1 | 0 | 3 | 0 |

## CONFERENCE PLAYOFFS

December 27, at Oakland
(Attendance 52,594)

### SCORING

| | | | | | |
|---|---|---|---|---|---|
| OAKLAND | 0 | 7 | 7 | 7 | —21 |
| MIAMI | 0 | 7 | 0 | 7 | —14 |

Second Quarter
Mia. Warfield, 16 yard pass from Griese
PAT—Yepremian (kick)
Oak. Biletnikoff, 22 yard pass from Lamonica PAT—Blanda (kick)

Third Quarter
Oak. Brown, 50 yard interception return
PAT—Blanda (kick)

Fourth Quarter
Oak. Sherman, 82 yard pass from Lamonica
PAT—Blanda (kick)
Mia. Richardson, 7 yard pass from Griese
PAT—Yepremian (kick)

### TEAM STATISTICS

| OAK. | | MIAMI |
|---|---|---|
| 12 | First Downs—Total | 16 |
| 5 | First Downs—Rushing | 5 |
| 7 | First Downs—Passing | 9 |
| 0 | First Downs—Penalty | 2 |
| 4 | Fumbles—Number | 2 |
| 2 | Fumbles—Lost Ball | 0 |
| 4 | Penalties—Number | 0 |
| 30 | Yards Penalized | 0 |
| 1 | Missed Field Goals | 2 |
| 52 | Offensive Plays—Total | 63 |
| 301 | Net Yards | 242 |
| 5.8 | Average Gain | 3.8 |
| 2 | Giveaways | 1 |
| 1 | Takeaways | 2 |
| −1 | Difference | +1 |

### INDIVIDUAL STATISTICS

| OAKLAND | No. | Yds. | Avg. | MIAMI | No. | Yds. | Avg. |
|---|---|---|---|---|---|---|---|
| **RUSHING** | | | | | | | |
| Hubbard | 18 | 58 | 3.2 | Kiick | 14 | 64 | 6.0 |
| Smith | 9 | 37 | 4.1 | Morris | 8 | 29 | 3.6 |
| Dixon | 8 | 31 | 3.9 | Csonka | 10 | 23 | 2.3 |
| Banaszak | 1 | −6 | −6.0 | Griese | 1 | 2 | 2.0 |
| | 36 | 120 | 3.3 | | 33 | 118 | 3.6 |
| **RECEIVING** | | | | | | | |
| Biletnikoff | 3 | 46 | 15.3 | Warfield | 4 | 62 | 15.5 |
| Chester | 2 | 47 | 23.5 | Kiick | 4 | 34 | 8.5 |
| Sherman | 1 | 82 | 82.0 | Richardson | 2 | 30 | 15.0 |
| Smith | 1 | 9 | 9.0 | Morris | 2 | 15 | 7.5 |
| Dixon | 1 | 3 | 3.0 | Twilley | 1 | 14 | 14.0 |
| | 8 | 187 | 23.4 | | 13 | 155 | 11.9 |
| **PUNTING** | | | | | | | |
| Eischeid | 4 | | 32.2 | Seiple | 5 | | 39.2 |
| **PUNT RETURNS** | | | | | | | |
| Atkinson | 1 | −1 | −1.0 | Scott | 1 | −1 | −1.0 |
| | | | | Anderson | 1 | −4 | −4.0 |
| | | | | | 2 | −5 | −2.5 |
| **KICKOFF RETURNS** | | | | | | | |
| Sherman | 1 | 22 | 22.0 | Ginn | 2 | 27 | 13.5 |
| Atkinson | 1 | 19 | 19.0 | Morris | 1 | 21 | 21.0 |
| Budness | 1 | 0 | 0.0 | Seiple | 1 | 8 | 8.0 |
| | 3 | 41 | 13.7 | | 4 | 56 | 14.0 |

**PASSING**

| OAKLAND | Att. | Comp. | Comp. Pct. | Yds. | Int. | Yds/ Att. | Yds/ Comp. | Yards Lost Tkld. |
|---|---|---|---|---|---|---|---|---|
| Lamonica | 16 | 8 | 50.0 | 187 | 0 | 11.7 | 23.4 | 0– 0 |
| **MIAMI** | | | | | | | | |
| Griese | 27 | 13 | 48.1 | 155 | 1 | 5.7 | 11.9 | 3–31 |

December 26, at Baltimore
(Attendance 49,694)

### SCORING

| | | | | | |
|---|---|---|---|---|---|
| BALTIMORE | 7 | 3 | 0 | 7 | —17 |
| CINCINNATI | 0 | 0 | 0 | 0 | — 0 |

First Quarter
Bal. Jefferson, 45 yard pass from Unitas
PAT—O'Brien (kick)

Second Quarter
Bal. O'Brien, 44 yard field goal

Fourth Quarter
Bal. Hinton, 53 yard pass from Unitas
PAT—O'Brien (kick)

### TEAM STATISTICS

| BALT. | | CIN. |
|---|---|---|
| 15 | First Downs—Total | 7 |
| 12 | First Downs—Rushing | 2 |
| 3 | First Downs—Passing | 5 |
| 0 | First Downs—Penalty | 0 |
| 0 | Fumbles—Number | 1 |
| 0 | Fumbles—Lost Ball | 0 |
| 6 | Penalties—Number | 1 |
| 63 | Yards Penalized | 5 |
| 2 | Missed Field Goals | 1 |
| 66 | Offensive Plays—Total | 46 |
| 299 | Net Yards | 139 |
| 4.5 | Average Gain | 3.0 |
| 0 | Giveaways | 1 |
| 1 | Takeaways | 0 |
| +1 | Difference | −1 |

### INDIVIDUAL STATISTICS

| BALTIMORE | No. | Yds. | Avg. | CINCINNATI | No. | Yds. | Avg. |
|---|---|---|---|---|---|---|---|
| **RUSHING** | | | | | | | |
| Bulaich | 25 | 116 | 4.6 | Robinson | 5 | 25 | 5.0 |
| Nowatzke | 10 | 25 | 2.5 | Carter | 2 | 16 | 8.0 |
| Unitas | 2 | 18 | 9.0 | Phillips | 10 | 12 | 1.2 |
| Hill | 3 | 11 | 3.7 | Lewis | 3 | 10 | 3.3 |
| Jefferson | 3 | 5 | 1.7 | Johnson | 2 | 0 | 0.0 |
| Havrilak | 3 | 0 | 0.0 | | 22 | 63 | 2.9 |
| Hinton | 1 | −5 | −5.0 | | | | |
| | 47 | 170 | 3.6 | | | | |
| **RECEIVING** | | | | | | | |
| Hinton | 3 | 86 | 28.7 | Myers | 4 | 66 | 16.5 |
| Jefferson | 2 | 51 | 25.5 | Phillips | 2 | 12 | 6.0 |
| Mackey | 1 | 8 | 8.0 | Thomas | 1 | 9 | 9.0 |
| | 6 | 145 | 24.2 | Johnson | 1 | 6 | 6.0 |
| | | | | | 8 | 93 | 11.6 |
| **PUNTING** | | | | | | | |
| Lee | 6 | | 38.3 | Lewis | 8 | | 39.1 |
| **PUNT RETURNS** | | | | | | | |
| Gardin | 7 | 28 | 4.0 | Parrish | 2 | 6 | 3.0 |
| **KICKOFF RETURNS** | | | | | | | |
| Nowatzke | 1 | 0 | 0.0 | Robinson | 2 | 29 | 14.5 |
| | | | | Lamb | 1 | 17 | 17.0 |
| | | | | | 3 | 46 | 15.3 |
| **INTERCEPTION RETURNS** | | | | | | | |
| M. Curtis | 1 | 0 | 0.0 | None | | | |

**PASSING**

| BALTIMORE | Att. | Comp. | Comp. Pct. | Yds. | Int. | Yds/ Att. | Yds/ Comp. | Yds Lost Tkld |
|---|---|---|---|---|---|---|---|---|
| Unitas | 17 | 6 | 35.3 | 145 | 0 | 8.5 | 24.2 | 2–16 |
| **CINCINNATI** | | | | | | | | |
| Carter | 20 | 7 | 35.0 | 64 | 1 | 3.2 | 9.1 | |
| Wyche | 1 | 1 | 100.0 | 29 | 0 | 29.0 | 29.0 | |
| | 21 | 8 | 38.1 | 93 | 1 | 4.4 | 11.6 | 3–17 |

1970 A.F.C. — Eastern Division 200

## BALTIMORE COLTS 11-2-1 Don McCafferty

| Scores of Each Game | | |
|---|---|---|
| 16 | San Diego | 14 |
| 24 | KANSAS CITY | 44 |
| 14 | Boston | 6 |
| 24 | Houston | 20 |
| 29 | N.Y. Jets | 22 |
| 27 | BOSTON | 3 |
| 35 | MIAMI | 0 |
| 13 | Green Bay | 10 |
| 17 | BUFFALO | 17 |
| 17 | Miami | 34 |
| 21 | CHICAGO | 20 |
| 29 | PHILADELPHIA | 10 |
| 20 | Buffalo | 14 |
| 35 | N.Y. JETS | 20 |

| Use Name | Pos. | Hgt | Wgt | Age | Int | Pts |
|---|---|---|---|---|---|---|
| Sam Ball | OT | 6'4" | 240 | 26 | | |
| Dennis Nelson | OT | 6'5" | 260 | 24 | | |
| Bob Vogel | OT | 6'5" | 250 | 28 | | |
| Cornelius Johnson | OG | 6'2" | 245 | 27 | | |
| Glenn Ressler | OG | 6'3" | 250 | 26 | | |
| Dan Sullivan | OG | 6'3" | 250 | 31 | | |
| John Williams | OG | 6'3" | 256 | 24 | | |
| Bill Curry | C | 6'2" | 235 | 27 | | |
| Tom Goode | C | 6'3" | 245 | 31 | | |
| Roy Hilton | DE | 6'6" | 240 | 25 | | |
| Billy Newsome | DE | 6'4" | 240 | 22 | | |
| Bubba Smith | DE | 6'7" | 295 | 25 | | |
| Jim Bailey | DT | 6'5" | 245 | 22 | | |
| Fred Miller | DT | 6'3" | 250 | 29 | | |
| Billy Ray Smith | DT | 6'4" | 250 | 35 | | |
| George Wright | DT | 6'3" | 260 | 23 | | |
| Mike Curtis | LB | 6'2" | 232 | 27 | 5 | |
| Bob Grant | LB | 6'2" | 225 | 24 | 2 | 6 |
| Ted Hendricks | LB | 6'7" | 215 | 22 | 1 | 6 |
| Ray May | LB | 6'1" | 230 | 25 | 1 | |
| Robbie Nichols | LB | 6'3" | 220 | 23 | | |
| Tom Curtis | DB | 6'1" | 196 | 22 | 1 | |
| Jim Duncan | DB | 6'2" | 220 | 24 | 2 | 6 |
| Ron Gardin | DB | 5'11" | 180 | 25 | | 6 |
| Jerry Logan | DB | 6'1" | 190 | 29 | 6 | 12 |
| Tommy Maxwell | DB | 6'2" | 195 | 23 | | |
| Charlie Stukes | DB | 6'3" | 212 | 26 | 3 | |
| Rick Volk | DB | 6'3" | 195 | 25 | 4 | |
| Earl Morrall | QB | 6'1" | 206 | 36 | | |
| Johnny Unitas | QB | 6'1" | 196 | 37 | | |
| Sam Havrilak | HB | 6'2" | 195 | 22 | | |
| Jack Maitland | HB | 6'1" | 210 | 22 | | 12 |
| Tom Matte | HB | 6' | 214 | 31 | | |
| Norm Bulaich | FB-HB | 6'1" | 218 | 23 | | 18 |
| Larry Conjar | FB | 6' | 214 | 24 | | |
| Jerry Hill | FB | 5'11" | 217 | 30 | | 12 |
| Tom Nowatzke | FB | 6'3" | 230 | 27 | | 6 |
| Eddie Hinton | WR | 6' | 200 | 23 | | 42 |
| Roy Jefferson | WR | 6'2" | 190 | 26 | | 42 |
| Jim O'Brien | WR | 6' | 195 | 23 | | 93 |
| Jimmy Orr | WR | 5'11" | 185 | 34 | | 12 |
| Ray Perkins | WR | 6' | 183 | 28 | | 6 |
| John Mackey | TE | 6'3" | 224 | 28 | | 18 |
| Tom Mitchell | TE | 6'2" | 215 | 26 | | 24 |
| David Lee | K | 6'4" | 230 | 26 | | |

## MIAMI DOLPHINS 10-4-0 Don Shula

| Scores of Each Game | | |
|---|---|---|
| 14 | Boston | 27 |
| 20 | Houston | 10 |
| 20 | OAKLAND | 13 |
| 20 | N.Y. Jets | 6 |
| 33 | Buffalo | 14 |
| 0 | CLEVELAND | 28 |
| 0 | Baltimore | 35 |
| 17 | Philadelphia | 24 |
| 21 | NEW ORLEANS | 10 |
| 34 | BALTIMORE | 17 |
| 20 | Atlanta | 7 |
| 37 | BOSTON | 20 |
| 16 | N.Y. JETS | 10 |
| 45 | BUFFALO | 7 |

| Use Name | Pos. | Hgt | Wgt | Age | Int | Pts |
|---|---|---|---|---|---|---|
| Doug Crusan | OT | 6'5" | 260 | 24 | | |
| Norm Evans | OT | 6'5" | 250 | 27 | | |
| Wayne Moore | OT | 6'6" | 265 | 25 | | |
| Bob Kuechenberg | OG | 6'3" | 255 | 22 | | |
| Jim Langer | OG | 6'2" | 240 | 22 | | |
| Larry Little | OG | 6'1" | 270 | 24 | | |
| Maxie Williams | OG | 6'4" | 250 | 30 | | |
| Bob DeMarco | C | 6'3" | 245 | 32 | | |
| Carl Mauck | C | 6'3" | 240 | 23 | | |
| Norm McBride | DE | 6'3" | 245 | 23 | | |
| Jim Riley | DE | 6'4" | 260 | 25 | | |
| Bill Stanfill | DE | 6'5" | 250 | 23 | | |
| Frank Cornish (from CHI) | DT | 6'6" | 285 | 26 | | |
| Manny Fernandez | DT | 6'2" | 250 | 24 | | |
| Bob Heinz | DT | 6'6" | 290 | 23 | | |
| John Richardson | DT | 6'2" | 260 | 25 | | |
| Nick Buoniconti | LB | 5'11" | 220 | 29 | | |
| Ted Davis | LB | 6'1" | 232 | 28 | 1 | |
| Mike Kolen | LB | 6'2" | 215 | 22 | | |
| Dick Palmer | LB | 6'2" | 220 | 22 | | |
| Jesse Powell | LB | 6'1" | 215 | 23 | | |
| Doug Swift | LB | 6'3" | 230 | 21 | | |
| Ed Weisacosky | LB | 6' | 230 | 26 | | |
| Dick Anderson | DB | 6'2" | 200 | 24 | 8 | |
| Dean Brown | DB | 5'10" | 170 | 23 | 1 | |
| Tim Foley | DB | 6' | 195 | 22 | | |
| Curtis Johnson | DB | 6'2" | 200 | 22 | 3 | |
| Lloyd Mumphord | DB | 5'11" | 180 | 23 | 5 | 12 |
| Bob Petrella | DB | 6' | 185 | 25 | | |
| Jake Scott | DB | 6' | 188 | 25 | 5 | 6 |
| Bill Darnall—Injury | | | | | | |
| Bob Griese | QB | 6'1" | 190 | 25 | | 12 |
| John Stofa | QB | 6'3" | 210 | 28 | | |
| Hubert Ginn | HB | 5'11" | 190 | 23 | | |
| Jim Kiick | HB | 5'11" | 220 | 24 | | 36 |
| Mercury Morris | HB | 5'10" | 190 | 23 | | 6 |
| Barry Pryor | HB | 6' | 215 | 24 | | |
| Larry Csonka | FB | 6'3" | 250 | 23 | | 36 |
| Stan Mitchell | FB | 6'2" | 210 | 26 | | 6 |
| Karl Noonan | WR | 6'3" | 205 | 26 | | 6 |
| Willie Richardson | WR | 6'2" | 198 | 30 | | 6 |
| Howard Twilley | WR | 5'10" | 180 | 26 | | 30 |
| Paul Warfield | WR | 6' | 190 | 27 | | 36 |
| Marv Fleming | TE | 6'4" | 235 | 28 | | |
| Jim Mandich | TE | 6'3" | 225 | 21 | | 6 |
| Larry Seiple | TE | 6' | 220 | 25 | | |
| Karl Kremser | K | 6' | 175 | 25 | | 2 |
| Garo Yepremian | K | 5'8" | 172 | 26 | | 97 |

## NEW YORK JETS 4-10-0 Weeb Ewbank

| Scores of Each Game | | |
|---|---|---|
| 21 | Cleveland | 31 |
| 31 | Boston | 21 |
| 31 | Buffalo | 34 |
| 6 | MIAMI | 20 |
| 22 | BALTIMORE | 29 |
| 6 | BUFFALO | 10 |
| 10 | N.Y. GIANTS | 22 |
| 17 | Pittsburgh | 21 |
| 31 | Los Angeles | 20 |
| 17 | BOSTON | 3 |
| 20 | MINNESOTA | 10 |
| 13 | OAKLAND | 14 |
| 10 | Miami | 16 |
| 20 | Baltimore | 35 |

| Use Name | Pos. | Hgt | Wgt | Age | Int | Pts |
|---|---|---|---|---|---|---|
| Dave Foley | OT | 6'5" | 255 | 22 | | |
| Winston Hill | OT | 6'4" | 285 | 28 | | |
| Roger Finnie | OG-OT | 6'3" | 245 | 24 | | |
| Tom Bayless | OG | 6'3" | 240 | 22 | | |
| Dave Herman | OG | 6'2" | 255 | 28 | | |
| Dave Middendorf | OG | 6'3" | 260 | 24 | | |
| Randy Rasmussen | OG | 6'2" | 255 | 25 | | |
| Pete Perreault | OT-OG | 6'3" | 248 | 31 | | |
| John Schmitt | C | 6'4" | 250 | 27 | | |
| Paul Crane | LB-C | 6'2" | 212 | 26 | | |
| Verlon Biggs | DE | 6'4" | 270 | 27 | | |
| Jimmie Jones | DE | 6'3" | 215 | 23 | | |
| Gerry Philbin | DE | 6'2' | 245 | 29 | | |
| Mark Lomas | DT-DE | 6'4" | 230 | 22 | | |
| John Elliott | DT | 6'4" | 244 | 25 | | 2 |
| John Little | DE-DT | 6'3" | 220 | 23 | | |
| Steve Thompson | DE-DT | 6'5" | 245 | 25 | | |
| Al Atkinson | LB | 6'1" | 230 | 27 | 3 | |
| Ralph Baker | LB | 6'3" | 235 | 28 | 2 | |
| John Ebersole | LB | 6'3" | 240 | 21 | | |
| Larry Grantham | LB | 6' | 210 | 31 | 3 | 6 |
| Dennis Onkotz | LB | 6'1" | 220 | 22 | | |
| Mike Battle | DB | 6'1" | 175 | 24 | | |
| John Dockery | DB | 6' | 186 | 25 | | |
| W.K. Hicks | DB | 6'1" | 195 | 27 | 8 | |
| Gus Holloman | DB | 6'3" | 195 | 24 | 3 | |
| Jim Hudson | DB | 6'2" | 210 | 27 | | |
| Cecil Leonard | DB | 5'11" | 160 | 24 | | |
| Steve Tannen | DB | 6'1" | 194 | 22 | 2 | 6 |
| Earlie Thomas | DB | 6'1" | 190 | 24 | 2 | 6 |
| Jim Richards—Military Service | | | | | | |
| Paul Seiler—Injury | | | | | | |
| Bob Davis | QB | 6'3" | 205 | 25 | | |
| Joe Namath | QB | 6'2" | 200 | 27 | | |
| Jim Turner | QB | 6'2" | 215 | 29 | | 85 |
| Al Woodall | QB | 6'5" | 205 | 24 | | |
| Emerson Boozer | HB | 5'11" | 195 | 27 | | 30 |
| Cliff McClain | HB | 6' | 217 | 22 | | |
| George Nock | HB | 5'10" | 200 | 24 | | 36 |
| Chuck Mercein | FB | 6'3" | 222 | 27 | | 6 |
| Matt Snell | FB | 6'2" | 220 | 28 | | 6 |
| Lee White | FB | 6'4" | 235 | 24 | | 6 |
| Eddie Bell | WR | 5'10" | 160 | 22 | | 12 |
| Rich Caster | WR | 6'5" | 222 | 21 | | 18 |
| Don Maynard | WR | 6' | 180 | 34 | | |
| Steve O'Neal | WR | 6'3" | 185 | 24 | | |
| George Sauer | WR | 6'1" | 195 | 26 | | 24 |
| Gary Arthur | TE | 6'5" | 230 | 22 | | |
| Pete Lammons | TE | 6'3" | 230 | 26 | | 12 |
| Wayne Stewart | TE | 6'7" | 213 | 23 | | |

## BUFFALO BILLS 3-10-1 Johnny Rauch

| Scores of Each Game | | |
|---|---|---|
| 10 | DENVER | 25 |
| 0 | LOS ANGELES | 19 |
| 34 | N.Y. JETS | 31 |
| 10 | Pittsburgh | 23 |
| 14 | MIAMI | 33 |
| 10 | N.Y. Jets | 6 |
| 45 | Boston | 10 |
| 14 | CINCINNATI | 43 |
| 17 | Baltimore | 17 |
| 13 | Chicago | 31 |
| 10 | BOSTON | 14 |
| 6 | N.Y. Giants | 20 |
| 14 | BALTIMORE | 20 |
| 7 | Miami | 45 |

| Use Name | Pos. | Hgt | Wgt | Age | Int | Pts |
|---|---|---|---|---|---|---|
| Levert Carr | OT | 6'5" | 260 | 26 | | |
| Paul Costa | OT | 6'4" | 255 | 28 | | |
| Jerry Gantt | OT | 6'4" | 266 | 21 | | |
| Art Laster | OT | 6'4" | 280 | 22 | | |
| Howard Kindig | C-OT | 6'6" | 264 | 29 | | |
| Richard Cheek | OG | 6'3" | 266 | 22 | | |
| Joe O'Donnell | OG | 6'2" | 262 | 27 | | |
| Jim Reilly | OG | 6'2" | 260 | 22 | | |
| Wayne Fowler | C | 6'3" | 260 | 21 | | |
| Frank Marchlewski | C | 6'2" | 240 | 26 | | |
| Al Cowlings | DE | 6'5" | 258 | 23 | | |
| Mike McBath | DE | 6'4" | 248 | 24 | | |
| Ron McDole | DE | 6'3" | 288 | 30 | | |
| Jim Dunaway | DT | 6'4" | 277 | 28 | | |
| Waddey Harvey | DT | 6'4" | 282 | 23 | | |
| Julian Nunamaker | DT | 6'3" | 252 | 24 | | |
| Bob Tatarek | DT | 6'4" | 260 | 24 | | |
| Al Andrews | LB | 6'3" | 216 | 26 | | |
| Edgar Chandler | LB | 6'3" | 235 | 24 | 1 | 6 |
| Jerald Collins | LB | 6'1" | 220 | 23 | | |
| Dick Cunningham | LB | 6'2" | 244 | 25 | | |
| Paul Guidry | LB | 6'3" | 233 | 26 | | |
| Mike McCaffrey | LB | 6'3" | 235 | 24 | | |
| Mike Stratton | LB | 6'3" | 240 | 28 | | |
| Jackie Allen | DB | 6'1" | 187 | 22 | | |
| Butch Byrd | DB | 6' | 196 | 28 | 4 | 6 |
| Ike Hill | DB | 5'10" | 180 | 23 | | |
| Robert James | DB | 6'1" | 177 | 23 | | |
| Tommy Pharr | DB | 5'10" | 187 | 23 | | |
| John Pitts | DB | 6'4" | 223 | 25 | 1 | |
| Pete Richardson | DB | 6'1" | 193 | 23 | 5 | |
| Max Anderson — Knee Injury | | | | | | |
| Dan Darragh | QB | 6'3" | 196 | 23 | | |
| James Harris | QB | 6'3" | 215 | 23 | | |
| Dennis Shaw | QB | 6'2" | 210 | 23 | | |
| Greg Jones | HB | 6'1" | 200 | 22 | | 12 |
| Lloyd Pate | HB | 6'1" | 205 | 24 | | 6 |
| O. J. Simpson | HB | 6'2" | 204 | 23 | | 36 |
| Bill Enyart | FB | 6'4" | 236 | 23 | | 6 |
| Wayne Patrick | FB | 6'2" | 254 | 24 | | 6 |
| Glenn Alexander | WR | 6'3" | 205 | 23 | | |
| Marlin Briscoe | WR | 5'10" | 177 | 24 | | 48 |
| Clyde Glosson | WR | 5'11" | 175 | 23 | | |
| Haven Moses | WR | 6'3" | 205 | 24 | | 12 |
| Austin Denney | TE | 6'2" | 230 | 26 | | |
| Willie Grate | TE | 6'4" | 225 | 24 | | 12 |
| Roland Moss (from SD) | HB-TE | 6'3" | 215 | 23 | | |
| Grant Guthrie | K | 6' | 210 | 22 | | 54 |
| Paul Maguire | K | 6' | 232 | 32 | | |

## BOSTON PATRIOTS 2-12-0 Clive Rush John Mazur

| Scores of Each Game | | |
|---|---|---|
| 27 | MIAMI | 14 |
| 21 | N.Y. JETS | 31 |
| 6 | Baltimore | 14 |
| 10 | Kansas City | 23 |
| 0 | N.Y. GIANTS | 16 |
| 3 | BALTIMORE | 27 |
| 10 | BUFFALO | 45 |
| 0 | St. Louis | 31 |
| 14 | SAN DIEGO | 16 |
| 3 | N.Y. Jets | 17 |
| 14 | Buffalo | 10 |
| 20 | Miami | 37 |
| 14 | MINNESOTA | 35 |
| 7 | Cincinnati | 45 |

| Use Name | Pos. | Hgt | Wgt | Age | Int | Pts |
|---|---|---|---|---|---|---|
| Tom Funchess | OT | 6'5" | 260 | 25 | | |
| Ezell Jones | OT | 6'4" | 255 | 23 | | |
| Tom Neville | OT | 6'4" | 255 | 27 | | |
| Len St. Jean | OG | 6'1" | 245 | 28 | | |
| Gary Bugenhagen | OT-OG | 6'2" | 250 | 25 | | |
| Angelo Loukas | OT-OG | 6'3" | 250 | 23 | | |
| Jon Morris | C | 6'4" | 255 | 27 | | |
| Mike Montler | OG-C | 6'4" | 270 | 26 | | |
| Ron Berger | DE | 6'8" | 275 | 26 | | |
| Ike Lassiter | DE | 6'5" | 270 | 29 | | |
| Dennis Wirgowski | DE | 6'5" | 255 | 22 | | |
| Mel Witt | DE | 6'3" | 250 | 24 | | |
| Houston Antwine | DT | 6' | 270 | 31 | | |
| Jim Hunt | DT | 5'11" | 255 | 31 | | |
| Rex Mirich | DT | 6'4" | 258 | 29 | | |
| Mike Ballou | LB | 6'3" | 235 | 22 | | |
| John Bramlett | LB | 6'2" | 220 | 29 | 1 | |
| Jim Cheyunski | LB | 6'2" | 220 | 24 | | |
| Ed Philpott | LB | 6'3" | 240 | 24 | 1 | |
| Marty Schottenheimer | LB | 6'3" | 225 | 27 | | |
| Fred Whittingham | LB | 6'1" | 240 | 31 | | |
| J.R. Williamson | LB | 6'2" | 220 | 28 | 1 | |
| Randy Beverly | DB | 5'11" | 185 | 26 | | |
| Larry Carwell | DB | 6'1" | 190 | 26 | | |
| Tom Janik | DB | 6'3" | 200 | 29 | | |
| Daryle Johnson | DB | 5'11" | 190 | 24 | 2 | |
| Art McMahon | DB | 5'11" | 190 | 24 | 1 | |
| John Outlaw | DB | 5'10" | 180 | 25 | | |
| Clarence Scott | DB | 6'2" | 205 | 26 | 1 | |
| Don Webb | DB | 5'10" | 195 | 31 | 1 | |
| Ed Toner — Injury | | | | | | |
| Joe Kapp | QB | 6'2" | 215 | 32 | | |
| Mike Taliaferro | QB | 6'2" | 205 | 28 | | |
| Sid Blanks | HB | 6' | 205 | 29 | | |
| Carl Garrett | HB | 5'11" | 210 | 23 | | 24 |
| Bob Gladieux (to BUF) | HB | 5'11" | 190 | 23 | | |
| Odell Lawson | HB | 6'2" | 218 | 22 | | |
| Jim Nance | FB | 6'1" | 240 | 27 | | 42 |
| Eddie Ray | TE-FB | 6'1" | 230 | 23 | | |
| Ginn Cappelletti | WR | 6' | 190 | 36 | | 30 |
| Charley Frazier | WR | 6' | 190 | 31 | | |
| Gayle Knief | WR | 6'3" | 205 | 23 | | 6 |
| Bill Rademacher | WR | 6'1" | 190 | 28 | | |
| Tom Richardson | WR | 6'2" | 195 | 25 | | |
| Ron Sellers | WR | 6'4" | 195 | 23 | | 24 |
| Bake Turner | WR | 6' | 180 | 30 | | 12 |
| Tom Beer | TE | 6'4" | 228 | 25 | | |
| Barry Brown | TE | 6'3" | 220 | 27 | | |
| Charlie Gogolak | K | 5'10" | 170 | 25 | | 11 |

## BALTIMORE COLTS

### RUSHING

| Last Name | No. | Yds | Avg | TD |
|---|---|---|---|---|
| Bulaich | 139 | 426 | 3.1 | 3 |
| Nowatzke | 73 | 248 | 3.4 | 1 |
| Maitland | 74 | 209 | 2.8 | 1 |
| Havrilak | 54 | 159 | 2.9 | 0 |
| Hill | 36 | 115 | 3.2 | 2 |
| Hinton | 5 | 58 | 11.6 | 2 |
| Jefferson | 4 | 47 | 11.8 | 0 |
| Matte | 12 | 43 | 3.6 | 0 |
| Unitas | 9 | 16 | 1.8 | 0 |
| Morrall | 2 | 6 | 3.0 | 0 |
| Perkins | 2 | 6 | 3.0 | 0 |
| Conjar | 1 | 3 | 3.0 | 0 |

### RECEIVING

| Last Name | No. | Yds | Avg | TD |
|---|---|---|---|---|
| Hinton | 47 | 733 | 16 | 5 |
| Jefferson | 44 | 749 | 17 | 7 |
| Mackey | 28 | 435 | 16 | 3 |
| Mitchell | 20 | 261 | 13 | 4 |
| Nowatzke | 16 | 93 | 6 | 0 |
| Havrilak | 14 | 141 | 10 | 0 |
| Bulaich | 11 | 123 | 11 | 0 |
| Orr | 10 | 199 | 20 | 2 |
| Perkins | 10 | 194 | 19 | 1 |
| Maitland | 9 | 67 | 7 | 1 |
| Hill | 8 | 62 | 8 | 0 |
| O'Brien | 1 | 28 | 28 | 0 |
| Matte | 1 | 2 | 2 | 0 |

### PUNT RETURNS

| Last Name | No. | Yds | Avg | TD |
|---|---|---|---|---|
| Gardin | 28 | 330 | 12 | 1 |
| Volk | 3 | 15 | 5 | 0 |
| Logan | 2 | 4 | 2 | 0 |
| T. Curtis | 3 | 2 | 1 | 0 |

### KICKOFF RETURNS

| Last Name | No. | Yds | Avg | TD |
|---|---|---|---|---|
| Duncan | 20 | 707 | 35 | 1 |
| Gardin | 11 | 265 | 24 | 0 |
| Nowatzke | 7 | 93 | 13 | 0 |
| Havrilak | 2 | 36 | 18 | 0 |
| Maitland | 1 | 28 | 28 | 0 |
| Grant | 1 | 21 | 21 | 0 |
| Jefferson | 1 | 11 | 11 | 0 |
| Newsome | 1 | 0 | 0 | 0 |
| Stukes | 1 | 0 | 0 | 0 |

### PASSING – PUNTING – KICKING Statistics

PASSING

| Last Name | Att | Comp | % | Yds | Yd/Att | TD | Int- | % | RK |
|---|---|---|---|---|---|---|---|---|---|
| Unitas | 321 | 166 | 52 | 2213 | 6.9 | 14 | 18- | 6 | 6 |
| Morrall | 93 | 51 | 55 | 792 | 8.5 | 9 | 4- | 4 | |
| Havrilak | 2 | 2 | 100 | 82 | 41.0 | 0 | 0- | 0 | |

PUNTING

| Last Name | No | Avg |
|---|---|---|
| Lee | 63 | 44.7 |

KICKING

| Last Name | XP | Att | % | FG | Att | % |
|---|---|---|---|---|---|---|
| O'Brien | 36 | 38 | 95 | 19 | 34 | 56 |

## MIAMI DOLPHINS

### RUSHING

| Last Name | No. | Yds | Avg | TD |
|---|---|---|---|---|
| Csonka | 193 | 874 | 4.5 | 6 |
| Kiick | 191 | 658 | 3.4 | 6 |
| Morris | 60 | 409 | 6.8 | 0 |
| Griese | 26 | 89 | 3.4 | 2 |
| Mitchell | 8 | 23 | 2.9 | 0 |
| Seiple | 2 | 21 | 10.5 | 0 |
| Warfield | 2 | 13 | 6.5 | 0 |
| Stofa | 2 | 5 | 2.5 | 0 |
| Pryor | 2 | 0 | 0.0 | 0 |
| Ginn | 5 | -1 | -0.2 | 0 |
| Noonan | 1 | -9 | -9.0 | 0 |

### RECEIVING

| Last Name | No. | Yds | Avg | TD |
|---|---|---|---|---|
| Kiick | 42 | 497 | 12 | 0 |
| Warfield | 28 | 703 | 25 | 6 |
| Twilley | 22 | 281 | 13 | 5 |
| Fleming | 18 | 205 | 11 | 0 |
| Morris | 12 | 149 | 12 | 0 |
| Csonka | 11 | 94 | 9 | 0 |
| Noonan | 10 | 186 | 19 | 1 |
| W. Richardson | 7 | 67 | 10 | 1 |
| Mitchell | 6 | 85 | 14 | 1 |
| Seiple | 2 | 14 | 7 | 0 |
| Mandich | 1 | 3 | 3 | 1 |

### PUNT RETURNS

| Last Name | No. | Yds | Avg | TD |
|---|---|---|---|---|
| Scott | 27 | 290 | 11 | 1 |
| Anderson | 1 | 6 | 6 | 0 |
| Morris | 2 | -1 | -1 | 0 |

### KICKOFF RETURNS

| Last Name | No. | Yds | Avg | TD |
|---|---|---|---|---|
| Morris | 28 | 812 | 29 | 1 |
| Scott | 4 | 117 | 29 | 0 |
| Ginn | 5 | 59 | 12 | 0 |
| Mitchell | 4 | 35 | 9 | 0 |
| Anderson | 1 | 8 | 8 | 0 |
| Seiple | 2 | 5 | 3 | 0 |
| Mandich | 2 | 0 | 0 | 0 |
| Brown | 1 | 0 | 0 | 0 |
| Foley | 1 | 0 | 0 | 0 |

### PASSING – PUNTING – KICKING Statistics

PASSING

| Last Name | Att | Comp | % | Yds | Yd/Att | TD | Int- | % | RK |
|---|---|---|---|---|---|---|---|---|---|
| Griese | 245 | 142 | 58 | 2019 | 8.2 | 12 | 17- | 7 | 4 |
| Stofa | 53 | 16 | 30 | 240 | 4.5 | 3 | 2- | 4 | |
| Kiick | 1 | 1 | 100 | 25 | 25.0 | 0 | 0- | 0 | |

PUNTING

| Last Name | No | Avg |
|---|---|---|
| Seiple | 58 | 41.2 |

KICKING

| Last Name | XP | Att | % | FG | Att | % |
|---|---|---|---|---|---|---|
| Yepremian | 31 | 31 | 100 | 22 | 29 | 76 |
| Kremser | 2 | 2 | 100 | 0 | 1 | 0 |

## NEW YORK JETS

### RUSHING

| Last Name | No. | Yds | Avg | TD |
|---|---|---|---|---|
| Boozer | 139 | 581 | 4.2 | 5 |
| Nock | 135 | 402 | 3.0 | 5 |
| Snell | 64 | 281 | 4.4 | 1 |
| White | 70 | 215 | 3.1 | 0 |
| Woodall | 28 | 110 | 3.9 | 0 |
| Mercein | 20 | 44 | 2.2 | 0 |
| O'Neal | 1 | 16 | 16.0 | 0 |
| Davis | 2 | 11 | 5.5 | 0 |
| Turner | 1 | 1 | 1.0 | 0 |
| Namath | 1 | -1 | -1.0 | 0 |
| Bell | 2 | -7 | -3.5 | 0 |

### RECEIVING

| Last Name | No. | Yds | Avg | TD |
|---|---|---|---|---|
| Maynard | 31 | 525 | 17 | 0 |
| Sauer | 31 | 510 | 16 | 4 |
| Boozer | 28 | 258 | 9 | 0 |
| Lammons | 25 | 316 | 13 | 2 |
| Bell | 21 | 246 | 12 | 2 |
| Caster | 19 | 393 | 21 | 3 |
| Nock | 18 | 146 | 8 | 1 |
| White | 12 | 125 | 10 | 1 |
| Mercein | 3 | 27 | 9 | 1 |
| Snell | 2 | 26 | 13 | 0 |
| McClain | 1 | 11 | 11 | 0 |
| Stewart | 1 | 7 | 7 | 0 |
| Battle | 1 | 2 | 2 | 0 |

### PUNT RETURNS

| Last Name | No. | Yds | Avg | TD |
|---|---|---|---|---|
| Battle | 19 | 117 | 6 | 0 |
| Bell | 7 | 33 | 5 | 0 |

### KICKOFF RETURNS

| Last Name | No. | Yds | Avg | TD |
|---|---|---|---|---|
| Battle | 40 | 891 | 22 | 0 |
| McClain | 4 | 70 | 18 | 0 |
| Bell | 3 | 61 | 20 | 0 |
| Leonard | 1 | 35 | 35 | 0 |
| Mercein | 4 | 32 | 8 | 0 |
| Nock | 1 | 18 | 18 | 0 |
| Caster | 1 | 0 | 0 | 0 |
| Onkotz | 1 | 0 | 0 | 0 |
| Tannen | 1 | -1 | -1 | 0 |

### PASSING – PUNTING – KICKING Statistics

PASSING

| Last Name | Att | Comp | % | Yds | Yd/Att | TD | Int- | % | RK |
|---|---|---|---|---|---|---|---|---|---|
| Woodall | 188 | 96 | 51 | 1265 | 6.7 | 9 | 9- | 5 | 9 |
| Namath | 179 | 90 | 50 | 1259 | 7.0 | 5 | 12- | 7 | 13 |
| Davis | 17 | 6 | 35 | 66 | 3.9 | 0 | 0- | 0 | |
| Bell | 1 | 0 | 0 | 0.0 | 0 | | 1- | 100 | |
| O'Neal | 1 | 1 | 100 | 2 | 2.0 | 0 | 0- | 0 | |

PUNTING

| Last Name | No | Avg |
|---|---|---|
| O'Neal | 73 | 40.1 |

KICKING

| Last Name | XP | Att | % | FG | Att | % |
|---|---|---|---|---|---|---|
| Turner | 28 | 28 | 100 | 19 | 35 | 54 |

## BUFFALO BILLS

### RUSHING

| Last Name | No. | Yds | Avg | TD |
|---|---|---|---|---|
| Simpson | 120 | 488 | 4.1 | 5 |
| Patrick | 66 | 259 | 3.9 | 1 |
| Shaw | 39 | 210 | 5.4 | 0 |
| Enyart | 58 | 196 | 3.4 | 0 |
| Pate | 46 | 162 | 3.5 | 1 |
| Jones | 31 | 113 | 3.6 | 1 |
| Darragh | 1 | 26 | 26.0 | 0 |
| Briscoe | 3 | 19 | 6.3 | 0 |
| Harris | 3 | -8 | -2.7 | 0 |

### RECEIVING

| Last Name | No. | Yds | Avg | TD |
|---|---|---|---|---|
| Briscoe | 57 | 1036 | 18 | 8 |
| Moses | 39 | 726 | 19 | 2 |
| Enyart | 35 | 235 | 7 | 1 |
| Pate | 19 | 103 | 5 | 0 |
| Patrick | 16 | 142 | 9 | 0 |
| Denney | 14 | 201 | 14 | 0 |
| Simpson | 10 | 139 | 14 | 0 |
| Jones | 8 | 89 | 11 | 0 |
| Grate | 7 | 147 | 21 | 2 |
| Alexander | 4 | 51 | 13 | 0 |
| Moss | 2 | 31 | 16 | 0 |
| Glosson | 2 | 16 | 8 | 0 |

### PUNT RETURNS

| Last Name | No. | Yds | Avg | TD |
|---|---|---|---|---|
| Pharr | 23 | 184 | 8 | 0 |
| Hill | 19 | 102 | 5 | 0 |
| Allen | 2 | 10 | 5 | 0 |
| Alexander | 1 | 2 | 2 | 0 |

### KICKOFF RETURNS

| Last Name | No. | Yds | Avg | TD |
|---|---|---|---|---|
| Simpson | 7 | 333 | 48 | 1 |
| Alexander | 12 | 204 | 17 | 0 |
| Hill | 9 | 165 | 18 | 0 |
| Jones | 7 | 162 | 23 | 1 |
| Moss | 7 | 131 | 19 | 0 |
| Glosson | 4 | 61 | 15 | 0 |
| Enyart | 3 | 60 | 20 | 0 |
| Patrick | 3 | 38 | 13 | 0 |
| Pate | 1 | 21 | 21 | 0 |
| Collins | 2 | 17 | 9 | 0 |
| Andrews | 1 | 16 | 16 | 0 |
| McCaffrey | 2 | 15 | 8 | 0 |
| Laster | 2 | 8 | 4 | 0 |
| McBath | 1 | 7 | 7 | 0 |
| Pharr | 1 | 6 | 6 | 0 |
| Costa | 1 | 0 | 0 | 0 |

### PASSING – PUNTING – KICKING Statistics

PASSING

| Last Name | Att | Comp | % | Yds | Yd/Att | TD | Int- | % | RK |
|---|---|---|---|---|---|---|---|---|---|
| Shaw | 321 | 178 | 55 | 2507 | 7.8 | 10 | 20- | 6 | 4 |
| Harris | 50 | 24 | 48 | 338 | 6.8 | 3 | 4- | 8 | |
| Darragh | 29 | 11 | 38 | 71 | 2.5 | 0 | 2- | 7 | |
| Simpson | 2 | 0 | 0 | 0.0 | 0 | | 0- | 0 | |

PUNTING

| Last Name | No | Avg |
|---|---|---|
| Maguire | 83 | 38.9 |

KICKING

| Last Name | XP | Att | % | FG | Att | % |
|---|---|---|---|---|---|---|
| Guthrie | 24 | 25 | 96 | 10 | 19 | 53 |

## BOSTON PATRIOTS

### RUSHING

| Last Name | No. | Yds | Avg | TD |
|---|---|---|---|---|
| Nance | 145 | 522 | 3.6 | 7 |
| Garrett | 88 | 272 | 3.1 | 4 |
| Lawson | 56 | 99 | 1.8 | 0 |
| Kapp | 20 | 71 | 3.6 | 0 |
| Blanks | 13 | 44 | 3.4 | 0 |
| Ray | 5 | 13 | 2.6 | 0 |
| Taliaferro | 3 | 11 | 3.7 | 0 |
| Gladieux | 4 | 8 | 2.0 | 0 |

### RECEIVING

| Last Name | No. | Yds | Avg | TD |
|---|---|---|---|---|
| Sellers | 38 | 550 | 14 | 4 |
| Turner | 28 | 428 | 15 | 2 |
| Garrett | 26 | 216 | 8 | 0 |
| Nance | 26 | 148 | 6 | 0 |
| Brown | 15 | 145 | 10 | 0 |
| Beer | 11 | 150 | 14 | 0 |
| Lawson | 11 | 113 | 10 | 0 |
| Frazier | 9 | 86 | 10 | 0 |
| Blanks | 5 | 49 | 10 | 0 |
| Rademacher | 4 | 51 | 13 | 0 |
| Knief | 3 | 39 | 13 | 1 |

### PUNT RETURNS

| Last Name | No. | Yds | Avg | TD |
|---|---|---|---|---|
| Garrett | 17 | 168 | 10 | 0 |
| Blanks | 9 | 83 | 9 | 0 |
| Carwell | 3 | 48 | 16 | 0 |
| Johnson | 2 | 6 | 3 | 0 |
| Lawson | 1 | 0 | 0 | 0 |

### KICKOFF RETURNS

| Last Name | No. | Yds | Avg | TD |
|---|---|---|---|---|
| Lawson | 25 | 546 | 22 | 0 |
| Garrett | 24 | 511 | 21 | 0 |
| Blanks | 7 | 152 | 22 | 0 |
| Carwell | 1 | 30 | 30 | 0 |
| Whittingham | 1 | 24 | 24 | 0 |
| Schottenheimer | 1 | 8 | 8 | 0 |
| Beer | 1 | 4 | 4 | 0 |
| Beverly | 1 | 0 | 0 | 0 |
| Brown | 1 | 0 | 0 | 0 |

### PASSING – PUNTING – KICKING Statistics

PASSING

| Last Name | Att | Comp | % | Yds | Yd/Att | TD | Int- | % | RK |
|---|---|---|---|---|---|---|---|---|---|
| Kapp | 219 | 98 | 45 | 1104 | 5.0 | 3 | 17- | 8 | 17 |
| Taliaferro | 173 | 78 | 45 | 871 | 5.0 | 4 | 11- | 6 | 16 |

PUNTING

| Last Name | No | Avg |
|---|---|---|
| Janik | 86 | 39.1 |

KICKING

| Last Name | XP | Att | % | FG | Att | % |
|---|---|---|---|---|---|---|
| Cappelletti | 12 | 13 | 92 | 6 | 15 | 40 |
| Gogolak | 5 | 5 | 100 | 2 | 7 | 29 |

| Scores of Each Game | | | Use Name | Pos. | Hgt | Wgt | Age | Int | Pts | Use Name | Pos. | Hgt | Wgt | Age | Int | Pts | Use Name | Pos. | Hgt | Wgt | Age | Int | Pts |
|---|---|---|---|---|---|---|---|---|---|---|---|---|---|---|---|---|---|---|---|---|---|---|---|

### CINCINNATI BENGALS 8-6-0 Paul Brown

| Score | Opponent | Opp | Player | Pos. | Hgt | Wgt | Age | Int | Pts | Player | Pos. | Hgt | Wgt | Age | Int | Pts | Player | Pos. | Hgt | Wgt | Age | Int | Pts |
|---|---|---|---|---|---|---|---|---|---|---|---|---|---|---|---|---|---|---|---|---|---|---|---|
| 31 | OAKLAND | 21 | Howard Fest | OT | 6'6" | 268 | 24 | | | Ken Avery | LB | 6'1" | 225 | 26 | 1 | | Virgil Carter | QB | 6'1" | 200 | 24 | | 12 |
| 3 | Detroit | 38 | Rufus Mayes | OT | 6'5" | 255 | 22 | | | Al Beauchamp | LB | 6'2" | 236 | 26 | 1 | 6 | Dave Lewis | QB | 6'2" | 210 | 24 | | |
| 13 | HOUSTON | 20 | Ernie Wright | OT | 6'4" | 270 | 30 | | | Bill Bergey | LB | 6'2" | 240 | 25 | 3 | | Sam Wyche | QB | 6'4" | 210 | 25 | | 12 |
| 27 | Cleveland | 30 | Guy Dennis | OG | 6'2" | 255 | 23 | | | Larry Ely | LB | 6'1" | 230 | 22 | | | Essex Johnson | HB | 5'9" | 200 | 23 | | 24 |
| 19 | KANSAS CITY | 27 | Pat Matson | OG | 6'1" | 245 | 26 | | | Wayne McClure | LB | 6'1" | 225 | 24 | | | Paul Robinson | HB | 6' | 200 | 25 | | 42 |
| 0 | Washington | 20 | Mike Wilson | OT-OG | 6'1" | 240 | 22 | | | Bill Peterson | LB | 6'3" | 230 | 25 | | | Paul Dunn | FB-HB | 6' | 210 | 22 | | |
| 10 | Pittsburgh | 21 | Bob Johnson | C | 6'5" | 265 | 24 | | | Al Coleman | DB | 6'1" | 183 | 25 | | | Doug Dressler | FB | 6'3" | 220 | 22 | | |
| 43 | Buffalo | 14 | Marty Baccaglio | DE | 6'3" | 245 | 25 | | | Sandy Durko | DB | 6'1" | 185 | 22 | | | Ron Lamb | FB | 6'2" | 230 | 25 | | |
| 14 | CLEVELAND | 10 | Royce Berry | DE | 6'3" | 248 | 24 | | 12 | Ken Dyer | DB | 6'3" | 186 | 24 | 3 | | Jess Phillips | HB-FB | 6'1" | 210 | 23 | | 30 |
| 34 | PITTSBURGH | 7 | Ron Carpenter | DE | 6'4" | 260 | 22 | | | Kenny Graham (to PIT) | DB | 6' | 205 | 28 | 3 | | Eric Crabtree | WR | 5'11" | 182 | 25 | | 12 |
| 26 | NEW ORLEANS | 6 | Nick Roman | DE | 6'3" | 230 | 22 | | | John Guillory | DB | 5'10" | 190 | 25 | | | Chip Myers | WR | 6'4" | 200 | 25 | | 6 |
| 17 | San Diego | 14 | Steve Chomyszak | DT | 6'5" | 265 | 25 | | | Lemar Parrish | DB | 5'11" | 185 | 22 | 5 | 18 | Speedy Thomas | WR | 6'1" | 178 | 25 | | 12 |
| 30 | Houston | 20 | Willie Jones | DT | 6'2" | 260 | 28 | | | Ken Riley | DB | 6' | 184 | 23 | 4 | | Bruce Coslet | TE | 6'3" | 230 | 24 | | 6 |
| 45 | BOSTON | 7 | Mike Reid | DT | 6'3" | 258 | 23 | | | Fletcher Smith | DB | 6'2" | 180 | 26 | 3 | | Mike Kelly | TE | 6'4" | 215 | 22 | | |
| | | | | | | | | | | | | | | | | | Bob Trumpy | TE | 6'6" | 225 | 25 | | 12 |
| | | | | | | | | | | Greg Cook—Shoulder Injury | | | | | | | Horst Muhlmann | K | 6'1" | 210 | 30 | | 108 |

### CLEVELAND BROWNS 7-7-0 Blanton Collier

| Score | Opponent | Opp | Player | Pos. | Hgt | Wgt | Age | Int | Pts | Player | Pos. | Hgt | Wgt | Age | Int | Pts | Player | Pos. | Hgt | Wgt | Age | Int | Pts |
|---|---|---|---|---|---|---|---|---|---|---|---|---|---|---|---|---|---|---|---|---|---|---|---|
| 31 | N.Y. JETS | 21 | Al Jenkins | OT | 6'2" | 255 | 24 | | | Billy Andrews | LB | 6' | 225 | 25 | 1 | 6 | Don Gault | QB | 6'2" | 190 | 24 | | |
| 31 | San Francisco | 34 | Bob McKay | OT | 6'5" | 260 | 22 | | | Tom Beutler | LB | 6'1" | 232 | 23 | | | Bill Nelsen | QB | 6' | 195 | 29 | | |
| 15 | PITTSBURGH | 7 | Dick Schafrath | OT | 6'3" | 258 | 34 | | | John Garlington | LB | 6'1" | 225 | 24 | 1 | | Mike Phipps | QB | 6'2" | 207 | 22 | | |
| 30 | CINCINNATI | 27 | Joe Taffoni | OT | 6'3" | 250 | 25 | | | Jim Houston | LB | 6'2" | 240 | 33 | 1 | | Ken Brown | HB | 6' | 205 | 24 | | |
| 24 | DETROIT | 41 | Jim Copeland | OG | 6'2" | 245 | 25 | | | Dale Lindsey | LB | 6'3" | 225 | 27 | 2 | 6 | Leroy Kelly | HB | 6' | 200 | 28 | | 48 |
| 28 | Miami | 0 | John Demarie | OG | 6'3" | 255 | 25 | | | Bob Matheson | LB | 6'4" | 240 | 25 | 1 | | Randy Minniear | HB | 6' | 210 | 26 | | 6 |
| 10 | SAN DIEGO | 27 | Gene Hickerson | OG | 6'3" | 248 | 35 | | | Erich Barnes | DB | 6'2" | 212 | 35 | 5 | 6 | Reece Morrison | HB | 6' | 205 | 24 | | 6 |
| 20 | Oakland | 23 | Fred Hoaglin | C | 6'4" | 250 | 26 | | | Ben Davis | DB | 5'11" | 185 | 24 | 1 | | Bo Scott | FB | 6'3" | 210 | 27 | | 66 |
| 10 | Cincinnati | 14 | Chuck Reynolds | C | 6'2" | 240 | 23 | | 2 | Mike Howell | DB | 6'1" | 190 | 27 | 1 | | Steve Engel | HB-FB | 6'1" | 218 | 22 | | |
| 28 | HOUSTON | 14 | Jack Gregory | DE | 6'6" | 250 | 25 | | | Ernie Kellerman | DB | 6' | 185 | 26 | 1 | | Gary Collins | WR | 6'4" | 210 | 29 | | 24 |
| 9 | Pittsburgh | 28 | Joe Jones | DE | 6'6" | 240 | 24 | | | Tom Schoen | DB | 5'11" | 185 | 24 | | | Fair Hooker | WR | 6'1" | 193 | 23 | | 12 |
| 21 | Houston | 10 | Ron Snidow | DE | 6'4" | 250 | 28 | | 2 | Rickey Stevenson | DB | 5'11" | 188 | 22 | | | Dave Jones | WR | 6'2" | 185 | 23 | | |
| 2 | DALLAS | 6 | Walter Johnson | DT | 6'3" | 275 | 27 | 1 | 2 | Freddie Summers | DB | 6'1" | 180 | 23 | | | Homer Jones | WR | 6'2" | 215 | 29 | | 12 |
| 27 | Denver | 13 | Joel Righetti | DT | 6'3" | 253 | 22 | | | Walt Sumner | DB | 6'1" | 180 | 23 | 4 | | Chip Glass | TE | 6'4" | 236 | 23 | | 12 |
| | | | Jerry Sherk | DT | 6'4" | 253 | 22 | | | | | | | | | | | Milt Morin | TE | 6'4" | 240 | 28 | | 6 |
| | | | Bill Yanchar | DT | 6'3" | 250 | 22 | | | | | | | | | | | Don Cockroft | K | 6'1" | 190 | 25 | | 70 |

### PITTSBURGH STEELERS 5-9-0 Chuck Noll

| Score | Opponent | Opp | Player | Pos. | Hgt | Wgt | Age | Int | Pts | Player | Pos. | Hgt | Wgt | Age | Int | Pts | Player | Pos. | Hgt | Wgt | Age | Int | Pts |
|---|---|---|---|---|---|---|---|---|---|---|---|---|---|---|---|---|---|---|---|---|---|---|---|
| 7 | HOUSTON | 19 | John Brown | OT | 6'2" | 255 | 31 | | | Chuck Allen | LB | 6'1" | 225 | 30 | 4 | | Terry Bradshaw | QB | 6'3" | 218 | 21 | | 6 |
| 13 | Denver | 16 | Mike Haggerty | OT | 6'4" | 240 | 24 | | | Carl Crennel | LB | 6'1" | 230 | 21 | | | Terry Hanratty | QB | 6'1" | 200 | 22 | | |
| 7 | Cleveland | 15 | Rick Sharp | OT | 6'3" | 262 | 22 | | | Henry Davis | LB | 6'1" | 225 | 23 | | | Dick Hoak | HB | 5'11" | 190 | 31 | | 6 |
| 23 | BUFFALO | 10 | Sam Davis | OG | 6'1" | 245 | 26 | | | Doug Fisher | LB | 6'1" | 225 | 23 | | | Preston Pearson | HB | 6'1" | 190 | 25 | | 12 |
| 7 | Houston | 3 | Bruce Van Dyke | OG | 6'2" | 240 | 30 | 2 | | Jerry Hillebrand | LB | 6'3" | 240 | 30 | 2 | | John Fuqua | FB-HB | 5'11" | 200 | 23 | | 54 |
| 14 | Oakland | 31 | Ralph Wenzel | OG | 6'3" | 250 | 27 | | | Andy Russell | LB | 6'3" | 225 | 28 | 3 | | Warren Bankston | FB | 6'4" | 225 | 23 | | 12 |
| 21 | CINCINNATI | 10 | Ray Mansfield | C | 6'3" | 240 | 29 | | | Brian Stenger | LB | 6'4" | 220 | 23 | | | Terry Cole | FB | 6'1" | 220 | 25 | | |
| 21 | N.Y. JETS | 17 | Jon Kolb | OT-C | 6'2" | 220 | 23 | | | Ocie Austin | DB | 6'3" | 200 | 23 | 1 | | Hubie Bryant | WR | 5'10" | 175 | 24 | | |
| 14 | KANSAS CITY | 31 | L. C. Greenwood | DE | 6'5" | 240 | 23 | | | Fred Barry | DB | 5'10" | 184 | 22 | | | Dave Kalina | WR | 6'3" | 205 | 23 | | |
| 7 | Cincinnati | 34 | Ben McGee | DE | 6'2" | 250 | 28 | | | Chuck Beatty | DB | 6'2" | 200 | 24 | 2 | 6 | Ron Shanklin | WR | 6'1" | 180 | 23 | | 24 |
| 28 | CLEVELAND | 9 | Lloyd Voss | DE | 6'4" | 256 | 28 | | | Mel Blount | DB | 6'3" | 205 | 22 | 1 | | Dave Smith | WR | 6'2" | 205 | 23 | | 12 |
| 12 | GREEN BAY | 20 | Dick Arndt | DT | 6'5" | 265 | 26 | | | Lee Calland | DB | 6' | 190 | 29 | 7 | | Jon Staggers | WR | 5'10" | 186 | 21 | | 6 |
| 16 | Atlanta | 27 | Joe Greene | DT | 6'4" | 270 | 23 | | | Clancy Oliver | DB | 6'1" | 180 | 22 | | | J. R. Wilburn | WR | 6'2" | 190 | 27 | | |
| 20 | Philadelphia | 30 | Chuck Hinton | DT | 6'5" | 248 | 31 | | | John Rowser | DB | 6'1" | 180 | 26 | 3 | | Bob Adams | TE | 6'2" | 225 | 24 | | |
| | | | Clarence Washington | DT | 6'3" | 265 | 23 | | | John Sodaski | DB | 6'1" | 197 | 22 | | | Dennis Hughes | TE | 6'1" | 220 | 22 | | 18 |
| | | | | | | | | | | | | | | | | | Gene Mingo | K | 6'1" | 210 | 31 | | 32 |
| | | | Rocky Bleier — Wounded in Military Service | | | | | | | Larry Gagner—Injury from automobile accident | | | | | | | Bobby Walden | K | 6' | 190 | 32 | | |
| | | | | | | | | | | | | | | | | | Allen Watson | K | 5'10" | 165 | 25 | | 22 |

### HOUSTON OILERS 3-10-1 Wally Lemm

| Score | Opponent | Opp | Player | Pos. | Hgt | Wgt | Age | Int | Pts | Player | Pos. | Hgt | Wgt | Age | Int | Pts | Player | Pos. | Hgt | Wgt | Age | Int | Pts |
|---|---|---|---|---|---|---|---|---|---|---|---|---|---|---|---|---|---|---|---|---|---|---|---|
| 19 | Pittsburgh | 7 | Elbert Drungo | OT | 6'5" | 250 | 27 | | | Garland Boyette | LB | 6'1" | 245 | 30 | 1 | | Charley Johnson | QB | 6' | 190 | 33 | | |
| 10 | MIAMI | 20 | Glen Ray Hines | OT | 6'5" | 265 | 26 | | | Claude Harvey | LB | 6'4" | 225 | 22 | | | Bob Naponic | QB | 6' | 190 | 23 | | |
| 20 | Cincinnati | 13 | Walt Suggs | OT | 6'5" | 260 | 31 | | | Jess Lewis | LB | 6'1" | 230 | 23 | | | Jerry Rhome | QB | 6' | 188 | 28 | | 6 |
| 20 | BALTIMORE | 24 | Ken Gray | OG | 6'2" | 250 | 34 | | | Ron Pritchard | LB | 6'1" | 235 | 23 | 2 | 2 | Woody Campbell | HB | 5'11" | 208 | 25 | | 6 |
| 3 | PITTSBURGH | 7 | Tom Regner | OG | 6'1" | 255 | 26 | | | Olen Underwood | LB | 6'1" | 220 | 28 | | | Mike Richardson | HB | 5'11" | 198 | 23 | | 18 |
| 31 | San Diego | 31 | Ron Saul | OG | 6'2" | 255 | 22 | | | Loyd Wainscott | LB | 6'1" | 235 | 23 | | | Joe Dawkins | FB-HB | 5'11" | 220 | 22 | | 12 |
| 0 | St. Louis | 44 | Doug Wilkerson | OG | 6'2" | 245 | 23 | | | George Webster | LB | 6'4" | 223 | 24 | | | Hoyle Granger | FB | 6'1" | 225 | 26 | | 6 |
| 9 | Kansas City | 24 | Hank Autry | C | 6'3" | 235 | 23 | | | Bob Atkins | DB | 6'3" | 215 | 24 | 1 | | Roy Hopkins | FB | 6'1" | 215 | 25 | | 18 |
| 20 | SAN FRANCISCO | 30 | Bobby Maples | C | 6'3" | 245 | 27 | | | Ken Houston | DB | 6'3" | 195 | 25 | 3 | | Tom Smiley | FB | 6'1" | 235 | 26 | | |
| 14 | Cleveland | 28 | Elvin Bethea | DE | 6'3" | 255 | 24 | | | Benny Johnson | DB | 5'11" | 178 | 22 | | | Jim Beirne | WR | 6'2" | 196 | 23 | | 6 |
| 31 | DENVER | 21 | Pat Holmes | DE | 6'5" | 250 | 30 | | | Leroy Mitchell | DB | 6'2" | 190 | 25 | 2 | | Mac Haik | WR | 6'1" | 196 | 24 | | |
| 10 | CLEVELAND | 21 | Spain Musgrove | DT-DE | 6'4" | 275 | 25 | | | Zeke Moore | DB | 6'2" | 198 | 26 | 6 | | Charlie Joiner | WR | 5'11" | 185 | 22 | | 18 |
| 20 | CINCINNATI | 30 | Lee Brooks | DT | 6'5" | 266 | 22 | | | Johnny Peacock | DB | 6'2" | 200 | 23 | 3 | 6 | Jerry LeVias | WR | 5'10" | 175 | 23 | | 30 |
| 10 | Dallas | 52 | Tom Domres | DT | 6'3" | 255 | 23 | | | | | | | | | | Paul Zaeske | WR | 6'2" | 200 | 24 | | |
| | | | Willie Parker | DT | 6'2" | 265 | 25 | | | | | | | | | | | Donnie Davis | TE | 6'4" | 225 | 30 | | |
| | | | | | | | | | | John Douglas—Injury | | | | | | | Alvin Reed | TE | 6'5" | 230 | 26 | | 12 |
| | | | | | | | | | | | | | | | | | Terry Stoepel | TE | 6'4" | 235 | 25 | | |
| | | | | | | | | | | | | | | | | | Roy Gerela | K | 5'10" | 185 | 22 | | 77 |
| | | | | | | | | | | | | | | | | | Spike Jones | K | 6'2" | 190 | 23 | | |

## CINCINNATI BENGALS

### RUSHING
| Last Name | No. | Yds | Avg | TD |
|---|---|---|---|---|
| Phillips | 163 | 648 | 4.0 | 4 |
| Robinson | 149 | 622 | 4.2 | 6 |
| E. Johnson | 65 | 273 | 4.2 | 2 |
| Carter | 34 | 246 | 7.2 | 2 |
| Wyche | 19 | 118 | 6.2 | 2 |
| Dressler | 18 | 77 | 4.3 | 0 |
| Lamb | 6 | 35 | 5.8 | 0 |
| Crabtree | 3 | 23 | 7.7 | 0 |
| Lewis | 2 | 8 | 4.0 | 0 |
| Thomas | 2 | 7 | 3.5 | 0 |

### RECEIVING
| Last Name | No. | Yds | Avg | TD |
|---|---|---|---|---|
| Myers | 32 | 542 | 17 | 1 |
| Phillips | 31 | 124 | 4 | 1 |
| Trumpy | 29 | 480 | 17 | 2 |
| Thomas | 21 | 257 | 12 | 2 |
| Crabtree | 19 | 231 | 12 | 2 |
| Robinson | 17 | 175 | 10 | 1 |
| E. Johnson | 15 | 190 | 13 | 2 |
| Coslet | 8 | 98 | 12 | 1 |

### PUNT RETURNS
| Last Name | No. | Yds | Avg | TD |
|---|---|---|---|---|
| Parrish | 23 | 194 | 8 | 1 |
| E. Johnson | 7 | 72 | 10 | 0 |
| Graham | 1 | 41 | 41 | 0 |
| Thomas | 4 | 20 | 5 | 0 |
| Robinson | 1 | 0 | 0 | 0 |
| Smith | 1 | 0 | 0 | 0 |

### KICKOFF RETURNS
| Last Name | No. | Yds | Avg | TD |
|---|---|---|---|---|
| Parrish | 16 | 482 | 30 | 1 |
| Robinson | 14 | 363 | 26 | 0 |
| E. Johnson | 3 | 68 | 23 | 0 |
| Dressler | 4 | 48 | 12 | 0 |
| Lamb | 2 | 41 | 21 | 0 |

### PASSING – PUNTING – KICKING Statistics
| PASSING | Att | Comp | % | Yds | Yd/Att | TD | Int– | % | RK |
|---|---|---|---|---|---|---|---|---|---|
| Carter | 278 | 143 | 51 | 1647 | 5.9 | 9 | 9– | 3 | 7 |
| Wyche | 57 | 26 | 46 | 411 | 7.2 | 3 | 2– | 4 | |
| Lewis | 4 | 3 | 75 | 39 | 9.8 | 0 | 0– | 0 | |

| PUNTING | No | Avg |
|---|---|---|
| Lewis | 79 | 46.2 |

| KICKING | XP | Att | % | FG | ATT | % |
|---|---|---|---|---|---|---|
| Muhlman | 33 | 33 | 100 | 25 | 37 | 68 |

## CLEVELAND BROWNS

### RUSHING
| Last Name | No. | Yds | Avg | TD |
|---|---|---|---|---|
| Kelly | 206 | 656 | 3.2 | 6 |
| Scott | 151 | 625 | 4.1 | 7 |
| Morrison | 73 | 175 | 2.4 | 0 |
| Phipps | 11 | 94 | 8.5 | 0 |
| Minniear | 12 | 39 | 3.3 | 1 |
| Morin | 1 | 2 | 2.0 | 0 |
| Nelsen | 7 | -4 | -0.6 | 0 |
| Brown | 1 | -8 | -8.0 | 0 |

### RECEIVING
| Last Name | No. | Yds | Avg | TD |
|---|---|---|---|---|
| Scott | 40 | 351 | 9 | 4 |
| Morin | 37 | 611 | 17 | 1 |
| Hooker | 28 | 490 | 18 | 2 |
| Collins | 26 | 351 | 14 | 4 |
| Kelly | 24 | 311 | 13 | 2 |
| Glass | 19 | 403 | 21 | 2 |
| H. Jones | 10 | 141 | 14 | 1 |
| Morrison | 5 | 95 | 19 | 1 |
| Minniear | 1 | -1 | -1 | 0 |

### PUNT RETURNS
| Last Name | No. | Yds | Avg | TD |
|---|---|---|---|---|
| Morrison | 15 | 133 | 9 | 0 |
| Sumner | 8 | 70 | 9 | 0 |
| Schoen | 8 | 18 | 2 | 0 |
| Kelly | 2 | 15 | 8 | 0 |
| Jenkins | 1 | 0 | 0 | 0 |

### KICKOFF RETURNS
| Last Name | No. | Yds | Avg | TD |
|---|---|---|---|---|
| H. Jones | 29 | 739 | 25 | 1 |
| Morrison | 7 | 153 | 22 | 0 |
| Brown | 2 | 44 | 22 | 0 |
| Schoen | 1 | 27 | 27 | 0 |
| Matheson | 2 | 21 | 11 | 0 |
| Righetti | 1 | 17 | 17 | 0 |
| Glass | 1 | 0 | 0 | 0 |
| Morin | 1 | 0 | 0 | 0 |

### PASSING – PUNTING – KICKING Statistics
| PASSING | Att | Comp | % | Yds | Yd/Att | TD | Int– | % | RK |
|---|---|---|---|---|---|---|---|---|---|
| Nelsen | 313 | 159 | 51 | 2156 | 6.9 | 16 | 16– | 5 | 8 |
| Phipps | 60 | 29 | 48 | 529 | 8.8 | 1 | 5– | 8 | |
| Gault | 19 | 2 | 11 | 67 | 3.5 | 0 | 3– | 16 | |

| PUNTING | No | Avg |
|---|---|---|
| Cockroft | 71 | 42.6 |

| KICKING | XP | Att | % | FG | ATT | % |
|---|---|---|---|---|---|---|
| Cockroft | 34 | 35 | 97 | 12 | 22 | 55 |

## PITTSBURGH STEELERS

### RUSHING
| Last Name | No. | Yds | Avg | TD |
|---|---|---|---|---|
| Fuqua | 138 | 691 | 5.0 | 7 |
| Pearson | 173 | 503 | 2.9 | 2 |
| Bradshaw | 32 | 233 | 7.3 | 1 |
| Bankston | 26 | 122 | 4.7 | 2 |
| Hoak | 40 | 115 | 2.9 | 1 |
| Bryant | 3 | 25 | 8.3 | 0 |
| Wilburn | 5 | 25 | 5.0 | 0 |
| Cole | 9 | 8 | 0.9 | 0 |
| Smith | 1 | 6 | 6.0 | 0 |
| Hanratty | 4 | -5 | -1.3 | 0 |
| Hughes | 1 | -8 | -8.0 | 0 |

### RECEIVING
| Last Name | No. | Yds | Avg | TD |
|---|---|---|---|---|
| Shanklin | 30 | 691 | 23 | 4 |
| Smith | 30 | 458 | 15 | 2 |
| Hughes | 24 | 332 | 14 | 3 |
| Fuqua | 23 | 289 | 13 | 2 |
| Bryant | 8 | 154 | 19 | 0 |
| Bankston | 7 | 30 | 4 | 0 |
| Staggers | 6 | 118 | 20 | 1 |
| Wilburn | 6 | 77 | 13 | 0 |
| Pearson | 6 | 71 | 12 | 0 |
| Hoak | 4 | 25 | 6 | 0 |
| Adams | 3 | 36 | 12 | 0 |
| Cole | 3 | 31 | 10 | 0 |

### PUNT RETURNS
| Last Name | No. | Yds | Avg | TD |
|---|---|---|---|---|
| Bryant | 37 | 159 | 4 | 0 |
| Staggers | 13 | 70 | 5 | 0 |
| Blount | 1 | 52 | 52 | 0 |

### KICKOFF RETURNS
| Last Name | No. | Yds | Avg | TD |
|---|---|---|---|---|
| Blount | 18 | 535 | 30 | 0 |
| Staggers | 14 | 333 | 24 | 0 |
| Pearson | 4 | 114 | 29 | 0 |
| Sharp | 1 | 9 | 9 | 0 |
| Wenzel | 1 | 6 | 6 | 0 |
| Calland | 1 | 0 | 0 | 0 |
| Washington | 1 | 0 | 0 | 0 |

### PASSING – PUNTING – KICKING Statistics
| PASSING | Att | Comp | % | Yds | Yd/Att | TD | Int– | % | RK |
|---|---|---|---|---|---|---|---|---|---|
| Bradshaw | 218 | 83 | 38 | 1410 | 6.5 | 6 | 24– | 11 | 15 |
| Hanratty | 163 | 64 | 39 | 842 | 5.2 | 5 | 8– | 5 | 14 |
| Hoak | 2 | 2 | 100 | 40 | 20.0 | 1 | 0– | 0 | |
| Walden | 1 | 1 | 100 | 20 | 20.0 | 0 | 0– | 0 | |

| PUNTING | No | Avg |
|---|---|---|
| Walden | 75 | 45.2 |
| Bradshaw | 3 | 17.3 |

| KICKING | XP | Att | % | FG | ATT | % |
|---|---|---|---|---|---|---|
| Mingo | 17 | 17 | 100 | 5 | 18 | 28 |
| Watson | 7 | 8 | 88 | 5 | 10 | 50 |

## HOUSTON OILERS

### RUSHING
| Last Name | No. | Yds | Avg | TD |
|---|---|---|---|---|
| Dawkins | 124 | 517 | 4.2 | 2 |
| Richardson | 103 | 368 | 3.6 | 2 |
| Hopkins | 57 | 207 | 3.6 | 3 |
| Campbell | 59 | 189 | 3.2 | 1 |
| Granger | 51 | 169 | 3.3 | 1 |
| Rhome | 9 | 54 | 6.0 | 1 |
| LeVias | 7 | 37 | 5.3 | 0 |
| Naponic | 3 | 12 | 4.0 | 0 |
| C. Johnson | 5 | 3 | 0.6 | 0 |
| Smiley | 1 | 0 | 0.0 | 0 |

### RECEIVING
| Last Name | No. | Yds | Avg | TD |
|---|---|---|---|---|
| Reed | 47 | 604 | 13 | 2 |
| LeVias | 41 | 529 | 13 | 5 |
| Richardson | 34 | 381 | 11 | 1 |
| Joiner | 28 | 416 | 15 | 3 |
| Haik | 17 | 190 | 11 | 0 |
| Beirne | 16 | 216 | 14 | 1 |
| Dawkins | 15 | 94 | 6 | 0 |
| Campbell | 15 | 78 | 5 | 0 |
| Hopkins | 14 | 142 | 10 | 0 |
| Granger | 11 | 118 | 11 | 0 |

### PUNT RETURNS
| Last Name | No. | Yds | Avg | TD |
|---|---|---|---|---|
| LeVias | 25 | 213 | 9 | 0 |
| Richardson | 10 | 30 | 3 | 0 |
| Houston | 4 | 13 | 3 | 0 |
| Beirne | 1 | 1 | 1 | 0 |
| Dawkins | 1 | 0 | 0 | 0 |

### KICKOFF RETURNS
| Last Name | No. | Yds | Avg | TD |
|---|---|---|---|---|
| LeVias | 26 | 598 | 23 | 0 |
| B. Johnson | 15 | 320 | 21 | 0 |
| Moore | 7 | 190 | 27 | 0 |
| Drungo | 1 | 25 | 25 | 0 |
| Hopkins | 1 | 20 | 20 | 0 |
| Lewis | 1 | 15 | 15 | 0 |
| Davis | 2 | 0 | 0 | 0 |
| Granger | 1 | 0 | 0 | 0 |
| Reed | 1 | 0 | 0 | 0 |

### PASSING – PUNTING – KICKING Statistics
| PASSING | Att | Comp | % | Yds | Yd/Att | TD | Int– | % | RK |
|---|---|---|---|---|---|---|---|---|---|
| C. Johnson | 281 | 144 | 51 | 1652 | 5.9 | 7 | 12– | 4 | 10 |
| Rhome | 168 | 88 | 52 | 1031 | 6.1 | 5 | 8– | 5 | 11 |
| Naponic | 20 | 6 | 30 | 85 | 4.3 | 0 | 2– | 10 | |
| LeVias | 1 | 0 | 0 | 0 | 0.0 | 0 | 1–100 | | |

| PUNTING | No | Avg |
|---|---|---|
| Jones | 84 | 42.4 |

| KICKING | XP | Att | % | FG | ATT | % |
|---|---|---|---|---|---|---|
| Gerela | 23 | 23 | 100 | 18 | 32 | 56 |

## OAKLAND RAIDERS 8-4-2 John Madden

**Scores of Each Game**

| |  | |
|---|---|---|
| 21 | Cincinnati | 31 |
| 27 | San Diego | 27 |
| 13 | Miami | 20 |
| 35 | DENVER | 23 |
| 34 | WASHINGTON | 20 |
| 31 | PITTSBURGH | 14 |
| 17 | Kansas City | 17 |
| 23 | CLEVELAND | 20 |
| 24 | Denver | 19 |
| 20 | SAN DIEGO | 17 |
| 14 | Detroit | 28 |
| 14 | N.Y. Jets | 13 |
| 20 | KANSAS CITY | 6 |
| 7 | SAN FRANCISCO | 38 |

| Use Name | Pos. | Hgt | Wgt | Age | Int | Pts |
|---|---|---|---|---|---|---|
| Harry Schuh | OT | 6'2" | 260 | 27 | | |
| Art Shell | OT | 6'5" | 255 | 23 | | |
| Bob Svihus | OT | 6'4" | 245 | 27 | | |
| George Buehler | OG | 6'2" | 260 | 23 | | |
| Jim Harvey | OG | 6'5" | 250 | 27 | | |
| Gene Upshaw | OG | 6'5" | 255 | 25 | | |
| Jim Otto | C | 6'2" | 248 | 32 | | |
| Tony Cline | DE | 6'2" | 230 | 22 | 1 | |
| Ben Davidson | DE | 6'8" | 280 | 30 | | |
| Carleton Oats | DT-DE | 6'2" | 260 | 27 | | |
| Al Dotson | DT | 6'4" | 260 | 27 | | |
| Tom Keating | DT | 6'3" | 247 | 27 | | |
| Art Thoms | DT | 6'5" | 250 | 23 | | |

| Use Name | Pos. | Hgt | Wgt | Age | Int | Pts |
|---|---|---|---|---|---|---|
| Duane Benson | LB | 6'2" | 215 | 25 | 1 | |
| Bill Budness | LB | 6'1" | 215 | 27 | | |
| Dan Conners | LB | 6'1" | 230 | 28 | | |
| Gerald Irons | LB | 6'2" | 230 | 23 | | |
| Bill Laskey | LB | 6'2" | 235 | 27 | 1 | |
| Gus Otto | LB | 6'2" | 220 | 27 | | |
| Carl Weathers | LB | 6'2" | 220 | 22 | | |
| Butch Atkinson | DB | 6' | 180 | 23 | 3 | |
| Willie Brown | DB | 6'1" | 190 | 29 | 3 | |
| Dave Grayson | DB | 5'10" | 187 | 31 | 1 | |
| Kent McCloughan | DB | 6'1" | 190 | 27 | 5 | |
| Jimmy Warren | DB | 5'11" | 175 | 31 | 2 | |
| Nemiah Wilson | DB | 6' | 160 | 27 | 2 | |
| Alvin Wyatt | DB | 5'10" | 185 | 22 | 6 | |

Roger Hagberg — died April 15, 1970  Auto Accident

| Use Name | Pos. | Hgt | Wgt | Age | Int | Pts |
|---|---|---|---|---|---|---|
| George Blanda | QB | 6'1" | 215 | 42 | | 84 |
| Daryle Lamonica | QB | 6'2" | 215 | 29 | | |
| Ken Stabler | QB | 6'3" | 194 | 24 | | |
| Pete Banaszak | HB | 5'11" | 200 | 26 | | 12 |
| Don Highsmith | HB | 6' | 200 | 22 | | |
| Charlie Smith | HB | 6'1" | 205 | 24 | | 30 |
| Larry Todd | HB | 6'1" | 185 | 27 | | |
| Hewritt Dixon | FB | 6'2" | 230 | 30 | | 12 |
| Marv Hubbard | FB | 6'1" | 215 | 24 | | 6 |
| Fred Biletnikoff | WR | 6'1" | 190 | 27 | | 42 |
| Drew Buie | WR | 6'2" | 178 | 23 | | |
| Rod Sherman | WR | 6' | 190 | 25 | | |
| Warren Wells | WR | 6'1" | 190 | 27 | | 66 |
| Ray Chester | TE | 6'3" | 220 | 22 | | 42 |
| Ted Koy | TE | 6'1" | 210 | 22 | | |
| Jacque MacKinnon | TE | 6'4" | 240 | 31 | | |
| Mike Eischeid | K | 6' | 190 | 29 | | |

## KANSAS CITY CHIEFS 7-5-2 Hank Stram

**Scores of Each Game**

| |  | |
|---|---|---|
| 10 | Minnesota | 27 |
| 44 | Baltimore | 24 |
| 13 | Denver | 26 |
| 23 | BOSTON | 10 |
| 27 | Cincinnati | 19 |
| 16 | DALLAS | 27 |
| 17 | OAKLAND | 17 |
| 24 | HOUSTON | 9 |
| 31 | Pittsburgh | 14 |
| 6 | ST. LOUIS | 6 |
| 26 | SAN DIEGO | 14 |
| 16 | DENVER | 0 |
| 6 | Oakland | 20 |
| 13 | San Diego | 31 |

| Use Name | Pos. | Hgt | Wgt | Age | Int | Pts |
|---|---|---|---|---|---|---|
| Dave Hill | OT | 6'5" | 260 | 29 | | |
| Sid Smith | OT | 6'4" | 260 | 22 | | |
| Jim Tyrer | OT | 6'6" | 270 | 31 | | |
| Ed Budde | OG | 6'5" | 260 | 29 | | |
| George Daney | OG | 6'3" | 240 | 23 | | |
| Mo Moorman | OG | 6'5" | 252 | 26 | | |
| E. J. Holub | C | 6'4" | 236 | 32 | | |
| Mike Oriard | C | 6'4" | 223 | 22 | | |
| Jack Rudnay | C | 6'3" | 240 | 22 | | |
| Aaron Brown | DE | 6'5" | 265 | 26 | | |
| Jerry Mays | DE | 6'4" | 250 | 30 | | |
| Marv Upshaw | DE | 6'3" | 245 | 23 | | |
| Buck Buchanan | DT | 6'7" | 275 | 30 | | |
| Curley Culp | DT | 6'1" | 265 | 24 | | |
| Bob Liggett | DT | 6'2" | 255 | 23 | | |

| Use Name | Pos. | Hgt | Wgt | Age | Int | Pts |
|---|---|---|---|---|---|---|
| Bobby Bell | LB | 6'4" | 228 | 30 | 3 | 6 |
| Chuck Hurston | LB | 6'6" | 240 | 27 | | |
| Willie Lanier | LB | 6'1" | 245 | 25 | 2 | |
| Jim Lynch | LB | 6'1" | 235 | 25 | | |
| Bob Stein | LB | 6'2" | 235 | 22 | | |
| Clyde Werner | LB | 6'4" | 225 | 22 | | |
| Caesar Belser | DB | 6' | 212 | 25 | | |
| Dave Hadley | DB | 5'9" | 186 | 21 | | |
| Jim Kearney | DB | 6'2" | 206 | 27 | 4 | |
| Jim Marsalis | DB | 5'11" | 194 | 24 | 4 | |
| Willie Mitchell | DB | 6'1" | 185 | 28 | | |
| Johnny Robinson | DB | 6' | 205 | 31 | 10 | 6 |
| Emmitt Thomas | DB | 6'2" | 192 | 27 | 5 | |

Remi Prudhomme—Injury
Goldie Sellers—Thigh Injury
Gene Trosch—Thigh Injury

| Use Name | Pos. | Hgt | Wgt | Age | Int | Pts |
|---|---|---|---|---|---|---|
| Len Dawson | QB | 6' | 190 | 36 | | |
| John Huarte | QB | 6' | 185 | 26 | | |
| Mike Livingston | QB | 6'3" | 212 | 24 | | |
| Warren McVea | HB | 5'10" | 182 | 24 | | |
| Ed Podolak | HB | 6'1" | 204 | 23 | | 24 |
| Wendell Hayes | FB | 6'2" | 220 | 29 | | 30 |
| Robert Holmes | FB | 5'9" | 220 | 24 | | 24 |
| Frank Pitts | WR | 6'2" | 200 | 26 | | 12 |
| Otis Taylor | WR | 6'2" | 215 | 27 | | 18 |
| Lewis Porter | WR | 5'11" | 178 | 23 | | |
| Gloster Richardson | WR | 6' | 200 | 27 | | 12 |
| Fred Arbanas | TE | 6'3" | 245 | 31 | | 6 |
| Billy Cannon | TE | 6'1" | 215 | 33 | | 12 |
| Morris Stroud | TE | 6'10" | 245 | 24 | | 6 |
| Jan Stenerud | K | 6'2" | 187 | 27 | | 116 |
| Jerrel Wilson | K | 6'4" | 222 | 28 | | |

## SAN DIEGO CHARGERS 5-6-3 Charlie Waller

**Scores of Each Game**

| |  | |
|---|---|---|
| 14 | BALTIMORE | 16 |
| 27 | OAKLAND | 27 |
| 10 | Los Angeles | 37 |
| 20 | GREEN BAY | 22 |
| 20 | Chicago | 31 |
| 31 | HOUSTON | 31 |
| 27 | Cleveland | 10 |
| 24 | DENVER | 21 |
| 16 | Boston | 14 |
| 17 | Oakland | 20 |
| 14 | Kansas City | 26 |
| 14 | CINCINNATI | 17 |
| 17 | Denver | 17 |
| 31 | KANSAS CITY | 13 |

| Use Name | Pos. | Hgt | Wgt | Age | Int | Pts |
|---|---|---|---|---|---|---|
| Terry Owens | OT | 6'6" | 275 | 26 | | |
| Russ Washington | OT | 6'6" | 295 | 23 | | |
| Bob Wells | OT | 6'4" | 280 | 25 | | |
| Ira Gordon | OG | 6'3" | 268 | 22 | | |
| Bill Lenkaitis | OG | 6'3" | 265 | 24 | | |
| Jim Schmedding | OG | 6'2" | 250 | 24 | | |
| Walt Sweeney | OG | 6'3" | 256 | 29 | | |
| Sam Gruneisen | C | 6'1" | 250 | 29 | | |
| Cal Withrow | C | 6' | 240 | 25 | | |
| Bob Briggs | DE | 6'4" | 276 | 25 | | |
| Joe Owens | DE | 6'2" | 235 | 23 | 2 | |
| Jeff Staggs | DE | 6'2" | 246 | 26 | | |
| Ron Billingsley | DT | 6'8" | 290 | 25 | | |
| Steve DeLong | DT | 6'3" | 252 | 27 | 1 | |
| Gene Ferguson | DT | 6'7" | 300 | 22 | | |
| Andy Rice | DT | 6'3" | 268 | 28 | | |
| Tom Williams | DT | 6'4" | 250 | 22 | | |

| Use Name | Pos. | Hgt | Wgt | Age | Int | Pts |
|---|---|---|---|---|---|---|
| Bob Babich | LB | 6'2" | 230 | 23 | | |
| Pete Barnes | LB | 6'3" | 247 | 25 | 3 | |
| Bob Bruggers | LB | 6'1" | 224 | 26 | | |
| Jack Protz | LB | 6'1" | 218 | 22 | | |
| Rick Redman | LB | 5'11" | 230 | 27 | | |
| Joe Beauchamp | DB | 6' | 185 | 26 | 1 | |
| Chuck Detwiler | DB | 6' | 185 | 23 | 6 | |
| Speedy Duncan | DB | 5'10" | 175 | 27 | | |
| Chris Fletcher | DB | 5'11" | 185 | 21 | | |
| Jim Hill | DB | 6'2" | 190 | 23 | | |
| Bob Howard | DB | 6'1" | 190 | 25 | 2 | |
| Jim Tolbert | DB | 6'3" | 207 | 26 | 2 | |

Ron Mix— Voluntarily Retired
Houston Ridge— Injury

| Use Name | Pos. | Hgt | Wgt | Age | Int | Pts |
|---|---|---|---|---|---|---|
| Wayne Clark | QB | 6'2" | 200 | 23 | | |
| Marty Domres | QB | 6'3" | 215 | 23 | | |
| John Hadl | QB | 6'1" | 218 | 30 | | 6 |
| Mike Garrett (from KC) | HB | 5'9" | 200 | 26 | | 12 |
| Dickie Post | HB | 5'9" | 190 | 24 | | 6 |
| Dave Smith | HB | 6'1" | 210 | 22 | | |
| Russ Smith | FB-HB | 6'1" | 212 | 26 | | 18 |
| Brad Hubbert | FB | 6'1" | 240 | 29 | | 6 |
| Jeff Queen | FB | 6'1" | 220 | 24 | | 12 |
| Gene Foster | HB-FB | 5'11" | 220 | 27 | | |
| Lance Alworth | WR | 6' | 180 | 30 | | 24 |
| Rick Eber | WR | 6' | 185 | 25 | | |
| Gary Garrison | WR | 6'1" | 193 | 26 | | 72 |
| Walker Gillette | WR | 6'5" | 198 | 23 | | |
| Willie Frazier | TE | 6'4" | 250 | 27 | | 48 |
| Art Strozier | TE | 6'2" | 220 | 24 | | |
| Mike Mercer | K | 6' | 215 | 34 | | 70 |
| Dennis Partee | K | 6'2" | 218 | 24 | | |

## DENVER BRONCOS 5-8-1 Lou Saban

**Scores of Each Game**

| |  | |
|---|---|---|
| 25 | Buffalo | 10 |
| 16 | PITTSBURGH | 13 |
| 26 | KANSAS CITY | 13 |
| 23 | Oakland | 35 |
| 24 | ATLANTA | 10 |
| 14 | San Francisco | 19 |
| 3 | WASHINGTON | 19 |
| 21 | San Diego | 24 |
| 19 | OAKLAND | 24 |
| 31 | New Orleans | 6 |
| 19 | Houston | 31 |
| 0 | Kansas City | 16 |
| 17 | SAN DIEGO | 17 |
| 13 | CLEVELAND | 27 |

| Use Name | Pos. | Hgt | Wgt | Age | Int | Pts |
|---|---|---|---|---|---|---|
| Sam Brunelli | OT | 6'1" | 270 | 27 | | |
| Mike Current | OT | 6'4" | 274 | 24 | | |
| Steve Alexakos | OG | 6'2" | 260 | 23 | | |
| George Goeddeke | OG | 6'3" | 253 | 25 | | |
| Mike Schnitker | OG | 6'3" | 245 | 23 | | |
| Bob Young | OG | 6'2" | 256 | 27 | | |
| Jay Bachman | C | 6'3" | 250 | 24 | | |
| Larry Kaminski | C | 6'2" | 245 | 25 | | |
| Walt Barnes | DE | 6'3" | 250 | 26 | | |
| Pete Duranko | DE | 6'2" | 250 | 26 | | |
| Rich Jackson | DE | 6'3" | 255 | 29 | | |
| Alden Roche | DE | 6'4" | 255 | 25 | | |
| Dave Costa | DT | 6'2" | 260 | 28 | | |
| Jerry Inman | DT | 6'3" | 256 | 30 | | |
| Paul Smith | DT | 6'3" | 256 | 25 | | |

John Huard—Injury

| Use Name | Pos. | Hgt | Wgt | Age | Int | Pts |
|---|---|---|---|---|---|---|
| Bill Butler | LB | 6'4" | 226 | 26 | | |
| Ken Criter | LB | 5'11" | 223 | 23 | | |
| Carl Cunningham | LB | 6'3" | 240 | 26 | | |
| Fred Forsberg | LB | 6'1" | 235 | 26 | | |
| Bill McKoy | LB | 6'3" | 235 | 22 | | |
| Chip Myrtle | LB | 6'2" | 225 | 25 | | |
| Dave Washington | LB | 6'5" | 215 | 21 | 2 | |
| Booker Edgerson | DB | 5'10" | 183 | 31 | | |
| Drake Garrett | DB | 5'9" | 183 | 24 | | |
| Cornell Gordon | DB | 6' | 187 | 29 | 3 | |
| Charlie Greer | DB | 6' | 205 | 24 | 4 | |
| Pete Jaquess | DB | 6' | 182 | 28 | | |
| Paul Martha | DB | 6' | 187 | 27 | 6 | |
| George Saimes | DB | 5'10" | 185 | 28 | | |
| Bill Thompson | DB | 6'1" | 200 | 23 | 2 | |
| Bob Wade | DB | 6'2" | 200 | 25 | 1 | |
| Alvin Mitchell | WR-DB | 6'3" | 195 | 26 | | |

| Use Name | Pos. | Hgt | Wgt | Age | Int | Pts |
|---|---|---|---|---|---|---|
| Pete Liske | QB | 6'2" | 206 | 29 | | 6 |
| Al Pastrana | QB | 6'1" | 190 | 25 | | 6 |
| Steve Tensi | QB | 6'5" | 210 | 27 | | |
| Floyd Little | HB | 5'10" | 196 | 28 | | 18 |
| Wandy Williams | HB | 6'1" | 190 | 24 | | |
| Bobby Anderson | FB-HB | 6' | 208 | 22 | | 24 |
| Willie Crenshaw | FB | 6'2" | 230 | 29 | | 36 |
| Clem Turner | FB | 6'1" | 236 | 25 | | 12 |
| Fran Lynch | HB-FB | 6'1" | 205 | 24 | | 6 |
| Al Denson | WR | 6'2" | 208 | 28 | | 12 |
| Mike Haffner | WR | 6'2" | 205 | 28 | | 6 |
| Jerry Hendren | WR | 6'2" | 187 | 22 | | |
| Bill Van Heusen | WR | 6'1" | 200 | 24 | | 12 |
| Bill Masters | TE | 6'5" | 240 | 24 | | 12 |
| Jim Whalen | TE | 6'2" | 210 | 26 | | 18 |
| Bobby Howfield | K | 5'9" | 180 | 33 | | 81 |

## OAKLAND RAIDERS

**RUSHING**

| Last Name | No. | Yds | Avg | TD |
|---|---|---|---|---|
| Dixon | 197 | 861 | 4.4 | 1 |
| Smith | 168 | 681 | 4.1 | 3 |
| Hubbard | 51 | 246 | 4.8 | 1 |
| Banaszak | 21 | 75 | 3.6 | 2 |
| Todd | 17 | 39 | 2.3 | 0 |
| Wells | 3 | 34 | 11.3 | 0 |
| Lamonica | 8 | 24 | 3.0 | 0 |
| Blanda | 2 | 4 | 2.0 | 0 |
| Sherman | 1 | 2 | 2.0 | 0 |
| Highsmith | 2 | 2 | 1.0 | 0 |
| Stabler | 1 | −4 | −4.0 | 0 |

**RECEIVING**

| Last Name | No. | Yds | Avg | TD |
|---|---|---|---|---|
| Biletnikoff | 45 | 768 | 17 | 7 |
| Wells | 43 | 935 | 22 | 11 |
| Chester | 42 | 556 | 13 | 7 |
| Dixon | 31 | 207 | 7 | 1 |
| Smith | 23 | 173 | 8 | 2 |
| Sherman | 18 | 285 | 16 | 0 |
| Todd | 5 | 51 | 10 | 0 |
| Buie | 2 | 52 | 26 | 0 |
| Banaszak | 1 | 2 | 2 | 0 |

**PUNT RETURNS**

| Last Name | No. | Yds | Avg | TD |
|---|---|---|---|---|
| Wyatt | 25 | 231 | 9 | 1 |
| Sherman | 8 | 65 | 8 | 0 |
| Atkinson | 4 | 12 | 3 | 0 |

**KICKOFF RETURNS**

| Last Name | No. | Yds | Avg | TD |
|---|---|---|---|---|
| Atkinson | 23 | 574 | 25 | 0 |
| Wyatt | 13 | 286 | 22 | 0 |
| Warren | 2 | 47 | 24 | 0 |
| Hubbard | 2 | 41 | 21 | 0 |
| Sherman | 2 | 39 | 20 | 0 |
| Thoms | 2 | 30 | 15 | 0 |

**PASSING – PUNTING – KICKING — Statistics**

| PASSING | Att | Comp | % | Yds | Yd/Att | TD | Int− | % | RK |
|---|---|---|---|---|---|---|---|---|---|
| Lamonica | 356 | 179 | 50 | 2516 | 7.1 | 22 | 15− | 4 | 1 |
| Blanda | 55 | 29 | 53 | 461 | 8.4 | 6 | 5− | 9 | |
| Stabler | 7 | 2 | 29 | 52 | 7.4 | 0 | 1− | 14 | |

| PUNTING | No | Avg |
|---|---|---|
| Eischeid | 79 | 39.5 |

| KICKING | XP | Att | % | FG | Att | % |
|---|---|---|---|---|---|---|
| Blanda | 36 | 36 | 100 | 16 | 29 | 55 |

## KANSAS CITY CHIEFS

**RUSHING**

| Last Name | No. | Yds | Avg | TD |
|---|---|---|---|---|
| Podolak | 168 | 749 | 4.5 | 3 |
| Hayes | 109 | 381 | 3.5 | 5 |
| McVea | 61 | 260 | 4.3 | 0 |
| Holmes | 63 | 206 | 3.3 | 3 |
| Pitts | 5 | 84 | 16.8 | 0 |
| Dawson | 11 | 46 | 4.2 | 0 |
| Livingston | 3 | 26 | 8.7 | 0 |
| Porter | 2 | 21 | 10.5 | 0 |
| Taylor | 3 | 13 | 4.3 | 0 |
| Cannon | 1 | 6 | 6.0 | 0 |
| Richardson | 1 | 4 | 4.0 | 0 |

**RECEIVING**

| Last Name | No. | Yds | Avg | TD |
|---|---|---|---|---|
| Taylor | 34 | 618 | 18 | 3 |
| Podolak | 26 | 307 | 12 | 1 |
| Hayes | 26 | 219 | 8 | 0 |
| Holmes | 23 | 173 | 8 | 1 |
| Pitts | 11 | 172 | 16 | 2 |
| Arbanas | 8 | 108 | 14 | 1 |
| Cannon | 7 | 125 | 18 | 2 |
| Richardson | 5 | 171 | 34 | 2 |
| McVea | 5 | 26 | 5 | 0 |
| Stroud | 4 | 86 | 22 | 1 |
| Porter | 1 | 29 | 29 | 0 |

**PUNT RETURNS**

| Last Name | No. | Yds | Avg | TD |
|---|---|---|---|---|
| Podolak | 23 | 311 | 14 | 0 |
| Mitchell | 4 | 33 | 8 | 0 |
| Porter | 1 | −3 | −3 | 0 |

**KICKOFF RETURNS**

| Last Name | No. | Yds | Avg | TD |
|---|---|---|---|---|
| Holmes | 19 | 535 | 28 | 0 |
| Podolak | 17 | 348 | 20 | 0 |
| McVea | 3 | 57 | 19 | 0 |
| Stein | 3 | 23 | 8 | 0 |
| Porter | 1 | 22 | 22 | 0 |
| Smith | 1 | 12 | 12 | 0 |

**PASSING**

| PASSING | Att | Comp | % | Yds | Yd/Att | TD | Int− | % | RK |
|---|---|---|---|---|---|---|---|---|---|
| Dawson | 262 | 141 | 54 | 1876 | 7.2 | 13 | 14− | 5 | 3 |
| Livingston | 22 | 11 | 50 | 122 | 5.6 | 0 | 1− | 5 | |
| Huarte | 2 | 0 | 0 | 0 | 0.0 | 0 | 1− | 50 | |
| Podolak | 2 | 2 | 100 | 40 | 20.0 | 0 | 0− | 0 | |
| McVea | 1 | 0 | 0 | 0 | 0.0 | 0 | 0− | 0 | |

| PUNTING | No | Avg |
|---|---|---|
| Wilson | 76 | 44.9 |

| KICKING | XP | Att | % | FG | Att | % |
|---|---|---|---|---|---|---|
| Stenerud | 26 | 26 | 100 | 30 | 42 | 71 |

## SAN DIEGO CHARGERS

**RUSHING**

| Last Name | No. | Yds | Avg | TD |
|---|---|---|---|---|
| Queen | 77 | 261 | 3.4 | 1 |
| Post | 74 | 225 | 3.0 | 1 |
| Garrett | 67 | 208 | 3.1 | 1 |
| Hadl | 28 | 188 | 6.7 | 1 |
| Hubbert | 49 | 175 | 3.6 | 1 |
| R. Smith | 52 | 163 | 3.1 | 3 |
| Frazier | 5 | 120 | 24.0 | 1 |
| Foster | 32 | 84 | 2.6 | 0 |
| D. Smith | 14 | 42 | 3.0 | 0 |
| Domres | 14 | 39 | 2.8 | 0 |
| Garrison | 4 | 7 | 1.8 | 0 |

**RECEIVING**

| Last Name | No. | Yds | Avg | TD |
|---|---|---|---|---|
| Garrison | 44 | 1006 | 23 | 12 |
| Frazier | 38 | 497 | 13 | 6 |
| Alworth | 35 | 608 | 17 | 4 |
| Queen | 20 | 236 | 12 | 1 |
| Garrett | 14 | 131 | 9 | 1 |
| Post | 13 | 113 | 9 | 0 |
| Foster | 10 | 92 | 9 | 0 |
| Hubbert | 7 | 44 | 6 | 0 |
| R. Smith | 5 | 44 | 9 | 0 |
| D. Smith | 4 | 65 | 16 | 0 |
| Eber | 2 | 43 | 22 | 0 |
| Strozier | 2 | 40 | 20 | 0 |
| Gillette | 2 | 21 | 11 | 0 |

**PUNT RETURNS**

| Last Name | No. | Yds | Avg | TD |
|---|---|---|---|---|
| Fletcher | 16 | 137 | 9 | 0 |
| R. Smith | 9 | 31 | 3 | 0 |
| Garrett | 3 | 30 | 10 | 0 |
| Duncan | 5 | 10 | 2 | 0 |
| Detwiler | 1 | −5 | −5 | 0 |

**KICKOFF RETURNS**

| Last Name | No. | Yds | Avg | TD |
|---|---|---|---|---|
| Duncan | 19 | 410 | 22 | 0 |
| Fletcher | 17 | 382 | 22 | 0 |
| Queen | 1 | 12 | 12 | 0 |
| R. Smith | 1 | 9 | 9 | 0 |
| Beauchamp | 1 | 0 | 0 | 0 |
| Hill | 1 | 0 | 0 | 0 |
| T. Owens | 1 | 0 | 0 | 0 |

**PASSING**

| PASSING | Att | Comp | % | Yds | Yd/Att | TD | Int− | % | RK |
|---|---|---|---|---|---|---|---|---|---|
| Hadl | 327 | 162 | 50 | 2388 | 7.3 | 22 | 15− | 5 | 2 |
| Domres | 55 | 28 | 51 | 491 | 8.9 | 2 | 4− | 7 | |
| Foster | 3 | 1 | 33 | 9 | 3.0 | 0 | 0− | 0 | |
| Clark | 2 | 1 | 50 | 48 | 24.0 | 0 | 0− | 0 | |

| PUNTING | No | Avg |
|---|---|---|
| Partee | 65 | 43.9 |
| Mercer | 8 | 35.4 |
| Hadl | 1 | 30.0 |

| KICKING | XP | Att | % | FG | Att | % |
|---|---|---|---|---|---|---|
| Mercer | 34 | 35 | 97 | 12 | 19 | 63 |

## DENVER BRONCOS

**RUSHING**

| Last Name | No. | Yds | Avg | TD |
|---|---|---|---|---|
| Little | 209 | 901 | 4.3 | 3 |
| Anderson | 83 | 368 | 4.4 | 4 |
| Crenshaw | 69 | 200 | 2.9 | 5 |
| Turner | 29 | 106 | 3.7 | 2 |
| Pastrana | 14 | 89 | 6.4 | 1 |
| Lynch | 20 | 81 | 4.1 | 1 |
| Liske | 7 | 42 | 6.0 | 1 |
| Tensi | 4 | 14 | 3.5 | 0 |
| Haffner | 1 | 1 | 1.0 | 0 |

**RECEIVING**

| Last Name | No. | Yds | Avg | TD |
|---|---|---|---|---|
| Denson | 47 | 646 | 14 | 2 |
| Whalen | 36 | 503 | 14 | 3 |
| Crenshaw | 18 | 105 | 6 | 1 |
| Little | 17 | 161 | 9 | 0 |
| Van Heusen | 16 | 382 | 24 | 2 |
| Haffner | 12 | 196 | 16 | 1 |
| Anderson | 9 | 140 | 16 | 0 |
| Masters | 9 | 83 | 9 | 2 |
| Turner | 8 | 23 | | 0 |
| Lynch | 7 | 6 | | 0 |
| Embree | 4 | | | 0 |

**PUNT RETURNS**

| Last Name | No. | Yds | Avg | TD |
|---|---|---|---|---|
| Thompson | 23 | 233 | 10 | 0 |
| Little | 22 | 187 | 9 | 0 |
| Greer | 14 | 123 | 9 | 0 |
| Jaquess | 4 | 13 | 3 | 0 |

**KICKOFF RETURNS**

| Last Name | No. | Yds | Avg | TD |
|---|---|---|---|---|
| Anderson | 21 | 520 | 25 | 0 |
| Hendren | 8 | 197 | 25 | 0 |
| Thompson | 9 | 188 | 21 | 0 |
| Little | 6 | 126 | 21 | 0 |
| Turner | 1 | 31 | 31 | 0 |
| Criter | 2 | 20 | 10 | 0 |
| Washington | 1 | 20 | 20 | 0 |
| Myrtle | 1 | 1 | 1 | 0 |
| Lynch | 0 | 11 | 0 | 0 |

**PASSING**

| PASSING | Att | Comp | % | Yds | Yd/Att | TD | Int− | % | RK |
|---|---|---|---|---|---|---|---|---|---|
| Liske | 238 | 112 | 47 | 1340 | 5.6 | 7 | 11− | 5 | 12 |
| Tensi | 80 | 38 | 48 | 539 | 6.7 | 3 | 8− | 10 | |
| Pastrana | 75 | 29 | 39 | 420 | 5.6 | 1 | 9− | 12 | |
| Anderson | 7 | 4 | 57 | 59 | 8.4 | 0 | 0− | 0 | |
| Little | 2 | 0 | 0 | 0 | 0.0 | 0 | 0− | 0 | |
| Van Heusen | 1 | 0 | 0 | 0 | 0.0 | 0 | 0− | 0 | |

| PUNTING | No | Avg |
|---|---|---|
| Van Heusen | 87 | 42.9 |

| KICKING | XP | Att | % | FG | Att | % |
|---|---|---|---|---|---|---|
| Howfield | 27 | 28 | 96 | 18 | 32 | 56 |

## NFC CHAMPIONSHIP GAME
January 3, at San Francisco
(Attendance 59,364)

### Two Interceptions Too Many

The opening round of the first NFC playoffs had produced two interesting games, as the Cowboys had beaten the Lions 5-0 on a field as muddy as a pigsty and the '49ers had edged the tough Vikings 17-14. In the conference championship, the Cowboys and '49ers would use different offensive styles with different results.

Dallas quarterback Craig Morton had a sore arm and could not match the passing ability of San Francisco's John Brodie, but the Cowboys did have two strong runners in rookie Duane Thomas and Walt Garrison, plus a top-notch offensive line to block for them. Neither offense did much in the first quarter, as Bruce Gossett of San Francisco booted a 16-yard field goal while Dallas' Mike Clark missed from the 40. The defensive deadlock continued into the second period, with Clark hitting on a 21 yard field goal to knot the first half score at 3-3.

The Cowboys got the first big break of the game in the third period. With Dallas end Larry Cole putting heavy pressure on him, Brodie rushed a pass over the middle which Lee Roy Jordan picked off at the San Francisco 13-yard line. Duane Thomas covered the ground to the end zone on the very next play, and Clark's extra point made the score 10-3. The '49ers drove right back into Dallas territory, but Mel Renfro intercepted a Brodie pass on the 18-yard line to extinguish that threat. The Cowboys then pounded their way downfield on the running of Thomas and Garrison, with a swing pass from Morton to Garrison covering the final five yards to the goal line.

Brodie then led his team on a 73-yard drive capped by a 26-yard scoring pitch to Dick Witcher; with Gossett's extra point, the '49ers trailed 17-10 with fifteen minutes left to play. The Dallas defense stood firm for the rest of the day, however, and the Cowboys headed off to the Super Bowl after failing in four previous playoff tries.

### SCORING

| | | | | |
|---|---|---|---|---|
| SAN FRANCISCO | 3 | 0 | 7 | 0—10 |
| DALLAS | 0 | 3 | 14 | 0—17 |

**First Quarter**
S.F. Gossett, 16 yard field goal

**Second Quarter**
Dal. Clark, 21 yard field goal

**Third Quarter**
Dal. Thomas, 13 yard rush
PAT—Clark (kick)
Dal. Garrison, 5 yard pass from Morton
PAT—Clark (kick)
S.F. Witcher, 26 yard pass from Brodie
PAT—Gossett (kick)

### TEAM STATISTICS

| S.F. | | DALLAS |
|---|---|---|
| 15 | First Downs—Total | 22 |
| 2 | First Downs—Rushing | 16 |
| 12 | First Downs—Passing | 5 |
| 1 | First Downs—Penalty | 1 |
| 1 | Fumbles—Number | 4 |
| 0 | Fumbles—Lost Ball | 1 |
| 5 | Penalties—Number | 7 |
| 51 | Yards Penalized | 75 |
| 1 | Missed Field Goals | 2 |
| 61 | Offensive Plays—Total | 75 |
| 307 | Net Yards | 319 |
| 5.0 | Average Gain | 4.3 |
| 2 | Giveaways | 1 |
| 1 | Takeaways | 2 |
| −1 | Difference | +1 |

### INDIVIDUAL STATISTICS

| SAN FRANCISCO | No | Yds | Avg. | DALLAS | No | Yds | Avg. |
|---|---|---|---|---|---|---|---|
| | | | | RUSHING | | | |
| Willard | 13 | 42 | 3.2 | Thomas | 27 | 143 | 5.3 |
| Cunningham | 5 | 14 | 2.8 | Garrison | 17 | 71 | 4.2 |
| Thomas | 1 | 5 | 5.0 | Welch | 5 | 27 | 5.4 |
| | 19 | 61 | 3.2 | Reeves | 2 | −12 | −6.0 |
| | | | | | 51 | 229 | 4.5 |
| | | | | RECEIVING | | | |
| Washington | 6 | 88 | 14.7 | Garrison | 3 | 51 | 17.0 |
| Cunningham | 4 | 34 | 8.5 | Thomas | 2 | 24 | 12.0 |
| Windsor | 3 | 70 | 23.3 | Rucker | 1 | 21 | 21.0 |
| Witcher | 3 | 41 | 13.7 | Ditka | 1 | 5 | 5.0 |
| Willard | 2 | 22 | 11.0 | | 7 | 101 | 14.4 |
| Kwalick | 1 | 7 | 7.0 | | | | |
| | 19 | 262 | 13.8 | | | | |
| | | | | PUNTING | | | |
| Spurrier | 5 | | 41.0 | Widby | 6 | | 40.2 |
| | | | | PUNT RETURNS | | | |
| B. Taylor | 2 | 5 | 2.5 | Hayes | 1 | 8 | 8.0 |
| | | | | Reeves | 1 | 0 | 0.0 |
| | | | | | 2 | 8 | 4.0 |
| | | | | KICKOFF RETURNS | | | |
| Thomas | 3 | 66 | 22.0 | Washington | 1 | 20 | 20.0 |
| Tucker | 1 | 23 | 23.0 | Waters | 1 | 16 | 16.0 |
| | 4 | 89 | 22.3 | Kiner | 1 | 10 | 10.0 |
| | | | | | 3 | 46 | 15.3 |
| | | | | INTERCEPTION RETURNS | | | |
| None | | | | Renfro | 1 | 19 | 19.0 |
| | | | | Jordan | 1 | 4 | 4.0 |
| | | | | | 2 | 23 | 11.5 |

| SAN FRANCISCO | PASSING Att. | Comp. | Comp. Pct. | Yds. | Int. | Yds/ Att. | Yds/ Comp. | Yards Lost Tackled |
|---|---|---|---|---|---|---|---|---|
| Brodie | 30 | 19 | 47.5 | 262 | 2 | 6.6 | 13.8 | 2—16 |
| DALLAS | | | | | | | | |
| Morton | 22 | 7 | 31.8 | 101 | 0 | 4.6 | 14.4 | 2—11 |

---

## AFC CHAMPIONSHIP GAME
January 3, at Baltimore
(Attendance 54,799)

### Two Old Men and One Crown

One old AFL team and one old NFL team squared off in the first AFC championship match. The Oakland Raiders got this far by beating the upcoming Miami Dolphins 21-14 in the first playoff round, while the Baltimore Colts arrived at this game fresh from a 17-0 whitewash of the Cincinnati Bengals. Before the game was over, it had developed into a duel of two of pro football's oldest quarterbacks, Johnny Unitas and George Blanda.

Baltimore scored the only points of the first quarter on Jim O'Brien's 16-yard field goal, as neither Unitas nor Oakland's Daryle Lamonica could spark the offense. Early in the second quarter, however, Lamonica pulled a thigh muscle when hit by Bubba Smith, so the forty-three-year-old Blanda had to take over at quarterback. By the time he entered the game, Baltimore had run its lead to 10-0 on a Norm Bulaich touchdown that Unitas had set up with a key pass to Eddie Hinton. When Blanda could drive his team only to the Baltimore 40-yard line, he simply kicked a field goal to net three points and drop the halftime score to 10-3.

The Raiders tied the score in the third quarter when Blanda hit Fred Biletnikoff with a 38-yard touchdown pass. Coolly directing his offense, Unitas brought the Colts back close enough for O'Brien to kick a field goal, and he engineered another long drive late in the period which Bulaich capped with his second touchdown.

Blanda responded in the final period by driving the Raiders 80 yards, with the final 15 yards coming on a pass to Warren Wells. The Raiders now trailed 20-17, but the Baltimore defense came through with clutch plays when needed. The Raiders twice were in scoring range of the Baltimore goal line, but both drives ended with Blanda passes getting intercepted in the end zone. The Colts finally iced the victory away when Unitas hit Ray Perkins, one of four wide receivers in on the play, with a 68-yard scoring pass which lengthened the final score to 27-17.

### SCORING

| | | | | |
|---|---|---|---|---|
| BALTIMORE | 3 | 7 | 10 | 7—27 |
| OAKLAND | 0 | 3 | 7 | 7—17 |

**First Quarter**
Balt. O'Brien, 16 yard field goal

**Second Quarter**
Balt. Bulaich, 2 yard rush
PAT—O'Brien (kick)
Oak. Blanda, 48 yard field goal

**Third Quarter**
Oak. Biletnikoff, 38 yard pass from Blanda
PAT—Blanda (kick)
Balt. O'Brien, 23 yard field goal
Balt. Bulaich, 11 yard rush
PAT—O'Brien (kick)

**Fourth Quarter**
Oak. Wells, 15 yard pass from Blanda
PAT—Blanda (kick)
Balt. Perkins, 68 yard pass from Unitas
PAT—O'Brien (kick)

### TEAM STATISTICS

| BALT. | | OAK. |
|---|---|---|
| 18 | First Downs—Total | 16 |
| 7 | First Downs—Rushing | 5 |
| 11 | First Downs—Passing | 10 |
| 0 | First Downs—Penalty | 1 |
| 0 | Fumbles—Number | 1 |
| 0 | Fumbles—Lost Ball | 1 |
| 2 | Penalties—Number | 2 |
| 10 | Yards Penalized | 20 |
| 2 | Missed Field Goals | 0 |
| 71 | Offensive Plays—Total | 63 |
| 363 | Net Yards | 336 |
| 5.1 | Average Gain | 5.3 |
| 0 | Giveaways | 4 |
| 4 | Takeaways | 0 |
| +4 | Difference | −4 |

### INDIVIDUAL STATISTICS

| BALTIMORE | No | Yds | Avg. | OAKLAND | No | Yds | Avg. |
|---|---|---|---|---|---|---|---|
| | | | | RUSHING | | | |
| Bulaich | 22 | 71 | 3.2 | Dixon | 10 | 51 | 5.1 |
| Nowatzke | 8 | 32 | 4.0 | Smith | 9 | 44 | 4.9 |
| Hill | 5 | 12 | 2.4 | Hubbard | 3 | 12 | 4.0 |
| Unitas | 2 | 9 | 4.5 | | 22 | 107 | 4.9 |
| Havrilak | 1 | 2 | 2.0 | | | | |
| | 38 | 126 | 3.3 | | | | |
| | | | | RECEIVING | | | |
| Hinton | 5 | 115 | 23.0 | Wells | 5 | 108 | 21.6 |
| Jefferson | 3 | 36 | 12.0 | Biletnikoff | 5 | 92 | 18.4 |
| Perkins | 2 | 80 | 40.0 | Dixon | 3 | 15 | 5.0 |
| Mackey | 1 | 14 | 14.0 | Chester | 2 | 36 | 18.0 |
| | 11 | 245 | 22.3 | Smith | 2 | 21 | 10.5 |
| | | | | Hubbard | 1 | 5 | 5.0 |
| | | | | | 18 | 277 | 15.4 |
| | | | | PUNTING | | | |
| Lee | 6 | | 45.3 | Eischeid | 5 | | 40.0 |
| | | | | PUNT RETURNS | | | |
| Gardin | 2 | 1 | 0.5 | Atkinson | 2 | 10 | 5.0 |
| | | | | KICKOFF RETURNS | | | |
| Duncan | 4 | 105 | 26.3 | Atkinson | 2 | 37 | 18.5 |
| | | | | Sherman | 1 | 23 | 23.0 |
| | | | | | 3 | 60 | 20.0 |
| | | | | INTERCEPTION RETURNS | | | |
| Logan | 1 | 16 | 16.0 | None | | | |
| May | 1 | 0 | 0.0 | | | | |
| Volk | 1 | 0 | 0.0 | | | | |
| | 3 | 16 | 5.3 | | | | |

| BALTIMORE | PASSING Att. | Comp. | Comp. Pct. | Yds. | Int. | Yds/ Att. | Yds/ Comp. | Yards Lost Tackled |
|---|---|---|---|---|---|---|---|---|
| Unitas | 30 | 11 | 36.7 | 245 | 0 | 8.2 | 22.3 | 3—8 |
| OAKLAND | | | | | | | | |
| Blanda | 32 | 17 | 53.0 | 271 | 3 | 8.5 | 15.9 | |
| Lamonica | 4 | 1 | 25.0 | 6 | 0 | 1.5 | 6.0 | |
| | 36 | 18 | 50.0 | 277 | 3 | 7.7 | 15.4 | 5—48 |

## Follow the Bouncing Ball

The first Super Bowl under the new merger arrangement ended in high drama after being, for most of the afternoon, a comedy of errors. Both the Dallas Cowboys and Baltimore Colts took turns giving the game away, but neither team would take it until the final seconds of play.

The strong defenses of both clubs dominated the first-quarter action, although the Cowboys did score on a 14-yard Mike Clark field goal. Another Clark field goal made the score 6-0 in the second quarter when the Colts tied the score on a fluke play. Baltimore quarterback Johnny Unitas threw a long pass down the center of the field to wide receiver Eddie Hinton; the ball bounced off Hinton's hands, back up into the air, grazed the fingertips of Dallas cornerback Mel Renfro, and came right down to the surprised John Mackey. Taking the ball around mid-field, Mackey sprinted the rest of the way to the end zone. The Cowboys blocked the Baltimore extra point, however, so the score remained tied at 6-6.

On the next Baltimore offensive series, a hard tackle by George Andrie forced Unitas to fumble the ball on his own 29-yard line and sent him out of the game with bruised ribs. Cowboy quarterback Craig Morton, operating with a sore arm, then moved his team down to the 7-yard line, from where a short pass to Duane Thomas scored the only Dallas touchdown of the day. Clark's conversion ran the score to 13-6, and neither offense could score again before the end of the half.

The Colts kept up the parade of mistakes when Jim Duncan fumbled the opening kickoff deep in Baltimore territory. The Cowboys then drove from the 31-yard line to the two-yard line on five plays, with Thomas' hard running the key element. With the ball in the shadows of the goal posts, Thomas took a handoff and fumbled the ball, the Colts recovering on the one-foot line.

With the threat erased, the third quarter settled into a pattern of offensive futility, with neither Morton nor Earl Morrall, filling in for the injured Unitas, able to ignite an attack. With only eight minutes left in the game, the Cowboys still clung to their 13-6 lead.

At that point, however, a Morton pass bounced off the fingers of fullback Walt Garrison into the hands of Colt safety Rick Volk, who returned the ball 17 yards to the Dallas three-yard line. In short order, Tom Nowatzke smashed over for the touchdown, and Jim O'Brien added the tying extra point.

Overtime seemed imminent late in the final quarter, but another Morton pass was intercepted with 1:09 left in the game. Mike Curtis stole the pass on the Dallas 41 and returned it to the 28. Two running plays ran the clock down, and then Jim O'Brien, Baltimore's rookie kicker, booted a 32-yard three-pointer to give the Colts an artistically flawed but nonetheless satisfying 16-13 victory.

| BALTIMORE | | DALLAS |
|---|---|---|
| | OFFENSE | |
| Hinton | WR | Hayes |
| Vogel | LT | Neely |
| Ressler | LG | Niland |
| Curry | C | Manders |
| Williams | RG | Nye |
| Sullivan | RT | Wright |
| Mackey | TE | Norman |
| Jefferson | WR | Rucker |
| Unitas | QB | Morton |
| Bulaich | RB | Thomas |
| Nowatzke | RB | Garrison |
| | DEFENSE | |
| Bubba Smith | LE | Cole |
| B. R. Smith | LT | Pugh |
| Miller | RT | Lilly |
| Hilton | RE | Andrie |
| May | LLB | Edwards |
| Curtis | MLB | Jordan |
| Hendricks | RLB | Howley |
| Stukes | LCB | Adderley |
| Duncan | RCB | Renfro |
| Logan | LS | Green |
| Volk | RS | Waters |

### SUBSTITUTES

**BALTIMORE**

Offense

| Ball | Maitland |
|---|---|
| Goode | Mitchell |
| Havrilak | Morrall |
| J. Hill | Perkins |
| Johnson | |

Defense

| Gardin | Newsome |
|---|---|
| Grant | Nichols |
| Maxwell | |

Kickers

| O'Brien | Lee |
|---|---|

**DALLAS**

Offense

| Asher | Homan |
|---|---|
| Ditka | Reeves |
| C. Hill | Welch |

Defense

| East | Lewis |
|---|---|
| Flowers | Stincic |
| Harris | Toomay |
| Kiner | Washington |

Kickers

| Clark | Widby |
|---|---|

### SCORING

| | 1 | 2 | 3 | 4 | |
|---|---|---|---|---|---|
| **BALTIMORE** | 0 | 6 | 0 | 10 | —16 |
| **DALLAS** | 3 | 10 | 0 | 0 | —13 |

**First Quarter**

Dall.  Clark, 14 yard field goal

**Second Quarter**

Dall.  Clark, 30 yard field goal

Balt.  Mackey, 75 yard pass from Unitas

  PAT — O'Brien (kick—blocked)

Dall.  Thomas, 7 yard pass from Morton

  PAT — Clark (kick)

**Fourth Quarter**

Balt.  Nowatzke, 2 yard rush

  PAT — O'Brien (kick)

Balt.  O'Brien, 32 yard field goal

### TEAM STATISTICS

| BALT. | | DALLAS |
|---|---|---|
| 14 | First Downs — Total | 10 |
| 4 | First Downs — Rushing | 4 |
| 6 | First Downs — Passing | 5 |
| 4 | First Downs — Penalty | 1 |
| 5 | Fumbles — Number | 1 |
| 3 | Fumbles — Lost Ball | 1 |
| 4 | Penalties — Number | 10 |
| 31 | Yards Penalized | 133 |
| 1 | Missed Field Goals | 0 |
| 56 | Offensive Plays | 59 |
| 329 | Net Yards | 215 |
| 5.9 | Average Gain | 3.7 |
| 6 | Giveaways | 4 |
| 4 | Takeaways | 6 |
| −2 | Difference | +2 |

### INDIVIDUAL STATISTICS

| BALTIMORE | No | Yds | Avg. | DALLAS | No | Yds | Avg. |
|---|---|---|---|---|---|---|---|
| | | | **RUSHING** | | | | |
| Nowatzke | 10 | 33 | 3.3 | Garrison | 12 | 65 | 5.4 |
| Bulaich | 18 | 28 | 1.6 | Thomas | 18 | 35 | 1.9 |
| Unitas | 1 | 4 | 4.0 | Morton | 1 | 2 | 2.0 |
| Havrilak | 1 | 3 | 3.0 | | 31 | 102 | 3.3 |
| Morrall | 1 | 1 | 1.0 | | | | |
| | 31 | 69 | 2.2 | | | | |
| | | | **RECEIVING** | | | | |
| Jefferson | 3 | 52 | 17.3 | Reeves | 5 | 46 | 9.2 |
| Mackey | 2 | 80 | 40.0 | Thomas | 4 | 21 | 5.3 |
| Hinton | 2 | 51 | 25.5 | Garrison | 2 | 19 | 9.5 |
| Havrilak | 2 | 27 | 13.5 | Hayes | 1 | 41 | 41.0 |
| Nowatzke | 1 | 45 | 45.0 | | 12 | 127 | 10.6 |
| Bulaich | 1 | 5 | 5.0 | | | | |
| | 11 | 260 | 23.6 | | | | |
| | | | **PUNTING** | | | | |
| Lee | 4 | | 41.5 | Widby | 9 | | 41.9 |
| | | | **PUNT RETURNS** | | | | |
| Gardin | 4 | 4 | 1.0 | Hayes | 3 | 9 | 3.0 |
| Logan | 1 | 8 | 8.0 | | | | |
| | 5 | 12 | 2.4 | | | | |
| | | | **KICKOFF RETURNS** | | | | |
| Duncan | 4 | 90 | 22.5 | Harris | 1 | 18 | 18.0 |
| | | | | Hill | 1 | 14 | 14.0 |
| | | | | Lewis | 1 | 2 | 2.0 |
| | | | | | 3 | 34 | 11.1 |
| | | | **INTERCEPTION RETURNS** | | | | |
| Volk | 1 | 30 | 30.0 | Howley | 2 | 22 | 11.0 |
| Logan | 1 | 14 | 14.0 | Renfro | 1 | 0 | 0.0 |
| Curtis | 1 | 13 | 13.0 | | 3 | 22 | 7.3 |
| | 3 | 57 | 19.0 | | | | |

**PASSING**

| BALTIMORE | Att | Comp | Comp Pct. | Yds. | Int | Yds/ Att. | Yds/ Comp | Yards Lost Tackled |
|---|---|---|---|---|---|---|---|---|
| Morrall | 15 | 7 | 46.7 | 147 | 1 | 9.8 | 21.0 | 0— 0 |
| Unitas | 9 | 3 | 33.3 | 88 | 2 | 9.8 | 29.3 | 0— 0 |
| Havrilak | 1 | 1 | 100.0 | 25 | 0 | 25.0 | 25.0 | 0— 0 |
| | 25 | 11 | 44.0 | 260 | 3 | 10.4 | 23.6 | 0— 0 |
| **DALLAS** | | | | | | | | |
| Morton | 26 | 12 | 46.2 | 127 | 3 | 4.9 | 10.6 | 2—14 |

# 1971 N.F.C.  With a Little Offensive Help

The long bomb and frequent passing had enlivened the game ever since Don Hutson and Sammy Baugh made their debuts in the 1930s and had become a way of offensive life since the days of Otto Graham and Bob Waterfield in the late 1940s. This year, however, defense had caught up. With most teams rigging up complex zone defenses which rendered long-passing quarterbacks impotent, scoring dropped and the field-goal kicker replaced the deep receiver as pro football's glamorous point producer. To counter the new defenses, pro offenses employed big, strong running backs and quarterbacks who could throw on the roll-out play and carry the ball occasionally. But a rule of thumb for this season was that the team with the better defense usually won; indeed, all four teams which made the playoffs had outstanding defenses which often overshadowed their offensive platoons.

## EASTERN DIVISION

**Dallas Cowboys**—For the first half of the season, coach Tom Landry alternated Craig Morton and Roger Staubach at quarterback; the Cowboys won four games and lost three. But starting with the eighth game, Landry gave the job full time to Staubach, and the team won its last seven games to move past the Redskins into first place. Both Dallas quarterbacks were fine passers, but Staubach gave the defense something extra to worry about by often running with the ball. By mid-season, defenses also had to worry about Duane Thomas running the ball. After sitting out the early games over a salary dispute, Thomas returned to the team in a sullen mood, but his ball-carrying fit right into the Dallas scheme of things.

**Washington Redskins**—When George Allen was hired as head coach, he immediately set out to trade for veteran players who would make no mistakes on the field. The resulting collection of football oldsters became known as the Over the Hill Gang. In a dazzling array of trades, Allen picked up Billy Kilmer, Roy Jefferson, Boyd Dowler, Clifton McNeil, Ron McDole, Verlon Biggs, Diron Talbert, Jack Pardee, Myron Pottios, Richie Petitbon, John Wilbur, and Speedy Duncan. Allen rigged together a defense which indeed made no errors, which delighted in forcing enemy offenses into fumbles and interceptions. The Washington attack started out fast but slumped when injuries erased Sonny Jurgensen, Charley Taylor, and Jerry Smith from the lineup and cut down on Larry Brown's effectiveness.

**Philadelphia Eagles**—Apparently on the way to another dismal season after losing their first three games, the Eagles fired head coach Jerry Williams and replaced him with young Ed Khayat. The Eagles lost their first two games under Khayat, but then went on to a 7-2 record. The defense triggered the reversal by jelling into one of the league's top units. On this surprising platoon, only Tim Rossovich and Bill Bradley had recognizable names; the others were parts of a nameless horde which swarmed over enemy players. The Eagles' offense, on the other hand, was feeble.

**St. Louis Cardinals**—Bob Hollway's first season as head coach flattened out into a 4-9-1 record and a disappointing fourth-place finish in the East. Hollway had coached the magnificent Viking defense as an assistant at Minnesota, but the St. Louis defense this season suffered from a variety of injuries and a slow adjustment to Hollway's new system. The Cardinal offense also sputtered, with neither Jim Hart nor Pete Beathard taking charge at quarterback.

**New York Giants**—The Giants had the worst defense in the NFC, totally unable to put pressure on enemy passers, while the secondary suffered from injuries and Bennie McRae's advanced years. Ron Johnson's knee injury ripped the heart out of the Giant running attack. In the passing department, quarterback Fran Tarkenton found tight end Bob Tucker a congenial target, but there was no deep threat to replace the traded Homer Jones.

## CENTRAL DIVISION

**Minnesota Vikings**—The Vikings' great defense again won first place in the Central Division, but the Minnesota offense just didn't have the power or direction to make the Vikings a complete team. At the quarterback spot, Gary Cuozzo, Bob Lee, and Norm Snead all rotated without any of them igniting a spark in the attack. Injuries to receivers Gene Washington and John Beasley also hurt the passing game, although Bob Grim rebounded from years of injuries to become a legitimate deep threat. Clint Jones, Dave Osborn, Jim Lindsey, Oscar Reed, and Bill Brown all were short-yardage runners, adept at grinding out yards behind the strong Viking front wall.

**Detroit Lions**—Blossoming into stardom in his fourth pro season was quarterback Greg Landry, a man with a strong passing arm plus the size and strength of a fullback in carrying the ball. Landry set a record for quarterbacks this season with 530 yards rushing. Second in the entire NFC in rushing yardage was Lion fullback Steve Owens, the powerful Heisman Trophy winner who had suffered through an injury-ruined rookie season last year. With Altie Taylor also picking up yardage on the ground, the Lions had the best running attack in the conference. The defense held the Lions back this season, with the front four unable to mount a pass rush now that Alex Karras had passed his prime and was cut loose before the season started. One tragic note of the season was the death of Chuck Hughes, who collapsed of a heart attack on the field in full view of millions.

**Chicago Bears**—Even with Gale Sayers still out with his bad knee, the Bears got off to a strong start. Middle linebacker Dick Butkus held the defense together with his outstanding play, and reserve quarterback Kent Nix was the offensive hero in the early going. After midseason, however, both Nix and Jack Concannon were injured, leaving the entire quarterbacking load on Bobby Douglass' shoulders. The Bears dropped six of their last seven, and coach Jim Dooley got the ax at the end of the season.

**Green Bay Packers**—Dan Devine, who left the University of Missouri to take over as head coach in Green Bay, suffered through a trying professional debut as his Packers blew an early lead and lost to the Giants 42-40 on opening day. To make matters worse, several players smashed into Devine on an out-of-bounds play and broke his leg. Getting through the rest of the season with the help of a crutch, Devine found little pleasing in the Packers' drop to last place in the Central Division. His hardest decision was to bench all-time great Ray Nitschke, and his greatest pleasure was the play of rookie fullback John Brockington, who led the NFC in rushing 1,105 yards.

## WESTERN DIVISION

**San Francisco '49ers**—Even with John Brodie suffering through an erratic season, the '49ers still had enough talent on both platoons to beat out the surprising Los Angeles Rams for first place in the West. Operating behind a top-notch offensive line, the '49ers running game prospered with Ken Willard's good year and a fine rookie performance from speedster Vic Washington. This took the pressure off Brodie, who still had Gene Washington, Ted Kwalick, and Dick Witcher to throw to. On defense, coach Dick Nolan stuck with one set of linemen and was rewarded with excellent seasons from Cedrick Hardman, Charlie Krueger, Earl Edwards, and Tommy Hart.

**Los Angeles Rams**—Long-time UCLA coach Tommy Prothro moved into the professional ranks by rebuilding the Rams and almost winning a divisional title. Prothro traded away Diron Talbert, Jack Pardee, Myron Pottios, Maxie Baughan, Richie Petitbon, Tommy Mason, Bob Brown, Wendell Tucker, and Billy Truax from last year's team and replaced them with younger players. The defense had eight new starters, with only Deacon Jones, Merlin Olsen, and Coy Bacon returning, but the new unit hung together well. On the offense, key new starters were Willie Ellison, who ran for a record 247 yards against New Orleans on December 5, Lance Rentzel, Bob Klein, and Harry Schuh.

**Atlanta Falcons**—The Falcons enjoyed their first season ever with an aggressive defense and a patchwork offense. The front four fielded two top linemen in Claude Humphrey and John Zook, linebacker Don Hansen's fine season made up for the loss of Tommy Nobis to a knee injury, and Ken Reaves starred in an underrated secondary which allowed the least passing yards in the Conference. On offense, the line improved into a good unit, with George Kunz and Mal Snider the top performers. The running attack lost its speed when a knee injury sidelined rookie Joe Profit, but Cannonball Butler, Art Malone, Harmon Wages, and free agent rookie Willie Belton ground out the yardage with straight-ahead power plays. Both of the wide receivers were rookies, Ken Burrow and Wes Chesson, but at quarterback the Falcons could field only journeymen Bob Berry and Dick Shiner.

**New Orleans Saints**—Rookie quarterback Archie Manning made a fine professional debut by scoring a touchdown on the last play of the game to beat the Rams 24-20 on opening day. Foot and leg problems kept him on the bench for much of the campaign, but Manning did show a strong arm and a talent for running with the ball. With Manning or Ed Hargett at quarterback, the New Orleans offense showed new punch. The line was improved with the addition of Glen Ray Hines, Don Morrison, and John Didion, and the receiving corps had always been the Saints' strongest department. At running back, second-year man Jim Strong, picked up from San Francisco, and rookies Bob Gresham and James Ford handled most of the running chores.

## FINAL TEAM STATISTICS

### OFFENSE

| | ATL. | CHI. | DALL. | DET. | G.B. | L.A. | MINN. | N.O. | N.Y.G. | PHIL. | ST.L. | S.F. | WASH. |
|---|---|---|---|---|---|---|---|---|---|---|---|---|---|
| **FIRST DOWNS:** | | | | | | | | | | | | | |
| Total | 221 | 189 | **288** | 269 | 208 | 234 | 198 | 242 | 236 | 201 | 212 | 257 | 212 |
| by Rushing | 99 | 75 | **135** | 131 | 115 | 105 | 89 | 105 | 86 | 65 | 86 | 113 | 77 |
| by Passing | 108 | 99 | **144** | 104 | 87 | 111 | 95 | 106 | 140 | 119 | 109 | 122 | 112 |
| by Penalty | 14 | 15 | 9 | **34** | 6 | 18 | 14 | 31 | 10 | 17 | 17 | 22 | 23 |
| **RUSHING:** | | | | | | | | | | | | | |
| Number | 494 | 365 | 512 | **532** | 500 | 460 | 484 | 452 | 394 | 407 | 417 | 498 | 477 |
| Yards | 1703 | 1434 | 2249 | **2376** | 2229 | 2139 | 1695 | 1711 | 1461 | 1248 | 1530 | 2129 | 1757 |
| Average Yards | 3.4 | 3.9 | 4.4 | 4.5 | 4.5 | **4.7** | 3.5 | 3.8 | 3.7 | 3.1 | 3.7 | 4.3 | 3.7 |
| Touchdowns | 12 | 6 | **25** | 15 | 18 | 15 | 14 | 18 | 11 | 6 | 8 | 12 | 8 |
| **PASSING:** | | | | | | | | | | | | | |
| Attempts | 285 | 443 | 361 | 299 | 254 | 370 | 334 | 387 | **462** | 390 | 385 | 391 | 334 |
| Completions | 167 | 186 | 206 | 157 | 121 | 185 | 157 | 182 | **268** | 200 | 170 | 209 | 182 |
| Completion Percentage | **58.6** | 42.0 | 57.1 | 52.5 | 47.6 | 50.0 | 47.0 | 47.0 | 58.0 | 51.3 | 44.2 | 53.5 | 54.5 |
| Passing Yards | 2495 | 2294 | 3037 | 2453 | 1842 | 2304 | 1910 | 2355 | **3062** | 2552 | 2656 | 2688 | 2391 |
| Avg. Yards per Attempt | **8.8** | 5.4 | 8.4 | 8.2 | 7.3 | 6.2 | 5.7 | 6.1 | 6.6 | 6.5 | 6.9 | 6.9 | 7.2 |
| Avg. Yards per Complet. | 14.9 | 12.3 | 14.7 | **15.6** | 15.2 | 12.5 | 12.2 | 12.9 | 11.4 | 12.8 | 15.6 | 12.9 | 13.1 |
| Times Tackled Passing | 31 | 49 | 32 | 31 | 18 | 26 | 28 | 50 | 40 | 26 | 19 | **11** | 17 |
| Yards Lost Tackled | 239 | 392 | 251 | 252 | 157 | 210 | 255 | 400 | 348 | 229 | 185 | **111** | 118 |
| Net Yards | 2256 | 1902 | **2786** | 2201 | 1685 | 2094 | 1655 | 1955 | 2714 | 2323 | 2471 | 2577 | 2273 |
| Touchdowns | 16 | 12 | **22** | 17 | 12 | 18 | 9 | 12 | 14 | 13 | 14 | 18 | 13 |
| Interceptions | 21 | 28 | 14 | 14 | 24 | **11** | 18 | 14 | 25 | 20 | 26 | 24 | 15 |
| Percent Intercepted | 7.4 | 6.3 | 3.9 | 4.7 | 9.4 | **3.0** | 5.4 | 3.6 | 5.4 | 5.1 | 6.8 | 6.1 | 4.5 |
| **PUNTS:** | | | | | | | | | | | | | |
| Number | 60 | 77 | 56 | 42 | 56 | 70 | **89** | 77 | 66 | 75 | 61 | 51 | 58 |
| Average Distance | 36.9 | 40.2 | 41.6 | 41.7 | 40.0 | 41.4 | 39.5 | 41.4 | 40.6 | **41.9** | 38.8 | 38.7 | 40.5 |
| **PUNT RETURNS:** | | | | | | | | | | | | | |
| Number | 37 | 36 | 31 | 23 | 38 | 35 | 27 | 16 | 19 | 24 | 30 | 39 | **45** |
| Yards | 174 | 262 | 248 | 194 | 177 | 172 | 164 | 100 | 122 | 172 | 234 | 268 | **427** |
| Average Yards | 4.7 | 7.3 | 8.0 | 8.4 | 4.7 | 4.9 | 6.1 | 6.3 | 6.4 | 7.2 | 7.8 | 6.9 | **9.5** |
| Touchdowns | 0 | 0 | 0 | 0 | 0 | 0 | 0 | 0 | 0 | 0 | 0 | 0 | 0 |
| **KICKOFF RETURNS:** | | | | | | | | | | | | | |
| Number | 59 | 59 | 50 | 51 | 58 | 54 | 41 | 56 | **63** | 49 | 58 | 46 | 43 |
| Yards | 1477 | 1325 | 1376 | 1233 | **1546** | 1322 | 960 | 1143 | 1416 | 1183 | 1363 | 1075 | 913 |
| Average Yards | 25.0 | 22.5 | **27.5** | 24.2 | 26.7 | 24.5 | 23.4 | 20.4 | 22.5 | 24.1 | 23.5 | 23.4 | 21.2 |
| Touchdowns | 0 | 0 | **2** | **2** | 1 | 1 | 0 | 0 | 1 | 0 | 1 | 0 | 0 |
| **INTERCEPTION RETURNS:** | | | | | | | | | | | | | |
| Number | 20 | 22 | 26 | 22 | 16 | 27 | 27 | 20 | 15 | 22 | 17 | 14 | **29** |
| Yards | 180 | 267 | 402 | 295 | 205 | 452 | **572** | 342 | 227 | 374 | 191 | 186 | 480 |
| Average Yards | 9.0 | 12.1 | 15.5 | 13.4 | 12.8 | 16.7 | **21.2** | 17.1 | 15.1 | 17.0 | 11.2 | 13.3 | 16.6 |
| Touchdowns | 1 | 0 | 0 | 3 | 0 | 2 | 1 | 1 | 1 | 1 | 1 | 0 | **5** |
| **PENALTIES:** | | | | | | | | | | | | | |
| Number | 79 | 78 | **94** | 69 | 61 | 79 | 70 | 85 | 77 | 81 | 66 | 88 | 80 |
| Yards | 723 | 746 | 952 | 738 | 568 | 642 | 661 | 869 | 640 | 838 | 643 | **961** | 801 |
| **FUMBLES:** | | | | | | | | | | | | | |
| Number | 39 | 28 | 30 | 35 | 29 | 32 | 25 | 29 | 37 | **21** | 35 | 33 | 32 |
| Number Lost | 15 | 18 | 21 | 19 | 20 | 18 | 12 | **11** | 20 | 15 | 20 | 18 | 20 |
| **POINTS:** | | | | | | | | | | | | | |
| Total | 274 | 185 | **406** | 341 | 274 | 313 | 245 | 266 | 228 | 221 | 231 | 300 | 276 |
| PAT Attempts | 34 | 20 | **50** | 39 | 33 | 37 | 25 | 31 | 30 | 24 | 24 | 33 | 27 |
| PAT Made | 29 | 20 | **50** | 39 | 32 | 37 | 25 | 29 | 30 | 23 | 24 | 33 | 27 |
| FG Attempts | 21 | 33 | 33 | 37 | 26 | 29 | 32 | 28 | 17 | 37 | 32 | 36 | **49** |
| FG Made | 13 | 15 | 18 | 22 | 14 | 18 | 22 | 17 | 6 | 18 | 21 | 23 | **29** |
| Percent FG Made | 61.9 | 45.5 | 54.5 | 59.5 | 53.8 | 62.1 | **68.8** | 60.7 | 35.3 | 48.6 | 65.6 | 63.9 | 59.2 |
| Safeties | 1 | 0 | 1 | 1 | 1 | 0 | **2** | 0 | 0 | 0 | 0 | 0 | 0 |

### DEFENSE

| | ATL. | CHI. | DALL. | DET. | G.B. | L.A. | MINN. | N.O. | N.Y.G. | PHIL. | ST.L. | S.F. | WASH. |
|---|---|---|---|---|---|---|---|---|---|---|---|---|---|
| **FIRST DOWNS:** | | | | | | | | | | | | | |
| Total | 237 | 234 | 200 | 210 | 230 | 239 | **194** | 260 | 228 | 251 | 244 | 199 | 213 |
| by Rushing | 114 | 99 | **59** | 97 | 104 | 91 | 88 | 129 | 104 | 104 | 109 | 80 | 73 |
| by Passing | 106 | 117 | 125 | 99 | 110 | 129 | **88** | 110 | 112 | 129 | 120 | 96 | 119 |
| by Penalty | 17 | 18 | 16 | 14 | 16 | 19 | 18 | 21 | **12** | 18 | 15 | 23 | 21 |
| **RUSHING:** | | | | | | | | | | | | | |
| Number | 500 | 509 | **353** | 432 | 489 | 455 | 447 | 495 | 449 | 450 | 486 | 408 | 408 |
| Yards | 2149 | 2116 | **1144** | 1842 | 1707 | 1658 | 1600 | 2200 | 2059 | 1962 | 1985 | 1668 | 1396 |
| Average Yards | 4.3 | 4.2 | **3.2** | 4.3 | 3.5 | 3.6 | 3.6 | 4.4 | 4.6 | 4.4 | 4.1 | 4.1 | 3.4 |
| Touchdowns | 19 | 14 | 8 | 15 | 7 | 11 | **2** | 18 | 12 | 16 | 10 | 4 | 7 |
| **PASSING:** | | | | | | | | | | | | | |
| Attempts | 343 | 362 | 421 | **306** | 353 | 387 | 405 | 333 | 333 | 407 | 375 | 341 | 411 |
| Completions | 164 | 192 | 209 | 163 | 186 | 200 | 206 | 175 | 173 | 220 | 212 | **152** | 191 |
| Completion Percentage | 47.8 | 53.0 | 49.6 | 53.3 | 52.7 | 51.7 | 50.9 | 52.6 | 52.0 | 54.1 | 56.5 | **44.6** | 46.5 |
| Passing Yards | **1895** | 2607 | 2660 | 2163 | 2469 | 2693 | 2022 | 2472 | 2458 | 2971 | 2546 | 2309 | 2448 |
| Avg. Yards per Attempt | 5.5 | 7.2 | 6.3 | 7.1 | 7.0 | 7.0 | **5.0** | 7.4 | 7.4 | 7.3 | 6.8 | 6.8 | 6.0 |
| Avg. Yards per Complet. | 11.6 | 13.6 | 12.7 | 13.3 | 13.3 | 13.5 | **9.8** | 14.1 | 14.2 | 13.5 | 12.0 | 15.2 | 12.8 |
| Times Tackled Passing | 31 | 28 | 43 | **18** | 19 | 37 | 27 | 24 | 18 | 32 | 20 | 38 | 36 |
| Yards Lost Tackled | 257 | 203 | 336 | **146** | 168 | 314 | 216 | 234 | 151 | 311 | 166 | 298 | 321 |
| Net Yards | **1638** | 2404 | 2324 | 2017 | 2301 | 2379 | 1806 | 2238 | 2307 | 2660 | 2380 | 2011 | 2127 |
| Touchdowns | **9** | 12 | 15 | 17 | 21 | 15 | 10 | 20 | 25 | 16 | 12 | 17 | 11 |
| Interceptions | 20 | 22 | 26 | 22 | 16 | 27 | 27 | 20 | 15 | 22 | 17 | 14 | **29** |
| Percent Intercepted | 5.8 | 6.1 | 6.2 | **7.2** | 4.5 | 7.0 | 6.7 | 6.1 | 4.5 | 5.4 | 4.5 | 4.1 | 7.1 |
| **PUNTS:** | | | | | | | | | | | | | |
| Number | 63 | 67 | 65 | 58 | 61 | 66 | **78** | **50** | 61 | 57 | 58 | 73 | 77 |
| Average Distance | 41.4 | 40.2 | 41.5 | 41.2 | 40.1 | **39.4** | 40.0 | 41.2 | 39.8 | 40.5 | 40.4 | 39.7 | 41.2 |
| **PUNT RETURNS:** | | | | | | | | | | | | | |
| Number | 26 | 31 | 26 | 18 | 23 | 27 | 47 | 43 | 50 | 40 | 24 | 19 | **17** |
| Yards | 117 | 172 | 231 | 111 | 169 | 67 | 336 | 251 | 319 | 372 | 160 | **44** | 87 |
| Average Yards | 4.5 | 5.5 | 8.9 | 6.2 | 7.3 | 2.5 | 7.1 | 5.8 | 6.4 | 9.3 | 6.7 | **2.3** | 5.1 |
| Touchdowns | 0 | 0 | 0 | 0 | 0 | 0 | 0 | 0 | 0 | 0 | 1 | 0 | 0 |
| **KICKOFF RETURNS:** | | | | | | | | | | | | | |
| Number | 52 | **32** | 70 | 70 | 56 | 57 | 49 | 54 | 45 | 48 | 54 | 61 | 61 |
| Yards | 1228 | **817** | 1681 | 1627 | 1248 | 1176 | 1077 | 1326 | 1063 | 1101 | 1318 | 1467 | 1066 |
| Average Yards | 23.6 | 25.5 | 24.0 | 23.2 | 22.3 | 20.6 | 22.0 | 24.6 | 23.6 | 22.9 | 24.4 | 24.0 | **17.5** |
| Touchdowns | 1 | 1 | **0** | **0** | **0** | 1 | **0** | 2 | **0** | 1 | 1 | **0** | **0** |
| **INTERCEPTION RETURNS:** | | | | | | | | | | | | | |
| Number | 21 | 28 | 14 | 14 | 24 | **11** | 18 | 14 | 25 | 20 | 26 | 24 | 15 |
| Yards | 242 | 465 | 304 | 207 | 449 | **83** | 204 | 171 | 377 | 359 | 358 | 385 | 284 |
| Average Yards | 11.5 | 16.6 | 21.7 | 14.8 | 18.7 | **7.5** | 11.3 | 12.2 | 15.1 | 18.0 | 13.8 | 16.0 | 18.9 |
| Touchdowns | **0** | 1 | 1 | 1 | 2 | 1 | 1 | 1 | 4 | 1 | **0** | 1 | 1 |
| **PENALTIES:** | | | | | | | | | | | | | |
| Number | 61 | 78 | 61 | 97 | 60 | 62 | 57 | **98** | 69 | 94 | 79 | 75 | 93 |
| Yards | 614 | 819 | 647 | 942 | 514 | 665 | 615 | **967** | 730 | 908 | 831 | 610 | 720 |
| **FUMBLES:** | | | | | | | | | | | | | |
| Number | 32 | 36 | **40** | 23 | 33 | 22 | 34 | 39 | 29 | 34 | 28 | 31 | 22 |
| Number Lost | 18 | 23 | **25** | 11 | 16 | 7 | 18 | **25** | 15 | **25** | 16 | 16 | 12 |
| **POINTS:** | | | | | | | | | | | | | |
| Total | 277 | 276 | 222 | 286 | 298 | 260 | **139** | 347 | 362 | 302 | 279 | 216 | 190 |
| PAT Attempts | 31 | 29 | 25 | 35 | 34 | 30 | **14** | 44 | 42 | 36 | 29 | 23 | 20 |
| PAT Made | 31 | 28 | 24 | 35 | 32 | 29 | **13** | 44 | 42 | 35 | 28 | 21 | 19 |
| FG Attempts | **23** | 41 | 25 | 25 | 37 | 32 | 32 | 26 | 32 | 33 | 39 | 33 | 33 |
| FG Made | 20 | 24 | 16 | **13** | 20 | 17 | 14 | **13** | 22 | 17 | 25 | 19 | 17 |
| Percent FG Made | 87.0 | 58.5 | 64.0 | 52.0 | 54.1 | 53.1 | **43.8** | 50.0 | 68.8 | 51.5 | 64.1 | 57.6 | 51.5 |
| Safeties | **0** | 1 | **0** | 1 | 1 | **0** | **0** | **0** | 1 | **0** | 1 | **0** | **0** |

## CONFERENCE PLAYOFFS

December 25 at Bloomington
(Attendance 47,307)

### SCORING

| | | | | | |
|---|---|---|---|---|---|
| **MINNESOTA** | **0** | **3** | **0** | **9** | **–12** |
| **DALLAS** | **3** | **3** | **14** | **0** | **–20** |

First Quarter
Dal. Clark, 26 yard field goal

Second Quarter
Min. Cox, 27 yard field goal
Dal. Clark, 44 yard field goal

Third Quarter
Dal. Thomas, 13 yard rush
PAT–Clark (kick)
Dal. Hayes, 9 yard pass from Staubach
PAT–Clark (kick)

Fourth Quarter
Min. Page, safety tackled Staubach in end zone
Min. Voigt, 6 yard pass from Cuozzo
PAT–Cox (kick)

### TEAM STATISTICS

| MINN. | | DALLAS |
|---|---|---|
| 17 | First Downs–Total | 10 |
| 5 | First Downs–Rushing | 5 |
| 12 | First Downs–Passing | 5 |
| 0 | First Downs–Penalty | 0 |
| 1 | Fumbles–Number | 0 |
| 1 | Fumbles–Lost Ball | 0 |
| 2 | Penalties–Number | 2 |
| 18 | Yards Penalized | 10 |
| 2 | Missed Field Goals | 0 |
| 64 | Offensive Plays–Total | 55 |
| 311 | Net Yards | 183 |
| 4.9 | Average Gain | 3.3 |
| 5 | Giveaways | 0 |
| 0 | Takeaways | 5 |
| –5 | Difference | +5 |

### INDIVIDUAL STATISTICS

| MINNESOTA | No. | Yds. | Avg. | DALLAS | No. | Yds. | Avg. |
|---|---|---|---|---|---|---|---|
| **RUSHING** | | | | | | | |
| Jones | 15 | 52 | 3.5 | D. Thomas | 21 | 66 | 3.1 |
| Lee | 3 | 28 | 9.3 | Hill | 14 | 28 | 2.0 |
| Osborn | 6 | 13 | 2.2 | Garrison | 2 | 2 | 1.0 |
| Lindsey | 1 | 6 | 6.0 | Staubach | 2 | 2 | 1.0 |
| Grim | 1 | 2 | 2.0 | | 39 | 98 | 2.5 |
| | 26 | 101 | 3.9 | | | | |
| **RECEIVING** | | | | | | | |
| Washington | 5 | 70 | 14.0 | Hayes | 3 | 31 | 10.3 |
| Grim | 4 | 74 | 18.5 | Alworth | 2 | 33 | 16.5 |
| Voigt | 4 | 46 | 11.5 | Ditka | 2 | 18 | 9.0 |
| Reed | 4 | –3 | –0.8 | Hill | 2 | 14 | 7.0 |
| Lindsey | 1 | 25 | 25.0 | D. Thomas | 1 | 3 | 3.0 |
| White | 1 | –2 | –2.0 | | 10 | 99 | 9.9 |
| | 19 | 210 | 11.1 | | | | |
| **PUNTING** | | | | | | | |
| Lee | 4 | | 43.5 | Widby | 7 | | 37.0 |
| **PUNT RETURNS** | | | | | | | |
| West | 2 | 6 | 3.0 | Waters | 2 | 37 | 18.5 |
| **KICKOFF RETURNS** | | | | | | | |
| Jones | 2 | 75 | 37.5 | I. Thomas | 2 | 31 | 15.5 |
| West | 2 | 74 | 37.0 | Harris | 1 | 21 | 21.0 |
| Bryant | 1 | 22 | 22.0 | | 3 | 52 | 17.3 |
| Brown | 1 | 17 | 17.0 | | | | |
| | 6 | 188 | 31.3 | | | | |
| **INTERCEPTION RETURNS** | | | | | | | |
| None | | | | Harris | 1 | 30 | 30.0 |
| | | | | Howley | 1 | 26 | 26.0 |
| | | | | Adderly | 1 | 8 | 8.0 |
| | | | | Jordan | 1 | 5 | 5.0 |
| | | | | | 4 | 69 | 17.3 |

**PASSING**

| MINNESOTA | Att. | Comp. | Comp. Pct. | Yds. | Int. | Yds/ Att. | Yds/ Comp. | Yds. Lost Tkld. |
|---|---|---|---|---|---|---|---|---|
| Cuozzo | 22 | 12 | 54.5 | 124 | 2 | 5.6 | 10.3 | 0– 0 |
| Lee | 16 | 7 | 43.8 | 86 | 2 | 5.4 | 12.3 | 0– 0 |
| | 38 | 19 | 50.0 | 210 | 4 | 5.5 | 11.1 | 0– 0 |
| **DALLAS** | | | | | | | | |
| Staubach | 14 | 10 | 71.4 | 99 | 0 | 7.1 | 9.9 | 2–14 |

December 26, at San Francisco
(Attendance 45,327)

### SCORING

| | | | | | |
|---|---|---|---|---|---|
| **SAN FRANCISCO** | **0** | **3** | **14** | **7** | **–24** |
| **WASHINGTON** | **7** | **3** | **3** | **7** | **–20** |

First Quarter
Was. Smith, 5 yard pass from Kilmer
PAT–Knight (kick)

Second Quarter
S.F. Gossett, 23 yard field goal
Was. Knight, 40 yard field goal

Third Quarter
S.F. G. Washington, 78 yard pass from Brodie PAT–Gossett (kick)
S.F. Windsor, 2 yard pass from Brodie
PAT–Gossett (kick)
Was. Knight, 36 yard field goal

Fourth Quarter
S.F. Hoskins, recovered fumble in end zone
PAT–Gossett (kick)
Was. Brown, 16 yard pass from Kilmer
PAT–Knight (kick)

### TEAM STATISTICS

| S.F. | | WASH. |
|---|---|---|
| 11 | First Downs–Total | 13 |
| 2 | First Downs–Rushing | 6 |
| 9 | First Downs–Passing | 5 |
| 0 | First Downs–Penalty | 2 |
| 0 | Fumbles – Number | 3 |
| 0 | Fumbles–Lost Ball | 2 |
| 3 | Penalties–Number | 4 |
| 41 | Yards Penalized | 55 |
| 0 | Missed Field Goals | 1 |
| 59 | Offensive Plays–Total | 67 |
| 285 | Net Yards | 192 |
| 4.8 | Average Gain | 2.9 |
| 0 | Giveaways | 3 |
| 3 | Takeaways | 0 |
| +3 | Difference | –3 |

### INDIVIDUAL STATISTICS

| SAN FRANCISCO | No. | Yds. | Avg. | WASHINGTON | No. | Yds. | Avg. |
|---|---|---|---|---|---|---|---|
| **RUSHING** | | | | | | | |
| V. Washington | 16 | 59 | 3.7 | Brown | 27 | 84 | 3.1 |
| Willard | 19 | 46 | 2.4 | Harraway | 10 | 28 | 2.8 |
| Schreiber | 4 | 7 | 1.8 | Kilmer | 1 | 0 | 0.0 |
| | 39 | 112 | 2.8 | Jefferson | 1 | –13 | –13.0 |
| | | | | | 39 | 99 | 2.5 |
| **RECEIVING** | | | | | | | |
| Kwalick | 3 | 26 | 8.7 | Brown | 6 | 62 | 10.3 |
| Witcher | 2 | 28 | 14.0 | Smith | 3 | 32 | 10.7 |
| G. Washington | 1 | 78 | 78.0 | Mason | 1 | 8 | 8.0 |
| Schreiber | 1 | 22 | 22.0 | Harraway | 1 | 4 | 4.0 |
| V. Washington | 1 | 10 | 10.0 | | 11 | 106 | 9.6 |
| Willard | 1 | 10 | 10.0 | | | | |
| Windsor | 1 | 2 | 2.0 | | | | |
| | 10 | 176 | 17.6 | | | | |
| **PUNTING** | | | | | | | |
| Spurrier | 10 | | 33.7 | Bragg | 5 | | 46.0 |
| **PUNT RETURNS** | | | | | | | |
| Fuller | 1 | 8 | 8.0 | Duncan | 2 | 11 | 5.5 |
| Simpson | 1 | 4 | 4.0 | Vactor | 1 | 47 | 47.0 |
| B. Taylor | 1 | 1 | 1.0 | | 3 | 58 | 19.3 |
| | 3 | 13 | 4.3 | | | | |
| **KICKOFF RETURNS** | | | | | | | |
| V. Washington | 4 | 79 | 19.8 | Duncan | 3 | 170 | 56.7 |
| Cunningham | 1 | 0 | 0.0 | McLinton | 1 | 19 | 19.0 |
| | 5 | 79 | 15.8 | | 4 | 189 | 47.3 |
| **INTERCEPTION RETURNS** | | | | | | | |
| R. Taylor | 1 | 17 | 17.0 | None | | | |

**PASSING**

| SAN FRANCISCO | Att. | Cmp. | Comp. Pct. | Yds. | Int. | Yds/ Att. | Yds/ Comp. | Yds Lost Tkld. |
|---|---|---|---|---|---|---|---|---|
| Brodie | 19 | 10 | 52.6 | 176 | 0 | 9.3 | 17.6 | 1– 3 |
| **WASHINGTON** | | | | | | | | |
| Kilmer | 27 | 11 | 40.7 | 106 | 1 | 3.9 | 9.6 | 1–13 |

## DALLAS COWBOYS 11-3-0 Tom Landry

| Scores of Each Game | | |
|---|---|---|
| 49 | Buffalo | 37 |
| 42 | Philadelphia | 7 |
| 16 | WASHINGTON | 20 |
| 20 | N.Y. GIANTS | 13 |
| 14 | New Orleans | 24 |
| 44 | NEW ENGLAND | 21 |
| 19 | Chicago | 23 |
| 16 | St. Louis | 13 |
| 20 | PHILADELPHIA | 7 |
| 13 | Washington | 0 |
| 28 | LOS ANGELES | 21 |
| 52 | N.Y. JETS | 10 |
| 42 | N.Y. Giants | 14 |
| 31 | ST. LOUIS | 12 |

| Use Name | Pos. | Hgt | Wgt | Age | Int | Pts |
|---|---|---|---|---|---|---|
| Forrest Gregg | OT | 6'4" | 250 | 38 | | |
| Tony Liscio | OT | 6'5" | 255 | 31 | | |
| Ralph Neely | OT | 6'5" | 265 | 27 | | |
| Don Talbert | OT | 6'5" | 255 | 31 | | |
| Rayfield Wright | OT | 6'7" | 255 | 26 | | |
| John Niland | OG | 6'4" | 245 | 27 | | |
| Blaine Nye | OG | 6'4" | 250 | 25 | | |
| Rodney Wallace | OG | 6'5" | 255 | 22 | | |
| John Fitzgerald | C | 6'5" | 250 | 23 | | |
| Dave Manders | C | 6'2" | 250 | 29 | | |
| George Andrie | DE | 6'7" | 250 | 31 | | |
| Larry Cole | DE | 6'4" | 255 | 24 | | |
| Tody Smith | DE | 6'5" | 245 | 22 | | |
| Pat Toomay | DE | 6'5" | 244 | 26 | | |
| Bill Gregory | DT | 6'5" | 255 | 21 | | |
| Bob Lilly | DT | 6'4" | 260 | 32 | | 6 |
| Jethro Pugh | DT | 6'6" | 260 | 27 | | |
| Lee Roy Caffey | LB | 6'3" | 250 | 31 | | |
| Dave Edwards | LB | 6'3" | 225 | 32 | 2 | |
| Chuck Howley | LB | 6'3" | 225 | 35 | 5 | |
| Lee Roy Jordan | LB | 6'2" | 220 | 30 | 2 | |
| D. D. Lewis | LB | 6'2" | 225 | 25 | 1 | |
| Tom Stincic | LB | 6'2" | 230 | 24 | | |
| Herb Adderley | DB | 6'1" | 200 | 32 | 6 | |
| Cornell Green | DB | 6'4" | 208 | 31 | 2 | |
| Cliff Harris | DB | 6' | 184 | 22 | 2 | |
| Mel Renfro | DB | 6' | 190 | 29 | 4 | |
| Ike Thomas | DB | 6'2" | 193 | 23 | | 12 |
| Mark Washington | DB | 5'10" | 183 | 23 | | |
| Charlie Waters | DB | 6'1" | 193 | 22 | 2 | |
| Bob Asher – Injury | | | | | | |
| Craig Morton | QB | 6'4" | 214 | 28 | | 6 |
| Roger Staubach | QB | 6'2" | 197 | 29 | | 12 |
| Dan Reeves | HB | 6'1" | 200 | 27 | | 1 |
| Claxton Welch | HB | 5'11" | 203 | 24 | | 8 |
| Joe Williams | HB | 6' | 195 | 24 | | 6 |
| Calvin Hill | FB-HB | 6'3" | 235 | 24 | | 66 |
| Duane Thomas | FB-HB | 6'1" | 210 | 24 | | 78 |
| Walt Garrison | FB | 6' | 205 | 27 | | 12 |
| Margene Adkins | WR | 5'10" | 183 | 24 | | |
| Lance Alworth | WR | 6' | 180 | 31 | | 12 |
| Bob Hayes | WR | 6' | 185 | 28 | | 48 |
| Gloster Richardson | WR | 6' | 200 | 28 | | 18 |
| Mike Ditka | TE | 6'3" | 225 | 31 | | 6 |
| Billy Truax | TE | 6'5" | 235 | 28 | | 6 |
| Mike Clark | K | 6'1" | 205 | 30 | | 86 |
| Toni Fritsch | K | 5'7" | 185 | 26 | | 17 |
| Ron Widby | K | 6'4" | 210 | 26 | | |

## WASHINGTON REDSKINS 9-4-1 George Allen

| Scores of Each Game | | |
|---|---|---|
| 24 | ST. LOUIS | 17 |
| 30 | N.Y. Giants | 3 |
| 20 | Dallas | 16 |
| 22 | HOUSTON | 13 |
| 20 | ST. LOUIS | 0 |
| 20 | Kansas City | 27 |
| 24 | NEW ORLEANS | 14 |
| 7 | PHILADELPHIA | 7 |
| 15 | Chicago | 16 |
| 0 | DALLAS | 13 |
| 20 | Philadelphia | 13 |
| 23 | N.Y. GIANTS | 7 |
| 38 | Los Angeles | 24 |
| 13 | CLEVELAND | 20 |

| Use Name | Pos. | Hgt | Wgt | Age | Int | Pts |
|---|---|---|---|---|---|---|
| Terry Hermeling | OT | 6'5" | 255 | 25 | | |
| Walt Rock | OT | 6'5" | 255 | 30 | | |
| Jim Snowden | OT | 6'3" | 255 | 29 | | |
| Mike Taylor | OT | 6'4" | 245 | 26 | | |
| Paul Laaveg | OG | 6'4" | 245 | 22 | | |
| Ray Schoenke | OG | 6'3" | 250 | 29 | | |
| John Wilbur | OG | 6'3" | 250 | 28 | | |
| George Burman | C-OG | 6'3" | 255 | 28 | | |
| Len Hauss | C | 6'2" | 235 | 29 | | |
| Verlon Biggs | DE | 6'4" | 270 | 28 | | |
| Jimmie Jones | DE | 6'3" | 215 | 24 | | |
| Ron McDole | DE | 6'3" | 288 | 31 | 3 | 6 |
| Bill Brundige | DT | 6'5" | 270 | 22 | | |
| Manny Sistrunk | DT | 6'5" | 265 | 24 | | |
| Diron Talbert | DT | 6'5" | 255 | 27 | | |
| Bob Grant | LB | 6'2" | 225 | 25 | | |
| Chris Hanburger | LB | 6'2" | 218 | 30 | 1 | 6 |
| Harold McLinton | LB | 6'2" | 235 | 24 | | |
| Jack Pardee | LB | 6'2" | 225 | 35 | 5 | 6 |
| Myron Pottios | LB | 6'2" | 232 | 31 | 1 | |
| Rusty Tillman | LB | 6'2" | 230 | 25 | | |
| Mike Bass | DB | 6' | 190 | 26 | 8 | 6 |
| Speedy Duncan | DB | 5'10" | 175 | 28 | 1 | 6 |
| Pat Fischer | DB | 5'10" | 170 | 31 | 3 | 6 |
| Jon Jaqua | DB | 6' | 190 | 23 | | |
| Brig Owens | DB | 5'11" | 190 | 28 | 2 | |
| Richie Petitbon | DB | 6'3" | 208 | 33 | 5 | |
| Ted Vactor | DB | 6' | 185 | 27 | | |
| Sonny Jurgensen | QB | 5'11" | 203 | 37 | | |
| Billy Kilmer | QB | 6' | 204 | 31 | | 12 |
| Sam Wyche | QB | 6'4" | 210 | 26 | | |
| Larry Brown | HB | 5'11" | 195 | 23 | | 36 |
| Bob Brunet | HB | 6'1" | 205 | 25 | | |
| Tommy Mason | FB-HB | 6' | 195 | 32 | | |
| Charlie Harraway | FB | 6'2" | 215 | 26 | | 12 |
| Mike Hull | FB | 6'3" | 220 | 26 | | |
| Jeff Jordan | HB-FB | 6'1" | 215 | 26 | | |
| Boyd Dowler | WR | 6'5" | 225 | 34 | | |
| Roy Jefferson | WR | 6'2" | 195 | 27 | | 24 |
| Bill Malinchak | WR | 6'1" | 200 | 27 | | |
| Clifton McNeil (from NYG) | WR | 6'2" | 187 | 31 | | 18 |
| Charley Taylor | WR | 6'3" | 210 | 30 | | 24 |
| Mack Alston | TE | 6'2" | 230 | 24 | | |
| Jerry Smith | TE | 6'2" | 208 | 28 | | 6 |
| Mike Bragg | K | 5'11" | 186 | 24 | | |
| Curt Knight | K | 6'1" | 190 | 28 | | 114 |

## PHILADELPHIA EAGLES 6-7-1 Jerry Williams Ed Khayat

| Scores of Each Game | | |
|---|---|---|
| 14 | Cincinnati | 37 |
| 7 | DALLAS | 42 |
| 3 | SAN FRANCISCO | 31 |
| 0 | MINNESOTA | 13 |
| 10 | Oakland | 34 |
| 23 | N.Y. GIANTS | 7 |
| 17 | DENVER | 16 |
| 7 | Washington | 7 |
| 7 | Dallas | 20 |
| 37 | St. Louis | 20 |
| 13 | WASHINGTON | 20 |
| 23 | Detroit | 20 |
| 19 | ST. LOUIS | 7 |
| 41 | N.Y. Giants | 28 |

| Use Name | Pos. | Hgt | Wgt | Age | Int | Pts |
|---|---|---|---|---|---|---|
| Wayde Key | OT | 6'4" | 245 | 24 | | |
| Steve Smith | OT | 6'5" | 250 | 27 | | 6 |
| Dick Stevens | OT | 6'4" | 240 | 23 | | |
| Henry Allison | OG | 6'2" | 255 | 24 | | |
| Jim Skaggs | OG | 6'2" | 250 | 31 | | |
| Tuufuli Uperesa | OG | 6'3" | 255 | 23 | | |
| Mike Evans | C | 6'5" | 250 | 24 | | |
| Mark Nordquist | OG-C | 6'4" | 245 | 25 | | |
| Don Brumm | DE | 6'3" | 245 | 28 | | |
| Richard Harris | DE | 6'4" | 260 | 23 | | |
| Mel Tom | DE | 6'4" | 250 | 30 | | |
| Mike Dirks | DT | 6'2" | 245 | 25 | | |
| Don Hultz | DT | 6'3" | 240 | 30 | 1 | |
| Gary Pettigrew | DT | 6'4" | 255 | 26 | | |
| Ernie Calloway | DE-DT | 6'6" | 240 | 23 | | |
| Dick Hart – Injury | | | | | | |
| Harry Jones – Injury | | | | | | |
| Bob Creech | LB | 6'3" | 222 | 22 | | |
| Bill Hobbs | LB | 6' | 220 | 25 | | 6 |
| Ike Kelley | LB | 5'11" | 224 | 27 | | |
| Ron Porter | LB | 6'3" | 232 | 26 | | |
| Tim Rossovich | LB | 6'4" | 240 | 25 | 1 | |
| Fred Whittingham | LB | 6'1" | 240 | 32 | | |
| Adrian Young | LB | 6'1" | 232 | 25 | | |
| Steve Zabel | TE-LB | 6'4" | 235 | 23 | 1 | 12 |
| Bill Bradley | DB | 5'11" | 190 | 24 | 11 | |
| Vern Davis | DB | 6'4" | 208 | 21 | | |
| Leroy Keyes | DB | 6'3" | 208 | 24 | 6 | |
| Al Nelson | DB | 5'11" | 186 | 27 | 2 | 12 |
| Steve Preece | DB | 6'1" | 195 | 24 | | |
| Nate Ramsey | DB | 6'1" | 200 | 30 | | |
| Jack Smith | DB | 6'4" | 204 | 23 | | |
| Jim Thrower | DB | 6'2" | 194 | 22 | | |
| Greg Barton – Canadian Football League | | | | | | |
| Rich Arrington | QB | 6'2" | 190 | 24 | | |
| Pete Liske | QB | 6'2" | 200 | 30 | | 6 |
| Jim Ward | QB | 6'2" | 200 | 27 | | |
| Tom Bailey | HB | 6'2" | 211 | 22 | | 6 |
| Ronnie Bull | FB-HB | 6' | 200 | 31 | | 6 |
| Sonny Davis | FB-HB | 5'11" | 215 | 23 | | 6 |
| Larry Watkins | FB-HB | 6'2" | 215 | 24 | | 6 |
| Lee Bouggess | FB | 6'2" | 210 | 23 | | 18 |
| Tom Woodeshick | FB | 6' | 222 | 29 | | 6 |
| Tony Baker (from NO) | FB | 5'11" | 225 | 26 | | 6 |
| Harold Carmichael | WR | 6'7" | 225 | 21 | | |
| Ben Hawkins | WR | 6' | 180 | 27 | | 30 |
| Harold Jackson | WR | 5'10" | 175 | 25 | | 18 |
| Billy Walik | WR | 5'11" | 180 | 23 | | |
| Kent Kramer | TE | 6'5" | 235 | 27 | | 6 |
| Gary Ballman | WR-TE | 6' | 210 | 31 | | |
| Fred Hill | WR-TE | 6'2" | 215 | 28 | | |
| Tom Dempsey | K | 6'1" | 264 | 30 | | 49 |
| Happy Feller | K | 5'11" | 185 | 22 | | 28 |
| Tom McNeill | K | 6'1" | 195 | 29 | | |

## ST. LOUIS CARDINALS 4-9-1 Bob Hollway

| Scores of Each Game | | |
|---|---|---|
| 17 | WASHINGTON | 24 |
| 17 | N.Y. JETS | 10 |
| 20 | N.Y. GIANTS | 21 |
| 26 | Atlanta | 9 |
| 0 | Washington | 20 |
| 14 | SAN FRANCISCO | 26 |
| 28 | Buffalo | 23 |
| 13 | DALLAS | 16 |
| 17 | San Diego | 20 |
| 20 | PHILADELPHIA | 37 |
| 24 | N.Y. Giants | 7 |
| 16 | GREEN BAY | 16 |
| 7 | Philadelphia | 19 |
| 12 | Dallas | 31 |

| Use Name | Pos. | Hgt | Wgt | Age | Int | Pts |
|---|---|---|---|---|---|---|
| Vern Emerson | OT | 6'5" | 260 | 25 | | |
| Ernie McMillan | OT | 6'6" | 255 | 33 | | |
| Bob Reynolds | OT | 6'6" | 265 | 30 | | |
| Dan Dierdorf | OG-OT | 6'4" | 265 | 22 | | |
| Irv Goode | OG | 6'4" | 255 | 30 | | |
| Chuck Hutchison | OG | 6'3" | 240 | 22 | | |
| Clyde Williams | OG | 6'2" | 250 | 31 | | |
| Tom Banks | C | 6'1" | 240 | 23 | | |
| Wayne Mulligan | C | 6'2" | 245 | 24 | | |
| Joe Schmiesing | DE | 6'4" | 260 | 26 | | |
| Chuck Walker | DE | 6'2" | 250 | 30 | | |
| Ron Yankowski | DE | 6'5" | 225 | 24 | | |
| Rolf Krueger | DT-DE | 6'4" | 250 | 24 | | |
| Paul Dickson | DT | 6'5" | 250 | 34 | | |
| Fred Heron | DT | 6'4" | 260 | 26 | | |
| Bob Rowe | DT | 6'4" | 260 | 26 | | |
| Terry Brown – Injury | | | | | | |
| Jim Hargrove | LB | 6'3" | 223 | 26 | | |
| Mike McGill | LB | 6'2" | 235 | 24 | 1 | |
| Terry Miller | LB | 6'2" | 225 | 25 | | |
| Rick Ogle | LB | 6'3" | 230 | 22 | | |
| Jamie Rivers | LB | 6'2" | 235 | 25 | | |
| Rocky Rosema | LB | 6'2" | 230 | 25 | | |
| Larry Stallings | LB | 6'2" | 230 | 29 | 1 | 6 |
| Jeff Allen | DB | 5'11" | 190 | 23 | | |
| Miller Farr | DB | 6'1" | 190 | 28 | 2 | |
| Dale Hackbart | DB | 6'3" | 220 | 35 | 1 | |
| George Hoey | DB | 5'10" | 170 | 24 | | 6 |
| Tom Longo | DB | 6'1" | 200 | 27 | | |
| Ted Provost | DB | 6'2" | 195 | 23 | | |
| Jerry Stovall | DB | 6'2" | 195 | 29 | 2 | |
| Norm Thompson | DB | 6'1" | 175 | 23 | 4 | |
| Roger Wehrli | DB | 6'1" | 195 | 23 | 2 | |
| Larry Willingham | DB | 6'1" | 190 | 22 | | |
| Larry Wilson | DB | 6' | 195 | 33 | 4 | |
| Pete Beathard | QB | 6'2" | 200 | 29 | | |
| Jim Hart | QB | 6'2" | 200 | 27 | | |
| Roy Shivers | HB | 6' | 200 | 29 | | 6 |
| Larry Stegent | HB | 6'1" | 200 | 23 | | |
| Paul White | HB | 6' | 200 | 23 | | |
| MacArthur Lane | FB-HB | 6' | 220 | 29 | | 18 |
| Cid Edwards | FB | 6'2" | 230 | 27 | | 24 |
| Johnny Roland | HB-FB | 6'2" | 215 | 28 | | |
| John Gilliam | WR | 6'1" | 195 | 26 | | 18 |
| Mel Gray | WR | 5'9" | 170 | 22 | | 24 |
| Freddie Hyatt | WR | 6'3" | 200 | 25 | | |
| Chuck Latourette | WR | 6' | 190 | 26 | | |
| Dave Williams | WR | 6'2" | 210 | 26 | | 6 |
| Jim McFarland | TE | 6'5" | 225 | 23 | | 12 |
| Jackie Smith | TE | 6'4" | 235 | 30 | | 24 |
| Jim Bakken | K | 6' | 195 | 30 | | 87 |

## NEW YORK GIANTS 4-10-0 Alex Webster

| Scores of Each Game | | |
|---|---|---|
| 42 | Green Bay | 40 |
| 3 | WASHINGTON | 30 |
| 21 | St. Louis | 20 |
| 13 | Dallas | 20 |
| 7 | BALTIMORE | 31 |
| 7 | Philadelphia | 23 |
| 10 | MINNESOTA | 17 |
| 35 | SAN DIEGO | 17 |
| 21 | Atlanta | 17 |
| 13 | Pittsburg | 17 |
| 7 | ST. LOUIS | 24 |
| 7 | Washington | 23 |
| 14 | DALLAS | 42 |
| 28 | PHILADELPHIA | 41 |

| Use Name | Pos. | Hgt | Wgt | Age | Int | Pts |
|---|---|---|---|---|---|---|
| Willie Young | OT | 6' | 265 | 28 | | |
| Charlie Harper | OG-OT | 6'2" | 250 | 27 | | |
| Bob Hyland | OG-OT | 6'5" | 250 | 26 | | |
| Steve Alexakos | OG | 6'2" | 260 | 24 | | |
| Doug Van Horn | OG | 6'2" | 245 | 27 | | |
| Wayne Walton | OG | 6'5" | 245 | 22 | | |
| Greg Larson | C | 6'2" | 250 | 32 | | |
| Fred Dryer | DE | 6'6" | 240 | 25 | | |
| Bob Lurtsema | DE | 6'6" | 250 | 29 | | |
| Henry Reed | DE | 6'3" | 230 | 22 | 1 | |
| Dave Tipton | DE | 6'6" | 240 | 22 | | |
| Dick Hanson | DT | 6'6" | 280 | 22 | | |
| Jim Kanicki | DT | 6'4" | 270 | 29 | | |
| Roland Lakes | DT | 6'4" | 263 | 31 | | |
| Dave Roller | DT | 6'2" | 240 | 21 | | |
| Jerry Shay | DT | 6'3" | 245 | 27 | | |
| Vern Vanoy | DT | 6'8" | 270 | 25 | | |
| John Douglas | LB | 6'2" | 225 | 26 | | |
| Jim Files | LB | 6'4" | 240 | 23 | 1 | |
| Ralph Heck | LB | 6'2" | 230 | 30 | 1 | 6 |
| Ron Hornsby | LB | 6'3" | 232 | 22 | | |
| Pat Hughes | LB | 6'2" | 240 | 24 | | |
| Pete Athas | WR-DB | 5'11" | 185 | 23 | 2 | 6 |
| Otto Brown | DB | 6'1" | 183 | 24 | | 6 |
| Scott Eaton | DB | 6'3" | 205 | 27 | 1 | |
| Richmond Flowers (from DAL) | DB | 6' | 180 | 24 | 1 | |
| Joe Green | DB | 5'11" | 195 | 24 | | 6 |
| Spider Lockhart | DB | 6'2" | 175 | 28 | 3 | |
| Bennie McRae | DB | 6'1" | 180 | 30 | | |
| Willie Williams | DB | 6' | 190 | 28 | | 5 |
| Randy Johnson | QB | 6'3" | 205 | 27 | | |
| Fran Tarkenton | QB | 6'1" | 190 | 31 | | 18 |
| Bobby Duhon | HB | 6' | 195 | 24 | | 6 |
| Ron Johnson | HB | 6'1" | 205 | 23 | | 6 |
| Rocky Thompson | HB | 5'11" | 200 | 23 | | 12 |
| Charlie Evans | FB | 6'1" | 215 | 23 | | 30 |
| Tucker Frederickson | FB | 6'3" | 220 | 28 | | 6 |
| Junior Coffey | HB-FB | 6'1" | 215 | 29 | | |
| Don Herrmann | WR | 6'2" | 195 | 24 | | 6 |
| Rich Houston | WR | 6'2" | 197 | 25 | | 24 |
| Coleman Zeno | WR | 6'4" | 210 | 24 | | |
| Joe Morrison | HB-FB-WR | 6'1" | 212 | 33 | | 6 |
| Dick Kotite | TE | 6'3" | 230 | 28 | | 12 |
| Bob Tucker | TE | 6'3" | 230 | 26 | | 24 |
| Tom Blanchard | K | 6' | 190 | 23 | | |
| Pete Gogolak | K | 6'2" | 190 | 29 | | 48 |

## DALLAS COWBOYS

### RUSHING

| Last Name | No. | Yds | Avg | TD |
|---|---|---|---|---|
| D. Thomas | 175 | 793 | 4.5 | 11 |
| Hill | 106 | 468 | 4.4 | 8 |
| Garrison | 127 | 429 | 3.4 | 1 |
| Staubach | 41 | 343 | 8.4 | 2 |
| Reeves | 17 | 79 | 4.6 | 0 |
| Williams | 21 | 67 | 3.2 | 1 |
| Welch | 14 | 51 | 3.6 | 1 |
| Hayes | 3 | 18 | 6.0 | 0 |
| Morton | 4 | 9 | 2.3 | 1 |
| Ditka | 2 | 2 | 1.0 | 0 |
| Alworth | 2 | −10 | −5.0 | 0 |

### RECEIVING

| Last Name | No. | Yds | Avg | TD |
|---|---|---|---|---|
| Garrison | 40 | 396 | 10 | 1 |
| Hayes | 35 | 840 | 24 | 8 |
| Alworth | 34 | 487 | 14 | 2 |
| Ditka | 30 | 360 | 12 | 1 |
| Hill | 19 | 244 | 13 | 3 |
| Truax | 15 | 232 | 15 | 1 |
| D. Thomas | 13 | 153 | 12 | 2 |
| Richardson | 8 | 170 | 21 | 3 |
| Adkins | 4 | 53 | 13 | 0 |
| Williams | 3 | 59 | 20 | 0 |
| Reeves | 3 | 25 | 8 | 0 |
| Welch | 1 | −1 | −1 | 0 |

### PUNT RETURNS

| Last Name | No. | Yds | Avg | TD |
|---|---|---|---|---|
| Harris | 17 | 129 | 8 | 0 |
| Waters | 9 | 109 | 12 | 0 |
| Adkins | 4 | 5 | 1 | 0 |
| Hayes | 1 | 5 | 5 | 0 |

### KICKOFF RETURNS

| Last Name | No. | Yds | Avg | TD |
|---|---|---|---|---|
| Harris | 29 | 823 | 28 | 0 |
| I. Thomas | 7 | 295 | 42 | 2 |
| Welch | 4 | 105 | 26 | 0 |
| D. Thomas | 2 | 64 | 32 | 0 |
| Ditka | 3 | 30 | 10 | 0 |
| Waters | 1 | 18 | 18 | 0 |
| Lewis | 1 | 15 | 15 | 0 |
| Hayes | 1 | 14 | 14 | 0 |
| Williams | 1 | 12 | 12 | 0 |
| Green | 1 | 0 | 0 | 0 |

### PASSING – PUNTING – KICKING

| PASSING | Att | Comp | % | Yds | Yd/Att | TD | Int− | % | RK |
|---|---|---|---|---|---|---|---|---|---|
| Staubach | 211 | 126 | 60 | 1882 | 8.9 | 15 | 4− | 2 | 1 |
| Morton | 143 | 78 | 55 | 1131 | 7.9 | 7 | 8− | 6 | 7 |
| Reeves | 5 | 2 | 40 | 24 | 4.8 | 0 | 1− | 20 | |
| Hill | 1 | 0 | 0 | 0 | 0.0 | 0 | 1−100 | | |
| D. Thomas | 1 | 0 | 0 | 0 | 0 | 0 | 0− 0 | | |

| PUNTING | No | Avg | | | | | | | |
|---|---|---|---|---|---|---|---|---|---|
| Widby | 56 | 41.6 | | | | | | | |

| KICKING | XP | Att | % | FG | Att | % | | | |
|---|---|---|---|---|---|---|---|---|---|
| Clark | 47 | 47 | 100 | 13 | 25 | 52 | | | |
| Fritsch | 2 | 2 | 100 | 5 | 8 | 63 | | | |
| Reeves | 1 | 1 | 100 | 0 | 0 | | | | |

## WASHINGTON REDSKINS

### RUSHING

| Last Name | No. | Yds | Avg | TD |
|---|---|---|---|---|
| Brown | 253 | 948 | 3.7 | 4 |
| Harraway | 156 | 635 | 4.1 | 2 |
| Mason | 31 | 85 | 2.7 | 0 |
| Jurgensen | 3 | 29 | 9.7 | 0 |
| Brunet | 10 | 27 | 2.7 | 0 |
| Jefferson | 2 | 13 | 6.5 | 0 |
| Hull | 2 | 8 | 4.0 | 0 |
| Kilmer | 17 | 5 | 0.3 | 2 |
| Smith | 1 | 5 | 5.0 | 0 |
| Wyche | 1 | 4 | 4.0 | 0 |
| Petitbon | 1 | −2 | −2.0 | 0 |

### RECEIVING

| Last Name | No. | Yds | Avg | TD |
|---|---|---|---|---|
| Jefferson | 47 | 701 | 15 | 4 |
| McNeil | 30 | 453 | 15 | 3 |
| Dowler | 26 | 352 | 14 | 0 |
| C. Taylor | 24 | 370 | 15 | 4 |
| Harraway | 20 | 121 | 6 | 0 |
| Smith | 16 | 227 | 14 | 1 |
| Brown | 16 | 176 | 11 | 2 |
| Mason | 12 | 109 | 9 | 0 |
| Alston | 5 | 87 | 17 | 0 |
| Brunet | 2 | 4 | 2 | 0 |

### PUNT RETURNS

| Last Name | No. | Yds | Avg | TD |
|---|---|---|---|---|
| Duncan | 22 | 233 | 11 | 0 |
| Vactor | 23 | 194 | 8 | 0 |

### KICKOFF RETURNS

| Last Name | No. | Yds | Avg | TD |
|---|---|---|---|---|
| Duncan | 27 | 724 | 27 | 0 |
| Jaqua | 6 | 78 | 13 | 0 |
| Bass | 4 | 61 | 15 | 0 |
| McLinton | 5 | 46 | 9 | 0 |
| Tillman | 1 | 4 | 4 | 0 |

### PASSING – PUNTING – KICKING

| PASSING | Att | Comp | % | Yds | Yd/Att | TD | Int− | % | RK |
|---|---|---|---|---|---|---|---|---|---|
| Kilmer | 306 | 166 | 54 | 2221 | 7.3 | 13 | 13− | 4 | 3 |
| Jurgensen | 28 | 16 | 57 | 170 | 7.1 | 0 | 2− | 7 | |

| PUNTING | No | Avg | | | | | | | |
|---|---|---|---|---|---|---|---|---|---|
| Bragg | 58 | 40.5 | | | | | | | |

| KICKING | XP | Att | % | FG | Att | % | | | |
|---|---|---|---|---|---|---|---|---|---|
| Knight | 27 | 27 | 100 | 29 | 49 | 59 | | | |

## PHILADELPHIA EAGLES

### RUSHING

| Last Name | No. | Yds | Avg | TD |
|---|---|---|---|---|
| Bull | 94 | 351 | 3.7 | 0 |
| Bouggess | 97 | 262 | 2.7 | 2 |
| Woodeshick | 66 | 188 | 2.8 | 0 |
| Baker | 46 | 174 | 3.8 | 0 |
| S. Davis | 47 | 163 | 3.5 | 1 |
| Watkins | 35 | 98 | 2.8 | 1 |
| Bailey | 5 | 41 | 1.8 | 1 |
| Jackson | 23 | 41 | 8.2 | 0 |
| Liske | 13 | 29 | 2.2 | 1 |
| Arrington | 5 | 23 | 4.6 | 0 |
| Hawkins | 4 | 8 | 2.0 | 0 |
| Zabel | 1 | −5 | −5.0 | 0 |

### RECEIVING

| Last Name | No. | Yds | Avg | TD |
|---|---|---|---|---|
| Jackson | 47 | 716 | 15 | 3 |
| Hawkins | 37 | 650 | 18 | 4 |
| Bouggess | 24 | 170 | 7 | 1 |
| Carmichael | 20 | 288 | 14 | 0 |
| Ballman | 13 | 238 | 18 | 0 |
| S. Davis | 11 | 46 | 4 | 0 |
| Baker | 10 | 80 | 8 | 1 |
| Bull | 9 | 75 | 8 | 1 |
| Hill | 7 | 92 | 13 | 0 |
| Bailey | 7 | 55 | 8 | 0 |
| Kramer | 6 | 65 | 11 | 1 |
| Watkins | 6 | 40 | 7 | 0 |
| Woodeshick | 6 | 36 | 6 | 1 |
| Zabel | 2 | 4 | 2 | 2 |

### PUNT RETURNS

| Last Name | No. | Yds | Avg | TD |
|---|---|---|---|---|
| Bradley | 18 | 118 | 7 | 0 |
| Walik | 5 | 48 | 10 | 0 |
| Hawkins | 1 | 6 | 6 | 0 |

### KICKOFF RETURNS

| Last Name | No. | Yds | Avg | TD |
|---|---|---|---|---|
| Walik | 14 | 369 | 26 | 0 |
| Nelson | 13 | 358 | 28 | 0 |
| Thrower | 12 | 299 | 25 | 0 |
| Jackson | 2 | 48 | 24 | 0 |
| S. Davis | 2 | 44 | 22 | 0 |
| Pettigrew | 2 | 37 | 19 | 0 |
| Harris | 2 | 28 | 14 | 0 |
| Kramer | 1 | 0 | 0 | 0 |
| Zabel | 1 | 0 | 0 | 0 |

### PASSING – PUNTING – KICKING

| PASSING | Att | Comp | % | Yds | Yd/Att | TD | Int− | % | RK |
|---|---|---|---|---|---|---|---|---|---|
| Liske | 269 | 143 | 53 | 1957 | 7.3 | 11 | 15− | 6 | 9 |
| Arrington | 118 | 55 | 47 | 576 | 4.9 | 2 | 5− | 4 | |
| Bull | 1 | 1 | 100 | 15 | 15.0 | 0 | 0− 0 | | |
| S. Davis | 1 | 0 | 0 | 0 | 0 | 0 | 0− 0 | | |
| Ward | 1 | 1 | 100 | 4 | 4.0 | 0 | 0− 0 | | |

| PUNTING | No | Avg | | | | | | | |
|---|---|---|---|---|---|---|---|---|---|
| McNeill | 73 | 42.0 | | | | | | | |
| Bradley | 2 | 38.0 | | | | | | | |

| KICKING | XP | Att | % | FG | Att | % | | | |
|---|---|---|---|---|---|---|---|---|---|
| Dempsey | 13 | 14 | 93 | 12 | 17 | 71 | | | |
| Feller | 10 | 10 | 100 | 6 | 20 | 30 | | | |

## ST. LOUIS CARDINALS

### RUSHING

| Last Name | No. | Yds | Avg | TD |
|---|---|---|---|---|
| Lane | 150 | 592 | 3.9 | 3 |
| Edwards | 108 | 316 | 2.9 | 4 |
| Roland | 78 | 278 | 3.6 | 0 |
| Shivers | 55 | 202 | 3.7 | 1 |
| Gray | 2 | 56 | 28.0 | 0 |
| Beethard | 4 | 29 | 7.3 | 0 |
| Latourette | 3 | 19 | 6.3 | 0 |
| Gilliam | 2 | 16 | 8.0 | 0 |
| Smith | 1 | 10 | 10.0 | 0 |
| Hart | 13 | 9 | 0.7 | 0 |
| White | 1 | 3 | 3.0 | 0 |

### RECEIVING

| Last Name | No. | Yds | Avg | TD |
|---|---|---|---|---|
| Gilliam | 42 | 837 | 20 | 3 |
| Lane | 29 | 298 | 10 | 0 |
| Smith | 21 | 379 | 18 | 4 |
| Gray | 18 | 534 | 30 | 4 |
| Roland | 15 | 108 | 7 | 0 |
| D. Williams | 12 | 182 | 15 | 1 |
| Edwards | 12 | 122 | 10 | 0 |
| Shivers | 10 | 76 | 8 | 0 |
| McFarland | 5 | 54 | 11 | 2 |
| Hyatt | 4 | 58 | 15 | 0 |
| Stegent | 1 | 12 | 12 | 0 |
| Reynolds | 1 | −4 | −4 | 0 |

### PUNT RETURNS

| Last Name | No. | Yds | Avg | TD |
|---|---|---|---|---|
| Willingham | 10 | 84 | 8 | 0 |
| Wehrli | 9 | 84 | 9 | 0 |
| Thompson | 5 | 27 | 5 | 0 |
| Gilliam | 1 | 21 | 21 | 0 |
| Roland | 3 | 10 | 3 | 0 |
| Stallings | 1 | 8 | 8 | 0 |
| Dickson | 1 | 0 | 0 | 0 |

### KICKOFF RETURNS

| Last Name | No. | Yds | Avg | TD |
|---|---|---|---|---|
| Gray | 30 | 740 | 25 | 0 |
| Hoey | 9 | 251 | 28 | 1 |
| Thompson | 7 | 182 | 26 | 0 |
| Willingham | 6 | 125 | 21 | 0 |
| Edwards | 2 | 41 | 21 | 0 |
| Roland | 2 | 24 | 12 | 0 |
| Dierdorf | 1 | 0 | 0 | 0 |
| Stegent | 1 | 0 | 0 | 0 |

### PASSING – PUNTING – KICKING

| PASSING | Att | Comp | % | Yds | Yd/Att | TD | Int− | % | RK |
|---|---|---|---|---|---|---|---|---|---|
| Hart | 243 | 110 | 45 | 1626 | 6.7 | 8 | 14− | 6 | 13 |
| Beethard | 141 | 60 | 43 | 1030 | 7.3 | 6 | 12− | 9 | 15 |
| Shivers | 1 | 0 | 0 | 0 | 0.0 | 0 | 0− 0 | | |

| PUNTING | No | Avg | | | | | | | |
|---|---|---|---|---|---|---|---|---|---|
| Latourette | 56 | 38.5 | | | | | | | |
| Bakken | 5 | 41.4 | | | | | | | |

| KICKING | XP | Att | % | FG | Att | % | | | |
|---|---|---|---|---|---|---|---|---|---|
| Bakken | 24 | 24 | 100 | 21 | 32 | 66 | | | |

## NEW YORK GIANTS

### RUSHING

| Last Name | No. | Yds | Avg | TD |
|---|---|---|---|---|
| Duhon | 93 | 344 | 3.7 | 1 |
| Frederickson | 64 | 242 | 3.8 | 0 |
| Thompson | 54 | 177 | 3.3 | 1 |
| Evans | 48 | 171 | 3.6 | 5 |
| Ron Johnson | 32 | 156 | 4.9 | 1 |
| Morrison | 38 | 131 | 3.4 | 0 |
| Tarkenton | 30 | 111 | 3.7 | 3 |
| Coffey | 22 | 70 | 3.2 | 0 |
| Randy Johnson | 6 | 29 | 4.8 | 0 |
| Zeno | 2 | 10 | 5.0 | 0 |
| Athas | 1 | 3 | 3.0 | 0 |
| Houston | 2 | 2 | 1.0 | 0 |
| Tucker | 1 | 1 | 1.0 | 0 |

### RECEIVING

| Last Name | No. | Yds | Avg | TD |
|---|---|---|---|---|
| Tucker | 59 | 791 | 13 | 4 |
| Morrison | 40 | 411 | 10 | 1 |
| Herrmann | 27 | 297 | 11 | 1 |
| Duhon | 25 | 266 | 11 | 0 |
| Houston | 24 | 426 | 18 | 4 |
| Frederickson | 21 | 114 | 5 | 1 |
| Thompson | 16 | 85 | 5 | 0 |
| Evans | 13 | 144 | 11 | 0 |
| Kotite | 10 | 146 | 15 | 2 |
| Ron Johnson | 6 | 47 | 8 | 0 |
| Zeno | 5 | 97 | 19 | 0 |
| Coffey | 5 | 20 | 4 | 0 |

### PUNT RETURNS

| Last Name | No. | Yds | Avg | TD |
|---|---|---|---|---|
| Duhon | 12 | 77 | 6 | 0 |
| Lockhart | 4 | 24 | 6 | 0 |
| Athas | 3 | 21 | 7 | 0 |

### KICKOFF RETURNS

| Last Name | No. | Yds | Avg | TD |
|---|---|---|---|---|
| Thompson | 36 | 947 | 26 | 1 |
| Duhon | 11 | 200 | 18 | 0 |
| Flowers | 8 | 156 | 20 | 0 |
| Green | 5 | 106 | 21 | 0 |
| Douglas | 1 | 7 | 7 | 0 |
| Dryer | 1 | 0 | 0 | 0 |
| Walton | 1 | 0 | 0 | 0 |

### PASSING – PUNTING – KICKING

| PASSING | Att | Comp | % | Yds | Yd/Att | TD | Int− | % | RK |
|---|---|---|---|---|---|---|---|---|---|
| Tarkenton | 386 | 226 | 59 | 2567 | 6.7 | 11 | 21− | 5 | 8 |
| Ran. Johnson | 74 | 41 | 55 | 477 | 6.5 | 3 | 3− | 4 | |
| Blanchard | 1 | 1 | 100 | 18 | 18.0 | 0 | 0− 0 | | |
| Duhon | 1 | 0 | 0 | 0 | 0.0 | 0 | 1−100 | | |

| PUNTING | No | Avg | | | | | | | |
|---|---|---|---|---|---|---|---|---|---|
| Blanchard | 66 | 40.6 | | | | | | | |

| KICKING | XP | Att | % | FG | Att | % | | | |
|---|---|---|---|---|---|---|---|---|---|
| Gogolak | 30 | 30 | 100 | 6 | 17 | 35 | | | |

## MINNESOTA VIKINGS 11-3-0   Bud Grant

**Scores of Each Game**

| | | |
|---|---|---|
| 16 | Detroit | 13 |
| 17 | CHICAGO | 20 |
| 19 | BUFFALO | 0 |
| 13 | Philadelphia | 0 |
| 24 | Green Bay | 13 |
| 10 | BALTIMORE | 3 |
| 17 | N.Y. Giants | 10 |
| 9 | SAN FRANCISCO | 13 |
| 3 | GREEN BAY | 0 |
| 23 | New Orleans | 10 |
| 24 | ATLANTA | 7 |
| 14 | San Diego | 30 |
| 29 | DETROIT | 10 |
| 27 | Chicago | 10 |

| Use Name | Pos. | Hgt | Wgt | Age | Int | Pts |
|---|---|---|---|---|---|---|
| Grady Alderman | OT | 6'2" | 247 | 32 | | |
| Doug Davis | OT | 6'4" | 250 | 27 | | |
| Ron Yary | OT | 6'6" | 255 | 25 | | |
| Pete Perreault | OG-OT | 6'3" | 248 | 32 | | |
| Roy Schmidt | OG | 6'3" | 250 | 29 | | |
| Milt Sunde | OG | 6'2" | 250 | 28 | | |
| Doug Sutherland | OG | 6'3" | 250 | 23 | | |
| Ed White | OG | 6'2" | 262 | 24 | | |
| Mick Tingelhoff | C | 6'1" | 237 | 31 | | |
| Godfrey Zaunbrecher | C | 6'2" | 235 | 23 | | |
| Carl Eller | DE | 6'6" | 247 | 29 | | |
| Jim Marshall | DE | 6'3" | 248 | 33 | | |
| John Ward | DE | 6'4" | 260 | 23 | | |
| Gary Larsen | DT | 6'5" | 260 | 31 | | |
| Alan Page | DT | 6'5" | 245 | 26 | | |
| Jerry Patton | DT | 6'3" | 260 | 25 | | |

| Use Name | Pos. | Hgt | Wgt | Age | Int | Pts |
|---|---|---|---|---|---|---|
| Carl Gersbach | LB | 6'1" | 230 | 24 | | |
| Wally Hilgenberg | LB | 6'3" | 230 | 28 | 2 | |
| Noel Jenke | LB | 6'1" | 218 | 24 | | |
| Lonnie Warwick | LB | 6'3" | 238 | 29 | | |
| Carl Winfrey | LB | 6' | 230 | 22 | | |
| Roy Winston | LB | 6'1" | 222 | 31 | 1 | 6 |
| Bobby Bryant | DB | 6' | 170 | 27 | 3 | |
| Karl Kassulke | DB | 6' | 195 | 29 | 2 | |
| Paul Krause | DB | 6'3" | 200 | 29 | 6 | |
| Ed Sharockman | DB | 6' | 200 | 31 | 6 | |
| Charlie West | DB | 6'1" | 197 | 25 | 7 | |
| Jeff Wright | DB | 5'11" | 190 | 22 | | |
| Nate Wright | DB | 5'11" | 180 | 23 | | |

John Beasley — Injury
Jim Vellone — Hodgkin's Disease

| Use Name | Pos. | Hgt | Wgt | Age | Int | Pts |
|---|---|---|---|---|---|---|
| Gary Cuozzo | QB | 6'1" | 195 | 30 | | |
| Bob Lee | QB | 6'2" | 195 | 25 | | 6 |
| Norm Snead | QB | 6'4" | 215 | 31 | | 6 |
| Clint Jones | HB | 6' | 205 | 26 | | 24 |
| Dave Osborn | HB | 6' | 208 | 28 | | 36 |
| Bill Brown | FB | 5'11" | 230 | 33 | | 12 |
| Leo Hayden | HB-FB | 6' | 212 | 23 | | |
| Jim Lindsey | HB-FB | 6'2" | 210 | 26 | | 6 |
| Oscar Reed | HB-FB | 5'11" | 222 | 27 | | 6 |
| Al Denson | WR | 6'2" | 208 | 29 | | |
| Bob Grim | WR | 6' | 195 | 26 | | 42 |
| John Henderson | WR | 6'3" | 195 | 28 | | |
| Gene Washington | WR | 6'3" | 208 | 27 | | |
| Bob Brown | TE | 6'3" | 225 | 28 | | |
| John Hilton | TE | 6'5" | 225 | 29 | | |
| Stu Voigt | TE | 6'1" | 220 | 23 | | 6 |
| Fred Cox | K | 5'10" | 200 | 32 | | 91 |

## DETROIT LIONS 7-6-1   Joe Schmidt

**Scores of Each Game**

| | | |
|---|---|---|
| 13 | MINNESOTA | 16 |
| 34 | New England | 7 |
| | ATLANTA | 38 |
| 3. | GREEN BAY | 28 |
| 31 | Houston | 7 |
| 23 | CHICAGO | 28 |
| 14 | Green Bay | 14 |
| 74 | Denver | 20 |
| 13 | LOS ANGELES | 21 |
| 28 | Chicago | 3 |
| 32 | KANSAS CITY | 21 |
| 20 | PHILADELPHIA | 23 |
| 10 | Minnesota | 29 |
| 27 | San Francisco | 31 |

| Use Name | Pos. | Hgt | Wgt | Age | Int | Pts |
|---|---|---|---|---|---|---|
| Rocky Freitas | OT | 6'6" | 280 | 25 | | |
| Ray Parson | OT | 6'4" | 250 | 24 | | |
| Jim Yarbrough | OT | 6'6" | 250 | 24 | | |
| Frank Gallagher | OG | 6'2" | 245 | 28 | | |
| Bob Kowalkowski | OG | 6'3" | 240 | 27 | | |
| Chuck Walton | OG | 6'3" | 255 | 30 | | |
| Dave Thompson | C-OG | 6'4" | 275 | 22 | | |
| Ed Flanagan | C | 6'3" | 240 | 27 | | |
| Larry Hand | DE | 6'4" | 250 | 31 | | |
| Jim Mitchell | DE | 6'3" | 245 | 22 | | |
| Joe Robb | DE | 6'3" | 245 | 34 | | |
| Bob Bell | DT | 6'4" | 250 | 23 | | 6 |
| Dick Evey | DT | 6'2" | 245 | 30 | | |
| Jerry Rush | DT | 6'4" | 265 | 29 | | |
| Larry Woods | DT | 6'6" | 260 | 23 | | |

| Use Name | Pos. | Hgt | Wgt | Age | Int | Pts |
|---|---|---|---|---|---|---|
| Ken Lee | LB | 6'4" | 230 | 22 | | |
| Mike Lucci | LB | 6'2" | 230 | 31 | 5 | 12 |
| Ed Mooney | LB | 6'2" | 225 | 26 | | |
| Paul Naumoff | LB | 6'1" | 215 | 26 | | |
| Wayne Walker | LB | 6'2" | 228 | 34 | 2 | 2 |
| Charlie Weaver | LB | 6'2" | 218 | 22 | | |
| Lem Barney | DB | 6' | 188 | 25 | 3 | 6 |
| Al Clark | DB | 6' | 180 | 23 | | |
| Dick LeBeau | DB | 6'1" | 185 | 34 | 6 | |
| Wayne Rasmussen | DB | 6'2" | 180 | 29 | 4 | |
| Tom Vaughn | DB | 5'11" | 190 | 28 | 1 | |
| Mike Weger | DB | 6'2" | 200 | 25 | 1 | 6 |
| Bobby Williams | DB | 6'1" | 200 | 29 | | |

Charlie Brown — Injury
Bill Cottrell — Injury
Nick Eddy — Knee Injury

| Use Name | Pos. | Hgt | Wgt | Age | Int | Pts |
|---|---|---|---|---|---|---|
| Greg Landry | QB | 6'4" | 205 | 24 | | 18 |
| Bill Munson | QB | 6'2" | 210 | 29 | | |
| Altie Taylor | HB | 5'10" | 196 | 23 | | 30 |
| Mickey Zofko | HB | 6'3" | 195 | 21 | | |
| Mel Farr | FB-HB | 6'2" | 210 | 26 | | 6 |
| Paul Gipson | FB-HB | 6' | 210 | 25 | | |
| Steve Owens | FB | 6'2" | 220 | 23 | | 60 |
| Bill Triplett | FB | 6'2" | 215 | 32 | | |
| *Chuck Hughes | WR | 5'11" | 175 | 28 | | |
| Ron Jessie | WR | 6' | 183 | 23 | | 14 |
| Earl McCullouch | WR | 5'11" | 175 | 25 | | 18 |
| Larry Walton | WR | 6'2" | 180 | 24 | | 30 |
| Craig Cotton | TE | 6'4" | 222 | 24 | | |
| Charlie Sanders | TE | 6'4" | 235 | 25 | | 30 |
| Errol Mann | K | 6' | 200 | 30 | | 103 |
| Herman Weaver | K | 6'4" | 210 | 22 | | |

*Died Oct. 24, 1971 — Heart Attack

## CHICAGO BEARS 6-8-0   Jim Dooley

**Scores of Each Game**

| | | |
|---|---|---|
| 17 | PITTSBURGH | 15 |
| 20 | Minnesota | 17 |
| 3 | Los Angeles | 17 |
| 35 | NEW ORLEANS | 14 |
| 0 | San Francisco | 13 |
| 28 | Detroit | 23 |
| 23 | DALLAS | 19 |
| 14 | GREEN BAY | 17 |
| 16 | WASHINGTON | 15 |
| 3 | DETROIT | 28 |
| 3 | Miami | 34 |
| 3 | Denver | 6 |
| 10 | Green Bay | 31 |
| 10 | MINNESOTA | 27 |

| Use Name | Pos. | Hgt | Wgt | Age | Int | Pts |
|---|---|---|---|---|---|---|
| Jeff Curchin | OT | 6'6" | 255 | 23 | | |
| Randy Jackson | OT | 6'5" | 245 | 27 | | |
| Steve Wright | OT | 6'6" | 250 | 29 | | |
| Jim Cadile | OG | 6'3" | 240 | 30 | | |
| Glenn Holloway | OG | 6'3" | 245 | 22 | | |
| Bob Newton | OT-OG | 6'4" | 250 | 22 | | |
| Rich Coady | C | 6'3" | 238 | 26 | | |
| Gene Hamlin | C | 6'3" | 245 | 25 | | |
| John Hoffman | DE | 6'7" | 260 | 28 | | |
| Willie Holman | DE | 6'4" | 250 | 26 | | |
| Tony McGee | DE | 6'4" | 250 | 22 | | |
| Ed O'Bradovich | DE | 6'3" | 255 | 31 | | |
| Dave Hale | DT | 6'7" | 260 | 24 | | |
| George Seals | DT | 6'2" | 260 | 28 | | 6 |
| Bill Staley | DT | 6'3" | 248 | 24 | | |

| Use Name | Pos. | Hgt | Wgt | Age | Int | Pts |
|---|---|---|---|---|---|---|
| Ross Brupbacher | LB | 6'3" | 215 | 23 | 2 | 6 |
| Doug Buffone | LB | 6'1" | 225 | 27 | 2 | |
| Dick Butkus | LB | 6'3" | 245 | 27 | 4 | 1 |
| Jimmy Gunn | LB | 6'1" | 215 | 22 | 1 | |
| Larry Rowden | LB | 6'2" | 220 | 21 | | |
| Charlie Ford | DB | 6'3" | 185 | 22 | 5 | |
| Cliff Hardy | DB | 6' | 187 | 24 | | |
| Bob Jeter | DB | 6'1" | 205 | 33 | 1 | |
| Garry Lyle | DB | 6'2" | 198 | 25 | 1 | |
| Jerry Moore | DB | 6'3" | 208 | 21 | | |
| Ron Smith | DB | 6'1" | 192 | 28 | 3 | |
| Joe Taylor | DB | 6'2" | 200 | 30 | 3 | |

Craig Baynham — Injury

| Use Name | Pos. | Hgt | Wgt | Age | Int | Pts |
|---|---|---|---|---|---|---|
| Jack Concannon | QB | 6'3" | 205 | 28 | | |
| Bobby Douglass | QB | 6'3" | 215 | 24 | | 19 |
| Kent Nix | QB | 6'1" | 195 | 27 | | |
| Joe Moore | HB | 6'1" | 205 | 22 | | |
| Cyril Pinder | HB | 6'2" | 222 | 24 | | 6 |
| Gale Sayers | HB | 6' | 198 | 28 | | |
| Don Shy | HB | 6'1" | 210 | 27 | | 12 |
| Jim Grabowski | FB | 6'2" | 220 | 27 | | |
| Jim Harrison | FB | 6'4" | 235 | 22 | | |
| Bill Tucker | FB | 6'2" | 220 | 27 | | |
| George Farmer | WR | 6'4" | 210 | 23 | | 30 |
| Dick Gordon | WR | 5'11" | 190 | 26 | | 30 |
| Jim Seymour | WR | 6'4" | 210 | 24 | | |
| Cecil Turner | WR | 5'10" | 170 | 27 | | |
| Ray Ogden | TE | 6'5" | 225 | 28 | | |
| Earl Thomas | TE | 6'3" | 224 | 22 | | |
| Bob Wallace | TE | 6'3" | 211 | 25 | | 12 |
| Bobby Joe Green | K | 5'11" | 175 | 33 | | |
| Mac Percival | K | 6'4" | 220 | 31 | | 63 |

## GREEN BAY PACKERS 4-8-2   Dan Devine

**Scores of Each Game**

| | | |
|---|---|---|
| 40 | N.Y. GIANTS | 42 |
| 34 | DENVER | 13 |
| 20 | CINCINNATI | 17 |
| 28 | Detroit | 31 |
| 13 | MINNESOTA | 24 |
| 13 | Los Angeles | 30 |
| 14 | DETROIT | 14 |
| 17 | Chicago | 14 |
| 0 | Minnesota | 3 |
| 21 | Atlanta | 28 |
| 21 | NEW ORLEANS | 29 |
| 16 | St. Louis | 16 |
| 31 | CHICAGO | 10 |
| 6 | Miami | 27 |

| Use Name | Pos. | Hgt | Wgt | Age | Int | Pts |
|---|---|---|---|---|---|---|
| Bill Hayhoe | OT | 6'8" | 258 | 24 | | |
| Dick Himes | OT | 6'4" | 244 | 25 | | |
| Francis Peay | OT | 6'5" | 250 | 27 | | |
| Dave Bradley | OG | 6'4" | 245 | 24 | | |
| Gale Gillingham | OG | 6'3" | 255 | 27 | | |
| Bill Lueck | OG | 6'3" | 235 | 25 | | |
| Randy Winkler | OG | 6'5" | 260 | 28 | | |
| Ken Bowman | C | 6'3" | 230 | 28 | | |
| Wimpy Winther | C | 6'4" | 260 | 23 | | |
| Cal Withrow | C | 6' | 240 | 26 | | |
| Lionel Aldridge | DE | 6'4" | 245 | 29 | | |
| Alden Roche | DE | 6'4" | 255 | 26 | | |
| Donnell Smith | DE | 6'4" | 245 | 22 | | |
| Clarence Williams | DE | 6'5" | 255 | 24 | | |
| Bob Brown | DT | 6'5" | 260 | 31 | | |
| Jim DeLisle | DT | 6'4" | 254 | 22 | | |
| Mike McCoy | DT | 6'5" | 284 | 22 | | |

| Use Name | Pos. | Hgt | Wgt | Age | Int | Pts |
|---|---|---|---|---|---|---|
| Fred Carr | LB | 6'5" | 238 | 25 | | |
| Jim Carter | LB | 6'3" | 235 | 22 | 1 | |
| Tommy Crutcher | LB | 6'3" | 235 | 29 | | |
| Ray Nitschke | LB | 6'3" | 235 | 35 | 1 | |
| Dave Robinson | LB | 6'3" | 245 | 30 | 3 | |
| Ken Ellis | DB | 5'10" | 190 | 23 | 6 | 6 |
| Charlie Hall | DB | 6'1" | 195 | 22 | | |
| Doug Hart | DB | 6' | 190 | 32 | 2 | 8 |
| Al Matthews | DB | 5'11" | 190 | 23 | 1 | |
| Al Randolph | DB | 6'2" | 196 | 27 | 1 | |
| Willie Wood | DB | 5'10" | 190 | 35 | 1 | |

| Use Name | Pos. | Hgt | Wgt | Age | Int | Pts |
|---|---|---|---|---|---|---|
| Zeke Bratkowski | QB | 6'2" | 215 | 39 | | 6 |
| Scott Hunter | QB | 6'2" | 205 | 23 | | 24 |
| Frank Patrick | QB | 6'7" | 225 | 24 | | |
| Bart Starr | QB | 6'1" | 190 | 38 | | 6 |
| Donny Anderson | HB | 6'3" | 210 | 28 | | 36 |
| Larry Krause | HB | 6' | 208 | 23 | | |
| Elijah Pitts | HB | 6'1" | 210 | 32 | | |
| Dave Hampton | FB-HB | 6' | 210 | 24 | | 30 |
| John Brockington | FB | 6' | 225 | 22 | | 30 |
| Perry Williams | FB | 6'2" | 220 | 24 | | |
| Carroll Dale | WR | 6'1" | 200 | 33 | | 24 |
| Dave Davis | WR | 6' | 175 | 23 | | |
| John Spilis | WR | 6'3" | 205 | 23 | | 6 |
| Len Garrett | TE | 6'3" | 230 | 22 | | |
| Rich McGeorge | TE | 6'4" | 235 | 22 | | 24 |
| Dave Conway | K | 6' | 195 | 25 | | 5 |
| Ken Duncan | K | 6'2" | 210 | 26 | | |
| Lou Michaels | K | 6'2" | 250 | 35 | | 43 |
| Tim Webster | K | 6' | 195 | 21 | | 26 |

## MINNESOTA VIKINGS

### RUSHING

| Last Name | No. | Yds | Avg | TD |
|---|---|---|---|---|
| Jones | 180 | 675 | 3.8 | 4 |
| Osborn | 123 | 349 | 2.8 | 5 |
| Lindsey | 46 | 182 | 4.0 | 0 |
| Reed | 50 | 182 | 3.6 | 1 |
| Bill Brown | 46 | 136 | 3.0 | 2 |
| Grim | 6 | 127 | 21.2 | 0 |
| Cuozzo | 15 | 24 | 1.6 | 0 |
| Lee | 11 | 14 | 1.3 | 1 |
| Snead | 6 | 6 | 1.0 | 1 |
| Denson | 1 | 0 | 0.0 | 0 |

### RECEIVING

| Last Name | No. | Yds | Avg | TD |
|---|---|---|---|---|
| Grim | 45 | 691 | 15 | 7 |
| Osborn | 25 | 195 | 8 | 1 |
| Voigt | 15 | 214 | 14 | 1 |
| Reed | 15 | 138 | 9 | 0 |
| Washington | 12 | 165 | 14 | 0 |
| Denson | 10 | 125 | 13 | 0 |
| Bill Brown | 10 | 94 | 9 | 0 |
| Jones | 9 | 98 | 11 | 0 |
| Lindsey | 8 | 31 | 4 | 0 |
| Bob Brown | 6 | 141 | 24 | 0 |
| Henderson | 2 | 18 | 9 | 0 |

### PUNT RETURNS

| Last Name | No. | Yds | Avg | TD |
|---|---|---|---|---|
| West | 18 | 94 | 5 | 0 |
| Grim | 7 | 44 | 6 | 0 |
| Bryant | 2 | 26 | 13 | 0 |

### KICKOFF RETURNS

| Last Name | No. | Yds | Avg | TD |
|---|---|---|---|---|
| West | 24 | 556 | 23 | 0 |
| Jones | 12 | 329 | 27 | 0 |
| Grim | 3 | 52 | 17 | 0 |
| Bryant | 1 | 23 | 23 | 0 |
| Voigt | 1 | 0 | 0 | 0 |

### PASSING – PUNTING – KICKING

**PASSING**

| Last Name | Att | Comp | % | Yds | Yd/Att | TD | Int– | % | RK |
|---|---|---|---|---|---|---|---|---|---|
| Cuozzo | 168 | 75 | 45 | 842 | 5.0 | 6 | 8– | 5 | 14 |
| Lee | 90 | 45 | 50 | 598 | 6.6 | 2 | 4– | 4 | |
| Snead | 75 | 37 | 49 | 470 | 6.3 | 1 | 6– | 8 | |
| Grim | 1 | 0 | 0 | 0 | 0.0 | 0 | 0– | 0 | |

**PUNTING**

| Last Name | No | Avg |
|---|---|---|
| Lee | 89 | 39.5 |

**KICKING**

| Last Name | XP | Att | % | FG | Att | % |
|---|---|---|---|---|---|---|
| Cox | 25 | 25 | 100 | 22 | 32 | 69 |

## DETROIT LIONS

### RUSHING

| Last Name | No. | Yds | Avg | TD |
|---|---|---|---|---|
| Owens | 246 | 1035 | 4.2 | 8 |
| Taylor | 174 | 736 | 4.2 | 4 |
| Landry | 76 | 530 | 7.0 | 3 |
| Farr | 22 | 64 | 2.9 | 0 |
| Gipson | 4 | 12 | 3.0 | 0 |
| Munson | 3 | 9 | 3.0 | 0 |
| Triplett | 4 | 4 | 1.0 | 0 |
| Jessie | 1 | 0 | 0.0 | 0 |
| McCullouch | 1 | −7 | −7.0 | 0 |
| L. Walton | 1 | −7 | −7.0 | 0 |

### RECEIVING

| Last Name | No. | Yds | Avg | TD |
|---|---|---|---|---|
| Owens | 32 | 350 | 11 | 2 |
| Sanders | 31 | 502 | 16 | 5 |
| L. Walton | 30 | 491 | 16 | 5 |
| Taylor | 26 | 270 | 10 | 1 |
| McCullouch | 21 | 552 | 26 | 3 |
| Cotton | 6 | 88 | 15 | 0 |
| Farr | 5 | 60 | 12 | 1 |
| Jessie | 4 | 87 | 22 | 0 |
| Hughes | 1 | 32 | 32 | 0 |
| Gipson | 1 | 21 | 21 | 0 |

### PUNT RETURNS

| Last Name | No. | Yds | Avg | TD |
|---|---|---|---|---|
| Barney | 14 | 122 | 9 | 0 |
| L. Walton | 6 | 38 | 6 | 0 |
| Vaughn | 2 | 30 | 15 | 0 |
| Thompson | 1 | 4 | 4 | 0 |

### KICKOFF RETURNS

| Last Name | No. | Yds | Avg | TD |
|---|---|---|---|---|
| Jessie | 16 | 470 | 29 | 2 |
| Barney | 9 | 222 | 25 | 0 |
| Clark | 8 | 216 | 27 | 0 |
| Williams | 4 | 112 | 28 | 0 |
| Gipson | 5 | 105 | 21 | 0 |
| Triplett | 3 | 70 | 23 | 0 |
| Parson | 2 | 26 | 13 | 0 |
| Mooney | 2 | 8 | 4 | 0 |
| Cotton | 1 | 4 | 4 | 0 |
| Rasmussen | 1 | 0 | 0 | 0 |

### PASSING – PUNTING – KICKING

**PASSING**

| Last Name | Att | Comp | % | Yds | Yd/Att | TD | Int– | % | RK |
|---|---|---|---|---|---|---|---|---|---|
| Landry | 261 | 136 | 52 | 2237 | 8.6 | 16 | 13– | 5 | 2 |
| Munson | 38 | 21 | 55 | 216 | 5.7 | 1 | 1– | 3 | |

**PUNTING**

| Last Name | No | Avg |
|---|---|---|
| H. Weaver | 42 | 41.7 |

**KICKING**

| Last Name | XP | Att | % | FG | Att | % |
|---|---|---|---|---|---|---|
| Mann | 37 | 37 | 100 | 22 | 37 | 60 |
| Walker | 2 | 2 | 100 | 0 | 0 | 0 |

## CHICAGO BEARS

### RUSHING

| Last Name | No. | Yds | Avg | TD |
|---|---|---|---|---|
| Shy | 116 | 420 | 3.6 | 2 |
| Pinder | 63 | 311 | 4.9 | 1 |
| Douglass | 39 | 284 | 7.3 | 3 |
| Grabowski | 51 | 149 | 2.9 | 0 |
| Joe Moore | 29 | 90 | 3.1 | 0 |
| Tucker | 32 | 82 | 2.6 | 0 |
| Sayers | 13 | 38 | 2.9 | 0 |
| Buffone | 1 | 19 | 19.0 | 0 |
| Harrison | 5 | 13 | 2.6 | 0 |
| Nix | 9 | 12 | 1.3 | 0 |
| Farmer | 1 | 11 | 11.0 | 0 |
| Concannon | 5 | 5 | 1.0 | 0 |
| Wallace | 1 | 0 | 0.0 | 0 |

### RECEIVING

| Last Name | No. | Yds | Avg | TD |
|---|---|---|---|---|
| Farmer | 46 | 737 | 16 | 5 |
| Gordon | 43 | 610 | 14 | 5 |
| Wallace | 27 | 400 | 15 | 2 |
| Shy | 19 | 163 | 9 | 0 |
| Grabowski | 17 | 100 | 6 | 0 |
| Tucker | 11 | 65 | 6 | 0 |
| Pinder | 10 | 51 | 5 | 0 |
| Seymour | 5 | 75 | 15 | 0 |
| Thomas | 3 | 40 | 13 | 0 |
| Joe Moore | 2 | 22 | 11 | 0 |
| Harrison | 2 | 18 | 9 | 0 |
| Turner | 1 | 13 | 13 | 0 |

### PUNT RETURNS

| Last Name | No. | Yds | Avg | TD |
|---|---|---|---|---|
| Smith | 26 | 194 | 7 | 0 |
| Turner | 9 | 63 | 7 | 0 |
| Lyle | 1 | 5 | 5 | 0 |

### KICKOFF RETURNS

| Last Name | No. | Yds | Avg | TD |
|---|---|---|---|---|
| Smith | 26 | 671 | 26 | 0 |
| Turner | 31 | 639 | 21 | 0 |
| Butkus | 2 | 15 | 8 | 0 |

### PASSING – PUNTING – KICKING

**PASSING**

| Last Name | Att | Comp | % | Yds | Yd/Att | TD | Int– | % | RK |
|---|---|---|---|---|---|---|---|---|---|
| Douglass | 225 | 91 | 40 | 1164 | 5.2 | 5 | 15– | 7 | 16 |
| Nix | 137 | 51 | 37 | 760 | 5.6 | 6 | 10– | 7 | |
| Concannon | 77 | 42 | 55 | 334 | 4.3 | 0 | 3– | 4 | |
| Green | 2 | 1 | 50 | 13 | 6.5 | 0 | 0– | 0 | |
| Shy | 1 | 1 | 100 | 23 | 23.0 | 1 | 0– | 0 | |
| Wallace | 1 | 0 | 0 | 0 | 0.0 | 0 | 0– | 0 | |

**PUNTING**

| Last Name | No | Avg |
|---|---|---|
| Green | 77 | 40.2 |

**KICKING**

| Last Name | XP | Att | % | FG | Att | % |
|---|---|---|---|---|---|---|
| Percival | 18 | 18 | 100 | 15 | 33 | 46 |
| Butkus | 1 | 1 | 100 | 0 | 0 | 0 |
| Douglass | 1 | 1 | 100 | 0 | 0 | 0 |

## GREEN BAY PACKERS

### RUSHING

| Last Name | No. | Yds | Avg | TD |
|---|---|---|---|---|
| Brockington | 216 | 1105 | 5.1 | 4 |
| Anderson | 186 | 757 | 4.1 | 5 |
| Hampton | 67 | 307 | 4.6 | 3 |
| Hunter | 21 | 50 | 2.4 | 4 |
| Starr | 3 | 11 | 3.7 | 1 |
| P. Williams | 3 | 4 | 1.3 | 0 |
| Bratkowski | 1 | 1 | 1.0 | 1 |
| Krause | 3 | −6 | −2.0 | 0 |

### RECEIVING

| Last Name | No. | Yds | Avg | TD |
|---|---|---|---|---|
| Dale | 31 | 598 | 19 | 4 |
| McGeorge | 27 | 463 | 17 | 4 |
| Anderson | 26 | 306 | 12 | 1 |
| Spilis | 14 | 281 | 20 | 1 |
| Brockington | 14 | 98 | 7 | 1 |
| Davis | 6 | 59 | 10 | 0 |
| Hampton | 3 | 37 | 12 | 1 |

### PUNT RETURNS

| Last Name | No. | Yds | Avg | TD |
|---|---|---|---|---|
| Ellis | 22 | 107 | 5 | 0 |
| Davis | 6 | 36 | 6 | 0 |
| Wood | 4 | 21 | 5 | 0 |
| Pitts | 5 | 13 | 3 | 0 |
| Randolph | 1 | 0 | 0 | 0 |

### KICKOFF RETURNS

| Last Name | No. | Yds | Avg | TD |
|---|---|---|---|---|
| Hampton | 46 | 1314 | 29 | 1 |
| Krause | 5 | 101 | 20 | 0 |
| Pitts | 2 | 41 | 21 | 0 |
| P. Williams | 2 | 41 | 21 | 0 |
| Davis | 1 | 22 | 22 | 0 |
| Ellis | 1 | 22 | 22 | 0 |
| Carter | 1 | 5 | 5 | 0 |

### PASSING – PUNTING – KICKING

**PASSING**

| Last Name | Att | Comp | % | Yds | Yd/Att | TD | Int– | % | RK |
|---|---|---|---|---|---|---|---|---|---|
| Hunter | 163 | 75 | 46 | 1210 | 7.4 | 7 | 17– | 10 | 11 |
| Starr | 45 | 24 | 53 | 286 | 6.4 | 0 | 3– | 7 | |
| Bratkowski | 37 | 19 | 51 | 298 | 8.1 | 4 | 3– | 8 | |
| Patrick | 5 | 1 | 20 | 39 | 7.8 | 0 | 1– | 20 | |
| Anderson | 4 | 2 | 50 | 9 | 2.3 | 1 | 0– | 0 | |

**PUNTING**

| Last Name | No | Avg |
|---|---|---|
| Anderson | 50 | 40.4 |
| Duncan | 6 | 36.0 |

**KICKING**

| Last Name | XP | Att | % | FG | Att | % |
|---|---|---|---|---|---|---|
| Michaels | 19 | 20 | 95 | 8 | 14 | 57 |
| Webster | 8 | 8 | 100 | 6 | 11 | 55 |
| Conway | 5 | 5 | 100 | 1 | 0 | |

## SAN FRANCISCO FORTY NINERS 9-5-0 Dick Nolan

**Scores of Each Game**

| | | |
|---|---|---|
| 17 | Atlanta | 20 |
| 38 | New Orleans | 20 |
| 31 | Philadelphia | 3 |
| 13 | LOS ANGELES | 20 |
| 13 | CHICAGO | 0 |
| 26 | St. Louis | 14 |
| 27 | NEW ENGLAND | 10 |
| 13 | Minnesota | 9 |
| 20 | NEW ORLEANS | 26 |
| 6 | Los Angeles | 17 |
| 24 | N.Y. Jets | 26 |
| 17 | KANSAS CITY | 26 |
| 24 | ATLANTA | 3 |
| 31 | DETROIT | 27 |

| Use Name | Pos. | Hgt | Wgt | Age | Int | Pts |
|---|---|---|---|---|---|---|
| Cas Banaszek | OT | 6'3" | 250 | 25 | | |
| Len Rohde | OT | 6'4" | 250 | 33 | | |
| John Watson | OT | 6'4" | 248 | 22 | | |
| Randy Beisler | OG | 6'4" | 255 | 26 | | |
| Elmer Collett | OG | 6'4" | 240 | 26 | | |
| Bob Hoskins | OG | 6'2" | 235 | 25 | | |
| Woody Peoples | OG | 6'2" | 247 | 28 | | |
| Forrest Blue | C | 6'5" | 260 | 25 | | 6 |
| Bill Belk | DE | 6'3" | 258 | 25 | | |
| Cedrick Hardman | DE | 6'3" | 255 | 22 | | |
| Tommy Hart | DE | 6'3" | 257 | 26 | | 6 |
| Earl Edwards | DT | 6'6" | 272 | 25 | | |
| Charlie Krueger | DT | 6'4" | 260 | 35 | | |
| Stan Hindman | DE-DT | 6'3" | 235 | 27 | | |

| Use Name | Pos. | Hgt | Wgt | Age | Int | Pts |
|---|---|---|---|---|---|---|
| Ed Beard | LB | 6'2" | 220 | 31 | | |
| Frank Nunley | LB | 6'2" | 232 | 25 | 1 | |
| Jim Sniadecki | LB | 6'2" | 220 | 24 | | |
| Skip Vanderbundt | LB | 6'3" | 230 | 24 | 1 | |
| Dave Wilcox | LB | 6'3" | 235 | 28 | | |
| Johnny Fuller | DB | 6' | 185 | 25 | 2 | |
| Tony Harris | DB | 6'2" | 190 | 22 | | |
| Jim Johnson | DB | 6'2" | 185 | 33 | 3 | |
| Mel Phillips | DB | 6' | 196 | 29 | | |
| Mike Simpson | DB | 5'11" | 175 | 24 | 1 | |
| Bruce Taylor | DB | 6' | 180 | 23 | 3 | 6 |
| Rosey Taylor | DB | 5'11" | 186 | 32 | 3 | |

| Use Name | Pos. | Hgt | Wgt | Age | Int | Pts |
|---|---|---|---|---|---|---|
| John Brodie | QB | 6'1" | 203 | 36 | | 18 |
| Steve Spurrier | QB | 6'2" | 200 | 26 | | |
| Doug Cunningham | HB | 5'11" | 192 | 25 | | 6 |
| John Isenbarger | HB | 6'3" | 205 | 23 | | |
| Vic Washington | HB | 5'10" | 196 | 25 | | 42 |
| Ken Willard | FB | 6'2" | 225 | 28 | | 30 |
| Larry Schreiber | HB-FB | 6' | 200 | 24 | | 7 |
| Preston Riley | WR | 6' | 180 | 23 | | |
| Gene Washington | WR | 6'1" | 185 | 24 | | 24 |
| Dick Witcher | WR | 6'3" | 204 | 26 | | 18 |
| Jimmy Thomas | HB-WR | 6'1" | 214 | 24 | | 6 |
| Ted Kwalick | TE | 6'4" | 220 | 24 | | 30 |
| Bob Windsor | TE | 6'4" | 230 | 28 | | |
| Bruce Gossett | K | 6'2" | 235 | 28 | | 101 |
| Jim McCann | K | 6'2" | 170 | 22 | | |

## LOS ANGELES RAMS 8-5-1 Tommy Prothro

| | | |
|---|---|---|
| 20 | New Orleans | 24 |
| 20 | ATLANTA | 20 |
| 17 | CHICAGO | 3 |
| 20 | San Francisco | 13 |
| 24 | Atlanta | 16 |
| 30 | GREEN BAY | 13 |
| 14 | MIAMI | 20 |
| 17 | Baltimore | 24 |
| 21 | Detroit | 13 |
| 17 | SAN FRANCISCO | 6 |
| 21 | Dallas | 28 |
| 45 | NEW ORLEANS | 28 |
| 24 | WASHINGTON | 38 |
| 23 | Pittsburgh | 14 |

| Use Name | Pos. | Hgt | Wgt | Age | Int | Pts |
|---|---|---|---|---|---|---|
| Rich Buzin | OT | 6'4" | 250 | 25 | | |
| Joe Carollo | OT | 6'2" | 265 | 31 | | |
| Charley Cowan | OT | 6'4" | 265 | 33 | | |
| Harry Schuh | OT | 6'2" | 260 | 28 | | |
| Mike LaHood | OG | 6'3" | 250 | 26 | | |
| Tom Mack | OG | 6'3" | 250 | 27 | | |
| Joe Scibelli | OG | 6'1" | 255 | 32 | | |
| Ken Iman | C | 6'1" | 240 | 32 | | |
| Rich Saul | OG-C | 6'3" | 235 | 23 | | |
| Deacon Jones | DE | 6'5" | 250 | 32 | | |
| Jack Youngblood | DE | 6'4" | 248 | 21 | | |
| Coy Bacon | DT-DE | 6'4" | 270 | 29 | 1 | |
| Bill Nelson | DT | 6'7" | 270 | 23 | | |
| Merlin Olsen | DT | 6'5" | 270 | 30 | | |
| Phil Olsen | DT | 6'5" | 265 | 23 | | |
| Greg Wojcik | DT | 6'6" | 268 | 25 | | |

| Use Name | Pos. | Hgt | Wgt | Age | Int | Pts |
|---|---|---|---|---|---|---|
| Ken Geddes | LB | 6'3" | 235 | 23 | | |
| Dean Halverson | LB | 6'2" | 212 | 25 | | |
| Marlin McKeever | LB | 6'1" | 235 | 31 | 4 | |
| Don Parish (from STL) | LB | 6'1" | 220 | 23 | | |
| John Pergine | LB | 6'1" | 225 | 24 | | |
| Jim Purnell | LB | 6'2" | 238 | 29 | 2 | |
| Jack Reynolds | LB | 6'1" | 232 | 23 | | |
| Isiah Robertson | LB | 6'3" | 225 | 22 | 4 | |
| Kermit Alexander | DB | 5'11" | 186 | 30 | 3 | 6 |
| Dave Elmendorf | DB | 6'1" | 195 | 22 | 2 | |
| Alvin Haymond | DB | 6' | 194 | 29 | | |
| Gene Howard | DB | 6' | 190 | 24 | 6 | 6 |
| Jim Nettles | DB | 5'9" | 177 | 29 | 5 | 6 |
| Clancy Williams | DB | 6'2" | 194 | 28 | | |

Jim Wilson — Injury  
Jim Ferguson — Injury

| Use Name | Pos. | Hgt | Wgt | Age | Int | Pts |
|---|---|---|---|---|---|---|
| Roman Gabriel | QB | 6'4" | 220 | 31 | | 12 |
| Jerry Rhome | QB | 6' | 188 | 29 | | |
| Willie Ellison | HB | 6'1" | 200 | 26 | | 24 |
| Larry Smith | HB | 6'3" | 220 | 23 | | 30 |
| Bob Thomas | HB | 5'10" | 200 | 22 | | |
| Travis Williams | HB | 6'1" | 210 | 25 | | 6 |
| Les Josephson | FB | 6' | 207 | 28 | | 30 |
| Lee White | FB | 6'4" | 235 | 25 | | |
| Matt Maslowski | WR | 6'3" | 210 | 21 | | 6 |
| David Ray | WR | 6' | 195 | 26 | | 91 |
| Lance Rentzel | WR | 6'2" | 202 | 27 | | 36 |
| Jack Snow | WR | 6'2" | 190 | 28 | | 30 |
| Pat Studstill | WR | 6'1" | 175 | 33 | | |
| Roger Williams | WR | 5'10" | 180 | 25 | | |
| Pat Curran | TE | 6'3" | 238 | 25 | | 6 |
| Bob Klein | TE | 6'5" | 235 | 24 | | 24 |

## ATLANTA FALCONS 7-6-1 Norm Van Bracklin

| | | |
|---|---|---|
| 20 | SAN FRANCISCO | 17 |
| 20 | Los Angeles | 20 |
| 38 | Detroit | 41 |
| 9 | ST. LOUIS | 26 |
| 16 | LOS ANGELES | 24 |
| 28 | NEW ORLEANS | 6 |
| 31 | Cleveland | 14 |
| 9 | Cincinnati | 6 |
| 17 | N.Y. GIANTS | 21 |
| 28 | GREEN BAY | 21 |
| 7 | Minnesota | 24 |
| 24 | OAKLAND | 13 |
| 3 | San Francisco | 24 |
| 24 | New Orleans | 20 |

| Use Name | Pos. | Hgt | Wgt | Age | Int | Pts |
|---|---|---|---|---|---|---|
| George Kunz | OT | 6'5" | 256 | 24 | | |
| Bill Sandeman | OT | 6'6" | 256 | 28 | | |
| Mal Snider | OT | 6'4" | 252 | 24 | | |
| Dick Enderle | OG | 6'1" | 248 | 23 | | |
| Andy Mauer | OG | 6'3" | 257 | 22 | | |
| Jim Miller | OG | 6'3" | 240 | 22 | | |
| John Matlock | C | 6'4" | 250 | 26 | | |
| Jeff Van Note | C | 6'2" | 244 | 25 | | |
| Claude Humphrey | DE | 6'5" | 248 | 27 | | |
| Mike Lewis | DE | 6'3" | 223 | 22 | | |
| Randy Marshall | DE | 6'5" | 237 | 24 | | |
| John Zook | DE | 6'5" | 248 | 23 | 2 | |
| Glen Condren | DT | 6'5" | 250 | 29 | | |
| Greg Lens | DT | 6'5" | 260 | 26 | | |
| John Small | LB-DT | 6'5" | 254 | 24 | | |

| Use Name | Pos. | Hgt | Wgt | Age | Int | Pts |
|---|---|---|---|---|---|---|
| Ron Acks | LB | 6'2" | 220 | 26 | 1 | |
| Grady Allen | LB | 6'3" | 230 | 25 | | |
| John Bramlett | LB | 6'2" | 220 | 30 | | |
| Greg Brezina | LB | 6'2" | 226 | 25 | 3 | |
| Don Hansen | LB | 6'3" | 220 | 27 | 3 | 6 |
| Rudy Kuechenberg | LB | 6'2" | 215 | 28 | | |
| Tommy Nobis | LB | 6'2" | 237 | 27 | | |
| Cleo Walker | LB | 6'3" | 220 | 23 | | |
| Ray Brown | DB | 6'2" | 198 | 22 | 3 | |
| Tom Hayes | DB | 6'1" | 193 | 25 | 3 | 18 |
| John Mallory | DB | 6' | 184 | 25 | | 6 |
| Tom McCauley | DB | 6'3" | 193 | 24 | 1 | |
| Tony Plummer | DB | 5'11" | 190 | 24 | | |
| Ken Reaves | DB | 6'3" | 203 | 26 | 6 | |
| Rudy Redmond | DB | 6' | 190 | 24 | | |
| Larry Shears | DB | 5'10" | 185 | 22 | | |

| Use Name | Pos. | Hgt | Wgt | Age | Int | Pts |
|---|---|---|---|---|---|---|
| Bob Berry | QB | 5'11" | 190 | 29 | | |
| Leo Hart | QB | 6'4" | 203 | 22 | | |
| Dick Shiner | QB | 6' | 195 | 29 | | 6 |
| Willie Belton | HB | 5'11" | 196 | 22 | | 6 |
| Cannonball Butler | HB | 5'10" | 200 | 28 | | 24 |
| Sonny Campbell | HB | 5'11" | 192 | 23 | | |
| Joe Profit | HB | 6' | 204 | 22 | | 6 |
| Art Malone | FB | 5'11" | 209 | 23 | | 48 |
| Harmon Wages | FB | 6'1" | 222 | 25 | | 12 |
| Ken Burrow | WR | 6' | 190 | 23 | | 36 |
| Wes Chesson | WR | 6'2" | 190 | 22 | | |
| Ray Jarvis | WR | 5'11" | 193 | 22 | | |
| Todd Snyder | WR | 6'2" | 184 | 22 | | |
| Mike Donohoe | TE | 6'3" | 228 | 26 | | |
| Jim Mitchell | TE | 6'2" | 225 | 23 | | 36 |
| Ray Poage | TE | 6'4" | 215 | 30 | | |
| Bill Bell | K | 6'1" | 190 | 23 | | 68 |
| Billy Lothridge | K | 6'1" | 200 | 27 | | |

## NEW ORLEANS SAINTS 4-8-2 J. D. Roberts

| | | |
|---|---|---|
| 24 | LOS ANGELES | 20 |
| 20 | SAN FRANCISCO | 38 |
| 13 | Houston | 13 |
| 14 | Chicago | 35 |
| 24 | DALLAS | 14 |
| 6 | Atlanta | 28 |
| 14 | Washington | 24 |
| 21 | OAKLAND | 21 |
| 26 | San Francisco | 20 |
| 10 | MINNESOTA | 23 |
| 29 | Green Bay | 21 |
| 28 | Los Angeles | 45 |
| 17 | CLEVELAND | 21 |
| 20 | ATLANTA | 24 |

| Use Name | Pos. | Hgt | Wgt | Age | Int | Pts |
|---|---|---|---|---|---|---|
| Glen Ray Hines | OT | 6'5" | 265 | 27 | | |
| Sam Holden | OT | 6'3" | 258 | 24 | | |
| Don Morrison | OT | 6'5" | 255 | 21 | | |
| Jake Kupp | OG | 6'3" | 248 | 29 | | |
| John Shinners | OG | 6'2" | 254 | 24 | | |
| Remi Pudhomme | C-OG | 6'3" | 250 | 29 | | |
| John Didion | C | 6'4" | 245 | 23 | | |
| Del Williams | C | 6'2" | 240 | 25 | | |
| Larry Estes | DE | 6'6" | 260 | 24 | | |
| Richard Neal | DE | 6'3" | 254 | 23 | | |
| Joe Owens | DE | 6'2" | 235 | 24 | | |
| Mike Walker | DE | 6'4" | 235 | 21 | | |
| Dan Goich | DT | 6'5" | 265 | 27 | | |
| Dave Long | DT | 6'4" | 245 | 26 | | |
| Bob Pollard | DT | 6'3" | 245 | 22 | | |
| Doug Mooers | DE-DT | 6'6" | 265 | 24 | | |

| Use Name | Pos. | Hgt | Wgt | Age | Int | Pts |
|---|---|---|---|---|---|---|
| Dick Absher | LB | 6'4" | 235 | 27 | 1 | |
| Wayne Colman | LB | 6'1" | 230 | 25 | 1 | |
| Carl Cunningham | LB | 6'3" | 240 | 27 | | |
| Jim Flanigan | LB | 6'3" | 240 | 26 | 1 | |
| Ray Hester | LB | 6'2" | 215 | 22 | | |
| Tom Roussel | LB | 6'3" | 235 | 26 | | |
| Richard Harvey | DB | 6'2" | 190 | 25 | | |
| Hugo Hollas | DB | 6'1" | 190 | 26 | 5 | |
| Delles Howell | DB | 6'1" | 195 | 24 | 5 | |
| Bivian Lee | DB | 6'3" | 200 | 23 | | |
| Dee Martin | DB | 6'1" | 190 | 22 | 3 | |
| Reynaud Moore | DB | 6'2" | 190 | 21 | | |
| Doug Wyatt | DB | 6'1" | 195 | 24 | 4 | 6 |

Leo Carroll — Injury  
John Huard — Injury  
Mike Morgan — Injury  
Joe Scarpati — Injury

| Use Name | Pos. | Hgt | Wgt | Age | Int | Pts |
|---|---|---|---|---|---|---|
| Edd Hargett | QB | 5'11" | 185 | 24 | | 6 |
| Archie Manning | QB | 6'3" | 204 | 22 | | 24 |
| Bob Gresham | HB | 5'11" | 193 | 23 | | 36 |
| Billy Harris | HB | 6' | 204 | 25 | | |
| Virgil Robinson | HB | 5'11" | 195 | 23 | | 12 |
| James Ford | FB-HB | 6' | 205 | 21 | | 12 |
| Hoyle Granger | FB | 6'1" | 225 | 27 | | 6 |
| Dave Kopay | HB-FB | 6'2" | 218 | 29 | | |
| Jim Strong | HB-FB | 6'1" | 204 | 24 | | 18 |
| Dan Abramowicz | WR | 6'1" | 195 | 26 | | 30 |
| Al Dodd | WR | 6' | 185 | 26 | | |
| Bob Newland | WR | 6'2" | 190 | 22 | | |
| Carlos Bell | TE | 6'5" | 238 | 22 | | |
| Don Burchfield | TE | 6'2" | 227 | 22 | | |
| Dave Parks | TE | 6'2" | 203 | 29 | | 30 |
| Skip Butler (to NYG) | K | 6'2" | 200 | 23 | | 8 |
| Charlie Durkee | K | 5'11" | 165 | 27 | | 72 |
| Julian Fagan | K | 6'3" | 205 | 23 | | |

## SAN FRANCISCO FORTY NINERS

### RUSHING
| Last Name | No. | Yds | Avg | TD |
|---|---|---|---|---|
| Willard | 216 | 855 | 4.0 | 4 |
| V. Washington | 191 | 811 | 4.2 | 3 |
| Schreiber | 34 | 180 | 5.3 | 0 |
| Cunningham | 25 | 98 | 3.9 | 1 |
| Kwalick | 6 | 62 | 10.3 | 0 |
| Brodie | 14 | 45 | 3.2 | 3 |
| Thomas | 3 | 36 | 12.0 | 1 |
| Isenbarger | 5 | 34 | 6.8 | 0 |
| Windsor | 1 | 21 | 21.0 | 0 |
| Spurrier | 1 | 2 | 2.0 | 0 |
| McCann | 2 | −15 | −7.5 | 0 |

### RECEIVING
| Last Name | No. | Yds | Avg | TD |
|---|---|---|---|---|
| Kwalick | 52 | 664 | 13 | 5 |
| G. Wash'gton | 46 | 884 | 19 | 4 |
| V. Wash'gton | 36 | 317 | 9 | 4 |
| Willard | 27 | 202 | 7 | 1 |
| Cunningham | 19 | 188 | 10 | 0 |
| Witcher | 18 | 250 | 14 | 3 |
| Schreiber | 3 | 79 | 26 | 1 |
| Riley | 3 | 39 | 13 | 0 |
| Thomas | 3 | 33 | 11 | 0 |
| Windsor | 2 | 32 | 16 | 0 |

### PUNT RETURNS
| Last Name | No. | Yds | Avg | TD |
|---|---|---|---|---|
| B. Taylor | 34 | 235 | 7 | 0 |
| Fuller | 3 | 31 | 10 | 0 |
| Riley | 1 | 2 | 2 | 0 |
| Vanderbundt | 1 | 0 | 0 | 0 |

### KICKOFF RETURNS
| Last Name | No. | Yds | Avg | TD |
|---|---|---|---|---|
| V. Wash'gton | 33 | 858 | 26 | 0 |
| Cunningham | 6 | 121 | 20 | 0 |
| Windsor | 4 | 66 | 17 | 0 |
| Beard | 1 | 21 | 21 | 0 |
| Kwalick | 2 | 9 | 5 | 0 |

### PASSING – PUNTING – KICKING
| PASSING | Att | Comp | % | Yds | Yd/Att | TD | Int− | % | RK |
|---|---|---|---|---|---|---|---|---|---|
| Brodie | 387 | 208 | 54 | 2642 | 6.8 | 18 | 24− | 6 | 6 |
| Spurrier | 4 | 1 | 25 | 46 | 11.5 | 0 | 0− | 0 | |

| PUNTING | No | Avg |
|---|---|---|
| McCann | 49 | 38.7 |
| Spurrier | 2 | 38.5 |

| KICKING | XP | Att | % | FG | Att | % |
|---|---|---|---|---|---|---|
| Gossett | 32 | 32 | 100 | 23 | 36 | 64 |
| Schreiber | 1 | 1 | 100 | 0 | 0 | 0 |

## LOS ANGELES RAMS

### RUSHING
| Last Name | No. | Yds | Avg | TD |
|---|---|---|---|---|
| Ellison | 211 | 1000 | 4.7 | 4 |
| Josephson | 99 | 449 | 4.5 | 3 |
| Smith | 91 | 404 | 4.4 | 5 |
| Rentzel | 14 | 113 | 8.1 | 1 |
| T. Williams | 18 | 103 | 5.7 | 0 |
| Gabriel | 18 | 48 | 2.7 | 2 |
| Klein | 3 | 21 | 7.0 | 0 |
| White | 2 | 11 | 5.5 | 0 |
| Rhome | 3 | 0 | 0.0 | 0 |
| Snow | 1 | −10 | −10.0 | 0 |

### RECEIVING
| Last Name | No. | Yds | Avg | TD |
|---|---|---|---|---|
| Rentzel | 38 | 534 | 14 | 5 |
| Snow | 37 | 666 | 18 | 5 |
| Ellison | 32 | 238 | 7 | 0 |
| Smith | 31 | 324 | 10 | 0 |
| Josephson | 26 | 230 | 9 | 2 |
| Klein | 14 | 160 | 11 | 4 |
| Maslowski | 3 | 82 | 27 | 1 |
| T. Williams | 3 | 68 | 23 | 0 |
| Curran | 1 | 2 | 2 | 1 |

### PUNT RETURNS
| Last Name | No. | Yds | Avg | TD |
|---|---|---|---|---|
| Haymond | 24 | 123 | 5 | 0 |
| Rentzel | 9 | 40 | 4 | 0 |
| Alexander | 1 | 5 | 5 | 0 |
| T. Williams | 1 | 4 | 4 | 0 |

### KICKOFF RETURNS
| Last Name | No. | Yds | Avg | TD |
|---|---|---|---|---|
| T. Williams | 25 | 743 | 30 | 1 |
| Haymond | 9 | 207 | 23 | 0 |
| Howard | 7 | 164 | 23 | 0 |
| R. Williams | 4 | 100 | 25 | 0 |
| Youngblood | 2 | 36 | 18 | 0 |
| Curran | 3 | 35 | 12 | 0 |
| LaHood | 1 | 25 | 25 | 0 |
| Thomas | 1 | 12 | 12 | 0 |
| Josephson | 1 | 0 | 0 | 0 |
| Saul | 1 | 0 | 0 | 0 |

### PASSING – PUNTING – KICKING
| PASSING | Att | Comp | % | Yds | Yd/Att | TD | Int− | % | RK |
|---|---|---|---|---|---|---|---|---|---|
| Gabriel | 352 | 180 | 51 | 2238 | 6.4 | 17 | 10− | 3 | 5 |
| Rhome | 18 | 5 | 28 | 66 | 5.6 | 1 | 1− | | 6 |

| PUNTING | No | Avg |
|---|---|---|
| Studstill | 70 | 41.4 |

| KICKING | XP | Att | % | FG | Att | % |
|---|---|---|---|---|---|---|
| Ray | 37 | 37 | 100 | 18 | 29 | 62 |

## ATLANTA FALCONS

### RUSHING
| Last Name | No. | Yds | Avg | TD |
|---|---|---|---|---|
| Butler | 186 | 594 | 3.2 | 2 |
| Malone | 120 | 438 | 3.7 | 6 |
| Wages | 64 | 266 | 4.2 | 1 |
| Belton | 56 | 237 | 4.2 | 1 |
| Campbell | 29 | 79 | 2.7 | 0 |
| Berry | 19 | 31 | 1.6 | 0 |
| Mitchell | 4 | 25 | 6.3 | 0 |
| Jarvis | 1 | 13 | 13.0 | 0 |
| Profit | 3 | 10 | 3.3 | 1 |
| Shiner | 10 | 9 | 0.9 | 1 |
| Burrow | 1 | 5 | 5.0 | 0 |
| Chesson | 1 | −4 | −4.0 | 0 |

### RECEIVING
| Last Name | No. | Yds | Avg | TD |
|---|---|---|---|---|
| Malone | 34 | 380 | 11 | 2 |
| Burrow | 33 | 741 | 22 | 6 |
| Mitchell | 33 | 593 | 18 | 5 |
| Chesson | 20 | 224 | 11 | 0 |
| Wages | 19 | 249 | 13 | 1 |
| Butler | 15 | 143 | 10 | 2 |
| Poage | 4 | 71 | 18 | 0 |
| Campbell | 3 | 40 | 13 | 0 |
| Belton | 3 | 22 | 7 | 0 |
| Mallory | 1 | 27 | 27 | 0 |
| Brezina | 1 | 3 | 3 | 0 |
| Kunz | 1 | 2 | 2 | 0 |

### PUNT RETURNS
| Last Name | No. | Yds | Avg | TD |
|---|---|---|---|---|
| Belton | 30 | 163 | 5 | 0 |
| McCauley | 1 | 8 | 8 | 0 |
| Mallory | 5 | 3 | 1 | 0 |
| Brown | 1 | 0 | 0 | 0 |

### KICKOFF RETURNS
| Last Name | No. | Yds | Avg | TD |
|---|---|---|---|---|
| Belton | 28 | 706 | 25 | 0 |
| Butler | 13 | 372 | 29 | 0 |
| Profit | 10 | 247 | 25 | 0 |
| Campbell | 4 | 95 | 24 | 0 |
| Wages | 1 | 21 | 21 | 0 |
| Enderle | 1 | 20 | 20 | 0 |
| Small | 1 | 12 | 12 | 0 |
| Matlock | 1 | 4 | 4 | 0 |

### PASSING – PUNTING – KICKING
| PASSING | Att | Comp | % | Yds | Yd/Att | TD | Int− | % | RK |
|---|---|---|---|---|---|---|---|---|---|
| Berry | 226 | 136 | 60 | 2005 | 8.9 | 11 | 16− | 7 | 4 |
| Shiner | 57 | 30 | 53 | 463 | 8.1 | 5 | 5− | | 9 |
| Hart | 1 | 0 | 0 | 0 | 0.0 | 0 | 0− | | |
| Lothridge | 1 | 1 | 100 | 27 | 27.0 | 0 | 0− | | |

| PUNTING | No | Avg |
|---|---|---|
| Lothridge | 44 | 37.3 |
| Bell | 16 | 36.1 |

| KICKING | XP | Att | % | FG | Att | % |
|---|---|---|---|---|---|---|
| Bell | 29 | 33 | 88 | 13 | 21 | 62 |

## NEW ORLEANS SAINTS

### RUSHING
| Last Name | No. | Yds | Avg | TD |
|---|---|---|---|---|
| Strong | 95 | 404 | 4.3 | 3 |
| Gresham | 127 | 383 | 3.0 | 6 |
| Ford | 93 | 379 | 4.1 | 2 |
| Manning | 33 | 172 | 5.2 | 4 |
| Granger | 32 | 139 | 4.3 | 1 |
| Robinson | 29 | 96 | 3.3 | 1 |
| Hargett | 9 | 24 | 2.7 | 1 |
| Dodd | 1 | 7 | 7.0 | 0 |
| Harris | 1 | 1 | 1.0 | 0 |
| Parks | 2 | −2 | −1.0 | 0 |
| Fagan | 1 | −17 | −17.0 | 0 |

### RECEIVING
| Last Name | No. | Yds | Avg | TD |
|---|---|---|---|---|
| Abramowicz | 37 | 657 | 18 | 5 |
| Parks | 35 | 568 | 16 | 5 |
| Newland | 21 | 319 | 15 | 0 |
| Gresham | 17 | 203 | 12 | 0 |
| Strong | 16 | 78 | 5 | 0 |
| Dodd | 15 | 298 | 20 | 0 |
| Robinson | 12 | 53 | 4 | 1 |
| Granger | 12 | 52 | 4 | 0 |
| Ford | 7 | 54 | 8 | 0 |
| Burchfield | 3 | 36 | 12 | 0 |
| Manning | 1 | −7 | −7 | 0 |

### PUNT RETURNS
| Last Name | No. | Yds | Avg | TD |
|---|---|---|---|---|
| Dodd | 13 | 88 | 7 | 0 |
| Moore | 2 | 12 | 6 | 0 |
| Abramowicz | 1 | 0 | 0 | 0 |

### KICKOFF RETURNS
| Last Name | No. | Yds | Avg | TD |
|---|---|---|---|---|
| Robinson | 19 | 443 | 23 | 0 |
| Dodd | 12 | 252 | 21 | 0 |
| Moore | 11 | 246 | 22 | 0 |
| Strong | 9 | 134 | 15 | 0 |
| Gresham | 3 | 60 | 20 | 0 |
| Burchfield | 1 | 5 | 5 | 0 |
| Absher | 1 | 3 | 3 | 0 |

### PASSING – PUNTING – KICKING
| PASSING | Att | Comp | % | Yds | Yd/Att | TD | Int− | % | RK |
|---|---|---|---|---|---|---|---|---|---|
| Hargett | 210 | 96 | 46 | 1191 | 5.7 | 6 | 5− | 2 | 10 |
| Manning | 177 | 86 | 49 | 1164 | 6.6 | 6 | 9− | 5 | 11 |

| PUNTING | No | Avg |
|---|---|---|
| Fagan | 77 | 41.4 |

| KICKING | XP | Att | % | FG | Att | % |
|---|---|---|---|---|---|---|
| Durkee | 24 | 25 | 96 | 16 | 23 | 70 |
| Butler | 5 | 6 | 83 | 1 | 5 | 20 |

# 1971 A.F.C. Aerial Oneupmanship

The old American Football League had never had an abundant supply of good quarterbacks, but the AFC now held the edge in that department over the NFC. The AFC had good veterans like Johnny Unitas and Len Dawson, men in their peak years like Joe Namath, John Hadl, Bob Griese, and Daryle Lamonica, and promising young passers like Jim Plunkett, Terry Bradshaw, Mike Phipps, and Dan Pastorini. After five years of the common draft, the AFC had picked the quarterback plums from the college crop, while the only exciting young passers in the NFC were Roger Staubach, Greg Landry, and Archie Manning.

## EASTERN DIVISION

**Miami Dolphins**— Although the Miami defense played surprisingly strong, the pride of the Dolphins was their versatile offense. Enemy defenses had to contend with an unheralded but solid line, a great deep receiver in Paul Warfield, a good short receiver in Howard Twilley, two relentless runners in Larry Csonka and Jim Kiick, a breakaway runner in Mercury Morris, and an enormously resourceful quarterback in young Bob Griese. Whenever the attack stalled, place kicker Garo Yepremian was deadly within the 50-yard line. With all this offensive firepower, the Dolphins raced evenly with the Colts through most of the season. Although assured of at least a wild-card berth in the playoffs, the Dolphins seemed to have conceded first place by losing to Baltimore on the next to last weekend, but a victory over Green Bay, plus the Colts' upset loss to New England, let the Dolphins slip into first place on the final day of the season.

**Baltimore Colts**—The Colts won the wild-card playoff spot on the strength of the conference's best defense and a strong offense. The defense had some problems at one cornerback slot, but the presence of stars Bubba Smith, Ted Hendricks, Mike Curtis, Ray May, Charlie Stukes, Rick Volk, and Jerry Logan glossed over any shortcomings in the other positions. The offense went with Earl Morrall at quarterback for the first half of the schedule, but Johnny Unitas recovered from an off-season Achilles tendon injury to reclaim the starting spot down the stretch. Although his arm was not what it once had been, Unitas still had enough guile to maneuver his way through the best defenses in the league.

**New England Patriots**—The Patriots had a brand-new name, a brand-new stadium in Foxboro, Massachusetts, to play in, and a talented new quarterback in rookie Jim Plunkett. In his professional debut, Plunkett threw two touchdown passes in leading the Patriots to a 20-6 upset victory over the Oakland Raiders, and the big rookie continued to impress friend and foe alike all season with his arm and poise. To catch Plunkett's passes, the Patriots signed little Randy Vataha, Plunkett's college teammate who had been cut by the Rams early in training camp. Other newcomers who made a good impression were rookie defensive tackle Julius Adams and ex-Dallas linebacker Steve Kiner.

**New York Jets**—The Jets again went through the season with many of their regulars missing from action. Injuries sidelined Joe Namath, Matt Snell, Gerry Philbin, and John Elliott for long stretches of time, George Sauer and Steve Thompson both quit football at their physical prime for other interests, and Verlon Biggs played out his option and signed with the Washington Redskins. Injuries so decimated the defensive line that coach Weeb Ewbank at one point talked Clovis Swinney out of his job selling cars to help the Jets out.

**Buffalo Bills**—For the second time in the last four years, scout Harvey Johnson stepped in as interim head coach under dismal conditions. This year, Johnny Rauch resigned before the season began, leaving Johnson to guide the dispirited Bills through a horrendous 1-13-0 campaign. Major problems during the year were injuries in the offensive line, where Johnson was forced to start five rookies and a second-year man, quarterback Dennis Shaw's serious regression from his good rookie showing, and a disorganized defense.

## CENTRAL DIVISION

**Cleveland Browns**—With Mike Phipps still not ready to take over as starting quarterback, Bill Nelsen took his aching knees into battle once more and took the Browns to the championship of the NFL's weakest division. The road to first place was a rocky one, with the Browns losing four straight mid-season games before going on a five-game winning streak. On paper, the Browns looked like a team evenly balanced between strengths and weaknesses. Leroy Kelly, Bo Scott, Milt Morin, Clarence Scott, Jack Gregory, and Walter Johnson fit comfortably into the asset column, but under the deficit heading were listed disorganization in the linebacking and secondary, advanced age in several offensive linemen, and the lack of a clutch wide receiver.

**Pittsburgh Steelers**—Dave Smith won a place on the roster of famous bloopers with his bonehead play of October 18. Sprinting to the end zone with a pass, Smith mistook the 5-yard line for the goal line and slammed the ball down on the ground, thinking that he had scored a touchdown. The referee noticed full well that Smith had never carried the ball across the goal line, and when the ball rolled through the end zone, he ruled it a touchback, gave the ball to Kansas City, and erased six points that Smith and the Steelers were already counting. But aside from that play, Smith enjoyed a fine season, as did fellow wide receiver Ron Shanklin and quarterback Terry Bradshaw.

**Houston Oilers**—Owner Bud Adams hired Ed Hughes, a man highly respected around the league, as his new head coach, but Adams quickly lost confidence in the coach and put him on the spot by firing one of his assistants in mid-season with no notice. The players rallied around Hughes late in the year and won their final three games after a very slow start. One of Hughes' moves during the season was to bench quarterback Charley Johnson and try rookies Lynn Dickey and Dan Pastorini at the position. Pastorini finally nailed down the starting job, showing good potential despite taking a steady pounding from defenders who sliced right through the porous Houston front wall.

**Cincinnati Bengals**—The Bengals slumped back into last place in the Central Division. Six of those losses, however, were by four points or less, so the Bengals were not nearly as lame as their record indicated. The Cincinnati attack again relied heavily on the run, with rookie Fred Willis and Essex Johnson taking over from Jess Phillips and Paul Robinson as the heavy-duty ball carriers. The need for a strong ground game was underlined by the weakened situation at quarterback. Greg Cook, the rookie marvel of 1970, still was out of action with a bad shoulder, and Virgil Carter missed several games with injuries.

## WESTERN DIVISION

**Kansas City Chiefs**—The Chiefs opened up their offense and won first place in the Western Division. Morris Stroud and rookie Elmo Wright developed into good receivers, giving Len Dawson two new targets to throw at and also taking some of the defense's attention away from Otis Taylor. No longer the only receiving threat on the team, Taylor enjoyed his best year as a pro, leading the NFL in yards gained on receptions. Ed Podolak spearheaded the running game and also contributed in the receiving and kick-returning departments. On defense, Jerry Mays' retirement weakened the front four, but the linebacking trio of Bobby Bell, Willie Lanier, and Jim Lynch plus the talented secondary kept the unit in fine condition.

**Oakland Raiders** — The Oakland Raiders finished out of first place in the Western Division for the first time in five years, but they still compiled a winning record despite several sizable difficulties during the course of the season. First of all, wide receiver Warren Wells, who was quarterback Daryle Lamonica's favorite deep threat , ran afoul of the law and had to sit out the entire season. Then Hewritt Dixon and Charlie Smith, the two starting running backs, were knocked out of action with injuries, and the advancing years started cutting down on the effectiveness of Tom Keating's and Ben Davidson in the defensive line. To remedy all these problems, coach John Madden promoted substitutes Marv Hubbard and Pete Banaszak to starters with fine results, and he rejuvenated the defense by giving lots of playing time to youngsters Tony Cline, Art Thoms, Harold Rice, Horace Jones and Phil Villapiano.

**San Diego Chargers**—The San Diego management had a new look at the start of the season as Sid Gillman decided to resume his coaching duties and Harland Svare came in as general manager. By mid-season, however, Gillman got into a disagreement with owner Eugene Klein and found himself out of work. Svare, meanwhile, found himself back on the field as head coach for the final four games. As usual, the San Diego defense leaked profusely, while the offense cranked out points at a rapid clip. The trade of Lance Alworth to Dallas gave the attack a new look, with rookie Billy Parks filling in with great results until he broke his arm late in the year.

**Denver Broncos**—Floyd Little's strong running cheered Lou Saban somewhat, but assorted other troubles made the coach's final half season a vexing one. Injuries erased starters Rich Jackson, Pete Duranko, Larry Kaminski, and Sam Brunelli and exposed the thinness of the Denver bench. None of the wide receivers on the team took up the slack left by the trade of Al Denson to Minnesota, and the quarterback situation was a highly unhealthy one. After several injury-filled seasons, quarterback Steve Tensi packed it all in, leaving ex-Packer Don Horn at the starting quarterback. After a lackluster first half, Horn went out with an injury, leaving only inexperienced Steve Ramsey as a passer. Nine games were enough for Saban this year, and assistant Jerry Smith took over as head man for the final five games.

## FINAL TEAM STATISTICS

### OFFENSE

| | BALT. | BUFF. | CIN. | CLEV. | DENV. | HOUS. | K.C. | MIAMI | N.ENG. | N.Y.J. | OAK. | PITT. | S.D. |
|---|---|---|---|---|---|---|---|---|---|---|---|---|---|
| **FIRST DOWNS:** | | | | | | | | | | | | | |
| Total | 242 | 185 | 236 | 231 | 217 | 201 | 240 | 232 | 190 | 202 | 258 | 226 | 264 |
| by Rushing | 123 | 68 | 109 | 89 | 102 | 62 | 108 | 121 | 85 | 115 | 128 | 98 | 86 |
| by Passing | 104 | 96 | 115 | 127 | 105 | 117 | 119 | 94 | 94 | 67 | 110 | 111 | 147 |
| by Penalty | 15 | 21 | 12 | 15 | 10 | 22 | 13 | 17 | 11 | 20 | 20 | 17 | 31 |
| **RUSHING:** | | | | | | | | | | | | | |
| Number | 512 | 320 | 462 | 461 | 512 | 361 | 487 | 486 | 419 | 485 | 473 | 416 | 390 |
| Yards | 2149 | 1337 | 2142 | 1558 | 2093 | 1106 | 1843 | 2429 | 1669 | 1888 | 2130 | 1758 | 1604 |
| Average Yards | 4.2 | 4.2 | 4.6 | 3.4 | 4.1 | 3.1 | 3.8 | 5.0 | 4.0 | 3.9 | 4.5 | 4.2 | 4.1 |
| Touchdowns | 23 | 6 | 14 | 19 | 9 | 10 | 14 | 11 | 7 | 12 | 19 | 10 | 11 |
| **PASSING:** | | | | | | | | | | | | | |
| Attempts | 344 | 401 | 365 | 376 | 358 | 423 | 337 | 293 | 330 | 278 | 348 | 414 | 450 |
| Completions | 176 | 202 | 214 | 188 | 175 | 194 | 183 | 156 | 159 | 119 | 174 | 214 | 244 |
| Completion Percentage | 51.2 | 50.4 | 58.6 | 50.0 | 48.9 | 45.9 | 54.3 | 53.2 | 48.2 | 42.8 | 50.0 | 51.7 | 54.2 |
| Passing Yards | 2152 | 2410 | 2427 | 2521 | 2243 | 2643 | 2694 | 2248 | 2206 | 1556 | 2363 | 2446 | 3305 |
| Avg. Yards per Attempt | 6.3 | 6.0 | 6.6 | 6.7 | 6.3 | 6.2 | 8.0 | 7.7 | 6.7 | 5.6 | 6.8 | 5.9 | 7.3 |
| Avg. Yards per Complet. | 12.2 | 11.9 | 11.3 | 13.4 | 12.8 | 13.6 | 14.7 | 14.4 | 13.9 | 13.1 | 13.6 | 11.4 | 13.5 |
| Times Tackled Passing | 27 | 49 | 40 | 22 | 22 | 31 | 35 | 25 | 36 | 23 | 24 | 37 | 19 |
| Yards Lost Tackled | 230 | 421 | 303 | 222 | 178 | 234 | 347 | 265 | 319 | 177 | 235 | 322 | 171 |
| Net Yards | 1922 | 1989 | 2124 | 2299 | 2065 | 2409 | 2347 | 1983 | 1887 | 1379 | 2128 | 2124 | 3134 |
| Touchdowns | 10 | 12 | 15 | 14 | 8 | 12 | 15 | 20 | 19 | 15 | 21 | 15 | 23 |
| Interceptions | 21 | 32 | 11 | 27 | 27 | 37 | 13 | 10 | 16 | 16 | 26 | 26 | 28 |
| Percent Intercepted | 6.1 | 8.0 | 3.0 | 7.2 | 7.5 | 8.7 | 3.9 | 3.4 | 4.8 | 5.8 | 7.5 | 6.3 | 6.2 |
| **PUNTS:** | | | | | | | | | | | | | |
| Number | 62 | 75 | 73 | 67 | 76 | 75 | 64 | 52 | 87 | 78 | 62 | 79 | 55 |
| Average Distance | 41.0 | 40.9 | 44.7 | 39.9 | 41.8 | 40.6 | 44.8 | 40.1 | 37.3 | 38.8 | 39.9 | 43.7 | 43.5 |
| **PUNT RETURNS:** | | | | | | | | | | | | | |
| Number | 43 | 44 | 25 | 40 | 41 | 32 | 33 | 41 | 31 | 25 | 29 | 35 | 37 |
| Yards | 351 | 343 | 145 | 359 | 320 | 198 | 150 | 432 | 181 | 155 | 182 | 264 | 215 |
| Average Yards | 8.2 | 7.8 | 5.8 | 9.0 | 7.8 | 6.2 | 4.5 | 10.5 | 5.8 | 6.2 | 6.3 | 7.5 | 5.8 |
| Touchdowns | 0 | 2 | 0 | 0 | 0 | 0 | 0 | 0 | 0 | 0 | 0 | 1 | 0 |
| **KICKOFF RETURNS:** | | | | | | | | | | | | | |
| Number | 32 | 74 | 43 | 46 | 44 | 59 | 47 | 32 | 64 | 55 | 54 | 49 | 49 |
| Yards | 679 | 1673 | 863 | 1065 | 960 | 1409 | 1031 | 806 | 1354 | 1168 | 1234 | 1120 | 1000 |
| Average Yards | 21.2 | 22.6 | 20.1 | 23.2 | 21.8 | 23.9 | 21.9 | 25.2 | 21.2 | 21.2 | 22.9 | 22.9 | 20.4 |
| Touchdowns | 0 | 0 | 0 | 0 | 0 | 0 | 0 | 1 | 0 | 0 | 0 | 0 | 0 |
| **INTERCEPTION RETURNS:** | | | | | | | | | | | | | |
| Number | 28 | 11 | 27 | 24 | 20 | 23 | 27 | 17 | 15 | 13 | 23 | 17 | 22 |
| Yards | 367 | 93 | 273 | 283 | 288 | 456 | 403 | 143 | 229 | 136 | 453 | 246 | 317 |
| Average Yards | 13.1 | 8.5 | 10.1 | 11.8 | 14.4 | 19.8 | 14.9 | 8.4 | 15.3 | 10.5 | 19.7 | 14.5 | 14.4 |
| Touchdowns | 1 | 0 | 2 | 0 | 1 | 5 | 3 | 0 | 2 | 0 | 2 | 1 | 2 |
| **PENALTIES:** | | | | | | | | | | | | | |
| Number | 57 | 74 | 82 | 68 | 67 | 91 | 72 | 65 | 67 | 70 | 81 | 88 | 81 |
| Yards | 529 | 691 | 921 | 612 | 781 | 856 | 734 | 632 | 657 | 672 | 869 | 898 | 895 |
| **FUMBLES:** | | | | | | | | | | | | | |
| Number | 26 | 33 | 29 | 29 | 25 | 24 | 23 | 22 | 26 | 30 | 26 | 37 | 30 |
| Number Lost | 11 | 16 | 12 | 18 | 12 | 14 | 13 | 13 | 16 | 10 | 13 | 16 | 15 |
| **POINTS:** | | | | | | | | | | | | | |
| Total | 313 | 184 | 284 | 285 | 203 | 251 | 302 | 315 | 238 | 212 | 344 | 246 | 311 |
| PAT Attempts | 36 | 21 | 32 | 34 | 18 | 29 | 32 | 33 | 29 | 27 | 43 | 28 | 37 |
| PAT Made | 35 | 20 | 32 | 34 | 18 | 26 | 32 | 33 | 28 | 26 | 41 | 27 | 36 |
| FG Attempts | 29 | 25 | 36 | 28 | 38 | 28 | 45 | 40 | 21 | 19 | 22 | 27 | 29 |
| FG Made | 20 | 12 | 20 | 15 | 25 | 17 | 26 | 28 | 12 | 8 | 15 | 17 | 17 |
| Percent FG Made | 69.0 | 48.0 | 55.6 | 53.6 | 65.8 | 60.7 | 57.8 | 70.0 | 57.1 | 42.1 | 68.2 | 63.0 | 58.6 |
| Safeties | 1 | 1 | 0 | 1 | 1 | 0 | 0 | 0 | 0 | 0 | 0 | 0 | 1 |

### DEFENSE

| | BALT. | BUFF. | CIN. | CLEV. | DENV. | HOUS. | K.C. | MIAMI | N.ENG. | N.Y.J. | OAK. | PITT. | S.D. |
|---|---|---|---|---|---|---|---|---|---|---|---|---|---|
| **FIRST DOWNS:** | | | | | | | | | | | | | |
| Total | 166 | 250 | 213 | 232 | 206 | 237 | 223 | 214 | 237 | 235 | 242 | 225 | 272 |
| by Rushing | 60 | 135 | 93 | 115 | 90 | 117 | 73 | 93 | 106 | 118 | 100 | 81 | 143 |
| by Passing | 95 | 101 | 102 | 100 | 91 | 97 | 125 | 111 | 111 | 101 | 122 | 132 | 114 |
| by Penalty | 11 | 14 | 18 | 17 | 25 | 23 | 25 | 10 | 20 | 16 | 20 | 12 | 15 |
| **RUSHING:** | | | | | | | | | | | | | |
| Number | 352 | 562 | 446 | 484 | 426 | 489 | 367 | 403 | 481 | 472 | 480 | 440 | 493 |
| Yards | 1113 | 2496 | 1778 | 2227 | 1834 | 1723 | 1300 | 1661 | 1918 | 2302 | 1751 | 1482 | 2296 |
| Average Yards | 3.2 | 4.4 | 4.0 | 4.6 | 4.3 | 3.5 | 3.5 | 4.1 | 4.0 | 4.9 | 3.6 | 3.4 | 4.7 |
| Touchdowns | 8 | 21 | 11 | 14 | 11 | 22 | 9 | 10 | 14 | 18 | 14 | 13 | 25 |
| **PASSING:** | | | | | | | | | | | | | |
| Attempts | 361 | 303 | 335 | 339 | 356 | 354 | 418 | 363 | 350 | 342 | 359 | 408 | 347 |
| Completions | 185 | 157 | 157 | 156 | 150 | 180 | 209 | 206 | 170 | 163 | 184 | 235 | 193 |
| Completion Percentage | 51.2 | 51.8 | 46.9 | 46.0 | 42.1 | 50.8 | 50.0 | 56.7 | 48.6 | 47.7 | 51.3 | 57.6 | 55.6 |
| Passing Yards | 2027 | 2333 | 2382 | 2170 | 2420 | 2416 | 2703 | 2293 | 2403 | 2285 | 2609 | 3060 | 2439 |
| Avg. Yards per Attempt | 5.6 | 7.7 | 7.1 | 6.4 | 6.8 | 6.8 | 6.5 | 6.3 | 6.9 | 6.7 | 7.3 | 7.5 | 7.0 |
| Avg. Yards per Complet. | 11.0 | 14.9 | 15.2 | 13.9 | 16.1 | 13.4 | 12.9 | 11.1 | 14.1 | 14.0 | 14.2 | 13.0 | 12.6 |
| Times Tackled Passing | 33 | 30 | 30 | 25 | 44 | 37 | 28 | 34 | 25 | 27 | 32 | 33 | 19 |
| Yards Lost Tackled | 288 | 225 | 254 | 203 | 435 | 344 | 235 | 293 | 249 | 230 | 223 | 294 | 177 |
| Net Yards | 1739 | 2108 | 2128 | 1967 | 1985 | 2072 | 2468 | 2000 | 2154 | 2055 | 2386 | 2766 | 2262 |
| Touchdowns | 9 | 20 | 19 | 12 | 18 | 11 | 11 | 10 | 16 | 17 | 15 | 16 | 15 |
| Interceptions | 28 | 11 | 27 | 24 | 20 | 23 | 27 | 17 | 15 | 13 | 23 | 17 | 22 |
| Percent Intercepted | 7.8 | 3.6 | 8.1 | 7.1 | 5.6 | 6.5 | 6.5 | 4.7 | 4.3 | 3.8 | 6.4 | 4.2 | 6.3 |
| **PUNTS:** | | | | | | | | | | | | | |
| Number | 88 | 66 | 73 | 66 | 67 | 76 | 67 | 72 | 66 | 65 | 59 | 77 | 67 |
| Average Distance | 38.9 | 39.0 | 40.9 | 42.4 | 45.7 | 42.2 | 40.7 | 40.7 | 38.8 | 38.1 | 41.7 | 41.5 | 43.7 |
| **PUNT RETURNS:** | | | | | | | | | | | | | |
| Number | 40 | 40 | 41 | 26 | 45 | 39 | 40 | 26 | 36 | 41 | 26 | 45 | 20 |
| Yards | 267 | 446 | 304 | 227 | 468 | 304 | 286 | 106 | 279 | 359 | 168 | 319 | 40 |
| Average Yards | 6.7 | 11.2 | 7.4 | 8.7 | 10.4 | 7.8 | 7.2 | 4.1 | 7.8 | 8.8 | 6.5 | 7.1 | 2.0 |
| Touchdowns | 0 | 0 | 1 | 0 | 0 | 0 | 0 | 0 | 1 | 0 | 0 | 0 | 0 |
| **KICKOFF RETURNS:** | | | | | | | | | | | | | |
| Number | 62 | 42 | 39 | 55 | 43 | 41 | 47 | 59 | 49 | 34 | 55 | 45 | 55 |
| Yards | 1345 | 971 | 1024 | 1252 | 1059 | 862 | 1071 | 1180 | 1427 | 906 | 1155 | 1002 | 1245 |
| Average Yards | 21.7 | 23.1 | 26.3 | 22.8 | 24.6 | 20.8 | 22.8 | 20.0 | 29.1 | 26.6 | 21.0 | 22.3 | 22.6 |
| Touchdowns | 0 | 0 | 0 | 0 | 0 | 0 | 0 | 0 | 1 | 1 | 0 | 0 | 0 |
| **INTERCEPTION RETURNS:** | | | | | | | | | | | | | |
| Number | 21 | 32 | 11 | 27 | 27 | 37 | 13 | 10 | 16 | 16 | 26 | 26 | 28 |
| Yards | 220 | 418 | 219 | 453 | 432 | 505 | 167 | 166 | 157 | 279 | 267 | 350 | 339 |
| Average Yards | 10.5 | 13.1 | 19.9 | 16.8 | 16.0 | 13.6 | 12.8 | 16.6 | 9.8 | 17.4 | 10.3 | 13.5 | 12.1 |
| Touchdowns | 1 | 3 | 1 | 2 | 2 | 3 | 0 | 1 | 1 | 1 | 0 | 1 | 4 |
| **PENALTIES:** | | | | | | | | | | | | | |
| Number | 67 | 89 | 72 | 86 | 78 | 75 | 71 | 62 | 60 | 81 | 80 | 81 | 84 |
| Yards | 687 | 883 | 722 | 772 | 771 | 916 | 751 | 569 | 559 | 814 | 832 | 784 | 887 |
| **FUMBLES:** | | | | | | | | | | | | | |
| Number | 22 | 17 | 21 | 31 | 36 | 31 | 16 | 38 | 35 | 35 | 26 | 27 | 27 |
| Number Lost | 13 | 11 | 12 | 16 | 20 | 14 | 6 | 14 | 14 | 14 | 17 | 18 | 10 |
| **POINTS:** | | | | | | | | | | | | | |
| Total | 140 | 394 | 265 | 273 | 275 | 330 | 208 | 174 | 325 | 299 | 278 | 292 | 341 |
| PAT Attempts | 18 | 45 | 32 | 30 | 32 | 37 | 21 | 21 | 35 | 37 | 30 | 32 | 44 |
| PAT Made | 17 | 45 | 31 | 30 | 32 | 36 | 20 | 21 | 34 | 35 | 30 | 30 | 44 |
| FG Attempts | 18 | 38 | 22 | 31 | 35 | 35 | 32 | 21 | 36 | 25 | 34 | 35 | 24 |
| FG Made | 5 | 25 | 14 | 21 | 17 | 24 | 20 | 9 | 27 | 14 | 22 | 22 | 11 |
| Percent FG Made | 27.8 | 65.8 | 63.6 | 67.7 | 48.6 | 68.9 | 62.5 | 42.9 | 75.0 | 56.0 | 64.7 | 62.9 | 45.8 |
| Safeties | 0 | 2 | 0 | 0 | 0 | 0 | 1 | 0 | 0 | 0 | 1 | 2 | 0 |

## CONFERENCE PLAYOFFS

December 25, at Kansas City
(Attendance 45,822)

### SCORING

| | | | | | | |
|---|---|---|---|---|---|---|
| KANSAS CITY | 10 | 0 | 7 | 7 | 0 | 0–24 |
| MIAMI | 0 | 10 | 7 | 7 | 0 | 3–27 |

First Quarter
K.C. Stenerud, 24 yard field goal
K.C. Podolak, 7 yard pass from Dawson
PAT–Stenerud (kick)

Second Quarter
Mia. Csonka, 1 yard rush
PAT–Yepremian (kick)
Mia. Yepremian, 14 yard field goal

Third Quarter
K.C. Otis, 1 yard rush
PAT–Stenerud (kick)
Mia. Kiick, 1 yard rush
PAT–Yepremian (kick)

Fourth Quarter
K.C. Podolak, 3 yard rush
PAT–Stenerud (kick)
Mia. Fleming, 5 yard pass from Griese
PAT–Yepremian (kick)

Second Overtime Period
Mia. Yepremian, 37 yard field goal 7:40

### TEAM STATISTICS

| K.C. | | MIAMI |
|---|---|---|
| 23 | First Downs–Total | 22 |
| 13 | First Downs–Rushing | 6 |
| 10 | First Downs–Passing | 14 |
| 0 | First Downs–Penalty | 2 |
| 2 | Fumbles–Number | 0 |
| 2 | Fumbles–Lost Ball | 0 |
| 6 | Penalties–Number | 5 |
| 44 | Yards Penalized | 26 |
| 3 | Missed Field Goals | 1 |
| 71 | Offensive Plays–Total | 78 |
| 451 | Net Yards | 407 |
| 6.4 | Average Gain | 5.2 |
| 4 | Giveaways | 2 |
| 2 | Takeaways | 4 |
| –2 | Difference | +2 |

### INDIVIDUAL STATISTICS

| KANSAS CITY | No. | Yds. | Avg. | MIAMI | No. | Yds. | Avg. |
|---|---|---|---|---|---|---|---|
| **RUSHING** | | | | | | | |
| Hayes | 22 | 100 | 4.5 | Csonka | 24 | 86 | 3.6 |
| Podolak | 17 | 85 | 5.0 | Kiick | 15 | 56 | 3.7 |
| Wright | 2 | 15 | 7.5 | Griese | 2 | 9 | 4.5 |
| Otis | 3 | 13 | 4.3 | Warfield | 2 | –7 | –3.5 |
| | 44 | 213 | 4.8 | | 43 | 144 | 3.3 |
| **RECEIVING** | | | | | | | |
| Podolak | 8 | 110 | 13.8 | Warfield | 7 | 140 | 20.0 |
| Wright | 3 | 104 | 34.7 | Twilley | 5 | 58 | 11.6 |
| Taylor | 3 | 12 | 4.0 | Fleming | 4 | 37 | 9.3 |
| Hayes | 3 | 6 | 2.0 | Kiick | 3 | 24 | 8.0 |
| Frazier | 1 | 14 | 14.0 | Mandich | 1 | 4 | 4.0 |
| | 18 | 246 | 13.7 | | 20 | 263 | 13.2 |
| **PUNTING** | | | | | | | |
| Wilson | 2 | | 51.0 | Seiple | 6 | | 40.0 |
| **PUNT RETURNS** | | | | | | | |
| Podolak | 2 | 1 | 0.5 | Scott | 1 | 18 | 18.0 |
| **KICKOFF RETURNS** | | | | | | | |
| Podolak | 3 | 154 | 52.0 | Morris | 2 | 61 | 30.5 |
| **INTERCEPTION RETURNS** | | | | | | | |
| Lanier | 1 | 17 | 17.0 | Scott | 1 | 13 | 13.0 |
| Lynch | 1 | 0 | 0.0 | Johnson | 1 | 0 | 0.0 |
| | 2 | 17 | 8.5 | | 2 | 13 | 6.5 |

**PASSING**

| KANSAS CITY | Att. | Comp. | Comp. Pct. | Yds. | Int. | Yds/ Att. | Yds/ Comp. | Yds Lost Tkld. |
|---|---|---|---|---|---|---|---|---|
| Dawson | 26 | 18 | 69.2 | 246 | 2 | 9.5 | 13.7 | 1–8 |
| Podolak | 1 | 0 | 0.0 | 0 | 0 | – | – | |
| | 27 | 18 | 66.7 | 246 | 2 | 9.1 | 13.7 | 1–8 |
| **MIAMI** | | | | | | | | |
| Griese | 35 | 20 | 57.1 | 263 | 2 | 7.5 | 13.2 | 0–0 |

December 26, at Cleveland
(Attendance 70,734)

### SCORING

| | | | | |
|---|---|---|---|---|
| CLEVELAND | 0 | 0 | 3 | 0– 3 |
| BALTIMORE | 0 | 14 | 3 | 3–20 |

Second Quarter
Balt. Nottingham, 1 yard rush
PAT–O'Brien (kick)
Balt. Nottingham, 7 yard rush
PAT–O'Brien (kick)

Third Quarter
Cle. Cockroft, 14 yard field goal
Balt. O'Brien, 42 yard field goal

Fourth Quarter
Balt. O'Brien, 15 yard field goal

### TEAM STATISTICS

| CLE. | | BALT. |
|---|---|---|
| 11 | First Downs–Total | 16 |
| 5 | First Downs–Rushing | 7 |
| 5 | First Downs–Passing | 8 |
| 1 | First Downs–Penalty | 1 |
| 6 | Fumbles–Number | 2 |
| 2 | Fumbles–Lost Ball | 2 |
| 3 | Penalties–Number | 5 |
| 16 | Yards Penalized | 43 |
| 2 | Missed Field Goals | 0 |
| 56 | Offensive Plays–Total | 64 |
| 165 | Net Yards | 271 |
| 2.9 | Average Gain | 4.2 |
| 5 | Giveaways | 3 |
| 3 | Takeaways | 5 |
| –2 | Difference | +2 |

### INDIVIDUAL STATISTICS

| CLEVELAND | No. | Yds. | Avg. | BALTIMORE | No. | Yds. | Avg. |
|---|---|---|---|---|---|---|---|
| **RUSHING** | | | | | | | |
| Kelly | 14 | 49 | 3.5 | Nottingham | 23 | 92 | 4.0 |
| Bo Scott | 8 | 25 | 3.1 | Matte | 16 | 26 | 1.6 |
| Nelsen | 2 | –5 | –2.5 | McCauley | 3 | 9 | 3.0 |
| | 24 | 69 | 2.9 | Nowatzke | 1 | 1 | 1.0 |
| | | | | | 43 | 128 | 3.0 |
| **RECEIVING** | | | | | | | |
| Bo Scott | 5 | 41 | 8.2 | Mitchell | 5 | 73 | 14.6 |
| Kelly | 4 | 24 | 6.0 | Matte | 3 | 22 | 7.3 |
| Hooker | 1 | 39 | 39.0 | Hinton | 2 | 30 | 15.0 |
| Morin | 1 | 16 | 16.0 | Perkins | 1 | 10 | 10.0 |
| Glass | 1 | 11 | 11.0 | Nottingham | 1 | 5 | 5.0 |
| | 12 | 131 | 10.9 | Havrilak | 1 | 3 | 3.0 |
| | | | | | 13 | 143 | 11.0 |
| **PUNTING** | | | | | | | |
| Cockroft | 5 | | 40.8 | Lee | 6 | | 37.2 |
| **PUNT RETURNS** | | | | | | | |
| Kelly | 3 | 71 | 23.7 | Volk | 4 | 27 | 6.8 |
| D. Jones | 1 | 3 | 3.0 | | | | |
| | 4 | 74 | 18.5 | | | | |
| **KICKOFF RETURNS** | | | | | | | |
| S. Brown | 2 | 34 | 17.0 | Pittman | 1 | 25 | 25.0 |
| Bo Scott | 1 | 30 | 30.0 | | | | |
| Morrison | 1 | 19 | 19.0 | | | | |
| Dieken | 1 | 15 | 15.0 | | | | |
| | 5 | 98 | 19.6 | | | | |
| **INTERCEPTION RETURNS** | | | | | | | |
| Snidow | 1 | 1 | 1.0 | Volk | 2 | 56 | 28.0 |
| C. Scott | Lat | 22 | – | Stukes | 1 | 23 | 23.0 |
| | 1 | 23 | 23.0 | | 3 | 89 | 29.7 |

**PASSING**

| CLEVE. | Att. | Cmp. | Pct. | Yds. | Int. | Yd/A | Yd/C | Tkld |
|---|---|---|---|---|---|---|---|---|
| Nelsen | 21 | 9 | 42.9 | 104 | 3 | 5.0 | 11.6 | |
| Phipps | 6 | 3 | 50.0 | 27 | 0 | 4.5 | 9.0 | |
| | 27 | 12 | 44.4 | 131 | 3 | 4.9 | 10.9 | 5–35 |
| **BALT.** | | | | | | | | |
| Unitas | 21 | 13 | 61.9 | 143 | 1 | 6.8 | 11.0 | 0– 0 |

**MIAMI DOLPHINS** 10-3-1 Don Shula

| Scores of Each Game | | |
|---|---|---|
| 10 | Denver | 10 |
| 29 | Buffalo | 14 |
| 10 | N.Y. JETS | 14 |
| 23 | Cincinnati | 13 |
| 41 | NEW ENGLAND | 3 |
| 30 | N.Y. Jets | 14 |
| 20 | Los Angeles | 14 |
| 34 | BUFFALO | 0 |
| 24 | PITTSBURGH | 21 |
| 17 | BALTIMORE | 14 |
| 34 | CHICAGO | 3 |
| 13 | New England | 34 |
| 3 | Baltimore | 14 |
| 27 | GREEN BAY | 6 |

| Use Name | Pos. | Hgt | Wgt | Age | Int | Pts |
|---|---|---|---|---|---|---|
| Doug Crusan | OT | 6'5" | 250 | 25 | | |
| Norm Evans | OT | 6'5" | 252 | 28 | | |
| Wayne Mass | OT | 6'4" | 240 | 25 | | |
| Bob Kuechenberg | OG | 6'3" | 247 | 23 | | |
| Jim Langer | OG | 6'2" | 250 | 23 | | |
| Larry Little | OG | 6'1" | 265 | 25 | | |
| Bob DeMarco | C | 6'3" | 250 | 33 | | |
| Vern Den Herder | DE | 6'6" | 250 | 22 | | |
| Jim Riley | DE | 6'4" | 250 | 26 | | |
| Bill Stanfill | DE | 6'5" | 250 | 24 | | |
| Frank Cornish | DT | 6'6" | 285 | 27 | | |
| Manny Fernandez | DT | 6'2" | 248 | 25 | | |
| John Richardson | DT | 6'2" | 248 | 26 | | |
| Bob Heinz | DE-DT | 6'6" | 270 | 24 | | |

Dick Palmer–Injury

| Use Name | Pos. | Hgt | Wgt | Age | Int | Pts |
|---|---|---|---|---|---|---|
| Nick Buoniconti | LB | 5'11" | 220 | 30 | 1 | |
| Dale Farley | LB | 6'3" | 235 | 22 | | |
| Mike Kolen | LB | 6'2" | 220 | 23 | | |
| Bob Matheson | LB | 6'4" | 240 | 26 | | |
| Jesse Powell | LB | 6'1" | 215 | 24 | | |
| Doug Swift | LB | 6'3" | 228 | 22 | 1 | |
| Dick Anderson | DB | 6'2" | 196 | 25 | 2 | |
| Tim Foley | DB | 6' | 194 | 23 | 4 | |
| Curtis Johnson | DB | 6'2" | 196 | 23 | 2 | 6 |
| Ray Jones | DB | 6' | 187 | 23 | | |
| Lloyd Mumphord | DB | 5'11" | 180 | 24 | | |
| Bob Petrella | DB | 6' | 190 | 26 | | |
| Jake Scott | DB | 6' | 188 | 26 | 7 | |

Dean Brown–Injury
Dick Daniels–Injury
Stan Mitchell–Injury

| Use Name | Pos. | Hgt | Wgt | Age | Int | Pts |
|---|---|---|---|---|---|---|
| Bob Griese | QB | 6'1" | 190 | 26 | | |
| George Mira | QB | 5'11" | 192 | 29 | | |
| Hubert Ginn | HB | 5'11" | 188 | 24 | | |
| Jim Kiick | HB | 5'11" | 215 | 25 | | 18 |
| Mercury Morris | HB | 5'10" | 190 | 24 | | 12 |
| Terry Cole | FB | 6'1" | 220 | 26 | | |
| Larry Csonka | FB | 6'3" | 237 | 24 | | 48 |
| Charlie Leigh | FB | 5'11" | 205 | 25 | | |
| Karl Noonan | WR | 6'3" | 198 | 27 | | |
| Otto Stowe | WR | 6'2" | 188 | 22 | | 6 |
| Howard Twilley | WR | 5'10" | 185 | 27 | | 24 |
| Paul Warfield | WR | 6' | 185 | 28 | | 66 |
| Marv Fleming | TE | 6'4" | 235 | 29 | | 12 |
| Jim Mandich | TE | 6'3" | 224 | 23 | | 6 |
| Larry Seiple | TE | 6' | 215 | 26 | | |
| Garo Yepremian | K | 5'8" | 165 | 27 | | 117 |

**BALTIMORE COLTS** 10-4-0 Don McCafferty

| Scores of Each Game | | |
|---|---|---|
| 22 | N.Y. JETS | 0 |
| 13 | CLEVELAND | 14 |
| 23 | New England | 3 |
| 43 | Buffalo | 0 |
| 31 | N.Y. Giants | 7 |
| 3 | Minnesota | 10 |
| 34 | PITTSBURGH | 21 |
| 24 | LOS ANGELES | 17 |
| 14 | N.Y. Jets | 13 |
| 14 | Miami | 17 |
| 37 | Oakland | 14 |
| 24 | BUFFALO | 0 |
| 14 | MIAMI | 3 |
| 17 | NEW ENGLAND | 21 |

| Use Name | Pos. | Hgt | Wgt | Age | Int | Pts |
|---|---|---|---|---|---|---|
| Lynn Larson | OT | 6'4" | 254 | 23 | | |
| Dennis Nelson | OT | 6'5" | 260 | 25 | | |
| Bob Vogel | OT | 6'5" | 250 | 29 | | |
| Cornelius Johnson | OG | 6'2" | 245 | 28 | | |
| Glenn Ressler | OG | 6'3" | 250 | 27 | | |
| Dan Sullivan | OG | 6'3" | 250 | 32 | | |
| John Williams | OG | 6'3" | 256 | 25 | | |
| Bill Curry | C | 6'2" | 236 | 28 | | |
| Ken Mendenhall | C | 6'3" | 235 | 23 | | |
| Roy Hilton | DE | 6'6" | 240 | 26 | | |
| Billy Newsome | DE | 6'4" | 240 | 23 | 2 | 6 |
| Bubba Smith | DE | 6'7" | 295 | 26 | | |
| Jim Bailey | DT | 6'5" | 245 | 23 | | |
| Rusty Ganas | DT | 6'4" | 257 | 21 | | |
| Fred Miller | DT | 6'3" | 250 | 30 | | |
| George Wright | DT | 6'3" | 260 | 24 | | |

| Use Name | Pos. | Hgt | Wgt | Age | Int | Pts |
|---|---|---|---|---|---|---|
| Tom Beutler | LB | 6'1" | 232 | 24 | | |
| Mike Curtis | LB | 6'2" | 232 | 28 | 3 | |
| Ted Hendricks | LB | 6'7" | 215 | 23 | 5 | 6 |
| Bill Laskey | LB | 6'2" | 235 | 28 | | |
| Ray May | LB | 6'1" | 230 | 26 | 1 | |
| Robbie Nichols | LB | 6'3" | 220 | 24 | | |
| Tom Nowatzke | FB-LB | 6'3" | 230 | 28 | 1 | |
| Tom Curtis | DB | 6'1" | 196 | 23 | | |
| Jim Duncan | DB | 6'2" | 200 | 25 | | |
| Lenny Dunlap | DB | 6'1" | 195 | 22 | | |
| Lonnie Hepburn | DB | 5'11" | 185 | 22 | | |
| Rex Kern | DB | 5'11" | 190 | 22 | | |
| Jerry Logan | DB | 6'1" | 190 | 30 | 4 | |
| Charlie Stukes | DB | 6'3" | 212 | 27 | 8 | |
| Rick Volk | DB | 6'3" | 195 | 26 | 4 | |

| Use Name | Pos. | Hgt | Wgt | Age | Int | Pts |
|---|---|---|---|---|---|---|
| Earl Morrall | QB | 6'1" | 206 | 37 | | |
| Johnny Unitas | QB | 6'1" | 196 | 38 | | |
| Tom Matte | HB | 6' | 214 | 32 | | 48 |
| Don McCauley | HB | 6'1" | 207 | 22 | | 12 |
| Charlie Pittman | HB | 6'1" | 200 | 23 | | |
| Don Nottingham | FB | 5'10" | 210 | 22 | | 36 |
| Norm Bulaich | HB-FB | 6'1" | 218 | 24 | | 60 |
| Sam Havrilak | WR | 6'2" | 195 | 23 | | |
| Eddie Hinton | WR | 6' | 200 | 24 | | 12 |
| Jim O'Brien | WR | 6' | 195 | 24 | | 95 |
| Ray Perkins | WR | 6' | 183 | 29 | | 24 |
| Willie Richardson | WR | 6'2" | 198 | 31 | | 12 |
| John Mackey | TE | 6'3" | 224 | 29 | | |
| Tom Mitchell | TE | 6'2" | 215 | 27 | | |
| David Lee | K | 6'4" | 230 | 27 | | |

**NEW ENGLAND PATRIOTS** 6-8-0 John Mazur

| Scores of Each Game | | |
|---|---|---|
| 20 | OAKLAND | 6 |
| 7 | DETROIT | 34 |
| 3 | BALTIMORE | 23 |
| 20 | N.Y. JETS | 0 |
| 3 | Miami | 41 |
| 21 | Dallas | 44 |
| 10 | San Francisco | 27 |
| 28 | HOUSTON | 20 |
| 38 | BUFFALO | 33 |
| 7 | Cleveland | 27 |
| 20 | Buffalo | 27 |
| 34 | MIAMI | 13 |
| 6 | N.Y. Jets | 13 |
| 21 | Baltimore | 17 |

| Use Name | Pos. | Hgt | Wgt | Age | Int | Pts |
|---|---|---|---|---|---|---|
| Mike Haggerty | OT | 6'4" | 250 | 25 | | |
| Mike Montler | OT | 6'4" | 270 | 27 | | |
| Tom Neville | OT | 6'4" | 255 | 28 | | |
| Bill Lenkaitis | OG | 6'3" | 265 | 25 | | |
| Len St. Jean | OG | 6'1" | 245 | 29 | | |
| Halvor Hagen | C-OG | 6'5" | 253 | 24 | | |
| Jon Morris | C | 6'4" | 255 | 28 | | |
| Ike Lassiter | DE | 6'5" | 270 | 30 | | |
| Art May | DE | 6'3" | 245 | 22 | | |
| Dennis Wirgowski | DE | 6'5" | 255 | 23 | | |
| Ron Berger | DT-DE | 6'8" | 275 | 27 | | |
| Julius Adams | DT | 6'3" | 258 | 23 | | |
| Houston Antwine | DT | 6' | 270 | 32 | | |
| Dave Rowe | DT | 6'6" | 280 | 26 | | |
| Bill Atessis | DE-DT | 6'3" | 240 | 22 | | |

Rick Cash–Injury
Joe Kapp–Holdout
J. R. Williamson–Injury

| Use Name | Pos. | Hgt | Wgt | Age | Int | Pts |
|---|---|---|---|---|---|---|
| Jim Cheyunski | LB | 6'2" | 220 | 25 | 1 | |
| Dennis Coleman | LB | 6'3" | 225 | 22 | | |
| Randy Edmunds | LB | 6'2" | 225 | 25 | | |
| Steve Kiner | LB | 6' | 219 | 24 | 4 | |
| Ed Philpott | LB | 6'3" | 240 | 25 | | |
| Ed Weisacosky | LB | 6' | 220 | 27 | | |
| Randy Beverly | DB | 5'11" | 205 | 27 | 2 | |
| Larry Carwell | DB | 6'1" | 200 | 27 | 5 | 6 |
| Phil Clark | DB | 6'2" | 208 | 26 | | |
| Rickie Harris | DB | 6' | 182 | 28 | | |
| Tom Janik | DB | 6'3" | 200 | 30 | | |
| Irv Mallory | DB | 6'1" | 196 | 22 | | |
| John Outlaw | DB | 5'10" | 175 | 26 | 3 | 6 |
| Perry Pruett | DB | 6'1" | 190 | 22 | | |
| Clarence Scott | DB | 6'2" | 205 | 27 | | |
| Don Webb | DB | 5'10" | 185 | 32 | | |
| Ron Gardin (from BAL) | WR-DB | 5'11" | 180 | 26 | | |

| Use Name | Pos. | Hgt | Wgt | Age | Int | Pts |
|---|---|---|---|---|---|---|
| Jim Plunkett | QB | 6'3" | 220 | 23 | | |
| Mike Taliaferro | QB | 6'2" | 205 | 29 | | |
| Carl Garrett | HB | 5'11" | 210 | 24 | | 12 |
| Bob Gladieux | HB | 5'11" | 190 | 24 | | |
| Jack Maitland | HB | 6'1" | 210 | 23 | | 6 |
| Odell Lawson | FB | 6'2" | 218 | 23 | | |
| Jim Nance | FB | 6'1" | 240 | 28 | | 30 |
| Hubie Bryant | WR | 5'10" | 168 | 25 | | 6 |
| Eric Crabtree (from CIN) | WR | 5'11" | 185 | 26 | | 18 |
| Reggie Rucker (from DAL-NYG) | WR | 6'2" | 190 | 23 | | 6 |
| Ron Sellers | WR | 6'4" | 195 | 24 | | 18 |
| Eric Stolberg | WR | 6'2" | 180 | 22 | | |
| Al Sykes | WR | 6'3" | 180 | 24 | | |
| Randy Vataha | WR | 5'10" | 180 | 22 | | 54 |
| Roland Moss | TE | 6'3" | 215 | 24 | | 12 |
| Tom Beer | OG-TE | 6'4" | 235 | 26 | | 18 |
| Charlie Gogolak | K | 5'10" | 170 | 26 | | 64 |

**NEW YORK JETS** 6-8-0 Weeb Ewbank

| Scores of Each Game | | |
|---|---|---|
| 0 | Baltimore | 22 |
| 10 | St. Louis | 17 |
| 14 | Miami | 10 |
| 0 | New England | 20 |
| 28 | BUFFALO | 17 |
| 14 | MIAMI | 30 |
| 21 | San Diego | 49 |
| 13 | KANSAS CITY | 10 |
| 13 | BALTIMORE | 14 |
| 20 | Buffalo | 7 |
| 21 | SAN FRANCISCO | 24 |
| 10 | Dallas | 52 |
| 13 | NEW ENGLAND | 6 |
| 35 | CINCINNATI | 21 |

| Use Name | Pos. | Hgt | Wgt | Age | Int | Pts |
|---|---|---|---|---|---|---|
| Winston Hill | OT | 6'4" | 285 | 29 | | |
| John Mooring | OT | 6'6" | 255 | 24 | | |
| Bob Svihus | OT | 6'4" | 245 | 28 | | |
| Dave Foley | C-OT | 6'5" | 255 | 23 | | |
| Dave Herman | OG | 6'2" | 255 | 29 | | |
| Roy Kirksey | OG | 6'1" | 265 | 23 | | |
| Randy Rasmussen | OG | 6'2" | 255 | 26 | | |
| John Schmitt | C | 6'4" | 250 | 28 | | |
| Paul Crane | LB-C | 6'2" | 212 | 27 | 1 | |
| Mark Lomas | DE | 6'4" | 230 | 23 | | |
| Gerry Philbin | DE | 6'2" | 245 | 30 | | |
| John Little | DT-DE | 6'3" | 220 | 24 | | |
| Steve Thompson | DT-DE | 6'5" | 245 | 25 | | |
| John Elliott | DT | 6'4" | 244 | 26 | | |
| Roger Finnie | DT | 6'3" | 245 | 25 | | |
| Chuck Hinton (from PIT) | DT | 6'5" | 264 | 32 | | |
| Scott Palmer | DT | 6'3" | 245 | 23 | | |
| Clovis Swinney | DT | 6'3" | 240 | 26 | | |

| Use Name | Pos. | Hgt | Wgt | Age | Int | Pts |
|---|---|---|---|---|---|---|
| Al Atkinson | LB | 6'1" | 230 | 28 | 2 | |
| Ralph Baker | LB | 6'3" | 235 | 29 | | 1 |
| Larry Grantham | LB | 6' | 210 | 32 | 1 | |
| John Ebersole | LB | 6'3" | 240 | 22 | | |
| Bill Zapalac | DE-LB | 6'4" | 225 | 23 | | |
| John Dockery | DB | 6' | 186 | 26 | 2 | |
| Chris Farasopoulos | DB | 5'11" | 190 | 22 | | |
| W.K. Hicks | DB | 6'1" | 195 | 28 | | 4 |
| Gus Holloman | DB | 6'3" | 195 | 25 | 2 | |
| Rich Sowells | DB | 6' | 175 | 22 | | |
| Steve Tannen | DB | 6'1" | 194 | 23 | | |
| Earlie Thomas | DB | 6'1" | 190 | 25 | | |
| Phil Wise | DB | 6' | 190 | 22 | 1 | |

Jim Richards–Military Service

| Use Name | Pos. | Hgt | Wgt | Age | Int | Pts |
|---|---|---|---|---|---|---|
| Bob Davis | QB | 6'3" | 205 | 26 | | 6 |
| Joe Namath | QB | 6'2" | 200 | 28 | | |
| Al Woodall | QB | 6'5" | 205 | 25 | | |
| Emerson Boozer | HB | 5'11" | 195 | 28 | | 36 |
| George Nock | HB | 5'10" | 200 | 25 | | 30 |
| Cliff McClain | FB-HB | 6' | 217 | 23 | | 12 |
| John Riggins | FB | 6'2" | 237 | 22 | | 18 |
| Matt Snell | FB | 6'2" | 220 | 29 | | |
| Steve Harkey | HB-FB | 6' | 215 | 22 | | |
| Eddie Bell | WR | 5'10" | 160 | 23 | | 6 |
| Rich Caster | WR | 6'5" | 222 | 22 | | 36 |
| Don Maynard | WR | 6' | 180 | 35 | | 12 |
| Steve O'Neal | WR | 6'3" | 185 | 25 | | |
| Vern Studdard | WR | 5'11" | 175 | 23 | | |
| Gary Arthur | TE | 6'5" | 230 | 23 | | |
| Pete Lammons | TE | 6'3" | 230 | 27 | | 6 |
| Wayne Stewart | TE | 6'7" | 213 | 24 | | |
| Bobby Howfield | K | 5'9" | 180 | 34 | | 49 |

**BUFFALO BILLS** 1-13-0 Harvey Johnson

| Scores of Each Game | | |
|---|---|---|
| 37 | DALLAS | 49 |
| 14 | MIAMI | 29 |
| 0 | Minnesota | 19 |
| 0 | BALTIMORE | 43 |
| 17 | N.Y. Jets | 28 |
| 3 | San Diego | 20 |
| 23 | ST. LOUIS | 28 |
| 0 | Miami | 34 |
| 33 | New England | 38 |
| 7 | N.Y. JETS | 20 |
| 27 | NEW ENGLAND | 20 |
| 0 | Baltimore | 24 |
| 14 | HOUSTON | 20 |
| 9 | Kansas City | 22 |

| Use Name | Pos. | Hgt | Wgt | Age | Int | Pts |
|---|---|---|---|---|---|---|
| Paul Costa | OT | 6'4" | 255 | 29 | | |
| Donnie Green | OT | 6'7" | 270 | 23 | | |
| Willie Young | OT | 6'4" | 270 | 23 | | |
| Bob Hews | DE-OT | 6'5" | 240 | 22 | | |
| Joe O'Donnell | OG | 6'2" | 262 | 28 | | |
| Mike Wilson | OG | 6'1" | 240 | 23 | | |
| Levert Carr | OT-OG | 6'5" | 260 | 27 | | |
| Bruce Jarvis | C | 6'7" | 246 | 22 | | |
| Howard Kindig | OT-C | 6'6" | 265 | 30 | | |
| Mike McBath | DE | 6'4" | 248 | 25 | | |
| Al Cowlings | DE | 6'5" | 258 | 24 | | |
| Louis Ross | DE | 6'6" | 238 | 24 | | |
| Cal Snowden | DE | 6'4" | 242 | 24 | | |
| Bill McKinley | LB-DE | 6'3" | 240 | 22 | | |
| Jim Dunaway | DT | 6'4" | 277 | 29 | | |
| Bob Tatarek | DT | 6'4" | 260 | 25 | | |

| Use Name | Pos. | Hgt | Wgt | Age | Int | Pts |
|---|---|---|---|---|---|---|
| Al Andrews | LB | 6'3" | 216 | 27 | 1 | |
| Edgar Chandler | LB | 6'3" | 235 | 25 | 1 | 2 |
| Jerald Collins | LB | 6'1" | 220 | 24 | | |
| Dick Cunningham | LB | 6'2" | 232 | 26 | | |
| Paul Guidry | LB | 6'3" | 233 | 27 | 1 | |
| Mike Stratton | LB | 6'3" | 240 | 29 | | |
| Chuck Hurston | LB | 6'6" | 240 | 28 | | |
| Jackie Allen | DB | 6'1" | 187 | 23 | | |
| Tim Beamer | DB | 5'11" | 185 | 23 | | |
| Tony Greene | DB | 5'10" | 170 | 22 | | |
| Robert James | DB | 6'1" | 185 | 24 | 4 | 6 |
| John Pitts | DB | 6'4" | 223 | 26 | 2 | |
| Pete Richardson | DB | 6'1" | 193 | 24 | 1 | |
| Alvin Wyatt | DB | 5'10" | 185 | 23 | 1 | 6 |

Richard Cheek – Knee Injury
Julian Nunamaker – Injury
Jim Reilly – Illness

| Use Name | Pos. | Hgt | Wgt | Age | Int | Pts |
|---|---|---|---|---|---|---|
| James Harris | QB | 6'3" | 215 | 24 | | |
| Dennis Shaw | QB | 6'2" | 210 | 24 | | |
| Max Anderson | HB | 5'8" | 180 | 26 | | |
| Greg Jones | HB | 6'1" | 200 | 23 | | 6 |
| O.J. Simpson | HB | 6'2" | 214 | 24 | | 30 |
| Jim Braxton | FB | 6'2" | 226 | 22 | | |
| Wayne Patrick | FB | 6'2" | 254 | 25 | | 6 |
| Marlin Briscoe | WR | 5'10" | 178 | 25 | | 30 |
| Bob Chandler | WR | 6' | 180 | 22 | | |
| J.D. Hill | WR | 6'1" | 193 | 22 | | 12 |
| Haven Moses | WR | 6'3" | 205 | 25 | | 12 |
| Ike Hill | DB-WR | 5'10" | 180 | 24 | | 12 |
| Austin Denney | TE | 6'2" | 230 | 27 | | |
| Ted Koy | TE | 6'1" | 210 | 23 | | 6 |
| Jan White | TE | 6'2" | 215 | 22 | | |
| Dave Chapple | K | 6' | 180 | 24 | | |
| Grant Guthrie | K | 6' | 210 | 23 | | 17 |
| Spike Jones | K | 6'2" | 190 | 24 | | |
| John Leypoldt | K | 6'2" | 224 | 25 | | 39 |

## MIAMI DOLPHINS

### RUSHING

| Last Name | No. | Yds | Avg | TD |
|---|---|---|---|---|
| Csonka | 195 | 1051 | 5.4 | 7 |
| Kiick | 162 | 738 | 4.6 | 3 |
| Morris | 57 | 315 | 5.5 | 1 |
| Warfield | 9 | 115 | 12.8 | 0 |
| Ginn | 22 | 97 | 4.4 | 0 |
| Griese | 26 | 82 | 3.2 | 0 |
| Leigh | 5 | 15 | 3.0 | 0 |
| Seiple | 1 | 14 | 14.0 | 0 |
| Cole | 3 | 11 | 3.7 | 0 |
| Mira | 6 | −9 | −1.5 | 0 |

### RECEIVING

| Last Name | No. | Yds | Avg | TD |
|---|---|---|---|---|
| Warfield | 43 | 996 | 23 | 11 |
| Kiick | 40 | 338 | 8 | 0 |
| Twilley | 23 | 349 | 15 | 4 |
| Fleming | 13 | 137 | 11 | 2 |
| Csonka | 13 | 113 | 9 | 1 |
| Noonan | 10 | 180 | 18 | 0 |
| Stowe | 5 | 68 | 14 | 1 |
| Morris | 5 | 16 | 3 | 0 |
| Mandich | 3 | 19 | 6 | 1 |
| Seiple | 1 | 32 | 32 | 0 |

### PUNT RETURNS

| Last Name | No. | Yds | Avg | TD |
|---|---|---|---|---|
| Scott | 33 | 318 | 10 | 0 |
| Anderson | 8 | 114 | 14 | 0 |

### KICKOFF RETURNS

| Last Name | No. | Yds | Avg | TD |
|---|---|---|---|---|
| Morris | 15 | 423 | 28 | 1 |
| Ginn | 10 | 252 | 25 | 0 |
| Leigh | 4 | 99 | 25 | 0 |
| Matheson | 3 | 32 | 11 | 0 |

### PASSING – PUNTING – KICKING

| PASSING | Att | Comp | % | Yds | Yd/Att | TD | Int− | % | RK |
|---|---|---|---|---|---|---|---|---|---|
| Griese | 263 | 145 | 55 | 2089 | 7.9 | 19 | 9− | 3 | 1 |
| Mira | 30 | 11 | 37 | 158 | 5.3 | 1 | 1− | 3 | |

| PUNTING | No | Avg |
|---|---|---|
| Seiple | 52 | 40.1 |

| KICKING | XP | Att | % | FG | Att | % |
|---|---|---|---|---|---|---|
| Yepremian | 33 | 33 | 100 | 28 | 40 | 70 |

## BALTIMORE COLTS

### RUSHING

| Last Name | No. | Yds | Avg | TD |
|---|---|---|---|---|
| Bulaich | 152 | 741 | 4.9 | 8 |
| Matte | 173 | 607 | 3.5 | 8 |
| Nottingham | 95 | 388 | 4.1 | 5 |
| McCauley | 58 | 246 | 4.2 | 2 |
| Hinton | 4 | 56 | 14.0 | 0 |
| Perkins | 5 | 35 | 7.0 | 0 |
| Richardson | 2 | 27 | 13.5 | 0 |
| Mackey | 3 | 18 | 6.0 | 0 |
| Morrall | 6 | 13 | 2.2 | 0 |
| Mitchell | 2 | 9 | 4.5 | 0 |
| Unitas | 9 | 5 | 0.6 | 0 |
| Pittman | 2 | 3 | 1.5 | 0 |
| Nowatzke | 1 | 1 | 1.0 | 0 |

### RECEIVING

| Last Name | No. | Yds | Avg | TD |
|---|---|---|---|---|
| Mitchell | 33 | 402 | 12 | 0 |
| Matte | 29 | 239 | 8 | 0 |
| Hinton | 25 | 436 | 17 | 2 |
| Bulaich | 25 | 229 | 9 | 2 |
| Perkins | 24 | 424 | 18 | 4 |
| Nottingham | 15 | 88 | 6 | 0 |
| Mackey | 11 | 143 | 13 | 0 |
| Richardson | 10 | 173 | 17 | 2 |
| McCauley | 3 | 6 | 2 | 0 |
| Havrilak | 1 | 12 | 12 | 0 |

### PUNT RETURNS

| Last Name | No. | Yds | Avg | TD |
|---|---|---|---|---|
| Volk | 22 | 118 | 5 | 0 |
| Dunlap | 8 | 112 | 14 | 0 |
| Kern | 3 | 19 | 6 | 0 |
| T. Curtis | 7 | 15 | 2 | 0 |
| Logan | 1 | 12 | 12 | 0 |

### KICKOFF RETURNS

| Last Name | No. | Yds | Avg | TD |
|---|---|---|---|---|
| Pittman | 14 | 330 | 24 | 0 |
| McCauley | 8 | 194 | 24 | 0 |
| Duncan | 3 | 102 | 34 | 0 |
| Dunlap | 1 | 28 | 28 | 0 |
| Logan | 1 | 16 | 16 | 0 |
| Stukes | 1 | 8 | 8 | 0 |
| Nowatzke | 1 | 1 | 1 | 0 |
| T. Curtis | 1 | 0 | 0 | 0 |
| Matte | 1 | 0 | 0 | 0 |
| Mitchell | 1 | 0 | 0 | 0 |

### PASSING – PUNTING – KICKING

| PASSING | Att | Comp | % | Yds | Yd/Att | TD | Int− | % | RK |
|---|---|---|---|---|---|---|---|---|---|
| Unitas | 176 | 92 | 52 | 942 | 5.4 | 3 | 9− | 5 | 10 |
| Morrall | 167 | 84 | 50 | 1210 | 7.3 | 7 | 12− | 7 | 9 |
| Matte | 1 | 0 | 0 | 0 | 0.0 | 0 | 0− | 0 | |

| PUNTING | No | Avg |
|---|---|---|
| Lee | 62 | 41.0 |

| KICKING | XP | Att | % | FG | Att | % |
|---|---|---|---|---|---|---|
| O'Brien | 35 | 36 | 97 | 20 | 29 | 69 |

## NEW ENGLAND PATRIOTS

### RUSHING

| Last Name | No. | Yds | Avg | TD |
|---|---|---|---|---|
| Garrett | 181 | 784 | 4.3 | 1 |
| Nance | 129 | 463 | 3.6 | 5 |
| Plunkett | 45 | 210 | 4.7 | 0 |
| Gladieux | 37 | 175 | 4.7 | 0 |
| Maitland | 13 | 25 | 1.9 | 1 |
| Crabtree | 3 | 12 | 4.0 | 0 |
| Lawson | 8 | 8 | 1.0 | 0 |
| Bryant | 4 | 1 | 0.3 | 0 |
| Rucker | 1 | 14 | 14.0 | 0 |
| Neville | 0 | −8 | 0.0 | 0 |

### RECEIVING

| Last Name | No. | Yds | Avg | TD |
|---|---|---|---|---|
| Vataha | 51 | 872 | 17 | 9 |
| Crabtree | 23 | 222 | 10 | 3 |
| Garrett | 22 | 265 | 12 | 1 |
| Nance | 18 | 95 | 5 | 0 |
| Sellers | 14 | 222 | 16 | 3 |
| Bryant | 14 | 212 | 15 | 1 |
| Beer | 12 | 191 | 16 | 3 |
| Moss | 9 | 124 | 14 | 1 |
| Gladieux | 6 | 60 | 10 | 0 |
| Rucker | 4 | 52 | 13 | 1 |
| Sykes | 1 | 15 | 15 | 0 |
| Maitland | 1 | 6 | 6 | 0 |

### PUNT RETURNS

| Last Name | No. | Yds | Avg | TD |
|---|---|---|---|---|
| Garrett | 8 | 124 | 16 | 0 |
| Gardin | 6 | 89 | 15 | 0 |
| Bryant | 10 | 24 | 2 | 0 |
| Harris | 5 | 19 | 4 | 0 |
| Gladieux | 4 | 0 | 0 | 0 |

### KICKOFF RETURNS

| Last Name | No. | Yds | Avg | TD |
|---|---|---|---|---|
| Garrett | 24 | 538 | 22 | 0 |
| Gardin | 14 | 321 | 23 | 0 |
| Bryant | 10 | 252 | 25 | 0 |
| Gladieux | 6 | 85 | 14 | 0 |
| Lawson | 2 | 47 | 24 | 0 |
| Rucker | 2 | 45 | 23 | 0 |
| Maitland | 2 | 40 | 20 | 0 |
| Mallory | 1 | 19 | 19 | 0 |
| Hagen | 1 | 7 | 7 | 0 |
| Janik | 1 | 0 | 0 | 0 |
| Webb | 1 | 0 | 0 | 0 |

### PASSING – PUNTING – KICKING

| PASSING | Att | Comp | % | Yds | Yd/Att | TD | Int− | % | RK |
|---|---|---|---|---|---|---|---|---|---|
| Plunkett | 328 | 158 | 48 | 2158 | 6.6 | 19 | 16− | 5 | 5 |
| Gladieux | 2 | 1 | 50 | 48 | 24.0 | 0 | 0− | 0 | |

| PUNTING | No | Avg |
|---|---|---|
| Janik | 87 | 37.3 |

| KICKING | XP | Att | % | FG | Att | % |
|---|---|---|---|---|---|---|
| Gogolak | 28 | 28 | 100 | 12 | 21 | 57 |

## NEW YORK JETS

### RUSHING

| Last Name | No. | Yds | Avg | TD |
|---|---|---|---|---|
| Riggins | 180 | 769 | 4.3 | 1 |
| Boozer | 188 | 618 | 3.3 | 5 |
| Davis | 18 | 154 | 8.6 | 1 |
| Nock | 48 | 137 | 2.9 | 3 |
| McClain | 12 | 108 | 9.0 | 2 |
| Harkey | 20 | 62 | 3.1 | 0 |
| Woodall | 13 | 26 | 2.0 | 0 |
| Caster | 2 | 10 | 5.0 | 0 |
| Maynard | 1 | 2 | 2.0 | 0 |
| Namath | 3 | −1 | −0.3 | 0 |
| Lammons | 0 | 3 | 0.0 | 0 |

### RECEIVING

| Last Name | No. | Yds | Avg | TD |
|---|---|---|---|---|
| Riggins | 36 | 231 | 6 | 2 |
| Caster | 26 | 454 | 17 | 6 |
| Maynard | 21 | 408 | 19 | 2 |
| Boozer | 11 | 120 | 11 | 1 |
| Lammons | 8 | 149 | 19 | 1 |
| Nock | 6 | 44 | 7 | 2 |
| Bell | 5 | 110 | 22 | 1 |
| Harkey | 5 | 28 | 6 | 0 |
| Arthur | 1 | 12 | 12 | 0 |

### PUNT RETURNS

| Last Name | No. | Yds | Avg | TD |
|---|---|---|---|---|
| Farasopoulos | 19 | 155 | 8 | 0 |
| Studdard | 4 | 3 | 1 | 0 |
| Hicks | 1 | 0 | 0 | 0 |
| Bell | 1 | −3 | −3 | 0 |

### KICKOFF RETURNS

| Last Name | No. | Yds | Avg | TD |
|---|---|---|---|---|
| Farasopoulos | 25 | 545 | 22 | 0 |
| Studdard | 15 | 329 | 22 | 0 |
| Wise | 8 | 210 | 26 | 0 |
| Nock | 5 | 71 | 14 | 0 |
| McClain | 1 | 11 | 11 | 0 |
| Harkey | 1 | 2 | 2 | 0 |

### PASSING – PUNTING – KICKING

| PASSING | Att | Comp | % | Yds | Yd/Att | TD | Int− | % | RK |
|---|---|---|---|---|---|---|---|---|---|
| Davis | 121 | 49 | 40 | 624 | 5.2 | 10 | 8− | 7 | |
| Woodall | 97 | 42 | 43 | 395 | 4.1 | 0 | 2− | 2 | |
| Namath | 59 | 28 | 47 | 537 | 9.1 | 5 | 6− | 10 | |
| O'Neal | 1 | 0 | 0 | 0 | 0.0 | 0 | 0− | 0 | |

| PUNTING | No | Avg |
|---|---|---|
| O'Neal | 78 | 38.8 |

| KICKING | XP | Att | % | FG | Att | % |
|---|---|---|---|---|---|---|
| Howfield | 25 | 26 | 96 | 8 | 19 | 42 |
| Baker | 1 | 1 | 100 | 0 | 0 | 0 |

## BUFFALO BILLS

### RUSHING

| Last Name | No. | Yds | Avg | TD |
|---|---|---|---|---|
| Simpson | 183 | 742 | 4.1 | 5 |
| Patrick | 79 | 332 | 4.2 | 1 |
| Braxton | 21 | 84 | 4.0 | 0 |
| Shaw | 14 | 82 | 5.9 | 0 |
| G. Jones | 16 | 53 | 3.3 | 0 |
| Harris | 6 | 42 | 7.0 | 0 |
| J. D. Hill | 1 | 2 | 2.0 | 0 |

### RECEIVING

| Last Name | No. | Yds | Avg | TD |
|---|---|---|---|---|
| Briscoe | 44 | 603 | 14 | 5 |
| Patrick | 36 | 327 | 9 | 0 |
| Moses | 23 | 470 | 20 | 2 |
| Simpson | 21 | 162 | 8 | 0 |
| Braxton | 18 | 141 | 8 | 0 |
| G. Jones | 16 | 113 | 7 | 1 |
| White | 13 | 130 | 10 | 0 |
| J. D. Hill | 11 | 216 | 20 | 2 |
| Koy | 10 | 133 | 13 | 1 |
| B. Chandler | 5 | 60 | 12 | 0 |
| I. Hill | 5 | 55 | 11 | 1 |

### PUNT RETURNS

| Last Name | No. | Yds | Avg | TD |
|---|---|---|---|---|
| Wyatt | 23 | 188 | 8 | 1 |
| I. Hill | 14 | 133 | 10 | 1 |
| Beamer | 7 | 22 | 3 | 0 |

### KICKOFF RETURNS

| Last Name | No. | Yds | Avg | TD |
|---|---|---|---|---|
| Wyatt | 30 | 762 | 25 | 0 |
| Beamer | 20 | 394 | 20 | 0 |
| I. Hill | 12 | 280 | 23 | 0 |
| Simpson | 4 | 107 | 27 | 0 |
| Braxton | 5 | 90 | 18 | 0 |
| G. Jones | 1 | 24 | 24 | 0 |
| Kindig | 2 | 16 | 8 | 0 |

### PASSING – PUNTING – KICKING

| PASSING | Att | Comp | % | Yds | Yd/Att | TD | Int− | % | RK |
|---|---|---|---|---|---|---|---|---|---|
| Shaw | 291 | 149 | 51 | 1813 | 6.2 | 11 | 26− | 9 | 11 |
| Harris | 103 | 51 | 50 | 512 | 5.0 | 1 | 6− | 6 | |
| Braxton | 3 | 1 | 33 | 49 | 16.3 | 0 | 0− | 0 | |
| Briscoe | 2 | 1 | 50 | 36 | 18.0 | 0 | 0− | 0 | |
| Simpson | 2 | 0 | 0 | 0 | 0.0 | 0 | 0− | 0 | |

| PUNTING | No | Avg |
|---|---|---|
| S. Jones | 72 | 41.2 |
| Chapple | 3 | 33.7 |

| KICKING | XP | Att | % | FG | Att | % |
|---|---|---|---|---|---|---|
| Leypoldt | 12 | 12 | 100 | 9 | 15 | 60 |
| Guthrie | 8 | 9 | 89 | 3 | 10 | 30 |

## CLEVELAND BROWNS 9-5-0  Nick Skorich

### Scores of Each Game

| | | |
|---|---|---|
| 31 | HOUSTON | 0 |
| 14 | Baltimore | 13 |
| 20 | OAKLAND | 34 |
| 27 | PITTSBURG | 17 |
| 27 | Cincinnati | 24 |
| 0 | DENVER | 27 |
| 14 | ATLANTA | 31 |
| 9 | Pittsburgh | 26 |
| 7 | Kansas City | 13 |
| 27 | NEW ENGLAND | 7 |
| 37 | Houston | 24 |
| 31 | CINCINNATI | 27 |
| 21 | New Orleans | 17 |
| 20 | Washington | 13 |

| Use Name | Pos. | Hgt | Wgt | Age | Int | Pts |
|---|---|---|---|---|---|---|
| Doug Dieken | OT | 6'5" | 237 | 22 | | 2 |
| Mitch Johnson | OT | 6'4" | 250 | 29 | | |
| Bob McKay | OT | 6'5" | 260 | 23 | | |
| Dick Schrafrath | OT | 6'3" | 258 | 35 | | |
| Jim Copeland | OG | 6'2" | 245 | 26 | | |
| John Demerie | OG | 6'3" | 255 | 26 | | |
| Gene Hickerson | OG | 6'3" | 248 | 36 | | |
| Mike Sikich | OG | 6'2" | 243 | 22 | | |
| Fred Hoaglin | C | 6'4" | 250 | 27 | | |
| Jack Gregory | DE | 6'6" | 250 | 26 | | |
| Joe Jones | DE | 6'6" | 246 | 23 | | |
| Bob Briggs | DT-DE | 6'4" | 276 | 26 | | |
| Walter Johnson | DT | 6'3" | 275 | 28 | | 6 |
| Jerry Sherk | DT | 6'4" | 253 | 23 | 2 | |
| Ron Snidow | DT | 6'4" | 250 | 29 | | |

| Use Name | Pos. | Hgt | Wgt | Age | Int | Pts |
|---|---|---|---|---|---|---|
| Billy Andrews | LB | 6' | 225 | 26 | 3 | |
| John Garlington | LB | 6'1" | 225 | 25 | 1 | |
| Charlie Hall | LB | 6'3" | 215 | 22 | | |
| Jim Houston | LB | 6'2" | 240 | 34 | | |
| Rick Kingrea | LB | 6'1" | 233 | 22 | | |
| Dale Lindsey | LB | 6'3" | 225 | 28 | 2 | |
| Erich Barnes | DB | 6'2" | 212 | 36 | | |
| Ben Davis | DB | 5'11" | 186 | 25 | 2 | |
| Mike Howell | DB | 6'1" | 190 | 28 | 2 | |
| Ernie Kellerman | DB | 6' | 185 | 27 | 3 | |
| Clarence Scott | DB | 6' | 175 | 22 | 4 | |
| Freddie Summers | DB | 6'1" | 180 | 24 | | |
| Walt Sumner | DB | 6'1" | 180 | 24 | 5 | |

| Use Name | Pos. | Hgt | Wgt | Age | Int | Pts |
|---|---|---|---|---|---|---|
| Bill Nelson | QB | 6' | 195 | 30 | | |
| Mike Phipps | QB | 6'2" | 207 | 23 | | |
| Ken Brown | HB | 5'10" | 205 | 25 | | |
| Leroy Kelly | HB | 6' | 200 | 29 | | 72 |
| Reece Morrison | HB | 6' | 205 | 25 | | |
| Bo Scott | FB | 6'3" | 210 | 28 | | 60 |
| Bo Cornell | FB | 6'1" | 217 | 22 | | |
| Stan Brown | WR | 5'9" | 184 | 22 | | |
| Gary Collins | WR | 6'4" | 210 | 30 | | 18 |
| Fair Hooker | WR | 6'1" | 193 | 24 | | 6 |
| Dave Jones | WR | 6'2" | 205 | 24 | | |
| Frank Pitts | WR | 6'2" | 200 | 27 | | 24 |
| Chip Glass | TE | 6'4" | 236 | 24 | | 6 |
| Milt Morin | TE | 6'4" | 240 | 29 | | 12 |
| Don Cockroft | K | 6'1" | 190 | 26 | | 79 |

## PITTSBURGH STEELERS 6-8-0  Chuck Noll

### Scores of Each Game

| | | |
|---|---|---|
| 15 | Chicago | 17 |
| 21 | CINCINNATI | 10 |
| 21 | SAN DIEGO | 17 |
| 17 | Cleveland | 27 |
| 16 | Kansas City | 38 |
| 23 | HOUSTON | 16 |
| 21 | Baltimore | 34 |
| 26 | CLEVELAND | 9 |
| 21 | Miami | 24 |
| 17 | N.Y. GIANTS | 13 |
| 10 | DENVER | 22 |
| 3 | Houston | 29 |
| 21 | Cincinnati | 13 |
| 14 | LOS ANGELES | 23 |

| Use Name | Pos. | Hgt | Wgt | Age | Int | Pts |
|---|---|---|---|---|---|---|
| John Brown | OT | 6'2" | 255 | 32 | | |
| Rick Sharp | OT | 6'3" | 265 | 23 | | |
| Jon Kolb | C-OT | 6'2" | 262 | 24 | | |
| Sam Davis | OG | 6'1" | 255 | 27 | | |
| Mel Holmes | OG | 6'3" | 250 | 21 | | |
| Gerry Mullins | OG | 6'3" | 235 | 22 | | |
| Bruce Van Dyke | OG | 6'2" | 255 | 27 | | |
| Jim Clack | C | 6'3" | 250 | 23 | | |
| Ray Mansfield | C | 6'3" | 255 | 30 | | |
| Bobby Maples | C | 6'3" | 245 | 28 | | |
| Bert Askson | DE | 6'3" | 220 | 25 | | |
| L.C. Greenwood | DE | 6'5" | 240 | 24 | | |
| Dwight White | DE | 6'4" | 250 | 22 | | |
| Ben McGee | DT-DE | 6'2" | 260 | 29 | | |
| Joe Greene | DT | 6'4" | 280 | 24 | | |
| Lloyd Voss | DT | 6'4" | 255 | 29 | | |

| Use Name | Pos. | Hgt | Wgt | Age | Int | Pts |
|---|---|---|---|---|---|---|
| Chuck Allen | LB | 6'1" | 227 | 31 | 3 | |
| Henry Davis | LB | 6'3" | 235 | 28 | | |
| Jack Ham | LB | 6'1" | 225 | 22 | 2 | |
| Andy Russell | LB | 6'3" | 225 | 29 | | |
| Brian Stenger | LB | 6'4" | 230 | 24 | | |
| Ralph Anderson | DB | 6'2" | 180 | 22 | 1 | |
| Ocie Austin | DB | 6'3" | 200 | 24 | | |
| Chuck Beatty | DB | 6'2" | 200 | 25 | | |
| Mel Blount | DB | 6'3" | 205 | 23 | 2 | |
| Lee Calland | DB | 6' | 190 | 30 | 2 | |
| Glen Edwards | DB | 6' | 185 | 24 | 1 | |
| John Rowser | DB | 6'1" | 185 | 27 | 4 | 6 |
| Mike Wagner | DB | 6'1" | 196 | 22 | 2 | |

Clarence Washington—Injury

| Use Name | Pos. | Hgt | Wgt | Age | Int | Pts |
|---|---|---|---|---|---|---|
| Terry Bradshaw | QB | 6'3" | 218 | 22 | | 30 |
| Terry Hanratty | QB | 6'1" | 200 | 23 | | 6 |
| Bob Leahy | QB | 6'2" | 205 | 25 | | |
| Rocky Bleier | HB | 5'11" | 205 | 25 | | |
| Jim Brumfield | HB | 6'1" | 195 | 24 | | |
| Preston Pearson | HB | 6'1" | 190 | 26 | | 18 |
| John Fuqua | FB-HB | 5'11" | 200 | 24 | | 30 |
| Warren Bankston | FB | 6'4" | 230 | 24 | | |
| Frank Lewis | WR | 6'1" | 196 | 24 | | |
| Ron Shanklin | WR | 6'1" | 180 | 24 | | 36 |
| Dave Smith | WR | 6'2" | 205 | 24 | | 30 |
| Jon Staggers | WR | 5'10" | 186 | 22 | | 6 |
| Al Young | WR | 6'1" | 195 | 22 | | |
| Bob Adams | TE | 6'2" | 225 | 25 | | |
| Larry Brown | TE | 6'4" | 225 | 22 | | 6 |
| Dennis Hughes | TE | 6'1" | 220 | 23 | | |
| Roy Gerela | K | 5'10" | 185 | 23 | | 78 |
| Bobby Walden | K | 6' | 190 | 33 | | |

## HOUSTON OILERS 4-9-1  Ed Hughes

### Scores of Each Game

| | | |
|---|---|---|
| 0 | Cleveland | 31 |
| 16 | KANSAS CITY | 20 |
| 13 | NEW ORLEANS | 13 |
| 13 | Washington | 22 |
| 7 | DETROIT | 31 |
| 16 | Pittsburgh | 23 |
| 10 | CINCINNATI | 6 |
| 20 | New England | 28 |
| 21 | Oakland | 41 |
| 13 | Cincinnati | 28 |
| 24 | CLEVELAND | 37 |
| 29 | PITTSBURGH | 3 |
| 20 | Buffalo | 14 |
| 49 | SAN DIEGO | 33 |

| Use Name | Pos. | Hgt | Wgt | Age | Int | Pts |
|---|---|---|---|---|---|---|
| Tom Funchess | OT | 6'5" | 260 | 26 | | |
| Sam Walton | OT | 6'5" | 270 | 28 | | |
| Gene Ferguson | OT | 6'7" | 300 | 23 | | |
| Walt Suggs | C-OT | 6'5" | 250 | 32 | | |
| Elbert Drungo | OG | 6'5" | 250 | 28 | | |
| Tom Regner | OG | 6'1" | 255 | 27 | | |
| Ron Saul | OG | 6'2" | 255 | 23 | | |
| Bob Young | OG | 6'2" | 256 | 28 | | |
| Jerry Sturm | C | 6'3" | 265 | 34 | | |
| Allen Aldridge | DE | 6'6" | 260 | 26 | | |
| Elvin Bethea | DE | 6'3" | 262 | 25 | | |
| Pat Holmes | DE | 6'6" | 250 | 31 | | |
| Scott Lewis | DE | 6'6" | 260 | 21 | | |
| Ron Billingsley | DT | 6'8" | 290 | 26 | | |
| Lee Brooks | DT | 6'5" | 266 | 23 | 1 | |
| Tom Domres (to DEN) | DT | 6'3" | 260 | 24 | | |
| Mike Tilleman | DT | 6'5" | 280 | 27 | | |

| Use Name | Pos. | Hgt | Wgt | Age | Int | Pts |
|---|---|---|---|---|---|---|
| Garland Boyette | LB | 6'1" | 235 | 31 | | 6 |
| Phil Croyle | LB | 6'3" | 220 | 23 | | |
| Dave Olerich | LB | 6'1" | 225 | 26 | | |
| Ron Pritchard | LB | 6'1" | 235 | 24 | | |
| George Webster | LB | 6'4" | 223 | 25 | | |
| Willie Alexander | DB | 6'2" | 195 | 21 | 4 | |
| Bob Atkins | DB | 6'3" | 210 | 25 | 1 | 6 |
| John Charles | DB | 6'1" | 200 | 27 | 5 | |
| Ken Houston | DB | 6'3" | 196 | 26 | 9 | 30 |
| Leroy Howard | DB | 5'11" | 175 | 22 | | |
| Benny Johnson | DB | 5'11" | 178 | 23 | | |
| Zeke Moore | DB | 6'2" | 196 | 27 | 3 | |

Roy Hopkins – Injury

| Use Name | Pos. | Hgt | Wgt | Age | Int | Pts |
|---|---|---|---|---|---|---|
| Lynn Dickey | QB | 6'4" | 218 | 21 | | |
| Charley Johnson | QB | 6' | 190 | 34 | | |
| Dan Pastorini | QB | 6'3" | 220 | 22 | | 18 |
| Woody Campbell | HB | 5'11" | 208 | 26 | | 6 |
| Andy Hopkins | HB | 5'10" | 187 | 22 | | |
| Dickie Post (from DEN) | HB | 5'9" | 190 | 25 | | 6 |
| Mike Richardson | HB | 5'11" | 196 | 24 | | |
| Ward Walsh | HB | 6' | 215 | 22 | | 6 |
| Robert Holmes (from KC) | FB | 5'9" | 220 | 25 | | 24 |
| Leroy Sledge | FB | 6'2" | 230 | 25 | | 6 |
| Joe Dawkins (to DEN) | HB-FB | 5'11" | 222 | 23 | | 12 |
| Jim Beirne | WR | 6'2" | 196 | 24 | | 6 |
| Ken Burrough | WR | 6'4" | 210 | 23 | | 6 |
| Linzy Cole | WR | 5'11" | 170 | 24 | | |
| Mac Haik | WR | 6'1" | 195 | 25 | | |
| Charlie Joiner | WR | 5'11" | 188 | 23 | | 42 |
| Alvin Reed | TE | 6'5" | 230 | 27 | | 6 |
| Floyd Rice | TE | 6'3" | 220 | 22 | | |
| Braden Beck | K | 6'2" | 200 | 27 | | 4 |
| Mark Moseley | K | 5'11" | 182 | 23 | | 73 |

## CINCINNATI BENGALS 4-10-0  Paul Brown

### Scores of Each Game

| | | |
|---|---|---|
| 37 | PHILADELPHIA | 14 |
| 10 | Pittsburgh | 21 |
| 17 | Green Bay | 20 |
| 13 | MIAMI | 23 |
| 24 | CLEVELAND | 27 |
| 27 | Oakland | 31 |
| 6 | Houston | 10 |
| 6 | ATLANTA | 9 |
| 24 | Denver | 10 |
| 28 | HOUSTON | 13 |
| 31 | SAN DIEGO | 0 |
| 27 | Cleveland | 31 |
| 13 | PITTSBURGH | 21 |
| 21 | N.Y. JETS | 35 |

| Use Name | Pos. | Hgt | Wgt | Age | Int | Pts |
|---|---|---|---|---|---|---|
| Howard Fest | OT | 6'6" | 268 | 25 | | |
| Vern Holland | OT | 6'5" | 270 | 23 | | |
| Rufus Mayes | OT | 6'5" | 255 | 23 | | |
| Ernie Wright | OT | 6'4" | 270 | 31 | | |
| Guy Dennis | OG | 6'2" | 255 | 24 | | |
| Steve Lawson | OG | 6'3" | 265 | 22 | | |
| Pat Matson | OG | 6'1" | 245 | 27 | | |
| Bob Johnson | C | 6'5" | 265 | 25 | | |
| Royce Berry | DE | 6'4" | 248 | 25 | | |
| Ron Carpenter | DE | 6'5" | 260 | 23 | | |
| Ken Dyer | DE | 6'5" | 262 | 24 | | |
| Nick Roman | DE | 6'3" | 230 | 23 | | |
| Steve Chomyszak | DT | 6'5" | 265 | 26 | | |
| Willie Jones | DT | 6'2" | 260 | 29 | | |
| Mike Reid | DT | 6'3" | 258 | 24 | | |

| Use Name | Pos. | Hgt | Wgt | Age | Int | Pts |
|---|---|---|---|---|---|---|
| Doug Adams | LB | 6' | 223 | 22 | | |
| Ken Avery | LB | 6'1" | 225 | 27 | | |
| Al Beauchamp | LB | 6'2" | 236 | 27 | 6 | 6 |
| Bill Bergey | LB | 6'2" | 240 | 26 | 1 | |
| Larry Ely | LB | 6'1" | 230 | 23 | | |
| Bill Peterson | LB | 6'3" | 230 | 26 | 1 | |
| Al Coleman | DB | 6'1" | 183 | 24 | 1 | |
| Neal Craig | DB | 6'1" | 185 | 23 | 1 | |
| Sandy Durko | DB | 6'3" | 185 | 23 | 4 | |
| Ken Dyer | DB | 6'3" | 190 | 25 | | |
| Jim Harris | DB | 5'11" | 173 | 25 | | |
| Lemar Parrish | DB | 5'11" | 185 | 23 | 7 | 12 |
| Ken Riley | DB | 6' | 184 | 24 | 5 | |
| Fletcher Smith | DB | 6'2" | 180 | 27 | 1 | |

Greg Cook—Shoulder Injury

| Use Name | Pos. | Hgt | Wgt | Age | Int | Pts |
|---|---|---|---|---|---|---|
| Ken Anderson | QB | 6'1" | 202 | 22 | | 6 |
| Virgil Carter | QB | 6'1" | 200 | 25 | 1 | |
| Dave Lewis | QB | 6'2" | 210 | 25 | | |
| Essex Johnson | HB | 5'9" | 195 | 24 | | 36 |
| Paul Robinson | HB | 6' | 200 | 26 | | 6 |
| Jess Phillips | HB | 6'1" | 210 | 24 | | 6 |
| Doug Dressler | FB | 6'3" | 220 | 23 | | |
| Ron Lamb | FB | 6'2" | 230 | 27 | | |
| Fred Willis | FB | 6' | 215 | 23 | | 42 |
| Mike Haffner | WR | 6'2" | 205 | 29 | | |
| Ed Marshall | WR | 6'5" | 200 | 23 | | |
| Chip Myers | WR | 6'4" | 200 | 26 | | 6 |
| Speedy Thomas | WR | 6'1" | 178 | 24 | | 12 |
| Bruce Coslet | TE | 6'3" | 230 | 25 | | 24 |
| Mike Kelley | TE | 6'4" | 215 | 23 | | |
| Bob Trumpy | TE | 6'6" | 225 | 26 | | 18 |
| Horst Muhlmann | K | 6'1" | 210 | 31 | | 91 |

## CLEVELAND BROWNS

### RUSHING
| Last Name | No. | Yds | Avg | TD |
|---|---|---|---|---|
| Kelly | 234 | 865 | 3.7 | 10 |
| B. Scott | 179 | 606 | 3.4 | 9 |
| K. Brown | 11 | 47 | 4.3 | 0 |
| Phipps | 6 | 35 | 5.8 | 0 |
| Cornell | 11 | 12 | 1.1 | 0 |
| Cockroft | 1 | 12 | 12.0 | 0 |
| Morin | 1 | 1 | 1.0 | 0 |
| Morrison | 5 | −2 | −0.4 | 0 |
| Nelsen | 13 | −18 | −1.4 | 0 |

### RECEIVING
| Last Name | No. | Yds | Avg | TD |
|---|---|---|---|---|
| Hooker | 45 | 649 | 14 | 1 |
| Morin | 40 | 581 | 15 | 2 |
| B. Scott | 30 | 233 | 8 | 1 |
| Pitts | 27 | 487 | 18 | 4 |
| Kelly | 25 | 252 | 10 | 2 |
| Collins | 15 | 231 | 15 | 3 |
| D. Jones | 4 | 66 | 17 | 0 |
| Cornell | 1 | 18 | 18 | 0 |
| Glass | 1 | 4 | 4 | 1 |

### PUNT RETURNS
| Last Name | No. | Yds | Avg | TD |
|---|---|---|---|---|
| Kelly | 30 | 292 | 10 | 0 |
| D. Jones | 9 | 63 | 7 | 0 |
| Kellerman | 1 | 4 | 4 | 0 |

### KICKOFF RETURNS
| Last Name | No. | Yds | Avg | TD |
|---|---|---|---|---|
| K. Brown | 15 | 330 | 22 | 0 |
| Morrison | 9 | 267 | 30 | 0 |
| Pitts | 9 | 238 | 26 | 0 |
| S. Brown | 7 | 157 | 22 | 0 |
| Houston | 1 | 21 | 21 | 0 |
| Cornell | 1 | 19 | 19 | 0 |
| Dieken | 1 | 16 | 16 | 0 |
| Kelly | 1 | 11 | 11 | 0 |
| Kellerman | 1 | 5 | 5 | 0 |
| Glass | 1 | 1 | 1 | 0 |

### PASSING – PUNTING – KICKING
| PASSING | Att | Comp | % | Yds | Yd/Att | TD | Int− | % | RK |
|---|---|---|---|---|---|---|---|---|---|
| Nelsen | 325 | 174 | 54 | 2319 | 7.1 | 13 | 23− | 7 | 5 |
| Phipps | 47 | 13 | 28 | 179 | 3.8 | 1 | 4 | 9 | |
| Kelly | 4 | 1 | 25 | 23 | 5.8 | 0 | 0− | 0 | |

| PUNTING | No | Avg |
|---|---|---|
| Cockroft | 62 | 40.5 |
| Collins | 5 | 32.4 |

| KICKING | XP | Att | % | FG | Att | % |
|---|---|---|---|---|---|---|
| Cockroft | 34 | 34 | 100 | 15 | 28 | 54 |

## PITTSBURGH STEELERS

### RUSHING
| Last Name | No. | Yds | Avg | TD |
|---|---|---|---|---|
| Fuqua | 155 | 625 | 4.0 | 4 |
| Pearson | 131 | 605 | 4.6 | 0 |
| Bankston | 70 | 274 | 3.9 | 0 |
| Bradshaw | 53 | 247 | 4.7 | 5 |
| Walden | 1 | 14 | 14.0 | 0 |
| Staggers | 1 | 5 | 5.0 | 0 |
| Hanratty | 1 | 3 | 3.0 | 1 |
| Shanklin | 2 | 1 | 0.5 | 0 |
| Leahy | 1 | −6 | −6.0 | 0 |
| Smith | 1 | −10 | −10.0 | 0 |

### RECEIVING
| Last Name | No. | Yds | Avg | TD |
|---|---|---|---|---|
| Shanklin | 49 | 652 | 13 | 6 |
| Fuqua | 49 | 427 | 9 | 1 |
| Smith | 47 | 663 | 14 | 5 |
| Pearson | 20 | 246 | 12 | 2 |
| Adams | 20 | 160 | 8 | 0 |
| Bankston | 17 | 148 | 9 | 0 |
| Staggers | 8 | 103 | 13 | 0 |
| Lewis | 3 | 44 | 15 | 0 |
| L. Brown | 1 | 3 | 3 | 1 |

### PUNT RETURNS
| Last Name | No. | Yds | Avg | TD |
|---|---|---|---|---|
| Staggers | 31 | 262 | 8 | 1 |
| Wagner | 2 | 2 | 1 | 0 |
| Edwards | 1 | 0 | 0 | 0 |
| Fuqua | 1 | 0 | 0 | 0 |

### KICKOFF RETURNS
| Last Name | No. | Yds | Avg | TD |
|---|---|---|---|---|
| Brumfield | 12 | 271 | 23 | 0 |
| Staggers | 10 | 261 | 26 | 0 |
| Pearson | 7 | 205 | 29 | 0 |
| Edwards | 9 | 198 | 22 | 0 |
| Bankston | 5 | 76 | 15 | 0 |
| Blount | 4 | 76 | 19 | 0 |
| Bleier | 1 | 21 | 21 | 0 |
| Clack | 1 | 12 | 12 | 0 |

### PASSING – PUNTING – KICKING
| PASSING | Att | Comp | % | Yds | Yd/Att | TD | Int− | % | RK |
|---|---|---|---|---|---|---|---|---|---|
| Bradshaw | 373 | 203 | 54 | 2259 | 6.1 | 13 | 22− | 6 | 8 |
| Hanratty | 29 | 7 | 24 | 159 | 5.5 | 2 | 3− | 10 | |
| Leahy | 11 | 3 | 27 | 18 | 1.6 | 0 | 1− | 9 | |
| Walden | 1 | 1 | 100 | 10 | 10.0 | 0 | 0− | 0 | |

| PUNTING | No | Avg |
|---|---|---|
| Walden | 79 | 43.7 |

| KICKING | XP | Att | % | FG | Att | % |
|---|---|---|---|---|---|---|
| Gerela | 27 | 27 | 100 | 17 | 27 | 63 |

## HOUSTON OILERS

### RUSHING
| Last Name | No. | Yds | Avg | TD |
|---|---|---|---|---|
| R. Holmes | 112 | 323 | 2.9 | 4 |
| Campbell | 96 | 259 | 2.7 | 1 |
| Pastorini | 26 | 140 | 5.4 | 3 |
| Dawkins | 42 | 135 | 3.2 | 2 |
| Walsh | 38 | 129 | 3.4 | 0 |
| Post | 40 | 86 | 2.2 | 0 |
| Sledge | 24 | 74 | 3.1 | 0 |
| Richardson | 17 | 33 | 1.9 | 0 |
| Dickey | 1 | 4 | 4.0 | 0 |
| Hopkins | 2 | 2 | 1.0 | 0 |
| C. Johnson | 2 | 0 | 0.0 | 0 |

### RECEIVING
| Last Name | No. | Yds | Avg | TD |
|---|---|---|---|---|
| Beirne | 38 | 550 | 14 | 1 |
| Joiner | 31 | 681 | 22 | 7 |
| Reed | 25 | 408 | 16 | 1 |
| Burrough | 25 | 370 | 15 | 1 |
| Campbell | 20 | 179 | 9 | 0 |
| R. Holmes | 19 | 154 | 8 | 0 |
| Post | 9 | 112 | 12 | 1 |
| Dawkins | 9 | 53 | 6 | 0 |
| Walsh | 6 | 36 | 6 | 1 |
| Sledge | 6 | 32 | 5 | 1 |
| Richardson | 4 | 17 | 4 | 0 |

### PUNT RETURNS
| Last Name | No. | Yds | Avg | TD |
|---|---|---|---|---|
| Cole | 14 | 107 | 8 | 0 |
| Houston | 16 | 91 | 6 | 0 |
| Rice | 2 | 0 | 0 | 0 |

### KICKOFF RETURNS
| Last Name | No. | Yds | Avg | TD |
|---|---|---|---|---|
| Cole | 32 | 834 | 26 | 0 |
| R. Holmes | 12 | 300 | 25 | 0 |
| Moore | 10 | 214 | 21 | 0 |
| Burrough | 8 | 157 | 20 | 0 |
| Post | 5 | 116 | 23 | 0 |
| Dawkins | 2 | 34 | 17 | 0 |
| Richardson | 1 | 26 | 26 | 0 |
| Joiner | 1 | 25 | 25 | 0 |
| Walsh | 1 | 24 | 24 | 0 |
| Rice | 1 | 0 | 0 | 0 |

### PASSING – PUNTING – KICKING
| PASSING | Att | Comp | % | Yds | Yd/Att | TD | Int− | % | RK |
|---|---|---|---|---|---|---|---|---|---|
| Pastorini | 270 | 127 | 47 | 1702 | 6.3 | 7 | 21− | 8 | 12 |
| C. Johnson | 94 | 46 | 49 | 592 | 6.3 | 3 | 7− | 7 | |
| Dickey | 57 | 19 | 33 | 315 | 5.5 | 0 | 9− | 16 | |
| Campbell | 2 | 2 | 100 | 34 | 17.0 | 2 | 0− | 0 | |

| PUNTING | No | Avg |
|---|---|---|
| Pastorini | 75 | 40.6 |

| KICKING | XP | Att | % | FG | Att | % |
|---|---|---|---|---|---|---|
| Moseley | 25 | 27 | 93 | 16 | 26 | 62 |
| Beck | 1 | 2 | 50 | 1 | 2 | 50 |

## CINCINNATI BENGALS

### RUSHING
| Last Name | No. | Yds | Avg | TD |
|---|---|---|---|---|
| Willis | 135 | 590 | 4.4 | 7 |
| E. Johnson | 85 | 522 | 6.1 | 4 |
| Phillips | 94 | 420 | 4.5 | 0 |
| Robinson | 49 | 213 | 4.3 | 1 |
| Dressler | 54 | 204 | 3.8 | 1 |
| Anderson | 22 | 125 | 5.7 | 1 |
| Carter | 8 | 42 | 5.3 | 0 |
| Lamb | 5 | 13 | 2.6 | 0 |
| Durko | 1 | 7 | 7.0 | 0 |
| Lewis | 6 | 6 | 1.0 | 0 |
| Thomas | 2 | −1 | −0.5 | 0 |

### RECEIVING
| Last Name | No. | Yds | Avg | TD |
|---|---|---|---|---|
| Trumpy | 40 | 531 | 13 | 3 |
| Myers | 27 | 286 | 11 | 1 |
| Willis | 24 | 223 | 9 | 0 |
| Thomas | 22 | 327 | 15 | 2 |
| Phillips | 22 | 125 | 6 | 1 |
| Coslet | 21 | 356 | 17 | 4 |
| Dressler | 19 | 145 | 8 | 0 |
| E. Johnson | 14 | 258 | 18 | 2 |
| Robinson | 8 | 47 | 6 | 0 |
| Marshall | 2 | 18 | 9 | 0 |
| Kelly | 1 | 9 | 9 | 0 |

### PUNT RETURNS
| Last Name | No. | Yds | Avg | TD |
|---|---|---|---|---|
| Parrish | 12 | 93 | 8 | 0 |
| E. Johnson | 3 | 28 | 9 | 0 |
| Durko | 6 | 14 | 2 | 0 |
| Thomas | 4 | 10 | 3 | 0 |

### KICKOFF RETURNS
| Last Name | No. | Yds | Avg | TD |
|---|---|---|---|---|
| Robinson | 18 | 335 | 19 | 0 |
| Parrish | 13 | 296 | 23 | 0 |
| Willis | 4 | 81 | 20 | 0 |
| Phillips | 2 | 49 | 25 | 0 |
| Lamb | 2 | 42 | 21 | 0 |
| E. Johnson | 2 | 40 | 20 | 0 |
| Dressler | 1 | 20 | 20 | 0 |
| Kelly | 1 | 0 | 0 | 0 |

### PASSING – PUNTING – KICKING
| PASSING | Att | Comp | % | Yds | Yd/Att | TD | Int− | % | RK |
|---|---|---|---|---|---|---|---|---|---|
| Carter | 222 | 138 | 62 | 1624 | 7.3 | 10 | 7− | 3 | 3 |
| Anderson | 131 | 72 | 55 | 777 | 5.9 | 5 | 4− | 3 | |
| Lewis | 10 | 3 | 30 | 18 | 1.8 | 0 | 0− | 0 | |
| Willis | 2 | 1 | 50 | 8 | 4.0 | 0 | 0− | 0 | |

| PUNTING | No | Avg |
|---|---|---|
| Lewis | 72 | 44.8 |
| Dressler | 1 | 34.0 |

| KICKING | XP | Att | % | FG | Att | % |
|---|---|---|---|---|---|---|
| Muhlmann | 31 | 31 | 100 | 20 | 36 | 56 |
| Carter | 1 | 1 | 100 | 0 | 0 | |

## KANSAS CITY CHIEFS 10-3-1 Hank Stram

**Scores of Each Game**

| | | |
|---|---|---|
| 14 | San Diego | 21 |
| 20 | Houston | 16 |
| 16 | Denver | 3 |
| 31 | SAN DIEGO | 10 |
| 38 | PITTSBURGH | 16 |
| 27 | WASHINGTON | 20 |
| 20 | Oakland | 20 |
| 10 | N.Y. Jets | 13 |
| 13 | CLEVELAND | 7 |
| 28 | DENVER | 10 |
| 21 | Detroit | 32 |
| 26 | San Francisco | 17 |
| 16 | OAKLAND | 14 |
| 22 | BUFFALO | 9 |

| Use Name | Pos. | Hgt | Wgt | Age | Int | Pts |
|---|---|---|---|---|---|---|
| Dave Hill | OT | 6'5" | 260 | 30 | | |
| Sid Smith | OT | 6'4" | 260 | 23 | | |
| Jim Tyrer | OT | 6'6" | 270 | 32 | | |
| Ed Budde | OG | 6'5" | 260 | 30 | | |
| George Daney | OG | 6'3" | 240 | 24 | | |
| Mo Moorman | OG | 6'5" | 252 | 27 | | |
| Mike Oriard | C | 6'4" | 223 | 23 | | |
| Jack Rudnay | C | 6'3" | 240 | 23 | | |
| Bruce Bergey | DE | 6'4" | 240 | 24 | | |
| Aaron Brown | DE | 6'5" | 265 | 27 | 1 | 6 |
| Marv Upshaw | DE | 6'3" | 245 | 24 | | |
| Buck Buchanan | DT | 6'7" | 275 | 31 | 1 | |
| Curley Culp | DT | 6'1" | 265 | 25 | | |
| Ed Lothamer | DT | 6'5" | 270 | 28 | | |
| Wilbur Young | DT | 6'6" | 305 | 22 | 1 | |
| Bobby Bell | LB | 6'4" | 228 | 31 | 1 | 6 |
| Willie Lanier | LB | 6'1" | 245 | 26 | 2 | |
| Jim Lynch | LB | 6'1" | 235 | 26 | 1 | |
| Bob Stein | DE-LB | 6'2" | 235 | 23 | 1 | |
| Nate Allen | DB | 5'10" | 170 | 23 | | |
| Caesar Belser | DB | 6' | 212 | 26 | | |
| Dave Hadley | DB | 5'9" | 186 | 22 | 1 | |
| Jim Kearney | DB | 6'2" | 206 | 28 | 3 | |
| Jim Marsalis | DB | 5'11" | 194 | 25 | 3 | |
| Kerry Reardon | DB | 5'11" | 180 | 22 | | |
| Johnny Robinson | DB | 6' | 205 | 32 | 4 | |
| Mike Sensibaugh | DB | 5'11" | 192 | 22 | | |
| Emmitt Thomas | DB | 6'2" | 192 | 28 | 8 | 6 |
| Len Dawson | QB | 6' | 190 | 37 | | |
| John Huarte | QB | 6' | 185 | 27 | | |
| Mike Livingston | QB | 6'3" | 212 | 25 | | |
| Mike Adamle | HB | 5'9" | 197 | 21 | | 6 |
| Warren McVea | HB | 5'10" | 182 | 25 | | 18 |
| Ed Podolak | HB | 6'1" | 202 | 24 | | 54 |
| Glenn Ellison | HB-FB | 6'1" | 215 | 22 | | |
| Wendell Hayes | FB | 6'2" | 220 | 30 | | 12 |
| Jim Otis | WR | 6' | 220 | 23 | | 12 |
| Dennis Homan | WR | 6'1" | 180 | 25 | | |
| Bruce Jankowski | WR | 5'11" | 185 | 22 | | |
| Otis Taylor | WR | 6'2" | 215 | 28 | | 48 |
| Elmo Wright | WR | 6' | 190 | 22 | | 18 |
| Willie Frazier (from HOU) | TE | 6'4" | 250 | 28 | | |
| Morris Stroud | TE | 6'10" | 255 | 25 | | 6 |
| Jan Stenerud | K | 6'2" | 187 | 28 | | 110 |
| Jerrel Wilson | K | 6'4" | 222 | 29 | | |

Clyde Werner—Knee Injury

## OAKLAND RAIDERS 8-4-2 John Madden

**Scores of Each Game**

| | | |
|---|---|---|
| 6 | New England | 20 |
| 34 | San Diego | 0 |
| 34 | Cleveland | 20 |
| 27 | Denver | 16 |
| 34 | PHILADELPHIA | 10 |
| 31 | CINCINNATI | 27 |
| 20 | KANSAS CITY | 20 |
| 21 | New Orleans | 21 |
| 41 | HOUSTON | 21 |
| 34 | San Diego | 33 |
| 14 | BALTIMORE | 37 |
| 13 | Atlanta | 24 |
| 14 | Kansas City | 16 |
| 21 | DENVER | 13 |

| Use Name | Pos. | Hgt | Wgt | Age | Int | Pts |
|---|---|---|---|---|---|---|
| Bob Brown | OT | 6'4" | 290 | 28 | | |
| Ron Mix | OT | 6'4" | 250 | 33 | | |
| Art Shell | OT | 6'5" | 255 | 24 | | |
| Paul Seiler | C-OT | 6'4" | 260 | 25 | | |
| George Buehler | OG | 6'2" | 260 | 24 | | |
| Jim Harvey | OG | 6'5" | 250 | 28 | | |
| Gene Upshaw | OG | 6'5" | 255 | 26 | | |
| Warren Koegel | C | 6'3" | 250 | 21 | | |
| Jim Otto | C | 6'2" | 248 | 33 | | |
| Tony Cline | DE | 6'3" | 230 | 31 | | |
| Ben Davidson | DE | 6'8" | 280 | 31 | | |
| Horace Jones | DE | 6'3" | 240 | 22 | | |
| Harold Rice | DE | 6'2" | 230 | 26 | | |
| Tom Gibson | DT | 6'6" | 290 | 23 | | |
| Tom Keating | DT | 6'3" | 247 | 28 | | |
| Carleton Oats | DT | 6'2" | 260 | 28 | | |
| Art Thomas | DT | 6'5" | 250 | 24 | | |
| Duane Benson | LB | 6'2" | 215 | 26 | | |
| Dan Conners | LB | 6'1" | 230 | 29 | 3 | |
| Gerald Irons | LB | 6'2" | 230 | 24 | | |
| Terry Mendenhall | LB | 6'1" | 210 | 22 | | |
| Gus Otto | LB | 6'2" | 220 | 28 | | |
| Greg Slough | LB | 6'3" | 230 | 23 | | |
| Phil Villapiano | LB | 6'2" | 210 | 22 | 2 | |
| Carl Weathers | LB | 6'2" | 220 | 23 | | |
| Butch Atkinson | DB | 6' | 180 | 24 | 4 | 6 |
| Willie Brown | DB | 6'1" | 190 | 30 | 2 | |
| Tommy Maxwell | DB | 6'2" | 195 | 24 | | |
| Jack Tatum | DB | 5'10" | 200 | 22 | 4 | |
| Jimmy Warren | DB | 5'11" | 175 | 32 | 2 | 12 |
| Nemiah Wilson | DB | 6' | 160 | 28 | 5 | |
| George Blanda | QB | 6'1" | 215 | 43 | | 86 |
| Daryle Lamonica | QB | 6'2" | 215 | 30 | | |
| Ken Stabler | QB | 6'3" | 194 | 25 | | 12 |
| Clarence Davis | HB | 5'10" | 190 | 22 | | 12 |
| Don Highsmith | HB | 6' | 200 | 23 | | 6 |
| Charlie Smith | HB | 6'1" | 205 | 25 | | 6 |
| Pete Banaszak | FB-HB | 5'11" | 210 | 27 | | 48 |
| Bill Enyart | FB | 6'4" | 235 | 24 | | |
| Marv Hubbard | FB | 6'1" | 215 | 25 | | 36 |
| Fred Biletnikoff | WR | 6'1" | 190 | 28 | | 54 |
| Drew Buie | WR | 6'2" | 178 | 24 | | 12 |
| Eldridge Dickey | WR | 5'10" | 198 | 25 | | 6 |
| Rod Sherman | WR | 6' | 190 | 26 | | 6 |
| Ray Chester | TE | 6'3" | 220 | 23 | | 42 |
| Bob Moore | TE | 6'3" | 220 | 22 | | |
| Jerry DePoyster | K | 6'1" | 205 | 25 | | |
| Mike Eischeid | K | 6' | 190 | 30 | | |

Hewitt Dixon — Injury
Warren Wells — Legal probation — ineligible
to play pro football.

## SAN DIEGO CHARGERS 6-8-0 Sid Gillman Harland Svare

**Scores of Each Game**

| | | |
|---|---|---|
| 21 | KANSAS CITY | 14 |
| 0 | OAKLAND | 34 |
| 17 | Pittsburg | 21 |
| 10 | Kansas City | 31 |
| 16 | Denver | 20 |
| 20 | BUFFALO | 3 |
| 49 | N.Y. JETS | 21 |
| 17 | N.Y. Giants | 35 |
| 20 | St. LOUIS | 17 |
| 33 | Oakland | 34 |
| 0 | Cincinnati | 31 |
| 30 | MINNESOTA | 14 |
| 45 | DENVER | 17 |
| 33 | Houston | 49 |

| Use Name | Pos. | Hgt | Wgt | Age | Int | Pts |
|---|---|---|---|---|---|---|
| Terry Owens | OT | 6'6" | 275 | 27 | | |
| Russ Washington | OT | 6'6" | 295 | 24 | | |
| Ira Gordon | OG-OT | 6'3" | 268 | 23 | | |
| Harris Jones | OG | 6'4" | 233 | 26 | | |
| Walt Sweeney | OG | 6'3" | 256 | 30 | | |
| Doug Wilkerson | OG | 6'2" | 245 | 24 | | |
| Sam Gruneisen | C | 6'1" | 250 | 30 | | |
| Carl Mauck | C | 6'3" | 234 | 24 | | |
| Jack Porter | C | 6'4" | 255 | 23 | | |
| West Grant (from BUF) | DE | 6'3" | 245 | 24 | | |
| Jeff Staggs | DE | 6'2" | 246 | 27 | | |
| Lee Thomas | DE | 6'5" | 246 | 24 | | |
| Steve DeLong | DT-DE | 6'3" | 252 | 28 | | |
| Ron East | DT | 6'4" | 242 | 28 | | |
| Kevin Hardy | DT | 6'5" | 260 | 26 | | |
| Andy Rice | DT | 6'3" | 268 | 29 | | |
| Gary Nowak | DT | 6'5" | 247 | 22 | | |
| Tom Williams | DT | 6'4" | 250 | 23 | | |
| Bob Babich | LB | 6'2" | 230 | 24 | | 6 |
| Pete Barnes | LB | 6'3" | 247 | 26 | 2 | 6 |
| Bob Bruggers | LB | 6'1" | 224 | 27 | | |
| Rick Redman | LB | 5'11" | 230 | 28 | 1 | |
| Mel Rogers | LB | 6'2" | 230 | 24 | | |
| John Tanner | LB | 6'4" | 222 | 26 | | |
| Ray White | LB | 6'1" | 225 | 22 | | 2 |
| Joe Beauchamp | DB | 6' | 185 | 27 | 4 | |
| Chuck Detwiler | DB | 6' | 185 | 24 | | |
| Chris Fletcher | DB | 5'11" | 185 | 22 | 3 | 6 |
| Jim Hill | DB | 6'2" | 190 | 24 | 2 | |
| Bob Howard | DB | 6'1" | 190 | 26 | 4 | |
| Bryant Salter | DB | 6'4" | 200 | 21 | 6 | |
| Jim Tolbert | DB | 6'3" | 207 | 27 | | |
| Marty Domres | QB | 6'3" | 215 | 24 | | |
| John Hadl | QB | 6'2" | 218 | 31 | | 6 |
| Mike Garrett | HB | 5'9" | 200 | 27 | | 42 |
| Mike Montgomery | HB | 6'2" | 202 | 22 | | 18 |
| Leon Burns | FB | 6'2" | 223 | 26 | | 6 |
| Jeff Queen | FB | 6'1" | 220 | 25 | | 42 |
| Eddie Ray | FB | 6'2" | 230 | 24 | | |
| Chuck Dicus | WR | 6' | 172 | 22 | | 6 |
| Gary Garrison | WR | 6'1" | 193 | 27 | | 36 |
| Walker Gillette | WR | 6'5" | 198 | 24 | | 12 |
| Jerry LeVias | WR | 5'10" | 178 | 24 | | 6 |
| Billy Parks | WR | 6'1" | 185 | 23 | | 24 |
| Pettis Norman | TE | 6'3" | 220 | 31 | | 6 |
| Art Strozier | TE | 6'2" | 220 | 25 | | |
| Dennis Partee | K | 6'2" | 218 | 25 | | 87 |

Rick Eber—Injury

## DENVER BRONCOS 4-9-1 Lou Saban Jerry Smith

**Scores of Each Game**

| | | |
|---|---|---|
| 10 | MIAMI | 10 |
| 13 | Green Bay | 34 |
| 3 | KANSAS CITY | 16 |
| 16 | OAKLAND | 27 |
| 20 | SAN DIEGO | 16 |
| 27 | Cleveland | 0 |
| 16 | Philadelphia | 17 |
| 20 | DETROIT | 24 |
| 10 | CINCINNATI | 24 |
| 10 | Kansas City | 28 |
| 22 | Pittsburg | 10 |
| 6 | CHICAGO | 3 |
| 17 | San Diego | 45 |
| 13 | Oakland | 21 |

| Use Name | Pos. | Hgt | Wgt | Age | Int | Pts |
|---|---|---|---|---|---|---|
| Sam Brunelli | OT | 6'1" | 270 | 28 | | |
| Mike Current | OT | 6'4" | 274 | 25 | | |
| Marv Montgomery | OT | 6'6" | 255 | 23 | | |
| Roger Shoals | OT | 6'4" | 260 | 32 | | |
| George Goeddeke | OG | 6'3" | 253 | 26 | | |
| Mike Schitkner | OG | 6'3" | 245 | 24 | | |
| Larron Jackson | OT-OG | 6'3" | 270 | 22 | | |
| Jay Bachman | C | 6'3" | 250 | 25 | | |
| Larry Kaminski | C | 6'2" | 245 | 26 | | |
| Tommy Lyons | C | 6'2" | 228 | 23 | | |
| Lyle Alzado | DE | 6'3" | 252 | 22 | | |
| Walt Barnes | DE | 6'3" | 250 | 27 | | |
| Rich Jackson | DE | 6'2" | 255 | 30 | | |
| Dave Costa | DT | 6'2" | 260 | 29 | | |
| Jerry Inman | DT | 6'3" | 256 | 31 | | |
| Paul Smith | DT | 6'3" | 256 | 26 | | |
| Carter Campbell | LB | 6'3" | 232 | 23 | | |
| Ken Criter | LB | 5'11" | 223 | 24 | | |
| Fred Forsberg | LB | 6'1" | 235 | 27 | 3 | 6 |
| Bill McKoy | LB | 6'3" | 235 | 23 | | |
| Chip Myrtle | LB | 6'2" | 225 | 26 | 3 | |
| Olen Underwood | LB | 6'1" | 220 | 29 | 1 | |
| Dave Washington | LB | 6'5" | 215 | 23 | 1 | |
| Butch Byrd | DB | 6' | 196 | 29 | | |
| Cornell Gordon | DB | 6' | 187 | 30 | 2 | |
| Charlie Greer | DB | 6' | 205 | 25 | 3 | |
| Leroy Mitchell | DB | 6'2" | 190 | 26 | 2 | |
| Randy Montgomery | DB | 5'11" | 182 | 24 | | |
| George Saimes | DB | 5'10" | 183 | 29 | | |
| Bill Thompson | DB | 6'1" | 200 | 24 | 5 | |
| Don Horn | QB | 6'2" | 195 | 26 | | |
| Steve Ramsey | QB | 6'2" | 210 | 23 | | |
| Floyd Little | HB | 5'10" | 196 | 29 | | 36 |
| Fran Lynch | FB-HB | 6'1" | 205 | 25 | | 8 |
| Clem Turner | FB | 6'1" | 236 | 26 | | |
| Bobby Anderson | HB-FB | 6' | 208 | 23 | | 24 |
| Gordon Bowdell | WR | 6'2" | 203 | 22 | | |
| Jack Gehrke | WR | 6' | 178 | 25 | | |
| Dwight Harrison | WR | 6'1" | 178 | 22 | | 12 |
| Jerry Simmons | WR | 6'1" | 190 | 28 | | 6 |
| Bill Van Heusen | WR | 6'1" | 200 | 25 | | |
| Bill Masters | TE | 6'5" | 240 | 27 | | 6 |
| John Mosier | TE | 6'3" | 220 | 23 | | |
| Jim Whalen (to PHI) | TE | 6'2" | 210 | 27 | | |
| Jim Turner | K | 6'2" | 205 | 30 | | 93 |

Tom Buckman — Injury
Pete Duranko — Injury

John Embree—Injury

## KANSAS CITY CHIEFS

### RUSHING

| Last Name | No. | Yds | Avg | TD |
|---|---|---|---|---|
| Podolak | 184 | 708 | 3.8 | 9 |
| Hayes | 132 | 537 | 4.1 | 1 |
| McVea | 68 | 288 | 4.2 | 3 |
| Otis | 49 | 184 | 3.8 | 0 |
| Adamle | 13 | 43 | 3.3 | 0 |
| Taylor | 1 | 25 | 25.0 | 0 |
| Dawson | 12 | 24 | 2.0 | 0 |
| Livingston | 5 | 11 | 2.2 | 0 |
| Frazier | 1 | -2 | -2.0 | 0 |
| Wright | 1 | -10 | -10.0 | 0 |

### RECEIVING

| Last Name | No. | Yds | Avg | TD |
|---|---|---|---|---|
| Taylor | 57 | 1110 | 19 | 7 |
| Podolak | 36 | 252 | 7 | 0 |
| Wright | 26 | 528 | 20 | 3 |
| Stroud | 22 | 454 | 21 | 1 |
| Hayes | 16 | 150 | 9 | 1 |
| Otis | 13 | 81 | 6 | 2 |
| Frazier | 10 | 154 | 15 | 0 |
| McVea | 5 | -3 | -1 | 0 |
| Homan | 2 | 47 | 24 | 0 |
| Smith | 1 | 12 | 12 | 0 |
| Adamle | 1 | 6 | 6 | 1 |

### PUNT RETURNS

| Last Name | No. | Yds | Avg | TD |
|---|---|---|---|---|
| Podolak | 14 | 84 | 6 | 0 |
| Homan | 10 | 61 | 6 | 0 |
| Reardon | 3 | 5 | 2 | 0 |
| Belser | 1 | 2 | 2 | 0 |
| Sensibaugh | 5 | -2 | 0 | 0 |

### KICKOFF RETURNS

| Last Name | No. | Yds | Avg | TD |
|---|---|---|---|---|
| Reardon | 12 | 308 | 26 | 0 |
| McVea | 9 | 177 | 20 | 0 |
| Adamle | 7 | 149 | 21 | 0 |
| Hayes | 4 | 75 | 19 | 0 |
| Sensibaugh | 4 | 71 | 18 | 0 |
| Podolak | 3 | 65 | 22 | 0 |
| Bergey | 1 | 15 | 15 | 0 |

### PASSING – PUNTING – KICKING

| PASSING | Att | Comp | % | Yds | Yd/Att | TD | Int- | % | RK |
|---|---|---|---|---|---|---|---|---|---|
| Dawson | 301 | 167 | 55 | 2504 | 8.3 | 15 | 13- | 4 | 2 |
| Livingston | 28 | 12 | 43 | 130 | 4.6 | 0 | 0- | 0 | |
| Huarte | 6 | 2 | 33 | 18 | 3.0 | 0 | 0- | 0 | |
| Podolak | 2 | 2 | 100 | 42 | 21.0 | 0 | 0- | 0 | |

| PUNTING | No | Avg |
|---|---|---|
| Wilson | 64 | 44.8 |

| KICKING | XP | Att | % | FG | Att | % |
|---|---|---|---|---|---|---|
| Stenerud | 32 | 32 | 100 | 26 | 44 | 59 |
| Stein | 0 | 0 | 0 | 0 | 1 | 0 |

## OAKLAND RAIDERS

### RUSHING

| Last Name | No. | Yds | Avg | TD |
|---|---|---|---|---|
| Hubbard | 181 | 867 | 4.8 | 5 |
| Banaszak | 137 | 563 | 4.1 | 8 |
| Davis | 54 | 321 | 5.9 | 2 |
| Highsmith | 76 | 307 | 4.0 | 1 |
| Buie | 2 | 32 | 16.0 | 0 |
| Stabler | 4 | 29 | 7.3 | 2 |
| Lamonica | 4 | 16 | 4.0 | 0 |
| Chester | 3 | 5 | 1.7 | 0 |
| Smith | 11 | 4 | 0.4 | 1 |
| DePoyster | 1 | -14 | -14.0 | 0 |

### RECEIVING

| Last Name | No. | Yds | Avg | TD |
|---|---|---|---|---|
| Biletnikoff | 61 | 929 | 15 | 9 |
| Chester | 28 | 442 | 16 | 7 |
| Hubbard | 22 | 167 | 8 | 1 |
| Davis | 15 | 97 | 6 | 0 |
| Banaszak | 13 | 128 | 10 | 0 |
| Sherman | 12 | 187 | 16 | 1 |
| Highsmith | 10 | 109 | 11 | 0 |
| Buie | 5 | 133 | 27 | 2 |
| Dickey | 4 | 78 | 20 | 1 |
| Smith | 2 | 67 | 34 | 0 |
| Moore | 2 | 26 | 13 | 0 |

### PUNT RETURNS

| Last Name | No. | Yds | Avg | TD |
|---|---|---|---|---|
| Atkinson | 20 | 159 | 8 | 0 |
| Maxwell | 6 | 21 | 4 | 0 |
| Sherman | 2 | 2 | 1 | 0 |
| Highsmith | 1 | 0 | 0 | 0 |

### KICKOFF RETURNS

| Last Name | No. | Yds | Avg | TD |
|---|---|---|---|---|
| Davis | 27 | 734 | 27 | 0 |
| Highsmith | 21 | 454 | 22 | 0 |
| Hubbard | 3 | 46 | 15 | 0 |
| Banaszak | 1 | 0 | 0 | 0 |
| Seiler | 1 | 0 | 0 | 0 |
| Smith | 1 | 0 | 0 | 0 |

### PASSING – PUNTING – KICKING

| PASSING | Att | Comp | % | Yds | Yd/Att | TD | Int- | % | RK |
|---|---|---|---|---|---|---|---|---|---|
| Lamonica | 242 | 118 | 49 | 1717 | 7.1 | 16 | 16- | 7 | 7 |
| Blanda | 58 | 32 | 55 | 378 | 6.5 | 4 | 6- | 10 | |
| Stabler | 48 | 24 | 50 | 268 | 5.6 | 1 | 4 | 8 | |

| PUNTING | No | Avg |
|---|---|---|
| DePoyster | 51 | 39.5 |
| Eischeid | 11 | 41.9 |

| KICKING | XP | Att | % | FG | Att | % |
|---|---|---|---|---|---|---|
| Blanda | 41 | 42 | 98 | 15 | 22 | 68 |

## SAN DIEGO CHARGERS

### RUSHING

| Last Name | No. | Yds | Avg | TD |
|---|---|---|---|---|
| Garrett | 140 | 591 | 4.2 | 4 |
| Queen | 95 | 318 | 3.3 | 4 |
| Montgomery | 60 | 226 | 3.8 | 1 |
| Burns | 61 | 223 | 3.7 | 1 |
| Parks | 5 | 77 | 15.4 | 0 |
| Hadl | 18 | 75 | 4.2 | 1 |
| LeVias | 4 | 73 | 18.3 | 0 |
| Ray | 2 | 15 | 7.5 | 0 |
| Partee | 1 | 7 | 7.0 | 0 |
| Norman | 1 | 1 | 1.0 | 0 |
| Domres | 1 | 0 | 0.0 | 0 |
| Garrison | 1 | 0 | 0.0 | 0 |
| Dicus | 1 | -2 | -2.0 | 0 |

### RECEIVING

| Last Name | No. | Yds | Avg | TD |
|---|---|---|---|---|
| Garrison | 42 | 889 | 21 | 6 |
| Parks | 41 | 609 | 15 | 4 |
| Garrett | 41 | 283 | 7 | 3 |
| Montgomery | 28 | 361 | 13 | 2 |
| Norman | 27 | 358 | 13 | 0 |
| Queen | 23 | 270 | 12 | 3 |
| LeVias | 21 | 265 | 13 | 1 |
| Gillette | 10 | 147 | 15 | 2 |
| Dicus | 6 | 89 | 15 | 1 |
| Burns | 3 | 22 | 7 | 0 |
| Strozier | 1 | 6 | 6 | 0 |
| Tanner | 1 | 6 | 6 | 0 |

### PUNT RETURNS

| Last Name | No. | Yds | Avg | TD |
|---|---|---|---|---|
| LeVias | 22 | 145 | 7 | 0 |
| Fletcher | 12 | 68 | 6 | 0 |
| Garrett | 3 | 2 | 1 | 0 |

### KICKOFF RETURNS

| Last Name | No. | Yds | Avg | TD |
|---|---|---|---|---|
| LeVias | 24 | 559 | 23 | 0 |
| Fletcher | 11 | 217 | 20 | 0 |
| Salter | 8 | 172 | 22 | 0 |
| Rogers | 1 | 20 | 20 | 0 |
| Burns | 2 | 19 | 10 | 0 |
| Sweeney | 1 | 13 | 13 | 0 |
| Thomas | 1 | 0 | 0 | 0 |
| Wilkerson | 1 | 0 | 0 | 0 |

### PASSING – PUNTING – KICKING

| PASSING | Att | Comp | % | Yds | Yd/Att | TD | Int- | % | RK |
|---|---|---|---|---|---|---|---|---|---|
| Hadl | 431 | 233 | 54 | 3075 | 7.1 | 21 | 25- | 6 | 4 |
| Domres | 12 | 7 | 58 | 97 | 8.1 | 1 | 3- | 25 | |
| Montgomery | 6 | 3 | 50 | 80 | 13.3 | 1 | 0- | 0 | |
| Garrett | 1 | 1 | 100 | 53 | 53.0 | 0 | 0- | 0 | |

| PUNTING | No | Avg |
|---|---|---|
| Partee | 55 | 43.5 |

| KICKING | XP | Att | % | FG | Att | % |
|---|---|---|---|---|---|---|
| Partee | 36 | 37 | 97 | 17 | 29 | 59 |

## DENVER BRONCOS

### RUSHING

| Last Name | No. | Yds | Avg | TD |
|---|---|---|---|---|
| Little | 284 | 1133 | 4.0 | 6 |
| Anderson | 139 | 533 | 3.8 | 3 |
| Lynch | 26 | 162 | 6.2 | 0 |
| Masters | 7 | 71 | 10.1 | 0 |
| C. Turner | 17 | 43 | 2.5 | 0 |
| Harrison | 5 | 36 | 7.2 | 0 |
| Mosier | 4 | 31 | 7.8 | 0 |
| Horn | 6 | 15 | 2.5 | 0 |
| Van Heusen | 1 | 10 | 10.0 | 0 |
| Simmons | 1 | 7 | 7.0 | 0 |
| Ramsey | 3 | 6 | 2.0 | 0 |
| Gehrke | 1 | 2 | 2.0 | 0 |

### RECEIVING

| Last Name | No. | Yds | Avg | TD |
|---|---|---|---|---|
| Anderson | 37 | 353 | 10 | 1 |
| Masters | 27 | 382 | 14 | 1 |
| Little | 26 | 255 | 10 | 0 |
| Simmons | 25 | 403 | 16 | 1 |
| Harrison | 19 | 265 | 14 | 2 |
| Gehrke | 14 | 254 | 18 | 0 |
| Whalen | 8 | 165 | 21 | 0 |
| C. Turner | 7 | 65 | 9 | 1 |
| Mosier | 3 | 36 | 12 | 0 |
| Lynch | 2 | 42 | 21 | 1 |
| Bowdell | 1 | 19 | 19 | 0 |
| Van Heusen | 1 | 10 | 10 | 0 |
| Washington | 1 | 0 | 0 | 0 |
| Schnitker | 1 | -11 | -11 | 0 |

### PUNT RETURNS

| Last Name | No. | Yds | Avg | TD |
|---|---|---|---|---|
| Thompson | 29 | 274 | 9 | 0 |
| Greer | 11 | 46 | 4 | 0 |
| Mitchell | 1 | 0 | 0 | 0 |

### KICKOFF RETURNS

| Last Name | No. | Yds | Avg | TD |
|---|---|---|---|---|
| Little | 7 | 199 | 28 | 0 |
| Anderson | 8 | 187 | 23 | 0 |
| Thompson | 5 | 105 | 21 | 0 |
| C. Turner | 5 | 100 | 20 | 0 |
| Criter | 5 | 81 | 16 | 0 |
| R. Montgomery | 4 | 80 | 20 | 0 |
| Bachman | 2 | 20 | 10 | 0 |
| Forsberg | 1 | 19 | 19 | 0 |
| Lynch | 0 | 19 | 0 | 0 |

### PASSING – PUNTING – KICKING

| PASSING | Att | Comp | % | Yds | Yd/Att | TD | Int- | % | RK |
|---|---|---|---|---|---|---|---|---|---|
| Ramsey | 178 | 84 | 47 | 1120 | 6.3 | 5 | 13- | 7 | 13 |
| Horn | 173 | 89 | 51 | 1056 | 6.1 | 3 | 14- | 8 | 14 |
| Anderson | 3 | 1 | 33 | 48 | 16.0 | 0 | 0- | 0 | |
| Gehrke | 2 | 1 | 50 | 19 | 9.5 | 0 | 0- | 0 | |
| Little | 1 | 0 | 0 | 0 | 0.0 | 0 | 0- | 0 | |
| Van Heusen | 1 | 0 | 0 | 0 | | 0 | 0- | 0 | |

| PUNTING | No | Avg |
|---|---|---|
| Van Heusen | 76 | 41.8 |

| KICKING | XP | Att | % | FG | Att | % |
|---|---|---|---|---|---|---|
| J. Turner | 18 | 18 | 100 | 25 | 38 | 66 |

# 1971 Championship Games

## Brodie's Mistake and Dallas' Defense

### SCORING

| | | | | |
|---|---|---|---|---|
| DALLAS | 0 | 7 | 0 | 7–14 |
| SAN FRANCISCO | 0 | 0 | 3 | 0– 3 |

Second Quarter
Dall.    Hill, 1 yard rush
PAT—Clark (kick)

Third Quarter
S.F.    Gossett, 28 yard field goal

Fourth Quarter
Dall.    D. Thomas, 2 yard rush
PAT—Clark (kick)

### TEAM STATISTICS

| DALLAS | | S.F. |
|---|---|---|
| 16 | First Downs—Total | 9 |
| 9 | First Downs—Rushing | 2 |
| 7 | First Downs—Passing | 7 |
| 0 | First Downs—Penalty | 0 |
| 2 | Fumbles—Number | 0 |
| 1 | Fumbles—Lost Ball | 0 |
| 2 | Penalties—Number | 1 |
| 30 | Yards Penalized | 12 |
| 3 | Missed Field Goals | 1 |
| 70 | Offensive Plays—Total | 47 |
| 244 | Net Yards | 239 |
| 3.5 | Average Gain | 5.1 |
| 1 | Giveaways | 3 |
| 3 | Takeaways | 1 |
| +2 | Difference | –2 |

The Cowboys and '49ers both won a return trip to the conference title game on the strength of a strong defense. Dallas had beaten the Vikings 20-12 to begin the playoffs, while the '49ers topped Washington 24-20 in the opening round, and the defensive units would decide the game today as they had last week.

Quarterbacks Roger Staubach and John Brodie made no headway against the psyched-up defenses in the first quarter. In the second period, however, Brodie committed a fatal error that the Cowboys capitalized on. Deep in his own territory, Brodie aimed a short screen pass to fullback Ken Willard without noticing Dallas' George Andrie lurking ominously on the scene. Once the ball was in the air, Andrie stepped in front of Willard, grabbed it, and lumbered down to the 1-yard line before being stopped. Calvin Hill carried the ball in, and Mike Clark's kick gave the Cowboys a 7-0 lead. Bruce Gossett put the '49ers on the scoreboard with a 28-yard field goal late in the period that cut the halftime Dallas lead down to 7-3.

The defensive units continued to dominate in the third period, and the slender Dallas lead looked as though it might hold up. In the fourth quarter, however, Roger Staubach went to work on some insurance points. Taking over on their own 20-yard line, the Cowboys drove downfield in a drive in which they converted four third-down situations into first downs. Staubach kept the drive alive with his scrambling, often creating time for his receivers to get open or finding room to run the ball himself. One key third-down play saw coach Tom Landry send tight end Mike Ditka into the lineup after '49er safety Mel Phillips was injured; Ditka promptly caught a clutch third-down pass against substitute safety Johnny Fuller. Duane Thomas sprinted around end for the final two yards, and the Dallas defense never let up for a second in preserving the 14-3 victory.

### INDIVIDUAL STATISTICS

#### RUSHING

| DALLAS | No | Yds | Avg. | SAN FRANCISCO | No | Yds | Avg. |
|---|---|---|---|---|---|---|---|
| Staubach | 8 | 55 | 6.9 | V. Washington | 10 | 58 | 5.8 |
| Garrison | 14 | 52 | 3.7 | Willard | 6 | 3 | 0.5 |
| D. Thomas | 15 | 44 | 2.9 | | 16 | 61 | 3.8 |
| Hill | 9 | 21 | 2.3 | | | | |
| | 46 | 172 | 3.7 | | | | |

#### RECEIVING

| | No | Yds | Avg. | | No | Yds | Avg. |
|---|---|---|---|---|---|---|---|
| Truax | 2 | 43 | 21.5 | G. Washington | 4 | 88 | 22.0 |
| Hayes | 2 | 22 | 11.0 | Kwalick | 4 | 52 | 13.0 |
| Alworth | 1 | 17 | 17.0 | V. Washington | 3 | 28 | 9.3 |
| Reeves | 1 | 17 | 17.0 | Willard | 1 | 6 | 6.0 |
| D. Thomas | 1 | 7 | 7.0 | Witcher | 1 | 6 | 6.0 |
| Ditka | 1 | 5 | 5.0 | Cunningham | 1 | 4 | 4.0 |
| Garrison | 1 | –8 | –8.0 | | 14 | 184 | 13.1 |
| | 9 | 103 | 11.4 | | | | |

#### PUNTING

| | No | | Avg. | | No | | Avg. |
|---|---|---|---|---|---|---|---|
| Widby | 6 | | 45.0 | Spurrier | 6 | | 38.2 |

#### PUNT RETURNS

| | No | Yds | Avg. | | No | Yds | Avg. |
|---|---|---|---|---|---|---|---|
| Hayes | 1 | 3 | 3.0 | Fuller | 2 | 10 | 5.0 |
| Harris | 1 | 1 | 1.0 | Taylor | 1 | 0 | 0.0 |
| | 2 | 4 | 2.0 | | 3 | 10 | 3.3 |

#### KICKOFF RETURNS

| | No | Yds | Avg. | | No | Yds | Avg. |
|---|---|---|---|---|---|---|---|
| Harris | 1 | 19 | 19.0 | V. Washington | 2 | 35 | 17.5 |
| | | | | Cunningham | 1 | 21 | 21.0 |
| | | | | | 3 | 56 | 18.7 |

#### INTERCEPTION RETURNS

| | No | Yds | Avg. | | | | |
|---|---|---|---|---|---|---|---|
| Jordan | 1 | 23 | 23.0 | None | | | |
| Andrie | 1 | 7 | 7.0 | | | | |
| Harris | 1 | 2 | 2.0 | | | | |
| | 3 | 32 | 10.7 | | | | |

#### PASSING

| DALLAS | Att. | Comp. | Comp. Pct. | Yds. | Int. | Yds/ Att. | Yds/ Comp. | Yards Lost Tackled |
|---|---|---|---|---|---|---|---|---|
| Staubach | 18 | 9 | 50.0 | 103 | 0 | 5.7 | 11.4 | 6–31 |

| SAN FRANCISCO | | | | | | | | |
|---|---|---|---|---|---|---|---|---|
| Brodie | 30 | 14 | 46.7 | 184 | 3 | 6.1 | 13.1 | 1– 6 |

---

## Good Strategy, Wrong Target

### SCORING

| | | | | |
|---|---|---|---|---|
| MIAMI | 7 | 0 | 7 | 7–21 |
| BALTIMORE | 0 | 0 | 0 | 0– 0 |

First Quarter
Miami    Warfield, 75 yard pass from Griese
PAT—Yepremian (kick)

Third Quarter
Miami    Anderson, 62 yard interception return
PAT—Yepremian (kick)

Fourth Quarter
Miami    Csonka, 5 yard rush
PAT—Yepremian (kick)

### TEAM STATISTICS

| MIAMI | | BALT. |
|---|---|---|
| 13 | First Downs—Total | 16 |
| 8 | First Downs—Rushing | 6 |
| 4 | First Downs—Passing | 10 |
| 1 | First Downs—Penalty | 0 |
| 0 | Fumbles—Number | 1 |
| 0 | Fumbles—Lost Ball | 0 |
| 1 | Penalties—Number | 2 |
| 12 | Yards Penalized | 20 |
| 0 | Missed Field Goals | 3 |
| 45 | Offensive Plays—Total | 68 |
| 286 | Net Yards | 302 |
| 6.4 | Average Gain | 4.4 |
| 1 | Giveaways | 3 |
| 3 | Takeaways | 1 |
| +2 | Difference | –2 |

The Dolphins had to guard against a letdown in this game as they were coming off an exhausting victory in the opening round of the playoffs. The Chiefs and Dolphins had battled back and forth all afternoon, with regulation time ending in a 24-24 tie. The two clubs fought through almost eighteen minutes of overtime before Garo Yepremian ended football's longest game with a 37-yard field goal.

The Colts, on the other hand, were coming off an easy 20-3 triumph over the Browns, so they were well rested physically and emotionally. Coach Don McCafferty planned to use a ball-control offense and a tight defense to defeat the Dolphins, but a 75-yard touchdown pass from Bob Griese to Paul Warfield early in the first quarter put Miami ahead 7-0 and put the pressure on Johnny Unitas and the Baltimore offense. But with starting backs Tom Matte and Norm Bulaich out of action with injuries, the Colts could not grind the yardage out against the quick Miami defense. The Colt defense also held up after the early Miami touchdown, and the half ended with the score 7-0.

With their ground attack getting no place against the Miami defense, the Colts went to the air in the third period. But while Griese had scored on a long bomb in the opening period, Unitas met disaster when he went for the bomb in the third quarter. Throwing deep for Eddie Hinton, Unitas undershot his man and instead hit Miami safety Dick Anderson. With his mates throwing blocks like experienced offensive players, Anderson weaved 62 yards with the ball for the second Miami touchdown.

Unitas had no luck crossing the Miami goal line for the rest of the afternoon, while the Dolphins scored a third touchdown on Larry Csonka's five-yard run which had been set up by a 50-yard pass to Warfield.

### INDIVIDUAL STATISTICS

#### RUSHING

| MIAMI | No | Yds | Avg. | BALTIMORE | No | Yds | Avg. |
|---|---|---|---|---|---|---|---|
| Kiick | 18 | 66 | 3.7 | McCauley | 15 | 50 | 3.3 |
| Csonka | 15 | 63 | 4.2 | Nottingham | 11 | 33 | 3.0 |
| Griese | 1 | 12 | 12.0 | Nowatzke | 2 | 5 | 2.5 |
| Morris | 1 | 3 | 3.0 | Unitas | 1 | 5 | 5.0 |
| | 35 | 144 | 4.1 | | 29 | 93 | 3.2 |

#### RECEIVING

| | No | Yds | Avg. | | No | Yds | Avg. |
|---|---|---|---|---|---|---|---|
| Warfield | 2 | 125 | 62.5 | Hinton | 6 | 98 | 16.3 |
| Twilley | 2 | 33 | 16.5 | Nottingham | 4 | 26 | 6.5 |
| | 4 | 158 | 39.5 | Perkins | 3 | 19 | 6.3 |
| | | | | Havrilak | 2 | 31 | 15.5 |
| | | | | McCauley | 2 | 24 | 12.0 |
| | | | | Mitchell | 1 | 14 | 14.0 |
| | | | | Mackey | 1 | 6 | 6.0 |
| | | | | Matte | 1 | 6 | 6.0 |
| | | | | | 20 | 224 | 11.2 |

#### PUNTING

| | No | | Avg. | | No | | Avg. |
|---|---|---|---|---|---|---|---|
| Seiple | 6 | | 42.7 | Lee | 3 | | 45.3 |

#### PUNT RETURNS

| | No | Yds | Avg. | | No | Yds | Avg. |
|---|---|---|---|---|---|---|---|
| Scott | 2 | 20 | 10.0 | Volk | 5 | 20 | 4.0 |

#### KICKOFF RETURNS

| | No | Yds | Avg. | | No | Yds | Avg. |
|---|---|---|---|---|---|---|---|
| Morris | 1 | 22 | 22.0 | Pittman | 2 | 58 | 29.0 |

#### INTERCEPTION RETURNS

| | No | Yds | Avg. | | No | Yds | Avg. |
|---|---|---|---|---|---|---|---|
| Anderson | 1 | 62 | 62.0 | Logan | 1 | 0 | 0.0 |
| Kolen | 1 | 11 | 11.0 | | | | |
| Scott | 1 | 0 | 0.0 | | | | |
| | 3 | 73 | 24.3 | | | | |

#### PASSING

| MIAMI | Att. | Comp. | Comp. Pct. | Yds. | Int. | Yds/ Att. | Yds/ Comp. | Yards Lost Tackled |
|---|---|---|---|---|---|---|---|---|
| Griese | 8 | 4 | 50.0 | 158 | 1 | 19.8 | 39.5 | 2–16 |

| BALTIMORE | | | | | | | | |
|---|---|---|---|---|---|---|---|---|
| Unitas | 36 | 20 | 55.6 | 224 | 3 | 6.3 | 11.2 | 3–15 |

## Finally Lassoing the Championship

The Cowboys had ended every season since 1966 with a loss in the playoffs, before finally losing last year in the Super Bowl to Baltimore. But now they were hopeful of kicking that habit with a new quarterback in charge of the offense. Since Roger Staubach had replaced Craig Morton as the starting passer halfway through the season, the Cowboys had won seven straight regular-season games and two playoff games. To end the doubts about their ability to win the big games, the Cowboys would have to beat the Miami Dolphins, an up-and-coming young team masterfully built by head coach Don Shula.

The young Dolphins made their first mistake in the opening period when fullback Larry Csonka muffed a handoff from quarterback Bob Griese on the Dallas 48-yard line. After Dallas recovered the fumble, Staubach led the Cowboys deep into Miami territory before settling for a Mike Clark field goal.

Even in the first quarter, Dallas consistently ate up yardage on the ground, with Duane Thomas and Walt Garrison carrying the ball through gaping holes cut open by Cowboy linemen. The Dallas defense, meanwhile, completely shut off the Miami running attack of Csonka and Jim Kiick. The Cowboys also mixed passes into their attack, and a seven-yard touchdown pass from Staubach to Lance Alworth capped a long Dallas drive in the second period. Although the Dolphins scored on a Garo Yepremian field goal, the Cowboys dominated the first half and took a 10-3 lead into the clubhouse at halftime.

After taking the second-half kickoff, the Cowboys ate up five minutes of the clock with a ball-control drive that featured strong running by Duane Thomas. A pitchout to Thomas for three yards scored the touchdown and opened the Dallas lead to 17-3.

Trailing by two touchdowns after three periods, the Dolphins desperately needed some offensive fireworks in the fourth quarter. Instead, they ran into disaster. With his team finally on the march, Griese lashed a pass at Kiick at mid-field. Cowboy linebacker Chuck Howley had been knocked down when the pass was thrown, but he jumped up and picked it off in front of Kiick. With a convoy of blockers in front of him, Howley chugged downfield with the ball before running out of gas on the Miami 9. Two running plays moved the ball to the 7, and then Staubach hit Mike Ditka in the end zone with a pass to put the game out of reach for the Dolphins. Mike Clark's extra point made the score 24-3, and although the Dolphins launched a drive deep into Dallas territory, a fumble by Griese ended the last Miami scoring threat of the day.

### DALLAS / MIAMI

| DALLAS | OFFENSE | MIAMI |
|---|---|---|
| Hayes | WR | Warfield |
| Liscio | LT | Crusan |
| Niland | LG | Kuechenberg |
| Manders | C | DeMarco |
| Nye | RG | Little |
| Wright | RT | Evans |
| Ditka | TE | Fleming |
| Alworth | WR | Twilley |
| Staubach | QB | Griese |
| D. Thomas | RB | Kiick |
| Garrison | RB | Csonka |

| DALLAS | DEFENSE | MIAMI |
|---|---|---|
| L. Cole | LE | Riley |
| Pugh | LT | Fernandez |
| Lillie | RT | Heinz |
| Andrie | RE | Stanfill |
| Edwards | LLB | Swift |
| Jordan | MLB | Buoniconti |
| Howley | RLB | Kolen |
| Adderley | LCB | Foley |
| Renfro | RCB | Johnson |
| Green | LS | Anderson |
| Harris | RS | Scott |

### SUBSTITUTES

**DALLAS**
Offense
| | |
|---|---|
| Fitzgerald | Truax |
| Hill | Welch |
| Reeves | Williams |

Defense
| | |
|---|---|
| Gregory | I. Thomas |
| Lewis | Toomay |
| Smith | Waters |
| Stincic | |

Kickers
| | |
|---|---|
| Clark | Widby |

**MIAMI**
Offense
| | |
|---|---|
| T. Cole | Moore |
| Ginn | Morris |
| Langer | Noonan |
| Mandich | Stowe |

Defense
| | |
|---|---|
| Cornish | Mumphord |
| Den Herder | Petrella |
| Matheson | Powell |

Kickers
| | |
|---|---|
| Yepremian | Seiple |

### SCORING

| | | | | |
|---|---|---|---|---|
| DALLAS | 3 | 7 | 7 | 7—24 |
| MIAMI | 0 | 3 | 0 | 0— 3 |

**First Quarter**
Dallas    Clark, 9 yard field goal

**Second Quarter**
Dallas    Alworth, 7 yard pass from
          Staubach    PAT — Clark (kick)
Miami     Yepremian, 31 yard field goal

**Third Quarter**
Dallas    D. Thomas, 3 yard rush
          PAT — Clark (kick)

**Fourth Quarter**
Dallas    Ditka, 7 yard pass from
          Staubach    PAT — Clark (kick)

### TEAM STATISTICS

| DALLAS | | MIAMI |
|---|---|---|
| 23 | First Downs — Total | 10 |
| 15 | First Downs — Rushing | 3 |
| 8 | First Downs — Passing | 7 |
| 0 | First Downs — Penalty | 0 |
| 1 | Fumbles — Number | 2 |
| 1 | Fumbles — Lost Ball | 2 |
| 3 | Penalties — Number | 0 |
| 15 | Yards Penalized | 0 |
| 0 | Missed Field Goals | 1 |
| 69 | Offensive Plays | 44 |
| 352 | Net Yards | 185 |
| 5.1 | Average Gain | 4.2 |
| 1 | Giveaways | 3 |
| 3 | Takeaways | 1 |
| +2 | Difference | -2 |

### INDIVIDUAL STATISTICS

**RUSHING**

| DALLAS | No | Yds | Avg. | MIAMI | No | Yds | Avg. |
|---|---|---|---|---|---|---|---|
| D. Thomas | 19 | 95 | 5.0 | Csonka | 9 | 40 | 4.4 |
| Garrison | 14 | 74 | 5.3 | Kiick | 10 | 40 | 4.0 |
| Hill | 7 | 25 | 3.6 | Griese | 1 | 0 | 0.0 |
| Staubach | 5 | 18 | 3.6 | | 20 | 80 | 4.0 |
| Ditka | 1 | 17 | 17.0 | | | | |
| Hayes | 1 | 16 | 16.0 | | | | |
| Reeves | 1 | 7 | 7.0 | | | | |
| | 48 | 252 | 5.3 | | | | |

**RECEIVING**

| DALLAS | No | Yds | Avg. | MIAMI | No | Yds | Avg. |
|---|---|---|---|---|---|---|---|
| D. Thomas | 3 | 17 | 5.7 | Warfield | 4 | 39 | 9.8 |
| Alworth | 2 | 28 | 14.0 | Kiick | 3 | 21 | 7.0 |
| Ditka | 2 | 28 | 14.0 | Csonka | 2 | 18 | 9.0 |
| Hayes | 2 | 23 | 11.5 | Fleming | 1 | 27 | 27.0 |
| Garrison | 2 | 11 | 5.5 | Twilley | 1 | 20 | 20.0 |
| Hill | 1 | 12 | 12.0 | Mandich | 1 | 9 | 9.0 |
| | 12 | 119 | 9.9 | | 12 | 134 | 11.2 |

**PUNTING**

| DALLAS | No | | Avg. | MIAMI | No | | Avg. |
|---|---|---|---|---|---|---|---|
| Widby | 5 | | 37.2 | Seiple | 5 | | 40.0 |

**PUNT RETURNS**

| DALLAS | No | Yds | Avg. | MIAMI | No | Yds | Avg. |
|---|---|---|---|---|---|---|---|
| Hayes | 1 | -1 | -1.0 | Scott | 1 | 21 | 21.0 |

**KICKOFF RETURNS**

| DALLAS | No | Yds | Avg. | MIAMI | No | Yds | Avg. |
|---|---|---|---|---|---|---|---|
| I. Thomas | 1 | 32 | 32.0 | Morris | 4 | 90 | 22.5 |
| Waters | 1 | 11 | 11.0 | Ginn | 1 | 32 | 32.0 |
| | 2 | 43 | 21.5 | | 5 | 122 | 24.4 |

**INTERCEPTION RETURNS**

| DALLAS | No | Yds | Avg. | MIAMI | | | |
|---|---|---|---|---|---|---|---|
| Howley | 1 | 41 | 41.0 | None | | | |

**PASSING**

| DALLAS | Att | Comp | Comp Pct. | Yds | Int | Yds/ Att. | Yds/ Comp | Yards Lost Tackled |
|---|---|---|---|---|---|---|---|---|
| Staubach | 19 | 12 | 63.2 | 119 | 0 | 6.3 | 9.9 | 2—19 |

| MIAMI | Att | Comp | Comp Pct. | Yds | Int | Yds/ Att. | Yds/ Comp | Yards Lost Tackled |
|---|---|---|---|---|---|---|---|---|
| Griese | 23 | 12 | 52.2 | 134 | 1 | 5.8 | 11.2 | 1—29 |

# 1972 N.F.C. Grounded but Not Stopped

In modern offensive football, the wide receiver was fast becoming an ornamental decoy, while the quarterback's main function was no longer passing the ball but handing it off. A record number of ten rushers carried the ball for 1,000 yards this year as the running back now was pro football's chief offensive weapon. The development of zone pass defenses had cut down on the air game's potency, so clubs more and more decided to move the ball on the ground in three- and four-yard chunks rather than going for twenty or thirty yards at a time with pass plays. An ever-increasing number of teams found that the best offense against a zone defense was two strong running backs and a strong-legged place kicker. Fading away into history were the days when long bombers like Van Brocklin, Unitas, and Lamonica captivated crowds and captured headlines with spectacular heaves.

## EASTERN DIVISION

**Washington Redskins**—George Allen's collection of misfits and rejects, known collectively as the Over the Hill Gang, stayed at a high level of enthusiasm all season and knocked the Dallas Cowboys out of first place in the Eastern Division for the first time since 1965. Allen's pride and joy was his defensive unit, which allowed the fewest points of any defense in the conference. The offense moved the ball well despite the absence of Sonny Jurgensen for most of the season with injuries; most of the time, substitute quarterback Bill Kilmer had only to hand off to halfback Larry Brown to keep the Skins on the march. Running at top speed and using his blockers well, Brown piled up a conference-leading total of 1,216 yards rushing despite sitting out the last two games of the season with an injury.

**Dallas Cowboys**—The Cowboys still had one of the deepest rosters in the NFL, but they dropped to second place in the East because they lacked the fine competitive edge they had last year. They lost to the Packers, Redskins, and '49ers during the season, and with a chance to take first place on the final day of the season they lost a listless 23-3 decision to New York and settled for the wild-card spot in the playoffs. The Cowboys did have several personnel problems. Duane Thomas' non-relations with his teammates forced the team to trade him to San Diego, a shoulder injury sidelined quarterback Roger Staubach for most of the season, a bad back took George Andrie out of the defensive line, and Bob Lilly's back hurt him all through the season.

**New York Giants**—Comebackers and newcomers led the Giants to a surprising winning season. The chief comeback was by halfback Ron Johnson, rebounding from a 1971 knee injury to carry the ball with his old authority and flair. Kicker Pete Gogolak also came back from a poor 1971 season to give the Giants a consistent three-point threat within the 40-yard line. Newcomers to the New York squad more than made up for the traded Fran Tarkenton and Fred Dryer. Quarterback Norm Snead led the NFC in passing statistics, but his main value was as a steady leader on offense. The defensive line improved immensely with the addition of end Jack Gregory from the Browns and rookie tackles John Mendenhall and Larry Jacobson.

**St. Louis Cardinals**—Despite top talent in some positions, the Cards stumbled through a season in which Gary Cuozzo, Tim Van Galder, and Jim Hart took turns as the starting quarterback, in which the defensive line had problems rushing opposing passers, and in which injuries sidelined linebackers Jamie Rivers, Jeff Staggs, and Mike McGill. Even though the Cards won their final two games, coach Bob Holloway got the ax after the season; departing of his own accord was safety Larry Wilson, retiring after a great thirteen-year pro career.

**Philadelphia Eagles**—The tough defense coach Ed Khayat had built last year was weakened by the trade of Tim Rossovich to San Diego because of a personality clash with the coach and by injuries to Ernie Calloway and Steve Zabel. The offensive had great receivers in Harold Jackson, Ben Hawkins, and Harold Carmichael but didn't have a quarterback who could consistently get the ball to them. Veteran Pete Liske had all the qualifications except a strong arm, while rookie John Reaves had a great arm but also the chronic rookie problem of inexperience. Rookie Po James played well at halfback, but the Eagles lacked the great back necessary in this era of running football.

## CENTRAL DIVISION

**Green Bay Packers**—In his second year as coach, Dan Devine took the Packers back to the top in the Central Division with a grinding defense and a methodical ball-control offense. The pride of the defense was the secondary of Ken Ellis, rookie Willie Buchanon, Jim Hill, and Al Matthews, four young speedsters who minimized the effect of Willie Wood's retirement. The Packers didn't have any stars like Willie Davis or Henry Jordan or a younger Ray Nitschke in the front lines, but the rebuilt front four and linebacking constantly frustrated enemy running attacks. Bart Starr's retirement left Scott Hunter in charge of the offense, although Starr remained as an assistant coach and called all the plays for Hunter. Even though his arm was not strong, Hunter kept the attack moving simply by handing off to back John Brockington and MacArthur Lane.

**Detroit Lions**—The Detroit offense steadily turned out points, ranking second in the league in point production, but the defense could not compete with the other units in Green Bay and Minnesota. Coach Joe Schmidt was swimming in offensive talents—a fine quarterback in Greg Landry, good runners in Steve Owens and Altie Taylor, a star receiver in Charlie Sanders, and one of the best offensive lines in the NFL. The chief defensive shortcoming was the lack of a strong pass rush. Despite taking defensive linemen Bob Bell and Herb Orvis as their first draft choices the last two years, the Lions had not rebuilt their line into a top unit. At the end of the year coach Schmidt resigned and defensive stars Wayne Walker and Dick LeBeau retired.

**Minnesota Vikings**—The Vikings solved their quarterback problems by getting Fran Tarkenton back from the Giants in a trade, but the defense slumped off from the super level it had been playing at. Injuries nagged Carl Eller, Alan Page, and Gary Larsen and made the Minnesota front four less fearsome than usual. Middle linebacker Lonnie Warwick missed eight games on the disabled list, and rookie Jeff Siemon showed much promise and made many mistakes. On offense, Tarkenton gave the team a major-league passer, but the receiving corps suffered because of Gene Washington's second straight injury-plagued season. The Viking running backs were all good for sure short yardage, but none of them ever threatened to break loose a long run.

**Chicago Bears**—The Bears had a completely schizophrenic offense, first in the NFL in rushing, last in passing. Quarterback Bobby Douglass was a big, strong lad who set a new record of 968 yards gained rushing by a quarterback, but his passes came infrequently and often shot wide of the intended receiver. Douglass, fullback Jim Harrison, and halfbacks Don Shy and Cyril Pinder moved the ball well on the ground, but enemy defenses paid a minimum of attention to the Chicago air game. For a while the all-out running attack worked, but once opposing teams got wise to the Bear game plan, Chicago lost six of their last seven games. Coach Abe Gibron's first year on the job saw Gale Sayers retire with a bad knee and Dick Butkus continue to play up to All-Pro standards with a knee that hurt him more and more with each game.

## WESTERN DIVISION

**San Francisco '49ers**—Heisman Trophy winner Steve Spurrier had done little else but punt in his past five seasons as a pro, but he stepped in for the injured John Brodie in mid-season and quarterbacked the '49ers to first place in the West. With a solid line to protect him and two great receivers in Gene Washington and Ted Kwalick to throw to, Spurrier engineered five San Francisco victories in the final six games, reaching his personal peak with five touchdown passes on November 19 against the Bears. On defense, the '49ers launched a ferocious pass rush despite disabling injuries to Cedrick Hardman and Earl Edwards; Tommy Hart and Charley Krueger responded with superior seasons to pick up the slack. The '49er playoff hopes soared in their final game when Brodie returned from the injured list to spark the team to a 20-17 victory over Minnesota.

**Atlanta Falcons**—The Falcons were strong at every position except quarterback, kicker, and defensive tackle, but these flaws kept the club from doing better than second place in the West. Quarterback Bob Berry had made the best of his limited talent, but coach Norm Van Brocklin had lost confidence in his ability to lead the Falcons to a title. Neither did kicker Bill Bell nor defensive tackles Glen Condren and Mike Lewis satisfy the coach. The Falcons did have a liberal supply of All-Stars in Claude Humphrey, John Zook, Tommy Nobis, Ken Reaves, George Kunz, Jim Mitchell, and Dave Hampton. Picked up from Green Bay, Hampton gained his 1,000th yard rushing of the year late in the final game. The game was stopped and the ball presented to Hampton. On his next carry Hampton lost five yards to finish at 995 yards for the year. Hampton, however, kept the ball.

**Los Angeles Rams**—With the death of owner Dan Reeves in April 1971, his family operated the club for a year and then sold the Rams to Robert Irsay. Before the 1972 season began, however, Irsay traded the Rams to Carroll Rosenbloom for his ownership of the Colts. Rosenbloom had grown accustomed to excellence from his Colt teams, but his first Ram squad disappointed him by finishing below .500 and in third place. Coach Tommy Prothro had daringly traded off Deacon Jones during the summer and replaced him with ex-Giant Fred Dryer, but leaks in the secondary hurt the defense more than the rebuilt front four. Quarterback Roman Gabriel's sore arm put a crimp in the offense, and five losses in the last six games cost Prothro his job.

**New Orleans Saints**—While the mid-1960s expansion teams in Atlanta, Miami, and Cincinnati had all achieved respectability, the Saints still had a look of a patchwork team created out of odds and ends. Coach J.D. Roberts had some topnotch players in quarterback Archie Manning, receiver Danny Abramowicz, tackle Glen Ray Hines, and rookie middle linebacker Joe Federspiel, but most of the roster was made up of journeymen and inexperienced youngsters. The distinguishing marks of the Saints this year were an uncanny ability to lose the ball on fumbles and interceptions and a morale problem in which the players expected one another to make errors and lose games.

## FINAL TEAM STATISTICS

### OFFENSE

| | ATL. | CHI. | DALL. | DET. | G.B. | L.A. | MINN. | N.O. | N.Y. | PHIL. | ST.L. | S.F. | WASH. |
|---|---|---|---|---|---|---|---|---|---|---|---|---|---|
| **FIRST DOWNS:** | | | | | | | | | | | | | |
| Total | 231 | 190 | 256 | 240 | 195 | 238 | 235 | 226 | 265 | 203 | 181 | 234 | 235 |
| by Rushing | 113 | 124 | 118 | 120 | 109 | 113 | 95 | 83 | 120 | 78 | 68 | 87 | 110 |
| by Passing | 101 | 54 | 126 | 97 | 72 | 108 | 127 | 123 | 124 | 110 | 102 | 129 | 106 |
| by Penalty | 17 | 12 | 12 | 23 | 14 | 17 | 13 | 20 | 21 | 15 | 11 | 18 | 19 |
| **RUSHING:** | | | | | | | | | | | | | |
| Number | 500 | 536 | 499 | 473 | 544 | 472 | 472 | 337 | 524 | 398 | 361 | 445 | 513 |
| Yards | 2092 | 2360 | 2124 | 2021 | 2127 | 2209 | 1740 | 1230 | 2022 | 1393 | 1229 | 1616 | 2082 |
| Average Yards | 4.2 | 4.4 | 4.3 | 4.3 | 3.9 | 4.7 | 3.7 | 3.6 | 3.9 | 3.5 | 3.4 | 3.6 | 4.1 |
| Touchdowns | 16 | 15 | 17 | 20 | 17 | 17 | 11 | 5 | 16 | 2 | 9 | 11 | 17 |
| **PASSING:** | | | | | | | | | | | | | |
| Attempts | 296 | 205 | 367 | 305 | 237 | 371 | 385 | 449 | 344 | 375 | 363 | 380 | 284 |
| Completions | 157 | 78 | 196 | 155 | 101 | 184 | 218 | 230 | 206 | 184 | 171 | 217 | 159 |
| Completion Percentage | 53.0 | 38.0 | 53.4 | 50.8 | 42.6 | 49.6 | 56.6 | 51.2 | 59.9 | 49.1 | 47.1 | 57.1 | 56.0 |
| Passing Yards | 2202 | 1283 | 2580 | 2283 | 1536 | 2282 | 2726 | 2781 | 2537 | 2527 | 2259 | 2888 | 2281 |
| Avg. Yards per Attempt | 7.4 | 6.3 | 7.0 | 7.5 | 6.5 | 6.2 | 7.1 | 6.2 | 7.4 | 6.7 | 6.2 | 7.6 | 8.0 |
| Avg. Yards per Complet. | 14.0 | 16.4 | 13.2 | 14.7 | 15.2 | 12.4 | 12.5 | 12.1 | 12.3 | 13.7 | 13.2 | 13.3 | 14.3 |
| Times Tackled Passing | 41 | 32 | 31 | 26 | 17 | 16 | 26 | 43 | 10 | 53 | 30 | 22 | 11 |
| Yards Lost Tackled | 283 | 175 | 238 | 149 | 124 | 136 | 203 | 347 | 76 | 457 | 221 | 153 | 88 |
| Net Yards | 1919 | 1108 | 2342 | 2134 | 1412 | 2146 | 2523 | 2434 | 2461 | 2070 | 2038 | 2735 | 2193 |
| Touchdowns | 13 | 9 | 16 | 19 | 7 | 13 | 19 | 18 | 20 | 10 | 11 | 27 | 21 |
| Interceptions | 15 | 13 | 23 | 18 | 9 | 22 | 13 | 21 | 15 | 20 | 23 | 24 | 15 |
| Percent Intercepted | 5.1 | 4.3 | 6.3 | 5.9 | 3.8 | 5.9 | 3.4 | 4.7 | 4.4 | 5.3 | 6.3 | 6.3 | 5.3 |
| **PUNTS:** | | | | | | | | | | | | | |
| Number | 61 | 67 | 51 | 43 | 65 | 53 | 62 | 71 | 47 | 63 | 73 | 64 | 59 |
| Average Distance | 42.8 | 41.2 | 38.2 | 40.3 | 41.8 | 44.2 | 42.8 | 40.8 | 42.7 | 40.3 | 39.4 | 39.7 | 38.5 |
| **PUNT RETURNS:** | | | | | | | | | | | | | |
| Number | 27 | 28 | 28 | 18 | 25 | 33 | 26 | 16 | 18 | 27 | 16 | 44 | 34 |
| Yards | 194 | 178 | 134 | 100 | 364 | 347 | 159 | 43 | 125 | 179 | 61 | 373 | 159 |
| Average Yards | 7.2 | 6.4 | 4.8 | 5.6 | 14.6 | 10.5 | 6.1 | 2.7 | 6.9 | 6.6 | 3.8 | 8.5 | 4.7 |
| Touchdowns | 0 | 0 | 0 | 0 | 2 | 0 | 0 | 0 | 0 | 0 | 0 | 0 | 0 |
| **KICKOFF RETURNS:** | | | | | | | | | | | | | |
| Number | 52 | 52 | 50 | 52 | 49 | 56 | 42 | 62 | 50 | 59 | 53 | 44 | 48 |
| Yards | 1039 | 1528 | 1080 | 1304 | 1141 | 1287 | 989 | 1312 | 1262 | 1375 | 1152 | 1041 | 1133 |
| Average Yards | 20.0 | 29.4 | 21.6 | 25.1 | 23.3 | 23.0 | 23.5 | 21.2 | 25.2 | 23.3 | 21.7 | 23.7 | 23.6 |
| Touchdowns | 0 | 2 | 0 | 0 | 0 | 0 | 0 | 0 | 1 | 0 | 0 | 1 | 0 |
| **INTERCEPTION RETURNS:** | | | | | | | | | | | | | |
| Number | 18 | 21 | 16 | 12 | 17 | 16 | 26 | 14 | 23 | 19 | 11 | 19 | 17 |
| Yards | 205 | 193 | 213 | 184 | 223 | 251 | 365 | 141 | 205 | 164 | 118 | 146 | 287 |
| Average Yards | 11.4 | 9.2 | 13.3 | 15.3 | 13.1 | 15.7 | 14.0 | 10.1 | 8.9 | 8.6 | 10.7 | 7.7 | 16.9 |
| Touchdowns | 1 | 0 | 1 | 1 | 1 | 1 | 2 | 0 | 2 | 0 | 0 | 3 | 1 |
| **PENALTIES:** | | | | | | | | | | | | | |
| Number | 73 | 74 | 90 | 48 | 63 | 78 | 51 | 69 | 57 | 76 | 64 | 73 | 78 |
| Yards | 650 | 574 | 841 | 417 | 610 | 648 | 440 | 585 | 512 | 690 | 582 | 664 | 721 |
| **FUMBLES:** Number | 42 | 40 | 27 | 17 | 22 | 24 | 32 | 33 | 32 | 37 | 43 | 30 | 27 |
| Number Lost | 19 | 22 | 15 | 7 | 10 | 9 | 19 | 16 | 14 | 18 | 16 | 13 | 11 |
| **POINTS:** | | | | | | | | | | | | | |
| Total | 269 | 225 | 319 | 339 | 304 | 291 | 301 | 215 | 331 | 145 | 193 | 353 | 336 |
| PAT Attempts | 31 | 27 | 36 | 40 | 29 | 31 | 34 | 26 | 39 | 12 | 22 | 43 | 42 |
| PAT Made | 31 | 27 | 36 | 39 | 29 | 31 | 34 | 24 | 34 | 11 | 19 | 41 | 40 |
| FG Attempts | 30 | 24 | 36 | 29 | 48 | 41 | 33 | 25 | 31 | 35 | 22 | 29 | 30 |
| FG Made | 16 | 12 | 21 | 20 | 33 | 24 | 21 | 11 | 21 | 20 | 14 | 18 | 14 |
| Percent FG Made | 53.3 | 50.0 | 58.3 | 69.0 | 68.8 | 58.5 | 63.6 | 44.0 | 67.7 | 57.1 | 63.6 | 62.1 | 46.7 |
| Safeties | 2 | 0 | 2 | 0 | 1 | 1 | 0 | 1 | 0 | 1 | 0 | 0 | 1 |

### DEFENSE

| | ATL. | CHI. | DALL. | DET. | G.B. | L.A. | MINN. | N.O. | N.Y. | PHIL. | ST.L. | S.F. | WASH. |
|---|---|---|---|---|---|---|---|---|---|---|---|---|---|
| **FIRST DOWNS:** | | | | | | | | | | | | | |
| Total | 221 | 224 | 217 | 239 | 209 | 235 | 200 | 251 | 218 | 268 | 276 | 221 | 223 |
| by Rushing | 122 | 96 | 81 | 126 | 85 | 101 | 103 | 107 | 101 | 137 | 119 | 96 | 95 |
| by Passing | 83 | 108 | 113 | 103 | 109 | 110 | 82 | 129 | 111 | 117 | 138 | 105 | 108 |
| by Penalty | 16 | 20 | 23 | 10 | 15 | 24 | 15 | 15 | 6 | 14 | 19 | 20 | 20 |
| **RUSHING:** | | | | | | | | | | | | | |
| Number | 504 | 476 | 428 | 491 | 443 | 438 | 454 | 482 | 402 | 544 | 548 | 446 | 427 |
| Yards | 2063 | 1751 | 1515 | 2204 | 1517 | 1762 | 2002 | 2089 | 1855 | 2266 | 2189 | 1847 | 1733 |
| Average Yards | 4.1 | 3.7 | 3.5 | 4.5 | 3.4 | 4.0 | 4.4 | 4.3 | 4.6 | 4.2 | 4.0 | 4.1 | 4.1 |
| Touchdowns | 16 | 11 | 7 | 14 | 14 | 9 | 13 | 15 | 9 | 22 | 11 | 12 | 12 |
| **PASSING:** | | | | | | | | | | | | | |
| Attempts | 301 | 342 | 382 | 312 | 340 | 363 | 331 | 367 | 333 | 318 | 365 | 366 | 367 |
| Completions | 137 | 180 | 187 | 171 | 174 | 181 | 169 | 213 | 182 | 175 | 221 | 169 | 186 |
| Completion Percentage | 45.5 | 52.6 | 49.0 | 54.8 | 51.2 | 49.9 | 51.1 | 58.0 | 54.7 | 55.0 | 60.5 | 46.2 | 50.7 |
| Passing Yards | 1911 | 2345 | 2508 | 2146 | 2209 | 2472 | 1791 | 2596 | 2571 | 2615 | 2733 | 2582 | 2130 |
| Avg. Yards per Attempt | 6.3 | 6.9 | 6.6 | 6.9 | 6.5 | 6.8 | 5.4 | 7.1 | 7.7 | 8.2 | 7.5 | 7.1 | 5.8 |
| Avg. Yards per Complet. | 13.9 | 13.0 | 13.4 | 12.5 | 12.7 | 13.7 | 10.6 | 12.2 | 14.1 | 14.9 | 12.4 | 15.3 | 11.5 |
| Times Tackled Passing | 24 | 23 | 32 | 21 | 29 | 42 | 21 | 24 | 37 | 17 | 22 | 46 | 35 |
| Yards Lost Tackled | 207 | 173 | 268 | 142 | 252 | 327 | 92 | 194 | 232 | 143 | 183 | 403 | 268 |
| Net Yards | 1704 | 2172 | 2240 | 2004 | 1957 | 2145 | 1699 | 2402 | 2339 | 2472 | 2550 | 2179 | 1862 |
| Touchdowns | 13 | 16 | 18 | 18 | 7 | 20 | 13 | 21 | 19 | 20 | 15 | 14 | 10 |
| Interceptions | 18 | 21 | 16 | 12 | 17 | 16 | 26 | 14 | 23 | 19 | 11 | 19 | 17 |
| Percent Intercepted | 6.0 | 6.1 | 4.2 | 3.8 | 5.0 | 4.4 | 7.9 | 3.8 | 6.9 | 6.0 | 3.0 | 5.2 | 4.6 |
| **PUNTS:** | | | | | | | | | | | | | |
| Number | 56 | 62 | 65 | 46 | 66 | 71 | 62 | 52 | 47 | 54 | 48 | 72 | 69 |
| Average Distance | 41.8 | 43.0 | 40.6 | 38.8 | 41.4 | 41.2 | 41.5 | 39.3 | 38.1 | 40.5 | 39.4 | 43.4 | 40.1 |
| **PUNT RETURNS:** | | | | | | | | | | | | | |
| Number | 30 | 24 | 15 | 26 | 32 | 22 | 35 | 36 | 27 | 26 | 37 | 20 | 19 |
| Yards | 239 | 126 | 41 | 321 | 225 | 54 | 317 | 281 | 171 | 137 | 144 | 70 | 39 |
| Average Yards | 8.0 | 5.3 | 2.7 | 12.3 | 7.0 | 2.5 | 9.1 | 7.8 | 6.3 | 5.3 | 3.9 | 3.5 | 2.1 |
| Touchdowns | 0 | 0 | 0 | 1 | 0 | 0 | 0 | 0 | 0 | 0 | 0 | 0 | 0 |
| **KICKOFF RETURNS:** | | | | | | | | | | | | | |
| Number | 48 | 42 | 52 | 68 | 46 | 54 | 62 | 50 | 63 | 41 | 40 | 66 | 53 |
| Yards | 1076 | 1025 | 1272 | 1593 | 932 | 999 | 1373 | 1129 | 1516 | 886 | 1037 | 1530 | 1191 |
| Average Yards | 22.4 | 24.4 | 24.5 | 23.4 | 20.3 | 18.5 | 22.1 | 22.6 | 24.1 | 21.6 | 25.9 | 23.2 | 22.5 |
| Touchdowns | 1 | 0 | 0 | 1 | 0 | 0 | 0 | 0 | 0 | 0 | 1 | 0 | 0 |
| **INTERCEPTION RETURNS:** | | | | | | | | | | | | | |
| Number | 15 | 13 | 23 | 23 | 9 | 22 | 13 | 21 | 15 | 20 | 23 | 24 | 15 |
| Yards | 206 | 104 | 302 | 294 | 69 | 439 | 116 | 349 | 192 | 198 | 289 | 240 | 160 |
| Average Yards | 13.7 | 8.0 | 13.1 | 16.3 | 7.7 | 20.0 | 8.9 | 16.6 | 12.8 | 9.9 | 12.6 | 10.0 | 10.7 |
| Touchdowns | 1 | 1 | 1 | 0 | 2 | 3 | 0 | 1 | 0 | 0 | 3 | 1 | 1 |
| **PENALTIES:** | | | | | | | | | | | | | |
| Number | 61 | 69 | 59 | 86 | 50 | 60 | 47 | 78 | 66 | 72 | 68 | 81 | 64 |
| Yards | 555 | 644 | 586 | 703 | 446 | 553 | 490 | 711 | 641 | 637 | 645 | 677 | 568 |
| **FUMBLES:** Number | 23 | 37 | 40 | 32 | 35 | 25 | 27 | 27 | 31 | 30 | 31 | 40 | 28 |
| Number Lost | 15 | 14 | 17 | 15 | 19 | 11 | 14 | 13 | 15 | 8 | 16 | 17 | 15 |
| **POINTS:** | | | | | | | | | | | | | |
| Total | 274 | 275 | 240 | 290 | 226 | 286 | 252 | 361 | 247 | 352 | 303 | 249 | 218 |
| PAT Attempts | 32 | 31 | 28 | 34 | 26 | 34 | 27 | 38 | 28 | 43 | 31 | 28 | 23 |
| PAT Made | 31 | 30 | 27 | 32 | 25 | 32 | 24 | 38 | 25 | 42 | 31 | 28 | 23 |
| FG Attempts | 31 | 27 | 34 | 34 | 27 | 30 | 35 | 43 | 29 | 25 | 47 | 29 | 33 |
| FG Made | 17 | 19 | 15 | 18 | 15 | 16 | 22 | 31 | 18 | 16 | 28 | 17 | 19 |
| Percent FG Made | 54.8 | 70.4 | 44.1 | 52.9 | 55.6 | 53.3 | 62.9 | 72.1 | 62.1 | 64.0 | 59.6 | 58.6 | 57.6 |
| Safeties | 0 | 1 | 0 | 0 | 0 | 1 | 0 | 1 | 0 | 2 | 1 | 1 | 0 |

## CONFERENCE PLAYOFFS

### December 23, at San Francisco (Attendance 59,746)

#### SCORING

| | | | | |
|---|---|---|---|---|
| SAN FRANCISCO | 7 | 14 | 7 | 0–28 |
| DALLAS | 3 | 10 | 0 | 17–30 |

First Quarter
- S.F. V. Washington, 97 yard kickoff return–PAT–Gossett (kick)
- DAL. Fritsch, 37 yard field goal

Second Quarter
- S.F. Schreiber, 1 yard rush PAT–Gossett (kick)
- S.F. Schreiber, 1 yard rush PAT–Gossett (kick)
- DAL. Fritsch, 45 yard field goal
- DAL. Alworth, 28 yard pass from Morton–PAT–Fritsch (kick)

Third Quarter
- S.F. Schreiber, 1 yard rush PAT–Gossett (kick)

Fourth Quarter
- DAL. Fritsch, 27 yard field goal
- DAL. Parks, 20 yard pass from Staubach–PAT–Fritsch (kick)
- DAL. Sellers, 10 yard pass from Staubach–PAT–Fritsch (kick)

#### TEAM STATISTICS

| S.F. | | DAL. |
|---|---|---|
| 13 | First Downs–Total | 22 |
| 7 | First Downs–Rushing | 5 |
| 6 | First Downs–Passing | 15 |
| 0 | First Downs–Penalty | 2 |
| 5 | Fumbles–Number | 4 |
| 1 | Fumbles–Lost Ball | 3 |
| 7 | Penalties–Number | 3 |
| 56 | Yards Penalized | 35 |
| 2 | Missed Field Goals | 0 |
| 59 | Offensive Plays | 77 |
| 261 | Net Yards | 402 |
| 4.4 | Average Gain | 5.2 |
| 3 | Giveaways | 5 |
| 5 | Takeaways | 3 |
| +2 | Difference | –2 |

#### INDIVIDUAL STATISTICS

| SAN FRANCISCO | No. | Yds. | Avg. | DALLAS | No. | Yds. | Avg. |
|---|---|---|---|---|---|---|---|
| **RUSHING** | | | | | | | |
| V. Washington | 10 | 56 | 5.6 | Hill | 18 | 125 | 6.9 |
| Schreiber | 26 | 52 | 2.0 | Staubach | 3 | 23 | 7.7 |
| Thomas | 1 | 3 | 3.0 | Garrison | 9 | 15 | 1.7 |
| | 37 | 111 | 3.0 | Morton | 1 | 2 | 2.0 |
| | | | | | 31 | 165 | 5.3 |
| **RECEIVING** | | | | | | | |
| Riley | 4 | 41 | 10.3 | Parks | 7 | 125 | 16.9 |
| G. Washington | 3 | 76 | 25.3 | Garrison | 3 | 24 | 8.0 |
| Schreiber | 3 | 20 | 6.7 | Alworth | 2 | 50 | 25.0 |
| V. Washington | 1 | 8 | 8.0 | Sellers | 2 | 21 | 10.5 |
| Kwalick | 1 | 5 | 5.0 | Montgomery | 2 | 19 | 9.5 |
| | 12 | 150 | 12.5 | Hayes | 1 | 13 | 13.0 |
| | | | | Ditka | 1 | 9 | 9.0 |
| | | | | Hill | 1 | 6 | 6.0 |
| | | | | Truax | 1 | 3 | 3.0 |
| | | | | | 20 | 270 | 13.5 |
| **PUNTING** | | | | | | | |
| McCann | 6 | | 37.3 | Bateman | 6 | | 41.8 |
| **PUNT RETURNS** | | | | | | | |
| Taylor | 1 | 5 | 5.0 | Waters | 1 | 2 | 2.0 |
| **KICKOFF RETURNS** | | | | | | | |
| V. Washington | 3 | 136 | 45.3 | Harris | 3 | 83 | 27.7 |
| Beard | 1 | 5 | 5.0 | | | | |
| McGill | 1 | 5 | 5.0 | | | | |
| | 5 | 146 | 29.2 | | | | |
| **INTERCEPTION RETURNS** | | | | | | | |
| Vanderbundt | 2 | 4 | 2.0 | Waters | 2 | 12 | 6.0 |

**PASSING**

| SAN FRANCISCO | Att. | Comp. | Comp. Pct. | Yds. | Int. | Yds/ Att. | Yds/ Comp. | Yards Lost Tackled |
|---|---|---|---|---|---|---|---|---|
| Brodie | 22 | 12 | 54.5 | 150 | 2 | 6.8 | 12.5 | 0– 0 |
| **DALLAS** | | | | | | | | |
| Morton | 21 | 8 | 38.1 | 96 | 2 | 4.6 | 12.0 | |
| Staubach | 20 | 12 | 60.0 | 174 | 0 | 8.7 | 14.5 | |
| | 41 | 20 | 48.8 | 270 | 2 | 6.6 | 13.5 | 5–33 |

### December 24, at Washington (Attendance 52,321)

#### SCORING

| | | | | |
|---|---|---|---|---|
| WASHINGTON | 0 | 10 | 0 | 6–16 |
| GREEN BAY | 0 | 3 | 0 | 0– 3 |

Second Quarter
- G.B. Marcol, 17 yard field goal
- WASH. Jefferson, 32 yard pass from Kilmer–PAT–Knight (kick)
- WASH. Knight, 42 yard field goal

Fourth Quarter
- WASH. Knight, 35 yard field goal
- WASH. Knight, 46 yard field goal

#### TEAM STATISTICS

| WASH. | | G.B. |
|---|---|---|
| 13 | First Downs–Total | 10 |
| 6 | First Downs–Rushing | 2 |
| 4 | First Downs–Passing | 8 |
| 3 | First Downs–Penalty | 0 |
| 1 | Fumbles–Number | 0 |
| 1 | Fumbles–Lost Ball | 0 |
| 4 | Penalties–Number | 6 |
| 39 | Yards Penalized | 54 |
| 0 | Missed Field Goals | 1 |
| 51 | Offensive Plays | 55 |
| 232 | Net Yards | 211 |
| 4.5 | Average Gain | 3.8 |
| 1 | Giveaways | 1 |
| 1 | Takeaways | 1 |
| 0 | Difference | 0 |

#### INDIVIDUAL STATISTICS

| WASHINGTON | No. | Yds. | Avg. | GREEN BAY | No. | Yds. | Avg. |
|---|---|---|---|---|---|---|---|
| **RUSHING** | | | | | | | |
| Brown | 25 | 101 | 4.0 | Lane | 14 | 56 | 4.0 |
| Harraway | 10 | 34 | 3.4 | Hunter | 2 | 13 | 6.5 |
| Kilmer | 1 | 3 | 3.0 | Brockington | 13 | 9 | 0.7 |
| | 36 | 138 | 3.8 | | 29 | 78 | 2.7 |
| **RECEIVING** | | | | | | | |
| Jefferson | 5 | 84 | 16.8 | Lane | 4 | 42 | 10.5 |
| Taylor | 2 | 16 | 8.0 | Dale | 2 | 28 | 14.0 |
| | 7 | 100 | 14.3 | Glass | 2 | 23 | 11.5 |
| | | | | Brockington | 2 | 17 | 8.5 |
| | | | | Staggers | 1 | 23 | 23.0 |
| | | | | Garrett | 1 | 17 | 17.0 |
| | | | | | 12 | 150 | 12.5 |
| **PUNTING** | | | | | | | |
| Bragg | 6 | | 46.5 | Widby | 8 | | 36.6 |
| **PUNT RETURNS** | | | | | | | |
| Haymond | 2 | 4 | 2.0 | Staggers | 3 | 20 | 6.7 |
| Vactor | 1 | 15 | 15.0 | Ellis | 1 | 13 | 13.0 |
| | 3 | 19 | 6.3 | | 4 | 33 | 8.3 |
| **KICKOFF RETURNS** | | | | | | | |
| Mul-Key | 2 | 60 | 30.0 | Thomas | 3 | 50 | 16.7 |
| | | | | Hudson | 1 | 12 | 12.0 |
| | | | | | 4 | 62 | 15.5 |
| **INTERCEPTION RETURNS** | | | | | | | |
| Hanburger | 1 | 15 | 15.0 | None | | | |

**PASSING**

| WASHINGTON | Att. | Comp. | Comp. Pct. | Yds. | Int. | Yds/ Att. | Yds/ Comp. | Yards Lost Tackled |
|---|---|---|---|---|---|---|---|---|
| Kilmer | 14 | 7 | 50.0 | 100 | 0 | 7.1 | 14.3 | 1– 6 |
| **GREEN BAY** | | | | | | | | |
| Hunter | 24 | 12 | 50.0 | 150 | 1 | 6.3 | 12.5 | 2–17 |

## WASHINGTON REDSKINS 11-3-0 George Allen

| Scores of Each Game | | |
|---|---|---|
| 24 | Minnesota | 21 |
| 24 | ST. LOUIS | 10 |
| 23 | New England | 24 |
| 14 | PHILADELPHIA | 0 |
| 33 | St. Louis | 3 |
| 24 | DALLAS | 20 |
| 23 | N.Y. Giants | 16 |
| 35 | N.Y. Jets | 17 |
| 27 | N.Y. GIANTS | 13 |
| 24 | ATLANTA | 13 |
| 21 | GREEN BAY | 16 |
| 23 | Philadelphia | 7 |
| 24 | Dallas | 34 |
| 17 | BUFFALO | 24 |

| Use Name | Pos. | Hgt | Wgt | Age | Int | Pts |
|---|---|---|---|---|---|---|
| Terry Hermeling | OT | 6'5" | 255 | 26 | | |
| Mitch Johnson | OT | 6'4" | 250 | 30 | | |
| Walt Rock | OT | 6'5" | 255 | 31 | | |
| Paul Laaveg | OG | 6'4" | 245 | 23 | | |
| John Wilbur | OG | 6'3" | 250 | 29 | | |
| Ray Schoenke | OT-OG | 6'3" | 250 | 30 | | |
| Len Hauss | C | 6'2" | 235 | 30 | | |
| George Burman | QG-C | 6'3" | 255 | 29 | | |
| Verlon Biggs | DE | 6'4" | 275 | 29 | | 6 |
| Mike Fanucci | DE | 6'4" | 225 | 22 | | |
| Jimmie Jones | DE | 6'3" | 215 | 25 | | |
| Ron McDole | DT-DE | 6'3" | 265 | 32 | | |
| Bill Brundige | DT | 6'5" | 270 | 23 | | |
| Manny Sistrunk | DT | 6'5" | 265 | 25 | | |
| Diron Talbert | DT | 6'5" | 255 | 28 | | |

Jim Snowden – Injury

| Use Name | Pos. | Hgt | Wgt | Age | Int | Pts |
|---|---|---|---|---|---|---|
| Chris Hamburger | LB | 6'2" | 218 | 31 | 4 | 6 |
| Harold McLinton | LB | 6'2" | 235 | 25 | 2 | |
| Jack Pardee | LB | 6'2" | 225 | 36 | | |
| Myron Pottios | LB | 6'2" | 232 | 32 | | |
| Rusty Tillman | LB | 6'2" | 230 | 26 | | |
| Mike Bass | DB | 6' | 190 | 27 | 3 | 6 |
| Speedy Duncan | DB | 5'10" | 180 | 29 | 1 | |
| Pat Fischer | DB | 5'10" | 170 | 32 | 4 | |
| Alvin Haymond | DB | 6' | 194 | 30 | | |
| Jon Jaqua | DB | 6' | 190 | 24 | | |
| Brig Owens | DB | 5'11" | 190 | 29 | 1 | |
| Richie Petitbon | DB | 6'3" | 208 | 34 | | |
| Jeff Severson | DB | 6'1" | 180 | 22 | | |
| Rosey Taylor | DB | 5'11" | 186 | 33 | 1 | |
| Ted Vactor | DB | 6' | 185 | 28 | 1 | |

Tommy Mason – Injury

| Use Name | Pos. | Hgt | Wgt | Age | Int | Pts |
|---|---|---|---|---|---|---|
| Sonny Jurgensen | QB | 5'11" | 203 | 38 | | |
| Billy Kilmer | QB | 6' | 204 | 32 | | |
| Sam Wyche | QB | 6'4" | 218 | 27 | | |
| Larry Brown | HB | 5'11" | 195 | 24 | | 72 |
| Bob Brunet | HB | 6'1" | 205 | 26 | | 12 |
| Herb Mul–Key | HB | 6' | 190 | 22 | | 6 |
| George Nock | HB | 5'10" | 200 | 26 | | |
| Charlie Harraway | FB | 6'2" | 215 | 27 | | 36 |
| Mike Hull | FB | 6'3" | 220 | 27 | | |
| Jeff Jordan | HB-FB | 6'1" | 215 | 27 | | |
| Roy Jefferson | WR | 6'2" | 195 | 28 | | 18 |
| Bill Malinchak | WR | 6'1" | 200 | 28 | | 8 |
| Clifton McNeil | WR | 6'2" | 187 | 32 | | |
| Charley Taylor | WR | 6'3" | 210 | 31 | | 42 |
| Mack Alston | TE | 6'2" | 230 | 25 | | |
| Jerry Smith | TE | 6'2" | 208 | 29 | | 42 |
| Mike Bragg | K | 5'11" | 186 | 25 | | |
| Curt Knight | K | 6'1" | 190 | 29 | | 82 |

## DALLAS COWBOYS 10-4-0 Tom Landry

| Scores of Each Game | | |
|---|---|---|
| 28 | PHILADELPHIA | 6 |
| 23 | N.Y. Giants | 14 |
| 13 | Green Bay | 16 |
| 17 | PITTSBURGH | 13 |
| 21 | Baltimore | 0 |
| 20 | Washington | 24 |
| 28 | DETROIT | 24 |
| 34 | San Diego | 28 |
| 33 | ST. LOUIS | 24 |
| 28 | Philadelphia | 7 |
| 10 | SAN FRANCISCO | 31 |
| 27 | St. Louis | 6 |
| 34 | WASHINGTON | 24 |
| 3 | N.Y. GIANTS | 23 |

| Use Name | Pos. | Hgt | Wgt | Age | Int | Pts |
|---|---|---|---|---|---|---|
| Ralph Neely | OT | 6'5" | 265 | 28 | | |
| Rayfield Wright | OT | 6'7" | 255 | 27 | | |
| Rodney Wallace | OG-OT | 6'5" | 255 | 23 | | |
| John Niland | OG | 6'4" | 245 | 28 | | 6 |
| Blaine Nye | OG | 6'4" | 250 | 26 | | |
| John Fitzgerald | C-OG | 6'5" | 250 | 24 | | |
| Dave Manders | C | 6'2" | 250 | 30 | | |
| George Andrie | DE | 6'7" | 250 | 32 | | |
| Larry Cole | DE | 6'4" | 250 | 25 | | |
| Tody Smith | DE | 6'5" | 245 | 23 | | |
| Pat Toomay | DE | 6'5" | 244 | 27 | | |
| Bill Gregory | DT | 6'5" | 255 | 22 | | |
| Bob Lilly | DT | 6'4" | 260 | 33 | | |
| Jethro Pugh | DT | 6'6" | 260 | 28 | | |

| Use Name | Pos. | Hgt | Wgt | Age | Int | Pts |
|---|---|---|---|---|---|---|
| John Babinecz | LB | 6'1" | 222 | 22 | | |
| Ralph Coleman | LB | 6'4" | 216 | 22 | | |
| Dave Edwards | LB | 6'3" | 225 | 33 | | |
| Chuck Howley | LB | 6'3" | 225 | 36 | 1 | |
| Lee Roy Jordan | LB | 6'2" | 220 | 31 | 2 | |
| Mike Keller | LB | 6'4" | 220 | 21 | | |
| D. D. Lewis | LB | 6'2" | 225 | 26 | 1 | |
| Herb Adderly | DB | 6'1" | 200 | 33 | | |
| Benny Barnes | DB | 6'1" | 190 | 21 | | |
| Cornell Green | DB | 6'4" | 208 | 32 | 2 | |
| Cliff Harris | DB | 6' | 184 | 23 | 3 | |
| Mel Renfro | DB | 6' | 190 | 30 | 1 | |
| Mark Washington | DB | 5'10" | 188 | 24 | | 2 |
| Charlie Waters | DB | 6'1" | 193 | 23 | 6 | 6 |

| Use Name | Pos. | Hgt | Wgt | Age | Int | Pts |
|---|---|---|---|---|---|---|
| Craig Morton | QB | 6'4" | 214 | 29 | | 12 |
| Roger Staubach | QB | 6'2" | 197 | 30 | | |
| Mike Montgomery | HB | 6'2" | 210 | 23 | | 18 |
| Dan Reeves | HB | 6'1" | 200 | 28 | | |
| Calvin Hill | FB-HB | 6'3" | 227 | 25 | | 54 |
| Robert Newhouse | FB-HB | 5'10" | 202 | 22 | | 6 |
| Walt Garrison | FB | 6' | 205 | 28 | | 60 |
| Bill Thomas | FB | 6'2" | 225 | 22 | | |
| Lance Alworth | WR | 6' | 180 | 32 | | 12 |
| Bob Hayes | WR | 6' | 185 | 29 | | |
| Billy Parks | WR | 6'1" | 185 | 24 | | 6 |
| Ron Sellers | WR | 6'4" | 195 | 25 | | 30 |
| Mike Ditka | TE | 6'3" | 225 | 32 | | 6 |
| Jean Fugett | TE | 6'3" | 220 | 20 | | |
| Billy Truax | TE | 6'5" | 240 | 29 | | |
| Marv Bateman | K | 6'4" | 213 | 22 | | |
| Toni Fritsch | K | 5'7" | 185 | 27 | | 99 |

## NEW YORK GIANTS 8-6-0 Alex Webster

| Scores of Each Game | | |
|---|---|---|
| 16 | Detroit | 30 |
| 14 | DALLAS | 23 |
| 27 | Philadelphia | 12 |
| 45 | NEW ORLEANS | 21 |
| 23 | San Francisco | 17 |
| 27 | ST. LOUIS | 21 |
| 16 | WASHINGTON | 23 |
| 29 | DENVER | 17 |
| 13 | Washington | 27 |
| 13 | St. Louis | 7 |
| 62 | PHILADELPHIA | 10 |
| 10 | Cincinnati | 13 |
| 13 | MIAMI | 23 |
| 23 | Dallas | 3 |

| Use Name | Pos. | Hgt | Wgt | Age | Int | Pts |
|---|---|---|---|---|---|---|
| Joe Taffoni | OT | 6'3" | 255 | 27 | | |
| Willie Young | OT | 6' | 265 | 29 | | |
| John Hill | C-OT | 6'2" | 245 | 22 | | |
| Mark Ellison | OG | 6'2" | 250 | 23 | | |
| Dick Enderle | OG | 6'1" | 250 | 24 | | |
| Doug Van Horn | OG | 6'2" | 245 | 28 | | |
| Bob Hyland | C-OT-OG | 6'5" | 255 | 27 | | |
| Greg Larson | C | 6'2" | 250 | 33 | | |
| Jack Gregory | DE | 6'6" | 250 | 27 | | |
| Henry Reed | DE | 6'3" | 230 | 23 | | |
| Larry Jacobsen | DT-DE | 6'6" | 260 | 22 | | |
| Dan Goich | DT | 6'4" | 250 | 28 | | |
| John Mendenhall | DT | 6'1" | 255 | 23 | | |
| Charlie Harper | DT | 6'2" | 250 | 28 | | |
| Dave Tipton | DE-DT | 6' | 240 | 23 | | |

| Use Name | Pos. | Hgt | Wgt | Age | Int | Pts |
|---|---|---|---|---|---|---|
| Carter Campbell | LB | 6'3" | 240 | 24 | | |
| John Douglas | LB | 6'2" | 228 | 27 | 1 | |
| Jim Files | LB | 6'4" | 240 | 24 | 2 | 6 |
| Ron Hornsby | LB | 6'3" | 232 | 23 | | |
| Pat Hughes | LB | 6'2" | 240 | 25 | 2 | |
| Pete Athas | DB | 5'11" | 185 | 24 | 4 | |
| Otto Brown | DB | 6'1" | 188 | 25 | 1 | |
| Chuck Crist | DB | 6'2" | 205 | 21 | 1 | |
| Richmond Flowers | DB | 6' | 180 | 25 | 4 | |
| Spider Lockhart | DB | 6'2" | 175 | 29 | 4 | 6 |
| Eldridge Small | DB | 6'1" | 190 | 22 | | |
| Willie Williams | DB | 6' | 190 | 29 | 4 | |

Scott Eaton – Injury
Jim Kanicki – Knee Injury

| Use Name | Pos. | Hgt | Wgt | Age | Int | Pts |
|---|---|---|---|---|---|---|
| Randy Johnson | QB | 6'3" | 205 | 28 | | 6 |
| Norm Snead | QB | 6'4" | 215 | 32 | | |
| Bobby Duhon | HB | 6' | 195 | 25 | | |
| Ron Johnson | HB | 6'1" | 205 | 24 | | 84 |
| Rocky Thompson | HB | 5'11" | 200 | 24 | | 6 |
| Vin Clements | FB | 6'3" | 210 | 23 | | |
| Charlie Evans | FB | 6'1" | 220 | 24 | | 30 |
| Joe Orduna | HB-FB | 6' | 195 | 24 | | 12 |
| Bob Grim | WR | 6' | 200 | 27 | | 6 |
| Don Herrmann | WR | 6'2" | 205 | 25 | | 30 |
| Rich Houston | WR | 6'2" | 195 | 26 | | 18 |
| Joe Morrison | HB-FB-WR | 6'1" | 212 | 34 | | |
| Dick Kotite | TE | 6'3" | 230 | 29 | | |
| Bob Tucker | TE | 6'3" | 230 | 27 | | 30 |
| Tom Gatewood | WR-TE | 6'3" | 215 | 21 | | |
| Tom Blanchard | K | 6' | 190 | 24 | | |
| Pete Gogolak | K | 6'2" | 190 | 30 | | 97 |

## ST. LOUIS CARDINALS 4-9-1 Bob Holloway

| Scores of Each Game | | |
|---|---|---|
| 10 | Baltimore | 3 |
| 10 | Washington | 24 |
| 19 | PITTSBURGH | 25 |
| 19 | Minnesota | 17 |
| 3 | WASHINGTON | 33 |
| 21 | N.Y. Giants | 27 |
| 10 | CHICAGO | 27 |
| 6 | Philadelphia | 6 |
| 24 | Dallas | 33 |
| 7 | N.Y. GIANTS | 13 |
| 10 | Miami | 31 |
| 6 | DALLAS | 27 |
| 24 | LOS ANGELES | 14 |
| 24 | PHILADELPHIA | 23 |

| Use Name | Pos. | Hgt | Wgt | Age | Int | Pts |
|---|---|---|---|---|---|---|
| Ernie McMillan | OT | 6'6" | 255 | 34 | | |
| Steve Wright | OT | 6'6" | 250 | 30 | | |
| Dan Dierdorf | OG-OT | 6'4" | 265 | 23 | | |
| Dave Bradley | OG | 6'4" | 245 | 25 | | |
| Conrad Dobler | OG | 6'3" | 250 | 21 | | |
| Chuck Hutchison | OG | 6'3" | 240 | 23 | | |
| Bob Young | OG | 6'2" | 260 | 29 | | |
| Wayne Mulligan | C | 6'2" | 245 | 25 | | |
| Tom Banks | OG-C | 6'1" | 240 | 24 | | |
| Tom Beckman | DE | 6'5" | 250 | 21 | | |
| Don Brumm | DE | 6'3" | 245 | 29 | | |
| Martin Imhof | DE | 6'6" | 255 | 22 | | |
| Ron Yankowski | DE | 6'5" | 225 | 25 | | |
| Fred Heron | DT | 6'4" | 240 | 27 | | |
| Scott Palmer | DT | 6'3" | 245 | 24 | | |
| John Richardson | DT | 6'2" | 250 | 28 | | |
| Bob Rowe | DT | 6'4" | 260 | 27 | | |

| Use Name | Pos. | Hgt | Wgt | Age | Int | Pts |
|---|---|---|---|---|---|---|
| Mark Arneson | LB | 6'2" | 220 | 22 | | |
| Steve Conley (from CIN) | LB | 6'2" | 225 | 23 | | |
| Jim Hargrove | LB | 6'3" | 225 | 27 | | |
| Mike McGill | LB | 6'2" | 235 | 25 | 2 | |
| Terry Miller | LB | 6'2" | 225 | 26 | | |
| Jamie Rivers | LB | 6'2" | 235 | 26 | | |
| Jeff Staggs | LB | 6'2" | 240 | 28 | 1 | |
| Larry Stallings | LB | 6'2" | 230 | 30 | | |
| Miller Farr | DB | 6'1" | 190 | 29 | 3 | |
| Dale Hackbart | DB | 6'3" | 210 | 36 | 1 | |
| Norm Thompson | DB | 6'1" | 175 | 24 | 1 | 12 |
| Eric Washington | DB | 6'2" | 190 | 22 | | |
| Roger Wehrli | DB | 6'1" | 195 | 24 | | |
| Larry Willingham | DB | 6'1" | 190 | 23 | | |
| Larry Wilson | DB | 6' | 195 | 34 | 3 | |

Jeff Allen – Injury
Larry Stegent – Injury

| Use Name | Pos. | Hgt | Wgt | Age | Int | Pts |
|---|---|---|---|---|---|---|
| Gary Cuozzo | QB | 6'1" | 195 | 31 | | |
| Jim Hart | QB | 6'2" | 200 | 28 | | |
| Tim Van Galder | QB | 6'1" | 190 | 28 | | |
| Danny Anderson | HB | 6'3" | 210 | 29 | | 36 |
| Craig Baynham | HB | 6'1" | 205 | 28 | | |
| Cannonball Butler | HB | 5'10" | 200 | 29 | | |
| Roy Shivers | HB | 6' | 200 | 30 | | |
| Leo Hayden | FB-HB | 6' | 210 | 24 | | 6 |
| Don Heater | FB-HB | 6'2" | 205 | 22 | | |
| Leon Burns | FB | 6'2" | 235 | 27 | | 12 |
| Tom Woodeshick | FB | 6' | 222 | 30 | | |
| Johnny Roland | HB-FB | 6'2" | 215 | 29 | | 24 |
| Walker Gillette | WR | 6'5" | 200 | 25 | | 12 |
| Mel Gray | WR | 5'9" | 170 | 23 | | |
| Freddie Hyatt | WR | 6'3" | 200 | 26 | | |
| Bobby Moore | WR | 6'2" | 210 | 22 | | 18 |
| Bob Wicks | WR | 6'3" | 195 | 22 | | |
| Jim McFarland | TE | 6'5" | 225 | 24 | | |
| Ara Person | TE | 6'2" | 220 | 23 | | |
| Jackie Smith | TE | 6'4" | 235 | 31 | | 12 |
| Jim Bakken | K | 6' | 195 | 31 | | 61 |

## PHILADELPHIA EAGLES 2-11-1 Ed Khayat

| Scores of Each Game | | |
|---|---|---|
| 6 | Dallas | 28 |
| 17 | CLEVELAND | 27 |
| 12 | N.Y. GIANTS | 27 |
| 0 | Washington | 14 |
| 3 | LOS ANGELES | 34 |
| 21 | Kansas City | 20 |
| 3 | New Orleans | 21 |
| 6 | ST. LOUIS | 6 |
| 18 | Houston | 17 |
| 7 | DALLAS | 28 |
| 10 | N.Y. Giants | 62 |
| 7 | WASHINGTON | 23 |
| 12 | CHICAGO | 21 |
| 23 | St. Louis | 24 |

| Use Name | Pos. | Hgt | Wgt | Age | Int | Pts |
|---|---|---|---|---|---|---|
| Wade Key | OT | 6'4" | 245 | 25 | | |
| Wayne Mass (from NE) | OT | 6'4" | 245 | 26 | | |
| Steve Smith | OT | 6'5" | 250 | 28 | | |
| Dick Stevens | OT | 6'4" | 240 | 24 | | |
| Henry Allison | OG | 6'2" | 255 | 25 | | |
| Tom Luken | OG | 6'3" | 253 | 22 | | |
| Jim Skaggs | OG | 6'2" | 250 | 32 | | |
| Vern Winfield | OG | 6'2" | 248 | 23 | | |
| Mark Nordquist | C-OG | 6'4" | 246 | 26 | | |
| Mike Evans | C | 6'5" | 250 | 26 | | |
| Jerry Sturm | C | 6'3" | 260 | 35 | | |
| Larry Estes | DE | 6'6" | 250 | 25 | | |
| Richard Harris | DE | 6'4" | 260 | 24 | | |
| Mel Tom | DE | 6'4" | 250 | 31 | | |
| Houston Antwine | DT | 6' | 270 | 33 | | |
| Don Hultz | DT | 6'3" | 240 | 31 | | |
| Gary Pettigrew | DT | 6'4" | 255 | 27 | | |
| Ernie Calloway | DE-DT | 6'6" | 255 | 24 | | |

| Use Name | Pos. | Hgt | Wgt | Age | Int | Pts |
|---|---|---|---|---|---|---|
| Dick Absher | LB | 6'4" | 235 | 28 | 1 | |
| Chuck Allen | LB | 6'1" | 225 | 32 | 1 | |
| John Bunting | LB | 6'1" | 220 | 22 | 1 | |
| Bill Cody | LB | 6'1" | 230 | 28 | | |
| Bob Creech | LB | 6'3" | 228 | 23 | | |
| Bill Overmeyer | LB | 6'3" | 220 | 23 | | |
| Ron Porter | LB | 6'3" | 232 | 27 | 2 | |
| John Sodaski | LB | 6'2" | 222 | 24 | | |
| Steve Zabel | LB | 6'4" | 235 | 24 | | |
| Kermit Alexander | DB | 5'11" | 186 | 31 | | |
| Jackie Allen | DB | 6'1" | 187 | 24 | | |
| Bill Bradley | DB | 5'11" | 190 | 25 | 9 | |
| Al Coleman | DB | 6'1" | 183 | 27 | | 2 |
| Pat Gibbs | DB | 5'10" | 188 | 22 | | |
| Leroy Keyes | DB | 6'3" | 208 | 25 | 2 | |
| Al Nelson | DB | 5'11" | 186 | 28 | | |
| Nate Ramsey | DB | 6'1" | 200 | 31 | 3 | |
| Jim Thrower | DB | 6'2" | 194 | 23 | | |

Lee Bouggess – Injury
Ike Kelly – Injury

| Use Name | Pos. | Hgt | Wgt | Age | Int | Pts |
|---|---|---|---|---|---|---|
| Rick Arrington | QB | 6'2" | 185 | 25 | | |
| Pete Liske | QB | 6'2" | 200 | 31 | | |
| John Reaves | QB | 6'3" | 210 | 22 | | 6 |
| Larry Crowe | HB | 6'1" | 198 | 22 | | |
| Po James | HB | 6'1" | 202 | 23 | | 6 |
| Tom Sullivan | HB | 6' | 190 | 22 | | |
| Sonny Davis | FB-HB | 5'11" | 215 | 24 | | |
| Tony Baker | FB | 5'11" | 225 | 27 | | |
| Larry Watkins | FB | 6'2" | 230 | 25 | | 6 |
| Tom Bailey | HB-FB | 6'2" | 211 | 23 | | |
| Harold Carmichael | WR | 6'7" | 225 | 22 | | 12 |
| Ben Hawkins | WR | 6' | 180 | 28 | | 6 |
| Harold Jackson | WR | 5'10" | 175 | 26 | | 24 |
| Billy Walik | WR | 5'11" | 180 | 24 | | 6 |
| Clark Hoss | TE | 6'8" | 235 | 23 | | |
| Kent Kramer | TE | 6'5" | 235 | 28 | | 6 |
| Gary Ballman | WR-TE | 6' | 215 | 32 | | |
| Tom Dempsey | K | 6'1" | 255 | 31 | | 71 |
| Tom McNeil | K | 6'1" | 195 | 30 | | |

## WASHINGTON REDSKINS

### Rushing
| Last Name | No. | Yds | Avg | TD |
|---|---|---|---|---|
| Brown | 285 | 1216 | 4.3 | 8 |
| Harraway | 148 | 567 | 3.8 | 6 |
| Mul-Key | 33 | 155 | 4.7 | 1 |
| Brunet | 30 | 82 | 2.7 | 2 |
| C. Taylor | 3 | 39 | 13.0 | 0 |
| Nock | 6 | 22 | 3.7 | 0 |
| Smith | 1 | 9 | 9.0 | 0 |
| Kilmer | 3 | -3 | -1.0 | 0 |
| Jurgensen | 4 | -5 | -1.3 | 0 |

### Receiving
| Last Name | No. | Yds | Avg | TD |
|---|---|---|---|---|
| C. Taylor | 49 | 673 | 14 | 7 |
| Jefferson | 35 | 550 | 16 | 3 |
| Brown | 32 | 473 | 15 | 4 |
| Smith | 21 | 353 | 17 | 7 |
| Harraway | 15 | 105 | 7 | 0 |
| Mul-Key | 4 | 66 | 17 | 0 |
| Alston | 2 | 53 | 27 | 0 |
| Brunet | 1 | 8 | 8 | 0 |

### Punt Returns
| Last Name | No. | Yds | Avg | TD |
|---|---|---|---|---|
| Vactor | 17 | 88 | 5 | 0 |
| Duncan | 11 | 70 | 6 | 0 |
| Haymond | 6 | 1 | 0 | 0 |

### Kickoff Returns
| Last Name | No. | Yds | Avg | TD |
|---|---|---|---|---|
| Duncan | 15 | 364 | 24 | 0 |
| Haymond | 10 | 291 | 29 | 0 |
| Mul-Key | 8 | 209 | 26 | 0 |
| Brunet | 8 | 190 | 24 | 0 |
| Bass | 2 | 22 | 11 | 0 |
| Vactor | 1 | 21 | 21 | 0 |
| Fanucci | 1 | 15 | 15 | 0 |
| McLinton | 1 | 15 | 15 | 0 |
| Tillman | 2 | 6 | 3 | 0 |

### Passing – Punting – Kicking
| PASSING | Att | Comp | % | Yds | Yd/Att | TD | Int- | % | RK |
|---|---|---|---|---|---|---|---|---|---|
| Kilmer | 225 | 120 | 53 | 1648 | 7.3 | 19 | 11- | 5 | 4 |
| Jurgensen | 59 | 39 | 66 | 633 | 10.7 | 2 | 4- | 7 | |

| PUNTING | No | Avg |
|---|---|---|
| Bragg | 59 | 38.5 |

| KICKING | XP | Att | % | FG | Att | % |
|---|---|---|---|---|---|---|
| Knight | 40 | 41 | 98 | 14 | 30 | 47 |

## DALLAS COWBOYS

### Rushing
| Last Name | No. | Yds | Avg | TD |
|---|---|---|---|---|
| Hill | 245 | 1036 | 4.2 | 6 |
| Garrison | 167 | 784 | 4.7 | 7 |
| Newhouse | 28 | 116 | 4.1 | 1 |
| Montgomery | 35 | 81 | 2.3 | 1 |
| Staubach | 6 | 45 | 7.5 | 0 |
| Morton | 8 | 26 | 3.3 | 2 |
| Reeves | 3 | 14 | 4.7 | 0 |
| Neely | 1 | 10 | 10.0 | 0 |
| Hayes | 2 | 8 | 4.0 | 0 |
| Alworth | 1 | 2 | 2.0 | 0 |
| Fugett | 3 | 2 | 0.7 | 0 |

### Receiving
| Last Name | No. | Yds | Avg | TD |
|---|---|---|---|---|
| Hill | 43 | 364 | 8 | 3 |
| Garrison | 37 | 390 | 11 | 4 |
| Sellers | 31 | 653 | 21 | 5 |
| Parks | 18 | 298 | 17 | 1 |
| Ditka | 17 | 198 | 12 | 1 |
| Hayes | 15 | 200 | 13 | 0 |
| Alworth | 15 | 195 | 13 | 2 |
| Montgomery | 8 | 131 | 16 | 1 |
| Fugett | 7 | 94 | 13 | 0 |
| Truax | 4 | 49 | 12 | 0 |
| Newhouse | 1 | 8 | 8 | 0 |

### Punt Returns
| Last Name | No. | Yds | Avg | TD |
|---|---|---|---|---|
| Harris | 19 | 78 | 4 | 0 |
| Waters | 9 | 56 | 6 | 0 |

### Kickoff Returns
| Last Name | No. | Yds | Avg | TD |
|---|---|---|---|---|
| Harris | 26 | 615 | 24 | 0 |
| Newhouse | 18 | 382 | 21 | 0 |
| Thomas | 2 | 50 | 25 | 0 |
| Waters | 2 | 18 | 9 | 0 |
| Montgomery | 1 | 15 | 15 | 0 |
| Fugett | 1 | 0 | 0 | 0 |

### Passing – Punting – Kicking
| PASSING | Att | Comp | % | Yds | Yd/Att | TD | Int- | % | RK |
|---|---|---|---|---|---|---|---|---|---|
| Morton | 339 | 185 | 55 | 2396 | 7.1 | 15 | 21- | 6 | 8 |
| Staubach | 20 | 9 | 45 | 98 | 4.9 | 0 | 2- | 10 | |
| Hill | 3 | 1 | 33 | 55 | 18.3 | 1 | 0- | 0 | |
| Montgomery | 3 | 1 | 33 | 31 | 10.3 | 0 | 0- | 0 | |
| Reeves | 2 | 0 | 0 | 0 | 0.0 | 0 | 0- | 0 | |

| PUNTING | No | Avg |
|---|---|---|
| Bateman | 51 | 38.2 |

| KICKING | XP | Att | % | FG | Att | % |
|---|---|---|---|---|---|---|
| Fritsch | 36 | 36 | 100 | 21 | 36 | 58 |

## NEW YORK GIANTS

### Rushing
| Last Name | No. | Yds | Avg | TD |
|---|---|---|---|---|
| Ron Johnson | 298 | 1182 | 4.0 | 9 |
| Evans | 91 | 317 | 3.5 | 4 |
| Clements | 46 | 221 | 4.8 | 0 |
| Orduna | 36 | 129 | 3.6 | 1 |
| Morrison | 9 | 36 | 4.0 | 0 |
| Thompson | 9 | 35 | 3.9 | 0 |
| Randy Johnson | 9 | 26 | 2.9 | 1 |
| Duhon | 9 | 23 | 2.6 | 0 |
| Snead | 10 | 21 | 2.1 | 0 |
| Blanchard | 1 | 17 | 17.0 | 0 |
| Herrmann | 3 | 9 | 3.0 | 0 |
| Tucker | 3 | 6 | 2.0 | 1 |

### Receiving
| Last Name | No. | Yds | Avg | TD |
|---|---|---|---|---|
| Tucker | 55 | 764 | 14 | 4 |
| Ron Johnson | 45 | 451 | 10 | 5 |
| Herrmann | 28 | 422 | 15 | 5 |
| Houston | 27 | 468 | 17 | 3 |
| Evans | 26 | 182 | 7 | 1 |
| Clements | 9 | 118 | 13 | 0 |
| Grim | 5 | 67 | 13 | 1 |
| Morrison | 5 | 39 | 8 | 0 |
| Orduna | 4 | 6 | 2 | 1 |
| Duhon | 2 | 20 | 10 | 0 |

### Punt Returns
| Last Name | No. | Yds | Avg | TD |
|---|---|---|---|---|
| Athas | 8 | 95 | 12 | 0 |
| Duhon | 2 | 20 | 10 | 0 |
| Grim | 1 | 7 | 10 | 0 |
| Mendenhall | 1 | 0 | 0 | 0 |

### Kickoff Returns
| Last Name | No. | Yds | Avg | TD |
|---|---|---|---|---|
| Thompson | 29 | 821 | 28 | 1 |
| Orduna | 12 | 244 | 20 | 0 |
| Small | 1 | 100 | 100 | 0 |
| Duhon | 2 | 47 | 24 | 0 |
| Douglas | 4 | 43 | 11 | 0 |
| Crist | 1 | 7 | 7 | 0 |
| Enderle | 1 | 0 | 0 | 0 |

### Passing – Punting – Kicking
| PASSING | Att | Comp | % | Yds | Yd/Att | TD | Int- | % | RK |
|---|---|---|---|---|---|---|---|---|---|
| Snead | 325 | 196 | 60 | 2307 | 7.1 | 17 | 12- | 4 | 2 |
| Ran Johnson | 17 | 10 | 59 | 230 | 13.5 | 3 | 3- | 18 | |
| Blanchard | 1 | 0 | 0 | 0 | 0.0 | 0 | 0- | 0 | |
| Ron Johnson | 1 | 0 | 0 | 0 | 0.0 | 0 | 0- | 0 | |

| PUNTING | No | Avg |
|---|---|---|
| Blanchard | 47 | 42.7 |

| KICKING | XP | Att | % | FG | Att | % |
|---|---|---|---|---|---|---|
| Gogolak | 34 | 38 | 89 | 21 | 31 | 68 |

## ST. LOUIS CARDINALS

### Rushing
| Last Name | No. | Yds | Avg | TD |
|---|---|---|---|---|
| Anderson | 153 | 536 | 3.5 | 4 |
| Roland | 105 | 414 | 3.9 | 2 |
| Burns | 26 | 69 | 2.7 | 2 |
| Moore | 9 | 44 | 4.9 | 0 |
| Baynham | 17 | 43 | 2.5 | 0 |
| Smith | 5 | 31 | 6.2 | 0 |
| Van Galder | 9 | 28 | 3.1 | 0 |
| Hart | 9 | 17 | 1.9 | 0 |
| Woodeshick | 5 | 14 | 2.8 | 0 |
| Shivers | 5 | 12 | 2.4 | 0 |
| Hayden | 8 | 11 | 1.4 | 1 |
| Cuozzo | 4 | 7 | 1.8 | 0 |
| Butler | 6 | 3 | 0.5 | 0 |
| Conley | 3 | 8 | 2.7 | 0 |

### Receiving
| Last Name | No. | Yds | Avg | TD |
|---|---|---|---|---|
| Roland | 38 | 321 | 8 | 2 |
| Gillette | 33 | 550 | 17 | 2 |
| Moore | 29 | 500 | 17 | 3 |
| Anderson | 28 | 298 | 11 | 2 |
| Smith | 26 | 407 | 16 | 2 |
| Burns | 6 | 24 | 4 | 0 |
| Gray | 3 | 62 | 21 | 0 |
| Hyatt | 2 | 32 | 16 | 0 |
| Shivers | 1 | 20 | 20 | 0 |
| Hayden | 1 | 17 | 17 | 0 |
| Baynham | 1 | 10 | 10 | 0 |
| Butler | 1 | 8 | 8 | 0 |
| Wicks | 1 | 8 | 8 | 0 |
| Woodeshick | 1 | 2 | 2 | 0 |

### Punt Returns
| Last Name | No. | Yds | Avg | TD |
|---|---|---|---|---|
| Willingham | 9 | 41 | 5 | 0 |
| Wehrli | 5 | 24 | 5 | 0 |
| Gray | 2 | -4 | -2 | 0 |

### Kickoff Returns
| Last Name | No. | Yds | Avg | TD |
|---|---|---|---|---|
| Moore | 20 | 437 | 22 | 0 |
| Gray | 17 | 378 | 22 | 0 |
| Willingham | 9 | 194 | 22 | 0 |
| Butler | 4 | 85 | 21 | 0 |
| Hyatt | 1 | 41 | 41 | 0 |
| Wehrli | 1 | 10 | 10 | 0 |
| Burns | 1 | 7 | 7 | 0 |

### Passing – Punting – Kicking
| PASSING | Att | Comp | % | Yds | Yd/Att | TD | Int- | % | RK |
|---|---|---|---|---|---|---|---|---|---|
| Cuozzo | 158 | 69 | 44 | 897 | 5.7 | 5 | 11- | 7 | 13 |
| Hart | 119 | 60 | 50 | 857 | 7.2 | 5 | 5- | 4 | |
| Van Galder | 79 | 40 | 51 | 434 | 5.5 | 1 | 7- | 9 | |
| Anderson | 3 | 2 | 67 | 71 | 23.7 | 0 | 0- | 0 | |
| Smith | 2 | 0 | 0 | 0 | 0.0 | 0 | 0- | 0 | |
| Wilson | 2 | 0 | 0 | 0 | 0.0 | 0 | 0- | 0 | |

| PUNTING | No | Avg |
|---|---|---|
| Anderson | 72 | 39.5 |
| Bakken | 1 | 26.0 |

| KICKING | XP | Att | % | FG | Att | % |
|---|---|---|---|---|---|---|
| Bakken | 19 | 21 | 90 | 14 | 22 | 64 |

## PHILADELPHIA EAGLES

### Rushing
| Last Name | No. | Yds | Avg | TD |
|---|---|---|---|---|
| James | 182 | 565 | 3.1 | 0 |
| Baker | 90 | 322 | 3.6 | 0 |
| Watkins | 67 | 262 | 3.9 | 1 |
| Reeves | 18 | 109 | 6.1 | 1 |
| Jackson | 9 | 76 | 8.4 | 0 |
| Bailey | 7 | 22 | 3.1 | 0 |
| Liske | 7 | 20 | 2.9 | 0 |
| Sullivan | 13 | 13 | 1.0 | 0 |
| Arrington | 1 | 2 | 2.0 | 0 |
| Crowe | 1 | 2 | 2.0 | 0 |
| Hawkins | 3 | 0 | 0.0 | 0 |

### Receiving
| Last Name | No. | Yds | Avg | TD |
|---|---|---|---|---|
| Jackson | 62 | 1048 | 17 | 4 |
| Hawkins | 30 | 512 | 17 | 1 |
| Carmichael | 20 | 276 | 14 | 2 |
| James | 20 | 156 | 8 | 1 |
| Baker | 16 | 114 | 7 | 0 |
| Kramer | 11 | 176 | 16 | 1 |
| Ballman | 9 | 183 | 20 | 0 |
| Watkins | 6 | -2 | 0 | 0 |
| Bailey | 5 | 32 | 6 | 0 |
| Sullivan | 4 | 17 | 4 | 0 |
| Walik | 1 | 15 | 15 | 1 |

### Punt Returns
| Last Name | No. | Yds | Avg | TD |
|---|---|---|---|---|
| Bradley | 22 | 155 | 7 | 0 |
| Winfield | 1 | 12 | 12 | 0 |
| Gibbs | 1 | 8 | 8 | 0 |
| Walik | 3 | 4 | 1 | 0 |

### Kickoff Returns
| Last Name | No. | Yds | Avg | TD |
|---|---|---|---|---|
| Nelson | 25 | 728 | 29 | 0 |
| Walik | 21 | 466 | 22 | 0 |
| Sullivan | 3 | 72 | 24 | 0 |
| Gibbs | 3 | 61 | 20 | 0 |
| Bradley | 2 | 22 | 11 | 0 |
| Pettigrew | 1 | 17 | 17 | 0 |
| Winfield | 3 | 9 | 3 | 0 |
| Overmyer | 1 | 0 | 0 | 0 |

### Passing – Punting – Kicking
| PASSING | Att | Comp | % | Yds | Yd/Att | TD | Int- | % | RK |
|---|---|---|---|---|---|---|---|---|---|
| Reaves | 224 | 108 | 48 | 1508 | 6.7 | 7 | 12- | 5 | 10 |
| Liske | 138 | 71 | 51 | 973 | 7.1 | 3 | 7- | 5 | |
| Arrington | 13 | 5 | 38 | 46 | 3.5 | 0 | 1- | 8 | |

| PUNTING | No | Avg |
|---|---|---|
| Bradley | 56 | 40.2 |
| McNeill | 7 | 41.4 |

| KICKING | XP | Att | % | FG | Att | % |
|---|---|---|---|---|---|---|
| Dempsey | 11 | 12 | 92 | 20 | 35 | 57 |

## GREEN BAY PACKERS 10-4-0  Dan Devine

**Scores of Each Game**

| | | |
|---|---|---|
| 26 | Cleveland | 10 |
| 14 | OAKLAND | 20 |
| 16 | DALLAS | 13 |
| 20 | CHICAGO | 17 |
| 24 | Detroit | 23 |
| 9 | ATLANTA | 10 |
| 13 | MINNESOTA | 27 |
| 34 | SAN FRANCISCO | 24 |
| 23 | Chicago | 17 |
| 23 | Houston | 10 |
| 16 | Washington | 21 |
| 33 | DETROIT | 7 |
| 23 | Minnesota | 7 |
| 30 | New Orleans | 20 |

| Use Name | Pos. | Hgt | Wgt | Age | Int | Pts |
|---|---|---|---|---|---|---|
| Bill Hayhoe | OT | 6'8" | 258 | 25 | | |
| Dick Himes | OT | 6'4" | 244 | 26 | | |
| Kevin Hunt | OT | 6'5" | 260 | 23 | | |
| Francis Peay | OT | 6'5" | 250 | 28 | | |
| Bill Lueck | OG | 6'3" | 235 | 26 | | |
| Mal Snider | OG | 6'4" | 250 | 25 | | |
| Keith Wortman | OG | 6'2" | 245 | 22 | | |
| Ken Bowman | C | 6'3" | 230 | 29 | | |
| Cal Withrow | C | 6' | 240 | 27 | | |
| Dave Pureifory | DE | 6'1" | 260 | 22 | | |
| Alden Roche | DE | 6'4" | 255 | 27 | | |
| Clarence Williams | DE | 6'5" | 255 | 25 | | 6 |
| Bob Brown | DT | 6'5" | 260 | 32 | | 2 |
| Gale Gillingham | OG | 6'3" | 255 | 28 | | |
| Mike McCoy | DT | 6'5" | 284 | 23 | | |
| Vern Vanoy | DT | 6'8" | 270 | 26 | | |

| Use Name | Pos. | Hgt | Wgt | Age | Int | Pts |
|---|---|---|---|---|---|---|
| Fred Carr | LB | 6'5" | 238 | 26 | | |
| Jim Carter | LB | 6'3" | 235 | 23 | 1 | |
| Tommy Crutcher | LB | 6'3" | 230 | 30 | | |
| Larry Hefner | LB | 6'2" | 215 | 23 | | |
| Ray Nitschke | LB | 6'3" | 235 | 36 | | |
| Dave Robinson | LB | 6'3" | 245 | 31 | 2 | |
| Willie Buchanon | DB | 6' | 190 | 21 | 4 | 6 |
| Ken Ellis | DB | 5'10" | 190 | 24 | 4 | 12 |
| Paul Gibson | DB | 6'2" | 195 | 24 | | |
| Charlie Hall | DB | 6'1" | 195 | 23 | | |
| Jim Hill | DB | 6'2" | 190 | 25 | 4 | |
| Bob Kroll | DB | 6'1" | 195 | 22 | | |
| Al Matthews | DB | 5'11" | 190 | 24 | 2 | |
| Ike Thomas | DB | 6'2" | 193 | 24 | | |

Larry Krause – Injury

| Use Name | Pos. | Hgt | Wgt | Age | Int | Pts |
|---|---|---|---|---|---|---|
| Scott Hunter | QB | 6'2" | 205 | 24 | | 30 |
| Frank Patrick | QB | 6'7" | 225 | 25 | | |
| Jerry Tagge | QB | 6'2" | 220 | 22 | | 6 |
| Bob Hudson | HB | 5'11" | 210 | 24 | | |
| MacArthur Lane | HB | 6' | 220 | 30 | | 18 |
| Dave Kopay | FB-HB | 6'2" | 218 | 30 | | |
| John Brockington | FB | 6'1" | 225 | 23 | | 54 |
| Perry Williams | FB | 6'2" | 220 | 25 | | |
| Carroll Dale | WR | 6'1" | 200 | 34 | | 6 |
| Dave Davis | WR | 6' | 175 | 24 | | 6 |
| Leland Glass | WR | 6' | 185 | 22 | | 6 |
| Jon Staggers | WR | 5'10" | 186 | 23 | | 12 |
| Len Garrett | TE | 6'3" | 230 | 23 | | |
| Pete Lammons | TE | 6'3" | 228 | 28 | | |
| Rich McGeorge | TE | 6'4" | 235 | 23 | | 12 |
| Chester Marcol | K | 6' | 190 | 23 | | 128 |
| Ron Widby | K | 6'4" | 210 | 27 | | |

## DETROIT LIONS 8-5-1  Joe Schmidt

| | | |
|---|---|---|
| 30 | N.Y. GIANTS | 16 |
| 10 | MINNESOTA | 34 |
| 38 | Chicago | 24 |
| 26 | Atlanta | 23 |
| 23 | GREEN BAY | 24 |
| 34 | SAN DIEGO | 20 |
| 24 | Dallas | 28 |
| 14 | CHICAGO | 0 |
| 14 | Minnesota | 16 |
| 27 | NEW ORLEANS | 14 |
| 37 | N.Y. JETS | 20 |
| 7 | Green Bay | 33 |
| 21 | Buffalo | 21 |
| 34 | Los Angeles | 17 |

| Use Name | Pos. | Hgt | Wgt | Age | Int | Pts |
|---|---|---|---|---|---|---|
| Rocky Freitas | OT | 6'6" | 270 | 26 | | |
| Gordon Jolley | OT | 6'5" | 230 | 23 | | |
| Jim Yarbrough | OT | 6'6" | 255 | 25 | | |
| Frank Gallagher | OG | 6'2" | 245 | 29 | | |
| Bob Kowalkowski | OG | 6'3" | 240 | 28 | | |
| Rocky Rasley | OG | 6'3" | 250 | 25 | | |
| Chuck Walton | OG | 6'3" | 255 | 31 | | |
| Ed Flanagan | C | 6'3" | 245 | 28 | | |
| Dave Thompson | OT-C | 6'4" | 275 | 23 | | |
| Gene Hamlin | C | 6'3" | 245 | 26 | | |
| Larry Hand | DE | 6'4" | 250 | 32 | | |
| Jim Mitchell | DE | 6'3" | 245 | 23 | 1 | |
| Herb Orvis | DE | 6'5" | 240 | 25 | | |
| Ken Sanders | DE | 6'5" | 225 | 22 | | |
| Bob Bell | DT | 6'4" | 250 | 24 | | |
| John Gordon | DT | 6'6" | 260 | 24 | | |
| Joe Schmiesing | DT | 6'4" | 260 | 27 | | |
| Bob Tatarek (from BUF) | DT | 6'4" | 270 | 26 | | |
| Larry Woods | DT | 6'6" | 260 | 24 | | |

| Use Name | Pos. | Hgt | Wgt | Age | Int | Pts |
|---|---|---|---|---|---|---|
| Mike Lucci | LB | 6'2" | 230 | 32 | 2 | |
| Paul Naumoff | LB | 6'1" | 215 | 27 | 1 | |
| Rick Ogle | LB | 6'3" | 230 | 23 | | |
| Wayne Walker | LB | 6'2" | 228 | 35 | | |
| Charlie Weaver | LB | 6'2" | 218 | 23 | 1 | |
| Adrian Young (from PHI) | LB | 6'1" | 232 | 26 | | |
| Lem Barney | DB | 6' | 188 | 26 | 3 | |
| Leon Jenkins | DB | 5'11" | 165 | 22 | | |
| Dick LeBeau | DB | 6'1" | 185 | 35 | | |
| Charlie Potts | DB | 6'3" | 210 | 23 | | |
| Al Randolph | DB | 6'2" | 205 | 28 | | |
| Wayne Rasmussen | DB | 6'2" | 180 | 30 | 2 | |
| Rudy Redmond | DB | 6' | 195 | 25 | 2 | 6 |
| Mike Weger | DB | 6'2" | 200 | 26 | | |

Sonny Campbell – Injury
Ed Mooney – Injury

| Use Name | Pos. | Hgt | Wgt | Age | Int | Pts |
|---|---|---|---|---|---|---|
| Greg Landry | QB | 6'4" | 210 | 25 | | 54 |
| Bill Munson | QB | 6'2" | 210 | 30 | | |
| Nick Eddy | HB | 6'1" | 210 | 28 | | 6 |
| Mel Farr | HB | 6'2" | 210 | 27 | | 18 |
| Altie Taylor | HB | 5'10" | 200 | 24 | | 36 |
| Mickey Zofko | HB | 6'3" | 195 | 22 | | 1 |
| Steve Owens | FB | 6'2" | 215 | 24 | | 24 |
| Bill Triplett | FB | 6'2" | 215 | 33 | | |
| Al Barnes | WR | 6'1" | 170 | 23 | | 6 |
| Ron Jessie | WR | 6' | 183 | 24 | | 24 |
| Earl McCullouch | WR | 5'11" | 175 | 26 | | 6 |
| Larry Walton | WR | 5'11" | 180 | 25 | | 36 |
| Craig Cotton | TE | 6'4" | 222 | 25 | | 6 |
| John Hilton | TE | 6'5" | 205 | 30 | | 6 |
| Charlie Sanders | TE | 6'4" | 225 | 26 | | 12 |
| Errol Mann | K | 6' | 200 | 31 | | 98 |
| Herman Weaver | K | 6'4" | 210 | 23 | | |

## MINNESOTA VIKINGS 7-7-0  Bud Grant

| | | |
|---|---|---|
| 21 | WASHINGTON | 24 |
| 34 | Detroit | 10 |
| 14 | MIAMI | 16 |
| 17 | ST. LOUIS | 19 |
| 23 | Denver | 20 |
| 10 | Chicago | 13 |
| 27 | GREEN BAY | 13 |
| 37 | NEW ORLEANS | 6 |
| 16 | DETROIT | 14 |
| 45 | Los Angeles | 41 |
| 10 | Pittsburgh | 23 |
| 23 | CHICAGO | 10 |
| 7 | GREEN BAY | 23 |
| 17 | San Francisco | 20 |

| Use Name | Pos. | Hgt | Wgt | Age | Int | Pts |
|---|---|---|---|---|---|---|
| Grady Alderman | OT | 6'2" | 247 | 33 | | |
| Doug Davis | OT | 6'4" | 250 | 28 | | |
| Ron Yary | OT | 6'6" | 255 | 26 | | |
| Ed White | OG | 6'2" | 262 | 25 | | |
| Milt Sunde | C-OG | 6'2" | 250 | 29 | | |
| John Ward | DE-OG | 6'4" | 250 | 24 | | |
| Mick Tingelhoff | C | 6'1" | 237 | 32 | | |
| Godfrey Zaunbrecher | C | 6'2" | 240 | 24 | | |
| Carl Eller | DE | 6'6" | 247 | 30 | | |
| Jim Marshall | DE | 6'4" | 248 | 34 | | |
| Bob Lurtsema | DT-DE | 6'6" | 250 | 30 | | |
| Gary Larsen | DT | 6'5" | 260 | 32 | | |
| Alan Page | DT | 6'5" | 245 | 27 | | |
| Doug Sutherland | DE-DT | 6'3" | 250 | 24 | | |

| Use Name | Pos. | Hgt | Wgt | Age | Int | Pts |
|---|---|---|---|---|---|---|
| Carl Gersbach | LB | 6'1" | 230 | 25 | | |
| Wally Hilgenberg | LB | 6'3" | 230 | 29 | 1 | 6 |
| Amos Martin | LB | 6'3" | 228 | 23 | | |
| Jeff Siemon | LB | 6'2" | 230 | 22 | 2 | |
| Lonnie Warwick | LB | 6'3" | 238 | 30 | 1 | |
| Roy Winston | LB | 6'1" | 222 | 32 | 3 | |
| Terry Brown | DB | 6'1" | 205 | 25 | | |
| Bobby Bryant | DB | 6' | 170 | 28 | 4 | 6 |
| Karl Kassulke | DB | 6' | 195 | 30 | 2 | |
| Paul Krause | DB | 6'3" | 200 | 30 | 6 | 12 |
| Ed Sharockman | DB | 6' | 200 | 32 | | |
| Charlie West | DB | 6'1" | 197 | 26 | 3 | |
| Jeff Wright | DB | 5'11" | 190 | 23 | 2 | |
| Nate Wright | DB | 5'11" | 180 | 24 | 2 | |

| Use Name | Pos. | Hgt | Wgt | Age | Int | Pts |
|---|---|---|---|---|---|---|
| Bob Lee | QB | 6'2" | 195 | 26 | | |
| Fran Tarkenton | QB | 6'1" | 190 | 32 | | |
| Clint Jones | HB | 6' | 205 | 27 | | 12 |
| Dave Osborn | HB | 6' | 208 | 29 | | 18 |
| Ed Marinaro | FB-HB | 6'2" | 212 | 22 | | 6 |
| Bill Brown | FB | 5'11" | 228 | 34 | | 48 |
| Oscar Reed | HB-FB | 5'11" | 222 | 28 | | 12 |
| Jim Lindsey | HB-FB | 6'2" | 210 | 27 | | |
| Calvin Demery | WR | 6' | 190 | 22 | | |
| John Gilliam | WR | 6'1" | 195 | 27 | | 42 |
| John Henderson | WR | 6'3" | 195 | 29 | | 12 |
| Gene Washington | WR | 6'3" | 208 | 28 | | 12 |
| John Beasley | TE | 6'3" | 228 | 27 | | 6 |
| Stu Voigt | TE | 6'1" | 220 | 24 | | 12 |
| Fred Cox | K | 5'10" | 200 | 33 | | 97 |
| Mike Eischeid | K | 6' | 190 | 31 | | |

## CHICAGO BEARS 4-9-1  Abe Gibron

| | | |
|---|---|---|
| 21 | ATLANTA | 37 |
| 13 | LOS ANGELES | 13 |
| 24 | DETROIT | 38 |
| 17 | Green Bay | 20 |
| 17 | Cleveland | 0 |
| 13 | MINNESOTA | 10 |
| 27 | St. Louis | 10 |
| 0 | Detroit | 14 |
| 17 | GREEN BAY | 14 |
| 21 | SAN FRANCISCO | 34 |
| 3 | CINCINNATI | 13 |
| 10 | Minnesota | 23 |
| 21 | Philadelphia | 12 |
| 21 | Oakland | 28 |

| Use Name | Pos. | Hgt | Wgt | Age | Int | Pts |
|---|---|---|---|---|---|---|
| Lionel Antoine | OT | 6'6" | 255 | 22 | | |
| Rich Buzin | OT | 6'4" | 250 | 26 | | |
| Randy Jackson | OT | 6'5" | 250 | 28 | | |
| Bob Asher | OG-OT | 6'5" | 250 | 24 | | |
| Jim Cadile | OG | 6'3" | 250 | 31 | | |
| Glen Holloway | OG | 6'3" | 250 | 23 | | |
| Ernie Janet | OG | 6'3" | 250 | 23 | | |
| Bob Newton | OG | 6'4" | 250 | 23 | | |
| Rich Coady | C | 6'3" | 245 | 27 | | |
| Steve DeLong | DE | 6'3" | 254 | 29 | | |
| Willie Holman | DE | 6'4" | 250 | 27 | | |
| Larry Horton | DT-DE | 6'4" | 248 | 23 | | |
| Bill Line | DT | 6'7" | 260 | 23 | | |
| Jim Osborne | DT | 6'3" | 250 | 22 | | |
| Andy Rice | DT | 6'3" | 268 | 30 | | |
| Bill Staley | DT | 6'3" | 250 | 25 | | |
| Tony McGee | DE-DT | 6'4" | 250 | 23 | | |

| Use Name | Pos. | Hgt | Wgt | Age | Int | Pts |
|---|---|---|---|---|---|---|
| Ross Brupbacher | LB | 6'3" | 215 | 24 | 1 | 6 |
| Doug Buffone | LB | 6'1" | 230 | 28 | 1 | |
| Jimmy Gunn | LB | 6'2" | 220 | 23 | | |
| Bill McKinney | LB | 6'1" | 226 | 27 | | |
| Bob Pifferini | LB | 6'2" | 226 | 22 | | |
| Larry Rowden | LB | 6'2" | 220 | 22 | | |
| Dick Butkus | C-LB | 6'3" | 245 | 28 | 2 | 1 |
| Craig Clemons | DB | 5'11" | 187 | 23 | | |
| Charlie Ford | DB | 6'3" | 185 | 23 | 7 | |
| Bob Jeter | DB | 6'1" | 200 | 34 | 2 | |
| Garry Lyle | DB | 6'2" | 198 | 26 | 2 | |
| Jerry Moore | DB | 6'3" | 208 | 22 | 1 | |
| Ron Smith | DB | 6'1" | 195 | 29 | 1 | 6 |
| Joe Taylor | DB | 6'2" | 200 | 31 | 4 | |

Joe Moore – Injury
Dave Hale – Injury

| Use Name | Pos. | Hgt | Wgt | Age | Int | Pts |
|---|---|---|---|---|---|---|
| Bobby Douglass | QB | 6'3" | 225 | 25 | | 48 |
| John Huarte | QB | 6' | 185 | 28 | | |
| Cyril Pinder | HB | 6'2" | 210 | 25 | | 18 |
| Gary Kosins | FB-HB | 6'1" | 215 | 23 | | 6 |
| Don Shy | FB-HB | 6'1" | 210 | 26 | | 6 |
| Jim Harrison | FB | 6'4" | 235 | 23 | | 18 |
| Roger Lawson | HB-FB | 6'2" | 215 | 22 | | 6 |
| George Farmer | WR | 6'4" | 214 | 24 | | 12 |
| Jim Seymour | WR | 6'4" | 210 | 25 | | 6 |
| Cecil Turner | WR | 5'10" | 176 | 26 | | |
| Bob Parsons | TE | 6'4" | 234 | 22 | | 6 |
| Earl Thomas | TE | 6'3" | 224 | 23 | | 24 |
| Bob Wallace | TE | 6'3" | 220 | 26 | | |
| Bobby Joe Green | K | 5'11" | 175 | 34 | | |
| Mac Percival | K | 6'4" | 220 | 32 | | 62 |

## GREEN BAY PACKERS

### RUSHING

| Last Name | No. | Yds | Avg | TD |
|---|---|---|---|---|
| Brockington | 274 | 1027 | 3.7 | 8 |
| Lane | 177 | 821 | 4.6 | 3 |
| P. Williams | 33 | 139 | 4.2 | 0 |
| Hudson | 15 | 62 | 4.1 | 0 |
| Kopay | 10 | 39 | 3.9 | 0 |
| Hunter | 22 | 37 | 1.7 | 5 |
| Glass | 2 | 13 | 6.5 | 0 |
| Davis | 2 | 0 | 0.0 | 0 |
| Tagge | 8 | −3 | −0.4 | 1 |
| Staggers | 1 | −8 | −8.0 | 0 |

### RECEIVING

| Last Name | No. | Yds | Avg | TD |
|---|---|---|---|---|
| Lane | 26 | 285 | 11 | 0 |
| Brockington | 19 | 243 | 13 | 1 |
| Dale | 16 | 317 | 20 | 1 |
| Glass | 15 | 261 | 17 | 1 |
| Staggers | 8 | 123 | 15 | 1 |
| Davis | 4 | 119 | 30 | 1 |
| Garrett | 4 | 66 | 17 | 0 |
| McGeorge | 4 | 50 | 13 | 2 |
| Kopay | 3 | 19 | 6 | 0 |
| Nitschke | 1 | 34 | 34 | 0 |
| Lammons | 1 | 19 | 19 | 0 |

### PUNT RETURNS

| Last Name | No. | Yds | Avg | TD |
|---|---|---|---|---|
| Ellis | 14 | 215 | 15 | 1 |
| Staggers | 9 | 148 | 16 | 1 |
| Glass | 1 | 1 | 1 | 0 |
| Hudson | 1 | 0 | 0 | 0 |

### KICKOFF RETURNS

| Last Name | No. | Yds | Avg | TD |
|---|---|---|---|---|
| Thomas | 21 | 572 | 27 | 0 |
| Staggers | 11 | 260 | 24 | 0 |
| Hudson | 11 | 247 | 22 | 0 |
| Kroll | 1 | 23 | 23 | 0 |
| Robinson | 1 | 20 | 20 | 0 |
| Ellis | 1 | 10 | 10 | 0 |
| P. Williams | 1 | 9 | 9 | 0 |
| Garrett | 1 | 0 | 0 | 0 |
| Wortman | 1 | 0 | 0 | 0 |

### PASSING – PUNTING – KICKING

| PASSING | Att | Comp | % | Yds | Yd/Att | TD | Int– | % | RK |
|---|---|---|---|---|---|---|---|---|---|
| Hunter | 199 | 86 | 43 | 1252 | 6.3 | 6 | 9– | 5 | 10 |
| Tagge | 29 | 10 | 34 | 154 | 5.3 | 0 | 0– | 0 | |
| Patrick | 4 | 1 | 25 | 9 | 2.3 | 0 | 0– | 0 | |
| Lane | 2 | 2 | 100 | 19 | 9.5 | 0 | 0– | 0 | |
| Widby | 2 | 2 | 100 | 102 | 51.0 | 0 | 0– | 0 | |
| Staggers | 1 | 0 | 0 | 0 | 0.0 | 0 | 0– | 0 | |

| PUNTING | No | Avg |
|---|---|---|
| Widby | 65 | 41.8 |

| KICKING | XP | Att | % | FG | Att | % |
|---|---|---|---|---|---|---|
| Marcol | 29 | 29 | 100 | 33 | 48 | 69 |

## DETROIT LIONS

### RUSHING

| Last Name | No. | Yds | Avg | TD |
|---|---|---|---|---|
| Taylor | 154 | 658 | 4.3 | 4 |
| Landry | 81 | 524 | 6.5 | 9 |
| Owens | 143 | 519 | 3.6 | 4 |
| Farr | 62 | 216 | 3.5 | 3 |
| Triplett | 17 | 48 | 2.8 | 0 |
| Zofko | 7 | 28 | 4.0 | 0 |
| Eddy | 8 | 28 | 3.5 | 0 |
| Munson | 1 | 0 | 0.0 | 0 |

### RECEIVING

| Last Name | No. | Yds | Avg | TD |
|---|---|---|---|---|
| Taylor | 29 | 250 | 9 | 2 |
| C. Sanders | 27 | 416 | 15 | 2 |
| L. Walton | 24 | 485 | 20 | 6 |
| Jessie | 24 | 424 | 18 | 4 |
| Owens | 15 | 100 | 7 | 0 |
| Farr | 10 | 132 | 13 | 0 |
| Cotton | 8 | 129 | 16 | 1 |
| Hilton | 5 | 133 | 27 | 1 |
| McCullouch | 5 | 96 | 19 | 1 |
| Barnes | 4 | 58 | 15 | 1 |
| Eddy | 2 | 46 | 23 | 1 |
| Zofko | 2 | 14 | 7 | 0 |

### PUNT RETURNS

| Last Name | No. | Yds | Avg | TD |
|---|---|---|---|---|
| Barney | 15 | 108 | 7 | 0 |
| L. Walton | 3 | −8 | −3 | 0 |

### KICKOFF RETURNS

| Last Name | No. | Yds | Avg | TD |
|---|---|---|---|---|
| Zofko | 26 | 616 | 24 | 0 |
| Jessie | 23 | 558 | 24 | 0 |
| Barney | 1 | 17 | 17 | 0 |
| Triplett | 1 | 12 | 12 | 0 |
| Orvis | 1 | 5 | 5 | 0 |
| L. Walton | 0 | 96 | 0 | 0 |

### PASSING – PUNTING – KICKING

| PASSING | Att | Comp | % | Yds | Yd/Att | TD | Int– | % | RK |
|---|---|---|---|---|---|---|---|---|---|
| Landry | 268 | 134 | 50 | 2066 | 7.7 | 18 | 17– | 6 | 6 |
| Munson | 35 | 20 | 57 | 194 | 5.5 | 1 | 1– | 3 | |
| Jessie | 1 | 0 | 0 | 0 | 0.0 | 0 | 0– | 0 | |
| McCullouch | 1 | 1 | 100 | 23 | 23.0 | 0 | 0– | 0 | |

| PUNTING | No | Avg |
|---|---|---|
| H. Weaver | 43 | 40.3 |

| KICKING | XP | Att | % | FG | Att | % |
|---|---|---|---|---|---|---|
| Mann | 38 | 39 | 97 | 20 | 29 | 69 |
| Zofko | 1 | 1 | 100 | 0 | 0 | 0 |

## MINNESOTA VIKINGS

### RUSHING

| Last Name | No. | Yds | Avg | TD |
|---|---|---|---|---|
| Reed | 151 | 639 | 4.2 | 2 |
| Bill Brown | 82 | 263 | 3.2 | 4 |
| Osborn | 82 | 261 | 3.2 | 2 |
| Marinaro | 66 | 223 | 3.4 | 0 |
| Tarkenton | 27 | 180 | 6.7 | 0 |
| Jones | 52 | 164 | 3.2 | 2 |
| Gilliam | 8 | 14 | 1.8 | 0 |
| Lindsey | 1 | 8 | 8.0 | 0 |
| Voigt | 1 | 1 | 1.0 | 1 |
| Krause | 1 | 0 | 0.0 | 0 |
| Eischeid | 1 | −13 | −13.0 | 0 |

### RECEIVING

| Last Name | No. | Yds | Avg | TD |
|---|---|---|---|---|
| Gilliam | 47 | 1035 | 22 | 7 |
| Reed | 30 | 205 | 7 | 0 |
| Beasley | 28 | 232 | 8 | 1 |
| Marinaro | 28 | 218 | 8 | 1 |
| Bill Brown | 22 | 298 | 14 | 4 |
| Osborn | 20 | 166 | 8 | 1 |
| Washington | 18 | 259 | 14 | 2 |
| Henderson | 10 | 190 | 19 | 2 |
| Voigt | 6 | 50 | 8 | 1 |
| Jones | 6 | 42 | 7 | 0 |
| Lindsey | 3 | 28 | 9 | 0 |
| White | 0 | 3 | 0 | 0 |

### PUNT RETURNS

| Last Name | No. | Yds | Avg | TD |
|---|---|---|---|---|
| West | 16 | 111 | 7 | 0 |
| Bryant | 10 | 48 | 5 | 0 |

### KICKOFF RETURNS

| Last Name | No. | Yds | Avg | TD |
|---|---|---|---|---|
| Gilliam | 14 | 369 | 26 | 0 |
| Jones | 12 | 327 | 27 | 0 |
| West | 9 | 196 | 22 | 0 |
| Bryant | 2 | 41 | 21 | 0 |
| Bill Brown | 3 | 37 | 12 | 0 |
| Lindsey | 1 | 17 | 17 | 0 |
| Voigt | 1 | 2 | 2 | 0 |

### PASSING – PUNTING – KICKING

| PASSING | Att | Comp | % | Yds | Yd/Att | TD | Int– | % | RK |
|---|---|---|---|---|---|---|---|---|---|
| Tarkenton | 378 | 215 | 57 | 2651 | 7.0 | 18 | 13– | 3 | 1 |
| Lee | 6 | 3 | 50 | 75 | 12.5 | 1 | 0– | 0 | |
| Krause | 1 | 0 | 0 | 0 | 0.0 | 0 | 0– | 0 | |

| PUNTING | No | Avg |
|---|---|---|
| Eischeid | 62 | 42.8 |

| KICKING | XP | Att | % | FG | Att | % |
|---|---|---|---|---|---|---|
| Cox | 34 | 34 | 100 | 21 | 33 | 64 |

## CHICAGO BEARS

### RUSHING

| Last Name | No. | Yds | Avg | TD |
|---|---|---|---|---|
| Douglass | 141 | 968 | 6.9 | 8 |
| Harrison | 167 | 622 | 3.7 | 2 |
| Shy | 91 | 342 | 3.8 | 1 |
| Pinder | 87 | 300 | 3.4 | 3 |
| Lawson | 33 | 106 | 3.2 | 1 |
| Butkus | 1 | 28 | 28.0 | 0 |
| Thomas | 5 | 13 | 2.6 | 0 |
| Kosins | 3 | 5 | 1.7 | 0 |
| Parsons | 1 | 0 | 0.0 | 0 |
| Turner | 3 | 0 | 0.0 | 0 |
| Huarte | 1 | −2 | −2.0 | 0 |
| Seymour | 1 | −9 | −9.0 | 0 |
| Farmer | 2 | −13 | −6.5 | 0 |

### RECEIVING

| Last Name | No. | Yds | Avg | TD |
|---|---|---|---|---|
| Thomas | 20 | 365 | 18 | 3 |
| Farmer | 14 | 380 | 27 | 2 |
| Seymour | 10 | 165 | 17 | 1 |
| Shy | 10 | 109 | 11 | 0 |
| Lawson | 8 | 120 | 15 | 0 |
| Harrison | 8 | 30 | 4 | 1 |
| Turner | 3 | 71 | 24 | 0 |
| Kosins | 2 | 15 | 8 | 1 |
| Pinder | 1 | 13 | 13 | 0 |
| Wallace | 1 | 9 | 9 | 0 |
| Parsons | 1 | 6 | 6 | 1 |

### PUNT RETURNS

| Last Name | No. | Yds | Avg | TD |
|---|---|---|---|---|
| Smith | 26 | 163 | 6 | 0 |
| Clemons | 2 | 15 | 8 | 0 |

### KICKOFF RETURNS

| Last Name | No. | Yds | Avg | TD |
|---|---|---|---|---|
| Smith | 30 | 924 | 31 | 1 |
| Turner | 16 | 409 | 26 | 0 |
| Clemons | 2 | 53 | 27 | 0 |
| Holloway | 1 | 28 | 28 | 0 |
| Butkus | 1 | 15 | 15 | 0 |
| Pinder | 1 | 14 | 14 | 0 |
| Horton | 1 | 3 | 3 | 0 |
| Thomas | 0 | 82 | 0 | 1 |

### PASSING – PUNTING – KICKING

| PASSING | Att | Comp | % | Yds | Yd/Att | TD | Int– | % | RK |
|---|---|---|---|---|---|---|---|---|---|
| Douglass | 198 | 75 | 38 | 1246 | 6.3 | 9 | 12– | 6 | 12 |
| Huarte | 5 | 2 | 40 | 14 | 2.8 | 0 | 0– | 0 | |
| Green | 2 | 1 | 50 | 23 | 11.5 | 0 | 1– | 50 | |

| PUNTING | No | Avg |
|---|---|---|
| Green | 67 | 41.2 |

| KICKING | XP | Att | % | FG | Att | % |
|---|---|---|---|---|---|---|
| Percival | 26 | 26 | 100 | 12 | 24 | 50 |
| Butkus | 1 | 1 | 100 | 0 | 0 | 0 |

## SAN FRANCISCO FORTY NINERS 8-5-1 Dick Nolan

| Scores of Each Game | | Use Name | Pos. | Hgt | Wgt | Age | Int | Pts |
|---|---|---|---|---|---|---|---|---|
| 34 | SAN DIEGO | 3 | Len Rohde | OT | 6'4" | 248 | 34 | | |
| 20 | Buffalo | 27 | John Watson | OT | 6'4" | 248 | 23 | | |
| 37 | New Orleans | 2 | Cas Banaszek | C-OT | 6'3" | 250 | 26 | | |
| 7 | Los Angeles | 31 | Randy Beisler | OG | 6'4" | 250 | 27 | | |
| 17 | N.Y. GIANTS | 23 | Elmer Collett | OG | 6'4" | 240 | 27 | | |
| 20 | NEW ORLEANS | 20 | Woody Peoples | OG | 6'2" | 258 | 29 | | |
| 49 | Atlanta | 14 | Forrest Blue | C | 6'5" | 260 | 26 | | |
| 24 | Green Bay | 34 | Bill Belk | DE | 6'3" | 253 | 26 | | |
| 24 | BALTIMORE | 21 | Cedrick Hardman | DE | 6'3" | 255 | 23 | | |
| 34 | Chicago | 21 | Tommy Hart | DE | 6'3" | 248 | 27 | 1 | |
| 31 | Dallas | 10 | Rolf Krueger | DT-DE | 6'4" | 253 | 25 | | |
| 16 | LOS ANGELES | 26 | Earl Edwards | DT | 6'6" | 262 | 26 | | |
| 20 | ATLANTA | 0 | Bob Hoskins | DT | 6'2" | 253 | 26 | | |
| 20 | MINNESOTA | 17 | Charlie Krueger | DT | 6'4" | 268 | 36 | | |

| Use Name | Pos. | Hgt | Wgt | Age | Int | Pts |
|---|---|---|---|---|---|---|
| Ed Beard | LB | 6'2" | 220 | 32 | 1 | |
| Marty Huff | LB | 6'2" | 234 | 23 | | |
| Frank Nunley | LB | 6'2" | 230 | 26 | 1 | |
| Dave Olerich | LB | 6'1" | 220 | 27 | | |
| Jim Sniadecki | LB | 6'2" | 230 | 25 | | |
| Skip Vanderbundt | LB | 6'3" | 224 | 25 | 2 | 18 |
| Dave Wilcox | LB | 6'3" | 240 | 29 | 3 | |
| Johnny Fuller | DB | 6' | 185 | 26 | 1 | |
| Windlan Hall | DB | 5'11" | 178 | 22 | 1 | |
| Jim Johnson | DB | 6'2" | 187 | 34 | 4 | |
| Ralph McGill | DB | 5'11" | 183 | 22 | | |
| Mel Phillips | DB | 6' | 194 | 30 | 1 | |
| Mike Simpson | DB | 5'11" | 168 | 25 | 2 | 6 |
| Bruce Taylor | DB | 6' | 187 | 24 | 2 | |

| Use Name | Pos. | Hgt | Wgt | Age | Int | Pts |
|---|---|---|---|---|---|---|
| John Brodie | QB | 6'1" | 203 | 37 | | 6 |
| Joe Reed | QB | 6'1" | 195 | 24 | | |
| Steve Spurrier | QB | 6'2" | 203 | 27 | | |
| John Isenbarger | HB | 6'3" | 205 | 24 | | 6 |
| Doug Cunningham | HB | 5'11" | 190 | 26 | | |
| Jimmy Thomas | HB | 6'1" | 214 | 25 | | 6 |
| Vic Washington | HB | 5'10" | 196 | 26 | | 30 |
| Ken Willard | FB | 6'2" | 216 | 29 | | 30 |
| Larry Schreiber | HB-FB | 6' | 200 | 25 | | 18 |
| Terry Beasley | WR | 5'10" | 184 | 21 | | |
| Preston Riley | WR | 6' | 180 | 24 | | 6 |
| Gene Washington | WR | 6'1" | 185 | 25 | | 72 |
| Ted Kwalick | TE | 6'4" | 223 | 25 | | 54 |
| Dick Witcher | TE | 6'3" | 204 | 27 | | 6 |
| Bruce Gossett | K | 6'2" | 228 | 29 | | 95 |
| Jim McCann | K | 6'2" | 163 | 23 | | |

## ATLANTA FALCONS 7-7-0 Norm Van Brocklin

| Scores of Each Game | | Use Name | Pos. | Hgt | Wgt | Age | Int | Pts |
|---|---|---|---|---|---|---|---|---|
| 37 | Chicago | 21 | Len Gotshalk | OT | 6'4" | 244 | 22 | | |
| 20 | New England | 21 | George Kunz | OT | 6'5" | 257 | 25 | | |
| 31 | LOS ANGELES | 3 | Bill Sandeman | OT | 6'6" | 252 | 26 | | |
| 23 | DETROIT | 26 | Dennis Havig | OG | 6'2" | 245 | 23 | | |
| 21 | New Orleans | 14 | Andy Maurer | OG | 6'3" | 265 | 23 | | |
| 10 | Green Bay | 9 | Jim Miller | OG | 6'3" | 240 | 23 | | |
| 14 | SAN FRANCISCO | 49 | Ted Fritsch | C | 6'2" | 240 | 22 | | |
| 7 | Los Angeles | 20 | Jeff Van Note | OG-C | 6'2" | 243 | 26 | | |
| 36 | NEW ORLEANS | 20 | Claude Humphrey | DE | 6'5" | 252 | 28 | 2 | |
| 13 | Washington | 24 | John Zook | DE | 6'5" | 243 | 24 | 6 | |
| 23 | DENVER | 20 | Chuck Walker (from STL) | DT-DE | 6'2" | 250 | 31 | | |
| 20 | HOUSTON | 10 | Glen Condren | DT | 6'5" | 250 | 30 | | |
| 0 | San Francisco | 20 | Rosie Manning | DT | 6'5" | 256 | 22 | | |
| 14 | KANSAS CITY | 17 | John Small | DT | 6'5" | 270 | 25 | | |
| | | | Mike Lewis | DE-DT | 6'3" | 244 | 23 | 1 | 2 |

| Use Name | Pos. | Hgt | Wgt | Age | Int | Pts |
|---|---|---|---|---|---|---|
| Grady Allen | LB | 6'3" | 230 | 26 | | |
| Duane Benson | LB | 6'2" | 215 | 27 | | |
| Greg Brezina | LB | 6'2" | 226 | 26 | | |
| Don Hansen | LB | 6'3" | 235 | 28 | 1 | |
| Noel Jenke | LB | 6'1" | 220 | 25 | | |
| Tommy Nobis | LB | 6'2" | 240 | 28 | 3 | 6 |
| Ray Brown | DB | 6'2" | 208 | 23 | 2 | |
| Ray Easterling | DB | 6' | 195 | 22 | | |
| Clarence Ellis | DB | 5'11" | 193 | 22 | 3 | |
| Willie Germany | DB | 6' | 192 | 23 | | |
| Tom Hayes | DB | 6'1" | 200 | 26 | 5 | |
| Tony Plummer | DB | 5'11" | 188 | 25 | | |
| Ken Reaves | DB | 6'3" | 210 | 27 | 3 | |
| Larry Shears | DB | 5'10" | 185 | 23 | | |

Harmon Wages — Knee Injury

| Use Name | Pos. | Hgt | Wgt | Age | Int | Pts |
|---|---|---|---|---|---|---|
| Bob Berry | QB | 5'11" | 185 | 30 | | 12 |
| Pat Sullivan | QB | 6'0" | 198 | 22 | | |
| Willie Belton | HB | 5'11" | 207 | 23 | | |
| Dave Hampton | HB | 6' | 210 | 25 | | 42 |
| Joe Profit | HB | 6' | 213 | 23 | | |
| Ron Lamb | FB | 6'2" | 225 | 28 | | |
| Art Malone | FB | 5'11" | 211 | 24 | | 60 |
| Eddie Ray | FB | 6'1" | 240 | 25 | | |
| Ken Burrow | WR | 6' | 190 | 24 | | 30 |
| Wes Chesson | WR | 6'2" | 195 | 23 | | 6 |
| Ray Jarvis | WR | 5'11" | 200 | 23 | | |
| Todd Snyder | TE | 6'2" | 226 | 22 | | |
| Larry Mialik | TE | 6'2" | 234 | 24 | | 24 |
| Jim Mitchell | TE | 6'2" | 234 | 24 | | 24 |
| Bill Bell | K | 6'1" | 192 | 24 | | 79 |
| John James | K | 6'3" | 197 | 23 | | |

## LOS ANGELES RAMS 6-7-1 Tommy Prothro

| Scores of Each Game | | Use Name | Pos. | Hgt | Wgt | Age | Int | Pts |
|---|---|---|---|---|---|---|---|---|
| 34 | NEW ORLEANS | 14 | Charley Cowan | OT | 6'4" | 250 | 23 | | |
| 13 | Chicago | 13 | Harry Schuh | OT | 6'2" | 260 | 29 | | |
| 3 | Atlanta | 31 | John Williams | OG-OT | 6'3" | 256 | 26 | | |
| 31 | SAN FRANCISCO | 7 | Mike LaHood | OG | 6'3" | 250 | 27 | | |
| 34 | Philadelphia | 3 | Tom Mack | OG | 6'3" | 250 | 28 | | |
| 15 | CINCINNATI | 12 | Joe Scibelli | OG | 6'1" | 255 | 33 | | |
| 17 | Oakland | 45 | Ken Iman | C | 6'1" | 240 | 33 | | |
| 20 | ATLANTA | 7 | Rich Saul | OG-C | 6'3" | 235 | 24 | | |
| 10 | DENVER | 16 | Coy Bacon | DE | 6'4" | 270 | 30 | | |
| 41 | MINNESOTA | 45 | Fred Dryer | DE | 6'6" | 240 | 26 | | |
| 16 | New Orleans | 19 | Jack Youngblood | DE | 6'4" | 250 | 22 | | |
| 26 | San Francisco | 16 | Larry Brooks | DT | 6'3" | 255 | 22 | | |
| 14 | St. Louis | 24 | Bill Nelson | DT | 6'7" | 270 | 24 | | |
| 17 | DETROIT | 34 | Merlin Olsen | DT | 6'5" | 270 | 31 | | |
| | | | Phil Olsen | DT | 6'5" | 265 | 24 | | |

| Use Name | Pos. | Hgt | Wgt | Age | Int | Pts |
|---|---|---|---|---|---|---|
| Ken Geddes | LB | 6'3" | 235 | 24 | | |
| Dean Halverson | LB | 6'2" | 212 | 26 | | |
| Marlin McKeever | LB | 6'1" | 235 | 32 | 2 | |
| John Pergine | LB | 6'1" | 225 | 25 | | |
| Jim Purnell | LB | 6'2" | 238 | 30 | 1 | |
| Jack Reynolds | LB | 6'1" | 232 | 24 | | |
| Isiah Robertson | LB | 6'3" | 225 | 23 | | |
| Al Clark | DB | 6' | 180 | 24 | 1 | |
| Dave Elmendorf | DB | 6'1" | 195 | 23 | 3 | |
| Gene Howard | DB | 6' | 190 | 25 | 3 | 6 |
| Jim Nettles | DB | 5'9" | 177 | 30 | 6 | |
| Clancy Williams | DB | 6'2" | 194 | 29 | | |
| Roger Williams | DB | 5'10" | 180 | 26 | | |

Travis Williams — Knee Injury

| Use Name | Pos. | Hgt | Wgt | Age | Int | Pts |
|---|---|---|---|---|---|---|
| Pete Beathard | QB | 6'2" | 200 | 30 | | |
| Roman Gabriel | QB | 6'4" | 220 | 32 | | 6 |
| Jim Bertelsen | HB | 5'11" | 205 | 22 | | 36 |
| Lawrence McCutcheon | HB | 6'1" | 205 | 22 | | |
| Larry Smith | HB | 6'3" | 220 | 24 | | 18 |
| Bob Thomas | HB | 5'10" | 200 | 23 | | 18 |
| Les Josephson | FB | 6'1" | 207 | 29 | | 6 |
| Willie Ellison | HB-FB | 6'1" | 200 | 27 | | 36 |
| Dick Gordon | WR | 5'11" | 190 | 27 | | 6 |
| John Love | WR | 5'11" | 185 | 27 | | 6 |
| David Ray | WR | 6' | 195 | 27 | | 103 |
| Lance Rentzel | WR | 6'2" | 202 | 28 | | 12 |
| Jack Snow | WR | 6'2" | 190 | 29 | | 24 |
| Joe Sweet | WR | 6'2" | 196 | 24 | | 8 |
| Pat Curran | TE | 6'3" | 238 | 26 | | |
| Bob Klein | TE | 6'5" | 235 | 25 | | 6 |
| Dave Chapple | K | 6' | 180 | 25 | | |

## NEW ORLEANS SAINTS 2-11-1 J. D. Roberts

| Scores of Each Game | | Use Name | Pos. | Hgt | Wgt | Age | Int | Pts |
|---|---|---|---|---|---|---|---|---|
| 14 | Los Angeles | 34 | Glen Ray Hines | OT | 6'5" | 265 | 28 | | |
| 17 | KANSAS CITY | 20 | Don Morrison | OT | 6'5" | 255 | 22 | | |
| 2 | SAN FRANCISCO | 37 | Craig Robinson | OT | 6'4" | 250 | 23 | | |
| 21 | N.Y. Giants | 45 | Carl Johnson | OG-OT | 6'3" | 240 | 22 | | |
| 20 | ATLANTA | 21 | Jake Kupp | OG | 6'3" | 248 | 30 | | |
| 20 | San Francisco | 20 | Royce Smith | OG | 6'3" | 245 | 23 | | |
| 21 | PHILADELPHIA | 3 | Del Williams | OG | 6'2" | 240 | 26 | | |
| 6 | Minnesota | 37 | John Didion | C | 6'4" | 245 | 24 | | |
| 20 | Atlanta | 36 | Bob Kuziel | C | 6'4" | 255 | 22 | | |
| 14 | Detroit | 27 | Wimpy Winther | C | 6'4" | 260 | 24 | | |
| 19 | LOS ANGELES | 16 | Mike Crangle | DE | 6'4" | 243 | 25 | | |
| 17 | N.Y. Jets | 18 | Richard Neal | DE | 6'3" | 254 | 24 | 6 | |
| 10 | NEW ENGLAND | 17 | Joe Owens | DE | 6'2" | 245 | 25 | 2 | |
| 20 | GREEN BAY | 30 | Faddie Tillman | DT-DE | 6'5" | 230 | 23 | | |
| | | | Dave Long | DT | 6'4" | 245 | 27 | | |
| | | | Doug Mooers | DT | 6'6" | 265 | 25 | | |
| | | | Bob Pollard | DT | 6'3" | 245 | 23 | | |

| Use Name | Pos. | Hgt | Wgt | Age | Int | Pts |
|---|---|---|---|---|---|---|
| Wayne Coleman | LB | 6'1" | 230 | 26 | | |
| Joe Federspiel | LB | 6'1" | 225 | 22 | | |
| Willie Hall | LB | 6'2" | 217 | 22 | | |
| Ray Hester | LB | 6'2" | 215 | 23 | | |
| Bill Hobbs | LB | 6' | 220 | 26 | | |
| Dick Palmer (from BUF) | LB | 6'2" | 232 | 24 | | |
| Tom Roussel | LB | 6'3" | 235 | 27 | 2 | |
| Tom Stincic | LB | 6'2" | 230 | 25 | | |
| Billy Hayes | DB | 6'1" | 175 | 25 | | |
| Hugo Hollas | DB | 6'1" | 190 | 27 | 1 | |
| Delles Howell | DB | 6'3" | 202 | 25 | 1 | |
| Ernie Jackson | DB | 5'10" | 173 | 22 | 3 | 6 |
| Bivian Lee | DB | 6'3" | 200 | 24 | 4 | |
| Tom Myers | DB | 5'11" | 184 | 21 | 3 | |
| Doug Wyatt | DB | 6'1" | 195 | 25 | | 6 |

Carlos Bell — Injury
Al Dodd — Injury
Dee Martin — Knee Injury

| Use Name | Pos. | Hgt | Wgt | Age | Int | Pts |
|---|---|---|---|---|---|---|
| Edd Hargett | QB | 5'11" | 190 | 25 | | |
| Archie Manning | QB | 6'3" | 204 | 23 | | 12 |
| Bob Gresham | HB | 5'11" | 195 | 24 | | 18 |
| Virgil Robinson | HB | 5'11" | 195 | 24 | | |
| Joe Williams | HB | 6' | 193 | 25 | | |
| James Ford | FB-HB | 6' | 200 | 22 | | |
| Bill Butler | FB | 6' | 218 | 22 | | 12 |
| Jim Strong | FB | 6'1" | 204 | 25 | | |
| Arthur Green | HB-FB | 5'11" | 198 | 24 | | |
| Dan Abramowicz | WR | 6'1" | 195 | 27 | | 42 |
| Margene Adkins | WR | 5'10" | 183 | 25 | | |
| Bob Newland | WR | 6'2" | 190 | 23 | | 12 |
| Cephus Weatherspoon | WR | 6'1" | 182 | 24 | | |
| Creston Whitaker | WR | 6'2" | 187 | 24 | | |
| Bob Brown | TE | 6'3" | 225 | 29 | | 6 |
| Dave Parks | TE | 6'2" | 203 | 30 | | 36 |
| Charlie Durkee | K | 5'11" | 165 | 29 | | 18 |
| Julian Fagan | K | 6'3" | 205 | 24 | | |
| Happy Feller | K | 5'11" | 185 | 23 | | 28 |
| Toni Linhart | K | 6' | 170 | 30 | | 11 |

## SAN FRANCISCO FORTY NINERS

### RUSHING

| Last Name | No. | Yds | Avg | TD |
|---|---|---|---|---|
| V. Washington | 141 | 468 | 3.3 | 3 |
| Schreiber | 118 | 420 | 3.6 | 2 |
| Willard | 100 | 345 | 3.5 | 4 |
| Thomas | 52 | 250 | 4.8 | 1 |
| Spurrier | 11 | 51 | 4.6 | 0 |
| Cunningham | 8 | 32 | 4.0 | 0 |
| Reed | 4 | 22 | 5.5 | 0 |
| Kwalick | 5 | 11 | 2.2 | 0 |
| Isenbarger | 3 | 9 | 3.0 | 0 |
| Brodie | 3 | 8 | 2.7 | 1 |

### RECEIVING

| Last Name | No. | Yds | Avg | TD |
|---|---|---|---|---|
| G. Wash'gton | 46 | 918 | 20 | 12 |
| V. Wash'gton | 43 | 393 | 9 | 1 |
| Kwalick | 40 | 751 | 19 | 9 |
| Schreiber | 31 | 283 | 9 | 1 |
| Willard | 24 | 131 | 5 | 1 |
| Thomas | 15 | 148 | 10 | 0 |
| Riley | 11 | 156 | 14 | 1 |
| Isenbarger | 3 | 66 | 22 | 1 |
| Witcher | 3 | 22 | 7 | 1 |
| Beasley | 1 | 20 | 20 | 0 |

### PUNT RETURNS

| Last Name | No. | Yds | Avg | TD |
|---|---|---|---|---|
| McGill | 22 | 219 | 10 | 0 |
| Taylor | 21 | 145 | 7 | 0 |
| Fuller | 1 | 9 | 9 | 0 |

### KICKOFF RETURNS

| Last Name | No. | Yds | Avg | TD |
|---|---|---|---|---|
| V. Washington | 27 | 771 | 29 | 1 |
| McGill | 10 | 192 | 19 | 0 |
| Schreiber | 2 | 41 | 21 | 0 |
| Nunley | 1 | 21 | 21 | 0 |
| Hoskins | 2 | 17 | 9 | 0 |
| Beard | 2 | -1 | -1 | 0 |

### PASSING – PUNTING – KICKING

**PASSING**

| Last Name | Att | Comp | % | Yds | Yd/Att | TD | Int– | % | RK |
|---|---|---|---|---|---|---|---|---|---|
| Spurrier | 269 | 147 | 55 | 1983 | 7.4 | 18 | 16– | 6 | 4 |
| Brodie | 110 | 70 | 64 | 905 | 8.2 | 9 | 8– | 7 | |
| Isenbarger | 1 | 0 | 0 | 0 | 0.0 | 0 | 0– | 0 | |

**PUNTING**

| Last Name | No | Avg |
|---|---|---|
| McCann | 64 | 39.7 |

**KICKING**

| Last Name | XP | Att | % | FG | Att | % |
|---|---|---|---|---|---|---|
| Gossett | 41 | 42 | 98 | 18 | 29 | 62 |

## ATLANTA FALCONS

### RUSHING

| Last Name | No. | Yds | Avg | TD |
|---|---|---|---|---|
| Hampton | 230 | 995 | 4.3 | 6 |
| Malone | 180 | 798 | 4.4 | 8 |
| Profit | 40 | 132 | 3.3 | 0 |
| Berry | 24 | 86 | 3.6 | 2 |
| Ray | 8 | 34 | 4.3 | 0 |
| Belton | 10 | 20 | 2.0 | 0 |
| Mitchell | 2 | 19 | 9.5 | 0 |
| Sullivan | 2 | 8 | 4.0 | 0 |
| Burrow | 3 | 3 | 1.0 | 0 |
| Bell | 1 | -3 | -3.0 | 0 |

### RECEIVING

| Last Name | No. | Yds | Avg | TD |
|---|---|---|---|---|
| Malone | 50 | 585 | 12 | 2 |
| Burrow | 29 | 492 | 17 | 5 |
| Mitchell | 28 | 470 | 17 | 4 |
| Hampton | 23 | 244 | 11 | 1 |
| Chesson | 18 | 338 | 19 | 1 |
| Profit | 3 | 22 | 7 | 0 |
| Snyder | 1 | 19 | 19 | 0 |
| Jarvis | 1 | 18 | 18 | 0 |
| Ray | 1 | 14 | 14 | 0 |
| Lamb | 1 | 10 | 10 | 0 |
| Belton | 1 | -1 | -1 | 0 |
| Berry | 1 | -9 | -9 | 0 |

### PUNT RETURNS

| Last Name | No. | Yds | Avg | TD |
|---|---|---|---|---|
| Belton | 17 | 110 | 6 | 0 |
| Brown | 8 | 71 | 9 | 0 |
| Ellis | 1 | 13 | 13 | 0 |
| Small | 1 | 0 | 0 | 0 |

### KICKOFF RETURNS

| Last Name | No. | Yds | Avg | TD |
|---|---|---|---|---|
| Hampton | 25 | 535 | 21 | 0 |
| Belton | 21 | 441 | 21 | 0 |
| Malone | 2 | 37 | 19 | 0 |
| Plummer | 1 | 21 | 21 | 0 |
| Germany | 2 | 5 | 3 | 0 |
| Chesson | 1 | 0 | 0 | 0 |

### PASSING – PUNTING – KICKING

**PASSING**

| Last Name | Att | Comp | % | Yds | Yd/Att | TD | Int– | % | RK |
|---|---|---|---|---|---|---|---|---|---|
| Berry | 277 | 154 | 56 | 2158 | 7.8 | 13 | 12– | 4 | 3 |
| Sullivan | 19 | 3 | 16 | 44 | 2.3 | 0 | 3– | 16 | |

**PUNTING**

| Last Name | No | Avg |
|---|---|---|
| James | 61 | 42.8 |

**KICKING**

| Last Name | XP | Att | % | FG | Att | % |
|---|---|---|---|---|---|---|
| Bell | 31 | 31 | 100 | 16 | 30 | 53 |

## LOS ANGELES RAMS

### RUSHING

| Last Name | No. | Yds | Avg | TD |
|---|---|---|---|---|
| Ellison | 170 | 764 | 4.5 | 5 |
| Bertelsen | 123 | 581 | 4.7 | 5 |
| Thomas | 77 | 433 | 5.6 | 3 |
| Smith | 60 | 276 | 4.6 | 2 |
| Josephson | 18 | 75 | 4.2 | 0 |
| Rentzel | 7 | 71 | 10.1 | 1 |
| Gabriel | 14 | 16 | 1.1 | 1 |
| Sweet | 1 | 1 | 1.0 | 0 |
| Beathard | 1 | -1 | -1.0 | 0 |
| Klein | 1 | -7 | -7.0 | 0 |

### RECEIVING

| Last Name | No. | Yds | Avg | TD |
|---|---|---|---|---|
| Snow | 30 | 590 | 20 | 4 |
| Bertelsen | 29 | 331 | 11 | 2 |
| Klein | 29 | 330 | 11 | 1 |
| Rentzel | 27 | 365 | 14 | 1 |
| Ellison | 23 | 141 | 6 | 1 |
| Smith | 15 | 186 | 12 | 1 |
| Josephson | 14 | 170 | 12 | 1 |
| Thomas | 11 | 95 | 9 | 0 |
| Gordon | 3 | 29 | 10 | 1 |
| Sweet | 2 | 26 | 13 | 1 |
| Love | 1 | 19 | 19 | 1 |

### PUNT RETURNS

| Last Name | No. | Yds | Avg | TD |
|---|---|---|---|---|
| Bertelson | 16 | 232 | 15 | 0 |
| Elmendorf | 3 | 56 | 19 | 0 |
| Love | 10 | 39 | 4 | 0 |
| Gordon | 4 | 20 | 5 | 0 |

### KICKOFF RETURNS

| Last Name | No. | Yds | Avg | TD |
|---|---|---|---|---|
| Ellison | 14 | 345 | 25 | 0 |
| Thomas | 8 | 212 | 27 | 0 |
| Love | 8 | 167 | 21 | 0 |
| R. Williams | 6 | 141 | 24 | 0 |
| Gordon | 4 | 141 | 35 | 0 |
| Bertelsen | 4 | 88 | 22 | 0 |
| Clark | 3 | 59 | 20 | 0 |
| Howard | 2 | 51 | 26 | 0 |
| Pergine | 3 | 46 | 15 | 0 |
| Curran | 4 | 37 | 9 | 0 |

### PASSING – PUNTING – KICKING

**PASSING**

| Last Name | Att | Comp | % | Yds | Yd/Att | TD | Int– | % | RK |
|---|---|---|---|---|---|---|---|---|---|
| Gabriel | 323 | 165 | 51 | 2027 | 6.3 | 12 | 15– | 5 | 9 |
| Beathard | 48 | 19 | 40 | 255 | 5.3 | 1 | 7– | 15 | |

**PUNTING**

| Last Name | No | Avg |
|---|---|---|
| Chapple | 53 | 44.2 |

**KICKING**

| Last Name | XP | Att | % | FG | Att | % |
|---|---|---|---|---|---|---|
| Ray | 31 | 31 | 100 | 24 | 41 | 59 |

## NEW ORLEANS SAINTS

### RUSHING

| Last Name | No. | Yds | Avg | TD |
|---|---|---|---|---|
| Gresham | 121 | 381 | 3.1 | 3 |
| Manning | 63 | 351 | 5.6 | 2 |
| Butler | 54 | 233 | 4.3 | 0 |
| Strong | 37 | 120 | 3.2 | 0 |
| J. Williams | 31 | 72 | 2.3 | 0 |
| Green | 14 | 51 | 3.6 | 0 |
| Ford | 11 | 28 | 2.5 | 0 |
| V. Robinson | 5 | 1 | 0.2 | 0 |
| Parks | 1 | -7 | -7.0 | 0 |

### RECEIVING

| Last Name | No. | Yds | Avg | TD |
|---|---|---|---|---|
| Newland | 47 | 579 | 12 | 2 |
| Abramowicz | 38 | 668 | 18 | 7 |
| Parks | 32 | 542 | 17 | 6 |
| Gresham | 29 | 192 | 7 | 0 |
| Butler | 25 | 226 | 9 | 2 |
| J. Williams | 16 | 116 | 7 | 0 |
| Strong | 14 | 123 | 9 | 0 |
| Brown | 11 | 175 | 16 | 1 |
| Adkins | 9 | 96 | 11 | 0 |
| Green | 7 | 49 | 7 | 0 |
| Ford | 1 | 9 | 9 | 0 |
| Whitaker | 1 | 6 | 6 | 0 |

### PUNT RETURNS

| Last Name | No. | Yds | Avg | TD |
|---|---|---|---|---|
| Myers | 9 | 43 | 5 | 0 |
| Adkins | 7 | 0 | 0 | 0 |

### KICKOFF RETURNS

| Last Name | No. | Yds | Avg | TD |
|---|---|---|---|---|
| Adkins | 43 | 1020 | 24 | 0 |
| Green | 8 | 187 | 23 | 0 |
| Strong | 4 | 53 | 13 | 0 |
| J. Williams | 2 | 23 | 12 | 0 |
| Butler | 1 | 14 | 14 | 0 |
| Hollas | 2 | 9 | 5 | 0 |
| Newland | 1 | 6 | 6 | 0 |

### PASSING – PUNTING – KICKING

**PASSING**

| Last Name | Att | Comp | % | Yds | Yd/Att | TD | Int– | % | RK |
|---|---|---|---|---|---|---|---|---|---|
| Manning | 448 | 230 | 51 | 2781 | 6.2 | 18 | 21– | 5 | 7 |
| Gresham | 1 | 0 | 0 | 0 | 0.0 | 0 | 0– | 0 | |

**PUNTING**

| Last Name | No | Avg |
|---|---|---|
| Fagan | 71 | 40.8 |

**KICKING**

| Last Name | XP | Att | % | FG | Att | % |
|---|---|---|---|---|---|---|
| Feller | 10 | 11 | 91 | 6 | 11 | 55 |
| Durkee | 9 | 9 | 100 | 3 | 9 | 33 |
| Linhart | 5 | 5 | 100 | 2 | 5 | 40 |

# 1972 A.F.C. Perfect From Start to Finish

Vince Lombardi's Packers had never done it. George Halas' Chicago Bears had come close but always fallen short. But Don Shula's Miami Dolphins did it; they went through the season unbeaten and untied and won three more games in the playoffs to finish with a perfect 17-0-0 record. The Bears had finished the 1934 and 1942 regular seasons with unblemished records, but both squads lost in the NFL championship game. Before the NFL split up into divisions, the Canton Bulldogs had gone undefeated in 1922 and 1923 and the Green Bay Packers in 1929, but each of those teams had been tied during the season. Paul Brown's Cleveland Browns breezed through the 1948 AAFC season without a loss or tie, but they had not been able to repeat that achievement after coming over to the NFL. The Dolphins were the first NFL team to compile an absolutely perfect record for a season, and they were a young team which had still not reached full development.

## EASTERN DIVISION

**Miami Dolphins**—Seven years ago the Dolphins had been created out of castoffs from the eight AFL teams; four years ago, they had finished on the bottom of the AFL's Eastern Division. But since Don Shula had taken over as coach in 1970, he had rebuilt, reorganized, and psyched the Dolphins into a powerhouse which rolled undefeated and untied through the 1973 season. The Miami defense was known as the "No-Name Defense," but those anonymous defenders allowed the fewest points in the NFL. After Bob Griese went out with an ankle injury in mid-season, veteran Earl Morrall stepped in at quarterback and kept the offense moving. The five Miami interior linemen—Norm Evans, Wayne Moore, Bob Keuchenberg, Larry Little, and Jim Langer—had all been cut loose by other pro teams, but the Dolphin blocking protected Morrall and cleared the way for runners Larry Csonka, Mercury Morris, and Jim Kiick. Csonka and Morris became the first teammates ever to gain 1,000 yards each in one season.

**New York Jets**—Quarterback Joe Namath stayed healthy all year and again wreaked havoc on defensive backs with his bullet passing, but the Jets nevertheless finished with a 7-7 record and out of the playoffs. The Jet defense unfortunately allowed points as readily as Namath and the offense could score them. None of the deep backs had a good year, while the front line was hurt by Gerry Philbin's disenchantment with coach Weeb Ewbank and John Elliott's slow recovery from knee surgery. The New York offensive cupboard was full. Running behind a line that was growing shopworn, John Riggins and Emerson Boozer balanced Namath's passing with consistently strong ball-carrying. But when Riggins and Boozer both went out of action late in the year with injuries, the Jet attack lost most of its spark.

**Baltimore Colts**—New owner Bob Irsay installed Joe Thomas as his general manager, and Thomas began ripping the team apart after it fell out of contention with four losses in the first five games. He fired coach Don McCafferty, ordered interim coach John Sandusky to bench veteran quarterback John Unitas in favor of younger Marty Domres, and one by one disposed of Baltimore veterans who had starred in the late 1960s and early 1970s. Before next season would begin, Thomas had traded off Unitas, Tom Matte, Dan Sullivan, Bill Curry, Bubba Smith, Fred Miller, Jerry Logan, Billy Newsome, Tom Nowatzke, and Norm Bulaich, and Bob Vogel retired.

**Buffalo Bills**—By the end of the opening game, starting offensive linemen Bruce Jarvis and Jim Reilly were out for the season with injuries. More blockers went onto the disabled list as the season progressed, and the Bills scoured the country for healthy offensive linemen to fill the breach. But even with the patchwork line, O. J. Simpson blossomed into stardom by running for 1,251 yards, the most in the NFL. Helping O. J. to prominence was head coach Lou Saban, who returned to the Bills with an offensive plan of going to Simpson twice as often as he had been used. Saban had quit the Bills after leading them to the AFL championship in 1965, but victories came harder with this Buffalo squad as only Walt Patulski, Don Croft, and Bobby James caused any excitement in the defensive platoon.

**New England Patriots**—General manager Upton Bell and head coach John Mazur battled with each other all season over how to build the Patriots. When the team won only three games all year, both Bell and Mazur were out of work by the end of the year. The biggest offensive problem was a deteriorating offensive line which exposed quarterback Jim Plunkett to severe punishment from enemy linemen. On defense, only Julius Adams and Jim Cheyunski provided any stability in the line and linebacking. Several veteran Patriots were lopped from the squad this year, as Jim Nance, Houston Antwine, Ron Sellers, and Don Webb all were casualties of a rebuilding program cursed with two dissenting architects. Before the season was over, coach Mazur had quit. In an unusual move to end an unusual season, the San Diego Chargers lent scout Phil Bengtson to the Patriots as interim head coach for the rest of the year.

## CENTRAL DIVISION

**Pittsburgh Steelers**—Pittsburgh fans thoroughly enjoyed the Steelers' drive to their first title of any sort. One group of fans dubbed themselves "Franco's Army" and adopted rookie fullback Franco Harris as their favorite. Harris' power running had given the Pittsburgh attack a new

dimension. Another group of fans, known as "Gerela's Gorillas," took place-kicker Roy Gerela as their idol. Appreciated by all Steeler fans were quarterback Terry Bradshaw and the very strong defensive unit. With both platoons playing well, the Steelers held a share of first place until December 3, when a 30-0 thumping of the Browns gave the team complete possession of the top rung in the division.

**Cleveland Browns**—The Browns' greatest asset was their ability to stay cool in pressure situations. Despite injuries in the defensive line, a chaotic linebacking situation, and problems in the offensive line, the Browns calmly beat the Bengals and Jets in the final two games to win the AFC wild-card berth in the playoffs. The partial retirement of Bill Nelsen put the quarterbacking burden squarely on Mike Phipps' shoulders, and the young passer responded with a season of steady progress as a leader. The Browns had strength at running back, with Leroy Kelly and Bo Scott, and in the secondary, where youngsters Clarence Scott and Tom Darden had become instant stars.

**Cincinnati Bengals**—The Bengals' season unfolded in three separate stages. First came the good start of four wins in the opening five games, then a mid-season slump of four losses in five games, and finally a late spurt of three wins in the last four games. Playing consistently well throughout the season was the Cincinnati defense, a unit strengthened by the addition of two top rookies in Sherman White and Tommy Casanova. Veteran Bengal defenders Mike Reid, Ron Carpenter, Bill Bergey, and Lemar Parrish shared with the rookies a wealth of talent, but the offense lacked the polished excellence of the defense; too many holes remained to be filled in this platoon. The Bengals needed a powerful running back and a speedy wide receiver, but few people bet against Paul Brown finding them in next year's draft as he had found his last one.

**Houston Oilers**—Owner Bud Adams used a long-term contract to lure head coach Bill Peterson away from Rice, but the new coach could not stop the deterioration of the Oilers. Outside of an early-season upset of the Jets, the Oilers served as the NFL's punching bag. Mid-season trades brought Fred Willis, Paul Robinson, and Dave Smith to Houston, but they could not help an offense plagued with a porous line. On defense, the team's two best linemen, Elvin Bethea and Mike Tilleman, demanded to be traded; two starting linebackers, George Webster and Ron Pritchard, were traded in mid-season.

## WESTERN DIVISION

**Oakland Raiders**—The Raiders had a knack for slipping new talent into the lineup while continuing to win without interruption. The defensive line, for instance, had been completely rebuilt in the last two seasons. Veterans like Ben Davidson, Tom Keating, and Carleton Oates had been eased aside in favor of youngsters Horace Jones, Art Thoms, Otis Sistrunk, and Tony Cline. The defense, meanwhile, suffered no letdown at all in stopping the run or pressuring the passer. At linebacker, the Raiders surrounded veteran Dan Conners with young outside men Phil Villipiano and Gerald Irons, and the secondary had veteran cornerbacks in Willie Brown and Nemiah Wilson and young safeties in George Atkinson and Jack Tatum. The offense had the same mixture of experience and youth, while the specialists ranged from rookie punt returner Cliff Branch to forty-four-year-old place-kicker George Blanda.

**Kansas City Chiefs**—Unable to win regularly at home, the Chiefs thus gave the Raiders only a weak challenge for the Western Division title. After years as an AFC power, the team was starting to crack under the weight of time. Safety Johnny Robinson retired, offensive linemen Ed Budde, Jim Tyrer, and Dave Hill were slowing down, and quarterback Len Dawson needed more rest. Other trouble spots for coach Hank Stram were receiver Elmo Wright's injury, a mediocre showing by the defensive ends, and a disappointing showing by rookie runner Jeff Kinney.

**Denver Broncos**—The Broncos followed the trend to hiring college coaches by signing John Ralston away from Stanford, but Ralston went out and traded for a veteran quarterback to lead the young Broncos on the field. Charley Johnson came over from Houston and gave the club a top passer and a poised offensive leader. With the Denver passing attack in good order, Floyd Little carried less of the offensive burden but still picked up 859 yards on the ground. Ralston traded away veteran defensive linemen Richard Jackson and Dave Costa, but the new unit of Lyle Alzado, Paul Smith, Pete Duranko, and Lloyd Voss kept pressure on opposing quarterbacks as the Broncos had their highest finish in ten years.

**San Diego Chargers**—Coach Harland Svare traded for some of the league's most famous oldsters and malcontents, bringing John Mackey, Deacon Jones, Lionel Aldridge, Dave Costa, Cid Edwards, Tim Rossovich, and Duane Thomas to San Diego. The Thomas deal was a complete washout, as Thomas' personal problems put him in no mood to play football. Injuries bothered Rossovich, and age had cut down on Mackey's skills, but the other acquisitions enjoyed good seasons in their new home. The defense suffered, however, when injuries decimated the secondary, and the offense was hurt by a difference in philosophy between quarterback John Hadl and offensive coach Bob Schnelker. Whereas Hadl had always run a wide-open passing attack, Schnelker insisted on a ball-control offense.

## FINAL TEAM STATISTICS

### OFFENSE

| | BALT. | BUFF. | CIN. | CLEV. | DENV. | HOUS. | K.C. | MIAMI | N.ENG. | N.Y. | OAK. | PITT. | S.D. |
|---|---|---|---|---|---|---|---|---|---|---|---|---|---|
| **FIRST DOWNS:** | | | | | | | | | | | | | |
| Total | 251 | 221 | 255 | 215 | 237 | 183 | 245 | 291 | 236 | 250 | 297 | 228 | 262 |
| by Rushing | 97 | 104 | 112 | 102 | 87 | 80 | 118 | 170 | 86 | 106 | 145 | 131 | 123 |
| by Passing | 124 | 98 | 122 | 101 | 132 | 88 | 116 | 102 | 126 | 117 | 122 | 79 | 116 |
| by Penalty | 30 | 19 | 21 | 12 | 18 | 15 | 11 | 19 | 24 | 27 | 30 | 18 | 23 |
| **RUSHING:** | | | | | | | | | | | | | |
| Number | 462 | 512 | 491 | 453 | 409 | 397 | 476 | 613 | 386 | 461 | 521 | 497 | 504 |
| Yards | 1894 | 2132 | 1996 | 1793 | 1838 | 1518 | 1915 | 2960 | 1532 | 2010 | 2376 | 2520 | 1995 |
| Average Yards | 4.1 | 4.2 | 4.1 | 4.0 | 4.5 | 3.8 | 4.0 | 4.8 | 4.0 | 4.4 | 4.6 | 5.1 | 4.0 |
| Touchdowns | 10 | 11 | 16 | 13 | 17 | 7 | 6 | 26 | 13 | 18 | 20 | 22 | 12 |
| **PASSING:** | | | | | | | | | | | | | |
| Attempts | 381 | 316 | 384 | 337 | 384 | 375 | 384 | 259 | 412 | 347 | 370 | 324 | 377 |
| Completions | 203 | 164 | 219 | 158 | 201 | 181 | 217 | 144 | 198 | 172 | 198 | 156 | 192 |
| Completion Percentage | 53.3 | 51.9 | 57.0 | 46.9 | 52.3 | 48.3 | 56.5 | 55.6 | 48.1 | 49.6 | 53.5 | 48.1 | 50.9 |
| Passing Yards | 2503 | 2012 | 2513 | 2135 | 2900 | 2045 | 2335 | 2235 | 2579 | 2930 | 2599 | 1958 | 2516 |
| Avg. Yards per Attempt | 6.6 | 6.4 | 6.5 | 6.3 | 7.6 | 5.5 | 6.1 | 8.6 | 6.3 | 8.4 | 7.0 | 6.0 | 6.7 |
| Avg. Yards per Complet. | 12.3 | 12.3 | 11.5 | 13.5 | 14.4 | 11.3 | 10.8 | 15.5 | 13.0 | 17.0 | 13.1 | 12.6 | 13.1 |
| Time Tackled Passing | 25 | 49 | 24 | 27 | 38 | 45 | 34 | 21 | 44 | 17 | 24 | 32 | 23 |
| Yards Lost Tackled | 210 | 411 | 192 | 219 | 266 | 372 | 297 | 159 | 452 | 153 | 230 | 247 | 212 |
| Net Yards | 2293 | 1601 | 2321 | 1916 | 2634 | 1673 | 2038 | 2076 | 2127 | 2777 | 2369 | 1711 | 2304 |
| Touchdowns | 15 | 16 | 10 | 13 | 19 | 10 | 20 | 17 | 10 | 21 | 23 | 12 | 15 |
| Interceptions | 12 | 24 | 11 | 19 | 23 | 23 | 20 | 12 | 28 | 22 | 15 | 12 | 28 |
| Percent Intercepted | 3.1 | 7.6 | 2.9 | 5.6 | 6.0 | 6.1 | 5.2 | 4.6 | 6.8 | 6.3 | 7.6 | 3.7 | 7.4 |
| **PUNTS:** | | | | | | | | | | | | | |
| Number | 57 | 80 | 66 | 81 | 60 | 85 | 66 | 44 | 75 | 51 | 55 | 66 | 45 |
| Average Distance | 42.1 | 38.8 | 42.1 | 43.2 | 40.1 | 41.0 | 44.8 | 39.4 | 38.1 | 39.3 | 36.9 | 43.6 | 40.3 |
| **PUNT RETURNS:** | | | | | | | | | | | | | |
| Number | 43 | 25 | 47 | 37 | 28 | 34 | 29 | 40 | 17 | 25 | 24 | 30 | 23 |
| Yards | 348 | 164 | 437 | 211 | 310 | 163 | 126 | 329 | 37 | 242 | 66 | 262 | 185 |
| Average Yards | 8.1 | 6.6 | 9.3 | 5.7 | 11.1 | 4.8 | 4.3 | 8.2 | 2.2 | 9.7 | 2.8 | 8.7 | 8.0 |
| Touchdowns | 0 | 0 | 2 | 0 | 1 | 0 | 0 | 0 | 0 | 1 | 0 | 0 | 0 |
| **KICKOFF RETURNS:** | | | | | | | | | | | | | |
| Number | 47 | 60 | 46 | 41 | 55 | 54 | 46 | 24 | 55 | 56 | 38 | 33 | 60 |
| Yards | 1321 | 1389 | 1018 | 933 | 1256 | 1093 | 1057 | 546 | 1293 | 1218 | 813 | 760 | 1273 |
| Average Yards | 28.1 | 23.2 | 22.1 | 22.8 | 22.8 | 20.2 | 23.0 | 22.8 | 23.5 | 21.8 | 21.4 | 23.0 | 21.2 |
| Touchdowns | 1 | 0 | 0 | 0 | 1 | 0 | 0 | 0 | 0 | 0 | 0 | 0 | 0 |
| **INTERCEPTION RETURNS:** | | | | | | | | | | | | | |
| Number | 23 | 23 | 20 | 13 | 10 | 6 | 24 | 26 | 10 | 19 | 25 | 28 | 24 |
| Yards | 331 | 369 | 326 | 154 | 109 | 93 | 396 | 286 | 223 | 282 | 328 | 395 | 310 |
| Average Yards | 14.4 | 16.0 | 16.3 | 11.8 | 10.9 | 15.5 | 16.5 | 11.0 | 22.3 | 14.8 | 13.1 | 14.1 | 12.9 |
| Touchdowns | 1 | 3 | 3 | 1 | 0 | 0 | 5 | 1 | 0 | 0 | 1 | 1 | 1 |
| **PENALTIES:** | | | | | | | | | | | | | |
| Number | 58 | 87 | 76 | 57 | 89 | 66 | 69 | 68 | 66 | 74 | 84 | 81 | 87 |
| Yards | 605 | 900 | 738 | 536 | 827 | 581 | 653 | 714 | 761 | 719 | 757 | 728 | 789 |
| **FUMBLES:** | | | | | | | | | | | | | |
| Number | 37 | 29 | 28 | 21 | 25 | 30 | 23 | 25 | 26 | 21 | 31 | 27 | 40 |
| Number Lost | 22 | 15 | 18 | 9 | 11 | 10 | 12 | 16 | 10 | 9 | 17 | 14 | 20 |
| **POINTS:** | | | | | | | | | | | | | |
| Total | 235 | 257 | 299 | 268 | 325 | 164 | 287 | 385 | 192 | 367 | 365 | 343 | 264 |
| PAT Attempts | 23 | 30 | 31 | 29 | 38 | 18 | 32 | 45 | 24 | 41 | 45 | 37 | 30 |
| PAT Made | 23 | 29 | 30 | 28 | 37 | 17 | 32 | 43 | 24 | 40 | 44 | 35 | 28 |
| FG Attempts | 39 | 24 | 40 | 27 | 29 | 21 | 36 | 37 | 16 | 37 | 26 | 41 | 31 |
| FG Made | 13 | 16 | 27 | 22 | 20 | 13 | 21 | 24 | 8 | 27 | 17 | 28 | 18 |
| Percent FG Made | 33.3 | 66.7 | 67.5 | 81.5 | 69.0 | 61.9 | 58.3 | 64.9 | 50.0 | 73.0 | 65.4 | 68.3 | 58.1 |
| Safeties | 0 | 0 | 1 | 0 | 0 | 0 | 0 | 0 | 0 | 0 | 0 | 1 | 1 |

### DEFENSE

| | BALT. | BUFF. | CIN. | CLEV. | DENV. | HOUS. | K.C. | MIAMI | N.ENG. | N.Y. | OAK. | PITT. | S.D. |
|---|---|---|---|---|---|---|---|---|---|---|---|---|---|
| **FIRST DOWNS:** | | | | | | | | | | | | | |
| Total | 233 | 249 | 207 | 240 | 251 | 263 | 227 | 186 | 288 | 255 | 227 | 228 | 244 |
| by Rushing | 111 | 125 | 98 | 130 | 102 | 147 | 93 | 76 | 143 | 121 | 97 | 88 | 99 |
| by Passing | 109 | 95 | 92 | 89 | 123 | 100 | 116 | 96 | 124 | 118 | 104 | 116 | 124 |
| by Penalty | 13 | 29 | 17 | 21 | 26 | 16 | 18 | 14 | 21 | 16 | 26 | 24 | 21 |
| **RUSHING:** | | | | | | | | | | | | | |
| Number | 515 | 532 | 406 | 520 | 439 | 546 | 453 | 389 | 548 | 476 | 469 | 445 | 435 |
| Yards | 1989 | 2241 | 1815 | 2333 | 1668 | 2591 | 1805 | 1548 | 2717 | 2072 | 1764 | 1715 | 1673 |
| Average Yards | 3.9 | 4.2 | 4.5 | 4.5 | 3.8 | 4.7 | 4.0 | 4.0 | 5.0 | 4.4 | 3.8 | 3.9 | 3.8 |
| Touchdowns | 15 | 26 | 11 | 13 | 15 | 23 | 12 | 8 | 27 | 16 | 9 | 6 | 18 |
| **PASSING:** | | | | | | | | | | | | | |
| Attempts | 313 | 308 | 350 | 310 | 397 | 324 | 368 | 348 | 326 | 363 | 348 | 411 | 358 |
| Completions | 178 | 131 | 167 | 160 | 206 | 174 | 186 | 178 | 175 | 186 | 166 | 206 | 201 |
| Completion Percentage | 56.9 | 42.5 | 47.7 | 51.6 | 51.9 | 53.7 | 50.5 | 51.1 | 53.7 | 51.2 | 47.7 | 50.1 | 56.1 |
| Passing Yards | 2555 | 2148 | 2033 | 1994 | 2540 | 2315 | 2483 | 2029 | 2634 | 2888 | 2363 | 2393 | 2441 |
| Avg. Yards per Attempt | 8.2 | 7.0 | 5.8 | 6.4 | 6.4 | 7.1 | 6.7 | 5.8 | 8.1 | 8.0 | 6.8 | 5.8 | 6.8 |
| Avg. Yards per Complet. | 14.4 | 16.4 | 12.2 | 12.5 | 12.3 | 13.3 | 13.3 | 11.4 | 15.1 | 15.5 | 14.2 | 11.6 | 12.1 |
| Time Tackled Passing | 25 | 22 | 38 | 38 | 41 | 24 | 32 | 33 | 15 | 27 | 27 | 40 | 26 |
| Yards Lost Tackled | 232 | 197 | 296 | 258 | 357 | 172 | 261 | 280 | 101 | 251 | 211 | 337 | 233 |
| Net Yards | 2323 | 1951 | 1737 | 1736 | 2183 | 2143 | 2222 | 1749 | 2533 | 2637 | 2152 | 2056 | 2208 |
| Touchdowns | 15 | 19 | 11 | 14 | 19 | 12 | 17 | 10 | 24 | 18 | 14 | 9 | 18 |
| Interceptions | 23 | 23 | 20 | 13 | 10 | 6 | 24 | 26 | 10 | 19 | 25 | 28 | 24 |
| Percent Intercepted | 7.3 | 7.5 | 5.7 | 4.2 | 2.5 | 1.9 | 6.5 | 7.5 | 3.1 | 5.2 | 7.2 | 6.8 | 6.7 |
| **PUNTS:** | | | | | | | | | | | | | |
| Number | 71 | 65 | 84 | 74 | 66 | 61 | 61 | 68 | 48 | 56 | 56 | 74 | 56 |
| Average Distance | 39.0 | 39.5 | 42.4 | 40.9 | 45.2 | 42.1 | 40.3 | 41.1 | 40.4 | 39.4 | 42.5 | 40.3 | 38.4 |
| **PUNT RETURNS:** | | | | | | | | | | | | | |
| Number | 29 | 39 | 26 | 46 | 28 | 31 | 38 | 17 | 34 | 23 | 28 | 37 | 17 |
| Yards | 204 | 329 | 152 | 357 | 249 | 299 | 328 | 67 | 366 | 239 | 215 | 169 | 157 |
| Average Yards | 7.0 | 8.4 | 5.8 | 7.8 | 8.9 | 9.6 | 8.6 | 3.9 | 10.8 | 10.4 | 7.7 | 4.6 | 9.2 |
| Touchdowns | 0 | 1 | 0 | 0 | 1 | 1 | 0 | 0 | 1 | 0 | 0 | 0 | 1 |
| **KICKOFF RETURNS:** | | | | | | | | | | | | | |
| Number | 50 | 29 | 44 | 50 | 54 | 28 | 43 | 56 | 32 | 47 | 59 | 54 | 53 |
| Yards | 1091 | 644 | 984 | 1198 | 1246 | 547 | 1083 | 1283 | 784 | 1386 | 1393 | 1190 | 1225 |
| Average Yards | 21.8 | 22.2 | 22.4 | 24.0 | 23.1 | 19.5 | 25.2 | 22.9 | 24.5 | 29.5 | 23.6 | 22.0 | 23.1 |
| Touchdowns | 0 | 0 | 0 | 0 | 0 | 0 | 0 | 0 | 0 | 1 | 1 | 0 | 1 |
| **INTERCEPTION RETURNS:** | | | | | | | | | | | | | |
| Number | 12 | 24 | 11 | 19 | 23 | 23 | 20 | 12 | 28 | 22 | 15 | 12 | 28 |
| Yards | 169 | 305 | 70 | 145 | 441 | 319 | 278 | 249 | 490 | 271 | 178 | 195 | 229 |
| Average Yards | 14.1 | 12.7 | 6.4 | 7.6 | 19.2 | 13.9 | 13.9 | 20.8 | 17.5 | 12.3 | 11.9 | 16.3 | 8.2 |
| Touchdowns | 0 | 1 | 0 | 0 | 6 | 3 | 0 | 2 | 2 | 1 | 0 | 1 | 0 |
| **PENALTIES:** | | | | | | | | | | | | | |
| Number | 84 | 72 | 69 | 63 | 83 | 79 | 66 | 70 | 88 | 86 | 83 | 77 | 75 |
| Yards | 826 | 685 | 581 | 557 | 784 | 741 | 643 | 659 | 862 | 856 | 801 | 712 | 679 |
| **FUMBLES:** | | | | | | | | | | | | | |
| Number | 22 | 20 | 30 | 39 | 27 | 29 | 35 | 32 | 23 | 21 | 22 | 37 | 26 |
| Number Lost | 13 | 8 | 9 | 16 | 12 | 18 | 19 | 20 | 14 | 12 | 12 | 20 | 10 |
| **POINTS:** | | | | | | | | | | | | | |
| Total | 252 | 377 | 229 | 249 | 350 | 380 | 254 | 171 | 446 | 324 | 248 | 175 | 344 |
| PAT Attempts | 30 | 47 | 24 | 27 | 41 | 40 | 30 | 21 | 54 | 37 | 27 | 18 | 41 |
| PAT Made | 27 | 47 | 23 | 27 | 39 | 39 | 29 | 18 | 54 | 36 | 26 | 17 | 41 |
| FG Attempts | 24 | 27 | 29 | 29 | 33 | 40 | 31 | 19 | 36 | 33 | 37 | 27 | 28 |
| FG Made | 15 | 16 | 20 | 20 | 21 | 33 | 15 | 9 | 22 | 22 | 20 | 16 | 19 |
| Percent FG Made | 62.5 | 59.3 | 69.0 | 69.0 | 63.6 | 82.5 | 48.4 | 47.4 | 61.1 | 66.7 | 54.1 | 59.3 | 67.9 |
| Safeties | 0 | 0 | 1 | 0 | 1 | 1 | 0 | 0 | 1 | 0 | 0 | 1 | 0 |

## CONFERENCE PLAYOFFS

### December 23, at Pittsburgh (Attendance 50,327)

#### SCORING

| | | | | |
|---|---|---|---|---|
| PITTSBURGH | 0 | 0 | 3 | 10–13 |
| OAKLAND | 0 | 0 | 0 | 7– 7 |

Third Quarter
PIT. Gerela, 18 yard field goal

Fourth Quarter
PIT. Gerela, 29 yard field goal
OAK. Stabler, 30 yard rush
PAT–Blanda (kick)
PIT. Harris, 60 yard pass from Bradshaw PAT–Gerela (kick)

#### TEAM STATISTICS

| PITT. | | OAK. |
|---|---|---|
| 13 | First Downs–Total | 13 |
| 7 | First Downs–Rushing | 9 |
| 6 | First Downs–Passing | 4 |
| 0 | First Downs–Penalty | 0 |
| 0 | Fumbles–Number | 3 |
| 0 | Fumbles–Lost Ball | 2 |
| 1 | Penalties–Number | 2 |
| 5 | Yards Penalized | 15 |
| 1 | Missed Field Goals | 0 |
| 64 | Offensive Plays | 65 |
| 252 | Net Yards | 216 |
| 3.9 | Average Gain | 3.3 |
| 1 | Giveaways | 4 |
| 4 | Takeaways | 1 |
| +3 | Difference | –3 |

#### INDIVIDUAL STATISTICS

| PITTSBURGH | No. | Yds. | Avg. | OAKLAND | No. | Yds. | Avg. |
|---|---|---|---|---|---|---|---|
| **RUSHING** | | | | | | | |
| Harris | 18 | 64 | 3.6 | Smith | 14 | 57 | 4.1 |
| Fuqua | 16 | 25 | 1.6 | Hubbard | 14 | 44 | 3.1 |
| Bradshaw | 2 | 19 | 9.5 | Stabler | 1 | 30 | 30.0 |
| | 36 | 108 | 3.0 | Davis | 2 | 7 | 3.5 |
| | | | | | 31 | 138 | 4.5 |
| **RECEIVING** | | | | | | | |
| Harris | 5 | 96 | 19.2 | Chester | 3 | 40 | 13.3 |
| Shanklin | 3 | 55 | 18.3 | Biletnikoff | 3 | 28 | 9.3 |
| Fuqua | 1 | 11 | 11.0 | Smith | 2 | 8 | 4.0 |
| McMakin | 1 | 9 | 9.0 | Banaszek | 1 | 12 | 12.0 |
| Young | 1 | 4 | 4.0 | Siani | 1 | 7 | 7.0 |
| | 11 | 175 | 15.9 | Otto | 1 | 5 | 5.0 |
| | | | | Hubbard | 1 | 2 | 2.0 |
| | | | | | 12 | 102 | 8.5 |
| **PUNTING** | | | | | | | |
| Walden | 6 | | 48.2 | DePoyster | 7 | | 45.1 |
| **PUNT RETURNS** | | | | | | | |
| Edwards | 3 | 39 | 13.0 | Atkinson | 1 | 37 | 37.0 |
| **KICKOFF RETURNS** | | | | | | | |
| Pearson | 1 | 21 | 21.0 | Davis | 1 | 26 | 26.0 |
| **INTERCEPTION RETURNS** | | | | | | | |
| Ham | 1 | 0 | 0.0 | Wilson | 1 | 7 | 7.0 |
| Russell | 1 | 0 | 0.0 | | | | |
| | 2 | 0 | 0.0 | | | | |

**PASSING**

| PITTSBURGH | Att. | Comp. | Comp. Pct. | Yds. | Int. | Yds/ Att. | Yds/ Comp. | Yards Lost Tackled |
|---|---|---|---|---|---|---|---|---|
| Bradshaw | 25 | 11 | 44.0 | 175 | 1 | 7.0 | 15.9 | 3–31 |
| **OAKLAND** | | | | | | | | |
| Lamonica | 18 | 6 | 33.0 | 45 | 2 | 2.5 | 7.5 | |
| Stabler | 12 | 6 | 50.0 | 57 | 0 | 4.8 | 9.5 | |
| | 30 | 12 | 40.0 | 102 | 2 | 3.4 | 8.5 | 4–24 |

### December 24, at Miami (Attendance 78,916)

#### SCORING

| | | | | |
|---|---|---|---|---|
| MIAMI | 10 | 0 | 0 | 10–20 |
| CLEVELAND | 0 | 0 | 7 | 7–14 |

First Quarter
MIA. Babb, 6 yard return of blocked punt PAT–Yepremiam (kick)
MIA. Yepremiam, 40 yard field goal

Third Quarter
CLE. Phipps, 5 yard rush
PAT – Cockroft (kick)

Fourth Quarter
MIA. Yepremiam, 46 yard field goal
CLE. Hooker, 27 yard pass from Phipps PAT–Cockroft (kick)
MIA. Kiick, 8 yard rush
PAT–Yepremiam (kick)

#### TEAM STATISTICS

| MIAMI | | CLEVE. |
|---|---|---|
| 17 | First Downs–Total | 15 |
| 11 | First Downs–Rushing | 9 |
| 4 | First Downs–Passing | 6 |
| 2 | First Downs–Penalty | 0 |
| 2 | Fumbles–Number | 2 |
| 2 | Fumbles–Lost Ball | 0 |
| 3 | Penalties–Number | 3 |
| 25 | Yards Penalized | 25 |
| 2 | Missed Field Goals | 0 |
| 64 | Offensive Plays | 57 |
| 272 | Net Yards | 283 |
| 4.3 | Average Gain | 5.0 |
| 2 | Giveaways | 5 |
| 5 | Takeaways | 2 |
| +3 | Difference | –3 |

#### INDIVIDUAL STATISTICS

| MIAMI | No. | Yds. | Avg. | CLEVELAND | No. | Yds. | Avg. |
|---|---|---|---|---|---|---|---|
| **RUSHING** | | | | | | | |
| Morris | 15 | 72 | 4.8 | Scott | 16 | 94 | 5.9 |
| Kiick | 14 | 50 | 3.6 | Phipps | 8 | 47 | 5.9 |
| Warfield | 2 | 41 | 20.5 | Brown | 4 | 13 | 3.3 |
| Csonka | 12 | 32 | 2.7 | Kelly | 4 | 11 | 2.8 |
| Morrall | 4 | 3 | 0.8 | | 32 | 165 | 5.2 |
| | 47 | 198 | 4.2 | | | | |
| **RECEIVING** | | | | | | | |
| Twilley | 3 | 33 | 11.0 | Scott | 4 | 30 | 7.5 |
| Warfield | 2 | 50 | 25.0 | Hooker | 3 | 53 | 17.7 |
| Kiick | 1 | 5 | 5.0 | Kelly | 1 | 27 | 27.0 |
| | 6 | 88 | 14.7 | Morin | 1 | 21 | 21.0 |
| | | | | | 9 | 131 | 14.6 |
| **PUNTING** | | | | | | | |
| Seiple | 5 | | 42.0 | Cockroft | 6 | | 34.7 |
| **PUNT RETURNS** | | | | | | | |
| Scott | 1 | 1 | 1.0 | Darden | 1 | 38 | 38.0 |
| | | | | Kelley | 1 | 8 | 8.0 |
| | | | | | 2 | 46 | 23.0 |
| **KICKOFF RETURNS** | | | | | | | |
| None | | | | Lefear | 3 | 56 | 18.7 |
| **INTERCEPTION RETURNS** | | | | | | | |
| Swift | 2 | 19 | 9.5 | None | | | |
| Anderson | 2 | 12 | 6.0 | | | | |
| Johnson | 1 | 33 | 33.0 | | | | |
| | 5 | 64 | 12.8 | | | | |

**PASSING**

| MIAMI | Att. | Comp. | Comp. Pct. | Yds. | Int. | Yds/ Att. | Yds/ Comp. | Yards Lost Tackled |
|---|---|---|---|---|---|---|---|---|
| Morrall | 13 | 6 | 46.2 | 88 | 0 | 6.8 | 14.7 | 4–14 |
| **CLEVELAND** | | | | | | | | |
| Phipps | 23 | 9 | 39.1 | 131 | 5 | 5.7 | 14.6 | 2–13 |

**MIAMI DOLPHINS 14-0-0 Don Shula**

| Scores of Each Game | | |
|---|---|---|
| 20 | Kansas City | 10 |
| 34 | HOUSTON | 13 |
| 16 | Minnesota | 14 |
| 27 | N.Y. Jets | 17 |
| 24 | SAN DIEGO | 10 |
| 24 | BUFFALO | 23 |
| 23 | Baltimore | 0 |
| 30 | Buffalo | 16 |
| 52 | NEW ENGLAND | 0 |
| 28 | N.Y. JETS | 24 |
| 31 | ST. LOUIS | 10 |
| 37 | New England | 21 |
| 23 | N.Y. Giants | 13 |
| 16 | BALTIMORE | 0 |

| Use Name | Pos. | Hgt | Wgt | Age | Int | Pts |
|---|---|---|---|---|---|---|
| Doug Crusan | OT | 6'5" | 250 | 26 | | |
| Norm Evans | OT | 6'5" | 252 | 29 | | |
| Wayne Moore | OT | 6'6" | 265 | 27 | | |
| Bob Kuechenberg | OG | 6'3" | 247 | 24 | | |
| Larry Little | OG | 6'1" | 265 | 26 | | |
| Al Jenkins | OT-OG | 6'2" | 245 | 26 | | |
| Jim Langer | C | 6'2" | 250 | 24 | | |
| Howard Kindig | OT-C | 6'6" | 260 | 31 | | |
| Vern Den Herder | DE | 6'6" | 250 | 23 | 1 | |
| Bill Stanfill | DE | 6'5" | 250 | 25 | | |
| Bob Matheson | LB-DE | 6'4" | 240 | 27 | | |
| Jim Dunaway | DT | 6'4" | 277 | 30 | | |
| Manny Fernandez | DT | 6'2" | 248 | 26 | | |
| Baldy Moore | DT | 6'5" | 265 | 26 | | |
| Bob Heinz | DE-DT | 6'6" | 270 | 25 | | |

| Use Name | Pos. | Hgt | Wgt | Age | Int | Pts |
|---|---|---|---|---|---|---|
| Larry Ball | LB | 6'6" | 225 | 22 | | |
| Nick Buoniconti | LB | 5'11" | 220 | 31 | 2 | |
| Mike Kolen | LB | 6'2" | 220 | 24 | 1 | |
| Jesse Powell | LB | 6'1" | 215 | 25 | | |
| Doug Swift | LB | 6'3" | 228 | 23 | 3 | |
| Dick Anderson | DB | 6'2" | 196 | 26 | 3 | 6 |
| Charlie Babb | DB | 6' | 190 | 22 | 1 | |
| Tim Foley | DB | 6' | 194 | 24 | 3 | |
| Curtis Johnson | DB | 6'2" | 196 | 24 | 3 | |
| Lloyd Mumphford | DB | 5'11" | 180 | 25 | 4 | 6 |
| Jake Scott | DB | 6' | 188 | 27 | 5 | |
| Karl Noonan – Knee Injury | | | | | | |
| Jim Riley – Knee Injury | | | | | | |

| Use Name | Pos. | Hgt | Wgt | Age | Int | Pts |
|---|---|---|---|---|---|---|
| Jim Del Gaizo | QB | 6'1" | 198 | 25 | | |
| Bob Griese | QB | 6'1" | 190 | 27 | | 6 |
| Earl Morrall | QB | 6'1" | 206 | 38 | | 6 |
| Hubert Ginn | HB | 5'11" | 188 | 25 | | 6 |
| Ed Jenkins | HB | 6'2" | 210 | 22 | | |
| Jim Kiick | HB | 5'11" | 215 | 26 | | 36 |
| Mercury Morris | HB | 5'10" | 190 | 25 | | 72 |
| Larry Csonka | FB | 6'3" | 237 | 25 | | 36 |
| Charlie Leigh | FB | 5'11" | 205 | 26 | | |
| Marlin Briscoe | WR | 5'10" | 178 | 26 | | 24 |
| Otto Stowe | WR | 6'2" | 188 | 23 | | 12 |
| Howard Twilley | WR | 5'10" | 185 | 28 | | 18 |
| Paul Warfield | WR | 6' | 185 | 29 | | 18 |
| Marv Fleming | TE | 6'4" | 235 | 30 | | 6 |
| Jim Mandich | TE | 6'3" | 224 | 24 | | 18 |
| Larry Seiple | TE | 6' | 215 | 27 | | |
| Billy Lothridge | K | 6'1" | 200 | 28 | | |
| Garo Yepremian | K | 5'8" | 172 | 28 | | 115 |

**NEW YORK JETS 7-7-0 Weeb Ewbank**

| Scores of Each Game | | |
|---|---|---|
| 41 | Buffalo | 24 |
| 44 | Baltimore | 34 |
| 20 | Houston | 26 |
| 17 | MIAMI | 27 |
| 41 | New England | 13 |
| 24 | BALTIMORE | 20 |
| 34 | NEW ENGLAND | 10 |
| 17 | WASHINGTON | 35 |
| 41 | BUFFALO | 3 |
| 24 | Miami | 28 |
| 20 | Detroit | 37 |
| 18 | NEW ORLEANS | 17 |
| 16 | Oakland | 24 |
| 10 | CLEVELAND | 26 |

| Use Name | Pos. | Hgt | Wgt | Age | Int | Pts |
|---|---|---|---|---|---|---|
| Winston Hill | OT | 6'4" | 270 | 30 | | |
| Bob Svihus | OT | 6'4" | 245 | 29 | | |
| John Mooring | C-OT | 6'6" | 255 | 25 | | |
| Roger Finnie | OG | 6'3" | 245 | 26 | | |
| Dave Herman | OG | 6'2" | 255 | 30 | | |
| Randy Rasmussen | OG | 6'2" | 255 | 27 | | 6 |
| Roy Kirksey | DT-OG | 6'1" | 265 | 24 | | |
| John Schmitt | C | 6'4" | 250 | 29 | | |
| Gerry Philbin | DE | 6'2" | 245 | 31 | | |
| Joey Jackson | DT-DE | 6'4" | 257 | 23 | | |
| Mark Lomas | DT-DE | 6'4" | 245 | 24 | | |
| John Elliott | DT | 6'4" | 244 | 27 | | |
| John Little | DT | 6'3" | 235 | 25 | | |
| Steve Thompson | DT | 6'5" | 237 | 27 | | |
| Ed Galigher | DE-DT | 6'4" | 255 | 21 | | |

| Use Name | Pos. | Hgt | Wgt | Age | Int | Pts |
|---|---|---|---|---|---|---|
| Al Atkinson | LB | 6'1" | 230 | 29 | 1 | |
| Ralph Baker | LB | 6'3" | 228 | 30 | 2 | |
| John Ebersole | LB | 6'3" | 227 | 23 | | |
| Larry Grantham | LB | 6' | 210 | 33 | | |
| Mike Taylor | LB | 6'1" | 230 | 22 | 1 | |
| Paul Crane | C-LB | 6'2" | 212 | 28 | 1 | |
| Bill Zapalac | DE-LB | 6'4" | 225 | 24 | 1 | |
| Chris Farasopoulos | DB | 5'11" | 190 | 23 | 2 | 6 |
| W. K. Hicks | DB | 6'1" | 195 | 29 | 1 | |
| Gus Holloman | DB | 6'3" | 195 | 26 | 1 | |
| Rich Sowells | DB | 6' | 175 | 23 | 2 | |
| Steve Tannen | DB | 6'1" | 194 | 24 | 7 | |
| Earlie Thomas | DB | 6'1" | 190 | 26 | 1 | |
| Phil Wise | DB | 6' | 190 | 23 | | |

| Use Name | Pos. | Hgt | Wgt | Age | Int | Pts |
|---|---|---|---|---|---|---|
| Bob Davis | QB | 6'3" | 205 | 27 | | |
| Joe Namath | QB | 6'2" | 200 | 29 | | |
| Hank Bjorklund | BH | 6'1" | 200 | 22 | | |
| Emerson Boozer | HB | 5'11" | 195 | 29 | | 84 |
| Cliff McClain | HB | 6' | 217 | 24 | | |
| John Riggins | FB | 6'2" | 233 | 23 | | 48 |
| Matt Snell | FB | 6'2" | 220 | 30 | | |
| Steve Harkey | HB-FB | 6' | 215 | 23 | | |
| Jerome Barkum | WR | 6'3" | 215 | 22 | | 12 |
| Eddie Bell | WR | 5'10" | 160 | 24 | | 12 |
| Don Maynard | WR | 6' | 180 | 36 | | 12 |
| Rocky Turner | WR | 6' | 190 | 22 | | |
| Rich Caster | TE | 6'5" | 228 | 23 | | 60 |
| Wayne Stewart | TE | 6'7" | 213 | 25 | | 6 |
| Bobby Howfield | K | 5'9" | 180 | 35 | | 121 |
| Steve O'Neal | K | 6'3" | 185 | 26 | | |

**BALTIMORE COLTS 5-9-0 Don McCafferty John Sandusky**

| Scores of Each Game | | |
|---|---|---|
| 3 | ST. LOUIS | 10 |
| 34 | N.Y. JETS | 44 |
| 17 | Buffalo | 0 |
| 20 | SAN DIEGO | 23 |
| 0 | DALLAS | 21 |
| 20 | N.Y. Jets | 24 |
| 0 | MIAMI | 23 |
| 24 | New England | 17 |
| 21 | San Francisco | 24 |
| 20 | Cincinnati | 19 |
| 31 | NEW ENGLAND | 0 |
| 35 | BUFFALO | 7 |
| 10 | Kansas City | 24 |
| 0 | Miami | 16 |

| Use Name | Pos. | Hgt | Wgt | Age | Int | Pts |
|---|---|---|---|---|---|---|
| Tom Drougas | OT | 6'4" | 257 | 22 | | |
| Dennis Nelson | OT | 6'5" | 260 | 26 | | |
| Bob Vogel | OT | 6'5" | 250 | 30 | | |
| Cornelius Johnson | OG | 6'2" | 245 | 29 | | |
| Glenn Ressler | OG | 6'3" | 250 | 28 | | |
| John Shinners | OG | 6'2" | 254 | 25 | | |
| Dan Sullivan | OG | 6'3" | 250 | 33 | | |
| Bill Curry | C | 6'2" | 236 | 29 | | |
| Ken Mendenhall | C | 6'3" | 235 | 24 | | |
| Dick Amman | DE | 6'5" | 234 | 21 | | |
| Roy Hilton | DE | 6'6" | 240 | 27 | | |
| Billy Newsome | DE | 6'4" | 250 | 24 | | |
| Chuck Hinton | DT | 6'5" | 264 | 33 | | |
| Fred Miller | DT | 6'3" | 250 | 31 | | |
| Jim Bailey | DE-DT | 6'5" | 255 | 24 | | |

| Use Name | Pos. | Hgt | Wgt | Age | Int | Pts |
|---|---|---|---|---|---|---|
| Mike Curtis | LB | 6'2" | 232 | 29 | 4 | 6 |
| Randy Edmunds | LB | 6'2" | 225 | 26 | | |
| Ted Hendricks | LB | 6'7" | 220 | 24 | 2 | |
| Bill Laskey | LB | 6'2" | 235 | 29 | | |
| Ray May | LB | 6'1" | 230 | 27 | 2 | |
| Stan White | LB | 6'1" | 225 | 22 | | |
| Lonnie Hepburn | DB | 5'11" | 180 | 23 | 1 | |
| Rex Kern | DB | 5'11" | 190 | 23 | | |
| Bruce Laird | DB | 6' | 185 | 22 | 1 | |
| Jerry Logan | DB | 6'1" | 190 | 31 | 4 | |
| Jack Mildren | DB | 6'1" | 200 | 22 | | |
| Nelson Munsey | DB | 6'1" | 185 | 24 | | 6 |
| Charlie Stukes | DB | 6'3" | 212 | 28 | 5 | |
| Rick Volk | DB | 6'3" | 195 | 27 | 4 | |
| Bubba Smith – Knee Injury | | | | | | |

| Use Name | Pos. | Hgt | Wgt | Age | Int | Pts |
|---|---|---|---|---|---|---|
| Marty Domres | QB | 6'3" | 220 | 25 | | 6 |
| Johnny Unitas | QB | 6'1" | 196 | 39 | | |
| Tom Matte | HB | 6' | 214 | 33 | | 6 |
| Don McCauley | HB | 6'1" | 207 | 23 | | 30 |
| Lydell Mitchell | HB | 5'11" | 204 | 23 | | 12 |
| Don Nottingham | FB | 5'10" | 210 | 23 | | 18 |
| Tom Nowatzke | FB | 6'3" | 230 | 29 | | |
| Norm Bulaich | HB-FB | 6'1" | 218 | 25 | | 6 |
| Glenn Doughty | WR | 6'2" | 204 | 21 | | |
| Willie Franklin | WR | 6'2" | 194 | 22 | | |
| Sam Havrilak | WR | 6'2" | 195 | 24 | | 36 |
| Eddie Hinton | WR | 6' | 200 | 25 | | 6 |
| Jim O'Brien | WR | 6' | 195 | 25 | | 75 |
| Cotton Speyrer | WR | 6' | 175 | 23 | | |
| Tom Mitchell | TE | 6'2" | 215 | 28 | | 24 |
| John Mosier | TE | 6'3" | 220 | 24 | | |
| David Lee | K | 6'4" | 230 | 28 | | |
| Boris Shlapak | K | 6' | 165 | 22 | | 4 |

**BUFFALO BILLS 4-9-1 Lou Saban**

| Scores of Each Game | | |
|---|---|---|
| 24 | N.Y. JETS | 41 |
| 27 | SAN FRANCISCO | 20 |
| 0 | BALTIMORE | 17 |
| 38 | NEW ENGLAND | 14 |
| 16 | Oakland | 28 |
| 23 | Miami | 24 |
| 21 | PITTSBURGH | 38 |
| 16 | MIAMI | 30 |
| 3 | N.Y. Jets | 41 |
| 27 | New England | 24 |
| 10 | Cleveland | 27 |
| 7 | Baltimore | 35 |
| 21 | DETROIT | 21 |
| 24 | Washington | 17 |

| Use Name | Pos. | Hgt | Wgt | Age | Int | Pts |
|---|---|---|---|---|---|---|
| Paul Costa | OT | 6'4" | 268 | 30 | | |
| Dave Foley | OT | 6'5" | 255 | 24 | | |
| Donnie Green | OT | 6'7" | 285 | 24 | | |
| Willie Young | OT | 6'4" | 270 | 24 | | |
| Bill Adams | OG | 6'2" | 250 | 22 | | |
| Dick Hart | OG | 6'2" | 250 | 29 | | |
| Reggie McKenzie | OG | 6'4" | 235 | 22 | | |
| Jeff Curchin | OT-OG | 6'6" | 255 | 24 | | |
| Remi Prudhomme (from NO) | C-OG | 6'4" | 250 | 30 | | |
| Tom Beard | C | 6'6" | 280 | 23 | | |
| Bruce Jarvis | C | 6'7" | 245 | 23 | | |
| John Matlock | C | 6'4" | 250 | 27 | | |
| Bobby Penchion | OG-C | 6'5" | 255 | 23 | | |
| Walt Patulski | DE | 6'6" | 252 | 22 | | |
| Louis Ross | DE | 6'6" | 242 | 25 | | |
| Al Cowlings | DT-DE | 6'5" | 250 | 25 | | |
| Frank Cornish | DT | 6'6" | 285 | 28 | | |
| Don Croft | DT | 6'3" | 252 | 23 | | |
| Steve Okoniewski | DT | 6'3" | 247 | 23 | | |
| Jerry Patton | DT | 6'3" | 250 | 26 | | |
| Mike McBath | DE-DT | 6'4" | 250 | 26 | | |

| Use Name | Pos. | Hgt | Wgt | Age | Int | Pts |
|---|---|---|---|---|---|---|
| Edgar Chandler | LB | 6'3" | 225 | 26 | | |
| Dick Cunningham | LB | 6'2" | 232 | 27 | | |
| Dale Farley | LB | 6'3" | 235 | 23 | 1 | |
| Paul Guidry | LB | 6'3" | 233 | 28 | 1 | |
| Ken Lee | LB | 6'4" | 232 | 23 | 6 | 6 |
| Jeff Lyman | LB | 6'2" | 230 | 22 | | |
| Andy Selfridge | LB | 6'4" | 218 | 23 | | |
| Mike Stratton | LB | 6'3" | 240 | 30 | 1 | |
| Dave Washington | TE-LB | 6'5" | 220 | 23 | 1 | |
| Leon Garror | DB | 6' | 180 | 24 | | |
| Tony Greene | DB | 5'10" | 170 | 23 | 3 | 6 |
| Robert James | DB | 6'1" | 185 | 25 | 1 | |
| John Pitts | DB | 6'4" | 215 | 27 | 1 | |
| John Saunders | DB | 6'3" | 202 | 22 | | |
| Maurice Tyler | DB | 6' | 188 | 22 | 4 | |
| Alvin Wyatt | DB | 5'10" | 180 | 24 | 4 | 6 |
| Mike Clark – Injury | | | | | | |
| Irv Goode – Knee Injury | | | | | | |

| Use Name | Pos. | Hgt | Wgt | Age | Int | Pts |
|---|---|---|---|---|---|---|
| Leo Hart | QB | 6'4" | 203 | 23 | | |
| Dennis Shaw | QB | 6'2" | 215 | 25 | | |
| Mike Taliaferro | QB | 6'2" | 205 | 30 | | |
| Randy Jackson | HB | 6' | 220 | 23 | | 6 |
| O. J. Simpson | HB | 6'2" | 214 | 25 | | 36 |
| Ted Koy | FB-HB | 6'1" | 215 | 24 | | |
| Jim Braxton | FB | 6'2" | 226 | 23 | | 36 |
| Wayne Patrick | FB | 6'2" | 245 | 26 | | 6 |
| Bob Chandler | WR | 6' | 180 | 23 | | 30 |
| Linzy Cole (from HOU) | WR | 5'11" | 170 | 24 | | |
| Dwight Harrison (from DEN) | WR | 6'1" | 178 | 23 | | |
| J. D. Hill | WR | 6'1" | 193 | 23 | | 30 |
| Bob Christiansen | TE | 6'4" | 230 | 23 | | |
| Jan White | TE | 6'2" | 216 | 23 | | 12 |
| Spike Jones | K | 6'2" | 190 | 25 | | |
| John Leypoldt | K | 6'2" | 224 | 26 | | 77 |
| Bill McKinley – Injury | | | | | | |
| Jim Reilly – Illness | | | | | | |

**NEW ENGLAND PATRIOTS 3-11-0 John Mazur Phil Bengtson**

| Scores of Each Game | | |
|---|---|---|
| 7 | CINCINNATI | 31 |
| 21 | ATLANTA | 20 |
| 24 | WASHINGTON | 23 |
| 14 | Buffalo | 38 |
| 13 | N.Y. JETS | 41 |
| 3 | Pittsburgh | 33 |
| 10 | N.Y. Jets | 34 |
| 17 | BALTIMORE | 24 |
| 0 | Miami | 52 |
| 24 | BUFFALO | 27 |
| 0 | Baltimore | 31 |
| 21 | MIAMI | 37 |
| 17 | New Orleans | 10 |
| 21 | Denver | 45 |

| Use Name | Pos. | Hgt | Wgt | Age | Int | Pts |
|---|---|---|---|---|---|---|
| Mike Montler | OT | 6'4" | 255 | 28 | | |
| Tom Neville | OT | 6'4" | 255 | 29 | | |
| Bob Reynolds | OT | 6'6" | 265 | 31 | | |
| Sam Adams | OG | 6'3" | 252 | 23 | | |
| Halvor Hagen | OG | 6'5" | 253 | 25 | | |
| Len St. Jean | OG | 6'1" | 250 | 30 | | |
| Bill Lenkaitis | C-OG | 6'3" | 260 | 26 | | |
| Jon Morris | C | 6'4" | 254 | 29 | | |
| Ron Berger | DE | 6'8" | 285 | 28 | | |
| Jim White | DE | 6'3" | 256 | 23 | | |
| Dennis Wirgowski | DT-DE | 6'5" | 250 | 24 | | |
| Rick Cash | DT | 6'5" | 260 | 25 | | |
| Dave Rowe | DT | 6'6" | 280 | 27 | | |
| Julius Adams | DE-DT | 6'3" | 260 | 24 | | |

| Use Name | Pos. | Hgt | Wgt | Age | Int | Pts |
|---|---|---|---|---|---|---|
| Ron Acks | LB | 6'2" | 220 | 27 | | |
| Dick Blanchard | LB | 6'3" | 225 | 23 | 1 | |
| Jim Cheyunski | LB | 6'2" | 225 | 26 | | |
| Ralph Cindrich | LB | 6'1" | 228 | 22 | | |
| Ron Kadziel | LB | 6'4" | 230 | 23 | | |
| Ed Weisacosky | LB | 6' | 220 | 28 | | |
| Ron Bolton | DB | 6'2" | 180 | 22 | | |
| Larry Carwell | DB | 6'1" | 190 | 28 | 1 | 6 |
| Rickie Harris | DB | 6' | 182 | 29 | 3 | |
| George Hoey | DB | 5'10" | 170 | 25 | 1 | |
| Honor Jackson | DB | 6'1" | 195 | 23 | 4 | |
| Art McMahon | DB | 5'11" | 190 | 26 | | |
| John Outlaw | DB | 5'10" | 180 | 27 | | |
| Clarence Scott | DB | 6'2" | 200 | 28 | | |

| Use Name | Pos. | Hgt | Wgt | Age | Int | Pts |
|---|---|---|---|---|---|---|
| Brian Dowling | QB | 6'2" | 210 | 25 | | 18 |
| Jim Plunkett | QB | 6'3" | 220 | 24 | | 6 |
| Carl Garrett | HB | 5'11" | 215 | 25 | | 30 |
| Bob Gladieux | HB | 5'11" | 195 | 25 | | |
| Jack Maitland | HB | 6'1" | 210 | 24 | | |
| Henry Matthews | HB | 6'3" | 203 | 23 | | |
| John Tarver | FB | 6'3" | 227 | 23 | | 12 |
| Josh Ashton | HB-FB | 6'1" | 205 | 23 | | 24 |
| Hubie Bryant | WR | 5'10" | 168 | 26 | | |
| Tom Reynolds | WR | 6'3" | 200 | 23 | | 12 |
| Reggie Rucker | WR | 6'2" | 190 | 24 | | 18 |
| Pat Studstill | WR | 6'1" | 175 | 34 | | |
| Randy Vataha | WR | 5'10" | 175 | 23 | | 12 |
| Tom Beer | TE | 6'4" | 235 | 27 | | |
| Bob Windsor | TE | 6'4" | 226 | 29 | | 6 |
| Charlie Gogolak | K | 5'10" | 170 | 27 | | 27 |
| Mike Walker | K | 6' | 190 | 22 | | 21 |

## MIAMI DOLPHINS

### RUSHING

| Last Name | No. | Yds | Avg | TD |
|---|---|---|---|---|
| Csonka | 213 | 1117 | 5.2 | 6 |
| Morris | 190 | 1000 | 5.3 | 12 |
| Kiick | 137 | 521 | 3.8 | 5 |
| Ginn | 27 | 142 | 5.3 | 1 |
| Leigh | 21 | 79 | 3.8 | 0 |
| Morrall | 17 | 67 | 3.9 | 1 |
| Warfield | 4 | 23 | 5.8 | 0 |
| Griese | 3 | 11 | 3.7 | 1 |
| DelGaizo | 1 | 0 | 0.0 | 0 |

### RECEIVING

| Last Name | No. | Yds | Avg | TD |
|---|---|---|---|---|
| Warfield | 29 | 606 | 21 | 3 |
| Kiick | 21 | 147 | 7 | 1 |
| Twilley | 20 | 364 | 18 | 3 |
| Briscoe | 16 | 279 | 17 | 4 |
| Morris | 15 | 168 | 11 | 0 |
| Stowe | 13 | 276 | 21 | 2 |
| Fleming | 13 | 156 | 12 | 1 |
| Mandich | 11 | 168 | 15 | 3 |
| Csonka | 5 | 48 | 10 | 0 |
| Ginn | 1 | 23 | 23 | 0 |

### PUNT RETURNS

| Last Name | No. | Yds | Avg | TD |
|---|---|---|---|---|
| Leigh | 22 | 210 | 10 | 0 |
| Scott | 13 | 100 | 8 | 0 |
| Anderson | 5 | 19 | 4 | 0 |

### KICKOFF RETURNS

| Last Name | No. | Yds | Avg | TD |
|---|---|---|---|---|
| Morris | 14 | 334 | 24 | 0 |
| Leigh | 6 | 153 | 26 | 0 |
| Matheson | 2 | 34 | 17 | 0 |
| Ginn | 1 | 25 | 25 | 0 |
| Briscoe | 1 | 0 | 0 | 0 |

### PASSING — PUNTING — KICKING

| PASSING | Att | Comp | % | Yds | Yd/Att | TD | Int– | % | RK |
|---|---|---|---|---|---|---|---|---|---|
| Morrall | 150 | 83 | 55 | 1360 | 9.1 | 11 | 7– | 5 | 1 |
| Griese | 97 | 53 | 55 | 638 | 6.6 | 4 | 4– | 4 |  |
| DelGaizo | 9 | 5 | 56 | 165 | 18.3 | 2 | 1– | 11 |  |
| Briscoe | 3 | 3 | 100 | 72 | 24.0 | 1 | 0– | 0 |  |

| PUNTING | No | Avg |
|---|---|---|
| Seiple | 36 | 39.9 |
| Lothridge | 4 | 37.5 |
| Anderson | 4 | 36.8 |

| KICKING | XP | Att | % | FG | Att | % |
|---|---|---|---|---|---|---|
| Yepremian | 43 | 45 | 96 | 24 | 37 | 65 |

## NEW YORK JETS

### RUSHING

| Last Name | No. | Yds | Avg | TD |
|---|---|---|---|---|
| Riggins | 207 | 944 | 4.6 | 7 |
| Boozer | 120 | 549 | 4.6 | 11 |
| McClain | 59 | 305 | 5.2 | 0 |
| Harkey | 45 | 129 | 2.9 | 0 |
| Bjorklund | 15 | 42 | 2.8 | 0 |
| Davis | 6 | 32 | 5.3 | 0 |
| Namath | 6 | 8 | 1.3 | 0 |
| Caster | 2 | 6 | 3.0 | 0 |
| Bell | 1 | –5 | –5.0 | 0 |

### RECEIVING

| Last Name | No. | Yds | Avg | TD |
|---|---|---|---|---|
| Caster | 39 | 833 | 21 | 10 |
| Bell | 35 | 629 | 18 | 2 |
| Maynard | 29 | 510 | 18 | 2 |
| Riggins | 21 | 230 | 11 | 1 |
| Barkum | 16 | 304 | 19 | 2 |
| Boozer | 11 | 142 | 13 | 3 |
| Harkey | 9 | 114 | 13 | 0 |
| McClain | 6 | 88 | 15 | 0 |
| Bjorklund | 4 | 54 | 14 | 0 |
| Stewart | 2 | 26 | 13 | 1 |

### PUNT RETURNS

| Last Name | No. | Yds | Avg | TD |
|---|---|---|---|---|
| Farasopoulos | 17 | 179 | 11 | 1 |
| Turner | 5 | 38 | 8 | 0 |
| Hicks | 3 | 25 | 8 | 0 |

### KICKOFF RETURNS

| Last Name | No. | Yds | Avg | TD |
|---|---|---|---|---|
| Farasopoulos | 26 | 627 | 24 | 0 |
| Wise | 9 | 211 | 23 | 0 |
| Bjorklund | 7 | 150 | 21 | 0 |
| Hicks | 4 | 73 | 24 | 0 |
| Turner | 3 | 57 | 19 | 0 |
| McClain | 2 | 45 | 23 | 0 |
| Kirksey | 2 | 33 | 17 | 0 |
| Snell | 1 | 14 | 14 | 0 |
| Zapalac | 1 | 8 | 8 | 0 |
| Barkum | 1 | 0 | 0 | 0 |

### PASSING — PUNTING — KICKING

| PASSING | Att | Comp | % | Yds | Yd/Att | TD | Int– | % | RK |
|---|---|---|---|---|---|---|---|---|---|
| Namath | 324 | 162 | 50 | 2816 | 8.7 | 19 | 21– | 6 | 8 |
| Davis | 22 | 10 | 46 | 114 | 5.2 | 2 | 1– | 5 |  |
| McClain | 1 | 0 | 0 | 0 | 0.0 | 0 | 0– | 0 |  |

| PUNTING | No | Avg |
|---|---|---|
| O'Neal | 51 | 39.3 |

| KICKING | XP | Att | % | FG | Att | % |
|---|---|---|---|---|---|---|
| Howfield | 40 | 41 | 98 | 27 | 37 | 73 |

## BALTIMORE COLTS

### RUSHING

| Last Name | No. | Yds | Avg | TD |
|---|---|---|---|---|
| McCauley | 178 | 675 | 3.8 | 2 |
| Nottingham | 123 | 466 | 3.8 | 3 |
| L. Mitchell | 45 | 215 | 4.8 | 1 |
| Matte | 33 | 137 | 4.2 | 0 |
| Domres | 30 | 137 | 4.6 | 1 |
| Bulaich | 27 | 109 | 4.0 | 1 |
| Havrilak | 12 | 72 | 6.0 | 2 |
| Doughty | 2 | 33 | 16.5 | 0 |
| Unitas | 3 | 15 | 5.0 | 0 |
| Nowatzke | 3 | 11 | 3.7 | 0 |
| O'Brien | 3 | 9 | 3.0 | 0 |
| Mildren | 3 | 8 | 2.7 | 0 |
| T. Mitchell | 0 | 7 | 0.0 | 0 |

### RECEIVING

| Last Name | No. | Yds | Avg | TD |
|---|---|---|---|---|
| T. Mitchell | 40 | 494 | 12 | 4 |
| Havrilak | 33 | 571 | 17 | 4 |
| McCauley | 30 | 256 | 9 | 2 |
| Nottingham | 25 | 191 | 7 | 0 |
| L. Mitchell | 18 | 147 | 8 | 1 |
| Matte | 14 | 182 | 13 | 1 |
| O'Brien | 11 | 263 | 24 | 2 |
| Hinton | 11 | 146 | 13 | 1 |
| Bulaich | 9 | 55 | 6 | 0 |
| Speyrer | 8 | 114 | 14 | 0 |
| Doughty | 3 | 31 | 10 | 0 |
| Mosier | 1 | 53 | 53 | 0 |

### PUNT RETURNS

| Last Name | No. | Yds | Avg | TD |
|---|---|---|---|---|
| Laird | 34 | 303 | 9 | 0 |
| Volk | 5 | 25 | 5 | 0 |
| Logan | 4 | 20 | 5 | 0 |

### KICKOFF RETURNS

| Last Name | No. | Yds | Avg | TD |
|---|---|---|---|---|
| Laird | 29 | 843 | 29 | 0 |
| McCauley | 13 | 377 | 29 | 1 |
| Bulaich | 1 | 62 | 62 | 0 |
| Nottingham | 2 | 38 | 19 | 0 |
| Mildren | 1 | 1 | 1 | 0 |
| Hendricks | 1 | 0 | 0 | 0 |

### PASSING — PUNTING — KICKING

| PASSING | Att | Comp | % | Yds | Yd/Att | TD | Int– | % | RK |
|---|---|---|---|---|---|---|---|---|---|
| Domres | 222 | 115 | 52 | 1392 | 6.3 | 11 | 6 | 3 | 6 |
| Unitas | 157 | 88 | 56 | 1111 | 7.1 | 4 | 6– | 4 | 4 |
| Havrilak | 1 | 0 | 0 | 0 | 0.0 | 0 | 0– | 0 |  |
| Mildren | 1 | 0 | 0 | 0 | 0.0 | 0 | 0– | 0 |  |

| PUNTING | No | Avg |
|---|---|---|
| Lee | 57 | 42.1 |

| KICKING | XP | Att | % | FG | Att | % |
|---|---|---|---|---|---|---|
| O'Brien | 24 | 24 | 100 | 13 | 31 | 42 |
| Shlapak | 4 | 4 | 100 | 0 | 8 | 0 |

## BUFFALO BILLS

### RUSHING

| Last Name | No. | Yds | Avg | TD |
|---|---|---|---|---|
| Simpson | 291 | 1251 | 4.3 | 6 |
| Braxton | 116 | 453 | 3.9 | 5 |
| Shaw | 35 | 138 | 3.9 | 0 |
| Patrick | 35 | 130 | 3.7 | 0 |
| Jackson | 17 | 57 | 3.4 | 0 |
| B. Chandler | 3 | 27 | 9.0 | 0 |
| L. Hart | 5 | 19 | 3.8 | 0 |
| Taliaferro | 5 | 19 | 3.8 | 0 |
| Jones | 2 | 18 | 9.0 | 0 |
| Hill | 1 | 11 | 11.0 | 0 |
| Harrison | 1 | 9 | 9.0 | 0 |
| Koy | 1 | 9 | 9.0 | 0 |

### RECEIVING

| Last Name | No. | Yds | Avg | TD |
|---|---|---|---|---|
| Hill | 52 | 754 | 15 | 5 |
| B. Chandler | 33 | 528 | 16 | 5 |
| Simpson | 27 | 198 | 7 | 0 |
| Braxton | 24 | 232 | 10 | 1 |
| White | 12 | 148 | 12 | 2 |
| Patrick | 8 | 42 | 5 | 1 |
| Jackson | 2 | 21 | 11 | 1 |
| Harrison | 1 | 16 | 16 | 0 |
| Koy | 1 | 9 | 9 | 0 |
| Washington | 1 | 4 | 4 | 0 |

### PUNT RETURNS

| Last Name | No. | Yds | Avg | TD |
|---|---|---|---|---|
| Wyatt | 11 | 85 | 8 | 0 |
| Cole | 7 | 35 | 5 | 0 |
| Hill | 4 | 24 | 6 | 0 |
| Greene | 2 | 18 | 9 | 0 |
| Harrison | 1 | 2 | 2 | 0 |

### KICKOFF RETURNS

| Last Name | No. | Yds | Avg | TD |
|---|---|---|---|---|
| Cole | 18 | 456 | 25 | 0 |
| Wyatt | 17 | 432 | 25 | 0 |
| Greene | 15 | 378 | 25 | 0 |
| Koy | 5 | 63 | 13 | 0 |
| Selfridge | 3 | 36 | 12 | 0 |
| Hill | 2 | 32 | 16 | 0 |
| Simpson | 1 | 21 | 21 | 0 |
| Braxton | 1 | 12 | 12 | 0 |
| Prudhomme | 1 | 0 | 0 | 0 |

### PASSING — PUNTING — KICKING

| PASSING | Att | Comp | % | Yds | Yd/Att | TD | Int– | % | RK |
|---|---|---|---|---|---|---|---|---|---|
| Shaw | 258 | 136 | 53 | 1666 | 6.5 | 14 | 17– | 7 | 9 |
| Taliaferro | 33 | 16 | 48 | 176 | 5.3 | 1 | 4– | 12 |  |
| L. Hart | 15 | 6 | 40 | 53 | 3.5 | 0 | 3– | 20 |  |
| Simpson | 8 | 5 | 63 | 113 | 14.1 | 1 | 0– | 0 |  |
| Jones | 2 | 1 | 50 | 4 | 2.0 | 0 | 0– | 0 |  |

| PUNTING | No | Avg |
|---|---|---|
| Jones | 80 | 38.8 |

| KICKING | XP | Att | % | FG | Att | % |
|---|---|---|---|---|---|---|
| Leypoldt | 29 | 30 | 97 | 16 | 24 | 67 |

## NEW ENGLAND PATRIOTS

### RUSHING

| Last Name | No. | Yds | Avg | TD |
|---|---|---|---|---|
| Ashton | 128 | 546 | 4.3 | 3 |
| Garrett | 131 | 488 | 3.7 | 5 |
| Plunkett | 36 | 230 | 6.4 | 1 |
| Tarver | 42 | 132 | 3.1 | 1 |
| Gladieux | 24 | 56 | 2.3 | 0 |
| Dowling | 7 | 35 | 5.0 | 3 |
| Maitland | 13 | 33 | 2.5 | 0 |
| Studstill | 1 | 11 | 11.0 | 0 |
| Rucker | 3 | 5 | 1.7 | 0 |
| Windsor | 1 | –4 | –4.0 | 0 |

### RECEIVING

| Last Name | No. | Yds | Avg | TD |
|---|---|---|---|---|
| Rucker | 44 | 681 | 15 | 3 |
| Windsor | 33 | 383 | 12 | 1 |
| Garrett | 30 | 410 | 14 | 0 |
| Vataha | 25 | 369 | 15 | 2 |
| Ashton | 22 | 207 | 9 | 1 |
| Gladieux | 19 | 192 | 10 | 0 |
| Tarver | 11 | 112 | 10 | 1 |
| T. Reynolds | 8 | 152 | 19 | 2 |
| Maitland | 4 | 33 | 8 | 0 |
| Beer | 2 | 40 | 20 | 0 |

### PUNT RETURNS

| Last Name | No. | Yds | Avg | TD |
|---|---|---|---|---|
| Garrett | 6 | 36 | 6 | 0 |
| Harris | 4 | 5 | 1 | 0 |
| Carwell | 5 | 2 | 0 | 0 |
| Gladieux | 2 | –6 | –3 | 0 |

### KICKOFF RETURNS

| Last Name | No. | Yds | Avg | TD |
|---|---|---|---|---|
| Garrett | 16 | 410 | 26 | 0 |
| Ashton | 15 | 309 | 21 | 0 |
| Rucker | 8 | 227 | 28 | 0 |
| Hoey | 9 | 210 | 23 | 0 |
| Matthews | 3 | 74 | 25 | 0 |
| Maitland | 3 | 48 | 16 | 0 |
| Beer | 1 | 15 | 15 | 0 |

### PASSING — PUNTING — KICKING

| PASSING | Att | Comp | % | Yds | Yd/Att | TD | Int– | % | RK |
|---|---|---|---|---|---|---|---|---|---|
| Plunkett | 355 | 169 | 48 | 2196 | 6.2 | 8 | 25– | 7 | 14 |
| Dowling | 54 | 29 | 54 | 383 | 7.1 | 2 | 1– | 2 |  |
| Garrett | 1 | 0 | 0 | 0 | 0.0 | 0 | 1– | 100 |  |
| Gladieux | 1 | 0 | 0 | 0 | 0.0 | 0 | 1– | 100 |  |
| Studstill | 1 | 0 | 0 | 0 | 0.0 | 0 | 0– | 0 |  |

| PUNTING | No | Avg |
|---|---|---|
| Studstill | 75 | 38.1 |

| KICKING | XP | Att | % | FG | Att | % |
|---|---|---|---|---|---|---|
| Walker | 15 | 15 | 100 | 2 | 8 | 25 |
| Gogolak | 9 | 9 | 100 | 6 | 8 | 75 |

## PITTSBURGH STEELERS 11-3-0 Chuck Noll

| Scores of Each Game | | |
|---|---|---|
| 34 | OAKLAND | 28 |
| 10 | Cincinnati | 15 |
| 25 | St. Louis | 19 |
| 13 | Dallas | 17 |
| 24 | HOUSTON | 7 |
| 33 | NEW ENGLAND | 3 |
| 38 | Buffalo | 21 |
| 40 | CINCINNATI | 17 |
| 16 | KANSAS CITY | 7 |
| 24 | Cleveland | 26 |
| 23 | MINNESOTA | 10 |
| 30 | CLEVELAND | 0 |
| 9 | Houston | 3 |
| 24 | San Diego | 2 |

| Use Name | Pos. | Hgt | Wgt | Age | Int | Pts |
|---|---|---|---|---|---|---|
| Gordon Gravelle | OT | 6'5" | 250 | 23 | | |
| Jon Kolb | OT | 6'2" | 262 | 25 | | |
| Gerry Mullins | OG-OT | 6'3" | 235 | 23 | | 6 |
| Sam Davis | OG | 6'1" | 255 | 28 | | |
| Bruce Van Dyke | OG | 6'2" | 255 | 28 | | |
| Mel Holmes | OT-OG | 6'3" | 250 | 22 | | |
| Jim Clack | C | 6'3" | 250 | 24 | | |
| Ray Mansfield | C | 6'3" | 255 | 31 | | |
| L.C. Greenwood | DE | 6'6" | 245 | 25 | | |
| Craig Hanneman | DE | 6'3" | 240 | 23 | | |
| Dwight White | DE | 6'4" | 255 | 23 | | |
| Steve Furness | DT | 6'4" | 255 | 21 | | |
| Joe Greene | DT | 6'4" | 270 | 25 | | |
| Ernie Holmes | DT | 6'3" | 260 | 24 | | |
| Ben McGee | DT | 6'2" | 260 | 30 | | |
| | | | | | | |
| Bob Adams — Injury | | | | | | |

| Use Name | Pos. | Hgt | Wgt | Age | Int | Pts |
|---|---|---|---|---|---|---|
| Ed Bradley | LB | 6'2" | 240 | 22 | | |
| Henry Davis | LB | 6'3" | 235 | 29 | 2 | 6 |
| Jack Ham | LB | 6'3" | 220 | 23 | 7 | 6 |
| Andy Russell | LB | 6'3" | 225 | 30 | | |
| Brian Stenger | LB | 6'4" | 230 | 25 | | |
| George Webster (from HOU) | LB | 6'4" | 223 | 26 | | |
| Carl Winfrey | LB | 6' | 230 | 23 | | |
| Ralph Anderson | DB | 6'2" | 180 | 23 | 3 | 2 |
| Chuck Beatty (to STL) | DB | 6'2" | 205 | 26 | 2 | |
| Mel Blount | DB | 6'3" | 205 | 24 | 3 | 6 |
| Lee Calland | DB | 6' | 190 | 31 | | |
| John Dockery | DB | 6' | 186 | 27 | | |
| Glen Edwards | DB | 6' | 185 | 25 | 1 | |
| John Rowser | DB | 6'1" | 185 | 28 | 4 | |
| Mike Wagner | DB | 6'1" | 196 | 23 | 6 | |
| | | | | | | |
| John Brown — Injury | | | | | | |

| Use Name | Pos. | Hgt | Wgt | Age | Int | Pts |
|---|---|---|---|---|---|---|
| Terry Bradshaw | QB | 6'3" | 218 | 23 | | 42 |
| Joe Gilliam | QB | 6'2" | 187 | 21 | | |
| Terry Hanratty | QB | 6'1" | 210 | 24 | | |
| Rocky Bleier | HB | 5'11" | 205 | 26 | | |
| Preston Pearson | HB | 6'1" | 205 | 27 | | |
| Franco Harris | FB-HB | 6'2" | 230 | 22 | | 66 |
| Warren Bankston | FB | 6'4" | 235 | 25 | | |
| Steve Davis | HB-FB | 6'1" | 218 | 22 | | 6 |
| John Fuqua | HB-FB | 5'11" | 200 | 25 | | 24 |
| Frank Lewis | WR | 6'1" | 196 | 25 | | 30 |
| Barry Pearson | WR | 5'11" | 185 | 22 | | |
| Ron Shanklin | WR | 6'1" | 180 | 25 | | 18 |
| Al Young | WR | 6'1" | 195 | 23 | | |
| Larry Brown | TE | 6'4" | 225 | 23 | | 6 |
| John McMakin | TE | 6'3" | 232 | 21 | | 6 |
| Roy Gerela | K | 5'10" | 185 | 24 | | 119 |
| Bobby Walden | K | 6' | 190 | 34 | | |

## CLEVELAND BROWNS 10-4-0 Nick Skorich

| Scores of Each Game | | |
|---|---|---|
| 10 | GREEN BAY | 26 |
| 27 | Philadelphia | 17 |
| 27 | CINCINNATI | 6 |
| 7 | KANSAS CITY | 31 |
| 0 | CHICAGO | 17 |
| 23 | Houston | 17 |
| 27 | Denver | 20 |
| 20 | HOUSTON | 0 |
| 21 | San Diego | 17 |
| 26 | PITTSBURGH | 24 |
| 27 | BUFFALO | 10 |
| 0 | Pittsburgh | 30 |
| 27 | Cincinnati | 24 |
| 26 | N.Y. Jets | 10 |

| Use Name | Pos. | Hgt | Wgt | Age | Int | Pts |
|---|---|---|---|---|---|---|
| Joe Carollo | OT | 6'2" | 265 | 32 | | |
| Doug Dieken | OT | 6'5" | 237 | 23 | | |
| Bob McKay | OT | 6'5" | 260 | 24 | | |
| Chris Morris | OT | 6'3" | 250 | 22 | | |
| John Demarie | C-OG-OT | 6'3" | 246 | 27 | | |
| Gene Hickerson | OG | 6'3" | 252 | 37 | | |
| Bubba Pena | OG | 6'2" | 250 | 23 | | |
| Craig Wycinsky | OG | 6'3" | 243 | 24 | | |
| Jim Copeland | C-OG | 6'2" | 243 | 27 | | |
| Bob DeMarco | C | 6'3" | 248 | 34 | | |
| Fred Hoaglin | C | 6'4" | 246 | 28 | | |
| Wes Grant | DE | 6'3" | 245 | 25 | | |
| Rich Jackson (from DEN) | DE | 6'3" | 255 | 31 | | |
| Nick Roman | DE | 6'3" | 235 | 24 | 1 | 6 |
| Ron Snidow | DE | 6'4" | 247 | 30 | | |
| Bob Briggs | DT-DE | 6'4" | 258 | 27 | 1 | 6 |
| Cotton Fest | DT | 6'2" | 255 | 22 | | |
| Walter Johnson | DT | 6'3" | 263 | 29 | 1 | |
| George Wright | DT | 6'3" | 265 | 25 | | |
| Jerry Sherk | DE-DT | 6'4" | 258 | 24 | | |

| Use Name | Pos. | Hgt | Wgt | Age | Int | Pts |
|---|---|---|---|---|---|---|
| Billy Andrews | LB | 6' | 220 | 27 | 1 | |
| John Garlington | LB | 6'1" | 218 | 26 | 1 | |
| Charlie Hall | LB | 6'3" | 220 | 23 | 1 | |
| Rick Kingrea | LB | 6'1" | 233 | 23 | | |
| Dale Lindsey | LB | 6'3" | 225 | 29 | | |
| Mel Long | LB | 6' | 228 | 25 | | |
| Jim Houston | DE-LB | 6'2" | 236 | 35 | | |
| Cliff Brooks | DB | 6'1" | 190 | 23 | | |
| Thom Darden | DB | 6'2" | 195 | 22 | 3 | |
| Ben Davis | DB | 5'11" | 180 | 26 | 3 | |
| Mike Howell (to MIA) | DB | 6'1" | 190 | 29 | 1 | |
| Bobby Majors | DB | 6'1" | 193 | 23 | | |
| Clarence Scott | DB | 6' | 180 | 23 | 6 | |
| Walt Sumner | DB | 6'1" | 195 | 25 | | |
| | | | | | | |
| Joe Jones — Knee Injury | | | | | | |

| Use Name | Pos. | Hgt | Wgt | Age | Int | Pts |
|---|---|---|---|---|---|---|
| Don Horn | QB | 6'2" | 195 | 27 | | |
| Bill Nelsen | QB | 6' | 195 | 31 | | |
| Mike Phipps | QB | 6'2" | 208 | 24 | | 30 |
| Leroy Kelly | HB | 6' | 202 | 30 | | 30 |
| Bill LeFear | HB | 5'11" | 197 | 22 | | |
| Ken Brown | FB-HB | 5'10" | 203 | 26 | | 12 |
| Bo Cornell | FB | 6'1" | 215 | 23 | | |
| Bo Scott | FB | 6'3" | 215 | 29 | | 12 |
| Charlie Brinkman | WR | 6'2" | 208 | 23 | | |
| Fair Hooker | WR | 6'1" | 190 | 25 | | 12 |
| Frank Pitts | WR | 6'2" | 200 | 28 | | 48 |
| Gloster Richardson | WR | 6' | 200 | 29 | | |
| Paul Staroba | WR | 6'3" | 204 | 23 | | 6 |
| Chip Glass | TE | 6'4" | 235 | 26 | | |
| Milt Morin | TE | 6'4" | 236 | 30 | | 6 |
| Don Cockroft | K | 6'1" | 195 | 27 | | 94 |

## CINCINNATI BENGALS 8-6-0 Paul Brown

| Scores of Each Game | | |
|---|---|---|
| 31 | New England | 7 |
| 15 | PITTSBURGH | 10 |
| 6 | Cleveland | 27 |
| 21 | DENVER | 10 |
| 23 | Kansas City | 16 |
| 30 | Los Angeles | 15 |
| 30 | HOUSTON | 7 |
| 17 | Pittsburgh | 40 |
| 14 | OAKLAND | 20 |
| 19 | BALTIMORE | 20 |
| 13 | Chicago | 3 |
| 13 | N.Y. GIANTS | 10 |
| 24 | CLEVELAND | 27 |
| 61 | Houston | 17 |

| Use Name | Pos. | Hgt | Wgt | Age | Int | Pts |
|---|---|---|---|---|---|---|
| Vern Holland | OT | 6'5" | 270 | 24 | | |
| Stan Walters | OT | 6'6" | 270 | 24 | | |
| Rufus Mayes | OG-OT | 6'5" | 260 | 24 | | |
| Guy Dennis | OG | 6'2" | 255 | 25 | | |
| Steve Lawson | OG | 6'3" | 265 | 23 | | |
| Pat Matson | OG | 6'1" | 245 | 28 | | |
| Howard Fest | OT-OG | 6'6" | 262 | 26 | | |
| Tom DeLeone | C-OG | 6'2" | 252 | 22 | | |
| Bob Johnson | C | 6'5" | 260 | 26 | | |
| Royce Berry | DE | 6'3" | 250 | 27 | | |
| Ron Carpenter | DE | 6'4" | 260 | 24 | | |
| Sherman White | DE | 6'5" | 255 | 23 | 2 | |
| Steve Chomyszak | DT | 6'5" | 270 | 27 | | |
| Ken Johnson | DT | 6'5" | 265 | 24 | | |
| Mike Reid | DT | 6'3" | 250 | 25 | | |

| Use Name | Pos. | Hgt | Wgt | Age | Int | Pts |
|---|---|---|---|---|---|---|
| Doug Adams | LB | 6' | 227 | 23 | 3 | |
| Ken Avery | LB | 6'1" | 230 | 28 | | |
| Al Beauchamp | LB | 6'2" | 237 | 28 | 1 | |
| Bill Bergey | LB | 6'2" | 243 | 27 | | |
| Tim Kearney | LB | 6'2" | 227 | 21 | | |
| Jim LeClair | LB | 6'2" | 226 | 21 | | |
| Bill Peterson | LB | 6'3" | 226 | 27 | | |
| Ron Pritchard (from HOU) | LB | 6'1" | 235 | 26 | | |
| Tommy Casanova | DB | 6'2" | 202 | 22 | 5 | 6 |
| Neal Craig | DB | 6'1" | 190 | 24 | 2 | 6 |
| Bernard Jackson | DB | 6' | 173 | 22 | 1 | |
| Ernie Kellerman | DB | 6' | 183 | 28 | | |
| Lemar Parrish | DB | 5'11" | 184 | 24 | 5 | 18 |
| Ken Riley | DB | 6' | 180 | 25 | 3 | |
| | | | | | | |
| Greg Cook — Shoulder Injury | | | | | | |
| Sandy Durko — Injury | | | | | | |

| Use Name | Pos. | Hgt | Wgt | Age | Int | Pts |
|---|---|---|---|---|---|---|
| Ken Anderson | QB | 6'1" | 211 | 23 | | 18 |
| Virgil Carter | QB | 6'1" | 198 | 26 | | 12 |
| Dave Lewis | QB | 6'2" | 218 | 26 | | |
| Essex Johnson | HB | 5'9" | 197 | 25 | | 36 |
| Reece Morrison (from CLE) | HB | 6' | 207 | 26 | | |
| Doug Dressler | HB | 6'3" | 226 | 24 | | 42 |
| Jess Phillips | HB-FB | 6'1" | 205 | 25 | | 6 |
| Drew Buie | WR | 6'2" | 185 | 25 | | |
| Charlie Joiner (from HOU) | WR | 5'11" | 188 | 24 | | 12 |
| Chip Myers | WR | 6'4" | 210 | 27 | | 18 |
| Speedy Thomas | WR | 6'1" | 170 | 25 | | 6 |
| Bruce Coslet | TE | 6'3" | 220 | 26 | | 6 |
| Mike Kelly | TE | 6'4" | 222 | 24 | | |
| Bob Trumpy | TE | 6'6" | 228 | 27 | | 12 |
| Pete Watson | TE | 6'1" | 210 | 22 | | |
| Horst Muhlmann | K | 6'1" | 220 | 32 | | 111 |

## HOUSTON OILERS 1-13-0 Bill Peterson

| Scores of Each Game | | |
|---|---|---|
| 17 | Denver | 30 |
| 13 | Miami | 34 |
| 26 | N.Y. JETS | 20 |
| 0 | OAKLAND | 34 |
| 7 | Pittsburgh | 24 |
| 17 | CLEVELAND | 23 |
| 7 | Cincinnati | 30 |
| 0 | Cleveland | 20 |
| 17 | PHILADELPHIA | 18 |
| 10 | GREEN BAY | 23 |
| 20 | San Diego | 34 |
| 10 | Atlanta | 20 |
| 3 | PITTSBURGH | 9 |
| 17 | CINCINNATI | 61 |

| Use Name | Pos. | Hgt | Wgt | Age | Int | Pts |
|---|---|---|---|---|---|---|
| Lavert Carr | OT | 6'5" | 260 | 28 | | |
| Gene Ferguson | OT | 6'7" | 300 | 24 | | |
| Tom Funchess | OT | 6'5" | 265 | 27 | | |
| Buzz Highsmith | C-OT | 6'4" | 255 | 29 | | |
| Soloman Freelon | OG | 6'2" | 250 | 21 | | |
| Ralph Miller | OG | 6'4" | 260 | 23 | | |
| Tom Regner | OG | 6'1" | 255 | 28 | | |
| Ron Saul | OG | 6'2" | 245 | 24 | | |
| Calvin Hunt | C | 6'3" | 245 | 24 | | |
| Guy Murdock | C | 6'2" | 245 | 21 | | |
| Allen Aldridge | DE | 6'6" | 260 | 27 | | |
| Elvin Bethea | DE | 6'3" | 262 | 26 | | |
| Council Rudolph | DE | 6'3" | 260 | 22 | | |
| Pat Holmes | DT-DE | 6'5" | 250 | 32 | | |
| Ron Billingsley | DT | 6'8" | 290 | 27 | | |
| Lee Brooks | DT | 6'5" | 255 | 24 | | |
| Mike Tilleman | DT | 6'5" | 280 | 28 | | |
| Greg Sampson | DE-DT | 6'6" | 260 | 21 | | |

| Use Name | Pos. | Hgt | Wgt | Age | Int | Pts |
|---|---|---|---|---|---|---|
| Garland Boyette | LB | 6'1" | 235 | 32 | | |
| Phil Croyle | LB | 6'3" | 220 | 24 | | |
| Rich Lewis | LB | 6'3" | 220 | 22 | | |
| Floyd Rice | LB | 6'3" | 225 | 23 | | |
| Guy Roberts | LB | 6'1" | 215 | 22 | | |
| Willie Alexander | DB | 6'2" | 195 | 22 | 1 | |
| Bob Atkins | DB | 6'3" | 210 | 26 | 2 | |
| John Charles | DB | 6'1" | 192 | 28 | 2 | |
| Ken Houston | DB | 6'3" | 195 | 27 | | |
| Benny Johnson | DB | 5'11" | 178 | 24 | 1 | |
| Zeke Moore | DB | 6'2" | 196 | 28 | | |
| Jim Tolbert | DB | 6'3" | 202 | 28 | | |
| | | | | | | |
| Lynn Dickey — Hip Injury | | | | | | |
| Elbert Drungo — Knee Injury | | | | | | |

| Use Name | Pos. | Hgt | Wgt | Age | Int | Pts |
|---|---|---|---|---|---|---|
| Ed Baker | QB | 6'2" | 198 | 23 | | |
| Kent Nix | QB | 6'1" | 195 | 28 | | |
| Dan Pastorini | QB | 6'3" | 215 | 23 | | 12 |
| Al Johnson | HB | 6' | 200 | 22 | | |
| Paul Robinson (from CIN) | HB | 6' | 198 | 27 | | 18 |
| Willie Rodgers | HB | 6' | 210 | 23 | | 12 |
| Ward Walsh (to GB) | HB | 6' | 210 | 23 | | 6 |
| Hoyle Granger | FB | 6'1" | 225 | 28 | | |
| Robert Holmes | FB | 5'9" | 220 | 26 | | |
| Fred Willis (from CIN) | FB | 6' | 212 | 24 | | 12 |
| Lewis Jolley | HB-FB | 6' | 210 | 22 | | |
| Ken Burrough | WR | 6'4" | 210 | 24 | | 24 |
| Rhett Dawson | WR | 6'1" | 185 | 23 | | 6 |
| Dave Smith (from PIT) | WR | 6'2" | 205 | 25 | | |
| Alvin Reed | TE | 6'5" | 235 | 28 | | |
| Jim Beirne | WR-TE | 6'2" | 196 | 25 | | 6 |
| Skip Butler | K | 6'2" | 200 | 24 | | 51 |
| Mark Moseley | K | 5'11" | 182 | 24 | | 5 |

## PITTSBURGH STEELERS

### RUSHING

| Last Name | No. | Yds | Avg | TD |
|---|---|---|---|---|
| Harris | 188 | 1055 | 5.6 | 10 |
| Fuqua | 150 | 665 | 4.4 | 4 |
| Bradshaw | 58 | 346 | 6.0 | 7 |
| P. Pearson | 67 | 264 | 3.9 | 0 |
| Steve Davis | 20 | 85 | 4.3 | 1 |
| Lewis | 3 | 68 | 22.7 | 0 |
| Bankston | 7 | 20 | 2.9 | 0 |
| Bleier | 1 | 17 | 17.0 | 0 |
| McMakin | 1 | 0 | 0.0 | 0 |
| Gilliam | 2 | 0 | 0.0 | 0 |

### RECEIVING

| Last Name | No. | Yds | Avg | TD |
|---|---|---|---|---|
| Shanklin | 38 | 669 | 18 | 3 |
| Lewis | 27 | 391 | 14 | 5 |
| McMakin | 21 | 277 | 13 | 1 |
| Harris | 21 | 180 | 9 | 1 |
| Fuqua | 18 | 152 | 8 | 0 |
| P. Pearson | 11 | 79 | 7 | 0 |
| Young | 6 | 86 | 14 | 0 |
| Brown | 1 | 13 | 13 | 1 |
| Bankston | 1 | 5 | 5 | 0 |
| Steve Davis | 1 | 5 | 5 | 0 |
| Mullins | 1 | 3 | 3 | 1 |

### PUNT RETURNS

| Last Name | No. | Yds | Avg | TD |
|---|---|---|---|---|
| Edwards | 22 | 202 | 9 | 0 |
| Lewis | 5 | 56 | 11 | 0 |
| Bleier | 2 | 1 | 1 | 0 |
| P. Pearson | 1 | 3 | 3 | 0 |

### KICKOFF RETURNS

| Last Name | No. | Yds | Avg | TD |
|---|---|---|---|---|
| P. Pearson | 13 | 292 | 22 | 0 |
| Steve Davis | 7 | 207 | 30 | 0 |
| Harris | 8 | 183 | 23 | 0 |
| Bleier | 2 | 40 | 20 | 0 |
| Bankston | 1 | 20 | 20 | 0 |
| Edwards | 1 | 18 | 18 | 0 |
| McMakin | 1 | 0 | 0 | 0 |

### PASSING – PUNTING – KICKING

| PASSING | Att | Comp | % | Yds | Yd/Att | TD | Int– | % | RK |
|---|---|---|---|---|---|---|---|---|---|
| Bradshaw | 308 | 147 | 48 | 1887 | 6.1 | 12 | 12– | 4 | 12 |
| Gilliam | 11 | 7 | 64 | 48 | 4.4 | 0 | 0– | 0 | |
| Hanratty | 4 | 2 | 50 | 23 | 5.8 | 0 | 0– | 0 | |
| Walden | 1 | 0 | 0 | 0 | 0.0 | 0 | 0– | 0 | |

| PUNTING | No | Avg |
|---|---|---|
| Walden | 65 | 43.8 |
| Gerela | 1 | 29.0 |

| KICKING | XP | Att | % | FG | Att | % |
|---|---|---|---|---|---|---|
| Gerela | 35 | 36 | 97 | 28 | 41 | 68 |

## CLEVELAND BROWNS

### RUSHING

| Last Name | No. | Yds | Avg | TD |
|---|---|---|---|---|
| Kelly | 224 | 811 | 3.6 | 4 |
| B. Scott | 123 | 571 | 4.6 | 2 |
| Phipps | 60 | 256 | 4.3 | 5 |
| Brown | 32 | 114 | 3.6 | 2 |
| Pitts | 3 | 29 | 9.7 | 0 |
| Cornell | 7 | 8 | 1.1 | 0 |
| Lefear | 3 | 6 | 2.0 | 0 |
| Nelsen | 1 | –2 | –2.0 | 0 |

### RECEIVING

| Last Name | No. | Yds | Avg | TD |
|---|---|---|---|---|
| Pitts | 36 | 620 | 17 | 8 |
| Hooker | 32 | 441 | 14 | 2 |
| Morin | 30 | 540 | 18 | 1 |
| Kelly | 23 | 204 | 9 | 1 |
| B. Scott | 23 | 172 | 8 | 0 |
| Brown | 5 | 64 | 13 | 0 |
| Glass | 5 | 61 | 12 | 0 |
| Cornell | 2 | 7 | 4 | 0 |
| Staroba | 1 | 19 | 19 | 1 |
| Richardson | 1 | 7 | 7 | 0 |

### PUNT RETURNS

| Last Name | No. | Yds | Avg | TD |
|---|---|---|---|---|
| Majors | 16 | 96 | 6 | 0 |
| Darden | 15 | 61 | 4 | 0 |
| Kelly | 5 | 40 | 8 | 0 |
| Sumner | 1 | 14 | 14 | 0 |

### KICKOFF RETURNS

| Last Name | No. | Yds | Avg | TD |
|---|---|---|---|---|
| Brown | 20 | 473 | 24 | 0 |
| Majors | 10 | 222 | 22 | 0 |
| Lefear | 6 | 138 | 23 | 0 |
| Johnson | 2 | 33 | 17 | 0 |

### PASSING – PUNTING – KICKING

| PASSING | Att | Comp | % | Yds | Yd/Att | TD | Int– | % | RK |
|---|---|---|---|---|---|---|---|---|---|
| Phipps | 305 | 144 | 47 | 1994 | 6.5 | 13 | 16– | 5 | 11 |
| Nelsen | 31 | 14 | 45 | 141 | 4.6 | 0 | 3– | 10 | |
| Kelly | 1 | 0 | 0 | 0 | 0.0 | 0 | 0– | 0 | |

| PUNTING | No | Avg |
|---|---|---|
| Cockroft | 81 | 43.2 |

| KICKING | XP | Att | % | FG | Att | % |
|---|---|---|---|---|---|---|
| Cockroft | 28 | 29 | 97 | 22 | 27 | 81 |

## CINCINNATI BENGALS

### RUSHING

| Last Name | No. | Yds | Avg | TD |
|---|---|---|---|---|
| E. Johnson | 212 | 825 | 3.9 | 4 |
| Dressler | 128 | 565 | 4.4 | 6 |
| Phillips | 48 | 207 | 4.3 | 1 |
| Anderson | 22 | 94 | 4.3 | 3 |
| Carter | 12 | 57 | 4.8 | 2 |
| Lewis | 1 | 15 | 15.0 | 0 |
| Joiner | 3 | 14 | 4.7 | 0 |
| Morrison | 1 | 2 | 2.0 | 0 |

### RECEIVING

| Last Name | No. | Yds | Avg | TD |
|---|---|---|---|---|
| Myers | 57 | 792 | 14 | 3 |
| Trumpy | 44 | 500 | 11 | 2 |
| Dressler | 39 | 348 | 9 | 1 |
| E. Johnson | 29 | 420 | 14 | 2 |
| Joiner | 24 | 439 | 18 | 2 |
| Thomas | 17 | 171 | 10 | 1 |
| Phillips | 10 | 50 | 5 | 0 |
| Coslet | 5 | 48 | 10 | 1 |
| Buie | 1 | 5 | 5 | 0 |

### PUNT RETURNS

| Last Name | No. | Yds | Avg | TD |
|---|---|---|---|---|
| Casanova | 30 | 289 | 10 | 1 |
| Parrish | 15 | 141 | 9 | 1 |
| E. Johnson | 2 | 7 | 4 | 0 |

### KICKOFF RETURNS

| Last Name | No. | Yds | Avg | TD |
|---|---|---|---|---|
| Jackson | 21 | 509 | 24 | 0 |
| Parrish | 15 | 348 | 23 | 0 |
| Joiner | 5 | 88 | 18 | 0 |
| Morrison | 3 | 67 | 22 | 0 |
| Casanova | 1 | 34 | 34 | 0 |
| Lewis | 1 | 15 | 15 | 0 |
| E. Johnson | 1 | 13 | 13 | 0 |
| Dennis | 1 | 11 | 11 | 0 |
| Kelly | 1 | 0 | 0 | 0 |

### PASSING – PUNTING – KICKING

| PASSING | Att | Comp | % | Yds | Yd/Att | Td | Int– | % | RK |
|---|---|---|---|---|---|---|---|---|---|
| Anderson | 301 | 171 | 57 | 1918 | 6.4 | 7 | 7– | 2 | 5 |
| Carter | 82 | 47 | 57 | 579 | 7.1 | 3 | 4– | 5 | |

| PUNTING | No | Avg |
|---|---|---|
| Lewis | 66 | 42.1 |

| KICKING | XP | Att | % | FG | Att | % |
|---|---|---|---|---|---|---|
| Muhlmann | 30 | 31 | 97 | 27 | 40 | 68 |

## HOUSTON OILERS

### RUSHING

| Last Name | No. | Yds | Avg | TD |
|---|---|---|---|---|
| Willis | 134 | 461 | 3.4 | 0 |
| Robinson | 107 | 449 | 4.2 | 3 |
| Pastorini | 38 | 205 | 5.4 | 2 |
| Rodgers | 71 | 204 | 2.9 | 2 |
| Granger | 42 | 175 | 4.2 | 0 |
| Holmes | 43 | 172 | 4.0 | 0 |
| Walsh | 8 | 36 | 4.5 | 0 |
| A. Johnson | 11 | 13 | 1.2 | 0 |
| Baker | 1 | 9 | 9.0 | 0 |
| Nix | 3 | 3 | 1.0 | 0 |

### RECEIVING

| Last Name | No. | Yds | Avg | TD |
|---|---|---|---|---|
| Willis | 45 | 297 | 7 | 2 |
| Smith | 30 | 316 | 11 | 0 |
| Burrough | 26 | 521 | 20 | 4 |
| Reed | 19 | 251 | 13 | 0 |
| Granger | 15 | 74 | 5 | 0 |
| Robinson | 14 | 112 | 8 | 0 |
| Beirne | 7 | 95 | 14 | 1 |
| Dawson | 6 | 78 | 13 | 1 |
| Rodgers | 6 | 61 | 10 | 0 |
| Holmes | 6 | 32 | 5 | 0 |
| A. Johnson | 6 | 24 | 4 | 0 |
| Walsh | 4 | 22 | 6 | 0 |

### PUNT RETURNS

| Last Name | No. | Yds | Avg | TD |
|---|---|---|---|---|
| Houston | 25 | 148 | 6 | 0 |
| Moore | 7 | 15 | 2 | 0 |
| A. Johnson | 2 | 0 | 0 | 0 |

### KICKOFF RETURNS

| Last Name | No. | Yds | Avg | TD |
|---|---|---|---|---|
| Rodgers | 17 | 335 | 20 | 0 |
| B. Johnson | 13 | 230 | 18 | 0 |
| Jolley | 11 | 267 | 24 | 0 |
| A. Johnson | 7 | 154 | 22 | 0 |
| Holmes | 2 | 39 | 20 | 0 |
| Moore | 1 | 22 | 22 | 0 |
| Granger | 1 | 5 | 5 | 0 |

### PASSING – PUNTING – KICKING

| PASSING | Att | Comp | % | Yds | Yd/Att | Td | Int– | % | RK |
|---|---|---|---|---|---|---|---|---|---|
| Pastorini | 299 | 144 | 48 | 1711 | 5.7 | 7 | 12– | 4 | 13 |
| Nix | 63 | 33 | 52 | 287 | 4.6 | 3 | 6– | 9 | |
| Baker | 10 | 4 | 40 | 47 | 4.7 | 0 | 4– | 40 | |
| Willis | 4 | 1 | 25 | 16 | 4.0 | 0 | 1– | 25 | |

| PUNTING | No | Avg |
|---|---|---|
| Pastorini | 82 | 41.2 |
| Butler | 3 | 35.0 |

| KICKING | XP | Att | % | FG | Att | % |
|---|---|---|---|---|---|---|
| Butler | 15 | 16 | 94 | 12 | 19 | 63 |
| Moseley | 2 | 2 | 100 | 1 | 2 | 50 |

| Scores of Each Game | | Use Name | Pos. | Hgt | Wgt | Age | Int | Pts |
|---|---|---|---|---|---|---|---|---|

## OAKLAND RAIDERS 10-3-1  John Madden

**Scores of Each Game**

| | | |
|---|---|---|
| 28 | Pittsburgh | 34 |
| 20 | Green Bay | 14 |
| 17 | SAN DIEGO | 17 |
| 34 | Houston | 0 |
| 28 | BUFFALO | 16 |
| 23 | DENVER | 30 |
| 45 | LOS ANGELES | 17 |
| 14 | Kansas City | 27 |
| 20 | Cincinnati | 14 |
| 37 | Denver | 20 |
| 26 | KANSAS CITY | 3 |
| 21 | San Diego | 19 |
| 24 | N.Y. JETS | 16 |
| 28 | CHICAGO | 21 |

| Use Name | Pos. | Hgt | Wgt | Age | Int | Pts |
|---|---|---|---|---|---|---|
| Bob Brown | OT | 6'4" | 280 | 29 | | |
| Art Shell | OT | 6'5" | 265 | 25 | | |
| Paul Seiler | C-OT | 6'4" | 260 | 26 | | |
| George Buehler | OG | 6'2" | 260 | 25 | | |
| Gene Upshaw | OG | 6'5" | 255 | 27 | | |
| John Vella | OG | 6'4" | 255 | 22 | | |
| Jim Otto | C | 6'2" | 255 | 34 | | |
| Dave Dalby | OG-C | 6'2" | 240 | 21 | | |
| Tony Cline | DE | 6'2" | 240 | 24 | 1 | |
| Horace Jones | DE | 6'3" | 240 | 23 | | |
| Tom Keating | DT | 6'3" | 247 | 29 | | |
| Carleton Oats | DT | 6'2" | 260 | 29 | | |
| Art Thoms | DT | 6'5" | 250 | 25 | 1 | |
| Otis Sistrunk | DE-DT | 6'4" | 255 | 24 | 1 | |

| Use Name | Pos. | Hgt | Wgt | Age | Int | Pts |
|---|---|---|---|---|---|---|
| Joe Carroll | LB | 6'1" | 220 | 22 | | |
| Dan Conners | LB | 6'1" | 230 | 30 | 1 | |
| Gerald Irons | LB | 6'2" | 230 | 25 | 2 | |
| Terry Mendenhall | LB | 6'1" | 210 | 23 | | |
| Gus Otto | LB | 6'2" | 220 | 29 | | |
| Greg Slough | LB | 6'3" | 230 | 24 | | |
| Phil Villapiano | LB | 6'1" | 222 | 23 | 3 | 6 |
| Butch Atkinson | DB | 6' | 180 | 25 | 4 | |
| Willie Brown | DB | 6'1" | 190 | 31 | 4 | |
| Tommy Maxwell | DB | 6'2" | 195 | 25 | | |
| Jack Tatum | DB | 5'10" | 200 | 23 | 4 | 6 |
| Skip Thomas | DB | 6'1" | 205 | 22 | | |
| Jimmy Warren | DB | 5'11" | 175 | 33 | | |
| Nemiah Wilson | DB | 6' | 165 | 29 | 4 | |

| Use Name | Pos. | Hgt | Wgt | Age | Int | Pts |
|---|---|---|---|---|---|---|
| George Blanda | QB | 6'1" | 215 | 44 | | 95 |
| Daryle Lamonica | QB | 6'2" | 215 | 31 | | |
| Ken Stabler | QB | 6'3" | 215 | 26 | | |
| Clarence Davis | HB | 5'10" | 190 | 23 | | 36 |
| Don Highsmith | HB | 6' | 200 | 24 | | 6 |
| Charlie Smith | HB | 6'1" | 205 | 26 | | 60 |
| Marv Hubbard | FB | 6'1" | 225 | 26 | | 24 |
| Peter Banaszak | HB-FB | 5'11" | 210 | 28 | | 6 |
| Jeff Queen | TE-FB | 6'11" | 220 | 25 | | |
| Fred Biletnikoff | WR | 6'1" | 190 | 29 | | 42 |
| Cliff Branch | WR | 5'11" | 170 | 24 | | |
| Mike Siani | WR | 6'2" | 195 | 22 | | 30 |
| Ray Chester | TE | 6'3" | 225 | 24 | | 48 |
| Bob Moore | TE | 6'3" | 220 | 23 | | 6 |
| Jerry DePoyster | K | 6'1" | 200 | 26 | | |

Ben Davidson — Heel Injury        Warren Koegel — Injury

## KANSAS CITY CHIEFS 8-6-0  Hank Stram

**Scores of Each Game**

| | | |
|---|---|---|
| 10 | MIAMI | 20 |
| 20 | New Orleans | 17 |
| 45 | Denver | 24 |
| 31 | Cleveland | 7 |
| 16 | CINCINNATI | 23 |
| 20 | PHILADELPHIA | 21 |
| 26 | San Diego | 14 |
| 27 | OAKLAND | 14 |
| 7 | Pittsburgh | 16 |
| 17 | SAN DIEGO | 27 |
| 3 | Oakland | 26 |
| 24 | DENVER | 21 |
| 24 | BALTIMORE | 10 |
| 17 | Atlanta | 14 |

| Use Name | Pos. | Hgt | Wgt | Age | Int | Pts |
|---|---|---|---|---|---|---|
| Dave Hill | OT | 6'5" | 260 | 31 | | |
| Sid Smith | OT | 6'4" | 260 | 24 | | |
| Jim Tyrer | OT | 6'6" | 280 | 33 | | |
| Ed Budde | OG | 6'5" | 265 | 31 | | |
| George Daney | OG | 6'3" | 240 | 25 | | |
| Larry Gagner | OG | 6'3" | 268 | 28 | | |
| Mo Moorman | OG | 6'5" | 252 | 28 | | |
| Mike Oriard | C | 6'4" | 223 | 24 | | |
| Jack Rudnay | C | 6'3" | 240 | 24 | | |
| Aaron Brown | DE | 6'5" | 255 | 28 | | |
| Marv Upshaw | DE | 6'3" | 260 | 25 | | |
| Wilbur Young | DT-DE | 6'6" | 285 | 23 | | |
| Buck Buchanan | DT | 6'7" | 270 | 32 | | |
| Curley Culp | DT | 6'1" | 265 | 26 | | |
| Ed Lothamer | DT | 6'5" | 270 | 29 | | |
| George Seals | DT | 6'2" | 260 | 29 | | |

| Use Name | Pos. | Hgt | Wgt | Age | Int | Pts |
|---|---|---|---|---|---|---|
| Bobby Bell | LB | 6'4" | 228 | 32 | 3 | 6 |
| Keith Best | LB | 6'3" | 220 | 22 | | |
| Willie Lanier | LB | 6'1" | 245 | 27 | 2 | |
| Jim Lynch | LB | 6'1" | 235 | 27 | | |
| Bob Stein | LB | 6'2" | 235 | 24 | | |
| Clyde Werner | LB | 6'4" | 225 | 24 | 1 | |
| Nate Allen | DB | 5'10" | 170 | 24 | 1 | |
| Jim Kearney | DB | 6'2" | 206 | 29 | 5 | 24 |
| Jim Marsalis | DB | 5'11" | 194 | 26 | 2 | |
| Larry Marshall | DB | 5'10" | 195 | 22 | | |
| Kerry Reardon | DB | 5'11" | 180 | 23 | | |
| Mike Sensibaugh | DB | 5'11" | 192 | 23 | 8 | |
| Emmitt Thomas | DB | 6'2" | 192 | 29 | 2 | |

Warren McVea—Knee Injury

| Use Name | Pos. | Hgt | Wgt | Age | Int | Pts |
|---|---|---|---|---|---|---|
| Len Dawson | QB | 6' | 190 | 38 | | |
| Mike Livingston | QB | 6'3" | 212 | 26 | | |
| Mike Adamle | HB | 5'9" | 197 | 22 | | 6 |
| Ed Podolak | HB | 6'1" | 204 | 25 | | 36 |
| Wendell Hayes | FB | 6'2" | 220 | 31 | | 18 |
| Jim Otis | FB | 6' | 220 | 24 | | |
| Jeff Kinney | HB-FB | 6'2" | 215 | 22 | | 6 |
| Dennis Homan | WR | 6'1" | 180 | 26 | | 6 |
| Bruce Jankowski | WR | 5'11" | 185 | 23 | | |
| Otis Taylor | WR | 6'3" | 215 | 29 | | 36 |
| Bob West | WR | 6'4" | 218 | 21 | | 18 |
| Elmo Wright | WR | 6' | 190 | 23 | | |
| Willie Frazier | TE | 6'4" | 234 | 29 | | 30 |
| Morris Stroud | TE | 6'10" | 255 | 26 | | 6 |
| Jan Stenerud | K | 6'2" | 187 | 29 | | 95 |
| Jerrel Wilson | K | 6'4" | 222 | 30 | | |

## DENVER BRONCOS 5-9-0  John Ralston

**Scores of Each Game**

| | | |
|---|---|---|
| 30 | HOUSTON | 17 |
| 14 | San Diego | 37 |
| 24 | KANSAS CITY | 45 |
| 10 | Cincinnati | 21 |
| 20 | MINNESOTA | 23 |
| 30 | Oakland | 23 |
| 20 | CLEVELAND | 27 |
| 17 | N.Y. Giants | 29 |
| 16 | Los Angeles | 10 |
| 20 | OAKLAND | 37 |
| 20 | Atlanta | 23 |
| 21 | Kansas City | 24 |
| 38 | SAN DIEGO | 13 |
| 45 | NEW ENGLAND | 21 |

| Use Name | Pos. | Hgt | Wgt | Age | Int | Pts |
|---|---|---|---|---|---|---|
| Mike Current | OT | 6'4" | 274 | 26 | | |
| Marv Montgomery | OT | 6'6" | 255 | 24 | 1 | |
| Rick Sharp | OT | 6'3" | 265 | 24 | | |
| George Goeddeke | OG-OT | 6'3" | 253 | 27 | | |
| Bill Cottrell | OG | 6'3" | 255 | 27 | | |
| Larron Jackson | OG | 6'3" | 270 | 23 | | |
| Mike Schnitker | OG | 6'3" | 245 | 25 | | |
| Tommy Lyons | C-OG | 6'2" | 228 | 24 | | |
| Larry Kaminski | C | 6'2" | 245 | 27 | | |
| Bobby Maples | C | 6'3" | 250 | 29 | | |
| Lyle Alzado | DE | 6'3" | 252 | 23 | | |
| John Hoffman (from STL) | DE | 6'7" | 260 | 29 | | |
| Lloyd Voss | DT-DE | 6'4" | 255 | 30 | | |
| Tom Domres | DT | 6'3" | 260 | 25 | | |
| Paul Smith | DT | 6'3" | 256 | 27 | | |
| Pete Duranko | DE-DT | 6'2" | 250 | 28 | | |

Walt Barnes — Injury

| Use Name | Pos. | Hgt | Wgt | Age | Int | Pts |
|---|---|---|---|---|---|---|
| Ken Criter | LB | 5'11" | 223 | 25 | | |
| Fred Forsberg | Lb | 6'1" | 235 | 28 | | |
| Bob Geddes | LB | 6'2" | 240 | 26 | | |
| Tom Graham | LB | 6'2" | 235 | 22 | 2 | |
| Bill McKoy | LB | 6'3" | 235 | 24 | | |
| Chip Myrtle | LB | 6'2" | 225 | 27 | | |
| Don Parish | LB | 6'1" | 220 | 24 | | |
| Mike Simone | LB | 6' | 210 | 22 | | |
| Cornell Gordon | DB | 6' | 187 | 31 | | |
| Charlie Greer | DB | 6' | 205 | 26 | 2 | 6 |
| Leroy Mitchell | DB | 6'2" | 190 | 27 | 3 | |
| Randy Montgomery | DB | 5'11" | 182 | 25 | 1 | |
| Steve Preece (from PHI) | DB | 6'1" | 195 | 25 | 1 | |
| George Saimes | DB | 5'10" | 188 | 30 | | |
| Bill Thompson | DB | 6'1" | 200 | 25 | 1 | |
| Bill West | DB | 5'10" | 185 | 24 | | |

Sam Brunelli — Injury
Jack Gehrke — Injury

| Use Name | Pos. | Hgt | Wgt | Age | Int | Pts |
|---|---|---|---|---|---|---|
| Mike Ernst | QB | 6'1" | 190 | 21 | | |
| Charley Johnson | QB | 6' | 190 | 35 | | |
| Steve Ramsey | QB | 6'2" | 210 | 24 | | 12 |
| Floyd Little | HB | 5'10" | 196 | 30 | | 78 |
| Fran Lynch | FB-HB | 6'1" | 205 | 26 | | 12 |
| Clem Turner | FB | 6'1" | 236 | 27 | | |
| Bobby Anderson | HB-FB | 6'2" | 215 | 24 | | 12 |
| Joe Dawkins | HB-FB | 5'11" | 223 | 24 | | 12 |
| Jim Krieg | WR | 5'9" | 172 | 23 | | |
| Haven Moses (from BUF) | WR | 6'3" | 205 | 26 | | 36 |
| Rod Sherman | WR | 6' | 190 | 27 | | 18 |
| Jerry Simmons | WR | 6'1" | 190 | 29 | | 12 |
| Bill Van Heusen | WR | 6'1" | 200 | 26 | | 6 |
| Bill Masters | TE | 6'5" | 240 | 28 | | 18 |
| Riley Odoms | TE | 6'4" | 230 | 22 | | 6 |
| Jim Turner | K | 6'2" | 205 | 31 | | 97 |

Jerry Inman — Injury

## SAN DIEGO CHARGERS 4-9-1  Harland Svare

**Scores of Each Game**

| | | |
|---|---|---|
| 3 | San Francisco | 34 |
| 37 | DENVER | 14 |
| 17 | Oakland | 17 |
| 23 | Baltimore | 20 |
| 24 | Miami | 24 |
| 20 | Detroit | 34 |
| 14 | KANSAS CITY | 26 |
| 28 | DALLAS | 34 |
| 17 | CLEVELAND | 21 |
| 27 | Kansas City | 17 |
| 34 | HOUSTON | 20 |
| 19 | OAKLAND | 21 |
| 13 | Denver | 38 |
| 2 | PITTSBURGH | 24 |

| Use Name | Pos. | Hgt | Wgt | Age | Int | Pts |
|---|---|---|---|---|---|---|
| Ira Gordon | OT | 6'3" | 268 | 24 | | |
| Terry Owens | OT | 6'6" | 268 | 28 | | |
| Russ Washington | OT | 6'6" | 294 | 25 | | |
| Ernie Wright | OT | 6'4" | 270 | 32 | | |
| Walt Sweeney | OG | 6'3" | 256 | 31 | | |
| Ralph Wenzel | OG | 6'3" | 250 | 29 | | |
| Doug Wilkerson | OG | 6'2" | 250 | 25 | | |
| Sam Gruneisen | C | 6'1" | 250 | 31 | | |
| Carl Mauck | C | 6'3" | 245 | 25 | 6 | |
| Lionel Aldridge | DE | 6'4" | 245 | 30 | | |
| Deacon Jones | DE | 6'5" | 250 | 33 | | |
| Cal Snowden | DE | 6'4" | 253 | 25 | | |
| Lee Thomas | DE | 6'5" | 246 | 25 | | |
| Dave Costa | DT | 6'2" | 260 | 30 | 2 | |
| Ron East | DT | 6'4" | 236 | 29 | | |
| Kevin Hardy | DT | 6'5" | 276 | 27 | | |
| Greg Wojcik | DT | 6'6" | 268 | 26 | | |

| Use Name | Pos. | Hgt | Wgt | Age | Int | Pts |
|---|---|---|---|---|---|---|
| John Andrews | LB | 6'3" | 225 | 23 | | |
| Bob Babich | LB | 6'2" | 230 | 25 | 2 | |
| Pete Barnes | LB | 6'3" | 240 | 27 | 1 | |
| Lee Roy Caffey | LB | 6'3" | 250 | 32 | 1 | |
| Pete Lazetich | LB | 6'3" | 245 | 22 | | |
| Rick Redman | LB | 5'11" | 222 | 29 | 1 | |
| Tim Rossovich | LB | 6'4" | 240 | 26 | 1 | |
| Ray White | LB | 6'1" | 242 | 23 | | |
| Joe Beauchamp | DB | 6' | 182 | 28 | 6 | 6 |
| Reggie Berry | DB | 6' | 190 | 23 | | |
| Chuck Detwiler | DB | 6' | 185 | 24 | | |
| Lenny Dunlap | DB | 6'1" | 195 | 23 | 5 | |
| Chris Fletcher | DB | 5'11" | 185 | 23 | | |
| Bob Howard | DB | 6'1" | 175 | 27 | | |
| Ray Jones | DB | 6' | 187 | 24 | | |
| Bryant Salter | DB | 6'4" | 194 | 22 | 7 | |

Harris Jones — Injury
Mel Rogers — Shoulder Injury

| Use Name | Pos. | Hgt | Wgt | Age | Int | Pts |
|---|---|---|---|---|---|---|
| Wayne Clark | QB | 6'2" | 200 | 25 | | |
| John Hadl | QB | 6'2" | 214 | 32 | 6 | |
| Mike Garrett | HB | 5'9" | 200 | 28 | | 42 |
| John Sykes | HB | 5'11" | 195 | 23 | | |
| Jesse Taylor | HB | 6' | 200 | 24 | | 6 |
| Oscar Dragon | FB-HB | 6' | 214 | 22 | | |
| Cid Edwards | FB | 6'2" | 230 | 28 | | 42 |
| Lee White | FB | 6'4" | 240 | 26 | | |
| Mike Carter | WR | 6'1" | 210 | 24 | | |
| Chuck Dicus | WR | 6' | 176 | 23 | | 12 |
| Gary Garrison | WR | 6'1" | 193 | 28 | | 42 |
| Jerry LeVias | WR | 5'10" | 178 | 25 | | |
| Dave Williams | WR | 6'2" | 200 | 27 | | 18 |
| John Mackey | TE | 6'3" | 224 | 30 | | |
| Pettis Norman | TE | 6'3" | 220 | 32 | | |
| Bill McClard | K | 5'10" | 202 | 20 | | 11 |
| Dennis Partee | K | 6'2" | 230 | 26 | | 71 |

Duane Thomas — Holdout

## OAKLAND RAIDERS

### Rushing

| Last Name | No. | Yds | Avg | TD |
|---|---|---|---|---|
| Hubbard | 219 | 1100 | 5.0 | 4 |
| Smith | 170 | 686 | 4.0 | 8 |
| Davis | 71 | 363 | 5.1 | 6 |
| Banaszak | 30 | 138 | 4.6 | 1 |
| Lamonica | 10 | 33 | 3.3 | 0 |
| Stabler | 6 | 27 | 4.5 | 0 |
| Highsmith | 9 | 11 | 1.2 | 1 |
| Queen | 4 | 10 | 2.5 | 0 |
| Branch | 1 | 5 | 5.0 | 0 |
| Chester | 1 | 3 | 3.0 | 0 |

### Receiving

| Last Name | No. | Yds | Avg | TD |
|---|---|---|---|---|
| Biletnikoff | 58 | 802 | 14 | 7 |
| Chester | 34 | 576 | 17 | 8 |
| Siani | 28 | 496 | 18 | 5 |
| Smith | 28 | 353 | 13 | 2 |
| Hubbard | 22 | 103 | 5 | 0 |
| Banaszak | 9 | 63 | 7 | 0 |
| Davis | 8 | 82 | 10 | 0 |
| Moore | 6 | 49 | 8 | 1 |
| Branch | 3 | 41 | 14 | 0 |
| Highsmith | 2 | 34 | 17 | 0 |

### Punt Returns

| Last Name | No. | Yds | Avg | TD |
|---|---|---|---|---|
| Atkinson | 10 | 33 | 3 | 0 |
| Branch | 12 | 21 | 2 | 0 |
| Maxwell | 2 | 12 | 6 | 0 |

### Kickoff Returns

| Last Name | No. | Yds | Avg | TD |
|---|---|---|---|---|
| Davis | 18 | 464 | 26 | 0 |
| Branch | 9 | 191 | 21 | 0 |
| Atkinson | 3 | 75 | 25 | 0 |
| Warren | 4 | 57 | 14 | 0 |
| Maxwell | 1 | 26 | 26 | 0 |
| Seiler | 1 | 0 | 0 | 0 |
| Slough | 1 | 0 | 0 | 0 |
| Smith | 1 | 0 | 0 | 0 |

### Passing — Punting — Kicking

| PASSING | Att | Comp | % | Yds | Yd/Att | TD | Int— | % | RK |
|---|---|---|---|---|---|---|---|---|---|
| Lamonica | 281 | 149 | 53 | 1998 | 7.1 | 18 | 12— | 4 | 2 |
| Stabler | 74 | 44 | 60 | 524 | 7.1 | 4 | 3— | 4 | |
| Blanda | 15 | 5 | 33 | 77 | 5.1 | 1 | 0— | 0 | |

| PUNTING | No. | Avg |
|---|---|---|
| DePoyster | 55 | 36.9 |

| KICKING | XP | Att | % | FG | Att | % |
|---|---|---|---|---|---|---|
| Blanda | 44 | 44 | 100 | 17 | 26 | 65 |

## KANSAS CITY CHIEFS

### Rushing

| Last Name | No. | Yds | Avg | TD |
|---|---|---|---|---|
| Podolak | 171 | 615 | 3.6 | 4 |
| Hayes | 128 | 536 | 4.2 | 0 |
| Adamle | 73 | 303 | 4.2 | 1 |
| Livingston | 14 | 133 | 9.5 | 0 |
| Kinney | 38 | 122 | 3.2 | 1 |
| Otis | 29 | 92 | 3.2 | 0 |
| Dawson | 15 | 75 | 5.0 | 0 |
| Wright | 1 | 24 | 24.0 | 0 |
| Taylor | 5 | 13 | 2.6 | 0 |
| West | 2 | 2 | 1.0 | 0 |

### Receiving

| Last Name | No. | Yds | Avg | TD |
|---|---|---|---|---|
| Taylor | 57 | 821 | 14 | 6 |
| Podolak | 46 | 345 | 8 | 2 |
| Hayes | 31 | 295 | 9 | 3 |
| Adamle | 15 | 76 | 5 | 0 |
| Frazier | 13 | 172 | 13 | 5 |
| Homan | 12 | 135 | 11 | 1 |
| Otis | 12 | 76 | 6 | 0 |
| Wright | 11 | 81 | 7 | 0 |
| West | 9 | 165 | 18 | 2 |
| Stroud | 4 | 80 | 20 | 1 |
| Kinney | 4 | 45 | 11 | 0 |
| Jankowski | 2 | 24 | 12 | 0 |
| Allen | 1 | 20 | 20 | 0 |

### Punt Returns

| Last Name | No. | Yds | Avg | TD |
|---|---|---|---|---|
| Marshall | 18 | 103 | 8 | 0 |
| Podolak | 8 | 11 | 1 | 0 |
| Homan | 2 | 9 | 5 | 0 |
| Reardon | 1 | 3 | 3 | 0 |

### Kickoff Returns

| Last Name | No. | Yds | Avg | TD |
|---|---|---|---|---|
| Marshall | 23 | 651 | 28 | 0 |
| Adamle | 8 | 185 | 23 | 0 |
| Podolak | 7 | 119 | 17 | 0 |
| Kinney | 4 | 63 | 16 | 0 |
| Reardon | 2 | 35 | 18 | 0 |
| Upshaw | 1 | 4 | 4 | 0 |
| Kearney | 1 | 0 | 0 | 0 |

### Passing — Punting — Kicking

| PASSING | Att | Comp | % | Yds | Yd/Att | TD | Int— | % | RK |
|---|---|---|---|---|---|---|---|---|---|
| Dawson | 305 | 175 | 57 | 1835 | 6.0 | 13 | 12— | 4 | 7 |
| Livingston | 78 | 41 | 53 | 480 | 6.2 | 7 | 8— | 10 | |
| Wilson | 1 | 1 | 100 | 20 | 20.0 | 0 | 0— | 0 | |

| PUNTING | No | Avg |
|---|---|---|
| Wilson | 66 | 44.8 |

| KICKING | XP | Att | % | FG | Att | % |
|---|---|---|---|---|---|---|
| Stenerud | 32 | 32 | 100 | 21 | 36 | 58 |

## DENVER BRONCOS

### Rushing

| Last Name | No. | Yds | Avg | TD |
|---|---|---|---|---|
| Little | 216 | 859 | 4.0 | 9 |
| Anderson | 72 | 319 | 4.4 | 1 |
| Dawkins | 56 | 243 | 4.3 | 2 |
| Lynch | 34 | 164 | 4.8 | 2 |
| Van Heusen | 3 | 76 | 25.3 | 1 |
| Odoms | 5 | 72 | 14.4 | 0 |
| Krieg | 1 | 63 | 63.0 | 0 |
| C. Turner | 5 | 16 | 3.2 | 0 |
| Ramsey | 6 | 15 | 2.5 | 2 |
| Moses | 2 | 11 | 5.5 | 0 |
| Ernst | 1 | 4 | 4.0 | 0 |
| Sherman | 1 | 2 | 2.0 | 0 |
| Johnson | 3 | 0 | 0.0 | 0 |
| Masters | 3 | -15 | -5.0 | 0 |

### Receiving

| Last Name | No. | Yds | Avg | TD |
|---|---|---|---|---|
| Sherman | 38 | 661 | 17 | 3 |
| Little | 28 | 367 | 13 | 4 |
| Masters | 25 | 393 | 16 | 3 |
| Anderson | 23 | 215 | 9 | 1 |
| Odoms | 21 | 320 | 15 | 1 |
| Moses | 18 | 284 | 16 | 6 |
| Dawkins | 18 | 242 | 13 | 0 |
| Simmons | 17 | 235 | 14 | 2 |
| Lynch | 7 | 75 | 11 | 0 |
| Krieg | 4 | 99 | 25 | 0 |
| Van Heusen | 4 | 59 | 15 | 0 |
| C. Turner | 1 | 10 | 10 | 0 |

### Punt Returns

| Last Name | No. | Yds | Avg | TD |
|---|---|---|---|---|
| Sherman | 10 | 89 | 9 | 0 |
| Thompson | 4 | 82 | 21 | 0 |
| Greer | 4 | 67 | 17 | 1 |
| Little | 8 | 64 | 8 | 0 |
| Simone | 1 | 5 | 5 | 0 |
| Krieg | 1 | 3 | 3 | 0 |

### Kickoff Returns

| Last Name | No. | Yds | Avg | TD |
|---|---|---|---|---|
| Montgomery | 29 | 756 | 26 | 1 |
| Dawkins | 15 | 357 | 24 | 0 |
| Little | 3 | 48 | 16 | 0 |
| Lynch | 3 | 45 | 15 | 0 |
| C. Turner | 1 | 25 | 25 | 0 |
| Krieg | 1 | 18 | 18 | 0 |
| Anderson | 1 | 13 | 13 | 0 |
| Simone | 1 | -6 | -6 | 0 |
| Preece | 1 | 0 | 0 | 0 |

### Passing — Punting — Kicking

| PASSING | Att | Comp | % | Yds | Yd/Att | TD | Int— | % | RK |
|---|---|---|---|---|---|---|---|---|---|
| Johnson | 238 | 132 | 55 | 1783 | 7.5 | 14 | 14— | 6 | 3 |
| Ramsey | 137 | 65 | 47 | 1050 | 7.7 | 3 | 9— | 7 | |
| Ernst | 4 | 1 | 25 | 10 | 2.5 | 0 | 0— | 0 | |
| Anderson | 3 | 1 | 33 | 14 | 4.7 | 1 | 0— | 0 | |
| Little | 2 | 2 | 100 | 43 | 21.5 | 1 | 0— | 0 | |

| PUNTING | No | Avg |
|---|---|---|
| Van Heusen | 60 | 40.1 |

| KICKING | XP | Att | % | FG | Att | % |
|---|---|---|---|---|---|---|
| J Turner | 37 | 37 | 100 | 20 | 29 | 69 |

## SAN DIEGO CHARGERS

### Rushing

| Last Name | No. | Yds | Avg | TD |
|---|---|---|---|---|
| Garrett | 272 | 1031 | 3.8 | 6 |
| Edwards | 157 | 679 | 4.3 | 5 |
| Hadl | 22 | 99 | 4.5 | 1 |
| L. White | 23 | 75 | 3.3 | 0 |
| Taylor | 13 | 58 | 4.5 | 0 |
| Dragon | 9 | 30 | 3.3 | 0 |
| Carter | 1 | 25 | 25.0 | 0 |
| Williams | 1 | 14 | 14.0 | 0 |
| Norman | 1 | 9 | 9.0 | 0 |
| Garrison | 2 | -6 | -3.0 | 0 |
| Clark | 2 | -8 | -4.0 | 0 |
| Dicus | 1 | -11 | -11.0 | 0 |

### Receiving

| Last Name | No. | Yds | Avg | TD |
|---|---|---|---|---|
| Garrison | 52 | 744 | 14 | 7 |
| Edwards | 40 | 557 | 14 | 2 |
| Garrett | 31 | 245 | 8 | 1 |
| Norman | 19 | 262 | 14 | 0 |
| Dicus | 18 | 227 | 13 | 2 |
| Williams | 14 | 315 | 23 | 3 |
| Mackey | 11 | 110 | 10 | 0 |
| L. White | 3 | 20 | 7 | 0 |
| Carter | 2 | 24 | 12 | 0 |
| LeVias | 1 | 8 | 8 | 0 |
| Hadl | 1 | 4 | 4 | 0 |

### Punt Returns

| Last Name | No. | Yds | Avg | TD |
|---|---|---|---|---|
| Dunlap | 19 | 179 | 9 | 0 |
| Garrett | 2 | 10 | 5 | 0 |
| Taylor | 1 | 5 | 5 | 0 |
| LeVias | 1 | -4 | -4 | 0 |

### Kickoff Returns

| Last Name | No. | Yds | Avg | TD |
|---|---|---|---|---|
| Taylor | 31 | 676 | 22 | 0 |
| Dunlap | 12 | 271 | 23 | 0 |
| Berry | 7 | 138 | 20 | 0 |
| Detwiler | 4 | 94 | 24 | 0 |
| Sykes | 2 | 44 | 22 | 0 |
| R. Jones | 3 | 41 | 14 | 0 |
| Beauchamp | 1 | 0 | 0 | 0 |
| Williams | 0 | 9 | 0 | 0 |

### Passing — Punting — Kicking

| PASSING | Att | Comp | % | Yds | Yd/Att | TD | Int— | % | RK |
|---|---|---|---|---|---|---|---|---|---|
| Hadl | 370 | 190 | 51 | 2449 | 6.6 | 15 | 26— | 7 | 10 |
| Clark | 6 | 2 | 33 | 67 | 11.2 | 0 | 2— | 33 | |
| Garrett | 1 | 0 | 0 | 0.0 | 0 | 0— | 0 | | |

| PUNTING | No | Avg |
|---|---|---|
| Partee | 45 | 40.3 |

| KICKING | XP | Att | % | FG | Att | % |
|---|---|---|---|---|---|---|
| Partee | 26 | 28 | 93 | 15 | 25 | 60 |
| McClard | 2 | 2 | 100 | 3 | 6 | 50 |

# 1972 Championship Games

## NFC CHAMPIONSHIP GAME
December 31, at Washington
(Attendance 53,129)

### No Stronger Than Its Weakest Link

#### SCORING

| | | | | |
|---|---|---|---|---|
| WASHINGTON | 0 | 10 | 16 | —26 |
| DALLAS | 0 | 3 | 0 | — 3 |

**Second Quarter**
Wash. Knight, 18 yard field goal
Wash. Taylor, 15 yard pass from Kilmer
PAT—Knight (Kick)
Dall. Fritsch, 35 yard field goal

**Fourth Quarter**
Wash. Taylor, 45 yard pass from Kilmer
PAT—Knight (Kick)
Wash. Knight, 39 yard field goal
Wash. Knight, 46 yard field goal
Wash. Knight, 45 yard field goal

#### TEAM STATISTICS

| WASH. | | DALLAS |
|---|---|---|
| 16 | First Downs—Total | 8 |
| 4 | First Downs—Rushing | 3 |
| 11 | First Downs—Passing | 3 |
| 1 | First Downs—Penalty | 2 |
| 2 | Fumbles—Number | 1 |
| 1 | Fumbles—Lost Ball | 1 |
| 4 | Penalties—Number | 4 |
| 38 | Yards Penalized | 30 |
| 0 | Missed Field Goals | 1 |
| 62 | Offensive Plays—Total | 45 |
| 316 | Net Yards | 169 |
| 5.1 | Average Gain | 3.8 |
| 1 | Giveaways | 1 |
| 1 | Takeaways | 1 |
| 0 | Difference | 0 |

The Cowboys and Redskins, arch-rivals in the Eastern Division, each made it to the NFC title game with a strong showing in the first round of the playoffs. The Redskins completely stifled the Packer running attack in a 16-3 triumph, while the Cowboys rallied in the fourth quarter to beat the '49ers 30-28. The two clubs had split their meetings during the regular season, and this match would decide the Super Bowl berth.

Roger Staubach, who had sat out most of the season with an injured shoulder but had returned to action in the come-from-behind victory over San Francisco the week before, started at quarterback for the Cowboys in place of Craig Morton. The Washington defense greeted him with a ferocious pass rush that kept him off balance all afternoon and prevented any second-half heroics.

The Washington offensive game plan called for attacking the Cowboys at their weak left cornerback spot, where Charley Waters, normally a safety, had beaten Herb Adderley out of a job. Leading 3-0 in the second quarter, the Redskins went to work on Waters. Charley Taylor beat him to haul in a 51-yard pass, and several plays later Kilmer hit Taylor with a 15-yard scoring pitch. The Cowboys answered with a drive deep into Washington territory, but when Calvin Hill overthrew Walt Garrison in the end zone on an option pass, they had to settle for a Toni Fritsch field goal.

Early in the third period Waters broke an arm, and coach Tom Landry put Mark Washington into the corner position and left the veteran Adderley on the bench. Taylor exploited Washington's inexperience in the fourth quarter by beating him for a 45-yard touchdown pass which gave the Redskins some breathing room. Forced to go to the air, the Cowboys could make no headway against the Redskin defense, and three Curt Knight field goals in the final quarter gave the Redskins a much savored 26-3 victory.

#### INDIVIDUAL STATISTICS

| WASHINGTON | No | Yds | Avg. | DALLAS | No | Yds | Avg. |
|---|---|---|---|---|---|---|---|
| **RUSHING** | | | | | | | |
| Brown | 30 | 88 | 2.9 | Staubach | 5 | 59 | 11.8 |
| Harraway | 11 | 19 | 1.7 | Hill | 9 | 22 | 2.4 |
| Kilmer | 3 | 15 | 5.0 | Garrison | 7 | 15 | 2.1 |
| | 44 | 122 | 2.8 | | 21 | 96 | 4.6 |
| **RECEIVING** | | | | | | | |
| Taylor | 7 | 146 | 20.9 | Sellers | 2 | 29 | 14.5 |
| Harraway | 3 | 13 | 4.3 | Garrison | 2 | 18 | 9.0 |
| Jefferson | 2 | 19 | 9.5 | Hill | 2 | 11 | 5.5 |
| Brown | 2 | 16 | 8.0 | Parks | 1 | 21 | 21.0 |
| | 14 | 194 | 13.9 | Alworth | 1 | 15 | 15.0 |
| | | | | Ditka | 1 | 4 | 4.0 |
| | | | | | 9 | 98 | 10.9 |
| **PUNTING** | | | | | | | |
| Bragg | 4 | | 36.0 | Bateman | 7 | | 43.1 |
| **PUNT RETURNS** | | | | | | | |
| Haymond | 4 | 10 | 2.5 | Waters | 3 | −5 | −1.7 |
| **KICKOFF RETURNS** | | | | | | | |
| None | | | | Harris | 2 | 29 | 14.5 |
| | | | | Newhouse | 1 | 25 | 25.0 |
| | | | | | 3 | 54 | 18.0 |

| WASHINGTON | Att. | Comp. | Comp. Pct. | Yds. | Int. | Yds/ Att. | Yds/ Comp. | Yards Lost Tackled |
|---|---|---|---|---|---|---|---|---|
| **PASSING** | | | | | | | | |
| Kilmer | 18 | 14 | 77.8 | 194 | 0 | 10.8 | 13.9 | 0— 0 |
| **DALLAS** | | | | | | | | |
| Staubach | 20 | 9 | 45.0 | 98 | 0 | 4.9 | 10.9 | 3—25 |
| Hill | 1 | 0 | 0.0 | 0 | 0 | — | — | |
| | 21 | 9 | 42.9 | 98 | 0 | 4.7 | 10.9 | 3—25 |

---

## AFC CHAMPIONSHIP GAME
December 31, at Pittsburgh
(Attendance 50,845)

### Simply Not Enough of Bradshaw

#### SCORING

| | | | | |
|---|---|---|---|---|
| PITTSBURGH | 7 | 0 | 3 | 7—17 |
| MIAMI | 0 | 7 | 7 | 7—21 |

**First Quarter**
Pitt. Mullins, Recovery of Pitt fumble in end zone
PAT—Gerela (kick)

**Second Quarter**
Miami Csonka, 9 yard pass from Morrall
PAT—Yepremian (kick)

**Third Quarter**
Pitt. Gerela, 14 yard field goal
Miami Kiick, 2 yard rush
PAT—Yepremian (kick)

**Fourth Quarter**
Miami Kiick, 3 yard rush
PAT—Yepremian (kick)
Pitt. Young, 12 yard pass from Bradshaw
PAT—Gerela (kick)

#### TEAM STATISTICS

| PITT. | | MIAMI |
|---|---|---|
| 13 | First Downs—Total | 19 |
| 6 | First Downs—Rushing | 11 |
| 6 | First Downs—Passing | 6 |
| 1 | First Downs—Penalty | 2 |
| 2 | Fumbles—Number | 0 |
| 0 | Fumbles—Lost Ball | 0 |
| 4 | Penalties—Number | 2 |
| 30 | Yards Penalized | 19 |
| 1 | Missed Field Goals | 0 |
| 48 | Offensive Plays—Total | 65 |
| 250 | Net Yards | 314 |
| 5.2 | Average Gain | 4.8 |
| 2 | Giveaways | 1 |
| 1 | Takeaways | 2 |
| −1 | Difference | +1 |

The Dolphins came into this game after a miracle season, while the Steelers came in after a miracle play. By beating Cleveland 20-14 last week in the start of the playoffs, the Dolphins ran their record to 15-0 for the season. The Steelers had a less shining record, but their spirits were high after beating the Raiders 13-7 in the opening round of the playoffs. In that game the Steelers scored the winning touchdown with five seconds left on a deflected pass which Franco Harris snagged in mid-air and carried across the goal line.

In the first quarter, after an extended drive into Miami territory, Terry Bradshaw fumbled on the three-yard line and Gerry Mullins fell on the ball as it rolled into the end zone. Although the Steelers took a 7-0 lead, the play was costly, as Bradshaw was knocked dizzy and had to be relieved by Terry Hanratty.

An alert play by punter Larry Seiple helped the Dolphins tie the score in the second quarter. Noticing that all the Steelers had dropped back to block for the return, Seiple crossed the defense up and ran with the ball, gaining 37 yards to the Pittsburgh 12-yard line. Two plays later Morrall hit Csonka with a scoring pass, and Garo Yepremian added the extra point.

As the second half began, Miami coach Don Shula put Bob Griese, out since October with a broken leg, in at quarterback to shake up his offense. The Steelers went ahead 10-7 on a Roy Gerela field goal, but Griese hit Paul Warfield with a 52-yard pass play which put the Dolphins in striking distance. Six plays later, Jim Kiick carried the ball in, and another Kiick touchdown in the fourth quarter lengthened the Miami lead to 21-10. Bradshaw returned to action for the final seven minutes of the game, but after leading the Steelers to one touchdown, he suffered two interceptions in his final three passes.

#### INDIVIDUAL STATISTICS

| PITTSBURGH | No | Yds | Avg. | MIAMI | No | Yds | Avg. |
|---|---|---|---|---|---|---|---|
| **RUSHING** | | | | | | | |
| Harris | 16 | 76 | 4.8 | Morris | 16 | 76 | 4.8 |
| Fuqua | 8 | 47 | 5.9 | Csonka | 24 | 68 | 2.8 |
| Bradshaw | 2 | 5 | 2.5 | Seiple | 1 | 37 | 37.0 |
| | 26 | 128 | 4.9 | Kiick | 8 | 12 | 1.5 |
| | | | | | 49 | 193 | 3.9 |
| **RECEIVING** | | | | | | | |
| Young | 4 | 54 | 13.5 | Fleming | 5 | 50 | 10.0 |
| Shanklin | 2 | 49 | 24.5 | Warfield | 2 | 63 | 31.5 |
| Harris | 2 | 3 | 1.5 | Csonka | 1 | 9 | 9.0 |
| McMakin | 1 | 22 | 22.0 | Mandich | 1 | 5 | 5.0 |
| Brown | 1 | 9 | 9.0 | Morris | 1 | −6 | −6.0 |
| | 10 | 137 | 13.7 | | 10 | 121 | 12.1 |
| **PUNTING** | | | | | | | |
| Walden | 4 | | 51.3 | Seiple | 4 | | 35.5 |
| **PUNT RETURNS** | | | | | | | |
| Edwards | 1 | 5 | 5.0 | None | | | |
| **KICKOFF RETURNS** | | | | | | | |
| P. Pearson | 2 | 63 | 31.5 | Morris | 1 | 23 | 23.0 |
| S. Davis | 1 | 22 | 22.0 | | | | |
| | 3 | 85 | 28.3 | | | | |
| **INTERCEPTION RETURNS** | | | | | | | |
| Edwards | 1 | 28 | 28.0 | Buoniconti | 1 | 6 | 6.0 |
| | | | | Kuler | 1 | 5 | 5.0 |
| | | | | | 2 | 11 | 5.5 |

| PITTSBURGH | Att. | Comp. | Comp. Pct. | Yds. | Int. | Yds/ Att. | Yds/ Comp. | Yards Lost Tackled |
|---|---|---|---|---|---|---|---|---|
| **PASSING** | | | | | | | | |
| Bradshaw | 10 | 5 | 50.0 | 80 | 2 | 8.0 | 16.0 | |
| Hanratty | 10 | 5 | 50.0 | 57 | 0 | 5.7 | 11.4 | |
| | 20 | 10 | 50.0 | 137 | 2 | 6.9 | 13.7 | 2—15 |
| **MIAMI** | | | | | | | | |
| Morrall | 11 | 7 | 63.6 | 51 | 1 | 4.6 | 7.3 | |
| Griese | 5 | 3 | 60.0 | 70 | 0 | 14.0 | 23.3 | |
| | 16 | 10 | 62.5 | 121 | 1 | 7.6 | 12.1 | 0— 0 |

# Super Perfect

The contrasts were interesting. The Miami Dolphins had swept through fourteen regular-season games and two playoff games without a loss and now had a chance to compile a perfect 17-0 record for the year. Under the thorough leadership of head coach Don Shula, the Dolphins had rebounded from last year's Super Bowl loss to Dallas to become a cool, mature, precise club, with programmed brutality on both platoons.

The Washington Redskins had mostly veteran players, but their style was not one of coolness. Coach George Allen strove to whip his men into a frenzy before every game, and he put a fanatical emphasis on this game. A loss in this game would spoil the entire season, he said, and he drilled his troops in Spartan fashion to prepare them for the younger Dolphins.

The Miami defense scuttled the Washington running attack right from the start, a reversal from last year's dissection of the Dolphin front wall by the Cowboys. Larry Brown and Charley Harraway found Miami tackle Manny Fernandez forever in their path, and quarterback Bill Kilmer suffered through a bad afternoon with his passing. The Dolphins picked off three passes, with safety Jake Scott making two of the interceptions.

The Dolphin attack moved well against the heralded Redskin defense, but three penalties prevented any score until late in the period. Just before the end of the quarter Howard Twilley beat Pat Fischer to the outside and hauled in a 28-yard Bob Griese touchdown pass which he carried in from the 5. Leading 7-0, the Dolphins continued to paralyze the Redskin offense in the second period and scored again late in the period. One minute before halftime Jim Kiick capped a long Miami drive by going over from the one-yard line, giving the Dolphins a solid 14-0 lead at intermission.

The Redskins finally got their offense rolling after taking the second-half kickoff. With Brown gaining on the ground and Kilmer completing three passes, the Redskins drove into Miami territory before the drive stalled. Curt Knight then lined up a comparitively easy 32-yard field goal, but his kick sailed wide to the right and the Dolphins took possession.

The Miami defense re-established its superiority through the second half as the Dolphin offense held onto the ball long enough on each possession to eat up valuable time. With two minutes left in the game, Garo Yepremian attempted a 42-yard field goal, only to have it blocked. When the ball bounced back to him, he picked it up and started to run toward the sidelines. With no football experience except kicking, Yepremian then attempted to pass the ball, only to have it slip out of his hands right to Mike Bass of the Redskins. Bass ran 49 yards with the aborted pass for Washington's only score of the day, but the Dolphins hung onto the 14-7 lead the rest of the way and became the first NFL team ever to go through a complete season with all wins.

| MIAMI | | WASHINGTON |
|---|---|---|
| | OFFENSE | |
| Warfield | WR | C. Taylor |
| W. Moore | LT | Hermeling |
| Kuechenberg | LG | Laaveg |
| Langer | C | Hauss |
| Little | RG | Wilbur |
| Evans | RT | Rock |
| Fleming | TE | Smith |
| Twilley | WR | Jefferson |
| Griese | QB | Kilmer |
| Kiick | RB | Brown |
| Csonka | RB | Harraway |
| | DEFENSE | |
| Den Herder | LE | McDole |
| Fernandez | LT | Brundige |
| Heinz | RT | Talbert |
| Stanfill | RE | Biggs |
| Swift | LLB | Pardee |
| Bouniconti | MLB | Pottios |
| Kolen | RLB | Hanburger |
| Mumphord | LCB | Fischer |
| Johnson | RCB | Bass |
| Anderson | LS | Owens |
| Scott | RS | R. Taylor |

**SUBSTITUTES**

MIAMI
| Offense | |
|---|---|
| Briscoe | Leigh |
| Crusan | Mandich |
| Ginn | Morrall |
| Jenkins | Morris |
| Kindig | |
| Defense | |
| Babb | M. Moore |
| Ball | Powell |
| Matheson | Stuckey |
| Kickers | |
| Seiple | Yepremian |

WASHINGTON
| Offense | |
|---|---|
| Alston | McNeil |
| Brunet | Mul-Key |
| Burman | Wyche |
| Hull | |
| Defense | |
| Fanucci | Severson |
| Haymond | Sistrunk |
| Jaqua | Tillman |
| McLinton | Vactor |
| Kickers | |
| Bragg | Knight |

## SCORING

| | | |
|---|---|---|
| **MIAMI** | | 7 7 0 0—14 |
| **WASHINGTON** | | 0 0 0 7— 7 |

First Quarter
Mia.    Twilley, 28 yd pass from Griese
        PAT — Yepremian (kick)    14:59

Second Quarter
Mia.    Kiick, 1 yard rush
        PAT — Yepremian (kick)    14:42

Fourth Quarter
Was.    Bass, 49 yard fumble return
        PAT — Knight    12:53

## TEAM STATISTICS

| MIAMI | | WASH. |
|---|---|---|
| 12 | First Downs — Total | 16 |
| 7 | First Downs — Rushing | 9 |
| 5 | First Downs — Passing | 7 |
| 0 | First Downs — Penalty | 0 |
| 2 | Fumbles — Number | 1 |
| 1 | Fumbles — Lost Ball | 0 |
| 3 | Penalties — Number | 3 |
| 35 | Yards Penalized | 25 |
| 50 | Total Offensive Plays | 66 |
| 253 | Total Net Yards | 228 |
| 5.1 | Average Gain | 3.5 |
| 1 | Missed Field Goals | 1 |
| 2 | Giveaways | 3 |
| 3 | Takeaways | 2 |
| +1 | Difference | −1 |

## INDIVIDUAL STATISTICS

| MIAMI | No | Yds | Avg. | WASHINGTON | No | Yds | Avg. |
|---|---|---|---|---|---|---|---|
| | | | **RUSHING** | | | | |
| Csonka | 15 | 112 | 7.5 | Brown | 22 | 72 | 3.3 |
| Kiick | 12 | 38 | 3.2 | Harraway | 10 | 37 | 3.7 |
| Morris | 10 | 34 | 3.4 | Kilmer | 2 | 18 | 9.0 |
| | 37 | 184 | 5.0 | Taylor | 1 | 8 | 8.0 |
| | | | | Smith | 1 | 6 | 6.0 |
| | | | | | 36 | 141 | 3.9 |
| | | | **RECEIVING** | | | | |
| Warfield | 3 | 36 | 12.0 | Jefferson | 5 | 50 | 10.0 |
| Kiick | 2 | 6 | 3.0 | Brown | 5 | 26 | 5.2 |
| Twilley | 1 | 28 | 28.0 | Taylor | 2 | 20 | 10.0 |
| Mandich | 1 | 19 | 19.0 | Smith | 1 | 11 | 11.0 |
| Csonka | 1 | −1 | −1.0 | Harraway | 1 | −3 | −3.0 |
| | 8 | 88 | 11.0 | | 14 | 104 | 7.4 |
| | | | **PUNTING** | | | | |
| Seiple | 7 | | 43.0 | Bragg | 5 | | 31.2 |
| | | | **PUNT RETURNS** | | | | |
| Scott | 2 | 4 | 2.0 | Haymond | 4 | 9 | 2.3 |
| | | | **KICKOFF RETURNS** | | | | |
| Morris | 2 | 33 | 16.5 | Haymond | 2 | 30 | 15.0 |
| | | | | Mul-Key | 1 | 15 | 15.0 |
| | | | | | 3 | 45 | 15.0 |
| | | | **INTERCEPTION RETURNS** | | | | |
| Scott | 2 | 63 | 31.5 | Owens | 1 | 0 | 0.0 |
| Buoniconti | 1 | 32 | 32.0 | | | | |
| | 3 | 95 | 31.7 | | | | |

### PASSING

| MIAMI | Att | Comp | Comp Pct. | Yds | Int | Yds/Att. | Yds/Comp | Yards Lost Tackled |
|---|---|---|---|---|---|---|---|---|
| Griese | 11 | 8 | 72.7 | 88 | 1 | 8.0 | 11.0 | 2—19 |
| **WASHINGTON** | | | | | | | | |
| Kilmer | 28 | 14 | 50.0 | 104 | 3 | 3.7 | 7.4 | 2—17 |

# 1973 N.F.C. Recession at the Concessions

When Congress passed a bill forbidding television blackouts of games sold out forty-eight hours ahead of time, the NFL reluctantly televised home games for the first time in years. This situation gave birth to a new football term, the "no-show," who was a fan holding a ticket for a sold-out game but instead watched it at home on TV. Ticket sales were not affected by the new ruling, but concession profits fell in the parks on days when unpleasant weather made the television set a much more comfortable way to view the game.

## EASTERN DIVISION

**Dallas Cowboys**—The Cowboys had injuries at several key positions but still made the playoffs. When newly acquired flanker Otto Stowe broke an ankle in mid-season, rookie Drew Pearson stepped into the starting lineup and began grabbing passes in all kinds of situations. A bad back made defensive tackle Bob Lilly's season a miserable one, but middle linebacker Lee Roy Jordan took charge of the defense with his first All-Pro season in an eleven-year pro career. Other added assets for coach Tom Landry were quarterback Roger Staubach's staying healthy for the entire season, Bob Hayes's recovery from an off-season to reclaim his starting wide-receiver job, and tight end Billy Joe DuPree's good rookie season.

**Washington Redskins**—The Over the Hill Gang was far from finished. Coach George Allen added Dave Robinson, Ken Houston, Alvin Reed, and Duane Thomas to his squad through a variety of trades. Robinson and Houston replaced the retired Jack Pardee and Roosevelt Taylor on the defensive unit, while Reed and Thomas gave the Skins all-star depth on offense. Thomas left his personal problems behind him when he reported to the Redskins, working hard to regain his top form of the 1971 season, but the superb running and blocking of backs Larry Brown and Charley Harraway kept Duane on the bench for most of the season. Veteran passing ace Sonny Jurgensen stayed healthy enough to share the quarterback job with Billy Kilmer, and their collective wisdom guided the Redskins attack.

**Philadelphia Eagles**—New head coach Mike McCormack ripped the Eagles apart and started all over again from scratch. To run the offense, he paid a high price to the Rams for Roman Gabriel, a quarterback who was used to winning. Ex-Colt Norm Bulaich and second-year man Tom Sullivan started at running back, tall Harold Carmichael and rookie Don Zimmerman won the wide-receiver jobs, and rookie Charley Young was an instant All-Pro at tight end. Operating behind a line with two fine rookies in Jerry Sisemore and Guy Morriss, Gabriel picked enemy defenses apart with precision passing and sharp play-calling. Coach McCormack had less success in rebuilding the defense. End Mel Tom was traded to Chicago after an argument with an assistant coach, cornerback Nate Ramsey was cut in mid-season, linebacker Ron Porter was traded to Minnesota, and knee injuries kayoed linebacker Steve Zabel and cornerback Al Nelson.

**St. Louis Cardinals**—New head coach Don Coryell succeeded in building a fine passing attack, but injuries and a bad defense held the Cards under .500 for the third straight season. Quarterback Jim Hart won the starting position and developed into a top passer, hitting wide receivers Mel Gray and Ahmad Rashad (previously known as Bobby Moore) with long bombs which had grown infrequent in 1970s pro football. But the St. Louis defense had problems stopping even mediocre attacks, despite a good rookie season from massive end Dave Butz. Late-season injuries crippled both platoons, with Hart and most of the offensive line out for the last few games of the year.

**New York Giants**—A perfect 6-0 record in pre-season play inflated Giant hopes to a vibrating level, but the cruel reality which followed turned the season into a nightmare. After opening with a win and tie in Yankee Stadium, the Giants for all purposes became a road team for the rest of the season. Yankee Stadium was shut for repairs, so the Giants held their practices in Jersey City and played their "home" games in the Yale Bowl in New Haven. The gypsy life disheartened the players, and the team lost seven straight games after leaving the old ball park. Coach Alex Webster announced his resignation before the final game, not a totally unexpected move.

## CENTRAL DIVISION

**Minnesota Vikings**—Fran Tarkenton finally began burying his image as a loser by leading the Vikings into the playoffs with a 12-2 record for the regular season. Aiding Tarkenton considerably was the front four of Carl Eller, Alan Page, Gary Larsen, and Jim Marshall, all of whom stayed healthy and gave the Minnesota defense its old devastating strength. The secondary lost safety Karl Kassulke when he was seriously hurt in a pre-season motorcycle accident, but the quartet of Bobby Bryant, Nate Wright, Paul Krause, and Jeff Wright threw an airtight cover on enemy receivers. The Viking offense had a new weapon in rookie Chuck Foreman, a slashing runner who also caught passes. At wide receiver, John Gilliam made fans forget the traded Gene Washington with his speed and sure hands. The Vikings had always had a defense, but now that they had an offense they outclassed their rivals in the Central Division.

**Detroit Lions**—High hopes for a divisional title flattened out into a disappointing second-place finish and bitter words from the owner and coach. The Lions compiled a 1-4-1 record in their first six games, with a 29-27 loss to Baltimore on October 21 the bitterest pill to swallow. Coach Don McCafferty said, "If we can't beat the Colts, we can't beat anybody." Owner William Clay Ford added, "I don't think they want to win—at least it doesn't look like it." The Lions responded with a 27-0 shutout of the Packers the next week, but a limp 20-0 loss to Washington on Thanksgiving Day brought another public blast from McCafferty. "We stunk out the joint," said the coach. We've got some losers on this ball club and they won't be around next year."

**Green Bay Packers**—The Packer defense had carried the team into the playoffs last year, but the one-dimensional Green Bay offense was too much of a load for the defense to carry this season. John Brockington and MacArthur Lane kept eating up the yardage on the ground, with Brockington gaining 1,000 yard for the third time in his three-year pro career. The Green Bay passing attack, however, was next to nonexistent. Coach Dan Devine gave youngsters Scott Hunter, Jim Del Gaizo, and Jerry Tagge each a shot at the quarterback job, but none of them took the pressure off the runners with a consistent passing game. The offensive line enjoyed its greatest success clearing the way for Brockington and Lane, with guard Gale Gillingham bouncing back from an injury-filled 1972 season to win All-Pro honors.

**Chicago Bears**—Dick Butkus scored the first touchdown of his pro career by falling on a Houston fumble in the end zone on October 28, but a bad knee made it increasingly hard for him to cover pass receivers coming out of the backfield. The problem with the Bears' offense had nothing to do with injuries; quarterback Bobby Douglass was a superior runner but simply could not pass well. Chicago fans singled Douglass out for insults whenever the Bears lost, calling on coach Abe Gibron to stick rookie quarterback Gary Huff into the lineup. Gibron stayed with Douglass until November 18, when he gave Huff his first extended chance. The inexperienced rookie threw four interceptions as the Lions crushed the Bears 30-7; the fans afterward booed Douglass but didn't call for Huff.

## WESTERN DIVISION

**Los Angeles Rams**—Carroll Rosenbloom had given Weeb Ewbank, Don Shula, and Don McCafferty their first head coaching positions while he owned the Colts, and he struck gold again this year with the Rams by hiring Chuck Knox as the head man. Knox led a team supposedly in need of an overhauling to a runaway title in the Western Division and a berth in the playoffs. The Los Angeles passing attack profited from two new faces brought in by Knox. Quarterback John Hadl came over from San Diego and receiver Harold Jackson from Philadelphia in major trades, and both men starred in their new surroundings. Two strong young runners, Larry McCutcheon and Jim Bertelsen, made Hadl's signal-calling task easier, with the excellent offensive line laboring anonymously for both the runners and passers. The defensive unit played up to the standards set by George Allen, although Merlin Olsen was the only starter left from that era. With little expected of them, the Rams won their first six games of the year and ran away from the other teams in the division.

**Atlanta Falcons**—With solid starters at every position except quarterback, the Falcons opened the season with a smashing triumph over the Saints in which Dick Shiner masterfully engineered the Atlanta attack. Shiner soon regressed into the mediocre form he had shown all his career, and coach Norm Van Brocklin next turned to Bob Lee at the position. An ex-Viking with little experience, Lee sparked the Falcons to a 41-0 victory over San Diego and a mid-season winning streak which made the team a prime candidate for the wild-card spot in the playoffs. December, however, brought bad times to the Falcons, as they lost to Buffalo and St. Louis.

**San Francisco '49ers**—Disappointment colored the '49ers season as the team finished a distant third in the West. Fullback Ken Willard publicly expressed his disappointment when benched at the start of the season. Bad knees turned receiver Gene Washington and cornerback Jim Johnson into disappointing performers. Quarterback John Brodie endured the bitterest season of all, finding himself on the bench behind Steve Spurrier and Joe Reed after the team got off to a slow start. The thirty-eight-year-old Brodie announced in mid-season that this would be his last campaign, and coach Dick Nolan gave him the starting nod in the season's finale against the Steelers, but a sore arm sent him out of the game in the first half.

**New Orleans Saints**—John North replaced J. D. Roberts as head coach in training camp, taking over a club that looked like one of the worst in the league. An opening-day trouncing by the Falcons embarrassed the team, but North patiently developed his defense into a good unit. The Saints beat the Bears on October 7 for their first victory, and they won four other games during the season, including an upset of the Washington Redskins. Young veterans Billy Newsome, Joe Owens, Joe Federspiel, Ernie Jackson, and Bivian Lee starred on the improved defensive platoon, while quarterback Archie Manning got some help on offense from end John Beasley, runner Jess Phillips and receiver Jubilee Dunbar, all picked up in trades.

## FINAL TEAM STATISTICS

(Other statistics not available at press time)

### OFFENSE

| | ATL. | CHI. | DALL. | DET. | G.B. | L.A. | MINN. | N.O. | N.Y. | PHIL. | ST.L. | S.F. | WASH. |
|---|---|---|---|---|---|---|---|---|---|---|---|---|---|
| **FIRST DOWNS:** | | | | | | | | | | | | | |
| Total | 240 | 193 | 281 | 237 | 187 | **294** | 246 | 207 | 239 | 267 | 238 | 251 | 232 |
| by Rushing | 123 | 97 | 139 | 122 | 98 | **177** | 135 | 100 | 83 | 103 | 96 | 97 | 76 |
| by Passing | 100 | 77 | 127 | 104 | 72 | 101 | 99 | 88 | 141 | **147** | 111 | 127 | 131 |
| by Penalty | 17 | 19 | 15 | 11 | 17 | 16 | 12 | 19 | 15 | 17 | **31** | 27 | 25 |
| **RUSHING:** | | | | | | | | | | | | | |
| Number | 518 | 496 | 542 | 496 | 527 | **659** | 538 | 497 | 456 | 417 | 416 | 422 | 459 |
| Yards | 2037 | 1907 | 2418 | 2133 | 1973 | **2925** | 2275 | 1842 | 1478 | 1791 | 1671 | 1743 | 1439 |
| Average Yards | 3.9 | 3.8 | **4.5** | 4.3 | 3.7 | 4.4 | 4.2 | 3.7 | 3.2 | 4.3 | 4.0 | 4.1 | 3.1 |
| Touchdowns | **18** | 11 | 17 | 17 | 10 | **18** | 14 | 5 | 11 | 9 | 13 | 15 | 9 |
| **PASSING:** | | | | | | | | | | | | | |
| Attempts | 320 | 303 | 321 | 325 | 255 | 271 | 298 | 338 | 412 | **479** | 394 | 466 | 372 |
| Completions | 168 | 136 | 192 | 171 | 119 | 144 | 179 | 163 | 230 | **275** | 210 | 233 | 209 |
| Completion Percentage | 52.5 | 44.9 | 59.8 | 52.6 | 46.7 | 53.1 | **60.1** | 48.2 | 55.8 | 57.4 | 53.3 | 50.0 | 56.2 |
| Passing Yards | 2362 | 1617 | 2602 | 2105 | 1503 | 2107 | 2234 | 1901 | 2762 | **3236** | 2592 | 2645 | 2560 |
| Avg. Yards per Attempt | 7.4 | 5.3 | **8.1** | 6.4 | 5.9 | 7.8 | 7.5 | 5.6 | 6.7 | 6.8 | 6.6 | 5.7 | 6.9 |
| Avg. Yards per Complet. | 14.1 | 11.9 | 13.6 | 12.3 | 12.6 | **14.6** | 12.5 | 11.7 | 12.0 | 11.8 | 12.3 | 11.4 | 12.2 |
| Times Tackled Passing | 41 | 49 | 43 | 27 | 27 | **17** | 32 | 37 | 28 | 34 | 27 | 27 | 31 |
| Yards Lost Tackled | 361 | 395 | 269 | 192 | 220 | **126** | 278 | 242 | 201 | 238 | 209 | 164 | 202 |
| Net Yards | 2001 | 1222 | 2333 | 1913 | 1283 | 1981 | 1956 | 1659 | 2561 | **2998** | 2383 | 2481 | 2358 |
| Touchdowns | 14 | 8 | **26** | 12 | 7 | 22 | 16 | 11 | 14 | 23 | 16 | 9 | 20 |
| Interceptions | 12 | 16 | 16 | 19 | 17 | 11 | **9** | 17 | 30 | 13 | 15 | 25 | 14 |
| Percent Intercepted | 3.8 | 5.3 | 5.0 | 5.8 | 6.7 | 4.1 | 3.0 | 5.0 | 7.3 | **2.7** | 3.8 | 5.4 | 3.8 |
| **PUNTS:** | | | | | | | | | | | | | |
| Number | 63 | **86** | 59 | 54 | 68 | 51 | 66 | 81 | 68 | 64 | 66 | 79 | 64 |
| Average Distance | 42.6 | 39.8 | 41.5 | 43.2 | 41.0 | 40.8 | 39.8 | 41.7 | 38.8 | 40.9 | 37.5 | **43.7** | 40.3 |
| **PUNT RETURNS:** | | | | | | | | | | | | | |
| Number | 48 | 37 | 28 | 35 | 30 | **51** | 28 | 22 | 21 | 15 | 27 | 37 | 40 |
| Yards | 429 | 204 | 174 | 289 | 137 | **478** | 140 | 218 | 160 | 116 | 192 | 393 | 331 |
| Average Yards | 8.9 | 5.5 | 6.2 | 8.3 | 4.6 | 9.4 | 5.0 | 9.9 | 7.6 | 7.7 | 7.1 | **10.6** | 8.3 |
| Touchdowns | 0 | **1** | 0 | 0 | 0 | 0 | 0 | 0 | 0 | 0 | 0 | 0 | 0 |
| **KICKOFF RETURNS:** | | | | | | | | | | | | | |
| Number | 53 | 59 | 33 | 50 | 53 | 36 | 35 | 47 | 56 | **63** | 58 | **63** | 43 |
| Yards | 1107 | 1344 | 725 | 1061 | 1189 | 915 | 752 | 947 | 1198 | **1441** | 1369 | 1301 | 1118 |
| Average Yards | 20.9 | 22.8 | 22.0 | 21.2 | 22.4 | 25.4 | 21.5 | 20.1 | 21.4 | 22.9 | 23.6 | 20.7 | **26.0** |
| Touchdowns | 0 | **1** | 0 | 0 | 0 | **1** | 0 | 0 | 0 | 0 | **1** | 0 | **1** |
| **INTERCEPTION RETURNS:** | | | | | | | | | | | | | |
| Number | 22 | 14 | 18 | 22 | 15 | 20 | 21 | 16 | 20 | 15 | 10 | 17 | **26** |
| Yards | 528 | 176 | 300 | 522 | 220 | 300 | 263 | 126 | 214 | 120 | 71 | 134 | **598** |
| Average Yards | **24.0** | 12.6 | 16.7 | 23.7 | 14.7 | 15.0 | 12.5 | 7.9 | 10.7 | 8.0 | 7.1 | 7.9 | 23.0 |
| Touchdowns | 2 | 0 | 2 | 1 | 3 | 1 | 2 | 0 | 0 | 1 | 0 | 0 | **4** |
| **PENALTIES:** | | | | | | | | | | | | | |
| Number | 66 | 86 | 83 | 64 | 68 | 54 | 55 | 58 | 67 | 61 | 61 | **93** | 81 |
| Yards | 598 | 817 | 762 | 584 | 653 | 606 | 482 | 516 | 586 | 566 | 594 | **903** | 771 |
| **FUMBLES:** | | | | | | | | | | | | | |
| Number | 40 | 40 | 25 | 30 | 23 | **21** | 29 | 34 | 23 | 41 | 36 | 32 | 32 |
| Number Lost | 21 | 26 | 12 | 14 | 11 | **9** | 17 | 17 | 10 | 15 | 14 | 14 | 18 |
| **POINTS:** | | | | | | | | | | | | | |
| Total | 318 | 195 | 382 | 271 | 202 | **388** | 296 | 163 | 226 | 310 | 286 | 262 | 325 |
| PAT Attempts | 34 | 22 | **46** | 30 | 20 | 42 | 33 | 16 | 25 | 34 | 31 | 26 | 37 |
| PAT Made | 34 | 21 | **45** | 28 | 19 | 40 | 33 | 16 | 25 | 34 | 31 | 26 | 37 |
| FG Attempts | 38 | 24 | 30 | 33 | 35 | **47** | 35 | 36 | 28 | 40 | 32 | 33 | 42 |
| FG Made | 26 | 14 | 19 | 21 | 21 | **30** | 21 | 17 | 17 | 24 | 23 | 26 | 22 |
| Percent FG Made | 68.4 | 58.3 | 63.3 | 63.6 | 60.0 | 63.8 | 60.0 | 47.2 | 60.7 | 60.0 | 71.9 | **78.8** | 52.4 |
| Safeties | 1 | 0 | 2 | 0 | 0 | **3** | 1 | 0 | 0 | 0 | 0 | 1 | 0 |

### DEFENSE

| | ATL. | CHI. | DALL. | DET. | G.B. | L.A. | MINN. | N.O. | N.Y. | PHIL. | ST.L. | S.F. | WASH. |
|---|---|---|---|---|---|---|---|---|---|---|---|---|---|
| **FIRST DOWNS:** | | | | | | | | | | | | | |
| Total | 212 | 247 | 208 | 245 | 230 | **173** | 220 | 271 | 240 | 286 | 307 | 242 | 233 |
| by Rushing | 104 | 138 | 83 | 127 | 114 | **71** | 105 | 131 | 126 | 136 | 135 | 112 | 89 |
| by Passing | 92 | 90 | 106 | 98 | 101 | **87** | 100 | 119 | 94 | 135 | 157 | 115 | 119 |
| by Penalty | 16 | 19 | 19 | 20 | **15** | **15** | **15** | 21 | 20 | **15** | **15** | **15** | 25 |
| **RUSHING:** | | | | | | | | | | | | | |
| Number | 520 | 563 | 435 | 501 | 506 | **366** | 450 | 556 | 497 | 513 | 504 | 513 | 480 |
| Yards | 2129 | 2509 | 1471 | 2117 | 1999 | **1270** | 1974 | 2402 | 2174 | 2423 | 2120 | 1963 | 1603 |
| Average Yards | 4.1 | 4.5 | 3.4 | 4.2 | 4.0 | 3.5 | 4.4 | 4.3 | 4.4 | 4.7 | 4.2 | 3.8 | **3.3** |
| Touchdowns | 12 | 19 | **5** | 10 | 13 | **5** | **5** | 17 | 21 | 22 | 16 | 11 | 8 |
| **PASSING:** | | | | | | | | | | | | | |
| Attempts | 324 | 303 | 352 | 332 | 327 | 328 | 377 | 337 | **275** | 370 | 417 | 383 | **406** |
| Completions | **151** | 156 | 187 | 173 | 180 | 179 | 198 | 176 | 161 | 219 | 252 | 194 | 203 |
| Completion Percentage | **46.6** | 51.5 | 53.1 | 52.1 | 55.0 | 54.6 | 52.5 | 52.2 | 58.5 | 59.2 | 60.4 | 50.7 | 50.0 |
| Passing Yards | **1619** | 1978 | 2301 | 2058 | 2050 | 2023 | 2124 | 2333 | 2252 | 2789 | 3226 | 2591 | 2531 |
| Avg. Yards per Attempt | **5.0** | 6.5 | 6.5 | 6.2 | 6.3 | 6.2 | 5.6 | 6.9 | 8.2 | 7.5 | 7.7 | 6.8 | 6.2 |
| Avg. Yards per Complet. | 10.7 | 12.7 | 12.3 | 11.9 | 11.4 | 11.3 | **10.7** | 13.3 | 14.0 | 12.7 | 12.8 | 13.4 | 12.5 |
| Times Tackled Passing | 29 | 32 | 40 | 33 | 25 | 45 | 30 | 24 | 35 | 21 | 29 | 32 | **53** |
| Yards Lost Tackled | 189 | 304 | 306 | 270 | 228 | 342 | 230 | 155 | 267 | 150 | 197 | 225 | **355** |
| Net Yards | **1430** | 1674 | 1995 | 1788 | 1822 | 1681 | 1894 | 2178 | 1985 | 2639 | 3029 | 2366 | 2176 |
| Touchdowns | 11 | 17 | 15 | 15 | 14 | 10 | **8** | 15 | 17 | 22 | 23 | 19 | 12 |
| Interceptions | 22 | 14 | 18 | 22 | 15 | 20 | 21 | 16 | 20 | 15 | 10 | 17 | **26** |
| Percent Intercepted | 6.8 | 4.6 | 5.1 | 6.6 | 4.6 | 6.1 | 5.6 | 4.7 | **7.3** | 4.1 | 2.4 | 4.4 | 6.4 |
| **PUNTS:** | | | | | | | | | | | | | |
| Number | 80 | 66 | 70 | 65 | 67 | **81** | 57 | 63 | 52 | 49 | 54 | 72 | **81** |
| Average Distance | 42.1 | 40.5 | 39.4 | 41.5 | 38.9 | 40.8 | 41.0 | 44.5 | 40.9 | 39.9 | 41.4 | 41.3 | **38.4** |
| **PUNT RETURNS:** | | | | | | | | | | | | | |
| Number | 30 | 40 | 29 | 30 | 41 | 24 | 41 | 49 | 32 | 35 | 23 | 46 | **14** |
| Yards | 185 | 294 | 152 | 166 | 300 | 261 | 271 | 587 | 379 | 376 | 186 | 367 | **104** |
| Average Yards | 6.1 | 7.4 | **5.2** | 5.5 | 7.3 | 10.9 | 6.5 | 11.9 | 11.8 | 10.8 | 8.1 | 8.0 | 7.4 |
| Touchdowns | **0** | **0** | 1 | **0** | **0** | **0** | 1 | 1 | **0** | **0** | **0** | **0** | **0** |
| **KICKOFF RETURNS:** | | | | | | | | | | | | | |
| Number | 58 | **33** | 53 | 59 | 40 | 68 | 58 | **33** | 43 | 55 | 57 | 52 | 62 |
| Yards | 1369 | 813 | 1320 | 1220 | 817 | 1318 | 1148 | **724** | 988 | 1246 | 1350 | 1151 | 1237 |
| Average Yards | 23.6 | 24.6 | 24.9 | 20.7 | 20.4 | 19.4 | **19.1** | 22.0 | 22.7 | 22.7 | 23.7 | 22.1 | 20.0 |
| Touchdowns | **0** | **0** | **0** | **0** | **0** | **0** | **0** | **0** | **0** | 1 | 1 | 1 | 1 |
| **INTERCEPTION RETURNS:** | | | | | | | | | | | | | |
| Number | 12 | 16 | 16 | 19 | 17 | 11 | **9** | 17 | 30 | 13 | 15 | 25 | 14 |
| Yards | **83** | 335 | 151 | 171 | 256 | 103 | 88 | 280 | 525 | 287 | 267 | 379 | 173 |
| Average Yards | **6.9** | 20.9 | 9.4 | 9.0 | 15.1 | 9.4 | 9.8 | 16.5 | 17.5 | 22.1 | 17.8 | 15.2 | 12.4 |
| Touchdowns | **0** | 1 | 1 | **0** | 1 | 1 | **0** | 3 | 3 | 1 | 2 | 1 | **0** |
| **PENALTIES:** | | | | | | | | | | | | | |
| Number | 58 | 77 | 52 | 68 | 54 | 61 | 58 | 69 | 58 | 73 | **95** | 77 | 86 |
| Yards | 562 | 672 | 516 | 606 | 483 | 566 | 633 | 751 | 484 | 692 | **892** | 754 | 708 |
| **FUMBLES:** | | | | | | | | | | | | | |
| Number | 29 | 35 | **44** | 31 | 34 | 29 | 36 | 32 | 32 | 31 | 31 | 23 | 35 |
| Number Lost | 15 | 19 | **23** | 11 | 18 | 18 | 15 | 14 | 12 | 15 | 17 | 15 | 18 |
| **POINTS:** | | | | | | | | | | | | | |
| Total | 224 | 334 | 203 | 247 | 259 | 178 | **168** | 312 | 362 | 393 | 365 | 319 | 198 |
| PAT Attempts | 24 | 37 | 23 | 26 | 28 | 17 | **15** | 36 | 42 | 47 | 42 | 32 | 21 |
| PAT Made | 23 | 35 | 23 | 25 | 28 | 16 | **15** | 35 | 42 | 45 | 41 | 32 | 21 |
| FG Attempts | 28 | 38 | 30 | 31 | **27** | **27** | 38 | 34 | 30 | 40 | 34 | 45 | 29 |
| FG Made | 19 | 25 | **14** | 22 | 19 | 20 | 21 | 19 | 22 | 22 | 24 | 31 | 17 |
| Percent FG Made | 67.9 | 65.8 | **46.7** | 71.0 | 70.4 | 74.1 | 55.3 | 55.9 | 73.3 | 55.0 | 70.6 | 68.9 | 58.6 |
| Safeties | **0** | 1 | **0** | **0** | 3 | **0** | **0** | 2 | 1 | **0** | **0** | 1 | **0** |

## CONFERENCE PLAYOFFS

### December 22, at Minnesota (Attendance 45,475)

#### SCORING

| | | | | |
|---|---|---|---|---|
| **MINNESOTA** | 0 | 3 | 7 | 17–27 |
| **WASHINGTON** | 0 | 7 | 3 | 10–20 |

Second Quarter
- Minn. Cox, 19 yard field goal
- Wash. Brown, 3 yard rush PAT–Knight (kick)

Third Quarter
- Minn. Brown, 2 yard rush PAT–Cox (kick)
- Wash. Knight, 52 yard field goal

Fourth Quarter
- Wash. Knight, 42 yard field goal
- Minn. Gilliam, 28 yard pass from Tarkenton PAT–Cox (kick)
- Minn. Gilliam, 6 yard pass from Tarkenton PAT–Cox (kick)
- Wash. Jefferson, 28 yard pass from Kilmer PAT–Knight (kick)
- Minn. Cox, 30 yard field goal

#### TEAM STATISTICS

| MINN. | | WASH. |
|---|---|---|
| 17 | First Downs–Total | 18 |
| 6 | First Downs–Rushing | 10 |
| 11 | First Downs–Passing | 7 |
| 0 | First Downs–Penalty | 1 |
| 2 | Fumbles–Number | 2 |
| 2 | Fumbles–Lost Ball | 1 |
| 2 | Penalties–Number | 0 |
| 9 | Yards Penalized | 0 |
| 0 | Missed Field Goals | 2 |
| 63 | Offensive Plays | 66 |
| 359 | Net Yards | 314 |
| 5.7 | Average Gain | 4.8 |
| 3 | Giveaways | 2 |
| 2 | Takeaways | 3 |
| –1 | Difference | +1 |

#### INDIVIDUAL STATISTICS

| MINNESOTA | No. | Yds. | Avg. | WASHINGTON | No. | Yds. | Avg. |
|---|---|---|---|---|---|---|---|
| **RUSHING** | | | | | | | |
| Reed | 17 | 95 | 5.6 | Brown | 29 | 115 | 4.0 |
| Foreman | 11 | 40 | 3.6 | Harraway | 13 | 40 | 3.1 |
| Marinaro | 1 | 3 | 3.0 | | 42 | 155 | 3.7 |
| Brown | 1 | 2 | 2.0 | | | | |
| Tarkenton | 4 | 1 | 0.3 | | | | |
| | 34 | 141 | 4.1 | | | | |
| **RECEIVING** | | | | | | | |
| Reed | 5 | 76 | 15.2 | Jefferson | 6 | 84 | 14.0 |
| Voigt | 3 | 39 | 13.0 | Taylor | 4 | 56 | 14.0 |
| Foreman | 3 | 23 | 7.7 | Brown | 2 | 13 | 6.5 |
| Gilliam | 2 | 36 | 18.0 | Harraway | 1 | 6 | 6.0 |
| Dale | 2 | 31 | 15.5 | | 13 | 159 | 12.2 |
| Lash | 1 | 17 | 17.0 | | | | |
| | 16 | 222 | 13.9 | | | | |
| **PUNTING** | | | | | | | |
| Eischeid | 6 | | 31.9 | Bragg | 4 | | 37.3 |
| **PUNT RETURNS** | | | | | | | |
| Bryant | 2 | 3 | 1.5 | Duncan | 3 | 8 | 2.7 |
| | | | | Mul-Key | 1 | 10 | 10.0 |
| | | | | | 4 | 18 | 4.5 |
| **KICKOFF RETURNS** | | | | | | | |
| Gilliam | 3 | 49 | 16.3 | Mul-Key | 3 | 69 | 23.0 |
| West | 2 | 78 | 39.0 | Brunet | 2 | 35 | 17.5 |
| | 5 | 127 | 25.4 | | 5 | 104 | 20.8 |
| **INTERCEPTION RETURNS** | | | | | | | |
| N. Wright | 1 | 26 | 26.0 | Bass | 1 | 28 | 28.0 |

**PASSING**

| MINNESOTA | Att. | Comp. | Comp. Pct. | Yds. | Int. | Yds/ Att. | Yds/ Comp. | Yards Lost Tackled |
|---|---|---|---|---|---|---|---|---|
| Tarkenton | 28 | 16 | 57.1 | 222 | 1 | 7.9 | 13.9 | 1–4 |
| **WASHINGTON** | | | | | | | | |
| Kilmer | 24 | 13 | 54.2 | 159 | 1 | 6.6 | 12.2 | 0–0 |

### December 23, at Irving, Tex. (Attendance 64,291)

#### SCORING

| | | | | |
|---|---|---|---|---|
| **DALLAS** | 14 | 3 | 0 | 10–27 |
| **LOS ANGELES** | 0 | 6 | 0 | 10–16 |

First Quarter
- Dall. Hill, 3 yard rush PAT–Fritsch (kick)
- Dall. Pearson, 4 yard pass from Staubach PAT–Fritsch (kick)

Second Quarter
- Dall. Fritsch, 39 yard field goal
- L.A. Ray, 33 yard field goal
- L.A. Ray, 37 yard field goal

Fourth Quarter
- L.A. Ray, 40 yard field goal
- L.A. Baker, 5 yard rush PAT–Ray (kick)
- Dall. Pearson, 83 yard pass from Staubach PAT–Fritsch (kick)
- Dall. Fritsch, 12 yard field goal

#### TEAM STATISTICS

| DALL. | | L.A. |
|---|---|---|
| 15 | First Downs–Total | 11 |
| 11 | First Downs–Rushing | 5 |
| 4 | First Downs–Passing | 5 |
| 0 | First Downs–Penalty | 1 |
| 2 | Fumbles–Number | 2 |
| 2 | Fumbles–Lost Ball | 2 |
| 5 | Penalties–Number | 2 |
| 44 | Yards Penalized | 20 |
| 0 | Missed Field Goals | 3 |
| 68 | Offensive Plays | 58 |
| 298 | Net Yards | 192 |
| 4.4 | Average Gain | 3.3 |
| 4 | Giveaways | 3 |
| 3 | Takeaways | 4 |
| –1 | Difference | +1 |

#### INDIVIDUAL STATISTICS

| DALLAS | No. | Yds. | Avg. | LOS ANGELES | No. | Yds. | Avg. |
|---|---|---|---|---|---|---|---|
| **RUSHING** | | | | | | | |
| Hill | 25 | 97 | 3.9 | McCutcheon | 13 | 48 | 3.7 |
| Staubach | 4 | 30 | 7.5 | Bertelsen | 12 | 37 | 3.1 |
| Garrison | 10 | 30 | 3.0 | Hadl | 2 | 10 | 5.0 |
| Newhouse | 6 | 5 | 0.8 | Baker | 1 | 5 | 5.0 |
| | 45 | 162 | 3.6 | Smith | 2 | –7 | –3.5 |
| | | | | | 30 | 93 | 3.1 |
| **RECEIVING** | | | | | | | |
| Pearson | 2 | 87 | 43.5 | Snow | 3 | 77 | 25.7 |
| Hill | 2 | 21 | 10.5 | Smith | 2 | 13 | 6.5 |
| Fuggett | 1 | 38 | 38.0 | Jackson | 1 | 40 | 40.0 |
| Hayes | 1 | 29 | 29.0 | McCutcheon | 1 | 3 | 3.0 |
| Garrison | 1 | 3 | 3.0 | | 7 | 133 | 19.0 |
| DuPree | 1 | 2 | 2.0 | | | | |
| | 8 | 180 | 22.5 | | | | |
| **PUNTING** | | | | | | | |
| Bateman | 7 | | 46.7 | Chapple | 5 | | 43.6 |
| **PUNT RETURNS** | | | | | | | |
| Richards | 2 | 3 | 1.5 | Bertelsen | 4 | 52 | 13.0 |
| | | | | Elmendorf | 1 | 1 | 1.0 |
| | | | | | 5 | 53 | 10.6 |
| **KICKOFF RETURNS** | | | | | | | |
| Waters | 1 | 23 | 23.0 | Scribner | 4 | 106 | 26.5 |
| Harris | 1 | 19 | 19.0 | Clark | 2 | 49 | 24.5 |
| | 2 | 42 | 21.0 | | 6 | 155 | 25.8 |
| **INTERCEPTION RETURNS** | | | | | | | |
| Jordan | 1 | 2 | 2.0 | Reynolds | 1 | 4 | 4.0 |
| | | | | Elmendorf | 1 | 0 | 0.0 |
| | | | | | 2 | 4 | 2.0 |

**PASSING**

| DALLAS | Att. | Comp. | Comp. Pct. | Yds. | Int. | Yds/ Att. | Yds/ Comp. | Yards Lost Tackled |
|---|---|---|---|---|---|---|---|---|
| Staubach | 16 | 8 | 50.0 | 180 | 2 | 11.3 | 22.5 | 7–44 |
| **LOS ANGELES** | | | | | | | | |
| Hadl | 23 | 7 | 30.4 | 133 | 1 | 5.8 | 19.0 | 5–34 |
| McCutcheon | 1 | 0 | 0.0 | 0 | 0 | – | – | 0– 0 |
| | 24 | 7 | 29.2 | 133 | 1 | 5.5 | 19.0 | 5–34 |

## DALLAS COWBOYS 10-4-0 Tom Landry

| Scores of Each Game | | |
|---|---|---|
| 20 | Chicago | 17 |
| 40 | NEW ORLEANS | 3 |
| 45 | ST. LOUIS | 10 |
| 7 | Washington | 14 |
| 31 | Los Angeles | 37 |
| 45 | N. Y. GIANTS | 28 |
| 16 | Philadelphia | 30 |
| 38 | CINCINNATI | 10 |
| 23 | N. Y. Giants | 10 |
| 31 | PHILADELPHIA | 10 |
| 7 | MIAMI | 14 |
| 22 | Denver | 10 |
| 27 | WASHINGTON | 7 |
| 30 | St. Louis | 3 |

| Use Name | Pos. | Hgt | Wgt | Age | Int | Pts |
|---|---|---|---|---|---|---|
| Ralph Neely | OT | 6'5" | 265 | 29 | | |
| Rodney Wallace | OT | 6'5" | 255 | 24 | | |
| Rayfield Wright | OT | 6'7" | 255 | 28 | | |
| John Niland | OG | 6'4" | 245 | 29 | | |
| Blaine Nye | OG | 6'4" | 250 | 27 | | |
| Jim Arneson | C-OG | 6'3" | 236 | 22 | | |
| Bruce Walton | C-OG | 6'6" | 250 | 22 | | |
| John Fitzgerald | C | 6'5" | 250 | 25 | | |
| Dave Manders | C | 6'2" | 250 | 31 | | |
| Larry Cole | DE | 6'4" | 250 | 26 | | |
| Harvey Martin | DE | 6'5" | 262 | 22 | | |
| Pat Toomay | DE | 6'5" | 244 | 28 | 1 | |
| Bill Gregory | DT | 6'5" | 255 | 23 | | |
| Bob Lilly | DT | 6'4" | 260 | 34 | | |
| Jethro Puth | DT | 6'6" | 260 | 29 | | |
| John Babinecz | LB | 6'1" | 222 | 23 | | |
| Rodrigo Barnes | LB | 6'1" | 215 | 23 | | |
| Dave Edwards | LB | 6'3" | 225 | 34 | | |
| Chuck Howley | LB | 6'3" | 225 | 27 | | |
| Lee Roy Jordan | LB | 6'2" | 220 | 32 | 6 | 6 |
| Mike Keller | LB | 6'4" | 220 | 22 | | |
| D. D. Lewis | LB | 6'2" | 225 | 27 | | 6 |
| Benny Barnes | DB | 6'1" | 190 | 22 | 1 | 4 |
| Cornell Green | DB | 6'4" | 208 | 33 | | |
| Cliff Harris | DB | 6' | 184 | 24 | 2 | |
| Mel Renfro | DB | 6' | 190 | 31 | 2 | 6 |
| Mark Washington | DB | 5'10" | 188 | 25 | 1 | |
| Charlie Waters | DB | 6'1" | 193 | 24 | 5 | |
| Craig Morton | QB | 6'4" | 214 | 30 | | |
| Roger Staubach | QB | 6'2" | 197 | 31 | | 18 |
| Cyril Pinder | HB | 6'2" | 210 | 26 | | |
| Les Strayhorn | HB | 5'10" | 205 | 22 | | 6 |
| Calvin Hill | FB-HB | 6'3" | 227 | 26 | | 36 |
| Walt Garrison | FB | 6' | 205 | 29 | | 48 |
| Robert Newhouse | HB-FB | 5'10" | 202 | 23 | | 12 |
| Larry Robinson | HB-FB | 6'4" | 210 | 22 | | |
| Bob Hayes | WR | 6' | 185 | 30 | | 18 |
| Mike Montgomery | WR | 6'2" | 210 | 24 | | 18 |
| Drew Pearson | WR | 6' | 175 | 22 | | 12 |
| Golden Richards | WR | 6' | 172 | 22 | | 6 |
| Otto Stowe | WR | 6'2" | 188 | 24 | | 36 |
| Billy Joe DuPree | TE | 6'4" | 225 | 23 | | 30 |
| Jean Fugett | TE | 6'3" | 220 | 21 | | 18 |
| Billy Truax | TE | 6'5" | 240 | 30 | | |
| Marv Bateman | K | 6'4" | 213 | 23 | | 1 |
| Mike Clark | K | 6'1" | 205 | 32 | | 4 |
| Toni Fritsch | K | 5'7" | 185 | 28 | | 97 |

## WASHINGTON REDSKINS 10-4-0 George Allen

| Scores of Each Game | | |
|---|---|---|
| 38 | SAN DIEGO | 0 |
| 27 | St. Louis | 34 |
| 28 | Philadelphia | 7 |
| 14 | DALLAS | 7 |
| 21 | N. Y. Giants | 3 |
| 31 | ST. LOUIS | 13 |
| 3 | New Orleans | 19 |
| 16 | Pittsburgh | 21 |
| 33 | SAN FRANCISCO | 9 |
| 22 | BALTIMORE | 14 |
| 20 | Detroit | 0 |
| 27 | N. Y. GIANTS | 24 |
| 7 | Dallas | 27 |
| 38 | PHILADELPHIA | 20 |

| Use Name | Pos. | Hgt | Wgt | Age | Int | Pts |
|---|---|---|---|---|---|---|
| Terry Hermeling | OT | 6'5" | 255 | 27 | | |
| Walt Rock | OT | 6'5" | 255 | 32 | | |
| George Starke | OT | 6'5" | 250 | 25 | | |
| Paul Laaveg | OG | 6'4" | 245 | 24 | | |
| Ray Schoenke | OG | 6'3" | 250 | 31 | | |
| John Wilbur | OG | 6'3" | 250 | 30 | | |
| Len Hauss | C | 6'2" | 235 | 31 | | |
| Dan Ryczek | C | 6'3" | 250 | 24 | | |
| Verlon Biggs | DE | 6'4" | 275 | 30 | | 6 |
| Jimmie Jones | DE | 6'3" | 215 | 26 | | |
| Ron McDole | DE | 6'3" | 265 | 33 | | |
| Bill Brundige | DT | 6'5" | 270 | 24 | | |
| Manny Sistrunk | DT | 6'5" | 265 | 26 | | |
| Diron Talbert | DT | 6'5" | 255 | 29 | | |
| Jon Jaqua – Injury | | | | | | |
| Chris Hanburger | LB | 6'2" | 218 | 32 | 1 | |
| Harold McLinton | LB | 6'2" | 235 | 26 | | |
| John Pergine | LB | 6'1" | 225 | 26 | | |
| Myron Pottios | LB | 6'2" | 232 | 33 | | |
| Dave Robinson | LB | 6'3" | 245 | 32 | 4 | 6 |
| Rusty Tillman | LB | 6'2" | 230 | 27 | | |
| Mike Bass | DB | 6' | 190 | 28 | 5 | 6 |
| Speedy Duncan | DB | 5'10" | 180 | 30 | 1 | |
| Pat Fischer | DB | 5'10" | 170 | 33 | 3 | |
| Ken Houston | DB | 6'3" | 198 | 28 | 6 | |
| Brig Owens | DB | 5'11" | 190 | 30 | 5 | 12 |
| Richie Petitbon | DB | 6'3" | 208 | 35 | | |
| Ted Vactor | DB | 6' | 185 | 29 | 1 | 6 |
| Larry Willis | DB | 5'11" | 170 | 24 | | |
| Rosey Taylor – Injury | | | | | | |
| Sonny Jurgensen | QB | 5'11" | 203 | 39 | | |
| Billy Kilmer | QB | 6' | 204 | 33 | | |
| Larry Brown | HB | 5'11" | 195 | 25 | | 84 |
| Bob Brunet | HB | 6'1" | 205 | 27 | | |
| Herb Mul-Key | HB | 6' | 190 | 23 | | 6 |
| Charlie Harraway | FB | 6'2" | 215 | 28 | | 24 |
| Mike Hull | FB | 6'3" | 220 | 28 | | |
| Duane Thomas | HB-FB | 6'1" | 215 | 26 | | |
| Frank Grant | WR | 5'11" | 180 | 23 | | 6 |
| Roy Jefferson | WR | 6'2" | 195 | 29 | | 6 |
| Bill Malinchak | WR | 6'1" | 200 | 29 | | |
| Charlie Taylor | WR | 6'3" | 210 | 32 | | 42 |
| Mike Hancock | TE | 6'4" | 220 | 23 | | 12 |
| Alvin Reed | TE | 6'5" | 235 | 29 | | |
| Jerry Smith | TE | 6'2" | 208 | 30 | | |
| Mike Bragg | K | 5'11" | 186 | 26 | | |
| Curt Knight | K | 6'1" | 190 | 30 | | 103 |

## PHILADELPHIA EAGLES 5-8-1 Mike McCormack

| Scores of Each Game | | |
|---|---|---|
| 23 | ST. LOUIS | 34 |
| 23 | N. Y. Giants | 23 |
| 7 | WASHINGTON | 28 |
| 26 | Buffalo | 27 |
| 27 | St. Louis | 24 |
| 21 | Minnesota | 28 |
| 30 | DALLAS | 16 |
| 24 | NEW ENGLAND | 23 |
| 27 | ATLANTA | 44 |
| 10 | Dallas | 31 |
| 20 | N. Y. GIANTS | 16 |
| 28 | San Francisco | 38 |
| 24 | N. Y. JETS | 23 |
| 20 | Washington | 38 |

| Use Name | Pos. | Hgt | Wgt | Age | Int | Pts |
|---|---|---|---|---|---|---|
| Jerry Sisemore | OT | 6'4" | 260 | 22 | | |
| Steve Smith | OT | 6'5" | 250 | 29 | | |
| Dick Stevens | OT | 6'4" | 240 | 25 | | |
| Wade Key | OG | 6'4" | 245 | 26 | | |
| Roy Kirksey | OG | 6'1" | 265 | 25 | | |
| Tom Luken | OG | 6'3" | 253 | 23 | | |
| Mark Nordquist | OG | 6'4" | 246 | 27 | | |
| Vern Winfield | OG | 6'2" | 248 | 24 | | |
| Mike Evans | C | 6'5" | 250 | 27 | | |
| Guy Morriss | C | 6'4" | 255 | 22 | | |
| Gerry Philbin | DE | 6'2" | 245 | 32 | | |
| Dennis Wirgowski | DE | 6'5" | 250 | 25 | 1 | |
| Will Wynn | DE | 6'4" | 240 | 24 | | 6 |
| Bill Dunstan | DT | 6'4" | 250 | 24 | | |
| Don Hultz | DT | 6'3" | 240 | 32 | | |
| Gary Pettigrew | DT | 6'4" | 255 | 28 | | |
| Richard Harris | DE-DT | 6'4" | 260 | 25 | | |
| John Bunting | LB | 6'1" | 220 | 23 | | |
| Dick Cunningham | LB | 6'2" | 238 | 28 | | |
| Dean Halverson | LB | 6'2" | 225 | 27 | | |
| Marlin McKeever | LB | 6'1" | 235 | 33 | | |
| Kevin Reilly | LB | 6'2" | 220 | 21 | | |
| Tom Roussel | LB | 6'3" | 235 | 28 | | |
| John Sodaski | LB | 6'1" | 222 | 25 | 1 | |
| Steve Zabel | LB | 6'4" | 235 | 25 | 2 | |
| Kermit Alexander | DB | 5'11" | 186 | 32 | | |
| Bill Bradley | DB | 5'11" | 190 | 26 | 4 | |
| Al Coleman | DB | 6'1" | 183 | 28 | | |
| Joe Lavender | DB | 6'4" | 190 | 24 | | |
| Randy Logan | DB | 6'1" | 195 | 22 | 5 | |
| Al Nelson | DB | 5'11" | 186 | 29 | | |
| John Outlaw | DB | 5'10" | 180 | 28 | 2 | 6 |
| Roman Gabriel | QB | 6'4" | 220 | 33 | | 6 |
| John Reaves | QB | 6'3" | 210 | 23 | | |
| Po James | HB | 6'1" | 202 | 24 | | 6 |
| Greg Oliver | HB | 6' | 192 | 24 | | |
| Tom Sullivan | HB | 6' | 190 | 23 | | 30 |
| Tom Bailey | FB-HB | 6'2" | 211 | 24 | | 6 |
| Lee Bouggess | FB | 6'2" | 210 | 25 | | 6 |
| Norm Bulaich | HB-FB | 6'1" | 218 | 26 | | 24 |
| Harold Carmichael | WR | 6'7" | 225 | 23 | | 54 |
| Stan Davis | WR | 5'10" | 180 | 23 | | |
| Ben Hawkins | WR | 6' | 180 | 29 | | |
| Bob Picard | WR | 6'1" | 195 | 23 | | |
| Don Zimmerman | WR | 6'3" | 195 | 23 | | 18 |
| Kent Kramer | TE | 6'5" | 235 | 29 | | |
| Charlie Young | TE | 6'4" | 230 | 22 | | 42 |
| Tom Dempsey | K | 6'1" | 255 | 32 | | 106 |
| Tom McNeill | K | 6'1" | 195 | 31 | | |

## ST. LOUIS CARDINALS 4-9-1 Don Coryell

| Scores of Each Game | | |
|---|---|---|
| 34 | Philadelphia | 23 |
| 34 | WASHINGTON | 27 |
| 10 | Dallas | 45 |
| 10 | OAKLAND | 17 |
| 24 | PHILADELPHIA | 27 |
| 13 | Washington | 31 |
| 35 | N. Y. GIANTS | 27 |
| 17 | DENVER | 17 |
| 21 | Green Bay | 25 |
| 13 | N. Y. Giants | 24 |
| 24 | Cincinnati | 42 |
| 16 | DETROIT | 20 |
| 32 | Atlanta | 10 |
| 3 | DALLAS | 30 |

| Use Name | Pos. | Hgt | Wgt | Age | Int | Pts |
|---|---|---|---|---|---|---|
| Dan Dierdorf | OT | 6'4" | 265 | 24 | | |
| Ernie McMillan | OT | 6'6" | 255 | 35 | | |
| Mike Taylor | OT | 6'4" | 255 | 28 | | |
| Tom Banks | OG | 6'1" | 240 | 25 | | |
| Ron Davis | OG | 6'2" | 235 | 22 | | |
| Conrad Dobler | OG | 6'3" | 250 | 22 | | |
| Roger Finnie | OG | 6'3" | 245 | 27 | | |
| Bob Young | OG | 6'2" | 260 | 30 | | |
| Tom Brahaney | C | 6'2" | 225 | 21 | | |
| Warren Koegel | C | 6'3" | 250 | 23 | | |
| Wayne Mulligan | C | 6'2" | 245 | 26 | | |
| Council Rudolph | DE | 6'3" | 260 | 23 | | |
| Ron Yankowski | DE | 6'5" | 240 | 26 | | |
| Dave Butz | DT-DE | 6'7" | 290 | 23 | | |
| Lee Brooks | DT | 6'5" | 265 | 25 | | |
| John Richardson | DT | 6'2" | 250 | 27 | | |
| Bob Rowe | DT | 6'4" | 260 | 28 | | |
| Bonnie Sloan | DT | 6'5" | 260 | 24 | | |
| Mark Arneson | LB | 6'2" | 220 | 23 | 1 | |
| Pete Barnes | LB | 6'3" | 240 | 28 | 1 | |
| Jack LeVeck | LB | 6' | 225 | 23 | | |
| Terry Miller | LB | 6'2" | 225 | 27 | | |
| Jamie Rivers | LB | 6'2" | 235 | 27 | 1 | |
| Jeff Staggs | LB | 6'2" | 240 | 29 | | |
| Larry Stallings | LB | 6'2" | 230 | 31 | 1 | |
| Dwayne Crump | DB | 5'11" | 180 | 23 | | |
| Chuck Detwiler | DB | 6' | 185 | 26 | 1 | |
| Clarence Duren | DB | 6'1" | 190 | 22 | 2 | |
| Norm Thompson | DB | 6'1" | 175 | 25 | | |
| Jim Tolbert | DB | 6'3" | 202 | 29 | 2 | |
| Eric Washington | DB | 6'2" | 190 | 23 | | |
| Roger Wehrli | DB | 6'1" | 195 | 25 | 1 | |
| Leon Burns – Injury | | | | | | |
| Jim Hart | QB | 6'2" | 215 | 29 | | |
| Gary Keithley | QB | 6'3" | 205 | 22 | | |
| Donny Anderson | HB | 6'3" | 210 | 30 | | 78 |
| Willie Belton | HB | 5'11" | 195 | 24 | | |
| Terry Metcalf | HB | 5'10" | 185 | 21 | | 12 |
| Eddie Moss | FB | 6' | 215 | 24 | | |
| Jim Otis | FB | 6' | 220 | 25 | | 6 |
| Leo Hayden | HB-FB | 6' | 210 | 25 | | |
| Don Shy | HB-FB | 6'1" | 210 | 27 | | 12 |
| Walker Gillette | WR | 6'5" | 200 | 26 | | 6 |
| Mel Gray | WR | 5'9" | 170 | 24 | | 42 |
| Don Maynard | WR | 6' | 180 | 37 | | |
| Marv Owens | WR | 5'11" | 205 | 23 | | |
| Ahmad Rashad | WR | 6'2" | 210 | 23 | | 18 |
| Gary Hammond | HB-WR | 5'11" | 180 | 24 | | |
| Jim McFarland | TE | 6'5" | 225 | 25 | | 6 |
| Jackie Smith | TE | 6'4" | 235 | 32 | | 6 |
| Jim Bakken | K | 6' | 200 | 32 | | 100 |

## NEW YORK GIANTS 2-11-1 Alex Webster

| Scores of Each Game | | |
|---|---|---|
| 34 | HOUSTON | 14 |
| 23 | PHILADELPHIA | 23 |
| 10 | Cleveland | 12 |
| 14 | GREEN BAY | 16 |
| 3 | WASHINGTON | 21 |
| 28 | Dallas | 45 |
| 27 | St. Louis | 35 |
| 0 | Oakland | 42 |
| 10 | DALLAS | 23 |
| 24 | St. LOUIS | 13 |
| 16 | Philadelphia | 20 |
| 24 | Washington | 27 |
| 6 | Los Angeles | 40 |
| 7 | MINNESOTA | 31 |

| Use Name | Pos. | Hgt | Wgt | Age | Int | Pts |
|---|---|---|---|---|---|---|
| Bart Buetow | OT | 6'5" | 250 | 22 | | |
| John Hill | OT | 6'2" | 245 | 23 | | |
| Joe Taffoni | OT | 6'3" | 255 | 28 | | |
| Willie Young | OT | 6' | 265 | 30 | | |
| Mark Ellison | OG | 6'2" | 250 | 24 | | |
| Dick Enderle | OG | 6'1" | 250 | 25 | | |
| Doug Van Horn | OG | 6'2" | 245 | 29 | | |
| Bob Hyland | OT-C | 6'5" | 255 | 28 | | |
| Greg Larson | C | 6'2" | 250 | 34 | | |
| Carter Campbell | DE | 6'3" | 240 | 25 | | |
| Jack Gregory | DE | 6'6" | 250 | 28 | | |
| Dave Tipton | DE | 6'6" | 240 | 24 | | |
| Rich Glover | DT | 6'1" | 240 | 22 | | |
| Dan Goich | DT | 6'4" | 250 | 29 | | |
| Larry Jacobson | DT | 6'6" | 260 | 23 | | |
| John Mendenhall | DT | 6'1" | 255 | 24 | | |
| John Douglas | LB | 6'2" | 228 | 28 | 1 | |
| Jim Files | LB | 6'4" | 240 | 25 | 1 | |
| Ron Hornsby | LB | 6'3" | 232 | 24 | | |
| Pat Hughes | LB | 6'2" | 240 | 26 | 3 | |
| Brian Kelley | LB | 6'3" | 222 | 22 | | |
| Henry Reed | LB | 6'3" | 230 | 24 | 1 | |
| Brad Van Pelt | LB | 6'5" | 235 | 22 | | |
| Pete Athas | DB | 5'11" | 185 | 27 | 5 | |
| Otto Brown | DB | 6'1" | 188 | 25 | | |
| Chuck Crist | DB | 6'2" | 205 | 22 | 2 | |
| Richmond Flowers | DB | 6' | 180 | 26 | 1 | |
| Spider Lockhart | DB | 6'2" | 175 | 30 | 2 | |
| Ron Lumpkin | DB | 6'2" | 200 | 22 | | |
| Eldridge Small | DB | 6'1" | 190 | 23 | | |
| Willie Williams | DB | 6' | 190 | 30 | 4 | |
| Randy Johnson | QB | 6'3" | 205 | 29 | | 6 |
| Norm Snead | QB | 6'4" | 215 | 33 | | |
| Ron Johnson | HB | 6'1" | 205 | 25 | | 54 |
| Jack Rizzo | HB | 5'10" | 195 | 24 | | |
| Rocky Thompson | HB | 5'11" | 200 | 25 | | |
| Joe Orduna | FB-HB | 6' | 195 | 25 | | 6 |
| Vin Clements | FB | 6'3" | 215 | 24 | | 12 |
| Charlie Evans | FB | 6'1" | 220 | 25 | | 6 |
| Johnny Roland | HB-FB | 6'2" | 220 | 30 | | 12 |
| Bob Grim | WR | 6' | 200 | 28 | | 12 |
| Don Herrmann | WR | 6'2" | 205 | 26 | | 12 |
| Rich Houston | WR | 6'2" | 195 | 27 | | |
| Walt Love | WR | 5'9" | 180 | 22 | | |
| Gary Ballman (to MIN) | TE | 6' | 215 | 33 | | |
| Tom Gatewood | TE | 6'3" | 215 | 22 | | |
| Bob Tucker | TE | 6'3" | 230 | 28 | | 30 |
| Tom Blanchard | K | 6' | 190 | 25 | | |
| Pete Gogolak | K | 6'2" | 190 | 31 | | 76 |
| Jim McCann | K | 6'2" | 163 | 24 | | |

## DALLAS COWBOYS

### RUSHING

| Last Name | No. | Yds | Avg | TD |
|---|---|---|---|---|
| Hill | 273 | 1142 | 4.2 | 6 |
| Garrison | 105 | 440 | 4.2 | 6 |
| Newhouse | 84 | 436 | 5.2 | 0 |
| Staubach | 46 | 250 | 5.4 | 3 |
| Strayhorn | 11 | 62 | 5.6 | 1 |
| Fugett | 1 | 34 | 34.0 | 0 |
| Stowe | 3 | 28 | 9.3 | 0 |
| Robinson | 2 | 17 | 8.5 | 0 |
| Pinder | 12 | 15 | 1.3 | 0 |
| Richards | 1 | 2 | 2.0 | 0 |
| DuPree | 2 | 2 | 1.0 | 0 |
| Morton | 2 | 0 | 0.0 | 0 |
| Montgomery | 1 | −10 | −10.0 | 0 |

### RECEIVING

| Last Name | No. | Yds | Avg | TD |
|---|---|---|---|---|
| Hill | 32 | 290 | 9 | 0 |
| DuPree | 29 | 392 | 14 | 5 |
| Garrison | 26 | 273 | 11 | 2 |
| Stowe | 23 | 389 | 17 | 6 |
| Pearson | 22 | 388 | 18 | 2 |
| Hayes | 22 | 360 | 16 | 3 |
| Montgomery | 14 | 164 | 12 | 3 |
| Fugett | 9 | 168 | 19 | 3 |
| Newhouse | 9 | 87 | 10 | 1 |
| Richards | 6 | 91 | 15 | 1 |

### PUNT RETURNS

| Last Name | No. | Yds | Avg | TD |
|---|---|---|---|---|
| Richards | 21 | 139 | 7 | 0 |
| Harris | 3 | 20 | 7 | 0 |
| Pearson | 2 | 13 | 7 | 0 |
| Montgomery | 2 | 2 | 1 | 0 |

### KICKOFF RETURNS

| Last Name | No. | Yds | Avg | TD |
|---|---|---|---|---|
| Montgomery | 6 | 175 | 29 | 0 |
| Pearson | 7 | 155 | 22 | 0 |
| Harris | 6 | 148 | 25 | 0 |
| Robinson | 4 | 86 | 22 | 0 |
| Newhouse | 3 | 62 | 21 | 0 |
| Richards | 3 | 44 | 15 | 0 |
| Strayhorn | 2 | 44 | 22 | 0 |
| Walton | 1 | 11 | 11 | 0 |
| Washington | 1 | 0 | 0 | 0 |

### PASSING – PUNTING – KICKING

| PASSING | Att | Comp | % | Yds | Yd/Att | TD | Int-% | RK |
|---|---|---|---|---|---|---|---|---|
| Staubach | 286 | 179 | 63 | 2428 | 8.5 | 23 | 15− 5 | 2 |
| Morton | 32 | 13 | 41 | 174 | 5.4 | 3 | 1− 3 | |
| Garrison | 1 | 0 | 0 | 0.0 | | 0 | 0− 0 | |
| Hill | 1 | 0 | 0 | 0.0 | | 0 | 0− 0 | |
| Montgomery | 1 | 0 | 0 | 0.0 | | 0 | 0− 0 | |

| PUNTING | No | Avg |
|---|---|---|
| Bateman | 55 | 41.6 |
| Montgomery | 4 | 39.5 |

| KICKING | XP | Att | % | FG | Att | % |
|---|---|---|---|---|---|---|
| Fritsch | 43 | 43 | 100 | 18 | 28 | 64 |
| Clark | 1 | 2 | 50 | 1 | 2 | 50 |
| Bateman | 1 | 1 | 100 | 0 | 0 | 0 |

## WASHINGTON REDSKINS

### RUSHING

| Last Name | No. | Yds | Avg | TD |
|---|---|---|---|---|
| Brown | 273 | 860 | 3.2 | 8 |
| Harraway | 128 | 452 | 3.5 | 1 |
| Thomas | 32 | 95 | 3.0 | 0 |
| Mul-Key | 8 | 20 | 2.5 | 0 |
| Kilmer | 9 | 10 | 1.1 | 0 |
| Jurgensen | 3 | 7 | 2.3 | 0 |
| Brunet | 2 | 4 | 2.0 | 0 |
| Jefferson | 1 | 1 | 1.0 | 0 |
| Hull | 2 | −3 | −1.5 | 0 |
| C. Taylor | 1 | −7 | −7.0 | 0 |

### RECEIVING

| Last Name | No. | Yds | Avg | TD |
|---|---|---|---|---|
| C. Taylor | 59 | 801 | 14 | 7 |
| Jefferson | 41 | 595 | 15 | 1 |
| Brown | 40 | 482 | 12 | 6 |
| Harraway | 32 | 291 | 9 | 3 |
| Smith | 19 | 215 | 11 | 0 |
| Reed | 9 | 124 | 14 | 0 |
| Thomas | 5 | 40 | 8 | 0 |
| Hancock | 2 | 3 | 2 | 2 |
| Grant | 1 | 12 | 12 | 1 |
| Jurgensen | 1 | −3 | −3 | 0 |

### PUNT RETURNS

| Last Name | No. | Yds | Avg | TD |
|---|---|---|---|---|
| Duncan | 28 | 228 | 8 | 0 |
| Mul-Key | 11 | 103 | 9 | 0 |
| Smith | 1 | 0 | 0 | 0 |

### KICKOFF RETURNS

| Last Name | No. | Yds | Avg | TD |
|---|---|---|---|---|
| Mul-Key | 36 | 1011 | 28 | 1 |
| Duncan | 4 | 65 | 16 | 0 |
| Tillman | 3 | 42 | 14 | 0 |

### PASSING – PUNTING – KICKING

| PASSING | Att | Comp | % | Yds | Yd/Att | TD | Int-% | RK |
|---|---|---|---|---|---|---|---|---|
| Kilmer | 227 | 122 | 54 | 1656 | 7.3 | 14 | 9− 4 | 6 |
| Jurgensen | 145 | 87 | 60 | 904 | 6.2 | 6 | 5− 3 | |

| PUNTING | No | Avg |
|---|---|---|
| Bragg | 64 | 40.3 |

| KICKING | XP | Att | % | FG | Att | % |
|---|---|---|---|---|---|---|
| Knight | 37 | 37 | 100 | 22 | 42 | 52 |

## PHILADELPHIA EAGLES

### RUSHING

| Last Name | No. | Yds | Avg | TD |
|---|---|---|---|---|
| Sullivan | 217 | 968 | 4.5 | 4 |
| Bulaich | 106 | 436 | 4.1 | 1 |
| James | 36 | 178 | 4.9 | 0 |
| Bailey | 20 | 91 | 4.6 | 0 |
| Carmichael | 3 | 42 | 14.0 | 0 |
| Bouggess | 15 | 34 | 2.3 | 0 |
| Young | 4 | 24 | 6.0 | 1 |
| Gabriel | 12 | 10 | 0.8 | 1 |
| Oliver | 1 | 6 | 6.0 | 0 |
| Reaves | 2 | 2 | 1.0 | 0 |
| Bradley | 1 | 0 | 0.0 | 0 |

### RECEIVING

| Last Name | No. | Yds | Avg | TD |
|---|---|---|---|---|
| Carmichael | 67 | 1116 | 17 | 9 |
| Young | 55 | 854 | 16 | 6 |
| Sullivan | 50 | 322 | 6 | 1 |
| Bulaich | 42 | 403 | 10 | 3 |
| Zimmerman | 22 | 220 | 10 | 3 |
| James | 17 | 94 | 6 | 0 |
| Bailey | 10 | 80 | 8 | 1 |
| Hawkins | 6 | 114 | 19 | 0 |
| Bouggess | 4 | 18 | 5 | 0 |
| Oliver | 1 | 9 | 9 | 0 |
| Davis | 1 | 6 | 6 | 0 |

### PUNT RETURNS

| Last Name | No. | Yds | Avg | TD |
|---|---|---|---|---|
| Bradley | 8 | 106 | 13 | 0 |
| Alexander | 5 | 10 | 2 | 0 |
| Davis | 2 | 0 | 0 | 0 |

### KICKOFF RETURNS

| Last Name | No. | Yds | Avg | TD |
|---|---|---|---|---|
| James | 16 | 413 | 26 | 0 |
| Sullivan | 12 | 280 | 23 | 0 |
| Nelson | 11 | 264 | 24 | 0 |
| Davis | 10 | 236 | 24 | 0 |
| Alexander | 9 | 189 | 21 | 0 |
| Coleman | 2 | 24 | 12 | 0 |
| Bailey | 2 | 18 | 9 | 0 |
| Oliver | 1 | 17 | 17 | 0 |

### PASSING – PUNTING – KICKING

| PASSING | Att | Comp | % | Yds | Yd/Att | TD | Int-% | RK |
|---|---|---|---|---|---|---|---|---|
| Gabriel | 460 | 270 | 59 | 3219 | 7.0 | 23 | 12− 3 | 1 |
| Reaves | 19 | 5 | 26 | 17 | 0.9 | 0 | 1− 5 | |

| PUNTING | No | Avg |
|---|---|---|
| McNeill | 46 | 40.9 |
| Bradley | 18 | 40.8 |

| KICKING | XP | Att | % | FG | Att | % |
|---|---|---|---|---|---|---|
| Dempsey | 34 | 34 | 100 | 24 | 40 | 60 |

## ST. LOUIS CARDINALS

### RUSHING

| Last Name | No. | Yds | Avg | TD |
|---|---|---|---|---|
| Anderson | 167 | 679 | 4.1 | 10 |
| Metcalf | 148 | 628 | 4.2 | 2 |
| Otis | 55 | 234 | 4.3 | 1 |
| Shy | 16 | 66 | 4.1 | 0 |
| Moss | 14 | 41 | 2.9 | 0 |
| Keithley | 8 | 29 | 3.6 | 0 |
| Hammond | 4 | 11 | 2.8 | 0 |
| Hart | 3 | −3 | −1.0 | 0 |
| Smith | 1 | −14 | −14.0 | 0 |

### RECEIVING

| Last Name | No. | Yds | Avg | TD |
|---|---|---|---|---|
| Smith | 41 | 600 | 15 | 1 |
| Anderson | 41 | 409 | 10 | 3 |
| Metcalf | 37 | 316 | 9 | 0 |
| Rashad | 30 | 409 | 14 | 3 |
| Gray | 29 | 513 | 18 | 7 |
| Gillette | 20 | 244 | 12 | 1 |
| Hammond | 4 | 39 | 10 | 0 |
| Shy | 3 | 15 | 5 | 1 |
| Otis | 2 | 19 | 10 | 0 |
| McFarland | 2 | 10 | 5 | 0 |
| Maynard | 1 | 18 | 18 | 0 |

### PUNT RETURNS

| Last Name | No. | Yds | Avg | TD |
|---|---|---|---|---|
| Wehrli | 9 | 92 | 10 | 0 |
| Hammond | 11 | 80 | 7 | 0 |
| Thompson | 6 | 18 | 3 | 0 |
| Belton | 1 | 2 | 2 | 0 |

### KICKOFF RETURNS

| Last Name | No. | Yds | Avg | TD |
|---|---|---|---|---|
| Shy | 16 | 445 | 28 | 1 |
| Hammond | 12 | 314 | 26 | 0 |
| Metcalf | 4 | 124 | 31 | 0 |
| Hayden | 5 | 98 | 20 | 0 |
| Belton | 3 | 83 | 28 | 0 |
| Moss | 4 | 78 | 20 | 0 |
| Gray | 4 | 73 | 18 | 0 |
| McFarland | 3 | 57 | 19 | 0 |
| Detwiler | 3 | 55 | 18 | 0 |
| Butz | 1 | 23 | 23 | 0 |
| Owens | 1 | 19 | 19 | 0 |
| Wehrli | 2 | 0 | 0 | 0 |

### PASSING – PUNTING – KICKING

| PASSING | Att | Comp | % | Yds | Yd/Att | TD | Int-% | RK |
|---|---|---|---|---|---|---|---|---|
| Hart | 320 | 178 | 56 | 2223 | 7.0 | 15 | 10− 3 | 4 |
| Keithley | 73 | 32 | 44 | 369 | 5.1 | 1 | 5− 7 | |
| Hammond | 1 | 0 | 0 | 0.0 | | 0 | 0− 0 | |

| PUNTING | No | Avg |
|---|---|---|
| Keithley | 66 | 37.5 |

| KICKING | XP | Att | % | FG | Att | % |
|---|---|---|---|---|---|---|
| Bakken | 31 | 31 | 100 | 23 | 32 | 72 |

## NEW YORK GIANTS

### RUSHING

| Last Name | No. | Yds | Avg | TD |
|---|---|---|---|---|
| Ron Johnson | 260 | 902 | 3.5 | 6 |
| Clements | 57 | 214 | 3.8 | 1 |
| Roland | 53 | 142 | 2.7 | 1 |
| Orduna | 36 | 104 | 2.9 | 1 |
| Evans | 34 | 77 | 2.3 | 1 |
| Randy Johnson | 4 | 24 | 6.0 | 1 |
| Snead | 4 | 13 | 3.3 | 0 |
| Thompson | 5 | 5 | 1.0 | 0 |
| Tucker | 1 | 4 | 4.0 | 0 |
| Rizzo | 1 | 3 | 3.0 | 0 |
| Grim | 1 | −10 | −10.0 | 0 |

### RECEIVING

| Last Name | No. | Yds | Avg | TD |
|---|---|---|---|---|
| Tucker | 50 | 681 | 14 | 5 |
| Herrmann | 43 | 520 | 12 | 2 |
| Grim | 37 | 593 | 16 | 2 |
| Ron Johnson | 32 | 377 | 12 | 3 |
| Roland | 22 | 190 | 9 | 1 |
| Clements | 15 | 129 | 9 | 1 |
| Evans | 13 | 100 | 8 | 0 |
| Houston | 8 | 90 | 11 | 0 |
| Orduna | 6 | 44 | 7 | 0 |
| Ballman | 3 | 38 | 13 | 0 |
| Hyland | 1 | 16 | 16 | 0 |
| Rizzo | 1 | 11 | 11 | 0 |
| Young | 1 | −5 | −5 | 0 |

### PUNT RETURNS

| Last Name | No. | Yds | Avg | TD |
|---|---|---|---|---|
| Athas | 20 | 153 | 8 | 0 |
| Crist | 1 | 7 | 7 | 0 |

### KICKOFF RETURNS

| Last Name | No. | Yds | Avg | TD |
|---|---|---|---|---|
| Love | 18 | 396 | 22 | 0 |
| Houston | 15 | 375 | 25 | 0 |
| Small | 11 | 207 | 19 | 0 |
| Orduna | 6 | 104 | 17 | 0 |
| Rizzo | 4 | 86 | 22 | 0 |
| Kelley | 2 | 30 | 15 | 0 |

### PASSING – PUNTING – KICKING

| PASSING | Att | Comp | % | Yds | Yd/Att | TD | Int-% | RK |
|---|---|---|---|---|---|---|---|---|
| Snead | 235 | 131 | 56 | 1483 | 6.3 | 7 | 22− 9 | 11 |
| Ran. Johnson | 177 | 99 | 56 | 1279 | 7.2 | 7 | 8− 5 | |

| PUNTING | No | Avg |
|---|---|---|
| Blanchard | 56 | 41.9 |
| McCann | 12 | 24.5 |

| KICKING | XP | Att | % | FG | Att | % |
|---|---|---|---|---|---|---|
| Gogolak | 25 | 25 | 100 | 17 | 28 | 61 |

## MINNESOTA VIKINGS 12-2-0 Bud Grant

Scores of Each Game:

| | | |
|---|---|---|
| 24 | OAKLAND | 16 |
| 22 | Chicago | 13 |
| 11 | GREEN BAY | 3 |
| 23 | Detroit | 9 |
| 17 | San Francisco | 13 |
| 28 | PHILADELPHIA | 21 |
| 10 | LOS ANGELES | 9 |
| 26 | CLEVELAND | 3 |
| 28 | DETROIT | 7 |
| 14 | Atlanta | 20 |
| 31 | CHICAGO | 13 |
| 0 | Cincinnati | 27 |
| 31 | Green Bay | 7 |
| 31 | N. Y. Giants | 7 |

| Use Name | Pos. | Hgt | Wgt | Age | Int | Pts |
|---|---|---|---|---|---|---|
| Grady Alderman | OT | 6'2" | 247 | 34 | | |
| Ron Yary | OT | 6'6" | 255 | 27 | | |
| Charlie Goodrum | OG-OT | 6'3" | 256 | 23 | | |
| Frank Gallagher (from ATL) | OG | 6'2" | 245 | 30 | | |
| Steve Lawson | OG | 6'3" | 265 | 24 | | |
| Milt Sunde | OG | 6'2" | 250 | 30 | | |
| John Ward | OG | 6'4" | 260 | 25 | | |
| Ed White | OG | 6'2" | 262 | 26 | | |
| Mick Tingelhoff | C | 6'1" | 237 | 33 | | |
| Godfrey Zaunbrecher | C | 6'2" | 240 | 25 | | |
| Carl Eller | DE | 6'6" | 247 | 31 | | |
| Jim Marshall | DE | 6'3" | 248 | 35 | | |
| Bob Lurtsema | DT-DE | 6'6" | 250 | 31 | | |
| Gary Larsen | DT | 6'5" | 260 | 33 | | |
| Alan Page | DT | 6'5" | 245 | 28 | | |
| Doug Sutherland | DT | 6'3" | 250 | 25 | | |
| Wally Hilgenberg | LB | 6'3" | 230 | 30 | 1 | 6 |
| Amos Martin | LB | 6'3" | 228 | 24 | | |
| Ron Porter | LB | 6'3" | 232 | 28 | | |
| Jeff Siemon | LB | 6'2" | 230 | 23 | 2 | |
| Roy Winston | LB | 6'1" | 222 | 33 | | 2 |
| Terry Brown | DB | 6'1" | 205 | 26 | 1 | 6 |
| Bobby Bryant | DB | 6' | 170 | 29 | 7 | 6 |
| Paul Krause | DB | 6'3" | 200 | 31 | 4 | |
| Al Randolph | DB | 6'2" | 205 | 29 | | |
| Charlie West | DB | 6'1" | 197 | 27 | | |
| Jeff Wright | DB | 5'11" | 190 | 24 | 3 | |
| Nate Wright | DB | 5'11" | 180 | 25 | 3 | |
| Bob Berry | QB | 5'11" | 185 | 31 | | |
| Fran Tarkenton | QB | 6'1" | 190 | 33 | | 6 |
| Brent McClanahan | HB | 5'10" | 202 | 22 | | |
| Dave Osborn | HB | 6' | 208 | 30 | | |
| Chuck Foreman | FB-HB | 6'2" | 216 | 22 | | 36 |
| Bill Brown | FB | 5'11" | 222 | 35 | | 24 |
| Ed Marinaro | HB-FB | 6'2" | 212 | 23 | | 24 |
| Oscar Reed | HB-FB | 5'11" | 222 | 29 | | 18 |
| Carroll Dale | WR | 6'1" | 200 | 35 | | |
| Rhett Dawson | WR | 6'1" | 185 | 24 | | |
| John Gilliam | WR | 6'1" | 195 | 28 | | 54 |
| Jim Lash | WR | 6'2" | 200 | 21 | | |
| Doug Kingswriter | TE | 6'2" | 222 | 23 | | |
| Stu Voigt | TE | 6'1" | 220 | 25 | | 12 |
| Fred Cox | K | 5'10" | 200 | 34 | | 96 |
| Mike Eischeid | K | 6' | 190 | 32 | | |

Karl Kassulke — Paralyzed in motorcycle accident

## DETROIT LIONS 6-7-1 Don McCafferty

Scores of Each Game:

| | | |
|---|---|---|
| 10 | Pittsburgh | 24 |
| 13 | Green Bay | 13 |
| 31 | ATLANTA | 6 |
| 9 | MINNESOTA | 23 |
| 13 | New Orleans | 20 |
| 27 | BALTIMORE | 29 |
| 34 | GREEN BAY | 0 |
| 30 | SAN FRANCISCO | 20 |
| 7 | Minnesota | 28 |
| 30 | Chicago | 7 |
| 0 | WASHINGTON | 20 |
| 20 | St. Louis | 16 |
| 40 | CHICAGO | 7 |
| 7 | Miami | 34 |

| Use Name | Pos. | Hgt | Wgt | Age | Int | Pts |
|---|---|---|---|---|---|---|
| Rocky Freitas | OT | 6'6" | 270 | 27 | | |
| Mike Haggerty | OT | 6'4" | 245 | 27 | | |
| Gordon Jolley | OT | 6'5" | 250 | 24 | | |
| Jim Yarbrough | OT | 6'6" | 265 | 26 | | |
| Guy Dennis | OG | 6'2" | 255 | 26 | | |
| Bob Kowalkowski | OG | 6'3" | 240 | 29 | | |
| Rocky Rasley | OG | 6'3" | 250 | 26 | | |
| Chuck Walton | OG | 6'3" | 255 | 32 | | |
| Ed Flanagan | C | 6'3" | 245 | 29 | | |
| Dave Thompson | OG-C | 6'4" | 275 | 24 | | |
| Larry Hand | DE | 6'4" | 250 | 33 | | |
| Jim Mitchell | DE | 6'3" | 245 | 24 | | |
| Ken Sanders | DE | 6'5" | 240 | 23 | | |
| Bob Bell | DT | 6'4" | 250 | 25 | | |
| Herb Orvis | DT | 6'5" | 240 | 26 | | |
| Ernie Price | DT | 6'4" | 255 | 22 | | |
| John Small | DT | 6'5" | 260 | 26 | | |
| Mike Hennigan | LB | 6'2" | 210 | 21 | | |
| Jim Laslavic | LB | 6'2" | 230 | 21 | | |
| Mike Lucci | LB | 6'2" | 230 | 33 | 4 | |
| Paul Naumoff | LB | 6'1" | 215 | 28 | | |
| Jim Teal | LB | 6'3" | 225 | 23 | | |
| Charlie Weaver | LB | 6'2" | 218 | 24 | 2 | |
| Lem Barney | DB | 6' | 188 | 27 | 4 | |
| Miller Farr | DB | 6'1" | 190 | 30 | 1 | |
| Willie Germany | DB | 6' | 192 | 24 | | |
| Dick Jauron | DB | 6' | 190 | 22 | 4 | 6 |
| Levi Johnson | DB | 6'3" | 190 | 22 | 5 | |
| Jim Thrower | DB | 6'2" | 194 | 24 | | |
| Mike Weger | DB | 6'2" | 200 | 27 | 2 | |
| Doug Wyatt | DB | 6'1" | 195 | 26 | | |
| Bill Cappleman | QB | 6'3" | 210 | 26 | | |
| Greg Landry | QB | 6'4" | 210 | 26 | | 12 |
| Bill Munson | QB | 6'2" | 210 | 31 | | |
| Mel Farr | HB | 6'2" | 210 | 28 | | 24 |
| Altie Taylor | HB | 5'10" | 200 | 25 | | 30 |
| Mickey Zofko | HB | 6'3" | 195 | 23 | | |
| Leon Crosswhite | FB | 6'2" | 215 | 22 | | 6 |
| Jim Hooks | FB | 5'11" | 225 | 21 | | |
| Steve Owens | FB | 6'2" | 215 | 25 | | 18 |
| Al Barnes | WR | 6'1" | 170 | 24 | | 6 |
| Ron Jessie | WR | 6' | 183 | 25 | | 24 |
| Earl McCullouch | WR | 5'11" | 175 | 27 | | 6 |
| Jim O'Brien | WR | 6' | 195 | 26 | | 38 |
| Larry Walton | WR | 5'11" | 180 | 26 | | 30 |
| John Hilton | TE | 6'5" | 225 | 31 | | 6 |
| Charlie Sanders | TE | 6'4" | 225 | 27 | | 12 |
| Errol Mann | K | 6' | 200 | 32 | | 53 |
| Herman Weaver | K | 6'4" | 210 | 24 | | |

Wayne Rasmussen — Injury
Rudy Redmond — Injury

## GREEN BAY PACKERS 5-7-2 Dan Devine

Scores of Each Game:

| | | |
|---|---|---|
| 23 | N. Y. JETS | 7 |
| 13 | DETROIT | 13 |
| 3 | Minnesota | 11 |
| 16 | N. Y. Giants | 14 |
| 10 | KANSAS CITY | 10 |
| 7 | Los Angeles | 24 |
| 0 | Detroit | 34 |
| 17 | CHICAGO | 31 |
| 25 | ST. LOUIS | 21 |
| 24 | New England | 33 |
| 6 | San Francisco | 20 |
| 30 | NEW ORLEANS | 10 |
| 7 | MINNESOTA | 31 |
| 21 | Chicago | 0 |

| Use Name | Pos. | Hgt | Wgt | Age | Int | Pts |
|---|---|---|---|---|---|---|
| Kent Branstetter | OT | 6'3" | 260 | 24 | | |
| Bill Hayhoe | OT | 6'8" | 258 | 26 | | |
| Dick Himes | OT | 6'4" | 244 | 27 | | |
| Mal Snider | OG-OT | 6'4" | 250 | 26 | | |
| Gale Gillingham | OG | 6'3" | 255 | 29 | | |
| Bill Lueck | OG | 6'3" | 235 | 27 | | |
| Keith Wortman | OG | 6'2" | 245 | 23 | | |
| Ken Bowman | C | 6'3" | 230 | 30 | | |
| Larry McCarren | C | 6'3" | 240 | 22 | | |
| Cal Withrow | C | 6' | 240 | 28 | | |
| Aaron Brown | DE | 6'5" | 270 | 29 | | |
| Dave Pureifory | DE | 6'1" | 260 | 23 | | |
| Alden Roche | DE | 6'4" | 255 | 28 | | |
| Clarence Williams | DE | 6'5" | 255 | 26 | | |
| Bob Brown | DT | 6'5" | 260 | 33 | | |
| Mike McCoy | DT | 6'5" | 284 | 24 | | |
| Carleton Oats | DT | 6'2" | 260 | 30 | | |
| Fred Carr | LB | 6'5" | 238 | 27 | | |
| Jim Carter | LB | 6'3" | 235 | 24 | 3 | 6 |
| Larry Hefner | LB | 6'3" | 230 | 24 | 1 | |
| Noel Jenke | LB | 6'1" | 225 | 26 | | |
| Tom MacLeod | LB | 6'3" | 220 | 22 | 2 | |
| Tom Toner | LB | 6'3" | 225 | 23 | 1 | |
| Hise Austin | DB | 6'4" | 195 | 24 | | |
| Willie Buchanan | DB | 6' | 190 | 22 | | |
| Ken Ellis | DB | 5'10" | 190 | 25 | 3 | 6 |
| Charlie Hall | DB | 6'1" | 195 | 24 | | |
| Jim Hill | DB | 6'2" | 190 | 25 | 3 | |
| Al Matthews | DB | 5'11" | 190 | 25 | 2 | 6 |
| Perry Smith | DB | 6'1" | 195 | 22 | | |
| Ike Thomas | WR-DB | 6'2" | 193 | 25 | | |
| Jim Del Gaizo | QB | 6'1" | 198 | 26 | | |
| Scott Hunter | QB | 6'2" | 205 | 25 | | 6 |
| Jerry Tagge | QB | 6'2" | 220 | 23 | | 12 |
| Don Highsmith | HB | 6' | 200 | 25 | | |
| Larry Krause | HB | 6' | 208 | 29 | | |
| MacArthur Lane | HB | 6'2" | 220 | 31 | | 12 |
| Ron McBride | HB | 6' | 200 | 24 | | |
| Les Goodman | FB-HB | 5'11" | 206 | 23 | | 6 |
| John Brockington | FB | 6'1" | 225 | 24 | | 18 |
| Perry Williams | FB | 6'2" | 220 | 26 | | 6 |
| Leland Glass | WR | 6' | 185 | 23 | | |
| Barry Smith | WR | 6'1" | 185 | 22 | | 12 |
| Jon Staggers | WR | 5'10" | 186 | 24 | | 24 |
| Paul Staroba | WR | 6'3" | 204 | 24 | | |
| Mike Donohoe | TE | 6'3" | 228 | 28 | | |
| Rich McGeorge | TE | 6'4" | 235 | 24 | | 6 |
| Chester Marcol | K | 6' | 190 | 24 | | 82 |
| Ron Widby | K | 6'4" | 220 | 28 | | |

Bob Kroll — Injury

## CHICAGO BEARS 3-11-0 Abe Gibron

Scores of Each Game:

| | | |
|---|---|---|
| 17 | DALLAS | 20 |
| 13 | MINNESOTA | 22 |
| 33 | Denver | 14 |
| 16 | New Orleans | 21 |
| 6 | Atlanta | 46 |
| 10 | NEW ENGLAND | 13 |
| 35 | HOUSTON | 14 |
| 31 | Green Bay | 17 |
| 7 | Kansas City | 19 |
| 7 | DETROIT | 30 |
| 13 | Minnesota | 31 |
| 0 | LOS ANGELES | 26 |
| 7 | Detroit | 40 |
| 0 | GREEN BAY | 21 |

| Use Name | Pos. | Hgt | Wgt | Age | Int | Pts |
|---|---|---|---|---|---|---|
| Lionel Antwine | OT | 6'6" | 255 | 23 | | |
| Bob Asher | OT | 6'5" | 250 | 25 | | |
| Randy Jackson | OT | 6'5" | 250 | 29 | | |
| Steve Kinney | OT | 6'5" | 255 | 24 | | |
| Glenn Holloway | OG | 6'3" | 255 | 24 | | |
| Ernie Janet | OG | 6'4" | 250 | 24 | | |
| Bob Newton | OG | 6'4" | 250 | 24 | | |
| Rich Coady | C | 6'3" | 235 | 28 | | |
| Willie Holman (to WAS) | DE | 6'4" | 250 | 28 | | |
| Gary Hrivnak | DE | 6'5" | 248 | 22 | | |
| Tony McGee | DE | 6'4" | 250 | 24 | | |
| Mel Tom (from PHI) | DE | 6'4" | 250 | 32 | | |
| Wally Chambers | DT | 6'6" | 250 | 22 | | |
| Dave Hale | DT | 6'7" | 255 | 26 | | |
| Jim Osborne | DT | 6'3" | 250 | 23 | | |
| Andy Rice | DT | 6'3" | 268 | 31 | | |
| Doug Buffone | LB | 6'1" | 225 | 29 | 3 | |
| Dick Butkus | LB | 6'3" | 245 | 29 | 1 | 6 |
| Gail Clark | LB | 6'2" | 227 | 22 | | |
| Jimmy Gunn | LB | 6'1" | 220 | 24 | | |
| Bob Pifferini | LB | 6'2" | 226 | 23 | | |
| Don Rives | LB | 6'2" | 215 | 22 | | |
| Adrian Young | LB | 6'1" | 232 | 27 | | |
| Craig Clemons | DB | 5'11" | 200 | 24 | 2 | |
| Allan Ellis | DB | 5'10" | 185 | 22 | 1 | |
| Charlie Ford | DB | 6'3" | 185 | 24 | 2 | |
| Bob Jeter | DB | 6'1" | 200 | 35 | | |
| Garry Lyle | DB | 6'2" | 198 | 27 | 5 | |
| Willie Roberts | DB | 6'1" | 190 | 25 | | |
| Joe Taylor | DB | 6'2" | 200 | 32 | | |
| Bobby Douglass | QB | 6'3" | 225 | 26 | | 30 |
| Gary Huff | QB | 6'1" | 200 | 22 | | |
| Carl Garrett | HB | 5'11" | 215 | 26 | | 30 |
| Joe Moore | HB | 6'1" | 205 | 24 | | |
| Reggie Sanderson | HB | 5'10" | 206 | 22 | | |
| Gary Kosins | FB-HB | 6'1" | 220 | 24 | | |
| Jim Harrison | FB | 6'4" | 235 | 24 | | 18 |
| Roger Lawson | HB-FB | 6'2" | 215 | 23 | | |
| George Farmer | WR | 6'4" | 214 | 25 | | 6 |
| Ike Hill | WR | 5'10" | 180 | 26 | | 12 |
| Dave Juenger | WR | 6'1" | 195 | 22 | | |
| Mike Reppond | WR | 6' | 180 | 22 | | |
| Tom Reynolds | WR | 6'3" | 200 | 24 | | |
| Cecil Turner | WR | 5'10" | 176 | 29 | | |
| Craig Cotton | TE | 6'4" | 222 | 26 | | |
| Bob Parsons | TE | 6'4" | 234 | 23 | | 6 |
| Earl Thomas | WR-TE | 6'3" | 215 | 24 | | 24 |
| Bobby Joe Green | K | 5'11" | 175 | 35 | | |
| Mac Percival | K | 6'4" | 220 | 33 | | 28 |
| Mirro Roder | K | 6'1" | 218 | 29 | | 35 |

## MINNESOTA VIKINGS

### RUSHING

| Last Name | No. | Yds | Avg | TD |
|---|---|---|---|---|
| Foreman | 182 | 801 | 4.4 | 4 |
| Reed | 100 | 401 | 4.0 | 3 |
| Marinaro | 95 | 302 | 3.2 | 2 |
| Osborn | 48 | 216 | 4.5 | 0 |
| B. Brown | 47 | 206 | 4.4 | 3 |
| Tarkenton | 41 | 202 | 4.9 | 1 |
| Gilliam | 5 | 71 | 14.2 | 1 |
| McClanahan | 17 | 69 | 4.1 | 0 |
| Berry | 2 | 5 | 2.5 | 0 |
| Voigt | 1 | 2 | 2.0 | 0 |

### RECEIVING

| Last Name | No. | Yds | Avg | TD |
|---|---|---|---|---|
| Gilliam | 42 | 907 | 22 | 8 |
| Foreman | 37 | 362 | 10 | 2 |
| Marinaro | 26 | 196 | 8 | 2 |
| Voigt | 23 | 318 | 14 | 2 |
| Reed | 19 | 122 | 6 | 0 |
| Dale | 14 | 192 | 14 | 0 |
| B. Brown | 5 | 22 | 4 | 1 |
| Osborn | 3 | 4 | 1 | 0 |
| Lash | 2 | 34 | 17 | 0 |
| Kingsriter | 2 | 27 | 14 | 0 |
| Dawson | 2 | 24 | 12 | 0 |
| Ward | 1 | 1 | 1 | 0 |

### PUNT RETURNS

| Last Name | No. | Yds | Avg | TD |
|---|---|---|---|---|
| Bryant | 25 | 140 | 6 | 0 |
| J. Wright | 2 | 0 | 0 | 0 |
| West | 1 | 0 | 0 | 0 |

### KICKOFF RETURNS

| Last Name | No. | Yds | Avg | TD |
|---|---|---|---|---|
| McClanahan | 16 | 410 | 26 | 0 |
| Gilliam | 10 | 174 | 17 | 0 |
| West | 3 | 104 | 35 | 0 |
| B. Brown | 3 | 35 | 12 | 0 |
| Reed | 2 | 29 | 15 | 0 |
| J. Wright | 1 | 0 | 0 | 0 |

### PASSING – PUNTING – KICKING

**PASSING**

| Last Name | Att | Comp | % | Yds | Yd/Att | TD | Int–% | RK |
|---|---|---|---|---|---|---|---|---|
| Tarkenton | 274 | 169 | 62 | 2113 | 7.7 | 15 | 7– 3 | 3 |
| Berry | 24 | 10 | 42 | 121 | 5.0 | 1 | 2– 8 | |

**PUNTING**

| Last Name | No | Avg |
|---|---|---|
| Eischeid | 66 | 39.8 |

**KICKING**

| Last Name | XP | Att | % | FG | Att | % |
|---|---|---|---|---|---|---|
| Cox | 33 | 33 | 100 | 21 | 35 | 60 |

## DETROIT LIONS

### RUSHING

| Last Name | No. | Yds | Avg | TD |
|---|---|---|---|---|
| Taylor | 176 | 719 | 4.1 | 5 |
| Owens | 113 | 401 | 3.5 | 1 |
| Mel Farr | 97 | 373 | 3.8 | 4 |
| Landry | 42 | 267 | 6.4 | 2 |
| Hooks | 19 | 110 | 5.8 | 0 |
| L. Walton | 4 | 74 | 18.5 | 0 |
| Munson | 10 | 33 | 3.3 | 0 |
| Zofko | 11 | 33 | 3.0 | 0 |
| Jessie | 5 | 31 | 6.2 | 1 |
| Crosswhite | 11 | 30 | 2.7 | 1 |
| C. Walton | 1 | 26 | 26.0 | 0 |
| H. Weaver | 1 | 18 | 18.0 | 0 |
| McCullouch | 2 | 12 | 6.0 | 0 |
| Barney | 2 | 9 | 4.5 | 0 |
| C. Sanders | 1 | −1 | −1.0 | 0 |
| Cappleman | 1 | −2 | −2.0 | 0 |

### RECEIVING

| Last Name | No. | Yds | Avg | TD |
|---|---|---|---|---|
| C. Sanders | 28 | 433 | 15 | 2 |
| Taylor | 27 | 252 | 9 | 0 |
| Mel Farr | 26 | 183 | 7 | 0 |
| Owens | 24 | 232 | 10 | 0 |
| L. Walton | 21 | 302 | 14 | 4 |
| Jessie | 20 | 364 | 18 | 3 |
| McCullouch | 9 | 179 | 20 | 1 |
| Hilton | 6 | 70 | 12 | 1 |
| Barnes | 3 | 43 | 14 | 1 |
| Zofko | 2 | 16 | 8 | 0 |
| O'Brien | 2 | 14 | 7 | 0 |
| C. Walton | 1 | 7 | 7 | 0 |
| Hooks | 1 | 6 | 6 | 0 |
| Crosswhite | 1 | 4 | 4 | 0 |

### PUNT RETURNS

| Last Name | No. | Yds | Avg | TD |
|---|---|---|---|---|
| Barney | 27 | 231 | 9 | 0 |
| Jauron | 6 | 49 | 8 | 0 |
| L. Walton | 1 | 9 | 9 | 0 |
| Teal | 1 | 0 | 0 | 0 |

### KICKOFF RETURNS

| Last Name | No. | Yds | Avg | TD |
|---|---|---|---|---|
| Jauron | 17 | 405 | 24 | 0 |
| Taylor | 12 | 295 | 25 | 0 |
| Jessie | 6 | 154 | 26 | 0 |
| Thrower | 3 | 54 | 18 | 0 |
| Hooks | 2 | 52 | 26 | 0 |
| Johnson | 3 | 51 | 17 | 0 |
| Barney | 1 | 28 | 28 | 0 |
| Jolley | 1 | 15 | 15 | 0 |
| Zofko | 1 | 7 | 7 | 0 |
| Barnes | 1 | 0 | 0 | 0 |
| Dennis | 1 | 0 | 0 | 0 |
| Germany | 1 | 0 | 0 | 0 |
| C. Weaver | 1 | 0 | 0 | 0 |

### PASSING – PUNTING – KICKING

**PASSING**

| Last Name | Att | Comp | % | Yds | Yd/Att | TD | Int–% | RK |
|---|---|---|---|---|---|---|---|---|
| Munson | 187 | 95 | 51 | 1129 | 6.0 | 9 | 8– 4 | 12 |
| Landry | 128 | 70 | 55 | 908 | 7.1 | 3 | 10– 8 | |
| Cappleman | 11 | 5 | 45 | 33 | 3.0 | 0 | 1– 9 | |
| Zofko | 1 | 1 | 100 | 35 | 35.0 | 0 | 0– 0 | |

**PUNTING**

| Last Name | No | Avg |
|---|---|---|
| H. Weaver | 54 | 43.2 |

**KICKING**

| Last Name | XP | Att | % | FG | Att | % |
|---|---|---|---|---|---|---|
| Mann | 14 | 14 | 100 | 13 | 19 | 68 |
| O'Brien | 14 | 14 | 100 | 8 | 14 | 57 |

## GREEN BAY PACKERS

### RUSHING

| Last Name | No. | Yds | Avg | TD |
|---|---|---|---|---|
| Brockington | 265 | 1144 | 4.3 | 3 |
| Lane | 170 | 528 | 3.1 | 1 |
| Goodman | 18 | 88 | 4.9 | 1 |
| P. Williams | 32 | 87 | 2.7 | 1 |
| Tagge | 15 | 62 | 4.1 | 2 |
| Staggers | 4 | 33 | 8.3 | 1 |
| Staroba | 1 | 11 | 11.0 | 0 |
| Krause | 1 | 8 | 8.0 | 0 |
| Highsmith | 7 | 7 | 1.0 | 0 |
| B. Smith | 1 | 5 | 5.0 | 0 |
| Hunter | 8 | 3 | 0.4 | 1 |
| Del Gaizo | 4 | 1 | 0.3 | 0 |

### RECEIVING

| Last Name | No. | Yds | Avg | TD |
|---|---|---|---|---|
| Lane | 27 | 255 | 9 | 1 |
| Staggers | 25 | 412 | 16 | 3 |
| McGeorge | 16 | 260 | 16 | 1 |
| Brockington | 16 | 128 | 8 | 0 |
| B. Smith | 15 | 233 | 16 | 2 |
| Glass | 11 | 119 | 11 | 0 |
| P. Williams | 5 | 44 | 9 | 0 |
| Goodman | 2 | 19 | 10 | 0 |
| Staroba | 1 | 23 | 23 | 0 |
| Donohoe | 1 | 10 | 10 | 0 |

### PUNT RETURNS

| Last Name | No. | Yds | Avg | TD |
|---|---|---|---|---|
| Staggers | 19 | 90 | 5 | 0 |
| Ellis | 11 | 47 | 4 | 0 |

### KICKOFF RETURNS

| Last Name | No. | Yds | Avg | TD |
|---|---|---|---|---|
| Thomas | 23 | 527 | 23 | 0 |
| Ellis | 12 | 319 | 27 | 0 |
| Krause | 11 | 244 | 22 | 0 |
| Lane | 2 | 31 | 16 | 0 |
| P. Williams | 1 | 24 | 24 | 0 |
| A. Brown | 2 | 19 | 10 | 0 |
| Highsmith | 1 | 18 | 18 | 0 |
| B. Brown | 1 | 7 | 7 | 0 |

### PASSING – PUNTING – KICKING

**PASSING**

| Last Name | Att | Comp | % | Yds | Yd/Att | TD | Int–% | RK |
|---|---|---|---|---|---|---|---|---|
| Tagge | 106 | 56 | 53 | 720 | 6.8 | 2 | 7– 7 | |
| Hunter | 84 | 35 | 42 | 442 | 5.3 | 2 | 4– 5 | |
| Del Gaizo | 62 | 27 | 44 | 318 | 5.1 | 2 | 6–10 | |
| Lane | 2 | 1 | 50 | 23 | 11.5 | 1 | 0– 0 | |
| Brockington | 1 | 0 | 0 | 0 | 0.0 | 0 | 0– 0 | |

**PUNTING**

| Last Name | No | Avg |
|---|---|---|
| Widby | 56 | 43.1 |
| Staroba | 12 | 31.1 |

**KICKING**

| Last Name | XP | Att | % | FG | Att | % |
|---|---|---|---|---|---|---|
| Marcol | 19 | 20 | 95 | 21 | 35 | 60 |

## CHICAGO BEARS

### RUSHING

| Last Name | No. | Yds | Avg | TD |
|---|---|---|---|---|
| Garrett | 175 | 655 | 3.7 | 5 |
| Douglass | 94 | 525 | 5.6 | 5 |
| Harrison | 100 | 374 | 3.7 | 1 |
| Moore | 58 | 191 | 3.3 | 0 |
| Lawson | 24 | 70 | 2.9 | 0 |
| Kosins | 24 | 65 | 2.7 | 0 |
| Huff | 11 | 22 | 2.0 | 0 |
| Sanderson | 3 | 8 | 2.7 | 0 |
| Farmer | 1 | 8 | 8.0 | 0 |
| Thomas | 1 | 5 | 5.0 | 0 |
| Parsons | 2 | 2 | 1.0 | 0 |
| Hill | 3 | −14 | −4.7 | 0 |

### RECEIVING

| Last Name | No. | Yds | Avg | TD |
|---|---|---|---|---|
| Thomas | 24 | 343 | 14 | 4 |
| Garrett | 23 | 292 | 13 | 0 |
| Harrison | 21 | 200 | 10 | 2 |
| Farmer | 15 | 219 | 15 | 1 |
| Cotton | 13 | 186 | 14 | 0 |
| Hill | 10 | 119 | 12 | 0 |
| Lawson | 9 | 60 | 7 | 0 |
| Reynolds | 7 | 127 | 18 | 0 |
| Sanderson | 5 | 23 | 5 | 0 |
| Kosins | 4 | 8 | 2 | 0 |
| Moore | 3 | 17 | 6 | 0 |
| Parsons | 2 | 23 | 12 | 1 |

### PUNT RETURNS

| Last Name | No. | Yds | Avg | TD |
|---|---|---|---|---|
| Hill | 36 | 204 | 6 | 1 |
| Moore | 1 | 0 | 0 | 0 |

### KICKOFF RETURNS

| Last Name | No. | Yds | Avg | TD |
|---|---|---|---|---|
| Hill | 27 | 637 | 24 | 1 |
| Garrett | 16 | 486 | 30 | 0 |
| Turner | 8 | 127 | 16 | 0 |
| Sanderson | 2 | 44 | 22 | 0 |
| Cotton | 2 | 15 | 8 | 0 |
| Parsons | 2 | 15 | 8 | 0 |
| Holloway | 1 | 8 | 8 | 0 |
| Osborne | 1 | 0 | 0 | 0 |
| Thomas | 0 | 12 | 0 | 0 |

### PASSING – PUNTING – KICKING

**PASSING**

| Last Name | Att | Comp | % | Yds | Yd/Att | TD | Int–% | RK |
|---|---|---|---|---|---|---|---|---|
| Douglass | 174 | 81 | 47 | 1057 | 6.1 | 5 | 7– 4 | 13 |
| Huff | 126 | 54 | 43 | 525 | 4.2 | 3 | 8– 6 | |
| Garrett | 1 | 0 | 0 | 0 | 0.0 | 0 | 0– 0 | |
| Hill | 1 | 1 | 100 | 35 | 35.0 | 0 | 0– 0 | |
| Thomas | 1 | 0 | 0 | 0 | 0.0 | 0 | 1–100 | |

**PUNTING**

| Last Name | No | Avg |
|---|---|---|
| Green | 82 | 40.5 |
| Parsons | 4 | 26.5 |

**KICKING**

| Last Name | XP | Att | % | FG | Att | % |
|---|---|---|---|---|---|---|
| Roder | 11 | 12 | 92 | 8 | 16 | 50 |
| Percival | 10 | 10 | 100 | 6 | 8 | 75 |

## LOS ANGELES RAMS 12-2-0 Chuck Knox

**Scores of Each Game**

| | | |
|---|---|---|
| 23 | Kansas City | 13 |
| 31 | ATLANTA | 0 |
| 40 | San Francisco | 20 |
| 31 | Houston | 26 |
| 37 | DALLAS | 31 |
| 24 | GREEN BAY | 7 |
| 9 | Minnesota | 10 |
| 13 | Atlanta | 15 |
| 29 | NEW ORLEANS | 7 |
| 31 | SAN FRANCISCO | 13 |
| 24 | New Orleans | 13 |
| 26 | Chicago | 0 |
| 40 | N. Y. GIANTS | 6 |
| 30 | CLEVELAND | 17 |

| Use Name | Pos. | Hgt | Wgt | Age | Int | Pts |
|---|---|---|---|---|---|---|
| Charley Cowan | OT | 6'4" | 265 | 35 | | |
| Harry Schuh | OT | 6'2" | 260 | 30 | | |
| John Williams | OT | 6'3" | 256 | 27 | | |
| Tom Mack | OG | 6'3" | 250 | 29 | | |
| Joe Scibelli | OG | 6'1" | 255 | 34 | | |
| Rich Saul | C-OG | 6'3" | 235 | 25 | | |
| Ken Iman | C | 6'1" | 240 | 34 | | |
| Fred Dryer | DE | 6'6" | 240 | 27 | | |
| Jack Youngblood | DE | 6'4" | 250 | 23 | | |
| Larry Brooks | DT | 6'3" | 255 | 23 | | |
| Bill Nelson | DT | 6'7" | 270 | 25 | | |
| Merlin Olsen | DT | 6'5" | 270 | 32 | | |
| Phil Olsen | DT | 6'5" | 265 | 25 | | |

| Use Name | Pos. | Hgt | Wgt | Age | Int | Pts |
|---|---|---|---|---|---|---|
| Ken Geddes | LB | 6'3" | 235 | 25 | | |
| Rick Kay | LB | 6'4" | 235 | 23 | | |
| Jack Reynolds | LB | 6'1" | 232 | 25 | 2 | |
| Isiah Robertson | LB | 6'3" | 225 | 24 | 3 | 6 |
| Bob Stein | LB | 6'2" | 235 | 25 | 1 | |
| Jim Youngblood | LB | 6'3" | 240 | 23 | 1 | |
| Cullen Bryant | DB | 6'1" | 210 | 22 | | 6 |
| Al Clark | DB | 6' | 180 | 25 | 1 | |
| Dave Elmendorf | DB | 6'1" | 195 | 24 | 1 | |
| Eddie McMillan | DB | 6' | 180 | 21 | 4 | |
| Steve Preece | DB | 6'1" | 195 | 26 | 2 | 6 |
| Charlie Stukes | DB | 6'3" | 212 | 29 | 5 | |
| Bill Drake | WR-DB | 6'1" | 195 | 23 | | |

| Use Name | Pos. | Hgt | Wgt | Age | Int | Pts |
|---|---|---|---|---|---|---|
| John Hadl | QB | 6'2" | 214 | 33 | | |
| James Harris | QB | 6'3" | 210 | 26 | | |
| Jim Bertelsen | HB | 5'11" | 205 | 23 | | 30 |
| Lawrence McCutcheon | HB | 6'1" | 205 | 23 | | 30 |
| Rob Scribner | HB | 6' | 200 | 22 | | |
| Larry Smith | HB | 6'3" | 220 | 25 | | 12 |
| Tony Baker | FB | 5'11" | 225 | 28 | | 42 |
| Cullen Bryant | FB | 6'1" | 218 | 22 | | |
| Les Josephson | FB | 6' | 207 | 30 | | 12 |
| Dick Gordon (to GB) | WR | 5'11" | 190 | 28 | | |
| Harold Jackson | WR | 5'1" | 175 | 27 | | 78 |
| David Ray | WR | 6' | 195 | 28 | | 130 |
| Rod Sherman | WR | 6' | 190 | 28 | | |
| Jack Snow | WR | 6'2" | 190 | 30 | | 12 |
| Joe Sweet | WR | 6'2" | 196 | 25 | | |
| Pat Curran | TE | 6'3" | 238 | 27 | | |
| Bob Klein | TE | 6'5" | 235 | 26 | | 12 |
| Dave Chapple | K | 6' | 180 | 26 | | |

## ATLANTA FALCONS 9-5-0 Norm Van Brocklin

| | | |
|---|---|---|
| 62 | New Orleans | 7 |
| 0 | Los Angeles | 31 |
| 6 | Detroit | 31 |
| 9 | SAN FRANCISCO | 13 |
| 46 | CHICAGO | 6 |
| 41 | San Diego | 0 |
| 17 | San Francisco | 3 |
| 15 | LOS ANGELES | 13 |
| 44 | Philadelphia | 27 |
| 20 | MINNESOTA | 14 |
| 28 | N. Y. Jets | 20 |
| 6 | BUFFALO | 17 |
| 10 | ST. LOUIS | 32 |
| 14 | NEW ORLEANS | 10 |

| Use Name | Pos. | Hgt | Wgt | Age | Int | Pts |
|---|---|---|---|---|---|---|
| Nick Bebout | OT | 6'5" | 260 | 22 | | |
| Len Gotshalk | OT | 6'4" | 260 | 23 | | |
| George Kunz | OT | 6'5" | 268 | 26 | | |
| Bill Sandeman | OT | 6'6" | 265 | 30 | | |
| Dennis Havig | OG | 6'2" | 256 | 24 | | |
| Andy Mauer | OG | 6'3" | 247 | 24 | | |
| Ted Fritsch | C | 6'2" | 240 | 23 | | |
| Jeff Van Note | C | 6'2" | 247 | 27 | | |
| Claude Humphrey | DE | 6'5" | 265 | 29 | 1 | |
| Greg Marx | DE | 6'4" | 260 | 23 | | |
| John Zook | DE | 6'3" | 250 | 25 | | |
| Mike Lewis | DT | 6'3" | 260 | 24 | | |
| Rosie Manning | DT | 6'5" | 256 | 23 | | |
| Mike Tilleman | DT | 6'5" | 278 | 29 | | |
| Chuck Walker | DT | 6'2" | 260 | 32 | 1 | |

| Use Name | Pos. | Hgt | Wgt | Age | Int | Pts |
|---|---|---|---|---|---|---|
| Duane Benson | LB | 6'2" | 215 | 28 | | |
| Greg Brezina | LB | 6'2" | 226 | 27 | 3 | |
| Don Hansen | LB | 6'3" | 228 | 29 | 1 | |
| Ken Mitchell | LB | 6'1" | 224 | 25 | | |
| Tommy Nobis | LB | 6'2" | 243 | 29 | | |
| Lonnie Warwick | LB | 6'3" | 240 | 31 | | |
| Ray Brown | DB | 6'2" | 202 | 24 | 6 | |
| Ray Easterling | DB | 6' | 195 | 23 | | |
| Clarence Ellis | DB | 5'11" | 190 | 23 | 2 | |
| Tom Hayes | DB | 6'1" | 198 | 27 | 4 | 12 |
| Rolland Lawrence | DB | 5'10" | 180 | 22 | 1 | |
| Tony Plummer | DB | 5'11" | 188 | 26 | 1 | 6 |
| Ken Reaves | DB | 6'3" | 210 | 28 | 2 | |

| Use Name | Pos. | Hgt | Wgt | Age | Int | Pts |
|---|---|---|---|---|---|---|
| Bob Lee | QB | 6'2" | 195 | 27 | | |
| Dick Shiner (to NE) | QB | 6' | 195 | 31 | | |
| Pat Sullivan | QB | 6' | 200 | 23 | | |
| Dave Hampton | HB | 6' | 210 | 26 | | 30 |
| Joe Washington | HB | 5'9" | 180 | 22 | | |
| Eddie Ray | FB | 6'1" | 240 | 26 | | 66 |
| Art Malone | FB | 5'11" | 216 | 25 | | 18 |
| Harmon Wages | FB | 6'1" | 212 | 27 | | 6 |
| Ken Burrow | WR | 6' | 190 | 25 | | 42 |
| Wes Chesson | WR | 6'2" | 195 | 24 | | 6 |
| Al Dodd | WR | 6' | 178 | 28 | | |
| Tom Geredine | WR | 6'2" | 195 | 23 | | 6 |
| Louis Neal | WR | 6'4" | 215 | 22 | | 6 |
| Larry Mialik | TE | 6'2" | 226 | 23 | | |
| Jim Mitchell | TE | 6'2" | 236 | 25 | | |
| John James | K | 6'3" | 197 | 24 | | |
| Nick Mike-Mayer | K | 5'8" | 186 | 23 | | 112 |

## SAN FRANCISCO FORTY-NINERS 5-9-0 Dick Nolan

| | | |
|---|---|---|
| 13 | Miami | 21 |
| 36 | Denver | 34 |
| 20 | LOS ANGELES | 40 |
| 13 | Atlanta | 9 |
| 13 | MINNESOTA | 17 |
| 40 | NEW ORLEANS | 0 |
| 3 | ATLANTA | 17 |
| 20 | Detroit | 30 |
| 9 | Washington | 33 |
| 13 | Los Angeles | 31 |
| 20 | GREEN BAY | 6 |
| 38 | PHILADELPHIA | 28 |
| 10 | New Orleans | 16 |
| 14 | PITTSBURGH | 37 |

| Use Name | Pos. | Hgt | Wgt | Age | Int | Pts |
|---|---|---|---|---|---|---|
| Cas Banaszek | OT | 6'3" | 250 | 27 | | |
| Len Rohde | OT | 6'4" | 248 | 35 | | |
| John Watson | OG-OT | 6'4" | 248 | 24 | | |
| Randy Beisler | OG | 6'4" | 244 | 28 | | |
| Ed Hardy | OG | 6'4" | 242 | 21 | | |
| Woody Peoples | OG | 6'2" | 250 | 30 | | |
| Forrest Blue | C | 6'5" | 260 | 27 | | |
| Jean Barrett | OT-C | 6'6" | 254 | 22 | | |
| Bill Belk | DE | 6'3" | 242 | 27 | | |
| Cedrick Hardman | DE | 6'3" | 255 | 24 | 2 | |
| Tommy Hart | DE | 6'3" | 248 | 28 | | |
| Bob Hoskins | DT | 6'2" | 250 | 27 | | |
| Charlie Krueger | DT | 6'4" | 254 | 37 | | |
| Rolf Krueger | DT | 6'4" | 253 | 26 | | |

| Use Name | Pos. | Hgt | Wgt | Age | Int | Pts |
|---|---|---|---|---|---|---|
| Willie Harper | LB | 6'2" | 215 | 23 | | |
| Charlie Hunt | LB | 6'2" | 212 | 22 | | |
| Frank Nunley | LB | 6'2" | 230 | 27 | 1 | |
| Dave Olerich | LB | 6'1" | 220 | 28 | | |
| Jim Sniadecki | LB | 6'2" | 228 | 26 | 1 | |
| Skip Vanderbundt | LB | 6'3" | 224 | 26 | 1 | |
| Dave Wilcox | LB | 6'3" | 234 | 30 | 2 | |
| Windlan Hall | DB | 5'11" | 175 | 23 | 1 | 12 |
| Jim Johnson | DB | 6'2" | 188 | 35 | 4 | |
| Ralph McGill | DB | 5'11" | 186 | 23 | | |
| Mel Phillips | DB | 6' | 190 | 31 | 1 | |
| Mike Simpson | DB | 5'11" | 170 | 26 | | |
| Bruce Taylor | DB | 6' | 180 | 25 | 6 | |

Terry Beasley — Shoulder Injury

| Use Name | Pos. | Hgt | Wgt | Age | Int | Pts |
|---|---|---|---|---|---|---|
| John Brodie | QB | 6'1" | 203 | 38 | | 6 |
| Joe Reed | QB | 6'1" | 192 | 25 | | |
| Steve Spurrier | QB | 6'2" | 200 | 28 | | 12 |
| Dave Atkins | HB | 6'1" | 202 | 24 | | 6 |
| Doug Cunningham | HB | 5'11" | 195 | 27 | | 6 |
| Jimmy Thomas | HB | 6'1" | 214 | 26 | | 6 |
| Vic Washington | HB | 5'10" | 196 | 27 | | 48 |
| Ken Willard | FB | 6'2" | 220 | 30 | | 12 |
| Randy Jackson | HB-FB | 6' | 220 | 24 | | |
| Larry Schreiber | HB-FB | 6' | 210 | 26 | | |
| Dan Abramowicz (from NO) | WR | 6'1" | 195 | 28 | | 6 |
| Ed Beverly | WR | 5'11" | 168 | 24 | | |
| John Isenbarger | WR | 6'3" | 196 | 25 | | |
| Gene Washington | WR | 6'1" | 185 | 26 | | 12 |
| Ted Kwalick | TE | 6'4" | 226 | 26 | | 30 |
| Dick Witcher | TE | 6'3" | 204 | 28 | | |
| Bruce Gossett | K | 6'2" | 228 | 30 | | 104 |
| Tom Wittum | K | 6'1" | 185 | 23 | | |

## NEW ORLEANS SAINTS 5-9-0 John North

| | | |
|---|---|---|
| 7 | ATLANTA | 62 |
| 3 | Dallas | 40 |
| 10 | Baltimore | 14 |
| 21 | CHICAGO | 16 |
| 20 | DETROIT | 13 |
| 0 | San Francisco | 40 |
| 19 | WASHINGTON | 3 |
| 13 | BUFFALO | 0 |
| 7 | Los Angeles | 29 |
| 14 | San Diego | 17 |
| 13 | LOS ANGELES | 24 |
| 10 | Green Bay | 30 |
| 16 | SAN FRANCISCO | 10 |
| 10 | Atlanta | 14 |

| Use Name | Pos. | Hgt | Wgt | Age | Int | Pts |
|---|---|---|---|---|---|---|
| Paul Ferson | OT | 6'5" | 260 | 23 | | |
| Carl Johnson | OT | 6'3" | 255 | 23 | | |
| Don Morrison | OT | 6'5" | 255 | 23 | | |
| Craig Robinson | OT | 6'4" | 250 | 24 | | |
| Jake Kupp | OG | 6'3" | 248 | 31 | | |
| Royce Smith | OG | 6'3" | 245 | 24 | | |
| Del Williams | OG | 6'2" | 240 | 27 | | |
| John Didion | C | 6'4" | 245 | 25 | | |
| Steve Baumgartner | DE | 6'7" | 260 | 22 | | |
| Billy Newsome | DE | 6'4" | 250 | 24 | 1 | |
| Joe Owens | DE | 6'2" | 245 | 25 | 1 | |
| Derland Moore | DT | 6'4" | 260 | 21 | 1 | |
| Bob Pollard | DT | 6'3" | 245 | 24 | | |
| Elex Price | DT | 6'3" | 260 | 23 | | |

| Use Name | Pos. | Hgt | Wgt | Age | Int | Pts |
|---|---|---|---|---|---|---|
| Wayne Colman | LB | 6'1" | 230 | 27 | | |
| Bob Creech | LB | 6'3" | 228 | 24 | | |
| Joe Federspiel | LB | 6'1" | 225 | 23 | 1 | |
| Willie Hall | LB | 6'2" | 225 | 23 | | |
| Ray Hester | LB | 6'2" | 215 | 24 | | |
| Rick Kingrea | LB | 6'1" | 233 | 24 | | |
| Dale Lindsey | LB | 6'3" | 225 | 30 | | |
| Jim Merlo | LB | 6'1" | 220 | 21 | 3 | |
| Dick Palmer | LB | 6'2" | 232 | 25 | | |
| Mike Fink | DB | 5'11" | 180 | 22 | | |
| Johnny Fuller | DB | 6' | 185 | 27 | 1 | |
| Ernie Jackson | DB | 5'10" | 175 | 23 | 3 | |
| Bivian Lee | DB | 6'3" | 200 | 25 | 3 | |
| Jerry Moore | DB | 6'3" | 208 | 23 | | |
| Tom Myers | DB | 5'11" | 184 | 22 | 3 | |
| Nate Ramsey | DB | 6'1" | 200 | 32 | | |

Ron Billingsley — Injury
Hugo Hollas — Knee Injury

| Use Name | Pos. | Hgt | Wgt | Age | Int | Pts |
|---|---|---|---|---|---|---|
| Bob Davis | QB | 6'3" | 205 | 27 | | |
| Archie Manning | QB | 6'3" | 215 | 24 | | 12 |
| Bobby Scott | QB | 6'1" | 200 | 24 | | |
| Henry Matthews | HB | 6'3" | 203 | 24 | | |
| Joe Profit (from ATL) | HB | 6' | 213 | 24 | | 12 |
| Howard Stevens | HB | 5'5" | 175 | 24 | | 12 |
| Jess Phillips | FB-HB | 6'1" | 210 | 26 | | |
| Bill Butler | FB | 6' | 210 | 23 | | 18 |
| Odell Lawson | FB | 6'2" | 205 | 25 | | |
| Lincoln Minor | HB-FB | 6'2" | 211 | 23 | | |
| Jubilee Dunbar | WR | 6' | 196 | 26 | | 24 |
| Freddie Hyatt | WR | 6'3" | 200 | 27 | | |
| Bob Newland | WR | 6'2" | 190 | 24 | | 24 |
| Preston Riley | WR | 6' | 180 | 25 | | |
| Speedy Thomas | WR | 6'1" | 170 | 26 | | |
| Doug Winslow | WR | 5'11" | 180 | 22 | | |
| Bert Askson | TE | 6'3" | 220 | 27 | | |
| John Beasley (from MIN) | TE | 6'3" | 228 | 28 | | 12 |
| Bob Brown | TE | 6'3" | 225 | 30 | | |
| Len Garrett (from GB) | TE | 6'3" | 230 | 24 | | |
| Mike Kelly | TE | 6'4" | 215 | 26 | | |
| Happy Feller | K | 5'11" | 185 | 24 | | 19 |
| Bill McClard | K | 5'10" | 202 | 21 | | 48 |
| Steve O'Neal | K | 6'3" | 185 | 27 | | |

## LOS ANGELES RAMS

### RUSHING

| Last Name | No. | Yds | Avg | TD |
|---|---|---|---|---|
| McCutcheon | 210 | 1097 | 5.2 | 2 |
| Bertelsen | 206 | 854 | 4.1 | 4 |
| Baker | 85 | 344 | 4.0 | 7 |
| Smith | 79 | 291 | 3.7 | 2 |
| Josephson | 36 | 174 | 4.8 | 2 |
| Scribner | 20 | 109 | 5.5 | 0 |
| Harris | 4 | 29 | 7.3 | 0 |
| Gordon | 2 | 15 | 7.5 | 0 |
| Preece | 1 | 11 | 11.0 | 1 |
| Hadl | 14 | 5 | 0.4 | 0 |
| Chapple | 1 | 0 | 0.0 | 0 |
| Jackson | 2 | −8 | −4.0 | 0 |

### RECEIVING

| Last Name | No. | Yds | Avg | TD |
|---|---|---|---|---|
| Jackson | 40 | 874 | 22 | 13 |
| McCutcheon | 30 | 289 | 10 | 3 |
| Klein | 21 | 277 | 13 | 2 |
| Bertelsen | 19 | 267 | 14 | 1 |
| Snow | 16 | 252 | 16 | 2 |
| Smith | 10 | 65 | 7 | 0 |
| Curran | 5 | 56 | 11 | 1 |
| Scribner | 2 | 19 | 10 | 0 |
| Sherman | 1 | 8 | 8 | 0 |

### PUNT RETURNS

| Last Name | No. | Yds | Avg | TD |
|---|---|---|---|---|
| Bertelsen | 26 | 258 | 10 | 0 |
| Elmendorf | 22 | 187 | 9 | 0 |
| Scribner | 3 | 32 | 11 | 0 |

### KICKOFF RETURNS

| Last Name | No. | Yds | Avg | TD |
|---|---|---|---|---|
| Bryant | 13 | 369 | 28 | 1 |
| Scribner | 11 | 314 | 29 | 0 |
| Clark | 2 | 80 | 40 | 0 |
| Gordon | 3 | 68 | 23 | 0 |
| Curran | 1 | 24 | 24 | 0 |
| Elmendorf | 2 | 23 | 12 | 0 |
| Smith | 1 | 16 | 16 | 0 |
| Bertelsen | 1 | 15 | 15 | 0 |
| McCutcheon | 1 | 6 | 6 | 0 |
| Klein | 1 | 0 | 0 | 0 |

### PASSING – PUNTING – KICKING

**PASSING**

| Last Name | Att | Comp | % | Yds | Yd/Att | TD | Int–% | RK |
|---|---|---|---|---|---|---|---|---|
| Hadl | 258 | 135 | 52 | 2008 | 7.8 | 22 | 11– 4 | 5 |
| Harris | 11 | 7 | 64 | 68 | 6.2 | 0 | 0– 0 | |
| Smith | 2 | 2 | 100 | 31 | 15.5 | 0 | 0– 0 | |

**PUNTING**

| Last Name | No | Avg |
|---|---|---|
| Chapple | 51 | 40.8 |

**KICKING**

| Last Name | XP | Att | % | FG | Att | % |
|---|---|---|---|---|---|---|
| Ray | 40 | 42 | 95 | 30 | 47 | 64 |

## ATLANTA FALCONS

### RUSHING

| Last Name | No. | Yds | Avg | TD |
|---|---|---|---|---|
| Hampton | 263 | 997 | 3.8 | 4 |
| Ray | 96 | 434 | 4.5 | 9 |
| Malone | 76 | 336 | 4.4 | 2 |
| Lee | 29 | 67 | 2.3 | 0 |
| Wages | 18 | 47 | 2.6 | 1 |
| Washington | 4 | 36 | 9.0 | 0 |
| J. Mitchell | 5 | 34 | 6.8 | 0 |
| Sullivan | 3 | 19 | 6.3 | 0 |
| Burrow | 2 | 17 | 8.5 | 0 |
| Shiner | 3 | −2 | −0.7 | 0 |
| Geredine | 1 | −3 | −3.0 | 0 |

### RECEIVING

| Last Name | No. | Yds | Avg | TD |
|---|---|---|---|---|
| J. Mitchell | 32 | 420 | 13 | 0 |
| Burrow | 31 | 567 | 18 | 7 |
| Hampton | 25 | 273 | 11 | 1 |
| Dodd | 19 | 291 | 15 | 0 |
| Ray | 19 | 192 | 10 | 2 |
| Malone | 19 | 177 | 9 | 1 |
| Geredine | 12 | 231 | 19 | 1 |
| Neal | 5 | 131 | 26 | 1 |
| Chesson | 2 | 36 | 18 | 1 |
| Mialik | 2 | 30 | 15 | 0 |
| Wages | 2 | 14 | 7 | 0 |

### PUNT RETURNS

| Last Name | No. | Yds | Avg | TD |
|---|---|---|---|---|
| Brown | 40 | 350 | 9 | 0 |
| Dodd | 8 | 69 | 9 | 0 |

### KICKOFF RETURNS

| Last Name | No. | Yds | Avg | TD |
|---|---|---|---|---|
| Washington | 20 | 432 | 22 | 0 |
| Hampton | 11 | 268 | 23 | 0 |
| Geredine | 9 | 211 | 23 | 0 |
| Plummer | 5 | 115 | 23 | 0 |
| Lawrence | 3 | 71 | 24 | 0 |
| Benson | 3 | 20 | 7 | 0 |
| Wages | 1 | 0 | 0 | 0 |

### PASSING – PUNTING – KICKING

**PASSING**

| Last Name | Att | Comp | % | Yds | Yd/Att | TD | Int–% | RK |
|---|---|---|---|---|---|---|---|---|
| Lee | 230 | 120 | 52 | 1786 | 7.8 | 10 | 8– 3 | 7 |
| Shiner | 68 | 36 | 53 | 432 | 6.4 | 3 | 4– 6 | |
| Sullivan | 26 | 14 | 54 | 175 | 6.7 | 1 | 0– 0 | |

**PUNTING**

| Last Name | No | Avg |
|---|---|---|
| James | 63 | 42.6 |

**KICKING**

| Last Name | XP | Att | % | FG | Att | % |
|---|---|---|---|---|---|---|
| Mike-Mayer | 34 | 34 | 100 | 26 | 38 | 68 |

## SAN FRANCISCO FORTY-NINERS

### RUSHING

| Last Name | No. | Yds | Avg | TD |
|---|---|---|---|---|
| V. Washington | 151 | 543 | 3.5 | 8 |
| Willard | 83 | 366 | 4.4 | 1 |
| Thomas | 56 | 259 | 4.6 | 1 |
| Cunningham | 44 | 165 | 3.8 | 1 |
| Schreiber | 42 | 163 | 3.9 | 0 |
| Reed | 15 | 85 | 5.7 | 0 |
| Wittum | 1 | 63 | 63.0 | 0 |
| Kwalick | 5 | 37 | 7.4 | 0 |
| Spurrier | 9 | 32 | 3.6 | 2 |
| Atkins | 4 | 19 | 4.8 | 1 |
| Brodie | 5 | 16 | 3.2 | 1 |
| Jackson | 6 | 10 | 1.7 | 0 |
| Isenbarger | 1 | −6 | −6.0 | 0 |

### RECEIVING

| Last Name | No. | Yds | Avg | TD |
|---|---|---|---|---|
| Kwalick | 47 | 729 | 16 | 5 |
| G. Washington | 37 | 606 | 16 | 2 |
| Abramowicz | 37 | 460 | 12 | 1 |
| V. Washington | 33 | 238 | 7 | 0 |
| Willard | 22 | 160 | 7 | 1 |
| Thomas | 19 | 157 | 8 | 0 |
| Cunningham | 15 | 118 | 8 | 0 |
| Schreiber | 12 | 98 | 8 | 0 |
| Isenbarger | 10 | 67 | 7 | 0 |
| Jackson | 1 | 20 | 20 | 0 |
| Witcher | 1 | 13 | 13 | 0 |
| Atkins | 1 | −3 | −3 | 0 |

### PUNT RETURNS

| Last Name | No. | Yds | Avg | TD |
|---|---|---|---|---|
| Taylor | 15 | 207 | 14 | 0 |
| McGill | 22 | 186 | 8 | 0 |

### KICKOFF RETURNS

| Last Name | No. | Yds | Avg | TD |
|---|---|---|---|---|
| V. Washington | 24 | 549 | 23 | 0 |
| McGill | 17 | 374 | 22 | 0 |
| Cunningham | 8 | 173 | 22 | 0 |
| Atkins | 3 | 93 | 31 | 0 |
| Thomas | 5 | 81 | 16 | 0 |
| Olerich | 2 | 17 | 9 | 0 |
| Hall | 1 | 14 | 14 | 0 |
| Simpson | 1 | 0 | 0 | 0 |
| Sniadecki | 1 | 0 | 0 | 0 |
| Willard | 1 | 0 | 0 | 0 |

### PASSING – PUNTING – KICKING

**PASSING**

| Last Name | Att | Comp | % | Yds | Yd/Att | TD | Int–% | RK |
|---|---|---|---|---|---|---|---|---|
| Brodie | 194 | 98 | 51 | 1126 | 5.8 | 3 | 12– 6 | 15 |
| Spurrier | 157 | 83 | 53 | 882 | 5.6 | 4 | 7– 4 | 14 |
| Reed | 114 | 51 | 45 | 589 | 5.2 | 2 | 6– 5 | |
| Isenbarger | 1 | 1 | 100 | 48 | 48.0 | 0 | 0– 0 | |

**PUNTING**

| Last Name | No | Avg |
|---|---|---|
| Wittum | 79 | 43.7 |

**KICKING**

| Last Name | XP | Att | % | FG | Att | % |
|---|---|---|---|---|---|---|
| Gossett | 26 | 26 | 100 | 26 | 33 | 79 |

## NEW ORLEANS SAINTS

### RUSHING

| Last Name | No. | Yds | Avg | TD |
|---|---|---|---|---|
| Phillips | 198 | 663 | 3.3 | 0 |
| Butler | 87 | 348 | 4.0 | 1 |
| Profit | 90 | 329 | 3.7 | 2 |
| Manning | 63 | 293 | 4.7 | 2 |
| Stevens | 45 | 183 | 4.1 | 1 |
| Lawson | 6 | 23 | 3.8 | 0 |
| Scott | 9 | 18 | 2.0 | 0 |
| Davis | 3 | 10 | 3.3 | 0 |
| Minor | 3 | 10 | 3.3 | 0 |
| Myers | 1 | 8 | 8.0 | 0 |
| Newland | 1 | 6 | 6.0 | 0 |
| Matthews | 4 | 4 | 1.0 | 0 |
| Dunbar | 3 | 3 | 1.0 | 0 |
| O'Neal | 2 | −1 | −0.5 | 0 |

### RECEIVING

| Last Name | No. | Yds | Avg | TD |
|---|---|---|---|---|
| Beasley | 32 | 283 | 9 | 2 |
| Newland | 29 | 489 | 17 | 4 |
| Dunbar | 23 | 447 | 19 | 4 |
| Phillips | 22 | 169 | 8 | 0 |
| Butler | 19 | 125 | 7 | 2 |
| Brown | 11 | 132 | 12 | 0 |
| Profit | 11 | 108 | 10 | 0 |
| Winslow | 4 | 45 | 11 | 0 |
| Stevens | 4 | 39 | 10 | 0 |
| Garrett | 2 | 38 | 15 | 0 |
| Matthews | 2 | 19 | 10 | 0 |
| Lawson | 2 | −5 | −3 | 0 |
| Minor | 1 | 5 | 5 | 0 |

### PUNT RETURNS

| Last Name | No. | Yds | Avg | TD |
|---|---|---|---|---|
| Stevens | 17 | 171 | 10 | 0 |
| Winslow | 5 | 47 | 9 | 0 |

### KICKOFF RETURNS

| Last Name | No. | Yds | Avg | TD |
|---|---|---|---|---|
| Stevens | 26 | 590 | 23 | 0 |
| Profit | 8 | 144 | 18 | 0 |
| Lawson | 7 | 118 | 17 | 0 |
| Fink | 5 | 81 | 16 | 0 |
| Moore | 1 | 14 | 14 | 0 |
| Jackson | 1 | 0 | 0 | 0 |

### PASSING – PUNTING – KICKING

**PASSING**

| Last Name | Att | Comp | % | Yds | Yd/Att | TD | Int–% | RK |
|---|---|---|---|---|---|---|---|---|
| Manning | 267 | 140 | 52 | 1642 | 6.2 | 10 | 12– 4 | 10 |
| Scott | 54 | 18 | 33 | 245 | 4.5 | 1 | 3– 6 | |
| Davis | 17 | 5 | 29 | 14 | 0.8 | 0 | 2– 12 | |

**PUNTING**

| Last Name | No | Avg |
|---|---|---|
| O'Neal | 81 | 41.7 |

**KICKING**

| Last Name | XP | Att | % | FG | Att | % |
|---|---|---|---|---|---|---|
| McClard | 9 | 9 | 100 | 13 | 24 | 54 |
| Feller | 7 | 7 | 100 | 4 | 12 | 33 |

# 1973 A.F.C. The Runningest Buffalo

Just as baseball fans had spent the year counting Hank Aaron's home runs as he closed in on Babe Ruth's one-year home run mark, football fans added up O. J. Simpson's rushing yardage week by week as he went after Jimmy Brown's one-year rushing mark of 1,863 yards. Simpson, the main ingredient in the Buffalo offense, excited the football world by running for a record 250 yards on opening day against New England. After seven games, he already had gained 1,000 yards, a goal coveted by runners for an entire season. With two games left on the schedule, O. J. had 1,584 yards and needed two good days to break the record. A good day of 219 yards against New England put him within shouting distance of the record. Needing 61 yards to set a new mark, Simpson quickly broke the record in the season's finale in cold, rainy New York. With a workhorse performance the rest of the day, he became the first runner ever to gain 2,000 yards in one season.

## EASTERN DIVISION

**Miami Dolphins**—The Dolphins were aiming at a second perfect season, but a tough 12-7 loss to Oakland in their second game brought an end to those hopes. But the Dolphins still had the cold, hard precision and flawless execution which made them the class of professional football. The offense still had Griese, Csonka, Warfield, Little, Langer, and company; the defense boasted of Stanfill, Buoniconti, Anderson, Scott, and the rest of the No Name Defense. Coach Don Shula again made sure that his players were hungry, and except for the loss to Oakland and a 16-3 upset by the Colts after Miami had clinched the Eastern crown, the Dolphins came close to another flawless season.

**Buffalo Bills**—When O. J. Simpson faced the reporters after breaking Jimmy Brown's single-season rushing mark, he began the meeting by introducing the offensive linemen one by one. They included Mike Montler, Reggie MacKenzie, Donnie Green, Dave Foley, and rookies Joe DeLamielleure and Paul Seymour. They were the reasons for O. J.'s success, so he figured they deserved to share in the glory. Simpson was not the entire story of the Bills' surge to a 9-5 record and second place in the East. Rookie quarterback Joe Ferguson played well, although his main task was handing off to Simpson. J. D. Hill and Bob Chandler gave the team a pair of fine wide receivers, and another receiver, Dwight Harrison, was converted into a starter in the secondary. Earl Edwards came from the '49ers in a trade and beefed up the front line of the defense.

**New England Patriots**—The defense could not stop a strong running attack, and good clubs simply cranked the yardage out against the Patriots on the ground. O. J. Simpson, for instance, enjoyed his two most productive days of his record season against New England. But even with the defensive problems, coach Chuck Fairbanks' first season was successful because of the fine rookie class the Patriots fielded. Guard John Hannah strengthened the blocking, Darryl Stingley won a starting wide-receiver job, Sam Cunningham added power to the running game, and little Mack Herron excited people on kick returns. Veteran receiver Reggie Rucker provided a bonus by developing into a star, but the kicking game still bothered the Pats, as rookie Jeff White booted a punt for -6 yards in one game and missed an extra point and an 18-yard field goal in a 24-23 loss to Philadelphia.

**New York Jets**—Weeb Ewbank's final year as head coach before retirement degenerated into a dismal 4-10 season. The defense played well through the campaign, but the offensive unit suffered from age, injury, and turmoil. Flanker Don Maynard was cut in the pre-season, while fullback John Riggins did not sign a contract until just before opening day and never did reach his best form. The offensive line slipped in its pass protection, exposing the Jet quarterbacks to enemy tacklers. Joe Namath went out of action with an injured shoulder against the Colts on September 23, and Al Woodall followed him onto the disabled list two weeks later to leave rookie free-agent Bill Demory as the team's only quarterback.

**Baltimore Colts**—A thorough housecleaning had swept out many veterans of recent years, as new head coach Howard Schnellenberger suffered through a 4-10 season in which few of his personnel shifts worked out very well. Second-year runner Lydell Mitchell did star in the backfield, but the offense was hurt by ex-Raider tight end Ray Chester's poor showing and by a confused quarterback situation. Rookie Bert Jones began the year as the starter, but veteran Marty Domres took over the position over the back part of the schedule; neither name could ignite much of a passing attack. The Colts enjoyed one moment of glory by beating the Dolphins late in the year.

## CENTRAL DIVISION

**Cincinnati Bengals**—The maturing of quarterback Ken Anderson and the addition of three talented rookies brought the Cincinnati offense up to the level of its topnotch defensive unit. With experience improving his poise, Anderson calmly executed the plays called by coach Paul Brown via messenger guards. Giving Brown and Anderson more to work with were rookies Isaac Curtis, Bobby Clark, and Lenvil Elliott, three swift and powerful freshmen. Curtis gave the Bengals a deep threat at wide receiver, while Clark provided power in the backfield

to go along with the speed of veteran Eassex Johnson. When injuries slowed up these two runners late in the season, Elliott broke into the lineup with a flair. The Bengal defense had been solid all along, so the team stormed into first place with a strong finish.

**Pittsburgh Steelers**—The Pittsburgh offense kept raking in points despite constant injuries to key players. Fullback Franco Harris missed the early going with a bad knee, and by the time he got back into action, halfback Frenchy Fuqua went out with a broken collarbone. Quarterback Terry Bradshaw starred until he suffered a shoulder separation in mid-season; Terry Hanratty then stepped in and kept the attack rolling until injured ribs put him out of commission. With third-stringer Joe Gilliam at quarterback, the Steelers rose up and beat the Washington Redskins 21-16. The defense turned in strong performances week after week, with Joe Greene, L. C. Greenwood, Andy Russell, Jack Ham, and Mike Wagner all candidates for All-Pro honors as the Steelers again made it to the playoffs.

**Cleveland Browns**—Age had turned the Browns into a mediocre team that finished third in the AFC Central Division. The Cleveland offensive unit especially creaked, with the line laboring under the weight of three thirty-three-year-old members. Fullback Bo Scott's injury and quarterback Mike Phipps' slower-than-expected development further slowed the attack, and the Browns' two first-round draft picks were of very little help. Receiver Steve Holden spent most of the season on the bench, while guard Pete Adams passed his rookie season on the disabled list. The Cleveland defense, however, held together well, aided immensely by ex-Charger Bob Babich's work at middle linebacker, and the Browns posted a winning record.

**Houston Oilers**—The Oilers had given coach Bill Peterson what was described as a "lifetime" pact to join the team in 1972, but his lifetime as Houston head coach ran out after five games of this season. With Peterson's two-year record at 1-18 after five straight losses this year, general manager Sid Gillman stepped out of the front office to take over as head coach. Hoping to recapture the magic of his years at San Diego, Gillman headed the Oilers for the remainder of the season, but could only manage one victory.

## WESTERN DIVISION

**Oakland Raiders**—The Raiders failed to score a touchdown in their first three games, so coach John Madden decided to bench quarterback Daryle Lamonica and replace him with lefty Ken Stabler. Whereas Lamonica excelled at throwing the long pass, Stabler thrived on running the ball-control offense preferred by coach Madden. With two strong runners in Marv Hubbard and Charlie Smith, two sure-handed receivers in Fred Biletnikoff and Mike Siani, and a superb front line, Stabler found many assets to manipulate in the Oakland attack. The defense had lots of old assets and one big addition in ex-Colt Bubba Smith. The Raider defense kept the team in the Western race early in the year, and the offense came through in victories over Kansas City and Denver in December to win first place and a playoff berth.

**Denver Broncos**—Bronco fans were amazed to find their club in the fight for first place all season long. In two years on the job, coach John Ralston had built a fine offense around the passing of veteran Charley Johnson and the running of star Floyd Little, with a solid line supporting both the air and ground games. The defense added two stand-out rookies in end Barney Chavous and cornerback Calvin Jones, and veteran tackle Paul Smith sparked the squad with his All-Pro performance at rushing enemy passers. On the last day of the season the Broncos faced Oakland in a face-to-face duel for the Western title. Trailing 14-10 in the fourth quarter, the Broncos gambled on a fake punt play on fourth down. Bill Van Heusen did not gain the needed yards. The Raiders took the ball over and scored a touchdown as the Broncos had to settle for second place in their first winning season ever.

**Kansas City Chiefs**—After a poor pre-season, the Kansas City defense played with its accustomed vigor in the regular season, but the offense had problems generating any steam at all. Veteran quarterback Len Dawson suffered from a variety of small hurts which kept him out of the lineup much of the time, and substitute Pete Beathard, in his second tour of duty in Kansas City, could not get the attack moving in early season trials. Coach Hank Stram finally turned to Mickey Livingston, who brought the offense back to life, and the Chiefs suddenly were in first place in late November. A 14-10 loss to Denver, however, knocked them out of first place, and a 37-7 beating at the hands of the Raiders ended any playoffs hopes for this year.

**San Diego Chargers**—The Chargers' attempt to regain respectability by bringing in old, established players failed miserably this year. Quarterback Johnny Unitas had little zip left in his arm after seventeen years with the Colts, and he wound up on the bench watching rookie Dan Fouts lead the attack. An injury to receiver Gary Garrison further hurt the offense, and coach Harland Svare unexplainedly benched runner Mike Garrett early in the season. Morale on the club plunged, and when receiver Dave Williams was released in mid-season, he called the team "a zoo." Svare resigned as coach after eight games to concentrate on front-office duties as general manager, turning over the reigns to assistant Ron Waller.

## FINAL TEAM STATISTICS

(Other statistics not available at press time)

### OFFENSE

| | BALT. | BUFF. | CIN. | CLEV. | DENV. | HOUS. | K.C. | MIAMI | N.ENG. | N.Y. | OAK. | PITT. | S.D. |
|---|---|---|---|---|---|---|---|---|---|---|---|---|---|
| **FIRST DOWNS:** | | | | | | | | | | | | | |
| Total | 218 | 219 | 252 | 200 | 253 | 193 | 208 | 215 | 237 | 222 | 288 | 217 | 198 |
| by Rushing | 121 | 152 | 124 | 107 | 111 | 89 | 106 | 111 | 97 | 95 | 129 | 111 | 88 |
| by Passing | 79 | 60 | 108 | 79 | 127 | 93 | 93 | 91 | 122 | 109 | 139 | 89 | 93 |
| by Penalty | 18 | 7 | 20 | 14 | 15 | 11 | 9 | 13 | 18 | 18 | 20 | 17 | 17 |
| **RUSHING:** | | | | | | | | | | | | | |
| Number | 536 | 605 | 515 | 506 | 487 | 386 | 511 | 507 | 454 | 453 | 547 | 555 | 431 |
| Yards | 2031 | 3088 | 2236 | 1968 | 1954 | 1388 | 1793 | 2521 | 1612 | 1864 | 2510 | 2143 | 1814 |
| Average Yards | 3.8 | 5.1 | 4.3 | 3.9 | 4.0 | 3.6 | 3.5 | 5.0 | 3.6 | 4.1 | 4.6 | 3.9 | 4.2 |
| Touchdowns | 9 | 20 | 13 | 12 | 16 | 9 | 11 | 16 | 15 | 7 | 14 | 12 | 9 |
| **PASSING:** | | | | | | | | | | | | | |
| Attempts | 300 | 213 | 332 | 308 | 378 | 411 | 313 | 256 | 380 | 373 | 353 | 309 | 363 |
| Completions | 137 | 96 | 180 | 152 | 196 | 225 | 173 | 133 | 195 | 181 | 205 | 140 | 161 |
| Completion Percentage | 45.7 | 45.1 | 54.2 | 49.4 | 51.9 | 54.7 | 55.3 | 52.0 | 51.3 | 48.5 | 58.1 | 45.3 | 44.4 |
| Passing Yards | 1746 | 1236 | 2439 | 1741 | 2706 | 2370 | 2039 | 1675 | 2581 | 2353 | 2611 | 2157 | 2129 |
| Avg. Yards per Attempt | 5.8 | 5.8 | 7.3 | 5.7 | 7.2 | 5.8 | 6.5 | 6.5 | 6.8 | 6.3 | 7.4 | 7.0 | 5.9 |
| Avg. Yards per Complet. | 12.7 | 12.9 | 13.6 | 11.5 | 13.8 | 10.5 | 11.8 | 12.6 | 13.2 | 13.0 | 12.7 | 15.4 | 13.2 |
| Times Tackled Passing | 32 | 31 | 24 | 45 | 27 | 43 | 39 | 13 | 37 | 37 | 45 | 30 | 37 |
| Yards Lost Tackled | 271 | 239 | 163 | 368 | 187 | 451 | 296 | 93 | 350 | 297 | 348 | 230 | 321 |
| Net Yards | 1475 | 997 | 2276 | 1373 | 2519 | 1919 | 1743 | 1582 | 2231 | 2056 | 2263 | 1927 | 1808 |
| Touchdowns | 14 | 4 | 18 | 10 | 22 | 11 | 10 | 17 | 13 | 16 | 16 | 20 | 9 |
| Interceptions | 25 | 14 | 12 | 20 | 20 | 27 | 13 | 12 | 17 | 22 | 18 | 26 | 30 |
| Percent Intercepted | 8.3 | 6.6 | 3.6 | 6.5 | 5.3 | 6.6 | 4.2 | 4.7 | 4.5 | 5.9 | 5.1 | 8.4 | 8.3 |
| **PUNTS:** | | | | | | | | | | | | | |
| Number | 62 | 66 | 68 | 82 | 69 | 85 | 80 | 48 | 61 | 74 | 69 | 62 | 72 |
| Average Distance | 38.7 | 40.3 | 41.0 | 40.5 | 45.1 | 38.8 | 45.5 | 42.3 | 37.7 | 37.1 | 45.3 | 41.1 | 41.1 |
| **PUNT RETURNS:** | | | | | | | | | | | | | |
| Number | 24 | 32 | 45 | 36 | 40 | 30 | 42 | 37 | 33 | 27 | 46 | 52 | 33 |
| Yards | 129 | 279 | 333 | 308 | 404 | 227 | 279 | 382 | 324 | 165 | 344 | 416 | 408 |
| Average Yards | 5.4 | 8.7 | 7.4 | 8.6 | 10.1 | 7.6 | 6.6 | 10.3 | 9.8 | 6.1 | 7.5 | 8.0 | 12.4 |
| Touchdowns | 0 | 1 | 0 | 0 | 0 | 0 | 0 | 0 | 0 | 0 | 1 | 0 | 2 |
| **KICKOFF RETURNS:** | | | | | | | | | | | | | |
| Number | 60 | 42 | 39 | 49 | 36 | 76 | 31 | 24 | 57 | 52 | 39 | 40 | 70 |
| Yards | 1343 | 972 | 876 | 1084 | 793 | 1799 | 725 | 523 | 1372 | 1061 | 937 | 843 | 1597 |
| Average Yards | 22.4 | 23.1 | 22.5 | 22.1 | 22.0 | 23.7 | 23.4 | 21.8 | 24.1 | 20.4 | 24.0 | 21.1 | 22.8 |
| Touchdowns | 1 | 2 | 0 | 0 | 0 | 1 | 0 | 0 | 1 | 1 | 0 | 0 | 0 |
| **INTERCEPTION RETURNS:** | | | | | | | | | | | | | |
| Number | 15 | 14 | 18 | 12 | 14 | 17 | 21 | 21 | 13 | 19 | 17 | 37 | 16 |
| Yards | 116 | 224 | 166 | 202 | 220 | 298 | 328 | 335 | 105 | 288 | 162 | 673 | 205 |
| Average Yards | 7.7 | 16.0 | 9.2 | 16.8 | 15.7 | 17.5 | 15.6 | 16.0 | 8.1 | 15.2 | 9.5 | 18.2 | 12.8 |
| Touchdowns | 1 | 1 | 0 | 1 | 2 | 0 | 1 | 2 | 0 | 2 | 0 | 3 | 1 |
| **PENALTIES:** | | | | | | | | | | | | | |
| Number | 57 | 75 | 83 | 70 | 83 | 95 | 83 | 52 | 50 | 62 | 82 | 84 | 74 |
| Yards | 483 | 744 | 799 | 620 | 745 | 900 | 797 | 416 | 550 | 575 | 759 | 817 | 628 |
| **FUMBLES:** | | | | | | | | | | | | | |
| Number | 16 | 27 | 25 | 34 | 21 | 43 | 36 | 22 | 51 | 32 | 29 | 36 | 41 |
| Number Lost | 13 | 13 | 14 | 17 | 9 | 25 | 18 | 16 | 25 | 17 | 16 | 14 | 21 |
| **POINTS:** | | | | | | | | | | | | | |
| Total | 226 | 259 | 286 | 234 | 354 | 199 | 231 | 343 | 258 | 240 | 292 | 347 | 188 |
| PAT Attempts | 26 | 28 | 32 | 24 | 41 | 22 | 23 | 38 | 31 | 27 | 32 | 37 | 22 |
| PAT Made | 22 | 28 | 31 | 24 | 40 | 22 | 21 | 38 | 25 | 27 | 31 | 36 | 20 |
| FG Attempts | 28 | 30 | 31 | 31 | 33 | 24 | 38 | 37 | 29 | 24 | 33 | 43 | 27 |
| FG Made | 16 | 21 | 21 | 22 | 22 | 15 | 24 | 25 | 15 | 17 | 23 | 29 | 12 |
| Percent FG Made | 57.1 | 70.0 | 67.7 | 71.0 | 66.7 | 62.5 | 63.2 | 67.6 | 51.7 | 70.8 | 69.7 | 67.4 | 44.4 |
| Safeties | 0 | 0 | 0 | 0 | 1 | 0 | 0 | 1 | 1 | 0 | 0 | 1 | 0 |

### DEFENSE

| | BALT. | BUFF. | CIN. | CLEV. | DENV. | HOUS. | K.C. | MIAMI | N.ENG. | N.Y. | OAK. | PITT. | S.D. |
|---|---|---|---|---|---|---|---|---|---|---|---|---|---|
| **FIRST DOWNS:** | | | | | | | | | | | | | |
| Total | 243 | 231 | 219 | 196 | 239 | 274 | 209 | 195 | 215 | 226 | 194 | 210 | 267 |
| by Rushing | 104 | 101 | 109 | 102 | 97 | 138 | 90 | 109 | 142 | 116 | 88 | 95 | 125 |
| by Passing | 123 | 112 | 97 | 79 | 121 | 114 | 95 | 78 | 67 | 101 | 92 | 91 | 124 |
| by Penalty | 16 | 18 | 13 | 15 | 21 | 22 | 24 | 8 | 6 | 9 | 14 | 24 | 18 |
| **RUSHING:** | | | | | | | | | | | | | |
| Number | 491 | 455 | 459 | 513 | 455 | 576 | 493 | 511 | 560 | 538 | 435 | 488 | 559 |
| Yards | 2089 | 1797 | 1807 | 2091 | 1795 | 2410 | 1956 | 1991 | 2850 | 2228 | 1470 | 1652 | 2264 |
| Average Yards | 4.3 | 3.9 | 3.9 | 4.1 | 3.9 | 4.2 | 4.0 | 3.9 | 5.1 | 4.1 | 3.4 | 3.4 | 4.1 |
| Touchdowns | 15 | 11 | 15 | 7 | 14 | 19 | 11 | 9 | 16 | 12 | 5 | 8 | 23 |
| **PASSING:** | | | | | | | | | | | | | |
| Attempts | 331 | 368 | 338 | 312 | 387 | 326 | 324 | 320 | 240 | 296 | 370 | 359 | 341 |
| Completions | 199 | 166 | 182 | 144 | 202 | 178 | 157 | 151 | 134 | 150 | 170 | 164 | 177 |
| Completion Percentage | 60.1 | 45.1 | 53.8 | 46.2 | 52.2 | 54.6 | 48.5 | 47.2 | 55.8 | 50.7 | 45.9 | 45.7 | 51.9 |
| Passing Yards | 2599 | 2394 | 2240 | 1984 | 2766 | 2466 | 1942 | 1604 | 1600 | 2148 | 1995 | 1923 | 2473 |
| Avg. Yards per Attempt | 7.9 | 6.5 | 6.6 | 6.4 | 7.1 | 7.6 | 6.0 | 5.0 | 6.7 | 7.3 | 5.4 | 5.4 | 7.3 |
| Avg. Yards per Complet. | 13.1 | 14.4 | 12.3 | 13.8 | 13.7 | 13.9 | 12.4 | 10.6 | 11.9 | 14.3 | 11.7 | 11.7 | 14.0 |
| Times Tackled Passing | 25 | 32 | 43 | 29 | 36 | 27 | 38 | 45 | 32 | 26 | 40 | 33 | 26 |
| Yards Lost Tackled | 200 | 276 | 342 | 248 | 326 | 229 | 323 | 314 | 262 | 198 | 305 | 251 | 219 |
| Net Yards | 2399 | 2118 | 1898 | 1736 | 2440 | 2237 | 1619 | 1290 | 1338 | 1950 | 1690 | 1672 | 2254 |
| Touchdowns | 16 | 12 | 9 | 16 | 15 | 26 | 11 | 5 | 11 | 18 | 12 | 11 | 18 |
| Interceptions | 15 | 14 | 18 | 12 | 14 | 17 | 21 | 21 | 13 | 19 | 17 | 37 | 16 |
| Percent Intercepted | 4.5 | 3.8 | 5.3 | 3.8 | 3.6 | 5.2 | 6.5 | 6.6 | 5.4 | 6.4 | 4.6 | 10.3 | 4.7 |
| **PUNTS:** | | | | | | | | | | | | | |
| Number | 47 | 63 | 77 | 78 | 69 | 62 | 84 | 76 | 62 | 67 | 90 | 75 | 60 |
| Average Distance | 37.4 | 39.8 | 41.7 | 40.4 | 43.3 | 39.6 | 42.9 | 38.5 | 40.5 | 40.9 | 43.1 | 42.4 | 43.1 |
| **PUNT RETURNS:** | | | | | | | | | | | | | |
| Number | 27 | 34 | 27 | 44 | 31 | 44 | 48 | 30 | 29 | 36 | 40 | 37 | 35 |
| Yards | 280 | 312 | 123 | 270 | 257 | 343 | 446 | 182 | 152 | 411 | 290 | 308 | 257 |
| Average Yards | 10.4 | 9.2 | 4.6 | 6.1 | 8.3 | 7.8 | 9.5 | 6.1 | 5.2 | 11.3 | 7.3 | 8.3 | 7.4 |
| Touchdowns | 0 | 1 | 0 | 0 | 0 | 0 | 0 | 0 | 0 | 1 | 0 | 0 | 0 |
| **KICKOFF RETURNS:** | | | | | | | | | | | | | |
| Number | 42 | 44 | 42 | 48 | 61 | 37 | 40 | 56 | 40 | 44 | 46 | 59 | 35 |
| Yards | 950 | 934 | 1170 | 1165 | 1244 | 811 | 1031 | 1202 | 963 | 1021 | 981 | 1357 | 862 |
| Average Yards | 22.6 | 21.2 | 27.9 | 24.3 | 20.4 | 21.9 | 25.8 | 21.5 | 24.1 | 23.2 | 21.4 | 23.0 | 24.6 |
| Touchdowns | 0 | 1 | 1 | 0 | 1 | 1 | 0 | 0 | 1 | 0 | 0 | 0 | 1 |
| **INTERCEPTION RETURNS:** | | | | | | | | | | | | | |
| Number | 25 | 14 | 12 | 20 | 20 | 27 | 13 | 12 | 17 | 22 | 18 | 26 | 30 |
| Yards | 336 | 149 | 198 | 271 | 331 | 357 | 151 | 190 | 385 | 296 | 187 | 512 | 532 |
| Average Yards | 13.4 | 10.6 | 16.5 | 13.6 | 16.6 | 13.2 | 11.6 | 15.8 | 22.6 | 13.5 | 10.4 | 19.7 | 17.7 |
| Touchdowns | 4 | 0 | 1 | 0 | 1 | 4 | 0 | 0 | 1 | 2 | 1 | 2 | 0 |
| **PENALTIES:** | | | | | | | | | | | | | |
| Number | 69 | 53 | 78 | 79 | 84 | 90 | 63 | 61 | 77 | 86 | 67 | 86 | 68 |
| Yards | 684 | 485 | 710 | 738 | 824 | 811 | 649 | 616 | 693 | 783 | 623 | 757 | 579 |
| **FUMBLES:** | | | | | | | | | | | | | |
| Number | 35 | 30 | 31 | 21 | 26 | 29 | 33 | 29 | 29 | 30 | 35 | 41 | 31 |
| Number Lost | 22 | 19 | 16 | 9 | 15 | 10 | 18 | 8 | 18 | 19 | 16 | 18 | 18 |
| **POINTS:** | | | | | | | | | | | | | |
| Total | 341 | 230 | 231 | 255 | 296 | 447 | 192 | 150 | 300 | 306 | 175 | 210 | 386 |
| PAT Attempts | 39 | 25 | 27 | 24 | 31 | 53 | 22 | 15 | 32 | 34 | 19 | 22 | 46 |
| PAT Made | 38 | 23 | 27 | 24 | 30 | 52 | 21 | 13 | 30 | 33 | 19 | 21 | 42 |
| FG Attempts | 33 | 34 | 23 | 46 | 35 | 42 | 27 | 27 | 32 | 34 | 30 | 29 | 38 |
| FG Made | 23 | 19 | 14 | 29 | 26 | 25 | 13 | 15 | 26 | 23 | 14 | 19 | 22 |
| Percent FG Made | 69.7 | 55.9 | 60.9 | 63.0 | 74.3 | 59.5 | 48.1 | 55.6 | 81.3 | 67.6 | 46.7 | 65.5 | 57.9 |
| Safeties | 0 | 0 | 0 | 0 | 1 | 1 | 0 | 1 | 0 | 0 | 0 | 0 | 1 |

## CONFERENCE PLAYOFFS

December 22, at Oakland (Attendance 51,110)

### SCORING

| | | | | | |
|---|---|---|---|---|---|
| OAKLAND | 7 | 3 | 13 | 10 | –33 |
| PITTSBURGH | 0 | 7 | 0 | 7 | –14 |

First Quarter
Oak. Hubbard, 1 yard rush
PAT–Blanda (kick)

Second Quarter
Oak. Blanda, 25 yard field goal
Pitt. B. Pearson, 4 yard pass from Bradshaw PAT–Gerela (kick)

Third Quarter
Oak. Blanda, 31 yard field goal
Oak. Blanda, 22 yard field goal
Oak. W. Brown, 54 yard interception return PAT–Blanda (kick)

Fourth Quarter
Oak. Blanda, 10 yard field goal
Pitt. Lewis, 26 yard pass from Bradshaw PAT–Gerela (kick)
Oak. Hubbard, 1 yard rush
PAT–Blanda (kick)

### TEAM STATISTICS

| OAK. | | PITT. |
|---|---|---|
| 24 | First Downs–Total | 15 |
| 14 | First Downs–Rushing | 2 |
| 8 | First Downs–Passing | 10 |
| 2 | First Downs–Penalty | 3 |
| 0 | Fumbles–Number | 1 |
| 0 | Fumbles–Lost Ball | 0 |
| 9 | Penalties–Number | 4 |
| 75 | Yards Penalized | 60 |
| 1 | Missed Field Goals | 0 |
| 74 | Offensive Plays | 46 |
| 361 | Net Yards | 223 |
| 4.8 | Average Gain | 4.8 |
| 0 | Giveaways | 3 |
| 3 | Takeaways | 0 |
| +3 | Difference | –3 |

### INDIVIDUAL STATISTICS

| OAKLAND | No | Yds | Avg. | PITTSBURGH | No | Yds | Avg. |
|---|---|---|---|---|---|---|---|
| **RUSHING** | | | | | | | |
| Hubbard | 20 | 91 | 4.6 | Harris | 10 | 29 | 2.9 |
| C. Smith | 17 | 73 | 4.3 | P. Pearson | 4 | 14 | 3.5 |
| C. Davis | 12 | 48 | 4.0 | Fuqua | 3 | 13 | 4.3 |
| Banaszak | 5 | 17 | 3.4 | Bradshaw | 3 | 9 | 3.0 |
| Moore | 1 | 3 | 3.0 | | 20 | 65 | 3.2 |
| | 55 | 232 | 4.2 | | | | |
| **RECEIVING** | | | | | | | |
| Siani | 5 | 68 | 13.6 | Lewis | 4 | 70 | 17.5 |
| Moore | 3 | 26 | 8.7 | Fuqua | 4 | 52 | 13.0 |
| C. Smith | 2 | 10 | 5.0 | B. Pearson | 2 | 7 | 3.5 |
| Hubbard | 1 | 17 | 17.0 | P. Pearson | 1 | 24 | 24.0 |
| Biletnikoff | 1 | 8 | 8.0 | Williams | 1 | 14 | 14.0 |
| Banaszak | 1 | 5 | 5.0 | | 12 | 167 | 13.9 |
| | 13 | 134 | 10.3 | | | | |
| **PUNTING** | | | | | | | |
| Guy | 2 | | 39.0 | Walden | 5 | | 41.6 |
| **PUNT RETURNS** | | | | | | | |
| Atkinson | 2 | 11 | 5.5 | Edwards | 1 | 20 | 20.0 |
| **KICKOFF RETURNS** | | | | | | | |
| C. Davis | 3 | 58 | 19.3 | P. Pearson | 4 | 79 | 19.8 |
| | | | | Steve Davis | 3 | 77 | 25.7 |
| | | | | | 7 | 156 | 22.3 |
| **INTERCEPTION RETURNS** | | | | | | | |
| W. Brown | 1 | 54 | 54.0 | None | | | |
| Atkinson | 1 | 8 | 8.0 | | | | |
| Villapiano | 1 | 0 | 0.0 | | | | |
| | 3 | 62 | 20.7 | | | | |

**PASSING**

| OAKLAND | Att. | Comp. | Comp. Pct. | Yds. | Int. | Yds/ Att. | Yds/ Comp. | Yards Lost Tackled |
|---|---|---|---|---|---|---|---|---|
| Stabler | 17 | 14 | 82.4 | 142 | 0 | 8.4 | 10.1 | 2–13 |
| **PITTSBURGH** | | | | | | | | |
| Bradshaw | 25 | 12 | 48.0 | 167 | 3 | 6.7 | 13.9 | 1– 9 |

December 23, at Miami (Attendance 80,047)

### SCORING

| | | | | | |
|---|---|---|---|---|---|
| MIAMI | 14 | 7 | 10 | 3 | –34 |
| CINCINNATI | 3 | 13 | 0 | 0 | –16 |

First Quarter
Mia. Warfield, 13 yard pass from Griese PAT–Yepremian (kick)
Cin. Muhlmann, 24 yard field goal
Mia. Csonka, 1 yard rush
PAT–Yepremian (kick)

Second Quarer
Mia. Morris, 4 yard rush
PAT–Yepremian (kick)
Cin. Craig, 45 yard interception return PAT–Muhlmann (kick)
Cin. Muhlmann, 46 yard field goal
Cin. Muhlmann, 12 yard field goal

Third Quarter
Mia. Mandich, 7 yard pass from Griese PAT–Yepremian (kick)
Mia. Yepremian, 50 yard field goal

Fourth Quarter
Mia. Yepremian, 46 yard field goal

### TEAM STATISTICS

| MIAMI | | CIN. |
|---|---|---|
| 27 | First Downs–Total | 11 |
| 18 | First Downs–Rushing | 5 |
| 9 | First Downs–Passing | 6 |
| 0 | First Downs–Penalty | 0 |
| 2 | Fumbles–Number | 0 |
| 1 | Fumbles–Lost Ball | 0 |
| 1 | Penalties–Number | 2 |
| 5 | Yards Penalized | 19 |
| 0 | Missed Field Goals | 0 |
| 71 | Offensive Plays | 50 |
| 400 | Net Yards | 194 |
| 5.6 | Average Gain | 3.9 |
| 3 | Giveaways | 1 |
| 1 | Takeaways | 3 |
| –2 | Difference | +2 |

### INDIVIDUAL STATISTICS

| MIAMI | No | Yds | Avg. | CINCINNATI | No | Yds | Avg. |
|---|---|---|---|---|---|---|---|
| **RUSHING** | | | | | | | |
| Morris | 20 | 106 | 5.3 | Clark | 7 | 40 | 5.7 |
| Csonka | 20 | 71 | 3.6 | Anderson | 3 | 26 | 8.8 |
| Kiick | 10 | 51 | 5.1 | E. Johnson | 2 | 17 | 8.5 |
| Leigh | 1 | 8 | 8.0 | Elliott | 7 | 15 | 2.1 |
| Nottingham | 1 | 5 | 5.0 | Curtis | 1 | –1 | –1.0 |
| | 52 | 241 | 4.6 | | 20 | 97 | 4.9 |
| **RECEIVING** | | | | | | | |
| Warfield | 4 | 95 | 23.8 | Elliott | 9 | 53 | 5.9 |
| Mandich | 3 | 28 | 9.3 | Joiner | 2 | 33 | 16.5 |
| Kiick | 3 | 19 | 6.3 | Clark | 2 | 18 | 9.0 |
| Briscoe | 1 | 17 | 17.0 | Curtis | 1 | 9 | 9.0 |
| | 11 | 159 | 14.5 | | 14 | 113 | 8.1 |
| **PUNTING** | | | | | | | |
| Seiple | 2 | | 49.0 | Lewis | 7 | | 36.3 |
| **PUNT RETURNS** | | | | | | | |
| Scott | 1 | 4 | 4.0 | Casanova | 1 | 15 | 15.0 |
| Anderson | 1 | 2 | 2.0 | Parrish | 1 | 11 | 11.0 |
| | 2 | 6 | 3.0 | | 2 | 26 | 13.0 |
| **KICKOFF RETURNS** | | | | | | | |
| Anderson | 1 | 14 | 14.0 | Parrish | 1 | 25 | 25.0 |
| Morris | 1 | 0 | 0.0 | Jackson | 1 | 17 | 17.0 |
| | 2 | 14 | 7.0 | | 2 | 42 | 21.0 |
| **INTERCEPTION RETURNS** | | | | | | | |
| Anderson | 1 | 19 | 19.0 | Craig | 1 | 45 | 45.0 |
| | | | | Casanova | 1 | 0 | 0.0 |
| | | | | | 2 | 45 | 22.5 |

**PASSING**

| MIAMI | Att. | Comp. | Comp. Pct. | Yds. | Int. | Yds/ Att. | Yds/ Comp. | Yards Lost Tackled |
|---|---|---|---|---|---|---|---|---|
| Griese | 18 | 11 | 61.1 | 159 | 1 | 8.8 | 14.5 | |
| Briscoe | 1 | 0 | 0.0 | 0 | 1 | – | – | |
| | 19 | 11 | 57.9 | 159 | 2 | 8.4 | 14.5 | 0– 0 |
| **CINCINNATI** | | | | | | | | |
| Anderson | 27 | 14 | 51.9 | 113 | 1 | 4.2 | 8.1 | 3–16 |

## MIAMI DOLPHINS 12-2 Don Shula

| Scores of Each Game | | |
|---|---|---|
| 21 | SAN FRANCISCO | 13 |
| 7 | Oakland | 12 |
| 44 | NEW ENGLAND | 23 |
| 31 | N. Y. JETS | 3 |
| 17 | Cleveland | 9 |
| 27 | BUFFALO | 6 |
| 30 | New England | 14 |
| 24 | N. Y. Jets | 14 |
| 44 | BALTIMORE | 0 |
| 17 | Buffalo | 0 |
| 14 | Dallas | 7 |
| 30 | PITTSBURGH | 26 |
| 3 | Baltimore | 16 |
| 34 | DETROIT | 7 |

| Use Name | Pos. | Hgt | Wgt | Age | Int | Pts |
|---|---|---|---|---|---|---|
| Doug Crusan | OT | 6'5" | 250 | 27 | | |
| Norm Evans | OT | 6'5" | 252 | 30 | | |
| Wayne Moore | OT | 6'6" | 265 | 28 | | |
| Willie Young | OT | 6'4" | 270 | 25 | | |
| Bob Kuechenberg | OG | 6'3" | 247 | 25 | | |
| Larry Little | OG | 6'1" | 265 | 27 | | |
| Ed Newman | OG | 6'2" | 245 | 22 | | |
| Jim Langer | C | 6'2" | 250 | 25 | | |
| Irv Goode | OG-C | 6'4" | 252 | 32 | | |
| Vern Den Herder | DE | 6'6" | 250 | 24 | | |
| Bill Stanfill | DE | 6'5" | 250 | 26 | | |
| Bob Heinz | DT-DE | 6'6" | 270 | 26 | | |
| Manny Fernandez | DT | 6'2" | 250 | 27 | | |
| Baldy Moore | DT | 6'2" | 265 | 27 | | |
| Larry Woods | DT | 6'6" | 260 | 25 | | |
| Larry Ball | LB | 6'6" | 225 | 23 | 1 | |
| Bruce Bannon | LB | 6'3" | 225 | 22 | | |
| Nick Buoniconti | LB | 5'11" | 220 | 32 | | 6 |
| Mike Kolen | LB | 6'2" | 220 | 25 | 2 | |
| Bob Matheson | LB-DE | 6'4" | 240 | 28 | | |
| Jesse Powell | LB | 6'1" | 215 | 26 | | |
| Doug Swift | LB | 6'3" | 228 | 24 | 1 | |
| Dick Anderson | DB | 6'2" | 196 | 27 | 8 | 12 |
| Charlie Babb | DB | 6' | 190 | 23 | | |
| Tim Foley | DB | 6' | 194 | 25 | 2 | 12 |
| Curtis Johnson | DB | 6'2" | 196 | 25 | 2 | 2 |
| Lloyd Mumphord | DB | 5'11" | 180 | 26 | | |
| Jake Scott | DB | 6' | 188 | 28 | 4 | |
| Henry Stuckey | DB | 6'1" | 190 | 23 | 1 | |
| Bob Griese | QB | 6'1" | 190 | 28 | | |
| Earl Morrall | QB | 6'1" | 206 | 39 | | |
| Jim Kiick | HB | 5'11" | 215 | 27 | | |
| Mercury Morris | HB | 5'10" | 190 | 26 | | 60 |
| Charlie Leigh | FB-HB | 5'11" | 205 | 27 | | 6 |
| Larry Csonka | FB | 6'3" | 237 | 26 | | 30 |
| Don Nottingham (from BAL) | FB | 5'10" | 210 | 24 | | 6 |
| Marlin Briscoe | WR | 5'10" | 178 | 27 | | 12 |
| Bo Rather | WR | 6'1" | 182 | 22 | | |
| Ron Sellers | WR | 6'4" | 195 | 26 | | |
| Howard Twilley | WR | 5'10" | 185 | 29 | | |
| Paul Warfield | WR | 6' | 185 | 30 | | 66 |
| Marv Fleming | TE | 6'4" | 235 | 31 | | |
| Jim Mandich | TE | 6'3" | 224 | 25 | | 24 |
| Larry Seiple | TE | 6' | 215 | 28 | | |
| Garo Yepremian | K | 5'8" | 175 | 29 | | 113 |

Jim Dunaway – Injury
Howard Kindig – Injury
Ed Jenkins – Injury

## BUFFALO BILLS 9-5 Lou Saban

| Scores of Each Game | | |
|---|---|---|
| 31 | New England | 13 |
| 7 | San Diego | 34 |
| 9 | N. Y. JETS | 7 |
| 27 | PHILADELPHIA | 26 |
| 31 | BALTIMORE | 13 |
| 6 | Miami | 27 |
| 23 | KANSAS CITY | 14 |
| 0 | New Orleans | 13 |
| 13 | CINCINNATI | 16 |
| 0 | MIAMI | 17 |
| 24 | Baltimore | 17 |
| 17 | Atlanta | 6 |
| 37 | NEW ENGLAND | 13 |
| 34 | N. Y. Jets | 14 |

| Use Name | Pos. | Hgt | Wgt | Age | Int | Pts |
|---|---|---|---|---|---|---|
| Dave Foley | OT | 6'5" | 255 | 25 | | |
| Donnie Green | OT | 6'7" | 272 | 25 | | |
| Mike Montler | C-OT | 6'4" | 255 | 29 | | |
| Joe DeLamielleure | OG | 6'3" | 254 | 22 | | |
| Reggie McKenzie | OG | 6'4" | 235 | 23 | | |
| Bobby Penchion | OG | 6'5" | 265 | 24 | | |
| Bruce Jarvis | C | 6'7" | 250 | 24 | | |
| Willie Parker | OG-C | 6'3" | 240 | 24 | | |
| Earl Edwards | DE | 6'6" | 262 | 27 | | |
| Halvor Hagen | DE | 6'5" | 245 | 26 | | |
| Walt Patulski | DE | 6'6" | 260 | 23 | | |
| Mike Kadish | DT | 6'5" | 265 | 23 | | |
| Bob Kampa | DT | 6'4" | 252 | 22 | | |
| Steve Okoniewski | DT | 6'3" | 247 | 24 | | |
| Jerry Patton | DT | 6'3" | 265 | 27 | | |
| Jeff Winans | DT | 6'5" | 265 | 21 | | |
| Jim Cheyunski | LB | 6'2" | 225 | 27 | 3 | |
| Phil Croyle (from HOU) | LB | 6'3" | 220 | 25 | | |
| Dale Farley | LB | 6'3" | 235 | 24 | | |
| Fred Forsberg (from DEN) | LB | 6'1" | 235 | 29 | 1 | |
| Merv Krakau | LB | 6'2" | 242 | 22 | | |
| Rich Lewis | LB | 6'3" | 220 | 23 | | |
| John Skorupan | LB | 6'2" | 214 | 22 | | |
| Bill Cahill | DB | 5'11" | 180 | 22 | | 6 |
| Leon Garror | DB | 6' | 180 | 25 | 1 | |
| Tony Greene | DB | 5'10" | 170 | 24 | 1 | |
| Dwight Harrison | DB | 6'1" | 178 | 24 | 5 | 6 |
| Robert James | DB | 6'1" | 185 | 26 | 1 | |
| Ernie Kellerman | DB | 6' | 183 | 29 | 2 | |
| Ken Stone (to WAS) | DB | 6'1" | 180 | 22 | | 6 |
| Donnie Walker | DB | 6'1" | 185 | 22 | 1 | |
| Joe Ferguson | QB | 6'1" | 190 | 23 | | 12 |
| Dennis Shaw | QB | 6'2" | 215 | 26 | | |
| Steve Jones | HB | 6' | 200 | 22 | | |
| O. J. Simpson | HB | 6'2" | 214 | 26 | | 72 |
| Pete Van Valkenberg | HB | 6'2" | 192 | 23 | | |
| Jim Braxton | FB | 6'2" | 243 | 24 | | 24 |
| Bo Cornell | FB | 6'1" | 215 | 24 | | |
| Larry Watkins | FB | 6'2" | 230 | 26 | | 18 |
| Bob Chandler | WR | 6' | 180 | 24 | | 19 |
| Wallace Francis | WR | 5'11" | 188 | 21 | | 12 |
| J. D. Hill | WR | 6'1" | 202 | 24 | | |
| Ray Jarvis | WR | 5'11" | 193 | 24 | | |
| Ted Koy | TE | 6'1" | 212 | 25 | | |
| Paul Seymour | TE | 6'5" | 260 | 23 | | |
| Dave Washington | TE | 6'5" | 220 | 24 | | |
| Spike Jones | K | 6'2" | 190 | 26 | | |
| John Leypoldt | K | 6'2" | 230 | 27 | | 90 |

Don Croft – Knee Injury

## NEW ENGLAND PATRIOTS 5-9 Chuck Fairbanks

| Scores of Each Game | | |
|---|---|---|
| 13 | BUFFALO | 31 |
| 7 | KANSAS CITY | 10 |
| 23 | Miami | 44 |
| 24 | BALTIMORE | 16 |
| 7 | N. Y. JETS | 9 |
| 13 | Chicago | 10 |
| 14 | MIAMI | 30 |
| 23 | Philadelphia | 24 |
| 13 | N. Y. Jets | 33 |
| 33 | GREEN BAY | 24 |
| 32 | Houston | 0 |
| 30 | SAN DIEGO | 14 |
| 13 | Buffalo | 37 |
| 13 | Baltimore | 18 |

| Use Name | Pos. | Hgt | Wgt | Age | Int | Pts |
|---|---|---|---|---|---|---|
| Tom Neville | OT | 6'4" | 255 | 30 | | |
| Leon Gray | OT | 6'3" | 256 | 21 | | |
| Bob Reynolds (to STL) | OT | 6'6" | 265 | 32 | | |
| Willie Banks | OG | 6'2" | 250 | 27 | | |
| Sam Adams | OT-OG | 6'3" | 252 | 24 | | |
| John Hannah | OG | 6'2" | 265 | 22 | | |
| Bill Lenkaitis | OG | 6'3" | 260 | 27 | | |
| Len St. Jean | OG | 6'1" | 250 | 31 | | |
| Jon Morris | C | 6'4" | 254 | 30 | | |
| Doug Dumler | C | 6'3" | 242 | 22 | | |
| Nate Dorsey | DE | 6'4" | 240 | 23 | | |
| Ray Hamilton | DE | 6'1" | 232 | 22 | | |
| Donnell Smith | DE | 6'4" | 245 | 24 | | |
| Julius Adams | DT-DE | 6'3" | 257 | 25 | | |
| Rick Cash | DT | 6'5" | 260 | 27 | | |
| Mel Lunsford | DT | 6'3" | 250 | 23 | | |
| Art Moore | DT | 6'5" | 253 | 22 | | |
| Dave Rowe | DT | 6'6" | 280 | 28 | | |
| Ron Acks | LB | 6'2" | 220 | 28 | 1 | |
| Edgar Chandler | LB | 6'3" | 225 | 27 | | |
| Will Foster | LB | 6'2" | 230 | 24 | | 6 |
| Bob Geddes | LB | 6'2" | 240 | 27 | | |
| Steve Kiner | LB | 6' | 218 | 26 | 2 | |
| Steve King | LB | 6'4" | 255 | 22 | | |
| Brian Stenger | LB | 6'4" | 230 | 26 | | |
| John Tanner | LB | 6'4" | 235 | 28 | | |
| Ralph Anderson | DB | 6'2" | 180 | 24 | 2 | |
| Ron Bolton | DB | 6'2" | 180 | 23 | 6 | |
| Greg Boyd | DB | 6'2" | 200 | 21 | | |
| Sandy Durko | DB | 6'1" | 185 | 25 | 3 | |
| George Hoey | DB | 5'10" | 170 | 26 | | |
| Honor Jackson (to NYG) | DB | 6'1" | 195 | 24 | 1 | |
| Don Martin | DB | 5'11" | 187 | 23 | | |
| Dave Mason | DB | 6' | 200 | 23 | | |
| Brian Dowling | QB | 6'2" | 200 | 26 | | |
| Jim Plunkett | QB | 6'3" | 220 | 25 | | 30 |
| Josh Ashton | HB | 6'1" | 205 | 24 | | |
| Mack Herron | HB | 5'5" | 170 | 25 | | 24 |
| Bob McCall | HB | 6' | 205 | 23 | | |
| Claxton Welch | HB | 5'11" | 203 | 26 | | |
| Paul Gipson | FB-HB | 6' | 210 | 26 | | |
| Sam Cunningham | FB | 6'3" | 215 | 23 | | 30 |
| John Tarver | FB | 6'3" | 227 | 24 | | 24 |
| Reggie Rucker | WR | 6'2" | 190 | 25 | | 18 |
| Darryl Stingley | WR | 6' | 190 | 21 | | 12 |
| Randy Vataha | WR | 5'10" | 175 | 24 | | 12 |
| Bob Adams | TE | 6'2" | 225 | 27 | | |
| John Mosier | TE | 6'3" | 220 | 25 | | |
| Bob Windsor | TE | 6'4" | 226 | 30 | | 24 |
| Bruce Barnes | K | 5'11" | 215 | 22 | | |
| Bill Bell | K | 6'1" | 192 | 25 | | 7 |
| Jeff White | K | 5'11" | 170 | 24 | | 63 |

Wayne Patrick – Knee Injury

## NEW YORK JETS 4-10 Weeb Ewbank

| Scores of Each Game | | |
|---|---|---|
| 7 | Green Bay | 23 |
| 34 | Baltimore | 10 |
| 7 | Buffalo | 9 |
| 3 | Miami | 31 |
| 9 | New England | 7 |
| 14 | Pittsburgh | 26 |
| 28 | DENVER | 40 |
| 14 | MIAMI | 24 |
| 33 | NEW ENGLAND | 13 |
| 14 | Cincinnati | 20 |
| 20 | ATLANTA | 28 |
| 20 | BALTIMORE | 17 |
| 23 | Philadelphia | 24 |
| 14 | BUFFALO | 34 |

| Use Name | Pos. | Hgt | Wgt | Age | Int | Pts |
|---|---|---|---|---|---|---|
| Winston Hill | OT | 6'4" | 280 | 31 | | |
| Bob Svihus | OT | 6'4" | 245 | 30 | | |
| Robert Woods | OT | 6'3" | 255 | 23 | | |
| John Mooring | C-OT | 6'6" | 255 | 26 | | |
| Dave Herman | OG | 6'2" | 255 | 31 | | |
| Randy Rasmussen | OG | 6'2" | 255 | 28 | | |
| Gary Puetz | OT-OG | 6'3" | 255 | 21 | | |
| Rick Harrell | C | 6'3" | 238 | 22 | | |
| John Schmitt | C | 6'4" | 250 | 30 | | |
| Ed Galigher | DE | 6'4" | 255 | 22 | | |
| Mark Lomas | DE | 6'4" | 250 | 25 | | |
| Joey Jackson | DT-DE | 6'4" | 270 | 24 | | |
| Richard Neal | DT-DE | 6'3" | 254 | 25 | | |
| John Little | DT | 6'3" | 250 | 26 | | |
| Steve Thompson | DT | 6'5" | 250 | 28 | | |
| John Elliott | DE-DT | 6'4" | 244 | 28 | | |
| Al Atkinson | LB | 6'1" | 230 | 30 | 1 | |
| Ralph Baker | LB | 6'3" | 228 | 31 | 4 | 6 |
| John Ebersole | LB | 6'3" | 235 | 24 | 1 | |
| Bill Ferguson | LB | 6'3" | 225 | 22 | | |
| Rob Spicer | LB | 6'4" | 227 | 22 | | |
| Mike Taylor | LB | 6'1" | 230 | 23 | | |
| Bill Zapalac | LB | 6'4" | 225 | 25 | | |
| Chris Farasopoulos | DB | 5'11" | 190 | 24 | 1 | |
| Delles Howell | DB | 6'3" | 200 | 26 | 4 | |
| Burgess Owens | DB | 6'2" | 200 | 22 | 1 | 6 |
| Rich Sowells | DB | 6' | 175 | 24 | 3 | 6 |
| Steve Tannen | DB | 6'1" | 194 | 25 | 1 | |
| Earlie Thomas | DB | 6'1" | 190 | 27 | 2 | |
| Phil Wise | DB | 6' | 190 | 24 | | 6 |
| Bill Demory | QB | 6'2" | 195 | 22 | | |
| Joe Namath | QB | 6'2" | 200 | 30 | | |
| Al Woodall | QB | 6'5" | 194 | 27 | | |
| Mike Adamle | HB | 5'9" | 197 | 23 | | |
| Hank Bjorklund | HB | 6'1" | 200 | 23 | | |
| Emerson Boozer | HB | 5'11" | 205 | 30 | | 36 |
| Cliff McClain | HB | 6' | 217 | 25 | | |
| Jim Nance | FB | 6'1" | 240 | 30 | | |
| John Riggins | FB | 6'2" | 230 | 24 | | 24 |
| Margene Adkins | WR | 5'10" | 183 | 26 | | |
| Jerome Barkum | WR | 6'3" | 215 | 23 | | 36 |
| Eddie Bell | WR | 5'10" | 160 | 25 | | 12 |
| David Knight | WR | 6'1" | 182 | 22 | | 6 |
| Rocky Turner | DB-WR | 6' | 200 | 23 | | |
| Dennis Cambal | TE | 6'3" | 228 | 24 | | |
| Rich Caster | TE | 6'5" | 228 | 24 | | 24 |
| Julian Fagan | K | 6'3" | 205 | 25 | | |
| Bobby Howfield | K | 5'9" | 180 | 36 | | 78 |

## BALTIMORE COLTS 4-10 Howard Schnellenberger

| Scores of Each Game | | |
|---|---|---|
| 14 | Cleveland | 24 |
| 10 | N. Y. JETS | 34 |
| 14 | NEW ORLEANS | 10 |
| 16 | New England | 24 |
| 13 | Buffalo | 31 |
| 29 | Detroit | 27 |
| 21 | OAKLAND | 34 |
| 27 | HOUSTON | 31 |
| 0 | Miami | 44 |
| 14 | Washington | 22 |
| 17 | BUFFALO | 24 |
| 17 | N. Y. Jets | 20 |
| 16 | MIAMI | 3 |
| 18 | NEW ENGLAND | 13 |

| Use Name | Pos. | Hgt | Wgt | Age | Int | Pts |
|---|---|---|---|---|---|---|
| Tom Drougas | OT | 6'4" | 257 | 23 | | |
| Dennis Nelson | OT | 6'5" | 260 | 27 | | |
| David Taylor | OT | 6'4" | 254 | 23 | | |
| Elmer Collett | OG | 6'4" | 240 | 28 | | |
| Cornelius Johnson | OG | 6'2" | 245 | 30 | | |
| Glenn Ressler | OG | 6'3" | 250 | 29 | | |
| Fred Hoaglin | C | 6'4" | 246 | 29 | | |
| Ken Mendenhall | C | 6'3" | 235 | 25 | | |
| Dan Neal | C | 6'4" | 240 | 24 | | |
| Mike Barnes | DE | 6'6" | 255 | 22 | | |
| Roy Hilton | DE | 6'6" | 240 | 28 | | |
| Dick Amman | DT-DE | 6'5" | 250 | 22 | | |
| Jim Bailey | DT | 6'5" | 255 | 25 | | |
| Joe Ehrmann | DT | 6'5" | 260 | 24 | | |
| Joe Schmiesing | DE-DT | 6'4" | 260 | 28 | | |
| Bill Windauer | DT | 6'3" | 245 | 23 | | |
| Stan Cherry | LB | 6'5" | 200 | 22 | | |
| Mike Curtis | LB | 6'2" | 232 | 30 | 2 | |
| Ted Hendricks | LB | 6'7" | 220 | 25 | 3 | 6 |
| Mike Kaczmarek | LB | 6'4" | 235 | 22 | 1 | |
| Ed Mooney | LB | 6'2" | 225 | 28 | | |
| Stan White | LB | 6'1" | 225 | 23 | 4 | 6 |
| Brian Herosian | DB | 6'3" | 200 | 22 | | |
| Rex Kern | DB | 5'11" | 190 | 24 | 2 | |
| Bruce Laird | DB | 6' | 185 | 23 | | |
| Jack Mildren | DB | 6'1" | 200 | 23 | | |
| Nelson Munsey | DB | 6'1" | 185 | 25 | | |
| Ray Oldham | DB | 6' | 200 | 22 | 2 | |
| Rick Volk | DB | 6'3" | 195 | 28 | 1 | |
| Marty Domres | QB | 6'3" | 220 | 26 | | 12 |
| Bert Jones | QB | 6'3" | 205 | 21 | | |
| Hubert Ginn (from MIA) | HB | 5'11" | 188 | 26 | | |
| Lydell Mitchell | HB | 5'11" | 204 | 24 | | 12 |
| Bill Olds | FB | 6'1" | 224 | 22 | | 12 |
| Don McCauley | HB-FB | 6'1" | 207 | 24 | | 12 |
| Glenn Doughty | WR | 6'2" | 204 | 22 | | 24 |
| Sam Havrilak | WR | 6'2" | 195 | 25 | | |
| Ollie Smith | WR | 6'2" | 195 | 24 | | |
| Cotton Speyrer | WR | 6' | 175 | 24 | | 30 |
| Tom Mitchell | TE-WR | 6'2" | 215 | 29 | | 24 |
| John Andrews | TE | 6'3" | 227 | 24 | | 6 |
| Ray Chester | TE | 6'3" | 235 | 25 | | 6 |
| George Hunt | K | 6'1" | 215 | 23 | | 70 |
| David Lee | K | 6'4" | 230 | 29 | | |

## MIAMI DOLPHINS

### RUSHING
| Last Name | No. | Yds | Avg | TD |
|---|---|---|---|---|
| Csonka | 219 | 1003 | 4.6 | 5 |
| Morris | 149 | 954 | 6.4 | 10 |
| Kiick | 76 | 257 | 3.4 | 0 |
| Nottingham | 52 | 252 | 4.8 | 1 |
| Leigh | 22 | 134 | 6.1 | 1 |
| Griese | 13 | 20 | 1.5 | 0 |
| Warfield | 1 | 15 | 15.0 | 0 |
| Morrall | 1 | 9 | 9.0 | 0 |
| Briscoe | 2 | -5 | -2.5 | 0 |

### RECEIVING
| Last Name | No. | Yds | Avg | TD |
|---|---|---|---|---|
| Briscoe | 30 | 447 | 15 | 2 |
| Warfield | 29 | 514 | 18 | 11 |
| Kiick | 27 | 208 | 8 | 0 |
| Mandich | 24 | 302 | 13 | 4 |
| Csonka | 7 | 22 | 3 | 0 |
| Morris | 4 | 51 | 13 | 0 |
| Leigh | 4 | 9 | 2 | 0 |
| Nottingham | 3 | 26 | 9 | 0 |
| Fleming | 3 | 22 | 7 | 0 |
| Sellers | 2 | 54 | 27 | 0 |
| Twilley | 2 | 30 | 15 | 0 |

### PUNT RETURNS
| Last Name | No. | Yds | Avg | TD |
|---|---|---|---|---|
| Scott | 22 | 266 | 12 | 0 |
| Leigh | 9 | 64 | 7 | 0 |
| Anderson | 6 | 52 | 9 | 0 |

### KICKOFF RETURNS
| Last Name | No. | Yds | Avg | TD |
|---|---|---|---|---|
| Leigh | 9 | 251 | 28 | 0 |
| Morris | 11 | 242 | 22 | 0 |
| Scott | 2 | 20 | 10 | 0 |
| Nottingham | 1 | 17 | 17 | 0 |
| Bannon | 1 | 10 | 10 | 0 |
| Seiple | 1 | 0 | 0 | 0 |

### PASSING – PUNTING – KICKING
| PASSING | Att | Comp | % | Yds | Yd/Att | TD | Int–% | RK |
|---|---|---|---|---|---|---|---|---|
| Griese | 218 | 116 | 53 | 1422 | 6.5 | 17 | 8–4 | 3 |
| Morrall | 38 | 17 | 45 | 253 | 6.7 | 0 | 4–11 | |

| PUNTING | No. | Avg |
|---|---|---|
| Seiple | 48 | 42.3 |

| KICKING | XP | Att | % | FG | Att | % |
|---|---|---|---|---|---|---|
| Yepremian | 38 | 38 | 100 | 25 | 37 | 68 |

## BUFFALO BILLS

### RUSHING
| Last Name | No. | Yds | Avg | TD |
|---|---|---|---|---|
| Simpson | 332 | 2003 | 6.0 | 12 |
| Braxton | 108 | 494 | 4.6 | 4 |
| Watkins | 98 | 414 | 4.2 | 0 |
| Ferguson | 48 | 147 | 3.1 | 2 |
| Van Valkenberg | 2 | 20 | 10.0 | 0 |
| Cornell | 4 | 13 | 3.3 | 0 |
| Steve Jones | 4 | 9 | 2.3 | 0 |
| Shaw | 4 | 2 | 0.5 | 0 |
| Chandler | 5 | -14 | -2.8 | 0 |

### RECEIVING
| Last Name | No. | Yds | Avg | TD |
|---|---|---|---|---|
| Chandler | 30 | 427 | 14 | 3 |
| Hill | 29 | 422 | 15 | 0 |
| Watkins | 12 | 86 | 7 | 1 |
| Seymour | 10 | 114 | 11 | 0 |
| Braxton | 6 | 101 | 17 | 0 |
| Simpson | 6 | 70 | 12 | 0 |
| R. Jarvis | 1 | 12 | 12 | 0 |
| Van Valkenberg | 1 | 7 | 7 | 0 |
| Ferguson | 1 | -3 | -3 | 0 |

### PUNT RETURNS
| Last Name | No. | Yds | Avg | TD |
|---|---|---|---|---|
| Walker | 25 | 210 | 8 | 0 |
| Cahill | 4 | 73 | 18 | 1 |
| Chandler | 2 | 5 | 3 | 0 |
| Hill | 1 | -9 | -9 | 0 |

### KICKOFF RETURNS
| Last Name | No. | Yds | Avg | TD |
|---|---|---|---|---|
| Francis | 23 | 687 | 30 | 2 |
| Jones | 6 | 116 | 19 | 0 |
| R. Jarvis | 5 | 84 | 17 | 0 |
| Cahill | 2 | 42 | 21 | 0 |
| Watkins | 1 | 18 | 18 | 0 |
| Parker | 1 | 16 | 16 | 0 |
| T. Greene | 1 | 7 | 7 | 0 |
| Cornell | 1 | 2 | 2 | 0 |
| Braxton | 1 | 0 | 0 | 0 |
| Van Valkenberg | 1 | 0 | 0 | 0 |

### PASSING – PUNTING – KICKING
| PASSING | Att | Comp | % | Yds | Yd/Att | TD | Int–% | RK |
|---|---|---|---|---|---|---|---|---|
| Ferguson | 164 | 73 | 45 | 939 | 5.7 | 4 | 10–6 | 13 |
| Shaw | 46 | 22 | 48 | 300 | 6.5 | 0 | 4–9 | |
| Simpson | 2 | 1 | 50 | -3 | -1.5 | 0 | 0–0 | |
| Chandler | 1 | 0 | 0 | 0 | 0.0 | 0 | 0–0 | |

| PUNTING | No | Avg |
|---|---|---|
| Spike Jones | 66 | 40.3 |

| KICKING | XP | Att | % | FG | Att | % |
|---|---|---|---|---|---|---|
| Leypoldt | 27 | 27 | 100 | 21 | 30 | 70 |
| Chandler | 1 | 1 | 100 | 0 | 0 | 0 |

## NEW ENGLAND PATRIOTS

### RUSHING
| Last Name | No. | Yds | Avg | TD |
|---|---|---|---|---|
| Cunningham | 155 | 516 | 3.3 | 4 |
| Tarver | 72 | 321 | 4.5 | 4 |
| Ashton | 93 | 305 | 3.3 | 0 |
| Plunkett | 44 | 209 | 4.8 | 5 |
| Herron | 61 | 200 | 3.3 | 2 |
| Stingley | 6 | 64 | 10.7 | 0 |
| McCall | 10 | 15 | 1.5 | 0 |
| B. Adams | 2 | 7 | 3.5 | 0 |
| Gipson | 5 | -1 | -0.2 | 0 |
| Rucker | 2 | -1 | -0.5 | 0 |
| Welch | 1 | -2 | -2.0 | 0 |
| Windsor | 1 | -6 | -6.0 | 0 |
| Vataha | 2 | -15 | -7.5 | 0 |

### RECEIVING
| Last Name | No. | Yds | Avg | TD |
|---|---|---|---|---|
| Rucker | 53 | 743 | 14 | 3 |
| Windsor | 23 | 348 | 15 | 4 |
| Stingley | 23 | 339 | 15 | 2 |
| Vataha | 20 | 341 | 17 | 2 |
| Herron | 18 | 265 | 15 | 1 |
| Cunningham | 15 | 144 | 10 | 1 |
| B. Adams | 14 | 197 | 14 | 0 |
| Ashton | 11 | 113 | 10 | 0 |
| Tarver | 9 | 41 | 5 | 0 |
| Welch | 6 | 22 | 4 | 0 |
| McCall | 3 | 18 | 6 | 0 |

### PUNT RETURNS
| Last Name | No. | Yds | Avg | TD |
|---|---|---|---|---|
| Herron | 27 | 282 | 10 | 0 |
| Durko | 3 | 21 | 7 | 0 |
| Stingley | 3 | 31 | 7 | 0 |

### KICKOFF RETURNS
| Last Name | No. | Yds | Avg | TD |
|---|---|---|---|---|
| Herron | 41 | 1092 | 27 | 1 |
| Stingley | 6 | 143 | 24 | 0 |
| Rucker | 5 | 103 | 21 | 0 |
| McCall | 2 | 17 | 9 | 0 |
| Tarver | 1 | 17 | 17 | 0 |
| Hannah | 1 | 0 | 0 | 0 |
| Windsor | 1 | 0 | 0 | 0 |

### PASSING – PUNTING – KICKING
| PASSING | Att | Comp | % | Yds | Yd/Att | TD | Int–% | RK |
|---|---|---|---|---|---|---|---|---|
| Plunkett | 376 | 193 | 51 | 2550 | 6.8 | 13 | 17–5 | 5 |

| PUNTING | No | Avg |
|---|---|---|
| Barnes | 55 | 38.8 |
| White | 6 | 27.2 |

| KICKING | XP | Att | % | FG | Att | % |
|---|---|---|---|---|---|---|
| White | 21 | 25 | 84 | 14 | 25 | 56 |
| Bell | 4 | 5 | 80 | 1 | 4 | 25 |

## NEW YORK JETS

### RUSHING
| Last Name | No. | Yds | Avg | TD |
|---|---|---|---|---|
| Boozer | 182 | 831 | 4.6 | 3 |
| Riggins | 134 | 482 | 3.6 | 4 |
| Adamle | 67 | 264 | 3.9 | 0 |
| Nance | 18 | 78 | 4.3 | 0 |
| Bjorkland | 22 | 72 | 3.3 | 0 |
| Woodall | 13 | 68 | 5.2 | 0 |
| Fagan | 2 | 47 | 23.5 | 0 |
| McClain | 8 | 32 | 4.0 | 0 |
| Barkum | 1 | 2 | 2.0 | 0 |
| Demory | 4 | -1 | -0.3 | 0 |
| Namath | 1 | -2 | -2.0 | 0 |
| Caster | 1 | -9 | -9.0 | 0 |

### RECEIVING
| Last Name | No. | Yds | Avg | TD |
|---|---|---|---|---|
| Barkum | 44 | 810 | 18 | 6 |
| Caster | 35 | 593 | 17 | 4 |
| Bell | 24 | 319 | 13 | 2 |
| Riggins | 23 | 158 | 7 | 0 |
| Boozer | 22 | 130 | 6 | 3 |
| Adamle | 9 | 63 | 7 | 0 |
| Adkins | 6 | 109 | 18 | 0 |
| Knight | 6 | 78 | 13 | 1 |
| McClain | 6 | 52 | 9 | 0 |
| Nance | 4 | 26 | 7 | 0 |
| Bjorkland | 2 | 15 | 8 | 0 |

### PUNT RETURNS
| Last Name | No. | Yds | Avg | TD |
|---|---|---|---|---|
| Farasopoulos | 14 | 111 | 8 | 0 |
| Turner | 11 | 54 | 5 | 0 |
| Tannen | 2 | 0 | 0 | 0 |

### KICKOFF RETURNS
| Last Name | No. | Yds | Avg | TD |
|---|---|---|---|---|
| Adkins | 31 | 615 | 20 | 0 |
| Bjorkland | 9 | 175 | 19 | 0 |
| Owens | 2 | 103 | 52 | 1 |
| McClain | 5 | 89 | 18 | 0 |
| Adamle | 5 | 79 | 16 | 0 |

### PASSING – PUNTING – KICKING
| PASSING | Att | Comp | % | Yds | Yd/Att | TD | Int–% | RK |
|---|---|---|---|---|---|---|---|---|
| Woodall | 201 | 101 | 50 | 1228 | 6.1 | 9 | 8–4 | 6 |
| Namath | 133 | 68 | 51 | 966 | 7.3 | 5 | 6–5 | |
| Demory | 39 | 12 | 31 | 159 | 4.1 | 2 | 8–21 | |

| PUNTING | No | Avg |
|---|---|---|
| Fagan | 74 | 37.1 |

| KICKING | XP | Att | % | FG | Att | % |
|---|---|---|---|---|---|---|
| Howfield | 27 | 27 | 100 | 17 | 24 | 71 |

## BALTIMORE COLTS

### RUSHING
| Last Name | No. | Yds | Avg | TD |
|---|---|---|---|---|
| L. Mitchell | 253 | 963 | 3.8 | 2 |
| McCauley | 144 | 514 | 3.6 | 2 |
| Domres | 32 | 126 | 3.9 | 2 |
| Olds | 26 | 100 | 3.8 | 2 |
| Doughty | 10 | 96 | 9.6 | 0 |
| Jones | 18 | 58 | 3.2 | 0 |
| Ginn | 16 | 47 | 2.9 | 0 |
| Mildren | 2 | 14 | 7.0 | 0 |
| Havrilak | 2 | 9 | 4.5 | 0 |
| Chester | 1 | 1 | 1.0 | 0 |
| Speyrer | 1 | 1 | 1.0 | 0 |
| Smith | 1 | -3 | -3.0 | 0 |
| Lee | 2 | -16 | -8.0 | 0 |
| Nelson | 0 | 3 | 0.0 | 0 |

### RECEIVING
| Last Name | No. | Yds | Avg | TD |
|---|---|---|---|---|
| Doughty | 25 | 587 | 23 | 4 |
| T. Mitchell | 25 | 313 | 13 | 4 |
| McCauley | 25 | 186 | 7 | 0 |
| Chester | 18 | 181 | 10 | 1 |
| Speyrer | 17 | 311 | 18 | 4 |
| L. Mitchell | 17 | 113 | 7 | 0 |
| Ginn | 3 | 2 | 1 | 0 |
| Olds | 2 | -4 | -2 | 0 |
| Smith | 1 | 37 | 37 | 0 |
| Havrilak | 1 | 9 | 9 | 0 |
| Andrews | 1 | 1 | 1 | 1 |

### PUNT RETURNS
| Last Name | No. | Yds | Avg | TD |
|---|---|---|---|---|
| Laird | 15 | 72 | 5 | 0 |
| Volk | 7 | 45 | 6 | 0 |
| Kern | 2 | 12 | 6 | 0 |

### KICKOFF RETURNS
| Last Name | No. | Yds | Avg | TD |
|---|---|---|---|---|
| Laird | 24 | 547 | 23 | 0 |
| Speyrer | 17 | 496 | 29 | 1 |
| Ginn | 9 | 198 | 22 | 0 |
| White | 1 | 17 | 17 | 0 |
| Volk | 2 | 16 | 8 | 0 |
| Olds | 3 | 14 | 5 | 0 |
| Andrews | 1 | 13 | 13 | 0 |
| Munsey | 1 | 13 | 13 | 0 |
| McCauley | 1 | 12 | 12 | 0 |

### PASSING – PUNTING – KICKING
| PASSING | Att | Comp | % | Yds | Yd/Att | TD | Int–% | RK |
|---|---|---|---|---|---|---|---|---|
| Domres | 191 | 93 | 49 | 1153 | 6.0 | 9 | 13–7 | 11 |
| Jones | 108 | 43 | 40 | 539 | 5.0 | 4 | 12–11 | |
| Speyrer | 1 | 1 | 100 | 54 | 54.0 | 1 | 0–0 | |

| PUNTING | No | Avg |
|---|---|---|
| Lee | 62 | 38.7 |

| KICKING | XP | Att | % | FG | Att | % |
|---|---|---|---|---|---|---|
| Hunt | 22 | 24 | 92 | 16 | 28 | 57 |

## CINCINNATI BENGALS 10-4-0 Paul Brown

| Scores of Each Game | | | Use Name | Pos. | Hgt | Wgt | Age | Int | Pts |
|---|---|---|---|---|---|---|---|---|---|
| 10 | Denver | 28 | Paul Brown | | | | | | |
| 24 | HOUSTON | 10 | Vern Holland | OT | 6'5" | 270 | 25 | | |
| 20 | San Diego | 13 | Rufus Mayes | OT | 6'5" | 260 | 25 | | |
| 10 | CLEVELAND | 17 | Stan Walters | OT | 6'6" | 270 | 25 | | |
| 9 | PITTSBURGH | 7 | Howard Fest | OG-OT | 6'6" | 262 | 27 | | |
| 14 | KANSAS CITY | 6 | Pat Matson | OG | 6'1" | 245 | 29 | | |
| 13 | Pittsburgh | 20 | John Shinners | OG | 6'2" | 254 | 26 | | |
| 10 | Dallas | 38 | Tom DeLeone | C | 6'2" | 252 | 23 | | |
| 16 | Buffalo | 13 | Bob Johnson | C | 6'5" | 260 | 27 | | |
| 20 | N. Y. JETS | 14 | Royce Berry | DE | 6'3" | 250 | 27 | | |
| 42 | ST. LOUIS | 24 | Ken Johnson | DE | 6'5" | 265 | 26 | | |
| 27 | MINNESOTA | 0 | Lee Thomas | DE | 6'5" | 246 | 26 | | |
| 34 | Cleveland | 17 | Sherman White | DE | 6'5" | 255 | 24 | | |
| 27 | Houston | 24 | Ron Carpenter | DT | 6'4" | 260 | 25 | | |
| | | | Steve Chomyszak | DT | 6'5" | 265 | 28 | | |
| | | | Mike Reid | DT | 6'3" | 255 | 26 | | |

| Use Name | Pos. | Hgt | Wgt | Age | Int | Pts |
|---|---|---|---|---|---|---|
| Doug Adams | LB | 6' | 222 | 24 | | |
| Ken Avery | LB | 6'1" | 227 | 29 | 1 | |
| Al Beauchamp | LB | 6'2" | 237 | 29 | 3 | |
| Bill Bergey | LB | 6'2" | 243 | 28 | 3 | |
| Tim Kearney | LB | 6'2" | 227 | 22 | | |
| Jim LeClair | LB | 6'2" | 226 | 22 | | |
| Ron Pritchard | LB | 6'1" | 235 | 26 | | |
| Lyle Blackwood | DB | 6' | 190 | 22 | | |
| Tommy Casanova | DB | 6'2" | 202 | 23 | 4 | |
| Neal Craig | DB | 6'1" | 190 | 25 | 2 | |
| Bernard Jackson | DB | 6'1" | 173 | 23 | 1 | |
| Bob Jones | DB | 6'1" | 194 | 22 | | |
| Lemar Parrish | DB | 5'11" | 185 | 25 | 2 | 6 |
| Ken Riley | DB | 6' | 180 | 26 | 2 | |

Virgil Carter — Broken Collarbone
Doug Dressler — Knee Injury

| Use Name | Pos. | Hgt | Wgt | Age | Int | Pts |
|---|---|---|---|---|---|---|
| Ken Anderson | QB | 6'1" | 211 | 24 | | |
| Greg Cook | QB | 6'3" | 215 | 26 | | |
| Mike Ernst | QB | 6'1" | 190 | 22 | | |
| Lenvil Elliott | HB | 6' | 200 | 21 | | 12 |
| Essex Johnson | HB | 5'9" | 200 | 26 | | 42 |
| Reece Morrison | HB | 6' | 207 | 27 | | |
| Booby Clark | FB | 6'2" | 245 | 22 | | 48 |
| Joe Wilson | HB-FB | 5'10" | 210 | 22 | | |
| Isaac Curtis | WR | 6' | 190 | 22 | | 54 |
| Tim George | WR | 6'5" | 225 | 21 | | |
| Charlie Joiner | WR | 5'11" | 188 | 25 | | |
| Chip Myers | WR | 6'4" | 210 | 28 | | |
| Bruce Coslet | TE | 6'3" | 227 | 27 | | |
| Al Chandler | TE | 6'2" | 233 | 22 | | |
| Bob Trumpy | TE | 6'6" | 228 | 28 | | 30 |
| Dave Lewis | K | 6'2" | 225 | 27 | | |
| Horst Muhlmann | K | 6'1" | 220 | 33 | | 94 |

## PITTSBURGH STEELERS 10-4-0 Chuck Noll

| Scores | | | Use Name | Pos. | Hgt | Wgt | Age | Int | Pts |
|---|---|---|---|---|---|---|---|---|---|
| 24 | DETROIT | 10 | Gordon Gravelle | OT | 6'5" | 250 | 24 | | |
| 33 | CLEVELAND | 6 | Glen Ray Hines | OT | 6'5" | 265 | 29 | | |
| 36 | Houston | 7 | Jon Kolb | OT | 6'2" | 262 | 26 | | |
| 38 | SAN DIEGO | 21 | Sam Davis | OG | 6'1" | 255 | 29 | | |
| 7 | Cincinnati | 19 | Mel Holmes | OG | 6'3" | 250 | 23 | | |
| 26 | N. Y. JETS | 14 | Bruce Van Dyke | OG | 6'2" | 255 | 29 | | |
| 20 | CINCINNATI | 13 | Gerry Mullins | OT-OG | 6'3" | 244 | 24 | | |
| 21 | WASHINGTON | 16 | Jim Clack | C | 6'3" | 250 | 25 | | |
| 17 | Oakland | 9 | Ray Mansfield | C | 6'3" | 260 | 32 | | |
| 13 | DENVER | 23 | L. C. Greenwood | DE | 6'5" | 245 | 26 | | |
| 16 | Cleveland | 21 | Dwight White | DE | 6'4" | 250 | 24 | 2 | 2 |
| 26 | Miami | 30 | Steve Furness | DT-DE | 6'4" | 255 | 22 | | |
| 33 | HOUSTON | 7 | Joe Greene | DT | 6'4" | 275 | 26 | | |
| 37 | San Francisco | 14 | Craig Hanneman | DT | 6'3" | 240 | 24 | | |
| | | | Ernie Holmes | DT | 6'3" | 260 | 25 | | |
| | | | Tom Keating | DT | 6'3" | 247 | 30 | | |

| Use Name | Pos. | Hgt | Wgt | Age | Int | Pts |
|---|---|---|---|---|---|---|
| Ed Bradley | LB | 6'2" | 240 | 23 | | |
| Henry Davis | LB | 6'3" | 235 | 30 | 2 | |
| Jack Ham | LB | 6'3" | 225 | 24 | 2 | 6 |
| Andy Russell | LB | 6'3" | 225 | 31 | 3 | 6 |
| Loren Toews | LB | 6'3" | 212 | 21 | 2 | |
| George Webster | LB | 6'4" | 223 | 27 | | |
| Mel Blount | DB | 6'3" | 205 | 25 | 4 | |
| John Dockery | DB | 6' | 186 | 28 | 1 | |
| Glen Edwards | DB | 6' | 185 | 26 | 6 | 6 |
| Dennis Meyer | DB | 5'11" | 186 | 22 | 6 | |
| John Rowser | DB | 6'1" | 185 | 29 | | |
| J.T. Thomas | DB | 6'2" | 196 | 22 | 1 | |
| Mike Wagner | DB | 6'1" | 196 | 24 | 8 | 6 |

Al Young — Illness

| Use Name | Pos. | Hgt | Wgt | Age | Int | Pts |
|---|---|---|---|---|---|---|
| Terry Bradshaw | QB | 6'3" | 218 | 24 | | 18 |
| Joe Gilliam | QB | 6'2" | 187 | 22 | | |
| Terry Hanratty | QB | 6'1" | 210 | 25 | | |
| Rocky Bleier | HB | 5'11" | 205 | 27 | | |
| Preston Pearson | HB | 6'1" | 205 | 28 | | 24 |
| Franco Harris | FB-HB | 6'2" | 230 | 23 | | 18 |
| Steve Davis | HB-FB | 6'1" | 218 | 23 | | 18 |
| John Fuqua | HB-FB | 5'11" | 205 | 26 | | 12 |
| Dave Davis | WR | 6' | 175 | 25 | | |
| Frank Lewis | WR | 6'1" | 196 | 25 | | 18 |
| Barry Pearson | WR | 5'11" | 185 | 23 | | 18 |
| Glenn Scolnik | WR | 6'3" | 190 | 22 | | |
| Ron Shanklin | WR | 6'1" | 180 | 26 | | 60 |
| Larry Brown | TE | 6'4" | 225 | 24 | | |
| John McMakin | TE | 6'3" | 232 | 22 | | 6 |
| Roy Gerela | K | 5'10" | 185 | 25 | | 123 |
| Bobby Walden | K | 6' | 190 | 35 | | |

## CLEVELAND BROWNS 7-5-2 Nick Skorich

| Scores | | | Use Name | Pos. | Hgt | Wgt | Age | Int | Pts |
|---|---|---|---|---|---|---|---|---|---|
| 24 | BALTIMORE | 14 | Joe Carollo | OT | 6'2" | 265 | 33 | | |
| 6 | Pittsburgh | 33 | Doug Dieken | OT | 6'5" | 254 | 24 | | |
| 12 | N. Y. GIANTS | 10 | Bob McKay | OT | 6'5" | 260 | 25 | | |
| 17 | Cincinnati | 10 | Chris Morris | OT | 6'3" | 250 | 23 | | |
| 9 | MIAMI | 17 | John Demarie | OG | 6'3" | 246 | 28 | | |
| 42 | HOUSTON | 13 | Chuck Hutchison | OG | 6'3" | 240 | 24 | | |
| 16 | SAN DIEGO | 16 | Gene Hickerson | OG | 6'3" | 252 | 38 | | |
| 3 | Minnesota | 26 | Jim Copeland | C-OG | 6'2" | 243 | 28 | | |
| 23 | Houston | 13 | Bob DeMarco | C | 6'2" | 248 | 35 | | |
| 7 | Oakland | 3 | Bob Briggs | DE | 6'4" | 258 | 28 | | |
| 21 | PITTSBURGH | 16 | Joe Jones | DE | 6'6" | 250 | 25 | | |
| 20 | Kansas City | 20 | Nick Roman | DE | 6'3" | 244 | 25 | | |
| 17 | CINCINNATI | 34 | Carl Barisich | DT | 6'4" | 255 | 22 | | |
| 17 | Los Angeles | 30 | Walter Johnson | DT | 6'3" | 265 | 30 | | |
| | | | Jerry Sherk | DT | 6'4" | 255 | 25 | | |

| Use Name | Pos. | Hgt | Wgt | Age | Int | Pts |
|---|---|---|---|---|---|---|
| Billy Andrews | LB | 6' | 220 | 28 | | |
| Bob Babich | LB | 6'2" | 230 | 26 | 1 | |
| John Garlington | LB | 6'1" | 218 | 27 | 1 | |
| Charlie Hall | LB | 6'3" | 225 | 24 | | |
| Mel Long | LB | 6' | 228 | 26 | | |
| Jim Romaniszyn | LB | 6'2" | 214 | 21 | | |
| Cliff Brooks | DB | 6'1" | 190 | 24 | | |
| Thom Darden | DB | 6'2" | 195 | 23 | 1 | |
| Ben Davis | DB | 5'11" | 180 | 27 | 2 | |
| Van Green | DB | 6'1" | 192 | 22 | | 6 |
| Clarence Scott | DB | 6' | 180 | 24 | 5 | 6 |
| Jim Stienke | DB | 5'11" | 188 | 22 | | |
| Walt Sumner | DB | 6'1" | 195 | 26 | 2 | |

Bubba Pena — Knee Injury

| Use Name | Pos. | Hgt | Wgt | Age | Int | Pts |
|---|---|---|---|---|---|---|
| Don Horn | QB | 6'2" | 195 | 28 | | |
| Mike Phipps | QB | 6'2" | 205 | 25 | | 30 |
| Leroy Kelly | HB | 6' | 202 | 31 | | 18 |
| Billy LeFear | HB | 5'11" | 197 | 23 | | |
| Greg Pruitt | HB | 5'10" | 186 | 22 | | 30 |
| Hugh McKinnis | FB | 6' | 225 | 25 | | |
| Bo Scott | FB | 6'3" | 215 | 30 | | 6 |
| Ken Brown | HB-FB | 5'10" | 203 | 27 | | |
| Steve Holden | WR | 6' | 192 | 22 | | |
| Fair Hooker | WR | 6'1" | 195 | 26 | | 12 |
| Frank Pitts | WR | 6'2" | 200 | 29 | | 24 |
| Gloster Richardson | WR | 6' | 200 | 30 | | 6 |
| Dave Sullivan | WR | 5'11" | 185 | 22 | | |
| Chip Glass | TE | 6'4" | 235 | 26 | | |
| Milt Morin | TE | 6'4" | 236 | 31 | | 6 |
| Ken Smith | TE | 6'4" | 225 | 22 | | |
| Don Cockroft | K | 6'1" | 195 | 28 | | 90 |

## HOUSTON OILERS 1-13-0 Bill Peterson   Sid Gillman

| Scores | | | Use Name | Pos. | Hgt | Wgt | Age | Int | Pts |
|---|---|---|---|---|---|---|---|---|---|
| 14 | N. Y. Giants | 34 | Levert Carr | OT | 6'5" | 260 | 29 | | |
| 10 | Cincinnati | 24 | Elbert Drungo | OT | 6'5" | 265 | 30 | | |
| 7 | PITTSBURGH | 36 | Tom Funchess | OT | 6'5" | 270 | 28 | | |
| 26 | LOS ANGELES | 31 | Kevin Hunt (from NE) | OT | 6'5" | 260 | 24 | | |
| 20 | DENVER | 48 | Soloman Freelon | OG | 6'2" | 250 | 22 | | |
| 13 | Cleveland | 42 | Brian Goodman | OG | 6'2" | 250 | 24 | | |
| 14 | Chicago | 35 | Al Jenkins | OG | 6'2" | 245 | 27 | | |
| 31 | Baltimore | 27 | Harris Jones | OG | 6'4" | 245 | 28 | | |
| 13 | CLEVELAND | 23 | Ralph Miller | OG | 6'4" | 240 | 24 | | |
| 14 | Kansas City | 38 | Ron Saul | OG | 6'2" | 255 | 25 | | |
| 0 | NEW ENGLAND | 32 | Bill Curry | C | 6'2" | 236 | 30 | | |
| 6 | OAKLAND | 17 | Sam Gruneisen | C | 6'1" | 250 | 32 | | |
| 7 | Pittsburgh | 33 | Calvin Hunt | C | 6'3" | 245 | 25 | | |
| 24 | CINCINNATI | 27 | Ron Lou | C | 6'2" | 235 | 22 | | |
| | | | Elvin Bethea | DE | 6'3" | 262 | 27 | | |
| | | | Mike Fanucci | DE | 6'4" | 240 | 23 | | |
| | | | Tody Smith | DE | 6'5" | 245 | 24 | | |
| | | | Wes Grant | DT-DE | 6'3" | 245 | 26 | | |
| | | | Al Cowlings | DT | 6'5" | 255 | 26 | | |
| | | | John Matuszak | DT | 6'8" | 290 | 22 | | |
| | | | Greg Sampson | DT | 6'6" | 260 | 22 | | |

| Use Name | Pos. | Hgt | Wgt | Age | Int | Pts |
|---|---|---|---|---|---|---|
| Gregg Bingham | LB | 6'1" | 227 | 22 | 2 | |
| Ralph Cindrich | LB | 6'1" | 228 | 23 | | |
| Paul Guidry | LB | 6'3" | 233 | 29 | | |
| Brian McConnell | LB | 6'4" | 207 | 23 | | |
| Guy Roberts | LB | 6'3" | 215 | 23 | 4 | |
| Ted Washington | LB | 6'1" | 240 | 25 | | |
| Willie Alexander | DB | 6'2" | 195 | 23 | 3 | |
| Bob Atkins | DB | 6'3" | 210 | 27 | | |
| Joe Blahak | DB | 5'9" | 182 | 23 | 2 | |
| John Charles | DB | 6'1" | 200 | 29 | | |
| Larry Eaglin | DB | 6' | 195 | 22 | | 6 |
| Alvin Haymond | DB | 6' | 194 | 31 | | |
| Benny Johnson | DB | 5'11" | 178 | 25 | | |
| Zeke Moore | DB | 6'2" | 196 | 29 | | |
| Jeff Severson | DB | 6'1" | 180 | 23 | 4 | |
| Alvin Wyatt | DB | 5'10" | 180 | 25 | | |

Jim Ford — Leg Injury
Willie Rogers — Knee Injury
Sid Smith — Injury

| Use Name | Pos. | Hgt | Wgt | Age | Int | Pts |
|---|---|---|---|---|---|---|
| Lynn Dickey | QB | 6'4" | 218 | 23 | | 1 |
| Edd Hargett | QB | 5'11" | 190 | 26 | | |
| Dan Pastorini | QB | 6'3" | 215 | 24 | | |
| Bob Gresham | HB | 5'11" | 195 | 25 | | 24 |
| Al Johnson | HB | 6' | 200 | 23 | | |
| Paul Robinson | HB | 6' | 195 | 28 | | 12 |
| George Amundson | FB-HB | 6'3" | 215 | 23 | | |
| Lewis Jolley | FB-HB | 6' | 210 | 23 | | |
| Bill Thomas | FB | 6'2" | 225 | 23 | | |
| Fred Willis | FB | 6' | 212 | 25 | | 30 |
| Jim Beirne | WR | 6'2" | 196 | 24 | | |
| Ken Burrough | WR | 6'4" | 210 | 25 | | 18 |
| Eddie Hinton | WR | 6' | 200 | 26 | | |
| Clifton McNeil | WR | 6'2" | 187 | 33 | | |
| Billy Parks | WR | 6'1" | 185 | 25 | | 6 |
| Dave Parks | TE | 6'2" | 203 | 31 | | 6 |
| Mack Alston | TE | 6'2" | 230 | 26 | | 24 |
| Ron Mayo | TE | 6'3" | 223 | 22 | | |
| Skip Butler | K | 6'2" | 200 | 25 | | 66 |
| Dave Green (to CIN) | K | 5'11" | 200 | 23 | | |

## CINCINNATI BENGALS

### RUSHING

| Last Name | No. | Yds | Avg | TD |
|---|---|---|---|---|
| E. Johnson | 195 | 997 | 5.1 | 4 |
| Clark | 254 | 988 | 3.9 | 8 |
| Elliott | 22 | 122 | 5.5 | 1 |
| Anderson | 26 | 97 | 3.7 | 0 |
| Wilson | 10 | 39 | 3.9 | 0 |
| Morrison | 3 | 11 | 3.7 | 0 |
| Lewis | 3 | −7 | −2.3 | 0 |
| Curtis | 2 | −11 | −5.5 | 0 |

### RECEIVING

| Last Name | No. | Yds | Avg | TD |
|---|---|---|---|---|
| Curtis | 45 | 843 | 19 | 9 |
| Clark | 45 | 347 | 8 | 0 |
| Trumpy | 29 | 435 | 15 | 5 |
| E. Johnson | 28 | 356 | 13 | 3 |
| Joiner | 13 | 214 | 16 | 0 |
| Coslet | 9 | 123 | 14 | 0 |
| Myers | 7 | 77 | 11 | 0 |
| George | 2 | 28 | 14 | 0 |
| Elliott | 1 | 12 | 12 | 1 |
| Morrison | 1 | 4 | 4 | 0 |

### PUNT RETURNS

| Last Name | No. | Yds | Avg | TD |
|---|---|---|---|---|
| Parrish | 25 | 200 | 8 | 0 |
| Casanova | 15 | 119 | 8 | 0 |
| Blackwood | 4 | 12 | 3 | 0 |
| Lewis | 1 | 2 | 2 | 0 |

### KICKOFF RETURNS

| Last Name | No. | Yds | Avg | TD |
|---|---|---|---|---|
| Jackson | 21 | 520 | 25 | 0 |
| Wilson | 8 | 173 | 22 | 0 |
| Parrish | 7 | 143 | 20 | 0 |
| Lewis | 2 | 40 | 20 | 0 |
| Coslet | 1 | 0 | 0 | 0 |

### PASSING – PUNTING – KICKING

**PASSING**

| Last Name | Att | Comp | % | Yds | Yd/Att | TD | Int–% | RK |
|---|---|---|---|---|---|---|---|---|
| Anderson | 329 | 179 | 54 | 2428 | 7.4 | 18 | 12– 4 | 1 |
| Cook | 3 | 1 | 33 | 11 | 3.7 | 0 | 0– 0 | |

**PUNTING**

| Last Name | No | Avg |
|---|---|---|
| Lewis | 68 | 41.0 |

**KICKING**

| Last Name | XP | Att | % | FG | Att | % |
|---|---|---|---|---|---|---|
| Muhlmann | 31 | 32 | 97 | 21 | 31 | 68 |

## PITTSBURGH STEELERS

### RUSHING

| Last Name | No. | Yds | Avg | TD |
|---|---|---|---|---|
| Harris | 188 | 698 | 3.7 | 3 |
| P. Pearson | 132 | 554 | 4.2 | 2 |
| Fuqua | 117 | 457 | 3.9 | 2 |
| Steve Davis | 67 | 266 | 4.0 | 2 |
| Bradshaw | 34 | 145 | 4.3 | 3 |
| Gilliam | 6 | 23 | 3.8 | 0 |
| Shanklin | 3 | 1 | 0.3 | 0 |
| Bleier | 3 | 0 | 0.0 | 0 |
| Hanratty | 3 | 0 | 0.0 | 0 |
| Walden | 1 | 0 | 0.0 | 0 |
| Lewis | 1 | −1 | −1.0 | 0 |

### RECEIVING

| Last Name | No. | Yds | Avg | TD |
|---|---|---|---|---|
| Shanklin | 30 | 711 | 24 | 10 |
| Lewis | 23 | 409 | 18 | 3 |
| B. Pearson | 23 | 317 | 14 | 3 |
| Fuqua | 17 | 150 | 9 | 0 |
| McMakin | 13 | 195 | 15 | 1 |
| P. Pearson | 11 | 173 | 16 | 2 |
| Harris | 10 | 69 | 7 | 0 |
| Steve Davis | 7 | 31 | 4 | 1 |
| Brown | 5 | 88 | 18 | 0 |
| D. Davis | 1 | 14 | 14 | 0 |

### PUNT RETURNS

| Last Name | No. | Yds | Avg | TD |
|---|---|---|---|---|
| Edwards | 34 | 336 | 10 | 0 |
| Meyer | 18 | 80 | 4 | 0 |

### KICKOFF RETURNS

| Last Name | No. | Yds | Avg | TD |
|---|---|---|---|---|
| Steve Davis | 15 | 404 | 27 | 0 |
| P. Pearson | 16 | 308 | 19 | 0 |
| Bleier | 3 | 47 | 16 | 0 |
| Harris | 1 | 23 | 23 | 0 |
| Fuqua | 1 | 22 | 22 | 0 |
| Hanneman | 1 | 20 | 20 | 0 |
| Edwards | 1 | 10 | 10 | 0 |
| Webster | 1 | 9 | 9 | 0 |
| Mansfield | 1 | 0 | 0 | 0 |

### PASSING – PUNTING – KICKING

**PASSING**

| Last Name | Att | Comp | % | Yds | Yd/Att | TD | Int–% | RK |
|---|---|---|---|---|---|---|---|---|
| Bradshaw | 180 | 89 | 49 | 1183 | 6.6 | 10 | 15– 8 | 8 |
| Hanratty | 69 | 31 | 45 | 643 | 9.3 | 8 | 5– 7 | |
| Gilliam | 60 | 20 | 33 | 331 | 5.5 | 2 | 6–10 | |

**PUNTING**

| Last Name | No | Avg |
|---|---|---|
| Walden | 62 | 41.1 |

**KICKING**

| Last Name | XP | Att | % | FG | Att | % |
|---|---|---|---|---|---|---|
| Gerela | 36 | 37 | 97 | 29 | 43 | 67 |

## CLEVELAND BROWNS

### RUSHING

| Last Name | No. | Yds | Avg | TD |
|---|---|---|---|---|
| Brown | 161 | 537 | 3.3 | 0 |
| Phipps | 60 | 395 | 6.6 | 5 |
| Kelly | 132 | 389 | 2.9 | 3 |
| Pruitt | 61 | 369 | 6.0 | 4 |
| LeFear | 26 | 135 | 5.2 | 0 |
| Bo Scott | 34 | 79 | 2.3 | 0 |
| McKinnis | 28 | 77 | 2.8 | 0 |
| Cockroft | 1 | −3 | −3.0 | 0 |
| Richardson | 3 | −10 | −3.3 | 0 |

### RECEIVING

| Last Name | No. | Yds | Avg | TD |
|---|---|---|---|---|
| Pitts | 31 | 317 | 10 | 4 |
| Morin | 26 | 417 | 16 | 1 |
| Brown | 22 | 187 | 9 | 0 |
| Hooker | 18 | 196 | 11 | 2 |
| Kelly | 15 | 180 | 12 | 0 |
| Richardson | 12 | 175 | 15 | 1 |
| Pruitt | 9 | 110 | 12 | 1 |
| Bo Scott | 6 | 23 | 4 | 1 |
| LeFear | 5 | 38 | 8 | 0 |
| Holden | 3 | 27 | 9 | 0 |
| McKinnis | 3 | 11 | 4 | 0 |
| Glass | 2 | 60 | 30 | 0 |

### PUNT RETURNS

| Last Name | No. | Yds | Avg | TD |
|---|---|---|---|---|
| Pruitt | 16 | 180 | 11 | 0 |
| Darden | 9 | 51 | 6 | 0 |
| LeFear | 7 | 51 | 7 | 0 |
| Holden | 2 | 19 | 10 | 0 |
| Kelly | 1 | 7 | 7 | 0 |
| Hall | 1 | 0 | 0 | 0 |

### KICKOFF RETURNS

| Last Name | No. | Yds | Avg | TD |
|---|---|---|---|---|
| Pruitt | 16 | 453 | 28 | 0 |
| Le Fear | 15 | 337 | 22 | 0 |
| Holden | 8 | 172 | 22 | 0 |
| Long | 6 | 87 | 15 | 0 |
| Romaniszyn | 2 | 21 | 11 | 0 |
| Dieken | 2 | 14 | 7 | 0 |

### PASSING – PUNTING – KICKING

**PASSING**

| Last Name | Att | Comp | % | Yds | Yd/Att | TD | Int–% | RK |
|---|---|---|---|---|---|---|---|---|
| Phipps | 299 | 148 | 49 | 1719 | 5.8 | 9 | 20– 7 | 9 |
| Horn | 8 | 4 | 50 | 22 | 2.8 | 1 | 0– 0 | |
| Pruitt | 1 | 0 | 0 | 0 | 0.0 | 0 | 0– 0 | |

**PUNTING**

| Last Name | No | Avg |
|---|---|---|
| Cockroft | 82 | 40.5 |

**KICKING**

| Last Name | XP | Att | % | FG | Att | % |
|---|---|---|---|---|---|---|
| Cockroft | 24 | 24 | 100 | 22 | 31 | 71 |

## HOUSTON OILERS

### RUSHING

| Last Name | No. | Yds | Avg | TD |
|---|---|---|---|---|
| Willis | 171 | 579 | 3.4 | 4 |
| Gresham | 104 | 400 | 3.8 | 2 |
| Robinson | 34 | 151 | 4.4 | 2 |
| Pastorini | 31 | 102 | 3.3 | 0 |
| Amundson | 15 | 56 | 3.7 | 0 |
| Thomas | 10 | 39 | 3.9 | 0 |
| Burrough | 5 | 38 | 7.6 | 1 |
| Alston | 1 | 13 | 13.0 | 0 |
| Dickey | 6 | 9 | 1.5 | 0 |
| Jolley | 7 | 6 | 0.9 | 0 |
| Hinton | 1 | −2 | −2.0 | 0 |
| Johnson | 1 | −3 | −3.0 | 0 |

### RECEIVING

| Last Name | No. | Yds | Avg | TD |
|---|---|---|---|---|
| Willis | 57 | 371 | 7 | 0 |
| B. Parks | 43 | 581 | 14 | 1 |
| Burrough | 43 | 577 | 13 | 2 |
| Gresham | 28 | 244 | 9 | 1 |
| Alston | 19 | 195 | 10 | 4 |
| Hinton | 13 | 202 | 16 | 1 |
| Amundson | 7 | 60 | 9 | 0 |
| Robinson | 7 | 46 | 7 | 0 |
| Jolley | 3 | 56 | 19 | 0 |
| D. Parks | 3 | 31 | 10 | 1 |
| Thomas | 1 | 4 | 4 | 0 |
| McNeil | 1 | 3 | 3 | 0 |

### PUNT RETURNS

| Last Name | No. | Yds | Avg | TD |
|---|---|---|---|---|
| Severson | 16 | 126 | 8 | 0 |
| Haymond | 14 | 101 | 7 | 0 |

### KICKOFF RETURNS

| Last Name | No. | Yds | Avg | TD |
|---|---|---|---|---|
| Gresham | 27 | 723 | 27 | 0 |
| Haymond | 28 | 703 | 25 | 0 |
| Hinton | 8 | 141 | 18 | 0 |
| Eaglin | 3 | 76 | 25 | 0 |
| Blahak | 2 | 41 | 21 | 0 |
| Jolley | 2 | 41 | 21 | 0 |
| Fanucci | 3 | 40 | 13 | 0 |
| Severson | 1 | 17 | 17 | 0 |

### PASSING – PUNTING – KICKING

**PASSING**

| Last Name | Att | Comp | % | Yds | Yd/Att | TD | Int–% | RK |
|---|---|---|---|---|---|---|---|---|
| Pastorini | 290 | 154 | 53 | 1482 | 5.1 | 5 | 17– 6 | 10 |
| Dickey | 120 | 71 | 59 | 888 | 7.4 | 6 | 10– 8 | |
| Willis | 1 | 0 | 0 | 0 | 0.0 | 0 | 0– 0 | |

**PUNTING**

| Last Name | No | Avg |
|---|---|---|
| Butler | 36 | 37.3 |
| Pastorini | 27 | 40.3 |
| Green | 22 | 39.5 |

**KICKING**

| Last Name | XP | Att | % | FG | Att | % |
|---|---|---|---|---|---|---|
| Butler | 21 | 21 | 100 | 15 | 24 | 63 |
| Dickey | 1 | 1 | 100 | 0 | 0 | 0 |

## OAKLAND RAIDERS 9-4-1 John Madden

### Scores of Each Game

| | | |
|---|---|---|
| 16 | Minnesota | 24 |
| 12 | MIAMI | 7 |
| 3 | Kansas City | 16 |
| 17 | St. Louis | 10 |
| 27 | SAN DIEGO | 17 |
| 23 | Denver | 23 |
| 34 | Baltimore | 21 |
| 42 | N. Y. GIANTS | 0 |
| 9 | PITTSBURGH | 17 |
| 3 | CLEVELAND | 7 |
| 31 | San Diego | 3 |
| 17 | Houston | 6 |
| 37 | KANSAS CITY | 7 |
| 21 | DENVER | 7 |

| Use Name | Pos. | Hgt | Wgt | Age | Int | Pts |
|---|---|---|---|---|---|---|
| Art Shell | OT | 6'5" | 265 | 26 | | |
| John Vella | OT | 6'4" | 255 | 23 | | |
| Bob Brown | OT | 6'4" | 280 | 30 | | |
| Paul Seiler | C-OT | 6'4" | 260 | 27 | | |
| George Buehler | OG | 6'2" | 260 | 26 | | |
| Gene Upshaw | OG | 6'5" | 255 | 28 | | |
| Dave Dalby | C-OG | 6'2" | 240 | 22 | | |
| Jim Otto | C | 6'2" | 255 | 35 | | |
| Tony Cline | DE | 6'2" | 240 | 25 | | |
| Horace Jones | DE | 6'3" | 255 | 24 | | |
| Bubba Smith | DE | 6'7" | 265 | 28 | | |
| Kelvin Korver | DT | 6'6" | 260 | 24 | 1 | |
| Otis Sistrunk | DT | 6'4" | 255 | 25 | | |
| Art Thoms | DT | 6'5" | 250 | 26 | | |
| Joe Carroll | LB | 6'1" | 220 | 23 | | |
| Dan Conners | LB | 6'1" | 230 | 31 | | |
| Gerald Irons | LB | 6'2" | 230 | 26 | 2 | |
| Monte Johnson | LB | 6'4" | 235 | 21 | | |
| Phil Villapiano | LB | 6'1" | 222 | 24 | 1 | |
| Gary Weaver | LB | 6'1" | 224 | 24 | | |
| Butch Atkinson | DB | 6' | 180 | 26 | 3 | 12 |
| Willie Brown | DB | 6'1" | 190 | 32 | 3 | |
| Tommy Maxwell | DB | 6'2" | 195 | 26 | | |
| Jack Tatum | DB | 5'10" | 200 | 24 | 1 | |
| Skip Thomas | DB | 6'1" | 205 | 23 | | |
| Jimmy Warren | DB | 5'11" | 175 | 34 | 1 | |
| Nemiah Wilson | DB | 6' | 165 | 30 | 3 | |
| Jackie Allen — Injury | | | | | | |
| George Blanda | QB | 6'1" | 215 | 45 | | 100 |
| Daryle Lamonica | QB | 6'2" | 215 | 32 | | |
| Ken Stabler | QB | 6'3" | 215 | 27 | | |
| Clarence Davis | HB | 5'10" | 190 | 24 | | 24 |
| Bob Hudson | HB | 5'11" | 205 | 25 | | |
| Charlie Smith | HB | 6'1" | 205 | 27 | | 30 |
| Marv Hubbard | FB | 6'1" | 225 | 27 | | 36 |
| Pete Banaszak | HB-FB | 5'11" | 210 | 29 | | |
| Jeff Queen | TE-FB | 6'1" | 220 | 27 | | |
| Fred Biletnikoff | WR | 6'1" | 190 | 30 | | 24 |
| Cliff Branch | WR | 5'11" | 170 | 25 | | 18 |
| Mike Siani | WR | 6'2" | 195 | 23 | | 18 |
| Steve Sweeney | WR | 6'5" | 240 | 29 | | 6 |
| Warren Bankston | TE | 6'4" | 235 | 26 | | |
| Bob Moore | TE | 6'3" | 220 | 24 | | 24 |
| Ray Guy | K | 6'3" | 190 | 23 | | |

## DENVER BRONCOS 7-5-2 John Ralston

### Scores of Each Game

| | | |
|---|---|---|
| 28 | CINCINNATI | 10 |
| 34 | SAN FRANCISCO | 36 |
| 14 | CHICAGO | 33 |
| 14 | Kansas City | 16 |
| 48 | Houston | 20 |
| 23 | OAKLAND | 23 |
| 40 | N. Y. Jets | 28 |
| 17 | St. Louis | 17 |
| 30 | SAN DIEGO | 19 |
| 23 | Pittsburgh | 13 |
| 14 | KANSAS CITY | 10 |
| 14 | DALLAS | 22 |
| 42 | San Diego | 28 |
| 7 | Oakland | 21 |

| Use Name | Pos. | Hgt | Wgt | Age | Int | Pts |
|---|---|---|---|---|---|---|
| Mike Askea | OT | 6'4" | 260 | 22 | | |
| Mike Current | OT | 6'4" | 274 | 27 | | |
| Larron Jackson | OT | 6'3" | 270 | 24 | | |
| Marv Montgomery | OT | 6'6" | 255 | 25 | | |
| Paul Howard | OG | 6'3" | 260 | 22 | | |
| Tommy Lyons | OG | 6'2" | 228 | 25 | | |
| Mike Schnitker | OG | 6'3" | 245 | 26 | | |
| Larry Kaminski | C | 6'2" | 245 | 28 | | |
| Bobby Maples | C | 6'3" | 250 | 30 | | |
| Lyle Alzado | DE | 6'3" | 252 | 24 | | |
| Barney Chavous | DE | 6'3" | 252 | 22 | | |
| John Grant | DE | 6'3" | 235 | 23 | | |
| Ed Smith | DE | 6'5" | 240 | 23 | | |
| Pete Duranko | DT | 6'2" | 250 | 29 | | |
| Jerry Inman | DT | 6'3" | 256 | 33 | | |
| Paul Smith | DT | 6'3" | 256 | 28 | | |
| Ken Criter | LB | 5'11" | 223 | 26 | | 2 |
| Tom Graham | LB | 6'2" | 235 | 23 | | |
| Tom Jackson | LB | 5'11" | 220 | 22 | | |
| Bill Laskey | LB | 6'2" | 235 | 30 | 2 | |
| Ray May (from BAL) | LB | 6'1" | 230 | 28 | 1 | |
| Jim O'Malley | LB | 6'1" | 230 | 22 | | |
| Mike Simone | LB | 6' | 210 | 23 | | |
| Charlie Greer | DB | 6' | 205 | 27 | 1 | |
| Dale Hackbart | DB | 6'3" | 210 | 37 | | |
| Calvin Jones | DB | 5'7" | 170 | 22 | 4 | |
| Leroy Mitchell | DB | 6'2" | 190 | 28 | | |
| Randy Montgomery | DB | 5'11" | 182 | 26 | | |
| John Pitts | DB | 6'4" | 218 | 28 | | |
| Bill Thompson | DB | 6'1" | 200 | 26 | 3 | 12 |
| Maurice Tyler | DB | 6' | 188 | 23 | | |
| Tom Domres — Injury | | | | | | |
| George Goeddeke — Injury | | | | | | |
| Chip Myrtle — Injury | | | | | | |
| Charley Johnson | QB | 6' | 190 | 36 | | |
| Steve Ramsey | QB | 6'2" | 210 | 25 | | |
| Bobby Anderson | HB | 6' | 208 | 25 | | 6 |
| Otis Armstrong | HB | 5'10" | 196 | 22 | | 6 |
| Floyd Little | HB | 5'10" | 196 | 31 | | 78 |
| Oliver Ross | FB-HB | 6' | 210 | 23 | | |
| Joe Dawkins | FB | 5'11" | 223 | 25 | | 12 |
| Fran Lynch | HB-FB | 6'1" | 205 | 27 | | |
| Haven Moses | WR | 6'3" | 205 | 27 | | 54 |
| Jerry Simmons | WR | 6'1" | 190 | 30 | | 6 |
| Bill Van Heusen | WR | 6'2" | 200 | 27 | | 6 |
| Gene Washington | WR | 6'3" | 205 | 29 | | 18 |
| Bill Masters | TE | 6'5" | 240 | 29 | | |
| Riley Odoms | TE | 6'4" | 230 | 23 | | 42 |
| Jim Turner | K | 6'2" | 205 | 32 | | 106 |

## KANSAS CITY CHIEFS 7-5-2 Hank Stram

### Scores of Each Game

| | | |
|---|---|---|
| 13 | LOS ANGELES | 23 |
| 10 | New England | 7 |
| 16 | OAKLAND | 3 |
| 16 | DENVER | 14 |
| 10 | Green Bay | 10 |
| 6 | Cincinnati | 14 |
| 6 | Buffalo | 23 |
| 19 | San Diego | 0 |
| 19 | CHICAGO | 7 |
| 38 | HOUSTON | 14 |
| 10 | Denver | 14 |
| 20 | CLEVELAND | 20 |
| 7 | Oakland | 37 |
| 33 | SAN DIEGO | 6 |

| Use Name | Pos. | Hgt | Wgt | Age | Int | Pts |
|---|---|---|---|---|---|---|
| Dave Hill | OT | 6'5" | 260 | 32 | | |
| Francis Peay | OT | 6'5" | 250 | 29 | | |
| Jim Tyrer | OT | 6'6" | 280 | 34 | | |
| Ed Budde | OG | 6'5" | 265 | 32 | | |
| George Daney | OG | 6'3" | 240 | 26 | | |
| Mo Moorman | OT-OG | 6'5" | 252 | 29 | | |
| Wayne Walton | OT-OG | 6'5" | 255 | 24 | | |
| Jack Rudnay | C | 6'3" | 240 | 25 | | |
| Mike Oriard | OG-C | 6'4" | 223 | 25 | | |
| Pat Holmes | DE | 6'5" | 250 | 33 | 1 | |
| John Lohmeyer | DE | 6'4" | 230 | 22 | | 6 |
| Marv Upshaw | DE | 6'3" | 260 | 26 | | |
| Wilbur Young | DE | 6'6" | 285 | 24 | | |
| Buck Buchanan | DT | 6'7" | 270 | 33 | 1 | |
| Curley Culp | DT | 6'1" | 265 | 27 | | |
| George Seals | DT | 6'2" | 260 | 30 | | |
| Bobby Bell | LB | 6'4" | 228 | 33 | 1 | |
| Willie Lanier | LB | 6'1" | 245 | 28 | 3 | 6 |
| Jim Lynch | LB | 6'1" | 235 | 28 | 1 | |
| Al Palewicz | LB | 6'1" | 215 | 23 | | |
| Clyde Werner | LB | 6'4" | 225 | 25 | | |
| Nate Allen | DB | 5'10" | 170 | 25 | 1 | |
| Doug Jones | DB | 6'2" | 202 | 23 | | |
| Jim Kearney | DB | 6'2" | 206 | 30 | 3 | |
| Jim Marsalis | DB | 5'11" | 194 | 27 | 2 | |
| Larry Marshall | DB | 5'10" | 195 | 23 | | |
| Kerry Reardon | DB | 5'11" | 180 | 24 | 2 | |
| Mike Sensibaugh | DB | 5'11" | 192 | 24 | 3 | |
| Emmitt Thomas | DB | 6'2" | 192 | 30 | 3 | |
| Cannonball Butler — Injury | | | | | | |
| Ernie Calloway — Knee Injury | | | | | | |
| Pete Beathard | QB | 6'2" | 200 | 31 | | 6 |
| Len Dawson | QB | 6' | 190 | 39 | | |
| Mike Livingston | QB | 6'3" | 212 | 27 | | 12 |
| Leroy Keyes | HB | 6'2" | 208 | 26 | | |
| Warren McVea | HB | 5'10" | 182 | 27 | | |
| Ed Podolak | HB | 6'1" | 205 | 26 | | 18 |
| Willie Ellison | FB-HB | 6'1" | 210 | 28 | | 12 |
| Wendell Hayes | FB | 6'2" | 220 | 32 | | 12 |
| Jeff Kinney | HB-FB | 6'2" | 215 | 22 | | 6 |
| Andy Hamilton | WR | 6'3" | 190 | 23 | | |
| Dan Kratzer | WR | 6'3" | 194 | 24 | | |
| Dave Smith | WR | 6'2" | 205 | 26 | | |
| Otis Taylor | WR | 6'3" | 215 | 30 | | 24 |
| Bob West | WR | 6'4" | 218 | 22 | | |
| Elmo Wright | WR | 6' | 190 | 24 | | 12 |
| Gary Butler | TE | 6'3" | 235 | 22 | | 12 |
| Morris Stroud | TE | 6'10" | 255 | 27 | | 12 |
| Jan Stenerud | K | 6'2" | 187 | 30 | | 93 |
| Jerrel Wilson | K | 6'4" | 222 | 31 | | |

## SAN DIEGO CHARGERS 2-11-1 Harland Svare  Ron Waller

### Scores of Each Game

| | | |
|---|---|---|
| 0 | Washington | 38 |
| 34 | BUFFALO | 7 |
| 13 | CINCINNATI | 20 |
| 21 | Pittsburgh | 38 |
| 17 | Oakland | 27 |
| 0 | ATLANTA | 41 |
| 16 | Cleveland | 16 |
| 0 | KANSAS CITY | 19 |
| 19 | Denver | 30 |
| 17 | NEW ORLEANS | 14 |
| 3 | OAKLAND | 31 |
| 14 | New England | 30 |
| 28 | DENVER | 42 |
| 6 | Kansas City | 33 |

| Use Name | Pos. | Hgt | Wgt | Age | Int | Pts |
|---|---|---|---|---|---|---|
| Ira Gordon | OT | 6'3" | 268 | 25 | | |
| Terry Owens | OT | 6'6" | 268 | 29 | | |
| Russ Washington | OT | 6'6" | 290 | 26 | | |
| Al Dennis | OG | 6'4" | 250 | 22 | | |
| Walt Sweeney | OG | 6'3" | 256 | 32 | | |
| Ralph Wenzel | OG | 6'3" | 250 | 30 | | |
| Doug Wilkerson | OG | 6'2" | 256 | 26 | | |
| Jay Douglas | C | 6'6" | 242 | 22 | | |
| Carl Mauck | C | 6'3" | 243 | 26 | | |
| Lionel Aldridge | DE | 6'4" | 245 | 31 | | |
| Coy Bacon | DE | 6'4" | 270 | 31 | | 6 |
| Deacon Jones | DE | 6'5" | 250 | 34 | | |
| Pete Lazetich | DE | 6'3" | 225 | 23 | | |
| Cal Snowden | DE | 6'4" | 253 | 26 | | |
| Dave Costa | DT | 6'2" | 260 | 31 | | |
| Greg Wojcik | DT | 6'4" | 243 | 30 | | |
| Carl Gersbach | LB | 6'1" | 230 | 26 | 1 | |
| Rick Redman | LB | 5'11" | 222 | 30 | 1 | |
| Floyd Rice (from HOU) | LB | 6'3" | 223 | 24 | 1 | 6 |
| Mel Rogers | LB | 6'2" | 230 | 26 | 1 | |
| Tim Rossovich | LB | 6'4" | 240 | 27 | 1 | |
| Mike Stratton | LB | 6'3" | 240 | 31 | 3 | |
| Joe Beauchamp | DB | 6' | 188 | 29 | | |
| Reggie Berry | DB | 6' | 190 | 24 | | |
| Lenny Dunlap | DB | 6'1" | 195 | 24 | | |
| Chris Fletcher | DB | 5'11" | 185 | 24 | | |
| Bob Howard | DB | 6'1" | 177 | 28 | 5 | |
| Willie McGee | DB | 5'11" | 175 | 23 | | |
| Bryant Salter | DB | 6'4" | 196 | 23 | 1 | |
| Ron Smith | DB | 6'1" | 195 | 30 | 1 | 12 |
| Ray White — Injury | | | | | | |
| Wayne Clark | QB | 6'2" | 205 | 26 | | |
| Dan Fouts | QB | 6'3" | 193 | 22 | | |
| Johnny Unitas | QB | 6'1" | 196 | 40 | | |
| Mike Garrett | HB | 5'9" | 200 | 29 | | 6 |
| Clint Jones | HB | 6' | 205 | 28 | | 6 |
| Bob Thomas | HB | 5'10" | 200 | 24 | | 6 |
| Cid Edwards | FB | 6'2" | 230 | 29 | | 6 |
| Robert Holmes | FB | 5'9" | 220 | 27 | | 42 |
| Gary Garrison | WR | 6'1" | 193 | 29 | | 12 |
| Ron Holliday | WR | 5'9" | 168 | 25 | 1 | |
| Jerry LeVias | WR | 5'10" | 178 | 26 | | 18 |
| Dave Williams (to PIT) | WR | 6'2" | 200 | 28 | | |
| Pettis Norman | TE | 6'3" | 226 | 23 | | |
| Gary Parris | TE | 6'2" | 226 | 23 | | |
| Jim Thaxton | TE | 6'2" | 240 | 24 | | 12 |
| Dennis Partee | K | 6'2" | 230 | 27 | | 9 |
| Ray Wersching | K | 5'11" | 210 | 23 | | 46 |

## OAKLAND RAIDERS

### RUSHING

| Last Name | No. | Yds | Avg | TD |
|---|---|---|---|---|
| Hubbard | 193 | 903 | 4.7 | 6 |
| C. Smith | 173 | 682 | 3.9 | 4 |
| Davis | 116 | 609 | 5.3 | 4 |
| Banaszak | 34 | 198 | 5.8 | 0 |
| Stabler | 21 | 101 | 4.8 | 0 |
| Guy | 1 | 21 | 21.0 | 0 |
| Hudson | 4 | 3 | 0.8 | 0 |
| Lamonica | 5 | −7 | −1.4 | 0 |

### RECEIVING

| Last Name | No. | Yds | Avg | TD |
|---|---|---|---|---|
| Biletnikoff | 48 | 660 | 14 | 4 |
| Siani | 45 | 742 | 16 | 3 |
| Moore | 34 | 375 | 11 | 4 |
| C. Smith | 28 | 260 | 9 | 1 |
| Branch | 19 | 290 | 15 | 3 |
| Hubbard | 15 | 116 | 8 | 0 |
| Davis | 7 | 76 | 11 | 0 |
| Banaszak | 6 | 31 | 5 | 0 |
| Sweeny | 2 | 52 | 26 | 1 |
| Hudson | 1 | 9 | 9 | 0 |

### PUNT RETURNS

| Last Name | No. | Yds | Avg | TD |
|---|---|---|---|---|
| Atkinson | 41 | 336 | 8 | 1 |
| Maxwell | 4 | 8 | 2 | 0 |
| Warren | 1 | 0 | 0 | 0 |

### KICKOFF RETURNS

| Last Name | No. | Yds | Avg | TD |
|---|---|---|---|---|
| Davis | 19 | 504 | 27 | 0 |
| Hudson | 14 | 350 | 25 | 0 |
| Banaszak | 3 | 48 | 16 | 0 |
| C. Smith | 2 | 23 | 12 | 0 |
| Bankston | 1 | 12 | 12 | 0 |

### PASSING – PUNTING – KICKING

| Last Name | Att | Comp | % | Yds | Yd/Att | TD | Int−% | RK |
|---|---|---|---|---|---|---|---|---|
| **PASSING** | | | | | | | | |
| Stabler | 260 | 163 | 63 | 1997 | 7.7 | 14 | 10− 4 | 2 |
| Lamonica | 93 | 42 | 45 | 614 | 6.6 | 2 | 8− 9 | |

| Last Name | No | Avg |
|---|---|---|
| **PUNTING** | | |
| Guy | 69 | 45.3 |

| Last Name | XP | Att | % | FG | Att | % |
|---|---|---|---|---|---|---|
| **KICKING** | | | | | | |
| Blanda | 31 | 31 | 100 | 23 | 33 | 70 |

## DENVER BRONCOS

### RUSHING

| Last Name | No. | Yds | Avg | TD |
|---|---|---|---|---|
| Little | 256 | 979 | 3.8 | 12 |
| Dawkins | 160 | 706 | 4.4 | 2 |
| Armstrong | 26 | 90 | 3.5 | 0 |
| Anderson | 19 | 61 | 3.2 | 1 |
| Odoms | 5 | 53 | 10.6 | 0 |
| Van Heusen | 4 | 34 | 8.5 | 0 |
| Moses | 3 | 25 | 8.3 | 1 |
| Ross | 5 | 21 | 4.2 | 0 |
| Johnson | 7 | −2 | −0.3 | 0 |
| Simmons | 1 | −4 | −4.0 | 0 |
| Masters | 1 | −9 | −9.0 | 0 |

### RECEIVING

| Last Name | No. | Yds | Avg | TD |
|---|---|---|---|---|
| Odoms | 43 | 629 | 15 | 7 |
| Little | 41 | 423 | 10 | 1 |
| Dawkins | 30 | 329 | 11 | 0 |
| Moses | 28 | 518 | 19 | 8 |
| Anderson | 15 | 153 | 10 | 0 |
| Simmons | 13 | 249 | 19 | 1 |
| Washington | 10 | 150 | 15 | 3 |
| Van Heusen | 8 | 149 | 19 | 1 |
| Masters | 5 | 65 | 13 | 0 |
| Armstrong | 2 | 43 | 22 | 1 |
| Jackson | 1 | −2 | −2 | 0 |

### PUNT RETURNS

| Last Name | No. | Yds | Avg | TD |
|---|---|---|---|---|
| Thompson | 30 | 366 | 12 | 0 |
| Tyler | 4 | 20 | 5 | 0 |
| Greer | 3 | 11 | 4 | 0 |
| Little | 1 | 7 | 7 | 0 |
| Criter | 1 | 0 | 0 | 0 |
| Mitchell | 1 | 0 | 0 | 0 |

### KICKOFF RETURNS

| Last Name | No. | Yds | Avg | TD |
|---|---|---|---|---|
| Armstrong | 20 | 472 | 24 | 0 |
| Dawkins | 10 | 222 | 22 | 0 |
| Thompson | 1 | 25 | 25 | 0 |
| Tyler | 1 | 23 | 23 | 0 |
| Montgomery | 1 | 22 | 22 | 0 |
| Lynch | 1 | 14 | 14 | 0 |
| Forsberg | 1 | 12 | 12 | 0 |
| Simone | 1 | 3 | 3 | 0 |

### PASSING – PUNTING – KICKING

| Last Name | Att | Comp | % | Yds | Yd/Att | TD | Int−% | RK |
|---|---|---|---|---|---|---|---|---|
| **PASSING** | | | | | | | | |
| Johnson | 346 | 184 | 53 | 2465 | 7.1 | 20 | 17− 5 | 3 |
| Ramsey | 27 | 10 | 37 | 194 | 7.2 | 2 | 2− 7 | |
| Anderson | 3 | 2 | 67 | 47 | 15.7 | 0 | 0− 0 | |
| Turner | 1 | 0 | 0 | 0 | 0.0 | 0 | 1−100 | |
| Van Heusen | 1 | 0 | 0 | 0 | 0.0 | 0 | 0− 0 | |

| Last Name | No | Avg |
|---|---|---|
| **PUNTING** | | |
| Van Heusen | 69 | 45.1 |

| Last Name | XP | Att | % | FG | Att | % |
|---|---|---|---|---|---|---|
| **KICKING** | | | | | | |
| Turner | 40 | 40 | 100 | 22 | 33 | 67 |

## KANSAS CITY CHIEFS

### RUSHING

| Last Name | No. | Yds | Avg | TD |
|---|---|---|---|---|
| Podolak | 210 | 721 | 3.4 | 3 |
| Ellison | 108 | 411 | 3.8 | 2 |
| Hayes | 95 | 352 | 3.7 | 2 |
| Kinney | 50 | 128 | 2.6 | 1 |
| Livingston | 19 | 94 | 4.9 | 2 |
| Dawson | 6 | 40 | 6.7 | 0 |
| Wright | 5 | 29 | 5.8 | 0 |
| Beathard | 6 | 16 | 2.7 | 1 |
| Butler | 2 | 10 | 5.0 | 0 |
| McVea | 4 | 5 | 1.3 | 0 |
| Keyes | 2 | 1 | 0.5 | 0 |
| Taylor | 4 | −14 | −3.5 | 0 |

### RECEIVING

| Last Name | No. | Yds | Avg | TD |
|---|---|---|---|---|
| Podolak | 55 | 445 | 8 | 0 |
| Taylor | 34 | 565 | 17 | 4 |
| Hayes | 18 | 134 | 7 | 0 |
| Wright | 16 | 252 | 16 | 2 |
| Stroud | 12 | 216 | 18 | 2 |
| Kinney | 11 | 126 | 11 | 0 |
| Ellison | 9 | 64 | 7 | 0 |
| Butler | 8 | 124 | 16 | 2 |
| West | 4 | 65 | 16 | 0 |
| Hamilton | 2 | 35 | 18 | 0 |
| Smith | 2 | 20 | 10 | 0 |
| Moorman | 1 | −1 | −1 | 0 |
| Keyes | 1 | −6 | −6 | 0 |

### PUNT RETURNS

| Last Name | No. | Yds | Avg | TD |
|---|---|---|---|---|
| Marshall | 29 | 180 | 6 | 0 |
| Podolak | 11 | 90 | 8 | 0 |
| Reardon | 2 | 9 | 5 | 0 |

### KICKOFF RETURNS

| Last Name | No. | Yds | Avg | TD |
|---|---|---|---|---|
| Marshall | 14 | 391 | 28 | 0 |
| McVea | 8 | 146 | 18 | 0 |
| Kinney | 5 | 130 | 26 | 0 |
| Reardon | 2 | 45 | 23 | 0 |
| Werner | 1 | 13 | 13 | 0 |
| West | 1 | 0 | 0 | 0 |

### PASSING – PUNTING – KICKING

| Last Name | Att | Comp | % | Yds | Yd/Att | TD | Int−% | RK |
|---|---|---|---|---|---|---|---|---|
| **PASSING** | | | | | | | | |
| Livingston | 145 | 75 | 52 | 916 | 6.3 | 6 | 7− 5 | 7 |
| Dawson | 101 | 66 | 65 | 725 | 7.2 | 2 | 5− 5 | |
| Beathard | 64 | 31 | 48 | 389 | 6.1 | 2 | 1− 2 | |
| Keyes | 1 | 0 | 0 | 0 | 0.0 | 0 | 0− 0 | |
| Podolak | 1 | 0 | 0 | 0 | 0.0 | 0 | 0− 0 | |
| Wilson | 1 | 1 | 100 | 9 | 9.0 | 0 | 0− 0 | |

| Last Name | No | Avg |
|---|---|---|
| **PUNTING** | | |
| Wilson | 80 | 45.5 |

| Last Name | XP | Att | % | FG | Att | % |
|---|---|---|---|---|---|---|
| **KICKING** | | | | | | |
| Stenerud | 21 | 23 | 91 | 24 | 38 | 63 |

## SAN DIEGO CHARGERS

### RUSHING

| Last Name | No. | Yds | Avg | TD |
|---|---|---|---|---|
| Edwards | 133 | 609 | 4.6 | 1 |
| Garrett | 114 | 467 | 4.1 | 0 |
| Holmes | 78 | 289 | 3.7 | 7 |
| C. Jones | 55 | 170 | 3.1 | 1 |
| Clark | 13 | 86 | 6.6 | 0 |
| Holliday | 6 | 70 | 11.7 | 0 |
| Thomas | 22 | 48 | 2.2 | 0 |
| LeVias | 2 | 33 | 16.5 | 0 |
| Fouts | 7 | 32 | 4.6 | 0 |
| Norman | 1 | 10 | 10.0 | 0 |

### RECEIVING

| Last Name | No. | Yds | Avg | TD |
|---|---|---|---|---|
| LeVias | 30 | 536 | 18 | 3 |
| Edwards | 25 | 164 | 7 | 0 |
| Holmes | 19 | 151 | 8 | 0 |
| Garrett | 15 | 124 | 8 | 1 |
| Garrison | 14 | 292 | 21 | 2 |
| Holliday | 14 | 182 | 13 | 0 |
| Norman | 13 | 200 | 15 | 0 |
| C. Jones | 7 | 126 | 18 | 0 |
| Thaxton | 7 | 119 | 17 | 2 |
| Dave Williams | 7 | 118 | 17 | 0 |
| Thomas | 7 | 51 | 7 | 1 |
| McGee | 3 | 67 | 22 | 0 |

### PUNT RETURNS

| Last Name | No. | Yds | Avg | TD |
|---|---|---|---|---|
| Smith | 27 | 352 | 13 | 2 |
| McGee | 6 | 56 | 9 | 0 |

### KICKOFF RETURNS

| Last Name | No. | Yds | Avg | TD |
|---|---|---|---|---|
| Smith | 36 | 947 | 26 | 0 |
| McGee | 20 | 423 | 21 | 0 |
| C. Jones | 10 | 217 | 22 | 0 |
| Rice | 2 | 17 | 9 | 0 |
| East | 1 | 8 | 8 | 0 |
| Rogers | 1 | 4 | 4 | 0 |
| Douglas | 1 | 0 | 0 | 0 |
| Wenzel | 1 | 0 | 0 | 0 |
| Holliday | 0 | −2 | 0 | 0 |

### PASSING – PUNTING – KICKING

| Last Name | Att | Comp | % | Yds | Yd/Att | TD | Int−% | RK |
|---|---|---|---|---|---|---|---|---|
| **PASSING** | | | | | | | | |
| Fouts | 194 | 87 | 45 | 1126 | 5.8 | 6 | 13− 7 | 12 |
| Clark | 90 | 40 | 44 | 532 | 5.9 | 0 | 9−10 | |
| Unitas | 76 | 34 | 45 | 471 | 6.2 | 3 | 7− 9 | |
| Holliday | 2 | 0 | 0 | 0 | 0.0 | 0 | 1−50 | |
| Garrett | 1 | 0 | 0 | 0 | 0.0 | 0 | 0− 0 | |

| Last Name | No | Avg |
|---|---|---|
| **PUNTING** | | |
| Partee | 72 | 41.1 |

| Last Name | XP | Att | % | FG | Att | % |
|---|---|---|---|---|---|---|
| **KICKING** | | | | | | |
| Wersching | 13 | 15 | 87 | 11 | 25 | 44 |
| Partee | 6 | 6 | 100 | 1 | 2 | 50 |
| Holliday | 1 | 1 | 100 | 0 | 0 | 0 |

# 1973 Championship Games

## Tarkenton's Winning Formula

### SCORING

| | | | | |
|---|---|---|---|---|
| DALLAS | 0 | 0 | 10 | 0—10 |
| MINNESOTA | 3 | 7 | 7 | 10—27 |

**First Quarter**
Minn.    Cox, 44 yard field goal

**Second Quarter**
Minn.    Foreman, 5 yard rush
         PAT—Cox (kick)

**Third Quarter**
Dall.    Richards, 63 yard punt return
         PAT—Fritsch (kick)
Minn.    Gilliam, 54 yard pass from Tarkenton
         PAT—Cox (kick)
Dall.    Fritsch, 17 yard field goal

**Fourth Quarter**
Minn.    Bryant, 63 yard interception return
         PAT—Cox (kick)
Minn.    Cox, 34 yard field goal

### TEAM STATISTICS

| DALLAS | | MINN. |
|---|---|---|
| 9 | First Downs—Total | 20 |
| 3 | First Downs—Rushing | 14 |
| 5 | First Downs—Passing | 6 |
| 1 | First Downs—Penalty | 0 |
| 2 | Fumbles—Number | 4 |
| 2 | Fumbles—Lost Ball | 3 |
| 2 | Penalties—Number | 3 |
| 20 | Yards Penalized | 33 |
| 0 | Missed Field Goals | 0 |
| 49 | Offensive Plays | 72 |
| 153 | Net Yards | 306 |
| 3.1 | Average Gain | 4.3 |
| 6 | Giveaways | 4 |
| 4 | Takeaways | 6 |
| −2 | Difference | +2 |

Fran Tarkenton was in his first playoffs in his thirteen-year career, and he celebrated last week by leading the Vikings to a 27-20 victory over the Redskins. Now he hoped to further destroy his image as a loser by beating the Cowboys, who had defeated the Rams 27-16 in the opening round of the playoffs.

The Vikings established a winning formula on offense in the first half by mixing unexpected passes with a strong running attack. The Minnesota blockers keyed on removing middle linebacker Lee Roy Jordan from all running plays, and with star tackle Bob Lilly out of action with a bad back, the Cowboys could not stop ball carriers Chuck Foreman and Oscar Reed. The Vikings controlled the ball for most of the first half, and their defense foiled the Cowboys whenever they got the ball.

Fred Cox scored Minnesota's first three points with a first-quarter field goal, and the Vikings added a touchdown in the second period on an 86-yard drive capped by Foreman's five-yard run.

The Dallas offense, playing without the injured Calvin Hill, could not crack the Minnesota defense until Golden Richards put the Cowboys on the scoreboard by returning a punt 63 yards for a touchdown. The Cowboys now had the momentum to take the lead, but Tarkenton deflated the Dallas hopes three plays later when he hit John Gilliam with a long bomb that went for a 54-yard touchdown. The Cowboys added a Toni Fritsch field goal late in the period to make the score 17-10 with fifteen minutes left.

Turnovers dominated the final period. The teams took turns giving the ball up until Bobby Bryant intercepted a Staubach pass and returned it 63 yards for a score. Another intercepted pass led to a Cox field goal which lengthened the Viking lead to 27-10. The Cowboys suffered the final indignity late in the game when Walt Garrison fumbled the ball away on the Minnesota two-yard line.

### INDIVIDUAL STATISTICS

| DALLAS | No | Yds | Avg. | MINNESOTA | No | Yds | Avg. |
|---|---|---|---|---|---|---|---|
| **RUSHING** | | | | | | | |
| Newhouse | 14 | 40 | 2.9 | Foreman | 19 | 76 | 4.0 |
| Staubach | 5 | 30 | 6.0 | Reed | 18 | 75 | 4.2 |
| Garrison | 5 | 9 | 1.8 | Osborn | 4 | 27 | 6.8 |
| Fugett | 1 | 1 | 1.0 | Tarkenton | 4 | 16 | 4.0 |
| | 25 | 80 | 3.2 | Brown | 2 | 9 | 4.5 |
| | | | | | 47 | 203 | 4.3 |
| **RECEIVING** | | | | | | | |
| Hayes | 2 | 25 | 12.5 | Foreman | 4 | 28 | 7.0 |
| Pearson | 2 | 24 | 12.0 | Gilliam | 2 | 63 | 31.5 |
| Montgomery | 2 | 15 | 7.5 | Voigt | 2 | 23 | 11.5 |
| DuPree | 1 | 20 | 20.0 | Lash | 1 | 11 | 11.0 |
| Garrison | 1 | 10 | 10.0 | Reed | 1 | 8 | 8.0 |
| Fugett | 1 | −1 | −1.0 | | 10 | 133 | 13.3 |
| Newhouse | 1 | −4 | −4.0 | | | | |
| | 10 | 89 | 8.9 | | | | |
| **PUNTING** | | | | | | | |
| Bateman | 4 | | 39.5 | Eischeid | 3 | | 43.3 |
| **PUNT RETURNS** | | | | | | | |
| Richards | 1 | 63 | 63.0 | Bryant | 1 | 0 | 0.0 |
| **KICKOFF RETURNS** | | | | | | | |
| Harris | 2 | 54 | 27.0 | West | 2 | 45 | 22.5 |
| Waters | 1 | 18 | 18.0 | Gilliam | 1 | 21 | 21.0 |
| | 3 | 72 | 24.0 | | 3 | 66 | 22.0 |
| **INTERCEPTION RETURNS** | | | | | | | |
| Waters | 1 | 1 | 1.0 | Bryant | 2 | 63 | 31.5 |
| | | | | J. Wright | 1 | 13 | 13.0 |
| | | | | Siemon | 1 | 0 | 0.0 |
| | | | | | 4 | 76 | 19.0 |

| DALLAS | Att. | Comp. | Comp. Pct. | Yds. | Int. | Yds/ Att. | Yds/ Comp. | Yards Lost Tackled |
|---|---|---|---|---|---|---|---|---|
| Staubach | 21 | 10 | 47.6 | 89 | 4 | 4.2 | 8.9 | 2—26 |
| **MINNESOTA** | | | | | | | | |
| Tarkenton | 21 | 10 | 47.6 | 133 | 1 | 6.3 | 13.3 | 4—30 |

---

## Bringing the Raiders Down to Earth

### SCORING

| | | | | |
|---|---|---|---|---|
| MIAMI | 7 | 7 | 3 | 10—27 |
| OAKLAND | 0 | 0 | 10 | 0—10 |

**First Quarter**
Miami    Csonka, 11 yard rush
         PAT—Yepremian (kick)

**Second Quarter**
Miami    Csonka, 2 yard rush
         PAT—Yepremian (kick)

**Third Quarter**
Oak.     Blanda, 21 yard field goal
Miami    Yepremian, 42 yard field goal
Oak.     Siani, 25 yard pass from Stabler
         PAT—Blanda (kick)

**Fourth Quarter**
Miami    Yepremian, 26 yard field goal
Miami    Csonka, 2 yard rush
         PAT—Yepremian (kick)

### TEAM STATISTICS

| MIAMI | | OAK. |
|---|---|---|
| 21 | First Downs—Total | 15 |
| 18 | First Downs—Rushing | 4 |
| 2 | First Downs—Passing | 8 |
| 1 | First Downs—Penalty | 2 |
| 1 | Fumbles—Number | 1 |
| 0 | Fumbles—Lost Ball | 0 |
| 3 | Penalties—Number | 3 |
| 26 | Yards Penalized | 35 |
| 0 | Missed Field Goals | 1 |
| 60 | Offensive Plays | 49 |
| 292 | Net Yards | 236 |
| 4.9 | Average Gain | 4.8 |
| 1 | Giveaways | 1 |
| 1 | Takeaways | 1 |
| 0 | Difference | 0 |

The Raiders had used a powerful running attack to beat the Steelers 33-14 in the AFC semifinal match, but the Dolphins, coming off a 34-16 victory over the Bengals, taught the Raiders a lesson about ball control in this AFC title match. Dolphin quarterback Bob Griese passed the ball only six times all game, relying instead on his powerful running backs to grind out the yardage. Larry Csonka and Mercury Morris plowed through gaping holes cut in the Oakland defense by the Miami blockers, and the Dolphins succeeded in eating up both yardage and the clock.

On the first series of the day, the Dolphins drove 64 yards to a touchdown, with the key play of the drive a 27-yard scramble by Griese on third-and-11 on the Oakland 38-yard line. Larry Csonka plowed over from the 11-yard line for the score.

The Raiders threatened in the first period when Ken Stabler hit Mike Siani with a pass deep in Miami territory, but a holding penalty nullified the play and extinguished the threat. The Dolphins, meanwhile, put together another long drive late in the half, and Csonka scored from the 2 after Griese had frozen the Raiders by faking a roll-out.

George Blanda put the Raiders on the scoreboard early in the second half with a 21-yard field goal, but Charley Leigh's 52-yard return of the kickoff led to Garo Yepremian's 42-yard three-pointer to make the score 17-3. Stabler started clicking on short passes late in the period, and his 25-yard scoring pitch to Siani narrowed the Miami lead to 17-10.

The Dolphins gave themselves some breathing room five minutes into the fourth quarter with a Yepremian field goal, and when the defensive unit stopped the Raiders on a fourth-and-inches try, the Miami attack ground out a final touchdown to run the winning margin to 27-10.

### INDIVIDUAL STATISTICS

| MIAMI | No | Yds | Avg. | OAKLAND | No | Yds | Avg. |
|---|---|---|---|---|---|---|---|
| **RUSHING** | | | | | | | |
| Csonka | 29 | 117 | 4.0 | Hubbard | 10 | 54 | 5.4 |
| Morris | 14 | 86 | 6.1 | C. Smith | 10 | 35 | 3.5 |
| Griese | 3 | 39 | 13.0 | C. Davis | 4 | 15 | 3.8 |
| Kiick | 6 | 12 | 2.0 | Banaszak | 2 | 3 | 1.5 |
| Nottingham | 1 | 12 | 12.0 | | 26 | 107 | 4.1 |
| | 53 | 266 | 5.0 | | | | |
| **RECEIVING** | | | | | | | |
| Warfield | 1 | 27 | 27.0 | C. Smith | 5 | 43 | 8.6 |
| Briscoe | 1 | 6 | 6.0 | Siani | 3 | 45 | 15.0 |
| Kiick | 1 | 1 | 1.0 | Biletnikoff | 2 | 15 | 7.5 |
| | 3 | 34 | 11.3 | Hubbard | 2 | 11 | 5.5 |
| | | | | Moore | 1 | 9 | 4.5 |
| | | | | C. Davis | 1 | 6 | 6.0 |
| | | | | | 15 | 129 | 8.6 |
| **PUNTING** | | | | | | | |
| Seiple | 1 | | 39.0 | Guy | 2 | | 51.0 |
| **PUNT RETURNS** | | | | | | | |
| Scott | 2 | 10 | 5.0 | Atkinson | 1 | 0 | 0.0 |
| **KICKOFF RETURNS** | | | | | | | |
| Leigh | 1 | 52 | 52.0 | C. Davis | 3 | 68 | 22.7 |
| Morris | 1 | 19 | 19.0 | C. Smith | 1 | 21 | 21.0 |
| Nottingham | 1 | 19 | 19.0 | | 4 | 89 | 22.3 |
| | 3 | 90 | 30.0 | | | | |
| **INTERCEPTION RETURNS** | | | | | | | |
| Matheson | 1 | 29 | 29.0 | W. Brown | 1 | 0 | 0.0 |

| MIAMI | Att. | Comp. | Comp. Pct. | Yds. | Int. | Yds/ Att. | Yds/ Comp. | Yards Lost Tackled |
|---|---|---|---|---|---|---|---|---|
| Griese | 6 | 3 | 50.0 | 34 | 1 | 5.7 | 11.3 | 1—8 |
| **OAKLAND** | | | | | | | | |
| Stabler | 23 | 15 | 65.2 | 129 | 1 | 5.6 | 8.6 | 0—0 |

## Dolphin Defense and Csonka Crashes

The Dolphins did not enjoy a perfect season this year, but they did play an almost perfect game against the Vikings in the Super Bowl. After receiving the opening kickoff, the Dolphins immediately set the tone of the day with a crunching 62-yard drive. With the Miami line ripping the famous Minnesota front four to shreds, Larry Csonka repeatedly burst through the middle for good yardage. On the tenth play of the drive, Csonka bulled into the end zone from five yards out; the Dolphins now had a 7-0 lead to nurse.

Viking quarterback Fran Tarkenton, a man eager to erase his image as a loser, could make no progress against the swarming Miami defense. The Dolphin line smothered the Minnesota running game, and the Dolphin zone defense made passing a very risky proposition. Tarkenton tried every play in the Viking playbook to no avail.

The Dolphins, meanwhile, did not stop with their seven-point lead. With Bob Griese passing very rarely, the Miami attack continued to move the ball on the ground. The Dolphin linemen habitually beat the Viking front four off the ball, slamming into them before they could react; Minnesota ends Carl Eller and Jim Marshall were taken out of almost every play. The second Dolphin touchdown came late in the opening quarter on a plunge by Jim Kiick, who had not scored all season. Garo Yepremian added the extra point, and the 14-0 lead looked close to impregnable.

Yepremian added a field goal in the second quarter to give the Dolphins a 17-0 halftime edge that understated the one-sidedness of the first half. The Vikings were not making out-and-out blunders; they simply were being beaten by better blocking and tackling. They did make a mistake on the second-half kickoff when a clipping penalty called back a long return by John Gilliam. The momentum which the return had given to the Vikings immediately shifted back to the Dolphins, and within seven minutes Csonka drove into the end zone for the third Miami touchdown.

With the decision no longer in doubt, the Vikings got onto the scoreboard in the fourth quarter on a touchdown run by Tarkenton. After Cox booted the extra point, the Vikings shocked Miami by recovering an on-side kick; once again, however, a penalty nullified the play and nipped a Minnesota rally before it could begin.

By the end of the day, the Dolphins again were undisputed champions of pro football, and Larry Csonka had set a Super Bowl rushing record with 145 hard-fought yards. With two straight championships to their credit, the Dolphins now drew comparisons with the Packers of Vince Lombardi's era. Although Marv Fleming, who played on both clubs, said, "This is the greatest team ever," the question joined the ranks of unanswerable sports fantasies.

### LINEUPS

| MIAMI | | MINNESOTA |
|---|---|---|
| **OFFENSE** | | |
| Warfield | WR | Dale |
| W. Moore | LT | Alderman |
| Kuechenberg | LG | White |
| Langer | C | Tingelhoff |
| Little | RG | Gallagher |
| Evans | RT | Yary |
| Mandich | TE | Voigt |
| Briscoe | WR | Gilliam |
| Griese | QB | Tarkenton |
| Morris | RB | Foreman |
| Csonka | RB | Reed |
| **DEFENSE** | | |
| Den Herder | LE | Eller |
| Fernandez | LT | Larsen |
| Heinz | RT | Page |
| Stanfill | RE | Marshall |
| Swift | LLB | Winston |
| Buoniconti | MLB | Siemon |
| Kolen | RLB | Hilgenberg |
| Mumphord | LCB | N. Wright |
| Johnson | RCB | Bryant |
| Anderson | LS | J. Wright |
| Scott | RS | Krause |

#### SUBSTITUTES

**MIAMI**

| **OFFENSE** | |
|---|---|
| Crusan | Morrall |
| Fleming | Newman |
| Goode | Nottingham |
| Kiick | Twilley |
| **DEFENSE** | |
| Babb | Matheson |
| Ball | M. Moore |
| Bannon | Stuckey |
| Foley | |
| **KICKERS** | |
| Seiple | Yepremian |

**MINNESOTA**

| **OFFENSE** | |
|---|---|
| B. Brown | Lash |
| Goodrum | Marinaro |
| Kingsriter | Osborn |
| **DEFENSE** | |
| T. Brown | Porter |
| Lurtsema | Sutherland |
| Martin | West |
| **KICKERS** | |
| Cox | Eischeid |

### SCORING

| MIAMI | 14 3 7 0—24 |
|---|---|
| MINNESOTA | 0 0 0 7— 7 |

**First Quarter**
Mia.  Csonka, 5 yard rush  9:33
  PAT — Yepremian (kick)
Mia.  Kiick, 1 yard rush  13:38
  PAT — Yepremian (kick)

**Second Quarter**
Mia.  Yepremian, 28 yard field goal  8:58

**Third Quarter**
Mia.  Csonka, 2 yard rush  6:16
  PAT — Yepremian (kick)

**Fourth Quarter**
Minn.  Tarkenton, 4 yard rush  1:35
  PAT — Cox (kick)

### TEAM STATISTICS

| MIAMI | | MINN. |
|---|---|---|
| 21 | First Downs — Total | 14 |
| 13 | First Downs — Rushing | 5 |
| 4 | First Downs — Passing | 8 |
| 4 | First Downs — Penalty | 1 |
| 1 | Fumbles — Number | 2 |
| 0 | Fumbles — Lost Ball | 1 |
| 1 | Penalties — Number | 7 |
| 4 | Yards Penalized | 65 |
| 0 | Missed Field Goals | 0 |
| 61 | Offensive Plays | 54 |
| 259 | Net Yards | 238 |
| 4.2 | Average Gain | 4.4 |
| 0 | Giveaways | 2 |
| 2 | Takeaways | 0 |
| +2 | Difference | −2 |

### INDIVIDUAL STATISTICS

**MIAMI**

**RUSHING**

| | No | Yds | Avg. |
|---|---|---|---|
| Csonka | 33 | 145 | 4.4 |
| Morris | 11 | 34 | 3.1 |
| Kiick | 7 | 10 | 1.4 |
| Griese | 2 | 7 | 3.5 |
| | 53 | 196 | 3.7 |

**RECEIVING**

| | No | Yds | Avg. |
|---|---|---|---|
| Warfield | 2 | 33 | 16.5 |
| Mandich | 2 | 21 | 10.5 |
| Briscoe | 2 | 19 | 9.5 |
| | 6 | 73 | 12.2 |

**PUNTING**

| | No | Yds | Avg. |
|---|---|---|---|
| Seiple | 3 | | 39.6 |

**PUNT RETURNS**

| | No | Yds | Avg. |
|---|---|---|---|
| Scott | 3 | 20 | 6.7 |

**KICKOFF RETURNS**

| | No | Yds | Avg. |
|---|---|---|---|
| Scott | 2 | 47 | 23.5 |

**INTERCEPTION RETURNS**

| | No | Yds | Avg. |
|---|---|---|---|
| Johnson | 1 | 10 | 10.0 |

**MINNESOTA**

**RUSHING**

| | No | Yds | Avg. |
|---|---|---|---|
| Reed | 11 | 32 | 2.9 |
| Foreman | 7 | 18 | 2.6 |
| Tarkenton | 4 | 17 | 4.3 |
| Marinaro | 1 | 3 | 3.0 |
| B. Brown | 1 | 2 | 2.0 |
| | 24 | 72 | 3.0 |

**RECEIVING**

| | No | Yds | Avg. |
|---|---|---|---|
| Foreman | 5 | 27 | 5.4 |
| Gilliam | 4 | 44 | 11.0 |
| Voigt | 3 | 46 | 15.3 |
| Marinaro | 2 | 39 | 19.5 |
| B. Brown | 1 | 9 | 9.0 |
| Kingsriter | 1 | 9 | 9.0 |
| Lash | 1 | 9 | 9.0 |
| Reed | 1 | −1 | −1.0 |
| | 18 | 182 | 10.1 |

**PUNTING**

| | No | Yds | Avg. |
|---|---|---|---|
| Eischeid | 5 | | 42.2 |

**KICKOFF RETURNS**

| | No | Yds | Avg. |
|---|---|---|---|
| Gilliam | 2 | 41 | 20.5 |
| West | 2 | 28 | 14.0 |
| | 4 | 69 | 17.3 |

**INTERCEPTION RETURNS**

None

**PASSING**

**MIAMI**

| | Att | Comp | Comp Pct. | Yds | Int | Yds/ Att. | Yds/ Comp | Yards Lost Tackled |
|---|---|---|---|---|---|---|---|---|
| Griese | 7 | 6 | 85.7 | 73 | 0 | 10.4 | 12.2 | 1—10 |

**MINNESOTA**

| | Att | Comp | Comp Pct. | Yds | Int | Yds/ Att. | Yds/ Comp | Yards Lost Tackled |
|---|---|---|---|---|---|---|---|---|
| Tarkenton | 28 | 18 | 64.3 | 182 | 1 | 6.5 | 10.1 | 2—16 |

# 1974 N.F.C. Internal and External Headaches

The summer was a troubled one for the N.F.L. The Players Association called a strike on July 1 for a variety of reasons, and veteran players spent the early part of training camp walking picket lines and working out in local playgrounds. While the early exhibition games went on with an overwhelming number of rookies and free agents, the World Football League opened shop as the newest alternative to the N.F.L. The twelve W.F.L. teams threw a lot of money around and signed to future contracts such N.F.L. stars as Larry Csonka, Paul Warfield, Jim Kiick, Calvin Hill, Kenny Stabler, Ted Hendricks, Bill Bergey, John Gilliam, Ted Kwalick, Tim Foley, Craig Morton, and Rayfield Wright, all scheduled for delivery in one to three years, after their N.F.L. contracts ran out.

The W.F.L. started play in July with mostly nondescript players and huge crowds in attendance. But by the time the N.F.L. strike ended in August, the W.F.L. was in big trouble. Those huge attendance figures turned out to be padded with thousands of freebies, and club owners found their reserves of capital rapidly shrinking. By September, franchises were shifting cities and clubs were going bankrupt, and players were going without paychecks—strong indications that the W.F.L. was a sinking ship and no threat at all to the established league.

## EASTERN DIVISION

**St. Louis Cardinals**—The Cards didn't figure as a contender this season, but six straight wins at the start of the schedule established them as the Cinderella club of the N.F.C. Coach Don Coryell had rigged together a potent offense last season, but his defense rebounded from a disappointing 1973 campaign to keep the Cards in every game by holding enemy scoring down. Big tackle Dave Butz missed most of the season with a knee injury, but the defense held together around an All-Pro performance by cornerback Roger Wehrli. The heart of the team, however, was the offense, which had breakaway potential both in the air and on the ground. A strong offensive line cleared the way for quick running back Terry Metcalf and protected quarterback Jim Hart while he zeroed in on speedster Mel Gray. The Cards made the playoffs for the first time since 1948, when the club was still based in Chicago.

**Washington Redskins**—Instead of an experienced, shopworn veteran, coach George Allen's prize acquisition this year was quarterback Joe Theismann, a star at Notre Dame seasoned by play in the Canadian Football League. But Theismann's main duty this season was running back punts, as veterans Billy Kilmer and Sonny Jurgensen continued to pilot the Redskin attack. Jurgensen particularly captured the public's fancy, as this 40-year-old passer with the protruding belly won several games in relief performances. The Redskins relied more than usual on the air game, as the running attack suffered from bad seasons by Larry Brown and Duane Thomas, plus Charlie Harraway's jump to the W.F.L. The defense was as tough as ever and brought the team home in a tie for first place.

**Dallas Cowboys**—After the Cowboys won their opening game and then lost four straight, fans and writers were saying prayers over the team's dead playoff chances. But the Cowboys didn't count themselves out and started the long fight back to catch the Cardinals and Redskins. One key game on that road was a November 17 confrontation in Washington, where the Redskins roared out to a 28–0 halftime lead; the Cowboys came back, 28–21, but fell short when Drew Pearson dropped a pass in the end zone late in the game. The two clubs met again on Thanksgiving Day, with the Redskins taking a 16–3 lead and knocking quarterback Roger Staubach out of action. Rookie Clint Longley then came into the fray and led the Cowboys to a 24–23 win with a 50-yard touchdown pass to Pearson with only 28 seconds left. But the Cowboys could not overcome their earlier disasters and didn't make the playoffs for the first time in nine years.

**Philadelphia Eagles**—Coach Mike McCormack had built the Eagles into an offensive power last year, and the addition of middle linebacker Bill Bergey from Cincinnati was expected to tighten up the defense enough to permit a shot at the playoffs. Four wins in the first five games kept the Eagles hot on the heels of first-place St. Louis, but then six straight losses ended any playoff hopes. The defense was much improved, but the offense went flat, with quarterback Roman Gabriel benched for the last three games in favor of rookie Mike Boryla.

**New York Giants**—The Giants had a new General Manager in former star player Andy Robustelli and a new head coach in Bill Arnsparger, who designed the famous Miami defense while an assistant under Don Shula. The new management drafted two fine rookie guards in John Hicks and Tom Mullen, and quarterback Craig Morton benefited from their pass protection after coming over from Dallas in an October trade. But despite improvements at some positions, the Giants still came up short at most positions and still had to practice in Jersey City, New Jersey and play home games in the Yale Bowl in New Haven, Connecticut. Without a real home, the Giants suffered through a 2–12 season, including a string of disheartening losses coming late in the fourth quarter.

## CENTRAL DIVISION

**Minnesota Vikings**—The Vikings used a familiar formula to quickly take charge of the Central Division. The blend of an overwhelming defense plus a versatile offense versed at ball-control had won divisional titles before, and again propelled the Vikings into the playoffs this season. The front four of Alan Page, Carl Eller, Jim Marshall, and Doug Sutherland put unrelenting pressure on enemy offenses, and the secondary didn't lose much when cornerback Bobby Bryant broke his arm and was replaced by rookie Jackie Wallace. The Viking offense had stars in all sectors, featuring quarterback Fran Tarkenton, running back Chuck Foreman, wide receiver John Gilliam, and tackle Ron Yary.

**Detroit Lions**—The season got off to a depressing start when head coach Don McCafferty died of a heart attack in training camp. With assistant Rick Forzano taking over the reigns, the Lions got off to a slow start in the regular season and seemed destined to finish in the lower ranks of the league. But the club righted itself and stayed in contention for a wildcard playoff berth into December before being eliminated. Bill Munson captured the starting quarterback's job in the preseason, but Greg Landry reclaimed the position late in the year when Munson suffered a dislocated shoulder.

**Green Bay Packers**—The Packer defense, bolstered by the addition of All-Pro linebacker Ted Hendricks from Baltimore, was one of the N.F.L.'s best, but the offense could generate little fireworks. Runners John Brockington and MacArthur Lane punched out less yards than had been expected, and young quarterback Jerry Tagge couldn't ignite a respectable passing attack. An October trade for John Hadl helped the offense somewhat, but not enough to give the Pack a winning season. Rumors of coach Dan Devine's impending dismissal circulated all season, but Devine beat the punch by resigning after the season to become head coach at Notre Dame.

**Chicago Bears**—The Bears beat Detroit in their opening game, but persistent quarterback problems quickly dragged the Bears down into another losing season. Neither Gary Huff nor Bobby Douglass was successful in putting points on the scoreboard, and coach Abe Gibron was fired after the season. The Bears were such a dull show that a game against the Giants on December 1 drew a crowd of 18,802 and a no-show total of 36,951. With Dick Butkus retired, the Bears simply had no big names to draw a crowd in bad weather.

## WESTERN DIVISION

**Los Angeles Rams**—Experts made the Rams the preseason favorite to reach the Super Bowl, but coach Chuck Knox's club never jelled into a powerhouse. They easily outdistanced the weak competition in the Western Division, but upset losses to clubs like New England and New Orleans belied the shaky base of the team's good record. One major change made by coach Knox was the trade of quarterback John Hadl to Green Bay in October and the elevation of sub James Harris to the starter's slot. The only black starting quarterback in the N.F.C., Harris had fine support from a strong offensive line, good receivers, and great running from Lawrence McCutcheon. The defense was the stingiest in the entire N.F.L. with end Jack Youngblood and tackle Larry Brooks making All-Pro, and with tackle Merlin Olsen still a formidable force.

**San Francisco '49ers**—The '49er offense sputtered under a veritable parade of quarterbacks. With John Brodie retired, Steve Spurrier was expected to start, but he suffered a shoulder separation in a preseason game. Joe Reed began the season in competent fashion but soon fell apart. Rookie Dennis Morrison then took his turn, and then 13th-draft-choice Tom Owen got a chance and saw considerable action in the latter part of the schedule. Veteran Norm Snead came over in a mid-season trade but could accomplish little more than the others in the parade. Rookie Wilbur Jackson injected some punch into the running game, but the defense suffered from Charlie Krueger's retirement, Jim Johnson's bad toe, and Mel Phillips' broken arm.

**New Orleans Saints**—Another mediocre season fanned recurrent rumors that quarterback Archie Manning was going to be traded to shore up several other positions. A flurry of quarterback trading in late October in the N.F.C. saw Manning stay in New Orleans, but coach John North was evidently not completely satisfied with his young passer. North sat Manning down for several games and started subs Bobby Scott and Larry Cipa.

**Atlanta Falcons**—The Falcons seemed ready to move into the playoff ranks for the first time, but instead the club degenerated into a dismal also-ran. Quarterbacks Bob Lee, Pat Sullivan, and Kim McQuilken could not move the offense, and the entire squad bristled under coach Norm Van Brocklin's stern regime. Rumors of the Dutchman's imminent firing ran wild in Atlanta, and a press conference in November saw Van Brocklin challenge a reporter to a fist fight. Van Brocklin was then canned with the team record at 2–6, and Atlanta fans were so disenchanted that there were 48,830 no-shows for the season's finale on December 15 against Green Bay.

## FINAL TEAM STATISTICS

### OFFENSE

| | ATL. | CHI. | DALL. | DET. | G.B. | L.A. | MINN. | N.O. | N.Y. | PHIL. | St.L. | S.F. | WASH |
|---|---|---|---|---|---|---|---|---|---|---|---|---|---|
| FIRST DOWNS: | | | | | | | | | | | | | |
| Total | 174 | 203 | **295** | 211 | 214 | 265 | 264 | 233 | 215 | 244 | 247 | 227 | 249 |
| by Rushing | 77 | 92 | **147** | 88 | 87 | 132 | 114 | 117 | 90 | 79 | 120 | 101 | 77 |
| by Passing | 86 | 96 | 129 | 114 | 108 | 112 | 136 | 91 | 107 | 141 | 117 | 104 | **156** |
| by Penalty | 11 | 15 | 19 | 9 | 19 | 21 | 14 | **25** | 18 | 24 | 10 | 22 | 16 |
| RUSHING: | | | | | | | | | | | | | |
| Number | 400 | 434 | 542 | 397 | 482 | **566** | 488 | 503 | 441 | 415 | 466 | 477 | 470 |
| Yards | 1493 | 1480 | **2454** | 1433 | 1571 | 2125 | 1856 | 1983 | 1496 | 1385 | 1956 | 1981 | 1443 |
| Average Yards | 3.7 | 3.4 | **4.5** | 3.6 | 3.3 | 3.8 | 3.8 | 3.9 | 3.4 | 3.3 | 4.2 | 4.2 | 3.1 |
| Touchdowns | 6 | 10 | **22** | 13 | 10 | 16 | 17 | 9 | 11 | 13 | 12 | 10 | 11 |
| PASSING: | | | | | | | | | | | | | |
| Attempts | 356 | 396 | **385** | 377 | 385 | 338 | 400 | 389 | 393 | **461** | 391 | 361 | 413 |
| Completions | 160 | 185 | 206 | 216 | 187 | 169 | 234 | 185 | 207 | **258** | 201 | 170 | 254 |
| Completion Percentage | 44.9 | 46.7 | 53.5 | 57.3 | 48.6 | 50.0 | 58.5 | 47.6 | 52.7 | 56.0 | 51.4 | 47.1 | **61.5** |
| Passing Yards | 1781 | 2079 | 2856 | 2475 | 2162 | 2368 | 2909 | 2037 | 2349 | 2531 | 2492 | 2281 | **2978** |
| Avg. Yards per Attempt | 5.0 | 5.3 | 7.4 | 6.6 | 5.6 | 7.0 | 7.3 | 5.2 | 6.0 | 5.5 | 6.4 | 6.3 | 7.2 |
| Avg. Yards per Complet. | 11.1 | 11.2 | 13.9 | 11.5 | 11.6 | **14.0** | 12.4 | 11.0 | 11.4 | 9.8 | 12.4 | 13.4 | 11.7 |
| Times Tackled Passing | 50 | 36 | 47 | 35 | 17 | 21 | 19 | 37 | 20 | 42 | **16** | 35 | 25 |
| Yards Lost Passing | 474 | 359 | 327 | 255 | **126** | 161 | 154 | 276 | 156 | 319 | 134 | 274 | 176 |
| Net Yards | 1307 | 1720 | 2529 | 2220 | 2036 | 2207 | 2755 | 1761 | 2193 | 2212 | 2358 | 2007 | **2802** |
| Touchdowns | 4 | 8 | 14 | 11 | 5 | 16 | **22** | 10 | 12 | 14 | 20 | 15 | **22** |
| Interceptions | 31 | 22 | 15 | 11 | 21 | 13 | 13 | 21 | 26 | 17 | **8** | 28 | 11 |
| Percent Intercepted | 8.7 | 5.6 | 3.9 | 2.9 | 5.5 | 3.8 | 3.3 | 5.4 | 6.6 | 3.7 | **2.1** | 7.8 | 2.7 |
| PUNTS: | | | | | | | | | | | | | |
| Number | **96** | 91 | 73 | 73 | 69 | 75 | 73 | 91 | 69 | 84 | 81 | 70 | 74 |
| Average Distance | 40.5 | 37.7 | 38.5 | 38.2 | 38.4 | 36.4 | 36.1 | **41.8** | 40.1 | 36.0 | 38.7 | 40.8 | 38.1 |
| PUNT RETURNS: | | | | | | | | | | | | | |
| Number | 51 | 44 | **62** | 34 | 42 | 53 | 43 | 43 | 41 | 37 | 52 | 44 | 46 |
| Yards | **635** | 248 | 573 | 429 | 416 | 507 | 320 | 415 | 408 | 339 | 512 | 398 | 453 |
| Average Yards | 12.5 | 5.6 | 9.2 | **12.6** | 9.9 | 9.6 | 7.4 | 9.7 | 10.0 | [illegible] | 9.8 | 9.9 | 9.8 |
| Touchdowns | 1 | 0 | 1 | 0 | **2** | 0 | 0 | 0 | 0 | 0 | 0 | 1 | 1 |
| KICKOFF RETURNS: | | | | | | | | | | | | | |
| Number | 60 | 57 | 49 | **62** | 49 | 40 | 50 | 53 | 59 | 48 | 50 | 51 | 45 |
| Yards | 1296 | 1256 | 1071 | 1293 | 1022 | 938 | 1090 | 1040 | **1458** | 1062 | 1203 | 1144 | 1166 |
| Average Yards | 21.6 | 22.0 | 21.9 | 20.9 | 20.9 | 23.5 | 21.8 | 19.6 | 24.7 | 22.1 | 24.1 | 22.4 | **25.9** |
| Touchdowns | 0 | 0 | 0 | 0 | 0 | **1** | 0 | 0 | 0 | 0 | **1** | 0 | **1** |
| INTERCEPTION RETURNS: | | | | | | | | | | | | | |
| Number | 17 | 18 | 13 | 17 | 23 | 22 | 22 | 16 | 15 | 18 | 16 | 20 | **26** |
| Yards | 210 | 293 | 110 | 266 | 278 | 340 | 282 | 179 | 91 | 176 | **372** | 247 | 328 |
| Average Yards | 12.4 | 16.3 | 8.5 | 15.6 | 12.1 | 15.5 | 12.8 | 11.2 | 6.1 | 9.8 | **23.3** | 12.4 | 13.1 |
| Touchdowns | 1 | 0 | 0 | **2** | 1 | **2** | 0 | 1 | 0 | 1 | **1** | 1 | **2** |
| PENALTIES: | | | | | | | | | | | | | |
| Number | 82 | **88** | 86 | 86 | 55 | 58 | 56 | 75 | 65 | 76 | 77 | 63 | 78 |
| Yards | 636 | 679 | 703 | 719 | 536 | 550 | 501 | 598 | 567 | **722** | 645 | 606 | 621 |
| FUMBLES: | | | | | | | | | | | | | |
| Number | 32 | 35 | 31 | 23 | 25 | 29 | 24 | 26 | 28 | 32 | 37 | 31 | **16** |
| Number Lost | 24 | 15 | 16 | 14 | 16 | 14 | **9** | 12 | 10 | 12 | **9** | 14 | **9** |
| POINTS: | | | | | | | | | | | | | |
| Total | 111 | 152 | 297 | 256 | 210 | 263 | 310 | 166 | 195 | 242 | 285 | 226 | **320** |
| PAT Attempts | 12 | 18 | 38 | 27 | 19 | 35 | **40** | 20 | 24 | 31 | 36 | 28 | 38 |
| PAT Made | 12 | 17 | **37** | 23 | 19 | 26 | 32 | 19 | 21 | 26 | 30 | 25 | 35 |
| FG Attempts | 16 | 13 | 21 | 32 | **39** | 16 | 20 | 16 | 19 | 16 | 22 | 24 | 31 |
| FG Made | 9 | 9 | 10 | 23 | **25** | 9 | 12 | 9 | 10 | 10 | 13 | 11 | 19 |
| Percent FG Made | 56.3 | 69.2 | 47.6 | **71.9** | 64.1 | 56.3 | 60.0 | 56.3 | 52.6 | 62.5 | 59.1 | 45.8 | 61.3 |
| Safeties | 0 | 0 | **1** | **1** | **1** | 0 | **1** | 0 | 0 | 0 | 0 | 0 | 0 |

### DEFENSE

| | ATL. | CHI. | DALL. | DET. | G.B. | L.A. | MINN. | N.O. | N.Y. | PHIL. | St.L. | S.F. | WASH. |
|---|---|---|---|---|---|---|---|---|---|---|---|---|---|
| FIRST DOWNS: | | | | | | | | | | | | | |
| Total | 238 | 231 | 199 | 270 | 218 | **186** | 230 | 226 | 291 | 248 | 249 | 232 | 210 |
| by Rushing | 140 | 104 | **63** | 127 | 93 | 66 | 100 | 104 | 134 | 105 | 108 | 113 | 79 |
| by Passing | **85** | 102 | 110 | 124 | 106 | 109 | 120 | 105 | 142 | 129 | 122 | 101 | 114 |
| by Penalty | 13 | 25 | 26 | 19 | 19 | 11 | **10** | 17 | 15 | 14 | 19 | 18 | 17 |
| RUSHING: | | | | | | | | | | | | | |
| Number | 627 | 519 | 417 | 486 | 465 | **381** | 437 | 447 | 521 | 460 | 461 | 503 | 414 |
| Yards | 2564 | 1739 | 1344 | 2102 | 1641 | **1302** | 1605 | 1758 | 1916 | 1797 | 1888 | 2033 | 1439 |
| Average Yards | 4.1 | 3.4 | **3.2** | 4.3 | 3.5 | 3.4 | 3.7 | 3.9 | 3.7 | 3.9 | 4.1 | 4.0 | 3.5 |
| Touchdowns | 19 | 17 | 8 | 17 | 10 | **4** | 12 | 11 | 15 | 14 | 15 | 13 | 7 |
| PASSING: | | | | | | | | | | | | | |
| Attempts | **302** | 329 | 349 | 405 | 383 | 381 | 396 | 369 | 415 | 434 | 413 | 339 | 399 |
| Completions | **136** | 174 | 178 | 219 | 188 | 194 | 214 | 193 | 245 | 230 | 230 | 178 | 197 |
| Completion Percentage | **45.0** | 52.9 | 51.0 | 54.1 | 49.1 | 50.9 | 54.0 | 52.3 | 59.0 | 53.0 | 55.7 | 52.5 | 49.4 |
| Passing Yards | **1847** | 2250 | 2451 | 2423 | 2254 | 2465 | 2569 | 2330 | 2688 | 2684 | 2581 | 2178 | 2102 |
| Avg. Yards per Attempt | 6.1 | 6.8 | 7.0 | 6.0 | 5.9 | 6.7 | 6.5 | 6.3 | 6.5 | 6.2 | 6.2 | 6.5 | 5.3 |
| Avg. Yards per Complet. | 13.6 | 12.9 | 13.8 | 11.1 | 12.0 | 12.7 | 12.0 | 12.1 | 11.0 | 11.7 | 11.2 | 12.2 | **10.7** |
| Times Tackled Passing | 31 | 25 | 37 | 24 | 28 | **44** | 31 | 37 | 25 | 28 | 35 | 28 | 31 |
| Yards Lost Passing | 275 | 171 | 332 | 187 | 254 | **363** | 267 | 291 | 147 | 211 | 218 | 247 | 256 |
| Net Yards | **1572** | 2079 | 2119 | 2236 | 2000 | 2102 | 2302 | 2039 | 2541 | 2473 | 2363 | 1931 | 1846 |
| Touchdowns | 13 | 12 | 17 | 13 | 10 | 16 | **8** | 17 | 22 | 9 | 11 | 14 | 13 |
| Interceptions | 17 | 18 | 13 | 17 | 23 | 22 | 22 | 16 | 15 | 18 | 16 | 20 | **25** |
| Percent Intercepted | 5.6 | 5.5 | 3.7 | 4.2 | 6.0 | 5.8 | 5.6 | 4.3 | 3.6 | 4.1 | 3.9 | 6.0 | 6.4 |
| PUNTS: | | | | | | | | | | | | | |
| Number | 84 | 77 | 93 | 62 | 84 | **95** | 75 | 77 | 65 | 73 | 85 | 74 | 80 |
| Average Distance | 38.3 | 38.5 | 39.9 | 37.2 | 36.6 | 41.2 | 37.1 | 42.5 | **36.2** | 39.1 | 39.2 | 39.5 | 38.4 |
| PUNT RETURNS: | | | | | | | | | | | | | |
| Number | 59 | 58 | **31** | 37 | 48 | 40 | 45 | 59 | 43 | 37 | 56 | 46 | 50 |
| Yards | 658 | 633 | 343 | 275 | 356 | 453 | 345 | 906 | 478 | **252** | 518 | 491 | 458 |
| Average Yards | 11.2 | 10.9 | 11.1 | 7.4 | 7.4 | 11.3 | 7.7 | 15.4 | 11.0 | **6.8** | 9.3 | 10.7 | 9.2 |
| Touchdowns | 1 | 1 | 1 | **0** | **0** | 1 | **0** | 2 | **0** | **0** | 1 | **0** | 1 |
| KICKOFF RETURNS: | | | | | | | | | | | | | |
| Number | **33** | 35 | 61 | 60 | 55 | 58 | 64 | 40 | 45 | 46 | 54 | 51 | 64 |
| Yards | 812 | **700** | 1194 | 1256 | 1156 | 1232 | 1116 | 894 | 1154 | 1028 | 1203 | 1099 | 1379 |
| Average Yards | 24.6 | 20.0 | 19.6 | 20.9 | 21.0 | 21.2 | **17.4** | 22.4 | 25.6 | 22.3 | 22.3 | 21.5 | 21.5 |
| Touchdowns | **0** | **0** | **0** | **0** | **0** | **0** | **0** | **0** | **0** | 1 | **0** | **0** | **0** |
| INTERCEPTION RETURNS: | | | | | | | | | | | | | |
| Number | 31 | 22 | 15 | 11 | 21 | 13 | 13 | 21 | 26 | 17 | **8** | 28 | 11 |
| Yards | 451 | 225 | 93 | 149 | 289 | 92 | 185 | 258 | 372 | 362 | **75** | 409 | **75** |
| Average Yards | 14.5 | 10.2 | **6.2** | 13.5 | 13.8 | 7.1 | 14.2 | 12.3 | 14.3 | 21.3 | 9.4 | 14.6 | 6.8 |
| Touchdowns | 1 | 1 | **0** | **0** | 1 | **0** | 1 | 2 | 2 | 1 | **0** | 1 | 1 |
| PENALTIES: | | | | | | | | | | | | | |
| Number | 54 | 74 | 69 | 71 | **88** | 82 | 70 | 77 | 80 | 86 | 80 | 85 | 69 |
| Yards | 449 | 601 | 657 | 566 | 715 | 772 | 660 | 690 | 616 | 722 | 654 | **830** | 529 |
| FUMBLES: | | | | | | | | | | | | | |
| Number | 26 | 28 | 31 | 23 | 19 | 15 | 25 | 37 | 28 | 36 | 24 | **38** | 28 |
| Number Lost | 12 | 14 | 13 | 13 | 12 | 3 | 11 | 19 | 10 | 16 | 9 | **20** | 15 |
| POINTS: | | | | | | | | | | | | | |
| Total | 271 | 279 | 235 | 270 | 206 | **181** | 195 | 263 | 299 | 217 | 218 | 236 | 196 |
| PAT Attempts | 34 | 33 | 28 | 30 | 23 | 22 | **21** | 34 | 39 | 26 | 27 | 29 | 24 |
| PAT Made | 31 | 29 | 28 | 28 | **17** | 19 | 18 | 29 | 32 | 25 | 26 | 26 | 22 |
| FG Attempts | 28 | 23 | 21 | 32 | 26 | **14** | 24 | 17 | 24 | 26 | **14** | 19 | 15 |
| FG Made | 12 | 16 | 13 | 20 | 17 | **10** | 17 | 10 | 11 | 12 | **10** | 12 | **10** |
| Percent FG Made | **42.9** | 69.6 | 61.9 | 62.5 | 65.4 | 71.4 | 70.7 | 58.8 | 45.8 | 46.2 | 71.4 | 63.2 | 66.7 |
| Safeties | **0** | 2 | **0** | 1 | **0** | **0** | **0** | **0** | **0** | **0** | **0** | **0** | **0** |

## CONFERENCE PLAYOFFS

December 21, at Minnesota (Attendance 44,626)

### SCORING

| | | | | | |
|---|---|---|---|---|---|
| MINNESOTA | 0 | 7 | 16 | 7 | – 30 |
| ST. LOUIS | 0 | 7 | 0 | 7 | – 14 |

Second Quarter
St.L. Thomas, 13 yard pass from Hart PAT–Bakken (kick)
Minn. Gilliam, 16 yard pass from Tarkenton PAT–Cox (kick)

Third Quarter
Minn. Cox, 37 yard field goal
Minn. N. Wright, 20 yard fumble return PAT–Cox (kick)
Minn. Gilliam, 38 yard pass from Tarkenton PAT-kick failed

Fourth Quarter
Minn. Foreman, 4 yard rush PAT–Cox (kick)
St.L. Metcalf, 11 yard rush PAT–Bakken (kick)

### TEAM STATISTICS

| MINN. | | St.L. |
|---|---|---|
| 19 | First Downs-Total | 17 |
| 12 | First Downs-Rushing | 6 |
| 7 | First Downs-Passing | 10 |
| 0 | First Downs-Penalty | 1 |
| 0 | Fumbles-Number | 2 |
| 0 | Fumbles-Lost Ball | 1 |
| 4 | Penalties-Number | 1 |
| 39 | Yards Penalized | 15 |
| 0 | Missed Field Goals | 1 |
| 66 | Offensive Plays | 67 |
| 363 | Net Yards | 284 |
| 5.5 | Average Gain | 4.2 |
| 2 | Giveaways | 2 |
| 2 | Takeaways | 2 |
| 0 | Difference | 0 |

### INDIVIDUAL STATISTICS

| MINNESOTA | No. | Yds. | Avg. | ST. LOUIS | No. | Yds. | Avg. |
|---|---|---|---|---|---|---|---|
| **RUSHING** | | | | | | | |
| Foreman | 23 | 114 | 5.0 | Metcalf | 15 | 55 | 3.7 |
| Osborn | 16 | 67 | 4.2 | Otis | 8 | 35 | 4.4 |
| Gilliam | 1 | 16 | 16.0 | Hart | 1 | 10 | 10.0 |
| Tarkenton | 2 | 0 | 2.0 | Willard | 1 | 0 | 0.0 |
| | 42 | 197 | 4.7 | | 25 | 100 | 4.0 |
| **RECEIVING** | | | | | | | |
| Foreman | 5 | 54 | 10.8 | Thomas | 6 | 64 | 10.7 |
| Osborn | 4 | 36 | 9.0 | Gray | 5 | 77 | 15.4 |
| Gilliam | 2 | 54 | 27.0 | Metcalf | 4 | 43 | 10.8 |
| Voigt | 2 | 25 | 12.5 | Hammond | 1 | 10 | 10.0 |
| | 13 | 169 | 13.0 | Smith | 1 | 7 | 7.0 |
| | | | | Otis | 1 | –1 | –1.0 |
| | | | | | 18 | 200 | 11.1 |
| **PUNTING** | | | | | | | |
| Eischeid | 5 | | 38.2 | Roberts | 7 | | 36.4 |
| **PUNT RETURNS** | | | | | | | |
| Wallace | 1 | 3 | 3.0 | Metcalf | 3 | 18 | 6.0 |
| **KICKOFF RETURNS** | | | | | | | |
| McCullum | 2 | 49 | 24.5 | Metcalf | 3 | 85 | 28.3 |
| Kingswriter | 1 | 0 | 1.0 | Hartle | 3 | 14 | 4.7 |
| | 3 | 49 | 16.3 | | 6 | 99 | 16.5 |
| **INTERCEPTION RETURNS** | | | | | | | |
| J. Wright | 1 | 18 | 18.0 | Wehrli | 1 | 10 | 10.0 |
| | | | | Arneson | 1 | 7 | 7.0 |
| | | | | | 2 | 17 | 8.5 |

**PASSING**

| MINNESOTA | Att. | Comp. | Comp. Pct. | Yds | Int | Yds/ Att. | Yds/ Comp. | Lost Tackled |
|---|---|---|---|---|---|---|---|---|
| Tarkenton | 23 | 13 | 56.5 | 169 | 2 | 7.3 | 13.0 | 1–3 |
| **ST. LOUIS** | | | | | | | | |
| Hart | 40 | 18 | 45.0 | 200 | 1 | 5.0 | 11.1 | 2-16 |

December 22, at Los Angeles (Attendance 80,118)

### SCORING

| | | | | |
|---|---|---|---|---|
| LOS ANGELES | 7 | 0 | 3 | 9–19 |
| WASHINGTON | 3 | 7 | 0 | 0–10 |

First Quarter
L.A. Klein, 10 yard pass from Harris PAT–Ray (kick)
Was. Bragg, 35 yard field goal

Second Quarter
Was. Denson, 1 yard rush PAT–Bragg (kick)

Third Quarter
L.A. Ray, 37 yard field goal

Fourth Quarter
L.A. Ray, 26 yard field goal
L.A. Robertson, 59 yard interception return PAT–bad center pass no attempt made

### TEAM STATISTICS

| L.A. | | WASH. |
|---|---|---|
| 14 | First Downs-Total | 13 |
| 8 | First Downs-Rushing | 4 |
| 6 | First Downs-Passing | 7 |
| 0 | First Downs-Penalty | 2 |
| 2 | Fumbles-Number | 3 |
| 0 | Fumbles-Lost Ball | 3 |
| 5 | Penalties-Number | 1 |
| 49 | Yards Penalized | 5 |
| 2 | Missed Field Goals | 0 |
| 66 | Offensive Plays | 58 |
| 226 | Net Yards | 218 |
| 3.4 | Average Gain | 3.8 |
| 2 | Giveaways | 6 |
| 6 | Takeaways | 2 |
| +4 | Difference | –4 |

### INDIVIDUAL STATISTICS

| LOS ANGELES | No. | Yds. | Avg. | WASHINGTON | No. | Yds. | Avg. |
|---|---|---|---|---|---|---|---|
| **RUSHING** | | | | | | | |
| McCutcheon | 26 | 71 | 2.7 | Brown | 18 | 39 | 2.2 |
| Bertelsen | 6 | 34 | 5.7 | Denson | 7 | 5 | 0.7 |
| Harris | 6 | 17 | 2.8 | Kilmer | 2 | 5 | 2.5 |
| Capelletti | 1 | 5 | 2.5 | | 27 | 49 | 1.8 |
| Baker | 2 | 2 | 1.0 | | | | |
| Scribner | 1 | 2 | 2.0 | | | | |
| | 42 | 131 | 3.1 | | | | |
| **RECEIVING** | | | | | | | |
| Jackson | 2 | 35 | 17.5 | Taylor | 4 | 79 | 19.8 |
| Klein | 2 | 23 | 11.5 | Evans | 4 | 31 | 7.8 |
| McCutcheon | 2 | 20 | 10.0 | J. Smith | 2 | 35 | 17.5 |
| Curran | 1 | 12 | 12.0 | Denson | 2 | 17 | 8.5 |
| Bertelsen | 1 | 5 | 5.0 | Grant | 1 | 15 | 15.0 |
| | 8 | 95 | 11.9 | | 13 | 177 | 13.6 |
| **PUNTING** | | | | | | | |
| Burke | 5 | | 43.0 | Bragg | 5 | | 45.2 |
| **PUNT RETURNS** | | | | | | | |
| Bertelsen | 1 | 10 | 10.0 | Theismann | 4 | 22 | 5.5 |
| Bryant | 1 | 6 | 6.0 | L. Jones | 1 | 9 | 9.0 |
| | 2 | 16 | 8.0 | | 5 | 31 | 6.2 |
| **KICKOFF RETURNS** | | | | | | | |
| Bryant | 3 | 82 | 27.3 | L. Jones | 4 | 76 | 19.0 |
| | | | | Cunningham | 1 | 19 | 19.0 |
| | | | | | 5 | 95 | 19.0 |
| **INTERCEPTION RETURNS** | | | | | | | |
| Robertson | 1 | 59 | 59.0 | Fischer | 1 | 17 | 17.0 |
| Reynolds | 1 | 12 | 12.0 | Stone | 1 | 7 | 7.0 |
| Simpson | 1 | 0 | 0.0 | | 2 | 24 | 12.0 |
| | 3 | 71 | 23.7 | | | | |

**PASSING**

| LOS ANGELES | Att. | Comp. | Comp. Pct. | Yds. | Int. | Yds/ Att. | Yds/ Comp. | Yards Lost Tackled |
|---|---|---|---|---|---|---|---|---|
| Harris | 24 | 8 | 33.3 | 95 | 2 | 4.0 | 11.9 | 0–0 |
| **WASHINGTON** | | | | | | | | |
| Kilmer | 18 | 7 | 38.9 | 99 | 0 | 5.5 | 14.1 | 0–0 |
| Jurgensen | 12 | 6 | 50.0 | 78 | 3 | 6.5 | 13.0 | 1–8 |
| | 30 | 13 | 43.3 | 177 | 3 | 5.9 | 13.6 | 1–8 |

# 1974 N.F.C. — Eastern Division

## ST. LOUIS CARDINALS 10-4-0 Don Coryell

| Scores of Each Game | | |
|---|---|---|
| 7 | PHILADELPHIA | 3 |
| 17 | Washington | 10 |
| 29 | CLEVELAND | 7 |
| 34 | San Francisco | 9 |
| 31 | DALLAS | 28 |
| 31 | Houston | 27 |
| 23 | WASHINGTON | 20 |
| 14 | Dallas | 17 |
| 24 | MINNESOTA | 28 |
| 13 | Philadelphia | 3 |
| 23 | N.Y. Giants | 21 |
| 13 | KANSAS CITY | 17 |
| 10 | New Orleans | 14 |
| 26 | N.Y. GIANTS | 14 |

| Use Name | Pos. | Hgt | Wgt | Age | Int | Pts |
|---|---|---|---|---|---|---|
| Dan Dierdorf | OT | 6'4" | 280 | 25 | | |
| Greg Kindle | OT | 6'4" | 265 | 23 | | |
| Ernie McMillan | OT | 6'6" | 265 | 36 | | |
| Conrad Dobler | OG | 6'3" | 255 | 23 | | |
| Bob Young | OG | 6'2" | 270 | 31 | | |
| Roger Finnie | OT-OG | 6'3" | 250 | 28 | | |
| Tom Banks | C | 6'1" | 240 | 26 | | |
| Tom Brahaney | C | 6'2" | 250 | 22 | | |
| Cal Withrow | C | 6' | 240 | 29 | | |
| Bob Crum | DE | 6'5" | 240 | 23 | | |
| Council Rudolph | DE | 6'3" | 245 | 24 | | |
| Ron Yankowski | DE | 6'5" | 235 | 27 | | 6 |
| Lee Brooks | DT-DE | 6'5" | 240 | 26 | | |
| Bob Bell | DT | 6'4" | 250 | 26 | | |
| Dave Butz | DT | 6'7" | 290 | 24 | | |
| Steve George | DT | 6'5" | 265 | 23 | | |
| Bob Rowe | DT | 6'4" | 245 | 29 | | |

| Use Name | Pos. | Hgt | Wgt | Age | Int | Pts |
|---|---|---|---|---|---|---|
| Mark Arneson | LB | 6'2" | 220 | 24 | | |
| Pete Barnes | LB | 6'3" | 235 | 29 | | |
| Greg Hartle | LB | 6'2" | 225 | 23 | | |
| Jack LeVeck | LB | 6' | 220 | 24 | | |
| Terry Miller | LB | 6'2" | 220 | 28 | | |
| Steve Neils | LB | 6'2" | 215 | 23 | | |
| Larry Stallings | LB | 6'2" | 230 | 32 | 2 | |
| Dwayne Crump | DB | 5'11" | 180 | 24 | 1 | |
| Clarence Duren | DB | 6'1" | 190 | 23 | 2 | |
| Ken Reaves (from NO) | DB | 6'3" | 210 | 29 | 1 | |
| Hurles Scales (from CHI) | DB | 6'1" | 200 | 23 | | |
| Scott Stringer | DB | 5'11" | 180 | 23 | | |
| Norm Thompson | DB | 6'1" | 180 | 26 | 6 | 6 |
| Jim Tolbert | DB | 6'3" | 210 | 30 | 2 | |
| Roger Wehrli | DB | 6'1" | 190 | 26 | 2 | 6 |

Ron Davis – Injury

| Use Name | Pos. | Hgt | Wgt | Age | Int | Pts |
|---|---|---|---|---|---|---|
| Jim Hart | QB | 6'2" | 210 | 30 | | 12 |
| Dennis Shaw | QB | 6'2" | 210 | 27 | | |
| Donny Anderson | HB | 6'3" | 215 | 31 | | 36 |
| Willie Belton | HB | 5'11" | 195 | 25 | | |
| Steve Jones (from BUF) | HB | 6' | 200 | 23 | | |
| Terry Metcalf | HB | 5'10" | 185 | 22 | | 48 |
| Eddie Moss | HB | 6' | 215 | 25 | | |
| Jim Otis | FB | 6' | 225 | 26 | | 6 |
| Ken Willard | FB | 6'2" | 215 | 31 | | 6 |
| J. V. Cain | WR | 6'4" | 225 | 23 | | 6 |
| Mel Gray | WR | 5'9" | 170 | 25 | | 36 |
| Gary Hammond | WR | 5'11" | 185 | 25 | | |
| Earl Thomas | WR | 6'3" | 215 | 25 | | 30 |
| Jim McFarland | TE | 6'5" | 225 | 26 | | |
| Jackie Smith | TE | 6'4" | 230 | 33 | | 18 |
| Sergio Albert | K | 6'3" | 195 | 22 | | |
| Jim Bakken | K | 6' | 200 | 33 | | 69 |
| Hal Roberts | K | 6'1" | 180 | 22 | | |

## WASHINGTON REDSKINS 10-4-0 George Allen

| Scores of Each Game | | |
|---|---|---|
| 13 | N.Y. Giants | 10 |
| 10 | St. Louis | 17 |
| 30 | DENVER | 3 |
| 17 | Cincinnati | 28 |
| 20 | MIAMI | 17 |
| 24 | N.Y. GIANTS | 3 |
| 20 | St. Louis | 23 |
| 17 | Green Bay | 6 |
| 27 | Philadelphia | 20 |
| 28 | DALLAS | 21 |
| 26 | PHILADELPHIA | 7 |
| 23 | Dallas | 24 |
| 23 | Los Angeles | 17 |
| 42 | CHICAGO | 0 |

| Use Name | Pos. | Hgt | Wgt | Age | Int | Pts |
|---|---|---|---|---|---|---|
| George Starke | OT | 6'5" | 250 | 26 | | |
| Jim Tyrer | OT | 6'6" | 270 | 35 | | |
| Paul Laaveg | OG | 6'4" | 250 | 25 | | |
| Ray Schoenke | OG | 6'3" | 250 | 32 | | |
| Walt Sweeney | OG | 6'3" | 254 | 33 | | |
| Fred Sturt | OT-OG | 6'4" | 255 | 23 | | |
| Len Hauss | C | 6'2" | 235 | 32 | | |
| Dan Ryczek | C | 6'3" | 245 | 25 | | |
| Verlon Biggs | DE | 6'4" | 275 | 31 | | |
| Martin Imhof | DE | 6'6" | 256 | 24 | | |
| Deacon Jones | DE | 6'5" | 272 | 35 | | 1 |
| Ron McDole | DE | 6'3" | 265 | 34 | | |
| Bill Brundige | DT | 6'5" | 270 | 25 | | |
| Dennis Johnson | DT | 6'4" | 260 | 22 | | |
| Manny Sistrunk | DT | 6'5" | 265 | 27 | | |
| Diron Talbert | DT | 6'5" | 255 | 30 | | |

Bob Brunet – Injury
Terry Hermeling – Injury

| Use Name | Pos. | Hgt | Wgt | Age | Int | Pts |
|---|---|---|---|---|---|---|
| Brad Dusek | LB | 6'2" | 214 | 23 | | |
| Chris Hanburger | LB | 6'2" | 218 | 33 | 4 | 6 |
| Harold McLinton | LB | 6'2" | 235 | 27 | 1 | 6 |
| Stu O'Dell | LB | 6'1" | 220 | 22 | | |
| John Pergine | LB | 6'1" | 225 | 27 | | |
| Dave Robinson | LB | 6'3" | 245 | 33 | 2 | |
| Russ Tillman | LB | 6'2" | 230 | 28 | | |
| Mike Varty | LB | 6'1" | 220 | 22 | | |
| Mike Bass | DB | 6' | 190 | 29 | 3 | 6 |
| Speedy Duncan | DB | 5'10" | 180 | 31 | | |
| Pat Fischer | DB | 5'10" | 170 | 34 | 3 | |
| Ken Houston | DB | 6'3" | 198 | 29 | 2 | 6 |
| Larry Jones | DB | 5'10" | 170 | 23 | | 6 |
| Brig Owens | DB | 5'11" | 190 | 31 | 4 | |
| Bryant Salter | DB | 6'4" | 196 | 24 | 1 | |
| Ken Stone | DB | 6'1" | 180 | 23 | 5 | |

Ted Vactor – Injury

| Use Name | Pos. | Hgt | Wgt | Age | Int | Pts |
|---|---|---|---|---|---|---|
| Sonny Jurgensen | QB | 5'11" | 203 | 40 | | |
| Billy Kilmer | QB | 6' | 204 | 34 | | |
| Joe Theismann | QB | 6' | 184 | 24 | | 6 |
| Larry Brown | HB | 5'11" | 195 | 26 | | 42 |
| Doug Cunningham | HB | 5'11" | 195 | 28 | | |
| Herb Mul-Key | HB | 6' | 190 | 24 | | |
| Larry Smith | HB | 6'3" | 220 | 26 | | 6 |
| Moses Denson | FB-HB | 6'1" | 215 | 30 | | 12 |
| Charlie Evans | FB | 6'1" | 220 | 26 | | 12 |
| Mike Hull | FB | 6'3" | 220 | 29 | | |
| Duane Thomas | HB-FB | 6'1" | 215 | 27 | | 36 |
| Frank Grant | WR | 5'11" | 180 | 24 | | 6 |
| Roy Jefferson | WR | 6'2" | 195 | 30 | | 24 |
| Bill Malinchak | WR | 6'1" | 200 | 30 | | |
| Charley Taylor | WR | 6'3" | 210 | 33 | | 30 |
| Mike Hancock | TE | 6'4" | 220 | 24 | | |
| Alvin Reed | TE | 6'5" | 235 | 30 | | 6 |
| Jerry Smith | TE | 6'2" | 208 | 31 | | 18 |
| Mike Bragg | K | 5'11" | 186 | 27 | | 10 |
| Mark Moseley | K | 5'11" | 205 | 26 | | 81 |

## DALLAS COWBOYS 8-6-0 Tom Landry

| Scores of Each Game | | |
|---|---|---|
| 24 | Atlanta | 0 |
| 10 | Philadelphia | 13 |
| 6 | N.Y. GIANTS | 14 |
| 21 | MINNESOTA | 23 |
| 28 | St. Louis | 31 |
| 31 | PHILADELPHIA | 24 |
| 21 | N.Y. Giants | 7 |
| 17 | ST. LOUIS | 14 |
| 20 | SAN FRANCISCO | 14 |
| 21 | Washington | 28 |
| 10 | Houston | 0 |
| 24 | WASHINGTON | 23 |
| 41 | CLEVELAND | 17 |
| 23 | Oakland | 27 |

| Use Name | Pos. | Hgt | Wgt | Age | Int | Pts |
|---|---|---|---|---|---|---|
| Ralph Neely | OT | 6'5" | 255 | 30 | | |
| Bruce Walton | OT | 6'6" | 252 | 23 | | |
| Rayfield Wright | OT | 6'7" | 260 | 29 | | |
| Gene Killian | OG | 6'4" | 250 | 21 | | |
| John Niland | OG | 6'4" | 255 | 30 | | |
| Blaine Nye | OG | 6'4" | 255 | 28 | | |
| Jim Arneson | C-OG | 6'3" | 252 | 23 | | |
| John Fitzgerald | C | 6'5" | 255 | 26 | | |
| Dave Manders | C | 6'2" | 250 | 32 | | |
| Larry Cole | DE | 6'4" | 250 | 27 | | |
| Too Tall Jones | DE | 6'9" | 260 | 23 | | |
| Harvey Martin | DE | 6'5" | 252 | 23 | | |
| Pat Toomay | DE | 6'5" | 250 | 29 | | |
| Bill Gregory | DT | 6'5" | 252 | 24 | | |
| Bob Lilly | DT | 6'4" | 260 | 35 | | |
| Jethro Pugh | DT | 6'6" | 250 | 30 | | |

| Use Name | Pos. | Hgt | Wgt | Age | Int | Pts |
|---|---|---|---|---|---|---|
| Dave Edwards | LB | 6'3" | 226 | 35 | | |
| Ken Hutcherson | LB | 6'1" | 220 | 22 | | |
| Lee Roy Jordan | LB | 6'2" | 226 | 33 | 2 | |
| D. D. Lewis | LB | 6'2" | 218 | 28 | 2 | |
| Cal Peterson | LB | 6'3" | 220 | 21 | | |
| Louie Walker | LB | 6'1" | 216 | 22 | | |
| Benny Barnes | DB | 6'1" | 192 | 23 | | |
| Cornell Green | DB | 6'4" | 212 | 34 | 2 | |
| Cliff Harris | DB | 6' | 190 | 25 | 3 | |
| Mel Renfro | DB | 6' | 192 | 32 | 1 | |
| Mark Washington | DB | 5'10" | 186 | 26 | 1 | |
| Charlie Waters | DB | 6'1" | 193 | 25 | 2 | |

Toni Fritsch – Knee Injury
Rodney Wallace – Injury
John Babinecz – Injury

| Use Name | Pos. | Hgt | Wgt | Age | Int | Pts |
|---|---|---|---|---|---|---|
| Clint Longley | QB | 6'1" | 193 | 22 | | |
| Roger Staubach | QB | 6'2" | 197 | 32 | | 18 |
| Doug Dennison | HB | 6'1" | 195 | 22 | | 24 |
| Dennis Morgan | HB | 5'11" | 200 | 22 | | 6 |
| Les Strayhorn | HB | 5'10" | 205 | 23 | | |
| Charles Young | HB | 6'1" | 210 | 21 | | |
| Calvin Hill | FB-HB | 6'3" | 230 | 27 | | 42 |
| Walt Garrison | FB | 6' | 205 | 30 | | 36 |
| Robert Newhouse | HB-FB | 5'10" | 205 | 24 | | 18 |
| Bob Hayes | WR | 6' | 190 | 31 | | 6 |
| Bill Houston | WR | 6'3" | 208 | 23 | | |
| Drew Pearson | WR | 6' | 183 | 23 | | 18 |
| Golden Richards | WR | 6' | 183 | 23 | | 30 |
| Billy Joe DuPree | TE | 6'4" | 228 | 24 | | 24 |
| Jean Fugett | TE | 6'3" | 226 | 22 | | 6 |
| Ron Howard | TE | 6'4" | 215 | 23 | | |
| Duane Carrell | K | 5'10" | 185 | 24 | | |
| Efren Herrera | K | 5'9" | 185 | 23 | | 57 |
| Mac Percival | K | 6'4" | 220 | 34 | | 10 |

## PHILADELPHIA EAGLES 7-7-0 Mike McCormack

| Scores of Each Game | | |
|---|---|---|
| 3 | St. Louis | 7 |
| 13 | DALLAS | 10 |
| 30 | BALTIMORE | 10 |
| 13 | San Diego | 7 |
| 35 | N.Y. GIANTS | 7 |
| 24 | Dallas | 31 |
| 10 | New Orleans | 14 |
| 0 | Pittsburgh | 27 |
| 20 | WASHINGTON | 27 |
| 3 | ST. LOUIS | 13 |
| 7 | Washington | 26 |
| 36 | GREEN BAY | 14 |
| 20 | N.Y. Giants | 7 |
| 28 | DETROIT | 17 |

| Use Name | Pos. | Hgt | Wgt | Age | Int | Pts |
|---|---|---|---|---|---|---|
| Herb Dobbins | OT | 6'4" | 260 | 23 | | |
| Jerry Sisemore | OT | 6'4" | 250 | 23 | | |
| Steve Smith | OT | 6'5" | 250 | 30 | | |
| Dick Stevens | OT | 6'4" | 245 | 26 | | |
| Wade Key | OG | 6'4" | 245 | 27 | | |
| Roy Kirksey | OG | 6'1" | 255 | 26 | | |
| Tom Luken | OG | 6'3" | 253 | 24 | | |
| Mark Nordquist | OG | 6'4" | 246 | 28 | | |
| Guy Morriss | C | 6'4" | 245 | 23 | | |
| Willie Cullars | DE | 6'5" | 250 | 23 | | |
| Joe Jones | DE | 6'6" | 250 | 26 | | |
| Will Wynn | DE | 6'4" | 245 | 25 | | 6 |
| Jim Cagle | DT | 6'5" | 255 | 22 | | |
| Bill Dunstan | DT | 6'4" | 250 | 25 | | 6 |
| Jerry Patton | DT | 6'3" | 265 | 28 | 1 | |
| Mitch Sutton | DT | 6'4" | 265 | 23 | | |

| Use Name | Pos. | Hgt | Wgt | Age | Int | Pts |
|---|---|---|---|---|---|---|
| Bill Bergey | LB | 6'2" | 250 | 29 | 5 | |
| John Bunting | LB | 6'1" | 220 | 24 | 2 | |
| Dean Halverson | LB | 6'2" | 230 | 28 | 1 | |
| Frank LeMaster | LB | 6'2" | 224 | 22 | | |
| Kevin Reilly | LB | 6'2" | 220 | 22 | | |
| Steve Zabel | LB | 6'4" | 234 | 26 | 2 | |
| Bill Bradley | DB | 5'11" | 190 | 27 | 2 | |
| Charlie Ford | DB | 6'3" | 195 | 25 | | |
| Joe Lavender | DB | 6'4" | 190 | 25 | 1 | 12 |
| Randy Logan | DB | 6'1" | 195 | 23 | 2 | |
| Larry Marshall (from MIN) | DB | 5'10" | 195 | 24 | | |
| John Outlaw | DB | 5'10" | 180 | 29 | 2 | |
| Artimus Parker | DB | 6'3" | 215 | 22 | | |
| Marion Reeves | DB | 6'1" | 195 | 22 | | |

Al Coleman – Injury

| Use Name | Pos. | Hgt | Wgt | Age | Int | Pts |
|---|---|---|---|---|---|---|
| Mike Boryla | QB | 6'3" | 200 | 23 | | |
| Roman Gabriel | QB | 6'4" | 220 | 34 | | |
| John Reaves | QB | 6'3" | 210 | 24 | | |
| Po James | HB | 6'1" | 202 | 25 | | 12 |
| Greg Oliver | HB | 6' | 192 | 25 | | |
| Tom Sullivan | HB | 6' | 190 | 24 | | 72 |
| Tom Bailey | FB-HB | 6'2" | 211 | 25 | | |
| Norm Bulaich | FB | 6'1" | 218 | 27 | | |
| Randy Jackson | FB | 6' | 220 | 25 | | |
| Harold Carmichael | WR | 6'7" | 225 | 24 | | 48 |
| Wes Chesson | WR | 6'2" | 190 | 25 | | |
| Bob Picard | WR | 6'1" | 195 | 24 | | |
| Charlie Smith | WR | 6'1" | 185 | 24 | | |
| Don Zimmerman | WR | 6'3" | 195 | 24 | | 12 |
| Kent Kramer | TE | 6'5" | 235 | 30 | | |
| Charlie Young | TE | 6'4" | 238 | 23 | | 18 |
| Tom Dempsey | K | 6'1" | 265 | 33 | | 56 |
| Merritt Kersey | K | 6'1" | 205 | 24 | | |

## NEW YORK GIANTS 2-12-0 Bill Arnsparger

| Scores of Each Game | | |
|---|---|---|
| 10 | WASHINGTON | 13 |
| 20 | NEW ENGLAND | 28 |
| 14 | Dallas | 6 |
| 7 | ATLANTA | 14 |
| 7 | Philadelphia | 35 |
| 3 | Washington | 24 |
| 7 | DALLAS | 21 |
| 33 | Kansas City | 27 |
| 20 | N.Y. JETS (OT) | 26 |
| 19 | Detroit | 20 |
| 21 | ST. LOUIS | 23 |
| 13 | Chicago | 16 |
| 7 | PHILADELPHIA | 20 |
| 14 | St. Louis | 26 |

| Use Name | Pos. | Hgt | Wgt | Age | Int | Pts |
|---|---|---|---|---|---|---|
| John Hill | OT | 6'2" | 245 | 24 | | |
| Doug Van Horn | OT | 6'2" | 245 | 30 | | |
| Willie Young | OT | 6' | 255 | 31 | | |
| Dick Enderle | OG | 6'1" | 250 | 26 | | |
| John Hicks | OG | 6'2" | 258 | 23 | | |
| Tom Mullen | OG | 6'3" | 245 | 22 | | |
| Karl Chandler | C | 6'5" | 250 | 22 | | |
| Bob Hyland | C | 6'5" | 255 | 29 | | |
| Rick Dvorak | DE | 6'4" | 235 | 22 | | |
| Jack Gregory | DE | 6'6" | 255 | 29 | | |
| Roy Hilton | DE | 6'6" | 240 | 29 | | 6 |
| George Hasenohrl | DT | 6'1" | 260 | 23 | | |
| Larry Jacobson | DT | 6'6" | 260 | 24 | | |
| John Mendenhall | DT | 6'1" | 255 | 25 | | |
| Gary Pettigrew | DT | 6'4" | 255 | 29 | | |
| Jim Pietrzak | DT | 6'5" | 260 | 21 | | |
| Andy Rice | DT | 6'3" | 268 | 32 | | |
| Carl Wafer | DT | 6'3" | 250 | 23 | | |

| Use Name | Pos. | Hgt | Wgt | Age | Int | Pts |
|---|---|---|---|---|---|---|
| Ron Hornsby | LB | 6'3" | 228 | 25 | 1 | |
| Pat Hughes | LB | 6'2" | 225 | 27 | 2 | |
| Brian Kelley | LB | 6'3" | 222 | 23 | 1 | |
| Henry Reed | LB | 6'3" | 230 | 25 | | |
| Andy Selfridge | LB | 6'4" | 220 | 25 | 1 | |
| Bill Singletary | LB | 6'2" | 230 | 23 | | |
| Brad Van Pelt | LB | 6'5" | 235 | 23 | 2 | |
| Pete Athas | DB | 5'11" | 185 | 26 | 2 | |
| Bobby Brooks | DB | 6'1" | 195 | 23 | | |
| Chuck Crist | DB | 6'2" | 205 | 23 | 3 | |
| Honor Jackson | DB | 6'1" | 195 | 25 | | |
| Spider Lockhart | DB | 6'2" | 175 | 31 | 2 | |
| Clyde Powers | DB | 6'1" | 195 | 23 | | |
| Eldridge Small | DB | 6'1" | 190 | 24 | 1 | |
| Jim Stienke | DB | 5'11" | 182 | 23 | | |

Terry Hermeling – Knee Injury

| Use Name | Pos. | Hgt | Wgt | Age | Int | Pts |
|---|---|---|---|---|---|---|
| Jim DelGaizo | QB | 6'1" | 190 | 27 | | |
| Craig Morton (from DAL) | QB | 6'4" | 210 | 31 | | |
| Norm Snead (to SF) | QB | 6'4" | 215 | 34 | | |
| Carl Summerell | QB | 6'4" | 208 | 22 | | |
| Steve Crosby | HB | 5'11" | 205 | 24 | | |
| Ron Johnson | HB | 6'1" | 205 | 26 | | 36 |
| Leon McQuay | HB | 5'9" | 195 | 24 | | 6 |
| Mickey Zofko (from DET) | HB | 6'3" | 195 | 24 | | |
| Joe Dawkins | FB | 5'11" | 220 | 26 | | 30 |
| Doug Kotar | HB-FB | 5'11" | 205 | 23 | | 24 |
| Don Clune | WR | 6'3" | 195 | 22 | | |
| Walker Gillette | WR | 6'5" | 200 | 27 | | 18 |
| Bob Grim | WR | 6' | 200 | 29 | | 12 |
| Don Herrmann | WR | 6'2" | 205 | 27 | | |
| Ray Rhodes | WR | 5'11" | 185 | 23 | | |
| Chip Glass | TE | 6'4" | 235 | 27 | | |
| Bob Tucker | TE | 6'3" | 230 | 29 | | 12 |
| Pete Gogolak | K | 6'2" | 190 | 32 | | 51 |
| Dave Jennings | K | 6'4" | 205 | 22 | | |

## ST. LOUIS CARDINALS

### RUSHING

| Last Name | No. | Yds | Avg | TD |
|---|---|---|---|---|
| Metcalf | 152 | 718 | 4.7 | 6 |
| Otis | 158 | 664 | 4.2 | 1 |
| Anderson | 90 | 316 | 3.5 | 3 |
| Willard | 40 | 175 | 4.4 | 0 |
| Belton | 12 | 49 | 4.1 | 0 |
| Hart | 10 | 21 | 2.1 | 2 |
| Moss | 4 | 13 | 3.3 | 0 |

### RECEIVING

| Last Name | No. | Yds | Avg | TD |
|---|---|---|---|---|
| Metcalf | 50 | 377 | 8 | 1 |
| Gray | 39 | 770 | 20 | 6 |
| Thomas | 34 | 513 | 15 | 5 |
| Smith | 25 | 413 | 17 | 3 |
| Otis | 19 | 109 | 6 | 0 |
| Anderson | 15 | 116 | 8 | 3 |
| Cain | 13 | 152 | 12 | 1 |
| Willard | 4 | 28 | 7 | 1 |
| Hammond | 2 | 14 | 7 | 0 |

### PUNT RETURNS

| Last Name | No. | Yds | Avg | TD |
|---|---|---|---|---|
| Metcalf | 26 | 340 | 13 | 0 |
| Hammond | 17 | 125 | 7 | 0 |
| Wehrli | 4 | 39 | 10 | 0 |
| Belton | 4 | 8 | 2 | 0 |
| Tolbert | 1 | 0 | 0 | 0 |

### KICKOFF RETURNS

| Last Name | No. | Yds | Avg | TD |
|---|---|---|---|---|
| Metcalf | 20 | 623 | 31 | 1 |
| Hammond | 11 | 268 | 24 | 0 |
| Moss | 8 | 133 | 17 | 0 |
| Belton | 5 | 111 | 22 | 0 |
| LeVeck | 2 | 32 | 16 | 0 |
| Reaves | 1 | 22 | 22 | 0 |
| Finnie | 1 | 8 | 8 | 0 |
| Cain | 1 | 5 | 5 | 0 |
| Crum | 1 | 1 | 1 | 0 |

### PASSING – PUNTING – KICKING

| PASSING | Att | Comp | % | Yds | Yd/Att | TD | Int–% | | RK |
|---|---|---|---|---|---|---|---|---|---|
| Hart | 388 | 200 | 52 | 2411 | 6.2 | 20 | 8– 2 | | 5 |
| Metcalf | 2 | 0 | 0 | 0 | 0.0 | 0 | 0– 0 | | |
| Hammond | 1 | 1 | 100 | 81 | 81.0 | 0 | 0– 0 | | |

| PUNTING | No | Avg | | | | | | | |
|---|---|---|---|---|---|---|---|---|---|
| Roberts | 81 | 38.7 | | | | | | | |

| KICKING | XP | Att | % | FG | Att | % | | | |
|---|---|---|---|---|---|---|---|---|---|
| Bakken | 30 | 36 | 83 | 13 | 22 | 59 | | | |

## WASHINGTON REDSKINS

### RUSHING

| Last Name | No. | Yds | Avg | TD |
|---|---|---|---|---|
| Brown | 163 | 430 | 2.6 | 3 |
| Denson | 103 | 391 | 3.8 | 0 |
| Thomas | 95 | 347 | 3.7 | 5 |
| L. Smith | 55 | 149 | 2.7 | 0 |
| Evans | 32 | 79 | 2.5 | 2 |
| Kilmer | 6 | 27 | 4.5 | 0 |
| Cunningham | 5 | 17 | 3.4 | 0 |
| Theismann | 3 | 12 | 4.0 | 1 |
| J. Smith | 1 | 5 | 5.0 | 0 |
| Mul-Key | 1 | 3 | 3.0 | 0 |
| Taylor | 1 | –1 | –1.0 | 0 |
| Jurgensen | 4 | –6 | –1.5 | 0 |
| Grant | 1 | –10 | –10.0 | 0 |

### RECEIVING

| Last Name | No. | Yds | Avg | TD |
|---|---|---|---|---|
| Taylor | 54 | 738 | 14 | 5 |
| J. Smith | 44 | 554 | 13 | 3 |
| Jefferson | 43 | 654 | 15 | 4 |
| Brown | 37 | 388 | 11 | 4 |
| Denson | 26 | 174 | 7 | 2 |
| L. Smith | 23 | 137 | 6 | 0 |
| Thomas | 10 | 31 | 3 | 1 |
| Grant | 9 | 196 | 22 | 1 |
| Reed | 4 | 36 | 9 | 1 |
| Evans | 2 | 44 | 22 | 0 |
| Cunningham | 2 | 26 | 13 | 0 |

### PUNT RETURNS

| Last Name | No. | Yds | Avg | TD |
|---|---|---|---|---|
| Theismann | 15 | 157 | 11 | 0 |
| Mul-Key | 13 | 140 | 11 | 0 |
| Houston | 6 | 81 | 14 | 1 |
| L. Jones | 8 | 54 | 7 | 0 |
| Duncan | 3 | 19 | 6 | 0 |
| Stone | 1 | 2 | 2 | 0 |

### KICKOFF RETURNS

| Last Name | No. | Yds | Avg | TD |
|---|---|---|---|---|
| L. Jones | 23 | 672 | 29 | 1 |
| Mul-Key | 10 | 285 | 29 | 0 |
| Evans | 4 | 60 | 15 | 0 |
| L. Smith | 2 | 57 | 29 | 0 |
| Denson | 2 | 49 | 25 | 0 |
| Bass | 1 | 22 | 22 | 0 |
| Ryczek | 1 | 11 | 11 | 0 |
| Tillman | 1 | 10 | 10 | 0 |
| Dusek | 1 | 0 | 0 | 0 |

### PASSING – PUNTING – KICKING

| PASSING | Att | Comp | % | Yds | Yd/Att | TD | Int–% | | RK |
|---|---|---|---|---|---|---|---|---|---|
| Kilmer | 234 | 137 | 59 | 1632 | 7.0 | 10 | 6– 3 | | 4 |
| Jurgensen | 167 | 107 | 64 | 1185 | 7.1 | 11 | 5– 3 | | 1 |
| Theismann | 11 | 9 | 82 | 145 | 13.2 | 1 | 0– 0 | | |
| Brown | 1 | 1 | 100 | 16 | 16.0 | 0 | 0– 0 | | |

| PUNTING | No | Avg | | | | | | | |
|---|---|---|---|---|---|---|---|---|---|
| Bragg | 74 | 38.1 | | | | | | | |

| KICKING | XP | Att | % | FG | Att | % | | | |
|---|---|---|---|---|---|---|---|---|---|
| Moseley | 27 | 29 | 93 | 18 | 30 | 60 | | | |
| Bragg | 7 | 8 | 88 | 1 | 1 | 100 | | | |
| D. Jones | 1 | 1 | 100 | 0 | 0 | — | | | |

## DALLAS COWBOYS

### RUSHING

| Last Name | No. | Yds | Avg | TD |
|---|---|---|---|---|
| Hill | 185 | 844 | 4.6 | 7 |
| Newhouse | 124 | 501 | 4.0 | 3 |
| Garrison | 113 | 429 | 3.8 | 5 |
| Staubach | 47 | 320 | 6.8 | 3 |
| Young | 33 | 205 | 6.2 | 0 |
| Strayhorn | 11 | 66 | 6.0 | 0 |
| Dennison | 16 | 52 | 3.3 | 4 |
| DuPree | 4 | 43 | 10.8 | 0 |
| Pearson | 3 | 6 | 2.0 | 0 |
| Waters | 1 | 6 | 6.0 | 0 |
| Richards | 1 | –5 | –5.0 | 0 |
| Longley | 4 | –13 | –3.2 | 0 |

### RECEIVING

| Last Name | No. | Yds | Avg | TD |
|---|---|---|---|---|
| Pearson | 62 | 1087 | 18 | 2 |
| Garrison | 34 | 253 | 7 | 1 |
| DuPree | 29 | 466 | 16 | 4 |
| Richards | 26 | 467 | 18 | 5 |
| Hill | 12 | 134 | 11 | 0 |
| Young | 11 | 73 | 7 | 0 |
| Newhouse | 9 | 67 | 7 | 0 |
| Hayes | 7 | 118 | 17 | 1 |
| Houston | 6 | 72 | 12 | 0 |
| Fugett | 4 | 60 | 15 | 1 |
| Dennison | 2 | 23 | 12 | 0 |
| Strayhorn | 2 | 12 | 6 | 0 |
| Barnes | 1 | 37 | 37 | 0 |
| Staubach | 1 | –13 | –13 | 0 |

### PUNT RETURNS

| Last Name | No. | Yds | Avg | TD |
|---|---|---|---|---|
| Morgan | 19 | 287 | 15 | 1 |
| Harris | 26 | 193 | 7 | 0 |
| Richards | 13 | 74 | 6 | 0 |
| Hayes | 2 | 11 | 6 | 0 |
| Waters | 1 | 8 | 8 | 0 |
| Renfro | 1 | 0 | 0 | 0 |

### KICKOFF RETURNS

| Last Name | No. | Yds | Avg | TD |
|---|---|---|---|---|
| Morgan | 35 | 823 | 24 | 0 |
| Young | 8 | 161 | 20 | 0 |
| Dennison | 3 | 54 | 18 | 0 |
| Strayhorn | 2 | 19 | 10 | 0 |
| Harris | 1 | 14 | 14 | 0 |

### PASSING – PUNTING – KICKING

| PASSING | Att | Comp | % | Yds | Yd/Att | TD | Int–% | | RK |
|---|---|---|---|---|---|---|---|---|---|
| Staubach | 360 | 190 | 53 | 2552 | 7.1 | 11 | 15– 4 | | 6 |
| Longley | 21 | 12 | 57 | 209 | 10.0 | 0 | 0– 0 | | |
| Carrell | 1 | 1 | 100 | 37 | 37.0 | 0 | 0– 0 | | |
| Pearson | 1 | 1 | 100 | 46 | 46.0 | 1 | 0– 0 | | |

| PUNTING | No | Avg | | | | | | | |
|---|---|---|---|---|---|---|---|---|---|
| Carrell | 40 | 39.8 | | | | | | | |

| KICKING | XP | Att | % | FG | Att | % | | | |
|---|---|---|---|---|---|---|---|---|---|
| Herrera | 33 | 33 | 100 | 8 | 13 | 62 | | | |
| Percival | 4 | 5 | 80 | 2 | 8 | 25 | | | |

## PHILADELPHIA EAGLES

### RUSHING

| Last Name | No. | Yds | Avg | TD |
|---|---|---|---|---|
| Sullivan | 244 | 760 | 3.1 | 11 |
| James | 67 | 276 | 4.1 | 2 |
| Bulaich | 50 | 152 | 3.0 | 0 |
| Gabriel | 14 | 76 | 5.4 | 0 |
| Young | 6 | 38 | 6.3 | 0 |
| Bailey | 10 | 32 | 3.2 | 0 |
| Boryla | 6 | 25 | 4.2 | 0 |
| Oliver | 7 | 19 | 2.7 | 0 |
| Reaves | 1 | 8 | 8.0 | 0 |
| Jackson | 7 | 3 | 0.4 | 0 |
| Kersey | 1 | 2 | 2.0 | 0 |
| Carmichael | 2 | –6 | –3.0 | 0 |

### RECEIVING

| Last Name | No. | Yds | Avg | TD |
|---|---|---|---|---|
| Young | 63 | 696 | 11 | 3 |
| Carmichael | 56 | 649 | 12 | 8 |
| Sullivan | 39 | 312 | 8 | 1 |
| James | 33 | 230 | 7 | 0 |
| Zimmerman | 30 | 368 | 12 | 2 |
| Bulaich | 28 | 204 | 7 | 0 |
| Bailey | 6 | 27 | 5 | 0 |
| Jackson | 2 | 17 | 9 | 0 |
| C. Smith | 1 | 28 | 28 | 0 |

### PUNT RETURNS

| Last Name | No. | Yds | Avg | TD |
|---|---|---|---|---|
| Bradley | 22 | 248 | 11 | 0 |
| Marshall | 13 | 118 | 9 | 0 |
| Reeves | 3 | 12 | 4 | 0 |
| C. Smith | 4 | 7 | 2 | 0 |

### KICKOFF RETURNS

| Last Name | No. | Yds | Avg | TD |
|---|---|---|---|---|
| Marshall | 20 | 468 | 23 | 0 |
| Jackson | 14 | 339 | 24 | 0 |
| James | 12 | 238 | 20 | 0 |
| Kramer | 2 | 39 | 20 | 0 |
| Kirksey | 1 | 19 | 19 | 0 |
| Bailey | 1 | 14 | 14 | 0 |
| Chesson | 1 | 1 | 1 | 0 |
| Zimmerman | 1 | 0 | 0 | 0 |

### PASSING – PUNTING – KICKING

| PASSING | Att | Comp | % | Yds | Yd/Att | TD | Int–% | | RK |
|---|---|---|---|---|---|---|---|---|---|
| Gabriel | 338 | 193 | 57 | 1867 | 5.5 | 9 | 12– 4 | | 8 |
| Boryla | 102 | 60 | 59 | 580 | 5.7 | 5 | 3– 3 | | |
| Reaves | 20 | 5 | 25 | 84 | 4.2 | 0 | 2–10 | | |
| Carmichael | 1 | 0 | 0 | 0 | 0.0 | 0 | 0– 0 | | |

| PUNTING | No | Avg | | | | | | | |
|---|---|---|---|---|---|---|---|---|---|
| Kersey | 82 | 36.1 | | | | | | | |
| Bradley | 2 | 33.5 | | | | | | | |

| KICKING | XP | Att | % | FG | Att | % | | | |
|---|---|---|---|---|---|---|---|---|---|
| Dempsey | 26 | 30 | 87 | 10 | 16 | 63 | | | |

## NEW YORK GIANTS

### RUSHING

| Last Name | No. | Yds | Avg | TD |
|---|---|---|---|---|
| Dawkins | 156 | 561 | 3.6 | 2 |
| Kotar | 106 | 396 | 3.7 | 4 |
| McQuay | 55 | 240 | 4.4 | 1 |
| Johnson | 97 | 218 | 2.2 | 4 |
| Crosby | 14 | 55 | 3.9 | 0 |
| Snead | 4 | 29 | 7.3 | 0 |
| Del Gaizo | 3 | 15 | 5.0 | 0 |
| Summerell | 2 | 8 | 4.0 | 0 |
| Zofko | 3 | 6 | 2.0 | 0 |
| Morton | 4 | 5 | 1.3 | 0 |
| Rhodes | 1 | –6 | –6.0 | 0 |

### RECEIVING

| Last Name | No. | Yds | Avg | TD |
|---|---|---|---|---|
| Dawkins | 46 | 332 | 7 | 3 |
| Tucker | 41 | 496 | 12 | 2 |
| Gillette | 29 | 466 | 16 | 3 |
| Grim | 28 | 466 | 17 | 2 |
| Johnson | 24 | 171 | 7 | 2 |
| Herrmann | 10 | 97 | 10 | 0 |
| Kotar | 10 | 57 | 6 | 0 |
| Rhodes | 9 | 138 | 15 | 0 |
| McQuay | 5 | 59 | 12 | 0 |
| Glass | 3 | 23 | 8 | 0 |
| Zofko | 3 | 15 | 5 | 0 |
| Crosby | 2 | 44 | 22 | 0 |

### PUNT RETURNS

| Last Name | No. | Yds | Avg | TD |
|---|---|---|---|---|
| Athas | 20 | 180 | 9 | 0 |
| Rhodes | 10 | 124 | 12 | 0 |
| McQuay | 7 | 81 | 12 | 0 |
| Kotar | 3 | 14 | 5 | 0 |
| Brooks | 1 | 9 | 9 | 0 |

### KICKOFF RETURNS

| Last Name | No. | Yds | Avg | TD |
|---|---|---|---|---|
| McQuay | 25 | 689 | 28 | 0 |
| Kotar | 15 | 350 | 23 | 0 |
| Dawkins | 4 | 154 | 39 | 0 |
| Brooks | 5 | 106 | 21 | 0 |
| Crosby | 2 | 47 | 24 | 0 |
| Small | 2 | 46 | 23 | 0 |
| Zofko | 3 | 33 | 11 | 0 |
| Rhodes | 1 | 27 | 27 | 0 |
| Kelley | 3 | 29 | 8 | 0 |
| Powers | 1 | 0 | 0 | 0 |

### PASSING – PUNTING – KICKING

| PASSING | Att | Comp | % | Yds | Yd/Att | TD | Int–% | | RK |
|---|---|---|---|---|---|---|---|---|---|
| Morton | 239 | 124 | 52 | 1522 | 6.4 | 9 | 13– 5 | | 9 |
| Snead | 159 | 97 | 61 | 983 | 6.2 | 5 | 8– 5 | | 9 |
| Del Gaizo | 32 | 12 | 38 | 165 | 5.2 | 0 | 3– 9 | | |
| Summerell | 13 | 6 | 46 | 59 | 4.5 | 0 | 3–23 | | |

| PUNTING | No | Avg | | | | | | | |
|---|---|---|---|---|---|---|---|---|---|
| Jennings | 68 | 39.8 | | | | | | | |
| Crosby | 1 | 60.0 | | | | | | | |

| KICKING | XP | Att | % | FG | Att | % | | | |
|---|---|---|---|---|---|---|---|---|---|
| Gogolak | 21 | 23 | 91 | 10 | 19 | 53 | | | |

## MINNESOTA VIKINGS 10-4-0 Bud Grant

**Scores of Each Game**

| | | |
|---|---|---|
| 32 | Green Bay | 17 |
| 7 | Detroit | 6 |
| 11 | CHIGAGO | 7 |
| 23 | Dallas | 21 |
| 51 | HOUSTON | 10 |
| 16 | DETROIT | 20 |
| 14 | NEW ENGLAND | 17 |
| 17 | Chicago | 0 |
| 28 | St. Louis | 24 |
| 7 | GREEN BAY | 19 |
| 17 | Los Angeles | 20 |
| 29 | NEW ORLEANS | 9 |
| 23 | ATLANTA | 10 |
| 35 | Kansas City | 15 |

| Use Name | Pos. | Hgt | Wgt | Age | Int | Pts |
|---|---|---|---|---|---|---|
| Grady Alderman | OT | 6'2" | 247 | 35 | | |
| Charlie Goodrum | OT | 6'3" | 256 | 24 | | |
| Steve Riley | OT | 6'6" | 258 | 21 | | |
| Ron Yary | OT | 6'6" | 255 | 28 | | |
| Steve Lawson | OG | 6'3" | 265 | 25 | | |
| Andy Mauer (From NO) | OG | 6'3" | 275 | 25 | | |
| Milt Sunde | OG | 6'2" | 250 | 31 | | |
| Ed White | OG | 6'2" | 280 | 27 | | |
| Scott Anderson | C | 6'4" | 234 | 23 | | |
| Mick Tingelhoff | C | 6'1" | 240 | 34 | | |
| Dave Boone | DE | 6'3" | 248 | 23 | | |
| Carl Eller | DE | 6'6" | 247 | 32 | | |
| Jim Marshall | DE | 6'3" | 240 | 36 | | |
| Bob Lurtsema | DT-DE | 6'6" | 250 | 32 | | |
| Gary Larsen | DT | 6'5" | 255 | 34 | | |
| Alan Page | DT | 6'5" | 245 | 29 | | |
| Doug Sutherland | DT | 6'3" | 250 | 26 | | |

| Use Name | Pos. | Hgt | Wgt | Age | Int | Pts |
|---|---|---|---|---|---|---|
| Matt Blair | LB | 6'5" | 230 | 23 | | |
| Wally Hilgenberg | LB | 6'3" | 230 | 31 | | 2 |
| Amos Martin | LB | 6'3" | 228 | 25 | 3 | 6 |
| Fred McNeill | LB | 6'2" | 230 | 22 | | |
| Jeff Siemon | LB | 6'2" | 230 | 24 | 2 | |
| Roy Winston | LB | 6'1" | 222 | 34 | | |
| Joe Blahak | DB | 5'9" | 188 | 24 | | |
| Terry Brown | DB | 6'1" | 205 | 27 | 2 | |
| Bobby Bryant | DB | 6' | 170 | 30 | | |
| Paul Krause | DB | 6'3" | 200 | 32 | 2 | |
| Randy Poltl | DB | 6'3" | 190 | 22 | | |
| Jackie Wallace | DB | 6'3" | 197 | 23 | 1 | |
| Jeff Wright | DB | 5'11" | 190 | 25 | 4 | |
| Nate Wright | DB | 5'11" | 180 | 26 | 6 | |

John Ward — Injury

| Use Name | Pos. | Hgt | Wgt | Age | Int | Pts |
|---|---|---|---|---|---|---|
| Bob Berry | QB | 5'11" | 185 | 32 | | |
| Fran Tarkenton | QB | 6'1" | 190 | 34 | | 12 |
| Brent McClanahan | HB | 5'11" | 202 | 23 | | 6 |
| Dave Osborn | HB | 6' | 208 | 31 | | 24 |
| Chuck Foreman | FB-HB | 6'2" | 207 | 23 | | 90 |
| Bill Brown | FB | 5'11" | 222 | 36 | | |
| Ed Marinaro | HB-FB | 6'2" | 212 | 24 | | 12 |
| Oscar Reed | HB-FB | 5'11" | 222 | 30 | | 6 |
| John Gilliam | WR | 6'1" | 195 | 29 | | 30 |
| John Holland | WR | 6' | 190 | 22 | | |
| Jim Lash | WR | 6'2" | 200 | 22 | | |
| Sam McCullum | WR | 6'2" | 203 | 21 | | 18 |
| Steve Craig | TE | 6'3" | 230 | 23 | | 6 |
| Doug Kingswriter | TE | 6'2" | 222 | 24 | | |
| Stu Voigt | TE | 6'1" | 225 | 26 | | 30 |
| Fred Cox | K | 5'10" | 200 | 35 | | 68 |
| Mike Eischeid | K | 6' | 190 | 33 | | |

## DETROIT LIONS 7-7-0 Don McCafferty - died of heart attack July 28, 1974 Rick Forzano

**Scores of Each Game**

| | | |
|---|---|---|
| 9 | Chicago | 17 |
| 6 | MINNESOTA | 7 |
| 19 | Green Bay | 21 |
| 13 | Los Angeles | 16 |
| 17 | SAN FRANCISCO | 14 |
| 20 | Minnesota | 16 |
| 19 | GREEN BAY | 17 |
| 4 | NEW ORLEANS | 14 |
| 13 | Oakland | 35 |
| 20 | N.Y. GIANTS | 19 |
| 34 | CHICAGO | 17 |
| 27 | DENVER | 31 |
| 23 | Cincinnati | 19 |
| 17 | Philadelphia | 28 |

| Use Name | Pos. | Hgt | Wgt | Age | Int | Pts |
|---|---|---|---|---|---|---|
| Rocky Freitas | OT | 6'6" | 270 | 28 | | |
| Gordon Jolley | OT | 6'5" | 250 | 25 | | |
| Jim Yarbrough | OT | 6'6" | 265 | 27 | | |
| Bob Kowalkowski | OG | 6'3" | 240 | 30 | | |
| Chuck Walton | OG | 6'3" | 256 | 33 | | |
| Daryl White | OG | 6'3" | 250 | 22 | | |
| Guy Dennis | C-OG | 6'2" | 255 | 27 | | |
| Ed Flanagan | C | 6'3" | 245 | 30 | | |
| Fred Rothwell | C | 6'3" | 240 | 21 | | |
| Larry Hand | DE | 6'4" | 250 | 31 | | |
| Ken Sanders | DE | 6'5" | 240 | 24 | | |
| Ernie Price | DT-DE | 6'4" | 255 | 23 | | |
| Billy Howard | DT | 6'4" | 245 | 24 | | |
| Herb Orvis | DT | 6'5" | 240 | 27 | | |
| Jim Mitchell | DE-DT | 6'3" | 245 | 25 | | 2 |
| John Small | LB-DT | 6'5" | 260 | 27 | | |

| Use Name | Pos. | Hgt | Wgt | Age | Int | Pts |
|---|---|---|---|---|---|---|
| Mike Hennigan | LB | 6'2" | 210 | 22 | | |
| Jim Laslavic | LB | 6'2" | 230 | 22 | 1 | |
| Paul Naumoff | LB | 6'1" | 215 | 29 | 1 | |
| Ed O'Neil | LB | 6'3" | 245 | 21 | | |
| Charlie Weaver | LB | 6'2" | 220 | 25 | 3 | |
| Lem Barney | DB | 6' | 190 | 28 | 4 | |
| Carl Capria | DB | 6'3" | 185 | 22 | | |
| Ben Davis | DB | 5'11" | 180 | 28 | 1 | |
| Bill Frohbose | DB | 6' | 185 | 22 | | |
| Dick Jauron | DB | 6' | 190 | 23 | 1 | |
| Levi Johnson | DB | 6'3" | 190 | 23 | 5 | 18 |
| Jim Thrower | DB | 6' | 185 | 25 | | |
| Charlie West | DB | 6'1" | 200 | 28 | 1 | |
| Doug Wyatt | DB | 6'1" | 195 | 27 | | |

Dick Cunningham — Injury
Mike Weger — Knee Injury

| Use Name | Pos. | Hgt | Wgt | Age | Int | Pts |
|---|---|---|---|---|---|---|
| Greg Landry | QB | 6'4" | 210 | 27 | | 6 |
| Bill Munson | QB | 6'2" | 210 | 32 | | 6 |
| Sam Wyche | QB | 6'4" | 220 | 29 | | |
| Dexter Bussey | HB | 6'1" | 195 | 22 | | |
| Jimmie Jones | HB | 5'10" | 205 | 24 | | 6 |
| Altie Taylor | HB | 5'10" | 200 | 26 | | 36 |
| Leon Crosswhite | FB | 6'2" | 215 | 24 | | 6 |
| Jim Hooks | FB | 5'11" | 225 | 22 | | |
| Steve Owens | FB | 6'2" | 215 | 26 | | 18 |
| Ray Jarvis | WR | 5'10" | 195 | 25 | | |
| Ron Jessie | WR | 6' | 185 | 26 | | 24 |
| Bob Pickard | WR | 6' | 185 | 21 | | 6 |
| Larry Walton | WR | 5'11" | 185 | 27 | | 18 |
| T. C. Blair | TE | 6'2" | 220 | 23 | | |
| Charlie Sanders | TE | 6'4" | 225 | 28 | | 18 |
| Errol Mann | K | 6' | 200 | 33 | | 92 |
| Herman Weaver | K | 6'4" | 210 | 25 | | |

## GREEN BAY PACKERS 6-8-0 Dan Devine

**Scores of Each Game**

| | | |
|---|---|---|
| 17 | MINNESOTA | 32 |
| 20 | Baltimore | 13 |
| 21 | DETROIT | 19 |
| 7 | BUFFALO | 27 |
| 17 | LOS ANGELES | 6 |
| 0 | Chicago | 10 |
| 17 | Detroit | 19 |
| 6 | WASHINGTON | 17 |
| 20 | CHICAGO | 3 |
| 19 | Minnesota | 7 |
| 34 | SAN DIEGO | 0 |
| 14 | Philadelphia | 36 |
| 6 | San Francisco | 7 |
| 3 | Atlanta | 10 |

| Use Name | Pos. | Hgt | Wgt | Age | Int | Pts |
|---|---|---|---|---|---|---|
| Dick Himes | OT | 6'4" | 260 | 28 | | |
| Lee Nystrom | OT | 6'5" | 260 | 23 | | |
| Harry Schuh | OT | 6'3" | 260 | 31 | | |
| Gale Gillingham | OG | 6'3" | 265 | 30 | | |
| Bill Lueck | OG | 6'3" | 250 | 28 | | |
| Bruce Van Dyke | OG | 6'2" | 255 | 30 | | |
| Keith Wortman | OG | 6'2" | 250 | 24 | | |
| Mal Snider | OT-OG | 6'4" | 250 | 27 | | |
| Larry McCarren | C | 6'3" | 248 | 23 | | |
| John Schmitt | C | 6'4" | 250 | 31 | | |
| Aaron Brown | DE | 6'5" | 270 | 30 | | |
| Mike Fannuci | DE | 6'4" | 242 | 24 | | |
| Dave Pureifory | DE | 6'1" | 255 | 24 | | |
| Alden Roche | DE | 6'4" | 255 | 29 | | |
| Clarence Williams | DE | 6'5" | 255 | 27 | | 1 |
| Mike McCoy | DT | 6'5" | 275 | 25 | | 1 |
| Steve Okoniewski | DT | 6'3" | 252 | 25 | | |

Ken Bowman — Back Injury

| Use Name | Pos. | Hgt | Wgt | Age | Int | Pts |
|---|---|---|---|---|---|---|
| Ron Acks | LB | 6'2" | 225 | 29 | | |
| Fred Carr | LB | 6'5" | 240 | 28 | 1 | |
| Jim Carter | LB | 6'3" | 245 | 25 | 1 | |
| Mark Cooney | LB | 6'4" | 230 | 22 | | |
| Larry Hefner | LB | 6'2" | 230 | 25 | | |
| Ted Hendricks | LB | 6'7" | 220 | 26 | 5 | 2 |
| Noel Jenke | LB | 6'1" | 225 | 27 | | |
| Willie Buchanon | DB | 6' | 190 | 23 | 4 | |
| Ken Ellis | DB | 5'10" | 190 | 26 | 3 | 6 |
| Charley Hall | DB | 6'1" | 190 | 25 | 2 | |
| Jim Hill | DB | 6'2" | 195 | 27 | 2 | |
| Dave Mason | DB | 6' | 195 | 24 | | |
| Al Matthews | DB | 5'11" | 190 | 26 | 3 | |
| Perry Smith | DB | 6'1" | 195 | 23 | | |

Bill Hayhoe — Injury
Tom Toner — Collarbone Injury
Ron Widby — Back Injury

| Use Name | Pos. | Hgt | Wgt | Age | Int | Pts |
|---|---|---|---|---|---|---|
| Jack Concannon | QB | 6'3" | 200 | 31 | | 6 |
| John Hadl (from LA) | QB | 6'2" | 214 | 34 | | |
| Jerry Tagge | QB | 6'2" | 215 | 24 | | |
| Larry Krause | HB | 6' | 208 | 26 | | |
| MacArthur Lane | HB | 6' | 220 | 32 | | 36 |
| Eric Torkelson | HB | 6'2" | 194 | 21 | | 6 |
| Les Goodman | FB-HB | 5'11" | 206 | 24 | | |
| Charlie Leigh (from MIA) | FB-HB | 5'11" | 206 | 28 | | |
| John Brockington | FB | 6'1" | 225 | 25 | | 30 |
| Barty Smith | FB | 6'4" | 240 | 22 | | |
| Steve Odom | WR | 5'8" | 165 | 21 | | 18 |
| Ken Payne | WR | 6'1" | 185 | 23 | | |
| Barry Smith | WR | 6'1" | 190 | 23 | | 6 |
| Jon Staggers | WR | 5'10" | 180 | 25 | | 6 |
| Mike Donohoe | TE | 6'3" | 230 | 29 | | |
| Rich McGeorge | TE | 6'4" | 230 | 25 | | |
| Chester Marcol | K | 6' | 190 | 25 | | 94 |
| Randy Walker | K | 5'10" | 177 | 22 | | |

## CHICAGO BEARS 4-10-0 Abe Gibron

**Scores of Each Game**

| | | |
|---|---|---|
| 17 | DETROIT | 9 |
| 21 | N.Y. JETS | 23 |
| 7 | Minnesota | 11 |
| 24 | NEW ORLEANS | 10 |
| 10 | Atlanta | 13 |
| 10 | GREEN BAY | 9 |
| 6 | Buffalo | 16 |
| 0 | MINNESOTA | 17 |
| 3 | Green Bay | 20 |
| 0 | SAN FRANCISCO | 34 |
| 17 | Detroit | 34 |
| 16 | N.Y. GIANTS | 13 |
| 21 | San Diego | 28 |
| 0 | Washington | 42 |

| Use Name | Pos. | Hgt | Wgt | Age | Int | Pts |
|---|---|---|---|---|---|---|
| Lionel Antoine | OT | 6'6" | 263 | 24 | | |
| Bob Asher | OT | 6'5" | 260 | 26 | | |
| Randy Jackson | OT | 6'4" | 247 | 30 | | |
| Steve Kinney | OT | 6'5" | 260 | 25 | | |
| Tom Forrest | OG | 6'2" | 255 | 22 | | |
| Mike Hoban | OG | 6'2" | 235 | 22 | | |
| Ernie Janet | OG | 6'4" | 255 | 23 | | |
| Bob Newton | OG | 6'4" | 260 | 25 | | |
| Rich Coady | C | 6'3" | 246 | 29 | | |
| Gary Hrivnak | DE | 6'5" | 254 | 23 | | |
| Mel Tom | DE | 6'4" | 242 | 33 | | |
| Richard Harris | DT-DE | 6'4" | 255 | 26 | | |
| Wally Chambers | DT | 6'6" | 255 | 23 | | |
| Dave Gallagher | DT | 6'4" | 256 | 22 | | |
| Don Hultz | DT | 6'3" | 240 | 33 | | |
| Jim Osborne | DT | 6'3" | 254 | 24 | | |

| Use Name | Pos. | Hgt | Wgt | Age | Int | Pts |
|---|---|---|---|---|---|---|
| Waymond Bryant | LB | 6'3" | 230 | 22 | 2 | |
| Doug Buffone | LB | 6'1" | 227 | 30 | 1 | |
| Jimmy Gunn | LB | 6'1" | 218 | 25 | | |
| Bob Pifferini | LB | 6'2" | 226 | 24 | | |
| Don Rives | LB | 6'2" | 220 | 23 | | |
| Craig Clemons | DB | 5'11" | 200 | 25 | 4 | |
| Allan Ellis | DB | 5'10" | 182 | 23 | 3 | |
| Norm Hodgins | DB | 6'1" | 190 | 22 | | |
| Bill Knox | DB | 5'9" | 193 | 23 | 2 | |
| Garry Lyle | DB | 6'2" | 193 | 28 | 3 | |
| Randy Montgomery | DB | 5'11" | 185 | 27 | 2 | |
| Joe Taylor | DB | 6'2" | 197 | 32 | 1 | |

Tom Reynolds – injury

| Use Name | Pos. | Hgt | Wgt | Age | Int | Pts |
|---|---|---|---|---|---|---|
| Joe Barnes | QB | 5'11" | 196 | 22 | | |
| Bobby Douglass | QB | 6'3" | 228 | 27 | | 6 |
| Gary Huff | QB | 6'1" | 194 | 23 | | 12 |
| Dave Gagnon | HB | 5'10" | 210 | 22 | | |
| Carl Garrett | HB | 5'11" | 205 | 27 | | 12 |
| Ken Grandberry | HB | 6' | 196 | 22 | | 12 |
| Clifton Taylor | HB | 5'11" | 200 | 22 | | 6 |
| Pete Van Valkenberg (from GB) | HB | 6'2" | 205 | 24 | | |
| Gary Kosins | FB-HB | 6'1" | 213 | 25 | | 6 |
| Jim Harrison | FB | 6'4" | 238 | 25 | | 6 |
| Perry Williams | FB | 6'2" | 227 | 22 | | 6 |
| George Farmer | WR | 6'4" | 214 | 26 | | |
| Ike Hill | WR | 5'10" | 180 | 27 | | 6 |
| Bo Rather | WR | 6'1" | 180 | 23 | | 18 |
| Charlie Wade | WR | 5'10" | 163 | 24 | | 6 |
| Wayne Wheeler | WR | 6'2" | 180 | 25 | | |
| Jim Kelly | TE | 6'4" | 210 | 23 | | |
| Fred Pagac | TE | 6' | 220 | 22 | | |
| Bob Parsons | TE | 6'4" | 234 | 24 | | 6 |
| Mirro Roder | K | 6'1" | 228 | 30 | | 44 |

## MINNESOTA VIKINGS

### RUSHING
| Last Name | No. | Yds | Avg | TD |
|---|---|---|---|---|
| Foreman | 199 | 777 | 3.9 | 9 |
| Osborn | 131 | 514 | 3.9 | 4 |
| Reed | 62 | 215 | 3.5 | 0 |
| Marinaro | 44 | 124 | 2.8 | 1 |
| Tarkenton | 21 | 120 | 5.7 | 2 |
| B. Brown | 19 | 41 | 2.2 | 0 |
| McClanahan | 9 | 41 | 4.6 | 1 |
| Gilliam | 2 | 16 | 8.0 | 0 |
| Berry | 1 | 8 | 8.0 | 0 |

### RECEIVING
| Last Name | No. | Yds | Avg | TD |
|---|---|---|---|---|
| Foreman | 53 | 586 | 11 | 6 |
| Lash | 32 | 631 | 20 | 0 |
| Voigt | 32 | 268 | 8 | 5 |
| Osborn | 29 | 196 | 7 | 0 |
| Gilliam | 26 | 578 | 22 | 5 |
| Marinaro | 17 | 132 | 8 | 1 |
| Reed | 15 | 99 | 7 | 1 |
| McCullum | 7 | 138 | 20 | 3 |
| Kingsriter | 5 | 89 | 18 | 0 |
| Holland | 5 | 84 | 17 | 0 |
| B. Brown | 5 | 41 | 8 | 0 |
| Craig | 4 | 26 | 7 | 1 |
| McClanahan | 3 | 35 | 12 | 0 |
| N. Wright | 1 | 6 | 6 | 0 |

### PUNT RETURNS
| Last Name | No. | Yds | Avg | TD |
|---|---|---|---|---|
| Wallace | 25 | 191 | 8 | 0 |
| McCullum | 12 | 86 | 7 | 0 |
| Hilgenberg | 1 | -2 | -2 | 0 |

### KICKOFF RETURNS
| Last Name | No. | Yds | Avg | TD |
|---|---|---|---|---|
| McClanahan | 23 | 549 | 24 | 0 |
| McCullum | 12 | 300 | 25 | 0 |
| Gilliam | 3 | 86 | 29 | 0 |
| Wallace | 2 | 31 | 16 | 0 |
| Foreman | 1 | 30 | 30 | 0 |
| B. Brown | 3 | 19 | 6 | 0 |
| Osborn | 1 | 14 | 14 | 0 |
| Marinaro | 1 | 5 | 5 | 0 |

### PASSING — PUNTING — KICKING
**PASSING**
| Last Name | Att | Comp | % | Yds | Yd/Att | TD | Int-% | RK |
|---|---|---|---|---|---|---|---|---|
| Tarkenton | 351 | 199 | 57 | 2598 | 7.4 | 1/ | 12-3 | 3 |
| Berry | 48 | 34 | 71 | 305 | 6.4 | 5 | 1-2 | |
| Eischeid | 1 | 1 | 100 | 6 | 6.0 | 0 | 0-0 | |

**PUNTING**
| Last Name | No | Avg |
|---|---|---|
| Eischeid | 73 | 36.1 |

**KICKING**
| Last Name | XP | Att | % | FG | Att | % |
|---|---|---|---|---|---|---|
| Cox | 32 | 39 | 82 | 12 | 20 | 60 |

## DETROIT LIONS

### RUSHING
| Last Name | No. | Yds | Avg | TD |
|---|---|---|---|---|
| Taylor | 150 | 532 | 3.5 | 5 |
| Owens | 97 | 374 | 3.9 | 3 |
| Jones | 32 | 147 | 4.6 | 1 |
| Hooks | 44 | 143 | 3.3 | 0 |
| Landry | 22 | 95 | 4.3 | 1 |
| Crosswhite | 12 | 49 | 4.1 | 1 |
| Munson | 18 | 40 | 2.2 | 1 |
| Bussey | 9 | 22 | 2.4 | 0 |
| Jessie | 6 | 17 | 2.8 | 1 |
| Pickard | 1 | 5 | 5.0 | 0 |
| L. Walton | 2 | 3 | 1.5 | 0 |
| Wyche | 1 | 0 | 0.0 | 0 |

### RECEIVING
| Last Name | No. | Yds | Avg | TD |
|---|---|---|---|---|
| Jessie | 54 | 781 | 14 | 3 |
| C. Sanders | 42 | 532 | 13 | 3 |
| L. Walton | 31 | 404 | 13 | 3 |
| Taylor | 30 | 293 | 10 | 1 |
| Owens | 24 | 158 | 7 | 0 |
| Hooks | 9 | 53 | 6 | 0 |
| Pickard | 8 | 88 | 11 | 1 |
| Jones | 4 | 35 | 9 | 0 |
| Bussey | 4 | 24 | 6 | 0 |
| Jarvis | 3 | 87 | 29 | 0 |
| Crosswhite | 3 | 31 | 10 | 0 |
| Munson | 1 | -6 | -6 | 0 |

### PUNT RETURNS
| Last Name | No. | Yds | Avg | TD |
|---|---|---|---|---|
| Jauron | 17 | 286 | 17 | 0 |
| Jarvis | 5 | 62 | 12 | 0 |
| Barney | 5 | 37 | 7 | 0 |
| West | 6 | 32 | 5 | 0 |
| Capria | 1 | 12 | 12 | 0 |

### KICKOFF RETURNS
| Last Name | No. | Yds | Avg | TD |
|---|---|---|---|---|
| Jones | 38 | 927 | 24 | 0 |
| Jarvis | 5 | 90 | 18 | 0 |
| West | 4 | 71 | 18 | 0 |
| Bussey | 5 | 59 | 12 | 0 |
| Jessie | 2 | 55 | 28 | 0 |
| L. Walton | 1 | 22 | 22 | 0 |
| Jauron | 2 | 21 | 11 | 0 |
| Dennis | 1 | 18 | 18 | 0 |
| Crosswhite | 1 | 11 | 11 | 0 |
| Johnson | 1 | 0 | 0 | 0 |

### PASSING — PUNTING — KICKING
**PASSING**
| Last Name | Att | Comp | % | Yds | Yd/Att | TD | Int-% | RK |
|---|---|---|---|---|---|---|---|---|
| Munson | 292 | 166 | 57 | 1874 | 6.4 | 8 | 7-2 | 6 |
| Landry | 82 | 49 | 60 | 572 | 7.0 | 3 | 3-4 | |
| L. Walton | 2 | 1 | 50 | 29 | 14.5 | 0 | 0-0 | |
| Wyche | 1 | 0 | 0 | 0 | 0.0 | 0 | 1-100 | |

**PUNTING**
| Last Name | No | Avg |
|---|---|---|
| H. Weaver | 72 | 38.5 |
| Mann | 1 | 18.0 |

**KICKING**
| Last Name | XP | Att | % | FG | Att | % |
|---|---|---|---|---|---|---|
| Mann | 23 | 26 | 88 | 23 | 32 | 72 |

## GREEN BAY PACKERS

### RUSHING
| Last Name | No. | Yds | Avg | TD |
|---|---|---|---|---|
| Brockington | 266 | 883 | 3.3 | 5 |
| Lane | 137 | 362 | 2.6 | 3 |
| Goodman | 20 | 101 | 5.1 | 0 |
| Odom | 6 | 66 | 11.0 | 1 |
| Torkelson | 13 | 60 | 4.6 | 0 |
| Tagge | 18 | 58 | 3.2 | 0 |
| Hadl | 19 | 25 | 1.3 | 0 |
| Barty Smith | 9 | 19 | 2.1 | 0 |
| Walker | 1 | 18 | 18.0 | 0 |
| Concannon | 3 | 7 | 2.3 | 1 |
| Leigh | 1 | 0 | 0.0 | 0 |

### RECEIVING
| Last Name | No. | Yds | Avg | TD |
|---|---|---|---|---|
| Brockington | 43 | 314 | 7 | 0 |
| Lane | 34 | 315 | 9 | 3 |
| Staggers | 32 | 450 | 14 | 0 |
| McGeorge | 30 | 440 | 15 | 6 |
| Barty Smith | 20 | 294 | 15 | 1 |
| Odom | 15 | 249 | 17 | 1 |
| Payne | 5 | 63 | 13 | 0 |
| Goodman | 5 | 19 | 4 | 0 |
| Torkelson | 2 | 10 | 5 | 0 |
| Donohue | 1 | 8 | 8 | 0 |

### PUNT RETURNS
| Last Name | No. | Yds | Avg | TD |
|---|---|---|---|---|
| Staggers | 22 | 222 | 10 | 1 |
| Odom | 15 | 191 | 13 | 1 |
| Ellis | 3 | 3 | 1 | 0 |
| Hefner | 1 | 0 | 0 | 0 |
| Torkelson | 1 | 0 | 0 | 0 |

### KICKOFF RETURNS
| Last Name | No. | Yds | Avg | TD |
|---|---|---|---|---|
| Odom | 31 | 713 | 23 | 0 |
| Leigh | 11 | 251 | 23 | 0 |
| Goodman | 4 | 49 | 12 | 0 |
| Torkelson | 1 | 20 | 20 | 0 |
| Okoniewski | 2 | 11 | 6 | 0 |
| Krause | 1 | 6 | 6 | 0 |

### PASSING — PUNTING — KICKING
**PASSING**
| Last Name | Att | Comp | % | Yds | Yd/Att | TD | Int-% | RK |
|---|---|---|---|---|---|---|---|---|
| Hadl | 299 | 142 | 48 | 1752 | 5.9 | 8 | 14-5 | 12 |
| Tagge | 146 | 70 | 48 | 709 | 4.9 | 1 | 10-7 | 15 |
| Concannon | 54 | 28 | 52 | 381 | 7.1 | 1 | 3-6 | |
| Lane | 1 | 0 | 0 | 0 | 0.0 | 0 | 0-0 | |

**PUNTING**
| Last Name | No | Avg |
|---|---|---|
| Walker | 69 | 38.4 |

**KICKING**
| Last Name | XP | Att | % | FG | Att | % |
|---|---|---|---|---|---|---|
| Marcol | 19 | 19 | 100 | 25 | 39 | 64 |

## CHICAGO BEARS

### RUSHING
| Last Name | No. | Yds | Avg | TD |
|---|---|---|---|---|
| Grandberry | 144 | 475 | 3.3 | 2 |
| Garrett | 96 | 346 | 3.6 | 1 |
| Douglass | 36 | 229 | 6.4 | 1 |
| Williams | 74 | 218 | 2.9 | 1 |
| Harrison | 36 | 94 | 2.6 | 1 |
| Huff | 23 | 37 | 1.6 | 2 |
| Kosins | 8 | 30 | 3.8 | 1 |
| Barnes | 1 | 19 | 19.0 | 0 |
| C. Taylor | 9 | 18 | 2.0 | 1 |
| Gagnon | 1 | 15 | 15.0 | 0 |
| Rather | 2 | 10 | 5.0 | 0 |
| Hodgins | 1 | 3 | 3.0 | 0 |
| Rives | 1 | 2 | 2.0 | 0 |
| Pagac | 1 | -1 | -1.0 | 0 |
| Wade | 1 | -15 | -15.0 | 0 |

### RECEIVING
| Last Name | No. | Yds | Avg | TD |
|---|---|---|---|---|
| Wade | 39 | 683 | 18 | 1 |
| Grandberry | 30 | 212 | 7 | 0 |
| Rather | 29 | 400 | 14 | 3 |
| Williams | 25 | 167 | 7 | 0 |
| Garrett | 16 | 132 | 8 | 1 |
| Kelly | 8 | 100 | 13 | 0 |
| Hill | 7 | 109 | 16 | 1 |
| Pagac | 6 | 79 | 13 | 0 |
| Wheeler | 5 | 59 | 12 | 1 |
| Farmer | 5 | 45 | 9 | 0 |
| Harrison | 5 | 38 | 8 | 0 |
| Gagnon | 4 | 20 | 5 | 0 |
| C. Taylor | 3 | 23 | 8 | 0 |
| Parsons | 2 | 9 | 5 | 1 |
| Kosins | 1 | 3 | 3 | 0 |

### PUNT RETURNS
| Last Name | No. | Yds | Avg | TD |
|---|---|---|---|---|
| Hill | 33 | 183 | 6 | 0 |
| Knox | 5 | 35 | 7 | 0 |
| Van Valkenburg | 4 | 22 | 6 | 0 |
| Hodgins | 2 | 8 | 4 | 0 |

### KICKOFF RETURNS
| Last Name | No. | Yds | Avg | TD |
|---|---|---|---|---|
| Grandberry | 22 | 568 | 26 | 0 |
| C. Taylor | 27 | 567 | 21 | 0 |
| Pagac | 3 | 53 | 18 | 0 |
| Van Valkenburg | 2 | 42 | 21 | 0 |
| Gagnon | 2 | 32 | 16 | 0 |
| Gallagher | 1 | 16 | 16 | 0 |
| Kinney | 1 | 0 | 0 | 0 |

### PASSING — PUNTING — KICKING
**PASSING**
| Last Name | Att | Comp | % | Yds | Yd/Att | TD | Int--% | RK |
|---|---|---|---|---|---|---|---|---|
| Huff | 283 | 142 | 50 | 1663 | 5.9 | 6 | 17-6 | 13 |
| Douglass | 100 | 41 | 41 | 387 | 3.9 | 2 | 4-4 | |
| Barnes | 9 | 2 | 22 | 29 | 3.2 | 0 | 1-11 | |
| Hill | 1 | 0 | 0 | 0 | 0.0 | 0 | 0-0 | |
| Hodgins | 1 | 0 | 0 | 0 | 0.0 | 0 | 0-0 | |
| Parsons | 1 | 0 | 0 | 0 | 0.0 | 0 | 0-0 | |
| Rather | 1 | 0 | 0 | 0 | 0.0 | 0 | 0-0 | |

**PUNTING**
| Last Name | No | Avg |
|---|---|---|
| Parsons | 90 | 37.9 |
| Barnes | 1 | 27.0 |

**KICKING**
| Last Name | XP | Att | % | FG | Att | % |
|---|---|---|---|---|---|---|
| Roder | 17 | 17 | 100 | 9 | 13 | 69 |

## LOS ANGELES RAMS 10-4-0 Chuck Knox

**Scores of Each Game**

| | | |
|---|---|---|
| 17 | Denver | 10 |
| 24 | NEW ORLEANS | 0 |
| 14 | New England | 20 |
| 16 | DETROIT | 13 |
| 6 | Green Bay | 17 |
| 37 | SAN FRANCISCO | 14 |
| 20 | N.Y. Jets | 13 |
| 15 | San Francisco | 13 |
| 21 | ATLANTA | 0 |
| 7 | New Orleans | 20 |
| 20 | MINNESOTA | 17 |
| 30 | Atlanta | 7 |
| 17 | WASHINGTON | 23 |
| 19 | BUFFALO | 14 |

| Use Name | Pos. | Hgt | Wgt | Age | Int | Pts |
|---|---|---|---|---|---|---|
| Charlie Cowan | OT | 6'4" | 265 | 36 | | |
| Tim Stokes | OT | 6'5" | 252 | 24 | | |
| John Williams | OT | 6'3" | 256 | 28 | | |
| Tom Mack | OG | 6'3" | 250 | 30 | | |
| Joe Scibelli | OG | 6'1" | 255 | 35 | | |
| Rich Saul | C-OG | 6'3" | 235 | 26 | | |
| Bill Curry | C | 6'2" | 235 | 31 | | |
| Ken Iman | C | 6'1" | 240 | 35 | | |
| Fred Dryer | DE | 6'6" | 240 | 28 | | |
| Jack Youngblood | DE | 6'4" | 255 | 24 | | |
| Cody Jones | DT-DE | 6'5" | 240 | 23 | | |
| Larry Brooks | DT | 6'3" | 255 | 24 | | |
| Bill Nelson | DT | 6'7" | 270 | 26 | | |
| Merlin Olsen | DT | 6'5" | 270 | 33 | | |
| Phil Olsen | DT | 6'5" | 265 | 26 | | |
| Ken Geddes | LB | 6'3" | 235 | 26 | 2 | |
| Jim Peterson | LB | 6'5" | 240 | 24 | | |
| Jack Reynolds | LB | 6'1" | 232 | 26 | | |
| Isiah Robertson | LB | 6'3" | 225 | 25 | 2 | |
| Bob Stein | LB | 6'2" | 235 | 26 | | |
| Jim Youngblood | LB | 6'3" | 240 | 24 | | |
| Al Clark | DB | 6' | 185 | 26 | | |
| Bill Drake | DB | 6'1" | 195 | 24 | | |
| Dave Elmendorf | DB | 6'1" | 195 | 25 | 7 | 12 |
| Eddie McMillan | DB | 6' | 190 | 22 | | |
| Tony Plummer | DB | 5'11" | 190 | 27 | | |
| Steve Preece | DB | 6'1" | 195 | 27 | 3 | |
| Bill Simpson | DB | 6'1" | 180 | 22 | 1 | |
| Charlie Stukes | DB | 6'3" | 212 | 30 | 7 | |
| James Harris | QB | 6'3" | 210 | 27 | | 30 |
| Ron Jaworski | QB | 6'2" | 185 | 23 | | 6 |
| Jim Bertelsen | HB | 5'11" | 205 | 24 | | 12 |
| Larry McCutcheon | HB | 6'1" | 205 | 24 | | 30 |
| Bob Scribner | HB | 6' | 200 | 23 | | 6 |
| Cullen Bryant | HB | 6'1" | 218 | 23 | | 6 |
| Tony Baker | FB | 5'11" | 215 | 29 | | 30 |
| Les Josephson | FB | 6' | 207 | 31 | | |
| John Cappelletti | HB-FB | 6'1" | 217 | 22 | | |
| Harold Jackson | WR | 5'10" | 175 | 28 | | 30 |
| Willie McGee | WR | 5'11" | 178 | 24 | | |
| Lance Rentzel | WR | 6'2" | 202 | 30 | | 6 |
| Jack Snow | WR | 6'2" | 190 | 31 | | 18 |
| Pat Curran | TE | 6'3" | 238 | 28 | | |
| Bob Klein | TE | 6'5" | 235 | 27 | | 24 |
| Terry Nelson | TE | 6'2" | 230 | 23 | | |
| Mike Burke | K | 5'10" | 188 | 24 | | 1 |
| Dave Chapple (to NE) | K | 6' | 195 | 27 | | |
| David Ray | K | 6' | 195 | 29 | | 52 |

Rick Kay – Knee Injury

## SAN FRANCISCO FORTY-NINERS 6-8-0 Dick Nolan

| | | |
|---|---|---|
| 17 | New Orleans | 13 |
| 16 | Atlanta | 10 |
| 3 | CINCINNATI | 21 |
| 9 | ST. LOUIS | 34 |
| 14 | Detroit | 17 |
| 14 | Los Angeles | 37 |
| 24 | OAKLAND | 35 |
| 13 | LOS ANGELES | 15 |
| 14 | Dallas | 20 |
| 34 | Chicago | 0 |
| 27 | ATLANTA | 0 |
| 0 | Cleveland | 7 |
| 7 | GREEN BAY | 6 |
| 35 | NEW ORLEANS | 2 |

| Use Name | Pos. | Hgt | Wgt | Age | Int | Pts |
|---|---|---|---|---|---|---|
| Cas Banaszek | OT | 6'3" | 255 | 28 | | |
| Keith Fahnhorst | OT | 6'6" | 255 | 22 | | |
| Len Rohde | OT | 6'4" | 248 | 36 | | |
| Jean Barrett | C-OT | 6'6" | 254 | 23 | | |
| Bobby Penchion | OG | 6'5" | 252 | 25 | | |
| Woody Peoples | OG | 6'2" | 252 | 31 | | |
| Randy Beisler | OT-OG | 6'4" | 247 | 29 | | |
| John Watson | OT-OG | 6'4" | 245 | 25 | | |
| Forrest Blue | C | 6'5" | 265 | 28 | | |
| Cedrick Hardman | DE | 6'3" | 258 | 25 | | |
| Tommy Hart | DE | 6'4" | 260 | 23 | | |
| Bill Belk | DT-DE | 6'3" | 248 | 28 | 6 | |
| Rolf Krueger | DT-DE | 6'4" | 253 | 27 | | |
| Mike Raines | DT-DE | 6'5" | 255 | 20 | | |
| Stan Hindman | DT | 6'3" | 245 | 30 | | |
| Bob Hoskins | DT | 6'2" | 250 | 28 | | |
| Bill Sandifer | DT | 6'6" | 278 | 22 | | |
| Willie Harper | LB | 6'2" | 220 | 24 | | |
| Tom Hull | LB | 6'3" | 230 | 22 | | |
| Billy McKoy | LB | 6'3" | 226 | 26 | | |
| Frank Nunley | LB | 6'2" | 234 | 28 | 4 | |
| Skip Vanderbundt | LB | 6'3" | 223 | 27 | 2 | |
| Dave Wilcox | LB | 6'3" | 240 | 31 | 1 | 6 |
| Caesar Belser | DB | 6' | 205 | 29 | | |
| Windlan Hall | DB | 5'11" | 175 | 24 | | |
| Hugo Hollas | DB | 6'1" | 190 | 29 | | |
| Mike Holmes | DB | 6'2" | 193 | 23 | 3 | |
| Jim Johnson | DB | 6'2" | 185 | 36 | 3 | |
| Ralph McGill | DB | 5'11" | 183 | 24 | 5 | |
| Mel Phillips | DB | 6' | 190 | 32 | 1 | |
| John Saunders | DB | 6'3" | 196 | 24 | | |
| Bruce Taylor | DB | 6' | 190 | 26 | 1 | |
| Dennis Morrison | QB | 6'3" | 211 | 23 | | |
| Tom Owen | QB | 6'1" | 194 | 21 | | 6 |
| Joe Reed | QB | 6'1" | 195 | 26 | | |
| Steve Spurrier | QB | 6'2" | 198 | 29 | | |
| Manfred Moore | HB | 6' | 194 | 23 | | 12 |
| Del Williams | HB | 6' | 195 | 23 | | 18 |
| Wilbur Jackson | HB | 6'1" | 215 | 22 | | 12 |
| Sammy Johnson | FB | 6' | 223 | 21 | | 12 |
| Larry Schreiber | HB-FB | 6' | 210 | 27 | | 24 |
| Danny Abramowicz | WR | 6'1" | 193 | 29 | | 6 |
| Terry Beasley | WR | 5'10" | 182 | 24 | | 18 |
| Mike Bettiga | WR | 6'3" | 193 | 24 | | |
| Gene Washington | WR | 6'1" | 185 | 27 | | 36 |
| Bob West | WR | 6'4" | 218 | 23 | | |
| Tom Mitchell | TE | 6'2" | 215 | 30 | | |
| Ted Kwalick | WR-TE | 6'4" | 228 | 27 | | 12 |
| Bruce Gossett | K | 6'2" | 230 | 31 | | 58 |
| Tom Wittum | K | 6'1" | 190 | 24 | | |

Ed Hardy — Injury

## NEW ORLEANS SAINTS 5-9-0 John North

| | | |
|---|---|---|
| 13 | SAN FRANCISCO | 17 |
| 0 | Los Angeles | 24 |
| 14 | ATLANTA | 13 |
| 10 | Chicago | 24 |
| 17 | Denver | 33 |
| 13 | Atlanta | 3 |
| 14 | PHILADELPHIA | 10 |
| 14 | Detroit | 19 |
| 0 | MIAMI | 21 |
| 20 | LOS ANGELES | 7 |
| 7 | PITTSBURGH | 28 |
| 9 | Minnesota | 29 |
| 14 | ST. LOUIS | 10 |
| 2 | San Francisco | 35 |

| Use Name | Pos. | Hgt | Wgt | Age | Int | Pts |
|---|---|---|---|---|---|---|
| Phil LaPorta | OT | 6'4" | 256 | 21 | | |
| John Mooring | OT | 6'5" | 255 | 27 | | |
| Don Morrison | OT | 6'5" | 260 | 24 | | |
| Jake Kupp | OG | 6'3" | 248 | 32 | | |
| Rocky Rasley | OG | 6'3" | 255 | 27 | | |
| Emanuel Zanders | OG | 6'1" | 263 | 23 | | |
| John Didion | C | 6'4" | 255 | 26 | | |
| Dave Thompson | OT-C | 6'4" | 260 | 25 | | |
| Steve Baumgartner | DE | 6'7" | 260 | 23 | | |
| Andy Dorris | DE | 6'4" | 230 | 23 | | |
| Billy Newsome | DE | 6'4" | 260 | 26 | | |
| Joe Owens | DE | 6'2" | 250 | 27 | | |
| Derland Moore | DT | 6'4" | 260 | 22 | | |
| Elex Price | DT | 6'3" | 260 | 24 | | |
| Bob Pollard | DE-DT | 6'3" | 250 | 25 | | |
| Don Coleman | LB | 6'2" | 222 | 21 | | |
| Wayne Colman | LB | 6'1" | 220 | 28 | 1 | |
| Joe Federspiel | LB | 6'1" | 235 | 24 | 1 | |
| Rick Kingrea | LB | 6'1" | 230 | 25 | | |
| Jim Merlo | LB | 6'1" | 225 | 22 | | |
| Rick Middleton | LB | 6'2" | 228 | 22 | | |
| Greg Boyd | DB | 6'2" | 200 | 22 | | |
| Chris Farasopolous | DB | 5'11" | 190 | 25 | 1 | |
| Johnny Fuller | DB | 6' | 185 | 28 | 1 | |
| Ernie Jackson | DB | 5'10" | 175 | 24 | 4 | |
| Bivian Lee | DB | 6'3" | 200 | 26 | | |
| Jerry Moore | DB | 6'3" | 208 | 24 | 1 | |
| Tom Myers | DB | 5'11" | 184 | 23 | 3 | |
| Terry Schmidt | DB | 6' | 180 | 22 | 4 | 6 |
| Mo Spencer (from StL) | DB | 6' | 175 | 22 | | |
| Larry Cipa | QB | 6'3" | 209 | 21 | | 6 |
| Archie Manning | QB | 6'3" | 215 | 25 | | 6 |
| Bobby Scott | QB | 6'1" | 200 | 25 | | |
| Alvin Maxon | HB | 5'11" | 205 | 21 | | 18 |
| Howard Stevens | HB | 5'5" | 165 | 24 | | 6 |
| Bill Butler | FB-HB | 6' | 210 | 27 | | |
| Jess Phillips | FB-HB | 6'1" | 210 | 27 | | 12 |
| Jack DeGrenier | FB | 6'1" | 225 | 22 | | |
| Odell Lawson | FB | 6' | 205 | 26 | | |
| Rod McNeill | FB | 6'2" | 220 | 23 | | 6 |
| Dave Davis | WR | 6' | 175 | 26 | | |
| Sam Havrilak | WR | 6'2" | 195 | 26 | | |
| Earl McCullouch | WR | 5'11" | 175 | 28 | | |
| Bob Newland | WR | 6'2" | 190 | 25 | | 12 |
| Joel Parker | WR | 6'5" | 212 | 22 | | 24 |
| Speedy Thomas | WR | 6'1" | 170 | 27 | | |
| Bob Wicks | WR | 6'3" | 205 | 24 | | |
| Richard Williams | WR | 5'11" | 170 | 22 | | |
| John Beasley | TE | 6'3" | 228 | 29 | | |
| Len Garrett | TE | 6'3" | 230 | 25 | | |
| Paul Seal | TE | 6'4" | 222 | 22 | | 24 |
| Tom Blanchard | K | 6' | 190 | 26 | | |
| Donnie Gibbs | K | 6'2" | 205 | 28 | | |
| Bill McClard | K | 5'10" | 202 | 22 | | 46 |

## ATLANTA FALCONS 3-11-0 Norm Van Brocklin Marion Campbell

| | | |
|---|---|---|
| 0 | DALLAS | 24 |
| 10 | SAN FRANCISCO | 16 |
| 3 | New Orleans | 14 |
| 14 | N.Y. Giants | 7 |
| 13 | CHICAGO | 10 |
| 3 | NEW ORLEANS | 14 |
| 17 | Pittsburgh | 24 |
| 7 | Miami | 42 |
| 0 | Los Angeles | 21 |
| 7 | BALTIMORE | 17 |
| 0 | San Francisco | 27 |
| 7 | LOS ANGELES | 30 |
| 10 | Minnesota | 23 |
| 10 | GREEN BAY | 3 |

| Use Name | Pos. | Hgt | Wgt | Age | Int | Pts |
|---|---|---|---|---|---|---|
| Nick Bebout | OT | 6'5" | 260 | 23 | | |
| George Kunz | OT | 6'5" | 268 | 27 | | |
| Dennis Havig | OG | 6'2" | 256 | 25 | | |
| Jim Miller | OG | 6'3" | 240 | 25 | | |
| Royce Smith | OG | 6'3" | 250 | 25 | | |
| Len Gotshalk | OT-OG | 6'4" | 260 | 24 | | |
| Ted Fritsch | C | 6'2" | 242 | 24 | | |
| Paul Ryczek | C | 6'2" | 230 | 22 | | |
| Jeff Van Note | C | 6'2" | 247 | 28 | | |
| Claude Humphrey | DE | 6'5" | 265 | 30 | | |
| John Zook | DE | 6'5" | 250 | 26 | 1 | |
| Larry Bailey | DT | 6'4" | 238 | 22 | | |
| Mike Lewis | DT | 6'3" | 260 | 24 | | |
| Rosie Manning | DT | 6'5" | 255 | 23 | | |
| Mike Tilleman | DT | 6'5" | 278 | 30 | | |
| Chuck Walker | DT | 6'2" | 260 | 33 | | |
| Greg Brezina | LB | 6'2" | 220 | 28 | 1 | |
| Don Hansen | LB | 6'3" | 228 | 30 | 1 | |
| Ken Mitchell | LB | 6'1" | 224 | 26 | | |
| Tommy Nobis | LB | 6'2" | 243 | 30 | 1 | |
| Dick Palmer | LB | 6'2" | 232 | 28 | | |
| Lonnie Warwick | DB | 6'3" | 240 | 32 | | |
| Ray Brown | DB | 6'2" | 202 | 25 | 8 | 6 |
| Rick Byas | DB | 5'9" | 180 | 23 | | |
| Ray Easterling | DB | 6' | 192 | 24 | | |
| Clarence Ellis | DB | 5'11" | 190 | 24 | 3 | |
| Tom Hayes | DB | 6'1" | 198 | 28 | 1 | |
| Rudy Holmes | DB | 5'10" | 178 | 21 | | |
| Rolland Lawrence | DB | 5'10" | 180 | 23 | 1 | |
| Bob Lee | QB | 6'2" | 200 | 28 | | 6 |
| Kim McQuilken | QB | 6'2" | 203 | 23 | | |
| Pat Sullivan | QB | 6' | 200 | 24 | | |
| Dave Hampton | HB | 6'2" | 207 | 27 | | 12 |
| Molly McGee | HB | 5'10" | 184 | 21 | | |
| Haskel Stanback | HB | 6' | 210 | 22 | | 6 |
| Vince Kendrick | FB | 6' | 223 | 22 | | |
| Eddie Ray | FB | 6'1" | 240 | 27 | | |
| Art Malone | HB-FB | 5'11" | 216 | 26 | | 12 |
| Ken Burrow | WR | 6' | 190 | 26 | | 6 |
| Al Dodd | WR | 6' | 178 | 29 | | 6 |
| Tom Geredine | WR | 6'2" | 190 | 24 | | |
| Louie Neal | WR | 6'4" | 215 | 23 | | |
| Gerald Tinker | WR | 5'9" | 170 | 23 | | 6 |
| Henry Childs (to NO) | TE | 6'2" | 223 | 23 | | |
| Larry Mialik | TE | 6'2" | 226 | 23 | | |
| Jim Mitchell | TE | 6'2" | 236 | 26 | | 6 |
| John James | K | 6'3" | 200 | 25 | | |
| Nick Mike-Mayer | K | 5'8" | 187 | 24 | | |

## LOS ANGELES RAMS

### RUSHING

| Last Name | No. | Yds | Avg | TD |
|---|---|---|---|---|
| McCutcheon | 236 | 1109 | 4.7 | 3 |
| Bertelsen | 127 | 419 | 3.3 | 2 |
| Cappelletti | 55 | 198 | 3.6 | 0 |
| Baker | 53 | 135 | 2.5 | 5 |
| Harris | 42 | 112 | 2.7 | 5 |
| Josephson | 11 | 35 | 3.2 | 0 |
| Jaworski | 7 | 34 | 4.9 | 1 |
| Bryant | 10 | 24 | 2.4 | 0 |
| Scribner | 9 | 24 | 2.7 | 0 |
| Snow | 1 | 13 | 13.0 | 0 |
| Jackson | 1 | 4 | 4.0 | 0 |
| T. Nelson | 1 | 3 | 3.0 | 0 |
| Preece | 1 | −4 | −4.0 | 0 |
| Rentzel | 1 | −9 | −9.0 | 0 |

### RECEIVING

| Last Name | No. | Yds | Avg | TD |
|---|---|---|---|---|
| McCutcheon | 39 | 408 | 11 | 2 |
| Jackson | 30 | 514 | 17 | 5 |
| Snow | 24 | 397 | 17 | 3 |
| Klein | 24 | 336 | 14 | 4 |
| Bertelsen | 20 | 175 | 9 | 0 |
| Rentzel | 18 | 396 | 22 | 1 |
| Cappelletti | 6 | 35 | 6 | 0 |
| Baker | 4 | 65 | 16 | 0 |
| Scribner | 2 | 28 | 14 | 1 |
| Bryant | 2 | 14 | 7 | 0 |

### PUNT RETURNS

| Last Name | No. | Yds | Avg | TD |
|---|---|---|---|---|
| Bryant | 17 | 171 | 10 | 0 |
| Elmendorf | 17 | 134 | 8 | 0 |
| Bertelsen | 11 | 132 | 12 | 0 |
| Scribner | 8 | 70 | 9 | 0 |

### KICKOFF RETURNS

| Last Name | No. | Yds | Avg | TD |
|---|---|---|---|---|
| Bryant | 23 | 617 | 27 | 1 |
| McGee | 12 | 288 | 24 | 0 |
| Cappelletti | 2 | 17 | 9 | 0 |
| Curran | 1 | 16 | 16 | 0 |
| Scribner | 1 | 0 | 0 | 0 |
| Youngblood | 1 | 0 | 0 | 0 |

### PASSING – PUNTING – KICKING

Statistics

| PASSING | Att | Comp | % | Yds | Yd/Att | TD | Int–% | RK |
|---|---|---|---|---|---|---|---|---|
| Harris | 198 | 106 | 54 | 1544 | 7.8 | 11 | 6– 3 | 2 |
| Jaworski | 24 | 10 | 42 | 144 | 6.0 | 0 | 1– 4 | |
| Burke | 1 | 0 | 0 | 0 | 0.0 | 0 | 0– 0 | |

| PUNTING | No | Avg |
|---|---|---|
| Chapple | 55 | 36.3 |
| Burke | 46 | 37.0 |

| KICKING | XP | Att | % | FG | Att | % |
|---|---|---|---|---|---|---|
| Ray | 25 | 31 | 81 | 9 | 16 | 56 |
| Burke | 1 | 3 | 33 | 0 | 0 | — |

## SAN FRANCISCO FORTY-NINERS

### RUSHING

| Last Name | No. | Yds | Avg | TD |
|---|---|---|---|---|
| Jackson | 174 | 705 | 4.1 | 0 |
| Schreiber | 174 | 634 | 3.6 | 3 |
| Johnson | 44 | 237 | 5.4 | 2 |
| Williams | 36 | 201 | 5.6 | 3 |
| Reed | 16 | 107 | 6.7 | 0 |
| Owen | 16 | 36 | 2.3 | 1 |
| Moore | 10 | 24 | 2.4 | 1 |
| Wittum | 1 | 13 | 13.0 | 0 |
| Washington | 2 | 4 | 2.0 | 0 |
| Morrison | 1 | 0 | 0.0 | 0 |
| Mitchell | 1 | −2 | −2.0 | 0 |
| Beasley | 1 | −3 | −3.0 | 0 |

### RECEIVING

| Last Name | No. | Yds | Avg | TD |
|---|---|---|---|---|
| Schreiber | 30 | 217 | 7 | 1 |
| Washington | 29 | 615 | 21 | 6 |
| Abramowicz | 25 | 369 | 15 | 1 |
| Jackson | 23 | 190 | 8 | 2 |
| Mitchell | 19 | 262 | 14 | 0 |
| Beasley | 15 | 253 | 15 | 3 |
| Kwalick | 13 | 231 | 18 | 2 |
| Johnson | 11 | 106 | 10 | 0 |
| Moore | 2 | 29 | 15 | 0 |
| Williams | 1 | 9 | 9 | 0 |

### PUNT RETURNS

| Last Name | No. | Yds | Avg | TD |
|---|---|---|---|---|
| McGill | 20 | 166 | 8 | 0 |
| Moore | 5 | 149 | 30 | 1 |
| Holmes | 9 | 45 | 5 | 0 |
| Taylor | 10 | 38 | 4 | 0 |

### KICKOFF RETURNS

| Last Name | No. | Yds | Avg | TD |
|---|---|---|---|---|
| Holmes | 25 | 612 | 25 | 0 |
| Moore | 18 | 398 | 22 | 0 |
| Jackson | 5 | 103 | 21 | 0 |
| Johnson | 2 | 31 | 16 | 0 |
| West | 1 | 0 | 0 | 0 |

### PASSING – PUNTING – KICKING

| PASSING | Att | Comp | % | Yds | Yd/Att | TD | Int–% | RK |
|---|---|---|---|---|---|---|---|---|
| Owen | 184 | 88 | 48 | 1327 | 7.2 | 10 | 15– 8 | 11 |
| Reed | 74 | 29 | 39 | 316 | 4.3 | 2 | 7–10 | |
| Morrison | 51 | 21 | 41 | 227 | 4.5 | 1 | 5–10 | |
| Spurrier | 3 | 1 | 33 | 2 | 0.7 | 0 | 0– 0 | |
| Abramowicz | 1 | 1 | 100 | 41 | 41.0 | 0 | 0– 0 | |

| PUNTING | No | Avg |
|---|---|---|
| Wittum | 68 | 41.2 |
| Gossett | 2 | 28.0 |

| KICKING | XP | Att | % | FG | Att | % |
|---|---|---|---|---|---|---|
| Gossett | 25 | 27 | 93 | 11 | 24 | 46 |

## NEW ORLEANS SAINTS

### RUSHING

| Last Name | No. | Yds | Avg | TD |
|---|---|---|---|---|
| Maxson | 165 | 714 | 4.3 | 2 |
| Phillips | 174 | 556 | 3.2 | 0 |
| Manning | 28 | 204 | 7.3 | 1 |
| Stevens | 43 | 190 | 4.4 | 1 |
| DeGrenier | 33 | 110 | 3.3 | 0 |
| McNeil | 22 | 90 | 4.1 | 1 |
| Butler | 21 | 74 | 3.5 | 0 |
| Cipa | 12 | 35 | 2.9 | 1 |
| Seal | 2 | 7 | 3.5 | 1 |
| Parker | 2 | 2 | 1.0 | 0 |
| Scott | 1 | 1 | 1.0 | 0 |

### RECEIVING

| Last Name | No. | Yds | Avg | TD |
|---|---|---|---|---|
| Maxon | 42 | 294 | 7 | 1 |
| Parker | 41 | 455 | 11 | 4 |
| Seal | 32 | 466 | 15 | 2 |
| Newland | 27 | 490 | 18 | 2 |
| Stevens | 13 | 81 | 6 | 0 |
| Phillips | 11 | 55 | 5 | 0 |
| Beasley | 5 | 85 | 17 | 0 |
| McNeil | 5 | 64 | 13 | 0 |
| DeGrenier | 4 | 13 | 3 | 0 |
| Butler | 2 | 3 | 2 | 0 |
| Havrilak | 1 | 23 | 23 | 0 |
| McCullouch | 1 | 5 | 5 | 0 |
| Thomas | 1 | 3 | 3 | 0 |

### PUNT RETURNS

| Last Name | No. | Yds | Avg | TD |
|---|---|---|---|---|
| Stevens | 37 | 376 | 10 | 0 |
| Farasopoulos | 3 | 36 | 12 | 0 |
| Jackson | 2 | 3 | 2 | 0 |
| McNeil | 1 | 0 | 0 | 0 |

### KICKOFF RETURNS

| Last Name | No. | Yds | Avg | TD |
|---|---|---|---|---|
| Stevens | 33 | 749 | 23 | 0 |
| Phillips | 7 | 124 | 18 | 0 |
| Jackson | 1 | 27 | 27 | 0 |
| Schmidt | 1 | 23 | 23 | 0 |
| Kingrea | 1 | 22 | 22 | 0 |
| Federspeil | 2 | 20 | 10 | 0 |
| Lawson | 1 | 20 | 20 | 0 |
| Middleton | 2 | 18 | 9 | 0 |
| Davis | 1 | 14 | 14 | 0 |
| Coleman | 2 | 13 | 7 | 0 |
| Butler | 1 | 12 | 12 | 0 |
| Spencer | 1 | −2 | −2 | 0 |

### PASSING – PUNTING – KICKING

| PASSING | Att | Comp | % | Yds | Yd/Att | TD | Int–% | RK |
|---|---|---|---|---|---|---|---|---|
| Manning | 261 | 134 | 51 | 1429 | 5.5 | 6 | 16– 6 | 14 |
| Scott | 71 | 31 | 44 | 366 | 5.2 | 4 | 4– 6 | |
| Cipa | 55 | 20 | 36 | 242 | 4.4 | 0 | 0– 0 | |
| McClard | 1 | 0 | 0 | 0 | 0.0 | 0 | 1–100 | |
| Parker | 1 | 0 | 0 | 0 | 0.0 | 0 | 0– 0 | |

| PUNTING | No | Avg |
|---|---|---|
| Blanchard | 88 | 42.1 |
| Gibbs | 3 | 33.0 |

| KICKING | XP | Att | % | FG | Att | % |
|---|---|---|---|---|---|---|
| McClard | 19 | 20 | 95 | 9 | 16 | 56 |

## ATLANTA FALCONS

### RUSHING

| Last Name | No. | Yds | Avg | TD |
|---|---|---|---|---|
| Hampton | 127 | 464 | 3.7 | 2 |
| Malone | 116 | 410 | 3.5 | 2 |
| Stanback | 57 | 235 | 4.1 | 1 |
| Ray | 46 | 139 | 3.0 | 0 |
| Lee | 19 | 99 | 5.2 | 1 |
| Kendrick | 17 | 71 | 4.2 | 0 |
| McGee | 7 | 30 | 4.3 | 0 |
| J. Mitchell | 3 | 21 | 7.0 | 0 |
| Sullivan | 3 | 19 | 6.3 | 0 |
| Tinker | 2 | 5 | 2.5 | 0 |
| McQuilken | 2 | 1 | 0.5 | 0 |
| Neal | 1 | −1 | −1.0 | 0 |

### RECEIVING

| Last Name | No. | Yds | Avg | TD |
|---|---|---|---|---|
| Burrow | 34 | 545 | 16 | 1 |
| J. Mitchell | 30 | 479 | 16 | 1 |
| Malone | 28 | 168 | 6 | 0 |
| Hampton | 13 | 111 | 9 | 0 |
| Dodd | 12 | 130 | 11 | 1 |
| Kendrick | 12 | 86 | 7 | 1 |
| Ray | 10 | 43 | 4 | 0 |
| Neal | 8 | 99 | 12 | 0 |
| Stanback | 8 | 39 | 5 | 0 |
| Geredine | 4 | 69 | 17 | 0 |
| Tinker | 1 | 12 | 12 | 0 |

### PUNT RETURNS

| Last Name | No. | Yds | Avg | TD |
|---|---|---|---|---|
| Dodd | 27 | 344 | 13 | 0 |
| Tinker | 14 | 195 | 14 | 1 |
| Brown | 9 | 96 | 11 | 0 |
| Fritsch | 1 | 0 | 0 | 0 |

### KICKOFF RETURNS

| Last Name | No. | Yds | Avg | TD |
|---|---|---|---|---|
| Tinker | 29 | 704 | 24 | 0 |
| Geredine | 9 | 219 | 24 | 0 |
| McGee | 8 | 167 | 21 | 0 |
| Byas | 5 | 136 | 27 | 0 |
| Mitchell | 4 | 36 | 9 | 0 |
| Easterling | 2 | 34 | 17 | 0 |
| Childs | 1 | 0 | 0 | 0 |
| Fritsch | 1 | 0 | 0 | 0 |
| Ryczek | 1 | 0 | 0 | 0 |

### PASSING – PUNTING – KICKING

| PASSING | Att | Comp | % | Yds | Yd/Att | TD | Int–% | RK |
|---|---|---|---|---|---|---|---|---|
| Lee | 172 | 78 | 45 | 852 | 5.5 | 3 | 14– 8 | 16 |
| Sullivan | 105 | 48 | 46 | 556 | 5.3 | 1 | 8– 8 | |
| McQuilken | 79 | 34 | 43 | 373 | 4.7 | 0 | 9–11 | |

| PUNTING | No | Avg |
|---|---|---|
| James | 96 | 40.5 |

| KICKING | XP | Att | % | FG | Att | % |
|---|---|---|---|---|---|---|
| Mike-Mayer | 12 | 12 | 100 | 9 | 16 | 56 |

# 1974 A.F.C. Same Game, Different Rules

The N.F.L. this year took some steps to return to its games the offensive fireworks that had been so common in the 1950's and 1960's. To promote more passing, the "bump-and-run" method of pass defense was closely regulated. To cut down on the number of field goals and increase the emphasis on touchdowns, the league fathers moved the goal posts back to the rear of the end zone, where they had stood all along in college ball and where they had stood in pro ball until being moved up to the goal line in 1933. Another change brought missed field goals that travel into the end zone back out to the line of scrimmage. And an extra sudden-death period was added for all tie games during the season, a measure heretofore reserved for playoff games. All these moves did produce some additional points and a couple of overtime games, but the main shift in tactics was to a new reliance on coffin-corner punting, with an eye to keeping opponents bottled up in a poor field position all game long.

## EASTERN DIVISION

**Miami Dolphins**—The signing of Larry Csonka, Paul Warfield, Jim Kiick, Tim Foley, and Bob Kuechenberg to future contracts with the new World Football League caused some bitterness in the Dolphin family; but coach Don Shula decided to play his best players regardless of where they might be in the future. When the Dolphins got off to a lack-lustre start, it was injuries, not dissension, at the heart of the team's problems. Csonka, Warfield, Wayne Moore, Doug Swift, Mercury Morris, and Manny Fernandez all suffered through injury-cursed seasons to throw the finely-tuned Dolphin machine out of gear. But subs like Nat Moore, Don Nottingham, and Ben Malone came through when thrown into the breach, and the Dolphins soon were playing in their usual championship style. A 35–28 victory over Buffalo on November 17 put Miami back into first place, and the A.F.C. held on to it the rest of the way.

**Buffalo Bills**—O.J. Simpson couldn't duplicate his record-setting performance of last year, but he still raced for 1125 yards despite a sore knee. The Buffalo attack had an added dimension this season, as young quarterback Joe Ferguson passed the ball much more often to wide receivers like ex-Cardinal Ahmad Rashad. A sound defense featuring backs Bobby James and Tony Greene complemented the powerful offense and helped boost the Bills into first place with a 29–28 win over New England on October 20. Although the Dolphins knocked the Bills out of the top slot one month later, Buffalo still marched into the playoffs as the wild-card team.

**New England Patriots**—The Pats began the season with a reorganized defense and an almost unbelievable stretch of good football. The Patriots beat the defending champion Dolphins 34–24 on opening day, and chalked up another big upset by upending the highly-touted Rams 20–14 two weeks later. The team's opening spurt brought in four straight wins and six out of the first seven. But then injuries started decimating the New England offense. Darryl Stingley, Reggie Rucker, Bob Windsor, and Sam Cunningham all went out of the lineup, and the crippled Patriot squad faltered badly down the stretch. But aside from the steady work of quarterback Jim Plunkett and defensive tackle Julius Adams, the star of the season was Mack Herron, the diminutive halfback who set a new record for total yardage gained in all categories combined for one season.

**New York Jets**—Charley Winner succeeded his father-in-law Weeb Ewbank as head coach this year, but a 1–7 start made it debatable if he would be staying very long in New York. But then Joe Namath led his mates to a 26–20 overtime win over the rival Giants, and the Jets suddenly came together. The team won its last six games to reach the .500 level and reclaim some of the dignity lost in the horrendous first part of the schedule.

**Baltimore Colts**—The year started on a down note, as All-Pro linebacker Ted Hendricks signed a future contract with the W.F.L. and was then traded at a dirt-cheap price to Green Bay by General Manager Joe Thomas. The personnel situation on the Colt roster was even worse than last season, and coach Howard Schnellenberger was fired after three games, with his fate sealed by an argument he had with owner Robert Irsay over whether Marty Domres or Bert Jones should play quarterback. Thomas doubled as coach for the rest of the year but could direct the team to only two wins.

## CENTRAL DIVISION

**Pittsburgh Steelers**—The Steelers' strong 6–0 preseason showing was less surprising than Joe Gilliam's winning the starting quarterback job away from Terry Bradshaw. Gilliam faltered in mid-season and was benched in favor of Bradshaw, but the Steelers had so much talent that they easily captured first place in the Central Division. The Steelers had a solid offensive line, a copious supply of wide receivers, a superb fullback in Franco Harris, and a brutally effective defense featuring Mean Joe Greene, L.C. Greenwood, Andy Russell, and Jack Ham. The biggest

bonus of the year was the play of halfback Rocky Bleier, who had recovered well enough from leg injuries suffered in the Vietnam war to claim a starting job in the offensive backfield.

**Cincinnati Bengals**—Passer Ken Anderson enjoyed a fine season, but a variety of circumstances reduced the Bengals to a 7–7 campaign. The defense never recovered from the loss of All-Pro middle linebacker Bill Bergey, whom coach Paul Brown traded to Philadelphia after he signed a future contract with the W.F.L. Injuries did in the offense. The backfield lost Booby Clark to foot and hand injuries and Essex Johnson to a bad knee, while the line suffered from Vern Holland's broken leg and Bob Johnson's broken ankle.

**Houston Oilers**—Coach Sid Gillman patched up the pitiful Oilers and turned out a respectable football team. The process needed time to take effect, as the Oilers won their opening game and then dropped five straight. During the early part of the campaign, Gillman also had to endure the efforts of defensive tackle John Matuszak to jump to the W.F.L. He actually did jump to the Houston Texans of that league, but was served with a restraining order right on the field in the middle of his first game. Soon after his return to the Oilers, Gillman sent him off to Kansas City in return for Curley Culp. A defensive front three of Elvin Bethea, Culp, and Tody Smith spearheaded a much improved defense that led the Oilers to six wins in their last eight games, including upsets over the Bills and Steelers. But despite his achievement of turning the Oilers around, Gillman resigned both his coach and General Manager positions after the season in a dispute with owner Bud Adams over how freely Gillman spent the team's money on a variety of "extravagant" arrangements such as an illegally-large taxi squad.

**Cleveland Browns**—The once-mighty Browns tumbled to their worst season ever, a humbling 4–10 campaign which dumped them ignominiously into the cellar in the Central Division. Five losses in the first six games took the Browns out of any playoff contention, and things improved only slightly the rest of the year. Little Greg Pruitt excited the fans, but the team in general was a dull loser that cost coach Nick Skorich his job.

## WESTERN DIVISION

**Oakland Raiders**—Quarterback Ken Stabler signed a future pact with the W.F.L., but he didn't let it cramp his style with the Raiders this year. The lefty passer guided the N.F.L.'s most explosive offense with the cool of a surgeon, throwing a league-leading 26 touchdown passes. His wide receivers were Fred Biletnikoff, with average speed but extraordinary moves, and Cliff Branch, a small sprinter who broke into the lineup when Mike Siani was injured. Power running came from big Marv Hubbard, and the versatile offensive line had All-Pro candidates in Gene Upshaw and Art Shell. With such an offense, the defense played far better than it had to for the Raiders to nail down the Western Division title. The offensive riches included 46-year-old George Blanda, whose place kicking left little to be desired and who got into the final game of the year at quarterback and threw a touchdown pass.

**Denver Broncos**—The Broncos hoped to challenge for a playoff berth, but they never climbed above a mediocre level during this season. A noteworthy game of this disappointing campaign was a 35–35 tie with the Pittsburgh Steelers on September 22, the first N.F.L. regular season game to go into overtime; an extra period resulted in no score, and the extra exertion may have contributed to both team's losing the next week. On the positive side for the Broncos, tight end Riley Odoms won All-Pro honors for his play, while second-year running back Otis Armstrong surprisingly blossomed into a dangerous runner, piling up a league-leading total of 1407 yards.

**Kansas City Chiefs**—The old Kansas City powerhouse that used to battle Oakland for the Western title every season was no more. Age was eating into the talent at almost all the positions, and only a handful of younger players showed a capacity for playing up to the standards of the old Chiefs. Rookie Woody Green did sparkle in his limited performances at running back, but his addition only balanced the mid-season loss of Ed Podolak with a thumb injury. The Chiefs endured their first losing season since 1963, but the gradual slide to this point prompted owner Lamar Hunt to fire Hank Stram, the only coach the team had since opening shop in Dallas 15 years before.

**San Diego Chargers**—Preseason training camp saw all-time great quarterback Johnny Unitas come into camp, work out for a few days, and then announce his retirement. New coach Tommy Prothro manned the passer's position with youngsters Dan Fouts and Jesse Freitas, and the young quarterbacks helped the Chargers win five games in a rebuilding season. The sturdiest building block Prothro could find was rookie Don Woods, an exciting runner whom the Green Bay Packers had cut loose on waivers before the season.

## FINAL TEAM STATISTICS

**OFFENSE**

| | BALT. | BUFF. | CIN. | CLEV. | DENV | HOUS. | K.C. | MIAMI | N.ENG | N.Y. | OAK. | PITT. | S.D. |
|---|---|---|---|---|---|---|---|---|---|---|---|---|---|
| **FIRST DOWNS:** | | | | | | | | | | | | | |
| Total | 244 | 220 | 260 | 223 | 258 | 200 | 224 | 272 | 255 | 234 | **284** | 251 | 245 |
| by Rushing | 110 | 118 | 115 | 104 | 120 | 76 | 92 | 134 | 123 | 96 | 127 | **136** | 113 |
| by Passing | 109 | 85 | 131 | 92 | 118 | 103 | 113 | 118 | 113 | 119 | **137** | 98 | 117 |
| by Penalty | 25 | 17 | 14 | **27** | 20 | 21 | 19 | 20 | 19 | 19 | 20 | 17 | 15 |
| **RUSHING:** | | | | | | | | | | | | | |
| Number | 450 | 545 | 445 | 461 | 486 | 421 | 469 | **570** | 520 | 444 | 561 | 546 | 508 |
| Yards | 1818 | 2094 | 1978 | 1924 | 2157 | 1361 | 1720 | 2191 | 2134 | 1625 | 2334 | **2417** | 2111 |
| Average Yards | 4.0 | 3.8 | **4.4** | 4.2 | 4.4 | 3.2 | 3.7 | 3.8 | 4.1 | 3.7 | 4.2 | 4.4 | 4.2 |
| Touchdowns | 13 | 11 | 14 | 14 | 20 | 16 | 10 | **25** | 21 | 12 | 15 | 19 | 15 |
| **PASSING:** | | | | | | | | | | | | | |
| Attempts | **425** | 251 | 353 | 367 | 329 | 363 | 395 | 283 | 359 | 369 | 335 | 386 | 349 |
| Completions | 221 | 128 | **224** | 179 | 184 | 203 | 211 | 171 | 177 | 194 | 186 | 166 | 165 |
| Completion Percentage | 52.0 | 51.0 | **63.5** | 48.8 | 55.9 | 55.9 | 53.4 | 60.4 | 49.3 | 52.6 | 55.5 | 43.0 | 47.3 |
| Passing Yards | 2424 | 1728 | **2804** | 2129 | 2660 | 2275 | 2421 | 2313 | 2514 | 2631 | 2561 | 2154 | 2479 |
| Avg. Yards per Attempt | 5.7 | 6.9 | 7.9 | 5.8 | 8.1 | 6.3 | 6.1 | **8.2** | 7.0 | 7.1 | 7.6 | 5.6 | 7.1 |
| Avg. Yards per Complet. | 11.0 | 13.5 | 12.5 | 11.9 | 14.5 | 11.2 | 11.5 | 13.5 | 14.2 | 13.6 | 13.8 | 13.0 | **15.0** |
| Times Tackled Passing | 49 | 33 | 37 | 48 | 46 | 33 | 37 | 31 | 21 | 19 | 24 | **18** | 23 |
| Yards Lost Tackled | 399 | 236 | 293 | 402 | 332 | 298 | 313 | 229 | **174** | 195 | 177 | 196 | 175 |
| Net Yards | 2025 | 1492 | **2511** | 1727 | 2328 | 1977 | 2108 | 2084 | 2340 | 2436 | 2384 | 1958 | 2304 |
| Touchdowns | 9 | 14 | 18 | 12 | 18 | 12 | 11 | 18 | 19 | 20 | **28** | 12 | 12 |
| Interceptions | 24 | 15 | **13** | 24 | 17 | 19 | 25 | 18 | 23 | 24 | 18 | 21 | 22 |
| Percent Intercepted | 5.7 | 6.0 | **3.7** | 6.5 | 5.2 | 5.2 | 6.3 | 6.4 | 6.4 | 6.5 | 5.4 | 5.4 | 6.3 |
| **PUNTS:** | | | | | | | | | | | | | |
| Number | 71 | 69 | 66 | **90** | 75 | 79 | 83 | 65 | 71 | 75 | 74 | 78 | 76 |
| Average Distance | 37.1 | 40.6 | 40.9 | 40.5 | 40.3 | 39.2 | 41.7 | 38.6 | 36.2 | 35.9 | **42.2** | 39.0 | 40.0 |
| **PUNT RETURNS:** | | | | | | | | | | | | | |
| Number | 42 | 56 | 52 | 52 | 43 | 41 | 44 | 46 | 40 | 53 | 45 | **67** | 37 |
| Yards | 253 | 460 | 632 | 523 | 474 | 495 | 296 | 520 | 533 | 425 | 517 | **774** | 287 |
| Average Yards | 6.0 | 8.2 | 12.2 | 10.1 | 11.0 | 12.1 | 6.7 | 11.3 | **13.3** | 8.0 | 11.5 | 11.6 | 7.8 |
| Touchdowns | 0 | 0 | **2** | 0 | 0 | 0 | 0 | 0 | 0 | 0 | 0 | 1 | 0 |
| **KICKOFF RETURNS:** | | | | | | | | | | | | | |
| Number | **66** | 50 | 54 | 60 | 54 | 62 | 56 | 49 | 58 | 61 | 50 | 42 | 55 |
| Yards | **1489** | 1128 | 1157 | 1375 | 1188 | 1419 | 1211 | 1118 | 1198 | 1307 | 1140 | 901 | 1142 |
| Average Yards | 22.6 | 22.6 | 21.4 | **22.9** | 22.0 | 22.9 | 21.6 | 22.8 | 20.7 | 21.4 | 22.8 | 21.5 | 20.8 |
| Touchdowns | 0 | 0 | 0 | **1** | 0 | 0 | 0 | 0 | 0 | 0 | 0 | 0 | 0 |
| **INTERCEPTION RETURNS:** | | | | | | | | | | | | | |
| Number | 10 | 20 | 9 | 24 | 22 | 21 | **28** | 16 | 24 | 17 | 27 | 25 | 15 |
| Yards | 87 | 413 | 110 | 336 | 311 | 313 | **531** | 139 | 294 | 278 | 378 | 320 | 273 |
| Average Yards | 8.7 | **20.7** | 12.2 | 14.0 | 14.1 | 14.9 | 19.0 | 8.7 | 12.3 | 16.4 | 14.0 | 12.8 | 18.2 |
| Touchdowns | 0 | 2 | 0 | 2 | 1 | 1 | **5** | 0 | 2 | 2 | 1 | 2 | 0 |
| **PENALTIES:** | | | | | | | | | | | | | |
| Number | 66 | 79 | 78 | 78 | 76 | 90 | 70 | 69 | 87 | 76 | 92 | **104** | 74 |
| Yards | 587 | 706 | 653 | 767 | 632 | 749 | 515 | 556 | 843 | 600 | 845 | **978** | 609 |
| **FUMBLES:** | | | | | | | | | | | | | |
| Number | 28 | 32 | 27 | 34 | 23 | 26 | 29 | 25 | 26 | 26 | **22** | 33 | 24 |
| Number Lost | 13 | 14 | 18 | 15 | 13 | 14 | 13 | 13 | 15 | **8** | 10 | 19 | 11 |
| **POINTS:** | | | | | | | | | | | | | |
| Total | 190 | 264 | 283 | 251 | 302 | 236 | 233 | 327 | 348 | 279 | **355** | 305 | 212 |
| PAT Attempts | 22 | 30 | 36 | 30 | 39 | 30 | 26 | 43 | 43 | 36 | **46** | 35 | 28 |
| PAT Made | 22 | 25 | 32 | 29 | 35 | 29 | 24 | 43 | 42 | 27 | **44** | 33 | 26 |
| FG Attempts | 20 | **33** | 18 | 16 | 21 | 19 | 24 | 15 | 22 | 18 | 17 | 29 | 16 |
| FG Made | 12 | 19 | 11 | 14 | 11 | 9 | 17 | 8 | 16 | 12 | 11 | **20** | 6 |
| Percent FG Made | 60.0 | 57.6 | 61.1 | **87.5** | 52.4 | 47.4 | **70.8** | **53.3** | 72.7 | 66.7 | 64.7 | 69.0 | 37.5 |
| Safeties | 0 | **1** | **1** | 0 | 0 | 0 | **1** | **1** | 0 | 0 | **1** | **1** | 0 |

**DEFENSE**

| | BALT. | BUFF. | CIN. | CLEV. | DENV | HOUS | K.C. | MIAMI | N.ENG. | N.Y. | OAK. | PITT. | S.D. |
|---|---|---|---|---|---|---|---|---|---|---|---|---|---|
| **FIRST DOWNS:** | | | | | | | | | | | | | |
| Total | 237 | 219 | 256 | 247 | 265 | 268 | 267 | 208 | 240 | 267 | 237 | **200** | 272 |
| by Rushing | 120 | 96 | 127 | 126 | 109 | 124 | 107 | **83** | 100 | 132 | 110 | 87 | 128 |
| by Passing | 101 | 97 | 109 | 95 | 135 | 129 | 141 | 117 | 129 | 112 | 106 | **83** | 127 |
| by Penalty | 16 | 26 | 20 | 26 | 21 | 15 | 19 | **8** | 11 | 23 | 21 | 30 | 17 |
| **RUSHING:** | | | | | | | | | | | | | |
| Number | 516 | 489 | 497 | 555 | 487 | 474 | 502 | **404** | 467 | 539 | 459 | 472 | 508 |
| Yards | 1961 | 1878 | 2152 | 2415 | 1808 | 2050 | 1801 | 1624 | **1587** | 2240 | 2108 | 1608 | 2160 |
| Average Yards | 3.8 | 3.8 | 4.3 | 4.4 | 3.7 | 4.3 | 3.6 | 4.0 | 3.4 | 4.2 | 4.6 | **3.4** | 4.3 |
| Touchdowns | 20 | 19 | 16 | 17 | 17 | 15 | 16 | **7** | 16 | 20 | 12 | **7** | 21 |
| **PASSING:** | | | | | | | | | | | | | |
| Attempts | 312 | 311 | 359 | **308** | 426 | 405 | 408 | 372 | 374 | 347 | 367 | 339 | 367 |
| Completions | 180 | 146 | 186 | **139** | 237 | 231 | 206 | 200 | 210 | 186 | 175 | 147 | 222 |
| Completion Percentage | 57.7 | 46.9 | 51.8 | 45.1 | 55.6 | 57.0 | 50.5 | 53.8 | 56.1 | 53.6 | 47.7 | **43.4** | 60.5 |
| Passing Yards | 2348 | 1898 | 2110 | 2259 | 2805 | 2724 | 2838 | 2452 | 2774 | 2249 | 2425 | **1872** | 2815 |
| Avg. Yards per Attempt | 7.5 | 6.1 | 5.9 | 7.3 | 6.6 | 6.7 | 7.0 | 6.6 | 7.4 | 6.5 | 6.6 | **5.5** | 7.7 |
| Avg. Yards per Complet. | 13.0 | 13.0 | 11.3 | 16.3 | 11.8 | **11.8** | 13.8 | 12.3 | 13.2 | 12.1 | 13.9 | 12.7 | 12.7 |
| Times Tackled Passing | 21 | 32 | 36 | 28 | 32 | 40 | 26 | 31 | 38 | 25 | 36 | **52** | 18 |
| Yards Lost Tackled | 183 | 287 | 320 | 234 | 222 | 349 | 175 | 270 | 294 | 192 | 314 | **406** | 145 |
| Net Yards | 2165 | 1611 | 1790 | 2025 | 2583 | 2375 | 2663 | 2182 | 2480 | 2057 | 2111 | **1466** | 2670 |
| Touchdowns | 16 | **11** | 13 | 22 | 14 | 19 | 22 | 14 | 17 | 14 | 12 | 14 | 13 |
| Interceptions | 10 | 20 | 9 | 24 | 22 | 21 | **28** | 16 | 24 | 17 | 27 | 25 | 15 |
| Percent Intercepted | 3.2 | 6.4 | 2.5 | **7.8** | 5.2 | 5.2 | 6.9 | 4.3 | 6.4 | 4.9 | 7.4 | 7.4 | 4.1 |
| **PUNTS:** | | | | | | | | | | | | | |
| Number | 67 | 77 | 81 | 76 | 70 | 70 | 80 | 70 | 75 | 71 | 73 | **91** | 66 |
| Average Distance | 38.4 | **37.1** | 37.8 | 38.0 | 42.6 | 39.1 | 40.1 | 39.2 | 38.4 | 37.2 | 39.9 | 41.2 | 40.6 |
| **PUNT RETURNS:** | | | | | | | | | | | | | |
| Number | 46 | 45 | 41 | 68 | 45 | 56 | 55 | 42 | 41 | **27** | 40 | 47 | 48 |
| Yards | 413 | 416 | 457 | 705 | 529 | 500 | 634 | **259** | 314 | 352 | 283 | 413 | 401 |
| Average Yards | 9.0 | 9.2 | 11.1 | 10.4 | 11.8 | 8.9 | 11.5 | **6.2** | 7.7 | 13.0 | 7.1 | 8.8 | 8.4 |
| Touchdowns | **0** | **0** | **0** | 1 | **0** | **0** | **0** | **0** | **0** | **0** | **0** | **0** | **0** |
| **KICKOFF RETURNS:** | | | | | | | | | | | | | |
| Number | 45 | 58 | 55 | 55 | 57 | 51 | 54 | 64 | 64 | 57 | 69 | 56 | **39** |
| Yards | **903** | 1345 | 1198 | 1345 | 1369 | 1111 | 1333 | 1222 | 1678 | 1395 | 1455 | 1275 | 960 |
| Average Yards | 20.1 | 23.2 | 21.8 | 24.5 | 24.0 | 21.8 | 24.7 | **19.1** | 26.2 | 24.5 | 21.1 | 22.8 | 24.6 |
| Touchdowns | **0** | **0** | **0** | 1 | 1 | **0** | **0** | **0** | 1 | **0** | **0** | **0** | **0** |
| **INTERCEPTION RETURNS:** | | | | | | | | | | | | | |
| Number | 24 | 15 | **13** | 24 | 17 | 19 | 25 | 18 | 23 | 24 | 18 | 21 | 22 |
| Yards | 384 | 183 | **140** | 423 | 304 | 238 | 336 | 320 | 331 | 452 | 276 | 222 | 311 |
| Average Yards | 16.0 | 12.2 | 10.8 | 17.6 | 17.9 | 12.5 | 13.4 | 17.8 | 14.4 | 18.8 | 15.3 | **10.6** | 14.1 |
| Touchdowns | 3 | 1 | **0** | 1 | 3 | **0** | 1 | 1 | 2 | 4 | 2 | 1 | 1 |
| **PENALTIES:** | | | | | | | | | | | | | |
| Number | 75 | 73 | 77 | 81 | 78 | **94** | 83 | 67 | 76 | 78 | 61 | 76 | 80 |
| Yards | 737 | 597 | 640 | 731 | 595 | **872** | 811 | 525 | 642 | 684 | 502 | 575 | 751 |
| **FUMBLES:** | | | | | | | | | | | | | |
| Number | 25 | 26 | 23 | 31 | 22 | 26 | 34 | 33 | 29 | 18 | 32 | **38** | 19 |
| Number Lost | 14 | 11 | 11 | 16 | 11 | 15 | 16 | 17 | 14 | 9 | 14 | **22** | 13 |
| **POINTS:** | | | | | | | | | | | | | |
| Total | 329 | 244 | 259 | 344 | 294 | 282 | 293 | 216 | 289 | 300 | 228 | **189** | 285 |
| PAT Attempts | 40 | 32 | 30 | 43 | 35 | 34 | 40 | 25 | 37 | 38 | 27 | **22** | 37 |
| PAT Made | 38 | 28 | 28 | 38 | 34 | 30 | **33** | 24 | 32 | 36 | 25 | **21** | 36 |
| FG Attempts | 27 | 15 | 22 | 23 | 24 | 23 | **14** | 21 | 18 | 24 | 22 | 17 | 20 |
| FG Made | 17 | 8 | 17 | 14 | 16 | 16 | **6** | 14 | 11 | 12 | 13 | 12 | 9 |
| Percent FG Made | 63.0 | 53.3 | 77.3 | 60.9 | 66.7 | 69.6 | **42.9** | 66.7 | 61.1 | 50.0 | 59.1 | 70.6 | 45.0 |
| Safeties | **0** | **0** | **0** | 3 | 1 | **0** | 1 | **0** | 1 | **0** | 1 | **0** | **0** |

## CONFERENCE PLAYOFFS

### December 21, at Oakland (Attendance 52,817)

#### SCORING

| | | | | |
|---|---|---|---|---|
| **OAKLAND** | 0 | 7 | 7 | 14–28 |
| **MIAMI** | 7 | 3 | 6 | 10–26 |

First Quarter
Mia. N. Moore, 89-yard kickoff return PAT–Yepremian (kick)

Second Quarter
Oak. C. Smith, 31 yard pass from Stabler PAT–Blanda (kick)
Mia. Yepremian, 33 yard field goal

Third Quarter
Oak. Biletnikoff, 13 yard pass from Stabler PAT–Blanda (kick)
Mia. Warfield, 16 yard pass from Griese PAT–kick missed

Fourth Quarter
Mia. Yepremian, 46 yard field goal
Oak. Branch, 72 yard pass from Stabler PAT–Blanda (kick)
Mia. Malone, 23 yard rush PAT–Yepremian (kick)
Oak. Davis, 8 yard pass from Stabler PAT–Blanda (kick)

#### TEAM STATISTICS

| OAK. | | MIAMI |
|---|---|---|
| 19 | First Downs-Total | 18 |
| 8 | First Downs-Rushing | 10 |
| 11 | First Downs-Passing | 6 |
| 0 | First Downs-Penalty | 2 |
| 0 | Fumbles-Number | 0 |
| 0 | Fumbles-Lost Ball | 0 |
| 3 | Penalties-Number | 3 |
| 59 | Yards Penalized | 15 |
| 0 | Missed Field Goals | 0 |
| 64 | Offensive Plays | 57 |
| 411 | Net Yards | 294 |
| 6.4 | Average Gain | 5.2 |
| 1 | Giveaways | 1 |
| 1 | Takeaways | 1 |
| 0 | Difference | 0 |

#### INDIVIDUAL STATISTICS

| OAKLAND | No. | Yds. | Avg. | MIAMI | No. | Yds. | Avg. |
|---|---|---|---|---|---|---|---|
| **RUSHING** | | | | | | | |
| Davis | 12 | 59 | 4.9 | Csonka | 24 | 114 | 4.8 |
| Hubbard | 14 | 55 | 3.9 | Malone | 14 | 83 | 5.9 |
| Banaszak | 3 | 14 | 4.7 | Griese | 2 | 14 | 7.0 |
| Stabler | 3 | 7 | 2.3 | Kiick | 1 | 2 | 2.0 |
| | 32 | 135 | 4.2 | | 41 | 213 | 5.2 |
| **RECEIVING** | | | | | | | |
| Biletnikoff | 8 | 122 | 15.3 | Warfield | 3 | 47 | 15.7 |
| Branch | 3 | 84 | 28.0 | N. Moore | 2 | 40 | 20.0 |
| Moore | 3 | 22 | 7.3 | Nottingham | 1 | 9 | 9.0 |
| C. Smith | 2 | 35 | 17.5 | Kiick | 1 | 5 | 5.0 |
| C. Davis | 2 | 16 | 8.0 | | 7 | 101 | 14.4 |
| Hubbard | 1 | 9 | 9.0 | | | | |
| Pitts | 1 | 5 | 5.0 | | | | |
| | 20 | 293 | 14.7 | | | | |
| **PUNTING** | | | | | | | |
| Guy | 7 | | 42.7 | Seiple | 6 | | 33.2 |
| **PUNT RETURNS** | | | | | | | |
| R. Smith | 3 | 16 | 5.3 | N. Moore | 2 | 5 | 2.5 |
| **KICKOFF RETURNS** | | | | | | | |
| Hart | 4 | 88 | 22.0 | N. Moore | 3 | 137 | 45.7 |
| R. Smith | 2 | 47 | 23.5 | Ginn | 2 | 46 | 23.0 |
| | 6 | 135 | 22.5 | | 5 | 183 | 36.6 |
| **INTERCEPTION RETURNS** | | | | | | | |
| Villapiano | 1 | 5 | 5.0 | | | | |

**PASSING**

| OAKLAND | Att. | Comp. | Comp. Pct. | Yds. | Int. | Yds/ Att. | Yds/ Comp. | Yards Lost Tackled |
|---|---|---|---|---|---|---|---|---|
| Stabler | 30 | 20 | 66.7 | 293 | 1 | 9.8 | 14.7 | 2–17 |
| **MIAMI** | | | | | | | | |
| Griese | 14 | 7 | 50.0 | 101 | 0 | 7.2 | 14.4 | 2–20 |

### December 22, at Pittsburgh (Attendance 48,321)

#### SCORING

| | | | | |
|---|---|---|---|---|
| **PITTSBURGH** | 3 | 26 | 0 | 3–32 |
| **BUFFALO** | 7 | 0 | 7 | 0–14 |

First Quarter
Pitt. Gerela, 21 yard field goal
Buf. Seymour, 22 yard pass from Ferguson PAT–Leypoldt (kick)

Second Quarter
Pit. Bleier, 27 yard pass from Bradshaw PAT–kick blocked
Pit. Harris, 1 yard rush PAT–Gerela (kick)
Pit. Harris, 4 yard rush PAT–kick blocked
Pit. Harris, 1 yard rush PAT–Gerela (kick)

Third Quarter
Buf. Simpson, 3 yard pass from Ferguson PAT–Leypoldt (kick)

Fourth Quarter
Pit. Gerela, 22 yard field goal

#### TEAM STATISTICS

| PITT. | | BUF. |
|---|---|---|
| 29 | First Downs-Total | 15 |
| 18 | First Downs-Rushing | 5 |
| 9 | First Downs-Passing | 10 |
| 2 | First Downs-Penalty | 0 |
| 2 | Fumbles-Number | 2 |
| 0 | Fumbles-Lost Ball | 1 |
| 2 | Penalties-Number | 3 |
| 10 | Yards Penalized | 15 |
| 0 | Missed Field Goals | 0 |
| 72 | Offensive Plays | 47 |
| 438 | Net Yards | 264 |
| 6.1 | Average Gain | 5.6 |
| 0 | Giveaways | 1 |
| 1 | Takeaways | 0 |
| +1 | Difference | –1 |

#### INDIVIDUAL STATISTICS

| PITTSBURGH | No. | Yds. | Avg. | BUFFALO | No. | Yds. | Avg. |
|---|---|---|---|---|---|---|---|
| **RUSHING** | | | | | | | |
| Harris | 24 | 74 | 3.1 | Simpson | 15 | 49 | 3.3 |
| Bradshaw | 5 | 48 | 9.6 | Braxton | 5 | 48 | 9.6 |
| Bleier | 14 | 45 | 3.2 | Ferguson | 1 | 3 | 3.0 |
| Steve Davis | 5 | 32 | 6.4 | | 21 | 100 | 4.8 |
| Swann | 2 | 24 | 12.0 | | | | |
| Gilliam | 1 | 12 | 12.0 | | | | |
| | 51 | 235 | 4.6 | | | | |
| **RECEIVING** | | | | | | | |
| Swann | 3 | 60 | 20.0 | Hill | 4 | 59 | 14.8 |
| Bleier | 3 | 54 | 18.0 | Simpson | 3 | 37 | 12.3 |
| Lewis | 2 | 18 | 9.0 | Seymour | 2 | 35 | 17.5 |
| Brown | 1 | 29 | 29.0 | Rashad | 1 | 25 | 25.0 |
| McMakin | 1 | 22 | 22.0 | Braxton | 1 | 8 | 8.0 |
| Shanklin | 1 | 15 | 15.0 | | 11 | 164 | 14.9 |
| Harris | 1 | 5 | 5.0 | | | | |
| | 12 | 203 | 16.9 | | | | |
| **PUNTING** | | | | | | | |
| Walden | 3 | | 38.7 | Bateman | 5 | | 39.4 |
| **PUNT RETURNS** | | | | | | | |
| Edwards | 2 | 13 | 6.5 | Walker | 2 | 11 | 5.5 |
| Swann | 2 | 12 | 6.0 | | | | |
| | 4 | 25 | 6.3 | | | | |
| **KICKOFF RETURNS** | | | | | | | |
| Blount | 2 | 56 | 28.0 | Francis | 6 | 118 | 19.7 |
| Steve Davis | 1 | 30 | 30.0 | | | | |
| | 3 | 86 | 28.7 | | | | |

**PASSING**

| PITTSBURGH | Att. | Comp. | Comp. Pct. | Yds | Int. | Yds/ Att. | Yds/ Comp. | Yards Lost Tackled |
|---|---|---|---|---|---|---|---|---|
| Bradshaw | 19 | 12 | 63.2 | 203 | 0 | 10.7 | 16.9 | 0–0 |
| Gilliam | 2 | 0 | 00.0 | 0 | 0 | – | – | 0–0 |
| | 21 | 12 | 57.1 | 203 | 0 | 9.7 | 16.9 | 0–0 |
| **BUFFALO** | | | | | | | | |
| Ferguson | 26 | 11 | 42.3 | 164 | 0 | 6.3 | 14.9 | 0–0 |

### MIAMI DOLPHINS 11-3-0 Don Shula

| Scores of Each Game | | |
|---|---|---|
| 24 | New England | 34 |
| 24 | Buffalo | 16 |
| 28 | San Diego | 21 |
| 21 | N.Y. JETS | 17 |
| 17 | Washington | 20 |
| 9 | KANSAS CITY | 3 |
| 17 | BALTIMORE | 7 |
| 42 | ATLANTA | 7 |
| 21 | New Orleans | 0 |
| 35 | BUFFALO | 28 |
| 14 | N.Y. Jets | 17 |
| 24 | CINCINNATI | 3 |
| 17 | Baltimore | 16 |
| 34 | NEW ENGLAND | 27 |

| Use Name | Pos. | Hgt | Wgt | Age | Int | Pts |
|---|---|---|---|---|---|---|
| Doug Crusan | OT | 6'5" | 250 | 28 | | |
| Norm Evans | OT | 6'5" | 250 | 31 | | |
| Tom Funchess | OT | 6'5" | 270 | 29 | | |
| Wayne Moore | OT | 6'6" | 265 | 29 | | |
| Tom Wickert | OT | 6'4" | 246 | 22 | | |
| Larry Little | OG | 6'1" | 265 | 28 | | |
| Ed Newman | OG | 6'2" | 245 | 23 | | |
| Bob Kuechenberg | OT-OG | 6'3" | 252 | 26 | | |
| Jim Langer | C | 6'2" | 253 | 26 | | |
| Irv Goode | OG-C | 6'4" | 262 | 33 | | |
| Vern Den Herder | DE | 6'6" | 252 | 25 | | |
| Bill Stanfill | DE | 6'5" | 252 | 27 | | |
| Don Reese | DT-DE | 6'6" | 255 | 22 | | |
| Randy Crowder | DT | 6'2" | 236 | 22 | | |
| Manny Fernandez | DT | 6'2" | 250 | 28 | | |
| Baldy Moore | DT | 6'2" | 265 | 28 | | |
| Bob Heinz | DE-DT | 6'6" | 265 | 27 | | |
| Larry Ball | LB | 6'6" | 235 | 24 | | |
| Bruce Bannon | LB | 6'3" | 225 | 23 | | |
| Nick Buoniconti | LB | 5'11" | 220 | 33 | 2 | |
| Mike Kolen | LB | 6'2" | 222 | 26 | 1 | |
| Bob Matheson | LB | 6'4" | 235 | 29 | 1 | |
| Doug Swift | LB | 6'3" | 226 | 25 | | |
| Dick Anderson | DB | 6'2" | 196 | 28 | 1 | |
| Charlie Babb | DB | 6' | 190 | 24 | | |
| Tim Foley | DB | 6' | 194 | 26 | 2 | 2 |
| Curtis Johnson | DB | 6'2" | 196 | 26 | | |
| Lloyd Mumphrey | DB | 5'11" | 176 | 27 | | |
| Jake Scott | DB | 6' | 188 | 29 | 8 | |
| Henry Stuckey | DB | 6'1" | 180 | 24 | 1 | |
| Jeris White | DB | 5'11" | 180 | 21 | | |
| Bob Griese | QB | 6'1" | 190 | 29 | | 6 |
| Earl Morrall | QB | 6'1" | 210 | 40 | | |
| Don Strock | QB | 6'5" | 216 | 23 | | |
| Hubert Ginn | HB | 5'11" | 185 | 27 | | 12 |
| Jim Kiick | HB | 5'11" | 214 | 28 | | 12 |
| Benny Malone | HB | 5'10" | 193 | 22 | | 18 |
| Mercury Morris | HB | 5'10" | 192 | 27 | | 12 |
| Larry Csonka | FB | 6'3" | 237 | 27 | | 54 |
| Don Nottingham | FB | 5'10" | 210 | 25 | | 48 |
| Melvin Baker | WR | 6' | 192 | 24 | | 12 |
| Marlin Briscoe | WR | 5'10" | 175 | 28 | | 6 |
| Nat Moore | WR | 5'9" | 180 | 22 | | 12 |
| Howard Twilley | WR | 5'10" | 185 | 30 | | 12 |
| Paul Warfield | WR | 6' | 188 | 31 | | 12 |
| Marv Fleming | TE | 6'4" | 230 | 32 | | 6 |
| Jim Mandich | TE | 6'3" | 224 | 26 | | 36 |
| Larry Seiple | TE | 6' | 214 | 29 | | |
| Garo Yepremian | K | 5'8" | 175 | 30 | | 67 |

### BUFFALO BILLS 9-5-0 Lou Saban

| Scores of Each Game | | |
|---|---|---|
| 21 | OAKLAND | 20 |
| 16 | MIAMI | 24 |
| 16 | N.Y. JETS | 12 |
| 27 | Green Bay | 7 |
| 27 | Baltimore | 14 |
| 30 | NEW ENGLAND | 28 |
| 16 | CHICAGO | 6 |
| 29 | New England | 28 |
| 9 | HOUSTON | 21 |
| 28 | Miami | 35 |
| 15 | Cleveland | 10 |
| 6 | BALTIMORE | 0 |
| 10 | N.Y. Jets | 20 |
| 14 | Los Angeles | 19 |

| Use Name | Pos. | Hgt | Wgt | Age | Int | Pts |
|---|---|---|---|---|---|---|
| Dave Foley | OT | 6'5" | 253 | 26 | | |
| Donnie Green | OT | 6'7" | 272 | 26 | | |
| Halvor Hagen | OT | 6'5" | 253 | 27 | | |
| Bill Adams | OG | 6'2" | 254 | 24 | | |
| Joe DeLamielleure | OG | 6'3" | 245 | 23 | | |
| Reggie McKenzie | OG | 6'4" | 242 | 24 | | |
| Bruce Jarvis | C | 6'7" | 250 | 25 | | |
| Nick Nighswander | C | 6' | 232 | 22 | | |
| Mike Montler | OT-C | 6'4" | 253 | 30 | | |
| Willie Parker | OG-C | 6'3" | 245 | 25 | | |
| Dave Costa | DE | 6'2" | 250 | 32 | | |
| Dave Means | DE | 6'4" | 235 | 22 | | |
| Walt Patulski | DE | 6'6" | 260 | 24 | | |
| Don Croft | DT | 6'3" | 254 | 25 | | |
| Mike Kadish | DT | 6'5" | 270 | 24 | | 2 |
| Jeff Yeates | DT | 6'3" | 240 | 23 | | |
| Earl Edwards | DE-DT | 6'6" | 256 | 28 | | |
| Doug Allen | LB | 6'2" | 228 | 22 | 1 | |
| Jim Cheyunski | LB | 6'2" | 220 | 28 | 1 | |
| Merv Krakau | LB | 6'2" | 237 | 23 | 1 | |
| Rich Lewis | LB | 6'3" | 215 | 24 | 1 | |
| John Skorupan | LB | 6'2" | 220 | 23 | | |
| Bo Cornell | FB-LB | 6'1" | 215 | 25 | | |
| Ted Koy | TE-LB | 6'1" | 210 | 26 | | |
| Dave Washington | TE-LB | 6'5" | 223 | 25 | 2 | 12 |
| Bill Cahill | DB | 5'11" | 170 | 23 | | |
| Neal Craig | DB | 6'1" | 190 | 26 | 1 | 6 |
| Tony Greene | DB | 5'10" | 170 | 25 | 9 | |
| Dwight Harrison | DB | 6'1" | 185 | 25 | 1 | |
| Robert James | DB | 6'1" | 184 | 27 | 3 | |
| Rex Kern | DB | 5'11" | 190 | 25 | | |
| Al Randolph | DB | 6'2" | 205 | 30 | | |
| Donnie Walker | DB | 6'1" | 180 | 23 | | |
| Jeff Winans – Injury | | | | | | |
| Joe Ferguson | QB | 6'1" | 180 | 24 | | 12 |
| Scott Hunter | QB | 6'2" | 205 | 26 | | |
| Gary Marangi | QB | 6'1" | 196 | 22 | | |
| Don Calhoun | HB | 6' | 198 | 22 | | |
| Clint Haserlig | HB | 6' | 190 | 22 | | |
| Gary Hayman | HB | 6'1" | 198 | 23 | | |
| Ed Jenkins (from NYG, to NE) | HB | 6'2" | 210 | 24 | | |
| Wayne Mosley | HB | 6' | 190 | 21 | | |
| O. J. Simpson | HB | 6'2" | 212 | 27 | | 24 |
| Jim Braxton | FB | 6'2" | 240 | 25 | | 24 |
| Larry Watkins | FB | 6'2" | 235 | 27 | | 12 |
| Bob Chandler | WR | 6' | 180 | 25 | | 6 |
| Wallace Francis | WR | 5'11" | 195 | 22 | | |
| J. D. Hill | WR | 6'1" | 190 | 25 | | 36 |
| Ahmad Rashad | WR | 6'2" | 200 | 24 | | 36 |
| Reuben Gant | TE | 6'4" | 230 | 22 | | |
| Paul Seymour | TE | 6'5" | 243 | 24 | | 12 |
| Marv Bateman (from DAL) | K | 6'4" | 210 | 24 | | |
| Spike Jones | K | 6'2" | 195 | 27 | | |
| John Leypoldt | K | 6'2" | 237 | 28 | | 82 |

### NEW ENGLAND PATRIOTS 7-7-0 Chuck Fairbanks

| Scores of Each Game | | |
|---|---|---|
| 34 | MIAMI | 24 |
| 28 | N.Y. Giants | 20 |
| 20 | LOS ANGELES | 14 |
| 42 | BALTIMORE | 3 |
| 24 | N.Y. Jets | 0 |
| 28 | Buffalo | 30 |
| 17 | Minnesota | 14 |
| 28 | BUFFALO | 29 |
| 14 | CLEVELAND | 21 |
| 16 | N.Y. JETS | 21 |
| 27 | Baltimore | 17 |
| 26 | Oakland | 41 |
| 17 | PITTSBURGH | 21 |
| 27 | Miami | 34 |

| Use Name | Pos. | Hgt | Wgt | Age | Int | Pts |
|---|---|---|---|---|---|---|
| Allen Gallaher | OT | 6'3" | 255 | 23 | | |
| Leon Gray | OT | 6'3" | 256 | 22 | | |
| Tom Neville | OT | 6'4" | 253 | 31 | | |
| Sam Adams | OG | 6'3" | 252 | 25 | | |
| Bill DuLac | OG | 6'4" | 260 | 23 | | |
| John Hannah | OG | 6'2" | 265 | 23 | | 6 |
| Doug Dumler | C | 6'3" | 242 | 23 | | |
| Jon Morris | C | 6'4" | 248 | 31 | | |
| Bill Lenkaitis | OG-C | 6'3" | 250 | 28 | | |
| Craig Hanneman | DE | 6'3" | 245 | 25 | | |
| Tony McGee | DE | 6'4" | 245 | 25 | | |
| Donnell Smith | DE | 6'4" | 252 | 25 | | |
| Julius Adams | DT-DE | 6'3" | 257 | 26 | | |
| Mel Lunsford | DT-DE | 6'3" | 260 | 24 | | |
| Ray Hamilton | NT | 6'1" | 246 | 23 | | |
| Art Moore | NT | 6'5" | 253 | 23 | | |
| Gail Clark | LB | 6'2" | 225 | 23 | | |
| Kent Carter | LB | 6'3" | 235 | 24 | | |
| Rodrigo Barnes (from DAL) | LB | 6'1" | 215 | 24 | | |
| Maury Damkroger | LB | 6'2" | 230 | 22 | | |
| Bob Geddes | LB | 6'2" | 240 | 28 | 2 | 6 |
| Sam Hunt | LB | 6'1" | 240 | 23 | 3 | |
| Steve King | LB | 6'4" | 230 | 23 | 1 | |
| Steve Nelson | LB | 6'2" | 230 | 23 | | |
| John Tanner | TE-LB | 6'4" | 235 | 29 | | 6 |
| George Webster | LB | 6'4" | 230 | 28 | | |
| Ron Bolton | DB | 6'2" | 170 | 24 | 7 | |
| Sandy Durko | DB | 6'1" | 186 | 26 | | |
| Prentice McCray | DB | 6'1" | 187 | 23 | 3 | |
| Dave McCurry | DB | 6'1" | 187 | 23 | | |
| Jim Massey | DB | 5'11" | 198 | 26 | | |
| Jack Mildren | DB | 6'1" | 200 | 24 | 3 | |
| Ken Pope | DB | 5'11" | 200 | 22 | | |
| Deac Sanders | DB | 6'1" | 178 | 24 | 5 | 6 |
| Neil Graff | QB | 6'3" | 200 | 24 | | |
| Jim Plunkett | QB | 6'3" | 212 | 26 | | 12 |
| Dick Shiner | QB | 6' | 210 | 32 | | |
| Josh Ashton | HB | 6'1" | 202 | 25 | | |
| Noe Gonzalez | HB | 6' | 210 | 23 | | |
| Mack Herron | HB | 5'5" | 175 | 26 | | 72 |
| Andy Johnson | HB | 6' | 204 | 21 | | |
| Sam Cunningham | FB | 6'3" | 224 | 24 | | 66 |
| John Tarver | FB | 6'3" | 220 | 25 | | 12 |
| Joe Wilson | HB-FB | 5'10" | 210 | 23 | | |
| Eddie Hinton | WR | 6' | 200 | 27 | | |
| Al Marshall | WR | 6'2" | 190 | 23 | | 6 |
| Reggie Rucker | WR | 6'2" | 190 | 26 | | 24 |
| Steve Schubert | WR | 5'10" | 185 | 23 | | 6 |
| Darryl Stingley | WR | 6' | 195 | 22 | | 12 |
| Joe Sweet | WR | 6'2" | 196 | 26 | | |
| Randy Vataha | WR | 5'10" | 170 | 25 | | 18 |
| Bob Adams | TE | 6'2" | 222 | 28 | | |
| Bob Windsor | TE | 6'4" | 225 | 31 | | 6 |
| Bruce Barnes | K | 5'11" | 212 | 23 | | |
| John Smith | K | 6' | 185 | 24 | | 90 |

### NEW YORK JETS 7-7-0 Charley Winner

| Scores of Each Game | | |
|---|---|---|
| 16 | Kansas City | 24 |
| 23 | Chicago | 21 |
| 12 | Buffalo | 16 |
| 17 | Miami | 21 |
| 0 | NEW ENGLAND | 24 |
| 20 | BALTIMORE | 35 |
| 13 | LOS ANGELES | 20 |
| 22 | HOUSTON | 27 |
| 26 | N.Y. Giants (OT) | 20 |
| 21 | New England | 16 |
| 17 | MIAMI | 14 |
| 27 | SAN DIEGO | 14 |
| 20 | BUFFALO | 10 |
| 45 | Baltimore | 38 |

| Use Name | Pos. | Hgt | Wgt | Age | Int | Pts |
|---|---|---|---|---|---|---|
| Gordie Browne | OT | 6'5" | 265 | 22 | | |
| Winston Hill | OT | 6'4" | 280 | 32 | | |
| Robert Woods | OT | 6'3" | 255 | 24 | | |
| Roger Bernhardt | OG | 6'4" | 244 | 24 | | |
| Randy Rasmussen | OG | 6'2" | 267 | 29 | | |
| Travis Roach | OG | 6'2" | 260 | 24 | | |
| Gary Puetz | OT-OG | 6'4" | 255 | 22 | | |
| Howard Kindig | C | 6'6" | 260 | 33 | | |
| Warren Koegel | C | 6'3" | 260 | 24 | | |
| Wayne Mulligan | C | 6'2" | 250 | 27 | | |
| Ed Galigher | DE | 6'4" | 260 | 23 | | |
| Mark Lomas | DE | 6'4" | 250 | 26 | | |
| John Little | DT-DE | 6'3" | 250 | 27 | | |
| Carl Barzilauskas | DT | 6'6" | 280 | 23 | | |
| Larry Woods | DT | 6'6" | 270 | 26 | | |
| Richard Neal | DE-DT | 6'3" | 260 | 26 | | |
| Joe Schmiesing | DE-DT | 6'4" | 256 | 29 | | |
| Al Atkinson | LB | 6'1" | 230 | 31 | | |
| Ralph Baker | LB | 6'3" | 228 | 32 | 2 | 6 |
| John Ebersole | LB | 6'3" | 235 | 25 | 3 | |
| Bill Ferguson | LB | 6'3" | 225 | 23 | | |
| Steve Reese | LB | 6'2" | 232 | 22 | | |
| Jamie Rivers | LB | 6'2" | 245 | 28 | 1 | |
| Delles Howell | DB | 6'3" | 200 | 27 | 2 | |
| Burgess Owens | DB | 6'2" | 200 | 23 | 3 | 12 |
| Rich Sowells | DB | 6' | 185 | 25 | 2 | |
| Steve Tannen | DB | 6'1" | 194 | 26 | 2 | |
| Earlie Thomas | DB | 6'1" | 190 | 28 | | |
| Phil Wise | DB | 6' | 190 | 25 | | |
| Roscoe Word | DB | 5'11" | 170 | 21 | 2 | |
| Bill Demory | QB | 6'2" | 195 | 23 | | |
| Joe Namath | QB | 6'2" | 200 | 31 | | 6 |
| Al Woodall | QB | 6'5" | 194 | 28 | | |
| Mike Adamle | HB | 5'9" | 193 | 24 | | 12 |
| Hank Bjorklund | HB | 6'1" | 200 | 24 | | |
| Emerson Boozer | HB | 5'11" | 205 | 31 | | 30 |
| Jazz Jackson | HB | 5'8" | 167 | 22 | | 12 |
| Bob Burns | FB | 6'3" | 212 | 22 | | 6 |
| John Riggins | FB | 6'2" | 230 | 25 | | 42 |
| Jerome Barkum | WR | 6'3" | 212 | 24 | | 18 |
| Eddie Bell | WR | 5'10" | 160 | 26 | | 6 |
| Dave Knight | WR | 6'1" | 182 | 23 | | 24 |
| Marv Owens | WR | 5'11" | 205 | 24 | | |
| Lou Piccone | WR | 5'9" | 175 | 25 | | |
| Willie Brister | TE | 6'4" | 236 | 22 | | |
| Rich Caster | TE | 6'5" | 228 | 25 | | 42 |
| Greg Gantt | K | 5'11" | 188 | 22 | | 1 |
| Bobby Howfield | K | 5'9" | 180 | 37 | | 26 |
| Pat Leahy | K | 6' | 200 | 23 | | 36 |

### BALTIMORE COLTS 2-12-0 Howard Schnellenberger Joe Thomas

| Scores of Each Game | | |
|---|---|---|
| 0 | Pittsburgh | 30 |
| 13 | GREEN BAY | 20 |
| 10 | Philadelphia | 30 |
| 3 | New England | 42 |
| 14 | BUFFALO | 27 |
| 35 | N.Y. Jets | 20 |
| 7 | Miami | 17 |
| 14 | CINCINNATI | 24 |
| 6 | DENVER | 17 |
| 17 | Atlanta | 7 |
| 17 | NEW ENGLAND | 27 |
| 0 | Buffalo | 6 |
| 16 | MIAMI | 17 |
| 38 | N.Y. JETS | 45 |

| Use Name | Pos. | Hgt | Wgt | Age | Int | Pts |
|---|---|---|---|---|---|---|
| Dennis Nelson | OT | 6'5" | 260 | 28 | | |
| Dave Simonson | OT | 6'6" | 246 | 22 | | |
| David Taylor | OT | 6'4" | 254 | 24 | | |
| Elmer Collett | OG | 6'4" | 240 | 29 | | |
| Robert Pratt | OG | 6'3" | 255 | 23 | | |
| Glenn Ressler | OG | 6'3" | 250 | 30 | | |
| Bob Van Duyne | OG | 6'5" | 235 | 22 | | |
| Ken Mendenhall | C | 6'3" | 240 | 25 | | |
| Dan Neal | C | 6'4" | 240 | 25 | | |
| Mike Barnes | DE | 6'6" | 255 | 23 | | |
| Fred Cook | DE | 6'4" | 235 | 22 | | |
| John Dutton | DE | 6'7" | 260 | 23 | | |
| Steve Williams | DE | 6'6" | 260 | 23 | | |
| Jim Bailey | DT | 6'5" | 255 | 26 | | |
| Joe Ehrmann | DT | 6'5" | 260 | 25 | | |
| Bill Windauer | DT | 6'3" | 245 | 24 | | |
| Tony Bertuca | LB | 6'2" | 225 | 24 | | |
| Mike Curtis | LB | 6'2" | 232 | 31 | 3 | |
| Dan Dickel | LB | 6'3" | 220 | 22 | 1 | |
| Tom MacLeod | LB | 6'3" | 230 | 23 | | |
| Danny Rhodes | LB | 6'2" | 220 | 23 | | |
| Stan White | LB | 6'1" | 225 | 24 | 1 | |
| Randy Hall | DB | 6'3" | 185 | 22 | | |
| Bruce Laird | DB | 6' | 185 | 24 | 1 | |
| Nelson Munsey | DB | 6'1" | 185 | 26 | | |
| Doug Nettles | DB | 6' | 177 | 23 | 1 | |
| Ray Oldham | DB | 6' | 200 | 23 | 1 | |
| Tim Rudnick | DB | 5'10" | 185 | 22 | | |
| Rick Volk | DB | 6'3" | 195 | 29 | 2 | |
| Marty Domres | QB | 6'3" | 222 | 27 | | 12 |
| Bert Jones | QB | 6'3" | 205 | 22 | | 24 |
| Bill Troup | QB | 6'5" | 220 | 23 | | |
| Lydell Mitchell | HB | 5'11" | 204 | 25 | | 42 |
| Joe Orduna | HB | 6' | 195 | 26 | | 6 |
| Bill Olds | FB | 6'1" | 224 | 23 | | 18 |
| Don McCauley | HB-FB | 6'1" | 214 | 25 | | 6 |
| Tim Berra | WR | 5'11" | 185 | 22 | | |
| Roger Carr | WR | 6'3" | 200 | 22 | | |
| Glenn Doughty | WR | 6'2" | 204 | 23 | | 12 |
| Freddie Scott | WR | 6'2" | 175 | 22 | | |
| Ollie Smith | WR | 6'2" | 195 | 25 | | |
| Cotton Speyrer | WR | 6' | 175 | 25 | | 6 |
| John Andrews | TE | 6'3" | 227 | 25 | | |
| Ray Chester | TE | 6'3" | 235 | 26 | | 6 |
| Ron Mayo | TE | 6'3" | 223 | 23 | | |
| David Lee | K | 6'4" | 230 | 30 | | |
| Toni Linhart | K | 6' | 178 | 32 | | 58 |

## MIAMI DOLPHINS

### Rushing

| Last Name | No. | Yds | Avg | TD |
|---|---|---|---|---|
| Csonka | 197 | 749 | 3.8 | 9 |
| Malone | 117 | 479 | 4.1 | 3 |
| Kiick | 86 | 274 | 3.2 | 1 |
| Nottingham | 66 | 273 | 4.1 | 8 |
| Morris | 56 | 214 | 3.8 | 1 |
| Ginn | 26 | 99 | 3.8 | 1 |
| Griese | 16 | 66 | 4.1 | 1 |
| Briscoe | 1 | 17 | 17.0 | 0 |
| N. Moore | 3 | 16 | 5.3 | 0 |
| Morrall | 1 | 11 | 11.0 | 0 |
| Strock | 1 | −7 | −7.0 | 0 |

### Receiving

| Last Name | No. | Yds | Avg | TD |
|---|---|---|---|---|
| N. Moore | 37 | 605 | 16 | 2 |
| Mandich | 33 | 374 | 11 | 6 |
| Warfield | 27 | 536 | 20 | 2 |
| Twilley | 24 | 256 | 11 | 2 |
| Kiick | 18 | 155 | 9 | 1 |
| Briscoe | 11 | 132 | 12 | 1 |
| Csonka | 7 | 35 | 5 | 0 |
| Baker | 4 | 121 | 30 | 2 |
| Nottingham | 3 | 40 | 13 | 0 |
| Morris | 2 | 27 | 14 | 1 |
| Malone | 2 | 26 | 13 | 0 |
| Ginn | 2 | 3 | 2 | 0 |
| Fleming | 1 | 3 | 3 | 1 |

### Punt Returns

| Last Name | No. | Yds | Avg | TD |
|---|---|---|---|---|
| Scott | 31 | 346 | 11 | 0 |
| N. Moore | 9 | 136 | 15 | 0 |
| Babb | 2 | 29 | 15 | 0 |
| Anderson | 3 | 9 | 3 | 0 |
| Stuckey | 1 | 0 | 0 | 0 |

### Kickoff Returns

| Last Name | No. | Yds | Avg | TD |
|---|---|---|---|---|
| N. Moore | 22 | 587 | 27 | 0 |
| Ginn | 12 | 235 | 20 | 0 |
| Malone | 6 | 159 | 27 | 0 |
| Matheson | 5 | 65 | 13 | 0 |
| Baker | 1 | 22 | 22 | 0 |
| Babb | 1 | 0 | 0 | 0 |

### Passing – Punting – Kicking

| PASSING | Att | Comp | % | Yds | Yd/Att | TD | Int–% | RK |
|---|---|---|---|---|---|---|---|---|
| Griese | 253 | 152 | 60 | 1968 | 7.8 | 16 | 15– 6 | 4 |
| Morrall | 27 | 17 | 63 | 301 | 11.1 | 2 | 3–11 | |
| Kiick | 1 | 1 | 100 | 13 | 13.0 | 0 | 0– 0 | |
| Moore | 1 | 1 | 100 | 31 | 31.0 | 0 | 0– 0 | |
| Briscoe | 1 | 0 | 0 | 0 | 0.0 | 0 | 0– 0 | |

| PUNTING | No | Avg |
|---|---|---|
| Seiple | 65 | 38.6 |

| KICKING | XP | Att | % | FG | Att | % |
|---|---|---|---|---|---|---|
| Yepremian | 43 | 43 | 100 | 8 | 15 | 53 |

## BUFFALO BILLS

### Rushing

| Last Name | No. | Yds | Avg | TD |
|---|---|---|---|---|
| Simpson | 270 | 1125 | 4.2 | 3 |
| Braxton | 146 | 543 | 3.7 | 4 |
| Watkins | 41 | 170 | 4.1 | 2 |
| Ferguson | 54 | 111 | 2.1 | 2 |
| Calhoun | 21 | 88 | 4.2 | 0 |
| Hayman | 7 | 31 | 4.4 | 0 |
| Marangi | 4 | 20 | 5.0 | 0 |
| Mosley | 2 | 6 | 3.0 | 0 |

### Receiving

| Last Name | No. | Yds | Avg | TD |
|---|---|---|---|---|
| Rashad | 36 | 433 | 12 | 4 |
| Hill | 32 | 572 | 18 | 6 |
| Braxton | 18 | 171 | 10 | 0 |
| Seymour | 15 | 246 | 16 | 2 |
| Simpson | 15 | 189 | 13 | 1 |
| Chandler | 7 | 88 | 13 | 1 |
| Calhoun | 2 | 10 | 5 | 0 |
| Jenkins | 1 | 12 | 12 | 0 |
| Watkins | 1 | 7 | 7 | 0 |
| Green | 1 | 0 | 0 | 0 |

### Punt Returns

| Last Name | No. | Yds | Avg | TD |
|---|---|---|---|---|
| Walker | 43 | 384 | 9 | 0 |
| Cahill | 10 | 62 | 6 | 0 |
| Hayman | 2 | 13 | 7 | 0 |
| Kern | 1 | 1 | 1 | 0 |

### Kickoff Returns

| Last Name | No. | Yds | Avg | TD |
|---|---|---|---|---|
| Francis | 37 | 947 | 26 | 0 |
| Calhoun | 6 | 90 | 15 | 0 |
| Cornell | 3 | 45 | 15 | 0 |
| Cahill | 1 | 26 | 26 | 0 |
| Walker | 1 | 20 | 20 | 0 |
| Craig | 1 | 0 | 0 | 0 |
| Rashad | 1 | 0 | 0 | 0 |

### Passing – Punting – Kicking

| PASSING | Att | Comp | % | Yds | Yd/Att | TD | Int–% | RK |
|---|---|---|---|---|---|---|---|---|
| Ferguson | 232 | 119 | 51 | 1588 | 6.8 | 12 | 12– 5 | 7 |
| Marangi | 18 | 9 | 50 | 140 | 7.8 | 2 | 3–17 | |
| Simpson | 1 | 0 | 0 | 0 | 0.0 | 0 | 0– 0 | |

| PUNTING | No | Avg |
|---|---|---|
| Bateman | 67 | 40.5 |
| Jones | 35 | 37.3 |

| KICKING | XP | Att | % | FG | Att | % |
|---|---|---|---|---|---|---|
| Leypoldt | 25 | 29 | 86 | 19 | 33 | 58 |

## NEW ENGLAND PATRIOTS

### Rushing

| Last Name | No. | Yds | Avg | TD |
|---|---|---|---|---|
| Herron | 231 | 824 | 3.6 | 7 |
| Cunningham | 166 | 811 | 4.9 | 9 |
| Plunkett | 30 | 161 | 5.4 | 2 |
| Tarver | 41 | 101 | 2.5 | 2 |
| Ashton | 26 | 99 | 3.8 | 0 |
| Stingley | 5 | 63 | 12.6 | 1 |
| Wilson | 15 | 57 | 3.8 | 0 |
| Vataha | 3 | 21 | 7.0 | 0 |
| Hinton | 1 | 1 | 1.0 | 0 |
| Johnson | 2 | −4 | −2.0 | 0 |

### Receiving

| Last Name | No. | Yds | Avg | TD |
|---|---|---|---|---|
| Herron | 38 | 474 | 13 | 5 |
| Rucker | 27 | 436 | 16 | 4 |
| Vataha | 25 | 561 | 22 | 3 |
| Cunningham | 22 | 214 | 10 | 2 |
| B. Adams | 17 | 244 | 14 | 0 |
| Windsor | 12 | 127 | 11 | 1 |
| Stingley | 10 | 139 | 14 | 1 |
| Tarver | 9 | 37 | 4 | 0 |
| Johnson | 8 | 147 | 18 | 0 |
| Wilson | 3 | 38 | 13 | 0 |
| Hinton | 2 | 36 | 18 | 0 |
| Tanner | 2 | 23 | 12 | 1 |
| Schubert | 1 | 21 | 21 | 1 |
| Marshall | 1 | 17 | 17 | 0 |

### Punt Returns

| Last Name | No. | Yds | Avg | TD |
|---|---|---|---|---|
| Herron | 35 | 517 | 15 | 0 |
| Schubert | 3 | 15 | 5 | 0 |
| Durko | 1 | 1 | 1 | 0 |
| Hinton | 1 | 0 | 0 | 0 |

### Kickoff Returns

| Last Name | No. | Yds | Avg | TD |
|---|---|---|---|---|
| Herron | 28 | 629 | 23 | 0 |
| Johnson | 15 | 303 | 20 | 0 |
| Schubert | 5 | 112 | 22 | 0 |
| Hinton | 3 | 83 | 28 | 0 |
| Wilson | 2 | 33 | 17 | 0 |
| Hunt | 1 | 21 | 21 | 0 |
| Tanner | 2 | 17 | 9 | 0 |
| Durko | 1 | 0 | 0 | 0 |
| D. Smith | 1 | 0 | 0 | 0 |

### Passing – Punting – Kicking

| PASSING | Att | Comp | % | Yds | Yd/Att | TD | Int–% | RK |
|---|---|---|---|---|---|---|---|---|
| Plunkett | 352 | 173 | 49 | 2457 | 7.0 | 19 | 22– 6 | 9 |
| Shiner | 6 | 3 | 50 | 37 | 6.2 | 0 | 1–17 | |
| Graff | 1 | 1 | 100 | 20 | 20.0 | 0 | 0– 0 | |

| PUNTING | No | Avg |
|---|---|---|
| B. Barnes | 45 | 35.6 |

| KICKING | XP | Att | % | FG | Att | % |
|---|---|---|---|---|---|---|
| J. Smith | 42 | 43 | 98 | 16 | 22 | 73 |

## NEW YORK JETS

### Rushing

| Last Name | No. | Yds | Avg | TD |
|---|---|---|---|---|
| Riggins | 169 | 680 | 4.0 | 5 |
| Boozer | 153 | 563 | 3.7 | 4 |
| Burns | 40 | 158 | 4.0 | 0 |
| Adamle | 28 | 93 | 3.3 | 2 |
| Jackson | 20 | 74 | 3.7 | 0 |
| Bjorklund | 23 | 57 | 2.5 | 0 |
| Barkum | 1 | 2 | 2.0 | 1 |
| Namath | 8 | 1 | 0.1 | 1 |
| Woodall | 2 | −3 | −1.5 | 0 |

### Receiving

| Last Name | No. | Yds | Avg | TD |
|---|---|---|---|---|
| Barkum | 41 | 524 | 13 | 3 |
| Knight | 40 | 579 | 15 | 4 |
| Caster | 38 | 745 | 20 | 7 |
| Riggins | 19 | 180 | 10 | 2 |
| Boozer | 14 | 161 | 12 | 1 |
| Bell | 13 | 126 | 10 | 1 |
| Burns | 11 | 83 | 8 | 1 |
| Adamle | 9 | 84 | 9 | 0 |
| Brister | 5 | 90 | 18 | 0 |
| Jackson | 2 | 44 | 22 | 1 |
| Bjorklund | 2 | 15 | 8 | 0 |

### Punt Returns

| Last Name | No. | Yds | Avg | TD |
|---|---|---|---|---|
| Word | 38 | 301 | 8 | 0 |
| Piccone | 9 | 75 | 8 | 0 |
| Jackson | 6 | 49 | 8 | 0 |

### Kickoff Returns

| Last Name | No. | Yds | Avg | TD |
|---|---|---|---|---|
| Piccone | 39 | 961 | 25 | 0 |
| Jackson | 4 | 100 | 25 | 0 |
| Bjorklund | 4 | 73 | 18 | 0 |
| Word | 4 | 69 | 17 | 0 |
| Burns | 3 | 52 | 17 | 0 |
| B. Owens | 3 | 35 | 12 | 0 |
| Adamle | 2 | 17 | 9 | 0 |
| Knight | 2 | 0 | 0 | 0 |

### Passing – Punting – Kicking

| PASSING | Att | Comp | % | Yds | Yd/Att | TD | Int–% | RK |
|---|---|---|---|---|---|---|---|---|
| Namath | 361 | 191 | 53 | 2616 | 7.2 | 20 | 22– 6 | 5 |
| Woodall | 8 | 3 | 38 | 15 | 1.9 | 0 | 2–25 | |

| PUNTING | No | Avg |
|---|---|---|
| Gantt | 75 | 35.9 |

| KICKING | XP | Att | % | FG | Att | % |
|---|---|---|---|---|---|---|
| Leahy | 18 | 19 | 95 | 6 | 11 | 55 |
| Howfield | 8 | 12 | 67 | 6 | 7 | 86 |
| Gantt | 1 | 2 | 50 | 0 | 0 | — |

## BALTIMORE COLTS

### Rushing

| Last Name | No. | Yds | Avg | TD |
|---|---|---|---|---|
| Mitchell | 214 | 757 | 3.5 | 5 |
| Olds | 129 | 475 | 3.7 | 1 |
| Jones | 39 | 279 | 7.2 | 2 |
| Domres | 22 | 145 | 6.6 | 2 |
| McCauley | 30 | 90 | 3.0 | 0 |
| Doughty | 7 | 51 | 7.3 | 0 |
| Scott | 2 | 12 | 6.0 | 0 |
| Andrews | 5 | 6 | 1.2 | 0 |
| Orduna | 2 | 3 | 1.5 | 1 |

### Receiving

| Last Name | No. | Yds | Avg | TD |
|---|---|---|---|---|
| Mitchell | 72 | 544 | 8 | 2 |
| Chester | 37 | 461 | 13 | 1 |
| Doughty | 24 | 300 | 13 | 2 |
| Carr | 21 | 405 | 19 | 0 |
| Olds | 21 | 153 | 7 | 2 |
| Scott | 18 | 317 | 18 | 0 |
| McCauley | 17 | 112 | 7 | 1 |
| Speyrer | 9 | 110 | 12 | 1 |
| Smith | 1 | 14 | 14 | 0 |
| Orduna | 1 | 8 | 8 | 0 |

### Punt Returns

| Last Name | No. | Yds | Avg | TD |
|---|---|---|---|---|
| Berra | 16 | 114 | 7 | 0 |
| Speyrer | 8 | 54 | 7 | 0 |
| Scott | 3 | 31 | 10 | 0 |
| Laird | 11 | 30 | 3 | 0 |
| Rudnick | 2 | 23 | 12 | 0 |
| Volk | 1 | 1 | 1 | 0 |
| Bertuca | 1 | 0 | 0 | 0 |

### Kickoff Returns

| Last Name | No. | Yds | Avg | TD |
|---|---|---|---|---|
| Speyrer | 22 | 539 | 25 | 0 |
| Laird | 19 | 499 | 26 | 0 |
| Berra | 13 | 259 | 20 | 0 |
| Orduna | 3 | 68 | 23 | 0 |
| Scott | 3 | 61 | 20 | 0 |
| Mayo | 2 | 23 | 12 | 0 |
| Andrews | 1 | 18 | 18 | 0 |
| McCauley | 1 | 17 | 17 | 0 |
| Rudnick | 1 | 5 | 5 | 0 |
| Oldham | 1 | 0 | 0 | 0 |

### Passing – Punting – Kicking

| PASSING | Att | Comp | % | Yds | Yd/Att | TD | Int–% | RK |
|---|---|---|---|---|---|---|---|---|
| Jones | 270 | 143 | 53 | 1610 | 6.0 | 8 | 12– 4 | 10 |
| Domres | 153 | 77 | 50 | 803 | 5.2 | 8 | 12– 8 | 15 |
| McCauley | 2 | 1 | 50 | 5 | 5.5 | 1 | 0– 0 | |

| PUNTING | No | Avg |
|---|---|---|
| Lee | 71 | 37.1 |

| KICKING | XP | Att | % | FG | Att | % |
|---|---|---|---|---|---|---|
| Linhart | 22 | 22 | 100 | 12 | 20 | 60 |

## PITTSBURGH STEELERS 10-3-1 Chuck Noll

### Scores of Each Game

| | | |
|---|---|---|
| 30 | BALTIMORE | 0 |
| 35 | Denver (OT) | 35 |
| 0 | OAKLAND | 17 |
| 13 | Houston | 7 |
| 34 | Kansas City | 24 |
| 20 | CLEVELAND | 16 |
| 24 | ATLANTA | 17 |
| 27 | PHILADELPHIA | 0 |
| 10 | Cincinnati | 17 |
| 26 | Cleveland | 16 |
| 28 | New Orleans | 7 |
| 10 | HOUSTON | 13 |
| 21 | New England | 17 |
| 27 | CINCINNATI | 3 |

| Use Name | Pos. | Hgt | Wgt | Age | Int | Pts |
|---|---|---|---|---|---|---|
| Gordon Gravelle | OT | 6'5" | 250 | 25 | | |
| Jon Kolb | OT | 6'2" | 262 | 27 | | |
| Dave Reavis | OT | 6'5" | 250 | 24 | | |
| Rick Druschel | OG-OT | 6'2" | 248 | 22 | | |
| Sam Davis | OG | 6'1" | 255 | 30 | | |
| Jim Clack | C-OG | 6'3" | 250 | 26 | | |
| Gerry Mullins | OT-OG | 6'3" | 244 | 25 | | 6 |
| Ray Mansfield | C | 6'3" | 260 | 33 | | |
| Mike Webster | OG-C | 6'1" | 232 | 22 | | |
| L. C. Greenwood | DE | 6'5" | 245 | 27 | | 2 |
| Dwight White | DE | 6'4" | 255 | 25 | | |
| Jim Wolf | DE | 6'2" | 230 | 22 | | |
| Charlie Davis | DT | 6'1" | 265 | 22 | | |
| Joe Greene | DT | 6'4" | 275 | 27 | 1 | |
| Ernie Holmes | DT | 6'3" | 260 | 26 | | |
| Steve Furness | DE-DT | 6'4" | 255 | 24 | | |

| Use Name | Pos. | Hgt | Wgt | Age | Int | Pts |
|---|---|---|---|---|---|---|
| Ed Bradley | LB | 6'2" | 240 | 24 | | |
| Jack Ham | LB | 6'3" | 225 | 25 | 5 | |
| Marv Kellum | LB | 6'2" | 225 | 22 | 1 | |
| Jack Lambert | LB | 6'4" | 215 | 22 | 2 | |
| Andy Russell | LB | 6'3" | 225 | 32 | 1 | |
| Loren Toews | LB | 6'3" | 212 | 22 | | |
| Jimmy Allen | DB | 6'2" | 194 | 22 | | |
| Mel Blount | DB | 6'3" | 205 | 26 | 2 | 6 |
| Dick Conn | DB | 6' | 185 | 23 | | |
| Glen Edwards | DB | 6' | 185 | 27 | 5 | 6 |
| Donnie Shell | DB | 5'11" | 190 | 22 | | 1 |
| J.T. Thomas | DB | 6'2" | 196 | 23 | 5 | 6 |
| Mike Wagner | DB | 6'1" | 210 | 25 | 2 | |

Henry Davis – Injury

| Use Name | Pos. | Hgt | Wgt | Age | Int | Pts |
|---|---|---|---|---|---|---|
| Terry Bradshaw | QB | 6'3" | 218 | 25 | | 12 |
| Joe Gilliam | QB | 6'2" | 187 | 23 | | 6 |
| Terry Hanratty | QB | 6'1" | 210 | 26 | | |
| Rocky Bleier | HB | 5'11" | 210 | 28 | | 12 |
| Preston Pearson | HB | 6'1" | 205 | 29 | | 24 |
| Franco Harris | FB-HB | 6'2" | 230 | 24 | | 36 |
| Reggie Harrison (from STL) | FB | 5'11" | 215 | 24 | | 6 |
| Steve Davis | HB-FB | 6'1" | 218 | 24 | | 18 |
| John Fuqua | HB-FB | 5'11" | 188 | 26 | | 12 |
| Reggie Garrett | WR | 6'1" | 172 | 22 | | |
| Frank Lewis | WR | 6'1" | 196 | 27 | | 24 |
| Ron Shanklin | WR | 6'1" | 190 | 27 | | 6 |
| John Stallworth | WR | 6'2" | 183 | 22 | | 6 |
| Lynn Swann | WR | 6' | 178 | 22 | | 18 |
| Larry Brown | TE | 6'4" | 230 | 25 | | 6 |
| Randy Grossman | TE | 6'1" | 215 | 20 | | |
| John McMakin | TE | 6'3" | 232 | 23 | | |
| Roy Gerela | K | 5'10" | 185 | 26 | | 93 |
| Bobby Walden | K | 6' | 190 | 26 | | |

## CINCINNATI BENGALS 7-7-0 Paul Brown

### Scores of Each Game

| | | |
|---|---|---|
| 33 | CLEVELAND | 7 |
| 17 | SAN DIEGO | 20 |
| 21 | San Francisco | 3 |
| 28 | WASHINGTON | 17 |
| 34 | Cleveland | 24 |
| 27 | Oakland | 30 |
| 21 | HOUSTON | 34 |
| 24 | Baltimore | 14 |
| 17 | PITTSBURGH | 10 |
| 3 | Houston | 20 |
| 33 | KANSAS CITY | 6 |
| 1 | Miami | 24 |
| 19 | DETROIT | 23 |
| 3 | Pittsburgh | 27 |

| Use Name | Pos. | Hgt | Wgt | Age | Int | Pts |
|---|---|---|---|---|---|---|
| Vern Holland | OT | 6'5" | 268 | 26 | | |
| Dave Lapham | OT | 6'3" | 255 | 22 | | |
| Rufus Mayes | OT | 6'5" | 258 | 26 | | |
| Stan Walters | OT | 6'6" | 262 | 26 | | |
| Howard Fest | OG-OT | 6'6" | 256 | 28 | | |
| Pat Matson | OG | 6'1" | 245 | 30 | | |
| John Shinners | OG | 6'2" | 255 | 27 | | |
| Bob Johnson | C | 6'5" | 262 | 28 | | |
| Royce Berry | DE | 6'3" | 250 | 28 | | |
| Ken Johnson | DE | 6'5" | 256 | 27 | | |
| Bob Maddox | DE | 6'5" | 232 | 25 | | 6 |
| Sherman White | DE | 6'5" | 255 | 25 | | |
| Ron Carpenter | DT | 6'4" | 260 | 26 | 2 | |
| Bill Kollar | DT | 6'3" | 255 | 21 | | |
| Mike Reid | DT | 6'3" | 255 | 27 | | |

| Use Name | Pos. | Hgt | Wgt | Age | Int | Pts |
|---|---|---|---|---|---|---|
| Doug Adams | LB | 6'1" | 226 | 25 | | |
| Ken Avery | LB | 6'1" | 227 | 30 | | |
| Al Beauchamp | LB | 6'2" | 232 | 30 | 1 | |
| Evan Jolitz | LB | 6'2" | 225 | 22 | | |
| Tim Kearney | LB | 6'2" | 230 | 23 | | |
| Vic Koegel | LB | 6' | 215 | 22 | | |
| Jim LeClair | LB | 6'2" | 235 | 23 | | |
| Ron Pritchard | LB | 6'1" | 230 | 27 | | |
| Lyle Blackwood | DB | 6' | 190 | 23 | | |
| Tommy Casanova | DB | 6'2" | 195 | 24 | 2 | |
| Bernard Jackson | DB | 6' | 178 | 24 | 1 | |
| Bob Jones | DB | 6'1" | 194 | 23 | | |
| Lemar Parrish | DB | 5'11" | 185 | 26 | | 18 |
| Ken Riley | DB | 6' | 182 | 27 | 5 | |
| Ken Sawyer | DB | 6' | 192 | 22 | | |

| Use Name | Pos. | Hgt | Wgt | Age | Int | Pts |
|---|---|---|---|---|---|---|
| Ken Anderson | QB | 6'1" | 211 | 25 | | 12 |
| Wayne Clark | QB | 6'2" | 203 | 27 | | 6 |
| Charlie Davis | HB | 5'11" | 200 | 22 | | |
| Lenvil Elliott | HB | 6' | 205 | 22 | | 12 |
| Essex Johnson | HB | 5'9" | 200 | 27 | | 6 |
| Booby Clark | FB | 6'2" | 245 | 23 | | 36 |
| Doug Dressler | FB | 6'3" | 228 | 26 | | 12 |
| Ed Williams | FB | 6'2" | 245 | 24 | | 24 |
| Isaac Curtis | WR | 6' | 193 | 23 | | 60 |
| Charlie Joiner | WR | 5'11" | 188 | 26 | | 6 |
| John McDaniel | WR | 6'1" | 193 | 22 | | |
| Chip Myers | WR | 6'5" | 205 | 29 | | 6 |
| Al Chandler | TE | 6'2" | 230 | 23 | | |
| Bruce Coslet | TE | 6'3" | 227 | 28 | | |
| Bob Trumpy | TE | 6'6" | 228 | 29 | | 12 |
| Dave Green | K | 5'11" | 208 | 24 | | |
| Horst Muhlmann | K | 6'1" | 220 | 34 | | 65 |

## HOUSTON OILERS 7-7-0 Sid Gillman

### Scores of Each Game

| | | |
|---|---|---|
| 21 | SAN DIEGO | 14 |
| 7 | Cleveland | 20 |
| 7 | KANSAS CITY | 17 |
| 7 | PITTSBURGH | 13 |
| 10 | Minnesota | 51 |
| 27 | ST. LOUIS | 31 |
| 34 | Cincinnati | 21 |
| 27 | N.Y. Jets | 22 |
| 21 | Buffalo | 9 |
| 20 | CINCINNATI | 3 |
| 0 | DALLAS | 10 |
| 13 | Pittsburgh | 10 |
| 14 | Denver | 37 |
| 28 | CLEVELAND | 24 |

| Use Name | Pos. | Hgt | Wgt | Age | Int | Pts |
|---|---|---|---|---|---|---|
| Elbert Drungo | OT | 6'5" | 265 | 31 | | |
| Kevin Hunt | OT | 6'5" | 260 | 25 | | |
| Greg Sampson | OT | 6'6" | 260 | 23 | | |
| Ronnie Carroll | OG | 6'2" | 265 | 25 | | |
| Curley Culp (from KC) | DT-OG | 6'1" | 265 | 28 | | |
| Soloman Freelon | OG | 6'2" | 250 | 23 | | |
| Brian Goodman | OG | 6'2" | 250 | 25 | | |
| Harris Jones | OG | 6'4" | 245 | 29 | | |
| Ron Saul | OG | 6'2" | 255 | 26 | | |
| Fred Hoaglin | C | 6'4" | 250 | 30 | | |
| Sid Smith | OT-C | 6'4" | 260 | 26 | | |
| Elvin Bethea | DE | 6'3" | 255 | 28 | | 6 |
| Ed Fisher | DE | 6'3" | 245 | 25 | | |
| Tody Smith | DE | 6'5" | 250 | 25 | 1 | |
| Jim White | DE | 6'3" | 255 | 25 | | |
| Al Cowlings | LB-DT | 6'5" | 245 | 27 | | |
| Bubba McCollum | DT | 6' | 250 | 22 | | |

Ron Lou – injury

| Use Name | Pos. | Hgt | Wgt | Age | Int | Pts |
|---|---|---|---|---|---|---|
| Duane Benson | LB | 6'2" | 215 | 29 | 2 | |
| Gregg Bingham | LB | 6'1" | 230 | 23 | 4 | |
| Ralph Cindrich (to DEN) | LB | 6'1" | 230 | 24 | | |
| Marvin Davis | LB | 6'4" | 235 | 22 | | |
| Steve Kiner | LB | 6' | 220 | 27 | 1 | |
| Guy Roberts | LB | 6'1" | 217 | 24 | | |
| Ted Washington | LB | 6'1" | 240 | 26 | | |
| Willie Alexander | DB | 6'2" | 190 | 24 | 2 | |
| Bob Atkins | DB | 6'3" | 210 | 28 | 6 | |
| John Charles | DB | 6'1" | 200 | 30 | | |
| Leonard Fairley | DB | 5'11" | 200 | 24 | | |
| Al Johnson | DB | 6' | 200 | 24 | | |
| Tommy Maxwell | DB | 6'2" | 195 | 27 | 2 | |
| Zeke Moore | DB | 6'2" | 196 | 30 | 2 | 6 |
| Jeff Severson | DB | 6'1" | 185 | 24 | 1 | |
| C. L. Whittington | DB | 6'1" | 200 | 22 | | |

| Use Name | Pos. | Hgt | Wgt | Age | Int | Pts |
|---|---|---|---|---|---|---|
| Lynn Dickey | QB | 6'4" | 210 | 24 | | |
| James Foote | QB | 6'2" | 210 | 22 | | |
| Dan Pastorini | QB | 6'3" | 205 | 25 | | |
| Ronnie Coleman | HB | 5'10" | 195 | 23 | | 6 |
| Bob Gresham | HB | 5'11" | 195 | 26 | | |
| Willie Rodgers | HB | 6' | 210 | 25 | | 30 |
| Vic Washington | HB | 5'10" | 196 | 28 | | 12 |
| Terry Wells | HB | 5'11" | 195 | 23 | | |
| George Amundson | FB | 6'2" | 215 | 23 | | 30 |
| Fred Willis | FB | 6' | 205 | 26 | | 24 |
| Ken Burrough | WR | 6'4" | 210 | 26 | | 12 |
| Billy Johnson | WR | 5'9" | 170 | 22 | | 18 |
| Mike Montgomery | WR | 6'2" | 210 | 25 | | 6 |
| Billy Parks | WR | 6'1" | 190 | 26 | | 6 |
| Mack Alston | TE | 6'2" | 230 | 27 | | 18 |
| Jerry Broadnax | TE | 6'2" | 225 | 23 | | |
| Jeff Queen | TE | 6'1" | 217 | 28 | | 6 |
| David Beverly | K | 6'2" | 180 | 24 | | |
| Skip Butler | K | 6'2" | 200 | 26 | | 56 |

## CLEVELAND BROWNS 4-10-0 Nick Skorich

### Scores of Each Game

| | | |
|---|---|---|
| 7 | Cincinnati | 33 |
| 20 | HOUSTON | 7 |
| 7 | St. Louis | 29 |
| 24 | OAKLAND | 40 |
| 24 | CINCINNATI | 34 |
| 16 | Pittsburgh | 20 |
| 23 | DENVER | 21 |
| 25 | San Diego | 36 |
| 21 | New England | 14 |
| 16 | PITTSBURGH | 26 |
| 10 | BUFFALO | 15 |
| 7 | SAN FRANCISCO | 0 |
| 17 | Dallas | 41 |
| 24 | Houston | 28 |

| Use Name | Pos. | Hgt | Wgt | Age | Int | Pts |
|---|---|---|---|---|---|---|
| Barry Darrow | OT | 6'7" | 260 | 24 | | |
| Doug Dieken | OT | 6'5" | 254 | 25 | | |
| Bob McKay | OT | 6'5" | 260 | 26 | | |
| Gerry Sullivan | OT | 6'4" | 250 | 22 | | |
| Pete Adams | OG | 6'4" | 260 | 23 | | |
| Jim Copeland | OG | 6'2" | 243 | 29 | | |
| John Demarie | OG | 6'3" | 246 | 29 | | |
| Glen Holloway | OG | 6'3" | 250 | 25 | | |
| Chuck Hutchison | OG | 6'3" | 250 | 25 | | |
| Tom DeLeone | C | 6'2" | 252 | 24 | | |
| Bob DeMarco | C | 6'3" | 248 | 36 | | |
| Mark Ilgenfritz | DE | 6'4" | 250 | 22 | | |
| Mike Seifert | DE | 6'3" | 245 | 23 | | |
| Carl Barisch | DT | 6'4" | 255 | 23 | | |
| Walter Johnson | DT | 6'3" | 265 | 31 | | |
| Jerry Sherk | DT | 6'4" | 255 | 26 | | |

| Use Name | Pos. | Hgt | Wgt | Age | Int | Pts |
|---|---|---|---|---|---|---|
| Billy Andrews | LB | 6' | 225 | 29 | 1 | |
| Bob Babich | LB | 6'2" | 230 | 27 | 1 | |
| John Garlington | LB | 6'1" | 218 | 28 | 2 | |
| Charlie Hall | LB | 6'3" | 225 | 25 | 3 | 6 |
| Mel Long | LB | 6' | 228 | 27 | | |
| Jim Romaniszyn | LB | 6'2" | 224 | 22 | | |
| Preston Anderson | DB | 6'1" | 183 | 22 | | |
| Cliff Brooks | DB | 6'1" | 190 | 25 | | |
| Eddie Brown | DB | 5'11" | 180 | 22 | 2 | |
| Thom Darden | DB | 6'2" | 195 | 24 | 8 | 6 |
| Van Green | DB | 6'1" | 192 | 23 | 2 | 6 |
| Clarence Scott | DB | 6' | 180 | 25 | 4 | |
| Walt Sumner | DB | 6'1" | 195 | 27 | | |

Ken Smith – Injury

| Use Name | Pos. | Hgt | Wgt | Age | Int | Pts |
|---|---|---|---|---|---|---|
| Mike Phipps | QB | 6'2" | 205 | 26 | | 6 |
| Brian Sipe | QB | 6'1" | 195 | 25 | | 24 |
| Ken Brown | HB | 5'10" | 203 | 28 | | 36 |
| Greg Pruitt | HB | 5'10" | 190 | 23 | | 30 |
| Billy LeFear | WR-HB | 5'11" | 197 | 24 | | |
| Hugh McKinnis | FB | 6' | 215 | 26 | | 12 |
| Bo Scott | FB | 6'3" | 215 | 31 | | |
| Jubilee Dunbar | WR | 6' | 196 | 27 | | |
| Tim George | WR | 6'5" | 210 | 22 | | |
| Ben Hawkins | WR | 6'1" | 180 | 30 | | |
| Steve Holden | WR | 6' | 198 | 23 | | 18 |
| Fair Hooker | WR | 6'1" | 195 | 27 | | 6 |
| Gloster Richardson | WR | 6' | 200 | 31 | | 12 |
| Dave Sullivan | WR | 5'11" | 185 | 23 | | |
| Milt Morin | TE | 6'4" | 236 | 32 | | 18 |
| Jim Thaxton (From SD) | TE | 6'2" | 240 | 25 | 1 | |
| Don Cockroft | K | 6'1" | 195 | 29 | | 71 |
| Chris Gartner | K | 6' | 170 | 24 | | |

## PITTSBURGH STEELERS

### RUSHING

| Last Name | No. | Yds | Avg | TD |
|---|---|---|---|---|
| Harris | 208 | 1006 | 4.8 | 5 |
| Bleier | 88 | 373 | 4.2 | 2 |
| Pearson | 70 | 317 | 4.5 | 4 |
| Steve Davis | 71 | 246 | 3.5 | 2 |
| Bradshaw | 34 | 224 | 6.6 | 2 |
| Fuqua | 50 | 156 | 3.1 | 2 |
| Gilliam | 14 | 41 | 2.9 | 1 |
| Harrison | 6 | 30 | 5.0 | 1 |
| Lewis | 2 | 25 | 12.5 | 0 |
| Swann | 1 | 14 | 14.0 | 0 |
| Hanratty | 1 | −6 | −6.0 | 0 |
| Stallworth | 1 | −9 | −9.0 | 0 |

### RECEIVING

| Last Name | No. | Yds | Avg | TD |
|---|---|---|---|---|
| Lewis | 30 | 365 | 12 | 4 |
| Harris | 23 | 200 | 9 | 1 |
| Shanklin | 19 | 324 | 17 | 1 |
| Brown | 17 | 190 | 11 | 1 |
| Stallworth | 16 | 269 | 17 | 1 |
| Grossman | 13 | 164 | 13 | 0 |
| Swann | 11 | 208 | 19 | 2 |
| Steve Davis | 11 | 152 | 14 | 1 |
| Pearson | 11 | 118 | 11 | 0 |
| Bleier | 7 | 87 | 12 | 0 |
| Fuqua | 6 | 68 | 11 | 0 |
| Mullins | 1 | 7 | 7 | 1 |
| Harrison | 1 | 2 | 2 | 0 |

### PUNT RETURNS

| Last Name | No. | Yds | Avg | TD |
|---|---|---|---|---|
| Swann | 41 | 577 | 14 | 1 |
| Edwards | 16 | 128 | 8 | 0 |
| Conn | 10 | 69 | 7 | 0 |

### KICKOFF RETURNS

| Last Name | No. | Yds | Avg | TD |
|---|---|---|---|---|
| Steve Davis | 12 | 269 | 22 | 0 |
| Pearson | 12 | 258 | 22 | 0 |
| Blount | 5 | 152 | 30 | 0 |
| Harrison | 4 | 72 | 18 | 0 |
| Bleier | 3 | 67 | 22 | 0 |
| Conn | 1 | 34 | 34 | 0 |
| Edwards | 2 | 31 | 16 | 0 |
| Swann | 2 | 11 | 6 | 0 |
| Allen | 1 | 7 | 7 | 0 |

### PASSING – PUNTING – KICKING

PASSING

| Last Name | Att | Comp | % | Yds | Yd/Att | TD | Int–% | RK |
|---|---|---|---|---|---|---|---|---|
| Gilliam | 212 | 96 | 45 | 1274 | 6.0 | 4 | 8– 4 | 12 |
| Bradshaw | 148 | 67 | 45 | 785 | 5.3 | 7 | 8–5 | 13 |
| Hanratty | 26 | 3 | 12 | 95 | 3.7 | 1 | 5–19 | |

PUNTING

| Last Name | No | Avg |
|---|---|---|
| Walden | 78 | 39.0 |

KICKING

| Last Name | XP | Att | % | FG | Att | % |
|---|---|---|---|---|---|---|
| Gersla | 33 | 35 | 94 | 20 | 29 | 69 |

## CINCINNATI BENGALS

### RUSHING

| Last Name | No. | Yds | Avg | TD |
|---|---|---|---|---|
| Davis | 72 | 375 | 5.2 | 0 |
| Elliott | 68 | 345 | 5.1 | 1 |
| Anderson | 43 | 314 | 7.3 | 2 |
| B. Clark | 99 | 312 | 3.2 | 5 |
| Dressler | 72 | 255 | 3.5 | 2 |
| Williams | 58 | 238 | 4.1 | 3 |
| Curtis | 8 | 62 | 7.8 | 0 |
| E. Johnson | 19 | 44 | 2.3 | 0 |
| Joiner | 4 | 20 | 5.0 | 0 |
| W. Clark | 1 | 8 | 8.0 | 1 |
| McDaniel | 1 | 5 | 5.0 | 0 |

### RECEIVING

| Last Name | No. | Yds | Avg | TD |
|---|---|---|---|---|
| Myers | 32 | 383 | 12 | 1 |
| Curtis | 30 | 633 | 21 | 10 |
| Dressler | 29 | 196 | 7 | 0 |
| Joiner | 24 | 390 | 16 | 1 |
| B. Clark | 23 | 194 | 8 | 1 |
| Trumpy | 21 | 330 | 16 | 2 |
| Davis | 19 | 171 | 9 | 0 |
| Elliott | 18 | 187 | 10 | 1 |
| Williams | 13 | 98 | 8 | 1 |
| E. Johnson | 8 | 85 | 11 | 1 |
| McDaniel | 2 | 79 | 40 | 0 |
| Coslet | 2 | 24 | 12 | 0 |
| Jackson | 1 | 22 | 22 | 0 |
| Chandler | 1 | 9 | 9 | 0 |
| Johnson | 1 | 3 | 3 | 0 |

### PUNT RETURNS

| Last Name | No. | Yds | Avg | TD |
|---|---|---|---|---|
| Parrish | 18 | 338 | 19 | 2 |
| Casanova | 24 | 265 | 11 | 0 |
| Blackwood | 10 | 29 | 3 | 0 |

### KICKOFF RETURNS

| Last Name | No. | Yds | Avg | TD |
|---|---|---|---|---|
| Jackson | 29 | 682 | 24 | 0 |
| Davis | 12 | 243 | 20 | 0 |
| McDaniel | 3 | 64 | 21 | 0 |
| Casanova | 1 | 48 | 48 | 0 |
| Parrish | 2 | 36 | 18 | 0 |
| Williams | 2 | 33 | 17 | 0 |
| Dressler | 3 | 32 | 11 | 0 |
| Blackwood | 1 | 17 | 17 | 0 |
| Elliott | 1 | 2 | 2 | 0 |

### PASSING – PUNTING – KICKING

PASSING

| Last Name | Att | Comp | % | Yds | Yd/Att | TD | Int–% | RK |
|---|---|---|---|---|---|---|---|---|
| Anderson | 328 | 213 | 65 | 2667 | 8.1 | 18 | 10– 3 | 1 |
| W. Clark | 22 | 9 | 41 | 98 | 4.5 | 0 | 3–14 | |
| Green | 2 | 1 | 50 | 22 | 11.0 | 0 | 0–0 | |
| Elliott | 1 | 1 | 100 | 17 | 17.0 | 0 | 0–0 | |

PUNTING

| Last Name | No | Avg |
|---|---|---|
| Green | 66 | 40.9 |

KICKING

| Last Name | XP | Att | % | FG | Att | % |
|---|---|---|---|---|---|---|
| Muhlmann | 32 | 35 | 91 | 11 | 18 | 61 |

## HOUSTON OILERS

### RUSHING

| Last Name | No. | Yds | Avg | TD |
|---|---|---|---|---|
| Rodgers | 122 | 413 | 3.4 | 5 |
| V. Washington | 74 | 281 | 3.8 | 2 |
| Willis | 74 | 239 | 3.2 | 3 |
| Coleman | 52 | 193 | 3.7 | 1 |
| Amundson | 59 | 138 | 2.3 | 4 |
| B. Johnson | 5 | 82 | 16.4 | 1 |
| Dickey | 3 | 7 | 2.3 | 0 |
| Queen | 2 | 7 | 3.5 | 0 |
| Gresham | 3 | 6 | 2.0 | 0 |
| Beverly | 1 | 4 | 4.0 | 0 |
| Burrough | 1 | 0 | 0.0 | 0 |
| Alston | 1 | −3 | −3.0 | 0 |
| Pastorini | 24 | −6 | −0.2 | 0 |

### RECEIVING

| Last Name | No. | Yds | Avg | TD |
|---|---|---|---|---|
| Burrough | 36 | 492 | 14 | 2 |
| B. Johnson | 29 | 388 | 13 | 2 |
| Willis | 25 | 130 | 5 | 1 |
| Rodgers | 24 | 153 | 6 | 0 |
| Parks | 20 | 330 | 17 | 1 |
| Amundson | 18 | 152 | 8 | 1 |
| Alston | 17 | 249 | 15 | 3 |
| V. Washington | 13 | 92 | 7 | 0 |
| Montgomery | 9 | 179 | 20 | 1 |
| Coleman | 4 | 9 | 2 | 0 |
| Broadnax | 3 | 69 | 23 | 0 |
| Gresham | 3 | 19 | 6 | 0 |
| Wells | 1 | 9 | 9 | 0 |
| Queen | 1 | 4 | 4 | 1 |

### PUNT RETURNS

| Last Name | No. | Yds | Avg | TD |
|---|---|---|---|---|
| B. Johnson | 30 | 409 | 14 | 0 |
| Severson | 11 | 86 | 8 | 0 |

### KICKOFF RETURNS

| Last Name | No. | Yds | Avg | TD |
|---|---|---|---|---|
| B. Johnson | 29 | 785 | 27 | 0 |
| Gresham | 9 | 180 | 20 | 0 |
| V. Washington | 7 | 177 | 25 | 0 |
| Severson | 6 | 108 | 18 | 0 |
| Coleman | 3 | 91 | 30 | 0 |
| Whittington | 3 | 37 | 12 | 0 |
| Amundson | 2 | 17 | 9 | 0 |
| A. Johnson | 1 | 14 | 14 | 0 |
| Saul | 1 | 10 | 10 | 0 |
| Jones | 1 | 0 | 0 | 0 |

### PASSING – PUNTING – KICKING

PASSING

| Last Name | Att | Comp | % | Yds | Yd/Att | TD | Int–% | RK |
|---|---|---|---|---|---|---|---|---|
| Pastorini | 247 | 140 | 57 | 1571 | 6.4 | 10 | 10– 4 | 5 |
| Dickey | 113 | 63 | 56 | 704 | 6.2 | 2 | 8– 7 | |
| Coleman | 2 | 0 | 0 | 0 | 0.0 | 0 | 0–0 | |
| Amundson | 1 | 0 | 0 | 0 | 0.0 | 0 | 1–100 | |

PUNTING

| Last Name | No | Avg |
|---|---|---|
| Beverly | 79 | 39.2 |

KICKING

| Last Name | XP | Att | % | FG | Att | % |
|---|---|---|---|---|---|---|
| Butler | 29 | 29 | 100 | 9 | 19 | 47 |

## CLEVELAND BROWNS

### RUSHING

| Last Name | No. | Yds | Avg | TD |
|---|---|---|---|---|
| Pruitt | 126 | 540 | 4.3 | 3 |
| McKinnis | 124 | 519 | 4.2 | 2 |
| K. Brown | 125 | 458 | 3.7 | 4 |
| Phipps | 39 | 279 | 7.2 | 1 |
| B. Scott | 23 | 86 | 3.7 | 0 |
| Sipe | 16 | 44 | 2.8 | 4 |
| Holden | 1 | 6 | 6.0 | 0 |
| LeFear | 6 | 2 | 0.3 | 0 |
| Thaxton | 1 | −10 | −10.0 | 0 |

### RECEIVING

| Last Name | No. | Yds | Avg | TD |
|---|---|---|---|---|
| McKinnis | 32 | 258 | 8 | 0 |
| Holden | 30 | 452 | 15 | 3 |
| K. Brown | 29 | 194 | 7 | 2 |
| Morin | 27 | 330 | 12 | 3 |
| Pruitt | 21 | 274 | 13 | 1 |
| Richardson | 9 | 266 | 30 | 2 |
| B. Scott | 7 | 22 | 3 | 0 |
| Dunbar | 6 | 74 | 12 | 0 |
| D. Sullivan | 5 | 92 | 18 | 0 |
| Thaxton | 4 | 71 | 18 | 0 |
| Hooker | 4 | 48 | 12 | 1 |
| LeFear | 4 | 21 | 5 | 0 |
| Green | 1 | 27 | 27 | 0 |

### PUNT RETURNS

| Last Name | No. | Yds | Avg | TD |
|---|---|---|---|---|
| Pruitt | 27 | 349 | 13 | 0 |
| Darden | 21 | 173 | 8 | 0 |
| LeFear | 2 | 1 | 1 | 0 |
| E. Brown | 2 | 0 | 0 | 0 |

### KICKOFF RETURNS

| Last Name | No. | Yds | Avg | TD |
|---|---|---|---|---|
| Pruitt | 22 | 606 | 28 | 1 |
| LeFear | 26 | 574 | 22 | 0 |
| E. Brown | 6 | 138 | 23 | 0 |
| Romaniszyn | 5 | 48 | 10 | 0 |
| K. Brown | 1 | 9 | 9 | 0 |

### PASSING – PUNTING – KICKING

PASSING

| Last Name | Att | Comp | % | Yds | Yd/Att | TD | Int–% | RK |
|---|---|---|---|---|---|---|---|---|
| Phipps | 256 | 117 | 46 | 1384 | 5.4 | 9 | 17–7 | 14 |
| Sipe | 108 | 59 | 55 | 603 | 5.6 | 1 | 7–7 | |
| Pruitt | 2 | 2 | 100 | 115 | 57.5 | 2 | 0–0 | |
| Cockroft | 1 | 1 | 100 | 27 | 27.0 | 0 | 0–0 | |

PUNTING

| Last Name | No | Avg |
|---|---|---|
| Cockroft | 90 | 40.5 |

KICKING

| Last Name | XP | Att | % | FG | Att | % |
|---|---|---|---|---|---|---|
| Cockroft | 29 | 30 | 97 | 14 | 16 | 88 |

## OAKLAND RAIDERS 12-2-0 John Madden

| Scores of Each Game | | |
|---|---|---|
| 20 | Buffalo | 21 |
| 27 | KANSAS CITY | 7 |
| 17 | Pittsburgh | 0 |
| 40 | Cleveland | 24 |
| 14 | SAN DIEGO | 10 |
| 30 | CINCINNATI | 27 |
| 35 | San Francisco | 24 |
| 28 | Denver | 17 |
| 35 | DETROIT | 13 |
| 17 | San Diego | 10 |
| 17 | DENVER | 20 |
| 41 | NEW ENGLAND | 26 |
| 7 | Kansas City | 6 |
| 27 | DALLAS | 23 |

| Use Name | Pos. | Hgt | Wgt | Age | Int | Pts |
|---|---|---|---|---|---|---|
| Henry Lawrence | OT | 6'4" | 268 | 22 | | |
| Harold Paul | OT | 6'5" | 245 | 24 | | |
| Art Shell | OT | 6'5" | 265 | 27 | | |
| John Vella | OT | 6'4" | 255 | 24 | | |
| George Buehler | OG | 6'2" | 260 | 27 | | |
| Dan Medlin | OG | 6'3" | 260 | 24 | | |
| Gene Upshaw | OG | 6'5" | 255 | 29 | | |
| Jim Otto | C | 6'2" | 255 | 36 | | |
| Dave Dalby | OG-C | 6'2" | 240 | 23 | | |
| Tony Cline | DE | 6'2" | 244 | 26 | | |
| Horace Jones | DE | 6'3" | 255 | 25 | | |
| Bubba Smith | DE | 6'7" | 265 | 29 | | |
| Kelvin Korver | DT | 6'6" | 270 | 25 | | |
| Otis Sistrunk | DT | 6'4" | 255 | 26 | 1 | 2 |
| Art Thoms | DT | 6'5" | 260 | 27 | | 6 |
| Dan Conners | LB | 6'1" | 230 | 32 | 3 | |
| Mike Dennery | LB | 6' | 222 | 24 | | |
| Gerald Irons | LB | 6'2" | 230 | 27 | 2 | |
| Monte Johnson | LB | 6'4" | 235 | 22 | 1 | |
| Phil Villapiano | LB | 6'1" | 222 | 25 | | |
| Gary Weaver | LB | 6'1" | 224 | 25 | | |
| Butch Atkinson | DB | 6' | 180 | 26 | 4 | |
| Willie Brown | DB | 6'1" | 195 | 33 | 1 | |
| Bob Prout | DB | 6'1" | 190 | 23 | | |
| Ron Smith | DB | 6'1" | 195 | 31 | | |
| Jack Tatum | DB | 5'10" | 200 | 25 | 4 | |
| Skip Thomas | DB | 6'1" | 205 | 24 | 6 | 6 |
| Jimmy Warren | DB | 5'11" | 175 | 35 | 2 | |
| Nemiah Wilson | DB | 6' | 165 | 31 | 3 | |
| George Blanda | QB | 6'2" | 215 | 46 | | 77 |
| Daryle Lamonica | QB | 6'2" | 215 | 33 | | |
| Larry Lawrence | QB | 6'1" | 208 | 25 | | |
| Ken Stabler | QB | 6'3" | 215 | 28 | | 6 |
| Clarence Davis | HB | 5'10" | 195 | 25 | | 18 |
| Harold Hart | HB | 6' | 206 | 21 | | 18 |
| Bob Hudson | HB | 5'11" | 205 | 26 | | |
| Charlie Smith | HB | 6'1" | 205 | 28 | | 12 |
| Mark van Eeghen | FB-HB | 6'1" | 215 | 22 | | |
| Warren Bankston | FB | 6'4" | 235 | 27 | | |
| Marv Hubbard | FB | 6'1" | 225 | 28 | | 24 |
| Pete Banaszak | HB-FB | 5'11" | 210 | 30 | | 30 |
| Fred Biletnikoff | WR | 6'1" | 190 | 31 | | 42 |
| Morris Bradshaw | WR | 6' | 198 | 21 | | |
| Cliff Branch | WR | 5'11" | 170 | 26 | | 78 |
| Frank Pitts | WR | 6'2" | 200 | 30 | | |
| Mike Siani | WR | 6'2" | 195 | 24 | | 6 |
| Dave Casper | TE | 6'4" | 250 | 22 | | 18 |
| Bob Moore | TE | 6'3" | 220 | 25 | | 12 |
| Ray Guy | K | 6'3" | 190 | 24 | | |
| George Jakowenko | K | 5'9" | 170 | 26 | | |

## DENVER BRONCOS 7-6-1 John Ralston

| Scores of Each Game | | |
|---|---|---|
| 10 | LOS ANGELES | 17 |
| 35 | PITTSBURGH (OT) | 35 |
| 3 | Washington | 30 |
| 17 | Kansas City | 14 |
| 33 | NEW ORLEANS | 17 |
| 27 | SAN DIEGO | 7 |
| 21 | Cleveland | 23 |
| 17 | OAKLAND | 28 |
| 17 | Baltimore | 6 |
| 34 | KANSAS CITY | 42 |
| 20 | Oakland | 17 |
| 31 | Detroit | 27 |
| 37 | HOUSTON | 14 |
| 0 | San Diego | 17 |

| Use Name | Pos. | Hgt | Wgt | Age | Int | Pts |
|---|---|---|---|---|---|---|
| Mike Current | OT | 6'4" | 270 | 28 | | |
| Claudie Minor | OT | 6'4" | 280 | 23 | | |
| Marv Montgomery | OT | 6'6" | 255 | 26 | | |
| LeFrancis Arnold | OG | 6'3" | 245 | 21 | | |
| Paul Howard | OG | 6'3" | 260 | 23 | | |
| Tommy Lyons | OG | 6'2" | 230 | 26 | | |
| Mike Schnitker | OG | 6'3" | 245 | 27 | | |
| Larron Jackson | OT-OG | 6'3" | 260 | 25 | | |
| Bobby Maples | C | 6'3" | 250 | 31 | | |
| Lyle Alzado | DE | 6'3" | 265 | 25 | | |
| Barney Chavous | DE | 6'3" | 252 | 23 | | |
| Steve Coleman | DE | 6'4" | 252 | 23 | | |
| John Grant | DE | 6'3" | 235 | 24 | | |
| Ed Smith | DE | 6'5" | 240 | 24 | 1 | |
| Pete Duranko | DT | 6'2" | 250 | 30 | | |
| Dan Goich | DT | 6'4" | 250 | 30 | | |
| Bob Kampa (from BUF) | DT | 6'4" | 245 | 23 | | |
| Paul Smith | DT | 6'3" | 256 | 29 | | |
| Ken Criter | LB | 5'11" | 223 | 27 | | |
| Randy Gradishar | LB | 6'3" | 233 | 22 | | |
| Tom Jackson | LB | 5'11" | 220 | 23 | 1 | |
| Bill Laskey | LB | 6'2" | 230 | 31 | 1 | |
| Ray May | LB | 6'1" | 230 | 29 | 2 | |
| Jim O'Malley | LB | 6'1" | 230 | 23 | | |
| Joe Rizzo | LB | 6'1" | 220 | 23 | | |
| Mike Simone | LB | 6' | 210 | 24 | | |
| Charlie Greer | DB | 6' | 205 | 28 | 1 | |
| Lonnie Hepburn | DB | 5'11" | 180 | 25 | | |
| Calvin Jones | DB | 5'7" | 170 | 23 | 5 | |
| John Pitts | DB | 6'4" | 218 | 29 | 1 | |
| John Rowser | DB | 6'1" | 190 | 30 | 4 | |
| Bill Thompson | DB | 6'1" | 200 | 27 | 5 | 6 |
| Maurice Tyler | DB | 6' | 188 | 24 | 1 | |
| John Hufnagel | QB | 6'1" | 194 | 23 | | |
| Charley Johnson | QB | 6' | 200 | 37 | | |
| Steve Ramsey | QB | 6'2" | 210 | 26 | | |
| Otis Armstrong | HB | 5'10" | 196 | 23 | | 72 |
| Floyd Little | HB | 5'10" | 196 | 32 | | 6 |
| Oliver Ross | HB | 6' | 210 | 24 | | |
| Jon Keyworth | FB | 6'3" | 230 | 23 | | 60 |
| Fran Lynch | HB-FB | 6'1" | 205 | 28 | | |
| Haven Moses | WR | 6'3" | 208 | 28 | | 12 |
| Jerry Simmons | WR | 6'1" | 190 | 31 | | 12 |
| Otto Stowe | WR | 6'2" | 188 | 25 | | 6 |
| Bill Van Heusen | WR | 6'1" | 200 | 28 | | 24 |
| Boyd Brown | TE | 6'4" | 216 | 22 | | |
| Bill Masters | TE | 6'5" | 240 | 30 | | |
| Riley Odoms | TE | 6'4" | 230 | 24 | | 36 |
| Jim Turner | K | 6'2" | 205 | 33 | | 68 |

Bobby Anderson – Broken Ankle

## KANSAS CITY CHIEFS 5-9-0 Hank Stram

| Scores of Each Game | | |
|---|---|---|
| 24 | N.Y. JETS | 16 |
| 7 | Oakland | 27 |
| 17 | Houston | 7 |
| 14 | DENVER | 17 |
| 24 | PITTSBURGH | 34 |
| 3 | Miami | 9 |
| 24 | San Diego | 14 |
| 21 | N.Y. GIANTS | 33 |
| 7 | SAN DIEGO | 14 |
| 42 | Denver | 34 |
| 6 | Cincinnati | 33 |
| 17 | St. Louis | 13 |
| 6 | OAKLAND | 7 |
| 15 | MINNESOTA | 35 |

| Use Name | Pos. | Hgt | Wgt | Age | Int | Pts |
|---|---|---|---|---|---|---|
| Tom Drougas (from DEN) | OT | 6'4" | 267 | 24 | | |
| Charlie Getty | OT | 6'4" | 260 | 22 | | |
| Dave Hill | OT | 6'5" | 260 | 33 | | |
| Jim Nicholson | OT | 6'6" | 260 | 24 | | |
| Francis Peay | OT | 6'5" | 250 | 30 | | |
| Wayne Walton | OG-OT | 6'5" | 255 | 25 | | |
| Ed Budde | OG | 6'5" | 265 | 33 | | |
| Tom Condon | OG | 6'3" | 240 | 21 | | |
| George Daney | OG | 6'3" | 240 | 27 | | |
| Tom Humphrey | C | 6'6" | 260 | 24 | | |
| Jack Rudnay | C | 6'3" | 240 | 26 | | |
| Bob Briggs | DE | 6'4" | 258 | 29 | | |
| Fred DeBernardi | DE | 6'6" | 250 | 25 | | |
| Marv Upshaw | DE | 6'3" | 260 | 27 | 1 | 6 |
| Wilbur Young | DE | 6'6" | 285 | 25 | 1 | 6 |
| Buck Buchanan | DT | 6'7" | 270 | 34 | | |
| Tom Keating | DT | 6'3" | 247 | 31 | | |
| John Matuszak | DT | 6'8" | 275 | 23 | | |
| Bobby Bell | LB | 6'4" | 228 | 34 | 1 | 6 |
| Tom Graham (from DEN) | LB | 6'2" | 235 | 24 | | |
| Willie Lanier | LB | 6'1" | 245 | 29 | 2 | 2 |
| Jim Lynch | LB | 6'1" | 235 | 29 | | |
| Al Palewicz | LB | 6'1" | 215 | 24 | | |
| Bob Thornbladh | LB | 6'1" | 220 | 22 | | |
| Clyde Werner | LB | 6'4" | 230 | 26 | 1 | |
| Nate Allen | DB | 5'10" | 170 | 26 | 1 | |
| Doug Jones | DB | 6'2" | 202 | 24 | 1 | |
| Jim Kearney | DB | 6'2" | 206 | 31 | | |
| Jim Marsalis | DB | 5'11" | 194 | 28 | | |
| Willie Osley | DB | 6' | 195 | 24 | | |
| Kerry Reardon | DB | 5'11" | 180 | 25 | 4 | |
| Mike Sensibaugh | DB | 5'11" | 192 | 25 | 4 | |
| Emmitt Thomas | DB | 6'2" | 192 | 31 | 12 | 12 |
| Dean Carlson | QB | 6'3" | 210 | 24 | | |
| Len Dawson | QB | 6' | 190 | 40 | | |
| David Jaynes | QB | 6'2" | 212 | 22 | | |
| Mike Livingston | QB | 6'3" | 212 | 28 | | |
| Woody Green | HB | 6'1" | 205 | 23 | | 24 |
| Cleo Miller | HB | 5'11" | 202 | 21 | | |
| Donnie Joe Morris | HB | 5'11" | 195 | 24 | | |
| Ed Podolak | HB | 6'1" | 205 | 27 | | 18 |
| Willie Ellison | FB-HB | 6'1" | 210 | 29 | | 12 |
| Wendell Hayes | FB | 6'2" | 220 | 33 | | 12 |
| Bill Thomas | FB | 6'2" | 225 | 24 | | |
| Jeff Kinney | HB-FB | 6'2" | 215 | 24 | | 6 |
| Larry Brunson | WR | 5'11" | 180 | 25 | | 12 |
| Andy Hamilton | WR | 6'3" | 190 | 24 | | |
| Barry Pearson | WR | 5'11" | 185 | 24 | | 6 |
| Otis Taylor | WR | 6'2" | 215 | 31 | | 12 |
| Elmo Wright | WR | 6' | 190 | 25 | | 12 |
| John Strada | TE | 6'3" | 230 | 22 | | |
| Morris Stroud | TE | 6'10" | 255 | 28 | | 12 |
| Jan Stenerud | K | 6'2" | 187 | 31 | | 75 |
| Jerrel Wilson | K | 6'4" | 222 | 32 | | |

Gary Butler – Knee Injury
John Lohmeyer – Injury

## SAN DIEGO CHARGERS 5-9-0 Tommy Prothro

| Scores of Each Game | | |
|---|---|---|
| 14 | Houston | 21 |
| 20 | Cincinnati | 17 |
| 21 | MIAMI | 28 |
| 7 | PHILADELPHIA | 13 |
| 10 | Oakland | 14 |
| 7 | Denver | 27 |
| 14 | KANSAS CITY | 24 |
| 36 | CLEVELAND | 25 |
| 14 | Kansas City | 7 |
| 10 | OAKLAND | 17 |
| 0 | Green Bay | 34 |
| 14 | N.Y. Jets | 27 |
| 28 | CHICAGO | 21 |
| 17 | DENVER | 0 |

| Use Name | Pos. | Hgt | Wgt | Age | Int | Pts |
|---|---|---|---|---|---|---|
| Terry Owens | OT | 6'6" | 260 | 30 | | |
| Brian Vertefeuille | OT | 6'3" | 252 | 23 | | |
| Russ Washington | OT | 6'6" | 290 | 27 | | |
| Mark Markovich | OG | 6'5" | 256 | 21 | | |
| Doug Wilkerson | OG | 6'2" | 256 | 27 | | |
| Ira Gordon | OT-OG | 6'3" | 265 | 26 | | |
| Jay Douglas | C | 6'6" | 260 | 23 | | |
| Carl Mauck | C | 6'3" | 243 | 27 | | |
| Coy Bacon | DE | 6'4" | 270 | 32 | | |
| Raymond Baylor | DE | 6'5" | 263 | 27 | | |
| Blenda Gay | DE | 6'5" | 250 | 23 | | 6 |
| Pete Lazetich | DE | 6'3" | 245 | 24 | | |
| Dave Tipton | DE | 6'6" | 240 | 25 | | |
| Bon Boatwright | DT | 6'5" | 262 | 22 | | |
| Bob Brown | DT | 6'5" | 290 | 34 | | |
| Dave Rowe | DT | 6'6" | 265 | 29 | | |
| John Teerlinck | DT | 6'5" | 245 | 23 | | |
| Charles Anthony | LB | 6'1" | 230 | 22 | 1 | |
| Fred Forsberg | LB | 6'1" | 225 | 30 | | |
| Carl Gersbach | LB | 6'1" | 230 | 27 | 1 | |
| Don Goode | LB | 6'2" | 234 | 23 | | |
| Mike Lee | LB | 6' | 232 | 23 | | |
| Chip Myrtle | LB | 6'2" | 225 | 29 | | |
| Floyd Rice | LB | 6'3" | 223 | 25 | 3 | |
| Mel Rogers | LB | 6'2" | 233 | 27 | | |
| Jeff Staggs | LB | 6'2" | 240 | 30 | | |
| Joe Beauchamp | DB | 6' | 188 | 30 | 1 | |
| Reggie Berry | DB | 6' | 185 | 25 | | |
| Danny Colbert | DB | 5'11" | 167 | 23 | | |
| Lenny Dunlap | DB | 6'1" | 198 | 25 | | |
| Chris Fletcher | DB | 5'11" | 182 | 25 | 4 | |
| George Hoey | DB | 5'10" | 180 | 27 | 1 | |
| Bob Howard | DB | 6'1" | 177 | 29 | 3 | |
| Sam Williams | DB | 6'2" | 192 | 22 | 1 | |
| Dan Fouts | QB | 6'3" | 193 | 23 | | 6 |
| Jesse Freitas | QB | 6'1" | 203 | 22 | | |
| Don Horn | QB | 6'2" | 195 | 29 | | |
| Glen Bonner | HB | 6'2" | 202 | 22 | | 24 |
| Bob Thomas | HB | 5'10" | 202 | 25 | | |
| Tommy Thompson | HB | 6'1" | 205 | 23 | | |
| Don Woods | HB | 6'1" | 210 | 23 | | 60 |
| Cid Edwards | FB | 6'2" | 230 | 30 | | |
| Bo Matthews | FB | 6'4" | 230 | 22 | | 24 |
| Jim Beirne | WR | 6'2" | 206 | 27 | | |
| Harrison Davis | WR | 6'4" | 220 | 22 | | 12 |
| Gary Garrison | WR | 6'1" | 195 | 30 | | 30 |
| Dick Gordon | WR | 5'11" | 190 | 29 | | |
| Jerry LeVias | WR | 5'10" | 177 | 27 | | |
| Dave Grannell | TE | 6'4" | 230 | 22 | | |
| Gary Parris | TE | 6'2" | 226 | 24 | | |
| Wayne Stewart | TE | 6'7" | 230 | 27 | | 6 |
| Dennis Partee | K | 6'2" | 209 | 28 | | 29 |
| Ray Wersching | K | 5'11" | 210 | 24 | | 15 |

Clint Jones – Injury
Reece Morrison – Injury

## OAKLAND RAIDERS

### RUSHING
| Last Name | No | Yds | Avg | TD |
|---|---|---|---|---|
| Hubbard | 188 | 865 | 4.6 | 4 |
| Davis | 129 | 554 | 4.3 | 2 |
| Banaszak | 80 | 272 | 3.4 | 5 |
| Hart | 51 | 268 | 5.3 | 2 |
| C. Smith | 64 | 194 | 3.0 | 1 |
| van Eeghen | 28 | 139 | 5.0 | 0 |
| L. Lawrence | 4 | 39 | 9.8 | 0 |
| Hudson | 1 | 12 | 12.0 | 0 |
| Bankston | 1 | 6 | 6.0 | 0 |
| Stabler | 12 | -2 | -0.2 | 0 |
| Lamonica | 2 | -3 | -1.5 | 0 |
| Pitts | 1 | -10 | -10.0 | 0 |

### RECEIVING
| Last Name | No. | Yds | Avg | TD |
|---|---|---|---|---|
| Branch | 60 | 1092 | 18 | 13 |
| Biletnikoff | 42 | 593 | 14 | 7 |
| Moore | 30 | 356 | 12 | 2 |
| Davis | 11 | 145 | 13 | 1 |
| Hubbard | 11 | 95 | 9 | 0 |
| Banaszak | 9 | 64 | 7 | 0 |
| C. Smith | 8 | 100 | 13 | 1 |
| van Eeghen | 4 | 33 | 8 | 0 |
| Casper | 4 | 26 | 7 | 3 |
| Siani | 3 | 30 | 10 | 1 |
| Pitts | 3 | 23 | 8 | 0 |
| Hart | 1 | 4 | 4 | 0 |

### PUNT RETURNS
| Last Name | No. | Yds | Avg | TD |
|---|---|---|---|---|
| R. Smith | 41 | 486 | 12 | 0 |
| Atkinson | 4 | 31 | 8 | 0 |

### KICKOFF RETURNS
| Last Name | No. | Yds | Avg | TD |
|---|---|---|---|---|
| Hart | 18 | 466 | 26 | 0 |
| R. Smith | 19 | 420 | 22 | 0 |
| Banaszak | 8 | 137 | 17 | 0 |
| Davis | 3 | 107 | 36 | 0 |
| Bankston | 1 | 10 | 10 | 0 |
| Bradshaw | 1 | 0 | 0 | 0 |

### PASSING – PUNTING – KICKING
| PASSING | Att | Comp | % | Yds | Yd/Att | TD | Int-% | RK |
|---|---|---|---|---|---|---|---|---|
| Stabler | 310 | 178 | 57 | 2469 | 8.0 | 26 | 12- 4 | 2 |
| L. Lawrence | 11 | 4 | 36 | 29 | 2.6 | 0 | 1- 9 | |
| Lamonica | 9 | 3 | 33 | 35 | 3.9 | 1 | 4- 44 | |
| Blanda | 4 | 1 | 25 | 28 | 7.0 | 1 | 0- 0 | |
| Guy | 1 | 0 | 0 | 0 | 0.0 | 0 | 1-100 | |

| PUNTING | No | Avg |
|---|---|---|
| Guy | 74 | 42.2 |

| KICKING | XP | Att | % | FG | Att | % |
|---|---|---|---|---|---|---|
| Blanda | 44 | 46 | 96 | 11 | 17 | 65 |

## DENVER BRONCOS

### RUSHING
| Last Name | No | Yds | Avg | TD |
|---|---|---|---|---|
| Armstrong | 263 | 1407 | 5.3 | 9 |
| Keyworth | 81 | 374 | 4.6 | 10 |
| Little | 117 | 312 | 2.7 | 1 |
| Odoms | 4 | 25 | 6.3 | 0 |
| Hufnagel | 2 | 22 | 11.0 | 0 |
| Moses | 2 | 16 | 8.0 | 0 |
| Ross | 3 | 8 | 2.7 | 0 |
| Stowe | 1 | 1 | 1.0 | 0 |
| Van Heusen | 1 | -1 | -1.0 | 0 |
| Ramsey | 5 | -2 | -0.4 | 0 |
| Lynch | 3 | -2 | -0.7 | 0 |
| Johnson | 4 | -3 | -0.7 | 0 |

### RECEIVING
| Last Name | No. | Yds | Avg | TD |
|---|---|---|---|---|
| Odoms | 42 | 639 | 15 | 6 |
| Armstrong | 38 | 405 | 11 | 3 |
| Moses | 34 | 559 | 16 | 2 |
| Little | 29 | 344 | 12 | 0 |
| Van Heusen | 16 | 421 | 26 | 4 |
| Keyworth | 12 | 109 | 9 | 0 |
| Simmons | 10 | 161 | 16 | 2 |
| Stowe | 2 | 9 | 5 | 1 |
| Ross | 1 | 13 | 13 | 0 |

### PUNT RETURNS
| Last Name | No. | Yds | Avg | TD |
|---|---|---|---|---|
| Thompson | 26 | 350 | 14 | 0 |
| Greer | 13 | 90 | 7 | 0 |
| Little | 4 | 34 | 9 | 0 |

### KICKOFF RETURNS
| Last Name | No. | Yds | Avg | TD |
|---|---|---|---|---|
| Armstrong | 16 | 386 | 24 | 0 |
| Thompson | 13 | 325 | 25 | 0 |
| Little | 8 | 171 | 21 | 0 |
| Ross | 7 | 117 | 17 | 0 |
| Keyworth | 4 | 85 | 21 | 0 |
| Brown | 3 | 56 | 19 | 0 |
| Criter | 3 | 48 | 16 | 0 |

### PASSING – PUNTING – KICKING
| PASSING | Att | Comp | % | Yds | Yd/Att | TD | Int-% | RK |
|---|---|---|---|---|---|---|---|---|
| Johnson | 244 | 136 | 56 | 1969 | 8.1 | 13 | 9- 4 | 3 |
| Ramsey | 74 | 41 | 55 | 580 | 7.8 | 5 | 7-10 | |
| Hufnagel | 10 | 6 | 60 | 70 | 7.0 | 0 | 1-10 | |
| Van Heusen | 1 | 1 | 100 | 41 | 41.0 | 0 | 0- 0 | |

| PUNTING | No | Avg |
|---|---|---|
| Van Heusen | 75 | 40.3 |

| KICKING | XP | Att | % | FG | Att | % |
|---|---|---|---|---|---|---|
| Turner | 35 | 38 | 92 | 11 | 21 | 52 |

## KANSAS CITY CHIEFS

### RUSHING
| Last Name | No | Yds | Avg | TD |
|---|---|---|---|---|
| Green | 135 | 509 | 3.8 | 3 |
| Podolak | 101 | 386 | 3.8 | 2 |
| Kinney | 63 | 249 | 4.0 | 0 |
| Hayes | 57 | 206 | 3.6 | 2 |
| Miller | 40 | 186 | 4.7 | 0 |
| Ellison | 37 | 114 | 3.1 | 2 |
| Livingston | 9 | 28 | 3.1 | 0 |
| Dawson | 11 | 28 | 2.5 | 0 |
| Wright | 3 | 26 | 8.7 | 1 |
| Carlson | 2 | 17 | 8.5 | 0 |
| Taylor | 1 | 6 | 6.0 | 0 |
| Pearson | 1 | 1 | 1.0 | 0 |
| Jaynes | 1 | 0 | 0.0 | 0 |
| B. Thomas | 3 | -3 | -1.0 | 0 |
| Brunson | 5 | -33 | -6.6 | 0 |

### RECEIVING
| Last Name | No. | Yds | Avg | TD |
|---|---|---|---|---|
| Podolak | 43 | 306 | 7 | 1 |
| Pearson | 27 | 387 | 14 | 1 |
| Green | 26 | 247 | 10 | 1 |
| Taylor | 24 | 375 | 16 | 2 |
| Brunson | 22 | 374 | 17 | 2 |
| Kinney | 18 | 105 | 6 | 1 |
| Miller | 14 | 149 | 11 | 0 |
| Wright | 13 | 209 | 16 | 1 |
| Stroud | 12 | 141 | 12 | 2 |
| Ellison | 5 | 64 | 13 | 0 |
| Hayes | 4 | 23 | 6 | 0 |
| Hamilton | 2 | 25 | 13 | 0 |
| Strada | 1 | 16 | 16 | 0 |

### PUNT RETURNS
| Last Name | No. | Yds | Avg | TD |
|---|---|---|---|---|
| Podolak | 15 | 134 | 9 | 0 |
| Brunson | 19 | 111 | 6 | 0 |
| Reardon | 4 | 30 | 8 | 0 |
| Green | 5 | 21 | 4 | 0 |
| Morris | 1 | 0 | 0 | 0 |

### KICKOFF RETURNS
| Last Name | No. | Yds | Avg | TD |
|---|---|---|---|---|
| B. Thomas | 25 | 571 | 23 | 0 |
| Miller | 14 | 310 | 22 | 0 |
| Brunson | 12 | 280 | 23 | 0 |
| Morris | 1 | 17 | 17 | 0 |
| Green | 1 | 16 | 16 | 0 |
| Keating | 1 | 10 | 10 | 0 |
| Humphrey | 1 | 7 | 7 | 0 |
| Jones | 1 | 0 | 0 | 0 |

### PASSING – PUNTING – KICKING
| PASSING | Att | Comp | % | Yds | Yd/Att | TD | Int-% | RK |
|---|---|---|---|---|---|---|---|---|
| Dawson | 235 | 138 | 59 | 1573 | 6.7 | 7 | 13- 6 | 8 |
| Livingston | 141 | 66 | 47 | 732 | 5.2 | 4 | 10- 7 | 16 |
| Carlson | 15 | 7 | 47 | 116 | 7.7 | 0 | 1- 7 | |
| Jaynes | 2 | 0 | 0 | 0 | 0.0 | 0 | 1-50 | |
| Wilson | 2 | 0 | 0 | 0 | 0.0 | 0 | 0- 0 | |

| PUNTING | No | Avg |
|---|---|---|
| Wilson | 83 | 41.7 |

| KICKING | XP | Att | % | FG | Att | % |
|---|---|---|---|---|---|---|
| Stenerud | 24 | 26 | 92 | 17 | 24 | 71 |

## SAN DIEGO CHARGERS

### RUSHING
| Last Name | No | Yds | Avg | TD |
|---|---|---|---|---|
| Woods | 227 | 1162 | 5.1 | 7 |
| Matthews | 95 | 328 | 3.5 | 4 |
| Edwards | 65 | 261 | 4.0 | 0 |
| Bonner | 66 | 199 | 3.0 | 3 |
| Fouts | 19 | 63 | 3.3 | 1 |
| Thomas | 21 | 56 | 2.7 | 0 |
| D. Gordon | 1 | 25 | 25.0 | 0 |
| Freitas | 6 | 16 | 2.7 | 0 |
| Thompson | 6 | 8 | 1.3 | 0 |
| Davis | 2 | -7 | -3.5 | 0 |

### RECEIVING
| Last Name | No. | Yds | Avg | TD |
|---|---|---|---|---|
| Garrison | 41 | 785 | 19 | 5 |
| Woods | 26 | 349 | 13 | 3 |
| Stewart | 19 | 283 | 15 | 1 |
| Davis | 18 | 432 | 24 | 2 |
| Edwards | 13 | 102 | 8 | 0 |
| Matthews | 12 | 90 | 8 | 0 |
| Bonner | 11 | 101 | 9 | 1 |
| LeVias | 9 | 105 | 12 | 0 |
| Beirne | 7 | 121 | 17 | 0 |
| Grannell | 3 | 51 | 17 | 0 |
| Parris | 3 | 36 | 12 | 0 |
| D. Gordon | 2 | 15 | 8 | 0 |
| Thomas | 1 | 9 | 9 | 0 |

### PUNT RETURNS
| Last Name | No. | Yds | Avg | TD |
|---|---|---|---|---|
| Colbert | 15 | 128 | 9 | 0 |
| LeVias | 5 | 41 | 8 | 0 |
| D. Gordon | 8 | 39 | 5 | 0 |
| Hoey | 4 | 38 | 10 | 0 |
| Davis | 4 | 34 | 9 | 0 |
| Beirne | 1 | 7 | 7 | 0 |

### KICKOFF RETURNS
| Last Name | No. | Yds | Avg | TD |
|---|---|---|---|---|
| D. Gordon | 14 | 354 | 25 | 0 |
| Thompson | 12 | 242 | 20 | 0 |
| Colbert | 10 | 215 | 22 | 0 |
| LeVias | 6 | 116 | 19 | 0 |
| Hoey | 3 | 73 | 24 | 0 |
| Woods | 3 | 61 | 20 | 0 |
| Thomas | 2 | 32 | 16 | 0 |
| Parris | 3 | 29 | 10 | 0 |
| Dunlap | 1 | 19 | 19 | 0 |
| Stewart | 1 | 1 | 1 | 0 |

### PASSING – PUNTING – KICKING
| PASSING | Att | Comp | % | Yds | Yd/Att | TD | Int-% | RK |
|---|---|---|---|---|---|---|---|---|
| Fouts | 237 | 115 | 49 | 1732 | 7.3 | 8 | 13- 6 | 11 |
| Freitas | 109 | 49 | 45 | 719 | 6.6 | 3 | 8- 7 | |
| Woods | 3 | 1 | 33 | 28 | 9.3 | 1 | 1-33 | |

| PUNTING | No | Avg |
|---|---|---|
| Partee | 76 | 40.0 |

| KICKING | XP | Att | % | FG | Att | % |
|---|---|---|---|---|---|---|
| Partee | 26 | 28 | 93 | 1 | 5 | 20 |
| Wersching | 0 | 0 | — | 5 | 11 | 45 |

## NFC CHAMPIONSHIP GAME
### December 29, at Minnesota
### (Attendance 47,404)

### SCORING

|  | | | | |
|---|---|---|---|---|
| MINNESOTA | 0 | 7 | 0 | 7—14 |
| LOS ANGELES | 0 | 3 | 0 | 7—10 |

**Second Quarter**
Minn.   Lash, 29 yard pass from Tarkenton. PAT—Cox (kick)
L.A.   Ray, 27 yard field goal

**Fourth Quarter**
Minn.   Osborn, 1 yard rush. PAT—Cox (kick)
L.A.   Jackson, 44 yard pass from Harris. PAT—Ray (kick)

### TEAM STATISTICS

| MINN. | | L.A. |
|---|---|---|
| 18 | First Downs—Total | 15 |
| 9 | First Downs—Rushing | 5 |
| 7 | First Downs—Passing | 10 |
| 2 | First Downs—Penalty | 0 |
| 5 | Fumbles—Number | 3 |
| 2 | Fumbles—Lost Ball | 3 |
| 2 | Penalties—Number | 7 |
| 20 | Yards Penalized | 70 |
| 0 | Missed Field Goals | 0 |
| 69 | Offensive Plays | 58 |
| 269 | Net Yards | 340 |
| 3.9 | Average Gain | 5.9 |
| 3 | Giveaways | 5 |
| 5 | Takeaways | 3 |
| +2 | Difference | −2 |

### Six Inches Short of Glory

The Vikings were looking for a third trip to the Super Bowl after beating the Cardinals 30–14 in the opening round of the playoffs. The Rams, on the other hand, were looking for their first Super Bowl ticket after beating the Redskins 19–10 for their first playoff victory since 1952. Both clubs rode strong defenses into this title match, but the Vikings had come through the pressure of post-season play before and for that reason were touted as the favorites in this game. Although both defensive units played up to championship standards, the offensive units looked tight under the pressure. Turnovers made the contest a sloppy affair, with the Vikings losing the ball three times and the Rams five times. Neither team could move the ball in the first period, with the Viking defense showing right from the start that it would hold Lawrence McCutcheon, the NFC's leading rusher, to way below his average yardage. The Vikings scored in the second period on a Fran Tarkenton-to-Jim Lash pass, and a David Ray field goal made the score 7–3 in favor of Minnesota at halftime. Minnesota's Mike Eischeid placed a coffin-corner punt out of bounds on the Los Angeles one-yard line early in the third period, and the Rams started a long trek upfield. Five plays later, quarterback James Harris hit Harold Jackson with a long pass that carried the ball 73 yards to the Minnesota 2-yard line, with a clutch tackle by safety Jeff Wright preventing a touchdown. John Cappelletti carried the ball to the six-inch line on the next play, but that was as close as the Rams would come. Guard Tom Mack was called for illegal motion before the next play, and the ball was moved back to around the five yard line. Harris ran for three yards on the next play, but then his pass into the end zone for tight end Pat Curran was tipped away by cornerback Jackie Wallace and picked off by linebacker Wally Hilgenberg. After their 99-yard drive had gone for naught, the Rams never again came close to taking the lead. The Vikings marched 80 yards in the fourth period, with Dave Osborn scoring from the one-yard line on a fourth-down play. A long touchdown pass from Harris to Jackson brought the Rams back to 14–10 late in the game, but the Viking pass rush crumpled the Rams' late attempts to score again.

### INDIVIDUAL STATISTICS

**RUSHING**

| MINNESOTA | No | Yds | Avg. | LOS ANGELES | No | Yds | Avg. |
|---|---|---|---|---|---|---|---|
| Foreman | 22 | 80 | 3.6 | Bertelsen | 14 | 65 | 4.6 |
| Osborn | 20 | 76 | 3.8 | McCutcheon | 12 | 32 | 2.7 |
| Tarkenton | 4 | 5 | 1.2 | Harris | 3 | 17 | 5.7 |
| Marinaro | 1 | 3 | 3.0 | Cappelletti | 3 | 8 | 2.7 |
|  | 47 | 164 | 3.5 | Baker | 1 | −1 | −1.0 |
|  | | | | | 33 | 121 | 3.7 |

**RECEIVING**

| MINNESOTA | No | Yds | Avg. | LOS ANGELES | No | Yds | Avg. |
|---|---|---|---|---|---|---|---|
| Voigt | 4 | 43 | 10.8 | Bertelsen | 5 | 53 | 10.6 |
| Lash | 2 | 40 | 20.0 | Jackson | 3 | 139 | 46.3 |
| Gilliam | 2 | 33 | 16.5 | McCutcheon | 2 | 22 | 11.0 |
| Marinaro | 1 | 6 | 6.0 | Snow | 1 | 19 | 19.0 |
| Osborn | 1 | 1 | 1.0 | Klein | 1 | 10 | 10.0 |
|  | 10 | 123 | 12.3 | Cappelletti | 1 | 5 | 5.0 |
|  | | | | | 13 | 248 | 19.1 |

**PUNTING**

| MINNESOTA | | | | LOS ANGELES | | | |
|---|---|---|---|---|---|---|---|
| Eischeid | 6 | | 39.2 | Burke | 5 | | 43.8 |

**PUNT RETURNS**

| MINNESOTA | No | Yds | Avg. | LOS ANGELES | No | Yds | Avg. |
|---|---|---|---|---|---|---|---|
| McCullum | 3 | 20 | 6.7 | Bryant | 3 | 18 | 6.0 |
| N. Wright | 1 | 3 | 3.0 | Scribner | 1 | 1 | 1.0 |
|  | 4 | 23 | 5.6 | Bertelsen | 1 | 0 | 0.0 |
|  | | | | | 5 | 19 | 3.8 |

**KICKOFF RETURNS**

| MINNESOTA | No | Yds | Avg. | LOS ANGELES | No | Yds | Avg. |
|---|---|---|---|---|---|---|---|
| McClanahan | 2 | 55 | 27.5 | Bryant | 3 | 57 | 19.0 |
| McCullum | 1 | 23 | 23.0 | | | | |
|  | 3 | 78 | 26.0 | | | | |

**INTERCEPTION RETURNS**

| MINNESOTA | No | Yds | Avg. | LOS ANGELES | No | Yds | Avg. |
|---|---|---|---|---|---|---|---|
| Poltl | 1 | 16 | 16.0 | Stukes | 1 | 0 | 0.0 |
| Hilgenberg | 1 | 0 | 0.0 | | | | |
|  | 2 | 16 | 8.0 | | | | |

**PASSING**

| MINNESOTA | Att. | Comp. | Comp. Pct. | Yds. | Int. | Yds/ Att. | Yds/ Comp. | Yards Lost Tackled |
|---|---|---|---|---|---|---|---|---|
| Tarkenton | 20 | 10 | 50.0 | 123 | 1 | 6.2 | 12.3 | 2—18 |

| LOS ANGELES | Att. | Comp. | Comp. Pct. | Yds. | Int. | Yds/ Att. | Yds/ Comp. | Yards Lost Tackled |
|---|---|---|---|---|---|---|---|---|
| Harris | 23 | 13 | 56.5 | 248 | 2 | 10.8 | 19.1 | 2—29 |

---

## AFC CHAMPIONSHIP GAME
### December 29, at Oakland
### (Attendance 53,515)

### SCORING

|  | | | | |
|---|---|---|---|---|
| OAKLAND | 3 | 0 | 7 | 3—13 |
| PITTSBURGH | 0 | 3 | 0 | 21—24 |

**First Quarter**
Oak.   Blanda, 40 yard field goal

**Second Quarter**
Pitt.   Gerela, 23 yard field goal

**Third Quarter**
Oak.   Branch, 38 yard pass from Stabler. PAT—Blanda (kick)

**Fourth Quarter**
Pitt.   Harris, 8 yard rush. PAT—Gerela (kick)
Pitt.   Swann, 6 yard pass from Bradshaw. PAT—Gerela (kick)
Oak.   Blanda, 24 yard field goal
Pitt.   Harris, 21 yard rush. PAT—Gerela (kick)

### TEAM STATISTICS

| OAK. | | PITT. |
|---|---|---|
| 15 | First Downs—Total | 20 |
| 0 | First Downs—Rushing | 11 |
| 13 | First Downs—Passing | 7 |
| 2 | First Downs—Penalty | 2 |
| 0 | Fumbles—Number | 3 |
| 0 | Fumbles—Lost Ball | 2 |
| 5 | Penalties—Number | 4 |
| 60 | Yards Penalized | 30 |
| 1 | Missed Field Goals | 1 |
| 59 | Offensive Plays | 68 |
| 278 | Net Yards | 305 |
| 4.7 | Average Gain | 4.5 |
| 3 | Giveaways | 3 |
| 3 | Takeaways | 3 |
| 0 | Difference | 0 |

### Near, but Not Far Enough

The Raiders were the popular choice to go on to the Super Bowl, after their fine regular season and then their stirring upset of the Miami Dolphins December 21, taking a 28–26 victory with a Ken Stabler-to-Clarence Davis touchdown pass with 26 seconds left in the game. With the Dolphin dynasty ended, the Raiders seemed the logical heir apparent, but the Steelers, fresh from a 32–14 dissection of Buffalo in the opening playoff round, disputed this line of succession. The key to the game was the Steeler defense, which completely nullified the Raider offense that had led the NFL in points scored. The Raiders found some room to move in the air, but the ground lanes were totally blocked off by the Pittsburgh linemen and linebackers. Conversely, the Oakland defense shut off the Pittsburgh passing game for most of the afternoon, but Steeler runners Franco Harris and Rocky Bleier were able to steadily eat up yardage behind the fine blocking of their offensive line. The Raiders scored in the opening period with George Blanda hitting a 40-yard field goal. Roy Gerela drilled one home from 23 yards in the second period to send the clubs off at halftime tied at 3–3. The Raiders took a 10–3 lead in the third quarter when Stabler whipped a 38-yard touchdown pass to Cliff Branch, one of the swift receiver's nine receptions of the day. The Oakland defense shut the Steelers out in the third period, and the Raiders seemed on the way to their second Super Bowl appearance. The opportunistic Steelers, however, were waiting to pounce on any Oakland errors. The Steelers knotted the game at 10–10 on Franco Harris's eight-yard touchdown carry, and then the defensive unit took over. Pittsburgh linebacker Jack Ham picked off a Stabler pass on the Oakland 33-yard line and carried it back all the way down to the nine yard line. Terry Bradshaw soon capitalized on this break by tossing a six-yard scoring pass to Lynn Swann, and now the Steelers were in charge and the Raiders forced to play "catch up" football. They closed the gap to 17–13 on a Blanda field goal, but Steeler rookie Jack Lambert intercepted a Stabler pass which Franco Harris soon converted into a 22-yard touchdown run, making the final score 24–13.

The frustration for Oakland was neatly summed up by John Madden, the head coach, when he said after the game, "It's really hard to come this far and lose."

### INDIVIDUAL STATISTICS

**RUSHING**

| OAKLAND | No | Yds | Avg. | PITTSBURGH | No | Yds | Avg. |
|---|---|---|---|---|---|---|---|
| C. Davis | 10 | 16 | 1.6 | Harris | 29 | 111 | 3.8 |
| Banaszak | 3 | 7 | 2.3 | Bleier | 18 | 98 | 5.4 |
| Hubbard | 7 | 6 | 0.9 | Bradshaw | 3 | 15 | 5.0 |
| Stabler | 1 | 0 | 0.0 | | 50 | 224 | 4.5 |
|  | 21 | 29 | 1.4 | | | | |

**RECEIVING**

| OAKLAND | No | Yds | Avg. | PITTSBURGH | No | Yds | Avg. |
|---|---|---|---|---|---|---|---|
| Branch | 9 | 186 | 20.7 | L. Brown | 2 | 37 | 18.5 |
| Moore | 4 | 32 | 8.0 | Bleier | 2 | 25 | 12.5 |
| Biletnikoff | 3 | 45 | 15.0 | Swann | 2 | 17 | 8.5 |
| C. Davis | 2 | 8 | 4.0 | Stallworth | 2 | 16 | 8.0 |
| Banaszak | 1 | 0 | 0.0 | | 8 | 95 | 11.9 |
|  | 19 | 271 | 4.3 | | | | |

**PUNTING**

| OAKLAND | | | | PITTSBURGH | | | |
|---|---|---|---|---|---|---|---|
| Guy | 5 | | 43.4 | Walden | 4 | | 41.0 |

**PUNT RETURNS**

| OAKLAND | No | Yds | Avg. | PITTSBURGH | No | Yds | Avg. |
|---|---|---|---|---|---|---|---|
| none | | | | Swann | 3 | 30 | 10.0 |
| | | | | Edwards | 1 | 15 | 15.0 |
| | | | | | 4 | 45 | 11.3 |

**KICKOFF RETURNS**

| OAKLAND | No | Yds | Avg. | PITTSBURGH | No | Yds | Avg. |
|---|---|---|---|---|---|---|---|
| Hart | 3 | 63 | 21.0 | S. Davis | 3 | 76 | 25.3 |
| R. Smith | 2 | 42 | 21.0 | Pearson | 1 | 28 | 28.0 |
|  | 5 | 105 | 21.0 | | 4 | 104 | 26.0 |

**INTERCEPTION RETURNS**

| OAKLAND | No | Yds | Avg. | PITTSBURGH | No | Yds | Avg. |
|---|---|---|---|---|---|---|---|
| Wilson | 1 | 37 | 37.0 | Ham | 2 | 19 | 9.5 |
|  | | | | Thomas | 1 | 37 | 37.0 |
|  | | | | | 3 | 56 | 18.7 |

**PASSING**

| OAKLAND | Att. | Comp. | Comp. Pct. | Yds. | Int. | Yds/ Att. | Yds/ Comp. | Yards Lost Tackled |
|---|---|---|---|---|---|---|---|---|
| Stabler | 36 | 19 | 52.8 | 271 | 3 | 7.5 | 14.3 | 2—22 |

| PITTSBURGH | Att. | Comp. | Comp. Pct. | Yds. | Int. | Yds/ Att. | Yds/ Comp. | Yards Lost Tackled |
|---|---|---|---|---|---|---|---|---|
| Bradshaw | 17 | 8 | 47.1 | 95 | 1 | 5.6 | 11.9 | 1—14 |

## Rooney's 42-Year Reward

This year's Super Bowl matchups included the Minnesota Vikings, twice losers of the NFL's big meal ticket, and the Pittsburgh Steelers, who were enjoying their first trip to the post season event. For the Vikings, already branded as a club unable to win the big one, the game was a matter of professional pride. The Steelers motivation came from the fact that they had finally pocketed their first conference title since 1933, the year the franchise began.

Many of the past Super Bowls have been conservative and relatively dull games, Super Bowl IX was no exception as both teams continued the same offensive pattern of trying to avoid costly mistakes rather than trying to break the game open. In fact, the only score of the first half was a safety, with the Steelers getting two points when Viking quarterback Fran Tarkenton botched a pitch-out deep in his own territory and had to fall on the ball in the end zone. The close 2–0 halftime score belied a key difference in the teams; the Pittsburgh defense, led by Joe Greene, had successfully shut down Viking running star Chuck Foreman, while the Steeler offensive line was opening up constant holes in the Viking front four to allow Franco Harris to go rushing through.

The break that the Steelers were waiting for came on the opening kickoff of the second half, when Minnesota's Bill Brown fumbled the ball and Pittsburgh's Marv Kellum recovered it on the Viking 30-yard line. Harris followed his offensive line the rest of the way, covering 24 yards in one carry and finally going over for the touchdown on a nine-yard sweep around left end. The 9–0 Steeler lead held up through the third period, but the Vikings came back with a strong challenge in the final period. A pass interference call on Mike Wagner gave the Vikes the ball on the Steeler five-yard line, but Foreman fumbled on the next play and Greene recovered for Pittsburgh. Four plays later, Matt Blair blocked Bobby Walden's punt, with Terry Brown falling on it in the end zone for a Viking touchdown. Fred Cox missed the extra point, and the Steeler defense steadfastly refused to let the Vikes close enough to go for the tying field goal. A 65-yard Pittsburgh drive culminating in a four-yard scoring pass from Terry Bradshaw to Larry Brown iced the game away with 3:31 left.

By the time the final gun sounded the Vikings had their third loss in three attempts, and the Steelers had a host of triumphs which included Franco Harris and his record-setting 158 yards rushing and the happiest owner in pro football in Art Rooney who, after 42 frustrating years, finally claimed his dream—a pro football championship.

### LINEUPS

| PITTSBURGH | OFFENSE | MINNESOTA |
|---|---|---|
| Lewis | WR | Lash |
| Kolb | LT | Goodrum |
| Clack | LG | Maurer |
| Mansfield | C | Tingelhoff |
| Mullins | RG | White |
| Gravelle | RT | Yary |
| L. Brown | TE | Voigt |
| Shanklin | WR | Gilliam |
| Bradshaw | QB | Tarkenton |
| Bleier | RB | Foreman |
| Harris | RB | Osborn |
| | DEFENSE | |
| Greenwood | LE | Eller |
| Greene | LT | Sutherland |
| Holmes | RT | Page |
| White | RE | Marshall |
| Ham | LLB | Winston |
| Lambert | MLB | Siemon |
| Russell | RLB | Hilgenberg |
| Thomas | LCB | N. Wright |
| Blount | RCB | Wallace |
| Wagner | LS | J. Wright |
| Edwards | RS | Krause |
| | SUBSTITUTES | |
| PITTSBURGH | OFFENSE | |
| Sam Davis | | McMakin |
| Steve Davis | | Pearson |
| Druschel | | Reaves |
| Garrett | | Swann |
| Grossman | | Stallworth |
| Harrison | | Webster |
| | DEFENSE | |
| Allen | | Furness |
| Bradley | | Kellum |
| Conn | | Shell |
| C. Davis | | Toews |
| | KICKERS | |
| Gerela | | Walden |
| **MINNESOTA** | OFFENSE | |
| Alderman | | Marinaro |
| Anderson | | McClanahan |
| B. Brown | | McCullum |
| Craig | | Reed |
| Kingsriter | | Sunde |
| Lawson | | |
| | DEFENSE | |
| Blair | | Martin |
| T. Brown | | McNeill |
| Larsen | | Poltl |
| Lurtsema | | |
| | KICKERS | |
| Cox | | Eischeid |

### SCORING

| | | |
|---|---|---|
| PITTSBURGH | 0 2 7 7 – 16 | |
| MINNESOTA | 0 0 0 6 – 6 | |

**Second Quarter**
Pitt.  Safety – Tarkenton tackled in end zone.  7:49

**Third Quarter**
Pitt.  Harris, 12 yard rush  1:35
PAT – Gerela (kick)

**Fourth Quarter**
Minn.  T. Brown, Recovered blocked punt in end zone.  4:27
Kick failed
Pitt.  L. Brown, 4 yard pass from Bradshaw  11:29
PAT – Gerela (kick)

### TEAM STATISTICS

| PITT. | | MINN. |
|---|---|---|
| 17 | First Downs-Total | 9 |
| 11 | First Downs-Rushing | 2 |
| 5 | First Downs-Passing | 5 |
| 1 | First Downs-Penalty | 2 |
| 4 | Fumbles-Number | 3 |
| 2 | Fumbles-Lost Ball | 2 |
| 8 | Penalties-Number | 4 |
| 122 | Yards Penalized | 18 |
| 1 | Missed Field Goals | 1 |
| 73 | Offensive Plays | 47 |
| 333 | Net Yards | 119 |
| 4.6 | Average Gain | 2.5 |
| 2 | Giveaways | 5 |
| 5 | Takeaways | 2 |
| +3 | Difference | –3 |

### INDIVIDUAL STATISTICS

#### RUSHING

| PITTSBURGH | No. | Yds. | Avg. | MINNESOTA | No. | Yds. | Avg. |
|---|---|---|---|---|---|---|---|
| Harris | 34 | 158 | 4.6 | Foreman | 12 | 18 | 1.5 |
| Bleier | 17 | 65 | 3.8 | Tarkenton | 1 | 0 | 0.0 |
| Bradshaw | 5 | 33 | 6.6 | Osborn | 8 | –1 | –0.1 |
| Swann | 1 | –7 | –7.0 | | 21 | 17 | 0.8 |
| | 57 | 249 | 4.4 | | | | |

#### RECEIVING

| PITTSBURGH | No. | Yds. | Avg. | MINNESOTA | No. | Yds. | Avg. |
|---|---|---|---|---|---|---|---|
| T. Brown | 3 | 49 | 16.3 | Foreman | 5 | 50 | 10.0 |
| Stallworth | 3 | 24 | 8.0 | Voigt | 2 | 31 | 15.5 |
| Bleier | 2 | 11 | 5.5 | Osborn | 2 | 7 | 3.5 |
| Lewis | 1 | 12 | 12.0 | Gilliam | 1 | 16 | 16.0 |
| | 9 | 96 | 10.7 | Reed | 1 | –2 | –2.0 |
| | | | | | 11 | 102 | 9.3 |

#### PUNTING

| | No. | | Avg. | | No. | | Avg. |
|---|---|---|---|---|---|---|---|
| Walden | 7 | | 34.7 | Eischeid | 6 | | 37.2 |

#### PUNT RETURNS

| | No. | Yds. | Avg. | | No. | Yds. | Avg. |
|---|---|---|---|---|---|---|---|
| Swann | 3 | 34 | 11.3 | McCullum | 3 | 11 | 3.7 |
| Edwards | 2 | 2 | 1.0 | N. Wright | 1 | 1 | 1.0 |
| | 5 | 36 | 7.2 | | 4 | 12 | 3.0 |

#### KICKOFF RETURNS

| | No. | Yds. | Avg. | | No. | Yds. | Avg. |
|---|---|---|---|---|---|---|---|
| Harrison | 2 | 17 | 8.5 | McCullum | 1 | 26 | 26.0 |
| Pearson | 1 | 15 | 15.0 | McClanahan | 1 | 22 | 22.0 |
| | 3 | 32 | 10.7 | B. Brown | 1 | 2 | 2.0 |
| | | | | | 3 | 50 | 16.7 |

#### INTERCEPTION RETURNS

| | No. | Yds. | Avg. | | |
|---|---|---|---|---|---|
| Wagner | 1 | 26 | 26.0 | none | |
| Blount | 1 | 10 | 10.0 | | |
| Greene | 1 | 10 | 10.0 | | |
| | 3 | 46 | 15.3 | | |

#### PASSING

| PITTSBURGH | Att. | Comp. | Comp. Pct. | Yds. | Int. | Yds/ Att. | Yds/ Comp. | Yards Lost Tackled |
|---|---|---|---|---|---|---|---|---|
| Bradshaw | 14 | 9 | 64.3 | 96 | 0 | 6.9 | 10.7 | 2–12 |
| **MINNESOTA** | | | | | | | | |
| Tarkenton | 26 | 11 | 42.3 | 102 | 3 | 3.9 | 9.3 | 0–0 |

# 1975 N.F.C. Striking Toward Freedom

The N.F.L. Players Association had struck during training camp in 1974 over the inability to reach agreement with the club owners on a contract, eventually going back to work without a settlement. In the training camps of 1975, the contract negotiations still dragged on, with Players Association president Ed Garvey unable to maintain a united front among his players. With the Rozelle Rule concerning free agent status the main bone of contention, the New England Patriots took the lead by striking on September 13, the Saturday before their final exhibition game. The Pats sat that game out, and by Wednesday, the Redskins, Jets, Giants, and Lions had joined them in striking. A truce was arranged on Thursday, September 18, so that the regular season got under way without a delay on Sunday. Only after the season did the players' fight to do away with the Rozelle Rule, which limited their freedom of movement in playing out their option, come to fruit. In the winter, federal judge Earl R. Larson ruled that the Rozelle Rule was an illegal monopolistic practice by the N.F.L. The lawyers' bills piled up for the league into 1976, as the owners appealed Larson's ruling and successfully beat back a legal challenge to the college and expansion drafts to be held for the upcoming season.

## EASTERN DIVISION

**St. Louis Cardinals**—The Cards started the season in lacklustre form, with losses to the Cowboys and Redskins among their first four decisions. But quarterback Jim Hart got his explosive offense rolling thereafter and won nine of the remaining ten games on the schedule to recapture first place in the East. The Cards took the top spot directly, beating both the Redskins and Cowboys down the stretch. The Cards trailed the Redskins 17-10 with 20 seconds remaining in the game on November 16 when Hart threw a pass to Mel Gray in the end zone. Gray dropped the ball when hit, but after conferring on the field for three minutes amidst pressure from both teams and the fans, the officials ruled that he had held on to it just long enough to make it a legal catch and a touchdown. Jim Bakken kicked the extra point to send the game into overtime, and he won it 20-17 with a field goal seven minutes into the extra period.

**Dallas Cowboys**—This was to be a rebuilding year for the Cowboys. After all, they had not made the playoffs last season, and from that squad, Calvin Hill had jumped to the W.F.L. and Bob Lilly, Walt Garrison, and Cornell Green had retired. But the expert observers did not take note of the depth on the Dallas roster and the marvelous collection of rookies that reported to the team. With holdover stars like Roger Staubach and Drew Pearson, a blossoming star like Robert Newhouse, and a serviceable pickup in veteran Preston Pearson, the offense kept rolling along in fine fashion, even spicing things up with an occasional shift into the shotgun formation. Oldsters like Mel Renfro, Lee Roy Jordan, and Jethro Pugh anchored the defense, but youngsters like Too Tall Jones and Harvey Martin provided much of the thunder. The Cowboys got off to a quick start, hit a midseason slump, and finished strong to capture a wildcard spot in the playoffs.

**Washington Redskins**—The Redskin defensive unit had the same tough veteran look of recent years, but the offense took on a more youthful appearance. Sonny Jurgensen was retired, young Frank Grant took over a wide receiver spot, and rookie Mike Thomas revitalized the running attack with 919 yards. With Jurgensen gone, Billy Kilmer handled almost all the quarterbacking and came through with high grades despite some injury problems. When the Skins won six of their first eight games, including triumphs over St. Louis and Dallas, a playoff berth seemed assured. But losses to St. Louis and Oakland cast a shadow over those hopes, and with the wildcard spot on the line on December 13, the Skins were crushed by the Cowboys 31-10. The dispirited club dropped the season's finale to the Eagles and went home, out of the playoffs for the first time in George Allen's reign. One highpoint of the disappointing campaign was Charley Taylor's moving into first place in the all-time list of pass receivers, surpassing Don Maynard's old mark.

**New York Giants**—Moving into Shea Stadium as temporary boarders with the Jets, the Giants began their second season under Bill Arnsbarger with a promising 23-14 victory over the Eagles. But the club lapsed back into mediocrity, losing three games, upsetting Buffalo 17-14, and then losing six of the next seven, including a 40-14 humiliation to the Green Bay Packers. The offense lost much of its zip at midseason, and the defense suffered because of John Mendenhall's bad ankle.

**Philadelphia Eagles**—The Eagles had no draft picks in the first six rounds of the college draft, and with no new help arriving, last year's late-season slump continued into this campaign. The team had top-notch performers at several positions, with tight end Charley Young and middle linebacker Bill Bergey among the very best at their positions. A weak pass rush and other soft spots, however, sent the Eagles to the bottom of the division. They did win four games, including two over the Redskins, and they did battle Dallas and St. Louis furiously before losing close decisions, but this was not enough to save coach Mike McCormick from the chopping block after the season.

## CENTRAL DIVISION

**Minnesota Vikings**—The only Viking weakness on paper seemed to be at wide receiver, where John Gilliam had jumped to the W.F.L.

But when Gilliam's Chicago team folded in September, he returned to the Vikes in time for the opening of the N.F.L. schedule. With his return, the Vikings excelled at all positions and ripped off ten straight victories at the start of the campaign to quickly ice away the Central Division title. The defensive unit, led by Carl Eller, Alan Page, Jeff Siemon, and Paul Krause, turned in its usual superb performance, and the offense produced the most points in the N.F.C., thanks greatly to Fran Tarkenton and Chuck Foreman. Tarkenton led the Conference in touchdown passes and moved past Johnny Unitas into first place in the all-time totals. Foreman enjoyed an exceptional season, scoring 22 touchdowns to tie Gale Sayers' old mark which O.J. Simpson also surpassed this year.

**Detroit Lions**—Pre-season predictions didn't hold out much hope for the Lions. Their top receiver, Ron Jessie, had played out his option and signed with Los Angeles, and the rest of the squad simply didn't measure up to the powers of the Conference. Three victories in the first four games fanned some sparks of hope, but the team faded in a blaze of injuries. Bill Munson and Greg Landry, the two top quarterbacks, both went on the shelf with injuries on October 26, and third-stringer Joe Reed filled in the rest of the way.

**Chicago Bears**—Jack Pardee came in as head coach, fresh from leading the Florida Blazers into the championship game of the W.F.L. last year. He promised a fresh look, but the same pale complexion showed on both the offensive and defensive units. The most glaring sore spot was quarterback, where Bobby Douglass started the season. He led the team to a 35-7 opening game loss and was soon on waivers. Gary Huff handled the controls through the bulk of the schedule, but rookie Bob Avellini finished the season at the helm, showing promise in a 42-17 triumph over New Orleans. Bright spots were Wally Chambers' great year in the defensive line and the influx of new talent in rookie runners Walter Payton and Roland Harper, rookie defensive end Mike Hartenstein, and tight end Greg Latta, a W.F.L. refugee.

**Green Bay Packers**—The naming of Bart Starr as head coach beckoned to the championship years of Vince Lombardi, but the old quarterback brought no magic with him this year. The Pack lost its first four games before upsetting Dallas 19-17 to get into the victory column. The Packers won three of their last five contests, but all came over weak opponents. Starr faced the same problem that plagued the departed Dan Devine—how to generate an offense. John Hadl was cursed with interceptions, and fullback John Brockington slipped in production.

## WESTERN DIVISION

**Los Angeles Rams**—The Rams had never jelled into the superpower that people expected, but they still had undeniable quality and depth in all sectors. The defensive unit, featuring Jack Youngblood and Isaiah Robertson, ranked next to the Minnesota outfit in frugality of points allowed. The offense had a solid line led by Tom Mack, fine receivers in Harold Jackson and Ron Jessie, and a stable of hard-charging runners like Larry McCutcheon, Cullen Bryant, Jim Bertelson, and John Cappelletti. James Harris at quarterback was just good enough to lead this club to a runaway victory in the Western Division. Coach Chuck Knox found riches on his bench when Harris injured his shoulder on December 14 and back-up Ron Jaworski took the team to a victory in the finale.

**San Francisco 49ers**—The early promise of the Dick Nolan regime petered out into the frustration of a lukewarm club with some hot flashes. After a weak start, the 49ers came alive in mid-season with three straight wins, including a 24-23 upset of the Rams. But then the club dropped its last four games of the schedule to slip out of contention for the playoffs and cost Nolan his job. The quarterback position was a recurring problem, with neither Steve Spurrier nor Norm Snead taking charge. Del Williams and Gene Washington provided some offensive flair, but the 49ers needed some new direction to turn their fortunes around.

**Atlanta Falcons**—The Falcons traded a lot to Baltimore for the first pick in the college draft, using that pick to take quarterback Steve Bartkowski. Bartkowski showed good potential despite an injured elbow and a less-than-sterling offensive unit around him. The main threat was Dave Hampton, who ran for 1002 yards. The defensive unit also had its problems, but had a coming star in cornerback Rolland Lawrence. The fans still seemed turned off after the rising expectations and ultimate turmoil of the Van Brocklin years, and a sparse audience of 29,444 saw the Falcons beat the Saints 14-7 on October 5.

**New Orleans Saints**—The Saints relapsed into pitifulness this season. They lost their first three games while scoring only 10 points, beat Green Bay 20-19, and then lost their next two games. Coach John North was canned at this point, and Ernie Hefferle took over on an interim basis. He made it look easy when the Saints beat Atlanta 23-7 in his first game in charge, but his club then found its true level and lost its last seven games. The end of the season saw Hank Stram sign on as the new head coach to try to build the Saints into the sort of power that the Kansas City Chiefs had been under him.

## FINAL TEAM STATISTICS

### OFFENSE

| | ATL. | CHI. | DALL. | DET. | G.B. | L.A. | MINN. | N.O. | N.Y. | PHIL. | ST.L. | S.F. | WASH. |
|---|---|---|---|---|---|---|---|---|---|---|---|---|---|
| **FIRST DOWNS:** | | | | | | | | | | | | | |
| Total | 225 | 190 | 288 | 241 | 211 | 273 | **314** | 215 | 229 | 237 | 276 | 240 | 272 |
| by Rushing | 87 | 74 | 132 | 111 | 84 | 134 | **142** | 109 | 95 | 84 | 131 | 86 | 97 |
| by Passing | 118 | 99 | 142 | 111 | 112 | 120 | **156** | 82 | 105 | 134 | 128 | 133 | 150 |
| by Penalty | 20 | 17 | 14 | 19 | 15 | 19 | 16 | 24 | **29** | 19 | 17 | 21 | 25 |
| **RUSHING:** | | | | | | | | | | | | | |
| Number | 465 | 441 | 571 | 532 | 431 | **585** | 556 | 463 | 482 | 461 | 555 | 422 | 444 |
| Yards | 1794 | 1653 | **2432** | 2147 | 1547 | 2371 | 2094 | 1642 | 1627 | 1702 | 2402 | 1598 | 1752 |
| Average Yards | 3.9 | 3.7 | 4.3 | 4.0 | 3.6 | 4.1 | 3.8 | 3.5 | 3.4 | 3.7 | **4.3** | 3.8 | 3.9 |
| Touchdowns | 12 | 11 | 17 | 10 | 14 | 18 | 18 | 9 | 17 | 3 | **19** | 12 | 9 |
| **PASSING:** | | | | | | | | | | | | | |
| Attempts | 388 | 356 | 376 | 362 | 394 | 334 | 446 | 392 | 379 | **458** | 355 | 450 | 448 |
| Completions | 165 | 191 | 207 | 183 | 212 | 181 | **281** | 181 | 193 | 238 | 187 | 234 | 229 |
| Completion Percentage | 42.5 | 53.7 | 55.1 | 50.6 | 53.8 | 54.2 | **63.0** | 46.2 | 50.9 | 52.0 | 52.7 | 52.0 | 51.1 |
| Passing Yards | 2361 | 2169 | 2835 | 2240 | 2400 | 2450 | **3121** | 1961 | 2457 | 2640 | 2619 | 2806 | 3092 |
| Avg. Yards per Attempt | 6.1 | 6.1 | **7.5** | 6.2 | 6.1 | 7.3 | 7.0 | 5.0 | 6.5 | 5.8 | 7.4 | 6.2 | 6.9 |
| Avg. Yards per Complet. | **14.3** | 11.4 | 13.7 | 12.2 | 11.3 | 13.5 | 11.1 | 10.8 | 12.7 | 11.1 | 14.0 | 12.0 | 13.5 |
| Times Tackled Passing | 32 | 32 | 39 | 41 | 42 | 30 | 29 | 53 | 49 | 30 | **8** | 33 | 27 |
| Yards Lost Passing | 294 | 330 | 242 | 323 | 328 | 255 | 260 | 416 | 355 | 200 | **66** | 246 | 175 |
| Net Yards | 2067 | 1839 | 2593 | 1917 | 2072 | 2195 | 2861 | 1545 | 2102 | 2440 | 2553 | 2560 | **2917** |
| Touchdowns | 18 | 9 | 19 | 15 | 11 | 14 | 27 | 8 | 11 | 19 | 20 | 15 | **28** |
| Interceptions | 29 | 23 | 17 | **12** | 22 | 17 | 14 | 24 | 18 | 23 | 20 | 19 | 29 |
| Percent Intercepted | 7.5 | 6.5 | 4.5 | 3.3 | 5.6 | 5.1 | **3.1** | 6.1 | 4.8 | 5.0 | 5.9 | 4.2 | 6.5 |
| **PUNTS:** | | | | | | | | | | | | | |
| Number | 89 | 94 | 68 | 81 | **95** | 73 | 73 | 92 | 86 | 83 | 64 | 67 | 72 |
| Average Distance | 41.5 | 39.0 | 39.4 | **41.9** | 35.8 | 39.4 | 41.1 | 41.0 | 39.0 | 38.9 | 37.7 | **41.9** | 40.6 |
| **PUNT RETURNS:** | | | | | | | | | | | | | |
| Number | 35 | 51 | 32 | 36 | 30 | 55 | 36 | 47 | 49 | 35 | 40 | **63** | 61 |
| Yards | 248 | 512 | 313 | 328 | 190 | 517 | 167 | 372 | 350 | 299 | 410 | **616** | 464 |
| Average Yards | 7.1 | 10.0 | 9.8 | 9.1 | 6.3 | 9.4 | 4.6 | 9.1 | 7.1 | 8.5 | **10.3** | 9.8 | 7.6 |
| Touchdowns | 0 | 0 | **1** | 0 | 0 | 0 | 0 | 0 | **1** | 0 | **1** | 0 | **1** |
| **KICKOFF RETURNS:** | | | | | | | | | | | | | |
| Number | 66 | **75** | 54 | 52 | 63 | 34 | 36 | 62 | 55 | 59 | 55 | 60 | 58 |
| Yards | 1217 | **1644** | 1158 | 1114 | 1398 | 764 | 787 | 1291 | 1250 | 1388 | 1337 | 1372 | 1296 |
| Average Yards | 18.4 | 21.9 | 21.4 | 21.4 | 22.2 | 22.5 | 21.9 | 20.8 | 22.7 | 23.5 | **24.3** | 22.9 | 22.3 |
| Touchdowns | 0 | 0 | **1** | 0 | **1** | 0 | 0 | 0 | 0 | 0 | **1** | 0 | 0 |
| **INTERCEPTION RETURNS:** | | | | | | | | | | | | | |
| Number | 25 | 13 | 25 | 20 | 14 | 22 | **28** | 16 | 16 | 26 | 22 | 11 | 18 |
| Yards | 342 | 241 | 346 | 315 | 174 | 372 | **404** | 305 | 117 | 344 | 249 | 138 | 335 |
| Average Yards | 13.7 | 18.5 | 13.8 | 15.8 | 12.4 | 16.9 | 14.4 | **19.1** | 7.3 | 13.2 | 11.3 | 12.5 | 18.6 |
| Touchdowns | 2 | 2 | **3** | 1 | 0 | 2 | 0 | 0 | 0 | 2 | 1 | 1 | 0 |
| **PENALTIES:** | | | | | | | | | | | | | |
| Number | 78 | **100** | 94 | 95 | 72 | 73 | 90 | 71 | 52 | 81 | 83 | 89 | 78 |
| Yards | 635 | **881** | 715 | 838 | 606 | 746 | 708 | 527 | 440 | 744 | 730 | 693 | 723 |
| **FUMBLES:** | | | | | | | | | | | | | |
| Number | 37 | 35 | **25** | 28 | 31 | 26 | 33 | 33 | 44 | 29 | 33 | 44 | 28 |
| Number Lost | 19 | 17 | 18 | 18 | 16 | **8** | 12 | 16 | 19 | 12 | 19 | 25 | 17 |
| **POINTS:** | | | | | | | | | | | | | |
| Total | 240 | 191 | 350 | 245 | 226 | 312 | **377** | 165 | 216 | 225 | 356 | 255 | 325 |
| PAT Attempts | 33 | 22 | 41 | 29 | 27 | 36 | **48** | 19 | 29 | 24 | 43 | 31 | 40 |
| PAT Made | 30 | 18 | 38 | 25 | 22 | 31 | **46** | 18 | 24 | 21 | 41 | 27 | 37 |
| FG Attempts | 10 | 23 | **35** | 21 | 17 | 26 | 17 | 21 | 11 | 29 | 24 | 28 | 25 |
| FG Made | 4 | 13 | **22** | 14 | 12 | 21 | 13 | 11 | 6 | 20 | 19 | 14 | 16 |
| Percent FG Made | 40.0 | 56.5 | 62.9 | 66.7 | 70.6 | **80.8** | 76.5 | 52.4 | 54.5 | 69.0 | 79.2 | 50.0 | 64.0 |
| Safeties | 0 | 1 | 0 | 2 | **3** | 1 | 2 | 0 | 0 | 0 | 0 | 0 | 0 |

### DEFENSE

| | ATL. | CHI. | DALL. | DET. | G.B. | L.A. | MINN. | N.O. | N.Y. | PHIL. | ST.L. | S.F. | WASH. |
|---|---|---|---|---|---|---|---|---|---|---|---|---|---|
| **FIRST DOWNS:** | | | | | | | | | | | | | |
| Total | 288 | 282 | 234 | 235 | 260 | 204 | **190** | 251 | 264 | 275 | 284 | 253 | 255 |
| by Rushing | 131 | 118 | 100 | 100 | 132 | **77** | **77** | 105 | 137 | 130 | 118 | 102 | 105 |
| by Passing | 142 | 143 | 113 | 116 | 112 | 103 | **93** | 125 | 120 | 123 | 142 | 130 | 128 |
| by Penalty | 15 | 21 | 21 | 19 | 16 | 24 | 20 | 21 | **7** | 22 | 24 | 21 | 22 |
| **RUSHING:** | | | | | | | | | | | | | |
| Number | 571 | 547 | 474 | 480 | 580 | 423 | **383** | 507 | 555 | 529 | 487 | 518 | 525 |
| Yards | 2277 | 2070 | 1699 | 1929 | 2339 | 1533 | **1532** | 1930 | 2422 | 2233 | 1925 | 1829 | 2047 |
| Average Yards | 4.0 | 3.8 | 3.6 | 4.0 | 4.0 | 3.6 | 4.0 | 3.8 | 4.4 | 4.2 | 4.0 | **3.5** | 3.9 |
| Touchdowns | 13 | 25 | 13 | 12 | 14 | **4** | 7 | 15 | 16 | 20 | 16 | 14 | 11 |
| **PASSING:** | | | | | | | | | | | | | |
| Attempts | 437 | 399 | 373 | 360 | 369 | 387 | 360 | **354** | 365 | 424 | 446 | 411 | 389 |
| Completions | 227 | 208 | **162** | 181 | 192 | 187 | 175 | 206 | 196 | 226 | 233 | 228 | 217 |
| Completion Percentage | 51.9 | 52.1 | **43.4** | 50.3 | 52.0 | 48.3 | 48.6 | 58.2 | 53.7 | 53.3 | 52.2 | 55.5 | 55.8 |
| Passing Yards | 2810 | 2825 | 2328 | 2377 | 2474 | 2126 | **1994** | 2587 | 2539 | 2658 | 2862 | 2521 | 2714 |
| Avg. Yards per Attempt | 6.4 | 7.1 | 6.2 | 6.6 | 6.7 | **5.5** | 5.5 | 7.3 | 6.6 | 6.3 | 6.4 | 6.1 | 7.0 |
| Avg. Yards per Complet. | 12.4 | 13.6 | 14.4 | 13.1 | 12.9 | **11.4** | 11.4 | 12.6 | 12.9 | 11.8 | 12.3 | 11.6 | 13.0 |
| Times Tackled Passing | 35 | 35 | 41 | 38 | 32 | 43 | **46** | 28 | 26 | 17 | 24 | 40 | 36 |
| Yards Lost Passing | 275 | 319 | 288 | 306 | 302 | 337 | **373** | 200 | 172 | 120 | 192 | 324 | 276 |
| Net Yards | 2535 | 2506 | 2040 | 2071 | 2172 | 1789 | **1621** | 2387 | 2367 | 2538 | 2670 | 2197 | 2438 |
| Touchdowns | 16 | 22 | 19 | 16 | 13 | **11** | 14 | 25 | 20 | 13 | 16 | 15 | 17 |
| Interceptions | 25 | 13 | 25 | 20 | 14 | 22 | **28** | 16 | 16 | 26 | 22 | 11 | 18 |
| Percent Intercepted | 5.7 | 3.0 | 6.6 | 5.6 | 3.8 | 5.7 | **7.8** | 4.5 | 4.4 | 6.1 | 5.0 | 2.7 | 4.6 |
| **PUNTS:** | | | | | | | | | | | | | |
| Number | 71 | 86 | 82 | 80 | 70 | **89** | **89** | 75 | 82 | 65 | 67 | 84 | 87 |
| Average Distance | 41.1 | 41.4 | 39.6 | **36.9** | 39.7 | 39.7 | 39.6 | 42.7 | 37.6 | 37.0 | 40.1 | 42.1 | 38.9 |
| **PUNT RETURNS:** | | | | | | | | | | | | | |
| Number | 52 | 49 | 37 | 41 | 45 | 45 | 51 | 61 | 39 | 58 | **34** | 43 | 38 |
| Yards | 389 | 303 | 261 | 524 | **222** | 401 | 419 | 679 | 364 | 530 | 329 | 490 | 240 |
| Average Yards | 7.5 | 6.2 | 7.1 | 12.8 | **4.9** | 8.9 | 8.2 | 11.1 | 9.3 | 9.1 | 9.7 | 11.4 | 6.3 |
| Touchdowns | **0** | **0** | **0** | 1 | **0** | **0** | **0** | 1 | 1 | 1 | **0** | **0** | **0** |
| **KICKOFF RETURNS:** | | | | | | | | | | | | | |
| Number | 45 | 43 | 66 | 53 | 49 | 64 | 69 | **42** | 46 | 51 | 71 | 48 | 64 |
| Yards | 1038 | **893** | 1576 | 1084 | 1051 | 1327 | 1345 | 1073 | 927 | 1149 | 1609 | 1061 | 1357 |
| Average Yards | 23.1 | 20.8 | 23.9 | 20.5 | 21.4 | 21.0 | **19.5** | 25.5 | 20.2 | 22.5 | 22.7 | 22.1 | 21.2 |
| Touchdowns | **0** | **0** | **0** | **0** | 1 | **0** | **0** | 1 | **0** | **0** | 1 | **0** | 1 |
| **INTERCEPTION RETURNS:** | | | | | | | | | | | | | |
| Number | 29 | 23 | 17 | **12** | 22 | 17 | 14 | 24 | 18 | 23 | 20 | 19 | 29 |
| Yards | 602 | 235 | 203 | **82** | 388 | 204 | 235 | 367 | 214 | 411 | 216 | 212 | 469 |
| Average Yards | 20.8 | 10.2 | 11.9 | **6.8** | 17.6 | 12.0 | 16.8 | 15.3 | 11.9 | 17.9 | 10.8 | 11.2 | 16.2 |
| Touchdowns | 1 | **0** | **0** | **0** | 2 | **0** | **0** | 2 | 1 | 2 | **0** | **0** | 4 |
| **PENALTIES:** | | | | | | | | | | | | | |
| Number | 78 | 78 | 63 | 94 | 73 | 85 | 91 | 77 | **97** | **97** | 82 | 86 | 89 |
| Yards | 721 | 723 | 639 | **874** | 544 | 626 | 681 | 726 | 755 | 784 | 679 | 702 | 772 |
| **FUMBLES:** | | | | | | | | | | | | | |
| Number | 25 | 29 | 43 | 30 | **44** | 31 | 29 | 43 | 22 | 30 | 26 | 34 | 27 |
| Number Lost | 12 | 14 | 19 | 17 | **27** | 18 | 13 | 22 | 8 | 18 | 15 | 16 | 19 |
| **POINTS:** | | | | | | | | | | | | | |
| Total | 289 | 379 | 268 | 262 | 285 | **135** | 180 | 360 | 306 | 302 | 276 | 286 | 276 |
| PAT Attempts | 31 | 48 | 32 | 31 | 32 | **15** | 21 | 48 | 39 | 36 | 33 | 34 | 33 |
| PAT Made | 28 | 47 | 31 | 26 | 30 | **13** | 19 | 44 | 37 | 32 | 27 | 31 | 27 |
| FG Attempts | 38 | 18 | 18 | 23 | 31 | 19 | 13 | **12** | 21 | 27 | 26 | 22 | 30 |
| FG Made | 25 | 14 | 13 | 16 | 21 | 10 | 9 | **8** | 11 | 18 | 15 | 17 | 17 |
| Percent FG Made | 65.8 | 77.8 | 72.2 | 69.6 | 67.7 | 52.6 | 69.2 | 66.7 | **52.4** | 66.7 | 57.7 | 77.3 | 56.7 |
| Safeties | **0** | 1 | **0** | 1 | **0** | 1 | 1 | 2 | 1 | **0** | **0** | **0** | **0** |

## CONFERENCE PLAYOFFS

December 27, at Los Angeles (Attendance 72,650)

### SCORING

**LOS ANGELES 14 14 0 7 – 35**
**ST. LOUIS 0 9 7 7 – 23**

First Quarter
- L.A. Jaworski, 5 yard rush PAT – Dempsey (kick)
- L.A. Youngblood, 47 yard interception return PAT – Dempsey (kick)

Second Quarter
- L.A. Simpson, 65 yard interception return PAT – Dempsey (kick)
- St.L. Otis, 3 yard rush PAT – Kick failed
- L.A. Jackson, 66 yard pass from Jaworski PAT – Dempsey (kick)
- St.L. Bakken, 29 yard field goal

Third Quarter
- St. L. M. Gray, 11 yard pass from Hart PAT – Bakken (kick)

Fourth Quarter
- L.A. Jessie, 2 yard fumble recovery PAT – Dempsey (kick)
- St.L. Jones, 3 yard rush PAT – Bakken (kick)

### TEAM STATISTICS

| L.A. | | ST.L. |
|---|---|---|
| 26 | First Downs – Total | 22 |
| 14 | First Downs – Rushing | 5 |
| 10 | First Downs – Passing | 16 |
| 2 | First Downs – Penalty | 1 |
| 5 | Fumbles – Number | 3 |
| 3 | Fumbles – Lost Ball | 2 |
| 5 | Penalties – Number | 6 |
| 38 | Yards Penalized | 70 |
| 1 | Missed Field Goals | 0 |
| 73 | Offensive Plays | 70 |
| 440 | Net Yards | 363 |
| 6.0 | Average Gain | 5.2 |
| 3 | Giveaways | 5 |
| 5 | Takeaways | 3 |
| +2 | Difference | -2 |

### INDIVIDUAL STATISTICS

| LOS ANGELES | No. | Yds. | Avg. | ST. LOUIS | No. | Yds. | Avg. |
|---|---|---|---|---|---|---|---|
| **RUSHING** | | | | | | | |
| McCutcheon | 37 | 202 | 5.5 | Otis | 12 | 38 | 3.2 |
| Scribner | 4 | 16 | 4.0 | Jones | 6 | 28 | 4.7 |
| Bryant | 3 | 12 | 4.0 | Metcalf | 8 | 27 | 3.4 |
| Jaworski | 8 | 7 | 0.9 | Latin | 1 | 2 | 2.0 |
| | 52 | 237 | 4.6 | | 27 | 95 | 3.5 |
| **RECEIVING** | | | | | | | |
| Jessie | 4 | 52 | 13.0 | Metcalf | 6 | 94 | 15.7 |
| McCutcheon | 3 | 8 | 2.7 | Otis | 4 | 52 | 13.0 |
| Jackson | 2 | 84 | 42.0 | M. Gray | 3 | 52 | 17.3 |
| Bryant | 2 | 26 | 13.0 | Harris | 2 | 33 | 16.5 |
| T. Nelson | 1 | 33 | 33.0 | Latin | 2 | 23 | 11.5 |
| | 12 | 203 | 16.9 | Jones | 2 | 19 | 9.5 |
| | | | | Cain | 2 | 17 | 8.5 |
| | | | | Smith | 1 | 1 | 1.0 |
| | | | | | 22 | 291 | 13.2 |
| **PUNTING** | | | | | | | |
| Carrell | 5 | | 31.6 | West | 6 | | 42.7 |
| **PUNT RETURNS** | | | | | | | |
| Scribner | 1 | 7 | 7.0 | Metcalf | 1 | 3 | 3.0 |
| Elmendorf | 1 | 0 | 0.0 | | | | |
| | 2 | 7 | 3.5 | | | | |
| **KICKOFF RETURNS** | | | | | | | |
| Bryant | 3 | 61 | 20.3 | Metcalf | 3 | 105 | 35.0 |
| Jessie | 1 | 17 | 17.0 | Hammond | 2 | 36 | 13.0 |
| Elmendorf | 1 | 12 | 12.0 | Crump | 1 | 28 | 28.0 |
| | 5 | 90 | 18.0 | Latin | 1 | 22 | 22.0 |
| | | | | | 7 | 191 | 27.3 |
| **INTERCEPTION RETURNS** | | | | | | | |
| Simpson | 2 | 83 | 41.5 | none | | | |
| Youngblood | 1 | 47 | 47.0 | | | | |
| | 3 | 130 | 43.3 | | | | |

**PASSING**

| | Att. | Comp. | Comp. Pct. | Yds | Int | Yds/ Att. | Yds/ Comp | Yards Lost Tackled |
|---|---|---|---|---|---|---|---|---|
| **LOS ANGELES** | | | | | | | | |
| Jaworski | 23 | 12 | 52.2 | 203 | 0 | 8.8 | 16.9 | 0-0 |
| **ST. LOUIS** | | | | | | | | |
| Hart | 41 | 22 | 53.7 | 291 | 3 | 7.1 | 13.2 | 2-23 |

December 28, at Minnesota (Attendance 46,425)

### SCORING

**MINNESOTA 0 7 0 7 – 14**
**DALLAS 0 0 7 10 – 17**

Second Quarter
- Min.. Foreman, 1 yard rush PAT – Cox (kick)

Third Quarter
- Dall. Dennison, 4 yard rush PAT – Fritsch (kick)

Fourth Quarter
- Dall. Fritsch, 24 yard field goal
- Minn. McClanahan, 1 yard rush PAT – Cox (kick)
- Dall. D. Pearson, 50 yard pass from Staubach PAT – Fritsch (kick)

### TEAM STATISTICS

| MINN. | | DALL. |
|---|---|---|
| 12 | First Downs – Total | 19 |
| 6 | First Downs – Rushing | 7 |
| 6 | First Downs – Passing | 11 |
| 0 | First Downs – Penalty | 1 |
| 2 | Fumbles – Number | 3 |
| 0 | Fumbles – Lost Ball | 1 |
| 7 | Penalties – Number | 4 |
| 60 | Yards Penalized | 30 |
| 1 | Missed Field Goals | 1 |
| 58 | Offensive Plays | 75 |
| 215 | Net Yards | 356 |
| 3.1 | Average Gain | 4.3 |
| 1 | Giveaways | 1 |
| 1 | Takeaways | 1 |
| 0 | Difference | 0 |

### INDIVIDUAL STATISTICS

| MINNESOTA | No. | Yds. | Avg. | DALLAS | No. | Yds. | Avg. |
|---|---|---|---|---|---|---|---|
| **RUSHING** | | | | | | | |
| Foreman | 18 | 56 | 3.1 | Dennison | 11 | 36 | 3.3 |
| Tarkenton | 3 | 32 | 10.7 | P. Pearson | 11 | 34 | 3.1 |
| McClanahan | 4 | 22 | 5.5 | Newhouse | 12 | 33 | 2.8 |
| Marinaro | 2 | 5 | 2.5 | Staubach | 7 | 24 | 3.4 |
| | 27 | 115 | 4.3 | Fuggett | 1 | 4 | 4.0 |
| | | | | | 42 | 131 | 3.1 |
| **RECEIVING** | | | | | | | |
| Marinaro | 5 | 64 | 12.8 | P. Pearson | 5 | 77 | 15.4 |
| Foreman | 4 | 42 | 10.5 | D. Pearson | 4 | 91 | 22.8 |
| Gilliam | 1 | 15 | 15.0 | Newhouse | 2 | 25 | 12.5 |
| Lash | 1 | 15 | 15.0 | Richards | 2 | 20 | 10.0 |
| Voigt | 1 | -1 | -1.0 | Fuggett | 2 | 13 | 6.5 |
| | 12 | 135 | 11.3 | DuPree | 1 | 17 | 17.0 |
| | | | | Dennison | 1 | 3 | 3.0 |
| | | | | | 17 | 246 | 14.4 |
| **PUNTING** | | | | | | | |
| Clabo | 7 | | 39.6 | Hoopes | 6 | | 38.5 |
| **PUNT RETURNS** | | | | | | | |
| McCullum | 3 | 4 | 1.3 | Richards | 2 | 13 | 6.5 |
| Bryant | 1 | 1 | 1.0 | Harris | 2 | 5 | 2.5 |
| | 4 | 5 | 1.3 | | 4 | 18 | 4.5 |
| **KICKOFF RETURNS** | | | | | | | |
| McClanahan | 2 | 38 | 19.0 | P. Pearson | 2 | 26 | 13.0 |
| McCullum | 1 | 3 | 3.0 | Dennison | 1 | 13 | 13.0 |
| Osborn | 1 | 0 | 0.0 | | 3 | 39 | 13.0 |
| | 4 | 41 | 10.3 | | | | |
| **INTERCEPTION RETURNS** | | | | | | | |
| none | | | | Renfro | 1 | 0 | 0.0 |

**PASSING**

| | Att. | Comp. | Comp. Pct. | Yds. | Int. | Yds/ Att. | Yds/ Comp | Yards Lost Tackled |
|---|---|---|---|---|---|---|---|---|
| **MINNESOTA** | | | | | | | | |
| Tarkenton | 26 | 12 | 46.2 | 135 | 1 | 15.2 | 11.3 | 4-35 |
| **DALLAS** | | | | | | | | |
| Staubach | 29 | 17 | 58.6 | 256 | 0 | 8.8 | 15.1 | 5-21 |

## ST. LOUIS CARDINALS 11-3 Don Coryell

| Scores of Each Game | | |
|---|---|---|
| 23 | ATLANTA | 20 |
| 31 | Dallas | *37 |
| 26 | N.Y. GIANTS | 14 |
| 17 | Washington | 27 |
| 31 | PHILADELPHIA | 20 |
| 20 | N.Y. Giants | 13 |
| 24 | NEW ENGLAND | 17 |
| 24 | Philadelphia | 23 |
| 20 | WASHINGTON | *17 |
| 37 | N.Y. Jets | 6 |
| 14 | BUFFALO | 32 |
| 31 | DALLAS | 17 |
| 34 | Chicago | 20 |
| 24 | Detroit | 13 |

| Use Name | Pos. | Hgt | Wgt | Age | Int | Pts |
|---|---|---|---|---|---|---|
| Dan Dierdorf | OT | 6'4" | 280 | 26 | | |
| Greg Kindle | OG-OT | 6'4" | 265 | 24 | | |
| Roger Finnie | OG-OT | 6'3" | 250 | 29 | | |
| Henry Allison | OG | 6'3" | 255 | 28 | | |
| Conrad Dobler | OG | 6'3" | 255 | 24 | | |
| Bob Young | OG | 6'2" | 270 | 32 | | |
| Tom Brahaney | C | 6'2" | 250 | 23 | | |
| Tom Banks | OG-C | 6'1" | 245 | 27 | | |
| Bob Bell | DE | 6'4" | 250 | 27 | | |
| Council Rudolph | DE | 6'3" | 245 | 25 | 1 | |
| Ron Yankowski | DE | 6'5" | 250 | 28 | | |
| Lee Brooks | DT | 6'5" | 250 | 27 | | |
| Charlie Davis | DT | 6'1" | 265 | 23 | | |
| Bob Rowe | DT | 6'4" | 270 | 30 | | |
| Mark Arneson | LB | 6'2" | 220 | 25 | 1 | |
| Pete Barnes | LB | 6'3" | 240 | 30 | 2 | |
| Greg Hartle | LB | 6'2" | 225 | 24 | | |
| Steve Neils | LB | 6'2" | 215 | 24 | | |
| Larry Stallings | LB | 6'2" | 230 | 33 | 1 | |
| Ray White | LB | 6'1" | 220 | 26 | | |
| Dwayne Crump | DB | 5'11" | 180 | 25 | | 6 |
| Clarence Duren | DB | 6'1" | 190 | 24 | 1 | |
| Tim Gray | DB | 6'1" | 200 | 22 | | |
| Ken Reaves | DB | 6'3" | 210 | 30 | 3 | |
| Norm Thompson | DB | 6'1" | 180 | 27 | 7 | 6 |
| Jim Tolbert | DB | 6'3" | 210 | 31 | | |
| Roger Wehrli | DB | 6'1" | 190 | 27 | 6 | 1 |
| Jim Hart | QB | 6'2" | 210 | 31 | | 6 |
| Gary Keithley | QB | 6'3" | 215 | 24 | | |
| Dennis Shaw | QB | 6'2" | 210 | 28 | | |
| Josh Ashton | HB | 6'1" | 205 | 26 | | |
| Steve Jones | HB | 6' | 200 | 24 | | 18 |
| Jerry Latin | HB | 5'10" | 190 | 22 | | 6 |
| Terry Metcalf | HB | 5'10" | 185 | 23 | | 78 |
| Eddie Moss | FB | 6' | 215 | 26 | | 6 |
| Jim Otis | FB | 6' | 225 | 27 | | 36 |
| Mel Gray | WR | 5'9" | 175 | 26 | | 66 |
| Gary Hammond | WR | 5'11" | 185 | 26 | | |
| Ike Harris | WR | 6'3" | 205 | 22 | | |
| Earl Thomas | WR | 6'3" | 220 | 26 | | 12 |
| J.V. Cain | TE | 6'4" | 225 | 24 | | 6 |
| Jackie Smith | TE | 6'4" | 230 | 34 | | 12 |
| Jeff West | TE | 6'3" | 220 | 22 | | |
| Jim Bakken | K | 6' | 200 | 34 | | 97 |

Steve George – Knee Injury

## DALLAS COWBOYS 10-4 Tom Landry

| Scores of Each Game | | |
|---|---|---|
| 18 | LOS ANGELES | 7 |
| 37 | ST. LOUIS | *31 |
| 36 | Detroit | 10 |
| 13 | N.Y. Giants | 7 |
| 17 | GREEN BAY | 19 |
| 20 | Philadelphia | 17 |
| 24 | Washington | *30 |
| 31 | KANSAS CITY | 34 |
| 34 | New England | 31 |
| 27 | PHILADELPHIA | 17 |
| 14 | N.Y. GIANTS | 3 |
| 17 | St. Louis | 31 |
| 31 | WASHINGTON | 10 |
| 31 | N.Y. Jets | 21 |

| Use Name | Pos. | Hgt | Wgt | Age | Int | Pts |
|---|---|---|---|---|---|---|
| Pat Donovan | OT | 6'4" | 250 | 22 | | |
| Ralph Neely | OT | 6'5" | 260 | 31 | | |
| Bruce Walton | OT | 6'6" | 252 | 24 | | |
| Rayfield Wright | OT | 6'7" | 260 | 29 | | |
| Burton Lawless | OG | 6'4" | 250 | 21 | | |
| Blaine Nye | OG | 6'4" | 255 | 29 | | |
| Herbert Scott | OG | 6'2" | 250 | 22 | | |
| Kyle Davis | C | 6'4" | 240 | 22 | | |
| John Fitzgerald | C | 6'5" | 255 | 27 | | |
| Too Tall Jones | DE | 6'9" | 260 | 24 | 1 | |
| Harvey Martin | DE | 6'5" | 257 | 24 | | |
| Randy White | LB-DT-DE | 6'4" | 245 | 22 | | |
| Larry Cole | DT | 6'4" | 250 | 28 | | |
| Bill Gregory | DT | 6'5" | 252 | 25 | 1 | |
| Jethro Pugh | DT | 6'6" | 250 | 31 | | |
| Bob Breunig | LB | 6'2" | 227 | 22 | | |
| Warren Capone | LB | 6'1" | 218 | 24 | | |
| Dave Edwards | LB | 6'3" | 225 | 36 | | |
| Thomas Henderson | LB | 6'2" | 220 | 22 | | 6 |
| Lee Roy Jordan | LB | 6'2" | 220 | 34 | 6 | |
| D.D. Lewis | LB | 6'2" | 218 | 29 | | |
| Cal Peterson | LB | 6'3" | 220 | 22 | 1 | |
| Benny Barnes | DB | 6'1" | 185 | 24 | | |
| Cliff Harris | DB | 6' | 190 | 25 | 3 | 6 |
| Randy Hughes | DB | 6'4" | 200 | 22 | 2 | 6 |
| Mel Renfro | DB | 6' | 190 | 33 | 4 | |
| Mark Washington | DB | 5'10" | 186 | 27 | 4 | |
| Charlie Waters | DB | 6'1" | 193 | 26 | 3 | 6 |
| Roland Woolsey | DB | 6'1" | 182 | 22 | | |
| Clint Longley | QB | 6'1" | 193 | 23 | | |
| Roger Staubach | QB | 6'2" | 197 | 33 | | 24 |
| Preston Pearson | HB | 6'1" | 205 | 30 | | 24 |
| Charley Young | HB | 6'1" | 210 | 22 | | 18 |
| Doug Dennison | FB-HB | 6'1" | 195 | 23 | | 42 |
| Scott Laidlaw | FB | 6' | 206 | 22 | | |
| Robert Newhouse | FB | 5'10" | 200 | 25 | | 12 |
| Percy Howard | WR | 6'4" | 210 | 23 | | |
| Drew Pearson | WR | 6' | 180 | 24 | | 48 |
| Golden Richards | WR | 6' | 183 | 24 | | 30 |
| Billy Joe DuPree | TE | 6'4" | 228 | 25 | | 6 |
| Ron Howard | TE | 6'4" | 225 | 24 | | |
| Jean Fugett | WR-TE | 6'3" | 226 | 23 | | 18 |
| Toni Fritsch | K | 5'7" | 195 | 30 | | 104 |
| Mitch Hoopes | K | 6'1" | 210 | 22 | | |

Efren Herrera – Injury

## WASHINGTON REDSKINS 8-6 George Allen

| Scores of Each Game | | |
|---|---|---|
| 41 | NEW ORLEANS | 3 |
| 49 | N.Y. GIANTS | 13 |
| 10 | Philadelphia | 26 |
| 27 | St. Louis | 17 |
| 10 | Houston | 13 |
| 23 | Cleveland | 7 |
| 30 | DALLAS | *24 |
| 21 | N.Y. Giants | 13 |
| 17 | St. Louis | *20 |
| 23 | OAKLAND | *26 |
| 31 | MINNESOTA | 30 |
| 30 | Atlanta | 27 |
| 10 | Dallas | 31 |
| 3 | PHILADELPHIA | 26 |

| Use Name | Pos. | Hgt | Wgt | Age | Int | Pts |
|---|---|---|---|---|---|---|
| Terry Hermeling | OT | 6'5" | 255 | 29 | | |
| George Starke | OT | 6'5" | 250 | 27 | | |
| Tim Stokes | OT | 6'5" | 250 | 25 | | |
| Paul Laaveg | OG | 6'4" | 250 | 26 | | |
| Walt Sweeney | OG | 6'3" | 254 | 34 | | |
| Ray Schoenke | OT-OG | 6'3" | 250 | 33 | | |
| Jim Arneson | C-OG | 6'3" | 252 | 24 | | |
| Len Hauss | C | 6'2" | 235 | 33 | | |
| Bob Kuziel | C | 6'4" | 255 | 25 | | |
| Dan Ryzcek | C | 6'3" | 245 | 26 | | |
| Dave Butz | DE | 6'7" | 297 | 25 | | |
| Ron McDole | DE | 6'3" | 265 | 35 | | 6 |
| Bill Brundige | DT | 6'5" | 270 | 26 | | |
| Dennis Johnson | DT | 6'4" | 260 | 23 | 1 | |
| Manny Sistrunk | DT | 6'5" | 265 | 28 | | |
| Diron Talbert | DT | 6'5" | 255 | 31 | | |
| Brad Dusek | LB | 6'2" | 214 | 24 | | 6 |
| Chris Hanburger | LB | 6'2" | 218 | 33 | 3 | |
| Harold McLinton | LB | 6'2" | 235 | 28 | | |
| John Pergine | LB | 6'1" | 225 | 28 | | 6 |
| Russ Tillman | LB | 6'2" | 230 | 29 | | |
| Pete Wysocki | LB | 6'2" | 225 | 26 | | |
| Mike Bass | DB | 6' | 190 | 30 | 4 | |
| Eddie Brown (from CLE) | DB | 5'11" | 185 | 23 | 1 | |
| Pat Fischer | DB | 5'10" | 170 | 35 | 3 | |
| Ken Houston | DB | 6'3" | 198 | 30 | 4 | |
| Brig Owens | DB | 5'11" | 190 | 32 | 1 | |
| Bryant Salter | DB | 6'4" | 196 | 25 | 1 | |
| Ken Stone | DB | 6'1" | 180 | 24 | | |
| Spencer Thomas | DB | 6'2" | 185 | 24 | | |
| Randy Johnson | QB | 6'3" | 205 | 31 | | |
| Billy Kilmer | QB | 6' | 204 | 35 | | 6 |
| Joe Theismann | QB | 6' | 184 | 25 | | |
| Larry Brown | HB | 5'11" | 195 | 27 | | 30 |
| Ralph Nelson | HB | 6'2" | 195 | 21 | | 6 |
| Mike Thomas | HB | 5'11" | 190 | 22 | | 42 |
| Bobby Anderson | HB | 6' | 208 | 27 | | |
| Bob Brunet | FB | 6'1" | 205 | 29 | | 6 |
| Moses Denson | FB | 6'1" | 215 | 31 | | |
| Frank Grant | WR | 5'11" | 180 | 25 | | 48 |
| Roy Jefferson | WR | 6'2" | 195 | 31 | | 12 |
| Larry Jones | WR | 5'10" | 170 | 24 | | 6 |
| Charley Taylor | WR | 6'3" | 210 | 34 | | 36 |
| Alvin Reed | TE | 6'5" | 235 | 31 | | 12 |
| Jerry Smith | TE | 6'2" | 208 | 32 | | 18 |
| Mike Bragg | K | 5'11" | 186 | 28 | | |
| Mark Moseley | K | 5'11" | 205 | 27 | | 85 |

Verlon Biggs – Knee Injury

Mike Hancock — Injury

Stu O'Dell — Shoulder Injury

## NEW YORK GIANTS 5-9 Bill Arnsparger

| Scores of Each Game | | |
|---|---|---|
| 23 | Philadelphia | 14 |
| 13 | Washington | 49 |
| 14 | St. Louis | 26 |
| 7 | DALLAS | 13 |
| 17 | Buffalo | 14 |
| 13 | ST. LOUIS | 20 |
| 35 | SAN DIEGO | 24 |
| 13 | WASHINGTON | 21 |
| 10 | PHILADELPHIA | 13 |
| 14 | Green Bay | 40 |
| 3 | Dallas | 14 |
| 0 | BALTIMORE | 21 |
| 28 | NEW ORLEANS | 14 |
| 26 | San Francisco | 23 |

| Use Name | Pos. | Hgt | Wgt | Age | Int | Pts |
|---|---|---|---|---|---|---|
| Dave Simonson | OT | 6'6" | 248 | 23 | | |
| Al Simpson | OT | 6'5" | 255 | 24 | | |
| Doug Van Horn | OT | 6'2" | 245 | 31 | | |
| Willie Young | OT | 6' | 255 | 32 | | |
| Dick Enderle | OG | 6'1" | 250 | 27 | | |
| John Hicks | OG | 6'2" | 258 | 24 | | |
| Tom Mullen | OG | 6'3" | 245 | 23 | | |
| Karl Chandler | C | 6'5" | 250 | 23 | | |
| Bob Hyland | C | 6'5" | 255 | 30 | | |
| Rick Dvorak | DE | 6'4" | 235 | 23 | | |
| Dave Gallagher | DE | 6'4" | 256 | 23 | | |
| Jack Gregory | DE | 6'6" | 255 | 30 | | |
| George Martin | DE | 6'4" | 245 | 22 | | |
| John Mendenhall | DT | 6'1" | 255 | 26 | | |
| Jim Pietrzak | DT | 6'5" | 260 | 22 | | |
| Bill Windauer (from MIA) | DT | 6'3" | 248 | 25 | | |
| Jimmy Gunn (from CHI) | LB | 6'1" | 218 | 26 | 1 | |
| Pat Hughes | LB | 6'2" | 225 | 28 | | |
| Brian Kelley | LB | 6'3" | 222 | 24 | 3 | |
| Bob Schmit | LB | 6'1" | 220 | 25 | | |
| Andy Selfridge | LB | 6'4" | 220 | 26 | | |
| Brad Van Pelt | LB | 6'5" | 235 | 24 | 3 | |
| Bobby Brooks | DB | 6'1" | 195 | 24 | 4 | |
| Rondy Colbert | DB | 5'9" | 165 | 21 | | 6 |
| Charlie Ford (from BUF) | DB | 6'3" | 185 | 26 | 1 | |
| Robert Giblin | DB | 6'2" | 205 | 22 | | |
| Spider Lockhart | DB | 6'2" | 175 | 32 | 1 | |
| Clyde Powers | DB | 6'1" | 195 | 24 | 3 | |
| Jim Stienke | DB | 5'11" | 182 | 24 | 2 | |
| Henry Stuckey | DB | 6'1" | 180 | 25 | | |
| Craig Morton | QB | 6'4" | 210 | 32 | | |
| Carl Summerell | QB | 6'4" | 208 | 23 | | |
| Mike Wells | QB | 6'5" | 225 | 24 | | |
| Steve Crosby | HB | 5'11" | 205 | 25 | | |
| Ron Johnson | HB | 6'1" | 205 | 27 | | 36 |
| Doug Kotar | HB | 5'11" | 205 | 24 | | 36 |
| Joe Dawkins | FB | 5'11" | 220 | 27 | | 12 |
| Larry Watkins | FB | 6'2" | 230 | 28 | | 18 |
| Marsh White | FB | 6'2" | 220 | 22 | | 6 |
| Danny Buggs | WR | 6'2" | 185 | 22 | | |
| Don Clune | WR | 6'3" | 195 | 23 | | |
| Walker Gillette | WR | 6'5" | 200 | 28 | | 12 |
| Ray Rhodes | WR | 5'11" | 185 | 24 | | 36 |
| Jim Obradovich | TE | 6'2" | 225 | 22 | | 6 |
| Bob Tucker | TE | 6'3" | 230 | 30 | | 6 |
| George Hunt | K | 6'1" | 215 | 25 | | 42 |
| Dave Jennings | K | 6'4" | 205 | 23 | | |

Larry Jacobson – Broken Ankle

## PHILADELPHIA EAGLES 4-10 Mike McCormack

| Scores of Each Game | | |
|---|---|---|
| 14 | N.Y. GIANTS | 23 |
| 13 | Chicago | 15 |
| 26 | WASHINGTON | 10 |
| 16 | Miami | 24 |
| 20 | St. Louis | 31 |
| 17 | DALLAS | 20 |
| 3 | LOS ANGELES | 42 |
| 23 | ST. LOUIS | 24 |
| 13 | N.Y. Giants | 10 |
| 17 | Dallas | 27 |
| 27 | SAN FRANCISCO | 17 |
| 0 | CINCINNATI | 31 |
| 10 | Denver | 25 |
| 26 | Washington | 3 |

| Use Name | Pos. | Hgt | Wgt | Age | Int | Pts |
|---|---|---|---|---|---|---|
| Jeff Bleamer | OT | 6'4" | 253 | 22 | | |
| Jerry Sisemore | OT | 6'4" | 260 | 24 | | |
| Stan Walters | OT | 6'6" | 270 | 27 | | |
| Ernie Janet (from GB) | OG | 6'4" | 255 | 26 | | |
| Wade Key | OG | 6'4" | 245 | 28 | | |
| Bill Lueck | OG | 6'3" | 250 | 29 | | |
| Tom Luken | OG | 6'3" | 253 | 25 | | |
| John Niland | OG | 6'4" | 250 | 31 | | |
| Ron Lou | C | 6'2" | 240 | 24 | | |
| Guy Morriss | C | 6'4" | 255 | 24 | | |
| Don Ratliff | DE | 6'5" | 250 | 25 | | |
| Blenda Gay | DE | 6'5" | 255 | 24 | | |
| Will Wynn | DE | 6'4" | 245 | 26 | | |
| Bill Dunstan | DT | 6'4" | 250 | 26 | | |
| Rich Glover | DT | 6'1" | 244 | 24 | | |
| Mitch Sutton | DT | 6'4" | 255 | 24 | | |
| Rosie Manning (from ATL) | DT | 6'5" | 259 | 24 | | |
| Bill Bergey | LB | 6'2" | 250 | 30 | 3 | |
| John Bunting | LB | 6'1" | 220 | 25 | 1 | |
| Steve Colavito | LB | 6' | 225 | 24 | | |
| Tom Ehlers | LB | 6'2" | 218 | 23 | | |
| Dean Halverson | LB | 6'2" | 230 | 29 | | |
| Frank LeMaster | LB | 6'2" | 230 | 23 | 4 | 6 |
| Jim Opperman | LB | 6'3" | 220 | 22 | | |
| Bill Bradley | DB | 5'11" | 190 | 28 | 5 | |
| Cliff Brooks | DB | 6'1" | 190 | 26 | | |
| Joe Lavender | DB | 6'4" | 190 | 26 | 3 | 6 |
| Randy Logan | DB | 6'1" | 195 | 24 | 1 | |
| Larry Marshall | DB | 5'10" | 195 | 25 | | |
| John Outlaw | DB | 5'10" | 180 | 30 | 5 | |
| Artimus Parker | DB | 6'3" | 215 | 23 | 4 | |
| Mike Boryla | QB | 6'3" | 200 | 24 | | |
| Roman Gabriel | QB | 6'4" | 220 | 35 | | 6 |
| Bill Troup | QB | 6'5" | 220 | 24 | | |
| Po James | HB | 6'1" | 202 | 26 | | 12 |
| Merritt Kersey | HB | 6'1" | 205 | 25 | | |
| James McAlister | HB | 6'1" | 205 | 23 | | 18 |
| Dennis Morgan | HB | 5'11" | 195 | 23 | | |
| Tom Sullivan | FB-HB | 6' | 190 | 25 | | |
| Art Malone | FB | 5'11" | 216 | 27 | | |
| John Tarver | FB | 6'3" | 220 | 26 | | |
| George Amundson | HB-FB | 6'3" | 215 | 24 | | |
| Harold Carmichael | WR | 6'7" | 225 | 25 | | 42 |
| Bob Picard | WR | 6'1" | 195 | 25 | | |
| Charlie Smith | WR | 6'1" | 185 | 25 | | 36 |
| Don Zimmerman | WR | 6'3" | 195 | 25 | | |
| Keith Krepfle | TE | 6'3" | 225 | 23 | | |
| Charlie Young | TE | 6'4" | 238 | 24 | | 18 |
| Spike Jones | K | 6'2" | 185 | 28 | | |
| Horst Muhlmann | K | 6'1" | 220 | 35 | | 81 |

Tom Bailey – Knee Injury

*Overtime

## ST. LOUIS CARDINALS

### RUSHING

| Last Name | No. | Yds | Avg | TD |
|---|---|---|---|---|
| Otis | 269 | 1076 | 4.0 | 5 |
| Metcalf | 165 | 816 | 4.9 | 9 |
| Jones | 54 | 275 | 5.1 | 2 |
| Latin | 35 | 165 | 4.7 | 1 |
| Ashton | 10 | 44 | 4.4 | 0 |
| Hammond | 3 | 13 | 4.3 | 0 |
| Moss | 4 | 12 | 3.0 | 1 |
| Hart | 11 | 7 | 0.6 | 1 |
| M. Gray | 1 | 6 | 6.0 | 0 |
| Shaw | 3 | -12 | -4.0 | 0 |

### RECEIVING

| Last Name | No. | Yds | Avg | TD |
|---|---|---|---|---|
| M. Gray | 48 | 926 | 19 | 11 |
| Metcalf | 43 | 378 | 9 | 2 |
| Thomas | 21 | 375 | 18 | 2 |
| Jones | 19 | 194 | 10 | 1 |
| Harris | 15 | 266 | 18 | 0 |
| Smith | 13 | 246 | 19 | 2 |
| Cain | 12 | 134 | 11 | 1 |
| Otis | 12 | 69 | 6 | 1 |
| Latin | 2 | 25 | 13 | 0 |
| Hammond | 2 | 6 | 3 | 0 |

### PUNT RETURNS

| Last Name | No. | Yds | Avg | TD |
|---|---|---|---|---|
| Metcalf | 23 | 285 | 12 | 1 |
| Hammond | 9 | 70 | 8 | 0 |
| M. Gray | 7 | 53 | 8 | 0 |
| Wehrli | 1 | 2 | 2 | 0 |

### KICKOFF RETURNS

| Last Name | No. | Yds | Avg | TD |
|---|---|---|---|---|
| Metcalf | 35 | 960 | 27 | 1 |
| Hammond | 13 | 254 | 20 | 0 |
| Smith | 1 | 25 | 25 | 0 |
| Moss | 1 | 21 | 21 | 0 |
| Hartle | 1 | 20 | 20 | 0 |
| T. Gray | 1 | 20 | 20 | 0 |
| Jones | 1 | 18 | 18 | 0 |
| Wehrli | 1 | 10 | 10 | 0 |
| Reaves | 1 | 9 | 9 | 0 |

### PASSING – PUNTING – KICKING

| PASSING | Att | Comp | % | Yds | Yd/Att | TD | Int–% | RK |
|---|---|---|---|---|---|---|---|---|
| Hart | 345 | 182 | 53 | 2507 | 7.3 | 19 | 19– 6 | 6 |
| Shaw | 8 | 4 | 50 | 61 | 7.6 | 0 | 1–13 | |
| Metcalf | 2 | 1 | 50 | 51 | 25.5 | 1 | 0– 0 | |

| PUNTING | No | Avg |
|---|---|---|
| West | 64 | 37.7 |

| KICKING | XP | Att | % | FG | Att | % |
|---|---|---|---|---|---|---|
| Bakken | 40 | 41 | 98 | 19 | 24 | 82 |

## DALLAS COWBOYS

### RUSHING

| Last Name | No. | Yds | Avg | TD |
|---|---|---|---|---|
| Newhouse | 209 | 930 | 4.4 | 2 |
| P. Pearson | 133 | 509 | 3.8 | 2 |
| Dennison | 111 | 383 | 3.5 | 7 |
| Staubach | 55 | 316 | 5.7 | 4 |
| Young | 50 | 225 | 4.5 | 2 |
| Richards | 3 | 18 | 6.0 | 0 |
| Hoopes | 1 | 13 | 13.0 | 0 |
| Longley | 3 | 12 | 4.0 | 0 |
| D. Pearson | 1 | 11 | 11.0 | 0 |
| Laidlaw | 3 | 10 | 3.3 | 0 |
| DuPree | 1 | 3 | 3.0 | 0 |
| Fugett | 1 | 2 | 2.0 | 0 |

### RECEIVING

| Last Name | No. | Yds | Avg | TD |
|---|---|---|---|---|
| D. Pearson | 46 | 822 | 18 | 8 |
| Fugett | 38 | 488 | 13 | 3 |
| Newhouse | 34 | 275 | 8 | 0 |
| P. Pearson | 27 | 353 | 13 | 2 |
| Richards | 21 | 451 | 22 | 4 |
| Young | 18 | 184 | 10 | 1 |
| Laidlaw | 11 | 100 | 9 | 0 |
| DuPree | 9 | 138 | 15 | 1 |
| Dennison | 2 | 5 | 3 | 0 |
| Breunig | 1 | 21 | 21 | 0 |

### PUNT RETURNS

| Last Name | No. | Yds | Avg | TD |
|---|---|---|---|---|
| Richards | 28 | 288 | 10 | 1 |
| Woolsey | 4 | 25 | 6 | 0 |

### KICKOFF RETURNS

| Last Name | No. | Yds | Avg | TD |
|---|---|---|---|---|
| P. Pearson | 16 | 391 | 24 | 0 |
| Dennison | 13 | 262 | 20 | 0 |
| Woolsey | 12 | 247 | 21 | 0 |
| Henderson | 4 | 130 | 33 | 1 |
| Young | 3 | 54 | 18 | 0 |
| P. Howard | 2 | 51 | 26 | 0 |
| Breunig | 2 | 13 | 7 | 0 |
| Peterson | 1 | 10 | 10 | 0 |
| Waters | 1 | 0 | 0 | 0 |

### PASSING – PUNTING – KICKING

| PASSING | Att | Comp | % | Yds | Yd/Att | TD | Int–% | RK |
|---|---|---|---|---|---|---|---|---|
| Staubach | 348 | 198 | 57 | 2666 | 7.7 | 17 | 16– 5 | 2 |
| Longley | 23 | 7 | 30 | 102 | 4.4 | 1 | 1– 4 | |
| Hoopes | 3 | 1 | 33 | 21 | 7.0 | 0 | 0– 0 | |
| Newhouse | 2 | 1 | 50 | 46 | 23.0 | 1 | 0– 0 | |

| PUNTING | No | Avg |
|---|---|---|
| Hoopes | 68 | 39.4 |

| KICKING | XP | Att | % | FG | Att | % |
|---|---|---|---|---|---|---|
| Fritsch | 38 | 40 | 95 | 22 | 35 | 63 |

## WASHINGTON REDSKINS

### RUSHING

| Last Name | No. | Yds | Avg | TD |
|---|---|---|---|---|
| M. Thomas | 235 | 919 | 3.9 | 4 |
| L. Brown | 97 | 352 | 3.6 | 3 |
| Denson | 56 | 195 | 3.5 | 0 |
| Nelson | 31 | 139 | 4.5 | 0 |
| Grant | 3 | 46 | 15.3 | 0 |
| Kilmer | 11 | 34 | 3.1 | 1 |
| Theismann | 3 | 34 | 11.3 | 0 |
| Brunet | 6 | 23 | 3.8 | 1 |
| R. Johnson | 2 | 10 | 5.0 | 0 |

### RECEIVING

| Last Name | No. | Yds | Avg | TD |
|---|---|---|---|---|
| Taylor | 53 | 744 | 14 | 6 |
| Grant | 41 | 776 | 19 | 8 |
| M. Thomas | 40 | 483 | 12 | 3 |
| Smith | 31 | 391 | 13 | 3 |
| L. Brown | 25 | 225 | 9 | 2 |
| Jefferson | 15 | 255 | 17 | 2 |
| Denson | 13 | 81 | 6 | 0 |
| Nelson | 5 | 58 | 12 | 1 |
| Pergine | 2 | 41 | 21 | 1 |
| Jones | 2 | 33 | 17 | 0 |
| Reed | 2 | 5 | 3 | 2 |

### PUNT RETURNS

| Last Name | No. | Yds | Avg | TD |
|---|---|---|---|---|
| Jones | 53 | 407 | 8 | 1 |
| E. Brown | 8 | 68 | 9 | 0 |
| Theismann | 2 | 5 | 3 | 0 |

### KICKOFF RETURNS

| Last Name | No. | Yds | Avg | TD |
|---|---|---|---|---|
| Jones | 47 | 1086 | 23 | 0 |
| E. Brown | 6 | 126 | 21 | 0 |
| Nelson | 5 | 107 | 21 | 0 |
| Brunet | 5 | 83 | 17 | 0 |
| Tillman | 1 | 4 | 4 | 0 |
| Grant | 0 | 16 | 0 | 0 |

### PASSING – PUNTING – KICKING

| PASSING | Att | Comp | % | Yds | Yd/Att | TD | Int–% | RK |
|---|---|---|---|---|---|---|---|---|
| Kilmer | 346 | 178 | 51 | 2440 | 7.1 | 23 | 16– 5 | 3 |
| Johnson | 79 | 41 | 52 | 556 | 7.0 | 4 | 10–13 | |
| Theismann | 22 | 10 | 46 | 96 | 4.4 | 1 | 3–14 | |
| Anderson | 1 | 0 | 0 | 0 | 0.0 | 0 | 0– 0 | |

| PUNTING | No | Avg |
|---|---|---|
| Bragg | 72 | 40.6 |

| KICKING | XP | Att | % | FG | Att | % |
|---|---|---|---|---|---|---|
| Moseley | 37 | 39 | 95 | 16 | 25 | 64 |

## NEW YORK GIANTS

### RUSHING

| Last Name | No. | Yds | Avg | TD |
|---|---|---|---|---|
| Dawkins | 129 | 438 | 3.4 | 2 |
| Kotar | 122 | 378 | 3.1 | 6 |
| Johnson | 116 | 351 | 3.0 | 5 |
| Watkins | 68 | 303 | 4.5 | 3 |
| White | 17 | 90 | 5.3 | 1 |
| Morton | 22 | 72 | 3.3 | 0 |
| Summerell | 3 | 4 | 1.3 | 0 |
| Buggs | 1 | 0 | 0.0 | 0 |
| Rhodes | 3 | -4 | -1.3 | 0 |
| Tucker | 1 | -5 | -5.0 | 0 |

### RECEIVING

| Last Name | No. | Yds | Avg | TD |
|---|---|---|---|---|
| Gillette | 43 | 600 | 14 | 2 |
| Tucker | 34 | 484 | 14 | 1 |
| Johnson | 34 | 280 | 8 | 1 |
| Rhodes | 26 | 537 | 21 | 6 |
| Dawkins | 24 | 245 | 10 | 0 |
| Kotar | 9 | 86 | 10 | 0 |
| Obradovich | 7 | 65 | 9 | 1 |
| Watkins | 7 | 43 | 6 | 0 |
| Clune | 5 | 97 | 19 | 0 |
| White | 3 | 15 | 5 | 0 |
| Hicks | 1 | 5 | 5 | 0 |

### PUNT RETURNS

| Last Name | No. | Yds | Avg | TD |
|---|---|---|---|---|
| Colbert | 27 | 238 | 9 | 1 |
| Buggs | 19 | 93 | 5 | 0 |
| Lockhart | 2 | 14 | 7 | 0 |
| Kotar | 1 | 5 | 5 | 0 |

### KICKOFF RETURNS

| Last Name | No. | Yds | Avg | TD |
|---|---|---|---|---|
| Colbert | 17 | 408 | 24 | 0 |
| Kotar | 17 | 405 | 24 | 0 |
| Buggs | 16 | 353 | 22 | 0 |
| Obradovich | 2 | 38 | 19 | 0 |
| Dawkins | 1 | 32 | 32 | 0 |
| Crosby | 1 | 14 | 14 | 0 |
| Selfridge | 1 | 0 | 0 | 0 |

### PASSING – PUNTING – KICKING

| PASSING | Att | Comp | % | Yds | Yd/Att | TD | Int–% | RK |
|---|---|---|---|---|---|---|---|---|
| Morton | 363 | 186 | 51 | 2359 | 6.5 | 11 | 16– 4 | 8 |
| Summerell | 16 | 7 | 44 | 98 | 6.1 | 0 | 2–13 | |

| PUNTING | No | Avg |
|---|---|---|
| Jennings | 76 | 40.9 |
| Hunt | 9 | 24.2 |
| Crosby | 1 | 28.0 |

| KICKING | XP | Att | % | FG | Att | % |
|---|---|---|---|---|---|---|
| Hunt | 24 | 29 | 83 | 6 | 11 | 55 |

## PHILADELPHIA EAGLES

### RUSHING

| Last Name | No. | Yds | Avg | TD |
|---|---|---|---|---|
| Sullivan | 173 | 632 | 3.7 | 0 |
| McAlister | 103 | 335 | 3.3 | 1 |
| Malone | 101 | 325 | 3.2 | 0 |
| James | 43 | 196 | 4.6 | 1 |
| Smith | 9 | 85 | 9.4 | 0 |
| Gabriel | 13 | 70 | 5.4 | 1 |
| Boryla | 8 | 33 | 4.1 | 0 |
| Tarver | 7 | 20 | 2.9 | 0 |
| Carmichael | 1 | 6 | 6.0 | 0 |
| Young | 2 | 1 | 0.5 | 0 |
| Jones | 1 | -1 | -1.0 | 0 |

### RECEIVING

| Last Name | No. | Yds | Avg | TD |
|---|---|---|---|---|
| Young | 49 | 659 | 13 | 3 |
| Carmichael | 49 | 639 | 13 | 7 |
| Smith | 37 | 515 | 14 | 6 |
| James | 32 | 267 | 8 | 1 |
| Sullivan | 28 | 276 | 10 | 0 |
| Malone | 20 | 120 | 6 | 0 |
| McAlister | 17 | 134 | 8 | 2 |
| Tarver | 5 | 14 | 3 | 0 |
| Krepfle | 1 | 16 | 16 | 0 |

### PUNT RETURNS

| Last Name | No. | Yds | Avg | TD |
|---|---|---|---|---|
| Marshall | 23 | 235 | 10 | 0 |
| Morgan | 8 | 60 | 8 | 0 |
| Bradley | 4 | 4 | 1 | 0 |

### KICKOFF RETURNS

| Last Name | No. | Yds | Avg | TD |
|---|---|---|---|---|
| Marshall | 22 | 557 | 25 | 0 |
| James | 13 | 311 | 24 | 0 |
| McAlister | 12 | 278 | 23 | 0 |
| Morgan | 7 | 170 | 24 | 0 |
| Sullivan | 3 | 42 | 14 | 0 |
| Opperman | 1 | 15 | 15 | 0 |
| Sisemore | 1 | 15 | 15 | 0 |

### PASSING – PUNTING – KICKING

| PASSING | Att | Comp | % | Yds | Yd/Att | TD | Int–% | RK |
|---|---|---|---|---|---|---|---|---|
| Gabriel | 292 | 151 | 52 | 1644 | 5.6 | 13 | 11– 4 | 7 |
| Boryla | 166 | 87 | 52 | 996 | 6.0 | 6 | 12– 7 | 14 |

| PUNTING | No | Avg |
|---|---|---|
| Jones | 68 | 40.3 |
| Kersey | 15 | 32.6 |

| KICKING | XP | Att | % | FG | Att | % |
|---|---|---|---|---|---|---|
| Muhlmann | 21 | 24 | 88 | 20 | 29 | 69 |

## MINNESOTA VIKINGS 12-2 Bud Grant

**Scores of Each Game**

| |  | |
|---|---|---|
| 27 | SAN FRANCISCO | 17 |
| 42 | Cleveland | 10 |
| 28 | CHICAGO | 3 |
| 29 | N.Y. JETS | 21 |
| 25 | DETROIT | 19 |
| 13 | Chicago | 9 |
| 28 | Green Bay | 17 |
| 38 | ATLANTA | 0 |
| 20 | New Orleans | 7 |
| 28 | SAN DIEGO | 13 |
| 30 | Washington | 31 |
| 24 | GREEN BAY | 3 |
| 10 | Detroit | 17 |
| 35 | Buffalo | 13 |

| Use Name | Pos. | Hgt | Wgt | Age | Int | Pts |
|---|---|---|---|---|---|---|
| Charlie Goodrum | OT | 6'3" | 256 | 25 | | |
| Steve Riley | OT | 6'6" | 258 | 22 | | |
| Ron Yary | OT | 6'6" | 255 | 29 | | |
| Steve Lawson | OG | 6'3" | 265 | 26 | | |
| Andy Mauer | OG | 6'3" | 275 | 26 | | |
| Ed White | OG | 6'2" | 270 | 28 | | |
| Mick Tingelhoff | C | 6'1" | 240 | 35 | | |
| John Ward | OG-C | 6'4" | 250 | 27 | | |
| Carl Eller | DE | 6'6" | 247 | 33 | 1 | |
| Jim Marshall | DE | 6'3" | 240 | 37 | | |
| Mark Mullaney | DE | 6'6" | 242 | 22 | | |
| Alan Page | DT | 6'5" | 245 | 30 | | |
| Doug Sutherland | DT | 6'3" | 250 | 27 | | |
| Bob Lurtsema | DE-DT | 6'6" | 250 | 33 | | |
| Matt Blair | LB | 6'5" | 230 | 24 | 1 | |
| Wally Hilgenberg | LB | 6'3" | 230 | 32 | 1 | |
| Amos Martin | LB | 6'3" | 228 | 26 | | |
| Fred McNeill | LB | 6'2" | 230 | 23 | 1 | |
| Jeff Siemon | LB | 6'2" | 235 | 25 | 3 | |
| Bob Stein (from SD) | LB | 6'2" | 235 | 27 | | |
| Roy Winston | LB | 6'1" | 222 | 35 | | |
| Pete Athas (from CLE) | DB | 5'11" | 185 | 27 | 1 | |
| Autry Beamon | DB | 6' | 190 | 21 | 1 | 2 |
| Joe Blahak | DB | 5'9" | 188 | 24 | 1 | 2 |
| Terry Brown | DB | 6'1" | 205 | 28 | 2 | 6 |
| Bobby Bryant | DB | 6' | 170 | 31 | 6 | |
| Paul Krause | DB | 6'3" | 200 | 33 | 10 | 6 |
| Jeff Wright | DB | 5'11" | 190 | 26 | | |
| Nate Wright | DB | 5'11" | 180 | 27 | | |
| Bob Berry | QB | 5'11" | 185 | 33 | | |
| Bob Lee | QB | 6'2" | 195 | 29 | | |
| Fran Tarkenton | QB | 6'1" | 190 | 35 | | 12 |
| Chuck Foreman | HB | 6'2" | 207 | 24 | | 132 |
| Ed Marinaro | FB-HB | 6'2" | 212 | 25 | | 24 |
| Brent McClanahan | FB-HB | 5'10" | 202 | 24 | | 6 |
| Robert Miller | FB | 5'11" | 204 | 22 | | 6 |
| Dave Osborn | FB | 6' | 208 | 32 | | 6 |
| John Gilliam | WR | 6'1" | 195 | 30 | | 42 |
| Clint Haslerig (from BUF) | WR | 6' | 194 | 23 | | |
| Jim Lash | WR | 6'2" | 200 | 23 | | 24 |
| Sam McCullum | WR | 6'2" | 203 | 22 | | |
| Steve Craig | TE | 6'3" | 230 | 24 | | |
| Doug Kingsriter | TE | 6'2" | 222 | 25 | | |
| Stu Voight | TE | 6'1" | 225 | 27 | | 24 |
| Neil Clabo | K | 6'2" | 200 | 22 | | |
| Fred Cox | K | 5'10" | 200 | 36 | | 85 |

## DETROIT LIONS 7-7 Rick Forzano

| |  | |
|---|---|---|
| 30 | GREEN BAY | 16 |
| 17 | Atlanta | 14 |
| 10 | DALLAS | 36 |
| 27 | CHICAGO | 7 |
| 19 | Minnesota | 25 |
| 8 | Houston | 24 |
| 28 | San Francisco | 17 |
| 21 | CLEVELAND | 10 |
| 13 | GREEN BAY | 10 |
| 21 | Kansas City | *24 |
| 0 | LOS ANGELES | 20 |
| 21 | Chicago | 25 |
| 17 | MINNESOTA | 10 |
| 13 | ST. LOUIS | 24 |

| Use Name | Pos. | Hgt | Wgt | Age | Int | Pts |
|---|---|---|---|---|---|---|
| Rocky Freitas | OT | 6'6" | 275 | 29 | | |
| Craig Hertwig | OT | 6'8" | 270 | 23 | | |
| Jim Yarbrough | OT | 6'6" | 265 | 28 | | |
| Lynn Boden | OG | 6'5" | 270 | 22 | | |
| Bob Kowalkowski | OG | 6'3" | 245 | 31 | | |
| Gordon Jolley | OT-OG | 6'5" | 245 | 26 | | |
| Guy Dennis | C-OG | 6'2" | 250 | 28 | | |
| Richard Hicks | C | 6'4" | 250 | 24 | | |
| Jon Morris | C | 6'4" | 250 | 32 | | |
| Ernie Price | DE | 6'4" | 245 | 24 | 2 | |
| Ken Sanders | DE | 6'5" | 245 | 25 | | |
| Larry Hand | DT-DE | 6'4" | 245 | 35 | 1 | |
| Doug English | DT | 6'5" | 245 | 22 | | |
| Herb Orvis | DT | 6'5" | 245 | 28 | | |
| Billy Howard | DE-DT | 6'4" | 255 | 25 | | |
| Jim Mitchell | DE-DT | 6'3" | 250 | 26 | | |
| Larry Ball | LB | 6'6" | 235 | 25 | | |
| Mike Hennigan | LB | 6'2" | 225 | 23 | | 6 |
| Jim Laslavic | LB | 6'2" | 225 | 23 | 2 | |
| Paul Naumoff | LB | 6'1" | 215 | 30 | 2 | |
| Ed O'Neil | LB | 6'3" | 235 | 22 | | 6 |
| Charlie Weaver | LB | 6'2" | 225 | 26 | 1 | |
| Lem Barney | DB | 6' | 190 | 29 | 5 | |
| Ben Davis | DB | 5'11" | 180 | 29 | 1 | 6 |
| Lenny Dunlap | DB | 6'1" | 200 | 26 | | |
| Dick Jauron | DB | 6' | 190 | 24 | 4 | |
| Levi Johnson | DB | 6'3" | 200 | 24 | 3 | 6 |
| Mike Weger | DB | 6'2" | 200 | 29 | 1 | |
| Charlie West | DB | 6'1" | 195 | 29 | | |

Steve Owens — Knee Injury
Larry Walton — Knee Injury
Jim Thrower — Knee Injury

| Use Name | Pos. | Hgt | Wgt | Age | Int | Pts |
|---|---|---|---|---|---|---|
| Jack Concannon | QB | 6'3" | 200 | 32 | | |
| Greg Landry | QB | 6'4" | 205 | 28 | | |
| Bill Munson | QB | 6'2" | 200 | 33 | | |
| Joe Reed | QB | 6'1" | 195 | 27 | | 6 |
| Dexter Bussey | HB | 6'1" | 210 | 23 | | 24 |
| Altie Taylor | HB | 5'10" | 200 | 27 | | 24 |
| Bobby Thompson | HB | 5'11" | 195 | 28 | | 6 |
| Jim Hooks | FB | 5'11" | 225 | 23 | | |
| Horace King | FB | 5'10" | 210 | 22 | | 12 |
| Marlin Briscoe (from SD) | WR | 5'10" | 180 | 29 | | 24 |
| George Farmer (from CHI) | WR | 6'4" | 214 | 27 | | |
| Dennis Franklin | WR | 6'1" | 185 | 22 | | |
| Ray Jarvis | WR | 5'11" | 190 | 26 | | 24 |
| Jon Staggers | WR | 5'10" | 185 | 26 | | 12 |
| Leonard Thompson | WR | 5'10" | 190 | 23 | | |
| John McMakin | TE | 6'3" | 225 | 24 | | |
| Charlie Sanders | TE | 6'4" | 230 | 29 | | 18 |
| Errol Mann | K | 6' | 205 | 34 | | 67 |
| Alan Pringle | K | 6' | 195 | 23 | | |
| Herman Weaver | K | 6'4" | 210 | 26 | | |

## GREEN BAY PACKERS 4-10 Bart Starr

| |  | |
|---|---|---|
| 16 | DETROIT | 30 |
| 13 | Denver | 23 |
| 7 | MIAMI | 31 |
| 19 | New Orleans | 20 |
| 19 | Dallas | 17 |
| 13 | PITTSBURGH | 16 |
| 17 | MINNESOTA | 28 |
| 14 | Chicago | 27 |
| 10 | Detroit | 13 |
| 40 | N.Y. GIANTS | 14 |
| 28 | CHICAGO | 7 |
| 3 | Minnesota | 24 |
| 5 | Los Angeles | 22 |
| 22 | ATLANTA | 13 |

| Use Name | Pos. | Hgt | Wgt | Age | Int | Pts |
|---|---|---|---|---|---|---|
| Ernie McMillan | OT | 6'6" | 265 | 37 | | |
| Dick Himes | OT | 6'4" | 260 | 29 | | |
| Bill Bain | OG | 6'4" | 270 | 23 | | |
| Pat Matson | OG | 6'1" | 245 | 31 | | |
| Bruce Van Dyke | OG | 6'2" | 255 | 31 | | |
| Keith Wortman | OG | 6'2" | 250 | 25 | | |
| Robert McCaffrey | C | 6'2" | 245 | 23 | | |
| Larry McCarren | C | 6'3" | 248 | 24 | | |
| Bill Cooke | DE | 6'5" | 250 | 24 | | |
| Dave Pureifory | DE | 6'1" | 255 | 25 | 4 | |
| Alden Roche | DE | 6'4" | 255 | 30 | | |
| Clarence Williams | DE | 6'5" | 255 | 28 | | |
| Mike McCoy | DT | 6'5" | 275 | 26 | 6 | |
| Steve Okoniewski | DT | 6'3" | 272 | 26 | | |
| Dave Roller | DT | 6'2" | 270 | 25 | | |

Bill Hayhoe — Broken Leg

| Use Name | Pos. | Hgt | Wgt | Age | Int | Pts |
|---|---|---|---|---|---|---|
| Ron Acks | LB | 6'2" | 225 | 30 | | |
| Fred Carr | LB | 6'5" | 240 | 29 | 3 | |
| Jim Carter | LB | 6'3" | 245 | 26 | | |
| Larry Hefner | LB | 6'2" | 230 | 26 | | |
| Tom Hull | LB | 6'3" | 230 | 23 | | |
| Tom Toner | LB | 6'3" | 235 | 25 | 1 | 2 |
| Gary Weaver | LB | 6'1" | 224 | 26 | | |
| Willie Buchanon | DB | 6' | 190 | 24 | | |
| Ken Ellis | DB | 5'10" | 195 | 27 | 1 | |
| Johnnie Gray | DB | 5'11" | 185 | 21 | 1 | |
| Charlie Hall | DB | 6'1" | 190 | 26 | | |
| Steve Luke | DB | 6'2" | 205 | 21 | | |
| Al Matthews | DB | 5'11" | 190 | 27 | 2 | |
| Hurles Scales | DB | 6'1" | 200 | 24 | | |
| Perry Smith | DB | 6'1" | 195 | 24 | 6 | |

Norm Hodgkins — Injury
Larry Krause — Shoulder Injury

| Use Name | Pos. | Hgt | Wgt | Age | Int | Pts |
|---|---|---|---|---|---|---|
| Carlos Brown | QB | 6'3" | 210 | 23 | | |
| John Hadl | QB | 6'2" | 214 | 35 | | |
| Don Milan | QB | 6'3" | 196 | 26 | | |
| Will Harrell | HB | 5'8" | 182 | 22 | | 18 |
| Eric Torkelson | HB | 6'2" | 195 | 22 | | 12 |
| Terry Wells | HB | 5'11" | 195 | 24 | | |
| John Brockington | FB | 6'1" | 225 | 26 | | 48 |
| Barty Smith | FB | 6'4" | 240 | 23 | | 30 |
| Kent Gaydos | WR | 6'6" | 228 | 25 | | |
| Steve Odom | WR | 5'8" | 174 | 22 | | 30 |
| Ken Payne | WR | 6'1" | 185 | 24 | | |
| Barry Smith | WR | 6'1" | 190 | 24 | | 6 |
| Gerald Tinker (from ATL) | WR | 5'9" | 175 | 24 | | 12 |
| Charlie Wade | WR | 5'10" | 163 | 25 | | |
| Bert Askson | TE | 6'3" | 225 | 29 | | |
| Rich McGeorge | TE | 6'4" | 230 | 26 | | 6 |
| David Beverly (from HOU) | K | 6'2" | 182 | 25 | | |
| Steve Broussard | K | 6' | 200 | 26 | | |
| Joe Danelo | K | 5'9" | 166 | 21 | | 53 |
| Chester Marcol | K | 6' | 190 | 26 | | 3 |

## CHICAGO BEARS 4-10 Jack Pardee

| |  | |
|---|---|---|
| 7 | BALTIMORE | 35 |
| 15 | PHILADELPHIA | 13 |
| 3 | Minnesota | 28 |
| 7 | Detroit | 27 |
| 3 | Pittsburgh | 34 |
| 9 | MINNESOTA | 13 |
| 13 | MIAMI | 46 |
| 27 | GREEN BAY | 14 |
| 3 | San Francisco | 31 |
| 10 | Los Angeles | 38 |
| 7 | Green Bay | 28 |
| 25 | DETROIT | 21 |
| 20 | ST. LOUIS | 34 |
| 42 | New Orleans | 17 |

| Use Name | Pos. | Hgt | Wgt | Age | Int | Pts |
|---|---|---|---|---|---|---|
| Lionel Antoine | OT | 6'6" | 263 | 25 | | |
| Bob Asher | OT | 6'5" | 260 | 27 | | |
| Jeff Sevy | OT | 6'5" | 250 | 24 | | |
| Noah Jackson | OG | 6'2" | 263 | 24 | | |
| Bob Newton | OG | 6'4" | 260 | 26 | | |
| Revie Sorey | OG | 6'2" | 260 | 21 | | |
| Mark Nordquist | C-OG | 6'4" | 246 | 29 | | |
| Dan Neal | C | 6'4" | 240 | 26 | | |
| Dan Peiffer | C | 6'3" | 250 | 24 | | |
| Richard Harris | DE | 6'4" | 255 | 27 | | |
| Mike Hartenstine | DE | 6'3" | 250 | 22 | 2 | |
| Gary Hrivnak | DE | 6'5" | 254 | 24 | | |
| Mel Tom | DE | 6'4" | 242 | 34 | | |
| Wally Chambers | DT | 6'6" | 255 | 24 | | |
| Jim Osborne | DT | 6'3" | 254 | 25 | | |
| Ron Rydalch | DT | 6'4" | 260 | 23 | | |
| Roger Stillwell | DT | 6'5" | 265 | 23 | | |
| John Babinecz | LB | 6'1" | 222 | 25 | 1 | |
| Waymond Bryant | LB | 6'3" | 230 | 23 | | |
| Doug Buffone | LB | 6'1" | 227 | 31 | 1 | |
| Larry Ely | LB | 6'1" | 230 | 27 | 1 | |
| Carl Gersbach | LB | 6'3" | 230 | 28 | 1 | |
| Bob Pifferini | LB | 6'2" | 226 | 25 | | |
| Don Rives | LB | 6'2" | 220 | 24 | | |
| Craig Clemons | DB | 5'11" | 200 | 26 | 2 | 6 |
| Earl Douthit | DB | 6'2" | 188 | 22 | | |
| Allan Ellis | DB | 5'10" | 182 | 24 | 2 | |
| Bill Knox | DB | 5'9" | 193 | 24 | | |
| Virgil Livers | DB | 5'8" | 176 | 23 | 2 | 6 |
| Doug Plank | DB | 6' | 197 | 22 | 2 | |
| Ted Vactor | DB | 6' | 185 | 31 | | |
| Nemiah Wilson | DB | 6' | 165 | 32 | | |
| Bob Avellini | QB | 6'2" | 197 | 22 | | 6 |
| Virgil Carter (from SD) | QB | 6'1" | 185 | 29 | | |
| Gary Huff | QB | 6'1" | 194 | 24 | | |
| Roland Harper | HB | 5'11" | 194 | 22 | | 6 |
| Johnny Musso | HB | 5'11" | 205 | 25 | | |
| Walter Payton | HB | 5'11" | 200 | 21 | | 42 |
| Mike Adamle | FB-HB | 5'9" | 193 | 25 | | 6 |
| Tom Donchez | FB | 6'2" | 216 | 22 | | |
| Cid Edwards | FB | 6'2" | 230 | 31 | | 6 |
| Bob Grim | WR | 6' | 200 | 30 | | 12 |
| Bo Rather | WR | 6'1" | 180 | 24 | | |
| Steve Schubert | WR | 5'10" | 185 | 24 | | |
| Ron Shanklin | WR | 6'1" | 190 | 28 | | |
| Gary Butler | TE | 6'3" | 235 | 24 | | |
| Greg Latta | TE | 6'3" | 226 | 22 | | 18 |
| Bob Parsons | TE | 6'4" | 234 | 25 | | 6 |
| Bob Thomas | K | 5'10" | 178 | 23 | | 57 |

*Overtime

## MINNESOTA VIKINGS

### RUSHING

| Last Name | No. | Yds | Avg | TD |
|---|---|---|---|---|
| Foreman | 280 | 1070 | 3.8 | 13 |
| Marinaro | 101 | 358 | 3.5 | 1 |
| McClanahan | 92 | 336 | 3.7 | 0 |
| Tarkenton | 16 | 108 | 6.8 | 2 |
| Osborn | 32 | 94 | 2.9 | 1 |
| Miller | 30 | 93 | 3.1 | 1 |
| Gilliam | 3 | 35 | 11.7 | 0 |
| Berry | 1 | 0 | 0.0 | 0 |
| Lee | 1 | 0 | 0.0 | 0 |

### RECEIVING

| Last Name | No. | Yds | Avg | TD |
|---|---|---|---|---|
| Foreman | 73 | 691 | 10 | 9 |
| Marinaro | 54 | 462 | 9 | 3 |
| Gilliam | 50 | 777 | 16 | 7 |
| Lash | 37 | 535 | 15 | 3 |
| Voigt | 34 | 363 | 11 | 4 |
| McClanahan | 18 | 141 | 8 | 1 |
| Craig | 6 | 68 | 11 | 0 |
| Miller | 4 | 35 | 9 | 0 |
| Haslerig | 2 | 28 | 14 | 0 |
| McCullum | 2 | 25 | 13 | 0 |
| Osborn | 1 | −4 | −4 | 0 |

### PUNT RETURNS

| Last Name | No. | Yds | Avg | TD |
|---|---|---|---|---|
| Bryant | 19 | 125 | 7 | 0 |
| McCullum | 12 | 22 | 2 | 0 |
| J. Wright | 1 | 22 | 22 | 0 |
| Athas | 6 | 37 | 6 | 0 |
| Beamon | 1 | 0 | 0 | 0 |
| Blair | 2 | −2 | −1 | 0 |

### KICKOFF RETURNS

| Last Name | No. | Yds | Avg | TD |
|---|---|---|---|---|
| McClanahan | 17 | 360 | 21 | 0 |
| McCullum | 9 | 221 | 25 | 0 |
| Athas | 6 | 95 | 16 | 0 |
| Miller | 5 | 93 | 19 | 0 |
| Marinaro | 5 | 71 | 14 | 0 |
| Osborn | 1 | 38 | 38 | 0 |
| Foreman | 1 | 4 | 4 | 0 |

### PASSING – PUNTING – KICKING

| PASSING | Att | Comp | % | Yds | Yd/Att | TD | Int−% | RK |
|---|---|---|---|---|---|---|---|---|
| Tarkenton | 425 | 273 | 64 | 2994 | 7.0 | 25 | 13− 3 | 1 |
| Lee | 14 | 5 | 36 | 103 | 7.4 | 2 | 1− 7 | |
| Berry | 6 | 3 | 50 | 24 | 4.0 | 0 | 0− 0 | |
| Lash | 1 | 0 | 0 | 0 | 0.0 | 0 | 0− 0 | |

| PUNTING | No | Avg |
|---|---|---|
| Clabo | 73 | 41.1 |

| KICKING | XP | Att | % | FG | Att | % |
|---|---|---|---|---|---|---|
| Cox | 46 | 48 | 96 | 13 | 17 | 76 |

## DETROIT LIONS

### RUSHING

| Last Name | No. | Yds | Avg | TD |
|---|---|---|---|---|
| Bussey | 157 | 696 | 4.4 | 2 |
| Taylor | 195 | 638 | 3.3 | 4 |
| B. Thompson | 51 | 268 | 5.3 | 1 |
| King | 61 | 260 | 4.3 | 2 |
| Reed | 34 | 193 | 5.7 | 1 |
| Landry | 20 | 92 | 4.6 | 0 |
| Staggers | 2 | 26 | 13.0 | 0 |
| Jarvis | 1 | 0 | 0.0 | 0 |
| Munson | 4 | −3 | −0.8 | 0 |
| Briscoe | 2 | −3 | −1.5 | 0 |
| Hooks | 4 | −8 | −2.0 | 0 |
| L. Thompson | 1 | −12 | −12.0 | 0 |

### RECEIVING

| Last Name | No. | Yds | Avg | TD |
|---|---|---|---|---|
| Sanders | 37 | 486 | 13 | 3 |
| Jarvis | 29 | 501 | 17 | 4 |
| Briscoe | 24 | 372 | 16 | 4 |
| Taylor | 21 | 111 | 5 | 0 |
| B. Thompson | 19 | 122 | 6 | 0 |
| Bussey | 14 | 175 | 13 | 2 |
| Staggers | 14 | 174 | 12 | 2 |
| King | 13 | 81 | 6 | 0 |
| Farmer | 8 | 118 | 15 | 0 |
| Franklin | 5 | 109 | 22 | 0 |
| McMakin | 2 | 43 | 22 | 0 |
| Hooks | 1 | 5 | 5 | 0 |

### PUNT RETURNS

| Last Name | No. | Yds | Avg | TD |
|---|---|---|---|---|
| West | 22 | 219 | 10 | 0 |
| Barney | 8 | 80 | 10 | 0 |
| Jauron | 6 | 29 | 5 | 0 |

### KICKOFF RETURNS

| Last Name | No. | Yds | Avg | TD |
|---|---|---|---|---|
| B. Thompson | 22 | 565 | 26 | 0 |
| L. Thompson | 12 | 271 | 23 | 0 |
| King | 6 | 117 | 20 | 0 |
| Weger | 3 | 42 | 14 | 0 |
| West | 2 | 41 | 21 | 0 |
| Bussey | 2 | 38 | 19 | 0 |
| Hooks | 2 | 8 | 4 | 0 |
| Dunlap | 1 | 19 | 19 | 0 |
| Hennigan | 1 | 13 | 13 | 0 |
| Dennis | 1 | 0 | 0 | 0 |

### PASSING – PUNTING – KICKING

| PASSING | Att | Comp | % | Yds | Yd/Att | TD | Int−% | RK |
|---|---|---|---|---|---|---|---|---|
| Reed | 191 | 86 | 45 | 1181 | 6.2 | 9 | 10− 5 | 10 |
| Munson | 109 | 65 | 60 | 626 | 5.7 | 5 | 2− 2 | |
| Landry | 56 | 31 | 55 | 403 | 7.2 | 1 | 0− 0 | |
| Concannon | 2 | 1 | 50 | 30 | 15.0 | 0 | 0− 0 | |
| Briscoe | 2 | 0 | 0 | 0 | 0.0 | 0 | 0− 0 | |
| King | 1 | 0 | 0 | 0 | 0.0 | 0 | 0− 0 | |
| H. Weaver | 1 | 0 | 0 | 0 | 0.0 | 0 | 0− 0 | |

| PUNTING | No | Avg |
|---|---|---|
| H. Weaver | 80 | 42.0 |
| Mann | 1 | 34.0 |

| KICKING | XP | Att | % | FG | Att | % |
|---|---|---|---|---|---|---|
| Mann | 25 | 29 | 86 | 14 | 21 | 67 |

## GREEN BAY PACKERS

### RUSHING

| Last Name | No. | Yds | Avg | TD |
|---|---|---|---|---|
| Brockington | 144 | 434 | 3.0 | 7 |
| Harrell | 121 | 359 | 3.0 | 1 |
| Barty Smith | 60 | 243 | 4.1 | 4 |
| Torkelson | 42 | 226 | 5.4 | 2 |
| Wells | 33 | 139 | 4.2 | 0 |
| Odom | 5 | 55 | 11.0 | 0 |
| Hadl | 20 | 47 | 2.4 | 0 |
| Milan | 4 | 41 | 10.3 | 0 |
| Tinker | 1 | 5 | 5.0 | 0 |
| Payne | 1 | −2 | −2.0 | 0 |

### RECEIVING

| Last Name | No. | Yds | Avg | TD |
|---|---|---|---|---|
| Payne | 58 | 766 | 13 | 0 |
| Harrell | 34 | 261 | 8 | 2 |
| Brockington | 33 | 242 | 8 | 1 |
| McGeorge | 32 | 458 | 14 | 1 |
| Barty Smith | 16 | 140 | 9 | 1 |
| Odom | 15 | 299 | 20 | 4 |
| Barry Smith | 6 | 77 | 13 | 1 |
| Torkelson | 6 | 37 | 6 | 0 |
| Wells | 6 | 11 | 2 | 0 |
| Tinker | 4 | 84 | 21 | 1 |
| Askson | 2 | 25 | 13 | 0 |

### PUNT RETURNS

| Last Name | No. | Yds | Avg | TD |
|---|---|---|---|---|
| Harrell | 21 | 136 | 7 | 0 |
| Ellis | 6 | 27 | 5 | 0 |
| Gray | 1 | 27 | 27 | 0 |
| Hall | 1 | 0 | 0 | 0 |
| Odom | 1 | 0 | 0 | 0 |

### KICKOFF RETURNS

| Last Name | No. | Yds | Avg | TD |
|---|---|---|---|---|
| Odom | 42 | 1034 | 25 | 1 |
| Luke | 6 | 91 | 15 | 0 |
| Torkelson | 5 | 89 | 18 | 0 |
| Harrell | 3 | 78 | 26 | 0 |
| Barty Smith | 4 | 53 | 13 | 0 |
| Wells | 1 | 26 | 26 | 0 |
| McGeorge | 1 | 17 | 17 | 0 |
| Bain | 1 | 10 | 10 | 0 |

### PASSING – PUNTING – KICKING

| PASSING | Att | Comp | % | Yds | Yd/Att | TD | Int−% | RK |
|---|---|---|---|---|---|---|---|---|
| Hadl | 353 | 191 | 54 | 2095 | 5.9 | 6 | 21− 6 | 13 |
| Milan | 32 | 15 | 47 | 181 | 5.7 | 1 | 1− 3 | |
| Harrell | 5 | 3 | 60 | 61 | 12.2 | 3 | 0− 0 | |
| Brown | 4 | 3 | 75 | 63 | 15.8 | 1 | 0− 0 | |

| PUNTING | No | Avg |
|---|---|---|
| Beverly | 78 | 37.7 |
| Broussard | 29 | 31.8 |

| KICKING | XP | ATT | % | FG | ATT | % |
|---|---|---|---|---|---|---|
| Danelo | 20 | 23 | 87 | 11 | 16 | 69 |
| Marcol | 0 | 0 | — | 1 | 1 | 100 |

## CHICAGO BEARS

### RUSHING

| Last Name | No. | Yds | Avg | TD |
|---|---|---|---|---|
| Payton | 196 | 679 | 3.5 | 7 |
| Harper | 100 | 453 | 4.5 | 1 |
| Adamle | 94 | 353 | 3.8 | 0 |
| Edwards | 27 | 73 | 2.7 | 0 |
| Musso | 6 | 33 | 5.5 | 0 |
| Rather | 4 | 24 | 6.0 | 0 |
| Huff | 5 | 7 | 1.4 | 0 |
| Avellini | 4 | −3 | −0.8 | 1 |

### RECEIVING

| Last Name | No. | Yds | Avg | TD |
|---|---|---|---|---|
| Rather | 39 | 685 | 18 | 2 |
| Payton | 33 | 213 | 7 | 0 |
| Grim | 28 | 374 | 13 | 2 |
| Harper | 27 | 191 | 7 | 0 |
| Latta | 16 | 202 | 13 | 3 |
| Adamle | 15 | 111 | 7 | 0 |
| Parsons | 13 | 184 | 14 | 1 |
| Edwards | 11 | 86 | 8 | 1 |
| Schubert | 5 | 68 | 14 | 0 |
| Jackson | 1 | 17 | 17 | 0 |
| Sevy | 1 | 6 | 6 | 0 |

### PUNT RETURNS

| Last Name | No. | Yds | Avg | TD |
|---|---|---|---|---|
| Livers | 42 | 456 | 11 | 0 |
| Schubert | 6 | 33 | 6 | 0 |
| Plank | 3 | 23 | 8 | 0 |
| Knox | 1 | 0 | 0 | 0 |

### KICKOFF RETURNS

| Last Name | No. | Yds | Avg | TD |
|---|---|---|---|---|
| Livers | 26 | 529 | 20 | 0 |
| Payton | 14 | 444 | 32 | 0 |
| Douthitt | 13 | 333 | 26 | 0 |
| Schubert | 9 | 146 | 16 | 0 |
| Knox | 4 | 67 | 17 | 0 |
| Harper | 4 | 67 | 17 | 0 |
| Adamle | 1 | 27 | 27 | 0 |
| Vactor | 1 | 25 | 25 | 0 |
| Rather | 1 | 6 | 6 | 0 |
| Osborne | 1 | 0 | 0 | 0 |

### PASSING – PUNTING – KICKING

| PASSING | Att | Comp | % | Yds | Yd/Att | TD | Int−% | RK |
|---|---|---|---|---|---|---|---|---|
| Huff | 205 | 114 | 56 | 1083 | 5.3 | 3 | 9− 4 | 12 |
| Avellini | 126 | 67 | 53 | 942 | 7.5 | 6 | 11− 9 | |
| Carter | 5 | 3 | 60 | 24 | 4.8 | 0 | 1−20 | |
| Adamle | 2 | 2 | 100 | 57 | 28.5 | 0 | 0− 0 | |
| Grim | 1 | 0 | 0 | 0 | 0.0 | 0 | 0− 0 | |
| Parsons | 1 | 0 | 0 | 0 | 0.0 | 0 | 0− 0 | |
| Payton | 1 | 0 | 0 | 0 | 0.0 | 0 | 1−100 | |

| PUNTING | No | Avg |
|---|---|---|
| Parsons | 93 | 39.0 |
| Payton | 1 | 39.0 |

| KICKING | XP | Att | % | FG | Att | % |
|---|---|---|---|---|---|---|
| Thomas | 18 | 22 | 82 | 13 | 23 | 57 |

## LOS ANGELES RAMS 12-2 Chuck Knox

| Scores of Each Game | | | Use Name | Pos. | Hgt | Wgt | Age | Int | Pts |
|---|---|---|---|---|---|---|---|---|---|
| 7 | Dallas | 18 | Charlie Cowan | OT | 6'4" | 265 | 37 | | |
| 23 | San Francisco | 14 | Doug France | OT | 6'5" | 260 | 22 | | |
| 24 | BALTIMORE | 13 | John Williams | OT | 6'3" | 256 | 29 | | |
| 13 | San Diego | *10 | Dennis Harrah | OG | 6'5" | 257 | 22 | | |
| 22 | ATLANTA | 7 | Tom Mack | OG | 6'3" | 250 | 31 | | |
| 38 | NEW ORLEANS | 14 | Joe Scibelli | OG | 6'1" | 255 | 36 | | |
| 42 | Philadelphia | 3 | Bob DeMarco | C | 6'3" | 245 | 37 | | |
| 23 | SAN FRANCISCO | 24 | Rich Saul | C | 6'3" | 235 | 27 | | |
| 16 | Atlanta | 7 | Al Cowlings | DE | 6'5" | 245 | 28 | | |
| 38 | CHICAGO | 10 | Fred Dryer | DE | 6'6" | 240 | 29 | 1 | 6 |
| 20 | Detroit | 0 | Mike Fanning | DE | 6'6" | 260 | 22 | | |
| 14 | New Orleans | 7 | Jack Youngblood | DE | 6'4" | 255 | 25 | | 2 |
| 22 | GREEN BAY | 5 | Larry Brooks | DT | 6'3" | 255 | 25 | | |
| 10 | PITTSBURGH | 3 | Cody Jones | DT | 6'5" | 240 | 24 | | |
| | | | Bill Nelson | DT | 6'7" | 270 | 27 | | |
| | | | Merlin Olsen | DT | 6'5" | 270 | 34 | | |

| Use Name | Pos. | Hgt | Wgt | Age | Int | Pts |
|---|---|---|---|---|---|---|
| Ken Geddes | LB | 6'3" | 235 | 27 | 1 | |
| Rick Kay | LB | 6'4" | 235 | 25 | | |
| Jim Peterson | LB | 6'5" | 240 | 25 | | 6 |
| Jack Reynolds | LB | 6'1" | 232 | 27 | 1 | |
| Isiah Robertson | LB | 6'3" | 225 | 26 | 4 | 6 |
| Jim Youngblood | LB | 6'3" | 240 | 25 | | |
| Al Clark | DB | 6' | 185 | 26 | | |
| Dave Elmendorf | DB | 6'1" | 195 | 26 | 4 | |
| Monte Jackson | DB | 5'11" | 190 | 22 | 2 | 6 |
| Eddie McMillan | DB | 6' | 190 | 23 | 3 | |
| Rod Perry | DB | 5'9" | 170 | 21 | | |
| Steve Preece | DB | 6'1" | 195 | 28 | | |
| Bill Simpson | DB | 6'1" | 180 | 23 | 6 | |
| | | | | | | |
| Charlie Stukes — Knee Injury | | | | | | |

| Use Name | Pos. | Hgt | Wgt | Age | Int | Pts |
|---|---|---|---|---|---|---|
| James Harris | QB | 6'3" | 210 | 28 | | 6 |
| Ron Jaworski | QB | 6'2" | 185 | 24 | | 12 |
| John Cappelletti | HB | 6'1" | 217 | 23 | | 36 |
| Larry McCutcheon | HB | 6'1" | 205 | 25 | | 18 |
| Rob Scribner | HB | 6' | 200 | 24 | | 12 |
| Jim Bertelsen | FB | 5'11" | 205 | 25 | | 18 |
| Cullen Bryant | FB | 6'1" | 240 | 24 | | 12 |
| Rod Phillips | TE-FB | 6' | 220 | 22 | | |
| Harold Jackson | WR | 5'10" | 175 | 29 | | 42 |
| Ron Jessie | WR | 6' | 185 | 27 | | 18 |
| Willie McGee | WR | 5'11" | 178 | 25 | | |
| Jack Snow | WR | 6'2" | 190 | 32 | | 6 |
| Bob Klein | TE | 6'5" | 235 | 28 | | 12 |
| Terry Nelson | TE | 6'2" | 230 | 23 | | |
| Duane Carrell | K | 5'10" | 185 | 25 | | |
| Tom Dempsey | K | 6'1" | 260 | 34 | | 94 |

## SAN FRANCISCO FORTY-NINERS 5-9 Dick Nolan

| Scores of Each Game | | | Use Name | Pos. | Hgt | Wgt | Age | Int | Pts |
|---|---|---|---|---|---|---|---|---|---|
| 17 | Minnesota | 27 | Cas Banaszek | OT | 6'3" | 255 | 29 | | |
| 14 | LOS ANGELES | 23 | Keith Fahnhorst | OT | 6'6" | 265 | 23 | | |
| 20 | Kansas City | 3 | Jeff Hart | OT | 6'5" | 266 | 21 | | |
| 3 | ATLANTA | 17 | Bobby Penchion | OG | 6'5" | 252 | 26 | | |
| 35 | NEW ORLEANS | 21 | Woody Peoples | OG | 6'2" | 252 | 32 | | |
| 16 | New England | 24 | John Watson | OT-OG | 6'4" | 245 | 26 | | |
| 17 | DETROIT | 28 | Bill Reid | C | 6'1" | 242 | 23 | | |
| 24 | Los Angeles | 23 | Jean Barrett | OG-C | 6'6" | 254 | 24 | | |
| 31 | CHICAGO | 3 | Cleveland Elam | DE | 6'3" | 254 | 23 | | |
| 16 | New Orleans | 6 | Cedrick Hardman | DE | 6'3" | 258 | 26 | | |
| 17 | Philadelphia | 27 | Tommy Hart | DE | 6'3" | 244 | 30 | | 6 |
| 13 | HOUSTON | 27 | Wayne Baker | DT | 6'6" | 270 | 22 | | |
| 9 | Atlanta | 31 | Bob Haskins | DT | 6'2" | 250 | 29 | | |
| 23 | N.Y. GIANTS | 26 | Bill Sandifer | DT | 6'6" | 278 | 23 | | |
| | | | Jimmy Webb | DT | 6'5" | 248 | 23 | | |

| Use Name | Pos. | Hgt | Wgt | Age | Int | Pts |
|---|---|---|---|---|---|---|
| Greg Collins | LB | 6'2" | 234 | 22 | | |
| Willie Harper | LB | 6'2" | 220 | 25 | | |
| Frank Nunley | LB | 6'2" | 234 | 29 | 1 | |
| Skip Vanderbundt | LB | 6'3" | 223 | 28 | 2 | |
| Dave Washington | LB | 6'5" | 223 | 26 | | 6 |
| Nate Allen | DB | 5'10" | 170 | 27 | 1 | 6 |
| Tim Anderson | DB | 6' | 192 | 26 | | |
| Windlan Hall | DB | 5'11" | 175 | 25 | | |
| Jim Johnson | DB | 6'2" | 185 | 37 | 2 | |
| Ralph McGill | DB | 5'11" | 183 | 25 | 1 | 6 |
| Mel Phillips | DB | 6' | 190 | 33 | 1 | |
| John Saunders | DB | 6'3" | 196 | 25 | | |
| Bruce Taylor | DB | 6' | 190 | 27 | 3 | |

| Use Name | Pos. | Hgt | Wgt | Age | Int | Pts |
|---|---|---|---|---|---|---|
| Tom Owen | QB | 6'1" | 194 | 22 | | |
| Norm Snead | QB | 6'4" | 215 | 35 | | 6 |
| Steve Spurrier | QB | 6'2" | 198 | 30 | | |
| Wilbur Jackson | HB | 6'1" | 215 | 23 | | |
| Kermit Johnson | HB | 6' | 195 | 24 | | |
| Manfred Moore | HB | 6' | 194 | 24 | | |
| Del Williams | FB | 6' | 195 | 24 | | 24 |
| Sammy Johnson | FB | 6' | 223 | 22 | | 18 |
| Larry Schreiber | FB | 6' | 209 | 28 | | 36 |
| Terry Beasley | WR | 5'10" | 182 | 25 | | |
| Bob Hayes | WR | 6' | 185 | 32 | | |
| Mike Holmes | WR | 6'2" | 193 | 24 | | 6 |
| Gene Washington | WR | 6'1" | 185 | 28 | | 54 |
| Len Garrett (from NO) | TE | 6'3" | 230 | 26 | | |
| Bill Larson | TE | 6'4" | 225 | 24 | | |
| Tom Mitchell | TE | 6'2" | 215 | 31 | | 18 |
| Steve Mike-Mayer | K | 6' | 178 | 27 | | 69 |
| Tom Wittum | K | 6'1" | 190 | 25 | | |

## ATLANTA FALCONS 4-10 Marion Campbell

| Scores of Each Game | | | Use Name | Pos. | Hgt | Wgt | Age | Int | Pts |
|---|---|---|---|---|---|---|---|---|---|
| 20 | St. Louis | 23 | Brent Adams | OT | 6'5" | 256 | 23 | | |
| 14 | DETROIT | 17 | Nick Bebout | OT | 6'5" | 267 | 24 | | |
| 14 | NEW ORLEANS | 7 | Len Gotshalk | OT | 6'4" | 253 | 25 | | |
| 17 | San Francisco | 3 | Dennis Havig | OG | 6'3" | 254 | 26 | | |
| 7 | Los Angeles | 22 | Larron Jackson | OG | 6'3" | 260 | 26 | | |
| 14 | CINCINNATI | 21 | Royce Smith | OG | 6'3" | 260 | 26 | | |
| 7 | New Orleans | 23 | Paul Ryczek | C | 6'2" | 238 | 23 | | |
| 0 | Minnesota | 38 | Jeff Van Note | C | 6'2" | 252 | 29 | | |
| 7 | LOS ANGELES | 16 | John Zook | DE | 6'5" | 248 | 27 | | |
| 35 | DENVER | 21 | Roy Hilton | DE | 6'6" | 250 | 30 | | |
| 34 | Oakland | *37 | Mike Lewis | DT | 6'3" | 258 | 25 | | |
| 27 | WASHINGTON | 30 | Jeff Merrow | DT | 6'4" | 230 | 22 | | |
| 31 | SAN FRANCISCO | 9 | Mike Tilleman | DT | 6'5" | 273 | 31 | | |
| 13 | Green Bay | 22 | Chuck Walker | DT | 6'2" | 250 | 33 | | |
| | | | | | | | | | |
| | | | Claude Humphrey — Knee Injury | | | | | | |

| Use Name | Pos. | Hgt | Wgt | Age | Int | Pts |
|---|---|---|---|---|---|---|
| Greg Brezina | LB | 6'2" | 220 | 29 | 4 | |
| Don Hansen | LB | 6'3" | 226 | 31 | 1 | |
| Fulton Kuykendall | LB | 6'5" | 225 | 22 | | |
| Tommy Nobis | LB | 6'2" | 232 | 31 | | |
| Ralph Ortega | LB | 6'2" | 220 | 22 | | |
| Carl Russ | LB | 6'2" | 227 | 22 | | |
| Ray Brown | DB | 6'2" | 208 | 26 | 4 | 6 |
| Rick Byas | DB | 5'9" | 172 | 24 | | |
| Ray Easterling | DB | 6' | 186 | 25 | 3 | |
| Tom Hayes | DB | 6'1" | 196 | 29 | 4 | |
| Bob Jones | DB | 6'1" | 193 | 24 | | |
| Rolland Lawrence | DB | 5'10" | .174 | 24 | 9 | 6 |
| Ron Mabra | DB | 5'10" | 164 | 24 | | |
| | | | | | | |
| Ted Fritsch — Knee Injury | | | | | | |
| Vince Kendrick — Knee Injury | | | | | | |
| Jim Miller — Knee Injury | | | | | | |

| Use Name | Pos. | Hgt | Wgt | Age | Int | Pts |
|---|---|---|---|---|---|---|
| Steve Bartkowski | QB | 6'4" | 213 | 22 | | 12 |
| Kim McQuilken | QB | 6'2" | 200 | 24 | | |
| Pat Sullivan | QB | 6' | 200 | 25 | | |
| Larry Crowe | HB | 6'1" | 198 | 25 | | |
| Dave Hampton | HB | 6' | 206 | 28 | | 36 |
| Mack Herron (from NE) | HB | 5'5" | 175 | 27 | | |
| Haskel Stanback | HB | 6' | 210 | 23 | | 30 |
| Brad Davis | FB | 5'11" | 208 | 22 | | |
| Monroe Eley | FB | 6'2" | 210 | 23 | | |
| Woody Thompson | FB | 6'1" | 228 | 23 | | |
| Oscar Reed | HB-FB | 5'11" | 222 | 31 | | |
| Ken Burrow | WR | 6' | 188 | 27 | | 12 |
| Wallace Francis | WR | 5'11" | 185 | 23 | | 24 |
| Alfred Jenkins | WR | 5'10" | 155 | 23 | | 36 |
| Frank Pitts | WR | 6'2" | 200 | 31 | | |
| Greg McCrary | TE | 6'3" | 230 | 24 | | |
| Jim Mitchell | TE | 6'2" | 235 | 27 | | 30 |
| John James | K | 6'3" | 197 | 26 | | |
| Nick Mike-Mayer | K | 5'8" | 185 | 25 | | 42 |

## NEW ORLEANS SAINTS 2-12 John North   Ernie Hefferle

| Scores of Each Game | | | Use Name | Pos. | Hgt | Wgt | Age | Int | Pts |
|---|---|---|---|---|---|---|---|---|---|
| 3 | Washington | 41 | John Hill | OT | 6'2" | 245 | 25 | | |
| 0 | CINCINNATI | 21 | Phil LaPorta | OT | 6'4" | 256 | 22 | | |
| 7 | Atlanta | 14 | Chris Morris | OT | 6'3" | 250 | 25 | | |
| 20 | GREEN BAY | 19 | Don Morrison | OT | 6'5" | 260 | 25 | | |
| 21 | San Francisco | 35 | Kurt Schumacher | OT | 6'3" | 260 | 22 | | |
| 14 | Los Angeles | 38 | Dave Thompson | C-OT | 6'4" | 260 | 26 | | |
| 23 | ATLANTA | 7 | Jake Kupp | OG | 6'3" | 248 | 33 | | |
| 10 | Oakland | 48 | Emanuel Zanders | OG | 6'1" | 260 | 24 | | |
| 7 | MINNESOTA | 20 | Tom Wickert | OT-OG | 6'4" | 246 | 23 | | |
| 6 | SAN FRANCISCO | 16 | Sylvester Croom | C | 6' | 235 | 20 | | |
| 16 | Cleveland | 17 | Lee Gross | C | 6'3" | 245 | 22 | | |
| 7 | LOS ANGELES | 14 | Steve Baumgartner | DE | 6'7" | 260 | 24 | | |
| 14 | N.Y. Giants | 28 | Andy Dorris | DE | 6'4" | 240 | 24 | | |
| 17 | CHICAGO | 42 | Elois Grooms | DE | 6'4" | 240 | 22 | | |
| | | | Joe Owens | DE | 6'2" | 250 | 28 | | |
| | | | Derland Moore | DT | 6'4" | 260 | 23 | | |
| | | | Bob Pollard | DT | 6'3" | 250 | 26 | | |
| | | | Elex Price | DT | 6'3" | 260 | 25 | | |

| Use Name | Pos. | Hgt | Wgt | Age | Int | Pts |
|---|---|---|---|---|---|---|
| Rusty Chambers | LB | 6'1" | 215 | 21 | | 6 |
| Don Coleman | LB | 6'2" | 222 | 22 | | |
| Joe Federspiel | LB | 6'1" | 235 | 25 | | |
| Rick Kingrea | LB | 6'1" | 230 | 26 | 1 | |
| Rick Middleton | LB | 6'2" | 228 | 23 | 1 | |
| Greg Westbrooks | LB | 6'2" | 215 | 22 | 1 | |
| Chuck Crist | DB | 6'2" | 205 | 24 | 3 | |
| Jim DeRatt | DB | 6' | 203 | 22 | | |
| Johnny Fuller | DB | 6' | 185 | 29 | | |
| Ernie Jackson | DB | 5'10" | 175 | 25 | 2 | |
| Bivian Lee | DB | 6'3" | 200 | 27 | 2 | |
| Tom Myers | DB | 5'11" | 184 | 24 | 5 | 6 |
| Terry Schmidt | DB | 6' | 177 | 23 | 1 | |
| Mo Spencer | DB | 6' | 175 | 23 | | |
| | | | | | | |
| Wayne Colman — Broken Arm | | | | | | |
| Dave Davis — Ankle Injury | | | | | | |
| Jim Merlo — Injury | | | | | | |
| Bob Newland — Injury | | | | | | |

| Use Name | Pos. | Hgt | Wgt | Age | Int | Pts |
|---|---|---|---|---|---|---|
| Larry Cipa | QB | 6'3" | 209 | 22 | | |
| Archie Manning | QB | 6'3" | 207 | 26 | | 6 |
| Bobby Scott | QB | 6'1" | 200 | 26 | | |
| Alvin Maxson | HB | 5'11" | 205 | 22 | | 18 |
| Steve Rogers | HB | 6'2" | 200 | 22 | | |
| Mike Strachan | HB | 6' | 195 | 22 | | 12 |
| Andrew Jones | FB | 6'2" | 213 | 22 | | 6 |
| Morris LaGrand (from KC) | FB | 6'1" | 220 | 24 | | |
| Rod McNeill | FB | 6'2" | 220 | 24 | | 24 |
| Larry Burton | WR | 6'1" | 190 | 23 | | 12 |
| Gil Chapman | WR | 5'9" | 180 | 22 | | |
| Andy Hamilton | WR | 6'3" | 190 | 25 | | |
| Don Herrmann | WR | 6'2" | 205 | 28 | | 6 |
| Joel Parker | WR | 6'5" | 212 | 23 | | 12 |
| Henry Childs | TE | 6'2" | 223 | 24 | | |
| Paul Seal | TE | 6'4" | 222 | 23 | | 6 |
| Tom Blanchard | K | 6' | 180 | 27 | | |
| Bill McClard | K | 5'10" | 202 | 23 | | 4 |
| Richie Szaro | K | 5'11" | 205 | 27 | | 47 |

*—Overtime

## LOS ANGELES RAMS

### Rushing

| Last Name | No. | Yds | Avg | TD |
|---|---|---|---|---|
| McCutcheon | 213 | 911 | 4.3 | 2 |
| Bryant | 117 | 467 | 4.0 | 2 |
| Bertelsen | 116 | 457 | 3.9 | 3 |
| Scribner | 42 | 216 | 5.1 | 2 |
| Cappelletti | 48 | 158 | 3.3 | 6 |
| Phillips | 17 | 69 | 4.1 | 0 |
| Harris | 18 | 45 | 2.5 | 1 |
| Jaworski | 12 | 33 | 2.8 | 0 |
| Jessie | 2 | 15 | 7.5 | 0 |

### Receiving

| Last Name | No. | Yds | Avg | TD |
|---|---|---|---|---|
| H. Jackson | 43 | 786 | 18 | 7 |
| Jessie | 41 | 547 | 13 | 3 |
| McCutcheon | 31 | 230 | 7 | 1 |
| Bryant | 20 | 229 | 12 | 0 |
| Klein | 16 | 237 | 15 | 2 |
| Bertelsen | 14 | 208 | 15 | 0 |
| McGee | 6 | 83 | 14 | 0 |
| Snow | 4 | 86 | 22 | 1 |
| Scribner | 2 | 28 | 14 | 0 |
| Phillips | 2 | 10 | 5 | 0 |
| Nelson | 1 | 5 | 5 | 0 |
| Cowan | 1 | 1 | 1 | 0 |

### Punt Returns

| Last Name | No. | Yds | Avg | TD |
|---|---|---|---|---|
| Scribner | 26 | 205 | 8 | 0 |
| Bertelsen | 11 | 143 | 13 | 0 |
| Elmendorf | 15 | 125 | 8 | 0 |
| Bryant | 2 | 47 | 24 | 0 |
| Simpson | 1 | −3 | −3 | 0 |

### Kickoff Returns

| Last Name | No. | Yds | Avg | TD |
|---|---|---|---|---|
| McGee | 17 | 404 | 24 | 0 |
| Bryant | 12 | 280 | 23 | 0 |
| Cappelletti | 3 | 39 | 13 | 0 |
| Scribner | 1 | 24 | 24 | 0 |
| Bertelsen | 1 | 17 | 17 | 0 |

### Passing – Punting – Kicking

| Passing | Att | Comp | % | Yds | Yd/Att | TD | Int–% | RK |
|---|---|---|---|---|---|---|---|---|
| Harris | 285 | 157 | 55 | 2148 | 7.5 | 14 | 15– 5 | 4 |
| Jaworski | 48 | 24 | 50 | 302 | 6.3 | 0 | 2– 4 | |
| McCutcheon | 1 | 0 | 0 | 0 | 0.0 | 0 | 0– 0 | |

| Punting | No | Avg |
|---|---|---|
| Carrell | 73 | 39.4 |

| Kicking | XP | Att | % | FG | Att | % |
|---|---|---|---|---|---|---|
| Dempsey | 31 | 36 | 86 | 21 | 26 | 81 |

## SAN FRANCISCO FORTY-NINERS

### Rushing

| Last Name | No. | Yds | Avg | TD |
|---|---|---|---|---|
| D. Williams | 117 | 631 | 5.4 | 3 |
| Schreiber | 134 | 337 | 2.5 | 5 |
| Jackson | 78 | 303 | 3.9 | 0 |
| S. Johnson | 55 | 185 | 3.4 | 2 |
| Spurrier | 15 | 91 | 6.1 | 0 |
| Snead | 9 | 30 | 3.3 | 1 |
| K. Johnson | 4 | 25 | 6.3 | 0 |
| Moore | 3 | 10 | 3.3 | 0 |
| Beasley | 1 | 5 | 5.0 | 0 |
| Owen | 1 | 1 | 1.0 | 0 |
| Hayes | 2 | −2 | −1.0 | 0 |
| Holmes | 1 | −4 | −4.0 | 0 |
| Washington | 1 | −4 | −4.0 | 0 |
| Wittum | 1 | −10 | −10.0 | 0 |

### Receiving

| Last Name | No. | Yds | Avg | TD |
|---|---|---|---|---|
| Washington | 44 | 735 | 17 | 9 |
| Schreiber | 40 | 289 | 7 | 1 |
| Williams | 34 | 370 | 11 | 1 |
| Mitchell | 25 | 366 | 15 | 3 |
| S. Johnson | 23 | 177 | 8 | 0 |
| Beasley | 20 | 297 | 15 | 0 |
| Jackson | 17 | 128 | 8 | 0 |
| Holmes | 16 | 220 | 14 | 1 |
| Hayes | 6 | 119 | 20 | 0 |
| Larson | 5 | 64 | 13 | 0 |
| Wittum | 2 | 29 | 15 | 0 |
| Moore | 1 | 11 | 11 | 0 |
| Fahnhorst | 1 | 1 | 1 | 0 |

### Punt Returns

| Last Name | No. | Yds | Avg | TD |
|---|---|---|---|---|
| McGill | 31 | 290 | 9 | 0 |
| Taylor | 16 | 166 | 10 | 0 |
| Moore | 16 | 160 | 10 | 0 |

### Kickoff Returns

| Last Name | No. | Yds | Avg | TD |
|---|---|---|---|---|
| Moore | 26 | 650 | 25 | 0 |
| S. Johnson | 17 | 400 | 24 | 0 |
| K. Johnson | 6 | 135 | 23 | 0 |
| Holmes | 2 | 59 | 30 | 0 |
| Baker | 4 | 45 | 11 | 0 |
| Hart | 2 | 28 | 14 | 0 |
| Williams | 1 | 24 | 24 | 0 |
| Hall | 1 | 18 | 18 | 0 |
| Fahnhorst | 1 | 13 | 13 | 0 |

### Passing – Punting – Kicking

| Passing | Att | Comp | % | Yds | Yd/Att | TD | Int–% | RK |
|---|---|---|---|---|---|---|---|---|
| Spurrier | 207 | 102 | 49 | 1151 | 5.6 | 5 | 7– 3 | 9 |
| Snead | 189 | 108 | 57 | 1337 | 7.1 | 9 | 10– 5 | 5 |
| Owen | 51 | 24 | 47 | 318 | 6.2 | 1 | 2– 4 | |
| S. Johnson | 2 | 0 | 0 | 0 | 0.0 | 0 | 0– 0 | |
| Washington | 1 | 0 | 0 | 0 | 0.0 | 0 | 0– 0 | |

| Punting | No | Avg |
|---|---|---|
| Wittum | 67 | 41.9 |

| Kicking | XP | Att | % | FG | Att | % |
|---|---|---|---|---|---|---|
| Mike-Mayer | 27 | 31 | 87 | 14 | 28 | 50 |

## ATLANTA FALCONS

### Rushing

| Last Name | No. | Yds | Avg | TD |
|---|---|---|---|---|
| Hampton | 250 | 1002 | 4.0 | 5 |
| Stanback | 105 | 440 | 4.2 | 5 |
| Herron | 62 | 274 | 4.4 | 0 |
| Thompson | 68 | 247 | 3.6 | 0 |
| Reed | 14 | 40 | 2.9 | 0 |
| McQuilken | 4 | 26 | 6.5 | 0 |
| Bartkowski | 14 | 15 | 1.1 | 2 |
| Francis | 2 | 12 | 6.0 | 0 |
| Sullivan | 6 | 9 | 1.5 | 0 |
| Tinker | 1 | 5 | 5.0 | 0 |
| Ely | 1 | 3 | 3.0 | 0 |

### Receiving

| Last Name | No. | Yds | Avg | TD |
|---|---|---|---|---|
| Jenkins | 38 | 767 | 20 | 6 |
| J. Mitchell | 34 | 536 | 16 | 4 |
| Burrow | 25 | 323 | 13 | 2 |
| Hampton | 21 | 195 | 9 | 1 |
| Stanback | 14 | 115 | 8 | 0 |
| Thompson | 14 | 92 | 7 | 0 |
| Francis | 13 | 270 | 21 | 4 |
| Tinker | 7 | 121 | 17 | 2 |
| Herron | 5 | 50 | 10 | 0 |
| Reed | 2 | 1 | 1 | 0 |
| Jones | 1 | 25 | 25 | 0 |

### Punt Returns

| Last Name | No. | Yds | Avg | TD |
|---|---|---|---|---|
| Herron | 22 | 183 | 8 | 0 |
| Eley | 7 | 61 | 9 | 0 |
| Jenkins | 6 | 38 | 6 | 0 |
| Tinker | 6 | 23 | 4 | 0 |
| Mabra | 4 | 20 | 5 | 0 |
| Brown | 2 | 12 | 6 | 0 |

### Kickoff Returns

| Last Name | No. | Yds | Avg | TD |
|---|---|---|---|---|
| Tinker | 13 | 307 | 24 | 0 |
| Francis | 14 | 265 | 19 | 0 |
| Herron | 13 | 264 | 20 | 0 |
| Eley | 8 | 131 | 16 | 0 |
| Byas | 5 | 94 | 19 | 0 |
| Lawrence | 4 | 80 | 20 | 0 |
| Thompson | 4 | 62 | 16 | 0 |
| McCrary | 3 | 48 | 16 | 0 |
| Jenkins | 1 | 24 | 24 | 0 |
| Reed | 2 | 17 | 9 | 0 |
| Davis | 1 | 0 | 0 | 0 |

### Passing – Punting – Kicking

| Passing | Att | Comp | % | Yds | Yd/Att | TD | Int–% | RK |
|---|---|---|---|---|---|---|---|---|
| Bartkowski | 255 | 115 | 45 | 1662 | 6.5 | 13 | 15– 6 | 11 |
| Sullivan | 70 | 28 | 40 | 380 | 5.4 | 3 | 5– 7 | |
| McQuilken | 61 | 20 | 33 | 253 | 4.2 | 1 | 9–15 | |
| James | 1 | 1 | 100 | 25 | 25.0 | 0 | 0– 0 | |
| Stanback | 1 | 1 | 100 | 41 | 41.0 | 1 | 0– 0 | |

| Punting | No | Avg |
|---|---|---|
| James | 89 | 41.5 |

| Kicking | XP | Att | % | FG | Att | % |
|---|---|---|---|---|---|---|
| Mike-Mayer | 30 | 33 | 91 | 4 | 10 | 40 |

## NEW ORLEANS SAINTS

### Rushing

| Last Name | No. | Yds | Avg | TD |
|---|---|---|---|---|
| Strachan | 161 | 668 | 4.1 | 2 |
| Maxson | 139 | 371 | 2.7 | 3 |
| McNeill | 61 | 206 | 3.4 | 2 |
| Manning | 33 | 186 | 5.6 | 1 |
| Jones | 42 | 108 | 2.6 | 1 |
| Rogers | 17 | 62 | 3.6 | 0 |
| LaGrand | 13 | 38 | 2.9 | 1 |
| Seal | 1 | 10 | 10.0 | 0 |
| Burton | 2 | 8 | 4.0 | 0 |
| Cipa | 6 | 2 | 0.3 | 0 |

### Receiving

| Last Name | No. | Yds | Avg | TD |
|---|---|---|---|---|
| Maxson | 41 | 234 | 6 | 0 |
| Strachan | 30 | 224 | 8 | 0 |
| Seal | 28 | 414 | 15 | 1 |
| McNeill | 18 | 138 | 8 | 2 |
| Burton | 16 | 305 | 19 | 2 |
| Hamilton | 12 | 210 | 18 | 0 |
| Childs | 10 | 179 | 18 | 0 |
| Jones | 10 | 52 | 5 | 0 |
| Parker | 9 | 123 | 14 | 2 |
| Herrmann | 3 | 47 | 16 | 1 |
| Chapman | 1 | 7 | 7 | 0 |
| Rogers | 1 | 2 | 2 | 0 |
| LaGrand | 1 | −1 | −1 | 0 |

### Punt Returns

| Last Name | No. | Yds | Avg | TD |
|---|---|---|---|---|
| Chapman | 17 | 207 | 12 | 0 |
| Schmidt | 11 | 76 | 7 | 0 |
| Myers | 10 | 70 | 7 | 0 |
| DeRatt | 2 | 17 | 9 | 0 |
| Spencer | 1 | 0 | 0 | 0 |

### Kickoff Returns

| Last Name | No. | Yds | Avg | TD |
|---|---|---|---|---|
| Chapman | 28 | 614 | 22 | 0 |
| McNeill | 10 | 276 | 28 | 0 |
| Maxson | 6 | 103 | 17 | 0 |
| Rogers | 6 | 98 | 16 | 0 |
| Strachan | 5 | 91 | 18 | 0 |
| Spencer | 5 | 68 | 14 | 0 |
| Schmidt | 2 | 54 | 27 | 0 |
| Chambers | 1 | 15 | 15 | 0 |

### Passing – Punting – Kicking

| Passing | Att | Comp | % | Yds | Yd/Att | TD | Int–% | RK |
|---|---|---|---|---|---|---|---|---|
| Manning | 338 | 159 | 47 | 1683 | 5.0 | 7 | 20– 6 | 15 |
| Cipa | 37 | 14 | 38 | 182 | 4.9 | 1 | 3– 8 | |
| Scott | 17 | 8 | 47 | 96 | 5.7 | 0 | 1– 6 | |

| Punting | No | Avg |
|---|---|---|
| Blanchard | 92 | 41.0 |

| Kicking | XP | Att | % | FG | Att | % |
|---|---|---|---|---|---|---|
| Szaro | 17 | 17 | 100 | 10 | 16 | 63 |

# 1975 A.F.C. Closing The Marketplace

The World Football League began its second year of play with some impressive new assets. Larry Csonka, Paul Warfield, and Jim Kiick reported to the Memphis club amidst much publicity, Calvin Hill and Ted Kwalick joined the Hawaii team, and John Gilliam played in the Chicago lineup. But other N.F.L. stars such as Kenny Stabler, L.C. Greenwood, and Curly Culp made haste to cancel their future contracts with W.F.L. clubs, and some of last year's stars of the new league, such as Tony Adams and Greg Latta, jumped at the chance to sign with N.F.L. teams. These departing players had taken an accurate reading of the league's pulse, for the massively bad publicity from last season carried over into 1975 and plunged the once-optimistic circuit into a new round of staggering debts and defaulted contracts. On October 22, 11 weeks into its 20-week schedule, the W.F.L. closed its doors and went out of business. Attendance for this second season averaged 13,371 per game and was fading, while new debts accumulated this year totaled up to about $10 million.

## EASTERN DIVISION

**Baltimore Colts**—The Colts seemed headed for another dismal season when they dropped four of their first five games, but they then beat the Jets 45-28 and roared through the rest of the schedule with the momentum of a runaway boulder. New coach Ted Marchibroda found the young talent under his command jelling into a top-flight unit in mid-season. Quarterback Bert Jones blossomed into one of the N.F.L.'s dangerous young passers, while Lydell Mitchell starred as a runner and receiver out of the backfield. The offensive line, bolstered by All-Pro tackle George Kunz from the Falcons, played far better than expected, and the defensive front four of Fred Cook, John Dutton, Joe Ehrmann, and Mike Barnes sacked quarterbacks with amazing regularity. The turnabout was so sudden that observers had to wonder when Cinderella was going to turn back into a pumpkin. On November 10, the Colts came back from a 21-0 deficit to beat the Bills 42-35. They upset the Dolphins in Miami 33-17 on November 23, and three weeks later climbed into a first-place tie by beating the Dolphins in Baltimore 10-7 in overtime. A 34-21 victory over New England in the final game clinched a playoff spot for the surprise team of the year.

**Miami Dolphins**—Coach Don Shula had other worries besides the defection of Larry Csonka, Paul Warfield, and Jim Kiick to the W.F.L. Injuries played havoc with his defensive platoon, striking down Dick Anderson, Nick Buoniconti, Bob Heinz, Manny Fernandez, and Bill Stanfill. But Shula managed to plug all the holes, getting good seasons out of odds and ends like Norm Bulaich, Don Nottingham, and Charlie Babb. After beating Buffalo 35-30 on October 26, the Dolphins looked home free for another divisional title. But the Oilers upset them 20-19 on November 16, and the Colts clobbered them 33-17 the next week. But worse than losing the game to the Colts was losing Bob Griese in that contest for the rest of the season with a toe injury. Forty-one year old Earl Morrall played well in leading the Dolphins to a 20-7 decision over New England but hurt his knee in the process. That left third-stringer Don Strock at quarterback. He engineered a 31-21 victory over Buffalo, but the red-hot Colts then took the 10-7 decision in an epic overtime contest. With two losses to the Colts, the Dolphins incredibly found themselves out of the playoffs.

**Buffalo Bills**—O.J. Simpson had reached the stage where he was in a class only with the greats of the past. Running behind the great Buffalo offensive line, the Juice rushed for 1817 yards and set a new record with 23 touchdowns scored for the season. Quarterback Joe Ferguson found it easier to pass against defenses keying on the running of Simpson and Jim Braxton. The only fly in the ointment was a defensive backfield which was decimated by injuries. After the Bills won five of their first six games, opponents began scoring points as fast as O.J. and company could put them on the board. Midseason losses to the Colts, Bengals, and Dolphins put an end to the playoff hopes for this year.

**New York Jets**—Two victories in the first three games fueled hopes for the Jets, but the defensive unit suddenly fell to pieces. After the promising start, the Jets lost to the Vikings 29-21, to the Dolphins 43-0, and to the Colts 45-28. Losses to the Bills and Vikings were followed by a 52-19 slaughter at the hands of the Colts, during which two Jets players broke into a fist fight on the sidelines. Coach Charley Winner got the axe and was replaced on an interim basis by Ken Shipp. One victory in five games was all Shipp could coax out of this squad with massive defensive problems and a mediocre season out of Joe Namath.

**New England Patriots**—The bad vibrations started with the strike in the final week of training camp and carried throughout the season. Jim Plunkett twice separated his shoulder, robbing the attack of leadership right at the start of the campaign. After the second injury, rookie Steve Grogan played so well that fans at Schaeffer Stadium booed Plunkett when he returned to the lineup. Mack Herron symbolized the turnaround in Patriot fortunes. After setting a record last season for total yardage, Herron fell out of favor with coach Chuck Fairbanks, found himself benched, and was waived to Atlanta late in the season.

## CENTRAL DIVISION

**Pittsburgh Steelers**—Despite a 37-0 triumph over San Diego to start the season, the Steelers looked better and better as the campaign wore on. After losing to Buffalo in their second game, the Steelers then tore through the league with 11 straight victories. The Pittsburgh defense smothered enemy attacks week after week, even while losing Joe Greene for a time with neck and groin injuries. Franco Harris led the offense with 1246 yards on the ground, but the performances of Terry Bradshaw, Lynn Swann, and the yeoman line ranked as high in excellence. The Steelers beat back challenges from the Oilers and Bengals to brand themselves the team to beat in the playoffs.

**Cincinnati Bengals**—Even with All-Pro defensive lineman Mike Reid retired to a career as a pianist, the Bengals had talent enough to threaten the Steelers in the Central Division. Paul Brown's men ran out to six quick wins but then lost 30-24 to the Steelers on November 2 to fall into a first place tie. They then dropped into second place by losing to the Browns the next week. Although they beat back the challenging Oilers 23-9 on November 30, the attempt to recapture first place failed by again bowing to the Steelers 35-14 on December 13. But a 47-17 shellacking of San Diego in the final game clinched a wildcard berth in the playoffs.

**Houston Oilers**—Bum Phillips thoroughly enjoyed his first year as head coach as the Oilers made a surprise run at a playoff berth. The Oilers won six of their first seven games, but inability to beat either the Steelers or Bengals condemned them to being an exciting also-ran. The defensive front three of Elvin Bethea, Curly Culp, and Tody Smith had new comfort in Robert Brazile, an excellent rookie linebacker. Operating behind a surprisingly strong line, quarterback Dan Pastorini got off lots of passes to Ken Burrough, while Ronnie Coleman and rookie Don Hardeman crunched out the yardage on the ground. The real star of the season, however, was Billy Johnson, a flashy little wide receiver and kick returner whose wobbly-leg victory dance after touchdowns turned on the fans and threatened spiking with extinction.

**Cleveland Browns**—The Browns had fallen on hardtimes, and the hiring of Forrest Gregg as head coach had no immediate effect on the situation. Nine losses at the start of the campaign horrified fans who had known only success until recently. An upset 35-23 victory over state-rival Cincinnati soothed some of the hurt, but few people would deny that the Browns were weaker at more positions than they were strong. Greg Pruitt and Reggie Rucker stood out as offensive threats among the rubble, while Jerry Sherk and rookie Mack Mitchell worked hard in the defensive line.

## WESTERN DIVISION

**Oakland Raiders**—The depth on the Raiders was such that the second unit could probably have played winning ball in the N.F.L. Despite Jim Otto's retirement and a bad knee which hobbled Kenny Stabler, the Oakland offensive machine rolled on with a strong line, five good running backs, and a complementary set of wide receivers in Cliff Branch and Fred Biletnikoff. The defense had a new recruit in All-Pro linebacker Ted Hendricks who was so strong that Bubba Smith was cut. George Blanda and Ray Guy gave Oakland an edge in kicking, while the specialty teams sparkled with kickoff returner Harold Hart and rookie punt receiver Neal Colzie. As expected, the Raiders easily captured the Western Division crown, but their plans to go all the way through the playoffs to the Super Bowl were soon thwarted by the Steelers.

**Denver Broncos**—The Broncos opened the season with two victories, but then fell into a rut which sank them below the .500 level. The ground game suffered when Otis Armstrong was injured, although second-year man Jon Keyworth assumed the heavy-duty running chores with some flair. At quarterback, veteran Charley Johnson failed to ignite the offense, lost his job to Steve Ramsey, then broke his collarbone after getting back into the lineup. At the end of this disappointing campaign, Johnson and Denver favorite Floyd Little retired after distinguished careers.

**Kansas City Chiefs**—New coach Paul Wiggins had to suffer through three straight losses at the start of the schedule, but the 42-10 upset over Oakland on national television got the Chiefs into the win column with a vengeance. The Chiefs did make a long-shot run at a playoff berth before dropping their last four games. Without a long string of injuries, the Chiefs might have stayed in the thick of the race. The offensive line was hurt and then Otis Taylor went out with a bad knee, and both Mickey Livingston and Len Dawson were kayoed with injuries, leaving W.F.L. ex-patriot Tony Adams running the offense at the end. Wiggins could look back on good performances from Willie Lanier, Emmitt Thomas, Jack Rudnay, and Woody Green, and count on better things to come from his spirited squad.

**San Diego Chargers**—Experts speculated as December began whether the Chargers would complete their schedule at 0-14, the first team ever to reach that mark. With a perfect record of 11 losses, the Chargers beat the Chiefs and ruined their chance at the record book. The Chargers had no offense at all, with the running game wiped out by injuries to Don Woods and Bo Matthews and with quarterbacks Don Fouts and Jesse Freitas unable to ignite any attack. The Chargers presented such a dull show that only 24,349 fans showed up on November 9 to see them lose to New England.

## FINAL TEAM STATISTICS

### OFFENSE

| | BALT. | BUFF. | CIN. | CLEV. | DENV. | HOUS. | K.C. | MIAMI | N.ENG. | N.Y. | OAK. | PITT. | S.D. |
|---|---|---|---|---|---|---|---|---|---|---|---|---|---|
| **FIRST DOWNS:** | | | | | | | | | | | | | |
| Total | 266 | 318 | 295 | 247 | 268 | 234 | 261 | 266 | 253 | 266 | 315 | 288 | 198 |
| by Rushing | 131 | 162 | 107 | 109 | 109 | 121 | 110 | 136 | 94 | 126 | 159 | 149 | 98 |
| by Passing | 114 | 132 | 166 | 114 | 137 | 90 | 128 | 108 | 133 | 111 | 139 | 125 | 89 |
| by Penalty | 21 | 24 | 22 | 24 | 22 | 23 | 23 | 22 | 26 | 29 | 17 | 14 | 11 |
| **RUSHING:** | | | | | | | | | | | | | |
| Number | 536 | 588 | 499 | 440 | 490 | 526 | 487 | 594 | 472 | 501 | 643 | 581 | 434 |
| Yards | 2217 | 2974 | 1819 | 1850 | 1993 | 2068 | 1847 | 2500 | 1845 | 2079 | 2573 | 2633 | 1801 |
| Average Yards | 4.1 | 5.1 | 3.6 | 4.2 | 4.1 | 3.9 | 3.8 | 4.2 | 3.9 | 4.1 | 4.0 | 4.5 | 4.1 |
| Touchdowns | 28 | 26 | 20 | 14 | 9 | 14 | 14 | 26 | 14 | 15 | 28 | 22 | 14 |
| **PASSING:** | | | | | | | | | | | | | |
| Attempts | 354 | 354 | 433 | 437 | 427 | 347 | 395 | 279 | 401 | 384 | 350 | 337 | 337 |
| Completions | 211 | 182 | 255 | 220 | 210 | 165 | 217 | 170 | 193 | 174 | 196 | 191 | 165 |
| Completion Percentage | 59.6 | 51.4 | 58.9 | 50.3 | 49.2 | 47.6 | 54.9 | 60.9 | 48.1 | 45.3 | 56.0 | 56.7 | 49.0 |
| Passing Yards | 2606 | 2661 | 3497 | 2297 | 2900 | 2099 | 2785 | 2196 | 2768 | 2468 | 2625 | 2544 | 1998 |
| Avg. Yards per Attempt | 7.4 | 7.5 | 8.1 | 5.3 | 7.0 | 6.0 | 7.1 | 7.8 | 6.9 | 6.4 | 7.5 | 6.7 | 5.9 |
| Avg. Yards per Complet. | 12.4 | 14.6 | 13.7 | 10.4 | 13.7 | 12.7 | 12.8 | 12.9 | 14.3 | 14.2 | 13.4 | 13.3 | 12.1 |
| Times Tackled Passing | 38 | 22 | 34 | 38 | 47 | 27 | 53 | 23 | 39 | 34 | 26 | 31 | 50 |
| Yards Lost Passing | 325 | 168 | 256 | 340 | 359 | 230 | 425 | 187 | 330 | 317 | 234 | 290 | 388 |
| Net Yards | 2281 | 2493 | 3241 | 1957 | 2541 | 1869 | 2360 | 2009 | 2438 | 2151 | 2391 | 2254 | 1610 |
| Touchdowns | 19 | 28 | 23 | 7 | 15 | 14 | 15 | 19 | 16 | 16 | 19 | 21 | 7 |
| Interceptions | 8 | 19 | 14 | 23 | 34 | 17 | 16 | 17 | 28 | 33 | 28 | 12 | 17 |
| Percent Intercepted | 2.3 | 5.4 | 3.2 | 5.3 | 8.0 | 4.9 | 4.1 | 6.1 | 7.0 | 8.6 | 8.0 | 3.6 | 5.0 |
| **PUNTS:** | | | | | | | | | | | | | |
| Number | 86 | 61 | 68 | 82 | 63 | 74 | 72 | 65 | 83 | 59 | 68 | 69 | 79 |
| Average Distance | 39.6 | 41.6 | 39.0 | 40.5 | 39.9 | 39.3 | 39.3 | 38.6 | 38.8 | 36.5 | 43.8 | 39.4 | 36.7 |
| **PUNT RETURNS:** | | | | | | | | | | | | | |
| Number | 42 | 33 | 48 | 40 | 41 | 43 | 37 | 43 | 33 | 22 | 58 | 54 | 38 |
| Yards | 439 | 278 | 267 | 294 | 470 | 620 | 303 | 509 | 262 | 116 | 688 | 548 | 442 |
| Average Yards | 10.5 | 8.4 | 5.6 | 7.4 | 11.5 | 14.4 | 8.2 | 11.8 | 7.9 | 5.3 | 11.9 | 10.1 | 11.6 |
| Touchdowns | 0 | 0 | 0 | 0 | 0 | 3 | 0 | 1 | 0 | 0 | 0 | 0 | 1 |
| **KICKOFF RETURNS:** | | | | | | | | | | | | | |
| Number | 52 | 62 | 46 | 67 | 59 | 54 | 62 | 40 | 66 | 74 | 51 | 38 | 69 |
| Yards | 1190 | 1457 | 1042 | 1526 | 1446 | 1144 | 1350 | 949 | 1250 | 1704 | 1324 | 815 | 1482 |
| Average Yards | 22.9 | 23.5 | 22.7 | 22.8 | 24.5 | 21.2 | 21.8 | 23.7 | 23.0 | 23.0 | 26.0 | 21.4 | 21.5 |
| Touchdowns | 0 | 0 | 0 | 0 | 0 | 1 | 0 | 0 | 1 | 0 | 1 | 1 | 0 |
| **INTERCEPTION RETURNS:** | | | | | | | | | | | | | |
| Number | 29 | 25 | 22 | 10 | 16 | 24 | 20 | 21 | 13 | 15 | 35 | 27 | 20 |
| Yards | 493 | 376 | 410 | 107 | 293 | 425 | 388 | 183 | 165 | 98 | 450 | 421 | 223 |
| Average Yards | 17.0 | 15.0 | 18.6 | 10.7 | 18.3 | 17.7 | 19.4 | 8.7 | 12.7 | 6.5 | 12.9 | 15.6 | 11.2 |
| Touchdowns | 4 | 2 | 2 | 1 | 1 | 0 | 0 | 0 | 1 | 0 | 0 | 0 | 0 |
| **PENALTIES:** | | | | | | | | | | | | | |
| Number | 80 | 90 | 88 | 85 | 92 | 100 | 82 | 74 | 89 | 99 | 101 | 89 | 84 |
| Yards | 760 | 748 | 783 | 851 | 790 | 849 | 658 | 575 | 719 | 799 | 951 | 756 | 705 |
| **FUMBLES:** | | | | | | | | | | | | | |
| Number | 18 | 24 | 31 | 35 | 28 | 28 | 38 | 20 | 43 | 24 | 31 | 34 | 32 |
| Number Lost | 10 | 15 | 20 | 14 | 14 | 17 | 18 | 9 | 22 | 8 | 20 | 20 | 12 |
| **POINTS:** | | | | | | | | | | | | | |
| Total | 395 | 420 | 340 | 218 | 254 | 293 | 282 | 357 | 258 | 258 | 375 | 373 | 189 |
| PAT Attempts | 52 | 57 | 45 | 24 | 28 | 34 | 31 | 46 | 33 | 32 | 48 | 46 | 22 |
| PAT Made | 51 | 51 | 40 | 21 | 23 | 31 | 30 | 46 | 33 | 27 | 44 | 44 | 21 |
| FG Attempts | 18 | 16 | 21 | 23 | 29 | 30 | 32 | 16 | 17 | 21 | 21 | 21 | 24 |
| FG Made | 10 | 9 | 10 | 17 | 21 | 18 | 22 | 13 | 9 | 13 | 13 | 17 | 12 |
| Percent FG Made | 55.6 | 56.3 | 47.6 | 73.9 | 72.4 | 60.0 | 68.8 | 81.3 | 52.9 | 61.9 | 61.9 | 81.0 | 50.0 |
| Safeties | 1 | 0 | 0 | 1 | 0 | 2 | 0 | 1 | 0 | 0 | 2 | 1 | 0 |

### DEFENSE

| | BALT. | BUFF. | CIN. | CLEV. | DENV. | HOUS. | K.C. | MIAMI | N.ENG. | N.Y. | OAK. | PITT. | S.D. |
|---|---|---|---|---|---|---|---|---|---|---|---|---|---|
| **FIRST DOWNS:** | | | | | | | | | | | | | |
| Total | 242 | 300 | 241 | 274 | 247 | 264 | 289 | 224 | 254 | 308 | 242 | 214 | 312 |
| by Rushing | 101 | 124 | 115 | 124 | 119 | 104 | 149 | 92 | 118 | 155 | 99 | 91 | 154 |
| by Passing | 124 | 151 | 107 | 125 | 106 | 137 | 121 | 113 | 120 | 133 | 113 | 97 | 139 |
| by Penalty | 17 | 25 | 19 | 25 | 22 | 23 | 19 | 19 | 16 | 20 | 30 | 26 | 19 |
| **RUSHING:** | | | | | | | | | | | | | |
| Number | 453 | 480 | 473 | 544 | 526 | 498 | 562 | 443 | 555 | 574 | 475 | 431 | 606 |
| Yards | 1821 | 1993 | 2194 | 2032 | 1974 | 1680 | 2724 | 1768 | 2220 | 2737 | 1785 | 1825 | 2442 |
| Average Yards | 4.0 | 4.2 | 4.6 | 3.7 | 3.8 | 3.4 | 4.8 | 4.0 | 4.0 | 4.8 | 3.8 | 4.2 | 4.0 |
| Touchdowns | 17 | 21 | 15 | 21 | 19 | 13 | 24 | 14 | 20 | 25 | 15 | 8 | 21 |
| **PASSING:** | | | | | | | | | | | | | |
| Attempts | 393 | 431 | 389 | 361 | 348 | 409 | 325 | 375 | 368 | 316 | 398 | 396 | 390 |
| Completions | 193 | 237 | 175 | 202 | 181 | 235 | 186 | 200 | 213 | 180 | 171 | 183 | 237 |
| Completion Percentage | 49.1 | 55.0 | 45.0 | 56.0 | 52.0 | 57.5 | 57.2 | 53.3 | 57.9 | 57.0 | 43.0 | 46.2 | 60.8 |
| Passing Yards | 2317 | 3355 | 2001 | 2889 | 2245 | 2800 | 2703 | 2335 | 2515 | 2860 | 2318 | 2194 | 2719 |
| Avg. Yards per Attempt | 5.9 | 7.6 | 5.1 | 8.0 | 6.5 | 6.9 | 8.3 | 6.2 | 6.8 | 9.1 | 5.8 | 5.5 | 7.0 |
| Avg. Yards per Complet. | 12.0 | 14.1 | 11.4 | 14.3 | 12.4 | 11.9 | 14.5 | 11.7 | 11.8 | 15.9 | 13.6 | 12.0 | 11.5 |
| Times Tackled Passing | 59 | 30 | 27 | 34 | 27 | 45 | 28 | 40 | 33 | 19 | 55 | 43 | 26 |
| Yards Lost Passing | 496 | 275 | 272 | 298 | 213 | 343 | 191 | 314 | 271 | 141 | 474 | 358 | 209 |
| Net Yards | 1821 | 3080 | 1729 | 2591 | 2032 | 2457 | 2512 | 2021 | 2244 | 2719 | 1844 | 1836 | 2510 |
| Touchdowns | 17 | 25 | 11 | 25 | 14 | 14 | 18 | 9 | 18 | 26 | 14 | 9 | 16 |
| Interceptions | 29 | 25 | 22 | 10 | 16 | 24 | 20 | 21 | 13 | 15 | 35 | 27 | 20 |
| Percent Intercepted | 7.4 | 5.8 | 5.7 | 2.8 | 4.6 | 5.9 | 6.2 | 5.6 | 3.5 | 4.7 | 8.8 | 6.8 | 5.1 |
| **PUNTS:** | | | | | | | | | | | | | |
| Number | 83 | 59 | 77 | 73 | 76 | 73 | 61 | 72 | 77 | 56 | 86 | 90 | 56 |
| Average Distance | 38.6 | 40.7 | 40.8 | 38.5 | 42.1 | 41.0 | 40.7 | 39.9 | 39.5 | 33.7 | 38.7 | 40.1 | 39.8 |
| **PUNT RETURNS:** | | | | | | | | | | | | | |
| Number | 51 | 29 | 42 | 45 | 39 | 47 | 36 | 34 | 42 | 22 | 35 | 36 | 48 |
| Yards | 513 | 179 | 386 | 469 | 534 | 356 | 503 | 373 | 513 | 208 | 265 | 199 | 373 |
| Average Yards | 10.1 | 6.2 | 9.2 | 10.4 | 13.7 | 7.6 | 14.0 | 11.0 | 12.2 | 9.5 | 7.6 | 5.5 | 7.8 |
| Touchdowns | 0 | 0 | 1 | 0 | 0 | 0 | 0 | 1 | 1 | 1 | 0 | 0 | 0 |
| **KICKOFF RETURNS:** | | | | | | | | | | | | | |
| Number | 70 | 64 | 66 | 48 | 57 | 61 | 59 | 65 | 46 | 52 | 68 | 64 | 40 |
| Yards | 1655 | 1496 | 1560 | 1279 | 1273 | 1355 | 1334 | 1549 | 1142 | 1203 | 1262 | 1304 | 1101 |
| Average Yards | 23.6 | 23.4 | 23.6 | 26.6 | 22.3 | 22.2 | 22.6 | 23.8 | 24.8 | 23.1 | 18.6 | 20.4 | 27.5 |
| Touchdowns | 1 | 0 | 0 | 1 | 0 | 0 | 0 | 1 | 0 | 0 | 0 | 0 | 0 |
| **INTERCEPTION RETURNS:** | | | | | | | | | | | | | |
| Number | 8 | 19 | 14 | 23 | 34 | 17 | 16 | 17 | 28 | 33 | 28 | 12 | 17 |
| Yards | 111 | 262 | 244 | 340 | 447 | 186 | 179 | 214 | 388 | 538 | 549 | 47 | 171 |
| Average Yards | 13.9 | 13.8 | 17.4 | 14.8 | 13.2 | 10.9 | 11.2 | 12.6 | 13.9 | 16.3 | 19.6 | 3.9 | 10.0 |
| Touchdowns | 0 | 0 | 1 | 1 | 1 | 0 | 1 | 1 | 1 | 4 | 2 | 0 | 1 |
| **PENALTIES:** | | | | | | | | | | | | | |
| Number | 79 | 80 | 91 | 89 | 88 | 91 | 99 | 82 | 103 | 93 | 63 | 85 | 81 |
| Yards | 700 | 651 | 821 | 735 | 779 | 892 | 934 | 716 | 759 | 798 | 527 | 700 | 686 |
| **FUMBLES:** | | | | | | | | | | | | | |
| Number | 29 | 42 | 40 | 26 | 37 | 38 | 40 | 23 | 31 | 25 | 14 | 22 | 34 |
| Number Lost | 12 | 20 | 22 | 16 | 16 | 19 | 22 | 9 | 16 | 13 | 6 | 10 | 14 |
| **POINTS:** | | | | | | | | | | | | | |
| Total | 269 | 355 | 246 | 372 | 307 | 226 | 341 | 222 | 358 | 433 | 255 | 162 | 345 |
| PAT Attempts | 36 | 47 | 30 | 48 | 35 | 27 | 44 | 27 | 42 | 57 | 32 | 19 | 40 |
| PAT Made | 35 | 46 | 26 | 45 | 34 | 21 | 40 | 25 | 37 | 53 | 30 | 15 | 35 |
| FG Attempts | 10 | 16 | 15 | 21 | 28 | 21 | 22 | 20 | 35 | 16 | 20 | 18 | 34 |
| FG Made | 6 | 9 | 12 | 13 | 21 | 13 | 11 | 11 | 23 | 12 | 11 | 11 | 22 |
| Percent FG Made | 60.0 | 56.3 | 80.0 | 61.9 | 75.0 | 61.9 | 50.0 | 55.0 | 65.7 | 75.0 | 55.0 | 61.1 | 64.7 |
| Safeties | 0 | 0 | 2 | 0 | 0 | 2 | 2 | 1 | 0 | 1 | 0 | 0 | 2 |

## CONFERENCE PLAYOFFS

### December 27, at Pittsburgh (Attendance 49,053)

**SCORING**

| | | | | | |
|---|---|---|---|---|---|
| PITTSBURGH | 7 | 0 | 7 | 14 | – 28 |
| BALTIMORE | 0 | 7 | 3 | 0 | – 10 |

First Quarter
- Pitt. Harris, 8 yard rush — PAT – Gerela (kick)

Second Quarter
- Balt. Doughty, 5 yard pass from Domres PAT – Linhart (kick)

Third Quarter
- Balt. Linhart, 21 yard field goal
- Pitt. Bleier, 7 yard rush — PAT – Gerela (kick)

Fourth Quarter
- Pitt. Bradshaw, 2 yard rush — PAT – Gerela (kick)
- Pitt. Russell, 93 yard fumble return — PAT – Gerela (kick)

**TEAM STATISTICS**

| PITT. | | BALT. |
|---|---|---|
| 16 | First Downs – Total | 10 |
| 13 | First Downs – Rushing | 4 |
| 3 | First Downs – Passing | 4 |
| 0 | First Downs – Penalty | 2 |
| 3 | Fumbles – Number | 2 |
| 3 | Fumbles – Lost Ball | 1 |
| 5 | Penalties – Number | 6 |
| 45 | Yards Penalized | 53 |
| 0 | Missed Field Goals | 0 |
| 59 | Offensive Plays | 68 |
| 287 | Net Yards | 154 |
| 4.9 | Average Gain | 2.3 |
| 5 | Giveaways | 3 |
| 3 | Takeaways | 5 |
| -2 | Difference | +2 |

**INDIVIDUAL STATISTICS**

| PITTSBURGH | No. | Yds. | Avg. | BALTIMORE | No. | Yds. | Avg. |
|---|---|---|---|---|---|---|---|
| **RUSHING** | | | | | | | |
| Harris | 27 | 153 | 5.7 | Mitchell | 26 | 63 | 2.4 |
| Bleier | 12 | 28 | 2.3 | Domres | 4 | 17 | 4.3 |
| Bradshaw | 3 | 22 | 7.3 | Olds | 5 | 6 | 1.2 |
| Collier | 1 | 8 | 8.0 | Jones | 2 | 6 | 3.0 |
| | 43 | 211 | 4.9 | McCauley | 3 | 3 | 1.0 |
| | | | | Carr | 1 | -13 | -13.0 |
| | | | | | 41 | 82 | 2.0 |
| **RECEIVING** | | | | | | | |
| Lewis | 3 | 65 | 31.7 | Mitchell | 4 | 20 | 5.0 |
| Swann | 2 | 15 | 7.5 | Doughty | 2 | 63 | 31.5 |
| Bleier | 2 | 14 | 7.0 | McCauley | 1 | 9 | 9.0 |
| L. Brown | 1 | 9 | 9.0 | Kennedy | 1 | 8 | 8.0 |
| | 8 | 103 | 12.9 | | 8 | 100 | 12.5 |
| **PUNTING** | | | | | | | |
| Walden | 4 | | 39.8 | Lee | 9 | | 40.1 |
| **PUNT RETURNS** | | | | | | | |
| Edwards | 2 | 22 | 11.0 | Stevens | 3 | 30 | 10.0 |
| Collier | 1 | 17 | 17.0 | Volk | 1 | 0 | 0.0 |
| D. Brown | 1 | 7 | 7.0 | | 4 | 30 | 7.5 |
| | 4 | 46 | 11.5 | | | | |
| **KICKOFF RETURNS** | | | | | | | |
| D. Brown | 2 | 53 | 26.5 | Laird | 4 | 86 | 21.5 |
| Harrison | 1 | 21 | 21.0 | McCauley | 1 | 17 | 17.0 |
| | 3 | 74 | 24.7 | | 5 | 103 | 20.6 |
| **INTERCEPTION RETURNS** | | | | | | | |
| Blount | 1 | 20 | 20.0 | Mumphord | 2 | 67 | 33.5 |
| Ham | 1 | 6 | 6.0 | | | | |
| | 2 | 26 | 13.0 | | | | |

**PASSING**

| PITTSBURGH | Att. | Comp. | Comp. Pct. | Yds. | Int. | Yds/ Att. | Yds/ Comp. | Yards Lost Tackled |
|---|---|---|---|---|---|---|---|---|
| Bradshaw | 13 | 8 | 61.6 | 103 | 2 | 7.9 | 12.9 | 3-27 |
| **BALTIMORE** | | | | | | | | |
| Jones | 11 | 6 | 54.5 | 91 | 0 | 8.3 | 11.4 | |
| Domres | 11 | 2 | 18.1 | 9 | 2 | 0.8 | 4.5 | |
| | 22 | 8 | 36.4 | 100 | 2 | 4.5 | 12.5 | 5-28 |

### December 28, at Oakland (Attendance 53,039)

**SCORING**

| | | | | | |
|---|---|---|---|---|---|
| OAKLAND | 3 | 14 | 7 | 7 | – 31 |
| CINCINNATI | 0 | 7 | 7 | 14 | – 28 |

First Quarter
- Oak. Blanda, 27 yard field goal

Second Quarter
- Oak. Siani, 9 yard pass from Stabler PAT – Blanda (kick)
- Cin. Fritts, 1 yard rush — PAT – Green (kick)
- Oak. Moore, 8 yard pass from Stabler PAT – Blanda (kick)

Third Quarter
- Oak. Banaszak, 6 yard rush — PAT – Blanda (kick)
- Cin. Elliott, 6 yard rush — PAT – Green (kick)

Fourth Quarter
- Oak. Casper, 2 yard pass from Stabler PAT – Blanda (kick)
- Cin. Joiner, 25 yard pass from Anderson PAT – Green (kick)
- Cin. Curtis, 14 yard pass from Anderson PAT – Green (kick)

**TEAM STATISTICS**

| OAK. | | CIN. |
|---|---|---|
| 27 | First Downs – Total | 17 |
| 9 | First Downs – Rushing | 8 |
| 15 | First Downs – Passing | 6 |
| 3 | First Downs – Penalty | 3 |
| 2 | Fumbles – Number | 1 |
| 1 | Fumbles – Lost Ball | 0 |
| 7 | Penalties – Number | 5 |
| 64 | Yards Penalized | 37 |
| 2 | Missed Field Goals | 0 |
| 75 | Offensive Plays | 57 |
| 358 | Net Yards | 258 |
| 4.8 | Average Gain | 4.5 |
| 2 | Giveaways | 0 |
| 0 | Takeaways | 2 |
| -2 | Difference | +2 |

**INDIVIDUAL STATISTICS**

| OAKLAND | No. | Yds. | Avg. | CINCINNATI | No. | Yds. | Avg. |
|---|---|---|---|---|---|---|---|
| **RUSHING** | | | | | | | |
| C. Davis | 16 | 63 | 3.9 | B. Clark | 8 | 46 | 5.8 |
| Banaszak | 17 | 62 | 3.6 | Elliott | 4 | 25 | 6.3 |
| Hubbard | 12 | 33 | 2.8 | Fritts | 6 | 14 | 2.3 |
| J. Phillips | 3 | 16 | 5.3 | Anderson | 3 | 12 | 4.0 |
| van Eeghen | 1 | 3 | 3.0 | Johnson | 3 | 0 | 0.0 |
| Stabler | 2 | -4 | -2.0 | Williams | 1 | 0 | 0.0 |
| | 51 | 173 | 3.4 | | 25 | 97 | 3.9 |
| **RECEIVING** | | | | | | | |
| Moore | 6 | 57 | 9.5 | B. Clark | 4 | 38 | 9.5 |
| Branch | 5 | 89 | 17.8 | Myers | 3 | 67 | 22.3 |
| Siani | 3 | 35 | 11.7 | Joiner | 3 | 60 | 20.0 |
| C. Davis | 2 | 16 | 8.0 | Curtis | 3 | 20 | 6.7 |
| Casper | 1 | 2 | 2.0 | Coslet | 2 | 14 | 7.0 |
| | 17 | 199 | 11.7 | Elliott | 1 | 9 | 9.0 |
| | | | | Trumpy | 1 | -7 | -7.0 |
| | | | | | 17 | 201 | 11.8 |
| **PUNTING** | | | | | | | |
| Guy | 1 | | 38.0 | D. Green | 6 | | 35.8 |
| **PUNT RETURNS** | | | | | | | |
| Colzie | 4 | 64 | 16.0 | Blackwood | 1 | 7 | 7.0 |
| **KICKOFF RETURNS** | | | | | | | |
| C. Davis | 4 | 93 | 23.3 | B. Jackson | 2 | 43 | 21.5 |
| Hart | 1 | 28 | 28.0 | Elliott | 1 | 18 | 18.0 |
| | 5 | 121 | 24.2 | Parish | 1 | 10 | 10.0 |
| | | | | | 4 | 71 | 17.8 |
| **INTERCEPTION RETURNS** | | | | | | | |
| none | | | | K. Riley | 1 | 34 | 34.0 |

**PASSING**

| OAKLAND | Att. | Comp. | Comp. Pct. | Yds. | Int. | Yds/ Att. | Yds/ Comp. | Yards Lost Tackled |
|---|---|---|---|---|---|---|---|---|
| Stabler | 23 | 17 | 73.9 | 199 | 1 | 8.7 | 11.7 | 4-14 |
| **CINCINNATI** | | | | | | | | |
| Anderson | 27 | 17 | 63.0 | 201 | 0 | 7.4 | 11.8 | 5-40 |

# 1975 A.F.C. — Eastern Division

## BALTIMORE COLTS 10-4 Ted Marchibroda

| Scores of Each Game | | |
|---|---|---|
| 35 | Chicago | 7 |
| 20 | OAKLAND | 31 |
| 13 | Los Angeles | 24 |
| 31 | BUFFALO | 38 |
| 10 | New England | 21 |
| 45 | N.Y. Jets | 28 |
| 21 | CLEVELAND | 7 |
| 42 | Buffalo | 35 |
| 52 | N.Y. JETS | 19 |
| 33 | Miami | 17 |
| 28 | KANSAS CITY | 14 |
| 21 | N.Y. Giants | 0 |
| 10 | MIAMI | 7 |
| 34 | NEW ENGLAND | 21 |

| Use Name | Pos. | Hgt | Wgt | Age | Int | Pts |
|---|---|---|---|---|---|---|
| Ed George | OT | 6'4" | 270 | 29 | | |
| George Kunz | OT | 6'5" | 266 | 28 | | |
| David Taylor | OT | 6'4" | 257 | 25 | | |
| Elmer Collett | OG | 6'4" | 246 | 30 | | |
| Ken Huff | OG | 6'4" | 260 | 22 | | |
| Robert Pratt | OG | 6'3" | 248 | 24 | | |
| Bob Van Duyne | OG | 6'5" | 245 | 23 | | |
| Forrest Blue | C | 6'5" | 265 | 29 | | |
| Ken Mendenhall | C | 6'3" | 250 | 26 | | |
| Fred Cook | DE | 6'4" | 247 | 23 | 1 | 6 |
| John Dutton | DE | 6'7" | 268 | 23 | | |
| Glenn Robinson | DE | 6'6" | 236 | 24 | | |
| Mike Barnes | DT | 6'6" | 260 | 24 | | |
| Joe Ehrmann | DT | 6'5" | 254 | 26 | | |
| Dave Pear | DT | 6'2" | 242 | 22 | | |
| Jim Cheyunski | LB | 6'2" | 220 | 29 | 2 | |
| Mike Curtis | LB | 6'2" | 232 | 32 | 1 | |
| Dan Dickel | LB | 6'3" | 230 | 23 | | |
| Derrel Luce | LB | 6'3" | 224 | 22 | | |
| Tom MacLeod | LB | 6'3" | 228 | 24 | 1 | |
| Mike Varty | LB | 6'1" | 225 | 23 | | |
| Stan White | LB | 6'1" | 220 | 25 | 8 | 6 |
| Bruce Laird | DB | 6' | 198 | 25 | 3 | 2 |
| Lloyd Mumphord | DB | 5'11" | 176 | 28 | 4 | |
| Nelson Munsey | DB | 6'1" | 198 | 27 | 3 | 6 |
| Doug Nettles | DB | 6' | 178 | 24 | | |
| Ray Oldham | DB | 6' | 190 | 24 | 2 | |
| Rick Volk | DB | 6'3" | 195 | 30 | | |
| Jackie Wallace | DB | 6'3" | 197 | 24 | 4 | 12 |
| Marty Domres | QB | 6'3" | 230 | 28 | | 6 |
| Bert Jones | QB | 6'3" | 212 | 23 | | 18 |
| Marshall Johnson | HB | 6'1" | 190 | 22 | | 12 |
| Lydell Mitchell | HB | 5'11" | 195 | 26 | | 90 |
| Howard Stevens | HB | 5'5" | 165 | 25 | | |
| Roosevelt Leaks | FB | 5'10" | 220 | 22 | | 6 |
| Bill Olds | FB | 6'1" | 222 | 24 | | 24 |
| Don McCauley | HB-FB | 6'1" | 216 | 26 | | 66 |
| Roger Carr | WR | 6'3" | 193 | 23 | | 12 |
| Glenn Doughty | WR | 6'2" | 202 | 24 | | 24 |
| Freddie Scott | WR | 6'2" | 170 | 23 | | |
| Ray Chester | TE | 6'3" | 236 | 27 | | 18 |
| Jimmie Kennedy | TE | 6'3" | 233 | 23 | | 6 |
| David Lee | K | 6'4" | 220 | 31 | | |
| Toni Linhart | K | 6' | 180 | 33 | | 81 |

Randy Hall – Foot Injury

## MIAMI DOLPHINS 10-4 Don Shula

| Scores of Each Game | | |
|---|---|---|
| 21 | OAKLAND | 31 |
| 22 | New England | 14 |
| 31 | Green Bay | 7 |
| 24 | PHILADELPHIA | 16 |
| 43 | N.Y. Jets | 0 |
| 35 | Buffalo | 30 |
| 46 | Chicago | 13 |
| 27 | N.Y. JETS | 7 |
| 19 | Houston | 20 |
| 17 | BALTIMORE | 33 |
| 20 | NEW ENGLAND | 7 |
| 31 | BUFFALO | 21 |
| 7 | Baltimore | 10 |
| 14 | DENVER | 13 |

| Use Name | Pos. | Hgt | Wgt | Age | Int | Pts |
|---|---|---|---|---|---|---|
| Darryl Carlton | OT | 6'6" | 260 | 22 | | |
| Norm Evans | OT | 6'5" | 250 | 32 | | |
| Wayne Moore | OT | 6'6" | 265 | 30 | | |
| Tom Drougas | OG-OT | 6'4" | 255 | 25 | | |
| Bob Kuechenberg | OG | 6'3" | 252 | 27 | | |
| Larry Little | OG | 6'1" | 265 | 29 | | |
| Ed Newman | OG | 6'2" | 245 | 24 | | |
| Jim Langer | C | 6'2" | 253 | 27 | | |
| Vern Den Herder | DE | 6'6" | 252 | 26 | | |
| Don Reese | DE | 6'6" | 255 | 23 | | 2 |
| Bill Stanfill | DE | 6'5" | 252 | 28 | | |
| Randy Crowder | DT | 6'2" | 236 | 23 | | |
| Manny Fernandez | DT | 6'2" | 250 | 29 | | |
| John Andrews | DE-DT | 6'6" | 250 | 23 | | |
| Rodrigo Barnes (from NE) | LB | 6'1" | 215 | 25 | | |
| Bruce Elia | LB | 6'1" | 222 | 22 | | |
| Mike Kolen | LB | 6'2" | 222 | 27 | 1 | |
| Bob Matheson | LB | 6'4" | 235 | 30 | 3 | |
| Earnest Rhone | LB | 6'2" | 212 | 22 | 2 | |
| Doug Swift | LB | 6'3" | 226 | 26 | | |
| Steve Towle | LB | 6'2" | 233 | 21 | 1 | |
| Charlie Babb | DB | 6' | 190 | 25 | 4 | |
| Tim Foley | DB | 6' | 194 | 27 | | |
| Barry Hill | DB | 6'3" | 185 | 22 | | |
| Curtis Johnson | DB | 6'2" | 196 | 27 | 4 | |
| Jake Scott | DB | 6' | 188 | 30 | 6 | |
| Jeris White | DB | 5'11" | 180 | 22 | | |
| Jim Del Gaizo | QB | 6'1" | 190 | 28 | | |
| Bob Griese | QB | 6'1" | 190 | 30 | | 6 |
| Earl Morrall | QB | 6'1" | 210 | 41 | | |
| Don Strock | QB | 6'5" | 216 | 24 | | 6 |
| Hubert Ginn | HB | 5'11" | 185 | 28 | | |
| Benny Malone | HB | 5'10" | 193 | 23 | | 18 |
| Mercury Morris | HB | 5'10" | 192 | 28 | | 24 |
| Larry Seiple | HB | 6' | 214 | 30 | | |
| Norm Bulaich | FB | 6'1" | 220 | 28 | | 60 |
| Don Nottingham | FB | 5'10" | 210 | 26 | | 72 |
| Stan Winfrey | FB | 5'11" | 223 | 22 | | |
| Nat Moore | WR | 5'9" | 180 | 23 | | 24 |
| Morris Owens | WR | 6' | 190 | 22 | | |
| Cotton Speyrer | WR | 6' | 175 | 26 | | |
| Howard Twilley | WR | 5'10" | 185 | 31 | | 24 |
| Freddie Solomon | HB-WR | 5'11" | 180 | 22 | | 18 |
| Jim Mandich | TE | 6'3" | 224 | 27 | | 24 |
| Jim McFarland | TE | 6'5" | 225 | 27 | | |
| Andre Tillman | TE | 6'5" | 230 | 22 | | |
| Garo Yepremian | K | 5'8" | 175 | 31 | | 79 |

Bob Heinz – Knee Injury

Dick Anderson – Knee Injury
Nick Buoniconti – Broken Finger

## BUFFALO BILLS 8-6 Lou Saban

| Scores of Each Game | | |
|---|---|---|
| 42 | N.Y. JETS | 14 |
| 30 | Pittsburgh | 21 |
| 38 | DENVER | 10 |
| 38 | Baltimore | 31 |
| 14 | N.Y. GIANTS | 17 |
| 30 | MIAMI | 35 |
| 24 | N.Y. Jets | 23 |
| 35 | BALTIMORE | 42 |
| 24 | Cincinnati | 33 |
| 45 | NEW ENGLAND | 31 |
| 32 | St. Louis | 14 |
| 21 | Miami | 31 |
| 34 | New England | 14 |
| 13 | MINNESOTA | 35 |

| Use Name | Pos. | Hgt | Wgt | Age | Int | Pts |
|---|---|---|---|---|---|---|
| Dave Foley | OT | 6'5" | 247 | 27 | | |
| Donnie Green | OT | 6'7" | 252 | 27 | | |
| Halvor Hagen | OT | 6'5" | 260 | 28 | | |
| Bill Adams | OG | 6'2" | 246 | 25 | | |
| Joe DeLamielleure | OG | 6'3" | 248 | 24 | | |
| Reggie McKenzie | OG | 6'4" | 244 | 25 | | |
| Mike Montler | C | 6'4" | 245 | 31 | | |
| Willie Parker | C | 6'3" | 252 | 26 | | |
| Mark Johnson | DE | 6'2" | 240 | 22 | | |
| Dave Means | DE | 6'4" | 235 | 23 | | |
| Walt Patulski | DE | 6'6" | 260 | 25 | | |
| Pat Toomay | DE | 6'5" | 244 | 30 | 1 | 6 |
| Jeff Winans | DE | 6'5" | 260 | 23 | | |
| Don Croft | DT | 6'3" | 260 | 26 | | |
| Earl Edwards | DT | 6'6" | 254 | 29 | | |
| Mike Kadish | DT | 6'5" | 270 | 25 | | 6 |
| Jeff Yeates | DT | 6'3" | 250 | 24 | | |
| Doug Allen | LB | 6'2" | 228 | 23 | | |
| Bo Cornell | LB | 6'1" | 222 | 26 | | |
| Merv Krakau | LB | 6'2" | 233 | 24 | 1 | |
| John McCrumbly | LB | 6'1" | 245 | 23 | | |
| Bob Nelson | LB | 6'4" | 232 | 22 | | |
| Tom Ruud | LB | 6'2" | 223 | 22 | | |
| John Skorupan | LB | 6'2" | 225 | 24 | 1 | |
| Steve Freeman | DB | 5'11" | 185 | 22 | 2 | 6 |
| Tony Greene | DB | 5'10" | 170 | 26 | 6 | |
| Dwight Harrison | DB | 6'1" | 186 | 26 | 8 | |
| Ed Jones | DB | 6' | 185 | 23 | 3 | |
| Royce McKinney | DB | 6'1" | 190 | 21 | | |
| Frank Oliver | DB | 6'1" | 189 | 23 | | |
| Ike Thomas | DB | 6'2" | 195 | 27 | 2 | |
| Joe Ferguson | QB | 6'1" | 184 | 25 | | 6 |
| Gary Marangi | QB | 6'1" | 203 | 23 | | |
| Gary Hayman | HB | 6'1" | 202 | 24 | | |
| O.J. Simpson | HB | 6'2" | 212 | 28 | | 138 |
| Jim Braxton | FB | 6'2" | 242 | 26 | | 78 |
| Steve Schnarr | FB | 6'2" | 218 | 22 | | |
| Dan Abramowicz | WR | 6'1" | 193 | 30 | | |
| Bob Chandler | WR | 6' | 180 | 26 | | 36 |
| J. D. Hill | WR | 6'1" | 185 | 26 | | 42 |
| John Holland | WR | 6' | 190 | 23 | | 6 |
| Vic Washington | DB-WR | 5'10" | 196 | 29 | | |
| Reuben Gant | TE | 6'4" | 230 | 23 | | 12 |
| Paul Seymour | TE | 6'5" | 246 | 25 | | 6 |
| Marv Bateman | K | 6'4" | 214 | 25 | | |
| John Leypoldt | K | 6'2" | 226 | 29 | | 78 |

Robert James – Knee Injury
Doug Jones – Knee Injury

Ahmad Rashad – Knee Injury

## NEW ENGLAND PATRIOTS 3-11 Chuck Fairbanks

| Scores of Each Game | | |
|---|---|---|
| 0 | HOUSTON | 7 |
| 14 | MIAMI | 22 |
| 7 | N.Y. Jets | 36 |
| 10 | Cincinnati | 27 |
| 21 | BALTIMORE | 10 |
| 24 | SAN FRANCISCO | 16 |
| 17 | St. Louis | 24 |
| 33 | San Diego | 19 |
| 31 | DALLAS | 34 |
| 31 | Buffalo | 45 |
| 7 | Miami | 20 |
| 28 | N.Y. JETS | 30 |
| 14 | BUFFALO | 34 |
| 21 | Baltimore | 34 |

| Use Name | Pos. | Hgt | Wgt | Age | Int | Pts |
|---|---|---|---|---|---|---|
| Leon Gray | OT | 6'3" | 256 | 23 | | |
| Shelby Jordan | OT | 6'7" | 260 | 23 | | |
| Sam Adams | OG | 6'3" | 252 | 26 | | |
| Steve Corbett | OG | 6'4" | 248 | 24 | | |
| Bill Du Lac | OG | 6'4" | 260 | 24 | | |
| John Hannah | OG | 6'2" | 265 | 24 | | |
| Doug Dumler | C | 6'3" | 242 | 24 | | |
| Bill Lenkaitis | C | 6'3" | 250 | 29 | | |
| Julius Adams | DE | 6'3" | 260 | 27 | | |
| Craig Hanneman | DE | 6'3" | 245 | 26 | | |
| Mel Lunsford | DE | 6'3" | 260 | 25 | | |
| Tony McGee | DE | 6'4" | 245 | 26 | | |
| Martin Imhoff | DE | 6'6" | 256 | 25 | | |
| Pete Cusick | NT | 6'1" | 255 | 22 | | |
| Ray Hamilton | NT | 6'1" | 245 | 24 | | 6 |
| Jerry Patton | DT | 6'3" | 255 | 29 | | |
| Dave Tipton (to SD) | DT | 6'1" | 255 | 21 | | |
| Maury Damkroger | LB | 6'2" | 230 | 23 | | |
| Bob Geddes | LB | 6'2" | 240 | 29 | | |
| Sam Hunt | LB | 6'1" | 240 | 24 | | |
| Steve King | LB | 6'4" | 230 | 24 | | |
| Steve Nelson | LB | 6'2" | 230 | 24 | 2 | |
| Kevin Reilly | LB | 6'2" | 220 | 23 | 1 | |
| Rod Shoate | LB | 6'1" | 211 | 22 | | |
| George Webster | LB | 6'4" | 230 | 29 | 1 | |
| Steve Zabel | LB | 6'4" | 230 | 27 | | |
| Ron Bolton | DB | 6'2" | 170 | 25 | 5 | |
| Dick Conn | DB | 6' | 185 | 24 | | |
| Bob Howard | DB | 6'1" | 177 | 30 | 3 | 6 |
| Durwood Keeton | DB | 5'10" | 180 | 23 | | |
| Jim Massey | DB | 5'11" | 198 | 27 | | |
| Prentice McCray | DB | 6'1" | 187 | 24 | | |
| Deac Sanders | DB | 6'1" | 178 | 25 | 1 | |
| Neil Graff | QB | 6'3" | 200 | 25 | | |
| Steve Grogan | QB | 6'4" | 200 | 22 | | 18 |
| Jim Plunkett | QB | 6'3" | 212 | 27 | | 6 |
| Don Calhoun (from BUF) | HB | 6' | 198 | 23 | | 12 |
| Andy Johnson | HB | 6' | 204 | 22 | | 24 |
| Leon McQuay | HB | 5'9" | 195 | 25 | | |
| Bobby Anderson | FB-HB | 6' | 208 | 27 | | |
| Allen Carter | FB | 5'11" | 208 | 22 | | 6 |
| Sam Cunningham | FB | 6'3" | 224 | 25 | | 48 |
| Steve Burks | WR | 6'5" | 211 | 22 | | |
| Darryl Stingley | WR | 6' | 195 | 23 | | 12 |
| Randy Vataha | WR | 5'10" | 170 | 26 | | 36 |
| Elmo Wright (from HOU) | WR | 6' | 190 | 26 | | |
| Russ Francis | TE | 6'6" | 240 | 22 | | 24 |
| Bob Windsor | TE | 6'4" | 225 | 32 | | |
| Mike Patrick | K | 6' | 213 | 22 | | |
| John Smith | K | 6' | 185 | 25 | | 60 |

Arthur Moore – Knee Injury
Joe Wilson – Ankle Injury

Al Marshall – Knee Injury
Tom Neville – Broken Leg

Leon Crosswhite – Foot Injury

## NEW YORK JETS 3-11 Charley Winner Ken Shipp

| Scores of Each Game | | |
|---|---|---|
| 14 | Buffalo | 42 |
| 30 | Kansas City | 24 |
| 36 | NEW ENGLAND | 7 |
| 21 | Minnesota | 29 |
| 0 | MIAMI | 43 |
| 28 | BALTIMORE | 45 |
| 23 | BUFFALO | 24 |
| 7 | Miami | 27 |
| 19 | Baltimore | 52 |
| 6 | ST. LOUIS | 37 |
| 7 | PITTSBURGH | 20 |
| 30 | New England | 28 |
| 16 | San Diego | 24 |
| 21 | DALLAS | 31 |

| Use Name | Pos. | Hgt | Wgt | Age | Int | Pts |
|---|---|---|---|---|---|---|
| Gordie Browne | OT | 6'5" | 265 | 23 | | |
| Winston Hill | OT | 6'4" | 280 | 33 | | |
| Robert Woods | OT | 6'3" | 255 | 25 | | |
| Gary Puetz | OG | 6'4" | 265 | 23 | | |
| Randy Rasmussen | OG | 6'2" | 267 | 30 | | |
| Darrell Austin | OT-OG | 6'4" | 250 | 23 | | |
| Wayne Mulligan | C | 6'2" | 250 | 28 | | |
| Joe Fields | OG-C | 6'2" | 240 | 21 | | |
| Richard Neal | DE | 6'3" | 260 | 27 | | |
| Billy Newsome | DE | 6'4" | 246 | 27 | | |
| Jim Bailey | DT | 6'5" | 255 | 27 | 1 | |
| Carl Barzilauskas | DT | 6'6" | 280 | 24 | | |
| Ed Galigher | DT | 6'4" | 253 | 24 | | |
| Larry Woods | DT | 6'6" | 270 | 27 | | |
| Ken Bernich | LB | 6'2" | 250 | 23 | | |
| John Ebersole | LB | 6'3" | 227 | 26 | 2 | |
| Rich Lewis | LB | 6'3" | 215 | 25 | | |
| Steve Reese | LB | 6'2" | 232 | 23 | | |
| Jamie Rivers | LB | 6'2" | 245 | 29 | | |
| Godwin Turk | LB | 6'3" | 230 | 24 | 2 | |
| Richard Wood | LB | 6'2" | 215 | 22 | | |
| Carl Capria | DB | 6'3" | 185 | 23 | | |
| Jerry Davis | DB | 5'11" | 182 | 24 | | |
| George Hoey (from DEN) | DB | 5'10" | 180 | 28 | | |
| Delles Howell | DB | 6'3" | 200 | 28 | 2 | |
| Burgess Owens | DB | 6'2" | 200 | 24 | 3 | |
| Bob Prout | DB | 6'1" | 183 | 24 | 1 | |
| Rich Sowells | DB | 6' | 180 | 26 | 1 | |
| Ed Taylor | DB | 6' | 170 | 22 | | |
| Donnie Walker | DB | 6'1" | 180 | 24 | | |
| Phil Wise | DB | 6' | 190 | 26 | 2 | |
| Roscoe Word | DB | 5'11" | 170 | 22 | 1 | |
| John Jones | QB | 6'1" | 180 | 23 | | |
| Joe Namath | QB | 6'2" | 200 | 32 | | |
| Emerson Boozer | HB | 5'11" | 205 | 32 | | 6 |
| Carl Garrett | HB | 5'11" | 205 | 28 | | 36 |
| Bob Gresham | HB | 5'11" | 195 | 27 | | 6 |
| Jazz Jackson | HB | 5'8" | 167 | 23 | | |
| John Riggins | FB | 6'2" | 225 | 26 | | 54 |
| Steve Davis | HB-FB | 6'1" | 218 | 25 | | 6 |
| Jerome Barkum | WR | 6'3" | 212 | 25 | | 30 |
| Eddie Bell | WR | 5'10" | 160 | 27 | | 24 |
| David Knight | WR | 6'1" | 175 | 24 | | |
| Lou Piccone | WR | 5'9" | 175 | 26 | | |
| Willie Brister | TE | 6'4" | 236 | 23 | | 6 |
| Rich Caster | TE | 6'5" | 228 | 26 | | 24 |
| Greg Gantt | K | 5'11" | 188 | 23 | | |
| Pat Leahy | K | 6' | 200 | 24 | | 66 |

Al Atkinson – Knee Injury
Mark Lomas – Foot Injury
Steve Tannen – Shoulder Injury

Al Woodall – Knee Injury

## BALTIMORE COLTS

### RUSHING

| Last Name | No. | Yds | Avg | TD |
|---|---|---|---|---|
| Mitchell | 289 | 1193 | 4.1 | 11 |
| Jones | 47 | 321 | 6.8 | 3 |
| Olds | 94 | 281 | 3.0 | 2 |
| McCauley | 60 | 196 | 3.3 | 10 |
| Leaks | 41 | 175 | 4.3 | 1 |
| Domres | 4 | 46 | 11.5 | 1 |
| Doughty | 1 | 5 | 5.0 | 0 |

### RECEIVING

| Last Name | No. | Yds | Avg | TD |
|---|---|---|---|---|
| Mitchell | 60 | 544 | 9 | 4 |
| Doughty | 39 | 666 | 17 | 4 |
| Chester | 38 | 457 | 12 | 3 |
| Olds | 30 | 194 | 7 | 2 |
| Carr | 23 | 517 | 23 | 2 |
| McCauley | 14 | 93 | 7 | 1 |
| Johnson | 4 | 115 | 29 | 2 |
| Kennedy | 2 | 15 | 8 | 1 |
| Leaks | 1 | 5 | 5 | 0 |

### PUNT RETURNS

| Last Name | No. | Yds | Avg | TD |
|---|---|---|---|---|
| Stevens | 36 | 396 | 11 | 0 |
| Wallace | 6 | 43 | 7 | 0 |

### KICKOFF RETURNS

| Last Name | No. | Yds | Avg | TD |
|---|---|---|---|---|
| Laird | 31 | 799 | 26 | 0 |
| Johnson | 7 | 134 | 19 | 0 |
| McCauley | 4 | 86 | 22 | 0 |
| Stevens | 3 | 71 | 24 | 0 |
| Pratt | 4 | 64 | 16 | 0 |
| Kennedy | 2 | 36 | 18 | 0 |
| Wallace | 1 | 0 | 0 | 0 |

### PASSING — PUNTING — KICKING

| PASSING | Att | Comp | % | Yds | Yd/Att | TD | Int-% | RK |
|---|---|---|---|---|---|---|---|---|
| Jones | 344 | 203 | 59 | 2483 | 7.2 | 18 | 8-2 | 3 |
| Domres | 10 | 8 | 80 | 123 | 12.3 | 1 | 0-0 | |

| PUNTING | No | Avg |
|---|---|---|
| Lee | 86 | 39.6 |

| KICKING | XP | Att | % | FG | Att | % |
|---|---|---|---|---|---|---|
| Linhart | 51 | 52 | 98 | 10 | 18 | 56 |

## MIAMI DOLPHINS

### RUSHING

| Last Name | No. | Yds | Avg | TD |
|---|---|---|---|---|
| Morris | 219 | 875 | 4.0 | 4 |
| Nottingham | 168 | 718 | 4.3 | 12 |
| Bulaich | 78 | 309 | 4.0 | 5 |
| Malone | 65 | 220 | 3.4 | 3 |
| Solomon | 4 | 87 | 21.8 | 0 |
| Ginn | 21 | 78 | 3.7 | 0 |
| Moore | 8 | 69 | 8.6 | 0 |
| Griese | 17 | 59 | 3.5 | 1 |
| Strock | 6 | 38 | 6.3 | 1 |
| Morrall | 4 | 33 | 8.3 | 0 |
| Winfrey | 3 | 10 | 3.3 | 0 |
| Seiple | 1 | 4 | 4.0 | 0 |

### RECEIVING

| Last Name | No. | Yds | Avg | TD |
|---|---|---|---|---|
| Moore | 40 | 705 | 18 | 4 |
| Bulaich | 32 | 276 | 9 | 5 |
| Twilley | 24 | 366 | 15 | 4 |
| Solomon | 22 | 339 | 15 | 2 |
| Mandich | 21 | 217 | 10 | 4 |
| Seiple | 10 | 84 | 8 | 0 |
| Nottingham | 9 | 66 | 7 | 0 |
| Tillman | 5 | 60 | 12 | 0 |
| Ginn | 3 | 21 | 7 | 0 |
| Malone | 2 | 47 | 24 | 0 |
| Morris | 2 | 15 | 8 | 0 |

### PUNT RETURNS

| Last Name | No. | Yds | Avg | TD |
|---|---|---|---|---|
| Solomon | 26 | 320 | 12 | 1 |
| Babb | 7 | 95 | 14 | 0 |
| Moore | 8 | 80 | 10 | 0 |
| Scott | 1 | 10 | 10 | 0 |
| Ginn | 1 | 4 | 4 | 0 |

### KICKOFF RETURNS

| Last Name | No. | Yds | Avg | TD |
|---|---|---|---|---|
| Solomon | 17 | 348 | 21 | 0 |
| Moore | 9 | 243 | 27 | 0 |
| Ginn | 9 | 235 | 26 | 0 |
| Nottingham | 3 | 80 | 27 | 0 |
| Winfrey | 1 | 25 | 25 | 0 |
| Malone | 1 | 18 | 18 | 0 |

### PASSING — PUNTING — KICKING

| PASSING | Att | Comp | % | Yds | Yd/Att | TD | Int-% | RK |
|---|---|---|---|---|---|---|---|---|
| Griese | 191 | 118 | 62 | 1693 | 8.9 | 14 | 13-7 | 5 |
| Strock | 45 | 26 | 58 | 230 | 5.1 | 2 | 2-4 | |
| Morrall | 43 | 26 | 61 | 273 | 6.4 | 3 | 2-5 | |

| PUNTING | No | Avg |
|---|---|---|
| Seiple | 65 | 38.6 |

| KICKING | XP | Att | % | FG | Att | % |
|---|---|---|---|---|---|---|
| Yepremian | 40 | 46 | 87 | 13 | 16 | 81 |

## BUFFALO BILLS

### RUSHING

| Last Name | No. | Yds | Avg | TD |
|---|---|---|---|---|
| Simpson | 329 | 1817 | 5.5 | 16 |
| Braxton | 186 | 823 | 4.4 | 9 |
| Ferguson | 23 | 82 | 3.6 | 1 |
| Marangi | 7 | 78 | 11.1 | 0 |
| Washington | 9 | 49 | 5.4 | 0 |
| Hayman | 10 | 30 | 3.0 | 0 |
| Haslerig | 2 | 9 | 4.5 | 0 |
| Chandler | 2 | 5 | 2.5 | 0 |
| Hill | 1 | 1 | 1.0 | 0 |

### RECEIVING

| Last Name | No. | Yds | Avg | TD |
|---|---|---|---|---|
| Chandler | 55 | 746 | 14 | 6 |
| Hill | 36 | 667 | 19 | 7 |
| Simpson | 28 | 426 | 15 | 7 |
| Braxton | 26 | 282 | 11 | 4 |
| Seymour | 19 | 268 | 14 | 1 |
| Gant | 9 | 107 | 12 | 2 |
| Holland | 7 | 144 | 21 | 1 |
| Washington | 2 | 21 | 11 | 0 |

### PUNT RETURNS

| Last Name | No. | Yds | Avg | TD |
|---|---|---|---|---|
| Hayman | 25 | 216 | 9 | 0 |
| Holland | 7 | 53 | 8 | 0 |
| Jones | 1 | 9 | 9 | 0 |

### KICKOFF RETURNS

| Last Name | No. | Yds | Avg | TD |
|---|---|---|---|---|
| Washington | 35 | 923 | 26 | 0 |
| Hayman | 8 | 179 | 22 | 0 |
| McKinney | 6 | 151 | 25 | 0 |
| Schnarr | 4 | 80 | 20 | 0 |
| Holland | 4 | 67 | 17 | 0 |
| Cornell | 3 | 38 | 13 | 0 |
| McKenzie | 1 | 15 | 15 | 0 |
| Ruud | 1 | 4 | 4 | 0 |

### PASSING — PUNTING — KICKING

| PASSING | Att | Comp | % | Yds | Yd/Att | TD | Int-% | RK |
|---|---|---|---|---|---|---|---|---|
| Ferguson | 321 | 169 | 53 | 2426 | 7.6 | 25 | 17-5 | 6 |
| Marangi | 33 | 13 | 39 | 235 | 7.1 | 3 | 2-6 | |

| PUNTING | No | Avg |
|---|---|---|
| Bateman | 61 | 41.6 |

| KICKING | XP | Att | % | FG | Att | % |
|---|---|---|---|---|---|---|
| Leypoldt | 51 | 57 | 89 | 9 | 16 | 56 |

## NEW ENGLAND PATRIOTS

### RUSHING

| Last Name | No. | Yds | Avg | TD |
|---|---|---|---|---|
| Cunningham | 169 | 666 | 3.9 | 6 |
| Johnson | 117 | 488 | 4.2 | 3 |
| Calhoun | 42 | 184 | 4.4 | 1 |
| Grogan | 30 | 110 | 3.7 | 3 |
| Carter | 22 | 95 | 4.3 | 0 |
| McQuay | 33 | 47 | 1.4 | 0 |
| Stingley | 6 | 39 | 6.5 | 0 |
| Plunkett | 4 | 7 | 1.8 | 1 |
| Vataha | 1 | 4 | 4.0 | 0 |
| Graff | 2 | 2 | 1.0 | 0 |
| Anderson | 1 | 1 | 1.0 | 0 |

### RECEIVING

| Last Name | No. | Yds | Avg | TD |
|---|---|---|---|---|
| Vataha | 46 | 720 | 16 | 6 |
| Francis | 35 | 636 | 18 | 4 |
| Cunningham | 32 | 253 | 8 | 2 |
| Johnson | 26 | 294 | 11 | 1 |
| Stingley | 21 | 378 | 18 | 2 |
| Burks | 6 | 158 | 26 | 0 |
| Windsor | 6 | 57 | 10 | 0 |
| Calhoun | 5 | 111 | 22 | 1 |
| Wright | 4 | 46 | 12 | 0 |
| McQuay | 4 | 27 | 7 | 0 |
| Carter | 2 | 39 | 20 | 0 |

### PUNT RETURNS

| Last Name | No. | Yds | Avg | TD |
|---|---|---|---|---|
| Stingley | 15 | 113 | 8 | 0 |
| Johnson | 6 | 60 | 10 | 0 |

### KICKOFF RETURNS

| Last Name | No. | Yds | Avg | TD |
|---|---|---|---|---|
| Carter | 32 | 879 | 28 | 1 |
| McQuay | 15 | 252 | 17 | 0 |
| Johnson | 10 | 188 | 19 | 0 |
| Burks | 4 | 65 | 16 | 0 |
| Stingley | 2 | 44 | 22 | 0 |
| Calhoun | 1 | 17 | 17 | 0 |

### PASSING — PUNTING — KICKING

| PASSING | Att | Comp | % | Yds | Yd/Att | TD | Int-% | RK |
|---|---|---|---|---|---|---|---|---|
| Grogan | 274 | 139 | 51 | 1976 | 7.2 | 11 | 18-7 | 11 |
| Plunkett | 92 | 36 | 39 | 571 | 6.2 | 3 | 7-8 | |
| Graff | 35 | 18 | 51 | 221 | 6.3 | 2 | 3-9 | |

| PUNTING | No | Avg |
|---|---|---|
| Patrick | 83 | 38.8 |

| KICKING | XP | Att | % | FG | Att | % |
|---|---|---|---|---|---|---|
| Smith | 33 | 33 | 100 | 9 | 17 | 53 |

## NEW YORK JETS

### RUSHING

| Last Name | No. | Yds | Avg | TD |
|---|---|---|---|---|
| Riggins | 238 | 1005 | 4.2 | 8 |
| Garrett | 122 | 566 | 4.6 | 5 |
| S. Davis | 70 | 290 | 4.1 | 1 |
| Gresham | 25 | 98 | 3.9 | 1 |
| Jones | 9 | 59 | 6.6 | 0 |
| Boozer | 20 | 51 | 2.6 | 0 |
| Jackson | 6 | 11 | 1.8 | 0 |
| Namath | 10 | 6 | 0.6 | 0 |
| Barkum | 1 | -7 | -7.0 | 0 |

### RECEIVING

| Last Name | No. | Yds | Avg | TD |
|---|---|---|---|---|
| Caster | 47 | 820 | 17 | 4 |
| Barkum | 36 | 549 | 15 | 5 |
| Riggins | 30 | 363 | 12 | 1 |
| Bell | 20 | 344 | 17 | 4 |
| Garrett | 19 | 180 | 10 | 1 |
| Piccone | 7 | 79 | 11 | 0 |
| S. Davis | 6 | 56 | 9 | 0 |
| Jackson | 5 | 54 | 11 | 0 |
| Gresham | 2 | 4 | 2 | 0 |
| Boozer | 1 | 16 | 16 | 1 |
| Brister | 1 | 3 | 3 | 0 |

### PUNT RETURNS

| Last Name | No. | Yds | Avg | TD |
|---|---|---|---|---|
| Piccone | 18 | 74 | 4 | 0 |
| Bell | 2 | 42 | 21 | 0 |
| Jackson | 1 | 0 | 0 | 0 |
| Sowells | 1 | 0 | 0 | 0 |

### KICKOFF RETURNS

| Last Name | No. | Yds | Avg | TD |
|---|---|---|---|---|
| Piccone | 26 | 637 | 25 | 0 |
| S. Davis | 20 | 483 | 24 | 0 |
| Garrett | 7 | 159 | 23 | 0 |
| Gresham | 7 | 153 | 22 | 0 |
| Taylor | 7 | 151 | 22 | 0 |
| Wood | 3 | 27 | 9 | 0 |
| Jackson | 2 | 52 | 26 | 0 |
| Word | 1 | 22 | 22 | 0 |
| Wise | 1 | 20 | 20 | 0 |

### PASSING — PUNTING — KICKING

| PASSING | Att | Comp | % | Yds | Yd/Att | TD | Int-% | RK |
|---|---|---|---|---|---|---|---|---|
| Namath | 326 | 157 | 48 | 2286 | 7.0 | 15 | 28-9 | 13 |
| Jones | 57 | 16 | 28 | 181 | 3.2 | 1 | 5-9 | |
| Gantt | 1 | 1 | 100 | 1 | 1.0 | 0 | 0-0 | |

| PUNTING | No | Avg |
|---|---|---|
| Gantt | 59 | 36.5 |

| KICKING | XP | Att | % | FG | Att | % |
|---|---|---|---|---|---|---|
| Leahy | 27 | 30 | 90 | 13 | 21 | 62 |

## PITTSBURGH STEELERS 12-2 Chuck Noll

| Scores of Each Game | | Use Name | Pos. | Hgt | Wgt | Age | Int | Pts |
|---|---|---|---|---|---|---|---|---|
| 37 | San Diego | 0 | Gordon Gravelle | OT | 6'5" | 255 | 26 | | |
| 21 | BUFFALO | 30 | Jon Kolb | OT | 6'2" | 262 | 28 | | |
| 42 | Cleveland | 6 | Dave Reavis | OT | 6'5" | 254 | 25 | | |
| 20 | DENVER | 9 | Sam Davis | OG | 6'1" | 250 | 31 | | |
| 34 | CHICAGO | 3 | Gerry Mullins | OT-OG | 6'3" | 240 | 26 | 6 | |
| 16 | Green Bay | 13 | Jim Clack | C-OG | 6'3" | 250 | 27 | | |
| 30 | Cincinnati | 24 | Ray Mansfield | C | 6'3" | 260 | 34 | | |
| 24 | HOUSTON | 17 | Mike Webster | OG-C | 6'1" | 245 | 23 | | |
| 28 | KANSAS CITY | 3 | John Banaszak | DE | 6'3" | 232 | 25 | | |
| 32 | Houston | 9 | L. C. Greenwood | DE | 6'5" | 245 | 28 | | |
| 20 | N.Y. Jets | 7 | Dwight White | DE | 6'4" | 255 | 26 | 2 | |
| 31 | CLEVELAND | 17 | Joe Greene | DT | 6'4" | 275 | 28 | | |
| 35 | CINCINNATI | 14 | Ernie Holmes | DT | 6'3" | 260 | 27 | | |
| 3 | Los Angeles | 10 | Steve Furness | DE-DT | 6'4" | 255 | 25 | | |

| Use Name | Pos. | Hgt | Wgt | Age | Int | Pts |
|---|---|---|---|---|---|---|
| Ed Bradley | LB | 6'2" | 232 | 25 | | |
| Jack Ham | LB | 6'3" | 225 | 26 | 1 | |
| Marv Kellum | LB | 6'2" | 225 | 23 | | |
| Jack Lambert | LB | 6'4" | 220 | 23 | 2 | |
| Andy Russell | LB | 6'2" | 220 | 33 | | |
| Loren Toews | LB | 6'3" | 222 | 23 | | |
| Jimmy Allen | DB | 6'2" | 194 | 23 | 2 | |
| Mel Blount | DB | 6'3" | 200 | 27 | 11 | |
| Dave Brown | DB | 6'1" | 200 | 22 | | |
| Glen Edwards | DB | 6' | 185 | 28 | 3 | |
| Donnie Shell | DB | 5'11" | 195 | 23 | 1 | |
| J. T. Thomas | DB | 6'2" | 196 | 24 | 3 | 6 |
| Mike Wagner | DB | 6'1" | 210 | 26 | 4 | |

| Use Name | Pos. | Hgt | Wgt | Age | Int | Pts |
|---|---|---|---|---|---|---|
| Terry Bradshaw | QB | 6'3" | 210 | 26 | | 18 |
| Joe Gilliam | QB | 6'2" | 187 | 24 | | |
| Terry Hanratty | QB | 6'1" | 205 | 27 | | |
| Rocky Bleier | HB | 5'11" | 210 | 29 | | 12 |
| Mike Collier | HB | 5'11" | 200 | 21 | | 24 |
| John Fuqua | HB | 5'11" | 200 | 28 | | 6 |
| Franco Harris | FB | 6'2" | 230 | 25 | | 66 |
| Reggie Harrison | FB | 5'11" | 215 | 25 | | 18 |
| Reggie Garrett | WR | 6'1" | 175 | 23 | | 6 |
| Frank Lewis | WR | 6'1" | 196 | 28 | | 12 |
| John Stallworth | WR | 6'2" | 185 | 23 | | 24 |
| Lynn Swann | WR | 6'1" | 180 | 23 | | 66 |
| Larry Brown | TE | 6'4" | 230 | 26 | | 6 |
| Randy Grossman | TE | 6'1" | 215 | 21 | | 6 |
| Roy Gerela | K | 5'10" | 190 | 27 | | 95 |
| Bobby Walden | K | 6' | 197 | 37 | | |

## CINCINNATI BENGALS 11-3 Paul Brown

| Scores of Each Game | | Use Name | Pos. | Hgt | Wgt | Age | Int | Pts |
|---|---|---|---|---|---|---|---|---|
| 24 | CLEVELAND | 17 | Vern Holland | OT | 6'5" | 268 | 27 | | |
| 21 | New Orleans | 0 | Al Krevis | OT | 6'6" | 263 | 23 | | |
| 21 | Houston | 19 | Rufus Mayes | OT | 6'5" | 265 | 27 | | |
| 27 | NEW ENGLAND | 10 | Howard Fest | OG | 6'6" | 262 | 29 | | |
| 14 | OAKLAND | 10 | Dave Lapham | OG | 6'3" | 258 | 23 | | |
| 21 | Atlanta | 14 | John Shinners | OG | 6'2" | 255 | 28 | | |
| 24 | PITTSBURGH | 30 | Bob Johnson | C | 6'5" | 255 | 29 | | |
| 17 | Denver | 16 | Ken Johnson | DE | 6'5" | 250 | 28 | | |
| 33 | BUFFALO | 24 | Sherman White | DE | 6'5" | 250 | 26 | | |
| 23 | Cleveland | 35 | Bob Brown | DT | 6'5" | 290 | 35 | | |
| 23 | HOUSTON | 19 | Ron Carpenter | DT | 6'4" | 260 | 27 | | |
| 31 | Philadelphia | 0 | Bill Kollar | DT | 6'3" | 250 | 22 | | |
| 14 | Pittsburgh | 35 | Baldy Moore | DT | 6'5" | 265 | 29 | | |
| 47 | SAN DIEGO | 17 | | | | | | | |

Royce Berry — Dislocated Wrist

| Use Name | Pos. | Hgt | Wgt | Age | Int | Pts |
|---|---|---|---|---|---|---|
| Al Beauchamp | LB | 6'2" | 232 | 31 | | |
| Glenn Cameron | LB | 6'2" | 230 | 22 | | |
| Brad Cousino | LB | 6' | 220 | 22 | | |
| Chris Devlin | LB | 6'3" | 222 | 21 | | |
| Bo Harris | LB | 6'3" | 230 | 22 | | |
| Jim LeClair | LB | 6'2" | 235 | 24 | 3 | |
| Ron Pritchard | LB | 6'1" | 230 | 28 | | |
| Lyle Blackwood | DB | 6'2" | 192 | 24 | 2 | |
| Tommy Casanova | DB | 6'1" | 195 | 25 | | |
| Marvin Cobb | DB | 6' | 185 | 22 | 4 | 6 |
| Ricky Davis | DB | 6'1" | 182 | 22 | 1 | |
| Bernard Jackson | DB | 6' | 178 | 25 | 5 | |
| Lemar Parrish | DB | 5'11" | 185 | 27 | 1 | |
| Ken Riley | DB | 6' | 182 | 28 | 6 | 6 |

| Use Name | Pos. | Hgt | Wgt | Age | Int | Pts |
|---|---|---|---|---|---|---|
| Ken Anderson | QB | 6'1" | 211 | 26 | | 12 |
| John Reaves | QB | 6'3" | 210 | 25 | | 12 |
| Lenvil Elliott | HB | 6' | 205 | 23 | | 24 |
| Stan Fritts | HB | 6'1" | 215 | 22 | | 60 |
| Essex Johnson | HB | 5'9" | 200 | 28 | | 12 |
| Booby Clark | FB | 6'2" | 245 | 24 | | 24 |
| Harold Henson | FB | 6'3" | 240 | 22 | | |
| Ed Williams | FB | 6'2" | 245 | 25 | | 18 |
| Isaac Curtis | WR | 6' | 193 | 24 | | 42 |
| Charlie Joiner | WR | 5'11" | 189 | 27 | | 30 |
| Chip Myers | WR | 6'4" | 205 | 30 | | 18 |
| John McDaniel | WR | 6'1" | 193 | 23 | | |
| Bruce Coslet | TE | 6'3" | 227 | 29 | | |
| Jack Novak | TE | 6'4" | 242 | 22 | | |
| Bob Trumpy | TE | 6'6" | 228 | 30 | | 6 |
| Dave Green | K | 5'11" | 208 | 25 | | 70 |

Charlie Davis — Knee Injury

## HOUSTON OILERS 10-4 Bum Phillips

| Scores of Each Game | | Use Name | Pos. | Hgt | Wgt | Age | Int | Pts |
|---|---|---|---|---|---|---|---|---|
| 7 | New England | 0 | Elbert Drungo | OT | 6'5" | 265 | 32 | | |
| 33 | SAN DIEGO | 17 | Kevin Hunt | OT | 6'5" | 260 | 26 | | |
| 19 | CINCINNATI | 21 | Greg Sampson | OT | 6'6" | 270 | 24 | | |
| 40 | Cleveland | 10 | Ed Fisher | OG | 6'3" | 245 | 26 | | |
| 13 | WASHINGTON | 10 | Conway Hayman | OG | 6'2" | 262 | 22 | | |
| 24 | DETROIT | 8 | Ron Saul | OG | 6'2" | 250 | 27 | | |
| 17 | Kansas City | 13 | Fred Hoaglin | C | 6'4" | 250 | 31 | | |
| 17 | Pittsburgh | 24 | Carl Mauck | C | 6'3" | 245 | 28 | | |
| 20 | MIAMI | 19 | Curley Culp | DG | 6'1" | 265 | 29 | 6 | |
| 9 | PITTSBURGH | 32 | Elvin Bethea | DE | 6'3" | 255 | 29 | 2 | |
| 19 | Cincinnati | 23 | Tody Smith | DE | 6'5" | 250 | 26 | | |
| 27 | San Francisco | 13 | Jim White | DE | 6'5" | 255 | 26 | | |
| 27 | Oakland | 26 | Bubba Smith | DT-DE | 6'7" | 265 | 30 | | |
| 21 | CLEVELAND | 10 | John Little | DE-DT | 6'3" | 250 | 28 | | |

Ronnie Carroll — Injury
Al Johnson — Ankle Injury
Lee Thomas — Injury

| Use Name | Pos. | Hgt | Wgt | Age | Int | Pts |
|---|---|---|---|---|---|---|
| Duane Benson | LB | 6'2" | 220 | 30 | | |
| Gregg Bingham | LB | 6'1" | 230 | 24 | 4 | |
| Robert Brazile | LB | 6'4" | 235 | 22 | | |
| Ralph Cindrich | LB | 6'1" | 230 | 25 | | |
| Steve Kiner | LB | 6' | 220 | 28 | 2 | |
| Guy Roberts | LB | 6'1" | 220 | 25 | | |
| Ted Thompson | LB | 6'1" | 215 | 22 | | |
| Ted Washington | LB | 6'1" | 240 | 27 | 3 | |
| Willie Alexander | DB | 6'2" | 190 | 25 | 3 | |
| Bob Atkins | DB | 6'3" | 210 | 29 | 4 | |
| Mark Cotney | DB | 5'11" | 200 | 23 | | |
| Willie Germany | DB | 6' | 192 | 26 | 2 | 6 |
| Zeke Moore | DB | 6'2" | 197 | 31 | 5 | |
| Greg Stemrick | DB | 5'11" | 185 | 23 | | |
| C. L. Whittington | DB | 6'1" | 200 | 23 | 1 | |

| Use Name | Pos. | Hgt | Wgt | Age | Int | Pts |
|---|---|---|---|---|---|---|
| Lynn Dickey | QB | 6'4" | 210 | 25 | | |
| Dan Pastorini | QB | 6'3" | 205 | 26 | | 6 |
| Ronnie Coleman | HB | 5'10" | 195 | 24 | | 30 |
| Willie Rogers | HB | 6' | 210 | 26 | | 8 |
| Don Hardeman | FB | 6'2" | 235 | 23 | | 30 |
| Robert Holmes | FB | 5'9" | 220 | 29 | | |
| Fred Willis | FB | 6' | 205 | 27 | | 12 |
| Jim Beirne | WR | 6'2" | 206 | 28 | | |
| Ken Burrough | WR | 6'4" | 210 | 27 | | 48 |
| Emmett Edwards | WR | 6'1" | 187 | 23 | | |
| Nate Hawkins | WR | 6'1" | 190 | 25 | | |
| Billy Johnson | WR | 5'9" | 170 | 23 | | 30 |
| Billy Parks | WR | 6'1" | 190 | 27 | | |
| Mack Alston | TE | 6'2" | 230 | 28 | | 24 |
| Willie Frazier | TE | 6'4" | 235 | 32 | | |
| John Sawyer | TE | 6'2" | 230 | 22 | | 6 |
| Skip Butler | K | 6'2" | 200 | 27 | | 85 |

## CLEVELAND BROWNS 3-11 Forrest Gregg

| Scores of Each Game | | Use Name | Pos. | Hgt | Wgt | Age | Int | Pts |
|---|---|---|---|---|---|---|---|---|
| 17 | Cincinnati | 24 | Barry Darrow | OT | 6'7" | 260 | 25 | | |
| 10 | MINNESOTA | 42 | Doug Dieken | OT | 6'5" | 252 | 26 | | |
| 6 | PITTSBURGH | 42 | Robert Jackson | OT | 6'5" | 245 | 22 | | |
| 10 | HOUSTON | 40 | Gerry Sullivan | OT | 6'4" | 250 | 23 | | |
| 15 | Denver | 16 | Chuck Hutchison | OG | 6'3" | 250 | 26 | | |
| 7 | WASHINGTON | 23 | Bob McKay | OG | 6'5" | 265 | 27 | | |
| 7 | Baltimore | 21 | Tom DeLeone | C | 6'2" | 248 | 25 | | |
| 10 | Detroit | 21 | John Demarie | C | 6'3" | 248 | 30 | | |
| 17 | Oakland | 38 | Joe Jones (from PHI) | DE | 6'6" | 250 | 27 | | |
| 35 | CINCINNATI | 23 | Ron East | DE | 6'4" | 250 | 32 | 2 | |
| 17 | NEW ORLEANS | 16 | Stan Lewis | DE | 6'4" | 240 | 21 | | |
| 17 | Pittsburgh | 31 | Mack Mitchell | DE | 6'7" | 245 | 23 | | |
| 40 | KANSAS CITY | 14 | Carl Barisich | DT | 6'4" | 255 | 24 | | |
| 10 | Houston | 21 | Walter Johnson | DT | 6'3" | 265 | 32 | | |
| | | | Jerry Sherk | DT | 6'4" | 250 | 27 | | |

| Use Name | Pos. | Hgt | Wgt | Age | Int | Pts |
|---|---|---|---|---|---|---|
| Dick Ambrose | LB | 6' | 235 | 22 | | |
| Bob Babich | LB | 6'2" | 230 | 28 | | |
| John Garlington | LB | 6'1" | 220 | 29 | | |
| Dave Graf | LB | 6'2" | 215 | 22 | 1 | |
| Charlie Hall | LB | 6'3" | 230 | 26 | 2 | 6 |
| Jack LeVeck | LB | 6' | 225 | 25 | | |
| Neal Craig | DB | 6'1" | 190 | 27 | 1 | |
| Van Green | DB | 6'1" | 192 | 24 | 1 | |
| Jim Hill | DB | 6'2" | 195 | 28 | 1 | 6 |
| Tony Peters | DB | 6'1" | 192 | 22 | 1 | |
| John Pitts (from DEN) | DB | 6'4" | 218 | 30 | 1 | |
| Clarence Scott | DB | 6' | 180 | 26 | 2 | |

Pete Adams — Knee Injury
Thom Darden — Knee Injury

| Use Name | Pos. | Hgt | Wgt | Age | Int | Pts |
|---|---|---|---|---|---|---|
| Will Cureton | QB | 6'3" | 200 | 25 | | |
| Mike Phipps | QB | 6'2" | 205 | 27 | | |
| Brian Sipe | QB | 6'1" | 190 | 26 | | |
| Ken Brown | HB | 5'10" | 203 | 29 | | 6 |
| Cleo Miller (from KC) | HB | 5'11" | 202 | 22 | | 6 |
| Larry Poole | HB | 6' | 195 | 23 | | |
| Greg Pruitt | HB | 5'10" | 190 | 24 | | 54 |
| Henry Hynoski | FB | 6' | 210 | 22 | | |
| Hugh McKinnis | FB | 6' | 220 | 27 | | 24 |
| Billy Pritchett | FB | 6'3" | 230 | 24 | | |
| Steve Holden | WR | 6' | 194 | 24 | | |
| Billy Lefear | WR | 5'11" | 197 | 25 | | |
| Willie Miller | WR | 5'9" | 172 | 28 | | 6 |
| Reggie Rucker | WR | 6'2" | 190 | 27 | | 18 |
| Milt Morin | TE | 6'4" | 240 | 33 | | |
| Garry Parris | TE | 6'2" | 226 | 25 | | |
| Oscar Roan | TE | 6'6" | 214 | 28 | | 18 |
| Don Cockroft | K | 6'1" | 195 | 30 | | 72 |

## PITTSBURGH STEELERS

### RUSHING

| Last Name | No. | Yds | Avg | TD |
|---|---|---|---|---|
| Harris | 262 | 1246 | 4.8 | 10 |
| Bleier | 140 | 528 | 3.8 | 2 |
| Fuqua | 74 | 285 | 3.9 | 1 |
| Bradshaw | 35 | 210 | 6.0 | 3 |
| Harrison | 43 | 191 | 4.4 | 3 |
| Collier | 21 | 124 | 5.9 | 3 |
| Lewis | 2 | 36 | 18.0 | 0 |
| Swann | 3 | 13 | 4.3 | 0 |
| Hanratty | 1 | 0 | 0.0 | 0 |

### RECEIVING

| Last Name | No. | Yds | Avg | TD |
|---|---|---|---|---|
| Swann | 49 | 781 | 16 | 11 |
| Harris | 28 | 214 | 8 | 1 |
| Stallworth | 20 | 423 | 21 | 4 |
| Fuqua | 18 | 146 | 8 | 0 |
| Lewis | 17 | 308 | 18 | 2 |
| L. Brown | 16 | 244 | 15 | 1 |
| Bleier | 15 | 65 | 4 | 0 |
| Garrett | 13 | 178 | 14 | 1 |
| Grossman | 11 | 135 | 12 | 1 |
| Shell | 2 | 39 | 20 | 0 |
| Collier | 1 | 7 | 7 | 0 |
| Harrison | 1 | 4 | 4 | 0 |

### PUNT RETURNS

| Last Name | No. | Yds | Avg | TD |
|---|---|---|---|---|
| Edwards | 25 | 267 | 11 | 0 |
| D. Brown | 22 | 217 | 10 | 0 |
| Swann | 7 | 64 | 9 | 0 |

### KICKOFF RETURNS

| Last Name | No. | Yds | Avg | TD |
|---|---|---|---|---|
| Collier | 22 | 523 | 24 | 1 |
| Blount | 8 | 139 | 17 | 0 |
| D. Brown | 6 | 126 | 21 | 0 |
| Harris | 1 | 27 | 27 | 0 |
| Fuqua | 1 | 0 | 0 | 0 |

### PASSING – PUNTING – KICKING

**PASSING**

| Last Name | Att | Comp | % | Yds | Yd/Att | TD | Int–% | RK |
|---|---|---|---|---|---|---|---|---|
| Bradshaw | 286 | 165 | 58 | 2055 | 7.2 | 18 | 9– 3 | 4 |
| Gilliam | 48 | 24 | 50 | 450 | 9.4 | 3 | 3– 6 | |
| Walden | 3 | 2 | 67 | 39 | 13.0 | 0 | 0– 0 | |

**PUNTING**

| Last Name | No | Avg |
|---|---|---|
| Walden | 69 | 39.4 |

**KICKING**

| Last Name | XP | Att | % | FG | Att | % |
|---|---|---|---|---|---|---|
| Gerela | 44 | 46 | 96 | 17 | 21 | 81 |

## CINCINNATI BENGALS

### RUSHING

| Last Name | No. | Yds | Avg | TD |
|---|---|---|---|---|
| Clark | 167 | 594 | 3.6 | 4 |
| Fritts | 94 | 375 | 4.0 | 8 |
| Elliott | 71 | 420 | 4.3 | 1 |
| Anderson | 49 | 188 | 3.8 | 2 |
| E. Johnson | 58 | 177 | 3.1 | 1 |
| Williams | 35 | 136 | 3.9 | 2 |
| Henson | 11 | 38 | 3.5 | 0 |
| Reaves | 6 | 13 | 2.2 | 2 |
| Coslet | 1 | 1 | 1.0 | 0 |
| McDaniel | 1 | −2 | −2.0 | 0 |
| Curtis | 6 | −9 | −1.5 | 0 |

### RECEIVING

| Last Name | No. | Yds | Avg | TD |
|---|---|---|---|---|
| Curtis | 44 | 934 | 21 | 7 |
| Clark | 42 | 334 | 8 | 0 |
| Joiner | 37 | 726 | 20 | 5 |
| Myers | 36 | 527 | 15 | 3 |
| E. Johnson | 25 | 196 | 8 | 1 |
| Trumpy | 22 | 276 | 13 | 1 |
| Elliott | 20 | 196 | 10 | 3 |
| Coslet | 10 | 117 | 12 | 0 |
| Williams | 10 | 96 | 10 | 1 |
| Fritts | 6 | 63 | 11 | 2 |
| Novak | 2 | 34 | 17 | 0 |
| Hensen | 1 | −2 | −2 | 0 |

### PUNT RETURNS

| Last Name | No. | Yds | Avg | TD |
|---|---|---|---|---|
| Blackwood | 23 | 123 | 5 | 0 |
| Parrish | 13 | 83 | 6 | 0 |
| Casanova | 11 | 60 | 6 | 0 |
| Cobb | 1 | 1 | 1 | 0 |

### KICKOFF RETURNS

| Last Name | No. | Yds | Avg | TD |
|---|---|---|---|---|
| Jackson | 25 | 587 | 24 | 0 |
| Elliott | 13 | 272 | 21 | 0 |
| Parrish | 4 | 114 | 29 | 0 |
| McDaniel | 3 | 69 | 23 | 0 |
| Cobb | 1 | 0 | 0 | 0 |
| Cousino | 1 | 0 | 0 | 0 |

### PASSING – PUNTING – KICKING

**PASSING**

| Last Name | Att | Comp | % | Yds | Yd/Att | TD | Int–% | RK |
|---|---|---|---|---|---|---|---|---|
| Anderson | 377 | 228 | 61 | 3169 | 8.4 | 21 | 11– 3 | 1 |
| Reaves | 51 | 25 | 49 | 297 | 5.8 | 2 | 3– 6 | |
| Fritts | 4 | 2 | 50 | 31 | 7.8 | 0 | 0– 0 | |
| Green | 1 | 0 | 0 | 0 | 0.0 | 0 | 0– 0 | |

**PUNTING**

| Last Name | No | Avg |
|---|---|---|
| Green | 68 | 39.0 |

**KICKING**

| Last Name | XP | Att | % | FG | Att | % |
|---|---|---|---|---|---|---|
| Green | 40 | 45 | 89 | 10 | 21 | 48 |

## HOUSTON OILERS

### RUSHING

| Last Name | No. | Yds | Avg | TD |
|---|---|---|---|---|
| Coleman | 175 | 790 | 4.5 | 5 |
| Hardeman | 166 | 648 | 3.9 | 5 |
| Willis | 118 | 420 | 3.6 | 2 |
| Pastorini | 23 | 97 | 4.2 | 1 |
| Rodgers | 18 | 55 | 3.1 | 1 |
| Holmes | 19 | 42 | 2.2 | 0 |
| Johnson | 5 | 17 | 3.4 | 0 |
| Dickey | 1 | 3 | 3.0 | 0 |
| Edwards | 1 | −4 | −4.0 | 0 |

### RECEIVING

| Last Name | No. | Yds | Avg | TD |
|---|---|---|---|---|
| Burrough | 53 | 1063 | 20 | 8 |
| Johnson | 37 | 393 | 11 | 0 |
| Willis | 20 | 104 | 5 | 0 |
| Alston | 18 | 165 | 9 | 4 |
| Coleman | 18 | 129 | 7 | 0 |
| Sawyer | 7 | 144 | 21 | 1 |
| Hardeman | 5 | 10 | 2 | 0 |
| Edwards | 2 | 22 | 11 | 0 |
| Hawkins | 1 | 32 | 32 | 0 |
| Beirne | 1 | 15 | 15 | 0 |
| Frazier | 1 | 9 | 9 | 0 |
| Parks | 1 | 8 | 8 | 0 |
| Holmes | 1 | 5 | 5 | 0 |

### PUNT RETURNS

| Last Name | No. | Yds | Avg | TD |
|---|---|---|---|---|
| Johnson | 40 | 612 | 15 | 3 |
| Cotney | 2 | 8 | 4 | 0 |
| Coleman | 1 | 0 | 0 | 0 |

### KICKOFF RETURNS

| Last Name | No. | Yds | Avg | TD |
|---|---|---|---|---|
| Johnson | 33 | 798 | 24 | 1 |
| Cotney | 10 | 189 | 19 | 0 |
| Coleman | 8 | 149 | 19 | 0 |
| Rodgers | 1 | 13 | 13 | 0 |
| Whittington | 1 | 0 | 0 | 0 |
| Thompson | 1 | −5 | −5 | 0 |

### PASSING – PUNTING – KICKING

**PASSING**

| Last Name | Att | Comp | % | Yds | Yd/Att | TD | Int–% | RK |
|---|---|---|---|---|---|---|---|---|
| Pastorini | 342 | 163 | 48 | 2053 | 6.0 | 14 | 16– 5 | 10 |
| Dickey | 4 | 2 | 50 | 46 | 11.5 | 0 | 1–25 | |
| Coleman | 1 | 0 | 0 | 0 | 0.0 | 0 | 0– 0 | |

**PUNTING**

| Last Name | No | Avg |
|---|---|---|
| Pastorini | 62 | 39.5 |

**KICKING**

| Last Name | XP | Att | % | FG | Att | % |
|---|---|---|---|---|---|---|
| Butler | 31 | 34 | 91 | 18 | 30 | 60 |

## CLEVELAND BROWNS

### RUSHING

| Last Name | No. | Yds | Avg | TD |
|---|---|---|---|---|
| Pruitt | 217 | 1067 | 4.9 | 8 |
| McKinnis | 71 | 259 | 3.6 | 4 |
| Pritchett | 75 | 199 | 2.7 | 0 |
| Poole | 17 | 114 | 6.7 | 0 |
| Phipps | 18 | 70 | 3.9 | 0 |
| Sipe | 9 | 60 | 6.7 | 0 |
| K. Brown | 16 | 45 | 2.8 | 1 |
| Hynoski | 7 | 38 | 5.4 | 0 |
| C. Miller | 13 | 23 | 1.8 | 1 |
| Cureton | 1 | 1 | 1.0 | 0 |
| W. Miller | 1 | −2 | −2.0 | 0 |
| Holden | 2 | −4 | −2.0 | 0 |

### RECEIVING

| Last Name | No. | Yds | Avg | TD |
|---|---|---|---|---|
| Rucker | 60 | 770 | 13 | 3 |
| Pruitt | 44 | 299 | 7 | 1 |
| Roan | 41 | 463 | 11 | 3 |
| Holden | 21 | 320 | 15 | 0 |
| McKinnis | 17 | 155 | 9 | 0 |
| Pritchett | 16 | 109 | 7 | 0 |
| W. Miller | 7 | 57 | 8 | 0 |
| Hynoski | 4 | 31 | 8 | 0 |
| Brown | 2 | 23 | 12 | 0 |
| C. Miller | 2 | 20 | 10 | 0 |
| Morin | 1 | 19 | 19 | 0 |
| Lefear | 1 | 14 | 14 | 0 |
| Parris | 1 | 12 | 12 | 0 |
| Poole | 1 | 5 | 5 | 0 |
| Craig | 1 | 1 | 1 | 0 |
| Green | 1 | −1 | −1 | 0 |

### PUNT RETURNS

| Last Name | No. | Yds | Avg | TD |
|---|---|---|---|---|
| Pruitt | 13 | 130 | 10 | 0 |
| W. Miller | 10 | 47 | 5 | 0 |
| Poole | 6 | 35 | 6 | 0 |
| Hynoski | 2 | 16 | 8 | 0 |
| Lefear | 1 | 14 | 14 | 0 |
| Green | 1 | 0 | 0 | 0 |

### KICKOFF RETURNS

| Last Name | No. | Yds | Avg | TD |
|---|---|---|---|---|
| Lefear | 13 | 412 | 32 | 0 |
| Pruitt | 14 | 302 | 22 | 0 |
| C. Miller | 12 | 241 | 20 | 0 |
| Hynoski | 8 | 194 | 24 | 0 |
| K. Brown | 7 | 126 | 18 | 0 |
| W. Miller | 4 | 94 | 24 | 0 |
| Poole | 2 | 65 | 33 | 0 |
| McKinnis | 3 | 39 | 13 | 0 |
| Ambrose | 1 | 3 | 3 | 0 |

### PASSING – PUNTING – KICKING

**PASSING**

| Last Name | Att | Comp | % | Yds | Yd/Att | TD | Int–% | RK |
|---|---|---|---|---|---|---|---|---|
| Phipps | 313 | 162 | 52 | 1749 | 5.6 | 4 | 19– 6 | 14 |
| Sipe | 88 | 45 | 51 | 427 | 4.9 | 1 | 3– 3 | |
| Cureton | 32 | 10 | 31 | 95 | 3.0 | 1 | 1– 3 | |
| Cockroft | 2 | 2 | 100 | 0 | 0.0 | 0 | 0– 0 | |
| Hynoski | 1 | 0 | 0 | 0 | 0.0 | 0 | 0– 0 | |
| W. Miller | 1 | 1 | 100 | 26 | 26.0 | 1 | 0– 0 | |

**PUNTING**

| Last Name | No | Avg |
|---|---|---|
| Cockroft | 82 | 40.5 |

**KICKING**

| Last Name | XP | Att | % | FG | Att | % |
|---|---|---|---|---|---|---|
| Cockroft | 21 | 24 | 88 | 17 | 23 | 74 |

## OAKLAND RAIDERS 11-3 John Madden

| Scores of Each Game | | |
|---|---|---|
| 31 | Miami | 21 |
| 31 | Baltimore | 20 |
| 6 | San Diego | 0 |
| 10 | KANSAS CITY | 42 |
| 10 | Cincinnati | 14 |
| 25 | SAN DIEGO | 0 |
| 42 | Denver | 17 |
| 48 | NEW ORLEANS | 10 |
| 38 | CLEVELAND | 17 |
| 26 | Washington | *23 |
| 37 | ATLANTA | *34 |
| 17 | DENVER | 10 |
| 26 | Houston | 27 |
| 28 | Kansas City | 20 |

| Use Name | Pos. | Hgt | Wgt | Age | Int | Pts |
|---|---|---|---|---|---|---|
| Henry Lawrence | OT | 6'4" | 278 | 23 | | |
| Art Shell | OT | 6'5" | 265 | 28 | | |
| John Vella | OT | 6'4" | 260 | 25 | | |
| George Buehler | OG | 6'2" | 270 | 28 | | |
| Dan Medlin | OG | 6'3" | 252 | 25 | | |
| Gene Upshaw | OG | 6'5" | 255 | 30 | | |
| Dave Dalby | C | 6'2" | 250 | 24 | | |
| Steve Sylvester | OG-C | 6'4" | 262 | 22 | | |
| Tony Cline | DE | 6'2" | 244 | 27 | | |
| Horace Jones | DE | 6'3" | 260 | 26 | | |
| Dave Rowe (from SD) | DT | 6'6" | 270 | 30 | | |
| Kelvin Korver | DT | 6'6" | 270 | 26 | | |
| Otis Sistrunk | DT | 6'4" | 273 | 27 | | |
| Art Thoms | DT | 6'5" | 250 | 28 | 1 | |
| Mike Dennery | LB | 6' | 226 | 25 | | |
| Willie Hall | LB | 6'2" | 220 | 25 | | 2 |
| Ted Hendricks | LB | 6'7" | 220 | 27 | 2 | 2 |
| Gerald Irons | LB | 6'2" | 236 | 28 | 1 | |
| Monte Johnson | LB | 6'4" | 240 | 23 | 1 | |
| Phil Villapiano | LB | 6'1" | 222 | 26 | 2 | |
| Butch Atkinson | DB | 6' | 185 | 27 | 4 | |
| Willie Brown | DB | 6'1" | 210 | 34 | 4 | |
| Neal Colzie | DB | 6'2" | 205 | 22 | 4 | |
| Charlie Phillips | DB | 6'2" | 215 | 22 | 6 | |
| Jack Tatum | DB | 5'10" | 206 | 26 | 4 | |
| Skip Thomas | DB | 6'1" | 205 | 25 | 6 | |
| George Blanda | QB | 6'2" | 215 | 47 | | 83 |
| Pete Beathard | QB | 6'2" | 205 | 33 | | |
| David Humm | QB | 6'2" | 184 | 23 | | |
| Larry Lawrence | QB | 6'1" | 208 | 26 | | |
| Ken Stabler | QB | 6'3" | 215 | 29 | | |
| Pete Banaszak | HB | 5'11" | 210 | 31 | | 96 |
| Louis Carter | HB | 5'11" | 200 | 22 | | |
| Clarence Davis | HB | 5'10" | 195 | 26 | | 30 |
| Harold Hart | HB | 6' | 206 | 22 | | 24 |
| Jess Phillips | FB-HB | 6'1" | 208 | 28 | | 6 |
| Marv Hubbard | FB | 6'1" | 235 | 29 | | 12 |
| Mark van Eeghen | FB | 6'1" | 225 | 23 | | 18 |
| Fred Biletnikoff | WR | 6'1" | 190 | 32 | | 12 |
| Morris Bradshaw | WR | 6' | 195 | 22 | | 24 |
| Cliff Branch | WR | 5'11" | 170 | 27 | | 54 |
| Mike Siani | WR | 6'2" | 195 | 25 | | |
| Dave Casper | TE | 6'4" | 228 | 23 | | 6 |
| Ted Kwalick | TE | 6'4" | 226 | 28 | | |
| Bob Moore | TE | 6'3" | 220 | 26 | | |
| Warren Bankston | FB-TE | 6'4" | 235 | 28 | | 6 |
| Ray Guy | K | 6'3" | 195 | 25 | | |

## DENVER BRONCOS 6-8 John Ralston

| Scores of Each Game | | |
|---|---|---|
| 37 | KANSAS CITY | 33 |
| 23 | GREEN BAY | 13 |
| 14 | Buffalo | 38 |
| 9 | Pittsburgh | 20 |
| 16 | CLEVELAND | 15 |
| 13 | Kansas City | 26 |
| 17 | OAKLAND | 42 |
| 16 | CINCINNATI | 17 |
| 27 | San Diego | 17 |
| 21 | Atlanta | 35 |
| 13 | SAN DIEGO | *10 |
| 10 | Oakland | 17 |
| 25 | PHILADELPHIA | 10 |
| 13 | Miami | 14 |

| Use Name | Pos. | Hgt | Wgt | Age | Int | Pts |
|---|---|---|---|---|---|---|
| Mike Current | OT | 6'4" | 258 | 29 | | |
| Claudie Minor | OT | 6'4" | 285 | 24 | | |
| Marv Montgomery | OT | 6'6" | 255 | 27 | | |
| Stan Rogers | OT | 6'4" | 255 | 23 | | |
| Brian Goodman | OG | 6'2" | 250 | 26 | | |
| Paul Howard | OG | 6'3" | 260 | 24 | | |
| Tommy Lyons | OG | 6'2" | 230 | 27 | | |
| Carl Schaukowitch | OG | 6'2" | 237 | 24 | | |
| Bobby Maples | C | 6'3" | 250 | 32 | | |
| Phil Olsen | DT-C | 6'5" | 260 | 27 | | |
| Barney Chavous | DE | 6'3" | 252 | 24 | | |
| Lyle Alzado | DT-DE | 6'3" | 265 | 26 | | |
| John Grant | DT-DE | 6'3" | 235 | 25 | | |
| Rubin Carter | DT | 6' | 256 | 22 | | |
| Paul Smith | DT | 6'3" | 256 | 30 | 6 | |

Ed Smith — Knee Injury

| Use Name | Pos. | Hgt | Wgt | Age | Int | Pts |
|---|---|---|---|---|---|---|
| Randy Gradishar | LB | 6'3" | 235 | 23 | 3 | 6 |
| Tom Jackson | LB | 5'11" | 220 | 24 | 2 | |
| Mike Lemon (from NO) | LB | 6'2" | 215 | 24 | | |
| Ray May | LB | 6'1" | 230 | 30 | 1 | |
| Jim O'Malley | LB | 6'1" | 230 | 24 | 1 | |
| Joe Rizzo | LB | 6'1" | 220 | 24 | | |
| Bob Swenson | LB | 6'3" | 220 | 22 | 1 | |
| Steve Haggerty | DB | 5'10" | 175 | 22 | | |
| Calvin Jones | DB | 5'7" | 170 | 24 | 1 | |
| Randy Poltl | DB | 6'3" | 190 | 23 | | |
| John Rowser | DB | 6'1" | 190 | 31 | 1 | |
| Jeff Severson | DB | 6'1" | 185 | 25 | | |
| Earlie Thomas | DB | 6'1" | 190 | 29 | 2 | |
| Bill Thompson | DB | 6'1" | 200 | 28 | 2 | |
| Louis Wright | DB | 6'2" | 195 | 22 | 2 | |

Clarence Ellis — Knee Injury

| Use Name | Pos. | Hgt | Wgt | Age | Int | Pts |
|---|---|---|---|---|---|---|
| John Hufnagel | QB | 6'1" | 194 | 24 | | |
| Charley Johnson | QB | 6' | 190 | 38 | | |
| Steve Ramsey | QB | 6'2" | 210 | 27 | | |
| Otis Armstrong | HB | 5'10" | 196 | 24 | | |
| Floyd Little | HB | 5'10" | 195 | 33 | | 24 |
| Fran Lynch | FB-HB | 6'1" | 205 | 29 | | 24 |
| Mike Franckowiak | FB | 6'3" | 220 | 22 | | |
| Al Haywood | FB | 5'11" | 215 | 27 | | |
| Jon Keyworth | FB | 6'3" | 230 | 23 | | 24 |
| Oliver Ross | HB-FB | 6' | 210 | 25 | | |
| Jack Dolbin | WR | 5'10" | 180 | 26 | | 24 |
| Haven Moses | WR | 6'3" | 208 | 29 | | 12 |
| Rick Upchurch | WR | 5'10" | 170 | 23 | | 18 |
| Bill Van Heusen | WR | 6'1" | 200 | 29 | | 6 |
| Bob Adams | TE | 6'2" | 220 | 29 | | |
| Boyd Brown | TE | 6'4" | 216 | 23 | | |
| Riley Odoms | TE | 6'4" | 230 | 25 | | 24 |
| Jim Turner | K | 6'2" | 205 | 34 | | 86 |

## KANSAS CITY CHIEFS 5-9 Paul Wiggin

| Scores of Each Game | | |
|---|---|---|
| 33 | Denver | 37 |
| 24 | N.Y. JETS | 30 |
| 3 | SAN FRANCISCO | 20 |
| 42 | OAKLAND | 10 |
| 12 | San Diego | 10 |
| 26 | DENVER | 13 |
| 13 | HOUSTON | 17 |
| 34 | Dallas | 31 |
| 3 | Pittsburgh | 28 |
| 24 | DETROIT | *21 |
| 14 | Baltimore | 28 |
| 20 | SAN DIEGO | 28 |
| 14 | Cleveland | 40 |
| 20 | Oakland | 28 |

| Use Name | Pos. | Hgt | Wgt | Age | Int | Pts |
|---|---|---|---|---|---|---|
| Gary Palmer | OT | 6'4" | 255 | 24 | | |
| Charlie Getty | OT | 6'4" | 260 | 23 | | |
| Jim Nicholson | OT | 6'6" | 260 | 25 | | |
| Bill Story | OT | 6'3" | 245 | 23 | | |
| Randy Beisler | OG | 6'4" | 244 | 30 | | |
| Roger Bernhardt | OG | 6'4" | 244 | 25 | | |
| Ed Budde | OG | 6'5" | 265 | 34 | | |
| Tom Condon | OG | 6'3" | 240 | 22 | | |
| Rocky Rasley | OG | 6'3" | 255 | 28 | | |
| Mike Wilson | OG | 6'1" | 250 | 27 | | |
| Charlie Ane | C | 6'1" | 233 | 23 | | |
| Jack Rudnay | C | 6'3" | 240 | 27 | | |
| John Lohmeyer | DE | 6'4" | 230 | 24 | | |
| Bob Maddox | DE | 6'5" | 232 | 26 | | |
| John Matuszak | DE | 6'8" | 275 | 24 | 6 | |
| Louis Ross | DE | 6'6" | 265 | 28 | | |
| Wilbur Young | DE | 6'6" | 285 | 26 | | |
| Buck Buchanan | DT | 6'7" | 270 | 35 | | |
| Larry Estes | DT | 6'6" | 250 | 28 | | |
| Tom Keating | DT | 6'3" | 247 | 32 | | |
| Marv Upshaw | DT | 6'3" | 260 | 28 | | |

| Use Name | Pos. | Hgt | Wgt | Age | Int | Pts |
|---|---|---|---|---|---|---|
| Ken Avery | LB | 6'1" | 227 | 31 | | |
| Tim Kearney | LB | 6'2" | 230 | 24 | | |
| Willie Lanier | LB | 6'1" | 245 | 30 | 5 | |
| Jim Lynch | LB | 6'1" | 225 | 30 | | |
| Al Palewicz | LB | 6'1" | 215 | 25 | | |
| Bill Peterson | LB | 6'3" | 225 | 30 | | |
| Hise Austin | DB | 6'4" | 187 | 24 | | |
| Jim Kearney | DB | 6'2" | 206 | 32 | | |
| Jim Marsalis | DB | 5'11" | 190 | 29 | 1 | |
| Don Martin | DB | 5'11" | 185 | 25 | | |
| Kerry Reardon | DB | 5'11" | 180 | 26 | 3 | |
| Mike Sensibaugh | DB | 5'11" | 192 | 26 | 5 | |
| Emmitt Thomas | DB | 6'2" | 192 | 32 | 6 | |

Clyde Werner — Tendon Injury

| Use Name | Pos. | Hgt | Wgt | Age | Int | Pts |
|---|---|---|---|---|---|---|
| Tony Adams | QB | 6' | 198 | 25 | | |
| Wayne Clark | QB | 6'2" | 203 | 28 | | |
| Len Dawson | QB | 6' | 190 | 41 | | |
| Mike Livingston | QB | 6'3" | 212 | 29 | | 12 |
| Woody Green | HB | 6'1" | 205 | 24 | | 36 |
| Ed Podolak | HB | 6'1" | 205 | 28 | | 30 |
| Charlie Thomas | HB | 5'9" | 180 | 24 | | |
| Doug Dressler (from NE) | FB | 6'3" | 228 | 27 | | 6 |
| MacArthur Lane | FB | 6'1" | 220 | 33 | | 12 |
| Jeff Kinney | HB-FB | 6'2" | 215 | 25 | | 12 |
| Larry Brunson | WR | 5'11" | 180 | 26 | | 12 |
| Reggie Craig | WR | 6' | 187 | 22 | | |
| Barry Pearson | WR | 5'11" | 185 | 25 | | 18 |
| Otis Taylor | WR | 6'2" | 215 | 32 | | |
| Bill Masters | TE | 6'5" | 240 | 31 | | 18 |
| Walter White | TE | 6'3" | 208 | 24 | | 18 |
| Jim McCann | K | 6'2" | 165 | 26 | | |
| Jan Stenerud | K | 6'2" | 187 | 32 | | 96 |
| Jerrel Wilson | K | 6'4" | 222 | 33 | | |

## SAN DIEGO CHARGERS 2-12 Tommy Prothro

| Scores of Each Game | | |
|---|---|---|
| 0 | PITTSBURGH | 37 |
| 17 | Houston | 33 |
| 0 | OAKLAND | 6 |
| 10 | LOS ANGELES | *13 |
| 10 | KANSAS CITY | 12 |
| 0 | Oakland | 25 |
| 24 | N.Y. Giants | 35 |
| 19 | NEW ENGLAND | 33 |
| 17 | DENVER | 27 |
| 13 | Minnesota | 28 |
| 10 | Denver | *13 |
| 28 | Kansas City | 20 |
| 24 | N.Y. JETS | 16 |
| 17 | Cincinnati | 47 |

| Use Name | Pos. | Hgt | Wgt | Age | Int | Pts |
|---|---|---|---|---|---|---|
| Terry Owens | OT | 6'6" | 264 | 31 | | |
| Billy Shields | OT | 6'7" | 260 | 22 | | |
| Russ Washington | OT | 6'6" | 285 | 28 | | |
| Booker Brown | OG | 6'2" | 257 | 22 | | |
| Ira Gordon | OG | 6'3" | 283 | 27 | | |
| Ralph Perretta | OG | 6'2" | 252 | 22 | | |
| Doug Wilkerson | OG | 6'2" | 262 | 28 | | |
| Ed Flanagan | C | 6'3" | 245 | 31 | | |
| Mark Markovich | C | 6'5" | 256 | 22 | | |
| Coy Bacon | DE | 6'4" | 278 | 33 | | |
| Fred Dean | DE | 6'3" | 220 | 23 | | |
| Gary Johnson | DT | 6'2" | 262 | 23 | | |
| Louie Kelcher | DT | 6'5" | 282 | 22 | | |
| John Teerlinck | DT | 6'5" | 250 | 24 | | |
| Greg Wojcik | DT | 6'6" | 270 | 32 | | |

| Use Name | Pos. | Hgt | Wgt | Age | Int | Pts |
|---|---|---|---|---|---|---|
| Billy Andrews | LB | 6' | 220 | 30 | | |
| Don Goode | LB | 6'2" | 225 | 24 | 1 | |
| Tom Graham | LB | 6'2" | 235 | 25 | 2 | |
| Drew Mahalic | LB | 6'4" | 225 | 22 | 1 | |
| Floyd Rice | LB | 6'3" | 235 | 26 | 1 | |
| Frank Tate | LB | 6'3" | 225 | 23 | | |
| Joe Beauchamp | DB | 6' | 184 | 31 | 1 | |
| Danny Colbert | DB | 5'11" | 176 | 24 | 2 | |
| Chris Fletcher | DB | 5'11" | 190 | 26 | 6 | |
| Mike Fuller | DB | 5'9" | 195 | 22 | 1 | 6 |
| Hal Stringert | DB | 5'11" | 180 | 23 | | |
| Maurice Tyler | DB | 6' | 190 | 25 | | |
| Mike Williams | DB | 5'10" | 180 | 21 | 4 | |
| Sam Williams | DB | 6'2" | 186 | 23 | 1 | |

Charles Anthony — Broken Leg
Jim Harrison — Injury
Ken Hutcherson — Leg Injury

| Use Name | Pos. | Hgt | Wgt | Age | Int | Pts |
|---|---|---|---|---|---|---|
| Dan Fouts | QB | 6'3" | 204 | 24 | | 12 |
| Jesse Freitas | QB | 6'1" | 192 | 23 | | |
| Bobby Douglass (from CHI) | HB-QB | 6'2" | 228 | 28 | | 6 |
| Dave Atkins | HB | 6'1" | 208 | 26 | | |
| Glen Bonner | HB | 6'2" | 202 | 23 | | |
| Charlie Smith | HB | 6'1" | 205 | 29 | | |
| Don Woods | HB | 6'1" | 214 | 24 | | 12 |
| Rickey Young | HB | 6'2" | 193 | 21 | | 36 |
| Tony Baker | FB | 5'11" | 215 | 30 | | 6 |
| Bo Matthews | FB | 6'4" | 230 | 23 | | 18 |
| Sam Scarber | FB | 6'2" | 232 | 27 | | 12 |
| Melvin Baker (from NO-NE) | WR | 6' | 192 | 25 | | |
| Gary Garrison | WR | 6'1" | 194 | 31 | | 12 |
| Dwight McDonald | WR | 6'2" | 187 | 24 | | 18 |
| Joe Sweet | WR | 6'2" | 196 | 27 | | |
| Chuck Bradley | TE | 6'6" | 232 | 24 | | |
| Craig Cotton | TE | 6'4" | 222 | 27 | | |
| Pat Curran | TE | 6'3" | 238 | 29 | | 1 |
| Denniss Partee | K | 6'2" | 225 | 29 | | |
| Ray Wersching | K | 5'11" | 222 | 25 | | 56 |

*Overtime

## OAKLAND RAIDERS

### RUSHING

| Last Name | No. | Yds | Avg | TD |
|---|---|---|---|---|
| Banaszak | 187 | 672 | 3.6 | 16 |
| van Eeghen | 136 | 597 | 4.4 | 2 |
| Davis | 112 | 486 | 4.3 | 4 |
| J. Phillips | 63 | 298 | 4.7 | 1 |
| Hubbard | 60 | 294 | 4.9 | 2 |
| Hart | 56 | 173 | 3.1 | 3 |
| Carter | 11 | 27 | 2.5 | 0 |
| Humm | 7 | 21 | 3.0 | 0 |
| Branch | 2 | 18 | 9.0 | 0 |
| Lawrence | 2 | −3 | −1.5 | 0 |
| Stabler | 6 | −5 | −0.8 | 0 |
| Bradshaw | 1 | −5 | −5.0 | 0 |

### RECEIVING

| Last Name | No. | Yds | Avg | TD |
|---|---|---|---|---|
| Branch | 51 | 893 | 18 | 9 |
| Biletnikoff | 43 | 587 | 14 | 2 |
| Moore | 19 | 175 | 9 | 0 |
| Siani | 17 | 294 | 17 | 0 |
| van Eeghen | 12 | 42 | 4 | 1 |
| Davis | 11 | 126 | 12 | 1 |
| Banaszak | 10 | 64 | 6 | 0 |
| Bradshaw | 7 | 180 | 26 | 4 |
| Hubbard | 7 | 81 | 12 | 0 |
| Hart | 6 | 27 | 5 | 0 |
| Casper | 5 | 71 | 14 | 1 |
| J. Phillips | 4 | 25 | 6 | 0 |
| Carter | 2 | 39 | 20 | 0 |
| Bankston | 2 | 21 | 11 | 1 |

### PUNT RETURNS

| Last Name | No. | Yds | Avg | TD |
|---|---|---|---|---|
| Colzie | 48 | 655 | 14 | 0 |
| Atkinson | 8 | 33 | 4 | 0 |
| Phillips | 2 | 0 | 0 | 0 |

### KICKOFF RETURNS

| Last Name | No. | Yds | Avg | TD |
|---|---|---|---|---|
| Hart | 17 | 518 | 31 | 1 |
| J. Phillips | 12 | 310 | 26 | 0 |
| Davis | 9 | 268 | 30 | 0 |
| van Eeghen | 7 | 112 | 16 | 0 |
| Atkinson | 2 | 60 | 30 | 0 |
| Banaszak | 2 | 24 | 12 | 0 |
| Bankston | 1 | 19 | 19 | 0 |
| Carter | 1 | 13 | 13 | 0 |

### PASSING – PUNTING – KICKING

| PASSING | Att | Comp | % | Yds | Yd/Att | TD | Int–% | RK |
|---|---|---|---|---|---|---|---|---|
| Stabler | 293 | 171 | 58 | 2296 | 7.8 | 16 | 24–8 | 8 |
| Humm | 38 | 18 | 47 | 246 | 6.5 | 3 | 2–5 | |
| Lawrence | 15 | 5 | 33 | 50 | 3.3 | 0 | 1–7 | |
| Blanda | 3 | 1 | 33 | 11 | 3.7 | 0 | 1–33 | |
| Guy | 1 | 1 | 100 | 22 | 22.0 | 0 | 0–0 | |

| PUNTING | No | Avg |
|---|---|---|
| Guy | 68 | 43.8 |

| KICKING | XP | Att | % | FG | Att | % |
|---|---|---|---|---|---|---|
| Blanda | 44 | 48 | 96 | 13 | 21 | 62 |

## DENVER BRONCOS

### RUSHING

| Last Name | No. | Yds | Avg | TD |
|---|---|---|---|---|
| Keyworth | 182 | 725 | 4.0 | 3 |
| Little | 125 | 445 | 3.6 | 2 |
| Lynch | 57 | 218 | 3.8 | 3 |
| Armstrong | 31 | 155 | 5.0 | 0 |
| Ross | 42 | 121 | 2.9 | 0 |
| Upchurch | 16 | 97 | 6.1 | 1 |
| Dolbin | 5 | 72 | 14.4 | 0 |
| Hufnagel | 8 | 47 | 5.9 | 0 |
| Ramsey | 6 | 38 | 6.3 | 0 |
| Odoms | 5 | 27 | 5.4 | 0 |
| Van Heusen | 2 | 26 | 13.0 | 0 |
| Johnson | 10 | 21 | 2.1 | 0 |
| Franckowiak | 1 | 1 | 1.0 | 0 |

### RECEIVING

| Last Name | No. | Yds | Avg | TD |
|---|---|---|---|---|
| Keyworth | 42 | 314 | 8 | 1 |
| Odoms | 40 | 544 | 14 | 3 |
| Moses | 29 | 505 | 17 | 2 |
| Little | 29 | 308 | 11 | 2 |
| Dolbin | 22 | 421 | 19 | 3 |
| Upchurch | 18 | 436 | 24 | 2 |
| Van Heusen | 15 | 246 | 16 | 0 |
| Ross | 7 | 69 | 10 | 0 |
| Lynch | 6 | 33 | 6 | 1 |
| Brown | 1 | 14 | 14 | 0 |
| Armstrong | 1 | 10 | 10 | 0 |

### PUNT RETURNS

| Last Name | No. | Yds | Avg | TD |
|---|---|---|---|---|
| Upchurch | 27 | 312 | 12 | 0 |
| Thompson | 13 | 158 | 12 | 0 |
| Lynch | 1 | 0 | 0 | 0 |

### KICKOFF RETURNS

| Last Name | No. | Yds | Avg | TD |
|---|---|---|---|---|
| Upchurch | 40 | 1084 | 27 | 0 |
| Little | 16 | 307 | 19 | 0 |
| Ross | 1 | 20 | 20 | 0 |
| Severson | 1 | 20 | 20 | 0 |
| Maples | 1 | 15 | 15 | 0 |

### PASSING – PUNTING – KICKING

| PASSING | Att | Comp | % | Yds | Yd/Att | TD | Int–% | RK |
|---|---|---|---|---|---|---|---|---|
| Ramsey | 233 | 128 | 55 | 1562 | 6.7 | 9 | 14–6 | 15 |
| Johnson | 142 | 65 | 46 | 1021 | 7.2 | 5 | 12–9 | |
| Hufnagel | 51 | 16 | 31 | 287 | 5.6 | 1 | 8–16 | |
| Van Heusen | 1 | 1 | 100 | 30 | 30.0 | 0 | 0–0 | |

| PUNTING | No | Avg |
|---|---|---|
| Van Heusen | 63 | 39.9 |

| KICKING | XP | Att | % | FG | Att | % |
|---|---|---|---|---|---|---|
| Turner | 23 | 26 | 88 | 21 | 28 | 75 |

## KANSAS CITY CHIEFS

### RUSHING

| Last Name | No. | Yds | Avg | TD |
|---|---|---|---|---|
| Green | 167 | 611 | 3.7 | 5 |
| Podolak | 102 | 351 | 3.4 | 3 |
| Lane | 79 | 311 | 3.9 | 2 |
| Kinney | 85 | 304 | 3.6 | 2 |
| Brunson | 2 | 89 | 44.5 | 0 |
| Livingston | 13 | 68 | 5.2 | 1 |
| Adams | 8 | 42 | 5.3 | 0 |
| Dressler | 6 | 24 | 4.0 | 0 |
| Dawson | 5 | 7 | 1.4 | 0 |
| White | 3 | −10 | −3.3 | 0 |

### RECEIVING

| Last Name | No. | Yds | Avg | TD |
|---|---|---|---|---|
| Podolak | 37 | 332 | 9 | 2 |
| Pearson | 36 | 608 | 17 | 3 |
| Lane | 25 | 202 | 8 | 0 |
| Masters | 24 | 314 | 13 | 3 |
| White | 23 | 559 | 24 | 3 |
| Brunson | 23 | 398 | 17 | 2 |
| Green | 23 | 215 | 9 | 1 |
| Kinney | 21 | 148 | 7 | 0 |
| Dressler | 3 | 6 | 2 | 1 |
| Craig | 1 | 10 | 10 | 0 |
| LaGrand | 1 | −1 | −1 | 0 |
| Adams | 1 | −7 | −7 | 0 |

### PUNT RETURNS

| Last Name | No. | Yds | Avg | TD |
|---|---|---|---|---|
| Thomas | 12 | 112 | 9 | 0 |
| Podolak | 13 | 96 | 7 | 0 |
| Reardon | 5 | 41 | 8 | 0 |
| Pearson | 2 | 31 | 16 | 0 |
| Craig | 4 | 19 | 5 | 0 |
| Brunson | 1 | 4 | 4 | 0 |

### KICKOFF RETURNS

| Last Name | No. | Yds | Avg | TD |
|---|---|---|---|---|
| Thomas | 22 | 516 | 24 | 0 |
| Green | 16 | 343 | 21 | 0 |
| Craig | 10 | 247 | 25 | 0 |
| Kinney | 2 | 39 | 20 | 0 |
| Dressler | 1 | 18 | 18 | 0 |
| Brunson | 1 | 8 | 8 | 0 |
| Peterson | 1 | 8 | 8 | 0 |

### PASSING – PUNTING – KICKING

| PASSING | Att | Comp | % | Yds | Yd/Att | TD | Int–% | RK |
|---|---|---|---|---|---|---|---|---|
| Livingston | 176 | 88 | 50 | 1245 | 7.1 | 8 | 6–3 | 7 |
| Dawson | 140 | 93 | 66 | 1095 | 7.8 | 5 | 4–3 | 2 |
| Adams | 77 | 36 | 47 | 445 | 5.8 | 2 | 4–5 | |
| Podolak | 1 | 0 | 0 | 0 | 0.0 | 0 | 1–100 | |
| White | 1 | 0 | 0 | 0 | 0.0 | 0 | 1–100 | |

| PUNTING | No | Avg |
|---|---|---|
| Wilson | 54 | 41.4 |
| McCann | 14 | 35.2 |
| Dressler | 4 | 25.0 |

| KICKING | XP | Att | % | FG | Att | % |
|---|---|---|---|---|---|---|
| Stenerud | 30 | 31 | 97 | 22 | 32 | 69 |

## SAN DIEGO CHARGERS

### RUSHING

| Last Name | No. | Yds | Avg | TD |
|---|---|---|---|---|
| Young | 138 | 577 | 4.2 | 5 |
| Woods | 87 | 317 | 3.6 | 2 |
| Matthews | 71 | 254 | 3.6 | 3 |
| Fouts | 23 | 170 | 7.4 | 2 |
| T. Baker | 42 | 131 | 3.1 | 1 |
| Bonner | 28 | 120 | 4.3 | 0 |
| Scarber | 15 | 68 | 4.5 | 1 |
| Freitas | 11 | 56 | 5.1 | 0 |
| Douglass | 10 | 42 | 4.2 | 0 |
| Douglass | 5 | 34 | 6.8 | 1 |
| Garrison | 3 | 30 | 10.0 | 0 |
| Curran | 3 | 21 | 7.0 | 0 |
| Carter | 2 | 11 | 5.5 | 0 |
| M. Baker | 1 | 21 | 21.0 | 0 |
| Atkins | 1 | 4 | 4.0 | 0 |

### RECEIVING

| Last Name | No. | Yds | Avg | TD |
|---|---|---|---|---|
| Curran | 45 | 619 | 14 | 0 |
| Garrison | 27 | 438 | 16 | 2 |
| Young | 21 | 166 | 8 | 1 |
| McDonald | 19 | 298 | 16 | 3 |
| Woods | 13 | 101 | 8 | 0 |
| Scarber | 12 | 68 | 6 | 1 |
| Matthews | 9 | 59 | 7 | 0 |
| Sweet | 8 | 147 | 18 | 0 |
| T. Baker | 6 | 27 | 5 | 0 |
| M. Baker | 2 | 26 | 13 | 0 |
| Bonner | 2 | 8 | 4 | 0 |
| Bradley | 1 | 42 | 42 | 0 |

### PUNT RETURNS

| Last Name | No. | Yds | Avg | TD |
|---|---|---|---|---|
| Fuller | 36 | 410 | 11 | 1 |
| Colbert | 2 | 32 | 16 | 0 |

### KICKOFF RETURNS

| Last Name | No. | Yds | Avg | TD |
|---|---|---|---|---|
| Fuller | 31 | 725 | 23 | 0 |
| Young | 15 | 323 | 22 | 0 |
| Smith | 8 | 222 | 28 | 0 |
| Andrews | 6 | 93 | 16 | 0 |
| Colbert | 5 | 91 | 18 | 0 |
| Curran | 3 | 28 | 9 | 0 |
| Markovich | 1 | 0 | 0 | 0 |

### PASSING – PUNTING – KICKING

| PASSING | Att | Comp | % | Yds | Yd/Att | TD | Int–% | RK |
|---|---|---|---|---|---|---|---|---|
| Fouts | 195 | 106 | 54 | 1396 | 7.2 | 2 | 10–5 | 12 |
| Freitas | 110 | 49 | 45 | 525 | 4.8 | 5 | 5–5 | |
| Douglass | 47 | 15 | 32 | 140 | 3.0 | 0 | 3–6 | |

| PUNTING | No | Avg |
|---|---|---|
| Partee | 79 | 36.8 |

| KICKING | XP | Att | % | FG | Att | % |
|---|---|---|---|---|---|---|
| Wersching | 20 | 21 | 95 | 12 | 24 | 50 |

# 1975 Championship Games

## SCORING

| | | | | | |
|---|---|---|---|---|---|
| LOS ANGELES | 0 | 0 | 0 | 7– | 7 |
| DALLAS | 7 | 14 | 13 | 3– | 37 |

**First Quarter**
Dall. P.Pearson, 18 yard pass from Staubach
PAT–Fritsch (kick)

**Second Quarter**
Dall. Richards, 4 yard pass from Staubach
PAT–Fritsch (kick)
Dall. P. Pearson, 15 yard pass from Staubach
PAT–Fritsch (kick)

**Third Quarter**
Dall. P. Pearson, 19 yard pass from Staubach
PAT–Fritsch (kick)
Dall. Fritsch, 40 yard field goal
Dall. Fritsch, 26 yard field goal

**Fourth Quarter**
L.A. Cappelletti, 1 yard rush
PAT–Dempsey (kick)
Dall. Fritsch, 26 yard field goal

## TEAM STATISTICS

| L.A. | | DALLAS |
|---|---|---|
| 9 | First Downs – Total | 24 |
| 1 | First Downs – Rushing | 8 |
| 7 | First Downs – Passing | 15 |
| 1 | First Downs – Penalty | 1 |
| 1 | Fumbles – Number | 1 |
| 0 | Fumbles – Lost Ball | 0 |
| 4 | Penalties – Number | 5 |
| 25 | Yards Penalized | 59 |
| 2 | Missed Field Goals | 0 |
| 45 | Offensive Plays | 78 |
| 118 | Net Yards | 441 |
| 2.6 | Average Gain | 5.7 |
| 3 | Giveaways | 1 |
| 1 | Takeaways | 3 |
| –2 | Difference | +2 |

## A Study in Contrasts

In the NFC semifinal match Los Angeles won easily over St. Louis, 35-23. By contrast, Dallas, the wild-card team, came back from a 14-10 deficit with 24 seconds left to play (a 50-yard TD bomb from Roger Staubach to Drew Pearson) to astonish Minnesota 17-14. But past performances went out the window in this championship game as the Cowboys totally humiliated the favorite Rams 37-7.

The game was one of the most lopsided ever staged in the playoffs, and represented a drastic difference in playing styles. While coach Chuck Knox's Rams played it close to the vest and suffered for it as a consequence, coach Tom Landry did just the opposite with Dallas. Leading 14-0 in the second quarter as the result of two touchdown passes by Staubach, Landry had the Cowboys go for broke rather than cautiously sit on the lead. Staubach connected to Preston Pearson on a 15-yard pass to run the score to 21-0 and then called several time outs to try and get into field goal range as the half ran out. The Rams play on the other hand was best typified by their choice on the first series of downs when the game opened. Facing third down and 15 from their 30, they elected to run a sweep. It was unsuccessful and they punted the ball away.

Dallas ran the score to 34-0 in the third quarter behind Staubach's fourth TD pass of the day, and two field goals by Toni Fritsch. In the 4th quarter the Rams scored a touchdown to avoid their first home field shutout in 30 years. Fritsch then added another field goal to make the final score 37-7.

Part of the Rams fall from grace following a 12-2 regular season was the inability of All-Pro ends Jack Youngblood and Fred Dryer to penetrate Staubach even once, and for Lawrence McCutcheon, Pro Bowl running back, to gain ten yards in 11 rushes. Also stopped cold was All-Pro wide receiver Harold Jackson, who had no completions for the day. As a final capper, last year's Pro Bowl Most Valuable Player, quarterback James Harris, suffering from an injured shoulder, was yanked early in the first quarter after throwing an interception.

## INDIVIDUAL STATISTICS

### RUSHING

| LOS ANGELES | No. | Yds | Avg. | DALLAS | No | Yds | Avg. |
|---|---|---|---|---|---|---|---|
| Jaworski | 2 | 12 | 6.0 | Newhouse | 16 | 64 | 4.0 |
| McCutcheon | 11 | 10 | 0.9 | Staubach | 7 | 54 | 7.7 |
| Cappelletti | 1 | 1 | 1.0 | Dennison | 13 | 35 | 2.7 |
| Scribner | 1 | 1 | 1.0 | P. Pearson | 7 | 20 | 2.9 |
| Bryant | 1 | –2 | –2.0 | Young | 6 | 17 | 2.8 |
| | 16 | 22 | 1.4 | Fuggett | 1 | 5 | 5.0 |
| | | | | | 50 | 195 | 3.9 |

### RECEIVING

| LOS ANGELES | No. | Yds | Avg. | DALLAS | No | Yds | Avg. |
|---|---|---|---|---|---|---|---|
| Jessie | 4 | 52 | 13.0 | P. Pearson | 7 | 123 | 17.6 |
| McCutcheon | 3 | 39 | 13.0 | D. Pearson | 5 | 46 | 9.2 |
| Nelson | 3 | 28 | 9.3 | Richards | 2 | 46 | 23.0 |
| Bryant | 1 | 28 | 28.0 | Fuggett | 2 | 5 | 2.5 |
| | 11 | 147 | 13.4 | Young | 1 | 15 | 15.0 |
| | | | | Dennison | 1 | 11 | 11.0 |
| | | | | | 18 | 246 | 13.7 |

### PUNTING

| | No | Avg. | | No | Avg. |
|---|---|---|---|---|---|
| Carrell | 7 | 35.4 | Hoopes | 4 | 34.8 |

### PUNT RETURNS

| | No | Yds | Avg. | | No | Yds | Avg. |
|---|---|---|---|---|---|---|---|
| Scribner | 2 | 3 | 1.5 | Richards | 3 | 17 | 5.7 |
| | | | | Harris | 1 | 9 | 9.0 |
| | | | | | 4 | 26 | 6.5 |

### KICKOFF RETURNS

| | No | Yds | Avg. | | No | Yds | Avg. |
|---|---|---|---|---|---|---|---|
| McGee | 5 | 103 | 20.6 | Dennison | 2 | 47 | 23.5 |
| Bryant | 2 | 49 | 24.5 | | | | |
| Jessie | 1 | 15 | 15.0 | | | | |
| | 8 | 167 | 20.9 | | | | |

### INTERCEPTION RETURNS

| | No | Yds | Avg. | | No | Yds | Avg. |
|---|---|---|---|---|---|---|---|
| Simpson | 1 | 37 | 37.0 | Lewis | 2 | 20 | 10.0 |
| | | | | C. Harris | 1 | 22 | 22.0 |
| | | | | | 3 | 42 | 14.0 |

### PASSING

| LOS ANGELES | Att | Comp | Comp Pct. | Yds | Int | Yds/ Att. | Yds/ Comp | Yards Lost Tackled |
|---|---|---|---|---|---|---|---|---|
| Jaworski | 22 | 11 | 50.0 | 147 | 2 | 6.7 | 13.4 | 5–51 |
| J. Harris | 2 | 0 | 00.0 | 0 | 1 | – | – | – |
| | 24 | 11 | 45.8 | 147 | 3 | 6.1 | 13.4 | 5–51 |

| DALLAS | Att | Comp | Comp Pct. | Yds | Int | Yds/ Att. | Yds/ Comp | Yards Lost Tackled |
|---|---|---|---|---|---|---|---|---|
| Staubach | 26 | 16 | 61.5 | 220 | 1 | 8.5 | 13.8 | 0–0 |
| Longley | 2 | 2 | 100.0 | 26 | 0 | 13.0 | 13.0 | 0–0 |
| | 28 | 18 | 64.3 | 246 | 1 | 8.8 | 13.7 | 0–0 |

---

## SCORING

| | | | | | |
|---|---|---|---|---|---|
| PITTSBURGH | 0 | 3 | 0 | 13– | 16 |
| OAKLAND | 0 | 0 | 0 | 10– | 10 |

**Second Quarter**
Pit. Gerela, 36 yard field goal

**Fourth Quarter**
Pit. Harris, 25 yard rush
PAT–Gerela (kick)
Oak. Siani, 14 yard pass from Stabler
PAT–Blanda (kick)
Pit. Stallworth, 20 yard pass from Bradshaw
PAT–Kick no good
Oak. Blanda, 41 yard field goal.

## TEAM STATISTICS

| PIT. | | OAK. |
|---|---|---|
| 16 | First Downs – Total | 18 |
| 5 | First Downs – Rushing | 3 |
| 10 | First Downs – Passing | 13 |
| 1 | First Downs – Penalty | 2 |
| 5 | Fumbles – Number | 4 |
| 5 | Fumbles – Lost Ball | 3 |
| 3 | Penalties – Number | 4 |
| 32 | Yards Penalized | 40 |
| 2 | Missed Field Goals | 1 |
| 64 | Offensive Plays | 76 |
| 332 | Net Yards | 321 |
| 5.2 | Average Gain | 4.2 |
| 8 | Giveaways | 5 |
| 5 | Takeaways | 8 |
| –3 | Difference | +3 |

## A Cold Reception

Oakland had done everything they could to prepare for Pittsburgh in the AFC Championship game. They went through the season with an 11-3 record and then held off Cincinnati 31-28 in the semifinal game. But they were met with an ice-covered and snow swept field and bone-chilling winds, plus the nearly impregnable defense of the Steelers. When the long afternoon came to a close they found themselves on the short end of a 16-10 score and another summer in which to think of the Super Bowl again.

Pittsburgh got ready for their second Super Bowl try by going through a 12-2 campaign and then stopping the Baltimore resurgence 28-10. The big plus for the Steelers was the return to fulltime duty after eight weeks of a hurting, defensive tackle Joe Greene.

When the first half came to a close, Pittsburgh led 3-0 as the result of a 36-yard field goal by Roy Gerela. In the third quarter the hard-hitting defensive battle continued with both teams unable to reach the scoreboard. Then, within a six minutes stretch of the final quarter Pittsburgh's Franco Harris bruised his way for 25 yards into the end zone, Oakland quarterback Ken Stabler hit Mike Siani with a 14-yard pass, and Terry Bradshaw, the Steeler's quarterback, hit John Stallworth with a 20-yard pass. Gerela's kick failed, and the score stood at 16-7.

By the time Oakland got on the board again there were 12 seconds left to play. Stabler had taken over the ball with 1:31 on the clock and drove his club from the Oakland 35 to the Pittsburgh 24. Ageless George Blanda, who had reached an NFL milestone during the season by scoring his 2000th career point, booted a 41-yard field goal to put the score at 16-10.

On the ensuing kickoff to Pittsburgh, Oakland went for the miracle by attempting a dribbler. Marv Hubbard recovered the ball for Oakland with seven seconds left. Stabler, at his own 45, threw a long bomb which hit Cliff Branch on the 15. But the Steelers were there to stop him as the season ran out for Oakland.

## INDIVIDUAL STATISTICS

### RUSHING

| PITTSBURGH | No | Yds | Avg. | OAKLAND | No | Yds | Avg. |
|---|---|---|---|---|---|---|---|
| Harris | 27 | 79 | 2.9 | Banaszak | 8 | 33 | 4.1 |
| Bradshaw | 2 | 22 | 11.0 | Hubbard | 10 | 30 | 3.0 |
| Bleier | 10 | 16 | 1.6 | Davis | 13 | 29 | 2.2 |
| | 39 | 117 | 3.0 | Phillips | 1 | 1 | 1.0 |
| | | | | | 32 | 93 | 2.9 |

### RECEIVING

| PITTSBURGH | No | Yds | Avg. | OAKLAND | No | Yds | Avg. |
|---|---|---|---|---|---|---|---|
| Harris | 5 | 58 | 11.6 | Siani | 5 | 80 | 18.0 |
| Grossman | 4 | 36 | 9.0 | Casper | 5 | 67 | 13.4 |
| Swann | 2 | 45 | 22.5 | Branch | 2 | 56 | 28.0 |
| Stallworth | 2 | 30 | 15.0 | Banaszak | 2 | 12 | 6.0 |
| Lewis | 1 | 33 | 33.0 | Moore | 2 | 12 | 6.0 |
| L. Brown | 1 | 13 | 13.0 | Hart | 1 | 16 | 16.0 |
| | 15 | 215 | 14.3 | Davis | 1 | 3 | 3.0 |
| | | | | | 18 | 246 | 13.7 |

### PUNTING

| | No | Avg. | | No | Avg. |
|---|---|---|---|---|---|
| Walden | 4 | 38.5 | Guy | 8 | 37.8 |

### PUNT RETURNS

| | No | Yds | Avg. | | No | Yds | Avg. |
|---|---|---|---|---|---|---|---|
| D. Brown | 2 | 28 | 14.0 | Siani | 1 | 0 | 0.0 |
| Collier | 1 | 0 | 0.0 | | | | |
| | 3 | 28 | 9.3 | | | | |

### KICKOFF RETURNS

| | No | Yds | Avg. | | No | Yds | Avg. |
|---|---|---|---|---|---|---|---|
| Collier | 2 | 57 | 28.5 | Davis | 3 | 56 | 18.7 |
| Harrison | 1 | 2 | 2.0 | Banaszak | 1 | 15 | 15.0 |
| | 3 | 59 | 19.7 | | 4 | 71 | 17.8 |

### INTERCEPTION RETURNS

| | No | Yds | Avg. | | No | Yds | Avg. |
|---|---|---|---|---|---|---|---|
| Wagner | 2 | 34 | 17.0 | Tatum | 2 | 8 | 4.0 |
| | | | | M. Johnson | 1 | 11 | 11.0 |
| | | | | | 3 | 19 | 6.3 |

### PASSING

| PITTSBURGH | Att | Comp | Comp Pct. | Yds | Int | Yds/ Att. | Yds/ Comp | Yards Lost Tackled |
|---|---|---|---|---|---|---|---|---|
| Bradshaw | 25 | 15 | 60.0 | 215 | 3 | 8.6 | 14.3 | 0–0 |

| OAKLAND | Att | Comp | Comp Pct. | Yds | Int | Yds/ Att. | Yds/ Comp | Yards Lost Tackled |
|---|---|---|---|---|---|---|---|---|
| Stabler | 42 | 18 | 42.9 | 246 | 2 | 5.9 | 13.7 | 2–18 |

# Swann's Song

Unlike past Super Bowl efforts, which had more fanfare off the field than on, this year's edition featured enough excitement to compete with the pre-game show. Favorite Pittsburgh, returning for the second time in two years, was facing Dallas, the first wildcard team to ever reach the NFL finals.

Through the first three quarters Dallas held a 10-7 lead. Then, at 3:32 of the final quarter, Reggie Harrison, a Pittsburgh reserve running back who plays on special teams, blocked a punt by Mitch Hoopes at the Dallas 9. The ball bounced off Harrison's face hard enough to wind up in the Dallas end zone, good enough for a two-point safety and run the score to 10-9. It was a play which was considered the turning point of the game. Roy Gerela put Pittsburgh in front for the first time with a 36-yard field at 6:19. A few minutes later Mike Wagner intercepted a Roger Staubach pass and returned it 19 yards to the Dallas 7. Terry Bradshaw was unable to get the touchdown, but Gerela booted an 18-yard field goal.

With the score 15-10, the game's hero, Lynn Swann, took a 59-yard pass from Bradshaw and ran it 5 yards into the end zone at 11:58. The kick failed and the stage was set for the final dramatics. The Cowboys drove 80 yards in five plays with under two minutes to play to make the score 21-17. On the drive, two passes of 30 and 11 yards from Staubach to Drew Pearson proved the key. Terry Hanratty replaced Bradshaw, who had been shaken up on his 64-yard pass to Swann, for Pittsburgh's last offensive series and found himself with fourth down and 9 to go on the Dallas 41. Only 1:28 was left to play and coach Chuck Noll decided to gamble, owing to the fact that Dallas had no time outs left. Rather than punt and risk the run back, he had the Steelers go for the run. They got two yards and Dallas took possession. Five plays later the game was over and Pittsburgh had its second straight Super Bowl triumph.

Dallas coach Tom Landry blamed the defeat on the blocked punt by Harrison, which he said changed the momentum of the game around. He may have been right, but Swann's performance—which earned him the game's Most Valuable Player award—was momentum enough for the Steelers. Hospitalized only two weeks earlier with a concussion, and dropping passes in practice, the fleet-footed receiver returned to catch four passes for an astonishing total of 161 yards—a Super Bowl record certain to stand for many years.

## LINEUPS

| PITTSBURGH | | DALLAS |
|---|---|---|
| | **OFFENSE** | |
| Stallworth | WR | Richards |
| Kolb | LT | Neely |
| Clack | LG | Lawless |
| Mansfield | C | Fitzgerald |
| Mullins | RG | Nye |
| Gravelle | RT | Wright |
| L. Brown | TE | Fugett |
| Swann | WR | D. Pearson |
| Bradshaw | QB | Staubach |
| Bleier | RB | P. Pearson |
| F. Harris | RB | Newhouse |
| | **DEFENSE** | |
| Greenwood | LE | Jones |
| Green | LT | Pugh |
| Holmes | RT | Cole |
| D. White | RE | Martin |
| Ham | LLB | D. Edwards |
| Lambert | MLB | Jordan |
| Russell | RLB | Lewis |
| Thomas | LCB | Washington |
| Blount | RCB | Renfro |
| Wagner | LS | Waters |
| G. Edwards | RS | C. Harris |

### SUBSTITUTES

**PITTSBURGH**

| OFFENSE | |
|---|---|
| Collier | Hanratty |
| S. Davis | Harrison |
| Fuqua | Lewis |
| Garrett | Reavis |
| Grossman | Webster |
| **DEFENSE** | |
| Allen | Furness |
| Banaszak | Kellum |
| Bradley | Shell |
| D. Brown | Toews |
| **KICKERS** | |
| Gerela | Walden |

**DALLAS**

| OFFENSE | |
|---|---|
| K. Davis | P. Howard |
| Dennison | R. Howard |
| Donovan | Scott |
| DuPree | Young |
| **DEFENSE** | |
| Barnes | Hughes |
| Breunig | Peterson |
| Capone | R. White |
| Gregory | Woolsey |
| Henderson | |
| **Kickers** | |
| Fritsch | Hoopes |

## SCORING

| | | | | | | | |
|---|---|---|---|---|---|---|---|
| **PITTSBURGH** | 7 | 0 | 0 | 14—21 |
| **DALLAS** | 7 | 3 | 0 | 7—17 |

**First Quarter**

| Dall. | D. Pearson, 29 yard pass from Staubach | 4:36 |
|---|---|---|
| | PAT — Fritsch (kick) | |
| Pitt. | Grossman, 7 yard pass from Bradshaw | 3:03 |
| | PAT — Gerela (kick) | |

**Second Quarter**

| Dall. | Fritsch, 36 yard field goal | 0:15 |
|---|---|---|

**Fourth Quarter**

| Pitt. | Safety — Harrison blocked punt out of end zone | 3:32 |
|---|---|---|
| Pitt. | Gerela, 36 yard field goal | 6:19 |
| Pitt. | Gerela, 18 yard field goal | 8:23 |
| Pitt. | Swann, 64 yard pass from Bradshaw | 11:58 |
| | PAT — Gerela (kick — failed) | |
| Dall. | P. Howard, 34 yard pass from Staubach | 13:12 |
| | PAT — Fritsch (kick) | |

## TEAM STATISTICS

| PITT. | | DALL. |
|---|---|---|
| 13 | First Downs — Total | 14 |
| 7 | First Downs — Rushing | 6 |
| 6 | First Downs — Passing | 8 |
| 0 | First Downs — Penalty | 0 |
| 4 | Fumbles — Number | 4 |
| 0 | Fumbles — Lost Ball | 0 |
| 0 | Penalties — Number | 2 |
| 0 | Yards Penalized | 20 |
| 2 | Missed Field Goals | 0 |
| 67 | Offensive Plays | 62 |
| 339 | Net Yards | 270 |
| 5.1 | Average Gain | 4.4 |
| 0 | Giveaways | 3 |
| 3 | Takeaways | 0 |
| +3 | Difference | -3 |

## INDIVIDUAL STATISTICS

| PITTSBURGH | No | Yds | Avg. | DALLAS | No | Yds | Avg. |
|---|---|---|---|---|---|---|---|
| | | | | **RUSHING** | | | |
| F. Harris | 27 | 82 | 3.0 | Newhouse | 16 | 56 | 3.5 |
| Bleier | 15 | 51 | 3.4 | Staubach | 5 | 22 | 4.4 |
| Bradshaw | 4 | 16 | 4.0 | Dennison | 5 | 16 | 3.2 |
| | 46 | 149 | 3.2 | P. Pearson | 5 | 14 | 2.8 |
| | | | | | 31 | 108 | 3.5 |
| | | | | **RECEIVING** | | | |
| Swann | 4 | 161 | 40.3 | P. Pearson | 5 | 53 | 10.6 |
| Stallworth | 2 | 8 | 4.0 | Young | 3 | 31 | 10.3 |
| F. Harris | 1 | 26 | 26.0 | D. Pearson | 2 | 59 | 29.5 |
| L. Brown | 1 | 7 | 7.0 | Newhouse | 2 | 12 | 6.0 |
| Grossman | 1 | 7 | 7.0 | P. Howard | 1 | 34 | 34.0 |
| | 9 | 209 | 23.2 | Fugett | 1 | 9 | 9.0 |
| | | | | Dennison | 1 | 6 | 6.0 |
| | | | | | 15 | 204 | 13.6 |
| | | | | **PUNTING** | | | |
| Walden | 4 | | 39.8 | Hoopes | 7 | | 35.0 |
| | | | | **PUNT RETURNS** | | | |
| D. Brown | 3 | 14 | 4.7 | Richards | 1 | 3 | 3.0 |
| G. Edwards | 2 | 17 | 8.5 | | | | |
| | 5 | 31 | 6.2 | | | | |
| | | | | **KICKOFF RETURNS** | | | |
| Blount | 3 | 64 | 21.3 | P. Pearson | 4 | 48 | 12.0 |
| Collier | 1 | 25 | 25.0 | Henderson | *0 | 48 | — |
| | 4 | 89 | 22.3 | | 4 | 96 | 24.0 |
| | | | | * = lateral | | | |
| | | | | **INTERCEPTION RETURNS** | | | |
| Thomas | 1 | 35 | 35.0 | none | | | |
| G. Edwards | 1 | 35 | 35.0 | | | | |
| Wagner | 1 | 19 | 19.0 | | | | |
| | 3 | 89 | 29.7 | | | | |

### PASSING

| PITTSBURGH | Att | Comp | Comp Pct. | Yds. | Int | Yds/ Att. | Comp | Yards Lost Tackled |
|---|---|---|---|---|---|---|---|---|
| Bradshaw | 19 | 9 | 47.4 | 209 | 0 | 11.0 | 23.2 | 2—19 |
| **DALLAS** | | | | | | | | |
| Staubach | 24 | 15 | 62.5 | 204 | 3 | 8.5 | 13.6 | 7—42 |

# 1976 N.F.C. THE VIKES — Bridesmaids, Again

## EASTERN DIVISION

**Dallas Cowboys** — Providing themselves beyond expectations with a trip to the Super Bowl the previous year, the Pokes rung up 11 victories and eight Pro Bowl selections (more than any team except Pittsburgh) on the way to a first-place finish that was tarnished by their first-round playoff failure against Los Angeles. Dallas' offense scored just 13 TD's in its last eight games, however, as the need for a breakaway running threat became more evident. While the pass catching chores appeared to be in good hands as Drew Pearson led the NFC in receptions and Billy Joe DuPree set a club record for catches by a tight end (42), only twice did a Cowboy rusher gain over 100 yards in a game.

**Washington Redskins** — After making four major trades and spending a bundle on free agents John Riggins, Calvin Hill and Jean Fugett before the season began, the pressure was on Head Coach George Allen to produce a winner. The Skins squeaked past St. Louis for the NFC "Wild Card" spot before Minnesota humiliated them in the playoffs. Critics remained divided all year on the question of who between Billy Kilmer and Joe Theismann should be the starting QB, but the feisty Kilmer emerged as the No. 1 man after engineering clutch victories down the stretch. As usual, the Skins' special teams were magnificent as Eddie Brown fell just a few yards short of an NFL punt return record and PK Mark Moseley led the NFC in scoring.

**St. Louis Cardinals** — Despite leading the league in offense and featuring three All-Pros in their offensive line, the 10-4 Cards failed to make the playoffs because of their two losses to conference rival Washington, also 10-4 for the year. The "Cardiac" crew won eight of its 10 games by seven points or less, four of them coming after halftime deficits. Their most dramatic victory came in Week No. 10 when they rallied from 15 points behind in the second half to nip the Rams 30-28 on Jim Bakken's 25-yard FG with four seconds left. But the next week at home against the Skins, the Cards suffered a costly emotional letdown, losing 16-10 after usually reliable WR Mel Gray dropped a last-minute endzone pass that would have won the game. After losing 19-14 the next week in Dallas, one play again stood out—an apparent pass interference penalty against TE J.V. Cain in the endzone with a minute remaining that was never called.

**Philadelphia Eagles** — Well-aware of the long-range drafting deficiencies caused by earlier trades for Roman Gabriel, Mike Boryla and Bill Bergey, rookie Head Coach Dick Vermeil announced at the beginning of the season it would take at least five years to turn things around in Philly. After Gabriel had trouble coming back from off-season knee surgery and Boryla finished the year with the lowest passing average per play among starting NFL QB's, the stage was set for the deal with L.A. that brought in strong-armed Ron Jaworski before the '77 season began. Each of the Eagles' four wins were against losing teams, and at one point in the second half of the season, they lost five straight and scored only 17 points.

**New York Giants** — Equipped with a flashy new stadium in New Jersey, the Giants couldn't help but be associated with the ill-fated WFL. In April they signed FB Larry Csonka, and after an 0-7 start, they replaced Head Coach Bill Arnsparger with Zonk's WFL mentor in Memphis, John McVay. The Giants finished 3-4 under McVay, good enough to win him a two-year contract. They finally won their first game the 10th week, upsetting Washington 12-9 behind a strong defense led by LB's Brad Van Pelt and Harry Carson. The offense, particularly the line, was weak all year, however, as Craig Morton's mediocre quarterbacking signalled his departure to Denver and Csonka and OT Tom Mullen were knocked out late in the season with knee injuries.

## CENTRAL DIVISION

**Minnesota Vikings** — Fighting off repeated claims that they were too old, the Vikes had another banner year, grabbing their eighth straight division title. After WR John Gilliam and RB Ed Marinaro became free agents and left the team, newcomer WR's Ahmad Rashad and Sammy White, the latter a brilliant rookie, picked up the slack offensively with more than 50 catches apiece. Multi-purpose RB Chuck Foreman led the team in receiving and rushing while Fran Tarkenton continued to capture all of the NFL's major passing records. But after their fourth frustrating Super Bowl loss, Foreman threatened not to return unless his salary increased and Tarkenton said he might retire to become another jock-turned-TV broadcaster.

**Chicago Bears** — Jack Pardee was named NFC Coach of the Year for piloting the Bears to a 7-7 finish, their best since '68. With a demanding schedule forcing them to take on six playoff qualifiers, they responded with two victories among the six—33-7 over Washington and 14-13 over Minnesota—as well as tough one-point losses to Oakland and Minnesota that would have been wins if not for faulty kicking. But aside from Walter Payton's 1,390 rushing yards, tops in the NFC, the Bears' offense remained unimaginative. The verdict was still out on second-year QB Bob Avellini, especially after he finished the season with a two-for 17 passing performance in a 28-14 loss to Denver. Sid Gillman, one of the game's great free-thinkers, was lured out of retirement after the season ended to become offensive coordinator.

**Detroit Lions** — Dissension and a rough 1-3 start cost Rick Forzano his head coaching job. Replacement Tommy Hudspeth got off on the right foot by opening up the offense with a double-wing, double-WR formation that shocked New England 30-10 the fifth week. But a pitiful offensive line and a dismal 1-6 road record that included losses to New Orleans and the New York Giants did little to secure Hudspeth's future. Behind OLB Charlie Weaver, the team's MVP, and linemen Jim Mitchell and Ken Sanders, the Lions' stunting defense remained strong, allowing the NFL's third lowest yardage total despite losing three tackles to surgery.

**Green Bay Packers** — Blessed with decent draft picks for the first time since '72, the Pack showed a very slight improvement, one more victory than '75, in Bart Starr's second season at the helm, and still needed help at almost every position when the year ended. Green Bay's five wins were all against sub-.500 teams, and it had to come from behind in the second half in four of them. QB Lynn Dickey, obtained from Houston before the season began in exchange for QB John Hadl and CB Ken Ellis, was respectable until a shoulder separation knocked him out of the last four games.

## WESTERN DIVISION

**Los Angeles Rams** — On the way to their fourth straight division title, the Rams featured a season-long battle among James Harris, Ron Jaworski and Pat Haden for the starting QB job. While nagging injuries continually hampered his competitors, Haden finally emerged as L.A.'s No. 1 man with five regular-season games left. A bountiful rushing attack headed by Lawrence McCutcheon and John Cappelletti was the key factor in the NFC's highest-scoring offense. Defensively, CB Monte Jackson's league-leading 10 interceptions spearheaded a sterling secondary that received strong assistance from a tough defensive line anchored by LT Merlin Olsen in his last season. The team's individual highlight was Harris' fourth-week, 436-yard passing performance in a 31-28 victory over Miami, the second-best ever by a Ram QB.

**San Francisco 49ers** — With Monte Clark replacing Dick Nolan as head coach, the Niners were the NFL's biggest surprise the first half of the season with a 6-1 record. They fell to 2-5 the second half, but finished the year with the conference's best defense, led by All-Pro DE Tommy Hart and his sack-happy cohorts, and a productive ground game featuring Delvin Williams and Wilbur Jackson. Monday night victories over L.A. and Minnesota were the strongest indicators of what appeared to be a long and happy coaching career in S.F. for Clark, but his falling out with the team's new owners after the season cut it short and paved the way for a strife-torn '77 campaign conducted by new GM Joe Thomas.

**New Orleans Saints** — New Head Coach Hank Stram had "Thunder and Lightning" in his offense in the form of rookie runners Tony Galbreath and Chuck Muncie, but a porous front wall offset their effectiveness as the Saints finished 4-10, two victories better than '75. QB's Bobby Scott and Bobby Douglass took over for Archie Manning, on the sidelines all season with tendonitis in his passing shoulder.

**Atlanta Falcons** — The Falcs lost four of their first five games, at which point GM Pat Peppler abruptly replaced Marion Campbell as head coach. A crucial blow to their offense was the knee injury that knocked QB Steve Bartkowski out of the lineup for nine games. The high point of their dreary 4-10 season came in the 11th week when they scored 17 points in the fourth quarter to upset playoff-bound Dallas 17-10. John James provided excellent punting all season while tiny WR Alfred Jenkins remained a constant long-range threat.

**Seattle Seahawks** — In their first season, the Seattle expansionites fared much better than their Tampa Bay counterparts, winning two games against the Bucs and Atlanta and coming up with close calls against Minnesota, St. Louis and Green Bay. On offense, QB Jim Zorn displayed great potential at times but threw too many interceptions while Steve Largent and Sherm Smith were pleasant surprises at WR and RB, respectively. The defense was a mess, however, giving up about 400 yards and 30 points a game.

**OFFENSE**

| | ATL. | CHI. | DALL. | DET. | G.B. | L.A. | MINN. | N.O. | N.Y. | PHIL. | ST.L. | S.F. | SEA. | WASH. |
|---|---|---|---|---|---|---|---|---|---|---|---|---|---|---|
| **FIRST DOWNS:** | | | | | | | | | | | | | | |
| Total | 191 | 201 | 269 | 259 | 210 | 265 | 294 | 226 | 216 | 220 | **307** | 242 | 239 | 255 |
| by Rushing | 78 | 115 | 111 | 123 | 99 | 143 | 125 | 92 | 98 | 109 | **140** | 131 | 75 | 114 |
| by Passing | 93 | 67 | 140 | 120 | 94 | 111 | **150** | 111 | 97 | 91 | 142 | 91 | 141 | 122 |
| by Penalty | 20 | 19 | 18 | 16 | 17 | 11 | 19 | 23 | 21 | 20 | **25** | 20 | 23 | 19 |
| **RUSHING:** | | | | | | | | | | | | | | |
| Number | 470 | 578 | 538 | 516 | 485 | **613** | 540 | 431 | 530 | 505 | 580 | 576 | 374 | 548 |
| Yards | 1689 | 2363 | 2147 | 2213 | 1722 | **2528** | 2003 | 1775 | 1904 | 2080 | 2301 | 2447 | 1416 | 2111 |
| Average Yards | 3.6 | 4.1 | 4.0 | **4.3** | 3.6 | 4.1 | 3.7 | 4.1 | 3.6 | 4.1 | 4.0 | 4.2 | 3.8 | 3.9 |
| Touchdowns | 10 | 20 | 16 | 9 | 15 | **23** | 18 | 16 | 11 | 8 | 17 | 14 | 14 | 10 |
| **PASSING:** | | | | | | | | | | | | | | |
| Attempts | 354 | 278 | 390 | 356 | 357 | 315 | 442 | 403 | 326 | 369 | 392 | 306 | **480** | 370 |
| Completions | 157 | 123 | 222 | 201 | 164 | 171 | **270** | 206 | 175 | 182 | 220 | 155 | 229 | 187 |
| Completion Pct. | 44.4 | 44.2 | 56.9 | 56.5 | 45.9 | 54.3 | **61.1** | 51.1 | 53.7 | 49.3 | 56.1 | 50.7 | 47.7 | 50.5 |
| Passing Yards | 1809 | 1705 | 2967 | 2630 | 2105 | 2629 | **3117** | 2353 | 2104 | 1844 | 2967 | 1963 | 2874 | 2288 |
| Avg. Yds. per Att. | 5.1 | 6.1 | 7.6 | 7.4 | 5.9 | **8.3** | 7.1 | 5.8 | 6.5 | 5.0 | 7.6 | 6.4 | 6.0 | 6.2 |
| Avg. Yds per Comp. | 11.5 | 13.9 | 13.4 | 13.1 | 12.8 | **15.4** | 11.5 | 11.4 | 12.0 | 10.1 | 13.5 | 12.7 | 12.6 | 12.2 |
| Times Tackled | 44 | 24 | 30 | 67 | 41 | 32 | 31 | 51 | 44 | 43 | **17** | 34 | 28 | 38 |
| Yds Lost Tackled | 395 | 225 | 230 | 490 | 375 | 288 | 262 | 369 | 312 | 352 | **132** | 325 | 225 | 303 |
| Net Yards | 1414 | 1480 | 2737 | 2140 | 1730 | 2341 | **2855** | 1984 | 1792 | 1492 | 2835 | 1638 | 2649 | 1985 |
| Touchdowns | 10 | 9 | 17 | **20** | 10 | 17 | 17 | 8 | 9 | 11 | 18 | 15 | 13 | **20** |
| Interceptions | 24 | 15 | 13 | 12 | 22 | 15 | **10** | 14 | 24 | 18 | 13 | 21 | 30 | 20 |
| Pct. Intercepted | 6.8 | 5.4 | 3.3 | 3.4 | 6.2 | 4.8 | **2.2** | 3.5 | 7.4 | 4.9 | 3.3 | 6.9 | 6.3 | 5.4 |
| **PUNTS:** | | | | | | | | | | | | | | |
| Number | **101** | 100 | 74 | 85 | 84 | 79 | 69 | **101** | 77 | 97 | 66 | 91 | 82 | 90 |
| Average Distance | **42.1** | 37.3 | 37.0 | 38.8 | 36.6 | 38.1 | 38.8 | 39.3 | 39.7 | 35.5 | 35.3 | 39.9 | 37.4 | 38.9 |
| **PUNT RETURNS:** | | | | | | | | | | | | | | |
| Number | 60 | 43 | 45 | 31 | 40 | 52 | 40 | 42 | 41 | 41 | 36 | **65** | 37 | 52 |
| Yards | 385 | 269 | 489 | 207 | 300 | 476 | 271 | 375 | 197 | 425 | 350 | 557 | 246 | **688** |
| Average Yards | 6.4 | 6.3 | 10.9 | 6.7 | 7.5 | 9.2 | 6.8 | 8.9 | 4.8 | 10.4 | 9.7 | 8.6 | 6.6 | **13.2** |
| Touchdowns | 0 | 0 | 0 | 0 | 0 | 0 | 0 | 0 | 0 | 0 | 0 | **2** | 0 | 1 |
| **KICKOFF RETURNS:** | | | | | | | | | | | | | | |
| Number | 60 | 51 | 42 | 47 | 65 | 44 | 42 | 62 | 53 | 58 | 54 | 38 | **79** | 50 |
| Yards | 1269 | 1087 | 1027 | 987 | 1361 | 1027 | 859 | 1173 | 1044 | 1148 | 1102 | 777 | **1605** | 1066 |
| Average Yards | 21.2 | 21.3 | **24.5** | 21.0 | 20.9 | 23.3 | 20.5 | 18.9 | 19.7 | 19.8 | 20.4 | 20.4 | 20.3 | 21.3 |
| Touchdowns | 0 | 0 | 0 | 0 | 0 | **1** | 0 | 0 | 0 | 0 | 0 | 0 | 0 | 0 |
| **INTERCEPTION RET:** | | | | | | | | | | | | | | |
| Number | 18 | 24 | 16 | 24 | 11 | **32** | 19 | 12 | 12 | 9 | 19 | 9 | 15 | 26 |
| Yards | 207 | 215 | 133 | **445** | 197 | 376 | 213 | 212 | 62 | 195 | 243 | 93 | 218 | 190 |
| Average Yards | 11.5 | 9.0 | 8.3 | 18.5 | 17.9 | 11.8 | 11.2 | 17.7 | 5.2 | **21.7** | 12.8 | 10.3 | 14.5 | 7.3 |
| Touchdowns | 0 | 2 | 0 | **3** | 2 | **3** | 0 | **3** | 0 | 0 | 1 | 0 | 1 | 0 |
| **PENALTIES:** | | | | | | | | | | | | | | |
| Number | 84 | **114** | 94 | 97 | 87 | 83 | 77 | 103 | 86 | 91 | 84 | 102 | 80 | 90 |
| Yards | 714 | **984** | 761 | 819 | 791 | 764 | 615 | 901 | 734 | 722 | 683 | 848 | 684 | 868 |
| **FUMBLES:** | | | | | | | | | | | | | | |
| Number | 30 | **24** | 26 | 38 | 37 | 29 | 33 | 32 | 27 | 33 | 44 | 30 | 30 | 36 |
| Number Lost | 17 | 13 | 16 | 21 | 23 | 21 | 19 | 18 | **12** | 14 | 24 | **12** | 18 | 23 |
| **POINTS:** | | | | | | | | | | | | | | |
| Total | 172 | 253 | 296 | 262 | 218 | **351** | 305 | 253 | 170 | 165 | 309 | 270 | 229 | 291 |
| PAT Attempts | 20 | 31 | 34 | 32 | 27 | 44 | 36 | 29 | 21 | 19 | 36 | 32 | 29 | 32 |
| PAT Made | 20 | 27 | 34 | 28 | 24 | **36** | 32 | 25 | 20 | 18 | 33 | 26 | 26 | 31 |
| FG Attempts | 21 | 25 | 23 | 24 | 19 | 26 | 31 | 23 | 21 | 16 | 27 | 28 | 16 | **34** |
| FG Made | 10 | 12 | 18 | 14 | 10 | 17 | 19 | 18 | 8 | 11 | 20 | 16 | 9 | **22** |
| Percent FG Made | 47.6 | 48.0 | **78.3** | 58.3 | 52.6 | 65.4 | 61.3 | **78.3** | 38.1 | 68.8 | 74.1 | 57.1 | 56.3 | 64.7 |
| Safeties | 1 | **2** | **2** | 0 | 1 | 0 | 0 | 0 | 0 | 0 | 0 | **2** | 1 | 1 |

**DEFENSE**

| | ATL. | CHI. | DALL. | DET. | G.B. | L.A. | MINN. | N.O. | N.Y. | PHIL. | ST.L. | S.F. | SEA. | WASH. |
|---|---|---|---|---|---|---|---|---|---|---|---|---|---|---|
| **FIRST DOWNS:** | | | | | | | | | | | | | | |
| Total | 257 | 250 | 246 | **191** | 262 | 213 | **207** | 275 | 251 | 262 | 239 | 218 | 323 | 215 |
| by Rushing | 143 | 104 | 113 | 94 | 132 | **79** | 103 | 129 | 120 | 113 | 111 | 94 | 166 | 109 |
| by Passing | 95 | 128 | 111 | **76** | 107 | 118 | 91 | 121 | 119 | 129 | 105 | 102 | 136 | 91 |
| by Penalty | 19 | 18 | 22 | 21 | 23 | 16 | 13 | 25 | **12** | 20 | 23 | 22 | 21 | 15 |
| **RUSHING:** | | | | | | | | | | | | | | |
| Number | 574 | 522 | 484 | 496 | 546 | **429** | 487 | **554** | 560 | 532 | 491 | 487 | 614 | 555 |
| Yards | 2577 | 1984 | 1821 | 1901 | 2288 | **1564** | 2096 | **2289** | 2203 | 2053 | 1979 | 1786 | 2876 | 2205 |
| Average Yards | 4.5 | 3.8 | 3.8 | 3.8 | 4.2 | **3.6** | 4.3 | 4.1 | 3.9 | 3.9 | 4.0 | 3.7 | 4.7 | 4.0 |
| Touchdowns | 22 | **10** | 12 | 13 | 17 | 11 | 14 | 22 | 14 | 16 | 19 | **10** | 20 | 12 |
| **PASSING:** | | | | | | | | | | | | | | |
| Attempts | 340 | 401 | 391 | **313** | 354 | 397 | 323 | 367 | 330 | 404 | 342 | 374 | 367 | 354 |
| Completions | 184 | 200 | 187 | **137** | 196 | 199 | 158 | 200 | 189 | 237 | 176 | 180 | 223 | 146 |
| Completion Pct. | 54.1 | 49.9 | 47.8 | 43.8 | 55.4 | 50.1 | 48.9 | 54.5 | 57.3 | 58.7 | 51.5 | 48.1 | 60.8 | **41.2** |
| Passing Yards | 2276 | 2612 | 2236 | 1904 | 2192 | 2487 | **1897** | 2514 | 2230 | 2688 | 2358 | 2349 | 2770 | 2241 |
| Avg. Yds. per Att. | 6.7 | 6.5 | **5.7** | 6.1 | 6.2 | 6.3 | 5.9 | 6.9 | 6.8 | 6.7 | 6.9 | 6.3 | 7.5 | 6.3 |
| Avg. Yds per Comp. | 12.4 | 13.1 | 12.0 | 13.9 | **11.2** | 12.5 | 12.0 | 12.6 | 11.8 | 11.3 | 13.4 | 13.1 | 12.4 | 15.4 |
| Times Tackled | 35 | 49 | 44 | 28 | 43 | 45 | 45 | 39 | 31 | 19 | 31 | **61** | 27 | 44 |
| Yds Lost Tackled | 275 | 395 | 327 | 218 | 357 | 395 | 322 | 312 | 242 | 138 | 248 | **573** | 246 | 324 |
| Net Yards | 2001 | 2217 | 1909 | 1686 | 1835 | 2092 | **1575** | 2202 | 1988 | 2550 | 2110 | 1776 | 2524 | 1917 |
| Touchdowns | 14 | 15 | 12 | 11 | 13 | 11 | **8** | 18 | 11 | 17 | 13 | 13 | 27 | 11 |
| Interceptions | 18 | 24 | 16 | 24 | 11 | **32** | 19 | 12 | 12 | 9 | 19 | 9 | 15 | 26 |
| Pct. Intercepted | 5.3 | 6.0 | 4.1 | 7.7 | 3.1 | **8.1** | 5.9 | 3.3 | 3.6 | 2.2 | 5.6 | 2.4 | 4.1 | 7.3 |
| **PUNTS:** | | | | | | | | | | | | | | |
| Number | 87 | 85 | 95 | 84 | 77 | 95 | 79 | 88 | 78 | 86 | 71 | **108** | 65 | 93 |
| Average Distance | 38.5 | 36.3 | 38.7 | 40.1 | 38.5 | 41.2 | 37.1 | 39.4 | 37.0 | 37.9 | 38.8 | 40.1 | **35.0** | 38.9 |
| **PUNT RETURNS:** | | | | | | | | | | | | | | |
| Number | 52 | 44 | **28** | 39 | 48 | 39 | 40 | 64 | 45 | 53 | 33 | 52 | 56 | 44 |
| Yards | 360 | 346 | **252** | 278 | 268 | 281 | 286 | 742 | 500 | 405 | 304 | 351 | 537 | 323 |
| Average Yards | 6.9 | 7.9 | 9.0 | 7.1 | **5.6** | 7.2 | 7.2 | 11.6 | 11.1 | 7.6 | 9.2 | 6.8 | 9.6 | 7.3 |
| Touchdowns | **0** | **0** | **0** | **0** | **0** | **0** | **0** | 1 | **0** | **0** | 1 | **0** | 1 | **0** |
| **KICKOFF RETURNS:** | | | | | | | | | | | | | | |
| Number | **38** | 54 | 62 | 55 | 44 | 70 | 66 | 54 | 39 | 44 | 66 | 46 | 47 | 63 |
| Yards | 934 | 969 | 1275 | 1188 | 784 | 1383 | 1209 | 1359 | **725** | 912 | 1623 | 924 | 1041 | 1028 |
| Average Yards | 24.6 | 17.9 | 20.6 | 21.6 | 17.8 | 19.8 | 18.3 | 25.2 | 18.6 | 20.7 | 24.6 | 20.1 | 22.1 | **16.3** |
| Touchdowns | **0** | **0** | **0** | **0** | **0** | **0** | **0** | **0** | **0** | **0** | 1 | **0** | **0** | **0** |
| **INTERCEPTION RET:** | | | | | | | | | | | | | | |
| Number | 24 | 15 | 13 | 12 | 22 | 15 | **10** | 14 | 24 | 18 | 13 | 21 | 30 | 20 |
| Yards | 469 | 213 | 155 | **121** | 362 | 211 | 185 | 140 | 249 | 189 | 134 | 253 | 388 | 149 |
| Average Yards | 19.5 | 14.2 | 11.9 | 10.1 | 16.5 | 14.1 | **18.5** | 10.0 | 10.4 | 10.5 | 10.3 | 12.0 | 12.9 | **7.5** |
| Touchdowns | 4 | **0** | 1 | **0** | 3 | **0** | **0** | 1 | 1 | 1 | **0** | 2 | 4 | **0** |
| **PENALTIES:** | | | | | | | | | | | | | | |
| Number | 102 | 86 | 71 | 88 | 104 | 82 | 76 | **105** | 104 | 105 | 83 | 94 | **106** | 95 |
| Yards | 868 | 699 | 643 | 696 | 914 | 747 | 653 | **883** | 835 | 907 | 708 | 906 | **926** | 818 |
| **FUMBLES:** | | | | | | | | | | | | | | |
| Number | 30 | 37 | 32 | 27 | 27 | 31 | 24 | **38** | 32 | 31 | 32 | 37 | 24 | **38** |
| Number Lost | 20 | 23 | 12 | 15 | 15 | 16 | 13 | **27** | 15 | 15 | 20 | 16 | 11 | 21 |
| **POINTS:** | | | | | | | | | | | | | | |
| Total | 312 | 216 | 194 | 220 | 299 | 190 | **176** | 346 | 250 | 286 | 267 | 190 | 429 | 217 |
| PAT Attempts | 40 | 25 | 25 | 25 | 34 | 22 | 22 | 44 | 27 | 35 | 34 | 25 | 53 | 23 |
| PAT Made | 32 | 25 | 23 | 25 | 29 | 20 | **14** | 36 | 26 | 33 | 31 | 20 | 51 | 22 |
| FG Attempts | 17 | 25 | **12** | 28 | 33 | 20 | 25 | 17 | 31 | 24 | 20 | 21 | 30 | 30 |
| FG Made | 12 | 13 | 7 | 15 | 22 | 12 | 10 | 14 | 20 | 13 | 10 | **6** | 20 | 19 |
| Percent FG Made | 70.6 | 52.0 | 58.3 | 53.6 | 66.7 | 60.0 | 40.0 | 82.4 | 64.5 | 54.2 | 50.0 | **28.6** | 66.7 | 63.3 |
| Safeties | 2 | 1 | **0** | **0** | **0** | 1 | **0** | 2 | 1 | 2 | 1 | 1 | **0** | **0** |

December 18, at Minnesota (Attendance 48,169)

### SCORING

| | | | | |
|---|---|---|---|---|
| **MINNESOTA** | 14 | 7 | 14 | 0–35 |
| **WASHINGTON** | 3 | 0 | 3 | 14–20 |

First Quarter
- Minn. — Voigt, 18 yard pass from Tarkenton PAT–Cox (kick)
- Wash. — Moseley, 47 yard field goal
- Minn. — S. White, 27 yard pass from Tarkenton PAT–Cox (kick)

Second Quarter
- Minn. — Foreman, 2 yard rush PAT–Cox (kick)

Third Quarter
- Minn. — Foreman, 30 yard rush PAT–Cox (kick)
- Wash. — Moseley, 35 yard field goal
- Minn. — S. White, 9 yard pass from Tarkenton PAT–Cox (kick)

Fourth Quarter
- Wash. — Grant, 12 yard pass from Kilmer PAT–Moseley (kick)
- Wash. — Jefferson, 3 yard pass from Kilmer PAT–Moseley (kick)

### TEAM STATISTICS

| MINN. | | WASH. |
|---|---|---|
| 21 | First Downs-Total | 19 |
| 11 | First Downs-Rushing | 3 |
| 9 | First Downs-Passing | 15 |
| 1 | First Downs-Penalties | 1 |
| 2 | Fumbles-Number | 0 |
| 0 | Fumbles-Lost Ball | 0 |
| 5 | Penalties-Number | 7 |
| 30 | Yards Penalized | 57 |
| 0 | Missed Field Goals | 1 |
| 69 | Offensive Plays | 68 |
| 384 | Net Yards | 365 |
| 5.6 | Average Gain | 5.4 |
| 2 | Giveaways | 2 |
| 2 | Takeaways | 2 |
| 0 | Difference | 0 |

### INDIVIDUAL STATISTICS

| MINNESOTA | No | Yds | Avg | WASHINGTON | No | Yds | Avg |
|---|---|---|---|---|---|---|---|
| **RUSHING** | | | | | | | |
| Foreman | 20 | 105 | 5.3 | Thomas | 11 | 45 | 4.1 |
| McClanahan | 20 | 101 | 5.1 | Riggins | 7 | 30 | 4.3 |
| Johnson | 2 | 11 | 5.5 | | 18 | 75 | 4.2 |
| Tarkenton | 1 | 3 | 3.0 | | | | |
| Miller | 2 | 1 | 0.5 | | | | |
| Lee | 1 | 0 | 1.0 | | | | |
| | 46 | 221 | 4.8 | | | | |
| **RECEIVING** | | | | | | | |
| S. White | 4 | 64 | 16.0 | Grant | 6 | 70 | 11.6 |
| Voigt | 4 | 42 | 10.5 | Fugett | 4 | 61 | 15.3 |
| McClanahan | 3 | 29 | 9.7 | Jefferson | 4 | 59 | 14.8 |
| Rashad | 1 | 35 | 35.0 | Hill | 4 | 31 | 7.8 |
| | 12 | 170 | 14.2 | Riggins | 4 | 29 | 7.3 |
| | | | | Thomas | 2 | 18 | 9.0 |
| | | | | Smith | 1 | 30 | 30.0 |
| | | | | L. Brown | 1 | 0 | 0.0 |
| | | | | | 26 | 298 | 11.5 |
| **PUNTING** | | | | | | | |
| Clabo | 6 | | 46.0 | Bragg | 6 | | 32.8 |
| **PUNT RETURNS** | | | | | | | |
| Willis | 2 | 12 | 6.0 | E. Brown | 6 | 55 | 9.2 |
| **KICKOFF RETURNS** | | | | | | | |
| Willis | 2 | 25 | 12.5 | E. Brown | 6 | 136 | 22.7 |
| Miller | 1 | 16 | 16.0 | | | | |
| Johnson | 1 | 0 | 0.0 | | | | |
| | 4 | 41 | 10.3 | | | | |
| **INTERCEPTION RETURNS** | | | | | | | |
| Bryant | 1 | 0 | 0.0 | Scott | 1 | 17 | 17.0 |
| N. Wright | 1 | 0 | 0.0 | Houston | 1 | 8 | 8.0 |
| | 2 | 0 | 0.0 | | 2 | 25 | 12.5 |

**PASSING**

| MINNESOTA | Att. | Comp. | Comp. Pct. | Yds. | Int. | Yds/ Att. | Yds. Comp. | Yards Lost Tackled |
|---|---|---|---|---|---|---|---|---|
| Tarkenton | 21 | 12 | 57.1 | 170 | 2 | 8.1 | 14.2 | 1–7 |
| Lee | 1 | 0 | 00.0 | | | | | |
| | 22 | 12 | 54.5 | 170 | 2 | 7.7 | 14.2 | 1–7 |
| **WASHINGTON** | | | | | | | | |
| Kilmer | 49 | 26 | 53.1 | 298 | 2 | 6.1 | 11.5 | 1–8 |

December 19, at Irving, Texas (Attendance 63,283)

### SCORING

| | | | | |
|---|---|---|---|---|
| **DALLAS** | 3 | 7 | 0 | 2–12 |
| **LOS ANGELES** | 0 | 7 | 0 | 7–14 |

First Quarter
- Dall. — Herrara, 44 yard field goal

Second Quarter
- L.A. — Haden, 4 yard rush PAT–Dempsey (kick)
- Dall. — Laidlaw, 1 yard rush PAT–Herrara (kick)

Fourth Quarter
- L.A. — McCutcheon, 1 yard rush PAT–Dempsey (kick)
- Dall. — Safety–R. Jackson, tackled in end zone

### TEAM STATISTICS

| DALLAS | | L.A. |
|---|---|---|
| 14 | First Downs-Total | 17 |
| 4 | First Downs-Rushing | 6 |
| 9 | First Downs-Passing | 8 |
| 1 | First Downs-Penalty | 3 |
| 3 | Fumbles-Number | 0 |
| 1 | Fumbles-Lost Ball | 0 |
| 6 | Penalties-Number | 8 |
| 34 | Yards Penalized | 94 |
| 0 | Missed Field Goals | 0 |
| 69 | Offensive Plays | 73 |
| 211 | Net Yards | 250 |
| 3.0 | Average Gain | 3.4 |
| 4 | Giveaways | 3 |
| 3 | Takeaways | 4 |
| −1 | Difference | +1 |

### INDIVIDUAL STATISTICS

| DALLAS | No | Yds | Avg. | LOS ANGELES | No | Yds | Avg. |
|---|---|---|---|---|---|---|---|
| **RUSHING** | | | | | | | |
| P. Pearson | 13 | 43 | 3.3 | McCutcheon | 21 | 58 | 2.8 |
| Newhouse | 9 | 25 | 2.8 | Cappelletti | 19 | 54 | 2.8 |
| Staubach | 2 | 8 | 4.0 | Haden | 8 | 16 | 2.0 |
| D. Pearson | 1 | 4 | 4.0 | R. Jackson | 1 | −8 | −8.0 |
| Dennison | 1 | 3 | 3.0 | | 49 | 120 | 2.4 |
| Laidlaw | 2 | 2 | 1.0 | | | | |
| | 28 | 85 | 3.0 | | | | |
| **RECEIVING** | | | | | | | |
| P. Pearson | 6 | 41 | 6.8 | H. Jackson | 6 | 116 | 19.3 |
| D. Pearson | 3 | 38 | 12.7 | Cappelletti | 2 | 15 | 7.5 |
| DuPree | 3 | 34 | 11.3 | Klein | 1 | 12 | 12.0 |
| Newhouse | 2 | 19 | 9.5 | McCutcheon | 1 | 9 | 9.0 |
| Johnson | 1 | 18 | 18.0 | | 10 | 152 | 15.2 |
| | 15 | 150 | 10.0 | | | | |
| **PUNTING** | | | | | | | |
| D. White | 6 | | 38.6 | R. Jackson | 7 | | 36.1 |
| **PUNT RETURNS** | | | | | | | |
| Johnson | 4 | 64 | 16 | Bryant | 2 | 23 | 11.5 |
| **KICKOFF RETURNS** | | | | | | | |
| Johnson | 2 | 49 | 24.5 | Bryant | 2 | 45 | 22.5 |
| | | | | Geredine | 1 | 26 | 26.0 |
| | | | | | 3 | 71 | 23.7 |
| **INTERCEPTION RETURNS** | | | | | | | |
| Barnes | 2 | 0 | 0.0 | Robertson | 1 | 15 | 15.0 |
| Waters | 1 | 9 | 9.0 | Elmendorf | 1 | 5 | 5.0 |
| | 3 | 9 | 3.0 | M. Jackson | 1 | 0 | 0.0 |
| | | | | | 3 | 20 | 6.7 |

**PASSING**

| DALLAS | Att. | Comp. | Comp. Pct. | Yds. | Int. | Yds/ Att. | Yds/ Comp. | Yards Lost Tackled |
|---|---|---|---|---|---|---|---|---|
| Staubach | 37 | 15 | 40.5 | 150 | 3 | 4.1 | 10.0 | 4–24 |
| **LOS ANGELES** | | | | | | | | |
| Haden | 21 | 10 | 47.6 | 152 | 3 | 7.2 | 15.2 | 3–22 |

# 1976 N.F.C. — Eastern Divison

## DALLAS COWBOYS 11-3 Tom Landry

| Scores of Each Game | | |
|---|---|---|
| 27 | PHILADELPHIA | 7 |
| 24 | New Orleans | 6 |
| 30 | BALTIMORE | 27 |
| 28 | Seattle | 13 |
| 24 | N.Y. Giants | 14 |
| 17 | St. Louis | 21 |
| 31 | CHICAGO | 21 |
| 20 | Washington | 7 |
| 9 | N.Y. GIANTS | 3 |
| 17 | BUFFALO | 10 |
| 10 | Atlanta | 17 |
| 19 | ST. LOUIS | 14 |
| 26 | Philadelphia | 7 |
| 14 | WASHINGTON | 27 |

| Use Name | Pos. | Hgt. | Wgt. | Age | Int | Pts. |
|---|---|---|---|---|---|---|
| Pat Donovan | OT | 6'4" | 250 | 23 | | |
| Ralph Neely | OT | 6'5" | 255 | 32 | | |
| Rayfield Wright | OT | 6'7" | 255 | 31 | | |
| Jim Eidson | OG-C | 6'3" | 264 | 22 | | |
| Burton Lawless | OG | 6'4" | 250 | 22 | | |
| Blaine Nye | OG | 6'4" | 255 | 30 | | |
| Tom Rafferty | OG-C | 6'3" | 250 | 22 | | |
| Herbert Scott | OG | 6'2" | 250 | 23 | | |
| John Fitzgerald | C | 6'5" | 252 | 28 | | |
| Too Tall Jones | DE | 6'9" | 265 | 25 | | |
| Harvey Martin | DE | 6'5" | 252 | 25 | 1 | |
| Greg Schaum | DE | 6'4" | 246 | 22 | | |
| Larry Cole | DT | 6'4" | 250 | 29 | | |
| Bill Gregory | DT | 6'5" | 252 | 26 | | |
| Jethro Pugh | DT | 6'6" | 248 | 32 | | |

Kyle Davis – Knee Injury

| Use Name | Pos. | Hgt. | Wgt. | Age | Int | Pts |
|---|---|---|---|---|---|---|
| Bob Breunig | LB | 6'2" | 228 | 23 | | |
| Mike Hegman | LB | 6'1" | 221 | 23 | | |
| Tim Henderson | LB | 6'2" | 223 | 23 | 2 | |
| Lee Roy Jordon | LB | 6'2" | 220 | 35 | | |
| D.D. Lewis | LB | 6'2" | 215 | 30 | | |
| Randy White | LB | 6'4" | 240 | 23 | | |
| Benny Barnes | DB | 6'1" | 190 | 25 | 1 | |
| Cliff Harris | DB | 6' | 190 | 27 | 3 | |
| Randy Hughes | DB | 6'4" | 210 | 23 | 1 | |
| Aaron Kyle | DB | 5'11" | 181 | 22 | 2 | |
| Beasley Reece | DB | 6'1" | 186 | 22 | | |
| Mel Renfro | DB | 6' | 190 | 34 | 3 | |
| Mark Washington | DB | 5'10" | 186 | 28 | 4 | |
| Charlie Waters | DB | 6'1" | 195 | 27 | 3 | |

| Use Name | Pos. | Hgt. | Wgt. | Age | Int | Pts |
|---|---|---|---|---|---|---|
| Roger Staubach | QB | 6'2" | 197 | 34 | | 18 |
| Danny White | QB | 6'2" | 180 | 24 | | |
| Doug Dennison | HB-FB | 6'1" | 208 | 24 | | 36 |
| Preston Pearson | HB | 6'1" | 208 | 31 | | 18 |
| Charley Young | HB | 6'1" | 220 | 23 | | 6 |
| Jim Jensen | FB | 6'3" | 230 | 22 | | |
| Scott Laidlaw | FB | 6' | 206 | 23 | | 24 |
| Robert Newhouse | FB-HB | 5'10" | 205 | 26 | | 18 |
| Butch Johnson | WR | 6'1" | 187 | 22 | | 12 |
| Drew Pearson | WR | 6' | 185 | 25 | | 42 |
| Golden Richards | WR | 6' | 190 | 25 | | 18 |
| Billy Joe DuPree | TE | 6'4" | 230 | 26 | | 12 |
| Jay Saldi | TE | 6'3" | 217 | 21 | | |
| Efren Herrera | K | 5'9" | 190 | 25 | | 88 |

Percy Howard – Injured

## WASHINGTON REDSKINS 10-4 George Allen

| Scores of Each Game | | |
|---|---|---|
| 19 | N.Y. GIANTS | 17 |
| 31 | SEATTLE | 7 |
| 20 | Philadelphia | *17 |
| 7 | Chicago | 33 |
| 30 | KANSAS CITY | 33 |
| 20 | DETROIT | 7 |
| 20 | ST. LOUIS | 10 |
| 7 | DALLAS | 20 |
| 24 | San Francisco | 21 |
| 9 | N.Y. Giants | 12 |
| 16 | St. Louis | 10 |
| 24 | PHILADELPHIA | 0 |
| 37 | N.Y. Jets | 16 |
| 27 | Dallas | 14 |

| Use Name | Pos. | Hgt. | Wgt. | Age | Int | Pts. |
|---|---|---|---|---|---|---|
| Terry Hermeling | OT | 6'5" | 255 | 30 | | |
| George Starke | OT | 6'5" | 249 | 28 | | |
| Tim Stokes | OT | 6'5" | 252 | 26 | | |
| Dan Nugent | OG | 6'3" | 250 | 23 | | |
| Ron Saul | OG | 6'2" | 254 | 28 | | |
| Ted Fritsch | C | 6'2" | 242 | 26 | | |
| Len Hauss | C | 6'2" | 235 | 34 | | |
| Bob Kuziel | C | 6'5" | 255 | 26 | | |
| Dallas Hickman | DE | 6'6" | 235 | 24 | | |
| Karl Lorch | DE | 6'3" | 260 | 26 | | |
| Ron McDole | DE | 6'3" | 265 | 36 | | 2 |
| Bill Brundige | DT-DE | 6'5" | 270 | 27 | | |
| Dave Butz | DT | 6'7" | 285 | 26 | | |
| Dennis Johnson | DT | 6'4" | 260 | 24 | 1 | |
| Diron Talbert | DT | 6'5" | 255 | 32 | | |

Paul Laaveg – Knee Injury
Ernie Janet – Groin Injury
Walt Sweeney – Knee Injury

| Use Name | Pos. | Hgt. | Wgt. | Age | Int | Pts |
|---|---|---|---|---|---|---|
| Brad Dusek | LB | 6'2" | 214 | 25 | 1 | 6 |
| Chris Hanburger | LB | 6'2" | 218 | 35 | 1 | |
| Harold McLinton | LB | 6'2" | 235 | 29 | 1 | |
| Stu O'Dell | LB | 6'1" | 220 | 24 | | |
| Russ Tillmann | LB | 6'2" | 230 | 30 | | |
| Pete Wysocki | LB | 6'2" | 225 | 27 | | |
| Eddie Brown | DB | 5'11" | 190 | 24 | 1 | 6 |
| Pat Fischer | DB | 5'10" | 170 | 36 | 5 | |
| Ken Houston | DB | 6'3" | 198 | 31 | 4 | |
| Joe Lavender | DB | 6'4" | 190 | 27 | 8 | |
| Brig Owens | DB | 5'11" | 190 | 33 | | |
| Jake Scott | DB | 6' | 188 | 31 | 4 | |
| Gerard Williams | DB | 6'1" | 184 | 24 | | |

| Use Name | Pos. | Hgt. | Wgt. | Age | Int | Pts |
|---|---|---|---|---|---|---|
| Billy Kilmer | QB | 6' | 204 | 36 | | |
| Joe Theismann | QB | 6' | 184 | 26 | | 6 |
| Larry Brown | HB | 5'11" | 195 | 28 | | |
| Bob Brunet | HB | 6'1" | 205 | 30 | | |
| Mike Thomas | HB | 5'11" | 190 | 23 | | 54 |
| Calvin Hill | FB | 6'3" | 227 | 29 | | 6 |
| John Riggins | FB | 6'2" | 230 | 27 | | 24 |
| Danny Buggs (from NYG) | WR | 6'2" | 185 | 23 | | |
| Brian Fryer | WR | 6'1" | 185 | 23 | | |
| Frank Grant | WR | 5'11" | 181 | 26 | | 30 |
| Roy Jefferson | WR | 6'2" | 195 | 32 | | 12 |
| Larry Jones | WR | 5'10" | 170 | 25 | | |
| Bill Malinchak | WR | 6'1" | 200 | 32 | | |
| Doug Winslow | WR | 5'11" | 181 | 25 | | |
| Jean Fugett | TE | 6'3" | 226 | 24 | | 36 |
| Jerry Smith | TE | 6'2" | 208 | 33 | | 12 |
| Mike Bragg | K | 5'11" | 186 | 29 | | |
| Mark Moseley | K | 5'11" | 205 | 28 | | 97 |

Charley Taylor – Shoulder Injury

## ST. LOUIS CARDINALS 10-4 Don Coryell

| Scores of Each Game | | |
|---|---|---|
| 30 | Seattle | 24 |
| 29 | GREEN BAY | 0 |
| 24 | San Diego | 43 |
| 27 | N.Y. GIANTS | 21 |
| 33 | PHILADELPHIA | 14 |
| 21 | DALLAS | 17 |
| 10 | Washington | 20 |
| 23 | SAN FRANCISCO | *20 |
| 17 | Philadelphia | 14 |
| 30 | Los Angeles | 28 |
| 10 | WASHINGTON | 16 |
| 14 | Dallas | 19 |
| 24 | BALTIMORE | 17 |
| 17 | N.Y. Giants | 14 |

| Use Name | Pos. | Hgt. | Wgt. | Age | Int | Pts. |
|---|---|---|---|---|---|---|
| Dan Dierdorf | OT | 6'4" | 280 | 27 | | |
| Roger Finnie | OT-OG | 6'3" | 250 | 30 | | |
| Brad Oates | OT | 6'6" | 270 | 22 | | |
| Henry Allison | OG | 6'3" | 255 | 29 | | |
| Conrad Dobler | OG | 6'3" | 255 | 25 | | |
| Keith Wortman | OG | 6'2" | 248 | 26 | | |
| Bob Young | OG | 6'2" | 270 | 33 | | |
| Tom Banks | C-OG | 6'1" | 245 | 28 | | |
| Tom Brahaney | C | 6'2" | 250 | 24 | | |
| Bob Bell | DE | 6'4" | 250 | 28 | | |
| Ron Yankowski | DE | 6'5" | 250 | 29 | | |
| John Zook | DE | 6'5" | 250 | 28 | | |
| Lee Brooks | DT | 6'5" | 250 | 28 | | |
| Charlie Davis | DT | 6'1" | 265 | 24 | | |
| Mike Dawson | DT | 6'4" | 270 | 22 | | |
| Steve Okoniewski | DT-DE | 6'3" | 267 | 27 | | |
| Marv Upshaw | DT | 6'3" | 260 | 29 | | |

Walt Patulski – Knee Injury
Bob Rowe – Back Injury

| Use Name | Pos. | Hgt. | Wgt. | Age | Int | Pts |
|---|---|---|---|---|---|---|
| Mark Arneson | LB | 6'2" | 220 | 26 | 1 | |
| Al Beauchamp | LB | 6'2" | 235 | 32 | | |
| Carl Gersbach | LB | 6'1" | 230 | 29 | | |
| Greg Hartle | LB | 6'2" | 225 | 25 | | |
| Tim Kearney (from TB) | LB | 6'2" | 228 | 25 | 1 | |
| Mike McDonald | LB | 6'2" | 215 | 23 | | |
| Mike McGraw | LB | 6'2" | 225 | 22 | | |
| Steve Neils | LB | 6'2" | 215 | 25 | | |
| Larry Stallings | LB | 6'2" | 230 | 34 | | |
| Ray White | LB | 6'1" | 220 | 27 | 2 | |
| Dwayne Crump | DB | 5'11" | 180 | 26 | | |
| Clarence Duren | DB | 6'1" | 190 | 25 | 1 | |
| Lee Nelson | DB | 5'10" | 185 | 22 | | |
| Ken Reaves | DB | 6'3" | 210 | 31 | 2 | |
| Mike Sensibaugh | DB | 5'11" | 190 | 27 | 4 | 6 |
| Jeff Severson | DB | 6'1" | 185 | 26 | | |
| Norm Thompson | DB | 6'1" | 180 | 28 | 4 | |
| Roger Wehrli | DB | 6'1" | 190 | 28 | | |

| Use Name | Pos. | Hgt. | Wgt. | Age | Int | Pts |
|---|---|---|---|---|---|---|
| Billy Donckers | QB | 6'1" | 205 | 25 | | |
| Jim Hart | QB | 6'2" | 210 | 32 | | |
| Steve Jones | HB | 6' | 200 | 25 | | 54 |
| Jerry Latin | HB | 5'10" | 190 | 23 | | 6 |
| Terry Metcalf | HB | 5'10" | 185 | 24 | | 42 |
| Wayne Morris | HB | 6' | 200 | 22 | | 24 |
| Eddie Moss | FB | 6' | 215 | 27 | | |
| Jim Otis | FB | 6' | 225 | 28 | | 12 |
| J.V. Cain | WR | 6'4" | 225 | 25 | | 30 |
| Mel Gray | WR | 5'9" | 175 | 27 | | 30 |
| Gary Hammond | WR | 5'11" | 185 | 27 | | |
| Ike Harris | WR | 6'3" | 205 | 25 | | 6 |
| Pat Tilley | WR | 5'10" | 175 | 23 | | 6 |
| Terry Joyce | TE | 6'6" | 230 | 22 | | |
| Jackie Smith | TE | 6'4" | 230 | 35 | | |
| Jim Bakken | K | 6' | 200 | 35 | | 93 |

## PHILADELPHIA EAGLES 4-10 Dick Vermeil

| Scores of Each Game | | |
|---|---|---|
| 7 | Dallas | 27 |
| 20 | N.Y. GIANTS | 7 |
| 17 | WASHINGTON | *20 |
| 14 | Atlanta | 13 |
| 14 | St. Louis | 33 |
| 13 | Green Bay | 28 |
| 12 | MINNESOTA | 31 |
| 10 | N.Y. Giants | 0 |
| 14 | ST. LOUIS | 17 |
| 3 | Cleveland | 24 |
| 7 | OAKLAND | 26 |
| 0 | Washington | 24 |
| 7 | DALLAS | 26 |
| 27 | SEATTLE | 10 |

| Use Name | Pos. | Hgt. | Wgt. | Age | Int | Pts. |
|---|---|---|---|---|---|---|
| Ed George | OT | 6'4" | 270 | 30 | | |
| Dennis Nelson | OT | 6'5" | 260 | 30 | | |
| Stan Walters | OT | 6'6" | 270 | 28 | | |
| Jeff Bleamer | OG-OT | 6'4" | 253 | 23 | | |
| Wade Key | OG | 6'4" | 245 | 29 | | |
| Jerry Sisemore | OG-OT | 6'4" | 260 | 25 | | |
| Dennis Franks | C | 6'1" | 236 | 23 | | |
| Guy Morriss | C | 6'4" | 255 | 25 | | |
| Blenda Gay | DE | 6'5" | 255 | 25 | | |
| Carl Hairston | DE | 6'3" | 245 | 23 | | |
| Bill Wynn | DE | 6'4" | 245 | 27 | | |
| Bill Dunstan | DT | 6'4" | 250 | 27 | | |
| Pete Lazetich | DT | 6'3" | 245 | 26 | | |
| Manny Sistrunk | DT | 6'5" | 275 | 29 | | |

Tom Luken – Knee Injury
John Niland – Knee Injury

| Use Name | Pos. | Hgt. | Wgt. | Age | Int | Pts |
|---|---|---|---|---|---|---|
| Bill Bergey | LB | 6'2" | 250 | 31 | 2 | |
| John Bunting | LB | 6'1" | 220 | 26 | | |
| Tom Ehlers | LB | 6'2" | 218 | 24 | 1 | |
| Frank LeMaster | LB | 6'2" | 231 | 24 | | |
| Drew Mahalic | LB | 6'4" | 228 | 23 | | |
| Terry Tautolo | LB | 6'2" | 234 | 22 | | |
| Bill Bradley | DB | 5'11" | 190 | 29 | 2 | |
| Mark Burke | DB | 6'1" | 175 | 22 | | |
| Tommy Campbell | DB | 6' | 188 | 26 | | |
| Al Clark | DB | 6' | 185 | 28 | 1 | |
| Randy Logan | DB | 6'1" | 195 | 25 | 1 | |
| Larry Marshall | DB | 5'10" | 195 | 26 | | |
| John Outlaw | DB | 5'10" | 180 | 30 | 2 | |
| Artimus Parker | DB | 6'3" | 200 | 24 | | |

Dean Halverson – Injured

| Use Name | Pos. | Hgt. | Wgt. | Age | Int | Pts |
|---|---|---|---|---|---|---|
| Mike Boryla | QB | 6'3" | 200 | 25 | | 12 |
| Roman Gabriel | QB | 6'4" | 220 | 36 | | |
| John Walton | QB | 6'2" | 210 | 28 | | |
| Dave Hampton (from ATL) | HB | 6' | 202 | 29 | | 6 |
| Mike Hogan | HB-FB | 6'2" | 205 | 21 | | |
| Herb Lusk | HB | 6' | 190 | 23 | | |
| James McAlister | HB | 6'1" | 205 | 24 | | |
| Tom Sullivan | HB | 6' | 190 | 26 | | 18 |
| Art Malone | FB | 5'11" | 216 | 28 | | 6 |
| Bill Olds (from SEA) | FB | 6'1" | 224 | 25 | | 6 |
| Harold Carmichael | WR | 6'7" | 225 | 26 | | 30 |
| Vince Papale | WR | 6'2" | 195 | 30 | | |
| Charlie Smith | WR | 6'1" | 185 | 26 | | 30 |
| Keith Krepfle | TE | 6'3" | 225 | 24 | | 6 |
| Charlie Young | TE | 6'4" | 238 | 25 | | |
| Spike Jones | K | 6'2" | 195 | 29 | | |
| Horst Muhlmann | K | 6'1" | 219 | 36 | | 51 |

## NEW YORK GIANTS 3-11 Bill Arnsparger (0-7), John McVay (3-4)

| Scores of Each Game | | |
|---|---|---|
| 17 | Washington | 19 |
| 7 | Philadelphia | 20 |
| 10 | Los Angeles | 24 |
| 21 | St. Louis | 27 |
| 14 | DALLAS | 24 |
| 7 | Minnesota | 24 |
| 0 | PITTSBURGH | 27 |
| 0 | PHILADELPHIA | 10 |
| 3 | Dallas | 9 |
| 12 | WASHINGTON | 9 |
| 13 | Denver | 14 |
| 28 | SEATTLE | 16 |
| 24 | DETROIT | 10 |
| 14 | ST. LOUIS | 17 |

| Use Name | Pos. | Hgt. | Wgt. | Age | Int | Pts. |
|---|---|---|---|---|---|---|
| Mike Gibbons | OT | 6'4" | 262 | 25 | | |
| Doug Van Horn | OT | 6'2" | 245 | 32 | | |
| Bill Ellenboggen | OG-OT | 6'4" | 260 | 25 | | |
| John Hicks | OG | 6'2" | 258 | 25 | | |
| Ron Mikolajczyk | OG | 6'3" | 275 | 26 | | |
| Tom Mullen | OG-OT | 6'3" | 250 | 24 | | |
| Al Simpson | OG-OT | 6'5" | 255 | 25 | | |
| Karl Chandler | C-OG | 6'5" | 250 | 24 | | |
| Ralph Hill | C | 6'1" | 245 | 26 | | |
| Troy Archer | DE | 6'4" | 250 | 21 | | |
| Rick Dvorak | DE | 6'4" | 245 | 24 | | |
| Jack Gregory | DE | 6'6" | 250 | 31 | | |
| George Martin | DE | 6'4" | 245 | 23 | | |
| Dave Gallagher | DT | 6'4" | 256 | 24 | 1 | |
| John Mendenhall | DT | 6'1" | 255 | 27 | 1 | |

Jim Pietrzak – Back Injury

| Use Name | Pos. | Hgt. | Wgt. | Age | Int | Pts |
|---|---|---|---|---|---|---|
| Harry Carson | LB | 6'2" | 228 | 22 | | |
| Brad Cousino | LB | 6' | 220 | 23 | | |
| Pat Hughes | LB | 6'2" | 225 | 29 | 1 | |
| Brian Kelley | LB | 6'3" | 222 | 25 | | |
| Dan Lloyd | LB | 6'2" | 225 | 22 | | |
| Bob Schmit | LB | 6'1" | 220 | 26 | | |
| John Tate | LB | 6'2" | 230 | 23 | | |
| Brad Van Pelt | LB | 6'5" | 235 | 25 | 2 | |
| Bobby Brooks | DB | 6'1" | 195 | 25 | 1 | |
| Bill Bryant | DB | 5'11" | 195 | 25 | | |
| Rondy Colbert | DB | 5'9" | 165 | 22 | | |
| Larry Mallory | DB | 5'11" | 185 | 24 | 1 | |
| Clyde Powers | DB | 6'1" | 195 | 25 | 1 | |
| Jim Stienke | DB | 5'11" | 182 | 25 | 2 | 6 |
| Henry Stuckey | DB | 6'1" | 180 | 26 | | |
| Rick Volk | DB | 6'3" | 195 | 31 | 2 | |

Charlie Ford – Knee Injury
Robert Giblin – Shoulder Injury

| Use Name | Pos. | Hgt. | Wgt. | Age | Int | Pts |
|---|---|---|---|---|---|---|
| Craig Morton | QB | 6'4" | 210 | 33 | | |
| Dennis Shaw | QB | 6'2" | 215 | 29 | | |
| Norm Snead | QB | 6'4" | 215 | 36 | | |
| Gordon Bell | HB | 5'9" | 180 | 22 | | 12 |
| Steve Crosby | HB | 5'11" | 205 | 26 | | |
| Bob Hammond | HB | 5'9" | 175 | 24 | | |
| Doug Kotar | HB | 5'11" | 205 | 25 | | 18 |
| Larry Csonka | FB | 6'3" | 237 | 29 | | 24 |
| Larry Watkins | FB | 6'2" | 230 | 29 | | 6 |
| Marsh White | FB | 6'2" | 220 | 23 | | 6 |
| Walker Gillette | WR | 6'5" | 200 | 29 | | 12 |
| Ed Marshall (from NYJ) | WR | 6'4" | 198 | 28 | | 18 |
| Ray Rhodes | WR | 5'11" | 185 | 25 | | 6 |
| Jim Robinson | WR | 5'9" | 170 | 23 | | 6 |
| Roger Wallace | WR | 5'11" | 180 | 24 | | |
| Gary Shirk | TE | 6'1" | 220 | 26 | | 6 |
| Bob Tucker | TE | 6'3" | 230 | 31 | | 6 |
| Joe Danelo | K | 5'9" | 166 | 22 | | 44 |
| Dave Jennings | K | 6'4" | 205 | 24 | | |

* – Overtime

## DALLAS COWBOYS

### RUSHING

| Last Name | No. | Yds | Avg | TD |
|---|---|---|---|---|
| Dennison | 153 | 542 | 3.5 | 6 |
| Newhouse | 116 | 450 | 3.9 | 3 |
| Laidlaw | 94 | 424 | 4.5 | 3 |
| P. Pearson | 68 | 233 | 3.4 | 1 |
| Young | 48 | 208 | 4.3 | 0 |
| Staubach | 43 | 184 | 4.3 | 3 |
| DuPree | 7 | 50 | 7.1 | 0 |
| D. Pearson | 2 | 20 | 10.0 | 0 |
| Saldi | 1 | 19 | 19.0 | 0 |
| D. White | 6 | 17 | 2.8 | 0 |

### RECEIVING

| Last Name | No. | Yds. | Avg | TD |
|---|---|---|---|---|
| D. Pearson | 58 | 806 | 14 | 6 |
| DuPree | 42 | 680 | 16 | 2 |
| Laidlaw | 38 | 325 | 9 | 1 |
| P. Pearson | 23 | 316 | 14 | 2 |
| Richards | 19 | 414 | 22 | 3 |
| Newhouse | 15 | 86 | 6 | 0 |
| Young | 11 | 134 | 12 | 1 |
| Dennison | 8 | 67 | 8 | 0 |
| Johnson | 5 | 84 | 17 | 2 |
| Barnes | 1 | 43 | 43 | 0 |
| Reece | 1 | 6 | 6 | 0 |
| Saldi | 1 | 6 | 6 | 0 |

### PUNT RETURNS

| Last Name | No. | Yds | Avg | TD |
|---|---|---|---|---|
| Johnson | 45 | 489 | 11 | 0 |

### KICKOFF RETURNS

| Last Name | No. | Yds | Avg | TD |
|---|---|---|---|---|
| Johnson | 28 | 693 | 25 | 0 |
| Jensen | 13 | 313 | 24 | 0 |
| Saldi | 1 | 9 | 9 | 0 |
| Henderson | 0 | 12 | 0 | 0 |

### PASSING – PUNTING – KICKING

| PASSING | Att | Comp | % | Yds | Yd/Att | TD | Int-% | RK |
|---|---|---|---|---|---|---|---|---|
| Staubach | 369 | 208 | 56 | 2715 | 7.4 | 14 | 11- 3 | 5 |
| D. White | 20 | 13 | 65 | 213 | 10.7 | 2 | 2- 10 | |
| D. Pearson | 1 | 1 | 100 | 39 | 39.0 | 1 | 0- 0 | |

| PUNTING | No | Avg |
|---|---|---|
| D. White | 70 | 38.4 |
| Herrera | 2 | 24.5 |

| KICKING | XP | Att | % | FG | Att | % |
|---|---|---|---|---|---|---|
| Herrera | 34 | 34 | 100 | 18 | 23 | 78 |

## WASHINGTON REDSKINS

### RUSHING

| Last Name | No. | Yds | Avg | TD |
|---|---|---|---|---|
| Thomas | 254 | 1101 | 4.3 | 5 |
| Riggins | 162 | 572 | 3.5 | 3 |
| Hill | 79 | 301 | 3.8 | 1 |
| Theismann | 17 | 97 | 5.7 | 1 |
| L. Brown | 20 | 56 | 2.8 | 0 |
| Fugett | 2 | 0 | 0.0 | 0 |
| Kilmer | 13 | -7 | -0.5 | 0 |
| Grant | 1 | -9 | -9.0 | 0 |

### RECEIVING

| Last Name | No. | Yds. | Avg | TD |
|---|---|---|---|---|
| Grant | 50 | 818 | 16 | 5 |
| Thomas | 28 | 290 | 10 | 4 |
| Jefferson | 27 | 364 | 13 | 2 |
| Fugett | 27 | 334 | 12 | 6 |
| Riggins | 21 | 172 | 8 | 1 |
| L. Brown | 17 | 98 | 6 | 0 |
| Hill | 7 | 100 | 14 | 0 |
| Smith | 7 | 75 | 11 | 2 |
| Buggs | 2 | 25 | 13 | 0 |
| Malinchak | 1 | 12 | 12 | 0 |

### PUNT RETURNS

| Last Name | No. | Yds | Avg | TD |
|---|---|---|---|---|
| E. Brown | 48 | 646 | 13 | 1 |
| Scott | 3 | 27 | 9 | 0 |
| Jones | 1 | 15 | 15 | 0 |

### KICKOFF RETURNS

| Last Name | No. | Yds | Avg | TD |
|---|---|---|---|---|
| E. Brown | 30 | 738 | 25 | 0 |
| Fryer | 9 | 166 | 18 | 0 |
| Brunet | 4 | 85 | 21 | 0 |
| Winslow | 2 | 32 | 16 | 0 |
| Jones | 1 | 16 | 16 | 0 |
| Owens | 1 | 15 | 15 | 0 |
| Tillman | 1 | 14 | 14 | 0 |
| Lorch | 1 | 0 | 0 | 0 |
| Wysocki | 1 | 0 | 0 | 0 |

### PASSING – PUNTING – KICKING

| PASSING | Att | Comp | % | Yds | Yd/Att | TD | Int-% | RK |
|---|---|---|---|---|---|---|---|---|
| Kilmer | 206 | 108 | 52 | 1252 | 6.1 | 12 | 10- 5 | 6 |
| Theismann | 163 | 79 | 49 | 1036 | 6.4 | 8 | 10- 6 | 9 |
| Hill | 1 | 0 | 0 | 0 | 0.0 | 0 | 0- 0 | |

| PUNTING | No | Avg |
|---|---|---|
| Bragg | 90 | 38.9 |

| KICKING | XP | Att | % | FG | Att | % |
|---|---|---|---|---|---|---|
| Moseley | 31 | 32 | 97 | 22 | 34 | 65 |

## ST. LOUIS CARDINALS

### RUSHING

| Last Name | No. | Yds | Avg | TD |
|---|---|---|---|---|
| Otis | 233 | 891 | 3.8 | 2 |
| Metcalf | 134 | 537 | 4.0 | 3 |
| Jones | 113 | 451 | 4.0 | 8 |
| Morris | 64 | 292 | 4.6 | 3 |
| Latin | 25 | 115 | 4.6 | 1 |
| Wehrli | 2 | 8 | 4.0 | 0 |
| Hart | 8 | 7 | 0.9 | 0 |
| Joyce | 1 | 0 | 0.0 | 0 |

### RECEIVING

| Last Name | No. | Yds. | Avg | TD |
|---|---|---|---|---|
| Harris | 52 | 782 | 15 | 1 |
| Gray | 36 | 686 | 19 | 5 |
| Metcalf | 33 | 388 | 12 | 4 |
| Jones | 29 | 152 | 5 | 1 |
| Tilley | 26 | 407 | 16 | 1 |
| Cain | 26 | 400 | 15 | 5 |
| Morris | 8 | 75 | 9 | 1 |
| Latin | 4 | 35 | 9 | 0 |
| Smith | 3 | 22 | 7 | 0 |
| Otis | 2 | 15 | 8 | 0 |
| Hammond | 1 | 5 | 5 | 0 |

### PUNT RETURNS

| Last Name | No. | Yds | Avg | TD |
|---|---|---|---|---|
| Metcalf | 17 | 188 | 11 | 0 |
| Tilley | 15 | 146 | 10 | 0 |
| Hammond | 3 | 16 | 5 | 0 |
| Neils | 1 | 0 | 0 | 0 |

### KICKOFF RETURNS

| Last Name | No. | Yds | Avg | TD |
|---|---|---|---|---|
| Latin | 16 | 357 | 22 | 0 |
| Metcalf | 16 | 325 | 20 | 0 |
| Morris | 9 | 181 | 20 | 0 |
| Smith | 3 | 63 | 21 | 0 |
| Crump | 3 | 57 | 19 | 0 |
| Hammond | 2 | 36 | 18 | 0 |
| Nelson | 1 | 43 | 43 | 0 |
| McGraw | 1 | 13 | 13 | 0 |
| Oates | 1 | 12 | 12 | 0 |
| Okoniewski | 1 | 12 | 12 | 0 |
| Severson | 1 | 3 | 3 | 0 |

### PASSING – PUNTING – KICKING

| PASSING | Att | Comp | % | Yds | Yd/Att | TD | Int-% | RK |
|---|---|---|---|---|---|---|---|---|
| Hart | 388 | 218 | 56 | 2946 | 7.6 | 18 | 13- 3 | 4 |
| Donckers | 1 | 1 | 100 | 16 | 16.0 | 0 | 0- 0 | |
| Metcalf | 1 | 0 | 0 | 0 | 0.0 | 0 | 0- 0 | |
| Wehrli | 1 | 0 | 0 | 0 | 0.0 | 0 | 0- 0 | |

| PUNTING | No | Avg |
|---|---|---|
| Joyce | 64 | 36.4 |

| KICKING | XP | Att | % | FG | Att | % |
|---|---|---|---|---|---|---|
| Bakken | 33 | 35 | 94 | 20 | 27 | 74 |

## PHILADELPHIA EAGLES

### RUSHING

| Last Name | No. | Yds | Avg | TD |
|---|---|---|---|---|
| Hogan | 123 | 561 | 4.6 | 0 |
| Sullivan | 99 | 399 | 4.0 | 2 |
| Hampton | 83 | 291 | 3.5 | 1 |
| McAlister | 68 | 265 | 3.9 | 0 |
| Lusk | 61 | 254 | 4.2 | 0 |
| Boryla | 29 | 166 | 5.7 | 2 |
| Olds | 38 | 129 | 3.4 | 1 |
| Smith | 9 | 25 | 2.8 | 1 |
| Malone | 2 | 14 | 7.0 | 1 |
| Young | 1 | 6 | 6.0 | 0 |
| Gabriel | 4 | 2 | 0.5 | 0 |
| Walton | 2 | 1 | 0.5 | 0 |

### RECEIVING

| Last Name | No. | Yds. | Avg | TD |
|---|---|---|---|---|
| Carmichael | 42 | 503 | 12 | 5 |
| Young | 30 | 374 | 12 | 0 |
| Smith | 27 | 412 | 15 | 4 |
| Hogan | 15 | 89 | 6 | 0 |
| Sullivan | 14 | 116 | 8 | 1 |
| Lusk | 13 | 119 | 9 | 0 |
| McAlister | 12 | 72 | 6 | 0 |
| Hampton | 12 | 57 | 5 | 0 |
| Olds | 9 | 29 | 3 | 0 |
| Krepfle | 6 | 80 | 13 | 1 |
| Malone | 1 | -3 | -3 | 0 |
| LeMaster | 1 | -4 | -4 | 0 |

### PUNT RETURNS

| Last Name | No. | Yds | Avg | TD |
|---|---|---|---|---|
| Marshall | 27 | 290 | 11 | 0 |
| Bradley | 9 | 64 | 7 | 0 |
| Clark | 4 | 57 | 14 | 0 |
| Burke | 1 | 14 | 14 | 0 |

### KICKOFF RETURNS

| Last Name | No. | Yds | Avg | TD |
|---|---|---|---|---|
| Marshall | 30 | 651 | 22 | 0 |
| McAlister | 9 | 172 | 19 | 0 |
| Lusk | 7 | 155 | 22 | 0 |
| Sullivan | 5 | 108 | 22 | 0 |
| Hampton | 3 | 46 | 15 | 0 |
| Olds | 1 | 11 | 11 | 0 |
| Ehlers | 1 | 8 | 8 | 0 |
| Bleamer | 1 | 0 | 0 | 0 |
| Smith | 1 | -3 | -3 | 0 |

### PASSING – PUNTING – KICKING

| PASSING | Att | Comp | % | Yds | Yd/Att | TD | Int-% | RK |
|---|---|---|---|---|---|---|---|---|
| Boryla | 246 | 123 | 50 | 1247 | 5.1 | 9 | 14- 6 | 12 |
| Gabriel | 92 | 46 | 50 | 476 | 5.2 | 2 | 2- 2 | |
| Walton | 28 | 12 | 43 | 125 | 4.5 | 0 | 2- 7 | |
| Carmichael | 2 | 0 | 0 | 0 | 0.0 | 0 | 0- 0 | |
| Jones | 1 | 1 | 100 | -4 | -4.0 | 0 | 0- 0 | |

| PUNTING | No | Avg |
|---|---|---|
| Jones | 94 | 36.6 |

| KICKING | XP | Att | % | FG | Att | % |
|---|---|---|---|---|---|---|
| Muhlmann | 18 | 19 | 95 | 11 | 16 | 69 |

## NEW YORK GIANTS

### RUSHING

| Last Name | No. | Yds | Avg | TD |
|---|---|---|---|---|
| Kotar | 185 | 731 | 4.0 | 3 |
| Csonka | 160 | 569 | 3.6 | 4 |
| Bell | 67 | 233 | 3.5 | 2 |
| White | 69 | 223 | 3.2 | 1 |
| Watkins | 26 | 96 | 3.7 | 1 |
| Morton | 15 | 48 | 3.2 | 0 |
| Rhodes | 2 | 10 | 5.0 | 0 |
| Mallory | 1 | 0 | 0.0 | 0 |
| Snead | 3 | -1 | -0.3 | 0 |
| Crosby | 1 | -1 | -1.0 | 0 |
| Gillette | 1 | -4 | -4.0 | 0 |

### RECEIVING

| Last Name | No. | Yds. | Avg | TD |
|---|---|---|---|---|
| Tucker | 42 | 498 | 12 | 1 |
| Kotar | 36 | 319 | 9 | 1 |
| Bell | 25 | 198 | 8 | 0 |
| Robinson | 18 | 249 | 14 | 1 |
| Rhodes | 16 | 305 | 19 | 1 |
| Gillette | 16 | 263 | 16 | 2 |
| Marshall | 8 | 166 | 21 | 3 |
| Csonka | 6 | 39 | 7 | 0 |
| Shirk | 4 | 52 | 13 | 1 |
| Watkins | 2 | 8 | 4 | 0 |
| White | 2 | 7 | 4 | 0 |

### PUNT RETURNS

| Last Name | No. | Yds | Avg | TD |
|---|---|---|---|---|
| Robinson | 24 | 106 | 4 | 0 |
| Colbert | 13 | 72 | 6 | 0 |
| Stienke | 3 | 18 | 6 | 0 |
| Bell | 1 | 1 | 1 | 0 |

### KICKOFF RETURNS

| Last Name | No. | Yds | Avg | TD |
|---|---|---|---|---|
| Robinson | 20 | 444 | 22 | 0 |
| Bell | 18 | 352 | 20 | 0 |
| Shirk | 6 | 109 | 18 | 0 |
| Kotar | 3 | 39 | 13 | 0 |
| Hammond | 2 | 44 | 22 | 0 |
| Colbert | 2 | 42 | 21 | 0 |
| Watkins | 1 | 9 | 9 | 0 |
| Carson | 1 | 5 | 5 | 0 |

### PASSING – PUNTING – KICKING

| PASSING | Att | Comp | % | Yds | Yd/Att | TD | Int-% | RK |
|---|---|---|---|---|---|---|---|---|
| Morton | 284 | 153 | 54 | 1865 | 6.6 | 9 | 20- 7 | 11 |
| Snead | 42 | 22 | 52 | 239 | 5.7 | 0 | 4- 10 | |

| PUNTING | No | Avg |
|---|---|---|
| Jennings | 74 | 41.3 |

| KICKING | XP | Att | % | FG | Att | % |
|---|---|---|---|---|---|---|
| Danelo | 20 | 21 | 95 | 8 | 21 | 38 |

## MINNESOTA VIKINGS 11-2-1 Bud Grant

### Scores of Each Game

| |  | |
|---|---|---|
| 40 | New Orleans | 9 |
| 10 | LOS ANGELES | *10 |
| 10 | Detroit | 9 |
| 17 | PITTSBURGH | 6 |
| 20 | CHICAGO | 19 |
| 24 | N.Y. GIANTS | 7 |
| 31 | Philadelphia | 12 |
| 13 | Chicago | 14 |
| 31 | DETROIT | 23 |
| 27 | SEATTLE | 21 |
| 17 | Green Bay | 10 |
| 16 | San Francisco | 20 |
| 20 | GREEN BAY | 9 |
| 29 | Miami | 7 |

| Use Name | Pos. | Hgt. | Wgt. | Age | Int | Pts |
|---|---|---|---|---|---|---|
| Bart Buetow | OT | 6'5" | 250 | 25 | | |
| Charlie Goodrum | OT | 6'3" | 256 | 26 | | |
| Steve Riley | OT | 6'6" | 258 | 23 | | |
| Ron Yary | OT | 6'6" | 255 | 30 | | |
| Wes Hamilton | OG | 6'3" | 255 | 23 | | |
| Ed White | OG | 6'2" | 270 | 29 | | |
| Mick Tingelhoff | C | 6'1" | 240 | 36 | | |
| Scott Anderson | C | 6'4" | 250 | 25 | | |
| Doug Dumler | C | 6'3" | 250 | 25 | | |
| Carl Eller | DE | 6'6" | 247 | 34 | | |
| Jim Marshall | DE | 6'3" | 240 | 39 | | |
| Mark Mullaney | DE | 6'6" | 242 | 23 | | |
| Alan Page | DT | 6'5" | 245 | 31 | | |
| Doug Sutherland | DT | 6'3" | 250 | 28 | | |
| James White | DT | 6'3" | 263 | 22 | | |
| Matt Blair | LB | 6'5" | 229 | 25 | 2 | |
| Wally Hilgenberg | LB | 6'3" | 229 | 33 | | |
| Amos Martin | LB | 6'3" | 228 | 27 | | |
| Fred McNeill | LB | 6'2" | 229 | 24 | | |
| Jeff Siemon | LB | 6'2" | 237 | 26 | 1 | |
| Roy Winston | LB | 6'1" | 222 | 36 | | |
| Nate Allen | DB | 5'10" | 174 | 28 | 3 | 6 |
| Autry Beamon | DB | 6'1" | 190 | 22 | 1 | |
| Bobby Bryant | DB | 6' | 170 | 32 | 2 | |
| Windlan Hall | DB | 5'11" | 175 | 26 | | |
| Paul Krause | DB | 6'3" | 200 | 34 | 2 | |
| Jeff Wright | DB | 5'11" | 190 | 27 | 1 | |
| Nate Wright | DB | 5'11" | 180 | 28 | 7 | |
| Bob Berry | QB | 5'11" | 185 | 34 | | |
| Bob Lee | QB | 6'2" | 195 | 30 | | |
| Fran Tarkenton | QB | 6'1" | 190 | 36 | | 6 |
| Chuck Foreman | HB | 6'2" | 207 | 25 | | 84 |
| Brent McClanahan | HB-FB | 5'10" | 202 | 25 | | 30 |
| Robert Miller | HB | 5'11" | 204 | 23 | | 6 |
| Bob Groce | FB | 6'2" | 210 | 22 | | |
| Sammy Johnson (from SF) | FB | 6' | 217 | 23 | | 12 |
| Mark Kellar | FB | 6' | 225 | 24 | | |
| Willie Spencer | FB | 6'3" | 235 | 23 | | |
| Bob Grim | WR | 6' | 188 | 31 | | |
| Ahmad Rashad | WR | 6'2" | 200 | 26 | | 18 |
| Sammy White | WR | 5'11" | 189 | 22 | | 60 |
| Leonard Willis | WR | 5'10" | 180 | 23 | | |
| Steve Craig | TE | 6'3" | 231 | 25 | | |
| Stu Voigt | TE | 6'1" | 225 | 28 | | 6 |
| Neil Clabo | K | 6'2" | 200 | 23 | | |
| Fred Cox | K | 5'10" | 200 | 37 | | 89 |

## CHICAGO BEARS 7-7 Jack Pardee

### Scores of Each Game

| |  | |
|---|---|---|
| 10 | DETROIT | 3 |
| 19 | San Francisco | 12 |
| 0 | ATLANTA | 10 |
| 33 | WASHINGTON | 7 |
| 19 | Minnesota | 20 |
| 12 | Los Angeles | 20 |
| 21 | Dallas | 31 |
| 14 | MINNESOTA | 13 |
| 27 | OAKLAND | 28 |
| 24 | GREEN BAY | 13 |
| 10 | Detroit | 14 |
| 16 | Green Bay | 10 |
| 34 | Seattle | 7 |
| 14 | DENVER | 28 |

| Use Name | Pos. | Hgt. | Wgt. | Age | Int | Pts |
|---|---|---|---|---|---|---|
| Lionel Antoine | OT | 6'6" | 266 | 26 | | |
| Dan Jiggetts | OT | 6'4" | 274 | 22 | | |
| Dennis Lick | OT | 6'3" | 271 | 22 | | |
| Jeff Sevy | OT-OG | 6'5" | 260 | 25 | | |
| Noah Jackson | OG | 6'2" | 265 | 25 | | |
| Revie Sorey | OG | 6'2" | 270 | 22 | | |
| John Ward (from TB) | OG-C | 6'4" | 269 | 28 | | |
| Dan Neal | C-OG | 6'4" | 257 | 27 | | |
| Don Peiffer | C | 6'3" | 254 | 25 | | |
| Royce Berry | DE | 6'3" | 239 | 30 | | |
| Mike Hartenstine | DE | 6'3" | 256 | 23 | | 6 |
| Jerry Meyers | DE | 6'4" | 245 | 22 | | |
| Roger Stillwell | DE | 6'5" | 254 | 24 | | |
| Wally Chambers | DT | 6'6" | 250 | 25 | 1 | |
| Jim Osborne | DT | 6'3" | 248 | 26 | | |
| Ron Rydalch | DT | 6'4" | 262 | 24 | | |
| Ross Brupbacher | LB | 6'3" | 220 | 28 | 7 | |
| Waymond Bryant | LB | 6'3" | 239 | 24 | 2 | |
| Doug Buffone | LB | 6'1" | 229 | 32 | | |
| Tom Hicks | LB | 6'4" | 235 | 23 | | |
| Jerry Muckensturm | LB | 6'4" | 226 | 22 | | |
| Dan Rives | LB | 6'2" | 230 | 25 | | |
| Craig Clemons | DB | 5'11" | 195 | 27 | 1 | |
| Allan Ellis | DB | 5'10" | 180 | 25 | 6 | 6 |
| Gary Fencik | DB | 6'1" | 190 | 22 | | |
| Bill Knox | DB | 5'9" | 190 | 25 | | |
| Virgil Livers | DB | 5'9" | 176 | 24 | 3 | |
| Doug Plank | DB | 6' | 198 | 23 | 4 | |
| Terry Schmidt | DB | 6' | 175 | 24 | | |
| Bob Avellini | QB | 6'2" | 211 | 23 | | 6 |
| Virgil Carter | QB | 6'1" | 190 | 30 | | |
| Gary Huff | QB | 6'1" | 199 | 25 | | |
| Mike Adamle | HB-FB | 5'9" | 198 | 26 | | 8 |
| Roland Harper | HB-FB | 6' | 215 | 23 | | 18 |
| Johnny Musso | HB | 5'11" | 201 | 26 | | |
| Walter Payton | HB | 5'11" | 203 | 22 | | 78 |
| Larry Schreiber | FB-HB | 6' | 205 | 29 | | |
| Brian Baschnagel | WR-DB | 6' | 195 | 22 | | |
| Randy Burks | WR | 6'2" | 170 | 23 | | 6 |
| Bo Rather | WR | 6'1" | 188 | 25 | | |
| Steve Schubert | WR | 5'10" | 187 | 25 | | |
| James Scott | WR | 6'1" | 185 | 24 | | 36 |
| Ron Shanklin | WR | 6'1" | 187 | 28 | | |
| Bob Bruer | TE | 6'5" | 230 | 23 | | |
| Gary Butler | TE | 6'3" | 235 | 25 | | |
| Greg Latta | TE | 6'3" | 228 | 23 | | |
| Bob Parsons | TE | 6'4" | 241 | 26 | | |
| Bob Thomas | K | 5'10" | 177 | 24 | | 63 |

Gary Hrivnak — Injury

## DETROIT LIONS 6-8 Rick Forzano (1-3), Tommy Hudspeth (5-5)

### Scores of Each Game

| |  | |
|---|---|---|
| 3 | Chicago | 10 |
| 24 | ATLANTA | 10 |
| 9 | MINNESOTA | 10 |
| 14 | Green Bay | 24 |
| 30 | NEW ENGLAND | 10 |
| 7 | Washington | 20 |
| 41 | Seattle | 14 |
| 27 | GREEN BAY | 6 |
| 23 | Minnesota | 31 |
| 16 | New Orleans | 17 |
| 14 | CHICAGO | 10 |
| 27 | BUFFALO | 14 |
| 10 | N.Y. Giants | 24 |
| 17 | LOS ANGELES | 20 |

| Use Name | Pos. | Hgt. | Wgt. | Age | Int | Pts |
|---|---|---|---|---|---|---|
| Russ Bolinger | OT | 6'5" | 255 | 21 | | |
| Rocky Freitas | OT | 6'6" | 275 | 30 | | |
| Craig Hertwig | OT | 6'8" | 270 | 24 | | |
| Jim Yarbrough | OT | 6'6" | 265 | 29 | | |
| Lynn Boden | OG | 6'5" | 270 | 23 | | |
| Bob Kowalkowski | OG | 6'3" | 245 | 32 | | |
| Ken Long | OG | 6'3" | 265 | 23 | | |
| Mark Markovich | C | 6'5" | 255 | 23 | | |
| Jon Morris | C | 6'4" | 250 | 33 | | |
| Billy Howard | DE | 6'4" | 255 | 26 | | |
| Jim Mitchell | DE | 6'3" | 250 | 27 | | |
| Ernie Price | DE | 6'4" | 245 | 25 | | |
| Ken Sanders | DE | 6'5" | 245 | 26 | | |
| Don Croft | DT | 6'3" | 258 | 27 | | |
| Doug English | DT | 6'5" | 245 | 23 | | |
| Larry Hand | DT | 6'4" | 245 | 36 | 1 | |
| Herb Orvis | DT | 6'5" | 245 | 29 | | |
| Jim Laslavic | LB | 6'2" | 240 | 24 | 2 | |
| Paul Naumoff | LB | 6'1" | 215 | 31 | | |
| Ed O'Neil | LB | 6'3" | 235 | 23 | 1 | 6 |
| Garth Ten Napel | LB | 6'1" | 210 | 22 | | |
| Charlie Weaver | LB | 6'2" | 225 | 27 | 2 | |
| John Woodcock | LB | 6'3" | 240 | 22 | | |
| Lem Barney | DB | 6' | 190 | 30 | 2 | 6 |
| Ben Davis | DB | 5'11" | 180 | 30 | 6 | |
| James Hunter | DB | 6'3" | 195 | 22 | 7 | 6 |
| Dick Jauron | DB | 6' | 190 | 25 | 2 | |
| Levi Johnson | DB | 6'3" | 200 | 25 | 6 | 6 |
| Maurice Tyler | DB | 6' | 188 | 26 | | |
| Charlie West | DB | 6'1" | 190 | 30 | 1 | |
| Gary Danielson | QB | 6'2" | 195 | 24 | | |
| Greg Landry | QB | 6'4" | 205 | 29 | | 6 |
| Joe Reed | QB | 6'1" | 195 | 28 | | 6 |
| Andy Bolton (from SEA) | HB | 6'1" | 205 | 22 | | |
| Dexter Bussey | HB | 6'1" | 210 | 24 | | 18 |
| Bobby Thompson | HB | 5'11" | 195 | 29 | | |
| Lawrence Gaines | FB | 6'1" | 240 | 24 | | 30 |
| Jim Hooks | FB | 5'11" | 225 | 24 | | |
| Horace King | FB | 5'10" | 210 | 23 | | |
| Dennis Franklin | WR | 6'1" | 185 | 23 | | |
| J.D. Hill | WR | 6'1" | 185 | 27 | | |
| Ray Jarvis | WR | 5'11" | 190 | 27 | | 30 |
| Bob Picard (from PHI.) | WR | 6'1" | 198 | 26 | | |
| Leonard Thompson | WR | 5'10" | 190 | 24 | | |
| Larry Walton | WR | 6' | 185 | 29 | | 18 |
| David Hill | TE | 6'2" | 220 | 22 | | 30 |
| Charlie Sanders | TE | 6'4" | 230 | 30 | | 30 |
| Benny Ricardo (from BUF) | K | 5'9" | 175 | 22 | | 54 |
| Herman Weaver | K | 6'4" | 210 | 27 | | |

## GREEN BAY PACKERS 5-9 Bart Starr

### Scores of Each Game

| |  | |
|---|---|---|
| 14 | SAN FRANCISCO | 26 |
| 0 | St. Louis | 29 |
| 7 | Cincinnati | 28 |
| 24 | DETROIT | 14 |
| 27 | SEATTLE | 20 |
| 28 | PHILADELPHIA | 13 |
| 14 | Oakland | 18 |
| 6 | Detroit | 27 |
| 32 | NEW ORLEANS | 27 |
| 13 | Chicago | 24 |
| 10 | MINNESOTA | 17 |
| 10 | CHICAGO | 16 |
| 9 | Minnesota | 20 |
| 24 | Atlanta | 20 |

| Use Name | Pos. | Hgt. | Wgt. | Age | Int | Pts |
|---|---|---|---|---|---|---|
| Dick Himes | OT | 6'4" | 260 | 30 | | |
| Mark Koncar | OT | 6'5" | 271 | 23 | | |
| Dick Enderle (from S.F.) | OG | 6'1" | 250 | 28 | | |
| Gale Gillingham | OG | 6'3" | 265 | 32 | | |
| Melvin Jackson | OG | 6'1" | 267 | 22 | | |
| Steve Knutson | OG | 6'3" | 254 | 24 | | |
| Bruce Van Dyke | OG | 6'2" | 255 | 32 | | |
| Bob Hyland | C | 6'5" | 255 | 31 | | |
| Larry McCarren | C | 6'3" | 248 | 24 | | |
| Bob Barber | DE | 6'3" | 240 | 24 | | |
| Dave Pureifory | DE | 6'1" | 255 | 27 | | |
| Alden Roche | DE | 6'4" | 255 | 31 | | |
| Clarence Williams | DE | 6'5" | 255 | 29 | | |
| Mike McCoy | DT | 6'5" | 275 | 27 | | |
| Dave Roller | DT | 6'2" | 270 | 26 | | |
| Ron Acks | LB | 6'2" | 225 | 31 | | |
| Fred Carr | LB | 6'5" | 240 | 30 | 1 | 6 |
| Jerry Dandridge | LB | 6'1" | 222 | 22 | | |
| Jim Gueno | LB | 6'2" | 220 | 22 | | |
| Don Hansen (from SEA) | LB | 6'3" | 228 | 32 | | |
| Bob Lally | LB | 6'2" | 230 | 24 | | |
| Tom Perko | LB | 6'3" | 233 | 22 | | |
| Tom Toner | LB | 6'3" | 235 | 26 | 1 | |
| Gary Weaver | LB | 6'1" | 225 | 27 | | |
| Willie Buchanan | DB | 6' | 190 | 25 | 2 | |
| Johnnie Gray | DB | 5'11" | 185 | 22 | 4 | 6 |
| Charlie Hall | DB | 6'1" | 190 | 28 | | |
| Steve Luke | DB | 6'2" | 205 | 22 | 2 | |
| Mike McCoy | DB | 5'11" | 183 | 23 | | |
| Perry Smith | DB | 6'1" | 195 | 25 | 1 | |
| Steve Wagner | DB | 6'2" | 198 | 22 | | |
| Carlos Brown | QB | 6'3" | 210 | 24 | | |
| Lynn Dickey | QB | 6'4" | 220 | 26 | | 6 |
| Randy Johnson (from WAS) | QB | 6'3" | 205 | 32 | | 6 |
| Will Harrell | HB | 5'9" | 182 | 23 | | 24 |
| Dave Osborn | HB | 6' | 208 | 33 | | |
| Clifton Taylor | HB | 6' | 195 | 24 | | 6 |
| Eric Torkelson | HB | 6'2" | 194 | 24 | | 12 |
| John Brockington | FB | 6'1" | 225 | 27 | | 12 |
| Barty Smith | FB | 6'4" | 240 | 24 | | 30 |
| Ken Starch | FB | 5'11" | 210 | 22 | | |
| Jessie Green | WR | 6'3" | 185 | 22 | | |
| Steve Odom | WR | 5'8" | 174 | 23 | | 12 |
| Ken Payne | WR | 6'1" | 185 | 25 | | 24 |
| Ollie Smith | WR | 6'2" | 200 | 27 | | 6 |
| Don Zimmerman (from PHI.) | WR | 6'3" | 195 | 26 | | |
| Bert Askon | TE | 6'3" | 225 | 30 | | 6 |
| Rich McGeorge | TE | 6'4" | 230 | 27 | | 6 |
| Randy Beverly | K | 6'2" | 180 | 26 | | |
| Chester Marcol | K | 6' | 190 | 26 | | 54 |

Jim Carter — Broken Arm

Don Milan — Broken Wrist
Gerald Tinker — Knee Injury

* — Overtime

## MINNESOTA VIKINGS

### Rushing

| Last Name | No. | Yds | Avg | TD |
|---|---|---|---|---|
| Foreman | 278 | 1155 | 4.2 | 13 |
| McClanhan | 130 | 382 | 2.9 | 4 |
| Miller | 67 | 286 | 4.3 | 0 |
| Johnson | 41 | 150 | 3.7 | 2 |
| Tarkenton | 27 | 45 | 1.7 | 1 |
| Kellar | 7 | 25 | 3.6 | 0 |
| Groce | 3 | 18 | 6.0 | 0 |
| Lee | 2 | 2 | 1.0 | 0 |
| Spencer | 4 | 2 | 0.5 | 0 |
| S. White | 5 | −10 | −2.0 | 0 |

### Receiving

| Last Name | No. | Yds | Avg | TD |
|---|---|---|---|---|
| Foreman | 55 | 567 | 10 | 1 |
| Rashad | 53 | 671 | 13 | 3 |
| S.White | 51 | 906 | 18 | 10 |
| McClanahan | 40 | 252 | 6 | 1 |
| Voigt | 28 | 303 | 11 | 1 |
| Miller | 23 | 181 | 8 | 1 |
| Grim | 9 | 108 | 12 | 0 |
| Johnson | 7 | 74 | 11 | 0 |
| Craig | 3 | 33 | 11 | 0 |
| Kellar | 2 | 22 | 11 | 0 |

### Punt Returns

| Last Name | No. | Yds | Avg | TD |
|---|---|---|---|---|
| Willis | 30 | 207 | 7 | 0 |
| Beamon | 7 | 19 | 3 | 0 |
| S.White | 3 | 45 | 15 | 0 |

### Kickoff Returns

| Last Name | No. | Yds | Avg | TD |
|---|---|---|---|---|
| Willis | 24 | 552 | 23 | 0 |
| S. White | 9 | 173 | 19 | 0 |
| Miller | 5 | 77 | 15 | 0 |
| Johnson | 2 | 35 | 18 | 0 |
| Kellar | 1 | 22 | 22 | 0 |
| Blair | 1 | 0 | 0 | 0 |

### Passing – Punting – Kicking

| PASSING | Att | Comp | % | Yds | Yd/Att | TD | Int–% | RK |
|---|---|---|---|---|---|---|---|---|
| Tarkenton | 412 | 255 | 62 | 2961 | 7.2 | 17 | 8–2 | 3 |
| Lee | 30 | 15 | 50 | 156 | 5.2 | 0 | 2–7 | |

| PUNTING | No | Avg |
|---|---|---|
| Clabo | 69 | 38.8 |

| KICKING | XP | Att | % | FG | Att | % |
|---|---|---|---|---|---|---|
| Cox | 32 | 36 | 89 | 19 | 31 | 61 |

## CHICAGO BEARS

### Rushing

| Last Name | No. | Yds | Avg | TD |
|---|---|---|---|---|
| Payton | 311 | 1390 | 4.5 | 13 |
| Harper | 147 | 625 | 4.3 | 2 |
| Musso | 57 | 200 | 3.5 | 4 |
| Adamle | 33 | 93 | 2.8 | 0 |
| Avellini | 18 | 58 | 3.2 | 1 |
| Schreiber | 4 | 15 | 3.8 | 0 |
| Rather | 1 | 4 | 4.0 | 0 |
| Parsons | 1 | 2 | 2.0 | 0 |
| Carter | 1 | 0 | 0.0 | 0 |
| Scott | 2 | −4 | −2.0 | 0 |
| Latta | 2 | −8 | −4.0 | 0 |
| Baschnagel | 1 | −12 | −12.0 | 0 |

### Receiving

| Last Name | No. | Yds | Avg | TD |
|---|---|---|---|---|
| Harper | 29 | 291 | 10 | 1 |
| Scott | 26 | 512 | 20 | 6 |
| Latta | 18 | 254 | 14 | 0 |
| Payton | 15 | 149 | 10 | 0 |
| Baschnagel | 13 | 226 | 17 | 0 |
| Rather | 5 | 33 | 7 | 0 |
| Schubert | 4 | 74 | 19 | 0 |
| Adamle | 4 | 28 | 7 | 1 |
| Musso | 4 | 26 | 7 | 0 |
| Shanklin | 2 | 32 | 16 | 0 |
| Burks | 1 | 55 | 55 | 1 |
| Schreiber | 1 | 16 | 16 | 0 |
| Parsons | 1 | 9 | 9 | 0 |

### Punt Returns

| Last Name | No. | Yds | Avg | TD |
|---|---|---|---|---|
| Livers | 28 | 205 | 7 | 0 |
| Schubert | 11 | 60 | 5 | 0 |
| Baschnagel | 2 | 2 | 1 | 0 |
| Adamle | 1 | 2 | 2 | 0 |
| Knox | 1 | 0 | 0 | 0 |

### Kickoff Returns

| Last Name | No. | Yds | Avg | TD |
|---|---|---|---|---|
| Baschnagel | 29 | 754 | 26 | 0 |
| Adamle | 11 | 179 | 16 | 0 |
| Harper | 6 | 119 | 20 | 0 |
| Musso | 2 | 18 | 9 | 0 |
| Livers | 1 | 14 | 14 | 0 |
| Schubert | 1 | 3 | 3 | 0 |
| Payton | 1 | 0 | 0 | 0 |

### Passing – Punting – Kicking

| PASSING | Att | Comp | % | Yds | Yd/Att | TD | Int–% | RK |
|---|---|---|---|---|---|---|---|---|
| Avellini | 271 | 118 | 44 | 1580 | 5.8 | 8 | 15–6 | 14 |
| Carter | 5 | 3 | 60 | 77 | 15.4 | 1 | 0–0 | |
| Parsons | 2 | 2 | 100 | 48 | 24.0 | 0 | 0–0 | |

| PUNTING | No | Avg |
|---|---|---|
| Parsons | 99 | 37.6 |

| KICKING | XP | Att | % | FG | Att | % |
|---|---|---|---|---|---|---|
| Thomas | 27 | 30 | 90 | 12 | 25 | 48 |

## DETROIT LIONS

### Rushing

| Last Name | No. | Yds | Avg | TD |
|---|---|---|---|---|
| Bussey | 196 | 858 | 4.4 | 3 |
| Gaines | 155 | 659 | 4.3 | 4 |
| King | 93 | 325 | 3.5 | 0 |
| Landry | 43 | 234 | 5.4 | 1 |
| Bolton | 15 | 71 | 4.7 | 0 |
| Reed | 11 | 63 | 5.7 | 1 |
| B.Thompson | 13 | 42 | 3.2 | 0 |
| Walton | 1 | 5 | 5.0 | 0 |
| L.Thompaon | 1 | 0 | 0.0 | 0 |
| H.Weaver | 1 | 0 | 0.0 | 0 |

### Receiving

| Last Name | No. | Yds | Avg | TD |
|---|---|---|---|---|
| Jarvis | 39 | 822 | 21 | 5 |
| C.Sanders | 35 | 545 | 16 | 5 |
| Bussey | 28 | 218 | 8 | 0 |
| Gaines | 23 | 130 | 6 | 1 |
| King | 21 | 163 | 8 | 0 |
| Walton | 20 | 293 | 15 | 3 |
| D.Hill | 19 | 249 | 13 | 5 |
| B.Thompson | 10 | 108 | 11 | 0 |
| L.Thompson | 3 | 52 | 17 | 0 |
| O'Neil | 1 | 32 | 32 | 1 |
| Franklin | 1 | 16 | 16 | 0 |
| J.D. Hill | 1 | 2 | 2 | 0 |

### Punt Returns

| Last Name | No. | Yds | Avg | TD |
|---|---|---|---|---|
| Barney | 23 | 191 | 8 | 0 |
| Hunter | 4 | 7 | 2 | 0 |
| West | 3 | 9 | 3 | 0 |
| Ten Napel | 1 | 0 | 0 | 0 |

### Kickoff Returns

| Last Name | No. | Yds | Avg | TD |
|---|---|---|---|---|
| B. Thompson | 22 | 431 | 20 | 0 |
| Hunter | 14 | 375 | 27 | 0 |
| Bolton | 15 | 280 | 19 | 0 |
| L.Thompson | 5 | 86 | 17 | 0 |
| King | 3 | 63 | 21 | 0 |
| Long | 2 | 18 | 9 | 0 |
| Bussey | 1 | 14 | 14 | 0 |

### Passing – Punting – Kicking

| PASSING | Att | Comp | % | Yds | Yd/Att | TD | Int–% | RK |
|---|---|---|---|---|---|---|---|---|
| Landry | 291 | 168 | 58 | 2191 | 7.5 | 17 | 8–3 | 2 |
| Reed | 62 | 32 | 52 | 425 | 6.9 | 3 | 3–5 | |
| H. Weaver | 2 | 1 | 50 | 14 | 7.0 | 0 | 0–0 | |
| J.D. Hill | 1 | 0 | 0 | 0 | 0.0 | 0 | 1–100 | |

| PUNTING | No | Avg |
|---|---|---|
| H. Weaver | 83 | 39.5 |
| Ricardo | 1 | 16.0 |

| KICKING | XP | Att | % | FG | Att | % |
|---|---|---|---|---|---|---|
| Ricardo | 21 | 23 | 91 | 11 | 18 | 61 |

## GREEN BAY PACKERS

### Rushing

| Last Name | No. | Yds | Avg | TD |
|---|---|---|---|---|
| Harrell | 130 | 435 | 3.3 | 3 |
| Brockington | 117 | 406 | 3.5 | 2 |
| B.Smith | 97 | 355 | 3.7 | 5 |
| Torkelson | 88 | 289 | 3.3 | 2 |
| Odom | 4 | 78 | 19.5 | 0 |
| Brown | 12 | 49 | 4.1 | 0 |
| Taylor | 14 | 47 | 3.4 | 1 |
| Johnson | 5 | 25 | 5.0 | 1 |
| Dickey | 11 | 19 | 1.7 | 1 |
| Osborn | 6 | 16 | 2.7 | 0 |
| Zimmerman | 1 | 3 | 3.0 | 0 |

### Receiving

| Last Name | No. | Yds | Avg | TD |
|---|---|---|---|---|
| Payne | 33 | 467 | 14 | 4 |
| McGeorge | 24 | 278 | 12 | 1 |
| Odom | 23 | 456 | 20 | 2 |
| O.Smith | 20 | 364 | 18 | 1 |
| Torkelson | 19 | 140 | 7 | 0 |
| Harrell | 17 | 201 | 12 | 1 |
| B.Smith | 11 | 88 | 8 | 0 |
| Brockington | 11 | 49 | 4 | 0 |
| Taylor | 2 | 21 | 11 | 0 |
| Hall | 1 | 18 | 18 | 0 |
| Zimmerman | 1 | 13 | 13 | 0 |
| Jackson | 1 | 8 | 8 | 0 |
| Askon | 1 | 2 | 2 | 1 |

### Punt Returns

| Last Name | No. | Yds | Avg | TD |
|---|---|---|---|---|
| Gray | 37 | 307 | 8 | 0 |
| Harrell | 3 | −7 | −2 | 0 |

### Kickoff Returns

| Last Name | No. | Yds | Avg | TD |
|---|---|---|---|---|
| Odom | 29 | 610 | 21 | 0 |
| M.C. McCoy | 18 | 457 | 25 | 0 |
| Torkelson | 6 | 123 | 21 | 0 |
| Taylor | 3 | 59 | 20 | 0 |
| Hyland | 3 | 31 | 10 | 0 |
| Osborn | 3 | 19 | 6 | 0 |
| Wagner | 1 | 27 | 27 | 0 |
| Gray | 1 | 23 | 23 | 0 |
| O.Smith | 1 | 12 | 12 | 0 |

### Passing – Punting – Kicking

| PASSING | Att | Comp | % | Yds | Yd/Att | TD | Int–% | RK |
|---|---|---|---|---|---|---|---|---|
| Dickey | 243 | 115 | 47 | 1465 | 6.0 | 7 | 14–6 | 13 |
| Brown | 74 | 26 | 35 | 333 | 4.5 | 2 | 6–8 | |
| Johnson | 35 | 21 | 60 | 249 | 7.1 | 0 | 1–3 | |
| Harrell | 4 | 1 | 25 | 40 | 10.0 | 1 | 1–25 | |
| Beverly | 1 | 1 | 100 | 18 | 18.0 | 0 | 0–0 | |

| PUNTING | No | Avg |
|---|---|---|
| Beverly | 83 | 37.0 |

| KICKING | XP | Att | % | FG | Att | % |
|---|---|---|---|---|---|---|
| Marcol | 24 | 27 | 89 | 10 | 19 | 53 |

## LOS ANGELES RAMS 10-3-1 Chuck Knox

| Scores of Each Game | | |
|---|---|---|
| 30 | Atlanta | 14 |
| 10 | Minnesota | *10 |
| 24 | N.Y. GIANTS | 10 |
| 31 | Miami | 28 |
| 0 | SAN FRANCISCO | 16 |
| 20 | CHICAGO | 12 |
| 16 | New Orleans | 10 |
| 45 | SEATTLE | 6 |
| 12 | Cincinnati | 20 |
| 28 | ST. LOUIS | 30 |
| 23 | San Francisco | 3 |
| 33 | NEW ORLEANS | 14 |
| 59 | ATLANTA | 0 |
| 20 | Detroit | 17 |

| Use Name | Pos. | Hgt. | Wgt. | Age | Int | Pts |
|---|---|---|---|---|---|---|
| Doug France | OT | 6'5" | 260 | 23 | | |
| Jackie Slater | OT | 6'4" | 252 | 22 | | |
| John Williams | OT | 6'3" | 256 | 30 | | |
| Dennis Harrah | OG | 6'5" | 257 | 23 | | |
| Greg Horton | OG | 6'4" | 245 | 25 | | |
| Tom Mack | OG | 6'3" | 250 | 32 | | |
| Geoff Reece | C | 6'4" | 247 | 24 | | |
| Rich Saul | C | 6'3" | 250 | 28 | | |
| Fred Dryer | DE | 6'6" | 240 | 30 | | |
| Mike Fanning | DE | 6'6" | 260 | 23 | | |
| Jack Youngblood | DE | 6'4" | 255 | 26 | | |
| Larry Brooks | DT | 6'3" | 255 | 26 | | |
| Cody Jones | DT | 6'5" | 240 | 25 | | |
| Merlin Olsen | DT | 6'5" | 270 | 35 | | |

| Use Name | Pos. | Hgt. | Wgt. | Age | Int | Pts |
|---|---|---|---|---|---|---|
| Carl Ekern | LB | 6'3" | 220 | 22 | | |
| Rick Kay | LB | 6'4" | 235 | 26 | 1 | |
| Kevin McLain | LB | 6'2" | 238 | 21 | | |
| Jack Reynolds | LB | 6'1" | 232 | 28 | | |
| Isiah Robertson | LB | 6'3" | 225 | 27 | 4 | |
| Mel Rogers | LB | 6'2" | 230 | 29 | | |
| Jim Youngblood | LB | 6'3" | 239 | 26 | 2 | |
| Dave Elmendorf | DB | 6'1" | 195 | 27 | 2 | |
| Monte Jackson | DB | 5'11" | 189 | 23 | 10 | 18 |
| Rod Perry | DB | 5'9" | 170 | 22 | 8 | |
| Steve Preece | DB | 6'1" | 195 | 29 | 1 | |
| Bill Simpson | DB | 6'1" | 180 | 24 | 4 | |
| Pat Thomas | DB | 5'9" | 180 | 22 | | |

| Use Name | Pos. | Hgt. | Wgt. | Age | Int | Pts |
|---|---|---|---|---|---|---|
| Pat Haden | QB | 5'11" | 182 | 23 | | 24 |
| James Harris | QB | 6'3" | 210 | 29 | | 12 |
| Ron Jaworski | QB | 6'2" | 185 | 25 | | 6 |
| John Cappelletti | HB-FB | 6'1" | 217 | 24 | | 12 |
| Lawrence McCutcheon | HB | 6'1" | 205 | 26 | | 66 |
| Rob Scribner | HB | 6' | 200 | 25 | | 6 |
| Jim Bertelsen | FB | 5'11" | 205 | 26 | | 12 |
| Cullen Bryant | FB | 6'1" | 235 | 25 | | 18 |
| Rod Phillips | FB | 6' | 220 | 23 | | 6 |
| Tom Geredine | WR | 6'2" | 189 | 26 | | 6 |
| Harold Jackson | WR | 5'10" | 175 | 30 | | 30 |
| Ron Jessie | WR | 6' | 185 | 28 | | 36 |
| Freeman Johns | WR | 6'1" | 175 | 22 | | |
| Dwight Scales | WR | 6'2" | 170 | 23 | | 6 |
| Bob Klein | TE | 6'5" | 235 | 29 | | 6 |
| Terry Nelson | TE | 6'2" | 230 | 25 | | |
| Tom Dempsey | K | 6'1" | 260 | 35 | | 87 |
| Rusty Jackson | K | 6'2" | 190 | 25 | | |

## SAN FRANCISCO FORTY NINERS 8-6 Monte Clark

| Scores of Each Game | | |
|---|---|---|
| 26 | Green Bay | 14 |
| 12 | CHICAGO | 19 |
| 37 | Seattle | 21 |
| 17 | N.Y. JETS | 6 |
| 16 | Los Angeles | 0 |
| 33 | NEW ORLEANS | 3 |
| 15 | ATLANTA | 0 |
| 20 | St. Louis | *23 |
| 21 | WASHINGTON | 24 |
| 16 | Atlanta | 21 |
| 3 | LOS ANGELES | 23 |
| 20 | MINNESOTA | 16 |
| 7 | San Diego | *13 |
| 27 | New Orleans | 7 |

| Use Name | Pos. | Hgt. | Wgt. | Age | Int | Pts |
|---|---|---|---|---|---|---|
| Cas Banaszek | OT | 6'3" | 247 | 30 | | |
| Jean Barrett | OT-C | 6'6" | 248 | 25 | | |
| Bill Cooke | OT | 6'5" | 250 | 25 | | |
| Keith Fahnhorst | OT | 6'6" | 256 | 24 | | |
| Steve Lawson | OG | 6'3" | 265 | 27 | | |
| Andy Mauer | OG | 6'3" | 275 | 27 | | |
| Mark Nordquist (from CHI.) | OG-C | 6'4" | 255 | 30 | | |
| John Watson | OG | 6'4" | 244 | 27 | | |
| Randy Cross | C | 6'3" | 247 | 22 | | |
| Tony Cline | DE | 6'2" | 244 | 28 | | |
| Cedrick Hardman | DE | 6'3" | 244 | 27 | | |
| Tommy Hart | DE | 6'3" | 249 | 31 | | 2 |
| Bill Sandifer | DE-DT | 6'6" | 260 | 24 | | |
| Cleveland Elam | DT | 6'4" | 252 | 24 | | 6 |
| Jimmy Webb | DT | 6'4" | 247 | 24 | | |

| Use Name | Pos. | Hgt. | Wgt. | Age | Int | Pts |
|---|---|---|---|---|---|---|
| Bruce Elia | LB | 6'1" | 217 | 23 | | |
| Willie Harper | LB | 6'2" | 208 | 26 | | |
| Dale Mitchell | LB | 6'3" | 223 | 23 | | |
| Frank Nunley | LB | 6'2" | 221 | 30 | 1 | |
| Skip Vanderbundt | LB | 6'3" | 222 | 29 | 2 | |
| Dave Washington | LB | 6'5" | 228 | 27 | | |
| Jim Johnson | DB | 6'2" | 187 | 38 | 1 | |
| Tony Leonard | DB | 5'11" | 170 | 23 | | 6 |
| Eddie Lewis | DB | 6' | 177 | 22 | | |
| Ralph McGill | DB | 5'11" | 178 | 26 | | 6 |
| Mel Phillips | DB | 6' | 184 | 34 | 2 | |
| Bruce Rhodes | DB | 6' | 187 | 24 | 3 | |
| Bruce Taylor | DB | 6' | 186 | 28 | | |

Bob Hoskins – Illness
Woody Peoples – Knee Injury
Bill Reid – Knee Injury

| Use Name | Pos. | Hgt. | Wgt. | Age | Int | Pts |
|---|---|---|---|---|---|---|
| Scott Bull | QB | 6'5" | 211 | 23 | | 12 |
| Marty Domres | QB | 6'4" | 220 | 29 | | |
| Jim Plunkett | QB | 6'3" | 219 | 28 | | |
| Paul Hofer | HB | 6' | 195 | 24 | | 6 |
| Kermit Johnson | HB | 6' | 202 | 24 | | 6 |
| Del Williams | HB | 6' | 197 | 25 | | 54 |
| Bob Ferrell | FB-HB | 6' | 208 | 23 | | 6 |
| Wilbur Jackson | FB | 6'1" | 219 | 24 | | 12 |
| Kenny Harrison | WR | 6' | 170 | 22 | | |
| Jim Lash (from MIN) | WR | 6'2" | 199 | 24 | | |
| Willie McGee | WR | 5'11" | 187 | 26 | | 24 |
| Steve Rivera | WR | 5'11" | 184 | 22 | | |
| Gene Washington | WR | 6'1" | 187 | 29 | | 36 |
| Tom Mitchell | TE | 6'2" | 226 | 32 | | 6 |
| Jim Obradovich | TE | 6'2" | 225 | 23 | | |
| Steve Mike-Mayer | K | 6' | 179 | 28 | | 74 |
| Tom Wittum | K | 6'1" | 191 | 26 | | |

## ATLANTA FALCONS 4-10 Marion Campbell (1-4) Pat Peppler (3-6)

| Scores of Each Game | | |
|---|---|---|
| 14 | LOS ANGELES | 30 |
| 10 | Detroit | 24 |
| 10 | Chicago | 0 |
| 13 | PHILADELPHIA | 14 |
| 0 | New Orleans | 30 |
| 17 | CLEVELAND | 20 |
| 0 | San Francisco | 15 |
| 23 | NEW ORLEANS | 20 |
| 13 | Seattle | 30 |
| 21 | SAN FRANCISCO | 16 |
| 17 | DALLAS | 10 |
| 14 | Houston | 20 |
| 0 | Los Angeles | 59 |
| 20 | GREEN BAY | 24 |

| Use Name | Pos. | Hgt. | Wgt. | Age | Int | Pts |
|---|---|---|---|---|---|---|
| Brent Adams | OT | 6'5" | 256 | 24 | | |
| Greg Kindle | OT | 6'4" | 265 | 25 | | |
| Phil McKinnely | OT | 6'4" | 248 | 22 | | |
| Dave Scott | OT | 6'4" | 285 | 22 | | |
| Len Gotshalk | OG | 6'4" | 259 | 26 | | |
| Larron Jackson | OG | 6'3" | 260 | 27 | | |
| Royce Smith | OG | 6'3" | 250 | 27 | | |
| Paul Ryczek | C | 6'2" | 230 | 24 | | |
| Jeff Van Note | C | 6'2" | 247 | 30 | | |
| Jim Weatherly | C | 6'3" | 245 | 24 | | |
| Jim Bailey | DE | 6'5" | 255 | 28 | | |
| Claude Humphrey | DE | 6'5" | 265 | 32 | | 2 |
| Jeff Merrow | DE-DT | 6'4" | 230 | 23 | | |
| Ron East | DT | 6'4" | 250 | 33 | | |
| Steve George | DT | 6'6" | 265 | 25 | | |
| Mike Lewis | DT | 6'3" | 261 | 27 | | |
| Mike Tilleman | DT | 6'5" | 278 | 32 | | |
| Bill Windauer | DT | 6'3" | 250 | 26 | | |

| Use Name | Pos. | Hgt. | Wgt. | Age | Int | Pts |
|---|---|---|---|---|---|---|
| Greg Brezina | LB | 6'1" | 221 | 30 | | |
| Jim Cope | LB | 6'1" | 235 | 23 | | |
| Fulton Kuykendall | LB | 6'5" | 225 | 23 | | |
| Dewey McClain | LB | 6'3" | 236 | 22 | 1 | |
| Tommy Nobis | LB | 6'2" | 243 | 32 | 1 | |
| Ralph Ortega | LB | 6'2" | 220 | 23 | | |
| Guy Roberts | LB | 6'1" | 220 | 26 | 1 | |
| Ray Brown | DB | 6'2" | 202 | 27 | 3 | |
| Rick Byas | DB | 5'9" | 180 | 25 | | |
| Ray Easterling | DB | 6' | 192 | 26 | 3 | |
| Bob Jones | DB | 6'2" | 193 | 25 | | |
| Rolland Lawrence | DB | 5'10" | 179 | 25 | 6 | |
| Ron Mabra | DB | 5'10" | 170 | 25 | | |
| Frank Reed | DB | 5'11" | 193 | 22 | 3 | |

Monroe Eley – Injury
Greg McCrary – Leg Injury

| Use Name | Pos. | Hgt. | Wgt. | Age | Int | Pts |
|---|---|---|---|---|---|---|
| Steve Bartkowski | QB | 6'4" | 213 | 23 | | 6 |
| Scott Hunter | QB | 6'2" | 205 | 28 | | 6 |
| Kim McQuilken | QB | 6'2" | 203 | 25 | | |
| Bubba Bean | HB | 5'11" | 195 | 22 | | 18 |
| Sonny Collins | HB | 6'1" | 196 | 23 | | |
| Mike Esposito | HB | 6' | 185 | 23 | | |
| Haskel Stanback | HB | 6' | 210 | 24 | | 24 |
| Brad Davis | FB | 5'10" | 200 | 23 | | |
| Billy Pritchett | FB | 6'3" | 233 | 25 | | 6 |
| Woody Thompson | FB | 6'1" | 228 | 24 | | |
| Karl Farmer | WR | 5'11" | 165 | 22 | | |
| Wallace Francis | WR | 5'11" | 190 | 24 | | |
| John Gilliam | WR | 6'1" | 187 | 31 | | 12 |
| Al Jenkins | WR | 5'10" | 172 | 24 | | 36 |
| Scott Piper | WR | 6'1" | 179 | 22 | | |
| Bob Adams | TE | 6'2" | 218 | 30 | | |
| Jim Mitchell | TE | 6'2" | 236 | 28 | | |
| John James | K | 6'3" | 200 | 27 | | |
| Nick Mike-Mayer | K | 5'8" | 187 | 26 | | 50 |

## NEW ORLEANS SAINTS 4-10 Hank Stram

| Scores of Each Game | | |
|---|---|---|
| 9 | MINNESOTA | 40 |
| 6 | DALLAS | 24 |
| 27 | Kansas City | 17 |
| 26 | HOUSTON | 31 |
| 30 | ATLANTA | 0 |
| 3 | San Francisco | 33 |
| 10 | LOS ANGELES | 16 |
| 20 | Atlanta | 23 |
| 27 | Green Bay | 32 |
| 17 | DETROIT | 16 |
| 51 | Seattle | 27 |
| 14 | Los Angeles | 33 |
| 6 | New England | 27 |
| 7 | SAN FRANCISCO | 27 |

| Use Name | Pos. | Hgt. | Wgt. | Age | Int | Pts |
|---|---|---|---|---|---|---|
| Jeff Hart | OT | 6'5" | 252 | 22 | | |
| Marv Montgomery (from DEN) | OT | 6'6" | 255 | 28 | | |
| Don Morrison | OT | 6'5" | 250 | 26 | | |
| Kurt Schumacher | OT | 6'3" | 246 | 23 | | |
| Terry Stieve | OG | 6'2" | 242 | 22 | | |
| Tom Wickert | OG-OT | 6'4" | 252 | 24 | | |
| Emanuel Zanders | OG | 6'1" | 248 | 25 | | |
| Lee Gross | C | 6'3" | 235 | 23 | | |
| John Hill | C | 6'2" | 246 | 26 | | |
| Steve Baumgartner | DE | 6'7" | 255 | 25 | | |
| Andy Dorris | DE | 6'4" | 240 | 25 | | |
| Elois Grooms | DE | 6'4" | 250 | 23 | | |
| Jeff Winans (from OAK) | DE | 6'5" | 260 | 24 | | |
| Derland Moore | DT | 6'4" | 253 | 24 | | |
| Bob Pollard | DT | 6'3" | 251 | 27 | | |
| Elex Price | DT | 6'3" | 253 | 26 | 1 | 6 |

| Use Name | Pos. | Hgt. | Wgt. | Age | Int | Pts |
|---|---|---|---|---|---|---|
| Ken Bordelon | LB | 6'4" | 236 | 22 | | |
| Warren Capone | LB | 6'1" | 220 | 25 | | 6 |
| Wayne Colman | LB | 6'1" | 215 | 30 | | |
| Joe Federspiel | LB | 6'1" | 230 | 26 | | |
| Rick Kingrea | LB | 6'1" | 222 | 27 | | |
| Jim Merlo | LB | 6'1" | 220 | 24 | 4 | 12 |
| Greg Westbrooks | LB | 6'2" | 217 | 23 | | |
| Pete Athas | DB | 5'11" | 185 | 28 | 2 | |
| Chuck Crist | DB | 6'2" | 205 | 25 | 1 | |
| Ernie Jackson | DB | 5'10" | 176 | 26 | 2 | |
| Benny Johnson | DB | 5'11" | 178 | 28 | | |
| Jim Kearney | DB | 6'2" | 196 | 33 | | |
| Tom Myers | DB | 5'11" | 170 | 25 | 1 | 6 |
| Mo Spencer | DB | 6' | 176 | 24 | 1 | |

Archie Manning – Shoulder Injury
Joel Parker – Injury
Louis Ross – Injury
Bob Stein – Injury

| Use Name | Pos. | Hgt. | Wgt. | Age | Int | Pts |
|---|---|---|---|---|---|---|
| Bobby Douglass | QB | 6'3" | 228 | 29 | | 12 |
| Bobby Scott | QB | 6'1" | 197 | 27 | | 6 |
| Alvin Maxson | HB | 5'11" | 201 | 24 | | 6 |
| Leon McQuay | HB | 5'9" | 200 | 26 | | |
| Mike Strachan | HB | 6' | 200 | 23 | | 12 |
| Tony Galbreath | FB-HB | 6' | 220 | 22 | | 48 |
| Andrew Jones | FB | 6'2" | 218 | 23 | | |
| Kim Jones | FB | 6'4" | 238 | 24 | | |
| Chuck Muncie | FB | 6'3" | 220 | 23 | | 12 |
| Larry Burton | WR | 6'1" | 193 | 24 | | 12 |
| Clarence Chapman | WR | 5'10" | 185 | 22 | | |
| Don Herrmann | WR | 6'2" | 193 | 29 | | |
| Tinker Owens | WR | 5'11" | 170 | 21 | | 6 |
| Henry Childs | TE | 6'2" | 220 | 25 | | 24 |
| Paul Seal | TE | 6'4" | 223 | 24 | | |
| Jim Thaxton | TE | 6'2" | 240 | 27 | | 6 |
| Tom Blanchard | K | 6' | 187 | 28 | | |
| Richie Szaro | K | 5'11" | 204 | 28 | | 79 |

## SEATTLE SEAHAWKS 2-12 Jack Patera

| Scores of Each Game | | |
|---|---|---|
| 24 | ST. LOUIS | 30 |
| 7 | Washington | 31 |
| 21 | SAN FRANCISCO | 37 |
| 13 | DALLAS | 28 |
| 20 | Green Bay | 27 |
| 13 | Tampa Bay | 10 |
| 14 | DETROIT | 41 |
| 6 | Los Angeles | 45 |
| 30 | ATLANTA | 13 |
| 21 | Minnesota | 27 |
| 27 | NEW ORLEANS | 51 |
| 16 | N.Y. Giants | 28 |
| 7 | CHICAGO | 34 |
| 10 | Philadelphia | 27 |

| Use Name | Pos. | Hgt. | Wgt. | Age | Int | Pts |
|---|---|---|---|---|---|---|
| Nick Bebout | OT | 6'5" | 260 | 25 | | |
| Norm Evans | OT | 6'5" | 250 | 33 | | |
| Gordon Jolley | OT-OG | 6'5" | 245 | 27 | | |
| Dave Simonson (from HOU) | OT | 6'6" | 250 | 24 | | |
| Ron Coder | OG | 6'4" | 250 | 22 | | |
| John Demarie | OG | 6'3" | 248 | 31 | | |
| Bob Newton | OG | 6'4" | 260 | 27 | | |
| Bobby Penchion | OG | 6'5" | 252 | 27 | | |
| Fred Hoaglin | C | 6'4" | 250 | 32 | | |
| Art Kuehn | C | 6'3" | 270 | 23 | | |
| Richard Harris | DE | 6'4" | 258 | 28 | | |
| Bob Lurtsema (from MIN.) | DE-DT | 6'6" | 250 | 34 | | |
| Dave Tipton | DE | 6'6" | 246 | 27 | | |
| Carl Barisich | DT | 6'4" | 255 | 25 | | |
| Steve Niehaus | DT | 6'4" | 270 | 21 | | |
| Larry Woods | DT | 6'6" | 268 | 28 | | |

| Use Name | Pos. | Hgt. | Wgt. | Age | Int | Pts |
|---|---|---|---|---|---|---|
| Ed Bradley | LB | 6'2" | 239 | 26 | 1 | |
| Randy Coffield | LB | 6'3" | 215 | 22 | | |
| Greg Collins | LB | 6'3" | 227 | 23 | | |
| Mike Curtis | LB | 6'2" | 232 | 33 | 2 | |
| Ken Geddes | LB | 6'3" | 235 | 28 | | |
| Sammy Green | LB | 6'2" | 228 | 21 | | |
| Lyle Blackwood | DB | 6' | 190 | 25 | | |
| Dave Brown | DB | 6'1" | 190 | 23 | 4 | 2 |
| Don Dufek | DB | 6' | 195 | 22 | | |
| Ernie Jones | DB | 6'3" | 180 | 23 | | |
| Al Matthews | DB | 5'11" | 190 | 28 | 3 | 6 |
| Eddie McMillan | DB | 6' | 190 | 24 | 1 | |
| Roland Woolsey | DB | 6'1" | 182 | 23 | 4 | |

Ken Hutcherson – Injury

| Use Name | Pos. | Hgt. | Wgt. | Age | Int | Pts |
|---|---|---|---|---|---|---|
| Bill Munson | QB | 6'2" | 205 | 34 | | |
| Steve Myer | QB | 6'2" | 188 | 22 | | |
| Jim Zorn | QB | 6'2" | 200 | 23 | | 24 |
| Ralph Nelson | HB | 6'2" | 195 | 22 | | 6 |
| Oliver Ross | HB-FB | 6' | 210 | 26 | | |
| Hugh McKinnis | FB | 6' | 219 | 28 | | 24 |
| Sherman Smith | FB | 6'4" | 217 | 21 | | 30 |
| Don Testerman | FB | 6'2" | 230 | 23 | | 12 |
| Don Clune | WR | 6'3" | 195 | 24 | | |
| Steve Largent | WR | 5'11" | 184 | 21 | | 24 |
| Sam McCullum | WR | 6'2" | 203 | 23 | | 24 |
| Steve Raible | WR | 6'2" | 195 | 22 | | 12 |
| Ron Howard | TE | 6'4" | 225 | 25 | | |
| John McMakin | TE | 6'3" | 225 | 25 | | 12 |
| Don Bitterlich | K | 5'7" | 166 | 22 | | 10 |
| Rick Engles | K | 5'11" | 170 | 22 | | |
| John Leypoldt (from BUF) | K | 6'2" | 230 | 30 | | 46 |

* – Overtime

## LOS ANGELES RAMS

### RUSHING

| Last Name | No. | Yds | Avg | TD |
|---|---|---|---|---|
| McCutcheon | 291 | 1168 | 4.0 | 9 |
| Cappelletti | 177 | 688 | 3.9 | 1 |
| Phillips | 34 | 206 | 6.1 | 1 |
| Bertelsen | 42 | 155 | 3.7 | 2 |
| Haden | 25 | 84 | 3.4 | 4 |
| Harris | 12 | 76 | 6.3 | 2 |
| Bryant | 21 | 64 | 3.0 | 2 |
| Jessie | 4 | 37 | 9.3 | 0 |
| H. Jackson | 1 | 15 | 15.0 | 0 |
| Jaworski | 2 | 15 | 7.5 | 1 |
| Scribner | 2 | 12 | 6.0 | 1 |
| Geredine | 1 | 8 | 8.0 | 0 |
| Preece | 1 | 0 | 0.0 | 0 |

### RECEIVING

| Last Name | No. | Yds | Avg | TD |
|---|---|---|---|---|
| H. Jackson | 39 | 751 | 19 | 5 |
| Jessie | 34 | 779 | 23 | 6 |
| Cappelletti | 30 | 302 | 10 | 1 |
| McCutcheon | 28 | 305 | 11 | 2 |
| Klein | 20 | 229 | 11 | 1 |
| Bertelsen | 6 | 33 | 6 | 0 |
| Nelson | 4 | 48 | 12 | 0 |
| Phillips | 4 | 23 | 6 | 0 |
| Scales | 3 | 105 | 35 | 1 |
| Bryant | 2 | 28 | 14 | 0 |
| Geredine | 1 | 23 | 23 | 1 |
| Harrah | 0 | 3 | 0 | 0 |

### PUNT RETURNS

| Last Name | No. | Yds | Avg | TD |
|---|---|---|---|---|
| Bryant | 29 | 321 | 11 | 0 |
| Bertelsen | 10 | 55 | 6 | 0 |
| Scribner | 8 | 54 | 7 | 0 |
| Scales | 4 | 46 | 12 | 0 |
| Johns | 1 | 0 | 0 | 0 |

### KICKOFF RETURNS

| Last Name | No. | Yds | Avg | TD |
|---|---|---|---|---|
| Bryant | 16 | 459 | 29 | 1 |
| Geredine | 9 | 181 | 20 | 0 |
| Thomas | 7 | 140 | 20 | 0 |
| Scales | 7 | 136 | 19 | 0 |
| Scribner | 3 | 54 | 18 | 0 |
| Johns | 2 | 56 | 28 | 0 |
| Nelson | 0 | 1 | 0 | 0 |

### PASSING – PUNTING – KICKING

| PASSING | Att | Comp | % | Yds | Yd/Att | TD | Int–% | RK |
|---|---|---|---|---|---|---|---|---|
| Harris | 158 | 91 | 58 | 1460 | 9.2 | 8 | 6– 4 | 1 |
| Haden | 105 | 60 | 57 | 896 | 8.5 | 8 | 4– 4 | |
| Jaworski | 52 | 20 | 39 | 273 | 5.3 | 1 | 5– 10 | |

| PUNTING | No | Avg |
|---|---|---|
| R. Jackson | 77 | 39.0 |

| KICKING | XP | Att | % | FG | Att | % |
|---|---|---|---|---|---|---|
| Dempsey | 36 | 44 | 82 | 17 | 26 | 65 |

## SAN FRANCISCO FORTY NINERS

### RUSHING

| Last Name | No. | Yds | Avg | TD |
|---|---|---|---|---|
| Williams | 248 | 1203 | 4.9 | 7 |
| Jackson | 200 | 792 | 4.0 | 1 |
| K. Johnson | 32 | 99 | 3.1 | 1 |
| Plunkett | 19 | 95 | 5.0 | 0 |
| Hofer | 18 | 74 | 4.1 | 0 |
| Bull | 15 | 66 | 4.4 | 2 |
| Ferrell | 9 | 28 | 3.1 | 1 |
| Domres | 4 | 18 | 4.5 | 0 |
| McGee | 3 | 12 | 4.0 | 0 |
| Lash | 3 | 5 | 1.7 | 0 |
| G. Washington | 1 | 3 | 3.0 | 0 |

### RECEIVING

| Last Name | No. | Yds | Avg | TD |
|---|---|---|---|---|
| G. Washington | 33 | 457 | 14 | 6 |
| Jackson | 33 | 324 | 10 | 1 |
| Williams | 27 | 283 | 10 | 2 |
| T. Mitchell | 20 | 240 | 12 | 1 |
| Lash | 17 | 242 | 14 | 0 |
| McGee | 13 | 269 | 21 | 4 |
| Hofer | 4 | 45 | 11 | 1 |
| Harris | 3 | 65 | 22 | 0 |
| K. Johnson | 1 | 11 | 11 | 0 |
| O'Bradovich | 1 | 11 | 11 | 0 |
| Ferrell | 1 | 9 | 9 | 0 |
| Rivera | 1 | 7 | 7 | 0 |

### PUNT RETURNS

| Last Name | No. | Yds | Avg | TD |
|---|---|---|---|---|
| Leonard | 35 | 293 | 8 | 1 |
| Rhodes | 16 | 142 | 9 | 0 |
| McGill | 10 | 103 | 10 | 1 |
| Taylor | 3 | 16 | 5 | 0 |
| Rivera | 1 | 3 | 3 | 0 |

### KICKOFF RETURNS

| Last Name | No. | Yds | Avg | TD |
|---|---|---|---|---|
| Leonard | 26 | 553 | 21 | 0 |
| Hofer | 5 | 91 | 18 | 0 |
| K. Johnson | 4 | 114 | 29 | 0 |
| T. Mitchell | 2 | 7 | 4 | 0 |
| Ferrell | 1 | 12 | 12 | 0 |

### PASSING – PUNTING – KICKING

| PASSING | Att | Comp | % | Yds | Yd/Att | TD | Int–% | RK |
|---|---|---|---|---|---|---|---|---|
| Plunkett | 243 | 126 | 52 | 1592 | 6.6 | 13 | 16– 7 | 8 |
| Bull | 48 | 21 | 44 | 252 | 5.3 | 2 | 4– 8 | |
| Domres | 14 | 7 | 50 | 101 | 7.2 | 0 | 1– 7 | |
| Williams | 1 | 1 | 100 | 18 | 18.0 | 0 | 0– 0 | |

| PUNTING | No | Avg |
|---|---|---|
| Wittum | 89 | 40.8 |

| KICKING | XP | Att | % | FG | Att | % |
|---|---|---|---|---|---|---|
| Mike-Mayer | 26 | 30 | 87 | 16 | 28 | 57 |

## ATLANTA FALCONS

### RUSHING

| Last Name | No. | Yds | Avg | TD |
|---|---|---|---|---|
| Bean | 124 | 428 | 3.5 | 2 |
| Stanback | 95 | 324 | 3.4 | 3 |
| Collins | 91 | 319 | 3.5 | 0 |
| Esposito | 60 | 317 | 5.3 | 2 |
| Thompson | 42 | 152 | 3.6 | 0 |
| Pritchett | 14 | 74 | 5.3 | 1 |
| Hunter | 14 | 41 | 2.9 | 1 |
| McQuilken | 9 | 26 | 2.9 | 0 |
| Mitchell | 1 | -6 | -6.0 | 0 |
| Bartkowski | 8 | -10 | -1.3 | 1 |

### RECEIVING

| Last Name | No. | Yds | Avg | TD |
|---|---|---|---|---|
| Jenkins | 41 | 710 | 17 | 6 |
| Gilliam | 21 | 292 | 14 | 2 |
| Stanback | 21 | 174 | 8 | 1 |
| Mitchell | 17 | 209 | 12 | 0 |
| Esposito | 17 | 88 | 5 | 0 |
| Bean | 16 | 148 | 9 | 1 |
| Thompson | 16 | 111 | 7 | 0 |
| Collins | 4 | 37 | 9 | 0 |
| Francis | 2 | 24 | 12 | 0 |
| Bob Adams | 1 | 15 | 15 | 0 |
| Pritchett | 1 | 1 | 1 | 0 |

### PUNT RETURNS

| Last Name | No. | Yds | Avg | TD |
|---|---|---|---|---|
| Lawrence | 54 | 372 | 7 | 0 |
| Byas | 1 | 8 | 8 | 0 |
| Esposito | 1 | 6 | 6 | 0 |
| Farmer | 1 | 0 | 0 | 0 |
| Mabra | 1 | 0 | 0 | 0 |
| Roberts | 1 | 0 | 0 | 0 |
| Jones | 1 | -1 | -1 | 0 |

### KICKOFF RETURNS

| Last Name | No. | Yds | Avg | TD |
|---|---|---|---|---|
| Lawrence | 21 | 521 | 25 | 0 |
| Byas | 12 | 270 | 23 | 0 |
| Francis | 9 | 156 | 17 | 0 |
| Collins | 7 | 141 | 20 | 0 |
| Mabra | 3 | 61 | 20 | 0 |
| Bean | 2 | 38 | 19 | 0 |
| Jones | 1 | 22 | 22 | 0 |
| Bob Adams | 1 | 21 | 21 | 0 |
| Stanback | 1 | 18 | 18 | 0 |
| Esposito | 1 | 12 | 12 | 0 |
| Ortega | 1 | 9 | 9 | 0 |
| Roberts | 1 | 0 | 0 | 0 |

### PASSING – PUNTING – KICKING

| PASSING | Att | Comp | % | Yds | Yd/Att | TD | Int–% | RK |
|---|---|---|---|---|---|---|---|---|
| McQuilken | 121 | 48 | 40 | 450 | 3.7 | 2 | 10– 8 | |
| Bartkowski | 120 | 57 | 48 | 677 | 5.6 | 2 | 4– 4 | |
| Hunter | 110 | 51 | 46 | 633 | 5.8 | 5 | 4– 4 | |
| Bean | 1 | 1 | 100 | 49 | 49.0 | 1 | 0– 0 | |
| Esposito | 1 | 0 | 00 | 0 | 0.0 | 0 | 0– 0 | |
| Jenkins | 1 | 0 | 00 | 0 | 0.0 | 0 | 1– 100 | |

| PUNTING | No | Avg |
|---|---|---|
| James | 101 | 42.1 |

| KICKING | XP | Att | % | FG | Att | % |
|---|---|---|---|---|---|---|
| Mike-Mayer | 20 | 20 | 100 | 10 | 21 | 48 |

## NEW ORLEANS SAINTS

### RUSHING

| Last Name | No. | Yds | Avg | TD |
|---|---|---|---|---|
| Muncie | 149 | 659 | 4.4 | 2 |
| Galbreath | 136 | 570 | 4.2 | 7 |
| Strachan | 66 | 258 | 3.9 | 2 |
| Maxson | 34 | 120 | 3.5 | 1 |
| Douglass | 21 | 92 | 4.4 | 2 |
| Scott | 12 | 48 | 4.0 | 1 |
| K. Jones | 6 | 21 | 3.5 | 0 |
| Childs | 1 | 16 | 16.0 | 0 |
| A. Jones | 1 | 2 | 2.0 | 0 |
| Burton | 3 | -4 | -1.3 | 0 |
| Seal | 2 | -7 | -3.5 | 0 |

### RECEIVING

| Last Name | No. | Yds | Avg | TD |
|---|---|---|---|---|
| Galbreath | 54 | 420 | 8 | 1 |
| Herrmann | 34 | 535 | 16 | 0 |
| Muncie | 31 | 272 | 9 | 0 |
| Childs | 26 | 349 | 13 | 3 |
| Burton | 18 | 297 | 17 | 2 |
| Owens | 12 | 241 | 20 | 1 |
| Seal | 9 | 72 | 8 | 0 |
| Thaxton | 7 | 112 | 16 | 1 |
| Maxson | 7 | 21 | 3 | 0 |
| Strachan | 6 | 22 | 4 | 0 |
| K. Jones | 1 | 14 | 14 | 0 |
| Douglass | 1 | -2 | -2 | 0 |

### PUNT RETURNS

| Last Name | No. | Yds | Avg | TD |
|---|---|---|---|---|
| Athas | 35 | 332 | 9 | 0 |
| Myers | 2 | 22 | 11 | 0 |
| Galbreath | 2 | 8 | 4 | 0 |
| McQuay | 2 | 5 | 3 | 0 |
| Crist | 1 | 8 | 8 | 0 |

### KICKOFF RETURNS

| Last Name | No. | Yds | Avg | TD |
|---|---|---|---|---|
| Galbreath | 20 | 399 | 20 | 0 |
| Maxson | 11 | 191 | 17 | 0 |
| Thaxton | 8 | 185 | 23 | 0 |
| McQuay | 8 | 151 | 19 | 0 |
| Muncie | 3 | 69 | 23 | 0 |
| Chapman | 3 | 63 | 21 | 0 |
| Athas | 2 | 68 | 34 | 0 |
| Schumacher | 2 | 17 | 9 | 0 |
| Capone | 2 | 0 | 0 | 0 |
| Hart | 1 | 12 | 12 | 0 |
| K. Jones | 1 | 12 | 12 | 0 |
| Childs | 1 | 6 | 6 | 0 |

### PASSING – PUNTING – KICKING

| PASSING | Att | Comp | % | Yds | Yd/Att | TD | Int–% | RK |
|---|---|---|---|---|---|---|---|---|
| Scott | 190 | 103 | 54 | 1065 | 5.6 | 4 | 6– 3 | 7 |
| Douglass | 213 | 103 | 48 | 1288 | 6.0 | 4 | 8– 4 | 10 |

| PUNTING | No | Avg |
|---|---|---|
| Blanchard | 101 | 39.3 |

| KICKING | XP | Att | % | FG | Att | % |
|---|---|---|---|---|---|---|
| Szaro | 25 | 29 | 86 | 18 | 23 | 78 |

## SEATTLE SEAHAWKS

### RUSHING

| Last Name | No. | Yds | Avg | TD |
|---|---|---|---|---|
| Smith | 119 | 537 | 4.5 | 4 |
| Zorn | 52 | 246 | 4.7 | 4 |
| Testerman | 67 | 246 | 3.7 | 1 |
| Nelson | 52 | 173 | 3.3 | 1 |
| McKinnis | 46 | 105 | 2.3 | 4 |
| Engles | 3 | 37 | 12.3 | 0 |
| Ross | 13 | 23 | 1.8 | 0 |
| Munson | 1 | 6 | 6.0 | 0 |
| Howard | 1 | 2 | 2.0 | 0 |
| Raible | 1 | 2 | 2.0 | 0 |
| Largent | 4 | -14 | -3.5 | 0 |

### RECEIVING

| Last Name | No. | Yds | Avg | TD |
|---|---|---|---|---|
| Largent | 54 | 705 | 13 | 4 |
| Howard | 37 | 422 | 11 | 0 |
| Smith | 36 | 384 | 11 | 1 |
| McCullum | 32 | 506 | 16 | 4 |
| Testerman | 25 | 232 | 9 | 1 |
| McKinnis | 13 | 148 | 11 | 0 |
| Nelson | 12 | 96 | 8 | 0 |
| McMakin | 9 | 158 | 18 | 2 |
| Raible | 4 | 126 | 32 | 1 |
| Clune | 4 | 67 | 17 | 0 |
| Ross | 2 | 22 | 11 | 0 |
| Blackwood | 1 | 8 | 8 | 0 |

### PUNT RETURNS

| Last Name | No. | Yds | Avg | TD |
|---|---|---|---|---|
| Blackwood | 19 | 132 | 7 | 0 |
| Brown | 11 | 74 | 7 | 0 |
| Largent | 4 | 36 | 9 | 0 |
| Woolsey | 2 | 5 | 3 | 0 |
| McMillan | 1 | -1 | -1 | 0 |

### KICKOFF RETURNS

| Last Name | No. | Yds | Avg | TD |
|---|---|---|---|---|
| Ross | 30 | 655 | 22 | 0 |
| Blackwood | 10 | 230 | 23 | 0 |
| Dufek | 9 | 177 | 20 | 0 |
| Largent | 8 | 156 | 20 | 0 |
| Smith | 5 | 78 | 16 | 0 |
| Testerman | 2 | 29 | 15 | 0 |

### PASSING – PUNTING – KICKING

| PASSING | Att | Comp | % | Yds | Yd/Att | TD | Int–% | RK |
|---|---|---|---|---|---|---|---|---|
| Zorn | 439 | 208 | 47 | 2571 | 5.9 | 12 | 27– 6 | 15 |
| Munson | 37 | 20 | 54 | 295 | 8.0 | 1 | 3– 8 | |
| Smith | 2 | 0 | 0 | 0 | | 0 | 0– 0 | |
| Engles | 1 | 1 | 100 | 8 | 8.0 | 0 | 0– 0 | |
| Largent | 1 | 0 | 0 | 0 | 0.0 | 0 | 0– 0 | |

| PUNTING | No | Avg |
|---|---|---|
| Engles | 80 | 38.3 |

| KICKING | XP | Att | % | FG | Att | % |
|---|---|---|---|---|---|---|
| Leypoldt | 22 | 25 | 88 | 8 | 15 | 53 |
| Bitterlich | 7 | 7 | 100 | 1 | 4 | 25 |

# 1976 A.F.C.  The Pats "Cinderella team" Almost Took It All

## EASTERN DIVISION

**Baltimore Colts** — The season started in turmoil with Coach Ted Marchibroda resigning just before the opener in a power struggle with GM Joe Thomas. When several assistants threatened to follow Marchibroda's lead and QB Bert Jones spoke publicly in his coach's defense, Thomas and Owner Bob Irsay quickly made amends with the coach. That was the beginning of the end for master builder Thomas, who was fired at the end of the season after five years at Baltimore. The Colts won eight of their first nine games and finished 11-3, edging New England for the division crown on the basis of a better intra-division record. Jones had a super year, passing for 24 TD's and a 102.6 rating. WR Roger Carr provided the deep threat, leading the league in reception yardage and average gain and ranking second in TD's. RB Lydell Mitchell placed second in AFC rushing and third in receptions. The Colts led the league in total offense, but a vulnerable defense was their undoing in the playoffs.

**New England Patriots** — The one-year rise from a 3-11 record to 11-3 and a "Wild Card" berth in the playoffs marked the Pats as the 1976 Cinderella team and Chuck Fairbanks as the Coach of the Year. Major reasons for the team's meteoric improvement were Steve Grogan, who proved himself an NFL-caliber QB in his first full season as a starter, and CB Mike Haynes, who was second in the AFC in punt return average and interceptions as Defensive Rookie of the Year. Led by RB's Sam Cunningham, Andy Johnson and Don Calhoun, the Pats ranked first in the league in yards per rush and second in scoring. Their 50 takeaways also were tops. After dropping their opener to Baltimore, the Pats beat overwhelming favorites Miami, Pittsburgh and Oakland in succession. Following mid-season upsets by Detroit and Miami, they won their last six games to reach the playoffs.

**Miami Dolphins** — After a 10-4 season in '75, Miami slipped to 6-8, Don Shula's first losing season as a head coach. A crippling series of injuries rocked the team, forcing 22 players to miss a total of 144 games. After a 6-0 preseason, Miami beat only one team above .500—a 10-3 upset of New England. The defense ranked only 26th in yards yielded, leaving too heavy a load for the offense. Rookie Duriel Harris led the NFL with a 32.9 kickoff return average.

**New York Jets** — Lou Holtz left North Carolina State to become the Jets' fourth head coach in four years, but his optimism turned sour and he unexpectedly resigned before the final game. Holtz inherited a sticky QB situation in which he had to choose between 33-year-old Joe Namath and rookie Richard Todd, who started six games and was the QB of record in the wins over Buffalo. Rookie free agent Clark Gaines became a starting RB in the seventh game and recorded four 100-yard games, outgaining all other NFL rookie runners and leading the club in receptions.

**Buffalo Bills** — O.J. Simpson's trade demands began a problem-filled year for the Bills. Simpson finally was coaxed back into the fold with a $2½ million contract over three years, but the team never recovered from the dispute. Added to the Bills' woes were the off-season departures of WR's Ahmad Rashad and J.D. Hill and defensive linemen Earl Edwards, Walt Patulski and Pat Toomay. RB Jim Braxton injured his knee in the opener and was lost for the season, as was QB Joe Ferguson, who suffered a back injury in the seventh game. A disillusioned Lou Saban resigned as head coach after five games with five years still remaining on a 10-year contract, and offensive line coach Jim Ringo replaced him. Things got even worse for Ringo. The Bills lost their last 10 games, nine under Ringo. Despite his slow start, Simpson led the NFL in rushing, but QB Gary Marangi finished last in AFC passing and the defense wasn't much better.

## CENTRAL DIVISION

**Pittsburgh Steelers** — The two-time defending Super Bowl champs found themselves in a deep hole after losing four of their first five games, but they regrouped and won their last nine games to grab the division title for the third year in a row. The manner in which the Steelers won those last nine was awe-inspiring, as they yielded only 28 points or an average of 3.1 per game. After going 19 games without a shutout, the Steel Curtain recorded five in the last eight games. Led by All-Pro MLB Jack Lambert, the defense had a string of 15 consecutive scoreless quarters and 22 periods in a row without allowing a TD. Injuries in the fifth and 10th games sidelined QB Terry Bradshaw for two games each, but rookie Mike Kruczek filled in remarkably well, starting six games during the winning streak, including both wins over Cincinnati. RB's Franco Harris and Rocky Bleier both rushed for more than 1,000 yards behind a talented offensive line.

**Cincinnati Bengals** — Leading the division by two games over Pittsburgh with only three to play, the Bengals lost to the Steelers and Raiders back-to-back and watched their playoff chances go down the drain. Despite a 10-4 record, their two losses to Pittsburgh were the deciding factor. Their fine defensive showing was led by DE Coy Bacon, who recorded a league-high 26 sacks after an off-season trade from San Diego for WR Charlie Joiner. CB Ken Riley led the AFC in interceptions, and SS Tom Casanova, MLB Jim LeClair and CB Lemar Parrish were named All-Pro on defense. Offensively, QB Ken Anderson played below his league-leading pace of the previous two years but WR Isaac Curtis and TE Bob Trumpy combined for 13 TD catches.

**Cleveland Browns** — Forrest Gregg guided the team to a surprising 9-5 record after a 3-11 mark in his first year. Although their schedule was relatively easy, the Browns nevertheless played well. Behind a sound offensive line which allowed only 19 sacks (second in NFL), Brian Sipe developed into a respected QB. RB Greg Pruitt reached 1,000 yards for the second year in a row despite recurring ankle sprains. All-Pro DT Jerry Sherk (12 sacks) led a defense which ranked fourth in the NFL against the run. The acquisitions of LB Gerald Irons and CB Ron Bolton solidified the defense, and FS Thom Darden rebounded from knee surgery to lead the club in interceptions. After a poor 1-3 start, the Browns won eight of their next nine games before losing the finale.

**Houston Oilers** — Injuries and a lack of depth precipitated a fall from a 10-4 record in '75 to 5-9 in '76. After roaring to a 4-1 start, Houston lost eight of its last nine games. It lost four games by four points or less, and two of those defeats prevented it from standing 6-0 after six weeks. The running attack was far below par, and disgruntled QB Dan Pastorini asked to be traded at midseason but was injured the next week. Vet John Hadl played well as backup QB, and WR Ken Burrough had an excellent year. Despite injuries to key players, the 3-4 defense ranked high, sparked by OLB Robert Brazile (named All-Pro in his second year), MG Curley Culp and DE Elvin Bethea (14½ sacks).

## WESTERN DIVISION

**Oakland Raiders** — Winning its fifth division title in a row, Oakland had the best record (13-1) in the NFL. Aside from a one-sided loss at New England, the defense was able to overcome a rash of injuries which sidelined three starters (Tony Cline, Horace Jones and Art Thoms) from the four-man front. Coach John Madden switched to a 3-4 alignment which gave up fewer points than in '75. Free agent John Matuszak was signed after the opener and became a starter at DE. However, the offense was primarily responsible for the team's success. QB Ken Stabler had an outstanding season, his 103.7 passer rating the sixth best of all-time. WR Cliff Branch's fine receiving stats were among the NFL's best, and RB Mark van Eeghen became only the third Raider ever to rush for 1,000 yards in a season, behind the blocking of LT Art Shell and LG Gene Upshaw.

**Denver Broncos** — Denver enjoyed the best season in its 17-year history but a crushing defeat at New England ended its playoff bid. Coach John Ralston, who had directed the team to its first three winning seasons during his five-year tenure, resigned under fire after the season. His successor was Red Miller, the offensive coordinator of the only team which scored more than 26 points against Denver all year. Denver ranked second in the AFC in points allowed and in rushing defense, led by LB's Tom Jackson and Randy Gradishar. The offense was less impressive, although RB Otis Armstrong gained 1,000 yards for the second time in his four-year career. Steve Ramsey held the QB job before falling into disfavor due to a poor performance in the Patriot game. Rick Upchurch averaged a league-high 13.7 yards per punt return with four TD's.

**San Diego Chargers** — After jumping off to a 4-2 start, the team lost six of its last eight games and finished 6-8, still a big improvement upon the 2-12 mark in '75. The defense ranked only 22nd overall, due largely to a weak pass defense. Guided by an offensive coordinator Bill Walsh, QB Dan Fouts had his best year, ranking 13th in NFL passing with more attempts than any other AFC QB. But he had only one accomplished WR in Charlie Joiner, who topped 1,000 yards in his first year as a Charger. The ground game ranked seventh in yardage per carry, with sophomore Rickey Young averaging 5.0.

**Kansas City Chiefs** — Four of K.C.'s five wins were against teams which finished with better records, including playoff-bound Washington. The offense ranked second in NFL passing yardage, as QB Mike Livingston finally cast aside the shadow of ex-teammate Len Dawson after eight years. Livingston had rapidly improving receivers in Walter White, Henry Marshall and Larry Brunson, and veteran RB MacArthur Lane led the NFL in receptions. The inexperienced defense was a different story, ranking 27th out of 28 teams overall.

**Tampa Bay Buccaneers** — The expansion team finished its first year without a win while Coach John McKay built for the future. It averaged only 8.9 points and was blanked five times, while giving up 29.4 points a game. The Bucs put a league-high 17 players on injured reserve, including six defensive starters. The play of veteran QB Steve Spurrier was so unimpressive that he was waived after the season ended. WR Morris Owens was the Bucs' most explosive offensive weapon, catching six TD passes.

## FINAL TEAM STATISTICS

### OFFENSE

| | BALT. | BUFF. | CIN. | CLEV. | DENV. | HOUS. | K.C. | MIAMI | N.ENG. | N.Y. | OAK. | PITT. | S.D. | T.B. |
|---|---|---|---|---|---|---|---|---|---|---|---|---|---|---|
| **FIRST DOWNS:** | | | | | | | | | | | | | | |
| Total | 301 | 250 | 238 | 260 | 239 | 199 | 275 | 267 | 260 | 220 | 303 | 271 | 256 | 191 |
| by Rushing | 133 | 135 | 114 | 119 | 106 | 71 | 103 | 122 | 150 | 104 | 137 | 163 | 111 | 71 |
| by Passing | 144 | 102 | 110 | 112 | 114 | 110 | 152 | 125 | 95 | 93 | 146 | 94 | 127 | 93 |
| by Penalty | 24 | 13 | 14 | 29 | 19 | 18 | 20 | 20 | 15 | 23 | 20 | 14 | 18 | 27 |
| **RUSHING:** | | | | | | | | | | | | | | |
| Number | 565 | 548 | 481 | 533 | 500 | 416 | 498 | 491 | 591 | 438 | 557 | 653 | 473 | 433 |
| Yards | 2303 | 2566 | 2109 | 2295 | 1932 | 1498 | 1873 | 2118 | 2948 | 1924 | 2285 | 2971 | 2040 | 1503 |
| Average Yards | 4.1 | 4.7 | 4.4 | 4.3 | 3.9 | 3.6 | 3.8 | 4.3 | 5.0 | 4.4 | 4.1 | 4.5 | 4.3 | 3.5 |
| Touchdowns | 26 | 11 | 15 | 9 | 14 | 6 | 18 | 15 | 24 | 10 | 14 | 33 | 13 | 5 |
| **PASSING:** | | | | | | | | | | | | | | |
| Attempts | 361 | 383 | 360 | 373 | 353 | 423 | 419 | 346 | 309 | 393 | 361 | 277 | 388 | 376 |
| Completions | 215 | 156 | 187 | 209 | 168 | 227 | 229 | 193 | 146 | 180 | 232 | 143 | 223 | 181 |
| Completion Pct. | 59.6 | 40.7 | 51.9 | 56.0 | 47.6 | 53.7 | 54.7 | 55.8 | 47.2 | 45.8 | 64.3 | 51.6 | 57.5 | 48.1 |
| Passing Yards | 3221 | 2084 | 2443 | 2399 | 2510 | 2429 | 3303 | 2604 | 1910 | 1989 | 3195 | 1935 | 2687 | 1926 |
| Avg. Yards per Att. | 8.9 | 5.4 | 6.8 | 6.4 | 7.1 | 5.7 | 7.9 | 7.5 | 6.2 | 5.1 | 8.9 | 7.0 | 6.9 | 5.1 |
| Avg. Yds per Comp. | 15.0 | 13.4 | 13.1 | 11.5 | 14.9 | 10.7 | 14.4 | 13.5 | 13.1 | 11.1 | 13.8 | 13.5 | 12.1 | 10.6 |
| Times Tackled | 30 | 33 | 37 | 19 | 48 | 39 | 42 | 37 | 19 | 45 | 28 | 27 | 46 | 50 |
| Yds Lost Tackled | 288 | 246 | 252 | 152 | 306 | 357 | 374 | 336 | 164 | 383 | 290 | 269 | 271 | 423 |
| Net Yards | 2933 | 1838 | 2191 | 2247 | 2204 | 2072 | 2929 | 2268 | 1746 | 1606 | 1905 | 1666 | 2416 | 1503 |
| Touchdowns | 24 | 16 | 21 | 21 | 15 | 17 | 15 | 15 | 18 | 7 | 33 | 10 | 17 | 9 |
| Interceptions | 10 | 17 | 15 | 15 | 22 | 19 | 17 | 15 | 20 | 28 | 18 | 12 | 18 | 20 |
| Pct. Intercepted | 2.8 | 4.4 | 4.2 | 4.0 | 6.2 | 4.5 | 4.1 | 4.3 | 6.5 | 7.1 | 5.0 | 4.3 | 4.6 | 5.3 |
| **PUNTS:** | | | | | | | | | | | | | | |
| Number | 59 | 87 | 76 | 69 | 84 | 100 | 68 | 62 | 67 | 81 | 67 | 76 | 82 | 92 |
| Average Distance | 39.7 | 42.3 | 39.5 | 37.4 | 35.1 | 35.3 | 41.1 | 38.2 | 40.1 | 39.7 | 41.6 | 39.2 | 38.7 | 39.3 |
| **PUNT RETURNS:** | | | | | | | | | | | | | | |
| Number | 40 | 33 | 54 | 49 | 51 | 48 | 34 | 35 | 48 | 40 | 50 | 71 | 45 | 43 |
| Yards | 315 | 220 | 343 | 369 | 640 | 504 | 429 | 415 | 628 | 289 | 553 | 636 | 490 | 366 |
| Average Yards | 7.9 | 6.7 | 6.4 | 7.5 | 12.5 | 10.5 | 12.6 | 11.9 | 13.1 | 7.2 | 11.1 | 9.0 | 10.9 | 8.5 |
| Touchdowns | 0 | 1 | 0 | 0 | 4 | 1 | 0 | 1 | 2 | 1 | 0 | 0 | 0 | 0 |
| **KICKOFF RETURNS:** | | | | | | | | | | | | | | |
| Number | 52 | 75 | 49 | 54 | 46 | 58 | 65 | 55 | 46 | 73 | 46 | 41 | 52 | 70 |
| Yards | 1072 | 1594 | 1046 | 1182 | 1075 | 1229 | 1538 | 1347 | 1087 | 1597 | 1025 | 855 | 1076 | 1488 |
| Average Yards | 20.6 | 21.3 | 21.3 | 21.9 | 23.4 | 21.2 | 23.7 | 24.5 | 23.6 | 21.9 | 22.3 | 20.9 | 20.7 | 21.3 |
| Touchdowns | 0 | 0 | 1 | 0 | 0 | 0 | 0 | 0 | 0 | 0 | 0 | 0 | 0 | 0 |
| **INTERCEPTION RET:** | | | | | | | | | | | | | | |
| Number | 15 | 19 | 26 | 21 | 24 | 11 | 23 | 11 | 23 | 11 | 16 | 22 | 20 | 9 |
| Yards | 211 | 293 | 330 | 234 | 452 | 176 | 161 | 144 | 505 | 146 | 128 | 262 | 299 | 99 |
| Average Yards | 14.1 | 15.4 | 12.7 | 11.1 | 18.8 | 16.0 | 7.0 | 13.1 | 22.0 | 13.3 | 8.0 | 11.9 | 15.0 | 11.0 |
| Touchdowns | 0 | 1 | 3 | 1 | 4 | 0 | 0 | 0 | 3 | 0 | 0 | 0 | 1 | 0 |
| **PENALTIES:** | | | | | | | | | | | | | | |
| Number | 92 | 91 | 79 | 107 | 105 | 99 | 97 | 70 | 102 | 71 | 107 | 111 | 78 | 109 |
| Yards | 786 | 797 | 700 | 1037 | 986 | 776 | 789 | 582 | 914 | 627 | 957 | 836 | 579 | 875 |
| **FUMBLES:** | | | | | | | | | | | | | | |
| Number | 25 | 45 | 38 | 45 | 23 | 25 | 32 | 14 | 28 | 44 | 21 | 40 | 28 | 30 |
| Number Lost | 18 | 26 | 20 | 22 | 12 | 14 | 16 | 8 | 16 | 25 | 11 | 19 | 13 | 17 |
| **POINTS:** | | | | | | | | | | | | | | |
| Total | 417 | 245 | 335 | 267 | 315 | 222 | 290 | 263 | 376 | 169 | 350 | 342 | 248 | 125 |
| PAT Attempts | 51 | 30 | 42 | 32 | 39 | 25 | 33 | 31 | 48 | 20 | 47 | 43 | 32 | 15 |
| PAT Made | 40 | 26 | 39 | 28 | 36 | 24 | 27 | 29 | 43 | 16 | 42 | 40 | 26 | 11 |
| FG Attempts | 27 | 24 | 27 | 28 | 21 | 27 | 38 | 23 | 25 | 16 | 19 | 26 | 20 | 17 |
| FG Made | 20 | 13 | 14 | 15 | 15 | 16 | 21 | 16 | 15 | 11 | 8 | 14 | 10 | 8 |
| Percent FG Made | 74.1 | 54.2 | 51.9 | 53.6 | 71.4 | 59.3 | 55.3 | 69.6 | 60.0 | 68.8 | 42.1 | 53.8 | 50.0 | 47.1 |
| Safeties | 1 | 0 | 1 | 1 | 0 | 0 | 1 | 0 | 0 | 0 | 1 | 1 | 0 | 0 |

### DEFENSE

| | BALT. | BUFF. | CIN. | CLEV. | DENV. | HOUS. | K.C. | MIAMI | N.ENG. | N.Y. | OAK. | PITT. | S.D. | T.B. |
|---|---|---|---|---|---|---|---|---|---|---|---|---|---|---|
| **FIRST DOWNS:** | | | | | | | | | | | | | | |
| Total | 229 | 262 | 234 | 244 | 222 | 226 | 309 | 268 | 258 | 277 | 261 | 182 | 259 | 284 |
| by Rushing | 83 | 128 | 116 | 109 | 90 | 117 | 161 | 125 | 102 | 135 | 98 | 69 | 113 | 136 |
| by Passing | 126 | 110 | 103 | 111 | 104 | 90 | 132 | 131 | 134 | 127 | 138 | 96 | 132 | 124 |
| by Penalty | 20 | 24 | 15 | 24 | 28 | 19 | 16 | 12 | 22 | 15 | 25 | 17 | 14 | 24 |
| **RUSHING:** | | | | | | | | | | | | | | |
| Number | 438 | 533 | 520 | 445 | 496 | 540 | 555 | 525 | 462 | 582 | 478 | 452 | 516 | 588 |
| Yards | 1844 | 2465 | 1912 | 1761 | 1709 | 2072 | 2861 | 2411 | 1847 | 2592 | 1903 | 1457 | 2048 | 2560 |
| Average Yards | 4.2 | 4.6 | 3.7 | 4.0 | 3.4 | 3.8 | 5.2 | 4.6 | 4.0 | 4.5 | 4.0 | 3.2 | 4.0 | 4.4 |
| Touchdowns | 11 | 19 | 11 | 15 | 14 | 13 | 24 | 14 | 12 | 14 | 17 | 5 | 10 | 23 |
| **PASSING:** | | | | | | | | | | | | | | |
| Attempts | 372 | 337 | 364 | 392 | 391 | 345 | 375 | 347 | 437 | 374 | 389 | 373 | 386 | 321 |
| Completions | 192 | 163 | 177 | 225 | 214 | 173 | 215 | 195 | 229 | 204 | 197 | 158 | 219 | 178 |
| Completion Pct. | 51.6 | 48.4 | 48.6 | 57.4 | 54.7 | 50.1 | 57.3 | 56.2 | 52.4 | 54.5 | 50.6 | 42.4 | 56.7 | 55.5 |
| Passing Yards | 2804 | 2475 | 2202 | 2353 | 2265 | 2259 | 2684 | 2863 | 2604 | 2468 | 2846 | 2179 | 2822 | 2412 |
| Avg. Yards per Att. | 7.5 | 7.3 | 6.0 | 6.0 | 5.8 | 6.5 | 7.2 | 8.3 | 6.0 | 6.6 | 7.3 | 5.8 | 7.3 | 7.5 |
| Avg. Yds per Comp. | 14.6 | 15.2 | 12.4 | 10.5 | 10.6 | 13.1 | 12.5 | 14.7 | 11.4 | 12.1 | 14.5 | 13.8 | 12.9 | 13.6 |
| Times Tackled | 56 | 28 | 46 | 32 | 32 | 50 | 22 | 20 | 47 | 16 | 46 | 41 | 23 | 24 |
| Yds Lost Tackled | 461 | 210 | 444 | 321 | 240 | 344 | 188 | 193 | 429 | 144 | 370 | 313 | 194 | 171 |
| Net Yards | 2343 | 2265 | 1758 | 2032 | 2025 | 1915 | 2496 | 2670 | 2175 | 2324 | 2476 | 1866 | 2628 | 2241 |
| Touchdowns | 16 | 18 | 13 | 18 | 8 | 17 | 25 | 20 | 16 | 25 | 13 | 9 | 21 | 19 |
| Interceptions | 15 | 19 | 26 | 21 | 24 | 11 | 23 | 11 | 23 | 11 | 16 | 22 | 20 | 9 |
| Pct. Intercepted | 4.0 | 5.6 | 7.1 | 5.4 | 6.1 | 3.2 | 6.1 | 3.2 | 5.3 | 2.9 | 4.1 | 5.9 | 5.2 | 2.8 |
| **PUNTS:** | | | | | | | | | | | | | | |
| Number | 79 | 72 | 86 | 71 | 91 | 96 | 64 | 63 | 75 | 66 | 87 | 94 | 66 | 65 |
| Average Distance | 36.9 | 38.5 | 38.2 | 37.4 | 37.3 | 38.7 | 39.1 | 41.2 | 38.8 | 40.5 | 38.9 | 37.5 | 41.2 | 39.3 |
| **PUNT RETURNS:** | | | | | | | | | | | | | | |
| Number | 33 | 52 | 41 | 45 | 43 | 60 | 39 | 34 | 37 | 55 | 38 | 36 | 45 | 71 |
| Yards | 231 | 878 | 323 | 517 | 372 | 659 | 376 | 272 | 288 | 458 | 264 | 206 | 601 | 754 |
| Average Yards | 7.0 | 16.9 | 7.9 | 11.5 | 8.7 | 11.0 | 9.6 | 8.0 | 7.8 | 8.3 | 6.9 | 5.7 | 13.4 | 10.6 |
| Touchdowns | 0 | 2 | 1 | 2 | 1 | 0 | 1 | 0 | 0 | 1 | 0 | 0 | 1 | 1 |
| **KICKOFF RETURNS:** | | | | | | | | | | | | | | |
| Number | 77 | 48 | 66 | 57 | 50 | 53 | 55 | 57 | 71 | 39 | 61 | 61 | 49 | 35 |
| Yards | 1716 | 1204 | 1616 | 1347 | 1208 | 1125 | 1263 | 1246 | 1569 | 899 | 1123 | 1284 | 1072 | 717 |
| Average Yards | 22.3 | 25.1 | 24.5 | 23.6 | 24.2 | 21.2 | 23.0 | 21.9 | 22.1 | 23.1 | 18.4 | 21.0 | 21.9 | 20.5 |
| Touchdowns | 0 | 0 | 0 | 1 | 0 | 0 | 0 | 0 | 0 | 0 | 0 | 0 | 0 | 0 |
| **INTERCEPTION RET:** | | | | | | | | | | | | | | |
| Number | 10 | 17 | 15 | 15 | 22 | 19 | 17 | 15 | 20 | 28 | 18 | 12 | 18 | 20 |
| Yards | 146 | 246 | 102 | 123 | 260 | 197 | 243 | 128 | 380 | 430 | 185 | 106 | 185 | 490 |
| Average Yards | 14.6 | 14.5 | 6.8 | 8.2 | 11.8 | 10.4 | 14.3 | 8.5 | 19.0 | 15.4 | 10.3 | 8.8 | 10.3 | 24.5 |
| Touchdowns | 1 | 0 | 0 | 0 | 1 | 0 | 1 | 0 | 0 | 3 | 0 | 0 | 1 | 4 |
| **PENALTIES:** | | | | | | | | | | | | | | |
| Number | 89 | 92 | 90 | 89 | 88 | 107 | 88 | 94 | 83 | 87 | 96 | 80 | 92 | 114 |
| Yards | 770 | 704 | 768 | 711 | 715 | 963 | 762 | 716 | 715 | 796 | 918 | 630 | 823 | 935 |
| **FUMBLES:** | | | | | | | | | | | | | | |
| Number | 32 | 37 | 34 | 24 | 23 | 33 | 35 | 31 | 37 | 36 | 26 | 42 | 24 | 33 |
| Number Lost | 21 | 23 | 15 | 11 | 13 | 17 | 20 | 18 | 27 | 21 | 9 | 24 | 11 | 19 |
| **POINTS:** | | | | | | | | | | | | | | |
| Total | 246 | 363 | 210 | 287 | 206 | 273 | 376 | 264 | 236 | 383 | 237 | 138 | 285 | 412 |
| PAT Attempts | 29 | 41 | 25 | 37 | 25 | 31 | 51 | 34 | 29 | 45 | 31 | 14 | 34 | 50 |
| PAT Made | 27 | 39 | 24 | 32 | 20 | 29 | 43 | 30 | 26 | 42 | 27 | 12 | 30 | 48 |
| FG Attempts | 20 | 30 | 22 | 19 | 28 | 29 | 18 | 21 | 17 | 29 | 17 | 24 | 34 | 31 |
| FG Made | 15 | 26 | 12 | 11 | 12 | 18 | 9 | 10 | 12 | 23 | 8 | 14 | 17 | 20 |
| Percent FG Made | 75.0 | 86.7 | 54.5 | 57.9 | 42.9 | 62.1 | 50.0 | 47.6 | 70.6 | 79.3 | 47.1 | 58.3 | 50.0 | 64.5 |
| Safeties | 0 | 0 | 0 | 0 | 0 | 2 | 0 | 0 | 0 | 1 | 0 | 0 | 0 | 2 |

## CONFERENCE PLAYOFFS

### December 18, at Oakland (Attendance 53,045)

#### SCORING

| | | | | |
|---|---|---|---|---|
| OAKLAND | 3 | 7 | 0 | 14–24 |
| NEW ENGLAND | 7 | 0 | 14 | 0–21 |

First Quarter
- N.E. — A. Johnson, 1 yard rush PAT–Smith (kick)
- Oak. — Mann, 40 yard field goal

Second Quarter
- Oak. — Biletnikoff, 31 yard pass from Stabler PAT–Mann (kick)

Third Quarter
- N.E. — Francis, 26 yard pass from Grogan PAT–Smith (kick)
- N.E. — J. Phillips, 3 yard rush PAT–Smith (kick)

Fourth Quarter
- Oak. — van Eeghen, 1 yard rush PAT–Mann (kick)
- Oak. — Stabler, 1 yard rush PAT–Mann (kick)

#### TEAM STATISTICS

| Oak. | | N.E. |
|---|---|---|
| 20 | First Downs-Total | 23 |
| 5 | First Downs-Rushing | 10 |
| 13 | First Downs-Passing | 6 |
| 2 | First Downs-Penalty | 7 |
| 1 | Fumbles-Number | 1 |
| 1 | Fumbles-Lost Ball | 1 |
| 11 | Penalties-Number | 10 |
| 93 | Yards Penalized | 83 |
| 0 | Missed Field Goals | 1 |
| 70 | Offensive Plays | 73 |
| 302 | Net Yards | 331 |
| 4.3 | Average Gain | 4.5 |
| 1 | Giveaways | 3 |
| 3 | Takeaways | 1 |
| +2 | Difference | –2 |

#### INDIVIDUAL STATISTICS

| OAKLAND | No | Yds | Avg. | NEW ENGLAND | No | Yds | Avg. |
|---|---|---|---|---|---|---|---|
| **RUSHING** | | | | | | | |
| van Eeghen | 11 | 39 | 3.5 | Cun'ham | 20 | 68 | 3.4 |
| C. Davis | 7 | 29 | 4.1 | Grogan | 7 | 35 | 5.0 |
| Banaszak | 4 | 28 | 7.0 | A. Johnson | 14 | 32 | 2.9 |
| Garrett | 1 | 4 | 4.0 | Calhoun | 5 | 17 | 3.4 |
| Stabler | 1 | 1 | 1.0 | J. Phillips | 3 | 12 | 4.0 |
| | 24 | 101 | 4.2 | | 49 | 164 | 3.3 |
| **RECEIVING** | | | | | | | |
| Biletnikoff | 9 | 137 | 15.2 | Francis | 4 | 96 | 24.0 |
| Casper | 4 | 47 | 11.8 | Stingley | 2 | 36 | 18.0 |
| Branch | 3 | 32 | 10.7 | Cun'ham | 2 | 14 | 7.0 |
| van Eeghen | 1 | 8 | 8.0 | A. Johnson | 2 | 13 | 6.5 |
| C. Davis | 1 | 5 | 5.0 | Briscoe | 1 | 7 | 7.0 |
| Garrett | 1 | 4 | 4.0 | Chandler | 1 | 1 | 1.0 |
| | 19 | 233 | 12.3 | | 12 | 167 | 13.9 |
| **PUNTING** | | | | | | | |
| Guy | 5 | | 37.8 | Patrick | 3 | | 44.0 |
| **PUNT RETURNS** | | | | | | | |
| Colzie | 3 | 53 | 17.7 | Haynes | 1 | 13 | 13.0 |
| **KICKOFF RETURNS** | | | | | | | |
| Garrett | 4 | 119 | 29.8 | J. Phillips | 4 | 67 | 16.8 |
| | | | | Webster | 1 | 0 | 0.0 |
| | | | | | 5 | 67 | 13.4 |
| **INTERCEPTION RETURNS** | | | | | | | |
| Thomas | 1 | 18 | 18.0 | none | | | |
| Johnson | 1 | 0 | 0.0 | | | | |
| | 2 | 18 | 9.0 | | | | |

**PASSING**

| OAKLAND | Att. | Comp. | Comp. Pct. | Yds. | Int. | Yds/ Att. | Yds/ Comp. | Yards Lost Tackled |
|---|---|---|---|---|---|---|---|---|
| Stabler | 32 | 19 | 59.4 | 233 | 0 | 7.3 | 12.3 | 4–32 |
| **NEW ENGLAND** | | | | | | | | |
| Grogan | 23 | 12 | 52.2 | 167 | 1 | 7.3 | 13.9 | |
| Francis | 1 | 0 | 0.0 | 0 | 1 | 0.0 | 0.0 | |
| | 24 | 12 | 50.0 | 167 | 2 | 7.0 | 13.9 | 0–0 |

### December 19, at Baltimore (Attendance 60,020)

#### SCORING

| | | | | |
|---|---|---|---|---|
| BALTIMORE | 7 | 0 | 0 | 7–14 |
| PITTSBURGH | 9 | 17 | 0 | 14–40 |

First Quarter
- Pitt. — Lewis, 76 yard pass from Bradshaw PAT–No Good
- Pitt. — Gerela, 45 yard field goal
- Balt. — Carr, 17 yard pass from Jones PAT–Linhart (kick)

Second Quarter
- Pitt. — Harrison, 1 yard rush PAT–Gerela (kick)
- Pitt. — Swann, 29 yard pass from Bradshaw PAT–Gerela (kick)
- Pitt. — Gerela, 25 yard field goal

Fourth Quarter
- Pitt. — Swan, 11 yard pass from Bradshaw PAT–Gerela (kick)
- Balt. — Leaks, 1 yard rush PAT–Linhart (kick)
- Pitt. — Harrison, 10 yard rush PAT–Gerela (kick)

#### TEAM STATISTICS

| BALT. | | PITT. |
|---|---|---|
| 16 | First Downs-Total | 29 |
| 4 | First Downs-Rushing | 12 |
| 8 | First Downs-Passing | 15 |
| 4 | First Downs-Penalty | 2 |
| 0 | Fumbles-Number | 2 |
| 0 | Fumbles-Lost Ball | 2 |
| 7 | Penalties-Number | 12 |
| 59 | Yards Penalized | 88 |
| 0 | Missed Field Goals | 0 |
| 53 | Offensive Plays | 65 |
| 170 | Net Yards | 526 |
| 3.2 | Average Gain | 8.1 |
| 2 | Giveaways | 2 |
| 2 | Takeaways | 2 |
| 0 | Difference | 0 |

#### INDIVIDUAL STATISTICS

| BALTIMORE | No. | Yds | Avg. | PITTSBURGH | No. | Yds | Avg. |
|---|---|---|---|---|---|---|---|
| Mitchell | 16 | 55 | 3.4 | Harris | 18 | 132 | 7.3 |
| Leaks | 4 | 12 | 3.0 | Fugua | 11 | 54 | 4.9 |
| Jones | 2 | 3 | 1.5 | Harrison | 10 | 40 | 4.0 |
| McCauley | 1 | 1 | 1.0 | Bleier | 1 | –1 | –1.0 |
| | 23 | 71 | 3.1 | | 40 | 225 | 5.6 |
| **RECEIVING** | | | | | | | |
| Mitchell | 5 | 42 | 8.4 | Swann | 5 | 77 | 15.4 |
| Chester | 3 | 42 | 14.0 | Harrison | 4 | 37 | 9.3 |
| Carr | 2 | 35 | 17.5 | Harris | 3 | 24 | 8.0 |
| Daughty | 1 | 25 | 25.0 | Lewis | 2 | 103 | 51.5 |
| | 11 | 144 | 13.1 | Fugua | 2 | 34 | 17.0 |
| | | | | Bell | 2 | 25 | 12.5 |
| | | | | Stallworth | 1 | 8 | 8.0 |
| | | | | | 19 | 308 | 16.2 |
| **PUNTING** | | | | | | | |
| D. Lee | 4 | | 40.5 | Walden | 1 | | 33.0 |
| **PUNT RETURNS** | | | | | | | |
| Stevens | 1 | 11 | 11.0 | Swann | 3 | 12 | 4.0 |
| **KICKOFF RETURNS** | | | | | | | |
| Stevens | 3 | 66 | 22.0 | Bell | 1 | 60 | 60.0 |
| H. Lee | 3 | 39 | 13.0 | Pough | 1 | 19 | 19.0 |
| Laird | 1 | 3 | 3.0 | | 2 | 79 | 39.5 |
| | 7 | 108 | 15.4 | | | | |
| **INTERCEPTION RETURNS** | | | | | | | |
| none | | | | Edwards | 1 | 26 | 26.0 |
| | | | | Wagner | 1 | 12 | 12.0 |
| | | | | | 2 | 38 | 19.0 |

**PASSING**

| BALTIMORE | Att. | Comp. | Comp. Pct. | Yds. | Int. | Yds/ Att. | Yds/ Comp. | Yards Lost Tackled |
|---|---|---|---|---|---|---|---|---|
| Jones | 25 | 11 | 44.0 | 144 | 2 | 5.8 | 13.1 | 5–45 |
| **PITTSBURGH** | | | | | | | | |
| Bradshaw | 18 | 14 | 77.7 | 264 | 0 | 14.7 | 18.9 | 1–1 |
| Kruczek | 6 | 5 | 83.3 | 44 | 0 | 7.3 | 8.8 | |
| | 24 | 19 | 79.2 | 308 | 0 | 12.8 | 16.2 | 1–1 |

**BALTIMORE COLTS** 11-3 Ted Marchibroda

| Scores of Each Game | | |
|---|---|---|
| 27 | New England | 13 |
| 28 | CINCINNATI | 27 |
| 27 | Dallas | 30 |
| 42 | TAMPA BAY | 17 |
| 28 | MIAMI | 14 |
| 31 | Buffalo | 13 |
| 20 | N.Y. Jets | 0 |
| 38 | HOUSTON | 14 |
| 37 | San Deigo | 21 |
| 14 | NEW ENGLAND | 21 |
| 17 | Miami | 16 |
| 33 | N.Y. JETS | 16 |
| 17 | St. Louis | 24 |
| 58 | BUFFALO | 20 |

| Use Name | Pos. | Hgt | Wgt | Age | Int | Pts |
|---|---|---|---|---|---|---|
| George Kunz | OT | 6'5" | 261 | 29 | | |
| David Taylor | OT | 6'4" | 264 | 26 | | |
| Elmer Collett | OG | 6'4" | 246 | 31 | | |
| Ken Huff | OG | 6'4" | 257 | 23 | | |
| Robert Pratt | OG | 6'4" | 248 | 25 | | |
| Bob Van Duyne | OG | 6'5" | 249 | 24 | | |
| Forrest Blue | C | 6'5" | 260 | 30 | | |
| Ken Mendenhall | C | 6'3" | 250 | 28 | | |
| Fred Cook | DE | 6'3" | 246 | 24 | 1 | |
| John Dutton | DE | 6'7" | 266 | 25 | | |
| Ron Fernandes | DE | 6'4" | 239 | 24 | | 2 |
| Mike Barnes | DT | 6'6" | 256 | 25 | | |
| Joe Ehrmann | DT | 6'5" | 254 | 27 | | |
| Ken Novak | DT | 6'7" | 275 | 22 | | |
| Jim Cheyunski | LB | 6'2" | 220 | 30 | | |
| Dan Dickel | LB | 6'3" | 230 | 24 | | |
| Derrel Luce | LB | 6'3" | 227 | 23 | 2 | 6 |
| Sanders Shiver | LB | 6'2" | 222 | 21 | | |
| Ed Simonini | LB | 6' | 220 | 22 | | |
| Stan White | LB | 6'1" | 223 | 26 | 3 | |
| Tim Baylor | DB | 6'6" | 191 | 22 | | |
| Randy Hall | DB | 6'3" | 194 | 24 | | |
| Bruce Laird | DB | 6' | 198 | 26 | | |
| Lloyd Mumphord | DB | 5'11" | 178 | 29 | 1 | |
| Nelson Munsey | DB | 6'1" | 191 | 28 | 1 | |
| Ray Oldham | DB | 6' | 192 | 25 | 2 | |
| Jackie Wallace | DB | 6'3" | 198 | 25 | 5 | |
| Bert Jones | QB | 6'3" | 212 | 24 | | 12 |
| Mike Kirkland | QB | 6'1" | 195 | 22 | | |
| Bill Troup | QB | 6'5" | 215 | 25 | | 6 |
| Lydell Mitchell | HB | 5'11" | 195 | 27 | | 48 |
| Howard Stevens | HB | 5'5" | 165 | 26 | | 6 |
| Roosevelt Leaks | FB | 5'10" | 225 | 23 | | 42 |
| Ron Lee | FB | 6'4" | 222 | 22 | | 6 |
| Don McCauley | FB-HB | 6'1" | 215 | 27 | | 66 |
| Roger Carr | WR | 6'3" | 196 | 24 | | 66 |
| Glenn Doughty | WR | 6'2" | 202 | 25 | | 30 |
| Freddie Scott | WR | 6'2" | 170 | 24 | | |
| Ricky Thompson | WR | 6' | 170 | 22 | | |
| Ray Chester | TE | 6'3" | 236 | 28 | | 18 |
| Jimmie Kennedy | TE | 6'3" | 230 | 24 | | |
| David Lee | K | 6'4" | 224 | 32 | | |
| Toni Linhart | K | 6' | 179 | 34 | | 109 |

Marshall Johnson – Knee Injury
Tom McLeod – Foot Injury
Doug Nettles – Shoulder Injury

**NEW ENGLAND PATRIOTS** 11-3 Chuck Fairbanks

| Scores of Each Game | | |
|---|---|---|
| 13 | BALTIMORE | 27 |
| 30 | MIAMI | 14 |
| 30 | Pittsburgh | 27 |
| 48 | OAKLAND | 17 |
| 10 | Detroit | 30 |
| 41 | N.Y. JETS | 7 |
| 26 | Buffalo | 22 |
| 3 | Miami | 10 |
| 20 | BUFFALO | 10 |
| 21 | Baltimore | 14 |
| 38 | N.Y. Jets | 24 |
| 38 | DENVER | 14 |
| 27 | NEW ORLEANS | 6 |
| 31 | Tampa Bay | 14 |

| Use Name | Pos. | Hgt | Wgt | Age | Int | Pts |
|---|---|---|---|---|---|---|
| Leon Gray | OT | 6'3" | 256 | 24 | | |
| Bob McKay | OT | 6'5" | 265 | 28 | | |
| Tom Neville | OT | 6'4" | 253 | 33 | | |
| Sam Adams | OG | 6'3" | 252 | 27 | | |
| John Hannah | OG | 6'2" | 265 | 25 | | |
| Fred Sturt | OG | 6'4" | 255 | 25 | | |
| Pete Brock | C-TE | 6'5" | 253 | 22 | | 6 |
| Bill Lenkaitis | C | 6'3" | 250 | 30 | | |
| Julius Adams | DE | 6'3" | 260 | 28 | | |
| Mel Lunsford | DE | 6'3" | 250 | 26 | | |
| Tony McGee | DE | 6'4" | 245 | 27 | | |
| Richard Bishop | NT | 6'1" | 275 | 26 | | |
| Ray Hamilton | NT | 6'1" | 245 | 25 | | |
| Art Moore | NT | 6'5" | 253 | 25 | | |
| Dave Tipton | NT | 6'1" | 250 | 22 | | |
| Pete Barnes | LB | 6'3" | 240 | 31 | | |
| Sam Hunt | LB | 6'1" | 240 | 25 | 2 | 6 |
| Steve King | LB | 6'4" | 225 | 25 | | |
| Steve Nelson | LB | 6'2" | 230 | 25 | 2 | |
| Jim Romaniszyn | LB | 6'2" | 220 | 24 | | |
| Donnie Thomas | LB | 6'2" | 245 | 23 | | |
| George Webster | LB | 6'4" | 230 | 30 | | |
| Steve Zabel | LB | 6'4" | 235 | 28 | | 1 |
| Doug Beaudoin | DB | 6'1" | 200 | 22 | | |
| Joe Blahak (from TB) | DB | 5'9" | 188 | 26 | | |
| Dick Conn | DB | 6' | 180 | 25 | | |
| Tim Fox | DB | 5'11" | 186 | 22 | 3 | |
| Willie Germany | DB | 6' | 192 | 27 | | |
| Mike Haynes | DB | 6'2" | 189 | 23 | 8 | 12 |
| Bob Howard | DB | 6'1" | 177 | 31 | 3 | |
| Prentice McCray | DB | 6'1" | 187 | 25 | 5 | 12 |
| Deac Sanders | DB | 6'1" | 178 | 26 | | |
| Steve Grogan | QB | 6'4" | 200 | 23 | | 78 |
| Tom Owen | QB | 6'1" | 194 | 23 | | |
| Don Calhoun | HB | 6' | 198 | 24 | | 6 |
| Ike Forte | HB | 6' | 196 | 22 | | 12 |
| Andy Johnson | HB | 6' | 204 | 23 | | 60 |
| Jess Phillips | HB-FB | 6'1" | 208 | 29 | | 6 |
| Sam Cunningham | FB | 6'3" | 224 | 26 | | 18 |
| Marlin Briscoe | WR | 5'10" | 180 | 30 | | 6 |
| Steve Burks | WR | 6'5" | 211 | 23 | | |
| Darryl Stingley | WR | 6' | 195 | 24 | | 24 |
| Randy Vataha | WR-DB | 5'10" | 170 | 27 | | 6 |
| Al Chandler | TE | 6'2" | 229 | 25 | | 18 |
| Russ Francis | TE | 6'6" | 240 | 23 | | 18 |
| Mike Patrick | K | 6' | 213 | 23 | | |
| John Smith | K | 6' | 185 | 26 | | 87 |

Steve Corbett – Neck Injury
Pete Kusick – Knee Injury
Craig Hanneman – Injury
Shelby Jordan – Declared Ineligible
Rod Shoate – Knee Injury

**MIAMI DOLPHINS** 6-8 Don Shula

| Scores of Each Game | | |
|---|---|---|
| 30 | Buffalo | 21 |
| 14 | New England | 30 |
| 16 | N.Y. JETS | 0 |
| 28 | LOS ANGELES | 31 |
| 14 | Baltimore | 28 |
| 17 | KANSAS CITY | *20 |
| 23 | Tampa Bay | 20 |
| 10 | NEW ENGLAND | 3 |
| 27 | N.Y. Jets | 7 |
| 3 | Pittsburgh | 14 |
| 16 | BALTIMORE | 17 |
| 13 | Cleveland | 17 |
| 45 | BUFFALO | 27 |
| 7 | MINNESOTA | 29 |

| Use Name | Pos. | Hgt | Wgt | Age | Int | Pts |
|---|---|---|---|---|---|---|
| Darryl Carlton | OT | 6'6" | 260 | 23 | | |
| Tom Drougas | OT | 6'4" | 255 | 26 | | |
| Wayne Moore | OT | 6'6" | 265 | 31 | | |
| Bob Kuechenberg | OG | 6'3" | 252 | 28 | | |
| Larry Little | OG | 6'1" | 265 | 30 | | |
| Mel Mitchell | OG | 6'3" | 260 | 23 | | |
| Ed Newman | OG | 6'2" | 245 | 25 | | |
| Jim Langer | C | 6'2" | 253 | 28 | | |
| John Andrews | DE | 6'6" | 251 | 24 | | |
| Vern Den Herder | DE | 6'6" | 252 | 27 | | |
| Wally Pesuit (from ATL) | DE | 6'4" | 260 | 22 | | |
| Don Reese | DE-DT | 6'6" | 255 | 24 | | |
| Bill Stanfill | DE | 6'5" | 252 | 29 | | |
| Randy Crowder | DT | 6'2" | 236 | 24 | | |
| Bob Heinz | DT | 6'6" | 265 | 29 | | |
| Nick Buoniconti | LB | 5'11" | 210 | 35 | | |
| Rusty Chambers (From N.O.) | LB | 6'1" | 215 | 22 | | |
| Mike Dennery | LB | 6' | 225 | 26 | | |
| Larry Gordon | LB | 6'4" | 230 | 23 | | |
| Bob Matheson | LB | 6'4" | 235 | 31 | 2 | |
| Andy Selfridge | LB | 6'4" | 220 | 27 | | |
| Steve Towle | LB | 6'2" | 233 | 22 | | |
| Dick Anderson | DB | 6'2" | 196 | 30 | 1 | |
| Charlie Babb | DB | 6' | 190 | 26 | 2 | |
| Ted Bachman (from SEA) | DB | 6' | 190 | 24 | | |
| Ken Ellis (from HOU) | DB | 5'10" | 190 | 28 | 2 | |
| Tim Foley | DB | 6' | 194 | 28 | | |
| Barry Hill | DB | 6'3" | 185 | 23 | | |
| Mike Holmes (from BUF.) | DB-WR | 6'2" | 198 | 25 | | |
| Curtis Johnson | DB | 6'2" | 196 | 28 | 1 | |
| Bryant Salter (to BAL) | DB | 6'4" | 196 | 26 | 1 | |
| Jeris White | DB | 5'11" | 180 | 23 | 2 | |
| Bob Griese | QB | 6'1" | 190 | 31 | | |
| Earl Morrall | QB | 6'1" | 210 | 42 | | |
| Don Strock | QB | 6'5" | 218 | 25 | | 6 |
| Gary Davis | HB | 5'10" | 202 | 21 | | 6 |
| Clayton Heath (From BUF.) | HB | 5'11" | 195 | 25 | | |
| Benny Malone | HB | 5'10" | 193 | 24 | | 24 |
| Norm Bulaich | FB-HB | 6'1" | 218 | 29 | | 24 |
| Don Nottingham | FB | 5'10" | 210 | 27 | | 18 |
| Stan Winfrey | FB | 5'11" | 223 | 23 | | 12 |
| Duriel Harris | WR | 5'11" | 175 | 21 | | 6 |
| Ike Hill | WR | 5'10" | 180 | 29 | | |
| Nat Moore | WR | 5'9" | 180 | 24 | | 24 |
| Freddie Solomon | WR | 5'11" | 181 | 23 | | 24 |
| Howard Twilley | WR | 5'10" | 185 | 32 | | 6 |
| Jim Mandich | TE | 6'3" | 224 | 28 | | 24 |
| Loaird McCreary | TE | 6'5" | 227 | 23 | | |
| Larry Seiple | TE | 6' | 214 | 31 | | 6 |
| Andre Tillman | TE | 6'5" | 230 | 23 | | 6 |
| Garo Yepremian | K | 5'8" | 175 | 32 | | 77 |

Manny Fernandez – Knee Injury
Mike Kolen – Knee Injury
Ernest Rhone – Knee Injury

**NEW YORK JETS** 3-11 Lou Holtz

| Scores of Each Game | | |
|---|---|---|
| 17 | Cleveland | 38 |
| 3 | Denver | 46 |
| 0 | Miami | 16 |
| 6 | San Francisco | 17 |
| 17 | BUFFALO | 14 |
| 7 | New England | 41 |
| 0 | BALTIMORE | 20 |
| 19 | Buffalo | 14 |
| 7 | MIAMI | 27 |
| 34 | TAMPA BAY | 0 |
| 24 | NEW ENGLAND | 38 |
| 16 | Baltimore | 33 |
| 16 | WASHINGTON | 37 |
| 3 | CINCINNATI | 42 |

| Use Name | Pos. | Hgt | Wgt | Age | Int | Pts |
|---|---|---|---|---|---|---|
| Winston Hill | OT | 6'4" | 272 | 34 | | |
| Al Krevis | OT | 6'6" | 263 | 24 | | |
| John Roman | OT | 6'4" | 248 | 24 | | |
| Robert Woods | OT | 6'3" | 259 | 26 | | |
| Gary Puetz | OG-OT | 6'4" | 267 | 24 | | |
| Randy Rasmussen | OG | 6'2" | 255 | 31 | | |
| Darrell Austin | C-OG | 6'4" | 252 | 24 | | |
| Joe Fields | C-OG | 6'2" | 245 | 22 | | |
| Richard Neal | DE | 6'3" | 263 | 28 | | |
| Billy Newsome | DE | 6'4" | 268 | 28 | | |
| Lawrence Pillers | DE | 6'3" | 250 | 23 | | |
| Carl Barzilauskas | DT | 6'6" | 265 | 25 | | |
| Larry Faulk | DT-DE | 6'3" | 249 | 23 | | |
| Ed Galigher | DT | 6'4" | 253 | 25 | | |
| Greg Buttle | LB | 6'3" | 235 | 22 | 2 | 6 |
| John Ebersole | LB | 6'3" | 235 | 27 | 1 | |
| Mike Hennigan | LB | 6'2" | 225 | 24 | | |
| Larry Keller | LB | 6'2" | 220 | 22 | 1 | |
| Bob Martin | LB | 6'1" | 217 | 22 | 2 | |
| Steve Poole | LB | 6'1" | 232 | 22 | | 6 |
| James Rosecrans | LB | 6'1" | 230 | 23 | | |
| Carl Russ | LB | 6'2" | 227 | 23 | | |
| Harry Howard | DB | 6' | 189 | 26 | | |
| Tommy Marvaso | DB | 6'1" | 190 | 22 | | |
| Burgess Owens | DB | 6'2" | 200 | 25 | | |
| Rich Sowells | DB | 6' | 181 | 27 | 2 | |
| Shafer Suggs | DB | 6'1" | 194 | 23 | 1 | |
| Ed Taylor | DB | 6' | 172 | 23 | 2 | |
| Phil Wise | DB | 6' | 202 | 27 | | |
| Steve Joachim | QB | 6'3" | 215 | 24 | | |
| Joe Namath | QB | 6'2" | 200 | 33 | | |
| Richard Todd | QB | 6'2" | 210 | 22 | | 6 |
| Clark Gaines | HB | 6'1" | 192 | 22 | | 30 |
| Louie Giammona | HB | 5'9" | 180 | 23 | | 6 |
| Bob Gresham | HB | 5'11" | 200 | 28 | | |
| Jazz Jackson | HB | 5'8" | 174 | 24 | | |
| Steve Rogers | HB | 6'2" | 205 | 23 | | |
| Allen Carter (from NE) | FB | 5'11" | 208 | 23 | | |
| Steve Davis | FB-HB | 6'1" | 210 | 26 | | 18 |
| Ed Marinaro | FB | 6'2" | 219 | 26 | | 12 |
| Jerome Barkum | WR | 6'3" | 212 | 26 | | 6 |
| Don Buckey | WR | 5'11" | 180 | 22 | | |
| Keith Denson | WR | 5'8" | 165 | 24 | | |
| Clint Haserlig | WR | 6' | 189 | 24 | | |
| David Knight | WR | 6'1" | 175 | 25 | | 12 |
| Lou Piccone | WR | 5'9" | 184 | 27 | | 6 |
| Howard Satterwhite | WR | 5'11" | 185 | 23 | | |
| Rich Caster | TE-WR | 6'5" | 224 | 27 | | 6 |
| Richard Osborne (from PHI.) | TE | 6'3" | 230 | 22 | | 6 |
| Duane Carrell | K | 5'10" | 185 | 26 | | |
| Pat Leahy | K | 6' | 200 | 25 | | 49 |

Mark Lomas – Knee Injury
Wayne Mulligan – Knee Injury
Don Coleman – Knee Injury

**BUFFALO BILLS** 2-12 Lou Saban (2-3) Jim Ringo (0-9)

| Scores of Each Game | | |
|---|---|---|
| 21 | Miami | 30 |
| 3 | HOUSTON | 13 |
| 14 | Tampa Bay | 9 |
| 50 | KANSAS CITY | 17 |
| 14 | N.Y. Jets | 17 |
| 13 | BALTIMORE | 31 |
| 22 | NEW ENGLAND | 26 |
| 14 | N.Y. JETS | 19 |
| 10 | New England | 20 |
| 10 | Dallas | 17 |
| 13 | SAN DIEGO | 34 |
| 14 | Detroit | 27 |
| 27 | Miami | 45 |
| 20 | Baltimore | 58 |

| Use Name | Pos. | Hgt | Wgt | Age | Int | Pts |
|---|---|---|---|---|---|---|
| Joe Devlin | OT | 6'5" | 258 | 22 | | |
| Dave Foley | OT | 6'5" | 247 | 28 | | |
| Donnie Green | OT | 6'7" | 252 | 28 | | |
| Bill Adams | OG-OT | 6'2" | 246 | 26 | | |
| Joe DeLamielleure | OG | 6'3" | 248 | 25 | | |
| Reggie McKenzie | OG | 6'4" | 242 | 26 | | |
| Mike Montler | C | 6'4" | 245 | 32 | | |
| Willie Parker | C-OG | 6'3" | 245 | 27 | | |
| Bob Patton | C | 6'1" | 245 | 22 | | |
| Mark Johnson | DE | 6'2" | 240 | 23 | | |
| Ken Jones | DE | 6'5" | 252 | 23 | | |
| Jeff Lloyd | DE | 6'6" | 255 | 22 | | |
| Marty Smith | DE | 6'3" | 250 | 22 | | |
| Sherman White | DE | 6'5" | 245 | 27 | 1 | |
| Mike Kadish | DT | 6'5" | 270 | 26 | | |
| Ben Williams | DT | 6'3" | 258 | 22 | | |
| Jeff Yeates (to ATL) | DT | 6'3" | 248 | 25 | | |
| Bo Cornell | LB | 6'1" | 222 | 27 | | |
| Dan Jilek | LB | 6'2" | 212 | 22 | 2 | |
| Merv Krakau | LB | 6'2" | 233 | 25 | 1 | |
| Bob Nelson | LB | 6'4" | 232 | 23 | | |
| Tom Ruud | LB | 6'2" | 223 | 23 | | |
| John Skorupan | LB | 6'2" | 221 | 25 | 1 | |
| Tim Anderson | DB | 6' | 194 | 27 | | |
| Cliff Brooks (from PHI & NYJ) | DB | 6'1" | 190 | 27 | | |
| Mario Clark | DB | 6'2" | 190 | 22 | 2 | |
| Steve Freeman | DB | 5'11" | 185 | 23 | | |
| Van Green (from CLE) | DB | 6'1" | 192 | 25 | | |
| Tony Greene | DB | 5'10" | 170 | 27 | 5 | 6 |
| Dwight Harrison | DB | 6'1" | 186 | 27 | 1 | |
| Doug Jones | DB | 6'2" | 205 | 26 | 3 | |
| Keith Moody | DB | 5'10" | 171 | 23 | 3 | 6 |
| Joe Ferguson | QB | 6'1" | 184 | 26 | | |
| Gary Marangi | QB | 6'1" | 203 | 24 | | 12 |
| Sam Wyche (from STL) | QB | 6'4" | 220 | 30 | | |
| Roland Hooks | HB | 6' | 197 | 23 | | |
| Darnell Powell | HB | 6' | 197 | 22 | | |
| Andy Reid | HB | 6' | 195 | 22 | | |
| O.J. Simpson | HB | 6'2" | 212 | 29 | | 54 |
| Vic Washington | HB | 5'10" | 195 | 30 | | |
| Jim Braxton | FB | 6'2" | 242 | 27 | | |
| Jeff Kinney (from K.C.) | FB-HB | 6'2" | 215 | 26 | | 6 |
| Eddie Ray | FB | 6'1" | 240 | 29 | | |
| Bob Chandler | WR | 6' | 180 | 27 | | 60 |
| Emmett Edwards (from HOU) | WR | 6'1" | 190 | 24 | | |
| Robert Gaddis | WR | 5'11" | 178 | 24 | | |
| John Holland | WR | 6' | 190 | 24 | | 18 |
| Fred Coleman | TE | 6'4" | 240 | 23 | | |
| Reuben Gant | TE-WR | 6'4" | 225 | 24 | | 18 |
| Paul Seymour | TE | 6'5" | 245 | 26 | | |
| Marv Bateman | K | 6'4" | 214 | 26 | | |
| George Jakowenko | K | 5'9" | 180 | 28 | | 57 |

Ron Holliday – Knee Injury
Robert James – Knee Injury

*—Overtime

## BALTIMORE COLTS

### RUSHING

| Last Name | No. | Yds | Avg | TD |
|---|---|---|---|---|
| Mitchell | 289 | 1200 | 4.2 | 5 |
| Leaks | 118 | 445 | 3.8 | 7 |
| McCauley | 69 | 227 | 3.3 | 9 |
| R. Lee | 41 | 220 | 5.4 | 1 |
| Jones | 38 | 214 | 5.6 | 2 |
| Doughty | 2 | 7 | 2.3 | 0 |
| Stevens | 1 | 3 | 3.0 | 1 |
| Troup | 5 | -1 | 0.2 | 1 |
| D. Lee | 1 | -12 | -12.0 | 0 |

### RECEIVING

| Last Name | No. | Yds | Avg | TD |
|---|---|---|---|---|
| Mitchell | 60 | 555 | 9 | 3 |
| Carr | 43 | 1112 | 26 | 11 |
| Doughty | 40 | 628 | 16 | 5 |
| McCauley | 34 | 347 | 10 | 2 |
| Chester | 24 | 467 | 19 | 3 |
| Leaks | 8 | 43 | 5 | 0 |
| Scott | 3 | 35 | 12 | 0 |
| Kennedy | 1 | 32 | 32 | 0 |
| Thompson | 1 | 11 | 11 | 0 |
| R. Lee | 1 | -9 | -9 | 0 |

### PUNT RETURNS

| Last Name | No. | Yds | Avg | TD |
|---|---|---|---|---|
| Stevens | 39 | 315 | 8 | 0 |
| R. Lee | 1 | 0 | 0 | 0 |

### KICKOFF RETURNS

| Last Name | No. | Yds | Avg | TD |
|---|---|---|---|---|
| Stevens | 30 | 710 | 24 | 0 |
| Laird | 7 | 143 | 20 | 0 |
| Kennedy | 4 | 64 | 16 | 0 |
| Wallace | 3 | 61 | 20 | 0 |
| R. Lee | 3 | 24 | 8 | 0 |
| Pratt | 1 | 21 | 21 | 0 |
| Scott | 1 | 20 | 20 | 0 |
| McCauley | 1 | 17 | 17 | 0 |
| Novak | 1 | 12 | 12 | 0 |
| Huff | 1 | 0 | 0 | 0 |

### PASSING – PUNTING – KICKING

| PASSING | Att | Comp | % | Yds | Yd/Att | TD | Int-% | RK |
|---|---|---|---|---|---|---|---|---|
| Jones | 343 | 207 | 60 | 3104 | 9.0 | 24 | 9— 3 | 2 |
| Troup | 18 | 8 | 44 | 117 | 6.5 | 0 | 1— 6 | |

| PUNTING | No | Avg | | | | | | |
|---|---|---|---|---|---|---|---|---|
| D. Lee | 59 | 39.7 | | | | | | |

| KICKING | XP | Att | % | FG | Att | % | | |
|---|---|---|---|---|---|---|---|---|
| Linhart | 48 | 50 | 96 | 20 | 27 | 74 | | |

## NEW ENGLAND PATRIOTS

### RUSHING

| Last Name | No. | Yds | Avg | TD |
|---|---|---|---|---|
| Cunningham | 172 | 824 | 4.8 | 3 |
| Calhoun | 129 | 721 | 5.6 | 1 |
| Johnson | 169 | 699 | 4.1 | 6 |
| Grogan | 60 | 397 | 6.6 | 12 |
| Phillips | 24 | 164 | 6.8 | 1 |
| Forte | 25 | 100 | 4.0 | 1 |
| Stingley | 8 | 45 | 5.6 | 0 |
| Francis | 2 | 12 | 6.0 | 0 |
| Burks | 1 | 2 | 2.0 | 0 |
| Patrick | 1 | -16 | -16.0 | 0 |

### RECEIVING

| Last Name | No. | Yds | Avg | TD |
|---|---|---|---|---|
| Johnson | 29 | 343 | 12 | 4 |
| Cunningham | 27 | 299 | 11 | 0 |
| Francis | 26 | 367 | 14 | 3 |
| Stingley | 17 | 370 | 22 | 4 |
| Calhoun | 12 | 56 | 5 | 0 |
| Vataha | 11 | 192 | 17 | 1 |
| Briscoe | 10 | 136 | 14 | 1 |
| Chandler | 5 | 49 | 10 | 3 |
| Forte | 3 | 9 | 3 | 1 |
| Burks | 2 | 27 | 14 | 0 |
| Phillips | 1 | 18 | 18 | 0 |
| Brock | 1 | 6 | 6 | 1 |

### PUNT RETURNS

| Last Name | No. | Yds | Avg | TD |
|---|---|---|---|---|
| Haynes | 45 | 608 | 14 | 2 |
| Beaudoin | 2 | 18 | 9 | 0 |
| Stingley | 1 | 2 | 2 | 0 |

### KICKOFF RETURNS

| Last Name | No. | Yds | Avg | TD |
|---|---|---|---|---|
| Phillips | 14 | 397 | 28 | 0 |
| Calhoun | 9 | 183 | 20 | 0 |
| Beaudoin | 6 | 134 | 22 | 0 |
| Forte | 3 | 62 | 21 | 0 |
| Conn | 2 | 29 | 15 | 0 |
| McKay | 1 | 23 | 23 | 0 |

### PASSING – PUNTING – KICKING

| PASSING | Att | Comp | % | Yds | Yd/Att | TD | Int-% | RK |
|---|---|---|---|---|---|---|---|---|
| Grogan | 302 | 145 | 48 | 1903 | 6.3 | 18 | 20— 7 | 12 |
| Owen | 5 | 1 | 20 | 7 | 1.4 | 0 | 0— 0 | |
| Johnson | 2 | 0 | 0 | 0 | 0.0 | 0 | 0— 0 | |

| PUNTING | No | Avg | | | | | | |
|---|---|---|---|---|---|---|---|---|
| Patrick | 67 | 40.1 | | | | | | |

| KICKING | XP | Att | % | FG | Att | % | | |
|---|---|---|---|---|---|---|---|---|
| Smith | 42 | 46 | 91 | 15 | 25 | 60 | | |
| Zabel | 1 | 1 | 100 | | | | | |

## MIAMI DOLPHINS

### RUSHING

| Last Name | No. | Yds | Avg | TD |
|---|---|---|---|---|
| Malone | 186 | 797 | 4.3 | 4 |
| Bulaich | 122 | 540 | 4.4 | 4 |
| Winfrey | 52 | 205 | 3.9 | 1 |
| Nottingham | 63 | 185 | 2.9 | 3 |
| Davis | 31 | 160 | 5.2 | 1 |
| Griese | 23 | 108 | 4.7 | 0 |
| Solomon | 4 | 60 | 15.0 | 1 |
| N. Moore | 4 | 36 | 9.0 | 0 |
| Seiple | 3 | 14 | 4.7 | 0 |
| Strock | 2 | 13 | 6.5 | 1 |
| Heath | 1 | 0 | 0.0 | 0 |

### RECEIVING

| Last Name | No. | Yds | Avg | TD |
|---|---|---|---|---|
| N. Moore | 33 | 625 | 19 | 4 |
| Bulaich | 28 | 151 | 5 | 0 |
| Solomon | 27 | 453 | 17 | 2 |
| Harris | 22 | 372 | 17 | 1 |
| Mandich | 22 | 260 | 12 | 4 |
| Twilley | 14 | 214 | 15 | 1 |
| Tillman | 13 | 130 | 10 | 1 |
| Seiple | 10 | 138 | 14 | 1 |
| Malone | 9 | 103 | 11 | 0 |
| Winfrey | 6 | 55 | 9 | 1 |
| Nottingham | 4 | 33 | 8 | 0 |
| McCreary | 2 | 51 | 26 | 0 |
| Davis | 2 | 8 | 4 | 0 |
| Holmes | 1 | 11 | 11 | 0 |

### PUNT RETURNS

| Last Name | No. | Yds | Avg | TD |
|---|---|---|---|---|
| Solomon | 13 | 205 | 16 | 1 |
| Harris | 9 | 79 | 9 | 0 |
| N. Moore | 8 | 72 | 9 | 0 |
| Babb | 3 | 38 | 13 | 0 |
| Anderson | 2 | 21 | 11 | 0 |

### KICKOFF RETURNS

| Last Name | No. | Yds | Avg | TD |
|---|---|---|---|---|
| Davis | 26 | 617 | 24 | 0 |
| Harris | 17 | 559 | 33 | 0 |
| Nottingham | 6 | 107 | 18 | 0 |
| Holmes | 4 | 90 | 23 | 0 |
| N. Moore | 2 | 28 | 14 | 0 |
| Winfrey | 2 | 24 | 12 | 0 |
| Solomon | 1 | 12 | 12 | 0 |
| Tillman | 1 | 0 | 0 | 0 |

### PASSING – PUNTING – KICKING

| PASSING | Att | Comp | % | Yds | Yd/Att | TD | Int-% | RK |
|---|---|---|---|---|---|---|---|---|
| Griese | 272 | 162 | 60 | 2097 | 7.7 | 11 | 12— 4 | 4 |
| Strock | 47 | 21 | 45 | 359 | 7.6 | 3 | 2— 4 | |
| Morrall | 26 | 10 | 39 | 148 | 5.7 | 1 | 1— 4 | |
| Solomon | 1 | 0 | 0 | 0 | 0.0 | 0 | 0— 0 | |

| PUNTING | No | Avg | | | | | | |
|---|---|---|---|---|---|---|---|---|
| Seiple | 62 | 38.2 | | | | | | |

| KICKING | XP | Att | % | FG | Att | % | | |
|---|---|---|---|---|---|---|---|---|
| Yepremian | 29 | 31 | 94 | 16 | 23 | 70 | | |

## NEW YORK JETS

### RUSHING

| Last Name | No. | Yds | Avg | TD |
|---|---|---|---|---|
| Gaines | 157 | 724 | 4.6 | 3 |
| Davis | 94 | 418 | 4.4 | 3 |
| Marinaro | 77 | 312 | 4.1 | 2 |
| Giammona | 39 | 158 | 3.8 | 1 |
| Todd | 28 | 107 | 3.8 | 1 |
| Gresham | 30 | 92 | 3.1 | 0 |
| Caster | 6 | 73 | 12.2 | 0 |
| Buttle | 1 | 26 | 26.0 | 0 |
| Piccone | 1 | 11 | 11.0 | 0 |
| Jackson | 1 | 6 | 6.0 | 0 |
| Namath | 2 | 5 | 2.5 | 0 |
| Carrell | 2 | 0 | 0.0 | 0 |

### RECEIVING

| Last Name | No. | Yds | Avg | TD |
|---|---|---|---|---|
| Gaines | 41 | 400 | 10 | 2 |
| Caster | 31 | 391 | 13 | 1 |
| Marinaro | 21 | 168 | 8 | 0 |
| Knight | 20 | 403 | 20 | 2 |
| Giammona | 15 | 145 | 10 | 0 |
| Piccone | 12 | 147 | 12 | 0 |
| Gresham | 11 | 66 | 6 | 0 |
| Davis | 8 | 57 | 7 | 0 |
| Satterwhite | 7 | 110 | 16 | 0 |
| Barkum | 5 | 54 | 11 | 1 |
| Buckey | 5 | 36 | 7 | 0 |
| Osborne | 2 | 9 | 5 | 1 |
| Jackson | 2 | 3 | 2 | 0 |

### PUNT RETURNS

| Last Name | No. | Yds | Avg | TD |
|---|---|---|---|---|
| Piccone | 21 | 173 | 8 | 1 |
| Giammona | 12 | 117 | 10 | 0 |
| Jackson | 6 | -1 | 0 | 0 |
| Marvaso | 1 | 0 | 0 | 0 |

### KICKOFF RETURNS

| Last Name | No. | Yds | Avg | TD |
|---|---|---|---|---|
| Piccone | 31 | 699 | 23 | 0 |
| Giammona | 23 | 527 | 23 | 0 |
| Jackson | 10 | 207 | 21 | 0 |
| Denson | 6 | 129 | 22 | 0 |
| Hennigan | 1 | 22 | 22 | 0 |
| Osborne | 1 | 8 | 8 | 0 |
| Gaines | 1 | 5 | 5 | 0 |

### PASSING – PUNTING – KICKING

| PASSING | Att | Comp | % | Yds | Yd/Att | TD | Int-% | RK |
|---|---|---|---|---|---|---|---|---|
| Namath | 230 | 114 | 50 | 1090 | 4.7 | 4 | 16— 7 | 14 |
| Todd | 162 | 65 | 40 | 870 | 5.4 | 3 | 12— 7 | 15 |
| Gresham | 1 | 1 | 100 | 29 | 29.0 | 0 | 0— 0 | |

| PUNTING | No | Avg | | | | | | |
|---|---|---|---|---|---|---|---|---|
| Carrell | 81 | 39.7 | | | | | | |

| KICKING | XP | Att | % | FG | Att | % | | |
|---|---|---|---|---|---|---|---|---|
| Leahy | 16 | 20 | 80 | 11 | 16 | 69 | | |

## BUFFALO BILLS

### RUSHING

| Last Name | No. | Yds | Avg | TD |
|---|---|---|---|---|
| Simpson | 290 | 1503 | 5.2 | 8 |
| Kinney | 118 | 482 | 4.1 | 1 |
| Marangi | 39 | 230 | 5.9 | 2 |
| Hooks | 25 | 116 | 4.6 | 0 |
| Ferguson | 18 | 81 | 4.5 | 0 |
| Washington | 22 | 65 | 3.0 | 0 |
| Ray | 24 | 56 | 2.3 | 0 |
| Powell | 11 | 40 | 3.6 | 0 |
| Braxton | 1 | 0 | 0.0 | 0 |
| Chandler | 1 | 0 | 0.0 | 0 |
| Edwards | 1 | 0 | 0.0 | 0 |

### RECEIVING

| Last Name | No. | Yds | Avg | TD |
|---|---|---|---|---|
| Chandler | 61 | 824 | 14 | 10 |
| Simpson | 22 | 259 | 12 | 1 |
| Seymour | 16 | 169 | 11 | 0 |
| Holland | 15 | 299 | 20 | 2 |
| Kinney | 14 | 78 | 6 | 0 |
| Gant | 12 | 263 | 23 | 3 |
| Hooks | 6 | 72 | 12 | 0 |
| Washington | 3 | 29 | 10 | 0 |
| Ray | 3 | 26 | 9 | 0 |
| Edwards | 2 | 53 | 27 | 0 |
| Montler | 1 | 6 | 6 | 0 |
| Powell | 1 | 6 | 6 | 0 |

### PUNT RETURNS

| Last Name | No. | Yds | Avg | TD |
|---|---|---|---|---|
| Moody | 16 | 166 | 10 | 1 |
| Hooks | 11 | 45 | 4 | 0 |
| Holland | 4 | 11 | 3 | 0 |
| Gaddis | 1 | 6 | 6 | 0 |

### KICKOFF RETURNS

| Last Name | No. | Yds | Avg | TD |
|---|---|---|---|---|
| Moody | 26 | 605 | 23 | 0 |
| Hooks | 23 | 521 | 23 | 0 |
| Ruud | 6 | 68 | 11 | 0 |
| Powell | 4 | 101 | 25 | 0 |
| Holland | 4 | 62 | 16 | 0 |
| Washington | 3 | 63 | 21 | 0 |
| Cornell | 2 | 32 | 16 | 0 |
| Gaddis | 1 | 16 | 16 | 0 |

### PASSING – PUNTING – KICKING

| PASSING | Att | Comp | % | Yds | Yd/Att | TD | Int-% | RK |
|---|---|---|---|---|---|---|---|---|
| Ferguson | 151 | 74 | 49 | 1086 | 7.2 | 9 | 1— 1 | 3 |
| Marangi | 232 | 82 | 35 | 998 | 4.3 | 7 | 16— 7 | 16 |
| Wyche | 1 | 1 | 100 | 5 | 5.0 | 0 | 0— 0 | |

| PUNTING | No | Avg | | | | | | |
|---|---|---|---|---|---|---|---|---|
| Bateman | 86 | 42.9 | | | | | | |

| KICKING | XP | Att | % | FG | Att | % | | |
|---|---|---|---|---|---|---|---|---|
| Jakowenko | 21 | 24 | 88 | 12 | 17 | 71 | | |

## PITTSBURGH STEELERS 10-4 Chuck Noll

**Scores of Each Game**

| | | |
|---|---|---|
| 28 | Oakland | 31 |
| 31 | CLEVELAND | 14 |
| 27 | NEW ENGLAND | 30 |
| 6 | Minnesota | 17 |
| 16 | Cleveland | 18 |
| 23 | CINCINNATI | 6 |
| 27 | N.Y. Giants | 0 |
| 23 | SAN DIEGO | 0 |
| 45 | Kansas City | 0 |
| 14 | MIAMI | 3 |
| 32 | HOUSTON | 16 |
| 7 | Cincinnati | 3 |
| 42 | TAMPA BAY | 0 |
| 21 | Houston | 0 |

| Use Name | Pos. | Hgt | Wgt | Age | Int | Pts |
|---|---|---|---|---|---|---|
| Gordon Gravelle | OT | 6'5" | 250 | 27 | | |
| Jon Kolb | OT | 6'2" | 262 | 29 | | |
| Jim Clack | OG | 6'3" | 250 | 28 | | |
| Sam Davis | OG | 6'1" | 255 | 32 | | |
| Gerry Mullins | OG-OT | 6'3" | 244 | 27 | | |
| Ray Mansfield | C | 6'3" | 260 | 35 | | |
| Ray Pinney | C-OT | 6'4" | 240 | 22 | | |
| Mike Webster | C | 6'1" | 250 | 24 | | |
| John Banaszak | DE | 6'3" | 244 | 26 | | |
| L.C. Greenwood | DE | 6'5" | 250 | 29 | | |
| Dwight White | DE | 6'4" | 255 | 27 | | |
| Gary Dunn | DT | 6'3" | 240 | 23 | | |
| Steve Furness | DT-DE | 6'4" | 255 | 25 | | |
| Joe Greene | DT | 6'4" | 275 | 29 | | |
| Ernie Holmes | DT | 6'3" | 260 | 28 | | |
| Jack Ham | LB | 6'3" | 225 | 27 | 2 | |
| Marv Kellum | LB | 6'2" | 225 | 24 | | |
| Jack Lambert | LB | 6'4" | 220 | 24 | 2 | |
| Andy Russell | LB | 6'3" | 225 | 34 | 1 | |
| Loren Toews | LB | 6'3" | 222 | 24 | | 2 |
| Jim Allen | DB | 6'2" | 194 | 24 | | |
| Mel Blount | DB | 6'3" | 205 | 28 | 6 | |
| Glen Edwards | DB | 6' | 185 | 29 | 6 | |
| Donnie Shell | DB | 5'11" | 190 | 24 | | |
| J.T. Thomas | DB | 6'2" | 196 | 25 | 2 | |
| Mike Wagner | DB | 6'1" | 200 | 27 | 2 | |
| Terry Bradshaw | QB | 6'3" | 200 | 27 | | 18 |
| Neil Graff (from SEA) | QB | 6'3" | 200 | 26 | | |
| Mike Kruczek | QB | 6'1" | 196 | 23 | | 12 |
| Rocky Bleier | HB | 5'11" | 210 | 30 | | 30 |
| Jack Deloplaine | HB | 5'10" | 205 | 22 | | 12 |
| John Fuqua | HB | 5'11" | 200 | 29 | | 6 |
| Franco Harris | FB | 6'2" | 225 | 26 | | 84 |
| Reggie Harrison | FB | 5'11" | 220 | 26 | | 24 |
| Theo Bell | WR | 5'11" | 180 | 22 | | 6 |
| Frank Lewis | WR | 6'1" | 196 | 29 | | 12 |
| Ernest Pough | WR | 6'1" | 174 | 24 | | 6 |
| John Stallworth | WR | 6'2" | 183 | 24 | | 18 |
| Lynn Swann | WR | 6' | 180 | 24 | | 18 |
| Larry Brown | TE | 6'4" | 229 | 27 | | |
| Bennie Cunningham | TE | 6'4" | 255 | 21 | | 6 |
| Randy Grossman | TE | 6'1" | 215 | 22 | | 6 |
| Roy Gerela | K | 5'10" | 185 | 28 | | 82 |
| Bobby Walden | K | 6' | 190 | 38 | | |

Mike Collier — Knee Injury
Reggie Garrett — Back Injury

## CINCINNATI BENGALS 10-4 Bill Johnson

**Scores of Each Game**

| | | |
|---|---|---|
| 17 | DENVER | 7 |
| 27 | Baltimore | 28 |
| 28 | GREEN BAY | 7 |
| 45 | Cleveland | 24 |
| 21 | TAMPA BAY | 0 |
| 6 | Pittsburgh | 23 |
| 27 | Houston | 7 |
| 21 | CLEVELAND | 27 |
| 20 | LOS ANGELES | 12 |
| 31 | HOUSTON | 27 |
| 27 | Kansas City | 24 |
| 3 | PITTSBURGH | 7 |
| 20 | Oakland | 35 |
| 42 | N.Y. Jets | 3 |

| Use Name | Pos. | Hgt | Wgt | Age | Int | Pts |
|---|---|---|---|---|---|---|
| Vern Holland | OT | 6'5" | 272 | 28 | | |
| Ron Hunt | OT | 6'6" | 274 | 21 | | |
| Rufus Mayes | OT | 6'5" | 268 | 28 | | |
| Glenn Bujnoch | OG | 6'5" | 260 | 22 | | |
| Greg Fairchild | OG-OT | 6'4" | 258 | 22 | | |
| Dave Lapham | OG | 6'4" | 258 | 24 | | |
| John Shinners | OG | 6'2" | 259 | 29 | | |
| Bob Johnson | C | 6'5" | 255 | 30 | | |
| Coy Bacon | DE | 6'4" | 270 | 34 | | 2 |
| Gary Burley | DE | 6'3" | 262 | 23 | | |
| Ken Johnson | DE | 6'5" | 262 | 29 | | |
| Bob Brown | DT | 6'5" | 280 | 36 | | |
| Ron Carpenter | DT | 6'4" | 265 | 28 | | |
| Bill Kollar | DT | 6'4" | 256 | 23 | | |
| Glenn Cameron | LB | 6'1" | 6'2" | 23 | | |
| Chris Devlin | LB | 6'3" | 228 | 22 | 1 | |
| Bo Harris | LB | 6'3" | 228 | 23 | 1 | |
| Jim LeClair | LB | 6'2" | 237 | 25 | 1 | |
| Ron Pritchard | LB | 6'1" | 226 | 29 | 1 | |
| Reggie Williams | LB | 6'1" | 230 | 21 | 1 | |
| Tommy Casanova | DB | 6'2" | 194 | 26 | 5 | 18 |
| Marvin Cobb | DB | 6' | 191 | 23 | 3 | |
| Bernard Jackson | DB | 6' | 179 | 26 | 1 | |
| Melvin Morgan | DB | 6' | 175 | 23 | | 6 |
| Lemar Parrish | DB | 5'11" | 180 | 28 | 2 | |
| Scott Perry | DB | 6' | 185 | 22 | | |
| Ken Riley | DB | 6' | 183 | 29 | 9 | 6 |
| Ken Anderson | QB | 6'1" | 210 | 27 | | 6 |
| John Reaves | QB | 6'3" | 202 | 26 | | |
| Tony Davis | HB | 5'10" | 210 | 23 | | 6 |
| Lenvil Elliott | HB | 6' | 207 | 24 | | 18 |
| Archie Griffin | HB | 5'9" | 191 | 22 | | 18 |
| Willie Shelby | HB | 5'10" | 190 | 23 | | 6 |
| Booby Clark | FB | 6'2" | 245 | 25 | | 48 |
| Stan Fritts | FB-HB | 6'1" | 215 | 23 | | 18 |
| Billy Brooks | WR | 6'3" | 215 | 23 | | |
| Isaac Curtis | WR | 6' | 195 | 25 | | 36 |
| John McDaniel | WR | 6'1" | 194 | 24 | | 6 |
| Pat McInally | WR | 6'6" | 200 | 23 | | |
| Chip Myers | WR | 6'4" | 208 | 31 | | 6 |
| Bruce Coslet | TE | 6'3" | 225 | 30 | | 12 |
| Bob Trumpy | TE | 6'6" | 231 | 31 | | 42 |
| Chris Bahr | K | 5'9" | 170 | 23 | | 81 |

## CLEVELAND BROWNS 9-5 Forrest Gregg

**Scores of Each Game**

| | | |
|---|---|---|
| 38 | N.Y. JETS | 17 |
| 14 | Pittsburgh | 31 |
| 13 | Denver | 44 |
| 24 | CINCINNATI | 45 |
| 18 | PITTSBURGH | 16 |
| 20 | Atlanta | 17 |
| 21 | SAN DIEGO | 17 |
| 6 | Cincinnati | 21 |
| 21 | Houston | 7 |
| 24 | PHILADELPHIA | 7 |
| 24 | Tampa Bay | 7 |
| 17 | MIAMI | 13 |
| 13 | HOUSTON | 10 |
| 14 | Kansas City | 39 |

| Use Name | Pos. | Hgt | Wgt | Age | Int | Pts |
|---|---|---|---|---|---|---|
| Barry Darrow | OT | 6'7" | 260 | 26 | | |
| Doug Dieken | OT | 6'5" | 252 | 27 | | |
| Henry Sheppard | OT-OG | 6'6" | 246 | 23 | | |
| Pete Adams | OG | 6'4" | 260 | 25 | | |
| Al Dennis | OG | 6'4" | 250 | 25 | | |
| Robert Jackson | OG | 6'5" | 245 | 23 | | |
| Tom DeLeone | C | 6'2" | 248 | 26 | | |
| Gerry Sullivan | C-OT | 6'4" | 250 | 24 | | |
| Earl Edwards | DE-DT | 6'6" | 256 | 30 | | |
| Joe Jones | DE | 6'6" | 250 | 28 | | 6 |
| Mack Mitchell | DE | 6'7" | 245 | 24 | | |
| Mike St. Clair | DE | 6'5" | 245 | 22 | | |
| Walter Johnson | DT | 6'3" | 265 | 33 | | |
| Jerry Sherk | DT | 6'4" | 250 | 28 | 1 | |
| Dick Ambrose | LB | 6' | 235 | 23 | | |
| Bob Babich | LB | 6'2" | 231 | 29 | 2 | |
| John Garlington | LB | 6'1" | 221 | 30 | | |
| Dave Graf | LB | 6'2" | 215 | 23 | | |
| Charlie Hall | LB | 6'3" | 230 | 27 | 1 | |
| Gerald Irons | LB | 6'2" | 230 | 29 | 1 | |
| Ron Bolton | DB | 6'2" | 170 | 26 | 3 | 6 |
| Terry Brown | DB | 6'1" | 205 | 29 | 1 | |
| Neil Craig | DB | 6'1" | 190 | 28 | 1 | |
| Bill Craven | DB | 5'11" | 190 | 24 | | |
| Thom Darden | DB | 6'2" | 193 | 26 | 7 | |
| Tony Peters | DB | 6'1" | 192 | 23 | | |
| Clarence Scott | DB | 6' | 180 | 27 | 4 | |
| Dave Mays | QB | 6'1" | 204 | 27 | | |
| Mike Phipps | QB | 6'2" | 205 | 28 | | |
| Brian Sipe | QB | 6'1" | 190 | 27 | | 1 |
| Brian Duncan | HB | 6' | 201 | 24 | | 6 |
| Cleo Miller | HB-FB | 5'11" | 202 | 23 | | 24 |
| Larry Poole | HB | 6' | 195 | 24 | | 6 |
| Greg Pruitt | HB | 5'10" | 190 | 25 | | 30 |
| Mike Pruitt | FB | 6' | 214 | 22 | | |
| Ricky Feacher (from NE) | WR | 5'10" | 174 | 22 | | |
| Steve Holden | WR | 6' | 194 | 25 | | 6 |
| Dave Logan | WR | 6'4" | 226 | 22 | | |
| Willie Miller | WR | 5'9" | 172 | 24 | | |
| Reggie Rucker | WR | 6' | 190 | 28 | | 48 |
| Paul Warfield | WR | 6' | 188 | 33 | | 36 |
| Gary Parris | TE | 6'2" | 226 | 26 | | |
| Oscar Roan | TE | 6'6" | 225 | 24 | | |
| Don Cockroft | K | 6'1" | 195 | 31 | | 72 |

Chuck Hutchinson — Knee Injury

Billy LeFear — Injury

## HOUSTON OILERS 5-9 Bum Phillips

**Scores of Each Game**

| | | |
|---|---|---|
| 20 | TAMPA BAY | 0 |
| 13 | Buffalo | 3 |
| 13 | OAKLAND | 14 |
| 31 | New Orleans | 26 |
| 17 | DENVER | 3 |
| 27 | San Diego | 30 |
| 7 | CINCINNATI | 27 |
| 14 | Baltimore | 38 |
| 7 | CLEVELAND | 21 |
| 27 | Cincinnati | 31 |
| 16 | Pittsburgh | 32 |
| 20 | ATLANTA | 14 |
| 0 | Cleveland | 13 |
| 0 | PITTSBURGH | 21 |

| Use Name | Pos. | Hgt | Wgt | Age | Int | Pts |
|---|---|---|---|---|---|---|
| Elbert Drungo | OT | 6'5" | 265 | 33 | | |
| Kevin Hunt | OT | 6'5" | 260 | 27 | | |
| Greg Sampson | OT | 6'6" | 270 | 25 | | |
| Bobby Simon | OT-OG | 6'3" | 252 | 23 | | |
| Ed Fisher | OG | 6'3" | 250 | 27 | | |
| Dennis Havig | OG | 6'2" | 256 | 27 | | |
| Conway Hayman | OG | 6'3" | 262 | 27 | | |
| Ron Lou | C | 6'2" | 242 | 25 | | |
| Carl Mauck | C | 6'3" | 250 | 29 | | |
| Elvin Bethea | DE | 6'3" | 255 | 30 | | |
| Albert Burton | DE | 6'5" | 270 | 24 | | |
| Joe Owens | DE | 6'2" | 245 | 29 | | |
| Bubba Smith | DE | 6'7" | 265 | 31 | | |
| Tody Smith (to BUF) | DE | 6'5" | 250 | 27 | | |
| Curley Culp | NT | 6'1" | 265 | 30 | | |
| John Little | NT | 6'3" | 250 | 29 | | |
| Duane Benson | LB | 6'2" | 225 | 31 | | |
| Gregg Bingham | LB | 6'1" | 230 | 25 | 2 | |
| Robert Brazile | LB | 6'4" | 238 | 23 | 1 | |
| Steve Kiner | LB | 6' | 225 | 29 | | |
| Tim Rossovich | LB | 6'4" | 240 | 30 | | |
| Ted Thompson | LB | 6'1" | 220 | 23 | | |
| Ted Washington | LB | 6'1" | 245 | 28 | | |
| Willie Alexander | DB | 6'2" | 195 | 26 | | |
| Bob Atkins | DB | 6'3" | 210 | 30 | | |
| Zeke Moore | DB | 6'2" | 195 | 32 | 1 | |
| Mike Reinfeldt (from OAK.) | DB | 6'2" | 178 | 23 | 1 | |
| Greg Stemrick | DB | 5'11" | 185 | 24 | 1 | |
| Mike Weger | DB | 6'2" | 200 | 30 | | |
| C.L. Whittington | DB | 6'1" | 200 | 24 | 5 | 6 |
| Sam Williams | DB | 6'2" | 192 | 24 | | |
| James Foote | QB | 6'2" | 210 | 24 | | |
| John Hadl | QB | 6'2" | 215 | 36 | | |
| Dan Pastorini | QB | 6'3" | 205 | 27 | | |
| Ronnie Coleman | HB | 5'10" | 198 | 25 | | 36 |
| Al Johnson | HB | 6' | 200 | 26 | | |
| Altie Taylor | HB | 5'10" | 200 | 28 | | |
| Joe Dawkins | FB | 5'11" | 220 | 28 | | 6 |
| Don Hardeman | FB | 6'2" | 235 | 24 | | 6 |
| Fred Willis | FB | 6' | 205 | 28 | | 18 |
| Mel Baker | WR | 6' | 182 | 26 | | |
| Mike Barber | WR-TE | 6'3" | 235 | 23 | | |
| Jim Beirne | WR | 6'2" | 208 | 29 | | |
| Ken Burrough | WR | 6'4" | 210 | 28 | | 42 |
| Billy Johnson | WR | 5'9" | 170 | 24 | | 24 |
| Earl Thomas | WR | 6'3" | 215 | 27 | | |
| Mack Alston | TE | 6'2" | 230 | 29 | | 6 |
| Alvis Darby (from SEA) | TE | 6'5" | 216 | 21 | | |
| John Sawyer | TE | 6'2" | 230 | 23 | | 6 |
| Skip Butler | K | 6'2" | 200 | 28 | | 72 |
| Leroy Clark | K | 5'11" | 200 | 26 | | |

Willie Frazier — Knee Injury
Willie Rogers — Injury

## PITTSBURGH STEELERS

### RUSHING

| Last Name | No. | Yds | Avg | TD |
|---|---|---|---|---|
| Harris | 289 | 1128 | 3.9 | 14 |
| Bleier | 220 | 1036 | 4.7 | 5 |
| Harrison | 54 | 235 | 4.4 | 4 |
| Bradshaw | 31 | 219 | 7.1 | 3 |
| Kruczek | 18 | 106 | 5.9 | 2 |
| Deloplaine | 17 | 91 | 5.4 | 2 |
| Fugua | 15 | 63 | 4.2 | 1 |
| Stallworth | 0 | 47 | — | 1 |
| Lewis | 2 | 24 | 12.0 | 1 |
| Pough | 2 | 8 | 4.0 | 0 |
| Walden | 3 | 7 | 2.3 | 0 |
| Bell | 1 | 5 | 5.0 | 0 |
| Swann | 1 | 2 | 2.0 | 0 |

### RECEIVING

| Last Name | No. | Yds | Avg | TD |
|---|---|---|---|---|
| Swann | 28 | 516 | 18 | 3 |
| Bleier | 24 | 294 | 12 | 0 |
| Harris | 23 | 151 | 7 | 0 |
| Lewis | 17 | 306 | 18 | 1 |
| Grossman | 15 | 181 | 12 | 1 |
| Stallworth | 9 | 111 | 12 | 2 |
| Pough | 8 | 161 | 20 | 1 |
| Brown | 7 | 97 | 14 | 0 |
| Cunningham | 5 | 49 | 10 | 1 |
| Bell | 3 | 43 | 14 | 1 |
| Harrison | 2 | 19 | 10 | 0 |
| Fugua | 1 | 4 | 4 | 0 |
| Deloplaine | 1 | 3 | 3 | 0 |

### PUNT RETURNS

| Last Name | No. | Yds | Avg | TD |
|---|---|---|---|---|
| Bell | 39 | 390 | 10 | 0 |
| Deloplaine | 17 | 150 | 9 | 0 |
| Fugua | 11 | 77 | 7 | 0 |
| Swann | 3 | 11 | 4 | 0 |
| Edwards | 1 | 8 | 8 | 0 |

### KICKOFF RETURNS

| Last Name | No. | Yds | Avg | TD |
|---|---|---|---|---|
| Pough | 18 | 369 | 21 | 0 |
| Deloplaine | 17 | 385 | 23 | 0 |
| Fugua | 4 | 75 | 19 | 0 |
| Harrison | 1 | 26 | 26 | 0 |
| Clack | 1 | 0 | 0 | 0 |

### PASSING – PUNTING – KICKING

| PASSING | Att | Comp | % | Yds | Yd/Att | TD | Int-% | RK |
|---|---|---|---|---|---|---|---|---|
| Bradshaw | 192 | 92 | 48 | 1177 | 6.1 | 10 | 9- 5 | 10 |
| Kruczek | 85 | 51 | 60 | 758 | 8.9 | 0 | 3- 4 | |

| PUNTING | No | Avg |
|---|---|---|
| Walden | 76 | 39.2 |

| KICKING | XP | Att | % | FG | Att | % |
|---|---|---|---|---|---|---|
| Gerella | 40 | 43 | 93 | 14 | 26 | 54 |

## CINCINNATI BENGALS

### RUSHING

| Last Name | No. | Yds | Avg | TD |
|---|---|---|---|---|
| Clark | 151 | 671 | 4.4 | 7 |
| Griffin | 138 | 625 | 4.5 | 3 |
| Elliott | 69 | 276 | 4.0 | 3 |
| Fritts | 47 | 200 | 4.3 | 3 |
| Davis | 36 | 178 | 4.9 | 1 |
| Anderson | 31 | 134 | 4.3 | 1 |
| Curtis | 3 | 29 | 9.7 | 0 |
| Shelby | 5 | 9 | 1.8 | 0 |
| Brooks | 1 | −13 | −13.0 | 0 |

### RECEIVING

| Last Name | No. | Yds | Avg | TD |
|---|---|---|---|---|
| Curtis | 41 | 766 | 19 | 6 |
| Clark | 23 | 158 | 7 | 1 |
| Elliott | 22 | 188 | 9 | 3 |
| Trumpy | 21 | 323 | 15 | 7 |
| Myers | 17 | 267 | 16 | 1 |
| Brooks | 16 | 191 | 12 | 0 |
| Griffin | 16 | 138 | 9 | 0 |
| McDaniel | 12 | 232 | 19 | 1 |
| Fritts | 9 | 75 | 8 | 0 |
| Coslet | 5 | 73 | 15 | 0 |
| Davis | 4 | 29 | 7 | 0 |
| Shelby | 1 | 3 | 3 | 0 |

### PUNT RETURNS

| Last Name | No. | Yds | Avg | TD |
|---|---|---|---|---|
| Shelby | 21 | 162 | 8 | 0 |
| Parrish | 20 | 122 | 6 | 0 |
| Casanova | 10 | 45 | 5 | 0 |
| Cobb | 3 | 14 | 5 | 0 |

### KICKOFF RETURNS

| Last Name | No. | Yds | Avg | TD |
|---|---|---|---|---|
| Shelby | 30 | 761 | 25 | 1 |
| Elliott | 5 | 98 | 20 | 0 |
| Davis | 4 | 21 | 5 | 0 |
| Parrish | 3 | 62 | 21 | 0 |
| Griffin | 3 | 56 | 19 | 0 |
| Hunt | 2 | 24 | 12 | 0 |
| Morgan | 1 | 14 | 14 | 0 |
| Fritts | 1 | 10 | 10 | 0 |

### PASSING – PUNTING – KICKING

| PASSING | Att | Comp | % | Yds | Yd/Att | TD | Int-% | RK |
|---|---|---|---|---|---|---|---|---|
| Anderson | 338 | 179 | 53 | 2367 | 7.0 | 19 | 14- 4 | 7 |
| Reaves | 22 | 8 | 36 | 76 | 3.5 | 2 | 1- 5 | |

| PUNTING | No | Avg |
|---|---|---|
| McInally | 76 | 39.5 |

| KICKING | XP | Att | % | FG | Att | % |
|---|---|---|---|---|---|---|
| Bahr | 39 | 42 | 93 | 14 | 27 | 52 |

## CLEVELAND BROWNS

### RUSHING

| Last Name | No. | Yds | Avg | TD |
|---|---|---|---|---|
| G. Pruitt | 209 | 1000 | 4.8 | 4 |
| C. Miller | 153 | 613 | 4.0 | 4 |
| Poole | 78 | 356 | 4.6 | 1 |
| M. Pruitt | 52 | 138 | 2.7 | 0 |
| Sipe | 18 | 71 | 3.9 | 0 |
| Duncan | 11 | 44 | 4.0 | 0 |
| Rucker | 2 | 30 | 15.0 | 0 |
| Phipps | 4 | 26 | 6.5 | 0 |
| Mays | 5 | 14 | 2.8 | 0 |
| Warfield | 1 | 3 | 3.0 | 0 |

### RECEIVING

| Last Name | No. | Yds | Avg | TD |
|---|---|---|---|---|
| Rucker | 49 | 676 | 14 | 8 |
| G. Pruitt | 45 | 341 | 8 | 1 |
| Warfield | 38 | 613 | 16 | 6 |
| C. Miller | 16 | 145 | 9 | 0 |
| Roan | 15 | 174 | 12 | 4 |
| Poole | 14 | 70 | 5 | 0 |
| Holden | 8 | 128 | 16 | 1 |
| M. Pruitt | 8 | 26 | 3 | 0 |
| Duncan | 6 | 49 | 8 | 1 |
| Logan | 5 | 104 | 21 | 0 |
| Parris | 5 | 73 | 15 | 0 |
| Feacher | 2 | 38 | 19 | 0 |

### PUNT RETURNS

| Last Name | No. | Yds | Avg | TD |
|---|---|---|---|---|
| Holden | 31 | 205 | 7 | 0 |
| Feacher | 13 | 142 | 11 | 0 |
| W. Miller | 5 | 22 | 4 | 0 |

### KICKOFF RETURNS

| Last Name | No. | Yds | Avg | TD |
|---|---|---|---|---|
| Feacher | 24 | 551 | 23 | 0 |
| Holden | 19 | 461 | 24 | 0 |
| Duncan | 6 | 145 | 24 | 0 |
| M. Pruitt | 6 | 106 | 18 | 0 |
| Poole | 3 | 62 | 21 | 0 |
| G. Pruitt | 1 | 27 | 27 | 0 |
| C. Miller | 1 | 23 | 23 | 0 |
| Ambrose | 1 | 16 | 16 | 0 |
| Jackson | 1 | 16 | 16 | 0 |
| Graf | 1 | 15 | 15 | 0 |
| W. Miller | 1 | 0 | 0 | 0 |

### PASSING – PUNTING – KICKING

| PASSING | Att | Comp | % | Yds | Yd/Att | TD | Int-% | RK |
|---|---|---|---|---|---|---|---|---|
| Sipe | 312 | 178 | 57 | 2113 | 6.8 | 17 | 14- 6 | 6 |
| Phipps | 37 | 20 | 54 | 146 | 3.9 | 3 | 0- 0 | |
| Mays | 20 | 9 | 45 | 101 | 5.1 | 0 | 1- 5 | |
| G. Pruitt | 3 | 2 | 67 | 39 | 13.0 | 1 | 0- 0 | |
| Cockroft | 1 | 0 | 0 | 0 | 0.0 | 0 | 0- 0 | |

| PUNTING | No | Avg |
|---|---|---|
| Cockroft | 64 | 38.9 |
| Mays | 2 | 45.5 |

| KICKING | XP | Att | % | FG | Att | % |
|---|---|---|---|---|---|---|
| Cockroft | 27 | 30 | 90 | 15 | 28 | 54 |
| Sipe | 1 | 1 | 100 | | | |

## HOUSTON OILERS

### RUSHING

| Last Name | No. | Yds | Avg | TD |
|---|---|---|---|---|
| Coleman | 171 | 684 | 4.0 | 2 |
| Willis | 148 | 542 | 3.7 | 2 |
| Hardeman | 32 | 114 | 3.6 | 1 |
| Dawkins | 31 | 61 | 2.0 | 1 |
| Pastorini | 11 | 45 | 4.1 | 0 |
| Burrough | 3 | 22 | 7.3 | 0 |
| Taylor | 5 | 11 | 2.2 | 0 |
| Hadl | 7 | 11 | 1.6 | 0 |
| B. Johnson | 6 | 6 | 1.0 | 0 |
| Baker | 1 | 2 | 2.0 | 0 |
| Butler | 1 | 0 | 0.0 | 0 |

### RECEIVING

| Last Name | No. | Yds | Avg | TD |
|---|---|---|---|---|
| Burrough | 51 | 932 | 18 | 7 |
| B. Johnson | 47 | 495 | 11 | 4 |
| Coleman | 40 | 247 | 6 | 3 |
| Willis | 32 | 255 | 8 | 1 |
| Alston | 19 | 174 | 9 | 1 |
| Sawyer | 18 | 208 | 12 | 1 |
| Hardeman | 7 | 25 | 4 | 0 |
| Thomas | 4 | 15 | 4 | 0 |
| Baker | 3 | 32 | 11 | 0 |
| Dawkins | 3 | 21 | 7 | 0 |
| Taylor | 2 | 15 | 8 | 0 |
| Stemrick | 1 | 10 | 10 | 0 |

### PUNT RETURNS

| Last Name | No. | Yds | Avg | TD |
|---|---|---|---|---|
| B. Johnson | 38 | 403 | 11 | 0 |
| Coleman | 7 | 91 | 13 | 1 |
| Whittington | 3 | 10 | 3 | 0 |

### KICKOFF RETURNS

| Last Name | No. | Yds | Avg | TD |
|---|---|---|---|---|
| B. Johnson | 26 | 579 | 22 | 0 |
| Taylor | 15 | 302 | 20 | 0 |
| A. Johnson | 8 | 150 | 19 | 0 |
| Hardeman | 7 | 171 | 24 | 0 |
| Baker | 1 | 15 | 15 | 0 |
| Beirne | 1 | 12 | 12 | 0 |

### PASSING – PUNTING – KICKING

| PASSING | Att | Comp | % | Yds | Yd/Att | TD | Int-% | RK |
|---|---|---|---|---|---|---|---|---|
| Pastorini | 309 | 167 | 54 | 1795 | 5.8 | 10 | 10- 3 | 9 |
| Hadl | 113 | 60 | 53 | 634 | 5.6 | 7 | 8- 7 | |
| Coleman | 1 | 0 | 0 | 0 | 0.0 | 0 | 1-100 | |

| PUNTING | No | Avg |
|---|---|---|
| Pastorini | 70 | 36.7 |
| Butler | 11 | 33.6 |
| Clark | 10 | 33.5 |
| Sawyer | 1 | 32.0 |

| KICKING | XP | Att | % | FG | Att | % |
|---|---|---|---|---|---|---|
| Butler | 24 | 24 | 100 | 16 | 27 | 59 |

## OAKLAND RAIDERS 13-1 John Madden

| Scores of Each Game | | |
|---|---|---|
| 31 | PITTSBURGH | 28 |
| 24 | Kansas City | 21 |
| 14 | Houston | 13 |
| 17 | New England | 48 |
| 27 | San Diego | 17 |
| 17 | Denver | 10 |
| 18 | GREEN BAY | 14 |
| 19 | DENVER | 6 |
| 28 | Chicago | 27 |
| 21 | KANSAS CITY | 10 |
| 26 | Philadelphia | 7 |
| 49 | TAMPA BAY | 16 |
| 35 | CINCINNATI | 20 |
| 24 | SAN DIEGO | 0 |

| Use Name | Pos. | Hgt | Wgt | Age | Int | Pts. |
|---|---|---|---|---|---|---|
| Henry Lawrence | OT | 6'4" | 273 | 24 | | |
| Art Shell | OT | 6'5" | 265 | 29 | | |
| John Vella | OT | 6'4" | 260 | 26 | | |
| George Buehler | OG | 6'2" | 270 | 29 | | |
| Dan Medlin | OG | 6'4" | 252 | 26 | | |
| Gene Upshaw | OG | 6'5" | 255 | 31 | | |
| Dave Dalby | C | 6'2" | 250 | 25 | | |
| Steve Sylvester | C | 6'4" | 262 | 23 | | |
| John Matuszak | DE | 6'8" | 275 | 25 | | |
| Herb McMath | DE | 6'4" | 245 | 21 | | |
| Charles Philyaw | DE | 6'9" | 270 | 22 | | |
| Dave Rowe | DT | 6'6" | 271 | 31 | | |
| Otis Sistrunk | DT | 6'4" | 273 | 28 | | |

Horace Jones – Knee Injury
Kelvin Korver – Knee Injury
Art Thoms – Knee Injury

| Use Name | Pos. | Hgt | Wgt | Age | Int | Pts |
|---|---|---|---|---|---|---|
| Rodrigo Barnes | LB | 6'1" | 215 | 26 | | |
| Greg Blankenship (to PIT) | LB | 6'1" | 212 | 22 | | |
| Rik Bonness | LB | 6'3" | 220 | 22 | | |
| Willie Hall | LB | 6'2" | 225 | 26 | 2 | |
| Ted Hendricks | LB | 6'7" | 220 | 28 | 1 | 2 |
| Monte Johnson | LB | 6'4" | 240 | 24 | 4 | |
| Floyd Rice | LB | 6'3" | 223 | 27 | | |
| Phil Villapiano | LB | 6'1" | 225 | 27 | 1 | |
| Butch Atkinson | DB | 6' | 185 | 29 | | |
| Willie Brown | DB | 6'1" | 210 | 35 | 3 | |
| Neal Colzie | DB | 6'2" | 205 | 23 | | |
| Charlie Phillips | DB | 6'2" | 215 | 23 | 1 | |
| Jack Tatum | DB | 5'10" | 206 | 27 | 2 | |
| Skip Thomas | DB | 6'1" | 205 | 26 | 2 | |

Marv Hubbard – Shoulder Injury
Frank Tate – Injury

| Use Name | Pos. | Hgt | Wgt | Age | Int | Pts |
|---|---|---|---|---|---|---|
| David Humm | QB | 6'2" | 184 | 24 | | |
| Mike Rae | QB | 6' | 190 | 25 | | 6 |
| Ken Stabler | QB | 6'3" | 215 | 30 | | 6 |
| Pete Banaszak | HB-FB | 5'11" | 210 | 32 | | 30 |
| Clarence Davis | HB | 5'10" | 195 | 27 | | 18 |
| Carl Garrett | HB | 5'11" | 205 | 29 | | 6 |
| Hubert Ginn | HB | 5'11" | 185 | 29 | | |
| Rick Jennings | HB | 5'9" | 180 | 23 | | |
| Manfred Moore (from TB) | HB | 6' | 199 | 25 | | |
| Terry Kunz | FB | 6'1" | 215 | 23 | | |
| Mark van Eeghen | FB | 6'2" | 225 | 24 | | 18 |
| Fred Biletnikoff | WR | 6'1" | 190 | 35 | | 42 |
| Morris Bradshaw | WR | 6' | 195 | 23 | | 6 |
| Cliff Branch | WR | 5'11" | 170 | 28 | | 72 |
| Mike Siani | WR | 6'2" | 195 | 26 | | 12 |
| Warren Bankston | TE | 6'4" | 235 | 29 | | 6 |
| Dave Casper | TE | 6'4" | 228 | 24 | | 60 |
| Ted Kwalick | TE | 6'4" | 225 | 29 | | |
| Ray Guy | K | 6'3" | 195 | 26 | | |
| Errol Mann (from DET) | K | 6' | 205 | 35 | | 59 |
| Fred Steinford | K | 5'11" | 180 | 22 | | 28 |

## DENVER BRONCOS 9-5 John Ralston

| Scores of Each Game | | |
|---|---|---|
| 7 | Cincinnati | 17 |
| 46 | N.Y. JETS | 3 |
| 44 | CLEVELAND | 13 |
| 26 | SAN DIEGO | 0 |
| 3 | Houston | 17 |
| 10 | OAKLAND | 17 |
| 35 | Kansas City | 26 |
| 6 | Oakland | 19 |
| 48 | TAMPA BAY | 13 |
| 17 | San Diego | 0 |
| 14 | N.Y. GIANTS | 13 |
| 14 | New England | 38 |
| 17 | KANSAS CITY | 16 |
| 28 | Chicago | 14 |

| Use Name | Pos. | Hgt | Wgt | Age | Int | Pts. |
|---|---|---|---|---|---|---|
| Bill Bain | OT | 6'4" | 270 | 24 | | |
| Glenn Hyde | OT | 6'3" | 250 | 25 | | |
| Claudie Minor | OT | 6'4" | 280 | 25 | | |
| Scott Parrish | OT | 6'6" | 270 | 23 | | |
| Tom Glassic | OG | 6'3" | 254 | 22 | | |
| Harvey Goodman | OG | 6'4" | 260 | 23 | | |
| Tommy Lyons | OG | 6'2" | 230 | 28 | | |
| Bobby Maples | C | 6'3" | 250 | 33 | | |
| Phil Olsen | C | 6'5" | 260 | 28 | | |
| Barney Chavous | DE | 6'3" | 252 | 25 | | |
| Paul Smith | DE | 6'3" | 256 | 31 | | |
| Jim White (from SEA) | DE | 6'3" | 260 | 27 | | |
| Lyle Alzado | DT | 6'3" | 252 | 27 | | |
| Rubin Carter | DT | 6' | 256 | 23 | | |
| John Grant | DT | 6'3" | 235 | 26 | | |
| Wayne Hammond | DT | 6'5" | 255 | 23 | | |
| Martin Imhof | DT | 6'6" | 255 | 26 | | |
| Randy Moore | DT | 6'2" | 241 | 22 | | |

| Use Name | Pos. | Hgt | Wgt | Age | Int | Pts |
|---|---|---|---|---|---|---|
| Rick Baska | LB | 6'3" | 225 | 24 | | |
| Larry Evans | LB | 6'2" | 216 | 23 | | |
| Randy Gradishar | LB | 6'3" | 233 | 24 | 3 | 6 |
| Tom Jackson | LB | 5'11" | 220 | 25 | 7 | 6 |
| Joe Rizzo | LB | 6'1" | 220 | 25 | 1 | |
| Bob Swenson | LB | 6'3" | 220 | 23 | 2 | |
| Godwin Turk | LB | 6'2" | 230 | 25 | | |
| Steve Foley | DB | 6'2" | 181 | 22 | 4 | |
| Billy Hardee | DB | 6' | 185 | 22 | | |
| Calvin Jones | DB | 5'7" | 169 | 25 | 2 | 6 |
| Chris Pane | DB | 5'11" | 181 | 23 | | |
| Randy Poltl | DB | 6'3" | 190 | 24 | 1 | 6 |
| John Rowser | DB | 6'1" | 190 | 32 | 4 | 12 |
| Bill Thompson | DB | 6'1" | 200 | 29 | | |
| Louis Wright | DB | 6'2" | 195 | 23 | | |

Paul Howard – Injury
Carl Schaukowitz – Injury

| Use Name | Pos. | Hgt | Wgt | Age | Int | Pts |
|---|---|---|---|---|---|---|
| Craig Penrose | QB | 6'3" | 222 | 23 | | |
| Steve Ramsey | QB | 6'2" | 210 | 28 | | |
| Norris Weese | QB | 6'1" | 195 | 25 | | |
| Otis Armstrong | HB | 5'10" | 196 | 25 | | 36 |
| Jim Kiick | HB | 5'11" | 215 | 30 | | 12 |
| Mike Franckowiak | FB | 6'3" | 220 | 23 | | |
| Jon Keyworth | FB | 6'3" | 230 | 25 | | 24 |
| Lonnie Perrin | FB | 6'1" | 222 | 24 | | 12 |
| Jack Dolbin | WR | 5'10" | 180 | 27 | | 6 |
| Haven Moses | WR | 6'3" | 208 | 30 | | 42 |
| John Schultz | WR | 5'10" | 182 | 23 | | |
| Rick Upchurch | WR | 5'10" | 170 | 24 | | 36 |
| Billy VanHeusen | WR | 6'1" | 200 | 30 | | |
| Boyd Brown | TE | 6'4" | 216 | 24 | | |
| Riley Odoms | TE | 6'4" | 230 | 26 | | 30 |
| Jim Turner | K | 6'2" | 205 | 35 | | 81 |

Fran Lynch – Knee Injury
Charlie Smith – Knee Injury

## SAN DIEGO CHARGERS 6-8 Tommy Prothro

| Scores of Each Game | | |
|---|---|---|
| 30 | Kansas City | 16 |
| 23 | Tampa Bay | 0 |
| 43 | ST. LOUIS | 24 |
| 0 | Denver | 26 |
| 17 | OAKLAND | 27 |
| 30 | HOUSTON | 27 |
| 17 | Cleveland | 21 |
| 0 | Pittsburgh | 23 |
| 21 | BALTIMORE | 37 |
| 0 | DENVER | 17 |
| 34 | Buffalo | 13 |
| 20 | KANSAS CITY | 23 |
| 13 | SAN FRANCISCO | *7 |
| 0 | Oakland | 24 |

| Use Name | Pos. | Hgt | Wgt | Age | Int | Pts. |
|---|---|---|---|---|---|---|
| Billy Shields | OT | 6'7" | 272 | 23 | | |
| Ron Singleton | OT | 6'7" | 245 | 24 | | |
| Russ Washington | OT | 6'6" | 290 | 29 | | |
| Charles Aiu | OG | 6'2" | 248 | 22 | | |
| Don Macek | OG | 6'3" | 253 | 22 | | |
| Ralph Perretta | OG-C | 6'2" | 252 | 23 | | |
| Doug Wilkerson | OG | 6'2" | 262 | 29 | | |
| Ed Flanagan | C | 6'3" | 245 | 32 | | |
| Fred Dean | DE | 6'3" | 226 | 24 | | |
| Leroy Jones | DE | 6'8" | 245 | 25 | 1 | |
| John Lee | DE | 6'2" | 247 | 23 | | |
| Charles DeJurnett | DT | 6'4" | 270 | 24 | | |
| Gary Johnson | DT | 6'2" | 262 | 24 | | |
| Louie Kelcher | DT | 6'5" | 282 | 23 | | |

Booker Brown – Illness
John Teerlinck – Knee Injury

| Use Name | Pos. | Hgt | Wgt | Age | Int | Pts |
|---|---|---|---|---|---|---|
| Don Goode | LB | 6'2" | 230 | 25 | 6 | |
| Tom Graham | LB | 6'2" | 235 | 26 | 3 | |
| Bob Horn | LB | 6'3" | 235 | 22 | 1 | |
| Woodrow Lowe | LB | 6' | 227 | 22 | 1 | |
| Rick Middleton | LB | 6'2" | 234 | 24 | | |
| Ray Preston | LB | 6' | 223 | 22 | | |
| Danny Colbert | DB | 5'11" | 182 | 25 | | |
| Chris Fletcher | DB | 5'11" | 189 | 27 | | |
| Mike Fuller | DB | 5'9" | 195 | 23 | 1 | 1 |
| Tom Hayes | DB | 6'1" | 198 | 30 | 2 | 6 |
| Hal Stringert | DB | 5'11" | 185 | 24 | 1 | |
| Jim Tolbert | DB | 6'3" | 210 | 32 | | |
| Mike Williams | DB | 5'10" | 181 | 22 | | |

| Use Name | Pos. | Hgt | Wgt | Age | Int | Pts |
|---|---|---|---|---|---|---|
| Dan Fouts | QB | 6'3" | 204 | 25 | | |
| Neal Jeffrey | QB | 6'1" | 180 | 23 | | |
| Clint Longley | QB | 6'1" | 195 | 24 | | |
| Mercury Morris | HB | 5'10" | 192 | 29 | | 12 |
| Joe Washington | HB | 5'10" | 184 | 22 | | |
| Rickey Young | HB | 6'2" | 193 | 22 | | 30 |
| Bo Matthews | FB | 6'4" | 230 | 24 | | 24 |
| Sam Scarber | FB | 6'2" | 232 | 28 | | 12 |
| Don Woods | FB-HB | 6'1" | 210 | 25 | | 24 |
| Eddie Bell | WR | 5'10" | 160 | 28 | | |
| Larry Dorsey | WR | 6'1" | 195 | 23 | | |
| Gary Garrison | WR | 6'1" | 190 | 32 | | 6 |
| Charlie Joiner | WR | 5'11" | 180 | 28 | | 42 |
| Dwight McDonald | WR | 6'2" | 187 | 25 | | 24 |
| Artie Owens | WR | 5'10" | 170 | 23 | | 6 |
| Chuck Bradley | TE | 6'6" | 255 | 25 | | |
| Pat Curran | TE | 6'3" | 238 | 30 | | 6 |
| Larry Mialik | TE | 6'2" | 226 | 26 | | |
| Jeff West | TE | 6'3" | 220 | 23 | | |
| Toni Fritsch | K | 5'7" | 195 | 31 | | 29 |
| Mitch Hoopes (to HOU) | K | 6'1" | 210 | 23 | | |
| Ray Wersching | K | 5'11" | 222 | 26 | | 26 |

## KANSAS CITY CHIEFS 5-9 Paul Wiggin

| Scores of Each Game | | |
|---|---|---|
| 16 | SAN DIEGO | 30 |
| 21 | OAKLAND | 24 |
| 17 | NEW ORLEANS | 27 |
| 17 | Buffalo | 50 |
| 33 | Washington | 30 |
| 20 | Miami | *17 |
| 26 | DENVER | 35 |
| 28 | Tampa Bay | 19 |
| 0 | PITTSBURGH | 45 |
| 10 | Oakland | 21 |
| 24 | CINCINNATI | 27 |
| 23 | San Diego | 20 |
| 16 | Denver | 17 |
| 39 | CLEVELAND | 14 |

| Use Name | Pos. | Hgt | Wgt | Age | Int | Pts. |
|---|---|---|---|---|---|---|
| Charlie Getty | OT | 6'4" | 260 | 24 | | |
| Matt Herkenhoff | OT | 6'4" | 255 | 25 | | |
| Jim Nicholson | OT | 6'6" | 261 | 26 | | |
| Ed Budde | OG | 6'5" | 265 | 35 | | |
| Tom Condon | OG | 6'3" | 240 | 23 | | |
| Rod Walters | OG | 6'3" | 258 | 22 | | |
| Charlie Ane | C | 6'1" | 233 | 24 | | |
| Orrin Olsen | C | 6'1" | 245 | 23 | | |
| Jack Rudnay | C | 6'3" | 240 | 28 | | |
| Larry Estes | DE-DT | 6'6" | 250 | 29 | | |
| John Lohmeyer | DE | 6'4" | 229 | 25 | 2 | |
| Whitney Paul | DE | 6'3" | 220 | 22 | | |
| Jim Wolf | DE | 6'3" | 250 | 24 | | |
| Wilbur Young | DE | 6'6" | 285 | 27 | | |
| Willie Lee | DT | 6'5" | 249 | 26 | | |
| Bob Maddox | DT | 6'5" | 248 | 27 | | |
| Keith Simons | DT | 6'3" | 254 | 22 | | |

| Use Name | Pos. | Hgt | Wgt | Age | Int | Pts |
|---|---|---|---|---|---|---|
| Billy Andrews | LB | 6' | 220 | 31 | 1 | |
| Jimbo Elrod | LB | 6' | 209 | 22 | 1 | |
| Willie Lanier | LB | 6'1" | 245 | 31 | 3 | |
| Jim Lynch | LB | 6'1" | 225 | 31 | 2 | |
| Dave Rozumek | LB | 6'2" | 215 | 22 | | |
| Clyde Werner | LB | 6'4" | 230 | 28 | | |
| Gary Barbaro | DB | 6'4" | 198 | 22 | 3 | |
| Tim Collier | DB | 6' | 166 | 22 | 2 | |
| Tim Gray | DB | 6'1" | 200 | 23 | 4 | |
| Kerry Reardon | DB | 5'11" | 180 | 27 | 5 | |
| Steve Taylor | DB | 6'3" | 204 | 22 | | |
| Emmitt Thomas | DB | 6'2" | 192 | 33 | 2 | |

Ken Avery – Injury
Randy Beisler – Injury
Roger Bernhardt – Injury

| Use Name | Pos. | Hgt | Wgt | Age | Int | Pts |
|---|---|---|---|---|---|---|
| Tony Adams | QB | 6' | 198 | 26 | | |
| Mike Livingston | QB | 6'3" | 212 | 30 | | 12 |
| Mike Nott | QB | 6'3" | 203 | 24 | | |
| Woody Green | HB | 6'1" | 205 | 25 | | 6 |
| Ed Podolak | HB | 6'1" | 205 | 29 | | 30 |
| Tommy Reamon | HB | 5'10" | 192 | 24 | | 30 |
| Glynn Harrison | FB | 5'11" | 190 | 22 | | |
| MacArthur Lane | FB | 6' | 220 | 34 | | 36 |
| Pat McNeil | FB | 5'9" | 208 | 22 | | |
| Larry Brunson | WR | 5'11" | 180 | 27 | | 6 |
| Reggie Craig | WR | 6' | 187 | 23 | | |
| Henry Marshall | WR | 6'2" | 205 | 22 | | 18 |
| Barry Pearson | WR | 5'11" | 185 | 26 | | |
| Lawrence Williams | WR | 5'10" | 175 | 22 | | |
| Bill Masters | TE | 6'5" | 240 | 32 | | 18 |
| Walter White | TE | 6'3" | 218 | 25 | | 42 |
| Jan Stenerud | K | 6'2" | 187 | 33 | | 90 |
| Jerrel Wilson | K | 6'4" | 222 | 34 | | |

## TAMPA BAY BUCCANEERS 0-14 John McKay

| Scores of Each Game | | |
|---|---|---|
| 0 | Houston | 20 |
| 0 | SAN DIEGO | 23 |
| 9 | BUFFALO | 14 |
| 17 | Baltimore | 42 |
| 0 | Cincinnati | 21 |
| 10 | SEATTLE | 13 |
| 20 | MIAMI | 23 |
| 19 | KANSAS CITY | 28 |
| 13 | Denver | 48 |
| 0 | N.Y. Jets | 34 |
| 7 | CLEVELAND | 24 |
| 16 | Oakland | 49 |
| 0 | Pittsburgh | 42 |
| 14 | NEW ENGLAND | 31 |

| Use Name | Pos. | Hgt | Wgt | Age | Int | Pts. |
|---|---|---|---|---|---|---|
| Mike Current | OT | 6'4" | 270 | 30 | | |
| Dave Reavis | OT | 6'5" | 250 | 26 | | |
| Steve Wilson | OT | 6'3" | 268 | 22 | | |
| Randy Young | OT | 6'5" | 250 | 22 | | |
| Steve Young | OT | 6'8" | 272 | 23 | | |
| Tom Alward | OG | 6'4" | 255 | 23 | | |
| Howard Fest | OG | 6'6" | 263 | 30 | | |
| Everett Little | OG | 6'4" | 265 | 22 | | |
| Dan Ryczek | C | 6'3" | 250 | 27 | | |
| Ed McAleney (from ATL) | DE | 6'2" | 235 | 22 | | |
| Council Rudolph | DE | 6'3" | 255 | 26 | | |
| Lee Roy Selmon | DE | 6'3" | 263 | 21 | | |
| Pat Toomay | DE | 6'5" | 244 | 31 | | |
| Larry Jameson | DT | 6'7" | 270 | 23 | | |
| Maulty Moore | DT | 6'5" | 265 | 30 | | |
| Dave Pear | DT | 6'2" | 248 | 23 | | |
| Dewey Selmon | DT | 6'1" | 254 | 22 | | |

Charlie Evans – Knee Injury
Kent Gaydos – Injury

| Use Name | Pos. | Hgt | Wgt | Age | Int | Pts |
|---|---|---|---|---|---|---|
| Larry Ball | LB | 6'6" | 235 | 26 | 1 | |
| Bert Cooper | LB | 6'1" | 242 | 24 | | |
| Jimmy Gunn | LB | 6'1" | 231 | 27 | | |
| Charlie Hunt | LB | 6'3" | 218 | 25 | | |
| Mike Lemon | LB | 6'2" | 220 | 25 | | |
| Cal Peterson | LB | 6'3" | 213 | 23 | 1 | |
| Jim Peterson | LB | 6'5" | 226 | 26 | | |
| Steve Reese | LB | 6'2" | 223 | 24 | | |
| Glenn Robinson | LB-DE | 6'6" | 245 | 24 | | |
| Jimmy Sims | LB | 6' | 195 | 25 | | |
| Richard Wood | LB | 6'2" | 215 | 23 | | |
| Mark Cotney | DB | 6' | 207 | 24 | 3 | |
| Ricky Davis | DB | 6' | 178 | 23 | | |
| Earl Douthit | DB | 6'2" | 188 | 23 | | |
| Curtis Jordan | DB | 6'2" | 182 | 22 | 2 | |
| Don Martin | DB | 5'11" | 185 | 26 | | |
| Frank Oliver | DB | 6' | 198 | 24 | | |
| Reggie Pierson (from DET.) | DB | 5'11" | 185 | 23 | | |
| Danny Reece | DB | 5'11" | 187 | 21 | | 6 |
| Ken Stone | DB | 6'1" | 180 | 25 | 2 | |
| Mike Washington | DB | 6'3" | 190 | 23 | | |
| Roscoe Word (from NYJ & BUF) | DB | 5'11" | 169 | 24 | | |

| Use Name | Pos. | Hgt | Wgt | Age | Int | Pts |
|---|---|---|---|---|---|---|
| Parnell Dickinson | QB | 6'2" | 185 | 23 | | |
| Terry Hanratty | QB | 6'1" | 205 | 28 | | |
| Larry Lawrence | QB | 6'1" | 208 | 27 | | |
| Steve Spurrier | QB | 6'2" | 205 | 31 | | |
| Louis Carter | HB | 5'11" | 209 | 23 | | 6 |
| Charlie Davis | HB | 5'11" | 200 | 24 | | 6 |
| Harold Hart | HB | 6' | 208 | 23 | | |
| Essex Johnson | HB | 5'9" | 200 | 29 | | 12 |
| Jimmy DuBose | FB | 5'11" | 217 | 21 | | |
| Vince Kendrick | FB | 6' | 239 | 24 | | |
| Rod McNeill (from NO) | FB | 6'2" | 215 | 25 | | |
| Ed Williams | FB | 6'2" | 245 | 26 | | 12 |
| Freddie Douglass | WR | 5'9" | 185 | 22 | | |
| Isaac Hagins | WR | 5'9" | 179 | 22 | | |
| Curtis Leak | WR | 5'11" | 180 | 22 | | |
| Lee McGriff | WR | 5'9" | 163 | 22 | | |
| John McKay | WR | 5'11" | 175 | 23 | | 6 |
| Morris Owens (from MIA) | WR | 6' | 190 | 23 | | 36 |
| Barry Smith | WR | 6'1" | 195 | 25 | | |
| Bob Moore | TE | 6'3" | 229 | 27 | | |
| Jack Novak | TE | 6'4" | 242 | 23 | | 6 |
| Fred Pagac | TE | 6' | 220 | 24 | | |
| Dave Green | K | 5'11" | 208 | 26 | | 35 |
| Mirro Roder | K | 6'1" | 218 | 32 | | |

*—Overtime

## OAKLAND RAIDERS

### RUSHING

| Last Name | No. | Yds. | Avg | TD |
|---|---|---|---|---|
| van Eeghen | 233 | 1012 | 4.3 | 3 |
| Davis | 114 | 516 | 4.5 | 3 |
| Banaszak | 114 | 370 | 3.2 | 5 |
| Garrett | 48 | 220 | 4.6 | 1 |
| Ginn | 10 | 53 | 5.3 | 0 |
| Rae | 10 | 37 | 3.7 | 1 |
| Kunz | 4 | 33 | 8.3 | 0 |
| Jennings | 10 | 22 | 2.2 | 0 |
| Branch | 3 | 12 | 4.0 | 0 |
| Casper | 1 | 5 | 5.0 | 0 |
| Bradshaw | 1 | 4 | 4.0 | 0 |
| Moore | 7 | 4 | 0.6 | 0 |
| Bankston | 1 | 3 | 3.0 | 0 |
| Guy | 1 | 0 | 0.0 | 0 |
| Stabler | 7 | -2 | -0.3 | 1 |

### RECEIVING

| Last Name | No. | Yds | Avg | TD |
|---|---|---|---|---|
| Casper | 53 | 691 | 13 | 10 |
| Branch | 46 | 1111 | 24 | 12 |
| Biletnikoff | 43 | 551 | 13 | 7 |
| Davis | 21 | 191 | 7 | 0 |
| van Eeghen | 17 | 173 | 10 | 0 |
| Banaszak | 15 | 74 | 5 | 0 |
| Siani | 11 | 173 | 16 | 2 |
| Garrett | 9 | 108 | 12 | 0 |
| Bankston | 5 | 73 | 15 | 1 |
| Moore | 5 | 46 | 9 | 0 |
| Kwalick | 4 | 15 | 4 | 0 |
| Bradshaw | 1 | 25 | 25 | 1 |
| Jennings | 1 | 10 | 10 | 0 |

### PUNT RETURNS

| Last Name | No. | Yds | Avg | TD |
|---|---|---|---|---|
| Colzie | 41 | 448 | 11 | 0 |
| Moore | 20 | 184 | 9 | 0 |
| Phillips | 2 | 7 | 4 | 0 |
| Jennings | 1 | 20 | 20 | 0 |

### KICKOFF RETURNS

| Last Name | No. | Yds | Avg | TD |
|---|---|---|---|---|
| Garrett | 18 | 388 | 22 | 0 |
| Jennings | 16 | 417 | 26 | 0 |
| Moore | 8 | 162 | 20 | 0 |
| Colzie | 6 | 115 | 19 | 0 |
| Bankston | 2 | 27 | 14 | 0 |
| Banaszak | 2 | 23 | 12 | 0 |
| Ginn | 1 | 27 | 27 | 0 |

### PASSING – PUNTING – KICKING

**PASSING**

| Last Name | Att | Comp | % | Yds | Yd/Att | TD | Int–% | RK |
|---|---|---|---|---|---|---|---|---|
| Stabler | 291 | 194 | 67 | 2737 | 9.4 | 27 | 17– 6 | 1 |
| Rae | 65 | 35 | 54 | 417 | 6.4 | 6 | 1– 2 | |
| Humm | 5 | 3 | 60 | 41 | 8.2 | 0 | 0– 0 | |

**PUNTING**

| Last Name | No | Avg |
|---|---|---|
| Guy | 67 | 41.6 |

**KICKING**

| Last Name | XP | Att | % | FG | Att | % |
|---|---|---|---|---|---|---|
| Mann | 35 | 37 | 95 | 8 | 21 | 38 |
| Steinfort | 16 | 19 | 84 | 4 | 8 | 50 |
| Guy | 0 | 1 | 0 | | | |

## DENVER BRONCOS

### RUSHING

| Last Name | No. | Yds. | Avg | TD |
|---|---|---|---|---|
| Armstrong | 247 | 1008 | 4.1 | 5 |
| Keyworth | 122 | 349 | 2.9 | 3 |
| Weese | 23 | 142 | 6.2 | 0 |
| Perrin | 37 | 118 | 3.2 | 2 |
| Kiick | 31 | 114 | 3.7 | 1 |
| Upchurch | 6 | 71 | 11.8 | 1 |
| Ramsey | 13 | 51 | 3.9 | 0 |
| Odoms | 3 | 36 | 12.0 | 2 |
| Franckowiak | 12 | 25 | 2.1 | 0 |
| Van Heusen | 1 | 20 | 20.0 | 0 |
| Dolbin | 2 | 5 | 2.5 | 0 |
| Penrose | 2 | -3 | -1.5 | 0 |
| Moses | 1 | -4 | -4.0 | 0 |

### RECEIVING

| Last Name | No. | Yds | Avg | TD |
|---|---|---|---|---|
| Armstrong | 39 | 457 | 12 | 1 |
| Odoms | 30 | 477 | 16 | 3 |
| Moses | 25 | 498 | 20 | 7 |
| Keyworth | 22 | 201 | 9 | 1 |
| Dolbin | 19 | 354 | 19 | 1 |
| Upchurch | 12 | 340 | 28 | 1 |
| Kiick | 10 | 78 | 8 | 1 |
| Franckowiak | 4 | 42 | 11 | 0 |
| Perrin | 4 | 35 | 9 | 0 |
| Schultz | 2 | 29 | 15 | 0 |
| Lyons | 1 | -1 | -1 | 0 |

### PUNT RETURNS

| Last Name | No. | Yds | Avg | TD |
|---|---|---|---|---|
| Upchurch | 39 | 536 | 14 | 4 |
| Thompson | 6 | 60 | 10 | 0 |
| Foley | 5 | 42 | 8 | 0 |
| Schultz | 1 | 2 | 2 | 0 |

### KICKOFF RETURNS

| Last Name | No. | Yds | Avg | TD |
|---|---|---|---|---|
| Upchurch | 22 | 514 | 23 | 0 |
| Perrin | 14 | 391 | 28 | 0 |
| Schultz | 3 | 82 | 27 | 0 |
| B. Brown | 3 | 41 | 14 | 0 |
| Franckowiak | 2 | 22 | 11 | 0 |
| Hyde | 1 | 17 | 17 | 0 |
| Goodman | 1 | 8 | 8 | 0 |

### PASSING – PUNTING – KICKING

**PASSING**

| Last Name | Att | Comp | % | Yds | Yd/Att | TD | Int–% | RK |
|---|---|---|---|---|---|---|---|---|
| Ramsey | 270 | 128 | 47 | 1931 | 7.2 | 11 | 13– 5 | 11 |
| Weese | 47 | 24 | 51 | 314 | 6.7 | 1 | 6– 13 | |
| Penrose | 36 | 16 | 44 | 265 | 7.4 | 3 | 3– 8 | |

**PUNTING**

| Last Name | No | Avg |
|---|---|---|
| Weese | 52 | 35.6 |
| Van Heusen | 31 | 35.3 |

**KICKING**

| Last Name | XP | Att | % | FG | Att | % |
|---|---|---|---|---|---|---|
| Turner | 36 | 39 | 92 | 15 | 21 | 71 |

## SAN DIEGO CHARGERS

### RUSHING

| Last Name | No. | Yds. | Avg | TD |
|---|---|---|---|---|
| Young | 162 | 802 | 5.0 | 4 |
| Woods | 126 | 450 | 3.6 | 3 |
| Morris | 50 | 256 | 5.1 | 2 |
| Scarber | 61 | 236 | 3.9 | 1 |
| Matthews | 46 | 199 | 4.3 | 3 |
| Fouts | 18 | 65 | 3.6 | 0 |
| Longley | 4 | 22 | 5.5 | 0 |
| Curran | 1 | 12 | 12.0 | 0 |
| Hoopes | 2 | 10 | 5.0 | 0 |
| Jeffrey | 1 | 0 | 0.0 | 0 |
| West | 1 | 0 | 0.0 | 0 |
| Dorsey | 1 | -12 | -12.0 | 0 |

### RECEIVING

| Last Name | No. | Yds | Avg | TD |
|---|---|---|---|---|
| Joiner | 50 | 1056 | 21 | 7 |
| Young | 47 | 441 | 9 | 1 |
| Woods | 34 | 224 | 7 | 1 |
| Curran | 33 | 349 | 11 | 1 |
| Scarber | 14 | 96 | 7 | 1 |
| Matthews | 12 | 81 | 7 | 0 |
| McDonald | 11 | 161 | 15 | 4 |
| Dorsey | 8 | 108 | 14 | 0 |
| Morris | 8 | 52 | 7 | 0 |
| Owens | 3 | 54 | 18 | 1 |
| Garrison | 2 | 58 | 29 | 1 |
| Bradley | 1 | 7 | 7 | 0 |

### PUNT RETURNS

| Last Name | No. | Yds | Avg | TD |
|---|---|---|---|---|
| Fuller | 33 | 436 | 13 | 0 |
| Bell | 7 | 31 | 4 | 0 |
| Williams | 5 | 23 | 5 | 0 |

### KICKOFF RETURNS

| Last Name | No. | Yds | Avg | TD |
|---|---|---|---|---|
| Owens | 25 | 551 | 22 | 0 |
| Fuller | 20 | 420 | 21 | 0 |
| Perretta | 2 | 24 | 12 | 0 |
| Middleton | 1 | 21 | 21 | 0 |
| Matthews | 1 | 19 | 19 | 0 |
| Bell | 1 | 18 | 18 | 0 |
| Preston | 1 | 16 | 16 | 0 |
| Horn | 1 | 7 | 7 | 0 |

### PASSING – PUNTING – KICKING

**PASSING**

| Last Name | Att | Comp | % | Yds | Yd/Att | TD | Int–% | RK |
|---|---|---|---|---|---|---|---|---|
| Fouts | 359 | 208 | 58 | 2535 | 7.1 | 14 | 15– 4 | 8 |
| Longley | 24 | 12 | 50 | 130 | 5.4 | 2 | 3– 13 | |
| Jeffrey | 2 | 2 | 100 | 11 | 5.5 | 0 | 0– 0 | |
| Woods | 2 | 1 | 50 | 11 | 5.5 | 1 | 0– 0 | |
| Joiner | 1 | 0 | 0 | 0 | 0.0 | 0 | 0– 0 | |

**PUNTING**

| Last Name | No | Avg |
|---|---|---|
| Hoopes | 49 | 37.7 |
| West | 38 | 40.7 |

**KICKING**

| Last Name | XP | Att | % | FG | Att | % |
|---|---|---|---|---|---|---|
| Fritsch | 11 | 14 | 79 | 6 | 12 | 50 |
| Wersching | 14 | 16 | 88 | 4 | 8 | 50 |
| Fuller | 1 | 1 | 100 | | | |

## KANSAS CITY CHIEFS

### RUSHING

| Last Name | No. | Yds. | Avg | TD |
|---|---|---|---|---|
| Lane | 162 | 542 | 3.3 | 5 |
| Podolak | 88 | 371 | 4.2 | 5 |
| Green | 73 | 322 | 4.4 | 1 |
| Reamon | 103 | 314 | 3.0 | 4 |
| Marshall | 5 | 101 | 20.2 | 1 |
| Livingston | 31 | 89 | 2.9 | 2 |
| Adams | 5 | 46 | 9.2 | 0 |
| Harrison | 16 | 41 | 2.6 | 0 |
| McNeil | 8 | 26 | 3.3 | 0 |
| White | 2 | 15 | 7.5 | 0 |
| Stenerud | 1 | 0 | 0.0 | 0 |
| Brunson | 3 | -1 | -0.3 | 0 |

### RECEIVING

| Last Name | No. | Yds | Avg | TD |
|---|---|---|---|---|
| Lane | 66 | 686 | 10 | 1 |
| White | 47 | 808 | 17 | 7 |
| Brunson | 33 | 656 | 20 | 1 |
| Marshall | 28 | 443 | 16 | 2 |
| Masters | 18 | 269 | 15 | 3 |
| Podolak | 13 | 156 | 12 | 0 |
| Reamon | 10 | 136 | 14 | 1 |
| Green | 9 | 100 | 11 | 0 |
| McNeil | 2 | 33 | 17 | 0 |
| Harrison | 1 | 12 | 12 | 0 |
| Williams | 1 | 9 | 9 | 0 |
| Getty | 1 | -5 | -5 | 0 |

### PUNT RETURNS

| Last Name | No. | Yds | Avg | TD |
|---|---|---|---|---|
| Brunson | 31 | 387 | 12 | 0 |
| Andrews | 1 | 38 | 38 | 0 |
| Reardon | 1 | 4 | 4 | 0 |
| Reamon | 1 | 0 | 0 | 0 |

### KICKOFF RETURNS

| Last Name | No. | Yds | Avg | TD |
|---|---|---|---|---|
| Williams | 25 | 688 | 28 | 0 |
| Reamon | 19 | 424 | 22 | 0 |
| Harrison | 13 | 278 | 21 | 0 |
| Green | 3 | 82 | 27 | 0 |
| Craig | 2 | 45 | 23 | 0 |
| McNeil | 2 | 22 | 11 | 0 |
| Marshall | 1 | 0 | 0 | 0 |

### PASSING – PUNTING – KICKING

**PASSING**

| Last Name | Att | Comp | % | Yds | Yd/Att | TD | Int–% | RK |
|---|---|---|---|---|---|---|---|---|
| Livingston | 338 | 189 | 56 | 2682 | 7.9 | 12 | 13– 4 | 5 |
| Adams | 71 | 36 | 51 | 575 | 8.1 | 3 | 4– 6 | |
| Nott | 10 | 4 | 40 | 46 | 4.6 | 0 | 0– 0 | |

**PUNTING**

| Last Name | No | Avg |
|---|---|---|
| Wilson | 65 | 42.0 |
| Nott | 1 | 35.0 |
| Stenerud | 1 | 28.0 |

**KICKING**

| Last Name | XP | Att | % | FG | Att | % |
|---|---|---|---|---|---|---|
| Stenerud | 27 | 33 | 82 | 21 | 38 | 55 |

## TAMPA BAY BUCCANEERS

### RUSHING

| Last Name | No. | Yds. | Avg | TD |
|---|---|---|---|---|
| Carter | 171 | 521 | 3.0 | 1 |
| Williams | 87 | 324 | 3.7 | 2 |
| Johnson | 47 | 166 | 3.5 | 1 |
| McNeill | 27 | 135 | 5.0 | 0 |
| C. Davis | 41 | 107 | 2.6 | 1 |
| Dickinson | 13 | 103 | 7.9 | .0 |
| DuBose | 20 | 62 | 3.1 | 0 |
| Spurrier | 12 | 48 | 4.0 | 0 |
| B. Moore | 2 | 23 | 11.5 | 0 |
| Pagac | 1 | 4 | 4.0 | 0 |
| Kendrick | 1 | 3 | 3.0 | 0 |
| Owens | 2 | 2 | 1.0 | 0 |
| Hanratty | 1 | 1 | 1.0 | 0 |
| Green | 1 | 0 | 0.0 | 0 |

### RECEIVING

| Last Name | No. | Yds | Avg | TD |
|---|---|---|---|---|
| Owens | 30 | 390 | 13 | 6 |
| Johnson | 25 | 201 | 8 | 1 |
| B. Moore | 24 | 289 | 12 | 0 |
| Williams | 23 | 166 | 7 | 0 |
| McKay | 20 | 302 | 15 | 1 |
| Carter | 20 | 135 | 7 | 0 |
| Novak | 8 | 130 | 16 | 1 |
| McNeill | 7 | 33 | 5 | 0 |
| DuBose | 5 | 26 | 5 | 0 |
| Smith | 4 | 88 | 22 | 0 |
| Douglass | 3 | 58 | 19 | 0 |
| C. Davis | 3 | 32 | 11 | 0 |
| Pagac | 2 | 15 | 8 | 0 |
| Green | 1 | 9 | 9 | 0 |
| Ryczek | 1 | 6 | 6 | 0 |

### PUNT RETURNS

| Last Name | No. | Yds | Avg | TD |
|---|---|---|---|---|
| Reece | 20 | 143 | 7 | 0 |
| Douglass | 4 | 78 | 20 | 0 |
| Cotney | 3 | 26 | 9 | 0 |
| Stone | 1 | 11 | 11 | 0 |
| Hagins | 1 | 2 | 2 | 0 |
| Word | 1 | -8 | -8 | 0 |

### KICKOFF RETURNS

| Last Name | No. | Yds | Avg | TD |
|---|---|---|---|---|
| McNeil | 17 | 384 | 23 | 0 |
| Carter | 15 | 300 | 20 | 0 |
| Johnson | 13 | 287 | 22 | 0 |
| Douglass | 7 | 167 | 24 | 0 |
| C. Davis | 4 | 73 | 18 | 0 |
| Word | 2 | 36 | 18 | 0 |
| Hagins | 2 | 35 | 18 | 0 |
| DuBose | 1 | 34 | 34 | 0 |
| Reece | 1 | 30 | 30 | 0 |
| Cooper | 1 | 22 | 22 | 0 |
| Pagac | 1 | 20 | 20 | 0 |
| Lemon | 1 | 2 | 2 | 0 |

### PASSING – PUNTING – KICKING

**PASSING**

| Last Name | Att | Comp | % | Yds | Yd/Att | TD | Int–% | RK |
|---|---|---|---|---|---|---|---|---|
| Spurrier | 311 | 156 | 50 | 1628 | 5.2 | 7 | 12– 4 | 13 |
| Dickinson | 39 | 15 | 38 | 210 | 5.4 | 1 | 5– 13 | |
| Hanratty | 14 | 6 | 43 | 32 | 2.3 | 0 | 1– 7 | |
| Carter | 5 | 2 | 40 | 24 | 4.8 | 1 | 0– 0 | |
| Lawrence | 5 | 0 | 0 | 0 | 0.0 | 0 | 2– 40 | |
| McGriff | 1 | 1 | 100 | 39 | 39.0 | 0 | 0– 0 | |
| R. Davis | 1 | 1 | 100 | -7 | -7.0 | 0 | 0– 0 | |

**PUNTING**

| Last Name | No | Avg |
|---|---|---|
| Green | 92 | 39.3 |

**KICKING**

| Last Name | XP | Att | % | FG | Att | % |
|---|---|---|---|---|---|---|
| Green | 11 | 14 | 79 | 8 | 14 | 57 |
| Roder | | | | 0 | 3 | 0 |

# 1976 Championship Games

## NFC CHAMPIONSHIP GAME
December 26, 1976 at Bloomington, Minn.
(Attendance 47,191)

### SCORING

| | | | | | |
|---|---|---|---|---|---|
| MINNESOTA | 7 | 3 | 7 | 7—24 | |
| LOS ANGELES | 0 | 0 | 13 | 0—13 | |

**First Quarter**
Minn.  Bryant, 90 yard blocked field goal return
PAT – Cox (kick)

**Second Quarter**
Minn.  Cox, 25 yard field goal

**Third Quarter**
Minn.  Foreman, 1 yard rush
PAT – Cox (kick
L.A.  McCutcheon, 10 yard rush
PAT – Kick no good
L.A.  H. Jackson, 5 yard pass from Haden
PAT – Dempsey (kick)

**Fourth Quarter**
Minn.  Johnson, 12 yard rush
PAT – Cox (kick)

### TEAM STATISTICS

| MINN. | | L.A. |
|---|---|---|
| 13 | First Downs—Total | 21 |
| 6 | First Downs—Rushing | 14 |
| 7 | First Downs—Passing | 7 |
| 0 | First Downs—Penalty | 0 |
| 1 | Fumbles— Number | 4 |
| 1 | Fumbles—Lost Ball | 2 |
| 4 | Penalty—Number | 3 |
| 32 | Yards Penalized | 33 |
| 0 | Missed Field Goals | 1 |
| 60 | Offensive Plays | 71 |
| 267 | Net Yards | 336 |
| 4.5 | Average Gain | 4.7 |
| 2 | Giveaways | 4 |
| 4 | Takeaways | 2 |
| +2 | Difference | -2 |

Minnesota never looked better while bombing Washington 35-20 in an NFC semi-final playoff bout that featured two TD's apiece by RB Chuck Foreman and WR Sammy White. Los Angeles, meanwhile, just barely got by Dallas 14-12 when the Pokes failed to take advantage of a blocked punt that put the ball on L.A.'s 17-yard line with 1:59 remaining. On this frosty Sunday in Bloomington, however, the Vikes, behind sore-kneed QB Fran Tarkenton, were no match for the Rams statistically except where it counted most—on the specialty teams. The end result was a 24-13 victory for Minnesota, enabling it to make its third visit to the Super Bowl in four years.

The game's biggest play occurred early in the first quarter after the Vikings' defense put the clamps on a strong Ram drive spearheaded by the running of Lawrence McCutcheon and John Cappelletti. With the ball spotted just inches short of Minnesota's goal-line on fourth down, Ram Head Coach Chuck Knox decided to play it safe with a field goal attempt by Tom Dempsey. Earlier in the year in a 10-10 overtime tie against the same Vikings, the Rams twice failed to score from one yard out after deciding not to kick field goals. Nate Allen, who had blocked Dempsey's overtime FG attempt in that earlier game, cleanly deflected the ball after charging in from the right side, and after it took a lucky bounce in the opposite direction, Bobby Bryant picked it up and scampered 90 yards for a TD with the closest Ram 15 yards behind.

Minnesota's Matt Blair followed suit with a second-quarter block of Rusty Jackson's punt after the latter dropped the snap, and it was soon 10-0 after Fred Cox's 25-yard field goal. The Rams' special team miseries continued when Dempsey failed to convert the extra point following their first TD of the game, and when they scored again late in the third quarter, after RE Fred Dryer blindsided Tarkenton and LE Jack Youngblood recovered the subsequent fumble to set up WR Harold Jackson's TD catch, their four-point deficit (17-13) meant the Rams would have to come up with more than a field goal to overtake the Vikes.

With Pat Haden at the controls, L. A. got as far as the Viking 39 with three minutes to go before failing to convert four aerial attempts, the last one intercepted by Bryant. Tarkenton connected with Foreman on a 57-yard safety-valve pass on third down to set up Sammy Johnson's clinching 12-yard TD. Foreman accounted for 119 yards on two plays, almost half of the Vikings' total offense. His brilliant 62-yard run set up Minnesota's second TD to put it ahead 17-0 in the third quarter.

Beside Tarkenton's injury, MLB Jeff Siemon didn't start but played the last three quarters with his legs heavily taped while WR White sat out most of the game with a fever. But that wasn't enough to keep the Rams from losing their third straight NFC Championship game.

### INDIVIDUAL STATISTICS

| MINNESOTA | No | Yds | Avg. | LOS ANGELES | No | Yds | Avg. |
|---|---|---|---|---|---|---|---|
| **RUSHING** | | | | | | | |
| Foreman | 15 | 118 | 7.9 | McCutcheon | 26 | 128 | 4.9 |
| Miller | 10 | 28 | 2.8 | Cappelletti | 16 | 59 | 3.7 |
| Johnson | 2 | 12 | 6.0 | Haden | 3 | 3 | 1.0 |
| McClanahan | 1 | 2 | 2.0 | Jessie | 1 | 3 | 3.0 |
| Tarkenton | 1 | -2 | -2.0 | | 46 | 193 | 4.2 |
| | 29 | 158 | 5.4 | | | | |
| **RECEIVING** | | | | | | | |
| Foreman | 5 | 81 | 16.2 | H Jackson | 4 | 70 | 17.5 |
| Rashad | 3 | 28 | 9.3 | Jessie | 2 | 60 | 30.0 |
| Miller | 3 | 24 | 8.0 | McCutcheon | 2 | 18 | 9.0 |
| Grim | 1 | 10 | 10.0 | Cappelletti | 1 | 13 | 13.0 |
| | 12 | 143 | 11.9 | | 9 | 161 | 17.9 |
| **PUNTING** | | | | | | | |
| Clabo | 8 | | 35.1 | R. Jackson | 7 | | 29.4 |
| **PUNT RETURNS** | | | | | | | |
| Willis | 3 | 20 | 6.7 | C. Bryant | 4 | 31 | 7.8 |
| | | | | Bertelsen | 3 | 19 | 6.3 |
| | | | | | 7 | 50 | 7.1 |
| **KICKOFF RETURNS** | | | | | | | |
| Willis | 3 | 69 | 23.0 | Geredine | 3 | 50 | 16.7 |
| | | | | C. Bryant | 1 | 21 | 21.0 |
| | | | | Scribner | 1 | 8 | 8.0 |
| | | | | | 5 | 79 | 15.8 |
| **INTERCEPTION RETURNS** | | | | | | | |
| B. Bryant | 2 | 17 | 8.5 | M. Jackson | 1 | 0 | 0.0 |

| | PASSING | | | | | | | |
|---|---|---|---|---|---|---|---|---|
| MINNESOTA | Att. | Comp. | Comp. Pct. | Yds. | Int. | Yds/ Att. | Yds/ Comp. | Yards Lost Tackled |
| Tarkenton | 27 | 12 | 44.4 | 143 | 1 | 5.3 | 11.9 | 4—34 |
| LOS ANGELES | | | | | | | | |
| Haden | 22 | 9 | 40.9 | 161 | 2 | 7.3 | 17.9 | 3—18 |

---

## AFC CHAMPIONSHIP GAME
December 26, 1976 at Oakland
(Attendance 53,739)

### SCORING

| | | | | | |
|---|---|---|---|---|---|
| OAKLAND | 3 | 14 | 7 | 0—24 | |
| PITTSBURGH | 0 | 7 | 0 | 0— 7 | |

**First Quarter**
Oak.  Mann, 39 yard field goal

**Second Quarter**
Oak.  C. Davis, 1 yard rush
PAT – Mann (kick)
Pitt.  Harrison, 3 yard rush
PAT – Mansfield (kick)
Oak.  Bankston, 4 yard pass from Stabler
PAT – Mann (kick)

**Third Quarter**
Oak.  Banaszak, 5 yard pass from Stabler
PAT – Mann (kick)

### TEAM STATISTICS

| OAK. | | PITT. |
|---|---|---|
| 15 | First Downs—Total | 13 |
| 7 | First Downs—Rushing | 3 |
| 7 | First Downs—Passing | 8 |
| 1 | First Downs—Penalty | 2 |
| 2 | Fumbles—Number | 1 |
| 0 | Fumbles —Lost Ball | 0 |
| 7 | Penalty—Number | 5 |
| 34 | Yards Penalized | 29 |
| 0 | Missed Field Goals | 0 |
| 69 | Offensive Plays | 59 |
| 220 | Net Yards | 237 |
| 3.2 | Average Gain | 4.0 |
| 0 | Giveaways | 1 |
| 1 | Takeaways | 0 |
| +1 | Difference | -1 |

Pittsburgh had a surprisingly easy time with Baltimore in the AFC semi-final, but its 40-14 victory proved costly as running backs Franco Harris and Rocky Bleier suffered rib and toe injuries, respectively, that kept them from playing Oakland in the AFC Championship Game. The Raiders' semi-final opponent, New England, was just one controversial penalty away from upsetting Oakland. Raider QB Ken Stabler engineered two late TD drives to edge the Pats 24-21, the last drive staying alive when New England NT Ray Hamilton was called for roughing Stabler on fourth down with 57 seconds remaining. Without Harris and Bleier, the Steelers were easy pickings for the Raiders as Oakland won 24-7 to end a string of six straight AFC title losses.

Forced into installing a one-back offense featuring Reggie Harrison, Steeler Head Coach Chuck Noll tried to help his confused QB Terry Bradshaw by calling all the Steelers' plays from the sidelines. Pittsburgh didn't get a first down until midway through the second quarter, at which time Oakland already led 10-0. The Raiders' rushers had a comparatively easy time, allowing Stabler to play-pass for Oakland's last two touchdowns. Willie Hall, the linebacker Raider Head Coach John Madden inserted into the starting lineup after converting to a 3-4 defense earlier in the year, set up Oakland's first TD with a brilliant 25-yard interception return to the Steelers' one-yard line. He also knocked down a pass, forced a fumble and made five unassisted tackles along with numerous assists.

Pittsburgh got on the scoreboard after an impressive second-quarter drive kept alive with the sharp third-down passing of Bradshaw but Stabler bounced right back with a demoralizing four-yard TD score to TE Warren Bankston 19 seconds before halftime. Stabler's longest pass of the day, 28 yards to WR Cliff Branch, was completed after he detected a safety blitz which earlier had thrown him for a 17-yard loss. The completion led to the second half's only score, a five-yard toss over the middle to RB Pete Banaszak on another adjusted pattern. On the play, Steeler LB Jack Ham got to Stabler, knocking a cap off Stabler's front tooth and delivering a big welt on his back that sent him to the sidelines. It didn't make much difference for the frustrated Steelers, however. Stabler's replacement, Mike Rae, ran out the clock as the Raiders relied on defense in the final period, and with no ground game to speak of, Bradshaw resorted to desperation passes in a futile attempt to get back in the game.

### INDIVIDUAL STATISTICS

| OAKLAND | No | Yds | Avg. | PITTSBURGH | No | Yds | Avg. |
|---|---|---|---|---|---|---|---|
| **RUSHING** | | | | | | | |
| van Eeghen | 22 | 66 | 3.0 | Harrison | 11 | 44 | 4.0 |
| C. Davis | 11 | 54 | 4.9 | Fuqua | 8 | 24 | 3.0 |
| Banaszak | 15 | 46 | 3.1 | Bradshaw | 1 | 4 | 4.0 |
| Garrett | 2 | 4 | 2.0 | Cunningham | 1 | 0 | 0.0 |
| Casper | 1 | -13.0 | -13.0 | | 21 | 72 | 3.4 |
| | 51 | 157 | 3.1 | | | | |
| **RECEIVING** | | | | | | | |
| Branch | 3 | 46 | 15.3 | Cunningham | 4 | 36 | 9.0 |
| Bankston | 2 | 11 | 5.5 | Swann | 3 | 58 | 19.3 |
| C. Davis | 2 | 7 | 3.5 | Fuqua | 2 | 11 | 5.5 |
| van Eeghen | 1 | 14 | 14.0 | Harrison | 2 | 10 | 5.0 |
| Banaszak | 1 | 5 | 5.0 | Brown | 1 | 32 | 32.0 |
| Casper | 1 | 5 | 5.0 | Stallworth | 1 | 18 | 18.0 |
| | 10 | 88 | 8.8 | Lewis | 1 | 11 | 11.0 |
| | | | | | 14 | 176 | 12.6 |
| **PUNTING** | | | | | | | |
| Guy | 7 | | 44.0 | Walden | 7 | | 37.3 |
| **PUNT RETURNS** | | | | | | | |
| Colzie | 2 | 19 | 8.5 | Bell | 2 | 14 | 7.0 |
| | | | | Swann | 1 | 4 | 4.0 |
| | | | | | 3 | 18 | 6.0 |
| **KICKOFF RETURNS** | | | | | | | |
| Garrett | 2 | 35 | 17.5 | Pough | 3 | 65 | 21.7 |
| | | | | Bell | 1 | 16 | 16.0 |
| | | | | Blount | 1 | 16 | 16.0 |
| | | | | | 5 | 97 | 19.4 |
| **INTERCEPTION RETURNS** | | | | | | | |
| Hall | 1 | 25 | 25.0 | none | | | |

| | PASSING | | | | | | | |
|---|---|---|---|---|---|---|---|---|
| OAKLAND | Att. | Comp. | Comp. Pct. | Yds. | Int. | Yds/ Att. | Yds/ Comp. | Yards Lost Tackled |
| Stabler | 16 | 10 | 62.5 | 88 | 0 | 5.5 | 8.8 | 2—25 |
| PITTSBURGH | | | | | | | | |
| Bradshaw | 35 | 14 | 40.0 | 176 | 1 | 5.0 | 12.6 | 3—11 |

# All the Silver

When the Oakland Raiders knocked off the defending NFL champion Pittsburgh Steelers, 24-7, to win the AFC, it seemed that coach John Madden and his Raiders would finally have their day in the sun. For all their frustration, the Raiders had won the Western Division title seven of eight times, but not since 1967, when they were humbled by Green Bay, have they appeared in the Super Bowl. Now all that remained in their way was Fran Tarkenton and the Minneota Vikings, three-time losers of the game's most valuable prize.

As things turned out, Minnesota proved hardly an opposition for the devastating Raiders as they rang up 266 yards on the ground and 163 yards in the air. Although the first quarter went scoreless, the Raiders were on top 16-0 at the half behind a field goal, a Ken Stabler pass, and Pete Banaszak's one-yard run. Errol Mann added another field goal in the third quarter and Tarkenton finally put Minnesota on the board to make the score 19-7 as the quarter ran out.

Whatever hopes the Vikings had for a comeback were soon dispelled as Banaszak again crossed the goal line 7:21 into the fourth quarter. A few minutes later Willie Brown intercepted a Tarkenton pass and ran the ball back 75 yards for a touchdown to make the score 32-7. With Bob Lee in the game for Tarkenton, the Vikings again got on the scoreboard, but it was simply a case of too little, too late.

Although Banaszak had scored two touchdowns and Clarence Davis rushed for a career-high 137 yards, the game's most valuable player honors went to Fred Biletnikoff, who caught four passes for 79 yards and set up three scores. The secret to the Raiders overwhelming victory was their ability to exploit the weak left side of the Vikings' line and to keep premier runner Chuck Foreman in check with only 44 yards in 17 attempts.

For the black and silver clad Raiders their dreams had finally become a reality. For the Vikings, the reality seemed more like a nightmare.

## LINEUPS

| OAKLAND | | MINNESOTA |
|---|---|---|
| | OFFENSE | |
| Branch | WR | Rashad |
| Shell | LT | Riley |
| Upshaw | LG | Goodrum |
| Dalby | C | Tinglehoff |
| Buehler | RG | E. White |
| Vella | RT | Yary |
| Casper | TE | Voigt |
| Biletnikoff | WR | S. White |
| Stabler | QB | Tarkenton |
| Davis | RB | Foreman |
| van Eeghen | RB | McClanahan |
| | DEFENSE | |
| Matuzek | LE | Eller |
| Rowe | LT | Sutherland |
| Sistrunk | RT | Page |
| M. Johnson | RE | Marshall |
| Villapiano | LLB | Blair |
| Willie Hall | MLB | Siemon |
| Hendricks | RLB | Hilgenberg |
| Thomas | LCB | N. Wright |
| Brown | RCB | Bryant |
| Tatum | FS | Krause |
| Atkinson | SS | J. Wright |

### SUBSTITUTES

**OAKLAND**

| | OFFENSE | |
|---|---|---|
| Banaszak | | Medlin |
| Bankston | | Moore |
| Bradshaw | | Rae |
| Garrett | | Siani |
| Humm | | Sylvester |
| Lawrence | | |
| | DEFENSE | |
| Barnes | | McMath |
| Bonness | | Phillips |
| Colzie | | Philyaw |
| Ginn | | Rice |
| | KICKERS | |
| Guy | | Mann |

**MINNESOTA**

| | OFFENSE | |
|---|---|---|
| Berry | | Hamilton |
| Bueton | | S. Johnson |
| Craig | | Lee |
| Dumler | | Miller |
| Grim | | Willis |
| Groce | | |
| | DEFENSE | |
| Allen | | McNeil |
| Beamon | | Mullaney |
| Windlan Hall | | J. White |
| Martin | | Winston |
| | KICKERS | |
| Clabo | | Cox |

## SCORING

| | | | | | |
|---|---|---|---|---|---|
| OAKLAND | 0 | 16 | 3 | 13—32 | |
| MINNESOTA | 0 | 0 | 7 | 7—14 | |

**Second Quarter**

| | | |
|---|---|---|
| Oak. | Mann, 24 yard field goal | 0:48 |
| Oak. | Casper, 1 yard pass from Stabler PAT—Mann (kick) | 7:50 |
| Oak. | Banaszak, 1 yard run PAT — Kick (no good) | 11:27 |

**Third Quarter**

| | | |
|---|---|---|
| Oak. | Mann, 40 yard field goal | 9:44 |
| Minn. | S. White, 8 yard pass from Tarkenton PAT—Cox (kick) | 14:13 |

**Fourth Quarter**

| | | |
|---|---|---|
| Oak. | Banaszak, 2 yard rush PAT — Mann (kick) | 7:21 |
| Oak. | Brown, 75 yard interception return PAT—Kick (no good) | 9:17 |
| Minn. | Voigt, 13 yard pass from Lee PAT — Cox (kick) | 14:35 |

## TEAM STATISTICS

| OAK. | | MINN. |
|---|---|---|
| 21 | First Downs—Total | 20 |
| 13 | First Downs—Rushing | 2 |
| 8 | First Downs—Passing | 15 |
| 0 | First Downs—Penalty | 3 |
| 0 | Fumbles—Number | 1 |
| 0 | Fumbles—Lost Ball | 1 |
| 4 | Penalties—Number | 2 |
| 30 | Yards Penalized | 25 |
| 1 | Missed Field Goals | 0 |
| 73 | Offensive Plays | 71 |
| 429 | Net Yards | 353 |
| 5.9 | Average Gain | 5.0 |
| 3 | Takeaways | 0 |
| 0 | Giveaways | 3 |
| +3 | Difference | -3 |

## INDIVIDUAL STATISTICS

### RUSHING

| OAKLAND | No | Yds | Avg. | MINNESOTA | No | Yds | Avg. |
|---|---|---|---|---|---|---|---|
| Davis | 16 | 137 | 8.6 | Foreman | 17 | 44 | 2.6 |
| van Eeghen | 18 | 73 | 4.1 | S. Johnson | 2 | 9 | 4.5 |
| Garrett | 4 | 19 | 4.8 | S. White | 1 | 7 | 7.0 |
| Banaszak | 10 | 19 | 1.9 | Lee | 1 | 4 | 4.0 |
| Ginn | 2 | 9 | 4.5 | Miller | 2 | 4 | 2.0 |
| Rae | 2 | 9 | 4.5 | McClanahan | 3 | 3 | 1.0 |
| | 52 | 266 | 5.1 | | 26 | 71 | 2.7 |

### RECEIVING

| OAKLAND | No | Yds | Avg. | MINNESOTA | No | Yds | Avg. |
|---|---|---|---|---|---|---|---|
| Biletnikoff | 4 | 79 | 19.8 | S. White | 5 | 77 | 15.4 |
| Casper | 4 | 70 | 17.5 | Foreman | 5 | 62 | 12.4 |
| Branch | 3 | 20 | 6.7 | Voigt | 4 | 49 | 12.3 |
| Garrett | 1 | 11 | 11.0 | Miller | 4 | 19 | 4.8 |
| | 12 | 180 | 15.0 | Rashad | 3 | 53 | 17.7 |
| | | | | S. Johnson | 3 | 26 | 8.7 |
| | | | | | 24 | 286 | 11.9 |

### PUNTING

| | No | Avg. | | No | Avg. |
|---|---|---|---|---|---|
| Guy | 4 | 40.5 | Clabo | 7 | 37.9 |

### PUNT RETURNS

| | No | Yds | Avg. | | No | Yds | Avg. |
|---|---|---|---|---|---|---|---|
| Colzie | 4 | 43 | 10.8 | Willis | 3 | 14 | 4.7 |

### KICKOFF RETURNS

| | No | Yds | Avg. | | No | Yds | Avg. |
|---|---|---|---|---|---|---|---|
| Garrett | 2 | 47 | 23.5 | S. White | 4 | 79 | 19.8 |
| Siani | 1 | 0 | 0.0 | Willis | 3 | 57 | 19.0 |
| | 3 | 47 | 15.7 | | 7 | 136 | 19.4 |

### INTERCEPTION RETURNS

| | No | Yds | Avg. | |
|---|---|---|---|---|
| Brown | 1 | 75 | 75.0 | none |
| Willie Hall | 1 | 16 | 16.0 | |
| | 2 | 91 | 45.5 | |

### PASSING

| OAKLAND | Att. | Comp | Comp Pct. | Yds. | Int. | Yds/ Att. | Yds/ Comp. | Yards Lost Tackled |
|---|---|---|---|---|---|---|---|---|
| Stabler | 19 | 12 | 63.2 | 180 | 0 | 9.5 | 15.0 | 2—17 |
| **MINNESOTA** | | | | | | | | |
| Tarkenton | 35 | 17 | 48.6 | 205 | 2 | 5.9 | 12.1 | 1—4 |
| Lee | 9 | 7 | 77.8 | 81 | 0 | 9.0 | 11.6 | |
| | 44 | 24 | 54.5 | 286 | 2 | 6.5 | 11.9 | 1—4 |

# 1977 N.F.C.   Freeing the Laborers

After lots of strident rhetoric and long negotiations, the NFL Players' Association and the league management reached a new labor agreement. Forged by union director Ed Garvey and management negotiator Sargent Karch, the new pact structured the rights of players for the next five years. For the fans, the highlight of the agreement was the preservation of the college draft and the modification of the free agent system. The new system provided for a specific set of draft choices which the signing team would give to the team losing the free agent, depending on the player's salary. Such a system gave football players much less freedom than their baseball counterparts enjoyed.

## EASTERN DIVISION

**Dallas Cowboys**—By trading for Seattle's first round draft pick, the Cowboys added halfback Tony Dorsett to their arsenal. Tom Landry brought the rookie from Pitt along slowly, but by midseason, Dorsett had given the Dallas offense a new dimension. The new running threat balanced the potent passing attack, with Roger Staubach throwing and Drew Pearson the ace receiver. The Cowboys used the firepower to win their first eight games and last four games in repeating as Eastern champs. Although Lee Roy Jordan retired, the defense prospered with star performances by Harvey Martin, Tom Henderson, Charlie Waters, and Cliff Harris. Landry further strengthened the defense by making a starting tackle of Randy White.

**Washington Redskins**—A 20-17 loss to the Giants was George Allen's first opening day loss in 12 years as an NFL head coach. The Redskin offense couldn't quite get into gear for two months, with the team record at 4-4 in November. The attack suffered from Roy Jefferson's retirement and John Riggins' knee injury in October. Allen's famed defense kept its edge despite its age and led the Skins to a late-season rush. With Joe Theismann starting most of the games at quarterback, Washington won five of their last six games. The only loss in that stretch was a 14-7 defeat by Dallas on Thanksgiving Day. That setback kept the Redskins out of the playoffs and contributed to Allen's departure.

**St. Louis Cardinals**—The grade A Cardinal offense stalled in the early going, resulting in three losses in the first four games. Once Don Coryell got his attack moving, the Cards ran off six straight victories to jump into the playoff race. Although speedsters Terry Metcalf and Mel Gray won most of the headlines, the heart of the offense was the front line which featured Dan Dierdorf, Conrad Dobler, and Tom Banks. Injuries in the secondary further exposed the team's Achilles heel. Although Roger Wehrli starred at cornerback, the Dolphins massacred the Cards 55-14 on Thanksgiving. The Cardinals then skidded to three more losses, culminating in an embarrassing defeat by Tampa Bay.

**Philadelphia Eagles**—In his second year in charge, Dick Vermeil found a quarterback around whom to build. A trade with the Rams brought Ron Jaworski and his rifle arm to Philadelphia. Although still short on talented bodies, Vermeil fashioned a team which battled the Eastern powers without flinching. Although they lost all six games to the Cowboys, Redskins, and Cardinals, the Eagles dropped five of those by six points or less. With Bill Bergey at its heart, the new 3-4 defense improved with time, winding up the year with a 27-0 thrashing of the Giants.

**New York Giants**—After sending Craig Morton to Denver in the off-season, the Giants cast around for a quarterback. Jerry Golsteyn began the season with an opening day 20-17 upset of the Redskins, but he played himself onto the bench before the end of September. CFL exile Joe Pisarcik ran the offense for most of the season, throwing erratically behind porous pass protection. With a 3-3 record in October, a 28-0 beating by the Cardinals on Monday night began a steep slide. The Giants lost six of their final eight games, dispelling the gloom only to beat Tampa Bay 10-0 and to wreak vengence on the Cards 27-7.

## CENTRAL DIVISION

**Minnesota Vikings**—The Vikings hit a reef when Fran Tarkenton broke a leg in a victory over the Bengals. Although in first place with a 6-3 record, the Vikes had to navigate the rest of the way without their leader. Veteran back-up Bob Lee engineered a split of the next two games. The Vikings fell behind the 49ers 24-0 in the third quarter, but rallied to a 28-27 victory behind the three touchdown passes of relief quarterback Tommy Kramer. One week later, Kramer started his first game but looked unsteady in a 35-13 loss. Going into the final weekend, the Vikings needed a victory to stay ahead of the hard-charging Chicago Bears. Traveling to Detroit, Lee started at QB as the Vikings won 30-21 and captured first place on the tiebreaker.

**Chicago Bears**—Walter Payton chased O.J. Simpson's single-season rushing record and carried the Bears into the playoff battle. Despite Payton's extraordinary season, the Bears stood at 3-5 after a 47-0 humiliation in Houston. From that point on, the Bears did not lose. Running behind the blocking of Revie Sorey, Payton set a single game record of 275 yards in a 10-7 victory over the Vikings. On the final Sunday, the Bears traveled to New Jersey in need of a victory to win a wild card spot. The icy field killed any chance Payton had for the rushing record, but the Bears struggled for the team goal. With the clock running low in the overtime period, Bob Thomas booted a field goal for a 12-9 victory which sent the Bears into the playoffs.

**Detroit Lions**—The Lions knew the heights and depths of NFL life. They looked miserable in a 37-0 loss at Dallas, then whipped the Chargers 20-0 in Detroit one week later. A balky offense frequently stalled as enemy pass rushers tormented Greg Landry. Injuries to runners Dexter Bussey and Lawrence Gaines further ruined the attack. The Lions put together a good record at home, but won only once on the road. A decisive 31-14 loss to the Bears on Thanksgiving Day effectively finished any playoff hopes, and the final game of the season ended Tommy Hudspeth's reign as head coach.

**Green Bay Packers**—Boos cascaded around Lambeau Field as the Packers put on a pitiful offensive show. In one mid-season stretch, the Packers lost to the Bears 26-0, were beaten by lowly Kansas City 20-10, and fell to the Rams 24-6. To make matters worse, quarterback Lynn Dickey suffered a broken leg on the last offensive play of the Rams game. Head coach Bart Starr turned to rookie David Whitehurst, and the youngster led his mates to two victories in the final three games.

**Tampa Bay Buccaneers**—After losing to the Seahawks in mid-season, the Bucs had a ticket for a second winless campaign. Head coach John McKay fielded a punchless offense which was shut out six times despite the addition of Ricky Bell and Anthony Davis, college stars under McKay at Southern California. Although still vulnerable to the pass, the new 3-4 defense shut down enemy rushers with strong work by Lee Roy Selmon and Dave Pear. With the loss string at 26 games, the Bucs traveled to New Orleans and stunned the Saints 33-14. The defense led the way with six interceptions. One week later, the Bucs treated their hometown fans to a 17-7 upset of the Cardinals to close out their second season.

## WESTERN DIVISION

**Los Angeles Rams**—Joe Namath brought his flamboyant style and aching knees to Los Angeles, but his time in the spotlight was short. After a tough Monday night loss to the Bears, he spent the rest of the year on the bench. Pat Haden took over at quarterback and guided the Rams to eight wins in his ten starts. The mobile young quarterback had a star runner in Lawrence McCutcheon, a star receiver in Harold Jackson, and a solid front line featuring guard Tom Mack. The defense lost Merlin Olsen to retirement but lost none of its strength, with Jack Youngblood, Isiah Robertson, and Monte Jackson named to All-Pro teams. Chuck Knox led his charges to a repeat Western title in his final season in Los Angeles.

**Atlanta Falcons**—New coach Leeman Bennett inspired the Atlanta defense to a record-breaking season. The Falcons allowed 129 points, a new low mark for the 14-game schedule. With Claude Humphrey starring up front and Rolland Lawrence in the secondary, the defense kept the Falcons in the playoff chase despite a sluggish offense. A pre-season knee injury kept quarterback Steve Bartkowski out of action for the first six games, but the Falcons still won four of those contests. Mid-season losses to the 49ers and Saints braked the momentum and began an easy glide back into the pack.

**San Francisco 49ers**—With a new owner in Edward DeBartolo, a new general manager in Joe Thomas, and a new coach in Ken Meyer, the 49ers looked terrible in the early going. Five straight losses out of the starting gate killed any playoff hopes, but a mid-season burst of four victories rekindled hopes of next year. A late relapse of losing dampened those hopes and cost Meyer his job as coach. Particularly discouraging was the 28-27 game with the Vikings, in which the 49ers had led 24-0.

**New Orleans Saints**—Head coach Hank Stram had a long-term building program in mind, but the miserable short-term results cost him his job after only two years. Archie Manning recovered enough shoulder strength to withstand waves of pass rushers pouring in on him. The defense had problems keeping the opponents out of the end zone. Richie Szaro provided several thrills with his place kicks. He booted a field goal which hit the right upright and bounced through at the gun for a 27-26 upset of the Rams. Two weeks later, he hit the left upright but saw the ball bounce back in a 10-7 overtime loss to the 49ers.

## FINAL TEAM STATISTICS

### OFFENSE

| | ATL. | CHI. | DALL. | DET. | G.B. | L.A. | MINN. | N.O. | NY G | PHIL. | ST. L. | S.F. | T.B. | WASH. |
|---|---|---|---|---|---|---|---|---|---|---|---|---|---|---|
| **FIRST DOWNS:** | | | | | | | | | | | | | | |
| Total | 198 | 247 | 272 | 218 | 195 | 270 | 245 | 223 | 201 | 211 | 247 | 219 | 168 | 227 |
| by Rushing | 102 | 141 | 118 | 94 | 81 | 139 | 110 | 115 | 105 | 98 | 114 | 126 | 84 | 79 |
| by Passing | 80 | 94 | 136 | 103 | 91 | 112 | 126 | 96 | 73 | 100 | 117 | 81 | 69 | 134 |
| by Penalty | 16 | 12 | 18 | 21 | 23 | 19 | 9 | 12 | 23 | 13 | 16 | 12 | 15 | 24 |
| **RUSHING:** | | | | | | | | | | | | | | |
| Number | 582 | 599 | 564 | 479 | 469 | 621 | 510 | 484 | 548 | 484 | 507 | 564 | 465 | 502 |
| Yards | 1890 | 2811 | 2369 | 1706 | 1464 | 2575 | 1821 | 2024 | 1897 | 1722 | 2042 | 2086 | 1424 | 1752 |
| Average Yards | 3.2 | 4.7 | 4.2 | 3.6 | 3.1 | 4.1 | 3.6 | 4.2 | 3.5 | 3.6 | 4.0 | 3.7 | 3.1 | 3.5 |
| Touchdowns | 9 | 18 | 21 | 11 | 5 | 19 | 9 | 14 | 11 | 10 | 19 | 16 | 4 | 4 |
| **PASSING:** | | | | | | | | | | | | | | |
| Attempts | 297 | 305 | 372 | 384 | 327 | 339 | 388 | 321 | 311 | 349 | 366 | 277 | 321 | 383 |
| Completions | 140 | 161 | 215 | 191 | 164 | 182 | 228 | 166 | 134 | 167 | 195 | 136 | 131 | 183 |
| Completion Pct. | 47.1 | 52.8 | 57.8 | 49.7 | 50.2 | 53.7 | 58.8 | 51.7 | 43.1 | 47.9 | 53.3 | 49.1 | 40.8 | 47.8 |
| Passing Yards | 1740 | 2070 | 2689 | 1959 | 2013 | 2253 | 2692 | 1933 | 1762 | 2198 | 2608 | 1797 | 1714 | 2284 |
| Avg. Yds per Att. | 5.9 | 6.8 | 7.2 | 5.1 | 6.2 | 6.6 | 6.9 | 6.0 | 5.7 | 6.3 | 7.1 | 6.5 | 5.3 | 6.0 |
| Avg. Yds per Comp. | 12.4 | 12.9 | 12.5 | 10.3 | 12.3 | 12.4 | 11.8 | 11.6 | 13.1 | 13.2 | 13.4 | 13.2 | 13.1 | 12.5 |
| Times Tackled | 40 | 26 | 33 | 54 | 32 | 25 | 35 | 46 | 46 | 47 | 15 | 36 | 48 | 52 |
| Yds Lost Tackled | 384 | 226 | 246 | 441 | 265 | 237 | 324 | 360 | 375 | 342 | 109 | 289 | 445 | 421 |
| Net Yards | 1356 | 1844 | 2443 | 1518 | 1748 | 2016 | 2368 | 1573 | 1387 | 1856 | 2499 | 1508 | 1269 | 1863 |
| Touchdowns | 8 | 11 | 18 | 7 | 6 | 16 | 19 | 13 | 6 | 18 | 14 | 9 | 3 | 15 |
| Interceptions | 16 | 18 | 10 | 16 | 21 | 11 | 22 | 21 | 22 | 21 | 21 | 17 | 30 | 16 |
| Pct. Intercepted | 5.4 | 5.9 | 2.7 | 4.2 | 6.4 | 3.2 | 5.7 | 6.5 | 7.1 | 6.0 | 5.7 | 6.1 | 9.3 | 4.2 |
| **PUNTS:** | | | | | | | | | | | | | | |
| Number | 106 | 82 | 83 | 101 | 86 | 73 | 83 | 87 | 100 | 95 | 72 | 80 | 99 | 91 |
| Average | 41.2 | 39.4 | 38.7 | 36.2 | 39.4 | 35.2 | 39.8 | 41.0 | 39.9 | 36.5 | 36.2 | 35.0 | 39.9 | 38.5 |
| **PUNT RETURNS:** | | | | | | | | | | | | | | |
| Number | 59 | 47 | 61 | 42 | 38 | 51 | 58 | 37 | 46 | 50 | 40 | 48 | 48 | 57 |
| Yards | 402 | 471 | 545 | 345 | 321 | 360 | 346 | 281 | 446 | 518 | 300 | 292 | 359 | 452 |
| Average Yards | 6.8 | 10.0 | 8.9 | 8.2 | 8.4 | 7.1 | 6.0 | 7.6 | 9.7 | 10.4 | 7.5 | 6.1 | 7.5 | 7.9 |
| Touchdowns | 0 | 1 | 0 | 1 | 1 | 0 | 0 | 0 | 1 | 0 | 0 | 0 | 0 | 0 |
| **KICKOFF RETURNS:** | | | | | | | | | | | | | | |
| Number | 34 | 57 | 44 | 58 | 51 | 33 | 45 | 63 | 54 | 45 | 59 | 49 | 43 | 47 |
| Yards | 621 | 1273 | 1071 | 1239 | 947 | 705 | 834 | 1355 | 1036 | 1110 | 1271 | 1174 | 914 | 1087 |
| Average Yards | 18.3 | 22.3 | 24.3 | 21.4 | 18.6 | 21.4 | 18.5 | 21.5 | 19.2 | 24.7 | 21.5 | 24.0 | 21.3 | 23.1 |
| Touchdowns | 0 | 1 | 0 | 1 | 1 | 0 | 0 | 1 | 0 | 1 | 0 | 1 | 0 | 0 |
| **INTERCEPTION RET:** | | | | | | | | | | | | | | |
| Number | 26 | 18 | 21 | 19 | 13 | 25 | 16 | 10 | 12 | 21 | 19 | 8 | 23 | 21 |
| Yards | 462 | 138 | 229 | 319 | 89 | 472 | 109 | 83 | 179 | 300 | 267 | 133 | 368 | 188 |
| Average Yards | 17.8 | 7.7 | 10.9 | 16.8 | 6.8 | 18.9 | 6.8 | 8.3 | 14.9 | 14.3 | 14.1 | 16.6 | 16.0 | 9.0 |
| Touchdowns | 2 | 0 | 1 | 1 | 1 | 1 | 0 | 1 | 2 | 0 | 1 | 0 | 3 | 0 |
| **PENALTIES:** | | | | | | | | | | | | | | |
| Number | 101 | 97 | 106 | 86 | 82 | 89 | 75 | 86 | 91 | 78 | 95 | 99 | 88 | 94 |
| Yards | 898 | 852 | 865 | 692 | 690 | 869 | 556 | 794 | 880 | 642 | 837 | 830 | 717 | 802 |
| **FUMBLES:** | | | | | | | | | | | | | | |
| Number | 28 | 36 | 26 | 26 | 24 | 32 | 36 | 20 | 27 | 31 | 31 | 27 | 30 | 26 |
| Number Lost | 9 | 17 | 14 | 14 | 9 | 17 | 24 | 11 | 12 | 17 | 16 | 8 | 16 | 14 |
| **POINTS:** | | | | | | | | | | | | | | |
| Total | 179 | 255 | 345 | 183 | 134 | 302 | 231 | 232 | 181 | 220 | 272 | 220 | 103 | 196 |
| PAT Attempts | 20 | 31 | 42 | 23 | 14 | 36 | 30 | 31 | 20 | 29 | 36 | 27 | 11 | 19 |
| PAT Made | 20 | 27 | 39 | 19 | 11 | 32 | 25 | 29 | 19 | 25 | 35 | 25 | 10 | 19 |
| FG Attempts | 30 | 27 | 29 | 19 | 21 | 30 | 17 | 12 | 23 | 15 | 16 | 19 | 17 | 37 |
| FG Made | 13 | 14 | 18 | 8 | 13 | 18 | 8 | 5 | 14 | 7 | 7 | 11 | 9 | 21 |
| Percent FG Made | 43.3 | 51.9 | 62.1 | 42.1 | 61.9 | 60.0 | 47.1 | 41.7 | 60.9 | 46.7 | 43.8 | 57.9 | 52.9 | 56.8 |
| Safeties | 0 | 0 | 0 | 1 | 0 | 0 | 1 | 1 | 0 | 0 | 0 | 0 | 0 | 0 |

### DEFENSE

| | ATL. | CHI. | DALL. | DET. | G.B. | L.A. | MINN. | N.O. | NY G | PHIL. | ST. L. | S.F. | T.B. | WASH. |
|---|---|---|---|---|---|---|---|---|---|---|---|---|---|---|
| **FIRST DOWNS:** | | | | | | | | | | | | | | |
| Total | 192 | 241 | 205 | 206 | 259 | 203 | 212 | 272 | 224 | 216 | 258 | 221 | 240 | 234 |
| by Rushing | 100 | 124 | 88 | 93 | 139 | 90 | 119 | 153 | 94 | 95 | 122 | 108 | 123 | 112 |
| by Passing | 76 | 106 | 94 | 103 | 105 | 94 | 80 | 103 | 109 | 106 | 120 | 93 | 106 | 102 |
| by Penalty | 16 | 11 | 23 | 10 | 15 | 19 | 13 | 16 | 21 | 15 | 16 | 20 | 11 | 20 |
| **RUSHING:** | | | | | | | | | | | | | | |
| Number | 504 | 541 | 457 | 521 | 583 | 462 | 548 | 623 | 519 | 523 | 513 | 551 | 581 | 537 |
| Yards | 1858 | 2157 | 1651 | 1905 | 2317 | 1698 | 2222 | 2729 | 1777 | 1917 | 2235 | 1869 | 2031 | 2039 |
| Average Yards | 3.7 | 4.0 | 3.6 | 3.7 | 4.0 | 3.7 | 4.1 | 4.4 | 3.4 | 3.7 | 4.4 | 3.4 | 3.5 | 3.8 |
| Touchdowns | 5 | 14 | 9 | 13 | 16 | 7 | 11 | 21 | 16 | 10 | 11 | 16 | 13 | 8 |
| **PASSING:** | | | | | | | | | | | | | | |
| Attempts | 320 | 377 | 371 | 302 | 319 | 370 | 312 | 290 | 328 | 358 | 376 | 270 | 337 | 380 |
| Completions | 141 | 182 | 154 | 161 | 186 | 180 | 149 | 154 | 185 | 183 | 198 | 139 | 190 | 167 |
| Completion Pct. | 44.1 | 48.3 | 41.5 | 53.3 | 58.3 | 48.6 | 47.8 | 53.1 | 56.4 | 51.1 | 52.7 | 51.5 | 56.4 | 43.9 |
| Passing Yards | 1775 | 2334 | 1991 | 2123 | 2042 | 2236 | 1835 | 2127 | 2399 | 2192 | 2476 | 1948 | 2141 | 2430 |
| Avg. Yds per Att. | 5.5 | 6.2 | 5.4 | 7.0 | 6.4 | 6.0 | 5.9 | 7.3 | 7.3 | 6.1 | 6.6 | 7.2 | 6.4 | 6.4 |
| Avg. Yds per Comp. | 12.6 | 12.8 | 12.9 | 13.2 | 11.0 | 12.4 | 12.3 | 13.8 | 13.0 | 12.0 | 12.5 | 14.0 | 11.3 | 14.6 |
| Times Tackled | 42 | 27 | 53 | 32 | 37 | 36 | 30 | 27 | 38 | 47 | 25 | 42 | 30 | 44 |
| Yds Lost Tackled | 391 | 207 | 429 | 256 | 323 | 359 | 254 | 234 | 303 | 316 | 209 | 360 | 246 | 359 |
| Net Yards | 1384 | 2127 | 1562 | 1867 | 1719 | 1877 | 1581 | 1893 | 2096 | 1876 | 2267 | 1588 | 1895 | 2071 |
| Touchdowns | 9 | 7 | 14 | 14 | 10 | 11 | 15 | 15 | 12 | 14 | 22 | 14 | 10 | 12 |
| Interceptions | 26 | 18 | 21 | 19 | 13 | 25 | 16 | 10 | 12 | 21 | 19 | 8 | 23 | 21 |
| Pct. Intercepted | 8.1 | 4.8 | 5.7 | 6.3 | 4.1 | 6.8 | 5.1 | 3.4 | 3.7 | 5.9 | 5.1 | 3.0 | 6.8 | 5.5 |
| **PUNTS:** | | | | | | | | | | | | | | |
| Number | 101 | 93 | 103 | 87 | 76 | 89 | 92 | 75 | 88 | 91 | 72 | 86 | 84 | 95 |
| Average | 36.3 | 39.1 | 37.1 | 39.5 | 36.5 | 38.7 | 38.2 | 38.8 | 38.9 | 38.7 | 39.5 | 37.5 | 39.9 | 36.6 |
| **PUNT RETURNS:** | | | | | | | | | | | | | | |
| Number | 58 | 42 | 36 | 62 | 53 | 29 | 42 | 51 | 67 | 45 | 33 | 47 | 71 | 50 |
| Yards | 519 | 216 | 280 | 535 | 311 | 116 | 507 | 604 | 680 | 244 | 157 | 444 | 469 | 228 |
| Average Yards | 8.9 | 5.1 | 7.8 | 8.6 | 5.9 | 4.0 | 12.1 | 11.8 | 10.1 | 5.4 | 4.8 | 9.4 | 6.6 | 4.6 |
| Touchdowns | 0 | 0 | 1 | 1 | 0 | 0 | 1 | 2 | 0 | 0 | 0 | 0 | 0 | 0 |
| **KICKOFF RETURNS:** | | | | | | | | | | | | | | |
| Number | 43 | 52 | 71 | 33 | 39 | 53 | 48 | 45 | 35 | 46 | 55 | 48 | 33 | 54 |
| Yards | 1021 | 1010 | 1614 | 741 | 786 | 1156 | 999 | 1075 | 895 | 940 | 1104 | 1025 | 699 | 1033 |
| Average Yards | 23.7 | 19.4 | 22.7 | 22.5 | 20.2 | 21.8 | 20.8 | 23.9 | 25.6 | 20.4 | 20.1 | 21.4 | 21.2 | 19.1 |
| Touchdowns | 1 | 1 | 0 | 0 | 0 | 0 | 2 | 0 | 1 | 0 | 0 | 1 | 0 | 0 |
| **INTERCEPTION RET:** | | | | | | | | | | | | | | |
| Number | 16 | 18 | 10 | 16 | 21 | 11 | 22 | 21 | 22 | 21 | 21 | 17 | 30 | 16 |
| Yards | 195 | 171 | 184 | 207 | 349 | 136 | 187 | 392 | 330 | 256 | 183 | 298 | 429 | 296 |
| Average Yards | 12.2 | 9.5 | 18.4 | 12.9 | 16.6 | 12.4 | 8.5 | 18.7 | 15.0 | 12.2 | 8.7 | 17.5 | 14.3 | 18.5 |
| Touchdowns | 0 | 1 | 0 | 1 | 1 | 0 | 0 | 4 | 2 | 0 | 1 | 1 | 3 | 1 |
| **PENALTIES:** | | | | | | | | | | | | | | |
| Number | 99 | 83 | 78 | 88 | 101 | 94 | 82 | 104 | 106 | 84 | 82 | 96 | 87 | 100 |
| Yards | 860 | 731 | 731 | 770 | 799 | 825 | 688 | 972 | 886 | 698 | 817 | 820 | 714 | 857 |
| **FUMBLES:** | | | | | | | | | | | | | | |
| Number | 35 | 27 | 22 | 32 | 27 | 26 | 23 | 29 | 47 | 24 | 19 | 21 | 34 | 28 |
| Number Lost | 22 | 13 | 10 | 16 | 11 | 16 | 13 | 15 | 20 | 13 | 12 | 10 | 18 | 12 |
| **POINTS:** | | | | | | | | | | | | | | |
| Total | 129 | 253 | 212 | 252 | 219 | 146 | 227 | 336 | 265 | 207 | 287 | 260 | 223 | 189 |
| PAT Attempts | 15 | 27 | 26 | 31 | 27 | 18 | 30 | 42 | 33 | 25 | 34 | 32 | 26 | 21 |
| PAT Made | 12 | 26 | 26 | 28 | 22 | 17 | 26 | 39 | 31 | 24 | 32 | 29 | 23 | 21 |
| FG Attempts | 16 | 29 | 15 | 24 | 23 | 18 | 17 | 24 | 22 | 26 | 26 | 22 | 27 | 29 |
| FG Made | 9 | 21 | 10 | 12 | 11 | 7 | 7 | 15 | 12 | 11 | 17 | 13 | 14 | 14 |
| Percent FG Made | 56.3 | 72.4 | 66.7 | 50.0 | 47.8 | 38.9 | 41.2 | 62.5 | 54.5 | 42.3 | 65.4 | 59.1 | 51.9 | 48.3 |
| Safeties | 0 | 1 | 0 | 1 | 1 | 0 | 0 | 0 | 0 | 0 | 0 | 0 | 1 | 0 |

## CONFERENCE PLAYOFFS

### December 26, at Irving, Texas (Attendance 62,920)

**SCORING**

| | | | | | |
|---|---|---|---|---|---|
| DALLAS | 7 | 10 | 17 | 3 | – 37 |
| CHICAGO | 0 | 0 | 0 | 7 | – 7 |

First Quarter
Dall. Dennison, 2 yard rush
PAT – Herrera (kick)

Second Quarter
Dall. DuPree, 26 yard pass from Staubach PAT – Herrera (kick)
Dall. Herrera, 21 yard field goal

Third Quarter
Dall. Dorsett, 22 yard rush
PAT – Herrera (kick)
Dall. Herrera, 31 yard field goal
Dall. Dorsett, 7 yard rush
PAT – Herrera (kick)

Fourth Quarter
Dall. Herrera, 27 yard field goal
Chi. Schubert, 34 yard pass from Avellini PAT – Thomas (kick)

**TEAM STATISTICS**

| DALLAS | | CHICAGO |
|---|---|---|
| 20 | First Downs – Total | 15 |
| 13 | First Downs – Rushing | 4 |
| 7 | First Downs – Passing | 9 |
| 0 | First Downs – Penalty | 2 |
| 2 | Fumbles – Number | 3 |
| 2 | Fumbles – Lost Ball | 3 |
| 3 | Penalties – Number | 4 |
| 35 | Yards Penalized | 43 |
| 0 | Missed Field Goals | 0 |
| 64 | Offensive Plays | 55 |
| 367 | Net Yards | 224 |
| 5.7 | Average Gain | 4.0 |
| 3 | Giveaways | 7 |
| 7 | Takeaways | 3 |
| +4 | Difference | -4 |

**INDIVIDUAL STATISTICS**

| DALLAS | No | Yds | Avg. | CHICAGO | No | Yds | Avg. |
|---|---|---|---|---|---|---|---|
| **RUSHING** | | | | | | | |
| Dorsett | 17 | 85 | 5.0 | Payton | 19 | 60 | 3.2 |
| Newhouse | 16 | 80 | 5.0 | Harper | 5 | 11 | 2.2 |
| Dennison | 8 | 40 | 5.0 | Earl | 2 | 6 | 3.0 |
| Staubach | 4 | 25 | 6.3 | Avellini | 1 | 4 | 4.0 |
| Brinson | 3 | 3 | 1.0 | | 27 | 81 | 3.0 |
| | 48 | 233 | 4.8 | | | | |
| **RECEIVING** | | | | | | | |
| D. Pearson | 2 | 38 | 19.0 | Schubert | 5 | 69 | 13.8 |
| Dorsett | 2 | 37 | 18.5 | Payton | 3 | 33 | 11.0 |
| DuPree | 1 | 28 | 28.0 | Scott | 3 | 29 | 9.7 |
| Newhouse | 1 | 13 | 13.0 | Latta | 2 | 25 | 12.5 |
| Richards | 1 | 12 | 12.0 | Earl | 1 | 15 | 15.0 |
| Brinson | 1 | 6 | 6.0 | Harper | 1 | 6 | 6.0 |
| | 8 | 134 | 16.8 | | 15 | 177 | 11.8 |
| **PUNTING** | | | | | | | |
| D. White | 3 | | 37.0 | Parsons | 6 | | 43.4 |
| **PUNT RETURNS** | | | | | | | |
| Johnson | 3 | 26 | 8.7 | Schubert | 1 | 7 | 7.0 |
| Hill | 1 | 12 | 12.0 | | | | |
| | 4 | 38 | 9.5 | | | | |
| **KICKOFF RETURNS** | | | | | | | |
| Brinson | 1 | 28 | 28.0 | Waltersch'd | 4 | 98 | 24.5 |
| Johnson | 1 | 16 | 16.0 | Payton | 3 | 57 | 19.0 |
| | 2 | 44 | 22.0 | Musso | 1 | 7 | 7.0 |
| | | | | | 8 | 162 | 20.3 |
| **INTERCEPTION RETURNS** | | | | | | | |
| Waters | 3 | 53 | 17.7 | Livers | 1 | 8 | 8.0 |
| Lewis | 1 | 23 | 23.0 | | | | |
| | 4 | 76 | 19.0 | | | | |

**PASSING**

| DALLAS | Att. | Comp. | Comp. Pct. | Yds. | Int. | Yds/ Att. | Yds/ Comp. | Yards Lost Tackled |
|---|---|---|---|---|---|---|---|---|
| Staubach | 13 | 8 | 61.5 | 134 | 1 | 10.3 | 16.8 | 2– 2 |
| **CHICAGO** | | | | | | | | |
| Avellini | 25 | 15 | 60.0 | 177 | 4 | 7.1 | 11.8 | 3–34 |

### December 26, at Los Angeles (Attendance 62,538)

**SCORING**

| | | | | | |
|---|---|---|---|---|---|
| LOS ANGELES | 0 | 0 | 0 | 7 | – 7 |
| MINNESOTA | 7 | 0 | 0 | 7 | – 14 |

First Quarter
Minn. Foreman, 5 yard rush
PAT – Cox (kick)

Fourth Quarter
Minn. Johnson, 1 yard rush
PAT – Cox (kick)
L.A. H. Jackson, 1 yard pass from Haden PAT – Septien (kick)

**TEAM STATISTICS**

| L.A. | | MINN. |
|---|---|---|
| 14 | First Downs – Total | 14 |
| 7 | First Downs – Rushing | 9 |
| 6 | First Downs – Passing | 4 |
| 1 | First Downs – Penalty | 1 |
| 1 | Fumbles – Number | 1 |
| 0 | Fumbles – Lost Ball | 0 |
| 2 | Penalties – Number | 7 |
| 15 | Yards Penalized | 50 |
| 1 | Missed Field Goals | 0 |
| 62 | Offensive Plays | 60 |
| 267 | Net Yards | 189 |
| 4.3 | Average Gain | 3.2 |
| 3 | Giveaways | 0 |
| 0 | Takeaways | 3 |
| -3 | Difference | +3 |

**INDIVIDUAL STATISTICS**

| LOS ANGELES | No | Yds | Avg. | MINNESOTA | No | Yds | Avg. |
|---|---|---|---|---|---|---|---|
| **RUSHING** | | | | | | | |
| McCutcheon | 16 | 102 | 6.4 | Foreman | 31 | 101 | 3.3 |
| Haden | 3 | 27 | 9.0 | Miller | 12 | 52 | 4.3 |
| Cappelletti | 7 | 11 | 1.6 | Johnson | 3 | 1 | 0.3 |
| Phillips | 1 | 9 | 9.0 | Lee | 3 | -10 | -3.3 |
| Nelson | 1 | 0 | 0.0 | | 49 | 144 | 2.9 |
| Tyler | 1 | 0 | 0.0 | | | | |
| | 29 | 149 | 5.1 | | | | |
| **RECEIVING** | | | | | | | |
| Nelson | 5 | 85 | 17.0 | Rashad | 2 | 37 | 18.5 |
| H. Jackson | 3 | 21 | 7.0 | Miller | 2 | 14 | 7.0 |
| McCutcheon | 2 | 15 | 7.5 | Foreman | 1 | 6 | 6.0 |
| Phillips | 2 | 0 | 0.0 | | 5 | 57 | 11.4 |
| Waddy | 1 | 5 | 5.0 | | | | |
| Cappelletti | 1 | 4 | 4.0 | | | | |
| | 14 | 130 | 9.3 | | | | |
| **PUNTING** | | | | | | | |
| Walker | 5 | | 37.6 | Clabo | 5 | | 40.8 |
| **PUNT RETURNS** | | | | | | | |
| Waddy | 3 | 17 | 5.7 | Moore | 2 | 30 | 15.0 |
| Bryant | 1 | 19 | 19.0 | | | | |
| Scales | 1 | 2 | 2.0 | | | | |
| | 5 | 38 | 7.6 | | | | |
| **KICKOFF RETURNS** | | | | | | | |
| Tyler | 2 | 43 | 21.5 | Moore | 1 | 15 | 15.0 |
| **INTERCEPTION RETURNS** | | | | | | | |
| none | | | | Krause | 1 | 14 | 14.0 |
| | | | | J. Wright | 1 | 3 | 3.0 |
| | | | | Allen | 1 | 0 | 0.0 |
| | | | | | 3 | 17 | 5.7 |

**PASSING**

| LOS ANGELES | Att. | Comp. | Comp. Pct. | Yds. | Int. | Yds/ Att. | Yds/ Comp. | Yards Lost Tackled |
|---|---|---|---|---|---|---|---|---|
| Haden | 32 | 14 | 43.8 | 130 | 3 | 4.1 | 9.3 | 1–12 |
| **MINNESOTA** | | | | | | | | |
| Lee | 10 | 5 | 50.0 | 57 | 0 | 5.7 | 11.8 | 1–12 |

# 1977 N.F.C. — Eastern Division

## DALLAS COWBOYS 12-2 Tom Landry

| Scores of Each Game | | |
|---|---|---|
| 16 | Minnesota | 10 |
| 41 | N.Y. GIANTS | 21 |
| 23 | TAMPA BAY | 7 |
| 30 | St. Louis | 24 |
| 34 | WASHINGTON | 16 |
| 16 | Philadelphia | 10 |
| 37 | DETROIT | 0 |
| 24 | N.Y. Giants | 10 |
| 17 | ST. LOUIS | 24 |
| 13 | Pittsburgh | 28 |
| 14 | Washington | 7 |
| 24 | PHILADELPHIA | 14 |
| 42 | San Francisco | 35 |
| 14 | DENVER | 6 |

| Use Name | Pos. | Hgt | Wgt | Age | Int | Pts |
|---|---|---|---|---|---|---|
| Pat Donovan | OT | 6'4" | 255 | 24 | | |
| Andy Frederick | OT | 6'6" | 241 | 22 | | |
| Ralph Neely | OT | 6'5" | 255 | 33 | | |
| Rayfield Wright | OT | 6'7" | 260 | 32 | | |
| Jim Cooper | OG-C | 6'5" | 252 | 21 | | |
| Burton Lawless | OG | 6'4" | 250 | 23 | | |
| Tom Rafferty | OG-C | 6'3" | 250 | 23 | | |
| Herbert Scott | OG | 6'2" | 250 | 24 | | |
| John Fitzgerald | C | 6'5" | 260 | 29 | | |
| Too Tall Jones | DE | 6'9" | 265 | 26 | | |
| Harvey Martin | DE | 6'5" | 252 | 26 | | |
| David Stalls | DE | 6'4" | 236 | 21 | | |
| Larry Cole | DT-DE | 6'4" | 260 | 30 | | |
| Bill Gregory | DT | 6'5" | 260 | 27 | | |
| Jethro Pugh | DT | 6'6" | 250 | 33 | | |
| Randy White | DT | 6'4" | 245 | 24 | | |
| Bob Breunig | LB | 6'2" | 227 | 24 | 1 | |
| Guy Brown | LB | 6'4" | 215 | 22 | | |
| Mike Hegman | LB | 6'1" | 225 | 24 | 1 | |
| Tom Henderson | LB | 6'2" | 220 | 24 | 3 | 6 |
| Bruce Huther | LB | 6'1" | 217 | 23 | | |
| D.D. Lewis | LB | 6'2" | 215 | 31 | 1 | |
| Benny Barnes | DB | 6'1" | 195 | 26 | | |
| Cliff Harris | DB | 6' | 192 | 28 | 5 | |
| Randy Hughes | DB | 6'4" | 208 | 24 | 2 | |
| Aaron Kyle | DB | 5'11" | 185 | 23 | 1 | |
| Mel Renfro | DB | 6' | 192 | 35 | 2 | |
| Mark Washington | DB | 5'10" | 187 | 29 | 2 | |
| Charlie Waters | DB | 6'1" | 198 | 28 | 3 | 6 |
| Glenn Carano | QB | 6'3" | 195 | 21 | | |
| Roger Staubach | QB | 6'2" | 202 | 35 | | 18 |
| Danny White | QB | 6'2" | 192 | 25 | | |
| Doug Dennison | HB | 6'1" | 204 | 25 | | 6 |
| Tony Dorsett | HB | 5'11" | 192 | 23 | | 78 |
| Preston Pearson | HB | 6'1" | 206 | 32 | | 30 |
| Larry Brinson | FB | 6' | 214 | 23 | | 6 |
| Scott Laidlaw | FB | 6' | 205 | 24 | | 6 |
| Robert Newhouse | FB | 5'10" | 205 | 27 | | 24 |
| Tony Hill | WR | 6'2" | 196 | 21 | | |
| Butch Johnson | WR | 6'1" | 191 | 23 | | 6 |
| Drew Pearson | WR | 6' | 183 | 26 | | 12 |
| Golden Richards | WR | 6' | 180 | 26 | | 18 |
| Billy Joe DuPree | TE | 6'4" | 226 | 27 | | 18 |
| Jay Saldi | TE | 6'3" | 224 | 22 | | 18 |
| Efren Herrera | K | 5'9" | 190 | 26 | | 93 |

Jim Eidson – Injury
Greg Schaum – Knee Injury
Charley Young – Knee Injury

Percy Howard – Injury

## WASHINGTON REDSKINS 9-5 George Allen

| Scores of Each Game | | |
|---|---|---|
| 17 | N.Y. Giants | 20 |
| 10 | ATLANTA | 6 |
| 24 | ST. LOUIS | 14 |
| 10 | Tampa Bay | 0 |
| 16 | Dallas | 34 |
| 6 | N.Y. GIANTS | 17 |
| 23 | PHILADELPHIA | 17 |
| 3 | Baltimore | 10 |
| 17 | Philadelphia | 14 |
| 10 | GREEN BAY | 9 |
| 7 | DALLAS | 14 |
| 10 | Buffalo | 0 |
| 26 | St. Louis | 20 |
| 17 | LOS ANGELES | 14 |

| Use Name | Pos. | Hgt | Wgt | Age | Int | Pts |
|---|---|---|---|---|---|---|
| George Starke | OT | 6'5" | 249 | 29 | | |
| Tim Stokes | OT | 6'5" | 252 | 27 | | |
| Tony Hermeling | •OG | 6'5" | 255 | 31 | | |
| Dan Nugent | OG | 6'3" | 250 | 24 | | |
| Ron Saul | OG | 6'2" | 254 | 29 | | |
| Ted Fritsch | C | 6'2" | 242 | 27 | | |
| Len Hauss | C | 6'2" | 235 | 35 | | |
| Bob Kuziel | C-OT | 6'5" | 255 | 27 | | |
| Dallas Hickman | DE | 6'6" | 235 | 25 | | |
| Dennis Johnson | DE | 6'4" | 260 | 25 | | |
| Karl Lorch | DE | 6'3" | 253 | 27 | | |
| Ron McDole | DE | 6'3" | 265 | 37 | 2 | |
| Bill Wynn | DE | 6'4" | 245 | 28 | | |
| Bill Brundige | DT | 6'5" | 270 | 28 | | |
| Dave Butz | DT | 6'7" | 285 | 27 | | |
| Diron Talbert | DT | 6'5" | 255 | 33 | | |
| Mike Curtis | LB | 6'2" | 232 | 34 | 1 | |
| Brad Dusek | LB | 6'2" | 214 | 26 | 1 | |
| Chris Hanburger | LB | 6'2" | 218 | 36 | | |
| Joe Harris | LB | 6'1" | 225 | 24 | | |
| Harold McLinton | LB | 6'2" | 235 | 30 | | |
| Stu O'Dell | LB | 6'1" | 220 | 25 | | |
| Rusty Tillman | LB | 6'2" | 230 | 31 | | |
| Pete Wysocki | LB | 6'2" | 225 | 28 | | |
| Eddie Brown | DB | 5'11" | 190 | 25 | 1 | |
| Pat Fischer | DB | 5'10" | 170 | 37 | | |
| Windlan Hall (from MIN) | DB | 5'11" | 175 | 27 | | |
| Ken Houston | DB | 6'3" | 198 | 32 | 5 | |
| Joe Lavender | DB | 6'4" | 190 | 28 | 4 | |
| Mark Murphy | DB | 6'4" | 210 | 22 | | |
| Brig Owens | DB | 5'11" | 190 | 34 | | |
| Jake Scott | DB | 6' | 188 | 32 | 3 | |
| Gerard Williams | DB | 6'1" | 184 | 25 | 4 | |
| Billy Kilmer | QB | 6' | 204 | 37 | | |
| Joe Theismann | QB | 6' | 184 | 27 | | 6 |
| Bob Brunet | HB | 6'1" | 205 | 31 | | |
| Clarence Harmon | HB | 5'11" | 190 | 21 | | 6 |
| Mike Thomas | HB | 5'11" | 190 | 24 | | 30 |
| Calvin Hill | FB | 6'3" | 227 | 30 | | 6 |
| Eddie Moss | FB | 6' | 215 | 28 | | |
| John Riggins | FB | 6'2" | 230 | 28 | | 12 |
| Danny Buggs | WR | 6'2" | 185 | 24 | | 6 |
| Frank Grant | WR | 5'11" | 181 | 27 | | 18 |
| Larry Jones | WR | 5'10" | 170 | 26 | | |
| Howard Satterwhite (to BAL) | WR | 5'11" | 185 | 24 | | |
| Charley Taylor | WR | 6'3" | 210 | 35 | | |
| Jean Fugett | TE | 6'3" | 226 | 25 | | 30 |
| Jerry Smith | TE | 6'2" | 208 | 34 | | |
| Mike Bragg | K | 5'11" | 186 | 30 | | |
| Mark Moseley | K | 5'11" | 205 | 29 | | 82 |

Brian Fryer – Injury

## ST. LOUIS CARDINALS 7-7 Don Coryell

| Scores of Each Game | | |
|---|---|---|
| 0 | Denver | 7 |
| 16 | CHICAGO | 13 |
| 14 | Washington | 24 |
| 24 | DALLAS | 30 |
| 21 | Philadelphia | 17 |
| 49 | NEW ORLEANS | 31 |
| 28 | N.Y. GIANTS | 0 |
| 27 | Minnesota | 7 |
| 24 | Dallas | 17 |
| 21 | PHILADELPHIA | 16 |
| 14 | MIAMI | 55 |
| 7 | N.Y. Giants | 27 |
| 20 | WASHINGTON | 26 |
| 7 | Tampa Bay | 17 |

| Use Name | Pos. | Hgt | Wgt | Age | Int | Pts |
|---|---|---|---|---|---|---|
| Dan Dierdorf | OT | 6'4" | 288 | 28 | | |
| Roger Finnie | OT | 6'3" | 248 | 31 | | |
| Brad Oates | OT | 6'6" | 274 | 23 | | |
| Dan Audick | OG | 6'3" | 244 | 22 | | |
| Conrad Dobler | OG | 6'3" | 253 | 26 | | 6 |
| Keith Wortman | OG-OT-C | 6'2" | 262 | 27 | | |
| Bob Young | OG | 6'2" | 279 | 34 | | |
| Tom Banks | C | 6'1" | 244 | 29 | | |
| Tom Brahaney | C | 6'2" | 246 | 25 | | |
| Bob Bell | DE | 6'4" | 257 | 29 | | |
| Ron Yankowski | DE | 6'5" | 258 | 30 | | |
| John Zook | DE | 6'5" | 254 | 29 | | |
| Charlie Davis | DT | 6'1" | 268 | 25 | | 6 |
| Mike Dawson | DT | 6'4" | 274 | 23 | | |
| Walt Patulski | DT | 6'6" | 267 | 27 | | |
| Kurt Allerman | LB | 6'3" | 222 | 22 | | |
| Mark Arneson | LB | 6'2" | 224 | 27 | 2 | |
| Tim Black | LB | 6'2" | 215 | 22 | | |
| Tim Kearney | LB | 6'2" | 225 | 26 | | |
| Marv Kellum | LB | 6'2" | 225 | 25 | 1 | |
| Steve Neils | LB | 6'2" | 218 | 26 | | |
| Eric Williams | LB | 6'2" | 217 | 22 | | |
| Carl Allen | DB | 6' | 185 | 21 | 1 | |
| Bill Bradley | DB | 5'11" | 190 | 30 | | |
| Rondy Colbert | DB | 5'9" | 165 | 23 | | |
| Robert Giblin | DB | 6'2" | 210 | 24 | | |
| Lee Nelson | DB | 5'10" | 183 | 23 | 4 | |
| Ken Reaves | DB | 6'3" | 208 | 32 | 2 | |
| Mike Sensibaugh | DB | 5'11" | 190 | 28 | 3 | 6 |
| Jeff Severson | DB | 6'1" | 185 | 27 | 1 | |
| Perry Smith | DB | 6'1" | 198 | 26 | | |
| Roger Wehrli | DB | 6'1" | 193 | 29 | 5 | |
| Billy Donckers | QB | 6'1" | 207 | 26 | | |
| Jim Hart | QB | 6'2" | 210 | 33 | | |
| Steve Pisarkiewicz | QB | 6'2" | 205 | 23 | | |
| Steve Jones | HB | 6' | 198 | 26 | | 18 |
| Jerry Latin | HB | 5'10" | 186 | 24 | | 12 |
| Terry Metcalf | HB | 5'10" | 185 | 25 | | 36 |
| Wayne Morris | FB | 6' | 208 | 23 | | 54 |
| Jim Otis | FB | 6' | 226 | 29 | | 12 |
| Mel Gray | WR | 5'9" | 178 | 28 | | 30 |
| Ike Harris | WR | 6'3" | 205 | 24 | | 18 |
| Ken Stone | WR-DB | 6'1" | 180 | 26 | | |
| Pat Tilley | WR | 5'10" | 171 | 24 | | |
| J.V. Cain | TE | 6'4" | 221 | 26 | | 12 |
| Jackie Smith | TE | 6'4" | 226 | 37 | | 6 |
| Jim Bakken | K | 6' | 198 | 36 | | 56 |
| Duane Carrell (from NYJ) | K | 5'10" | 178 | 27 | | |
| Terry Joyce | K | 6'6" | 227 | 23 | | |

Ray White – Knee Injury

## PHILADELPHIA EAGLES 5-9 Dick Vermeil

| Scores of Each Game | | |
|---|---|---|
| 13 | TAMPA BAY | 3 |
| 0 | Los Angeles | 20 |
| 13 | Detroit | 17 |
| 28 | N.Y. Giants | 10 |
| 17 | ST. LOUIS | 21 |
| 10 | DALLAS | 16 |
| 17 | Washington | 23 |
| 28 | NEW ORLEANS | 7 |
| 14 | WASHINGTON | 17 |
| 16 | St. Louis | 21 |
| 6 | New England | 14 |
| 14 | Dallas | 24 |
| 17 | N.Y. GIANTS | 14 |
| 27 | N.Y. JETS | 0 |

| Use Name | Pos. | Hgt | Wgt | Age | Int | Pts |
|---|---|---|---|---|---|---|
| Ed George | OT | 6'4" | 270 | 31 | | |
| Donnie Green | OT | 6'7" | 261 | 29 | | |
| Dennis Nelson | OT | 6'5" | 260 | 31 | | |
| Stan Walters | OT | 6'6" | 270 | 29 | | |
| Wade Key | OG | 6'4" | 245 | 30 | | |
| Tom Luken | OG | 6'3" | 253 | 27 | | |
| Jerry Sisemore | OG | 6'4" | 260 | 26 | | |
| Dennis Franks | C | 6'1" | 236 | 24 | | |
| Guy Morriss | C | 6'4" | 255 | 26 | | |
| Lem Burnham | DE | 6'4" | 228 | 30 | | |
| Carl Hairston | DE | 6'3" | 245 | 24 | | |
| Manny Sistrunk | DE | 6'5" | 276 | 30 | | |
| Art Thoms | DE-NT | 6'5" | 250 | 30 | | |
| Johnny Jackson | NT | 6'2" | 250 | 24 | | |
| Charles Johnson | NT | 6'3" | 262 | 25 | | |
| Pete Lazetich | NT | 6'3" | 245 | 27 | | |
| Bill Bergey | LB | 6'2" | 245 | 32 | 2 | |
| John Bunting | LB | 6'1" | 220 | 27 | | |
| Tom Ehlers | LB | 6'2" | 218 | 25 | | |
| Frank LeMaster | LB | 6'2" | 231 | 25 | | |
| Drew Mahalic | LB | 6'4" | 225 | 24 | | |
| James Reed | LB | 6'2" | 230 | 22 | | |
| Terry Tautolo | LB | 6'2" | 235 | 23 | | |
| Herman Edwards | DB | 6' | 194 | 23 | 6 | |
| Eric Johnson | DB | 6'1" | 192 | 25 | | |
| Randy Logan | DB | 6'1" | 195 | 26 | 5 | |
| Larry Marshall | DB | 5'10" | 195 | 27 | | |
| Mark Mitchell | DB | 6'1" | 180 | 22 | | |
| John Outlaw | DB | 5'10" | 180 | 31 | 2 | |
| Deac Sanders | DB | 6'1" | 178 | 27 | 6 | |
| Roman Gabriel | QB | 6'4" | 225 | 37 | | |
| Ron Jaworski | QB | 6'2" | 195 | 26 | | 30 |
| John Walton | QB | 6'2" | 210 | 29 | | |
| Herb Lusk | HB | 6' | 190 | 24 | | 18 |
| Wilbert Montgomery | HB | 5'10" | 195 | 22 | | 18 |
| Tom Sullivan | HB | 6' | 190 | 27 | | 12 |
| James Betterson | FB | 6' | 210 | 23 | | 6 |
| Cleveland Franklin | FB | 6'2" | 216 | 22 | | |
| Mike Hogan | FB | 6'2" | 215 | 22 | | 6 |
| Harold Carmichael | WR | 6'7" | 225 | 27 | | 42 |
| Wally Henry | WR | 5'8" | 170 | 22 | | |
| Vince Papale | WR | 6'2" | 195 | 31 | | |
| Larry Sievers | WR | 6'4" | 204 | 23 | | |
| Charlie Smith | WR | 6'1" | 185 | 27 | | 24 |
| Keith Krepfle | TE | 6'3" | 225 | 25 | | 18 |
| Richard Osborne | TE | 6'3" | 230 | 23 | | |
| Ove Johannson | K | 5'10" | 175 | 29 | | 4 |
| Spike Jones | K | 6'2" | 195 | 30 | | |
| Nick Mike-Mayer (from ATL) | K | 5'8" | 187 | 27 | | 44 |
| Horst Muhlmann | K | 6'1" | 211 | 37 | | 26 |

## NEW YORK GIANTS 5-9 John McVay

| Scores of Each Game | | |
|---|---|---|
| 20 | WASHINGTON | 17 |
| 21 | Dallas | 41 |
| 3 | Atlanta | 17 |
| 10 | PHILADELPHIA | 28 |
| 20 | SAN FRANCISCO | 17 |
| 17 | Washington | 6 |
| 0 | St. Louis | 28 |
| 13 | DALLAS | 24 |
| 10 | Tampa Bay | 0 |
| 7 | CLEVELAND | 21 |
| 13 | Cincinnati | 30 |
| 27 | ST. LOUIS | 7 |
| 14 | Philadelphia | 17 |
| 9 | CHICAGO | *12 |

| Use Name | Pos. | Hgt | Wgt | Age | Int | Pts |
|---|---|---|---|---|---|---|
| Mike Gibbons | OT | 6'4" | 262 | 26 | | |
| Gordon Gravelle | OT | 6'5" | 252 | 28 | | |
| Ron Mikolajczyk | OG | 6'3" | 275 | 27 | | |
| Tom Mullen | OT | 6'3" | 250 | 25 | | |
| Brad Benson | OG | 6'3" | 255 | 21 | | |
| Bill Ellenbogen | OG-OT | 6'5" | 255 | 26 | | |
| John Hicks | OG | 6'2" | 258 | 26 | | |
| Doug Van Horn | OG-OT | 6'2" | 243 | 33 | | |
| Karl Chandler | C | 6'5" | 250 | 25 | | |
| Ralph Hill | C | 6'1" | 245 | 27 | | |
| Jack Gregory | DE | 6'6" | 250 | 32 | | |
| Gary Jeter | DE | 6'4" | 250 | 22 | | |
| George Martin | DE | 6'4" | 245 | 24 | 1 | 6 |
| Troy Archer | DT | 6'4" | 250 | 22 | | |
| John Mendenhall | DT | 6'1" | 255 | 28 | | |
| Jim Pietrzak | DT | 6'5" | 260 | 24 | | |
| J.T. Turner | DT | 6'3" | 250 | 24 | | |
| Harry Carson | LB | 6'2" | 235 | 23 | | |
| Brian Kelley | LB | 6'3" | 222 | 26 | 1 | |
| Dan Lloyd | LB | 6'2" | 225 | 23 | | |
| Frank Marion | LB | 6'3" | 230 | 26 | | |
| Andy Selfridge | LB | 6'4" | 220 | 28 | | |
| Brad Van Pelt | LB | 6'5" | 235 | 26 | 2 | |
| Bill Bryant | DB | 5'11" | 195 | 26 | 3 | 6 |
| Ernie Jones | DB | 6'3" | 180 | 24 | 1 | |
| Larry Mallory | DB | 5'11" | 185 | 25 | 1 | |
| Clyde Powers | DB | 6'1" | 195 | 26 | 1 | |
| Beasley Reece | DB | 6'1" | 186 | 23 | | |
| Ray Rhodes | DB | 5'11" | 185 | 26 | 2 | |
| Jim Stienke | DB | 5'11" | 182 | 26 | | |
| Randy Dean | QB | 6'3" | 195 | 22 | | |
| Jerry Golsteyn | QB | 6'4" | 210 | 23 | | |
| Joe Pisarcik | QB | 6'4" | 220 | 25 | | 12 |
| Gordon Bell | HB | 5'9" | 180 | 23 | | |
| Bob Hammond | HB | 5'10" | 170 | 25 | | 24 |
| Harold Hart | HB | 6' | 211 | 24 | | |
| Doug Kotar | HB | 5'11" | 203 | 26 | | 12 |
| Larry Csonka | FB | 6'3" | 233 | 30 | | 6 |
| Willie Spencer | FB | 6'3" | 235 | 24 | | 18 |
| Larry Watkins | FB | 6'2" | 230 | 30 | | |
| Ed Marshall | WR | 6'5" | 200 | 29 | | |
| Emery Moorehead | WR | 6'2" | 210 | 23 | | 6 |
| Johnny Perkins | WR | 6'2" | 205 | 24 | | |
| Jim Robinson | WR | 5'9" | 170 | 24 | | 18 |
| Boyd Brown | TE | 6'4" | 216 | 25 | | |
| Al Dixon | TE | 6'5" | 220 | 23 | | |
| Gary Shirk | TE | 6'1" | 220 | 27 | | 12 |
| Joe Danelo | K | 5'9" | 166 | 23 | | 61 |
| Dave Jennings | K | 6'4" | 203 | 25 | | |

Dave Gallagher – Voluntary Retirement
Dick Leavitt – Knee Injury

Marsh White – Wrist Injury

*—Overtime

## DALLAS COWBOYS

### Rushing

| Last Name | No | Yds | Avg | TD |
|---|---|---|---|---|
| Dorsett | 208 | 1007 | 4.8 | 12 |
| Newhouse | 180 | 721 | 4.0 | 3 |
| P. Pearson | 89 | 341 | 3.8 | 1 |
| Staubach | 51 | 171 | 3.4 | 1 |
| Dennison | 12 | 60 | 5.0 | 1 |
| Brinson | 8 | 28 | 3.5 | 1 |
| D. Pearson | 2 | 22 | 11.0 | 0 |
| Laidlaw | 9 | 15 | 1.7 | 0 |
| DuPree | 3 | 9 | 3.0 | 0 |
| D. White | 1 | -2 | -2.0 | 0 |
| Johnson | 1 | -3 | -3.0 | 0 |

### Receiving

| Last Name | No | Yds | Avg | TD |
|---|---|---|---|---|
| D. Pearson | 48 | 870 | 18 | 0 |
| P. Pearson | 46 | 535 | 12 | 4 |
| Dorsett | 29 | 273 | 9 | 1 |
| DuPree | 28 | 347 | 12 | 3 |
| Richards | 17 | 225 | 13 | 3 |
| Newhouse | 16 | 106 | 7 | 1 |
| Johnson | 12 | 135 | 11 | 1 |
| Saldi | 11 | 108 | 10 | 2 |
| Laidlaw | 5 | 60 | 12 | 1 |
| Hill | 2 | 21 | 11 | 0 |
| Dennison | 1 | 9 | 9 | 0 |

### Punt Returns

| Last Name | No | Yds | Avg | TD |
|---|---|---|---|---|
| Johnson | 50 | 423 | 8 | 0 |
| Hill | 10 | 124 | 12 | 0 |
| Harris | 1 | -2 | -2 | 0 |

### Kickoff Returns

| Last Name | No | Yds | Avg | TD |
|---|---|---|---|---|
| Johnson | 22 | 536 | 24 | 0 |
| Brinson | 17 | 409 | 24 | 0 |
| Hill | 3 | 64 | 21 | 0 |
| Dennison | 1 | 30 | 30 | 0 |
| DuPree | 0 | 24 | — | 0 |
| Henderson | 1 | 8 | 8 | 0 |

### Passing

| Last Name | Att | Comp | % | Yds | Yd/Att | TD | Int-% | RK |
|---|---|---|---|---|---|---|---|---|
| Staubach | 361 | 210 | 58 | 2620 | 7.3 | 18 | 9- 2 | 1 |
| D. White | 10 | 4 | 40 | 35 | 3.5 | 0 | 1- 10 | |
| Dorsett | 1 | 1 | 100 | 34 | 34.0 | 0 | 0- 0 | |

### Punting

| Last Name | No | Avg |
|---|---|---|
| D. White | 80 | 39.6 |
| Herrera | 2 | 22.0 |

### Kicking

| Last Name | XP | Att | % | FG | Att | % |
|---|---|---|---|---|---|---|
| Herrera | 39 | 41 | 95 | 18 | 29 | 62 |

## WASHINGTON REDSKINS

### Rushing

| Last Name | No | Yds | Avg | TD |
|---|---|---|---|---|
| Thomas | 228 | 806 | 3.5 | 3 |
| Harmon | 94 | 310 | 3.3 | 0 |
| Hill | 69 | 257 | 3.7 | 0 |
| Riggins | 68 | 203 | 3.0 | 0 |
| Theismann | 29 | 149 | 5.1 | 1 |
| Kilmer | 10 | 20 | 2.0 | 0 |
| Brunet | 3 | 6 | 2.0 | 0 |
| Jones | 1 | 1 | 1.0 | 0 |

### Receiving

| Last Name | No | Yds | Avg | TD |
|---|---|---|---|---|
| Fuggett | 36 | 631 | 17 | 5 |
| Grant | 34 | 480 | 14 | 3 |
| Thomas | 28 | 245 | 9 | 2 |
| Buggs | 26 | 341 | 13 | 1 |
| Hill | 18 | 154 | 9 | 1 |
| Taylor | 14 | 158 | 11 | 0 |
| Harmon | 14 | 119 | 9 | 1 |
| Riggins | 7 | 95 | 14 | 2 |
| Jones | 5 | 55 | 11 | 0 |
| Smith | 1 | 6 | 6 | 0 |

### Punt Returns

| Last Name | No | Yds | Avg | TD |
|---|---|---|---|---|
| Brown | 57 | 452 | 8 | 0 |

### Kickoff Returns

| Last Name | No | Yds | Avg | TD |
|---|---|---|---|---|
| Brown | 34 | 852 | 25 | 0 |
| Murphy | 3 | 44 | 15 | 0 |
| Tillman | 3 | 39 | 13 | 0 |
| Jones | 2 | 42 | 21 | 0 |
| Brunet | 2 | 40 | 20 | 0 |
| Moss | 2 | 35 | 18 | 0 |
| Harmon | 1 | 18 | 18 | 0 |
| Buggs | 0 | 17 | — | 0 |

### Passing

| Last Name | Att | Comp | % | Yds | Yd/Att | TD | Int-% | RK |
|---|---|---|---|---|---|---|---|---|
| Kilmer | 201 | 99 | 49 | 1187 | 5.9 | 8 | 7- 4 | 6 |
| Thiesmann | 182 | 84 | 46 | 1097 | 6.0 | 7 | 9- 5 | 11 |

### Punting

| Last Name | No | Avg |
|---|---|---|
| Bragg | 91 | 38.5 |

### Kicking

| Last Name | XP | Att | % | FG | Att | % |
|---|---|---|---|---|---|---|
| Moseley | 19 | 19 | 100 | 21 | 37 | 57 |

## ST. LOUIS CARDINALS

### Rushing

| Last Name | No | Yds | Avg | TD |
|---|---|---|---|---|
| Metcalf | 149 | 739 | 5.0 | 4 |
| Morris | 165 | 661 | 4.0 | 8 |
| Otis | 99 | 334 | 3.4 | 2 |
| Latin | 56 | 208 | 3.7 | 2 |
| Jones | 24 | 77 | 3.2 | 3 |
| Wehrli | 1 | 19 | 19.0 | 0 |
| Hart | 11 | 18 | 1.6 | 0 |
| Gray | 1 | -1 | -1.0 | 0 |
| Joyce | 1 | -13 | -13.0 | 0 |
| Carrell | 2 | -15 | -7.5 | 0 |

### Receiving

| Last Name | No | Yds | Avg | TD |
|---|---|---|---|---|
| Harris | 40 | 547 | 14 | 3 |
| Gray | 38 | 782 | 21 | 5 |
| Metcalf | 34 | 403 | 12 | 2 |
| Cain | 25 | 328 | 13 | 2 |
| Morris | 24 | 222 | 9 | 1 |
| Jones | 12 | 66 | 6 | 0 |
| Latin | 9 | 89 | 10 | 0 |
| Tilley | 5 | 64 | 13 | 0 |
| J. Smith | 5 | 49 | 10 | 1 |
| Otis | 2 | 18 | 9 | 0 |
| Stone | 1 | 40 | 40 | 0 |

### Punt Returns

| Last Name | No | Yds | Avg | TD |
|---|---|---|---|---|
| Metcalf | 14 | 108 | 8 | 0 |
| Tilley | 13 | 111 | 9 | 0 |
| Bradley | 11 | 77 | 7 | 0 |
| Nelson | 1 | 4 | 4 | 0 |
| Severson | 1 | 0 | 0 | 0 |

### Kickoff Returns

| Last Name | No | Yds | Avg | TD |
|---|---|---|---|---|
| Metcalf | 32 | 772 | 24 | 0 |
| Jones | 8 | 132 | 17 | 0 |
| Bradley | 7 | 75 | 19 | 0 |
| Latin | 3 | 79 | 26 | 0 |
| Nelson | 3 | 68 | 23 | 0 |
| Allerman | 2 | 39 | 20 | 0 |
| Morris | 2 | 39 | 20 | 0 |
| Otis | 1 | 16 | 16 | 0 |
| Wortman | 1 | 15 | 15 | 0 |
| Oates | 1 | 11 | 11 | 0 |
| J. Smith | 1 | 15 | 15 | 0 |
| P. Smith | 1 | 10 | 10 | 0 |

### Passing

| Last Name | Att | Comp | % | Yds | Yd/Att | TD | Int-% | RK |
|---|---|---|---|---|---|---|---|---|
| Hart | 355 | 186 | 52 | 2542 | 7.2 | 13 | 20- 6 | 7 |
| Donckers | 5 | 5 | 100 | 38 | 7.6 | 0 | 0- 0 | |
| Metcalf | 5 | 3 | 60 | 27 | 5.4 | 1 | 1- 20 | |
| Joyce | 1 | 1 | 100 | 1 | 1.0 | 0 | 0- 0 | |

### Punting

| Last Name | No | Avg |
|---|---|---|
| Carrell | 63 | 36.7 |
| Joyce | 22 | 38.7 |

### Kicking

| Last Name | XP | Att | % | FG | Att | % |
|---|---|---|---|---|---|---|
| Bakken | 35 | 36 | 97 | 7 | 16 | 44 |

## PHILADELPHIA EAGLES

### Rushing

| Last Name | No | Yds | Avg | TD |
|---|---|---|---|---|
| Hogan | 155 | 546 | 3.5 | 0 |
| Sullivan | 125 | 363 | 2.9 | 0 |
| Betterson | 62 | 233 | 3.8 | 1 |
| Lusk | 52 | 229 | 4.4 | 2 |
| Montgomery | 45 | 183 | 4.1 | 2 |
| Jaworski | 40 | 127 | 3.2 | 5 |
| Lemaster | 1 | 30 | 30.0 | 0 |
| Smith | 2 | 13 | 6.5 | 0 |
| Franklin | 1 | 0 | 0.0 | 0 |
| Henry | 1 | -2 | -2.0 | 0 |

### Receiving

| Last Name | No | Yds | Avg | TD |
|---|---|---|---|---|
| Carmichael | 46 | 665 | 15 | 7 |
| Smith | 33 | 464 | 14 | 4 |
| Krepfle | 27 | 530 | 20 | 3 |
| Sullivan | 26 | 223 | 9 | 2 |
| Hogan | 19 | 118 | 6 | 1 |
| Lusk | 5 | 102 | 20 | 1 |
| Betterson | 4 | 41 | 10 | 0 |
| Montgomery | 3 | 18 | 6 | 0 |
| Henry | 2 | 16 | 8 | 0 |
| Papale | 1 | 15 | 15 | 0 |
| Osborne | 1 | 6 | 6 | 0 |

### Punt Returns

| Last Name | No | Yds | Avg | TD |
|---|---|---|---|---|
| Marshall | 46 | 489 | 11 | 0 |
| Henry | 2 | 25 | 13 | 0 |
| Mitchell | 2 | 4 | 2 | 0 |

### Kickoff Returns

| Last Name | No | Yds | Avg | TD |
|---|---|---|---|---|
| Montgomery | 23 | 619 | 27 | 1 |
| Marshall | 20 | 455 | 23 | 0 |
| Lusk | 1 | 23 | 23 | 0 |
| Betterson | 1 | 13 | 13 | 0 |

### Passing

| Last Name | Att | Comp | % | Yds | Yd/Att | TD | Int-% | RK |
|---|---|---|---|---|---|---|---|---|
| Jaworski | 346 | 166 | 48 | 2183 | 6.3 | 18 | 21- 6 | 10 |
| Gabriel | 3 | 1 | 33 | 15 | 5.0 | 0 | 0- 0 | |

### Punting

| Last Name | No. | Avg |
|---|---|---|
| Jones | 93 | 37.2 |
| Mike-Mayer | 1 | 23.0 |

### Kicking

| Last Name | XP | Att | % | FG | Att | % |
|---|---|---|---|---|---|---|
| Muhlmann | 17 | 19 | 89 | 3 | 8 | 38 |
| Mike-Mayer | 14 | 14 | 100 | 10 | 22 | 45 |
| Johansson | 1 | 3 | 33 | 1 | 4 | 25 |

## NEW YORK GIANTS

### Rushing

| Last Name | No | Yds | Avg | TD |
|---|---|---|---|---|
| Hammond | 154 | 577 | 3.7 | 3 |
| Kotar | 132 | 480 | 3.6 | 2 |
| Csonka | 134 | 464 | 3.5 | 1 |
| Spencer | 62 | 184 | 3.0 | 3 |
| Watkins | 19 | 71 | 3.7 | 0 |
| Bell | 16 | 63 | 3.9 | 0 |
| Pisarcik | 27 | 57 | 2.1 | 2 |
| Moorehead | 1 | 5 | 5.0 | 0 |
| Golsteyn | 3 | -4 | -1.3 | 0 |

### Receiving

| Last Name | No | Yds | Avg | TD |
|---|---|---|---|---|
| Robinson | 22 | 422 | 19 | 3 |
| Perkins | 20 | 279 | 14 | 0 |
| Hammond | 19 | 136 | 7 | 0 |
| Shirk | 16 | 280 | 18 | 2 |
| Kotar | 15 | 73 | 5 | 0 |
| Moorehead | 12 | 143 | 12 | 1 |
| Marshall | 7 | 178 | 25 | 0 |
| Dixon | 6 | 78 | 13 | 0 |
| Bell | 4 | 33 | 8 | 0 |
| Spencer | 4 | 20 | 5 | 0 |
| Csonka | 2 | 20 | 10 | 0 |
| Watkins | 1 | 9 | 9 | 0 |

### Punt Returns

| Last Name | No | Yds | Avg | TD |
|---|---|---|---|---|
| Hammond | 32 | 334 | 10 | 1 |
| Robinson | 7 | 87 | 12 | 0 |
| Steinke | 5 | 30 | 6 | 0 |
| Bell | 1 | 0 | 0 | 0 |
| Reece | 1 | -5 | -5 | 0 |

### Kickoff Returns

| Last Name | No | Yds | Avg | TD |
|---|---|---|---|---|
| Hammond | 19 | 419 | 22 | 0 |
| Bell | 12 | 235 | 20 | 0 |
| Reece | 7 | 159 | 23 | 0 |
| Moorehead | 4 | 65 | 16 | 0 |
| Spencer | 3 | 44 | 15 | 0 |
| Shirk | 3 | 38 | 13 | 0 |
| Kotar | 2 | 36 | 18 | 0 |
| Kelley | 1 | 20 | 20 | 0 |
| Hill | 1 | 11 | 11 | 0 |
| Selfridge | 1 | 9 | 9 | 0 |
| Mallory | 1 | 0 | 0 | 0 |

### Passing

| Last Name | Att | Comp | % | Yds | Yd/Att | TD | Int-% | RK |
|---|---|---|---|---|---|---|---|---|
| Pisarcik | 241 | 103 | 43 | 1346 | 5.6 | 4 | 14- 6 | 13 |
| Golsteyn | 70 | 31 | 44 | 416 | 5.9 | 2 | 8- 11 | |

### Punting

| Last Name | No | Avg |
|---|---|---|
| Jennings | 100 | 39.9 |

### Kicking

| Last Name | XP | Att | % | FG | Att | % |
|---|---|---|---|---|---|---|
| Danelo | 19 | 20 | 95 | 14 | 23 | 61 |

# 1977 N.F.C. — Central Division

## MINNESOTA VIKINGS 9-5 Bud Grant

| Scores of Each Game | | |
|---|---|---|
| 10 | DALLAS | 16 |
| 9 | Tampa Bay | 3 |
| 19 | GREEN BAY | 7 |
| 14 | DETROIT | 7 |
| 22 | CHICAGO | 16 |
| 3 | Los Angeles | 35 |
| 14 | Atlanta | 7 |
| 7 | ST. LOUIS | 27 |
| 42 | CINCINNATI | 10 |
| 7 | Chicago | 10 |
| 13 | Green Bay | 6 |
| 28 | SAN FRANCISCO | 27 |
| 13 | Oakland | 35 |
| 30 | Detroit | 21 |

| Use Name | Pos. | Hgt | Wgt | Age | Int | Pts |
|---|---|---|---|---|---|---|
| Bart Buetow | OT | 6'5" | 250 | 26 | | |
| Steve Riley | OT | 6'6" | 258 | 24 | | |
| Ron Yary | OT | 6'6" | 255 | 31 | | |
| Charlie Goodrum | OG | 6'3" | 256 | 27 | | |
| Wes Hamilton | OG | 6'3" | 255 | 24 | | |
| Dennis Swilley | OG-OT | 6'3" | 241 | 22 | | |
| Ed White | OG-OT | 6'2" | 270 | 30 | | |
| Doug Dumler | C | 6'3" | 242 | 26 | | |
| Mick Tinglehoff | C | 6'1" | 240 | 37 | | |
| Carl Eller | DE | 6'6" | 247 | 35 | | 2 |
| Joey Jackson | DE-DT | 6'4" | 262 | 28 | | |
| Jim Marshall | DE | 6'3" | 240 | 39 | | |
| Mark Mullaney | DE | 6'6" | 242 | 24 | | |
| Alan Page | DT | 6'5" | 245 | 32 | | |
| Doug Sutherland | DT | 6'3" | 250 | 29 | | |
| James White | DT | 6'3" | 263 | 23 | | |
| Matt Blair | LB | 6'5" | 229 | 26 | 1 | 6 |
| Wally Hilgenberg | LB | 6'3" | 229 | 34 | | |
| Fred McNeill | LB | 6'2" | 229 | 25 | 1 | |
| Jeff Siemon | LB | 6'2" | 237 | 27 | 1 | |
| Scott Studwell | LB | 6'2" | 224 | 23 | 1 | |
| Nate Allen | DB | 5'10" | 174 | 29 | 1 | |
| Joe Blahak | DB | 5'9" | 185 | 27 | | |
| Bobby Bryant | DB | 6' | 170 | 33 | 4 | |
| Tom Hannon | DB | 5'11" | 193 | 22 | | |
| Paul Krause | DB | 6'3" | 205 | 35 | 2 | |
| Phil Wise | DB | 6' | 193 | 28 | 1 | |
| Jeff Wright | DB | 5'11" | 190 | 28 | 1 | |
| Nate Wright | DB | 5'11" | 180 | 29 | 3 | 6 |
| Tommy Kramer | QB | 6'1" | 199 | 22 | | |
| Bob Lee | QB | 6'2" | 195 | 31 | | |
| Fran Tarkenton | QB | 6'1" | 185 | 37 | | |
| Chuck Foreman | HB | 6'2" | 207 | 26 | | 54 |
| Sammy Johnson | HB-FB | 6' | 226 | 24 | | 12 |
| Manfred Moore | HB | 6' | 200 | 26 | | |
| Mark Kellar | FB | 6' | 225 | 25 | | |
| Brent McClanahan | FB | 5'10" | 202 | 26 | | 18 |
| Robert Miller | FB | 5'11" | 204 | 24 | | |
| Bob Grim | WR | 6' | 188 | 32 | | |
| Ahmad Rashad | WR | 6'2" | 200 | 27 | | 12 |
| Sammy White | WR | 5'11" | 189 | 23 | | 54 |
| Steve Craig | TE | 6'3" | 231 | 26 | | |
| Bob Tucker (from NYG) | TE | 6'3" | 230 | 32 | | 12 |
| Stu Voigt | TE | 6'1" | 225 | 29 | | 6 |
| Neil Clabo | K | 6'2" | 200 | 24 | | |
| Fred Cox | K | 5'10" | 200 | 38 | | 49 |

## CHICAGO BEARS 9-5 Jack Pardee

| Scores of Each Game | | |
|---|---|---|
| 30 | DETROIT | 20 |
| 13 | St. Louis | 16 |
| 24 | NEW ORLEANS | 42 |
| 24 | LOS ANGELES | 23 |
| 16 | Minnesota | 22 |
| 10 | ATLANTA | 16 |
| 26 | Green Bay | 0 |
| 0 | Houston | 47 |
| 28 | KANSAS CITY | 27 |
| 10 | MINNESOTA | 7 |
| 31 | Detroit | 14 |
| 10 | Tampa Bay | 0 |
| 21 | GREEN BAY | 10 |
| 12 | N.Y. Giants | *9 |

| Use Name | Pos. | Hgt | Wgt | Age | Int | Pts |
|---|---|---|---|---|---|---|
| Ted Albrecht | OT-OG | 6'4" | 253 | 22 | | |
| Dan Jiggetts | OT | 6'4" | 276 | 23 | | |
| Dennis Lick | OT | 6'3" | 268 | 23 | | |
| Jeff Sevy | OT-DT-DE | 6'5" | 261 | 26 | | |
| Fred Dean | OG | 6'3" | 253 | 22 | | |
| Noah Jackson | OG | 6'2" | 273 | 26 | | |
| Revie Sorey | OG | 6'2" | 259 | 23 | | |
| Dan Neal | C-OG | 6'4" | 248 | 28 | | |
| Dan Peiffer | C | 6'3" | 251 | 26 | | |
| Mike Hartenstine | DE | 6'3" | 257 | 24 | | |
| Jerry Meyers | DE-DT | 6'4" | 245 | 23 | | |
| Billy Newsome | DE | 6'4" | 250 | 29 | | |
| Wally Chambers | DT-DE | 6'6" | 259 | 26 | | |
| Jim Osborne | DT | 6'3" | 251 | 27 | | |
| Don Rydalch | DT | 6'4" | 257 | 25 | | |
| Roger Stilwell | DT-DE | 6'6" | 258 | 25 | | |
| Waymond Bryant | LB | 6'3" | 239 | 25 | | |
| Doug Buffone | LB | 6'1" | 227 | 33 | 1 | |
| Gary Campbell | LB | 6'1" | 218 | 25 | | |
| Tom Hicks | LB | 6'4" | 225 | 24 | 1 | |
| Jerry Muckensturm | LB | 6'4" | 226 | 23 | | |
| Don Rives | LB | 6'2" | 231 | 26 | | |
| Mel Rogers | LB | 6'2" | 230 | 30 | | |
| Craig Clemons | DB | 5'11" | 191 | 28 | | |
| Allan Ellis | DB | 5'10" | 175 | 26 | 6 | |
| Gary Fencik | DB | 6'1" | 192 | 23 | 4 | |
| Virgil Livers | DB | 5'9" | 178 | 25 | 2 | |
| Doug Plank | DB | 6' | 201 | 24 | 4 | |
| Terry Schmidt | DB | 6' | 176 | 25 | | |
| Mike Spivey | DB | 6' | 194 | 23 | | |
| Len Walterscheid | DB | 5'11" | 190 | 22 | | |
| Bob Avellini | QB | 6'2" | 206 | 24 | | 6 |
| Vince Evans | QB | 6'2" | 216 | 22 | | |
| Mike Phipps | QB | 6'2" | 211 | 29 | | |
| Art Best | HB | 6'1" | 205 | 24 | | |
| Johnny Musso | HB-FB | 5'11" | 196 | 27 | | 12 |
| Walter Payton | HB | 5'11" | 205 | 23 | | 96 |
| Robin Earl | FB | 6'5" | 247 | 22 | | 6 |
| Roland Harper | FB | 6' | 209 | 24 | | |
| Brian Baschnagel | WR | 6' | 193 | 23 | | 6 |
| Bo Rather | WR | 6'1" | 189 | 26 | | 12 |
| Steve Rivera (from SF) | WR | 5'11" | 183 | 23 | | |
| Steve Schubert | WR | 5'10" | 188 | 26 | | 6 |
| James Scott | WR | 6'1" | 191 | 25 | | 18 |
| Chuck Bradley (from SD) | TE | 6'6" | 239 | 26 | | |
| Greg Latta | TE | 6'3" | 230 | 24 | | 24 |
| Bob Parsons | TE | 6'4" | 232 | 27 | | |
| Bob Thomas | K | 5'10" | 174 | 25 | | 69 |

Lionel Antoine – Knee Injury
Larry Schreiber – Injury

## DETROIT LIONS 6-8 Tommy Hudspeth

| Scores of Each Game | | |
|---|---|---|
| 20 | Chicago | 30 |
| 23 | NEW ORLEANS | 19 |
| 17 | PHILADELPHIA | 13 |
| 7 | Minnesota | 14 |
| 10 | GREEN BAY | 6 |
| 7 | San Francisco | 28 |
| 0 | Dallas | 37 |
| 20 | SAN DIEGO | 0 |
| 6 | Atlanta | 17 |
| 16 | TAMPA BAY | 7 |
| 14 | CHICAGO | 31 |
| 9 | Green Bay | 10 |
| 13 | Baltimore | 10 |
| 21 | MINNESOTA | 30 |

| Use Name | Pos. | Hgt | Wgt | Age | Int | Pts |
|---|---|---|---|---|---|---|
| Rocky Freitas | OT | 6'6" | 275 | 31 | | |
| Craig Hertwig | OT | 6'8" | 270 | 25 | | |
| Dave Simonsen | OT | 6'6" | 248 | 25 | | |
| Jim Yarbrough | OT | 6'6" | 270 | 30 | | |
| Gary Anderson | OG | 6'3" | 250 | 21 | | |
| Lynn Boden | OG | 6'5" | 270 | 24 | | |
| Russ Bolinger | OG-OT | 6'5" | 255 | 22 | | |
| Mark Markovich | OG-C | 6'5" | 255 | 24 | | |
| Mel Mitchell | OG-C | 6'3" | 260 | 24 | | |
| Jon Morris | C | 6'4" | 250 | 34 | | |
| Jim Mitchell | DE | 6'3" | 250 | 28 | | |
| Ernie Price | DE | 6'4" | 245 | 26 | | |
| Ken Sanders | DE | 6'5" | 245 | 27 | | |
| John Woodcock | DE | 6'3" | 240 | 23 | | |
| Doug English | DT | 6'5" | 255 | 24 | | 2 |
| Larry Hand | DT | 6'4" | 245 | 37 | | |
| Herb Orvis | DT | 6'5" | 255 | 30 | | |
| Tony Daykin | LB | 6'1" | 215 | 22 | | |
| Jim Laslavic | LB | 6'2" | 240 | 25 | 1 | |
| Mike McGraw | LB | 6'2" | 225 | 23 | | |
| Paul Naumoff | LB | 6'1" | 215 | 32 | | |
| Ed O'Neil | LB | 6'3" | 235 | 24 | | 6 |
| Garth Ten Napel | LB | 6'1" | 215 | 23 | | |
| Charlie Weaver | LB | 6'2" | 225 | 28 | 1 | |
| Len Barney | DB | 6' | 190 | 31 | 3 | |
| James Hunter | DB | 6'3" | 195 | 23 | 6 | |
| Dick Jauron | DB | 6' | 190 | 26 | 3 | |
| Levi Johnson | DB | 6'3" | 200 | 26 | 2 | |
| Reggie Pinkney | DB | 5'11" | 190 | 22 | 2 | 6 |
| Randy Rich (to DEN) | DB | 5'10" | 175 | 23 | | |
| Charlie West | DB | 6'1" | 195 | 31 | 1 | |
| Walt Williams | DB | 6' | 185 | 23 | | |
| Gary Danielson | QB | 6'2" | 195 | 25 | | |
| Greg Landry | QB | 6'4" | 205 | 30 | | |
| Joe Reed | QB | 6'1" | 195 | 29 | | |
| Andy Bolton | HB | 6'1" | 205 | 23 | | |
| Dexter Bussey | HB | 6'1" | 210 | 25 | | 30 |
| Rick Kane | HB | 5'11" | 200 | 22 | | 24 |
| Eddie Payton (from CLE) | HB | 5'8" | 175 | 26 | | 12 |
| Glenn Capriola | FB | 5'11" | 219 | 22 | | |
| Marv Hubbard | FB | 6'1" | 235 | 31 | | 6 |
| Horace King | FB | 5'10" | 210 | 24 | | 6 |
| Luther Blue | WR | 5'11" | 190 | 21 | | 6 |
| J.D. Hill | WR | 6'1" | 185 | 28 | | 6 |
| Ray Jarvis | WR | 5'11" | 190 | 28 | | 6 |
| Leonard Thompson | WR-HB | 5'10" | 190 | 25 | | 12 |
| David Hill | TE | 6'2" | 220 | 23 | | 12 |
| Bill Larson (from WAS) | TE | 6'4" | 225 | 23 | | |
| Charlie Sanders | TE | 6'4" | 230 | 31 | | 6 |
| Mitch Hoopes | K | 6'1" | 204 | 24 | | |
| Steve Mike-Mayer | K | 6' | 180 | 29 | | 43 |
| Wilbur Summers | K | 6'4" | 220 | 23 | | |

Lawrence Gaines – Knee Injury
Ken Long – Injury
Benny Ricardo – Shoulder Injury

## GREEN BAY PACKERS 4-10 Bart Starr

| Scores of Each Game | | |
|---|---|---|
| 24 | New Orleans | 20 |
| 10 | HOUSTON | 16 |
| 7 | Minnesota | 19 |
| 7 | CINCINNATI | 17 |
| 6 | Detroit | 10 |
| 13 | Tampa Bay | 0 |
| 0 | CHICAGO | 26 |
| 10 | Kansas City | 20 |
| 6 | LOS ANGELES | 24 |
| 9 | Washington | 10 |
| 6 | MINNESOTA | 13 |
| 10 | DETROIT | 9 |
| 10 | Chicago | 21 |
| 16 | SAN FRANCISCO | 14 |

| Use Name | Pos. | Hgt | Wgt | Age | Int | Pts |
|---|---|---|---|---|---|---|
| Dick Himes | OT | 6'4" | 260 | 31 | | |
| Steve Knutson | OT-OG | 6'3" | 254 | 25 | | |
| Greg Koch | OT | 6'4" | 265 | 22 | | |
| Mark Koncar | OT | 6'5" | 268 | 24 | | |
| Dennis Havig | OG | 6'2" | 251 | 28 | | |
| Melvin Jackson | OG | 6'1" | 267 | 23 | | |
| Bob Kowalkowski | OG | 6'3" | 245 | 33 | | |
| Rick Scribner | OG | 6'4" | 257 | 21 | | |
| Darrel Gofourth | C | 6'3" | 260 | 22 | | |
| Larry McCarren | C | 6'3" | 248 | 25 | | |
| Bob Barber | DE-DT | 6'3" | 240 | 25 | | |
| Mike Butler | DE | 6'5" | 265 | 23 | | |
| Ezra Johnson | DE | 6'4" | 240 | 21 | | |
| Clarence Williams | DE-DT | 6'5" | 255 | 30 | | |
| Herb McMath | DT | 6'4" | 250 | 22 | | |
| Dave Pureifory | DT | 6'1" | 255 | 28 | | |
| Dave Roller | DT | 6'2" | 270 | 27 | | |
| Fred Carr | LB | 6'5" | 240 | 31 | 1 | |
| Jim Carter | LB | 6'3" | 245 | 28 | | |
| Jim Cheyunski | LB | 6'2" | 220 | 31 | | |
| Jim Gueno | LB | 6'2" | 220 | 23 | | |
| Don Hansen | LB | 6'3" | 228 | 33 | | |
| Blane Smith | LB | 6'3" | 238 | 23 | | |
| Tom Toner | LB | 6'3" | 235 | 27 | 1 | |
| Gary Weaver | LB | 6'1" | 225 | 28 | | |
| Willie Buchanon | DB | 6' | 190 | 26 | 2 | 6 |
| Johnnie Gray | DB | 5'11" | 185 | 23 | 1 | |
| Steve Luke | DB | 6'2" | 205 | 23 | 4 | |
| Mike McCoy | DB | 5'11" | 183 | 24 | 4 | |
| Tim Moresco | DB | 5'11" | 176 | 22 | | |
| Terry Randolph | DB | 6' | 184 | 22 | | |
| Steve Wagner | DB | 6'2" | 208 | 23 | | |
| Lynn Dickey | QB | 6'4" | 220 | 27 | | |
| Brian Dowling | QB | 6'2" | 210 | 30 | | |
| David Whitehurst | QB | 6'2" | 204 | 22 | | 6 |
| Will Harrell | HB | 5'9" | 182 | 24 | | 12 |
| Terdell Middleton | HB | 6' | 195 | 22 | | 6 |
| Nate Simpson | HB | 5'10" | 176 | 22 | | |
| Jim Culbreath | FB | 6' | 209 | 24 | | |
| Barty Smith | FB | 6'4" | 240 | 25 | | 18 |
| Eric Torkelson | FB | 6'2" | 194 | 25 | | 6 |
| Keith Hartwig (from MIN) | WR | 6' | 186 | 23 | | |
| Steve Odom | WR | 5'8" | 174 | 24 | | 18 |
| Ken Payne (to PHI) | WR | 6'1" | 185 | 26 | | 6 |
| Ollie Smith | WR | 6'2" | 200 | 28 | | |
| Aundra Thompson | WR-HB | 6' | 186 | 24 | | |
| Randy Vataha | WR | 5'10" | 170 | 28 | | |
| Bert Askon | TE | 6'3" | 225 | 31 | | |
| Rich McGeorge | TE | 6'4" | 230 | 28 | | 6 |
| David Beverly | K | 6'2" | 180 | 27 | | |
| Chester Marcol | K | 6' | 190 | 27 | | 50 |

## TAMPA BAY BUCCANEERS 2-12 John McKay

| Scores of Each Game | | |
|---|---|---|
| 3 | Philadelphia | 13 |
| 3 | MINNESOTA | 9 |
| 7 | Dallas | 23 |
| 0 | WASHINGTON | 10 |
| 23 | Seattle | 30 |
| 0 | GREEN BAY | 13 |
| 10 | San Francisco | 20 |
| 0 | Los Angeles | 31 |
| 0 | N.Y. GIANTS | 10 |
| 7 | Detroit | 16 |
| 0 | ATLANTA | 17 |
| 0 | CHICAGO | 10 |
| 33 | New Orleans | 14 |
| 17 | ST. LOUIS | 7 |

| Use Name | Pos. | Hgt | Wgt | Age | Int | Pts |
|---|---|---|---|---|---|---|
| Darryl Carlton | OT | 6'6" | 270 | 24 | | |
| Blanchard Carter | OT | 6'4" | 250 | 22 | | |
| Dave Reavis | OT-OG | 6'5" | 250 | 27 | | |
| Randy Johnson | OG | 6'2" | 255 | 24 | | |
| Dan Medlin | OG | 6'4" | 255 | 27 | | |
| Steve Wilson | OG-C | 6'3" | 265 | 23 | | |
| Jeff Winans | OG-OT | 6'5" | 265 | 25 | | |
| Dan Ryczek | C | 6'3" | 250 | 28 | | |
| Charley Hannah | DE | 6'5" | 250 | 22 | | |
| Glenn Robinson | DE | 6'6" | 245 | 25 | | |
| Council Rudolph | DE | 6'3" | 255 | 27 | | |
| Lee Roy Selmon | DE | 6'3" | 260 | 22 | | |
| Greg Johnson (from BAL & CHI) | DT NT-DE | 6'4" | 240 | 23 | 1 | 6 |
| Bill Kollar | NT | 6'4" | 256 | 24 | | |
| Dave Pear | NT | 6'2" | 250 | 24 | | |
| Rik Bonness | LB | 6'3" | 220 | 23 | | |
| Paul Harris | LB | 6'3" | 225 | 22 | | |
| Cecil Johnson | LB | 6'2" | 220 | 22 | 1 | |
| Mike Lemon | LB | 6'2" | 220 | 26 | | |
| Dave Lewis | LB | 6'4" | 230 | 22 | 2 | |
| Dewey Selmon | LB | 6'1" | 250 | 23 | 2 | |
| Richard Wood | LB | 6'2" | 215 | 24 | 4 | 12 |
| Cedric Brown | DB | 6'1" | 190 | 23 | 2 | |
| Mark Cotney | DB | 6' | 205 | 25 | 1 | |
| Curtis Jordan | DB | 6'2" | 185 | 23 | 1 | |
| Reggie Pierson | DB | 5'11" | 185 | 24 | | |
| Danny Reece | DB | 5'11" | 190 | 22 | | |
| Mike Washington | DB | 6'3" | 190 | 24 | 5 | 6 |
| Jeris White | DB | 5'11" | 180 | 24 | 4 | |
| Jeb Blount | QB | 6'3" | 200 | 23 | | |
| Parnell Dickinson | QB | 6'2" | 185 | 24 | | |
| Randy Hedberg | QB | 6'3" | 200 | 22 | | |
| Gary Huff | QB | 6'1" | 195 | 26 | | |
| Louis Carter | HB | 5'11" | 209 | 24 | | 12 |
| Anthony Davis | HB | 5'10" | 190 | 24 | | 6 |
| Jack Wender | HB | 6' | 210 | 23 | | |
| Ricky Bell | FB | 6'2" | 220 | 21 | | 6 |
| Jimmy DuBose | FB | 5'11" | 215 | 22 | | |
| Ed Williams | FB | 6'2" | 245 | 27 | | |
| Isaac Hagins | WR | 5'9" | 180 | 23 | | |
| John McKay | WR | 5'11" | 185 | 24 | | |
| Larry Mucker | WR | 5'11" | 190 | 22 | | |
| Morris Owens | WR | 6' | 190 | 24 | | 18 |
| George Ragsdale | WR-HB | 5'11" | 185 | 23 | | |
| Gary Butler | TE | 6'3" | 235 | 26 | | |
| Bob Moore | TE | 6'3" | 225 | 28 | | |
| Dana Nafziger | TE | 6'1" | 220 | 23 | | |
| Jack Novak | TE | 6'4" | 240 | 24 | | |
| Charles Waddell | TE | 6'5" | 235 | 24 | | |
| Dave Green | K | 5'11" | 205 | 27 | | 17 |
| Allan Leavitt | K | 5'11" | 176 | 21 | | 20 |
| Larry Swider | K | 6'2" | 193 | 22 | | |

Mike Boryla – Knee Injury

Howard Fest – Injury
Tody Smith – Injury

*—Overtime

## MINNESOTA VIKINGS

### RUSHING

| Last Name | No. | Yds | Avg | TD |
|---|---|---|---|---|
| Foreman | 270 | 1112 | 4.1 | 6 |
| McClanahan | 95 | 324 | 3.4 | 1 |
| Johnson | 55 | 217 | 3.9 | 2 |
| Miller | 46 | 152 | 3.3 | 0 |
| Kellar | 7 | 15 | 2.1 | 0 |
| Tarkenton | 15 | 6 | 0.4 | 0 |
| Kramer | 10 | 3 | 0.3 | 0 |
| Lee | 12 | −8 | −0.7 | 0 |

### RECEIVING

| Last Name | No. | Yds | Avg | TD |
|---|---|---|---|---|
| Rashad | 51 | 681 | 13 | 2 |
| S. White | 41 | 760 | 19 | 9 |
| Foreman | 38 | 308 | 8 | 3 |
| McClanahan | 34 | 276 | 8 | 2 |
| Miller | 27 | 246 | 9 | 0 |
| Voigt | 20 | 212 | 11 | 1 |
| Tucker | 15 | 200 | 13 | 2 |
| Johnson | 4 | 21 | 5 | 0 |
| Grim | 3 | 65 | 22 | 0 |
| Craig | 1 | 14 | 14 | 0 |

### PUNT RETURNS

| Last Name | No. | Yds | Avg | TD |
|---|---|---|---|---|
| Moore | 47 | 277 | 6 | 0 |
| Grim | 11 | 69 | 6 | 0 |

### KICKOFF RETURNS

| Last Name | No. | Yds | Avg | TD |
|---|---|---|---|---|
| Moore | 24 | 524 | 22 | 0 |
| S. White | 7 | 113 | 16 | 0 |
| Miller | 5 | 66 | 13 | 0 |
| McClanahan | 4 | 90 | 23 | 0 |
| Kellar | 3 | 37 | 12 | 0 |
| Grim | 1 | 4 | 4 | 0 |
| Swilley | 1 | 0 | 0 | 0 |

### PASSING – PUNTING – KICKING Statistics

| Last Name | Att | Comp | % | Yds | Yd/Att | TD | Int– % | RK |
|---|---|---|---|---|---|---|---|---|
| PASSING | | | | | | | | |
| Tarkenton | 258 | 155 | 60 | 1734 | 6.7 | 9 | 14– 5 | 3 |
| Lee | 72 | 42 | 58 | 522 | 7.3 | 4 | 4– 6 | |
| Kramer | 57 | 30 | 53 | 425 | 7.5 | 5 | 4– 7 | |
| Krause | 1 | 1 | 100 | 11 | 11.0 | 1 | 0– 0 | |

| Last Name | No | Avg |
|---|---|---|
| PUNTING | | |
| Clabo | 83 | 39.8 |

| Last Name | XP | Att | % | FG | Att | % |
|---|---|---|---|---|---|---|
| KICKING | | | | | | |
| Cox | 25 | 29 | 86 | 8 | 17 | 47 |

## CHICAGO BEARS

### RUSHING

| Last Name | No. | Yds | Avg | TD |
|---|---|---|---|---|
| Payton | 339 | 1852 | 5.5 | 14 |
| Harper | 120 | 457 | 3.8 | 0 |
| Earl | 56 | 233 | 4.2 | 1 |
| Musso | 37 | 132 | 3.6 | 2 |
| Avellini | 37 | 109 | 2.9 | 1 |
| Best | 6 | 20 | 3.3 | 0 |
| Rather | 2 | 8 | 4.0 | 0 |
| Baschnagel | 1 | 0 | 0.0 | 0 |
| Evans | 1 | 0 | 0.0 | 0 |

### RECEIVING

| Last Name | No. | Yds | Avg | TD |
|---|---|---|---|---|
| Scott | 50 | 809 | 16 | 3 |
| Payton | 27 | 269 | 10 | 2 |
| Latta | 26 | 335 | 13 | 4 |
| Harper | 19 | 142 | 8 | 0 |
| Rather | 17 | 294 | 17 | 2 |
| Schubert | 8 | 119 | 15 | 0 |
| Earl | 6 | 32 | 5 | 0 |
| Baschnagel | 4 | 50 | 13 | 0 |
| Musso | 3 | 13 | 4 | 0 |
| Rivera | 1 | 7 | 7 | 0 |

### PUNT RETURNS

| Last Name | No. | Yds | Avg | TD |
|---|---|---|---|---|
| Schubert | 31 | 291 | 9 | 1 |
| Walterscheid | 6 | 59 | 10 | 0 |
| Livers | 6 | 46 | 8 | 0 |
| Baschnagel | 3 | 54 | 18 | 0 |
| Rivera | 3 | 7 | 2 | 0 |
| Plank | 1 | 21 | 21 | 0 |

### KICKOFF RETURNS

| Last Name | No. | Yds | Avg | TD |
|---|---|---|---|---|
| Baschnagel | 23 | 557 | 24 | 0 |
| Evans | 13 | 253 | 19 | 0 |
| Best | 6 | 127 | 21 | 0 |
| Musso | 5 | 100 | 20 | 0 |
| Walterscheid | 3 | 59 | 20 | 0 |
| Harper | 3 | 44 | 15 | 0 |
| Payton | 2 | 95 | 48 | 0 |
| Earl | 2 | 38 | 19 | 0 |

### PASSING – PUNTING – KICKING Statistics

| Last Name | Att | Comp | % | Yds | Yd/Att | TD | Int– % | RK |
|---|---|---|---|---|---|---|---|---|
| PASSING | | | | | | | | |
| Avellini | 293 | 154 | 53 | 2004 | 6.8 | 11 | 18– 6 | 9 |
| Phipps | 5 | 3 | 60 | 5 | 1.0 | 0 | 0– 0 | |
| Parsons | 4 | 4 | 100 | 61 | 15.3 | 0 | 0– 0 | |
| Harper | 2 | 0 | 0 | 0 | 0.0 | 0 | 0– 0 | |
| Baschnagel | 1 | 0 | 0 | 0 | 0.0 | 0 | 0– 0 | |

| Last Name | No | Avg |
|---|---|---|
| PUNTING | | |
| Parsons | 80 | 40.4 |

| Last Name | XP | Att | % | FG | Att | % |
|---|---|---|---|---|---|---|
| KICKING | | | | | | |
| Thomas | 27 | 30 | 90 | 14 | 27 | 52 |

## DETROIT LIONS

### RUSHING

| Last Name | No. | Yds | Avg | TD |
|---|---|---|---|---|
| King | 155 | 521 | 3.4 | 1 |
| Kane | 124 | 421 | 3.4 | 4 |
| Bussey | 85 | 338 | 4.0 | 4 |
| Hubbard | 38 | 150 | 3.9 | 1 |
| Landry | 25 | 99 | 4.0 | 0 |
| Thompson | 31 | 91 | 2.9 | 1 |
| Danielson | 7 | 62 | 8.9 | 0 |
| Payton | 4 | 13 | 3.3 | 0 |
| D. Hill | 4 | 10 | 2.5 | 0 |
| Bolton | 3 | 4 | 1.3 | 0 |
| Reed | 1 | 3 | 3.0 | 0 |
| Summers | 1 | 0 | 0.0 | 0 |
| Blue | 1 | −6 | −6.0 | 0 |

### RECEIVING

| Last Name | No. | Yds | Avg | TD |
|---|---|---|---|---|
| King | 40 | 238 | 6 | 0 |
| D. Hill | 32 | 465 | 14 | 2 |
| Jarvis | 28 | 353 | 13 | 1 |
| J.D. Hill | 24 | 247 | 10 | 1 |
| Kane | 18 | 186 | 10 | 0 |
| C. Sanders | 14 | 170 | 12 | 1 |
| Bussey | 11 | 116 | 11 | 1 |
| Blue | 8 | 90 | 11 | 1 |
| Thompson | 7 | 42 | 6 | 0 |
| Hubbard | 6 | 36 | 6 | 0 |
| Payton | 2 | 10 | 5 | 0 |
| Bolton | 1 | 6 | 6 | 0 |

### PUNT RETURNS

| Last Name | No. | Yds | Avg | TD |
|---|---|---|---|---|
| Payton | 30 | 290 | 10 | 1 |
| Jauron | 11 | 41 | 4 | 0 |
| Rich | 2 | 18 | 9 | 0 |
| Kane | 1 | 13 | 13 | 0 |
| Blue | 1 | 0 | 0 | 0 |

### KICKOFF RETURNS

| Last Name | No. | Yds | Avg | TD |
|---|---|---|---|---|
| Payton | 22 | 548 | 25 | 1 |
| Kane | 16 | 376 | 24 | 0 |
| Bolton | 6 | 86 | 14 | 0 |
| Thompson | 5 | 84 | 17 | 0 |
| Rich | 5 | 73 | 15 | 0 |
| Hunter | 4 | 95 | 24 | 0 |
| Blue | 1 | 24 | 24 | 0 |
| Hubbard | 1 | 18 | 18 | 0 |
| Boden | 1 | 14 | 14 | 0 |
| Woodcock | 1 | 12 | 12 | 0 |

### PASSING – PUNTING – KICKING Statistics

| Last Name | Att | Comp | % | Yds | Yd/Att | TD | Int– % | RK |
|---|---|---|---|---|---|---|---|---|
| PASSING | | | | | | | | |
| Landry | 240 | 135 | 56 | 1359 | 5.7 | 6 | 7– 3 | 4 |
| Danielson | 100 | 42 | 42 | 445 | 4.5 | 1 | 5– 5 | |
| Reed | 40 | 13 | 33 | 150 | 3.8 | 0 | 4– 10 | |
| Summers | 1 | 1 | 100 | 5 | 5.0 | 0 | 0– 0 | |
| Thompson | 1 | 0 | 0 | 0 | 0.0 | 0 | 0– 0 | |
| D. Hill | 1 | 0 | 0 | 0 | 0.0 | 0 | 0– 0 | |
| Payton | 1 | 0 | 0 | 0 | 0.0 | 0 | 0– 0 | |

| Last Name | No | Avg |
|---|---|---|
| PUNTING | | |
| Summers | 93 | 36.8 |
| Hoopes | 6 | 39.2 |

| Last Name | XP | Att | % | FG | Att | % |
|---|---|---|---|---|---|---|
| KICKING | | | | | | |
| Mike-Mayer | 19 | 21 | 90 | 8 | 19 | 42 |

## GREEN BAY PACKERS

### RUSHING

| Last Name | No. | Yds | Avg | TD |
|---|---|---|---|---|
| Ba. Smith | 166 | 554 | 3.3 | 2 |
| Torkelson | 103 | 309 | 3.0 | 1 |
| Simpson | 60 | 204 | 3.4 | 0 |
| Harrell | 60 | 140 | 2.3 | 1 |
| Middleton | 35 | 97 | 2.8 | 0 |
| Whitehurst | 14 | 55 | 3.9 | 1 |
| Culbreath | 12 | 53 | 4.4 | 0 |
| Dickey | 5 | 24 | 4.8 | 0 |
| Odom | 1 | 6 | 6.0 | 0 |
| Beverly | 2 | −3 | −1.5 | 0 |

### RECEIVING

| Last Name | No. | Yds | Avg | TD |
|---|---|---|---|---|
| Ba. Smith | 37 | 340 | 9 | 1 |
| Odom | 27 | 549 | 20 | 3 |
| O. Smith | 22 | 357 | 16 | 0 |
| Harrell | 19 | 194 | 10 | 0 |
| McGeorge | 17 | 142 | 8 | 1 |
| Torkelson | 11 | 107 | 10 | 0 |
| Vataha | 10 | 109 | 11 | 0 |
| Payne | 7 | 99 | 14 | 1 |
| Simpson | 5 | 19 | 4 | 0 |
| Askon | 2 | 51 | 26 | 0 |
| Thompson | 2 | 12 | 6 | 0 |
| Culbreath | 2 | 6 | 3 | 0 |
| Middleton | 1 | 27 | 27 | 0 |

### PUNT RETURNS

| Last Name | No. | Yds | Avg | TD |
|---|---|---|---|---|
| Harrell | 28 | 253 | 9 | 1 |
| Gray | 10 | 68 | 7 | 0 |

### KICKOFF RETURNS

| Last Name | No. | Yds | Avg | TD |
|---|---|---|---|---|
| Odom | 23 | 468 | 20 | 0 |
| Wagner | 6 | 62 | 10 | 0 |
| Culbreath | 5 | 82 | 16 | 0 |
| Middleton | 4 | 141 | 35 | 1 |
| Thompson | 4 | 82 | 21 | 0 |
| Harrell | 3 | 48 | 16 | 0 |
| Torkelson | 2 | 36 | 18 | 0 |
| Moresco | 1 | 15 | 15 | 0 |
| Gofourth | 1 | 13 | 13 | 0 |
| Gueno | 1 | 0 | 0 | 0 |
| Simpson | 1 | 0 | 0 | 0 |

### PASSING – PUNTING – KICKING Statistics

| Last Name | Att | Comp | % | Yds | Yd/Att | TD | Int– % | RK |
|---|---|---|---|---|---|---|---|---|
| PASSING | | | | | | | | |
| Dickey | 220 | 113 | 51 | 1346 | 6.1 | 5 | 14– 6 | 12 |
| Whitehurst | 105 | 50 | 48 | 634 | 6.0 | 1 | 7– 7 | |
| Harrell | 1 | 1 | 100 | 33 | 33.0 | 0 | 0– 0 | |
| Dowling | 1 | 0 | 0 | 0 | 0.0 | 0 | 0– 0 | |

| Last Name | No. | Avg |
|---|---|---|
| PUNTING | | |
| Beverly | 85 | 39.9 |

| Last Name | XP | Att | % | FG | Att | % |
|---|---|---|---|---|---|---|
| KICKING | | | | | | |
| Marcol | 11 | 14 | 79 | 13 | 21 | 62 |

## TAMPA BAY BUCCANEERS

### RUSHING

| Last Name | No. | Yds | Avg | TD |
|---|---|---|---|---|
| Bell | 148 | 436 | 2.9 | 1 |
| Davis | 95 | 297 | 3.1 | 1 |
| DuBose | 71 | 284 | 4.0 | 0 |
| Williams | 63 | 198 | 3.1 | 0 |
| L. Carter | 59 | 117 | 2.0 | 2 |
| Hedberg | 9 | 35 | 3.9 | 0 |
| Blount | 5 | 26 | 5.2 | 0 |
| Ragsdale | 3 | 21 | 7.0 | 0 |
| Huff | 8 | 10 | 1.3 | 0 |
| Hagins | 1 | 2 | 2.0 | 0 |
| Green | 1 | 0 | 0.0 | 0 |
| Owens | 2 | −2 | −1.0 | 0 |

### RECEIVING

| Last Name | No. | Yds | Avg | TD |
|---|---|---|---|---|
| Owens | 34 | 655 | 19 | 3 |
| Hagins | 15 | 196 | 13 | 0 |
| McKay | 12 | 164 | 14 | 0 |
| DuBose | 11 | 89 | 8 | 0 |
| Bell | 11 | 88 | 8 | 0 |
| Williams | 10 | 67 | 7 | 0 |
| L. Carter | 10 | 65 | 7 | 0 |
| Nafziger | 9 | 119 | 13 | 0 |
| Davis | 8 | 91 | 11 | 0 |
| Mucker | 4 | 59 | 15 | 0 |
| Reece | 2 | 59 | 30 | 0 |
| Novak | 2 | 24 | 12 | 0 |
| Ragsdale | 2 | 17 | 9 | 0 |
| Butler | 1 | 21 | 21 | 0 |

### PUNT RETURNS

| Last Name | No. | Yds | Avg | TD |
|---|---|---|---|---|
| Reece | 31 | 274 | 9 | 0 |
| Hagins | 17 | 85 | 5 | 0 |

### KICKOFF RETURNS

| Last Name | No. | Yds | Avg | TD |
|---|---|---|---|---|
| Hagins | 21 | 493 | 23 | 0 |
| Davis | 15 | 277 | 18 | 0 |
| Reece | 3 | 72 | 24 | 0 |
| Ragsdale | 3 | 68 | 23 | 0 |
| Nafziger | 1 | 4 | 4 | 0 |

### PASSING – PUNTING – KICKING Statistics

| Last Name | Att | Comp | % | Yds | Yd/Att | TD | Int– % | RK |
|---|---|---|---|---|---|---|---|---|
| PASSING | | | | | | | | |
| Huff | 138 | 67 | 49 | 889 | 6.4 | 3 | 13– 9 | |
| Hedberg | 90 | 25 | 28 | 244 | 2.7 | 0 | 10– 11 | |
| Blount | 89 | 37 | 42 | 522 | 5.9 | 0 | 7– 8 | |
| Green | 2 | 2 | 100 | 59 | 29.5 | 0 | 0– 0 | |
| L. Carter | 2 | 0 | 0 | 0 | 0.0 | 0 | 0– 0 | |

| Last Name | No | Avg |
|---|---|---|
| PUNTING | | |
| Green | 98 | 40.3 |

| Last Name | XP | Att | % | FG | Att | % |
|---|---|---|---|---|---|---|
| KICKING | | | | | | |
| Leavitt | 5 | 5 | 100 | 5 | 10 | 50 |
| Green | 5 | 6 | 83 | 4 | 7 | 71 |

# 1977 N.F.C. — Western Division

## LOS ANGELES RAMS 10-4 Chuck Knox

### Scores of Each Game

| | | |
|---|---|---|
| 6 | Atlanta | 17 |
| 20 | PHILADELPHIA | 0 |
| 34 | SAN FRANCISCO | 14 |
| 23 | Chicago | 24 |
| 14 | NEW ORLEANS | 7 |
| 35 | MINNESOTA | 3 |
| 26 | New Orleans | 27 |
| 31 | TAMPA BAY | 0 |
| 24 | Green Bay | 6 |
| 23 | San Francisco | 10 |
| 9 | Cleveland | 0 |
| 20 | OAKLAND | 14 |
| 23 | ATLANTA | 7 |
| 14 | Washington | 17 |

| Use Name | Pos. | Hgt | Wgt | Age | Int | Pts |
|---|---|---|---|---|---|---|
| Doug France | OT | 6'5" | 272 | 24 | | |
| Winston Hill | OT | 6'4" | 272 | 35 | | |
| Jeff Williams | OT | 6'4" | 256 | 22 | | |
| John Williams | OT | 6'3" | 265 | 31 | | |
| Dennis Harrah | OG | 6'5" | 257 | 24 | | |
| Greg Horton | OG | 6'4" | 245 | 26 | | |
| Tom Mack | OG | 6'3" | 250 | 33 | | |
| Jackie Slater | C | 6'4" | 270 | 23 | | |
| Rick Nuzum | C | 6'3" | 250 | 29 | | |
| Rich Saul | | | | | | |
| Al Cowlings | DE-DT | 6'5" | 245 | 30 | | |
| Fred Dryer | DE | 6'6" | 240 | 31 | | |
| Jack Youngblood | DE | 6'4" | 242 | 27 | | |
| Larry Brooks | DT | 6'3" | 255 | 27 | | |
| Mike Fanning | DT | 6'6" | 260 | 24 | | |
| Cody Jones | DT-DE | 6'5" | 240 | 26 | | |

| Use Name | Pos. | Hgt | Wgt | Age | Int | Pts |
|---|---|---|---|---|---|---|
| Bob Brudzinski | LB | 6'4" | 230 | 22 | 2 | |
| Carl Ekern | LB | 6'3" | 220 | 23 | | |
| Kevin McLain | LB | 6'2" | 227 | 22 | | |
| Bob Pifferini | LB | 6'2" | 226 | 27 | | |
| Jack Reynolds | LB | 6'1" | 232 | 29 | | |
| Isiah Robertson | LB | 6'3" | 225 | 28 | 1 | |
| Jim Youngblood | LB | 6'3" | 239 | 27 | 2 | 6 |
| Nolan Cromwell | DB | 6'1" | 196 | 22 | | |
| Dave Elmendorf | DB | 6'1" | 195 | 28 | 2 | |
| Monte Jackson | DB | 5'11" | 189 | 24 | 5 | |
| Rod Perry | DB | 5'9" | 170 | 23 | 1 | |
| Bill Simpson | DB | 6'1" | 180 | 25 | 6 | |
| Pat Thomas | DB | 5'9" | 180 | 23 | 5 | |
| Jackie Wallace | DB | 6'3" | 198 | 26 | 1 | |

Willie Miller — Elbow Injury
Rob Scribner — Thigh Injury

| Use Name | Pos. | Hgt | Wgt | Age | Int | Pts |
|---|---|---|---|---|---|---|
| Vince Ferragamo | QB | 6'3" | 208 | 23 | | |
| Pat Haden | QB | 5'11" | 182 | 24 | | 12 |
| Joe Namath | QB | 6'2" | 200 | 34 | | |
| Sonny Collins | HB | 6'1" | 195 | 24 | | |
| Lawrence McCutcheon | HB | 6'1" | 205 | 27 | | 54 |
| Wendell Tyler | HB | 5'10" | 188 | 22 | | 18 |
| Cullen Bryant | FB | 6'1" | 235 | 26 | | |
| John Cappelletti | FB-HB | 6'1" | 217 | 25 | | 36 |
| Jim Jodat | FB | 5'11" | 210 | 23 | | 12 |
| Rod Phillips | FB | 6' | 220 | 24 | | 6 |
| Harold Jackson | WR | 5'10" | 175 | 31 | | 36 |
| Ron Jessie | WR | 6' | 185 | 29 | | |
| Freeman Johns | WR | 6'1" | 175 | 23 | | |
| Dwight Scales | WR | 6'2" | 170 | 24 | | 6 |
| Billy Waddy | WR | 5'11" | 185 | 23 | | 6 |
| Terry Nelson | TE | 6'2" | 230 | 26 | | 18 |
| Charlie Young | TE | 6'4" | 235 | 26 | | 6 |
| Raphael Septien | K | 5'9" | 171 | 23 | | 86 |
| Glenn Walker | K | 6'1" | 210 | 25 | | |

## ATLANTA FALCONS 7-7 Leeman Bennett

| | | |
|---|---|---|
| 17 | LOS ANGELES | 6 |
| 6 | Washington | 10 |
| 17 | N.Y. GIANTS | 3 |
| 7 | San Francisco | 0 |
| 0 | Buffalo | 3 |
| 16 | Chicago | 10 |
| 7 | MINNESOTA | 14 |
| 3 | SAN FRANCISCO | 10 |
| 17 | DETROIT | 6 |
| 20 | New Orleans | 21 |
| 17 | Tampa Bay | 0 |
| 10 | NEW ENGLAND | 16 |
| 7 | Los Angeles | 23 |
| 35 | NEW ORLEANS | 7 |

| Use Name | Pos. | Hgt | Wgt | Age | Int | Pts |
|---|---|---|---|---|---|---|
| Bob Adams | OT | 6'2" | 218 | 31 | | |
| Warren Bryant | OT | 6'6" | 270 | 21 | | |
| Phil McKinnely | OT-TE | 6'4" | 248 | 24 | | |
| Greg Kindle | OG | 6'4" | 265 | 26 | | |
| Dave Scott | OG | 6'5" | 285 | 23 | | |
| R.C. Thielemann | OG-C | 6'4" | 247 | 22 | | |
| Paul Ryczek | C | 6'2" | 230 | 25 | | |
| Jeff Van Note | OG-C | 6'2" | 247 | 31 | | |
| Edgar Fields | DE | 6'2" | 255 | 23 | | |
| Claude Humphrey | DE | 6'5" | 265 | 33 | | |
| Jeff Merrow (to OAK) | DE-LB | 6'4" | 230 | 24 | | |
| Jeff Yeates | DE-OG | 6'3" | 248 | 26 | | |
| Jim Bailey | DT | 6'5" | 260 | 29 | | |
| Wilson Faumuina | DT | 6'5" | 275 | 23 | | |
| Bob Jordan | DT | 6'6" | 255 | 22 | | |
| Mike Lewis | DT | 6'3" | 261 | 28 | | |
| Mike Tilleman | DT | 6'5" | 278 | 32 | | |

| Use Name | Pos. | Hgt | Wgt | Age | Int | Pts |
|---|---|---|---|---|---|---|
| Greg Brezina | LB | 6'1" | 221 | 31 | | |
| Rick Kay (from LA) | LB | 6'4" | 235 | 27 | | |
| Fulton Kuykendall | LB | 6'5" | 225 | 24 | | |
| Ron McCartney | LB | 6'1" | 220 | 23 | | |
| Dewey McClain | LB | 6'2" | 220 | 24 | 4 | 6 |
| Ralph Ortega | LB | 6'1" | 222 | 22 | 2 | 6 |
| Robert Pennywell | LB | 6'2" | 218 | 22 | | |
| Andy Spiva | DB | 6'2" | 202 | 28 | 5 | |
| Ray Brown | DB | 5'9" | 180 | 26 | 3 | 6 |
| Rick Byas | DB | 6' | 192 | 27 | 4 | |
| Ray Easterling | DB | 5'10" | 179 | 26 | 7 | |
| Rolland Lawrence | DB | 6' | 185 | 24 | | |
| Tom Moriarty | DB | 5'11" | 193 | 23 | | |
| Frank Reed | | | | | | |

Len Gotschalk — Knee Injury
Bubba Bean — Knee Injury

| Use Name | Pos. | Hgt | Wgt | Age | Int | Pts |
|---|---|---|---|---|---|---|
| Steve Bartkowski | QB | 6'4" | 213 | 24 | | |
| Scott Hunter | QB | 6'2" | 205 | 29 | | 6 |
| June Jones | QB | 6'4" | 200 | 24 | | |
| Kim McQuilken | QB | 6'2" | 203 | 26 | | |
| Mike Esposito | HB-DB | 6' | 183 | 24 | 1 | |
| Secedrick McIntyre | HB | 5'10" | 190 | 23 | | 6 |
| Haskel Stanback | HB | 6' | 210 | 25 | | 36 |
| Monroe Eley | FB | 6'2" | 210 | 28 | | 6 |
| Billy Ray Pritchett | FB | 6'3" | 230 | 26 | | |
| Woody Thompson | FB | 6'1" | 228 | 25 | | 6 |
| Karl Farmer | WR | 5'11" | 165 | 23 | | |
| Wallace Francis | WR | 5'11" | 190 | 25 | | 24 |
| Al Jenkins | WR | 5'11" | 172 | 25 | | 6 |
| Billy Ryckman | WR | 5'11" | 172 | 22 | | 6 |
| Grey McCrary | TE | 6'3" | 230 | 25 | | 6 |
| Jim Mitchell | TE | 6'2" | 236 | 29 | | |
| John James | K | 6'3" | 200 | 28 | | |
| Fred Steinfort | K | 5'11" | 180 | 23 | | 31 |

## SAN FRANCISCO FORTY-NINERS 5-9 Ken Meyer

| | | |
|---|---|---|
| 0 | Pittsburgh | 27 |
| 15 | MIAMI | 19 |
| 14 | Los Angeles | 34 |
| 0 | ATLANTA | 7 |
| 17 | N.Y. Giants | 20 |
| 28 | DETROIT | 7 |
| 20 | TAMPA BAY | 10 |
| 10 | Atlanta | 3 |
| 10 | New Orleans | 7 |
| 10 | LOS ANGELES | 23 |
| 20 | NEW ORLEANS | 17 |
| 27 | Minnesota | 28 |
| 35 | DALLAS | 42 |
| 14 | Green Bay | 16 |

| Use Name | Pos. | Hgt | Wgt | Age | Int | Pts |
|---|---|---|---|---|---|---|
| John Ayers | OT-OG | 6'5" | 247 | 24 | | |
| Cas Banaszak | OT | 6'3" | 252 | 31 | | |
| Jean Barrett | OT-C | 6'6" | 250 | 26 | | |
| Keith Fahnhorst | OT | 6'6" | 263 | 25 | | |
| Ron Singleton | OG | 6'7" | 245 | 25 | | |
| Steve Lawson | OG | 6'3" | 257 | 28 | | |
| Johnny Miller | OG | 6'1" | 247 | 23 | | |
| Woody Peoples | OG | 6'2" | 250 | 34 | | |
| Randy Cross | C | 6'3" | 250 | 23 | | |
| Tony Cline | DE | 6'2" | 237 | 29 | | |
| Cedric Hardman | DE | 6'3" | 244 | 28 | | |
| Tommy Hart | DE | 6'3" | 246 | 32 | | |
| Bill Cooke | DT-DE | 6'5" | 243 | 26 | | |
| Cleveland Elam | DT | 6'4" | 251 | 25 | | |
| Ed Galigher | DT | 6'4" | 247 | 26 | | |
| Jimmy Webb | DT | 6'5" | 245 | 25 | | |

| Use Name | Pos. | Hgt | Wgt | Age | Int | Pts |
|---|---|---|---|---|---|---|
| Mike Baldassin | LB | 6'1" | 218 | 22 | | 6 |
| Ed Bradley | LB | 6'2" | 225 | 27 | | |
| Bruce Elia | LB | 6'1" | 220 | 24 | | |
| Willie Harper | LB | 6'2" | 205 | 27 | 1 | |
| Dale Mitchell | LB | 6'3" | 225 | 24 | | |
| Howard Stidham | LB | 6'2" | 214 | 22 | | |
| Skip Vanderbundt | LB | 6'3" | 225 | 30 | 1 | |
| Dave Washington | LB | 6'5" | 230 | 28 | 2 | |
| Stan Black | DB | 6' | 196 | 21 | | |
| Mike Burns | DB | 6' | 181 | 23 | | |
| Tony Leonard | DB | 5'11" | 165 | 24 | 1 | |
| Eddie Lewis | DB | 6' | 174 | 23 | | |
| Al Matthews | DB | 5'11" | 190 | 29 | | |
| Ralph McGill | DB | 5'11" | 180 | 27 | 1 | |
| Mel Phillips | DB | 6' | 185 | 35 | 2 | |
| Bruce Taylor | DB | 6' | 178 | 29 | | |

Bruce Rhodes — Injury

| Use Name | Pos. | Hgt | Wgt | Age | Int | Pts |
|---|---|---|---|---|---|---|
| Scott Bull | QB | 6'5" | 215 | 24 | | |
| Steve DeBerg | QB | 6'2" | 205 | 23 | | |
| Jim Plunkett | QB | 6'3" | 207 | 29 | | 6 |
| Paul Hofer | HB | 6' | 193 | 25 | | |
| Dave Williams | HB-FB | 6'2" | 200 | 23 | | 6 |
| Del Williams | HB | 6' | 195 | 26 | | 54 |
| Bob Ferrell | FB | 6' | 219 | 24 | | 6 |
| Wilbur Jackson | FB | 6'1" | 213 | 25 | | 42 |
| Kenny Harrison | WR | 6' | 164 | 23 | | 6 |
| Jim Lash | WR | 6'2" | 200 | 25 | | |
| Willie McGee | WR | 5'11" | 178 | 27 | | |
| Gene Washington | WR | 6'1" | 180 | 30 | | 30 |
| Tom Mitchell | TE | 6'2" | 225 | 33 | | |
| Jim Obradovich | TE | 6'2" | 227 | 24 | | |
| Paul Seal | TE | 6'4" | 223 | 25 | | 6 |
| Ray Wersching | K | 5'11" | 210 | 27 | | 53 |
| Tom Wittum | K | 6'1" | 198 | 27 | | 5 |

## NEW ORLEANS SAINTS 3-11 Hank Stram

| | | |
|---|---|---|
| 20 | GREEN BAY | 24 |
| 19 | Detroit | 23 |
| 42 | Chicago | 24 |
| 0 | SAN DIEGO | 14 |
| 7 | Los Angeles | 14 |
| 31 | St. Louis | 49 |
| 27 | LOS ANGELES | 26 |
| 7 | Philadelphia | 28 |
| 7 | SAN FRANCISCO | 10 |
| 21 | ATLANTA | 20 |
| 17 | San Francisco | 20 |
| 13 | N.Y. JETS | 16 |
| 14 | TAMPA BAY | 33 |
| 7 | Atlanta | 35 |

| Use Name | Pos. | Hgt | Wgt | Age | Int | Pts |
|---|---|---|---|---|---|---|
| Dave Hubbard | OT | 6'7" | 270 | 21 | | |
| Dave Lafary | OT | 6'7" | 280 | 22 | | |
| Marv Montgomery | OT | 6'6" | 255 | 29 | | |
| Don Morrison | OT | 6'5" | 250 | 27 | | |
| Mike Watson | OT | 6'6" | 272 | 21 | | |
| Robert Woods (from NYJ) | OT-OG | 6'3" | 259 | 27 | | |
| Kurt Schumacher | OG | 6'3" | 246 | 24 | | |
| Terry Stieve | OG | 6'2" | 242 | 23 | | |
| Emanuel Zanders | OG | 6'1" | 248 | 26 | | |
| Lee Gross | C | 6'3" | 235 | 24 | | |
| John Hill | C | 6'2" | 246 | 27 | | |
| John Watson | C-OG | 6'4" | 244 | 28 | | |
| Joe Campbell | DE | 6'6" | 254 | 22 | | |
| Elois Grooms | DE | 6'4" | 250 | 24 | | 6 |
| Bob Pollard | DE-DT | 6'3" | 236 | 28 | | 6 |
| Oakley Dalton | DT | 6'6" | 285 | 25 | | |
| Mike Fultz | DT | 6'5" | 278 | 23 | | |
| Derland Moore | DT | 6'4" | 253 | 25 | | |
| Elex Price | DT | 6'3" | 265 | 27 | | |

| Use Name | Pos. | Hgt | Wgt | Age | Int | Pts |
|---|---|---|---|---|---|---|
| Ken Bordelon | LB | 6'4" | 226 | 23 | | |
| Joe Federspiel | LB | 6'1" | 230 | 27 | | |
| Pat Hughes | LB | 6'2" | 225 | 30 | 1 | |
| Rick Kingrea | LB | 6'1" | 222 | 28 | | |
| Jim Merlo | LB | 6'1" | 220 | 25 | 1 | 6 |
| Greg Westbrooks | LB | 6'2" | 217 | 24 | | |
| Wade Bosarge | DB | 5'10" | 175 | 21 | | |
| Craig Cassady | DB | 5'11" | 175 | 23 | | |
| Clarence Chapman | DB | 5'10" | 185 | 23 | 1 | 6 |
| Chuck Crist | DB | 6'2" | 205 | 26 | 4 | |
| Ernie Jackson | DB | 5'10" | 176 | 27 | 1 | |
| Jim Marsalis | DB | 5'11" | 190 | 31 | 1 | |
| Tom Myers | DB | 5'11" | 180 | 26 | 1 | 6 |
| Jimmy Stewart | DB | 5'11" | 190 | 22 | | |

Mo Spencer — Neck Injury

| Use Name | Pos. | Hgt | Wgt | Age | Int | Pts |
|---|---|---|---|---|---|---|
| Bobby Douglass | QB | 6'3" | 228 | 30 | | |
| Archie Manning | QB | 6'3" | 200 | 28 | | 30 |
| Bobby Scott | QB | 6'1" | 197 | 28 | | |
| Greg Boykin | HB | 6' | 225 | 23 | | |
| Chuck Muncie | HB-FB | 6'3" | 220 | 24 | | 42 |
| Mike Strachan | HB | 6' | 200 | 24 | | |
| Tony Galbreath | FB | 6' | 230 | 23 | | 18 |
| Kim Jones | FB | 6'4" | 243 | 25 | | |
| Larry Burton | WR | 5'11" | 193 | 25 | | |
| John Gilliam (from CHI) | WR | 6'1" | 187 | 32 | | 6 |
| Don Herrmann | WR | 6'2" | 193 | 30 | | |
| Richard Mauti | WR | 6' | 190 | 23 | | |
| Joel Parker | WR | 6'5" | 215 | 25 | | |
| Leonard Willis (to BUF) | WR | 5'10" | 180 | 24 | | |
| Henry Childs | TE | 6'2" | 220 | 26 | | 54 |
| Jim Thaxton | TE-WR | 6'2" | 242 | 28 | | 6 |
| Tom Blanchard | K | 6' | 180 | 29 | | |
| Richie Szaro | K | 5'11" | 204 | 29 | | 44 |

Tinker Owens — Knee Injury

## LOS ANGELES RAMS

### RUSHING

| Last Name | No. | Yds. | Avg | TD |
|---|---|---|---|---|
| McCutcheon | 294 | 1238 | 4.2 | 7 |
| Cappelletti | 178 | 598 | 3.4 | 5 |
| Tyler | 61 | 317 | 5.2 | 3 |
| Phillips | 37 | 183 | 4.9 | 1 |
| Haden | 29 | 106 | 3.7 | 2 |
| Bryant | 6 | 42 | 7.0 | 0 |
| Waddy | 2 | 34 | 17.0 | 0 |
| Nelson | 3 | 31 | 10.3 | 0 |
| Jodat | 5 | 15 | 3.0 | 1 |
| H. Jackson | 1 | 6 | 6.0 | 0 |
| Namath | 4 | 5 | 1.3 | 0 |
| Ferragamo | 1 | 0 | 0.0 | 0 |

### RECEIVING

| Last Name | No. | Yds | Avg | TD |
|---|---|---|---|---|
| H. Jackson | 48 | 666 | 14 | 6 |
| Nelson | 31 | 401 | 13 | 3 |
| Cappelletti | 28 | 228 | 8 | 1 |
| McCutcheon | 25 | 274 | 11 | 2 |
| Waddy | 23 | 355 | 15 | 1 |
| Jessie | 9 | 139 | 15 | 0 |
| Scales | 5 | 104 | 21 | 1 |
| Young | 5 | 35 | 7 | 1 |
| Bryant | 4 | 28 | 7 | 0 |
| Wallace | 1 | 13 | 13 | 0 |
| Phillips | 1 | 5 | 5 | 0 |
| Tyler | 1 | 3 | 3 | 0 |
| Jodat | 1 | 2 | 2 | 1 |

### PUNT RETURNS

| Last Name | No. | Yds | Avg | TD |
|---|---|---|---|---|
| Waddy | 31 | 219 | 7 | 0 |
| Bryant | 20 | 141 | 7 | 0 |

### KICKOFF RETURNS

| Last Name | No. | Yds | Avg | TD |
|---|---|---|---|---|
| Tyler | 24 | 523 | 22 | 0 |
| Jodat | 6 | 129 | 22 | 0 |
| Bryant | 2 | 35 | 18 | 0 |
| Phillips | 1 | 10 | 10 | 0 |
| Ekern | 1 | 8 | 8 | 0 |

### PASSING – PUNTING – KICKING

**PASSING**

| Last Name | Att | Comp | % | Yds | Yd/Att | TD | Int– % | RK |
|---|---|---|---|---|---|---|---|---|
| Haden | 215 | 122 | 56 | 1551 | 7.2 | 11 | 6– 3 | 2 |
| Namath | 107 | 50 | 47 | 606 | 5.7 | 3 | 5– 5 | |
| Ferragamo | 15 | 9 | 60 | 83 | 5.5 | 2 | 0– 0 | |
| Walker | 1 | 1 | 100 | 13 | 13.0 | 0 | 0– 0 | |

**PUNTING**

| Last Name | No | Avg |
|---|---|---|
| Walker | 73 | 35.2 |

**KICKING**

| Last Name | XP | Att | % | FG | Att | % |
|---|---|---|---|---|---|---|
| Septien | 32 | 35 | 91 | 18 | 30 | 60 |

## ATLANTA FALCONS

### RUSHING

| Last Name | No. | Yds. | Avg | TD |
|---|---|---|---|---|
| Stanback | 247 | 873 | 3.5 | 6 |
| Thompson | 132 | 478 | 3.6 | 1 |
| Eley | 97 | 273 | 2.8 | 1 |
| Esposito | 34 | 101 | 3.0 | 0 |
| Hunter | 28 | 70 | 2.5 | 1 |
| McIntyre | 13 | 65 | 5.0 | 0 |
| Bartkowski | 18 | 13 | 0.7 | 0 |
| Jenkins | 2 | 7 | 3.5 | 0 |
| Pritchett | 3 | 7 | 2.3 | 0 |
| Francis | 4 | 6 | 1.5 | 0 |
| Farmer | 1 | 4 | 4.0 | 0 |
| McQuilken | 2 | −1 | −0.5 | 0 |
| Mitchell | 1 | −6 | −6.0 | 0 |

### RECEIVING

| Last Name | No. | Yds | Avg | TD |
|---|---|---|---|---|
| Jenkins | 39 | 677 | 17 | 4 |
| Stanback | 30 | 261 | 9 | 0 |
| Francis | 26 | 390 | 15 | 1 |
| Mitchell | 17 | 178 | 10 | 0 |
| Thompson | 12 | 56 | 5 | 0 |
| Eley | 9 | 60 | 7 | 0 |
| McCrary | 2 | 48 | 24 | 1 |
| Farmer | 2 | 39 | 20 | 0 |
| McIntyre | 1 | 27 | 27 | 1 |
| Ryckman | 1 | 5 | 5 | 0 |
| Esposito | 1 | −1 | −1 | 0 |

### PUNT RETURNS

| Last Name | No. | Yds | Avg | TD |
|---|---|---|---|---|
| Lawrence | 51 | 352 | 7 | 0 |
| Ryckman | 7 | 40 | 6 | 0 |
| Byas | 1 | 10 | 10 | 0 |

### KICKOFF RETURNS

| Last Name | No. | Yds | Avg | TD |
|---|---|---|---|---|
| Farmer | 21 | 419 | 20 | 0 |
| Moriarty | 8 | 136 | 17 | 0 |
| Francis | 1 | 22 | 22 | 0 |
| Eley | 1 | 16 | 16 | 0 |
| McIntyre | 1 | 15 | 15 | 0 |
| Lawrence | 1 | 13 | 13 | 0 |
| Ryckman | 1 | 0 | 0 | 0 |

### PASSING – PUNTING – KICKING

**PASSING**

| Last Name | Att | Comp | % | Yds | Yd/Att | TD | Int– % | RK |
|---|---|---|---|---|---|---|---|---|
| Hunter | 151 | 70 | 46 | 898 | 6.0 | 2 | 3– 2 | |
| Bartkowski | 136 | 64 | 47 | 796 | 5.9 | 5 | 13– 10 | |
| McQuilkin | 7 | 5 | 71 | 47 | 6.7 | 1 | 0– 0 | |
| Jones | 1 | 1 | 100 | −1 | −1.0 | 0 | 0– 0 | |
| Esposito | 1 | 0 | 0 | 0 | 0.0 | 0 | 0– 0 | |
| James | 1 | 0 | 0 | 0 | 0.0 | 0 | 0– 0 | |

**PUNTING**

| Last Name | No | Avg |
|---|---|---|
| James | 105 | 41.4 |

**KICKING**

| Last Name | XP | Att | % | FG | Att | % |
|---|---|---|---|---|---|---|
| Steinfort | 13 | 13 | 100 | 6 | 11 | 55 |

## SAN FRANCISCO FORTY-NINERS

### RUSHING

| Last Name | No. | Yds. | Avg | TD |
|---|---|---|---|---|
| Del Williams | 268 | 931 | 3.5 | 7 |
| Jackson | 179 | 780 | 4.4 | 7 |
| Ferrell | 41 | 160 | 3.9 | 1 |
| Hofer | 34 | 106 | 3.1 | 0 |
| Plunkett | 28 | 71 | 2.5 | 1 |
| Bull | 5 | 20 | 4.0 | 0 |
| Harrison | 6 | 15 | 2.5 | 0 |
| Da. Williams | 2 | 6 | 3.0 | 0 |
| McGee | 1 | −3 | −3.0 | 0 |

### RECEIVING

| Last Name | No. | Yds | Avg | TD |
|---|---|---|---|---|
| G. Washington | 32 | 638 | 20 | 5 |
| Jackson | 22 | 169 | 8 | 0 |
| Del Williams | 20 | 179 | 9 | 2 |
| T. Mitchell | 19 | 226 | 12 | 0 |
| Harrison | 15 | 217 | 14 | 1 |
| Seal | 13 | 230 | 18 | 1 |
| Hofer | 5 | 46 | 9 | 0 |
| Lash | 3 | 22 | 7 | 0 |
| McGee | 2 | 27 | 14 | 0 |
| O'Bradovich | 2 | 16 | 8 | 0 |
| Ferrell | 2 | 12 | 6 | 0 |
| Cline | 1 | 15 | 15 | 0 |

### PUNT RETURNS

| Last Name | No. | Yds | Avg | TD |
|---|---|---|---|---|
| Leonard | 22 | 154 | 7 | 0 |
| Black | 13 | 38 | 3 | 0 |
| Da. Williams | 1 | 60 | 60 | 0 |
| Elia | 1 | 1 | 1 | 0 |
| Baldassin | 1 | 0 | 0 | 0 |

### KICKOFF RETURNS

| Last Name | No. | Yds | Avg | TD |
|---|---|---|---|---|
| Hofer | 36 | 871 | 24 | 0 |
| Da. Williams | 4 | 122 | 31 | 0 |
| Ferrell | 3 | 35 | 12 | 0 |
| Leonard | 1 | 68 | 68 | 0 |
| O'Bradovich | 1 | 9 | 9 | 0 |
| Del Williams | 1 | 9 | 9 | 0 |

### PASSING – PUNTING – KICKING

**PASSING**

| Last Name | Att | Comp | % | Yds | Yd/Att | TD | Int– % | RK |
|---|---|---|---|---|---|---|---|---|
| Plunkett | 248 | 128 | 52 | 1693 | 6.8 | 9 | 14– 6 | 8 |
| Bull | 24 | 7 | 29 | 89 | 3.7 | 0 | 2– 8 | |
| Wittum | 3 | 1 | 33 | 15 | 5.0 | 0 | 0– 0 | |
| Harrison | 1 | 0 | 0 | 0 | 0.0 | 0 | 0– 0 | |
| Del Williams | 1 | 0 | 0 | 0 | 0.0 | 0 | 1–100 | |

**PUNTING**

| Last Name | No | Avg |
|---|---|---|
| Wittum | 77 | 36.4 |

**KICKING**

| Last Name | XP | Att | % | FG | Att | % |
|---|---|---|---|---|---|---|
| Wersching | 23 | 23 | 100 | 10 | 17 | 59 |
| Wittum | 2 | 4 | 50 | 1 | 2 | 50 |

## NEW ORLEANS SAINTS

### RUSHING

| Last Name | No. | Yds. | Avg | TD |
|---|---|---|---|---|
| Muncie | 201 | 811 | 4.0 | 6 |
| Galbreath | 168 | 644 | 3.8 | 3 |
| Strachan | 55 | 271 | 4.9 | 0 |
| Manning | 39 | 270 | 6.9 | 5 |
| Douglass | 2 | 23 | 11.5 | 0 |
| Jones | 8 | 23 | 2.9 | 0 |
| Scott | 4 | 11 | 2.8 | 0 |
| Thaxton | 1 | −3 | −3.0 | 0 |
| Boykin | 5 | −9 | −1.8 | 0 |
| Herrmann | 1 | −17 | −17.0 | 0 |

### RECEIVING

| Last Name | No. | Yds | Avg | TD |
|---|---|---|---|---|
| Galbreath | 41 | 265 | 7 | 0 |
| Childs | 33 | 518 | 16 | 9 |
| Herrmann | 32 | 408 | 13 | 0 |
| Muncie | 21 | 248 | 12 | 1 |
| Thaxton | 14 | 211 | 15 | 1 |
| Gilliam | 11 | 133 | 12 | 1 |
| Mauti | 4 | 71 | 18 | 0 |
| Strachan | 3 | 26 | 9 | 0 |
| Boykin | 3 | 21 | 7 | 0 |
| Burton | 1 | 13 | 13 | 0 |
| Jones | 1 | 9 | 9 | 0 |
| Parker | 1 | 7 | 7 | 0 |
| Grooms | 1 | 3 | 3 | 1 |

### PUNT RETURNS

| Last Name | No. | Yds | Avg | TD |
|---|---|---|---|---|
| Mauti | 37 | 281 | 8 | 0 |

### KICKOFF RETURNS

| Last Name | No. | Yds | Avg | TD |
|---|---|---|---|---|
| Mauti | 27 | 609 | 23 | 0 |
| Chapman | 15 | 385 | 26 | 1 |
| Willis | 8 | 148 | 19 | 0 |
| Boykin | 5 | 76 | 15 | 0 |
| Campbell | 2 | 33 | 17 | 0 |
| Jones | 2 | 23 | 12 | 0 |
| Kingrea | 2 | 21 | 11 | 0 |
| Stewart | 1 | 33 | 33 | 0 |
| Muncie | 1 | 19 | 19 | 0 |
| Thaxton | 0 | 8 | – | 0 |

### PASSING – PUNTING – KICKING

**PASSING**

| Last Name | Att | Comp | % | Yds | Yd/Att | TD | Int– % | RK |
|---|---|---|---|---|---|---|---|---|
| Manning | 205 | 113 | 55 | 1284 | 6.3 | 8 | 9– 4 | 5 |
| Scott | 82 | 36 | 44 | 516 | 6.3 | 3 | 8– 10 | |
| Douglass | 31 | 16 | 52 | 130 | 4.2 | 1 | 3– 10 | |
| Blanchard | 3 | 1 | 33 | 3 | 1.0 | 1 | 1– 38 | |

**PUNTING**

| Last Name | No | Avg |
|---|---|---|
| Blanchard | 82 | 42.4 |
| Scott | 3 | 31.7 |

**KICKING**

| Last Name | XP | Att | % | FG | Att | % |
|---|---|---|---|---|---|---|
| Szaro | 29 | 31 | 94 | 5 | 12 | 42 |

# 1977 A.F.C.   Seeing is Believing

Perhaps the most controversial team of the year was the Zebras. Game officials came under unusually harsh criticism for a number of close calls at key moments of games. The Oilers claimed that poor officiating cost them two games, while Joe Greene of Pittsburgh was furious enough to threaten physical violence after officials penalized the Steelers 17 times in a game against the Colts. In the important Patriots-Colts game and in the Raiders-Broncos battle for the A.F.C. crown, quick whistles on apparent fumbles whipped up the winds of protest. Regardless of the criticisms, no one impugned the integrity of the officials, who did their best to police a lot of action.

## EASTERN DIVISION

**Baltimore Colts**—A late-season losing streak put their title in jeopardy, but the Colts repeated as Eastern champs. The explosive Baltimore offense led the team to nine victories in the first ten games. The arm of Bert Jones, the versatility of Lydell Mitchell, and the blocking of George Kunz paved the way for impressive triumphs over the Dolphins and Steelers. The defense also had stars in pass rusher John Dutton and ball hawk Lyle Blackwood, a pick-up from Seattle. Ahead of the pack by two games, the Colts suddenly lost to the Broncos, Dolphins, and Lions to enter the final weekend tied for first with Miami. Before a supportive hometown crowd, the Colts beat the Patriots 30-24 to earn first place on the tiebreaker formula.

**Miami Dolphins**—Given a taste of losing last season, Don Shula whipped his Dolphins back into the playoff race. Shula rebuilt his defense, partly out of necessity. Nick Buoniconti retired to be a full-time lawyer, while Don Reese and Randy Crowder were kept busy with federal drug charges. Into the breach stepped rookies A.J. Duhe, Bob Baumhower, and Kim Bokamper, all impressive starters. The offense still churned out points behind the sterling efforts of Bob Griese, Nat Moore, Larry Little, and Jim Langer. An impressive 55-14 victory over the Cardinals on Thanksgiving Day cost the Dolphins the services of Vern Den Herder and Charlie Babb, both injured for the rest of the year. One week later, they whipped the front-running Colts 17-6 on Monday night, but a loss to the Patriots ultimately cost the Dolphins a trip to the playoffs.

**New England Patriots**—The holdout of star linemen Leon Gray and John Hannah took away the team's peace of mind. Although Gray and Hannah returned to the field after sitting out three games, the talented Patriots sauntered through the first nine games without much fire. Their 5-4 record included a solid victory over the unbeaten Colts and losses to the lowly Jets and Bills. Recognizing their under-achievement, the Pats went on a tear in search of a wild card spot. Four straight victories brought them into a showdown with the Colts on the final Sunday. Leading 21-3 in the third quarter, the Pats left the field in anguish as the Colts rallied for a 30-24 decision.

**Buffalo Bills**—Head coach Jim Ringo took a long time winning his first game. The loser of nine straight after taking over last season, Ringo watched his team drop the first four games this year before upsetting the Falcons 3-0. Ringo was stuck with offensive and defensive units that made errors at key times, reaching new depths in a 56-17 humiliation in Seattle. The Bills lost their offensive meal ticket in that game when O.J. Simpson suffered a knee injury which required surgery. One week later, the Bills upset the Patriots 24-14, as reserve halfback Roland Hooks ran for 155 yards behind the blocking of Joe DeLamielleure and the rest of the Electric Company front line.

**New York Jets**—With Joe Namath gone, the Jets searched for a new identity. Rookie coach Walt Michaels brought in a host of useful rookie players, with Marvin Powell, Wesley Walker, Dan Alexander, and Scott Dierking playing on offense, Joe Klecko on defense, and Bruce Harper on the specialty squads. All these newcomers underwent a serious dose of losing in their New York debuts. The Jets began their year with a 20-0 loss to the Oilers and ended it with a 27-0 trouncing by the Eagles. Between those bookends, the Jets lost a lot of close decisions and won upset victories over the Patriots and Steelers.

## CENTRAL DIVISION

**Pittsburgh Steelers**—No longer the awesome titans of 1974-75, the Steelers still battled their way to a Central Division title. Losses to the Raiders, Oilers, Colts, and Broncos left the Steelers at 4-4 and questioned their ability to beat the big boys. With no one taking charge in the Central, however, the Steelers took the lead with four straight triumphs. On December 11, Chuck Noll's men ran into an ambush in Cincinnati. In two degree weather, the Steelers and Bengals struggled in the cold to a 17-10 Cincinnati decision. The only playoff hope for the Steelers was to win their final game and hope that the Bengals lost their finale. The Steelers did beat San Diego, and the Bengals did their part by losing to the Oilers.

**Cincinnati Bengals**—The Bengals swung like a pendulum in the early going. They lost to the Browns 13-3 on opening day, beat Seattle 42-20 a week later, and then dropped a 24-3 decision to the Chargers. Inconsistent in the early fall, they started winning in November. In a gritty contest in two degree weather, the Bengals whipped the Steelers 17-10 on December 11. That victory ensured the Bengals of first place on a tiebreaker formula should they beat the Oilers in their final game. Unfortunately, quarterback Ken Anderson spent a miserable afternoon in the Astrodome, throwing incompletions and dodging Houston pass rushers with limited success. With a heartbreaking 21-16 loss, the Bengals dropped the trophy they had fought for in the cold.

**Houston Oilers**—Although out of the playoff race, the Oilers charged down the stretch as one of the NFL's toughest clubs. Bum Phillips was reaping the results of his careful molding process. The Oilers jumped out to three victories in their first four games, including a 27-10 decision over the Steelers. A mid-season cold spell, however, whipped away any fantasies of post-season glory. A 47-0 feast at the expense of the Bears started the Houston hot streak. The Oilers ended the year by knocking the Bengals out of the playoffs with a 21-16 decision.

**Cleveland Browns**—The Browns couldn't sustain their jackrabbit start and fell far off the pace by the end of the race. At the halfway point, they led the Central field with a 5-2 record, capped by a 44-7 massacre of Kansas City. Things turned bad from that point on, but the Browns still clung to first place for almost another month. They dropped back-to-back games with the Bengals and Steelers, losing quarterback Brian Sipe in the Pittsburgh game with a separated shoulder. Although reserve QB Dave Mays led the Browns to a 21-7 victory over the Jets in his first start, four losses at the end of the schedule sent the Browns reeling into last place. Head coach Forrest Gregg lost his job one week from the end, falling just shy of three years on the job.

## WESTERN DIVISION

**Denver Broncos**—With Red Miller's arrival came the birth of the Orange Crush defense and an epidemic of Broncomania. The new head coach combined a stingy defense with a conservative error-free offense to take Denver to the playoffs for the first time ever. The defense captured the imagination of the city and gave enemy offenses a nasty time. The 3-4 unit got All-Pro caliber play from Lyle Alzado, Rubin Carter, Randy Gradishar, Tom Jackson, Louie Wright, and Bill Thompson. The offense had little flair but did have an inspirational leader in quarterback Craig Morton, who came to Denver in a minor trade and thrived in Miller's system. Victories over the Raiders, Steelers, and Colts convinced all observers that these upstarts were for real.

**Oakland Raiders**—The defending Super Bowl champs lost only three games but had to settle for a wild card playoff berth behind the phenomenal Broncos. The Raiders split their two meetings with Denver only to fall to second place with losses to the Chargers and Rams. The Oakland offense counted heavily on Mark van Eeghen, who ran for over 1,200 yards behind the blocking of Gene Upshaw, Art Shell, and Dave Casper. Although still formidable, the defense lost an edge when Phil Villipiano went out with a knee injury after only two games.

**San Diego Chargers**—After a 24-0 loss to the Raiders on opening day, the Chargers won three games which they allowed a total of 10 points. An excellent young line led by Louie Kelcher laid the groundwork for the defensive resurgence. The offense had less success, as Dan Fouts stayed at home in a salary dispute. James Harris played quarterback most of the season, but both he and back-up Bill Munson were knocked out with injuries in a loss to the Broncos. Little-used Cliff Olander started the next game and engineered a stunning 12-7 upset of the champion Raiders. Fouts then settled his problems with management and led the Chargers to two victories in the remaining four games.

**Seattle Seahawks**—The Seahawks compiled the best second-year record of any modern NFL expansion team. A crew of young offensive linemen gave Sherman Smith enough room to run impressively, and Jim Zorn got enough time to connect frequently with Steve Largent. Head coach Jack Patera still had lots of work left on his defensive unit, but they did rise to the occasion several times. The Seahawks thrashed Buffalo 56-17 at home, and they whipped the Jets 17-0 on the road. Victories over Kansas City and Cleveland ensured an escape from the Western basement.

**Kansas City Chiefs**—Only last year, team owner Lamar Hunt had given head coach Paul Wiggin a new three-year contract at a healthy raise. Seven games into this season, Hunt fired Wiggin. The Chiefs got off to a miserable start, dropping their first five games with a pushover defense. A 44-7 loss to the Browns finally sent Wiggin into exile. Tom Bettis took over as interim head coach and inspired his charges to a 20-10 victory over the Packers in his first game. The Chiefs lost the next six, however, including a 34-31 decision to Seattle which wrapped up last place.

## FINAL TEAM STATISTICS

### OFFENSE

| | BALT. | BUFF. | CIN. | CLEV. | DENV. | HOU. | K.C. | MIA. | N.E. | NY J | OAK. | PIT. | S.D. | SEA. |
|---|---|---|---|---|---|---|---|---|---|---|---|---|---|---|
| FIRST DOWNS: | | | | | | | | | | | | | | |
| Total | 269 | 246 | 248 | 271 | 223 | 228 | 228 | 267 | 247 | 195 | 305 | 266 | 235 | 251 |
| by Rushing | 111 | 93 | 110 | 119 | 101 | 112 | 95 | 143 | 132 | 83 | 156 | 122 | 93 | 116 |
| by Passing | 136 | 141 | 112 | 119 | 107 | 91 | 101 | 107 | 101 | 96 | 125 | 124 | 121 | 116 |
| by Penalty | 22 | 12 | 26 | 33 | 15 | 25 | 23 | 17 | 14 | 16 | 24 | 20 | 21 | 19 |
| RUSHING: | | | | | | | | | | | | | | |
| Number | 566 | 450 | 488 | 510 | 523 | 509 | 456 | 519 | 603 | 437 | 681 | 581 | 488 | 461 |
| Yards | 2123 | 1861 | 1861 | 2200 | 2043 | 1989 | 1843 | 2366 | 2303 | 1618 | 2627 | 2258 | 1761 | 1964 |
| Average Yards | 3.8 | 4.1 | 3.8 | 4.3 | 3.9 | 3.9 | 4.0 | 4.6 | 3.8 | 3.7 | 3.9 | 3.9 | 3.6 | 4.3 |
| Touchdowns | 17 | 3 | 10 | 9 | 16 | 15 | 13 | 18 | 13 | 6 | 20 | 20 | 10 | 12 |
| PASSING: | | | | | | | | | | | | | | |
| Attempts | 395 | 458 | 385 | 377 | 313 | 347 | 374 | 311 | 305 | 360 | 324 | 341 | 369 | 387 |
| Completions | 224 | 221 | 192 | 208 | 163 | 181 | 190 | 182 | 160 | 170 | 184 | 173 | 206 | 175 |
| Completion Pct. | 56.7 | 48.3 | 49.9 | 55.2 | 52.1 | 52.2 | 50.8 | 58.5 | 52.5 | 47.2 | 56.8 | 50.7 | 55.8 | 45.2 |
| Passing Yards | 2686 | 2803 | 2550 | 2374 | 2265 | 2107 | 2514 | 2264 | 2162 | 2286 | 2338 | 2632 | 2442 | 2459 |
| Avg. Yds Per Att. | 6.8 | 6.1 | 6.6 | 6.3 | 7.2 | 6.1 | 6.7 | 7.3 | 7.1 | 6.4 | 7.2 | 7.7 | 6.6 | 6.4 |
| Avg. Yds Per Comp. | 12.0 | 12.7 | 13.3 | 11.4 | 13.9 | 11.6 | 13.2 | 12.4 | 13.5 | 13.4 | 12.7 | 15.2 | 11.9 | 14.1 |
| Times Tackled | 26 | 36 | 31 | 24 | 50 | 23 | 48 | 36 | 14 | 35 | 25 | 27 | 24 | 21 |
| Yds Lost Tackled | 221 | 273 | 217 | 199 | 402 | 232 | 421 | 303 | 155 | 284 | 229 | 245 | 198 | 131 |
| Net Yards | 2465 | 2530 | 2333 | 2175 | 1863 | 1875 | 2093 | 1961 | 2007 | 2002 | 2109 | 2387 | 2244 | 2328 |
| Touchdowns | 17 | 12 | 12 | 19 | 15 | 14 | 11 | 22 | 17 | 14 | 21 | 17 | 11 | 23 |
| Interceptions | 12 | 24 | 16 | 31 | 12 | 21 | 26 | 14 | 21 | 26 | 24 | 21 | 20 | 32 |
| Pct. Intercepted | 3.0 | 5.2 | 4.2 | 8.2 | 3.8 | 6.1 | 7.0 | 4.5 | 6.9 | 7.2 | 7.4 | 6.2 | 5.4 | 8.3 |
| PUNTS: | | | | | | | | | | | | | | |
| Number | 84 | 83 | 70 | 62 | 91 | 79 | 89 | 58 | 68 | 76 | 59 | 73 | 73 | 64 |
| Average | 37.4 | 38.9 | 41.3 | 39.0 | 39.2 | 38.4 | 39.4 | 36.9 | 34.6 | 37.6 | 43.3 | 36.3 | 37.1 | 38.0 |
| PUNT RETURNS: | | | | | | | | | | | | | | |
| Number | 42 | 32 | 41 | 38 | 58 | 36 | 36 | 40 | 43 | 38 | 37 | 46 | 46 | 32 |
| Yards | 323 | 380 | 328 | 322 | 712 | 539 | 236 | 315 | 429 | 540 | 373 | 389 | 521 | 217 |
| Average Yards | 7.7 | 11.9 | 8.0 | 8.5 | 12.3 | 15.0 | 6.6 | 7.9 | 10.0 | 12.6 | 10.1 | 8.5 | 11.3 | 6.8 |
| Touchdowns | 0 | 2 | 0 | 0 | 1 | 2 | 0 | 0 | 0 | 0 | 0 | 0 | 1 | 0 |
| KICKOFF RETURNS: | | | | | | | | | | | | | | |
| Number | 48 | 60 | 46 | 53 | 34 | 46 | 63 | 38 | 39 | 61 | 49 | 45 | 39 | 71 |
| Yards | 912 | 1238 | 886 | 1075 | 732 | 1056 | 1284 | 1011 | 1051 | 1374 | 909 | 995 | 734 | 1502 |
| Average Yards | 19.0 | 20.6 | 19.7 | 20.3 | 21.5 | 23.0 | 20.4 | 26.6 | 26.9 | 22.5 | 18.6 | 22.1 | 18.8 | 21.2 |
| Touchdowns | 0 | 0 | 0 | 0 | 0 | 1 | 0 | 1 | 3 | 0 | 0 | 0 | 0 | 0 |
| INTERCEPTION RET: | | | | | | | | | | | | | | |
| Number | 30 | 21 | 16 | 23 | 25 | 26 | 21 | 15 | 19 | 11 | 26 | 31 | 21 | 25 |
| Yards | 434 | 329 | 238 | 430 | 491 | 429 | 348 | 124 | 194 | 153 | 352 | 374 | 317 | 356 |
| Average Yards | 14.5 | 15.7 | 14.9 | 18.7 | 19.6 | 16.5 | 16.6 | 8.3 | 10.2 | 13.9 | 13.5 | 12.1 | 15.1 | 14.2 |
| Touchdowns | 0 | 1 | 2 | 3 | 2 | 1 | 2 | 0 | 0 | 1 | 0 | 0 | 2 | 1 |
| PENALTIES: | | | | | | | | | | | | | | |
| Number | 77 | 87 | 89 | 125 | 91 | 106 | 82 | 59 | 112 | 62 | 89 | 122 | 97 | 76 |
| Yards | 620 | 866 | 859 | 1046 | 883 | 835 | 706 | 432 | 931 | 508 | 747 | 973 | 813 | 656 |
| FUMBLES: | | | | | | | | | | | | | | |
| Number | 24 | 36 | 37 | 34 | 28 | 30 | 33 | 22 | 28 | 24 | 22 | 41 | 29 | 27 |
| Number Lost | 14 | 20 | 16 | 22 | 15 | 17 | 21 | 13 | 15 | 14 | 16 | 28 | 11 | 14 |
| POINTS: | | | | | | | | | | | | | | |
| Total | 295 | 160 | 238 | 269 | 274 | 299 | 225 | 313 | 278 | 191 | 351 | 283 | 222 | 282 |
| PAT Attempts | 35 | 19 | 26 | 31 | 34 | 36 | 29 | 41 | 33 | 21 | 42 | 37 | 25 | 37 |
| PAT Made | 32 | 17 | 25 | 30 | 31 | 29 | 27 | 37 | 33 | 18 | 39 | 34 | 21 | 33 |
| FG Attempts | 26 | 17 | 27 | 23 | 19 | 25 | 18 | 22 | 21 | 25 | 28 | 14 | 23 | 18 |
| FG Made | 17 | 9 | 19 | 17 | 13 | 16 | 8 | 10 | 15 | 15 | 20 | 9 | 17 | 9 |
| Percent FG Made | 65.4 | 52.9 | 70.4 | 73.9 | 68.4 | 64.0 | 44.4 | 45.5 | 71.4 | 60.0 | 71.4 | 64.3 | 73.9 | 50.0 |
| Safeties | 1 | 1 | 0 | 1 | 0 | 3 | 0 | 0 | 1 | 1 | 0 | 0 | 0 | 0 |

### DEFENSE

| | BALT. | BUFF. | CIN. | CLEV. | DENV. | HOU. | K.C. | MIA. | N.E. | NY J | OAK. | PIT. | S.D. | SEA. |
|---|---|---|---|---|---|---|---|---|---|---|---|---|---|---|
| FIRST DOWNS: | | | | | | | | | | | | | | |
| Total | 210 | 260 | 253 | 261 | 217 | 247 | 304 | 227 | 215 | 283 | 204 | 228 | 228 | 295 |
| by Rushing | 78 | 134 | 113 | 113 | 77 | 103 | 169 | 101 | 86 | 137 | 86 | 80 | 102 | 152 |
| by Passing | 116 | 98 | 113 | 116 | 234 | 124 | 113 | 117 | 111 | 131 | 105 | 112 | 105 | 125 |
| by Penalty | 16 | 28 | 27 | 32 | 17 | 20 | 22 | 9 | 18 | 15 | 13 | 36 | 21 | 18 |
| RUSHING: | | | | | | | | | | | | | | |
| Number | 423 | 589 | 525 | 524 | 470 | 522 | 632 | 467 | 452 | 575 | 408 | 493 | 508 | 596 |
| Yards | 798 | 2405 | 1897 | 2098 | 1531 | 1815 | 2971 | 1749 | 1605 | 2245 | 1754 | 1723 | 1927 | 2485 |
| Average Yards | 4.3 | 4.1 | 3.6 | 4.0 | 3.3 | 3.5 | 4.7 | 3.7 | 3.6 | 3.9 | 4.3 | 3.5 | 3.8 | 4.2 |
| Touchdowns | 11 | 21 | 15 | 14 | 5 | 11 | 23 | 12 | 8 | 14 | 7 | 9 | 11 | 21 |
| PASSING: | | | | | | | | | | | | | | |
| Attempts | 382 | 316 | 351 | 340 | 426 | 379 | 333 | 414 | 356 | 377 | 367 | 357 | 380 | 349 |
| Completions | 181 | 155 | 196 | 184 | 235 | 192 | 175 | 226 | 188 | 215 | 177 | 157 | 172 | 199 |
| Completion Pct. | 47.4 | 49.1 | 55.8 | 54.1 | 55.2 | 50.7 | 52.7 | 54.6 | 52.8 | 57.0 | 48.2 | 40.0 | 45.3 | 57.0 |
| Passing Yards | 2549 | 2213 | 2453 | 2298 | 2556 | 2431 | 2244 | 2393 | 2504 | 2587 | 2503 | 2254 | 2088 | 2464 |
| Avg. Yds Per Att. | 6.7 | 7.0 | 7.0 | 6.8 | 6.0 | 6.4 | 6.7 | 5.8 | 7.0 | 6.9 | 6.8 | 6.3 | 5.5 | 7.1 |
| Avg. Yds Per Comp. | 14.1 | 14.3 | 12.5 | 12.5 | 10.9 | 12.7 | 12.8 | 10.6 | 13.3 | 12.0 | 14.1 | 14.4 | 12.1 | 12.4 |
| Times Tackled | 47 | 17 | 25 | 31 | 35 | 32 | 25 | 20 | 58 | 26 | 35 | 32 | 44 | 18 |
| Yds Lost Tackled | 359 | 165 | 226 | 281 | 312 | 289 | 222 | 160 | 471 | 184 | 281 | 285 | 363 | 131 |
| Net Yards | 2190 | 2048 | 2227 | 2017 | 2244 | 2142 | 2022 | 2233 | 2033 | 2403 | 2222 | 1969 | 1725 | 2333 |
| Touchdowns | 10 | 17 | 14 | 15 | 11 | 12 | 15 | 10 | 16 | 23 | 17 | 16 | 14 | 19 |
| Interceptions | 30 | 21 | 16 | 23 | 25 | 26 | 21 | 15 | 19 | 11 | 26 | 31 | 21 | 25 |
| Pct. Intercepted | 7.9 | 6.7 | 4.6 | 6.8 | 5.9 | 6.9 | 6.3 | 3.6 | 5.3 | 2.9 | 7.1 | 8.7 | 5.5 | 7.2 |
| PUNTS: | | | | | | | | | | | | | | |
| Number | 81 | 73 | 75 | 70 | 95 | 77 | 63 | 67 | 78 | 73 | 74 | 79 | 76 | 54 |
| Average | 36.2 | 36.2 | 37.6 | 37.7 | 40.7 | 40.8 | 41.0 | 38.5 | 39.1 | 38.2 | 37.6 | 40.3 | 40.6 | 36.0 |
| PUNT RETURNS: | | | | | | | | | | | | | | |
| Number | 44 | 42 | 38 | 31 | 55 | 46 | 50 | 29 | 33 | 46 | 31 | 34 | 40 | 42 |
| Yards | 481 | 604 | 260 | 558 | 397 | 340 | 703 | 267 | 270 | 448 | 217 | 380 | 378 | 389 |
| Average Yards | 10.9 | 14.4 | 6.8 | 18.0 | 7.2 | 7.4 | 14.1 | 9.2 | 8.2 | 9.7 | 7.0 | 11.2 | 9.5 | 9.3 |
| Touchdowns | 1 | 0 | 0 | 3 | 0 | 0 | 0 | 0 | 0 | 0 | 0 | 1 | 0 | 0 |
| KICKOFF RETURNS: | | | | | | | | | | | | | | |
| Number | 60 | 40 | 48 | 50 | 50 | 63 | 44 | 59 | 52 | 45 | 63 | 48 | 47 | 50 |
| Yards | 1514 | 814 | 1029 | 986 | 1084 | 1331 | 958 | 1281 | 1086 | 946 | 997 | 1080 | 952 | 1240 |
| Average Yards | 25.2 | 20.3 | 21.4 | 19.7 | 21.7 | 21.1 | 21.8 | 21.7 | 20.9 | 21.0 | 15.8 | 22.5 | 20.3 | 24.8 |
| Touchdowns | 2 | 1 | 0 | 0 | 0 | 0 | 1 | 0 | 0 | 1 | 0 | 0 | 0 | 0 |
| INTERCEPTION RET: | | | | | | | | | | | | | | |
| Number | 12 | 24 | 16 | 31 | 12 | 21 | 26 | 14 | 21 | 26 | 24 | 21 | 20 | 32 |
| Yards | 298 | 326 | 192 | 351 | 172 | 253 | 390 | 238 | 279 | 420 | 373 | 299 | 109 | 592 |
| Average Yards | 24.8 | 13.6 | 12.0 | 11.3 | 14.3 | 12.0 | 15.0 | 17.0 | 13.3 | 16.2 | 15.5 | 14.2 | 5.5 | 18.5 |
| Touchdowns | 1 | 0 | 0 | 0 | 0 | 1 | 3 | 0 | 2 | 0 | 2 | 1 | 0 | 3 |
| PENALTIES: | | | | | | | | | | | | | | |
| Number | 78 | 71 | 103 | 117 | 97 | 97 | 105 | 82 | 71 | 89 | 82 | 82 | 87 | 96 |
| Yards | 618 | 638 | 768 | 979 | 718 | 791 | 929 | 644 | 610 | 788 | 717 | 784 | 831 | 794 |
| FUMBLES: | | | | | | | | | | | | | | |
| Number | 27 | 21 | 34 | 32 | 28 | 39 | 39 | 37 | 20 | 37 | 31 | 28 | 28 | 20 |
| Number Lost | 17 | 12 | 23 | 16 | 14 | 28 | 23 | 18 | 10 | 17 | 21 | 13 | 10 | 11 |
| POINTS: | | | | | | | | | | | | | | |
| Total | 221 | 313 | 235 | 267 | 148 | 230 | 349 | 197 | 217 | 300 | 230 | 243 | 205 | 373 |
| PAT Attempts | 27 | 39 | 29 | 32 | 18 | 26 | 42 | 23 | 26 | 39 | 29 | 29 | 26 | 43 |
| PAT Made | 24 | 37 | 26 | 27 | 16 | 24 | 37 | 21 | 22 | 34 | 23 | 27 | 25 | 42 |
| FG Attempts | 21 | 21 | 18 | 22 | 22 | 22 | 28 | 20 | 21 | 21 | 19 | 21 | 13 | 31 |
| FG Made | 11 | 14 | 11 | 16 | 8 | 16 | 20 | 12 | 13 | 10 | 11 | 14 | 8 | 23 |
| Percent FG Made | 52.4 | 66.7 | 61.7 | 72.7 | 36.4 | 72.7 | 71.4 | 60.0 | 61.9 | 47.6 | 57.9 | 66.7 | 61.5 | 74.2 |
| Safeties | 1 | 0 | 1 | 0 | 0 | 1 | 0 | 1 | 0 | 1 | 0 | 0 | 0 | 2 |

## CONFERENCE PLAYOFFS

### December 24, at Baltimore (Attendance 60,753)

**SCORING**

| | | | | | | | |
|---|---|---|---|---|---|---|---|
| BALT. | 0 | 10 | 7 | 14 | 0 | 0 | – 31 |
| OAK. | 7 | 0 | 14 | 10 | 0 | 6 | – 37 |

First Quarter
- Oak. Davis, 30 yard rush PAT – Mann (kick)

Second Quarter
- Balt. Laird, 61 yard interception return PAT – Linhart (kick)
- Balt. Linhart, 35 yard field goal

Third Quarter
- Oak. Casper, 8 yard pass from Stabler PAT – Mann (kick)
- Balt. Johnson, 87 yard kickoff return PAT – Linhart (kick)
- Oak. Casper, 10 yard pass from Stabler PAT – Mann (kick)

Fourth Quarter
- Balt. R. Lee, 1 yard rush PAT – Linhart (kick)
- Oak. Banazak, 1 yard rush PAT – Mann (kick)
- Balt. R. Lee, 13 yard rush PAT – Linhart (kick)
- Oak. Mann, 22 yard field goal

Second Overtime
- Oak. Casper, 10 yard pass from Stabler PAT – none attempted

**TEAM STATISTICS**

| BALT. | | OAK. |
|---|---|---|
| 22 | First Downs – Total | 28 |
| 10 | First Downs – Rushing | 8 |
| 8 | First Downs – Passing | 17 |
| 4 | First Downs – Penalty | 3 |
| 1 | Fumbles – Number | 4 |
| 0 | Fumbles – Lost Ball | 2 |
| 8 | Penalties – Number | 7 |
| 82 | Yards Penalized | 65 |
| 0 | Missed Field Goals | 1 |
| 82 | Offensive Plays | 89 |
| 301 | Net Yards | 491 |
| 3.7 | Average Gain | 5.5 |
| 0 | Giveaways | 4 |
| 4 | Takeaways | 0 |
| 14 | Difference | -4 |

**INDIVIDUAL STATISTICS**

| BALTIMORE | No | Yds | Avg. | OAKLAND | No | Yds | Avg. |
|---|---|---|---|---|---|---|---|
| **RUSHING** | | | | | | | |
| Mitchell | 23 | 67 | 2.9 | v. Eeghen | 19 | 76 | 4.0 |
| R. Lee | 11 | 46 | 4.2 | Davis | 16 | 48 | 3.0 |
| Leaks | 8 | 35 | 4.4 | Banaszak | 11 | 37 | 3.4 |
| Jones | 6 | 30 | 5.0 | Garrett | 1 | 6 | 6.0 |
| McCauley | 2 | 9 | 4.5 | | 47 | 167 | 3.6 |
| | 50 | 187 | 3.7 | | | | |
| **RECEIVING** | | | | | | | |
| Mitchell | 3 | 39 | 13.0 | Biletnikoff | 7 | 88 | 12.6 |
| Scott | 2 | 45 | 22.5 | Branch | 6 | 113 | 18.8 |
| R. Lee | 2 | 22 | 11.0 | Casper | 4 | 70 | 17.5 |
| McCauley | 2 | 11 | 5.5 | v. Eeghen | 2 | 39 | 19.5 |
| Chester | 1 | 30 | 30.0 | Davis | 2 | 35 | 17.5 |
| Doughty | 1 | 20 | 20.0 | | 21 | 345 | 16.4 |
| Pratt | 1 | -3 | -3.0 | | | | |
| | 12 | 164 | 13.7 | | | | |
| **PUNTING** | | | | | | | |
| D. Lee | 12 | | 36.5 | Guy | 8 | | 46.8 |
| **PUNT RETURNS** | | | | | | | |
| Blackwood | 2 | 6 | 3.0 | Colzie | 5 | 42 | 8.4 |
| Johnson | 1 | 16 | 16.0 | Bradshaw | 1 | 0 | 0.0 |
| | 3 | 22 | 7.3 | | 6 | 42 | 7.0 |
| **KICKOFF RETURNS** | | | | | | | |
| Johnson | 3 | 134 | 44.7 | Garrett | 5 | 169 | 33.8 |
| McCauley | 1 | 25 | 25.0 | Davis | 1 | 17 | 17.0 |
| Blackwood | 1 | 17 | 17.0 | | 6 | 186 | 31.0 |
| Nettles | 1 | 17 | 17.0 | | | | |
| | 6 | 193 | 32.2 | | | | |
| **INTERCEPTION RETURNS** | | | | | | | |
| Laird | 2 | 61 | 30.5 | none | | | |

**PASSING**

| | Att | Comp | Comp. Pct. | Yds | Int | Yds/ Att. | Yds/ Comp | Yards Lost Tackled |
|---|---|---|---|---|---|---|---|---|
| **BALTIMORE** | | | | | | | | |
| Jones | 26 | 12 | 46.2 | 164 | 0 | 6.3 | 13.7 | 6-50 |
| **OAKLAND** | | | | | | | | |
| Stabler | 40 | 21 | 52.5 | 345 | 2 | 8.6 | 16.4 | 2-21 |

### December 24, at Denver (Attendance 75,011)

**SCORING**

| | | | | | |
|---|---|---|---|---|---|
| DENVER | 7 | 7 | 7 | 13 | – 34 |
| PITTSBURGH | 0 | 14 | 0 | 7 | – 21 |

First Quarter
- Denv. Lytle, 7 yard rush PAT – Turner (kick)

Second Quarter
- Pitt. Bradshaw, 1 yard rush PAT – Gerela (kick)
- Denv. Armstong, 10 yard rush PAT – Turner (kick)
- Pitt. Harris, 1 yard rush PAT – Gerela (kick)

Third Quarter
- Denv. Odoms, 30 yard pass from Morton PAT – Turner (kick)

Fourth Quarter
- Pitt. Brown, 1 yard pass from Bradshaw PAT – Gerela (kick)
- Denv. Turner, 44 yard field goal
- Denv. Turner, 25 yard field goal
- Denv. Dolbin, 34 yard pass from Morton PAT – Turner (kick)

**TEAM STATISTICS**

| DENVER | | PITTS. |
|---|---|---|
| 15 | First Downs – Total | 18 |
| 5 | First Downs – Rushing | 10 |
| 9 | First Downs – Passing | 8 |
| 1 | First Downs – Penalty | 0 |
| 3 | Fumbles – Number | 2 |
| 1 | Fumbles – Lost Ball | 1 |
| 3 | Penalties – Number | 10 |
| 20 | Yards Penalized | 67 |
| 0 | Missed Field Goals | 0 |
| 61 | Offensive Plays | 76 |
| 258 | Net Yards | 307 |
| 4.2 | Average Gain | 4.0 |
| 0 | Giveaways | 3 |
| 3 | Takeaways | 0 |
| +3 | Difference | -3 |

**INDIVIDUAL STATISTICS**

| DENVER | No | Yds | Avg. | PITTSBURGH | No | Yds | Avg. |
|---|---|---|---|---|---|---|---|
| **RUSHING** | | | | | | | |
| Armstrong | 11 | 44 | 4.0 | Harris | 28 | 92 | 3.3 |
| Lytle | 12 | 26 | 2.2 | Bradshaw | 4 | 21 | 5.3 |
| Keyworth | 5 | 20 | 4.0 | Bleier | 7 | 14 | 2.0 |
| Jensen | 4 | 13 | 3.3 | | 39 | 127 | 3.3 |
| Morton | 5 | 0 | 0.0 | | | | |
| | 37 | 103 | 2.8 | | | | |
| **RECEIVING** | | | | | | | |
| Odoms | 5 | 43 | 8.6 | Stallworth | 4 | 80 | 20.0 |
| Moses | 2 | 45 | 22.5 | Harris | 4 | 20 | 5.0 |
| Jensen | 2 | 33 | 16.5 | Cunningham | 3 | 42 | 14.0 |
| Dolbin | 1 | 34 | 34.0 | Maxson | 3 | 11 | 3.7 |
| Armstrong | 1 | 9 | 9.0 | Bleier | 2 | 10 | 5.0 |
| | 11 | 164 | 14.9 | Grossman | 1 | 7 | 7.0 |
| | | | | Swann | 1 | 6 | 6.0 |
| | | | | Brown | 1 | 1 | 1.0 |
| | | | | | 19 | 177 | 9.3 |
| **PUNTING** | | | | | | | |
| Dilts | 5 | | 37.6 | Engles | 5 | | 40.8 |
| **PUNT RETURNS** | | | | | | | |
| Thompson | 2 | 5 | 2.5 | Smith | 4 | 31 | 7.8 |
| Schultz | 1 | 4 | 4.0 | | | | |
| Upchurch | 1 | 3 | 3.0 | | | | |
| | 4 | 12 | 3.0 | | | | |
| **KICKOFF RETURNS** | | | | | | | |
| Upchurch | 3 | 48 | 19.3 | Smith | 4 | 80 | 20.0 |
| Schultz | 1 | 27 | 27.0 | Maxson | 1 | 24 | 24.0 |
| | 4 | 85 | 21.3 | | 5 | 104 | 20.8 |
| **INTERCEPTION RETURNS** | | | | | | | |
| T. Jackson | 2 | 49 | 24.5 | none | | | |
| B. Jackson | 1 | 15 | 15.0 | | | | |
| | 3 | 64 | 31.3 | | | | |

**PASSING**

| | Att | Comp | Comp. Pct. | Yds | Int | Yds/ Att. | Yds/ Comp | Yards Lost Tackled |
|---|---|---|---|---|---|---|---|---|
| **DENVER** | | | | | | | | |
| Morton | 23 | 11 | 47.8 | 164 | 0 | 7.1 | 14.9 | 1-9 |
| **PITTSBURGH** | | | | | | | | |
| Bradshaw | 37 | 19 | 51.4 | 177 | 3 | 4.8 | 9.3 | 0 |

1977 A.F.C. — Eastern Division
326

## BALTIMORE COLTS 10-4 Ted Marchibroda

| Scores of Each Game | | |
|---|---|---|
| 29 | Seattle | 14 |
| 20 | N.Y. Jets | 12 |
| 17 | BUFFALO | 14 |
| 45 | MIAMI | 28 |
| 17 | Kansas City | 6 |
| 3 | New England | 17 |
| 31 | PITTSBURGH | 21 |
| 10 | WASHINGTON | 3 |
| 31 | Buffalo | 13 |
| 33 | N.Y. JETS | 12 |
| 13 | Denver | 27 |
| 6 | Miami | 17 |
| 10 | DETROIT | 13 |
| 30 | NEW ENGLAND | 24 |

| Use Name | Pos. | Hgt | Wgt | Age | Int | Pts |
|---|---|---|---|---|---|---|
| Wade Griffin | OT | 6'5" | 231 | 23 | | |
| George Kunz | OT | 6'5" | 262 | 30 | | |
| David Taylor | OT | 6'4" | 264 | 27 | | |
| Elmer Collett | OG | 6'4" | 241 | 32 | | |
| Ken Huff | OG | 6'4" | 262 | 24 | | |
| Robert Pratt | OG | 6'4" | 248 | 26 | | 6 |
| Bob Van Duyne | OG-OT | 6'5" | 244 | 25 | | |
| Forrest Blue | C | 6'5" | 260 | 31 | | |
| Ken Mendenhall | C | 6'3" | 250 | 29 | | |
| Fred Cook | DE | 6'3" | 243 | 25 | | |
| John Dutton | DE | 6'7" | 266 | 26 | | |
| Ron Fernandes | DE | 6'4" | 255 | 25 | | |
| Mike Barnes | DT | 6'6" | 256 | 26 | | |
| Joe Ehrmann | DT | 6'5" | 264 | 28 | | |
| Ken Novak | DT | 6'7" | 264 | 23 | | |
| Dan Dickel | LB | 6'3" | 230 | 25 | | |
| Derrel Luce | LB | 6'3" | 227 | 24 | | |
| Tom McCleod | LB | 6'3" | 224 | 26 | 2 | |
| Sanders Shiver | LB | 6'2" | 222 | 22 | | |
| Ed Simonini | LB | 6' | 210 | 23 | 1 | |
| Stan White | LB | 6'1" | 223 | 27 | 7 | |
| Tim Baylor | DB | 6'6" | 191 | 23 | | |
| Lyle Blackwood | DB | 6' | 190 | 26 | 10 | |
| Bruce Laird | DB | 6' | 198 | 27 | 3 | |
| Lloyd Mumphord | DB | 5'11" | 178 | 30 | | |
| Nelson Munsey | DB | 6'1" | 186 | 29 | 3 | |
| Doug Nettles | DB | 6' | 178 | 26 | 1 | 2 |
| Ray Oldham | DB | 6' | 192 | 26 | | |
| Norm Thompson | DB | 6'1" | 180 | 29 | 3 | |
| Bert Jones | QB | 6'3" | 212 | 25 | | 12 |
| Mike Kirkland | QB | 6'1" | 195 | 23 | | |
| Bill Troup | QB | 6'5" | 215 | 26 | | |
| Don McCauley | HB-FB | 6'1" | 215 | 28 | | 48 |
| Lydell Mitchell | HB | 5'11" | 198 | 28 | | 42 |
| Howard Stevens | HB | 5'5" | 165 | 27 | | |
| Roosevelt Leaks | FB | 5'10" | 225 | 24 | | 24 |
| Ron Lee | FB | 6'4" | 228 | 23 | | 18 |
| Roger Carr | WR | 6'3" | 196 | 25 | | 6 |
| Glenn Doughty | WR | 6'1" | 205 | 26 | | 24 |
| Perry Griggs | WR | 5'10" | 182 | 23 | | |
| Marshall Johnson | WR | 6'1" | 190 | 24 | | |
| Freddie Scott | WR | 6'2" | 175 | 25 | | 12 |
| Ricky Thompson | WR | 6' | 176 | 23 | | |
| Mack Alston | TE | 6'2" | 230 | 30 | | |
| Ray Chester | TE | 6'3" | 236 | 29 | | 18 |
| Jimmie Kennedy | TE | 6'3" | 230 | 25 | | |
| David Lee | K | 6'4" | 216 | 33 | | |
| Toni Linhart | K | 6' | 179 | 35 | | 83 |

Delles Howell – Injury

## MIAMI DOLPHINS 10-4 Don Shula

| Scores of Each Game | | |
|---|---|---|
| 13 | Buffalo | 0 |
| 19 | San Francisco | 15 |
| 27 | HOUSTON | 7 |
| 28 | Baltimore | 45 |
| 21 | N.Y. JETS | 17 |
| 31 | SEATTLE | 13 |
| 13 | SAN DIEGO | 14 |
| 14 | N.Y. Jets | 10 |
| 17 | NEW ENGLAND | 5 |
| 17 | Cincinnati | 23 |
| 55 | St. Louis | 14 |
| 17 | BALTIMORE | 6 |
| 10 | New England | 14 |
| 31 | BUFFALO | 14 |

| Use Name | Pos. | Hgt | Wgt | Age | Int | Pts |
|---|---|---|---|---|---|---|
| Mike Current | OT | 6'4" | 270 | 31 | | |
| Wayne Moore | OT | 6'6" | 265 | 32 | | |
| Steve Young | OT | 6'8" | 270 | 24 | | |
| Bob Kuechenberg | OG-C | 6'3" | 255 | 29 | | |
| Larry Little | OG-OT | 6'1" | 265 | 31 | | |
| Ed Newman | OG | 6'2" | 245 | 26 | | |
| Wally Pesuit | OG-OT | 6'4" | 250 | 23 | | |
| Jim Langer | C | 6'2" | 253 | 29 | | |
| John Alexander | DE | 6'2" | 250 | 21 | | |
| Vern Den Herder | DE | 6'6" | 252 | 28 | | |
| A.J. Duhe | DE | 6'4" | 247 | 21 | | |
| Rick Dvorak (from NYG) | DE | 6'4" | 245 | 25 | | |
| Carl Barisich | NT | 6'4" | 255 | 26 | | |
| Bob Baumhower | NT | 6'5" | 258 | 22 | | |
| Bob Heinz | NT-DE | 6'6" | 260 | 30 | | |
| Bill Windauer | NT | 6'3" | 250 | 27 | | |
| Larry Ball | LB | 6'6" | 235 | 27 | | |
| Kim Bokamper | LB | 6'6" | 245 | 22 | | |
| Rusty Chambers | LB | 6'1" | 220 | 23 | | |
| Larry Gordon | LB | 6'4" | 230 | 24 | 1 | |
| Mike Kolen | LB | 6'2" | 222 | 29 | | |
| Bob Matheson | LB | 6'4" | 235 | 32 | 1 | |
| Earnest Rhone | LB | 6'2" | 212 | 24 | | |
| Guy Roberts | LB | 6'1" | 220 | 27 | | |
| Steve Towle | LB | 6'2" | 233 | 23 | | |
| Dick Anderson | DB | 6'2" | 196 | 31 | | |
| Charlie Babb | DB | 6' | 190 | 27 | 1 | |
| Charles Cornelius | DB | 5'9" | 176 | 25 | | |
| Tim Foley | DB | 6' | 194 | 29 | 3 | |
| Curtis Johnson | DB | 6'2" | 196 | 29 | 4 | |
| Vern Roberson | DB | 6'1" | 195 | 25 | 1 | |
| Norris Thomas | DB | 5'11" | 170 | 23 | 3 | |
| Rick Volk | DB | 6'3" | 195 | 32 | 1 | |
| Bob Griese | QB | 6'1" | 190 | 32 | | |
| Don Strock | QB | 6'5" | 218 | 26 | | |
| Gary Davis | HB | 5'10" | 202 | 22 | | 18 |
| Benny Malone | HB | 5'10" | 193 | 25 | | 30 |
| Nat Moore | HB-WR | 5'9" | 180 | 25 | | 78 |
| Norm Bulaich | FB | 6'1" | 218 | 30 | | 24 |
| Leroy Harris | FB | 5'9" | 220 | 23 | | 24 |
| Don Nottingham | FB | 5'10" | 210 | 28 | | 12 |
| Stan Winfrey (from TB) (to BUF) | FB | 5'11" | 223 | 24 | | |
| Terry Anderson | WR | 5'9" | 182 | 22 | | |
| Duriel Harris | WR | 5'11" | 175 | 22 | | 30 |
| Freddie Solomon | WR | 5'11" | 181 | 24 | | 12 |
| Jim Mandich | TE-WR | 6'3" | 214 | 29 | | |
| Loaird McCreary | TE-WR | 6'5" | 227 | 24 | | 6 |
| Larry Seiple | TE-WR | 6' | 214 | 32 | | |
| Andre Tillman | TE | 6'5" | 230 | 24 | | 12 |
| Mike Michel | K | 5'10" | 177 | 23 | | |
| Garo Yepremian | K | 5'8" | 175 | 33 | | 67 |

Manny Fernandez – Knee Injury
Bill Stanfill – Injury

## NEW ENGLAND PATRIOTS 9-5 Chuck Fairbanks

| Scores of Each Game | | |
|---|---|---|
| 21 | KANSAS CITY | 17 |
| 27 | Cleveland | 30 |
| 27 | N.Y. Jets | 30 |
| 31 | SEATTLE | 0 |
| 24 | San Diego | 20 |
| 17 | BALTIMORE | 3 |
| 24 | N.Y. JETS | 13 |
| 14 | BUFFALO | 24 |
| 5 | Miami | 17 |
| 20 | Buffalo | 7 |
| 14 | PHILADELPHIA | 6 |
| 16 | Atlanta | 10 |
| 14 | MIAMI | 10 |
| 24 | Baltimore | 30 |

| Use Name | Pos. | Hgt | Wgt | Age | Int | Pts |
|---|---|---|---|---|---|---|
| Leon Gray | OT | 6'3" | 255 | 25 | | |
| Shelby Jordan | OT | 6'7" | 260 | 25 | | |
| Bob McKay | OT | 6'5" | 265 | 29 | | |
| Tom Neville | OT | 6'4" | 255 | 34 | | |
| Sam Adams | OG | 6'3" | 255 | 28 | | |
| Pete Brock | OG-C | 6'5" | 260 | 23 | | |
| John Hannah | OG | 6'2" | 265 | 26 | | |
| Fred Sturt | OG | 6'4" | 255 | 26 | | |
| Bob Hyland | C | 6'5" | 255 | 32 | | |
| Bill Lenkaitis | C | 6'3" | 252 | 31 | | |
| Julius Adams | DE | 6'3" | 260 | 29 | | |
| Greg Boyd | DE | 6'6" | 270 | 24 | | |
| Mel Lunsford | DE | 6'3" | 260 | 27 | | |
| Tony McGee | DE | 6'4" | 250 | 28 | | |
| Richard Bishop | NT | 6'1" | 260 | 27 | | |
| Ray Hamilton | NT | 6'1" | 250 | 26 | | |
| Art Moore | NT | 6'5" | 260 | 26 | | |
| Pete Barnes | LB | 6'3" | 240 | 32 | 1 | |
| Ray Costict | LB | 6' | 214 | 22 | | |
| Sam Hunt | LB | 6'1" | 250 | 26 | 2 | |
| Steve King | LB | 6'4" | 228 | 26 | | |
| Steve Nelson | LB | 6'2" | 228 | 26 | | |
| Rod Shoate | LB | 6'1" | 215 | 24 | | |
| Steve Zabel | LB | 6'4" | 228 | 29 | | |
| Doug Beaudoin | DB | 6'1" | 195 | 23 | | |
| Raymond Clayborn | DB | 6'1" | 181 | 22 | | 20 |
| Dick Conn | DB | 6' | 185 | 26 | | |
| Tim Fox | DB | 5'11" | 190 | 23 | 3 | |
| Mike Haynes | DB | 6'2" | 195 | 24 | 5 | |
| Bob Howard | DB | 6'1" | 175 | 32 | 4 | |
| Prentice McCray | DB | 6'1" | 190 | 24 | 4 | |
| Steve Grogan | QB | 6'4" | 205 | 24 | | 6 |
| Tom Owen | QB | 6'1" | 200 | 24 | | |
| Don Calhoun | HB-FB | 6' | 215 | 25 | | 24 |
| Ike Forte | HB | 6' | 202 | 23 | | 12 |
| Horace Ivory | HB | 6' | 197 | 23 | | |
| Sam Cunningham | FB | 6'3" | 230 | 27 | | 30 |
| Jess Phillips | FB | 6'1" | 208 | 30 | | 6 |
| Steve Burks | WR | 6'5" | 210 | 24 | | |
| Stanley Morgan | WR | 5'11" | 180 | 22 | | 18 |
| Darryl Stingley | WR | 6' | 193 | 25 | | 36 |
| Don Westbrook | WR | 5'10" | 188 | 24 | | |
| Al Chandler | TE | 6'2" | 228 | 26 | | |
| Russ Francis | TE | 6'6" | 240 | 24 | | 24 |
| Don Hasselbeck | TE | 6'7" | 245 | 23 | | 24 |
| Mike Patrick | K | 6' | 195 | 24 | | |
| John Smith | K | 6' | 190 | 27 | | 78 |

Pete Cusick – Knee Injury
Andy Johnson – Knee Injury
Jim Romaniszyn – Injury

## BUFFALO BILLS 3-11 Jim Ringo

| Scores of Each Game | | |
|---|---|---|
| 0 | MIAMI | 13 |
| 6 | Denver | 26 |
| 14 | Baltimore | 17 |
| 19 | N.Y. JETS | 24 |
| 3 | ATLANTA | 0 |
| 16 | CLEVELAND | 27 |
| 17 | Seattle | 56 |
| 24 | New England | 14 |
| 13 | BALTIMORE | 31 |
| 7 | NEW ENGLAND | 20 |
| 20 | Oakland | 14 |
| 0 | WASHINGTON | 10 |
| 14 | N.Y. Jets | 10 |
| 14 | Miami | 31 |

| Use Name | Pos. | Hgt | Wgt | Age | Int | Pts |
|---|---|---|---|---|---|---|
| Joe Devlin | OT | 6'5" | 258 | 23 | | |
| Dave Foley | OT | 6'5" | 247 | 29 | | |
| Ken Jones | OT | 6'5" | 252 | 24 | | |
| Bill Adams | OG | 6'2" | 246 | 27 | | |
| Joe DeLamielleure | OG | 6'3" | 248 | 26 | | |
| Reggie McKenzie | OG | 6'4" | 242 | 27 | | |
| Willie Parker | C | 6'3" | 245 | 28 | | |
| Connie Zelencik | C-OG | 6'4" | 245 | 22 | | |
| Phil Dokes | DE | 6'5" | 258 | 21 | | |
| Greg Morton | DE | 6'1" | 230 | 23 | | |
| Sherman White | DE | 6'5" | 250 | 28 | | |
| Ben Williams | DE | 6'3" | 258 | 23 | | |
| Bill Dunstan | DT | 6'4" | 250 | 28 | | |
| Mike Kadish | DT | 6'5" | 270 | 27 | | |
| John Little | DT | 6'3" | 250 | 30 | | |
| Greg Collins | LB | 6'3" | 227 | 24 | | |
| Bo Cornell | LB | 6'1" | 222 | 28 | | 6 |
| Dan Jilek | LB | 6'2" | 219 | 23 | | |
| Merv Krakau | LB | 6'2" | 248 | 26 | | |
| Bob Nelson | LB | 6'4" | 232 | 24 | | |
| Shane Nelson | LB | 6'1" | 222 | 22 | | |
| Tom Ruud | LB | 6'2" | 223 | 24 | | |
| John Skorupan | LB | 6'2" | 221 | 26 | | |
| Mario Clark | DB | 6'2" | 190 | 23 | 7 | |
| Steve Freeman | DB | 5'11" | 185 | 24 | 1 | |
| Tony Greene | DB | 5'10" | 170 | 28 | 9 | 2 |
| Dwight Harrison | DB | 6'1" | 186 | 28 | 2 | |
| Doug Jones | DB | 6'2" | 205 | 27 | 2 | 6 |
| Keith Moody | DB | 5'10" | 171 | 24 | | 6 |
| Charles Romes | DB | 6'1" | 191 | 23 | | |
| Fred Besana | QB | 6'4" | 200 | 23 | | |
| Joe Ferguson | QB | 6'1" | 184 | 27 | | 12 |
| Ken Johnson | QB | 6'2" | 205 | 26 | | |
| Curtis Brown | HB | 5'10" | 203 | 22 | | 6 |
| Mike Collier | HB | 5'11" | 200 | 23 | | |
| Reuben Gibson | HB | 6' | 196 | 22 | | |
| Roland Hooks | HB | 6' | 197 | 24 | | |
| O.J. Simpson | HB | 6'2" | 212 | 30 | | |
| Jim Braxton | FB | 6'2" | 240 | 28 | | 12 |
| Mike Franckowiak | FB | 6'3" | 218 | 24 | | |
| Mel Baker | WR | 6' | 190 | 27 | | |
| Bob Chandler | WR | 6' | 180 | 28 | | 24 |
| Reggie Craig (from CLE) | WR | 6' | 190 | 24 | | |
| John Holland | WR | 6' | 190 | 25 | | |
| John Kimbrough | WR | 5'10" | 165 | 23 | | 18 |
| Lou Piccone | WR | 5'9" | 184 | 28 | | 12 |
| Reuben Gant | TE | 6'4" | 225 | 25 | | 12 |
| Paul Seymour | TE | 6'5" | 245 | 27 | | |
| Marv Bateman | K | 6'4" | 215 | 27 | | |
| Carson Long | K | 5'10" | 210 | 22 | | 34 |
| Neil O'Donoghue | K | 6'6" | 204 | 24 | | 10 |

## NEW YORK JETS 3-11 Walt Michaels

| Scores of Each Game | | |
|---|---|---|
| 0 | Houston | 20 |
| 12 | BALTIMORE | 20 |
| 30 | NEW ENGLAND | 27 |
| 24 | Buffalo | 19 |
| 17 | Miami | 21 |
| 27 | OAKLAND | 28 |
| 13 | New England | 24 |
| 10 | MIAMI | 14 |
| 0 | SEATTLE | 17 |
| 12 | Baltimore | 33 |
| 20 | PITTSBURGH | 23 |
| 16 | New Orleans | 13 |
| 10 | BUFFALO | 14 |
| 0 | Philadelphia | 27 |

| Use Name | Pos. | Hgt | Wgt | Age | Int | Pts |
|---|---|---|---|---|---|---|
| Jeff Bleamer | OT-OG | 6'4" | 253 | 24 | | |
| Ken Helms | OT-C | 6'4" | 265 | 22 | | |
| Marvin Powell | OT | 6'5" | 264 | 22 | | |
| Gary Puetz | OT-OG | 6'4" | 265 | 25 | | |
| Dan Alexander | OG | 6'4" | 245 | 22 | | |
| Darrell Austin | OG-C | 6'4" | 252 | 25 | | |
| Randy Rasmussen | OG | 6'2" | 255 | 32 | | |
| John Roman | OG-OT | 6'4" | 251 | 25 | | |
| Joe Fields | C-OG | 6'2" | 245 | 23 | | |
| Al Burton | DE | 6'5" | 265 | 25 | | |
| John Hennessy | DE | 6'3" | 246 | 22 | | |
| Richard Neal | DE | 6'3" | 256 | 29 | | |
| Lawrence Pillers | DE | 6'3" | 257 | 24 | | |
| Carl Barzilauskas | DT | 6'6" | 270 | 26 | | |
| Joe Klecko | DT | 6'3" | 256 | 23 | | |
| Tank Marshall | DT | 6'4" | 245 | 22 | | |
| Abdul Salaam | DT | 6'3" | 260 | 24 | | |
| Greg Buttle | LB | 6'3" | 229 | 23 | 2 | 6 |
| John Ebersole | LB | 6'3" | 235 | 28 | 1 | |
| Mike Hennigan | LB | 6'2" | 215 | 25 | | |
| Jim Jerome | LB | 6'4" | 225 | 23 | | |
| Larry Keller | LB | 6'2" | 225 | 23 | 1 | |
| Bob Martin | LB | 6'1" | 223 | 23 | 1 | |
| Al Palewicz | LB | 6'1" | 217 | 27 | | |
| Carl Russ | LB | 6'2" | 227 | 24 | | |
| Billy Hardee | DB | 6' | 185 | 23 | 1 | |
| Ron Mabra | DB | 5'10" | 164 | 26 | | |
| Tommy Marvaso | DB | 6'1" | 191 | 23 | | |
| Burgess Owens | DB | 6'2" | 195 | 26 | 3 | |
| Artimus Parker | DB | 6'3" | 200 | 25 | 1 | |
| Ken Schroy | DB | 6'2" | 191 | 24 | | |
| Shafer Suggs | DB | 6'1" | 200 | 24 | | |
| Ed Taylor | DB | 6' | 176 | 24 | 1 | |
| Maurice Tyler | DB | 6' | 190 | 27 | | |
| Marty Domres | QB | 6'4" | 220 | 30 | | |
| Matt Robinson | QB | 6'2" | 196 | 22 | | |
| Richard Todd | QB | 6'2" | 205 | 23 | | 12 |
| Bruce Harper | HB-WR | 5'8" | 174 | 22 | | 6 |
| Kevin Long | HB | 6'1" | 205 | 22 | | |
| Charlie White | HB-FB | 6' | 222 | 24 | | 12 |
| Scott Dierking | FB | 5'10" | 215 | 22 | | 6 |
| Clark Gaines | FB-HB | 6'1" | 201 | 23 | | 24 |
| Tom Newton | FB | 6' | 205 | 23 | | |
| Rich Caster | WR | 6'5" | 230 | 28 | | 6 |
| Shelton Diggs | WR | 6'1" | 190 | 22 | | |
| David Knight | WR | 6'1" | 170 | 26 | | |
| Wesley Walker | WR | 6' | 172 | 22 | | 18 |
| Jerome Barkum | TE | 6'3" | 217 | 27 | | 36 |
| Bob Raba | TE | 6'1" | 222 | 22 | | |
| Pat Leahy | K | 6' | 190 | 26 | | 63 |
| Chuck Ramsey | K | 6'2" | 195 | 25 | | |

Don Coleman – Knee Injury
Louie Giammona – Knee Injury

## BALTIMORE COLTS

### Rushing
| Last Name | No. | Yds | Avg | TD |
|---|---|---|---|---|
| Mitchell | 301 | 1159 | 3.9 | 3 |
| R. Lee | 84 | 346 | 4.1 | 3 |
| Leaks | 59 | 237 | 4.0 | 3 |
| McCauley | 83 | 234 | 2.8 | 6 |
| Jones | 28 | 146 | 5.2 | 2 |
| Doughty | 2 | 11 | 5.5 | 0 |
| D. Lee | 2 | -2 | -1.0 | 0 |
| Troup | 7 | -8 | -1.1 | 0 |

### Receiving
| Last Name | No. | Yds | Avg | TD |
|---|---|---|---|---|
| Mitchell | 71 | 620 | 9 | 4 |
| McCauley | 51 | 495 | 10 | 2 |
| Chester | 31 | 556 | 18 | 3 |
| Doughty | 28 | 435 | 16 | 4 |
| Scott | 18 | 267 | 15 | 2 |
| Carr | 11 | 199 | 18 | 1 |
| R. Lee | 10 | 60 | 6 | 0 |
| Leaks | 3 | 39 | 13 | 1 |
| R. Thompson | 1 | 15 | 15 | 0 |

### Punt Returns
| Last Name | No. | Yds | Avg | TD |
|---|---|---|---|---|
| Stevens | 34 | 301 | 9 | 0 |
| Blackwood | 7 | 22 | 3 | 0 |
| Oldham | 1 | 0 | 0 | 0 |

### Kickoff Returns
| Last Name | No. | Yds | Avg | TD |
|---|---|---|---|---|
| Laird | 24 | 541 | 23 | 0 |
| Stevens | 11 | 216 | 20 | 0 |
| McCauley | 5 | 67 | 13 | 0 |
| Blackwood | 1 | 24 | 24 | 0 |
| Huff | 1 | 15 | 15 | 0 |
| Johnson | 1 | 15 | 15 | 0 |
| Griggs | 1 | 12 | 12 | 0 |
| Kennedy | 1 | 9 | 9 | 0 |
| Shiver | 1 | 7 | 7 | 0 |
| Griffin | 1 | 6 | 6 | 0 |
| Doughty | 1 | 0 | 0 | 0 |

### Passing
| Last Name | Att | Comp | % | Yds | Yd/Att | TD | Int- | % | RK |
|---|---|---|---|---|---|---|---|---|---|
| Jones | 393 | 224 | 57 | 2686 | 6.8 | 17 | 11- | 3 | 3 |
| Troup | 2 | 0 | 0 | 0 | 0.0 | 0 | 1- | 50 | |

### Punting
| Last Name | No | Avg |
|---|---|---|
| D. Lee | 82 | 38.3 |

### Kicking
| Last Name | XP | Att | % | FG | Att | % |
|---|---|---|---|---|---|---|
| Linhart | 32 | 35 | 91 | 17 | 26 | 65 |

## MIAMI DOLPHINS

### Rushing
| Last Name | No. | Yds | Avg | TD |
|---|---|---|---|---|
| Malone | 129 | 615 | 4.8 | 5 |
| Davis | 126 | 533 | 4.2 | 2 |
| L. Harris | 91 | 417 | 4.6 | 4 |
| Bulaich | 91 | 416 | 4.6 | 4 |
| Nottingham | 44 | 214 | 4.9 | 2 |
| N. Moore | 14 | 89 | 6.4 | 1 |
| Solomon | 6 | 43 | 7.2 | 0 |
| Griese | 16 | 30 | 1.9 | 0 |
| T. Anderson | 1 | 11 | 11.0 | 0 |
| Michel | 1 | -2 | -2.0 | 0 |

### Receiving
| Last Name | No. | Yds | Avg | TD |
|---|---|---|---|---|
| N. Moore | 52 | 765 | 15 | 12 |
| D. Harris | 34 | 601 | 18 | 5 |
| Bulaich | 25 | 180 | 7 | 0 |
| Tillman | 17 | 169 | 10 | 2 |
| Davis | 14 | 151 | 11 | 1 |
| Solomon | 12 | 181 | 15 | 1 |
| Nottingham | 8 | 58 | 7 | 0 |
| L. Harris | 7 | 29 | 4 | 0 |
| Mandich | 6 | 63 | 11 | 0 |
| Malone | 4 | 58 | 15 | 0 |
| McCreary | 2 | 10 | 5 | 1 |
| Seiple | 1 | -1 | -1 | 0 |

### Punt Returns
| Last Name | No. | Yds | Avg | TD |
|---|---|---|---|---|
| Solomon | 32 | 285 | 9 | 0 |
| D. Anderson | 4 | 3 | 1 | 0 |
| Babb | 2 | 10 | 5 | 0 |
| Davis | 1 | 11 | 17 | 0 |
| T. Anderson | 1 | 6 | 6 | 0 |

### Kickoff Returns
| Last Name | No. | Yds | Avg | TD |
|---|---|---|---|---|
| Davis | 14 | 414 | 30 | 0 |
| Solomon | 10 | 273 | 27 | 1 |
| T. Anderson | 7 | 167 | 24 | 0 |
| D. Harris | 4 | 91 | 23 | 0 |
| Nottingham | 2 | 36 | 18 | 0 |
| McCreary | 1 | 30 | 30 | 0 |

### Passing
| Last Name | Att | Comp | % | Yds | Yd/Att | TD | Int- | % | RK |
|---|---|---|---|---|---|---|---|---|---|
| Griese | 307 | 180 | 59 | 2252 | 7.3 | 22 | 13- | 4 | 1 |
| Strock | 4 | 2 | 50 | 12 | 3.0 | 0 | 1- | 25 | |

### Punting
| Last Name | No | Avg |
|---|---|---|
| Michel | 35 | 38.2 |
| Seiple | 22 | 36.4 |

### Kicking
| Last Name | XP | Att | % | FG | Att | % |
|---|---|---|---|---|---|---|
| Yepremian | 37 | 40 | 93 | 10 | 22 | 45 |
| Michel | 0 | 1 | 0 | | | |

## NEW ENGLAND PATRIOTS

### Rushing
| Last Name | No. | Yds | Avg | TD |
|---|---|---|---|---|
| Cunningham | 270 | 1015 | 3.8 | 4 |
| Calhoun | 198 | 727 | 3.7 | 4 |
| Grogan | 61 | 324 | 5.3 | 1 |
| Forte | 62 | 157 | 2.5 | 2 |
| Stingley | 3 | 33 | 11.0 | 1 |
| Phillips | 5 | 27 | 5.4 | 1 |
| Morgan | 1 | 10 | 10.0 | 0 |
| Ivory | 3 | 10 | 3.3 | 0 |

### Receiving
| Last Name | No. | Yds | Avg | TD |
|---|---|---|---|---|
| Cunningham | 42 | 370 | 9 | 1 |
| Stingley | 39 | 657 | 17 | 5 |
| Morgan | 21 | 443 | 21 | 3 |
| Francis | 16 | 229 | 14 | 4 |
| Calhoun | 13 | 152 | 12 | 0 |
| Hasselbeck | 9 | 76 | 8 | 4 |
| Forte | 8 | 88 | 11 | 0 |
| Chandler | 7 | 68 | 10 | 0 |
| Burks | 5 | 79 | 16 | 0 |

### Punt Returns
| Last Name | No. | Yds | Avg | TD |
|---|---|---|---|---|
| Haynes | 24 | 200 | 8 | 0 |
| Morgan | 16 | 220 | 14 | 0 |
| Forte | 2 | 9 | 5 | 0 |
| Beaudoin | 1 | 0 | 0 | 0 |

### Kickoff Returns
| Last Name | No. | Yds | Avg | TD |
|---|---|---|---|---|
| Clayborn | 28 | 869 | 31 | 3 |
| Phillips | 6 | 93 | 16 | 0 |
| Beaudoin | 4 | 73 | 18 | 0 |
| McKay | 1 | 16 | 16 | 0 |

### Passing
| Last Name | Att | Comp | % | Yds | Yd/Att | TD | Int- | % | RK |
|---|---|---|---|---|---|---|---|---|---|
| Grogan | 305 | 160 | 52 | 2162 | 7.1 | 17 | 21- | 7 | 7 |

### Punting
| Last Name | No | Avg |
|---|---|---|
| Patrick | 65 | 36.2 |

### Kicking
| Last Name | XP | Att | % | FG | Att | % |
|---|---|---|---|---|---|---|
| Smith | 33 | 33 | 100 | 15 | 21 | 71 |

## BUFFALO BILLS

### Rushing
| Last Name | No. | Yds | Avg | TD |
|---|---|---|---|---|
| Simpson | 126 | 557 | 4.4 | 0 |
| Hooks | 128 | 497 | 3.9 | 0 |
| Braxton | 113 | 372 | 3.3 | 1 |
| Ferguson | 41 | 279 | 6.8 | 2 |
| Collier | 31 | 116 | 3.7 | 0 |
| Brown | 8 | 34 | 4.3 | 0 |
| Piccone | 1 | 6 | 6.0 | 0 |
| Franckowiak | 1 | 0 | 0.0 | 0 |
| Bateman | 1 | 0 | 0.0 | 0 |

### Receiving
| Last Name | No. | Yds | Avg | TD |
|---|---|---|---|---|
| Chandler | 60 | 745 | 12 | 4 |
| Braxton | 43 | 461 | 11 | 1 |
| Gant | 41 | 646 | 16 | 2 |
| Piccone | 17 | 240 | 14 | 2 |
| Hooks | 16 | 195 | 12 | 0 |
| Simpson | 16 | 138 | 9 | 0 |
| Kimbrough | 10 | 207 | 21 | 2 |
| Holland | 8 | 107 | 13 | 0 |
| Brown | 5 | 20 | 4 | 1 |
| Collier | 3 | 23 | 8 | 0 |
| Seymour | 2 | 21 | 11 | 0 |
| Craig | 1 | 5 | 5 | 0 |

### Punt Returns
| Last Name | No. | Yds | Avg | TD |
|---|---|---|---|---|
| Moody | 15 | 196 | 13 | 1 |
| Kimbrough | 16 | 184 | 12 | 1 |
| Craig | 1 | 0 | 0 | 0 |
| Willis | 1 | 0 | 0 | 0 |

### Kickoff Returns
| Last Name | No. | Yds | Avg | TD |
|---|---|---|---|---|
| Moody | 30 | 636 | 21 | 0 |
| Kimbrough | 15 | 346 | 23 | 0 |
| Piccone | 4 | 89 | 22 | 0 |
| Collier | 4 | 55 | 14 | 0 |
| Brown | 3 | 66 | 22 | 0 |
| Romes | 1 | 18 | 18 | 0 |
| B. Nelson | 1 | 10 | 10 | 0 |
| Dunstan | 1 | 9 | 9 | 0 |
| Franckowiak | 1 | 9 | 9 | 0 |

### Passing
| Last Name | Att | Comp | % | Yds | Yd/Att | TD | Int- | % | RK |
|---|---|---|---|---|---|---|---|---|---|
| Ferguson | 457 | 221 | 48 | 2803 | 6.1 | 12 | 24- | 5 | 13 |
| Simpson | 1 | 0 | 0 | 0 | 0.0 | 0 | 0- | 0 | |

### Punting
| Last Name | No | Avg |
|---|---|---|
| Bateman | 81 | 39.9 |

### Kicking
| Last Name | XP | Att | % | FG | Att | % |
|---|---|---|---|---|---|---|
| Long | 13 | 14 | 93 | 7 | 11 | 64 |
| O'Donoghue | 4 | 5 | 80 | 2 | 6 | 33 |
| Klaban | 0 | 2 | 0 | | | |

## NEW YORK JETS

### Rushing
| Last Name | No. | Yds | Avg | TD |
|---|---|---|---|---|
| Gaines | 158 | 595 | 3.8 | 3 |
| Dierking | 79 | 315 | 4.0 | 0 |
| Harper | 44 | 198 | 4.5 | 0 |
| Long | 56 | 170 | 3.0 | 1 |
| White | 50 | 151 | 3.0 | 1 |
| Todd | 24 | 46 | 1.9 | 2 |
| Robinson | 5 | 45 | 9.0 | 0 |
| Newton | 8 | 39 | 4.9 | 0 |
| Keller | 1 | 25 | 25.0 | 0 |
| Walker | 3 | 25 | 8.3 | 0 |
| Domres | 4 | 23 | 5.8 | 0 |
| Diggs | 1 | 16 | 16.0 | 0 |
| Caster | 2 | -15 | -7.5 | 0 |

### Receiving
| Last Name | No. | Yds | Avg | TD |
|---|---|---|---|---|
| Gaines | 55 | 469 | 9 | 1 |
| Walker | 35 | 740 | 21 | 3 |
| Barkum | 26 | 450 | 17 | 6 |
| Harper | 21 | 209 | 10 | 1 |
| Caster | 10 | 205 | 21 | 1 |
| Knight | 7 | 129 | 18 | 0 |
| Newton | 5 | 33 | 7 | 0 |
| Long | 5 | 17 | 3 | 0 |
| Dierking | 4 | 29 | 7 | 1 |
| White | 2 | 5 | 3 | 1 |

### Punt Returns
| Last Name | No. | Yds | Avg | TD |
|---|---|---|---|---|
| Harper | 34 | 425 | 13 | 0 |
| Schroy | 3 | 38 | 13 | 0 |
| Hardee | 1 | 17 | 17 | 0 |

### Kickoff Returns
| Last Name | No. | Yds | Avg | TD |
|---|---|---|---|---|
| Harper | 42 | 1035 | 25 | 0 |
| Hardee | 7 | 148 | 21 | 0 |
| Dierking | 6 | 91 | 15 | 0 |
| Raba | 4 | 64 | 16 | 0 |
| Marvaso | 2 | 36 | 18 | 0 |

### Passing
| Last Name | Att | Comp | % | Yds | Yd/Att | TD | Int- | % | RK |
|---|---|---|---|---|---|---|---|---|---|
| Todd | 265 | 133 | 50 | 1863 | 7.0 | 11 | 17- | 6 | 10 |
| Robinson | 54 | 20 | 37 | 310 | 5.7 | 2 | 8- | 15 | |
| Domres | 40 | 17 | 43 | 113 | 2.8 | 1 | 1- | 3 | |
| Harper | 1 | 0 | 0 | 0 | 0.0 | 0 | 0- | 0 | |

### Punting
| Last Name | No | Avg |
|---|---|---|
| Ramsey | 62 | 37.1 |

### Kicking
| Last Name | XP | Att | % | FG | Att | % |
|---|---|---|---|---|---|---|
| Leahy | 18 | 21 | 86 | 15 | 25 | 60 |

## PITTSBURGH STEELERS 9-5 Chuck Noll

| Scores of Each Game | | |
|---|---|---|
| 27 | SAN FRANCISCO | 0 |
| 7 | OAKLAND | 16 |
| 28 | Cleveland | 14 |
| 10 | Houston | 27 |
| 20 | CINCINNATI | 14 |
| 27 | HOUSTON | 10 |
| 21 | Baltimore | 31 |
| 7 | Denver | 21 |
| 35 | CLEVELAND | 31 |
| 28 | DALLAS | 13 |
| 23 | N.Y. Jets | 20 |
| 30 | SEATTLE | 20 |
| 10 | Cincinnati | 17 |
| 10 | San Diego | 9 |

| Use Name | Pos. | Hgt | Wgt | Age | Int | Pts |
|---|---|---|---|---|---|---|
| Larry Brown | OT-TE | 6'4" | 245 | 28 | | |
| Jon Kolb | OT | 6'2" | 262 | 30 | | |
| Jim Clack | OG-C | 6'3" | 250 | 29 | | |
| Sam Davis | OG | 6'1" | 255 | 33 | | |
| Gerry Mullins | OG-OT | 6'3" | 244 | 28 | | |
| Ted Peterson | C-OT-OG | 6'5" | 244 | 22 | | |
| Ray Pinney | C-OT | 6'4" | 240 | 23 | | |
| Mike Webster | C | 6'1" | 250 | 25 | | |
| John Banaszak | DE | 6'3" | 244 | 27 | | |
| L.C. Greenwood | DE | 6'5" | 250 | 30 | | |
| Dwight White | DE | 6'4" | 255 | 28 | 2 | |
| Steve Furness | DT-DE | 6'4" | 255 | 26 | | |
| Joe Greene | DT | 6'4" | 264 | 30 | | |
| Ernie Holmes | DT | 6'3" | 260 | 29 | | |
| Robin Cole | LB-DE | 6'2" | 220 | 21 | | |
| Brad Cousino | LB | 6' | 215 | 24 | | |
| Jack Ham | LB | 6'3" | 225 | 28 | 4 | |
| Dave LaCrosse | LB | 6'3" | 210 | 21 | | |
| Jack Lambert | LB | 6'4" | 220 | 25 | 1 | |
| Loren Toews | LB | 6'3" | 222 | 25 | | 2 |
| Dennis Winston | LB | 6' | 228 | 21 | 2 | |
| Jim Allen | DB | 6'2" | 194 | 25 | 5 | |
| Mel Blount | DB | 6'3" | 205 | 29 | 6 | |
| Tony Dungy | DB-QB | 6' | 188 | 21 | 3 | |
| Glen Edwards | DB | 6' | 185 | 30 | 3 | |
| Brent Sexton | DB | 6'1" | 190 | 24 | | |
| Donnie Shell | DB | 5'11" | 190 | 25 | 3 | |
| J.T. Thomas | DB | 6'2" | 196 | 26 | 2 | |
| Mike Wagner | DB | 6'1" | 200 | 28 | | |
| Terry Bradshaw | QB | 6'3" | 215 | 28 | | 18 |
| Neil Graff | QB | 6'3" | 205 | 27 | | |
| Mike Kruczek | QB | 6'1" | 201 | 24 | | |
| Cliff Stoudt | QB | 6'4" | 218 | 22 | | |
| Rocky Bleier | HB | 5'11" | 210 | 31 | | 24 |
| Jack Deloplaine | HB | 5'10" | 205 | 23 | | |
| Alvin Mason | HB | 5'11" | 201 | 25 | | |
| Laverne Smith | HB | 5'10" | 193 | 22 | | |
| Franco Harris | FB | 6'2" | 225 | 27 | | 66 |
| Reggie Harrison | FB | 5'11" | 220 | 27 | | |
| Sidney Thornton | FB | 5'11" | 230 | 22 | | 12 |
| Frank Lewis | WR | 6'1" | 196 | 30 | | 6 |
| Ernest Pough | WR | 6'1" | 174 | 25 | | |
| Jim Smith | WR | 6'2" | 205 | 22 | | |
| John Stallworth | WR | 6'2" | 183 | 25 | | 42 |
| Lynn Swann | WR | 6' | 180 | 25 | | 42 |
| Bennie Cunningham | TE | 6'4" | 247 | 22 | | 12 |
| Randy Grossman | TE | 6'1" | 225 | 23 | | |
| Rick Engles (from SEA) | K | 5'11" | 180 | 23 | | |
| Roy Gerela | K | 5'10" | 185 | 29 | | 61 |
| Bobby Walden | K | 6' | 197 | 39 | | |

Gary Dunn – Knee Injury

Thao Bell – Leg Injury
John Fuqua – Broken Finger

## CINCINNATI BENGALS 8-6 Bill Johnson

| Scores of Each Game | | |
|---|---|---|
| 3 | CLEVELAND | 13 |
| 43 | SEATTLE | 20 |
| 3 | San Diego | 24 |
| 17 | Green Bay | 7 |
| 14 | Pittsburgh | 20 |
| 13 | DENVER | 24 |
| 13 | HOUSTON | 10 |
| 10 | Cleveland | 7 |
| 10 | Minnesota | 42 |
| 23 | MIAMI | 17 |
| 30 | N.Y. GIANTS | 13 |
| 27 | Kansas City | 7 |
| 17 | PITTSBURGH | 10 |
| 16 | Houston | 21 |

| Use Name | Pos. | Hgt | Wgt | Age | Int | Pts |
|---|---|---|---|---|---|---|
| Vern Holland | OT | 6'5" | 265 | 29 | | |
| Ron Hunt | OT | 6'6" | 255 | 22 | | |
| Rufus Mayes | OT | 6'5" | 256 | 29 | | |
| Glenn Bujnoch | OG | 6'5" | 251 | 23 | | 6 |
| Greg Fairchild | OG-C | 6'4" | 257 | 23 | | |
| Dave Lapham | OG-OT-C | 6'4" | 259 | 25 | | |
| John Shinners | OG | 6'2" | 259 | 30 | | |
| Bob Johnson | C | 6'5" | 256 | 31 | | |
| Ken Johnson | DE | 6'5" | 258 | 30 | | |
| Coy Bacon | DE | 6'4" | 265 | 35 | | |
| Gary Burley | DE | 6'3" | 265 | 24 | | |
| Ron Carpenter | DT | 6'4" | 265 | 29 | | |
| Eddie Edwards | DT | 6'5" | 256 | 23 | | |
| Walter Johnson | DT | 6'3" | 265 | 34 | | |
| Wilson Whitley | DT | 6'3" | 264 | 22 | | |
| Glenn Cameron | LB | 6'2" | 217 | 24 | | |
| Bo Harris | LB | 6'3" | 221 | 24 | 2 | |
| Jim LeClair | LB | 6'2" | 238 | 26 | 2 | |
| Ray Phillips | LB | 6'4" | 221 | 23 | | |
| Ron Pritchard | LB | 6'1" | 208 | 30 | | |
| Reggie Williams | LB | 6'1" | 228 | 22 | 3 | 12 |
| Jerry Anderson | DB | 5'11" | 198 | 23 | | |
| Tommy Casanova | DB | 6'2" | 196 | 27 | 1 | |
| Marvin Cobb | DB | 6' | 191 | 24 | 2 | |
| Melvin Morgan | DB | 6' | 186 | 24 | 1 | |
| Lemar Parrish | DB | 5'11" | 183 | 29 | 3 | 6 |
| Scott Perry | DB | 6' | 182 | 23 | | |
| Ken Riley | DB | 6' | 185 | 30 | 2 | |
| Ken Anderson | QB | 6'1" | 212 | 28 | | 12 |
| John Reeves | QB | 6'3" | 210 | 27 | | |
| Mike Wells | QB | 6'5" | 225 | 26 | | |
| Lenvil Elliott | HB | 6' | 208 | 25 | | 6 |
| Archie Griffin | HB | 5'9" | 193 | 23 | | |
| Willie Shelby | HB | 5'11" | 198 | 24 | | 6 |
| Booby Clark | FB | 6'2" | 242 | 26 | | 6 |
| Tony Davis | FB | 5'10" | 210 | 24 | | 12 |
| Pete Johnson | FB | 6' | 240 | 23 | | 24 |
| Billy Brooks | WR | 6'3" | 202 | 24 | | 24 |
| Isaac Curtis | WR | 6' | 192 | 26 | | 12 |
| Steve Holden (from CLE) | WR | 6' | 200 | 26 | | |
| John McDaniel | WR | 6'1" | 197 | 25 | | |
| Pat McInally | WR | 6'6" | 210 | 24 | | 18 |
| Mike Cobb | TE | 6'5" | 248 | 21 | | |
| Jim Corbett | TE | 6'4" | 214 | 22 | | 6 |
| Bob Trumpy | TE | 6'6" | 228 | 32 | | 6 |
| Rick Walker | TE | 6'3" | 237 | 22 | | |
| Chris Bahr | K | 5'9" | 168 | 24 | | 82 |

Chris Devlin – Leg Injury

## HOUSTON OILERS 8-6 Bum Phillips

| Scores of Each Game | | |
|---|---|---|
| 20 | N.Y. JETS | 0 |
| 16 | Green Bay | 10 |
| 7 | Miami | 27 |
| 27 | PITTSBURGH | 10 |
| 23 | CLEVELAND | 24 |
| 27 | Pittsburgh | 10 |
| 10 | Cincinnati | 13 |
| 47 | CHICAGO | 0 |
| 29 | Oakland | 34 |
| 22 | Seattle | 10 |
| 34 | KANSAS CITY | 20 |
| 14 | DENVER | 24 |
| 19 | Cleveland | 15 |
| 21 | CINCINNATI | 16 |

| Use Name | Pos. | Hgt | Wgt | Age | Int | Pts |
|---|---|---|---|---|---|---|
| Conway Hayman | OT | 6'3" | 260 | 28 | | |
| Kevin Hunt | OT-OG | 6'5" | 260 | 28 | | |
| Greg Sampson | OT | 6'6" | 270 | 26 | | |
| Morris Towns | OT | 6'4" | 275 | 23 | | |
| Elbert Drungo | OG | 6'5" | 265 | 34 | | |
| Ed Fisher | OG-C | 6'3" | 250 | 28 | | |
| George Reihner | OG | 6'4" | 263 | 22 | | |
| David Carter | C | 6'2" | 225 | 24 | | |
| Carl Mauck | C | 6'3" | 250 | 30 | | |
| Steve Baumgartner (from NO) | DE-DT | 6'7" | 255 | 26 | | |
| Elvin Bethea | DE | 6'3" | 255 | 31 | | |
| Andy Dorris (from SEA) | DE | 6'4" | 240 | 26 | | |
| Ernest Kirk | DE | 6'2" | 265 | 25 | 1 | |
| James Young | DE | 6'2" | 260 | 27 | | 4 |
| Curly Culp | NT | 6'1" | 265 | 31 | 1 | |
| Ken Kennard | NT-DE | 6'2" | 245 | 22 | | 2 |
| Gregg Bingham | LB | 6'1" | 230 | 26 | 2 | 6 |
| Robert Brazile | LB | 6'4" | 238 | 24 | 3 | |
| Steve Kiner | LB | 6' | 225 | 30 | 1 | |
| Art Stringer | LB | 6'1" | 223 | 23 | 1 | |
| Ted Thompson | LB | 6'1" | 220 | 24 | | |
| Ted Washington | LB | 6'1" | 245 | 29 | 3 | |
| Willie Alexander | DB | 6'2" | 195 | 27 | 3 | 6 |
| Bill Currier | DB | 6' | 190 | 22 | 2 | |
| Al Johnson | DB | 6' | 200 | 27 | | |
| Kurt Knoff | DB | 6'2" | 188 | 23 | | |
| Zeke Moore | DB | 6'2" | 195 | 33 | 3 | 6 |
| Mike Reinfeldt | DB | 6'2" | 195 | 24 | 5 | |
| Rich Sowells | DB | 6' | 180 | 28 | | |
| Greg Stemrick | DB | 5'11" | 185 | 25 | 1 | 6 |
| Mike Weger | DB | 6'2" | 200 | 31 | | |
| Tom Dunivan | QB | 6'3" | 210 | 23 | | |
| John Hadl | QB | 6'2" | 215 | 37 | | 6 |
| Dan Pastorini | QB | 6'3" | 205 | 28 | | 12 |
| Ronnie Coleman | HB | 5'10" | 198 | 26 | | 36 |
| Mike Voight | HB | 6' | 214 | 23 | | |
| Rob Carpenter | FB | 6'1" | 214 | 22 | | 6 |
| Don Hardeman | FB | 6'2" | 235 | 25 | | 18 |
| Tim Wilson | FB | 6'3" | 220 | 23 | | 18 |
| Warren Anderson | WR | 6'2" | 195 | 22 | | |
| Ken Burrough | WR | 6'4" | 210 | 29 | | 48 |
| Eddie Foster | WR | 5'10" | 185 | 23 | | |
| Gary Garrison | WR | 6'1" | 194 | 33 | | |
| Billy Johnson | WR | 5'9" | 170 | 25 | | 42 |
| Mike Barber | TE | 6'3" | 235 | 24 | | 6 |
| Jimmie Giles | TE | 6'3" | 225 | 22 | | |
| Skip Butler | K | 6'2" | 200 | 29 | | 2 |
| Tom Dempsey | K | 6'1" | 260 | 36 | | 20 |
| Toni Fritsch | K | 5'7" | 189 | 32 | | 55 |
| Cliff Parsley | K | 6'1" | 211 | 22 | | |

C.L. Whittington – Injury
Fred Willis – Injury

## CLEVELAND BROWNS 6-8 Forrest Gregg (6-7), Dick Modzelewski (0-1)

| Scores of Each Game | | |
|---|---|---|
| 13 | Cincinnati | 3 |
| 30 | NEW ENGLAND | 27 |
| 14 | PITTSBURGH | 28 |
| 10 | OAKLAND | 26 |
| 24 | Houston | 23 |
| 27 | Buffalo | 16 |
| 44 | KANSAS CITY | 7 |
| 7 | CINCINNATI | 10 |
| 7 | Pittsburgh | 10 |
| 21 | N.Y. Giants | 7 |
| 0 | LOS ANGELES | 9 |
| 14 | San Diego | 37 |
| 15 | HOUSTON | 19 |
| 19 | Seattle | 20 |

| Use Name | Pos. | Hgt | Wgt | Age | Int | Pts |
|---|---|---|---|---|---|---|
| Barry Darrow | OT | 6'7" | 260 | 27 | | |
| Doug Dieken | OT | 6'5" | 252 | 28 | | |
| Bob Lingenfelter | OT | 6'7" | 277 | 23 | | |
| Al Dennis | OG | 6'4" | 250 | 26 | | |
| Robert Jackson | OG | 6'5" | 250 | 24 | | |
| Henry Sheppard | OG | 6'6" | 246 | 24 | | |
| Tom DeLeone | C | 6'2" | 248 | 27 | | |
| Gerry Sullivan | C | 6'4" | 250 | 25 | | |
| Joe Jones | DE | 6'6" | 250 | 29 | | |
| Mack Mitchell | DE | 6'7" | 245 | 25 | | |
| Mike St. Clair | DE | 6'5" | 245 | 23 | | |
| Earl Edwards | DT | 6'6" | 256 | 31 | | |
| Steve Okoniewski (from STL) | DT | 6'3" | 255 | 28 | | |
| Jerry Sherk | DT | 6'4" | 250 | 29 | | 2 |
| Mickey Sims | DT | 6'5" | 282 | 22 | | |
| Dick Ambrose | LB | 6' | 235 | 24 | | |
| Bob Babich | LB | 6'2" | 231 | 30 | | |
| John Garlington | LB | 6'1" | 221 | 31 | | |
| Dave Graf | LB | 6'2" | 215 | 24 | | |
| Charlie Hall | LB | 6'3" | 235 | 28 | 1 | |
| Gerald Irons | LB | 6'2" | 230 | 30 | 3 | 6 |
| Mark Johnson | LB | 6'2" | 236 | 24 | | |
| Ron Bolton | DB | 6'2" | 170 | 27 | 3 | |
| Thom Darden | DB | 6'2" | 193 | 27 | 6 | 6 |
| Oliver Davis | DB | 6'1" | 200 | 23 | 3 | |
| Ken Ellis | DB | 5'10" | 195 | 29 | | |
| Ricky Jones | DB | 6'1" | 195 | 22 | 1 | |
| Tony Peters | DB | 6'1" | 192 | 24 | 2 | |
| Clarence Scott | DB | 6' | 180 | 28 | 3 | 6 |
| Roland Woolsey | DB | 6'1" | 182 | 24 | 1 | |
| Terry Luck | QB | 6'3" | 205 | 23 | | 6 |
| Gary Marangi | QB | 6'1" | 203 | 25 | | |
| Dave Mays | QB | 6'1" | 204 | 28 | | |
| Brian Sipe | QB | 6'1" | 190 | 28 | | |
| Larry Poole | HB | 6' | 195 | 25 | | 24 |
| Greg Pruitt | HB | 5'10" | 190 | 26 | | 24 |
| Brian Duncan | FB-HB | 6' | 201 | 25 | | 6 |
| Cleo Miller | FB | 5'11" | 202 | 24 | | 30 |
| Mike Pruitt | FB | 6' | 214 | 23 | | 6 |
| Ricky Feacher | WR | 5'10" | 174 | 23 | | |
| Dave Logan | WR | 6'4" | 226 | 23 | | 6 |
| Reggie Rucker | WR | 6'2" | 190 | 29 | | 12 |
| Paul Warfield | WR | 6' | 188 | 34 | | 12 |
| Lawrence Williams (from KC) | WR | 5'10" | 173 | 23 | | 6 |
| Gary Parris | TE | 6'2" | 226 | 27 | | 30 |
| Oscar Roan | TE | 6'6" | 214 | 25 | | 12 |
| Don Cockroft | K | 6'1" | 195 | 32 | | 81 |
| Greg Coleman | K | 6' | 178 | 22 | | |

Pete Adams – Injury

Bill Craven – Injury

## PITTSBURGH STEELERS

### RUSHING

| Last Name | No. | Yds | Avg | TD |
|---|---|---|---|---|
| Harris | 300 | 1162 | 3.9 | 11 |
| Bleier | 135 | 465 | 3.4 | 4 |
| Harrison | 36 | 175 | 4.9 | 0 |
| Bradshaw | 31 | 171 | 5.5 | 3 |
| Thornton | 27 | 103 | 3.8 | 2 |
| Maxson | 18 | 56 | 3.1 | 0 |
| L. Smith | 14 | 55 | 3.9 | 0 |
| Stallworth | 6 | 47 | 7.8 | 0 |
| Dungy | 3 | 8 | 2.7 | 0 |
| Deloplaine | 2 | 7 | 3.5 | 0 |
| Swann | 2 | 6 | 3.0 | 0 |
| Graff | 5 | 3 | 0.6 | 0 |
| Kruczek | 1 | 0 | 0.0 | 0 |
| Walden | 1 | 0 | 0.0 | 0 |

### RECEIVING

| Last Name | No. | Yds | Avg | TD |
|---|---|---|---|---|
| Swann | 50 | 789 | 16 | 7 |
| Stallworth | 44 | 784 | 18 | 7 |
| Cunningham | 20 | 347 | 17 | 2 |
| Bleier | 18 | 161 | 9 | 0 |
| Lewis | 11 | 263 | 24 | 1 |
| Harris | 11 | 62 | 6 | 0 |
| Maxson | 5 | 70 | 14 | 0 |
| Grossman | 5 | 57 | 11 | 0 |
| J. Smith | 4 | 80 | 20 | 0 |
| Harrison | 3 | 11 | 4 | 0 |
| Thornton | 1 | 5 | 5 | 0 |
| Pough | 1 | 3 | 3 | 0 |

### PUNT RETURNS

| Last Name | No. | Yds | Avg | TD |
|---|---|---|---|---|
| J. Smith | 36 | 294 | 8 | 0 |
| Swann | 9 | 88 | 10 | 0 |
| Deloplaine | 1 | 7 | 7 | 0 |

### KICKOFF RETURNS

| Last Name | No. | Yds | Avg | TD |
|---|---|---|---|---|
| J. Smith | 16 | 381 | 24 | 0 |
| L. Smith | 16 | 365 | 23 | 0 |
| Pough | 7 | 111 | 16 | 0 |
| Maxson | 5 | 120 | 24 | 0 |
| Deloplaine | 1 | 18 | 18 | 0 |

### PASSING – PUNTING – KICKING

| PASSING | Att | Comp | % | Yds | Yd/Att | TD | Int– | % | RK |
|---|---|---|---|---|---|---|---|---|---|
| Bradshaw | 314 | 162 | 52 | 2523 | 8.0 | 17 | 19– | 6 | 5 |
| Graff | 12 | 6 | 50 | 47 | 3.9 | 0 | 0– | 0 | |
| Dungy | 8 | 3 | 38 | 43 | 5.4 | 0 | 2– | 25 | |
| Kruczek | 7 | 2 | 29 | 19 | 2.7 | 0 | 0– | 0 | |

| PUNTING | No | Avg |
|---|---|---|
| Walden | 67 | 37.0 |
| Engles | 9 | 34.0 |

| KICKING | XP | Att | % | FG | Att | % |
|---|---|---|---|---|---|---|
| Gerela | 34 | 37 | 92 | 9 | 14 | 64 |

## CINCINNATI BENGALS

### RUSHING

| Last Name | No. | Yds | Avg | TD |
|---|---|---|---|---|
| P. Johnson | 153 | 585 | 3.8 | 4 |
| Griffin | 137 | 549 | 4.0 | 0 |
| Elliott | 65 | 269 | 4.1 | 0 |
| Clark | 68 | 226 | 3.3 | 1 |
| K. Anderson | 26 | 128 | 4.9 | 2 |
| Davis | 27 | 81 | 3.0 | 2 |
| Casanova | 1 | 20 | 20.0 | 0 |
| Bujnoch | 1 | 4 | 4.0 | 1 |
| McInally | 1 | 4 | 4.0 | 0 |
| Ma. Cobb | 1 | 0 | 0.0 | 0 |
| Reaves | 5 | 0 | 0.0 | 0 |
| Corbett | 1 | –1 | –1.0 | 0 |
| Brooks | 2 | –4 | –2.0 | 0 |

### RECEIVING

| Last Name | No. | Yds | Avg | TD |
|---|---|---|---|---|
| Brooks | 39 | 772 | 20 | 4 |
| Elliott | 29 | 238 | 8 | 1 |
| Griffin | 28 | 240 | 9 | 0 |
| Curtis | 20 | 338 | 17 | 2 |
| Trumpy | 18 | 251 | 14 | 1 |
| McInally | 17 | 258 | 15 | 3 |
| McDaniel | 12 | 148 | 12 | 0 |
| Davis | 9 | 83 | 9 | 0 |
| Corbett | 7 | 127 | 18 | 1 |
| Clark | 7 | 33 | 5 | 0 |
| P. Johnson | 5 | 49 | 10 | 0 |
| Walker | 1 | 13 | 13 | 0 |

### PUNT RETURNS

| Last Name | No. | Yds | Avg | TD |
|---|---|---|---|---|
| Davis | 19 | 220 | 12 | 0 |
| Shelby | 11 | 54 | 5 | 0 |
| Parrish | 4 | 30 | 8 | 0 |
| Holden | 3 | 14 | 5 | 0 |
| Casanova | 1 | 6 | 6 | 0 |
| Ma. Cobb | 1 | 4 | 4 | 0 |
| Williams | 1 | 0 | 0 | 0 |
| J. Anderson | 1 | 0 | 0 | 0 |

### KICKOFF RETURNS

| Last Name | No. | Yds | Avg | TD |
|---|---|---|---|---|
| Shelby | 19 | 403 | 21 | 0 |
| Griffin | 9 | 192 | 21 | 0 |
| J. Anderson | 8 | 129 | 16 | 0 |
| Davis | 3 | 42 | 14 | 0 |
| Holden | 2 | 42 | 21 | 0 |
| Elliott | 1 | 23 | 23 | 0 |
| Parrish | 1 | 23 | 23 | 0 |
| Ma. Cobb | 1 | 15 | 15 | 0 |
| P. Johnson | 1 | 11 | 11 | 0 |
| Fairchild | 1 | 6 | 6 | 0 |

### PASSING – PUNTING – KICKING

| PASSING | Att | Comp | % | Yds | Yd/Att | TD | Int– | % | RK |
|---|---|---|---|---|---|---|---|---|---|
| K. Anderson | 323 | 166 | 51 | 2145 | 6.6 | 11 | 11– | 3 | 6 |
| Reeves | 59 | 24 | 41 | 383 | 6.5 | 0 | 5– | 9 | |
| Griffin | 1 | 1 | 100 | 18 | 18.0 | 1 | 0– | 0 | |
| McInally | 1 | 1 | 100 | 4 | 4.0 | 0 | 0– | 0 | |
| Ma. Cobb | 1 | 0 | 0 | 0 | 0.0 | 0 | 0– | 0 | |

| PUNTING | No | Avg |
|---|---|---|
| McInally | 67 | 41.8 |
| Bahr | 2 | 44.0 |

| KICKING | XP | Att | % | FG | Att | % |
|---|---|---|---|---|---|---|
| Bahr | 25 | 26 | 97 | 19 | 27 | 70 |

## HOUSTON OILERS

### RUSHING

| Last Name | No. | Yds | Avg | TD |
|---|---|---|---|---|
| Coleman | 185 | 660 | 3.6 | 5 |
| Carpenter | 144 | 652 | 4.5 | 1 |
| Wilson | 99 | 343 | 3.5 | 3 |
| Hardeman | 42 | 162 | 3.9 | 2 |
| B. Johnson | 6 | 102 | 17.0 | 1 |
| Pastorini | 18 | 39 | 2.2 | 2 |
| Voight | 7 | 20 | 2.9 | 0 |
| Burrough | 4 | 10 | 2.5 | 0 |
| Hadl | 3 | 11 | 3.7 | 1 |
| Giles | 1 | –10 | –10.0 | 0 |

### RECEIVING

| Last Name | No. | Yds | Avg | TD |
|---|---|---|---|---|
| Burrough | 43 | 816 | 19 | 8 |
| Carpenter | 23 | 156 | 7 | 0 |
| Coleman | 22 | 115 | 5 | 1 |
| B. Johnson | 20 | 412 | 21 | 3 |
| Wilson | 20 | 107 | 5 | 0 |
| Giles | 17 | 147 | 9 | 0 |
| Foster | 15 | 208 | 14 | 0 |
| Hardeman | 11 | 47 | 4 | 1 |
| Barber | 9 | 94 | 10 | 1 |
| Garrison | 1 | 5 | 5 | 0 |

### PUNT RETURNS

| Last Name | No. | Yds | Avg | TD |
|---|---|---|---|---|
| B. Johnson | 35 | 539 | 15 | 2 |
| Stemrick | 1 | 0 | 0 | 0 |

### KICKOFF RETURNS

| Last Name | No. | Yds | Avg | TD |
|---|---|---|---|---|
| B. Johnson | 25 | 630 | 25 | 1 |
| Anderson | 8 | 182 | 23 | 0 |
| Voight | 8 | 156 | 20 | 0 |
| Wilson | 2 | 33 | 17 | 0 |
| Foster | 1 | 31 | 31 | 0 |
| Stringer | 1 | 15 | 15 | 0 |
| Thompson | 1 | 9 | 9 | 0 |

### PASSING – PUNTING – KICKING

| PASSING | Att | Comp | % | Yds | Yd/Att | TD | Int– | % | RK |
|---|---|---|---|---|---|---|---|---|---|
| Pastorini | 319 | 169 | 53 | 1987 | 6.2 | 13 | 18– | 6 | 8 |
| Hadl | 24 | 11 | 46 | 76 | 3.2 | 0 | 3– | 13 | |
| Coleman | 3 | 1 | 33 | 44 | 14.7 | 1 | 0– | 0 | |
| Burrough | 1 | 0 | 0 | 0 | 0.0 | 0 | 0– | 0 | |

| PUNTING | No | Avg |
|---|---|---|
| Parsley | 77 | 39.4 |

| KICKING | XP | Att | % | FG | Att | % |
|---|---|---|---|---|---|---|
| Fritsch | 19 | 20 | 95 | 12 | 16 | 75 |
| Dempsey | 8 | 11 | 73 | 4 | 6 | 67 |
| Butler | 2 | 3 | 67 | 0 | 3 | 0 |
| Pastorini | 0 | 1 | 0 | | | |

## CLEVELAND BROWNS

### RUSHING

| Last Name | No. | Yds | Avg | TD |
|---|---|---|---|---|
| G. Pruitt | 236 | 1086 | 4.6 | 3 |
| Miller | 163 | 756 | 4.6 | 4 |
| M. Pruitt | 47 | 205 | 4.4 | 1 |
| Poole | 38 | 118 | 3.1 | 1 |
| Williams | 2 | 30 | 15.0 | 1 |
| Duncan | 5 | 16 | 3.2 | 0 |
| Sipe | 10 | 14 | 1.4 | 0 |
| Rucker | 2 | 6 | 3.0 | 0 |
| Warfield | 1 | 2 | 2.0 | 0 |
| Mays | 4 | 2 | 0.5 | 0 |
| Luck | 3 | –2 | –0.7 | 0 |
| Coleman | 1 | –3 | –3.0 | 0 |

### RECEIVING

| Last Name | No. | Yds | Avg | TD |
|---|---|---|---|---|
| Miller | 41 | 291 | 7 | 1 |
| G. Pruitt | 37 | 471 | 13 | 1 |
| Rucker | 36 | 565 | 16 | 2 |
| Parris | 21 | 213 | 10 | 5 |
| Logan | 19 | 284 | 15 | 1 |
| Warfield | 18 | 251 | 14 | 2 |
| Poole | 17 | 137 | 8 | 3 |
| Roan | 13 | 136 | 11 | 2 |
| Williams | 7 | 94 | 13 | 0 |
| M. Pruitt | 3 | 12 | 4 | 0 |
| Duncan | 1 | 5 | 5 | 1 |
| Luck | 1 | 4 | 4 | 1 |

### PUNT RETURNS

| Last Name | No. | Yds | Avg | TD |
|---|---|---|---|---|
| Woolsey | 32 | 290 | 9 | 0 |
| Feacher | 2 | 15 | 8 | 0 |

### KICKOFF RETURNS

| Last Name | No. | Yds | Avg | TD |
|---|---|---|---|---|
| Williams | 25 | 518 | 21 | 0 |
| Duncan | 15 | 298 | 20 | 0 |
| Feacher | 11 | 219 | 20 | 0 |
| M. Pruitt | 6 | 131 | 22 | 0 |
| Ellis | 5 | 80 | 16 | 0 |
| Jackson | 1 | 21 | 21 | 0 |
| Ambrose | 1 | 20 | 20 | 0 |
| Babich | 1 | 14 | 14 | 0 |
| Woolsey | 1 | 2 | 2 | 0 |

### PASSING – PUNTING – KICKING

| PASSING | Att | Comp | % | Yds | Yd/Att | TD | Int– | % | RK |
|---|---|---|---|---|---|---|---|---|---|
| Sipe | 195 | 112 | 57 | 1233 | 6.3 | 9 | 14– | 7 | 9 |
| Mays | 121 | 55 | 45 | 797 | 6.6 | 6 | 10– | 8 | |
| Luck | 50 | 25 | 50 | 316 | 6.3 | 1 | 7– | 14 | |
| G. Pruitt | 9 | 4 | 44 | 28 | 3.1 | 3 | 0– | 0 | |
| Logan | 2 | 0 | 0 | 0 | 0.0 | 0 | 0– | 0 | |

| PUNTING | No. | Avg |
|---|---|---|
| Coleman | 61 | 39.2 |
| Cockroft | 1 | 30.0 |

| KICKING | XP | Att | % | FG | Att | % |
|---|---|---|---|---|---|---|
| Cockroft | 30 | 31 | 97 | 17 | 23 | 74 |

## DENVER BRONCOS 12-2 Red Miller

| Scores of Each Game | | |
|---|---|---|
| 7 | ST. LOUIS | 0 |
| 26 | BUFFALO | 6 |
| 24 | Seattle | 13 |
| 23 | KANSAS CITY | 7 |
| 30 | Oakland | 7 |
| 24 | Cincinnati | 13 |
| 14 | OAKLAND | 24 |
| 21 | PITTSBURGH | 7 |
| 17 | San Diego | 14 |
| 14 | Kansas City | 7 |
| 27 | BALTIMORE | 13 |
| 24 | Houston | 14 |
| 17 | SAN DIEGO | 9 |
| 6 | Dallas | 14 |

| Use Name | Pos. | Hgt | Wgt | Age | Int | Pts |
|---|---|---|---|---|---|---|
| Henry Allison (from STL) | OT-OG | 6'3" | 263 | 30 | | |
| Glenn Hyde | OT | 6'3" | 255 | 26 | | |
| Andy Maurer | OT | 6'3" | 265 | 28 | | |
| Claudie Minor | OT | 6'4" | 280 | 26 | | |
| Bill Bryan | OG | 6'2" | 246 | 22 | | |
| Tom Glassic | OG | 6'3" | 248 | 23 | | |
| Paul Howard | OG | 6'3" | 260 | 26 | | |
| Steve Schindler | OG | 6'3" | 252 | 23 | | |
| Bobby Maples | C | 6'3" | 250 | 34 | | |
| Mike Montler | C | 6'4" | 250 | 33 | | |
| Lyle Alzado | DE | 6'3" | 250 | 28 | | |
| Barney Chevous | DE | 6'3" | 250 | 26 | | |
| Brison Manor | DE | 6'4" | 247 | 25 | | |
| Paul Smith | DE | 6'3" | 250 | 32 | 1 | |
| Rubin Carter | NT | 6' | 254 | 24 | | |
| John Grant | NT | 6'3" | 246 | 27 | | |

Bill Bain – Knee Injury
Randy Moore – Injury

| Use Name | Pos. | Hgt | Wgt | Age | Int | Pts |
|---|---|---|---|---|---|---|
| Rick Baska | LB | 6'3" | 224 | 25 | | |
| Larry Evans | LB | 6'2" | 218 | 24 | 1 | |
| Randy Gradishar | LB | 6'3" | 231 | 25 | 3 | |
| Tom Jackson | LB | 5'11" | 224 | 26 | 4 | 6 |
| Rob Nairne | LB | 6'4" | 220 | 23 | | |
| Joe Rizzo | LB | 6'1" | 220 | 23 | 3 | |
| Bob Swenson | LB | 6'3" | 223 | 24 | 1 | |
| Goodwin Turk | LB | 6'2" | 230 | 26 | | |
| Steve Foley | DB | 6'2" | 190 | 23 | 3 | |
| Bernard Jackson | DB | 6' | 181 | 27 | 1 | |
| Chris Pane | DB | 5'11" | 185 | 24 | | |
| Randy Poltl | DB | 6'3" | 188 | 25 | | |
| Larry Riley | DB | 5'10" | 189 | 22 | | |
| Bill Thompson | DB | 6'1" | 200 | 30 | 5 | |
| Louis Wright | DB | 6'2" | 195 | 24 | 3 | 6 |

| Use Name | Pos. | Hgt | Wgt | Age | Int | Pts |
|---|---|---|---|---|---|---|
| Craig Morton | QB | 6'4" | 214 | 34 | | 24 |
| Craig Penrose | QB | 6'3" | 205 | 24 | | |
| Norris Weese | QB | 6'1" | 193 | 26 | | 6 |
| Otis Armstrong | HB | 5'10" | 197 | 26 | | 24 |
| Jim Kiick (to WAS) | HB | 5'11" | 215 | 31 | | |
| Rob Lytle | HB | 6'1" | 198 | 22 | | 12 |
| Jim Jensen | FB-TE | 6'3" | 240 | 23 | | 6 |
| Jon Keyworth | FB | 6'3" | 234 | 26 | | 6 |
| Lonnie Perrin | FB | 6'1" | 224 | 25 | | 24 |
| Jack Dolbin | WR | 5'10" | 183 | 28 | | 18 |
| Haven Moses | WR | 6'3" | 200 | 31 | | 24 |
| John Schultz | WR | 5'10" | 183 | 24 | | |
| Rick Upchurch | WR | 5'10" | 180 | 25 | | 24 |
| Ron Egloff | TE | 6'5" | 227 | 21 | | |
| Riley Odoms | TE | 6'4" | 232 | 27 | | 18 |
| Buck Dilts | K | 5'9" | 190 | 23 | | |
| Jim Turner | K | 6'2" | 212 | 36 | | 76 |

## OAKLAND RAIDERS 11-3 John Madden

| Scores of Each Game | | |
|---|---|---|
| 24 | SAN DIEGO | 0 |
| 16 | Pittsburgh | 7 |
| 37 | Kansas City | 28 |
| 26 | Cleveland | 10 |
| 7 | DENVER | 30 |
| 28 | N.Y. Jets | 27 |
| 24 | Denver | 14 |
| 44 | SEATTLE | 7 |
| 34 | HOUSTON | 29 |
| 7 | San Diego | 12 |
| 34 | BUFFALO | 13 |
| 14 | Los Angeles | 20 |
| 35 | MINNESOTA | 13 |
| 21 | KANSAS CITY | 20 |

| Use Name | Pos. | Hgt | Wgt | Age | Int | Pts |
|---|---|---|---|---|---|---|
| Henry Lawrence | OT-OG | 6'4" | 270 | 25 | | |
| Art Shell | OT | 6'5" | 275 | 30 | | |
| John Vella | OT | 6'4" | 260 | 27 | | |
| George Buehler | OG | 6'2" | 270 | 30 | | |
| Everett Little | OG | 6'4" | 265 | 23 | | |
| Mickey Marvin | OG | 6'4" | 270 | 21 | | |
| Gene Upshaw | OG | 6'5" | 255 | 32 | | |
| Dave Dalby | C | 6'2" | 250 | 26 | | |
| Steve Sylvester | C-OT-OG | 6'4" | 260 | 24 | | |
| John Matuszak | DE | 6'8" | 270 | 26 | | |
| Charles Philyaw | DE | 6'9" | 270 | 23 | | |
| Otis Sistrunk | DE | 6'4" | 270 | 29 | 1 | |
| Pat Toomay | DE | 6'5" | 245 | 32 | | |
| Mike McCoy | NT | 6'5" | 275 | 28 | | |
| Dave Rowe | NT | 6'6" | 270 | 32 | | |

Kelvin Korver – Knee Injury

| Use Name | Pos. | Hgt | Wgt | Age | Int | Pts |
|---|---|---|---|---|---|---|
| Jeff Barnes | LB | 6'2" | 215 | 22 | | |
| Willie Hall | LB | 6'2" | 225 | 27 | 1 | 6 |
| Ted Hendricks | LB | 6'7" | 220 | 29 | | 2 |
| Monte Johnson | LB | 6'4" | 240 | 25 | 2 | |
| Rod Martin | LB | 6'2" | 215 | 23 | | |
| Randy McClanahan | LB | 6'5" | 225 | 22 | | |
| Floyd Rice | LB | 6'3" | 225 | 28 | 2 | |
| Phil Villapiano | LB | 6'1" | 225 | 28 | | |
| Butch Atkinson | DB | 6' | 185 | 30 | 2 | |
| Willie Brown | DB | 6'1" | 210 | 36 | 4 | |
| Neal Colzie | DB | 6'2" | 205 | 24 | 3 | |
| Lester Hayes | DB | 6' | 208 | 22 | 1 | |
| Steve Jackson | DB | 6'1" | 192 | 22 | 1 | |
| Charlie Phillips | DB | 6'2" | 215 | 24 | 2 | |
| Jack Tatum | DB | 5'10" | 205 | 28 | 6 | |
| Skip Thomas | DB | 6' | 205 | 27 | 1 | |
| Jimmie Warren | DB | 5'11" | 175 | 38 | | |

Terry Kunz – Injury

| Use Name | Pos. | Hgt | Wgt | Age | Int | Pts |
|---|---|---|---|---|---|---|
| David Humm | QB | 6'2" | 185 | 25 | | |
| Mike Rae | QB | 6' | 190 | 26 | | 6 |
| Ken Stabler | QB | 6'3" | 215 | 31 | | |
| Clarence Davis | HB | 5'10" | 195 | 28 | | 30 |
| Carl Garrett | HB | 5'11" | 205 | 30 | | 18 |
| Hubert Ginn | HB | 5'11" | 185 | 30 | | |
| Pete Banaszak | FB-HB | 5'11" | 210 | 33 | | 30 |
| Terry Robiskie | FB | 6'1" | 210 | 22 | | 6 |
| Mark van Eeghen | FB | 6'2" | 225 | 25 | | 42 |
| Fred Biletnikoff | WR | 6'1" | 190 | 34 | | 30 |
| Morris Bradshaw | WR | 6' | 196 | 24 | | |
| Cliff Branch | WR | 5'11" | 170 | 29 | | 36 |
| Rick Jennings (from TB, SF) | WR-HB | 5'9" | 180 | 24 | | |
| Mike Siani | WR | 6'2" | 195 | 27 | | 12 |
| Warren Bankston | TE | 6'4" | 235 | 30 | | |
| Dave Casper | TE | 6'4" | 230 | 25 | | 36 |
| Ted Kwalick | TE | 6'4" | 225 | 30 | | |
| Ray Guy | K | 6'3" | 195 | 27 | | |
| Errol Mann | K | 6' | 205 | 36 | | 99 |

## SAN DIEGO CHARGERS 7-7 Tommy Prothro

| Scores of Each Game | | |
|---|---|---|
| 0 | Oakland | 24 |
| 23 | Kansas City | 7 |
| 24 | CINCINNATI | 3 |
| 14 | New Orleans | 0 |
| 20 | NEW ENGLAND | 24 |
| 16 | KANSAS CITY | 21 |
| 14 | Miami | 13 |
| 0 | Detroit | 20 |
| 14 | DENVER | 17 |
| 12 | OAKLAND | 7 |
| 30 | Seattle | 28 |
| 37 | CLEVELAND | 14 |
| 9 | Denver | 17 |
| 9 | PITTSBURGH | 10 |

| Use Name | Pos. | Hgt | Wgt | Age | Int | Pts |
|---|---|---|---|---|---|---|
| Booker Brown | OT | 6'2" | 257 | 24 | | |
| Billy Shields | OT | 6'7" | 254 | 24 | | |
| Russ Washington | OT | 6'6" | 290 | 30 | | |
| Charles Aiu | OG | 6'2" | 254 | 23 | | |
| Don Macek | OG-C | 6'3" | 253 | 23 | | |
| Doug Wilkerson | OG | 6'3" | 257 | 30 | | |
| Ralph Perretta | C | 6'2" | 250 | 24 | | |
| Bob Rush | C | 6'5" | 258 | 21 | | |
| Fred Dean | DE | 6'3" | 226 | 25 | 1 | 12 |
| Leroy Jones | DE | 6'8" | 274 | 26 | 1 | 6 |
| John Lee | DE | 6'2" | 253 | 24 | | |
| Charles DeJurnett | DT-DE | 6'4" | 270 | 25 | | |
| Gary Johnson | DT | 6'2" | 254 | 25 | | |
| Louie Kelcher | DT | 6'5" | 282 | 24 | | |

| Use Name | Pos. | Hgt | Wgt | Age | Int | Pts |
|---|---|---|---|---|---|---|
| Don Goode | LB | 6'2" | 231 | 26 | | |
| Tom Graham | LB | 6'2" | 235 | 27 | | |
| Bob Horn | LB | 6'3" | 237 | 23 | 1 | |
| Woodrow Lowe | LB | 6' | 227 | 23 | 1 | |
| Rick Middleton | LB | 6'2" | 228 | 25 | | |
| Ray Preston | LB | 6' | 215 | 23 | | |
| Jerome Dove | DB | 6'2" | 186 | 23 | 1 | |
| Clarence Duren | DB | 6'1" | 190 | 26 | 4 | |
| Mike Fuller | DB | 5'9" | 188 | 24 | 5 | 12 |
| Pete Shaw | DB | 5'10" | 184 | 23 | | |
| Hal Stringert | DB | 5'11" | 185 | 25 | 4 | |
| Mike Williams | DB | 5'10" | 180 | 23 | 3 | |

Danny Colbert – Injury

| Use Name | Pos. | Hgt | Wgt | Age | Int | Pts |
|---|---|---|---|---|---|---|
| Dan Fouts | QB | 6'3" | 204 | 26 | | |
| James Harris | QB | 6'3" | 217 | 30 | | 12 |
| Neal Jeffrey | QB | 6'1" | 180 | 24 | | |
| Bill Munson | QB | 6'2" | 205 | 36 | | |
| Cliff Olander | QB | 6'5" | 196 | 22 | | |
| Hank Bauer | HB | 5'10" | 195 | 23 | | 6 |
| Joe Washington | HB | 5'10" | 182 | 23 | | |
| Rickey Young | HB | 6'2" | 198 | 23 | | 24 |
| Larry Barnes | FB-HB | 5'11" | 220 | 23 | | |
| Bo Matthews | FB | 6'4" | 230 | 25 | | |
| Clarence Williams | FB | 5'9" | 198 | 22 | | 12 |
| Don Woods | FB | 6'1" | 209 | 26 | | 12 |
| Larry Dorsey | WR | 6'1" | 195 | 24 | | 12 |
| Charlie Joiner | WR | 5'11" | 188 | 29 | | 36 |
| Dwight McDonald | WR | 6'2" | 187 | 26 | | |
| Artie Owens | WR | 5'10" | 174 | 24 | | |
| Johnnie Rodgers | WR | 5'10" | 180 | 26 | | |
| Pat Curran | TE | 6'3" | 238 | 31 | | |
| Bob Klein | TE | 6'5" | 245 | 30 | | 6 |
| Jeff West | TE | 6'3" | 211 | 24 | | |
| Rolf Benirschke | K | 6' | 165 | 22 | | 72 |

## SEATTLE SEAHAWKS 5-9 Jack Patera

| Scores of Each Game | | |
|---|---|---|
| 14 | BALTIMORE | 29 |
| 20 | Cincinnati | 42 |
| 13 | DENVER | 24 |
| 0 | New England | 31 |
| 30 | TAMPA BAY | 23 |
| 13 | Miami | 31 |
| 56 | BUFFALO | 17 |
| 7 | Oakland | 44 |
| 17 | N.Y. Jets | 0 |
| 10 | HOUSTON | 22 |
| 28 | SAN DIEGO | 30 |
| 20 | Pittsburgh | 30 |
| 34 | Kansas City | 31 |
| 20 | CLEVELAND | 19 |

| Use Name | Pos. | Hgt | Wgt | Age | Int | Pts |
|---|---|---|---|---|---|---|
| Steve August | OT | 6'5" | 254 | 22 | | |
| Nick Bebout | OT | 6'5" | 260 | 26 | | |
| Norm Evans | OT | 6'5" | 250 | 34 | | |
| Ron Coder | OG | 6'4" | 250 | 23 | | |
| Gordon Jolley | OG-OT | 6'5" | 245 | 28 | | |
| Tom Lynch | OG | 6'5" | 260 | 22 | | |
| Bob Newton | OG | 6'4" | 260 | 28 | | |
| Art Kuehn | C | 6'3" | 255 | 24 | | |
| Geoff Reece | C | 6'4" | 247 | 25 | | |
| John Yarno | C | 6'5" | 251 | 22 | | |
| Dennis Boyd | DE-DT | 6'6" | 255 | 21 | | |
| Richard Harris | DE | 6'4" | 258 | 29 | | |
| Horace Jones | DE | 6'3" | 255 | 28 | | |
| Alden Roche | DE | 6'4" | 255 | 32 | | |
| Ron East | DT | 6'4" | 248 | 34 | | |
| Bob Lurtsema | DT-DE | 6'6" | 250 | 35 | | |
| Steve Niehaus | DT-DE | 6'4" | 270 | 22 | | |
| Bill Sandifer | DT | 6'6" | 262 | 25 | | |

| Use Name | Pos. | Hgt | Wgt | Age | Int | Pts |
|---|---|---|---|---|---|---|
| Terry Beeson | LB | 6'3" | 240 | 21 | | |
| Pete Cronan | LB | 6'2" | 238 | 22 | | |
| Ken Geddes | LB | 6'3" | 235 | 29 | 3 | |
| Sammy Green | LB | 6'2" | 230 | 22 | 1 | |
| Mike Jones | LB | 6'2" | 214 | 23 | | |
| Amos Martin | LB | 6'3" | 228 | 28 | | |
| Charles McShane | LB | 6'3" | 230 | 23 | | |
| Autry Beamon | DB | 6'1" | 190 | 23 | 6 | 6 |
| Dave Brown | DB | 6'1" | 190 | 24 | 4 | 6 |
| Don Dufek | DB | 6' | 195 | 23 | 2 | |
| Doug Long | DB | 6' | 189 | 22 | | |
| Eddie McMillan | DB | 6' | 190 | 25 | 4 | |
| Walter Packer | DB | 5'10" | 174 | 21 | | |
| Steve Preece | DB | 6'1" | 195 | 30 | 4 | |
| Cornell Webster | DB | 6' | 180 | 22 | 1 | |

Randy Coffield – Injury

| Use Name | Pos. | Hgt | Wgt | Age | Int | Pts |
|---|---|---|---|---|---|---|
| Sam Adkins | QB | 6'2" | 214 | 22 | | |
| Steve Myer | QB | 6'2" | 188 | 23 | | |
| Jim Zorn | QB | 6'2" | 200 | 24 | | 6 |
| Al Hunter | HB | 5'11" | 195 | 22 | | 6 |
| David Sims | HB | 6'3" | 216 | 21 | | 48 |
| Sherman Smith | HB-FB | 6'4" | 216 | 22 | | 36 |
| Tony Benjamin | FB | 6'3" | 225 | 21 | | |
| Ed Marinaro | FB-HB | 6'2" | 207 | 27 | | |
| Don Testerman | FB | 6'2" | 235 | 24 | | 30 |
| Duke Fergerson | WR | 6'1" | 193 | 23 | | 12 |
| Steve Largent | WR | 5'11" | 184 | 22 | | 60 |
| Sam McCullum | WR | 6'2" | 203 | 24 | | 6 |
| Steve Raible | WR | 6'2" | 195 | 23 | | |
| Ron Howard | TE | 6'4" | 240 | 26 | | 6 |
| Fred Rayhle | TE | 6'5" | 216 | 23 | | |
| John Sawyer | TE | 6'2" | 230 | 24 | | |
| John Leypoldt | K | 6'2" | 230 | 31 | | 60 |
| Herman Weaver | K | 6'4" | 210 | 28 | | |

## KANSAS CITY CHIEFS 2-12 Paul Wiggin (1-6), Tom Bettis (1-6)

| Scores of Each Game | | |
|---|---|---|
| 17 | New England | 21 |
| 7 | SAN DIEGO | 23 |
| 28 | OAKLAND | 37 |
| 7 | Denver | 23 |
| 6 | BALTIMORE | 17 |
| 21 | San Diego | 16 |
| 7 | Cleveland | 44 |
| 20 | GREEN BAY | 10 |
| 27 | Chicago | 28 |
| 7 | DENVER | 14 |
| 2 | Houston | 34 |
| 7 | CINCINNATI | 27 |
| 31 | SEATTLE | 34 |
| 20 | Oakland | 21 |

| Use Name | Pos. | Hgt | Wgt | Age | Int | Pts |
|---|---|---|---|---|---|---|
| Matt Herkenhoff | OT | 6'4" | 255 | 26 | | |
| Jim Nicholson | OT | 6'6" | 275 | 27 | | |
| Tom Wickert (from DET) | OT-OG | 6'4" | 248 | 25 | | |
| Tom Condon | OG | 6'3" | 240 | 24 | | |
| Charlie Getty | OG-OT | 6'4" | 260 | 25 | | |
| Darius Helton | OG | 6'2" | 260 | 22 | | |
| Bob Simmons | OG-OT | 6'4" | 260 | 23 | | |
| Charlie Ane | C | 6'1" | 233 | 25 | | |
| Jack Rudnay | C | 6'3" | 240 | 29 | | |
| Larry Estes | DE | 6'6" | 250 | 30 | | |
| John Lohmeyer | DE-DT | 6'4" | 229 | 26 | | 2 |
| Whitney Paul | DE | 6'3" | 220 | 23 | 1 | |
| Wilbur Young | DE | 6'6" | 290 | 28 | | |
| Cliff Frazier | DT | 6'4" | 265 | 22 | | |
| Willie Lee | DT | 6'5" | 249 | 27 | | 6 |
| Keith Simons | DT | 6'3" | 254 | 23 | | |

Rod Walters – Injury

| Use Name | Pos. | Hgt | Wgt | Age | Int | Pts |
|---|---|---|---|---|---|---|
| Billy Andrews | LB | 6' | 220 | 32 | | |
| Ray Burks | LB | 6'3" | 217 | 22 | | |
| Jimbo Elrod | LB | 6' | 223 | 23 | | |
| Tom Howard | LB | 6'2" | 208 | 23 | 1 | |
| Willie Lanier | LB | 6'1" | 245 | 32 | | |
| Jim Lynch | LB | 6'1" | 225 | 32 | 3 | |
| Otis Rodgers | LB | 6'3" | 230 | 23 | | |
| Dave Rozumek | LB | 6'2" | 212 | 23 | | |
| Gary Barbaro | DB | 6'4" | 198 | 23 | 8 | 6 |
| Tim Collier | DB | 6' | 166 | 23 | 2 | 6 |
| Ricky Davis | DB | 6'1" | 180 | 24 | | |
| Chris Golub | DB | 6'2" | 196 | 22 | | |
| Tim Gray | DB | 6'1" | 200 | 24 | 2 | 12 |
| Gary Green | DB | 5'11" | 184 | 21 | 3 | |
| Emitt Thomas | DB | 6'2" | 192 | 34 | 1 | |
| Ricky Wesson | DB | 5'9" | 163 | 22 | | |

| Use Name | Pos. | Hgt | Wgt | Age | Int | Pts |
|---|---|---|---|---|---|---|
| Tony Adams | QB | 6' | 198 | 27 | | |
| Mike Livingston | QB | 6'3" | 211 | 31 | | 6 |
| Mark Vitali | QB | 6'5" | 209 | 22 | | |
| Ted McKnight | HB | 6'1" | 203 | 23 | | |
| Arnold Morgado | HB | 6' | 210 | 24 | | |
| Ed Podolak | HB | 6'1" | 205 | 30 | | 30 |
| Tony Reed | HB | 5'11" | 197 | 22 | | 12 |
| Mark Bailey | FB | 6'3" | 237 | 22 | | 18 |
| John Brockington (from GB) | FB | 6'1" | 225 | 28 | | 12 |
| MacArthur Lane | FB | 6' | 220 | 35 | | 6 |
| Pat McNeil | FB | 5'9" | 208 | 23 | | |
| Larry Brunson | WR | 5'11" | 180 | 28 | | |
| Gerald Butler | WR | 6'4" | 205 | 23 | | |
| Henry Marshall | WR | 6'2" | 205 | 23 | | 24 |
| Charlie Wade | WR | 5'10" | 163 | 27 | | |
| Edwin Bechman | TE | 6'4" | 223 | 22 | | |
| Tony Samuels | TE | 6'4" | 229 | 22 | | |
| Walter White | TE | 6'3" | 218 | 26 | | 30 |
| Jan Stenerud | K | 6'2" | 187 | 34 | | 51 |
| Jerrel Wilson | K | 6'4" | 222 | 35 | | |

Woody Green – Knee Injury

## DENVER BRONCOS

**RUSHING**

| Last Name | No. | Yds | Avg | TD |
|---|---|---|---|---|
| Armstrong | 130 | 489 | 3.8 | 4 |
| Perrin | 110 | 456 | 4.1 | 3 |
| Lytle | 104 | 408 | 3.9 | 1 |
| Keyworth | 83 | 311 | 3.7 | 1 |
| Jensen | 40 | 143 | 3.6 | 1 |
| Morton | 31 | 125 | 4.0 | 4 |
| Weese | 11 | 56 | 5.1 | 1 |
| Penrose | 4 | 24 | 6.0 | 0 |
| Upchurch | 1 | 19 | 19.0 | 1 |
| Dolbin | 2 | 12 | 6.0 | 0 |
| Kiick | 1 | 1 | 1.0 | 0 |
| Dilts | 1 | 0 | 0.0 | 0 |
| Moses | 5 | -1 | -0.2 | 0 |

**RECEIVING**

| Last Name | No. | Yds | Avg | TD |
|---|---|---|---|---|
| Odoms | 37 | 429 | 12 | 3 |
| Moses | 27 | 539 | 20 | 4 |
| Dolbin | 26 | 443 | 17 | 3 |
| Armstrong | 18 | 128 | 7 | 0 |
| Lytle | 17 | 198 | 12 | 1 |
| Upchurch | 12 | 245 | 20 | 2 |
| Keyworth | 11 | 48 | 4 | 0 |
| Perrin | 6 | 106 | 18 | 1 |
| Jensen | 4 | 63 | 16 | 0 |
| Egloff | 2 | 27 | 14 | 0 |
| Kiick | 2 | 14 | 7 | 0 |
| Turner | 1 | 25 | 25 | 1 |

**PUNT RETURNS**

| Last Name | No. | Yds | Avg | TD |
|---|---|---|---|---|
| Upchurch | 51 | 653 | 13 | 1 |
| Pane | 6 | 48 | 8 | 0 |
| Schultz | 1 | 11 | 11 | 0 |

**KICKOFF RETURNS**

| Last Name | No. | Yds | Avg | TD |
|---|---|---|---|---|
| Upchurch | 20 | 456 | 23 | 0 |
| Schultz | 6 | 135 | 23 | 0 |
| Perrin | 3 | 72 | 24 | 0 |
| Pane | 1 | 16 | 16 | 0 |
| Keyworth | 1 | 15 | 15 | 0 |
| Hyde | 1 | 15 | 15 | 0 |
| Grant | 1 | 8 | 8 | 0 |
| Nairne | 1 | 1 | 1 | 0 |
| Dolbin | 0 | 14 | — | 0 |

**PASSING – PUNTING – KICKING**

PASSING

| Last Name | Att | Comp | % | Yds | Yd/Att | TD | Int- | % | RK |
|---|---|---|---|---|---|---|---|---|---|
| Morton | 254 | 131 | 42 | 1929 | 7.6 | 14 | 8- | 3 | 2 |
| Penrose | 39 | 21 | 54 | 217 | 5.6 | 0 | 4- | 10 | |
| Weese | 20 | 11 | 55 | 119 | 6.0 | 1 | 0- | 0 | |

PUNTING

| Last Name | No | Avg |
|---|---|---|
| Dilts | 90 | 39.2 |
| Weese | 1 | 38.0 |

KICKING

| Last Name | XP | Att | % | FG | Att | % |
|---|---|---|---|---|---|---|
| Turner | 31 | 34 | 91 | 13 | 19 | 68 |

## OAKLAND RAIDERS

**RUSHING**

| Last Name | No. | Yds | Avg | TD |
|---|---|---|---|---|
| van Eeghen | 324 | 1273 | 3.9 | 7 |
| Davis | 194 | 787 | 4.1 | 5 |
| Banaszak | 67 | 214 | 3.2 | 5 |
| Garrett | 53 | 175 | 3.3 | 1 |
| Robiskie | 22 | 100 | 4.5 | 1 |
| Rae | 13 | 75 | 5.8 | 1 |
| Ginn | 5 | 6 | 1.2 | 0 |
| Stabler | 3 | -3 | -3.0 | 0 |

**RECEIVING**

| Last Name | No. | Yds | Avg | TD |
|---|---|---|---|---|
| Casper | 48 | 584 | 12 | 6 |
| Branch | 33 | 540 | 16 | 6 |
| Biletnikoff | 33 | 446 | 14 | 5 |
| Siani | 24 | 344 | 14 | 2 |
| Davis | 16 | 124 | 8 | 0 |
| van Eeghen | 15 | 135 | 9 | 0 |
| Garrett | 8 | 61 | 8 | 2 |
| Bradshaw | 5 | 90 | 18 | 0 |
| Banaszak | 2 | 14 | 7 | 0 |

**PUNT RETURNS**

| Last Name | No. | Yds | Avg | TD |
|---|---|---|---|---|
| Colzie | 32 | 334 | 10 | 0 |
| Jennings | 12 | 71 | 6 | 0 |

**KICKOFF RETURNS**

| Last Name | No. | Yds | Avg | TD |
|---|---|---|---|---|
| Garrett | 21 | 420 | 20 | 0 |
| Jennings | 7 | 153 | 22 | 0 |
| Banaszak | 7 | 119 | 17 | 0 |
| Robiskie | 6 | 83 | 14 | 0 |
| Ginn | 3 | 74 | 25 | 0 |
| Davis | 3 | 63 | 21 | 0 |
| Hayes | 3 | 57 | 19 | 0 |
| Bankston | 1 | 0 | 0 | 0 |
| McCoy | 1 | 0 | 0 | 0 |

**PASSING – PUNTING – KICKING**

PASSING

| Last Name | Att | Comp | % | Yds | Yd/Att | TD | Int- | % | RK |
|---|---|---|---|---|---|---|---|---|---|
| Stabler | 294 | 169 | 58 | 2176 | 7.4 | 20 | 20- | 7 | 4 |
| Rae | 30 | 15 | 50 | 162 | 5.4 | 1 | 4- | 13 | |

PUNTING

| Last Name | No | Avg |
|---|---|---|
| Guy | 59 | 43.3 |

KICKING

| Last Name | XP | Att | % | FG | Att | % |
|---|---|---|---|---|---|---|
| Mann | 39 | 42 | 93 | 20 | 29 | 71 |

## SAN DIEGO CHARGERS

**RUSHING**

| Last Name | No. | Yds | Avg | TD |
|---|---|---|---|---|
| Young | 157 | 543 | 3.5 | 4 |
| Woods | 118 | 405 | 3.4 | 1 |
| J. Washington | 62 | 217 | 3.5 | 0 |
| C. Williams | 50 | 215 | 4.3 | 2 |
| Matthews | 43 | 193 | 4.5 | 0 |
| Barnes | 24 | 70 | 2.9 | 0 |
| Rodgers | 3 | 44 | 14.7 | 0 |
| Olander | 7 | 30 | 4.3 | 0 |
| Harris | 10 | 13 | 1.3 | 2 |
| Fouts | 6 | 13 | 2.2 | 0 |
| Fuller | 1 | 7 | 7.0 | 1 |
| Bauer | 4 | 4 | 1.0 | 0 |
| Owens | 1 | 3 | 3.0 | 0 |
| Curran | 1 | 2 | 2.0 | 0 |
| Munson | 1 | 2 | 2.0 | 0 |

**RECEIVING**

| Last Name | No. | Yds | Avg | TD |
|---|---|---|---|---|
| Young | 48 | 423 | 9 | 0 |
| Joiner | 35 | 542 | 15 | 6 |
| J. Washington | 31 | 244 | 8 | 0 |
| Klein | 20 | 244 | 12 | 1 |
| Woods | 18 | 218 | 12 | 1 |
| McDonald | 13 | 174 | 13 | 0 |
| Rodgers | 12 | 187 | 16 | 0 |
| Dorsey | 10 | 198 | 20 | 2 |
| Curran | 10 | 123 | 12 | 0 |
| Matthews | 3 | 41 | 14 | 0 |
| C. Williams | 3 | 20 | 7 | 0 |
| Bauer | 1 | 15 | 15 | 1 |
| Barnes | 1 | 10 | 10 | 0 |
| West | 1 | 3 | 3 | 0 |

**PUNT RETURNS**

| Last Name | No. | Yds | Avg | TD |
|---|---|---|---|---|
| Fuller | 28 | 360 | 13 | 1 |
| Rodgers | 15 | 158 | 11 | 0 |
| Dove | 1 | 3 | 3 | 0 |
| M. Williams | 1 | 0 | 0 | 0 |
| C. Williams | 1 | 0 | 0 | 0 |

**KICKOFF RETURNS**

| Last Name | No. | Yds | Avg | TD |
|---|---|---|---|---|
| C. Williams | 24 | 481 | 20 | 0 |
| Owens | 8 | 132 | 17 | 0 |
| Rodgers | 4 | 66 | 17 | 0 |
| Woods | 1 | 27 | 27 | 0 |
| Middleton | 1 | 20 | 20 | 0 |
| Joiner | 1 | 8 | 8 | 0 |

**PASSING – PUNTING – KICKING**

PASSING

| Last Name | Att | Comp | % | Yds | Yd/Att | TD | Int- | % | RK |
|---|---|---|---|---|---|---|---|---|---|
| Harris | 211 | 109 | 52 | 1240 | 5.9 | 5 | 11- | 5 | 12 |
| Fouts | 109 | 69 | 63 | 869 | 8.0 | 4 | 6- | 6 | |
| Munson | 31 | 20 | 65 | 225 | 7.3 | 1 | 1- | 3 | |
| Olander | 16 | 7 | 44 | 76 | 4.8 | 0 | 2- | 13 | |
| J. Washington | 1 | 1 | 100 | 32 | 32.0 | 1 | 0- | 0 | |
| Woods | 1 | 0 | 0 | 0 | 0.0 | 0 | 0- | 0 | |

PUNTING

| Last Name | No | Avg |
|---|---|---|
| West | 72 | 37.6 |

KICKING

| Last Name | XP | Att | % | FG | Att | % |
|---|---|---|---|---|---|---|
| Benirschke | 21 | 24 | 88 | 17 | 23 | 74 |

## SEATTLE SEAHAWKS

**RUSHING**

| Last Name | No. | Yds | Avg | TD |
|---|---|---|---|---|
| Smith | 163 | 763 | 4.7 | 4 |
| Testerman | 119 | 459 | 3.9 | 1 |
| Sims | 99 | 369 | 3.7 | 5 |
| Hunter | 32 | 179 | 5.6 | 1 |
| Zorn | 25 | 141 | 5.6 | 1 |
| Benjamin | 13 | 48 | 3.7 | 0 |
| Adkins | 3 | 6 | 2.0 | 0 |
| Myer | 6 | 1 | 0.2 | 0 |
| Weaver | 1 | -2 | -2.0 | 0 |

**RECEIVING**

| Last Name | No. | Yds | Avg | TD |
|---|---|---|---|---|
| Largent | 33 | 643 | 19 | 10 |
| Testerman | 31 | 219 | 7 | 4 |
| Smith | 30 | 419 | 14 | 2 |
| Fergersen | 19 | 374 | 20 | 2 |
| Howard | 17 | 177 | 10 | 1 |
| Sims | 12 | 176 | 15 | 3 |
| Sawyer | 10 | 105 | 11 | 0 |
| McCullum | 9 | 198 | 22 | 1 |
| Raible | 5 | 79 | 16 | 0 |
| Hunter | 5 | 42 | 8 | 0 |
| Benjamin | 4 | 27 | 7 | 0 |

**PUNT RETURNS**

| Last Name | No. | Yds | Avg | TD |
|---|---|---|---|---|
| Packer | 20 | 131 | 7 | 0 |
| Ferguson | 8 | 54 | 7 | 0 |
| Largent | 4 | 32 | 8 | 0 |

**KICKOFF RETURNS**

| Last Name | No. | Yds | Avg | TD |
|---|---|---|---|---|
| Hunter | 36 | 820 | 23 | 0 |
| Packer | 13 | 280 | 22 | 0 |
| Fergerson | 11 | 240 | 22 | 0 |
| Sims | 4 | 52 | 13 | 0 |
| Smith | 3 | 56 | 19 | 0 |
| Raible | 2 | 19 | 10 | 0 |
| Dufek | 1 | 21 | 21 | 0 |
| Testerman | 1 | 14 | 14 | 0 |

**PASSING – PUNTING – KICKING**

PASSING

| Last Name | Att | Comp | % | Yds | Yd/Att | TD | Int- | % | RK |
|---|---|---|---|---|---|---|---|---|---|
| Zorn | 251 | 104 | 41 | 1687 | 6.7 | 16 | 19- | 8 | 14 |
| Myer | 130 | 70 | 54 | 729 | 5.6 | 6 | 12- | 9 | |
| Sims | 4 | 1 | 25 | 43 | 10.8 | 1 | 1- | 25 | |
| Preece | 1 | 0 | 0 | 0 | 0.0 | 0 | 0- | 0 | |
| Smith | 1 | 0 | 0 | 0 | 0.0 | 0 | 0- | 0 | |

PUNTING

| Last Name | No | Avg |
|---|---|---|
| Weaver | 58 | 39.5 |

KICKING

| Last Name | XP | Att | % | FG | Att | % |
|---|---|---|---|---|---|---|
| Leypoldt | 33 | 37 | 89 | 9 | 18 | 50 |

## KANSAS CITY CHIEFS

**RUSHING**

| Last Name | No. | Yds | Avg | TD |
|---|---|---|---|---|
| Podolak | 133 | 550 | 4.1 | 5 |
| Reed | 126 | 505 | 4.0 | 2 |
| Bailey | 66 | 266 | 4.0 | 2 |
| Brockington | 65 | 186 | 2.9 | 1 |
| Lane | 25 | 79 | 3.2 | 1 |
| Livingston | 19 | 78 | 4.1 | 1 |
| McNight | 11 | 74 | 6.7 | 0 |
| Burks | 1 | 51 | 51.0 | 0 |
| Adams | 5 | 21 | 4.2 | 0 |
| Morgado | 3 | 12 | 4.0 | 0 |
| Marshall | 7 | 11 | 1.6 | 0 |
| Brunson | 2 | 8 | 4.0 | 0 |
| White | 2 | -3 | -1.5 | 0 |

**RECEIVING**

| Last Name | No. | Yds | Avg | TD |
|---|---|---|---|---|
| White | 48 | 674 | 14 | 5 |
| Podolak | 32 | 313 | 10 | 0 |
| Marshall | 23 | 445 | 19 | 4 |
| Brockington | 21 | 223 | 11 | 1 |
| Brunson | 20 | 295 | 15 | 0 |
| Bailey | 17 | 206 | 12 | 1 |
| Reed | 12 | 125 | 10 | 0 |
| Samuels | 5 | 65 | 13 | 0 |
| Lane | 3 | 40 | 13 | 0 |
| Morgado | 2 | 21 | 11 | 0 |
| McKnight | 1 | 11 | 11 | 0 |
| Beckman | 1 | 3 | 3 | 0 |

**PUNT RETURNS**

| Last Name | No. | Yds | Avg | TD |
|---|---|---|---|---|
| Green | 14 | 115 | 8 | 0 |
| Brunson | 20 | 108 | 5 | 0 |
| Podolak | 2 | 13 | 7 | 0 |

**KICKOFF RETURNS**

| Last Name | No. | Yds | Avg | TD |
|---|---|---|---|---|
| McNight | 12 | 305 | 25 | 0 |
| Reed | 11 | 239 | 22 | 0 |
| Brunson | 11 | 216 | 20 | 0 |
| Wesson | 7 | 129 | 18 | 0 |
| Bailey | 3 | 46 | 15 | 0 |
| Getty | 1 | 15 | 15 | 0 |
| Burks | 1 | 15 | 15 | 0 |

**PASSING – PUNTING – KICKING**

PASSING

| Last Name | Att | Comp | % | Yds | Yd/Att | TD | Int- | % | RK |
|---|---|---|---|---|---|---|---|---|---|
| Livingston | 282 | 143 | 51 | 1823 | 6.5 | 9 | 15- | 5 | 11 |
| Adams | 92 | 47 | 51 | 691 | 7.5 | 2 | 11- | 12 | |

PUNTING

| Last Name | No | Avg |
|---|---|---|
| Wilson | 88 | 39.9 |

KICKING

| Last Name | XP | Att | % | FG | Att | % |
|---|---|---|---|---|---|---|
| Stenerud | 27 | 28 | 96 | 8 | 18 | 44 |

# 1977 Championship Games

## NFC CHAMPIONSHIP GAME

January 1, at Irving, Tex.
(Attendance: 61,968)

### SCORING

| | | | | |
|---|---|---|---|---|
| DALLAS | 6 | 10 | 0 | 7—23 |
| MINNESOTA | 0 | 6 | 0 | 0— 6 |

**First Quarter**
Dallas — Richards, 32 yard pass from Staubach
PAT — Kick (no good)

**Second Quarter**
Dallas — Newhouse, 5 yard rush
PAT — Herrera (Kick)
Minn. — Cox, 12 yard field goal
Minn. — Cox, 37 yard field goal
Dallas — Herrera, 21 yard field goal

**Fourth Quarter**
Dallas — Dorsett, 11 yard rush
PAT — Herrera (Kick)

### TEAM STATISTICS

| DALLAS | | MINN. |
|---|---|---|
| 16 | First Downs—Total | 12 |
| 7 | First Downs—Rushing | 4 |
| 7 | First Downs—Passing | 6 |
| 2 | First Downs—Penalty | 2 |
| 1 | Fumbles—Number | 5 |
| 1 | Fumbles—Lost Ball | 3 |
| 5 | Penalty—Number | 5 |
| 84 | Yards Penalized | 32 |
| 0 | Missed Field Goals | 0 |
| 66 | Offensive Plays | 63 |
| 328 | Net Yards | 214 |
| 4.8 | Average Gain | 3.4 |
| 2 | Giveaways | 4 |
| 4 | Takeaways | 2 |
| +2 | Difference | -2 |

### SCORING

| | | | | |
|---|---|---|---|---|
| DENVER | 7 | 0 | 7 | 6—20 |
| OAKLAND | 3 | 0 | 0 | 14—17 |

**First Quarter**
Oak. — Mann, 20 yard field goal
Den. — Moses, 74 yard pass from Morton
PAT — Turner (kick)

**Third Quarter**
Den. — Keyworth, 1 yard rush
PAT — Turner (kick)

**Fourth Quarter**
Oak. — Casper, 7 yard pass from Stabler
PAT — Mann (kick)
Den. — Moses, 12 yard pass from Morton
PAT — No kick—pass failed
Oak. — Casper, 17 yard pass from Stabler
PAT — Mann (kick)

### TEAM STATISTICS

| DENVER | | OAKLAND |
|---|---|---|
| 16 | First Downs—Total | 20 |
| 6 | First Downs—Rushing | 6 |
| 8 | First Downs—Passing | 11 |
| 2 | First Downs—Penalty | 3 |
| 2 | Fumbles—Number | 0 |
| 0 | Fumbles—Lost Ball | 0 |
| 8 | Penalty—Number | 2 |
| 46 | Yards Penalized | 6 |
| 3 | Missed Field Goals | 1 |
| 58 | Offensive Plays | 72 |
| 308 | Net Yards | 298 |
| 5.3 | Average Gain | 4.1 |
| 1 | Giveaways | 1 |
| 1 | Takeaways | 1 |
| 0 | Difference | 0 |

## NFC CHAMPIONSHIP GAME

As expected, Dallas had no trouble at all with a young, inexperienced Chicago Bear team that turned the ball over seven times in the Pokes' 37-7 NFC semifinal victory in Irving. But it was a different story in Los Angeles that same day as Minnesota took advantage of a sloppy, mud-infested field to upset the playoff-jinxed Rams 14-7. The Cowboys proceeded to start the new year off on the right foot with a convincing 23-6 victory over the Vikes to put themselves in the Super Bowl.

The Vikings were no match for a Dallas defense led by linemen Harvey Martin, and Ed Jones and OLB Tom Henderson. After holding the Bears' Walter payton to only 60 rushing yards the week before, the Cowboys' "flex" limited Chuck Foreman to just 59. Two minutes into the first quarter, Martin tackled RB Robert Miller hard enough to cause a fumble which the big end recovered on Minnesota's 39-yard line to set up the Cowboys' first score. Robert Newhouse, who enjoyed his second-straight 80-yard playoff game, powered his way to the 32-yard line and the QB Roger Staubach took over, faking a quick screen and throwing long to WR Golden Richards in the endzone. Minnesota's Carl Eller blocked the extra point, but on the Cowboys' next TD drive, the Vikes' usually reliable specialty teams failed to stop punter Danny White's fake and subsequent 14-yard run for a first down. A defensive holding call on FS Paul Krause moved the ball deeper into Viking territory and Newhouse responded with a five-yard TD romp to make it 13-0.

Martin recovered two fumbles while his opposite number, Jones, was an imposing force against the run. Also helping out defensively was a strong secondary effort that kept the Vikes' top receiver, Ahmad Rashad, under wraps all day with double-team coverage.

## AFC CHAMPIONSHIP GAME

January 1, at Denver
(Attendance: 75,004)

The defending Super Bowl champion Raiders just barely made it to AFC title game with a 37-31 overtime victory at Baltimore in one of the most exciting contests of all-time. The leader changed hands six times and Raider Errol Mann tied the score for the last time when he booted a 22-yard field goal with 26 seconds left in regulation following a clutch 42-yard reception by TE Dave Casper. Casper later scored the game winner on a 10-yard Ken Stabler pass 43 seconds into the second overtime, ending the third longest game in NFL history.

Meanwhile, Denver got past its first hurdle with a 34-21 win over Pittsburgh, after breaking open a 21-21 tie with 13 unanswered points in the fourth quarter. Just as it had done all season, the Broncos' Orange Crush defense provided good field position by forcing four turnovers, including two interceptions by All-Pro OLB Tom Jackson.

Because Oakland had more experience and the Cinderella Broncos were still somewhat of an unknown quantity in many observers' eyes, the Raiders were rated as slight favorites over the team which had beaten them to the AFC West crown. As Oakland repeatedly tried to run to the outside and failed because of the superb lateral movement of the Bronco defense, the momentum swung toward Denver. Although Oakland had taken an early lead on Mann's 20-yard field goal, QB Craig Morton struck two plays later on a 74-yard TD bomb to WR Haven Moses.

After leading 7-3 at halftime, Denver was driving for another score midway through the third quarter when perhaps the most controversial play of the season occurred. With first-and-goal at the Raider two, Rob Lytle took a handoff and vaulted over the left side of his offensive line. He was met head-on by safety Jack Tatum, who jarred the ball loose while Lytle was in mid-air. Raider MG Mike McCoy picked up the loose ball and began to run, but the play was whistled dead. The officials, apparently screened from the fumble, ruled that Denver should keep the ball. Jon Keyworth scored from the one on the next play, and Denver had a 14-3 lead.

Whether that disputed "non-fumble" would have changed the outcome of the game will be debated for years, but it certainly put Oakland at a big disadvantage. The Raiders closed the gap on Stabler's seven-yard TD pass to Casper, but the Morton-Moses duo clicked again on a 12-yard scoring pass. Oakland once again trimmed the deficit to three on a 17-yard pass to the reliable Casper with 3:16 remaining, but Denver ran out the clock using Lonnie Perrin and Otis Armstrong.

### INDIVIDUAL STATISTICS

| DALLAS | No | Yds | Avg. | MINNESOTA | No | Yds | Avg. |
|---|---|---|---|---|---|---|---|
| **RUSHING** | | | | | | | |
| Newhouse | 15 | 81 | 5.4 | Foreman | 21 | 59 | 2.8 |
| Dorsett | 19 | 71 | 3.7 | Miller | 8 | 5 | 0.6 |
| D. White | 1 | 14 | 14.0 | S. Johnson | 1 | 2 | 2.0 |
| Staubach | 4 | 4 | 1.0 | | 30 | 66 | 2.2 |
| | 39 | 170 | 4.3 | | | | |
| **RECEIVING** | | | | | | | |
| D. Pearson | 4 | 62 | 15.5 | Foreman | 5 | 36 | 7.2 |
| P. Pearson | 3 | 48 | 16.0 | S. White | 3 | 46 | 15.3 |
| Richards | 2 | 34 | 17.0 | Rashad | 3 | 18 | 6.0 |
| Newhouse | 2 | 5 | 2.5 | Miller | 2 | 39 | 19.5 |
| DuPree | 1 | 16 | 16.0 | Voigt | 1 | 19 | 19.0 |
| | 12 | 165 | 13.8 | | 14 | 158 | 11.3 |
| **PUNTING** | | | | | | | |
| D. White | 8 | | 36.6 | Clabo | 8 | | 34.7 |
| **PUNT RETURNS** | | | | | | | |
| Hill | 3 | 44 | 14.7 | Moore | 3 | 2 | 0.7 |
| B. Johnson | 2 | 13 | 6.5 | | | | |
| | 5 | 57 | 11.4 | | | | |
| **KICKOFF RETURNS** | | | | | | | |
| Brinson | 3 | 36 | 12.0 | Moore | 3 | 74 | 24.7 |
| | | | | S. White | 1 | 37 | 37.0 |
| | | | | Kellar | 1 | 11 | 11.0 |
| | | | | | 5 | 122 | 24.4 |
| **INTERCEPTION RETURNS** | | | | | | | |
| Henderson | 1 | 1 | 1.0 | N. Wright | 1 | 0 | 0.0 |

#### PASSING

| DALLAS | Att. | Comp. | Comp. Pct. | Yds. | Int. | Yds/ Att. | Yds/ Comp. | Yards Lost Tackled |
|---|---|---|---|---|---|---|---|---|
| Staubach | 23 | 12 | 52.2 | 165 | 1 | 7.2 | 13.8 | 2—7 |
| **MINNESOTA** | | | | | | | | |
| Lee | 31 | 14 | 45.2 | 158 | 1 | 5.1 | 11.3 | 2—10 |

### INDIVIDUAL STATISTICS

| DENVER | No | Yds | Avg. | OAKLAND | No | Yds | Avg. |
|---|---|---|---|---|---|---|---|
| **RUSHING** | | | | | | | |
| Perrin | 11 | 42 | 3.8 | van Eeghen | 20 | 71 | 3.6 |
| Lytle | 7 | 26 | 3.7 | Banaszak | 7 | 22 | 3.1 |
| Keyworth | 8 | 19 | 2.4 | Davis | 9 | 1 | 0.1 |
| Armstrong | 7 | 16 | 2.3 | | 36 | 94 | 2.6 |
| Jensen | 1 | 2 | 2.0 | | | | |
| Morton | 2 | -4 | -2.0 | | | | |
| Moses | 1 | -10 | -10.0 | | | | |
| | 37 | 91 | 2.5 | | | | |
| **RECEIVING** | | | | | | | |
| Moses | 5 | 168 | 33.6 | Casper | 5 | 71 | 14.2 |
| Perrin | 2 | 20 | 10.0 | Biletnikoff | 4 | 38 | 9.5 |
| Jensen | 1 | 20 | 20.0 | Branch | 3 | 59 | 19.7 |
| Odoms | 1 | 13 | 13.0 | van Eeghen | 2 | 8 | 4.0 |
| Keyworth | 1 | 3 | 3.0 | Bradshaw | 1 | 25 | 25.0 |
| | 10 | 224 | 22.4 | Siani | 1 | 12 | 12.0 |
| | | | | Banaszak | 1 | 2 | 2.0 |
| | | | | | 17 | 215 | 12.6 |
| **PUNTING** | | | | | | | |
| Dilts | 4 | | 40.8 | Guy | 5 | | 36.0 |
| **PUNT RETURNS** | | | | | | | |
| Upchurch | 2 | 12 | 6.0 | Garrett | 2 | 5 | 2.5 |
| **KICKOFF RETURNS** | | | | | | | |
| Upchurch | 2 | 33 | 16.5 | Garrett | 3 | 111 | 37.0 |
| Schultz | 1 | 20 | 20.0 | Davis | 1 | 25 | 25.0 |
| Lytle | 1 | 14 | 14.0 | | 4 | 136 | 36.0 |
| | 4 | 67 | 16.8 | | | | |
| **INTERCEPTION RETURNS** | | | | | | | |
| Swenson | 1 | 14 | 14.0 | Rice | 1 | 11 | 11.0 |

#### PASSING

| DENVER | Att. | Comp. | Comp. Pct. | Yds. | Int. | Yds/ Att. | Yds/ Comp | Yards Lost Tackled |
|---|---|---|---|---|---|---|---|---|
| Morton | 20 | 10 | 50.0 | 224 | 1 | 11.2 | 22.4 | 1—7 |
| **OAKLAND** | | | | | | | | |
| Stabler | 35 | 17 | 48.6 | 215 | 1 | 6.1 | 12.6 | 1—11 |

# Orange Crushed

Orange was undoubtedly the NFL's most popular color during the 77' season, but after the Dallas Cowboys swept past the Denver Broncos 27-10 in the first Super Bowl played indoors, the game's most vivid scenes had been painted in a solid shade of black and blue.

Most responsible for this setting were the imposing members of the Cowboys' defensive line—safety Randy Hughes notwithstanding—as they ripped away at the left side of Denver's offensive line and pressured quarterback Craig Morton into a miserable performance.

Morton, the NFL's Comeback Player of the Year, completed as many passes to the Cowboys as his own teammates, unintentionally entering his name into the less-distinguished portion of the Super Bowl record book.

In addition to his four interceptions, the game featured the most Super Bowl penalties ever by both teams (20 for 154 yards) as well as most fumbles, both teams (10).

Thanks, however, to the Pokes' inability to capitalize on more than a few scoring opportunities in the first half, as well as Bronco Head Coach Red Miller's decision to replace Morton with Norris Weese with 6:40 left in the third quarter, the game was kept from becoming a Super Bore.

Four plays after Hughes snatched a Morton pass on the Denver 29, Tony Dorsett's three-yard sprint off left tackle put the Cowboys on the scoreboard first with 10:31 gone in the first quarter.

Efren Herrera's 35-yard three-pointer following another interception finished up the first-period scoring, and he also provided the second quarter's only score with a 43-yarder after blowing three straight field goal attempts.

Jim Turner's 47-yarder that barely made it over the cross-bar gave the Broncos their first score early in the third quarter, but the Cowboys extended their lead to 20-3 after a stunning 45-yard TD reception by Butch Johnson as he dove across the goal line to snare QB Roger Staubach's pass.

With Weese adding much-needed mobility to the Denver attack, the Broncs scored their first TD of the game on Rob Lytle's one-yard plunge, one play after ex-Cowboy Jim Jensen galloped 16 yards with a Weese pitchout.

But the game's second exceptional TD reception—Golden Richards' 29-yard, over-the-head catch of Robert Newhouse's option pass while rolling left—made sure the Cinderella Broncos would turn back into a normal old orange pumpkin, at least until next year.

For the first time in Super Bowl history, co-winners were selected as MVP's—White (five tackles, one assist) and DE Harvey Martin (two tackles, two sacks, one deflection).

And while Staubach called a clever game, emphasizing a counteraction passing attack away from Denver's pursuit toward the middle, Dallas' Doomsday defense—and all those black and blue marks—really told the story.

## LINEUPS

| DALLAS | | DENVER |
|---|---|---|
| | **OFFENSE** | |
| Richards | WR | Dolbin |
| Neely | LT | Maurer |
| Scott | LG | Glassic |
| Fitzgerald | C | Montler |
| Rafferty | RG | Howard |
| Donovan | RT | Minor |
| DuPree | TE | Odoms |
| D. Pearson | WR | Moses |
| Staubach | QB | Morton |
| Dorsett | RB | Armstrong |
| Newhouse | RB | Keyworth |
| | **DEFENSE** | |
| Jones | LE | Chavous |
| Pugh | LT-NT | Carter |
| R. White | RT-RE | Alzado |
| Martin | RE-LLB | Swenson |
| Henderson | LLB-LLB | Rizzo |
| Bruenig | MLB-RLB | Gradishar |
| Lewis | RLB-RLB | Jackson |
| Barnes | LCB | L. Wright |
| Kyle | RCB | Foley |
| Waters | SS | Thompson |
| Harris | FS-WS | Jackson |

### SUBSTITUTES

| DALLAS | **OFFENSE** | |
|---|---|---|
| Brinson | Hill | P. Pearson |
| Carano | Johnson | Saldi |
| Cooper | Laidlaw | D. White |
| Dennison | Lawless | R. Wright |
| Frederick | | |
| | **DEFENSE** | |
| Brown | Hegman | Renfro |
| Cole | Hughes | Stalls |
| Gregory | Huther | Washington |
| | **KICKER** | |
| | Herrera | |

| DENVER | **OFFENSE** | |
|---|---|---|
| Allison | Lytle | Schindler |
| Egloff | Maples | Schultz |
| Hyde | Penrose | Upchurch |
| Jensen | Perrin | Weese |
| | **DEFENSE** | |
| Evans | Nairne | Riley |
| Grant | Poltl | Smith |
| Jackson | Rich | Turk |
| Manor | | |
| | **KICKERS** | |
| Dilts | | Turner |

## SCORING

| | | | | |
|---|---|---|---|---|
| DALLAS | 10 | 3 | 7 | 7—27 |
| DENVER | 0 | 0 | 10 | 0—10 |

**First Quarter**
Dallas  Dorsett, 3 yard rush  10:31
  PAT — Herrera (kick)
Dallas  Herrera, 35 yard field goal  13:29

**Second Quarter**
Dallas  Herrera, 43 yard field goal  3:44

**Third Quarter**
Denver  Turner, 47 yard field goal  2:28
Dallas  Johnson, 45 yard pass from  8:01
  Staubach  PAT — Herrera (kick)
Denver  Lytle, 1 yard rush  9:21
  PAT — Turner (kick)

**Fourth Quarter**
Dallas  Richards, 29 yard pass  7:56
  from Newhouse
  PAT — Herrera (kick)

## TEAM STATISTICS

| DALLAS | | DENVER |
|---|---|---|
| 17 | First Downs—Total | 11 |
| 8 | First Downs—Rushing | 8 |
| 8 | First Downs—Passing | 1 |
| 1 | First Downs—Penalty | 2 |
| 6 | Fumbles—Number | 4 |
| 2 | Fumbles—Lost Ball | 4 |
| 12 | Penalties—Number | 8 |
| 94 | Yards Penalized | 60 |
| 3 | Missed Field Goals | 0 |
| 71 | Offensive Plays | 58 |
| 325 | Net Yards | 156 |
| 4.6 | Average Gain | 2.7 |
| 2 | Giveaways | 8 |
| 8 | Takeaways | 2 |
| +6 | Differnece | -6 |

## INDIVIDUAL STATISTICS

| DALLAS | | | | DENVER | | | |
|---|---|---|---|---|---|---|---|
| | No | Yds | Avg. | | No | Yds | Avg. |
| | | | **RUSHING** | | | | |
| Dorsett | 15 | 66 | 4.4 | Lytle | 10 | 35 | 3.5 |
| Newhouse | 14 | 55 | 3.9 | Armstrong | 7 | 27 | 3.9 |
| D. White | 1 | 13 | 13.0 | Weese | 3 | 26 | 8.7 |
| P. Pearson | 3 | 11 | 3.7 | Jensen | 1 | 16 | 16.0 |
| Staubach | 3 | 6 | 2.6 | Keyworth | 5 | 9 | 1.8 |
| Laidlaw | 1 | 1 | 1.0 | Perrin | 3 | 8 | 2.7 |
| Johnson | 1 | -9 | -9.0 | | 29 | 121 | 4.2 |
| | 38 | 143 | 3.8 | | | | |
| | | | **RECEIVING** | | | | |
| P. Pearson | 5 | 37 | 7.4 | Dolbin | 2 | 24 | 12.0 |
| DuPree | 4 | 66 | 16.5 | Odoms | 2 | 9 | 4.5 |
| Newhouse | 3 | -1 | -0.3 | Moses | 1 | 21 | 21.0 |
| Johnson | 2 | 53 | 26.5 | Upchurch | 1 | 9 | 9.0 |
| Richards | 2 | 38 | 19.0 | Jensen | 1 | 5 | 5.0 |
| Dorsett | 2 | 11 | 5.5 | Perrin | 1 | -7 | -7.0 |
| D. Pearson | 1 | 13 | 13.0 | | 8 | 61 | 7.6 |
| | 19 | 217 | 11.4 | | | | |
| | | | **PUNTING** | | | | |
| D. White | 5 | | 41.6 | Dilts | 4 | | 38.2 |
| | | | **PUNT RETURNS** | | | | |
| Hill | 1 | 0 | 0.0 | Upchurch | 3 | 22 | 7.3 |
| | | | | Schultz | 1 | 0 | 0.0 |
| | | | | | 4 | 2 | 5.5 |
| | | | **KICKOFF RETURNS** | | | | |
| Johnson | 2 | 29 | 14.5 | Upchurch | 3 | 94 | 31.3 |
| Brinson | 1 | 22 | 22.0 | Schultz | 2 | 62 | 31.0 |
| | 3 | 51 | 17.0 | Jensen | 1 | 17 | 17.0 |
| | | | | | 6 | 173 | 28.8 |
| | | | **INTERCEPTION RETURNS** | | | | |
| Washington | 1 | 27 | 27.0 | none | | | |
| Kyle | 1 | 19 | 19.0 | | | | |
| Barnes | 1 | 0 | 0.0 | | | | |
| Hughes | 1 | 0 | 0.0 | | | | |
| | 4 | 46 | 11.5 | | | | |

### PASSING

| DALLAS | Att. | Comp. | Comp. Pct. | Yds | Int. | Yds/ Att. | Yds/ Comp. | Yards Lost Tackled |
|---|---|---|---|---|---|---|---|---|
| Staubach | 25 | 17 | 68.0 | 183 | 0 | 7.5 | 10.8 | |
| D. White | 2 | 1 | 50.0 | 5 | 0 | 2.5 | 5.0 | |
| Newhouse | 1 | 1 | 100.0 | 29 | 0 | 29.0 | 29.0 | |
| | 28 | 19 | 67.9 | 217 | 0 | 7.8 | 11.4 | 5—35 |
| **DENVER** | | | | | | | | |
| Morton | 15 | 4 | 26.7 | 39 | 4 | 2.6 | 9.8 | 2—20 |
| Weese | 10 | 4 | 40.0 | 22 | 0 | 2.2 | 5.5 | 2— 6 |
| | 25 | 8 | 32.0 | 61 | 4 | 2.4 | 7.6 | 4—26 |

The rebirth of the forward pass took another step forward with a change in the rule about "chucking." Previously, receivers were fair game for shots from defenders all the way downfield until the pass was released. With this year's rule change, defenders could hit receivers only within five yards of the line of scrimmage. Slender speedsters had only to find their way five yards downfield and then could run pass patterns without a physical beating. Together with a liberalized rule on pass blocking, this change aimed to restore the aerial circus which had flourished before zone defenses had grounded pro offenses.

## EASTERN DIVISION

**Dallas Cowboys**—The pre-season pundits said that Dallas would win easily. They were half right. The Cowboys repeated as Eastern champs, but only after a two-month trance almost cost them their crown. Coach Tom Landry lost old pros Ralph Neely and Mel Renfro to retirement, but he still enjoyed an embarassment of riches. Roger Staubach piloted a versatile offense which featured Tony Dorsett's running, a fine corps of receivers, and a superb line starring Billy Joe DuPree and Herbert Scott. The Doomsday Defense shone from front to back, with Randy White, Cliff Harris, and Charlie Waters only the brightest of the stars. Nevertheless, the defending Super Bowl champs sleepwalked into November. By the fifth week of the season, they trailed the Redskins by two games. Back to back losses to the Vikings and Dolphins in October dropped the record to 6-4 and put a playoff berth in doubt. Suddenly, they awoke and again played inspired football. With the Redskins faltering, Dallas and Washington met on Thanksgiving Day with first place at stake. It was no contest, with the Cowboys asserting 37-10 dominance. With victories in their last six games, the Cowboys were hitting their stride as they entered the playoffs.

**Philadelphia Eagles**—The eagles found the key to the playoffs sitting on their bench. Wilbert Montgomery had returned kicks as a rookie last year, but rarely lined up with the offensive unit. Coach Dick Vermeil made Montgomery his starting halfback and was rewarded with the Eagles' best running threat in years. With the ground game established, quarterback Ron Jaworski could pass more selectively and more effectively. Harold Carmichael gained the most yardage of any N.F.C. receiver while running his record pass receiving string to 96 games. Linebacker Bill Bergey led the strong 3-4 defense which sparked the Eagles' resurgence in recent years under Vermeil. The season began with disappointing losses to the Rams and Redskins, but then three straight triumphs boosted the Eagles into contention. Several close calls went the Eagles' way in their quest. A last-minute fumble gave them a victory over the Giants on November 19 when defeat was all but sealed. They went into their final game with a two game losing streak and with any hope of a playoff spot depending on both the Vikings and Packers losing. The Vikings and Packers both lost, the Eagles whipped the Giants 20-3, and Philadelphia was in the playoffs for the first time since 1960.

**Washington Redskins**—The Jack Pardee era burst onto the Washington scene with a quick blast of glory. Pardee took charge of a squad weakened by retirements of Pat Fischer, Len Hauss, Jerry Smith, Charley Taylor, and Brig Owens, and had no high draft choices with which to rebuild. Pardee obtained Lemar Parrish and Coy Bacon from the Bengals to shore up the defense and made Joe Theismann the first-string quarterback. The results were immediate, six victories at the start of the season, including a Monday night decision over Dallas. With visions of a Super Bowl already dancing, the dream began to crumble. The veteran defense started showing its age, and the offense lost its knack at scoring points. By mid-season, Pardee tried old-timer Billy Kilmer at quarterback, and some reports of grumbling by the players turned up. Their shot at first place was in their own hands on Thanksgiving, but the Redskins were no match for the Cowboys. Mired in a losing streak, the last chance at a wild card berth went up in smoke with a final-game loss to the Bears 14-10.

**St. Louis Cardinals**—When the Cardinals hired 62-year-old Bud Wilkinson as head coach, fans worried. They did not want to see a legend from the past dragged down by the sullen realities of a new age. Wilkinson had last coached in 1963, when he ended his fabulously successful career at the University of Oklahoma. The fear came true for two months, as the once-powerful Cardinals lost their first eight games. Sometimes overlooked was the absence of many of St. Louis' past offensive weapons. Terry Metcalf jumped to the Canadian Football League, J.V. Cain ripped an Achilles tendon, and Ike Harris and Conrad Dobler were traded to the Saints. Injuries further decimated both offense and defense. With critics shaking their heads and the injured reserve list bulging, Wilkinson engineered a surgence of the Cardinals, leading them to victory in six of their final eight contests. Wilkinson had a lackluster crew of runners, but his offensive line, featuring Dan Dierdorf, Bob Young, and Tom Banks, kept quarterback Jim Hart well protected.

**New York Giants**—Defensive tackle John Mendenhall said over the summer, "I'm looking forward to the season to see what disappointments it will bring." The season would start out pleasantly for the Giants, but would result in a chokingly bitter disappointment. The Giants ran out to a 3-1 start, their best beginning in ten years. Halfway into the schedule, their good defense had them in playoff contention despite an unimaginative offense. On November 19, they brought a three game losing streak into their battle with the Eagles in Giants' stadium. With under a minute left, the Giants led 17-12, they had possession of the ball, and the Eagles had no more time outs. Instead of falling down with the ball, quarterback Joe Pisarcik attempted to run the clock out with a handoff to Larry Csonka. With the horror of a nightmare, the handoff was botched, the ball bounced free, and Eagle cornerback Herman Edwards scooped it up and dashed 26 yards for a touchdown. The Giants lost 19-17 and suffered a firestorm of press and fan criticism. Assistant coach Bob Gibson, who had called for the play, was fired, the first scapegoat tossed to the fans. Gibson's scalp was not enough, as more than a decade of frustration found its focus in that one loss. The Giants wound up losing seven of their last eight games, and both head coach John McVay and general manager Andy Robustelli followed Gibson into unemployment.

## CENTRAL DIVISION

**Minnesota Vikings**—Bud Grant surveyed his aging squad and devised a formula to keep the Vikings in the running in the NFL's weakest division. Even with All-Pro Matt Blair at linebacker, the defense lacked the fury of the past, so Grant traded Alan Page to Chicago and used Carl Eller and Paul Krause less. Younger men thus got their chance on the Minnesota defense. The offense had lost its ability to run the ball, so Grant turned Fran Tarkenton's passing arm loose. The 38-year-old quarterback showered passes on stellar wide receivers Sammy White and Ahmad Rashad and on backs Rickey Young and Chuck Foreman. The Vikes got off to a 3-4 start which dropped them three games out of first place, but consecutive victories over Green Bay and Dallas shot them back into contention. Climbing back into a first place tie with the Packers, they traveled to Green Bay on November 26 and battled to a 10-10 deadlock. Still tied for first place, both clubs lost their final two games, so the divisional title went to the Vikings because of their victory over the Packers during the season. The title, the cheapest in the league, nevertheless tasted sweet to Tarkenton and Mick Tingelhoff, two veterans in their final season.

**Green Bay Packers**—"The Pack is back," blared Green Bay supporters as Bart Starr's charges built up a three game lead in the Central Division with a 6-1 start. A mean front four of Ezra Johnson, Mike Butler, Carl Barzilauskas, and Dave Roller led an improving defense which also featured Willie Buchanon at cornerback. Two new weapons spearheaded the offense. Rookie James Lofton burned defenses with his speed at wide receiver, giving young quarterback David Whitehurst a long-distance target. Second-year halfback Terdell Middleton won a starting job and blended quickness and power. A loss in Minnesota on October 22 tempered the euphoria in Green Bay, and a 42-14 trouncing by the Cowboys in Milwaukee on November 12 visibly shook their confidence. With their offense stalled, the Packers blew several opportunities to win a playoff spot. They could manage only a 10-10 tie with the Vikings on November 26, they lost to the Bears 10-0 on December 10, and they killed off their final hopes with a 31-14 defeat at the hands of the Rams on the final day of the season.

**Detroit Lions**—New head coach Monte Clark kept a lot of rookies on his squad, but nevertheless had to be disappointed with a 1-6 start. Quarterback Greg Landry was sacked with alarming regularity in the early games, a victim of immobile, battle-scarred knees. Unable to improve the pass blocking, Clark turned to Gary Danielson, an inexperienced quarterback with good legs. From the sixth game on, Danielson started at QB, and he showed steady progress as time passed. With the ex-WFLer passing and with Dexter Bussey running with authority, the Lions won six of their last nine games, including impressive triumphs over the Broncos and Vikings. On defense, rookie end Al Baker made the Silver Rush one of the league's best pass rushing outfits.

**Chicago Bears**—Under new coach Neill Armstrong, the Bears looked like a playoff team at the start of the year, a playoff team at the end of the year, and a doormat in the middle. As a result, the Bears did not make the playoffs. Bolstered by end Tommy Hart from San Francisco, the Bear defense mauled the Cardinals, 49ers, and Lions in three season-opening victories. The peerless Walter Payton ran with abandon and made up the bulk of the offense, with help from fullback Roland Harper. After the strong start, the Bears lost eight straight games. Opponents keyed on Payton and found no threat in Bob Avellini's passing. After a two-month dry spell, the Bears again remembered how to win, closing the year by dashing the playoff hopes of the Packers and Redskins.

**FINAL TEAM STATISTICS**

**OFFENSE**

| | ATL. | CHI. | DALL. | DET. | G.B. | L.A. | MINN. | N.O. | NYG. | PHIL. | ST.L. | S.F. | T.B. | WASH. |
|---|---|---|---|---|---|---|---|---|---|---|---|---|---|---|
| FIRST DOWNS: | | | | | | | | | | | | | | |
| Total | 253 | 262 | **342** | 269 | 226 | 301 | 308 | 295 | 246 | 271 | 281 | 257 | 238 | 261 |
| by Rushing | 90 | 136 | **146** | 105 | 105 | 128 | 102 | 119 | 125 | 143 | 103 | 117 | 111 | 99 |
| by Passing | 133 | 99 | 167 | 141 | 101 | 148 | **176** | 154 | 101 | 112 | 158 | 106 | 101 | 134 |
| by Penalty | 30 | 27 | 29 | 23 | 20 | 25 | 30 | 22 | 20 | 16 | 20 | **34** | 26 | 28 |
| RUSHING: | | | | | | | | | | | | | | |
| Number | 533 | **634** | 625 | 525 | 550 | 609 | 505 | 512 | 580 | 587 | 554 | 585 | 549 | 537 |
| Yards | 1660 | 2526 | **2783** | 2163 | 2023 | 2308 | 1536 | 1845 | 2304 | 2456 | 1954 | 2091 | 2098 | 2082 |
| Average Yards | 3.1 | 4.0 | **4.5** | 4.1 | 3.7 | 3.8 | 3.0 | 3.6 | 4.0 | 4.2 | 3.5 | 3.6 | 3.8 | 3.9 |
| Touchdowns | 13 | 19 | **22** | 12 | 16 | 12 | 10 | 17 | 12 | 16 | 14 | 14 | 16 | 10 |
| PASSING: | | | | | | | | | | | | | | |
| Attempts | 449 | 352 | 449 | 429 | 357 | 466 | **592** | 479 | 382 | 401 | 508 | 435 | 361 | 438 |
| Completions | 221 | 186 | 251 | 247 | 180 | 236 | **352** | 294 | 176 | 207 | 252 | 190 | 151 | 212 |
| Completion Pct. | 49.2 | 52.8 | 55.9 | 57.6 | 50.4 | 50.6 | 59.5 | **61.4** | 46.1 | 51.6 | 49.6 | 43.7 | 41.8 | 48.4 |
| Passing Yards | 2883 | 2221 | 3405 | 2746 | 2358 | 3109 | **3528** | 3452 | 2428 | 2485 | 3357 | 2306 | 2171 | 2978 |
| Avg.Yds per Att. | 4.8 | 5.0 | **6.6** | 4.8 | 5.3 | 5.8 | 5.2 | 6.1 | 5.1 | 5.0 | 6.0 | 4.1 | 4.1 | 5.3 |
| Avg. Yds per Comp. | 13.1 | 11.9 | 13.6 | 11.1 | 13.1 | 13.2 | 10.0 | 11.7 | 13.8 | 12.0 | 13.3 | 12.1 | **14.4** | 14.1 |
| Times Tackled | 56 | 34 | 33 | 47 | 37 | 34 | 30 | 37 | 38 | 41 | **22** | 42 | 52 | 46 |
| Yds Lost Tackled | 481 | 288 | 229 | 444 | 274 | 235 | 285 | 301 | 283 | 288 | **186** | 350 | 468 | 413 |
| Net Yards | 2402 | 1933 | 3176 | 2302 | 2084 | 2874 | **3243** | 3153 | 2145 | 2197 | 3171 | 1956 | 1703 | 2565 |
| Touchdowns | 11 | 7 | **25** | 19 | 11 | 13 | **25** | 17 | 13 | 16 | 16 | 9 | 12 | 17 |
| Interceptions | 23 | 28 | 17 | 18 | 18 | 22 | 34 | **16** | 27 | **16** | 21 | 36 | 18 | 21 |
| Pct. Intercepted | 5.1 | 8.0 | 3.8 | 4.2 | 5.0 | 4.7 | 5.7 | **3.3** | 7.1 | 4.0 | 4.1 | 8.3 | 5.0 | 4.8 |
| PUNTS: | | | | | | | | | | | | | | |
| Number | **110** | 96 | 77 | 87 | 106 | 85 | 85 | 86 | 95 | 92 | 102 | 97 | 102 | 104 |
| Average | 38.4 | 37.0 | 39.9 | 42.0 | 35.5 | 36.1 | 36.4 | 41.1 | **42.1** | 36.8 | 37.4 | 36.9 | 40.1 | 39.0 |
| PUNT RETURNS: | | | | | | | | | | | | | | |
| Number | 42 | 41 | 63 | 47 | 46 | **67** | 49 | 36 | 48 | 48 | 51 | 47 | 62 | 54 |
| Yards | 345 | 286 | 502 | 430 | 393 | **711** | 239 | 242 | 274 | 416 | 395 | 323 | 512 | 527 |
| Average Yards | 8.2 | 7.0 | 8.0 | 9.1 | 8.5 | **10.6** | 4.9 | 6.7 | 5.7 | 8.7 | 7.7 | 6.9 | 8.3 | 9.8 |
| Touchdowns | 0 | **1** | 0 | 0 | 0 | 0 | 0 | 0 | 0 | **1** | **1** | 0 | 0 | **1** |
| KICKOFF RET.: | | | | | | | | | | | | | | |
| Number | 59 | 61 | 47 | 51 | 52 | 52 | 55 | 65 | 60 | 54 | 55 | **73** | 56 | 58 |
| Yards | 1332 | 1358 | 896 | 1129 | 1085 | 1055 | 1057 | 1384 | 1081 | 1134 | 1148 | **1421** | 1095 | 1352 |
| Average Yards | 22.6 | 22.3 | 19.1 | 22.1 | 20.9 | 20.3 | 19.2 | 21.3 | 18.0 | 21.0 | 20.9 | 19.5 | 19.6 | **23.3** |
| Touchdowns | **1** | 0 | 0 | 0 | **1** | 0 | 0 | 0 | 0 | 0 | 0 | **1** | 0 | **1** |
| INTERCEPT RET.: | | | | | | | | | | | | | | |
| Number | 12 | 17 | 23 | 22 | 27 | 28 | 22 | 21 | 21 | 28 | 26 | 18 | **29** | 22 |
| Yards | 159 | 216 | 316 | 292 | 344 | 427 | 192 | 319 | **438** | 271 | 249 | 283 | 312 | 189 |
| Average Yards | 13.3 | 12.7 | 13.7 | 13.3 | 12.7 | 15.3 | 8.7 | 15.2 | **20.9** | 9.7 | 9.6 | 15.7 | 10.8 | 8.6 |
| Touchdowns | 0 | 1 | 0 | 1 | 2 | **5** | 0 | 1 | 1 | 2 | 0 | 1 | 0 | 0 |
| PENALTIES: | | | | | | | | | | | | | | |
| Number | 130 | 101 | 96 | 125 | 99 | 133 | 113 | 112 | 101 | **94** | 106 | 115 | 100 | 116 |
| Yards | 1083 | 958 | 816 | 1003 | **776** | 1169 | 817 | 1044 | 1016 | 805 | 890 | 930 | 860 | 978 |
| FUMBLES: | | | | | | | | | | | | | | |
| Number | 41 | **22** | 36 | 35 | 35 | 39 | 34 | 32 | 23 | 39 | 28 | 56 | 35 | 31 |
| Number Lost | 18 | **8** | 18 | 15 | 24 | 22 | 17 | 15 | 12 | 22 | 14 | 27 | 20 | 16 |
| POINTS: | | | | | | | | | | | | | | |
| Total | 240 | 253 | **384** | 290 | 249 | 316 | 294 | 281 | 264 | 270 | 248 | 219 | 241 | 273 |
| PAT Attempts | 27 | 29 | **48** | 33 | 31 | 33 | 37 | 35 | 29 | 36 | 31 | 25 | 29 | 31 |
| PAT Made | 26 | 26 | **46** | 32 | 30 | 31 | 36 | 33 | 27 | 30 | 27 | 24 | 25 | 30 |
| FG Attempts | 26 | 22 | 26 | 28 | 19 | **43** | 19 | 25 | 29 | 17 | 22 | 23 | 24 | 30 |
| FG Made | 16 | 17 | 16 | 20 | 11 | **29** | 12 | 12 | 21 | 8 | 11 | 15 | 14 | 19 |
| Percent FG Made | 61.5 | **77.3** | 61.5 | 71.4 | 57.9 | 67.4 | 63.2 | 48.0 | 72.4 | 47.1 | 50.0 | 65.2 | 58.3 | 63.3 |
| Safeties | **2** | 1 | 1 | 0 | 0 | 0 | 0 | 1 | 0 | 0 | 1 | 0 | 0 | 0 |

**DEFENSE**

| | ATL. | CHI. | DALL. | DET. | G.B. | L.A. | MINN. | N.O. | NYG. | PHIL. | ST.L. | S.F. | T.B. | WASH. |
|---|---|---|---|---|---|---|---|---|---|---|---|---|---|---|
| FIRST DOWNS: | | | | | | | | | | | | | | |
| Total | 267 | 282 | 232 | 276 | 302 | **229** | 278 | 286 | 316 | 248 | 286 | 298 | 256 | 283 |
| by Rushing | 117 | 128 | **83** | 115 | 137 | 89 | 120 | 129 | 155 | 92 | 131 | 128 | 109 | 131 |
| by Passing | **113** | 134 | 128 | 125 | 143 | **113** | 137 | 130 | 127 | 136 | 131 | 133 | 131 | 133 |
| by Penalty | 37 | 20 | 21 | 36 | 22 | 27 | 21 | 27 | 34 | 20 | 24 | 37 | **16** | 19 |
| RUSHING: | | | | | | | | | | | | | | |
| Number | 578 | 568 | **477** | 565 | 620 | 505 | 559 | 579 | 640 | 505 | 588 | 649 | 595 | 625 |
| Yards | 2067 | 2174 | **1721** | 2184 | 2439 | 1845 | 2116 | 2420 | 2656 | 1862 | 2396 | 2365 | 2049 | 2536 |
| Average Yards | 3.6 | 3.8 | 3.6 | 3.9 | 3.9 | 3.7 | 3.8 | 4.2 | 4.2 | 3.7 | 4.1 | 3.6 | **3.4** | 4.1 |
| Touchdowns | 21 | 15 | 13 | 18 | 19 | 11 | 20 | **9** | 25 | 11 | 15 | 17 | 12 | 15 |
| PASSING: | | | | | | | | | | | | | | |
| Attempts | 444 | 436 | 432 | **350** | 463 | 399 | 442 | 418 | 443 | 443 | 428 | 413 | 419 | 409 |
| Completions | 215 | 239 | 202 | 191 | 254 | **188** | 240 | 215 | 210 | 228 | 212 | 219 | 241 | 197 |
| Completion Pct. | 48.4 | 54.8 | **46.8** | 54.6 | 54.9 | 47.1 | 54.3 | 51.4 | 47.4 | 51.5 | 49.5 | 53.0 | 57.5 | 48.2 |
| Passing Yards | 2789 | 2857 | 2730 | 2781 | 2910 | **2449** | 2917 | 2700 | 2637 | 2986 | 2641 | 2948 | 2535 | 2701 |
| Avg.Yds per Att. | 4.8 | 5.3 | 4.7 | 5.7 | 4.9 | **4.5** | 5.7 | 5.5 | 5.1 | 5.9 | 5.1 | 5.9 | 5.0 | 5.4 |
| Avg. Yds per Comp. | 13.0 | 12.0 | 13.5 | 14.6 | 11.5 | 13.0 | 12.2 | 12.6 | 12.6 | 13.1 | 12.5 | 13.5 | **10.5** | 13.7 |
| Times Tackled | 47 | 40 | **58** | 55 | 48 | 47 | 33 | 33 | 29 | 29 | 37 | 35 | 33 | 35 |
| Yds Lost Tackled | 425 | 351 | 442 | **482** | 386 | 401 | 227 | 236 | 251 | 213 | 290 | 289 | 256 | 323 |
| Net Yards | 2364 | 2506 | 2288 | 2299 | 2524 | **2048** | 2690 | 2464 | 2386 | 2773 | 2351 | 2659 | 2279 | 2378 |
| Touchdowns | 11 | 16 | 11 | 19 | 16 | 15 | 15 | 21 | **10** | 17 | 19 | 20 | 13 | 11 |
| Interceptions | 12 | 17 | 23 | 22 | 27 | 28 | 22 | 21 | 21 | 28 | 26 | 18 | **29** | 22 |
| Pct. Intercepted | 2.7 | 3.9 | 5.3 | 6.3 | 5.8 | **7.0** | 5.0 | 5.0 | 4.7 | 6.3 | 6.1 | 4.4 | 6.9 | 5.4 |
| PUNTS: | | | | | | | | | | | | | | |
| Number | **108** | 96 | **108** | 87 | 90 | 104 | 92 | 71 | 90 | 83 | 94 | 87 | 97 | 105 |
| Average | 36.6 | **35.8** | 39.4 | 40.2 | 37.9 | 38.0 | 36.2 | 40.2 | 37.1 | 39.1 | 38.9 | 40.2 | 40.4 | 37.0 |
| PUNT RETURNS: | | | | | | | | | | | | | | |
| Number | 54 | 45 | **40** | 54 | 51 | 38 | 52 | 59 | 61 | 47 | 59 | 46 | 62 | 48 |
| Yards | 305 | 295 | 311 | 467 | 286 | **223** | 541 | 539 | 624 | 354 | 575 | 356 | 447 | 328 |
| Average Yards | 5.6 | 6.6 | 7.8 | 8.6 | **5.6** | 5.9 | 10.4 | 9.1 | 10.2 | 7.5 | 9.7 | 7.7 | 7.2 | 6.8 |
| Touchdowns | 0 | 0 | 0 | 0 | 0 | 1 | 0 | 0 | 0 | 1 | 0 | 0 | 0 | 2 |
| KICKOFF RET.: | | | | | | | | | | | | | | |
| Number | 49 | 52 | 73 | 69 | 52 | 64 | 61 | 53 | 55 | 56 | 51 | **47** | 49 | 55 |
| Yards | 1141 | 1146 | 1709 | 1424 | 1015 | 1335 | 1297 | 1035 | 1197 | 1154 | 1142 | **928** | 1146 | 965 |
| Average Yards | 23.3 | 22.0 | 23.4 | 20.6 | 19.5 | 20.9 | 21.3 | 19.5 | 21.8 | 20.6 | 22.4 | 19.7 | 23.4 | **17.5** |
| Touchdowns | 0 | 0 | 0 | 0 | 0 | 1 | 0 | 0 | 0 | 0 | 2 | 0 | 0 | 0 |
| INTERCEPT RET.: | | | | | | | | | | | | | | |
| Number | 23 | 28 | 17 | 18 | 18 | 22 | 34 | **16** | 27 | **16** | 21 | 36 | 18 | 21 |
| Yards | 252 | 312 | 176 | **75** | 262 | 269 | 424 | 198 | 376 | 131 | 303 | 608 | 235 | 480 |
| Average Yards | 11.0 | 11.1 | 10.4 | **4.2** | 14.6 | 12.2 | 12.5 | 12.4 | 13.9 | 8.1 | 14.4 | 16.9 | 13.1 | 22.9 |
| Touchdowns | 2 | 1 | 1 | 0 | 1 | 0 | 2 | 1 | 2 | 0 | 1 | 1 | 1 | 1 |
| PENALTIES: | | | | | | | | | | | | | | |
| Number | 116 | 101 | 95 | **128** | 116 | 100 | 110 | 110 | 113 | 104 | 96 | 154 | 101 | 91 |
| Yards | 1010 | 801 | 783 | 1043 | 949 | 755 | 1013 | 929 | 862 | 884 | 809 | 1301 | 963 | 830 |
| FUMBLES: | | | | | | | | | | | | | | |
| Number | 46 | 32 | 27 | 41 | 40 | 33 | 35 | 37 | 36 | 40 | 34 | **50** | 32 | 20 |
| Number Lost | 25 | 16 | 13 | 19 | 20 | 15 | 21 | 20 | 18 | 20 | 16 | **27** | 14 | 10 |
| POINTS: | | | | | | | | | | | | | | |
| Total | 290 | 274 | **208** | 300 | 269 | 245 | 306 | 298 | 298 | 250 | 296 | 350 | 259 | 283 |
| PAT Attempts | 36 | 32 | **25** | 39 | 36 | 28 | 39 | 33 | 38 | 30 | 37 | 40 | 27 | 30 |
| PAT Made | 35 | 28 | **23** | 38 | 36 | 26 | 33 | 32 | 32 | 28 | 35 | 39 | **23** | 29 |
| FG Attempts | 23 | 19 | 22 | **13** | 18 | 26 | 19 | 33 | 26 | 26 | 18 | 38 | 32 | 34 |
| FG Made | 13 | 16 | 11 | 8 | **5** | 17 | 13 | 22 | 12 | 14 | 13 | 23 | 24 | 24 |
| Percent FG Made | 56.5 | 84.2 | 50.0 | 61.5 | **27.8** | 65.4 | 68.4 | 66.7 | 46.2 | 53.8 | 72.2 | 60.5 | 75.0 | 70.6 |
| Safeties | 0 | 0 | 1 | 2 | 1 | 0 | 0 | 1 | 1 | 0 | 0 | 1 | 1 | 1 |

**Tampa Bay Buccaneers**—The Bucs finished last once again, but this season bore no resemblence to the past two joke-filled campaigns. The Bucs won five games, stayed in playoff contention into November, and genuinely worried opponents for the first time. John McKay's building program yielded its first harvest, a tenacious defense which burst into prominence with surprising suddenness. Lee Roy Selmon blossomed into an All-Pro end, and the tough 3-4 defense led the way to impressive victories over the Vikings and Falcons. The offense had not yet risen to the excellence of the defense, but rookie quarterback Doug Williams held out hope for the future. With a 4-4 record at mid-season, the Bucs succumbed to a rash of injuries and their inexperience, losing seven of their final eight. Nevertheless, the progress was startling.

## WESTERN DIVISION

**Los Angeles Rams**—Because Chuck Knox hadn't gotten the team into the Super Bowl, the Rams hired George Allen as head coach. All Allen got the Rams into was turmoil, as owner Carroll Rosenbloom fired Allen two games into the pre-season schedule. During his short tenure, four players left camp in salary disputes, massive discontent brewed among the players in camp, and Rosenbloom was upset by Allen's alleged over-reaching for authority. Assistant coach Ray Malavasi took over as head coach and tried to soothe everyone's feelings. Despite the commotion and Lawrence McCutcheon's lingering thigh injury, the talent-deep Rams bolted out of the gate with seven straight victories and coasted home to their sixth Western title in a row. The defensive unit ranked with the N.F.L.'s best, with All-Pro performances from linemen Jack Youngblood and Larry Brooks, linebacker Jim Youngblood, and small cornerbacks Pat Thomas and Rod Perry. The offense suffered only from comparison with the sterling defense. Quarterback Pat Haden had a robust platoon of backs and ends, and he operated behind a top-notch line featuring Doug France, Dennis Harrah, and Tom Mack. The accurate toe of rookie placekicker Frank Corral topped the offense nicely.

**Atlanta Falcons**—Leeman Bennett took his overachieving Falcons into the playoffs for the first time in their history. The defense used a lot of blitzing and came up with big plays that kept the Falcons in several close games. The offense began the year with a new quarterback in June Jones, who unseated Steve Bartkowski in the pre-season. After three games, however, Bartkowski reclaimed his job. Thus inspired, Bartkowski guided the Falcons to a series of last-minute victories. On November 12, a 57-yard bomb from Barkowski to Alfred Jackson with ten seconds left gave the Falcons a 20-17 triumph over the Saints. Two weeks later, the Falcons again beat the Saints 20-17 on a touchdown pass with five seconds left. Two weeks after that, Tim Mazzetti booted a field goal at the gun to beat Washington by another 20-17 score.

**New Orleans Saints**—An opening day victory over the Vikings began Dick Nolan's regime on an up note. Although injuries thinned out an already sparse squad, the Saints nevertheless rose to a 5-4 mark before slumping at the back of the schedule. Guards Conrad Dobler and Emanuel Zanders both went out with injuries in September, and the running attack could never get rolling behind the patched line. Quarterback Archie Manning, however, got enough blocking to unleash a consistently dangerous passing attack. Although rookie Wes Chandler took a while to get comfortable at wide receiver, ex-Cardinal Ike Harris prospered right away. The highlight of the year was a 10-3 upset over the unbeaten Rams on October 22.

**San Francisco 49ers**—General manager Joe Thomas overhauled the 49ers by hiring a new head coach in Pete McCulley, sending a bundle of draft choices to Buffalo for O.J. Simpson, and trading off Del Williams, Tommy Hart, and Woody Peoples. During the pre-season, changes continued. Wilbur Jackson, Jean Barrett, and Willie Harper went out with knee injuries, and coach McCulley shockingly cut quarterback Jim Plunkett and receiver Gene Washington. The 49ers thus entered the season with a large cache of rookies. O.J. unfortunately was coming off a knee operation and had passed his peak as a runner. Thomas showed signs of panic when, with an 1-8 record, McCulley was canned and replaced by assistant Fred O'Conner. In O'Conner's first game at the helm, Simpson hurt his shoulder and went to the sidelines for the year. With the worst offense and defense in the league, the 49ers saw growing numbers of empty seats at each game. In the season finale, quarterbacks Steve DeBerg and Scott Bull both were injured, forcing O'Connor to use defensive back Bruce Threadgill and receiver Freddie Solomon as QB against the Lions. With the 2-14 record finally set, owner Eddie DeBartolo pushed the rebuilding program ahead by firing Thomas.

# 1978 N.F.C. — Eastern Division

## DALLAS COWBOYS 12-4-0 Tom Landry

| Scores of Each Game | | |
|---|---|---|
| 38 | BALTIMORE | 0 |
| 34 | N.Y. Giants | 24 |
| 14 | Los Angeles | 27 |
| 21 | ST. LOUIS | 12 |
| 5 | Washington | 9 |
| 24 | N.Y. GIANTS | 3 |
| 24 | St. Louis | *21 |
| 14 | PHILADELPHIA | 7 |
| 10 | MINNESOTA | 21 |
| 16 | Miami | 23 |
| 42 | Green Bay | 14 |
| 27 | NEW ORLEANS | 7 |
| 37 | WASHINGTON | 10 |
| 17 | NEW ENGLAND | 10 |
| 31 | Philadelphia | 13 |
| 30 | N.Y. Jets | 7 |

| Use Name | Pos. | Hgt. | Wgt. | Age | Int. | Pts. |
|---|---|---|---|---|---|---|
| Pat Donovan | OT | 6'4" | 255 | 25 | | |
| Andy Frederick | OT | 6'6" | 245 | 23 | | |
| Rayfield Wright | OT | 6'7" | 260 | 33 | | |
| Burton Lawless | OG | 6'4" | 250 | 24 | | |
| Tom Rafferty | OG | 6'3" | 250 | 24 | | |
| Tom Randall | OG | 6'5" | 245 | 22 | | |
| Herbert Scott | OG | 6'2" | 250 | 25 | | |
| Jim Cooper | C-OG | 6'5" | 252 | 22 | | |
| John Fitzgerald | C | 6'5" | 260 | 30 | | |
| Too Tall Jones | DE | 6'9" | 265 | 27 | | |
| Harvey Martin | DE | 6'5" | 252 | 27 | 1 | |
| Larry Bethea | DT | 6'5" | 254 | 22 | | |
| Larry Cole | DT-DE | 6'4" | 260 | 31 | 1 | |
| Jethro Pugh | DT | 6'6" | 250 | 34 | | |
| David Stalls | DT-DE | 6'4" | 236 | 22 | | |
| Randy White | DT | 6'4" | 245 | 25 | | |
| Bob Breunig | LB | 6'2" | 227 | 25 | 1 | |
| Guy Brown | LB | 6'4" | 215 | 23 | | |
| Mike Hegman | LB | 6'1" | 225 | 25 | | |
| Tom Henderson | LB | 6'2" | 220 | 25 | | |
| Bruce Huther | LB | 6'1" | 217 | 24 | | |
| D.D. Lewis | LB | 6'2" | 215 | 32 | | |
| Benny Barnes | DB | 6'1" | 195 | 27 | 5 | |
| Cliff Harris | DB | 6' | 192 | 29 | 4 | |
| Randy Hughes | DB | 6'4" | 208 | 25 | 2 | |
| Aaron Kyle | DB | 5'11" | 185 | 24 | 3 | |
| Dennis Thurman | DB | 5'11" | 170 | 22 | 2 | |
| Mark Washington | DB | 5'11" | 187 | 30 | | |
| Charlie Waters | DB | 6'1" | 198 | 29 | 4 | |
| Glenn Carano | QB | 6'3" | 195 | 22 | | |
| Roger Staubach | QB | 6'2" | 202 | 36 | | 6 |
| Danny White | QB | 6'2" | 192 | 26 | | |
| Alois Blackwell | HB | 5'10" | 195 | 23 | | |
| Doug Dennison | HB | 6'1" | 204 | 26 | | 6 |
| Tony Dorsett | HB | 5'11" | 192 | 24 | | 60 |
| Preston Pearson | HB | 6'1" | 206 | 33 | | |
| Larry Brinson | FB | 6' | 214 | 24 | | 12 |
| Scott Laidlaw | FB | 6' | 205 | 25 | | 24 |
| Robert Newhouse | FB | 5'10" | 205 | 28 | | 60 |
| Tony Hill | WR | 6'2" | 196 | 22 | | 36 |
| Butch Johnson | WR | 6'1" | 191 | 24 | | |
| Drew Pearson | WR | 6' | 183 | 27 | | 18 |
| Robert Steele | WR | 6'4" | 196 | 22 | | |
| Billy Joe DuPree | TE | 6'4" | 226 | 28 | | 54 |
| Jay Saldi | TE | 6'3" | 224 | 23 | | 12 |
| Jackie Smith | TE | 6'4" | 232 | 38 | | |
| Rafael Septien | K | 5'9" | 171 | 24 | | 94 |

## PHILADELPHIA EAGLES 9-7-0 Dick Vermeil

| Scores of Each Game | | |
|---|---|---|
| 14 | LOS ANGELES | 16 |
| 30 | Washington | 35 |
| 24 | New Orleans | 17 |
| 17 | MIAMI | 3 |
| 17 | Baltimore | 14 |
| 14 | New England | 24 |
| 17 | WASHINGTON | 10 |
| 7 | Dallas | 14 |
| 10 | ST. LOUIS | 16 |
| 10 | GREEN BAY | 3 |
| 17 | N.Y. JETS | 9 |
| 19 | N.Y. Giants | 17 |
| 14 | St. Louis | 10 |
| 27 | Minnesota | 28 |
| 13 | DALLAS | 31 |
| 20 | N.Y. GIANTS | 3 |

| Use Name | Pos. | Hgt. | Wgt. | Age | Int. | Pts. |
|---|---|---|---|---|---|---|
| Ed George | OT | 6'4" | 270 | 32 | | |
| Jerry Sisemore | OT | 6'4" | 260 | 27 | | |
| Stan Walters | OT | 6'6" | 270 | 30 | | |
| Wade Key | OG | 6'4" | 245 | 31 | | |
| Tom Luken | OG | 6'3" | 253 | 28 | | |
| Woody Peoples | OG | 6'2" | 250 | 35 | | |
| Dennis Franks | C | 6'1" | 245 | 25 | | |
| Guy Morriss | C | 6'4" | 255 | 27 | | |
| Len Burnham | DE | 6'4" | 240 | 31 | | |
| Carl Hairston | DE | 6'3" | 245 | 25 | | |
| Dennis Harrison | DE | 6'8" | 275 | 22 | 1 | |
| Manny Sistrunk | DE | 6'5" | 275 | 31 | | |
| Ken Clarke | NT | 6'2" | 255 | 22 | | |
| Charles Johnson | NT | 6'3" | 262 | 26 | | |
| Bill Bergey | LB | 6'2" | 245 | 33 | 4 | |
| John Bunting | LB | 6'1" | 220 | 28 | 1 | |
| Frank LeMaster | LB | 6'2" | 231 | 26 | 3 | 6 |
| Drew Mahalic | LB | 6'4" | 225 | 25 | 1 | |
| Mike Osborn | LB | 6'5" | 235 | 22 | | |
| Ray Phillips (from CIN) | LB | 6'3" | 221 | 24 | | |
| Terry Tautolo | LB | 6'2" | 235 | 24 | | |
| Reggie Wilkes | LB | 6'4" | 230 | 22 | | |
| Herman Edwards | DB | 6' | 194 | 24 | 7 | 6 |
| Bob Howard | DB | 6'1" | 175 | 33 | 3 | |
| Eric Johnson | DB | 6'1" | 192 | 26 | | |
| Randy Logan | DB | 6'1" | 195 | 27 | 2 | |
| John Outlaw | DB | 5'10" | 180 | 32 | | |
| Deac Sanders | DB | 6'1" | 175 | 28 | 5 | 6 |
| John Sciarra | DB-QB | 5'11" | 185 | 24 | 1 | 12 |
| Charles Williams | DB | 6'1" | 180 | 24 | | |
| Ron Jaworski | QB | 6'2" | 195 | 27 | | |
| John Walton | QB | 6'2" | 210 | 30 | | |
| Billy Campfield | HB | 5'11" | 185 | 22 | | |
| Louie Giammona | HB | 5'9" | 180 | 25 | | |
| Herb Lusk | HB | 6' | 190 | 25 | | 18 |
| Wilbert Montgomery | HB | 5'10" | 195 | 23 | | 60 |
| Larry Barnes (from SD, STL) | FB | 5'11" | 220 | 24 | | 6 |
| James Betterson | FB | 6' | 210 | 24 | | |
| Cleveland Franklin | FB | 6'2" | 216 | 23 | | |
| Mike Hogan | FB | 6'2" | 215 | 23 | | 30 |
| Harold Carmichael | WR | 6'7" | 225 | 28 | | 48 |
| Wally Henry | WR | 5'8" | 170 | 23 | | 6 |
| Oren Middlebrook | WR | 6'2" | 185 | 23 | | |
| Vince Papale | WR | 6'2" | 195 | 32 | | |
| Ken Payne | WR | 6'1" | 185 | 27 | | 6 |
| Charlie Smith | WR | 6'1" | 185 | 28 | | 12 |
| Keith Krepfle | TE | 6'3" | 225 | 26 | | 18 |
| Bill Larson | TE | 6'4" | 220 | 24 | | |
| Richard Osborne | TE | 6'3" | 230 | 24 | | |
| Rick Engles | K | 5'11" | 180 | 24 | | |
| Mitch Hoopes | K | 6'1" | 204 | 25 | | |
| Mike Michel | K | 5'10" | 177 | 24 | | 9 |
| Nick Mike-Mayer | K | 5'8" | 187 | 28 | | 45 |

## WASHINGTON REDSKINS 8-8-0 Jack Pardee

| Scores of Each Game | | |
|---|---|---|
| 16 | New England | 14 |
| 35 | PHILADELPHIA | 30 |
| 28 | St. Louis | 10 |
| 23 | N.Y. JETS | 3 |
| 9 | DALLAS | 5 |
| 21 | Detroit | 19 |
| 10 | Philadelphia | 17 |
| 6 | N.Y. Giants | 17 |
| 38 | SAN FRANCISCO | 20 |
| 17 | Baltimore | 21 |
| 16 | N.Y. GIANTS | *13 |
| 17 | ST. LOUIS | 27 |
| 10 | Dallas | 37 |
| 0 | MIAMI | 16 |
| 17 | Atlanta | 20 |
| 10 | CHICAGO | 14 |

| Use Name | Pos. | Hgt. | Wgt. | Age | Int. | Pts. |
|---|---|---|---|---|---|---|
| Jim Harlan | OT | 6'4" | 250 | 24 | | |
| Terry Hermeling | OT | 6'5" | 255 | 32 | | |
| George Starke | OT | 6'5" | 250 | 30 | | |
| Jeff Williams | OT | 6'4" | 255 | 23 | | |
| Fred Dean | OG | 6'3" | 253 | 23 | | |
| Dan Nugent | OG | 6'3" | 250 | 25 | | |
| Ron Saul | OG | 6'3" | 254 | 30 | | |
| Ted Fritsch | C | 6'2" | 242 | 28 | | |
| Bob Kuziel | C | 6'5" | 255 | 28 | | |
| Coy Bacon | DE | 6'4" | 265 | 36 | | |
| Karl Lorch | DE | 6'3" | 258 | 28 | | |
| Ron McDole | DE | 6'3" | 265 | 38 | 1 | |
| Perry Brooks | DT | 6'3" | 260 | 23 | | |
| Dave Butz | DT | 6'7" | 285 | 28 | 1 | |
| Bob Heinz | DT | 6'6" | 260 | 31 | | |
| Diron Talbert | DT | 6'5" | 255 | 34 | | |
| Mike Curtis | LB | 6'2" | 232 | 35 | 1 | |
| Brad Dusek | LB | 6'2" | 214 | 27 | 1 | 6 |
| Chris Hanburger | LB | 6'2" | 218 | 37 | | |
| Dallas Hickman | LB-DE | 6'6" | 235 | 26 | | |
| Don Hover | LB | 6'2" | 222 | 23 | | |
| Harold McClinton | LB | 6'2" | 235 | 31 | | |
| Pete Wysocki | LB | 6'2" | 225 | 29 | | |
| Don Harris | DB | 6'2" | 185 | 24 | | |
| Ken Houston | DB | 6'3" | 198 | 33 | 2 | |
| Joe Lavender | DB | 6'4" | 190 | 29 | 1 | |
| Mark Murphy | DB | 6'4" | 210 | 23 | | |
| Lemar Parrish | DB | 5'11" | 183 | 30 | 4 | |
| Jake Scott | DB | 6' | 188 | 33 | 7 | |
| Gerard Williams | DB | 6'1" | 184 | 26 | 4 | 6 |
| Bill Brundige-Knee Injury | | | | | | |
| Billy Kilmer | QB | 6' | 204 | 38 | | |
| Kim McQuilken | QB | 6'2" | 203 | 27 | | |
| Joe Theismann | QB | 6' | 190 | 28 | | 6 |
| Ike Forte | HB | 6' | 196 | 24 | | |
| Tony Green | HB | 5'9" | 185 | 21 | | 18 |
| Clarence Harmon | HB-FB | 5'11" | 190 | 22 | | 6 |
| Benny Malone (from MIA) | HB | 5'10" | 193 | 26 | | 6 |
| Mike Thomas | HB | 5'11" | 190 | 25 | | 30 |
| John Riggins | FB | 6'2" | 230 | 29 | | 30 |
| Terry Anderson (from MIA) | WR | 5'9" | 182 | 23 | | |
| Danny Buggs | WR | 6'2" | 185 | 25 | | 12 |
| John McDaniel | WR | 6'1" | 197 | 26 | | 24 |
| J.T. Smith (to KC) | WR | 6'2" | 185 | 22 | | |
| Ricky Thompson | WR | 6' | 176 | 24 | | 6 |
| Jean Fugett | TE | 6'4" | 230 | 26 | | 42 |
| Reggie Haynes | TE | 6'2" | 229 | 23 | | |
| Mike Bragg | K | 5'11" | 186 | 31 | | |
| Mark Moseley | K | 5'11" | 205 | 30 | | 87 |

## ST. LOUIS CARDINALS 6-10-0 Bud Wilkinson

| Scores of Each Game | | |
|---|---|---|
| 10 | Chicago | 17 |
| 6 | NEW ENGLAND | 16 |
| 10 | WASHINGTON | 28 |
| 12 | Dallas | 21 |
| 10 | Miami | 24 |
| 17 | BALTIMORE | 30 |
| 21 | DALLAS | *24 |
| 10 | N.Y. Jets | 23 |
| 16 | Philadelphia | 10 |
| 20 | N.Y. GIANTS | 10 |
| 16 | San Francisco | 10 |
| 27 | Washington | 17 |
| 10 | PHILADELPHIA | 14 |
| 21 | DETROIT | 14 |
| 0 | N.Y. Giants | 17 |
| 42 | ATLANTA | 21 |

| Use Name | Pos. | Hgt. | Wgt. | Age | Int. | Pts. |
|---|---|---|---|---|---|---|
| Dan Dierdorf | OT | 6'4" | 288 | 29 | | |
| Roger Finnie | OT | 6'3" | 248 | 32 | | |
| Keith Wortman | OT-OG | 6'2" | 262 | 28 | | |
| George Collins | OG | 6'2" | 248 | 22 | | |
| Tom Mullen | OG | 6'3" | 250 | 26 | | |
| Terry Stieve | OG | 6'2" | 245 | 24 | | |
| Bob Young | OG-C | 6'2" | 279 | 35 | | |
| Tom Banks | C-OG | 6'1" | 245 | 30 | | |
| Tom Brahaney | C | 6'2" | 246 | 26 | | |
| Bob Bell | DE | 6'4" | 257 | 30 | | |
| Bob Pollard | DE | 6'3" | 251 | 29 | | |
| Ron Yankowski | DE | 6'5" | 258 | 31 | | |
| John Zook | DE | 6'5" | 254 | 30 | | |
| Charlie Davis | NT | 6'1" | 268 | 26 | | |
| Mike Dawson | NT | 6'4" | 274 | 24 | | |
| Keith Simons | NT | 6'3" | 254 | 24 | | |
| Kurt Allerman | LB | 6'3" | 222 | 23 | | |
| Mark Arneson | LB | 6'2" | 224 | 28 | | |
| John Barefield | LB | 6'2" | 224 | 23 | | |
| Randy Gill (to TB) | LB | 6'2" | 230 | 22 | | |
| Tim Kearney | LB | 6'2" | 221 | 27 | 1 | |
| Steve Neils | LB | 6'2" | 218 | 27 | 1 | |
| Curtis Townsend | LB | 6'1" | 229 | 23 | | |
| Greg Westbrooks (to OAK) | LB | 6'3" | 217 | 25 | | |
| Eric Williams | LB | 6'2" | 217 | 23 | 1 | |
| Carl Allen | DB | 6' | 186 | 22 | 6 | |
| Doug Greene | DB | 6'2" | 205 | 22 | | |
| Ken Greene | DB | 6'2 | 203 | 22 | | |
| Lee Nelson | DB | 5'10" | 185 | 24 | 1 | |
| Mike Sensibaugh | DB | 5'11" | 190 | 29 | 3 | 6 |
| Perry Smith | DB | 6' | 190 | 27 | 3 | |
| Ken Stone | DB | 6'1" | 180 | 27 | 9 | |
| Roger Wehrli | DB | 6' | 193 | 30 | 4 | |
| Roland Woolsey | DB | 6'1" | 182 | 25 | | |
| J.V. Cain-Achilles Injury | | | | | | |
| Robert Giblin-Injury | | | | | | |
| Jim Hart | QB | 6'2" | 210 | 34 | | 12 |
| Mark Manges | QB | 6'2" | 210 | 22 | | |
| Steve Pisarkiewicz | QB | 6'2" | 205 | 24 | | |
| Gordon Bell | HB | 5'9" | 180 | 24 | | |
| Ted Farmer | HB | 5'11" | 175 | 24 | | |
| Will Harrell | HB | 5'9" | 182 | 25 | | 6 |
| Steve Jones | HB | 6' | 198 | 27 | | 12 |
| Wayne Morris | HB-FB | 6' | 208 | 24 | | 12 |
| Willie Shelby | HB | 5'11" | 198 | 25 | | |
| Jim Otis | FB | 6' | 226 | 30 | | 48 |
| Warren Anderson | WR | 6'2" | 195 | 23 | | |
| Jim Childs | WR | 6'2" | 194 | 22 | | 6 |
| Mel Gray | WR | 5'9" | 173 | 29 | | 12 |
| Tommy Southard (to HOU) | WR | 6' | 185 | 23 | | |
| Dave Stief | WR | 6'3 | 195 | 22 | | 24 |
| Pat Tilley | WR | 5'10 | 171 | 25 | | 18 |
| Al Chandler (from NE) | TE | 6'2" | 229 | 27 | | 24 |
| Eason Ramson | TE | 6'2 | 220 | 22 | | 6 |
| Jim Thaxton | TE | 6'3 | 242 | 29 | | 6 |
| Jim Bakken | K | 6' | 198 | 37 | | 60 |
| Steve Little | K | 6' | 180 | 22 | | |
| Mike Wood (from MIN) | K | 5'11" | 199 | 23 | | |

## NEW YORK GIANTS 6-10-0 John McVay

| Scores of Each Game | | |
|---|---|---|
| 19 | Tampa Bay | 13 |
| 24 | DALLAS | 34 |
| 26 | KANSAS CITY | 10 |
| 27 | SAN FRANCISCO | 10 |
| 20 | Atlanta | 23 |
| 3 | Dallas | 24 |
| 17 | TAMPA BAY | 14 |
| 17 | WASHINGTON | 6 |
| 17 | New Orleans | 28 |
| 10 | St. Louis | 20 |
| 13 | Washington | *16 |
| 17 | PHILADELPHIA | 19 |
| 17 | Buffalo | 41 |
| 17 | LOS ANGELES | 20 |
| 17 | ST. LOUIS | 0 |
| 3 | Philadelphia | 20 |

| Use Name | Pos. | Hgt. | Wgt. | Age | Int. | Pts. |
|---|---|---|---|---|---|---|
| Bill Bain (from DEN) | OT | 6'4" | 270 | 26 | | |
| Brad Benson | OT-OG-C | 6'3" | 258 | 22 | | |
| Gordon Gravelle | OT | 6'5" | 252 | 29 | | |
| Gordon King | OT | 6'6" | 275 | 22 | | |
| Ron Mikolajczyk | OT | 6'3" | 275 | 28 | | |
| Jim Pietrzak | OT-C | 6'5" | 260 | 25 | | |
| J.T. Turner | OG | 6'3" | 250 | 25 | | |
| Doug Van Horn | OG | 6'2" | 245 | 34 | | |
| Jim Clack | C | 6'3" | 250 | 30 | | |
| Leo Tierney (from CLE) | C | 6'3" | 248 | 24 | | |
| Jack Gregory | DE | 6'6" | 250 | 33 | | 6 |
| George Martin | DE | 6'4" | 245 | 25 | | 6 |
| Troy Archer | DT | 6'4" | 250 | 23 | | |
| Larry Gillard | DT | 6'4" | 270 | 23 | | |
| Gary Jeter | DT-DE | 6'4" | 260 | 23 | | |
| Jim Krahl | DT | 6'5" | 252 | 22 | | |
| John Mendenhall | DT | 6'1" | 255 | 29 | | |
| Harry Carson | LB | 6'2 | 235 | 24 | 3 | |
| Randy Coffield | LB | 6'3 | 215 | 24 | | |
| Brian Kelley | LB | 6'3" | 222 | 27 | 1 | |
| Dan Lloyd | LB | 6'2 | 225 | 24 | | |
| Frank Marion | LB | 6'3 | 228 | 27 | | |
| John Skorupan | LB | 6'3" | 225 | 27 | | |
| Brad Van Pelt | LB | 6'5" | 235 | 27 | 3 | |
| Bill Bryant (to PHI) | DB | 5'11" | 195 | 27 | | |
| Terry Jackson | DB | 5'10" | 197 | 22 | 7 | 6 |
| Ernie Jones | DB | 6'3" | 180 | 25 | 3 | |
| Larry Mallory | DB | 5'11" | 185 | 26 | | |
| Odis McKinney | DB | 6'2" | 187 | 21 | 1 | |
| Beasley Reese | DB | 6'1" | 193 | 24 | | |
| Ray Rhodes | DB | 5'11" | 185 | 27 | 3 | |
| Maurice Tyler | DB | 6' | 190 | 28 | | 6 |
| Fred Besana | QB | 6'4" | 205 | 24 | | |
| Randy Dean | QB | 6'3" | 195 | 23 | | |
| Jerry Golsteyn | QB | 6'4" | 210 | 24 | | |
| Joe Pisarcik | QB | 6'4" | 220 | 26 | | 6 |
| Bob Hammond | HB | 5'10" | 170 | 26 | | 18 |
| Doug Kotar | HB | 5'11" | 205 | 27 | | 12 |
| Billy Taylor | HB | 6' | 215 | 22 | | |
| Larry Csonka | FB | 6'3" | 235 | 31 | | 36 |
| Dan Doornink | FB | 6'3" | 210 | 22 | | 6 |
| Willie Spencer | FB | 6'4" | 235 | 25 | | 12 |
| Emery Moorehead | WR | 6'2" | 210 | 24 | | |
| Johnny Perkins | WR | 6'2" | 205 | 24 | | 18 |
| Ernest Pugh | WR | 6'1 | 174 | 26 | | |
| Jim Robinson | WR | 5'9 | 170 | 25 | | 12 |
| James Thompson | WR | 6' | 178 | 25 | | |
| Al Dixon | TE | 6'5" | 220 | 24 | | 18 |
| Gary Shirk | TE | 6'1" | 220 | 28 | | 12 |
| Joe Danelo | K | 5'9" | 166 | 24 | | 90 |
| Dave Jennings | K | 6'4" | 205 | 26 | | |

*—Overtime

## DALLAS COWBOYS

### RUSHING

| Last Name | No. | Yds. | Avg. | TD |
|---|---|---|---|---|
| Dorsett | 290 | 1325 | 4.6 | 7 |
| Newhouse | 140 | 584 | 4.2 | 8 |
| Laidlaw | 75 | 312 | 4.2 | 3 |
| Staubach | 42 | 182 | 4.3 | 1 |
| P. Pearson | 25 | 104 | 4.2 | 0 |
| Brinson | 18 | 96 | 5.3 | 2 |
| Dennison | 14 | 75 | 5.4 | 1 |
| Blackwell | 9 | 37 | 4.1 | 0 |
| D. Pearson | 3 | 29 | 9.7 | 0 |
| Hill | 3 | 17 | 5.7 | 0 |
| DuPree | 1 | 15 | 15.0 | 0 |
| D. White | 5 | 7 | 1.4 | 0 |

### RECEIVING

| Last Name | No. | Yds. | Avg. | TD |
|---|---|---|---|---|
| P. Pearson | 47 | 526 | 11 | 0 |
| Hill | 46 | 823 | 18 | 6 |
| D. Pearson | 44 | 714 | 16 | 3 |
| Dorsett | 37 | 378 | 10 | 2 |
| DuPree | 34 | 509 | 15 | 9 |
| Newhouse | 20 | 176 | 9 | 2 |
| Johnson | 12 | 155 | 13 | 0 |
| Laidlaw | 6 | 108 | 18 | 1 |
| Saldi | 3 | 8 | 3 | 2 |
| Dennison | 1 | 6 | 6 | 0 |

### PUNT RETURNS

| Last Name | No. | Yds. | Avg. | TD |
|---|---|---|---|---|
| Johnson | 51 | 401 | 8 | 0 |
| Hill | 11 | 101 | 9 | 0 |
| Thurman | 1 | 0 | 0 | 0 |

### KICKOFF RETURNS

| Last Name | No. | Yds. | Avg. | TD |
|---|---|---|---|---|
| Johnson | 29 | 603 | 21 | 0 |
| Brinson | 6 | 93 | 16 | 0 |
| Blackwell | 3 | 70 | 23 | 0 |
| Dennison | 3 | 63 | 21 | 0 |
| Thurman | 3 | 42 | 14 | 0 |
| R. White | 1 | 15 | 15 | 0 |
| Lawless | 1 | 10 | 10 | 0 |
| Saldi | 1 | 0 | 0 | 0 |

### PASSING – PUNTING – KICKING

| PASSING | Att. | Comp. | % | Yds. | Yd./Att. | TD | Int.–% | | RK |
|---|---|---|---|---|---|---|---|---|---|
| Staubach | 413 | 231 | 56 | 3190 | 7.7 | 25 | 16– | 4 | 1 |
| D. White | 34 | 20 | 59 | 215 | 6.3 | 0 | 1– | 3 | |
| Dorsett | 1 | 0 | 0 | 0 | 0.0 | 0 | 0– | 0 | |
| Hill | 1 | 0 | 0 | 0 | 0.0 | 0 | 0– | 0 | |

| PUNTING | No. | Avg. |
|---|---|---|
| D. White | 76 | 40.5 |

| KICKING | XP | Att. | % | FG | Att. | % |
|---|---|---|---|---|---|---|
| Septien | 46 | 47 | 98 | 16 | 26 | 62 |

## PHILADELPHIA EAGLES

### RUSHING

| Last Name | No. | Yds. | Avg. | TD |
|---|---|---|---|---|
| Montgomery | 259 | 1220 | 4.7 | 9 |
| Hogan | 145 | 607 | 4.2 | 4 |
| Campfield | 61 | 247 | 4.0 | 0 |
| Franklin | 60 | 167 | 2.8 | 0 |
| Jaworski | 30 | 79 | 2.6 | 0 |
| Betterson | 11 | 32 | 2.9 | 0 |
| LeMaster | 2 | 29 | 14.5 | 0 |
| Carmichael | 1 | 21 | 21.0 | 0 |
| Payne | 1 | 17 | 17.0 | 0 |
| Engles | 1 | 16 | 16.0 | 0 |
| Barnes | 4 | 12 | 3.0 | 1 |
| Sciarra | 8 | 11 | 1.4 | 2 |
| Giammona | 4 | 6 | 1.5 | 0 |
| Michel | 1 | 0 | 0.0 | 0 |
| Walton | 2 | 0 | 0.0 | 0 |

### RECEIVING

| Last Name | No. | Yds. | Avg. | TD |
|---|---|---|---|---|
| Carmicheal | 55 | 1072 | 20 | 8 |
| Montgomery | 34 | 195 | 8 | 1 |
| Hogan | 31 | 164 | 5 | 1 |
| Krepfle | 26 | 374 | 14 | 3 |
| Campfield | 15 | 101 | 7 | 0 |
| Payne | 13 | 238 | 18 | 1 |
| Osborne | 13 | 195 | 11 | 0 |
| Smith | 11 | 142 | 13 | 2 |
| Franklin | 7 | 46 | 7 | 0 |
| Barnes | 2 | 13 | 7 | 0 |
| Betterson | 2 | 8 | 4 | 0 |

### PUNT RETURNS

| Last Name | No. | Yds. | Avg. | TD |
|---|---|---|---|---|
| Sciarra | 37 | 251 | 7 | 0 |
| Henry | 11 | 165 | 15 | 1 |
| Giammona | 0 | 1 | — | 0 |

### KICKOFF RETURNS

| Last Name | No. | Yds. | Avg. | TD |
|---|---|---|---|---|
| Campfield | 18 | 368 | 20 | 0 |
| Giammona | 12 | 245 | 20 | 0 |
| Betterson | 7 | 185 | 26 | 0 |
| Montgomery | 6 | 154 | 26 | 0 |
| Lusk | 3 | 61 | 20 | 0 |
| Henry | 3 | 54 | 18 | 0 |
| Tautolo | 3 | 45 | 15 | 0 |
| Barnes | 2 | 22 | 11 | 0 |

### PASSING – PUNTING – KICKING

| PASSING | Att. | Comp. | % | Yds. | Yd./Att. | TD | Int.–% | | RK |
|---|---|---|---|---|---|---|---|---|---|
| Jaworski | 398 | 206 | 52 | 2487 | 6.3 | 16 | 16– | 4 | 5 |
| Engles | 1 | 1 | 100 | -2 | -2.0 | 0 | 0– | 0 | |
| Sciarra | 1 | 0 | 0 | 0 | 0.0 | 0 | 0– | 0 | |
| Walton | 1 | 0 | 0 | 0 | 0.0 | 0 | 0– | 0 | |

| PUNTING | No. | Avg. |
|---|---|---|
| Michel | 58 | 35.8 |
| Engles | 33 | 39.6 |

| KICKING | XP | Att. | % | FG | Att. | % |
|---|---|---|---|---|---|---|
| Mike-Mayer | 21 | 22 | 95 | 8 | 17 | 47 |
| Michel | 9 | 12 | 75 | | | |

## WASHINGTON REDSKINS

### RUSHING

| Last Name | No. | Yds. | Avg. | TD |
|---|---|---|---|---|
| Riggins | 248 | 1014 | 4.1 | 5 |
| Thomas | 161 | 533 | 3.3 | 3 |
| Theismann | 37 | 177 | 4.8 | 1 |
| Harmon | 34 | 141 | 4.1 | 0 |
| Malone | 33 | 110 | 3.3 | 1 |
| Green | 22 | 82 | 3.7 | 1 |
| McDaniel | 2 | 25 | 12.5 | 0 |
| Haynes | 1 | 13 | 13.0 | 0 |
| Forte | 4 | 4 | 1.0 | 0 |
| Kilmer | 1 | 1 | 1.0 | 0 |

### RECEIVING

| Last Name | No. | Yds. | Avg. | TD |
|---|---|---|---|---|
| Buggs | 36 | 575 | 16 | 2 |
| Thomas | 35 | 387 | 11 | 2 |
| McDaniel | 34 | 577 | 17 | 4 |
| Riggins | 31 | 299 | 10 | 0 |
| Fugett | 25 | 367 | 15 | 7 |
| Thompson | 23 | 350 | 15 | 1 |
| Harmon | 11 | 112 | 10 | 1 |
| Green | 4 | 89 | 22 | 0 |
| Malone | 3 | 29 | 10 | 0 |
| Haynes | 2 | 32 | 16 | 0 |
| Anderson | 1 | 56 | 56 | 0 |
| Murphy | 1 | 13 | 13 | 0 |

### PUNT RETURNS

| Last Name | No. | Yds. | Avg. | TD |
|---|---|---|---|---|
| Green | 42 | 443 | 10 | 1 |
| Anderson | 5 | 47 | 9 | 0 |
| Smith | 4 | 33 | 8 | 0 |
| Harmon | 1 | 5 | 5 | 0 |
| Parrish | 1 | 4 | 4 | 0 |
| Forte | 1 | -5 | -5 | 0 |

### KICKOFF RETURNS

| Last Name | No. | Yds. | Avg. | TD |
|---|---|---|---|---|
| Green | 34 | 870 | 26 | 1 |
| Forte | 11 | 243 | 22 | 0 |
| Anderson | 10 | 227 | 23 | 0 |
| Harris | 6 | 99 | 17 | 0 |
| Harmon | 3 | 52 | 17 | 0 |
| Smith | 1 | 18 | 18 | 0 |

### PASSING – PUNTING – KICKING

| PASSING | Att. | Comp. | % | Yds. | Yd./Att. | TD | Int.–% | | RK |
|---|---|---|---|---|---|---|---|---|---|
| Theismann | 390 | 187 | 48 | 2593 | 6.7 | 13 | 18– | 5 | 8 |
| Kilmer | 46 | 23 | 50 | 316 | 6.9 | 4 | 3– | 7 | |
| Bragg | 2 | 2 | 100 | 69 | 34.5 | 0 | 0– | 0 | |

| PUNTING | No. | Avg. |
|---|---|---|
| Bragg | 103 | 39.4 |

| KICKING | XP | Att. | % | FG | Att. | % |
|---|---|---|---|---|---|---|
| Moseley | 30 | 31 | 97 | 19 | 30 | 63 |

## ST. LOUIS CARDINALS

### RUSHING

| Last Name | No. | Yds. | Avg. | TD |
|---|---|---|---|---|
| Otis | 197 | 664 | 3.4 | 8 |
| Morris | 174 | 631 | 3.6 | 1 |
| Jones | 105 | 392 | 3.7 | 2 |
| Harrell | 35 | 134 | 3.8 | 0 |
| Gray | 5 | 51 | 10.2 | 1 |
| Tilley | 1 | 32 | 32.0 | 0 |
| Bell | 7 | 23 | 3.3 | 0 |
| Hart | 11 | 11 | 1.0 | 2 |
| Ramson | 2 | 8 | 4.0 | 0 |
| Shelby | 2 | 5 | 2.5 | 0 |
| Farmer | 1 | 4 | 4.0 | 0 |
| Little | 1 | 0 | 0.0 | 0 |
| Wehrli | 1 | 0 | 0.0 | 0 |
| Pisarkiewicz | 5 | -1 | -0.2 | 0 |
| Stief | 1 | -8 | -8.0 | 0 |

### RECEIVING

| Last Name | No. | Yds. | Avg. | TD |
|---|---|---|---|---|
| Tilley | 62 | 900 | 15 | 3 |
| Gray | 44 | 871 | 20 | 1 |
| Morris | 33 | 298 | 9 | 1 |
| Jones | 27 | 217 | 8 | 0 |
| Stief | 24 | 477 | 20 | 4 |
| Ramson | 23 | 238 | 10 | 1 |
| Chandler | 16 | 190 | 12 | 4 |
| Otis | 8 | 38 | 5 | 0 |
| Childs | 4 | 50 | 13 | 1 |
| Thaxton | 3 | 31 | 10 | 1 |
| Bell | 3 | 28 | 9 | 0 |
| Harrell | 3 | 5 | 2 | 0 |
| Shelby | 1 | 11 | 11 | 0 |

### PUNT RETURNS

| Last Name | No. | Yds. | Avg. | TD |
|---|---|---|---|---|
| Harrell | 21 | 196 | 9 | 1 |
| Bell | 8 | 177 | 22 | 0 |
| Shelby | 9 | 211 | 23 | 0 |
| Tilley | 2 | 8 | 4 | 0 |
| Southard | 2 | -2 | -1 | 0 |
| Woolsey | 1 | 4 | 4 | 0 |
| Smith | 1 | 0 | 0 | 0 |

### KICKOFF RETURNS

| Last Name | No. | Yds. | Avg. | TD |
|---|---|---|---|---|
| Harrell | 19 | 389 | 21 | 0 |
| Shelby | 9 | 211 | 23 | 0 |
| Bell | 8 | 177 | 22 | 0 |
| Childs | 4 | 77 | 19 | 0 |
| Morris | 3 | 66 | 22 | 0 |
| Nelson | 3 | 58 | 19 | 0 |
| Southard | 2 | 47 | 24 | 0 |
| Woolsey | 1 | 25 | 25 | 0 |
| Townsend | 1 | 13 | 13 | 0 |
| Westbrooks | 1 | 12 | 12 | 0 |
| Stone | 1 | 3 | 3 | 0 |

### PASSING – PUNTING – KICKING

| PASSING | Att. | Comp. | % | Yds. | Yd./Att. | TD | Int.–% | | RK |
|---|---|---|---|---|---|---|---|---|---|
| Hart | 477 | 240 | 50 | 3121 | 6.5 | 16 | 18– | 4 | 6 |
| Pisarkiewicz | 29 | 10 | 35 | 164 | 5.7 | 0 | 3– | 10 | |
| Stief | 1 | 1 | 100 | 43 | 43.0 | 0 | 0– | 0 | |
| Wood | 1 | 1 | 100 | 29 | 29.0 | 0 | 0– | 0 | |

| PUNTING | No. | Avg. |
|---|---|---|
| Little | 46 | 38.0 |
| Wood | 82 | 36.8 |
| Bakken | 4 | 36.8 |

| KICKING | XP | Att. | % | FG | Att. | % |
|---|---|---|---|---|---|---|
| Bakken | 27 | 30 | 90 | 11 | 22 | 50 |

## NEW YORK GIANTS

### RUSHING

| Last Name | No. | Yds. | Avg. | TD |
|---|---|---|---|---|
| Kotar | 149 | 625 | 4.2 | 1 |
| Hammond | 131 | 554 | 4.2 | 0 |
| Csonka | 91 | 311 | 3.4 | 6 |
| Doornink | 60 | 306 | 5.1 | 1 |
| Taylor | 73 | 250 | 3.4 | 0 |
| Dean | 14 | 94 | 6.7 | 0 |
| Pisarcik | 17 | 68 | 4.0 | 1 |
| Spencer | 38 | 61 | 1.6 | 2 |
| Pough | 3 | 33 | 11.0 | 0 |
| Perkins | 1 | 3 | 3.00 | 0 |
| Kelley | 1 | 2 | 2.0 | 0 |
| Jennings | 1 | 0 | 0.0 | 0 |
| Goldsteyn | 1 | -3 | -3.0 | 0 |

### RECEIVING

| Last Name | No. | Yds. | Avg. | TD |
|---|---|---|---|---|
| Robinson | 32 | 620 | 19 | 2 |
| Perkins | 32 | 514 | 16 | 3 |
| Kotar | 22 | 225 | 10 | 1 |
| Hammond | 20 | 173 | 9 | 2 |
| Dixon | 18 | 376 | 21 | 3 |
| Doornink | 12 | 66 | 6 | 0 |
| Shirk | 10 | 127 | 13 | 2 |
| Taylor | 9 | 70 | 8 | 0 |
| Thompson | 7 | 113 | 16 | 0 |
| Csonka | 7 | 73 | 10 | 0 |
| Moorehead | 3 | 45 | 15 | 0 |
| Spencer | 2 | 25 | 13 | 0 |
| Pough | 1 | 2 | 2 | 0 |
| Kelley | 1 | -1 | -1 | 0 |

### PUNT RETURNS

| Last Name | No. | Yds. | Avg. | TD |
|---|---|---|---|---|
| Hammond | 22 | 157 | 7 | 0 |
| Robinson | 19 | 106 | 6 | 0 |
| Jackson | 4 | 1 | 0 | 0 |
| Thompson | 2 | 4 | 2 | 0 |
| Tyler | 1 | 6 | 6 | 0 |

### KICKOFF RETURNS

| Last Name | No. | Yds. | Avg. | TD |
|---|---|---|---|---|
| Pough | 15 | 313 | 21 | 0 |
| Hammond | 15 | 290 | 19 | 0 |
| Taylor | 11 | 192 | 17 | 0 |
| Shirk | 5 | 63 | 13 | 0 |
| Skorupan | 4 | 52 | 13 | 0 |
| Kotar | 3 | 51 | 17 | 0 |
| Moorehead | 2 | 52 | 26 | 0 |
| Reece | 2 | 40 | 20 | 0 |
| Spencer | 1 | 14 | 14 | 0 |
| Marion | 1 | 12 | 12 | 0 |
| Tyler | 1 | 2 | 2 | 0 |

### PASSING – PUNTING – KICKING

| PASSING | Att. | Comp. | % | Yds. | Yd./Att. | TD | Int.–% | | RK |
|---|---|---|---|---|---|---|---|---|---|
| Pisarcik | 301 | 143 | 48 | 2096 | 7.0 | 12 | 23– | 8 | 13 |
| Dean | 39 | 19 | 49 | 188 | 4.8 | 1 | 3– | 8 | |
| Goldsteyn | 40 | 12 | 30 | 110 | 2.8 | 0 | 1– | 3 | |
| Mallory | 1 | 1 | 100 | 35 | 35.0 | 0 | 0– | 0 | |
| Jennings | 1 | 1 | 100 | -1 | -1.0 | 0 | 0– | 0 | |

| PUNTING | No. | Avg. |
|---|---|---|
| Jennings | 95 | 42.1 |

| KICKING | XP | Att. | % | FG | Att. | % |
|---|---|---|---|---|---|---|
| Danelo | 27 | 29 | 93 | 11 | 29 | 72 |

## MINNESOTA VIKINGS 8-7-1 Bud Grant

| Scores of Each Game | | |
|---|---|---|
| 24 | New Orleans | 31 |
| 12 | DENVER | *9 |
| 10 | TAMPA BAY | 16 |
| 24 | Chicago | 20 |
| 24 | Tampa Bay | 7 |
| 28 | Seattle | 29 |
| 17 | LOS ANGELES | 34 |
| 21 | GREEN BAY | 7 |
| 21 | Dallas | 10 |
| 17 | DETROIT | 7 |
| 17 | CHICAGO | 14 |
| 7 | SAN DIEGO | 13 |
| 10 | Green Bay | *10 |
| 28 | PHILADELPHIA | 27 |
| 14 | Detroit | 45 |
| 20 | Oakland | 27 |

| Use Name | Pos. | Hgt. | Wgt. | Age | Int. | Pts. |
|---|---|---|---|---|---|---|
| Frank Myers | OT | 6'5" | 255 | 22 | | |
| Steve Riley | OT | 6'6" | 258 | 25 | | |
| Ron Yary | OT | 6'6" | 255 | 32 | | |
| Charlie Goodrum | OG | 6'3" | 256 | 28 | | |
| Wes Hamilton | OG | 6'3" | 255 | 25 | | |
| Bob Lingenfelter | OG-OT | 6'7" | 277 | 24 | | |
| Dennis Swilley | OG | 6'3" | 241 | 23 | | |
| Jim Hough | C | 6'2" | 267 | 22 | | |
| Mick Tingelhoff | C | 6'1" | 240 | 38 | | |
| Carl Eller | DE | 6'6" | 247 | 36 | | |
| Randy Holloway | DE | 6'5" | 245 | 23 | | |
| Jim Marshall | DE | 6'3" | 240 | 40 | | |
| Mark Mullaney | DE | 6'6" | 242 | 25 | | |
| Lyman Smith | DT | 6'5" | 250 | 21 | | |
| Doug Sutherland | DT | 6'3" | 250 | 30 | | |
| James White | DT | 6'3" | 263 | 24 | | |
| Matt Blair | LB | 6'5" | 229 | 26 | 3 | 6 |
| Wally Hilgenberg | LB | 6'3" | 229 | 35 | | |
| Fred McNeill | LB | 6'2" | 229 | 26 | 2 | 6 |
| Jeff Siemon | LB | 6'3" | 237 | 28 | | |
| Scott Studwell | LB | 6'2" | 224 | 24 | | |
| Nate Allen | DB | 5'11" | 174 | 30 | | |
| Bobby Bryant | DB | 6'1" | 170 | 34 | 7 | |
| Tom Hannon | DB | 5'11" | 193 | 23 | 2 | |
| Paul Krause | DB | 6'3" | 205 | 36 | | |
| Nelson Munsey | DB | 6'1" | 186 | 30 | | |
| John Turner | DB | 6' | 199 | 22 | 1 | |
| Phil Wise | DB | 6' | 193 | 29 | 2 | |
| Nate Wright | DB | 5'11" | 180 | 31 | 5 | |
| Tommy Kramer | QB | 6'1" | 199 | 23 | | |
| Bob Lee | QB | 6'2" | 195 | 32 | | |
| Fran Tarkenton | QB | 6'1" | 185 | 38 | | 6 |
| Brent McClanahan | HB | 5'10" | 202 | 27 | | |
| Robert Miller | HB | 5'11" | 204 | 25 | | 18 |
| Rickey Young | HB | 6'2" | 198 | 24 | | 36 |
| Chuck Foreman | FB-HB | 6'2" | 207 | 27 | | 42 |
| Sammy Johnson | FB | 6'1" | 226 | 25 | | |
| Mark Kellar | FB | 6' | 225 | 26 | | |
| Kevin Miller | WR | 5'10" | 180 | 23 | | 6 |
| Ahmad Rashad | WR | 6'2" | 200 | 28 | | 48 |
| Harry Washington | WR | 6' | 180 | 22 | | |
| Sammy White | WR | 5'11" | 189 | 24 | | 54 |
| Steve Craig | TE | 6'3" | 231 | 27 | | |
| Bob Tucker | TE | 6'3" | 230 | 33 | | |
| Stu Voigt | TE | 6'1" | 225 | 30 | | |
| Greg Coleman | K | 6' | 178 | 23 | | |
| Rich Danmeier | K | 6' | 183 | 26 | | 72 |

## GREEN BAY PACKERS 8-7-1 Bart Starr

| Scores of Each Game | | |
|---|---|---|
| 13 | Detroit | 7 |
| 28 | NEW ORLEANS | 17 |
| 3 | OAKLAND | 28 |
| 24 | San Diego | 3 |
| 35 | DETROIT | 14 |
| 24 | CHICAGO | 14 |
| 45 | SEATTLE | 28 |
| 7 | Minnesota | 21 |
| 9 | TAMPA BAY | 7 |
| 3 | Philadelphia | 10 |
| 14 | DALLAS | 42 |
| 3 | Denver | 16 |
| 10 | MINNESOTA | *10 |
| 17 | Tampa Bay | 7 |
| 0 | Chicago | 14 |
| 14 | Los Angeles | 31 |

| Use Name | Pos. | Hgt. | Wgt. | Age | Int. | Pts. |
|---|---|---|---|---|---|---|
| Greg Koch | OT | 6'4" | 265 | 23 | | |
| Gerald Skinner | OT | 6'4" | 260 | 23 | | |
| Tim Stokes | OT | 6'5" | 252 | 28 | | |
| Derrel Gofourth | OG | 6'3" | 260 | 23 | | |
| Leotis Harris | OG | 6'1" | 267 | 23 | | |
| Melvin Jackson | OG | 6'1" | 267 | 24 | | |
| Randy Pass | OG-C | 6'3" | 247 | 23 | | |
| Larry McCarren | C | 6'3" | 248 | 26 | | |
| Rich Nuzum | C | 6'4" | 238 | 26 | | |
| Bob Barber | DE | 6'3" | 240 | 26 | | |
| Mike Butler | DE | 6'5" | 265 | 24 | | |
| Ezra Johnson | DE | 6'4" | 240 | 22 | | |
| Carl Barzilauskas | DT | 6'6" | 265 | 27 | 1 | |
| Terry Jones | DT | 6'2" | 259 | 21 | | |
| Dave Roller | DT | 6'2" | 270 | 28 | | |
| John Anderson | LB | 6'3" | 221 | 22 | 5 | |
| Jim Carter | LB | 6'3" | 245 | 29 | | |
| Frank Chesley | LB | 6'3" | 219 | 23 | | |
| Mike Douglass | LB | 6' | 224 | 23 | | |
| Jim Gueno | LB | 6'2" | 220 | 24 | | |
| Mike Hunt | LB | 6'2" | 240 | 21 | 1 | |
| Danny Johnson | LB | 6'1" | 216 | 23 | | |
| Paul Rudzinski | LB | 6'1" | 220 | 22 | | |
| Gary Weaver | LB | 6'1" | 225 | 29 | | |
| Willie Buchanon | DB | 6' | 190 | 27 | 9 | 6 |
| Johnnie Gray | DB | 5'11" | 185 | 24 | 3 | |
| Estus Hood | DB | 5'11" | 180 | 22 | 3 | |
| Steve Luke | DB | 6'2" | 205 | 24 | 2 | 6 |
| Mike McCoy | DB | 5'11" | 183 | 25 | 3 | |
| Howard Sampson | DB | 5'10" | 185 | 22 | | |
| Steve Wagner | DB | 6'2" | 208 | 24 | | |
| Bobby Douglass | QB | 6'3" | 228 | 31 | | |
| Neil Graff | QB | 6'3" | 205 | 28 | | |
| Dennis Sproul | QB | 6'2" | 210 | 22 | | |
| David Whitehurst | QB | 6'2" | 204 | 23 | | 6 |
| Terdell Middleton | HB | 6' | 195 | 23 | | 72 |
| Nate Simpson | HB | 5'11" | 190 | 23 | | |
| Eric Torkelson | HB | 6'2" | 194 | 26 | | |
| Jim Culbreath | FB | 6' | 210 | 25 | | |
| Reggie Harrison | FB | 5'11" | 220 | 28 | | |
| Walt Landers | FB | 6' | 214 | 25 | | 6 |
| Barty Smith | FB | 6'4" | 240 | 26 | | 24 |
| James Lofton | WR | 6'3" | 187 | 22 | | 36 |
| Steve Odom | WR | 5'8" | 174 | 25 | | 12 |
| Willie Taylor | WR | 6'1" | 179 | 22 | | |
| Audra Thompson | WR | 6' | 186 | 25 | | 12 |
| Walter Tullis | WR | 6' | 170 | 25 | | |
| Paul Coffman | TE | 6'3" | 218 | 22 | | |
| Rich McGeorge | TE | 6'4" | 230 | 29 | | 6 |
| David Beverly | K | 6'2" | 180 | 28 | | |
| Chester Marcol | K | 6' | 190 | 28 | | 63 |

Lynn Dickey – Leg Injury
Mark Koncar – Leg Injury

## DETROIT LIONS 7-9-0 Monte Clark

| Scores of Each Game | | |
|---|---|---|
| 7 | GREEN BAY | 13 |
| 15 | Tampa Bay | 7 |
| 0 | CHICAGO | 19 |
| 16 | Seattle | 28 |
| 14 | Green Bay | 35 |
| 19 | WASHINGTON | 21 |
| 0 | Atlanta | 14 |
| 31 | SAN DIEGO | 14 |
| 21 | Chicago | 17 |
| 7 | Minnesota | 17 |
| 34 | TAMPA BAY | 23 |
| 17 | Oakland | 29 |
| 17 | DENVER | 14 |
| 14 | St. Louis | 21 |
| 45 | MINNESOTA | 14 |
| 33 | SAN FRANCISCO | 14 |

| Use Name | Pos. | Hgt. | Wgt. | Age | Int. | Pts. |
|---|---|---|---|---|---|---|
| Karl Baldischwiler | OT | 6'5" | 265 | 22 | | |
| Bill Fifer (to NO) | OT | 6'4" | 250 | 22 | | |
| Donnie Green | OT | 6'7" | 261 | 30 | | |
| Brad Oates | OT | 6'6" | 274 | 24 | | |
| Lynn Boden | OG | 6'5" | 260 | 25 | | |
| Homer Elias | OG | 6'3" | 255 | 23 | | |
| Amos Fowler | OG | 6'3" | 250 | 22 | | |
| Donnie Hickman (from WAS) | OG | 6'2" | 260 | 23 | | |
| Willie Brock | C | 6'3" | 246 | 22 | | |
| Karl Chandler | C-OG | 6'5" | 250 | 26 | | |
| Mike Montler | C | 6'4" | 250 | 34 | | |
| Larry Tearry | C | 6'3" | 260 | 22 | | |
| Al Baker | DE | 6'6" | 260 | 21 | | |
| Dave Pureifory (from CIN) | DE | 6'1" | 255 | 29 | | |
| Ken Sanders | DE | 6'5" | 245 | 28 | | |
| Bill Cooke (from SEATTLE) | DT | 6'5" | 250 | 27 | | |
| Doug English | DT | 6'5" | 255 | 25 | | |
| Dave Gallagher | DT | 6'4" | 256 | 26 | | |
| Dan Gray | DT | 6'6" | 240 | 22 | | |
| John Woodcock | DT | 6'3" | 240 | 24 | | |
| Tony Daykin | LB | 6'1" | 215 | 23 | | |
| Dan Dickel | LB | 6'3" | 230 | 26 | | |
| Paul Naumoff | LB | 6'1" | 215 | 33 | 1 | |
| Ed O'Neil | LB | 6'3" | 235 | 25 | 4 | |
| Dave Washington | LB | 6'6" | 230 | 29 | | |
| Charlie Weaver | LB | 6'2" | 225 | 29 | 3 | |
| Jim Allen | DB | 6'2" | 195 | 26 | 5 | 6 |
| Luther Bradley | DB | 6'2" | 195 | 23 | 3 | 6 |
| Mike Burns | DB | 6' | 180 | 24 | 1 | |
| James Hunter | DB | 6'3" | 195 | 24 | 2 | |
| Reggie Pinkney | DB | 5'11" | 190 | 23 | 1 | |
| Bruce Rhodes | DB | 6' | 190 | 26 | 1 | |
| Tony Sumler | DB | 5'10" | 185 | 22 | | |
| Walt Williams | DB | 6' | 185 | 24 | 1 | |
| Gary Danielson | QB | 6'2" | 195 | 26 | | |
| Greg Landry | QB | 6'4" | 205 | 31 | | |
| Joe Reed | QB | 6'1" | 195 | 30 | | |
| Andy Bolton | HB | 6'1" | 205 | 24 | | |
| Dexter Bussey | HB | 6'1" | 210 | 26 | | 36 |
| Ken Callicutt | HB | 6' | 190 | 23 | | |
| Rick Kane | HB | 5'11" | 200 | 23 | | 12 |
| Lawrence Gaines | FB | 6'1" | 240 | 24 | | 6 |
| Horace King | FB | 5'10" | 210 | 25 | | 36 |
| Luther Blue | WR | 5'11" | 190 | 22 | | 12 |
| Ray Jarvis | WR | 6'1" | 190 | 29 | | |
| Willie McGee | WR | 5'11" | 178 | 28 | | |
| Freddie Scott | WR | 6'2" | 175 | 26 | | 12 |
| Jessie Thompson | WR | 6'1" | 185 | 22 | | 24 |
| Leonard Thompson | WR | 5'10" | 190 | 26 | | 24 |
| Bill Gay | TE | 6'5" | 225 | 23 | | |
| David Hill | TE | 6'2" | 220 | 24 | | 24 |
| Benny Ricardo | K | 5'10" | 175 | 24 | | 92 |
| Tom Skladany | K | 6' | 165 | 23 | | |

Russ Bolinger – Knee Injury
Levi Johnson – Achilles Injury
Mark Markovich – Knee Injury
Jim Yarbrough – Achilles Injury
J.D. Hill – Achilles Injury
Gene Washington – Achilles Injury

## CHICAGO BEARS 7-8-0 Neill Armstrong

| Scores of Each Game | | |
|---|---|---|
| 17 | ST. LOUIS | 10 |
| 16 | San Francisco | 13 |
| 19 | Detroit | 0 |
| 20 | MINNESOTA | 24 |
| 19 | OAKLAND | *25 |
| 14 | Green Bay | 24 |
| 7 | Denver | 16 |
| 19 | Tampa Bay | 33 |
| 17 | DETROIT | 21 |
| 29 | SEATTLE | 31 |
| 14 | Minnesota | 17 |
| 13 | ATLANTA | 7 |
| 14 | TAMPA BAY | 3 |
| 7 | San Diego | 40 |
| 14 | GREEN BAY | 0 |
| 14 | Washington | 10 |

| Use Name | Pos. | Hgt. | Wgt. | Age | Int. | Pts. |
|---|---|---|---|---|---|---|
| Ted Albrecht | OT | 6'4" | 255 | 23 | | |
| Lionel Antoine | OT | 6'6" | 267 | 28 | | |
| Dan Jiggetts | OT | 6'4" | 276 | 24 | | |
| Dennis Lick | OT | 6'3" | 268 | 24 | | |
| Noah Jackson | OG | 6'2" | 273 | 27 | | |
| Jeff Sevy | OG | 6'5" | 261 | 27 | | |
| Revie Sorey | OG | 6'2" | 259 | 24 | | |
| Jon Morris | C | 6'4" | 250 | 35 | | |
| Dan Neal | C | 6'4" | 248 | 29 | | |
| Tommy Hart | DE | 6'4" | 246 | 33 | | |
| Mike Hartenstine | DE | 6'3" | 257 | 25 | | |
| Jerry Meyers | DT | 6'4" | 245 | 24 | | |
| Jim Osborne | DT | 6'3" | 251 | 28 | | |
| Alan Page (from MINN) | DT | 6'4" | 245 | 33 | | |
| Ron Rydalch | DT | 6'4" | 257 | 26 | | |
| Brad Shearer | DT | 6'3" | 254 | 23 | | |
| Doug Buffone | LB | 6'1" | 227 | 34 | 3 | |
| Gary Campbell | LB | 6'1" | 218 | 26 | | |
| Chris Devlin (from CIN) | LB | 6'2" | 228 | 24 | | |
| Bruce Herron | LB | 6'2" | 220 | 24 | | |
| Tom Hicks | LB | 6'4" | 225 | 25 | | |
| Jerry Muckensturm | LB | 6'4" | 226 | 24 | | |
| Don Rives | LB | 6'2" | 231 | 27 | 2 | |
| Gary Fencik | DB | 6'1" | 192 | 24 | 4 | |
| Wentford Gaines (from PIT) | DB | 6' | 185 | 25 | 1 | |
| Virgil Livers | DB | 5'9" | 178 | 26 | 3 | 6 |
| Doug Plank | DB | 6' | 201 | 25 | 1 | |
| Terry Schmidt | DB | 6' | 176 | 26 | 2 | |
| Mike Spivey | DB | 6' | 194 | 24 | | 6 |
| Len Walterscheid | DB | 5'11" | 185 | 23 | 1 | |
| Bob Avellini | QB | 6'2" | 206 | 25 | | 12 |
| Vince Evans | QB | 6'2" | 216 | 23 | | |
| Mike Phipps | QB | 6'3" | 211 | 30 | | |
| Art Best | HB | 6'1" | 205 | 25 | | |
| Walter Payton | HB | 5'11" | 205 | 24 | | 66 |
| Robin Earl | FB | 6'5" | 245 | 23 | | |
| Roland Harper | FB | 6' | 209 | 25 | | 48 |
| Mike Morgan | FB | 5'11" | 218 | 22 | | |
| John Skibinski | FB | 6' | 218 | 23 | | |
| Brian Baschnagel | WR | 6' | 184 | 24 | | |
| Bo Rather (to MIAMI) | WR | 6'1" | 189 | 27 | | |
| Golden Richards (from DAL) | WR | 6' | 180 | 27 | | |
| Steve Schubert | WR | 5'10" | 188 | 27 | | 6 |
| James Scott | WR | 6'1" | 191 | 26 | | 30 |
| Mike Cobb | TE | 6'5" | 248 | 22 | | |
| Greg Latta | TE | 6'3" | 230 | 25 | | |
| Bob Parsons | TE | 6'5" | 232 | 28 | | |
| Bob Thomas | K | 5'10" | 174 | 26 | | 77 |

Johnny Musso – Knee Injury
Steve Rivera – Injury
Waymond Bryant – Shoulder Injury
Allan Ellis – Knee Injury
Walt Patulski – Back Injury

## TAMPA BAY BUCCANEERS 5-11-0 John McKay

| Scores of Each Game | | |
|---|---|---|
| 13 | N.Y. GIANTS | 19 |
| 7 | DETROIT | 15 |
| 16 | Minnesota | 10 |
| 14 | ATLANTA | 9 |
| 7 | MINNESOTA | 24 |
| 30 | Kansas City | 13 |
| 14 | N.Y. Giants | 17 |
| 33 | CHICAGO | 19 |
| 7 | Green Bay | 9 |
| 23 | Los Angeles | 26 |
| 23 | Detroit | 34 |
| 31 | BUFFALO | 10 |
| 3 | Chicago | 14 |
| 7 | GREEN BAY | 17 |
| 3 | San Francisco | 6 |
| 10 | NEW ORLEANS | 17 |

| Use Name | Pos. | Hgt. | Wgt. | Age | Int. | Pts. |
|---|---|---|---|---|---|---|
| Darryl Carlton | OT | 6'6" | 270 | 25 | | |
| Rocky Freitas | OT | 6'6" | 275 | 32 | | |
| Dave Reavis | OT | 6'5" | 250 | 28 | | |
| Greg Horton (from LA) | OG | 6'4" | 245 | 27 | | |
| Randy Johnson | OG | 6'2" | 255 | 25 | | |
| Dan Medlin | OG | 6'4" | 255 | 28 | | |
| Brett Moritz | OG | 6'5" | 250 | 23 | | |
| Gary Puetz (from NYJ) | OG-OT | 6'4" | 265 | 26 | | |
| Kurt Schumacher | OG | 6'3" | 255 | 25 | | |
| Jeff Winans | OG-OT | 6'5" | 265 | 26 | | |
| Steve Wilson | C | 6'3" | 265 | 24 | | |
| Wally Chambers | DE | 6'6" | 250 | 27 | 1 | |
| Charles Hannah | DE | 6'5" | 250 | 23 | | |
| Bill Kollar | DE-MG | 6'4" | 256 | 25 | | |
| Lee Roy Selmon | DE | 6'3" | 260 | 23 | | |
| Randy Crowder | MG-DE | 6'2" | 245 | 26 | | |
| Dave Pear | MG | 6'2" | 250 | 25 | | |
| Rik Bonness | LB | 6'3" | 220 | 24 | | |
| Aaron Brown | LB | 6'2" | 235 | 22 | 1 | |
| Paul Harris (from MINN) | LB | 6'3" | 215 | 23 | | |
| Earl Inmon | LB | 6'1" | 215 | 24 | | |
| Cecil Johnson | LB | 6'2" | 220 | 23 | 2 | |
| Dave Lewis | LB | 6'4" | 230 | 23 | 3 | |
| Dana Nafziger | LB | 6'1" | 220 | 24 | | |
| Dewey Selmon | LB | 6'1" | 250 | 24 | 1 | |
| Richard Wood | LB | 6'2" | 215 | 25 | | |
| Jerry Anderson | DB | 5'11" | 195 | 24 | | |
| Cedric Brown | DB | 6'1" | 190 | 24 | 6 | |
| Billy Cesare | DB | 5'11" | 190 | 23 | | |
| Mark Cotney | DB | 6' | 205 | 26 | 2 | |
| Curtis Jordan | DB | 6'2" | 185 | 24 | 3 | |
| Danny Reece | DB | 5'11" | 190 | 23 | 1 | |
| Mike Washington | DB | 6'3" | 190 | 25 | 5 | 6 |
| Jeris White | DB | 5'11" | 180 | 25 | 5 | |
| Mike Boryla | QB | 6'3" | 200 | 27 | | |
| Gary Huff | QB | 6'1" | 195 | 27 | | |
| Mike Rae (from OAK) | QB | 6' | 190 | 27 | | |
| Doug Williams | QB | 6'4" | 215 | 23 | | 6 |
| Ricky Bell | HB | 6'2" | 220 | 23 | | 36 |
| Louis Carter | HB | 5'11" | 210 | 25 | | 6 |
| Dave Farmer | HB | 6' | 205 | 24 | | |
| George Ragsdale | HB | 5'11" | 185 | 24 | | 12 |
| Charlie White | HB | 6' | 222 | 25 | | |
| Johnny Davis | FB | 6'1" | 235 | 22 | | 18 |
| Jimmy DuBose | FB | 5'11" | 215 | 23 | | 24 |
| Karl Farmer | WR | 5'11" | 165 | 24 | | |
| Larry Franklin | WR | 6'1" | 185 | 23 | | |
| Frank Grant (from WAS) | WR | 5'11" | 181 | 28 | | |
| Isaac Hagins | WR | 5'9" | 180 | 24 | | |
| John McKay | WR | 5'11" | 185 | 25 | | 6 |
| Larry Mucher | WR | 5'11" | 190 | 23 | | |
| Morris Owens | WR | 6' | 190 | 25 | | 30 |
| Alvis Darby | TE | 6'5" | 225 | 23 | | |
| Jim Giles | TE | 6'3" | 225 | 23 | | 12 |
| Jim O'Bradovich | TE | 6'2" | 227 | 28 | | 18 |
| Dave Green | K | 5'11" | 205 | 28 | | 3 |
| Neil O'Donohue | K | 6'6" | 205 | 25 | | 64 |

Booker Brown – Knee Injury
Randy Hedberg – Elbow Injury

*—Overtime

## MINNESOTA VIKINGS

### RUSHING

| Last Name | No. | Yds. | Avg. | TD |
|---|---|---|---|---|
| Foreman | 237 | 749 | 3.2 | 5 |
| Young | 134 | 417 | 3.1 | 1 |
| R. Miller | 70 | 213 | 3.0 | 3 |
| Johnson | 11 | 41 | 3.7 | 0 |
| Kellar | 11 | 34 | 3.1 | 0 |
| S. White | 5 | 30 | 6.0 | 0 |
| McClanahan | 10 | 26 | 2.6 | 0 |
| Coleman | 2 | 22 | 11.0 | 0 |
| Kramer | 1 | 10 | 10.0 | 0 |
| Tarkenton | 24 | −6 | −0.3 | 1 |

### RECEIVING

| Last Name | No. | Yds. | Avg. | TD |
|---|---|---|---|---|
| Young | 88 | 704 | 8 | 5 |
| Rashad | 66 | 769 | 12 | 8 |
| Foreman | 61 | 396 | 7 | 2 |
| S. White | 53 | 741 | 14 | 9 |
| Tucker | 47 | 540 | 12 | 0 |
| R. Miller | 22 | 230 | 11 | 0 |
| Voigt | 4 | 52 | 13 | 0 |
| Craig | 4 | 31 | 8 | 0 |
| Kellar | 3 | −5 | −2 | 0 |
| McClanahan | 2 | 11 | 6 | 0 |
| K. Miller | 1 | 35 | 35 | 1 |
| Washington | 1 | 24 | 24 | 0 |

### PUNT RETURNS

| Last Name | No. | Yds. | Avg. | TD |
|---|---|---|---|---|
| K. Miller | 48 | 239 | 5 | 0 |
| S. White | 1 | 0 | 0 | 0 |

### KICKOFF RETURNS

| Last Name | No. | Yds. | Avg. | TD |
|---|---|---|---|---|
| K. Miller | 40 | 854 | 21 | 0 |
| Washington | 4 | 71 | 18 | 0 |
| S. White | 3 | 50 | 17 | 0 |
| McClanahan | 3 | 38 | 13 | 0 |
| R. Miller | 2 | 23 | 12 | 0 |
| Kellar | 1 | 13 | 13 | 0 |
| Young | 1 | 8 | 8 | 0 |
| Craig | 1 | 0 | 0 | 0 |

### PASSING – PUNTING – KICKING

| PASSING | Att. | Comp. | % | Yds. | Yd./Att. | TD | Int.–% | RK |
|---|---|---|---|---|---|---|---|---|
| Tarkenton | 572 | 345 | 60 | 3468 | 6.1 | 25 | 32– 6 | 4 |
| Kramer | 16 | 5 | 31 | 50 | 3.1 | 0 | 1– 6 | |
| Lee | 4 | 2 | 50 | 10 | 2.5 | 0 | 1– 25 | |

| PUNTING | No. | Avg. |
|---|---|---|
| Coleman | 51 | 39.0 |

| KICKING | XP | Att. | % | FG | Att. | % |
|---|---|---|---|---|---|---|
| Danmeier | 36 | 37 | 97 | 12 | 19 | 63 |

## GREEN BAY PACKERS

### RUSHING

| Last Name | No. | Yds. | Avg. | TD |
|---|---|---|---|---|
| Middleton | 284 | 1116 | 3.9 | 11 |
| Smith | 154 | 567 | 3.7 | 4 |
| Culbreath | 30 | 92 | 3.1 | 0 |
| Whitehurst | 28 | 67 | 2.4 | 1 |
| Simpson | 27 | 58 | 2.1 | 0 |
| Landers | 7 | 40 | 5.7 | 0 |
| B. Douglass | 4 | 27 | 6.8 | 0 |
| Thompson | 4 | 25 | 6.3 | 0 |
| Torkelson | 6 | 18 | 3.0 | 0 |
| Lofton | 3 | 13 | 4.3 | 0 |
| Beverly | 1 | 0 | 0.0 | 0 |
| Sproul | 2 | 0 | 0.0 | 0 |

### RECEIVING

| Last Name | No. | Yds. | Avg. | TD |
|---|---|---|---|---|
| Lofton | 46 | 818 | 18 | 6 |
| Smith | 37 | 256 | 7 | 0 |
| Middleton | 34 | 332 | 10 | 1 |
| Thompson | 26 | 527 | 20 | 2 |
| McGeorge | 23 | 247 | 11 | 1 |
| Culbreath | 7 | 78 | 11 | 0 |
| Odom | 4 | 60 | 15 | 1 |
| Torkelson | 2 | 36 | 18 | 0 |
| Simpson | 1 | 4 | 4 | 0 |

### PUNT RETURNS

| Last Name | No. | Yds. | Avg. | TD |
|---|---|---|---|---|
| Odom | 33 | 298 | 9 | 0 |
| Gray | 11 | 95 | 9 | 0 |
| Sampson | 1 | 0 | 0 | 0 |
| Tullis | 1 | 0 | 0 | 0 |

### KICKOFF RETURNS

| Last Name | No. | Yds. | Avg. | TD |
|---|---|---|---|---|
| Odom | 25 | 677 | 27 | 1 |
| Thompson | 6 | 124 | 21 | 0 |
| Wagner | 6 | 84 | 14 | 0 |
| Culbreath | 4 | 58 | 15 | 0 |
| Hood | 3 | 74 | 25 | 0 |
| Sampson | 1 | 23 | 23 | 0 |
| Middleton | 1 | 22 | 22 | 0 |
| E. Johnson | 1 | 14 | 14 | 0 |
| Gueno | 1 | 9 | 9 | 0 |
| Landers | 1 | 0 | 0 | 0 |
| Lofton | 1 | 0 | 0 | 0 |
| McGeorge | 1 | 0 | 0 | 0 |
| Smith | 1 | 0 | 0 | 0 |

### PASSING – PUNTING – KICKING

| PASSING | Att. | Comp. | % | Yds. | Yd./Att. | TD | Int.–% | RK |
|---|---|---|---|---|---|---|---|---|
| Whitehurst | 328 | 168 | 51 | 2093 | 6.4 | 10 | 17– 5 | 10 |
| Sproul | 13 | 5 | 39 | 87 | 6.7 | 0 | 0– 0 | |
| B. Douglass | 12 | 5 | 42 | 90 | 7.5 | 1 | 1– 8 | |
| Beverly | 2 | 2 | 100 | 88 | 44.0 | 0 | 0– 0 | |
| Lofton | 2 | 0 | 0 | 0 | 0.0 | 0 | 0– 0 | |

| PUNTING | No. | Avg. |
|---|---|---|
| Beverly | 106 | 35.5 |

| KICKING | XP | Att. | % | FG | Att. | % |
|---|---|---|---|---|---|---|
| Marcol | 30 | 30 | 100 | 11 | 19 | 58 |

## DETROIT LIONS

### RUSHING

| Last Name | No. | Yds. | Avg. | TD |
|---|---|---|---|---|
| Bussey | 225 | 924 | 4.1 | 5 |
| King | 155 | 660 | 4.3 | 4 |
| Gaines | 54 | 178 | 3.3 | 1 |
| Kane | 44 | 153 | 3.5 | 2 |
| Danielson | 22 | 93 | 4.2 | 0 |
| Scott | 4 | 53 | 13.3 | 0 |
| Landry | 5 | 29 | 5.8 | 0 |
| O'Neil | 1 | 25 | 25.0 | 0 |
| Hill | 3 | 12 | 4.0 | 0 |
| Blue | 5 | 9 | 1.8 | 0 |
| Daykin | 1 | 8 | 8.0 | 0 |
| L. Thompson | 1 | 7 | 7.0 | 0 |
| J. Thompson | 2 | 7 | 3.5 | 0 |
| Bolton | 2 | 5 | 2.5 | 0 |
| Reed | 1 | 0 | 0.0 | 0 |

### RECEIVING

| Last Name | No. | Yds. | Avg. | TD |
|---|---|---|---|---|
| Hill | 53 | 633 | 12 | 4 |
| King | 48 | 396 | 8 | 2 |
| Scott | 37 | 564 | 15 | 2 |
| Blue | 31 | 350 | 11 | 2 |
| Bussey | 31 | 275 | 9 | 1 |
| J. Thompson | 18 | 175 | 10 | 4 |
| Kane | 16 | 161 | 10 | 0 |
| L. Thompson | 10 | 167 | 17 | 4 |
| Gaines | 2 | 16 | 8 | 0 |
| Jarvis | 1 | 9 | 9 | 0 |

### PUNT RETURNS

| Last Name | No. | Yds. | Avg. | TD |
|---|---|---|---|---|
| J. Thompson | 16 | 161 | 10 | 0 |
| Scott | 8 | 55 | 7 | 0 |
| Blue | 7 | 59 | 8 | 0 |
| L. Thompson | 3 | 19 | 6 | 0 |
| Hunter | 2 | 21 | 11 | 0 |
| Williams | 1 | 1 | 1 | 0 |

### KICKOFF RETURNS

| Last Name | No. | Yds. | Avg. | TD |
|---|---|---|---|---|
| J. Thompson | 14 | 346 | 25 | 0 |
| L. Thompson | 8 | 207 | 26 | 0 |
| Kane | 8 | 156 | 20 | 0 |
| Blue | 7 | 170 | 24 | 0 |
| Scott | 3 | 72 | 24 | 0 |
| Callicutt | 2 | 12 | 6 | 0 |
| Hunter | 1 | 21 | 21 | 0 |
| McGee | 1 | 0 | 0 | 0 |

### PASSING – PUNTING – KICKING

| PASSING | Att. | Comp. | % | Yds. | Yd./Att. | TD | Int.–% | RK |
|---|---|---|---|---|---|---|---|---|
| Danielson | 351 | 199 | 57 | 2294 | 6.5 | 18 | 17– 5 | 3 |
| Landry | 77 | 48 | 62 | 452 | 5.9 | 1 | 1– 1 | |
| Skladany | 1 | 0 | 0 | 0 | 0.0 | 0 | 0– 0 | |

| PUNTING | No. | Avg. |
|---|---|---|
| Skladany | 86 | 42.5 |

| KICKING | XP | Att. | % | FG | Att. | % |
|---|---|---|---|---|---|---|
| Ricardo | 32 | 33 | 97 | 20 | 28 | 71 |

## CHICAGO BEARS

### RUSHING

| Last Name | No. | Yds. | Avg. | TD |
|---|---|---|---|---|
| Payton | 333 | 1395 | 4.2 | 11 |
| Harper | 240 | 992 | 4.1 | 6 |
| Avellini | 34 | 54 | 1.6 | 2 |
| Phipps | 13 | 34 | 2.6 | 0 |
| Evans | 6 | 23 | 3.8 | 0 |
| Earl | 3 | 17 | 5.7 | 0 |
| Best | 2 | 11 | 5.5 | 0 |
| Parsons | 1 | 0 | 0.0 | 0 |
| Baschnagel | 2 | 0 | 0.0 | 0 |

### RECEIVING

| Last Name | No. | Yds. | Avg. | TD |
|---|---|---|---|---|
| Payton | 50 | 480 | 10 | 0 |
| Harper | 43 | 340 | 8 | 2 |
| Scott | 42 | 759 | 18 | 5 |
| Richards | 28 | 381 | 14 | 0 |
| Latta | 15 | 159 | 11 | 0 |
| Schubert | 4 | 51 | 13 | 0 |
| Rather | 2 | 55 | 28 | 0 |
| Baschnagel | 2 | 29 | 15 | 0 |
| Cobb | 1 | 7 | 7 | 0 |
| Earl | 1 | 1 | 1 | 0 |

### PUNT RETURNS

| Last Name | No. | Yds. | Avg. | TD |
|---|---|---|---|---|
| Schubert | 27 | 229 | 9 | 1 |
| Livers | 10 | 31 | 3 | 0 |
| Walterscheid | 3 | 24 | 8 | 0 |
| Baschnagel | 1 | 2 | 2 | 0 |

### KICKOFF RETURNS

| Last Name | No. | Yds. | Avg. | TD |
|---|---|---|---|---|
| Baschnagel | 20 | 455 | 23 | 0 |
| Walterscheid | 11 | 335 | 31 | 0 |
| Gaines | 10 | 240 | 24 | 0 |
| Morgan | 5 | 110 | 22 | 0 |
| Schubert | 4 | 80 | 20 | 0 |
| Earl | 3 | 48 | 16 | 0 |
| Skibinski | 3 | 36 | 12 | 0 |
| Spivey | 2 | 34 | 17 | 0 |
| Latta | 2 | 14 | 7 | 0 |
| Muckensturm | 1 | 6 | 6 | 0 |

### PASSING – PUNTING – KICKING

| PASSING | Att. | Comp. | % | Yds. | Yd./Att. | TD | Int.–% | RK |
|---|---|---|---|---|---|---|---|---|
| Avellini | 264 | 141 | 53 | 1718 | 6.5 | 5 | 16– 6 | 11 |
| Phipps | 83 | 44 | 53 | 465 | 5.6 | 2 | 10– 12 | |
| Evans | 3 | 1 | 33 | 38 | 12.7 | 0 | 1– 33 | |
| Harper | 1 | 0 | 0 | 0 | 0.0 | 0 | 0– 0 | |
| Parsons | 1 | 0 | 0 | 0 | 0.0 | 0 | 0– 0 | |

| PUNTING | No. | Avg. |
|---|---|---|
| Parsons | 96 | 37.0 |

| KICKING | XP | Att. | % | FG | Att. | % |
|---|---|---|---|---|---|---|
| Thomas | 26 | 28 | 93 | 17 | 22 | 77 |

## TAMPA BAY BUCCANEERS

### RUSHING

| Last Name | No. | Yds. | Avg. | TD |
|---|---|---|---|---|
| Bell | 185 | 679 | 3.7 | 6 |
| Davis | 97 | 370 | 3.8 | 3 |
| DuBose | 93 | 358 | 3.8 | 4 |
| Carter | 81 | 275 | 3.4 | 1 |
| Rae | 20 | 186 | 9.3 | 0 |
| Ragsdale | 25 | 121 | 4.8 | 1 |
| C. White | 11 | 42 | 3.8 | 0 |
| Mucker | 5 | 35 | 7.0 | 0 |
| Williams | 27 | 23 | 0.9 | 1 |
| Huff | 3 | 10 | 3.3 | 0 |
| Green | 1 | 0 | 0.0 | 0 |
| Giles | 1 | −1 | −1.0 | 0 |

### RECEIVING

| Last Name | No. | Yds. | Avg. | TD |
|---|---|---|---|---|
| Owens | 32 | 640 | 20 | 5 |
| Giles | 23 | 324 | 14 | 2 |
| Carter | 19 | 139 | 7 | 0 |
| Bell | 15 | 122 | 8 | 0 |
| O'Bradovich | 14 | 219 | 16 | 3 |
| Grant | 14 | 204 | 15 | 0 |
| Mucker | 13 | 271 | 21 | 0 |
| McKay | 9 | 166 | 18 | 1 |
| Hagins | 6 | 65 | 11 | 0 |
| Davis | 5 | 13 | 3 | 0 |
| Ragsdale | 3 | 41 | 14 | 1 |
| C. White | 2 | 31 | 16 | 0 |
| Reece | 1 | 25 | 25 | 0 |
| DuBose | 1 | 3 | 3 | 0 |

### PUNT RETURNS

| Last Name | No. | Yds. | Avg. | TD |
|---|---|---|---|---|
| Reece | 44 | 393 | 9 | 0 |
| Mucker | 7 | 49 | 7 | 0 |
| Cotney | 5 | 38 | 8 | 0 |
| Hagins | 4 | 23 | 6 | 0 |
| C. Brown | 2 | 9 | 5 | 0 |

### KICKOFF RETURNS

| Last Name | No. | Yds. | Avg. | TD |
|---|---|---|---|---|
| Ragsdale | 24 | 555 | 23 | 0 |
| Reece | 11 | 240 | 22 | 0 |
| Carter | 6 | 97 | 16 | 0 |
| Giles | 5 | 60 | 12 | 0 |
| Hagins | 4 | 69 | 17 | 0 |
| O'Bradovich | 3 | 48 | 16 | 0 |
| Mucker | 2 | 9 | 5 | 0 |

### PASSING – PUNTING – KICKING

| PASSING | Att. | Comp. | % | Yds. | Yd./Att. | TD | Int.–% | RK |
|---|---|---|---|---|---|---|---|---|
| Williams | 194 | 73 | 38 | 1170 | 6.0 | 7 | 8– 4 | 12 |
| Rae | 118 | 57 | 48 | 705 | 6.0 | 4 | 7– 6 | |
| Huff | 36 | 15 | 42 | 169 | 4.7 | 1 | 3– 8 | |
| Carter | 5 | 2 | 40 | 87 | 17.4 | 0 | 0– 0 | |
| Boryla | 5 | 2 | 40 | 15 | 3.0 | 0 | 0– 0 | |
| Green | 3 | 2 | 67 | 25 | 8.3 | 0 | 0– 0 | |

| PUNTING | No. | Avg. |
|---|---|---|
| Green | 100 | 40.9 |

| KICKING | XP | Att. | % | FG | Att. | % |
|---|---|---|---|---|---|---|
| O'Donohue | 25 | 29 | 86 | 13 | 23 | 57 |

## LOS ANGELES RAMS 12-4-0 Ray Malavasi

**Scores of Each Game**

| | | |
|---|---|---|
| 16 | Philadelphia | 14 |
| 10 | ATLANTA | 0 |
| 27 | DALLAS | 14 |
| 10 | Houston | 6 |
| 26 | New Orleans | 20 |
| 27 | SAN FRANCISCO | 10 |
| 34 | Minnesota | 17 |
| 3 | NEW ORLEANS | 10 |
| 7 | Atlanta | 15 |
| 26 | TAMPA BAY | 23 |
| 10 | PITTSBURGH | 7 |
| 31 | San Francisco | 28 |
| 19 | Cleveland | 30 |
| 20 | N.Y. Giants | 17 |
| 19 | CINCINNATI | 20 |
| 31 | GREEN BAY | 14 |

| Use Name | Pos. | Hgt. | Wgt. | Age | Int. | Pts. |
|---|---|---|---|---|---|---|
| Doug France | OT | 6'5" | 272 | 25 | | |
| Jackie Slater | OT-OG | 6'4" | 270 | 24 | | |
| John Williams | OT | 6'3" | 265 | 32 | | |
| Ed Fulton | OG | 6'3" | 250 | 23 | | |
| Dennis Harrah | OG | 6'5" | 257 | 25 | | |
| Tom Mack | OG | 6'3" | 250 | 34 | | |
| Dan Ryczek | C | 6'3" | 250 | 29 | | |
| Rich Saul | C | 6'3" | 250 | 30 | | |
| Doug Smith | C-OG | 6'3" | 250 | 21 | | |
| Reggie Doss | DE | 6'4" | 267 | 21 | | |
| Fred Dryer | DE | 6'6" | 240 | 32 | | |
| Jack Youngblood | DE | 6'4" | 242 | 28 | | |
| Larry Brooks | DT | 6'3" | 255 | 28 | | |
| Mike Fanning | DT | 6'6" | 260 | 25 | | |
| Cody Jones | DT | 6'5" | 240 | 27 | | |
| Bob Brudzinski | LB | 6'4" | 231 | 23 | 1 | 6 |
| Carl Ekern | LB | 6'3" | 220 | 24 | | |
| Kevin McLain | LB | 6'2" | 227 | 23 | | |
| Jack Reynolds | LB | 6'1" | 232 | 30 | | |
| Isiah Robertson | LB | 6'3" | 225 | 29 | | 6 |
| Jim Youngblood | LB | 6'3" | 239 | 28 | 2 | |
| Eddie Brown | DB | 5'11" | 190 | 26 | | |
| Nolan Cromwell | DB | 6'1" | 197 | 23 | 1 | 12 |
| Dave Elmendorf | DB | 6'1" | 195 | 29 | 3 | |
| Dwayne O'Steen | DB | 6'1" | 190 | 23 | | |
| Rod Perry | DB | 5'9" | 170 | 24 | 8 | 18 |
| Bill Simpson | DB | 6'1" | 180 | 26 | 5 | |
| Pat Thomas | DB | 5'9" | 180 | 24 | 8 | 6 |
| Jackie Wallace | DB | 6'3" | 198 | 27 | | |
| Vince Ferragamo | QB | 6'3" | 208 | 24 | | |
| Pat Haden | QB | 5'11" | 182 | 25 | | |
| John Cappelletti | HB | 6'1" | 220 | 26 | | 24 |
| Jerry Latin (from St.L) | HB | 5'10" | 186 | 25 | | |
| Larry Marshall (from KC) | HB | 5'10" | 195 | 28 | | |
| Lawrence McCutcheon | HB | 6'1" | 205 | 28 | | 12 |
| Wendell Tyler | HB | 5'10" | 188 | 23 | | |
| Cullen Bryant | FB | 6'1" | 234 | 27 | | 42 |
| Jim Jodat | FB | 5'11" | 210 | 24 | | |
| Rod Phillips | FB | 6' | 220 | 25 | | |
| Preston Dennard | WR | 6'1" | 185 | 22 | | |
| Ron Jessie | WR | 6' | 185 | 30 | | 24 |
| Willie Miller | WR | 5'9" | 172 | 31 | | 30 |
| Dwight Scales | WR | 6'2" | 170 | 25 | | 6 |
| Ron Smith | WR | 6' | 185 | 21 | | |
| Billy Waddy | WR | 5'11" | 185 | 24 | | 6 |
| Terry Nelson | TE | 6'2" | 230 | 27 | | 6 |
| Charlie Young | TE | 6'4" | 235 | 27 | | |
| Frank Corral | K | 6'2" | 220 | 23 | | 118 |
| Glenn Walker | K | 6'1" | 210 | 26 | | |

## ATLANTA FALCONS 9-7-0 Leeman Bennett

**Scores of Each Game**

| | | |
|---|---|---|
| 20 | HOUSTON | 14 |
| 0 | Los Angeles | 10 |
| 16 | CLEVELAND | 24 |
| 9 | Tampa Bay | 14 |
| 23 | N.Y. GIANTS | 20 |
| 7 | Pittsburgh | 31 |
| 14 | DETROIT | 0 |
| 20 | San Francisco | 17 |
| 15 | LOS ANGELES | 7 |
| 21 | SAN FRANCISCO | 10 |
| 20 | New Orleans | 17 |
| 7 | Chicago | 13 |
| 20 | NEW ORLEANS | 17 |
| 7 | Cincinnati | 37 |
| 20 | WASHINGTON | 17 |
| 21 | St. Louis | 42 |

| Use Name | Pos. | Hgt. | Wgt. | Age | Int. | Pts. |
|---|---|---|---|---|---|---|
| Warren Bryant | OT | 6'6" | 270 | 22 | | |
| Mike Kenn | OT | 6'6" | 257 | 22 | | |
| Phil McKinnely | OT-OG | 6'4" | 248 | 24 | | |
| Marv Montgomery | OT | 6'6" | 255 | 30 | | |
| Dave Scott | OG | 6'4" | 285 | 24 | | |
| R.C. Thielemann | OG | 6'4" | 247 | 23 | | |
| Paul Ryczek | C | 6'2" | 230 | 26 | | |
| Jeff Van Note | C | 6'2" | 247 | 32 | | |
| Edgar Fields | DE-DT | 6'2" | 255 | 24 | | |
| Claude Humphrey | DE | 6'5" | 265 | 34 | | |
| Jeff Merrow | DE | 6'4" | 230 | 25 | | |
| Jeff Yeates | DE | 6'3" | 248 | 27 | | |
| Jim Bailey | DT | 6'5" | 260 | 30 | | |
| Wilson Faumuina | DT | 6'5" | 275 | 24 | 1 | |
| Mike Lewis | DT | 6'3" | 261 | 29 | | |
| Greg Brezina | LB | 6'1" | 221 | 32 | | |
| Ron McCartney | LB | 6'1" | 220 | 24 | | |
| Dewey McClain | LB | 6'3" | 236 | 24 | | |
| Fulton Kuykendall | LB | 6'5" | 225 | 25 | | |
| Ralph Ortega | LB | 6'2" | 220 | 25 | | |
| Robert Pennywell | LB | 6'1" | 222 | 23 | | |
| Steve Stewart | LB | 6'2" | 217 | 22 | | |
| Garth Ten Napel | LB | 6'1" | 215 | 24 | | |
| Rick Byas | DB | 5'9" | 180 | 27 | 2 | 6 |
| Ray Easterling | DB | 6' | 192 | 28 | 1 | |
| Bob Glazebrook | DB | 6'1" | 200 | 22 | | |
| Rolland Lawrence | DB | 5'10" | 179 | 27 | 6 | |
| Ernie Jackson | DB | 5'10" | 176 | 28 | | |
| Tom Moriarty | DB | 6' | 185 | 25 | | 6 |
| Tom Pridemore | DB | 5'10" | 186 | 22 | 1 | |
| Frank Reed | DB | 5'11" | 193 | 24 | 1 | |
| Jim Stienke | DB | 5'11" | 182 | 27 | | |
| Steve Bartkowski | QB | 6'4" | 213 | 25 | | 12 |
| Scott Hunter | QB | 6'2" | 205 | 30 | | |
| June Jones | QB | 6'4" | 200 | 25 | | |
| Bubba Bean | HB-FB | 5'11" | 195 | 24 | | 24 |
| Mike Esposito | HB | 6'" | 183 | 25 | | |
| Ricky Patton | HB | 5'11" | 185 | 24 | | 12 |
| Ray Strong | HB | 5'9" | 184 | 22 | | 12 |
| George Franklin | FB | 6'3" | 226 | 24 | | |
| Haskel Stanback | FB | 6' | 210 | 26 | | 30 |
| Wallace Francis | WR | 5'11" | 190 | 26 | | 18 |
| Alfred Jackson | WR | 5'11" | 176 | 23 | | 12 |
| Al Jenkins | WR | 5'10" | 172 | 26 | | |
| Dennis Pearson | WR | 5'11" | 177 | 23 | | 6 |
| Billy Ryckman | WR | 5'11" | 172 | 23 | | 12 |
| Lewis Gilbert | TE | 6'4" | 225 | 22 | | |
| Jim Mitchell | TE | 6'2" | 236 | 30 | | 12 |
| Ken Moore | TE | 6'4" | 232 | 24 | | |
| James Wright | TE | 6'3" | 240 | 22 | | |
| John James | K | 6'2" | 200 | 29 | | |
| Tim Mazzetti | K | 6'1" | 175 | 22 | | 57 |
| Fred Steinfort | K | 5'11" | 180 | 26 | | 17 |

Brent Adams-Knee Injury
Andy Spiva-Knee Injury

## NEW ORLEANS SAINTS 7-9-0 Dick Nolan

**Scores of Each Game**

| | | |
|---|---|---|
| 31 | MINNESOTA | 24 |
| 17 | Green Bay | 28 |
| 17 | PHILADELPHIA | 24 |
| 20 | Cincinnati | 18 |
| 20 | LOS ANGELES | 26 |
| 16 | CLEVELAND | 24 |
| 14 | San Francisco | 7 |
| 7 | Los Angeles | 3 |
| 28 | N.Y. GIANTS | 17 |
| 14 | Pittsburgh | 20 |
| 17 | ATLANTA | 20 |
| 7 | Dallas | 27 |
| 17 | Atlanta | 20 |
| 24 | SAN FRANCISCO | 13 |
| 12 | HOUSTON | 17 |
| 17 | Tampa Bay | 10 |

| Use Name | Pos. | Hgt. | Wgt. | Age | Int. | Pts. |
|---|---|---|---|---|---|---|
| Kevin Hunt | OT | 6'5" | 260 | 29 | | |
| Mark Meseroll | OT | 6'5" | 270 | 23 | | |
| J.T. Taylor | OT | 6'4" | 265 | 22 | | |
| John Watson | OT | 6'4" | 244 | 29 | | |
| Robert Woods | OT | 6'4" | 259 | 28 | | |
| Gary Anderson (from DET) | OG | 6'3" | 250 | 22 | | |
| Conrad Dobler | OG | 6'3" | 255 | 27 | | |
| Dave Lafary | OG | 6'7" | 280 | 23 | | |
| Fred Sturt (from NE) | OG | 6'4" | 255 | 27 | | |
| Emanuel Sanders | OG | 6'1" | 248 | 27 | | |
| John Hill | C | 6'2" | 246 | 28 | | |
| Joe Campbell | DE | 6'6" | 254 | 23 | | |
| Elois Groom | DE | 6'4" | 250 | 25 | | |
| Richard Neal | DE | 6'3" | 263 | 30 | | |
| Don Reese | DE | 6'6" | 250 | 26 | | |
| Barry Bennett | DT | 6'5" | 257 | 22 | | |
| Mike Fultz | DT | 6'5" | 278 | 24 | | |
| Derland Moore | DT | 6'4" | 253 | 26 | | |
| Elex Price | DT | 6'3" | 265 | 28 | | |
| Ron Crosby | LB | 6'3" | 225 | 23 | | |
| Joe Federspiel | LB | 6'1" | 230 | 28 | 2 | |
| Pat Hughes | LB | 6'2" | 225 | 31 | 2 | |
| Rick Kingrea | LB | 6'1" | 222 | 29 | | |
| Jim Merlo | LB | 6'1" | 220 | 26 | | |
| Rusty Rebowe | LB | 5'10" | 213 | 22 | | |
| Floyd Rice | LB | 6'3" | 225 | 29 | | |
| Skip Vanderbundt | LB | 6'3" | 225 | 31 | | |
| Ray Brown | DB | 6'2" | 202 | 29 | 4 | |
| Clarence Chapman | DB | 5'10" | 185 | 24 | 2 | |
| Eric Felton | DB | 6'" | 200 | 22 | 1 | |
| Ralph McGill | DB | 5'11" | 180 | 28 | | |
| Tom Myers | DB | 5'11" | 180 | 27 | 6 | 6 |
| Don Schwartz | DB | 6'1" | 191 | 22 | | |
| Mo Spencer | DB | 6' | 176 | 26 | 4 | |
| Ed Burns | QB | 6'3" | 210 | 23 | | |
| Archie Manning | QB | 6'3" | 200 | 29 | | 6 |
| Bobby Scott | QB | 6'1" | 197 | 29 | | |
| Chuck Muncie | HB | 6'3" | 220 | 25 | | 42 |
| Mike Strachan | HB | 6' | 200 | 25 | | 24 |
| James Van Wagner | HB | 6' | 202 | 23 | | |
| Tony Galbreath | FB | 6'3" | 230 | 24 | | 42 |
| Jack Holmes | FB | 5'11" | 210 | 23 | | |
| Kim Jones | FB | 6'4" | 235 | 26 | | |
| Wes Chandler | WR | 5'11" | 186 | 22 | | 12 |
| Ike Harris | WR | 6'3" | 205 | 25 | | 24 |
| Richard Mauti | WR | 6' | 190 | 24 | | 12 |
| Tinker Owens | WR | 5'11" | 170 | 23 | | 12 |
| Henry Childs | TE | 6'2" | 220 | 27 | | 24 |
| Larry Hardy | TE | 6'3" | 230 | 22 | | |
| Brooks Williams | TE | 6'4" | 226 | 23 | | |
| Tom Blanchard | K | 6' | 180 | 30 | | |
| Tom Jurich | K | 5'10" | 185 | 22 | | 2 |
| John Leypoldt (from SEA) | K | 6'2" | 230 | 32 | | 10 |
| Steve Mike-Mayer | K | 6'" | 180 | 30 | | 36 |
| Richie Szaro | K | 5'11" | 204 | 30 | | 21 |

Ken Bordelon-Knee Injury
Jimmy Stewart-Knee Injury
Mike Watson-Knee Injury

## SAN FRANCISCO FORTY-NINERS 2-14-0 Pete McCulley, Fred O'Connor

**Scores of Each Game**

| | | |
|---|---|---|
| 7 | Cleveland | 24 |
| 13 | CHICAGO | 16 |
| 19 | Houston | 20 |
| 10 | N.Y. Giants | 27 |
| 28 | CINCINNATI | 12 |
| 10 | Los Angeles | 27 |
| 7 | NEW ORLEANS | 14 |
| 17 | ATLANTA | 20 |
| 20 | Washington | 38 |
| 10 | Atlanta | 21 |
| 10 | ST. LOUIS | 16 |
| 28 | LOS ANGELES | 31 |
| 7 | PITTSBURGH | 24 |
| 9 | New Orleans | 24 |
| 6 | TAMPA BAY | 3 |
| 14 | Detroit | 33 |

| Use Name | Pos. | Hgt. | Wgt. | Age | Int. | Pts. |
|---|---|---|---|---|---|---|
| John Ayers | OT-OG | 6'5" | 247 | 25 | | |
| Keith Fahnhorst | OT | 6'6" | 263 | 26 | | |
| Ron Singleton | OT | 6'7" | 275 | 26 | | |
| Walt Downing | OG | 6'3" | 254 | 22 | | |
| Ernie Hughes | OG | 6'3" | 250 | 23 | | |
| Steve Knutson | OG-OT | 6'3" | 254 | 26 | | |
| Randy Cross | C | 6'3" | 250 | 24 | | |
| Kyle Davis | C | 6'2" | 240 | 25 | | |
| Fred Quillan | C | 6'5" | 240 | 22 | | |
| Cedrick Hardman | DE | 6'4" | 244 | 29 | | |
| Willie McCray | DE | 6'5" | 234 | 25 | | |
| Archie Reese | DE | 6'3" | 263 | 22 | | |
| Cleveland Elam | DT-DE | 6'4" | 251 | 26 | | |
| Ed Galigher | DT | 6'4" | 247 | 27 | | |
| Jimmy Webb | DT | 6'5" | 245 | 26 | | |
| Mike Baldassin | LB | 6'1" | 218 | 23 | | |
| Ed Bradley | LB | 6'2" | 225 | 28 | | |
| Dan Bunz | LB | 6'4" | 230 | 22 | 1 | |
| Bruce Elia | LB | 6'1" | 220 | 25 | | |
| Joe Harris | LB | 6'1" | 225 | 25 | | |
| Dean Moore | LB | 6'2" | 210 | 23 | | |
| Mark Nichols | LB | 6'3" | 225 | 21 | 1 | |
| Chuck Crist | DB | 6'2" | 205 | 27 | 6 | |
| Bob Jury | DB | 6'1" | 188 | 22 | | |
| Anthony Leonard (to DET) | DB | 5'11" | 165 | 25 | 4 | 6 |
| Eddie Lewis | DB | 6' | 174 | 24 | 3 | |
| Wonder Monds | DB | 6'3" | 215 | 26 | | |
| Ricky Odom (from KC) | DB | 6' | 183 | 21 | 2 | |
| Vern Roberson | DB | 6'1" | 195 | 26 | 1 | |
| Bruce Threadgill | DB-QB | 6' | 190 | 22 | | |
| Scott Bull | QB | 6'5 | 211 | 25 | | 6 |
| Steve DeBerg | QB | 6'2 | 205 | 24 | | 6 |
| Paul Hofer | HB | 6' | 193 | 26 | | 42 |
| O.J. Simpson | HB | 6'2" | 212 | 31 | | 18 |
| Elliott Walker | HB | 5'11" | 193 | 21 | | |
| Dave Williams | HB | 6'2" | 200 | 24 | | 6 |
| Greg Boykin | FB | 6' | 225 | 24 | | |
| Earl Carr | FB | 6' | 224 | 23 | | |
| Bob Ferrell | FB | 6' | 219 | 25 | | 6 |
| Elmo Boyd (to GB) | WR | 6' | 164 | 24 | | 6 |
| Kenny Harrison | WR | 6' | 188 | 24 | | |
| Larry Jones | WR | 5'10" | 170 | 27 | | |
| Terry LeCount | WR | 5'10" | 172 | 22 | | |
| Mike Shumann | WR | 6'" | 175 | 22 | | |
| Freddie Solomon | WR-QB | 5'11" | 181 | 25 | | 18 |
| Jack Steptoe | WR | 6'1" | 175 | 22 | | 6 |
| Lon Boyett | TE | 6'6" | 240 | 24 | | |
| Rick DeSimone | TE | 6'3" | 213 | 22 | | |
| Ken McAfee | TE | 6'5" | 250 | 22 | | 6 |
| Paul Seal | TE | 6'4" | 223 | 26 | | 12 |
| Mike Connell | K | 6'1" | 200 | 22 | | |
| Ray Wersching | K | 5'11" | 210 | 28 | | 69 |

Jean Barrett-Foot Injury
Willie Harper-Knee Injury
Wilber Jackson-Knee Injury
Johnny Miller-Elbow Injury

## LOS ANGELES RAMS

### RUSHING

| Last Name | No. | Yds. | Avg. | TD |
|---|---|---|---|---|
| Bryant | 178 | 658 | 3.7 | 7 |
| Cappelletti | 174 | 604 | 3.5 | 3 |
| McCutcheon | 118 | 420 | 3.6 | 0 |
| Haden | 33 | 206 | 6.2 | 0 |
| Jodat | 26 | 100 | 3.8 | 0 |
| Phillips | 28 | 81 | 2.9 | 0 |
| Latin | 24 | 72 | 3.0 | 0 |
| Nelson | 6 | 67 | 11.2 | 1 |
| Tyler | 14 | 45 | 3.2 | 0 |
| Waddy | 5 | 31 | 6.2 | 0 |
| Cromwell | 1 | 16 | 16.0 | 1 |
| Ferragamo | 2 | 10 | 5.0 | 0 |
| Young | 2 | 6 | 3.0 | 0 |
| Miller | 1 | -7 | -7.0 | 0 |

### RECEIVING

| Last Name | No. | Yds. | Avg. | TD |
|---|---|---|---|---|
| Miller | 50 | 767 | 15 | 5 |
| Jessie | 49 | 752 | 15 | 4 |
| Cappelletti | 41 | 382 | 9 | 1 |
| Nelson | 23 | 344 | 15 | 0 |
| Young | 18 | 213 | 12 | 0 |
| Waddy | 14 | 258 | 18 | 1 |
| McCutcheon | 12 | 76 | 6 | 2 |
| Bryant | 8 | 76 | 10 | 0 |
| Phillips | 7 | 48 | 7 | 0 |
| Scales | 5 | 105 | 21 | 0 |
| Dennard | 3 | 35 | 12 | 0 |
| Jodat | 3 | 21 | 7 | 0 |
| Tyler | 2 | 17 | 9 | 0 |
| R. Smith | 1 | 15 | 15 | 0 |
| Latin | 1 | 3 | 3 | 0 |

### PUNT RETURNS

| Last Name | No. | Yds. | Avg. | TD |
|---|---|---|---|---|
| Wallace | 52 | 618 | 12 | 0 |
| Waddy | 10 | 45 | 5 | 0 |
| Marshall | 6 | 51 | 9 | 0 |
| Bryant | 3 | 27 | 9 | 0 |
| Brown | 1 | 13 | 13 | 0 |
| Cromwell | 1 | 8 | 8 | 0 |

### KICKOFF RETURNS

| Last Name | No. | Yds. | Avg. | TD |
|---|---|---|---|---|
| Latin | 24 | 515 | 22 | 0 |
| Jodat | 22 | 447 | 20 | 0 |
| Marshall | 9 | 223 | 25 | 0 |
| Phillips | 3 | 52 | 17 | 0 |
| Tyler | 2 | 31 | 16 | 0 |
| D. Smith | 1 | 8 | 8 | 0 |

### PASSING – PUNTING – KICKING

PASSING

| Last Name | Att. | Comp. | % | Yds. | Yd./Att. | TD | Int.–% | RK |
|---|---|---|---|---|---|---|---|---|
| Haden | 444 | 229 | 52 | 2995 | 6.8 | 13 | 19– 4 | 7 |
| Ferragamo | 20 | 7 | 35 | 114 | 5.7 | 0 | 2– 10 | |
| McCutcheon | 1 | 0 | 0 | 0 | 0.0 | 0 | 0– 0 | |
| Walker | 1 | 0 | 0 | 0 | 0.0 | 0 | 0– 0 | |

PUNTING

| Last Name | No. | Avg. |
|---|---|---|
| Walker | 83 | 37.0 |

KICKING

| Last Name | XP | Att. | % | FG | Att. | % |
|---|---|---|---|---|---|---|
| Corral | 31 | 33 | 94 | 29 | 43 | 67 |

## ATLANTA FALCONS

### RUSHING

| Last Name | No. | Yds. | Avg. | TD |
|---|---|---|---|---|
| Bean | 193 | 707 | 3.7 | 3 |
| Stanback | 188 | 588 | 3.1 | 5 |
| Patton | 68 | 206 | 3.0 | 1 |
| Strong | 30 | 99 | 3.3 | 2 |
| Bartkowski | 33 | 60 | 1.8 | 2 |
| Esposito | 7 | 21 | 3.0 | 0 |
| Pearson | 1 | 1 | 1.0 | 0 |
| Jones | 10 | -3 | -0.3 | 0 |
| Franklin | 1 | -8 | -8.0 | 0 |
| Francis | 2 | -11 | -5.5 | 0 |

### RECEIVING

| Last Name | No. | Yds. | Avg. | TD |
|---|---|---|---|---|
| Francis | 45 | 695 | 15 | 3 |
| Ryckman | 45 | 679 | 15 | 2 |
| Mitchell | 32 | 366 | 11 | 2 |
| Bean | 31 | 209 | 7 | 1 |
| A. Jackson | 26 | 526 | 20 | 2 |
| Stanback | 12 | 108 | 9 | 0 |
| Patton | 10 | 90 | 9 | 1 |
| Strong | 7 | 56 | 8 | 0 |
| Pearson | 5 | 71 | 14 | 0 |
| Esposito | 3 | 10 | 3 | 0 |
| Jenkins | 2 | 28 | 14 | 0 |
| Wright | 2 | 26 | 13 | 0 |
| Franklin | 1 | 19 | 19 | 0 |

### PUNT RETURNS

| Last Name | No. | Yds. | Avg. | TD |
|---|---|---|---|---|
| Ryckman | 28 | 227 | 8 | 0 |
| A. Jackson | 11 | 89 | 8 | 0 |
| Byas | 2 | 12 | 6 | 0 |
| Lawrence | 1 | 17 | 17 | 0 |

### KICKOFF RETURNS

| Last Name | No. | Yds. | Avg. | TD |
|---|---|---|---|---|
| Pearson | 25 | 662 | 27 | 1 |
| Franklin | 11 | 258 | 24 | 0 |
| A. Jackson | 11 | 225 | 21 | 0 |
| Pridemore | 4 | 71 | 18 | 0 |
| Strong | 3 | 50 | 17 | 0 |
| Wright | 2 | 31 | 16 | 0 |
| Fields | 2 | 21 | 11 | 0 |
| Mitchell | 1 | 14 | 14 | 0 |

### PASSING – PUNTING – KICKING

PASSING

| Last Name | Att. | Comp. | % | Yds. | Yd./Att. | TD | Int.–% | RK |
|---|---|---|---|---|---|---|---|---|
| Bartkowski | 369 | 187 | 51 | 2489 | 6.8 | 10 | 18– 5 | 9 |
| Jones | 79 | 34 | 43 | 394 | 5.0 | 1 | 4– 5 | |
| Bean | 1 | 0 | 0 | 0 | 0.0 | 0 | 0– 0 | |

PUNTING

| Last Name | No. | Avg. |
|---|---|---|
| James | 109 | 38.8 |

KICKING

| Last Name | XP | Att. | % | FG | Att. | % |
|---|---|---|---|---|---|---|
| Mazzetti | 18 | 18 | 100 | 13 | 16 | 81 |
| Steinfort | 8 | 9 | 89 | 3 | 10 | 30 |

## NEW ORLEANS SAINTS

### RUSHING

| Last Name | No. | Yds. | Avg. | TD |
|---|---|---|---|---|
| Galbreath | 186 | 635 | 3.4 | 5 |
| Muncie | 160 | 557 | 3.5 | 7 |
| Strachan | 108 | 388 | 3.6 | 4 |
| Manning | 38 | 202 | 5.3 | 1 |
| Jones | 9 | 31 | 3.4 | 0 |
| Harris | 2 | 22 | 11.0 | 0 |
| Chandler | 2 | 10 | 5.0 | 0 |
| Holmes | 2 | 4 | 2.0 | 0 |
| Scott | 1 | 0 | 0.0 | 0 |
| Blanchard | 2 | 0 | 0.0 | 0 |
| Childs | 2 | -4 | -2.0 | 0 |

### RECEIVING

| Last Name | No. | Yds. | Avg. | TD |
|---|---|---|---|---|
| Galbreath | 74 | 582 | 8 | 2 |
| Childs | 53 | 869 | 16 | 4 |
| Harris | 40 | 590 | 15 | 4 |
| Owens | 40 | 446 | 11 | 2 |
| Chandler | 35 | 472 | 14 | 2 |
| Muncie | 26 | 233 | 9 | 0 |
| Strachan | 10 | 51 | 5 | 0 |
| Mauti | 8 | 69 | 9 | 2 |
| Hardy | 5 | 131 | 26 | 1 |
| Jones | 2 | 10 | 5 | 0 |
| Van Wagner | 1 | -1 | -1 | 0 |

### PUNT RETURNS

| Last Name | No. | Yds. | Avg. | TD |
|---|---|---|---|---|
| Chandler | 34 | 233 | 7 | 0 |
| McGill | 1 | 5 | 5 | 0 |
| Schwartz | 1 | 4 | 4 | 0 |

### KICKOFF RETURNS

| Last Name | No. | Yds. | Avg. | TD |
|---|---|---|---|---|
| Chandler | 32 | 760 | 24 | 0 |
| Mauti | 17 | 388 | 23 | 0 |
| Chapman | 9 | 149 | 17 | 0 |
| Schwartz | 3 | 51 | 17 | 0 |
| Hardy | 2 | 3 | 2 | 0 |
| Holmes | 1 | 18 | 18 | 0 |
| Rice | 1 | 15 | 15 | 0 |

### PASSING – PUNTING – KICKING

PASSING

| Last Name | Att. | Comp. | % | Yds. | Yd./Att. | TD | Int.–% | RK |
|---|---|---|---|---|---|---|---|---|
| Manning | 471 | 291 | 62 | 3416 | 7.3 | 17 | 16– 3 | 2 |
| Scott | 5 | 3 | 60 | 36 | 7.2 | 0 | 0– 0 | |
| Harris | 1 | 0 | 0 | 0 | 0.0 | 0 | 0– 0 | |
| Muncie | 1 | 0 | 0 | 0 | 0.0 | 0 | 0– 0 | |
| Strachan | 1 | 0 | 0 | 0 | 0.0 | 0 | 0– 0 | |

PUNTING

| Last Name | No. | Avg. |
|---|---|---|
| Blanchard | 84 | 42.0 |

KICKING

| Last Name | XP | Att. | % | FG | Att. | % |
|---|---|---|---|---|---|---|
| Mike-Mayer | 18 | 18 | 100 | 6 | 13 | 46 |
| Szaro | 9 | 9 | 100 | 4 | 6 | 67 |
| Leypoldt | 4 | 5 | 80 | 2 | 3 | 67 |
| Jurich | 2 | 2 | 100 | 0 | 3 | 0 |

## SAN FRANCISCO FORTY-NINERS

### RUSHING

| Last Name | No. | Yds. | Avg. | TD |
|---|---|---|---|---|
| Simpson | 161 | 593 | 3.7 | 1 |
| Ferrell | 125 | 471 | 3.8 | 1 |
| Hofer | 121 | 465 | 3.8 | 7 |
| Boykin | 102 | 361 | 3.5 | 2 |
| Bull | 29 | 100 | 3.4 | 1 |
| Solomon | 14 | 70 | 5.0 | 1 |
| DeBerg | 15 | 20 | 1.3 | 1 |
| Williams | 15 | 18 | 1.2 | 0 |
| Carr | 1 | 2 | 2.0 | 0 |
| Elia | 1 | 0 | 0.0 | 0 |
| Jones | 1 | -9 | -9.0 | 0 |

### RECEIVING

| Last Name | No. | Yds. | Avg. | TD |
|---|---|---|---|---|
| Solomon | 31 | 458 | 15 | 2 |
| MacAfee | 22 | 205 | 9 | 1 |
| Seal | 21 | 370 | 18 | 2 |
| Simpson | 21 | 172 | 8 | 2 |
| Boykin | 19 | 112 | 6 | 0 |
| Harrison | 16 | 320 | 20 | 0 |
| Ferrell | 16 | 123 | 8 | 0 |
| Hofer | 12 | 170 | 14 | 0 |
| LeCount | 10 | 131 | 13 | 0 |
| Williams | 10 | 63 | 6 | 0 |
| Boyd | 9 | 115 | 13 | 1 |
| Steptoe | 2 | 46 | 23 | 1 |
| Jones | 1 | 21 | 21 | 0 |

### PUNT RETURNS

| Last Name | No. | Yds. | Avg. | TD |
|---|---|---|---|---|
| Leonard | 18 | 140 | 8 | 0 |
| Steptoe | 11 | 129 | 12 | 0 |
| Jones | 10 | 86 | 9 | 0 |
| Solomon | 9 | 35 | 4 | 0 |
| Shumann | 8 | 40 | 5 | 0 |
| Roberson | 1 | 7 | 7 | 0 |

### KICKOFF RETURNS

| Last Name | No. | Yds. | Avg. | TD |
|---|---|---|---|---|
| Williams | 34 | 745 | 22 | 1 |
| Hofer | 18 | 386 | 21 | 0 |
| LeCount | 5 | 91 | 18 | 0 |
| Hughes | 4 | 53 | 13 | 0 |
| Nichols | 3 | 39 | 13 | 0 |
| Boykin | 3 | 37 | 12 | 0 |
| Walker | 2 | 25 | 13 | 0 |
| Downing | 2 | 13 | 7 | 0 |
| Ferrell | 1 | 24 | 24 | 0 |
| Quillan | 1 | 8 | 8 | 0 |

### PASSING – PUNTING – KICKING

PASSING

| Last Name | Att. | Comp. | % | Yds. | Yd./Att. | TD | Int.–% | RK |
|---|---|---|---|---|---|---|---|---|
| DeBerg | 302 | 137 | 45 | 1570 | 5.2 | 8 | 22– 7 | 14 |
| Bull | 121 | 48 | 40 | 651 | 5.4 | 1 | 11– 9 | |
| Solomon | 10 | 5 | 50 | 85 | 8.5 | 0 | 1– 10 | |
| Threadgill | 2 | 0 | 0 | 0 | 0.0 | 0 | 2–100 | |

PUNTING

| Last Name | No. | Avg. |
|---|---|---|
| Connell | 96 | 37.3 |

KICKING

| Last Name | XP | Att. | % | FG | Att. | % |
|---|---|---|---|---|---|---|
| Wersching | 24 | 25 | 96 | 15 | 23 | 65 |

# 1978 A.F.C.  Rozelle's Second Wild Card

Pete Rozelle engineered changes in the league schedule and playoffs which would answer some critics and also equalize competition among the teams. Some fans had complained that teams had lumped several pre-season games in with regular season games in season ticket plans. Rozelle responded by increasing the regular schedule from 14 to 16 games. Despite the extra two games, the N.F.L. record book was not rewritten en masse, as some had feared. In addition to expanding the schedule, the league arranged for the weaker teams to face a larger proportion of losing teams and for the stronger teams to face a steady diet of tough opponents. Although some critics claimed that this plan rewarded failure and penalized success, rebuilding clubs found their road to the playoffs shortened by this arrangement. Rozelle also created a second "wild card" playoff berth in each division, thus keeping a fistful of teams in playoff contention well into December.

A secondary aspect of the increased schedule was the booking of several Thursday and Sunday night games. Fans were treated to extra editions of ABC'S "Monday Night Football" on these other nights of the week.

freshman year with 123 rushing yards against the Colts to put himself over the 1,000-yard mark.

**Baltimore Colts**—After three straight Eastern Division titles, the fall was far and the thud loud. Even before the season started, the Colt offense lost its key moving parts. Tight end Raymond Chester and wide receiver Freddie Scott were traded off during the summer, and after a bitter salary holdout, running back Lydell Mitchell was swapped to San Diego for Joe Washington. Worst of all, quarterback Bert Jones suffered a separated shoulder in a pre-season game. The season began in humiliating fashion, with losses to Dallas 38-0 and to Miami 42-0. When Jones came back for the seventh game, he promptly reinjured his shoulder. Three weeks later, he returned to engineer an upset over the Redskins. One week later, he led the Colts to a victory over Seattle but again was injured and went off for the year. Without him, the Colts lost their last five games. With the worst offense and defense in the A.F.C., the Colts were fortunate to win five games.

## EASTERN DIVISION

**New England Patriots**—The talented Patriots had always found a way to sabotage their Super Bowl plans. This year, they had to go to extreme lengths to accomplish it. When receiver Darryl Stingley was paralyzed in a pre-season game, the Pats sublimated their grief, obtained Harold Jackson from the Rams, and headed into the season undaunted. When Julius Adams was injured in the opening game, the team kept its spirit. The Pats won eight of their first ten games with a wide array of weapons. Although quarterback Steve Grogan was an erratic passer, he frequently hit tight end Russ Francis and wide receiver Stanley Morgan. The New England running game gained the most yardage in the league, with All-Pro lineman Leon Gray and John Hannah clearing the way for a large corps of powerful runners. The defense worked well together and enjoyed an All-Pro performance by Mike Haynes. Even the traditional Patriot late-season slump couldn't knock the Patriots out of the playoffs. What finally did break their momentum were the events of December 18, the final day of the season. Coach Chuck Fairbanks chose the afternoon of his team's Monday night game in Miami to inform them that he would be leaving the Pats after the season and joining the University of Colorado. Owner Billy Sullivan blew his top and, in a melodramatic scene worthy of daytime television, ordered Fairbanks out of the New England dressing room before the game. The Pats took a 23-3 beating that night and headed into the playoffs with their spirits dragging.

**Miami Dolphins**—The big winner of the O.J. Simpson trade was the Dolphins. When the 49ers obtained O.J. from the Bills, they sent incumbent halfback Del Williams to Miami. Instead of running behind the patchwork 49er line, Williams flourished behind the blocking of stars Bob Kuechenberg, Jim Langer, and Larry Little. The strong ground attack kept the Dolphins afloat even when Bob Griese missed the first five games with a knee injury. Although not as strong as the Miami teams of the early 1970's, this club won its last three games to earn a wild-card playoff berth.

**New York Jets**—A new Mad Bomber delighted New York rather than terrorized it. When quarterback Richard Todd broke a collarbone in the Jets' fourth game, seldom-used reserve Matt Robinson stepped into the lineup and excited fans with his willingness to throw the long pass. In Wesley Walker, he had one of the NFL's premier deep receivers. With runners Kevin Long and Scott Dierking blossoming behind a maturing line, the New York offense carried the surprising Jets into playoff contention. The new 3-4 defense was not yet of playoff caliber, but the special teams showcased stars in kicker Pat Leahy and returner Bruce Harper. The Jets were knocked out of the post-season picture only on December 10, when they staged a 24-point forth quarter to tie the game but lost to the Browns 37-34 in overtime.

**Buffalo Bills**—After their dismal 1977 campaign, the Bills started fresh in 1978. Chuck Knox took over as head coach with a track record of success with the Rams. Longtime meal ticket O.J. Simpson returned to his native West Coast, bringing to Buffalo a package of draft choices from San Francisco. Knox fielded a young defense with prominent rookie starters in Dee Hardison and Lucius Sanford. On offense, he gave QB Joe Ferguson a new target by obtaining veteran Frank Lewis from the Steelers. Rookie halfback Terry Miller stepped into O.J.'s shoes and, after a slow start, learned to use the blocking of linemen like Joe DeLamielleure to good advantage. On November 26, Miller ran for 208 yards in a victory over the Giants, and he capped his

## CENTRAL DIVISION

**Pittsburgh Steelers**—The Steelers lost one game to the Oilers, they lost one game to the Rams, and they spent the rest of the season demonstrating football excellence to the NFL. The Steel Curtain defense allowed the fewest points in the league. If Joe Greene was dropping off a bit because of age, L.C. Greenwood, Jam Ham, Jack Lambert, and Mel Blount still played peerless defense. The offense began with a sturdy line and had burly Franco Harris for its overland routes. QB Terry Bradshaw silenced his critics from the past by leading the NFL in touchdown passes, aided in this feat by superb wide receivers Lynn Swann and John Stallworth. The dynastic mentality of the Steelers kept them on top even while trading off Jim Clack, Ernie Holmes, Glen Edwards, and Frank Lewis and losing Bobby Walden to retirement and J.T. Thomas to a blood disorder. With the best record in the league, the Steelers charged into the playoffs with a 21-17 victory over Denver, their upcoming opponents, an encouraging tuneup.

**Houston Oilers**—The Oilers sent several draft picks and tight end Jimmie Giles to Tampa Bay for the Bucs' number one position in the college draft. Houston got a bargain, as they used the pick to acquire Earl Campbell, a 225-pound running back from the University of Texas. Often compared to Jimmy Brown as a package of speed and power, Campbell led the NFL in rushing and helped the Oilers into the playoffs for the first time in nine years. To go with his ball-control offense, coach Bum Phillips had his 3-4 defense in good shape, led by Elvin Bethea, Curly Culp, and Robert Brazile. A bread-and-butter team with little flash, the Oilers played 13 games decided by seven points or less. The most satisfying of their ten victories was a 24-17 triumph over the Steelers on Monday night, October 23. A loss to the Steelers on December 3 disappointed the Oilers, but a potential rematch in the playoffs loomed on the horizon.

**Cleveland Browns**—The first 240 minutes of Sam Rutigliano's tenure as head coach were glorious. The Browns won their first three games and battled the Steelers to a deadlock after four quarters on September 24. The Steelers won that game 15-9 on a razzle-dazzle pass play, and the Browns proceeded into a slump which dropped them back into the pack. Rutigliano took pride in his offense, with Brian Sipe finding Reggie Rucker and tight end Ozzie Newsome frequently with passes. Greg Pruitt ran for over 900 yards despite missing four games with a calf injury. The defense showcased an All-Pro safetyman in Thom Darden, but the pass rush fell shy of playoff quality.

**Cincinnati Bengals**—An 0-5 start prompted GM Paul Brown to fire his hand-picked coaching successor, Bill Johnson. Some critics claimed that Johnson suffered from excessive meddling by the front office, but a more telling problem was quarterback Ken Anderson's absence for the first four games with a broken finger. Under new coach Homer Rice, the Bengals lost their first three games but then began to show improvement. The Bengals ambushed Houston 28-13 on October 29 to break into the winning column. Rice's big change was scrapping the 3-4 defense which Johnson had installed at the start of the season. The new front four of Gary Burley, Wilson Whitley, Eddie Edwards, and rookie Ross Browner pressured quarterbacks into distraction the last leg of the season. The Bengals salvaged their pride with a closing rush, beating the Falcons, Rams, and cross-state rival Browns in their final three games. Old faces disappeared from the Bengal roster, as Tommy Casanova retired into the medical profession and Bob Trumpy retired into the broadcast booth.

FINAL TEAM STATISTICS

OFFENSE

| | BALT. | BUFF. | CIN. | CLEV. | DENV. | HOU. | K.C. | MIA. | N.E. | N.Y. J | OAK. | PIT. | S.D. | SEA. |
|---|---|---|---|---|---|---|---|---|---|---|---|---|---|---|
| FIRST DOWNS: | | | | | | | | | | | | | | |
| Total | 249 | 274 | 271 | 293 | 294 | 276 | 287 | 270 | 322 | 277 | 309 | 316 | 315 | **345** |
| by Rushing | 95 | 132 | 105 | 133 | 129 | 135 | 160 | 119 | **181** | 131 | 116 | 133 | 116 | 150 |
| by Passing | 124 | 113 | 141 | 130 | 137 | 119 | 98 | 135 | 125 | 128 | 164 | 149 | **171** | 156 |
| by Penalty | 30 | 29 | 25 | 30 | 28 | 22 | 29 | 16 | 16 | 18 | 29 | 34 | 28 | **39** |
| RUSHING: | | | | | | | | | | | | | | |
| Number | 532 | 556 | 526 | 559 | 601 | 603 | 663 | 548 | **671** | 562 | 577 | 641 | 590 | 561 |
| Yards | 2044 | 2381 | 2131 | 2488 | 2451 | 2476 | 2986 | 2366 | **3165** | 2250 | 2186 | 2297 | 2096 | 2394 |
| Average Yards | 3.8 | 4.3 | 4.1 | 4.5 | 4.1 | 4.1 | 4.5 | 4.3 | **4.7** | 4.0 | 3.8 | 3.6 | 3.6 | 4.3 |
| Touchdowns | 9 | 15 | 10 | 17 | 15 | 19 | 19 | 18 | **30** | 21 | 18 | 16 | 16 | 28 |
| PASSING: | | | | | | | | | | | | | | |
| Attempts | 383 | 388 | 470 | 442 | 391 | 373 | 370 | 379 | 390 | 388 | 433 | 380 | **477** | 467 |
| Completions | 202 | 203 | 250 | 236 | 217 | 201 | 204 | 226 | 196 | 193 | 251 | 212 | **271** | 261 |
| Completion Pct. | 52.7 | 52.3 | 53.2 | 53.4 | 55.5 | 53.9 | 55.1 | **59.6** | 50.3 | 49.7 | 58.0 | 55.8 | 56.8 | 55.9 |
| Passing Yards | 2543 | 2503 | 3039 | 3137 | 2710 | 2473 | 2032 | 2707 | 3006 | 2957 | 3095 | 2961 | **3566** | 3401 |
| Avg. Yds per Att. | 4.8 | 5.4 | 5.4 | 6.0 | 5.4 | 6.0 | 4.7 | 6.1 | **6.8** | 6.1 | 5.8 | 6.7 | 6.6 | 6.1 |
| Avg. Yds per Comp. | 12.6 | 12.3 | 12.2 | 13.3 | 12.5 | 12.3 | 10.0 | 12.0 | **15.3** | 15.3 | 12.3 | 14.0 | 13.2 | 13.0 |
| Times Tackled | 49 | 30 | 38 | 35 | 48 | **17** | 21 | 27 | 24 | 43 | 39 | 25 | 32 | 44 |
| Yds Lost Tackled | 480 | 254 | 298 | 278 | 332 | **135** | 198 | 238 | 206 | 350 | 368 | 262 | 191 | 284 |
| Net Yards | 2063 | 2249 | 2741 | 2859 | 2378 | 2338 | 1834 | 2469 | 2800 | 2607 | 2727 | 2699 | **3375** | 3117 |
| Touchdowns | 17 | 21 | 14 | 22 | 17 | 16 | 7 | 24 | 15 | 19 | 16 | **28** | 26 | 15 |
| Interceptions | 30 | 17 | 30 | 21 | 17 | 17 | **16** | 18 | 25 | 28 | 31 | 22 | 30 | 22 |
| Pic. Intercepted | 7.8 | 4.4 | 6.4 | 4.8 | 4.3 | 4.6 | **4.3** | 4.7 | 6.4 | 7.2 | 7.2 | 5.8 | 6.3 | 4.7 |
| PUNTS: | | | | | | | | | | | | | | |
| Number | 94 | 89 | 95 | 79 | **96** | 92 | 80 | 81 | 61 | 74 | 83 | 66 | 75 | 69 |
| Average | 37.4 | 37.9 | **42.4** | 39.1 | 36.4 | 38.5 | 40.6 | 40.3 | 35.0 | 40.1 | 41.7 | 40.0 | 36.3 | 36.4 |
| PUNT RETURNS: | | | | | | | | | | | | | | |
| Number | 35 | 40 | **59** | 39 | 51 | 46 | 45 | 41 | 47 | 33 | 47 | 58 | 57 | 40 |
| Yards | 219 | 375 | 264 | 317 | 582 | 416 | 488 | 341 | 520 | 413 | 310 | 451 | **590** | 342 |
| Average Yards | 6.3 | 9.4 | 4.5 | 8.1 | 11.4 | 9.0 | 10.8 | 8.3 | 11.1 | **12.5** | 6.6 | 7.8 | 10.4 | 8.6 |
| Touchdowns | 0 | **1** | 0 | 0 | **1** | 0 | 0 | 0 | 0 | **1** | 0 | 0 | 0 | 0 |
| KICK OFF RET.: | | | | | | | | | | | | | | |
| Number | **74** | 66 | 58 | 72 | 42 | 58 | 61 | 53 | 55 | 67 | 60 | 44 | 58 | 67 |
| Yards | 1648 | 1316 | 1164 | **1697** | 952 | 1304 | 1456 | 1132 | 1172 | 1509 | 1233 | 1043 | 1252 | 1510 |
| Average Yards | 22.3 | 19.9 | 20.1 | 23.6 | 22.7 | 22.5 | **23.9** | 21.4 | 21.3 | 22.5 | 20.6 | 23.7 | 21.6 | 22.5 |
| Touchdowns | **1** | **1** | 0 | 0 | 0 | 0 | 0 | 0 | 0 | 0 | 0 | **1** | 0 | 0 |
| INTERCEPT. RET.: | | | | | | | | | | | | | | |
| Number | 17 | 14 | 20 | 27 | 31 | 17 | 21 | **32** | 22 | 23 | 28 | 27 | 22 | 22 |
| Yards | 249 | 290 | 319 | 353 | 307 | 199 | 274 | **458** | 358 | 389 | 407 | 289 | 191 | 193 |
| Average Yards | 14.6 | **20.7** | 16.0 | 13.1 | 9.9 | 11.7 | 13.0 | 14.3 | 16.3 | 16.9 | 14.5 | 10.7 | 8.7 | 8.8 |
| Touchdowns | 2 | 1 | **3** | 1 | 1 | 0 | 0 | 2 | 1 | 1 | 1 | 0 | 2 | 1 |
| PENALTIES: | | | | | | | | | | | | | | |
| Number | 90 | 120 | 110 | 128 | 132 | 102 | 110 | **74** | 92 | 102 | 108 | 109 | 98 | 94 |
| Yards | 771 | 1103 | 956 | 1170 | 1092 | 833 | 1048 | **603** | 852 | 854 | 948 | 948 | 748 | 789 |
| FUMBLES: | | | | | | | | | | | | | | |
| Number | 38 | 34 | 36 | 50 | 28 | 35 | 32 | 24 | 35 | **22** | 27 | 35 | 37 | 36 |
| Number Lost | 17 | 17 | 19 | 29 | 17 | 21 | 18 | 12 | 21 | **9** | 12 | 17 | 21 | 19 |
| POINTS: | | | | | | | | | | | | | | |
| Total | 239 | 302 | 252 | 334 | 282 | 283 | 243 | **372** | 358 | 359 | 311 | 356 | 355 | 345 |
| PAT Attempts | 31 | 39 | 29 | 40 | 35 | 35 | 26 | 45 | **46** | 42 | 39 | 45 | 43 | 44 |
| PAT Made | 27 | 36 | 26 | 37 | 31 | 31 | 25 | 41 | 42 | 41 | 33 | **44** | 37 | 40 |
| FG Attempts | 17 | 13 | **30** | 28 | 22 | 18 | **30** | 23 | 24 | **30** | 20 | 26 | 22 | 21 |
| FG Made | 8 | 10 | 16 | 19 | 11 | 14 | 20 | 19 | 12 | **22** | 12 | 12 | 18 | 13 |
| Percent FG Made | 47.1 | 76.9 | 53.3 | 67.9 | 50.0 | 77.8 | 66.7 | **82.6** | 50.0 | 73.3 | 60.0 | 46.2 | 81.8 | 61.9 |
| Safeties | 1 | 1 | **2** | 0 | 1 | 0 | 1 | **2** | **2** | 0 | 1 | 0 | 0 | 1 |

DEFENSE

| | BALT. | BUFF. | CIN. | CLEV. | DENV. | HOU. | K.C. | MIA. | N.E. | N.Y. J | OAK. | PIT. | S.D. | SEA. |
|---|---|---|---|---|---|---|---|---|---|---|---|---|---|---|
| FIRST DOWNS: | | | | | | | | | | | | | | |
| Total | 291 | 305 | 269 | 329 | **251** | 292 | 284 | 298 | 258 | 324 | 299 | 265 | 273 | 331 |
| by Rushing | 153 | 171 | 121 | 116 | 106 | 120 | 138 | 120 | **100** | 157 | 125 | 106 | 114 | 153 |
| by Passing | 119 | **104** | 118 | 175 | 120 | 144 | 122 | 156 | 143 | 146 | 140 | 119 | 141 | 160 |
| by Penalty | 19 | 30 | 30 | 38 | 25 | 28 | 24 | 22 | **15** | 21 | 34 | 40 | 18 | 18 |
| RUSHING: | | | | | | | | | | | | | | |
| Number | 662 | 677 | 607 | 563 | 549 | 556 | 602 | 543 | 511 | 600 | 583 | 513 | **510** | 551 |
| Yards | 3010 | 3228 | 2396 | 2149 | 1979 | 2072 | 2384 | 2261 | 1852 | 2701 | 2183 | **1774** | 2208 | 2513 |
| Average Yards | 4.5 | 4.8 | 3.9 | 3.8 | 3.6 | 3.7 | 4.0 | 4.2 | 3.6 | 4.5 | 3.7 | **3.5** | 4.3 | 4.6 |
| Touchdowns | 21 | 23 | 16 | 19 | 12 | 14 | 21 | 15 | 14 | 20 | 15 | **11** | 12 | 20 |
| PASSING: | | | | | | | | | | | | | | |
| Attempts | 357 | **317** | 396 | 489 | 438 | 428 | 365 | 437 | 425 | 447 | 448 | 442 | 441 | 460 |
| Completions | 191 | **167** | 193 | 265 | 246 | 240 | 219 | 256 | 235 | 260 | 234 | 221 | 237 | 263 |
| Completion Pct. | 53.5 | 52.7 | **48.7** | 54.2 | 56.2 | 56.1 | 60.0 | 58.6 | 55.3 | 58.2 | 52.2 | 50.0 | 53.7 | 57.2 |
| Passing Yards | 3125 | **2156** | 2520 | 3435 | 2712 | 3125 | 2820 | 3251 | 3059 | 3052 | 2916 | 2755 | 2825 | 3225 |
| Avg. Yds per Att. | 7.5 | 5.8 | 5.2 | 6.2 | 5.3 | 6.1 | 6.6 | 6.1 | 6.0 | 6.0 | 5.7 | 4.9 | **4.8** | 6.2 |
| Avg. Yds per Comp. | 16.4 | 12.9 | 13.1 | 13.0 | **11.0** | 13.0 | 12.9 | 12.7 | 13.0 | 11.7 | 12.5 | 12.5 | 11.9 | 12.3 |
| Times Tackled | 30 | 22 | 33 | 31 | 30 | 37 | 29 | 41 | 35 | 22 | 29 | 44 | **54** | 25 |
| Yds Lost Tackled | 224 | 196 | 284 | 232 | 242 | 283 | 238 | 343 | 296 | 229 | 205 | 361 | **974** | 220 |
| Net Yards | 2901 | **1960** | 2236 | 3203 | 2470 | 2842 | 2582 | 2908 | 2763 | 2823 | 2711 | 2394 | 2351 | 3005 |
| Touchdowns | 29 | 20 | 14 | 20 | **9** | 17 | 17 | 15 | 21 | 21 | 17 | 10 | 23 | 21 |
| Interceptions | 17 | 14 | 20 | 27 | 31 | 17 | 21 | **32** | 22 | 23 | 28 | 27 | 22 | 22 |
| Pic. Intercepted | 4.8 | 4.4 | 5.1 | 5.5 | 7.1 | 4.0 | 5.8 | **7.3** | 5.8 | 5.1 | 6.3 | 6.1 | 5.0 | 4.8 |
| PUNTS: | | | | | | | | | | | | | | |
| Number | 80 | 71 | **108** | 82 | 88 | 81 | 76 | 74 | 78 | 70 | 90 | 82 | 99 | 67 |
| Average | **35.7** | 36.5 | 41.6 | 38.4 | 39.9 | 42.7 | 39.9 | 37.0 | 39.5 | 37.4 | 39.5 | 39.4 | 38.5 | 37.4 |
| PUNT RETURNS: | | | | | | | | | | | | | | |
| Number | 53 | 48 | 58 | 41 | 48 | 53 | 50 | 42 | **29** | 52 | 38 | 38 | 37 | 36 |
| Yards | 460 | 492 | 564 | 366 | **226** | 517 | 538 | 303 | 272 | 609 | 309 | 239 | 356 | 371 |
| Average Yards | 8.7 | 9.2 | 9.7 | 8.9 | **4.7** | 9.8 | 10.8 | 7.2 | 9.4 | 11.7 | 8.1 | 6.3 | 9.6 | 10.3 |
| Touchdowns | 0 | 1 | 0 | 0 | 0 | 1 | 0 | 0 | 0 | 0 | 0 | 0 | 1 | 0 |
| KICK OFF RET.: | | | | | | | | | | | | | | |
| Number | 52 | 58 | 49 | 72 | 52 | 61 | 54 | 70 | 69 | 64 | **51** | 60 | 69 | 66 |
| Yards | 1271 | 1191 | 1105 | 1469 | 1223 | 1360 | 1087 | 1469 | 1576 | 1417 | **992** | 1336 | 1457 | 1328 |
| Average Yards | 24.4 | 20.5 | 22.6 | 20.4 | 23.5 | 22.3 | 20.1 | 21.0 | 22.8 | 22.1 | **19.5** | 22.3 | 21.1 | 20.1 |
| Touchdowns | 1 | 0 | 0 | 1 | 0 | 0 | 0 | 0 | 1 | 0 | 0 | 0 | 0 | 1 |
| INTERCEPT. RET.: | | | | | | | | | | | | | | |
| Number | 30 | 17 | 30 | 21 | 17 | 17 | **16** | 18 | 25 | 28 | 31 | 22 | 30 | 22 |
| Yards | 529 | 219 | 211 | 343 | 195 | **174** | 209 | 224 | 252 | 470 | 374 | 212 | 470 | 300 |
| Average Yards | 17.6 | 12.9 | **7.0** | 16.3 | 11.5 | 10.2 | 13.1 | 12.4 | 10.1 | 16.8 | 12.1 | 9.6 | 15.7 | 13.6 |
| Touchdowns | 3 | 1 | 2 | 2 | 0 | 0 | 1 | 0 | 1 | 2 | 1 | 0 | 2 | 1 |
| PENALTIES: | | | | | | | | | | | | | | |
| Number | 114 | 98 | 123 | 131 | 114 | 99 | 99 | 99 | 81 | 98 | 93 | 109 | 99 | **125** |
| Yards | 1006 | 941 | 1074 | **1110** | 894 | 940 | 921 | 865 | 683 | 855 | 793 | 987 | 862 | 997 |
| FUMBLES: | | | | | | | | | | | | | | |
| Number | 36 | 27 | 36 | 35 | 27 | 28 | 30 | **37** | 34 | 34 | 29 | 33 | 32 | 34 |
| Number Lost | 20 | 16 | 17 | 18 | 13 | 17 | 14 | **21** | **21** | 17 | 15 | **21** | 16 | 17 |
| POINTS: | | | | | | | | | | | | | | |
| Total | 421 | 354 | 284 | 356 | 198 | 298 | 327 | 254 | 286 | 364 | 283 | **195** | 309 | 358 |
| PAT Attempts | 54 | 46 | 34 | 41 | **21** | 34 | 40 | 30 | 38 | 45 | 35 | 22 | 40 | 43 |
| PAT Made | 53 | 43 | 30 | 36 | **21** | 33 | 33 | 28 | 31 | 40 | 31 | **21** | 36 | 41 |
| FG Attempts | 24 | 21 | 23 | 29 | 27 | 32 | 18 | 21 | **19** | 24 | 17 | 26 | 22 | 27 |
| FG Made | 14 | 11 | 16 | 22 | 17 | 19 | 14 | 14 | **9** | 18 | 14 | 14 | 11 | 19 |
| Percent FG Made | 58.3 | 52.4 | 69.9 | 75.9 | 63.0 | 59.4 | 77.8 | 66.7 | **47.4** | 75.0 | 82.4 | 53.8 | 50.0 | 70.4 |
| Safeties | 1 | 1 | 1 | 1 | 0 | 2 | 0 | 2 | 0 | 0 | 0 | 0 | 0 | 1 |

## WESTERN DIVISION

**Denver Broncos**—The Orange Crush defense still came down hard enough on enemy offenses to boost the Broncos into first place. The fine-tuned unit, featuring Lyle Alzado, Randy Gradishar, Tom Jackson, Louis Wright, and Bill Thompson, allowed on average fewer than 13 points per game. The Denver offense had to work hard to score much more than that for the Broncos. Craig Morton's performance fell off from the heights of 1977, sharing some time at quarterback with Norris Weese and Craig Penrose. Nevertheless, with Riley Odoms and Haven Moses available as receivers and with six running backs getting substantial playing time, the Broncos went 7-1 in the Division and finished 10-6. The most explosive weapon for the Broncos was Rick Upchurch, who ran back kickoffs and punts with productive abandon. As the regular season ended, the most impressive statistic about the Broncos was that they had never lost two games in a row under the two-year reign of head coach Red Miller.

**Oakland Raiders**—Little cracks in the championship veneer of the Raiders led to their missing the playoffs for the first time in seven years. They lost both meetings with the Broncos, their main rival in the Division. With a playoff spot on the line, they went into a three game losing spin in November and December. The first of those losses was a 17-16 decision to Seattle in which an extra point was missed. The aging offensive line allowed more frequent sacks of QB Ken Stabler, and Stabler's aging arm went long less successfully and threw the most interceptions in the A.F.C. This list of horrors must not obscure the fact that the Raiders were still a winning team, although not a playoff team. Dave Casper excelled at tight end, Mark van Eeghen ran for over 1,000 yards, and rookie Art Whittington prospered at halfback after Clarence Davis and Terry Robiskie both went out with injuries. At the season's end, head coach John Madden resigned for health reasons, although sceptics looked to see if Dr. Al Davis had signed the prescription.

**San Diego Chargers**—Loaded with talent, the Chargers stumbled out to a 1-3 start, at which point head coach Tommy Prothro quit. Don Coryell, one-time coach at San Diego State and recently deposed choreographer of the St. Louis Cardinals offensive ballet, replaced Prothro. The team did not turn around immediately, but over the second half of the schedule, it roared to a 7-1 record and was considered the best team not to make the playoffs. As in St. Louis, Coryell cranked up an all-out passing attack. Dan Fouts had long distance targets in Charlie Joiner and rookie John Jefferson, and he could dump short passes to halfback Lydell Mitchell, a pre-season acquisition from the Colts. The pass rush by defensive linemen Fred Dean, Louie Kelcher, Gary Johnson, and Leroy Jones disrupted enemy passing attacks regularly. The Chargers left their calling card by ending the season with a 45-24 thrashing of the playoff-bound Oilers in Houston.

**Seattle Seahawks**—Finishing with a rush, the Seahawks amassed a winning record in their third year of operation. Coach Jack Patera didn't have a complete team of talented players, but he had enough pieces to make the Seahawks an exciting show. Quarterback Jim Zorn flung left-handed passes with a passion, making Steve Largent the A.F.C.'s leading receiver and leading his mates to several upsets. They beat the Vikings 29-28 on October 8 with an Efren Herrera field goal as time ran out. Two weeks later, they throttled the Raiders 27-7. Over the last five weeks, the Seahawks won four times, including another victory over the Raiders which severely wounded their playoff hopes. Relatively unnoticed in the aerial blitz was halfback David Sims' 15 touchdowns, the most in the league.

**Kansas City Chiefs**—After compiling the worst record in the N.F.L. in 1977, the Chiefs brought in Marv Levy to take charge of the rebuilding. Veteran players Ed Podolak, Willie Lanier, Jim Lynch, and Jerrell Wilson departed, taking with them past memories of Chief glory. Levy first restructured the defense, putting in a 3-4 system and installing high draft choices Art Still, Sylvester Hicks, and Gary Spani as starters. To help his young defense, Levy planned a ball-control offense which would run the ball endlessly. The wing-T formation he ordered used three running backs and only one wide receiver, and the Chiefs indeed lived and died with the run. A victory on opening day raised hopes prematurely, as six straight defeats followed. By late season, the Chiefs were ready for some moments of glory, whipping the Chargers 23-0 and beating Buffalo 14-10 the next week.

**NEW ENGLAND PATRIOTS** 11-5-0 Chuck Fairbanks, Ron Erhardt

| Scores of Each Game | | |
|---|---|---|
| 14 | WASHINGTON | 16 |
| 16 | St. Louis | 6 |
| 27 | BALTIMORE | 34 |
| 21 | Oakland | 14 |
| 28 | SAN DIEGO | 23 |
| 24 | PHILADELPHIA | 14 |
| 10 | Cincinnati | 7 |
| 33 | MIAMI | 24 |
| 55 | N.Y. JETS | 21 |
| 14 | Buffalo | 10 |
| 23 | HOUSTON | 26 |
| 19 | N.Y. Jets | 17 |
| 35 | Baltimore | 14 |
| 10 | Dallas | 17 |
| 26 | BUFFALO | 24 |
| 3 | Miami | 23 |

| Use Name | Pos. | Hgt. | Wgt. | Age | Int. | Pts. |
|---|---|---|---|---|---|---|
| Leon Gray | OT | 6'3" | 256 | 26 | | |
| Shelby Jordan | OT | 6'7" | 260 | 26 | | |
| Bob McKay | OT | 6'5" | 265 | 30 | | |
| Dwight Wheeler | OT | 6'3" | 255 | 23 | | |
| Sam Adams | OG | 6'3" | 260 | 29 | | |
| Bob Cryder | OG | 6'4" | 265 | 21 | | |
| Terry Falcon | OG | 6'3" | 260 | 23 | | |
| John Hannah | OG | 6'2" | 265 | 27 | | |
| Pete Brock | C | 6'5" | 260 | 24 | | |
| Bill Lenkaitis | C | 6'3" | 250 | 32 | | |
| Julius Adams | DE | 6'3" | 260 | 30 | | |
| Richard Bishop | DE-NT | 6'1" | 260 | 28 | | |
| Greg Boyd | DE | 6'6" | 265 | 25 | | |
| Mel Lunsford | DE | 6'3" | 250 | 28 | | |
| Tony McGee | DE | 6'4" | 245 | 29 | | |
| Greg Schaum | DE | 6'4" | 245 | 24 | | |
| Ray Hamilton | NT | 6'1" | 245 | 27 | | |
| Ernie Holmes | NT | 6'3" | 260 | 30 | | |

| Use Name | Pos. | Hgt. | Wgt. | Age | Int. | Pts. |
|---|---|---|---|---|---|---|
| Ray Costict | LB | 6' | 218 | 23 | | |
| Mike Hawkins | LB | 6'2" | 232 | 22 | | |
| Sam Hunt | LB | 6'1" | 240 | 27 | | |
| Steve King | LB | 6'4" | 230 | 27 | | |
| Merv Krakau (from BUF) | LB | 6'2" | 230 | 27 | | |
| Steve Nelson | LB | 6'2" | 230 | 27 | 5 | |
| Rod Shoate | LB | 6'1" | 211 | 25 | | |
| Steve Zabel | LB | 6'4" | 235 | 30 | 1 | |
| Doug Beaudoin | DB | 6'1" | 190 | 24 | 3 | |
| Sidney Brown | DB | 6' | 186 | 22 | | |
| Ray Clayborn | DB | 6'1" | 190 | 23 | 4 | |
| Dick Conn | DB | 6' | 180 | 27 | 1 | |
| Tim Fox | DB | 5'11" | 186 | 24 | 2 | |
| Mike Haynes | DB | 6'2" | 189 | 25 | 6 | 6 |
| Prentice McCray | DB | 6'1" | 187 | 27 | | |

Pete Cusick – Knee Injury
Jim Romaniszyn – Injury
Darryl Stingley – Spinal Injury

| Use Name | Pos. | Hgt. | Wgt. | Age | Int. | Pts. |
|---|---|---|---|---|---|---|
| Matt Cavanaugh | QB | 6'1" | 210 | 21 | | |
| Steve Grogan | QB | 6'4" | 200 | 25 | | 30 |
| Tom Owen | QB | 6'1" | 194 | 25 | | |
| Horace Ivory | HB | 6' | 198 | 24 | | 66 |
| Andy Johnson | HB | 6' | 204 | 25 | | 18 |
| James McAlister | HB | 6'1" | 205 | 26 | | 12 |
| Don Calhoun | FB-HB | 6' | 212 | 26 | | 6 |
| Sam Cunningham | FB | 6'3" | 230 | 28 | | 48 |
| Mosi Tatupu | FB | 6' | 229 | 23 | | |
| Harold Jackson | WR | 5'10" | 175 | 32 | | 36 |
| Stanley Morgan | WR | 5'10" | 176 | 23 | | 30 |
| Carlos Pennywell | WR | 6'2" | 180 | 22 | | |
| Don Westbrook | WR | 5'10" | 184 | 25 | | |
| Russ Francis | TE | 6'6" | 240 | 25 | | 24 |
| Don Hasselbeck | TE | 6'7" | 242 | 24 | | |
| Nick Lowery | K | 6'4" | 190 | 22 | | 7 |
| Mike Patrick | K | 6' | 213 | 25 | | |
| David Posey | K | 5'10" | 167 | 22 | | 62 |
| John Smith | K | 6' | 185 | 28 | | 9 |
| Jerrel Wilson | K | 6'4" | 222 | 36 | | |

**MIAMI DOLPHINS** 11-5-0 Don Shula

| Scores of Each Game | | |
|---|---|---|
| 20 | N.Y. Jets | 33 |
| 42 | Baltimore | 0 |
| 31 | BUFFALO | 24 |
| 3 | Philadelphia | 17 |
| 24 | ST. LOUIS | 10 |
| 21 | CINCINNATI | 0 |
| 28 | San Diego | 21 |
| 24 | New England | 33 |
| 26 | BALTIMORE | 8 |
| 23 | DALLAS | 16 |
| 25 | Buffalo | 24 |
| 30 | Houston | 35 |
| 13 | N.Y. JETS | 24 |
| 16 | Washington | 0 |
| 23 | OAKLAND | 6 |
| 23 | NEW ENGLAND | 3 |

| Use Name | Pos. | Hgt. | Wgt. | Age | Int. | Pts. |
|---|---|---|---|---|---|---|
| Mike Current | OT | 6'4" | 270 | 32 | | |
| Eric Laasko | OT-OG | 6'4" | 265 | 21 | | |
| Wayne Moore | OT | 6'6" | 265 | 33 | | |
| Bob Kuechenberg | OG-OT | 6'3" | 255 | 30 | | |
| Larry Little | OG-OT | 6'1" | 265 | 32 | | |
| Mel Mitchell | OG-OT-C | 6'2" | 260 | 25 | | |
| Ed Newman | OG | 6'2" | 245 | 27 | | |
| Wally Pesuit | OG-C | 6'4" | 250 | 24 | | |
| Jim Langer | C | 6'2" | 253 | 30 | | |
| John Alexander | DE | 6'2" | 250 | 22 | | |
| Doug Betters | DE | 6'7" | 250 | 22 | | |
| Vern Den Herder | DE | 6'6" | 252 | 29 | | 6 |
| A.J. Duhe | DE | 6'4" | 247 | 22 | | |
| Bob Simpson | DE | 6'5" | 235 | 24 | | |
| Carl Barisich | NT | 6'4" | 255 | 27 | | |
| Bob Baumhower | NT | 6'5" | 258 | 23 | 1 | |

| Use Name | Pos. | Hgt. | Wgt. | Age | Int. | Pts. |
|---|---|---|---|---|---|---|
| Larry Ball | LB | 6'6" | 235 | 28 | | |
| Kim Bokamper | LB | 6'6" | 245 | 23 | 1 | |
| Rusty Chambers | LB | 6'1" | 220 | 24 | 1 | |
| Sean Clancy | LB | 6'4" | 218 | 21 | | |
| Larry Gordon | LB | 6'4" | 230 | 25 | 3 | |
| Bob Matheson | LB | 6'4" | 235 | 33 | | |
| Earnest Rhone | LB | 6'2" | 212 | 25 | 2 | |
| Steve Towle | LB | 6'2" | 233 | 24 | 1 | |
| Charlie Babb | DB | 6' | 190 | 28 | 3 | 6 |
| Charles Cornelius | DB | 5'9" | 178 | 26 | 1 | |
| Tim Foley | DB | 6' | 194 | 30 | 6 | |
| Curtis Johnson | DB | 6'2" | 196 | 30 | 3 | |
| Gerald Small | DB | 5'11" | 187 | 22 | 4 | 6 |
| Norris Thomas | DB | 5'11" | 175 | 24 | 2 | 6 |
| Rich Volk | DB | 6'3" | 195 | 33 | 4 | |

Don Nottingham – Shoulder Injury
Steve Young – Ankle Injury

| Use Name | Pos. | Hgt. | Wgt. | Age | Int. | Pts. |
|---|---|---|---|---|---|---|
| Guy Benjamin | QB | 6'4" | 210 | 23 | | |
| Bob Griese | QB | 6'1" | 190 | 33 | | |
| Don Strock | QB | 6'5" | 220 | 27 | | |
| Gary Davis | HB | 5'10" | 202 | 23 | | 18 |
| Del Williams | HB | 6' | 195 | 27 | | 48 |
| Jim Braxton | FB | 6'2" | 240 | 29 | | 12 |
| Norm Bulaich | FB | 6'1" | 212 | 31 | | 12 |
| Leroy Harris | FB | 5'9" | 220 | 24 | | 12 |
| Jimmy Cefalo | WR | 5'11" | 190 | 21 | | 18 |
| Duriel Harris | WR | 5'11" | 175 | 23 | | 18 |
| Nat Moore | WR | 5'9" | 180 | 26 | | 60 |
| Bruce Hardy | TE | 6'5" | 235 | 22 | | 12 |
| Loaird McCreary | TE | 6'5" | 227 | 25 | | 12 |
| Andre Tillman | TE | 6'5" | 230 | 25 | | 18 |
| George Roberts | K | 6' | 172 | 23 | | |
| Garo Yepremian | K | 5'8" | 175 | 34 | | 98 |

**NEW YORK JETS** 8-8-0 Walt Michaels

| Scores of Each Game | | |
|---|---|---|
| 33 | MIAMI | 20 |
| 21 | Buffalo | 20 |
| 17 | SEATTLE | 24 |
| 3 | Washington | 23 |
| 17 | PITTSBURGH | 28 |
| 45 | BUFFALO | 14 |
| 33 | Baltimore | 10 |
| 23 | ST. LOUIS | 10 |
| 21 | New England | 55 |
| 31 | Denver | 28 |
| 9 | Philadelphia | 17 |
| 17 | NEW ENGLAND | 19 |
| 24 | Miami | 13 |
| 24 | BALTIMORE | 16 |
| 34 | Cleveland | *37 |
| 7 | DALLAS | 30 |

| Use Name | Pos. | Hgt. | Wgt. | Age | Int. | Pts. |
|---|---|---|---|---|---|---|
| Marvin Powell | OT | 6'5" | 264 | 23 | | |
| John Roman | OT | 6'4" | 251 | 26 | | |
| Chris Ward | OT | 6'3" | 269 | 22 | | |
| Dan Alexander | OG | 6'4" | 245 | 23 | | |
| Darrell Austin | OG-C | 6'4" | 252 | 26 | | |
| Randy Rasmussen | OG | 6'2" | 255 | 33 | | |
| Stan Waldemore | OG-OT | 6'4" | 257 | 23 | | |
| Joe Fields | C | 6'2" | 245 | 24 | | |
| Joe Klecko | DE | 6'3" | 256 | 24 | | |
| Lawrence Pillers | DE | 6'3" | 257 | 25 | | |
| Gregg Robinson | DE-NT | 6'6" | 255 | 22 | | |
| Joe Moreino | NT-DE | 6'6" | 246 | 23 | | |
| Joe Pellegrini | NT | 6'2" | 270 | 22 | | |
| Abdul Salaam | NT | 6'3" | 260 | 25 | | |

| Use Name | Pos. | Hgt. | Wgt. | Age | Int. | Pts. |
|---|---|---|---|---|---|---|
| Greg Buttle | LB | 6'3" | 229 | 24 | 2 | |
| John Hennessy | LB-DE | 6'3" | 246 | 23 | | |
| Mike Hennigan | LB | 6'2" | 215 | 26 | 3 | |
| Larry Keller | LB | 6'2" | 225 | 24 | 1 | |
| Bob Martin | LB | 6'1" | 223 | 24 | 2 | |
| Mark Merrill | LB | 6'4" | 237 | 23 | | |
| Mike Mock | LB | 6'1" | 225 | 23 | | |
| Blake Whitlach | LB | 6'1" | 233 | 22 | | |
| Reggie Grant | DB | 5'9" | 185 | 22 | | |
| Bobby Jackson | DB | 5'9" | 175 | 21 | 5 | |
| Tim Moresco | DB | 5'11" | 176 | 23 | | |
| Burgess Owens | DB | 6'2" | 195 | 27 | 5 | 6 |
| Larry Riley | DB | 5'10" | 195 | 23 | | |
| Ken Schroy | DB | 6'2" | 191 | 25 | | |
| Shafer Suggs | DB | 6'1" | 200 | 25 | 3 | |
| Ed Taylor | DB | 6' | 176 | 25 | 2 | |

| Use Name | Pos. | Hgt. | Wgt. | Age | Int. | Pts. |
|---|---|---|---|---|---|---|
| Matt Robinson | QB | 6'2" | 196 | 23 | | |
| Pat Ryan | QB | 6'3" | 205 | 22 | | |
| Richard Todd | QB | 6'2" | 205 | 24 | | |
| Bruce Harper | HB | 5'8" | 174 | 23 | | 30 |
| Kevin Long | HB | 6'1" | 205 | 23 | | 60 |
| Darnell Powell | HB | 5'11" | 200 | 24 | | 6 |
| Scott Dierking | FB | 5'10" | 215 | 23 | | 24 |
| Jim Earley | FB | 6'1" | 230 | 22 | | |
| Clark Gaines | FB | 6'1" | 201 | 24 | | 12 |
| Tom Newton | FB | 6' | 205 | 24 | | 12 |
| Kevin Bell | WR | 5'10" | 180 | 23 | | |
| Derrick Gaffney | WR | 6'1" | 175 | 23 | | 18 |
| Bobby Jones | WR | 5'11" | 180 | 23 | | |
| Bruce Stephens | WR | 5'9" | 170 | 21 | | |
| Wesley Walker | WR | 6' | 172 | 23 | | 48 |
| Jerome Barkum | TE | 6'3" | 217 | 28 | | 18 |
| Mark Iwanowski | TE | 6'4" | 230 | 22 | | |
| Bob Raba | TE | 6'1" | 222 | 23 | | |
| Mickey Shuler | TE | 6'3" | 229 | 22 | | 18 |
| Pat Leahy | K | 6' | 190 | 27 | | 107 |
| Chuck Ramsey | K | 6'2" | 195 | 26 | | |

**BUFFALO BILLS** 5-11-0 Chuck Knox

| Scores of Each Game | | |
|---|---|---|
| 17 | PITTSBURGH | 28 |
| 20 | N.Y. JETS | 21 |
| 24 | Miami | 31 |
| 24 | BALTIMORE | 17 |
| 28 | KANSAS CITY | 13 |
| 14 | N.Y. Jets | 45 |
| 10 | Houston | 17 |
| 5 | CINCINNATI | 0 |
| 20 | Cleveland | 41 |
| 10 | NEW ENGLAND | 14 |
| 24 | MIAMI | 25 |
| 10 | Tampa Bay | 31 |
| 41 | N.Y. GIANTS | 17 |
| 10 | Kansas City | 14 |
| 24 | New England | 26 |
| 21 | Baltimore | 14 |

| Use Name | Pos. | Hgt. | Wgt. | Age | Int. | Pts. |
|---|---|---|---|---|---|---|
| Joe Devlin | OT | 6'5" | 250 | 24 | | |
| Elbert Drungo | OT | 6'5" | 265 | 35 | | |
| Craig Hertwig | OT | 6'8" | 270 | 26 | | |
| Ken Jones | OT | 6'5" | 250 | 25 | | |
| Bill Adams | OG | 6'2" | 246 | 28 | | |
| Joe DeLamielleure | OG | 6'3" | 245 | 27 | | |
| Reggie McKenzie | OG | 6'4" | 242 | 28 | | |
| Will Grant | C | 6'3" | 248 | 24 | | |
| Willie Parker | C | 6'3" | 245 | 29 | | |
| Scott Hutchinson | DE | 6'4" | 243 | 22 | | |
| Sherman White | DE | 6'5" | 250 | 29 | | |
| Ben Williams | DE | 6'3" | 245 | 24 | | |
| Phil Dokes | DT | 6'5" | 255 | 22 | | |
| Dee Hardison | DT | 6'4" | 269 | 22 | | |
| Mekeli Ieremia | DT | 6'2" | 244 | 24 | | |
| Dennis Johnson | DT | 6'4" | 265 | 26 | | |
| Mike Kadish | DT | 6'5" | 270 | 28 | | |

| Use Name | Pos. | Hgt. | Wgt. | Age | Int. | Pts. |
|---|---|---|---|---|---|---|
| Doug Becker (from CHI) | LB | 6' | 222 | 22 | | |
| Mario Celotto | LB | 6'3" | 234 | 22 | | |
| Tom Ehlers | LB | 6'2" | 218 | 26 | | |
| Tom Graham | LB | 6'2" | 235 | 28 | | |
| Dan Jilek | LB | 6'2" | 225 | 24 | | |
| Randy McClanahan | LB | 6'5" | 225 | 23 | | |
| Shane Nelson | LB | 6'1" | 225 | 23 | 3 | |
| Lucius Sanford | LB | 6'2" | 216 | 22 | 1 | |
| Mario Clark | DB | 6'2" | 195 | 24 | 5 | |
| Steve Freeman | DB | 5'11" | 185 | 25 | | |
| Tony Greene | DB | 5'10" | 175 | 29 | 3 | |
| Doug Jones | DB | 6'2" | 205 | 28 | | |
| Eddie McMillan | DB | 6' | 190 | 26 | | |
| Keith Moody | DB | 5'10" | 170 | 25 | | 6 |
| Charles Romes | DB | 6'1" | 190 | 24 | 2 | 6 |
| Marvin Switzer | DB | 6' | 192 | 23 | | |

Mike Collier – Foot Injury
John Holland – Knee Injury
Phil Olsen – Knee Injury
Connie Zelencik – Injury

| Use Name | Pos. | Hgt. | Wgt. | Age | Int. | Pts. |
|---|---|---|---|---|---|---|
| Joe Ferguson | QB | 6'1" | 195 | 28 | | |
| Dave Mays | QB | 6'1" | 204 | 29 | | |
| Bill Munson | QB | 6'2" | 205 | 37 | | |
| Roland Hooks | HB | 6' | 195 | 25 | | 18 |
| Terry Miller | HB | 5'10" | 196 | 22 | | 42 |
| Steve Powell | HB | 5'11" | 186 | 22 | | |
| Curtis Brown | FB | 5'10" | 203 | 23 | | 30 |
| Dennis Johnson | FB | 6'3" | 220 | 22 | | 12 |
| Bob Chandler | WR | 6' | 180 | 29 | | 30 |
| Mike Levenseller (to TB) | WR | 6'1" | 180 | 22 | | |
| Frank Lewis | WR | 6'1" | 196 | 31 | | 42 |
| Lou Piccone | WR | 5'9" | 175 | 29 | | 14 |
| Larry Walton | WR | 6' | 180 | 30 | | 6 |
| Leonard Willis | WR | 5'11" | 185 | 25 | | |
| Mike Franckowiak | TE | 6'3" | 225 | 25 | | |
| Reuben Gant | TE | 6'4" | 225 | 26 | | 30 |
| Tom Dempsey | K | 6'1" | 260 | 31 | | 66 |
| Rusty Jackson | K | 6'2" | 195 | 27 | | |

**BALTIMORE COLTS** 5-11-0 Ted Marchibroda

| Scores of Each Game | | |
|---|---|---|
| 0 | Dallas | 38 |
| 0 | MIAMI | 42 |
| 34 | New England | 27 |
| 17 | Buffalo | 24 |
| 14 | PHILADELPHIA | 17 |
| 30 | St. Louis | 17 |
| 10 | N.Y. JETS | 33 |
| 7 | DENVER | 6 |
| 8 | Miami | 26 |
| 21 | WASHINGTON | 17 |
| 17 | Seattle | 14 |
| 24 | CLEVELAND | 45 |
| 14 | NEW ENGLAND | 35 |
| 16 | N.Y. Jets | 24 |
| 13 | Pittsburgh | 35 |
| 14 | BUFFALO | 21 |

| Use Name | Pos. | Hgt. | Wgt. | Age | Int. | Pts. |
|---|---|---|---|---|---|---|
| Wade Griffin | OT | 6'5" | 231 | 24 | | |
| George Kunz | OT | 6'5" | 262 | 31 | | |
| Don Morrison | OT | 6'5" | 250 | 28 | | |
| Bob Van Duyne | OT | 6'5" | 244 | 26 | | |
| Ron Baker | OG | 6'4" | 247 | 23 | | |
| Ken Huff | OG | 6'4" | 262 | 25 | | |
| Robert Pratt | OG | 6'4" | 248 | 27 | | |
| Forrest Blue | C | 6'5" | 260 | 32 | | |
| Ken Mendenhall | C | 6'3" | 250 | 30 | | |
| Geoff Reece | C | 6'4" | 247 | 26 | | |
| Fred Cook | DE | 6'3" | 243 | 26 | | |
| John Dutton | DE | 6'7" | 266 | 27 | | |
| Mike Ozdowski | DE | 6'5" | 243 | 22 | | |
| Mike Barnes | DT | 6'6" | 256 | 27 | | |
| Joe Ehrmann | DT | 6'5" | 254 | 29 | | |
| Greg Marshall | DT | 6'3" | 257 | 21 | | |
| Herb Orvis | DT | 6'5" | 255 | 31 | | |
| Dave Rowe (from OAK) | DT | 6'7" | 270 | 33 | | |

| Use Name | Pos. | Hgt. | Wgt. | Age | Int. | Pts. |
|---|---|---|---|---|---|---|
| Derrel Luce | LB | 6'3" | 227 | 25 | 1 | 6 |
| Tom MacLeod | LB | 6'3" | 224 | 27 | | |
| Stu O'Dell | LB | 6'1" | 220 | 26 | | |
| Calvin O'Neal | LB | 6'1" | 235 | 23 | | |
| Sanders Shiver | LB | 6'2" | 222 | 23 | | |
| Ed Simonini | LB | 6' | 210 | 24 | 2 | |
| Stan White | LB | 6'1" | 223 | 28 | 1 | |
| Mike Woods | LB | 6'2" | 227 | 23 | | |
| Tim Baylor | DB | 6'6" | 201 | 24 | | |
| Lyle Blackwood | DB | 6' | 190 | 27 | 4 | 12 |
| Dwight Harrison | DB | 6'1" | 185 | 29 | | |
| Bruce Laird | DB | 6' | 198 | 28 | | |
| Lloyd Mumphord | DB | 5'11" | 178 | 31 | 2 | |
| Doug Nettles | DB | 6' | 178 | 27 | 1 | |
| Norm Thompson | DB | 6'1" | 180 | 30 | 6 | |

Ron Fernandes – Knee Injury
David Taylor – Ankle Injury

| Use Name | Pos. | Hgt. | Wgt. | Age | Int. | Pts. |
|---|---|---|---|---|---|---|
| Bert Jones | QB | 6'3" | 212 | 26 | | |
| Mike Kirkland | QB | 6'1" | 195 | 24 | | |
| Bill Troup | QB | 6'5" | 215 | 27 | | 6 |
| Don McCauley | HB-FB | 6'1" | 215 | 29 | | 30 |
| Joe Washington | HB | 5'10" | 182 | 24 | | 12 |
| Don Hardeman | FB | 6'2" | 235 | 26 | | |
| Roosevelt Leaks | FB | 5'10" | 225 | 25 | | 24 |
| Ron Lee | FB | 6'4" | 228 | 24 | | 12 |
| Randy Burke | WR | 6'1" | 186 | 23 | | |
| Gerald Butler | WR | 6'4" | 212 | 24 | | |
| Roger Carr | WR | 6'3" | 200 | 26 | | 36 |
| Glenn Doughty | WR | 6'1" | 205 | 27 | | 18 |
| Marshall Johnson | WR | 6'1" | 196 | 25 | | |
| Mike Siani | WR | 6'2" | 195 | 28 | | 6 |
| Mack Alston | TE | 6'2" | 238 | 31 | | 12 |
| Reese McCall | TE | 6'7" | 232 | 22 | | 12 |
| David Lee | K | 6'4" | 216 | 34 | | |
| Toni Linhart | K | 5'11" | 179 | 36 | | 51 |

*—Overtime

## RUSHING / RECEIVING / PUNT RETURNS / KICKOFF RETURNS / PASSING – PUNTING – KICKING

### NEW ENGLAND PATRIOTS

**RUSHING**

| Last Name | No. | Yds. | Avg. | TD |
|---|---|---|---|---|
| Cunningham | 199 | 768 | 3.9 | 8 |
| Ivory | 141 | 693 | 4.9 | 11 |
| Johnson | 147 | 675 | 4.6 | 3 |
| Grogan | 81 | 539 | 6.7 | 5 |
| Calhoun | 76 | 391 | 5.1 | 1 |
| McAlister | 19 | 77 | 4.1 | 2 |
| Morgan | 2 | 11 | 5.5 | 0 |
| Jackson | 1 | 7 | 7.0 | 0 |
| Tatupu | 3 | 6 | 2.0 | 0 |
| Wilson | 1 | 0 | 0.0 | 0 |
| Westbrook | 1 | −2 | −2.0 | 0 |

**RECEIVING**

| Last Name | No. | Yds. | Avg. | TD |
|---|---|---|---|---|
| Francis | 39 | 543 | 14 | 4 |
| Jackson | 37 | 743 | 20 | 6 |
| Morgan | 34 | 820 | 24 | 5 |
| Cunningham | 31 | 297 | 10 | 0 |
| Johnson | 26 | 267 | 10 | 0 |
| Ivory | 14 | 122 | 9 | 0 |
| Hasselbeck | 7 | 107 | 15 | 0 |
| Westbrook | 3 | 38 | 13 | 0 |
| Calhoun | 3 | 29 | 10 | 0 |
| Pennywell | 1 | 28 | 28 | 0 |
| McAlister | 1 | 12 | 12 | 0 |

**PUNT RETURNS**

| Last Name | No. | Yds. | Avg. | TD |
|---|---|---|---|---|
| Morgan | 32 | 335 | 11 | 0 |
| Haynes | 14 | 183 | 13 | 0 |
| Cohn | 1 | 2 | 2 | 0 |

**KICKOFF RETURNS**

| Last Name | No. | Yds. | Avg. | TD |
|---|---|---|---|---|
| Clayborn | 27 | 636 | 24 | 0 |
| McAlister | 10 | 186 | 19 | 0 |
| Ivory | 7 | 165 | 24 | 0 |
| Westbrook | 7 | 125 | 18 | 0 |
| Cohn | 1 | 26 | 26 | 0 |
| Morgan | 1 | 17 | 17 | 0 |
| Tatupu | 1 | 17 | 17 | 0 |
| Wheeler | 1 | 0 | 0 | 0 |

**PASSING**

| Last Name | Att. | Comp. | % | Yds. | Yd./Att. | TD | Int.–% | RK |
|---|---|---|---|---|---|---|---|---|
| Grogan | 362 | 181 | 50 | 2824 | 7.8 | 15 | 23– 6 | 10 |
| Owen | 26 | 15 | 58 | 182 | 7.0 | 0 | 2– 8 | |
| Johnson | 2 | 0 | 0 | 0 | 0.0 | 0 | 0– 0 | |

**PUNTING**

| Last Name | No. | Avg. |
|---|---|---|
| Wilson | 54 | 35.6 |
| Patrick | 7 | 30.9 |

**KICKING**

| Last Name | XP | Att. | % | FG | Att. | % |
|---|---|---|---|---|---|---|
| Posey | 29 | 31 | 94 | 11 | 22 | 50 |
| Smith | 6 | 7 | 86 | 1 | 1 | 100 |
| Lowery | 7 | 7 | 100 | 0 | 1 | 0 |

### MIAMI DOLPHINS

**RUSHING**

| Last Name | No. | Yds. | Avg. | TD |
|---|---|---|---|---|
| Wiliams | 272 | 1258 | 4.6 | 8 |
| L. Harris | 123 | 512 | 4.2 | 2 |
| Davis | 62 | 313 | 5.0 | 3 |
| Bulaich | 40 | 196 | 4.9 | 2 |
| Braxton | 50 | 121 | 2.4 | 2 |
| Strock | 10 | 23 | 2.3 | 0 |
| Griese | 9 | 10 | 1.1 | 0 |
| Benjamin | 1 | −2 | −2.0 | 0 |
| N. Moore | 4 | −3 | −0.8 | 0 |
| Roberts | 1 | −7 | −7.0 | 0 |

**RECEIVING**

| Last Name | No. | Yds. | Avg. | TD |
|---|---|---|---|---|
| N. Moore | 48 | 645 | 13 | 10 |
| D. Harris | 45 | 645 | 15 | 3 |
| Tillman | 31 | 398 | 13 | 3 |
| L. Harris | 25 | 211 | 8 | 0 |
| Davis | 24 | 218 | 9 | 0 |
| Williams | 18 | 192 | 11 | 0 |
| Bulaich | 16 | 92 | 6 | 0 |
| Braxton | 9 | 85 | 9 | 0 |
| Cefalo | 6 | 145 | 24 | 3 |
| Hardy | 4 | 32 | 8 | 2 |
| McCreary | 3 | 27 | 9 | 2 |
| Den Herder | 1 | 7 | 7 | 1 |

**PUNT RETURNS**

| Last Name | No. | Yds. | Avg. | TD |
|---|---|---|---|---|
| Cefalo | 28 | 232 | 8 | 0 |
| Babb | 9 | 57 | 6 | 0 |
| Davis | 2 | 36 | 18 | 0 |
| N. Moore | 1 | 11 | 11 | 0 |
| Cornelius | 1 | 5 | 5 | 0 |

**KICKOFF RETURNS**

| Last Name | No. | Yds. | Avg. | TD |
|---|---|---|---|---|
| D. Harris | 29 | 657 | 23 | 0 |
| Davis | 13 | 251 | 19 | 0 |
| Cefalo | 2 | 40 | 20 | 0 |
| Hardy | 2 | 27 | 14 | 0 |

**PASSING**

| Last Name | Att. | Comp. | % | Yds. | Yd./Att. | TD | Int.–% | RK |
|---|---|---|---|---|---|---|---|---|
| Griese | 235 | 148 | 63 | 1791 | 7.6 | 11 | 11– 5 | 3 |
| Strock | 135 | 72 | 53 | 825 | 6.1 | 12 | 6– 4 | |
| Benjamin | 8 | 6 | 75 | 91 | 11.4 | 1 | 1– 13 | |
| Williams | 1 | 0 | 0 | 0 | 0.0 | 0 | 0– 0 | |

**PUNTING**

| Last Name | No. | Avg. |
|---|---|---|
| Roberts | 81 | 40.3 |

**KICKING**

| Last Name | XP | Att. | % | FG | Att. | % |
|---|---|---|---|---|---|---|
| Yepremian | 41 | 45 | 91 | 19 | 23 | 83 |

### NEW YORK JETS

**RUSHING**

| Last Name | No. | Yds. | Avg. | TD |
|---|---|---|---|---|
| Long | 214 | 954 | 4.5 | 10 |
| Dierking | 170 | 681 | 4.0 | 4 |
| Harper | 58 | 303 | 5.2 | 2 |
| Gaines | 44 | 154 | 3.5 | 2 |
| D. Powell | 20 | 77 | 3.9 | 1 |
| Newton | 11 | 45 | 4.1 | 2 |
| M. Robinson | 28 | 23 | 0.8 | 0 |
| Todd | 14 | 18 | 1.3 | 0 |
| Gaffney | 2 | −2 | −1.0 | 0 |
| Walner | 1 | −3 | −3.0 | 0 |

**RECEIVING**

| Last Name | No. | Yds. | Avg. | TD |
|---|---|---|---|---|
| Walker | 48 | 1169 | 24 | 8 |
| Gaffney | 38 | 691 | 18 | 3 |
| Barkum | 28 | 391 | 14 | 3 |
| Long | 26 | 204 | 8 | 0 |
| Dierking | 19 | 152 | 8 | 0 |
| Harper | 13 | 196 | 15 | 2 |
| Shuler | 11 | 67 | 6 | 3 |
| Newton | 5 | 48 | 10 | 0 |
| Gaines | 3 | 23 | 8 | 0 |
| Jones | 1 | 18 | 18 | 0 |
| Roman | 1 | −2 | −2 | 0 |

**PUNT RETURNS**

| Last Name | No. | Yds. | Avg. | TD |
|---|---|---|---|---|
| Harper | 30 | 378 | 13 | 1 |
| Schroy | 3 | 35 | 12 | 0 |

**KICKOFF RETURNS**

| Last Name | No. | Yds. | Avg. | TD |
|---|---|---|---|---|
| Harper | 55 | 1280 | 23 | 0 |
| D. Powell | 3 | 50 | 17 | 0 |
| Stephens | 3 | 42 | 14 | 0 |
| Gaines | 3 | 33 | 11 | 0 |
| Bell | 2 | 66 | 33 | 0 |
| Shuler | 1 | 12 | 12 | 0 |
| Schroy | 0 | 26 | — | 0 |

**PASSING**

| Last Name | Att. | Comp. | % | Yds. | Yd./Att. | TD | Int.–% | RK |
|---|---|---|---|---|---|---|---|---|
| M. Robinson | 266 | 124 | 47 | 2002 | 7.5 | 13 | 16– 6 | 9 |
| Todd | 107 | 60 | 56 | 849 | 7.9 | 6 | 10– 9 | |
| Ryan | 14 | 9 | 64 | 106 | 7.6 | 0 | 2– 14 | |
| Dierking | 1 | 0 | 0 | 0 | 0.0 | 0 | 0– 0 | |

**PUNTING**

| Last Name | No. | Avg. |
|---|---|---|
| Ramsey | 74 | 40.1 |

**KICKING**

| Last Name | XP | Att. | % | FG | Att. | % |
|---|---|---|---|---|---|---|
| Leahy | 41 | 42 | 98 | 22 | 30 | 73 |

### BUFFALO BILLS

**RUSHING**

| Last Name | No. | Yds. | Avg. | TD |
|---|---|---|---|---|
| Miller | 238 | 1060 | 4.5 | 7 |
| Brown | 128 | 591 | 4.6 | 4 |
| Hooks | 76 | 358 | 4.7 | 2 |
| Johnson | 55 | 222 | 4.0 | 2 |
| Ferguson | 27 | 76 | 2.8 | 0 |
| Gant | 1 | 14 | 14.0 | 0 |
| Jackson | 1 | −13 | −13.0 | 0 |

**RECEIVING**

| Last Name | No. | Yds. | Avg. | TD |
|---|---|---|---|---|
| Chandler | 44 | 581 | 13 | 5 |
| Lewis | 41 | 735 | 18 | 7 |
| Gant | 34 | 408 | 12 | 5 |
| Miller | 22 | 246 | 11 | 0 |
| Brown | 18 | 130 | 7 | 0 |
| Hooks | 15 | 110 | 7 | 1 |
| Johnson | 10 | 83 | 8 | 0 |
| Piccone | 7 | 71 | 10 | 2 |
| Walton | 4 | 66 | 17 | 1 |
| Willis | 2 | 41 | 21 | 0 |
| Ferguson | 1 | −6 | −6 | 0 |

**PUNT RETURNS**

| Last Name | No. | Yds. | Avg. | TD |
|---|---|---|---|---|
| Moody | 19 | 240 | 13 | 1 |
| Piccone | 14 | 88 | 6 | 0 |
| Levenseller | 3 | 35 | 12 | 0 |
| Hooks | 3 | 12 | 4 | 0 |
| Brown | 1 | 0 | 0 | 0 |

**KICKOFF RETURNS**

| Last Name | No. | Yds. | Avg. | TD |
|---|---|---|---|---|
| Brown | 17 | 428 | 25 | 1 |
| Moody | 18 | 371 | 21 | 0 |
| Johnson | 10 | 204 | 20 | 0 |
| Hooks | 7 | 124 | 18 | 0 |
| Frankowiak | 5 | 60 | 12 | 0 |
| Powell | 3 | 53 | 18 | 0 |
| Piccone | 3 | 51 | 17 | 0 |
| Miller | 1 | 17 | 17 | 0 |
| Hutchinson | 1 | 8 | 8 | 0 |
| Willis | 1 | 0 | 0 | 0 |

**PASSING**

| Last Name | Att. | Comp. | % | Yds. | Yd./Att. | TD | Int.–% | RK |
|---|---|---|---|---|---|---|---|---|
| Ferguson | 330 | 175 | 53 | 2136 | 6.5 | 16 | 15– 5 | 7 |
| Munson | 43 | 24 | 56 | 328 | 7.6 | 4 | 2– 5 | |
| Mays | 15 | 4 | 27 | 39 | 2.6 | 1 | 0– 0 | |

**PUNTING**

| Last Name | No. | Avg. |
|---|---|---|
| Jackson | 87 | 38.8 |

**KICKING**

| Last Name | XP | Att. | % | FG | Att. | % |
|---|---|---|---|---|---|---|
| Dempsey | 36 | 38 | 95 | 10 | 13 | 77 |

### BALTIMORE COLTS

**RUSHING**

| Last Name | No. | Yds. | Avg. | TD |
|---|---|---|---|---|
| Washington | 240 | 956 | 4.0 | 0 |
| R. Lee | 81 | 374 | 4.6 | 1 |
| Leaks | 83 | 266 | 3.2 | 2 |
| Hardeman | 48 | 244 | 5.1 | 0 |
| McCauley | 44 | 107 | 2.4 | 5 |
| Jones | 9 | 38 | 4.2 | 0 |
| Kirkland | 8 | 35 | 4.4 | 0 |
| Troup | 18 | 25 | 1.4 | 1 |
| Doughty | 1 | −1 | −1.0 | 0 |

**RECEIVING**

| Last Name | No. | Yds. | Avg. | TD |
|---|---|---|---|---|
| Washington | 45 | 377 | 8 | 1 |
| McCauley | 34 | 296 | 9 | 0 |
| Carr | 30 | 629 | 21 | 6 |
| Doughty | 25 | 390 | 16 | 3 |
| Alston | 18 | 210 | 12 | 1 |
| R. Lee | 13 | 109 | 8 | 1 |
| McCall | 11 | 160 | 15 | 1 |
| Hardeman | 10 | 88 | 9 | 0 |
| Leaks | 9 | 111 | 12 | 2 |
| Siani | 6 | 151 | 25 | 1 |
| Johnson | 1 | 22 | 22 | 0 |

**PUNT RETURNS**

| Last Name | No. | Yds. | Avg. | TD |
|---|---|---|---|---|
| Johnson | 25 | 143 | 6 | 0 |
| Washington | 7 | 37 | 5 | 0 |
| McCall | 1 | 37 | 37 | 0 |
| Blackwood | 1 | 2 | 2 | 0 |
| Burke | 1 | 0 | 0 | 0 |

**KICKOFF RETURNS**

| Last Name | No. | Yds. | Avg. | TD |
|---|---|---|---|---|
| Washington | 19 | 499 | 26 | 1 |
| Johnson | 41 | 927 | 23 | 0 |
| McCauley | 7 | 150 | 21 | 0 |
| Hardeman | 3 | 36 | 12 | 0 |
| Blackwood | 1 | 18 | 18 | 0 |
| Morrison | 1 | 6 | 6 | 0 |
| Burke | 1 | 2 | 2 | 0 |
| Van Duyne | 1 | 0 | 0 | 0 |
| O'Dell | 0 | 10 | — | 0 |

**PASSING**

| Last Name | Att. | Comp. | % | Yds. | Yd./Att. | TD | Int.–% | RK |
|---|---|---|---|---|---|---|---|---|
| Troup | 296 | 154 | 52 | 1882 | 6.4 | 10 | 21– 7 | 14 |
| Jones | 42 | 27 | 64 | 370 | 8.8 | 4 | 1– 2 | |
| Kirkland | 41 | 19 | 46 | 211 | 5.2 | 1 | 8– 20 | |
| Washington | 4 | 2 | 50 | 80 | 20.0 | 2 | 0– 0 | |

**PUNTING**

| Last Name | No. | Avg. |
|---|---|---|
| D. Lee | 92 | 38.2 |

**KICKING**

| Last Name | XP | Att. | % | FG | Att. | % |
|---|---|---|---|---|---|---|
| Linhart | 27 | 31 | 87 | 8 | 17 | 47 |

## PITTSBURGH STEELERS 14-2-0  Chuck Noll

| Scores of Each Game | |
|---|---|
| 28 | Buffalo 17 |
| 21 | SEATTLE 10 |
| 28 | Cincinnati 3 |
| 15 | CLEVELAND *9 |
| 28 | N.Y. Jets 17 |
| 31 | ATLANTA 7 |
| 34 | Cleveland 14 |
| 17 | HOUSTON 24 |
| 27 | KANSAS CITY 24 |
| 20 | NEW ORLEANS 14 |
| 7 | Los Angeles 10 |
| 7 | CINCINNATI 6 |
| 24 | San Francisco 7 |
| 13 | Houston 3 |
| 35 | BALTIMORE 13 |
| 21 | Denver 17 |

| Use Name | Pos. | Hgt. | Wgt. | Age | Int. | Pts. |
|---|---|---|---|---|---|---|
| Larry Brown | OT | 6'4" | 245 | 29 | | |
| Jon Kolb | OT | 6'2" | 262 | 31 | | |
| Ray Pinney | OT | 6'4" | 240 | 24 | | |
| Steve Courson | OG | 6'1" | 260 | 22 | | |
| Sam Davis | OG | 6'1" | 255 | 34 | | |
| Gerry Mullins | OG | 6'3" | 244 | 29 | | |
| Ted Petersen | C-OT | 6'5" | 244 | 23 | | |
| Mike Webster | C | 6'1" | 250 | 26 | | |
| Fred Anderson | DE-DT | 6'5" | 235 | 23 | | |
| L.C. Greenwood | DE | 6'5" | 250 | 31 | | |
| Dwight White | DE | 6'4" | 255 | 29 | | |
| John Banaszak | DT-DE | 6'3" | 244 | 28 | | |
| Tom Beasley | DT | 6'5" | 253 | 24 | | |
| Gary Dunn | DT | 6'3" | 247 | 25 | | |
| Steve Furness | DT-DE | 6'4" | 255 | 27 | | |
| Joe Greene | DT | 6'4" | 264 | 31 | | |
| Robin Cole | LB | 6'2" | 220 | 22 | | |
| Jack Ham | LB | 6'3" | 225 | 29 | 3 | |
| Jack Lambert | LB | 6'4" | 220 | 26 | 4 | |
| Loren Toews | LB | 6'3" | 222 | 26 | 1 | |
| Dennis Winston | LB | 6' | 228 | 22 | | |
| Larry Anderson | DB | 5'11" | 177 | 21 | | 6 |
| Mel Blount | DB | 6'3" | 205 | 30 | 4 | |
| Tony Dungy | DB | 6' | 188 | 22 | 6 | |
| Ron Johnson | DB | 5'10" | 200 | 22 | 4 | |
| Ray Oldham (from BAL) | DB | 6' | 192 | 27 | | |
| Donnie Shell | DB | 5'11" | 190 | 26 | 3 | 6 |
| Nat Terry (to DET) | DB | 5'11" | 165 | 22 | | |
| Mike Wagner | DB | 6'1" | 200 | 29 | 2 | |
| Terry Bradshaw | QB | 6'3" | 215 | 29 | | 6 |
| Mike Kruczek | QB | 6'1" | 205 | 25 | | |
| Cliff Stoudt | QB | 6'4" | 218 | 23 | | |
| Rocky Bleier | HB | 5'11" | 210 | 32 | | 36 |
| Jack Deloplaine (from WAS) | HB | 5'10" | 205 | 24 | | |
| Alvin Maxson (to TB, HOU, NYG) | HB | 5'11" | 205 | 26 | | |
| Rick Moser | HB | 6' | 210 | 21 | | |
| Sidney Thornton | HB-FB | 5'11" | 230 | 23 | | 18 |
| Franco Harrris | FB | 6'2" | 225 | 28 | | 48 |
| Theo Bell | WR | 5'11" | 180 | 24 | | 6 |
| Randy Reutershan | WR | 5'10" | 182 | 23 | | |
| Jim Smith | WR | 6'2" | 205 | 23 | | 12 |
| John Stallworth | WR | 6'2" | 183 | 26 | | 54 |
| Lynn Swann | WR | 6' | 180 | 26 | | 66 |
| Bennie Cunningham | TE | 6'4" | 247 | 23 | | 12 |
| Randy Grossman | TE | 6'1" | 215 | 24 | | 6 |
| Jim Mandich | TE | 6'3" | 214 | 30 | | |
| Craig Colquitt | K | 6'2" | 182 | 24 | | |
| Roy Gerela | K | 5'10" | 185 | 30 | | 80 |

Laverne Smith-Leg Injury
J.T. Thomas-Illness

## HOUSTON OILERS 10-6-0  Bum Phillips

| Scores of Each Game | |
|---|---|
| 14 | Atlanta 20 |
| 20 | Kansas City 17 |
| 20 | SAN FRANCISCO 19 |
| 6 | LOS ANGELES 10 |
| 16 | Cleveland 13 |
| 17 | Oakland 21 |
| 17 | BUFFALO 10 |
| 24 | Pittsburgh 17 |
| 13 | Cincinnati 28 |
| 14 | CLEVELAND 10 |
| 26 | New England 23 |
| 35 | MIAMI 30 |
| 17 | CINCINNATI 10 |
| 3 | PITTSBURGH 13 |
| 17 | New Orleans 12 |
| 24 | SAN DIEGO 45 |

| Use Name | Pos. | Hgt. | Wgt. | Age | Int. | Pts. |
|---|---|---|---|---|---|---|
| Larry Harris | OT | 6'3" | 274 | 24 | | |
| Conway Hayman | OT-OG | 6'3" | 260 | 29 | | |
| Greg Sampson | OT | 6'6" | 270 | 27 | | |
| Morris Towns | OT | 6'4" | 275 | 24 | | |
| Ed Fisher | OG | 6'3" | 250 | 29 | | |
| George Reihner | OG | 6'4" | 263 | 23 | | |
| John Schumacher | OG | 6'3" | 275 | 22 | | |
| David Carter | C | 6'2" | 225 | 24 | | |
| Carl Mauck | C | 6'4" | 250 | 31 | | |
| Steve Baumgartner | DE-LB | 6'7" | 275 | 27 | | |
| Elvin Bethea | DE | 6'3" | 255 | 32 | | |
| Jimmy Dean | DE | 6'4" | 252 | 23 | | |
| Andy Dorris | DE | 6'4" | 240 | 27 | | |
| James Young | DE | 6'2" | 260 | 27 | | |
| Curley Culp | MG | 6'1" | 265 | 32 | | |
| Ken Kennard | MG | 6'2" | 245 | 23 | | |
| Gregg Bingham | LB | 6'1" | 230 | 27 | | |
| Robert Brazile | LB | 6'4" | 238 | 25 | 1 | |
| Steve Kiner | LB | 6' | 225 | 31 | 1 | |
| Art Stringer | LB | 6'1" | 223 | 24 | 1 | |
| Ted Thompson | LB | 6'1" | 220 | 25 | | |
| Ted Washington | LB | 6'1" | 245 | 30 | | |
| Willie Alexander | DB | 6'3" | 195 | 28 | 5 | |
| Bill Currier | DB | 6' | 190 | 23 | 1 | |
| Al Johnson | DB | 6' | 200 | 28 | | |
| Kurt Knoff | DB | 6'2" | 188 | 24 | 1 | |
| Mike Reinfeldt | DB | 6'2" | 195 | 25 | 1 | |
| Greg Stemrick | DB | 5'11" | 185 | 26 | 3 | |
| C.L. Whittington | DB | 6'1" | 200 | 26 | 1 | |
| J.C. Wilson | DB | 6' | 177 | 22 | 2 | |
| Tom Dunivan | QB | 6'3" | 210 | 24 | | |
| Gifford Nielsen | QB | 6'4" | 205 | 23 | | |
| Dan Pastorini | QB | 6'3" | 205 | 29 | | |
| Earl Campbell | HB-FB | 5'11" | 224 | 23 | | 78 |
| Ronnie Coleman | HB | 5'10" | 198 | 27 | | 12 |
| Anthony Davis (to LA) | HB | 5'10" | 190 | 26 | | |
| Brian Duncan | HB | 6' | 201 | 26 | | |
| Larry Poole | HB | 6' | 195 | 26 | | |
| Robert Turner | HB | 5'11" | 200 | 24 | | |
| Rob Carpenter | FB | 6'1" | 214 | 23 | | 30 |
| Tim Wilson | FB | 6'3" | 220 | 24 | | 26 |
| Ken Burrough | WR | 6'4" | 210 | 30 | | 12 |
| Rich Caster | WR | 6'5" | 230 | 29 | | 30 |
| Johnnie Dirden | WR | 6' | 190 | 26 | | |
| Billy Johnson | WR | 5'9" | 170 | 26 | | |
| Guido Merkens | WR-DB | 6'1" | 200 | 23 | | |
| Mike Renfro | WR | 6' | 184 | 23 | | 12 |
| Robert Woods | WR | 5'7" | 170 | 23 | | 12 |
| Mike Barber | TE | 6'3" | 235 | 25 | | 18 |
| Conrad Rucker | TE | 6'3" | 260 | 23 | | |
| Toni Fritsch | K | 5'7" | 195 | 33 | | 73 |
| Cliff Parsley | K | 6'1" | 211 | 23 | | |

Eddie Foster – Knee Injury
Mike Voight – Injury

## CLEVELAND BROWNS 8-8-0  Sam Rutigliano

| Scores of Each Game | |
|---|---|
| 24 | SAN FRANCISCO 7 |
| 13 | CINCINNATI *10 |
| 24 | Atlanta 16 |
| 9 | Pittsburgh *15 |
| 13 | HOUSTON 16 |
| 24 | New Orleans 16 |
| 14 | PITTSBURGH 34 |
| 3 | Kansas City 17 |
| 41 | BUFFALO 20 |
| 10 | Houston 14 |
| 7 | DENVER 19 |
| 45 | Baltimore 24 |
| 30 | LOS ANGELES 19 |
| 24 | Seattle 47 |
| 37 | N.Y. JETS *34 |
| 16 | Cincinnati 48 |

| Use Name | Pos. | Hgt. | Wgt. | Age | Int. | Pts. |
|---|---|---|---|---|---|---|
| Leo Biedermann | OT | 6'7" | 254 | 22 | | |
| Barry Darrow | OT | 6'7" | 260 | 28 | | |
| Doug Dieken | OT | 6'5" | 252 | 29 | | |
| George Buehler (from OAK) | OG | 6'2" | 270 | 31 | | |
| Greg Fairchild | OG | 6'4" | 257 | 24 | | |
| Bob Jackson | OG | 6'5" | 250 | 25 | | |
| Henry Sheppard | OG | 6'6" | 246 | 25 | | |
| Tom DeLeone | C | 6'2" | 248 | 28 | | |
| Gerry Sullivan | C-OT | 6'4" | 250 | 26 | | |
| Joe Jones | DE | 6'6" | 250 | 30 | | |
| Mack Mitchell | DE | 6'7" | 245 | 26 | | |
| Mike St. Clair | DE | 6'5" | 245 | 24 | | |
| Earl Edwards | DT | 6'6" | 256 | 32 | | |
| Ken Novak | DT | 6'7" | 264 | 24 | | |
| Jerry Sherk | DT | 6'4" | 250 | 30 | | |
| Mickey Sims | DT | 6'5" | 282 | 23 | | |
| Jesse Turnbow | DT | 6'7" | 272 | 21 | | |
| Dick Ambrose | LB | 6' | 235 | 25 | 2 | |
| Bob Babich | LB | 6'2" | 231 | 31 | | |
| Dave Graf | LB | 6'2" | 215 | 25 | | |
| Charlie Hall | LB | 6'3" | 235 | 29 | 1 | |
| Gerald Irons | LB | 6'2" | 230 | 31 | 2 | |
| Robert Jackson | LB | 6'1" | 230 | 24 | | |
| Clay Matthews | LB | 6'2" | 230 | 22 | 1 | |
| Ron Belton | DB | 6'2" | 170 | 28 | | |
| Thom Darden | DB | 6'2" | 193 | 28 | 10 | |
| Oliver Davis | DB | 6'1" | 200 | 24 | 6 | 6 |
| Ricky Jones | DB | 6'1" | 195 | 23 | | |
| Tom London | DB | 6'1" | 197 | 24 | | |
| Tony Peters | DB | 6'1" | 192 | 25 | 2 | |
| Randy Rich (from OAK) | DB | 5'10" | 181 | 24 | | |
| Clarence Scott | DB | 6' | 180 | 29 | 3 | |
| Johnny Evans | QB | 6'1" | 197 | 22 | | |
| Mark Miller | QB | 6'2" | 176 | 22 | | 6 |
| Brian Sipe | QB | 6'1" | 190 | 29 | | 18 |
| Larry Collins | HB | 5'11" | 189 | 23 | | 6 |
| Cleo Miller | HB-FB | 6' | 202 | 26 | | 6 |
| Greg Pruitt | HB | 5'10" | 190 | 27 | | 30 |
| Tom Sullivan | HB | 6' | 190 | 28 | | |
| Calvin Hill | FB-HB | 6'3" | 227 | 31 | | 42 |
| Mike Pruitt | FB | 6' | 214 | 24 | | 30 |
| Ricky Feacher | WR | 5'10" | 174 | 24 | | |
| Dave Logan | WR | 6'4" | 226 | 24 | | 24 |
| Reggie Rucker | WR | 6'2" | 190 | 30 | | 48 |
| Keith Wright | WR | 5'10" | 172 | 22 | | |
| Ozzie Newsome | TE | 6'2" | 226 | 22 | | 24 |
| Gary Parris | TE | 6'2" | 226 | 28 | | |
| Oscar Roan | TE | 6'6" | 214 | 26 | | |
| Don Cockroft | K | 6'1" | 195 | 33 | | 94 |

## CINCINNATI BENGALS 4-12-0  Bill Johnson, Homer Rice

| Scores of Each Game | |
|---|---|
| 23 | KANSAS CITY 24 |
| 10 | Cleveland *13 |
| 3 | PITTSBURGH 28 |
| 18 | NEW ORLEANS 20 |
| 12 | San Francisco 28 |
| 0 | Miami 21 |
| 3 | NEW ENGLAND 10 |
| 0 | Buffalo 5 |
| 28 | HOUSTON 13 |
| 13 | San Diego 22 |
| 21 | OAKLAND 34 |
| 6 | Pittsburgh 7 |
| 10 | Houston 17 |
| 37 | ATLANTA 7 |
| 20 | Los Angeles 19 |
| 48 | CLEVELAND 16 |

| Use Name | Pos. | Hgt. | Wgt. | Age | Int. | Pts. |
|---|---|---|---|---|---|---|
| Vern Holland | OT | 6'5" | 265 | 30 | | |
| Ron Hunt | OT | 6'6" | 255 | 23 | | |
| Rufus Mayes | OT | 6'5" | 256 | 30 | | |
| Mike Wilson | OT | 6'5" | 280 | 23 | | |
| Glenn Bujnoch | OG | 6'5" | 251 | 24 | | |
| Mark Donahue | OG | 6'3" | 261 | 22 | | |
| Dave Lapham | OG | 6'4" | 259 | 26 | | |
| Blair Bush | C | 6'3" | 254 | 21 | | |
| Bob Johnson | C | 6'5" | 256 | 32 | | |
| Ross Browner | DE | 6'3" | 262 | 24 | | |
| Gary Burley | DE | 6'3" | 265 | 25 | | |
| Eddie Edwards | DT-DE | 6'4" | 256 | 24 | 1 | |
| Ted Vincent | DT | 6'4" | 262 | 22 | | |
| Wilson Whitley | DT | 6'3" | 264 | 23 | | |
| Glenn Cameron | LB | 6'1" | 217 | 25 | | |
| Tom DePaso | LB | 6'2" | 222 | 22 | | |
| Tom Dinkel | LB | 6'3" | 246 | 22 | 1 | |
| Bo Harris | LB | 6'3" | 221 | 25 | | |
| Jim LeClair | LB | 6'2" | 238 | 27 | 1 | |
| Tom Ruud | LB | 6'2" | 230 | 25 | | |
| Rod Shumon | LB | 6'1" | 225 | 22 | 1 | |
| Reggie Williams | LB | 6'1" | 228 | 23 | 1 | |
| Lou Breeden | DB | 5'11" | 185 | 24 | 3 | |
| Marvin Cobb | DB | 6' | 191 | 25 | 1 | |
| Ray Griffin | DB | 5'10" | 186 | 22 | | |
| Dick Jauron | DB | 6' | 190 | 27 | 4 | 6 |
| Melvin Morgan | DB | 6' | 186 | 25 | 1 | |
| Scott Perry | DB | 6' | 182 | 24 | 3 | 18 |
| Ken Riley | DB | 6' | 185 | 31 | 3 | |
| Ken Anderson | QB | 6'1" | 210 | 29 | | 6 |
| Rob Hertel | QB | 6'2" | 192 | 23 | | |
| John Reaves | QB | 6'2" | 210 | 28 | | |
| Lenvil Elliott | HB | 6' | 208 | 26 | | |
| Archie Griffin | HB | 5'9" | 193 | 24 | | 18 |
| Deacon Turner | HB | 5'11" | 212 | 23 | | |
| Booby Clark | FB | 6'2" | 245 | 27 | | |
| Tony Davis | FB | 5'10" | 210 | 25 | | 12 |
| Pete Johnson | FB | 6' | 240 | 24 | | 42 |
| Billy Brooks | WR | 6'3" | 202 | 25 | | 12 |
| Isaac Curtis | WR | 6' | 192 | 27 | | 18 |
| Dennis Law | WR | 6'1" | 180 | 24 | | |
| Pat McInally | WR | 6'6" | 210 | 25 | | |
| Don Bass | TE | 6'2" | 218 | 23 | | 30 |
| Jim Corbett | TE | 6'3" | 221 | 24 | | |
| Rich Walker | TE | 6'3" | 237 | 23 | | 12 |
| Chris Bahr | K | 5'9" | 170 | 25 | | 74 |

*—Overtime

## PITTSBURGH STEELERS

### Rushing

| Last Name | No. | Yds. | Avg. | TD |
|---|---|---|---|---|
| Harris | 310 | 1082 | 3.5 | 8 |
| Bleier | 165 | 633 | 3.8 | 5 |
| Thornton | 71 | 264 | 3.7 | 2 |
| Moser | 42 | 153 | 3.6 | 0 |
| Bradshaw | 32 | 93 | 2.9 | 1 |
| Deloplaine | 11 | 49 | 4.5 | 0 |
| Maxson | 4 | 9 | 2.3 | 0 |
| Swann | 1 | 7 | 7.0 | 0 |
| Kruczek | 5 | 7 | 1.4 | 0 |

### Receiving

| Last Name | No. | Yds. | Avg. | TD |
|---|---|---|---|---|
| Swann | 61 | 880 | 14 | 11 |
| Stallworth | 41 | 798 | 20 | 9 |
| Grossman | 37 | 448 | 12 | 1 |
| Harris | 22 | 144 | 7 | 0 |
| Bleier | 17 | 168 | 10 | 1 |
| Cunningham | 16 | 321 | 20 | 2 |
| Smith | 6 | 83 | 14 | 2 |
| Bell | 6 | 53 | 9 | 1 |
| Thornton | 5 | 66 | 13 | 1 |
| Moser | 1 | -1 | -1 | 0 |
| Bradshaw | 0 | 1 | — | 0 |

### Punt Returns

| Last Name | No. | Yds. | Avg. | TD |
|---|---|---|---|---|
| Reutershan | 20 | 148 | 7 | 0 |
| Bell | 21 | 152 | 7 | 0 |
| Smith | 9 | 65 | 7 | 0 |
| Terry | 7 | 80 | 11 | 0 |
| Shell | 1 | 6 | 6 | 0 |

### Kickoff Returns

| Last Name | No. | Yds. | Avg. | TD |
|---|---|---|---|---|
| L. Anderson | 37 | 930 | 25 | 1 |
| Terry | 7 | 145 | 21 | 0 |
| Maxson | 3 | 50 | 17 | 0 |
| Thornton | 1 | 37 | 37 | 0 |
| Deloplaine | 1 | 19 | 19 | 0 |
| Smith | 1 | 16 | 16 | 0 |
| Moser | 1 | 8 | 8 | 0 |
| Mullins | 1 | 0 | 0 | 0 |

### Passing – Punting – Kicking

| PASSING | Att. | Comp. | % | Yds. | Yd./Att. | TD | Int.–% | RK |
|---|---|---|---|---|---|---|---|---|
| Bradshaw | 368 | 207 | 56 | 2915 | 7.9 | 28 | 20–5 | 1 |
| Kruczek | 11 | 5 | 46 | 46 | 4.2 | 0 | 2–18 | |
| Harris | 1 | 0 | 0 | 0 | 0.0 | 0 | 0–0 | |

| PUNTING | No. | Avg. |
|---|---|---|
| Colquitt | 66 | 40.0 |

| KICKING | XP | Att. | % | FG | Att. | % |
|---|---|---|---|---|---|---|
| Gerela | 44 | 45 | 98 | 12 | 26 | 46 |

## HOUSTON OILERS

### Rushing

| Last Name | No. | Yds. | Avg. | TD |
|---|---|---|---|---|
| Campbell | 302 | 1450 | 4.8 | 13 |
| T. Wilson | 126 | 431 | 3.4 | 0 |
| Carpenter | 82 | 348 | 4.2 | 5 |
| Coleman | 61 | 188 | 3.1 | 1 |
| Caster | 5 | 32 | 6.4 | 0 |
| Barber | 2 | 14 | 7.0 | 0 |
| Pastorini | 18 | 11 | 0.6 | 0 |
| Renfro | 1 | 9 | 9.0 | 0 |
| Davis | 3 | 7 | 2.3 | 0 |
| Woods | 2 | 4 | 2.0 | 0 |
| Duncan | 1 | 0 | 0.0 | 0 |
| Burrough | 3 | -11 | -3.7 | 0 |

### Receiving

| Last Name | No. | Yds. | Avg. | TD |
|---|---|---|---|---|
| Burrough | 47 | 624 | 13 | 2 |
| Barber | 32 | 513 | 16 | 3 |
| Renfro | 26 | 339 | 13 | 2 |
| Caster | 20 | 316 | 16 | 5 |
| Coleman | 19 | 246 | 13 | 1 |
| Carpenter | 17 | 150 | 9 | 0 |
| T. Wilson | 15 | 91 | 6 | 1 |
| Campbell | 12 | 48 | 4 | 0 |
| Woods | 6 | 96 | 16 | 2 |
| Rucker | 2 | 38 | 19 | 0 |
| Duncan | 2 | 0 | 0 | 0 |
| B. Johnson | 1 | 10 | 10 | 0 |
| Merkens | 1 | 6 | 6 | 0 |
| Sampson | 1 | -4 | -4 | 0 |

### Punt Returns

| Last Name | No. | Yds. | Avg. | TD |
|---|---|---|---|---|
| Coleman | 16 | 142 | 9 | 0 |
| Merkens | 13 | 132 | 10 | 0 |
| Woods | 9 | 82 | 9 | 0 |
| B. Johnson | 8 | 60 | 8 | 0 |
| Thompson | 0 | 2 | — | 0 |

### Kickoff Returns

| Last Name | No. | Yds. | Avg. | TD |
|---|---|---|---|---|
| Dirden | 32 | 780 | 24 | 0 |
| Poole | 4 | 107 | 27 | 0 |
| Davis | 4 | 98 | 25 | 0 |
| B. Johnson | 4 | 73 | 18 | 0 |
| Turner | 4 | 69 | 17 | 0 |
| Woods | 3 | 59 | 20 | 0 |
| Coleman | 2 | 40 | 20 | 0 |
| Duncan | 2 | 38 | 19 | 0 |
| T. Wilson | 2 | 29 | 15 | 0 |
| Carpenter | 1 | 11 | 11 | 0 |

### Passing – Punting – Kicking

| PASSING | Att. | Comp. | % | Yds. | Yd./Att. | TD | Int.–% | RK |
|---|---|---|---|---|---|---|---|---|
| Pastorini | 368 | 199 | 54 | 2473 | 6.7 | 16 | 17–5 | 8 |
| Nielsen | 4 | 2 | 50 | 0 | 0.0 | 0 | 0–0 | |
| Burrough | 1 | 0 | 0 | 0 | 0.0 | 0 | 0–0 | |

| PUNTING | No. | Avg. |
|---|---|---|
| Parsley | 91 | 38.9 |

| KICKING | XP | Att. | % | FG | Att. | % |
|---|---|---|---|---|---|---|
| Fritsch | 31 | 32 | 97 | 14 | 18 | 78 |

## CLEVELAND BROWNS

### Rushing

| Last Name | No. | Yds. | Avg. | TD |
|---|---|---|---|---|
| G. Pruitt | 176 | 960 | 5.5 | 3 |
| M. Pruitt | 135 | 560 | 4.1 | 5 |
| C. Miller | 89 | 336 | 3.8 | 1 |
| Hill | 80 | 289 | 3.6 | 1 |
| Newsome | 13 | 96 | 7.4 | 2 |
| Sipe | 28 | 87 | 3.1 | 3 |
| Collins | 22 | 64 | 2.9 | 1 |
| M. Miller | 7 | 63 | 9.0 | 1 |
| Rucker | 2 | 14 | 7.0 | 0 |
| Evans | 2 | 12 | 6.0 | 0 |
| T. Sullivan | 5 | 7 | 1.4 | 0 |

### Receiving

| Last Name | No. | Yds. | Avg. | TD |
|---|---|---|---|---|
| Rucker | 43 | 893 | 21 | 8 |
| Newsome | 38 | 589 | 16 | 2 |
| G. Pruitt | 38 | 292 | 8 | 2 |
| Logan | 37 | 585 | 16 | 4 |
| Hill | 25 | 334 | 13 | 6 |
| C. Miller | 20 | 152 | 8 | 0 |
| M. Pruitt | 20 | 112 | 6 | 0 |
| Wright | 8 | 76 | 10 | 0 |
| Feacher | 4 | 76 | 19 | 0 |
| T. Sullivan | 1 | 20 | 20 | 0 |
| Collins | 1 | 4 | 4 | 0 |
| Parris | 1 | 4 | 4 | 0 |

### Punt Returns

| Last Name | No. | Yds. | Avg. | TD |
|---|---|---|---|---|
| Wright | 37 | 288 | 7 | 0 |
| Newsome | 2 | 29 | 15 | 0 |

### Kickoff Returns

| Last Name | No. | Yds. | Avg. | TD |
|---|---|---|---|---|
| Wright | 30 | 789 | 26 | 0 |
| Collins | 32 | 709 | 22 | 0 |
| T. Sullivan | 4 | 90 | 23 | 0 |
| Rich | 2 | 43 | 22 | 0 |
| G. Pruitt | 1 | 31 | 31 | 0 |
| B. Jackson | 1 | 19 | 19 | 0 |
| C. Miller | 1 | 15 | 15 | 0 |
| Rucker | 1 | 1 | 1 | 0 |

### Passing – Punting – Kicking

| PASSING | Att. | Comp. | % | Yds. | Yd./Att. | TD | Int.–% | RK |
|---|---|---|---|---|---|---|---|---|
| Sipe | 399 | 222 | 56 | 2906 | 7.3 | 21 | 15–4 | 4 |
| M. Miller | 39 | 13 | 33 | 212 | 5.4 | 1 | 4–10 | |
| Evans | 1 | 1 | 100 | 19 | 19.0 | 0 | 0–0 | |
| G. Pruitt | 3 | 0 | 0 | 0 | 0.0 | 0 | 2–67 | |

| PUNTING | No. | Avg. |
|---|---|---|
| Evans | 79 | 39.1 |

| KICKING | XP | Att. | % | FG | Att. | % |
|---|---|---|---|---|---|---|
| Cochroft | 37 | 40 | 93 | 19 | 28 | 68 |

## CINCINNATI BENGALS

### Rushing

| Last Name | No. | Yds. | Avg. | TD |
|---|---|---|---|---|
| P. Johnson | 180 | 762 | 4.2 | 7 |
| A. Griffin | 132 | 484 | 3.7 | 0 |
| Turner | 84 | 333 | 4.0 | 0 |
| Clark | 40 | 187 | 4.7 | 0 |
| Anderson | 29 | 167 | 5.8 | 1 |
| Elliott | 29 | 75 | 2.6 | 0 |
| Davis | 21 | 57 | 2.7 | 2 |
| Reaves | 6 | 50 | 8.3 | 0 |
| Dinkel | 1 | 20 | 20.0 | 0 |
| Curtis | 1 | 1 | 1.0 | 0 |
| Hertel | 1 | 0 | 0.0 | 0 |
| Law | 1 | -1 | -1.0 | 0 |
| Bass | 1 | -4 | -4.0 | 0 |

### Receiving

| Last Name | No. | Yds. | Avg. | TD |
|---|---|---|---|---|
| Curtis | 47 | 737 | 16 | 3 |
| A. Griffin | 35 | 284 | 8 | 3 |
| P. Johnson | 31 | 236 | 8 | 0 |
| Brooks | 30 | 506 | 17 | 2 |
| Bass | 27 | 447 | 17 | 4 |
| McInally | 15 | 189 | 13 | 0 |
| Corbett | 12 | 187 | 16 | 0 |
| Walker | 12 | 126 | 11 | 2 |
| Elliott | 12 | 100 | 8 | 0 |
| Clark | 11 | 73 | 7 | 0 |
| Turner | 11 | 50 | 5 | 0 |
| Law | 5 | 81 | 16 | 0 |
| Davis | 2 | 23 | 11 | 0 |

### Punt Returns

| Last Name | No. | Yds. | Avg. | TD |
|---|---|---|---|---|
| Davis | 22 | 130 | 6 | 0 |
| Law | 25 | 106 | 4 | 0 |
| Breeden | 6 | -12 | -2 | 0 |
| Jauron | 3 | 32 | 11 | 0 |
| Bass | 3 | 8 | 3 | 0 |

### Kickoff Returns

| Last Name | No. | Yds. | Avg. | TD |
|---|---|---|---|---|
| R. Griffin | 37 | 787 | 21 | 0 |
| Bass | 7 | 138 | 20 | 0 |
| A. Griffin | 4 | 94 | 24 | 0 |
| Davis | 3 | 51 | 17 | 0 |
| Law | 2 | 30 | 15 | 0 |
| Turner | 1 | 24 | 24 | 0 |
| Corbett | 1 | 15 | 15 | 0 |
| Breeden | 1 | 12 | 12 | 0 |
| Clark | 1 | 11 | 11 | 0 |
| Vincent | 1 | 2 | 2 | 0 |

### Passing – Punting – Kicking

| PASSING | Att. | Comp. | % | Yds. | Yd./Att. | TD | Int.–% | RK |
|---|---|---|---|---|---|---|---|---|
| Anderson | 319 | 173 | 54 | 2219 | 7.0 | 10 | 22–7 | 12 |
| Reaves | 144 | 74 | 51 | 790 | 5.5 | 3 | 8–6 | |
| A. Griffin | 3 | 2 | 67 | 21 | 7.0 | 0 | 0–0 | |
| Hertel | 4 | 1 | 25 | 9 | 2.3 | 0 | 0–0 | |

| PUNTING | No. | Avg. |
|---|---|---|
| McInally | 91 | 43.1 |
| Bahr | 4 | 27.0 |

| KICKING | XP | Att. | % | FG | Att. | % |
|---|---|---|---|---|---|---|
| Bahr | 26 | 29 | 90 | 16 | 30 | 53 |

| Scores of Each Game | | Use Name | Pos. | Hgt. | Wgt. | Age | Int. | Pts. |
|---|---|---|---|---|---|---|---|---|

## DENVER BRONCOS 10-6-0  Red Miller

| | | | Use Name | Pos. | Hgt. | Wgt. | Age | Int. | Pts. |
|---|---|---|---|---|---|---|---|---|---|
| 14 | OAKLAND | 6 | Bill Bain | OT | 6'4" | 270 | 26 | | |
| 9 | Minnesota | *12 | Glenn Hyde | OT | 6'3" | 250 | 27 | | |
| 27 | SAN DIEGO | 14 | Claudie Minor | OT | 6'4" | 280 | 27 | | |
| 23 | Kansas City | *17 | Tom Neville | OT | 6'4" | 253 | 35 | | |
| 28 | SEATTLE | 7 | Tom Glassic | OG | 6'3" | 254 | 24 | | |
| 0 | San Diego | 23 | Paul Howard | OG | 6'3" | 260 | 27 | | |
| 16 | CHICAGO | 7 | Steve Schindler | OG | 6'3" | 260 | 24 | | |
| 6 | Baltimore | 7 | Bill Bryan | C | 6'2" | 244 | 23 | | |
| 20 | Seattle | *17 | Bobby Maples | C | 6'3" | 250 | 35 | | |
| 28 | N.Y. JETS | 31 | Lyle Alzado | DE | 6'3" | 250 | 29 | | |
| 19 | Cleveland | 7 | Barney Chavous | DE | 6'3" | 252 | 27 | | |
| 16 | GREEN BAY | 3 | Brison Manor | DE | 6'4" | 248 | 26 | | |
| 14 | Detroit | 17 | Paul Smith | DE | 6'3" | 256 | 33 | | |
| 21 | Oakland | 6 | Rubin Carter | NT | 6' | 256 | 25 | | |
| 24 | KANSAS CITY | 3 | John Grant | NT | 6'3" | 246 | 28 | | |
| 17 | PITTSBURGH | 21 | Don Latimer | NT | 6'3" | 265 | 23 | | |

| Use Name | Pos. | Hgt. | Wgt. | Age | Int. | Pts. |
|---|---|---|---|---|---|---|
| Larry Evans | LB | 6'2" | 216 | 25 | | |
| Randy Gradishar | LB | 6'3" | 233 | 26 | 4 | 6 |
| Tom Jackson | LB | 5'11" | 220 | 27 | 3 | 6 |
| Rob Nairne | LB | 6'4" | 220 | 24 | | |
| Joe Rizzo | LB | 6'1" | 220 | 27 | 3 | |
| Bob Swenson | LB | 6'3" | 220 | 25 | 1 | |
| Godwin Turk | LB | 6'3" | 230 | 27 | 2 | |
| Steve Foley | DB | 6'2" | 185 | 24 | 6 | |
| Maurice Harvey | DB | 5'10" | 190 | 22 | | |
| Bernard Jackson | DB | 6' | 178 | 28 | 6 | |
| Chris Pane | DB | 5'11" | 180 | 25 | | |
| Bill Thompson | DB | 6'1" | 200 | 31 | 4 | 6 |
| Charlie West | DB | 6'1" | 190 | 32 | | |
| Louie Wright | DB | 6'2" | 195 | 25 | 2 | |
| Jim Jensen-Knee Injury | | | | | | |

| Use Name | Pos. | Hgt. | Wgt. | Age | Int. | Pts. |
|---|---|---|---|---|---|---|
| Craig Morton | QB | 6'4" | 210 | 35 | | |
| Craig Penrose | QB | 6'3" | 205 | 25 | | |
| Norris Weese | QB | 6'1" | 195 | 27 | | 6 |
| Otis Armstrong | HB | 5'10" | 196 | 27 | | 12 |
| Rob Lytle | HB | 6'1" | 195 | 23 | | 12 |
| Dave Preston | HB | 5'10" | 195 | 23 | | 12 |
| Larry Canada | FB | 6'2" | 235 | 23 | | 18 |
| Jon Keyworth | FB | 6'3" | 230 | 27 | | 24 |
| Lonnie Perrin | FB | 6'1" | 222 | 26 | | 30 |
| Jack Dolbin | WR | 5'10" | 183 | 29 | | |
| Vince Kinney | WR | 6'2" | 190 | 22 | | |
| Haven Moses | WR | 6'3" | 200 | 32 | | 30 |
| John Schultz | WR | 5'10" | 182 | 25 | | |
| Rick Upchurch | WR | 5'10" | 170 | 26 | | 12 |
| Ron Egloff | TE | 6'5" | 238 | 22 | | 6 |
| Bob Moore | TE | 6'3" | 225 | 29 | | |
| Riley Odoms | TE | 6'4" | 230 | 28 | | 36 |
| Bucky Dilts | K | 5'9" | 183 | 24 | | |
| Jim Turner | K | 6'2" | 205 | 37 | | 64 |

## OAKLAND RAIDERS 9-7-0  John Madden

| | | | Use Name | Pos. | Hgt. | Wgt. | Age | Int. | Pts. |
|---|---|---|---|---|---|---|---|---|---|
| 6 | Denver | 14 | Henry Lawrence | OT | 6'4" | 270 | 26 | | |
| 21 | San Diego | 20 | Lindsey Mason | OT | 6'5" | 260 | 23 | | |
| 28 | Green Bay | 3 | Art Shell | OT | 6'5" | 275 | 31 | | |
| 14 | NEW ENGLAND | 21 | Mickey Marvin | OG | 6'4" | 270 | 22 | | |
| 25 | Chicago | *19 | Gene Upshaw | OG | 6'5" | 255 | 33 | | |
| 21 | HOUSTON | 17 | Dave Dalby | C | 6'2" | 250 | 27 | | |
| 28 | KANSAS CITY | 6 | Steve Sylvester | C-OG-OT | 6'4" | 260 | 25 | | |
| 7 | Seattle | 27 | Dave Browning | DE | 6'5" | 245 | 22 | | |
| 23 | SAN DIEGO | 27 | John Matuszak | DE | 6'8" | 275 | 27 | | |
| 20 | Kansas City | 10 | Charles Philyaw | DE-MG | 6'9" | 275 | 24 | | |
| 34 | Cincinnati | 21 | Pat Toomay | DE | 6'5" | 245 | 33 | | |
| 29 | DETROIT | 17 | Mike McCoy | MG | 6'5" | 275 | 29 | | |
| 16 | SEATTLE | 17 | Otis Sistrunk | MG-DE | 6'4" | 270 | 30 | | |
| 6 | DENVER | 21 | | | | | | | |
| 6 | Miami | 23 | | | | | | | |
| 27 | MINNESOTA | 20 | | | | | | | |

| Use Name | Pos. | Hgt. | Wgt. | Age | Int. | Pts. |
|---|---|---|---|---|---|---|
| Jeff Barnes | LB | 6'2" | 215 | 23 | | |
| Willie Hall | LB | 6'2" | 225 | 28 | 2 | |
| Ted Hendricks | LB | 6'7" | 220 | 30 | 3 | |
| John Huddleston | LB | 6'3" | 230 | 24 | | |
| Monte Johnson | LB | 6'4" | 240 | 26 | 1 | |
| Rod Martin | LB | 6'2" | 205 | 24 | | |
| Phil Villipiano | LB | 6'2" | 225 | 29 | 2 | |
| Robert Watts | LB | 6'3" | 218 | 24 | | |
| Willie Brown | DB | 6'1" | 210 | 37 | 1 | |
| Neal Colzie | DB | 6'2" | 205 | 25 | 3 | 6 |
| Mike Davis | DB | 6'2" | 200 | 22 | 1 | |
| Lester Hayes | DB | 6' | 208 | 23 | 4 | |
| Monte Jackson | DB | 5'11" | 189 | 25 | 2 | |
| Charlie Phillips | DB | 6'2" | 215 | 25 | 6 | 18 |
| Jack Tatum | DB | 5'10" | 205 | 29 | 3 | |
| Bob Nelson-Injury | | | | | | |
| Sam Scarber-Injury | | | | | | |
| John Vella-Chest Injury | | | | | | |

| Use Name | Pos. | Hgt. | Wgt. | Age | Int. | Pts. |
|---|---|---|---|---|---|---|
| David Humm | QB | 6'2" | 185 | 26 | | |
| Jim Plunkett | QB | 6'3" | 207 | 30 | | |
| Ken Stabler | QB | 6'3" | 215 | 32 | | |
| Pete Banaszak | HB | 5'11" | 210 | 34 | | |
| Clarence Davis | HB | 5'10" | 195 | 29 | | |
| Harold Hart | HB | 6' | 205 | 25 | | |
| Art Whittington | HB | 5'11" | 180 | 22 | | 42 |
| Terry Robiskie | FB-HB | 6'1" | 210 | 23 | | 12 |
| Booker Russell | FB | 6'2" | 230 | 22 | | |
| Mark van Eeghen | FB | 6'2" | 225 | 26 | | 60 |
| Fred Biletnikoff | WR | 6'1" | 190 | 35 | | 24 |
| Morris Bradshaw | WR | 6' | 195 | 25 | | 12 |
| Cliff Branch | WR | 5'11" | 170 | 30 | | 6 |
| Larry Brunson | WR | 5'11" | 180 | 29 | | |
| Joe Stewart | WR | 5'11" | 180 | 22 | | |
| Warren Bankston | TE | 6'4" | 235 | 31 | | |
| Dave Casper | TE | 6'4" | 230 | 26 | | 60 |
| Ray Chester | TE | 6'3" | 235 | 30 | | 12 |
| Derrick Ramsey | TE | 6'4" | 220 | 21 | | |
| Jim Breech | K | 5'6" | 165 | 22 | | |
| Ray Guy | K | 6'3" | 195 | 28 | | |
| Errol Mann | K | 6' | 205 | 37 | | 69 |

## SAN DIEGO CHARGERS 9-7-0  Tommy Prothro, Don Coryell

| | | | Use Name | Pos. | Hgt. | Wgt. | Age | Int. | Pts. |
|---|---|---|---|---|---|---|---|---|---|
| 24 | Seattle | 20 | Milton Hardaway | OT | 6'9" | 309 | 23 | | |
| 20 | OAKLAND | 21 | Billy Shields | OT | 6'7" | 254 | 25 | | |
| 14 | Denver | 27 | Russ Washington | OT | 6'6" | 290 | 31 | | |
| 3 | GREEN BAY | 24 | Charles Aiu (to SEA) | OG | 6'2" | 250 | 24 | | |
| 23 | New England | 28 | Dan Audick | OG | 6'3" | 255 | 23 | | |
| 23 | DENVER | 0 | Ed White | OG | 6'2" | 270 | 31 | | |
| 21 | MIAMI | 28 | Doug Wilkerson | OG | 6'2" | 257 | 31 | | |
| 14 | Detroit | 31 | Don Macek | C-OG | 6'3" | 253 | 24 | | |
| 27 | Oakland | 23 | Ralph Perretta | C | 6'2" | 250 | 25 | | |
| 22 | CINCINNATI | 13 | Mark Slater | C | 6'1" | 252 | 23 | | |
| 29 | KANSAS CITY | *23 | Fred Dean | DE | 6'3" | 228 | 26 | | |
| 13 | Minnesota | 7 | Leroy Jones | DE | 6'8" | 265 | 27 | | |
| 0 | Kansas City | 23 | John Lee | DE | 6'2" | 253 | 25 | | |
| 40 | CHICAGO | 7 | Wilbur Young | DE | 6'6" | 290 | 29 | | |
| 37 | SEATTLE | 10 | Charles DeJurnett | DT | 6'4" | 270 | 26 | | |
| 45 | Houston | 24 | Gary Johnson | DT | 6'2" | 254 | 26 | 1 | 6 |
| | | | Louie Kelcher | DT | 6'5" | 282 | 25 | 1 | |

| Use Name | Pos. | Hgt. | Wgt. | Age | Int. | Pts. |
|---|---|---|---|---|---|---|
| Don Goode | LB | 6'2" | 225 | 27 | 1 | |
| Bob Horn | LB | 6'3" | 237 | 24 | 1 | |
| Jim Laslavic | LB | 6'2" | 240 | 26 | | |
| Woodrow Lowe | LB | 6' | 227 | 24 | 1 | |
| Rick Middleton | LB | 6'2" | 228 | 26 | 1 | |
| Ray Preston | LB | 6' | 215 | 24 | | |
| Jerome Dove | DB | 6' | 186 | 24 | 1 | |
| Glen Edwards | DB | 6' | 185 | 31 | 3 | |
| Mike Fuller | DB | 5'9" | 188 | 25 | 4 | 6 |
| Keith King | DB | 6'4" | 226 | 23 | 1 | |
| Pete Shaw | DB | 5'10" | 184 | 24 | 2 | |
| Hal Stringert | DB | 5'11" | 185 | 26 | 2 | |
| Mike Williams | DB | 5'10" | 180 | 24 | 3 | |
| Bob Rush-Knee Injury | | | | | | |

| Use Name | Pos. | Hgt. | Wgt. | Age | Int. | Pts. |
|---|---|---|---|---|---|---|
| Dan Fouts | QB | 6'3" | 204 | 27 | | 12 |
| James Harris | QB | 6'3" | 217 | 31 | | |
| Cliff Olander | QB | 6'5" | 196 | 23 | | |
| Hank Bauer | HB | 5'10" | 204 | 24 | | 54 |
| Lydell Mitchell | HB | 5'11" | 198 | 29 | | 30 |
| Clarence Williams | HB | 5'9" | 198 | 23 | | |
| Ricky Anderson | FB | 6'1" | 211 | 25 | | |
| Bo Matthews | FB | 6'4" | 230 | 26 | | |
| Don Woods | FB | 6'1" | 209 | 27 | | 18 |
| Larry Burton | WR | 6'1" | 193 | 26 | | 18 |
| John Jefferson | WR | 6'1" | 190 | 22 | | 78 |
| Charlie Joiner | WR | 5'11" | 188 | 30 | | 6 |
| Dwight McDonald | WR | 6'2" | 187 | 27 | | 6 |
| Artie Owens | WR | 5'10" | 174 | 25 | | |
| Johnny Rodgers | WR | 5'10" | 180 | 27 | | |
| Pat Curran | TE | 6'3" | 235 | 32 | | 12 |
| Bob Klein | TE | 6'5" | 245 | 31 | | 12 |
| Greg McCrary (from WAS) | TE | 6'3" | 230 | 26 | | 6 |
| Jeff West | TE | 6'3" | 211 | 25 | | |
| Rolf Benirshke | K | 6' | 170 | 23 | | 91 |

## SEATTLE SEAHAWKS 9-7-0  Jack Patera

| | | | Use Name | Pos. | Hgt. | Wgt. | Age | Int. | Pts. |
|---|---|---|---|---|---|---|---|---|---|
| 10 | SAN DIEGO | 24 | Steve August | OT | 6'5" | 254 | 23 | | |
| 10 | Pittsburgh | 21 | Nick Bebout | OT | 6'5" | 260 | 27 | | |
| 24 | N.Y. Jets | 17 | Louis Bullard | OT | 6'6" | 265 | 22 | | |
| 28 | DETROIT | 16 | Norm Evans | OT | 6'5" | 250 | 35 | | |
| 7 | Denver | 28 | Ron Coder | OG | 6'4" | 250 | 24 | | |
| 29 | MINNESOTA | 28 | Tom Lynch | OG | 6'5" | 260 | 23 | | |
| 28 | Green Bay | 45 | Bob Newton | OG | 6'4" | 260 | 29 | | |
| 27 | OAKLAND | 7 | Art Kuehn | C | 6'3" | 255 | 25 | | |
| 17 | DENVER | *20 | John Yarno | C | 6'5" | 251 | 23 | | |
| 31 | Chicago | 29 | Bill Gregory | DE | 6'5" | 260 | 28 | | |
| 14 | BALTIMORE | 17 | Dave Kraayeveld | DE-DT | 6'5" | 255 | 22 | | |
| 13 | Kansas City | 10 | Ernie Price (from DET) | DE | 6'4" | 245 | 27 | | |
| 17 | Oakland | 16 | Alden Roche | DE | 6'4" | 255 | 33 | | |
| 47 | CLEVELAND | 24 | Dennis Boyd | DT | 6'6" | 250 | 23 | | |
| 10 | San Diego | 37 | Steve Niehaus | DT | 6'4" | 255 | 23 | | |
| 23 | KANSAS CITY | 19 | Bill Sandifer | DT-DE | 6'6" | 260 | 26 | | |

| Use Name | Pos. | Hgt. | Wgt. | Age | Int. | Pts. |
|---|---|---|---|---|---|---|
| Terry Beeson | LB | 6'3" | 240 | 22 | | |
| Keith Butler | LB | 6'4" | 225 | 22 | | |
| Pete Cronan | LB | 6'2" | 238 | 23 | 2 | |
| Ken Geddes | LB | 6'3" | 235 | 30 | | |
| Sammy Green | LB | 6'2" | 230 | 23 | 1 | |
| Charles McShane | LB | 6'3" | 230 | 24 | | |
| Autry Beamon | DB | 6'1" | 190 | 24 | 4 | |
| Dave Brown | DB | 6'1" | 190 | 25 | 3 | |
| John Harris | DB | 6'2" | 200 | 22 | 4 | |
| Kerry Justin | DB | 5'11" | 175 | 24 | | |
| Doug Long | DB | 6' | 189 | 23 | | |
| Keith Simpson | DB | 6'1" | 195 | 22 | 2 | 6 |
| Cornell Webster | DB | 6' | 180 | 23 | 5 | |
| Don Dufek-Knee Injury | | | | | | |

| Use Name | Pos. | Hgt. | Wgt. | Age | Int. | Pts. |
|---|---|---|---|---|---|---|
| Sam Adkins | QB | 6'2" | 214 | 23 | | |
| Steve Myer | QB | 6'2" | 188 | 24 | | |
| Jim Zorn | QB | 6'2" | 200 | 25 | | 36 |
| Rufus Crawford | HB | 5'10" | 180 | 23 | | |
| Al Hunter | HB | 5'11" | 195 | 23 | | 12 |
| David Sims | HB | 6'3" | 216 | 22 | | 90 |
| Tony Benjamin | FB | 6'3" | 225 | 22 | | |
| Sherman Smith | FB | 6'4" | 225 | 23 | | 42 |
| Don Testerman | FB | 6'2" | 230 | 25 | | |
| Duke Fergerson | WR | 6'1" | 193 | 24 | | |
| Steve Largent | WR | 5'11" | 184 | 23 | | 48 |
| Sam McCullum | WR | 6'2" | 203 | 25 | | 18 |
| Steve Raible | WR | 6'2" | 195 | 24 | | 6 |
| Ron Howard | TE | 6'4" | 240 | 27 | | 6 |
| Brian Peets | TE | 6'4" | 225 | 22 | | |
| John Sawyer | TE | 6'2" | 230 | 25 | | |
| Efren Herrera | K | 5'9" | 190 | 27 | | 79 |
| Herman Weaver | K | 6'4" | 210 | 29 | | |

## KANSAS CITY CHIEFS 4-12-0  Marv Levy

| | | | Use Name | Pos. | Hgt. | Wgt. | Age | Int. | Pts. |
|---|---|---|---|---|---|---|---|---|---|
| 24 | Cincinnati | 3 | Larry Brown | OT | 6'5" | 260 | 23 | | |
| 17 | HOUSTON | 20 | Charlie Getty | OT-OG | 6'4" | 260 | 26 | | |
| 10 | N.Y. Giants | 26 | Matt Herkenhoff | OT | 6'5" | 257 | 25 | | |
| 17 | DENVER | *23 | Jim Nicholson | OT | 6'6" | 275 | 28 | | |
| 13 | Buffalo | 28 | Tom Condon | OG | 6'3" | 240 | 25 | | |
| 13 | TAMPA BAY | 30 | Bob Simmons | OG | 6'4" | 260 | 24 | | |
| 6 | Oakland | 28 | Rod Walters | OG-OT | 6'3" | 258 | 24 | | |
| 17 | CLEVELAND | 3 | Charlie Ane | C | 6'1" | 233 | 26 | | |
| 24 | Pittsburgh | 27 | Jack Rudnay | C | 6'3" | 240 | 30 | | |
| 10 | OAKLAND | 20 | Sylvester Hicks | DE | 6'4" | 248 | 23 | | |
| 23 | San Diego | *29 | Dave Lindstrom | DE | 6'6" | 249 | 23 | | |
| 10 | SEATTLE | 13 | Art Still | DE | 6'7" | 252 | 22 | | |
| 23 | SAN DIEGO | 0 | Stan Johnson | NT | 6'4" | 275 | 23 | | |
| 14 | BUFFALO | 10 | Jeff Lloyd | NT | 6'6" | 255 | 24 | | |
| 3 | Denver | 24 | Don Parrish | NT | 6'2" | 255 | 23 | | |
| 9 | Seattle | 23 | | | | | | | |

| Use Name | Pos. | Hgt. | Wgt. | Age | Int. | Pts. |
|---|---|---|---|---|---|---|
| Jimbo Elrod | LB | 6' | 223 | 24 | | |
| Tom Howard | LB | 6'2" | 208 | 24 | 1 | |
| Charles Jackson | LB | 6'3" | 236 | 23 | | |
| Whitney Paul | LB | 6'3" | 220 | 24 | 3 | |
| Dave Rozumek | LB | 6'1" | 212 | 24 | 2 | |
| Clarence Sanders | LB | 6'4" | 228 | 25 | | |
| Gary Spani | LB | 6'2" | 230 | 22 | | |
| Gary Barbaro | DB | 6'4" | 198 | 24 | 3 | |
| Ted Burgmeier | DB | 5'10" | 185 | 22 | | |
| Tim Collier | DB | 6' | 166 | 24 | 3 | |
| Tim Gray | DB | 6'1" | 200 | 25 | 6 | |
| Gary Green | DB | 5'11" | 184 | 21 | 1 | |
| Ray Milo | DB | 5'11" | 178 | 24 | | |
| Clyde Powers | DB | 6'1" | 195 | 27 | | |
| Emmitt Thomas | DB | 6'2" | 192 | 35 | 2 | |
| Ricky Davis-Shoulder Injury | | | | | | |
| Darius Helton-Shoulder Injury | | | | | | |
| Willie Lee-Knee Injury | | | | | | |

| Use Name | Pos. | Hgt. | Wgt. | Age | Int. | Pts. |
|---|---|---|---|---|---|---|
| Tony Adams | QB | 6' | 198 | 28 | | |
| Mike Livingston | QB | 6'3" | 210 | 32 | | 6 |
| Dennis Shaw | QB | 6'2" | 215 | 31 | | |
| Horace Belton | HB | 5'9" | 200 | 23 | | |
| Ted McKnight | HB | 6'1" | 203 | 24 | | 42 |
| Eddie Payton | HB | 5'8" | 175 | 27 | | |
| Tony Reed | HB | 5'11" | 197 | 23 | | 36 |
| Mark Bailey | FB | 6'3" | 237 | 23 | | |
| MacArthur Lane | FB-HB | 6' | 220 | 36 | | |
| Arnold Morgado | FB | 6'1" | 210 | 25 | | 42 |
| Larry Dorsey | WR | 6'1" | 195 | 25 | | 12 |
| Bill Kollar | WR | 5'11" | 187 | 22 | | |
| Henry Marshall | WR | 6'2" | 205 | 24 | | 12 |
| Jerrold McRae | WR | 6'1" | 201 | 23 | | |
| Ed Beckman | TE | 6'4" | 240 | 27 | | |
| Andre Samuels | TE | 6'4" | 229 | 25 | | |
| Walter White | TE | 6'3" | 218 | 27 | | 6 |
| Zenon Andrusyshyn | K | 6'2" | 210 | 31 | | |
| Jan Stenerud | K | 6'2" | 187 | 35 | | 85 |

*—Overtime

## DENVER BRONCOS

### RUSHING
| Last Name | No. | Yds. | Avg. | TD |
|---|---|---|---|---|
| Perrin | 108 | 455 | 4.2 | 4 |
| Keyworth | 112 | 444 | 4.0 | 3 |
| Armstrong | 112 | 381 | 3.4 | 1 |
| Canada | 79 | 365 | 4.6 | 3 |
| Lytle | 81 | 341 | 4.2 | 2 |
| Preston | 66 | 296 | 4.5 | 1 |
| Morton | 17 | 71 | 4.2 | 1 |
| Weese | 17 | 48 | 2.8 | 1 |
| Upchurch | 5 | 31 | 6.2 | 0 |
| Foley | 1 | 14 | 14.0 | 0 |
| Odoms | 2 | 5 | 5.0 | 0 |
| Penrose | 1 | 0 | 0.0 | 0 |

### RECEIVING
| Last Name | No. | Yds. | Avg. | TD |
|---|---|---|---|---|
| Odoms | 54 | 829 | 15 | 6 |
| Moses | 37 | 744 | 20 | 5 |
| Dolbin | 24 | 284 | 12 | 0 |
| Preston | 24 | 199 | 8 | 1 |
| Keyworth | 21 | 166 | 8 | 1 |
| Upchurch | 17 | 210 | 12 | 1 |
| Armstrong | 12 | 98 | 8 | 1 |
| Perrin | 10 | 54 | 5 | 1 |
| Canada | 6 | 37 | 6 | 0 |
| Lytle | 6 | 37 | 6 | 0 |
| Egloff | 4 | 33 | 8 | 1 |
| Kinney | 1 | 23 | 23 | 0 |
| Turner | 1 | -4 | -4 | 0 |

### PUNT RETURNS
| Last Name | No. | Yds. | Avg. | TD |
|---|---|---|---|---|
| Upchurch | 36 | 493 | 14 | 1 |
| Preston | 10 | 68 | 7 | 0 |
| West | 3 | 20 | 7 | 0 |
| Thompson | 1 | 3 | 3 | 0 |
| Pane | 1 | -2 | -2 | 0 |

### KICKOFF RETURNS
| Last Name | No. | Yds. | Avg. | TD |
|---|---|---|---|---|
| Perrin | 12 | 256 | 21 | 0 |
| B. Jackson | 9 | 209 | 23 | 0 |
| Upchurch | 8 | 222 | 28 | 0 |
| Preston | 7 | 154 | 22 | 0 |
| Keyworth | 2 | 24 | 12 | 0 |
| Pane | 1 | 29 | 29 | 0 |
| West | 1 | 24 | 24 | 0 |
| Schultz | 1 | 20 | 20 | 0 |
| Turk | 1 | 14 | 14 | 0 |

### PASSING
| Last Name | Att. | Comp. | % | Yds. | Yd./Att. | TD | Int.-% | RK |
|---|---|---|---|---|---|---|---|---|
| Morton | 267 | 146 | 55 | 1802 | 6.8 | 11 | 8- 3 | 5 |
| Weese | 87 | 55 | 63 | 723 | 8.3 | 4 | 5- 6 | |
| Penrose | 37 | 16 | 43 | 185 | 5.0 | 2 | 4-11 | |

### PUNTING
| Last Name | No. | Avg. |
|---|---|---|
| Dilts | 96 | 36.4 |

### KICKING
| Last Name | XP | Att. | % | FG | Att. | % |
|---|---|---|---|---|---|---|
| Turner | 31 | 35 | 89 | 11 | 22 | 50 |

## OAKLAND RAIDERS

### RUSHING
| Last Name | No. | Yds. | Avg. | TD |
|---|---|---|---|---|
| van Eeghen | 270 | 1080 | 4.0 | 9 |
| Whittington | 172 | 661 | 3.8 | 7 |
| Robiskie | 49 | 189 | 3.9 | 2 |
| Banaszak | 43 | 137 | 3.2 | 0 |
| Russell | 11 | 65 | 5.9 | 0 |
| Hart | 7 | 44 | 6.3 | 0 |
| Bradshaw | 1 | 5 | 5.0 | 0 |
| Casper | 1 | 5 | 5.0 | 0 |
| C. Davis | 14 | 4 | 0.3 | 0 |
| Stabler | 4 | 0 | 0.0 | 0 |
| Humm | 5 | -4 | -0.8 | 0 |

### RECEIVING
| Last Name | No. | Yds. | Avg. | TD |
|---|---|---|---|---|
| Casper | 62 | 852 | 14 | 9 |
| Branch | 49 | 709 | 15 | 1 |
| Bradshaw | 40 | 552 | 14 | 2 |
| van Eeghen | 27 | 291 | 11 | 0 |
| Whittington | 23 | 106 | 5 | 0 |
| Biletnikoff | 20 | 285 | 14 | 2 |
| Chester | 13 | 146 | 11 | 2 |
| Banaszak | 7 | 78 | 11 | 0 |
| Robiskie | 5 | 51 | 10 | 0 |
| C. Davis | 4 | 24 | 6 | 0 |
| Hart | 1 | 1 | 1 | 0 |

### PUNT RETURNS
| Last Name | No. | Yds. | Avg. | TD |
|---|---|---|---|---|
| Colzie | 47 | 310 | 7 | 0 |

### KICKOFF RETURNS
| Last Name | No. | Yds. | Avg. | TD |
|---|---|---|---|---|
| Whittington | 23 | 473 | 21 | 0 |
| Hart | 11 | 252 | 23 | 0 |
| Ramsey | 7 | 125 | 18 | 0 |
| Brunson | 6 | 154 | 26 | 0 |
| Stewart | 4 | 120 | 30 | 0 |
| Robiskie | 3 | 58 | 19 | 0 |
| Chester | 2 | 27 | 14 | 0 |
| Russell | 2 | -3 | -2 | 0 |
| Colzie | 1 | 15 | 15 | 0 |
| Mason | 1 | 12 | 12 | 0 |

### PASSING
| Last Name | Att. | Comp. | % | Yds. | Yd./Att. | TD | Int.-% | RK |
|---|---|---|---|---|---|---|---|---|
| Stabler | 406 | 237 | 58 | 2944 | 7.3 | 16 | 30- 7 | 11 |
| Humm | 26 | 14 | 54 | 151 | 5.8 | 0 | 1- 4 | |
| Casper | 1 | 0 | 0 | 0 | 0.0 | 0 | 0- 0 | |

### PUNTING
| Last Name | No. | Avg. |
|---|---|---|
| Guy | 81 | 42.7 |

### KICKING
| Last Name | XP | Att. | % | FG | Att. | % |
|---|---|---|---|---|---|---|
| Mann | 33 | 38 | 87 | 12 | 20 | 60 |

## SAN DIEGO CHARGERS

### RUSHING
| Last Name | No. | Yds. | Avg. | TD |
|---|---|---|---|---|
| Mitchell | 214 | 820 | 3.8 | 3 |
| Woods | 151 | 514 | 3.4 | 3 |
| Bauer | 85 | 304 | 3.6 | 8 |
| Matthews | 71 | 286 | 4.0 | 0 |
| C. Williams | 27 | 76 | 2.8 | 0 |
| Fouts | 20 | 43 | 2.2 | 2 |
| McCrary | 2 | 18 | 9.0 | 0 |
| Anderson | 3 | 11 | 3.7 | 0 |
| Jefferson | 1 | 7 | 7.0 | 0 |
| Harris | 10 | 7 | 0.7 | 0 |
| Rodgers | 1 | 5 | 5.0 | 0 |
| West | 1 | 0 | 0.0 | 0 |
| Olander | 1 | -3 | -3.0 | 0 |

### RECEIVING
| Last Name | No. | Yds. | Avg. | TD |
|---|---|---|---|---|
| Mitchell | 57 | 500 | 9 | 2 |
| Jefferson | 56 | 1001 | 18 | 13 |
| Klein | 34 | 413 | 12 | 2 |
| Woods | 34 | 295 | 9 | 0 |
| Joiner | 33 | 607 | 18 | 1 |
| Matthews | 11 | 78 | 7 | 0 |
| Bauer | 10 | 78 | 8 | 1 |
| Owens | 9 | 188 | 21 | 0 |
| Curran | 9 | 92 | 10 | 2 |
| Burton | 5 | 127 | 25 | 3 |
| Rodgers | 5 | 47 | 9 | 0 |
| McDonald | 3 | 84 | 28 | 1 |
| McCrary | 1 | 29 | 29 | 0 |
| C. Williams | 1 | 17 | 17 | 0 |
| Anderson | 1 | -3 | -3 | 0 |

### PUNT RETURNS
| Last Name | No. | Yds. | Avg. | TD |
|---|---|---|---|---|
| Fuller | 39 | 436 | 11 | 0 |
| Rodgers | 11 | 88 | 8 | 0 |
| Shaw | 4 | 46 | 12 | 0 |
| Owens | 1 | 20 | 20 | 0 |
| Goode | 1 | 0 | 0 | 0 |
| M. Williams | 1 | 0 | 0 | 0 |

### KICKOFF RETURNS
| Last Name | No. | Yds. | Avg. | TD |
|---|---|---|---|---|
| Owens | 20 | 524 | 26 | 0 |
| Rodgers | 11 | 287 | 26 | 0 |
| C. Williams | 6 | 143 | 24 | 0 |
| Anderson | 6 | 83 | 14 | 0 |
| Fuller | 5 | 109 | 22 | 0 |
| Woods | 2 | 37 | 19 | 0 |
| Horn | 2 | 27 | 14 | 0 |
| Preston | 1 | 15 | 15 | 0 |
| Klein | 1 | 13 | 13 | 0 |
| Macek | 1 | 6 | 6 | 0 |
| Middleton | 1 | 5 | 5 | 0 |
| Slater | 1 | 3 | 3 | 0 |
| Stringert | 1 | 0 | 0 | 0 |

### PASSING
| Last Name | Att. | Comp. | % | Yds. | Yd./Att. | TD | Int.-% | RK |
|---|---|---|---|---|---|---|---|---|
| Fouts | 381 | 224 | 59 | 2999 | 7.9 | 24 | 20- 5 | 2 |
| Harris | 88 | 42 | 48 | 518 | 5.9 | 2 | 9-10 | |
| Olander | 8 | 5 | 63 | 49 | 6.1 | 0 | 1-13 | |

### PUNTING
| Last Name | No. | Avg. |
|---|---|---|
| West | 73 | 37.3 |

### KICKING
| Last Name | XP | Att. | % | FG | Att. | % |
|---|---|---|---|---|---|---|
| Benirshke | 37 | 43 | 86 | 18 | 22 | 82 |

## SEATTLE SEAHAWKS

### RUSHING
| Last Name | No. | Yds. | Avg. | TD |
|---|---|---|---|---|
| Smith | 165 | 805 | 4.9 | 6 |
| Sims | 174 | 752 | 4.3 | 14 |
| Hunter | 105 | 348 | 3.3 | 2 |
| Zorn | 59 | 290 | 4.9 | 6 |
| Testerman | 43 | 155 | 3.6 | 0 |
| Crawford | 8 | 19 | 2.4 | 0 |
| Raible | 2 | 13 | 6.5 | 0 |
| Myer | 2 | 10 | 5.0 | 0 |
| Benjamin | 1 | 7 | 7.0 | 0 |
| Weaver | 2 | -5 | -2.5 | 0 |

### RECEIVING
| Last Name | No. | Yds. | Avg. | TD |
|---|---|---|---|---|
| Largent | 71 | 1168 | 17 | 8 |
| McCullum | 37 | 525 | 14 | 3 |
| Sims | 30 | 195 | 7 | 1 |
| Smith | 28 | 366 | 13 | 1 |
| Raible | 22 | 316 | 14 | 1 |
| Howard | 18 | 251 | 14 | 1 |
| Testerman | 17 | 143 | 8 | 0 |
| Hunter | 12 | 172 | 14 | 0 |
| Fergerson | 11 | 116 | 11 | 0 |
| Sawyer | 9 | 101 | 11 | 0 |
| Crawford | 4 | 25 | 6 | 0 |
| Peets | 1 | 14 | 14 | 0 |
| Benjamin | 1 | 9 | 9 | 0 |

### PUNT RETURNS
| Last Name | No. | Yds. | Avg. | TD |
|---|---|---|---|---|
| Crawford | 34 | 284 | 8 | 0 |
| Harris | 5 | 58 | 12 | 0 |
| Geddes | 1 | 0 | 0 | 0 |

### KICKOFF RETURNS
| Last Name | No. | Yds. | Avg. | TD |
|---|---|---|---|---|
| Hunter | 16 | 385 | 24 | 0 |
| Crawford | 35 | 829 | 24 | 0 |
| Fergerson | 10 | 236 | 24 | 0 |
| Long | 4 | 35 | 9 | 0 |
| Testerman | 1 | 19 | 19 | 0 |
| Boyd | 1 | 6 | 6 | 0 |

### PASSING
| Last Name | Att. | Comp. | % | Yds. | Yd./Att. | TD | Int.-% | RK |
|---|---|---|---|---|---|---|---|---|
| Zorn | 443 | 248 | 56 | 3283 | 7.4 | 15 | 20- 5 | 6 |
| Myer | 22 | 11 | 50 | 94 | 4.3 | 0 | 2- 9 | |
| Sims | 1 | 1 | 100 | 15 | 15.0 | 0 | 0- 0 | |
| Weaver | 1 | 1 | 100 | 9 | 9.0 | 0 | 0- 0 | |

### PUNTING
| Last Name | No. | Avg. |
|---|---|---|
| Weaver | 66 | 37.0 |
| Herrera | 3 | 24.3 |

### KICKING
| Last Name | XP | Att. | % | FG | Att. | % |
|---|---|---|---|---|---|---|
| Herrera | 40 | 44 | 91 | 13 | 21 | 62 |

## KANSAS CITY CHIEFS

### RUSHING
| Last Name | No. | Yds. | Avg. | TD |
|---|---|---|---|---|
| Reed | 206 | 1053 | 5.1 | 5 |
| McKnight | 104 | 627 | 6.0 | 6 |
| Morgado | 160 | 593 | 3.7 | 7 |
| Bailey | 83 | 298 | 3.6 | 0 |
| Lane | 52 | 277 | 5.3 | 0 |
| Belton | 24 | 79 | 3.3 | 0 |
| Livingston | 23 | 49 | 2.1 | 1 |
| Adams | 9 | 15 | 1.7 | 0 |
| Andrusyshyn | 1 | 0 | 0.0 | 0 |
| Marshall | 1 | -5 | -5.0 | 0 |

### RECEIVING
| Last Name | No. | Yds. | Avg. | TD |
|---|---|---|---|---|
| Reed | 48 | 483 | 10 | 1 |
| White | 42 | 340 | 8 | 1 |
| Lane | 36 | 279 | 8 | 0 |
| Marshall | 26 | 433 | 17 | 2 |
| McKnight | 14 | 83 | 6 | 1 |
| Belton | 11 | 88 | 8 | 0 |
| Dorsey | 9 | 169 | 19 | 2 |
| Morgado | 7 | 47 | 7 | 0 |
| Samuels | 6 | 97 | 16 | 0 |
| Bailey | 5 | 13 | 3 | 0 |

### PUNT RETURNS
| Last Name | No. | Yds. | Avg. | TD |
|---|---|---|---|---|
| Payton | 32 | 364 | 11 | 0 |
| Marshall | 6 | 51 | 9 | 0 |
| Burgmeier | 4 | 59 | 15 | 0 |
| Green | 1 | 6 | 6 | 0 |
| Sanders | 1 | 5 | 5 | 0 |
| Dorsey | 1 | 3 | 3 | 0 |

### KICKOFF RETURNS
| Last Name | No. | Yds. | Avg. | TD |
|---|---|---|---|---|
| Payton | 30 | 775 | 26 | 0 |
| Belton | 9 | 227 | 25 | 0 |
| Morgado | 5 | 100 | 20 | 0 |
| Beckman | 3 | 74 | 25 | 0 |
| McKnight | 3 | 65 | 22 | 0 |
| Sanders | 2 | 15 | 8 | 0 |
| Green | 1 | 27 | 27 | 0 |
| Paul | 1 | 0 | 0 | 0 |

### PASSING
| Last Name | Att. | Comp. | % | Yds. | Yd./Att. | TD | Int.-% | RK |
|---|---|---|---|---|---|---|---|---|
| Livingston | 290 | 159 | 55 | 1573 | 5.4 | 5 | 13- 5 | 13 |
| Adams | 79 | 44 | 56 | 415 | 5.3 | 2 | 3- 4 | |
| White | 1 | 1 | 100 | 44 | 44.0 | 0 | 0- 0 | |

### PUNTING
| Last Name | No. | Avg. |
|---|---|---|
| Andrusyshym | 79 | 41.1 |

### KICKING
| Last Name | XP | Att. | % | FG | Att. | % |
|---|---|---|---|---|---|---|
| Stenerud | 25 | 26 | 96 | 20 | 30 | 67 |

# 1978 N.F.C. PLAYOFFS

December 24 at Atlanta (Attendance 49,447)

### SCORING

| | | | | |
|---|---|---|---|---|
| **PHIL.** | **6** | **0** | **7** | **0–13** |
| **ATL.** | **0** | **0** | **0** | **14–14** |

First Quarter
- Phil. — Carmichael 13 yard pass from Jaworski
  PAT – kick failed (Michel)

Third Quarter
- Phil. — Montgomery 1 yard rush
  PAT – Michel (kick)

Fourth Quarter
- Atl. — Mitchell 19 yard pass from Bartkowski
  PAT – Mazzetti (kick)
- Atl. — Francis 37 yard pass from Bartkowski
  PAT – Mazzetti (kick)

### TEAM STATISTICS

| PHIL. | | ATL. |
|---|---|---|
| 15 | First Downs | 14 |
| 32–53 | Rushes–Yards | 27–75 |
| 164 | Passing Yards | 223 |
| 95 | Return Yards | 14 |
| 19–35–0 | Passing | 18–32–2 |
| 9–33.7 | Punting | 7–33.1 |
| 3–2 | Fumbles–Lost | 3–3 |
| 5–60 | Penalties–Yards | 6–63 |
| 2 | Giveaways | 5 |
| 5 | Takeaways | 2 |
| +3 | Difference | −3 |

### INDIVIDUAL STATISTICS

**RUSHING**

| PHILADELPHIA | No. | Yds. | Avg. | ATLANTA | No. | Yds. | Avg. |
|---|---|---|---|---|---|---|---|
| Hogan | 14 | 37 | 2.2 | Stanback | 16 | 58 | 3.3 |
| Montgomery | 16 | 19 | 1.2 | Bean | 9 | 14 | 1.6 |
| Jaworski | 1 | 3 | 3.0 | Bartkowski | 2 | 3 | 1.5 |
| Campfield | 1 | 0 | 0.0 | | | | |

**RECEIVING**

| PHILADELPHIA | No. | Yds. | Avg. | ATLANTA | No. | Yds. | Avg. |
|---|---|---|---|---|---|---|---|
| Smith | 7 | 108 | 15.4 | Francis | 6 | 135 | 22.5 |
| Carmichael | 5 | 45 | 9.0 | Bean | 4 | 44 | 11.0 |
| Osborne | 3 | 15 | 5.0 | Mitchell | 3 | 35 | 11.7 |
| Middlebrook | 1 | 11 | 11.0 | Stanback | 2 | 7 | 3.5 |
| Payne | 1 | 10 | 10.0 | Pearson | 1 | 13 | 13.0 |
| Hogan | 1 | 6 | 6.0 | Ryckman | 1 | 5 | 5.0 |
| Montgomery | 1 | −5 | −5.0 | Jackson | 1 | 4 | 4.0 |

**PASSING**

| | Att. | Comp. | Comp. Pct. | Yds. | Int. | Yds./ Att. | Yds./ Comp. |
|---|---|---|---|---|---|---|---|
| **PHILADELPHIA** | | | | | | | |
| Jaworski | 35 | 19 | 54.3 | 190 | 0 | 5.4 | 10.0 |
| **ATLANTA** | | | | | | | |
| Bartkowski | 32 | 18 | 56.3 | 243 | 2 | 7.6 | 13.5 |

December 30 at Dallas (Attendance (69,338)

### SCORING

| | | | | |
|---|---|---|---|---|
| **ATL.** | **7** | **13** | **0** | **0–20** |
| **DAL.** | **10** | **3** | **7** | **7–27** |

First Quarter
- Dal. — Septien 34 yard field goal
- Atl. — Bean 14 yard rush
  PAT – Mazzetti (kick)
- Dal. — Laidlaw 12 yard rush
  PAT – Septien (kick)

Second Quarter
- Atl. — Mazzetti 42 yard field goal
- Dal. — Septien 48 yard field goal
- Atl. — Francis 17 yard pass from Bartkowski
  PAT – Mazzetti (kick)
- Atl. — Mazzetti 22 yard field goal

Third Quarter
- Dal. — Smith 2 yard pass from White
  PAT – Septien (kick)

Fourth Quarter
- Dal. — Laidlaw 1 yard rush
  PAT – Septien (kick)

### TEAM STATISTICS

| ATL | | DAL. |
|---|---|---|
| 16 | First Downs | 26 |
| 36–164 | Rushes–Yards | 37–148 |
| 52 | Passing Yards | 221 |
| 0 | Return Yards | 69 |
| 8–23–3 | Passing | 17–37–1 |
| 6–37.5 | Punting | 3–36.0 |
| 0–0 | Fumbles–Lost | 6–3 |
| 7–69 | Penalties–Yards | 7–65 |
| 3 | Giveaways | 4 |
| 4 | Takeaways | 3 |
| +1 | Difference | −1 |

### INDIVIDUAL STATISTICS

**RUSHING**

| ATLANTA | No. | Yds. | Avg. | DALLAS | No. | Yds. | Avg. |
|---|---|---|---|---|---|---|---|
| Bean | 17 | 72 | 4.2 | Laidlaw | 17 | 66 | 3.9 |
| Stanbach | 9 | 62 | 6.9 | Dorsett | 14 | 65 | 4.6 |
| Franklin | 8 | 24 | 3.0 | DuPree | 1 | 20 | 20.0 |
| Esposito | 2 | 6 | 3.0 | Staubach | 1 | 3 | 3.0 |
| | | | | P. Pearson | 1 | −2 | −2.0 |
| | | | | White | 3 | −4 | −1.3 |

**RECEIVING**

| ATLANTA | No. | Yds. | Avg. | DALLAS | No. | Yds. | Avg. |
|---|---|---|---|---|---|---|---|
| Francis | 6 | 66 | 11.0 | D. Pearson | 4 | 75 | 18.8 |
| Ryckman | 1 | 22 | 22.0 | DuPree | 5 | 59 | 11.8 |
| Esposito | 1 | 7 | 7.0 | Smith | 3 | 38 | 12.7 |
| | | | | Hill | 3 | 36 | 12.0 |
| | | | | Laidlaw | 1 | 15 | 15.0 |
| | | | | Dorsett | 1 | 9 | 9.0 |

**PASSING**

| | Att. | Comp. | Comp. Pct. | Yds. | Int. | Yds./ Att. | Yds./ Comp. |
|---|---|---|---|---|---|---|---|
| **ATLANTA** | | | | | | | |
| Bartkowski | 23 | 8 | 34.8 | 95 | 3 | 4.1 | 11.9 |
| **DALLAS** | | | | | | | |
| Staubach | 17 | 7 | 41.2 | 105 | 0 | 6.2 | 15.0 |
| White | 20 | 10 | 50.0 | 127 | 1 | 6.4 | 12.7 |

December 31 at Los Angeles (Attendance 69,631)

### SCORING

| | | | | |
|---|---|---|---|---|
| **MIN.** | **3** | **7** | **0** | **0–10** |
| **L.A.** | **0** | **10** | **14** | **10–34** |

First Quarter
- Min. — Danmeier 42 yard field goal

Second Quarter
- L.A. — Miller 9 yard pass from Haden
  PAT – Corral (kick)
- L.A. — Corral 43 yard field goal
- Min. — Rashad 1 yard pass from Tarkenton
  PAT – Danmeier (kick)

Third Quarter
- L.A. — Bryant 3 yard rush
  PAT – Corral (kick)
- L.A. — Jessie 27 yard pass from Haden
  PAT – Corral (kick)

Fourth Quarter
- L.A. — Corral 28 yard field goal
- L.A. — Jodat 3 yard rush
  PAT – Corral (kick)

### TEAM STATISTICS

| MINN. | | L.A. |
|---|---|---|
| 12 | First Downs | 25 |
| 16–36 | Rushes–Yards | 48–200 |
| 208 | Passing yards | 209 |
| 10 | Return Yards | 99 |
| 18–38–2 | Passing | 15–29–1 |
| 6–41.3 | Punting | 4–31.0 |
| 2–0 | Fumbles–Lost | 1–0 |
| 2–12 | Penalties–Yards | 4–35 |
| 2 | Giveaways | 1 |
| 1 | Takeaways | 2 |
| −1 | Difference | +1 |

### INDIVIDUAL STATISTICS

**RUSHING**

| MINNESOTA | No. | Yds. | Avg. | LOS ANGELES | No. | Yds. | Avg. |
|---|---|---|---|---|---|---|---|
| Foreman | 13 | 31 | 2.4 | Bryant | 27 | 100 | 3.7 |
| Kellar | 2 | 7 | 3.5 | Cappelletti | 10 | 44 | 4.4 |
| Tarkenton | 1 | −2 | −2.0 | Davis | 4 | 17 | 4.3 |
| | | | | Haden | 2 | 15 | 7.5 |
| | | | | Phillips | 2 | 10 | 5.0 |
| | | | | Waddy | 1 | 9 | 9.0 |
| | | | | Jodat | 1 | 3 | 3.0 |
| | | | | Nelson | 1 | 2 | 2.0 |

**RECEIVING**

| MINNESOTA | No. | Yds. | Avg. | LOS ANGELES | No. | Yds. | Avg. |
|---|---|---|---|---|---|---|---|
| Rashad | 7 | 84 | 12.0 | Jessie | 6 | 108 | 18.0 |
| Young | 4 | 49 | 12.3 | Young | 2 | 30 | 15.0 |
| Tucker | 4 | 48 | 12.0 | Miller | 2 | 29 | 14.5 |
| Foreman | 3 | 38 | 12.7 | Nelson | 1 | 13 | 13.0 |
| | | | | Bryant | 2 | 13 | 6.5 |
| | | | | Waddy | 1 | 10 | 10.0 |
| | | | | Cappelletti | 1 | 6 | 6.0 |

**PASSING**

| | Att. | Comp. | Comp. Pct. | Yds. | Int. | Yds./ Att. | Yds./ Comp. |
|---|---|---|---|---|---|---|---|
| **MINNESOTA** | | | | | | | |
| Tarkenton | 37 | 18 | 48.6 | 219 | 2 | 5.9 | 12.2 |
| **LOS ANGELES** | | | | | | | |
| Haden | 29 | 15 | 51.7 | 209 | 1 | 7.2 | 13.9 |

# 1978 A.F.C. PLAYOFFS

## SCORING

| | | | | |
|---|---|---|---|---|
| HOU. | 7 | 0 | 0 | 10–17 |
| MIA. | 7 | 0 | 0 | 2–9 |

**First Quarter**
Mia. — Tillman 13 yard pass from Griese
    PAT-Yepremian (kick)
Hou. — Wilson 12 yard pass from Pastorini
    PAT-Fritsch (kick)

**Fourth Quarter**
Hou. — Fritsch 35 yard field goal
Hou. — Campbell 1 yard rush
    PAT-Fritsch (kick)
Mia. — Safety–Pastorini ran out of end zone

## TEAM STATISTICS

| HOU. | | MIA. |
|---|---|---|
| 23 | First Downs | 14 |
| 45–165 | Rushes–Yards | 25–91 |
| 290 | Passing Yards | 118 |
| 15 | Return Yards | 24 |
| 20–30–0 | Passing | 12–30–3 |
| 5–44.0 | Punting | 5–48.6 |
| 3–1 | Fumbles-Lost | 2–2 |
| 5–37 | Penalties–Yards | 1–5 |
| 1 | Giveaways | 5 |
| 5 | Takeaways | 1 |
| +4 | Difference | –4 |

## INDIVIDUAL STATISTICS

**HOUSTON**     **MIAMI**

| | No. | Yds. | Avg. | | No. | Yds. | Avg. |
|---|---|---|---|---|---|---|---|
| **RUSHING** | | | | | | | |
| Campbell | 26 | 84 | 3.0 | L. Harris | 9 | 43 | 4.8 |
| Wilson | 14 | 76 | 5.4 | Williams | 13 | 41 | 3.2 |
| Poole | 1 | 12 | 12.0 | Moore | 1 | 7 | 7.0 |
| Coleman | 1 | 2 | 2.0 | Bulaich | 2 | 0 | 0.0 |
| Pastorini | 3 | –9 | –3.0 | | | | |
| **RECEIVING** | | | | | | | |
| Burrough | 6 | 103 | 17.2 | D. Harris | 4 | 42 | 10.5 |
| Wilson | 5 | 40 | 8.0 | Moore | 2 | 28 | 14.0 |
| Barber | 4 | 112 | 28.0 | Tillman | 2 | 24 | 12.0 |
| Woods | 2 | 22 | 11.0 | Bulaich | 2 | 14 | 7.0 |
| Campbell | 1 | 13 | 13.0 | L. Harris | 1 | 21 | 21.0 |
| Caster | 1 | 11 | 11.0 | Williams | 1 | 8 | 8.0 |
| Coleman | 1 | 5 | 5.0 | | | | |

**PASSING**

**HOUSTON**

| | Att. | Comp. | Comp. Pct. | Yds. | Int. | Yds./ Att. | Yds./ Comp. |
|---|---|---|---|---|---|---|---|
| Pastorini | 29 | 20 | 68.9 | 306 | 0 | 10.6 | 15.3 |
| Barber | 1 | | 0.0 | 0 | 0 | 0.0 | 0.0 |

**MIAMI**

| | Att. | Comp. | Comp. Pct. | Yds. | Int. | Yds./ Att. | Yds./ Comp. |
|---|---|---|---|---|---|---|---|
| Griese | 28 | 11 | 39.3 | 114 | 2 | 4.1 | 10.4 |
| Strock | 2 | 1 | 50.0 | 23 | 1 | 16.5 | 23.0 |

---

## SCORING

| | | | | |
|---|---|---|---|---|
| DEN. | 3 | 7 | 0 | 0–10 |
| PIT. | 6 | 13 | 0 | 14–33 |

**First Quarter**
Den. — Turner 37 yard field goal
Pit. — Harris 1 yard rush
    PAT – Kick failed

**Second Quarter**
Pit. — Harris 18 yard rush
    PAT – Gerela (kick)
Pit. — Gerela 24 yard field goal
Den. — Preston 3 yard rush
    PAT – Turner (kick)
Pit. — Gerela 27 yard field goal

**Fourth Quarter**
Pit. — Stallworth 45 yard pass from Bradshaw
    PAT – Gerela (kick)
Pit. — Swann 38 yard pass from Bradshaw
    PAT – Gerela (kick)

## TEAM STATISTICS

| DEN. | | PIT. |
|---|---|---|
| 15 | First Downs | 24 |
| 27–87 | Rushes–Yards | 40–153 |
| 131 | Passing Yards | 272 |
| 110 | Return Yards | 93 |
| 12–22–0 | Passing | 16–29–1 |
| 6–34.0 | Punting | 2–36.0 |
| 2–2 | Fumbles-Lost | 4–1 |
| 8–104 | Penalties–Yards | 11–88 |
| 2 | Giveaways | 2 |
| 2 | Takeaways | 2 |
| 0 | Difference | 0 |

## INDIVIDUAL STATISTICS

**DENVER**     **PITTSBURGH**

| | No. | Yds. | Avg. | | No. | Yds. | Avg. |
|---|---|---|---|---|---|---|---|
| **RUSHING** | | | | | | | |
| Weese | 4 | 43 | 10.8 | Harris | 24 | 105 | 4.4 |
| Preston | 4 | 14 | 3.5 | Bleier | 8 | 26 | 3.3 |
| Keyworth | 6 | 12 | 2.0 | Moser | 2 | 6 | 3.0 |
| Lytle | 5 | 6 | 1.2 | J. Smith | 1 | 4 | 4.0 |
| Perrin | 6 | 6 | 1.0 | Deloplaine | 1 | 4 | 4.0 |
| Armstrong | 1 | 3 | 3.0 | Bradshaw | 2 | 4 | 2.0 |
| Canada | 1 | 3 | 3.0 | Thornton | 2 | 4 | 2.0 |
| **RECEIVING** | | | | | | | |
| Dolbin | 4 | 77 | 19.3 | Stallworth | 10 | 156 | 15.6 |
| Moses | 2 | 33 | 16.5 | Grossman | 4 | 64 | 16.0 |
| Preston | 2 | 19 | 9.5 | Swann | 2 | 52 | 26.0 |
| Perrin | 2 | 16 | 8.0 | | | | |
| Odoms | 1 | 24 | 24.0 | | | | |
| Lytle | 1 | –1 | –1.0 | | | | |

**PASSING**

**DENVER**

| | Att. | Comp. | Comp. Pct. | Yds. | Int. | Yds./ Att. | Yds./ Comp. |
|---|---|---|---|---|---|---|---|
| Morton | 5 | 3 | 60.0 | 34 | 0 | 6.8 | 11.3 |
| Weese | 16 | 8 | 50.0 | 118 | 0 | 7.4 | 14.8 |

**PITTSBURGH**

| | Att. | Comp. | Comp. Pct. | Yds. | Int. | Yds./ Att. | Yds./ Comp. |
|---|---|---|---|---|---|---|---|
| Bradshaw | 29 | 16 | 55.2 | 272 | 1 | 9.4 | 17.0 |

---

## SCORING

| | | | | |
|---|---|---|---|---|
| HOU. | 0 | 21 | 3 | 7–31 |
| N.E. | 0 | 0 | 7 | 7–14 |

**Second Quarter**
Hou. — Burrough 71 yard pass from Pastorini
    PAT – Fritsch (kick)
Hou. — Barber 19 yard pass from Pastorini
    PAT – Fritsch (kick)
Hou. — Barber 13 yard pass from Pastorini
    PAT – Fritsch (kick)

**Third Quarter**
Hou. — Fritsch 30 yard field goal
N.E. — Jackson 24 yard pass from Johnson
    PAT – Posey (kick)

**Fourth Quarter**
N.E. — Francis 24 yard pass from Owen
    PAT – Posey (kick)
Hou. — Campbell 2 yard rush
    PAT – Fritsch (kick)

## TEAM STATISTICS

| HOU. | | N.E. |
|---|---|---|
| 21 | First Downs | 15 |
| 54–174 | Rushes–Yards | 20–83 |
| 170 | Passing Yards | 180 |
| 105 | Return Yards | 142 |
| 12–15–1 | Passing | 16–35–3 |
| 5–34.8 | Punting | 4–43.3 |
| 1–0 | Fumbles-Lost | 2–0 |
| 2–25 | Penalties-Yards | 8–92 |
| 1 | Giveaways | 3 |
| 3 | Takeaways | 1 |
| +2 | Difference | –2 |

## INDIVIDUAL STATISTICS

**HOUSTON**     **NEW ENGLAND**

| | No. | Yds. | Avg. | | No. | Yds. | Avg. |
|---|---|---|---|---|---|---|---|
| **RUSHING** | | | | | | | |
| Campbell | 27 | 118 | 4.4 | Cunningham | 10 | 42 | 4.2 |
| T. Wilson | 14 | 26 | 1.9 | Grogan | 1 | 16 | 16.0 |
| Coleman | 7 | 19 | 2.7 | Johnson | 6 | 14 | 2.3 |
| Duncan | 2 | 7 | 3.5 | Ivory | 3 | 11 | 3.7 |
| Poole | 3 | 7 | 2.3 | | | | |
| Nielson | 1 | –3 | –3.0 | | | | |
| **RECEIVING** | | | | | | | |
| Barber | 5 | 83 | 16.6 | Francis | 8 | 101 | 12.6 |
| Burrough | 3 | 91 | 30.3 | Cunningham | 3 | 28 | 9.3 |
| Caster | 2 | 12 | 6.0 | Morgan | 2 | 37 | 18.5 |
| Campbell | 1 | 10 | 10.0 | Johnson | 2 | 16 | 8.0 |
| Woods | 1 | 4 | 4.0 | Jackson | 1 | 24 | 24.0 |

**PASSING**

**HOUSTON**

| | Att. | Comp. | Comp. Pct. | Yds. | Int. | Yds./ Att. | Yds./ Comp. |
|---|---|---|---|---|---|---|---|
| Pastorini | 15 | 12 | 80.0 | 200 | 1 | 13.3 | 16.7 |

**NEW ENGLAND**

| | Att. | Comp. | Comp. Pct. | Yds. | Int. | Yds./ Att. | Yds./ Comp. |
|---|---|---|---|---|---|---|---|
| Grogan | 12 | 3 | 25.0 | 38 | 2 | 3.2 | 12.7 |
| Owen | 22 | 12 | 54.5 | 144 | 1 | 6.5 | 12.0 |
| Johnson | 1 | 1 | 100.0 | 24 | 0 | 24.0 | 24.0 |

## NFC CHAMPIONSHIP GAME
January 7, 1979 at Los Angeles
(Attendance 71,086)

### SCORING

| | | | | | |
|---|---|---|---|---|---|
| DALLAS | 0 | 0 | 7 | 21–28 | |
| LOS ANGELES | 0 | 0 | 0 | 0– 0 | |

**Third Quarter**
Dal.    Dorsett 5 yard rush
     PAT – Septien (kick)

**Fourth Quarter**
Dal.    Laidlaw 4 yard pass from Staubach
     PAT – Septien (kick)
Dal.    DuPree 11 yard pass from Staubach
     PAT – Septien (kick)
Dal.    Henderson 68 yard interception return
     PAT – Septien (kick)

### TEAM STATISTICS

| DALL. | | L. A. |
|---|---|---|
| 16 | First Downs | 15 |
| 33–126 | Rushes-Yards | 31–81 |
| 109 | Passing Yards | 96 |
| 163 | Return Yards | 22 |
| 13–25–2 | Passing | 14–35–5 |
| 8–35.0 | Punting | 5–39.0 |
| 2–1 | Fumbles-Lost | 3–2 |
| 10–85 | Penalties-Yards | 5–40 |
| 3 | Giveaways | 7 |
| 7 | Takeaways | 3 |
| +4 | Difference | –4 |

Three times in the past four years, Chuck Knox had led the Rams into the NFC title game only to be turned back from the gates of the Super Bowl. This year, Knox was gone and the Rams again went down to defeat in the next-to-last weekend of the season.

The sterling Los Angeles defense did its part in the first half, shutting out the Dallas offense. The Ram attack, however, failed to score any points against the Doomsday Defense of Dallas. At halftime, neither team had scored, and observers waited to see who would first cash in on their opponent's mistakes.

The Cowboys cashed in. Midway through the third period, Ram quarterback Pat Haden shot a pass at tight end Terry Nelson, only to have Dallas safety Charlie Waters pick it off. Waters presented Roger Staubach & Co. with the ball on the Los Angeles 10-yard line, and Tony Dorsett shortly broke into the end zone with the first points of the day.

The Rams responded with their biggest offensive threat of the day. They reached the Dallas 13-yard line but lost the ball on a failed fourth-and-one power play. Later in the period, Charlie Waters intercepted another Haden pass, giving Dallas possession 20 yards from the end zone. Just shy of a minute into the fourth quarter, Staubach hit Scott Laidlaw with a short touchdown pass to run the lead to a formidable 14-0

The Rams tried futilely to come back under sub QB Vince Ferragamo, who came in when Haden broke his right thumb in the third quarter. The Cowboys held the Rams off and posted two more touchdowns in the final three minutes. Staubach hit Billy Joe DuPree with a short scoring pass, and Thomas Henderson intercepted a Ferragamo pass and bolted 68 yards to score.

## INDIVIDUAL STATISTICS

### DALLAS / LOS ANGELES

#### RUSHING

| DALLAS | No. | Yds. | Avg. | LOS ANGELES | No. | Yds. | Avg. |
|---|---|---|---|---|---|---|---|
| Dorsett | 17 | 101 | 5.9 | Bryant | 20 | 52 | 2.6 |
| Laidlaw | 10 | 20 | 2.0 | Haden | 2 | 20 | 10.0 |
| Staubach | 3 | 7 | 2.3 | Cappelletti | 3 | 19 | 6.3 |
| Newhouse | 1 | 4 | 4.0 | Phillips | 3 | 2 | 0.7 |
| DuPree | 1 | 3 | 3.0 | Jodat | 2 | –5 | –2.5 |
| Smith | 1 | –9 | –9.0 | Waddy | 1 | –7 | –7.0 |
| | 33 | 126 | 3.8 | | 31 | 81 | 2.6 |

#### RECEIVING

| DALLAS | No. | Yds. | Avg. | LOS ANGELES | No. | Yds. | Avg. |
|---|---|---|---|---|---|---|---|
| DuPree | 3 | 48 | 16.0 | Jessie | 4 | 42 | 10.5 |
| Johnson | 2 | 19 | 9.5 | Miller | 3 | 96 | 32.0 |
| D. Pearson | 2 | 19 | 9.5 | Waddy | 2 | 23 | 11.5 |
| Dorsett | 2 | 15 | 7.5 | Bryant | 2 | 2 | 1.0 |
| P. Pearson | 2 | 12 | 6.0 | Scales | 1 | 18 | 18.0 |
| Hill | 1 | 9 | 9.0 | Cappelletti | 1 | 15 | 15.0 |
| Laidlaw | 1 | 4 | 4.0 | Nelson | 1 | 10 | 10.0 |
| | 13 | 126 | 9.7 | | 14 | 206 | 13.9 |

#### PUNTING

| DALLAS | No. | Yds. | Avg. | LOS ANGELES | No. | Yds. | Avg. |
|---|---|---|---|---|---|---|---|
| D. White | 8 | | 35.0 | Walker | 5 | | 39.0 |

#### PUNT RETURNS

| DALLAS | No. | Yds. | Avg. | LOS ANGELES | No. | Yds. | Avg. |
|---|---|---|---|---|---|---|---|
| Johnson | 4 | 40 | 10.0 | Wallace | 2 | 22 | 11.0 |

#### KICKOFF RETURNS

| DALLAS | No. | Yds. | Avg. | LOS ANGELES | No. | Yds. | Avg. |
|---|---|---|---|---|---|---|---|
| none | | | | Jodat | 3 | 59 | 19.7 |
| | | | | Marshall | 2 | 47 | 23.5 |
| | | | | | 5 | 106 | 21.2 |

#### INTERCEPTION RETURNS

| DALLAS | No. | Yds. | Avg. | LOS ANGELES | No. | Yds. | Avg. |
|---|---|---|---|---|---|---|---|
| Waters | 2 | 49 | 24.5 | Thomas | 1 | 0 | 0.0 |
| Henderson | 1 | 68 | 68.0 | Cromwell | 1 | 0 | 0.0 |
| Harris | 1 | 5 | 5.0 | | 2 | 0 | 0.0 |
| Hughes | 1 | 1 | 1.0 | | | | |
| | 5 | 123 | 24.6 | | | | |

#### PASSING

| DALLAS | Att. | Comp. | Comp. Pct. | Yds. | Int. | Yds./ Att. | Yds./ Comp. |
|---|---|---|---|---|---|---|---|
| Staubach | 25 | 13 | 52.0 | 126 | 2 | 5.0 | 9.7 |

| LOS ANGELES | Att. | Comp. | Comp. Pct. | Yds. | Int. | Yds./ Att. | Yds./ Comp. |
|---|---|---|---|---|---|---|---|
| Haden | 19 | 7 | 36.8 | 76 | 3 | 4.0 | 10.0 |
| Ferragamo | 16 | 7 | 43.8 | 130 | 2 | 8.1 | 18.6 |

---

## AFC CHAMPIONSHIP GAME
January 7, 1979 at Pittsburgh
(Attendance 50,725)

### SCORING

| | | | | | |
|---|---|---|---|---|---|
| HOUSTON | 0 | 3 | 2 | 0– 5 | |
| PITTSBURGH | 14 | 17 | 3 | 0–34 | |

**First Quarter**
Pit.    Harris 7 yard rush
     PAT – Gerela (kick)
Pit.    Bleier 15 yard rush
     PAT – Gerela (kick)

**Second Quarter**
Hou.    Fritsch 19 yard field goal
Pit.    Swann 29 yard pass from Bradshaw
     PAT – Gerela (kick)
Pit.    Stallworth 17 yard pass from Bradshaw PAT – Gerela (kick)
Pit.    Gerela 37 yard field goal

**Third Quarter**
Pit.    Gerela 22 yard field goal
Hou.    Safety–Bleier tackled in end zone

### TEAM STATISTICS

| HOU. | | PITT. |
|---|---|---|
| 10 | First Downs | 21 |
| 26–72 | Rushes-Yards | 47–179 |
| 70 | Passing Yards | 200 |
| 179 | Return Yards | 217 |
| 12–26–5 | Passing | 11–19–2 |
| 6–39.5 | Punting | 1–53.0 |
| 6–4 | Fumbles-Lost | 6–3 |
| 5–48 | Penalties-Yards | 4–32 |
| 9 | Giveaways | 5 |
| 5 | Takeaways | 9 |
| –4 | Difference | +4 |

The setting was Three Rivers Stadium in Pittsburgh in a cold, steady rain. The principles were the time-tested Steelers and the upstart Houston Oilers. The result was a romp.

The Oilers had come this far on Earl Campbell's running, Dan Pastorini's passing, and a tough defense. The slippery footing negated Campbell, the Steel Curtain stifled Pastorini, and the Pittsburgh offense broke the Oiler defense.

The Steelers acclimated themselves to the weather right from the start. Twice in the first quarter, they drove for touchdowns, with Franco Harris and Rocky Bleier scoring the points.

Until late in the second quarter, the only points of the period were a Houston field goal. Then, within the last 48 seconds, the Steelers scored 17 points. Terry Bradshaw hit Lynn Swann with a 29-yard touchdown pass to run the score to 21-3. Oiler returner Johnnie Dirden fumbled the ensuing kickoff, Rick Moser recovered for Pittsburgh, and Bradshaw immediately threw to John Stallworth for another score. After the kickoff, Ronnie Coleman fumbled on the first play from scrimmage, giving the Steelers a chance to add three more points before time expired.

The shell-shocked Oilers returned for the second half with an insurmountable deficit. With the weather and playing field continuing to deteriorate, the only points of the second half were a Pittsburgh field goal and a safety by the Houston defense.

The confrontation between Earl Campbell and Franco Harris was defused by the rain, with Campbell running for 62 yards and Harris 51. In every team category, however, including the score, the Steelers were far superior.

## INDIVIDUAL STATISTICS

### HOUSTON / PITTSBURGH

#### RUSHING

| HOUSTON | No. | Yds. | Avg. | PITTSBURGH | No. | Yds. | Avg. |
|---|---|---|---|---|---|---|---|
| Campbell | 22 | 62 | 2.8 | Harris | 20 | 51 | 2.6 |
| Woods | 1 | 9 | 9.0 | Bleier | 10 | 45 | 4.5 |
| T. Wilson | 2 | 6 | 3.0 | Bradshaw | 7 | 29 | 4.1 |
| Coleman | 1 | –5 | –5.0 | Deloplaine | 3 | 28 | 9.3 |
| | 26 | 72 | 2.8 | Thornton | 3 | 22 | 7.3 |
| | | | | Moser | 3 | 7 | 2.3 |
| | | | | Kruczek | 1 | –3 | –3.0 |
| | | | | | 47 | 179 | 3.8 |

#### RECEIVING

| HOUSTON | No. | Yds. | Avg. | PITTSBURGH | No. | Yds. | Avg. |
|---|---|---|---|---|---|---|---|
| Caster | 5 | 44 | 8.8 | Swann | 4 | 98 | 24.5 |
| T. Wilson | 5 | 33 | 6.6 | Bleier | 4 | 42 | 10.5 |
| Coleman | 1 | 15 | 15.0 | Grossman | 2 | 43 | 21.5 |
| Campbell | 1 | 4 | 4.0 | Stallworth | 1 | 17 | 17.0 |
| | 12 | 96 | 8.0 | | 11 | 200 | 18.2 |

#### PUNTING

| HOUSTON | No. | Yds. | Avg. | PITTSBURGH | No. | Yds. | Avg. |
|---|---|---|---|---|---|---|---|
| Parsley | 6 | | 39.5 | Colquitt | 1 | | 53.0 |

#### PUNT RETURNS

| HOUSTON | No. | Yds. | Avg. | PITTSBURGH | No. | Yds. | Avg. |
|---|---|---|---|---|---|---|---|
| none | | | | Bell | 6 | 91 | 15.1 |

#### KICKOFF RETURNS

| HOUSTON | No. | Yds. | Avg. | PITTSBURGH | No. | Yds. | Avg. |
|---|---|---|---|---|---|---|---|
| Dirden | 3 | 72 | 26.0 | Deloplaine | 1 | 21 | 21.0 |
| Merkens | 2 | 57 | 28.5 | L. Anderson | 1 | 15 | 15.0 |
| Woods | 2 | 33 | 16.5 | | 2 | 36 | 18.0 |
| Duncan | 1 | 17 | 17.0 | | | | |
| | 8 | 179 | 22.4 | | | | |

#### INTERCEPTION RETURNS

| HOUSTON | No. | Yds. | Avg. | PITTSBURGH | No. | Yds. | Avg. |
|---|---|---|---|---|---|---|---|
| Alexander | 1 | 0 | 0.0 | Toews | 1 | 35 | 35.0 |
| Stemrick | 1 | 0 | 0.0 | Johnson | 1 | 34 | 34.0 |
| | 2 | 0 | 0.0 | Blount | 1 | 16 | 16.0 |
| | | | | Shell | 1 | 5 | 5.0 |
| | | | | Ham | 1 | 0 | 0.0 |
| | | | | | 5 | 90 | 18.0 |

#### PASSING

| HOUSTON | Att. | Comp. | Comp. Pct. | Yds. | Int. | Yds./ Att. | Yds./ Comp. |
|---|---|---|---|---|---|---|---|
| Pastorini | 26 | 15 | 57.7 | 96 | 5 | 3.7 | 6.4 |

| PITTSBURGH | Att. | Comp. | Comp. Pct. | Yds. | Int. | Yds./ Att. | Yds./ Comp. |
|---|---|---|---|---|---|---|---|
| Bradshaw | 19 | 11 | 57.8 | 200 | 2 | 10.5 | 18.2 |

# Steeling the Rubber Match

Champions clashed, both two-time Super Bowl winners and both symbols of excellence. If the Cowboys were perceived as slightly flashier, the Steelers were perceived as slightly more physical. Three years ago, the Steelers had beaten the Cowboys for the crown. Now the Cowboys were the defending champs.

The Cowboys looked like champs in their opening drive until they fumbled on a razzle-dazzle play in Pittsburgh territory. Six plays later, Terry Bradshaw threw to John Stallworth for a 7-0 Steeler lead. Later in the period, Harvey Martin caused Bradshaw to fumble, and three plays later, Roger Staubach evened the score with a pass to Tony Hill.

Dallas went ahead early in the second quarter when Mike Hegman picked up Bradshaw's fumble and raced 37 yards to score. Two minutes later, John Stallworth broke Aaron Kyle's tackle on a short pass and ran for a 75-yard TD. Just before the halftime break, the Steelers went ahead on a Bradshaw-to-Bleier pass.

The Cowboys drove into Steeler territory in the third quarter, but when Jackie Smith dropped a pass while open in the end zone, they had to settle for three points.

The Steelers increased their four-point lead in the final quarter. A pass interference call against Benny Barnes moved the Steelers deep into Dallas territory, and then the classy Pittsburgh front line opened the way for Franco Harris to rumble 22 yards to score. On the following kickoff, Randy White fumbled a short kick. Bradshaw threw to Swann in the end zone on the next play to run the score to 35-17 with about six minutes left. Although Staubach rallied the Cowboys to two touchdowns in the final minutes, the Steelers, led by MVP Bradshaw, had secured their third Super Bowl title.

## LINEUPS

| PITTSBURGH | | DALLAS |
|---|---|---|
| | OFFENSE | |
| Stallworth | WR | Hill |
| Kolb | LT | Donovan |
| Davis | LG | Scott |
| Webster | C | Fitzgerald |
| Mullins | RG | Rafferty |
| Pinney | RT | Wright |
| Grossman | TE | DuPree |
| Swann | WR | D. Pearson |
| Bradshaw | QB | Staubach |
| Bleier | RB | Newhouse |
| Harris | RB | Dorsett |
| | DEFENSE | |
| Greenwood | LE | Jones |
| Greene | LT | Cole |
| Furness | RT | R. White |
| Banaszak | RE | Martin |
| Ham | LLB | Henderson |
| Lambert | MLB | Breunig |
| Toews | RLB | Lewis |
| Johnson | LCB | Barnes |
| Blount | RCB | Kyle |
| Shell | SS | Waters |
| Wagner | FS | Harris |

### SUBSTITUTES

| PITTSBURGH | | |
|---|---|---|
| | OFFENSE | |
| Bell | | Mandich |
| Brown | | Moser |
| Courson | | Peterson |
| Cunningham | | Smith |
| Deloplaine | | Stoudt |
| Kruczek | | Thornton |
| | DEFENSE | |
| F. Anderson | | Dunn |
| L. Anderson | | Oldham |
| Beasley | | White |
| Cole | | Winston |
| Dungy | | |
| | KICKERS | |
| Colquitt | | Gerela |

| DALLAS | | |
|---|---|---|
| | OFFENSE | |
| Blackwell | | Lawless |
| Brinson | | P. Pearson |
| Carano | | Randall |
| Cooper | | Smith |
| Frederick | | Steele |
| Johnson | | D. White |
| Laidlaw | | |
| | DEFENSE | |
| Bethea | | Pugh |
| Brown | | Stalls |
| Hegman | | Thurman |
| Hughes | | Washington |
| Huther | | |
| | KICKERS | |
| Septien | | |

## SCORING

| | | | | | |
|---|---|---|---|---|---|
| PITTSBURGH | 7 | 14 | 0 | 14 | 35 |
| DALLAS | 7 | 7 | 3 | 14 | 31 |

**First Quarter**
Pit.   Stallworth 28 yard pass from Bradshaw
  PAT – Gerela (kick)
Dal.   Hill 39 yard pass from Staubach
  PAT – Septien (kick)

**Second Quarter**
Dal.   Hegman 37 yard fumble return
  PAT – Septien (kick)
Pit.   Stallworth 75 yard pass from Bradshaw
  PAT – Gerela (kick)
Pit.   Bleier 7 yard pass from Bradshaw
  PAT – Gerela (kick)

**Third Quarter**
Dal.   Septien 27 yard field goal

**Fourth Quarter**
Pit.   Harris 22 yard rush
  PAT – Gerela (kick)
Pit.   Swann 18 yard pass from Bradshaw
  PAT – Gerela (kick)
Dal.   DuPree 7 yard pass from Staubach
  PAT – Septien (kick)
Dal.   Johnson 4 yard pass from Staubach
  PAT – Septien (kick)

## TEAM STATISTICS

| PIT. | | DAL. |
|---|---|---|
| 19 | First Downs–Total | 20 |
| 2 | First Downs–Rushing | 6 |
| 15 | First Downs–Passing | 13 |
| 2 | First Downs–Penalty | 1 |
| 2 | Fumbles–Number | 3 |
| 2 | Fumbles Lost | 2 |
| 5 | Penalties–Number | 9 |
| 35 | Yards Penalized | 89 |
| 1 | Missed Field Goals | 0 |
| 58 | Offensive Plays | 67 |
| 357 | Net Yards | 330 |
| 6.2 | Average Gain | 4.9 |
| 3 | Giveaways | 3 |
| 3 | Takeaways | 3 |
| 0 | Difference | 0 |

## INDIVIDUAL STATISTICS

### RUSHING

| PITTSBURGH | No. | Yds. | Avg. | DALLAS | No. | Yds. | Avg. |
|---|---|---|---|---|---|---|---|
| Harris | 20 | 68 | 3.4 | Dorsett | 16 | 96 | 6.0 |
| Bleier | 2 | 3 | 1.5 | Staubach | 4 | 37 | 9.3 |
| Bradshaw | 2 | −5 | −2.5 | Laidlaw | 3 | 12 | 4.0 |
| | 24 | 66 | 2.8 | P. Pearson | 1 | 6 | 6.0 |
| | | | | Newhouse | 8 | 3 | 0.4 |
| | | | | | 32 | 154 | 4.8 |

### RECEIVING

| PITTSBURGH | No. | Yds. | Avg. | DALLAS | No. | Yds. | Avg. |
|---|---|---|---|---|---|---|---|
| Swann | 7 | 124 | 17.7 | Dorsett | 5 | 44 | 8.8 |
| Stallworth | 3 | 115 | 38.3 | D. Pearson | 4 | 73 | 18.3 |
| Grossman | 3 | 29 | 9.7 | Hill | 2 | 49 | 24.5 |
| Bell | 2 | 21 | 10.5 | Johnson | 2 | 30 | 15.0 |
| Harris | 1 | 22 | 22.0 | DuPree | 2 | 17 | 8.5 |
| Bleier | 1 | 7 | 7.0 | P. Pearson | 2 | 15 | 7.5 |
| | 17 | 318 | 18.7 | | 17 | 228 | 13.4 |

### PUNTING

| PITTSBURGH | No. | Yds. | Avg. | DALLAS | No. | Yds. | Avg. |
|---|---|---|---|---|---|---|---|
| Colquitt | 3 | | 43.0 | D. White | 5 | | 39.6 |

### PUNT RETURNS

| PITTSBURGH | No. | Yds. | Avg. | DALLAS | No. | Yds. | Avg. |
|---|---|---|---|---|---|---|---|
| Bell | 4 | 27 | 6.3 | Johnson | 2 | 33 | 16.5 |

### KICKOFF RETURNS

| PITTSBURGH | No. | Yds. | Avg. | DALLAS | No. | Yds. | Avg. |
|---|---|---|---|---|---|---|---|
| L. Anderson | 3 | 45 | 15.0 | Johnson | 3 | 63 | 21.0 |
| | | | | Brinson | 2 | 41 | 20.5 |
| | | | | R. White | 1 | 0 | 0.0 |
| | | | | | 6 | 104 | 17.3 |

### INTERCEPTION RETURNS

| PITTSBURGH | No. | Yds. | Avg. | DALLAS | No. | Yds. | Avg. |
|---|---|---|---|---|---|---|---|
| Blount | 1 | 13 | 13.0 | Lewis | 1 | 21 | 21.0 |

### PASSING

| PITTSBURGH | Att. | Comp. | Comp. Pct. | Yds. | Int. | Yds./Att. | Yds./Comp. | Yards Lost Tackled |
|---|---|---|---|---|---|---|---|---|
| Bradshaw | 30 | 17 | 56.7 | 318 | 1 | 10.6 | 18.7 | 4—27 |
| DALLAS | | | | | | | | |
| Staubach | 30 | 17 | 56.7 | 228 | 1 | 7.6 | 13.4 | 5—52 |

# 1979 N.F.C. ... Never to Lose Their Crowns

Many seasons ago, A.E. Housman wrote a poem mourning an athlete who died young. Those feelings were stirred with unusual frequency in 1979. In April, a car accident killed Atlanta linebacker Andy Spiva and seriously injured teammate Garth Ten Napel. In June, Giants defensive tackle Troy Archer lost his life in a car accident in New Jersey, not far from Giants Stadium. One month later, St. Louis tight end J.V. Cain keeled over on the training field and died from heart failure.

Two other NFL players almost fell to the Grim Reaper this year. Chicago quarterback Vince Evans contracted a staph infection in early October and was critically ill for several days. San Diego kicker Rolf Benirschke had been steadily losing weight until he collapsed after a game in late September. He was hospitalized with Crohn's disease, an intestinal disorder, and only extensive surgery saved his life. Although neither returned to action this year, both would recover and play again.

## EASTERN DIVISION

**Dallas Cowboys**—Holes in the Cowboy defense raised hopes in Philadelphia and Washington. Jethro Pugh had retired, Too Tall Jones decided to quit football for a boxing career, and Charlie Waters tore up a knee in the pre-season. The Dallas defenders rallied around Randy White and Bob Breunig, however, and the Cowboys shot out to a 7-1 record. Roger Staubach piloted the offense to its usual high production. Suddenly, as November began, the Cowboys fell into a dive. They lost four out of five games, including meetings with the Eagles and Redskins. After the loss to the Cowboys, coach Tom Landry cut linebacker Thomas Henderson for a supposedly lackadaisical attitude. With the troops in disorder, the Cowboys regrouped for a stretch run. They beat the Giants and the Eagles, and faced the Redskins on the final Sunday of the season with a playoff berth at issue. Washington led 34-21 with just under seven minutes left when Staubach went to work. He threw a touchdown pass to Ron Springs with three minutes left, and after the defense held the Redskins, he hit Tony Hill with a scoring pass 39 seconds from the end. Rafael Septien's kick made the score 35-34 and put the Cowboys into the playoffs, the final showcase for the retiring Staubach.

**Philadelphia Eagles**—The Eagles showed their maturity when Bill Bergey injured a knee in the third game of the season. With their leader out for the year, the young defense stayed tough and kept the Eagles in playoff contention. Middle guard Charles Johnson stepped into the leadership gap with inspired play. The offense did its share with star performances from Ron Jaworski, Wilbert Montgomery, Harold Carmichael, Keith Krepfle, and Stan Walters. Despite a three-game losing streak in mid-season, the Eagles beat Dallas on Monday night television and clinched a playoff berth with a 44-7 trouncing of the Lions on December 2. One week later, they lost a rematch with the Cowboys, costing Dick Vermeil & Co. a clear shot at first place in the East. Despite a closing victory over Houston, the Eagles had to settle for one of the NFC wild-card slots.

**Washington Redskins**—Jack Pardee's rebuilding program was supposed to get results only after a few years, but the refurbished defense kept the Redskins in the playoff race. Three young linebackers played behind a good pass-rushing line and in front of a hawkish secondary featuring Lemar Parrish and Ken Houston. The offense relied on a strong ground game and the accurate toe of Mark Moseley. The Skins beat both the Cowboys and Eagles during the year and traveled to Texas Stadium on December 16 to end the season. With a playoff berth at stake, the Redskins took a 17-0 lead over the Cowboys in the first half, but fell behind 21-17 in the third quarter. Fighting the tide of momentum, the Skins surged ahead 34-21 in the fourth quarter. With the taste of playoffs on their lips, the Redskins were thrown out of the banquet. The Cowboys rallied for two touchdowns in the final four minutes to win the game 35-34. A 42-6 Chicago Bear victory earlier in the day meant that the Skins were nosed out of the playoffs by the Bears on a point-differential tie-breaker.

**New York Giants**—Coach Ray Perkins inspired hope in the fans, but by early October, they had almost lost the faith. Five losses at the start of the year promised continued futility, but then the Giants began to win. Rookie quarterback Phil Simms stepped into the starting lineup in game six and led the way to an upset victory over unbeaten Tampa Bay. The defense featured linebackers Brad Van Pelt and Harry Carson, while the offense breathed new life with the arrival of Simms and fellow rookie Earnest Gray as a deep passing threat. Unheralded Billy Taylor replaced Larry Csonka and ran the ball as well as the departed star had done. A 14-6 victory over the Redskins on November 25 was the high-water point of the season, as the Giants failed to win any of their three final games.

**St. Louis Cardinals**—A new star come on stage in St. Louis as an old legend exited. Rookie halfback Ottis Anderson ran for 193 yards on opening day against Dallas, and he kept running through NFL defenses for a season total of 1,605 yards. His way was cleared by a line which lost Dan Dierdorf for most of the year with a knee injury, but which still showcased the skills of veterans Tom Banks and Bob Young. Despite the reborn running attack, the Cards lost close games regularly because of defensive breakdowns. Veteran cornerback Roger Wehrli turned in his usual All-Pro performance, but his young mates had much to learn about the pro game. Coach Bud Wilkinson had a strained relationship with team president Bill Bidwill, and when the two quarreled over who should play quarterback in the final three games, Wilkinson was canned. Larry Wilson took over as interim coach, used Steve Pisarkiewicz at QB at Bidwill desired, and led the Cards to two victories. The finale, however, was a 42-6 embarrassment in Chicago.

## CENTRAL DIVISION

**Tampa Bay Buccaneers**—Not long ago, they were the butts of tactless jokes. This year, the Buccaneers stepped into Cinderella's slippers. With Lee Roy Selmon and David Lewis leading a ferocious defense, the Bucs won the first five games of their favorable schedule. While the other Central Division teams stumbled, the Buccaneers took a commanding lead by mid-season. The offense relied on Ricky Bell's running but did not measure up to the defense. Needing one victory to clinch a playoff berth, the Bucs lost three games in a row to the Bears, 49ers, and Chiefs, scoring a total of 10 points in three weeks. The playoff spot which seemed so secure a month earlier was on the line as the Buccaneers hosted the Chiefs in the final Sunday of the schedule. The Tampa Bay defense crushed any thoughts of choking and instead dominated the Kansas City offense. The Bucs could score only on Neil O'Donoghue's fourth-period field goal, but the defense made it stand up for a 3-0 triumph and a ticket to the playoffs.

**Chicago Bears**—The Bears shuffled quarterbacks, lost fullback Roland Harper with a bad knee, and had their receiver corps decimated by injuries. They also had the peerless Walter Payton and a hard-nosed defense, and they parlayed these assets into a wild-card playoff berth. Once November began, the Bears hit their stride. The offense depended on Payton to control the ball, while safetyman Gary Fencik led the defense to a series of good outings. Although the Lions embarrassed them 20-0 on Thanksgiving Day, the Bears kept driving. By beating Tampa Bay and Green Bay, they went into the final weekend with a slight chance of making the playoffs. Washington had to lose to Dallas, and the Bears had to beat St. Louis and run up a big score to have a better point differential for the season than the Redskins. On the morning of the game, the players learned that team president George Halas, Jr. had died in his sleep. Inspired by many things, the Bears destroyed the Cardinals 42-6, and when Dallas beat the Redskins 35-34, the Bears were in the playoffs.

**Minnesota Vikings**—The exodus of familiar faces continued, with Fran Tarkenton, Mick Tingelhoff, and Carl Eller no longer around. Coach Bud Grant had kept the Vikings in contention through the recent rebuilding years, but he couldn't prevent a losing season this year, the first since 1967. To add to the changes, Chuck Foreman was eased out of the lineup by rookie Ted Brown. Tommy Kramer settled in admirably at quarterback and found inviting targets in Ahmad Rashad and Sammy White. The ground game, however, was weak enough to hamstring the attack's efficiency. Although Matt Blair was at his peak at linebacker, the defense did not hold a candle to the Viking squads of the early 1970's. More Viking stand-bys bid farewell at the end of season, with Jim Marshall taking a 282-consecutive-game record into retirement along with Wally Hilgenberg and Paul Krause.

**Green Bay Packers**—As Bart Starr heard increasing calls for his firing, none of his efforts could prevent a Packer disintegration in the second half of the schedule. The offense suffered from an anemic running attack. Rookie fullback Eddie Lee Ivery starred in the pre-season, but he injured his knee two minutes into the opening game and went out for the year. Veteran fullback Barty Smith stepped in, but a knee injury sent him to the sidelines in October. Halfback Terdell Middleton could not repeat his sterling performance of last year because of an assortment of nagging injuries. The defense suffered from the trade of Willie Buchanon to San Diego and the knee injury which ended Carl Barzilauskas' career in October. With seven losses in the final nine games, the campaign ended with the Packers in retreat and with their leadership in question.

**Detroit Lions**—The pre-season polls fingered the Lions as favorites to win the Central Division title. Unfortunately, quarterback Gary Danielson suffered a severe knee injury in the final pre-season game,

FINAL TEAM STATISTICS

**OFFENSE**

| | ATL. | CHI. | DALL. | DET. | G.B. | L.A. | MINN. | N.O. | N.Y. | PHIL. | ST.L. | S.F. | T.B. | WASH. |
|---|---|---|---|---|---|---|---|---|---|---|---|---|---|---|
| FIRST DOWNS: | | | | | | | | | | | | | | |
| Total | 303 | 262 | **339** | 227 | 279 | 299 | 311 | 315 | 223 | 292 | 305 | 336 | 267 | 298 |
| by Rushing | 126 | 140 | 122 | 85 | 121 | 134 | 112 | **160** | 82 | 122 | 145 | 120 | 107 | 126 |
| by Passing | 150 | 98 | 195 | 131 | 133 | 138 | 168 | 135 | 111 | 150 | 136 | **200** | 137 | 144 |
| by Penalty | 27 | 24 | 22 | 11 | 25 | 27 | **31** | 20 | 30 | 20 | 24 | 16 | 23 | 28 |
| RUSHING: | | | | | | | | | | | | | | |
| Number | 500 | **627** | 578 | 441 | 483 | 592 | 487 | 551 | 498 | 567 | 566 | 480 | 609 | 609 |
| Yards | 2200 | 2486 | 2375 | 1677 | 1861 | 2460 | 1764 | 2476 | 1820 | 2421 | **2582** | 1932 | 2437 | 2328 |
| Average Yards | 4.4 | 4.0 | 4.1 | 3.8 | 3.9 | 4.2 | 3.6 | 4.5 | 3.7 | 4.3 | **4.6** | 4.0 | 4.0 | 3.8 |
| Touchdowns | 15 | 17 | 15 | 11 | 14 | 16 | 9 | **28** | 12 | 17 | 24 | 17 | 13 | 17 |
| PASSING: | | | | | | | | | | | | | | |
| Attempts | 479 | 373 | 503 | 452 | 444 | 456 | 566 | 428 | 401 | 410 | 492 | **602** | 434 | 401 |
| Completions | 251 | 195 | 287 | 218 | 240 | 242 | 315 | 257 | 190 | 209 | 248 | **361** | 183 | 235 |
| Completion Pct | 52.4 | 52.3 | 57.1 | 48.2 | 54.1 | 53.1 | 55.7 | **60.0** | 47.4 | 51.0 | 50.4 | 60.0 | 42.2 | 58.6 |
| Passing Yards | 3127 | 2429 | **3883** | 2775 | 3057 | 3032 | 3397 | 3291 | 2419 | 2882 | 2870 | 3760 | 2700 | 2839 |
| Avg. Yds. per Att. | 5.1 | 5.3 | 6.6 | 4.6 | 5.5 | 5.4 | 5.2 | **7.1** | 4.3 | 5.9 | 4.9 | 5.9 | 5.9 | 5.9 |
| Avg. Yds per Comp. | 12.5 | 12.5 | 13.5 | 12.7 | 12.7 | 12.5 | 10.8 | 12.8 | 12.7 | 13.8 | 11.6 | 10.4 | **14.8** | 12.1 |
| Times Tackled | 54 | 31 | 41 | 51 | 47 | 39 | 37 | 17 | 59 | 34 | 39 | 17 | **12** | 34 |
| Yds Lost Tackled | 398 | 278 | 290 | 439 | 376 | 359 | 258 | 140 | 465 | 272 | 268 | 119 | **88** | 263 |
| Net Yards | 2729 | 2151 | 3593 | 2336 | 2681 | 2673 | 3139 | 3151 | 1954 | 2610 | 2602 | **3641** | 2612 | 2576 |
| Touchdowns | 19 | 16 | **29** | 14 | 15 | 19 | 23 | 16 | 15 | 21 | 12 | 18 | 19 | 20 |
| Interceptions | 23 | 16 | **13** | 27 | 22 | 29 | 24 | 22 | 22 | **13** | 24 | 21 | 26 | 15 |
| Pct. Intercepted | 4.8 | 4.3 | **2.6** | 6.0 | 5.0 | 6.4 | 4.2 | 5.1 | 5.5 | 3.2 | 4.9 | 3.5 | 6.0 | 3.7 |
| PUNTS: | | | | | | | | | | | | | | |
| Number | 84 | 93 | 76 | 98 | 69 | 95 | 91 | 69 | **104** | 76 | 81 | 72 | 95 | 78 |
| Average | 39.2 | 37.5 | 41.7 | 40.1 | 40.4 | 39.3 | 39.0 | 39.5 | **42.7** | 38.9 | 37.8 | 36.5 | 38.7 | 38.4 |
| PUNT RETURNS: | | | | | | | | | | | | | | |
| Number | 26 | 39 | 51 | 45 | 28 | 58 | 57 | 30 | 28 | 57 | 48 | 44 | **71** | 33 |
| Yards | 188 | 334 | 334 | 372 | 141 | 330 | 288 | 231 | 109 | **544** | 368 | 314 | 438 | 271 |
| Average Yards | 7.2 | 8.6 | 6.5 | 8.3 | 5.0 | 5.7 | 5.1 | 7.7 | 3.9 | **9.5** | 7.7 | 7.1 | 6.2 | 8.2 |
| Touchdowns | 0 | **1** | 0 | 0 | 0 | 0 | 0 | 0 | 0 | 0 | 0 | 0 | 0 | 0 |
| KICKOFF RET.: | | | | | | | | | | | | | | |
| Number | 73 | 51 | 68 | **78** | 61 | 66 | 61 | 66 | 67 | 56 | 71 | 75 | 51 | 55 |
| Yards | 1370 | 1054 | 1316 | 1569 | 1295 | 1292 | 1380 | 1319 | 1255 | 1261 | **1609** | 1538 | 959 | 1145 |
| Average Yards | 18.8 | 20.7 | 19.4 | 20.1 | 21.2 | 19.6 | 22.6 | 20.0 | 18.7 | 22.5 | **22.7** | 20.5 | 18.8 | 20.8 |
| Touchdowns | 0 | **1** | 0 | 0 | **1** | 0 | 0 | 0 | 0 | **1** | **1** | **1** | 0 | 0 |
| INTERCEPT. RET.: | | | | | | | | | | | | | | |
| Number | 15 | 29 | **13** | 14 | 18 | 25 | 22 | 26 | 21 | 22 | 18 | 15 | 14 | 26 |
| Yards | 224 | 402 | 193 | **73** | 243 | 355 | 351 | 351 | 165 | 266 | 288 | 171 | 238 | 250 |
| Average Yards | 14.9 | 13.9 | 14.8 | **5.2** | 13.5 | 14.2 | 16.0 | 13.5 | 7.9 | 12.1 | 16.0 | 11.4 | 17.0 | 9.6 |
| Touchdowns | 2 | 2 | 0 | 1 | 0 | 2 | 0 | 2 | 1 | 0 | 1 | 0 | 1 | 1 |
| PENALTIES: | | | | | | | | | | | | | | |
| Number | 107 | 100 | 100 | 110 | 93 | 98 | 96 | 93 | 122 | 90 | 107 | 95 | 102 | **86** |
| Yards | 1026 | 816 | 845 | 897 | 681 | 743 | 787 | 812 | 1047 | **680** | 954 | 853 | 905 | 749 |
| FUMBLES: | | | | | | | | | | | | | | |
| Number | 31 | **21** | 34 | 37 | 37 | 38 | 40 | 24 | 34 | 38 | 42 | 37 | 25 | **21** |
| Number Lost | 20 | 13 | 21 | 19 | 22 | 20 | 17 | 14 | 18 | 16 | 21 | 18 | 15 | **10** |
| POINTS: | | | | | | | | | | | | | | |
| Total | 300 | 306 | **371** | 219 | 246 | 323 | 259 | 370 | 237 | 339 | 307 | 308 | 273 | 348 |
| PAT Attempts | 37 | 37 | 45 | 27 | 31 | 40 | 31 | **46** | 30 | 39 | 40 | 36 | 35 | 39 |
| PAT Made | 31 | 34 | 40 | 25 | 24 | 36 | 28 | **44** | 28 | 36 | 31 | 32 | 30 | 39 |
| FG Attempts | 25 | 27 | 29 | 18 | 20 | 25 | 22 | 21 | 20 | 31 | 26 | 24 | 19 | **33** |
| FG Made | 13 | 16 | 19 | 10 | 12 | 13 | 13 | 16 | 9 | 23 | 12 | 20 | 11 | **25** |
| Percent FG Made | 52.0 | 59.3 | 65.5 | 55.6 | 60.0 | 52.0 | 59.1 | 76.2 | 45.0 | 74.2 | 46.2 | **83.3** | 57.9 | 75.8 |
| Safeties | 1 | 1 | **2** | 1 | 0 | 1 | 0 | 1 | 1 | 0 | 0 | 0 | 0 | 0 |

**DEFENSE**

| | ATL. | CHI. | DALL. | DET. | G.B. | L.A. | MINN. | N.O. | N.Y. | PHIL. | ST.L. | S.F. | T.B. | WASH. |
|---|---|---|---|---|---|---|---|---|---|---|---|---|---|---|
| FIRST DOWNS: | | | | | | | | | | | | | | |
| Total | 311 | 272 | 259 | 311 | 327 | 266 | 297 | 334 | 322 | 274 | 302 | 326 | **247** | 320 |
| by Rushing | 109 | **100** | 105 | 142 | 162 | 115 | 148 | 147 | 130 | 128 | 125 | 136 | 116 | 126 |
| by Passing | 177 | 148 | 134 | 128 | 146 | 133 | 133 | 168 | 159 | 125 | 149 | 160 | **111** | 165 |
| by Penalty | 25 | 24 | 20 | 41 | 19 | 18 | **16** | 19 | 33 | 21 | 28 | 30 | 20 | 29 |
| RUSHING: | | | | | | | | | | | | | | |
| Number | 555 | 519 | **500** | 638 | 639 | 548 | 583 | 521 | 618 | 515 | 567 | 544 | 539 | 541 |
| Yards | 2163 | 1978 | 2115 | 2515 | 2885 | 1997 | 2526 | 2469 | 2452 | 2271 | 2204 | 2213 | **1873** | 2154 |
| Average Yards | 3.9 | 3.8 | 4.2 | 3.9 | 4.5 | 3.6 | 4.3 | 4.7 | 4.0 | 4.4 | 3.9 | 4.1 | **3.5** | 4.0 |
| Touchdowns | 29 | **9** | 15 | 22 | 14 | 13 | 24 | 22 | 14 | 16 | 18 | 24 | 13 | 21 |
| PASSING: | | | | | | | | | | | | | | |
| Attempts | 487 | 458 | 435 | **402** | 440 | 454 | 424 | 488 | 463 | 459 | 478 | 441 | 436 | 470 |
| Completions | 268 | 222 | **207** | 220 | 249 | 220 | 229 | 265 | 253 | 243 | 258 | 262 | 250 | 234 |
| Completion Pct | 55.0 | 48.5 | **47.6** | 54.7 | 56.6 | 48.5 | 54.0 | 54.3 | 54.6 | 52.9 | 54.0 | 59.4 | 57.3 | 49.8 |
| Passing Yards | 3799 | 2908 | 2833 | 2787 | 3041 | 3007 | 2965 | 3457 | 3154 | 2798 | 3067 | 3407 | **2405** | 3339 |
| Avg. Yds. per Att. | 7.0 | 5.0 | 5.2 | 5.5 | 5.8 | 5.1 | 5.9 | 5.7 | 5.9 | 4.9 | 5.7 | 6.8 | **4.4** | 5.8 |
| Avg. Yds per Comp. | 14.2 | 13.1 | 13.7 | 12.7 | 12.2 | 13.7 | 13.0 | 13.1 | 12.5 | 11.6 | 11.9 | 13.0 | **9.6** | 14.3 |
| Times Tackled | 29 | 47 | 43 | 45 | 35 | **52** | 30 | 46 | 32 | 45 | 28 | 29 | 40 | 47 |
| Yds Lost Tackled | 203 | 380 | 362 | 345 | 279 | **451** | 268 | 391 | 228 | 324 | 194 | 227 | 329 | 347 |
| Net Yards | 3596 | 2528 | 2471 | 2442 | 2762 | 2556 | 2697 | 3066 | 2926 | 2474 | 2873 | 3180 | **2076** | 2992 |
| Touchdowns | 17 | 21 | 21 | 15 | 21 | 24 | **14** | 24 | 22 | 18 | 22 | 25 | **14** | 18 |
| Interceptions | 15 | **29** | 13 | 14 | 18 | 25 | 22 | 26 | 21 | 22 | 18 | 15 | 14 | 26 |
| Pct. Intercepted | 3.1 | **6.3** | 3.0 | 3.5 | 4.1 | 5.5 | 5.2 | 5.3 | 4.5 | 4.8 | 3.8 | 3.4 | 3.2 | 5.5 |
| PUNTS: | | | | | | | | | | | | | | |
| Number | 73 | 90 | 96 | 83 | 64 | **108** | 93 | 71 | 80 | 85 | 90 | 74 | 104 | 70 |
| Average | 37.3 | 37.8 | 40.8 | 40.0 | 39.3 | 40.3 | 34.7 | 38.4 | **36.7** | 39.8 | 39.2 | 38.1 | 41.1 | 40.7 |
| PUNT RETURNS: | | | | | | | | | | | | | | |
| Number | 41 | 54 | 34 | 57 | 43 | 59 | 48 | 32 | 60 | 34 | 45 | 37 | 47 | **29** |
| Yards | 259 | 404 | 252 | 440 | 305 | 405 | 354 | 223 | 447 | 200 | 378 | 262 | 270 | **135** |
| Average Yards | 6.3 | 7.5 | 7.4 | 7.7 | 7.1 | 6.9 | 7.4 | 7.0 | 7.5 | 5.9 | 8.4 | 7.1 | 5.7 | **4.7** |
| Touchdowns | 0 | 0 | 0 | 1 | 0 | 0 | 0 | 0 | 0 | 0 | 0 | 0 | 0 | 0 |
| KICKOFF RET.: | | | | | | | | | | | | | | |
| Number | 61 | 59 | 68 | 51 | 50 | 58 | 59 | 76 | **44** | 69 | 57 | 68 | 55 | 76 |
| Yards | 1312 | 1252 | 1578 | 987 | 999 | 1303 | 1070 | 1523 | **900** | 1265 | 1332 | 1367 | 1254 | 1280 |
| Average Yards | 21.5 | 21.2 | 23.2 | 19.4 | 20.0 | 22.5 | 18.1 | 20.0 | 20.5 | 18.3 | 23.4 | 20.1 | 22.8 | **16.8** |
| Touchdowns | 0 | 0 | 1 | 1 | 0 | 0 | 0 | 0 | 0 | 0 | 1 | 0 | 0 | 0 |
| INTERCEPT. RET.: | | | | | | | | | | | | | | |
| Number | 23 | 16 | 13 | 27 | 22 | **29** | 24 | 22 | 22 | 13 | 24 | 21 | 26 | 15 |
| Yards | 362 | 240 | 114 | 396 | 247 | 387 | 308 | 199 | **449** | 132 | 301 | 355 | 324 | 82 |
| Average Yards | 15.7 | 15.0 | 8.8 | 14.7 | 11.2 | 13.3 | 12.8 | 9.0 | **20.4** | 10.2 | 12.5 | 16.9 | 12.5 | 5.5 |
| Touchdowns | **2** | 0 | 1 | **2** | **2** | 0 | **2** | 1 | 1 | 0 | 1 | **2** | 1 | 0 |
| PENALTIES: | | | | | | | | | | | | | | |
| Number | 98 | 104 | 70 | 118 | 106 | 105 | 93 | 98 | 105 | 86 | 92 | **119** | 100 | 76 |
| Yards | 815 | 864 | 704 | 972 | 912 | **993** | 786 | 871 | 800 | 681 | 744 | 858 | 870 | 617 |
| FUMBLES: | | | | | | | | | | | | | | |
| Number | 35 | 25 | 20 | 30 | 30 | 38 | 23 | 32 | 36 | 20 | 40 | 33 | **45** | 34 |
| Number Lost | 21 | 14 | 10 | 12 | 14 | 16 | 11 | 16 | 17 | 11 | 19 | 19 | **24** | 21 |
| POINTS: | | | | | | | | | | | | | | |
| Total | 388 | 249 | 313 | 365 | 316 | 309 | 337 | 360 | 323 | 282 | 358 | 416 | **237** | 295 |
| PAT Attempts | 47 | **31** | 38 | 42 | 36 | 38 | 42 | 46 | 39 | 34 | 43 | 54 | 28 | 39 |
| PAT Made | 44 | **27** | 34 | 41 | 32 | 35 | 32 | 45 | 35 | 33 | 41 | 46 | 25 | 37 |
| FG Attempts | 29 | 20 | 27 | 36 | 33 | 21 | 24 | **17** | 35 | 23 | 31 | **17** | 24 | **17** |
| FG Made | 20 | 12 | 17 | 24 | 20 | 14 | 15 | 11 | 18 | 15 | 19 | 14 | 14 | **8** |
| Percent FG Made | 69.0 | 60.0 | 63.0 | 66.7 | 60.6 | 66.7 | 62.5 | 64.7 | 51.4 | 65.2 | 61.3 | 82.4 | 58.3 | **47.1** |
| Safeties | 1 | 0 | 0 | 0 | 1 | 2 | 1 | 0 | 0 | 0 | 1 | 2 | 1 | 0 |

leaving coach Monte Clark without a seasoned QB. Although Danielson's loss was expected to hurt the offense, the entire team sagged from the blow and seemed to lose its will. Clark shuffled his defensive lineup, but no combination could prevent a demoralizing eight-game losing skid which began on the last day of September and ended with an upset 20-0 thrashing of the Bears on Thanksgiving Day. What the Lions had most of all to be thankful for was their number-one position in the upcoming college draft.

## WESTERN DIVISION

**Los Angeles Rams**—With a roster deep in talent, the Rams nevertheless had to scramble in the weak Western Division. Before the season started, guard Tom Mack had retired and halfback John Cappelletti went to the sidelines with a groin injury. As the season progressed, injuries struck at the Los Angeles wide receivers and cornerbacks. Despite good offensive and defensive lines featuring Jack Youngblood, Larry Brooks, Dennis Harrah, and Rich Saul, the Rams had a tepid 5-6 record in mid-November. To make matters worse, quarterback Pat Haden had broken a finger, leaving the QB job to inexperienced Vince Ferragamo. Taking over for the final four games, Ferragamo led the Rams to three victories and a playoff spot. Although Ferragamo showed a talent for throwing the long ball, the Ram offense relied on the running of Wendell Tyler and Cullen Bryant. The defense feasted on enemy quarterbacks all season and hoped to continue that diet in the playoffs.

**New Orleans Saints**—For the pro football fans of New Orleans, it was heady stuff. The Saints were battling for first place in the West well into December. Coach Dick Nolan had put together a first-rate offense. The line enjoyed the return of guards Emanuel Zanders and Conrad Dobler from injuries, and quarterback Archie Manning had a pair of dangerous receivers in Wes Chandler and Ike Harris. On the ground, Chuck Muncie carried the ball with speed, power, and heart. Nolan even added Garo Yepremian as place kicker after the Dolphins cut him loose. The defense, unfortunately, did not measure up despite Tommy Myers' brilliant season. With high-scoring games the rule, the Saints compiled a 7-6 record as of the start of December and were tied with the Rams for first place. On December 3, the Saints hosted Oakland and bolted to a 28-7 lead in the second quarter. Six minutes into the third quarter, the Saints led 35-14, but the defense could not stand its ground. The Raiders ran off 28 unanswered points and won the game 42-35. A 35-0 loss to San Diego one week later ended the playoff dreams, but the Saints kept their spirit and beat the Rams 29-14 to end the season at .500, the first Saint squad ever to do it.

**Atlanta Falcons**—One year ago, the Falcons won the close games and made it into the playoffs. This year, they lost the close games and finished with a losing record. Coach Leeman Bennett had reason to expect improvement from his team this season. Rookie fullback William Andrews ran for over 100 yards in his first two games and gave the attack a new threat. Alfred Jenkins came back from an injury to start at wide receiver. On defense, however, the Falcons could not stop enemy passing attacks. After two victories to open the schedule, the Falcons lost six of their next seven matches. Four of those losses were by a margin of five points or less, and another was a 50-19 trouncing by the Raiders. On November 11, they sleepwalked through a 24-3 debacle in New Jersey. Although they beat the streaking San Diego Chargers late in the year, the Falcons chalked up the season as a major disappointment.

**San Francisco 49ers**—The 49ers hired Bill Walsh away from Stanford University to rebuild the team as head coach and general manager. Walsh spent the year rummaging through the rubble he inherited and through the waiver list for serviceable football players. While doing this, the 49ers lost their first seven games and won only twice all season. The defense was manned by a horde of new faces, and errors of inexperience led to many enemy scores. On offense, Walsh emphasized the pass and turned young quarterback Steve DeBerg loose. DeBerg set new NFL records for passing attempts and completions in a season. For O. J. Simpson, the premier runner of the 1970's, it was a last hurrah. He lost his starting job to Paul Hofer in mid-season, and by announcing his plan to retire at the end of the season, he was able to make token appearances over the last leg of the schedule and reap a harvest of cheers and affection from appreciative fans.

# 1979 N.F.C. — Eastern Division

## DALLAS COWBOYS 11-5-0 Tom Landry

| Scores of Each Game | | |
|---|---|---|
| 22 | St. Louis | 21 |
| 21 | San Francisco | 13 |
| 24 | CHICAGO | 20 |
| 7 | Cleveland | 26 |
| 38 | CINCINNATI | 13 |
| 36 | Minnesota | 20 |
| 30 | LOS ANGELES | 6 |
| 22 | ST. LOUIS | 13 |
| 3 | Pittsburgh | 14 |
| 16 | N.Y. Giants | 14 |
| 21 | PHILADELPHIA | 31 |
| 20 | Washington | 34 |
| 24 | HOUSTON | 30 |
| 28 | N.Y. GIANTS | 7 |
| 24 | Philadelphia | 17 |
| 35 | WASHINGTON | 34 |

| Use Name | Pos. | Hgt. | Wgt. | Age | Int. | Pts. |
|---|---|---|---|---|---|---|
| Jim Cooper | OT | 6'5" | 260 | 23 | | |
| Pat Donovan | OT | 6'4" | 250 | 26 | | |
| Andy Frederick | OT | 6'6" | 255 | 24 | | |
| Rayfield Wright | OT | 6'7" | 260 | 34 | | |
| Burton Lawless | OG | 6'4" | 255 | 25 | | |
| Tom Rafferty | OG | 6'3" | 250 | 25 | | |
| Herbert Scott | OG | 6'2" | 252 | 26 | | |
| John Fitzgerald | C | 6'5" | 260 | 31 | | |
| Robert Shaw | C-OG | 6'4" | 245 | 22 | | |
| Larry Cole | DE-DT | 6'4" | 252 | 32 | | |
| John Dutton | DE | 6'7" | 265 | 28 | | |
| Harvey Martin | DE | 6'5" | 250 | 28 | | 2 |
| Bruce Thornton | DE-DT | 6'5" | 265 | 21 | 1 | |
| Larry Bethea | DT | 6'5" | 254 | 23 | | |
| David Stalls | DT | 6'4" | 245 | 23 | | |
| Randy White | DT | 6'4" | 250 | 26 | | |

| Use Name | Pos. | Hgt. | Wgt. | Age | Int. | Pts. |
|---|---|---|---|---|---|---|
| Bob Breunig | LB | 6'2" | 225 | 26 | | |
| Guy Brown | LB | 6'4" | 228 | 24 | | |
| Mike Hegman | LB | 6'1" | 225 | 26 | | |
| Tom Henderson | LB | 6'2" | 220 | 26 | | |
| Bruce Huther | LB | 6'1" | 220 | 25 | | |
| D.D. Lewis | LB | 6'2" | 215 | 33 | 2 | |
| Benny Barnes | DB | 6'1" | 195 | 28 | 2 | 6 |
| Cliff Harris | DB | 6' | 192 | 30 | 2 | |
| Randy Hughes | DB | 6'4" | 207 | 26 | 2• | |
| Aaron Kyle | DB | 5'11" | 185 | 25 | 2 | |
| Wade Manning | DB | 5'11" | 190 | 24 | | |
| Aaron Mitchell | DB | 6'1" | 196 | 22 | 1 | |
| Dennis Thurman | DB | 5'11" | 170 | 23 | 1 | |

Too Tall Jones – Voluntarily Retired
Charlie Waters – Knee Injury

| Use Name | Pos. | Hgt. | Wgt. | Age | Int. | Pts. |
|---|---|---|---|---|---|---|
| Glenn Carano | QB | 6'3" | 202 | 23 | | |
| Roger Staubach | QB | 6'2" | 202 | 37 | | |
| Danny White | QB | 6'2" | 192 | 27 | | |
| Alois Blackwell | HB | 5'10" | 195 | 24 | | |
| Tony Dorsett | HB | 5'11" | 190 | 25 | | 42 |
| Preston Pearson | HB | 6'1" | 206 | 34 | | 12 |
| Ron Springs | HB | 6'1" | 200 | 22 | | 18 |
| Larry Brinson | FB | 6' | 214 | 25 | | |
| Scott Laidlaw | FB | 6' | 205 | 26 | | 18 |
| Robert Newhouse | FB | 5'10" | 215 | 29 | | 24 |
| Tony Hill | WR | 6'2" | 198 | 23 | | 60 |
| Butch Johnson | WR | 6'1" | 192 | 25 | | 6 |
| Drew Pearson | WR | 6' | 183 | 28 | | 48 |
| Steve Wilson | WR | 5'10" | 192 | 22 | | |
| Doug Cosbie | TE | 6'6" | 230 | 23 | | |
| Billy Joe DuPree | TE | 6'4" | 229 | 29 | | 30 |
| Jay Saldi | TE | 6'3" | 227 | 24 | | 6 |
| Raphael Septien | K | 5'9" | 171 | 25 | | 97 |

## PHILADELPHIA EAGES 11-5-0 Dick Vermeil

| Scores of Each Game | | |
|---|---|---|
| 23 | N.Y. GIANTS | 17 |
| 10 | ATLANTA | 14 |
| 26 | New Orleans | 14 |
| 17 | N.Y. Giants | 13 |
| 17 | PITTSBURGH | 14 |
| 28 | WASHINGTON | 17 |
| 24 | St. Louis | 20 |
| 7 | Washington | 17 |
| 13 | Cincinnati | 37 |
| 19 | CLEVELAND | 24 |
| 31 | Dallas | 21 |
| 16 | ST. LOUIS | 13 |
| 21 | Green Bay | 10 |
| 44 | DETROIT | 7 |
| 17 | DALLAS | 24 |
| 26 | Houston | 20 |

| Use Name | Pos. | Hgt. | Wgt. | Age | Int. | Pts. |
|---|---|---|---|---|---|---|
| Rufus Mayes | OT | 6'5" | 256 | 31 | | |
| Jerry Sisemore | OT | 6'4" | 260 | 28 | | |
| Stan Walters | OT | 6'6" | 270 | 31 | | |
| Wade Key | OG | 6'4" | 245 | 32 | | |
| Woody Peoples | OG | 6'2" | 252 | 36 | | |
| Petey Perot | OG | 6'2" | 261 | 22 | | |
| Guy Morriss | C | 6'4" | 255 | 28 | | |
| Mark Slater | C | 6'1" | 257 | 24 | | |
| Lem Burnham | DE | 6'4" | 240 | 32 | | |
| Carl Hairston | DE | 6'3" | 260 | 26 | | |
| Dennis Harrison | DE | 6'8" | 275 | 23 | | |
| Claude Humphrey | DE | 6'5" | 265 | 35 | | |
| Manny Sistrunk | DE | 6'5" | 275 | 32 | | |
| Ken Clarke | MG | 6'2" | 255 | 23 | | |
| Charles Johnson | MG | 6'3" | 262 | 27 | | |

Vince Papale – Shoulder Injury

| Use Name | Pos. | Hgt. | Wgt. | Age | Int. | Pts. |
|---|---|---|---|---|---|---|
| Bill Bergey | LB | 6'2" | 245 | 34 | 1 | |
| John Bunting | LB | 6'1" | 220 | 29 | 2 | |
| Al Chesley | LB | 6'3" | 240 | 22 | 2 | |
| Frank LeMaster | LB | 6'2" | 231 | 27 | | |
| Ray Phillips | LB | 6'4" | 217 | 25 | | |
| Jerry Robinson | LB | 6'2" | 216 | 22 | | |
| Terry Tautolo | LB | 6'2" | 235 | 25 | | |
| Reggie Wilkes | LB | 6'4" | 235 | 23 | 2 | |
| Richard Blackmore | DB | 5'10" | 174 | 23 | | |
| Herman Edwards | DB | 6' | 194 | 25 | 3 | |
| Bob Howard | DB | 6'1" | 175 | 34 | 3 | |
| Al Latimer | DB | 5'11" | 172 | 21 | | |
| Randy Logan | DB | 6'1" | 195 | 28 | 3 | |
| Henry Monroe | DB | 5'11" | 180 | 22 | | |
| Deac Sanders | DB | 6'1" | 175 | 29 | | |
| John Sciarra | DB | 5'11" | 185 | 25 | 2 | |
| Brenard Wilson | DB | 6' | 170 | 24 | 4 | |

| Use Name | Pos. | Hgt. | Wgt. | Age | Int. | Pts. |
|---|---|---|---|---|---|---|
| Ron Jaworski | QB | 6'2" | 195 | 28 | | 12 |
| John Walton | QB | 6'2" | 210 | 31 | | |
| Billy Campfield | HB | 5'11" | 205 | 23 | | 24 |
| Louie Giammona | HB | 5'9" | 180 | 26 | | |
| Wilbert Montgomery | HB | 5'10" | 195 | 24 | | 84 |
| Larry Barnes | FB | 5'11" | 220 | 25 | | 6 |
| Earl Carr | FB | 6' | 224 | 24 | | |
| Leroy Harris | FB | 5'9" | 230 | 25 | | 12 |
| Harold Carmichael | WR | 6'7" | 225 | 29 | | 66 |
| Scott Fitzkee | WR | 6' | 187 | 22 | | 6 |
| Wally Henry | WR | 5'8" | 170 | 24 | | |
| Jerrold McRae | LWR | 6' | 187 | 24 | | |
| Charlie Smith | WR | 6'1" | 185 | 29 | | 6 |
| Keith Krepfle | TE | 6'3" | 225 | 27 | | 18 |
| John Spagnola | TE | 6'4" | 240 | 22 | | |
| Tony Franklin | K | 5'8" | 182 | 22 | | 105 |
| Max Runager | K | 6'1" | 189 | 23 | | |

## WASHINGTON REDSKINS 10-6-0 Jack Pardee

| Scores of Each Game | | |
|---|---|---|
| 27 | HOUSTON | 29 |
| 27 | Detroit | 24 |
| 27 | N.Y. GIANTS | 0 |
| 17 | St. Louis | 7 |
| 16 | Atlanta | 7 |
| 17 | Philadelphia | 28 |
| 13 | Cleveland | 9 |
| 17 | PHILADELPHIA | 7 |
| 10 | NEW ORLEANS | 14 |
| 7 | Pittsburgh | 38 |
| 30 | ST. LOUIS | 28 |
| 34 | DALLAS | 20 |
| 6 | N.Y. Giants | 14 |
| 38 | GREEN BAY | 21 |
| 28 | CINCINNATI | 14 |
| 34 | Dallas | 35 |

| Use Name | Pos. | Hgt. | Wgt. | Age | Int. | Pts. |
|---|---|---|---|---|---|---|
| Terry Hermeling | OT | 6'5" | 255 | 33 | | |
| George Starke | OT | 6'5" | 250 | 31 | | |
| Fred Dean | OG | 6'3" | 253 | 24 | | |
| Greg Dubinetz | OG | 6'4" | 260 | 25 | | |
| Ron Saul | OG | 6'2" | 254 | 31 | | |
| Jeff Williams | OG-OT | 6'4" | 260 | 24 | | |
| Ted Fritsch | C-OG | 6'2" | 247 | 29 | | |
| Bob Kuziel | C | 6'5" | 255 | 29 | | |
| Coy Bacon | DE | 6'4" | 265 | 37 | | |
| Joe Jones | DE | 6'6" | 250 | 31 | | |
| Karl Lorch | DE | 6'3" | 258 | 29 | 1 | 6 |
| Paul Smith | DE | 6'3" | 255 | 34 | | |
| Perry Brooks | DT | 6'3" | 260 | 24 | | |
| Dave Butz | DT | 6'7" | 285 | 29 | | |
| Diron Talbert | DT | 6'5" | 255 | 35 | | |

| Use Name | Pos. | Hgt. | Wgt. | Age | Int. | Pts. |
|---|---|---|---|---|---|---|
| Monte Coleman | LB | 6'2" | 220 | 21 | 1 | |
| Brad Dusek | LB | 6'2" | 227 | 28 | 1 | |
| Dallas Hickman | LB-DE | 6'6" | 236 | 27 | | |
| Don Hover | LB | 6'2" | 227 | 24 | | 6 |
| Rich Milot | LB | 6'4" | 225 | 22 | | |
| Neal Olkewicz | LB | 6' | 218 | 22 | 1 | |
| Pete Wysocki | LB | 6'2" | 224 | 30 | 1 | |
| Don Harris | DB | 6'2" | 185 | 25 | | |
| Ken Houston | DB | 6'3" | 198 | 34 | 1 | |
| Joe Lavender | DB | 6'4" | 190 | 30 | 6 | |
| Mark Murphy | DB | 6'4" | 210 | 24 | 3 | |
| Lemar Parrish | DB | 5'11" | 177 | 31 | 9 | |
| Tony Peters | DB | 6'1" | 185 | 26 | 1 | |
| Ray Waddy | DB | 5'11" | 175 | 23 | 1 | |

Gary Anderson – Ankle Injury
Dan Nugent – Back Injury
Dan Testerman – Knee Injury

| Use Name | Pos. | Hgt. | Wgt. | Age | Int. | Pts. |
|---|---|---|---|---|---|---|
| Kim McQuilken | QB | 6'2" | 203 | 28 | | |
| Fred Martensen | QB | 6'2" | 195 | 25 | | |
| Joe Theismann | QB | 6' | 195 | 29 | | 24 |
| Ike Forte | HB | 6' | 211 | 25 | | 6 |
| Bob Hammond (from NYG) | HB | 5'10" | 170 | 27 | | |
| Buddy Hardeman | HB | 6' | 190 | 24 | | 6 |
| Clarence Harmon | HB-FB | 5'11" | 213 | 23 | | 30 |
| Benny Malone | HB | 5'10" | 193 | 27 | | 24 |
| John Riggins | FB | 6'2" | 230 | 30 | | 72 |
| Danny Buggs | WR | 6'2" | 185 | 26 | | 6 |
| Chris DeFrance | WR | 6'1" | 205 | 22 | | |
| Dennis Law | WR | 6'1" | 175 | 24 | | |
| John McDaniel | WR | 6'1" | 197 | 27 | | 12 |
| Ricky Thompson | WR | 6' | 177 | 25 | | 24 |
| Phil DuBois | TE | 6'2" | 220 | 22 | | |
| Jean Fugett | TE | 6'3" | 230 | 27 | | 18 |
| Grady Richardson | TE | 6'4" | 225 | 27 | | |
| Don Warren | TE | 6'4" | 229 | 23 | | |
| Mike Bragg | K | 5'11" | 186 | 32 | | |
| Mark Moseley | K | 5'11" | 205 | 31 | | **114** |

## NEW YORK GIANTS 6-10-0 Ray Perkins

| Scores of Each Game | | |
|---|---|---|
| 17 | Philadelphia | 23 |
| 14 | ST. LOUIS | 27 |
| 0 | Washington | 27 |
| 13 | PHILADELPHIA | 17 |
| 14 | New Orleans | 24 |
| 17 | TAMPA BAY | 14 |
| 32 | SAN FRANCISCO | 16 |
| 21 | Kansas City | 17 |
| 20 | Los Angeles | 14 |
| 14 | DALLAS | 16 |
| 24 | ATLANTA | 3 |
| 3 | Tampa Bay | 31 |
| 14 | WASHINGTON | 6 |
| 7 | Dallas | 28 |
| 20 | St. Louis | 29 |
| 7 | BALTIMORE | 31 |

| Use Name | Pos. | Hgt. | Wgt. | Age | Int. | Pts. |
|---|---|---|---|---|---|---|
| Brad Benson | OT | 6'3" | 258 | 23 | | |
| Gus Coppens | OT | 6'5" | 270 | 24 | | |
| Gordon King | OT | 6'6" | 275 | 23 | | |
| Ron Mikolajczyk | OT | 6'3" | 275 | 29 | | |
| Tom Neville | OT | 6'4" | 250 | 36 | | |
| Dan Fowler | OG | 6'5" | 260 | 23 | | |
| Roy Simmons | OG | 6'3" | 264 | 22 | | |
| J.T. Turner | OG | 6'3" | 250 | 26 | | |
| Doug Van Horn | OG | 6'2" | 245 | 35 | | |
| Jim Clack | C | 6'3" | 250 | 31 | | |
| Keith Eck | C-OG | 6'5" | 255 | 23 | | |
| Gary Jeter | DE | 6'4" | 260 | 24 | | |
| George Martin | DE | 6'4" | 245 | 26 | | |
| Mike McCoy | DT | 6'5" | 275 | 30 | | |
| John Mendenhall | DT | 6'1" | 255 | 30 | | |
| Calvin Miller | DT-DE | 6'2" | 250 | 25 | | |
| Phil Tabor | DT | 6'4" | 255 | 22 | | |
| Jeff Weston | DT | 6'5" | 250 | 22 | | |

| Use Name | Pos. | Hgt. | Wgt. | Age | Int. | Pts. |
|---|---|---|---|---|---|---|
| Harry Carson | LB | 6'2" | 235 | 25 | 3 | 6 |
| Randy Coffield | LB | 6'3" | 215 | 25 | | |
| Brian Kelley | LB | 6'3" | 222 | 28 | 3 | |
| Dan Lloyd | LB | 6'2" | 225 | 25 | 2 | |
| Frank Marion | LB | 6'3" | 228 | 28 | | |
| John Skorupan | LB | 6'2" | 225 | 28 | | 2 |
| Brad Van Pelt | LB | 6'5" | 235 | 28 | | |
| Alan Caldwell | DB | 6' | 176 | 23 | 2 | |
| Terry Jackson | DB | 5'10" | 197 | 23 | 3 | 6 |
| Ernie Jones | DB | 6'3" | 180 | 26 | 2 | 6 |
| Otis McKinney | DB | 6'2" | 187 | 22 | 1 | |
| Ray Oldham | DB | 6' | 192 | 28 | 2 | |
| Beasley Reece | DB | 6'1" | 195 | 25 | 1 | |
| Ray Rhodes | DB | 5'11" | 185 | 28 | 2 | |

Larry Gillard – Knee Injury
Troy Archer – Died in Auto Accident in June

| Use Name | Pos. | Hgt. | Wgt. | Age | Int. | Pts. |
|---|---|---|---|---|---|---|
| Randy Dean | QB | 6'3" | 195 | 24 | | 6 |
| Joe Pisarcik | QB | 6'4" | 220 | 27 | | |
| Dave Rader | QB | 6'3" | 211 | 22 | | |
| Phil Simms | QB | 6'3" | 216 | 23 | | 6 |
| Doug Kotar | HB | 5'11" | 205 | 28 | | 18 |
| Emery Moorehead | HB-FB | 6'2" | 210 | 25 | | |
| George Franklin | FB | 6'3" | 225 | 25 | | |
| Eddie Hicks | FB | 6'2" | 210 | 24 | | |
| Ken Johnson | FB | 6'2" | 220 | 22 | | 6 |
| Billy Taylor | FB-HB | 6' | 215 | 23 | | 66 |
| Earnest Gray | WR | 6'3" | 195 | 22 | | 24 |
| Johnny Perkins | WR | 6'2" | 205 | 26 | | 24 |
| Jim Robinson | WR | 5'9" | 170 | 26 | | |
| Dwight Scales | WR | 6'2" | 182 | 26 | | |
| Gene Washington | WR | 5'9" | 170 | 26 | | |
| Al Dixon (to KC) | TE | 6'5" | 220 | 25 | | |
| Cleveland Jackson | TE | 6'4" | 230 | 22 | | |
| Loaird McCreary | TE | 6'5" | 227 | 26 | | |
| Tom Mullady | TE | 6'3" | 232 | 22 | | |
| Gary Shirk | TE | 6'1" | 220 | 29 | | 12 |
| Joe Danelo | K | 5'9" | 166 | 25 | | 55 |
| Dave Jennings | K | 6'4" | 205 | 27 | | |

## ST. LOUIS CARDINALS 5-11-0 Bud Wilkinson, Larry Wilson

| Scores of Each Game | | |
|---|---|---|
| 21 | DALLAS | 22 |
| 27 | N.Y. Giants | 14 |
| 21 | PITTSBURGH | 24 |
| 7 | WASHINGTON | 17 |
| 0 | Los Angeles | 21 |
| 24 | Houston | 17 |
| 20 | PHILADELPHIA | 24 |
| 13 | Dallas | 22 |
| 20 | CLEVELAND | 38 |
| 37 | MINNESOTA | 7 |
| 28 | Washington | 30 |
| 13 | Philadelphia | 16 |
| 28 | Cincinnati | 34 |
| 13 | SAN FRANCISCO | 10 |
| 29 | N.Y. GIANTS | 20 |
| 6 | Chicago | 42 |

| Use Name | Pos. | Hgt. | Wgt. | Age | Int. | Pts. |
|---|---|---|---|---|---|---|
| Joe Bostic | OT | 6'3" | 265 | 22 | | |
| Dan Dierdorf | OT | 6'4" | 288 | 30 | | |
| Brad Oates | OT | 6'6" | 275 | 25 | | |
| Keith Wortman | OT | 6'2" | 275 | 29 | | |
| George Collins | OG | 6'2" | 248 | 23 | | |
| Terry Stieve | OG | 6'2" | 263 | 25 | | |
| Bob Young | OG | 6'2" | 279 | 36 | | |
| Tom Banks | C-OG | 6'1" | 245 | 31 | | |
| Tom Brahaney | C | 6'2" | 246 | 27 | | |
| Chuck Brown | C-OG | 6'1" | 235 | 22 | | |
| Mike Dawson | DE | 6'4" | 274 | 25 | | |
| Bob Pollard | DE | 6'3" | 251 | 30 | | |
| Jim Ramey | DE | 6'4" | 247 | 22 | | |
| Bob Rozier | DE | 6'3" | 240 | 24 | | |
| Ron Yankowski | DE | 6'5" | 258 | 32 | | |
| John Zook | DE | 6'5" | 254 | 31 | | |
| Charlie Davis | NT | 6'1" | 275 | 27 | | |
| Keith Simons | NT | 6'3" | 254 | 25 | | |

| Use Name | Pos. | Hgt. | Wgt. | Age | Int. | Pts. |
|---|---|---|---|---|---|---|
| Kurt Allerman | LB | 6'3" | 222 | 24 | | |
| Mark Arneson | LB | 6'2" | 224 | 29 | | 6 |
| John Barefield | LB | 6'2" | 224 | 24 | | |
| Sean Clancy | LB | 6'4" | 218 | 22 | | |
| Calvin Favron | LB | 6'1" | 225 | 22 | | |
| Chris Garlich | LB | 6'1" | 220 | 22 | | |
| Tim Kearney | LB | 6'2" | 221 | 28 | | |
| Steve Neils | LB | 6'2" | 218 | 28 | | 6 |
| Eric Williams | LB | 6'2" | 225 | 24 | 1 | |
| Carl Allen | DB | 6' | 186 | 23 | 5 | |
| Roy Green | DB | 5'11" | 190 | 22 | | 6 |
| Ken Greene | DB | 6'3" | 203 | 23 | 3 | |
| Steve Henry | DB | 6'2" | 190 | 22 | | |
| Lee Nelson | DB | 5'10" | 185 | 25 | | |
| Perry Smith | DB | 6'1" | 190 | 28 | 1 | |
| Ken Stone | DB | 6'1" | 180 | 28 | 6 | |
| Roger Wehrli | DB | 6'1" | 193 | 31 | 2 | 6 |

J.V. Cain – Died of Heart Failure in July

| Use Name | Pos. | Hgt. | Wgt. | Age | Int. | Pts. |
|---|---|---|---|---|---|---|
| Jim Hart | QB | 6'2" | 210 | 35 | | |
| Mike Loyd | QB | 6'2" | 216 | 23 | | |
| Steve Pisarkiewicz | QB | 6'2" | 205 | 25 | | |
| Ottis Anderson | HB | 6'2" | 210 | 22 | | 60 |
| Will Harrell | HB | 5'9" | 182 | 26 | | |
| Robert Hawkins | HB | 6' | 195 | 22 | | |
| Thomas Lott | HB | 5'11" | 205 | 22 | | |
| Randy Love | HB | 6'1" | 205 | 22 | | |
| Theotis Brown | FB | 6'2" | 225 | 22 | | 42 |
| Wayne Morris | FB | 6' | 208 | 25 | | 54 |
| Rod Phillips | FB | 6' | 220 | 26 | | 6 |
| Jim Childs | WR | 6'2" | 194 | 23 | | |
| Mel Gray | WR | 5'9" | 173 | 30 | | 6 |
| Dave Stief | WR | 6'3" | 195 | 23 | | |
| Pat Tilley | WR | 5'10" | 171 | 26 | | 36 |
| Al Chandler (to NE) | TE | 6'2" | 229 | 28 | | 12 |
| Bill Murrell | TE | 6'3" | 220 | 23 | | |
| Richard Osborne | TE | 6'3" | 230 | 25 | | |
| Gary Parris | TE | 6'2" | 226 | 29 | | 1 |
| Steve Little | K | 6' | 180 | 23 | | 54 |

## DALLAS COWBOYS

### RUSHING

| Last Name | No. | Yds. | Avg. | TD |
|---|---|---|---|---|
| Dorsett | 250 | 1107 | 4.4 | 6 |
| Newhouse | 124 | 449 | 3.6 | 3 |
| Springs | 67 | 248 | 3.7 | 2 |
| Laidlaw | 69 | 236 | 3.4 | 3 |
| Staubach | 37 | 172 | 4.6 | 0 |
| Brinson | 14 | 48 | 3.4 | 0 |
| D. Pearson | 3 | 27 | 9.0 | 0 |
| D. White | 1 | 25 | 25.0 | 0 |
| DuPree | 2 | 19 | 9.5 | 0 |
| Hill | 2 | 18 | 9.0 | 0 |
| P. Pearson | 7 | 14 | 2.0 | 1 |
| Johnson | 1 | 13 | 13.0 | 0 |
| Saldi | 1 | −1 | −1.0 | 0 |

### RECEIVING

| Last Name | No. | Yds. | Avg. | TD |
|---|---|---|---|---|
| Hill | 60 | 1062 | 18 | 10 |
| D. Pearson | 55 | 1026 | 19 | 8 |
| Dorsett | 45 | 375 | 8 | 1 |
| DuPree | 29 | 324 | 11 | 5 |
| P. Pearson | 26 | 333 | 13 | 1 |
| Springs | 25 | 251 | 10 | 1 |
| Laidlaw | 12 | 59 | 5 | 0 |
| Newhouse | 7 | 55 | 8 | 1 |
| Johnson | 6 | 105 | 18 | 1 |
| Cosbie | 5 | 36 | 7 | 0 |
| Wilson | 3 | 76 | 25 | 0 |

### PUNT RETURNS

| Last Name | No. | Yds. | Avg. | TD |
|---|---|---|---|---|
| Wilson | 35 | 236 | 7 | 0 |
| Manning | 10 | 55 | 6 | 0 |
| Hill | 6 | 43 | 7 | 0 |

### KICKOFF RETURNS

| Last Name | No. | Yds. | Avg. | TD |
|---|---|---|---|---|
| Springs | 38 | 780 | 21 | 0 |
| Wilson | 19 | 328 | 17 | 0 |
| Manning | 7 | 145 | 21 | 0 |
| Brinson | 2 | 23 | 12 | 0 |
| Hill | 1 | 32 | 32 | 0 |
| Huther | 1 | 8 | 8 | 0 |

### PASSING

| Last Name | Att. | Comp. | % | Yds. | Yd./Att. | TD | Int.-% | RK |
|---|---|---|---|---|---|---|---|---|
| Staubach | 461 | 267 | 58 | 3586 | 7.8 | 27 | 11- 2 | 1 |
| D. White | 39 | 19 | 49 | 267 | 6.9 | 1 | 2- 5 | |
| Springs | 3 | 1 | 33 | 30 | 10.0 | 1 | 0- 0 | |

### PUNTING

| Last Name | No. | Avg. |
|---|---|---|
| D. White | 76 | 41.7 |

### KICKING

| Last Name | XP | Att. | % | FG | Att. | % |
|---|---|---|---|---|---|---|
| Septien | 40 | 44 | 90 | 19 | 29 | 66 |

## PHILADELPHIA EAGLES

### RUSHING

| Last Name | No. | Yds. | Avg. | TD |
|---|---|---|---|---|
| Montgomery | 338 | 1512 | 4.5 | 9 |
| Harris | 107 | 504 | 4.7 | 2 |
| Campfield | 30 | 165 | 5.5 | 3 |
| Jaworski | 43 | 119 | 2.8 | 2 |
| Barnes | 25 | 74 | 3.0 | 1 |
| Giammona | 15 | 38 | 2.5 | 0 |
| LeMaster | 1 | 15 | 15.0 | 0 |
| Carmichael | 1 | 0 | 0.0 | 0 |
| Carr | 1 | −1 | −1.0 | 0 |
| Walton | 6 | −5 | −0.8 | 0 |

### RECEIVING

| Last Name | No. | Yds. | Avg. | TD |
|---|---|---|---|---|
| Carmichael | 52 | 872 | 17 | 11 |
| Krepfle | 41 | 760 | 19 | 3 |
| Montgomery | 41 | 494 | 12 | 5 |
| Smith | 24 | 399 | 17 | 1 |
| Harris | 22 | 107 | 5 | 0 |
| Campfield | 16 | 115 | 7 | 0 |
| Fitzkee | 8 | 105 | 13 | 1 |
| Spagnola | 2 | 24 | 12 | 0 |
| Barnes | 1 | 6 | 6 | 0 |
| Carr | 1 | 2 | 2 | 0 |
| McRae | 1 | −2 | −2 | 0 |

### PUNT RETURNS

| Last Name | No. | Yds. | Avg. | TD |
|---|---|---|---|---|
| Sciarra | 16 | 182 | 11 | 0 |
| Henry | 35 | 320 | 9 | 0 |
| Giammona | 5 | 42 | 8 | 0 |
| Blackmore | 1 | 0 | 0 | 0 |

### KICKOFF RETURNS

| Last Name | No. | Yds. | Avg. | TD |
|---|---|---|---|---|
| Henry | 28 | 668 | 24 | 0 |
| Giammona | 15 | 294 | 20 | 0 |
| Campfield | 7 | 251 | 36 | 1 |
| Wilson | 2 | 0 | 0 | 0 |
| Barnes | 1 | 23 | 23 | 0 |
| Latimer | 1 | 18 | 18 | 0 |
| Montgomery | 1 | 6 | 6 | 0 |
| Smith | 1 | 1 | 1 | 0 |

### PASSING

| Last Name | Att. | Comp. | % | Yds. | Yd./Att. | TD | Int.-% | RK |
|---|---|---|---|---|---|---|---|---|
| Jaworski | 374 | 190 | 51 | 2669 | 7.1 | 18 | 12- 3 | 3 |
| Walton | 36 | 19 | 53 | 213 | 5.9 | 3 | 1- 3 | |

### PUNTING

| Last Name | No. | Avg. |
|---|---|---|
| Runager | 74 | 39.6 |
| Franklin | 1 | 32.0 |

### KICKING

| Last Name | XP | Att. | % | FG | Att. | % |
|---|---|---|---|---|---|---|
| Franklin | 39 | 36 | 92 | 23 | 31 | 74 |

## WASHINGTON REDSKINS

### RUSHING

| Last Name | No. | Yds. | Avg. | TD |
|---|---|---|---|---|
| Riggins | 260 | 1153 | 4.4 | 9 |
| Malone | 176 | 472 | 2.7 | 3 |
| Harmon | 65 | 267 | 4.1 | 0 |
| Theismann | 46 | 181 | 3.9 | 4 |
| Forte | 25 | 125 | 5.0 | 1 |
| Hardeman | 31 | 124 | 4.0 | 0 |
| Hammond | 2 | 5 | 2.5 | 0 |
| McQuilken | 2 | −3 | −1.5 | 0 |

### RECEIVING

| Last Name | No. | Yds. | Avg. | TD |
|---|---|---|---|---|
| Buggs | 46 | 631 | 14 | 1 |
| Harmon | 32 | 434 | 14 | 5 |
| Riggins | 28 | 163 | 6 | 3 |
| Warren | 26 | 303 | 12 | 0 |
| McDaniel | 25 | 357 | 14 | 2 |
| Thompson | 22 | 368 | 17 | 4 |
| Hardeman | 21 | 197 | 9 | 1 |
| Malone | 13 | 137 | 11 | 1 |
| Fugett | 10 | 128 | 13 | 3 |
| Forte | 10 | 105 | 11 | 0 |
| Hammond | 2 | 16 | 8 | 0 |

### PUNT RETURNS

| Last Name | No. | Yds. | Avg. | TD |
|---|---|---|---|---|
| Hardeman | 24 | 207 | 9 | 0 |
| Hammond | 13 | 75 | 6 | 0 |
| Harmon | 1 | 10 | 10 | 0 |
| Peters | 1 | 0 | 0 | 0 |

### KICKOFF RETURNS

| Last Name | No. | Yds. | Avg. | TD |
|---|---|---|---|---|
| Hammond | 25 | 544 | 22 | 0 |
| Hardeman | 19 | 404 | 21 | 0 |
| Forte | 8 | 211 | 26 | 0 |
| Harris | 6 | 80 | 13 | 0 |
| Harmon | 5 | 63 | 13 | 0 |

### PASSING

| Last Name | Att. | Comp. | % | Yds. | Yd./Att. | TD | Int.-% | RK |
|---|---|---|---|---|---|---|---|---|
| Theismann | 395 | 233 | 59 | 2797 | 7.1 | 20 | 13- 3 | 2 |
| Hardeman | 2 | 1 | 50 | 30 | 15.0 | 0 | 1- 50 | |
| McQuilken | 4 | 1 | 25 | 12 | 3.0 | 0 | 1- 25 | |

### PUNTING

| Last Name | No. | Avg. |
|---|---|---|
| Bragg | 78 | 38.4 |

### KICKING

| Last Name | XP | Att. | % | FG | Att. | % |
|---|---|---|---|---|---|---|
| Moseley | 39 | 39 | 100 | 25 | 33 | 76 |

## NEW YORK GIANTS

### RUSHING

| Last Name | No. | Yds. | Avg. | TD |
|---|---|---|---|---|
| Taylor | 198 | 700 | 3.5 | 7 |
| Kotar | 160 | 616 | 3.9 | 3 |
| Johnson | 62 | 168 | 2.7 | 0 |
| Simms | 29 | 166 | 5.7 | 1 |
| Moorehead | 36 | 95 | 2.6 | 0 |
| Dean | 8 | 56 | 7.0 | 1 |
| Jennings | 2 | 11 | 5.5 | 0 |
| Pisarcik | 1 | 6 | 6.0 | 0 |
| Gray | 2 | 2 | 1.0 | 0 |

### RECEIVING

| Last Name | No. | Yds. | Avg. | TD |
|---|---|---|---|---|
| Shirk | 31 | 471 | 15 | 2 |
| Gray | 28 | 537 | 19 | 4 |
| Taylor | 28 | 253 | 9 | 4 |
| Kotar | 25 | 230 | 9 | 0 |
| Perkins | 20 | 337 | 17 | 4 |
| Johnson | 16 | 108 | 7 | 1 |
| Scales | 14 | 222 | 16 | 0 |
| Robinson | 13 | 146 | 11 | 0 |
| Moorehead | 9 | 62 | 7 | 0 |
| Dixon | 2 | 18 | 9 | 0 |
| Van Pelt | 1 | 20 | 20 | 0 |
| C. Jackson | 1 | 7 | 7 | 0 |
| McCreary | 1 | 7 | 7 | 0 |
| Danelo | 1 | 1 | 1 | 0 |

### PUNT RETURNS

| Last Name | No. | Yds. | Avg. | TD |
|---|---|---|---|---|
| Robinson | 6 | 29 | 5 | 0 |
| Scales | 2 | 3 | 2 | 0 |
| Reece | 1 | 8 | 8 | 0 |
| T. Jackson | 1 | 5 | 5 | 0 |

### KICKOFF RETURNS

| Last Name | No. | Yds. | Avg. | TD |
|---|---|---|---|---|
| Robinson | 7 | 140 | 20 | 0 |
| Taylor | 6 | 131 | 22 | 0 |
| Reece | 6 | 81 | 14 | 0 |
| Hicks | 3 | 51 | 17 | 0 |
| Kotar | 2 | 39 | 20 | 0 |
| Moorehead | 1 | 16 | 16 | 0 |
| Marion | 1 | 14 | 14 | 0 |
| Coffield | 1 | 12 | 12 | 0 |
| Gray | 1 | 0 | 0 | 0 |
| Lloyd | 1 | 0 | 0 | 0 |

### PASSING

| Last Name | Att. | Comp. | % | Yds. | Yd./Att. | TD | Int.-% | RK |
|---|---|---|---|---|---|---|---|---|
| Simms | 265 | 134 | 51 | 1743 | 6.6 | 13 | 14- 5 | 10 |
| Pisarcik | 108 | 43 | 40 | 537 | 5.0 | 2 | 6- 6 | |
| Dean | 26 | 11 | 42 | 91 | 3.5 | 0 | 2- 8 | |
| Jennings | 2 | 2 | 100 | 48 | 24.0 | 0 | 0- 0 | |

### PUNTING

| Last Name | No. | Avg. |
|---|---|---|
| Jennings | 104 | 42.7 |

### KICKING

| Last Name | XP | Att. | % | FG | Att. | % |
|---|---|---|---|---|---|---|
| Danelo | 28 | 29 | 97 | 9 | 20 | 45 |

## ST. LOUIS CARDINALS

### RUSHING

| Last Name | No. | Yds. | Avg. | TD |
|---|---|---|---|---|
| Anderson | 331 | 1605 | 4.8 | 6 |
| Morris | 106 | 387 | 3.7 | 8 |
| T. Brown | 73 | 318 | 4.4 | 7 |
| Harrell | 19 | 100 | 5.3 | 0 |
| Phillips | 3 | 50 | 16.7 | 1 |
| Lott | 11 | 50 | 4.5 | 0 |
| Gray | 4 | 41 | 10.3 | 0 |
| Pisarkiewicz | 11 | 20 | 1.8 | 0 |
| Hart | 6 | 11 | 1.8 | 0 |
| Little | 2 | 0 | 0.0 | 0 |

### RECEIVING

| Last Name | No. | Yds. | Avg. | TD |
|---|---|---|---|---|
| Tilley | 57 | 938 | 17 | 6 |
| Anderson | 41 | 308 | 8 | 2 |
| Morris | 35 | 237 | 7 | 1 |
| Gray | 25 | 447 | 18 | 1 |
| T. Brown | 25 | 191 | 8 | 0 |
| Stief | 22 | 324 | 15 | 0 |
| Parris | 14 | 174 | 12 | 0 |
| Childs | 8 | 93 | 12 | 0 |
| Osborne | 7 | 37 | 5 | 0 |
| Chandler | 6 | 51 | 9 | 2 |
| Harrell | 3 | 33 | 11 | 0 |
| Murrell | 2 | 20 | 10 | 0 |
| Lott | 2 | 8 | 4 | 0 |
| Green | 1 | 15 | 15 | 0 |
| Hart | 1 | −4 | −4 | 0 |

### PUNT RETURNS

| Last Name | No. | Yds. | Avg. | TD |
|---|---|---|---|---|
| Harrell | 32 | 205 | 6 | 0 |
| Green | 8 | 42 | 5 | 0 |
| Nelson | 4 | 88 | 22 | 0 |
| Lott | 4 | 33 | 8 | 0 |

### KICKOFF RETURNS

| Last Name | No. | Yds. | Avg. | TD |
|---|---|---|---|---|
| Green | 41 | 1005 | 25 | 1 |
| Harrell | 22 | 497 | 23 | 0 |
| Barefield | 3 | 62 | 21 | 0 |
| Allerman | 2 | 16 | 8 | 0 |
| Lott | 1 | 19 | 19 | 0 |
| Favron | 1 | 10 | 10 | 0 |
| Garlich | 1 | 0 | 0 | 0 |

### PASSING

| Last Name | Att. | Comp. | % | Yds. | Yd./Att. | TD | Int.-% | RK |
|---|---|---|---|---|---|---|---|---|
| Hart | 378 | 194 | 51 | 2218 | 5.9 | 9 | 20- 5 | 12 |
| Pisarkiewicz | 109 | 52 | 48 | 621 | 5.7 | 3 | 4- 4 | |
| Little | 3 | 2 | 67 | 31 | 10.3 | 0 | 0- 0 | |
| Anderson | 1 | 0 | 0 | 0 | 0.0 | 0 | 0- 0 | |
| Harrell | 1 | 0 | 0 | 0 | 0.0 | 0 | 0- 0 | |

### PUNTING

| Last Name | No. | Avg. |
|---|---|---|
| Little | 79 | 38.7 |

### KICKING

| Last Name | XP | Att. | % | FG | Att. | % |
|---|---|---|---|---|---|---|
| Little | 24 | 32 | 75 | 10 | 19 | 53 |

## TAMPA BAY BUCCANEERS 10-6-0 John McKay

| Scores of Each Game | | |
|---|---|---|
| 31 | DETROIT | 16 |
| 29 | Baltimore | *26 |
| 21 | Green Bay | 10 |
| 21 | LOS ANGELES | 6 |
| 17 | Chicago | 13 |
| 14 | N.Y. Giants | 17 |
| 14 | NEW ORLEANS | 42 |
| 21 | GREEN BAY | 3 |
| 12 | Minnesota | 10 |
| 14 | Atlanta | 17 |
| 16 | Detroit | 14 |
| 31 | N.Y. GIANTS | 3 |
| 22 | MINNESOTA | 23 |
| 0 | CHICAGO | 14 |
| 7 | San Francisco | 23 |
| 3 | KANSAS CITY | 0 |

| Use Name | Pos. | Hgt. | Wgt. | Age | Int. | Pts. |
|---|---|---|---|---|---|---|
| Darryl Carlton | OT | 6'6" | 285 | 26 | | |
| Charles Hannah | OT | 6'6" | 255 | 24 | | |
| Dave Reavis | OT | 6'5" | 265 | 29 | | |
| Darrell Austin | OG-C | 6'4" | 250 | 27 | | |
| Greg Horton | OG | 6'4" | 250 | 28 | | |
| Greg Roberts | OG | 6'3" | 255 | 22 | | |
| George Yarno | OG | 6'2" | 255 | 22 | | |
| Steve Wilson | C | 6'3" | 270 | 25 | | |
| Wally Chambers | DE | 6'6" | 250 | 28 | | |
| Bill Kollar | DE-MG | 6'4" | 250 | 26 | | |
| Reggie Lewis | DE-MG | 6'3" | 260 | 23 | | |
| Gene Sanders | DE-MG | 6'3" | 270 | 22 | | |
| Lee Roy Selmon | DE | 6'3" | 255 | 24 | | 6 |
| Randy Crowder | MG | 6'2" | 250 | 27 | | |
| David Logan | MG-DE | 6'2" | 250 | 22 | | |

| Use Name | Pos. | Hgt. | Wgt. | Age | Int. | Pts. |
|---|---|---|---|---|---|---|
| Rik Bonness | LB | 6'3" | 215 | 25 | | |
| Aaron Brown | LB | 6'2" | 235 | 23 | | |
| Cecil Johnson | LB | 6'2" | 230 | 24 | | |
| Dave Lewis | LB | 6'4" | 240 | 24 | 2 | 6 |
| Dana Nafziger | LB | 6'1" | 225 | 25 | | |
| Dewey Selmon | LB | 6'1" | 245 | 25 | | |
| Richard Wood | LB | 6'2" | 225 | 26 | 2 | |
| Cedric Brown | DB | 6'1" | 205 | 25 | 3 | |
| Billy Cesare | DB | 5'11" | 190 | 24 | | |
| Mark Cotney | DB | 6' | 205 | 27 | 1 | |
| Curtis Jordan | DB | 6'2" | 210 | 25 | | |
| Danny Reece | DB | 5'11" | 190 | 24 | | |
| Mike Washington | DB | 6'3" | 205 | 26 | 3 | 6 |
| Jeris White | DB | 5'11" | 185 | 26 | 3 | |

Jerry Anderson – Injury
Randy Johnson – Injury
Dave Green – Achilles Injury

| Use Name | Pos. | Hgt. | Wgt. | Age | Int. | Pts. |
|---|---|---|---|---|---|---|
| Chuck Fusina | QB | 6'1" | 200 | 22 | | |
| Mike Rae | QB | 6' | 195 | 28 | | |
| Doug Williams | QB | 6'4" | 215 | 24 | | 12 |
| Rick Berns | HB | 6'2" | 200 | 23 | | |
| Jerry Eckwood | HB | 6' | 195 | 24 | | 12 |
| George Ragsdale | HB | 5'11" | 185 | 25 | | |
| Ricky Bell | FB-HB | 6'2" | 220 | 24 | | 54 |
| Johnny Davis | FB | 6'1" | 235 | 23 | | 12 |
| Tony Davis | FB | 5'10" | 215 | 26 | | |
| Isaac Hagins | WR | 5'9" | 180 | 25 | | 18 |
| Gordon Jones | WR | 6' | 190 | 22 | | 6 |
| Larry Mucker | WR | 5'11" | 195 | 24 | | 30 |
| Morris Owens | WR | 6' | 200 | 26 | | |
| Jim Giles | TE | 6'3" | 240 | 24 | | 42 |
| Jim Obradovich | TE | 6'2" | 230 | 26 | | 6 |
| Tom Blanchard | K | 6' | 180 | 31 | | |
| Neil O'Donoghue | K | 6'6" | 205 | 26 | | 63 |

Jimmy DuBose – Knee Injury

## CHICAGO BEARS 10-6-0 Neill Armstrong

| Scores of Each Game | | |
|---|---|---|
| 6 | GREEN BAY | 3 |
| 26 | MINNESOTA | 7 |
| 20 | Dallas | 24 |
| 16 | Miami | 31 |
| 13 | TAMPA BAY | 17 |
| 7 | Buffalo | 0 |
| 7 | NEW ENGLAND | 27 |
| 27 | Minnesota | 30 |
| 28 | San Francisco | 27 |
| 35 | DETROIT | 7 |
| 27 | LOS ANGELES | 23 |
| 23 | N.Y. JETS | 13 |
| 0 | Detroit | 20 |
| 14 | Tampa Bay | 0 |
| 15 | Green Bay | 14 |
| 42 | ST. LOUIS | 6 |

| Use Name | Pos. | Hgt. | Wgt. | Age | Int. | Pts. |
|---|---|---|---|---|---|---|
| Ted Albrecht | OT | 6'4" | 250 | 24 | | |
| Dan Jiggetts | OT | 6'4" | 269 | 25 | | |
| Dennis Lick | OT | 6'3" | 265 | 25 | | |
| Lynn Boden | OG | 6'5" | 260 | 26 | | |
| Noah Jackson | OG | 6'2" | 270 | 28 | | |
| Revie Sorey | OG | 6'2" | 263 | 25 | | |
| Tony Ardizzone | C | 6'3" | 241 | 22 | | |
| Dan Neal | C | 6'4" | 251 | 30 | | |
| Dan Hampton | DE | 6'5" | 252 | 21 | | |
| Al Harris | DE | 6'5" | 236 | 22 | | |
| Tommy Hart | DE | 6'4" | 246 | 34 | | |
| Mike Hartenstine | DE | 6'3" | 240 | 26 | | |
| Jerry Meyers | DT | 6'4" | 257 | 25 | | |
| Jim Osborne | DT | 6'3" | 246 | 29 | | |
| Alan Page | DT | 6'5" | 228 | 34 | | |
| Ron Rydalch | DT | 6'4" | 256 | 27 | | |

| Use Name | Pos. | Hgt. | Wgt. | Age | Int. | Pts. |
|---|---|---|---|---|---|---|
| Doug Buffone | LB | 6'1" | 217 | 35 | 2 | |
| Gary Campbell | LB | 6'1" | 221 | 27 | 1 | |
| Bruce Herron | LB | 6'2" | 219 | 25 | | |
| Tom Hicks | LB | 6'4" | 235 | 26 | 3 | 6 |
| Lee Kunz | LB | 6'2" | 221 | 22 | | |
| Mark Merrill (from NYJ) | LB | 6'4" | 237 | 24 | | |
| Jerry Muckensturm | LB | 6'4" | 219 | 25 | 1 | |
| Allan Ellis | DB | 5'10" | 174 | 28 | 3 | |
| Gary Fencik | DB | 6'1" | 192 | 25 | 6 | |
| Wentford Gaines | DB | 6' | 186 | 26 | 1 | |
| Virgil Livers | DB | 5'9" | 184 | 27 | 2 | |
| Doug Plank | DB | 6' | 197 | 26 | 3 | |
| Terry Schmidt | DB | 6' | 179 | 27 | 6 | 6 |
| Mike Spivey | DB | 6' | 195 | 25 | | |
| Len Walterscheid | DB | 5'11" | 189 | 24 | 1 | |

Lionel Antoine – Knee Injury
Roland Harper – Knee Injury
Brad Shearer – Knee Injury

| Use Name | Pos. | Hgt. | Wgt. | Age | Int. | Pts. |
|---|---|---|---|---|---|---|
| Bob Avellini | QB | 6'2" | 209 | 26 | | |
| Vince Evans | QB | 6'2" | 210 | 24 | | 6 |
| Mike Phipps | QB | 6'3" | 203 | 31 | | |
| Jack Deloplaine (to PIT) | HB | 5'10" | 205 | 25 | | |
| Willie McClendon | HB | 6'1" | 205 | 21 | | 6 |
| Walter Payton | HB-FB | 5'11" | 204 | 25 | | 96 |
| Robin Earl | FB | 6'5" | 240 | 24 | | |
| Lonnie Perrin (from WAS) | FB | 6'1" | 222 | 27 | | |
| John Skibinski | FB | 6' | 224 | 24 | | |
| Dave Williams | FB | 6'2" | 215 | 25 | | 36 |
| Brian Baschnagel | WR | 6' | 180 | 25 | | 12 |
| Kris Haines (from WAS) | WR | 5'11" | 183 | 22 | | |
| Golden Richards | WR | 6' | 180 | 28 | | 6 |
| Steve Schubert | WR | 5'10" | 186 | 28 | | 6 |
| James Scott | WR | 6'1" | 191 | 27 | | 18 |
| Harry Washington | WR | 6' | 180 | 23 | | |
| Rickey Watts | WR | 6'1" | 204 | 22 | | 24 |
| Mike Cobb | TE | 6'5" | 240 | 23 | | |
| Greg Latta | TE | 6'3" | 235 | 26 | | |
| Bob Parsons | TE | 6'5" | 225 | 29 | | |
| Bob Thomas | K | 5'10" | 175 | 27 | | 82 |

## MINNESOTA VIKINGS 7-9-0 Bud Grant

| Scores of Each Game | | |
|---|---|---|
| 28 | SAN FRANCISCO | 22 |
| 7 | Chicago | 26 |
| 12 | MIAMI | 27 |
| 27 | GREEN BAY | *21 |
| 13 | Detroit | 10 |
| 20 | DALLAS | 36 |
| 7 | N.Y. Jets | 14 |
| 30 | CHICAGO | 27 |
| 10 | TAMPA BAY | 12 |
| 7 | St. Louis | 37 |
| 7 | Green Bay | 19 |
| 14 | DETROIT | 7 |
| 23 | Tampa Bay | 22 |
| 21 | Los Angeles | *27 |
| 10 | BUFFALO | 3 |
| 23 | New England | 27 |

| Use Name | Pos. | Hgt. | Wgt. | Age | Int. | Pts. |
|---|---|---|---|---|---|---|
| Frank Myers | OT | 6'5" | 255 | 23 | | |
| Steve Riley | OT | 6'6" | 258 | 26 | | |
| Ron Yary | OT | 6'6" | 255 | 33 | | |
| Charlie Goodrum | OG | 6'3" | 256 | 29 | | |
| Wes Hamilton | OG | 6'3" | 255 | 26 | | |
| Jim Hough | OG-C | 6'2" | 267 | 23 | | |
| Dave Huffman | C-OG | 6'6" | 255 | 22 | | |
| Dennis Swilley | C | 6'3" | 241 | 24 | | |
| Randy Holloway | DE | 6'5" | 245 | 24 | | |
| Jim Marshall | DE | 6'3" | 240 | 41 | | |
| Mark Mullaney | DE | 6'6" | 242 | 26 | | |
| Steve Niehaus | DT | 6'4" | 255 | 24 | | |
| Dave Roller | DT | 6'2" | 270 | 29 | | |
| Doug Sutherland | DT | 6'3" | 250 | 31 | | |
| James White | DT | 6'3" | 263 | 25 | | |

| Use Name | Pos. | Hgt. | Wgt. | Age | Int. | Pts. |
|---|---|---|---|---|---|---|
| Matt Blair | LB | 6'5" | 229 | 27 | 3 | |
| Wally Hilgenberg | LB | 6'3" | 229 | 36 | | |
| Derrel Luce | LB | 6'3" | 227 | 26 | | |
| Fred McNeill | LB | 6'2" | 229 | 27 | | |
| Jeff Siemon | LB | 6'3" | 237 | 29 | | |
| Scott Studwell | LB | 6'2" | 224 | 25 | 1 | |
| Nate Allen (to DET.) | DB | 5'10" | 174 | 31 | 1 | |
| Tim Baylor | DB | 6'6" | 190 | 25 | | |
| Bobby Bryant | DB | 6' | 170 | 35 | 2 | |
| Tom Hannon | DB | 5'11" | 193 | 24 | 4 | |
| Kurt Knoff | DB | 6'2" | 188 | 25 | 2 | |
| Paul Krause | DB | 6'3" | 205 | 37 | 3 | |
| Keith Nord | DB | 6' | 197 | 22 | | |
| John Turner | DB | 6' | 199 | 23 | 2 | |
| Phil Wise | DB | 6' | 193 | 30 | | |
| Nate Wright | DB | 5'11" | 180 | 31 | 4 | |

Ken Novak – Injury
Lyman Smith – Injury

| Use Name | Pos. | Hgt. | Wgt. | Age | Int. | Pts. |
|---|---|---|---|---|---|---|
| Steve Dils | QB | 6'1" | 190 | 23 | | |
| Tommy Kramer | QB | 6'1" | 199 | 24 | | 6 |
| John Reaves | QB | 6'3" | 210 | 29 | | |
| Jimmy Edwards | HB | 5'9" | 185 | 26 | | |
| Brent McClanahan | HB | 5'10" | 202 | 28 | | |
| Robert Miller | HB | 5'11" | 204 | 26 | | 12 |
| Rickey Young | HB | 6'2" | 195 | 25 | | 42 |
| Ted Brown | FB-HB | 5'10" | 198 | 22 | | 6 |
| Chuck Foreman | FB | 6'2" | 207 | 28 | | 12 |
| Doug Cunningham | WR | 6'2" | 195 | 23 | | |
| Terry LeCount (from SF) | WR | 5'10" | 172 | 23 | | 12 |
| Kevin Miller | WR | 5'10" | 180 | 24 | | |
| Ahmad Rashad | WR | 6'2" | 200 | 29 | | 54 |
| Robert Steele | WR | 6'4" | 196 | 23 | | |
| Sammy White | WR | 5'11" | 189 | 25 | | 24 |
| Bob Tucker | TE | 6'3" | 230 | 34 | | 12 |
| Stu Voigt | TE | 6'1" | 225 | 31 | | 12 |
| Greg Coleman | K | 6' | 178 | 24 | | |
| Rick Danmeier | K | 6' | 183 | 27 | | 67 |

## GREEN BAY PACKERS 5-11-0 Bart Starr

| Scores of Each Game | | |
|---|---|---|
| 3 | Chicago | 6 |
| 28 | NEW ORLEANS | 19 |
| 10 | TAMPA BAY | 21 |
| 21 | Minnesota | *27 |
| 27 | NEW ENGLAND | 14 |
| 7 | Atlanta | 25 |
| 24 | DETROIT | 16 |
| 3 | Tampa Bay | 21 |
| 7 | Miami | 27 |
| 22 | N.Y. JETS | 27 |
| 19 | MINNESOTA | 7 |
| 12 | Buffalo | 19 |
| 10 | PHILADELPHIA | 21 |
| 21 | Washington | 38 |
| 14 | CHICAGO | 15 |
| 18 | Detroit | 13 |

| Use Name | Pos. | Hgt. | Wgt. | Age | Int. | Pts. |
|---|---|---|---|---|---|---|
| Greg Koch | OT | 6'4" | 265 | 24 | | |
| Mark Koncar | OT | 6'5" | 268 | 26 | | |
| Tim Stokes | OT | 6'5" | 252 | 29 | | |
| Steve Young | OT | 6'8" | 270 | 26 | | |
| Derrel Gofourth | OG | 6'3" | 260 | 24 | | |
| Leotis Harris | OG | 6'1" | 267 | 24 | | |
| Melvin Jackson | OG | 6'1" | 267 | 25 | | |
| Larry McCarren | C | 6'3" | 248 | 27 | | |
| Mike Wellman | C | 6'3" | 253 | 23 | | |
| Bob Barber | DE | 6'3" | 240 | 27 | | |
| Mike Butler | DE | 6'5" | 265 | 25 | | 6 |
| Ezra Johnson | DE | 6'4" | 240 | 23 | | |
| Carl Barzilauskas | DT | 6'6" | 265 | 28 | | |
| Earl Edwards | DT | 6'6" | 260 | 33 | | |
| Charles Johnson | DT | 6'1" | 262 | 22 | 1 | |
| Terry Jones | DT | 6'2" | 259 | 22 | | |
| Casey Merrill | DT-DE | 6'4" | 255 | 22 | | |

| Use Name | Pos. | Hgt. | Wgt. | Age | Int. | Pts. |
|---|---|---|---|---|---|---|
| John Anderson | LB | 6'3" | 230 | 23 | | 4 |
| Mike Douglass | LB | 6' | 224 | 24 | 3 | |
| Jim Gueno | LB | 6'2" | 220 | 25 | | |
| Mike Hunt | LB | 6'2" | 240 | 22 | 1 | |
| Joe McLaughlin | LB | 6'1" | 235 | 22 | | |
| Paul Rudzinski | LB | 6'1" | 220 | 23 | | |
| Davie Simmons | LB | 6'4" | 218 | 22 | | |
| Steve Stewart | LB | 6'2" | 220 | 23 | | |
| Gary Weaver | LB | 6'1" | 225 | 30 | | |
| Rich Wingo | LB | 6'1" | 230 | 23 | 2 | |
| Johnnie Gray | DB | 5'11" | 185 | 25 | 5 | |
| Estus Hood | DB | 5'11" | 180 | 23 | 2 | |
| Steve Luke | DB | 6'2" | 205 | 25 | 1 | |
| Mike McCoy | DB | 5'11" | 183 | 26 | 3 | |
| Howard Sampson | DB | 5'10" | 185 | 23 | | |
| Wylie Turner | DB | 5'10" | 182 | 22 | | |
| Steve Wagner | DB | 6'2" | 208 | 25 | | |

Rick Nuzum – Calf Injury

| Use Name | Pos. | Hgt. | Wgt. | Age | Int. | Pts. |
|---|---|---|---|---|---|---|
| Lynn Dickey | QB | 6'4" | 220 | 29 | | |
| David Whitehurst | QB | 6'2" | 204 | 24 | | 24 |
| Ricky Patton (from ATL) | HB | 5'11" | 189 | 25 | | |
| Nate Simpson | HB-FB | 5'11" | 201 | 24 | | 6 |
| Terdell Middleton | HB | 6' | 195 | 24 | | 18 |
| Steve Atkins | FB-HB | 6' | 216 | 23 | | 6 |
| Jim Culbreath | FB | 6' | 210 | 26 | | |
| Eddie Lee Ivery | FB | 6'1" | 210 | 22 | | |
| Sammy Johnson (from PHI) | FB | 6'1" | 226 | 26 | | |
| Walt Landers | FB | 6' | 214 | 26 | | 6 |
| Barty Smith | FB | 6'4" | 240 | 27 | | 24 |
| Eric Torkelson | FB | 6'2" | 194 | 27 | | 18 |
| Ron Cassidy | WR | 6' | 185 | 22 | | |
| Bobby Kimball | WR | 6'1" | 190 | 22 | | |
| James Lofton | WR | 6'3" | 187 | 23 | | 24 |
| Steve Odom (to N.Y. GIANTS) | WR | 5'8" | 174 | 26 | | |
| Aundra Thompson | WR | 6' | 186 | 26 | | 24 |
| Walter Tullis | WR | 6' | 170 | 26 | | 6 |
| Paul Coffman | TE | 6'3" | 218 | 23 | | 24 |
| John Thompson | TE | 6'3" | 228 | 22 | | |
| David Beverly | K | 6'2" | 180 | 29 | | |
| Tom Birney | K | 6'4" | 220 | 23 | | 28 |
| Chester Marcol | K | 6' | 190 | 29 | | 28 |

## DETROIT LIONS 2-14-0 Monte Clark

| Scores of Each Game | | |
|---|---|---|
| 16 | Tampa Bay | 31 |
| 24 | WASHINGTON | 27 |
| 10 | N.Y. Jets | 31 |
| 24 | ATLANTA | 23 |
| 10 | MINNESOTA | 13 |
| 17 | New England | 24 |
| 16 | Green Bay | 24 |
| 7 | New Orleans | 17 |
| 17 | BUFFALO | 20 |
| 7 | Chicago | 35 |
| 14 | TAMPA BAY | 16 |
| 7 | Minnesota | 14 |
| 20 | CHICAGO | 0 |
| 7 | Philadelphia | 44 |
| 10 | MIAMI | 28 |
| 13 | GREEN BAY | 18 |

| Use Name | Pos. | Hgt. | Wgt. | Age | Int. | Pts. |
|---|---|---|---|---|---|---|
| Karl Baldischwiler | OT | 6'5" | 265 | 23 | | |
| Keith Dorney | OT | 6'5" | 265 | 21 | | |
| Don Morrison | OT-C | 6'5" | 259 | 29 | | |
| Russ Bolinger | OG | 6'5" | 250 | 24 | | |
| Homer Elias | OG | 6'3" | 255 | 24 | | |
| Amos Fowler | OG | 6'3" | 250 | 23 | | |
| Wally Posuit | OG-C | 6'4" | 250 | 25 | | |
| Karl Chandler | C | 6'5" | 250 | 27 | | |
| Dennis Franks | C | 6'1" | 245 | 26 | | |
| Larry Tearry | C | 6'3" | 260 | 23 | | |
| Al Baker | DE | 6'6" | 260 | 22 | | |
| Bill Gay | DE | 6'3" | 225 | 24 | | 6 |
| Dave Pureifory | DE | 6'1" | 255 | 30 | | |
| Ken Sanders | DE | 6'5" | 245 | 29 | | |
| Cleveland Elam | DT | 6'4" | 251 | 27 | | |
| Doug English | DT | 6'5" | 260 | 26 | | 2 |
| Dave Gallagher | DT | 6'4" | 255 | 27 | | |

Gary Danielson – Knee Injury
Dan Gray – Injury
Mark Markovich – Injury
Jesse Thompson – Illness

| Use Name | Pos. | Hgt. | Wgt. | Age | Int. | Pts. |
|---|---|---|---|---|---|---|
| Jon Brooks | LB | 6'2" | 215 | 22 | | |
| Garry Cobb | LB | 6'2" | 210 | 22 | | |
| Eddie Cole | LB | 6'2" | 235 | 22 | | |
| Ken Fantetti | LB | 6'2" | 230 | 22 | | |
| James Harrell | LB | 6'1" | 215 | 22 | | |
| Ed O'Neil | LB | 6'3" | 235 | 26 | | |
| Dave Washington | LB | 6'5" | 230 | 30 | | |
| Charlie Weaver | LB | 6'2" | 225 | 30 | 1 | |
| Jim Allen | DB | 6'2" | 195 | 27 | 4 | |
| Luther Bradley | DB | 6'2" | 195 | 24 | 4 | |
| Ken Ellis (to LA) | DB | 5'10" | 180 | 31 | | |
| James Hunter | DB | 6'3" | 195 | 25 | 3 | |
| Ernie Jackson | DB | 5'10" | 175 | 29 | | |
| Doug Jones | DB | 6'2" | 205 | 29 | | |
| Tony Leonard | DB | 5'11" | 175 | 26 | | |
| Eddie Lewis (from SF) | DB | 6' | 174 | 25 | | |
| Dave Parkin | DB | 6' | 190 | 23 | | |
| Don Patterson | DB | 5'11" | 175 | 21 | | |
| Jimmy Stewart | DB | 5'11" | 190 | 24 | | |
| Walt Williams | DB | 6' | 185 | 25 | 2 | 6 |

John Woodcock – Back Injury

| Use Name | Pos. | Hgt. | Wgt. | Age | Int. | Pts. |
|---|---|---|---|---|---|---|
| Jerry Golsteyn (to BAL) | QB | 6'4" | 210 | 25 | | |
| Scott Hunter | QB | 6'2" | 205 | 31 | | 6 |
| Jeff Komlo | QB | 6'2" | 205 | 23 | | 12 |
| Joe Reed | QB | 6'1" | 190 | 31 | | |
| Dexter Bussey | HB | 6'1" | 195 | 27 | | 6 |
| Ken Callicut | HB | 6' | 190 | 24 | | |
| Rick Kane | HB | 5'11" | 200 | 24 | | 30 |
| Lawrence Gaines | FB | 6'1" | 230 | 25 | | |
| Horace King | FB | 5'10" | 205 | 26 | | 6 |
| Bo Robinson | FB | 6'2" | 225 | 23 | | 12 |
| John Arnold | WR | 5'10" | 175 | 23 | | |
| Luther Blue | WR | 5'11" | 180 | 23 | | 6 |
| Freddie Scott | WR | 6'2" | 180 | 27 | | 30 |
| Leonard Thompson | WR | 5'10" | 190 | 27 | | 12 |
| Gene Washington | WR | 6'1" | 180 | 31 | | 6 |
| Robert Woods | WR | 5'7" | 170 | 24 | | |
| David Hill | TE | 6'2" | 230 | 25 | | 18 |
| Ulysses Norris | TE | 6'4" | 225 | 22 | | 6 |
| Benny Ricardo | K | 5'10" | 170 | 25 | | 55 |
| Larry Swider | K | 6'2" | 195 | 24 | | |
| Tom Skladany | K | 6' | 195 | 24 | | |

*Overtime

## TAMPA BAY BUCCANEERS

### RUSHING

| Last Name | No. | Yds. | Avg. | TD |
|---|---|---|---|---|
| Bell | 283 | 1263 | 4.5 | 7 |
| Eckwood | 194 | 690 | 3.6 | 2 |
| J. Davis | 59 | 221 | 3.7 | 2 |
| Williams | 35 | 119 | 3.4 | 2 |
| Berns | 23 | 102 | 4.4 | 0 |
| Mucker | 4 | 16 | 4.0 | 0 |
| Jones | 1 | 12 | 12.0 | 0 |
| Giles | 2 | 7 | 3.5 | 0 |
| Ragsdale | 6 | 5 | 0.8 | 0 |
| Rae | 1 | 2 | 2.0 | 0 |
| Blanchard | 1 | 0 | 0.0 | 0 |

### RECEIVING

| Last Name | No. | Yds. | Avg. | TD |
|---|---|---|---|---|
| Giles | 40 | 579 | 15 | 7 |
| Hagins | 39 | 692 | 18 | 3 |
| Bell | 25 | 248 | 10 | 2 |
| Eckwood | 22 | 268 | 12 | 0 |
| Owens | 20 | 377 | 19 | 0 |
| Mucker | 14 | 268 | 19 | 5 |
| Obradovich | 6 | 63 | 11 | 1 |
| J. Davis | 5 | 57 | 11 | 0 |
| Berns | 5 | 40 | 8 | 0 |
| Jones | 4 | 80 | 20 | 1 |
| Ragsdale | 3 | 28 | 9 | 0 |

### PUNT RETURNS

| Last Name | No. | Yds. | Avg. | TD |
|---|---|---|---|---|
| Reece | 70 | 431 | 6 | 0 |
| T. Davis | 1 | 7 | 7 | 0 |

### KICKOFF RETURNS

| Last Name | No. | Yds. | Avg. | TD |
|---|---|---|---|---|
| Ragsdale | 34 | 675 | 20 | 0 |
| Hagins | 9 | 196 | 22 | 0 |
| T. Davis | 4 | 33 | 8 | 0 |
| Nafziger | 2 | 36 | 18 | 0 |
| Reece | 1 | 13 | 13 | 0 |
| Berns | 1 | 6 | 6 | 0 |

### PASSING – PUNTING – KICKING

| PASSING | Att. | Comp. | % | Yds. | Yd./Att. | TD | Int.–% | RK |
|---|---|---|---|---|---|---|---|---|
| Williams | 397 | 166 | 42 | 2448 | 6.2 | 18 | 24– 6 | 13 |
| Rae | 36 | 17 | 47 | 252 | 7.0 | 1 | 2– 6 | |
| Eckwood | 1 | 0 | 0 | 0 | 0.0 | 0 | 0– 0 | |

| PUNTING | No. | Avg. |
|---|---|---|
| Blanchard | 93 | 39.6 |

| KICKING | XP | Att. | % | FG | Att. | % |
|---|---|---|---|---|---|---|
| O'Donoghue | 30 | 35 | 86 | 11 | 19 | 58 |

## CHICAGO BEARS

### RUSHING

| Last Name | No. | Yds. | Avg. | TD |
|---|---|---|---|---|
| Payton | 369 | 1610 | 4.4 | 14 |
| Williams | 127 | 401 | 3.2 | 1 |
| McClendon | 37 | 160 | 4.3 | 1 |
| Earl | 35 | 132 | 3.8 | 0 |
| Evans | 12 | 72 | 6.0 | 1 |
| Phipps | 27 | 51 | 1.9 | 0 |
| Deloplaine | 7 | 18 | 2.6 | 0 |
| Perrin | 7 | 18 | 2.6 | 0 |
| Buffone | 1 | 14 | 14.0 | 0 |
| Avellini | 3 | 10 | 3.3 | 0 |
| Skibinski | 3 | 10 | 3.3 | 0 |
| Watts | 1 | −6 | −6.0 | 0 |

### RECEIVING

| Last Name | No. | Yds. | Avg. | TD |
|---|---|---|---|---|
| Williams | 42 | 354 | 8 | 5 |
| Payton | 31 | 313 | 10 | 2 |
| Baschnagel | 30 | 452 | 15 | 2 |
| Watts | 24 | 421 | 18 | 3 |
| Scott | 21 | 382 | 18 | 3 |
| Latta | 15 | 131 | 9 | 0 |
| Earl | 8 | 56 | 7 | 0 |
| Cobb | 6 | 91 | 15 | 0 |
| McClendon | 6 | 27 | 5 | 0 |
| Richards | 5 | 107 | 21 | 1 |
| Schubert | 2 | 29 | 15 | 0 |
| Deloplaine | 2 | 13 | 7 | 0 |
| Perrin | 1 | 27 | 27 | 0 |
| Buffone | 1 | 22 | 22 | 0 |
| Skibinski | 1 | 4 | 4 | 0 |

### PUNT RETURNS

| Last Name | No. | Yds. | Avg. | TD |
|---|---|---|---|---|
| Schubert | 25 | 238 | 10 | 1 |
| Walterscheid | 14 | 96 | 7 | 0 |

### KICKOFF RETURNS

| Last Name | No. | Yds. | Avg. | TD |
|---|---|---|---|---|
| Walterscheid | 19 | 427 | 23 | 0 |
| Watts | 14 | 289 | 21 | 1 |
| Baschnagel | 12 | 260 | 22 | 0 |
| Perrin | 4 | 86 | 22 | 0 |
| Schubert | 2 | 45 | 23 | 0 |
| McClendon | 1 | 12 | 12 | 0 |
| Latta | 1 | 8 | 8 | 0 |
| Herron | 1 | 0 | 0 | 0 |

### PASSING – PUNTING – KICKING

| PASSING | Att. | Comp. | % | Yds. | Yd./Att. | TD | Int.–% | RK |
|---|---|---|---|---|---|---|---|---|
| Phipps | 255 | 134 | 53 | 1535 | 6.0 | 9 | 8– 3 | 7 |
| Evans | 63 | 32 | 51 | 508 | 8.1 | 4 | 5– 8 | |
| Avellini | 51 | 27 | 53 | 310 | 6.1 | 2 | 3– 6 | |
| Payton | 1 | 1 | 100 | 54 | 54.0 | 1 | 0– 0 | |
| Parsons | 2 | 1 | 50 | 22 | 11.0 | 0 | 0– 0 | |
| Baschnagel | 1 | 0 | 0 | 0 | 0.0 | 0 | 0– 0 | |

| PUNTING | No. | Avg. |
|---|---|---|
| Parsons | 92 | 37.9 |

| KICKING | XP | Att. | % | FG | Att. | % |
|---|---|---|---|---|---|---|
| Thomas | 34 | 37 | 92 | 16 | 27 | 59 |

## MINNESOTA VIKINGS

### RUSHING

| Last Name | No. | Yds. | Avg. | TD |
|---|---|---|---|---|
| Young | 188 | 708 | 3.8 | 3 |
| Brown | 130 | 551 | 4.2 | 1 |
| Foreman | 87 | 223 | 2.6 | 2 |
| Kramer | 32 | 138 | 4.3 | 1 |
| R. Miller | 35 | 109 | 3.1 | 2 |
| McClanahan | 14 | 29 | 2.1 | 0 |
| S. White | 1 | 6 | 6.0 | 0 |

### RECEIVING

| Last Name | No. | Yds. | Avg. | TD |
|---|---|---|---|---|
| Rashad | 80 | 1156 | 15 | 9 |
| Young | 72 | 519 | 7 | 4 |
| S. White | 42 | 715 | 17 | 4 |
| Brown | 31 | 197 | 6 | 0 |
| Tucker | 24 | 223 | 9 | 2 |
| Foreman | 19 | 147 | 8 | 0 |
| Voigt | 15 | 139 | 9 | 2 |
| McClanahan | 10 | 57 | 6 | 0 |
| R. Miller | 9 | 60 | 7 | 0 |
| LeCount | 6 | 119 | 20 | 2 |
| Cunningham | 5 | 50 | 10 | 0 |
| Steele | 1 | 10 | 10 | 0 |
| Edwards | 1 | 2 | 2 | 0 |
| Kramer | 0 | 3 | – | 0 |

### PUNT RETURNS

| Last Name | No. | Yds. | Avg. | TD |
|---|---|---|---|---|
| Edwards | 33 | 186 | 6 | 0 |
| K. Miller | 18 | 85 | 5 | 0 |
| Nord | 3 | 11 | 4 | 0 |
| Bryant | 1 | 7 | 7 | 0 |
| Turner | 1 | 0 | 0 | 0 |
| Allen | 1 | −1 | −1 | 0 |

### KICKOFF RETURNS

| Last Name | No. | Yds. | Avg. | TD |
|---|---|---|---|---|
| Edwards | 44 | 1103 | 25 | 0 |
| Brown | 8 | 186 | 23 | 0 |
| McClanahan | 3 | 53 | 18 | 0 |
| R. Miller | 3 | 38 | 13 | 0 |
| Steele | 1 | 0 | 0 | 0 |
| Studwell | 1 | 0 | 0 | 0 |
| Voigt | 1 | 0 | 0 | 0 |

### PASSING – PUNTING – KICKING

| PASSING | Att. | Comp. | % | Yds. | Yd./Att. | TD | Int.–% | RK |
|---|---|---|---|---|---|---|---|---|
| Kramer | 566 | 315 | 56 | 3397 | 6.0 | 23 | 24– 4 | 6 |

| PUNTING | No. | Avg. |
|---|---|---|
| Coleman | 90 | 39.5 |

| KICKING | XP | Att. | % | FG | Att. | % |
|---|---|---|---|---|---|---|
| Danmeier | 28 | 30 | 93 | 13 | 22 | 59 |

## GREEN BAY PACKERS

### RUSHING

| Last Name | No. | Yds. | Avg. | TD |
|---|---|---|---|---|
| Middleton | 131 | 495 | 3.8 | 2 |
| Torkelson | 98 | 401 | 4.1 | 3 |
| Atkins | 42 | 239 | 5.7 | 1 |
| Simpson | 66 | 235 | 3.6 | 1 |
| Smith | 57 | 201 | 3.5 | 3 |
| Patton | 40 | 135 | 3.4 | 0 |
| Whitehurst | 18 | 73 | 4.1 | 4 |
| Landers | 17 | 41 | 2.4 | 0 |
| Ivery | 3 | 24 | 8.0 | 0 |
| Wagner | 1 | 16 | 16.0 | 0 |
| Dickey | 5 | 13 | 2.6 | 0 |
| Culbreath | 5 | 8 | 1.6 | 0 |
| Lofton | 1 | −1 | −1.0 | 0 |
| A. Thompson | 2 | −18 | −9.0 | 0 |

### RECEIVING

| Last Name | No. | Yds. | Avg. | TD |
|---|---|---|---|---|
| Coffman | 56 | 711 | 13 | 4 |
| Lofton | 54 | 968 | 18 | 4 |
| A. Thompson | 25 | 395 | 16 | 3 |
| Smith | 19 | 155 | 8 | 1 |
| Torkelson | 19 | 139 | 7 | 0 |
| Middleton | 18 | 155 | 9 | 1 |
| Simpson | 11 | 46 | 4 | 0 |
| Tullis | 10 | 173 | 17 | 1 |
| Atkins | 10 | 89 | 9 | 0 |
| Cassidy | 6 | 102 | 17 | 0 |
| Patton | 6 | 41 | 7 | 0 |
| Landers | 5 | 60 | 12 | 1 |
| Gueno | 1 | 23 | 23 | 0 |

### PUNT RETURNS

| Last Name | No. | Yds. | Avg. | TD |
|---|---|---|---|---|
| Odom | 24 | 106 | 4 | 0 |
| Gray | 13 | 61 | 5 | 0 |

### KICKOFF RETURNS

| Last Name | No. | Yds. | Avg. | TD |
|---|---|---|---|---|
| Odom | 44 | 949 | 22 | 0 |
| A. Thompson | 15 | 346 | 23 | 1 |
| McCoy | 11 | 248 | 23 | 0 |
| Sampson | 4 | 61 | 15 | 0 |
| Wellman | 1 | 10 | 10 | 0 |
| Wagner | 1 | 8 | 8 | 0 |

### PASSING – PUNTING – KICKING

| PASSING | Att. | Comp. | % | Yds. | Yd./Att. | TD | Int.–% | RK |
|---|---|---|---|---|---|---|---|---|
| Whitehurst | 322 | 179 | 56 | 2247 | 7.0 | 10 | 18– 6 | 11 |
| Dickey | 119 | 60 | 50 | 787 | 6.6 | 5 | 4– 3 | |
| Beverly | 2 | 1 | 50 | 23 | 11.5 | 0 | 0– 0 | |
| Lofton | 1 | 0 | 0 | 0 | 0.0 | 0 | 0– 0 | |

| PUNTING | No. | Avg. |
|---|---|---|
| Beverly | 69 | 40.4 |

| KICKING | XP | Att. | % | FG | Att. | % |
|---|---|---|---|---|---|---|
| Birney | 7 | 10 | 70 | 7 | 9 | 78 |
| Marcol | 16 | 18 | 89 | 4 | 10 | 40 |
| Anderson | 1 | 2 | 50 | 1 | 1 | 100 |

## DETROIT LIONS

### RUSHING

| Last Name | No. | Yds. | Avg. | TD |
|---|---|---|---|---|
| Bussey | 144 | 625 | 4.3 | 1 |
| Kane | 94 | 332 | 3.5 | 4 |
| Robinson | 87 | 302 | 3.5 | 2 |
| King | 39 | 160 | 4.1 | 1 |
| Komlo | 30 | 107 | 3.6 | 2 |
| Gaines | 23 | 55 | 2.4 | 0 |
| G. Washington | 1 | 24 | 24.0 | 0 |
| Thompson | 5 | 24 | 4.8 | 0 |
| Scott | 6 | 21 | 3.5 | 0 |
| Hill | 1 | 15 | 15.0 | 0 |
| Reed | 2 | 11 | 5.5 | 0 |
| Callicut | 3 | 6 | 2.0 | 0 |
| S. Hunter | 2 | 3 | 1.5 | 1 |
| Golsteyn | 1 | 0 | 0.0 | 0 |
| O'Neil | 1 | 0 | 0.0 | 0 |
| Swider | 1 | 0 | 0.0 | 0 |
| Blue | 1 | −8 | −8.0 | 0 |

### RECEIVING

| Last Name | No. | Yds. | Avg. | TD |
|---|---|---|---|---|
| Scott | 62 | 929 | 15 | 5 |
| Hill | 47 | 569 | 12 | 3 |
| Thompson | 24 | 451 | 19 | 2 |
| King | 18 | 150 | 8 | 0 |
| Bussey | 15 | 102 | 7 | 0 |
| G. Washington | 14 | 192 | 14 | 1 |
| Robinson | 14 | 118 | 8 | 0 |
| Kane | 9 | 104 | 12 | 1 |
| Blue | 8 | 102 | 13 | 1 |
| Norris | 4 | 43 | 11 | 1 |
| Callicut | 2 | 16 | 8 | 0 |
| Bolinger | 1 | −1 | −1 | 0 |

### PUNT RETURNS

| Last Name | No. | Yds. | Avg. | TD |
|---|---|---|---|---|
| Arnold | 19 | 164 | 9 | 0 |
| Thompson | 9 | 117 | 13 | 0 |
| Ellis | 8 | 43 | 5 | 0 |
| Callicut | 4 | 25 | 6 | 0 |
| Woods | 2 | 12 | 6 | 0 |
| Leonard | 1 | 7 | 7 | 0 |
| Pesuit | 1 | 5 | 5 | 0 |
| Lewis | 1 | −1 | −1 | 0 |

### KICKOFF RETURNS

| Last Name | No. | Yds. | Avg. | TD |
|---|---|---|---|---|
| Arnold | 23 | 539 | 23 | 0 |
| Callicut | 24 | 406 | 17 | 0 |
| Kane | 13 | 281 | 22 | 0 |
| Thompson | 6 | 151 | 25 | 0 |
| Leonard | 3 | 70 | 23 | 0 |
| King | 2 | 36 | 18 | 0 |
| Woods | 2 | 34 | 17 | 0 |
| Fanetti | 2 | 18 | 9 | 0 |
| Blue | 1 | 26 | 26 | 0 |
| Robinson | 1 | 8 | 8 | 0 |
| Gay | 1 | 0 | 0 | 0 |

### PASSING – PUNTING – KICKING

| PASSING | Att. | Comp. | % | Yds. | Yd./Att. | TD | Int.–% | RK |
|---|---|---|---|---|---|---|---|---|
| Komlo | 368 | 183 | 50 | 2238 | 6.1 | 11 | 23– 6 | 14 |
| S. Hunter | 41 | 18 | 44 | 321 | 7.8 | 1 | 1– 2 | |
| Reed | 32 | 14 | 44 | 164 | 5.1 | 2 | 1– 3 | |
| Golsteyn | 9 | 2 | 22 | 16 | 1.8 | 0 | 2– 22 | |
| Swider | 1 | 1 | 100 | 36 | 36.0 | 0 | 0– 0 | |
| Skladany | 1 | 0 | 0 | 0 | 0.0 | 0 | 0– 0 | |

| PUNTING | No. | Avg. |
|---|---|---|
| Swider | 88 | 40.0 |
| Skladany | 10 | 40.6 |

| KICKING | XP | Att. | % | FG | Att. | % |
|---|---|---|---|---|---|---|
| Ricardo | 25 | 26 | 96 | 10 | 18 | 56 |

## LOS ANGELES RAMS 9-7-0 Ray Malavasi

| Scores of Each Game | | |
|---|---|---|
| 17 | OAKLAND | 24 |
| 13 | Denver | 9 |
| 27 | SAN FRANCISCO | 24 |
| 6 | Tampa Bay | 21 |
| 21 | ST. LOUIS | 0 |
| 35 | New Orleans | 17 |
| 6 | Dallas | 30 |
| 16 | SAN DIEGO | 40 |
| 14 | N.Y. GIANTS | 20 |
| 24 | Seattle | 0 |
| 23 | Chicago | 27 |
| 20 | ATLANTA | 14 |
| 26 | San Francisco | 20 |
| 27 | MINNESOTA | *21 |
| 34 | Atlanta | 13 |
| 14 | NEW ORLEANS | 29 |

| Use Name | Pos. | Hgt. | Wgt. | Age | Int. | Pts. |
|---|---|---|---|---|---|---|
| Doug France | OT | 6′5″ | 288 | 26 | | |
| Gordon Gravelle (from NYG) | OT | 6′5″ | 252 | 30 | | |
| Jackie Slater | OT | 6′4″ | 269 | 25 | | |
| John Williams | OT-OG | 6′3″ | 256 | 33 | | |
| Brent Adams | OG-OT | 6′5″ | 256 | 27 | | |
| Bill Bain | OG | 6′4″ | 270 | 27 | | |
| Dennis Harrah | OG | 6′5″ | 251 | 26 | | |
| Kent Hill | OG | 6′5″ | 260 | 22 | | |
| Dan Ryczek | C | 6′3″ | 245 | 30 | | |
| Rich Saul | C | 6·3″ | 243 | 31 | | |
| Doug Smith | C-OG | 6′3″ | 250 | 22 | | |
| Reggie Doss | DE | 6′4″ | 267 | 22 | | |
| Fred Dryer | DE | 6′6″ | 230 | 33 | | |
| Jerry Wilkinson | DE | 6′9″ | 255 | 23 | | |
| Jack Youngblood | DE | 6′4″ | 243 | 29 | | |
| Larry Brooks | DT | 6′3″ | 255 | 29 | | |
| Bill Dunstan | DT | 6′4″ | 250 | 30 | | |
| Mike Fanning | DT | 6′6″ | 248 | 26 | | |
| George Andrews | LB | 6′3″ | 226 | 23 | | |
| Bob Brudzinski | LB | 6′4″ | 231 | 24 | 1 | |
| Joe Harris (from MIN) | LB | 6′1″ | 225 | 26 | | 6 |
| Kevin McLain | LB | 6′2″ | 227 | 24 | | |
| Jack Reynolds | LB | 6′1″ | 231 | 31 | | 6 |
| Greg Westbrooks (from OAK) | LB | 6′3″ | 215 | 26 | | |
| Jim Youngblood | LB | 6′3″ | 231 | 29 | 5 | 12 |
| Eddie Brown | DB | 5′11″ | 190 | 27 | 3 | |
| Nolan Cromwell | DB | 6′1″ | 197 | 24 | 5 | 6 |
| Dave Elmendorf | DB | 6′1″ | 196 | 30 | 3 | |
| Sid Justin | DB | 5′10″ | 170 | 25 | 1 | 6 |
| Ricky Odom | DB | 6′ | 183 | 22 | | |
| Dwayne O'Steen | DB | 6′1″ | 190 | 24 | 4 | |
| Rod Perry | DB | 5′9″ | 177 | 25 | 8 | 18 |
| Jeff Severson | DB | 6′1″ | 185 | 29 | | |
| Ivory Sully | DB | 6′ | 193 | 22 | | |
| Pat Thomas | DB | 6′9″ | 184 | 25 | 3 | |
| Jackie Wallare | DB | 6′3″ | 196 | 28 | | |
| Vince Ferragamo | QB | 6′3″ | 207 | 25 | | |
| Pat Haden | QB | 5′11″ | 180 | 26 | | |
| Bob Lee | QB | 6′2″ | 195 | 33 | | |
| Jeff Rutledge | QB | 6′2″ | 200 | 22 | | |
| Eddie Hill | HB | 6′2″ | 197 | 22 | | 12 |
| Lawrence McCutcheon | HB | 6′1″ | 205 | 29 | | |
| Wendell Tyler | HB | 5′10″ | 188 | 24 | | 60 |
| Cullen Bryant | FB | 6′1″ | 234 | 28 | | 30 |
| Jim Judat | FB | 5′11″ | 207 | 25 | | 6 |
| Elvis Peacock | FB | 6′1″ | 220 | 22 | | |
| Preston Dennard | WR | 6′1″ | 185 | 23 | | 24 |
| Drew Hill | WR | 5′9″ | 170 | 22 | | 6 |
| Ron Jessie | WR | 6′ | 181 | 31 | | 12 |
| Willie Miller | WR | 5′9″ | 172 | 32 | | 6 |
| Ron Smith | WR | 6′ | 185 | 22 | | 6 |
| Billy Waddy | WR | 5′11″ | 180 | 25 | | 18 |
| Terry Nelson | TE | 6′2″ | 241 | 28 | | 18 |
| Charlie Young | TE | 6′4″ | 234 | 28 | | 12 |
| Ken Clark | K | 6′2″ | 197 | 31 | | |
| Frank Corral | K | 6′2″ | 220 | 24 | | 75 |

John Cappelletti – Groin Injury
Anthony Davis – Broken Rib
Carl Ekern – Knee Injury
Cody Jones – Achilles Injury

## NEW ORLEANS SAINTS 8-8-0 Dick Nolan

| Scores of Each Game | | |
|---|---|---|
| 34 | ATLANTA | *40 |
| 19 | Green Bay | 28 |
| 14 | PHILADELPHIA | 26 |
| 30 | San Francisco | 21 |
| 24 | N.Y. GIANTS | 14 |
| 17 | LOS ANGELES | 35 |
| 42 | Tampa Bay | 14 |
| 17 | DETROIT | 7 |
| 14 | Washington | 10 |
| 3 | Denver | 10 |
| 31 | SAN FRANCISCO | 20 |
| 24 | Seattle | 38 |
| 37 | Atlanta | 6 |
| 35 | OAKLAND | 42 |
| 0 | SAN DIEGO | 35 |
| 29 | Los Angeles | 14 |

| Use Name | Pos. | Hgt. | Wgt. | Age | Int. | Pts. |
|---|---|---|---|---|---|---|
| Roger Finnie | OT | 6′3″ | 250 | 33 | | |
| J.T. Taylor | OT | 6′4″ | 265 | 23 | | |
| John Watson | OT | 6′4″ | 244 | 30 | | |
| Robert Woods | OT | 6′3″ | 259 | 29 | | |
| Conrad Dobler | OG | 6′3″ | 255 | 28 | | |
| Dave Lafary | OG | 6′7″ | 280 | 24 | | |
| Fred Sturt | OG | 6′4″ | 255 | 28 | | |
| Emanuel Zanders | OG | 6′1″ | 248 | 28 | | |
| John Hill | C | 6′2″ | 246 | 29 | | |
| Jim Pietrzak (from NYG) | C-OT | 6′5″ | 260 | 26 | | |
| Joe Campbell | DE | 6′6″ | 254 | 24 | | |
| Elois Grooms | DE | 6′4″ | 250 | 26 | 1 | 2 |
| Don Reese | DE | 6′6″ | 250 | 27 | | |
| Barry Bennett | DT | 6′4″ | 257 | 23 | | |
| Mike Fultz | DT | 6′5″ | 278 | 25 | | |
| Derland Moore | DT | 6′4″ | 253 | 27 | | |
| Elex Price | DT | 6′3″ | 265 | 29 | | |
| Ken Bordelon | LB | 6′4″ | 226 | 25 | 2 | 6 |
| Joe Federspiel | LB | 6′1″ | 230 | 29 | 1 | |
| Pat Hughes | LB | 6′2″ | 225 | 32 | 4 | |
| Jim Kovach | LB | 6′2″ | 225 | 23 | | |
| Reggie Mathis | LB | 6′2″ | 220 | 23 | | |
| Jim Merlo | LB | 6′1″ | 220 | 27 | | |
| Ray Brown | DB | 6′2″ | 202 | 30 | 1 | |
| Clarence Chapman | CB | 5′10″ | 185 | 25 | 2 | |
| Eric Felton | DB | 6′ | 200 | 23 | 4 | |
| David Gray | DB | 6′ | 190 | 24 | 1 | |
| Ralph McGill | DB | 5′11″ | 178 | 29 | 1 | |
| Tom Myers | DB | 5′11″ | 180 | 28 | 7 | 6 |
| Ricky Ray | DB | 5′11″ | 180 | 22 | | |
| Don Schwartz | DB | 6′1″ | 191 | 23 | 2 | |
| Ed Burns | QB | 6′3″ | 210 | 24 | | |
| Archie Manning | QB | 6′3″ | 200 | 30 | | 12 |
| Bobby Scott | QB | 6′1″ | 197 | 30 | | |
| Chuck Muncie | HB-FB | 6′3″ | 233 | 26 | | 66 |
| Mike Strachan | HB | 6′ | 200 | 26 | | 36 |
| Wayne Wilson | HB | 6′3″ | 208 | 21 | | |
| Tony Galbreath | FB | 6′1″ | 230 | 25 | | 67 |
| Jack Holmes | FB | 5′11″ | 210 | 26 | | |
| Kim Jones | FB | 6′4″ | 235 | 27 | | |
| Wes Chandler | WR | 5′11″ | 186 | 23 | | 36 |
| Ike Harris | WR | 6′3″ | 210 | 26 | | 12 |
| Richard Mauti | WR | 6′ | 190 | 25 | | |
| Tinker Owens | WR | 5′11″ | 170 | 24 | | 6 |
| Henry Childs | TE | 6′2″ | 220 | 28 | | 30 |
| Larry Hardy | TE | 6′3″ | 230 | 23 | | 6 |
| Brooks Williams | TE | 6′4″ | 226 | 24 | | |
| Russell Erxleben | K | 6′4″ | 219 | 22 | | 10 |
| Rick Partridge | K | 6′1″ | 175 | 22 | | |
| Garo Yepremian | K | 5′8″ | 175 | 35 | | 75 |

Mike Watson – Injury

## ATLANTA FALCONS 6-10-0 Leeman Bennett

| Scores of Each Game | | |
|---|---|---|
| 40 | New Orleans | *34 |
| 14 | Philadelphia | 10 |
| 17 | DENVER | *20 |
| 23 | Detroit | 24 |
| 7 | WASHINGTON | 16 |
| 25 | GREEN BAY | 7 |
| 19 | Oakland | 50 |
| 15 | San Francisco | 20 |
| 28 | SEATTLE | 31 |
| 17 | TAMPA BAY | 14 |
| 3 | N.Y. Giants | 24 |
| 14 | Los Angeles | 20 |
| 6 | NEW ORLEANS | 37 |
| 28 | San Diego | 26 |
| 13 | LOS ANGELES | 34 |
| 31 | SAN FRANCISCO | 21 |

| Use Name | Pos. | Hgt. | Wgt. | Age | Int. | Pts. |
|---|---|---|---|---|---|---|
| Warren Bryant | OT | 6′6″ | 270 | 23 | | |
| Mike Kenn | OT | 6′6″ | 257 | 23 | | |
| Phil McKinnely | OT | 6′4″ | 248 | 25 | | |
| Pat Howell | OG | 6′5″ | 253 | 22 | | |
| Dave Scott | OG | 6′4″ | 285 | 25 | | |
| R.C. Thielemann | OG | 6′4″ | 247 | 24 | | |
| Chuck Correal | C | 6′3″ | 247 | 23 | | |
| Paul Ryczek | C | 6′2″ | 230 | 27 | | |
| Jeff Van Note | C | 6′2″ | 247 | 33 | | |
| Jeff Merrow | DE | 6′4″ | 230 | 26 | | |
| Don Smith | DE | 6′5″ | 248 | 22 | | |
| Jeff Yeates | DE-DT | 6′3″ | 236 | 28 | | |
| Wilson Faumuina | DT | 6′5″ | 275 | 25 | | |
| Edgar Fields | DT-DE | 6′2″ | 255 | 25 | | |
| Mike Lewis | DT | 6′3″ | 261 | 30 | | 2 |
| Mike Zele | DT | 6′3″ | 236 | 23 | | |
| Greg Brezina | LB | 6′1″ | 221 | 33 | | |
| Brian Cabral | LB | 6′ | 209 | 23 | | |
| Tony Daykin | LB | 6′1″ | 215 | 24 | | |
| Fulton Kuykendall | LB | 6′5″ | 225 | 26 | | |
| Ron McCartney | LB | 6′1″ | 220 | 25 | | |
| Dewey McClain | LB | 6′3″ | 236 | 25 | | |
| Robert Pennywell | LB | 6′1″ | 222 | 24 | 1 | 6 |
| Joel Williams | LB | 6′ | 215 | 22 | | |
| Rick Byas | DB | 5′9″ | 180 | 28 | 1 | 6 |
| Ray Easterling | DB | 6′ | 192 | 29 | 2 | |
| Bob Glazebrook | DB | 6′1″ | 200 | 23 | | |
| Jerome King | DB | 5′10″ | 173 | 24 | | |
| Rolland Lawrence | DB | 5′10″ | 179 | 28 | 6 | 6 |
| Tom Moriarty | DB | 6′ | 185 | 26 | | |
| Tom Pridemore | DB | 5′10″ | 186 | 23 | 2 | |
| Frank Reed | DB | 5′11″ | 193 | 25 | 2 | |
| Steve Bartkowski | QB | 6′4″ | 213 | 26 | | 12 |
| Larry Fortner | QB | 6′4″ | 212 | 23 | | |
| June Jones | QB | 6′4″ | 200 | 26 | | |
| Mike Moroski | QB | 6′4″ | 200 | 21 | | 6 |
| Bubba Bean | HB | 5′11″ | 195 | 25 | | 6 |
| Lynn Cain | HB | 6′1″ | 205 | 23 | | 24 |
| Haskel Stanback | HB-FB | 6′ | 210 | 27 | | 30 |
| Ray Strong | HB | 5′9″ | 184 | 23 | | |
| William Andrews | FB | 6′ | 200 | 23 | | 30 |
| James Mayberry | FB | 5′11″ | 210 | 21 | 1 | 12 |
| Wallace Francis | WR | 5′11″ | 190 | 27 | | 48 |
| Alfred Jackson | WR | 5′11″ | 176 | 24 | | |
| Al Jenkins | WR | 5′10″ | 172 | 27 | | 18 |
| Dennis Pearson | WR | 5′11″ | 177 | 24 | | |
| Billy Ryckman | WR | 5′11″ | 172 | 24 | | 12 |
| Russ Mikeska | TE | 6′3″ | 225 | 23 | | |
| Jim Mitchell | TE | 6′2″ | 236 | 31 | | 12 |
| John James | K | 6′3″ | 200 | 30 | | |
| Tim Mazzetti | K | 6′1″ | 175 | 23 | | 70 |

Mike Esposito – Shoulder Injury
Lewis Gilbert – Knee Injury
James Wright – Knee Injury
Garth Ten Napel – Injured in Auto Accident in April
Andy Spiva – Died in Auto Accident in April

## SAN FRANCISCO FORTY-NINERS 2-14-0 Bill Walsh

| Scores of Each Game | | |
|---|---|---|
| 22 | Minnesota | 28 |
| 13 | DALLAS | 21 |
| 24 | Los Angeles | 27 |
| 21 | NEW ORLEANS | 30 |
| 9 | San Diego | 31 |
| 24 | SEATTLE | 35 |
| 16 | N.Y. Giants | 32 |
| 20 | ATLANTA | 15 |
| 27 | CHICAGO | 28 |
| 10 | Oakland | 23 |
| 20 | New Orleans | 31 |
| 28 | DENVER | 38 |
| 20 | LOS ANGELES | 26 |
| 10 | St. Louis | 13 |
| 23 | TAMPA BAY | 7 |
| 21 | Atlanta | 31 |

| Use Name | Pos. | Hgt. | Wgt. | Age | Int. | Pts. |
|---|---|---|---|---|---|---|
| Jean Barrett | OT | 6′6″ | 250 | 28 | | |
| Keith Fahnhorst | OT | 6′6″ | 263 | 27 | | |
| Ron Singleton | OT | 6′7″ | 267 | 27 | | |
| John Ayers | OG | 6′5″ | 247 | 26 | | |
| Randy Cross | OG | 6′3″ | 255 | 25 | | |
| Walt Downing | OG-C | 6′3″ | 254 | 23 | | |
| Fred Quillan | C | 6′5″ | 254 | 23 | | |
| Dwaine Board | DE | 6′5″ | 245 | 22 | | |
| Al Cowlings | DE | 6′5″ | 222 | 32 | | |
| Cedrick Hardman | DE | 6·3″ | 244 | 30 | | |
| Archie Reese | DE | 6′3″ | 262 | 23 | | |
| Ed Galigher | DT | 6′4″ | 255 | 28 | | |
| Ruben Vaughen | DT | 6′2″ | 264 | 23 | | |
| Ted Vincent | DT | 6′4″ | 265 | 23 | | |
| Jimmy Webb | DT | 6′5″ | 245 | 27 | | |
| Dan Bunz | LB | 6′4″ | 230 | 23 | 1 | |
| Gordy Ceresino | LB | 6′ | 224 | 21 | | |
| Willie Harper | LB | 6′2″ | 215 | 29 | | |
| Scott Hilton | LB | 6′4″ | 225 | 25 | | |
| Bob Martin (from NYJ) | LB | 6′1″ | 214 | 25 | | |
| Jeff McIntyre | LB | 6′3″ | 232 | 23 | | |
| Dave Morton | LB | 6′2″ | 224 | 24 | | |
| Bob Nelson | LB | 6′4″ | 230 | 26 | | |
| Thomas Seabron | LB | 6′3″ | 215 | 22 | | |
| Ron Shumon | LB | 6′1″ | 234 | 23 | | |
| John Bristor | DB | 6′ | 188 | 23 | | |
| Charles Cornelius | DB | 5′9″ | 178 | 27 | 3 | |
| Tony Dungy | DB | 6′ | 190 | 23 | | |
| Tim Gray | DB | 6′1″ | 200 | 26 | 1 | |
| Dwight Hicks | DB | 6′1″ | 189 | 23 | 5 | |
| Charles Johnson | DB | 5′10″ | 180 | 23 | | |
| Eric Johnson | DB | 6′1″ | 192 | 27 | | |
| Melvin Morgan | DB | 6′ | 180 | 26 | 1 | |
| Gerard Williams | DB | 6′1″ | 184 | 27 | 4 | |
| Steve Deberg | QB | 6′2″ | 205 | 25 | | |
| Joe Montana | QB | 6′2″ | 200 | 23 | | |
| Lenvil Elliott | HB-FB | 6′ | 210 | 27 | | 18 |
| Phil Francis | HB-FB | 6′1″ | 215 | 22 | | 6 |
| Paul Hofer | HB | 6′ | 195 | 27 | | 54 |
| O.J. Simpson | HB | 6′2″ | 212 | 32 | | 18 |
| Bob Ferrell | FB | 6′ | 213 | 26 | | |
| Mike Hogan | FB | 6′2″ | 215 | 24 | | |
| Wilbur Jackson | FB | 6′1″ | 219 | 27 | | 12 |
| Dwight Clark | WR | 6′3″ | 205 | 22 | | |
| James Owens | WR-HB-DB | 5′11″ | 188 | 24 | | 6 |
| Mike Shumann | WR | 6′ | 175 | 23 | | 24 |
| Freddie Solomon | WR | 5′11″ | 188 | 26 | | 48 |
| Bob Bruer | TE | 6′5″ | 235 | 26 | | 6 |
| Ken MacAfee | TE | 6′5″ | 245 | 23 | | 24 |
| Eason Ramson | TE | 6′2″ | 234 | 23 | | |
| Paul Seal | TE | 6′4″ | 227 | 27 | | |
| Dan Melville | K | 6′ | 185 | 23 | | |
| Ray Wersching | K | 5′11″ | 210 | 29 | | 92 |

Mike Baldassin – Injury
Lon Boyett – Injury
Ed Bradley – Broken Ankle
Scott Bull – Knee Injury
Ernie Hughes – Knee Injury
Bob Jury – Shoulder Injury

Steve Knutson – Knee Injury
Johnny Miller – Knee Injury

* – Overtime

## LOS ANGELES RAMS

### RUSHING

| Last Name | No. | Yds. | Avg. | TD |
|---|---|---|---|---|
| Tyler | 218 | 1109 | 5.1 | 9 |
| Bryant | 177 | 619 | 3.5 | 5 |
| McCutcheon | 73 | 243 | 3.3 | 0 |
| Peacock | 52 | 224 | 4.3 | 0 |
| E. Hill | 29 | 114 | 3.9 | 1 |
| Haden | 16 | 97 | 6.1 | 0 |
| Dennard | 4 | 32 | 8.0 | 0 |
| Rutledge | 5 | 27 | 5.4 | 0 |
| Jodat | 6 | 6 | 1.0 | 0 |
| Cromwell | 1 | 5 | 5.0 | 1 |
| Miller | 1 | 4 | 4.0 | 0 |
| Clark | 1 | 3 | 3.0 | 0 |
| Ferragamo | 3 | −2 | −0.7 | 0 |
| Lee | 4 | −5 | −1.3 | 0 |
| Nelson | 2 | −16 | −8.0 | 0 |

### RECEIVING

| Last Name | No. | Yds. | Avg. | TD |
|---|---|---|---|---|
| Dennard | 43 | 766 | 18 | 4 |
| Tyler | 32 | 308 | 10 | 1 |
| Bryant | 31 | 227 | 7 | 0 |
| Nelson | 25 | 293 | 12 | 3 |
| Peacock | 21 | 261 | 12 | 0 |
| McCutcheon | 19 | 101 | 5 | 0 |
| R. Smith | 16 | 300 | 19 | 1 |
| Waddy | 14 | 220 | 16 | 3 |
| Young | 13 | 144 | 11 | 2 |
| Jessie | 11 | 169 | 15 | 2 |
| Miller | 8 | 111 | 14 | 1 |
| D. Hill | 4 | 94 | 24 | 1 |
| E. Hill | 4 | 36 | 9 | 1 |
| Andrews | 1 | 2 | 2 | 0 |

### PUNT RETURNS

| Last Name | No. | Yds. | Avg. | TD |
|---|---|---|---|---|
| Brown | 56 | 332 | 6 | 0 |
| D. Hill | 1 | 0 | 0.0 | 0 |
| Justin | 1 | −2 | −2.0 | 0 |

### KICKOFF RETURNS

| Last Name | No. | Yds. | Avg. | TD |
|---|---|---|---|---|
| D. Hill | 40 | 803 | 20 | 0 |
| E. Hill | 15 | 305 | 20 | 0 |
| Brown | 5 | 103 | 21 | 0 |
| Peacock | 3 | 46 | 15 | 0 |
| Jodat | 2 | 19 | 10 | 0 |
| Tyler | 1 | 16 | 16 | 0 |

### PASSING – PUNTING – KICKING

| PASSING | Att. | Comp. | % | Yds. | Yd./Att. | TD | Int.–% | RK |
|---|---|---|---|---|---|---|---|---|
| Haden | 290 | 163 | 56 | 1854 | 6.4 | 11 | 14– 5 | 8 |
| Lee | 22 | 11 | 50 | 243 | 11.1 | 2 | 1– 5 | |
| Ferragamo | 110 | 53 | 48 | 778 | 7.1 | 5 | 10– 9 | |
| Rutledge | 32 | 13 | 41 | 125 | 3.9 | 1 | 4–13 | |
| Clark | 2 | 2 | 100 | 32 | 16.0 | 0 | 0– 0 | |

| PUNTING | No. | Avg. |
|---|---|---|
| Clark | 93 | 40.1 |

| KICKING | XP | Att. | % | FG | Att. | % |
|---|---|---|---|---|---|---|
| Corral | 36 | 39 | 92 | 13 | 25 | 52 |

## NEW ORLEANS SAINTS

### RUSHING

| Last Name | No. | Yds. | Avg. | TD |
|---|---|---|---|---|
| Muncie | 238 | 1198 | 5.0 | 11 |
| Galbreath | 189 | 708 | 3.7 | 9 |
| Strachan | 62 | 276 | 4.5 | 6 |
| Manning | 35 | 186 | 5.3 | 2 |
| Holmes | 17 | 68 | 4.0 | 0 |
| Wilson | 5 | 26 | 5.2 | 0 |
| Harris | 2 | 9 | 4.5 | 0 |
| Jones | 3 | 5 | 1.7 | 0 |

### RECEIVING

| Last Name | No. | Yds. | Avg. | TD |
|---|---|---|---|---|
| Chandler | 65 | 1069 | 16 | 6 |
| Galbreath | 58 | 484 | 8 | 1 |
| Childs | 51 | 846 | 17 | 5 |
| Muncie | 40 | 308 | 8 | 0 |
| Harris | 25 | 395 | 16 | 2 |
| Owens | 7 | 72 | 10 | 1 |
| Holmes | 3 | 19 | 6 | 0 |
| Strachan | 3 | 9 | 3 | 0 |
| Mauti | 2 | 64 | 32 | 0 |
| Williams | 2 | 22 | 11 | 0 |
| Hardy | 1 | 3 | 3 | 1 |

### PUNT RETURNS

| Last Name | No. | Yds. | Avg. | TD |
|---|---|---|---|---|
| Mauti | 27 | 218 | 8 | 0 |
| Chandler | 3 | 13 | 4 | 0 |

### KICKOFF RETURNS

| Last Name | No. | Yds. | Avg. | TD |
|---|---|---|---|---|
| Mauti | 36 | 801 | 22 | 0 |
| Wilson | 11 | 230 | 21 | 0 |
| Holmes | 8 | 120 | 15 | 0 |
| Chandler | 7 | 136 | 19 | 0 |
| Williams | 2 | 12 | 6 | 0 |
| Kovach | 1 | 10 | 10 | 0 |
| Owens | 1 | 10 | 10 | 0 |

### PASSING – PUNTING – KICKING

| PASSING | Att. | Comp. | % | Yds. | Yd./Att. | TD | Int.–% | RK |
|---|---|---|---|---|---|---|---|---|
| Manning | 420 | 252 | 60 | 3169 | 7.6 | 15 | 20– 5 | 4 |
| Scott | 2 | 2 | 100 | 12 | 6.0 | 0 | 0– 0 | |
| Galbreath | 3 | 2 | 67 | 70 | 23.3 | 0 | 1–33 | |
| Muncie | 2 | 1 | 50 | 40 | 20.0 | 1 | 0– 0 | |
| Erxleben | 1 | 0 | 0 | 0 | | 0 | 1–100 | |

| PUNTING | No. | Avg. |
|---|---|---|
| Partridge | 57 | 40.9 |
| Chandler | 8 | 31.0 |
| Erxleben | 4 | 37.0 |

| KICKING | XP | Att. | % | FG | Att. | % |
|---|---|---|---|---|---|---|
| Yepremian | 39 | 40 | 98 | 12 | 16 | 75 |
| Galbreath | 1 | 2 | 50 | 2 | 3 | 67 |
| Erxleben | 4 | 4 | 100 | 2 | 2 | 100 |

## ATLANTA FALCONS

### RUSHING

| Last Name | No. | Yds. | Avg. | TD |
|---|---|---|---|---|
| Andrews | 239 | 1023 | 4.3 | 3 |
| Bean | 88 | 393 | 4.5 | 1 |
| Cain | 63 | 295 | 4.7 | 2 |
| Stanback | 36 | 202 | 5.6 | 5 |
| Mayberry | 45 | 193 | 4.3 | 1 |
| Bartkowski | 14 | 36 | 2.6 | 2 |
| Moroski | 3 | 31 | 10.3 | 1 |
| Jones | 6 | 19 | 3.2 | 0 |
| Strong | 2 | 7 | 3.5 | 0 |
| James | 1 | 0 | 0.0 | 0 |

### RECEIVING

| Last Name | No. | Yds. | Avg. | TD |
|---|---|---|---|---|
| Francis | 74 | 1013 | 14 | 8 |
| Jenkins | 50 | 858 | 17 | 3 |
| Andrews | 39 | 309 | 8 | 2 |
| Mitchell | 16 | 118 | 7 | 2 |
| Cain | 15 | 181 | 12 | 2 |
| Stanback | 13 | 89 | 7 | 0 |
| Bean | 12 | 137 | 11 | 0 |
| Jackson | 11 | 156 | 14 | 0 |
| Pearson | 7 | 119 | 17 | 0 |
| Mayberry | 7 | 48 | 7 | 0 |
| Ryckman | 4 | 59 | 15 | 2 |
| Glazebrook | 1 | 20 | 20 | 0 |
| Mikeska | 1 | 14 | 14 | 0 |
| Strong | 1 | 6 | 6 | 0 |

### PUNT RETURNS

| Last Name | No. | Yds. | Avg. | TD |
|---|---|---|---|---|
| Pearson | 12 | 115 | 10 | 0 |
| Ryckman | 12 | 72 | 6 | 0 |
| McClain | 1 | 2 | 2 | 0 |
| Glazebrook | 1 | −1 | −1 | 0 |

### KICKOFF RETURNS

| Last Name | No. | Yds. | Avg. | TD |
|---|---|---|---|---|
| Pearson | 30 | 570 | 19 | 0 |
| Strong | 15 | 343 | 23 | 0 |
| Pridemore | 9 | 111 | 12 | 0 |
| Cain | 7 | 149 | 21 | 0 |
| Stanback | 6 | 109 | 18 | 0 |
| Mayberry | 4 | 49 | 12 | 0 |
| Jackson | 1 | 20 | 20 | 0 |
| Byas | 1 | 19 | 19 | 0 |

### PASSING – PUNTING – KICKING

| PASSING | Att. | Comp. | % | Yds. | Yd./Att. | TD | Int.–% | RK |
|---|---|---|---|---|---|---|---|---|
| Bartkowski | 380 | 204 | 54 | 2505 | 6.6 | 17 | 20– 5 | 9 |
| Moroski | 15 | 8 | 53 | 97 | 6.5 | 0 | 0– 0 | |
| Jones | 83 | 38 | 46 | 505 | 6.1 | 2 | 3– 4 | |
| James | 1 | 1 | 100 | 20 | 20.0 | 0 | 0– 0 | |

| PUNTING | No. | Avg. |
|---|---|---|
| James | 83 | 39.7 |

| KICKING | XP | Att. | % | FG | Att. | % |
|---|---|---|---|---|---|---|
| Mazzetti | 31 | 37 | 84 | 13 | 25 | 52 |

## SAN FRANCISCO FORTY-NINERS

### RUSHING

| Last Name | No. | Yds. | Avg. | TD |
|---|---|---|---|---|
| Hofer | 123 | 615 | 5.0 | 7 |
| Simpson | 120 | 460 | 3.8 | 3 |
| Jackson | 114 | 375 | 3.3 | 2 |
| Elliott | 33 | 135 | 4.1 | 3 |
| Francis | 31 | 118 | 3.8 | 1 |
| Solomon | 6 | 85 | 14.2 | 0 |
| Owens | 7 | 33 | 4.7 | 0 |
| Ferrell | 8 | 33 | 4.1 | 0 |
| Hogan | 9 | 31 | 3.4 | 0 |
| Montana | 3 | 22 | 7.3 | 0 |
| Shumann | 1 | 19 | 19.0 | 0 |
| DeBerg | 17 | 10 | 0.6 | 0 |
| Melville | 3 | 0 | 0.0 | 0 |
| Bruer | 5 | −4 | −0.8 | 0 |

### RECEIVING

| Last Name | No. | Yds. | Avg. | TD |
|---|---|---|---|---|
| Hofer | 58 | 662 | 11 | 2 |
| Solomon | 57 | 807 | 14 | 7 |
| Jackson | 53 | 422 | 8 | 0 |
| Shumann | 39 | 452 | 12 | 4 |
| Francis | 32 | 198 | 6 | 0 |
| Bruer | 26 | 254 | 10 | 1 |
| MacAfee | 24 | 266 | 11 | 4 |
| Elliott | 23 | 197 | 9 | 0 |
| Clark | 18 | 232 | 13 | 0 |
| Owens | 10 | 121 | 12 | 0 |
| Hogan | 9 | 65 | 7 | 0 |
| Simpson | 7 | 46 | 7 | 0 |
| Seal | 3 | 34 | 11 | 0 |
| Ferrell | 2 | 4 | 2 | 0 |

### PUNT RETURNS

| Last Name | No. | Yds. | Avg. | TD |
|---|---|---|---|---|
| Solomon | 23 | 142 | 6 | 0 |
| Hicks | 13 | 120 | 9 | 0 |
| Dungy | 8 | 52 | 7 | 0 |

### KICKOFF RETURNS

| Last Name | No. | Yds. | Avg. | TD |
|---|---|---|---|---|
| Owens | 41 | 1002 | 24 | 1 |
| Elliott | 9 | 170 | 19 | 0 |
| Hofer | 8 | 124 | 16 | 0 |
| Francis | 7 | 103 | 15 | 0 |
| Ferrell | 6 | 78 | 13 | 0 |
| Hicks | 2 | 36 | 18 | 0 |
| Bruer | 1 | 20 | 20 | 0 |
| Barrett | 1 | 5 | 5 | 0 |

### PASSING – PUNTING – KICKING

| PASSING | Att. | Comp. | % | Yds. | Yd./Att. | TD | Int.–% | RK |
|---|---|---|---|---|---|---|---|---|
| DeBerg | 578 | 347 | 60 | 3652 | 6.3 | 17 | 21– 4 | 5 |
| Montana | 23 | 13 | 57 | 96 | 4.2 | 1 | 0– 0 | |
| Solomon | 1 | 1 | 100 | 12 | 12.0 | 0 | 0– 0 | |

| PUNTING | No. | Avg. |
|---|---|---|
| Melville | 71 | 37.0 |

| KICKING | XP | Att. | % | FG | Att. | % |
|---|---|---|---|---|---|---|
| Wersching | 32 | 35 | 91 | 20 | 24 | 83 |

# 1979 A.F.C. The Shouting Above

Discord rang in the halls of several N.F.L. teams. In New England, the Patriots sued Chuck Fairbanks to prevent him from leaving to coach the University of Oklahoma team. The court battle languished into the warm weather, when the Patriots gave up the fight and named Ron Erhardt their new head coach.

In New Jersey, the Giants were ripped by a feud within the Mara family. After the 1978 management was cleared out, Wellington and Tim Mara couldn't agree on new leadership. After some unseemly squabbling and intervention by Pete Rozelle, they made George Young, an assistant to Don Shula in Miami, the new general manager.

In Los Angeles, the headlines came in rapid succession. Early in the year, owner Carroll Rosenbloom sought and received permission from his fellow owners to move the Rams from the Los Angeles Coliseum to Anaheim Stadium in 1980. Although the geographical distance was not far, the citizens and leaders of Los Angeles raised the hue and cry against their "betrayal." In the spring, Rosenbloom drowned accidentally at his Florida home. Majority ownership went to his widow, Georgia, while his son Steve, a team executive, held a minority interest. The two Rosenblooms struggled bitterly for power, with Georgia finally firing Steve. Cast out by his stepmother, Steve found refuge as a high executive with the New Orleans Saints.

## EASTERN DIVISION

**Miami Dolphins**—Two heroes from the glorious past boosted the Dolphins back into first place in the East. Larry Csonka returned to Miami as a free agent after a four-year exile in the W.F.L. and in New Jersey with the Giants. Csonka's running power and a tough defense shot the Dolphins out to a fast start in the playoff race. Young nose tackle Bob Baumhower led the defense with an All-Star performance. A hamstring injury bothered quarterback Bob Griese at the start of the year, and when the offense faltered in mid-season, coach Don Shula turned to Don Strock to run the attack. On November 25, Shula brought Griese off the bench in the second quarter against the Colts. The veteran led the Dolphins to a 28-24 victory. Four days later, the Patriots came to Miami for a first-place showdown. Strock started the game but didn't generate much offense. Griese came into the fray in the second half, directing the offense to 26 points and a 39-24 triumph. The Dolphins then sewed up first place with an easy game against the Lions.

**New England Patriots**—As usual, the Patriots had mountains of talent ready to erupt into a championship. As usual, the Patriots sputtered far short of their goal. The offense had a great passing attack and a stable of good runners. The offensive line suffered from the trade of Leon Gray to the Oilers, but still enjoyed the talents of John Hannah. The defense combined a strong pass rush with a swarm of young blue-chip secondary men such as Mike Haynes. New coach Ron Erhardt had the Pats in first place in mid-November with an 8-4 record. On November 25, the Bills rocked the Patriots with a 16-13 overtime upset, dropping New England into a first-place tie with Miami. Against the Dolphins on the following Thursday night, the Pats blew a first half lead and dropped a 39-24 decision. With signs of choking in full view, the Patriots went to Shea Stadium in New York on December 9. The Pats had demolished the Jets 56-3 in September, but the Jets had the last laugh. They edged the Patriots 27-26 to kill any New England hopes for a playoff berth.

**New York Jets**—Despite last year's strong finish, coach Walt Michaels made basic changes in both his offensive and defensive units. Michaels reinstalled the 4-3 defense and manned it with a large class of promising rookies. Marty Lyons, Stan Blinka, Mike McKibben, and Johnny Lynn started for most of the campaign, while Mark Gastineau and Donald Dykes also saw considerable action. Unfortunately, the young defense was easy meat at first for enemy passers, allowing 56 points to the Patriots and 46 to the Bills in September. On the offense, Matt Robinson won the quarterback job in the pre-season, but jammed his thumb before the opening game. Richard Todd stepped in the second week as QB, and despite barrages of boos, stayed at the helm the rest of the season. With star receiver Wesley Walker out much of the time with injuries, the Jet attack concentrated on the ground. Marvin Powell and his line mates cleared the way for the unheralded Jet backs to lead the NFL in rushing yardage. With the offense taking charge, the Jets won their last three games to finish at .500 for the second straight year.

**Buffalo Bills**—The Bills lost the big fish, but reeled in several other prizes. They used their number-one position in the college draft to pick Ohio State linebacker Tom Cousineau, but the young star chose instead to play with Montreal in the Canadian Football League. Nevertheless, the Bills unveiled two other freshman gems in receiver Jerry Butler and linebacker Jim Haslett. Butler helped the offense to a blistering start, scoring 51 points against the Bengals and 46 points against the Jets in September. The aerial circus of Joe Ferguson, Frank Lewis, and Butler masked a weak running attack in the early going. Once defenses realized that Terry Miller and the other runners could be lightly covered, the Buffalo offense cooled off rapidly. The new 3-4 defense kept the Bills close to the top, only one game out of first place as December began. Three straight losses at the end of the schedule, however, finished any playoff ambitions.

**Baltimore Colts**—The Colts put on a better show off the field than on it. Owner Bob Irsay repeatedly threatened to move the Colts to another city because the state would not improve Municipal Stadium. He accused quarterback Bert Jones of malingering on the sidelines with a sore shoulder. He frequently threatened to fire coach Ted Marchibroda. When Toni Linhart missed three field goals on September 16, Irsay rewarded his efforts with a $10,000 raise, while Marchibroda put him on waivers the next day. On the field, as Bert Jones went, so went the Colts. Jones hurt his shoulder in an opening day loss to Kansas City, sitting out the next six games. With Greg Landry at QB, the Colts dropped five of those six games. Jones then returned to the field and led the Colts to consecutive victories over the Bills, Patriots, and Bengals. Jones reinjured his shoulder in the Bengals game and went out for the year. Landry came back and guided the team to five losses in the remaining six games.

## CENTRAL DIVISION

**Pittsburgh Steelers**—With four victories to open the season, the Steelers reasserted their dominance in the A.F.C. Occasional lapses, however, demonstrated their humanity and made them struggle to hold off challengers to their perch. Losses to the Eagles, Bengals, and Chargers dropped them into a first-place tie with Houston at 9-3. On November 25, they hosted the rising Cleveland Browns and went into overtime to take a 33-30 decision. One week later, they beat Cincinnati while the Oilers were losing. The Steelers thus took a one-game lead into the Astrodome for a Monday night confrontation on December 10. The physical Oilers outmuscled the Steelers and won the game 20-17, creating another tie going into the final weekend. The veteran Steelers geared up for the visiting Buffalo Bills. With habitual winners named Greene, Bradshaw, Harris, Swann, Stallworth, Greenwood, Lambert, Shell, and Webster on the job, the Steelers throttled Buffalo 28-0 to retain first place for another year.

**Houston Oilers**—Bum Phillips and his troops kept banging at the throne room door, but the Steelers wouldn't open up. Earl Campbell charged his way to a second rushing title in two years, leading an offense which suffered because of Dan Pastorini's bad shoulder. Leon Gray beefed up the blocking after arriving in a trade with New England. Age chipped away at the front line of the defense, but Robert Brazile and Mike Reinfeldt kept the back lines in top order. An early confrontation with the Steelers ended in a disappointing 38-7 loss, but the Oilers stayed on the heels of their quarry. They climbed into a first-place tie with the Steelers in November but dropped off the pace by losing to the Browns 14-7 on December 2. One week later, they launched a savage pass rush to beat the Steelers 20-17. To take first place on the final weekend, the Oilers had to beat the Eagles while the Steelers lost to the Bills. Instead, Pittsburgh won, Houston lost, and the Oilers again went into the playoffs as a wild-card team.

**Cleveland Browns**—The Browns began the season with a 25-22 overtime victory over the Jets, with Don Cockroft kicking field goals with four seconds left in regulation time and with 15 seconds left in overtime. They then beat the Chiefs 27-24 on a touchdown pass with 57 seconds left on the clock. One week later, Cockroft booted a field goal with under two minutes left for a 13-10 triumph over the Colts. On September 24, the Browns blew out the Cowboys 26-7 on Monday night television. During that moment of victory, halfback Greg Pruitt injured a knee, and he never fully recovered. With their offensive ace sidelined, the Browns doggedly stayed in the race. Brian Sipe, Mike Pruitt, and Ozzie Newsome developed into top offensive weapons. The Browns bolstered the defense by obtaining end Lyle Alzado from Denver, but veteran tackle Jerry Sherk offset the gain by missing a lot of time with injuries. Thom Darden led a solid secondary. An overtime loss to the Steelers on November 25 severely hurt the Browns' playoff hopes. Although they rallied to beat Houston on December 2, the Raiders and Bengals beat the Browns in the final two games to seal their fate.

**Cincinnati Bengals**—Head coach Homer Rice led the Bengals to a strong finish last year, but he couldn't prevent a miserable beginning this year. The Bengals dropped their first six games before rising up to upset the Steelers 34-10. Although several of their losses were by close scores, the final standings would show only four victories for Cincinnati. The Bengal defense made enemy offenses healthy, with

FINAL TEAM STATISTICS

**OFFENSE**

| | BALT. | BUFF. | CIN. | CLEV. | DENV. | HOU. | K.C. | MIA. | N.E. | N.Y. J. | OAK. | PIT. | S.D. | SEA. |
|---|---|---|---|---|---|---|---|---|---|---|---|---|---|---|
| FIRST DOWNS: | | | | | | | | | | | | | | |
| Total | 291 | 252 | 289 | 350 | 306 | 268 | 241 | 297 | 318 | 299 | 321 | 337 | 330 | 315 |
| by Rushing | 97 | 83 | 138 | 125 | 130 | 149 | 122 | 126 | 132 | 153 | 102 | 141 | 114 | 121 |
| by Passing | 158 | 147 | 131 | 189 | 149 | 100 | 91 | 140 | 159 | 126 | 191 | 179 | 192 | 171 |
| by Penalty | 36 | 22 | 20 | 36 | 27 | 19 | 28 | 31 | 27 | 20 | 28 | 17 | 24 | 23 |
| RUSHING: | | | | | | | | | | | | | | |
| Number | 515 | 474 | 560 | 504 | 525 | 616 | 569 | 561 | 604 | 634 | 491 | 561 | 481 | 500 |
| Yards | 1674 | 1621 | 2329 | 2281 | 2036 | 2571 | 2316 | 2187 | 2252 | 2646 | 1763 | 2603 | 1668 | 1967 |
| Average Yards | 3.3 | 3.4 | 4.2 | 4.5 | 3.9 | 4.2 | 4.1 | 3.9 | 3.7 | 4.2 | 3.6 | 4.6 | 3.5 | 3.9 |
| Touchdowns | 12 | 11 | 23 | 16 | 13 | 24 | 18 | 19 | 16 | 23 | 13 | 25 | 25 | 24 |
| PASSING: | | | | | | | | | | | | | | |
| Attempts | 550 | 465 | 426 | 545 | 476 | 386 | 361 | 416 | 475 | 369 | 513 | 492 | 541 | 523 |
| Completions | 313 | 241 | 228 | 289 | 260 | 195 | 190 | 235 | 237 | 190 | 311 | 272 | 338 | 292 |
| Completion Pct. | 56.9 | 51.8 | 53.5 | 53.0 | 54.6 | 50.5 | 52.6 | 56.5 | 49.9 | 51.5 | 60.6 | 55.3 | 62.5 | 55.8 |
| Passing Yards | 3575 | 3603 | 2821 | 3838 | 3433 | 2494 | 1953 | 3018 | 3600 | 2864 | 3704 | 3877 | 4138 | 3791 |
| Avg. Yds per Att. | 5.3 | 6.3 | 4.7 | 5.9 | 6.0 | 5.4 | 4.1 | 6.2 | 6.1 | 6.5 | 6.2 | 7.0 | 6.8 | 6.6 |
| Avg. Yds per Comp. | 11.4 | 15.0 | 12.4 | 13.3 | 13.2 | 12.8 | 10.3 | 12.8 | 15.2 | 15.1 | 11.9 | 14.3 | 12.2 | 13.0 |
| Times Tackled | 52 | 43 | 63 | 43 | 43 | 32 | 42 | 29 | 49 | 32 | 36 | 27 | 31 | 23 |
| Yds Lost Tackled | 403 | 387 | 511 | 347 | 327 | 238 | 293 | 255 | 382 | 266 | 293 | 222 | 223 | 201 |
| Net Yards | 3172 | 3216 | 2310 | 3491 | 3106 | 2256 | 1660 | 2763 | 3218 | 2598 | 3411 | 3655 | 3915 | 3590 |
| Touchdowns | 18 | 14 | 17 | 28 | 18 | 17 | 7 | 20 | 30 | 16 | 27 | 26 | 24 | 20 |
| Interceptions | 19 | 15 | 15 | 27 | 23 | 21 | 18 | 22 | 23 | 25 | 23 | 26 | 25 | 18 |
| Pct. Intercepted | 3.5 | 3.2 | 3.5 | 5.0 | 4.8 | 5.4 | 5.0 | 5.3 | 4.8 | 6.8 | 4.5 | 5.3 | 4.6 | 3.4 |
| PUNTS: | | | | | | | | | | | | | | |
| Number | 101 | 96 | 91 | 71 | 89 | 93 | 90 | 71 | 84 | 73 | 70 | 68 | 75 | 70 |
| Average | 36.2 | 38.2 | 40.4 | 40.1 | 39.9 | 40.6 | 43.1 | 39.5 | 36.2 | 40.8 | 42.0 | 40.2 | 36.5 | 38.4 |
| PUNT RETURNS: | | | | | | | | | | | | | | |
| Number | 49 | 38 | 42 | 41 | 43 | 38 | 58 | 34 | 37 | 36 | 35 | 63 | 52 | 34 |
| Yards | 391 | 318 | 316 | 345 | 401 | 221 | 612 | 337 | 311 | 314 | 179 | 523 | 488 | 281 |
| Average Yards | 8.0 | 8.4 | 7.5 | 8.4 | 9.3 | 5.8 | 10.6 | 9.9 | 8.4 | 8.7 | 5.1 | 8.3 | 9.4 | 8.3 |
| Touchdowns | 1 | 0 | 0 | 0 | 0 | 0 | 2 | 1 | 1 | 0 | 0 | 0 | 0 | 0 |
| KICKOFF RET.: | | | | | | | | | | | | | | |
| Number | 70 | 59 | 81 | 75 | 50 | 67 | 51 | 51 | 66 | 76 | 65 | 51 | 50 | 70 |
| Yards | 1402 | 1131 | 1560 | 1531 | 966 | 1234 | 1004 | 1148 | 1239 | 1561 | 1475 | 987 | 1066 | 1444 |
| Average Yards | 20.0 | 19.2 | 19.3 | 20.4 | 19.3 | 18.4 | 19.7 | 22.5 | 18.8 | 20.5 | 22.7 | 19.4 | 21.3 | 20.6 |
| Touchdowns | 0 | 0 | 0 | 0 | 0 | 0 | 0 | 0 | 0 | 0 | 1 | 0 | 0 | 0 |
| INTERCEPT RET.: | | | | | | | | | | | | | | |
| Number | 23 | 24 | 20 | 16 | 19 | 34 | 23 | 23 | 20 | 21 | 24 | 27 | 28 | 17 |
| Yards | 382 | 370 | 260 | 278 | 189 | 618 | 437 | 285 | 352 | 239 | 313 | 200 | 562 | 284 |
| Average Yards | 16.6 | 15.4 | 13.0 | 17.4 | 9.9 | 18.2 | 19.0 | 12.4 | 17.6 | 11.4 | 13.0 | 7.4 | 20.1 | 16.7 |
| Touchdowns | 1 | 2 | 1 | 1 | 0 | 1 | 1 | 0 | 1 | 2 | 3 | 1 | 2 | 1 |
| PENALTIES: | | | | | | | | | | | | | | |
| Number | 137 | 104 | 88 | 83 | 116 | 109 | 108 | 79 | 99 | 109 | 119 | 108 | 108 | 104 |
| Yards | 12.39 | 887 | 744 | 709 | 996 | 947 | 971 | 651 | 864 | 876 | 1024 | 866 | 908 | 903 |
| FUMBLES: | | | | | | | | | | | | | | |
| Number | 36 | 32 | 24 | 29 | 34 | 31 | 31 | 27 | 29 | 26 | 34 | 47 | 31 | 31 |
| Number Lost | 21 | 19 | 14 | 17 | 17 | 11 | 18 | 15 | 16 | 13 | 15 | 26 | 10 | 18 |
| POINTS: | | | | | | | | | | | | | | |
| Total | 271 | 268 | 337 | 359 | 289 | 362 | 238 | 341 | 411 | 337 | 365 | 416 | 411 | 378 |
| PAT Attempts | 33 | 30 | 43 | 44 | 36 | 43 | 29 | 40 | 49 | 42 | 45 | 52 | 52 | 46 |
| PAT Made | 31 | 25 | 40 | 38 | 32 | 41 | 28 | 36 | 46 | 35 | 41 | 50 | 47 | 43 |
| FG Attempts | 28 | 33 | 23 | 29 | 21 | 25 | 23 | 29 | 33 | 30 | 27 | 30 | 26 | 23 |
| FG Made | 14 | 21 | 13 | 17 | 13 | 21 | 12 | 21 | 23 | 16 | 18 | 18 | 16 | 19 |
| Percent FG Made | 50.0 | 63.6 | 56.5 | 58.6 | 61.9 | 84.0 | 52.2 | 72.4 | 69.7 | 53.3 | 66.7 | 60.0 | 61.5 | 82.6 |
| Safeties | 0 | 0 | 0 | 0 | 1 | 0 | 0 | 1 | 1 | 1 | 0 | 0 | 2 | 1 |

**DEFENSE**

| | BALT. | BUFF. | CIN. | CLEV. | DENV. | HOU. | K.C. | MIA. | N.E. | N.Y. J. | OAK. | PIT. | S.D. | SEA. |
|---|---|---|---|---|---|---|---|---|---|---|---|---|---|---|
| FIRST DOWNS: | | | | | | | | | | | | | | |
| Total | 265 | 273 | 334 | 307 | 273 | 304 | 297 | 238 | 283 | 331 | 319 | 260 | 268 | 350 |
| by Rushing | 106 | 137 | 133 | 136 | 100 | 125 | 102 | 87 | 118 | 107 | 137 | 95 | 117 | 146 |
| by Passing | 130 | 117 | 175 | 158 | 146 | 158 | 169 | 135 | 139 | 198 | 150 | 135 | 132 | 171 |
| by Penalty | 29 | 19 | 26 | 13 | 27 | 21 | 26 | 16 | 26 | 26 | 32 | 30 | 19 | 33 |
| RUSHING: | | | | | | | | | | | | | | |
| Number | 559 | 617 | 528 | 577 | 502 | 522 | 522 | 484 | 495 | 502 | 534 | 506 | 475 | 533 |
| Yards | 2306 | 2481 | 2219 | 2604 | 1693 | 2225 | 1847 | 1702 | 1770 | 1706 | 2374 | 1709 | 1907 | 2375 |
| Average Yards | 4.1 | 4.0 | 4.2 | 4.5 | 3.4 | 4.3 | 3.5 | 3.5 | 3.6 | 3.4 | 4.4 | 3.4 | 4.0 | 4.5 |
| Touchdowns | 15 | 18 | 22 | 25 | 16 | 19 | 8 | 9 | 22 | 13 | 17 | 9 | 19 | 23 |
| PASSING: | | | | | | | | | | | | | | |
| Attempts | 411 | 382 | 492 | 468 | 512 | 465 | 528 | 418 | 467 | 570 | 471 | 480 | 472 | 508 |
| Completions | 203 | 193 | 275 | 271 | 296 | 242 | 296 | 230 | 246 | 339 | 247 | 226 | 261 | 317 |
| Completion Pct. | 49.4 | 50.5 | 55.9 | 57.9 | 57.8 | 52.0 | 56.1 | 55.0 | 52.7 | 59.5 | 52.4 | 47.1 | 55.3 | 62.4 |
| Passing Yards | 3080 | 2713 | 3908 | 3289 | 3321 | 3186 | 3404 | 3051 | 3065 | 4288 | 3366 | 2912 | 2881 | 3739 |
| Avg. Yds per Att. | 6.2 | 6.3 | 7.1 | 6.1 | 6.0 | 5.4 | 5.5 | 6.0 | 4.9 | 7.0 | 6.2 | 4.8 | 5.0 | 6.4 |
| Avg. Yds per Comp. | 15.2 | 14.1 | 14.2 | 12.1 | 11.2 | 13.2 | 11.5 | 13.3 | 12.5 | 12.7 | 13.6 | 12.9 | 11.0 | 11.8 |
| Times Tackled | 39 | 23 | 32 | 31 | 19 | 51 | 38 | 36 | 57 | 22 | 33 | 49 | 42 | 37 |
| Yds Lost Tackled | 312 | 183 | 216 | 243 | 162 | 421 | 280 | 314 | 512 | 173 | 254 | 351 | 332 | 280 |
| Net Yards | 2768 | 2530 | 3692 | 3046 | 3159 | 2765 | 3124 | 2737 | 2553 | 4115 | 3112 | 2561 | 2549 | 3459 |
| Touchdowns | 23 | 14 | 27 | 14 | 11 | 18 | 22 | 17 | 13 | 31 | 21 | 19 | 11 | 21 |
| Interceptions | 23 | 24 | 20 | 16 | 19 | 34 | 23 | 23 | 20 | 21 | 24 | 27 | 28 | 17 |
| Pct. Intercepted | 5.6 | 6.3 | 4.1 | 3.4 | 3.7 | 7.3 | 4.4 | 5.5 | 4.3 | 3.7 | 5.1 | 5.6 | 5.9 | 3.3 |
| PUNTS: | | | | | | | | | | | | | | |
| Number | 95 | 92 | 71 | 80 | 88 | 73 | 88 | 77 | 94 | 69 | 63 | 100 | 83 | 69 |
| Average | 40.0 | 38.2 | 39.6 | 41.4 | 42.1 | 41.0 | 38.8 | 37.9 | 38.7 | 36.6 | 37.7 | 40.0 | 40.7 | 37.9 |
| PUNT RETURNS: | | | | | | | | | | | | | | |
| Number | 43 | 61 | 48 | 45 | 52 | 64 | 49 | 25 | 28 | 33 | 40 | 31 | 34 | 42 |
| Yards | 296 | 555 | 325 | 375 | 480 | 726 | 315 | 131 | 317 | 260 | 416 | 276 | 204 | 289 |
| Average Yards | 6.9 | 9.1 | 6.8 | 8.3 | 9.2 | 11.3 | 6.4 | 5.2 | 11.3 | 7.9 | 10.4 | 8.9 | 6.0 | 6.9 |
| Touchdowns | 1 | 1 | 0 | 0 | 0 | 1 | 0 | 0 | 1 | 0 | 1 | 0 | 0 | 0 |
| KICKOFF RET.: | | | | | | | | | | | | | | |
| Number | 57 | 54 | 63 | 70 | 57 | 69 | 51 | 69 | 80 | 70 | 67 | 81 | 72 | 70 |
| Yards | 1065 | 1142 | 1258 | 1324 | 1173 | 1310 | 1017 | 1518 | 1621 | 1529 | 1290 | 1668 | 1535 | 1238 |
| Average Yards | 18.7 | 21.1 | 20.0 | 18.9 | 20.6 | 19.0 | 19.9 | 22.0 | 20.3 | 21.8 | 19.3 | 20.6 | 21.3 | 17.7 |
| Touchdowns | 0 | 0 | 0 | 0 | 1 | 0 | 0 | 0 | 0 | 1 | 0 | 0 | 1 | 0 |
| INTERCEPT RET.: | | | | | | | | | | | | | | |
| Number | 19 | 15 | 15 | 27 | 23 | 21 | 18 | 22 | 23 | 25 | 23 | 26 | 25 | 18 |
| Yards | 321 | 161 | 305 | 315 | 291 | 290 | 209 | 382 | 417 | 414 | 473 | 401 | 279 | 185 |
| Average Yards | 16.9 | 10.7 | 20.3 | 11.7 | 12.7 | 13.8 | 11.6 | 17.4 | 18.1 | 16.6 | 20.6 | 15.4 | 11.2 | 10.3 |
| Touchdowns | 1 | 0 | 2 | 1 | 1 | 1 | 0 | 3 | 0 | 0 | 3 | 1 | 1 | 1 |
| PENALTIES: | | | | | | | | | | | | | | |
| Number | 112 | 106 | 101 | 118 | 118 | 103 | 118 | 107 | 102 | 98 | 106 | 94 | 100 | 117 |
| Yards | 1014 | 788 | 871 | 1018 | 1033 | 920 | 1018 | 834 | 902 | 888 | 1018 | 732 | 812 | 1045 |
| FUMBLES: | | | | | | | | | | | | | | |
| Number | 25 | 31 | 39 | 38 | 30 | 29 | 34 | 29 | 35 | 34 | 35 | 32 | 30 | 39 |
| Number Lost | 16 | 17 | 24 | 16 | 18 | 16 | 14 | 15 | 23 | 19 | 22 | 15 | 18 | 16 |
| POINTS: | | | | | | | | | | | | | | |
| Total | 351 | 279 | 421 | 352 | 262 | 331 | 262 | 257 | 326 | 383 | 337 | 262 | 246 | 372 |
| PAT Attempts | 42 | 34 | 52 | 42 | 31 | 40 | 32 | 30 | 39 | 46 | 43 | 31 | 32 | 46 |
| PAT Made | 37 | 27 | 49 | 34 | 31 | 37 | 31 | 26 | 36 | 39 | 39 | 28 | 28 | 42 |
| FG Attempts | 28 | 31 | 27 | 35 | 26 | 28 | 21 | 26 | 26 | 29 | 22 | 26 | 12 | 29 |
| FG Made | 20 | 16 | 20 | 22 | 15 | 18 | 13 | 15 | 18 | 22 | 12 | 16 | 8 | 18 |
| Percent FG Made | 71.4 | 51.6 | 74.1 | 62.9 | 57.7 | 64.3 | 61.9 | 57.7 | 69.2 | 75.9 | 54.5 | 61.5 | 66.7 | 62.1 |
| Safeties | 1 | 0 | 0 | 0 | 0 | 0 | 0 | 0 | 1 | 1 | 2 | 0 | 1 | 0 |

their pass defense particularly heartening to quarterbacks. On offense, Ken Anderson directed one of the worst passing attacks in the NFL. The Bengals had cause for hope in rookies Jack Thompson, Charles Alexander, and Dan Ross, but for Rice, it was exit, stage left.

## WESTERN DIVISION

**San Diego Chargers**—Air Coryell began regular service this year. Known for his exciting offenses in St. Louis, coach Don Coryell gave quarterback Dan Fouts a mandate to throw the ball endlessly. At the end of the season, Fouts had a new NFL record for passing yardage in a season, and the Chargers had captured first place in the West. Fouts had two superb targets in fleet receivers Charlie Joiner and John Jefferson. Rookie tight end Kellen Winslow provided a third receiving threat until he broke a leg in October. Coryell made some adjustments on his defensive unit. He obtained cornerback Willie Buchanon from the Packers to shore up the secondary, and when tackle Louie Kelcher injured a knee in pre-season, Coryell inserted veteran Wilbur Young into the starting lineup. Young played the best ball of his career and combined with Fred Dean as a ferocious pass rushing duo. A stretch run of six victories in seven weeks, including victories over Pittsburgh and Denver, wrapped up the trip to the playoffs.

**Denver Broncos**—The Orange Crush wasn't the same after Lyle Alzado was shipped to Cleveland because of a salary dispute. Although the defense featured stars like Randy Gradishar, Louie Wright, and Bill Thompson, it could not pressure passers as it had in the past. Nevertheless, the Broncos had bigger problems on offense. Coach Red Miller made Norris Weese his starting quarterback, but after six weeks of sporadic offense, Miller reinstalled Craig Morton as his starter. Despite their weaknesses, the Broncos held a share of first place until December 8, when the Seahawks beat them 28-23. On the final weekend, the Broncos journeyed to San Diego and were whipped 17-7. Only a loss by Oakland during the weekend salvaged a wild-card berth for the Bronks, who lost two games in a row for the first time ever under coach Miller.

**Oakland Raiders**—Tom Flores had a tough act to follow, and he stumbled on his entrance. Despite missing out on the playoffs last season, the John Madden years harvested glory and excellence. With Flores the new head coach, the Raiders lost three of their first four games. The veteran Oakland defense then strung together several outstanding performances and put the Raiders back into the playoff chase. Flores tinkered with his offense, installing a double tight end offense in mid-season. With two stars in Dave Casper and Ray Chester, the new arrangement controlled the ball for long stretches of time. Any playoff hopes looked dead when the Raiders lost to the Chiefs 24-21 on November 18, dropping them to 6-6. Valiantly, the Raiders then beat Denver, New Orleans, and Cleveland to put themselves in a long shot position to win a wild-card berth on the final weekend. It wasn't to be, as the Seahawks ended the dream with a 29-24 upset.

**Seattle Seahawks**—The Seahawks carted a three-ring circus around the league, combining high-wire thrills with clownish pratfalls. Preseason experts labeled the young Seattle squad as playoff contenders, but a 1-4 start showed that they were not yet ready for such heady circles. To go with a porous defense, coach Jack Patera fielded a daring offense which flirted with greatness. The Seahawks frequently delighted their fans by going for the yardage on fourth down, and fake field goals stood the fans up several times during the season. On October 29, the Seahawks beat the Falcons 31-28 by using a quarterback draw on fourth-and-five, an onside kick, and a 20 yard pass play to kicker Efren Herrera on a fake field goal. Six days later, the Rams held the Seahawks to a total offense of minus seven yards in a 24-0 smothering. Seattle played with enough consistency to win five of its last six games. On December 8, the Seahawks beat Denver 28-23 to knock the Broncos out of first place. Eight days later, Jim Zorn threw for 314 yards in a 29-24 victory which ended Oakland's playoff hopes and gave the Seahawks their second winning season.

**Kansas City Chiefs**—Marv Levy's rebuilding plan showed results, as the Chiefs won four of their first six games and held on to finish at a respectable 7-9. The miserable defense which Levy had inherited had improved rapidly, as shown by a 14-0 opening victory over the Colts and five other games in which the enemy scored under 10 points. The offense had less to show for its efforts, but rookie quarterback Steve Fuller held out promise for the future. On the special teams, rookie Bob Grupp led the N.F.L. in punting, and J.T. Smith broke two punt returns open for touchdowns.

## MIAMI DOLPHINS 10-6-0 Don Shula

| Scores of Each Game | | |
|---|---|---|
| 9 | Buffalo | 7 |
| 19 | SEATTLE | 10 |
| 27 | Minnesota | 12 |
| 31 | CHICAGO | 16 |
| 27 | N.Y. Jets | 33 |
| 3 | Oakland | 13 |
| 17 | BUFFALO | 7 |
| 13 | New England | 28 |
| 27 | GREEN BAY | 7 |
| 6 | HOUSTON | 9 |
| 19 | BALTIMORE | 0 |
| 24 | Cleveland | *30 |
| 28 | Baltimore | 24 |
| 39 | NEW ENGLAND | 24 |
| 28 | Detroit | 10 |
| 24 | N.Y. JETS | 27 |

| Use Name | Pos. | Hgt. | Wgt. | Age | Int. | Pts. |
|---|---|---|---|---|---|---|
| Mike Current | OT | 6'4" | 270 | 33 | | |
| Jon Giesler | OT | 6'5" | 255 | 22 | | |
| Cleveland Green | OT | 6'3" | 265 | 21 | | |
| Bob Kuechenberg | OT-OG | 6'3" | 255 | 31 | | |
| Eric Laasko | OG-OT | 6'4" | 265 | 22 | | |
| Larry Little | OG-OT | 6'1" | 265 | 33 | | |
| Ed Newman | OG | 6'2" | 245 | 28 | | |
| Jeff Toews | OG-C | 6'3" | 255 | 21 | | |
| Mark Dennard | C | 6'1" | 250 | 23 | | |
| Jim Langer | C | 6'2" | 257 | 31 | | |
| Doug Betters | DE | 6'7" | 250 | 23 | | |
| Vern Den Herder | DE-NT | 6'6" | 252 | 30 | | |
| A.J. Duhe | DE | 6'4" | 247 | 23 | | |
| Carl Barisch | NT | 6'4" | 255 | 28 | | |
| Bob Baumhower | NT | 6'5" | 258 | 24 | | |
| Kim Bokamper | LB | 6'6" | 245 | 24 | 1 | |
| Rusty Chambers | LB | 6'1" | 220 | 25 | 1 | |
| Larry Gordon | LB | 6'4" | 230 | 26 | 2 | |
| Mel Land | LB | 6'3" | 243 | 23 | | |
| Bob Matheson | LB | 6'4" | 235 | 34 | 1 | |
| Ralph Ortega | LB | 6'2" | 220 | 26 | | |
| Earnest Rhone | LB | 6'2" | 226 | 26 | 2 | |
| Steve Towle | LB | 6'2" | 233 | 25 | 1 | |
| Charlie Babb | DB | 6' | 190 | 29 | 1 | |
| Doug Bessillieu | DB | 6'1" | 199 | 23 | | |
| Glenn Blackwood | DB | 6' | 183 | 22 | | |
| Neal Colzie | DB | 6'2" | 190 | 26 | 5 | |
| Tim Foley | DB | 6' | 194 | 31 | 2 | |
| Mike Kozlowski | DB | 6' | 187 | 23 | | |
| Gerald Small | DB | 5'11" | 187 | 23 | 5 | |
| Ed Taylor (from NYJ) | DB | 6' | 175 | 26 | | |
| Norris Thomas | DB | 5'11" | 175 | 26 | 2 | |
| Guy Benjamin | QB | 6'4" | 210 | 24 | | |
| Bob Griese | QB | 6'1" | 190 | 34 | | |
| Don Strock | QB | 6'5" | 220 | 28 | | |
| Gary Davis | HB | 5'10" | 202 | 24 | | 6 |
| Tony Nathan | HB-FB | 6' | 201 | 22 | | 18 |
| Del Williams | HB | 6' | 195 | 28 | | 24 |
| Norm Bulaich | FB-HB | 6'1" | 212 | 32 | | 18 |
| Larry Csonka | FB | 6'3" | 235 | 32 | | 78 |
| Steve Howell | FB-TE | 6'2" | 222 | 22 | | |
| Bob Torrey (from NYG) | FB | 6'4" | 230 | 22 | | 6 |
| Jimmy Cefalo | WR | 5'11" | 190 | 22 | | 18 |
| Duriel Harris | WR | 5'11" | 180 | 24 | | 18 |
| Nat Moore | WR | 5'9" | 180 | 27 | | 36 |
| Bruce Hardy | TE-QB | 6'5" | 235 | 23 | | 18 |
| Ronnie Lee | TE | 6'3" | 242 | 22 | | |
| George Roberts | K | 6' | 172 | 24 | | |
| Uwe von Schamann | K | 6' | 200 | 23 | | 99 |

Bo Rather – Injury
Andre Tillman – Broken Leg

## NEW ENGLAND PATRIOTS 9-7-0 Ron Erhardt

| Scores of Each Game | | |
|---|---|---|
| 13 | PITTSBURGH | *16 |
| 56 | N.Y. JETS | 3 |
| 20 | Cincinnati | 14 |
| 27 | SAN DIEGO | 21 |
| 14 | Green Bay | 27 |
| 24 | DETROIT | 17 |
| 27 | Chicago | 7 |
| 28 | MIAMI | 13 |
| 26 | Baltimore | 31 |
| 26 | Buffalo | 6 |
| 10 | Denver | 45 |
| 50 | BALTIMORE | 21 |
| 13 | BUFFALO | *16 |
| 24 | Miami | 39 |
| 26 | N.Y. Jets | 27 |
| 27 | MINNESOTA | 23 |

| Use Name | Pos. | Hgt. | Wgt. | Age | Int. | Pts. |
|---|---|---|---|---|---|---|
| Shelby Jordan | OT | 6'7" | 260 | 27 | | |
| Gary Puetz (from PHI) | OT-OG | 6'4" | 265 | 27 | | |
| Dwight Wheeler | OT | 6'3" | 255 | 24 | | |
| Sam Adams | OG | 6'3" | 260 | 30 | | |
| Bob Cryder | OG | 6'4" | 265 | 22 | | |
| Terry Falcon | OG | 6'3" | 260 | 24 | | |
| John Hannah | OG | 6'2" | 265 | 28 | | |
| Pete Brock | C-OT-OG-TE | 6'5" | 260 | 25 | | |
| Bill Lenkaitis | C | 6'3" | 255 | 33 | | |
| Julius Adams | DE | 6'3" | 263 | 31 | | |
| Richard Bishop | DE-NT | 6'1" | 260 | 29 | | |
| Mark Buben | DE-NT | 6'3" | 260 | 22 | | |
| Mel Lunsford | DE-NT | 6'3" | 260 | 29 | | |
| Tony McGee | DE | 6'4" | 250 | 30 | | |
| Ray Hamilton | NT | 6'1" | 245 | 28 | | |
| Ray Costict | LB | 6' | 218 | 24 | 1 | |
| Bob Golic | LB | 6'2 | 240 | 21 | | |
| Mike Hawkins | LB | 6'2" | 232 | 23 | 2 | 6 |
| Sam Hunt | LB | 6'1" | 253 | 28 | | |
| Steve Kiner | LB | 6'4" | 230 | 28 | | |
| Bill Matthews | LB | 6'2" | 235 | 23 | | |
| Steve Nelson | LB | 6'2" | 230 | 28 | 1 | |
| Rod Shoate | LB | 6'1" | 215 | 26 | 1 | |
| John Zamberlin | LB | 6'2" | 232 | 23 | | |
| Doug Beaudoin | DB | 6'1" | 190 | 25 | 1 | |
| Ray Clayborn | DB | 6'1" | 190 | 24 | 5 | |
| Dick Conn | DB | 6' | 180 | 28 | | |
| Tim Fox | DB | 5'11" | 190 | 25 | 2 | |
| Mike Haynes | DB | 6'2" | 195 | 26 | 3 | |
| Prentice McCray | DB | 6'1" | 190 | 28 | 3 | |
| Rick Sanford | DB | 6'1" | 192 | 22 | 1 | 6 |
| Mark Washington | DB | 5'10" | 187 | 31 | | |
| Matt Cavanaugh | QB | 6'1" | 210 | 22 | | |
| Steve Grogan | QB | 6'4" | 208 | 26 | | 12 |
| Tom Owen | QB | 6'1" | 194 | 26 | | |
| Horace Ivory | HB | 6' | 198 | 25 | | 18 |
| Allan Clark | HB | 5'10" | 186 | 22 | | 12 |
| Andy Johnson | HB | 6' | 204 | 26 | | 6 |
| Don Calhoun | FB-HB | 6' | 212 | 27 | | 36 |
| Sam Cunningham | FB | 6'3" | 230 | 29 | | 30 |
| Mosi Tatupu | FB | 6' | 229 | 24 | | |
| Harold Jackson | WR | 5'10" | 175 | 33 | | 42 |
| Ray Jarvis | WR | 5'11" | 190 | 30 | | 6 |
| Stanley Morgan | WR | 5'10" | 180 | 24 | | 18 |
| Carlos Pennywell | WR | 6'2" | 180 | 23 | | 6 |
| Don Westbrook | WR | 5'10" | 184 | 26 | | 6 |
| Russ Francis | TE | 6'6" | 242 | 26 | | 30 |
| Don Hasselbeck | TE | 6'7" | 245 | 25 | | |
| Eddie Hare | K | 6'4" | 209 | 22 | | |
| John Smith | K | 6' | 185 | 29 | | **115** |

Sidney Brown–Injury

## NEW YORK JETS 8-8-0 Walt Michaels

| Scores of Each Game | | |
|---|---|---|
| 22 | CLEVELAND | *25 |
| 3 | New England | 56 |
| 31 | DETROIT | 10 |
| 31 | Buffalo | 46 |
| 33 | MIAMI | 27 |
| 8 | Baltimore | 10 |
| 14 | MINNESOTA | 7 |
| 28 | OAKLAND | 19 |
| 24 | Houston | *27 |
| 27 | Green Bay | 22 |
| 12 | BUFFALO | 14 |
| 13 | Chicago | 23 |
| 7 | Seattle | 30 |
| 30 | BALTIMORE | 17 |
| 27 | NEW ENGLAND | 26 |
| 27 | Miami | 24 |

| Use Name | Pos. | Hgt. | Wgt. | Age | Int. | Pts. |
|---|---|---|---|---|---|---|
| Marvin Powell | OT | 6'5" | 268 | 24 | | |
| John Roman | OT | 6'4" | 251 | 27 | | |
| Chris Ward | OT | 6'3" | 270 | 23 | | |
| Dan Alexander | OG | 6'4" | 255 | 24 | | |
| Eric Cunningham | OG | 6'3" | 257 | 22 | | |
| Randy Rasmussen | OG | 6'2" | 255 | 34 | | |
| Stan Waldemore | OG-OT-C | 6'4" | 257 | 24 | | |
| Joe Fields | C | 6'2" | 253 | 25 | | |
| Ed McGlasson | C | 6'4" | 248 | 23 | | |
| Mark Gastineau | DE | 6'5" | 257 | 22 | | |
| Marty Lyons | DE | 6'5" | 245 | 22 | | |
| Lawrence Pillers | DE | 6'3" | 260 | 26 | | |
| Joe Klecko | DT | 6'3" | 262 | 25 | | |
| Joe Pellegrini | DT | 6'2" | 266 | 23 | | |
| Abdul Salaam | DT | 6'3" | 260 | 26 | | |
| Bob Winkel | DT-DE | 6'4" | 246 | 23 | | |
| Stan Blinka | LB | 6'2" | 230 | 22 | 2 | |
| Greg Buttle | LB | 6'3" | 232 | 25 | 2 | |
| Ron Crosby | LB | 6'3" | 225 | 24 | | |
| John Hennessy | LB-DE | 6'3" | 236 | 24 | | |
| Mike McKibben | LB | 6'3" | 228 | 22 | 1 | |
| John Sullivan | LB | 6'1" | 221 | 22 | | |
| Donald Dykes | DB | 5'11" | 188 | 24 | | |
| Bobby Jackson | DB | 5'9" | 175 | 22 | 4 | 6 |
| Johnny Lynn | DB | 6' | 190 | 22 | 2 | 6 |
| Tim Moresco | DB | 5'11" | 180 | 24 | | 2 |
| Burgess Owens | DB | 6'2" | 200 | 28 | 6 | |
| Ken Schroy | DB | 6'2" | 196 | 26 | 1 | |
| Shafer Suggs | DB | 6'1" | 204 | 26 | 3 | 6 |
| Pat Ryan | QB | 6'3" | 205 | 23 | | |
| Matt Robinson | QB | 6'2" | 198 | 24 | | 6 |
| Richard Todd | QB | 6'2" | 203 | 25 | | 30 |
| Woody Bennett | HB | 6'2" | 217 | 24 | | 6 |
| Scott Dierking | HB-FB | 5'10" | 215 | 24 | | 18 |
| Bruce Harper | HB | 65'8" | 177 | 24 | | 12 |
| Clark Gaines | FB-HB | 6'2" | 209 | 25 | | |
| Kevin Long | FB-HB | 6'1" | 214 | 24 | | 42 |
| Tom Newton | FB | 6' | 213 | 25 | | 36 |
| Paul Darby | WR | 5'10" | 192 | 22 | | |
| Roger Farmer | WR | 6'3" | 195 | 23 | | |
| Derrick Gaffney | WR | 6'1" | 180 | 24 | | 6 |
| Bobby Jones | WR | 5'11" | 180 | 24 | | 6 |
| Wesley Walker | WR | 6' | 175 | 24 | | 30 |
| Jerome Barkum | TE | 6'3" | 225 | 29 | | 24 |
| Bob Raba | TE | 6'1" | 225 | 24 | | |
| Mickey Shuler | TE | 6'3" | 229 | 23 | | 18 |
| Dave Jacobs | K | 5'7" | 151 | 22 | | 25 |
| Pat Leahy | K | 6' | 195 | 28 | | 36 |
| Toni Linhart | K | 6' | 179 | 37 | | 32 |
| Chuck Ramsey | K | 6'2" | 189 | 27 | | |
| Richie Szaro | K | 5'11" | 204 | 31 | | 2 |

Larry Keller – Knee Injury
Mike Hennigan – Knee Injury
Mike Mock – Injury
Darnell Powell – Injury

## BUFFALO BILLS 7-9-0 Chuck Knox

| Scores of Each Game | | |
|---|---|---|
| 7 | MIAMI | 9 |
| 51 | CINCINNATI | 24 |
| 19 | San Diego | 27 |
| 46 | N.Y. JETS | 31 |
| 31 | Baltimore | 13 |
| 0 | CHICAGO | 7 |
| 7 | Miami | 17 |
| 13 | BALTIMOR | 14 |
| 20 | Detroit | 17 |
| 6 | NEW ENGLAND | 26 |
| 14 | N.Y. Jets | 12 |
| 19 | GREEN BAY | 12 |
| 16 | New England | *13 |
| 16 | DENVER | 19 |
| 3 | Minnesota | 10 |
| 0 | Pittsburgh | 28 |

| Use Name | Pos. | Hgt. | Wgt. | Age | Int. | Pts. |
|---|---|---|---|---|---|---|
| Jon Borchardt | OT | 6'5" | 255 | 22 | | |
| Joe Devlin | OT | 6'5" | 250 | 25 | | |
| Ken Jones | OT | 6'5" | 250 | 26 | | |
| Joe DeLamielleure | OG | 6'3" | 245 | 28 | | |
| Ed Fulton | OG | 6'3" | 250 | 24 | | |
| Reggie McKenzie | OG | 6'4" | 242 | 29 | | |
| Will Grant | C | 6'4" | 248 | 25 | | |
| Willie Parker | C | 6'3" | 245 | 30 | | |
| Tim Vogler | C-OG | 6'3" | 245 | 22 | | |
| Dee Hardison | DE-NT | 6'4" | 269 | 23 | | |
| Scott Hutchinson | DE | 6'4" | 243 | 23 | | |
| Ken Johnson | DE | 6'5" | 253 | 24 | | |
| Sherman White | DE | 6'5" | 250 | 30 | | |
| Ben Williams | DE-NT | 6'3" | 245 | 25 | | |
| Mike Kadish | NT | 6'5" | 270 | 29 | | |
| Fred Smerlas | NT | 6'3" | 270 | 22 | | 6 |
| Jim Haslett | LB | 6'3" | 232 | 23 | 2 | |
| Tom Higgins | LB | 6'1" | 235 | 25 | | |
| Dan Jilek | LB | 6'2" | 225 | 25 | | |
| Chris Keating | LB | 6'2" | 223 | 21 | | |
| Shane Nelson | LB | 6'1" | 225 | 24 | 1 | |
| Isiah Robertson | LB | 6'3" | 225 | 30 | 2 | 6 |
| Lucius Sanford | LB | 6'2" | 216 | 23 | 2 | 6 |
| Mario Clark | DB | 6'2" | 195 | 25 | 5 | |
| Steve Freeman | DB | 5'11" | 185 | 26 | 3 | 6 |
| Doug Greene | DB | 6'2" | 205 | 23 | 1 | |
| Tony Greene | DB | 5'10" | 175 | 30 | 1 | |
| Keith Moody | DB | 5'10" | 170 | 26 | | |
| Jeff Nixon | DB | 6'3" | 190 | 22 | 6 | |
| Charles Romes | DB | 6'1" | 190 | 25 | 1 | 6 |
| Joe Ferguson | QB | 6'1" | 195 | 29 | | 6 |
| Dan Manucci | QB | 6'2" | 194 | 21 | | |
| Bill Munson | QB | 6'2" | 205 | 38 | | |
| Roland Hooks | HB-FB | 6' | 195 | 26 | | 36 |
| Terry Miller | HB | 5'10" | 196 | 23 | | 6 |
| Steve Powell | HB | 5'11" | 186 | 23 | | |
| Curtis Brown | FB | 5'10" | 203 | 24 | | 24 |
| Mike Collier | FB | 5'11" | 200 | 25 | | 12 |
| Dennis Johnson | FB | 6'3" | 220 | 23 | | |
| Jerry Butler | WR | 6' | 178 | 21 | | 24 |
| Bob Chandler | WR | 6' | 180 | 30 | | |
| Dan Fulton | WR | 6'2" | 180 | 22 | | |
| Frank Lewis | WR | 6'1" | 196 | 32 | | 12 |
| Lou Piccone | WR | 5'9" | 175 | 30 | | 12 |
| Leonard Willis | WR | 5'11" | 185 | 26 | | |
| Reuben Gant | TE | 6'4" | 225 | 27 | | 12 |
| Ron Howard | TE | 6'4" | 230 | 28 | | |
| Joe Shipp | TE | 6'4" | 225 | 24 | | 6 |
| Tom Dempsey | K | 6'1" | 249 | 32 | | 11 |
| Rusty Jackson | K | 6'2" | 195 | 28 | | |
| Nick Mike-Mayer | K | 5'9" | 185 | 29 | | 17 |

Phil Dokes – Shoulder Injury
Tom Ehlers – Pinched Nerve
Mekeli Ieremia – Knee Injury
Connie Zelencik – Knee Injury
Phil Olsen – Knee Injury

## BALTIMORE COLTS 5-11-0 Ted Marchibroda

| Scores of Each Game | | |
|---|---|---|
| 0 | Kansas City | 14 |
| 26 | TAMPA BAY | *29 |
| 10 | Cleveland | 13 |
| 13 | Pittsburgh | 17 |
| 13 | BUFFALO | 31 |
| 10 | N.Y. JETS | 8 |
| 16 | HOUSTON | 28 |
| 14 | Buffalo | 13 |
| 31 | NEW ENGLAND | 26 |
| 38 | CINCINNATI | 28 |
| 0 | Miami | 19 |
| 21 | New England | 50 |
| 24 | MIAMI | 28 |
| 17 | N.Y. Jets | 30 |
| 7 | KANSAS CITY | 10 |
| 31 | N.Y. Giants | 7 |

| Use Name | Pos. | Hgt. | Wgt. | Age | Int. | Pts. |
|---|---|---|---|---|---|---|
| Wade Griffin | OT | 6'5" | 231 | 25 | | |
| Jeff Hart | OT | 6'5" | 263 | 23 | | |
| David Taylor | OT | 6'4" | 263 | 29 | | |
| Ron Baker | OG | 6'4" | 251 | 24 | | |
| Ken Huff | OG | 6'4" | 252 | 26 | | |
| Robert Pratt | OG | 6'4" | 246 | 28 | | |
| Bob Van Duyne | OG | 6'5" | 238 | 27 | | |
| Lee Gross | C | 6'3" | 235 | 26 | | |
| Ken Mendenhall | C | 6'3" | 248 | 31 | | |
| Fred Cook | DE | 6'3" | 243 | 27 | | |
| Ron Fernandes | DE | 6'4" | 258 | 27 | | |
| Greg Fields | DE | 6'7" | 256 | 24 | | |
| Mike Ozdowski | DE | 6'5" | 236 | 23 | | |
| Mike Barnes | DT | 6'6" | 256 | 28 | | |
| Joe Ehrmann | DT | 6'5" | 259 | 30 | | |
| Jim Krahl | DT | 6'5" | 252 | 23 | | |
| Herb Orvis | DT | 6'5" | 245 | 32 | | |
| Barry Krauss | LB | 6'3" | 238 | 22 | | |
| Sanders Shiver | LB | 6'2" | 228 | 24 | 4 | |
| Ed Simonini | LB | 6' | 214 | 25 | | |
| Stan White | LB | 6'1" | 225 | 29 | 1 | |
| Mike Woods | LB | 6'2" | 231 | 24 | | |
| Steve Zabel | LB | 6'4" | 228 | 31 | | |
| Lyle Blackwood | DB | 6' | 189 | 28 | 4 | |
| Larry Braziel | DB | 6' | 192 | 24 | 4 | 12 |
| Nesby Glasgow | DB | 5'10" | 182 | 22 | 1 | 6 |
| Dwight Harrison | DB | 6'1" | 186 | 30 | 2 | |
| Bruce Laird | DB | 6' | 197 | 29 | 3 | |
| Doug Nettles | DB | 6' | 184 | 28 | 2 | |
| Reggie Pinkney | DB | 5'11" | 186 | 24 | | |
| Norm Thompson | DB | 6'1" | 180 | 31 | 2 | |
| Bert Jones | QB | 6'3" | 201 | 27 | | 6 |
| Greg Landry | QB | 6'4" | 210 | 32 | | |
| Don McCauley | HB-FB | 6'1" | 208 | 30 | | 36 |
| Joe Washington | HB | 5'10" | 182 | 25 | | 42 |
| Cleveland Franklin | FB | 6'2" | 216 | 24 | | |
| Ben Garry | FB | 6' | 209 | 23 | | |
| Don Hardeman | FB | 6'2" | 235 | 27 | | 24 |
| Roosevelt Leaks | FB | 5'10" | 226 | 26 | | 6 |
| Randy Burke | WR | 6'2" | 186 | 24 | | |
| Roger Carr | WR | 6'3" | 198 | 27 | | 6 |
| Brian DeRoo | WR | 6'3" | 190 | 23 | | 6 |
| Glenn Doughty | WR | 6'1" | 204 | 28 | | 12 |
| Mike Siani | WR | 6'2" | 199 | 29 | | 12 |
| Mack Alston | TE | 6'2" | 232 | 32 | | 6 |
| Reese McCall | TE | 6'7" | 238 | 23 | | 24 |
| Bucky Dilts | K | 5'9" | 183 | 25 | | |
| Steve Mike-Mayer | K | 6' | 180 | 31 | | 61 |

Stu O'Dell – Injury
Dave Rowe – Arm Injury
Ron Lee – Back Injury
George Kunz – Voluntarily Retired

*—Overtime

## MIAMI DOLPHINS

### Rushing

| Last Name | No. | Yds. | Avg. | TD |
|---|---|---|---|---|
| Csonka | 220 | 837 | 3.8 | 12 |
| Williams | 184 | 703 | 3.8 | 3 |
| Davis | 98 | 383 | 3.9 | 1 |
| Nathan | 16 | 68 | 4.3 | 0 |
| Torrey | 13 | 61 | 4.7 | 1 |
| Bulaich | 9 | 37 | 4.1 | 2 |
| Griese | 11 | 30 | 2.7 | 0 |
| Moore | 3 | 22 | 7.3 | 0 |
| Harris | 1 | 20 | 20.0 | 0 |
| Strock | 3 | 18 | 6.0 | 0 |
| Howell | 3 | 8 | 2.7 | 0 |

### Receiving

| Last Name | No. | Yds. | Avg. | TD |
|---|---|---|---|---|
| Moore | 48 | 840 | 18 | 6 |
| Harris | 42 | 798 | 19 | 3 |
| Davis | 34 | 215 | 6 | 0 |
| Hardy | 30 | 386 | 13 | 3 |
| Williams | 21 | 175 | 8 | 1 |
| Nathan | 17 | 213 | 13 | 2 |
| Csonka | 16 | 75 | 5 | 1 |
| Cefalo | 12 | 223 | 19 | 3 |
| Bulaich | 8 | 53 | 7 | 1 |
| Howell | 3 | 23 | 8 | 0 |
| Lee | 2 | 14 | 7 | 0 |
| Torrey | 2 | 3 | 2 | 0 |

### Punt Returns

| Last Name | No. | Yds. | Avg. | TD |
|---|---|---|---|---|
| Nathan | 28 | 306 | 11 | 1 |
| Kozlowski | 3 | 21 | 7 | 0 |
| Cefalo | 2 | 10 | 5 | 0 |
| Babb | 1 | 0 | 0 | 0 |

### Kickoff Returns

| Last Name | No. | Yds. | Avg. | TD |
|---|---|---|---|---|
| Nathan | 45 | 1016 | 23 | 0 |
| Kozlowski | 4 | 85 | 21 | 0 |
| Davis | 2 | 27 | 14 | 0 |
| Bessillieu | 0 | 20 | — | 0 |

### Passing

| Last Name | Att. | Comp. | % | Yds. | Yd./Att. | TD | Int.-% | RK |
|---|---|---|---|---|---|---|---|---|
| Griese | 310 | 176 | 57 | 2160 | 7.0 | 14 | 16- 5 | 10 |
| Strock | 100 | 56 | 56 | 830 | 8.3 | 6 | 6- 6 | |
| Benjamin | 4 | 3 | 75 | 28 | 7.0 | 0 | 0- 0 | |
| Hardy | 1 | 0 | 0 | 0 | 0.0 | 0 | 0- 0 | |
| Williams | 1 | 0 | 0 | 0 | 0.0 | 0 | 0- 0 | |

### Punting

| Last Name | No. | Avg. |
|---|---|---|
| Roberts | 69 | 40.2 |
| von Schamann | 1 | 31.0 |

### Kicking

| Last Name | XP | Att. | % | FG | Att. | % |
|---|---|---|---|---|---|---|
| von Schamann | 36 | 40 | 90 | 21 | 29 | 72 |

## NEW ENGLAND PATRIOTS

### Rushing

| Last Name | No. | Yds. | Avg. | TD |
|---|---|---|---|---|
| Cunningham | 159 | 563 | 3.5 | 5 |
| Ivory | 143 | 522 | 3.7 | 1 |
| Calhoun | 137 | 456 | 3.3 | 5 |
| Grogan | 64 | 368 | 5.8 | 2 |
| Johnson | 43 | 132 | 3.1 | 1 |
| Clark | 19 | 84 | 4.4 | 2 |
| Tatupu | 23 | 71 | 3.1 | 0 |
| Morgan | 7 | 39 | 5.6 | 0 |
| Jacison | 3 | 12 | 4.0 | 0 |
| Westbrook | 2 | 8 | 4.0 | 0 |
| Hare | 1 | 0 | | 0 |
| Owen | 2 | -1 | -0.5 | 0 |
| Cavanaugh | 1 | -2 | -2.0 | 0 |

### Receiving

| Last Name | No. | Yds. | Avg. | TD |
|---|---|---|---|---|
| Jackson | 45 | 1013 | 23 | 7 |
| Morgan | 44 | 1002 | 23 | 12 |
| Francis | 39 | 557 | 14 | 5 |
| Cunningham | 29 | 236 | 8 | 0 |
| Ivory | 23 | 216 | 9 | 2 |
| Calhoun | 15 | 66 | 4 | 1 |
| Hasselbeck | 13 | 158 | 12 | 0 |
| Westbrook | 9 | 173 | 19 | 1 |
| Johnson | 9 | 68 | 8 | 0 |
| Pennywell | 4 | 35 | 9 | 1 |
| Clark | 2 | 35 | 18 | 0 |
| Jarvis | 2 | 30 | 15 | 0 |
| Tatupu | 2 | 9 | 5 | 0 |

### Punt Returns

| Last Name | No. | Yds. | Avg. | TD |
|---|---|---|---|---|
| Morgan | 29 | 289 | 10 | 1 |
| Haynes | 5 | 16 | 3 | 0 |
| Westbrook | 2 | 5 | 3 | 0 |
| Sanford | 1 | 1 | 1 | 0 |

### Kickoff Returns

| Last Name | No. | Yds. | Avg. | TD |
|---|---|---|---|---|
| Clark | 37 | 816 | 22 | 0 |
| Westbrook | 11 | 151 | 14 | 0 |
| Sanford | 10 | 179 | 18 | 0 |
| Tatupu | 3 | 15 | 5 | 0 |
| Clayborn | 2 | 33 | 17 | 0 |
| Washington | 1 | 18 | 18 | 0 |
| Ivory | 1 | 15 | 15 | 0 |
| Morgan | 1 | 12 | 12 | 0 |

### Passing

| Last Name | Att. | Comp. | % | Yds. | Yd./Att. | TD | Int.-% | RK |
|---|---|---|---|---|---|---|---|---|
| Grogan | 423 | 206 | 49 | 3286 | 7.8 | 28 | 20- 5 | 5 |
| Owen | 47 | 27 | 57 | 248 | 5.3 | 2 | 3- 6 | |
| Westbrook | 2 | 2 | 100 | 52 | 26.0 | 0 | 0- 0 | |
| Cavanaugh | 1 | 1 | 100 | 10 | 10.0 | 0 | 0- 0 | |
| Hare | 1 | 1 | 100 | 4 | 4.0 | 0 | 0- 0 | |
| Jackson | 1 | 0 | 0 | 0 | 0.0 | 0 | 0- 0 | |

### Punting

| Last Name | No. | Avg. |
|---|---|---|
| Hare | 83 | 36.6 |

### Kicking

| Last Name | XP | Att. | % | FG | Att. | % |
|---|---|---|---|---|---|---|
| Smith | 46 | 49 | 94 | 23 | 33 | 70 |

## NEW YORK JETS

### Rushing

| Last Name | No. | Yds. | Avg. | TD |
|---|---|---|---|---|
| Gaines | 186 | 905 | 4.9 | 0 |
| Dierking | 186 | 767 | 4.1 | 3 |
| Long | 116 | 442 | 3.8 | 7 |
| Harper | 65 | 282 | 4.3 | 0 |
| Newton | 37 | 145 | 3.9 | 6 |
| Todd | 36 | 93 | 2.6 | 5 |
| Jones | 1 | 4 | 4.0 | 0 |
| Bennett | 2 | 4 | 2.0 | 1 |
| Robinson | 3 | 4 | 1.3 | 1 |
| Ramsey | 2 | 0 | 0.0 | 0 |

### Receiving

| Last Name | No. | Yds. | Avg. | TD |
|---|---|---|---|---|
| Gaffney | 32 | 534 | 17 | 1 |
| Gaines | 29 | 219 | 8 | 0 |
| Barkum | 27 | 401 | 15 | 4 |
| Walker | 23 | 569 | 25 | 5 |
| Jones | 19 | 379 | 20 | 1 |
| Harper | 17 | 250 | 15 | 2 |
| Shuler | 16 | 225 | 14 | 3 |
| Dierking | 10 | 121 | 12 | 0 |
| Long | 10 | 115 | 12 | 0 |
| Newton | 4 | 33 | 8 | 0 |
| Raba | 2 | 9 | 5 | 0 |
| Bennett | 1 | 9 | 9 | 0 |

### Punt Returns

| Last Name | No. | Yds. | Avg. | TD |
|---|---|---|---|---|
| Harper | 33 | 290 | 9 | 0 |
| Schroy | 2 | 24 | 12 | 0 |
| Darby | 1 | 0 | 0 | 0 |

### Kickoff Returns

| Last Name | No. | Yds. | Avg. | TD |
|---|---|---|---|---|
| Harper | 55 | 1158 | 21 | 0 |
| Jones | 7 | 140 | 20 | 0 |
| Schroy | 6 | 179 | 30 | 0 |
| Gaines | 2 | 29 | 15 | 0 |
| Hennessy | 2 | 15 | 8 | 0 |
| Raba | 1 | 18 | 18 | 0 |
| Shuler | 1 | 15 | 15 | 0 |
| Bennett | 1 | 7 | 7 | 0 |
| Newton | 1 | 0 | 0 | 0 |

### Passing

| Last Name | Att. | Comp. | % | Yds. | Yd./Att. | TD | Int.-% | RK |
|---|---|---|---|---|---|---|---|---|
| Todd | 334 | 171 | 51 | 2660 | 8.0 | 16 | 16- 4 | |
| Robinson | 31 | 17 | 55 | 191 | 6.2 | 0 | 2- 7 | |
| Ryan | 4 | 2 | 50 | 13 | 3.3 | 0 | 1- 25 | |

### Punting

| Last Name | No. | Avg. |
|---|---|---|
| Ramsey | 73 | 40.8 |

### Kicking

| Last Name | XP | Att. | % | FG | Att. | % |
|---|---|---|---|---|---|---|
| Leahy | 12 | 15 | 80 | 8 | 13 | 62 |
| Linhart | 14 | 18 | 78 | 6 | 14 | 43 |
| Jacobs | 10 | 11 | 91 | 5 | 9 | 56 |
| Szaro | 2 | 2 | 100 | 0 | 2 | 0 |

## BUFFALO BILLS

### Rushing

| Last Name | No. | Yds. | Avg. | TD |
|---|---|---|---|---|
| Brown | 172 | 574 | 3.3 | 1 |
| Miller | 139 | 484 | 3.5 | 1 |
| Hooks | 89 | 320 | 3.6 | 6 |
| Collier | 34 | 130 | 3.8 | 2 |
| Ferguson | 22 | 68 | 3.1 | 1 |
| Powell | 10 | 29 | 2.9 | 0 |
| Butler | 2 | 13 | 6.5 | 0 |
| D. Johnson | 3 | 5 | 1.7 | 0 |
| Mike-Myer | 1 | 4 | 4.0 | 0 |
| Lewis | 2 | -6 | -3.0 | 0 |

### Receiving

| Last Name | No. | Yds. | Avg. | TD |
|---|---|---|---|---|
| Lewis | 54 | 1082 | 20 | 2 |
| Butler | 48 | 834 | 17 | 4 |
| Brown | 39 | 401 | 10 | 3 |
| Piccone | 33 | 556 | 17 | 2 |
| Hooks | 26 | 254 | 10 | 0 |
| Gant | 19 | 245 | 13 | 2 |
| Miller | 10 | 111 | 11 | 0 |
| Collier | 7 | 43 | 6 | 0 |
| Shipp | 3 | 43 | 14 | 1 |
| Fulton | 2 | 34 | 17 | 0 |

### Punt Returns

| Last Name | No. | Yds. | Avg. | TD |
|---|---|---|---|---|
| Moody | 38 | 318 | 8 | 0 |

### Kickoff Returns

| Last Name | No. | Yds. | Avg. | TD |
|---|---|---|---|---|
| Moody | 27 | 556 | 21 | 0 |
| Miller | 8 | 160 | 20 | 0 |
| Collier | 7 | 129 | 18 | 0 |
| Powell | 6 | 97 | 16 | 0 |
| Willis | 4 | 92 | 23 | 0 |
| Brown | 3 | 42 | 14 | 0 |
| Piccone | 3 | 41 | 14 | 0 |
| Keating | 1 | 14 | 14 | 0 |

### Passing

| Last Name | Att. | Comp. | % | Yds. | Yd./Att. | TD | Int.-% | RK |
|---|---|---|---|---|---|---|---|---|
| Ferguson | 458 | 238 | 52 | 3572 | 7.8 | 14 | 15- 3 | 8 |
| Munson | 7 | 3 | 43 | 31 | 4.4 | 0 | 0- 0 | |

### Punting

| Last Name | No. | Avg. |
|---|---|---|
| Jackson | 96 | 38.2 |

### Kicking

| Last Name | XP | Att. | % | FG | Att. | % |
|---|---|---|---|---|---|---|
| Mike-Mayer | 17 | 18 | 94 | 20 | 29 | 69 |
| Dempsey | 8 | 11 | 73 | 1 | 4 | 25 |

## BALTIMORE COLTS

### Rushing

| Last Name | No. | Yds. | Avg. | TD |
|---|---|---|---|---|
| Washington | 242 | 884 | 3.7 | 4 |
| Hardeman | 109 | 292 | 2.7 | 3 |
| McCauley | 59 | 168 | 2.8 | 3 |
| Leaks | 49 | 145 | 3.0 | 1 |
| Landry | 31 | 115 | 3.7 | 0 |
| Garry | 13 | 41 | 3.2 | 0 |
| Jones | 10 | 40 | 4.0 | 1 |
| White | 1 | 3 | 3.0 | 0 |
| Dilts | 1 | -14 | -14.0 | 0 |

### Receiving

| Last Name | No. | Yds. | Avg. | TD |
|---|---|---|---|---|
| Washington | 82 | 750 | 9 | 3 |
| McCauley | 55 | 575 | 11 | 3 |
| McCall | 37 | 536 | 15 | 4 |
| Doughty | 35 | 510 | 15 | 2 |
| Carr | 27 | 400 | 15 | 1 |
| Hardeman | 25 | 115 | 5 | 1 |
| Siani | 15 | 214 | 14 | 2 |
| Leaks | 14 | 119 | 9 | 0 |
| Alston | 10 | 114 | 11 | 1 |
| Burke | 6 | 151 | 25 | 0 |
| DeRoo | 4 | 82 | 21 | 1 |
| Garry | 3 | 9 | 3 | 0 |

### Punt Returns

| Last Name | No. | Yds. | Avg. | TD |
|---|---|---|---|---|
| Glasgow | 44 | 352 | 8 | 1 |
| Blackwood | 4 | -1 | 0 | 0 |
| Thompson | 1 | 40 | 40 | 0 |

### Kickoff Returns

| Last Name | No. | Yds. | Avg. | TD |
|---|---|---|---|---|
| Glasgow | 50 | 1126 | 23 | 0 |
| Garry | 8 | 135 | 17 | 0 |
| Blackwood | 3 | 41 | 14 | 0 |
| Laird | 3 | 34 | 11 | 0 |
| McCauley | 2 | 29 | 15 | 0 |
| Hart | 1 | 16 | 16 | 0 |
| Van Duyne | 1 | 12 | 12 | 0 |
| Griffin | 1 | 8 | 8 | 0 |
| Washington | 1 | 1 | 1 | 0 |

### Passing

| Last Name | Att. | Comp. | % | Yds. | Yd./Att. | TD | Int.-% | RK |
|---|---|---|---|---|---|---|---|---|
| Landry | 457 | 270 | 59 | 2932 | 6.4 | 15 | 15- 3 | |
| Jones | 92 | 43 | 47 | 643 | 7.0 | 3 | 3- 3 | |
| Washington | 1 | 0 | 0 | 0 | 0.0 | 0 | 1-100 | |

### Punting

| Last Name | No. | Avg. |
|---|---|---|
| Dilts | 99 | 36.9 |

### Kicking

| Last Name | XP | Att. | % | FG | Att. | % |
|---|---|---|---|---|---|---|
| Mike-Mayer | 28 | 29 | 97 | 11 | 20 | 55 |

## PITTSBURGH STEELERS 12-4-0 Chuck Noll

### Scores of Each Game

| | | |
|---|---|---|
| 16 | New England | *13 |
| 38 | HOUSTON | 7 |
| 24 | St. Louis | 21 |
| 17 | BALTIMORE | 13 |
| 14 | Philadelphia | 17 |
| 51 | Cleveland | 35 |
| 10 | Cincinnati | 34 |
| 42 | DENVER | 7 |
| 14 | DALLAS | 3 |
| 38 | WASHINGTON | 7 |
| 30 | Kansas City | 3 |
| 7 | San Diego | 35 |
| 33 | CLEVELAND | *30 |
| 37 | CINCINNATI | 17 |
| 17 | Houston | 20 |
| 28 | BUFFALO | 0 |

| Use Name | Pos. | Hgt. | Wgt. | Age | Int. | Pts. |
|---|---|---|---|---|---|---|
| Larry Brown | OT-TE | 6'4" | 245 | 30 | | 6 |
| Jon Kolb | OT | 6'2" | 262 | 32 | | |
| Ted Petersen | OT-C | 6'5" | 244 | 24 | | |
| Sam Davis | OG | 6'1" | 255 | 35 | | |
| Gerry Mullins | OG | 6'3" | 244 | 30 | | |
| Steve Courson | OG | 6'1" | 260 | 23 | | |
| Thom Dornbrook | C-OG | 6'2" | 240 | 22 | | |
| Mike Webster | C | 6'1" | 250 | 27 | | |
| John Banaszak | DE-DT | 6'3" | 244 | 29 | 1 | |
| L. C. Greenwood | DE | 6'5" | 250 | 32 | | |
| Dwight White | DE | 6'4" | 255 | 30 | | |
| Tom Beasley | DT | 6'5" | 253 | 25 | | |
| Gary Dunn | DT-DE | 6'3" | 247 | 6 | | |
| Steve Furness | DT-DE | 6'4" | 255 | 28 | | |
| Joe Greene | DT | 6'4" | 260 | 32 | | |
| Robin Cole | LB | 6'2" | 220 | 23 | | |
| Tom Graves | LB | 6'3" | 228 | 23 | | |
| Jack Ham | LB | 6'3" | 225 | 30 | 2 | |
| Jack Lambert | LB | 6'4" | 220 | 27 | 6 | |
| Loren Toews | LB | 6'3" | 222 | 27 | | |
| Zack Valentine | LB | 6'2" | 220 | 22 | | |
| Dennis Winston | LB | 6' | 228 | 23 | 3 | 6 |
| Larry Anderson | DB | 5'11" | 177 | 22 | 1 | |
| Mel Blount | DB | 6'3" | 205 | 31 | 3 | |
| Ron Johnson | DB | 5'10" | 200 | 23 | 1 | |
| Donnie Shell | DB | 5'11" | 190 | 27 | 5 | |
| J.T. Thomas | DB | 6'2" | 196 | 28 | | |
| Mike Wagner | DB | 6'1" | 200 | 30 | 4 | |
| Dwayne Woodruff | DB | 5'11" | 189 | 22 | 1 | |
| Terry Bradshaw | QB | 6'3" | 215 | 30 | | |
| Mike Kruczek | QB | 6'1" | 205 | 26 | | |
| Cliff Stoudt | QB | 6'4" | 218 | 24 | | |
| Anthony Anderson | HB | 6' | 197 | 22 | | 6 |
| Rocky Bleier | HB | 5'11" | 210 | 33 | | 24 |
| Rick Moser | HB | 6' | 210 | 22 | | 6 |
| Sidney Thornton | HB-FB | 5'11" | 230 | 24 | | 60 |
| Franco Harris | FB | 6'2" | 225 | 29 | | 72 |
| Greg Hawthorne | FB | 6'2" | 225 | 22 | | 6 |
| Theo Bell | WR | 5'11" | 180 | 25 | | |
| Jim Smith | WR | 6'2" | 205 | 24 | | 12 |
| John Stallworth | WR | 6'2" | 183 | 27 | | 48 |
| Lynn Swann | WR | 6' | 180 | 27 | | 36 |
| Bennie Cunningham | TE | 6'4" | 247 | 24 | | 24 |
| Randy Grossman | TE | 6'1" | 215 | 25 | | 6 |
| Matt Bahr | K | 5'10" | 165 | 23 | | 104 |
| Craig Colquitt | K | 6'2" | 182 | 25 | | |

Fred Anderson – Broken Hand
Ray Pinney – Stomach Injury

## HOUSTON OILERS 11-5-0 Bum Phillips

### Scores of Each Game

| | | |
|---|---|---|
| 29 | Washington | 27 |
| 7 | Pittsburgh | 38 |
| 20 | KANSAS CITY | 6 |
| 30 | Cincinnati | *27 |
| 31 | CLEVELAND | 10 |
| 17 | ST. LOUIS | 24 |
| 28 | Baltimore | 16 |
| 14 | Seattle | 34 |
| 27 | N.Y. JETS | *24 |
| 9 | Miami | 6 |
| 31 | OAKLAND | 17 |
| 42 | CINCINNATI | 21 |
| 30 | Dallas | 24 |
| 7 | Cleveland | 14 |
| 20 | PITTSBURGH | 17 |
| 20 | PHILADELPHIA | 26 |

| Use Name | Pos. | Hgt. | Wgt. | Age | Int. | Pts. |
|---|---|---|---|---|---|---|
| Leon Gray | OT | 6'3" | 260 | 27 | | |
| Wesley Phillips | OT | 6'5" | 275 | 25 | | |
| Morris Towns | OT | 6'4" | 275 | 25 | | |
| Ed Fisher | OG | 6'3" | 250 | 30 | | |
| Conway Hayman | OG-OT | 6'3" | 270 | 30 | | |
| Tom Randall | OG | 6'5" | 245 | 23 | | |
| George Reihner | OG | 6'4" | 263 | 24 | | |
| David Carter | C | 6'2" | 225 | 26 | | |
| Carl Mauck | C | 6'3" | 250 | 32 | | |
| Jessie Baker | DE | 6'5" | 265 | 22 | | 6 |
| Elvin Bethea | DE | 6'3" | 255 | 33 | | |
| Andy Dorris | DE | 6'4" | 240 | 28 | | |
| James Young | DE | 6'2" | 260 | 29 | | |
| Curley Culp | MG | 6'1" | 265 | 33 | | |
| Ken Kennard | MG | 6'2" | 245 | 24 | | |
| Mike Stensrud | MG | 6'5" | 270 | 23 | | |
| Steve Baumgartner | LB | 6'7" | 245 | 28 | | |
| Gregg Bingham | LB | 6'1" | 230 | 28 | 3 | |
| Robert Brazile | LB | 6'4" | 238 | 26 | 2 | |
| Jimbo Elrod | LB | 6' | 223 | 25 | | |
| Daryl Hunt | LB | 6'3" | 220 | 22 | | |
| Mike Murphy | LB | 6'2" | 222 | 22 | | |
| Art Stringer | LB | 6'1" | 223 | 25 | 2 | |
| Ted Thompson | LB | 6'1" | 220 | 26 | | |
| Ted Washington | LB | 6'1" | 245 | 31 | | |
| Willie Alexander | DB | 6'2" | 195 | 29 | 2 | |
| Bill Currier | DB | 6' | 195 | 24 | | |
| Carter Hartwig | DB | 6' | 185 | 23 | 2 | |
| Charles Jefferson | DB | 6'2" | 178 | 22 | | |
| Vernon Perry | DB | 6'2" | 211 | 25 | 3 | |
| Mike Reinfeldt | DB | 6'2" | 195 | 26 | 12 | |
| Greg Stemrick | DB | 5'11" | 185 | 27 | 2 | |
| J.C. Wilson | DB | 6' | 177 | 23 | 6 | 6 |
| Gifford Nielsen | QB | 6'4" | 205 | 24 | | |
| Dan Pastorini | QB | 6'3" | 205 | 30 | | |
| Earl Campbell | HB | 5'11" | 224 | 24 | | 114 |
| Ronnie Coleman | HB | 5'10" | 198 | 28 | | 6 |
| Kenny King | HB | 5'11" | 203 | 22 | | |
| Rob Carpenter | FB-HB | 6'1" | 214 | 24 | | 24 |
| Booby Clark | FB | 6'2" | 245 | 28 | | |
| Tim Wilson | FB | 6'3" | 220 | 25 | | 18 |
| Ken Burrough | WR | 6'4" | 210 | 31 | | 36 |
| Rich Caster | WR | 6'5" | 230 | 30 | | 6 |
| Richard Ellender | WR | 5'11" | 171 | 22 | | |
| Eddie Foster | WR | 5'10" | 185 | 25 | | |
| Jeff Groth (from MIAMI) | WR | 5'10" | 172 | 22 | | |
| Billy Johnson | WR | 5'9" | 170 | 27 | | 6 |
| Guido Merkens | WR-QB | 6'1" | 200 | 24 | | 6 |
| Mike Renfro | WR | 6' | 184 | 24 | | 12 |
| Mike Barber | TE | 6'3" | 235 | 26 | | 18 |
| Conrad Rucker | TE | 6'3" | 260 | 24 | | |
| Toni Fritsch | K | 5'7" | 195 | 34 | | 104 |
| Cliff Parsley | K | 6'1" | 211 | 24 | | |

Greg Sampson – Illness
John Schumacher – Back Injury
C.L. Whittington – Injury

## CLEVELAND BROWNS 9-7-0 Sam Rutigliano

### Scores of Each Game

| | | |
|---|---|---|
| 25 | N.Y. Jets | *22 |
| 27 | Kansas City | 24 |
| 13 | BALTIMORE | 10 |
| 26 | DALLAS | 7 |
| 10 | Houston | 31 |
| 35 | PITTSBURGH | 51 |
| 9 | WASHINGTON | 13 |
| 28 | CINCINNATI | 27 |
| 38 | St. Louis | 20 |
| 24 | Philadelphia | 19 |
| 24 | SEATTLE | 29 |
| 30 | MIAMI | *24 |
| 30 | Pittsburgh | *33 |
| 14 | HOUSTON | 7 |
| 14 | Oakland | 19 |
| 12 | Cincinnati | 16 |

| Use Name | Pos. | Hgt. | Wgt. | Age | Int. | Pts. |
|---|---|---|---|---|---|---|
| Doug Dieken | OT | 6'5" | 252 | 30 | | |
| Matt Miller | OT | 6'6" | 270 | 23 | | |
| Henry Sheppard | OT | 6'6" | 263 | 26 | | |
| George Buehler | OG | 6'2" | 270 | 32 | | |
| Bob Jackson | OG | 6'5" | 260 | 26 | | |
| Cody Risien | OG | 6'7" | 255 | 22 | | |
| Tom DeLeone | C | 6'2" | 248 | 29 | | |
| Gerry Sullivan | C-OT | 6'4" | 250 | 27 | | |
| Lyle Alzado | DE | 6'3" | 250 | 30 | | |
| Jack Gregory | DE | 6'6" | 255 | 34 | | |
| Mike St. Clair | DE | 6'5" | 253 | 25 | | |
| Henry Bradley | DT | 6'2" | 265 | 25 | | |
| Rich Dimler | DT | 6'6" | 260 | 23 | | |
| Jerry Sherk | DT | 6'4" | 250 | 31 | | |
| Mickey Sims | DT | 6'5" | 270 | 24 | | |
| Dick Ambrose | LB | 6' | 235 | 26 | 1 | |
| Dave Graf | LB | 6'2" | 221 | 26 | | |
| Charlie Hall | LB | 6'3" | 235 | 30 | 2 | |
| Gerald Irons | LB | 6'2" | 230 | 32 | | |
| Robert Jackson | LB | 6'1" | 230 | 25 | | |
| Clay Matthews | LB | 6'2" | 230 | 23 | 1 | |
| Ron Bolton | DB | 6'2" | 170 | 29 | 3 | |
| Clinton Burrell | DB | 6'2" | 192 | 22 | | |
| Thom Darden | DB | 6'2" | 193 | 29 | 5 | 6 |
| Oliver Davis | DB | 6'1" | 205 | 25 | 1 | |
| Lawrence Johnson | DB | 6' | 204 | 21 | | |
| Ricky Jones | DB | 6'1" | 215 | 24 | | |
| Randy Rich | DB | 5'10" | 181 | 25 | | |
| Clarence Scott | DB | 6' | 190 | 30 | 3 | |
| Johnny Evans | QB | 6'1" | 197 | 23 | | |
| Mark Miller | QB | 6'2" | 176 | 23 | | |
| Brian Sipe | QB | 6'1" | 195 | 30 | | 12 |
| Doug Dennison | HB | 5'7" | 205 | 27 | | |
| Dino Hall | HB | 5'7" | 165 | 23 | | 6 |
| Calvin Hill | HB-FB | 6'3" | 227 | 32 | | 18 |
| Cleo Miller | HB-FB | 5'11" | 214 | 26 | | 6 |
| Pat Moriarty | HB | 6' | 195 | 24 | | 12 |
| Greg Pruitt | HB | 5'10" | 190 | 28 | | 6 |
| Mike Pruitt | FB | 6' | 225 | 25 | | 66 |
| Willie Adams | WR. | 6'2" | 194 | 23 | | |
| Ricky Feacher | WR | 5'10" | 174 | 25 | | 6 |
| Dave Logan | WR | 6'4" | 216 | 25 | | 42 |
| Reggie Rucker | WR | 6'2" | 190 | 31 | | 36 |
| John Smith | WR | 6' | 175 | 23 | | |
| Keith Wright | WR | 5'10" | 175 | 23 | | |
| Ozzie Newsome | TE | 6'2" | 232 | 23 | | 54 |
| Curtis Weathers | TE | 6'5" | 220 | 22 | | |
| Don Cockroft | K | 6'1" | 195 | 34 | | 89 |

Rickey Anderson – Knee Injury
Larry Collins – Knee Injury

## CINCINNATI BENGALS 4-12-0 Homer Rice

### Scores of Each Game

| | | |
|---|---|---|
| 0 | Denver | 10 |
| 24 | Buffalo | 51 |
| 14 | NEW ENGLAND | 20 |
| 27 | HOUSTON | *30 |
| 13 | Dallas | 38 |
| 7 | KANSAS CITY | 10 |
| 34 | PITTSBURGH | 10 |
| 27 | Cleveland | 28 |
| 37 | PHILADELPHIA | 13 |
| 28 | Baltimore | 38 |
| 24 | SAN DIEGO | 26 |
| 21 | Houston | 42 |
| 34 | ST. LOUIS | 28 |
| 17 | Pittsburgh | 37 |
| 14 | Washington | 28 |
| 16 | CLEVELAND | 12 |

| Use Name | Pos. | Hgt. | Wgt. | Age | Int. | Pts. |
|---|---|---|---|---|---|---|
| Vern Holland | OT | 6'5" | 267 | 31 | | |
| Max Montoya | OT | 6'5" | 278 | 23 | | |
| Mike Wilson | OT | 6'5" | 280 | 24 | | |
| Glenn Bujnoch | OG | 6'5" | 255 | 25 | | |
| Barney Cotton | OG | 6'5" | 261 | 22 | | |
| Mark Donahue | OG | 6'3" | 251 | 23 | | |
| Dave Lapham | OG-C | 6'4" | 258 | 27 | | |
| Blair Bush | C | 6'3" | 252 | 22 | | |
| Bob Johnson | C | 6'5" | 223 | 33 | | |
| Ross Browner | DE | 6'3" | 261 | 25 | | |
| Gary Burley | DE | 6'3" | 269 | 26 | | |
| Mack Mitchell | DE | 6'7" | 253 | 27 | | |
| Eddie Edwards | DT | 6'5" | 256 | 25 | | |
| Mike White | DT | 6'5" | 266 | 22 | | |
| Wilson Whitley | DT | 6'3" | 265 | 24 | 1 | |
| Glenn Cameron | LB | 6'1" | 230 | 26 | | |
| Tom DePaso | LB | 6'2" | 223 | 23 | | |
| Tom Dinkel | LB | 6'3" | 246 | 23 | | |
| Bo Harris | LB | 6'3" | 226 | 26 | | |
| Howie Kurnick | LB | 6'2" | 219 | 22 | | 6 |
| Jim LeClair | LB | 6'2" | 234 | 28 | 1 | 6 |
| Tom Ruud | LB | 6'2" | 226 | 26 | | |
| Reggie Williams | LB | 6'1" | 228 | 24 | 2 | |
| Lou Breeden | DB | 5'11" | 187 | 25 | | |
| Jim Browner | DB | 6'1" | 209 | 23 | 1 | |
| Scott Bork | DB | 6'2" | 193 | 23 | | |
| Marvin Cobb | DB | 6' | 188 | 26 | 3 | |
| Ray Griffin | DB | 5'10" | 183 | 23 | 4 | 6 |
| Dick Jauron | DB | 6' | 184 | 28 | 6 | |
| Vaughn Lusby | DB | 5'10" | 178 | 23 | | |
| Scott Perry | DB | 6' | 180 | 25 | 1 | |
| Ken Riley | DB | 6' | 183 | 32 | 1 | |
| Ken Anderson | QB | 6'1" | 208 | 30 | | 12 |
| Jack Thompson | QB | 6'3" | 217 | 23 | | 30 |
| Charles Alexander | HB-HB | 6'1" | 221 | 22 | | 6 |
| Archie Griffin | HB | 5'9" | 184 | 25 | | 12 |
| Nathan Poole | HB | 5'8" | 210 | 22 | | |
| Deacon Turner | HB | 5'11" | 210 | 24 | | 6 |
| Pete Johnson | FB | 6' | 259 | 25 | | 90 |
| Don Bass | WR-TE | 6'2" | 218 | 24 | | 18 |
| Billy Brooks | WR | 6'3" | 202 | 26 | | 6 |
| Isaac Curtis | WR | 6'1" | 192 | 28 | | 48 |
| Steve Kreider | WR | 6'3" | 192 | 21 | | |
| Mike Levenseller | WR | 6'1" | 180 | 23 | | |
| Pat McInally | WR | 6'6" | 209 | 26 | | |
| Jim Corbett | TE | 6'4" | 217 | 24 | | |
| Dan Ross | TE | 6'4" | 238 | 22 | | 6 |
| Rick Walker | TE | 6'3" | 235 | 24 | | 6 |
| Chris Bahr | K | 5'9" | 172 | 26 | | 79 |

*—Overtime

## PITTSBURGH STEELERS

### RUSHING

| Last Name | No. | Yds. | Avg. | TD |
|---|---|---|---|---|
| Harris | 267 | 1186 | 4.4 | 11 |
| Thornton | 118 | 585 | 5.0 | 6 |
| Bleier | 92 | 434 | 4.7 | 4 |
| Hawthorne | 28 | 123 | 4.4 | 1 |
| A. Anderson | 18 | 118 | 6.6 | 0 |
| Bradshaw | 21 | 83 | 4.0 | 0 |
| Moser | 11 | 33 | 3.0 | 1 |
| Kruczek | 4 | 20 | 5.0 | 0 |
| Smith | 1 | 12 | 12.0 | 0 |
| Swann | 1 | 9 | 9.0 | 0 |

### RECEIVING

| Last Name | No. | Yds. | Avg. | TD |
|---|---|---|---|---|
| Stallworth | 70 | 1183 | 17 | 8 |
| Swann | 41 | 808 | 20 | 5 |
| Cunningham | 36 | 512 | 14 | 4 |
| Harris | 36 | 291 | 8 | 1 |
| Bleier | 31 | 277 | 9 | 0 |
| Smith | 17 | 243 | 14 | 2 |
| Thornton | 16 | 231 | 14 | 4 |
| Grossman | 12 | 217 | 18 | 1 |
| Hawthorne | 8 | 47 | 6 | 0 |
| Bell | 3 | 61 | 20 | 0 |
| Moser | 1 | 6 | 6 | 0 |
| Brown | 1 | 1 | 1 | 1 |

### PUNT RETURNS

| Last Name | No. | Yds. | Avg. | TD |
|---|---|---|---|---|
| Smith | 16 | 146 | 9 | 0 |
| Bell | 45 | 378 | 8 | 0 |
| Dornbrook | 1 | 0 | 0 | 0 |
| Swann | 1 | −1 | −1 | 0 |

### KICKOFF RETURNS

| Last Name | No. | Yds. | Avg. | TD |
|---|---|---|---|---|
| L. Anderson | 34 | 732 | 22 | 0 |
| A. Anderson | 13 | 200 | 15 | 0 |
| Hawthorne | 2 | 46 | 23 | 0 |
| Moser | 1 | 6 | 6 | 0 |
| Cole | 1 | 3 | 3 | 0 |

### PASSING – PUNTING – KICKING

| PASSING | Att. | Comp. | % | Yds. | Yd./Att. | TD | Int.–% | | RK |
|---|---|---|---|---|---|---|---|---|---|
| Bradshaw | 472 | 259 | 55 | 3724 | 7.9 | 26 | 25– | 5 | 6 |
| Kruczek | 20 | 13 | 65 | 153 | 7.7 | 0 | 1– | 5 | |

| PUNTING | No. | Avg. |
|---|---|---|
| Colquitt | 68 | 40.2 |

| KICKING | XP | Att. | % | FG | Att. | % |
|---|---|---|---|---|---|---|
| Bahr | 50 | 52 | 96 | 18 | 30 | 60 |

## HOUSTON OILERS

### RUSHING

| Last Name | No. | Yds. | Avg. | TD |
|---|---|---|---|---|
| Campbell | 368 | 1697 | 4.6 | 19 |
| Carpenter | 92 | 355 | 3.9 | 3 |
| T. Wilson | 84 | 319 | 3.8 | 2 |
| Coleman | 21 | 81 | 3.9 | 0 |
| Clark | 22 | 51 | 2.3 | 0 |
| Caster | 4 | 25 | 6.3 | 0 |
| Pastorini | 15 | 23 | 1.5 | 0 |
| King | 3 | 9 | 3.0 | 0 |
| Nielsen | 5 | 7 | 1.4 | 0 |
| Barber | 2 | 4 | 2.0 | 0 |

### RECEIVING

| Last Name | No. | Yds. | Avg. | TD |
|---|---|---|---|---|
| Burrough | 40 | 752 | 19 | 6 |
| T. Wilson | 29 | 208 | 7 | 1 |
| Barber | 27 | 377 | 14 | 3 |
| Caster | 18 | 239 | 13 | 1 |
| Renfro | 16 | 323 | 20 | 2 |
| Carpenter | 16 | 116 | 7 | 1 |
| Campbell | 16 | 94 | 6 | 0 |
| Coleman | 12 | 114 | 10 | 1 |
| Johnson | 6 | 108 | 18 | 1 |
| Clark | 6 | 58 | 10 | 0 |
| Rucker | 4 | 40 | 10 | 0 |
| Merkens | 3 | 44 | 15 | 0 |
| Ellender | 1 | 15 | 15 | 1 |
| Groth | 1 | 6 | 6 | 0 |

### PUNT RETURNS

| Last Name | No. | Yds. | Avg. | TD |
|---|---|---|---|---|
| Ellender | 31 | 203 | 7 | 0 |
| Johnson | 4 | 17 | 4 | 0 |
| Merkens | 2 | 6 | 3 | 0 |
| Coleman | 1 | −5 | −5 | 0 |

### KICKOFF RETURNS

| Last Name | No. | Yds. | Avg. | TD |
|---|---|---|---|---|
| Ellender | 24 | 514 | 21 | 0 |
| Coleman | 16 | 321 | 20 | 0 |
| Hartwig | 13 | 328 | 18 | 0 |
| Johnson | 4 | 37 | 9 | 0 |
| Carpenter | 2 | 34 | 17 | 0 |
| T. Wilson | 2 | 30 | 15 | 0 |
| Merkens | 2 | 22 | 11 | 0 |
| Groth | 1 | 21 | 21 | 0 |
| King | 1 | 17 | 17 | 0 |
| Caster | 1 | 0 | 0 | 0 |
| Sternrick | 1 | 0 | 0 | 0 |

### PASSING – PUNTING – KICKING

| PASSING | Att. | Comp. | % | Yds. | Yd./Att. | TD | Int.–% | | RK |
|---|---|---|---|---|---|---|---|---|---|
| Pastorini | 324 | 163 | 50 | 2090 | 6.5 | 14 | 18– | 6 | 13 |
| Nielsen | 61 | 32 | 53 | 404 | 6.6 | 3 | 3– | 5 | |
| Burrough | 1 | 0 | 0 | 0 | 0.0 | 0 | 0– | 0 | |

| PUNTING | No. | Avg. |
|---|---|---|
| Parsley | 93 | 40.6 |

| KICKING | XP | Att. | % | FG | Att. | % |
|---|---|---|---|---|---|---|
| Fritsch | 41 | 43 | 95 | 21 | 25 | 84 |

## CLEVELAND BROWNS

### RUSHING

| Last Name | No. | Yds. | Avg. | TD |
|---|---|---|---|---|
| M. Pruitt | 264 | 1294 | 4.9 | 9 |
| G. Pruitt | 62 | 233 | 3.8 | 0 |
| C. Miller | 39 | 213 | 5.5 | 1 |
| Hill | 53 | 193 | 3.6 | 1 |
| Sipe | 45 | 178 | 4.0 | 2 |
| D. Hall | 22 | 152 | 6.9 | 1 |
| Moriarty | 14 | 11 | 0.8 | 2 |
| Newsome | 1 | 6 | 6.0 | 0 |
| Adams | 2 | 4 | 2.0 | 0 |
| Feacher | 1 | −1 | −1.0 | 0 |
| Mark Miller | 1 | −2 | −2.0 | 0 |

### RECEIVING

| Last Name | No. | Yds. | Avg. | TD |
|---|---|---|---|---|
| Logan | 59 | 982 | 17 | 7 |
| Newsome | 55 | 781 | 14 | 9 |
| Rucher | 43 | 749 | 17 | 6 |
| M. Pruitt | 41 | 372 | 9 | 2 |
| Hill | 38 | 381 | 10 | 2 |
| C. Miller | 26 | 251 | 10 | 0 |
| G. Pruitt | 14 | 155 | 11 | 1 |
| Feacher | 7 | 103 | 15 | 1 |
| D Hall | 2 | 14 | 7 | 0 |
| Moriarty | 1 | 17 | 17 | 0 |
| Weathers | 1 | 14 | 14 | 0 |
| Wright | 1 | 13 | 13 | 0 |
| Adams | 1 | 6 | 6 | 0 |

### PUNT RETURNS

| Last Name | No. | Yds. | Avg. | TD |
|---|---|---|---|---|
| D. Hall | 29 | 295 | 10 | 0 |
| Wright | 12 | 50 | 4 | 0 |

### KICKOFF RETURNS

| Last Name | No. | Yds. | Avg. | TD |
|---|---|---|---|---|
| D. Hall | 50 | 1014 | 20 | 0 |
| Wright | 15 | 402 | 27 | 0 |
| Feacher | 2 | 51 | 26 | 0 |
| Rich | 2 | 10 | 5 | 0 |
| G. Pruitt | 1 | 22 | 22 | 0 |
| B. Jackson | 1 | 18 | 18 | 0 |
| C. Miller | 1 | 14 | 14 | 0 |
| Matt Miller | 1 | 0 | 0 | 0 |
| Moriarty | 1 | 0 | 0 | 0 |
| Weathers | 1 | 0 | 0 | 0 |

### PASSING – PUNTING – KICKING

| PASSING | Att. | Comp. | % | Yds. | Yd./Att. | TD | Int.–% | | RK |
|---|---|---|---|---|---|---|---|---|---|
| Sipe | 535 | 286 | 54 | 3793 | 7.1 | 28 | 26– | 5 | 9 |
| Mark Miller | 8 | 2 | 25 | 31 | 3.9 | 0 | 1– | 13 | |
| Evans | 2 | 1 | 50 | 14 | 7.0 | 0 | 0– | 0 | |

| PUNTING | No. | Avg. |
|---|---|---|
| Evans | 69 | 41.2 |

| KICKING | XP | Att. | % | FG | Att. | % |
|---|---|---|---|---|---|---|
| Cockroft | 38 | 43 | 88 | 17 | 29 | 59 |

## CINCINNATI BENGALS

### RUSHING

| Last Name | No. | Yds. | Avg. | TD |
|---|---|---|---|---|
| P. Johnson | 243 | 865 | 3.6 | 14 |
| A. Griffin | 140 | 688 | 4.9 | 0 |
| Alexander | 88 | 286 | 3.3 | 1 |
| Anderson | 28 | 235 | 8.4 | 2 |
| Thompson | 21 | 116 | 5.5 | 5 |
| Turner | 28 | 86 | 3.1 | 1 |
| Bass | 4 | 35 | 8.8 | 0 |
| McInally | 1 | 18 | 18.0 | 0 |
| Dinkel | 2 | 14 | 7.0 | 0 |
| Kreider | 2 | 0 | 0.0 | 0 |
| Poole | 1 | −3 | −3.0 | 0 |
| Curtis | 2 | −11 | −5.5 | 0 |

### RECEIVING

| Last Name | No. | Yds. | Avg. | TD |
|---|---|---|---|---|
| Bass | 58 | 724 | 13 | 3 |
| A. Griffin | 43 | 417 | 10 | 2 |
| Ross | 41 | 516 | 13 | 1 |
| Curtis | 32 | 605 | 19 | 8 |
| P. Johnson | 24 | 154 | 6 | 1 |
| Alexander | 11 | 91 | 8 | 0 |
| Brooks | 8 | 214 | 27 | 1 |
| Corbett | 3 | 34 | 11 | 0 |
| Kreider | 3 | 20 | 7 | 0 |
| Turner | 2 | 18 | 9 | 0 |
| McInally | 1 | 24 | 24 | 0 |
| Walker | 1 | 14 | 14 | 1 |
| Poole | 1 | −10 | −10 | 0 |

### PUNT RETURNS

| Last Name | No. | Yds. | Avg. | TD |
|---|---|---|---|---|
| Lusby | 32 | 260 | 8 | 0 |
| Levenseller | 8 | 46 | 6 | 0 |
| Jauron | 1 | 10 | 10 | 0 |
| Burk | 1 | 0 | 0 | 0 |

### KICKOFF RETURNS

| Last Name | No. | Yds. | Avg. | TD |
|---|---|---|---|---|
| Turner | 55 | 1149 | 21 | 0 |
| Poole | 7 | 128 | 18 | 0 |
| Lusby | 6 | 92 | 15 | 0 |
| J. Browner | 6 | 87 | 15 | 0 |
| Kurnick | 4 | 60 | 15 | 0 |
| R. Browner | 2 | 29 | 15 | 0 |
| R. Griffin | 1 | 15 | 15 | 0 |

### PASSING – PUNTING – KICKING

| PASSING | Att. | Comp. | % | Yds. | Yd./Att. | TD | Int.–% | | RK |
|---|---|---|---|---|---|---|---|---|---|
| Anderson | 339 | 189 | 56 | 2340 | 6.9 | 16 | 10– | 3 | 3 |
| Thompson | 87 | 39 | 45 | 481 | 5.5 | 1 | 5– | 6 | |

| PUNTING | No. | Avg. |
|---|---|---|
| McInally | 89 | 41.3 |

| KICKING | XP | Att. | % | FG | Att. | % |
|---|---|---|---|---|---|---|
| Bahr | 40 | 42 | 95 | 13 | 23 | 57 |

## SAN DIEGO CHARGERS 12-4-0 Don Coryell

| Scores of Each Game | | |
|---|---|---|
| 33 | Seattle | 16 |
| 30 | OAKLAND | 10 |
| 27 | BUFFALO | 19 |
| 21 | New England | 27 |
| 31 | SAN FRANCISCO | 9 |
| 0 | Denver | 7 |
| 20 | SEATTLE | 10 |
| 40 | Los Angeles | 16 |
| 22 | Oakland | 45 |
| 20 | Kansas City | 14 |
| 26 | Cincinnati | 24 |
| 35 | PITTSBURGH | 7 |
| 28 | KANSAS CITY | 7 |
| 26 | ATLANTA | 28 |
| 35 | New Orleans | 0 |
| 17 | DENVER | 7 |

| Use Name | Pos. | Hgt. | Wgt. | Age | Int. | Pts. |
|---|---|---|---|---|---|---|
| Dan Audick | OT-OG | 6'3" | 253 | 24 | | |
| Billy Shields | OT | 6'7" | 275 | 26 | | |
| Russ Washington | OT | 6'6" | 288 | 32 | | |
| Don Macek | OG-C | 6'3" | 253 | 25 | | |
| Ed White | OG | 6'2" | 271 | 32 | | |
| Doug Wilkerson | OG | 6'2" | 263 | 32 | | |
| Ralph Perretta | C | 6'2" | 251 | 26 | | |
| Bob Rush | C | 6'5" | 264 | 23 | | |
| Fred Dean | DE | 6'3" | 230 | 27 | | |
| Leroy Jones | DE | 6'8" | 260 | 28 | | |
| John Lee | DE | 6'2" | 259 | 26 | | |
| Charles DeJurnett | DT | 6'4" | 260 | 27 | | |
| Gary Johnson | DT | 6'2" | 252 | 27 | | |
| Louie Kelcher | DT | 6'5" | 282 | 26 | | |
| Wilbur Young | DT | 6'6" | 290 | 30 | | 8 |

| Use Name | Pos. | Hgt. | Wgt. | Age | Int. | Pts. |
|---|---|---|---|---|---|---|
| Don Goode | LB | 6'3" | 231 | 28 | 1 | |
| Bob Horn | LB | 6'3" | 230 | 25 | 2 | |
| Keith King | LB | 6'4" | 230 | 24 | | |
| Woodrow Lowe | LB | 6' | 227 | 25 | 5 | 12 |
| Ray Preston | LB | 6' | 218 | 25 | 5 | |
| Cliff Thrift | LB | 6'2" | 232 | 23 | | |
| Willie Buchanon | DB | 6' | 195 | 28 | | |
| Jerome Dove | DB | 6'2" | 193 | 25 | | |
| Frank Duncan | DB | 6'1" | 188 | 22 | | |
| Glenn Edwards | DB | 6' | 183 | 32 | 4 | |
| Mike Fuller | DB | 5'9" | 182 | 26 | 4 | |
| Pete Shaw | DB | 5'10" | 178 | 25 | 3 | |
| Hal Stringert | DB | 5'11" | 187 | 27 | | |
| Mike Williams | DB | 5'10" | 179 | 25 | 4 | |

Pat Curran – Injury
Milton Hardaway – Knee Injury
Jim Laslavic – Knee Injury
Dwight McDonald – Injury

| Use Name | Pos. | Hgt. | Wgt. | Age | Int. | Pts. |
|---|---|---|---|---|---|---|
| Dan Fouts | QB | 6'3" | 210 | 28 | | 12 |
| James Harris | QB | 6'3" | 221 | 32 | | |
| Cliff Olander | QB | 6'5" | 187 | 24 | | 1 |
| Hank Bauer | HB | 5'10" | 200 | 25 | | 48 |
| Lydell Mitchell | HB | 5'11" | 198 | 30 | | 6 |
| Artie Owens | HB | 5'10" | 182 | 26 | | 12 |
| Mike Thomas | HB | 5'11" | 190 | 26 | | 6 |
| Bo Mathews | FB | 6'4" | 222 | 27 | | 6 |
| Clarence Williams | FB-HB | 5'9" | 195 | 24 | | 72 |
| Don Woods | FB | 6'1" | 208 | 28 | | |
| Larry Burton | WR | 6'1" | 195 | 27 | | |
| John Floyd | WR | 6'1" | 195 | 22 | | 6 |
| John Jefferson | WR | 6'1" | 198 | 23 | | 60 |
| Charlie Joiner | WR | 5'11" | 183 | 31 | | 24 |
| Bob Klein | TE | 6'5" | 237 | 32 | | 30 |
| Greg McCrary | TE | 6'3" | 235 | 27 | | 2 |
| Jeff West | TE | 6'3" | 210 | 26 | | |
| Kellen Winslow | TE-WR | 6'5" | 252 | 21 | | 12 |
| Rolf Benirschke | K | 6' | 171 | 24 | | 24 |
| Roy Gerela | K | 5'10" | 185 | 31 | | 9 |
| Mike Wood (from St.L) | K | 5'11" | 199 | 24 | | 73 |

## DENVER BRONCOS 10-6-0 Red Miller

| Scores of Each Game | | |
|---|---|---|
| 10 | CINCINNATI | 0 |
| 9 | LOS ANGELES | 13 |
| 20 | Atlanta | *17 |
| 37 | SEATTLE | 34 |
| 3 | Oakland | 27 |
| 7 | SAN DIEGO | 0 |
| 24 | Kansas City | 10 |
| 7 | Pittsburgh | 42 |
| 20 | KANSAS CITY | 3 |
| 10 | NEW ORLEANS | 3 |
| 45 | NEW ENGLAND | 10 |
| 38 | San Francisco | 28 |
| 10 | OAKLAND | 14 |
| 19 | Buffalo | 16 |
| 23 | Seattle | 28 |
| 7 | San Diego | 17 |

| Use Name | Pos. | Hgt. | Wgt. | Age | Int. | Pts. |
|---|---|---|---|---|---|---|
| Kelvin Clark | OT | 6'3" | 245 | 23 | | |
| Claudie Minor | OT | 6'4" | 280 | 28 | | |
| Dave Studdard | OT-TE | 6'4" | 255 | 23 | | 6 |
| Tom Glassic | OG | 6'3" | 254 | 25 | | |
| Paul Howard | OG | 6'3" | 260 | 28 | | |
| Glenn Hyde | OG-OT | 6'3" | 252 | 28 | | |
| Ken Brown | C | 6'1" | 245 | 25 | | |
| Bill Bryan | C | 6'2" | 244 | 24 | | |
| Barney Chavous | DE | 6'3" | 252 | 28 | | |
| John Grant | DE | 6'3" | 246 | 29 | | |
| Brison Manor | DE | 6'4" | 248 | 27 | | |
| Bruce Radford | DE | 6'5" | 252 | 23 | | |
| Rubin Carter | NT | 6' | 253 | 26 | | 6 |
| Kit Lathrop (to GB) | NT | 6'5" | 253 | 23 | | |
| Don Latimer | NT | 6'3" | 265 | 24 | | |

| Use Name | Pos. | Hgt. | Wgt. | Age | Int. | Pts. |
|---|---|---|---|---|---|---|
| Larry Evans | LB | 6'2" | 214 | 26 | | |
| Randy Gradishar | LB | 6'3" | 231 | 27 | | |
| Tom Jackson | LB | 5'11" | 220 | 28 | 1 | |
| Rob Nairne | LB | 6'4" | 220 | 25 | | 6 |
| Joe Rizzo | LB | 6'1" | 220 | 28 | 2 | |
| Jim Ryan | LB | 6'1" | 212 | 22 | | |
| Bob Swenson | LB | 6'3" | 222 | 26 | 3 | 6 |
| Butch Atkinson | DB | 6' | 185 | 32 | | |
| Steve Foley | DB | 6'2" | 190 | 25 | 6 | |
| Bernard Jackson | DB | 6' | 180 | 29 | | |
| Chris Pane | DB | 5'11" | 188 | 26 | | |
| Bill Thompson | DB | 6'1" | 200 | 32 | 4 | 6 |
| Charlie West | DB | 6'1" | 195 | 33 | 1 | |
| Louis Wright | DB | 6'2" | 200 | 26 | 2 | 6 |

Maurice Harvey – Knee Injury
James Wright — Knee Injury

| Use Name | Pos. | Hgt. | Wgt. | Age | Int. | Pts. |
|---|---|---|---|---|---|---|
| Craig Morton | QB | 6'4" | 211 | 36 | | 6 |
| Craig Penrose | QB | 6'3" | 211 | 26 | | |
| Norris Weese | QB | 6'1" | 195 | 28 | | 18 |
| Otis Armstrong | HB | 5'10" | 196 | 28 | | 18 |
| Zachary Dixon (to NYG) | HB | 6' | 200 | 23 | | |
| Rob Lytle | HB | 6'1" | 195 | 24 | | 24 |
| Dave Preston | HB | 5'10" | 195 | 24 | | 12 |
| Larry Canada | FB | 6'2" | 238 | 24 | | |
| Jim Jensen | FB | 6'3" | 230 | 25 | | 12 |
| Jon Keyworth | FB | 6'3" | 230 | 28 | | 6 |
| Jack Dolbin | WR | 5'10" | 180 | 30 | | |
| Vince Kinney | WR | 6'2" | 190 | 23 | | |
| Haven Moses | WR | 6'3" | 200 | 33 | | 36 |
| Rick Upchurch | WR | 5'10" | 170 | 27 | | 42 |
| Steve Watson | WR | 6'4" | 192 | 22 | | |
| Ron Egloff | TE | 6'5" | 238 | 23 | | |
| Riley Odoms | TE | 6'4" | 230 | 29 | | 6 |
| Luke Prestridge | K | 6'4" | 235 | 22 | | |
| Fred Steinfort | K | 5'11" | 180 | 25 | | |
| Jim Turner | K | 6'2" | 205 | 38 | | 71 |

## OAKLAND RAIDERS 9-7-0 Tom Flores

| Scores of Each Game | | |
|---|---|---|
| 24 | Los Angeles | 17 |
| 10 | San Diego | 30 |
| 10 | Seattle | 27 |
| 7 | Kansas City | 35 |
| 27 | DENVER | 3 |
| 13 | MIAMI | 3 |
| 50 | ATLANTA | 19 |
| 19 | N.Y. Jets | 28 |
| 45 | SAN DIEGO | 22 |
| 23 | SAN FRANCISCO | 10 |
| 17 | Houston | 31 |
| 21 | KANSAS CITY | 24 |
| 14 | Denver | 10 |
| 42 | New Orleans | 35 |
| 19 | CLEVELAND | 14 |
| 24 | SEATTLE | 29 |

| Use Name | Pos. | Hgt. | Wgt. | Age | Int. | Pts. |
|---|---|---|---|---|---|---|
| Bruce Davis | OT | 6'6" | 280 | 23 | | |
| Henry Lawrence | OT | 6'4" | 270 | 27 | | |
| Art Shell | OT | 6'5" | 275 | 32 | | |
| John Vella | OT | 6'4" | 260 | 29 | | |
| Mickey Marvin | OG | 6'4" | 270 | 23 | | |
| Dan Medlin | OG | 6'4" | 250 | 29 | | |
| Steve Sylvester | OG-OT-C | 6'4" | 260 | 26 | | |
| Gene Upshaw | OG | 6'5" | 255 | 34 | | |
| Dave Dalby | C | 6'2" | 250 | 28 | | |
| Joe Bell | DE | 6'3" | 250 | 23 | | |
| Dave Browning | DE | 6'5" | 245 | 23 | | |
| Willie Jones | DE | 6'4" | 240 | 21 | | |
| John Matuszak | DE | 6'8" | 275 | 28 | | |
| Charles Philyaw | DE-NT | 6'9" | 290 | 25 | | |
| Pat Toomay | DE | 6'5" | 245 | 34 | | |
| Reggie Kinlaw | NT | 6'2" | 240 | 22 | | |
| Dave Pear | NT | 6'2" | 250 | 26 | | |

| Use Name | Pos. | Hgt. | Wgt. | Age | Int. | Pts. |
|---|---|---|---|---|---|---|
| Jeff Barnes | LB | 6'2" | 215 | 24 | 1 | |
| Ted Hendricks | LB | 6'7" | 220 | 31 | 1 | 6 |
| John Huddleston | LB | 6'3" | 230 | 25 | | |
| Monte Johnson | LB | 6'4" | 240 | 27 | 1 | 6 |
| Rod Martin | LB | 6'2" | 210 | 25 | | |
| Phil Villapiano | LB | 6'2" | 225 | 30 | | |
| Rufus Bess | DB | 5'9" | 180 | 22 | 1 | |
| Mike Davis | DB | 6'2" | 200 | 23 | 2 | |
| Lester Hayes | DB | 6' | 195 | 24 | 7 | 12 |
| Monte Jackson | DB | 5'11" | 190 | 26 | 2 | |
| Charlie Phillips | DB | 6'2" | 215 | 26 | 4 | |
| Jack Tatum | DB | 5'10" | 205 | 30 | 2 | |
| Henry Williams | DB | 5'10" | 180 | 22 | 3 | |

Lindsey Mason – Knee Injury
Otis Sistrunk – Injury

| Use Name | Pos. | Hgt. | Wgt. | Age | Int. | Pts. |
|---|---|---|---|---|---|---|
| David Humm | QB | 6'2" | 190 | 27 | | |
| Jim Plunkett | QB | 6'3" | 205 | 31 | | |
| Ken Stabler | QB | 6'3" | 210 | 33 | | |
| Clarence Hawkins | HB | 6' | 205 | 23 | | 6 |
| Derrick Jensen | HB-FB | 6'1" | 225 | 23 | | 6 |
| Ira Matthews | HB | 5'8" | 175 | 22 | | 6 |
| Terry Robiskie | HB-FB | 6'1" | 210 | 24 | | |
| Art Whittington | HB | 5'11" | 185 | 23 | | 12 |
| Todd Christensen (from NYG) | FB | 6'3" | 230 | 23 | | |
| Booker Russell | FB | 6'2" | 230 | 23 | | 24 |
| Mark van Eeghen | FB | 6'2" | 225 | 27 | | 54 |
| Morris Bradshaw | WR | 6' | 195 | 26 | | |
| Cliff Branch | WR | 5'11" | 170 | 31 | | 36 |
| Larry Brunson | WR | 5'11" | 180 | 30 | | 6 |
| Rich Martini | WR | 6'2" | 185 | 23 | | 12 |
| Joe Stewart | WR | 5'11" | 180 | 23 | | |
| Dave Casper | TE | 6'4" | 230 | 27 | | 18 |
| Ray Chester | TE | 6'3" | 235 | 31 | | 48 |
| Derrick Ramsey | TE | 6'4" | 220 | 22 | | 18 |
| Jim Breech | K | 5'6" | 155 | 23 | | 95 |
| Ray Guy | K | 6'3" | 190 | 29 | | |

## SEATTLE SEAHAWKS 9-7-0 Jack Patera

| Scores of Each Game | | |
|---|---|---|
| 16 | SAN DIEGO | 33 |
| 10 | Miami | 19 |
| 27 | OAKLAND | 10 |
| 34 | Denver | 37 |
| 6 | KANSAS CITY | 24 |
| 35 | San Francisco | 24 |
| 10 | San Diego | 20 |
| 34 | HOUSTON | 14 |
| 31 | Atlanta | 28 |
| 0 | LOS ANGELES | 24 |
| 29 | Cleveland | 24 |
| 38 | NEW ORLEANS | 24 |
| 30 | N.Y. JETS | 7 |
| 21 | Kansas City | 37 |
| 28 | DENVER | 23 |
| 29 | Oakland | 24 |

| Use Name | Pos. | Hgt. | Wgt. | Age | Int. | Pts. |
|---|---|---|---|---|---|---|
| Steve August | OT | 6'5" | 254 | 24 | | |
| Nick Bebout | OT | 6'5" | 260 | 28 | | |
| Louis Bullard | OT | 6'6" | 265 | 23 | | |
| Bill Fifer | OT | 6'4" | 250 | 23 | | |
| Jeff Sevy | OT | 6'5" | 260 | 28 | | |
| Ron Coder | OG-OT | 6'4" | 250 | 25 | | |
| Tom Lynch | OG | 6'5" | 260 | 24 | | |
| Bob Newton | OG | 6'4" | 260 | 30 | | |
| Art Kuehn | C | 6'3" | 255 | 26 | | |
| John Yarno | C | 6'5" | 251 | 24 | | |
| Mark Bell | DE | 6'4" | 240 | 22 | | |
| Dennis Boyd | DE | 6'6" | 255 | 23 | | |
| Carl Eller | DE | 6'6" | 247 | 37 | | |
| Bill Gregory | DE | 6'5" | 260 | 29 | | |
| Ernie Price (to CLE) | DE | 6'4" | 245 | 28 | | |
| Bill Cooke | DT | 6'5" | 250 | 28 | | |
| Robert Hardy | DT | 6'2" | 250 | 23 | | |
| Manu Tuiasosopo | DT | 6'3" | 252 | 22 | | |

| Use Name | Pos. | Hgt. | Wgt. | Age | Int. | Pts. |
|---|---|---|---|---|---|---|
| Terry Beeson | LB | 6'3" | 240 | 23 | 1 | |
| Keith Butler | LB | 6'4" | 225 | 23 | 1 | |
| Pete Cronan | LB | 6'2" | 238 | 24 | | |
| Sammy Green | LB | 6'2" | 230 | 24 | 1 | 6 |
| Michael Jackson | LB | 6'1" | 220 | 22 | | |
| Charles McShane | LB | 6'3" | 230 | 25 | | |
| Joe Norman | LB | 6'1" | 220 | 22 | | |
| Larry Polowski | LB | 6'3" | 235 | 21 | | |
| Autry Beamon | DB | 6'1" | 190 | 25 | 1 | |
| Dave Brown | DB | 6'1" | 190 | 26 | 5 | |
| Don Dufek | DB | 6' | 195 | 25 | | |
| John Harris | DB | 6'2" | 200 | 23 | 2 | |
| Kerry Justin | DB | 5'11" | 175 | 24 | 1 | |
| Mike O'Brien | DB | 6'1" | 195 | 23 | | |
| Keith Simpson | DB | 6'1" | 195 | 23 | 4 | |
| Cornell Webster | DB | 6' | 180 | 24 | 1 | 6 |

Bill Sandifer – Knee Injury
John Sawyer – Hamstring Injury

| Use Name | Pos. | Hgt. | Wgt. | Age | Int. | Pts. |
|---|---|---|---|---|---|---|
| Sam Adkins | QB | 6'2" | 214 | 24 | | |
| Steve Myer | QB | 6'2" | 200 | 25 | | |
| Jim Zorn | QB | 6'2" | 200 | 26 | | 12 |
| Tony Green (from NYG) | HB | 5'9" | 185 | 22 | | |
| Al Hunter | HB | 5'11" | 195 | 24 | | 6 |
| Jeff Moore | HB | 6' | 195 | 23 | | 12 |
| David Sims | HB | 6'3" | 216 | 23 | | |
| Sherman Smith | HB-FB | 6'4" | 225 | 24 | | 90 |
| Tony Benjamin | FB | 6'3" | 225 | 23 | | |
| Dan Doornink | FB | 6'3" | 210 | 23 | | 54 |
| Duke Fergerson | WR | 6'1" | 185 | 25 | | |
| Jessie Green | WR | 6'3" | 194 | 25 | | |
| Steve Largent | WR | 5'11" | 184 | 24 | | 54 |
| Sam McCullum | WR | 6'2" | 203 | 26 | | 24 |
| Steve Raible | WR | 6'2" | 195 | 25 | | 6 |
| Mark Bell | TE | 6'4" | 235 | 22 | | |
| Brian Peets | TE | 6'4" | 225 | 23 | | 6 |
| Efren Herrera | K | 5'9" | 190 | 28 | | 100 |
| Herman Weaver | K | 6'4" | 210 | 30 | | |

## KANSAS CITY CHIEFS 7-9-0 Marv Levy

| Scores of Each Game | | |
|---|---|---|
| 14 | BALTIMORE | 0 |
| 24 | CLEVELAND | 27 |
| 6 | Houston | 20 |
| 35 | OAKLAND | 7 |
| 24 | Seattle | 6 |
| 10 | Cincinnati | 7 |
| 10 | DENVER | 24 |
| 17 | N.Y. GIANTS | 21 |
| 3 | Denver | 20 |
| 14 | SAN DIEGO | 20 |
| 3 | PITTSBURGH | 30 |
| 24 | Oakland | 21 |
| 7 | San Diego | 28 |
| 37 | SEATTLE | 21 |
| 10 | Baltimore | 7 |
| 0 | Tampa Bay | 3 |

| Use Name | Pos. | Hgt. | Wgt. | Age | Int. | Pts. |
|---|---|---|---|---|---|---|
| Larry Brown | OT | 6'5" | 264 | 24 | | |
| Charlie Getty | OT | 6'4" | 269 | 27 | | |
| Matt Herkenhoff | OT | 6'4" | 255 | 28 | | |
| Jim Nicholson | OT | 6'6" | 275 | 29 | | |
| John Choma | OG | 6'5" | 241 | 24 | | |
| Tom Condon | OG | 6'3" | 254 | 26 | | |
| Bob Simmons | OG | 6'4" | 260 | 25 | | |
| Rod Walters | OG-OT | 6'3" | 258 | 25 | | |
| Charlie Ane | C | 6'1" | 237 | 27 | | |
| Jack Rudnay | C | 6'3" | 240 | 31 | | |
| Curtis Anderson | DE | 6'6" | 250 | 22 | | |
| Mike Bell | DE | 6'4" | 255 | 22 | | |
| Sylvester Hicks | DE | 6'4" | 252 | 24 | | |
| Dave Linstrom | DE | 6'6" | 257 | 24 | | |
| Art Still | DE | 6'7" | 252 | 23 | | |
| Ken Kremer | NT-DE | 6'4" | 250 | 22 | | |
| Don Parrish | NT | 6'2" | 255 | 24 | | |

| Use Name | Pos. | Hgt. | Wgt. | Age | Int. | Pts. |
|---|---|---|---|---|---|---|
| Jerry Blanton | LB | 6'1" | 225 | 23 | | |
| Tom Howard | LB | 6'2" | 208 | 25 | 1 | |
| Charles Jackson | LB | 6'2" | 236 | 24 | | |
| Frank Manumaleuga | LB | 6'2" | 245 | 23 | 1 | |
| Whitney Paul | LB | 6'3" | 220 | 25 | 1 | |
| Cal Peterson | LB | 6'3" | 220 | 26 | | |
| Dave Rozumek | LB | 6'1" | 222 | 25 | | |
| Gary Spani | LB | 6'2" | 230 | 23 | | |
| Gary Barbaro | DB | 6'4" | 204 | 25 | 7 | 6 |
| M.L. Carter | DB | 5'9" | 173 | 23 | 3 | |
| Herb Christopher | DB | 5'10" | 190 | 25 | 2 | |
| Tim Collier | DB | 6' | 174 | 25 | 2 | |
| Gary Green | DB | 5'11" | 184 | 23 | 5 | |
| Gerald Jackson | DB | 6'1" | 195 | 23 | 1 | |
| Horace Perkins | DB | 5'11" | 180 | 25 | | |
| Jerry Reece | DB | 6'3" | 192 | 24 | | |

Bill Kellar – Shoulder Injury
Clyde Powers – Knee Injury
Mark Bailey – Voluntarily Retired

| Use Name | Pos. | Hgt. | Wgt. | Age | Int. | Pts. |
|---|---|---|---|---|---|---|
| Steve Fuller | QB | 6'4" | 198 | 22 | | 6 |
| Bill Kenney | QB | 6'4" | 210 | 24 | | |
| Mike Livingston | QB | 6'3" | 210 | 33 | | |
| Horace Belton | HB | 5'8" | 200 | 24 | | 6 |
| Ben Cowins | HB | 6' | 192 | 23 | | |
| Earl Gant | HB | 6' | 207 | 22 | | 6 |
| Tony Reed | HB | 5'11" | 197 | 24 | | 6 |
| Wilbert Haslip | FB | 5'11" | 212 | 22 | | |
| Ted McKnight | FB-HB | 6'1" | 205 | 25 | | 48 |
| Arnold Morgado | FB-HB | 6' | 210 | 26 | | 24 |
| Mike Williams | FB | 6'3" | 222 | 21 | | 18 |
| Johnnie Dirden | WR | 6' | 190 | 27 | | |
| Steve Gaunty | WR | 5'10" | 175 | 20 | | 6 |
| Henry Marshall | WR | 6'2" | 205 | 25 | | 12 |
| Stan Rome | WR | 6'5" | 205 | 23 | | |
| J.T. Smith | WR | 6'2" | 185 | 23 | | 30 |
| Ed Beckman | TE | 6'4" | 226 | 24 | | |
| Tony Samuels | TE | 6'4" | 229 | 24 | | 6 |
| Walter White | TE | 6'3" | 218 | 28 | | |
| Bob Grupp | K | 5'11" | 193 | 24 | | |
| Jan Stenerud | K | 6'2" | 187 | 36 | | 64 |

* – Overtime

## SAN DIEGO CHARGERS

### RUSHING

| Last Name | No. | Yds. | Avg. | TD |
|---|---|---|---|---|
| C. Williams | 200 | 752 | 3.8 | 12 |
| Thomas | 91 | 353 | 3.9 | 1 |
| Mitchell | 63 | 211 | 3.3 | 0 |
| Owens | 40 | 151 | 3.8 | 1 |
| Matthews | 30 | 112 | 3.7 | 1 |
| Fouts | 26 | 49 | 1.9 | 2 |
| Bauer | 22 | 28 | 1.3 | 8 |
| Harris | 6 | 26 | 4.3 | 0 |
| Fuller | 1 | 0 | 0.0 | 0 |
| West | 1 | −2 | −2.0 | 0 |
| Joiner | 1 | −12 | −12.0 | 0 |

### RECEIVING

| Last Name | No. | Yds. | Avg. | TD |
|---|---|---|---|---|
| Joiner | 72 | 1008 | 14 | 4 |
| Jefferson | 61 | 1090 | 18 | 10 |
| C. Williams | 51 | 352 | 7 | 0 |
| Klein | 37 | 424 | 12 | 5 |
| Thomas | 32 | 388 | 12 | 0 |
| Winslow | 25 | 255 | 10 | 2 |
| Mitchell | 19 | 159 | 8 | 1 |
| Owens | 15 | 176 | 12 | 1 |
| Floyd | 10 | 152 | 15 | 1 |
| Matthews | 7 | 40 | 6 | 0 |
| McCrary | 5 | 32 | 6 | 0 |
| Burton | 4 | 62 | 16 | 0 |

### PUNT RETURNS

| Last Name | No. | Yds. | Avg. | TD |
|---|---|---|---|---|
| Fuller | 46 | 448 | 10 | 0 |
| M. Williams | 3 | 19 | 6 | 0 |
| Shaw | 2 | 21 | 11 | 0 |
| Goode | 1 | 0 | 0 | 0 |

### KICKOFF RETURNS

| Last Name | No. | Yds. | Avg. | TD |
|---|---|---|---|---|
| Owens | 35 | 791 | 23 | 0 |
| Fuller | 6 | 115 | 19 | 0 |
| Bauer | 4 | 92 | 23 | 0 |
| C. Williams | 1 | 19 | 19 | 0 |
| Mitchell | 1 | 15 | 15 | 0 |
| Thrift | 1 | 11 | 11 | 0 |
| Parretta | 1 | 9 | 9 | 0 |
| Matthews | 1 | 4 | 4 | 0 |
| Woods | 0 | 10 | — | 0 |

### PASSING – PUNTING – KICKING

PASSING

| Last Name | Att. | Comp. | % | Yds. | Yd./Att. | TD | Int.–% | RK |
|---|---|---|---|---|---|---|---|---|
| Fouts | 530 | 332 | 63 | 4082 | 7.7 | 24 | 24– 5 | 1 |
| Harris | 9 | 5 | 56 | 38 | 4.2 | 0 | 1– 11 | |
| Thomas | 1 | 1 | 100 | 18 | 18.0 | 0 | 0– 0 | |
| Fuller | 1 | 0 | 0 | 0 | 0.0 | 0 | 0– 0 | |

PUNTING

| Last Name | No. | Avg. |
|---|---|---|
| West | 75 | 36.5 |

KICKING

| Last Name | XP | ATT | % | FG | ATT | % |
|---|---|---|---|---|---|---|
| Wood | 34 | 37 | 92 | 13 | 21 | 62 |
| Benirschke | 12 | 13 | 92 | 4 | 4 | 100 |
| Gerela | 0 | 0 | — | 1 | 7 | 14 |

## DENVER BRONCOS

### RUSHING

| Last Name | No. | Yds. | Avg. | TD |
|---|---|---|---|---|
| Armstrong | 108 | 453 | 4.2 | 2 |
| Jensen | 106 | 400 | 3.8 | 1 |
| Lytle | 102 | 371 | 3.6 | 4 |
| Keyworth | 81 | 323 | 4.0 | 1 |
| Preston | 43 | 169 | 3.9 | 1 |
| Canada | 36 | 143 | 4.0 | 0 |
| Weese | 18 | 116 | 6.4 | 3 |
| Prestridge | 1 | 29 | 29.0 | 0 |
| Upchurch | 3 | 17 | 5.7 | 0 |
| Morton | 23 | 13 | 0.6 | 1 |
| Dixon | 3 | 9 | 3.0 | 0 |
| Odoms | 1 | −7 | −7.0 | 0 |

### RECEIVING

| Last Name | No. | Yds. | Avg. | TD |
|---|---|---|---|---|
| Upchurch | 64 | 937 | 15 | 7 |
| Moses | 54 | 943 | 18 | 6 |
| Odoms | 40 | 638 | 16 | 1 |
| Jensen | 19 | 144 | 8 | 1 |
| Preston | 19 | 137 | 7 | 1 |
| Keyworth | 18 | 132 | 7 | 0 |
| Armstrong | 14 | 138 | 10 | 1 |
| Lytle | 13 | 93 | 7 | 0 |
| Watson | 6 | 83 | 14 | 0 |
| Egloff | 5 | 70 | 14 | 0 |
| Dolbin | 3 | 74 | 25 | 0 |
| Canada | 3 | 36 | 12 | 0 |
| Turner | 1 | 6 | 6 | 0 |
| Studdard | 1 | 2 | 2 | 1 |

### PUNT RETURNS

| Last Name | No. | Yds. | Avg. | TD |
|---|---|---|---|---|
| Upchurch | 30 | 304 | 10 | 0 |
| Preston | 7 | 78 | 11 | 0 |
| Pane | 5 | 20 | 4 | 0 |
| West | 1 | −1 | −1 | 0 |

### KICKOFF RETURNS

| Last Name | No. | Yds. | Avg. | TD |
|---|---|---|---|---|
| Pane | 18 | 354 | 20 | 0 |
| Preston | 13 | 336 | 26 | 0 |
| Upchurch | 5 | 79 | 16 | 0 |
| B. Jackson | 4 | 53 | 13 | 0 |
| Dixon | 3 | 53 | 18 | 0 |
| Canada | 3 | 31 | 10 | 0 |
| Grant | 1 | 25 | 25 | 0 |
| Armstrong | 1 | 21 | 21 | 0 |
| Kinney | 1 | 14 | 14 | 0 |
| Egloff | 1 | 0 | 0 | 0 |

### PASSING – PUNTING – KICKING

PASSING

| Last Name | Att. | Comp. | % | Yds. | Yd./Att. | TD | Int.–% | RK |
|---|---|---|---|---|---|---|---|---|
| Morton | 370 | 204 | 55 | 2626 | 7.1 | 16 | 19– 5 | 11 |
| Weese | 97 | 53 | 55 | 731 | 7.5 | 1 | 3– 3 | |
| Penrose | 5 | 2 | 40 | 44 | 8.8 | 0 | 1– 20 | |
| Keyworth | 1 | 1 | 100 | 32 | 32.0 | 1 | 0– 0 | |
| Preston | 1 | 0 | 0 | 0 | 0.0 | 0 | 0– 0 | |
| Prestridge | 1 | 0 | 0 | 0 | 0.0 | 0 | 0– 0 | |
| Upchurch | 1 | 0 | 0 | 0 | 0.0 | 0 | 0– 0 | |

PUNTING

| Last Name | No. | Avg. |
|---|---|---|
| Prestridge | 89 | 39.9 |

KICKING

| Last Name | XP | Att. | % | FG | Att. | % |
|---|---|---|---|---|---|---|
| Turner | 32 | 34 | 94 | 13 | 21 | 62 |

## OAKLAND RAIDERS

### RUSHING

| Last Name | No. | Yds. | Avg. | TD |
|---|---|---|---|---|
| van Eeghen | 223 | 818 | 3.7 | 7 |
| Whittington | 109 | 397 | 3.6 | 2 |
| Jensen | 73 | 251 | 3.4 | 0 |
| Russell | 33 | 190 | 5.8 | 4 |
| Hawkins | 21 | 72 | 3.4 | 0 |
| Plunkett | 3 | 18 | 6.0 | 0 |
| Robiskie | 10 | 14 | 1.4 | 0 |
| Branch | 1 | 4 | 4.0 | 0 |
| Matthews | 2 | 3 | 1.5 | 0 |
| Stabler | 16 | −4 | −0.3 | 0 |

### RECEIVING

| Last Name | No. | Yds. | Avg. | TD |
|---|---|---|---|---|
| Branch | 59 | 844 | 14 | 6 |
| Chester | 58 | 712 | 12 | 8 |
| Casper | 57 | 771 | 13 | 3 |
| van Eeghen | 51 | 474 | 9 | 2 |
| Martini | 24 | 259 | 11 | 2 |
| Whittington | 19 | 240 | 13 | 0 |
| Ramsey | 13 | 161 | 12 | 3 |
| Jensen | 7 | 23 | 3 | 1 |
| Russell | 6 | 79 | 13 | 0 |
| Brunson | 5 | 49 | 10 | 1 |
| Robiskie | 5 | 36 | 7 | 0 |
| Bradshaw | 3 | 28 | 9 | 0 |
| Hawkins | 2 | 24 | 12 | 1 |
| Stewart | 1 | 3 | 3 | 0 |
| Dalby | 1 | 1 | 1 | 0 |

### PUNT RETURNS

| Last Name | No. | Yds. | Avg. | TD |
|---|---|---|---|---|
| Matthews | 32 | 165 | 5 | 0 |
| Brunson | 2 | 8 | 4 | 0 |
| M. Davis | 1 | 6 | 6 | 0 |

### KICKOFF RETURNS

| Last Name | No. | Yds. | Avg. | TD |
|---|---|---|---|---|
| Brunson | 17 | 441 | 26 | 0 |
| Matthews | 35 | 873 | 25 | 1 |
| Whittington | 5 | 46 | 9 | 0 |
| Russell | 3 | 21 | 7 | 0 |
| Stewart | 2 | 63 | 32 | 0 |
| Hawkins | 1 | 25 | 25 | 0 |
| Robiskie | 1 | 6 | 6 | 0 |
| Jensen | 1 | 0 | 0 | 0 |

### PASSING – PUNTING – KICKING

PASSING

| Last Name | Att. | Comp. | % | Yds. | Yd./Att. | TD | Int.–% | RK |
|---|---|---|---|---|---|---|---|---|
| Stabler | 498 | 304 | 61 | 3615 | 7.3 | 26 | 22– 4 | 2 |
| Plunkett | 15 | 7 | 47 | 89 | 5.9 | 1 | 1– 7 | |

PUNTING

| Last Name | No. | Avg. |
|---|---|---|
| Guy | 69 | 42.6 |

KICKING

| Last Name | XP | Att. | % | FG | Att. | % |
|---|---|---|---|---|---|---|
| Breech | 41 | 45 | 91 | 18 | 27 | 67 |

## SEATTLE SEAHAWKS

### RUSHING

| Last Name | No. | Yds. | Avg. | TD |
|---|---|---|---|---|
| Smith | 194 | 775 | 4.0 | 11 |
| Doornink | 152 | 500 | 3.3 | 8 |
| Zorn | 46 | 279 | 6.1 | 2 |
| Hunter | 34 | 174 | 5.1 | 1 |
| Moore | 44 | 168 | 3.8 | 2 |
| Sims | 20 | 53 | 2.7 | 0 |
| Benjamin | 5 | 13 | 2.6 | 0 |
| Adkins | 2 | 11 | 5.5 | 0 |
| Myer | 1 | 0 | 0.0 | 0 |
| Weaver | 2 | −6 | −3.0 | 0 |

### RECEIVING

| Last Name | No. | Yds. | Avg. | TD |
|---|---|---|---|---|
| Largent | 66 | 1237 | 19 | 9 |
| Doornink | 54 | 432 | 8 | 1 |
| Smith | 48 | 499 | 10 | 4 |
| McCullum | 46 | 739 | 16 | 4 |
| Peets | 25 | 293 | 12 | 1 |
| Raible | 20 | 252 | 13 | 1 |
| Moore | 14 | 128 | 9 | 0 |
| Hunter | 7 | 77 | 11 | 0 |
| Sims | 4 | 28 | 7 | 0 |
| Bell | 2 | 20 | 10 | 0 |
| Fergerson | 2 | 12 | 6 | 0 |
| Webster | 1 | 39 | 39 | 0 |
| Herrera | 1 | 20 | 20 | 0 |
| J. Green | 1 | 9 | 9 | 0 |
| Benjamin | 1 | 6 | 6 | 0 |

### PUNT RETURNS

| Last Name | No. | Yds. | Avg. | TD |
|---|---|---|---|---|
| T. Green | 19 | 138 | 7 | 0 |
| Moore | 10 | 90 | 9 | 0 |
| Harris | 8 | 70 | 9 | 0 |

### KICKOFF RETURNS

| Last Name | No. | Yds. | Avg. | TD |
|---|---|---|---|---|
| Moore | 31 | 641 | 21 | 0 |
| T. Green | 32 | 651 | 20 | 0 |
| Hunter | 15 | 299 | 20 | 0 |
| Benjamin | 2 | 33 | 17 | 0 |
| Harris | 1 | 21 | 21 | 0 |
| Doornink | 1 | 13 | 13 | 0 |

### PASSING – PUNTING – KICKING

PASSING

| Last Name | Att. | Comp. | % | Yds. | Yd./Att. | TD | Int.–% | RK |
|---|---|---|---|---|---|---|---|---|
| Zorn | 505 | 285 | 56 | 3661 | 7.3 | 20 | 18– 4 | 4 |
| Weaver | 4 | 3 | 75 | 73 | 18.3 | 0 | 0– 0 | |
| Myer | 8 | 2 | 25 | 28 | 3.5 | 0 | 0– 0 | |
| Smith | 1 | 1 | 100 | 11 | 11.0 | 0 | 0– 0 | |
| Sims | 2 | 1 | 50 | 18 | 9.0 | 0 | 0– 0 | |
| Adkins | 3 | 0 | 0 | 0 | 0.0 | 0 | 0– 0 | |

PUNTING

| Last Name | No. | Avg. |
|---|---|---|
| Weaver | 66 | 40.2 |
| Herrera | 1 | 36.0 |

KICKING

| Last Name | XP | Att. | % | FG | Att. | % |
|---|---|---|---|---|---|---|
| Herrera | 43 | 46 | 93 | 19 | 23 | 83 |

## KANSAS CITY CHIEFS

### RUSHING

| Last Name | No. | Yds. | Avg. | TD |
|---|---|---|---|---|
| McKnight | 153 | 755 | 4.9 | 8 |
| Reed | 113 | 446 | 3.9 | 1 |
| Fuller | 50 | 264 | 5.3 | 1 |
| Williams | 69 | 261 | 3.8 | 1 |
| Morgado | 75 | 231 | 3.1 | 4 |
| Gant | 56 | 196 | 3.5 | 1 |
| Belton | 44 | 134 | 3.0 | 1 |
| Marshall | 2 | 34 | 17.0 | 1 |
| Livingston | 3 | 2 | 0.7 | 0 |
| Haslip | 2 | 1 | 0.5 | 0 |
| Manumaleuga | 1 | −3 | −3.0 | 0 |
| Rome | 1 | −5 | −5.0 | 0 |

### RECEIVING

| Last Name | No. | Yds. | Avg. | TD |
|---|---|---|---|---|
| McKnight | 38 | 226 | 6 | 0 |
| Reed | 34 | 352 | 10 | 0 |
| Smith | 33 | 444 | 14 | 3 |
| Marshall | 21 | 332 | 16 | 1 |
| Williams | 16 | 129 | 8 | 2 |
| Gant | 15 | 101 | 7 | 0 |
| Samuels | 14 | 147 | 11 | 0 |
| Gaunty | 5 | 87 | 17 | 1 |
| Morgado | 5 | 55 | 11 | 0 |
| Belton | 4 | 44 | 11 | 0 |
| White | 3 | 15 | 5 | 0 |
| Beckman | 2 | 21 | 11 | 0 |

### PUNT RETURNS

| Last Name | No. | Yds. | Avg. | TD |
|---|---|---|---|---|
| Smith | 58 | 612 | 11 | 2 |

### KICKOFF RETURNS

| Last Name | No. | Yds. | Avg. | TD |
|---|---|---|---|---|
| Belton | 22 | 463 | 21 | 0 |
| Gaunty | 12 | 271 | 23 | 0 |
| Dirden | 7 | 154 | 22 | 0 |
| Gant | 4 | 75 | 19 | 0 |
| McKnight | 2 | 34 | 17 | 0 |
| Haslip | 1 | 7 | 7 | 0 |
| Collier | 1 | 0 | 0 | 0 |
| Morgado | 1 | 0 | 0 | 0 |
| Peterson | 1 | 0 | 0 | 0 |

### PASSING – PUNTING – KICKING

PASSING

| Last Name | Att. | Comp. | % | Yds. | Yd./Att. | TD | Int.–% | RK |
|---|---|---|---|---|---|---|---|---|
| Fuller | 270 | 146 | 54 | 1484 | 5.5 | 6 | 14– 5 | 14 |
| Livingston | 90 | 44 | 49 | 469 | 5.2 | 1 | 4– 4 | |
| Grupp | 1 | 0 | 0 | 0 | 0.0 | 0 | 0– 0 | |

PUNTING

| Last Name | No. | Avg. |
|---|---|---|
| Grupp | 89 | 43.6 |

KICKING

| Last Name | XP | Att. | % | FG | Att. | % |
|---|---|---|---|---|---|---|
| Stenerud | 28 | 29 | 97 | 12 | 23 | 52 |

December 23 at Philadelphia (Attendance 69, 397)

### SCORING

| | | | | |
|---|---|---|---|---|
| **CHICAGO** | 7 | 10 | 0 | 0–17 |
| **PHILADELPHIA** | 7 | 3 | 7 | 10–27 |

First Quarter
Phi. Carmichael, 17 yard pass from Jaworski.
PAT – Franklin (kick)
Chi. Payton, 2 yard rush
PAT – Thomas (kick)

Second Quarter
Phi. Franklin, 29 yard field goal
Chi. Payton, 1 yard rush
PAT – Thomas (kick)
Chi. Thomas, 30 yard field goal

Third Quarter
Phi. Carmichael, 29 yard pass from Jaworski
PAT – Franklin (kick)

Fourth Quarter
Phi. Campfield, 63 yard pass from Jaworski
PAT – Franklin (kick)
Phi. Franklin, 34 yard field goal

### TEAM STATISTICS

| CHI. | | PHI. |
|---|---|---|
| 15 | First Downs–Total | 18 |
| 7 | First Downs–Rushing | 8 |
| 7 | First Downs–Passing | 8 |
| 1 | First Downs–Penalty | 2 |
| 1 | Fumbles–Number | 4 |
| 1 | Fumbles–Lost Ball | 2 |
| 4 | Penalties–Number | 4 |
| 35 | Yards Penalized | 46 |
| 1 | Missed Field Goals | 0 |
| 60 | Offensive Plays | 63 |
| 241 | Net Yards | 315 |
| 4.0 | Average Gain | 5.0 |
| 3 | Giveaways | 3 |
| 3 | Takeaways | 3 |
| 0 | Difference | 0 |

### INDIVIDUAL STATISTICS

**RUSHING**

| CHICAGO | No. | Yds. | Avg. | PHILADELPHIA | No. | Yds. | Avg. |
|---|---|---|---|---|---|---|---|
| Payton | 16 | 67 | 4.2 | Montgomery | 26 | 87 | 3.3 |
| Williams | 10 | 23 | 2.3 | Harris | 8 | 33 | 4.1 |
| McClendon | 2 | 6 | 3.0 | Jaworski | 3 | 19 | 6.3 |
| Phipps | 1 | 3 | 3.0 | | 37 | 139 | 3.8 |
| | 29 | 99 | 3.4 | | | | |

**RECEIVING**

| CHICAGO | No. | Yds. | Avg. | PHILADELPHIA | No. | Yds. | Avg. |
|---|---|---|---|---|---|---|---|
| Payton | 3 | 52 | 17.3 | Carmichael | 6 | 111 | 18.5 |
| Watts | 3 | 42 | 14.0 | Campfield | 2 | 70 | 35.0 |
| Baschnagel | 3 | 38 | 12.7 | Montgomery | 2 | 0 | 0.0 |
| Latta | 2 | 6 | 3.0 | Harris | 1 | 15 | 15.0 |
| Williams | 2 | 4 | 2.0 | Smith | 1 | 8 | 8.0 |
| | 13 | 142 | 10.9 | | 12 | 204 | 17.0 |

**PUNTING**

| CHICAGO | No. | | Avg. | PHILADELPHIA | No. | | Avg. |
|---|---|---|---|---|---|---|---|
| Parsons | 6 | | 39.0 | Runager | 4 | | 40.5 |

**PUNT RETURNS**

| CHICAGO | No. | Yds. | Avg. | PHILADELPHIA | No. | Yds. | Avg. |
|---|---|---|---|---|---|---|---|
| none | | | | Henry | 4 | 51 | 12.8 |

**KICKOFF RETURNS**

| CHICAGO | No. | Yds. | Avg. | PHILADELPHIA | No. | Yds. | Avg. |
|---|---|---|---|---|---|---|---|
| Walterscheid | 3 | 66 | 22.0 | Henry | 3 | 76 | 25.3 |
| Watts | 2 | 31 | 15.5 | | | | |
| Baschnagel | 1 | 27 | 27.0 | | | | |
| | 6 | 124 | 20.7 | | | | |

**INTERCEPTION RETURNS**

| CHICAGO | No. | Yds. | Avg. | PHILADELPHIA | No. | Yds. | Avg. |
|---|---|---|---|---|---|---|---|
| Ellis | 1 | 25 | 25.0 | Edwards | 1 | 5 | 5.0 |
| | | | | Howard | 1 | 0 | 0.0 |
| | | | | | 2 | 5 | 2.5 |

**PASSING**

| | Att. | Comp. | Comp. Pct. | Yds. | Int. | Yds./Att. | Yds./Comp. |
|---|---|---|---|---|---|---|---|
| **CHICAGO** | | | | | | | |
| Phipps | 30 | 13 | 43.3 | 142 | 2 | 4.6 | 10.9 |
| **PHILADELPHIA** | | | | | | | |
| Jaworski | 23 | 12 | 52.2 | 204 | 1 | 8.9 | 17.0 |

December 29 at Tampa (Attendance 71,402)

### SCORING

| | | | | |
|---|---|---|---|---|
| **PHILADELPHIA** | 0 | 7 | 3 | 7–17 |
| **TAMPA BAY** | 7 | 10 | 0 | 7–24 |

First Quarter
T.B. Bell, 3 yard rush
PAT–O'Donoghue (kick)

Second Quarter
T.B. O'Donoghue, 40 yard field goal
T.B. Bell, 1 yard rush
PAT–O'Donoghue (kick)
Phi. Smith, 11 yard pass from Jaworski
PAT–Franklin (kick)

Third Quarter
Phi. Franklin, 43 yard field goal

Fourth Quarter
T.B. Giles, 9 yard pass from Williams
PAT–O'Donoghue (kick)
Phi. Carmichael, 37 yard pass from Jaworski
PAT–Franklin (kick)

### TEAM STATISTICS

| PHI. | | T.B. |
|---|---|---|
| 15 | First Downs–Total | 17 |
| 4 | First Downs–Rushing | 12 |
| 9 | First Downs–Passing | 4 |
| 2 | First Downs–Penalty | 1 |
| 2 | Fumbles–Number | 0 |
| 1 | Fumbles–Lost Ball | 0 |
| 8 | Penalties–Number | 9 |
| 62 | Yards Penalized | 105 |
| 1 | Missed Field Goals | 0 |
| 58 | Offensive Plays | 70 |
| 227 | Net Yards | 318 |
| 3.9 | Average Gain | 4.5 |
| 1 | Giveaways | 1 |
| 1 | Takeaways | 1 |
| 0 | Difference | 0 |

### INDIVIDUAL STATISTICS

**RUSHING**

| PHILADELPHIA | No. | Yds. | Avg. | TAMPA BAY | No. | Yds. | Avg. |
|---|---|---|---|---|---|---|---|
| Montgomery | 13 | 35 | 2.7 | Bell | 38 | 142 | 3.7 |
| Harris | 4 | 13 | 3.3 | Eckwood | 8 | 19 | 2.4 |
| Jaworski | 1 | 0 | 0.0 | Williams | 6 | 19 | 3.2 |
| | 18 | 48 | 2.7 | J. Davis | 3 | 6 | 2.0 |
| | | | | | 55 | 186 | 3.4 |

**RECEIVING**

| PHILADELPHIA | No. | Yds. | Avg. | TAMPA BAY | No. | Yds. | Avg. |
|---|---|---|---|---|---|---|---|
| Montgomery | 4 | 35 | 8.8 | Giles | 3 | 43 | 14.3 |
| Carmichael | 3 | 92 | 30.7 | Hagins | 2 | 34 | 17.0 |
| Smith | 3 | 49 | 16.3 | Mucker | 1 | 34 | 34.0 |
| Krepfle | 3 | 23 | 7.7 | Owens | 1 | 21 | 21.0 |
| Harris | 1 | 2 | 2.0 | | 7 | 132 | 17.1 |
| Campfield | 1 | −2 | −2.0 | | | | |
| | 15 | 199 | 13.3 | | | | |

**PUNTING**

| PHILADELPHIA | No. | | Avg. | TAMPA BAY | No. | | Avg. |
|---|---|---|---|---|---|---|---|
| Runager | 5 | | 44.2 | Blanchard | 5 | | 42.6 |

**PUNT RETURNS**

| PHILADELPHIA | No. | Yds. | Avg. | TAMPA BAY | No. | Yds. | Avg. |
|---|---|---|---|---|---|---|---|
| Henry | 4 | 48 | 12.0 | Reece | 3 | 33 | 11.0 |

**KICKOFF RETURNS**

| PHILADELPHIA | No. | Yds. | Avg. | TAMPA BAY | No. | Yds. | Avg. |
|---|---|---|---|---|---|---|---|
| Henry | 3 | 72 | 24.0 | Hagins | 3 | 59 | 19.7 |
| Giammona | 1 | 15 | 15.0 | T. Davis | 1 | 0 | 0.0 |
| | 4 | 87 | 21.8 | | 4 | 59 | 14.8 |

**INTERCEPTION RETURNS**

| PHILADELPHIA | No. | Yds. | Avg. | TAMPA BAY | No. | Yds. | Avg. |
|---|---|---|---|---|---|---|---|
| Robinson | 1 | 37 | 37.0 | none | | | |

**PASSING**

| | Att. | Comp. | Comp. Pct. | Yds. | Int. | Yds. Att. | Yds. Comp. |
|---|---|---|---|---|---|---|---|
| **PHILADEL-PHIA** | | | | | | | |
| Jaworski | 38 | 15 | 39.5 | 199 | 0 | 5.2 | 13.3 |
| **TAMPA BAY** | | | | | | | |
| Williams | 15 | 7 | 46.7 | 132 | 1 | 8.8 | 17.1 |

December 30 at Irving, Tex. (Attendance 64,792)

### SCORING

| | | | | |
|---|---|---|---|---|
| **LOS ANGELES** | 0 | 14 | 0 | 7–21 |
| **DALLAS** | 2 | 3 | 7 | 7–19 |

First Quarter
Dal. Safety, Ferragamo tackled in end zone

Second Quarter
L.A. Tyler, 20 yard pass from Ferragamo
PAT – Corral (kick)
Dal. Septien, 33 yard field goal
L.A. R. Smith, 43 yard pass from Ferragamo
PAT – Corral (kick)

Third Quarter
Dal. Springs, 1 yard rush
PAT – Septien (kick)

Fourth Quarter
Dal. Saldi, 2 yard pass from Staubach
PAT – Septien (kick)
L.A. Waddy, 50 yard pass from Ferragamo
PAT – Corral (kick)

### TEAM STATISTICS

| L.A. | | DAL. |
|---|---|---|
| 16 | First Downs–Total | 17 |
| 8 | First Downs–Rushing | 8 |
| 7 | First Downs–Passing | 8 |
| 1 | First Downs–Penalty | 1 |
| 0 | Fumbles–Number | 0 |
| 0 | Fumbles–Lost Ball | 0 |
| 6 | Penalties–Number | 6 |
| 44 | Yards Penalized | 55 |
| 1 | Missed Field Goals | 0 |
| 61 | Offensive Plays | 64 |
| 361 | Net Yards | 306 |
| 5.9 | Average Gain | 4.8 |
| 2 | Giveaways | 1 |
| 1 | Takeaways | 2 |
| −1 | Difference | −1 |

### INDIVIDUAL STATISTICS

**RUSHING**

| LOS ANGELES | No. | Yds. | Avg. | DALLAS | No. | Yds. | Avg. |
|---|---|---|---|---|---|---|---|
| Tyler | 19 | 82 | 4.3 | Dorsett | 19 | 87 | 4.6 |
| Bryant | 17 | 67 | 3.9 | DuPree | 1 | 27 | 27.0 |
| Cromwell | 1 | 7 | 7.0 | Newhouse | 7 | 21 | 3.0 |
| Waddy | 1 | 3 | 3.0 | Springs | 5 | 20 | 4.0 |
| Ferragamo | 1 | 0 | 0.0 | Staubach | 1 | 3 | 3.0 |
| | 39 | 159 | 4.1 | P. Pearson | 1 | −2 | −2.0 |
| | | | | | 34 | 156 | 4.6 |

**RECEIVING**

| LOS ANGELES | No. | Yds. | Avg. | DALLAS | No. | Yds. | Avg. |
|---|---|---|---|---|---|---|---|
| Waddy | 3 | 97 | 32.3 | D. Pearson | 4 | 87 | 21.8 |
| R. Smith | 2 | 55 | 27.5 | DuPree | 2 | 26 | 13.0 |
| Tyler | 2 | 40 | 20.0 | Saldi | 2 | 17 | 8.5 |
| Dennard | 1 | 15 | 15.0 | P. Pearson | 2 | 15 | 7.5 |
| Bryant | 1 | 3 | 3.0 | Johnson | 1 | 3 | 3.0 |
| | 9 | 210 | 23.3 | Springs | 1 | 2 | 2.0 |
| | | | | Hill | 1 | 0 | 0.0 |
| | | | | | 13 | 150 | 11.5 |

**PUNTING**

| LOS ANGELES | No. | | Avg. | DALLAS | No. | | Avg. |
|---|---|---|---|---|---|---|---|
| Clark | 5 | | 41.4 | D. White | 8 | | 36.8 |

**PUNT RETURNS**

| LOS ANGELES | No. | Yds. | Avg. | DALLAS | No. | Yds. | Avg. |
|---|---|---|---|---|---|---|---|
| E. Brown | 3 | 17 | 5.7 | Wilson | 1 | 8 | 8.0 |
| | | | | Manning | 1 | 2 | 2.0 |
| | | | | | 2 | 10 | 5.0 |

**KICKOFF RETURNS**

| LOS ANGELES | No. | Yds. | Avg. | DALLAS | No. | Yds. | Avg. |
|---|---|---|---|---|---|---|---|
| E. Hill | 3 | 64 | 21.3 | Springs | 3 | 61 | 20.3 |
| Jodat | 1 | 12 | 12.0 | Wilson | 1 | 18 | 18.0 |
| | 4 | 76 | 19.0 | | 4 | 79 | 19.8 |

**INTERCEPTION RETURNS**

| LOS ANGELES | No. | Yds. | Avg. | DALLAS | No. | Yds. | Avg. |
|---|---|---|---|---|---|---|---|
| E. Brown | 1 | 21 | 21.0 | Harris | 1 | 22 | 22.0 |
| | | | | Thurman | 1 | 18 | 18.0 |
| | | | | | 2 | 40 | 20.0 |

**PASSING**

| | Att. | Comp. | Comp. Pct. | Yds. | Int. | Yds. Att. | Yds. Comp. |
|---|---|---|---|---|---|---|---|
| **LOS ANGELES** | | | | | | | |
| Ferragamo | 21 | 9 | 42.9 | 210 | 2 | 10.0 | 23.3 |
| **DALLAS** | | | | | | | |
| Staubach | 28 | 13 | 46.4 | 150 | 1 | 5.4 | 11.5 |
| Springs | 1 | 0 | 0.0 | 0 | 0 | 0.0 | 0.0 |

## Game 1

December 23 at Houston (Attendance 48,776)

### SCORING

| | | | | | |
|---|---|---|---|---|---|
| DENVER | 7 | 0 | 0 | 0– | 7 |
| HOUSTON | 3 | 7 | 0 | 3– | 13 |

**First Quarter**
Hou. — Fritsch, 31 yard field goal
Denv. — Preston, 7 yard pass from Morton
PAT – Turner (kick)

**Second Quarter**
Hou. — Campbell, 3 yard rush
PAT – Fritsch (kick)

**Fourth Quarter**
Hou. — Fritsh, 20 yard field goal

### TEAM STATISTICS

| DENV. | | HOU. |
|---|---|---|
| 17 | First Downs–Total | 15 |
| 7 | First Downs–Rushing | 8 |
| 9 | First Downs–Passing | 6 |
| 1 | First Downs–Penalty | 1 |
| 1 | Fumbles–Number | 0 |
| 0 | Fumbles–Lost Ball | 0 |
| 7 | Penalties–Number | 2 |
| 70 | Yards Penalized | 19 |
| 1 | Missed Field Goals | 0 |
| 65 | Offensive Plays | 65 |
| 216 | Net Yards | 282 |
| 3.3 | Average Gain | 4.3 |
| 1 | Giveaways | 2 |
| 2 | Takeaways | 1 |
| –1 | Difference | –1 |

### INDIVIDUAL STATISTICS

**RUSHING**

| DENVER | No. | Yds. | Avg. | HOUSTON | No. | Yds. | Avg. |
|---|---|---|---|---|---|---|---|
| Armstrong | 12 | 51 | 4.3 | Carpenter | 16 | 59 | 3.7 |
| Canada | 4 | 29 | 7.3 | Campbell | 16 | 50 | 3.1 |
| Preston | 9 | 24 | 2.7 | T. Wilson | 8 | 21 | 2.6 |
| Jensen | 4 | 5 | 1.3 | Coleman | 2 | 5 | 2.5 |
| Upchurch | 1 | 3 | 3.0 | | 42 | 135 | 3.2 |
| Morton | 2 | 0 | 0.0 | | | | |
| | 32 | 112 | 3.5 | | | | |

**RECEIVING**

| DENVER | No. | Yds. | Avg. | HOUSTON | No. | Yds. | Avg. |
|---|---|---|---|---|---|---|---|
| Preston | 4 | 40 | 10.0 | T. Wilson | 4 | 53 | 13.3 |
| Moses | 3 | 47 | 15.7 | Carpenter | 3 | 26 | 8.7 |
| Armstrong | 2 | 22 | 11.0 | Coleman | 1 | 41 | 41.0 |
| Odom | 2 | 3 | 1.5 | Barber | 1 | 31 | 31.0 |
| Egloff | 1 | 17 | 17.0 | Campbell | 1 | 7 | 7.0 |
| Jensen | 1 | 11 | 11.0 | | 10 | 158 | 15.8 |
| Canada | 1 | 4 | 4.0 | | | | |
| | 14 | 144 | 10.3 | | | | |

**PUNTING**

| | No. | Yds. | Avg. | | No. | Yds. | Avg. |
|---|---|---|---|---|---|---|---|
| Prestridge | 6 | | 44.4 | Parsley | 5 | | 43.2 |

**PUNT RETURNS**

| | No. | Yds. | Avg. | | No. | Yds. | Avg. |
|---|---|---|---|---|---|---|---|
| Upchurch | 2 | 25 | 12.5 | Ellender | 5 | 42 | 8.4 |

**KICKOFF RETURNS**

| | No. | Yds. | Avg. | | No. | Yds. | Avg. |
|---|---|---|---|---|---|---|---|
| Preston | 3 | 56 | 18.7 | Hartwig | 1 | 26 | 26.0 |
| Upchurch | 1 | 27 | 27.0 | | | | |
| | 4 | 83 | 20.7 | | | | |

**INTERCEPTION RETURNS**

| | No. | Yds. | Avg. | | No. | Yds. | Avg. |
|---|---|---|---|---|---|---|---|
| Thompson | 1 | 12 | 12.0 | Bingham | 1 | 15 | 15.0 |
| Swenson | 1 | 0 | 0.0 | | | | |
| | 2 | 12 | 6.0 | | | | |

**PASSING**

| DENVER | Att. | Comp. | Comp. Pct. | Yds. | Int. | Yds./ Att. | Yds./ Comp. |
|---|---|---|---|---|---|---|---|
| Morton | 27 | 14 | 51.9 | 144 | 1 | 5.3 | 10.3 |

| HOUSTON | Att. | Comp. | Comp. Pct. | Yds. | Int. | Yds./ Att. | Yds./ Comp. |
|---|---|---|---|---|---|---|---|
| Pastorini | 18 | 8 | 44.4 | 149 | 1 | 8.3 | 18.7 |
| Nielsen | 4 | 2 | 50.0 | 9 | 1 | 2.3 | 4.5 |
| | 22 | 10 | 45.5 | 158 | 2 | 7.2 | 15.8 |

## Game 2

December 29 at San Diego (Attendance 51,192)

### SCORING

| | | | | | |
|---|---|---|---|---|---|
| HOUSTON | 0 | 10 | 7 | 0– | 17 |
| SAN DIEGO | 7 | 0 | 7 | 0– | 14 |

**First Quarter**
S.D. — C. Williams, 1 yard rush
PAT – Wood (kick)

**Second Quarter**
Hou. — Fritsch, 26 yard field goal
Hou. — Clark, 1 yard rush
PAT – Fritsch (kick)

**Third Quarter**
S.D. — Mitchell, 8 yard rush
PAT – Wood (kick)
Hou. — Renfro, 47 yard pass from Nielsen
PAT – Fritsch (kick)

### TEAM STATISTICS

| HOU. | | S.D. |
|---|---|---|
| 15 | First Downs–Total | 25 |
| 9 | First Downs–Rushing | 6 |
| 5 | First Downs–Passing | 17 |
| 1 | First Downs–Penalty | 2 |
| 0 | Fumbles–Number | 0 |
| 0 | Fumbles–Lost Ball | 0 |
| 5 | Penalties–Number | 6 |
| 45 | Yards Penalized | 30 |
| 0 | Missed Field Goals | 1 |
| 59 | Offensive Plays | 68 |
| 259 | Net Yards | 380 |
| 4.4 | Average Gain | 5.6 |
| 1 | Giveaways | 5 |
| 5 | Takeaways | 1 |
| –4 | Difference | –4 |

### INDIVIDUAL STATISTICS

**RUSHING**

| HOUSTON | No. | Yds. | Avg. | SAN DIEGO | No. | Yds. | Avg. |
|---|---|---|---|---|---|---|---|
| Carpenter | 18 | 67 | 3.7 | Mitchell | 8 | 33 | 4.1 |
| T. Wilson | 11 | 39 | 3.5 | Williams | 11 | 30 | 2.7 |
| Clark | 9 | 30 | 3.3 | | 19 | 63 | 3.3 |
| Nielsen | 2 | 12 | 6.0 | | | | |
| | 40 | 148 | 3.7 | | | | |

**RECEIVING**

| HOUSTON | No. | Yds. | Avg. | SAN DIEGO | No. | Yds. | Avg. |
|---|---|---|---|---|---|---|---|
| Carpenter | 4 | 23 | 5.8 | Klein | 5 | 41 | 8.2 |
| T. Wilson | 3 | 16 | 5.3 | Joiner | 4 | 81 | 20.3 |
| Renfro | 1 | 47 | 47.0 | Jefferson | 4 | 70 | 17.5 |
| Coleman | 1 | 13 | 13.0 | Williams | 4 | 30 | 7.5 |
| Barber | 1 | 12 | 12.0 | Mitchell | 4 | 26 | 6.5 |
| | 10 | 111 | 11.1 | Floyd | 3 | 51 | 17.0 |
| | | | | McCrary | 1 | 34 | 34.0 |
| | | | | | 25 | 333 | 13.3 |

**PUNTING**

| | No. | Yds. | Avg. | | No. | Yds. | Avg. |
|---|---|---|---|---|---|---|---|
| Parsley | 6 | | 40.7 | West | 2 | | 32.0 |

**PUNT RETURNS**

| | No. | Yds. | Avg. | | No. | Yds. | Avg. |
|---|---|---|---|---|---|---|---|
| Ellender | 1 | 25 | 25.0 | Fuller | 3 | 29 | 9.7 |

**KICKOFF RETURNS**

| | No. | Yds. | Avg. | | No. | Yds. | Avg. |
|---|---|---|---|---|---|---|---|
| Hartwig | 2 | 37 | 18.5 | Owens | 3 | 60 | 20.0 |
| Ellender | 1 | 16 | 16.0 | Bauer | 1 | 24 | 24.0 |
| | 3 | 53 | 17.7 | | 4 | 84 | 21.0 |

**INTERCEPTION RETURNS**

| | No. | Yds. | Avg. | | No. | Yds. | Avg. |
|---|---|---|---|---|---|---|---|
| Perry | 4 | 0 | 0.0 | M. Williams | 1 | 0 | 0.0 |
| J.C. Wilson | 1 | 3 | 3.0 | | | | |
| Reinfeldt | 0 | 8 | — | | | | |
| | 5 | 11 | 2.2 | | | | |

**PASSING**

| HOUSTON | Att. | Comp. | Comp. Pct. | Yds. | Int. | Yds./ Att. | Yds./ Comp. |
|---|---|---|---|---|---|---|---|
| Nielsen | 19 | 10 | 52.6 | 111 | 1 | 5.8 | 11.1 |

| SAN DIEGO | Att. | Comp. | Comp. Pct. | Yds. | Int. | Yds./ Att. | Yds./ Comp. |
|---|---|---|---|---|---|---|---|
| Fouts | 47 | 25 | 53.2 | 333 | 5 | 7.1 | 13.3 |

## Game 3

December 30 at Pittsburgh (Attendance 50,214)

### SCORING

| | | | | | |
|---|---|---|---|---|---|
| MIAMI | 0 | 0 | 7 | 7– | 14 |
| PITTSBURGH | 20 | 0 | 7 | 7– | 34 |

**First Quarter**
Pit. — Thornton, 1 yard rush
PAT – Bahr (kick)
Pit. — Stallworth, 17 yard pass from Bradshaw
PAT – kick failed
Pit. — Swann, 20 yard pass from Bradshaw
PAT–Bahr (kick)

**Third Quarter**
Mia. — Harris, 7 yard pass from Griese
PAT–von Schamann (kick)
Pit. — Bleier, 1 yard rush
PAT–Bahr (kick)

**Fourth Quarter**
Pit. — Harris, 5 yard rush
PAT–Bahr (kick)
Mia. — Csonka, 1 yard rush
PAT–von Schamann (kick)

### TEAM STATISTICS

| MIA. | | PIT. |
|---|---|---|
| 16 | First Downs–Total | 27 |
| 2 | First Downs–Rushing | 14 |
| 11 | First Downs–Passing | 12 |
| 3 | First Downs–Penalty | 1 |
| 0 | Fumbles–Number | 3 |
| 0 | Fumbles–Lost Ball | 3 |
| 4 | Penalties–Number | 8 |
| 35 | Yards Penalized | 41 |
| 0 | Missed Field Goals | 0 |
| 65 | Offensive Plays | 72 |
| 249 | Net Yards | 379 |
| 3.8 | Average Gain | 5.3 |
| 2 | Giveaways | 3 |
| 3 | Takeaways | 2 |
| –1 | Difference | –1 |

### INDIVIDUAL STATISTICS

**RUSHING**

| MIAMI | No. | Yds. | Avg. | PITTSBURGH | No. | Yds. | Avg. |
|---|---|---|---|---|---|---|---|
| Csonka | 10 | 20 | 2.0 | Harris | 21 | 83 | 4.0 |
| Davis | 2 | 12 | 6.0 | Thornton | 12 | 52 | 4.3 |
| Williams | 8 | 1 | 0.1 | Hawthrone | 2 | 15 | 7.5 |
| Griese | 1 | 1 | 1.0 | Bleier | 4 | 13 | 3.3 |
| Roberts | 1 | –9 | –9.0 | A. Anderson | 1 | –4 | –4.0 |
| | 22 | 25 | 1.1 | | 40 | 159 | 4.0 |

**RECEIVING**

| MIAMI | No. | Yds. | Avg. | PITTSBURGH | No. | Yds. | Avg. |
|---|---|---|---|---|---|---|---|
| Williams | 6 | 26 | 4.3 | Stallworth | 6 | 86 | 14.3 |
| Moore | 5 | 93 | 18.6 | Harris | 5 | 32 | 6.4 |
| Harris | 3 | 61 | 20.3 | Smith | 4 | 41 | 10.3 |
| Nathan | 3 | 27 | 9.0 | Swann | 3 | 37 | 12.3 |
| Davis | 2 | 24 | 12.0 | Thornton | 3 | 34 | 11.3 |
| Hardy | 2 | 12 | 6.0 | | 21 | 230 | 10.5 |
| Torrey | 1 | 0 | 0.0 | | | | |
| | 22 | 243 | 11.5 | | | | |

**PUNTING**

| | No. | Yds. | Avg. | | No. | Yds. | Avg. |
|---|---|---|---|---|---|---|---|
| Roberts | 4 | | 36.3 | Colquitt | 2 | | 29.5 |

**PUNT RETURNS**

| | No. | Yds. | Avg. | | No. | Yds. | Avg. |
|---|---|---|---|---|---|---|---|
| none | | | | Bell | 3 | 31 | 10.3 |
| | | | | Woodruff | 1 | 0 | 0.0 |
| | | | | | 4 | 31 | 7.8 |

**KICKOFF RETURNS**

| | No. | Yds. | Avg. | | No. | Yds. | Avg. |
|---|---|---|---|---|---|---|---|
| Nathan | 4 | 73 | 18.3 | L. Anderson | 1 | 26 | 26.0 |
| Davis | 2 | 14 | 7.0 | Hawthorne | 1 | 20 | 20.0 |
| | 6 | 87 | 14.5 | | 2 | 46 | 23.0 |

**INTERCEPTION RETURNS**

| | No. | Yds. | Avg. | | No. | Yds. | Avg. |
|---|---|---|---|---|---|---|---|
| none | | | | Winston | 1 | 3 | 3.0 |
| | | | | Woodruff | 1 | 0 | 0.0 |
| | | | | | 2 | 3 | 1.5 |

**PASSING**

| MIAMI | Att. | Comp. | Comp. Pct. | Yds. | Int. | Yds./ Att. | Yds./ Comp. |
|---|---|---|---|---|---|---|---|
| Griese | 26 | 14 | 53.8 | 118 | 1 | 4.5 | 8.4 |
| Strock | 14 | 8 | 57.1 | 125 | 1 | 8.9 | 17.4 |
| | 40 | 22 | 55.0 | 243 | 2 | 6.1 | 11.5 |

| PITTSBURGH | Att. | Comp. | Comp. Pct. | Yds. | Int. | Yds./ Att. | Yds./ Comp. |
|---|---|---|---|---|---|---|---|
| Bradshaw | 31 | 21 | 67.7 | 230 | 0 | 7.4 | 10.5 |

# 1979 CHAMPIONSHIP GAMES

## NFC CHAMPIONSHIP GAME
January 6, 1980 at Tampa
(Attendance 72,033)

### SCORING

| | | | | |
|---|---|---|---|---|
| LOS ANGELES | 0 | 6 | 0 | 3– 9 |
| TAMPA BAY | 0 | 0 | 0 | 0– 0 |

Second Quarter
L.A.　　Corral, 19 yard field goal
L.A.　　Corral, 21 yard field goal

Fourth Quarter
L.A.　　Corral, 23 yard field goal

### TEAM STATISTICS

| L.A. | | T.B. |
|---|---|---|
| 23 | First Downs–Total | 7 |
| 13 | First Downs–Rushing | 4 |
| 8 | First Downs–Passing | 3 |
| 2 | First Downs–Penalty | 0 |
| 1 | Fumbles–Number | 1 |
| 1 | Fumbles–Lost Ball | 0 |
| 3 | Penalties–Number | 4 |
| 20 | Yards Penalized | 45 |
| 1 | Missed Field Goals | 0 |
| 77 | Offensive Plays | 54 |
| 369 | Net Yards | 177 |
| 4.8 | Average Gain | 3.3 |
| 1 | Giveaways | 1 |
| 1 | Takeaways | 1 |
| 0 | Difference | 0 |

Under the sun in Tampa, the Buccaneers took the field with the best wishes of most of America. The Bucs were the Horatio Alger of the N.F.L., rising from their abject station two years ago to being one victory away from the Super Bowl. The part of America that loves underdogs loved the Buccaneers.

The Los Angeles Rams planned to spoil the scenario and play out their own Cinderella fantasy. Longtime champions of the N.F.L. West, they had failed ever to make it into the Super Bowl. This year's squad squeaked into the playoffs with a 9-7 record and small prospects. In a major surprise, they beat Dallas in the first round to come into this match.

Both clubs brought formidable defenses into the game, and both lived up to their reputations. Despite the warm climate, the game was played out on the lines of trench warfare which was long the fashion in such outposts as Chicago, Green Bay, and Detroit. The Rams ran the ball as often as possible, and with their offensive line beating the Tampa Bay linemen and linebackers, Cullen Bryant and Wendell Tyler ate up yardage in small but steady mouthfuls. The Rams controlled the ball for almost 21 minutes of the first half. Despite the ground gaining, the Rams could score only on a pair of Frank Corral field goals in the second quarter. The Bucs, on the other hand, made no headway against the Los Angeles defense. Quarterback Doug Williams missed his first eight passes and could not move his team in the few opportunities he had. At halftime, Horatio Alger trailed, 6-0.

With the Bucs clearly off-key in this pressure situation, they lost their quarterback in the third period when Williams injured his arm. Sub QB Mike Rae did guide the Bucs within scoring distance once in the third quarter, but a fourth-down pass went astray. The Bucs launched no further scoring threats, and a Frank Corral field goal in the fourth quarter made the final score 9-0.

## AFC CHAMPIONSHIP GAME
January 6, 1980 at Pittsburgh

Two titans clashed head-on, with the thunderclaps drawing a huge television audience. All eyes were on a match which was expected to produce this year's Super Bowl champion. The Steelers and the Oilers had met twice already this season. The Steelers had won in Three Rivers Stadium in September by a 38-7 margin, while the Oilers triumphed 20-17 in December in the Astrodome.

The Pittsburgh defense nullified Houston's big weapon all afternoon. Earl Campbell had won his second rushing title in two pro seasons, but the Steel Curtain keyed on him and held him to 15 yards. With their ground game thwarted, the Oilers had to rely on the pass to move the ball.

The Oilers scored early in the game on a pass, but it was thrown by Pittsburgh quarterback Terry Bradshaw. On the sixth play of the game, safety Vernon Perry grabbed the pass and dashed 75 yards to the end zone. The kick made the score 7-0.

Never one to panic, Bradshaw cooly directed the Pittsburgh offense along its usual game plan. By the end of the first quarter, the Houston lead was cut to 7-3. Toni Fritsch added a field goal early in the second quarter, but Bradshaw threw touchdown passes to Bennie Cunningham and John Stallworth for a 17-10 edge at halftime.

The key play of the game occurred in the third period. With a first down six yards from a touchdown, Dan Pastorini lofted a pass deep into the right corner of the end zone. Houston receiver Mike Renfro caught the pass as he was skidding beyond the back line of the end zone. The officials ruled that he had not kept his feet within the line as he caught the ball. After a hot dispute, the Oilers failed to score on the next two plays, and Toni Fritsch kicked a field goal. With their lead intact, the Steelers added 10 points in the fourth quarter and shut the Oilers out the rest of the way for a 27-13 triumph.

### SCORING

| | | | | |
|---|---|---|---|---|
| HOUSTON | 7 | 3 | 0 | 3–13 |
| PITTSBURGH | 3 | 14 | 0 | 10–27 |

First Quarter
Hou.　　Perry, 75 yard interception return
　　　　PAT – Fritsch (kick)
Pit.　　Bahr, 21 yard field goal

Second Quarter
Hou.　　Fritsch, 27 yard field goal
Pit.　　Cunningham, 16 yard pass from Bradshaw
　　　　PAT – Bahr (kick)
Pit.　　Stallworth, 20 yard pass from Bradshaw
　　　　PAT – Bahr (kick)

Fourth Quarter
Hou.　　Fritsch, 23 yard field goal
Pit.　　Bahr, 39 yard field goal
Pit.　　Bleier, 4 yard rush
　　　　PAT – Bahr (kick)

### TEAM STATISTICS

| HOUS. | | PITTS. |
|---|---|---|
| 11 | First Downs–Total | 22 |
| 2 | First Downs–Rushing | 9 |
| 7 | First Downs–Passing | 13 |
| 2 | First Downs–Penalty | 0 |
| 4 | Fumbles–Number | 1 |
| 2 | Fumbles–Lost Ball | 1 |
| 2 | Penalties–Number | 5 |
| 10 | Yards Penalized | 34 |
| 0 | Missed Field Goals | 1 |
| 52 | Offensive Plays | 69 |
| 227 | Net Yards | 358 |
| 4.4 | Average Gain | 5.2 |
| 3 | Giveaways | 2 |
| 2 | Takeaways | 3 |
| –1 | Difference | +1 |

### INDIVIDUAL STATISTICS

| LOS ANGELES | | | | TAMPA BAY | | | |
|---|---|---|---|---|---|---|---|
| | No. | Yds. | Avg. | | No. | Yds. | Avg. |
| **RUSHING** | | | | | | | |
| Bryant | 18 | 106 | 6.0 | Bell | 20 | 59 | 3.0 |
| Tyler | 28 | 86 | 3.1 | Mucker | 1 | 24 | 24.0 |
| McCutcheon | 6 | 26 | 4.3 | Eckwood | 2 | 5 | 2.5 |
| Ferragamo | 1 | –2 | –2.0 | J. Davis | 2 | 4 | 2.0 |
| | 53 | 216 | 4.1 | Rae | 1 | 0 | 0.0 |
| | | | | | 26 | 92 | 3.5 |
| **RECEIVING** | | | | | | | |
| Bryant | 4 | 39 | 10.8 | Hagins | 2 | 42 | 21.0 |
| Dennard | 3 | 56 | 18.7 | Bell | 2 | 12 | 6.0 |
| Young | 3 | 39 | 13.0 | Mucker | 1 | 42 | 42.0 |
| Nelson | 1 | 15 | 15.0 | | 5 | 96 | 19.2 |
| Tyler | 1 | 14 | 14.0 | | | | |
| | 12 | 163 | 13.6 | | | | |
| **PUNTING** | | | | | | | |
| Clark | 5 | | 37.2 | Blanchard | 8 | | 37.1 |
| **PUNT RETURNS** | | | | | | | |
| E. Brown | 6 | 67 | 11.2 | Reece | 2 | 14 | 7.0 |
| | | | | Johnson | 1 | 0 | 0.0 |
| | | | | | 3 | 14 | 4.7 |
| **KICKOFF RETURNS** | | | | | | | |
| E. Hill | 1 | 27 | 27.0 | Hagins | 4 | 106 | 26.5 |
| **INTERCEPTION RETURNS** | | | | | | | |
| Jim Youngbl'd | 1 | 10 | 10.0 | none | | | |

**PASSING**

| LOS ANGELES | Att. | Comp. | Comp. Pct. | Yds. | Int. | Yds./ Att. | Yds./ Comp. |
|---|---|---|---|---|---|---|---|
| Ferragamo | 23 | 12 | 52.2 | 163 | 0 | 7.1 | 13.6 |
| **TAMPA BAY** | | | | | | | |
| Williams | 13 | 2 | 15.4 | 12 | 1 | 0.9 | 6.0 |
| Rae | 13 | 2 | 15.4 | 42 | 0 | 3.2 | 21.0 |
| Eckwood | 1 | 1 | 100.0 | 42 | 0 | 42.0 | 42.0 |
| | 27 | 5 | 18.5 | 96 | 1 | 3.6 | 19.2 |

### INDIVIDUAL STATISTICS

| HOUSTON | | | | PITTSBURGH | | | |
|---|---|---|---|---|---|---|---|
| | No. | Yds. | Avg. | | No. | Yds. | Avg. |
| **RUSHING** | | | | | | | |
| Campbell | 17 | 15 | 0.9 | Harris | 21 | 85 | 4.0 |
| T. Wilson | 4 | 9 | 2.3 | Bleier | 13 | 52 | 4.0 |
| Caster | 1 | 0 | 0.0 | Bradshaw | 1 | 25 | 25.0 |
| | 22 | 24 | 1.1 | Thornton | 1 | –1 | –1.0 |
| | | | | | 36 | 161 | 4.5 |
| **RECEIVING** | | | | | | | |
| T. Wilson | 7 | 60 | 8.6 | Harris | 6 | 50 | 8.3 |
| Carpenter | 5 | 23 | 4.6 | Swann | 4 | 64 | 16.0 |
| Renfro | 3 | 52 | 17.3 | Stallworth | 3 | 52 | 17.3 |
| Coleman | 2 | 46 | 23.0 | Bleier | 3 | 39 | 13.0 |
| Merkens | 1 | 12 | 12.0 | Cunningham | 2 | 14 | 7.0 |
| Campbell | 1 | 11 | 11.0 | | 18 | 219 | 12.2 |
| Barber | 1 | 8 | 8.0 | | | | |
| | 20 | 212 | 10.6 | | | | |
| **PUNTING** | | | | | | | |
| Parsley | 4 | | 30.0 | Colquitt | 3 | | 51.0 |
| **PUNT RETURNS** | | | | | | | |
| Ellender | 3 | 8 | 2.7 | Bell | 3 | 8 | 2.7 |
| **KICKOFF RETURNS** | | | | | | | |
| Ellender | 4 | 47 | 11.8 | L. Anderson | 4 | 82 | 20.5 |
| Hartwig | 1 | 13 | 13.0 | | | | |
| Carpenter | 1 | 4 | 4.0 | | | | |
| | 6 | 64 | 10.7 | | | | |
| **INTERCEPTION RETURNS** | | | | | | | |
| Perry | 1 | 75 | 75.0 | Woodruff | 1 | 0 | 0.0 |

**PASSING**

| HOUSTON | Att. | Comp. | Comp. Pct. | Yds. | Int. | Yds./ Att. | Yds./ Comp. |
|---|---|---|---|---|---|---|---|
| Pastorini | 28 | 19 | 67.9 | 203 | 1 | 7.3 | 10.7 |
| Nielsen | 1 | 1 | 100.0 | 9 | 0 | 9.0 | 9.0 |
| | 29 | 20 | 68.9 | 212 | 1 | 7.3 | 10.6 |
| **PITTSBURGH** | | | | | | | |
| Bradshaw | 30 | 18 | 60.0 | 219 | 1 | 7.3 | 12.2 |

# Super Bowl XIV   Four Rings in Four Tries

According to the common wisdom, the Los Angeles Rams had snuck into this game only to be cannon fodder for the Pittsburgh Steelers. The Rams, after all, had only the sixth best record in the N.F.C. The Steelers, on the other hand, had been to the Super Bowl three times before and won each time. Although star linebacker Jack Ham was out with an ankle injury, the battle-hardened Steelers took the field at their prime.

The Steelers scored on their first possession, with Matt Bahr kicking a 41-yard field goal. The Rams then took the kickoff and drove downfield, scoring on Cullen Bryant's plunge from the one. Pittsburgh responded by scoring on the next possession to go ahead 10-7 early in the second quarter. While the Steelers could score no more in the first half, the Rams got two field goals from Frank Corral to go ahead 13-10 at halftime.

With an upset in the wind, the Steelers took charge on a 47-yard touchdown pass from Terry Bradshaw to Lynn Swann early in the third quarter. The Rams refused to recognize any shift in momentum. Vince Ferragamo threw to Billy Waddy for a 50 yard gain, and on the next play, halfback Lawrence McCutcheon threw a 24-yard scoring pass to Ron Smith. Although Corral missed the extra point, the Rams led 19-17 after three quarters.

In the fourth quarter, the Steelers played like champions. Less than three minutes into the period, John Stallworth beat the L.A. secondary and hauled in a long bomb for a 73-yard TD pass. With the score now 24-19 against them, the Rams began a drive with under nine minutes left. They drove from their own 16 yard line to the Pittsburgh 32-yard line. Ferragamo then shot a pass at Ron Smith, but Jack Lambert picked it off. Bradshaw then used a long pass to Stallworth and a pass interference call to drive the Steelers to the clinching touchdown in a 31-19 triumph.

## LINEUPS

| LOS ANGELES | | PITTSBURGH |
|---|---|---|
| | OFFENSE | |
| Waddy | WR | Stallworth |
| France | LT | Kolb |
| K. Hill | LG | Davis |
| Saul | C | Webster |
| Harrah | RG | Mullins |
| Slater | RT | Brown |
| Nelson | TE | Cunningham |
| Dennard | WR | Swann |
| Ferragamo | QB | Bradshaw |
| Tyler | RB | Harris |
| Bryant | RB | Bleier |
| | DEFENSE | |
| Jack Youngblood | LE | Greenwood |
| Fanning | LT | Greene |
| Brooks | RT | Dunn |
| Dryer | RE | Banaszak |
| Jim Youngblood | LLB | Winston |
| Reynolds | MLB | Lambert |
| Brudzinski | RLB | Cole |
| Thomas | LCB | Johnson |
| Perry | RCB | Blount |
| Elmendorf | SS | Shell |
| Cromwell | FS | Thomas |
| | SUBSTITUTES | |
| **LOS ANGELES** | | |
| | OFFENSE | |
| Bain | Jodat | Ryczek |
| Gravelle | Lee | R. Smith |
| D. Hill | McCutc'n | Young |
| E. Hill | Rutledge | |
| | DEFENSE | |
| Andrews | Harris | Wallace |
| E. Brown | O'Steen | Westbrooks |
| Doss | Sully | Wilkinson |
| Ellis | | |
| | KICKERS | |
| Clark | | Corral |
| **PITTSBURGH** | | |
| | OFFENSE | |
| A. Anderson | Grossman | Petersen |
| Bell | Hawth'ne | Smith |
| Courson | Kruczek | Stoudt |
| Dornbrook | Moser | Thornton |
| | DEFENSE | |
| L. Anderson | Graves | Valentine |
| Beasley | Ham | White |
| Furness | Toews | Woodruff |
| | KICKERS | |
| Bahr | | Colquitt |

## SCORING

| | | | | |
|---|---|---|---|---|
| LOS ANGELES | 7 | 6 | 6 | 0– 19 |
| PITTSBURGH | 3 | 7 | 7 | 14– 31 |

**First Quarter**
Pit.  Bahr, 41 yard field goal
L.A.  Bryant, 1 yard rush
        PAT – Corral (kick)

**Second Quarter**
Pit.  Harris, 1 yard rush
        PAT – Bahr (kick)
L.A.  Corral, 31 yard field goal
L.A.  Corral, 45 yard field goal

**Third Quarter**
Pit.  Swann, 47 yard pass from Bradshaw
        PAT – Bahr (kick)
L.A.  R. Smith, 24 yard pass from McCutcheon
        PAT – kick failed

**Fourth Quarter**
Pit.  Stallworth, 73 yard pass from Bradshaw
        PAT – Bahr (kick)
Pit.  Harris, 1 yard rush
        PAT – Bahr (kick)

## TEAM STATISTICS

| L.A. | | PITT. |
|---|---|---|
| 16 | First Downs–Total | 19 |
| 6 | First Downs–Rushing | 8 |
| 9 | First Downs–Passing | 10 |
| 1 | First Downs–Penalty | 1 |
| 0 | Fumbles–Number | 0 |
| 0 | Fumbles–Lost Ball | 0 |
| 2 | Penalties–Number | 6 |
| 26 | Yards Penalized | 65 |
| 0 | Missed Field Goals | 0 |
| 59 | Offensive Plays | 58 |
| 301 | Net Yards | 393 |
| 5.1 | Average Gain | 6.8 |
| 1 | Giveaways | 3 |
| 3 | Takeaways | 1 |
| +2 | Difference | –2 |

## INDIVIDUAL STATISTICS

| LOS ANGELES | No. | Yds. | Avg. | PITTSBURGH | No. | Yds. | Avg. |
|---|---|---|---|---|---|---|---|
| | | | | **RUSHING** | | | |
| Tyler | 17 | 60 | 3.5 | Harris | 20 | 46 | 2.3 |
| Bryant | 6 | 30 | 5.0 | Bleier | 10 | 25 | 2.5 |
| McCutcheon | 5 | 10 | 2.0 | Bradshaw | 3 | 9 | 3.0 |
| Ferragamo | 1 | 7 | 7.0 | Thornton | 4 | 4 | 1.0 |
| | 29 | 107 | 3.7 | | 37 | 84 | 2.3 |
| | | | | **RECEIVING** | | | |
| Waddy | 3 | 75 | 25.0 | Swann | 5 | 79 | 15.8 |
| Bryant | 3 | 21 | 7.0 | Stallworth | 3 | 121 | 40.3 |
| Tyler | 3 | 20 | 6.7 | Harris | 3 | 66 | 22.0 |
| Dennard | 2 | 32 | 16.0 | Cunningham | 2 | 21 | 10.5 |
| Nelson | 2 | 20 | 10.0 | Thornton | 1 | 22 | 22.0 |
| D. Hill | 1 | 28 | 28.0 | | 14 | 309 | 22.1 |
| R. Smith | 1 | 24 | 24.0 | | | | |
| McCutcheon | 1 | 16 | 16.0 | | | | |
| | 16 | 236 | 14.8 | | | | |
| | | | | **PUNTING** | | | |
| Clark | 5 | | 44.0 | Colquitt | 2 | | 42.5 |
| | | | | **PUNT RETURNS** | | | |
| E. Brown | 1 | 4 | 4.0 | Bell | 2 | 17 | 8.5 |
| | | | | Smith | 2 | 14 | 7.0 |
| | | | | | 4 | 31 | 7.8 |
| | | | | **KICKOFF RETURNS** | | | |
| E. Hill | 3 | 47 | 15.7 | L. Anderson | 5 | 162 | 32.4 |
| Judat | 2 | 32 | 16.0 | | | | |
| Andrews | 1 | 0 | 0.0 | | | | |
| | 6 | 79 | 13.2 | | | | |
| | | | | **INTERCEPTION RETURNS** | | | |
| Elmendorf | 1 | 10 | 10.0 | Lambert | 1 | 16 | 16.0 |
| E. Brown | 1 | 6 | 6.0 | | | | |
| Perry | 1 | –1 | –1.0 | | | | |
| Thomas | 0 | 6 | — | | | | |
| | 3 | 21 | 7.0 | | | | |

### PASSING

| LOS ANGELES | Att. | Comp. | Comp. Pct. | Yds. | Int. | Yds./ Att. | Yds./ Comp. | Yards Lost Tackled |
|---|---|---|---|---|---|---|---|---|
| Ferragamo | 25 | 15 | 60.0 | 212 | 1 | 8.5 | 14.1 | |
| McCutcheon | 1 | 1 | 100.0 | 24 | 0 | 24.0 | 24.0 | |
| | 26 | 16 | 61.5 | 23.6 | 1 | 12.9 | 14.8 | 4-42 |
| **PITTSBURGH** | | | | | | | | |
| Bradshaw | 21 | 14 | 66.7 | 309 | 3 | 14.7 | 22.1 | 0-0 |

| Use Name (Nickname) - Positions | Team by Year | See Section | Hgt. | Wgt. | College | Int | Pts |
|---|---|---|---|---|---|---|---|
| Abramowicz, Dan WR-OE | 67-73NO 73-74SF 75Buf | 2 | 6'1" | 195 | Xavier-Ohio | | 234 |
| Acks, Ron LB | 68-71Atl 72-73NE 74-76GB | | 6'2" | 223 | Illinois | 2 | 6 |
| Adamle, Mike HB-FB | 71-72KC 73-74NYJ 75-76Chi | 23 | 5'9" | 196 | Northwestern | | 38 |
| Adams, Bill OG-OT | 72-78Buf | | 6'2" | 248 | Holy Cross | | |
| Adams, Bob TE-OT | 69-71Pit 72JJ 73-74NE 75Den 76-77Atl | 2 | 6'2" | 222 | U. of Pacific | | |
| Adams, Brent OT-OG | 75-77Atl 78KJ 79LA | | 6'5" | 256 | Tenn-Chattanooga | | |
| Adams, Doug LB | 71-74Cin | | 6' | 225 | Ohio State | 3 | |
| Adams, Julius DE-DT | 71-85,87NE | | 6'3" | 262 | Texas Southern | | |
| Adams, Pete OG | 74Cle 75KJ 76Cle 77JJ | | 6'4" | 260 | Southern Calif. | | |
| Adams, Sam OG | 72-80NE 81NO | | 6'3" | 256 | Prairie View | | |
| Adams, Tony QB | 75-78KC 87Min | 12 | 6' | 198 | Utah State | | |
| Adkins, Margene WR | 70-71Dal 72NO 73NYJ 75WFL | 23 | 5'10" | 183 | Henderson J.C. | | |
| Aiu, Charles OG | 76-78SD 78Sea | | 6'2" | 251 | Hawaii | | |
| Albert, Sergio K | 74StL | | 6'3" | 195 | U.S. International | | |
| Albrecht, Ted OT-OG | 77-81Chi 82KJ | | 6'4" | 251 | California | | |
| Alexakos, Steve OG | 70Den 71NYG | | 6'2" | 260 | San Diego State | | |
| Alexander, Glenn WR | 70Buf | | 6'3" | 205 | Grambling | | |
| Alexander, John DE | 77-78Mia | | 6'2" | 250 | Rutgers | | |
| Alexander, Willie DB | 71-79Hou | | 6'2" | 194 | Alcorn State | 23 | 6 |
| Allen, Doug LB | 74-75Buf | | 6'2" | 228 | Penn State | 1 | |
| Allen, George | HC66-70LA HC71-77Was | | | | Alma, Marquette, | | |
| | | | | | Michigan | | |
| Allen, Grady LB | 68-72Atl | | 6'3" | 226 | Texas A&M | 2 | |
| Allen, Jackie DB | 69OakA 70-71Buf 72Phi 73JJ | | 6'1" | 187 | Baylor | | |
| Allen, Jeff DB | 71StL 72JJ | | 5'11' | 190 | Iowa State | | |
| Allen, Jim DB | 74-77Pit 78-81Det | | 6'2" | 194 | U.C.L.A. | 31 | 6 |
| Allen, Nate DB | 71-74KC 75SF 76-79Min 79Det | | 5'10" | 172 | Texas Southern | 9 | 12 |
| Allison, Henry OG-OT | 71-72Phi 75-77StL 77Den | | 6'3" | 257 | San Diego State | | |
| Alston, Mack TE | 70-72Was 73-76Hou 77-80Bal | 2 | 6'2" | 231 | Md. Eastern Shore | | 90 |
| Alward, Tom OG | 76TB | | 6'4" | 255 | Nebraska | | |
| Alzado, Lyle DE-DT | 71-78Den 79-81Cle 82-84Raid | | 6'3" | 254 | Yankton | | 2 |
| Ambrose, Dick (Bam Bam) LB | 75-83Cle 84NJ | | 6' | 232 | Virginia | 5 | |
| Amman, Dick DE-DT | 72-73Bal | | 6'5" | 242 | Florida State | | |
| Amundson, George FB-HB | 73-74Hou 75Phi | 2 | 6'3" | 215 | Iowa State | | 30 |
| Anderson, Bobby HB-FB | 70-73Den 74BN 75Was | 23 | 6' | 208 | Colorado | | 66 |
| Anderson, Dick DB | 68-69MiaA 70-74Mia 75KJ 76-77Mia | 3 | 6'2" | 198 | Colorado | 34 | 24 |
| Anderson, Donny HB | 66-71GB 72-74StL | 234 | 6'3" | 212 | Texas Tech | | 336 |
| Anderson, Gary OG | 77-78Det 78NO 79NJ 80Was | | 6'3" | 253 | Stanford | | |
| | 83-85USFL | | | | | | |
| Anderson, Jerry DB | 77Cin 78TB 79JJ | | 5'11" | 196 | Oklahoma | | |
| Anderson, Ken QB | 71-86Cin | 12 | 6'1" | 210 | Augustana (Ill.) | | 120 |
| Anderson, Preston DB | 74Cle | | 6'1" | 183 | Rice | | |
| Anderson, Ralph (Sticks) DB | 71-72Pit 73NE | | 6'2" | 180 | West Texas State | 6 | 2 |
| Anderson, Rickey FB | 78SD 79KJ | | 6'1" | 211 | S. Carolina State | | |
| Anderson, Scott C | 74-76Min | | 6'4" | 242 | Missouri | | |
| Anderson, Terry WR | 77-78Mia 78Was 80SF | | 5'9" | 182 | Bethune-Cookman | | |
| Anderson, Tim DB | 75SF 76Buf | | 6' | 193 | Ohio State | | |
| Anderson, Warren WR | 77Hou 78StL | | 6'2" | 195 | West Virginia St. | | |
| Andrews, Al LB | 70-71Buf | | 6'3" | 216 | New Mexico State | 1 | |
| Andrews, Billy LB | 67-74Cle 75SD 76-77 KC | | 6' | 223 | Southeastern La. | 7 | 6 |
| Andrews, John TE-HB | 72SD 73-74Bal | | 6'3" | 222 | Indiana | | 6 |
| Andrews, John DE-DT | 75-76Mia | | 6'6" | 251 | Morgan State | | |
| Andrusyshyn, Zenon K | 78KC 79-82CFL 83-85USFL | 4 | 6'2" | 210 | California | | |
| Ane, Charlie C | 75-80KC 81GB | | 6'1" | 234 | Michigan State | | |
| Anthony, Charles LB | 74SD 75KJ | | 6'1" | 230 | Southern Calif. | 1 | |
| Antoine, Lionel OT | 72-76Chi 77KJ 78Chi 79KJ | | 6'6" | 262 | Southern Illinois | | |
| Archer, Troy DT-DE | 76-78NYG | | 6'4" | 250 | Colorado | | 6 |
| | 1979 — Died in automobile accident | | | | | | |
| Ardizzane, Tony C | 79Chi | | 6'3" | 241 | Northwestern | | |
| Armstrong, Otis HB | 73-80Den | 23 | 5'10" | 196 | Purdue | | 192 |
| Arneson, Jim OG-C | 73-74Dal 75Was | | 6'3" | 247 | Arizona | | |
| Arneson, Mark LB | 72-80StL | | 6'2" | 222 | Arizona | 5 | 6 |
| Arnold, Francis OG | 74Den | | 6'3" | 295 | Oregon | | |
| Arnsparger, Bill | HC74-76NYG | | | | Miami-Ohio | | |
| Arrington, Rick QB | 70-72Phi | 1 | 6'2" | 187 | Tulsa | | 6 |
| Arthur, Gary TE | 70-77NYJ | | 6'5" | 254 | Miami-Ohio | | |
| Asher, Bob OT-OG | 70Dal 71JJ 72-75Chi | | 6'5" | 254 | Vanderbilt | | |
| Ashton, Josh HB-FB | 72-74NE 75StL | 2 | 6'1" | 204 | Tulsa | | 24 |
| Askea, Mike OT | 73Den | | 6'4" | 260 | Stanford | | |
| Askson, Bert TE-DE | 71Pit 73NO 74WFL 75-77GB | | 6'3" | 223 | Texas Southern | | 6 |
| Atessis, Bill DE-DT | 71NE | | 6'3" | 240 | Texas | | |
| Athas, Pete DB-WR | 71-74NYG 75Cle 75Min 76NO | 3 | 5'11" | 185 | Tennessee | 16 | 6 |
| Atkins, Bob DB | 68-69StL 70-76Hou | | 6'3" | 211 | Grambling | 19 | 6 |
| Atkins, Dave HB | 73SF 75SD | | 6'1" | 205 | Texas-El Paso | | 6 |
| Atkinson, Al LB | 65-69NY-A 70-74 NYJ 75KJ | | 6'1" | 229 | Villanova | 21 | |
| Atkinson, Butch DB | 68-69OakA 70-77Oak 79Den | 3 | 6' | 182 | Morris Brown | 30 | 42 |
| Austin, Darrell OG-C-OT | 75-78NYJ 79-80TB 81ZJ | | 6'4" | 252 | South Carolina | | |
| Austin, Hise LB | 73KC 74WFL 75GB | | 6'4" | 191 | Prairie View | | |
| Austin, Ocie DB | 69Bal 70-71Pit | | 6'3" | 200 | Utah State | 3 | |
| Avellini, Bob QB | 75-84Chi 84NYJ | 12 | 6'2" | 208 | Maryland | | 30 |
| Avery, Ken LB | 67-68NYG 69CinA 70-74Cin 75KC 76JJ | | 6'1" | 225 | Southern Miss. | 2 | |
| Babb, Charlie DB | 72-79Mia | | 6' | 190 | Memphis State | 12 | 6 |
| Babich, Bob LB | 70-72SD 73-78Cle | | 6'2" | 231 | Miami-Ohio | 6 | 6 |
| Babinecz, John LB | 72-73Dal 74JJ 75Chi | | 6'1" | 222 | Villanova | 1 | |
| Bachman, Ted DB | 76Sea 76Mia | | 6' | 190 | New Mexico State | | |
| Bacon, Coy DE-DT | 68-72LA 73-75SD 76-77Cin 78-81Was | | 6'4" | 269 | Jackson State | 2 | 10 |
| | 83USFL | | | | | | |
| Bailey, Jim DT-DE | 70-74Bal 75NYJ 76-78 Atl | | 6'4" | 253 | Kansas | 1 | |
| Bailey, Larry DT | 74Atl | | 6'4" | 238 | U. of Pacific | | |
| Bailey, Mark FB | 77-78KC 80KJ | 2 | 6'3" | 237 | Long Beach State | | 18 |
| Bailey, Tom HB-FB | 71-74Phi 75KJ | 2 | 6'2" | 211 | Florida State | | 12 |
| Baker, Ed QB | 72Hou | | 6'2" | 198 | Lafayette | | |
| Baker, John DE | 70NYG | | 6'5" | 260 | Norfolk State | | |
| Baker, Melvin WR | 74Mia 75NO 75NE 75SD 76Hou 77Buf | | 6' | 189 | Texas Southern | | 12 |
| Baker, Tony FB-HB | 68-71NO 71-72Phi 73-74LA 75SD | 2 | 5'11" | 224 | Iowa State | | 102 |
| Baker, Wayne DT | 75SF | | 6'6" | 270 | Brigham Young | | |
| Baldassin, Mike LB | 77-78SF 79JJ | | 6'1" | 218 | Washington | | 6 |
| Ball, Larry LB | 72-74Mia 75Det 76TB 77-78Mia | | 6'6" | 232 | Louisville | 2 | 6 |
| Ballou, Mike LB | 70Bos | | 6'3" | 235 | U.C.L.A. | | |
| Banaszak, John DE-DT | 75-81Pit 83-85USFL | | 6'3" | 242 | Eastern Michigan | 1 | |
| Banaszak, Pete HB-FB | 66-69OakA 70-78Oak | 2 | 5'11" | 206 | Miami (Fla.) | | 312 |
| Banaszek, Cas OT-C | 68-77SF | | 6'3" | 249 | Northwestern | | |
| Banks, Tom C-OG | 71-80StL 83-84USFL | | 6'1" | 243 | Auburn | | |
| Banks, Willie OG | 68-69Was 70NYG 73NE | | 6'2" | 240 | Alcorn State | | |
| Bankston, Warren TE-FB | 69-72Pit 73-78Oak | 2 | 6'4" | 233 | Tulane | | 30 |
| Bannon, Bruce LB | 73-74Mia | | 6'3" | 225 | Penn State | | |
| Barber, Bob DE-DT | 76-79GB 80-81CFL 83USFL | | 6'3" | 240 | Grambling | | |
| Barefield, John LB | 78-80StL 83-85USFL | | 6'2" | 224 | Texas A&I | | |
| Barisich, Carl NT-DT | 73-75Cle 76Sea 77-80Mia 81NYG | | 6'4" | 255 | Princeton | | |

| Use Name (Nickname) - Positions | Team by Year | See Section | Hgt. | Wgt. | College | Int | Pts |
|---|---|---|---|---|---|---|---|
| Barkum, Jerome TE-WR | 72-83NYJ | 2 | 6'3" | 218 | Jackson State | | 240 |
| Barnes, Al WR | 72-73Det 74WFL | | 6'1" | 170 | New Mexico State | | 12 |
| Barnes, Benny DB | 72-83Dal | | 6'1" | 192 | Stanford | 11 | 16 |
| Barnes, Bruce K | 73-74NE | 4 | 5'11" | 214 | U.C.L.A. | | |
| Barnes, Joe QB | 74Chi | | 5'11" | 196 | Texas Tech | | |
| Barnes, Larry FB-HB | 77-78SD 78StL 78-79Phi 80LJ | 2 | 5'11" | 220 | Tennessee State | | 12 |
| Barnes, Mike DT-DE | 73-81Bal | | 6'6" | 256 | Miami (Fla.) | | |
| Barnes, Pete LB | 67-68Hou 69-72SD 73-75StL 76-77NE | | 6'3" | 242 | Southern U. | 15 | 6 |
| Barnes, Rodrigo LB | 73-74Dal 74-75NE 75Mia 76Oak | | 6'1" | 215 | Rice | | |
| Barney, Lem DB | 67-77Det | 34 | 6'1" | 189 | Jackson State | 56 | 66 |
| Barrett, Jean OT-C-OG | 73-77SF 78FJ 79-80SF | | 6'6" | 251 | Tulsa | | |
| Barry, Fred DB | 70Pit | | 5'10" | 184 | Boston U. | | |
| Barzilauskas, Carl DT | 74-77NYJ 78-79GB | | 6'6" | 271 | Indiana | 1 | |
| Baska, Rick LB | 76-77Den | | 6'3" | 225 | U.C.L.A. | | |
| Bass, Mike DB | 67Det 69-73Was | | 6' | 190 | Michigan | 30 | 24 |
| Bateman, Marv K | 72-74Dal 74-77Buf | 4 | 6'4" | 213 | Utah | | 1 |
| Baumgartner, Steve DE-LB-DT | 73-77NO 77-79Hou | | 6'7" | 256 | Purdue | | |
| Bayless, Tom OG | 70NYJ | | 6'3" | 240 | Purdue | | |
| Baylor, Raymond DE | 74SD | | 6'5" | 263 | Texas Southern | | |
| Baylor, Tim DB | 76-78Bal 79Min | | 6'6" | 195 | Morgan State | | |
| Beamer, Tim DB | 71Buf | | 5'11" | 185 | Johnson C. Smith | | |
| Beamon, Autry DB | 75-76Min 77-79Sea 80-81Cle | | 6'1" | 190 | East Texas State | 13 | 8 |
| Bean, Bubba HB-FB | 76-79Atl 80KJ | 2 | 5'11" | 195 | Texas A&M | | 48 |
| Beard, Tom C | 72Buf | | 6'6" | 280 | Michigan State | | |
| Beasley, John TE | 67-70Min 71JJ 72-73Min 73-74NO | 2 | 6'3" | 229 | California | | 84 |
| Beasley, Terry WR | 72SF 73SJ 74-75SF | 2 | 5'10" | 183 | Auburn | | 18 |
| Beatty, Chuck DB | 69-72Pit 72StL | | 6'2" | 203 | North Texas | 4 | 6 |
| Beauchamp, Al LB | 68-69CinA 70-75Cin 76StL | | 6'2" | 235 | Southern U. | 15 | 18 |
| Beauchamp, Joe DB | 66-69SD-A 70-75SD | | 6' | 185 | Iowa State | 23 | 18 |
| Beaudoin, Doug DB | 76-79NE 80Mia 81SD 83-85USFL | | 6'1" | 193 | Minnesota | 4 | |
| Bebout, Nick OT | 73-75Atl 76-79Sea 80Min | | 6'5" | 261 | Wyoming | | |
| Beck, Braden K | 71Hou | | 6'2" | 200 | Stanford | | 4 |
| Becker, Doug LB | 78Chi 78Buf | | 6' | 222 | Notre Dame | | |
| Beckman, Tom DE | 72StL | | 6'5" | 250 | Michigan | | |
| Beirne, Jim WR-TE | 68-69HouA 70-73Hou 74SD 75-76Hou | 2 | 6'2" | 198 | Purdue | | 68 |
| Beisler, Randy OG-DE-OT | 66-68Phi 69-74SF | | 6'4" | 249 | Indiana | 1 | |
| Belk, Bill DE-DT | 68-74SF | | 6'3" | 248 | Md. Eastern Shore | 1 | 12 |
| Bell, Bill K | 71-72Atl 73NE | 5 | 6'1" | 191 | Kansas | | 154 |
| Bell, Bob DE-DT | 71-73Det 74-78StL | | 6'4" | 252 | Cincinnati | | 6 |
| Bell, Carlos TE | 71NO 72JJ | | 6'5" | 238 | Houston | | |
| Bell, Eddie WR | 70-75NYJ 76SD | 2 | 5'10" | 160 | Idaho State | | 72 |
| Bell, Gordon HB | 76-77NYG 78StL | 23 | 5'9" | 180 | Michigan | | 12 |
| Bell, Joe DE | 79Oak | | 6'3" | 250 | Norfolk State | | |
| Bell, Kevin WR | 78NYJ | | 5'10" | 180 | Lamar | | |
| Belser, Ceaser DB-LB | 68-69KC-A 70-71KC 74SD | | 6' | 211 | Ark.-Pine Bluff | | |
| Belton, Horace HB | 78-80KC 81KJ | 23 | 5'8" | 200 | Southeastern La. | | 18 |
| Belton, Willie HB | 71-72Atl 73-74StL | 23 | 5'11" | 198 | Md. Eastern Shore | | 6 |
| Benjamin, Tony FB | 77-79Sea | | 6'3" | 225 | Duke | | |
| Benson, Duane LB | 67-69OakA 70-71Oak 72-73Atl | | 6'2" | 217 | Hamline | 3 | |
| Berger, Ron DE-DT | 69BosA 70Bos 71-72NE | | 6'8" | 278 | Wayne State | | |
| Bergey, Bill LB | 69CinA 70-73Cin 74-80Phi 81KJ | | 6'2" | 245 | Arkansas State | 27 | |
| Bergey, Bruce DE | 71KC 72-73CFL 74-75WFL | | 6'4" | 240 | U.C.L.A. | | |
| Bernhardt, Roger OG | 74NYJ 75KC 76JJ | | 6'4" | 244 | Kansas | | |
| Bernich, Ken LB | 75NYJ | | 6'2" | 250 | Auburn | | |
| Berra, Tim WR | 74Bal | | 5'11" | 185 | Massachusetts | | |
| Berry, Bob QB | 65-67Min 68-72Atl 73-76Min | 12 | 5'11" | 189 | Oregon | | 24 |
| Berry, Reggie DB | 72-74SD | | 6' | 188 | Long Beach State | | |
| Berry, Royce DE | 69CinA 70-74Cin 75BW 76Chi | | 6'3" | 247 | Houston | | 12 |
| Bertelsen, Jim FB-HB | 72-76LA | 23 | 5'11" | 205 | Texas | | 108 |
| Bertuca, Tony LB | 74Bal | | 6'2" | 225 | Chico State | | |
| Besana, Fred QB | 77Buf 78NYG 83-85USFL | | 6'4" | 203 | California | | |
| Best, Art HB | 77-78Chi 80NYG | | 6'1" | 205 | Kent State | | |
| Best, Keith LB | 72KC | | 6'3" | 220 | Kansas State | | |
| Bethea, Elvin DE | 68-69HouA 70-83Hou | | 6'3" | 257 | N. Carolina A&T | | 8 |
| Betterson, James FB | 77-78Phi | 2 | 6' | 210 | North Carolina | | 6 |
| Bettiga, Mike WR | 74SF | | 6'3" | 193 | Humboldt State | | |
| Beutler, Tom LB | 70Cle 71Bal | | 6'1" | 232 | Toledo | | |
| Beverly, David K | 74-75Hou 75-80GB | 4 | 6'2" | 180 | Auburn | | |
| Beverly, Ed WR | 73SF | | 5'11" | 168 | Arizona State | | |
| Biedermann, Leo OT | 78Cle 82CFL 83USFL | | 6'7" | 254 | California | | |
| Biggs, Verlon DE-DT | 65-69NY-A 70NYJ 71-74Was 75KJ | | 6'4" | 267 | Jackson State | 1 | 12 |
| Biletnikoff, Fred WR-FL | 65-69OakA 70-78Oak | 2 | 6'1" | 190 | Florida State | | 462 |
| Billingsley, Ron DT-DE | 67-69SD-A 70SD | | 6'8" | 278 | Wyoming | | |
| Bingham, Gregg LB | 73-84Hou | | 6'1" | 229 | Purdue | 21 | 6 |
| Birney, Tom K | 79-80GB | 5 | 6'4" | 220 | Michigan State | | 60 |
| Bishop, Richard NT-DE-DT | 76-81NE 82Mia 83LA | | 6'1" | 263 | Louisville | | |
| Bitterlich, Don K | 76Sea | | 5'7" | 166 | Temple | | 10 |
| Bjorklund, Hank HB | 72-74NYJ | 2 | 6'1" | 200 | Princeton | | |
| Black, Stan DB | 77SF | | 6' | 196 | Mississippi State | | |
| Black, Tim LB | 77StL | | 6'2" | 215 | Baylor | | |
| Blackwell, Alois HB | 78-79Dal 80JJ | | 5'10" | 195 | Houston | | |
| Blahak, Joe DB | 73Hou 74-75Min 76TB 76NE 77Min | | 5'9" | 187 | Nebraska | 3 | 2 |
| Blair, Matt LB | 74-85Min | | 6'5" | 232 | Iowa State | 16 | 12 |
| Blair, T.C. TE | 74Det | | 6'4" | 220 | Tulsa | | |
| Blanchard, Dick LB | 72NE | | 6'3" | 225 | Tulsa | 1 | |
| Blanchard, Tom K | 71-73NYG 74-78NO 79-81TB | 4 | 6' | 185 | Oregon | | |
| Blankenship, Greg LB | 76Oak 76Pit | | 6'1" | 212 | Hayward State | | |
| Bleamer, Jeff OT-OG | 75-76Phi 77NYJ | | 6'4" | 253 | Penn State | | |
| Bleier, Rocky HB | 68Pit 69MS 70inj from MS 71-80Pit | 2 | 5'11" | 207 | Notre Dame | | 150 |
| Blount, Jeb QB | 77TB | 1 | 6'3" | 200 | Tulsa | | |
| Blount, Mel DB | 70-83Pit | 3 | 6'3" | 205 | Southern U. | 57 | 24 |
| Blue, Forrest C-OT | 68-74SF 75-78Bal | | 6'5" | 259 | Auburn | | 6 |
| Blue, Luther WR | 77-79Det 80Phi | 2 | 5'11" | 185 | Iowa State | | 24 |
| Boatwright, Ron DT | 74SD | | 6'5" | 262 | Oklahoma State | | |
| Boden, Lynn OG-OT | 75-78Det 79Chi | | 6'5" | 266 | S. Dakota State | | |
| Bolton, Andy HB | 76Sea 76-78Det | | 6'1" | 205 | Fisk | | |
| Bolton, Ron DB | 72-75NE 76-82Cle | | 6'2" | 172 | Virginia State | 35 | 6 |
| Bonner, Glen HB | 74-75SD | 2 | 6'2" | 202 | Washington | | 24 |
| Bonness, Rik LB | 76Oak 77-80TB | | 6'5" | 219 | Nebraska | | |
| Boone, Dave DE | 74Min | | 6'3" | 248 | Eastern Michigan | | |
| Boozer, Emerson HB | 66-69NY-A 70-75NYJ | 23 | 5'11" | 203 | Md. Eastern Shore | | 390 |
| Bordelon, Ken LB | 76-77NO 78KJ 79-82NO 83LJ | | 6'4" | 228 | Louisiana State | 3 | 6 |
| Boryla, Mike QB | 74-76Phi 77KJ 78TB | 12 | 6'3" | 200 | Stanford | | 12 |
| Bosarge, Wade DB | 77Mia 77NO | | 5'10" | 175 | Tulsa | | |
| Bouggess, Lee FB | 70-71Phi 72JJ 73Phi | 2 | 6'2" | 210 | Louisville | | 48 |

| Use Name (Nickname) - Positions | Team by Year | See Section | Hgt. | Wgt. | College | Int | Pts |
|---|---|---|---|---|---|---|---|
| Bowdell, Gordon WR | 71Den | | 6'2" | 203 | Michigan | | |
| Boyd, Elmo WR | 78SF 78GB | | 6' | 188 | Eastern Kentucky | | 6 |
| Boyd, Greg DB | 73NO 74NE | | 6'2" | 201 | Arizona | | |
| Boyett, Lon TE | 78SF 79JJ | | 6'6" | 240 | Northridge State | | |
| Boykin, Greg FB-HB | 77NO 78SF | 2 | 6' | 225 | Northwestern | | 12 |
| Bradley, Bill DB | 69-76Phi 77StL | 34 | 5'11" | 190 | Texas | 34 | 6 |
| Bradley, Chuck TE | 75-77SD 77Chi | | 6'6" | 243 | Oregon | | |
| Bradley, Dave OG | 69-71GB 72StL | | 6'4" | 245 | Penn State | | |
| Bradley, Ed LB | 72-75Pit 76Sea 77-78SF 79BN | | 6'2" | 234 | Wake Forest | 1 | |
| Bradshaw, Morris WR | 74-81Oak 82NE 84USFL | 2 | 6' | 196 | Ohio State | | 78 |
| Bradshaw, Terry QB | 70-83Pit | 12 | 6'3" | 215 | Louisiana Tech | | 192 |
| Bragg, Mike K | 68-79Was 80Bal | 4 | 5'11" | 186 | Richmond | | 10 |
| Brahaney, Tom C | 73-81StL | | 6'2" | 245 | Oklahoma | | |
| Branch, Cliff WR | 72-81Oak 82-85Raid 86LJ | 2 | 5'11" | 170 | Colorado | | 402 |
| Bransletter, Kent OT | 73GB | | 6'3" | 260 | Houston | | |
| Braxton, Jim FB | 71-78Buf 78Mia | 2 | 6'2" | 238 | West Virginia | | 186 |
| Brazile, Robert LB | 75-84Hou | | 6'4" | 241 | Jackson State | 13 | |
| Breunig, Bob LB | 75-84Dal | | 6'2" | 226 | Arizona State | 9 | |
| Brezina, Greg LB | 68-69Atl 70KJ 71-79Atl | | 6'2" | 222 | Houston | 12 | |
| Briggs, Bob DE-DT | 68-69SD-A 70SD 71-73Cle 74KC | | 6'4" | 267 | Heidelberg | 1 | 12 |
| Brinkman, Charlie WR | 72Cle | | 6'2" | 208 | Louisville | | |
| Brinson, Larry FB | 77-79Dal 80Sea 81KJ | 23 | 6' | 214 | Florida | | 24 |
| Briscoe, Marlin WR-QB | 68DenA 69Buf-A 70-71Buf | 12 | 5'10" | 178 | Nebraska-Omaha | | 198 |
| | 72-74Mia 75SD 76Det 76NE | | | | | | |
| Brister, Willie TE | 74-75NYJ | | 6'4" | 236 | Southern U. | | |
| Bristor, John DB | 79SF | | 6' | 188 | Waynesburg | | |
| Broadnax, Jerry TE | 74Hou 75WFL | | 6'2" | 225 | Southern U. | | |
| Brock, Willie C | 78Det | | 6'3" | 246 | Colorado | | |
| Brockington, John FB | 71-77GB 77KC | 2 | 6'1" | 225 | Ohio State | | 204 |
| Brooks, Billy WR | 76-79Cin 81SD 81Hou | 2 | 6'3" | 204 | Oklahoma | | 42 |
| Brooks, Bobby DB | 74-76NYG | | 6'1" | 195 | Bishop | 5 | |
| Brooks, Cliff DB | 72-74Cle 75-76Phi 76NYJ 76Buf | | 6'1" | 190 | Tennessee State | | |
| Brooks, Larry DT | 72-82LA | | 6'3" | 255 | Virginia State | | |
| Brooks, Lee DT | 70-72Hou 73-76StL | | 6'5" | 256 | Texas | 1 | |
| Broussard, Steve K | 75GB | 4 | 6' | 200 | Southern Miss. | | |
| Brown, Aaron DE | 66KC-A 67LJ 68-69KC-A 70-72KC | | 6'5" | 263 | Minnesota | 1 | 6 |
| | 73-74GB | | | | | | |
| Brown, Bob TE | 69-70StL 71Min 72-73NO | 2 | 6'3" | 225 | Alcorn State | | 6 |
| Brown, Bob DT-DE | 66-73GB 74SD 75-76Cin | | 6'5" | 268 | Ark.-Pine Bluff | | 2 |
| Brown, Booker OT-OG | 75SD 76IL 77SD 78KJ | | 6'2" | 257 | Southern Calif. | | |
| Brown, Boyd TE | 74-76Den 77NYG | | 6'4" | 216 | Alcorn State | | |
| Brown, Carlos QB | 75-76GB | 1 | 6'3" | 210 | U. of Pacific | | |
| Brown, Charlie WR | 70Det 71JJ | | 6'2" | 195 | Northern Arizona | | |
| Brown, Chuck C-OG | 79StL | | 6'1" | 235 | Houston | | |
| Brown, Dean DB | 69Cle 70Mia 71JJ | | 5'10" | 170 | Ft. Valley State | 1 | |
| Brown, Eddie DB | 74-75Cle 75-77Was 78-79LA 83-84 | 3 | 5'11" | 187 | Tennessee | 6 | 6 |
| | 83-84USFL | | | | | | |
| Brown, Ken HB-FB | 70-75Cle | 23 | 5'10" | 204 | none | | 54 |
| Brown, Ken C | 79Den 80GB | | 6'1" | 245 | New Mexico | | |
| Brown, Larry HB | 69-76Was | 2 | 5'11" | 195 | Kansas State | | 330 |
| Brown, Larry TE-OT | 71-84Pit | 2 | 6'4" | 246 | Kansas | | 30 |
| Brown, Larry OT | 78-79KC | | 6'5" | 262 | Miami (Fla.) | | |
| Brown, Otto DB | 69Dal 70-73NYG | | 6'1" | 187 | Prairie View | 2 | 6 |
| Brown, Ray DB | 71-77Atl 78-80NO | 3 | 6'2" | 203 | West Texas State | 38 | 12 |
| Brown, Sidney DB | 78NE | | 6' | 186 | Oklahoma | | |
| Brown, Stan WR | 71Cle | | 5'9" | 184 | Purdue | | |
| Brown, Terry DB-WR | 69-70StL 71JJ 72-75Min 76Cle | | 6'1" | 206 | Oklahoma State | 7 | 12 |
| Browne, Gordie OT | 74-75NYJ | | 6'5" | 265 | Boston College | | |
| Brumfield, Jim HB | 71Pit | | 6'1" | 195 | Indiana State | | |
| Brundige, Bill DT-DE | 70-77Was 78KJ | | 6'5" | 270 | Colorado | | |
| Brunet, Bob HB-FB | 68-73Was 74FJ 75-77Was | 2 | 6'1" | 205 | Louisiana Tech | | 24 |
| Brunson, Larry WR | 74-77KC 78-79Oak 80Den | 23 | 5'11" | 180 | Colorado | | 36 |
| Brunson, Mike WR | 70Atl | | 6'1" | 187 | Arizona State | | |
| Brupbacher, Ross LB | 70-72Chi 74WFL 76Chi | | 6'3" | 216 | Texas A&M | 12 | 12 |
| Bryant, Bill (Boone) DB | 76-78NYG 78Phi | | 5'11" | 195 | Grambling | 3 | 6 |
| Bryant, Bobby DB | 68-80Min | 3 | 6' | 171 | South Carolina | 51 | 24 |
| Bryant, Hubie WR | 70Pit 71-72NE | 23 | 5'10" | 170 | Minnesota | | 6 |
| Bryant, Waymond LB | 74-77Chi 78SJ | | 6'3" | 235 | Tennessee State | 4 | |
| Buchanon, Willie DB | 72-78GB 79-82SD | | 6' | 189 | San Diego State | 28 | 18 |
| Buckey, Don WR | 76NYJ | | 5'11" | 180 | N. Carolina State | | |
| Buehler, George OG | 69OakA 70-78Oak 78-79Cle | | 6'2" | 264 | Stanford | | |
| Buetow, Bart (The Mad Scientist) | 73NYG 76-77Min | | 6'5" | 250 | Minnesota | | |
| Buffone, Doug LB | 66-79Chi | | 6'1" | 227 | Louisville | 24 | 6 |
| Buggs, Danny WR | 75-76NYG 76-79Was 80CFL | 2 | 6'2" | 185 | West Virginia | | 24 |
| Buie, Drew WR | 69OakA 70-71Oak 72Cin | | 6'2" | 180 | Catawba | | 12 |
| Bulaich, Norm HB-FB | 70-72Bal 73-74Phi 75-79Mia | 2 | 6'1" | 217 | Texas Christian | | 246 |
| Bull, Scott QB | 76-78 SF 79KJ | 12 | 6'5" | 212 | Arkansas | | 18 |
| Bunting, John LB | 72-82Phi 83-85USFL | | 6'1" | 220 | North Carolina | 8 | |
| Burchfield, Don TE | 71NO | | 6'2" | 227 | Ball State | | |
| Burgmeier, Ted DB | 78KC | | 5'10" | 185 | Notre Dame | | |
| Burk, Scott DB | 79Cin | | 6'2" | 193 | Oklahoma State | | |
| Burke, Mark DB | 76Phi | | 6'1" | 175 | West Virginia | | |
| Burke, Mike K | 74LA | 4 | 5'10" | 188 | Miami (Fla.) | | 1 |
| Burks, Randy WR | 76Chi | | 5'11" | 170 | Southeastern Okla. | | 6 |
| Burks, Ray LB | 77KC | | 6'3" | 217 | U.C.L.A. | | |
| Burks, Steve WR | 75-77NE | 2 | 6'5" | 211 | Arkansas State | | |
| Burnham, Lem DE | 77-79Phi 80KJ | | 6'4" | 236 | U.S. International | | |
| Burns, Bob FB | 72NYJ | 2 | 6'3" | 212 | Georgia | | 6 |
| Burns, Ed QB | 78-80NO | | 6'3" | 210 | Nebraska | | |
| Burns, Leon FB | 71SD 72StL 73JJ | 2 | 6'2" | 229 | Long Beach State | | 18 |
| Burns, Mike DB | 77SF 78Det | | 6' | 180 | Southern Calif. | 1 | |
| Burrough, Ken WR | 70NO 71-81Hou 82BN | 2 | 6'4" | 210 | Texas Southern | | 300 |
| Burrow, Jim DB | 76GB | | 5'11" | 181 | Nebraska | | |
| Burrow, Ken WR | 71-75Atl | 2 | 6' | 190 | San Diego State | | 126 |
| Burton, Al DE | 76-77Hou 77NYJ | | 6'5" | 267 | Bethune-Cookman | | |
| Burton, Larry WR | 75-77NO 78-79SD | 2 | 6'1" | 192 | Purdue | | 42 |
| Bussey, Dexter HB-FB | 74-84Det | 2 | 6'1" | 209 | Oklahoma, | | 138 |
| | | | | | Texas-Arlington | | |
| Butler, Bill FB | 72-74NO | 2 | 6'2" | 212 | Kansas State | | 30 |
| Butler, Bill LB | 70Den | | 6'4" | 226 | Northridge State | | |
| Butler, Gary TE | 73KC 74KJ 75-76Chi 77TB | | 6'3" | 235 | Rice | | 12 |
| Butler, Gerald WR | 77KC 78Bal | | 6'4" | 209 | Nicholls State | | |
| Butler, Skip K | 71NO 71NYG 72-77Hou | 45 | 6'2" | 200 | Texas-Arlington | | 340 |
| Buzin, Rich OT | 68-70NYG 71LA 72Chi | | 6'4" | 250 | Penn State | | |
| Byas, Rick DB | 74-80Atl | | 5'9" | 179 | Wayne State | 6 | 16 |
| Cagle, Jim DT | 74Phi | | 6'5" | 255 | Georgia | | |
| Cahill, Bill DB | 73-74Buf | | 5'11" | 175 | Washington | | 6 |
| Cain, J.V. TE-WR | 74-77StL 78FJ | 2 | 6'4" | 224 | Colorado | | 54 |
| | 1979 — Died of heart failure | | | | | | |

| Use Name (Nickname) - Positions | Team by Year | See Section | Hgt. | Wgt. | College | Int | Pts |
|---|---|---|---|---|---|---|---|
| Caldwell, Alan DB | 79NYG | | 6' | 176 | North Carolina | 2 | |
| Calhoun, Don FB-HB | 74-75Buf 75-81NE 82Phi 84USFL | 2 | 6' | 208 | Kansas State | | 150 |
| Calloway, Ernie DT-DE | 69-72Phi 73KJ | | 6'6" | 244 | Texas Southern | | |
| Cambal, Dennis TE | 73NYJ | | 6'3" | 228 | William & Mary | | |
| Campbell, Carter LB-DE | 70SF 71Den 72-73NYG | | 6'3" | 232 | Weber State | | |
| | 74-75WFL | | | | | | |
| Campbell, Joe DE-NT | 77-80NO 80-81Oak 81TB | | 6'6" | 253 | Maryland | | |
| Campbell, Sonny HB | 70-71Atl 72JJ | 2 | 5'11" | 192 | Northern Arizona | | 12 |
| Campbell, Tommy DB | 76Phi | | 6' | 188 | Iowa State | | |
| Canada, Larry FB | 78-79Den 80KJ 81Den 83-85USFL | 2 | 6'2" | 233 | Wisconsin | | 42 |
| Capone, Warren LB | 75Dal 76NO | | 6'1" | 218 | Louisiana State | | 6 |
| Cappelletti, John HB-FB | 74-78LA 79LJ 80-83SD | 2 | 6'1" | 218 | Penn State | | 168 |
| Cappelman, Bill QB | 70Min 73Det | | 6'3" | 210 | Florida State | | |
| Capria, Carl DB | 74Det 75NYJ | | 6'3" | 185 | Purdue | | |
| Capriola, Glenn FB | 77Det | | 5'11" | 219 | Boston College | | |
| Carlson, Dean QB | 74KC | | 6'3" | 210 | Iowa State | | |
| Carlton, Darryl OT | 75-76Mia 77-79TB | | 6'6" | 271 | Tampa | | |
| Carmichael, Harold WR | 71-83Phi 84Dal | 2 | 6'7" | 225 | Southern U. | | 474 |
| Carpenter, Ron DT-DE | 70-77Cin | | 6'4" | 261 | N. Carolina State | | 2 |
| Carr, Earl FB | 78SF 79Phi | | 6' | 224 | Florida | | |
| Carr, Fred LB | 68-77GB | | 6'5" | 239 | Texas-El Paso | 8 | 6 |
| Carr, Levert OT-DT-OG | 69SD-A 70-71Buf 72-73Hou | | 6'5" | 258 | North Central | | |
| Carr, Roger WR | 74-81Bal 82Sea 83SD | 2 | 6'3" | 196 | Louisiana Tech | | 186 |
| Carrell, Duane K | 74Dal 75LA 76-77NYJ 77StL | 4 | 5'10" | 184 | Florida State | | |
| Carroll, Joe LB | 72-73Oak | | 6'1" | 220 | Pittsburgh | | |
| Carroll, Ronnie OG | 74Hou | | 6'2" | 265 | Sam Houston St. | | |
| Carter, Allen FB | 75-76NE 76NYJ | 3 | 5'11" | 208 | Southern Calif. | | 6 |
| Carter, Blanchard OT | 77TB | | 6'4" | 250 | Nevada-Las Vegas | | |
| Carter, Jim LB | 70-75GB 76BA 77-78GB | | 6'3" | 240 | Minnesota | 6 | 6 |
| Carter, Kent LB | 74NE | | 6'3" | 235 | Southern Calif. | | |
| Carter, Louis HB | 75Oak 76-78TB | 2 | 5'11" | 207 | Maryland | | 24 |
| Carter, Mike WR | 70GB 72SD | | 6'1" | 210 | Sacramento State | | |
| Carter, Virgil QB | 68-69Chi 70-72Cin 73AJ 74WFL 75SD | 12 | 6'1" | 192 | Brigham Young | | 49 |
| | 75-76Chi | | | | | | |
| Casanova, Tommy DB | 72-77Cin | 3 | 6'2" | 197 | Louisiana State | 17 | 24 |
| Cash, Rick DE-DT | 69Atl 69-70LA 71JJ 72-73NE | | 6'5" | 260 | Missouri, | | |
| | | | | | NE Missouri St. | | |
| Casper, Dave TE | 74-80Oak 80-82Hou 83Min 84Raid | 2 | 6'4" | 232 | Notre Dame | | 318 |
| Cassady, Craig DB | 77NO | | 5'11" | 175 | Ohio State | | |
| Caster, Rich TE-WR | 70-77NYJ 78-80Hou 81NO | 2 | 6'5" | 228 | Jackson State | | 270 |
| | 81-82Was | | | | | | |
| Ceresino, Gordy LB | 79SF | | 6' | 224 | Stanford | | |
| Chambers, Rusty LB | 75-76NO 76-80Mia | | 6'1" | 218 | Tulane | 2 | 6 |
| 1981 — Died in automobile accident | | | | | | | |
| Chambers, Wally DT-DE | 73-77Chi 78-79TB | | 6'6" | 253 | Eastern Kentucky | 2 | |
| Chandler, Al TE | 73-74Cin 76-78NE 78-79StL 79NE | 2 | 6'2" | 229 | Oklahoma | | 54 |
| Chandler, Bob WR | 71-79Buf 80-81Oak 82Raid | 2 | 6' | 180 | Southern Calif. | | 289 |
| Chandler, Edgar LB | 68-69BufA 70-72Buf 73NE | | 6'3" | 227 | Georgia | 2 | 8 |
| Chandler, Karl C-OG | 74-77NYG 78-79Det | | 6'5" | 250 | Princeton | | |
| Chapman, Clarence DB | 76-80NO 80-81Cin 83-84USFL | 3 | 5'10" | 185 | Eastern Michigan | 5 | 6 |
| | 85Det | | | | | | |
| Chapman, Gil WR | 75NO | 2 | 5'9" | 180 | Michigan | | |
| Chapple, Dave K | 71Buf 72-74LA 74NE | 3 | 6' | 184 | Cal.-Santa Barbara | | |
| Charles, John DB | 67-69BosA 70Min 71-74Hou | | 6'1" | 199 | Purdue | 16 | 12 |
| Chavous, Barney DE | 73-85Den | | 6'3" | 254 | S. Carolina State | | 8 |
| Cheek, Richard OG | 70Buf 71KJ | | 6'3" | 266 | Auburn | | |
| Cherry, Stan LB | 73Bal | | 6'5" | 200 | Morgan State | | |
| Chesley, Frank LB | 78GB | | 6'3" | 219 | Wyoming | | |
| Chesson, Wes WR | 71-73Atl 74Phi | 2 | 6'2" | 192 | Duke | | |
| Chester, Ray TE | 70-72Oak 73-77Bal 78-81Oak 83USFL | 2 | 6'3" | 232 | Morgan State | | 288 |
| Cheyunski, Jim LB | 68-69BosA 70Bos 71-72NE | | 6'2" | 222 | Syracuse | 9 | |
| | 73-74Buf 75-76Bal 77GB | | | | | | |
| Childs, Henry TE | 74Atl 74-80NO 81LA 84GB | 2 | 6'2" | 222 | Kansas City C.C. | | 174 |
| Childs, Jim WR | 78-79StL | 2 | 6'2" | 194 | Cal. Poly.-S.L.O. | | 6 |
| Chomyszak, Steve DT-C-OT | 66NY-A 66-69CinA 70-73Cin | | 6'5" | 270 | Syracuse | | |
| Christiansen, Bob TE | 72Buf | | 6'4" | 230 | U.C.L.A. | | |
| Cindrich, Ralph LB | 72NE 73-74Hou 74Den 75Hou | | 6'1" | 229 | Pittsburgh | | |
| Cipa, Larry QB | 74-75NO | 1 | 6'3" | 209 | Michigan | | 6 |
| Clabo, Neil K | 75-77Min | 4 | 6'2" | 200 | Tennessee | | |
| Clack, Jim C-OG | 71-77Pit 78-81NYG | | 6'3" | 250 | Wake Forest | | |
| Clancy, Sean LB | 78Mia 79StL | | 6'4" | 218 | Amherst | | |
| Clark, Al DB | 71Det 72-75LA 76Phi | | 6' | 183 | Eastern Michigan | 3 | |
| Clark, Booby FB | 73-78Cin 79-80Hou | 2 | 6'2" | 245 | Bethune-Cookman | | 162 |
| Clark, Gail LB | 73Chi 74NE | | 6'2" | 226 | Michigan State | | |
| Clark, Ken K | 79LA | 4 | 6'2" | 197 | St. Mary's (N.S.) | | |
| Clark, Leroy K | 76Hou | | 5'11" | 200 | Prairie View | | |
| Clark, Wayne QB | 70,72-73SD 74Cin 75KC | 1 | 6'2" | 203 | U.S. International | | 6 |
| Clements, Vin FB | 72-73NYG 74-75WFL | 2 | 6'3" | 213 | Connecticut | | 12 |
| Clemons, Craig DB | 72-77Chi | | 5'11" | 195 | Iowa | 9 | 6 |
| Cline, Tony DE | 75Oak 76-77SF | | 6'2" | 239 | Miami (Fla.) | 3 | |
| Clune, Don WR | 74-75NYG 76Sea | | 6'3" | 195 | Pennsylvania | | |
| Coady, Rich C-TE | 70-74Chi | | 6'3" | 240 | Memphis State | | |
| Cobb, Marvin DB | 75-79Cin 80Pit 80Min | | 6' | 189 | Southern Calif. | 13 | 6 |
| Cobb, Mike TE | 77Cin 78-81Chi 83-84USFL | 2 | 6'5" | 244 | Michigan State | | |
| Cockroft, Don K | 68-80Cle | 45 | 6'1" | 193 | Adams State | | 1080 |
| Coder, Ron OG-OT | 76-79Sea 80StL 81KJ 84-85USFL | | 6'4" | 250 | Penn State | | |
| Coffield, Randy LB | 76-77Sea 78-79NYG | | 6'3" | 215 | Florida State | | |
| Colavito, Steve LB | 75Phi | | 6' | 225 | Wake Forest | | |
| Colbert, Danny DB | 74-76SD 77JJ | | 5'11" | 175 | Tulsa | 2 | |
| Colbert, Rondy DB | 75-76NYG 77StL | 3 | 5'9" | 185 | Lamar | | 6 |
| Cole, Eddie LB | 79-80Det | | 6'2" | 235 | Mississippi | | 2 |
| Cole, Larry DE-DT | 68-80Dal | | 6'4" | 252 | Air Force, Hawaii | 4 | 24 |
| Cole, Linzy WR | 70Chi 71-72Hou 72Buf | 3 | 5'11" | 170 | Texas Christian | | |
| Coleman, Al DB | 68Min 69CinA 70-71Cin 72-73Phi 74JJ | | 6'1" | 185 | Jackson State, | 1 | 2 |
| | | | | | Tennessee State | | |
| Coleman, Dennis LB | 71NE | | 6'3" | 225 | Mississippi | | |
| Coleman, Don LB | 74-75NO 76-77KJ | | 6'2" | 220 | Michigan | | |
| Coleman, Fred TE | 76Buf | | 6'4" | 240 | Northeast La. | | |
| Coleman, Ralph LB | 72Dal | | 6'4" | 216 | N. Carolina A&T | | |
| Coleman, Ronnie HB | 74-81Hou | 23 | 5'10" | 197 | Alabama A&M | | 138 |
| Coleman, Steve DE | 74Den | | 6'4" | 252 | Delaware State | | |
| Collett, Elmer OG | 67-72SF 73-77Bal | | 6'4" | 241 | San Fran. State | | |
| Collier, Mike HB-FB | 75Pit 76KJ 77Buf 78FJ 79Buf | 23 | 5'11" | 200 | Morgan State | | 36 |
| Collins, Greg LB | 75SF 76Sea 77Buf | | 6'3" | 229 | Notre Dame | | |
| Collins, Gerald LB | 69BufA 70-71Buf | | 6'1" | 220 | Western Michigan | | |
| Collins, Larry HB | 78Cle 79KJ 80NO 83USFL | 3 | 5'11" | 190 | Texas A&I | | 6 |
| Collins, Sonny HB | 76Atl 77LA | 2 | 6'1" | 196 | Kentucky | | |
| Colman, Wayne LB | 68-69Phi 69-74NO 75BA 76NO | | 6'1" | 227 | Temple | 3 | |
| Colzie, Neal DB | 75-78Oak 79Mia 80-83TB 85USFL | 3 | 6'2" | 200 | Ohio State | 25 | 12 |
| Condon, Tom OG | 74-84KC | | 6'3" | 255 | Boston College | | |
| Conley, Steve WR | 72Cin 72StL | | 6'2" | 225 | Kansas | | |
| Conn, Dick DB | 74Pit 75WFL 75-79NE | | 6' | 183 | Georgia | 1 | |

| Use Name (Nickname) - Positions | Team by Year | See Section | Hgt. | Wgt. | College | Int | Pts |
|---|---|---|---|---|---|---|---|
| Conway, Dave K | 71GB | | 6' | 195 | Texas | | 5 |
| Cook, Fred DE | 74-80Bal | | 6'3" | 244 | Southern Miss. | 2 | 6 |
| Cooke, Bill DT-DE-OT | 75GB 76-77SF 78Sea 78Det 79-80Sea | | 6'5" | 249 | Massachusetts | | |
| Cooney, Mark LB | 74GB | | 6'4" | 230 | Colorado | | |
| Cooper, Bert LB | 76TB | | 6'1" | 242 | Florida State | | |
| Cope, Jim LB | 76Atl | | 6'1" | 235 | Ohio State | | |
| Copeland, Jim OG-C | 67-74Cle | | 6'2" | 242 | Virginia | | |
| Coppens, Gus OT | 79NYG | | 6'5" | 270 | U.C.L.A. | | |
| Corbett, Jim TE | 77-80Cin | 2 | 6'4" | 218 | Pittsburgh | | 6 |
| Corbett, Steve OG | 75NE 76ZJ | | 6'4" | 248 | Boston College | | |
| Cornelius, Charles DB | 77-78Mia 79-80SF | | 5'9" | 178 | Bethune-Cookman | 4 | |
| Cornell, Bo LB-FB | 71-72Cle 73-77Buf | | 6'1" | 217 | Washington | | 6 |
| Coslet, Bruce TE | 69-76Cin HC90-93NYJ | 2 | 6'3" | 228 | U. of Pacific | | 54 |
| Costict, Ray LB | 77-79NE 80KJ 83USFL | | 6' | 217 | Mississippi State | 1 | |
| Cotton, Craig TE | 69-72Det 73Chi 74WFL 75SD | 2 | 6'4" | 222 | Youngstown State | | 6 |
| Cousina, Brad LB | 75Cin 76NYG 77Pit | | 6' | 218 | Miami-Ohio | | |
| Cowins, Ben HB | 79KC | | 6' | 192 | Arkansas | | |
| Cowings, Al DE-DT-LB | 70-72Buf 73-74Hou 75,77LA 79SF | | 6'5" | 247 | Southern Calif. | | |
| Cox, Fred K | 63-77Min | 45 | 5'10" | 200 | Pittsburgh | | 1365 |
| Craig, Neal DB | 71-73Cin 74Buf 75-76Cle | | 6'1" | 189 | Fisk | 8 | 12 |
| Craig, Reggie WR | 75-76KC 77Cle 77Buf | | 6' | 188 | Arkansas | | |
| Craig, Steve TE | 74-78Min | 2 | 6'3" | 231 | Northwestern | | 6 |
| Crangle, Mike DE | 72NO | | 6'4" | 243 | Tennessee-Martin | | |
| Craven, Bill DB | 76Cle 77JJ | | 5'11" | 190 | Harvard | | |
| Crawford, Rufus HB | 78Sea | 3 | 5'10" | 180 | Virginia State | | |
| Creech, Bob LB | 71-72Phi 73NO | | 6'3" | 226 | Texas Christian | | |
| Crennel, Carl LB | 70Pit | | 6'1" | 230 | West Virginia | | |
| Crist, Chuck DB | 72-74NYG 75-77NO 78SF | | 6'2" | 205 | Penn State | 20 | |
| Criter, Ken LB | 69DenA 70-74Den | | 5'11" | 223 | Wisconsin | | 2 |
| Croft, Don DT | 72Buf 73KJ 74-75Buf 76Det | | 6'3" | 256 | Texas-El Paso | | |
| Croom, Sylvester C | 75NO | | 6' | 235 | Alabama | | |
| Crosby, Steve HB | 74-76NYG | | 5'11" | 205 | Ft. Hays State | | |
| Crosswhite, Leon FB | 73-74Det 75FJ | | 6'2" | 215 | Oklahoma | | 12 |
| Crowder, Randy DT-NT-DE | 74-76Mia 78-80TB 81-82KJ<br>77 — Ineligible to play pro football | | 6'2" | 242 | Penn State | | |
| Crowe, Larry HB | 72Phi 75Atl | | 6'1" | 198 | Texas Southern | | |
| Croyle, Phil LB | 71-73Hou 73Buf | | 6'3" | 220 | California | | |
| Crum, Bob DE | 74StL | | 6'5" | 240 | Arizona | | |
| Crump, Dwayne DB | 73-76StL | | 5'11" | 180 | Fresno State | 1 | 6 |
| Crusan, Doug OT | 66-69MiaA 70-74Mia | | 6'5" | 253 | Indiana | | |
| Csonka, Larry FB | 68-69MiaA 70-74Mia 75WFL 76-78NYG 79Mia | 2 | 6'3" | 238 | Syracuse | | 408 |
| Culbreath, Jim FB | 77-79GB 80Phi 80NYG | 2 | 6' | 210 | Oklahoma | | |
| Cullers, Willie DE | 74NYG | | 6'5" | 250 | Kansas | | |
| Culp, Curley DT-NT-OT | 68-69KC-A 70-74KC 74-80Hou 80-81Det | | 6'1" | 265 | Arizona State | | |
| Cunningham, Dick LB-OT | 67-69BufA 70-72Buf 73Phi 74JJ | | 6'2" | 238 | Arkansas | | |
| Cunningham, Doug HB | 67-73SF 74Was | 23 | 5'11" | 191 | Mississippi | | 60 |
| Cunningham, Doug WR | 79Min | | 6'2" | 195 | Rice | | |
| Cunningham, Sam (Bam) FB | 73-79NE 80HO 81-82NE | 2 | 6'3" | 226 | Southern Calif. | | 294 |
| Curchin, Jeff OT-OG | 70-71Chi 72Buf | | 6'6" | 256 | Florida State | | |
| Cureton, Will QB | 75Cle | 1 | 6'3" | 200 | East Texas State | | |
| Curran, Pat TE | 69-74LA 75-78SD 79JJ | 2 | 6'3" | 238 | Iowa State, Lakeland | | 37 |
| Current, Mike OT | 67MiaA 67-69DenA 70-75Den 76TB 77-79Mia | | 6'4" | 267 | Ohio State | | |
| Curtis, Isaac WR | 73-84Cin | 2 | 6' | 192 | California, San Diego State | | 318 |
| Curtis, Mike LB-FB | 65-75Bal 76Sea 77-78Was | | 6'2" | 232 | Duke | 25 | 18 |
| Curtis, Tom DB | 70-71Bal | | 6'1" | 196 | Michigan | | |
| Cusick, Pete NT | 75NE 76-78KJ | | 6'1" | 255 | Ohio State | | |
| Dalby, Dave C-OG | 72-81Oak 82-85Raid | | 6'2" | 248 | U.C.L.A. | | |
| Dalton, Oakley DT | 77NO | | 6'6" | 285 | Jackson State | | |
| Damkroger, Maury LB | 74-75NE | | 6'2" | 230 | Nebraska | | |
| Dandridge, Jerry LB | 76GB | | 6'1" | 222 | Memphis State | | |
| Danelo, Joe K | 75GB 76-82NYG 83-84Buf | 5 | 5'9" | 165 | Washington State | | 639 |
| Daney, George OG | 67-69KC-A 70-74KC | | 6'3" | 240 | Detroit, Texas-El Paso | | 6 |
| Darby, Alvis TE | 76Sea 76Hou 78TB | | 6'5" | 221 | Florida | | |
| Darby, Paul WR | 79-80NYJ | | 5'10" | 192 | SW Texas State | | 6 |
| Darden, Thom DB | 72-74Cle 75KJ 76-81Cle | 3 | 6'2" | 193 | Michigan | 45 | 18 |
| Darrow, Barry OT | 74-78Cle | | 6'7" | 260 | Montana | | |
| Davis, Anthony HB | 77TB 78Hou 78LA 79JJ 83USFL | 2 | 5'10" | 190 | Southern Calif. | | 6 |
| Davis, Ben DB | 67-73Cle 74-76Det | 3 | 5'11" | 183 | Defiance | 19 | 12 |
| Davis, Bob QB | 67-69HouA 70-72NYJ 73NO 74-75WFL | 12 | 6'3" | 205 | Virginia | | 12 |
| Davis, Brad FB | 75-76Atl | | 5'10" | 204 | Louisiana State | | 12 |
| Davis, Butch DB | 70Chi | | 5'11" | 183 | Missouri | 1 | |
| Davis, Charlie HB | 74Cin 75KJ 76TB | 2 | 5'11" | 200 | Colorado | | 6 |
| Davis, Charlie DT-NT | 74Pit 75-79StL 80Hou 84USFL | | 6'1" | 269 | Texas Christian | | 6 |
| Davis, Clarence HB | 71-78Oak | 23 | 5'10" | 191 | Southern Calif. | | 168 |
| Davis, Dave WR | 71-72GB 73Pit 74NO 75BN | 2 | 6' | 175 | Tennessee State | | 6 |
| Davis, Dick HB-FB | 70Den 70NO | 2 | 5'11" | 215 | Nebraska | | |
| Davis, Gary HB | 76-79Mia 80-81TB 81Cle | 23 | 5'10" | 203 | Cal. Poly.-S.L.O. | | 48 |
| Davis, Harrison WR | 74SD | 2 | 6'4" | 220 | Virginia | | 12 |
| Davis, Henry LB | 68-69NYG 70-73Pit 74JJ | | 6'3" | 235 | Grambling | 4 | 6 |
| Davis, Jerry DB | 75NYJ | | 5'11" | 182 | Morris Brown | | |
| Davis, Kyle C | 75Dal 76KJ 78SF | | 6'4" | 240 | Oklahoma | | |
| Davis, Marvin LB | 74Hou | | 6'4" | 235 | Southern U. | | |
| Davis, Ricky DB | 75Cin 76TB 77KC 78AJ | | 6'1" | 180 | Alabama | 1 | |
| Davis, Ron OG | 73StL 74JJ | | 6'2" | 235 | Virginia State | | |
| Davis, Sam OG-OT | 67-79Pit 80-81KJ | | 6'1" | 251 | Allen | | |
| Davis, Sonny HB-FB | 71-72Phi | 2 | 5'11" | 215 | Tennessee State | | 6 |
| Davis, Stan WR | 73Phi | | 5'10" | 180 | Memphis State | | |
| Davis, Steve FB-HB | 72-74Pit 75-76NYJ | 23 | 6'1" | 216 | Delaware State | | 66 |
| Davis, Tony FB-HB | 76-78Cin 79-81TB 83USFL | 23 | 5'10" | 211 | Nebraska | | 36 |
| Davis, Vern DB | 71Phi | | 6'4" | 208 | Western Michigan | | |
| Dawkins, Joe FB-HB | 70-71Hou 71-73Den 74-75NYG 76Hou | 23 | 5'11" | 221 | Wisconsin | | 96 |
| Dawson, Rhett WR | 72Hou 73Min | | 6'1" | 185 | Florida State | | 6 |
| Daykin, Tony LB | 77-78Det 79-81Atl | | 6'1" | 215 | Georgia Tech | | |
| Dean, Fred OG | 77Chi 78-80Was 81BA 82Was 83-85USFL | 3 | 6'3" | 253 | Texas Southern | | |
| Dean, Jimmy DE | 78Hou | | 6'4" | 252 | Texas A&M | | |
| Dean, Randy QB | 77-79NYG | 1 | 6'3" | 195 | Northwestern | | 6 |
| DeBernardi, Fred DE | 74KC | | 6'4" | 250 | Texas-El Paso | | |
| DeFrance, Chris WR | 79Was | | 6'1" | 205 | Arizona State | | |
| DeGrener, Jack FB | 74NO | 2 | 6'1 | 225 | Texas-Arlington | | |
| DeLamielleure, Joe OG | 73-79Buf 80-84Cle 85Buf | | 6'3" | 250 | Michigan State | | |
| DeLeone, Tom C-OG | 72-73Cin 74-84Cle | | 6'2" | 250 | Ohio State | | |
| Del Gaizo, Jim QB | 72Mia 73GB 74NYG 75Mia | 1 | 6'1" | 194 | Temple | | |
| DeLisle, Jim DT | 71GB | | 6'4" | 254 | Wisconsin | | |
| Deloplaine, Jack HB | 76-77Pit 78Was 78Pit 79Chi 79Pit | 2 | 5'10" | 205 | Salem | | 12 |

| Use Name (Nickname) - Positions | Team by Year | See Section | Hgt. | Wgt. | College | Int | Pts |
|---|---|---|---|---|---|---|---|
| Demarie, John OG-OT-C | 67-75Cle 76Sea | | 6'3" | 250 | Louisiana State | | |
| Demery, Calvin WR | 72Min | | 6' | 190 | Arizona State | | |
| Demory, Bill QB | 73-74NYJ | 1 | 6'2" | 195 | Arizona | | |
| Dempsey, Tom K | 69-70NO 71-74Phi 75-76LA 77Hou 78-79Buf | 5 | 6'1" | 260 | Palomar J.C. | | 729 |
| Den Herder, Vern DE-NT | 71-81Mia | | 6'6" | 251 | Central Iowa | 1 | 6 |
| Dennery, Mike LB | 74-75Oak 76Mia | | 6' | 224 | Southern Miss. | | 2 |
| Dennis, Al OG | 73SD 76-77Cle | | 6'4" | 250 | Grambling | | |
| Dennis, Guy OG-C | 69CinA 70-72Cin 73-75Det | | 6'2" | 254 | Florida | | |
| Dennison, Doug HB-FB | 74-78Dal 79Cle 80CFL 83-84USFL | 2 | 6'1" | 202 | Kutztown | | 114 |
| Denson, Keith WR | 76NYJ | | 5'8" | 165 | San Diego State | | |
| Denson, Moses FB-HB | 74-75Was | 2 | 6'1" | 215 | Md. Eastern Shore | | 12 |
| DePaso, Tom LB | 78-79Cin | | 6'2" | 223 | Penn State | | |
| DePoyster, Jerry K | 68Det 71-72Oak | 45 | 6'1" | 202 | Wyoming | | 27 |
| DeRatt, Jimmy DB | 75NO | | 6' | 203 | North Carolina | | |
| DeSimone, Rick TE | 78SF | | 6'3" | 213 | Northridge State | | |
| Detwiler, Chuck DB | 70-72SD 73StL 74-75WFL | | 6' | 185 | Utah State | 1 | 6 |
| Devine, Dan | HC71-74GB | | | | Minnesota-Duluth | | |
| Devlin, Chris LB | 75-76Cin 77FJ 78Cin 78Chi | | 6'2" | 226 | Penn State | 1 | |
| Dickel, Dan LB | 74-77Bal 78Det | | 6'3" | 225 | Iowa | 1 | |
| Dickey, Lynn QB | 71Hou 72PJ 73-75Hou 76-77GB 78BL 79-85GB | 12 | 6'4" | 210 | Kansas State | | 55 |
| Dickinson, Parnell QB | 76-77TB | 1 | 6'2" | 185 | Miss. Valley St. | | |
| Dicus, Chuck WR | 71-72SD | 2 | 6' | 174 | Arkansas | | 18 |
| Didion, John C-LB | 69-70Was 71-74NO | | 6'4" | 247 | Oregon State | | |
| Dieken, Doug OT | 71-84Cle | | 6'5" | 250 | Illinois | | 8 |
| Dierdorf, Dan OT-OG-C | 71-83StL | | 6'4" | 281 | Michigan | | |
| Diggs, Sheldon WR | 77NYJ | | 6'1" | 190 | Southern Calif. | | |
| Dilts, Bucky K | 77-78Den 79Bal | 4 | 5'9" | 185 | Georgia | | |
| Dirden, Johnnie WR | 78Hou 79KC 81Pit 83-84USFL | 3 | 6' | 188 | Sam Houston St. | | |
| Dobbins, Herb OT | 74Phi | | 6'4" | 260 | San Diego State | | |
| Dobler, Conrad OG | 72-77StL 78-79NO 80-81Buf | | 6'3" | 254 | Wyoming | | 6 |
| Dockery, John DB | 68-69NY-A 70-71NYJ 72-73Pit | | 6' | 186 | Harvard | 8 | |
| Dodd, Al WR-DB | 67Chi 69-71NO 72JJ 73-74Atl | 23 | 6' | 180 | Northwestern La. | | 24 |
| Dokes, Phil DT-DE | 77-78Buf 79SJ 83-84USFL | | 6'5" | 257 | Oklahoma State | | |
| Dolbin, Jack WR | 75-79Den | 2 | 5'10" | 181 | Wake Forest | | 48 |
| Domres, Marty QB | 69SD-A 70-71SD 72-75Bal 76SF 77NYJ | 12 | 6'4" | 219 | Columbia | | 60 |
| Domres, Tom DT-DE | 68-69HouA 70-71Hou 71-72Den 73JJ | | 6'3" | 257 | Wisconsin | | 6 |
| Donahue, Mark OG | 78-79Cin | | 6'3" | 256 | Michigan | | |
| Donchez, Tom FB | 75Chi | | 6'2" | 216 | Penn State | | |
| Donckers, Billy QB | 76-77StL | | 6'1" | 206 | San Diego State | | |
| Donohue, Mike TE | 68,70-71Atl 73-74GB | 2 | 6'3" | 228 | San Francisco | | 12 |
| Donovan, Pat OT | 75-83Dal | | 6'4" | 253 | Stanford | | |
| Dorris, Andy DE | 73-76NO 77Sea 77-81Hou | | 6'4" | 238 | New Mexico State | | |
| Dorsey, Larry WR | 76-77SD 78KC | 2 | 6'1" | 195 | Tennessee State | | 24 |
| Dorsey, Nate DE | 73NE | | 6'4" | 240 | Miss. Valley St. | | |
| Doughty, Glenn WR | 72-79Bal | 2 | 6'1" | 204 | Michigan | | 144 |
| Douglas, Jay C | 73-74SD | | 6'6" | 251 | Memphis State | | |
| Douglas, John LB | 70-73NYG 74WFL | | 6'2" | 227 | Missouri | 2 | |
| Douglass, Bobby QB | 69-75Chi 75SD 76-77NO 78GB | 12 | 6'3" | 224 | Kansas | | 133 |
| Douglass, Freddie WR | 76TB | | 5'9" | 185 | Arkansas | | |
| Douthit, Earl DB | 75Chi 76TB | | 6'2" | 188 | Iowa | | |
| Dove, Jerome DB | 77-80GB | | 6'2" | 190 | Colorado State | 2 | |
| Dowling, Brian QB | 72-73NE 74-75WFL 77GB | 1 | 6'2" | 207 | Yale | | 18 |
| Dragon, Oscar HB-FB | 72SD | | 6' | 214 | Arizona State | | |
| Drake, Bill DB-WR | 73-74LA | | 6'1" | 195 | Oregon | | |
| Dressler, Doug FB | 70-72Cin 73KJ 74Chi 75NE 75KC | 2 | 6'3" | 225 | Ohio State | | 66 |
| Drougas, Tom OT-OG | 72-73Bal 74Den 74KC 75-76Mia | | 6'4" | 258 | Oregon | | |
| Drungo, Elbert OT-OG | 69HouA 70-71Hou 72KJ 73-77Hou | | 6'5" | 260 | Tennessee State | | |
| Druschel, Rich OT-OG | 74Pit | | 6'2" | 248 | N. Carolina State | | |
| Dryer, Fred DE | 69-71NYG 72-81LA | | 6'6" | 238 | San Diego State | 1 | 10 |
| Dubinetz, Greg OG | 79Was | | 6'4" | 260 | Yale | | |
| DuBose, Jimmy FB | 76-78TB 79KJ | 2 | 5'11" | 216 | Florida | | |
| Duhon, Bobby HB | 68NYG 69KJ 70-72NYG | 23 | 6' | 194 | Tulane | | 36 |
| DuLac, Bill OG | 74-75NE | | 6'4" | 260 | Eastern Michigan | | |
| Dumier, Doug C | 73-75NE 76-77Min | | 6'3" | 243 | Nebraska | | |
| Dunbar, Jubilee WR | 73NO 74Cle | 2 | 6' | 196 | Southern U. | | 24 |
| Duncan, Brian HB-FB | 76-77Cle 78Hou | | 6' | 201 | S.M.U. | | 12 |
| Duncan, Jim DB | 69-71Bal | 3 | 6'2" | 200 | Md. Eastern Shore | 2 | 12 |
| Duncan, Ken K | 71GB | | 6'2" | 210 | Tulsa | | |
| Dungy, Tony DB-QB | 77-78Pit 79SF | | 6' | 189 | Minnesota | 9 | |
| Dunivan, Tom QB | 77-78Hou | | 6'3" | 210 | Texas Tech | | |
| Dunlap, Lenny DB | 71Bal 72-74SD 75Det | 3 | 6'1" | 197 | North Texas | 5 | |
| Dunn, Paul HB-FB | 70Cin | | 6' | 210 | U.S. International | | |
| Dunstan, Bill DT | 73-76Phi 77Buf 79LA | | 6'4" | 250 | Utah State | | 6 |
| DuPree, Billy Joe TE | 73-83Dal | 2 | 6'4" | 227 | Michigan State | | 252 |
| Duranko, Pete DE-DT | 67-69Den-A 70Den 71JJ | | 6'2" | 249 | Notre Dame | | |
| Duren, Clarence DB | 73-76StL 77SD | | 6'1" | 190 | California | 10 | |
| Durko, Sandy DB | 70-71Cin 72JJ 73-74NE | | 6'1" | 185 | Southern Calif. | 7 | |
| Dusek, Brad LB | 74-81Was | | 6'2" | 217 | Texas A&M | 4 | 18 |
| Dusenberry, Bill DB | 70NO | | 6'2" | 198 | Johnson C. Smith | | |
| Dvorak, Rick DE | 74-77NYG 77Mia | | 6'4" | 240 | Wichita State | | |
| Eaglin, Larry DB | 73Hou | | 6'3" | 195 | S.F. Austin State | | 6 |
| Earl, Robin FB-TE | 77-82Chi 84-85USFL | 2 | 6'5" | 242 | Washington | | 30 |
| Earley, Jim FB | 78NYJ | | 6'1" | 230 | Michigan State | | |
| East, Ron DT-DE | 67-70Dal 71-73SD 74WFL 75Cle 76Atl 77Sea | | 6'4" | 244 | Montana State | | 2 |
| Easterling, Ray DB | 72-79Atl 80JJ | | 6' | 192 | Richmond | 13 | |
| Ebersole, John LB | 70-77NYJ | | 6'3" | 234 | Penn State | 8 | |
| Eck, Keith C-OG | 79NYG 80IL | | 6'5" | 255 | U.C.L.A. | | |
| Edwards, Cid FB | 66-71StL 72-74SD 75Chi | 2 | 6'2" | 230 | Tennessee State | | 114 |
| Edwards, Earl DE-DT | 69-72SF 73-75Buf 76-78Cle 79GB | | 6'6" | 261 | Wichita State | | |
| Edwards, Emmett WR | 75-76Hou 76Buf | | 6'1" | 189 | Kansas | | |
| Edwards, Glen DB | 71-77Pit 78-81SD 83USFL | 3 | 6' | 184 | Florida A&M | 39 | 18 |
| Edwards, Jimmy HB | 79Min | 3 | 5'9" | 185 | Northeast La. | | |
| Ehlers, Tom LB | 75-77Phi 78Buf 79XJ | | 6'2" | 218 | Kentucky | 1 | |
| Ehrmann, Joe DT | 73-80Bal 81-82Det 83-85USFL | | 6'5" | 256 | Syracuse | 1 | |
| Eidson, Jim OG-C | 76Dal 77JJ | | 6'3" | 264 | Mississipi State | | 1 |
| Eischeid, Mike K | 66-69OakA 70-71Oak 72-74Min | 4 | 6' | 190 | Upper Iowa | | 70 |
| Elam, Cleveland DT-DE | 75-78SF 79Det | | 6'4" | 252 | Tennessee State | | 6 |
| Eley, Monroe FB | 75Atl 76JJ 77Atl | 2 | 6'2" | 210 | Arizona State | | 6 |
| Elia, Bruce LB | 75Mia 76-78SF | | 6'1" | 220 | Ohio State | | |
| Ellenbogen, Bill OG-OT | 76-77NYG | | 6'5" | 258 | Virginia Tech | | |
| Ellender, Rich WR | 79Hou | 3 | 5'11" | 171 | McNeese State | | |
| Eller, Carl DE | 64-78Min 79Sea | | 6'6" | 252 | Minnesota | 1 | 10 |
| Elliott, John DT-DE-LB | 67-69NY-A 70-73NYJ 74WFL | | 6'4" | 244 | Texas | | 2 |
| Elliott, Lenvil HB-FB | 73-78Cin 79-81SF | 23 | 6' | 207 | N.E. Missouri St. | | 108 |
| Ellis, Allan DB | 73-77Chi 78KJ 79-80Chi 81SD | | 5'10" | 179 | U.C.L.A. | 22 | 6 |
| Ellis, Clarence DB | 72-74Atl 75KJ | | 5'11" | 191 | Notre Dame | 8 | |

| Use Name (Nickname) - Positions | Team by Year | See Section | Hgt. | Wgt. | College | Int | Pts |
|---|---|---|---|---|---|---|---|
| Ellis, Ken DB | 70-75GB 76Hou 76Mia 77Cle 79Det 79LA | 3 | 5'10" | 191 | Southern U. | 22 | 30 |
| Ellison, Glenn HB-FB | 71Oak | | 6'1" | 215 | Arkansas | | |
| Ellison, Mark OG | 72-73NYG | | 6'2" | 250 | Dayton | | |
| Ellison, Willie HB-FB | 67-72LA 73-79KC | 23 | 6'1" | 204 | Texas Southern | | 180 |
| Elmendorf, Dave DB | 71-79LA | 3 | 6'1" | 195 | Texas A&M | 27 | 12 |
| Elrod, Jimbo LB | 76-78KC 79Hou | | 6' | 220 | Oklahoma | 1 | |
| Ely, Larry LB | 70-71Cin 74WFL 75Chi | | 6'1" | 230 | Iowa | 1 | |
| Emerson, Vern OT | 69-71StL | | 6'5" | 260 | Minnesota-Duluth | | |
| Enderle, Dick OG | 69-71Atl 72-75NYG 76SF 76GB | | 6'1" | 250 | Minnesota | | |
| Engel, Steve HB-FB | 70Cle | | 6'1" | 218 | Colorado | | |
| Engels, Rick K | 76-77Sea 77Pit 78Phi | 4 | 5'11" | 177 | Tulsa | | |
| Enyart, Bill FB | 69BufA 70Buf 71Oak 72KJ | 2 | 6'4" | 236 | Oregon State | | 24 |
| Ernst, Mike QB | 72Cin 73Den | | 6'1" | 190 | Fullerton State | | |
| Esposito, Mike HB | 76-78Atl 79SJ | 2 | 6' | 183 | Boston College | 1 | 12 |
| Estes, Larry DE-DT | 70-71NO 72Phi 74-75WFL 75-77KC | | 6'6" | 255 | Alcorn State | | |
| Evans, Charlie FB | 71-73NYG 74Was 76KJ | 2 | 6'1" | 219 | Southern Calif. | | 78 |
| Evans, Johnny K-QB | 78-80Cle | 4 | 6'1" | 197 | N. Carolina State | | |
| Evans, Larry LB | 76-82Den 83SD | | 6'2" | 218 | Mississippi | 3 | |
| Evans, Mike C | 68-73Phi | | 6'5" | 250 | Boston College | | |
| Evans, Norm OT | 65Hou 66-75Mia 76-78Sea | | 6'5" | 248 | Texas Christian | | 6 |
| Fagan, Julian K | 70-72NO 73NYJ | 4 | 6'3" | 205 | Mississippi | | |
| Fairbanks, Chuck | HC73-78NE | | | | Michigan State | | |
| Fairchild, Greg OG-C-OT | 76-77Cin 78Cle 78-79CFL 83-84USFL | | 6'4" | 257 | Tulsa | | |
| Fairley, Leonard DB | 74Hou | | 5'11" | 200 | Alcorn State | | |
| Falcon, Terry OG-OT | 78-79NE 80NYG 83USFL | | 6'3" | 260 | Montana | | |
| Fanning, Mike DT-DE-NT | 75-81LA 83Det 84Sea | | 6'6" | 257 | Notre Dame | | 2 |
| Fanucci, Mike DE | 72Was 73Hou 74GB | | 6'4" | 236 | Arizona State | | |
| Farasopoulos, Chris DB | 71-73NYJ 74NO | 3 | 5'11" | 190 | Brigham Young | 4 | 6 |
| Farber, Hap LB | 70Min 70NO | | 6'1" | 220 | Mississippi | | |
| Farmer, Dave HB | 78TB | | 6' | 205 | Southern Calif. | | |
| Farmer, George WR | 70-75Chi 75Det | 2 | 6'4" | 212 | U.C.L.A. | | 60 |
| Farmer, Karl WR | 76-77Atl 78TB | | 5'11" | 165 | Pittsburgh | | |
| Farmer, Roger WR | 79NYJ | | 6'3" | 195 | Baker | | |
| Farmer, Ted HB | 78StL | | 5'11" | 175 | Oregon | | |
| Farr, Mel HB | 67-73Det | 2 | 6'2" | 208 | U.C.L.A. | | 216 |
| Faumuina, Wilson DT-DE-NT | 77-81Atl | | 6'5" | 275 | San Jose State | 1 | |
| Federspiel, Joe LB | 72-80NO 81Bal 83USFL | | 6'1" | 230 | Kentucky | 5 | |
| Feller, Happy K | 71Phi 72-73NO | 5 | 5'11" | 185 | Texas | | 75 |
| Felton, Eric DB | 78-79NO 80NYG 81SJ | | 6' | 200 | Texas Tech | 5 | |
| Fergerson, Duke WR | 77-79Sea 80Buf | 2 | 6'1" | 189 | San Diego State | | 12 |
| Ferguson, Bill LB | 73-74NYJ | | 6'3" | 225 | San Diego State | | |
| Ferguson, Gene OT-DT | 69SD-A 70SD 71-72Hou | | 6'7" | 302 | Norfolk State | | |
| Fernandes, Ron DE | 76-77Bal 78KJ 79Bal 80IL 83USFL | | 6'4" | 251 | Eastern Michigan | | 2 |
| Fernandez, Manny DT-NT | 66-69MiaA 70-75Mia 76-77KJ | | 6'2" | 250 | Utah | | |
| Ferrell, Bob FB-HB | 76-80SF | 2 | 6' | 216 | U.C.L.A. | | 18 |
| Fersen, Paul OT | 73NO | | 6'5" | 260 | Georgia | | |
| Fest, Cotton DT | 72Cle | | 6'2" | 255 | Dayton | | |
| Fest, Howard OG-OT-C | 66-69CinA 70-75Cin 76TB 77JJ | | 6'6" | 263 | Texas | | |
| Fields, Edgar DE-DT | 77-80Atl 81Det | | 6'2" | 255 | Texas A&M | | |
| Fifer, Bill OT | 78Det 78NO 79Sea | | 6'4" | 250 | West Texas State | | |
| Files, Jim LB | 70-73NYG | | 6'4" | 240 | Oklahoma | | |
| Fink, Mike DB | 73NO | | 5'11" | 180 | Missouri | | |
| Finnie, Roger OT-OG-DT | 69NY-A 70-72NYJ 73-78StL 79NO | | 6'3" | 247 | Florida A&M | | |
| Fisher, Ed OG-DE-C | 74-82Hou 85USFL | | 6'3" | 249 | Arizona State | | |
| Fitzgerald, John C-OG | 71-80Dal 81KJ | | 6'5" | 255 | Boston College | | |
| Flanagan, Ed C | 65-74Det 75-76SD | | 6'3" | 246 | Purdue | | |
| Fletcher, Chris DB | 70-76SD | 3 | 5'11" | 186 | Temple | 13 | 6 |
| Flowers, Richmond DB-WR | 69-71Dal 71-73NYG 74-75WFL | | 6' | 181 | Tennessee | 6 | |
| Foley, Dave OT-C | 70-71NYJ 72-77Buf | | 6'5" | 252 | Ohio State | | |
| Foley, Tim DB | 70-80Mia | | 6' | 194 | Purdue | 22 | 14 |
| Foote, James QB | 74,76Hou | | 6'2" | 210 | Delaware Valley | | |
| Ford, Charlie DB | 71-73Chi 74Phi 75Buf 75NYG 76KJ | | 6'3" | 187 | Houston | 15 | |
| Ford, James HB-FB | 71-72NO 73LJ | 2 | 6' | 203 | Texas Southern | | 12 |
| Foreman, Chuck HB-FB | 73-79Min 80NE | 2 | 6'2" | 209 | Miami (Fla.) | | 456 |
| Forrest, Tom OG | 74Chi | | 6'2" | 255 | Cincinnati | | |
| Forsberg, Fred LB | 68DenA 70-73Den 73Buf 74SD | | 6'1" | 233 | Washington | 5 | 6 |
| Forte, Ike HB | 76-77NE 78-80Was 81NYG | 23 | 6' | 203 | Arkansas | | 42 |
| Fortner, Larry QB | 79-80Atl | | 6'4" | 212 | Miami-Ohio | | |
| Forzano, Rick | HC74-76Det | | | | Kent State | | |
| Foster, Eddie WR | 77Hou 78KJ 79Hou | 2 | 5'10" | 185 | Houston | | |
| Foster, Will LB | 73NE | | 6'2" | 230 | Eastern Michigan | | 6 |
| Fowler, Dan OG | 79NYG | | 6'5" | 260 | Kentucky | | |
| Fowler, Wayne C | 70Buf | | 6'3" | 260 | Richmond | | |
| France, Doug OT | 75-81LA 83Hou 84SJ | | 6'5" | 270 | Ohio State | | |
| Francis, Jon HB | 87LA | 2 | 5'11" | 207 | Boise State | | 12 |
| Francis, Wallace WR | 73-74Buf 75-81Atl | 23 | 5'11" | 190 | Ark.-Pine Bluff | | 180 |
| Franckowiak, Mike FB-TE | 75-76Den 77-78Buf | | 6'3" | 221 | Central Michigan | | |
| Franco, Brian K | 87Cle | | 5'8" | 165 | Penn State | | 11 |
| Franklin, Cleveland FB | 77-78Phi 79-82Bal | 2 | 6'2" | 216 | Baylor | | 18 |
| Franklin, Dennis WR | 75-76Det | | 6'1" | 185 | Michigan | | |
| Franklin, George FB | 78Atl 79NYG | | 6'3" | 226 | Texas A&I | | |
| Franklin, Larry WR | 78TB | | 6'1" | 185 | Jackson State | | |
| Franklin, Willie WR | 72Bal | | 6'2" | 195 | Oklahoma | | |
| Franks, Dennis C | 76-78Phi 79Det | | 6'1" | 241 | Michigan | | |
| Frazier, Cliff DT | 77KC | | 6'4" | 265 | U.C.L.A. | | |
| Freelon, Solomon OG | 72-74Hou | | 6'2" | 250 | Grambling | | |
| Freitas, Jesse QB | 74-75SD | 1 | 6'1" | 198 | San Diego State | | |
| Freitas, Rocky OT | 68-77Det 78TB | | 6'6" | 271 | Oregon State | | |
| Fritsch, Ted C | 72-74Atl 75KJ 76-79Was | | 6'2" | 242 | St. Norbert | | |
| Fritsch, Toni K | 71-73Dal 74KJ 75Dal 76SD 77-81Hou 82NO 84-85USFL | 5 | 5'7" | 190 | none | | 758 |
| Fritts, Stan HB-FB | 75-76Cin | 2 | 6'1" | 215 | N. Carolina State | | 78 |
| Fronbose, Bill DB | 74Det | | 6' | 185 | Miami (Fla.) | | |
| Fryer, Brian WR | 76Was 77JJ | | 6'1" | 185 | Alberta | | |
| Fugett, Jean TE-WR | 72-75Dal 76-79Was | 2 | 6'3" | 225 | Amherst | | 168 |
| Fuller, Johnny DB | 68-72SF 73-75NO | 3 | 6' | 182 | Lamar | 8 | |
| Fuller, Mike DB | 75-80SD 81-82Cin | 3 | 5'9" | 187 | Auburn | 17 | 25 |
| Fulton, Ed OG | 78LA 79Buf 80-82CFL 84-85USFL | | 6'3" | 250 | Maryland | | |
| Fultz, Mike DT | 77-80NO 81Mia 81Bal | | 6'5" | 278 | Nebraska | | |
| Funchess, Tom OT | 68-69BosA 70Bos 71-73Hou 74Mia | | 6'5" | 264 | Jackson State | | |
| Fuqua, John (Frenchy) HB-FB | 69NYG 70-76Pit 77BG | 23 | 5'11" | 200 | Morgan State | | 144 |
| Furness, Steve DT-DE | 72-80Pit 81Det | | 6'4" | 255 | Rhode Island | | |
| Gaddis, Robert WR | 76Buf | | 5'11" | 178 | Miss. Valley St. | | |
| Gagnon, Dave HB | 74Chi | | 5'10" | 210 | Ferris State | | |
| Gaines, Clark FB-HB | 76-80NYJ 81-82KC | 2 | 6'1" | 206 | Wake Forest | | 84 |
| Gaines, Lawrence FB | 76Det 77KJ 78-79Det | 2 | 6'1" | 237 | Wyoming | | 36 |
| Gaines, Wentford DB | 78Pit 78-80Chi | | 6' | 185 | Cincinnati | 2 | |
| Galigher, Ed DE-DT | 72-76NYJ 77-79SF | | 6'4" | 253 | U.C.L.A. | | |
| Gallagher, Allen OT | 74NE | | 6'3" | 255 | Southern Calif. | | |
| Gallagher, Dave DT-DE | 74Chi 75-76NYG 77VR 78-79Det | | 6'4" | 256 | Michigan | 1 | |
| Gallagher, Frank OG | 67-72Det 73Atl 73Min | | 6'2" | 243 | North Carolina | | |
| Gallegos, Chan QB | 72Oak | | 5'9" | 175 | San Jose State | | |
| Ganas, Rusty DT | 71Bal | | 6'4" | 257 | South Carolina | | |
| Gant, Reuben TE-WR | 74-80Buf | 2 | 6'4" | 226 | Oklahoma State | | 90 |
| Gantt, Greg K | 74-75NYJ | 4 | 5'11" | 188 | Alabama | | 11 |
| Gantt, Jerry OT | 70Buf | | 6'4" | 266 | N. Car. Central | | |
| Gardin, Ron DB-WR | 70-71Bal 73NE | 3 | 5'11" | 180 | Arizona | | 6 |
| Garlich, Chris LB | 79StL | | 6'1" | 220 | Missouri | | |
| Garlington, John LB | 68-77Cle | | 6'1" | 222 | Louisiana State | 9 | |
| Garrett, Carl HB | 69BosA 70Bos 71-72NE 73-74Chi 75NYJ 76-77Oak | 23 | 5'11" | 209 | N. Mex. Highlands | | 210 |
| Garrett, Len TE | 71-73GB 73-75NO 75SF | | 6'3" | 230 | N. Mex. Highlands | | |
| Garrett, Reggie WR | 74-75Pit 76XJ | 2 | 6'1" | 174 | Eastern Michigan | | 6 |
| Garrison, Gary WR | 66-69SD-A 70-76SD 77Hou | 2 | 6'1" | 194 | San Diego State | | 348 |
| Garrison, Walt FB-HB | 66-74Dal | 23 | 6' | 204 | Oklahoma State | | 234 |
| Garror, Leon DB | 72-73Buf | | 6' | 180 | Alcorn State | 1 | |
| Garry, Ben FB | 79-80Bal | | 6' | 215 | Southern Miss. | | |
| Gartner, Chris K | 74Cle | | 6' | 170 | Indiana | | |
| Gatewood, Tom TE-WR | 72-73NYG | | 6'3" | 215 | Notre Dame | | |
| Gault, Don QB | 70Cle | | 6'2" | 190 | Hofstra | | |
| Gaunty, Steve WR | 79KC | | 5'10" | 175 | Northern Colorado | | 6 |
| Gay, Blenda DE | 74SD 75-76Phi died due to knife wound — Dec. 1976 | | 6'5" | 254 | Fayetteville St. | | 6 |
| Gaydos, Kent WR | 75GB 76JJ | | 6'6" | 228 | Florida State | | |
| Geddes, Bob LB | 72Den 73-75NE | | 6'2" | 240 | U.C.L.A. | 2 | 6 |
| Geddes, Ken LB | 71-75LA 76-78Sea | | 6'3" | 235 | Nebraska | 6 | |
| George, Ed OT | 75Bal 76-78Phi | | 6'4" | 270 | Wake Forest | | |
| George, Steve DT | 74StL 75KJ 76Atl | | 6'6" | 265 | Houston | | |
| George, Tim WR | 73Cin 74Cle | | 6'5" | 218 | Whittier | | |
| Geredine, Tom WR | 73-74Atl 76LA | 23 | 6'2" | 191 | NE Missouri St. | | 12 |
| Gerela, Roy K | 69HouA 70Hou 71-78Pit 79SD | 45 | 5'10" | 185 | New Mexico State | | 903 |
| Germany, Willie DB | 72Atl 73Det 74WFL 75Hou 76NE | | 6' | 192 | Morgan State | 2 | 6 |
| Gersbach, Carl LB | 70Phi 71-72Min 73-74SD 75Chi 76StL | | 6'1" | 230 | West Chester | 3 | |
| Getty, Charlie OT-OG | 74-82KC 83GB | | 6'4" | 265 | Penn State | | |
| Giammona, Louie HB | 76NYJ 77KJ 78-82Phi 83USFL | 23 | 5'9" | 180 | Utah State | | 54 |
| Gibbons, Mike OT | 76-77NYG | | 6'4" | 262 | Southwestern Okla. | | |
| Gibbs, Donnie K | 74NO | | 6'2" | 205 | Texas Christian | | |
| Gibbs, Pat DB | 72Phi | | 5'10" | 188 | Lamar | | |
| Giblin, Robert DE | 75NYG 76SJ 77StL 78JJ | | 6'2" | 208 | Houston | | |
| Gibson, Paul DB | 72GB | | 6'2" | 195 | Texas-El Paso | | |
| Gibson, Rueben HB | 77Buf | | 6' | 196 | Memphis State | | |
| Gibson, Tom DT | 71Oak | | 6'6" | 290 | Texas El-Paso | | |
| Gill, Randy LB | 78StL 78TB | | 6'2" | 230 | San Jose State | | |
| Gillard, Larry DT | 78NYG 79KJ | | 6'4" | 270 | Mississippi State | | |
| Gillette, Walker WR | 70-71SD 72-73StL 74-76NYG | 2 | 6'5" | 200 | Richmond | | 72 |
| Gilliam, Joe QB | 72-75Pit | 1 | 6'2" | 187 | Tennessee State | | 6 |
| Gilliam, John WR-HB | 67-68NO 69-71StL 72-75Min 76Atl 77Chi 77NO | 23 | 6'1" | 192 | S. Carolina State | | 312 |
| Gillingham, Gale OG-OT | 66-76GB | | 6'3" | 257 | Minnesota | | |
| Ginn, Hubert HB | 70-73Mia 73Bal 74-75Mia 76-77Oak | 23 | 5'11" | 187 | Florida A&M | | 18 |
| Gipson, Paul HB-FB | 69-70Atl 71Det 73NE | 2 | 6' | 208 | Houston | | 24 |
| Gladieux, Bob (Harpo) HB | 69BosA 70Bos 70Buf 71-72NE | 2 | 5'11" | 191 | Notre Dame | | |
| Glass, Chip TE | 69-73Cle 74NYG | 2 | 6'4" | 236 | Florida State | | 30 |
| Glass, Leland WR | 72-73GB | 2 | 6' | 185 | Oregon | | 6 |
| Glassic, Tom OG | 76-83Den | | 6'3" | 254 | Virginia | | |
| Glossen, Clyde WR | 70Buf | | 5'11" | 175 | Texas-El Paso | | |
| Glover, Rich DT | 73NYG 74WFL 75Phi | | 6'1" | 242 | Nebraska | | |
| Goeddeke, George OG-OT-C | 67-69DenA 70-72Den 73JJ | | 6'3" | 250 | Notre Dame | | |
| Gofourth, Derrel OG-C | 77-82GB | | 6'3" | 260 | Oklahoma State | | |
| Goich, Dan DT-DE | 69-70Det 71NO 72-73NYG 74Den | | 6'4" | 258 | California | | |
| Golub, Chris DB | 77KC | | 6'2" | 196 | Kansas | | |
| Gonzalez, Noe HB | 74NE | | 6' | 210 | SW Texas State | | |
| Goode, Don LB | 74-79SD 80-81Cle | | 6'2" | 230 | Kansas | 10 | |
| Goodman, Brian OG | 73-74Hou 75Den | | 6'2" | 250 | U.C.L.A. | | |
| Goodman, Harvey OG | 76Den | | 6'4" | 260 | Colorado | | |
| Goodman, Les HB-FB | 73-74GB | 2 | 5'11" | 206 | Yankton | | 6 |
| Goodrum, Charlie OT-OG | 73-74Min | | 6'3" | 256 | Florida A&M | | |
| Gordon, Dick WR-OE | 65-71Chi 72-73LA 73GB 74SD | 23 | 5'11" | 190 | Michigan State | | 216 |
| Gordon, Ira OG-OT | 70-75SD | | 6'3" | 270 | Kansas State | | |
| Gordon, John DT | 72Det | | 6'6" | 260 | Hawaii | | |
| Gordon, Larry LB | 76-82Mia Died 1983 — heart attack | | 6'4" | 230 | Arizona State | 8 | 2 |
| Gotshalk, Len OT-OG | 72-76Atl 77KJ | | 6'4" | 255 | Humboldt State | | |
| Gradishar, Randy LB | 74-83Den | | 6'3" | 232 | Ohio State | 20 | 24 |
| Graf, Dave LB | 75-79Cle 81Was | | 6'2" | 217 | Penn State | 1 | |
| Graff, Neil QB | 74-75NE 76Sea 76-77Pit 78GB | 1 | 6'3" | 202 | Wisconsin | | |
| Graham, Tom LB | 72-74Den 74KC 75-77SD 78Buf | | 6'2" | 235 | Oregon | 7 | |
| Grandberry, Ken HB | 74Chi | 2 | 6' | 198 | Washington State | | 12 |
| Grannell, Dave TE | 74SD | | 6'4" | 230 | Arizona State | | |
| Grant, Bob LB | 68-70Bal 71Was | | 6'2" | 225 | Wake Forest | 5 | 6 |
| Grant, Bud OE-DE | 51-52Phi 53CFL HC67-83, 85Min 49-51 played in N.B.A. | | 6'3" | 199 | Minnesota | | |
| Grant, Frank WR | 73-78Was 78TB | 2 | 5'11" | 181 | Southern Colorado | | 108 |
| Grant, John NT-DE-DT | 73-79Den | | 6'3" | 241 | Southern Calif. | | |
| Grant, Reggie DB | 78NYJ | | 5'9" | 185 | Oregon | | |
| Grant, Wes DE-DT | 71Cle 71SD 72Cle 73Hou | | 6'3" | 245 | U.C.L.A. | | |
| Gravelle, Gordon OT | 72-76Pit 77-79NYG 79La | | 6'5" | 251 | Brigham Young | | |
| Graves, Tom LB | 79Pit | | 6'3" | 228 | Michigan State | | |
| Gray, Dan DT | 78Det 79JJ | | 6'6" | 240 | Rutgers | | |
| Gray, David DB | 79NO | | 6' | 187 | San Diego State | 1 | |
| Gray, Johnnie DB | 75-83GB | 3 | 5'11" | 185 | Fullerton State | 22 | 6 |
| Gray, Leon OT | 73-78NE 79-81Hou 82-83NO | | 6'3" | 257 | Jackson State | | |
| Gray, Mel WR | 71-82StL 84USFL | 23 | 5'9" | 173 | Missouri | | 276 |
| Gray, Tim DB | 75StL 76-78KC 79SF | | 6'1" | 200 | Texas A&M | 13 | 12 |
| Green, Arthur HB-FB | 72NO | | 5'11" | 198 | Albany State (Ga.) | | |
| Green, Dave K | 73Hou 73-75Cin 76-78TB 79FJ | 45 | 5'11" | 206 | Ohio U. | | 125 |
| Green, Donnie OT | 71-76Buf 77Phi 78Det | | 6'7" | 266 | Purdue | | |
| Green, Jessie WR | 76GB 79-80Sea | | 6'3" | 191 | Tulsa | | 6 |
| Green, Joe DB | 70-71NYG | | 5'11" | 195 | Bowling Green | | 6 |
| Green, Sammy LB | 76-79Sea 80Hou 83USFL | | 6'2" | 230 | Florida | 3 | 6 |
| Green, Tony HB | 78Was 79NYG 79Sea | 3 | 5'9" | 185 | Florida | | 18 |
| Green, Van DB | 73-76Cle 76Buf | | 6'1" | 192 | Shaw | 3 | 12 |
| Green, Woody HB | 74-76KC 77KJ | 2 | 6'1" | 205 | Arizona State | | 66 |
| Greene, Joe (Mean Joe) DT | 69-81Pit | | 6'4" | 269 | North Texas | 1 | |
| Greene, Tony DB | 71-79Buf | | 5'10" | 171 | Maryland | 37 | 14 |
| Greenwood, L.C. DE | 69-81Pit | | 6'5" | 246 | Ark.-Pine Bluff | | 2 |

| Use Name (Nickname) - Positions | Team by Year | See Section | Hgt. | Wgt. | College | Int | Pts |
|---|---|---|---|---|---|---|---|
| Greer, Charlie DB | 66-69DenA 70-74Den | 3 | 6' | 205 | Colorado | 17 | 1 |
| Gregory, Bill DT-DE | 71-77Dal 78-80Sea | | 6'5" | 256 | Wisconsin | 2 | |
| Gregory, Jack DE | 67-71Cle 72-78NYG 79Cle | | 6'6" | 251 | Tenn.-Chattanooga, Delta State | 1 | |
| Gresham, Bob HB | 71-72NO 73-74Hou 75-76NYJ | 23 | 5'11" | 196 | West Virginia | | 84 |
| Griese, Bob QB | 67-69MiaA 70-80Mia | 12 | 6'1" | 190 | Purdue | | 42 |
| Griffin, Archie HB | 76-82Cin 84USFL | 2 | 5'9" | 188 | Ohio State | | 78 |
| Griffin, Wade OT | 77-81Bal 82ZJ | | 6'5" | 260 | Mississippi | | |
| Griggs, Perry WR | 77Bal | | 5'10" | 182 | Baylor | | |
| Grim, Bob WR-DB | 67-71Min 72-74NYG 75Chi 76-77Min | 23 | 6' | 196 | Oregon State | | 96 |
| Groce, Bob FB | 76Min | | 6'2" | 210 | Macalester | | |
| Gross, Lee C | 75-77NO 79Bal | | 6'3" | 237 | Auburn | | |
| Grossman, Randy TE | 74-81Pit | 2 | 6'1" | 218 | Temple | | 30 |
| Gueno, Jim LB | 76-80GB | | 6'2" | 220 | Tulane | | |
| Gunn, Jimmy LB | 70-75Chi 75NYG 76TB | | 6'1" | 220 | Southern Calif. | 2 | |
| Guthrie, Grant K | 70-71Buf | 5 | 6' | 210 | Florida State | | 71 |
| Guy, Ray K | 73-81Oak 82-86Raid | 4 | 6'3" | 195 | Southern Miss. | | 1 |
| Haden, Pat QB | 76-81LA | 12 | 5'11" | 183 | Southern Calif. | | 36 |
| Hagen, Halvor OT-C-OG-DE | 69-70Dal 71-72NE 73-75Buf | | 6'5" | 252 | Weber State | | |
| Haggerty, Steve DB | 75Den | | 5'10" | 175 | Nevada-Las Vegas | | |
| Hagins, Isaac WR | 76-80TB | 23 | 5'9" | 180 | Southern U. | | 30 |
| Hall, Charlie LB | 71-80Cle | | 6'3" | 228 | Houston | 13 | 12 |
| Hall, Charlie DB | 71-76GB | | 6'1" | 193 | Pittsburgh | 2 | |
| Hall, Randy DB | 74Bal 75FJ 76Bal | | 6'3" | 190 | Idaho | | |
| Hall, Willie LB | 72-73NO 75-78Oak | | 6'2" | 223 | Southern Calif. | 5 | 6 |
| Hall, Windian DB | 72-75SF 76-77Min 77Was | | 5'11" | 176 | Arizona State | 2 | 12 |
| Halverson, Dean LB | 68LA 70Atl 71-72LA 73-75Phi 76JJ | | 6'2" | 221 | Washington | 1 | |
| Ham, Jack LB | 71-82Pit | | 6'3" | 224 | Penn State | 32 | 12 |
| Hamilton, Andy WR | 73-74KC 75NO | 2 | 6'3" | 190 | Louisiana State | | |
| Hamilton, Ray (Sugar Bear) NT-DT-DE | 73-81NE | | 6'1" | 244 | Oklahoma | | 6 |
| Hamlin, Gene C | 70Was 71Chi 72Det | | 6'3" | 245 | Western Michigan | | |
| Hammond, Bob HB | 76-79NYG 79-80Was | 23 | 5'10" | 171 | Morgan State | | 48 |
| Hammond, Gary WR-HB | 73-76StL | 3 | 5'11" | 184 | S.M.U. | | |
| Hammond, Wayne DT | 76Den | | 6'5" | 255 | Montana State | | |
| Hampton, Dave HB-FB | 69-71GB 72-76Atl 76Phi | 23 | 6' | 207 | Wyoming | | 204 |
| Hanburger, Chris LB | 65-78Was | | 6'2" | 218 | North Carolina | 19 | 30 |
| Hancock, Mike TE | 73-74Was 75JJ | | 6'4" | 220 | Idaho State | | 12 |
| Hand, Larry DE-DT | 65-77Det | | 6'5" | 247 | Appalachian State | 5 | 18 |
| Hannah, John OG | 73-85NE | | 6'2" | 265 | Alabama | | 6 |
| Hanneman, Craig DE-DT | 72-73Pit 74-75NE 76JJ | | 6'3" | 243 | Oregon State | | |
| Hanratty, Terry QB | 69-75Pit 76TB | 1 | 6'1" | 206 | Notre Dame | | 6 |
| Hansen, Don LB | 66-67Min 69-75Atl 76Sea 76-77GB | | 6'3" | 227 | Illinois | 10 | 6 |
| Hanson, Dick DT | 71NYG | | 6'6" | 280 | N. Dakota State | | |
| Hardaway, Milton OT | 78SD 79KJ | | 6'9" | 309 | Oklahoma State | | |
| Hardee, Billy DB | 76Den 77NYJ 78-82CFL 84-85USFL | | 6' | 185 | Virginia Tech | 1 | |
| Hardeman, Buddy HB | 78CFL 79-80Was 83USFL | 2 | 6' | 196 | Iowa State | | 6 |
| Hardeman, Don (Jaws) FB | 75-77Hou 78-79Bal | 2 | 6'2" | 235 | Texas A&I | | 78 |
| Harden, Lee DB | 70GB | | 5'11" | 195 | Texas El-Paso | | |
| Hardman, Cedrick DE | 70-79SF 80-81Oak 83USFL | | 6'3" | 250 | North Texas State | | 8 |
| Hardy, Cliff DB | 71Chi | | 6' | 187 | Michigan State | | |
| Hardy, Ed OG | 73SF 74JJ | | 6'4" | 242 | Jackson State | | |
| Hardy, Kevin DT-DE | 68SF 69DJ 70GB 71-72SD | | 6'5" | 271 | Notre Dame | | |
| Hare, Eddie K | 79NE | 4 | 6'4" | 209 | Tulsa | | |
| Hargett, Edd QB | 69-72NO 73Hou 74-75WFL | 1 | 5'11" | 187 | Texas A&M | | 6 |
| Hargrove, Jim LB | 67Min 68MS 69-70Min 71-72StL | | 6'3" | 229 | Howard Payne | 1 | 6 |
| Harky, Steve HB-FB | 71-72NYJ | 2 | 6' | 215 | Georgia Tech | | |
| Harlan, Jim OT | 78Was | | 6'4" | 250 | Howard Payne | | |
| Harper, Roland FB-HB | 75-78Chi 79KJ 80-82Chi | 2 | 6' | 208 | Louisiana Tech | | 108 |
| Harper, Willie LB | 73-77SF 78KJ 79-83SF 84-85USFL | | 6'2" | 214 | Nebraska | 3 | |
| Harraway, Charlie FB | 66-68Cle 69-73Was 74WFL | 2 | 6'2" | 221 | San Jose State | | 162 |
| Harrell, Rick C | 73NYJ | | 6'3" | 238 | Clemson | | |
| Harrell, Willard HB | 75-77GB 78-84StL | 23 | 5'9" | 182 | U. of Pacific | | 96 |
| Harris, Bo LB | 75-82Cin | | 6'3" | 225 | Louisiana State | 7 | 6 |
| Harris, Cliff DB | 70-79Dal | 3 | 6' | 188 | Ouachita Baptist | 29 | 6 |
| Harris, Don DB | 78-80Was 80NYG 81CFL 83USFL | | 6'2" | 185 | Rutgers | | |
| Harris, Franco FB-HB | 72-83Pit 84Sea | 2 | 6'2" | 227 | Penn State | | 600 |
| Harris, Ike WR | 75-77StL 78-81NO | 2 | 6'3" | 207 | Iowa State | | 96 |
| Harris, James QB | 69BufA 70-71Buf 73-76LA 77-81SD | 12 | 6'3" | 215 | Grambling | | 60 |
| Harris, Jim DB | 70Was 71Cin | | 5'11" | 173 | Howard Payne | | |
| Harris, Joe LB | 75-76CFL 77Was 78SF 79Min 79-81LA 82Bal 83USFL | | 6'1" | 225 | Georgia Tech | 2 | 18 |
| Harris, Larry OT | 78Hou | | 6'3" | 274 | Oklahoma State | | |
| Harris, Leroy FB | 77-78Mia 79-80Phi 81BA 82Phi | 2 | 5'9" | 226 | Arkansas State | | 84 |
| Harris, Paul LB | 77TB 78Min 78TB | | 6'3" | 220 | Alabama | | |
| Harris, Richard DE-DT | 71-73Phi 74-75Chi 76-77Sea | 2 | 6'4" | 258 | Grambling | | |
| Harris, Tony DB | 71SF | | 6'2" | 190 | Toledo | | |
| Harrison, Dwight DB-WR | 71-72Den 72-77Buf | 2 | 6'1" | 183 | Texas A&I | 19 | 18 |
| Harrison, Glynn FB | 76KC | | 5'11" | 190 | Georgia | | |
| Harrison, Jim FB | 71-74Chi | 2 | 6'4" | 236 | Missouri | | 42 |
| Harrison, Kenny WR | 76-78SF 80Was | 2 | 6' | 176 | S.M.U. | | 6 |
| Harrison, Reggie (Booby) FB | 74StL 74-77Pit 78GB | 2 | 5'11" | 218 | Cincinnati | | 48 |
| Hart, Harold HB | 74-75Oak 76JJ 77NYG 78Oak | 23 | 6' | 207 | Texas Southern | | 42 |
| Hart, Jeff OT | 75SF 76NO 79-83Bal 84-85USFL | | 6'5" | 266 | Oregon State | | |
| Hart, Jim QB | 66-83StL 84Was | 12 | 6'2" | 206 | Southern Illinois | | 96 |
| Hart, Leo QB | 71Atl 72Buf | | 6'4" | 203 | Duke | | |
| Hart, Tommy DE-LB | 68-77SF 78-79Chi 80NO | | 6'3" | 244 | Morris Brown | 2 | 14 |
| Hartle, Greg LB | 74-76StL | | 6'2" | 225 | Newberry | | |
| Hartwig, Keith WR | 77Min 77GB | | 6' | 186 | Arizona | | |
| Harvey, Claude LB | 70Hou | | 6'4" | 225 | Prairie View | | |
| Harvey, Richard DB | 70Phi 71NO | | 6'2" | 190 | Jackson State | | |
| Hasenhorl, George DT | 74NYG | | 6'1" | 260 | Ohio State | | |
| Haselrig, Clint HB-WR | 74-75Buf 75Min 76NYJ | | 6' | 191 | Michigan | | |
| Haslip, Wilbert FB | 79KC 83USFL | | 5'11" | 212 | Hawaii | | |
| Hauss, Len C | 64-77Was | | 6'2" | 234 | Georgia | | |
| Haverdick, Dave DT | 70Det | | 6'4" | 245 | Morehead State | | |
| Havig, Dennis OG | 72-75Atl 76Hou 77GB | | 6'2" | 253 | Colorado | | |
| Havrilak, Sam WR-HB-DB | 69-73Bal 74NO | 2 | 6'2" | 195 | Bucknell | | 42 |
| Hawkins, Clarence HB | 79Oak | | 6' | 205 | Florida A&M | | 6 |
| Hawkins, Nate WR | 75Hou | | 6'1" | 190 | Nevada-Las Vegas | | |
| Hawkins, Robert HB | 79StL | | 6' | 195 | Kentucky | | |
| Hayden, Leo HB-FB | 71Min 72-73StL | | 6' | 211 | Ohio State | | 6 |
| Hayes, Billy DB | 72NO | | 6'1" | 175 | San Diego State | | |
| Hayes, Bob WR-OE | 65-74Dal 75SF | 23 | 6' | 187 | Florida A&M | | 456 |
| Hayes, Ed DB | 70Phi | | 6'1" | 185 | Morgan State | 1 | |
| Hayes, Tom DB | 71-75Atl 76SD | | 6'1" | 197 | San Diego State | 19 | 36 |
| Hayhoe, Bill OT | 69-73GB 74JJ 75BL | | 6'8" | 258 | Southern Calif. | | |
| Hayman, Conway OG-OT | 75-80Hou | | 6'3" | 264 | Delaware | | |
| Hayman, Gary HB | 74-75Buf | 3 | 6'1" | 200 | Penn State | | |

| Use Name (Nickname) - Positions | Team by Year | See Section | Hgt. | Wgt. | College | Int | Pts |
|---|---|---|---|---|---|---|---|
| Haynes, Reggie TE | 78Was | | 6'2" | 229 | Nevada-Las Vegas | | |
| Haywood, Al FB | 75Den | | 5'11" | 215 | Bethune-Cookman | | |
| Heater, Don HB | 72StL | | 6'2" | 205 | Montana Tech | | |
| Heath, Clayton HB | 76Buf 76Mia | | 5'11" | 195 | Wake Forest | | |
| Hedberg, Randy QB | 77TB 78EJ | 1 | 6'3" | 200 | Minot State | | |
| Hefferle, Ernie | HC75NO | | | | Duquesne | | |
| Hefner, Larry LB | 72-75GB | | 6'2" | 226 | Clemson | 1 | |
| Heinz, Bob DT-DE-NT | 69MiaA 70-74Mia 75KJ 76-77Mia 78Was | | 6'6" | 268 | U. of Pacific | | |
| Helms, Ken OT-C | 77NYJ | | 6'4" | 265 | Georgia | | |
| Helton, Darius OG | 77KC 78SJ | | 6'2" | 260 | N. Carolina Central | | |
| Henderson, Tom (Hollywood) LB | 75-79Dal 80SF 80Hou 81BQ | | 6'2" | 221 | Langston | 4 | 14 |
| Hendren, Jerry WR | 70Den | | 6'2" | 187 | Idaho | | |
| Hendricks, Ted (Mad Stork) LB | 69-73Bal 74GB 75-81Oak 82-83Raid | | 6'7" | 222 | Miami (Fla.) | 26 | 34 |
| Hennessy, John LB-DE | 77-78NYJ | | 6'3" | 243 | Michigan | | |
| Hennigan, Mike LB | 73-75Det 76-78NYJ 79KJ | | 6'2" | 217 | Tennessee Tech | 3 | |
| Henson, Champ FB | 75Cin | | 6'3" | 240 | Ohio State | | |
| Hepburn, Lonnie DB | 71-72Bal 74Den | | 5'11" | 182 | Texas Southern | 1 | |
| Hermeling, Terry OT-OG-DE | 70-73Was 74KJ 75-80Was | | 6'5" | 255 | Nevada-Reno | | |
| Herosian, Brian DB | 73Bal | | 6'3" | 200 | Connecticut | | |
| Herrera, Efren K | 74Dal 75JJ 76-77Dal 78-81Sea 82Buf 84USFL | 5 | 5'9" | 189 | U.C.L.A. | | 604 |
| Herrmann, Don WR | 69-74NYG 75-77NO | 2 | 6'2" | 199 | Waynesburg | | 96 |
| Herron, Mack HB | 73-75NE 75Atl | 23 | 5'5" | 174 | Kansas State | | 96 |
| Hertel, Rob QB | 78Cin 80Phi | | 6'2" | 195 | Southern Calif. | | |
| Hertwig, Craig OT | 75-77Det 78Buf | | 6'8" | 270 | Georgia | | |
| Hester, Ray LB | 71-73NO | | 6'2" | 215 | Tulane | | |
| Hews, Bob OT-DE | 71Buf | | 6'5" | 240 | Princeton | | |
| Hickman, Dallas DE-LB | 76-80Was 81Bal 81Was | | 6'6" | 238 | California | | |
| Hickman, Donnie OG | 78Was 78Det | | 6'2" | 260 | Southern Calif. | | |
| Hicks, Eddie FB-HB | 79-80NYG | | 6'2" | 210 | East Carolina | | |
| Hicks, John OG | 74-77NYG | | 6'2" | 258 | Ohio State | | |
| Hicks, R.W. C | 75Det | | 6'4" | 250 | Humboldt State | | |
| Hicks, Sylvester DE | 78-81KC | | 6'4" | 251 | Tennessee State | | |
| Hicks, Tom LB | 76-80Chi | | 6'4" | 233 | Illinois | 4 | 7 |
| Higgins, Tom LB | 79Buf | | 6'1" | 235 | N. Carolina State | | |
| Highsmith, Don HB | 70-72Oak 73GB 74-75WFL | 2 | 6' | 200 | Michigan State | | 12 |
| Hilgenberg, Wally LB-OG | 64-66Det 67JJ 68-79Min | | 6'3" | 230 | Iowa | 8 | 14 |
| Hill, Barry DB | 73-76Mia | | 6'3" | 185 | Iowa State | | |
| Hill, Calvin HB-FB | 69-74Dal 75WFL 76-77Was 78-81Cle | 2 | 6'3" | 228 | Yale | | 390 |
| Hill, Ike WR-DB | 70-71Buf 73-74Chi 76Mia | 23 | 5'10" | 180 | Catawba | | 30 |
| Hill, J.D. WR | 71-75Buf 76-77Det 78FJ | 2 | 6'1" | 190 | Arizona State | | 126 |
| Hill, Jim DB | 69SD-A 70-71SD 72-74GB 75Cle | | 6'2" | 192 | Texas A&I | 19 | 6 |
| Hill, John C-OT | 72-74NYG 75-84NO 85SF | | 6'2" | 249 | Lehigh | | |
| Hill, Ralph C | 76-77NYG | | 6'1" | 245 | Florida A&M | | |
| Hilton, Roy DE | 65-73Bal 74NYG 75Atl | | 6'6" | 240 | Jackson State | 1 | 12 |
| Hilton, Scott LB | 79-80SF | | 6'4" | 228 | none | | |
| Himes, Dick OT | 68-77GB | | 6'4" | 251 | Ohio State | | |
| Hinton, Eddie WR | 69-72Bal 73Hou 74NE | 2 | 6' | 200 | Oklahoma | | 72 |
| Hoaglin, Fred C | 66-72Cle 73Bal 74-75Hou 76Sea | | 6'4" | 246 | Pittsburgh | | |
| Hoban, Mike OG | 74Chi | | 6'2" | 235 | Michigan | | |
| Hobbs, Bill LB | 69-71Phi 72NO | | 6' | 218 | Texas A&M | | 6 |
| Hodgins, Norm DB | 74Chi 75JJ | | 6'1" | 190 | Louisiana State | | |
| Hoey, George DB | 71StL 72-73NE 74SD 75Den 75NYJ | | 5'10" | 174 | Michigan | | |
| Hofer, Paul HB | 76-81SF | 23 | 6' | 194 | Mississippi | | 126 |
| Hogan, Mike FB-HB | 76-78Phi 79SF 80NYG 80Phi | 2 | 6'2" | 213 | Tenn.-Chattanooga | | 48 |
| Holden, Sam OT | 71NO | | 6'3" | 258 | Grambling | | |
| Holden, Steve WR | 73-77Cle 77Cin | 23 | 6' | 195 | Arizona State | | 24 |
| Holland, John WR | 74Min 75-77Buf 78KJ | 2 | 6' | 190 | Tennessee State | | 24 |
| Holland, Vern OT | 71-79Cin 80Det 80NYG | | 6'5" | 268 | Tennessee State | | |
| Hollas, Hugo DB | 70-72NO 73KJ 74SF | | 6'1" | 190 | Rice | 11 | |
| Holliday, Ron WR | 73SD 74-75WFL 76KJ | 2 | 5'9" | 168 | Pittsburgh | | 1 |
| Holloman, Gus DB | 68-69DenA 70-74NYJ | 4 | 6'3" | 195 | Houston | | |
| Holloway, Glenn OG | 70-73Chi 74Cle | | 6'3" | 249 | North Texas | | |
| Hollway, Bob | HC71-72StL | | | | Michigan | | |
| Holman, Willie DE-DT | 68-73Chi 73Was | | 6'4" | 250 | S. Carolina State | | |
| Holmes, Ernie (Fats) DT-NT | 72-77Pit 78NE | | 6'3" | 260 | Texas Southern | | |
| Holmes, Mel OG-OT | 71-73Pit | | 6'3" | 250 | N. Carolina A&T | | |
| Holmes, Mike DB-WR | 74-75SF 76Buf 76Mia 77-82CFL 83USFL | 23 | 6'2" | 195 | Texas Southern | 3 | 6 |
| Holmes, Robert FB | 68-69KC-A 70-71KC 71-72Hou 73SD 74WFL 75Hou | 23 | 5'9" | 220 | Southern U. | | 162 |
| Holmes, Rudy DB | 74Atl | | 5'10" | 178 | Duke | | |
| Holtz, Lou | HC76NYJ | | | | Kent State | | |
| Homan, Dennis WR | 68-70Dal 71-72KC | 2 | 6'1" | 180 | Alabama | | 2 |
| Hooker, Fair WR | 69-74Cle 75WFL | 2 | 6'1" | 198 | Arizona State | | 48 |
| Hooks, Jim FB | 73-76Det | 2 | 5'11" | 225 | Central St.-Ohio | | |
| Hooks, Roland HB-FB | 76-82Buf 83KJ | 23 | 6' | 196 | N. Carolina State | | 90 |
| Hoopes, Mitch K | 75Dal 76SD 76Hou 77Det 78Phi 83USFL | 4 | 6'1" | 207 | Arizona | | |
| Hopkins, Andy HB | 71Hou | | 5'10" | 187 | S.F. Austin State | | |
| Horn, Don QB | 67-70GB 71Den 72-73Cle 74SD | 1 | 6'2" | 195 | Washington State, San Diego State | | 6 |
| Hornsby, Ron LB | 71-74NYG | | 6'3" | 231 | Southeastern La. | | |
| Horton, Greg OG-C | 76-78LA 78-79TB 80LA 83-84USFL | | 6'4" | 246 | Colorado | | |
| Horton, Larry DE-DT | 72Chi | | 6'2" | 248 | Iowa | | |
| Hoskins, Bob DT-OG | 70-75SF 76IL | | 6'2" | 246 | Wichita State | | |
| Hoss, Clark TE | 72Phi | | 6'8" | 235 | Oregon State | | |
| Houston, Bill WR | 74Dal | | 6'3" | 208 | Jackson State | | |
| Houston, Ken DB | 67-69HouA 70-72Hou 73-80Was | 3 | 6'3" | 196 | Prairie View | 49 | 72 |
| Houston, Rich WR | 69-73NYG | 23 | 6'2" | 196 | East Texas State | | 42 |
| Hover, Don LB | 78-79Was | | 6'2" | 225 | Washington State | | 6 |
| Howard, Billy DE-DT | 74-76Det | | 6'4" | 252 | Alcorn State | | |
| Howard, Bob DB | 67-69SD-A 70-74SD 75-77NE 78-79Phi | | 6'1" | 181 | San Diego State | 37 | 6 |
| Howard, Gene DB | 68-70NO 71-72LA | 3 | 6' | 190 | Langston | 14 | 12 |
| Howard, Harry DB | 76NYJ | | 6' | 189 | Ohio State | | |
| Howard, Leroy DB | 71Hou | | 5'11" | 175 | Bishop | | |
| Howard, Percy WR | 75Dal 76-77JJ | | 6'4" | 210 | Austin Peay | | |
| Howard, Ron TE | 74-75Dal 76-78Sea 79Buf | 2 | 6'4" | 229 | Seattle | | 12 |
| Howell, Delles DB | 70-72NO 73-75NYJ 77JJ | | 6'3" | 199 | Grambling | 17 | |
| Howfield, Bobby K | 68-69DenA 70Den 71-74NYJ | 5 | 5'9" | 180 | none | | 487 |
| Hrivnak, Gary DE | 73-75Chi 76JJ | | 6'5" | 252 | Purdue | | |
| Hubbard, Dave OT | 77NO | | 6'7" | 270 | Brigham Young | | |
| Hubbard, Marv FB | 69OakA 70-75Oak 76SJ 77Det | 2 | 6'1" | 224 | Colgate | | 144 |
| Huddleston, John LB | 78-79Oak | | 6'3" | 230 | Utah | | |
| Hudson, Bob HB | 72GB 73-74Oak | 3 | 5'11" | 207 | Northeast La. | | |
| Huff, Gary QB | 73-76Chi 77-78TB 80SF 85USFL | 12 | 6'1" | 197 | Florida State | | 12 |
| Huff, Marty LB | 72SF | | 6'2" | 234 | Michigan | | |

| Use Name (Nickname) - Positions | Team by Year | See Section | Hgt. | Wgt. | College | Int | Pts |
|---|---|---|---|---|---|---|---|
| Hufnagel, John QB | 74-75Den | 1 | 6'1" | 194 | Penn State | | |
| Hughes, Dennis TE | 70-71Pit | 2 | 6'1" | 220 | Georgia | | 18 |
| Hughes, Pat LB-C | 70-76NYG 77-79NO | | 6'2" | 231 | Boston U. | 15 | |
| Hughes, Randy DB | 75-80Dal 81SJ | | 6'4" | 207 | Oklahoma | 9 | 6 |
| Hull, Mike FB-TE | 68-70Chi 71-74Was | 2 | 6'3" | 220 | Southern Calif. | | 6 |
| Hull, Tom LB | 74SF 75GB | | 6'3" | 230 | Penn State | | |
| Humm, David QB | 75-79Oak 80Buf 81-82Bal 83-84Raid | 1 | 6'2" | 188 | Nebraska | | |
| Humphrey, Claude DE | 68-78Atl 79-81Phi | | 6'5" | 258 | Tennessee State | 2 | 10 |
| Humphrey, Tom C | 74KC | | 6'6" | 260 | Abilene Christian | | |
| Hunt, Calvin C | 71Phi 72-73Hou | | 6'3" | 244 | Baylor | | |
| Hunt, Charlie LB | 73SF 75WFL 76TB | | 6'2" | 215 | Florida State | | |
| Hunt, Ervin DB | 70GB | | 6'2" | 190 | Fresno State | | |
| Hunt, George K | 73Bal 75NYG | 5 | 6'1" | 215 | Tennessee | | 112 |
| Hunt, Kevin OT-OG | 72GB 73NE 73-77Hou 78NO | | 6'5" | 260 | Doane | | |
| Hunt, Mike LB | 78-80GB | | 6'2" | 240 | Minnesota | 2 | |
| Hunt, Ron OT | 76-78Cin | | 6'6" | 261 | Oregon | | |
| Hunt, Sam LB | 74-80NE | | 6'1" | 248 | S.F. Austin State | 7 | 6 |
| Hunter, Al HB | 77-80Sea | 23 | 5'11" | 195 | Notre Dame | | 24 |
| Hunter, James DB | 76-82Det | | 6'3" | 195 | Grambling | 27 | 6 |
| Hunter, Scott QB | 71-73GB 74Buf 76-78Atl 79Det | 12 | 6'2" | 205 | Alabama | | 78 |
| Hutcherson, Ken LB | 74Dal 75SD 76JJ | | 6'1" | 219 | Livingston | | |
| Hutchinson, Chuck OG | 70-72StL 73-75Cle 76KJ | | 6'3" | 242 | Ohio State | | |
| Hyatt, Freddie WR | 68-72StL 73NO | | 6'3" | 203 | Auburn | | |
| Hyland, Bob C-OG-OT | 67-69GB 70Chi 71-75NYG 76GB 77NE | | 6'5" | 253 | Boston College | | |
| Hynoski, Henry FB | 75Cle | | 6' | 210 | Temple | | |
| Iremia, Mekell DT | 78Buf 79-80KJ | | 6'2" | 244 | Brigham Young | | |
| Ilgenfritz, Mark OT-OG-C | 74Cle 75WFL | | 6'4" | 250 | Vanderbilt | | |
| Imhof, Martin DE-DT | 72StL 74Was 75NE 76Den | | 6'6" | 256 | San Diego State | | |
| Inmon, Earl LB | 78TB | | 6'1" | 215 | Bethune-Cookman | | |
| Irons, Gerald LB | 70-75Oak 76-79Cle | | 6'2" | 231 | Md. Eastern Shore | 13 | 6 |
| Isenbarger, John HB-WR | 70-73SF 74WFL | 2 | 6'3" | 203 | Indiana | | 12 |
| Ivory, Horace HB | 77-81NE 81-82Sea | 23 | 6' | 198 | Oklahoma | | 108 |
| Iwanowski, Mark TE | 78NYJ | | 6'4" | 230 | Pennsylvania | | |
| Jackson, Bernard DB | 72-76Cin 77-80Den 80SD | 3 | 6' | 178 | Washington State | 17 | |
| Jackson, Bob OG-OT-C | 75-81Cle | | 6'5" | 253 | Duke | | |
| Jackson, Ernie DB | 72-77NO 78Atl 79Det | | 5'10" | 175 | Duke | 15 | 6 |
| Jackson, Gerald DB | 79KC | | 6'1" | 195 | Mississippi State | 1 | |
| Jackson, Harold WR | 68LA 69-72Phi 73-77LA 78-81NE 82Min 83Sea | 2 | 5'10" | 175 | Jackson State | | 456 |
| Jackson, Honor DB | 72-73NE 73-74NYG | | 6'1" | 195 | Pacific | 5 | |
| Jackson, Jazz HB | 74-76NYJ | 2 | 5'8" | 169 | Western Kentucky | | 12 |
| Jackson, Joey DE-DT | 72-73NYJ 74-75WFL 77Min | | 6'4" | 263 | New Mexico State | | |
| Jackson, Johnny NT | 77Phi | | 6'2" | 250 | Southern U. | | |
| Jackson, Larron OG-OT | 71-74Den 75-76Atl | | 6'3" | 265 | Missouri | | |
| Jackson, Melvin OG | 76-80GB | | 6'1" | 267 | Southern Calif. | | |
| Jackson, Monte DB | 75-77LA 78-81Oak 82Raid 83LA | | 5'11" | 193 | San Diego State | 23 | 24 |
| Jackson, Noah OG | 75-83Chi 84TB | | 6'2" | 267 | Tampa | | |
| Jackson, Randy OT | 67-74Chi | | 6'5" | 247 | Florida | | |
| Jackson, Randy HB-FB | 72Buf 73SF 74Phi | 2 | 6' | 220 | Wichita State | | 6 |
| Jackson, Rusty K | 76LA 78-79Buf | 4 | 6'2" | 193 | Louisiana State | | |
| Jackson, Steve DB | 77Oak | | 6'1" | 192 | Louisiana State | 1 | |
| Jackson, Tom LB | 73-86Den | | 5'11" | 221 | Louisville | 20 | 18 |
| Jackson, Wilbur FB-HB | 74-77SF 78KJ 79SF 80-82Was | 2 | 6'1" | 217 | Alabama | | 102 |
| Jacobsen, Larry DT-DE | 72-74NYG 75BN | | 6'6" | 260 | Nebraska | | |
| Jakowenko, George K | 74Oak 76Buf | 5 | 5'9" | 175 | Syracuse | | 57 |
| James, John K | 72-81Atl 82Det 82-84Hou | 4 | 6'3" | 198 | Florida | | |
| James, Po HB | 72-75Phi | 23 | 6'1" | 202 | New Mexico State | | 36 |
| James, Robert DB-WR | 69BufA 70-74Buf 75-76KJ | | 6'1" | 182 | Fisk | 9 | 6 |
| Jameson, Larry DT | 76TB | | 6'7" | 270 | Indiana | | |
| Janet, Ernie OG | 72-74Chi 75GB 75Phi 76GJ | | 6'4" | 253 | Washington | | |
| Jankowski, Bruce WR | 71-72KC | | 5'11" | 185 | Ohio State | | |
| Jaqua, Jon DB | 70-72Was 73JJ | | 6' | 190 | Lewis and Clark | 1 | |
| Jarvis, Bruce C | 71-74Buf | | 6'7" | 248 | Washington | | |
| Jarvis, David QB | 74KC | | 6'2" | 212 | Kansas | | |
| Jarvis, Ray WR | 71-72Atl 73Buf 74-78Det 79NE | 2 | 6'1" | 192 | Norfolk State | | 66 |
| Jauron, Dick DB | 73-77Det 78-80Cin 81KJ | 3 | 6' | 189 | Yale | 25 | 12 |
| Jefferson, Charles DB | 79-80Hou | | 6' | 178 | McNeese State | | |
| Jefferson, Roy WR-FL-OE | 65-69Pit 70Bal 71-76Was | 23 | 6'2" | 194 | Utah | | 318 |
| Jeffrey, Neal QB | 76-77SD | | 6'1" | 180 | Baylor | | |
| Jenkins, Al OG-OT-DE-DT | 69-70Cle 72Mia 73Hou | | 6'2" | 250 | Tulsa | | |
| Jenkins, Alfred WR | 75-83Atl | 2 | 5'10" | 170 | Morris Brown | | 240 |
| Jenkins, Ed HB | 72Mia 73JJ 74NYG 74Buf 74NE | | 6'2" | 210 | Holy Cross | | |
| Jenkins, Leon DB | 72Det | | 5'11" | 165 | West Virginia | | |
| Jennings, Rick HB-WR | 76Oak 77TB 77SF 77Oak | | 5'9" | 180 | Maryland | | |
| Jensen, Jim FB-TE | 76Dal 77Den 78KJ 79-80Den 81-82GB | 2 | 6'3" | 232 | Iowa | | 42 |
| Jerome, Jim LB | 77NYJ | | 6'4" | 225 | Syracuse | | |
| Jessie, Ron WR | 71-74Det 75-79LA 80-81Buf | 23 | 6' | 183 | Kansas | | 182 |
| Jiggetts, Dan OT-OG | 76-82Chi 84USFL | | 6'4" | 272 | Harvard | | |
| Jilek, Dan LB | 76-79Buf | | 6'2" | 220 | Michigan | 2 | |
| Joachim, Steve QB | 76NYJ | | 6'3" | 215 | Temple | | |
| Johannson, Ove K | 77Phi | | 5'10" | 175 | Abilene Christian | | 4 |
| Johns, Freeman WR | 76-77LA | | 6'1" | 175 | S.M.U. | | |
| Johnson, Al DB-HB | 72-74Hou 75NJ 76-78Hou | | 6' | 200 | Cincinnati | | |
| Johnson, Andy HB | 74-76NE 77KJ 78-81NE 83USFL | 23 | 6' | 204 | Georgia | | 132 |
| Johnson, Benny DB | 70-73Hou 74WFL 76NO | 3 | 5'11" | 178 | Johnson C. Smith | 1 | |
| Johnson, Bill K | 70NYG | 4 | 6'4" | 208 | Livingston | | |
| Johnson, Bob C | 68-69CinA 70-79Cin | | 6'5" | 257 | Tennessee | | |
| Johnson, Carl OT-OG | 72-73NO | | 6'3" | 248 | Nebraska | | |
| Johnson, Cornelius OG | 68-73Bal | | 6'2" | 245 | Virginia Union | | |
| Johnson, Danny LB | 78GB | | 6'1" | 216 | Tennessee State | | |
| Johnson, Dennis DT-DE | 74-77Was 78Buf | | 6'4" | 261 | Delaware | 2 | |
| Johnson, Dennis FB-TE | 78-79Buf 80NYG 83-85USFL | 2 | 6'3" | 220 | Mississippi State | | 12 |
| Johnson, Eric DB | 74-75WFL 77-78Phi 79SF 83-84USFL | | 6'1" | 192 | Washington State | | |
| Johnson, Essex HB | 68-69CinA 70-75Cin 76TB | 23 | 5'9" | 197 | Grambling | | 186 |
| Johnson, Greg DT-NT-DE | 77Bal 77Chi 77TB | | 6'4" | 240 | Florida State | 1 | 6 |
| Johnson, Ken DE-DT | 71-77Cin | | 6'5" | 261 | Indiana | | |
| Johnson, Ken QB | 74WFL 77Buf 78-82CFL 83-84USFL | | 6'2" | 205 | Colorado | | |
| Johnson, Ken FB | 79NYG 83USFL | | 6'2" | 220 | Miami (Fla.) | | 6 |
| Johnson, Kermit HB | 75-76SF | 2 | 6' | 201 | U.C.L.A. | | 6 |
| Johnson, Len C-OG | 70NYG | | 6'2" | 250 | St. Cloud State | | |
| Johnson, Levi DB | 73-77Det 78FJ | | 6'3" | 196 | Texas A&I | 21 | 30 |
| Johnson, Mark DE-LB | 75-76Buf 77Cle | | 6'2" | 239 | Missouri | | |
| Johnson, Marshall WR-HB | 75Bal 76KJ 77-78Bal | 3 | 6'1" | 192 | Houston | | 12 |
| Johnson, Monte LB | 73-79Oak 80KJ | | 6'4" | 239 | Nebraska | 10 | 6 |
| Johnson, Randy QB | 66-70Atl 71-73NYG 74WFL 75Was 76GB | 12 | 6'3" | 202 | Texas A&I | | 60 |

| Use Name (Nickname) - Positions | Team by Year | See Section | Hgt. | Wgt. | College | Int | Pts |
|---|---|---|---|---|---|---|---|
| Johnson, Randy OG | 77-78TB 79JJ | | 6'2" | 255 | Georgia | | |
| Johnson, Ron HB | 69Cle 70-75NYG | 2 | 6'1" | 205 | Michigan | | 330 |
| Johnson, Sammy FB-HB | 74-76SF 76-78Min 79Phi 79GB | 2 | 6' | 224 | North Carolina | | 54 |
| Johnson, Stan NT | 78KC | | 6'4" | 275 | Tennessee State | | |
| Johnson, Walter DT | 65-76Cle 77Cin | | 6'3" | 268 | Los Angeles State | 2 | 14 |
| Joiner, Charlie WR | 69HouA 70-72Hou 72-75Cin 76-86SD | 2 | 5'11" | 184 | Grambling | | 390 |
| Jolitz, Evan LB | 74Cin | | 6'2" | 225 | Cincinnati | | |
| Jolley, Gordon OT-OG | 72-75Det 76-77Sea | | 6'5" | 244 | Utah | | |
| Jolley, Lexis HB-FB | 72-73Hou | | 6' | 210 | North Carolina | | |
| Jones, Andrew FB | 75-76NO | 2 | 6'2" | 216 | Washington State | | 6 |
| Jones, Bert QB | 73-81Bal 82LA | 12 | 6'3" | 210 | Louisiana State | | 84 |
| Jones, Bob WR | 73-74Cin 75-76Atl | | 6'1" | 194 | Virginia Union | | |
| Jones, Calvin DB | 73-76Den | | 5'7" | 170 | Washington | 12 | 6 |
| Jones, Clint HB | 67-72Min 73SD 74JJ | 23 | 6' | 206 | Michigan State | | 126 |
| Jones, Cody DT-DE-NT | 74-78LA 79FJ 80-82LA | | 6'5" | 243 | San Jose State | | |
| Jones, Dave WR | 69-71Cle | | 6'2" | 185 | Kansas State | | |
| Jones, Doug DB | 73-74KC 75KJ 76-78Buf 79Det | | 6'2" | 204 | Northridge State | 6 | |
| Jones, Ed DB | 75Buf | | 6' | 185 | Rutgers | 3 | |
| Jones, Ernie DB | 76Sea 77-79NYG | | 6'3" | 180 | Miami (Fla.) | 6 | 6 |
| Jones, Greg HB | 70-71Buf | 2 | 6'1" | 200 | U.C.L.A. | | 18 |
| Jones, Harris OG-C | 71SD 72JJ 73-74Hou | | 6'4" | 241 | Johnson C. Smith | | |
| Jones, Horace DE | 71-75Oak 76KJ 77Sea | | 6'3" | 251 | Louisville | | |
| Jones, Jimmie DE | 69NY-A 70NYJ 71-73Was | | 6'3" | 215 | Wichita State | | |
| Jones, Jimmie HB-FB | 74Det | 23 | 5'10" | 205 | U.C.L.A. | | 6 |
| Jones, Joe (Turkey) DE | 70-71Cle 72KJ 73Cle 74-75Phi 75-78Cle 79-80Was | | 6'6" | 249 | Tennessee State | | 6 |
| Jones, John QB | 75NYJ | 1 | 6'1" | 180 | Fisk | | |
| Jones, June QB | 77-79Atl 80NJ 81Atl HC94-95Atl | 1 | 6'4" | 200 | Portland State | | |
| Jones, Kim FB | 76-79NO | 2 | 6'4" | 238 | Colorado State | | |
| Jones, Larry WR-DB | 74-77Was 78SF | 3 | 5'10" | 170 | NE Missouri St. | | 12 |
| Jones, Leroy DE | 76-83SD | | 6'8" | 263 | Norfolk State | 2 | 6 |
| Jones, Mike LB | 77Sea | | 6'2" | 214 | Jackson State | | |
| Jones, Ray DB | 70Phi 71Mia 72SD | | 6' | 187 | Southern U. | 2 | |
| Jones, Spike K | 70Hou 71-74Buf 75-77Phi | 4 | 6'2" | 191 | Georgia | | |
| Jones, Steve HB | 73-74Buf 74-78StL | 2 | 6' | 199 | Duke | | 102 |
| Jordan, Bob DT | 77Atl | | 6'6" | 255 | Memphis State | | |
| Jordan, Jeff HB-FB | 70LA 71-72Was | | 6'1" | 215 | Washington | | |
| Joyce, Terry K-TE | 76-77StL | 4 | 6'6" | 229 | Missouri Southern | | |
| Juenger, Dave WR | 73Chi | | 6'1" | 195 | Ohio U. | | |
| Jurich, Tom K | 78NO | | 5'10" | 185 | Northern Arizona | | 2 |
| Jury, Bob DB | 78SF 79SJ | | 6'1" | 188 | Pittsburgh | | |
| Kaczmarek, Mike LB | 73Bal | | 6'4" | 235 | Southern Illinois | | |
| Kadish, Mike DT-NT | 73-81Buf | | 6'5" | 270 | Notre Dame | | 8 |
| Kadziel, Ron LB | 72NE | | 6'4" | 230 | Stanford | | |
| Kalina, Dave WR | 70Pit | | 6'3" | 205 | Miami (Fla.) | | |
| Kaminski, Larry C | 68-69DenA 70-73Den | | 6'2" | 244 | Purdue | | |
| Kampa, Bob DT | 73-74Buf | | 6'4" | 249 | California | | |
| Kay, Rick LB | 73LA 74KJ 75-77LA 77Atl | | 6'4" | 235 | Colorado | 1 | |
| Kearney, Jim DB | 65-66Det 67-69KC-A 70-75KC 76NO | | 6'2" | 204 | Prairie View | 23 | 30 |
| Kearney, Tim LB | 72-74Cin 75KC 76TB 76-81StL | | 6'2" | 225 | Northern Michigan | 3 | |
| Keating, Tom DT | 64-65BufA 66-67OakA 68FJ 69OakA 70-72Oak 73Pit 74-75KC | | 6'3" | 246 | Michigan | | |
| Keeton, Durwood DB | 75NE | | 5'10" | 180 | Oklahoma | | |
| Keithly, Gary QB | 73, 75StL | 1 4 | 6'3" | 210 | Texas-El Paso | | |
| Kelcher, Louie DT-NT | 75-83SD 84SF | | 6'5" | 290 | S.M.U. | 2 | |
| Kellar, Mark FB | 76-78Min | 2 | 6' | 225 | Northern Illinois | | |
| Keller, Larry LB | 76-78NYJ 79KJ | | 6'2" | 223 | Houston | 3 | |
| Keller, Mike LB | 72-73Dal | | 6'4" | 220 | Michigan | | |
| Kelley, Brian LB | 73-83NYG | | 6'3" | 222 | Cal. Lutheran | 15 | |
| Kellum, Marv TE | 74-76Pit 77StL | | 6'2" | 225 | Wichita State | 2 | |
| Kelly, Jim TE | 74Chi | | 6'4" | 210 | Tennessee State | | |
| Kelly, Mike TE | 70-72Cin 73NO | | 6'4" | 217 | Davidson | | |
| Kendrick, Vince FB | 74Atl 75KJ 76TB | 2 | 6' | 231 | Florida | | 6 |
| Kennedy, Jimmie TE | 75-77Bal | | 6'5" | 231 | Colorado State | | 6 |
| Kern, Rex DB | 71-73Bal 74Buf | | 5'11" | 190 | Ohio State | 2 | |
| Kersey, Merritt HB-K | 74-75Phi | 4 | 6'1" | 205 | West Chester | | |
| Key, Wade OG-OT | 70-79Phi | | 6'4" | 245 | SW Texas State | | |
| Keyes, Leroy HB-DB | 69-72Phi 73KC | 2 | 6'3" | 208 | Purdue | 8 | 18 |
| Keyworth, Jon FB | 74-80Den | 2 | 6'3" | 231 | Colorado | | 150 |
| Kiick, Jim HB | 68-69MiaA 70-74Mia 75WFL 76-77Den 77Was | 2 | 5'11" | 215 | Wyoming | | 198 |
| Killan, Gene OG | 74Dal | | 6'4" | 250 | Tennessee | | |
| Kilmer, Billy QB | 61-62SF 63BL 64, 66SF 67-70NO 71-78Was | 12 | 6' | 201 | U.C.L.A. | | 132 |
| Kimball, Bobby WR | 79-80GB | | 6'1" | 190 | Oklahoma | | |
| Kimbrough, John WR | 77Buf | 2 | 5'10" | 165 | St. Cloud State | | 18 |
| Kindle, Greg OT-OG | 74-75StL 76-77Atl | | 6'4" | 265 | Tennessee State | | |
| Kiner, Steve LB | 70Dal 71, 73NE 74-78Hou | | 6' | 221 | Tennessee | 10 | 2 |
| King, Horace FB-HB | 75-83Det | 2 | 5'10" | 208 | Georgia | | 84 |
| King, Keith LB-DB | 78-81SD | | 6'4" | 229 | Colorado State | 4 | |
| King, Steve LB | 73-81NE | | 6'4" | 232 | Tulsa | 1 | |
| Kingrea, Rick LB | 71-72Cle 73-78NO | | 6'1" | 228 | Tulane | 1 | |
| Kingsriter, Doug TE | 73-75Min | | 6'2" | 222 | Minnesota | | |
| Kinney, Jeff HB-FB | 72-76KC 76Buf | 2 | 6'2" | 215 | Nebraska | | 36 |
| Kinney, Steve OT | 73-74Chi | | 6'5" | 257 | Utah State | | |
| Kinney, Vince WR | 78-79Den 83USFL | | 6'2" | 190 | Maryland | | |
| Kirk, Ernest DE | 77Hou | | 6'2" | 265 | Howard Payne | 1 | |
| Kirkland, Mike QB | 76-78Bal | 1 | 6'1" | 195 | Arkansas | | |
| Kirnsey, Roy OG-OT | 71-72NYJ 73-74Phi | | 6'1" | 235 | Md. Eastern Shore | | |
| Klein, Bob TE | 69-76LA 77-79SD | 2 | 6'5" | 237 | Southern Calif. | | 138 |
| Knief, Gayle WR | 70Bos | | 6'3" | 205 | Morningside | | 6 |
| Knight, Curt K | 69-73Was | 5 | 6'1" | 190 | North Texas, Texas, Texas-El Paso | | 475 |
| Knight, David WR | 73-77NYJ | 2 | 6'1" | 177 | William & Mary | | 42 |
| Knoff, Kurt DB | 77-78Hou 79-82Min | | 6'2" | 191 | Kansas | 10 | 6 |
| Knox, Bill DB | 74-76Chi | | 5'9" | 192 | Purdue | 2 | |
| Knutson, Steve OG-OT | 76-77GB 78SF 79KJ | | 6'3" | 254 | Southern Calif. | | |
| Koegel, Vic LB | 75Cin | | 6' | 215 | Ohio State | | |
| Koegel, Warren C | 71Oak 72JJ 73Cin 74NYJ | | 6'3" | 253 | Penn State | | |
| Kolb, Jon OT-C | 69-81Pit | | 6'2" | 256 | Oklahoma State | | |
| Kolen, Mike LB | 70-75Mia 76KJ 77Mia | | 6'2" | 220 | Auburn | 5 | |
| Kollar, Bill DE-DT-NT | 74-76Cin 77-81TB | | 6'4" | 253 | Montana State | | |
| Koncar, Mike OT | 76-77GB 78KJ 79-81GB 82Hou | | 6'5" | 269 | Colorado | | |
| Korver, Kelvin DT | 73-75Oak 76-77KJ | | 6'6" | 267 | Northwestern | 1 | |
| Kosins, Gary HB-FB | 72-74Chi | 2 | 6'1" | 216 | Dayton | | 12 |
| Kotar, Doug HB | 74-79NYG 80KJ 81NYG | 23 | 5'11" | 205 | Kentucky | | 26 |
| Kowalkowski, Bob OG | 66-76Det 77GB | | 6'3" | 243 | Virginia | | |
| Koy, Ted LB-TE-HB-FB | 70Oak 71-74Buf | 2 | 6'1" | 211 | Texas | | 6 |
| Kraayeveld, Dave DE-DT | 78Sea | | 6'5" | 255 | Milton, Wisconsin | | |

| Use Name (Nickname) - Positions | Team by Year | See Section | Hgt. | Wgt. | College | Int | Pts |
|---|---|---|---|---|---|---|---|
| Krahl, Jim DT | 78NYG 79-80Bal 80SF | | 6'5" | 252 | Texas Tech | | |
| Krakau, Merv LB | 73-78Buf 78NE 83USFL | | 6'2" | 237 | Iowa State | 3 | |
| Kramer, Kent TE | 66SF 67NO 69-70Min 71-74Phi | 2 | 6'5" | 234 | Minnesota | | 48 |
| Kratzer, Don WR | 73KC | | 6'3" | 194 | Missouri Valley | | |
| Krause, Larry HB | 70-71GB 72JJ 73-74GB 75SU | 3 | 6' | 208 | St. Norbert | | 6 |
| Krause, Paul DB-FL | 64-67Was 68-79Min | | 6'3" | 199 | Iowa | 81 | 42 |
| Krepfle, Keith TE | 75-81Phi 82Atl | 2 | 6'3" | 227 | Iowa State | | 114 |
| Krevis, Al OT | 75Cin 76NYJ | | 6'5" | 263 | Boston College | | |
| Krieg, Jim WR | 72Den | | 5'9" | 172 | Washinton | | |
| Kroll, Bob DB | 72GB 73JJ | | 6'1" | 195 | Northern Michigan | | |
| Kruczek, Mike QB | 76-79Pit 80Was | 12 | 6'1" | 202 | Boston College | | 12 |
| Krueger, Rolf DE-DT | 69-72StL 72-74SF | | 6'4" | 251 | Texas A&M | | |
| Kuechenberg, Bob OG-OT-C | 70-83Mia 84JJ | | 6'3" | 253 | Notre Dame | | |
| Kunz, George OT | 69-74Atl 75-78Bal 79VR 80Bal | | 6'5" | 260 | Notre Dame | | |
| Kunz, Terry FB | 76Oak 77JJ | | 6'1" | 215 | Colorado | | |
| Kupp, Jake OG | 64-65Dal 66Was 67Atl 67-75NO | | 6'3" | 240 | Washington | | |
| Kurnick, Howie LB | 79Cin 80KJ | | 6'2" | 219 | Cincinnati | | 6 |
| Kuziel, Bob C-OT | 72NO 74WFL 75-80Was | | 6'5" | 255 | Pittsburgh | | |
| Kwalick, Ted TE-WR | 69-74SF 75WFL 75-77Oak | 2 | 6'4" | 226 | Penn State | | 138 |
| Kyle, Aaron DB | 76-79Dal 80-82Den | | 5'11" | 185 | Wyoming | 11 | 2 |
| Laaveg, Paul OG | 70-75Was 76KJ | | 6'4" | 247 | Iowa | | |
| LaCrosse, Dave LB | 77Pit | | 6'3" | 210 | Wake Forest | | |
| LaGrand, Morris FB | 75KC 75NO | | 6'1" | 220 | Tampa | | 6 |
| LaHood, Mike OG | 69LA 70StL 71-72LA | | 6'3" | 250 | Wyoming | | |
| Laidlaw, Scott FB | 75-79Dal 80NYG | 2 | 6' | 205 | Stanford | | 72 |
| Laird, Bruce DB | 72-81Bal 82-83SD 84-85USFL | 3 | 6' | 193 | American Inter. | 19 | 2 |
| Lally, Bob LB | 76GB | | 6'2" | 230 | Cornell | | |
| Lamb, Ron LB | 68DenA 68-69CinA 71-72Cin 72Atl | 2 | 6'2" | 227 | South Carolina | | |
| Lambert, Jack LB | 74-84Pit | | 6'4" | 220 | Kent State | 28 | |
| Landers, Walt FB | 78-79GB | | 6' | 214 | Clark Atlanta | | 12 |
| Landry, Greg QB | 68-78Det 79-81Bal 83-84USFL 84Chi | 12 | 6'4" | 207 | Massachusetts | | 132 |
| Lane, MacArthur HB-FB | 68-71StL 72-74GB 75-78KC | 2 | 6' | 220 | Utah State | | 222 |
| Langer, Jim C-OG | 70-79Mia 80-81Min | | 6'2" | 251 | S. Dakota State | | |
| Lanier, Willie LB | 67-69KC-A 70-77KC | | 6'1" | 245 | Morgan State | 27 | 14 |
| Lapham, Dave OG-OT-C | 74-83Cin 84-85USFL | | 6'4" | 259 | Syracuse | | |
| LaPorta, Phil OT | 74-75NO | | 6'4" | 256 | Penn State | | |
| Larson, Bill TE | 75SF 77Was 77Det 78Phi 80Den 80-81GB | | 6'4" | 224 | Colorado State | | 6 |
| Larson, Lynn OT | 71Bal | | 6'4" | 254 | Kansas State | | |
| Lash, Jim WR | 73-76Min 76-77SF | 2 | 6'2" | 200 | Northwestern | 1 | 24 |
| Laskey, Bill LB | 65BufA 66-67OakA 68FJ 69OakA 70Oak 71-72Bal 73-74Den | | 6'2" | 237 | Michigan | 7 | |
| Laslavic, Jim LB | 73-77Det 78SD 79KJ 80-81SD 82GB | | 6'2" | 237 | Penn State | 8 | |
| Laster, Art OT | 70Buf | | 6'4" | 280 | Md. Eastern Shore | | |
| Latimer, Don NT | 78-83Den 84USFL | | 6'3" | 259 | Miami (Fla.) | 1 | 6 |
| Latin, Jerry HB | 75-78StL 78LA | 23 | 5'10" | 188 | Northern Illinois | | 24 |
| Latta, Greg TE | 75-80Chi | 2 | 6'3" | 227 | Morgan State | | 42 |
| Lavender, Joe (Big Bird) DB | 73-75Phi 76-82Was | | 6'4" | 189 | San Diego State | 33 | 24 |
| Law, Dennis WR | 78Cin 79Was | 3 | 6'1" | 179 | East Tennessee St. | | |
| Lawless, Burton OG | 75-79Dal 80Det 81Mia | | 6'4" | 252 | Florida | | |
| Lawrence, Larry QB | 74-75Oak 76TB | 1 | 6'1" | 208 | Iowa | | |
| Lawrence, Rolland DB | 73-80Atl 81LJ | 3 | 5'10" | 179 | Tabor | 39 | 12 |
| Lawson, Odell FB-HB | 70Bos 71NE 73-74NO | 23 | 6'2" | 212 | Langston | | |
| Lawson, Roger HB-FB | 72-73Chi | 2 | 6'2" | 215 | Western Michigan | | |
| Lawson, Steve OG | 71-72Cin 73-75Min 76-77SF | | 6'3" | 264 | Kansas | | |
| Lazetich, Pete DE-DT-NT-LB | 72-74SD 76-77Phi | | 6'3" | 241 | Stanford | | |
| Leahy, Bob QB | 71Pit | | 6'2" | 205 | Emporia State | | |
| Leak, Curtis, WR | 76TB | | 5'11" | 180 | Johnson C. Smith | | |
| Leaks, Roosevelt FB | 75-79Bal 80-83Buf | 2 | 5'10" | 225 | Texas | | 192 |
| Leavitt, Allan K | 77Atl 77TB | 5 | 5'11" | 176 | Georgia | | 20 |
| Leavitt, Dick OT | 76NYG 77KJ | | 6'3" | 285 | Bowdoin | | |
| LeClair, Jim LB | 72-83Cin 84-85USFL | | 6'3" | 234 | North Dakota | 10 | 6 |
| Lee, Bivian DB | 71-75NO | | 6'3" | 200 | Prairie View | 9 | |
| Lee, Bob QB | 69-72Min 73-74Atl 75-78Min 79-80LA | 12 4 | 6'2" | 195 | Arizona State, U. of Pacific | | 18 |
| Lee, David K | 66-78Bal | 4 | 6'4" | 223 | Louisiana Tech | | |
| Lee, John DE | 76-80SD 81NE 83-84USFL | | 6'2" | 255 | Nebraska | | |
| Lee, Ken LB | 71Det 72Buf | | 6'4" | 231 | Washington | 6 | 6 |
| Lee, Mike LB | 74SD | | 6' | 232 | Nevada-Las Vegas | | |
| Lee, Ron FB | 76-78Bal 79XJ | 2 | 6'4" | 226 | West Virginia | | 36 |
| Lee, Willie DT | 76-77KC 78KJ | | 6'5" | 249 | Bethune-Cookman | | 6 |
| LeFear, Billy HB-WR | 72-75Cle 76JJ | 23 | 5'11" | 197 | Henderson State | | |
| Leigh, Charlie FB-HB | 68-69Cle 71-74Mia 74GB | 23 | 5'11" | 203 | none | | 12 |
| LeMaster, Frank LB | 74-82Phi 83SJ | | 6'2" | 232 | Kentucky | 10 | 18 |
| Lemon, Mike LB | 75NO 75Den 76-77TB | | 6'2" | 218 | Kansas | | |
| Lenkaitis, Bill C-OG | 68-69SD-A 70SD 71-81NE | | 6'3" | 255 | Penn State | | |
| Lens, Greg DT | 70-71Atl | | 6'5" | 260 | Trinity (Texas) | | |
| Leonard, Cecil DB | 69NY-A 70NYJ | | 5'11" | 165 | Tuskegee | | |
| Leonard, Tony DB | 76-78SF 78-79Det | 3 | 5'11" | 169 | Virginia Union | 5 | 12 |
| LeVeck, Jack LB | 73-74StL 75Cle | | 6' | 224 | Ohio U. | | |
| Levenseller, Mike WR | 78Buf 78TB 79-80Cin | | 6'1" | 180 | Washington State | | |
| LeVias, Jerry WR | 69HouA 70Hou 71-74SD | 23 | 5'10" | 177 | S.M.U. | | 84 |
| Lewis, Dave QB-K | 70-73Cin | 4 | 6'2" | 216 | Stanford | | |
| Lewis, D.D. LB | 68Dal 69MS 70-81Dal | | 6'2" | 218 | Mississippi State | 8 | 6 |
| Lewis, Eddie DB | 76-79SF 79-80Det | | 6' | 175 | Kansas | 3 | |
| Lewis, Frank WR | 71-77Pit 78-83Buf | 2 | 6'1" | 196 | Grambling | | 246 |
| Lewis, Jess LB | 70Hou | | 6'1" | 230 | Oregon State | | |
| Lewis, Mike DT-DE-NT | 71-79Atl 80GB | | 6'3" | 255 | Ark.-Pine Bluff | 1 | 4 |
| Lewis, Rich LB | 72Hou 73-74Buf 75NYJ | | 6'3" | 217 | Portland State | | |
| Lewis, Scott DE | 71Hou | | 6'6" | 260 | Grambling | | |
| Lewis, Stan DE | 75Cle | | 6'4" | 240 | Wayne State-Neb. | | |
| Leypoldt, John K | 71-76Buf 76-78Sea 78NO | 5 | 6'2" | 229 | none | | 482 |
| Liggett, Bob DT | 70KC | | 6'2" | 255 | Nebraska | | |
| Line, Bill DT | 72Chi | | 6'7" | 260 | S.M.U. | | |
| Lingenfelter, Bob OT-OG | 77Cle 78Min | | 6'7" | 277 | Nebraska | | |
| Linhart, Toni K | 72NO 74-79Bal 79NYJ | 5 | 6' | 178 | none | | 425 |
| Little, Everett OG | 76TB 77Oak | | 6'4" | 265 | Houston | | |
| Little, Floyd HB | 67-69Den-A 70-75Den | 23 | 5'10" | 196 | Syracuse | | 324 |
| Little, John DT-DE-NT | 70-74NYJ 75-76Hou 77Buf | | 6'3" | 241 | Oklahoma State | | |
| Little, Larry OG-OT-DT | 67-68SD 69MiaA 70-80Mia | | 6'1" | 266 | Bethune-Cookman | | |
| Little, Steve K | 78-80StL | 45 | 6' | 180 | Arkansas | | 80 |
| Livers, Virgil DB | 75-79Chi 80KJ 83-84USFL | 3 | 5'9" | 178 | Western Kentucky | 12 | 12 |
| Livingston, Mike QB | 68-69KC-A 70-79KC 80Min 83USFL | 12 | 6'3" | 211 | S.M.U. | | 48 |
| Lloyd, Dan LB | 76-79NYG 80-81IL 83USFL | | 6'2" | 225 | Washington | 2 | |
| Lloyd, Jeff DE-NT | 76Buf 78KC | | 6'6" | 255 | West Texas State | | |
| Lockhart, Carl (Spider) DB | 65-75NYG | 3 | 6'2" | 176 | North Texas | 41 | 18 |
| Logan, Randy DB | 73-83Phi | | 6'1" | 195 | Michigan | 23 | |
| Lohmeyer, John DE-DT | 73KC 74JJ 75-77KC | | 6'4" | 230 | Kansas State | | 10 |
| Lomas, Mark DE-DT | 70-74NYJ 75FJ 76NYJ | | 6'4" | 241 | Northern Arizona | | |
| London, Tom DB | 78Cle | | 6'1" | 197 | N. Carolina State | | |

| Use Name (Nickname) - Positions | Team by Year | See Section | Hgt. | Wgt. | College | Int | Pts |
|---|---|---|---|---|---|---|---|
| Long, Carson K | 77Buf | 5 | 5'10" | 210 | Pittsburgh | | 34 |
| Long, Doug LB | 77-78Sea | | 6' | 189 | Whitworth | | |
| Long, Ken OG | 76Det 77JJ | | 6'3" | 265 | Purdue | | |
| Long, Kevin FB-HB | 77-81NYJ 83-84USFL | 2 | 6'1" | 212 | South Carolina | | 168 |
| Long, Mel LB | 72-74Cle | | 6' | 228 | Toledo | | |
| Longley, Clint QB | 74-75Dal 76SD | 1 | 6'1" | 194 | Abilene Christian | | |
| Longo, Tom DB | 69-70NYG 71StL | | 6'1" | 199 | Notre Dame | | |
| Lorch, Karl DE-DT | 76-81Was 83-85USFL | | 6'3" | 258 | Southern Calif. | 1 | 6 |
| Lott, Thomas HB | 79StL 83USFL | | 5'11" | 205 | Oklahoma | | |
| Lou, Ron C | 73Hou 74JJ 75Phi 76Hou | | 6'2" | 240 | Arizona State | | |
| Love, Walt WR | 73NYG | | 5'9" | 180 | Westminister (Pa.) | | |
| Luce, Derrel LB | 75-78Bal 79-80Min 80Det | | 6'3" | 226 | Baylor | 3 | 12 |
| Luck, Terry QB | 77Cle | 1 | 6'3" | 205 | Nebraska | | 6 |
| Lueck, Bill OG | 68-74GB 75Phi | | 6'3" | 239 | Arizona | | |
| Luke, Steve DB | 75-80GB | | 6'2" | 205 | Ohio State | 10 | 6 |
| Luken, Tom OG | 72-75Phi 76KJ 77-78Phi | | 6'3" | 253 | Purdue | | |
| Lumpkin, Ron DB | 73NYG | | 6'2" | 200 | Arizona State | | |
| Lunsford, Mel DE-DT-NT | 73-80NE 83USFL | | 6'3" | 256 | Central St.-Ohio | | |
| Lurtsema, Bob DE-DT | 67-71NYG 72-76Min 76-77Sea | | 6'6" | 250 | Michigan Tech, Western Michigan | 1 | |
| Lusby, Vaughn DB | 79Cin 80Chi | 3 | 5'10" | 180 | Arkansas | | |
| Lusk, Herb HB | 76-78Phi | 2 | 6' | 190 | Long Beach State | | 18 |
| Lyle, Garry DB-HB | 68-74Chi | | 6'2" | 197 | George Washington | 12 | |
| Lyman, Jeff LB | 72Buf | | 6'2" | 230 | Brigham Young | | |
| Lynch, Fran HB-FB | 67-69DenA 70-75Den 76KJ | 2 | 6'1" | 203 | Hofstra | | 86 |
| Lynch, Jim LB | 67-69KC-A 70-77KC | | 6'1" | 232 | Notre Dame | 17 | 6 |
| Lyons, Dicky DB | 70NO | | 6' | 190 | Kentucky | 1 | |
| Lyons, Tommy OG-C | 71-76Den | | 6'2" | 229 | Georgia | | |
| Mabra, Ron DB | 75-76Atl 77NYJ | | 5'10" | 166 | Howard | | |
| MacAfee, Ken TE | 78-79SF | 2 | 6'5" | 248 | Notre Dame | | 30 |
| Mack, Tom OG | 66-78LA | | 6'3" | 249 | Michigan | | |
| MacLeod, Tom LB | 73GB 74-75Bal 76FJ 77-78Bal | | 6'3" | 225 | Minnesota | 5 | |
| Madden, John | HC69OakA HC70-78Oak | | | | Cal. Poly.-S.L.O. | | |
| Maddox, Bob DE-DT | 74Cin 75-77KC | | 6'5" | 237 | Frostburg State | | 6 |
| Mahalic, Drew LB | 75SD 76-78Phi | | 6'4" | 226 | Notre Dame | 2 | |
| Maitland, Jack HB | 70Bal 71-72NE | 2 | 6'1" | 210 | Williams | | 18 |
| Majors, Bobby DB | 72Cle | | 6'1" | 193 | Tennessee | | |
| Malavasi, Ray | HC66DenA HC 78-82LA | | | | Army, Mississippi State | | |
| Malinchak, Bill WR-OE | 66-69Det 70-74, 76Was | 2 | 6'1" | 198 | Indiana | | 32 |
| Mallory, Irvin DB | 71NE | | 6'1" | 196 | Virginia Union | | |
| Mallory, Larry DB | 76-78NYG | | 5'11" | 185 | Tennessee State | 2 | |
| Malone, Art FB-HB | 70-74Atl 75-76Phi | 2 | 5'11" | 213 | Arizona State | | 150 |
| Malone, Benny HB | 74-78Mia 78-79Was | 2 | 5'10" | 193 | Arizona State | | 120 |
| Manders, Dave C | 64-66Dal 67JJ 68-74Dal | | 6'2" | 247 | Michigan State | | |
| Mandich, Jim TE-WR | 70-77Mia 78Pit | 2 | 6'3" | 222 | Michigan | | 138 |
| Manges, Mark QB | 78StL | | 6'2" | 210 | Maryland | | |
| Mann, Errol K | 68GB 69-76Det 76-78Oak | 5 | 6' | 202 | North Dakota | | 846 |
| Manning, Archie QB | 71-75NO 76SJ 77-82NO 82-83Hou 83-84Min | 12 | 6'3" | 205 | Mississippi | | 108 |
| Manning, Rosie DT | 72-75Atl 75Phi | | 6'5" | 257 | Northeastern Okla. | | |
| Mansfield, Ray C-DT | 63Phi 64-76Pit | | 6'3" | 252 | Washington | | |
| Maples, Bobby C-LB | 65-69HouA 70Hou 71Pit 72-78Den | | 6'3" | 247 | Baylor | 1 | |
| Marangi, Gary QB | 74-76Buf 77Cle | 12 | 6'1" | 201 | Boston College | | 12 |
| Marcol, Chester K | 72-80GB 80Hou | 5 | 6' | 190 | Hillsdale | | 525 |
| Marinaro, Ed HB-FB | 72-75Min 76NYJ 77Sea | 2 | 6'2" | 212 | Cornell | | 78 |
| Markovich, Mark C-OG | 74-75SD 76-77Det 78KJ 79JJ | | 6'5" | 256 | Penn State | | |
| Marsalis, Jim DB | 69KC-A 70-75KC 77NO | | 5'11" | 193 | Tennessee State | 15 | |
| Marshall, Al WR | 74NE 75KJ | | 6'2" | 190 | Boise State | | 6 |
| Marshall, Ed WR | 71Cin 74-75WFL 76NYJ 76-77NYG | 2 | 6'5" | 199 | Cameron | | 18 |
| Marshall, Greg DT | 78Bal | | 6'3" | 257 | Oregon State | | |
| Marshall, Larry DB-HB | 72-73KC 74Min 74-77Phi 78KC 78LA | 3 | 5'10" | 195 | Md. Eastern Shore | | |
| Marshall, Randy DE | 70-71Atl | | 6'5" | 237 | Linfield | | 6 |
| Marshall, Tank DT | 77NYJ | | 6'4" | 245 | Texas A&M | | |
| Martin, Amos LB | 72-76Min 77Sea | | 6'3" | 228 | Louisville | 3 | 6 |
| Martin, Bob LB | 76-79NYJ 79SF | | 6'1" | 219 | Nebraska | 5 | |
| Martin, Dee DB | 71NO 72KJ | | 6'1" | 190 | Kentucky State | 3 | |
| Martin, Don DB | 73NE 75KC 76TB | | 5'11" | 186 | Yale | | |
| Martin, Harvey DE | 73-83Dal | | 6'5" | 254 | East Texas State | 2 | 4 |
| Marvaso, Tommy DB | 76-77NYJ | | 6'1" | 191 | Cincinnati | | |
| Marx, Greg DE | 73Atl | | 6'4" | 260 | Notre Dame | | |
| Maslowski, Matt WR | 71LA | | 6'3" | 210 | Cal.-San Diego | | 6 |
| Mason, Dave DB | 73NE 74GB | | 6' | 198 | Nebraska | | |
| Mass, Wayne OT | 68-70Chi 71Mia 72Phi | | 6'4" | 243 | Clemson | | |
| Massey, Jim DB | 74-75NE | | 5'11" | 198 | Linfield | | |
| Masters, Bill TE | 67-69BufA 70-74Den 75-76KC | 2 | 6'5" | 236 | Louisiana State | | 90 |
| Matheson, Bob LB-DE | 67-70Cle 71-79Mia | | 6'4" | 238 | Duke | 12 | |
| Matlock, John C-OT | 67NY-A 68CinA 70-71Atl 72Buf | | 6'4" | 250 | Miami (Fla.) | | |
| Matson, Pat OG | 66-67DenA 68-69CinA 70-74Cin 75GB | | 6'1" | 246 | Oregon | | |
| Matthews, Al DB | 70-75GB 76Sea 77SF | | 5'11" | 190 | Texas A&I | 13 | 12 |
| Matthews, Bo FB | 74-79SD 80-81NYG 81Mia 83-84USFL | 2 | 6'4" | 227 | Colorado | | 72 |
| Matthews, Henry HB | 72NE 73NO | | 6'3" | 203 | Michigan State | | |
| Matuszak, John (Tooz) DE-DT | 73-74Hou 74WFL 75KC 76-81Oak 82JJ | | 6'8" | 278 | Missouri, Tampa | | 6 |
| Mauck, Carl C | 69Bal 70Mia 71-74SD 75-81Hou | | 6'3" | 245 | Southern Illinois | | 6 |
| Maurer, Andy OG-OT | 70-73Atl 74NO 74-75Min 76SF 77Den | | 6'3" | 265 | Oregon | | |
| Maxson, Alvin HB | 74-76NO 77-78Pit 78TB 78Hou 78NYG | 23 | 5'11" | 203 | S.M.U. | | 42 |
| Maxwell, Bruce HB-FB | 70Det | | 6'1" | 220 | Arkansas | | |
| Maxwell, Tommy DB | 69-70Bal 71-73Oak 74Hou | | 6'2" | 195 | Texas A&M | 5 | |
| May, Art DE | 71NE | | 6'3" | 245 | Tuskegee | | |
| May, Ray LB | 67-69Pit 70-73Bal 73-75Den | | 6'1" | 230 | Southern Calif. | 13 | 6 |
| Mayes, Rufus OT-OG | 69Chi 70-78Cin 79Phi | | 6'5" | 259 | Ohio State | | |
| Mayo, Ron TE | 73Hou 74Bal | | 6'3" | 223 | Morgan State | | |
| Mays, Dave QB | 76-77Cle 78Buf | 1 | 6'1" | 204 | Texas Southern | | |
| Mazur, John | HC70Bos HC71-72NE | | | | Notre Dame | | |
| Mazzetti, Tim K | 78-80Atl 83-85USFL | 5 | 6'1" | 175 | Pennsylvania | | 230 |
| McAleney, Ed DE | 76Atl 76TB | | 6'2" | 235 | Massachusetts | | |
| McAlister, James HB | 75-76Phi 78NE | 23 | 6'1" | 205 | U.C.L.A. | | 30 |
| McBath, Mike DE-OT-DT | 68-69BufA 70-72Buf | | 6'4" | 248 | Penn State | | |
| McBride, Ron HB | 73GB | | 6' | 200 | Missouri | | |
| McCaffrey, Mike LB | 70Buf | | 6'3" | 235 | California | | |
| McCaffrey, Robert C | 75GB | | 6'2" | 245 | Southern Calif. | | |
| McCall, Bob HB | 73NE | | 6' | 205 | Arizona | | |
| McCann, Jim K | 71-72SF 73NYG 75KC | 4 | 6'2" | 165 | Arizona State | | |
| McCarren, Larry C | 73-84GB | | 6'3" | 246 | Illinois | | |
| McCartney, Ron LB | 77-79Atl | | 6'1" | 220 | Tennessee | | |
| McCauley, Don HB-FB | 71-81Bal | 23 | 6'1" | 211 | North Carolina | | 348 |
| McCauley, Tom DB-WR | 69-71Atl | | 6'3" | 187 | North Carolina | 2 | 6 |
| McClain, Cliff HB-FB | 70-73NYJ | 2 | 6' | 217 | S. Carolina State | | 12 |
| McClain, Dewey LB | 76-80Atl 83-84USFL | | 6'3" | 236 | EC Oklahoma | 1 | |

| Use Name (Nickname) - Positions | Team by Year | See Section | Hgt. | Wgt. | College | Int | Pts |
|---|---|---|---|---|---|---|---|
| McClanahan, Brent HB-FB | 73-79Min | 23 | 5'10" | 202 | Arizona State | | 60 |
| McClanahan, Randy LB | 77Oak 78Buf 80-81Oak | | 6'5" | 225 | Southwestern La. | 1 | |
| McClard, Bill K | 72SD 73-75NO | 5 | 5'10" | 202 | Arkansas | | 109 |
| McCollum, Bubba DT | 74Hou | | 6' | 250 | Kentucky | | |
| McConnell, Brian LB | 73Hou | | 6'4" | 207 | Michigan State | | |
| McCormack, Mike OT-OG-DT | 51NYY 52-53MS 54-62Cle HC73-75Phi HC80-81Bal HC82Sea | | 6'4" | 246 | Kansas | | |
| McCoy, Mike DT-NT | 70-75GB 77-78Oak 79-80NYG 80Det | | 6'5" | 278 | Notre Dame | 1 | 6 |
| McCrary, Greg TE | 75Atl 76LJ 77Atl 78Was 78-80SD 81Was | 2 | 6'3" | 233 | Clark Atlanta | | 26 |
| McCray, Prentice DB | 74-80NE 80Det | | 6'1" | 188 | Arizona State | 15 | 12 |
| McCray, Willie DE | 78SF | | 6'5" | 234 | Alabama, Troy State | | |
| McCreary, Loaird TE-WR | 76-78Mia 79NYG 84USFL | | 6'5" | 227 | Tennessee State | | 18 |
| McCrumbly, John LB | 75Buf | | 6'1" | 245 | Texas A&M | | |
| McCulley, Pete | HC78SF | | | | Louisiana Tech | | |
| McCullouch, Earl WR | 68-73Det 74NO 75WFL | 2 | 5'11" | 175 | Southern Calif. | | 114 |
| McCullum, Sam WR | 74-75Min 76-81Sea 82-83Min | 2 | 6'2" | 198 | Montana State | | 156 |
| McCurry, Dave DB | 74NE | | 6'1" | 187 | Iowa State | | |
| McCutcheon, Lawrence HB-FB | 72-79LA 80Den 80Sea 81Buf | 2 | 6'1" | 205 | Colorado State | | 234 |
| McDaniel, John WR | 74-77Cin 78-80Was | 2 | 6'1" | 196 | Lincoln (Mo.) | | 42 |
| McDonald, Dwight WR | 75-78SD 79JJ | 2 | 6'2" | 187 | San Diego State | | 48 |
| McDonald, Mike LB | 76StL | | 6'2" | 215 | Catawba | | |
| McFarland, Jim TE | 70-74StL 75Mia | | 6'5" | 225 | Nebraska | | 18 |
| McGee, Molly HB | 74Atl | | 5'10" | 184 | Rhode Island | | |
| McGee, Tony DE-DT | 71-73Chi 74-81NE 82-84Was | | 6'4" | 248 | Wyoming, Bishop | | |
| McGee, Willie WR | 73SD 74-75LA 76-77SF 78Det | 23 | 5'11" | 179 | Alcorn State | | 24 |
| McGeorge, Rich TE | 70-78GB | 2 | 6'4" | 232 | Elon | | 78 |
| McGill, Mike LB | 68-70Min 71-72StL | | 6'2" | 236 | Notre Dame | 3 | 6 |
| McGill, Ralph DB | 72-77SF 78-79NO | 3 | 5'11" | 181 | Tulsa | 8 | 12 |
| McGraw, Mike LB | 76StL 77Det | | 6'2" | 225 | Wyoming | | |
| McGriff, Lee WR | 76TB | | 5'9" | 163 | Florida | | |
| McIntyre, Secedrick HB | 77Atl | | 5'10" | 190 | Auburn | | 6 |
| McKay, Bob OT-OG | 70-75Cle 76-78NE | | 6'5" | 262 | Texas | | |
| McKay, John (J.K.) WR | 76-78TN | 2 | 5'11" | 182 | Southern Calif. | | 12 |
| McKay, John | HC76-84TB | | | | Oregon | | |
| McKenzie, Reggie OG | 72-82Buf 83-84Sea | | 6'4" | 252 | Michigan | | |
| McKinley, Bill DE-LB | 71Buf 72JJ | | 6'1" | 240 | Arizona | | |
| McKinnely, Phil OT-TE-OG | 76-80Atl 81LA 82Chi 84-85USFL | | 6'4" | 248 | U.C.L.A. | | |
| McKinney, Bill LB | 72Chi | | 6'1" | 226 | West Texas State | | |
| McKinney, Royce DB | 75Buf | | 6'1" | 190 | Kentucky State | | |
| McKinnis, Hugh FB | 73-75Cle 76Sea | 2 | 6' | 220 | Arizona State | | 60 |
| McKnight, Ted HB-FB | 77-81KC 82Buf | 2 | 6'1" | 209 | Minnesota-Duluth | | 138 |
| McKoy, Bill LB | 70-72Den 74SF | | 6'3" | 233 | Purdue | | |
| McLain, Kevin LB | 76-79LA 83-84USFL | | 6'2" | 230 | Colorado State | | |
| McLinton, Harold LB | 69-78Was | | 6'2" | 235 | Southern U. | 3 | 6 |
| McMakin, John TE | 72-74Pit 75Det 76Sea | 2 | 6'3" | 229 | Clemson | | 24 |
| McMath, Herb DT-DE | 76Oak 77GB | | 6'4" | 248 | Morningside | | |
| McMillan, Eddie LB | 73-75LA 76-77Sea 78Buf | | 6' | 189 | Florida State | 12 | |
| McNeill, Fred LB | 74-85Min | | 6'2" | 229 | U.C.L.A. | 7 | 6 |
| McNeil, Pat FB | 76-77KC | | 5'9" | 208 | Baylor | | |
| McNeill, Rod FB | 74-76NO 76TB | 23 | 6'2" | 218 | Southern Calif. | | 30 |
| McNeill, Tom K | 67-69NO 70Min 71-73Phi | 4 | 6'1" | 195 | Baylor, S.F. Austin State | | |
| McQuay, Leon HB | 74NYG 75NE 76NO | 23 | 5'9" | 197 | Tampa | | 6 |
| McQuilken, Kim QB | 74-77Atl 78-80Was 83USFL | 1 | 6'2" | 203 | Lehigh | | |
| McRae, Jerrold WR | 78KC 79Phi | | 6' | 194 | Tennessee State | | |
| McShane, Charles LB | 77-79Sea | | 6'3" | 230 | Cal. Lutheran | | |
| McVay, John | HC76-78NYG | | | | Miami-Ohio | | |
| McVea, Warren HB-WR | 68CinA 69KC-A 70-71KC 72KJ 73KC | 23 | 5'10" | 182 | Houston | | 78 |
| Means, Dave DE | 74-75Buf | | 6'4" | 235 | SW Missouri St. | | |
| Medlin, Dan OG | 74-76Oak 77-78TB 79Oak | | 6'3" | 254 | N. Carolina State | | |
| Melville, Dan K | 79SF | 4 | 6' | 185 | California | | |
| Mendenhall, John DT | 72-79NYG 80Det | | 6'1" | 255 | Grambling | 1 | |
| Mendenhall, Ken C | 71-80Bal | | 6'3" | 242 | Oklahoma | | |
| Mendenhall, Terry LB | 71-72Oak | | 6'1" | 210 | San Diego State | | |
| Merlo, Jim LB | 73-74NO 75JJ 76-79NO | | 6'1" | 221 | Stanford | 8 | 18 |
| Merrow, Jeff DE-DT-LB | 75-77Atl 77Oak 78-83Atl | | 6'4" | 236 | West Virginia | | |
| Meserol, Mark OT | 78NO 80JJ | | 6'5" | 270 | Florida State | | |
| Metcalf, Terry HB-WR | 73-77StL 78-80CFL 81Was | 23 | 5'10" | 185 | Long Beach State | | 216 |
| Meyer, Dennis DB | 73Pit | | 5'11" | 186 | Arkansas State | | |
| Meyer, Ken | HC77SF | | | | Denison | | |
| Meyers, Jerry DE-DT | 76-79Chi 80KC | | 6'4" | 249 | Northern Illinois | | |
| Mialik, Larry TE | 72-74Atl 76SD | | 6'2" | 226 | Wisconsin | | |
| Michaels, Walt LB | 51GB 52-61Cle 63NYG HC77-82NYJ | | 6' | 231 | Washington & Lee | | |
| Michel, Mike K | 77Mia 78Phi | 45 | 5'10" | 177 | Stanford | | 9 |
| Middlebrook, Oren WR | 78Phi | | 6'2" | 185 | Arkansas State | | |
| Middleton, Rick LB | 74-75NO 76-78SD | | 6'2" | 229 | Ohio State | 2 | |
| Mike-Mayer, Nick K | 73-77Atl 77-78Phi 79-82Buf | 5 | 5'8" | 186 | Temple | | 571 |
| Mike-Mayer, Steve K | 75-76SF 77Det 78NO 79-80Bal | 5 | 6' | 180 | Maryland | | 362 |
| Mikolajczyk, Ron OT-OG | 72-73CFL 74-75WFL 76-79NYG 83-84USFL | | 6'3" | 275 | Tampa | | |
| Milan, Don QB | 75GB 76BW | 1 | 6'3" | 196 | Cal. Poly.-S.L.O. | | |
| Mildren, Jack DB | 72-73Bal 74NE | | 6'1" | 200 | Oklahoma | 3 | |
| Miller, Calvin NT-DT-DE | 79NYG 80Atl | | 6'2" | 260 | Oklahoma State | | |
| Miller, Cleo HB-FB | 74-75KC 75-82Cle 83-84USFL | 23 | 5'11" | 207 | Ark.-Pine Bluff | | 102 |
| Miller, Jim OG | 71-72,74Atl | | 6'3" | 240 | Iowa | | |
| Miller, Johnny OG | 77SF 78EJ 79KJ | | 6'1" | 247 | Livingstone | | |
| Miller, Kevin WR | 78-80Min 83USFL | 3 | 5'10" | 181 | Louisville | | 6 |
| Miller, Mark QB | 78-79Cle 80GB 83USFL | 1 | 6'2" | 176 | Bowling Green | | 6 |
| Miller, Red | HC77-80Den | | | | Western Illinois | | |
| Miller, Robert HB-FB | 75-80Min | 2 | 5'11" | 204 | Kansas | | 48 |
| Miller, Terry LB | 71-74StL | | 6'2" | 224 | Illinois | | |
| Miller, Willie WR | 75-76Cle 77EJ 78-82LA | 2 | 5'9" | 172 | Colorado State | | 96 |
| Milo, Ray DB | 78KC | | 5'11" | 178 | New Mexico State | | |
| Minor, Claudie OT | 74-82Den | | 6'4" | 279 | San Diego State | | |
| Mitchell, Dale LB | 76-77SF | | 6'3" | 224 | Southern Calif. | | |
| Mitchell, Jim TE | 69-79Atl | 2 | 6'2" | 234 | Prairie View | | 186 |
| Mitchell, Jim DE-DT | 70-77Det | | 6'3" | 247 | Virginia State | 1 | 2 |
| Mitchell, Ken LB | 73-74Atl | | 6'1" | 224 | Nevada-Las Vegas | | |
| Mitchell, Leroy DB | 67-68BosA 69BQ 70Hou 71-73Den | | 6'2" | 192 | Texas Southern | 19 | 6 |
| Mitchell, Lydell HB | 72-77Bal 78-79SD 80LA | 2 | 5'11" | 199 | Penn State | | 282 |
| Mitchell, Mack DE | 75-78Cle 79Cin 84USFL | | 6'7" | 246 | Houston | | 2 |
| Mitchell, Mark DB | 77Phi | | 6'1" | 180 | Tulane | | |
| Mitchell, Mel OG-C-OT | 76-77Mia 77Det 78Mia 80Min | | 6'3" | 260 | Tennessee State | | |
| Mitchell, Tom TE-WR | 66OakA 68-73Bal 74-77SF | 2 | 6'2" | 219 | Bucknell | | 144 |
| Mock, Mike LB | 78NYJ 79JJ | | 6'1" | 225 | Texas Tech | | |
| Monds, Wonder DB | 78SF | | 6'3" | 215 | Nebraska | | |
| Monroe, Henry DB | 79Phi | | 5'11" | 180 | Mississippi | | |
| Montgomery, Marv OT | 71-76Den 76-77NO 78Atl | | 6'6" | 255 | Southern Calif. | 1 | |
| Montgomery, Mike HB-WR | 71SD 72-73Dal 74Hou | 2 | 6'2" | 208 | Kansas State | | 60 |

| Use Name (Nickname) - Positions | Team by Year | See Section | Hgt. | Wgt. | College | Int | Pts |
|---|---|---|---|---|---|---|---|
| Montgomery, Randy DB | 71-73Den 74Chi | 3 | 5'11" | 183 | Weber State | 2 | 6 |
| Montgomery, Ross FB | 69-70Chi | 2 | 6'3" | 220 | Texas Christian | | |
| Montler, Mike C-OT-OG | 69BosA 70Bos 71-72NE 73-76Buf 77Den 78Det | | 6'4" | 256 | Colorado | | |
| Moody, Keith DB | 76-79Buf 80Oak 83USFL | 3 | 5'10" | 171 | Syracuse | 3 | 18 |
| Mooers, Doug DT-DE | 71-72NO | | 6'6" | 265 | Whittier | | |
| Mooney, Ed LB | 68-71Det 72JJ 73Bal | | 6'2" | 231 | Texas Tech | | |
| Moore, Art NT-DT | 73-74NE 75KJ 76-77NE | | 6'5" | 255 | Tulsa | | |
| Moore, Bob TE | 71-75Oak 76-77TB 78Den | 2 | 6'3" | 222 | Stanford | | 42 |
| Moore, Dean LB | 78SF 83-84USFL | | 6'2" | 210 | Iowa | | |
| Moore, Derland DT-NT-DE | 73-86NO 86NYJ | | 6'4" | 260 | Oklahoma | 1 | |
| Moore, Jerry DB | 71-72Chi 73-74NO | | 6'3" | 208 | Arkansas | 2 | |
| Moore, Joe HB | 71Chi 72JJ 73Chi | 2 | 6'1" | 205 | Missouri | | |
| Moore, Ken TE | 78Atl | | 6'4" | 232 | Northern Illinois | | |
| Moore, Manfred HB | 74-75SF 76TB 76Oak 77Min | 3 | 6' | 197 | Southern Calif. | | 12 |
| Moore, Maulty DT | 72-74Mia 75Cin 76TB | | 6'5" | 265 | Bethune-Cookman | | |
| Moore, Randy DT | 76Den 77JJ | | 6'2" | 241 | Arizona | | |
| Moore, Reynaud DB | 71NO | | 6'2" | 190 | U.C.L.A. | | |
| Moore, (Solomon) Wayne OT | 70-78Mia | | 6'6" | 265 | Lamar | | |
| Moore, Zeke DB | 67-69HouA 70-77Hou | 3 | 6'2" | 195 | Lincoln (Mo.) | 24 | 24 |
| Mooring, John OT-C | 71-73NYJ 74NO | | 6'6" | 255 | Tampa | | |
| Moorman, Mo OG-OT | 68-69KC-A 70-73KC | | 6'5" | 252 | Kentucky, Texas A&M | | |
| Moreino, Joe NT-DE | 78NYJ | | 6'6" | 246 | Idaho State | | |
| Moresco, Tim DB | 77GB 78-80NYJ | | 5'11" | 178 | Syracuse | | 2 |
| Morgado, Arnold FB-HB | 77-80KC | 2 | 6' | 209 | Hawaii | | 96 |
| Morgan, Dennis HB | 74Dal 75Phi | 3 | 5'11" | 198 | Western Illinois | | 6 |
| Morgan, Melvin DB | 76-78Cin 79-80SF | | 6' | 183 | Miss. Valley St. | 3 | 6 |
| Morgan, Mike FB | 78Chi | | 5'11" | 218 | Wisconsin | | |
| Moriarty, Pat HB | 79Cle | | 6' | 195 | Georgia Tech | | 12 |
| Moriarty, Tom DB | 77-79Atl 80Pit 81Atl 83-84USFL | | 6' | 183 | Bowling Green | | 6 |
| Morin, Milt TE | 66-75Cle | 2 | 6'4" | 243 | Massachusetts | | 96 |
| Moritz, Brett OG | 78TB | | 6'5" | 250 | Army, Nebraska | | |
| Morris, Chris OT | 72-73Cle 75NO | | 6'3" | 250 | Indiana | | |
| Morris, Donny Joe HB | 74KC | | 5'11" | 195 | North Texas | | |
| Morris, Jon C | 64-69BosA 70Bos 71-74NE 75-77Det 78Chi | | 6'4" | 247 | Holy Cross | | |
| Morris, Mercury HB | 69MiaA 70-75Mia 76SD | 23 | 5'10" | 190 | West Texas State | | 210 |
| Morrison, Dennis QB | 74SF | 1 | 6'3" | 211 | Kansas State | | |
| Morrison, Don OT-C | 71-77NO 78Bal 79Det | | 6'5" | 255 | Texas-Arlington | | |
| Morrison, Reece HB | 68-72Cle 72-73Cin 74JJ | 23 | 6' | 206 | SW Texas State | | 24 |
| Mortenson, Fred QB | 79Was 83-85USFL | | 6'2" | 195 | Arizona State | | |
| Morton, Craig QB | 65-74Dal 74-76NYG 77-82Den | 12 | 6'4" | 213 | California | | 72 |
| Morton, Dave LB | 79SF | | 6'2" | 224 | U.C.L.A. | | |
| Morton, Greg DE | 77Buf | | 6'1" | 230 | Michigan | | |
| Moseley, Mark K | 70Phi 71-72Hou 74-86Was 86Cle | 5 | 5'11" | 200 | Texas A&M, S.F. Austin State | | 1382 |
| Mosely, Wayne HB | 74Buf | | 6' | 190 | Alabama A&M | | |
| Moses, Haven WR | 68-69BufA 70-72Buf 72-81Den | 2 | 6'3" | 204 | San Diego State | | 342 |
| Mosler, John TE | 71Den 72Bal 73NE | | 6'3" | 220 | Kansas | | |
| Moss, Eddie FB-HB | 73-76StL 77Was | | 6' | 215 | SE Missouri St. | | 6 |
| Moss, Roland TE-FB | 69Bal 70SD 70Buf 71NE | 2 | 6'3" | 215 | Toledo | | 12 |
| Muckensturm, Jerry LB | 76-80Chi 81SJ 82-83Chi | | 6'4" | 223 | Arkansas State | 3 | |
| Mucker, Larry WR | 77-80TB | 2 | 5'11" | 191 | Arizona State | | 30 |
| Muhlmann, Horst K | 69CinA 70-74Cin 75-77Phi | 5 | 6'1" | 215 | none | | 707 |
| Mul-Key, Herb HB | 72-74Was | 23 | 6' | 190 | none | | 12 |
| Mullen, Tom OG-OT | 74-77NYG 78StL | | 6'3" | 248 | SW Missouri St. | | |
| Mulligan, Wayne C | 69-73StL 74-75NYJ 76JJ | | 6'2" | 246 | Clemson | | |
| Mullins, Gerry OG-OT | 71-79Pit | | 6'3" | 242 | Southern Calif. | | 18 |
| Mumphord, Lloyd DB | 69MiaA 70-74Mia 75-78Bal | | 5'11" | 179 | Texas Southern | 21 | 18 |
| Munsey, Nelson DB | 72-77Bal 78Min | | 6'1" | 188 | Wyoming | 7 | 12 |
| Munson, Bill QB | 64-67LA 68-75Det 76Sea 77SD 78-79Buf | 12 | 6'2" | 203 | Utah State | | 18 |
| Murdock, Guy C | 72Hou | | 6'2" | 245 | Michigan | | |
| Murphy, Mike LB | 79Hou 83-84USFL | | 6'2" | 222 | SW Missouri St. | | |
| Murrell, Bill TE | 79StL | | 6'3" | 220 | Winston-Salem St. | | |
| Musso, Johnny (Italian Stallion) HB-FB | 75-77Chi 78KJ | 2 | 5'11" | 201 | Alabama | | 38 |
| Myer, Steve QB | 76-79Sea 80XJ | 1 | 6'2" | 191 | New Mexico | | |
| Myers, Chip WR-FL | 67SF 69CinA 70-76Cin | 2 | 6'4" | 203 | Northwestern Okla. | | 72 |
| Myers, Frank OT | 78-79Min | | 6'5" | 255 | Texas A&M | | |
| Myers, Tom DB | 72-82NO 84-85USFL | | 5'11" | 181 | Syracuse | 36 | 30 |
| Myrtle, Chip LB-TE | 67-69DenA 70-72Den 73JJ 74SD | | 6'4" | 224 | Maryland | 4 | 2 |
| Nafziger, Dana LB-TE | 77-79TB 80KJ 81-82TB | | 6'1" | 222 | Cal. Poly.-S.L.O. | | |
| Namath, Joe (Broadway Joe)QB | 65-69NY-A 70-76NYJ 77LA | 12 | 6'2" | 198 | Alabama | | 48 |
| Naponic, Bob QB | 70Hou | | 6' | 190 | Illinois | | |
| Naumoff, Paul LB | 67-78Det | | 6'1" | 216 | Tennessee | 6 | |
| Neal, Dan C-OG | 73-74Bal 75-83Chi | | 6'4" | 250 | Kentucky | | |
| Neal, Lewis WR | 73-74Atl | 2 | 6'4" | 215 | Prairie View | | 6 |
| Neal, Richard DE-DT | 69-72NO 73-77NYJ 78NO | | 6'3" | 258 | Southern U. | | 6 |
| Neely, Ralph OT | 65-77Dal | | 6'5" | 261 | Oklahoma | | |
| Neils, Steve LB | 74-80StL | | 6'2" | 217 | Minnesota | 1 | 6 |
| Nelson, Bill DT | 71-75LA | | 6'7" | 270 | Oregon State | | |
| Nelson, Dennis OT | 70-74Bal 76-77Phi | | 6'5" | 260 | Illinois State | | |
| Nelson, Ralph HB | 75Was 76Sea | 2 | 6'2" | 195 | none | | 12 |
| Nelson, Shane LB | 77-82Buf | | 6'1" | 226 | Baylor | 4 | |
| Nelson, Terry TE | 74-80LA | 2 | 6'2" | 233 | Ark.-Pine Bluff | | 42 |
| Nettles, Doug DB | 74-79Bal 80NYG | | 6' | 179 | Vanderbilt | 5 | 2 |
| Neville, Tom OT | 65-69BosA 70Bos 71-74NE 75BL 76-77NE 78Den 79NYG | | 6'4" | 252 | Mississippi State | | |
| Newhouse, Robert FB-HB | 72-83Dal | 2 | 5'10" | 209 | Houston | | 216 |
| Newland, Bob WR | 71-74NO 75JJ | 2 | 6'2" | 190 | Oregon | | 48 |
| Newman, Ed OG | 73-84Mia | | 6'2" | 249 | Fla. Atlantic, Duke | | |
| Newsome, Billy DE | 70-72Bal 73-74NO 75-76NYG 77Chi | | 6'4" | 251 | Grambling | 3 | 6 |
| Newton, Bob OG-OT | 71-75Chi 76-81Sea 83-84USFL | | 6'4" | 257 | Nebraska | | |
| Nichols, Mark LB | 78SF | | 6'3" | 225 | Colorado State | 1 | |
| Nichols, Robbie LB | 70-71Bal | | 6'3" | 220 | Tulsa | | |
| Nicholson, Jim OT | 74-79KC 80KJ 81SF | | 6'6" | 269 | Michigan State | | |
| Niehaus, Steve DT-DE | 76-78Sea 79Min | | 6'4" | 263 | Notre Dame | | |
| Niland, John OG | 66-74Dal 75Phi 76KJ | | 6'4" | 247 | Iowa | | 6 |
| Nix, Kent QB | 67-69Pit 70-71Chi 72Hou | 12 | 6'1" | 195 | Texas Christian | | 12 |
| Nobis, Tommy LB | 66-76Atl | | 6'2" | 237 | Texas | 12 | 12 |
| Nock, George HB | 69NY-A 70-71NYJ 72Was | 2 | 5'10" | 200 | Morgan State | | 66 |
| Nordquist, Mark OG-C | 68-74Phi 75-76Chi 76SF | | 6'4" | 245 | U. of Pacific | | |
| Nott, Mike QB | 76KC | | 6'3" | 203 | Santa Clara | | |
| Nottingham, Don FB | 71-73Bal 73-77Mia 78SJ | 2 | 5'10" | 210 | Kent State | | 210 |
| Novak, Gary DT | 71SD | | 6'5" | 247 | Michigan State | | |
| Novak, Jack TE | 75Cin 76-77TB | 2 | 6'4" | 241 | Wisconsin | | 6 |
| Novak, Ken DT | 76-77Bal 78Cle 79JJ | | 6'7" | 268 | Purdue | | |
| Nugent, Dan OG | 76-78Was 79XJ 80Was | | 6'3" | 250 | Auburn | | |
| Nunamaker, Julian DE-DT | 69BufA 70Buf 71JJ | | 6'3" | 251 | Tennessee-Martin | | |
| Nunley, Frank (Fudgehammer) LB | 67-76SF | | 6'2" | 230 | Michigan | | 14 |

| Use Name (Nickname) - Positions | Team by Year | See Section | Hgt. | Wgt. | College | Int | Pts |
|---|---|---|---|---|---|---|---|
| Nuzum, Rick C | 77LA 78GB 79LJ | | 6'4" | 238 | Kentucky | | |
| Nye, Blaine OG | 68-76Dal | | 6'4" | 252 | Stanford | | |
| Nystrom, Lee OT | 74GB | | 6'5" | 260 | Macalester | | |
| Nyvall, Vic HB | 70NO | | 5'10" | 185 | Northwestern La. | | |
| Oates, Brad OT-OG | 76-77StL 78Det 79-80StL | | 6'6" | 274 | Duke, Brigham Young | | |
| Obradovich, Jim TE | 75NYG 76-77SF 78-83TB | 2 | 6'2" | 227 | Southern Calif. | | 42 |
| O'Brien, Jim WR-K | 70-72Bal 73Det | 2 5 | 6' | 195 | Cincinnati | | 301 |
| O'Brien, Mike DB | 79Sea 83USFL | | 6'1" | 195 | California | | |
| O'Connor, Fred | HC78SF | | | | East Stroudsburg | | |
| O'Dell, Stu LB | 74Was 75SJ 76-77Was 78Bal 79JJ | | 6'1" | 220 | Indiana | | |
| Odom, Ricky DB | 78KC 78SF 79LA | | 6' | 183 | Southern Calif. | 2 | |
| Odom, Steve WR | 74-79GB 79NYG | 23 | 5'8" | 173 | Utah | | 90 |
| Odoms, Riley TE | 72-83Den | 2 | 6'4" | 231 | Houston | | 264 |
| Ogle, Rick LB | 71StL 72Det | | 6'3" | 230 | Colorado | | |
| Okoniewski, Steve DT-DE | 72-73Buf 74-75GB | | 6'3" | 257 | Montana | | |
| Olander, Cliff QB | 77-79SD 80-81NYG | | 6'5" | 191 | New Mexico State | | 1 |
| Oldham, Ray DB | 73-78Bal 78Pit 79NYG 80-82Det | | 6' | 193 | Middle Tenn. St. | 14 | 12 |
| Olds, Bill FB | 73-75Bal 76Sea 76Phi | 2 | 6'1" | 224 | Nebraska | | 60 |
| Olerich, Dave LB-TE | 67-68SF 69-70StL 71Hou 72-73SF | | 6'1" | 221 | San Francisco | | |
| Oliver, Frank DB | 75Buf 76TB | | 6' | 194 | Kentucky State | | |
| Oliver, Greg HB | 73-74Phi | | 6' | 192 | Trinity (Texas) | | |
| Olsen, Orrin C | 76KC | | 6'1" | 245 | Brigham Young | | |
| Olsen, Phil DT-C | 71-74LA 75-76Den 78KJ | | 6'5" | 263 | Utah State | | |
| O'Malley, Jim LB | 73-75Den | | 6'1" | 230 | Notre Dame | 1 | |
| O'Neal, Calvin LB | 78Bal | | 6'1" | 235 | Michigan | | |
| O'Neal, Steve WR-K | 69NY-A 70-72NYJ 73NO | 4 | 6'3" | 185 | Texas A&M | | |
| O'Neil, Ed LB | 74-79Det 80GB | | 6'3" | 236 | Penn State | 5 | 18 |
| Onkontz, Dennis LB | 70NYJ | | 6'1" | 220 | Penn State | | |
| Opperman, Jim LB | 75Phi | | 6'3" | 220 | Colorado State | | |
| Orduna, Joe HB-FB | 72-73NYG 74Bal | 2 | 6' | 195 | Nebraska | | 24 |
| Oriard, Mike C-OG | 70-73KC | | 6'4" | 223 | Notre Dame | | |
| Ortega, Ralph LB | 75-78Atl 79-80Mia | | 6'2" | 200 | Florida | 5 | 6 |
| Orvis, Herb DT-DE | 72-77Det 78-81Bal | | 6'5" | 248 | Colorado | | |
| Osborn, Dave HB | 65-75Min 76GB | 2 | 6' | 206 | North Dakota | | 216 |
| Osborn, Mike LB | 78Phi | | 6'5" | 235 | Kansas State | | |
| Osborne, Jim DT | 72-84Chi | | 6'3" | 251 | Southern U. | | 2 |
| Osborne, Richard TE | 76Phi 76NYJ 77-78Phi 79StL | 2 | 6'3" | 230 | Texas A&M | | 6 |
| Osley, Willie DB | 74KC | | 6' | 195 | Illinois | | |
| Otis, Jim FB | 70NO 71-72KC 73-78StL | 2 | 6' | 223 | Ohio State | | 132 |
| Outlaw, John DB | 69BosA 70Bos 71-72NE 73, 75-78Phi | | 5'10" | 180 | Jackson State | 14 | 12 |
| Overmeyer, Bill LB | 72Phi | | 6'3" | 220 | Ashland | | |
| Owen, Tom QB | 74-75SF 76-81NE 82Was 83NYG | 1 | 6'1" | 195 | Wichita State | | 6 |
| Owens, Artie WR-HB | 76-79SD 80Buf 80NO 83USFL | 23 | 5'10" | 176 | West Virginia | | 18 |
| Owens, Brig DB | 66-77Was | | 5'11" | 190 | Cincinnati | 36 | 32 |
| Owens, Burgess DB | 73-79NYJ 80-81Oak 82Raid | | 6'2" | 199 | Miami (Fla.) | 30 | 36 |
| Owens, Joe DE | 70SD 71-75NO 76Hou | | 6'2" | 244 | Alcorn State | 1 | 4 |
| Owens, Marv WR | 73StL 74NYJ | | 5'11" | 205 | San Diego State | | |
| Owens, Morris WR | 75-76Mia 76-79TB | 2 | 6' | 192 | Arizona State | | 84 |
| Owens, Steve FB | 70-74Det 75KJ | 2 | 6'2" | 217 | Oklahoma | | 132 |
| Owens, Terry OT | 66-69SD-A 70-75SD | | 6'6" | 263 | Jacksonville St. | | |
| Owens, Tinker WR | 76NO 77KJ 78-80NO 81KJ | 2 | 5'11" | 170 | Oklahoma | | 24 |
| Ozdowski, Mike DE | 78-81Bal | | 6'5" | 242 | Virginia | | |
| Packer, Walter DB | 77Sea | | 5'10" | 174 | Mississippi State | | |
| Pagac, Fred TE | 74Chi 75WFL 76TB | | 6' | 220 | Ohio State | | |
| Page, Alan DT | 67-78Min 78-81Chi | | 6'5" | 244 | Notre Dame | 2 | 24 |
| Palewicz, Al LB | 73-75KC 77 NYJ | | 6'1" | 215 | Miami (Fla.) | | |
| Palmer, Dick LB | 70Mia 71JJ 72Buf 72-73NO 74 Atl | | 6'2" | 229 | Kentucky | | |
| Palmer, Gary OT-DT | 75KC | | 6'4" | 255 | Kansas | | |
| Palmer, Scott DT | 71NYJ 72StL | | 6'3" | 243 | Texas | | |
| Pane, Chris DB | 76-79Den | | 5'11" | 184 | New Mexico | | |
| Papale, Vince WR | 76-78Phi 79SJ | | 6'2" | 195 | St. Joseph's-Pa. | | |
| Parish, Don LB | 70-71StL 71LA 72Den | | 6'1" | 220 | Stanford | 1 | 6 |
| Parker, Artimus DB | 74-76Phi | | 6'3" | 208 | Southern Calif. | 5 | |
| Parker, Joel WR | 74-75NO 76JJ 77NO | 2 | 6'5" | 213 | Forida | | 36 |
| Parker, Kenny DB | 70NYG | | 6'1" | 190 | Fordham | | |
| Parker, Willie C | 73-79Buf 80Det | | 6'3" | 245 | North Texas | | |
| Parker, Dave DB | 79Det | | 6' | 190 | Utah State | | |
| Parks, Billy WR | 71SD 72Dal 73-75Hou | 2 | 6'1" | 187 | Long Beach State | | 42 |
| Parris, Gary TE | 73-74SD 75-78Cle 79-80StL | 2 | 6'2" | 226 | Florida State | | 31 |
| Parrish, Lemar DB | 70-77Cin 78-81Was 82Buf | 3 | 5'11" | 180 | Lincoln (Mo.) | 47 | 78 |
| Parrish, Scott OT | 76Den | | 6'6" | 270 | Utah State | | |
| Parsley, Cliff K | 77-82Hou | 4 | 6'1" | 213 | Oklahoma State | | |
| Parson, Ray OT | 71Det | | 6'4" | 250 | Minnesota | | |
| Parsons, Bob K-TE | 72-83Chi 84-85USFL | 4 | 6'5" | 230 | Penn State | | |
| Partee, Dennis K | 68-69SD-A 70-75SD | 45 | 6'2" | 218 | S.M.U. | | 380 |
| Pass, Randy OG-C | 78GB | | 6'3" | 247 | Georgia Tech | | |
| Pastorini, Dan QB | 71-79Hou 80Oak 81LA 82-83Phi | 12 4 | 6'3" | 208 | Santa Clara | | 48 |
| Pastrana, Al QB | 69DenA 70Den | 1 | 6'1" | 190 | Maryland | | 6 |
| Pate, Lloyd HB | 70Buf | 2 | 6'1" | 205 | Cincinnati | | 6 |
| Patera, Jack LB-OG | 55-57Bal 58-59ChiC 60-61Dal HC76-82Sea | | 6'1" | 234 | Oregon | | |
| Patrick, Frank QB | 70-72GB | | 6'7" | 225 | Nebraska | | |
| Patrick, Mike K | 75-78NE | 4 | 6' | 209 | Mississippi State | | |
| Patrick, Wayne FB | 68-69BufA 70-72Buf 73KJ | 2 | 6'2" | 241 | Louisville | | 36 |
| Patterson, Don DB | 79Det 80NYG | | 5'11" | 175 | Georgia Tech | | |
| Patton, Bob C | 76Buf | | 6'1" | 245 | Delaware | | |
| Patton, Jerry DT | 71Min 72-73Buf 74Pit 75NE | | 6'3" | 261 | Nebraska | 1 | |
| Patulski, Walt DE | 72-75Buf 76KJ 77StL 78XJ | | 6'6" | 260 | Notre Dame | | |
| Paul, Harold OT | 74Oak | | 6'5" | 245 | Oklahoma | | |
| Payne, Ken WR | 74-77GB 77-78Phi | 2 | 6'1" | 185 | Langston | | 36 |
| Pear, Dave NT-DT | 75Bal 76-78TB 79-80Oak | | 6'2" | 248 | Washington | | |
| Pearson, Barry WR | 72-73Pit 74-76KC | 2 | 5'11" | 185 | Northwestern | | 42 |
| Pearson, Dennis WR | 78-79Atl 80KJ | 3 | 5'11" | 177 | San Deigo State | | 6 |
| Pearson, Drew WR | 73-83Dal | 2 | 6' | 184 | Tulsa | | 300 |
| Pearson, Preston HB-DB | 67-69Bal 70-74Pit 75-80Dal | 23 | 6'1" | 200 | Illinois | | 198 |
| Peay, Francis OT | 66-67NYG 68-72GB 73-74KC | | 6'5" | 250 | Missouri | | |
| Peets, Brian TE | 76-79Sea 80BL 81SF | 2 | 6'4" | 225 | U. of Pacific | | 6 |
| Peiffer, Dan C | 75-77Chi 80Was 81KJ | | 6'3" | 252 | SE Missouri St. | | |
| Pellegrini, Joe DT-NT | 78-79NYJ | | 6'2" | 268 | Idaho | | |
| Pena, Bubba OG | 72Cle 73KJ | | 6'2" | 250 | Massachusetts | | |
| Penchion, Bobby OG-C | 72-73Buf 74-75SF 76Sea | | 6'5" | 256 | Alcorn State | | |
| Pennywell, Carlos WR | 78-81NE | 2 | 6'2" | 180 | Grambling | | 18 |
| Pennywell, Robert LB | 77-80Atl 83-85USFL | | 6'1" | 222 | Grambling | 3 | 12 |
| Penrose, Craig QB | 76-79Den 80NYJ 83-84USFL | 1 | 6'3" | 211 | San Diego State | | |
| Peoples, Woody OG | 68-75SF 76XJ 77SF 78-80Phi | | 6'2" | 251 | Grambling | | |
| Peppler, Pat | HC76Atl | | | | Michigan State | | |
| Percival, Mac K | 67-73Chi 74Dal | 5 | 6'4" | 219 | Texas Tech | | 466 |
| Pergine, John LB | 69-72LA 73-75Was | | 6'1" | 225 | Notre Dame | | 6 |
| Perkins, Horace DB | 79KC | | 5'11" | 180 | Colorado | | |
| Perko, Tom LB | 76GB | | 6'3" | 233 | Pittsburgh | | |
| Perretta, Ralph C-OG | 75-79SD 80NYG 80SD | | 6'2" | 251 | Purdue | | |
| Perrin, Lonnie FB | 76-78Den 79Was 79Chi | 23 | 6'1" | 222 | Illinois | | 66 |
| Perry, Rod DB | 75-82LA 83-84Cle | | 5'9" | 178 | Colorado | 30 | 24 |
| Perry, Scott DB | 76-79Cin 80SF 80SD | | 6' | 182 | Williams | 4 | 18 |
| Person, Ara TE | 72StL | | 6'2" | 220 | Morgan State | | |
| Pesuit, Wally OG-C-DE-OT | 76Atl 76-78Mia 79-80Det 83-84USFL | | 6'4" | 252 | Kentucky | | |
| Peters, Tony DB | 75-77Cle 79-82Was 83SL 84Was | | 6'1" | 187 | Oklahoma | 14 | |
| Peterson, Bill LB-TE | 68-69CinA 70-72Cin 75KC | | 6'3" | 228 | San Jose State | 5 | |
| Peterson, Bill | HC72-73Hou | | | | Ohio Northern | | |
| Peterson, Cal LB | 74-75Dal 76TB 79-81KC 82Raid | | 6'3" | 220 | U.C.L.A. | 2 | |
| Peterson, Jim LB | 74-75LA 76TB | | 6'5" | 235 | San Diego State | | |
| Pettigrew, Gary DT-DE | 66-73Phi 74NYG | | 6'4" | 252 | Stanford | | |
| Pharr, Tommy DB | 70Buf | | 5'10" | 187 | Mississippi State | | |
| Phillips, Charlie DB | 75-79Oak 80KJ | | 6'2" | 215 | Southern Calif. | 19 | 18 |
| Phillips, Jess HB-FB-DB | 68-69CinA 70-72Cin 73-74NO 75Oak 76-77NE | 23 | 6'1" | 208 | Michigan State | 3 | 90 |
| Phillips, Mel DB | 66-77SF | | 6' | 191 | N. Carolina A&T | 12 | 6 |
| Phillips, Ray LB | 77-78Cin 78-81Phi 83-84USFL | | 6'4" | 224 | Nebraska | 1 | |
| Phillips, Rod FB-TE | 75-78LA 79-80StL | 2 | 6' | 220 | Jackson State | | 18 |
| Phillips, Wesley OT | 79Hou 79-80CFL 83USFL | | 6'5" | 275 | Lenoir Rhyne | | |
| Philyaw, Charles (King Kong) DE-NT | 76-79Oak 83-84USFL | | 6'9" | 276 | Texas Southern | | |
| Phipps, Mike QB | 70-76Cle 77-81Chi | 12 | 6'3" | 208 | Purdue | | 78 |
| Picard, Bob WR | 73-76Phi 76Det | | 6'1" | 196 | Eastern Washington | | |
| Piccone, Lou WR | 74-76NYJ 77-82Buf | 23 | 5'9" | 177 | W. Liberty State | | 44 |
| Pickard, Bob WR | 74Det | | 6' | 190 | Xavier-Ohio | | 6 |
| Pierce, Danny HB-FB | 70Was | | 6'3" | 215 | Memphis State | | |
| Pierson, Reggie DB | 76Det 76-77TB | | 5'11" | 185 | Oklahoma State | | |
| Pietrzak, Jim C-DT-OT | 74-75NYG 76NYJ 77-79NYG 79-84NO 87KC | | 6'5" | 260 | Eastern Michigan | | |
| Pifferini, Bob LB | 72-75Chi 77LA | | 6'2" | 226 | U.C.L.A. | | |
| Pinder, Cyril HB-LB | 68-70Phi 71-72Chi 73Dal 74-75WFL | 2 | 6'2" | 218 | Illinois | | 42 |
| Pinkney, Reggie DB | 77-78Det 79-81Bal | | 5'11" | 188 | East Carolina | 4 | 6 |
| Piper, Scott WR | 76Atl | | 6'1" | 179 | Arizona | | |
| Pisarkiewicz, Steve QB | 77-79StL 80GB 82CFL 83,85USFL | 1 | 6'2" | 205 | Missouri | | |
| Pittman, Charlie HB | 70StL 71Bal | | 6'1" | 200 | Penn State | | |
| Pitts, Frank WR-DE-FL | 65-69KC-A 70KC 71-73Cle 74Oak 75Atl | 2 | 6'2" | 198 | Southern U. | | 174 |
| Pitts, John DB | 67-69BufA 70-72Buf 73-74Den 75Cle | | 6'4" | 218 | Arizona State | 10 | |
| Plank, Doug DB | 75-82Chi 84USFL | | 6' | 200 | Ohio State | 15 | 2 |
| Plummer, Tony DB | 70StL 71-73Atl 74LA | | 5'11" | 189 | U. of Pacific | 1 | 6 |
| Plunkett, Jim QB | 71-75NE 76-77SF 78-81Oak 82-86Raid 87SJ | 12 | 6'3" | 215 | Stanford | | 84 |
| Podolak, Ed HB | 69KC-A 70-77KC | 23 | 6'1" | 204 | Iowa | | 240 |
| Pollard, Bob DT-DE | 71-77NO 78-81StL | | 6'3" | 248 | Weber State | | 6 |
| Poll, Randy DB | 74Min 75-77Den | | 6'3" | 190 | Stanford | 1 | 6 |
| Polowski, Larry LB | 79Sea | | 6'3" | 235 | Boise State | | |
| Poole, Larry HB | 75-77Cle 78Hou | 2 | 6' | 195 | Kent State | | 30 |
| Poole, Steve LB | 76NYJ | | 6'1" | 232 | Tennessee | | 6 |
| Pope, Ken DB | 74NE | | 5'11" | 200 | Oklahoma | | |
| Porter, Jack C | 71SD | | 6'4" | 255 | Oklahoma | | |
| Porter, Lewis WR | 70KC | | 5'11" | 178 | Southern U. | | |
| Porter, Ron LB | 67-69Bal 69-72Phi 73Min 74WFL | | 6'3" | 232 | Idaho | 3 | |
| Posey, David K | 78NE | 5 | 5'10" | 167 | Florida | | 52 |
| Potts, Charlie DB | 72Det | | 6'3" | 210 | Purdue | | |
| Pough, Ernest WR | 76-77Pit 78NYG | 23 | 6'1" | 174 | Texas Southern | | 6 |
| Powell, Darnell HB | 77Buf 78NYJ 79JJ | 2 | 5'11" | 199 | Tenn.-Chattanooga | | 6 |
| Powell, Jesse LB | 69MiaA 70-73Mia | | 6'1" | 214 | West Texas State | | |
| Powell, Steve HB | 78-79Buf | | 5'11" | 186 | NE Missouri St. | | |
| Powers, Clyde DB | 74-77NYG 78KC 79KJ | | 6'1" | 195 | Oklahoma | 5 | |
| Pratt, Robert OG | 74-81Bal 83-85Sea | | 6'4" | 249 | North Carolina | | 6 |
| Preece, Steve DB | 69NO 70-72Phi 72Den 73-76LA 77Sea | | 6'1" | 195 | Oregon State | 14 | 18 |
| Price, Elex DT | 73-80NO | | 6'3" | 262 | Alcorn State | 1 | 12 |
| Price, Ernie DE-DT | 73-78Det 78-79Sea 79Cle 83-84USFL | | 6'4" | 248 | Texas A&I | | 2 |
| Pringle, Alan K | 75Det | | 6' | 195 | Rice | | |
| Pritchard, Ron LB | 69HouA 70-72Hou 72-77Cin | | 6'1" | 231 | Arizona State | 3 | 2 |
| Pritchett, Billy Ray FB | 75Cle 76-77Atl | 2 | 6'3" | 231 | West Texas State | | 6 |
| Profit, Joe HB | 71-73Atl 73NO | 2 | 6' | 210 | Northeast La. | | 18 |
| Prothro, Tommy | HC71-72LA HC74-78SD | | | | Duke | | |
| Protz, Jack LB | 70SD | | 6'1" | 218 | Syracuse | | |
| Prout, Bob DB | 74Oak 75NYJ | | 6'1" | 187 | Knox | 1 | |
| Provost, Ted DB | 70Min 71StL | | 6'2" | 195 | Ohio State | | |
| Pruett, Perry DB | 71NE | | 6'1" | 190 | North Texas | | |
| Pruitt, Greg HB | 73-81Cle 82-84Raid | 23 | 5'10" | 190 | Oklahoma | | 282 |
| Puetz, Gary OG-OT | 73-78NYJ 78TB 79Phi 79-81NE 82Was | | 6'4" | 263 | Valparaiso | | |
| Pugh, Jethro DT-DE | 65-78Dal | | 6'6" | 256 | Elizabeth City St. | 1 | 4 |
| Pureifory, Dave DE-DT | 72-77GB 78Cin 78-82Det 83-85USFL | | 6'1" | 256 | Eastern Michigan | | 4 |
| Queen, Jeff FB-TE | 69SD-A 70-71SD 72-73Oak 74Hou | 2 | 6'1" | 221 | Morgan State | | 60 |
| Raba, Rob TE | 77-79NYJ 80Bal 81Was | | 6'1" | 224 | Maryland | | |
| Rader, Dave QB | 79NYG | | 6'3" | 211 | Tulsa | | |
| Rae, Mike QB | 76-78Oak 78-80TB 81Was 83-85USFL | 12 | 6' | 193 | Southern Calif | | 12 |
| Ragsdale, George HB-WR | 77-79TB 80SJ 83-84USFL | 23 | 5'11" | 185 | N. Carolina A&T | | 12 |
| Raible, Steve WR | 76-81Sea | 2 | 6'2" | 195 | Georgia Tech | | 24 |
| Raines, Mike DT-DE | 74SF 75-82CFL 83-84USFL | | 6'5" | 255 | Alabama | | |
| Ralston, John | HC72-76Den | | | | California | | |
| Ramsey, Steve QB | 70NO 71-76Den | 12 | 6'2" | 210 | North Texas | | 12 |
| Randall, Tom OG | 78Dal 79Hou | | 6'5" | 245 | Iowa State | | |
| Randolph, Al DB | 66-70SF 71GB 72Det 73Cin 74Buf | | 6'2" | 199 | Iowa | 11 | 8 |
| Randolph, Terry DB | 77GB | | 6' | 184 | American Inter. | | |
| Rashad, Ahmad WR | 72-73StL 74Buf 75KJ 76-82Min 1972 — played as Bobby Moore | 2 | 6'2" | 202 | Oregon | | 276 |
| Rasley, Rocky OG | 69-70, 72-73Det 74NO 75KC | | 6'3" | 252 | Oregon State | | |
| Rasmussen, Randy OG | 67-69NY-A 70-81NYJ | | 6'2" | 256 | Kearney State | | 6 |
| Rather, Bo WR | 73Mia 74-78Chi 78Mia 79JJ | 2 | 6'1" | 185 | Michigan | | 42 |
| Ratiff, Don DB | 75Phi | | 6'5" | 250 | Maryland | | |
| Ray, David WR-K | 69-74LA | 5 | 6' | 195 | Alabama | | 497 |
| Ray, Eddie FB-TE | 70Bos 71SD 72-74Atl 76Buf | 2 | 6'1" | 237 | Louisiana State | | 66 |
| Rayhle, Fred TE | 77Sea | | 6'5" | 216 | Tenn.-Chattanooga | | |
| Reamon, Tommy HB | 76KC | 2 | 5'10" | 192 | Missouri | | 30 |
| Reardon, Kerry DB | 71-76KC | | 5'11" | 180 | Iowa | 14 | |
| Reaves, John QB | 72-74Phi 75-78Cin 79Min 81Hou 83-85USFL 87TB | 12 | 6'3" | 209 | Florida | | 18 |
| Reaves, Ken DB | 66-73Atl 74NO 74-77StL | | 6'3" | 206 | Norfolk State | 37 | 6 |
| Reavis, Dave OT-OG | 74-75Pit 76-83TB | | 6'5" | 257 | Arkansas | | |
| Rebowe, Rusty LB | 78NO | | 5'10" | 213 | Nicholls State | | |
| Redmond, Rudy LB | 69-71Atl 72Det 73JJ | | 6' | 190 | U. of Pacific | 8 | 6 |
| Reece, Danny DB | 76-80TB | 3 | 5'11" | 190 | Southern Calif. | 1 | 6 |

| Use Name (Nickname) - Positions | Team by Year | See Section | Hgt. | Wgt. | College | Int | Pts |
|---|---|---|---|---|---|---|---|
| Reece, Geoff C | 76LA 77Sea 78Bal | | 6'4" | 247 | Washington State | | |
| Reed, Alvin TE | 67-69HouA 70-72Hou 73-75Was | 2 | 6'5" | 232 | Prairie View | | 84 |
| Reed, Frank DB | 76-80Atl 83USFL | | 5'11" | 193 | Washington | 6 | 6 |
| Reed, Henry LB-DE | 71-74NYG | | 6'3" | 230 | Weber State | 3 | |
| Reed, James LB | 77Phi | | 6'2" | 230 | California | | |
| Reed, Joe QB | 72-74SF 75-79Det | 12 | 6'1" | 194 | Mississippi State | | 12 |
| Reed, Oscar HB-FB | 68-74Min 75Atl | 2 | 5'11" | 222 | Colorado State | | 66 |
| Reed, Tony HB | 77-80KC 81Den | 2 | 5'11" | 197 | Colorado | | 60 |
| Reese, Don DE-DT | 74-76Mia 78-80NO 81SD 85USFL | | 6'6" | 254 | Jackson State | | 8 |
| | 1977 — Ineligible to play pro football | | | | | | |
| Reese, Steve LB | 74-75NYJ 76TB | | 6'2" | 229 | Louisville | | |
| Reeves, Marion DB | 74Phi | | 6'1" | 195 | Clemson | | |
| Reid, Andy HB | 76Buf | | 6' | 195 | Georgia | | |
| Reid, Bill C | 75SF 76KJ | | 6'1" | 242 | Stanford | | |
| Reid, Mike DT | 70-74Cin | | 6'3" | 255 | Penn State | | |
| Reihner, George OG | 77-79Hou 80KJ 82Hou | | 6'4" | 263 | Penn State | | |
| Reilly, Kevin LB | 73-74Phi 75NE | | 6'2" | 220 | Villanova | 1 | |
| Reinfeldt, Mike DB | 76Oak 76-83Hou | | 6'2" | 192 | Wis.-Milwaukee | 26 | 6 |
| Renfro, Mel DB-HB | 64-77Dal | 3 | 6' | 191 | Oregon | 52 | 36 |
| Reppond, Mike WR | 73Chi | | 6' | 180 | Arkansas | | |
| Ressler, Glenn OG-C-OT-DT | 65-74Bal | | 6'3" | 247 | Penn State | | |
| Reutershan, Randy WR | 78Pit | | 5'10" | 182 | Pittsburgh | | |
| Reynolds, Jack (Hacksaw) LB | 70-80LA 81-84SF | | 6'1" | 232 | Tennessee | 6 | 6 |
| Reynolds, Tom WR | 72NE 73Chi 74JJ | 2 | 6'3" | 200 | San Diego State | | 12 |
| Rhodes, Bruce DB | 76SF 77JJ 78Det | | 6' | 189 | San Fran. State | 4 | |
| Rhodes, Danny LB | 74Bal | | 6'2" | 220 | Arkansas | | |
| Rhodes, Ray DB-WR | 74-79NYG 80SF | 2 | 5'11" | 185 | Tulsa | 8 | 42 |
| Rhone, Earnest LB | 75Mia 76KJ 77-84Mia | | 6'2" | 220 | Henderson State | 14 | |
| Rice, Andy DT | 66-67KC-A 67-69HouA 70-71SD | | 6'3" | 268 | Texas Southern | | |
| | 72-73Chi 74NYG | | | | | | |
| Rice, Floyd LB-TE | 71-73Hou 73-75SD 76-77Oak 78NO | | 6'3" | 224 | Alcorn State | 7 | 6 |
| Rice, Harold DE | 71Oak | | 6'2" | 230 | Tennessee State | | |
| Rice, Homer | HC78-79Cin | | | | Centre | | |
| Rich, Randy DB | 77Det 77Den 78Oak 78-79Cle | | 5'10" | 178 | New Mexico | | |
| Richards, Golden WR | 73-78Dal 78-79Chi | 23 | 6' | 181 | Hawaii | | 108 |
| Richardson, Gloster WR | 67-69KC-A 70KC 71Dal | 2 | 6' | 200 | Jackson State | | 108 |
| | 72-74Cle | | | | | | |
| Richardson, Grady TE | 74-75WFL 79-80Was 83USFL | | 6'4" | 225 | Fullerton State | | |
| Richardson, John DT | 67-69MiaA 70-71Mia 72-73StL | | 6'2" | 254 | U.C.L.A. | | |
| Richardson, Mike HB | 69HouA 70-71Hou | 2 | 5'11" | 193 | S.M.U. | | 20 |
| Richardson, Pete DB | 69BufA 70-71Buf | | 6'1" | 197 | Dayton | 8 | |
| Riggins, John FB | 71-75NYJ 76-79Was 80HO 81-85Was | 2 | 6'2" | 232 | Kansas State | | 696 |
| Riley, Ken DB | 69CinA 70-83Cin | | 6' | 183 | Florida A&M | 65 | 30 |
| Riley, Larry DB | 77Den 78NYJ | | 5'10" | 192 | Salem | | |
| Riley, Preston WR | 70-72SF 73NO | 2 | 6' | 180 | Memphis State | | 6 |
| Riley, Steve OT | 74-84Min | | 6'6" | 258 | Southern Calif. | | |
| Rivera, Steve WR | 76-77SF 77Chi 78JJ | | 5'11" | 184 | California | | |
| Rivers, Jamie LB | 68-73StL 74-75NYJ | | 6'2" | 238 | Bowling Green | 4 | |
| Rives, Don LB | 73-78Chi | | 6'2" | 225 | Texas Tech | 2 | |
| Rizzo, Jack HB | 73NYG | | 5'10" | 195 | Lehigh | | |
| Rizzo, Joe LB | 74-80Den | | 6'1" | 220 | Kings Point | 9 | |
| Roach, Travis OG | 74NYJ | | 6'2" | 260 | Texas | | |
| Roan, Oscar TE | 75-78Cle | 2 | 6'6" | 214 | S.M.U. | | 54 |
| Roberson, Vern DB | 77Mia 78SF | | 6'1" | 195 | Grambling | 2 | |
| Roberts, Gary OG | 70Atl | | 6'2" | 242 | Purdue | | |
| Roberts, Guy LB | 72-75Hou 76Atl 77Mia | | 6'1" | 218 | Maryland | 5 | |
| Roberts, Hal K | 72StL | 4 | 6'1" | 180 | Houston | | |
| Roberts J.D. | HC72-74NO | | | | Oklahoma | | |
| Roberts, Willie DB | 73Chi | | 6'1" | 190 | Houston | | |
| Robertson, Isiah LB | 71-78LA 79-82Buf | | 6'3" | 225 | Southern U. | 25 | 24 |
| Robinson, Craig OT | 72-73NO | | 6'4" | 250 | Houston | | |
| Robinson, Glenn DE-LB | 75Bal 76-77TB | | 6'6" | 242 | Oklahoma State | | |
| Robinson, Gregg DE-NT | 78NYJ | | 6'6" | 255 | Dartmouth | | |
| Robinson, Jim WR | 76-79NYG 80SF 81LJ | 23 | 5'9" | 170 | Georgia Tech | | 36 |
| Robinson, Larry HB-FB | 73Dal | | 6'4" | 210 | Tennessee | | |
| Robinson, Paul HB | 68-69CinA 70-72Cin 72-73Hou 74WFL | 23 | 6' | 199 | Arizona | | 156 |
| Robinson, Virgil HB | 71-72NO | 2 | 5'11" | 195 | Grambling | | 12 |
| Robiskie, Terry FB-HB | 77-79Oak 80-81Mia | 2 | 6'1" | 210 | Louisiana State | | 30 |
| Roche, Alden DE | 70Den 71-76GB 77-78Sea | | 6'4" | 255 | Southern U. | | |
| Roder, Mirro K | 73-74Chi 76TB | 5 | 6'1" | 221 | none | | 79 |
| Rodgers, Johnny WR | 77-78SD | 23 | 5'10" | 180 | Nebraska | | |
| Rodgers, Otis LB | 77KC | | 6'3" | 230 | Iowa State | | |
| Rodgers, Willie HB-FB | 72Hou 73KJ 74-75Hou 76JJ | 2 | 6' | 210 | Kentucky | | 50 |
| Rogers, Mel LB | 71SD 72SJ 73-74SD 75WFL 76LA 77Chi | | 6'2" | 231 | Florida A&M | 1 | |
| Rogers, Stan OT | 75Den | | 6'4" | 255 | Maryland | | |
| Rogers, Steve HB | 75NO 76NYJ | | 6'2" | 203 | Louisiana State | | |
| Roller, Dave DT | 71NYG 74-75WFL 75-78GB 79-80Min | | 6'2" | 270 | Kentucky | | |
| Roman, John OT-OG | 76-82NYJ | | 6'4" | 255 | Idaho State | | |
| Roman, Nick DE | 70-71Cin 72-73Cle | | 6'3" | 235 | Ohio State | 1 | 6 |
| Romaniszyn, Jim LB | 73-74Cle 76NE 77-78JJ | | 6'2" | 219 | Edinboro | | |
| Rosecrans, James LB | 76NYJ | | 6'1" | 230 | Penn State | | |
| Ross, Louis DE | 71-72Buf 74WFL 75KC 76JJ | | 6'6" | 248 | S. Carolina State | | |
| Ross, Oliver HB-FB | 73-75Den 76Sea | 23 | 6' | 210 | Alabama A&M | | |
| Rossovich, Tim LB-DE | 68-71Phi 72-73SD 74-75WFL | | 6'4" | 245 | Southern Calif. | 3 | |
| Rothwell, Fred C | 74Det | | 6'3" | 240 | Kansas State | | |
| Roussel, Tom LB | 68-70Was 71-72NO 73Phi | | 6'3" | 235 | Southern Miss. | 2 | |
| Rowden, Larry DB | 71-72Chi | | 6'2" | 220 | Houston | | |
| Rowe, Bob DT-DE | 67-75StL 76XJ | | 6'4" | 258 | Western Michigan | 2 | 6 |
| Rowe, Dave DT-NT | 67-70NO 71-73NE 74-75SD | | 6'6" | 273 | Penn State | | |
| Rowser, John DB | 67-69GB 70-73Pit 74-76Den | | 6'1" | 185 | Michigan | 26 | 24 |
| Rozier, Bob DE | 79StL | | 6'3" | 240 | California | | |
| Rozumek, Dave LB | 76-79KC | | 6'1" | 215 | New Hampshire | 2 | |
| Rucker, Conrad TE | 78-79Hou 80TB 80LA | | 6'3" | 255 | Southern U. | | |
| Rucker, Reggie WR | 70-71Dal 71NYG 71-74NE 75-81Cle | 2 | 6'2" | 190 | Boston U. | | 264 |
| Rudnay, Jack C | 70-82KC | | 6'3" | 240 | Northwestern | | |
| Rudnick, Tim DB | 74Bal | | 5'10" | 185 | Notre Dame | | |
| Rudolph, Council DE | 72Hou 73-75StL 76-77TB | | 6'3" | 255 | Kentucky State | 1 | |
| Rudzinski, Paul LB | 78-80GB 81XJ | | 6'1" | 220 | Michigan State | 1 | |
| Russ, Carl LB | 75Atl 76-77NYJ | | 6'2" | 227 | Michigan | | |
| Russell, Andy LB | 63Pit 64-65MS 66-76Pit | | 6'3" | 221 | Missouri | 18 | 13 |
| Ruud, Tom LB | 75-77Buf 78-79Cin | | 6'2" | 225 | Nebraska | | |
| Ryckman, Billy WR | 77-79Atl 80KJ 83USFL | 23 | 5'11" | 172 | Louisiana Tech | | 30 |
| Ryczek, Dan C | 73-75Was 76-77TB 78-79LA 87Phi | | 6'3" | 246 | Virginia | | |
| Ryczek, Paul C | 74-79Atl 81NO | | 6'2" | 231 | Virginia | | |
| Rydalch, Ron DT | 75-80Chi | | 6'4" | 259 | Utah | | |
| St. Clair, Mike DE | 76-79Cle 80-82Cin 84-85USFL | | 6'5" | 249 | Grambling | | 6 |
| Salaam, Abdul DT-DE | 76-83NYJ | | 6'3" | 262 | Kent State | | |
| | 1976 — Played as Lary Faulk | | | | | | |
| Salter, Bryant DB | 71-73SD 74-75Was 76Mia 76Bal | | 6'4" | 196 | Pittsburgh | 17 | |

| Use Name (Nickname) - Positions | Team by Year | See Section | Hgt. | Wgt. | College | Int | Pts |
|---|---|---|---|---|---|---|---|
| Sampson, Greg OT-DT-DE | 72-78Hou 79IL | | 6'6" | 266 | Stanford | | |
| Sampson, Howard DB | 78-79GB | | 5'10" | 185 | Arkansas | | |
| Samuels, Tony TE | 76-80KC 80TB 81KJ 83USFL | 2 | 6'4" | 230 | Bethune-Cookman | | 18 |
| Sanders, Charlie TE | 68-77Det | 2 | 6'4" | 227 | Minnesota | | 186 |
| Sanders, Clarence LB | 78,80KC | | 6'4" | 229 | Cincinnati | | |
| Sanders, Deac DB | 74-76NE 77-79Phi | | 6'1" | 177 | South Dakota | 17 | 12 |
| Sanders, Ken DE | 72-79Det 80-81Min | | 6'5" | 242 | Howard Payne | | |
| Sanderson, Reggie HB | 73Chi | | 5'10" | 206 | Stanford | | |
| Sandfer, Dill DT-DE | 74-76SF 77-78Sea 79KJ | | 6'6" | 268 | U.C.L.A. | | |
| Satterwhite, Howard WR | 76NYJ 77Was 77Bal | | 5'11" | 185 | Sam Houston St. | | |
| Saul, Rich C-OG-OT-LB | 70-81LA | | 6'3" | 241 | Michigan State | | |
| Saul, Ron OG | 70-75Hou 76-81Was | | 6'2" | 254 | Michigan State | | |
| Saunders, John DB | 72Buf 74-75SF | | 6'3" | 198 | Toledo | | |
| Sawyer, Ken DB | 74Cin | | 6' | 192 | Syracuse | | |
| Scales, Hurles DB | 74Chi 74StL 75GB | | 6'1" | 200 | North Texas | | |
| Scarber, Sam FB | 75-76SD 77KJ | 2 | 6'2" | 232 | New Mexico | | 24 |
| Schaukowitz, Carl OG | 75Den 76JJ | | 6'2" | 237 | Penn State | | |
| Schaum, Greg DE | 76Dal 77KJ 78NE | | 6'4" | 246 | Michigan State | | |
| Schindler, Steve OG | 77-78Den 79KJ | | 6'3" | 256 | Boston College | | |
| Schmidt, Terry DB | 74-75NO 76-84Chi | | 6' | 178 | Ball State | 26 | 18 |
| Schmiesing, Joe DT-DE | 68-71StL 72Det 73Bal 74NYJ | | 6'4" | 253 | Minnesota, | | |
| | | | | | New Mexico State | | |
| Schmit, Bob LB | 75-76NYG | | 6'1" | 220 | Nebraska | | |
| Schnarr, Steve FB | 75Buf | | 6'2" | 216 | Otterbein | | |
| Schnellenberger, Howard | HC73-74Bal | | | | Kentucky | | |
| Schnitker, Mike OG | 69DenA 70-74Den | | 6'3" | 243 | Colorado | | |
| Schoen, Tom DB | 70Cle | | 5'11" | 185 | Notre Dame | | |
| Schreiber, Larry HB-FB | 71-75SF 76Chi 77JJ | 2 | 6' | 206 | Tennessee Tech | | 85 |
| Schubert, Steve WR | 74NE 75-79Chi | 23 | 5'10" | 187 | Massachusetts | | 24 |
| Schultz, John WR | 76-78Den | | 5'10" | 182 | Maryland | | |
| Schumacher, Kurt OG-OT | 75-77NO 78TB | | 6'3" | 252 | Ohio State | | |
| Scoinik, Glenn WR | 73Pit | | 6'3" | 190 | Indiana | | |
| Scott, Bo FB | 69-74Cle | 23 | 6'3" | 213 | Ohio State | | 144 |
| Scott, Bobby QB | 73-82NO 83USFL | 12 | 6'1" | 198 | Tennessee | | 6 |
| Scott, Clarence DB | 71-83Cle | | 6' | 183 | Kansas State | 39 | 18 |
| Scott, Clarence DB | 69BosA 70Bos 71-72NE | | 6'2" | 204 | Morgan State | 1 | |
| Scott, Dave OG-OT | 76-82Atl | | 6'4" | 276 | Kansas | | |
| Scott, Freddie WR | 74-77Bal 78-83Det 84USFL | 2 | 6'2" | 178 | Amherst | | 126 |
| Scott, Herbert OG | 75-84Dal | | 6'2" | 254 | Virginia Union | | |
| Scott, Jake DB | 70-75Mia 76-78Was | 3 | 6' | 188 | Georgia | 49 | 6 |
| Scott, James WR | 76-80Chi 81CFL 82Chi | 2 | 6'1" | 190 | Henderson J.C. | | 120 |
| Scribner, Rick OG | 77GB | | 6'4" | 257 | Idaho State | | |
| Scribner, Rob HB | 73-76LA 77LJ | 23 | 6' | 200 | U.C.L.A. | | 24 |
| Seabron, Thomas LB | 79-80SF 80StL | | 6'3" | 215 | Michigan | | |
| Seal, Paul TE | 74-76NO 77-79SF | 2 | 6'4" | 223 | Michigan | | 48 |
| Seifert, Mike DE | 74Cle | | 6'3" | 245 | Wisconsin | | |
| Seiler, Paul OT-C | 67NY-A 68MS 69NY-A 70JJ | | 6'4" | 258 | Notre Dame | | |
| | 71-73Oak 74-75WFL | | | | | | |
| Seiple, Larry TE-HB-K | 67-69MiaA 70-77Mia | 2 4 | 6' | 213 | Kentucky | | 42 |
| Seivers, Larry WR | 77Phi | | 6'4" | 204 | Tennessee | | |
| Selfridge, Andy LB | 72Buf 74-75NYG 76Mia 77NYG | | 6'4" | 220 | Virginia | 1 | |
| Sellers, Ron WR | 69BosA 70Bos 71NE 72Dal 73Mia | 2 | 6'4" | 196 | Florida State | | 108 |
| Selmon, Dewey LB-DT | 76-80TB 81LJ 82SD | | 6'1" | 246 | Oklahoma | 3 | |
| Sensibaugh, Mike DB | 71-75KC 76-78StL | | 5'11" | 191 | Ohio State | 27 | 12 |
| Severson, Jeff DB | 72Was 73-74Hou 75Den 76-77StL | 3 | 6'1" | 183 | Long Beach State | 6 | |
| | 79LA | | | | | | |
| Sevy, Jeff OT-OG-DT-DE | 75-78Chi79-80Sea83-84USFL | | 6'5" | 259 | California | | |
| Sexton, Brent DB | 77Pit | | 6'1" | 190 | Elon | | |
| Seymour, Jim WR | 70-72Chi | 2 | 6'4" | 210 | Notre Dame | | 30 |
| Seymour, Paul TE | 73-77Buf | 2 | 6'5" | 250 | Michigan | | 18 |
| Shanklin, Ron WR | 70-74Pit 75-76Chi | 2 | 6'1" | 183 | North Texas | | 144 |
| Sharp, Rich OT | 70-71Pit 72Den | | 6'3" | 264 | Washington | | |
| Shaw, Bob WR | 70NO | | 6' | 194 | Winston-Salem St. | | |
| Shaw, Dennis QB | 70-73Buf 74-75StL 76NYG 78KC | 12 | 6'2" | 213 | San Diego State | | |
| | 84USFL | | | | | | |
| Shears, Larry DB | 71-72Atl | | 5'10" | 185 | Lincoln (Mo.) | | |
| Shelby, Willie HB | 76-77Cin 78StL | 3 | 5'11" | 195 | Alabama | 12 | |
| Shell, Art OT | 68-69OakA 70-81Oak 82Raid HC89-94Raid | | 6'5" | 267 | Md. Eastern Shore | | |
| Sheppard, Henry OG-OT | 76-81Cle | | 6'6" | 255 | S.M.U. | | |
| Sherk, Jerry DT-DE-NT | 70-81Cle | | 6'4" | 252 | Oklahoma State | 3 | 2 |
| Sherman, Rod WR-FL | 67Oak A 68CinA 69OakA | 23 | 6' | 190 | Southern Calif. | | 40 |
| | 70-71Oak 72Den 73LA | | | | | | |
| Shinners, John OG | 69-71NO 72Bal 73-77Cin | | 6'2" | 255 | Xavier-Ohio | | |
| Shipp, Joe TE | 79Buf | | 6'4" | 225 | Southern Calif. | | 6 |
| Shipp, Ken | HC75NYJ | | | | Middle Tenn. St. | | |
| Shirk, Gary TE | 74-75WFL 76-82NYG 84-85USFL | 2 | 6'1" | 220 | Morehead State | | 66 |
| Shoate, Rod LB | 75NE 76KJ 77-81NE 83-84USFL | | 6'1" | 214 | Oklahoma | 5 | 6 |
| Shumon, Ron LB | 78Cin 79SF | | 6'1" | 230 | Wichita State | 1 | |
| Shy, Don HB-FB | 67-68Pit 69-70NO 70-72Chi 73StL | 23 | 6'1" | 209 | San Diego State | | 84 |
| Siani, Mike WR | 72-77Oak 78-80Bal | 2 | 6'2" | 196 | Villanova | | 102 |
| Siemon, Jeff LB | 72-82Min | | 6'2" | 235 | Stanford | 11 | |
| Sikich, Mike OG | 71Cle | | 6'2" | 243 | Northwestern | | |
| Simon, Bobby OT-OG | 76Hou | | 6'3" | 252 | Grambling | | |
| Simone, Mike LB | 72-74Den | | 6' | 210 | Stanford | | |
| Simonini, Ed LB | 76-81Bal 82NO | | 6' | 210 | Texas A&M | 3 | |
| Simons, Keith NT-DT | 76-77KC 78-79StL | | 6'3" | 254 | Minnesota | | |
| Simonson, Dave OT | 74Bal 75NYG 76Hou 76Sea 77Det | | 6'6" | 248 | Minnesota | | |
| Simpson, Al OT-OG | 75-76NYG | | 6'5" | 255 | Colorado State | | |
| Simpson, Bill DB | 74-78LA 79VR 80-82Buf | | 6'1" | 184 | Michigan State | 33 | 2 |
| Simpson, Bob DE | 78Mia | | 6'5" | 235 | Colorado | | |
| Simpson, Mike DB | 70-73SF | | 5'11" | 172 | Houston | 3 | 6 |
| Simpson, Nate HB-FB | 77-79GB | 2 | 5'11" | 189 | Tennessee State | | 6 |
| Simpson, O.J. (Juice) HB | 69BufA 70-77Buf78-79SF | 23 | 6'2" | 211 | Southern Calif. | | 456 |
| Sims, David HB | 77-79Sea | 2 | 6'3" | 216 | Georgia Tech | | 138 |
| Sims, Jimmy LB | 76TB | | 6' | 195 | Southern Calif. | | |
| Sims, Mickey DT | 77-79Cle | | 6'5" | 278 | S. Carolina State | | |
| Singletary, Bill LB | 74NYG | | 6'2" | 230 | Temple | | |
| Singleton, Ron OT | 76SD 77-80SF | | 6'7" | 260 | Grambling | | |
| Sipe, Brian QB | 74-83Cle 84-85USFL | 12 | 6'1" | 193 | San Diego State | | 67 |
| Sisemore, Jerry OT-OG | 73-84Phi | | 6'4" | 261 | Texas | | |
| Sistrunk, Manny DT-DE | 70-75Was 76-79Phi | | 6'5" | 269 | Ark.-Pine Bluff | | |
| Sistrunk, Otis DT-DE-NT | 72-78Oak 79JJ | | 6'4" | 265 | none | 3 | 2 |
| Siwek, Mike DT | 70StL | | 6'3" | 260 | Western Michigan | | |
| Skinner, Gerald OT | 78GB | | 6'4" | 260 | Arkansas | | |
| Skorupan, John LB | 73-77Buf 78-80NYG | | 6'2" | 222 | Penn State | 2 | 2 |
| Sledge, Leroy FB | 71Hou | | 6'2" | 230 | Bakersfield J.C. | | 6 |
| Sloan, Ronnie OT | 73StL | | 6'5" | 260 | Austin Peay | | |
| Slough, Greg LB | 71-72Oak | | 6'3" | 230 | Southern Calif. | | |
| Small, Eldridge DB | 72-74NYG | | 6'1" | 190 | Texas A&I | 1 | |
| Small, John LB-DT | 70-72Atl 73-74Det 75JJ | | 6'5" | 260 | The Citadel | | |

| Use Name (Nickname) - Positions | Team by Year | See Section | Hgt. | Wgt. | College | Int | Pts |
|---|---|---|---|---|---|---|---|
| Smith, Barry WR | 73-75GB 76TB | 2 | 6'1" | 190 | Florida State | | 24 |
| Smith, Barty FB | 74-80GB | 2 | 6'4" | 240 | Richmond | | 126 |
| Smith, Blane LB | 77GB | | 6'3" | 238 | Purdue | | |
| Smith, Bubba DE-DT | 67-71Bal 72KJ 73-74Oak 75-76Hou | | 6'7" | 280 | Michigan State | | |
| Smith, Charlie HB | 68-69Oak 70-74Oak 75SD 76KJ | 23 | 6'1" | 205 | Utah | | 204 |
| Smith, Charlie WR | 74-81Phi 83-84USFL | 2 | 6'1" | 185 | Grambling | | 150 |
| Smith, Dave WR | 70-72Pit 72Hou 72KC | 2 | 6'2" | 205 | Indiana State | | 42 |
| Smith, Donnell DE | 71GB 73-74NE | | 6'4" | 247 | Southern U. | | |
| Smith, Ed DE | 73-74Den 75KJ | | 6'5" | 241 | Colorado College | 1 | |
| Smith, Jack DB | 71Phi | | 6'4" | 204 | Troy State | | |
| Smith, Jerry OG-LB | 52-53SF 54-55MS 56SF 56GB HC71Den | | 6'1" | 230 | Wisconsin | | |
| Smith, Jerry TE-WR | 65-77Was | 2 | 6'2" | 209 | Arizona State | | 360 |
| Smith, John K | 74-83NE | 5 | 6' | 186 | King Alfred's (U.K.), Southampton U. (U.K.) | | 692 |
| Smith, John WR | 79Cle | | 6' | 175 | Tennessee State | | |
| Smith, Ken TE | 73Cle 74JJ | | 6'4" | 225 | New Mexico | | |
| Smith, Larry HB | 69-73LA 74Was | 2 | 6'3" | 220 | Florida | | 96 |
| Smith, Laverne HB | 77Pit 78LJ | | 5'10" | 193 | Kansas | | |
| Smith, Lyman DT | 78Min 79JJ | | 6'5" | 250 | Duke | | |
| Smith, Marty DE | 76Buf | | 6'3" | 250 | Louisville | | |
| Smith, Ollie WR | 73-74Bal 76-77GB | 2 | 6'2" | 198 | Tennessee | | 6 |
| Smith, Paul DT-DE | 68-69DenA 70-78Den 79-80Was | | 6'3" | 254 | New Mexico | 2 | 6 |
| Smith, Perry DB | 73-76GB 77-79StL 80-81Den | | 6'1" | 193 | Colorado State | 13 | |
| Smith, Ron DB-FL-HB | 65Chi 66-67Atl 68-69LA 70-72Chi 73SD 74Oak | 23 | 6'1" | 191 | Wisconsin | 13 | 36 |
| Smith, Royce OG | 72-73NO 74-76Atl | | 6'3" | 250 | Georgia | | |
| Smith, Sherman HB-FB | 76-82Sea 83SD | 2 | 6'4" | 223 | Miami-Ohio | | 228 |
| Smith, Sid C-OT | 70-72KC 73JJ 74Hou | | 6'4" | 260 | Southern Calif. | | |
| Smith, Steve OT-DE-TE | 66Pit 68-70Min 71-74Phi | | 6'5" | 246 | Michigan | | 6 |
| Smith, Tody DE | 71-72Dal 73-76Hou 76Buf 77JJ | | 6'5" | 248 | Southern Calif. | 1 | |
| Sniadecki, Jim LB | 69-73SF 74-75WFL | | 6'2" | 224 | Indiana | 1 | |
| Snider, Mal OG-OT | 69-71Atl 72-74GB | | 6'5" | 250 | Stanford | | |
| Snow, Jack WR-DE | 65-75LA | 2 | 6'2" | 195 | Notre Dame | | 270 |
| Snowden, Cal DE | 69-70StL 71Buf 72-73SD | | 6'4" | 247 | Indiana | | |
| Snyder, Todd WR | 70-72Atl | 2 | 6'2" | 187 | Ohio U. | | 12 |
| Sodaski, John LB-DB | 70-72Pit 73Phi | | 6'1" | 214 | Villanova | 1 | |
| Sorey, Revie OG | 75-81Chi 82JJ 83Chi | | 6'2" | 262 | Illinois | | |
| Southard, Tommy WR | 78StL 78Hou | | 6' | 185 | Furman | | |
| Sowells, Rich DB | 71-76NYJ 77Hou | | 6' | 179 | Alcorn State | 10 | 6 |
| Spencer, Mo DB | 74-76NO 77ZJ 78NO | | 6' | 176 | N. Car. Central | 5 | |
| Spencer, Willie FB | 76Min 77-78NYG | 2 | 6'3" | 235 | none | | 30 |
| Speyrer, Cotton WR | 72-74Bal 75Mia | 23 | 6' | 175 | Texas | | 36 |
| Spicer, Bob LB | 73NYJ | | 6'4" | 227 | Indiana | | |
| Spills, John WR | 69-71GB | 2 | 6'3" | 205 | Northern Illinois | | 6 |
| Spiva, Andy LB | 77Atl 78KJ | | 6'2" | 218 | Tennessee | | |
| Sprout, Dennis QB | 78GB | | 6'2" | 210 | Arizona State | | |
| Spurrier, Steve QB | 67-75SF 76TB | 12 4 | 6'2" | 202 | Florida | | 12 |
| Stabler, Ken (Snake) QB | 70-79Oak 80-81Hou 82-84NO | 12 | 6'3" | 210 | Alabama | | 24 |
| Staggers, Jon WR | 70-71Pit 72-74GB 75Det | 23 | 5'10" | 185 | Missouri | | 66 |
| Staggs, Jeff LB-DE | 67-69SD-A 70-71SD 73-74StL 74SD | | 6'2" | 242 | Brigham Young, San Diego State | 3 | |
| Staley, Bill DT | 68-69CinA 70-72Chi | | 6'3" | 249 | Utah State | | |
| Stanback, Haskel HB-FB | 74-79Atl | 2 | 6' | 210 | Tennessee | | 156 |
| Stanfill, Bill DE | 69MiaA 70-76Mia 77ZJ | | 6'5" | 251 | Georgia | 2 | 12 |
| Starch, Ken FB | 76GB | | 5'11" | 210 | Wisconsin | | |
| Starke, George OT | 73-84Was | | 6'5" | 252 | Columbia | | |
| Staroba, Paul WR | 72Cle 73GB | | 6'3" | 204 | Michigan | | 6 |
| Staubach, Roger (The Dodger) QB | 69-79Dal | 12 | 6'2" | 198 | Navy | | 120 |
| Steele, Robert WR | 78Dal 79Min | | 6'4" | 196 | North Alabama | | |
| Stegent, Larry HB | 71StL 72SJ | | 6'1" | 200 | Texas A&M | | |
| Stein, Bob LB-DE | 69KC-A 70-72KC 73-74LA 75SD 75Min 76JJ | | 6'2" | 235 | Minnesota | 2 | |
| Steinfort, Fred K | 76Oak 77-78Atl 79-81Den 82Buf | 5 | 5'11" | 180 | Boston College | | 304 |
| Stemrick, Greg DB | 75-82Hou 83NO | | 5'11" | 185 | Colorado State | 15 | 6 |
| Stenerud, Jan K | 67-69KC-A 70-79KC 80-83GB 84-85Min | 5 | 6'2" | 188 | Montana State | | 1699 |
| Stenger, Brian LB | 69-72Pit 73NE | | 6'4" | 226 | Notre Dame | 3 | |
| Stephens, Bruce WR | 78NYJ | | 5'9" | 170 | Columbia | | |
| Steptoe, Jack WR | 78SF 84USFL | | 6'1" | 175 | Utah | | 6 |
| Stevens, Dick OT | 70-74Phi | | 6'4" | 241 | Baylor | | |
| Stevens, Howard WR | 73-74NO 75-77Bal | 23 | 5'5" | 167 | Louisville | | 24 |
| Stevenson, Ricky DB | 70Cle | | 5'11" | 188 | Arizona | | |
| Stewart, Jimmy DB | 77NO 78KJ 79Det 80LJ | | 5'11" | 190 | Tulsa | | |
| Stewart, Joe WR | 78-79Oak | | 5'11" | 180 | Missouri | | |
| Stewart, Steve LB | 78Atl 79GB | | 6'2" | 219 | Minnesota | | |
| Stewart, Wayne TE | 69NY-A 70-72NYJ 74SD | 2 | 6'7" | 214 | California | | 12 |
| Stidham, Howard LB | 77SF | | 6'2" | 214 | Tennessee Tech | | |
| Stienke, Jim DB | 73Cle 74-77NYG 78Atl | | 5'11" | 183 | SW Texas State | 4 | 6 |
| Stillwell, Roger DT-DE | 75-77Chi | | 6'5" | 259 | Stanford | | |
| Stincic, Tom LB | 69-71Dal 72NO | | 6'2" | 229 | Michigan | 1 | |
| Stingley, Darryl WR | 73-77NE 78XJ 1978- Paralyzed in game | 2 | 6' | 194 | Purdue | | 96 |
| Stokes, Tim OT | 74LA 75-77Was 78-80GB 81NYG 81-82GB | | 6'5" | 252 | Oregon | | |
| Stolberg, Eric WR | 71NE | | 6'2" | 180 | Indiana | | |
| Stone, Ken DB-WR | 72Buf 73-75Was 76TB 77-80StL | | 6'1" | 180 | Vanderbilt | 27 | 6 |
| Story, Bill OT | 75KC | | 6'3" | 245 | Southern Illinois | | |
| Stowe, Otto WR | 71-72Mia 73Dal 74Den | 2 | 6'2" | 188 | Iowa State | | 12 |
| Strachan, Mike HB | 75-80NO | 2 | 6' | 199 | Iowa State | | 84 |
| Strada, John TE | 74KC | | 6'3" | 230 | William Jewell | | |
| Strayhorn, Les HB | 73-74Dal | | 5'10" | 205 | East Carolina | | 6 |
| Stringer, Art LB | 77-81Hou | | 6'1" | 223 | Ball State | 4 | |
| Stringert, Hal DB | 75-80SD | | 5'11" | 185 | Hawaii | 8 | |
| Strong, Jim HB-FB | 70SF 71-72NO | 2 | 6'1" | 204 | Houston | | 18 |
| Stroud, Morris TE | 69KC-A 70-74KC | 2 | 6'10" | 250 | Clark Atlanta | | 42 |
| Strozier, Art TE | 70-71SD | | 6'2" | 220 | Kansas State | | |
| Stuckey, Henry DB | 73-74Mia 75-76NYG | | 6'1" | 180 | Missouri | 2 | |
| Studdard, Vern WR | 71NYJ | | 5'11" | 175 | Mississippi | | |
| Stukes, Charlie DB | 67-72Bal 73-74LA 75KJ | | 6'3" | 212 | Md. Eastern Shore | 32 | 6 |
| Sturt, Fred OG | 74Was 76-78NE 78-81NO | | 6'4" | 255 | Bowling Green | | |
| Suggs, Shafer DB | 76-80NYJ 80Cin 81CFL 83USFL | | 6'1" | 200 | Ball State | 7 | 6 |
| Sullivan, Dave WR | 73-74Cle | | 5'11" | 185 | Virginia | | |
| Sullivan, Gerry C-OT-OG | 74-81Cle 84-85USFL | | 6'4" | 250 | Illinois | | |
| Sullivan, Jim DT-DE | 70Atl | | 6'4" | 240 | Lincoln (Mo.) | | |
| Sullivan, John LB | 79-80NYJ | | 6'1" | 223 | Illinois | | |
| Sullivan, Pat QB | 72-75Atl | 1 | 6' | 200 | Auburn | | |
| Sullivan, Tom (Silky) HB-FB | 72-77Phi 78Cle | 23 | 6' | 190 | Miami (Fla.) | | 132 |
| Sumler, Tony DB | 78Det | | 5'10" | 185 | Wichita State | | |
| Summerell, Carl QB | 74-75NYG | 1 | 6'4" | 208 | East Carolina | | |
| Summers, Freddie DB | 69-71Cle | | 6'1" | 180 | Wake Forest | | |
| Sumers, Wilbur K | 77Det | 4 | 6'4" | 220 | Louisville | | |
| Sumner, Walt DB | 69-74Cle | | 6'1" | 188 | Florida State | 15 | 6 |

| Use Name (Nickname) - Positions | Team by Year | See Section | Hgt. | Wgt. | College | Int | Pts |
|---|---|---|---|---|---|---|---|
| Sutherland, Doug DT-OG-DE | 70NO 71-80Min 81Sea | | 6'3" | 250 | Wis.-Superior | | |
| Sutton, Mitch DT | 74-75Phi | | 6'4" | 260 | Kansas | | |
| Swann, Lynn WR | 74-82Pit | 23 | 6' | 180 | Southern Calif. | | 318 |
| Sweeney, Steve WR | 73Oak | | 6'3" | 205 | California | | |
| Sweet, Joe WR | 72-73LA 74NE 75SD | 2 | 6'2" | 196 | Tennessee State | | 8 |
| Swenson, Bob LB | 75-79Den 80BA 81-83Den 84KJ | | 6'3" | 222 | California | 11 | 6 |
| Swift, Doug LB | 70-75Mia | | 6'3" | 228 | Amherst | 5 | |
| Swinney, Clovis DT | 70NO 71NYJ | | 6'3" | 240 | Arkansas State | | |
| Switzer, Marvin DB | 78Buf | | 6' | 192 | Kansas State | | |
| Sykes, Al WR | 71NE | | 6'3" | 180 | Florida A&M | | |
| Sykes, John HB | 72SD | | 5'11" | 195 | Morgan State | | |
| Sylvester, Steve C-OG-OT | 75-81Oak 82-83Raid | | 6'4" | 261 | Notre Dame | | |
| Szaro, Richie K | 75-78NO 79NYJ | 5 | 5'11" | 204 | Harvard | | 193 |
| Taffoni, Joe OT-OG | 67-70Cle 72-73NYG | | 6'3" | 251 | West Virginia, Tenn.-Martin | | |
| Tagge, Jerry QB | 72-74GB | 12 | 6'2" | 218 | Nebraska | | 18 |
| Talbert, Diron DT-DE | 67-70LA 71-80Was | | 6'5" | 252 | Texas | | |
| Tannen, Steve DB | 70-74NYJ 75SJ | | 6'1" | 194 | Florida | 12 | 6 |
| Tanner, John LB | 71SD 73-74NE | | 6'4" | 231 | Tennessee Tech | | 6 |
| Tarver, John FB | 72-74NE 75Phi | 2 | 6'3" | 224 | Colorado | | 48 |
| Tatarek, Bob DT | 68-69BufA 70-72Buf 72Det | | 6'4" | 260 | Miami (Fla.) | | |
| Tate, Frank LB | 75SD 76JJ | | 6'3" | 225 | N. Car. Central | | |
| Tate, John LB | 76NYG | | 6'2" | 230 | Jackson State | | |
| Tatum, Jack DB | 71-79Oak 80Hou | | 5'10" | 203 | Ohio State | 37 | 6 |
| Taylor, Altie HB | 69-75Det 76Hou | 23 | 5'10" | 199 | Utah State | | 180 |
| Taylor, Bruce DB | 70-77SF | 3 | 6' | 184 | Boston U. | 18 | 12 |
| Taylor, Charley WR-HB-OE | 64-75Was 76SJ 77Was | 2 | 6'3" | 210 | Arizona State | | 540 |
| Taylor, Clifton HB | 74,76GB | 3 | 6' | 198 | Memphis State | | 12 |
| Taylor, David OT | 73-77Bal 78NJ 79Bal | | 6'4" | 260 | Catawba | | |
| Taylor, Ed DB | 75-79NYJ 79-81Mia 83USFL | | 6' | 174 | Memphis State | 8 | |
| Taylor, Jesse HB | 72SD | 3 | 6' | 200 | Cincinnati | | 6 |
| Taylor, Joe DB | 67-74Chi | | 6'2" | 189 | N. Carolina A&T | 15 | |
| Taylor, Mike OT | 68-69Pit 69-70NO 71Was 73StL | | 6'4" | 247 | Southern Calif. | | |
| Taylor, Mike LB | 72-73NYJ 74WFL | | 6'1" | 230 | Michigan | 1 | |
| Taylor, Otis WR-FL-OE | 65-69KC-A 70-75KC | 2 | 6'2" | 215 | Prairie View | | 360 |
| Taylor, Steve DB | 76KC | | 6'3" | 204 | Kansas | | |
| Taylor, Willie WR | 78GB | | 6'1" | 179 | Pittsburgh | | |
| Tearry, Larry C | 78-79Det | | 6'3" | 260 | Wake Forest | | |
| Teel, Jim LB | 73Det | | 6'3" | 225 | Purdue | | |
| Teerlinck, John DT | 74-75SD 76KJ | | 6'5" | 248 | Western Illinois | | |
| Ten Napel, Garth LB | 76-77Det 78Atl 79AA | | 6'1" | 213 | Texas A&M | | |
| Terry, Nat DB | 78Pit 78Det | | 5'11" | 165 | Florida State | | |
| Testerman, Don FB | 76-78Sea 79KJ 80Mia | 2 | 6'2" | 231 | Clemson | | 42 |
| Thaxton, Jim TE-WR | 73-74SD 74Cle 76-77NO 78StL | 2 | 6'2" | 241 | Tennessee State | 1 | 30 |
| Thomas, Bill FB | 72Dal 73Hou 74KC | 3 | 6'2" | 225 | Boston College | | |
| Thomas, Bob HB | 71-72LA 73-74SD | 2 | 5'10" | 201 | Arizona State | | 24 |
| Thomas, Charlie HB | 75KC | | 5'9" | 180 | Tennessee State | | |
| Thomas, Donnie LB | 76NE | | 6'2" | 245 | Indiana | | |
| Thomas, Duane HB-FB | 70-71Dal 72HO 73-74Was | 2 | 6'1" | 215 | West Texas State | | 144 |
| Thomas, Earl WR-TE | 71-73Chi 74-75StL 76Hou | 2 | 6'3" | 219 | Houston | | 90 |
| Thomas, Earlie DB | 70-74NYJ 75Den | | 6'1" | 190 | Colorado State | 7 | 6 |
| Thomas, Emmitt DB | 66-69KC-A 70-78KC | 3 | 6'2" | 192 | Bishop | 58 | 30 |
| Thomas, Ike DB-WR | 71Dal 71-73GB 74-75WFL 75Buf | 3 | 6'2" | 194 | Bishop | 2 | 12 |
| Thomas, Jimmy HB-WR | 69-73SF | 2 | 6'1" | 215 | Texas-Arlington | | 72 |
| Thomas, Joe | HC74Bal | | | | Ohio Northern | | |
| Thomas, J.T. DB | 73-77Pit 78IL 79-81Pit 82Den | | 6'2" | 196 | Florida State | 20 | 12 |
| Thomas, Lee DE | 71-72SD 73Cin 75LJ | | 6'5" | 246 | Jackson State | | |
| Thomas, Mike HB | 75-78Was 79-80SD | 2 | 5'11" | 190 | Nevada-Las Vegas | | 180 |
| Thomas, Pat DB | 76-82LA | | 5'9" | 183 | Texas A&M | 26 | 6 |
| Thomas, Skip (Dr. Death) DB | 72-77Oak | | 6'1" | 205 | Southern Calif. | 17 | 6 |
| Thomas, Speedy WR | 69CinA 70-72Cin 73-74NO | 2 | 6'1" | 174 | Utah | | 54 |
| Thomas, Spencer DB | 75Was | | 6'2" | 185 | Washburn | | |
| Thompson, Billy DB | 69DenA 70-81Den | 3 | 6'1" | 200 | Md. Eastern Shore | 40 | 42 |
| Thompson, Bobby HB | 75-76Det | 23 | 5'11" | 195 | Oklahoma | | 6 |
| Thompson, Dave OT-C-OG | 71-73Det 74-75NO | | 6'4" | 271 | Clemson | | |
| Thompson, James WR | 78NYG | | 6' | 178 | Memphis State | | |
| Thompson, Jesse WR | 78Det 79IL 80Det 81FJ | 2 | 6'1" | 185 | California | | 24 |
| Thompson, Norm DB | 71-76StL 77-79Bal | | 6'1" | 179 | Utah | 33 | 24 |
| Thompson, Ricky WR | 76-77Bal 78-81Was 82StL | 2 | 6' | 176 | Baylor | | 84 |
| Thompson (born Symonds), Rocky HB | 71-73NYG | 23 | 5'11" | 200 | West Texas State | | 18 |
| Thompson, Steve DT-DE | 68-69NY-A 70NYJ 71VR 72-73NYJ 74WFL | | 6'5" | 244 | Washington | | |
| Thompson, Ted LB | 75-84Hou | | 6'1" | 220 | S.M.U. | | 4 |
| Thompson, Tommy HB | 74SD | | 6'1" | 205 | Southern Illinois | | |
| Thompson, Woody FB | 75-77Atl | 2 | 6'1" | 228 | Miami (Fla.) | | 6 |
| Thoms, Art DT-DE-NT | 69OakA 70-75Oak 76KJ 77Phi | | 6'5" | 251 | Syracuse | 2 | 6 |
| Thornbladh, Bob LB | 74KC | | 6'1" | 220 | Michigan | | |
| Threadgill, Bruce DB-QB | 78SF 79-82CFL 84-85USFL | | 6' | 190 | Mississippi State | | |
| Thrower, Jim DB | 70-72Phi 73-74Det 75KJ | | 6'2" | 194 | East Texas State | | |
| Tierney, Leo C | 78Cle 78NYG | | 6'3" | 248 | Georgia Tech | | |
| Tillman, Mike DT | 66Min 67-70NO 71-72Hou 73-76Atl | | 6'5" | 275 | Montana | | |
| Tillman, Andre TE | 75-78Mia 79BL | 2 | 6'5" | 230 | Texas Tech | | 36 |
| Tillman, Faddie DE-DT | 72NO | | 6'5" | 230 | Boise State | | |
| Tillman, Rusty LB | 70-77Was | | 6'2" | 230 | Northern Arizona | | |
| Tinker, Gerald WR | 74-75Atl 75GB 76KJ | 3 | 5'9" | 173 | Kent State | | 18 |
| Tipton, Dave DE-DT | 71-73NYG 74-75SD 75NE 76Sea | | 6'6" | 242 | Stanford | | |
| Tipton, Dave NT-DT | 75NE 75SD 76NE 77CFL 83-85USFL | | 6'1" | 253 | Western Illinois | | |
| Tolbert, Jim DB | 66-69SD-A 70-71SD 72Hou 73-75StL 76SD | | 6'3" | 207 | Lincoln (Mo.) | 10 | |
| Tom, Mel DE | 67-73Phi 73-75Chi | | 6'4" | 247 | Hawaii, San Jose St. | | 2 |
| Toner, Tom LB | 73GB 74BC 75-77GB | | 6'3" | 233 | Idaho State | 4 | 2 |
| Toomay, Pat DE | 70-74Dal 75Buf 76TB 77-79Oak | | 6'4" | 245 | Vanderbilt | 2 | 6 |
| Torkelson, Eric HB-FB | 74-79GB 80LJ 81GB | 2 | 6'2" | 196 | Connecticut | | 54 |
| Torrey, Bob FB | 79NYG 79Mia 80Phi | | 6'4" | 231 | Penn State | | 6 |
| Towle, Steve LB | 75-80Mia 81LJ | | 6'2" | 233 | Kansas | 3 | |
| Townsend, Curtis DB | 78StL | | 6'1" | 229 | Arkansas | | |
| Troup, Bill QB | 74Bal 75Phi 76-79Bal 80GB | 12 | 6'5" | 218 | South Carolina | | 12 |
| Trumpy, Bob TE-WR | 68-69CinA 70-77Cin | 2 | 6'6" | 226 | Illinois, Utah | | 210 |
| Tucker, Bob TE | 70-77NYG 77-80Min | 2 | 6'3" | 230 | Bloomsburg | | 168 |
| Tullis, Walter WR | 78-79GB 83USFL | 2 | 6' | 170 | Delaware State | | 6 |
| Turk, Goodwin LB | 75NYJ 76-78Den | | 6'3" | 230 | Southern U. | 4 | |
| Tumbow, Jesse DT | 78Cle | | 6'7" | 272 | Tenessee | | |
| Turner, Cecil WR | 68-73Chi | 23 | 5'10" | 172 | Cal. Poly.-S.L.O. | | 36 |
| Turner, Clem FB | 69CinA 70-72Den | 2 | 6'1" | 238 | Cincinnati | | 18 |
| Turner, Deacon HB | 78-80Cin | 23 | 5'11" | 211 | San Diego State | | 12 |
| Turner, Jim K | 64-69NY-A 70NYJ 71-79Den | 5 | 6'2" | 206 | Utah State | | 1439 |
| Turner, Robert HB | 78Hou | | 5'11" | 200 | Oklahoma State | | |
| Turner, Rocky WR-DB | 72-73NYJ | | 6' | 195 | Tenn.-Chattanooga | | |

| Use Name (Nickname) - Positions | Team by Year | See Section | Hgt. | Wgt. | College | Int | Pts |
|---|---|---|---|---|---|---|---|
| Turner, Wylie DB | 79-80GB | | 5'10" | 182 | Angelo State | 2 | |
| Twilley, Howard WR | 66-69MiaA 70-76Mia | 2 | 5'10" | 183 | Tulsa | | 138 |
| Tyler, Maurice DB | 72Buf 73-74Den 75SD 76Det 77NYJ 78NYG 80CFL 83-84USFL | | 6' | 189 | Morgan State | 5 | 6 |
| Upchurch, Rick WR | 75-83Den | 23 | 5'10" | 175 | Minnesota | | 210 |
| Uperesa, Tuufuli OG | 71Phi | | 6'3" | 255 | Montana | | |
| Upshaw, Gene OG-OT | 67-69OakA 70-81Oak | | 6'5" | 255 | Texas A&I | | |
| Upshaw, Marv DE-DT | 68-69Cle 70-75KC 76StL | | 6'3" | 253 | Trinity (Texas) | 2 | 6 |
| Vactor, Ted DB | 69-73Was 74JJ 75Chi | 3 | 6' | 185 | Nebraska | 2 | 6 |
| Vanderbundt, Skip LB | 69-77SF 78NO | | 6'3" | 227 | Oregon State | 14 | 18 |
| Van Duyne, Bob OG-OT | 74-80Bal 81-82CFL 83-84USFL | | 6'5" | 243 | Idaho | | |
| Van Dyke, Bruce OG | 66Phi 67-73Pit 74-76GB | | 6'2" | 248 | Missouri | | |
| van Eeghen, Mark FB-HB | 74-81Oak 82-83NE | 2 | 6'2" | 223 | Colgate | | 252 |
| Van Galder, Tim QB | 72StL | 1 | 6'1" | 190 | Iowa State | | |
| Van Heusen, Bill WR-K | 68-69DenA 70-76Den | 2 4 | 6'1" | 200 | Maryland | | 72 |
| Van Horn, Doug OG-OT | 66Det 68-79NYG | | 6'2" | 245 | Ohio State | | |
| Van Note, Jeff C-OG-LB | 69-86Atl | | 6'2" | 248 | Kentucky | | |
| Vanoy, Vern DT | 71NYG 72GB | | 6'3" | 270 | Kansas | | |
| Van Pelt, Brad LB | 73-83NYG 84-85Raid 86Cle | | 6'5" | 235 | Michigan State | 20 | |
| Van Valkenberg, Pete HB | 73Buf 74GB 74Chi | | 6'2" | 194 | Brigham Young | | |
| Van Wagner, James HB | 78NO | | 6' | 202 | Michigan Tech | | |
| Varty, Mike LB | 74Was 75Bal | | 6'1" | 223 | Northwestern | | |
| Vataha, Randy WR | 71-76NE 77GB | 2 | 5'10" | 173 | Stanford | | 138 |
| Vella, John OT | 72-77Oak 78Chest Injury 79Oak 80Min | | 6'4" | 258 | Southern Calif. | | |
| Vermeil, Dick | HC76-82Phi | | | | San Jose State | | |
| Verteteulle, Brian OT | 74SD | | 6'3" | 252 | Idaho State | | |
| Villapiano, Phil LB | 71-79Oak 80-83Buf | | 6'1" | 222 | Bowling Green | 11 | 8 |
| Vincent, Ted DT | 78Cin 79-80SF | | 6'4" | 264 | Wichita State | | |
| Vinyard, Kenny K | 70Atl | 5 | 5'10" | 190 | Texas Tech | | 50 |
| Vitali, Mark QB | 77KC | | 6'5" | 209 | Purdue | | |
| Voight, Mike HB | 77Hou 78JJ | | 6' | 214 | North Carolina | | |
| Voigt, Stu TE | 70-80Min | 2 | 6'1" | 223 | Wisconsin | | 108 |
| Volk, Rick DB | 67-75Bal 76NYG 77-78Mia | 3 | 6'3" | 195 | Michigan | 38 | 6 |
| Waddell, Charles TE | 77TB | | 6'5" | 235 | North Carolina | | |
| Wade, Charlie WR | 74Chi 75GB 77KC | 2 | 5'10" | 163 | Tennessee State | | 6 |
| Wafer, Carl DT | 74NYG | | 6'3" | 250 | Tennessee State | | |
| Wages, Harmon FB-HB | 69-71Atl 72KJ 73Atl | 2 | 6'1" | 214 | Florida | | 60 |
| Wagner, Mike DB | 71-80Pit | | 6'1" | 200 | Western Illinois | 36 | 6 |
| Wagner, Steve DB | 76-79GB 80Phi 81SJ | | 6'2" | 206 | Wisconsin | | |
| Walden, Bobby K | 64-67Min 68-77Pit | 4 | 6' | 192 | Georgia | | |
| Walik, Billy WR | 70-72Phi | 3 | 5'11" | 180 | Villanova | | 6 |
| Walker, Chuck DT-DE | 64-72StL 72-75Atl | | 6'2" | 249 | Duke | 1 | |
| Walker, Cleo LB-C | 70GB 71Atl | | 6'3" | 220 | Louisville | | |
| Walker, Donnie DB | 73-74Buf 75NYJ | 3 | 6'1" | 182 | Central St.-Ohio | 1 | |
| Walker, Elliott HB | 78SF | | 5'11" | 193 | Pittsburgh | | |
| Walker, Glen K | 77-78LA 83USFL | 4 | 6'1" | 210 | Southern Calif. | | |
| Walker, Louie LB | 74Dal | | 6'1" | 216 | Colorado State | | |
| Walker, Mike K | 73NE | 5 | 6' | 190 | none | | 21 |
| Walker, Mike DE | 71NO | | 6'4" | 235 | Tulane | | |
| Walker, Randy K | 74GB 75JJ | 4 | 5'10" | 177 | Northwestern La. | | |
| Wallace, Bob TE-WR | 68-72Chi | 2 | 6'3" | 213 | Texas-El Paso | | 54 |
| Wallace, Jackie DB | 74Min 75-76Bal 77-79LA | 3 | 6'3" | 197 | Arizona | 10 | 12 |
| Wallace, Rodney OG-OT | 71-73Dal 74JJ | | 6'5" | 255 | New Mexico | | |
| Wallace, Roger WR | 76NYG | | 5'11" | 180 | Bowling Green | | |
| Walsh, Ward HB | 71-72Hou 72GB | 2 | 6' | 213 | Colorado | | 12 |
| Walters, Rod OG-OT | 76KC 77JJ 78-80KC 80Mia 80Det 84-85USFL | | 6'3" | 258 | Iowa | | |
| Walters, Stan OT | 72-74Cin 75-83Phi | | 6'6" | 271 | Syracuse | | |
| Walton, Bruce OT-OG-C | 73-75Dal | | 6'6" | 251 | U.C.L.A. | | |
| Walton, Chuck OG | 67-74Det | | 6'3" | 253 | Iowa State | | |
| Walton, John QB | 75WFL 76-79Phi 83-85USFL | 1 | 6'2" | 210 | Elizabeth City St. | | |
| Walton, Larry WR | 69-74Det 75KJ 76Det 78Buf | 2 | 6' | 181 | Arizona State | | 168 |
| Walton, Wayne OT-OG | 71NYG 73-74KC | | 6'5" | 252 | Abilene Christian | | |
| Ward, John OG-C-DE | 70-73Min 74LJ 75Min 76TB 76Chi | | 6'4" | 258 | Oklahoma State | | |
| Warfield, Paul WR | 64-69Cle 70-74Mia 75WFL 76-77Cle | 2 | 6' | 188 | Ohio State | | 516 |
| Washington, Dave LB-TE | 70-71Den 72-74Buf 75-77SF | | 6'5" | 224 | Alcorn State | 6 | 20 |
| Washington, Eric DB | 72-73StL | | 6'2" | 190 | Texas-El Paso | | |
| Washington, Gene WR | 67-72Min 73Den | 2 | 6'3" | 212 | Michigan State | | 156 |
| Washington, Gene WR | 69-77SF 78FJ 79Det | 2 | 6'1" | 185 | Stanford | | 360 |
| Washington, Gene WR | 79NYG | | 5'9" | 170 | Georgia | | |
| Washington, Harry WR | 78Min 79Chi | | 6' | 180 | Colorado State | | |
| Washington, Joe HB | 73Atl | | 5'9" | 180 | Illinois State | | |
| Washington, Mark DB | 70-78Dal 79NE | | 5'10" | 187 | Morgan State | 13 | 8 |
| Washington, Russ OT | 68-69SD-A 70-82SD | | 6'7" | 290 | Missouri | | |
| Washington, Ted LB | 73-82Hou | | 6'1" | 244 | Miss. Valley St. | | |
| Washington, Vic HB-DB-WR | 71-73SF 74Hou 75-76Buf | 23 | 5'10" | 196 | Wyoming | | 132 |
| Waters, Charlie DB | 70-78Dal 79KJ 80-81Dal | | 6'1" | 195 | Clemson | 41 | 18 |
| Watkins, Larry FB-HB | 69Det 70-72Phi 73-74Buf 75-77NYG | 2 | 6'2" | 226 | Alcorn State | | 78 |
| Watson, Allen K | 70Pit | 5 | 5'10" | 165 | Newport-Wales | | 22 |
| Watson, John OT-OG-C | 71-76SF 77-79NO | | 6'4" | 246 | Oklahoma | | |
| Watson, Mike OT | 77NO 78KJ 79JJ | | 6'6" | 272 | Miami-Ohio | | |
| Watson, Pete TE | 72Cin | | 6'1" | 210 | Tufts | | |
| Watts, Robert LB | 78Oak | | 6'3" | 218 | Boston College | | |
| Weatherly, Jim C | 76Atl | | 6'3" | 245 | none | | |
| Weathers, Carl LB | 70-71Oak | | 6'2" | 220 | San Diego State | | |
| Weatherspoon, Cephus WR | 72NO | | 6'1" | 182 | Fort Lewis | | |
| Weaver, Charlie LB | 71-80Det 81Was | | 6'2" | 223 | Southern Calif. | 15 | |
| Weaver, Gary LB | 73-74Oak 75-79GB | | 6'1" | 225 | Fresno State | | |
| Weaver, Herman K | 70-76Det 77-80Sea 83USFL | 4 | 6'4" | 210 | Tennessee | | |
| Webb, Jimmy DT-DE | 75-80SF 81SD | | 6'5" | 246 | Mississippi State | | |
| Webster, Cornell DB | 77-80Sea | | 6' | 180 | Tulsa | 8 | 6 |
| Webster, George LB | 67-69HouA 70-72Hou 72-73Pit 74-76NE | | 6'4" | 225 | Michigan State | 5 | |
| Webster, Tim K | 71GB | 5 | 6' | 195 | Arkansas | | 26 |
| Weese, Norris QK | 76-79Den | 12 4 | 6'1" | 195 | Mississippi | | 30 |
| Weger, Mike DB | 67-73Det 74JJ 75Det 76-77Hou | | 6'2" | 197 | Bowling Green | 17 | 12 |
| Wehrli, Roger DB | 69-82StL | 3 | 6'1" | 193 | Missouri | 40 | 19 |
| Welch, Claxton HB-FB | 69-71Dal 73NE | 2 | 5'11" | 202 | Oregon | | 12 |
| Wellman, Mike C | 79-80GB | | 6'3" | 253 | Kansas | | |
| Wells, Mike QB | 75-76NYG 77Cin | | 6'5" | 225 | Illinois | | |
| Wells, Terry HB | 74Hou 75GB | 2 | 5'11" | 195 | Southern Miss. | | |
| Wender, Jack HB | 77TB | | 6' | 210 | Fresno State | | |
| Werner, Clyde LB | 70KC 71KJ 72-74KC 75FJ 76KC | | 6'4" | 227 | Washington | 2 | |
| Wesson, Ricky DB | 77KC | | 5'9" | 163 | S.M.U. | | |
| West, Bill DB | 72Den | | 5'10" | 185 | Tennessee State | | |
| West, Bob WR | 72-73KC 74SF | 2 | 6'4" | 218 | San Diego State | | 18 |
| West, Charlie DB | 68-73Min 74-77Det 78-79Den | 3 | 6'1" | 194 | Texas-El Paso | 15 | 6 |
| Westbrook, Don WR | 77-81NE | 2 | 5'10" | 185 | Nebraska | | 18 |

| Use Name (Nickname) - Positions | Team by Year | See Section | Hgt. | Wgt. | College | Int | Pts |
|---|---|---|---|---|---|---|---|
| Westbrooks, Greg LB | 75-77NO 78StL 78-79Oak 79LA | | 6'2" | 217 | Colorado | 1 | |
| Wheeler, Wayne WR | 74Chi | | 6'2" | 180 | Alabama | | 6 |
| Whitaker, Creston WR | 72NO | | 6'2" | 187 | North Texas | | |
| White, Charlie HB-FB | 77NYJ 78TB | 2 | 6' | 222 | Bethune-Cookman | | 12 |
| White, Daryl OG | 74Det | | 6'3" | 250 | Nebraska | | |
| White, Dwight DE | 71-80Pit | | 6'4" | 253 | East Texas State | 4 | 4 |
| White, Ed OG-OT | 69-77Min 78-85SD | | 6'2" | 270 | California | | |
| White, James (Duck) DT-NT | 76-83Min | | 6'3" | 265 | Oklahoma State | 1 | |
| White, Jan TE | 71-72Buf | 2 | 6'2" | 216 | Ohio State | | 12 |
| White, Jeff K | 73NE | 5 | 5'11" | 170 | Texas-El Paso | | 63 |
| White, Jeris DB | 74-76Mia 77-79TB 80-82Was | | 5'11" | 183 | Hawaii | 19 | |
| White, Jim DE | 72NE 74-75Hou 76Sea 76Den | | 6'3" | 257 | Colorado State | | |
| White, Lee FB | 68-69NY-A 70NYJ 72LA 72SD | 2 | 6'4" | 238 | Weber State | | 6 |
| White, Marsh FB | 75-76NYG 77BN | 2 | 6'2" | 220 | Arkansas | | 12 |
| White, Paul HB | 70-71StL | | 6' | 200 | Texas-El Paso | | |
| White, Ray LB | 71-72SD 73JJ 75-76StL 77KJ | | 6'1" | 227 | Syracuse | 2 | 2 |
| White, Sherman DE | 72-75Cin 76-83Buf | | 6'5" | 251 | California | 2 | 2 |
| White, Stan LB | 72-79Bal 80-82Det 83-84USFL | | 6'1" | 224 | Ohio State | 34 | 12 |
| White, Walter TE | 75-79KC | 2 | 6'3" | 216 | Maryland | | 96 |
| Whitlach, Blake LB | 78NYJ | | 6'1" | 233 | Louisiana State | | |
| Whittington, C.L. DB | 74-76Hou 77JJ 78Hou 79JJ | | 6'1" | 200 | Prairie View | 7 | 6 |
| Wickert, Tom OT-OG | 74Mia 75-76NO 77Det 77KC | | 6'4" | 248 | Washington State | | |
| Wicks, Bob WR | 72StL 74NO | | 6'3" | 200 | Utah State | | |
| Widby, Ron K | 68-71Dal 72-73BB 74KJ 1967-68 — Played in A.B.A. | 4 | 6'4" | 212 | Tennessee | | |
| Wilkerson, Doug OG | 70Hou 71-84SD | | 6'2" | 256 | N. Car. Central | | |
| Wilkinson, Bud | HC78-79StL | | | | Minnesota | | |
| Williams, Charles DB | 78Phi | | 6'1" | 180 | Jackson State | | |
| Williams, Clarence (Sweeney) DE | 70-77GB | | 6'5" | 255 | Prairie View | 1 | 6 |
| Williams, Clarence HB-FB | 77-81SD | 23 | 5'9" | 194 | South Carolina | | 114 |
| Williams, Dave WR-FL | 67-71StL 72-73SD 73Pit | 2 | 6'2" | 205 | Washington | | 150 |
| Williams, Dave FB-HB | 77-78SF 79-81Chi | 23 | 6'2" | 210 | Colorado | | 66 |
| Williams, Del OG-C | 67-73NO | | 6'2" | 242 | Florida State | | |
| Williams, Delvin HB | 74-77SF 78-80Mia 81GB | 2 | 6' | 197 | Kansas | | 234 |
| Williams, Donnie WR | 70LA | | 6'3" | 210 | Prairie View | | |
| Williams, Ed FB | 74-75Cin 76-77TB | 2 | 6'2" | 245 | Langston | | 54 |
| Williams, Gerard DB | 76-78Was 79SF 80StL 80SF | | 6'1" | 184 | Langston | 13 | 6 |
| Williams, Jeff OG-OT | 77LA 78-80Was 81SD 82Chi | | 6'4" | 258 | Rhode Island | | |
| Williams, Joe HB | 71Dal 72NO | 2 | 6' | 194 | Wyoming | | 6 |
| Williams, John OT-OG-DE | 68-71Bal 72-79LA | | 6'3" | 257 | Minnesota | | |
| Williams, Lawrence WR | 76-77KC 77Cle | 3 | 5'10" | 174 | Texas Tech | | 6 |
| Williams, Mike DB | 75-82SD 83LA | | 5'10" | 181 | Louisiana State | 24 | |
| Williams, Perry FB | 69-73GB 74Chi | 2 | 6'2" | 220 | Purdue | | 12 |
| Williams, Richard WR | 72NO | | 5'11" | 170 | Abilene Christian | | |
| Williams, Roger DB-WR | 71-72LA | | 5'10" | 180 | Grambling | | |
| Williams, Sam DB | 74-75SD 76Hou | | 6'2" | 190 | California | 2 | |
| Williams, Steve DE | 74Bal | | 6'6" | 260 | Western Carolina | | |
| Williams, Tom DT | 70-71SD | | 6'4" | 250 | Cal.-Davis | | |
| Willingham, Larry DB | 71-72StL | | 6'1" | 190 | Auburn | | |
| Willis, Fred FB | 71-72Cin 72-76Hou 77JJ | 2 | 6' | 209 | Boston College | | 138 |
| Willis, Larry DB | 73Was | | 5'11" | 170 | Texas-El Paso | | |
| Willis, Leonard WR | 76Min 77NO 77-79Buf 83-85USFL | 3 | 5'11" | 183 | Ohio State | | |
| Wilson, Joe HB | 73Cin 74NE 75NJ | 2 | 5'10" | 210 | Holy Cross | | |
| Wilson, Mike OG-OT | 69CinA 70Cin 71Buf 75KC | | 6'1" | 243 | Dayton | | |
| Wilson, Nemiah DB | 65-67DenA 68-69OakA 70-74Oak 75Chi | | 6' | 166 | Grambling | 27 | 24 |
| Winans, Jeff DE-OG-OT-DT | 73-75Buf 76Oak 76NO 77-78TB 80JJ | | 6'5" | 263 | Southern Calif. | | |
| Windauer, Bill DT-NT | 73-74Bal 75Mia 75BYG 76Atl 77Mia | | 6'3" | 248 | Iowa | | |
| Windsor, Bob TE | 67-71SF 72-75NE | 2 | 6'4" | 227 | Kentucky | | 90 |
| Winfield, Vern OG | 72-73Phi | | 6'2" | 248 | Minnesota | | |
| Winfrey, Carl LB | 71Min 72Pit | | 6' | 230 | Wisconsin | | |
| Winfrey, Stan FB | 75-76Mia 77TB 79Mia 79Buf | 2 | 5'11" | 223 | Arkansas State | | 12 |
| Winkel, Bob DT-DE | 79-80NYJ | | 6'4" | 251 | Kentucky | | |
| Winslow, Doug WR | 73NO 74-75WFL 76Was | | 5'11" | 181 | Drake | | |
| Winther, Wimpy C | 71GB 72NO | | 6'3" | 260 | Mississippi | | |
| Wirgowski, Dennis DE-DT | 70Bos 71-72NE 73Phi | | 6'5" | 253 | Purdue | 1 | |
| Wise, Phil DB | 71-76NYJ 77-79Min | | 6' | 192 | Nebraska-Omaha | 6 | 6 |
| Withrow, Phil C | 70SD 71-73GB 74StL | | 6' | 240 | Kentucky | | |
| Wittum, Tom K | 73-77SF | 4 | 6'1" | 191 | Northern Illinois | | 5 |
| Wocjik, Greg DT | 71LA 72-73SD 74WFL 75SD | | 6'6" | 268 | Southern Calif. | | |
| Wolf, Jim DE | 74Pit 76KC | | 6'3" | 240 | Prairie View | | |
| Woodall, Al QB | 69NY-A 70-71NYJ 72JJ 73-74NYJ 75KJ | 12 | 6'5" | 202 | Duke | | |
| Woodcock, John DE-DT-LB | 76-78Det 79XJ 80Det 81-82SD | | 6'3" | 246 | New Mexico, Hawaii | | |
| Woods, Don HB-FB | 74-80SD 80SF | 2 | 6'1" | 209 | New Mexico | | 126 |
| Woods, Larry DT | 71-72Det 73Mia 74-75NYJ 76Sea | | 6'6" | 265 | Tennessee State | | |
| Woods, Mike LB | 78-81Bal | | 6'2" | 233 | Cincinnati | 1 | |
| Woods, Robert OT-OG | 73-77NYJ 77-80NO 81Was 83-85USFL | | 6'3" | 258 | Tennessee State | | |
| Woods, Robert WR | 78Hou 79Det | | 5'7" | 170 | Grambling | | 12 |
| Woolsey, Roland DB | 75Dal 76Sea 77Cle 78StL | 3 | 6'1" | 182 | Boise State | 5 | |
| Word, Roscoe DB | 74-76NYJ 76Buf 76TB | 3 | 5'11" | 170 | Jackson State | 3 | |
| Wortman, Keith OT-OG | 72-75GB 76-81StL | | 6'2" | 259 | Nebraska | | |
| Wright, Elmo WR | 71-74KC 75Hou 75NE | 2 | 6' | 190 | Houston | | 42 |
| Wright, George DT | 70-71Bal 72Cle | | 6'3" | 262 | Sam Houston St. | | |
| Wright, Jeff DB | 71-77Min | | 5'11" | 190 | Minnesota | 11 | |
| Wright, Keith WR | 78-80Cle | 23 | 5'10" | 174 | Memphis State | | 18 |
| Wright, Nate DB | 69Atl 69-70StL 71-80Min | | 5'11" | 180 | San Diego State | 35 | 6 |
| Wright, Rayfield OT-TE | 67-79Dal | | 6'7" | 254 | Ft. Valley State | | 6 |
| Wyatt, Alvin DB | 70Oak 71-72Buf 73Hou 74-75WFL | 3 | 5'10" | 183 | Bethune-Cookman | 5 | 18 |
| Wyatt, Doug DB | 70-72NO 73-74Det | | 6'1" | 195 | Tulsa | 8 | 12 |
| Wyche, Sam QB | 68-69CinA 70Cin 71-72Was 74Det 76StL 76Buf HC84-91Cin HC92-95TB | 12 | 6'4" | 214 | Furman | | 18 |
| Wycinski, Craig OG | 72Cle | | 6'3" | 243 | Michigan | | |
| Wynn, Will DB | 73-76Phi 77Was | | 6'4" | 244 | Tennessee State | | 12 |
| Wysocki, Pete LB | 75-80Was | | 6'2" | 225 | Western Michigan | 1 | |
| Yanchar, Bill DT | 70Cle | | 6'3" | 250 | Purdue | | |
| Yankowski, Ron DE | 71-80StL | | 6'5" | 244 | Kansas State | | 6 |
| Yarbrough, Jim OT | 69-77Det 78FJ | | 6'6" | 261 | Florida | | |
| Yary, Ron OT | 68-81Min 82LA | | 6'6" | 256 | Southern Calif. | | |
| Yeates, Jeff DE-DT-OG | 74-76Buf 76-84Atl | | 6'3" | 249 | Boston College | 1 | |
| Yepremian, Garo K | 66-67Det 70-78Mia 79NO 80-81TB | 5 | 5'8" | 172 | none | | 1074 |
| Young, Adrian LB | 68-72Phi 72Det 73Chi | | 6'1" | 230 | Southern Calif. | | |
| Young, Al WR | 71-72Pit 73IL | | 6'1" | 195 | S. Carolina State | | |
| Young, Bob OG-DT | 66-69DenA 70Den 71Hou 72-79StL 80Hou 81NO | | 6'2" | 269 | Texas, Howard Payne, SW Texas State | | |
| Young, Charley HB | 74-76Dal 77KJ | 2 | 6'1" | 213 | N. Carolina State | | 24 |
| Young, Charle TE | 73-76Phi 77-79LA 80-82SF 83-85Sea | 2 | 6'4" | 235 | Southern Calif. | | 168 |
| Young, James DE | 77-79Hou | | 6'2" | 260 | Texas Southern | | 4 |
| Young, Randy OT | 76TB | | 6'5" | 250 | Iowa State | | |
| Young, Rickey HB | 75-77SD 78-83Min | 2 | 6'2" | 196 | Jackson State | | 234 |

| Use Name (Nickname)-Positions | Team by Year | See Section | Hgt. | Wgt. | College | Int | Pts |
|---|---|---|---|---|---|---|---|
| Young, Steve OT | 76TB 77Mia 78NJ 79GB | | 6'8" | 271 | Colorado | | |
| Young, Wilbur DE-DT | 71-77KC 78-80SD 81Was 81-82SD 84-85USFL | | 6'6" | 289 | William Penn | 1 | 14 |
| Young, Willie (Sugar Bear) OT | 66-75NYG | | 6' | 259 | Grambling | | |
| Young, Willie OT | 71-72Buf 73Mia | | 6'4" | 270 | Alcorn State | | 4 |
| Youngblood, Jack DE | 71-84LA | | 6'4" | 247 | Florida | | |
| Youngblood, Jim LB | 73-84LA | | 6'3" | 235 | Tennessee Tech | 14 | 30 |
| Zabel, Steve LB-TE | 70-74Phi 75-78NE 79Bal | 2 | 6'4" | 233 | Oklahoma | 6 | 19 |
| Zanders, Emanuel OG | 74-80NO 81Chi | | 6'1" | 251 | Jackson State | | |

| Use Name (Nickname)-Positions | Team by Year | See Section | Hgt. | Wgt. | College | Int | Pts |
|---|---|---|---|---|---|---|---|
| Zapalas, Bill LB-DE | 71-73NYJ | | 6'4" | 225 | Texas | | |
| Zaunbrechner, Godfrey C | 71-73Min | | 6'4" | 238 | Louisiana State | | |
| Zelencik, Connie C-OG | 77Buf 78JJ 79KJ | | 6'4" | 245 | Purdue | | |
| Zeno, Coleman WR | 71NYG | | 6'4" | 210 | Grambling | | |
| Zimmerman, Don WR | 73-76Phi 76GB | 2 | 6'3" | 195 | Northeast La. | | 30 |
| Zotko, Mickey HB | 71-74Det 74NYG | 3 | 6'3" | 195 | Auburn | | 1 |
| Zook, John DE | 69-75Atl 76-79StL | | 6'5" | 248 | Kansas | 4 | 8 |

Lifetime Statistics- 1970- 1979 Players   Section 1 — PASSING
(All men with 25 or more passing attempts)

| Name | Years | Att. | Comp. | Comp. Pct. | Yards | Yds./ Att. | TD | Int. | Pct. Int. |
|---|---|---|---|---|---|---|---|---|---|
| Tony Adams | 75-78,87 | 408 | 212 | 52.0 | 2733 | 6.7 | 12 | 27 | 6.6 |
| Ken Anderson | 71-84 | 4475 | 2654 | 59.3 | 32838 | 7.3 | 197 | 160 | 3.6 |
| Rick Arrington | 70-72 | 204 | 97 | 47.5 | 950 | 4.7 | 3 | 9 | 4.4 |
| Bob Avellini | 75-84 | 1110 | 560 | 50.5 | 7111 | 6.4 | 33 | 69 | 6.2 |
| Bob Berry | 65-76 | 1173 | 661 | 56.4 | 9197 | 7.8 | 64 | 64 | 5.5 |
| Jeb Blount | 77 | 89 | 37 | 41.6 | 522 | 5.9 | 0 | 7 | 7.9 |
| Mike Boryla | 74-76,78 | 519 | 272 | 52.4 | 2838 | 5.5 | 20 | 29 | 5.6 |
| Terry Bradshaw | 70-83 | 3901 | 2105 | 54.0 | 27989 | 7.2 | 212 | 210 | 5.4 |
| Marlin Briscoe | 68-76 | 233 | 97 | 41.6 | 1697 | 7.3 | 14 | 14 | 6.0 |
| Carlos Brown | 75-76 | 78 | 29 | 37.2 | 396 | 5.1 | 3 | 6 | 7.7 |
| Scott Bull | 76-78 | 193 | 76 | 39.4 | 992 | 5.1 | 3 | 17 | 8.8 |
| Virgil Carter | 68-72,75-76 | 785 | 425 | 54.1 | 5063 | 6.4 | 29 | 31 | 3.9 |
| Larry Cipa | 74-75 | 92 | 34 | 37.0 | 424 | 4.6 | 1 | 3 | 3.3 |
| Wayne Clark | 70,72-75 | 120 | 52 | 43.3 | 745 | 6.2 | 0 | 14 | 11.7 |
| Will Cureton | 75 | 32 | 10 | 31.3 | 95 | 3.0 | 1 | 1 | 3.1 |
| Bob Davis | 67-73 | 324 | 137 | 42.3 | 1553 | 4.8 | 14 | 23 | 7.1 |
| Randy Dean | 77-79 | 65 | 30 | 46.2 | 279 | 4.3 | 1 | 5 | 7.7 |
| Jim Del Gaizo | 72-75 | 103 | 44 | 32.7 | 648 | 6.3 | 4 | 10 | 9.7 |
| Bill Demory | 73-74 | 39 | 12 | 30.8 | 159 | 4.1 | 2 | 8 | 20.5 |
| Lynn Dickey | 71-77,79-85 | 3125 | 1747 | 55.9 | 23322 | 7.5 | 141 | 179 | 5.7 |
| Parnell Dickinson | 76-77 | 39 | 15 | 38.5 | 210 | 5.4 | 1 | 5 | 12.8 |
| Marty Domres | 69-77 | 809 | 399 | 49.3 | 4904 | 6.1 | 27 | 50 | 6.2 |
| Bobby Douglass | 69-77 | 1178 | 507 | 43.0 | 6493 | 5.5 | 36 | 64 | 5.4 |
| Brian Dowling | 72-73,77 | 55 | 29 | 52.7 | 383 | 7.0 | 2 | 1 | 1.8 |
| Jesse Freitas | 74-75 | 219 | 98 | 44.7 | 1244 | 5.7 | 8 | 13 | 5.9 |
| Joe Gilliam | 72-75,83 | 331 | 147 | 44.4 | 2103 | 6.4 | 9 | 17 | 5.1 |
| Neil Graff | 74-78 | 48 | 25 | 52.1 | 288 | 6.0 | 2 | 3 | 6.3 |
| Bob Griese | 67-80 | 3429 | 1926 | 56.2 | 25092 | 7.3 | 192 | 172 | 5.0 |
| Pat Haden | 76-81 | 1363 | 731 | 53.6 | 9296 | 6.8 | 52 | 60 | 4.4 |
| Terry Hanratty | 69-76 | 431 | 165 | 38.3 | 2510 | 5.8 | 24 | 35 | 8.1 |
| Edd Hargett | 69-73 | 437 | 205 | 46.9 | 2727 | 6.2 | 11 | 10 | 2.3 |
| James Harris | 69-71,73-81 | 1149 | 607 | 52.8 | 8136 | 7.1 | 45 | 59 | 5.1 |
| Jim Hart | 66-84 | 5076 | 2593 | 51.1 | 34665 | 6.8 | 209 | 247 | 4.9 |
| Randy Hedberg | 77 | 90 | 25 | 27.8 | 244 | 2.7 | 0 | 10 | 11.1 |
| Don Horn | 67-74 | 465 | 232 | 49.9 | 3369 | 7.2 | 20 | 36 | 7.7 |
| Gary Huff | 73-78,80 | 788 | 392 | 49.7 | 4329 | 5.5 | 16 | 50 | 6.3 |
| John Hufnagel | 74-75 | 61 | 22 | 36.1 | 357 | 5.9 | 1 | 9 | 14.8 |
| David Humm | 75-84 | 137 | 63 | 46.0 | 753 | 5.5 | 3 | 8 | 5.8 |
| Scott Hunter | 71-74,76-79 | 748 | 335 | 44.8 | 4756 | 6.4 | 23 | 38 | 5.1 |
| Randy Johnson | 66-73,75-76 | 1286 | 647 | 50.3 | 8329 | 6.5 | 51 | 90 | 7.0 |
| Bert Jones | 73-82 | 2551 | 1430 | 56.1 | 18190 | 7.1 | 124 | 101 | 4.0 |
| John Jones | 75 | 57 | 16 | 28.1 | 181 | 3.2 | 1 | 5 | 8.8 |
| June Jones | 77-79,81 | 166 | 75 | 45.2 | 923 | 5.6 | 3 | 7 | 4.2 |
| Gary Keithley | 73,75 | 73 | 32 | 43.8 | 369 | 5.1 | 1 | 5 | 6.8 |
| Billy Kilmer | 61-78 | 2984 | 1585 | 53.1 | 20495 | 6.9 | 152 | 146 | 4.9 |
| Mike Kirkland | 76-78 | 41 | 19 | 46.3 | 211 | 5.2 | 1 | 8 | 19.5 |
| Mike Kruczek | 76-80 | 154 | 93 | 60.4 | 1185 | 7.7 | 0 | 8 | 5.2 |
| Greg Landry | 68-81,84 | 2300 | 1276 | 55.5 | 16052 | 7.0 | 98 | 103 | 4.5 |
| Larry Lawrence | 74-76 | 31 | 9 | 29.0 | 79 | 2.5 | 0 | 4 | 12.9 |
| Bob Lee | 69-80 | 730 | 368 | 50.4 | 5034 | 6.9 | 30 | 40 | 5.5 |
| Mike Livingston | 68-80 | 1751 | 912 | 52.1 | 11295 | 6.5 | 56 | 83 | 4.7 |
| Clint Longley | 74-76 | 68 | 31 | 45.6 | 441 | 6.5 | 5 | 4 | 5.9 |
| Mike Loyd | 79-80 | 28 | 5 | 17.9 | 49 | 1.8 | 0 | 1 | 3.6 |
| Terry Luck | 77 | 50 | 25 | 50.0 | 316 | 6.3 | 1 | 7 | 14.0 |
| Archie Manning | 71-75,77-84 | 3642 | 2011 | 55.2 | 23911 | 6.6 | 125 | 173 | 4.8 |
| Gary Marangi | 74-77 | 283 | 104 | 36.7 | 1373 | 4.9 | 12 | 21 | 7.4 |
| Dave Mays | 76-78 | 156 | 80 | 51.3 | 937 | 6.0 | 7 | 11 | 7.1 |
| Kim McQuilkin | 74-80 | 272 | 108 | 39.7 | 1135 | 4.1 | 4 | 29 | 10.7 |
| Don Milan | 75-76 | 32 | 15 | 48.9 | 181 | 5.7 | 1 | 1 | 3.1 |
| Mark Miller | 78-80 | 47 | 15 | 31.9 | 243 | 5.2 | 1 | 5 | 10.6 |
| Dennis Morrison | 74 | 51 | 21 | 41.2 | 227 | 4.5 | 1 | 5 | 9.8 |
| Craig Morton | 65-82 | 3786 | 2053 | 54.2 | 27908 | 7.4 | 183 | 187 | 4.9 |
| Bill Munson | 64-79 | 1982 | 1070 | 54.0 | 12896 | 6.5 | 84 | 80 | 4.0 |
| Steve Myer | 76-79 | 160 | 83 | 51.9 | 851 | 5.3 | 6 | 14 | 8.8 |
| Joe Namath | 65-77 | 3762 | 1886 | 50.1 | 27663 | 7.4 | 173 | 220 | 5.8 |
| Kent Nix | 67-72 | 652 | 301 | 46.2 | 3644 | 5.6 | 23 | 49 | 7.5 |
| Tom Owen | 74-81 | 349 | 170 | 48.7 | 2300 | 6.6 | 14 | 26 | 7.5 |
| Dan Pastorini | 71-83 | 3055 | 1556 | 50.9 | 18515 | 6.1 | 103 | 161 | 5.3 |
| Al Pastrana | 69-70 | 75 | 29 | 38.7 | 420 | 5.6 | 1 | 9 | 12.0 |
| Craig Penrose | 76-80 | 117 | 55 | 47.0 | 711 | 6.1 | 5 | 12 | 10.3 |
| Mike Phipps | 70-81 | 1799 | 886 | 49.3 | 10506 | 5.8 | 55 | 108 | 8.2 |
| Steve Pisarkiewicz | 77-80 | 143 | 64 | 44.8 | 804 | 5.6 | 3 | 7 | 4.9 |
| Jim Plunkett | 71-86 | 3701 | 1943 | 52.5 | 25882 | 7.0 | 164 | 198 | 5.3 |
| Mike Rae | 76-81 | 249 | 124 | 49.8 | 1536 | 6.2 | 12 | 14 | 5.6 |
| Steve Ramsey | 70-76 | 921 | 456 | 49.5 | 6437 | 7.0 | 35 | 58 | 6.3 |
| John Reaves | 72-79,81,87 | 616 | 286 | 46.4 | 3617 | 5.9 | 17 | 34 | 5.5 |
| Joe Reed | 72-79 | 513 | 225 | 46.8 | 2825 | 5.5 | 18 | 31 | 6.0 |
| Bobby Scott | 73-81 | 500 | 237 | 47.4 | 2781 | 5.6 | 15 | 28 | 5.6 |
| Dennis Shaw | 70-76,78 | 924 | 489 | 52.9 | 6347 | 6.9 | 35 | 68 | 7.4 |
| Brian Sipe | 74-83 | 3439 | 1944 | 56.5 | 23713 | 6.9 | 154 | 159 | 4.6 |
| Steve Spurrier | 67-76 | 1151 | 597 | 51.9 | 6878 | 6.0 | 40 | 60 | 5.3 |
| Ken Stabler | 70-84 | 3793 | 2270 | 59.8 | 27938 | 7.4 | 194 | 222 | 5.9 |
| Roger Staubach | 69-79 | 2958 | 1685 | 57.0 | 22700 | 7.7 | 153 | 109 | 3.7 |
| Pat Sullivan | 72-75 | 220 | 93 | 42.3 | 1155 | 5.3 | 5 | 16 | 7.3 |
| Carl Summerell | 74-75 | 29 | 13 | 44.8 | 157 | 5.4 | 0 | 5 | 17.2 |
| Jerry Tagge | 72-74 | 281 | 136 | 48.4 | 1583 | 5.6 | 3 | 17 | 6.0 |
| Bill Troup | 74-80 | 328 | 166 | 50.6 | 2047 | 6.2 | 10 | 26 | 7.9 |
| Tim Van Galder | 72 | 79 | 40 | 50.6 | 434 | 5.5 | 1 | 7 | 8.9 |
| John Walton | 76-79 | 65 | 31 | 47.7 | 338 | 5.2 | 3 | 3 | 4.6 |
| Norris Weese | 76-79 | 251 | 143 | 57.0 | 1887 | 7.5 | 7 | 14 | 5.6 |
| Al Woodall | 69-71,73-74 | 503 | 246 | 48.9 | 2970 | 5.9 | 18 | 23 | 4.6 |
| Sam Wyche | 68-72,74,76 | 222 | 116 | 52.7 | 1748 | 7.9 | 12 | 9 | 4.6 |

Lifetime Statistics- 1970- 1979 Players Section 2 - RUSHING and RECEIVING
(All men with 25 or more rushing attempts or 10 or more receptions) 388

| | | RUSHING | | | | RECEIVING | | | |
|---|---|---|---|---|---|---|---|---|---|
| Name | Years | Att. | Yards | Avg. | TD | Rec. | Yards | Avg. | TD |
| Dan Abramowicz | 67-75 | 6 | 95 | 15.8 | 0 | 369 | 5686 | 15.4 | 39 |
| Mike Adamle | 71-76 | 308 | 1149 | 3.7 | 4 | 53 | 368 | 6.9 | 2 |
| Bob Adams | 69-71, 73-77 | 2 | 7 | 3.5 | 0 | 61 | 732 | 12.0 | 0 |
| Tony Adams | 75-78,87 | 38 | 155 | 4.1 | 0 | 1 | -7 | -7.0 | 0 |
| Margene Adkins | 70-73 | | | | | 19 | 258 | 13.6 | 0 |
| Mack Alston | 70-80 | 2 | 10 | 5.0 | 0 | 108 | 1247 | 11.5 | 15 |
| George Amundson | 73-75 | 74 | 194 | 2.6 | 4 | 25 | 212 | 8.5 | 1 |
| Bobby Anderson | 70-73,75 | 314 | 1282 | 4.1 | 9 | 84 | 861 | 10.3 | 2 |
| Donny Anderson | 66-74 | 1197 | 4696 | 3.9 | 41 | 209 | 2548 | 12.2 | 14 |
| Ken Anderson | 71-86 | 397 | 2220 | 5.6 | 20 | | | | |
| Otis Armstrong | 73-80 | 1023 | 4453 | 4.4 | 25 | 131 | 1302 | 9.9 | 7 |
| Josh Ashton | 72-75 | 257 | 894 | 3.9 | 3 | 33 | 320 | 9.7 | 1 |
| Bob Avellini | 75-84 | 104 | 225 | 2.2 | 5 | | | | |
| Mark Bailey | 77-78 | 149 | 564 | 3.8 | 2 | 22 | 219 | 10.0 | 1 |
| Tom Bailey | 71-75 | 42 | 186 | 3.9 | 15 | 28 | 194 | 6.9 | 1 |
| Tony Baker | 68-75 | 536 | 2087 | 3.9 | 15 | 82 | 685 | 8.4 | 2 |
| Pete Banaszak | 66-78 | 964 | 3772 | 3.9 | 47 | 121 | 1022 | 8.4 | 5 |
| Warren Bankston | 69-78 | 167 | 684 | 4.1 | 3 | 38 | 283 | 7.4 | 2 |
| Jerome Barkum | 72-83 | 3 | -3 | -1.0 | 0 | 326 | 4789 | 14.7 | 40 |
| Larry Barnes | 77-79 | 53 | 156 | 2.9 | 2 | 4 | 29 | 7.3 | 0 |
| Bubba Bean | 76, 78-79 | 405 | 1528 | 3.8 | 6 | 59 | 494 | 8.4 | 2 |
| John Beasley | 67-70, 72-74 | | | | | 151 | 1607 | 10.6 | 13 |
| Terry Beasley | 72, 74-75 | 2 | 2 | 1.0 | 0 | 38 | 570 | 15.0 | 3 |
| Jim Beirne | 68-76 | 1 | 3 | 3.0 | 0 | 142 | 2011 | 14.2 | 11 |
| Eddie Bell | 70-76 | 3 | -12 | -4.0 | 0 | 118 | 1774 | 15.0 | 12 |
| Gordon Bell | 76-78 | 90 | 319 | 3.5 | 2 | 32 | 259 | 8.1 | 0 |
| Horace Belton | 79-80 | 136 | 486 | 3.6 | 3 | 20 | 226 | 11.3 | 0 |
| Willie Belton | 71-74 | 78 | 306 | 3.9 | 1 | 4 | 21 | 5.3 | 0 |
| Bob Berry | 65-76 | 109 | 409 | 3.8 | 4 | | | | |
| Jim Bertelsen | 72-76 | 614 | 2466 | 4.0 | 16 | 88 | 1014 | 11.5 | 2 |
| James Betterson | 77-78 | 73 | 265 | 3.6 | 1 | 6 | 49 | 8.2 | 0 |
| Fred Biletnikoff | 65-78 | | | | | 589 | 8974 | 15.2 | 76 |
| Hank Bjorklund | 72-74 | 60 | 171 | 2.9 | 0 | 8 | 84 | 10.5 | 0 |
| Rocky Bleier | 68-69, 71-80 | 928 | 3865 | 4.2 | 23 | 136 | 1294 | 9.5 | 2 |
| Luther Blue | 77-80 | 7 | -5 | -0.7 | 0 | 47 | 542 | 11.5 | 4 |
| Glen Bonner | 74-75 | 94 | 319 | 3.4 | 3 | 13 | 109 | 8.4 | 1 |
| Emerson Boozer | 66-75 | 1291 | 5135 | 4.0 | 52 | 139 | 1488 | 10.7 | 12 |
| Mike Boryla | 74-76, 78 | 43 | 224 | 5.2 | 2 | | | | |
| Lee Bouggess | 70-71, 73 | 271 | 697 | 2.6 | 5 | 78 | 589 | 7.6 | 3 |
| Greg Boykin | 77-78 | 107 | 352 | 3.3 | 2 | 22 | 133 | 6.0 | 0 |
| Morris Bradshaw | 74-82 | 2 | -1 | -0.5 | 0 | 90 | 1416 | 15.7 | 12 |
| Terry Bradshaw | 70-83 | 444 | 2257 | 5.1 | 32 | 0 | 1 | — | 0 |
| Cliff Branch | 72-84 | 11 | 70 | 6.4 | 0 | 501 | 8685 | 17.3 | 67 |
| Jim Braxton | 71-78 | 741 | 2890 | 3.9 | 25 | 144 | 1473 | 10.2 | 6 |
| Larry Brinson | 77-80 | 56 | 229 | 4.1 | 4 | 1 | 9 | 9.0 | 0 |
| Marlin Briscoe | 68-76 | 49 | 336 | 3.9 | 3 | 224 | 3537 | 15.8 | 30 |
| John Brockington | 71-77 | 1347 | 5185 | 3.8 | 30 | 157 | 1297 | 8.3 | 4 |
| Billy Brooks | 76-81 | 3 | -17 | -5.7 | 0 | 96 | 1720 | 17.9 | 7 |
| Bob Brown | 69-73 | 1 | 8 | 8.0 | 0 | 28 | 448 | 16.0 | 1 |
| Ken Brown | 70-75 | 346 | 1193 | 3.4 | 7 | 58 | 468 | 8.1 | 2 |
| Larry Brown | 69-76 | 1530 | 5875 | 3.8 | 35 | 238 | 2485 | 10.4 | 20 |
| Larry Brown | 71-81 | | | | | 48 | 636 | 13.3 | 5 |
| Bob Brunet | 68-77 | 131 | 406 | 3.1 | 3 | 24 | 200 | 8.3 | 1 |
| Larry Brunson | 74-80 | 12 | 63 | 5.3 | 0 | 104 | 1787 | 17.2 | 6 |
| Hubie Bryant | 70-72 | 7 | 26 | 3.7 | 0 | 22 | 366 | 16.6 | 1 |
| Danny Buggs | 75-79 | 1 | 0 | 0.0 | 0 | 110 | 1572 | 14.3 | 4 |
| Norm Bulaich | 70-79 | 814 | 3362 | 4.1 | 30 | 224 | 1766 | 7.9 | 11 |
| Scott Bull | 76-78 | 49 | 186 | 3.8 | 3 | | | | |
| Steve Burke | 75-77 | 1 | 2 | 2.0 | 0 | 13 | 264 | 20.3 | 0 |
| Bob Burns | 74 | 40 | 158 | 4.0 | 0 | 11 | 83 | 7.5 | 1 |
| Leon Burns | 71-72 | 87 | 292 | 3.4 | 3 | 9 | 44 | 4.9 | 0 |
| Ken Burrough | 70-81 | 17 | 63 | 3.7 | 1 | 421 | 7102 | 16.9 | 49 |
| Ken Burrow | 71-75 | 6 | 25 | 4.2 | 0 | 152 | 2668 | 17.6 | 21 |
| Larry Burton | 75-79 | 5 | 4 | 0.8 | 0 | 44 | 804 | 18.3 | 7 |
| Dexter Bussey | 74-84 | 1203 | 5105 | 4.2 | 18 | 193 | 1616 | 8.4 | 5 |
| Bill Butler | 72-74 | 162 | 655 | 4.0 | 1 | 46 | 354 | 7.7 | 4 |
| J.V. Cain | 74-77 | | | | | 76 | 1014 | 13.3 | 9 |
| Don Calhoun | 74-83 | 860 | 3559 | 4.1 | 23 | 84 | 624 | 7.4 | 2 |
| Sonny Campbell | 70-71 | 57 | 195 | 3.4 | 2 | 10 | 132 | 13.2 | 0 |
| Larry Canada | 78-81 | 148 | 621 | 4.2 | 6 | 12 | 110 | 9.2 | 1 |
| John Cappelletti | 74-83 | 824 | 2751 | 3.3 | 24 | 135 | 1233 | 9.1 | 4 |
| Harold Carmichael | 71-84 | 9 | 64 | 7.1 | 0 | 589 | 8985 | 15.2 | 79 |
| Roger Carr | 74-83 | 1 | -8 | -8.0 | 0 | 271 | 5071 | 18.7 | 31 |
| Louis Carter | 75-78 | 322 | 940 | 2.9 | 4 | 51 | 378 | 7.4 | 0 |
| Virgil Carter | 68-72,75-76 | 109 | 640 | 5.9 | 8 | | | | |
| Dave Casper | 74-84 | 6 | 27 | 4.5 | 0 | 378 | 5216 | 13.8 | 52 |
| Rich Caster | 70-82 | 23 | 119 | 5.2 | 0 | 322 | 5515 | 17.1 | 45 |
| Al Chandler | 73-74,76-79 | | | | | 35 | 367 | 10.5 | 9 |
| Bob Chandler | 71-81 | 11 | 18 | 1.6 | 0 | 370 | 5243 | 14.2 | 48 |
| Wes Chesson | 71-74 | 1 | -4 | -4.0 | 0 | 40 | 598 | 15.0 | 2 |
| Ray Chester | 70-81 | 5 | 9 | 1.8 | 0 | 364 | 5013 | 13.8 | 48 |
| Henry Childs | 74-81 | 4 | 12 | 3.0 | 1 | 223 | 3401 | 15.3 | 28 |
| Jim Childs | 78-79 | | | | | 12 | 143 | 11.9 | 1 |
| Booby Clark | 73-80 | 802 | 3032 | 3.8 | 25 | 157 | 1197 | 7.6 | 2 |
| Vin Clements | 72-73 | 103 | 435 | 4.2 | 1 | 24 | 247 | 10.3 | 1 |
| Mike Cobb | 77-81 | | | | | 11 | 134 | 12.2 | 0 |
| Ronnie Coleman | 74-81 | 770 | 2769 | 3.6 | 16 | 150 | 1239 | 8.3 | 6 |
| Mike Collier | 75, 77, 79 | 86 | 370 | 4.3 | 5 | 11 | 73 | 6.6 | 0 |
| Sonny Collins | 76-77 | 91 | 319 | 3.5 | 0 | 4 | 37 | 9.3 | 0 |
| Jim Corbett | 77-80 | 1 | -1 | -1.0 | 0 | 25 | 376 | 15.0 | 1 |
| Bruce Coslet | 69-76 | 1 | 1 | 1.0 | 0 | 61 | 878 | 14.4 | 9 |
| Craig Cotton | 69-73, 75 | | | | | 28 | 409 | 14.6 | 1 |
| Steve Craig | 74-78 | | | | | 18 | 172 | 9.6 | 1 |
| Larry Csonka | 68-74, 76-79 | 1891 | 8081 | 4.3 | 64 | 106 | 820 | 7.7 | 4 |
| Jim Culbreath | 77-80 | 48 | 156 | 3.3 | 0 | 9 | 84 | 9.3 | 0 |
| Doug Cunningham | 67-74 | 406 | 1515 | 3.7 | 10 | 137 | 1171 | 8.5 | 0 |
| Sam Cunningham | 73-82 | 1385 | 5453 | 3.9 | 43 | 210 | 1905 | 9.1 | 6 |
| Pat Curran | 69-78 | 30 | 127 | 4.2 | 0 | 106 | 1266 | 11.9 | 5 |
| Isaac Curtis | 73-84 | 25 | 56 | 2.2 | 0 | 416 | 7101 | 17.1 | 53 |
| Anthony Davis | 77-78 | 98 | 304 | 3.1 | 1 | 8 | 91 | 11.4 | 0 |
| Bob Davis | 67-73 | 52 | 332 | 6.4 | 2 | | | | |
| Charlie Davis | 74-76 | 113 | 482 | 4.3 | 1 | 22 | 203 | 9.2 | 0 |
| Clarence Davis | 71-78 | 804 | 3640 | 4.5 | 26 | 99 | 865 | 8.7 | 2 |
| Dave Davis | 71-74 | 2 | 0 | 0.0 | 0 | 11 | 192 | 17.5 | 1 |
| Dick Davis | 70 | 27 | 94 | 3.5 | 0 | 4 | 29 | 7.3 | 0 |

| | | RUSHING | | | | RECEIVING | | | |
|---|---|---|---|---|---|---|---|---|---|
| Name | Years | Att. | Yards | Avg. | TD | Rec. | Yards | Avg. | TD |
| Gary Davis | 76-81 | 324 | 1410 | 4.4 | 7 | 83 | 671 | 8.1 | 1 |
| Harrison Davis | 74 | 2 | -7 | -7.0 | 0 | 18 | 432 | 24.0 | 2 |
| Sonny Davis | 71-72 | 47 | 163 | 3.5 | 1 | 11 | 46 | 4.2 | 0 |
| Steve Davis | 72-76 | 322 | 1305 | 4.1 | 9 | 33 | 301 | 9.1 | 2 |
| Tony Davis | 76-81 | 91 | 345 | 3.8 | 5 | 27 | 250 | 9.3 | 1 |
| Joe Dawkins | 70-76 | 698 | 2661 | 3.8 | 13 | 145 | 1316 | 9.1 | 3 |
| Jack DeGrener | 74 | 33 | 110 | 3.3 | 0 | 4 | 13 | 3.3 | 0 |
| Jack Deloplaine | 76-79 | 37 | 165 | 4.5 | 2 | 3 | 16 | 5.3 | 0 |
| Doug Dennison | 74-79 | 306 | 1112 | 3.6 | 19 | 14 | 110 | 7.9 | 0 |
| Moses Denson | 74-75 | 159 | 586 | 3.7 | 0 | 39 | 255 | 6.5 | 2 |
| Lynn Dickey | 71-77,79-85 | 140 | 121 | 0.9 | 9 | | | | |
| Chuck Dicus | 71-72 | 2 | -13 | -6.5 | 0 | 24 | 316 | 13.2 | 3 |
| Al Dodd | 67,69-71,73-74 | 9 | 50 | 5.6 | 0 | 111 | 1803 | 16.2 | 3 |
| Jack Dolbin | 75-79 | 9 | 89 | 9.9 | 0 | 94 | 1579 | 16.8 | 7 |
| Marty Domres | 69-77 | 130 | 679 | 5.2 | 10 | | | | |
| Mike Donohue | 70-71,73-74 | | | | | 10 | 106 | 10.6 | 2 |
| Larry Dorsey | 76-78 | 1 | -12 | -12.0 | 0 | 27 | 475 | 17.6 | 4 |
| Glenn Doughty | 72-79 | 26 | 202 | 7.8 | 0 | 219 | 3547 | 16.2 | 24 |
| Bobby Douglass | 69-78 | 410 | 2654 | 6.5 | 22 | 1 | -2 | -2.0 | 0 |
| Doug Dressler | 70-72,74-75 | 278 | 1125 | 4.0 | 9 | 90 | 695 | 7.7 | 2 |
| Jimmy DuBose | 76-79 | 184 | 704 | 3.8 | 4 | 17 | 118 | 6.9 | 0 |
| Bobby Duhon | 68,70-72 | 221 | 840 | 3.8 | 4 | 68 | 717 | 10.5 | 1 |
| Jubilee Dunbar | 73-74 | 3 | 3 | 1.0 | 0 | 29 | 521 | 18.0 | 4 |
| Billy Joe DuPree | 73-83 | 26 | 178 | 6.9 | 1 | 267 | 3565 | 13.4 | 41 |
| Cid Edwards | 68-75 | 698 | 3006 | 4.3 | 15 | 144 | 1491 | 10.4 | 4 |
| Monroe Eley | 75-77 | 98 | 276 | 2.8 | 1 | 9 | 60 | 6.7 | 0 |
| Lenvil Elliot | 73-81 | 440 | 1900 | 4.3 | 8 | 159 | 1484 | 9.3 | 10 |
| Willie Ellison | 67-74 | 801 | 3426 | 4.3 | 24 | 104 | 888 | 8.5 | 6 |
| Bill Enyart | 69-71 | 105 | 387 | 3.7 | 1 | 54 | 421 | 7.8 | 3 |
| Mike Esposito | 76-78 | 101 | 439 | 4.3 | 2 | 21 | 97 | 4.6 | 0 |
| Charlie Evans | 71-74 | 205 | 644 | 3.1 | 12 | 54 | 470 | 8.7 | 1 |
| George Farmer | 70-75 | 4 | 6 | 1.5 | 0 | 119 | 1995 | 16.8 | 10 |
| Mel Farr | 67-73 | 739 | 3072 | 4.2 | 26 | 146 | 1374 | 9.4 | 10 |
| Duke Fergerson | 77-80 | | | | | 35 | 543 | 15.5 | 2 |
| Bob Ferrell | 76-80 | 183 | 692 | 3.8 | 3 | 21 | 148 | 7.0 | 0 |
| James Ford | 71-72 | 104 | 407 | 3.9 | 2 | 8 | 63 | 7.9 | 0 |
| Chuck Foreman | 73-80 | 1556 | 5950 | 3.8 | 53 | 350 | 3156 | 9.0 | 23 |
| Ike Forte | 76-81 | 165 | 511 | 3.1 | 5 | 39 | 387 | 9.9 | 2 |
| Eddie Foster | 77,79 | | | | | 15 | 208 | 13.9 | 0 |
| Wallace Francis | 73-81 | 10 | 27 | 2.7 | 1 | 244 | 3695 | 15.1 | 27 |
| Cleveland Franklin | 77-82 | 208 | 635 | 3.1 | 3 | 36 | 258 | 7.2 | 0 |
| Stan Fritts | 75-76 | 141 | 575 | 4.1 | 11 | 15 | 138 | 9.2 | 2 |
| Jean Fugett | 72-79 | 7 | 38 | 5.4 | 0 | 156 | 2270 | 14.6 | 28 |
| Frenchy Fuqua | 69-76 | 719 | 3031 | 4.2 | 21 | 135 | 1247 | 9.2 | 3 |
| Clark Gaines | 76-82 | 582 | 2552 | 4.4 | 8 | 166 | 1438 | 8.7 | 6 |
| Lawrence Gaines | 76,78-79 | 232 | 892 | 3.8 | 5 | 25 | 146 | 5.8 | 1 |
| Reuben Gant | 74-80 | 1 | 14 | 14.0 | 0 | 127 | 1850 | 14.6 | 15 |
| Carl Garrett | 69-77 | 1031 | 4197 | 4.1 | 28 | 182 | 1931 | 10.6 | 7 |
| Reggie Garrett | 74-75 | | | | | 13 | 178 | 13.7 | 1 |
| Gary Garrison | 66-77 | 12 | 29 | 2.4 | 0 | 405 | 7538 | 18.6 | 58 |
| Walt Garrison | 66-74 | 899 | 3886 | 4.3 | 30 | 182 | 1794 | 9.9 | 9 |
| Tom Geredine | 73-74,76 | 2 | 5 | 2.5 | 0 | 17 | 323 | 19.0 | 2 |
| Louie Giammona | 76,78-82 | 201 | 682 | 3.4 | 7 | 46 | 444 | 9.7 | 2 |
| Walker Gillette | 70-76 | 1 | -4 | -4.0 | 0 | 153 | 2291 | 15.0 | 12 |
| John Gilliam | 67-77 | 35 | 293 | 8.4 | 2 | 382 | 7056 | 18.5 | 48 |
| Hubert Ginn | 70-77 | 132 | 521 | 3.9 | 3 | 9 | 49 | 5.4 | 0 |
| Paul Gipson | 69-71,73 | 123 | 491 | 4.0 | 1 | 21 | 240 | 11.4 | 3 |
| Bob Gladieux | 69-72 | 65 | 239 | 3.7 | 0 | 25 | 252 | 10.1 | 0 |
| Chip Glass | 69-74 | | | | | 34 | 642 | 18.9 | 5 |
| Leland Glass | 72-73 | 2 | 13 | 6.5 | 0 | 26 | 380 | 14.6 | 1 |
| Les Goodman | 73-74 | 38 | 189 | 5.0 | 1 | 7 | 38 | 5.4 | 0 |
| Dick Gordon | 65-74 | 15 | 90 | 6.0 | 0 | 243 | 3594 | 14.8 | 36 |
| Ken Grandberry | 74 | 144 | 475 | 3.3 | 2 | 30 | 212 | 7.1 | 0 |
| Frank Grant | 73-78 | 5 | 27 | 5.4 | 0 | 149 | 2486 | 16.7 | 18 |
| Mel Gray | 71-82 | 15 | 154 | 10.3 | 1 | 351 | 6644 | 18.9 | 45 |
| Woody Green | 74-76 | 375 | 1442 | 3.8 | 9 | 58 | 562 | 9.7 | 2 |
| Bob Gresham | 71-76 | 410 | 1360 | 3.3 | 12 | 90 | 728 | 8.1 | 1 |
| Bob Griese | 67-80 | 261 | 994 | 3.8 | 7 | | | | |
| Archie Griffin | 76-82 | 691 | 2808 | 4.1 | 7 | 192 | 1607 | 8.4 | 6 |
| Bob Grim | 67-77 | 8 | 137 | 17.1 | 0 | 194 | 2914 | 15.0 | 16 |
| Randy Grossman | 74-81 | | | | | 119 | 1514 | 12.7 | 5 |
| Pat Haden | 76-81 | 124 | 609 | 4.9 | 6 | | | | |
| Isaac Hagins | 76-80 | 4 | 26 | 6.5 | 0 | 83 | 1317 | 14.7 | 5 |
| Andy Hamilton | 73-75 | | | | | 16 | 270 | 16.9 | 0 |
| Bob Hammond | 76-80 | 332 | 1401 | 4.2 | 3 | 65 | 528 | 8.1 | 3 |
| Dave Hampton | 69-76 | 1148 | 4536 | 4.0 | 25 | 119 | 1156 | 9.7 | 6 |
| Buddy Hardeman | 79-80 | 71 | 256 | 3.6 | 0 | 37 | 375 | 10.1 | 1 |
| Don Hardeman | 75-79 | 397 | 1460 | 3.7 | 11 | 58 | 285 | 4.9 | 2 |
| Steve Harky | 71-72 | 65 | 191 | 2.9 | 0 | 14 | 142 | 10.1 | 0 |
| Roland Harper | 75-78,80-82 | 757 | 3044 | 4.0 | 15 | 128 | 1013 | 7.9 | 3 |
| Charlie Harraway | 66-73 | 822 | 3019 | 3.7 | 20 | 158 | 1304 | 8.3 | 7 |
| Willard Harrell | 75-84 | 429 | 1391 | 3.2 | 10 | 127 | 1135 | 8.9 | 4 |
| Franco Harris | 72-84 | 2949 | 12120 | 4.1 | 91 | 307 | 2287 | 7.4 | 9 |
| Ike Harris | 73-81 | 4 | 31 | 17.6 | 0 | 211 | 3305 | 15.7 | 16 |
| James Harris | 69-71,73-81 | 121 | 367 | 3.0 | 10 | | | | |
| Leroy Harris | 77-82 | 442 | 1813 | 4.1 | 13 | 72 | 571 | 7.9 | 1 |
| Dwight Harrison | 71-77 | 6 | 45 | 7.5 | 0 | 20 | 281 | 14.1 | 2 |
| Jim Harrison | 71-74 | 272 | 1009 | 3.7 | 3 | 31 | 248 | 8.0 | 3 |
| Kenny Harrison | 76-78,80 | 8 | 4 | 0.5 | 0 | 42 | 668 | 15.9 | 1 |
| Reggie Harrison | 74-78 | 134 | 631 | 4.7 | 8 | 7 | 36 | 5.1 | 0 |
| Harold Hart | 74-75,77-78 | 114 | 485 | 4.3 | 5 | 8 | 32 | 4.0 | 0 |
| Jim Hart | 66-84 | 159 | 207 | 1.3 | 16 | 1 | -4 | -4.0 | 0 |
| Sam Havrilak | 69-74 | 73 | 289 | 4.0 | 3 | 51 | 761 | 14.9 | 4 |
| Bob Hayes | 65-75 | 24 | 68 | 2.8 | 2 | 371 | 7414 | 20.0 | 71 |
| Don Herriman | 69-77 | 4 | -8 | -2.0 | 0 | 234 | 3039 | 13.0 | 16 |
| Mack Herron | 73-75 | 354 | 1298 | 3.7 | 9 | 61 | 789 | 12.9 | 6 |
| Don Highsmith | 70-73 | 94 | 327 | 3.5 | 2 | 12 | 143 | 11.9 | 0 |
| Calvin Hill | 69-74,76-81 | 1452 | 6083 | 4.2 | 42 | 271 | 2861 | 10.6 | 23 |
| Ike Hill | 70-74,76 | 3 | -14 | -4.7 | 0 | 22 | 283 | 12.9 | 2 |
| J.D. Hill | 71-77 | 3 | 14 | 4.7 | 0 | 185 | 2880 | 15.6 | 21 |
| Eddie Hinton | 69-74 | 12 | 110 | 9.2 | 2 | 111 | 1822 | 16.4 | 10 |
| Paul Hofer | 76-81 | 416 | 1746 | 4.2 | 16 | 147 | 1634 | 11.1 | 5 |
| Mike Hogan | 76-80 | 466 | 1835 | 3.9 | 6 | 79 | 482 | 6.1 | 2 |
| Steve Holden | 73-77 | 3 | 2 | 0.7 | 0 | 62 | 927 | 15.0 | 4 |
| John Holland | 74-77 | | | | | 35 | 634 | 18.1 | 3 |

389

Lifetime Statistics- 1970- 1979 Players Section 2 - RUSHING and RECEIVING

(All men with 25 or more rushing attempts or 10 or more receptions)

| | | RUSHING | | | | RECEIVING | | | |
|---|---|---|---|---|---|---|---|---|---|
| Name | Years | Att. | Yards | Avg. | TD | Rec. | Yards | Avg. | TD |
| Ron Holiday | 73 | 6 | 70 | 11.7 | 0 | 14 | 182 | 13.0 | 0 |
| Mike Holmes | 74-76 | 1 | -4 | -4.0 | 0 | 17 | 231 | 13.6 | 1 |
| Robert Holmes | 68-73, 75 | 639 | 2510 | 3.9 | 23 | 113 | 982 | 8.7 | 4 |
| Dennis Homan | 68-72 | 2 | -3 | -1.5 | 0 | 37 | 619 | 16.7 | 2 |
| Fair Hooker | 69-74 | | | | | 129 | 1845 | 14.3 | 8 |
| Jim Hooks | 73-76 | 67 | 245 | 3.7 | 0 | 11 | 64 | 5.8 | 0 |
| Roland Hooks | 76-82 | 399 | 1684 | 4.2 | 12 | 96 | 950 | 9.9 | 3 |
| Rich Houston | 69-73 | 3 | 13 | 4.3 | 0 | 65 | 1121 | 17.2 | 7 |
| Ron Howard | 74-79 | 1 | 2 | 2.0 | 0 | 72 | 850 | 11.8 | 2 |
| Marv Hubbard | 69-75,77 | 951 | 4544 | 4.8 | 23 | 85 | 628 | 7.4 | 1 |
| Gary Huff | 73-78,80 | 50 | 86 | 1.7 | 2 | | | | |
| Dennis Hughes | 70-71 | 1 | -4 | -4.0 | 0 | 24 | 332 | 13.8 | 3 |
| Mike Hull | 68-74 | 77 | 207 | 2.7 | 1 | 29 | 127 | 4.4 | 0 |
| Al Hunter | 77-80 | 180 | 715 | 4.0 | 4 | 27 | 331 | 12.3 | 0 |
| Scott Hunter | 71-74,76-79 | 95 | 204 | 2.1 | 13 | | | | |
| John Isenbarger | 70-73 | 27 | 80 | 3.0 | 0 | 21 | 291 | 13.9 | 2 |
| Horace Ivory | 77-82 | 351 | 1425 | 4.1 | 15 | 54 | 471 | 8.7 | 2 |
| Harold Jackson | 68-83 | 33 | 181 | 5.5 | 0 | 579 | 10372 | 17.9 | 76 |
| Jazz Jackson | 74-76 | 27 | 91 | 3.4 | 0 | 9 | 101 | 11.2 | 1 |
| Randy Jackson | 72-74 | 30 | 73 | 2.3 | 0 | 15 | 58 | 3.9 | 1 |
| Wilbur Jackson | 74-82 | 971 | 3852 | 4.0 | 13 | 184 | 1592 | 8.7 | 4 |
| Po James | 72-75 | 328 | 1215 | 3.7 | 4 | 102 | 747 | 7.3 | 2 |
| Ray Jarvis | 71-79 | 2 | 13 | 6.5 | 0 | 104 | 1832 | 17.6 | 11 |
| Roy Jefferson | 65-76 | 25 | 188 | 7.5 | 0 | 451 | 7539 | 16.7 | 52 |
| Alfred Jenkins | 75-83 | 2 | 7 | 3.5 | 0 | 359 | 6258 | 17.4 | 40 |
| Jim Jensen | 76-77,79-82 | 283 | 1126 | 4.0 | 4 | 80 | 651 | 8.1 | 3 |
| Ron Jessie | 71-81 | 19 | 91 | 4.8 | 2 | 265 | 4278 | 16.1 | 26 |
| Andy Johnson | 74-76,78-81 | 491 | 2017 | 4.1 | 13 | 161 | 1807 | 11.2 | 9 |
| Dennis Johnson | 78-80 | 58 | 227 | 3.9 | 2 | 10 | 83 | 8.3 | 0 |
| Essex Johnson | 68-76 | 722 | 3236 | 4.5 | 19 | 146 | 1742 | 11.9 | 12 |
| Kermit Johnson | 75-76 | 36 | 124 | 3.4 | 1 | 1 | 11 | 11.0 | 0 |
| Randy Johnson | 66-73,75-76 | 114 | 573 | 5.0 | 10 | | | | |
| Ron Johnson | 69-75 | 1203 | 4307 | 3.6 | 40 | 213 | 1977 | 9.3 | 15 |
| Sammy Johnson | 74-79 | 206 | 830 | 4.0 | 9 | 45 | 378 | 8.4 | 0 |
| Charlie Joiner | 69-86 | 8 | 22 | 2.8 | 0 | 750 | 12146 | 16.2 | 65 |
| Andrew Jones | 75-76 | 43 | 110 | 2.6 | 1 | 10 | 52 | 5.2 | 0 |
| Bert Jones | 73-82 | 247 | 1429 | 5.8 | 14 | | | | |
| Clint Jones | 67-73 | 602 | 2178 | 3.6 | 20 | 38 | 431 | 11.3 | 0 |
| Greg Jones | 70-71 | 47 | 166 | 3.5 | 1 | 24 | 202 | 8.4 | 1 |
| Jimmie Jones | 74 | 32 | 147 | 4.6 | 1 | 4 | 35 | 8.8 | 0 |
| Kim Jones | 76-79 | 26 | 80 | 3.1 | 0 | 4 | 33 | 8.3 | 0 |
| Steve Jones | 73-78 | 300 | 1204 | 4.0 | 15 | 87 | 629 | 7.2 | 2 |
| Mark Kellar | 76-78 | 25 | 74 | 3.0 | 0 | 5 | 17 | 3.4 | 0 |
| Vince Kendrick | 74, 76 | 18 | 74 | 4.1 | 0 | 12 | 86 | 7.2 | 1 |
| Leroy Keyes | 69-73 | 125 | 369 | 3.0 | 3 | 30 | 270 | 9.0 | 0 |
| Jon Keyworth | 74-80 | 699 | 2653 | 3.4 | 22 | 141 | 1057 | 7.5 | 3 |
| Jim Kiick | 68-74, 76-77 | 1029 | 3759 | 3.7 | 29 | 233 | 2302 | 9.9 | 4 |
| Billy Kilmer | 61-78 | 362 | 1509 | 4.2 | 21 | | | | |
| John Kimbrough | 77 | | | | | 10 | 207 | 20.7 | 2 |
| Horace King | 75-83 | 549 | 2081 | 3.8 | 9 | 197 | 1573 | 8.0 | 5 |
| Jeff Kinney | 72-76 | 353 | 1285 | 3.6 | 5 | 68 | 502 | 7.4 | 1 |
| Bob Klein | 69-79 | 4 | 14 | 3.5 | 0 | 219 | 2687 | 12.3 | 23 |
| David Knight | 73-77 | | | | | 73 | 1189 | 16.3 | 7 |
| Gary Kosins | 72-74 | 35 | 100 | 2.9 | 1 | 7 | 26 | 3.7 | 1 |
| Doug Kotar | 74-79,81 | 900 | 3380 | 3.8 | 20 | 126 | 1022 | 8.1 | 1 |
| Ted Koy | 70-74 | 1 | 9 | 9.0 | 0 | 11 | 142 | 12.9 | 1 |
| Kent Kramer | 66-67,69-74 | | | | | 45 | 586 | 12.8 | 8 |
| Keith Krepfle | 75-83 | 1 | 2 | 2.0 | 0 | 152 | 2425 | 16.0 | 19 |
| Mike Kruczek | 76-80 | 37 | 138 | 3.7 | 2 | | | | |
| Ted Kwalick | 69-77 | 19 | 175 | 9.2 | 0 | 168 | 2570 | 15.3 | 23 |
| Scott Laidlaw | 75-80 | 255 | 1007 | 3.9 | 9 | 74 | 668 | 9.0 | 3 |
| Ron Lamb | 68-69,71-72 | 49 | 128 | 2.6 | 0 | 8 | 97 | 12.1 | 0 |
| Greg Landry | 68-81,84 | 430 | 2655 | 6.2 | 21 | | | | |
| MacArthur Lane | 68-78 | 1206 | 4656 | 3.9 | 30 | 287 | 2786 | 9.7 | 7 |
| Jim Lash | 73-77 | 3 | 5 | 1.7 | 0 | 91 | 1464 | 16.1 | 3 |
| Jerry Latin | 75-78 | 130 | 560 | 4.3 | 4 | 16 | 152 | 9.5 | 0 |
| Greg Latta | 75-80 | 2 | -8 | -4.0 | 0 | 90 | 1081 | 12.0 | 7 |
| Odell Lawson | 70-71,73-74 | 70 | 130 | 1.9 | 0 | 13 | 108 | 8.3 | 0 |
| Roger Lawson | 72-73 | 57 | 176 | 3.1 | 1 | 17 | 180 | 10.6 | 0 |
| Roosevelt Leaks | 75-83 | 663 | 2406 | 3.6 | 28 | 71 | 590 | 8.3 | 4 |
| Bob Lee | 69-80 | 92 | 197 | 2.1 | 3 | | | | |
| Ron Lee | 76-78 | 206 | 940 | 4.6 | 5 | 24 | 160 | 6.7 | 1 |
| Billy LeFear | 72-75 | 35 | 143 | 4.1 | 0 | 10 | 73 | 7.3 | 0 |
| Charlie Leigh | 68-69,71-74 | 72 | 372 | 5.2 | 2 | 9 | -4 | -0.4 | 0 |
| Jerry LeVias | 69-74 | 19 | 161 | 8.5 | 0 | 144 | 2139 | 14.9 | 14 |
| Frank Lewis | 71-83 | 12 | 146 | 12.1 | 1 | 397 | 6724 | 16.9 | 40 |
| Floyd Little | 67-75 | 1641 | 6323 | 3.9 | 43 | 215 | 2417 | 11.2 | 9 |
| Mike Livingston | 68-80 | 156 | 682 | 4.4 | 7 | | | | |
| Kevin Long | 77-81 | 564 | 2190 | 3.9 | 25 | 74 | 539 | 7.3 | 3 |
| Herb Lusk | 76-78 | 113 | 483 | 4.3 | 2 | 18 | 221 | 12.3 | 1 |
| Fran Lynch | 67-75 | 304 | 1258 | 4.1 | 12 | 35 | 357 | 10.2 | 2 |
| Ken MacAfee | 78-79 | | | | | 46 | 471 | 10.2 | 5 |
| Jack Maitland | 70-72 | 100 | 267 | 2.7 | 2 | 14 | 106 | 7.6 | 1 |
| Bill Malinchak | 66-74,76 | | | | | 35 | 508 | 14.5 | 4 |
| Art Malone | 70-76 | 635 | 2457 | 3.9 | 19 | 161 | 1465 | 9.1 | 6 |
| Benny Malone | 74-79 | 706 | 2693 | 3.8 | 19 | 33 | 400 | 12.1 | 1 |
| Jim Mandich | 70-78 | | | | | 121 | 1406 | 11.6 | 23 |
| Archie Manning | 71-75,77-84 | 346 | 2197 | 6.4 | 18 | 1 | -7 | -7.0 | 0 |
| Gary Marangi | 74-77 | 50 | 328 | 6.6 | 2 | | | | |
| Ed Marinaro | 72-77 | 383 | 1319 | 3.4 | 4 | 146 | 1176 | 8.1 | 7 |
| Ed Marshall | 71, 76-77 | | | | | 17 | 362 | 21.3 | 3 |
| Bill Masters | 67-76 | 18 | 114 | 6.3 | 0 | 169 | 2268 | 13.4 | 15 |
| Bo Matthews | 74-81 | 424 | 1566 | 3.7 | 11 | 75 | 488 | 6.5 | 0 |
| Alvin Maxson | 74-78 | 360 | 1270 | 3.5 | 6 | 95 | 619 | 6.5 | 1 |
| James McAlister | 75-76,78 | 190 | 677 | 3.6 | 3 | 30 | 218 | 7.3 | 2 |
| Don McCauley | 71-81 | 770 | 2627 | 3.4 | 40 | 333 | 3026 | 9.1 | 17 |
| Cliff McClain | 70-73 | 79 | 445 | 5.6 | 2 | 13 | 151 | 11.6 | 0 |
| Brent McClanahan | 73-79 | 367 | 1207 | 3.3 | 6 | 107 | 772 | 7.2 | 4 |
| Greg McCrary | 75,77-81 | 2 | 18 | 9.0 | 0 | 22 | 228 | 10.4 | 3 |
| Earl McCullough | 68-74 | 8 | 29 | 3.6 | 0 | 124 | 2319 | 18.7 | 19 |
| Sam McCullum | 74-83 | | | | | 274 | 4017 | 14.7 | 26 |
| Lawrence McCutcheon | 72-81 | 1521 | 6578 | 4.3 | 26 | 198 | 1799 | 9.1 | 13 |
| John McDaniel | 74-80 | 4 | 28 | 7.0 | 0 | 89 | 1547 | 17.4 | 7 |
| Dwight McDonald | 75-78 | | | | | 46 | 717 | 15.6 | 8 |
| Willie McGee | 73-78 | 4 | 9 | 2.3 | 0 | 24 | 446 | 18.6 | 4 |
| Rich McGeorge | 70-78 | 1 | 3 | 3.0 | 0 | 175 | 2370 | 13.5 | 13 |

| | | RUSHING | | | | RECEIVING | | | |
|---|---|---|---|---|---|---|---|---|---|
| Name | Years | Att. | Yards | Avg. | TD | Rec. | Yards | Avg. | TD |
| Pat McInally | 76-81 | 4 | -5 | -1.3 | 0 | 57 | 808 | 14.2 | 5 |
| John McKay | 76-78 | | | | | 41 | 632 | 7.2 | 2 |
| Hugh McKinnis | 73-76 | 269 | 960 | 3.6 | 10 | 65 | 572 | 8.8 | 0 |
| Ted McKnight | 77-82 | 528 | 2344 | 4.4 | 22 | 99 | 717 | 7.2 | 1 |
| John McMakin | 72-76 | 1 | 0 | 0.0 | 0 | 45 | 673 | 15.0 | 4 |
| Rod McNeill | 74-76 | 110 | 428 | 3.9 | 3 | 30 | 235 | 7.8 | 2 |
| Leon McQuay | 74-76 | 88 | 287 | 3.3 | 1 | 9 | 86 | 9.6 | 0 |
| Warren McVea | 68-71,73 | 248 | 1186 | 4.8 | 11 | 38 | 358 | 9.4 | 2 |
| Terry Metcalf | 73-77,81 | 766 | 3498 | 4.6 | 24 | 245 | 2457 | 10.0 | 9 |
| Cleo Miller | 74-82 | 593 | 2491 | 4.2 | 16 | 140 | 1175 | 8.4 | 1 |
| Robert Miller | 75-80 | 275 | 951 | 3.5 | 7 | 95 | 771 | 8.1 | 1 |
| Willie Miller | 75-76,78-82 | 5 | -2 | -0.4 | 0 | 112 | 1786 | 15.9 | 15 |
| Jim Mitchell | 69-79 | 26 | 187 | 7.2 | 1 | 305 | 4358 | 14.3 | 28 |
| Lydell Mitchell | 72-80 | 1675 | 6534 | 3.9 | 27 | 376 | 3203 | 8.5 | 17 |
| Tom Mitchell | 66,68-77 | 3 | 14 | 4.7 | 0 | 239 | 3181 | 13.3 | 24 |
| Mike Montgomery | 71-74 | 96 | 291 | 3.1 | 2 | 59 | 835 | 14.2 | 7 |
| Ross Montgomery | 69-70 | 77 | 281 | 3.6 | 0 | 16 | 83 | 5.2 | 0 |
| Bob Moore | 71-78 | 2 | 23 | 11.5 | 0 | 115 | 1270 | 11.0 | 7 |
| Joe Moore | 71,73 | 87 | 281 | 3.2 | 0 | 8 | 39 | 7.8 | 0 |
| Arnold Morgado | 77-80 | 284 | 956 | 3.4 | 15 | 19 | 150 | 7.9 | 1 |
| Milt Morin | 66-75 | 5 | 41 | 8.2 | 0 | 271 | 4208 | 15.5 | 16 |
| Mercury Morris | 69-76 | 804 | 4133 | 5.1 | 31 | 54 | 543 | 10.1 | 1 |
| Reece Morrison | 68-73 | 160 | 526 | 3.3 | 2 | 14 | 210 | 15.0 | 2 |
| Craig Morton | 65-81 | 215 | 627 | 2.9 | 12 | | | | |
| Haven Moses | 68-81 | 18 | 43 | 2.4 | 1 | 448 | 8091 | 18.1 | 56 |
| Roland Moss | 69-71 | | | | | 11 | 155 | 14.1 | 1 |
| Larry Mucker | 77-80 | 9 | 51 | 5.7 | 0 | 33 | 635 | 19.2 | 5 |
| Herb Mul-Key | 72-74 | 42 | 178 | 4.2 | 1 | 4 | 66 | 16.5 | 0 |
| Bill Munson | 64-79 | 130 | 548 | 4.2 | 3 | 1 | -6 | -6.0 | 0 |
| Johnny Musso | 75-77 | 100 | 365 | 3.7 | 6 | 7 | 39 | 5.6 | 0 |
| Chip Myers | 67,69-76 | | | | | 220 | 3092 | 14.1 | 12 |
| Joe Namath | 65-77 | 71 | 140 | 2.0 | 7 | | | | |
| Lewis Neal | 73-74 | 1 | -1 | -1.0 | 0 | 13 | 230 | 17.7 | 10 |
| Ralph Nelson | 75-76 | 83 | 312 | 3.8 | 1 | 17 | 154 | 9.1 | 1 |
| Terry Nelson | 74-80 | 12 | 85 | 7.1 | 1 | 87 | 1113 | 12.8 | 6 |
| Robert Newhouse | 72-83 | 1160 | 4784 | 4.1 | 31 | 120 | 956 | 8.0 | 5 |
| Bob Newland | 71-74 | 1 | 6 | 6.0 | 0 | 124 | 1877 | 15.1 | 0 |
| Kent Nix | 67-72 | 43 | 145 | 3.4 | 2 | | | | |
| George Nock | 69-72 | 192 | 556 | 2.9 | 8 | 24 | 190 | 7.9 | 3 |
| Don Nottingham | 71-78 | 611 | 2496 | 4.1 | 34 | 67 | 502 | 7.5 | 0 |
| Jack Novak | 75-77 | | | | | 12 | 188 | 15.7 | 1 |
| Jim Obradovich | 75-83 | | | | | 56 | 661 | 11.8 | 7 |
| Jim O'Brien | 70-73 | 3 | 9 | 3.0 | 0 | 14 | 305 | 21.8 | 2 |
| Steve Odom | 74-79 | 16 | 205 | 12.8 | 1 | 84 | 1613 | 19.2 | 11 |
| Riley Odoms | 72-83 | 25 | 211 | 8.4 | 2 | 396 | 5755 | 14.5 | 41 |
| Bill Olds | 73-76 | 287 | 985 | 3.4 | 6 | 62 | 372 | 6.0 | 4 |
| Joe Orduna | 72-74 | 74 | 236 | 3.2 | 3 | 11 | 58 | 5.3 | 1 |
| Dave Osborn | 65-76 | 1179 | 4336 | 3.7 | 29 | 173 | 1412 | 8.2 | 7 |
| Richard Osborne | 76-79 | | | | | 23 | 197 | 8.6 | 1 |
| Jim Otis | 70-78 | 1160 | 4350 | 3.8 | 19 | 90 | 549 | 6.1 | 3 |
| Artie Owens | 76-80 | 41 | 154 | 3.8 | 1 | 27 | 418 | 15.5 | 2 |
| Morris Owens | 75-79 | 4 | 0 | 0.0 | 0 | 116 | 2062 | 17.8 | 14 |
| Steve Owens | 70-74 | 635 | 2451 | 3.9 | 20 | 99 | 861 | 8.7 | 2 |
| Tinker Owens | 76-80 | | | | | 60 | 785 | 13.1 | 4 |
| Joel Parker | 74-77 | 2 | 2 | 1.0 | 0 | 51 | 585 | 11.5 | 6 |
| Billy Parks | 71-75 | 5 | 77 | 15.4 | 0 | 123 | 1826 | 14.8 | 7 |
| Gary Parris | 73-80 | | | | | 45 | 512 | 11.4 | 5 |
| Bob Parsons | 72-81 | 8 | 2 | 0.3 | 0 | 19 | 231 | 12.2 | 4 |
| Dan Pastorini | 71-83 | 216 | 685 | 3.2 | 8 | | | | |
| Lloyd Pate | 70 | 46 | 162 | 3.1 | 1 | 19 | 103 | 5.4 | 0 |
| Wayne Patrick | 68-72 | 264 | 1084 | 4.1 | 5 | 96 | 745 | 7.8 | 1 |
| Ken Payne | 74-78 | 2 | 15 | 7.5 | 0 | 116 | 1633 | 14.1 | 6 |
| Barry Pearson | 72-76 | 1 | 1 | 1.0 | 0 | 86 | 1212 | 14.1 | 7 |
| Dennis Pearson | 78-80 | 1 | 1 | 1.0 | 0 | 12 | 190 | 15.8 | 0 |
| Drew Pearson | 73-83 | 21 | 189 | 9.0 | 0 | 489 | 7822 | 16.0 | 48 |
| Preston Pearson | 67-80 | 941 | 3609 | 3.8 | 13 | 254 | 3095 | 12.2 | 17 |
| Brian Peets | 78-81 | | | | | 27 | 312 | 11.6 | 1 |
| Carlos Pennywell | 78-81 | 1 | 3 | 3.0 | 0 | 12 | 143 | 11.9 | 3 |
| Lonnie Perrin | 76-79 | 262 | 1047 | 4.0 | 9 | 21 | 222 | 10.6 | 2 |
| Jess Phillips | 68-77 | 888 | 3568 | 4.0 | 13 | 114 | 694 | 6.1 | 2 |
| Rod Phillips | 75-80 | 121 | 595 | 4.9 | 3 | 14 | 86 | 6.1 | 0 |
| Mike Phipps | 70-81 | 254 | 1278 | 5.0 | 13 | | | | |
| Lou Piccone | 74-82 | 2 | 17 | 8.5 | 0 | 100 | 1380 | 13.8 | 6 |
| Cyril Pinder | 68-73 | 428 | 1709 | 4.0 | 7 | 67 | 556 | 8.3 | 0 |
| Frank Pitts | 68-75 | 28 | 257 | 9.2 | 1 | 175 | 2897 | 16.6 | 27 |
| Jim Plunkett | 71-86 | 323 | 1337 | 4.1 | 14 | | | | |
| Ed Podolak | 69-77 | 1157 | 4451 | 3.8 | 34 | 288 | 2456 | 8.5 | 6 |
| Larry Poole | 75-78 | 133 | 588 | 4.4 | 2 | 32 | 212 | 6.6 | 3 |
| Ernest Pough | 76-78 | 5 | 41 | 8.3 | 0 | 10 | 166 | 16.6 | 1 |
| Darnell Powell | 76,78-79 | 31 | 117 | 3.8 | 1 | 1 | 6 | 6.0 | 0 |
| Billy Ray Pritchett | 75-77 | 92 | 290 | 3.2 | 1 | 17 | 110 | 6.5 | 0 |
| Joe Profit | 71-73 | 133 | 471 | 3.5 | 3 | 14 | 130 | 9.3 | 0 |
| Greg Pruitt | 73-84 | 1196 | 5672 | 4.7 | 27 | 328 | 3069 | 9.4 | 18 |
| Jeff Queen | 69-74 | 178 | 596 | 3.3 | 5 | 54 | 658 | 12.2 | 5 |
| Mike Rae | 76-81 | 44 | 300 | 6.8 | 2 | | | | |
| George Ragsdale | 77-80 | 34 | 147 | 4.3 | 1 | 8 | 86 | 10.8 | 1 |
| Steve Raible | 76-81 | 3 | 15 | 5.0 | 0 | 68 | 1017 | 15.0 | 3 |
| Steve Ramsey | 70-76 | 33 | 108 | 3.3 | 2 | | | | |
| Ahmad Rashad | 72-74,76-82 | 10 | 52 | 5.2 | 0 | 495 | 6831 | 13.8 | 44 |
| Bo Rather | 73-78 | 9 | 46 | 5.1 | 0 | 92 | 1467 | 15.9 | 7 |
| Eddie Ray | 70-74,76 | 181 | 691 | 3.8 | 9 | 33 | 275 | 8.3 | 2 |
| Tommy Reaman | 76 | 103 | 314 | 3.0 | 4 | 10 | 136 | 13.6 | 1 |
| John Reaves | 72-79,81 | 44 | 195 | 4.4 | 3 | | | | |
| Alvin Reed | 67-75 | 1 | 0 | 0.0 | 0 | 214 | 2983 | 13.9 | 14 |
| Joe Reed | 72-79 | 84 | 484 | 5.8 | 2 | | | | |
| Oscar Reed | 68-75 | 504 | 2008 | 4.0 | 8 | 94 | 677 | 7.2 | 3 |
| Tony Reed | 77-81 | 581 | 2340 | 4.0 | 8 | 172 | 1699 | 9.9 | 2 |
| Tom Reynolds | 72-73 | | | | | 15 | 279 | 18.6 | 2 |
| Ray Rhodes | 74-80 | 6 | 0 | 0.0 | 0 | 51 | 980 | 19.2 | 7 |
| Golden Richards | 73-79 | 5 | 15 | 3.0 | 0 | 122 | 2136 | 17.5 | 17 |
| Gloster Richardson | 67-74 | 5 | -8 | -1.8 | 0 | 92 | 1976 | 21.5 | 18 |
| Mike Richardson | 69-71 | 125 | 452 | 3.6 | 2 | 38 | 398 | 10.5 | 1 |
| John Riggins | 71-79,81-85 | 2916 | 11352 | 3.9 | 104 | 250 | 2090 | 8.4 | 12 |
| Preston Riley | 70-72 | | | | | 21 | 331 | 15.8 | 1 |
| Oscar Roan | 75-78 | | | | | 69 | 773 | 11.2 | 9 |

(All men with 25 or more rushing attempts or 10 or more receptions)

| Name | Years | RUSHING | | | | RECEIVING | | | |
| --- | --- | --- | --- | --- | --- | --- | --- | --- | --- |
| | | Att. | Yards | Avg. | TD | Rec. | Yards | Avg. | TD |
| Jim Robinson | 76-80 | | | | | 85 | 1437 | 16.9 | 6 |
| Paul Robinson | 68-73 | 737 | 2947 | 4.0 | 24 | 90 | 612 | 6.8 | 2 |
| Virgil Robinson | 71-72 | 34 | 97 | 2.9 | 1 | 12 | 53 | 4.4 | 1 |
| Terry Robiskie | 77-81 | 159 | 549 | 3.5 | 5 | 23 | 147 | 6.4 | 0 |
| Johnny Rodgers | 77-78 | 4 | 49 | 12.3 | 0 | 17 | 234 | 13.8 | 0 |
| Willie Rodgers | 72-75 | 211 | 672 | 3.2 | 8 | 30 | 214 | 7.1 | 0 |
| Oliver Ross | 73-76 | 63 | 173 | 2.7 | 0 | 10 | 104 | 10.4 | 0 |
| Reggie Rucker | 70-81 | 12 | 68 | 5.7 | 0 | 447 | 7065 | 15.8 | 44 |
| Billy Ryckman | 77-80 | | | | | 50 | 743 | 14.9 | 4 |
| Tony Samuels | 77-81 | | | | | 33 | 419 | 12.7 | 2 |
| Sam Scarber | 75-76,78 | 76 | 304 | 4.0 | 2 | 26 | 164 | 6.3 | 2 |
| Larry Schreiber | 71-76 | 506 | 1794 | 3.5 | 10 | 117 | 982 | 8.4 | 4 |
| Steve Schubert | 74-79 | | | | | 24 | 362 | 15.1 | 1 |
| Bo Scott | 69-74 | 554 | 2124 | 3.8 | 18 | 112 | 826 | 7.4 | 7 |
| Bobby Scott | 73-81 | 30 | 74 | 2.5 | 1 | | | | |
| Freddie Scott | 74-83 | 25 | 191 | 7.6 | 1 | 262 | 4270 | 16.3 | 20 |
| James Scott | 76-82 | 2 | -4 | -2.0 | 0 | 177 | 3202 | 18.1 | 20 |
| Rob Scribner | 73-76 | 73 | 361 | 4.9 | 3 | 6 | 75 | 12.5 | 1 |
| Paul Seal | 74-79 | 5 | 10 | 2.0 | 1 | 106 | 1586 | 14.9 | 7 |
| Larry Seiple | 67-77 | 15 | 145 | 9.7 | 0 | 73 | 934 | 12.8 | 7 |
| Ron Sellers | 69-73 | | | | | 112 | 2184 | 19.5 | 18 |
| Jim Seymour | 70-72 | 1 | -9 | -9.0 | 0 | 21 | 385 | 18.3 | 5 |
| Paul Seymour | 73-77 | | | | | 62 | 818 | 13.2 | 3 |
| Ron Shanklin | 70-76 | 5 | 2 | 0.4 | 0 | 168 | 3079 | 18.3 | 24 |
| Dennis Shaw | 70-76, 78 | 95 | 420 | 4.4 | 0 | | | | |
| Rod Sherman | 67-73 | 4 | 20 | 5.0 | 0 | 105 | 1576 | 15.0 | 5 |
| Gary Shirk | 76-82 | | | | | 130 | 1640 | 12.6 | 11 |
| Don Shy | 67-73 | 457 | 1577 | 3.5 | 10 | 76 | 835 | 11.0 | 3 |
| Mike Siani | 72-80 | | | | | 158 | 2618 | 16.6 | 17 |
| Nate Simpson | 77-79 | 153 | 497 | 3.2 | 1 | 17 | 69 | 4.1 | 0 |
| O.J. Simpson | 69-79 | 2404 | 11236 | 4.7 | 61 | 203 | 2142 | 10.5 | 14 |
| David Sims | 77-79 | 293 | 1174 | 4.0 | 19 | 46 | 399 | 8.7 | 4 |
| Brian Sipe | 74-83 | 223 | 762 | 3.4 | 11 | | | | |
| Barry Smith | 73-76 | 10 | 24 | 2.4 | 0 | 46 | 692 | 15.0 | 4 |
| Barty Smith | 74-80 | 544 | 1942 | 3.6 | 18 | 120 | 979 | 8.2 | 3 |
| Charlie Smith | 68-75 | 858 | 3351 | 3.9 | 24 | 141 | 1596 | 11.3 | 10 |
| Charlie Smith | 74-81 | 27 | 161 | 6.0 | 1 | 218 | 3349 | 15.4 | 24 |
| Dave Smith | 70-73 | 2 | -4 | -2.0 | 0 | 109 | 1457 | 13.4 | 7 |
| Jerry Smith | 65-77 | 8 | 56 | 7.0 | 0 | 421 | 5496 | 13.1 | 60 |
| Larry Smith | 69-74 | 528 | 2027 | 3.3 | 11 | 149 | 1176 | 7.9 | 5 |
| Ollie Smith | 73-74, 76-77 | 1 | -3 | -3.0 | 0 | 44 | 772 | 17.5 | 1 |
| Ron Smith | 65-74 | 8 | 42 | 5.3 | 0 | 11 | 227 | 20.6 | 0 |
| Sherman Smith | 76-83 | 834 | 3520 | 4.2 | 28 | 217 | 2393 | 11.0 | 10 |
| Jack Snow | 65-75 | 2 | 3 | 1.5 | 0 | 340 | 6012 | 17.7 | 45 |
| Todd Snyder | 70-72 | | | | | 24 | 330 | 13.8 | 2 |
| Willie Spencer | 76-78 | 104 | 247 | 2.4 | 5 | 6 | 45 | 7.5 | 0 |
| Cotton Spreyer | 72-75 | 1 | 1 | 1.0 | 0 | 34 | 535 | 15.7 | 5 |
| John Spilis | 69-71 | | | | | 27 | 446 | 16.5 | 1 |
| Steve Spurrier | 67-76 | 61 | 258 | 4.2 | 2 | | | | |
| Ken Stabler | 70-84 | 118 | 93 | 0.8 | 4 | | | | |
| Jon Staggers | 70-75 | 8 | 56 | 7.0 | 1 | 93 | 1370 | 14.7 | 7 |
| Haskel Stanback | 74-79 | 728 | 2662 | 3.7 | 25 | 98 | 786 | 8.0 | 1 |
| Roger Staubach | 69-79 | 410 | 2264 | 5.4 | 20 | 1 | -13 | -13.0 | 0 |
| Howard Stevens | 73-77 | 89 | 376 | 4.2 | 4 | 17 | 120 | 7.1 | 0 |
| Wayne Stewart | 74 | | | | | 19 | 283 | 14.9 | 1 |
| Darryl Stingley | 73-77 | 28 | 244 | 8.7 | 2 | 110 | 1883 | 17.1 | 14 |
| Otto Stowe | 71-74 | 4 | 29 | 7.3 | 0 | 43 | 742 | 17.3 | 10 |
| Steve Strachan | 85-88 | 52 | 174 | 3.3 | 0 | 7 | 61 | 8.7 | 0 |
| Jim Strong | 70-72 | 134 | 527 | 3.9 | 3 | 30 | 201 | 6.7 | 0 |
| Morris Stroud | 69-74 | | | | | 54 | 977 | 18.1 | 7 |
| Tom Sullivan | 72-78 | 876 | 3142 | 3.6 | 17 | 162 | 1286 | 7.9 | 5 |
| Lynn Swann | 74-82 | 11 | 72 | 6.5 | 0 | 336 | 5462 | 16.3 | 51 |
| Joe Sweet | 72-75 | 1 | 1 | 1.0 | 0 | 10 | 173 | 17.3 | 1 |
| Jerry Tagge | 72-74 | 41 | 117 | 2.9 | 3 | | | | |
| John Tarver | 72-75 | 162 | 562 | 3.5 | 7 | 34 | 214 | 6.3 | 1 |
| Altie Taylor | 69-76 | 1170 | 4308 | 3.7 | 24 | 175 | 1538 | 8.8 | 6 |
| Charley Taylor | 64-75, 77 | 442 | 1488 | 3.4 | 11 | 649 | 9110 | 14.0 | 79 |
| Otis Taylor | 65-75 | 30 | 161 | 5.4 | 3 | 410 | 7306 | 17.8 | 57 |
| Don Testerman | 76-78, 80 | 230 | 865 | 3.8 | 2 | 73 | 604 | 8.3 | 5 |

| Name | Years | RUSHING | | | | RECEIVING | | | |
| --- | --- | --- | --- | --- | --- | --- | --- | --- | --- |
| | | Att. | Yards | Avg. | TD | Rec. | Yards | Avg. | TD |
| Jim Thaxton | 73-74, 76-78 | 2 | -13 | -6.5 | 0 | 35 | 544 | 15.5 | 5 |
| Bob Thomas | 71-74 | 120 | 537 | 4.5 | 3 | 19 | 155 | 8.2 | 1 |
| Duane Thomas | 70-71, 73-74 | 453 | 2038 | 4.5 | 21 | 38 | 297 | 7.8 | 3 |
| Earl Thomas | 71-76 | 6 | 18 | 3.0 | 0 | 106 | 1651 | 15.6 | 14 |
| Jimmy Thomas | 69-73 | 165 | 824 | 5.0 | 4 | 67 | 923 | 13.8 | 8 |
| Mike Thomas | 75-80 | 1087 | 4196 | 3.9 | 19 | 192 | 2011 | 10.5 | 11 |
| Speedy Thomas | 69-72, 74 | 8 | 22 | 2.8 | 1 | 19 | 122 | 6.4 | 0 |
| Bobby Thompson | 75-76 | 64 | 310 | 4.8 | 1 | 29 | 230 | 7.9 | 0 |
| Jesse Thompson | 78,80 | 3 | 3 | 1.0 | 0 | 29 | 312 | 10.8 | 4 |
| Ricky Thompson | 76-81 | | | | | 97 | 1480 | 15.3 | 14 |
| Rocky Thompson | 71-73 | 68 | 217 | 3.2 | 1 | 16 | 85 | 5.3 | 0 |
| Woody Thompson | 75-77 | 242 | 877 | 3.6 | 1 | 42 | 259 | 6.2 | 0 |
| Andre Tillman | 75-78 | | | | | 66 | 757 | 11.5 | 6 |
| Eric Torkelson | 74-81 | 351 | 1307 | 3.7 | 8 | 59 | 469 | 7.9 | 0 |
| Bill Troup | 74-78,80 | 30 | 16 | 0.5 | 2 | | | | |
| Bob Trumpy | 68-77 | 1 | -1 | -1.0 | 0 | 298 | 4600 | 15.4 | 35 |
| Bob Tucker | 70-80 | 6 | 6 | 1.0 | 1 | 422 | 5421 | 12.8 | 27 |
| Walter Tullis | 78-79 | | | | | 10 | 173 | 17.3 | 1 |
| Cecil Turner | 68-73 | 8 | 13 | 1.6 | 0 | 21 | 364 | 17.3 | 2 |
| Clem Turner | 69-72 | 74 | 270 | 3.6 | 2 | 21 | 114 | 5.4 | 1 |
| Deacon Turner | 78-80 | 142 | 549 | 3.9 | 1 | 25 | 141 | 5.6 | 1 |
| Howard Twilley | 66-76 | | | | | 212 | 3064 | 14.5 | 23 |
| Rick Upchurch | 75-84 | 49 | 349 | 7.1 | 3 | 267 | 4369 | 16.4 | 24 |
| Mark van Eeghen | 74-83 | 1652 | 6651 | 4.0 | 37 | 174 | 1583 | 9.1 | 4 |
| Bill Van Heusen | 68-76 | 13 | 171 | 13.2 | 1 | 82 | 1684 | 20.5 | 11 |
| Randy Vataha | 71-77 | 6 | -2 | -0.3 | 0 | 188 | 3164 | 16.8 | 23 |
| Stu Voigt | 70-80 | 2 | 3 | 1.5 | 0 | 177 | 1919 | 10.8 | 17 |
| Charlie Wade | 74-75,77 | 1 | -15 | -15.0 | 0 | 39 | 683 | 17.5 | 1 |
| Harmon Wages | 68-71,73 | 332 | 1321 | 4.0 | 5 | 85 | 765 | 9.0 | 5 |
| Bob Wallace | 68-72 | 8 | 45 | 5.6 | 0 | 109 | 1403 | 12.9 | 9 |
| Ward Walsh | 71-72 | 46 | 165 | 3.6 | 0 | 10 | 58 | 5.8 | 1 |
| Larry Walton | 69-74,76,78 | 12 | 101 | 8.4 | 1 | 172 | 2682 | 15.6 | 27 |
| Paul Warfield | 64-74,76-77 | 22 | 204 | 9.6 | 0 | 427 | 8565 | 20.1 | 85 |
| Gene Washington | 67-73 | | | | | 182 | 3237 | 17.8 | 26 |
| Gene Washington | 69-77,79 | 6 | 23 | 3.8 | 0 | 385 | 6856 | 17.8 | 60 |
| Vic Washington | 71-76 | 588 | 2208 | 3.8 | 16 | 130 | 1090 | 8.4 | 5 |
| Larry Watkins | 69-77 | 448 | 1711 | 3.8 | 12 | 51 | 284 | 5.6 | 1 |
| Norris Weese | 76-79 | 69 | 362 | 5.2 | 5 | | | | |
| Claxton Welch | 69-71,73 | 26 | 83 | 3.2 | 2 | 7 | 21 | 3.0 | 0 |
| Terry Wells | 74-75 | 33 | 139 | 4.2 | 0 | 7 | 20 | 2.9 | 0 |
| Bob West | 72-74 | 2 | 2 | 1.0 | 0 | 13 | 230 | 17.7 | 2 |
| Don Westbrook | 77-81 | 3 | 6 | 2.0 | 0 | 23 | 393 | 17.1 | 3 |
| Charlie White | 77-78 | 61 | 193 | 3.2 | 1 | 4 | 36 | 9.0 | 1 |
| Jan White | 71-72 | | | | | 25 | 276 | 11.1 | 2 |
| Lee White | 68-72 | 123 | 389 | 3.2 | 0 | 16 | 143 | 8.9 | 1 |
| Marsh White | 75-76 | 86 | 313 | 3.6 | 2 | 5 | 22 | 4.4 | 0 |
| Walter White | 75-79 | 4 | 12 | 3.0 | 0 | 163 | 2396 | 14.7 | 16 |
| Clarence Williams | 77-81 | 394 | 1327 | 3.4 | 17 | 93 | 727 | 7.8 | 2 |
| Dave Williams | 67-73 | 6 | 69 | 11.5 | 0 | 183 | 2768 | 15.1 | 25 |
| Dave Williams | 77-81 | 172 | 501 | 2.9 | 1 | 92 | 675 | 7.3 | 7 |
| Delvin Williams | 74-81 | 1312 | 5598 | 4.3 | 33 | 152 | 1415 | 9.3 | 6 |
| Ed Williams | 74-77 | 243 | 896 | 3.7 | 7 | 56 | 427 | 7.6 | 2 |
| Joe Williams | 71-72 | 52 | 139 | 2.7 | 1 | 19 | 175 | 9.2 | 0 |
| Perry Williams | 69-74 | 177 | 547 | 3.1 | 1 | 37 | 285 | 7.7 | 0 |
| Fred Willis | 71-76 | 780 | 2831 | 3.6 | 18 | 203 | 1380 | 6.8 | 5 |
| Joe Wilson | 73-75 | 25 | 96 | 3.8 | 0 | 3 | 38 | 12.7 | 0 |
| Bob Windsor | 67-75 | 9 | 57 | 6.3 | 0 | 185 | 2307 | 12.5 | 14 |
| Stan Winfrey | 75-77 | 55 | 225 | 4.1 | 1 | 6 | 55 | 9.2 | 1 |
| Al Woodall | 69-71,73-74 | 60 | 214 | 3.6 | 0 | | | | |
| Don Woods | 74-80 | 763 | 3087 | 4.0 | 16 | 145 | 1358 | 9.4 | 5 |
| Elmo Wright | 71-75 | 10 | 69 | 6.9 | 0 | 70 | 1116 | 15.9 | 6 |
| Keith Wright | 78-80 | | | | | 12 | 151 | 12.6 | 3 |
| Sam Wyche | 68-72,74,76 | 45 | 303 | 6.7 | 3 | 1 | 5 | 5.0 | 0 |
| Charley Young | 74-76 | 131 | 638 | 4.9 | 2 | 40 | 391 | 9.8 | 2 |
| Charle Young | 73-85 | 16 | 80 | 5.0 | 1 | 418 | 5106 | 12.2 | 27 |
| Rickey Young | 75-83 | 1011 | 3666 | 3.6 | 23 | 408 | 3285 | 8.1 | 16 |
| Steve Zabel | 70-79 | 1 | -5 | -5.0 | 0 | 10 | 123 | 12.3 | 3 |
| Don Zimmerman | 73-76 | 1 | 3 | 3.0 | 0 | 53 | 601 | 11.3 | 5 |

391

Lifetime Statistics- 1970-1979 Section 3 — **PUNT RETURNS and KICKOFF RETURNS**

(All men with 25 or more punt returns or 25 or more kickoff returns)

| | | PUNT RETURNS | | | | KICKOFF RETURNS | | | |
|---|---|---|---|---|---|---|---|---|---|
| Name | Years | No. | Yards | Avg. | TD | No. | Yards | Avg. | TD |
| Mike Adamle | 71-76 | 1 | 2 | 2.0 | 0 | 34 | 636 | 18.7 | 0 |
| Margene Adkins | 70-73 | 15 | 49 | 3.3 | 0 | 81 | 1784 | 22.0 | 0 |
| Bobby Anderson | 70-75 | | | | | 30 | 720 | 24.0 | 0 |
| Dick Anderson | 68-77 | 40 | 272 | 6.8 | 0 | 7 | 114 | 16.3 | 0 |
| Donny Anderson | 66-74 | 15 | 222 | 14.8 | 1 | 34 | 759 | 22.3 | 0 |
| Otis Armstrong | 73-80 | | | | | 37 | 879 | 23.8 | 0 |
| John Arnold | 79-80 | 47 | 368 | 7.6 | 0 | 32 | 684 | 21.4 | 0 |
| Pete Athas | 71-76 | 92 | 818 | 8.9 | 0 | 8 | 163 | 20.4 | 0 |
| Butch Atkinson | 68-77,79 | 148 | 1247 | 8.4 | 3 | 76 | 1893 | 24.9 | 0 |
| Gordon Bell | 76-78 | 16 | 102 | 6.4 | 0 | 38 | 764 | 20.1 | 0 |
| Horace Belton | 78-80 | | | | | 37 | 800 | 21.6 | 0 |
| Willie Belton | 71-74 | 52 | 283 | 5.4 | 0 | 57 | 1341 | 23.5 | 0 |
| Jim Bertelsen | 72-76 | 74 | 810 | 10.9 | 0 | 6 | 120 | 20.0 | 0 |
| Mel Blount | 70-82 | 1 | 52 | 52.0 | 0 | 36 | 911 | 25.3 | 0 |
| Emerson Boozer | 66-75 | | | | | 37 | 872 | 23.6 | 1 |
| Bill Bradley | 69-77 | 122 | 953 | 7.8 | 0 | 27 | 564 | 20.9 | 0 |
| Larry Brinson | 77-80 | | | | | 25 | 525 | 21.0 | 0 |
| Eddie Brown | 74-79 | 172 | 1511 | 8.8 | 1 | 81 | 1957 | 24.2 | 0 |
| Ken Brown | 70-75 | | | | | 44 | 973 | 22.1 | 0 |
| Ray Brown | 71-80 | 60 | 539 | 9.0 | 0 | | | | |
| Larry Brunson | 74-80 | 75 | 630 | 8.4 | 0 | 87 | 2022 | 23.2 | 0 |
| Cullen Bryant | 73-84 | 71 | 707 | 10.0 | 0 | 69 | 1813 | 26.3 | 3 |
| Bobby Bryant | 68-80 | 69 | 404 | 5.9 | 0 | 22 | 437 | 19.9 | 0 |
| Hubie Bryant | 73-75 | 19 | 218 | 11.5 | 0 | 48 | 1266 | 26.4 | 2 |
| Allen Carter | 75-76 | | | | | 33 | 898 | 27.2 | 1 |
| Tommy Casanova | 72-77 | 91 | 784 | 8.7 | 1 | 2 | 82 | 41.0 | 0 |
| Clarence Chapman | 76-81,85 | | | | | 35 | 768 | 21.9 | 1 |
| Gill Chapman | 75 | 17 | 207 | 12.2 | 0 | 28 | 614 | 21.9 | 0 |
| Rondy Colbert | 75-77 | 40 | 310 | 7.8 | 1 | 19 | 450 | 23.7 | 0 |
| Linzy Cole | 70-72 | 35 | 225 | 6.4 | 0 | 50 | 1290 | 25.8 | 0 |
| Ronnie Coleman | 74-81 | 25 | 228 | 9.1 | 1 | 29 | 601 | 20.7 | 0 |
| Mike Collier | 75,77-79 | | | | | 33 | 707 | 21.4 | 1 |
| Larry Collins | 78,80 | | | | | 32 | 709 | 22.2 | 0 |
| Neal Colzie | 75-83 | 170 | 1759 | 10.3 | 0 | 7 | 130 | 18.6 | 0 |
| Rufus Crawford | 78 | 34 | 284 | 8.4 | 0 | 35 | 829 | 23.7 | 0 |
| Doug Cunningham | 67-74 | 30 | 272 | 9.1 | 0 | 68 | 1613 | 23.7 | 0 |
| Thom Darden | 72-81 | 45 | 285 | 6.3 | 0 | 1 | -1 | -1.0 | 0 |
| Ben Davis | 67-68,70-76 | 27 | 240 | 8.9 | 1 | 35 | 860 | 24.6 | 0 |
| Clarence Davis | 71-78 | | | | | 79 | 2140 | 27.1 | 0 |
| Gary Davis | 76-81 | 3 | 47 | 15.7 | 0 | 104 | 2341 | 22.5 | 0 |
| Steve Davis | 72-76 | | | | | 54 | 1363 | 25.2 | 0 |
| Tony Davis | 76-81 | 42 | 357 | 8.5 | 0 | 21 | 256 | 12.2 | 0 |
| Joe Dawkins | 70-76 | 1 | 0 | 0.0 | 0 | 32 | 799 | 25.0 | 0 |
| Johnnie Dirden | 78-81 | | | | | 42 | 979 | 22.3 | 0 |
| Al Dodd | 67,69-71,73-74 | 80 | 744 | 9.3 | 0 | 38 | 776 | 20.4 | 0 |
| Bobby Duhon | 68,70-72 | 40 | 286 | 7.2 | 1 | 40 | 716 | 17.9 | 0 |
| Lenny Dunlap | 71-75 | 27 | 291 | 10.8 | 0 | 15 | 337 | 22.5 | 0 |
| Glen Edwards | 71-81 | 104 | 959 | 9.2 | 0 | 13 | 257 | 19.8 | 0 |
| Jimmy Edwards | 79 | 33 | 186 | 5.6 | 0 | 44 | 1103 | 25.1 | 0 |
| Richard Ellender | 79 | 31 | 203 | 6.5 | 0 | 24 | 514 | 21.4 | 0 |
| Lenvil Elliott | 73-81 | | | | | 47 | 877 | 18.7 | 0 |
| Ken Ellis | 70-77,79 | 71 | 469 | 6.6 | 1 | 41 | 882 | 21.5 | 0 |
| Willie Ellison | 67-74 | | | | | 42 | 1011 | 24.1 | 0 |
| Dave Elmendorf | 71-79 | 57 | 502 | 8.8 | 0 | 2 | 23 | 11.5 | 0 |
| Chris Farasopoulos | 71-74 | 53 | 481 | 9.1 | 1 | 51 | 1172 | 23.0 | 0 |
| Chris Fletcher | 70-76 | 28 | 205 | 7.3 | 0 | 28 | 599 | 21.4 | 0 |
| Ike Forte | 76-81 | 3 | 4 | 1.3 | 0 | 26 | 630 | 24.2 | 0 |
| Wallace Francis | 73-81 | | | | | 84 | 2077 | 24.0 | 2 |
| Johnny Fuller | 68-75 | 25 | 114 | 4.6 | 0 | 10 | 186 | 18.6 | 0 |
| Mike Fuller | 75-82 | 252 | 2660 | 10.6 | 2 | 79 | 1701 | 21.5 | 0 |
| Frenchy Fuqua | 69-76 | 12 | 77 | 6.4 | 0 | 26 | 496 | 19.1 | 0 |
| Ron Gardin | 70-71,73 | 34 | 419 | 12.3 | 1 | 25 | 586 | 23.4 | 0 |
| Carl Garrett | 69-77 | 43 | 487 | 11.3 | 0 | 154 | 3704 | 24.1 | 0 |
| Walt Garrison | 66-74 | | | | | 41 | 813 | 19.8 | 0 |
| Tom Geredine | 73-74,76 | | | | | 27 | 611 | 22.6 | 0 |
| Louie Giammona | 76,78-81 | 18 | 167 | 9.3 | 0 | 58 | 1167 | 20.1 | 0 |
| John Gillam | 67-77 | 23 | 94 | 4.1 | 0 | 74 | 1884 | 25.5 | 2 |
| Hubert Ginn | 70-77 | 1 | 4 | 4.0 | 0 | 50 | 1105 | 22.1 | 0 |
| Dick Gordon | 65-74 | 31 | 148 | 4.8 | 0 | 79 | 1925 | 24.4 | 0 |
| Johnnie Gray | 75-83 | 85 | 656 | 7.7 | 0 | 21 | 317 | 15.1 | 0 |
| Mel Gray | 71-81 | 9 | 49 | 5.4 | 0 | 51 | 1191 | 23.4 | 0 |
| Tony Green | 71-79 | 61 | 581 | 9.5 | 1 | 66 | 1521 | 23.0 | 1 |
| Charlie Greer | 68-74 | 55 | 426 | 7.7 | 1 | 2 | 41 | 20.5 | 0 |
| Bob Gresham | 71-76 | | | | | 46 | 1116 | 24.3 | 1 |
| Bob Grim | 67-77 | 59 | 282 | 4.8 | 0 | 26 | 549 | 21.1 | 0 |
| Isaac Hagins | 76-80 | 22 | 110 | 5.0 | 0 | 40 | 875 | 21.9 | 0 |
| Bob Hammond | 76-80 | 67 | 566 | 8.4 | 1 | 61 | 1297 | 21.3 | 0 |
| Gary Hammond | 73-76 | 40 | 291 | 7.3 | 0 | 38 | 872 | 22.9 | 0 |
| Dave Hampton | 69-76 | | | | | 113 | 2923 | 25.9 | 3 |
| Willard Harrell | 75-84 | 123 | 854 | 6.9 | 2 | 97 | 1921 | 19.8 | 0 |
| Cliff Harris | 70-79 | 66 | 418 | 6.3 | 0 | 63 | 1622 | 25.7 | 0 |
| Harold Hart | 74-78 | | | | | 46 | 1236 | 26.9 | 1 |
| Bob Hayes | 64-75 | 104 | 1158 | 11.1 | 3 | 23 | 581 | 25.3 | 0 |
| Gary Hayman | 74-75 | 27 | 229 | 8.5 | 0 | 8 | 179 | 22.4 | 0 |
| Mack Herron | 73-75 | 84 | 982 | 11.7 | 0 | 82 | 1985 | 24.2 | 1 |
| Ike Hill | 70-71,73-74,76 | 102 | 622 | 6.1 | 2 | 21 | 445 | 21.2 | 0 |
| Paul Hofer | 76-81 | | | | | 68 | 1474 | 21.7 | 0 |
| Steve Holden | 73-77 | 36 | 238 | 6.6 | 0 | 29 | 675 | 23.3 | 0 |
| Mike Holmes | 74-76 | 9 | 45 | 5.0 | 0 | 31 | 761 | 24.5 | 0 |
| Robert Holmes | 68-73,75 | | | | | 35 | 928 | 26.5 | 0 |
| Roland Hooks | 76-82 | 43 | 302 | 7.0 | 0 | 48 | 969 | 20.2 | 0 |
| Ken Houston | 67-80 | 51 | 333 | 6.5 | 0 | 3 | 80 | 26.7 | 0 |
| Rich Houston | 69-73 | | | | | 35 | 800 | 22.9 | 0 |
| Gene Howard | 68-72 | 22 | 129 | 5.9 | 0 | 41 | 975 | 23.8 | 0 |
| Bob Hudson | 72-74 | 1 | 0 | 0.0 | 0 | 25 | 597 | 23.9 | 0 |
| Al Hunter | 77-80 | | | | | 78 | 1717 | 22.0 | 0 |
| Horace Ivory | 77-82 | | | | | 70 | 1696 | 24.2 | 1 |
| Bernard Jackson | 72-80 | | | | | 118 | 2709 | 23.0 | 0 |
| Po James | 72-75 | | | | | 41 | 962 | 23.5 | 0 |
| Dick Jauron | 73-80 | 44 | 447 | 10.2 | 0 | 19 | 426 | 22.4 | 0 |
| Roy Jefferson | 65-76 | 58 | 436 | 7.5 | 1 | 5 | 91 | 18.2 | 0 |
| Ron Jessie | 71-81 | | | | | 47 | 1237 | 26.3 | 2 |
| Andy Johnson | 74-76,78-81 | 6 | 60 | 10.0 | 0 | 28 | 544 | 19.4 | 0 |
| Benny Johnson | 70-73,76 | | | | | 28 | 550 | 19.6 | 0 |
| Essex Johnson | 68-76 | 51 | 303 | 5.9 | 0 | 49 | 1036 | 21.1 | 0 |
| Marshall Johnson | 75,77-78 | 25 | 147 | 5.9 | 0 | 49 | 1076 | 22.0 | 0 |

| | | PUNT RETURNS | | | | KICKOFF RETURNS | | | |
|---|---|---|---|---|---|---|---|---|---|
| Name | Years | No. | Yards | Avg. | TD | No. | Yards | Avg. | TD |
| Clint Jones | 67-73 | | | | | 99 | 2426 | 24.5 | 1 |
| Jimmie Jones | 74 | | | | | 38 | 927 | 24.4 | 0 |
| Larry Jones | 74-78 | 72 | 562 | 7.8 | 1 | 73 | 1816 | 24.9 | 1 |
| Doug Kotar | 74-79,81 | 4 | 19 | 4.8 | 0 | 42 | 920 | 21.9 | 0 |
| Larry Krause | 70-71,73-74 | | | | | 35 | 864 | 24.7 | 1 |
| Bruce Laird | 72-83 | 61 | 405 | 6.6 | 0 | 152 | 3728 | 24.5 | 0 |
| Jerry Latin | 75-78 | | | | | 43 | 951 | 22.1 | 0 |
| Dennis Law | 78-79 | 25 | 106 | 4.2 | 0 | 2 | 30 | 15.0 | 0 |
| Rolland Lawrence | 73-80 | 109 | 734 | 6.7 | 0 | 29 | 685 | 23.6 | 0 |
| Odell Lawson | 70-71,73-74 | 1 | 0 | 0.0 | 0 | 28 | 613 | 21.9 | 0 |
| Billy LeFear | 72-75 | 10 | 56 | 5.6 | 0 | 60 | 1461 | 24.4 | 0 |
| Charlie Leigh | 68-69,71-74 | 50 | 368 | 7.4 | 0 | 46 | 1082 | 23.5 | 0 |
| Tony Leonard | 76-79 | 76 | 594 | 7.8 | 1 | 30 | 691 | 23.0 | 0 |
| Jerry LeVais | 69-74 | 88 | 687 | 7.8 | 0 | 94 | 2213 | 23.5 | 0 |
| Floyd Little | 67-75 | 81 | 893 | 11.0 | 2 | 104 | 2523 | 24.3 | 0 |
| Virgil Livers | 75-79 | 86 | 738 | 8.6 | 0 | 27 | 543 | 20.1 | 0 |
| Spider Lockhart | 65-75 | 64 | 328 | 5.1 | 0 | 1 | 19 | 19.0 | 0 |
| Larry Marshall | 72-78 | 162 | 1466 | 9.0 | 0 | 138 | 3396 | 24.6 | 0 |
| Alvin Maxson | 74-78 | | | | | 25 | 464 | 18.6 | 0 |
| James McAlister | 75-76,78 | | | | | 31 | 636 | 20.5 | 0 |
| Don McCauley | 71-81 | | | | | 45 | 967 | 22.5 | 1 |
| Brent McClanahan | 73-79 | | | | | 66 | 1500 | 22.7 | 0 |
| Ralph McGill | 72-79 | 106 | 969 | 9.1 | 1 | 27 | 566 | 21.0 | 0 |
| Rod McNeill | 74-76 | 1 | 0 | 0.0 | 0 | 27 | 660 | 24.4 | 0 |
| Leon McQuay | 74-76 | 9 | 86 | 9.6 | 0 | 48 | 1092 | 22.8 | 0 |
| Warren McVea | 68-71,73 | | | | | 47 | 1008 | 21.4 | 0 |
| Terry Metcalf | 73-77,81 | 84 | 936 | 11.4 | 1 | 120 | 3087 | 25.7 | 2 |
| Cleo Miller | 74-82 | | | | | 34 | 660 | 19.4 | 0 |
| Kevin Miller | 78-80 | 66 | 324 | 4.9 | 0 | 40 | 854 | 21.4 | 0 |
| Randy Montgomery | 71-74 | | | | | 33 | 836 | 25.3 | 1 |
| Keith Moody | 76-80 | 88 | 920 | 10.5 | 3 | 109 | 2318 | 21.3 | 0 |
| Manfred Moore | 74-77 | 88 | 770 | 8.8 | 1 | 76 | 1734 | 22.8 | 0 |
| Zeke Moore | 67-77 | 8 | 93 | 11.6 | 0 | 64 | 1618 | 25.3 | 1 |
| Dennis Morgan | 74-75 | 27 | 347 | 12.9 | 1 | 42 | 993 | 23.6 | 0 |
| Mercury Morris | 69-76 | 27 | 171 | 6.3 | 0 | 111 | 2947 | 26.5 | 3 |
| Reece Morrison | 68-73 | 26 | 182 | 7.0 | 0 | 32 | 727 | 22.7 | 0 |
| Herb Mul-Key | 72-74 | 24 | 243 | 10.1 | 0 | 54 | 1505 | 27.4 | 1 |
| Steve Odom | 74-79 | 73 | 595 | 8.2 | 1 | 194 | 4251 | 21.9 | 2 |
| Artie Owens | 76-80 | 1 | 20 | 20.0 | 0 | 96 | 2155 | 22.4 | 0 |
| Lemar Parrish | 70-82 | 131 | 1205 | 9.2 | 4 | 61 | 1504 | 24.7 | 1 |
| Dennis Pearson | 78-80 | 12 | 115 | 9.6 | 0 | 55 | 1232 | 22.4 | 1 |
| Preston Pearson | 67-80 | 7 | 40 | 5.7 | 0 | 114 | 2801 | 24.6 | 2 |
| Lonnie Perrin | 76-79 | | | | | 33 | 805 | 24.4 | 0 |
| Jess Phillips | 68-77 | 2 | 16 | 8.0 | 0 | 45 | 1048 | 23.3 | 0 |
| Lou Piccone | 74-82 | 73 | 482 | 6.6 | 1 | 111 | 2559 | 23.1 | 0 |
| Ed Podolak | 69-77 | 86 | 739 | 8.6 | 0 | 34 | 697 | 20.5 | 0 |
| Ernest Pough | 76-78 | | | | | 40 | 793 | 19.8 | 0 |
| Greg Pruitt | 73-84 | 194 | 2007 | 10.3 | 1 | 106 | 2514 | 23.7 | 1 |
| George Ragsdale | 77-79 | | | | | 61 | 1298 | 21.2 | 0 |
| Danny Reece | 76-80 | 222 | 1554 | 7.0 | 0 | 23 | 483 | 21.0 | 0 |
| Mel Renfro | 64-77 | 109 | 842 | 7.7 | 1 | 85 | 2246 | 26.4 | 2 |
| Golden Richards | 73-79 | 62 | 501 | 8.1 | 1 | 3 | 44 | 14.7 | 0 |
| Jim Robinson | 76-80 | 59 | 364 | 6.2 | 0 | 27 | 584 | 21.6 | 0 |
| Paul Robinson | 68-73 | 2 | 1 | 0.5 | 0 | 40 | 924 | 23.1 | 0 |
| Johnny Rodgers | 77-78 | 26 | 246 | 9.5 | 0 | 15 | 353 | 23.5 | 0 |
| Oliver Ross | 73-76 | | | | | 38 | 792 | 20.8 | 0 |
| Billy Ryckman | 77-80 | 47 | 339 | 7.2 | 0 | 1 | 0 | 0.0 | 0 |
| Steve Schubert | 74-79 | 103 | 866 | 8.4 | 3 | 21 | 586 | 18.4 | 0 |
| Bo Scott | 69-74 | | | | | 25 | 722 | 28.9 | 0 |
| Jake Scott | 70-78 | 130 | 1357 | 10.4 | 1 | 6 | 137 | 22.8 | 0 |
| Rob Scribner | 73-76 | 45 | 361 | 8.0 | 0 | 16 | 392 | 24.5 | 0 |
| Jeff Severson | 72-79 | 28 | 212 | 7.6 | 0 | 9 | 148 | 16.4 | 0 |
| Willie Shelby | 76-78 | 42 | 304 | 7.2 | 0 | 58 | 1375 | 23.7 | 1 |
| Rod Sherman | 67-73 | 27 | 212 | 7.9 | 0 | 8 | 145 | 18.1 | 0 |
| Don Shy | 67-73 | 29 | 202 | 7.0 | 0 | 26 | 618 | 23.8 | 0 |
| O.J. Simpson | 69-79 | | | | | 33 | 990 | 30.0 | 1 |
| Charlie Smith | 68-75 | | | | | 30 | 659 | 22.0 | 0 |
| Ron Smith | 65-74 | 235 | 1788 | 7.6 | 2 | 275 | 6922 | 25.2 | 3 |
| Cotton Speyrer | 72-75 | 8 | 54 | 6.8 | 0 | 39 | 1035 | 26.5 | 1 |
| Jon Staggers | 70-75 | 94 | 792 | 8.4 | 3 | 35 | 854 | 24.4 | 0 |
| Howard Stevens | 73-77 | 163 | 1559 | 9.6 | 0 | 103 | 2336 | 22.7 | 0 |
| Tom Sullivan | 72-78 | | | | | 27 | 592 | 21.9 | 0 |
| Lynn Swann | 74-82 | 61 | 739 | 12.1 | 1 | 3 | 11 | 3.7 | 0 |
| Altie Taylor | 69-76 | | | | | 27 | 597 | 22.1 | 0 |
| Bruce Taylor | 70-77 | 142 | 1323 | 9.3 | 0 | 12 | 190 | 15.8 | 0 |
| Clifton Taylor | 74,76 | | | | | 30 | 626 | 20.9 | 0 |
| Jesse Taylor | 72 | 1 | 0 | 0.0 | 0 | 31 | 676 | 21.8 | 0 |
| Bill Thomas | 72-74 | | | | | 27 | 621 | 23.0 | 0 |
| Emmitt Thomas | 66-78 | 11 | 64 | 5.8 | 0 | 29 | 673 | 23.2 | 0 |
| Ike Thomas | 71-75 | | | | | 51 | 1394 | 27.3 | 0 |
| Billy Thompson | 69-81 | 157 | 1814 | 11.6 | 0 | 46 | 1156 | 25.1 | 0 |
| Bobby Thompson | 75-76 | | | | | 44 | 996 | 22.6 | 0 |
| Rocky Thompson | 71-73 | | | | | 65 | 1768 | 27.2 | 2 |
| Gerald Tinker | 74-75 | 20 | 218 | 10.9 | 1 | 42 | 1011 | 24.1 | 0 |
| Cecil Turner | 68-73 | 27 | 114 | 4.2 | 0 | 108 | 2616 | 24.2 | 4 |
| Deacon Turner | 78-80 | | | | | 65 | 1346 | 20.7 | 0 |
| Rick Upchurch | 75-83 | 248 | 3008 | 12.3 | 8 | 95 | 2355 | 24.8 | 0 |
| Ted Vactor | 69-75 | 42 | 290 | 6.9 | 0 | 30 | 746 | 24.9 | 0 |
| Rick Volk | 67-78 | 84 | 548 | 6.5 | 0 | 2 | 16 | 8.0 | 0 |
| Billy Walik | 70-72 | 28 | 130 | 4.6 | 0 | 67 | 1640 | 24.5 | 0 |
| Donnie Walker | 73-75 | 68 | 594 | 8.7 | 0 | 1 | 20 | 20.0 | 0 |
| Jackie Wallace | 74-79 | 83 | 852 | 10.3 | 0 | 6 | 92 | 15.3 | 0 |
| Vic Washington | 71-76 | | | | | 129 | 3341 | 25.9 | 1 |
| Roger Wehrli | 69-81 | 42 | 310 | 7.4 | 0 | 5 | 38 | 7.6 | 0 |
| Charlie West | 68-79 | 158 | 1099 | 7.0 | 1 | 85 | 2127 | 25.0 | 0 |
| Clarence Williams | 77-81 | 1 | 0 | 0.0 | 0 | 35 | 690 | 19.7 | 0 |
| Dave Williams | 77-81 | 1 | 60 | 60.0 | 0 | 88 | 2019 | 22.9 | 3 |
| Lawrence Williams | 76-77 | | | | | 50 | 1206 | 24.1 | 0 |
| Leonard Willis | 76-79 | 30 | 207 | 6.9 | 0 | 37 | 792 | 21.4 | 0 |
| Roland Woolsey | 75-78 | 39 | 324 | 8.3 | 0 | 14 | 274 | 19.6 | 0 |
| Roscoe Word | 74-76 | 39 | 293 | 7.5 | 0 | 7 | 127 | 18.1 | 0 |
| Keith Wright | 78-80 | 78 | 467 | 6.0 | 0 | 70 | 1767 | 25.2 | 0 |
| Alvin Wyatt | 70-73 | 59 | 504 | 8.5 | 2 | 60 | 1480 | 24.7 | 0 |
| Mickey Zofko | 71-74 | | | | | 30 | 656 | 21.9 | 0 |

| Name | Years | No. | Avg. | Name | Years | No. | Avg. |
|---|---|---|---|---|---|---|---|
| Donny Anderson | 66-74 | 387 | 39.6 | Terry Joyce | 76-77 | 86 | 37.0 |
| Zenon Andrusyshyn | 78 | 79 | 41.1 | Gary Keithly | 73, 75 | 66 | 37.5 |
| Bruce Barnes | 73-74 | 100 | 37.4 | Merrit Kersey | 74-75 | 97 | 32.5 |
| Lem Barney | 67-77 | 113 | 35.5 | Bob Lee | 69-80 | 156 | 39.7 |
| Marv Bateman | 72-77 | 401 | 40.9 | David Lee | 66-78 | 838 | 40.6 |
| | | | | | | | |
| David Beverly | 74-80 | 586 | 38.1 | David Lewis | 70-73 | 285 | 43.7 |
| Tom Blanchard | 71-81 | 819 | 41.3 | Steve Little | 78-80 | 125 | 38.5 |
| Bill Bradley | 69-77 | 213 | 39.0 | Jim McCann | 71-73,75 | 139 | 37.6 |
| Mike Bragg | 68-80 | 978 | 39.8 | Tom McNeill | 69-73 | 317 | 41.1 |
| Steve Broussard | 75 | 29 | 31.8 | Dan Melville | 79 | 71 | 37.0 |
| | | | | | | | |
| Mike Burke | 74 | 46 | 37.0 | Mike Michel | 77-78 | 93 | 36.7 |
| Skip Butler | 71-77 | 50 | 36.4 | Steve O'Neal | 69-73 | 337 | 40.7 |
| Duane Carrell | 74-77 | 257 | 38.9 | Cliff Parsley | 77-81 | 407 | 39.8 |
| Dave Chapple | 71-74 | 162 | 40.2 | Bob Parsons | 72-83 | 884 | 38.6 |
| Neil Clabo | 75-77 | 225 | 39.9 | Dennis Partee | 68-75 | 519 | 41.3 |
| | | | | | | | |
| Ken Clark | 79 | 93 | 40.1 | Dan Pastorini | 71-81 | 316 | 39.7 |
| Don Cockroft | 68-80 | 651 | 40.3 | Mike Patrick | 75-78 | 222 | 38.2 |
| Fred Cox | 63-77 | 70 | 38.7 | Hal Roberts | 74 | 81 | 38.7 |
| Jerry DePoyster | 68,71-72 | 106 | 38.2 | Larry Seiple | 67-77 | 633 | 40.0 |
| Bucky Dilts | 77-79 | 285 | 37.5 | Steve Spurrier | 67-76 | 230 | 38.3 |
| | | | | | | | |
| Mike Eischeid | 66-74 | 564 | 41.3 | Wilbur Summers | 77 | 93 | 36.8 |
| Rick Engels | 76-78 | 122 | 38.4 | Bill Van Heusen | 68-76 | 574 | 41.7 |
| Johnny Evans | 78-80 | 214 | 39.5 | Bobby Walden | 64-77 | 974 | 41.6 |
| Julian Fagan | 70-73 | 299 | 40.5 | Glenn Walker | 77-78 | 156 | 36.1 |
| Greg Gantt | 74-75 | 134 | 36.2 | Randy Walker | 74 | 69 | 38.4 |
| | | | | | | | |
| Roy Gerela | | | | Herman Weaver | 70-80 | 635 | 40.3 |
| Dave Green | 73-78 | 424 | 40.1 | Norris Weese | 76-79 | 53 | 35.7 |
| Ray Guy | 73-86 | 1052 | 42.3 | Tom Wittum | 73-77 | 303 | 41.9 |
| Eddie Hare | 79 | 83 | 36.6 | | | | |
| Gus Holloman | 68-74 | 47 | 38.7 | | | | |
| | | | | | | | |
| Mitch Hoopes | 75-78 | 123 | 38.7 | | | | |
| Rusty Jackson | 76,78-79 | 260 | 38.7 | | | | |
| John James | 72-84 | 1083 | 40.6 | | | | |
| Bill Johnson | 70 | 43 | 39.5 | | | | |
| Spike Jones | 70-77 | 592 | 39.1 | | | | |

Lifetime Statistics - 1970-1979    Section 5 - KICKING
(All men with 10 or more PAT or field goal attempts)

| Name | Years | PAT | PAT Att. | PAT Pct. | FG | FG Att. | FG Pct. |
|---|---|---|---|---|---|---|---|
| Bill Bell | 71-73 | 64 | 69 | 93 | 30 | 55 | 55 |
| Tom Birney | 79-80 | 21 | 28 | 75 | 13 | 21 | 62 |
| Skip Butler | 71-77 | 127 | 133 | 95 | 71 | 132 | 54 |
| Don Cockroft | 68-80 | 432 | 457 | 95 | 216 | 328 | 66 |
| Fred Cox | 63-77 | 519 | 539 | 96 | 282 | 455 | 62 |
| | | | | | | | |
| Joe Danelo | 75-84 | 240 | 250 | 96 | 133 | 228 | 58 |
| Tom Dempsey | 69-79 | 252 | 282 | 89 | 159 | 258 | 62 |
| Jerry DePoyster | 68, 71-72 | 18 | 20 | 90 | 3 | 15 | 20 |
| Happy Feller | 71-73 | 27 | 28 | 96 | 16 | 43 | 37 |
| Toni Fritsch | 71-73, 75-82 | 287 | 300 | 96 | 157 | 231 | 68 |
| | | | | | | | |
| Roy Gerela | 69-79 | 351 | 365 | 96 | 184 | 306 | 60 |
| Dave Green | 73-78 | 56 | 65 | 86 | 23 | 43 | 54 |
| Grant Guthrie | 70-71 | 32 | 34 | 94 | 13 | 29 | 45 |
| Efren Herrera | 74,76-82 | 256 | 268 | 96 | 116 | 171 | 69 |
| Bobby Howfield | 68-74 | 193 | 201 | 96 | 98 | 166 | 59 |
| | | | | | | | |
| George Hunt | 73, 75 | 46 | 53 | 87 | 22 | 39 | 56 |
| George Jakowenko | 74, 76 | 21 | 24 | 88 | 12 | 17 | 71 |
| Curt Knight | 69-73 | 172 | 175 | 98 | 101 | 175 | 58 |
| Allan Leavitt | 77 | 5 | 5 | 100 | 5 | 10 | 50 |
| John Leypoldt | 71-78 | 203 | 222 | 91 | 93 | 154 | 60 |
| | | | | | | | |
| Toni Linhart | 72,74-79 | 200 | 213 | 94 | 75 | 127 | 59 |
| Steve Little | 78-80 | 41 | 51 | 80 | 13 | 27 | 48 |
| Carson Long | 77 | 13 | 14 | 93 | 7 | 11 | 64 |
| Errol Mann | 68-78 | 315 | 333 | 95 | 177 | 276 | 64 |
| Chester Marcol | 72-80 | 156 | 167 | 93 | 121 | 196 | 62 |

| Name | Years | PAT | PAT Att. | PAT Pct. | FG | FG Att. | FG Pct. |
|---|---|---|---|---|---|---|---|
| Tim Mazzetti | 78-80 | 95 | 104 | 91 | 45 | 68 | 66 |
| Bill McClard | 72-75 | 31 | 32 | 97 | 26 | 51 | 51 |
| Mike Michel | 77-78 | 9 | 13 | 69 | | | |
| Nick Mike-Mayer | 73-82 | 226 | 234 | 97 | 115 | 204 | 56 |
| Steve Mike-Mayer | 75-80 | 161 | 175 | 92 | 67 | 131 | 51 |
| | | | | | | | |
| Mark Moseley | 70-86 | 482 | 511 | 94 | 300 | 457 | 66 |
| Horst Muhlmann | 69-77 | 245 | 257 | 95 | 154 | 239 | 64 |
| Jim O'Brien | 70-73 | 109 | 112 | 97 | 60 | 108 | 56 |
| Dennis Partee | 68-75 | 165 | 175 | 94 | 71 | 121 | 59 |
| Mac Percival | 67-74 | 163 | 167 | 98 | 101 | 190 | 53 |
| | | | | | | | |
| David Posey | 78 | 29 | 31 | 94 | 11 | 22 | 50 |
| David Ray | 69-74 | 167 | 175 | 95 | 110 | 178 | 62 |
| Mirro Roder | 73-74,76 | 28 | 29 | 97 | 17 | 32 | 53 |
| John Smith | 74-83 | 308 | 326 | 95 | 128 | 191 | 67 |
| Fred Steinfort | 76-81,83 | 122 | 129 | 95 | 63 | 114 | 55 |
| | | | | | | | |
| Jan Stenerud | 67-85 | 580 | 601 | 97 | 373 | 558 | 67 |
| Rich Szaro | 75-79 | 82 | 88 | 93 | 37 | 59 | 63 |
| Jim Turner | 64-79 | 521 | 544 | 96 | 304 | 488 | 62 |
| Kenny Vinyard | 70 | 23 | 26 | 88 | 9 | 25 | 36 |
| Mike Walker | 72 | 15 | 15 | 100 | 2 | 8 | 25 |
| | | | | | | | |
| Allen Watson | 70 | 7 | 8 | 88 | 5 | 10 | 50 |
| Tim Webster | 71 | 8 | 8 | 100 | 6 | 11 | 55 |
| Jeff White | 73 | 21 | 25 | 84 | 14 | 25 | 56 |
| Garo Yepremian | 66-67, 70-81 | 444 | 464 | 96 | 210 | 313 | 67 |

# 1980-1995
# NEW CHALLENGES, NEW TRIUMPHS

By winning the final two Super Bowls of the 1980s to add to their Super Bowl victories after the 1981 and 1984 seasons, the San Francisco 49ers ascended to the title of "Team of the '80s." Led by quarterback Joe Montana and wide receiver Jerry Rice, the 49ers' offense kept them a step in front of the competition. Nevertheless, most observers ranked San Francisco behind the Steelers' 1970s dynasty and the Lombardi-led Packers of the 1960s. The earlier powerhouses were usually given the edge in defense and because their superiority over their contemporaries was greater. A computer simulation by NFL Films during the 1989 season even awarded the "greatest team" ever mantle to the 1978 Steelers over the 1988 49ers.

The Washington Redskins and Chicago Bears were consistently strong through the 1980s and the New York Giants, Denver Broncos and several other clubs had their moments. The influence of the draft and the possibility of new free-agent rules seem likely to continue the diversity of strength throughout the league for some time to come.

## Experiments

In 1986, the NFL tried a novel experiment with television instant replay, first attempted by the USFL, to allow officials in the booth to overrule on-field officials. As suspected, the replays proved the field officials were usually right, some replays were inconclusive and the process slowed the already long games. Nevertheless, the process was approved by most fans. Somewhat grudgingly, the NFL owners have extended instant replay each year since then.

To speed up games, which were averaging over three hours, halftimes were cut to 13 minutes once teams reached their lockerrooms and rules concerning timeouts and the 30-second clock were tightened before the 1990 season. Several teams, particularly Cincinnati and Buffalo, experimented with no-huddle offenses to keep opponents from changing defensive personnel, and this also tended to speed up games. On the other hand, the tendency for more passing lengthened the elapsed time because of the frequent clock stoppages.

## The Three-Dollar League

Eight years after the WFL debacle, the NFL faced a new and more serious challenge. The United States Football League began operations in the spring of 1983 with twelve franchises: Arizona Wranglers, Birmingham Stallions, Boston Breakers, Chicago Blitz, Denver Gold, Los Angeles Express, Michigan Panthers, New Jersey Generals, Oakland Raiders, Philadelphia Stars, Tampa Bay Bandits and Washington Federals. The new league avoided direct confrontation at the gate with the NFL by playing its games from March to July, but it went head-to-head with the established league in attempting you sign "name" college stars. It was successful there, in that it signed Heisman Trophy winners Herschel Walker, Mike Rozier and Doug Flutie in each of its three seasons. Aside for the loss of a few talented athletes, the NFL's major difficulty was that the presence of an alternative league sent player salaries skyrocketing.

Aided by a modest TV contract with cable network ESPN, the USFL pronounced its first season a success and added six new teams in '84: Houston Gamblers, Jacksonville Bulls, Memphis Showboats, Oklahoma Outlaws, Pittsburgh Maulers and San Antonio Gunslingers. The Breakers franchise shifted to New Orleans. In the league's third season, the Breakers moved to Portland, the Stars to Baltimore, and the Federals to Orlando. Michigan combined with Oakland, and Pittsburgh, Oklahoma and Chicago quit altogether.

After three years, the USFL had begun to resemble the WFL in its hordes of unheralded players, its small presence in the media, its frequent franchise shifts, and its large financial losses.

Then, against the wishes of some of its owners, the USFL voted to play its fourth season in the fall of 1986 — opposite the NFL. That season, however, was never played. It soon became obvious that the USFL's hopes rested on a $1.69 billion suit, charging the NFL with excerising monopolistic practices to keep the USFL from gaining a lucrative TV contract. In July 1986, a federal jury in New York found the NFL was indeed a monopoly, but that the USFL's problems were of its own making. The damage award of $1 (trebled to $3) meant that the USFL — with $150 million is debts — was finished, although it was not until early 1988 when the USFL lost its last appeal that the final coffin nail was hammered home.

## TV Holds Sway

A five-year contract with the three television networks signed in 1981 provided a $656 million package for broadcast rights. Under this pact, each team received about $5 million annually in TV revenue. Expanded playoffs and parity-minded scheduling sought to put the best show possible on the field and on television.

Nevertheless, pro football's TV ratings fell. Some argued overexposure; others blamed a general decline in network viewing caused by cable TV. In March 1987, Rozelle announces a new three-year, $1.428 billion TV contract that included CBS, NBC, ABC and, for the first time, ESPN. The $476 million annual yield, though down 3.4 percent from 1986, kept most teams in the black.

For the 1990 season, the NFL again expanded its TV base. This was done in part by adding TNT, a new cable network to its cable coverage. Under the contract, TNT broadcast Sunday night games through the first half of the season and ESPN televised them during the second half. CBS and NBC were pacified for slipping ratings by extending the regular season to 17 weeks, with each team receiving a bye during the season. And ABC, whose Monday Night Football remained a prime-time staple, was rewarded with a playoff game by adding a third wild-card teams to the postseason. Through its various contracts the NFL stood to reap $3.6 billion.

## Player Movement

The 1977 agreement with the NFLPA governed the game for five years, but Rozelle and the owners again faced Ed Garvey and

a list of demands as the 1982 expiration approached. The players offered some radical proposals for a new labor contract. Of the many features, the most prominant was that the players receive their salaries out of a pool made up of 55 percent of the team's gross receipts from tickets and television. Out of this pool, the salary share of each player would be set by a formula based on years in the league and incentive clauses. The players also wanted a less restrictive free-agent arrangement. The owners flatly rejected setting aside any fixed portion of their receipts for the players, and once again, hard negotiations proceeded under careful threats of a strike.

The players made good on the threats, walking off of the field two weeks into the 1982 season. For 57 days, negotiations dragged on. America spent its first October without NFL football since 1919. The parties reached a new arrangement on November 16, leaving pro football structurally unchanged. Although there would be more money for the players, none of the novel proposals of the union were adopted. Play resumed less than a week later amid fears of fan resentment. Attendance was down in some cities, but, by the time the Super Bowl rolled around, the fan backlash had played itself out.

In 1987, new contract negotiations brought new exasperation to fans because of a 24-day players' strike in what many called a "season of unreason." After the season's first two games, the players walked out with a variety of demands. In 1982, it was the players who had stopped the season, but this time the owners were prepared. After only one week off, games were continued with what the owners called "replacement players" and what the NFLPA termed "scabs." For three weeks, the replacements performed to the constant carping of fans, media, union players and some NFL coaches. Attendance dropped and much of the play was ragged but the games counted in the standings. Union players soon began crossing the picket lines. Finally, the union gave in — a crushing defeat — vowing to pursue their goals in the courts.The fans came back almost immediately, and by the end of the season attendance was back to normal. But wounds had been opened between players and management that will take years to heal.

In 1989, as part of its strategy to win free agency for players through antitrust action in the courts, the NFLPA decertified itself as the sole bargaining agent for the players. In the meantime, the NFL came up with a limited free-agent plan — the so-called Plan B. Under this system, teams can protect about two-thirds of their rosters while opening the remaining one-third to free agency by leaving them unprotected until April 1 of every year. Although Plan B has benefitted marginal players and some in the higher-age brackets, only a few of those signing with new teams have made an impact on the championship races.

Despite a great deal of discussion, suggestions such as salary caps (particularly for first-year players) have yet to be implemented. In addition to the high cost of signing college seniors, the NFL was forced to drop is rule against signing underclassmen, a policy that had been in effect since the 1920s. Rather than face still another court fight — one it would surely lose — the league agreed to make underclassmen who announced their intention to turn professional eligible for the draft. The success of such players as Detroit's Barry Sanders proved that some college juniors were ready to compete in the NFL.

## Trouble in the ranks

At the start of the 1980s, Rozelle also found himself locked in combat with one of the NFL management lodge brothers. Al Davis,

the principle owner of the Oakland Raiders, took the NFL to court in a lawsuit that could change the face of pro football as much as the demands of the NFL Players Association. The chain reaction began with the decision of the Los Angeles Rams to move to Anaheim, a suburban city that was still within metropolitan Los Angeles, for the 1980 season. Davis, meanwhile, was having trouble negotiating a contract with the Oakland Stadium authorities. Davis claimed that the abandoned Los Angeles Coliseum had made a better offer than the Oakland officials, so he announced his decision to move the Raiders to Los Angeles for the 1981 season. Possibly the biggest lure for Davis was the prospect of major profits in Los Angeles through pay television.

Davis quickly found out that his decision could not so easily be carried out. An NFL bylaw provided that a franchise could not move unless 21 of the 28 owners gave their approval. The owners turned thumbs down on the proposal, citing the proximity of Anaheim to Los Angeles. A furious and frustrated Davis then turned to the courts. Joined by the Los Angeles Coliseum, the Raiders sued the NFL in federal court, claiming that the league bylaws on moving franchises violated U.S. antitrust laws. While waiting for the trial to come up on the court calendar, Davis relished the Super Bowl XV triumph of his Raiders and the presentation of the trophy by Rozelle, now his bitter personal enemy.

The first trial ended in a hung jury in 1981, but the court delay had forced the Raiders to stay in Oakland for that season. When the case was retried in the spring of 1982, the jury found that the NFL rule did violate the law and that Davis was entitled to move his team to Los Angeles. With league control thus weakened, the Baltimore Colts moved to Indianapolis for the 1984 season without seeking league approval. After the 1987 season, St. Louis Cardinals owner Bill Bidwell received league approval to move his franchise to Phoenix.

## Comings and Goings

Regardless of labor and internal problems, an NFL franchise was still a prestige purchase. Real-estate developer Alex Spanos became the majority owner of the San Diego Chargers in the 1984 for $40 million, car dealer Norman Braman paid $65 million for the Philadelphia Eagles in 1985, the New England Patriots were sold to Remington manufacturer Victor Kiam in 1987 for $90 million, and the Seattle Seahawks went for $80 million to real estate executive Ken Behring in 1988.

The most publicized sale was that of the Dallas Cowboys to oilman Jerry Jones for $140 million. Jones purchased the team from H.R. "Bum" Bright who had headed an 11-person limited partnership that had bought the Cowboys from their original owner, Clint Murchison Jr., in 1984 for $80 million. Under Bright, the Cowboys had become a losing team on the field. Jones startled the football world by ousting team president Tex Schramm and coach Tom Landry, the two men who had guided the Cowboys since the team's entrance into the NFL. As his new head coach, Jones hired Jimmy Johnson, his Arkansas roommate when both played for the Razorbacks about the time the Cowboys were being born. After a disastrous 1-15 first season, Johnson, formerly a highly successfully college coach at Miami (Fla.), bought the Cowboys to a .500 season in 1990.

The Chicago Bears also underwent an ownership change when George Halas died in 1983. Pro football's winningest coach and the man who created the Bears in 1922 and is a charter member of the Pro Football Hall of Fame, Halas was arguably the most

important contributor to the NFL's ultimate success. Control of the team passed to his son-in-law Edward McCaskey and grandson Michael McCaskey.

There have been many suggestions that the league should realign along more logical divisions (for example, move Arizona out of the Eastern Division and Atlanta out of the West. Another complaint, specifically from television executives, is that the NFC has most of the country's largest markets. Unfortunately, any realignment suggestions run into arguments about ancient (and lucrative) rivalries.

However, while true expansion waited, in 1989 the league established the World League of American Football (WLAF) with teams in both Europe and North America that began play in March 1991. Schramm was named president, but he was later succeeded by Mike Lynn, the Vikings' general manager.

It was hoped that the new league would function as a farm system for the NFL, open new markets and eventually serve as a base for international expansion. The World League lasted two seasons, and then was revived in 1995.

## Goodbye, Pete; Hello, Paul

Early in 1989, Pete Rozelle announced his intention to retire as commissioner after 29 years. "We must replace the irreplaceable man," Giants owner Wellington Mara commented. The favorite to succeed Rozelle was Saints general manager Jim Finks, but he was unable to muster enough votes. The owners split into two camps, the "Old Guard" who favored Finks and the "Young Turks" who wanted a younger, more market-conscious commissioner. Finally, in October 1989, the owners were able to agree on league counsel Paul Tagliabue as the new commissioner. His first, and perhaps most important, job was to negotiate the new TV contracts with the networks and cable companies. That he was once again able to increase revenue got his term in office off to a rousing start.

However, Tagliabue said from the start that a new collective bargaining agreement with the players would be his No. 1 priority. In the next three years, more than 20 suits were filed by the owners and players, although the games continued to be played and players continued to be paid according to terms of the expired 1982 agreement.

In September 1992, Judge David Doty from the Federal District Court in Minneapolis declared the NFL's Plan B form of free agency illegal. In another decision, Doty proclaimed four players, including Philadelphia's Keith Jackson, the best tight end in the league, as immediate free agents. Throughout the 1992 season, the two sides worked on reaching a new agreement. Just when things looked like they were going to fall apart, Doty gave the two sides 24 hours to reach a settlement, or else he would do it himself. They did. .

## A New Era

First was an end to all the litigation and lawsuits. Players were awarded free agency after five years in the league, assuming their contracts had expired, with a restricted form of free agency for three- and four-year veterans. And the draft was cut to eight rounds, allowing more players free agency in another form.

The owners won, too. They gained a salary cap aimed at controlling their costs and giving them financial stability.

As the 1993 offseason got under way, Reggie White led nearly 400 players into the new era of free agency. Some of the biggest names to change teams included Ronnie Lott, Jeff Hostetler and Jim McMahon.

The new agreement will last until 1999, meaning strikes would not be a threat until the end of the century.

The 1993 season ended much as it began — with a Dallas Super Bowl victory over Buffalo. On the field it was the Year of the Kicker, with field goals sailing through uprights at a record pace and percentage.

Miami's Don Shula surpassed the legendary George Halas as the NFL's all-time winningest head coach. Shula ended the season with 327 lifetime victories.

When the year began, Tagliabue said his three goals were peace with the players, a new television contract and expansion. The commissioner went 3 for 3, hitting home runs on all three issues.

Free agency worked well, with 120 players switching teams while salaries rose 51 percent over 1992 to an average of $737,850 per player. Old faces in new places added badly needed life to the NFL.

The story of the new TV contract was that CBS got outfoxed by upstart Fox Network. Fox paid a whopping $1.58 billion for the rights to televise NFC games, and CBS, which had televised NFL games since 1956, was left out in the cold. The overall TV contract was $4.35 billion, which also upped the salary cap for future years.

The NFL also announced two new expansion teams that would begin play in 1995 — the Carolina Panthers and Jacksonville Jaguars. The Carolina franchise wasn't much of a surprise because the market is hot and the ownership group headed by former Colt receiver Jerry Richardson was rock-solid. But when Jacksonville became the 30th franchise a month later, on November 30, eyebrows were raised because St. Louis and Baltimore were shut out. Shoe magnate Wayne Weaver was the one who persuaded NFL owners that the growing Southeast was a better choice than the former NFL locales.

In 1994, the NFL used a two-point conversion for the first time. Other new rule changes, such as moving kickoffs back to the 30-yard line, moving the placement of missed field goals to the spot the ball was kicked from and a no-chucking rule once receivers got five yards off the line of scrimmage increased scoring considerably. Three receivers caught more than 100 passes, including Minnesota's Cris Carter, who caught 122 balls.

But the season was somewhat overshadowed by O.J. Simpson, the Pro Football Hall of Famer, who was charged with the June 12th murder of his former wife and her friend. Simpson's highly publicized trial began the week of Super Bowl XXIX and continued through the 1995 offseason.

In 1995, more off-field happenings overshadowed the news on the field, and nothing more so than what has come to be known as "franchise free agency." The Rams, after 49 years in Los Angeles, moved to St. Louis, and the Raiders, following 13 years in Los Angeles, packed up and went back to Oakland. But the moving continued, with the Cleveland Browns announcing their move to Baltimore midway through the '95 campaign and the Oilers playing all season with the knowledge that Nashville, Tenn. woukd probably be their next home. And, once the season had ended, the Seattle Seahawks announced they would move to Los Angeles.

Two new cities gained NFL teams in 1995, too — the expansion Carolina Panthers and Jacksonville Jaguars. Carolina won a record seven games, while Jacksonville, with four wins, also broke the previous expansion record for victories.

The free agent system in the NFL gave the players much less freedom than their baseball counterparts. As a result, several players staged long holdouts in attempts to win salary increases from their teams. The Rams had a rash of discontent after they announced a big-money contract for rookie Johnnie Johnson. Four veteran players, making no more money than the rookie, stayed away from camp for over a month while insisting upon renegotiation of their contracts. The Rams stood firm, and Jim Youngblood, Jack Youngblood, and Larry Brooks all returned in time for the opening game. Dennis Harrah came back for the second game.

The New England Patriots had a similar situation on their hands. Sam Cunningham, Mike Haynes, Richard Bishop, and Tom Owens all boycotted training camp while negotiating contracts. Haynes and Bishop didn't report until late September, Owen didn't suit up until early November, and Cunningham held out for the entire season.

Other noteworthy holdouts included John Riggins of the Redskins, who sat out all of 1980, and Fred Dean of the San Diego Chargers, who held out two weeks into the season.

## EASTERN DIVISION

**Philadelphia Eagles—**With an unusual comeback in their final game, the Eagles won first place in the East. They soared to an 11-1 record in late November, combining offensive and defensive excellence. The leak-proof defense blended experience and youth. Bill Bergey returned from a knee injury to play with gusto, while Charles Johnson, Carl Hairston, Randy Logan, and Jerry Robinson all ripened into star defenders. The offense suffered from Wilbert Montgomery's visits to sick bay, but Ron Jaworski stepped up the air attack to compensate. With a playoff bid locked up, the Eagles went into a skid which put first place in jeopardy. If they lost by 25 points or more to Dallas on Demcember 21, the Cowboys would finish in first place under tie-breaker rules. Early in the fourth period, the Cowboys took a 35-10 lead and threatened to pour it on. The Eagles bore down and closed the gap to 35-27 by the end. Harold Carmichael was shaken up in the second quarter of the game and did not catch a pass, ending his receiving streak at 127 games.

**Dallas Cowboys—**When Tom Landry predicted an 8-8 finish for his Cowboys, he may have been shucking his opposition. Roger Staubach had retired, leaving the fine-tuned offense in the hands of apprentice Danny White. Novices also manned three of the four secondary positions, adding to Landry's anxiety. Everything worked out fine for the master coach. White kept the offense moving, even showing a talent for running the two-minute drill. Star blockers Herbert Scott and Pat Donovan helped White and runner Tony Dorsett do their job. The young secondary made mistakes, but it held together under the leadership of tackle Randy White and linebacker Bob Breunig. Too Tall Jones returned from his boxing sojourn to beef up the defensive line. The Broncos darkened Landry's mood by blasting the Cowboys 41-20 on September 14, but Cowboy class asserted itself over the long haul. Five victories in the last six games fell just shy of taking first place, but did earn a wild-card ticket into the playoffs.

**Washington Redskins—**When John Riggins left camp in a salary dispute, he took much of the Redskin offense with him. Without the big fullback, the Skins could not control the ball as they had in recent years. Even with rookie Art Monk juicing up the receiving, the attack moved only in spurts. A long slump by kicker Mark Moseley only worsened the problem. A 1-5 start sparked rumors of coach Jack Pardee's impending demise. A 23-0 pasting of St. Louis on October 19 raised some hopes, but an embarrassing 24-0 loss to the Eagles on November 16 deflated the team's spirit. Brightening the dark days was the Washington secondary, which led the NFC in interceptions. Pardee rallied his team for a late spurt. They beat the Chargers 40-17 on December 7, then ended the year with victories over the Giants and Cardinals. The spurt, however, did not save Pardee's job.

**St. Louis Cardinals—**Jim Hanifan had helped Don Coryell build a contender in St. Louis in the mid-1970's, and now he returned to run another renewal program. The Cards lost their first three games, but then whipped the Eagles and Saints to encourage their new coach. For the rest of the year, however, the club won only three times. A weak defense dragged the team down, with a feeble pass rush the main culprit. On offense, Hanifan had a blue chip in Ottis Anderson, a devastating runner for the second straight year. He ran for 1,352 yards behind a patched-up forward line. Veterans Bob Young and Tom Banks were sent packing, while injuries claimed Keith Wortman and Terry Stieve. Dan Dierdorf did return from a knee injury to lay a foundation for the new offensive line. Tragedy touched the Cardinals when kicker Steve Little was crippled in a car accident in October, only a few days after being cut from the team.

**New York Giants—**A 41-35 triumph over the Cardinals on opening day had New York fans celebrating the return of good times. That optimism wilted in the heat of an eight-game losing streak in which the Giants played spiritless football. The secondary was manned by young players who made mistakes in bunches, while the offense looked as if it had punched itself out in the first round. The Giants did end the string with a lively 38-35 victory over the Cowboys, but such savory moments were few. Injuries did contribute to the team's poor showing. Doug Kotar missed the entire season and was joined by Billy Taylor for part of the season. The strong linebacking corps was depleted by Dan Lloyd's bout with cancer and by early-season knee injuries to Brian Kelley and Harry Carson. No one could claim, however, that injuries were the only cause.

## CENTRAL DIVISION

**Minnesota Vikings—**Bud Grant recaptured past Viking glory by taking this young squad to the playoffs. Over the first half of the season, the Vikes played like a retooling also-ran. In building a 3-5 record, the running game reaped a sparse harvest, and quarterback Tommy Kramer threw a bushel of interceptions. On the back half of the schedule, the Vikings played sound fundamental football and battled back into the playoff race. They trounced front-running Detroit 34-0 on November 9, and moved into a first-place tie one week later. By beating the Buccaneers 21-10 on December 7, the Vikes moved into first place alone. One week later, they sewed up a playoff spot with a miraculous pass play. Trailing the Browns 23-22 with five seconds left on the clock, Kramer heaved the ball from midfield toward the end zone. The ball was tipped into the air and grabbed by Ahmad Rashad, who stepped over the goal line. Even with a loss on the final weekend, the Vikings took first place over the Lions on tiebreaking rules.

**Detroit Lions—**Everything was just right for winning a playoff berth. The Lions had a stunning new runner in rookie Billy Sims, they had quarterback Gary Danielson back in good health, they had an easy schedule, and they were part of the N.F.L.'s weakest division. The plan worked for four weeks. After a 43-28 trouncing by the Falcons on October 5, the Lions struggled to hold onto first place. Four mid-season losses in five games dropped them into a dogfight with the Vikings for the top spot. Two late losses scratched the Lions from the playoff picture. On Thanksgiving Day, they led the Bears 17-3 entering the fourth quarter, only to have the Bears knot the score with a touchdown and conversion as the clock ran out. When the Bears won the coin toss for overtime, Chicago's Dave Williams took the kickoff and ran 95 yards to end the game. Ten days later, Roy Green of St. Louis ran a punt back for a touchdown late in the final quarter to beat the Lions 24-23. Detroit came back to win its final two games, but the Vikings had already sewn up first place.

**Chicago Bears—**The Bears had everything except a passing attack. Their solid defense featured all-star performances by Dan Hampton, veteran Alan Page, and Gary Fencik. Walter Payton carried the freight on the ground in peerless fashion, assisted by fullback Roland Harper, who rebounded from knee surgery. Because the Bears could not throw the ball, they did not repeat as a playoff team. Mike Phipps had driven the Bears to the playoffs last year with a conservative and error-free job at quarterback. In this year's early games, Phipps had problems moving the offense and suffered a plague of interceptions. Vince Evans took over as a starter on October 19 and juiced up the attack with his bazooka arm and strong running. After a shaky mid-season, the Bears won three of their last four games, including an overtime victory over the Lions on Thanksgiving Day and a 61-7 drubbing of the Packers ten days later.

**Tampa Bay Buccaneers—**The clock struck twelve for John McKay's Cinderella team. The Bucs fell out of the playoffs by posting a 1-6-1 record against other Central Division teams and by losing six of their last seven games. The offense suffered from Ricky Bell's injury-spoiled year, but the fate of the Bucs fell with the quality of the defense. The front line suffered the end of Wally Chambers' career and an early knee injury to Randy Crowder. McKay, however, put much of the blame on the heralded linebacking corps which did not play up to its clippings. Lee Roy Selmon continued to grow in skill and stature, but the rest of the defensive unit could not follow suit. The Bucs often made costly mistakes, twice killing last minute drives in close games with mental errors.

**Green Bay Packers—**The high point came on opening day, when kicker Chester Marcol grabbed his blocked field goal and scooted to a touchdown for a 12-6 overtime victory over Chicago. Three losses followed, including a 51-21 beating by the Rams. Rumors flourished that Bart Starr was about to go as coach and general manager, but he held onto his jobs for the course of the season. Starr didn't get much

FINAL TEAM STATISTICS

OFFENSE

| | ATL. | CHI. | DALL. | DET. | G.B. | L.A. | MINN. | N.O. | NYG | PHIL. | ST. L. | S.F. | T.B. | WASH. |
|---|---|---|---|---|---|---|---|---|---|---|---|---|---|---|
| FIRST DOWNS: | | | | | | | | | | | | | | |
| Total | 336 | 286 | **337** | 308 | 307 | 316 | 324 | 285 | 261 | 326 | 281 | 298 | 281 | 279 |
| by Rushing | **145** | 139 | 143 | 143 | 119 | 144 | 100 | 80 | 100 | 118 | 123 | 105 | 102 | 109 |
| by Passing | 166 | 121 | 171 | 143 | 164 | 157 | **191** | 183 | 136 | 186 | 137 | 171 | 154 | 148 |
| by Penalty | 25 | 26 | 23 | 22 | 24 | 15 | **33** | 22 | 25 | 22 | 21 | 22 | 25 | 22 |
| RUSHING: | | | | | | | | | | | | | | |
| Number | 559 | 579 | 595 | 572 | 493 | **615** | 433 | 348 | 483 | 527 | 519 | 415 | 477 | 517 |
| Yards | 2405 | 2440 | 2378 | 2599 | 1806 | **2799** | 1642 | 1362 | 1730 | 1995 | 2183 | 1743 | 1839 | 2016 |
| Average Yards | 4.3 | 4.2 | 4.0 | 4.5 | 3.7 | **4.6** | 3.8 | 3.9 | 3.6 | 3.8 | 4.2 | 4.2 | 3.9 | 3.9 |
| Touchdowns | 15 | 22 | **26** | 21 | 13 | 17 | 14 | 9 | 10 | 19 | 19 | 10 | 9 | 12 |
| PASSING: | | | | | | | | | | | | | | |
| Attempts | 467 | 404 | 449 | 423 | 511 | 451 | 574 | 566 | 514 | 477 | 470 | **597** | 530 | 486 |
| Completions | 259 | 209 | 265 | 248 | 289 | 261 | 331 | 334 | 245 | 275 | 239 | **363** | 256 | 284 |
| Completion Pct. | 55.5 | 51.7 | 59.0 | 58.6 | 56.6 | 57.9 | 57.7 | 59.0 | 47.7 | 57.7 | 50.9 | **60.8** | 48.3 | 58.4 |
| Passing Yards | 3568 | 2669 | 3356 | 3287 | 3651 | 3441 | 3934 | **4010** | 2931 | 3771 | 3063 | 3799 | 3414 | 3171 |
| Avg. Yds. per Att. | 6.5 | 5.5 | 6.5 | 6.3 | 5.9 | 6.7 | 6.0 | 6.0 | 4.7 | **6.9** | 5.2 | 5.7 | 5.8 | 5.4 |
| Avg Yds per Comp. | **13.8** | 12.8 | 12.7 | 13.3 | 12.6 | 13.2 | 11.9 | 12.0 | 12.0 | 13.7 | 12.8 | 10.5 | 13.3 | 11.2 |
| Times Tackled | 35 | 33 | 31 | 45 | 43 | 29 | 41 | 46 | 47 | 32 | 50 | 30 | **24** | 36 |
| Yds Lost Tackled | 324 | 274 | 252 | 346 | 360 | 234 | 246 | 362 | 322 | 247 | 387 | 222 | **194** | 333 |
| Net Yards | 3244 | 2395 | 3104 | 2941 | 3291 | 3207 | **3688** | 3648 | 2609 | 3524 | 2676 | 3577 | 3220 | 2838 |
| Touchdowns | **31** | 13 | 30 | 13 | 15 | **31** | 22 | 26 | 19 | 28 | 16 | 27 | 20 | 17 |
| Interceptions | 17 | 25 | 25 | **12** | 29 | 23 | 23 | 22 | 25 | **12** | 24 | 26 | 17 | 18 |
| Pct. Intercepted | 3.6 | 6.2 | 5.6 | 2.8 | 5.7 | 5.1 | 4.0 | 3.9 | 4.9 | **2.5** | 5.1 | 4.4 | 3.2 | 3.7 |
| PUNTS: | | | | | | | | | | | | | | |
| Number | 79 | 79 | 71 | 73 | 87 | 77 | 81 | 89 | 94 | 76 | **100** | 77 | 89 | 85 |
| Average | 39.1 | 40.6 | 40.9 | 41.6 | 38.2 | 39.0 | 38.8 | 39.3 | **44.8** | 38.8 | 41.1 | 40.9 | 41.8 | 39.2 |
| PUNT RETURNS: | | | | | | | | | | | | | | |
| Number | 53 | 41 | 55 | 56 | 37 | 47 | 34 | 22 | 37 | **63** | 50 | 45 | 57 | 48 |
| Yards | 536 | 277 | 556 | 463 | 297 | 315 | 251 | 176 | 302 | **560** | 399 | 409 | 313 | 487 |
| Average Yards | 10.1 | 6.8 | 10.1 | 8.3 | 8.0 | 6.7 | 7.4 | 8.0 | 8.2 | 8.9 | 8.0 | 9.1 | 5.5 | **10.1** |
| Touchdowns | 0 | 0 | 0 | 0 | 0 | 0 | 0 | 0 | 0 | 0 | 1 | **2** | 0 | 0 |
| KICKOFF RET.: | | | | | | | | | | | | | | |
| Number | 53 | 56 | 58 | 57 | 73 | 53 | 63 | **88** | 71 | 53 | 65 | 75 | 67 | 57 |
| Yards | 958 | 1153 | 1259 | 1169 | 1415 | 979 | 1386 | **1973** | 1319 | 955 | 1297 | 1385 | 1294 | 1204 |
| Average Yards | 18.1 | 20.6 | 21.7 | 20.5 | 19.4 | 18.5 | 22.0 | **22.4** | 18.6 | 18.0 | 20.0 | 18.5 | 19.3 | 21.1 |
| Touchdowns | 0 | **1** | 0 | **1** | 0 | **1** | **1** | 0 | 0 | 0 | 0 | **1** | 0 | 0 |
| INTERCEPT RET.: | | | | | | | | | | | | | | |
| Number | 26 | 17 | 27 | 23 | 13 | 25 | 24 | 12 | 18 | 25 | 20 | 17 | 15 | **33** |
| Yards | 313 | 162 | 523 | 168 | 92 | **546** | 296 | 196 | 113 | 170 | 327 | 186 | 179 | 319 |
| Average Yards | 12.0 | 9.5 | 19.4 | 7.3 | 7.1 | **21.8** | 12.3 | 16.3 | 6.3 | 6.8 | 16.4 | 10.9 | 11.9 | 9.7 |
| Touchdowns | 0 | 1 | 3 | 1 | 0 | **4** | 2 | 0 | 0 | 0 | 1 | 0 | 1 | 1 |
| PENALTIES: | | | | | | | | | | | | | | |
| Number | 91 | 100 | 109 | 104 | **84** | 118 | 90 | 98 | 98 | 96 | 103 | 109 | 90 | 114 |
| Yards | 861 | 842 | 908 | 844 | **697** | 973 | 717 | 837 | 962 | 809 | 922 | 933 | 840 | 1008 |
| FUMBLES: | | | | | | | | | | | | | | |
| Number | 32 | 23 | 26 | 40 | 36 | 29 | **15** | 28 | 33 | 29 | 24 | 39 | 28 | 35 |
| Number Lost | 9 | 14 | 14 | 19 | 12 | 13 | **3** | 13 | 18 | 16 | 13 | 14 | 21 | 18 |
| POINTS: | | | | | | | | | | | | | | |
| Total | 405 | 304 | **454** | 334 | 231 | 424 | 317 | 291 | 249 | 384 | 299 | 320 | 271 | 261 |
| PAT Attempts | 49 | 37 | **60** | 36 | 28 | 54 | 39 | 37 | 29 | 48 | 37 | 40 | 32 | 30 |
| PAT Made | 46 | 35 | **59** | 35 | 24 | 52 | 33 | 33 | 27 | 48 | 35 | 33 | 31 | 27 |
| FG Attempts | 27 | 18 | 17 | **42** | 20 | 30 | 26 | 22 | 24 | 31 | 23 | 19 | 23 | 33 |
| FG Made | 19 | 13 | 11 | **27** | 11 | 16 | 16 | 12 | 16 | 16 | 14 | 15 | 16 | 18 |
| Percent FG Made | 70.4 | 72.2 | 64.7 | 64.3 | 55.0 | 53.3 | 61.5 | 54.5 | 66.7 | 51.6 | 60.9 | **78.9** | 69.6 | 54.5 |
| Safeties | **1** | **1** | **1** | **1** | 0 | 0 | **1** | 0 | 0 | 0 | 0 | **1** | 0 | 0 |

DEFENSE

| | ATL. | CHI. | DALL. | DET. | G.B. | L.A. | MINN. | N.O. | NYG | PHIL. | ST. L. | S.F. | T.B. | WASH. |
|---|---|---|---|---|---|---|---|---|---|---|---|---|---|---|
| FIRST DOWNS: | | | | | | | | | | | | | | |
| Total | 298 | 285 | 286 | **265** | 316 | 281 | 330 | 360 | 336 | 270 | 311 | 341 | 313 | 298 |
| by Rushing | 100 | 111 | 98 | 100 | 136 | 112 | 135 | 178 | 156 | **87** | 115 | 137 | 126 | 144 |
| by Passing | 175 | 149 | 160 | 143 | 166 | 141 | 170 | 155 | 160 | 157 | 176 | 185 | 168 | **127** |
| by Penalty | 23 | 25 | 28 | 22 | **14** | 28 | 25 | 27 | 20 | 26 | 20 | 19 | 19 | 27 |
| RUSHING: | | | | | | | | | | | | | | |
| Number | 441 | 506 | 469 | 449 | 565 | **445** | 531 | 630 | 584 | **445** | 547 | 556 | 548 | 585 |
| Yards | 1670 | 2015 | 2069 | **1599** | 2399 | 1945 | 2456 | 3106 | 2507 | 1618 | 2059 | 2218 | 2101 | 2524 |
| Average Yards | 3.8 | 4.0 | 4.4 | **3.6** | 4.2 | 4.4 | 4.6 | 4.9 | 4.3 | 3.6 | 3.8 | 4.0 | 3.8 | 4.3 |
| Touchdowns | **8** | 10 | 15 | 9 | 19 | 13 | 15 | 28 | 31 | **8** | 17 | 20 | 20 | 16 |
| PASSING: | | | | | | | | | | | | | | |
| Attempts | 564 | 451 | 484 | 462 | 460 | 510 | 499 | 445 | 448 | 543 | 531 | 495 | 516 | **392** |
| Completions | 333 | 238 | 231 | 256 | 259 | 245 | 283 | 255 | 255 | 265 | 287 | 327 | 328 | **187** |
| Completion Pct. | 59.0 | 52.8 | **47.7** | 55.4 | 56.3 | 48.0 | 56.7 | 57.3 | 56.9 | 48.8 | 54.0 | 66.1 | 63.6 | **47.7** |
| Passing Yards | 3990 | 3271 | 3568 | 3234 | 3617 | 3097 | 3644 | 3341 | 3469 | 3180 | 3616 | 3958 | 3477 | **2504** |
| Avg. Yds. per Att. | 5.9 | 5.8 | 6.1 | 5.8 | 6.9 | **4.6** | 6.4 | 6.6 | 6.8 | 4.8 | 5.8 | **8.0** | 6.1 | 5.0 |
| Avg Yds per Comp. | 12.0 | 13.7 | 15.5 | 12.6 | 14.0 | 12.6 | 12.9 | 13.1 | 13.6 | 12.0 | 12.6 | 12.1 | **10.6** | 13.4 |
| Times Tackled | 46 | 46 | 43 | 44 | 34 | **56** | 30 | 27 | 28 | 44 | 38 | 31 | 24 | 43 |
| Yds Lost Tackled | 396 | 379 | 358 | 300 | 234 | **496** | 244 | 229 | 224 | 355 | 291 | 207 | 173 | 333 |
| Net Yards | 3594 | 2892 | 3210 | 2934 | 3383 | 2601 | 3400 | 3112 | 3245 | 2825 | 3325 | **3751** | 3304 | **2171** |
| Touchdowns | 24 | 20 | 21 | **14** | 19 | 23 | 24 | 31 | 22 | 16 | 23 | 29 | 17 | 17 |
| Interceptions | 26 | 17 | 27 | 23 | 13 | 25 | 24 | 12 | 18 | 25 | 20 | 17 | 15 | **33** |
| Pct. Intercepted | 4.6 | 3.8 | 5.6 | 5.0 | 2.8 | 4.9 | 4.8 | 2.7 | 4.0 | 4.6 | 3.7 | 3.4 | 2.9 | **8.4** |
| PUNTS: | | | | | | | | | | | | | | |
| Number | 85 | 82 | 76 | **93** | 83 | 90 | 71 | 64 | 70 | 89 | 89 | 67 | 89 | 84 |
| Average | 41.3 | 39.0 | 43.5 | 41.6 | 39.1 | 42.1 | 39.3 | 38.5 | 40.3 | 41.3 | 40.1 | **38.2** | 42.0 | 40.7 |
| PUNT RETURNS: | | | | | | | | | | | | | | |
| Number | 36 | 46 | **32** | 38 | 50 | 42 | 42 | 48 | 58 | 35 | 62 | 48 | 54 | 52 |
| Yards | 240 | 415 | **215** | 300 | 342 | 353 | 259 | 490 | 506 | 224 | 645 | 530 | 529 | 351 |
| Average Yards | 6.7 | 9.0 | 6.7 | 7.9 | 6.8 | 8.4 | **6.2** | 10.2 | 8.7 | 6.4 | 10.4 | 11.0 | 9.8 | 6.8 |
| Touchdowns | 0 | 0 | 0 | 1 | 0 | 0 | 0 | 1 | 0 | 0 | 1 | 0 | 1 | 0 |
| KICKOFF RET.: | | | | | | | | | | | | | | |
| Number | 73 | 58 | 73 | 64 | **52** | 78 | 62 | 58 | **52** | 70 | 57 | 58 | 62 | 60 |
| Yards | 1579 | 1251 | 1568 | 1289 | **902** | 1553 | 1048 | 1159 | 1047 | 1307 | 1142 | 1203 | 1417 | 1102 |
| Average Yards | 21.6 | 21.6 | 21.5 | 20.1 | 17.3 | 19.9 | **16.9** | 20.0 | 20.1 | 18.7 | 20.0 | 20.7 | 22.9 | 18.4 |
| Touchdowns | 0 | 0 | 0 | 3 | 0 | 0 | 0 | 0 | 1 | 0 | 0 | 0 | 1 | 1 |
| INTERCEPT RET.: | | | | | | | | | | | | | | |
| Number | 17 | 25 | 25 | **12** | 29 | 23 | 23 | 22 | 25 | **12** | 24 | 26 | 17 | 18 |
| Yards | **143** | 161 | 179 | 173 | 483 | 307 | 187 | 217 | 376 | 220 | 246 | 319 | 185 | 219 |
| Average Yards | 8.4 | **6.4** | 7.2 | 14.4 | 16.7 | 13.3 | 8.1 | 9.9 | 15.0 | 18.3 | 10.3 | 12.3 | 10.9 | 12.2 |
| Touchdowns | **0** | 1 | 1 | 1 | 4 | 1 | 1 | **0** | 1 | 1 | 1 | 2 | **0** | 1 |
| PENALTIES: | | | | | | | | | | | | | | |
| Number | 101 | **129** | 106 | 98 | 109 | 83 | 111 | 79 | 108 | 87 | 101 | 92 | 117 | 90 |
| Yards | 919 | **1109** | 989 | 815 | 872 | 778 | 914 | 690 | 862 | 789 | 919 | 826 | 1077 | 766 |
| FUMBLES: | | | | | | | | | | | | | | |
| Number | 33 | 32 | 33 | 20 | 27 | 30 | 33 | 27 | **48** | 27 | 27 | 34 | 32 | 25 |
| Number Lost | 16 | 14 | 20 | 11 | 14 | 17 | 14 | 12 | **23** | 10 | 14 | 17 | 13 | 12 |
| POINTS: | | | | | | | | | | | | | | |
| Total | 272 | 264 | 311 | 272 | 371 | 289 | 308 | 487 | 425 | **222** | 350 | 415 | 341 | 293 |
| PAT Attempts | 32 | 31 | 38 | 31 | 43 | 38 | 40 | 60 | 55 | **26** | 42 | 52 | 40 | 36 |
| PAT Made | 30 | 30 | 38 | 30 | 36 | 34 | 32 | 56 | 51 | **24** | 41 | 50 | 39 | 36 |
| FG Attempts | 25 | 27 | 28 | 21 | 27 | 20 | 20 | 31 | 24 | 26 | 33 | 26 | 33 | **17** |
| FG Made | 16 | 14 | 15 | 16 | 25 | **9** | 12 | 23 | 14 | 14 | 17 | 17 | 20 | 13 |
| Percent FG Made | 64.0 | 51.9 | 53.6 | 76.2 | 92.6 | **45.0** | 60.0 | 74.2 | 58.3 | 53.8 | 51.5 | 65.4 | 60.6 | 76.5 |
| Safeties | 1 | 0 | 0 | 1 | 1 | 0 | 0 | 1 | 1 | 0 | 0 | 1 | 1 | 1 |

help from his two first-round draft picks. Defensive tackle Bruce Clark played in Canada, while linebacker George Cumby went out with a knee injury in early November. Injuries also took key young veterans Mark Koncar and Rich Wingo out of the lineup for practically the entire year. The Packers had one of the NFL's brightest stars in receiver James Lofton, but the rest of the squad had a dreary overtone. The Packers slunk away with four straight losses at the end of the year, including a 61-7 humiliation at the hands of the Bears.

## WESTERN DIVISION

**Atlanta Falcons**—After a slow start, the Falcons whipped unbeaten San Francisco and Detroit and then roared into the playoffs with a strong defense and versatile offense. Steve Bartkowski blossomed into a dangerous offensive leader, showering passes on rookie tight end Junior Miller and veteran wide receivers Al Jenkins and Wallace Francis. William Andrews and Lynn Cain combined for over 2,000 yards on the ground, moving behind a strong line that featured Mike Kenn and Jeff Van Note. The defense revived with the spirited play of rookie linebackers Buddy Curry and Al Richardson. With coach Leeman Bennett keeping all the ingredients in balance, the Falcons began a winning streak in mid-October that ended only with an overtime loss to the Rams on the final day of the season. Even with that loss, the Falcons had the first Divisional championship in their history.

**Los Angeles Rams**—For the first time since 1972, the Rams finished out of first place in the West. They did, however, win a wildcard playoff berth with five victories in their last six games. On opening day, the Rams debuted in Anaheim by losing to the Lions 41-20. In that game, quarterback Pat Haden broke his right thumb and gave way to Vince Ferragamo. A hero in last year's playoffs, Ferragamo had lost the QB job to Haden in pre-season but made good on this second chance. As usual, the Ram defense made life miserable for enemy passers, with Jack Youngblood leading the pass rush and with Pat Thomas and Nolan Cromwell prowling the secondary. The offensive line propped the attack up, with Doug France, Kent Hill, and Rich Saul the standouts on a top unit. Injuries struck the running back corps. Star runner Wendell Tyler was injured in a summer car accident, returned only in mid-season, and quickly went off for the year with an elbow injury. Elvis Peacock played halfback for most of the year until injuring a knee late in the campaign. Coach Ray Malavasi simply delved into his reserves and came up with two fine rookie runners in Jewerl Thomas and Mike Guman.

**San Francisco '49ers**—After winning only two games last year, the 49ers bolted out to three straight victories at the start of the season. The realities of rebuilding then set in, but the 49ers did string together three more successes later in the fall. Bill Walsh tried lots of new faces on defense, with the Rams and Cowboys running up big scores in October. On offense, the 49ers threw the ball a lot. Steve DeBerg did the passing during the early win streak, but by the end of the year, Joe Montana had captured the starting QB job with his mobility and intelligent play. Second-year receiver Dwight Clark won a starting job with sure hands and quick moves, while rookie fullback Earl Cooper ran for power and hauled in lots of passes. Halfback Paul Hofer was off to an excellent year when a knee injury felled him in October.

**New Orleans Saints**—The promise of 1979 was choked by the brutal failure of 1980. The Saints began losing on opening day and pursued it with a vengence. With an atrocious defense and widespread griping, the Saints quickly settled into a listless, defeatist style of football. Head coach Dick Nolan traded runner Chuck Muncie to San Diego after some personal friction, but that move only reduced the New Orleans running game to puny proportions. With their team self-destructing every Sunday, fans rechristened the team the Aints and took to wearing paper bags over their heads at games. The Saints reached their nadir on November 24, when they walked through a 27-7 beating at the hands of the Rams on Monday night television. Nolan was fired after that game, and Dick Stanfel took over for the balance of the season. On December 7, the Saints took a 35-7 halftime lead over the 49ers, but wound up losing 38-35 in overtime. With a perfect record closing in on them, the Saints escaped history by beating the Jets 21-20 on December 14. A fall-from-ahead loss to the Patriots one week later closed out a memorable year.

## PHILADELPHIA EAGLES 12-4-0 Dick Vermeil

| Scores of Each Game | | |
|---|---|---|
| 27 | DENVER | 6 |
| 42 | Minnesota | 7 |
| 35 | N.Y.GIANTS | 3 |
| 14 | St. Louis | 24 |
| 24 | WASHINGTON | 14 |
| 31 | N.Y. Giants | 16 |
| 17 | DALLAS | 10 |
| 17 | CHICAGO | 14 |
| 27 | Seattle | 20 |
| 34 | New Orleans | 21 |
| 24 | Washington | 0 |
| 10 | OAKLAND | 7 |
| 21 | San Diego | 22 |
| 17 | ATLANTA | 20 |
| 17 | ST. LOUIS | 3 |
| 27 | Dallas | 35 |

| Use Name | Pos. | Hgt. | Wgt. | Age | Int. | Pts. |
|---|---|---|---|---|---|---|
| Steve Kenney | OT | 6'4" | 262 | 24 | | |
| Jerry Sisemore | OT | 6'4" | 265 | 29 | | |
| Stan Walters | OT | 6'6" | 275 | 32 | | |
| Ron Baker | OG | 6'4" | 250 | 25 | | |
| Woody Peoples | OG | 6'2" | 260 | 37 | | |
| Petey Perot | OG | 6'2" | 261 | 23 | | |
| Guy Morriss | C | 6'4" | 255 | 29 | | |
| Mark Slater | C | 6'1" | 257 | 25 | | |
| Thomas Brown | DE | 6'4" | 240 | 23 | | |
| Carl Hairston | DE | 6'3" | 260 | 27 | 1 | |
| Dennis Harrison | DE | 6'8" | 275 | 24 | | |
| Claude Humphrey | DE | 6'5" | 258 | 36 | | |
| Ken Clarke | NT | 6'2" | 260 | 24 | | |
| Charles Johnson | NT | 6'3" | 262 | 28 | 3 | |
| Bill Bergey | LB | 6'2" | 245 | 35 | 1 | |
| John Bunting | LB | 6'1" | 220 | 30 | | |
| Al Chesley | LB | 6'3" | 240 | 23 | | |
| Frank LeMaster | LB | 6'2" | 238 | 28 | 1 | |
| Ray Phillips | LB | 6'4" | 230 | 26 | | |
| Jerry Robinson | LB | 6'2" | 218 | 23 | 2 | 6 |
| Reggie Wilkes | LB | 6'4" | 230 | 24 | 1 | |
| Richard Blackmore | DB | 5'10" | 174 | 24 | 2 | |
| Herman Edwards | DB | 6' | 190 | 26 | 3 | |
| Zac Henderson | DB | 6'1" | 190 | 25 | | |
| Randy Logan | DB | 6'1" | 195 | 29 | 1 | |
| John Sciarra | DB | 5'11" | 185 | 26 | | |
| Steve Wagner | DB | 6'2" | 208 | 26 | | |
| Brenard Wilson | DB | 6' | 175 | 25 | 6 | |
| Roynell Young | DB | 6'1" | 181 | 22 | 4 | |
| Rob Hertel | QB | 6'2" | 198 | 25 | | |
| Ron Jaworski | QB | 6'2" | 196 | 29 | | 6 |
| Joe Pisarcik | QB | 6'4" | 220 | 28 | | |
| Billy Campfield | HB | 5'11" | 205 | 24 | | 18 |
| Zachary Dixon (to BAL) | HB | 6' | 200 | 24 | | |
| Louie Giammona | HB | 5'9" | 180 | 27 | | 30 |
| Wilbert Montgomery | HB | 5'10" | 195 | 25 | | 60 |
| Jim Culbreath (to NYG) | FB | 6' | 210 | 27 | | |
| Perry Harrington | FB-HB | 5'11" | 210 | 22 | | 6 |
| Leroy Harris | FB | 5'9" | 230 | 26 | | 24 |
| Bob Torrey | FB | 6'4" | 232 | 23 | | |
| Luther Blue | WR | 5'11" | 180 | 24 | | |
| Harold Carmichael | WR | 6'7" | 225 | 30 | | 54 |
| Scott Fitzkee | WR | 6' | 187 | 23 | | 12 |
| Wally Henry | WR | 5'8" | 180 | 25 | | |
| Rodney Parker | WR | 6'1" | 190 | 27 | | 6 |
| Charlie Smith | WR | 6'1" | 185 | 30 | | 18 |
| Ken Dunek | TE | 6'6" | 235 | 23 | | |
| Lewis Gilbert (to SF) | TE | 6'4" | 225 | 24 | | |
| Keith Krepfle | TE | 6'3" | 230 | 28 | | 24 |
| John Spagnola | TE | 6'4" | 240 | 23 | | 18 |
| Tony Franklin | K | 5'8" | 182 | 23 | | 96 |
| Max Runager | K | 6'1" | 189 | 24 | | |

Larry Barnes – Thigh Injury
Lem Burnham – Knee Injury

## DALLAS COWBOYS 12-4-0 Tom Landry

| Scores of Each Game | | |
|---|---|---|
| 17 | Washington | 3 |
| 20 | Denver | 41 |
| 28 | TAMPA BAY | 17 |
| 28 | Green Bay | 7 |
| 24 | N.Y. GIANTS | 3 |
| 59 | SAN FRANCISCO | 14 |
| 10 | Philadelphia | 17 |
| 42 | SAN DIEGO | 31 |
| 27 | St. Louis | 24 |
| 35 | N.Y. Giants | 38 |
| 31 | ST. LOUIS | 21 |
| 14 | WASHINGTON | 10 |
| 51 | SEATTLE | 7 |
| 19 | Oakland | 13 |
| 14 | Los Angeles | 38 |
| 35 | PHILADELPHIA | 27 |

| Use Name | Pos. | Hgt. | Wgt. | Age | Int. | Pts. |
|---|---|---|---|---|---|---|
| Jim Cooper | OT | 6'5" | 260 | 24 | | |
| Pat Donovan | OT | 6'4" | 250 | 27 | | |
| Andy Frederick | OT | 6'6" | 255 | 25 | | |
| Kurt Petersen | OG | 6'4" | 251 | 23 | | |
| Tom Rafferty | OG | 6'3" | 250 | 26 | | |
| Herbert Scott | OG | 6'2" | 252 | 27 | | |
| Norm Wells | OG | 6'5" | 261 | 22 | | |
| John Fitzgerald | C | 6'5" | 260 | 32 | | |
| Robert Shaw | C | 6'4" | 245 | 23 | | |
| Too Tall Jones | DE | 6'9" | 260 | 29 | | |
| Harvey Martin | DE | 6'5" | 250 | 29 | | |
| Bruce Thornton | DE-DT | 6'5" | 265 | 22 | | |
| Larry Bethea | DT | 6'5" | 254 | 24 | | |
| Larry Cole | DT | 6'4" | 252 | 33 | 1 | 6 |
| John Dutton | DT | 6'7" | 265 | 29 | 1 | 6 |
| Randy White | DT | 6'4" | 250 | 27 | | |
| Bob Breunig | LB | 6'2" | 225 | 27 | 3 | |
| Guy Brown | LB | 6'4" | 228 | 25 | | |
| Anthony Dickerson | LB | 6'2" | 214 | 23 | 2 | |
| Mike Hegman | LB | 6'1" | 225 | 27 | 2 | 6 |
| Bruce Huther | LB | 6'1" | 220 | 26 | | |
| D.D. Lewis | LB | 6'2" | 215 | 34 | | |
| Bill Roe | LB | 6'3" | 230 | 22 | | |
| Benny Barnes | DB | 6'1" | 195 | 29 | 1 | |
| Dextor Clinkscale | DB | 5'11" | 189 | 22 | | |
| Randy Hughes | DB | 6'4" | 207 | 27 | | |
| Eric Hurt | DB | 5'11" | 171 | 23 | | |
| Wade Manning | DB | 5'11" | 190 | 25 | | |
| Aaron Mitchell | DB | 6'1" | 196 | 23 | 3 | |
| Roland Solomon (to BUFF) | DB | 6' | 196 | 24 | | |
| Dennis Thurman | DB | 5'11" | 170 | 24 | 5 | 6 |
| Charlie Waters | DB | 6'1" | 200 | 31 | 5 | |
| Steve Wilson | DB | 5'10" | 192 | 23 | 4 | |
| Glenn Carano | QB | 6'3" | 202 | 24 | | |
| Gary Hogeboom | QB | 6'4" | 201 | 22 | | |
| Danny White | QB | 6'2" | 192 | 28 | | 6 |
| Tony Dorsett | HB | 5'11" | 190 | 26 | | 66 |
| James Jones | HB-FB | 5'10" | 201 | 21 | | |
| Preston Pearson | HB | 6'1" | 196 | 35 | | 12 |
| Robert Newhouse | FB | 5'10" | 215 | 30 | | 36 |
| Timmy Newsome | FB | 6'1" | 227 | 22 | | 12 |
| Ron Springs | FB | 6'1" | 200 | 23 | | 42 |
| Tony Hill | WR | 6'2" | 198 | 24 | | 48 |
| Butch Johnson | WR | 6'1" | 192 | 26 | | 24 |
| Drew Pearson | WR | 6' | 183 | 29 | | 36 |
| Doug Cosbie | TE | 6'6" | 230 | 24 | | 6 |
| Billy Joe DuPree | TE | 6'4" | 229 | 30 | | 42 |
| Jay Saldi | TE-WR | 6'3" | 227 | 25 | | 6 |
| Rafael Septien | K | 5'9" | 171 | 26 | | 92 |

## WASHINGTON REDSKINS 6-10-0 Jack Pardee

| Scores of Each Game | | |
|---|---|---|
| 3 | DALLAS | 17 |
| 23 | N.Y. Giants | 21 |
| 21 | Oakland | 24 |
| 0 | SEATTLE | 14 |
| 14 | Philadelphia | 24 |
| 17 | Denver | 20 |
| 23 | ST. LOUIS | 0 |
| 22 | NEW ORLEANS | 14 |
| 14 | MINNESOTA | 39 |
| 21 | Chicago | 35 |
| 0 | PHILADELPHIA | 24 |
| 10 | Dallas | 14 |
| 6 | Atlanta | 10 |
| 40 | SAN DIEGO | 17 |
| 16 | N.Y. GIANTS | 13 |
| 31 | St. Louis | 7 |

| Use Name | Pos. | Hgt. | Wgt. | Age | Int. | Pts. |
|---|---|---|---|---|---|---|
| Terry Hermeling | OT | 6'5" | 255 | 34 | | |
| Jerry Scanlan | OT | 6'5" | 270 | 23 | | |
| George Starke | OT | 6'5" | 250 | 32 | | |
| Gary Anderson | OG | 6'3" | 259 | 24 | | |
| Fred Dean | OG | 6'3" | 253 | 25 | | |
| Dan Nugent | OG | 6'3" | 250 | 27 | | |
| Ron Saul | OG | 6'2" | 254 | 32 | | |
| Jeff Williams | OG-OT | 6'4" | 255 | 25 | | |
| Jeff Bostic | C | 6'2" | 246 | 21 | | |
| Bob Kuziel | C | 6'5" | 255 | 30 | | |
| Dan Peiffer | C | 6'3" | 251 | 29 | | |
| Coy Bacon | DE | 6'4" | 265 | 38 | | |
| Dallas Hickman | DE-LB | 6'6" | 242 | 28 | | |
| Joe Jones | DE | 6'6" | 250 | 32 | | |
| Karl Lorch | DE | 6'3" | 258 | 30 | | |
| Perry Brooks | DT | 6'3" | 260 | 25 | | |
| Dave Butz | DT | 6'7" | 285 | 30 | | |
| Paul Smith | DT | 6'3" | 255 | 35 | 1 | |
| Diron Talbert | DT | 6'5" | 255 | 36 | | |
| Monte Coleman | LB | 6'2" | 230 | 22 | 3 | |
| Brad Dusek | LB | 6'2" | 223 | 29 | | |
| Rich Milot | LB | 6'4" | 230 | 23 | 4 | |
| Neal Olkewicz | LB | 6' | 227 | 23 | | |
| Pete Wysocki | LB | 6'2" | 224 | 31 | | |
| Ken Houston | DB | 6'3" | 202 | 35 | | |
| Joe Lavender | DB | 6'4" | 185 | 31 | 6 | 6 |
| Mark Murphy | DB | 6'4" | 210 | 25 | 6 | |
| Mike Nelms | DB | 6'1" | 185 | 25 | | |
| Lemar Parrish | DB | 5'11 | 170 | 32 | 7 | |
| Tony Peters | DB | 6'1" | 177 | 27 | 4 | |
| Ray Waddy | DB | 5'11" | 175 | 24 | | |
| Jeris White | DB | 5'11" | 188 | 27 | 2 | |
| Mike Kruczek | QB | 6'1" | 205 | 27 | | |
| Kim McQuilken | QB | 6'2" | 203 | 29 | | |
| Joe Theismann | QB | 6' | 195 | 30 | | 18 |
| Rickey Claitt | HB-FB | 5'10" | 206 | 23 | | 12 |
| Ike Forte | HB | 6' | 202 | 26 | | 12 |
| Bob Hammond | HB | 5'10" | 170 | 28 | | 6 |
| Buddy Hardeman | HB | 6' | 202 | 25 | | |
| Clarence Harmon | HB-FB | 5'11" | 209 | 24 | | 48 |
| Wilbur Jackson | FB | 6'1" | 219 | 28 | | 24 |
| Kenny Harrison | WR | 6' | 170 | 26 | | |
| John McDaniel | WR | 6'1" | 198 | 28 | | |
| Zion McKinney | WR | 6' | 200 | 22 | | |
| Art Monk | WR | 6'3" | 209 | 22 | | 18 |
| Ricky Thompson | WR | 6' | 177 | 26 | | 30 |
| Phil DuBois | TE | 6'2" | 221 | 23 | | |
| Grady Richardson | TE | 6'4" | 225 | 28 | | |
| Rick Walker | TE | 6'3" | 235 | 25 | | 6 |
| Don Warren | TE | 6'4" | 236 | 24 | | |
| Mike Connell | K | 6'1" | 200 | 24 | | |
| Mark Moseley | K | 5'11" | 205 | 32 | | 81 |

John Riggins – Holdout

## ST. LOUIS CARDINALS 5-11-0 Jim Hanifan

| Scores of Each Game | | |
|---|---|---|
| 35 | N.Y.GIANTS | 41 |
| 21 | San Francisco | *24 |
| 7 | Detroit | 20 |
| 24 | PHILADELPHIA | 14 |
| 40 | New Orleans | 7 |
| 13 | LOS ANGELES | 21 |
| 0 | Washington | 23 |
| 17 | Baltimore | 10 |
| 24 | DALLAS | 27 |
| 27 | ATLANTA | *33 |
| 21 | Dallas | 31 |
| 13 | KANSAS CITY | 21 |
| 23 | N.Y. Giants | 7 |
| 24 | DETROIT | 23 |
| 3 | Philadelphia | 17 |
| 7 | WASHINGTON | 31 |

| Use Name | Pos. | Hgt. | Wgt. | Age | Int. | Pts. |
|---|---|---|---|---|---|---|
| George Collins | OT-OG | 6'2" | 260 | 24 | | |
| Dan Dierdorf | OT | 6'4" | 288 | 31 | | |
| Mark Goodspeed | OT | 6'5" | 270 | 23 | | |
| Brad Oates (to KC) | OT | 6'6" | 275 | 26 | | |
| Keith Wortman | OT | 6'2" | 275 | 30 | | |
| Tom Banks | OG-C | 6'1" | 245 | 32 | | |
| Joe Bostic | OG-OT | 6'3" | 265 | 23 | | |
| Ron Coder | OG | 6'4" | 250 | 26 | | |
| Barney Cotton | OG | 6'5" | 265 | 23 | | |
| Tom Brahaney | C | 6'2" | 246 | 28 | | |
| Randy Clark | C-OG-OT | 6'3" | 254 | 23 | | |
| Curtis Greer | DE | 6'4" | 252 | 22 | | |
| Stafford Mays | DE | 6'2" | 242 | 22 | | |
| Bob Pollard | DE | 6'3" | 252 | 31 | | |
| Ron Yankowski | DE | 6'5" | 258 | 33 | | |
| Bill Acker | NT | 6'2" | 255 | 24 | | |
| Rush Brown | NT | 6'2" | 257 | 26 | 1 | |
| Mike Dawson | NT | 6'4" | 275 | 26 | | |
| Oudious Lee | NT | 6'1" | 253 | 24 | | |
| Mark Arneson | LB | 6'2" | 224 | 30 | | |
| Charlie Baker | LB | 6'2" | 217 | 22 | | |
| John Barefield | LB | 6'2" | 224 | 25 | | |
| Kirby Criswell | LB | 6'5" | 238 | 23 | | |
| Calvin Favron | LB | 6'1" | 225 | 23 | | |
| Tim Kearney | LB | 6'2" | 221 | 29 | 1 | |
| Jeff McIntyre | LB | 6'3" | 232 | 24 | | |
| Steve Neils | LB | 6'2" | 218 | 29 | | |
| Eric Williams | LB | 6'2" | 225 | 25 | 2 | |
| Carl Allen | DB | 6' | 186 | 24 | 3 | 6 |
| Tim Collier | DB | 6' | 174 | 26 | 2 | |
| Roy Green | DB | 5'11" | 190 | 23 | 1 | 6 |
| Ken Greene | DB | 6'3" | 203 | 24 | 4 | |
| Lee Nelson | DB | 5'10" | 185 | 26 | | |
| Ken Stone | DB | 6'1" | 180 | 29 | 5 | |
| Roger Wehrli | DB | 6'1" | 193 | 32 | 1 | |
| Jim Hart | QB | 6'2" | 210 | 36 | | |
| Rusty Lisch | QB | 6'3" | 213 | 23 | | |
| Mike Loyd | QB | 6'2" | 216 | 24 | | |
| Ottis Anderson | HB | 6'2" | 215 | 23 | | 54 |
| Will Harrell | HB | 5'9" | 182 | 27 | | 18 |
| Randy Love | HB | 6'1" | 205 | 23 | | |
| Theotis Brown | FB | 6'2" | 225 | 23 | | 12 |
| Wayne Morris | FB | 6' | 208 | 26 | | 42 |
| Rod Phillips | FB | 6' | 221 | 27 | | |
| Mark Bell | WR | 5'9" | 175 | 23 | | |
| Mel Gray | WR | 5'9" | 171 | 31 | | 18 |
| Jeff Lee | WR | 6'2" | 195 | 25 | | |
| Dave Stief | WR | 6'3" | 195 | 24 | | |
| Pat Tilley | WR | 5'10" | 171 | 27 | | 36 |
| Chris Combs | TE | 6'4" | 239 | 22 | | 6 |
| Doug Marsh | TE | 6'3" | 236 | 22 | | 24 |
| Gary Parris | TE | 6'2" | 226 | 30 | | |
| Steve Little | K | 6' | 180 | 24 | | 26 |
| Neil O'Donoghue | K | 6'6" | 210 | 27 | | 51 |
| Larry Swider | K | 6'2" | 195 | 25 | | |

Terry Stieve – Knee Injury

## NEW YORK GIANTS 4-12-0 Ray Perkins

| Scores of Each Game | | |
|---|---|---|
| 41 | St. Louis | 35 |
| 21 | WASHINGTON | 23 |
| 3 | Philadelphia | 35 |
| 7 | LOS ANGELES | 28 |
| 3 | Dallas | 24 |
| 16 | PHILADELPHIA | 31 |
| 7 | San Diego | 44 |
| 9 | DENVER | 14 |
| 13 | Tampa Bay | 30 |
| 38 | DALLAS | 35 |
| 27 | GREEN BAY | 21 |
| 0 | San Francisco | 12 |
| 7 | ST. LOUIS | 23 |
| 27 | Seattle | 21 |
| 13 | Washington | 16 |
| 17 | OAKLAND | 33 |

| Use Name | Pos. | Hgt. | Wgt. | Age | Int. | Pts. |
|---|---|---|---|---|---|---|
| Brad Benson | OT | 6'3" | 258 | 24 | | |
| Vern Holland (from DET) | OT | 6'5" | 267 | 32 | | |
| Gordon King | OT | 6'6" | 275 | 24 | | |
| Jeff Weston | OT | 6'5" | 255 | 23 | | |
| Terry Falcon | OG-OT | 6'3" | 260 | 25 | | |
| Roy Simmons | OG | 6'3" | 264 | 23 | | |
| John Sinnott | OG-OT | 6'4" | 275 | 22 | | |
| J.T. Turner | OG | 6'3" | 255 | 27 | | |
| Jim Clack | C | 6'3" | 250 | 32 | | |
| Kelly Saalfeld | C | 6'3" | 246 | 24 | | |
| Steve Tobin | C | 6'4" | 258 | 23 | | |
| Gary Jeter | DE | 6'4" | 260 | 25 | | |
| Chris Linnin | DE | 6'4" | 255 | 23 | | |
| Dale Markham | DE | 6'8" | 280 | 23 | | |
| George Martin | DE-TE | 6'4" | 245 | 27 | | 6 |
| Myron Lapka | NT-DE | 6'4" | 255 | 24 | | |
| Curtis McGriff | NT | 6'5" | 270 | 22 | | |
| George Small | NT | 6'2" | 260 | 23 | | |
| Phil Tabor | NT | 6'4" | 255 | 23 | | |
| Ben Apuna | LB | 6'1" | 222 | 23 | | |
| Phil Cancik | LB | 6'1" | 225 | 23 | | |
| Harry Carson | LB | 6'2" | 240 | 26 | | |
| Brian Kelley | LB | 6'3" | 222 | 29 | | |
| Frank Marion | LB | 6'3" | 228 | 29 | 1 | |
| Joe McLaughlin | LB | 6'1" | 235 | 23 | | |
| John Skorupan | LB | 6'2" | 225 | 29 | | |
| Kevin Turner | LB | 6'2" | 225 | 23 | | |
| Brad Van Pelt | LB | 6'5" | 235 | 29 | 3 | |
| Whip Walton | LB | 6'2" | 225 | 25 | | |
| Mike Whittington | LB | 6'2" | 220 | 22 | | |
| Kervin Wyatt | LB | 6'2" | 235 | 22 | | |
| Tony Blount | DB | 6'1" | 195 | 21 | | |
| Mike Dennis | DB | 5'10" | 190 | 21 | 5 | |
| Eric Felton | DB | 6' | 200 | 24 | | |
| Don Harris | DB | 6'2" | 185 | 26 | | |
| Mark Haynes | DB | 5'11" | 185 | 21 | 1 | |
| Bud Hebert | DB | 6' | 190 | 23 | 1 | |
| Steve Henry | DB | 6'2" | 190 | 23 | 1 | |
| Terry Jackson | DB | 5'10" | 197 | 24 | 1 | |
| Doug Nettles | DB | 6' | 180 | 29 | | |
| Don Patterson | DB | 5'11" | 175 | 22 | | |
| Beasley Reece | DB | 6'1" | 195 | 26 | 3 | |
| Gary Woolford | DB | 6' | 182 | 26 | 2 | |
| Scott Brunner | QB | 6'5" | 200 | 23 | | |
| Cliff Olander | QB | 6'5" | 187 | 25 | | |
| Phil Simms | QB | 6'3" | 216 | 24 | | 6 |
| Art Best | HB | 6'1" | 205 | 27 | | |
| Alvin Garrett | HB-WR | 5'7" | 178 | 23 | | 6 |
| Larry Heater | HB | 5'11" | 205 | 22 | | 18 |
| Billy Taylor | HB-FB | 6' | 215 | 24 | | 24 |
| Eddie Hicks | FB-HB | 6'2" | 210 | 25 | | |
| Mike Hogan (to PHIL) | FB | 6'2" | 215 | 25 | | 12 |
| Scott Laidlaw | FB | 6' | 205 | 27 | | |
| Bo Matthews | FB | 6'4" | 222 | 28 | | |
| Leon Perry | FB | 5'11" | 225 | 23 | | 12 |
| Nate Rivers | FB | 6'3" | 215 | 25 | | |
| Mike Friede (from DET) | WR | 6'3" | 200 | 22 | | |
| Earnest Gray | WR | 6'3" | 195 | 23 | | 60 |
| Nate Johnson | WR | 5'11" | 192 | 23 | | |
| Johnny Perkins | WR | 6'2" | 205 | 27 | | 18 |
| Danny Pittman | WR | 6'2" | 205 | 22 | | |
| Dennis Johnson | TE | 6'3" | 220 | 24 | | |
| Tom Mullady | TE | 6'3" | 232 | 23 | | 12 |
| Gary Shirk | TE | 6'1" | 220 | 30 | | 6 |
| Joe Danelo | K | 5'9" | 166 | 26 | | 75 |
| Dave Jennings | K | 6'4" | 205 | 28 | | |

Keith Eck – Illness
Doug Kotar – Knee Injury
Dan Lloyd – Illness

*—Overtime

## PHILADELPHIA EAGLES

### RUSHING

| Last Name | No. | Yds. | Avg. | TD |
|---|---|---|---|---|
| Montgomery | 193 | 778 | 4.0 | 8 |
| Giammona | 97 | 361 | 3.7 | 4 |
| Harris | 104 | 341 | 3.3 | 3 |
| Harrington | 32 | 166 | 5.2 | 1 |
| Campfield | 44 | 120 | 2.7 | 1 |
| Jaworski | 27 | 95 | 3.5 | 1 |
| Smith | 5 | 33 | 6.6 | 0 |
| LeMaster | 2 | 21 | 10.5 | 0 |
| Fitzkee | 1 | 15 | 15.0 | 0 |
| Sciarra | 3 | 11 | 3.7 | 0 |
| Dixon | 2 | 8 | 4.0 | 0 |
| Culbreath | 1 | 3 | 3.0 | 0 |
| Krepfle | 1 | 2 | 2.0 | 0 |
| Pisarcik | 3 | −3 | −1.0 | 0 |

### RECEIVING

| Last Name | No. | Yds. | Avg. | TD |
|---|---|---|---|---|
| Montgomery | 50 | 407 | 8 | 2 |
| Carmichael | 48 | 815 | 17 | 9 |
| Smith | 47 | 825 | 18 | 3 |
| Krepfle | 30 | 450 | 15 | 4 |
| Campfield | 26 | 275 | 11 | 2 |
| Spagnola | 18 | 193 | 11 | 3 |
| Giammona | 17 | 178 | 11 | 1 |
| Harris | 15 | 207 | 14 | 1 |
| Parker | 9 | 148 | 16 | 1 |
| Fitzkee | 6 | 169 | 28 | 2 |
| Henry | 4 | 68 | 17 | 0 |
| Harrington | 3 | 24 | 8 | 0 |
| Gilbert | 1 | 7 | 7 | 0 |
| Dixon | 1 | 5 | 5 | 0 |

### PUNT RETURNS

| Last Name | No. | Yds. | Avg. | TD |
|---|---|---|---|---|
| Sciarra | 36 | 330 | 9 | 0 |
| Henry | 26 | 222 | 9 | 0 |
| Giammona | 1 | 8 | 8 | 0 |

### KICKOFF RETURNS

| Last Name | No. | Yds. | Avg. | TD |
|---|---|---|---|---|
| Campfield | 26 | 540 | 21 | 0 |
| Henry | 7 | 154 | 22 | 0 |
| Giammona | 7 | 82 | 12 | 0 |
| Harrington | 6 | 104 | 17 | 0 |
| Dixon | 2 | 30 | 15 | 0 |
| Montgomery | 1 | 23 | 23 | 0 |
| Blue | 1 | 16 | 16 | 0 |
| Baker | 1 | 6 | 6 | 0 |
| Clarke | 1 | 0 | 0 | 0 |
| Spagnola | 1 | 0 | 0 | 0 |

### PASSING – PUNTING – KICKING

**PASSING**

| Last Name | Att. | Comp. | % | Yds. | Yd./Att. | TD | Int.–% | | RK |
|---|---|---|---|---|---|---|---|---|---|
| Jaworski | 451 | 257 | 57 | 3529 | 7.8 | 27 | 12– | 3 | 1 |
| Pisarcik | 22 | 15 | 68 | 187 | 8.5 | 0 | 0– | 0 | |
| Giammona | 3 | 3 | 100 | 55 | 18.3 | 1 | 0– | 0 | |
| Montgomery | 1 | 0 | 0 | 0 | 0.0 | 0 | 0– | 0 | |

**PUNTING**

| Last Name | No. | Avg. |
|---|---|---|
| Runager | 75 | 39.3 |

**KICKING**

| Last Name | XP | Att. | % | FG | Att. | % |
|---|---|---|---|---|---|---|
| Franklin | 48 | 48 | 100 | 16 | 31 | 52 |

## DALLAS COWBOYS

### RUSHING

| Last Name | No. | Yds. | Avg. | TD |
|---|---|---|---|---|
| Dorsett | 278 | 1185 | 4.3 | 11 |
| Newhouse | 118 | 451 | 3.8 | 6 |
| Springs | 89 | 326 | 3.7 | 6 |
| J. Jones | 41 | 135 | 3.3 | 0 |
| D. White | 27 | 114 | 4.2 | 1 |
| Newsome | 25 | 79 | 3.2 | 2 |
| D Pearson | 2 | 30 | 15.0 | 0 |
| Hill | 4 | 27 | 6.8 | 0 |
| DuPree | 4 | 19 | 4.8 | 0 |
| P. Pearson | 3 | 6 | 2.0 | 0 |
| Carano | 4 | 6 | 1.5 | 0 |

### RECEIVING

| Last Name | No. | Yds. | Avg. | TD |
|---|---|---|---|---|
| Hill | 60 | 1055 | 18 | 8 |
| D. Pearson | 43 | 568 | 13 | 6 |
| Dorsett | 34 | 263 | 8 | 0 |
| DuPree | 29 | 312 | 11 | 7 |
| Saldi | 25 | 311 | 12 | 1 |
| P. Pearson | 20 | 213 | 11 | 2 |
| Johnson | 19 | 263 | 14 | 4 |
| Springs | 15 | 212 | 14 | 1 |
| Newhouse | 8 | 75 | 9 | 0 |
| J. Jones | 5 | 39 | 8 | 0 |
| Newsome | 4 | 43 | 11 | 0 |
| Cosbie | 2 | 11 | 6 | 1 |
| D. White | 1 | −9 | −9 | 0 |

### PUNT RETURNS

| Last Name | No. | Yds. | Avg. | TD |
|---|---|---|---|---|
| J. Jones | 54 | 548 | 10 | 0 |
| Solomon | 1 | 8 | 8 | 0 |

### KICKOFF RETURNS

| Last Name | No. | Yds. | Avg. | TD |
|---|---|---|---|---|
| J. Jones | 32 | 720 | 23 | 0 |
| Newsome | 12 | 293 | 24 | 0 |
| Wilson | 7 | 139 | 20 | 0 |
| Hurt | 4 | 71 | 18 | 0 |
| Saldi | 1 | 23 | 23 | 0 |
| Cosbie | 1 | 13 | 13 | 0 |
| Waters | 1 | 0 | 0 | 0 |

### PASSING – PUNTING – KICKING

**PASSING**

| Last Name | Att. | Comp. | % | Yds. | Yd./Att. | TD | Int.–% | | RK |
|---|---|---|---|---|---|---|---|---|---|
| D. White | 436 | 260 | 60 | 3287 | 7.5 | 28 | 25– | 6 | 7 |
| Carano | 12 | 5 | 42 | 69 | 5.8 | 0 | 0– | 0 | |
| Dorsett | 1 | 0 | 0 | 0 | 0.0 | 0 | 0– | 0 | |

**PUNTING**

| Last Name | No. | Avg. |
|---|---|---|
| D. White | 71 | 40.9 |

**KICKING**

| Last Name | XP | Att. | % | FG | Att. | % |
|---|---|---|---|---|---|---|
| Septien | 59 | 60 | 98 | 11 | 17 | 65 |

## WASHINGTON REDSKINS

### RUSHING

| Last Name | No. | Yds. | Avg. | TD |
|---|---|---|---|---|
| Jackson | 176 | 708 | 4.0 | 3 |
| Harmon | 128 | 484 | 3.8 | 4 |
| Hammond | 45 | 265 | 5.9 | 0 |
| Claitt | 57 | 215 | 3.8 | 1 |
| Theismann | 29 | 175 | 6.0 | 3 |
| Hardeman | 40 | 132 | 3.3 | 0 |
| Forte | 30 | 51 | 1.7 | 1 |
| Kruczek | 9 | 5 | 0.6 | 0 |
| Walker | 1 | −8 | −8.0 | 0 |
| Harrison | 2 | −11 | −5.5 | 0 |

### RECEIVING

| Last Name | No. | Yds. | Avg. | TD |
|---|---|---|---|---|
| Monk | 58 | 797 | 14 | 3 |
| Harmon | 54 | 534 | 10 | 4 |
| Warren | 31 | 323 | 10 | 0 |
| Jackson | 27 | 279 | 10 | 1 |
| Hammond | 24 | 203 | 9 | 1 |
| Thompson | 22 | 313 | 14 | 5 |
| Hardeman | 16 | 178 | 11 | 0 |
| Forte | 15 | 174 | 12 | 1 |
| McDaniel | 14 | 154 | 11 | 0 |
| Walker | 10 | 88 | 9 | 1 |
| Harrison | 8 | 66 | 8 | 0 |
| Claitt | 3 | 34 | 11 | 1 |
| DuBois | 1 | 16 | 16 | 0 |
| Coleman | 1 | 12 | 12 | 0 |

### PUNT RETURNS

| Last Name | No. | Yds. | Avg. | TD |
|---|---|---|---|---|
| Nelms | 48 | 487 | 10 | 0 |

### KICKOFF RETURNS

| Last Name | No. | Yds. | Avg. | TD |
|---|---|---|---|---|
| Nelms | 38 | 810 | 21 | 0 |
| Jackson | 8 | 204 | 26 | 0 |
| Forte | 4 | 114 | 29 | 0 |
| McKinney | 2 | 48 | 24 | 0 |
| Claitt | 2 | 18 | 9 | 0 |
| Monk | 1 | 10 | 10 | 0 |
| Anderson | 1 | 0 | 0 | 0 |
| Thompson | 1 | 0 | 0 | 0 |

### PASSING – PUNTING – KICKING

**PASSING**

| Last Name | Att. | Comp. | % | Yds. | Yd./Att. | TD | Int.–% | | RK |
|---|---|---|---|---|---|---|---|---|---|
| Theisman | 454 | 262 | 58 | 2962 | 6.5 | 17 | 16– | 4 | 8 |
| Kruczek | 31 | 22 | 71 | 209 | 6.7 | 0 | 2– | 7 | |
| Hardeman | 1 | 0 | 0 | 0 | 0.0 | 0 | 0– | 0 | |

**PUNTING**

| Last Name | No. | Avg. |
|---|---|---|
| Connell | 85 | 39.2 |

**KICKING**

| Last Name | XP | Att. | % | FG | Att. | % |
|---|---|---|---|---|---|---|
| Moseley | 27 | 30 | 90 | 18 | 33 | 55 |

## ST. LOUIS CARDINALS

### RUSHING

| Last Name | No. | Yds. | Avg. | TD |
|---|---|---|---|---|
| Anderson | 301 | 1352 | 4.5 | 9 |
| Morris | 117 | 456 | 3.9 | 6 |
| T. Brown | 40 | 186 | 4.7 | 1 |
| Harrell | 42 | 170 | 4.0 | 3 |
| Hart | 9 | 11 | 1.2 | 0 |
| Phillips | 2 | 6 | 3.0 | 0 |
| Love | 1 | 3 | 3.0 | 0 |
| Loyd | 6 | 2 | 0.3 | 0 |
| Gray | 1 | −3 | −3.0 | 0 |

### RECEIVING

| Last Name | No. | Yds. | Avg. | TD |
|---|---|---|---|---|
| Tilley | 68 | 966 | 14 | 6 |
| Gray | 40 | 709 | 18 | 3 |
| Anderson | 36 | 308 | 9 | 0 |
| Marsh | 22 | 269 | 12 | 4 |
| T. Brown | 21 | 290 | 14 | 1 |
| Stief | 16 | 165 | 10 | 0 |
| Morris | 15 | 110 | 7 | 1 |
| Harrell | 9 | 52 | 6 | 0 |
| Bell | 8 | 123 | 15 | 0 |
| Combs | 2 | 52 | 26 | 1 |
| J. Lee | 2 | 19 | 10 | 0 |

### PUNT RETURNS

| Last Name | No. | Yds. | Avg. | TD |
|---|---|---|---|---|
| Green | 16 | 168 | 11 | 1 |
| Bell | 21 | 195 | 9 | 0 |
| Harrell | 11 | 31 | 3 | 0 |
| Nelson | 1 | 5 | 5 | 0 |
| Allen | 1 | 0 | 0 | 0 |

### KICKOFF RETURNS

| Last Name | No. | Yds. | Avg. | TD |
|---|---|---|---|---|
| Green | 32 | 745 | 23 | 0 |
| Harrell | 19 | 348 | 18 | 0 |
| Love | 3 | 46 | 15 | 0 |
| Stone | 3 | 34 | 11 | 0 |
| Phillips | 2 | 28 | 14 | 0 |
| T. Brown | 2 | 26 | 13 | 0 |
| Clark | 2 | 14 | 7 | 0 |
| Nelson | 1 | 29 | 29 | 0 |
| Collins | 1 | 0 | 0 | 0 |
| Baker | 0 | 27 | — | 0 |

### PASSING – PUNTING – KICKING

**PASSING**

| Last Name | Att. | Comp. | % | Yds. | Yd./Att. | TD | Int.–% | | RK |
|---|---|---|---|---|---|---|---|---|---|
| Hart | 425 | 228 | 54 | 2946 | 6.9 | 16 | 20– | 5 | 12 |
| Loyd | 28 | 5 | 18 | 49 | 1.8 | 0 | 1– | 4 | |
| Lisch | 17 | 6 | 35 | 68 | 4.0 | 0 | 3– | 18 | |

**PUNTING**

| Last Name | No. | Avg. |
|---|---|---|
| Swider | 99 | 41.5 |

**KICKING**

| Last Name | XP | Att. | % | FG | Att. | % |
|---|---|---|---|---|---|---|
| O'Donoghue | 18 | 18 | 100 | 11 | 15 | 73 |
| Little | 17 | 19 | 89 | 3 | 8 | 38 |

## NEW YORK GIANTS

### RUSHING

| Last Name | No. | Yds. | Avg. | TD |
|---|---|---|---|---|
| Taylor | 147 | 580 | 3.9 | 4 |
| Heater | 111 | 360 | 3.2 | 3 |
| Perry | 59 | 272 | 4.6 | 1 |
| Simms | 36 | 190 | 5.3 | 1 |
| Matthews | 64 | 180 | 2.8 | 0 |
| Hogan | 34 | 90 | 2.6 | 2 |
| Hicks | 19 | 50 | 2.6 | 0 |
| Garrett | 9 | 31 | 3.4 | 0 |
| Brunner | 10 | 18 | 1.8 | 0 |
| Laidlaw | 5 | 10 | 2.0 | 0 |
| Pittman | 1 | −7 | −7.0 | 0 |

### RECEIVING

| Last Name | No. | Yds. | Avg. | TD |
|---|---|---|---|---|
| Gray | 52 | 777 | 15 | 10 |
| Taylor | 33 | 253 | 8 | 0 |
| Mullady | 28 | 391 | 14 | 2 |
| Pittman | 25 | 308 | 12 | 0 |
| Friede | 22 | 371 | 17 | 0 |
| Shirk | 21 | 211 | 10 | 1 |
| Matthews | 19 | 86 | 5 | 0 |
| Perkins | 14 | 193 | 14 | 3 |
| Heater | 10 | 139 | 14 | 0 |
| Perry | 8 | 84 | 11 | 1 |
| Garrett | 5 | 69 | 14 | 1 |
| Hogan | 5 | 46 | 9 | 0 |
| Laidlaw | 2 | 16 | 8 | 0 |
| Hicks | 1 | 4 | 4 | 0 |
| Martin | 1 | 4 | 4 | 1 |

### PUNT RETURNS

| Last Name | No. | Yds. | Avg. | TD |
|---|---|---|---|---|
| Garrett | 35 | 287 | 8 | 0 |
| Reece | 2 | 15 | 8 | 0 |

### KICKOFF RETURNS

| Last Name | No. | Yds. | Avg. | TD |
|---|---|---|---|---|
| Reece | 24 | 471 | 20 | 0 |
| Garrett | 28 | 527 | 19 | 0 |
| Heater | 5 | 103 | 21 | 0 |
| N. Johnson | 5 | 89 | 18 | 0 |
| Pittman | 2 | 41 | 21 | 0 |
| Haynes | 2 | 40 | 20 | 0 |
| McLaughlin | 2 | 27 | 14 | 0 |
| Laidlaw | 1 | 18 | 18 | 0 |
| Lapka | 1 | 3 | 3 | 0 |
| Wyatt | 1 | 0 | 0 | 0 |

### PASSING – PUNTING – KICKING

**PASSING**

| Last Name | Att. | Comp. | % | Yds. | Yd./Att. | TD | Int.–% | | RK |
|---|---|---|---|---|---|---|---|---|---|
| Simms | 402 | 193 | 48 | 2321 | 5.8 | 15 | 19– | 5 | 15 |
| Brunner | 112 | 52 | 46 | 610 | 5.5 | 4 | 6– | 5 | |

**PUNTING**

| Last Name | No. | Avg. |
|---|---|---|
| Jennings | 94 | 44.8 |

**KICKING**

| Last Name | XP | Att. | % | FG | Att. | % |
|---|---|---|---|---|---|---|
| Danelo | 27 | 28 | 96 | 16 | 24 | 67 |

## MINNESOTA VIKINGS 9-7-0 Bud Grant

| Scores of Each Game | | |
|---|---|---|
| 24 | ATLANTA | 23 |
| 7 | PHILADELPHIA | 42 |
| 34 | Chicago | 14 |
| 7 | Detroit | 27 |
| 17 | PITTSBURGH | 23 |
| 13 | CHICAGO | 7 |
| 0 | Cincinnati | 14 |
| 3 | Green Bay | 16 |
| 39 | Washington | 14 |
| 34 | DETROIT | 0 |
| 38 | TAMPA BAY | 30 |
| 13 | GREEN BAY | 25 |
| 23 | New Orleans | 20 |
| 21 | Tampa Bay | 10 |
| 28 | CLEVELAND | 23 |
| 16 | Houston | 20 |

| Use Name | Pos. | Hgt. | Wgt. | Age | Int. | Pts. |
|---|---|---|---|---|---|---|
| Nick Bebout | OT | 6'5" | 260 | 29 | | |
| Dave Huffman | OT-OG-C | 6'6" | 258 | 23 | | |
| Steve Riley | OT | 6'6" | 258 | 27 | | |
| John Vella | OT | 6'4" | 260 | 30 | | |
| Ron Yary | OT | 6'6" | 255 | 34 | | |
| Brent Boyd | OG | 6'3" | 260 | 23 | | |
| Wes Hamilton | OG | 6'3" | 266 | 27 | | |
| Jim Hough | OG-C | 6'2" | 270 | 24 | | |
| Mel Mitchell | OG | 6'3" | 260 | 27 | | |
| Jim Langer | C | 6'2" | 253 | 32 | | |
| Dennis Swilley | C | 6'3" | 241 | 25 | | |
| Randy Holloway | DE | 6'5" | 252 | 25 | | 2 |
| Doug Martin | DE | 6'3" | 258 | 23 | | |
| Mark Mullaney | DE | 6'6" | 242 | 27 | | |
| Ken Sanders | DE | 6'5" | 245 | 30 | | |
| Dave Roller | DT | 6'2" | 270 | 30 | | |
| Doug Sutherland | DT | 6'3" | 250 | 32 | | |
| James White | DT | 6'3" | 263 | 26 | | |
| Matt Blair | LB | 6'5" | 237 | 29 | 3 | |
| Dennis Johnson | LB | 6'3" | 231 | 22 | | |
| Henry Johnson | LB | 6'1" | 235 | 22 | | |
| Fred McNeill | LB | 6'2" | 226 | 28 | | |
| Jeff Siemon | LB | 6'2" | 237 | 30 | | |
| Scott Studwell | LB | 6'2" | 224 | 26 | 1 | |
| Larry Brune | DB | 6'2" | 202 | 27 | 2 | |
| Bobby Bryant | DB | 6' | 177 | 36 | 3 | |
| Tom Hannon | DB | 5'11" | 190 | 25 | 4 | 6 |
| Kurt Knoff | DB | 6'2" | 202 | 26 | 3 | 6 |
| Keith Nord | DB | 6' | 193 | 23 | | 6 |
| Willie Teal | DB | 5'10" | 195 | 23 | | |
| John Turner | DB | 6' | 199 | 24 | 6 | |
| Nate Wright | DB | 5'11" | 180 | 32 | 2 | |
| Steve Dils | QB | 6'1" | 192 | 24 | | |
| Tommy Kramer | QB | 6'1" | 204 | 25 | | 6 |
| Mike Livingston | QB | 6'3" | 215 | 34 | | |
| Robert Miller | HB | 5'11" | 204 | 27 | | 6 |
| Eddie Payton | HB | 5'8" | 175 | 29 | | |
| Rickey Young | HB | 6'2" | 195 | 26 | | 30 |
| Ted Brown | FB | 5'10" | 200 | 23 | | 60 |
| Doug Paschal | FB | 6'2" | 219 | 22 | | 6 |
| Terry LeCount | WR | 5'10" | 187 | 24 | | |
| Kevin Miller | WR | 5'10" | 184 | 25 | | |
| Ahmad Rashad | WR | 6'2" | 200 | 30 | | 30 |
| Sammy White | WR | 5'11" | 189 | 26 | | 30 |
| Bob Bruer (from SF) | TE | 6'5" | 235 | 27 | | |
| Joe Senser | TE | 6'4" | 238 | 24 | | 42 |
| Bob Tucker | TE | 6'3" | 230 | 35 | | 6 |
| Stu Voigt | TE | 6'1" | 225 | 32 | | |
| Greg Coleman | K | 6' | 184 | 25 | | |
| Rick Danmeier | K | 6' | 204 | 28 | | 81 |

## DETROIT LIONS 9-7-0 Monte Clark

| Scores of Each Game | | |
|---|---|---|
| 41 | Los Angeles | 20 |
| 29 | Green Bay | 7 |
| 20 | ST. LOUIS | 7 |
| 27 | MINNESOTA | 7 |
| 28 | Atlanta | 43 |
| 24 | NEW ORLEANS | 13 |
| 7 | Chicago | 24 |
| 17 | Kansas City | 20 |
| 17 | SAN FRANCISCO | 13 |
| 0 | Minnesota | 34 |
| 9 | BALTIMORE | 10 |
| 24 | Tampa Bay | 10 |
| 17 | CHICAGO | *23 |
| 23 | St. Louis | 24 |
| 27 | TAMPA BAY | 14 |
| 24 | GREEN BAY | 3 |

| Use Name | Pos. | Hgt. | Wgt. | Age | Int. | Pts. |
|---|---|---|---|---|---|---|
| Karl Baldischwiler | OT | 6'5" | 260 | 24 | | |
| Chris Dieterich | OT-OG | 6'3" | 255 | 22 | | |
| Keith Dorney | OT | 6'5" | 260 | 22 | | |
| Mike Whited | OT | 6'4" | 250 | 22 | | |
| Russ Bolinger | OG | 6'5" | 255 | 25 | | |
| Homer Elias | OG-OT | 6'3" | 255 | 25 | | |
| Tommie Ginn | OG-C | 6'3" | 250 | 22 | | |
| Burton Lawless | OG | 6'4" | 255 | 26 | | |
| Amos Fowler | C | 6'3" | 250 | 24 | | |
| Willie Parker | C | 6'3" | 245 | 31 | | |
| Wally Pesuit | C | 6'4" | 250 | 26 | | |
| Tom Turnure | C | 6'4" | 250 | 23 | | |
| Al Baker | DE | 6'6" | 245 | 23 | 1 | |
| Dave Pureifory | DE | 6'1" | 255 | 31 | | |
| William Gay | DT-DE | 6'5" | 250 | 25 | | |
| Mike McCoy (from NYG) | DT | 6'5" | 275 | 31 | | |
| John Mendenhall | DT | 6'1" | 255 | 31 | | |
| Tom Tuinei | DT | 6'4" | 250 | 22 | | |
| John Woodcock | DT | 6'3" | 250 | 26 | | |
| Garry Cobb | LB | 6'2" | 225 | 23 | | |
| Eddie Cole | LB | 6'2" | 235 | 23 | | 2 |
| Ken Fantetti | LB | 6'2" | 230 | 23 | 1 | |
| James Harrell | LB | 6'1" | 220 | 23 | | |
| Derrel Luce (from MIN) | LB | 6'3" | 225 | 27 | | |
| Davie Simmons | LB | 6'4" | 218 | 23 | | |
| Charlie Weaver | LB | 6'2" | 225 | 31 | 1 | |
| Stan White | LB | 6'1" | 225 | 30 | 2 | |
| Jim Allen | DB | 6'2" | 190 | 28 | 6 | |
| Luther Bradley | DB | 6'2" | 190 | 25 | 1 | |
| James Hunter | DB | 6'3" | 195 | 26 | 6 | |
| Eddie Lewis | DB | 6' | 175 | 26 | | |
| Prentice McCray (from NE) | DB | 6'1" | 190 | 29 | | |
| Ray Oldham | DB | 6' | 190 | 29 | 3 | 6 |
| Wayne Smith | DB | 6' | 170 | 23 | 1 | |
| Walt Williams | DB | 6' | 185 | 26 | 1 | |
| Gary Danielson | QB | 6'2" | 195 | 28 | | 12 |
| Eric Hipple | QB | 6'2" | 200 | 22 | | |
| Jeff Komlo | QB | 6'2" | 200 | 24 | | |
| Ken Callicutt | HB | 6' | 195 | 25 | | |
| Rick Kane | HB | 5'11" | 200 | 25 | | |
| Billy Sims | HB | 6' | 210 | 24 | | 96 |
| Dexter Bussey | FB | 6'1" | 210 | 28 | | 18 |
| Horace King | FB | 5'10" | 205 | 27 | | 12 |
| Bo Robinson | FB | 6'2" | 225 | 24 | | |
| John Arnold | WR | 5'10" | 175 | 24 | | |
| Freddie Scott | WR | 6'2" | 180 | 28 | | 30 |
| Jesse Thompson | WR | 6'1" | 185 | 24 | | |
| Leonard Thompson | WR | 5'10" | 190 | 28 | | 18 |
| Ray Williams | WR | 5'9" | 170 | 21 | | 18 |
| David Hill | TE | 6'2" | 230 | 26 | | 6 |
| Ulysses Norris | TE | 6'4" | 230 | 23 | | |
| Eddie Murray | K | 5'10" | 165 | 24 | | 116 |
| Tom Skladany | K | 6' | 195 | 25 | | |

Doug English – Voluntarily Retired

## CHICAGO BEARS 7-9-0 Neill Armstrong

| Scores of Each Game | | |
|---|---|---|
| 6 | Green Bay | *12 |
| 22 | NEW ORLI ANS | 3 |
| 14 | MINNESOTA | 34 |
| 3 | Pittsburgh | 38 |
| 23 | TAMPA BAY | 0 |
| 7 | Minnesota | 13 |
| 24 | DETROIT | 7 |
| 14 | Philadelphia | 17 |
| 21 | Cleveland | 27 |
| 35 | WASHINGTON | 21 |
| 6 | HOUSTON | 10 |
| 17 | Atlanta | 28 |
| 23 | Detroit | *17 |
| 61 | GREEN BAY | 7 |
| 14 | CINCINNATI | *17 |
| 14 | Tampa Bay | 13 |

| Use Name | Pos. | Hgt. | Wgt. | Age | Int. | Pts. |
|---|---|---|---|---|---|---|
| Ted Albrecht | OT | 6'4" | 250 | 25 | | |
| Dan Jiggetts | OT | 6'4" | 270 | 26 | | |
| Dennis Lick | OT | 6'3" | 265 | 26 | | |
| Noah Jackson | OG | 6'2" | 265 | 29 | | |
| Rocco Moore | OG-OT | 6'5" | 276 | 25 | | |
| Revie Sorey | OG | 6'2" | 260 | 26 | | |
| Dan Neal | C | 6'4" | 255 | 31 | | |
| Paul Tabor | C-OG | 6'4" | 241 | 23 | | |
| Dan Hampton | DE | 6'5" | 255 | 22 | | |
| Al Harris | DE | 6'5" | 240 | 23 | | |
| Mike Hartenstine | DE | 6'3" | 243 | 27 | | |
| Jim Osborne | DT | 6'3" | 245 | 30 | | |
| Alan Page | DT | 6'5" | 225 | 35 | 1 | 8 |
| Ron Rydalch | DT | 6'4" | 260 | 28 | | |
| Brad Shearer | DT | 6'3" | 247 | 25 | | |
| Gary Campbell | LB | 6'1" | 220 | 28 | 3 | |
| Bruce Herron | LB | 6'2" | 220 | 26 | | |
| Tom Hicks | LB | 6'4" | 235 | 27 | 1 | |
| Lee Kunz | LB | 6'2" | 225 | 23 | | |
| Jerry Muckensturm | LB | 6'4" | 220 | 26 | 2 | |
| Otis Wilson | LB | 6'2" | 222 | 22 | 2 | |
| Dave Becker | DB | 6'2" | 190 | 23 | | |
| Allan Ellis | DB | 5'10" | 177 | 29 | 1 | |
| Gary Fencik | DB | 6'1" | 197 | 26 | 1 | |
| Wentford Gaines | DB | 6' | 185 | 27 | | |
| Jonathan Hoke | DB | 5'11" | 175 | 23 | | |
| Vaughn Lusby | DB | 5'10" | 181 | 24 | | |
| Doug Plank | DB | 6' | 202 | 27 | 1 | |
| Terry Schmidt | DB | 6' | 177 | 28 | 1 | |
| Mike Ulmer | DB | 6' | 190 | 25 | | |
| Len Walterscheid | DB | 5'11" | 190 | 25 | 4 | 6 |
| Bob Avellini | QB | 6'2" | 210 | 27 | | |
| Vince Evans | QB | 6'2" | 212 | 25 | | 48 |
| Mike Phipps | QB | 6'3" | 209 | 32 | | 12 |
| Willie McClendon | HB | 6'1" | 205 | 22 | | 6 |
| Walter Payton | HB | 5'11" | 202 | 26 | | 42 |
| Roland Harper | FB | 6' | 210 | 27 | | 30 |
| John Skibinski | FB | 6' | 222 | 25 | | |
| Matt Suhey | FB | 5'11" | 212 | 22 | | |
| Dave Williams | FB | 6'2" | 217 | 26 | | 6 |
| Brian Baschnagel | WR | 6' | 184 | 26 | | 12 |
| Kris Haines | WR | 5'11" | 180 | 23 | | |
| James Scott | WR | 6'1" | 190 | 28 | | 18 |
| Rickey Watts | WR | 6'1" | 203 | 23 | | 12 |
| Mike Cobb | TE | 6'5" | 243 | 24 | | |
| Robin Earl | TE | 6'5" | 240 | 25 | | 18 |
| Robert Fisher | TE | 6'3" | 240 | 22 | | 12 |
| Greg Latta | TE | 6'3" | 225 | 27 | | |
| Bob Parsons | TE | 6'4" | 225 | 30 | | |
| Bob Thomas | K | 5'10" | 175 | 28 | | 74 |

Virgil Livers – Knee Injury

## TAMPA BAY BUCCHANEERS 5-10-1 John McKay

| Scores of Each Game | | |
|---|---|---|
| 17 | Cincinnati | 12 |
| 10 | LOS ANGELES | 9 |
| 17 | Dallas | 28 |
| 27 | CLEVELAND | 34 |
| 0 | Chicago | 23 |
| 14 | GREEN BAY | *14 |
| 14 | Houston | 20 |
| 24 | San Francisco | 23 |
| 30 | N.Y. GIANTS | 13 |
| 21 | PITTSBURGH | 24 |
| 30 | Minnesota | 38 |
| 10 | DETROIT | 24 |
| 20 | Green Bay | 17 |
| 10 | MINNESOTA | 21 |
| 14 | Detroit | 27 |
| 13 | CHICAGO | 14 |

| Use Name | Pos. | Hgt. | Wgt. | Age | Int. | Pts. |
|---|---|---|---|---|---|---|
| Darrell Austin | OT-OG | 6'4" | 255 | 28 | | |
| Charley Hannah | OT | 6'5" | 260 | 25 | | |
| Dave Reavis | OT | 6'5" | 260 | 30 | | |
| Greg Roberts | OG | 6'3" | 260 | 23 | | |
| Gene Sanders | OG | 6'3" | 260 | 23 | | |
| Ray Snell | OG | 6'3" | 255 | 22 | | |
| George Yarno | OG | 6'2" | 255 | 23 | | |
| Jim Leonard | C | 6'3" | 250 | 22 | | |
| Steve Wilson | C | 6'3" | 265 | 26 | | |
| Bill Kollar | DE-NT | 6'4" | 250 | 27 | | |
| Reggie Lewis | DE | 6'3" | 255 | 24 | | |
| Lee Roy Selmon | DE | 6'3" | 250 | 25 | | |
| David Stalls | DE | 6'4" | 255 | 24 | | |
| Randy Crowder | NT | 6'2" | 250 | 28 | | |
| David Logan | NT | 6'2" | 250 | 23 | | 6 |
| Bruce Radford | NT-DE | 6'5" | 260 | 24 | | |
| Rik Bonness | LB | 6'3" | 220 | 26 | | |
| Scot Brantley | LB | 6'1" | 230 | 22 | 1 | |
| Aaron Brown | LB | 6'2" | 235 | 24 | | |
| Andy Hawkins | LB | 6'2" | 215 | 22 | | |
| Cecil Johnson | LB | 6'2" | 230 | 25 | | |
| Dave Lewis | LB | 6'4" | 245 | 25 | 1 | |
| Dewey Selmon | LB | 6'1" | 240 | 26 | | |
| Richard Wood | LB | 6'2" | 230 | 27 | 3 | 6 |
| Cedric Brown | DB | 6'1" | 205 | 26 | 1 | 6 |
| Neal Colzie | DB | 6'2" | 195 | 27 | 1 | |
| Mark Cotney | DB | 6' | 205 | 28 | 3 | |
| Curtis Jordan | DB | 6'2" | 205 | 26 | | |
| Danny Reece | DB | 5'11" | 195 | 25 | | |
| Norris Thomas | DB | 5'11" | 185 | 26 | 1 | |
| Mike Washington | DB | 6'3" | 200 | 27 | 4 | |
| Chuck Fusina | QB | 6'1" | 195 | 23 | | |
| Mike Rae | QB | 6' | 200 | 29 | | |
| Doug Williams | QB | 6'4" | 215 | 25 | | 24 |
| Rick Berns | HB | 6'2" | 205 | 24 | | |
| Gary Davis | HB | 5'10" | 200 | 25 | | |
| Jerry Eckwood | HB | 6' | 200 | 25 | | 18 |
| Ricky Bell | FB-HB | 6'2" | 215 | 25 | | 18 |
| Johnny Davis | FB | 6'1" | 235 | 24 | | 6 |
| Tony Davis | FB | 5'10" | 210 | 27 | | 6 |
| Isaac Hagins | WR | 5'9" | 180 | 26 | | 12 |
| Kevin House | WR | 6'1" | 175 | 22 | | 30 |
| Gordon Jones | WR | 6' | 190 | 23 | | 30 |
| Larry Mucker | WR | 5'11" | 190 | 25 | | |
| Mike Shumann | WR | 6' | 175 | 24 | | 6 |
| Jimmie Giles | TE | 6'3" | 245 | 25 | | 24 |
| Jim Obradovich | TE | 6'2" | 230 | 27 | | |
| Tom Blanchard | K | 6' | 185 | 32 | | |
| Garo Yepremian | K | 5'8" | 175 | 36 | | 79 |

Dana Nafziger – Knee Injury
George Ragsdale – Shoulder Injury

## GREEN BAY PACKERS 5-10-1 Bart Starr

| Scores of Each Game | | |
|---|---|---|
| 12 | CHICAGO | *6 |
| 7 | DETROIT | 29 |
| 21 | Los Angeles | 51 |
| 7 | DALLAS | 28 |
| 14 | CINCINNATI | 9 |
| 14 | Tampa Bay | *14 |
| 21 | Cleveland | 26 |
| 16 | MINNESOTA | 3 |
| 20 | Pittsburgh | 22 |
| 23 | SAN FRANCISCO | 16 |
| 21 | N.Y. Giants | 27 |
| 25 | Minnesota | 13 |
| 17 | TAMPA BAY | 20 |
| 7 | Chicago | 61 |
| 3 | HOUSTON | 22 |
| 3 | Detroit | 24 |

| Use Name | Pos. | Hgt. | Wgt. | Age | Int. | Pts. |
|---|---|---|---|---|---|---|
| Buddy Aydelette | OT | 6'4" | 250 | 24 | | |
| Greg Koch | OT | 6'4" | 265 | 25 | | |
| Mark Koncar | OT | 6'5" | 268 | 27 | | |
| Tim Stones | OT | 6'5" | 252 | 30 | | |
| Karl Swanke | OT-C | 6'6" | 251 | 22 | | |
| Derrell Gofourth | OG | 6'3" | 260 | 25 | | |
| Leotis Harris | OG | 6'1" | 267 | 25 | | |
| Melvin Jackson | OG | 6'1" | 267 | 26 | | |
| Syd Kitson | OG | 6'4" | 252 | 21 | | |
| Ken Brown | C | 6'1" | 245 | 26 | | |
| Larry McCarren | C | 6'3" | 248 | 28 | | |
| Mike Wellman | C | 6'3" | 253 | 24 | | |
| Mike Butler | DE | 6'5" | 265 | 26 | | |
| Ezra Johnson | DE | 6'4" | 240 | 24 | | |
| Kit Lathrop | DE | 6'5" | 253 | 24 | | |
| Casey Merrill | DE | 6'4" | 255 | 23 | | |
| Rich Dimler | NT | 6'6" | 260 | 24 | | |
| Charles Johnson | NT | 6'1" | 262 | 23 | | |
| Terry Jones | NT | 6'2" | 259 | 23 | | |
| Mike Lewis | NT | 6'3" | 260 | 31 | | |
| Kurt Allerman | LB | 6'3" | 222 | 25 | | |
| John Anderson | LB | 6'3" | 221 | 24 | | |
| Bruce Beekley | LB | 6'2" | 225 | 23 | | |
| Brian Cabral | LB | 6' | 224 | 24 | | |
| George Cumby | LB | 6' | 215 | 24 | | |
| Mike Douglass | LB | 6' | 224 | 25 | | |
| Jim Gueno | LB | 6'2" | 220 | 26 | | |
| Mike Hunt | LB | 6'2" | 240 | 23 | | |
| Ed O'Neil | LB | 6'3" | 235 | 27 | | |
| Paul Rudzinski | LB | 6'1" | 220 | 24 | 1 | |
| Johnnie Gray | DB | 5'11" | 185 | 26 | 5 | |
| Estus Hood | DB | 5'11" | 180 | 24 | 1 | |
| Mike Jolly | DB | 6'3" | 185 | 22 | 2 | |
| Mark Lee | DB | 5'11" | 187 | 22 | | |
| Steve Luke | DB | 6'2" | 205 | 26 | 1 | |
| Mike McCoy | DB | 5'11" | 183 | 27 | 1 | |
| Mark Murphy | DB | 6'2" | 199 | 22 | | |
| Wylie Turner | DB | 5'10" | 182 | 23 | 2 | |
| Lynn Dickey | QB | 6'4" | 220 | 30 | | 6 |
| Mark Miller | QB | 6'2" | 176 | 24 | | |
| Steve Pisarkiewicz | QB | 6'2" | 205 | 26 | | |
| Bill Troup | QB | 6'5" | 220 | 29 | | |
| David Whitehurst | QB | 6'2" | 204 | 25 | | |
| Harlan Huckleby | HB | 6'1" | 199 | 22 | | 6 |
| Eddie Lee Ivery | HB-FB | 6'1" | 210 | 23 | | 24 |
| Terdell Middleton | HB | 6' | 195 | 25 | | 12 |
| Vickey Ray Anderson | FB | 6' | 205 | 24 | | |
| Steve Atkins | FB | 6' | 216 | 24 | | 12 |
| Gerry Ellis | FB | 5'11" | 215 | 22 | | 48 |
| Barty Smith | FB | 6'4" | 240 | 28 | | |
| Ron Cassidy | WR | 6' | 185 | 23 | | |
| Bobby Kimball | WR | 6'1" | 190 | 23 | | |
| James Lofton | WR-DB | 6'3" | 187 | 24 | | 24 |
| Fred Nixon | WR | 5'11" | 191 | 21 | | |
| Aundra Thompson | WR | 6' | 186 | 27 | | 12 |
| Paul Coffman | TE | 6'3" | 218 | 24 | | 18 |
| Bill Larson (from DEN) | TE | 6'4" | 225 | 26 | | 6 |
| John Thompson | TE | 6'3" | 228 | 23 | | |
| David Beverly | K | 6'2" | 180 | 30 | | |
| Tom Birney | K | 6'4" | 220 | 24 | | 32 |
| Chester Marcol (to HOU) | K | 6' | 190 | 30 | | 23 |
| Jan Stenerud | K | 6'2" | 190 | 37 | | 12 |

Eric Torkelson – Leg Injury
Rich Wingo – Back Injury

*—Overtime

## MINNESOTA VIKINGS

### Rushing

| Last Name | No. | Yds. | Avg. | TD |
|---|---|---|---|---|
| Brown | 219 | 912 | 4.2 | 8 |
| Young | 130 | 351 | 2.7 | 3 |
| Kramer | 31 | 115 | 3.7 | 1 |
| R. Miller | 27 | 98 | 3.6 | 1 |
| S. White | 4 | 65 | 16.3 | 0 |
| Paschal | 15 | 53 | 3.5 | 1 |
| Dils | 3 | 26 | 8.7 | 0 |
| Payton | 2 | 15 | 7.5 | 0 |
| Rashad | 1 | 8 | 8.0 | 0 |
| Senser | 1 | −1 | −1.0 | 0 |

### Receiving

| Last Name | No. | Yds. | Avg. | TD |
|---|---|---|---|---|
| Rashad | 69 | 1095 | 16 | 5 |
| Young | 64 | 499 | 8 | 2 |
| Brown | 62 | 623 | 10 | 2 |
| S. White | 53 | 887 | 17 | 5 |
| Senser | 42 | 447 | 11 | 7 |
| Tucker | 15 | 173 | 12 | 1 |
| LeCount | 13 | 168 | 13 | 0 |
| R. Miller | 10 | 19 | 2 | 0 |
| Paschal | 2 | 18 | 9 | 0 |
| Yary | 1 | 5 | 5 | 0 |

### Punt Returns

| Last Name | No. | Yds. | Avg. | TD |
|---|---|---|---|---|
| Payton | 34 | 251 | 7 | 0 |

### Kickoff Returns

| Last Name | No. | Yds. | Avg. | TD |
|---|---|---|---|---|
| Payton | 53 | 1184 | 22 | 0 |
| Paschal | 4 | 66 | 17 | 0 |
| Bruer | 2 | 20 | 10 | 0 |
| Nord | 1 | 70 | 70 | 1 |
| R. Miller | 1 | 23 | 23 | 0 |
| Boyd | 1 | 20 | 20 | 0 |
| Yary | 1 | 3 | 3 | 0 |

### Passing – Punting – Kicking

| PASSING | Att. | Comp. | % | Yds. | Yd./Att. | TD | Int.–% | RK |
|---|---|---|---|---|---|---|---|---|
| Kramer | 522 | 299 | 57 | 3582 | 6.9 | 19 | 23– 4 | 9 |
| Dils | 51 | 32 | 63 | 352 | 6.9 | 3 | 0– 0 | |
| Senser | 1 | 0 | 0 | 0 | 0.0 | 0 | 0– 0 | |

| PUNTING | No. | Avg. |
|---|---|---|
| Coleman | 81 | 38.8 |

| KICKING | XP | Att. | % | FG | Att. | % |
|---|---|---|---|---|---|---|
| Danmeier | 33 | 38 | 87 | 16 | 26 | 62 |

## DETROIT LIONS

### Rushing

| Last Name | No. | Yds. | Avg. | TD |
|---|---|---|---|---|
| Sims | 313 | 1303 | 4.2 | 13 |
| Bussey | 145 | 720 | 5.0 | 3 |
| Danielson | 48 | 232 | 4.8 | 2 |
| Kane | 31 | 125 | 4.0 | 0 |
| Scott | 5 | 86 | 17.2 | 1 |
| L. Thompson | 6 | 61 | 10.2 | 0 |
| King | 18 | 57 | 3.2 | 1 |
| R. Williams | 2 | 17 | 8.5 | 1 |
| Robinson | 3 | 2 | 0.7 | 0 |
| J. Thompson | 1 | −4 | −4.0 | 0 |

### Receiving

| Last Name | No. | Yds. | Avg. | TD |
|---|---|---|---|---|
| Scott | 53 | 834 | 16 | 4 |
| Sims | 51 | 621 | 12 | 3 |
| Hill | 39 | 424 | 11 | 1 |
| Bussey | 39 | 364 | 9 | 0 |
| L. Thompson | 19 | 511 | 27 | 3 |
| King | 19 | 184 | 10 | 1 |
| J. Thompson | 11 | 137 | 13 | 0 |
| R. Williams | 10 | 146 | 15 | 1 |
| Kane | 5 | 26 | 5 | 0 |
| Callicutt | 1 | 19 | 19 | 0 |

### Punt Returns

| Last Name | No. | Yds. | Avg. | TD |
|---|---|---|---|---|
| R. Williams | 27 | 259 | 10 | 0 |
| Arnold | 28 | 204 | 7 | 0 |
| Callicutt | 1 | 0 | 0 | 0 |

### Kickoff Returns

| Last Name | No. | Yds. | Avg. | TD |
|---|---|---|---|---|
| Kane | 23 | 495 | 22 | 0 |
| Callicutt | 16 | 301 | 19 | 0 |
| R. Williams | 9 | 228 | 25 | 1 |
| Arnold | 9 | 145 | 16 | 0 |

### Passing – Punting – Kicking

| PASSING | Att. | Comp. | % | Yds. | Yd./Att. | TD | Int.–% | RK |
|---|---|---|---|---|---|---|---|---|
| Danielson | 417 | 244 | 59 | 3223 | 7.7 | 13 | 11– 3 | 5 |
| Komlo | 4 | 2 | 50 | 26 | 6.5 | 0 | 1– 25 | |
| Skladany | 2 | 2 | 100 | 38 | 19.0 | 0 | 0– 0 | |

| PUNTING | No. | Avg. |
|---|---|---|
| Skladany | 72 | 42.2 |

| KICKING | XP | Att. | % | FG | Att. | % |
|---|---|---|---|---|---|---|
| Murray | 35 | 36 | 97 | 27 | 42 | 64 |

## CHICAGO BEARS

### Rushing

| Last Name | No. | Yds. | Avg. | TD |
|---|---|---|---|---|
| Payton | 317 | 1460 | 4.6 | 6 |
| Harper | 113 | 404 | 3.6 | 5 |
| Evans | 60 | 306 | 5.1 | 8 |
| McClendon | 10 | 88 | 8.8 | 1 |
| Williams | 26 | 57 | 2.2 | 0 |
| Skibinski | 13 | 54 | 4.2 | 0 |
| Suhey | 22 | 45 | 2.0 | 0 |
| Phipps | 15 | 38 | 2.5 | 2 |
| Parsons | 2 | 4 | 2.0 | 0 |
| Watts | 1 | −16 | −16.0 | 0 |

### Receiving

| Last Name | No. | Yds. | Avg. | TD |
|---|---|---|---|---|
| Payton | 46 | 367 | 8 | 1 |
| Scott | 36 | 696 | 19 | 3 |
| Baschnagel | 28 | 396 | 14 | 2 |
| Watts | 22 | 444 | 20 | 2 |
| Williams | 22 | 132 | 6 | 0 |
| Earl | 18 | 223 | 12 | 3 |
| Fisher | 12 | 203 | 17 | 2 |
| Suhey | 7 | 60 | 9 | 0 |
| Harper | 7 | 31 | 4 | 0 |
| Skibinski | 5 | 18 | 4 | 0 |
| Haines | 4 | 83 | 21 | 0 |
| Cobb | 2 | 16 | 8 | 0 |

### Punt Returns

| Last Name | No. | Yds. | Avg. | TD |
|---|---|---|---|---|
| Walterscheid | 33 | 239 | 7 | 0 |
| Lusby | 4 | 14 | 4 | 0 |
| Watts | 2 | 20 | 10 | 0 |
| Suhey | 1 | 4 | 4 | 0 |
| Plank | 1 | 0 | 0 | 0 |

### Kickoff Returns

| Last Name | No. | Yds. | Avg. | TD |
|---|---|---|---|---|
| Williams | 27 | 666 | 25 | 1 |
| Suhey | 19 | 406 | 21 | 0 |
| Fisher | 3 | 32 | 11 | 0 |
| Walterscheid | 1 | 12 | 12 | 0 |
| Watts | 1 | 12 | 12 | 0 |
| Earl | 1 | 11 | 11 | 0 |
| McClendon | 1 | 11 | 11 | 0 |
| Herron | 1 | 5 | 5 | 0 |
| Haines | 1 | 0 | 0 | 0 |
| Ulmer | 1 | −2 | −2 | 0 |

### Passing – Punting – Kicking

| PASSING | Att. | Comp. | % | Yds. | Yd./Att. | TD | Int.–% | RK |
|---|---|---|---|---|---|---|---|---|
| Evans | 278 | 148 | 53 | 2039 | 7.3 | 11 | 16– 6 | 14 |
| Phipps | 122 | 61 | 50 | 630 | 5.2 | 2 | 9– 7 | |
| Parsons | 1 | 0 | 0 | 0 | 0.0 | 0 | 0– 0 | |
| Payton | 3 | 0 | 0 | 0 | 0.0 | 0 | 0– 0 | |

| PUNTING | No. | Avg. |
|---|---|---|
| Parsons | 79 | 40.6 |

| KICKING | XP | Att. | % | FG | Att. | % |
|---|---|---|---|---|---|---|
| Thomas | 35 | 37 | 95 | 13 | 18 | 72 |

## TAMPA BAY BUCCANEERS

### Rushing

| Last Name | No. | Yds. | Avg. | TD |
|---|---|---|---|---|
| Bell | 174 | 599 | 3.4 | 2 |
| Eckwood | 149 | 504 | 3.4 | 2 |
| Williams | 58 | 370 | 6.4 | 4 |
| Berns | 39 | 131 | 3.4 | 0 |
| J. Davis | 39 | 130 | 3.3 | 1 |
| House | 1 | 32 | 32.0 | 0 |
| Hagins | 3 | 24 | 8.0 | 0 |
| T. Davis | 5 | 24 | 4.8 | 0 |
| G. Davis | 7 | 21 | 3.0 | 0 |
| Fusina | 1 | 14 | 14.0 | 0 |
| Jones | 1 | −10 | −10.0 | 0 |

### Receiving

| Last Name | No. | Yds. | Avg. | TD |
|---|---|---|---|---|
| Jones | 48 | 669 | 14 | 5 |
| Eckwood | 47 | 475 | 10 | 1 |
| Bell | 38 | 292 | 8 | 1 |
| Giles | 33 | 602 | 18 | 4 |
| House | 24 | 531 | 22 | 5 |
| Hagins | 23 | 364 | 16 | 2 |
| T. Davis | 12 | 115 | 10 | 1 |
| Obradovich | 11 | 152 | 14 | 0 |
| G. Davis | 9 | 79 | 9 | 0 |
| Schumann | 4 | 75 | 19 | 1 |
| J. Davis | 4 | 17 | 4 | 0 |
| Mucker | 2 | 37 | 19 | 0 |
| Berns | 1 | 6 | 6 | 0 |

### Punt Returns

| Last Name | No. | Yds. | Avg. | TD |
|---|---|---|---|---|
| Reece | 57 | 313 | 6 | 0 |

### Kickoff Returns

| Last Name | No. | Yds. | Avg. | TD |
|---|---|---|---|---|
| G. Davis | 44 | 951 | 22 | 0 |
| Reece | 7 | 128 | 18 | 0 |
| Obradovich | 6 | 46 | 9 | 0 |
| Hagins | 4 | 82 | 21 | 0 |
| T. Davis | 4 | 58 | 15 | 0 |
| Berns | 1 | 19 | 19 | 0 |
| Jordan | 1 | 0 | 0 | 0 |

### Passing – Punting – Kicking

| PASSING | Att. | Comp. | % | Yds. | Yd./Att. | TD | Int.–% | RK |
|---|---|---|---|---|---|---|---|---|
| Williams | 521 | 254 | 49 | 3396 | 6.5 | 20 | 16– 3 | 11 |
| Fusina | 4 | 2 | 50 | 18 | 4.5 | 0 | 1– 25 | |
| Eckwood | 4 | 0 | 0 | 0 | 0.0 | 0 | 0– 0 | |
| Hannah | 1 | 0 | 0 | 0 | 0.0 | 0 | 0– 0 | |

| PUNTING | No. | Avg. |
|---|---|---|
| Blanchard | 88 | 42.3 |

| KICKING | XP | Att. | % | FG | Att. | % |
|---|---|---|---|---|---|---|
| Yepremian | 31 | 32 | 97 | 16 | 23 | 70 |

## GREEN BAY PACKERS

### Rushing

| Last Name | No. | Yds. | Avg. | TD |
|---|---|---|---|---|
| Ivery | 202 | 831 | 4.1 | 3 |
| Ellis | 126 | 545 | 4.3 | 5 |
| Atkins | 67 | 216 | 3.2 | 1 |
| Middleton | 56 | 155 | 2.8 | 2 |
| Beverly | 6 | 21 | 3.5 | 0 |
| Huckleby | 6 | 11 | 1.8 | 0 |
| Dickey | 19 | 11 | 0.6 | 0 |
| V. Anderson | 4 | 5 | 1.3 | 0 |
| A. Thompson | 5 | 5 | 1.0 | 0 |
| Coffman | 1 | 3 | 3.0 | 0 |
| Smith | 1 | 3 | 3.0 | 0 |

### Receiving

| Last Name | No. | Yds. | Avg. | TD |
|---|---|---|---|---|
| Lofton | 71 | 1226 | 17 | 4 |
| Ivery | 50 | 481 | 10 | 1 |
| Ellis | 48 | 496 | 10 | 3 |
| Coffman | 42 | 496 | 12 | 3 |
| A. Thompson | 40 | 609 | 15 | 2 |
| Middleton | 13 | 59 | 5 | 0 |
| Atkins | 7 | 49 | 7 | 1 |
| Cassidy | 5 | 109 | 22 | 0 |
| Larson | 5 | 44 | 9 | 1 |
| Nixon | 4 | 78 | 20 | 0 |
| Huckleby | 3 | 11 | 4 | 0 |
| V. Anderson | 2 | 2 | 1 | 0 |

### Punt Returns

| Last Name | No. | Yds. | Avg. | TD |
|---|---|---|---|---|
| Cassidy | 17 | 139 | 8 | 0 |
| Nixon | 11 | 85 | 8 | 0 |
| Lee | 5 | 32 | 6 | 0 |
| Gray | 4 | 41 | 10 | 0 |

### Kickoff Returns

| Last Name | No. | Yds. | Avg. | TD |
|---|---|---|---|---|
| Lee | 30 | 589 | 20 | 0 |
| A. Thompson | 15 | 283 | 19 | 0 |
| McCoy | 14 | 261 | 19 | 0 |
| Nixon | 6 | 160 | 27 | 0 |
| Gray | 5 | 63 | 13 | 0 |
| Huckleby | 3 | 59 | 20 | 0 |

### Passing – Punting – Kicking

| PASSING | Att. | Comp. | % | Yds. | Yd./Att. | TD | Int.–% | RK |
|---|---|---|---|---|---|---|---|---|
| Dickey | 478 | 278 | 58 | 3529 | 7.4 | 15 | 25– 5 | 10 |
| Whitehurst | 15 | 5 | 33 | 55 | 3.7 | 0 | 1– 7 | |
| Troup | 12 | 4 | 33 | 48 | 4.0 | 0 | 3– 25 | |
| Pisarkiewicz | 5 | 2 | 40 | 19 | 3.8 | 0 | 0– 0 | |
| Beverly | 1 | 0 | 0 | 0 | 0.0 | 0 | 0– 0 | |

| PUNTING | No. | Avg. |
|---|---|---|
| Beverly | 86 | 38.3 |
| Marcol | 1 | 33.0 |

| KICKING | XP | Att. | % | FG | Att. | % |
|---|---|---|---|---|---|---|
| Birney | 14 | 18 | 78 | 6 | 12 | 50 |
| Marcol | 8 | 10 | 80 | 3 | 4 | 75 |
| Stenerud | 3 | 3 | 100 | 3 | 5 | 60 |

## ATLANTA FALCONS 12-4-0 Leeman Bennett

| Scores of Each Game | | |
|---|---|---|
| 23 | Minnesota | 24 |
| 37 | New England | 21 |
| 17 | MIAMI | 20 |
| 20 | San Francisco | 17 |
| 43 | DETROIT | 28 |
| 7 | N.Y. JETS | 14 |
| 41 | New Orleans | 14 |
| 13 | LOS ANGELES | 10 |
| 30 | Buffalo | 14 |
| 33 | St. Louis | *27 |
| 31 | NEW ORLEANS | 13 |
| 28 | CHICAGO | 17 |
| 10 | WASHINGTON | 6 |
| 20 | Philadelphia | 17 |
| 35 | SAN FRANCISCO | 10 |
| 17 | Los Angeles | *20 |

| Use Name | Pos. | Hgt. | Wgt. | Age | Int. | Pts. |
|---|---|---|---|---|---|---|
| Warren Bryant | OT | 6'6" | 270 | 24 | | |
| Mike Kenn | OT | 6'6" | 257 | 24 | | |
| Phil McKinnely | OT | 6'4" | 248 | 26 | | |
| Chuck Herman | OG | 6'3" | 250 | 21 | | |
| Pat Howell | OG | 6'5" | 253 | 23 | | |
| Dave Scott | OG | 6'4" | 265 | 26 | | |
| R.C. Thielemann | OG | 6'4" | 247 | 25 | | |
| Chuck Correal | C | 6'3" | 247 | 24 | | |
| Jeff Van Note | C | 6'2" | 247 | 34 | | |
| Edgar Fields | DE | 6'2" | 255 | 26 | | |
| Jeff Merrow | DE | 6'4" | 230 | 27 | | |
| Matthew Teague | DE | 6'5" | 240 | 21 | | |
| Jeff Yeates | DE | 6'3" | 248 | 29 | 1 | |
| Wilson Faumuina | NT | 6'5" | 275 | 26 | | |
| Calvin Miller | NT | 6'2" | 270 | 26 | | |
| Don Smith | NT-DE | 6'5" | 248 | 23 | | |
| Mike Zele | NT | 6'3" | 236 | 24 | | |

Bubba Bean – Knee Injury
Ray Easterling – Injury
June Jones — Ankle Injury

| Use Name | Pos. | Hgt. | Wgt. | Age | Int. | Pts. |
|---|---|---|---|---|---|---|
| Jon Brooks (to LA) | LB | 6'2" | 215 | 23 | | |
| Buddy Curry | LB | 6'3" | 221 | 22 | 3 | 6 |
| Tony Daykin | LB | 6'1" | 215 | 25 | | |
| Fulton Kuykendall | LB | 6'5" | 225 | 27 | | |
| Jim Laughlin | LB | 6' | 212 | 22 | 1 | |
| Dewey McClain | LB | 6'3" | 236 | 26 | | |
| Robert Pennywell | LB | 6'1" | 222 | 25 | | |
| Al Richardson | LB | 6'2" | 206 | 22 | 7 | 6 |
| Stan Sytsma | LB | 6'2" | 220 | 24 | | |
| Joel Williams | LB | 6'1" | 215 | 23 | 2 | 8 |
| Rick Byas | DB | 5'9" | 180 | 29 | | |
| Bob Glazebrook | DB | 6'1" | 200 | 24 | 2 | |
| Kenny Johnson | DB | 5'10" | 176 | 22 | 4 | |
| Earl Jones | DB | 6' | 178 | 23 | 1 | |
| Jerome King (to NYG) | DB | 5'10" | 173 | 25 | | |
| Rolland Lawrence | DB | 5'10" | 179 | 29 | 3 | |
| Tom Pridemore | DB | 5'10" | 186 | 24 | 2 | |
| Frank Reed | DB | 5'11" | 193 | 26 | | 6 |

Dennis Pearson – Knee Injury
Billy Ryckman – Knee Injury

| Use Name | Pos. | Hgt. | Wgt. | Age | Int. | Pts. |
|---|---|---|---|---|---|---|
| Steve Bartkowski | QB | 6'4" | 213 | 27 | | 12 |
| Larry Fortner | QB | 6'4" | 212 | 24 | | |
| Mike Moroski | QB | 6'4" | 200 | 22 | | |
| Anthony Anderson | HB | 6' | 197 | 23 | | |
| Lynn Cain | HB | 6'1" | 205 | 24 | | 54 |
| Ray Strong | HB | 5'9" | 184 | 24 | | 6 |
| William Andrews | FB | 6' | 200 | 24 | | 30 |
| Quinn Jones | FB | 6'1" | 215 | 24 | | |
| James Mayberry | FB | 5'11" | 210 | 22 | | |
| Wallace Francis | WR | 5'11" | 190 | 28 | | 42 |
| Alfred Jackson | WR | 5'11" | 176 | 25 | | 42 |
| Alfred Jenkins | WR | 5'10" | 172 | 28 | | 36 |
| Mike Smith | WR | 5'10" | 194 | 22 | | |
| Reggie Smith | WR | 5'4" | 168 | 24 | | |
| Russ Mikeska | TE | 6'3" | 225 | 24 | | |
| Junior Miller | TE | 6'4" | 235 | 22 | | 54 |
| John James | K | 6'3" | 200 | 31 | | |
| Tim Mazzetti | K | 6'1" | 175 | 24 | | 103 |

## LOS ANGELES RAMS 11-5-0 Ray Malavasi

| Scores of Each Game | | |
|---|---|---|
| 20 | DETROIT | 41 |
| 9 | Tampa Bay | 10 |
| 51 | GREEN BAY | 21 |
| 28 | N.Y. Giants | 7 |
| 48 | SAN FRANCISCO | 26 |
| 21 | St. Louis | 13 |
| 31 | San Francisco | 17 |
| 10 | Atlanta | 13 |
| 45 | NEW ORLEANS | 31 |
| 14 | MIAMI | 35 |
| 17 | New England | 14 |
| 27 | New Orleans | 7 |
| 38 | N.Y. JETS | 13 |
| 7 | Buffalo | *10 |
| 38 | DALLAS | 14 |
| 20 | ATLANTA | *17 |

| Use Name | Pos. | Hgt. | Wgt. | Age | Int. | Pts. |
|---|---|---|---|---|---|---|
| Doug France | OT | 6'5" | 270 | 27 | | |
| Irv Pankey | OT | 6'4" | 269 | 22 | | |
| Jackie Slater | OT | 6'4" | 271 | 26 | | |
| Bill Bain | OG | 6'4" | 277 | 28 | | |
| Dennis Harrah | OG-C | 6'5" | 255 | 27 | | |
| Kent Hill | OG | 6'5" | 260 | 23 | | |
| Greg Horton | OG-C | 6'4" | 248 | 29 | | |
| Ed McGlasson | OG-C | 6'4" | 248 | 24 | | |
| Doug Smith | OG-C | 6'3" | 255 | 23 | | |
| Rich Saul | C | 6'3" | 245 | 32 | | |
| Reggie Doss | DE | 6'4" | 267 | 23 | | |
| Fred Dryer | DE | 6'6" | 231 | 34 | | |
| Jack Youngblood | DE | 6'4" | 244 | 30 | | |
| Larry Brooks | DT | 6'3" | 253 | 30 | | |
| Mike Fanning | DT | 6'6" | 252 | 27 | | |
| Cody Jones | DT | 6'5" | 244 | 29 | | |
| Phil Murphy | DT | 6'5" | 280 | 22 | | |

| Use Name | Pos. | Hgt. | Wgt. | Age | Int. | Pts. |
|---|---|---|---|---|---|---|
| George Andrews | LB | 6'3" | 223 | 24 | | |
| Bob Brudzinski | LB | 6'4" | 229 | 25 | | |
| Carl Ekern | LB | 6'3" | 223 | 26 | | |
| Joe Harris | LB | 6'1" | 224 | 27 | | |
| Jack Reynolds | LB | 6'1" | 227 | 32 | 1 | |
| Greg Westbrooks (from OAK) | LB | 6'3" | 220 | 27 | | |
| Jim Youngblood | LB | 6'3" | 231 | 30 | 1 | 6 |
| Nolan Cromwell | DB | 6'1" | 198 | 25 | 8 | 7 |
| Jeff Delaney | DB | 6' | 195 | 23 | 2 | |
| LeRoy Irvin | DB | 5'11" | 180 | 22 | 2 | |
| Johnnie Johnson | DB | 6'1" | 185 | 23 | 3 | 6 |
| Rod Perry | DB | 5'9" | 182 | 26 | 5 | 6 |
| Lucious Smith | DB | 5'10" | 190 | 23 | | |
| Ivory Sully | DB | 6' | 193 | 23 | | |
| Pat Thomas | DB | 5'9" | 182 | 26 | 3 | |

| Use Name | Pos. | Hgt. | Wgt. | Age | Int. | Pts. |
|---|---|---|---|---|---|---|
| Vince Ferragamo | QB | 6'3" | 212 | 26 | | 6 |
| Pat Haden | QB | 5'11" | 185 | 27 | | |
| Bob Lee | QB | 6'2" | 190 | 34 | | |
| Jeff Rutledge | QB | 6'1" | 202 | 23 | | |
| Mike Guman | HB-FB | 6'2" | 210 | 22 | | 24 |
| Eddie Hill | HB | 6'2" | 197 | 23 | | |
| Lydell Mitchell | HB | 5'11" | 198 | 31 | | |
| Elvis Peacock | HB-FB | 6'1" | 208 | 23 | | 54 |
| Jewerl Thomas | HB-FB | 5'10" | 223 | 22 | | 18 |
| Wendell Tyler | HB | 5'10" | 195 | 25 | | |
| Cullen Bryant | FB | 6'1" | 236 | 29 | | 36 |
| Preston Dennard | WR | 6'1" | 183 | 24 | | 36 |
| Drew Hill | WR | 5'9" | 170 | 23 | | 18 |
| Willie Miller | WR | 5'9" | 172 | 33 | | 48 |
| Jeff Moore | WR | 6'1" | 200 | 23 | | 6 |
| Billy Waddy | WR | 5'11" | 188 | 26 | | 30 |
| Walt Arnold | TE | 6'3" | 225 | 22 | | 6 |
| Victor Hicks | TE | 6'3" | 250 | 23 | | 18 |
| Terry Nelson | TE | 6'2" | 240 | 29 | | |
| Conrad Rucker (from TB) | TE | 6'3" | 245 | 25 | | |
| Frank Corral | K | 6'2" | 228 | 25 | | 99 |

## SAN FRANCISCO FORTY-NINERS 6-10-0 Bill Walsh

| Scores of Each Game | | |
|---|---|---|
| 26 | New Orleans | 23 |
| 24 | ST. LOUIS | *21 |
| 37 | N.Y. Jets | 27 |
| 17 | ATLANTA | 20 |
| 26 | Los Angeles | 48 |
| 14 | Dallas | 59 |
| 17 | LOS ANGELES | 31 |
| 23 | TAMPA BAY | 24 |
| 13 | Detroit | 17 |
| 16 | Green Bay | 23 |
| 13 | Miami | 17 |
| 12 | N.Y. GIANTS | 0 |
| 21 | NEW ENGLAND | 17 |
| 38 | NEW ORLEANS | *35 |
| 10 | Atlanta | 35 |
| 13 | BUFFALO | 18 |

| Use Name | Pos. | Hgt. | Wgt. | Age | Int. | Pts. |
|---|---|---|---|---|---|---|
| Jean Barrett | OT | 6'6" | 250 | 29 | | |
| Ken Bungarda | OT | 6'6" | 270 | 23 | | |
| Keith Fahnhorst | OT | 6'6" | 263 | 28 | | |
| Ron Singleton | OT | 6'7" | 267 | 28 | | |
| John Ayers | OG | 6'5" | 255 | 27 | | |
| Randy Cross | OG | 6'3" | 255 | 26 | | |
| Walt Downing | OG-C | 6'3" | 254 | 24 | | |
| Ernie Hughes | OG | 6'3" | 255 | 25 | | |
| Fred Quillan | C | 6'5" | 260 | 24 | | |
| Dwaine Board | DE | 6'5" | 245 | 23 | | |
| Mel Land | DE | 6'3" | 242 | 24 | | |
| Lawrence Pillers (from NYJ) | DE-DT | 6'3" | 260 | 27 | | |
| Jim Stuckey | DE | 6'4" | 251 | 22 | | 2 |
| Jimmy Webb | DE | 6'5" | 245 | 28 | | |
| Mike Calhoun (from TB) | DT-DE | 6'4" | 260 | 23 | | |
| Jim Krahl (from BAL) | DT | 6'5" | 252 | 24 | | |
| Archie Reese | DT | 6'3" | 262 | 24 | | |
| Ken Times | DT | 6'2" | 246 | 24 | | |
| Ted Vincent | DT | 6'4" | 265 | 24 | | |
| George Visger | DT | 6'4" | 250 | 21 | | |

| Use Name | Pos. | Hgt. | Wgt. | Age | Int. | Pts. |
|---|---|---|---|---|---|---|
| Dan Bunz | LB | 6'4" | 225 | 24 | | |
| Willie Harper | LB | 6'2" | 215 | 30 | | |
| Scott Hilton | LB | 6'4" | 230 | 26 | | |
| Bobby Leopold | LB | 6'1" | 215 | 22 | 2 | |
| Craig Puki | LB | 6'1" | 231 | 23 | 1 | |
| Thomas Seabron (TO STL) | LB | 6'3" | 215 | 23 | | |
| Terry Tautolo | LB | 6'2" | 235 | 26 | 1 | |
| Keena Turner | LB | 6'2" | 219 | 21 | 2 | |
| Ricky Churchman | DB | 6'1" | 193 | 22 | 4 | |
| Charles Cornelius | DB | 5'9" | 178 | 28 | | |
| Dwight Hicks | DB | 6'1" | 189 | 24 | 4 | |
| Charles Johnson | DB | 5'10" | 180 | 24 | 1 | |
| Al Latimer | DB | 5'11" | 172 | 22 | | |
| Melvin Morgan | DB | 6' | 186 | 27 | | |
| Scott Perry (to SD) | DB | 6' | 180 | 26 | | |
| Ray Rhodes | DB | 5'11" | 185 | 29 | 1 | |
| Gerard Williams (from STL) | DB | 6'1" | 184 | 28 | 1 | |
| Herb Williams | DB | 6' | 198 | 22 | | |

| Use Name | Pos. | Hgt. | Wgt. | Age | Int. | Pts. |
|---|---|---|---|---|---|---|
| Steve DeBerg | QB | 6'2" | 205 | 26 | | |
| Gary Huff | QB | 6'1" | 200 | 29 | | |
| Joe Montana | QB | 6'2" | 200 | 24 | | 12 |
| Lenvil Elliott | HB | 6' | 210 | 28 | | 18 |
| Paul Hofer | HB | 6' | 195 | 28 | | 18 |
| Ricky Patton | HB | 5'11" | 192 | 26 | | |
| Don Woods (from SD) | HB-FB | 6'1" | 204 | 29 | | |
| Jerry Aldridge | FB | 6'2" | 220 | 24 | | |
| Earl Cooper | FB | 6'2" | 227 | 22 | | 54 |
| Bob Ferrell | FB | 6' | 219 | 27 | | |
| Phil Francis | FB | 6'1" | 215 | 23 | | |
| Terry Anderson | WR | 5'9" | 182 | 25 | | |
| Dwight Clark | WR | 6'3" | 205 | 23 | | 48 |
| James Owens | WR | 5'11" | 188 | 25 | | 6 |
| Jim Robinson | WR | 5'9" | 170 | 27 | | |
| Freddie Solomon | WR | 5'11" | 188 | 27 | | 60 |
| Eason Ramson | TE | 6'2" | 234 | 24 | | 12 |
| Charlie Young | TE | 6'4" | 234 | 29 | | 12 |
| Jim Miller | K | 5'11" | 183 | 23 | | |
| Ray Wersching | K | 5'11" | 210 | 30 | | 78 |

## NEW ORLEANS SAINTS 1-15-0 Dick Nolan, Dick Stanfel

| Scores of Each Game | | |
|---|---|---|
| 23 | SAN FRANCISCO | 26 |
| 3 | Chicago | 22 |
| 26 | BUFFALO | 35 |
| 16 | Miami | 21 |
| 7 | ST. LOUIS | 40 |
| 13 | Detroit | 24 |
| 14 | ATLANTA | 41 |
| 14 | Washington | 22 |
| 31 | Los Angeles | 45 |
| 21 | PHILADELPHIA | 34 |
| 13 | Atlanta | 31 |
| 7 | LOS ANGELES | 27 |
| 20 | MINNESOTA | 23 |
| 35 | San Francisco | *38 |
| 21 | N.Y. Jets | 20 |
| 27 | NEW ENGLAND | 38 |

| Use Name | Pos. | Hgt. | Wgt. | Age | Int. | Pts. |
|---|---|---|---|---|---|---|
| Stan Brock | OT | 6'6" | 275 | 22 | | |
| Dave Lafary | OT-OG | 6'7" | 280 | 25 | | |
| J.T. Taylor | OT | 6'4" | 265 | 24 | | |
| Larry Coombs | OG-C | 6'4" | 260 | 23 | | |
| Fred Sturt | OG | 6'4" | 255 | 29 | | |
| Robert Woods | OG-OT | 6'3" | 259 | 30 | | |
| Emanuel Zanders | OG | 6'1" | 248 | 29 | | |
| John Hill | C | 6'2" | 246 | 30 | | |
| Jim Pietrzak | C | 6'5" | 260 | 27 | | |
| Elois Grooms | DE | 6'4" | 250 | 27 | 1 | |
| Tommy Hart | DE | 6'4" | 246 | 35 | | |
| Steve Parker | DE | 6'6" | 265 | 23 | | |
| Don Reese | DE | 6'6" | 250 | 28 | | 6 |
| Barry Bennett | DT | 6'4" | 257 | 24 | | |
| Mike Fultz | DT | 6'5" | 278 | 26 | | |
| Derland Moore | DT | 6'4" | 253 | 28 | | |
| Elex Price | DT | 6'3" | 265 | 30 | | 6 |

| Use Name | Pos. | Hgt. | Wgt. | Age | Int. | Pts. |
|---|---|---|---|---|---|---|
| Ken Bordelon | LB | 6'4" | 226 | 26 | | |
| Chuck Evans | LB | 6'3" | 235 | 23 | | |
| Joe Federspiel | LB | 6'1" | 230 | 30 | | |
| Stan Holloway | LB | 6'2" | 218 | 22 | | |
| Jim Kovach | LB | 6'2" | 225 | 24 | 1 | |
| Reggie Mathis | LB | 6'2" | 220 | 24 | 1 | |
| Dave Washington | LB | 6'5" | 225 | 31 | | |
| Ray Brown | DB | 6'2" | 202 | 31 | 2 | |
| Clarence Chapman (to CIN) | DB | 5'10" | 185 | 26 | | |
| James Marshall | DB | 6' | 187 | 27 | 2 | |
| Tom Myers | DB | 5'11" | 180 | 29 | 5 | |
| Ricky Ray | DB | 5'11" | 180 | 23 | | |
| Don Schwartz | DB | 6'1" | 191 | 24 | | |
| Dave Waymer | DB | 6'1" | 195 | 22 | | |

| Use Name | Pos. | Hgt. | Wgt. | Age | Int. | Pts. |
|---|---|---|---|---|---|---|
| Guy Benjamin | QB | 6'4" | 210 | 25 | | |
| Ed Burns | QB | 6'3" | 210 | 25 | | |
| Archie Manning | QB | 6'3" | 200 | 31 | | |
| Bobby Scott | QB | 6'1" | 197 | 31 | | |
| Larry Collins | HB | 5'11" | 190 | 25 | | |
| Jack Holmes | HB-FB | 5'11" | 210 | 27 | | 18 |
| Jimmy Rogers | HB | 5'10" | 190 | 25 | | 18 |
| Mike Strachan | HB | 6' | 198 | 27 | | |
| Tony Galbreath | FB | 6' | 230 | 26 | | 30 |
| Wayne Wilson | FB | 6'3" | 208 | 22 | | 12 |
| Gordon Banks | WR | 5'9" | 175 | 22 | | |
| Wes Chandler | WR | 5'11" | 186 | 24 | | 36 |
| Tom Donovan | WR | 5'11" | 179 | 23 | | |
| Ike Harris | WR | 6'3" | 210 | 27 | | 36 |
| Rich Mauti | WR | 6' | 190 | 26 | | |
| Tinker Owens | WR | 5'11" | 170 | 25 | | |
| Henry Childs | TE | 6'2" | 220 | 29 | | 36 |
| Larry Hardy | TE | 6'3" | 230 | 24 | | |
| Brooks Williams | TE | 6'4" | 226 | 25 | | 12 |
| Russell Erxleben | K | 6'4" | 219 | 23 | | 8 |
| Benny Ricardo | K | 5'10" | 170 | 26 | | 61 |

*—Overtime

## ATLANTA FALCONS

### RUSHING

| Last Name | No. | Yds. | Avg. | TD |
|---|---|---|---|---|
| Andrews | 265 | 1308 | 4.9 | 4 |
| Cain | 235 | 914 | 3.9 | 8 |
| Mayberry | 18 | 88 | 4.9 | 0 |
| Strong | 6 | 42 | 7.0 | 1 |
| Bartkowski | 25 | 35 | 1.4 | 2 |
| James | 1 | 13 | 13.0 | 0 |
| Anderson | 6 | 5 | 0.8 | 0 |
| Francis | 1 | 2 | 2.0 | 0 |
| J. Miller | 2 | −2 | −1.0 | 0 |

### RECEIVING

| Last Name | No. | Yds. | Avg. | TD |
|---|---|---|---|---|
| Jenkins | 57 | 1026 | 18 | 6 |
| Francis | 54 | 862 | 16 | 7 |
| Andrews | 51 | 456 | 9 | 1 |
| J. Miller | 46 | 584 | 13 | 9 |
| Cain | 24 | 223 | 9 | 1 |
| Jackson | 23 | 412 | 18 | 7 |
| Mayberry | 3 | 1 | 0 | 0 |
| Mikeska | 1 | 4 | 4 | 0 |

### PUNT RETURNS

| Last Name | No. | Yds. | Avg. | TD |
|---|---|---|---|---|
| Johnson | 23 | 281 | 12 | 0 |
| R. Smith | 27 | 262 | 10 | 0 |
| Lawrence | 3 | −7 | −2 | 0 |

### KICKOFF RETURNS

| Last Name | No. | Yds. | Avg. | TD |
|---|---|---|---|---|
| R. Smith | 25 | 512 | 21 | 0 |
| Strong | 10 | 168 | 17 | 0 |
| Anderson | 7 | 97 | 14 | 0 |
| Jackson | 3 | 70 | 23 | 0 |
| M. Smith | 3 | 58 | 19 | 0 |
| Pridemore | 3 | 39 | 13 | 0 |
| Fields | 1 | 11 | 11 | 0 |
| Daykin | 1 | 3 | 3 | 0 |

### PASSING – PUNTING – KICKING Statistics

| PASSING | Att. | Comp. | % | Yds. | Yd./Att. | TD | Int.–% | RK |
|---|---|---|---|---|---|---|---|---|
| Bartkowski | 463 | 257 | 56 | 3544 | 7.7 | 31 | 16– 4 | 3 |
| James | 1 | 0 | 0 | 0 | 0.0 | 0 | 1–100 | |
| Moroski | 3 | 2 | 67 | 24 | 8.0 | 0 | 0– 0 | |

| PUNTING | No. | Avg. |
|---|---|---|
| James | 79 | 39.1 |

| KICKING | XP | Att. | % | FG | Att. | % |
|---|---|---|---|---|---|---|
| Mazzetti | 46 | 49 | 94 | 19 | 27 | 70 |

## LOS ANGELES RAMS

### RUSHING

| Last Name | No. | Yds. | Avg. | TD |
|---|---|---|---|---|
| Bryant | 183 | 807 | 4.4 | 3 |
| Peacock | 164 | 777 | 4.7 | 7 |
| J. Thomas | 65 | 427 | 6.6 | 2 |
| Guman | 100 | 410 | 4.1 | 4 |
| Tyler | 30 | 157 | 5.2 | 0 |
| E. Hill | 39 | 120 | 3.1 | 0 |
| Ferragamo | 15 | 34 | 2.3 | 1 |
| Dennard | 2 | 20 | 10.0 | 0 |
| Hicks | 1 | 19 | 19.0 | 0 |
| Mitchell | 7 | 16 | 2.3 | 0 |
| Haden | 3 | 12 | 4.0 | 0 |
| D. Hill | 1 | 4 | 4.0 | 0 |
| Cromwell | 2 | 0 | 0.0 | 0 |
| Lee | 1 | −1 | −1.0 | 0 |
| Waddy | 1 | −1 | −1.0 | 0 |
| Miller | 1 | −2 | −2.0 | 0 |

### RECEIVING

| Last Name | No. | Yds. | Avg. | TD |
|---|---|---|---|---|
| Bryant | 53 | 386 | 7 | 3 |
| Waddy | 38 | 670 | 18 | 5 |
| Dennard | 36 | 596 | 17 | 6 |
| Peacock | 25 | 213 | 9 | 2 |
| Hicks | 23 | 318 | 14 | 3 |
| Miller | 22 | 358 | 16 | 8 |
| D. Hill | 19 | 416 | 22 | 2 |
| Guman | 14 | 131 | 9 | 0 |
| Moore | 10 | 168 | 17 | 1 |
| Arnold | 5 | 75 | 15 | 1 |
| J. Thomas | 5 | 30 | 6 | 0 |
| E. Hill | 4 | 29 | 7 | 0 |
| Nelson | 3 | 22 | 7 | 0 |
| Mitchell | 2 | 21 | 11 | 0 |
| Tyler | 2 | 8 | 4 | 0 |

### PUNT RETURNS

| Last Name | No. | Yds. | Avg. | TD |
|---|---|---|---|---|
| Irvin | 42 | 296 | 7 | 0 |
| Waddy | 2 | 10 | 5 | 0 |
| Guman | 2 | 6 | 3 | 0 |
| J. Johnson | 1 | 3 | 3 | 0 |

### KICKOFF RETURNS

| Last Name | No. | Yds. | Avg. | TD |
|---|---|---|---|---|
| D. Hill | 43 | 880 | 21 | 1 |
| Sully | 4 | 36 | 9 | 0 |
| Guman | 2 | 25 | 13 | 0 |
| J. Thomas | 2 | 21 | 11 | 0 |
| P. Thomas | 1 | 12 | 12 | 0 |
| Irvin | 1 | 5 | 5 | 0 |

### PASSING – PUNTING – KICKING Statistics

| PASSING | Att. | Comp. | % | Yds. | Yd./Att. | TD | Int.–% | RK |
|---|---|---|---|---|---|---|---|---|
| Ferragamo | 404 | 240 | 59 | 3199 | 7.9 | 30 | 19– 5 | 2 |
| Haden | 41 | 19 | 46 | 185 | 4.5 | 0 | 4– 10 | |
| Cromwell | 1 | 0 | 0 | 0 | 0.0 | 0 | 0– 0 | |
| Guman | 1 | 1 | 100 | 31 | 31.0 | 1 | 0– 0 | |
| Rutledge | 4 | 1 | 25 | 26 | 6.5 | 0 | 0– 0 | |

| PUNTING | No. | Avg. |
|---|---|---|
| Corral | 76 | 39.5 |

| KICKING | XP | Att. | % | FG | Att. | % |
|---|---|---|---|---|---|---|
| Corral | 51 | 52 | 98 | 16 | 30 | 53 |

## SAN FRANCISCO FORTY-NINERS

### RUSHING

| Last Name | No. | Yds. | Avg. | TD |
|---|---|---|---|---|
| Cooper | 171 | 720 | 4.2 | 5 |
| Elliott | 76 | 341 | 4.5 | 2 |
| Hofer | 60 | 293 | 4.9 | 1 |
| Woods | 54 | 239 | 4.4 | 0 |
| Montana | 32 | 77 | 2.4 | 2 |
| Solomon | 8 | 56 | 7.0 | 0 |
| Francis | 7 | 36 | 5.1 | 0 |
| DeBerg | 6 | 4 | 0.7 | 0 |
| Patton | 1 | 1 | 1.0 | 0 |
| Ramson | 2 | −2 | −1.0 | 0 |
| Miller | 2 | −12 | −6.0 | 0 |

### RECEIVING

| Last Name | No. | Yds. | Avg. | TD |
|---|---|---|---|---|
| Cooper | 83 | 567 | 7 | 4 |
| Clark | 82 | 991 | 12 | 8 |
| Solomon | 48 | 658 | 14 | 8 |
| Hofer | 41 | 467 | 11 | 2 |
| Young | 29 | 325 | 11 | 2 |
| Elliott | 27 | 285 | 11 | 1 |
| Ramson | 21 | 179 | 9 | 2 |
| Woods | 20 | 171 | 9 | 0 |
| Owens | 9 | 133 | 15 | 0 |
| Francis | 3 | 23 | 8 | 0 |

### PUNT RETURNS

| Last Name | No. | Yds. | Avg. | TD |
|---|---|---|---|---|
| Solomon | 27 | 298 | 11 | 2 |
| Hicks | 12 | 58 | 5 | 0 |
| Robinson | 3 | 36 | 12 | 0 |
| Churchman | 2 | 16 | 8 | 0 |
| Ferrell | 1 | 1 | 1 | 0 |

### KICKOFF RETURNS

| Last Name | No. | Yds. | Avg. | TD |
|---|---|---|---|---|
| Owens | 31 | 726 | 23 | 1 |
| Elliott | 18 | 321 | 18 | 0 |
| Anderson | 6 | 104 | 17 | 0 |
| Francis | 5 | 60 | 12 | 0 |
| Solomon | 4 | 61 | 15 | 0 |
| Patton | 4 | 43 | 11 | 0 |
| Johnson | 2 | 10 | 5 | 0 |
| Ramson | 1 | 18 | 18 | 0 |
| Tautolo | 1 | 16 | 16 | 0 |
| Young | 1 | 14 | 14 | 0 |
| Hughes | 1 | 10 | 10 | 0 |
| Hofer | 1 | 2 | 2 | 0 |

### PASSING – PUNTING – KICKING Statistics

| PASSING | Att. | Comp. | % | Yds. | Yd./Att. | TD | Int.–% | RK |
|---|---|---|---|---|---|---|---|---|
| Montana | 273 | 176 | 65 | 1795 | 6.6 | 15 | 9– 3 | 4 |
| DeBerg | 321 | 186 | 58 | 1998 | 6.2 | 12 | 17– 5 | 13 |
| Solomon | 1 | 0 | 0 | 0 | 0.0 | 0 | 0– 0 | |
| Woods | 2 | 1 | 50 | 6 | 3.0 | 0 | 0– 0 | |

| PUNTING | No. | Avg. |
|---|---|---|
| Miller | 77 | 40.9 |

| KICKING | XP | Att. | % | FG | Att. | % |
|---|---|---|---|---|---|---|
| Wersching | 33 | 39 | 85 | 15 | 19 | 79 |

## NEW ORLEANS SAINTS

### RUSHING

| Last Name | No. | Yds. | Avg. | TD |
|---|---|---|---|---|
| Rogers | 80 | 366 | 4.6 | 1 |
| Galbreath | 81 | 308 | 3.8 | 3 |
| Wilson | 63 | 188 | 3.0 | 1 |
| Manning | 23 | 166 | 7.2 | 0 |
| Holmes | 38 | 119 | 3.1 | 2 |
| Strachan | 20 | 41 | 2.1 | 0 |
| Chandler | 1 | 9 | 9.0 | 0 |
| Mauti | 1 | 2 | 2.0 | 0 |
| Banks | 1 | −5 | −5.0 | 0 |

### RECEIVING

| Last Name | No. | Yds. | Avg. | TD |
|---|---|---|---|---|
| Chandler | 65 | 975 | 15 | 6 |
| Galbreath | 57 | 470 | 8 | 2 |
| Harris | 37 | 692 | 19 | 6 |
| Childs | 34 | 463 | 14 | 6 |
| Wilson | 31 | 241 | 8 | 1 |
| Holmes | 29 | 226 | 8 | 1 |
| Rogers | 27 | 267 | 10 | 2 |
| Williams | 26 | 351 | 14 | 2 |
| Hardy | 13 | 197 | 15 | 0 |
| Strachan | 5 | 60 | 12 | 0 |
| T. Owens | 1 | 26 | 26 | 0 |
| Mauti | 1 | 10 | 10 | 0 |
| Banks | 1 | 7 | 7 | 0 |

### PUNT RETURNS

| Last Name | No. | Yds. | Avg. | TD |
|---|---|---|---|---|
| Mauti | 11 | 111 | 10 | 0 |
| Chandler | 8 | 36 | 5 | 0 |
| Waymer | 3 | 29 | 10 | 0 |

### KICKOFF RETURNS

| Last Name | No. | Yds. | Avg. | TD |
|---|---|---|---|---|
| Mauti | 31 | 798 | 26 | 0 |
| Rogers | 41 | 930 | 23 | 0 |
| Wilson | 9 | 159 | 18 | 0 |
| Galbreath | 6 | 86 | 14 | 0 |
| Holloway | 1 | 0 | 0 | 0 |

### PASSING – PUNTING – KICKING Statistics

| PASSING | Att. | Comp. | % | Yds. | Yd./Att. | TD | Int.–% | RK |
|---|---|---|---|---|---|---|---|---|
| Manning | 509 | 309 | 61 | 3716 | 7.3 | 23 | 20– 4 | 6 |
| Scott | 33 | 16 | 49 | 200 | 6.1 | 2 | 1– 3 | |
| Benjamin | 17 | 7 | 41 | 28 | 1.7 | 0 | 1– 0 | |
| Chandler | 1 | 1 | 100 | 43 | 43.0 | 0 | 0– 0 | |
| Erxleben | 1 | 0 | 0 | 0 | 0.0 | 0 | 0– 0 | |
| Galbreath | 2 | 0 | 0 | 0 | 0.0 | 0 | 0– 0 | |
| Holmes | 3 | 1 | 33 | 23 | 7.7 | 1 | 0– 0 | |

| PUNTING | No. | Avg. |
|---|---|---|
| Erxleben | 89 | 39.3 |

| KICKING | XP | Att. | % | FG | Att. | % |
|---|---|---|---|---|---|---|
| Ricardo | 31 | 34 | 91 | 10 | 17 | 59 |
| Erxleben | 2 | 2 | 100 | 2 | 5 | .40 |

The newest pro football lawsuit began when Al Davis decided to move the Raiders from Oakland to the Los Angeles Coliseum for this season. Davis claimed he could not reach a new stadium contract in Oakland, but he was apparently lured by the possibilities of pay television in Los Angeles. Commissioner Pete Rozelle pointed to the NFL rule requiring 21 of the team owners to approve any shift of a franchise. The owners turned thumbs down on the move, and Davis filed a lawsuit in which he claimed that this rule was illegal because it violated antitrust laws. With the case mired in the courts, Davis resigned himself to a 1980 season in Oakland. Raider fans showed their protest by staying outside the stadium in thousands for the first five minutes of a Monday night game on December 1. Bitter words and charges flew back and forth between Davis and Rozelle, making their possible meeting at a Super Bowl trophy award presentation a much-anticipated event.

## EASTERN DIVISION

**Buffalo Bills**—Chuck Knox worked his magic to take the Bills to the playoffs for the first time since 1974. The first-place finish coincided with the arrival of Joe Cribbs, a sleek rookie runner. The improved running attack plus occasional use of the shotgun formation juiced up the Buffalo offense. The defense shut enemy attacks down with a precision secondary and outstanding play by nose tackle Fred Smerlas. The Bills started quick with five straight victories, the fifth being a 26-24 upset of the unbeaten Chargers in San Diego. After a mid-season slump, the Bills regained their stride just as the rival Patriots were breaking down. Five victories in the final seven games included a 28-13 decision over the Steelers, a 10-7 overtime triumph over the Rams, and an 18-13 beating of the 49ers which sewed up first place on the final Sunday.

**New England Patriots**—All they didn't have was heart. Despite some hold-out problems, the Patriots had a full arsenal of weapons and were in the thick of the playoff chase in early November. In first place with a 7-2 record, the Pats fell on their faces as the weather grew colder. They lost close games to the Oilers and Rams to fall one game off the pace in the East. The Pats regrouped and reignited their potent offense in a 47-21 trouncing of the Colts. With hope that the swoon was over, the Pats went to San Francisco to face the 4-8 49ers. With the chips on the table, the Patriots folded, dropping an error-filled 21-17 decision. Still only one game behind Buffalo, the Patriots flew to Miami for a Monday night game. The Patriots played very conservative football and lost the game in overtime. Although the Pats revived to beat first-place Buffalo and the Saints, the comeback came too late. The only harvest of the season was all-star attention for John Hannah, Stanley Morgan, Steve Nelson, and Mike Haynes, and a shaky hold on his job for head coach Ron Erhardt.

**Miami Dolphins**—Two old heroes faded into history, taking with them Miami's playoff hopes for this year. Larry Csonka demanded renegotiation of his contract after his 1979 performance, but the Dolphins instead cut him loose. Without him, the Dolphins lacked a pile-driving short-yardage runner. The other legend, quarterback Bob Griese, had an ailing right shoulder which grew steadily worse. In three come-from-behind victories in September, Griese twice came off the bench to engineer fourth quarter rallies. After a 30-17 loss to the Colts on October 5, Griese went to the sidelines for good. The offense stumbled for a while, but by the later stages of the campaign, rookie David Woodley had brought a youthful verve to the QB position. Despite a rebuilt secondary, the Miami defense continued at a high level, leading the team to impressive victories over the Bills and Patriots. But with the mid-season changes and an intangible lack of enthusiasm, the Dolphins missed out on the playoffs with a break-even record.

**Baltimore Colts**—With Bert Jones back in good health, the Colts made a run at the playoffs. After two injury-spoiled seasons, Jones directed an offense which had rookie help in halfback Curtis Dickey and wide receiver Ray Butler. With a 4-2 record, the Colts stood only one game out of first place in October. The defense, however, sabotaged any Baltimore playoff hopes with weak play. Bruce Laird led a competent secondary, but the front four played inconsistently. The Colts dropped four of their final five games, but the single victory was a 28-24 upset over the first-place Bills. Head coach Mike McCormack debuted in Baltimore with a squad that won only two games at home all season. Baltimore fans responded with the lowest attendance in the NFL, capped by a paultry 16,941 fans on hand for the Colts' final game.

**New York Jets**—High hopes ran unchecked through the pre-season. The Jets had resolved their quarterback question by sending Matt Robinson to Denver and making Richard Todd the offensive leader.

The league-leading running game returned intact, and the passing attack had a new explosive weapon in rookie Johnny Lam Jones, a world-class runner. Although the defense looked like the weak link on the team, it had played well enough during the later stages of last year to fuel optimism. By early October, the Jets were 0-5 and the biggest disappointment of the year. On offense, Jones dropped an alarming number of passes, Wesley Walker, Clark Gaines, and Randy Rasmusson, went out in mid-season with injuries, and Todd played with uncertainty. The defense earned even more jeers, with the inexperienced secondary an easy mark for enemy sharpshooters. The high hopes fell to a masochistic low on December 14, as a New York audience watched the Jets lose to the winless Saints.

## CENTRAL DIVISION

**Cleveland Browns**—The Kardiac Kids, they were called, and the Browns indeed raised pulses with a series of games that were in contention into the final minute. Thanks to Brian Sipe, the Browns won enough of them to dethrone the Steelers as Central Division champions. Sipe repeatedly completed clutch passes while keeping his interception total low. The Cleveland passing attack thrived despite an unbalanced running game. Mike Pruitt provided muscle at fullback, but neither injury-scarred Greg Pruitt nor Heisman Trophy rookie Charles White was much of a running threat at halfback. Head Coach Sam Rutigliano had in recent years brought in leaders for each of his lines, guard Joe DeLamiellure from Buffalo and defensive end Lyle Alzado from Denver. Rutigliano switched to the 3-4 defense this season, but Jerry Sherk's knee injury in the first game hurt the pass rush badly. The key victory of the year was a 17-14 triumph over the Oilers on November 30. Although the Browns and Oilers finished with identical 11-5 records, the Browns captured first place on tie-breaking calculations.

**Houston Oilers**—After the Steelers had ousted the Oilers from the playoffs last season, Bum Phillips promised to "kick in" the door to the AFC title. Although the Steelers failed to make the playoffs this year, the Browns cut in line ahead of the Oilers and entered the throne room. Phillips had spared no cost in beefing up his squad for this campaign. He swapped quarterback Dan Pastorini to Oakland for crafty Ken Stabler, obtained veteran guard Bob Young from the Cardinals, and sent a package of draft choices to the Raiders in October for tight end Dave Casper. With receiver Ken Burrough injured for much of the year and with Stabler's arm on the wane, the Houston offense used double tight ends and relied more than ever on the running of Earl Campbell. Enemy defenses knew that the Oilers would rely on straight-ahead muscle football. A frustrating 31-17 loss to the Steelers on opening day ushered the Oilers to a slow start, but a revival in mid-October put them back into the race. Their fate was sealed by losses to the Jets and Browns in November, but the Oilers had the satisfaction of knocking the Steelers out of the playoffs with a 6-0 beating on Thursday night, December 4. When the dust cleared at the end of the schedule, the Oilers again had to settle for a wild-card ticket to the playoffs.

**Pittsburgh Steelers**—After a 4-1 start, age and injuries brought the Steelers down from their pedestal of excellence. Sam Adams sat out the entire year while John Stallworth went out after two games. Jon Kolb and Steve Courson missed half the schedule, Franco Harris and Lynn Swann each lost three games to injuries, and Terry Bradshaw and Jack Lambert each spent some time in sick bay. Chuck Noll deployed his deep bench, but the casualty list was too long to overcome. Although Lambert and Donnie Shell kept their play at an all-star level, the duo of L.C. Greenwood and Joe Greene slowed down noticeably. With Terry Bradshaw passing effectively, the Steelers climbed back into the race with a mid-season winning streak, but a loss to Buffalo on November 23 spelled the beginning of the end. The true backbreaker was a 6-0 struggle which the Steelers lost to the Oilers on December 4. Instead of a fifth Super Bowl appearance, the Steelers got to go home for Christmas.

**Cincinnati Bengals**—General manager Paul Browns hired Forrest Gregg to be head coach with the style of a first sergeant. Gregg made the tail-ender Bengals competitive in the early going. They lost two close games, then upset the champion Steelers 30-28. After two more close losses, they traveled to Pittsburgh and again whipped the Steelers. After beating the Vikings a week later, the Bengals fell off into a five-week slump. Gregg got his best results with the defense, which played well in the newly installed 3-4 setup. The offense had tougher going. Pete Johnson provided ball control running, but numerous injuries plagued quarterback Ken Anderson. After the dry spell, the Bengals won three of their last four games to raise hopes that they may someday climb out of the basement in the strong Central Division.

FINAL TEAM STATISTICS

**OFFENSE**

| | BALT. | BUFF. | CIN. | CLEV. | DENV. | HOU. | K.C. | MIA. | N.E. | NY J | OAK. | PIT. | S.D. | SEA. |
|---|---|---|---|---|---|---|---|---|---|---|---|---|---|---|
| **FIRST DOWNS:** | | | | | | | | | | | | | | |
| Total | 327 | 317 | 283 | 336 | 286 | 329 | 270 | 284 | 319 | 289 | 281 | 308 | **372** | 302 |
| by Rushing | 128 | 134 | 111 | 102 | 107 | **155** | 130 | 107 | 139 | 124 | 108 | 111 | 106 | 114 |
| by Passing | 174 | 157 | 147 | 207 | 158 | 152 | 122 | 149 | 154 | 146 | 149 | 177 | **244** | 166 |
| by Penalty | 25 | 26 | 25 | 27 | 21 | 22 | 18 | **28** | 26 | 19 | 24 | 20 | 22 | 22 |
| **RUSHING:** | | | | | | | | | | | | | | |
| Number | 527 | **603** | 513 | 436 | 480 | 573 | 552 | 492 | 588 | 470 | 541 | 512 | 509 | 456 |
| Yards | 2078 | 2222 | 2069 | 1673 | 1865 | **2635** | 1873 | 1876 | 2240 | 1873 | 2146 | 1986 | 1879 | 1783 |
| Average Yards | 3.9 | 3.7 | 4.0 | 3.8 | 3.9 | **4.6** | 3.4 | 3.8 | 3.8 | 4.0 | 4.0 | 3.9 | 3.7 | 3.9 |
| Touchdowns | **20** | 17 | 9 | 15 | 16 | 18 | 15 | 9 | 19 | 17 | 14 | 15 | 18 | 13 |
| **PASSING:** | | | | | | | | | | | | | | |
| Attempts | 493 | 461 | 510 | 554 | 467 | 463 | 401 | 492 | 413 | 481 | 456 | 484 | **594** | 517 |
| Completions | 272 | 262 | 281 | 337 | 262 | 296 | 237 | 267 | 240 | 265 | 235 | 250 | **350** | 287 |
| Completion Pct. | 55.2 | 56.8 | 55.1 | 60.8 | 56.1 | **63.9** | 59.1 | 54.3 | 58.1 | 55.1 | 51.5 | 51.7 | 58.9 | 55.5 |
| Passing Yards | 3409 | 2936 | 3102 | 4132 | 3107 | 3271 | 2869 | 2953 | 3395 | 3335 | 3294 | 3832 | **4741** | 3494 |
| Avg. Yds per Att. | 5.9 | 5.7 | 5.2 | 6.8 | 5.4 | 6.1 | 5.3 | 5.1 | **7.3** | 5.8 | 5.8 | 6.9 | 7.2 | 5.5 |
| Avg Yds per Comp. | 12.5 | 11.2 | 11.0 | 12.3 | 11.9 | 11.1 | 12.1 | 11.1 | 14.2 | 12.6 | 14.0 | **15.3** | 13.6 | 12.2 |
| Times Tackled | 36 | **20** | 37 | 23 | 44 | 27 | 57 | 31 | 25 | 42 | 47 | 37 | 32 | 51 |
| Yds Lost Tackled | 281 | **186** | 287 | 217 | 330 | 264 | 421 | 265 | 200 | 326 | 395 | 264 | 210 | 398 |
| Net Yards | 3128 | 2750 | 2815 | 3915 | 2777 | 3007 | 2448 | 2688 | 3195 | 3009 | 2899 | 3568 | **4531** | 3096 |
| Touchdowns | 25 | 20 | 17 | **30** | 14 | 15 | 15 | 21 | 27 | 17 | 23 | 26 | **30** | 18 |
| Interceptions | 24 | 19 | 25 | **14** | 25 | 28 | **14** | 26 | 27 | 30 | 24 | 24 | 26 | 23 |
| Pct. Intercepted | 4.9 | 4.1 | 4.9 | **2.5** | 5.4 | 6.0 | 3.5 | 5.3 | 6.5 | 6.2 | 5.3 | 5.0 | 4.4 | 4.4 |
| **PUNTS:** | | | | | | | | | | | | | | |
| Number | 84 | 74 | **87** | 66 | 70 | 67 | 85 | 79 | 63 | 74 | 71 | 66 | 61 | 70 |
| Average | 38.1 | 38.2 | 39.7 | 38.3 | **43.9** | 40.7 | 39.0 | 41.5 | 38.0 | 41.8 | 43.6 | 40.2 | 38.5 | 40.4 |
| **PUNT RETURNS:** | | | | | | | | | | | | | | |
| Number | 26 | 39 | 39 | 35 | 42 | 48 | 40 | 32 | **60** | 33 | 49 | 45 | 41 | 41 |
| Yards | 188 | 259 | 252 | 170 | 408 | 384 | **581** | 213 | 513 | 269 | 421 | 391 | 335 | 349 |
| Average Yards | 7.2 | 6.6 | 6.5 | 4.9 | 9.7 | 8.0 | **14.5** | 6.7 | 8.6 | 8.2 | 8.6 | 8.7 | 8.2 | 8.5 |
| Touchdowns | 0 | 0 | 0 | 0 | 0 | 0 | **2** | 0 | 1 | 0 | 0 | 0 | 0 | 1 |
| **KICKOFF RET.:** | | | | | | | | | | | | | | |
| Number | 67 | 47 | 68 | 63 | 62 | 53 | 62 | 61 | 56 | **74** | 62 | 65 | 62 | 73 |
| Yards | 1383 | 827 | 1199 | 1308 | 1290 | 981 | 1249 | 1234 | 1281 | **1491** | 1180 | 1350 | 1135 | 1489 |
| Average Yards | 20.6 | 17.6 | 17.6 | 20.8 | 20.8 | 18.5 | 20.1 | 20.2 | **22.9** | 20.1 | 19.0 | 20.8 | 18.3 | 20.4 |
| Touchdowns | 0 | 0 | 0 | 0 | 0 | 0 | 0 | 0 | 1 | 0 | **2** | 0 | 0 | 0 |
| **INTERCEPT RET.:** | | | | | | | | | | | | | | |
| Number | 17 | 24 | 20 | 22 | 16 | 26 | 28 | 28 | 24 | 23 | **35** | 26 | 20 | 23 |
| Yards | 310 | 334 | 255 | 266 | 343 | 313 | 364 | 198 | 288 | 293 | **501** | 260 | 270 | 95 |
| Average Yards | 18.2 | 13.9 | 12.8 | 12.1 | **21.4** | 12.0 | 13.0 | 7.1 | 12.0 | 12.7 | 14.3 | 10.0 | 13.5 | 4.1 |
| Touchdowns | 1 | **2** | **2** | 0 | **2** | 0 | **2** | 0 | 1 | **2** | **2** | 0 | **2** | 0 |
| **PENALTIES:** | | | | | | | | | | | | | | |
| Number | 104 | 90 | 118 | 117 | 93 | 101 | **74** | **74** | 79 | 103 | 98 | 111 | 109 | 109 |
| Yards | 914 | 731 | 949 | 1042 | 899 | 838 | 591 | **567** | 696 | 767 | 929 | 933 | 912 | 901 |
| **FUMBLES:** | | | | | | | | | | | | | | |
| Number | 23 | 36 | 22 | 24 | 25 | 33 | 42 | 33 | **19** | 27 | 38 | 38 | 40 | 38 |
| Number Lost | 13 | 22 | **8** | 14 | 12 | 19 | 16 | 16 | 9 | 11 | 20 | 18 | 22 | 15 |
| **POINTS:** | | | | | | | | | | | | | | |
| Total | 355 | 320 | 244 | 357 | 310 | 295 | 319 | 266 | **441** | 302 | 364 | 352 | 418 | 291 |
| Pat Attempts | 46 | 40 | 28 | 45 | 33 | 34 | 37 | 32 | 52 | 37 | 44 | 42 | 50 | 33 |
| Pat Made | 43 | 37 | 27 | 39 | 32 | 31 | 37 | 32 | **51** | 36 | 41 | 39 | 46 | 33 |
| FG Attempts | 23 | 23 | 29 | 26 | 34 | 25 | 26 | 23 | 34 | 22 | **37** | 28 | 36 | 31 |
| FG Made | 12 | 13 | 15 | 16 | **26** | 20 | 20 | 14 | **26** | 14 | 19 | 19 | 24 | 20 |
| Percent FG Made | 52.2 | 56.5 | 51.7 | 61.5 | 76.5 | **80.0** | 76.9 | 60.9 | 76.5 | 63.6 | 51.4 | 67.9 | 66.7 | 64.5 |
| Safeties | 0 | **2** | **2** | 0 | 1 | 0 | 0 | 0 | 0 | 1 | 1 | **2** | 0 | 0 |

**DEFENSE**

| | BALT. | BUFF. | CIN. | CLEV. | DENV. | HOU. | K.C. | MIA. | N.E. | NY J | OAK. | PIT. | S.D. | SEA. |
|---|---|---|---|---|---|---|---|---|---|---|---|---|---|---|
| **FIRST DOWNS:** | | | | | | | | | | | | | | |
| Total | 338 | **251** | 286 | 340 | 303 | 259 | 328 | 309 | 270 | 348 | 319 | 302 | 284 | 301 |
| by Rushing | 140 | 109 | 111 | 105 | 125 | **94** | 136 | 107 | 118 | 127 | 108 | 101 | 101 | 129 |
| by Passing | 164 | **120** | 154 | 197 | 158 | 147 | 179 | 185 | 141 | 198 | 181 | 171 | 156 | 147 |
| by Penalty | 34 | 22 | 21 | 38 | 20 | 18 | 13 | 17 | **11** | 23 | 30 | 30 | 27 | 25 |
| **RUSHING:** | | | | | | | | | | | | | | |
| Number | 574 | 486 | 469 | 485 | 554 | **444** | 536 | 530 | 482 | 508 | 501 | 486 | 478 | 550 |
| Yards | 2210 | 1819 | **1680** | 1761 | 2120 | 1811 | 2206 | 2018 | 1876 | 1951 | 1726 | 1762 | 1842 | 2067 |
| Average Yards | 3.9 | 3.7 | 3.6 | 3.6 | 3.8 | 4.1 | 4.1 | 3.8 | 3.9 | 3.8 | **3.4** | 3.6 | 3.9 | 3.8 |
| Touchdowns | 20 | 14 | 13 | 12 | 10 | **8** | 17 | 13 | 12 | 20 | 19 | 9 | 18 | 17 |
| **PASSING:** | | | | | | | | | | | | | | |
| Attempts | 476 | **433** | 491 | 536 | 448 | 454 | 523 | 505 | 458 | 544 | 524 | 532 | 519 | 462 |
| Completions | 260 | **240** | 284 | 336 | 270 | 246 | 278 | 290 | 266 | 337 | 296 | 280 | 300 | 267 |
| Completion Pct. | 54.6 | 55.4 | 57.8 | 62.7 | 60.3 | 54.2 | 53.2 | 57.4 | 58.1 | 61.9 | 56.5 | **52.6** | 57.8 | 57.8 |
| Passing Yards | 3576 | **2561** | 3426 | 4089 | 3449 | 3053 | 3393 | 3439 | 3232 | 3899 | 3731 | 3517 | 3324 | 3280 |
| Avg. Yds per Att. | 6.6 | **4.9** | **7.0** | 6.8 | 6.4 | 5.7 | 5.6 | 6.0 | 5.8 | 6.4 | 5.7 | 6.1 | 4.9 | 6.4 |
| Avg Yds per Comp. | 13.8 | **10.7** | 12.1 | 12.2 | 12.8 | 12.4 | 12.2 | 11.9 | 12.2 | 11.6 | 12.6 | 12.6 | 11.1 | 12.3 |
| Times Tackled | 30 | 33 | 35 | 32 | 39 | 34 | 37 | 27 | 44 | 28 | 54 | 18 | **60** | 26 |
| Yds Lost Tackled | 240 | 279 | 302 | 224 | 324 | 252 | 284 | 233 | 346 | 235 | 419 | 145 | **475** | 170 |
| Net Yards | 3336 | **2282** | 3124 | 3865 | 3125 | 2801 | 3109 | 3206 | 2886 | 2664 | 3312 | 3372 | 2849 | 3101 |
| Touchdowns | 21 | **15** | 22 | 23 | 20 | 16 | 25 | 21 | 28 | 27 | 17 | 25 | 18 | 28 |
| Interceptions | 17 | 24 | 20 | 22 | 16 | 26 | 28 | 28 | 24 | 23 | **35** | 26 | 20 | 23 |
| Pct. Intercepted | 3.6 | 5.5 | 4.1 | 4.1 | 3.6 | 5.7 | 5.4 | 5.5 | 5.2 | 4.2 | **6.7** | 4.9 | 3.9 | 5.0 |
| **PUNTS:** | | | | | | | | | | | | | | |
| Number | 72 | 82 | 72 | 63 | 70 | 78 | 66 | 72 | **92** | 63 | 87 | 73 | 86 | 66 |
| Average | 39.7 | 39.3 | 38.5 | 37.4 | 41.6 | 40.9 | 42.2 | **37.3** | 41.0 | 39.9 | 38.9 | 40.7 | 40.4 | 40.2 |
| **PUNT RETURNS:** | | | | | | | | | | | | | | |
| Number | 49 | 34 | 46 | 38 | 52 | 40 | 44 | 42 | **28** | 46 | 34 | 34 | 43 | 42 |
| Yards | 357 | **204** | 478 | 245 | 443 | 394 | 289 | 339 | 237 | 369 | 268 | 217 | 359 | 476 |
| Average Yards | 7.3 | **6.0** | 10.4 | 6.4 | 8.5 | 9.9 | 6.6 | 8.1 | 8.5 | 8.0 | 7.9 | 6.4 | 8.3 | 11.3 |
| Touchdowns | 1 | 0 | 0 | 0 | 1 | 0 | 0 | 0 | 0 | 1 | 0 | 0 | 0 | 0 |
| **KICKOFF RET.:** | | | | | | | | | | | | | | |
| Number | 54 | **52** | 57 | 71 | 55 | 68 | 61 | 53 | 89 | 54 | 66 | 68 | 75 | 64 |
| Yards | 1062 | 1051 | 1180 | **1018** | 1187 | 1265 | 1253 | 1210 | 1649 | 1207 | 1315 | 1339 | 1617 | 1223 |
| Average Yards | 19.7 | 20.2 | 20.7 | **14.3** | 21.6 | 18.6 | 20.5 | 22.8 | 18.5 | 22.4 | 19.9 | 19.7 | 21.6 | 19.1 |
| Touchdowns | 1 | 0 | 1 | 0 | 0 | 0 | 0 | 0 | 0 | 0 | 0 | 0 | 0 | 0 |
| **INTERCEPT RET.:** | | | | | | | | | | | | | | |
| Number | 24 | 19 | 25 | **14** | 25 | 28 | **14** | 26 | 27 | 30 | 24 | 24 | 26 | 23 |
| Yards | 378 | 193 | 351 | 270 | 388 | 424 | **130** | 386 | 369 | 408 | 153 | 226 | 419 | 170 |
| Average Yards | 15.8 | 10.2 | 14.0 | 19.3 | 15.5 | 15.1 | 9.3 | 14.8 | 13.7 | 13.6 | **6.4** | 9.4 | 16.1 | 7.4 |
| Touchdowns | 1 | 1 | **0** | 2 | 2 | 2 | **0** | 1 | **0** | 1 | **0** | 2 | 1 | 2 |
| **PENALTIES:** | | | | | | | | | | | | | | |
| Number | 98 | 97 | 106 | 96 | 101 | 101 | 82 | **108** | 92 | 90 | 102 | 93 | 104 | 103 |
| Yards | 775 | 805 | 809 | 766 | 850 | 763 | 617 | **923** | 833 | 872 | 922 | 806 | 880 | 876 |
| **FUMBLES:** | | | | | | | | | | | | | | |
| Number | 32 | 37 | **44** | 23 | 26 | 22 | 26 | 31 | 31 | 26 | 34 | 23 | 39 | 33 |
| Number Lost | 17 | 20 | **22** | 10 | 12 | 13 | 15 | 17 | 10 | 9 | 17 | 14 | 18 | 11 |
| **POINTS:** | | | | | | | | | | | | | | |
| Total | 387 | 260 | 312 | 310 | 323 | **251** | 336 | 305 | 325 | 395 | 306 | 313 | **327** | 408 |
| Pat Attempts | 47 | 31 | 38 | 37 | 34 | **27** | 42 | 36 | 40 | 51 | 37 | 37 | 40 | 47 |
| Pat Made | 45 | 29 | 36 | 32 | 32 | **26** | 39 | 33 | 39 | 50 | 36 | 34 | 39 | 45 |
| FG Attempts | 30 | **20** | 27 | 29 | 40 | 29 | 30 | 25 | **20** | 24 | 24 | 29 | 34 | 33 |
| FG Made | 20 | 15 | 16 | 18 | 29 | 21 | 15 | 18 | 14 | **13** | 14 | 19 | 16 | 25 |
| Percent FG Made | 66.7 | 75.0 | 59.3 | 62.1 | 72.5 | 72.4 | 50.0 | 72.0 | 70.0 | 54.2 | 58.3 | 65.5 | **47.1** | 75.8 |
| Safeties | 0 | 0 | 0 | 1 | 0 | 0 | 0 | 1 | 2 | 0 | 0 | 0 | 0 | 3 |

## WESTERN DIVISION

**San Diego Chargers**—After four weeks of play, the Chargers had beaten each of the other Western teams. A letdown followed, with the Chargers losing four of their next six games, but Don Coryell rallied his club to a second straight divisional title. The soul of the Chargers was its all-out passing attack. Don Fouts threw the ball often and accurately, making Kellen Winslow, John Jefferson, and Charlie Joiner all 1,000-yard receivers. To balance the attack, the Chargers obtained runner Chuck Muncie from the Saints in late September. The offensive line kept the offense moving despite losing Russ Washington to a knee injury in mid-October. The defense launched a great pass rush, with Fred Dean, Gary Johnson, Louie Kelcher, and Leroy Jones applying the pressure. To get into the playoffs, the Chargers won five of their last six games, culminating in a 26-17 victory over the Steelers on the final Monday night of the schedule.

**Oakland Raiders**—The Raiders brought lots of new faces into training camp, most notably quarterback Dan Pastorini. Lightly regarded because of the wholesale changes, the Raiders lived up to these predictions by dropping three of their first five games. To make matters worse, Pastorini went out for the year with a broken leg suffered in the third loss. Into the lineup came Jim Plunkett, whose career had floundered badly in recent years. Playing error-free ball, Plunkett sparked the Raiders into a six-game winning streak which shot them back into the Western race. Plunkett was the glamour boy of the resurgence, but the Oakland defense was its heart. Game after game, the defense would come up with a clutch big play to stymie enemy drives. Leading this crew of pirates was linebacker Ted Hendricks and sticky-fingered back Lester Hayes. Over the last month of the campaign, the Raiders and Chargers battled for the lead. The Raiders wrapped up a playoff berth with a final victory over the Giants, but settled for a wild-card spot when the Chargers beat Pittsburgh and took first place on the tiebreaker rules.

**Kansas City Chiefs**—With their offensive line chewed up by injuries, the Chiefs lost their first four games of the season. After the blockers healed, however, the Chiefs won eight of twelve games to forge ahead out of the Western basement. Head coach Marv Levy had built a fine defense, with all-stars in end Art Still, cornerback Gary Green, and safety Gary Barbaro. Oakland and Houston both lost matches with the rising Chiefs. The offense was slowly becoming more versatile, with reserve quarterback Bill Kenney doing well in the last three games while Steve Fuller was hurt. J.T. Smith kept up his fine punt returning, while young Nick Lowery wrested the kicking job away from old-timer Jan Stenerud.

**Denver Broncos**—For the second year in a row, coach Red Miller turned the Denver offense over to a young quarterback. Matt Robinson came from the Jets with a reputation as a dangerous passer, but he started the season as if overwhelmed by doubt. Although the Broncos beat Dallas 41-20 on September 14, they had a 1-3 record at the end of the month. In the next two games, veteran Craig Morton came off the bench to take the Broncos to victory. From that point on, Morton started and Robinson worked mostly as a kick holder. By late November, the Broncos were 7-5 and trailed the Chargers and Raiders by only one game. With their fate in their own hands, they dropped the ball. They lost to Oakland 9-3 on Monday night, December 1. One week later, they were beaten by the Chiefs 31-14, and they followed that by losing again to the Raiders 24-21. The defense held together around linebacker Randy Gradishar after the loss of Bob Swenson and Joe Rizzo to injuries. Otis Armstrong was forced to retire in mid-season by a spinal condition, and coach Miller would not return when new owners bought the club during the off-season.

**Seattle Seahawks**—The Seahawks angered their fans by losing all of their eight home games. Although they broke even on the road, the 4-12 season was a bitter disappointment after two promising .500 years. The collapse cursed all sectors of the team. The offense gained little yardage on the ground after Sherman Smith ripped up a knee in the third game of the season. The offensive line also fell down on its pass protection, subjecting quarterback Jim Zorn to steady pressure from opposing linemen. While dodging tacklers, Zorn delivered the ball to Steve Largent with accustomed frequency. The defense played poorly despite good work by linebacker Michael Jackson and rookie end Jacob Green. Although they started the year well enough, the Seahawks ended it with a demoralizing nine-game losing streak, including a 51-7 beating by the Cowboys.

**BUFFALO BILLS** 11-5-0 Chuck Knox

| Scores of Each Game | | |
|---|---|---|
| 17 | MIAMI | 7 |
| 20 | N.Y. JETS | 10 |
| 35 | New Orleans | 26 |
| 24 | OAKLAND | 7 |
| 26 | San Diego | 24 |
| 12 | BALTIMORE | 17 |
| 14 | Miami | 17 |
| 31 | NEW ENGLAND | 13 |
| 14 | ATLANTA | 30 |
| 31 | N.Y. Jets | 24 |
| 14 | Cincinnati | 0 |
| 28 | PITTSBURGH | 13 |
| 24 | Baltimore | 28 |
| 10 | LOS ANGELES | *7 |
| 2 | New England | 24 |
| 18 | San Francisco | 13 |

| Use Name | Pos. | Hgt. | Wgt. | Age | Int. | Pts. |
|---|---|---|---|---|---|---|
| Joe Devlin | OT | 6'5" | 250 | 26 | | |
| Dee Hardison | OT | 6'4" | 269 | 24 | | |
| Ken Jones | OT | 6'5" | 250 | 27 | | |
| Jon Borchardt | OG-OT | 6'5" | 255 | 23 | | |
| Conrad Dobler | OG | 6'3" | 255 | 29 | | |
| Ed Fulton | OG | 6'3" | 250 | 25 | | |
| Reggie McKenzie | OG | 6'4" | 242 | 30 | | |
| Will Grant | C | 6'3" | 248 | 26 | | |
| Jim Ritcher | C | 6'3" | 251 | 22 | | |
| Tim Vogler | C | 6'3" | 245 | 23 | | |
| Scott Hutchinson | DE | 6'4" | 243 | 24 | | |
| Darrell Irvin | DE | 6'4" | 255 | 23 | | |
| Ken Johnson | DE | 6'5" | 253 | 25 | | 2 |
| Sherman White | DE | 6'5" | 250 | 31 | 1 | |
| Ben Williams | DE | 6'3" | 245 | 26 | | |
| Mike Kadish | NT | 6'5" | 270 | 30 | | |
| Fred Smerlas | NT | 6'3" | 270 | 23 | | |
| Jim Haslett | LB | 6'3" | 232 | 24 | 2 | |
| Chris Keating | LB | 6'2" | 223 | 22 | | |
| Shane Nelson | LB | 6'1" | 225 | 25 | | |
| Ervin Parker | LB | 6'4" | 225 | 22 | | |
| Isiah Robertson | LB | 6'3" | 225 | 31 | 2 | |
| Lucius Sanford | LB | 6'2" | 216 | 24 | | 6 |
| Phil Villapiano | LB | 6'2" | 225 | 31 | | |
| Rufus Bess | DB | 5'9" | 180 | 23 | | |
| Larry Carter | DB | 5'11" | 185 | 23 | | |
| Mario Clark | DB | 6'2" | 195 | 26 | 1 | |
| Steve Freeman | DB | 5·11" | 185 | 27 | 7 | 6 |
| Doug Greene | DB | 6'2" | 205 | 24 | | |
| Rod Kush | DB | 6' | 188 | 23 | | |
| Jeff Nixon | DB | 6'3" | 190 | 23 | 5 | 6 |
| Charles Romes | DB | 6'1" | 190 | 26 | 2 | |
| Bill Simpson | DB | 6'1" | 191 | 28 | 4 | 2 |
| Joe Ferguson | QB | 6'1" | 195 | 30 | | |
| David Humm | QB | 6'2" | 190 | 28 | | |
| Dan Manucci | QB | 6'2" | 194 | 22 | | |
| Joe Cribbs | HB | 5'11" | 190 | 22 | | 72 |
| Roland Hooks | HB | 6' | 195 | 27 | | 6 |
| Terry Miller | HB | 5'10" | 196 | 24 | | |
| Curtis Brown | FB | 5'10' | 203 | 25 | | 18 |
| Roosevelt Leaks | FB | 5'10" | 225 | 27 | | 18 |
| Jerry Butler | WR | 6' | 178 | 22 | | 36 |
| Duke Fergerson | WR | 6'1" | 185 | 26 | | |
| Ron Jessie | WR | 6' | 181 | 32 | | 6 |
| Mike Kirtman | WR | 6'1" | 180 | 24 | | |
| Frank Lewis | WR | 6'1" | 196 | 33 | | 36 |
| Artie Owens (to NO) | WR | 5'10" | 182 | 27 | | |
| Lou Piccone | WR | 5'9" | 175 | 31 | | |
| Mark Brammer | TE | 6'3" | 238 | 22 | | 24 |
| Reuben Gant | TE | 6'4" | 225 | 28 | | 6 |
| Greg Cater | K | 6' | 191 | 23 | | |
| Nick Mike-Mayer | K | 5'8" | 185 | 30 | | 76 |

Mikeli Ieremia – Knee Injury

**NEW ENGLAND PATRIOTS** 10-6-0 Ron Erhardt

| Scores of Each Game | | |
|---|---|---|
| 34 | CLEVELAND | 17 |
| 21 | ATLANTA | 37 |
| 37 | Seattle | 31 |
| 23 | DENVER | 14 |
| 21 | N.Y. Jets | 11 |
| 34 | MIAMI | 0 |
| 37 | Baltimore | 21 |
| 13 | Buffalo | 31 |
| 34 | N.Y. JETS | 21 |
| 34 | Houston | 38 |
| 14 | LOS ANGELES | 17 |
| 47 | BALTIMORE | 21 |
| 17 | San Francisco | 21 |
| 13 | Miami | *16 |
| 24 | BUFFALO | 2 |
| 38 | New Orleans | 27 |

| Use Name | Pos. | Hgt. | Wgt. | Age | Int. | Pts. |
|---|---|---|---|---|---|---|
| Shelby Jordan | OT | 6'7" | 260 | 28 | | |
| Gary Puetz | OT | 6'4" | 265 | 28 | | |
| Dwight Wheeler | OT | 6'3" | 255 | 25 | | |
| Sam Adams | OG | 6'3" | 260 | 31 | | |
| Bob Cryder | OG | 6'4" | 265 | 23 | | |
| John Hannah | OG | 6'2" | 265 | 29 | | |
| Pete Brock | C-OT | 6'5" | 260 | 26 | | |
| Bill Lenkaitis | C | 6'3" | 255 | 34 | | |
| Julius Adams | DE | 6'3" | 263 | 32 | | |
| Mel Lunsford | DE | 6'3" | 260 | 30 | | |
| Doug McDougald | DE | 6'5" | 271 | 23 | | |
| Tony McGee | DE | 6'4" | 250 | 31 | | |
| Richard Bishop | NT-DE | 6'1" | 260 | 30 | | |
| Ray Hamilton | NT | 6'1" | 245 | 29 | | |
| Steve McMichael | NT | 6'2" | 245 | 22 | | |
| Bob Golic | LB | 6'2" | 240 | 22 | | |
| Mike Hawkins | LB | 6'2" | 232 | 24 | 2 | |
| Sam Hunt | LB | 6'1" | 270 | 29 | | |
| Steve King | LB | 6'4" | 230 | 29 | | |
| Bill Matthews | LB | 6'2" | 235 | 24 | 1 | |
| Larry McGrew | LB | 6'4" | 231 | 23 | | |
| Steve Nelson | LB | 6'2" | 230 | 29 | 3 | |
| Rod Shoate | LB | 6'1" | 215 | 27 | 3 | 6 |
| John Zamberlin | LB | 6'2" | 232 | 24 | | |
| Raymond Clayborn | DB | 6'1" | 190 | 25 | 5 | |
| Bill Currier | DB | 6' | 195 | 25 | | |
| Tim Fox | DB | 5'11" | 190 | 26 | 4 | |
| Mike Haynes | DB | 6'2" | 195 | 27 | 1 | 6 |
| Roland James | DB | 6'2" | 189 | 22 | 4 | 6 |
| Rick Sanford | DB | 6'1" | 192 | 23 | 1 | 6 |
| Matt Cavanaugh | QB | 6'1" | 210 | 23 | | |
| Steve Grogan | QB | 6'4" | 208 | 27 | | 6 |
| Tom Owen | QB | 6'1" | 194 | 27 | | |
| Allan Clark | HB | 5'10" | 186 | 23 | | 12 |
| Vagas Ferguson | HB | 6'1" | 194 | 23 | | 12 |
| Horace Ivory | HB | 6' | 198 | 26 | | 18 |
| Andy Johnson | HB | 6' | 204 | 27 | | 18 |
| Don Calhoun | FB | 6' | 212 | 28 | | 54 |
| Chuck Foreman | FB | 6'2" | 212 | 29 | | 6 |
| Mosi Tatupu | FB | 6' | 229 | 25 | | 18 |
| Preston Brown | WR | 5'10" | 184 | 22 | | |
| Harold Jackson | WR | 5'10" | 175 | 34 | | 30 |
| Stanley Morgan | WR | 5'11" | 180 | 25 | | 36 |
| Carlos Pennywell | WR | 6'2" | 180 | 24 | | 6 |
| Don Westbrook | WR | 5'10" | 185 | 27 | | |
| Russ Francis | TE | 6'6" | 242 | 27 | | 48 |
| Don Hasselbeck | TE | 6'7" | 245 | 26 | | 24 |
| Mike Hubach | K | 5'10" | 185 | 22 | | |
| John Smith | K | 6' | 185 | 30 | | 129 |

Mark Buben – Injury
Ray Costict – Knee Injury
Steve Schindler – Knee Injury
Jimmy Stewart – Hamstring Injury
Sam Cunningham – Holdout

**MIAMI DOLPHINS** 8-8-0 Don Shula

| Scores of Each Game | | |
|---|---|---|
| 7 | Buffalo | 17 |
| 17 | CINCINNATI | 16 |
| 20 | Atlanta | 17 |
| 21 | NEW ORLEANS | 16 |
| 17 | BALTIMORE | 30 |
| 0 | New England | 34 |
| 17 | BUFFALO | 14 |
| 14 | N.Y. Jets | 17 |
| 10 | Oakland | 16 |
| 35 | Los Angeles | 14 |
| 17 | SAN FRANCISCO | 13 |
| 24 | SAN DIEGO | *27 |
| 10 | Pittsburgh | 23 |
| 16 | NEW ENGLAND | *13 |
| 24 | Baltimore | 14 |
| 17 | N.Y. JETS | 24 |

| Use Name | Pos. | Hgt. | Wgt. | Age | Int. | Pts. |
|---|---|---|---|---|---|---|
| Jon Giesler | OT | 6'5" | 260 | 33 | | |
| Cleveland Green | OT | 6'3" | 265 | 22 | | |
| Eric Laasko | OT | 6'4' | 265 | 23 | | |
| Thom Dornbrook | OG-C | 6'2" | 240 | 23 | | |
| Bob Kuechenberg | OG-OT | 6'3" | 255 | 32 | | |
| Larry Little | OG-OT | 6'1" | 260 | 34 | | |
| Ed Newman | OG | 6'2" | 255 | 29 | | |
| Jeff Toews | OG | 6'3" | 255 | 22 | | |
| Mark Dennard | C | 6'1" | 252 | 24 | | |
| Dwight Stephenson | C | 6'2" | 255 | 22 | | |
| Bill Barnett | DE-NT | 6'4" | 255 | 24 | | |
| Doug Betters | DE | 6'7" | 260 | 24 | | |
| Vern Den Herder | DE | 6'6" | 252 | 31 | | |
| Carl Barisich | NT | 6'4" | 255 | 29 | | |
| Bob Baumhower | NT | 6'5" | 260 | 25 | | |
| Kim Bokamper | LB | 6'6" | 247 | 25 | 1 | |
| Rusty Chambers | LB | 6'1" | 220 | 26 | | |
| A. J. Duhe | LB-DE | 6'4" | 252 | 24 | | |
| Larry Gordon | LB | 6'4" | 230 | 27 | 1 | |
| Ralph Ortega | LB | 6'2" | 225 | 27 | 1 | |
| Earnest Rhone | LB | 6'2" | 224 | 27 | 3 | |
| Steve Shull | LB | 6'1" | 218 | 22 | | |
| Steve Towle | LB | 6'2" | 230 | 26 | | |
| Jeff Allen | DB | 5'11" | 185 | 22 | | |
| Doug Beaudoin | DB | 6'1" | 190 | 26 | | |
| Don Bessillieu | DB | 6'1" | 200 | 24 | 4 | 6 |
| Glenn Blackwood | DB | 6' | 183 | 23 | 3 | |
| Billy Cesare | DB | 5'11" | 195 | 25 | | |
| Tim Foley | DB | 6' | 198 | 32 | | |
| Don McNeal | DB | 5'11" | 192 | 22 | 5 | |
| Gerald Small | DB | 5'11" | 192 | 24 | 7 | |
| Ed Taylor | DB | 6' | 175 | 27 | 3 | |
| Bob Griese | QB | 6'1" | 190 | 35 | | |
| Don Strock | QB | 6'5" | 220 | 29 | | |
| David Woodley | QB | 6'2" | 196 | 21 | | 18 |
| Pete Woods | QB | 6'3" | 214 | 24 | | |
| Nick Giaquinto | HB | 5'11" | 204 | 25 | | 12 |
| Rick Moser | HB | 6' | 210 | 23 | | |
| Tony Nathan | HB | 6' | 206 | 23 | | 36 |
| Del Williams | HB | 6' | 200 | 29 | | 12 |
| Woody Bennett (from NYJ) | FB | 6'2" | 222 | 25 | | 6 |
| Steve Howell | FB | 6'2" | 230 | 23 | | 6 |
| Terry Robiskie | FB | 6'1" | 210 | 25 | | 12 |
| Don Testerman | FB | 6'2" | 230 | 27 | | |
| Elmer Bailey | WR | 6' | 195 | 22 | | |
| Jimmy Cefalo | WR | 5'11" | 188 | 23 | | 6 |
| Duriel Harris | WR | 5'11" | 184 | 25 | | 12 |
| Nat Moore | WR | 5'9" | 188 | 28 | | 42 |
| Bruce Hardy | TE | 6'5" | 230 | 24 | | 12 |
| Ronnie Lee | TE | 6'3" | 235 | 23 | | 12 |
| Joe Rose | TE | 6'3" | 225 | 23 | | |
| George Roberts | K | 6' | 184 | 25 | | |
| Uwe von Schamann | K | 6' | 188 | 24 | | 74 |

Mike Kozlowski–Ankle Injury

**BALTIMORE COLTS** 7-9-0 Mike McCormack

| Scores of Each Game | | |
|---|---|---|
| 17 | N.Y. Jets | 14 |
| 17 | PITTSBURGH | 20 |
| 16 | Houston | 21 |
| 35 | N.Y. JETS | 21 |
| 30 | Miami | 17 |
| 17 | Buffalo | 12 |
| 21 | NEW ENGLAND | 37 |
| 10 | ST. LOUIS | 17 |
| 31 | Kansas City | 24 |
| 27 | CLEVELAND | 28 |
| 10 | Detroit | 9 |
| 21 | New England | 47 |
| 28 | BUFFALO | 24 |
| 33 | Cincinnati | 34 |
| 14 | MIAMI | 24 |
| 28 | KANSAS CITY | 38 |

| Use Name | Pos. | Hgt. | Wgt. | Age | Int. | Pts. |
|---|---|---|---|---|---|---|
| Wade Griffin | OT | 6'5" | 245 | 26 | | |
| Jeff Hart | OT | 6'5" | 265 | 26 | | |
| George Kunz | OT | 6'5" | 275 | 33 | | |
| Chris Foote | OG-C | 6'3" | 250 | 23 | | |
| Ken Huff | OG | 6'4" | 258 | 27 | | |
| Robert Pratt | OG | 6'4" | 243 | 29 | | |
| Bob Van Duyne | OG | 6'5' | 247 | 28 | | |
| Ray Donaldson | C-OG | 6'3" | 252 | 22 | | |
| Ken Mendenhall | C | 6'3" | 238 | 32 | | |
| Fred Cook | DE | 6'3" | 252 | 28 | | |
| Greg Fields | DE | 6'7" | 262 | 25 | | |
| Mike Ozdowski | DE | 6'5" | 247 | 24 | | |
| Mike Barnes | DT | 6'6" | 251 | 29 | | |
| Joe Ehrmann | DT | 6'5" | 252 | 31 | 1 | |
| Gary Don Johnson | DT | 6'4" | 263 | 24 | | |
| Herb Orvis | DT | 6'5" | 255 | 33 | | |
| Steve Heimkreiter | LB | 6'2" | 226 | 23 | | |
| Ricky Jones | LB | 6'1" | 215 | 25 | | |
| Barry Krauss | LB | 6'3" | 238 | 23 | | |
| Sanders Shiver | LB | 6'2" | 228 | 25 | 1 | 6 |
| Ed Simonini | LB | 6' | 206 | 26 | | |
| Ed Smith | LB | 6'2" | 217 | 23 | | |
| Mike Woods | LB | 6'2" | 237 | 25 | 1 | |
| Kim Anderson | DB | 5'11" | 182 | 23 | 2 | |
| Lyle Blackwood | DB | 6' | 188 | 29 | 1 | |
| Larry Braziel | DB | 6' | 195 | 25 | 2 | |
| Nesby Glasgow | DB | 5'10" | 185 | 23 | 4 | |
| Derrick Hatchett | DB | 5'11" | 180 | 22 | | |
| Bruce Laird | DB | 6' | 194 | 30 | 5 | |
| Reggie Pinkney | DB | 5'11" | 187 | 25 | | |
| Bert Jones | QB | 6'3" | 209 | 28 | | 12 |
| Greg Landry | QB | 6'4" | 210 | 33 | | 6 |
| Curtis Dickey | HB-FB | 6'1" | 201 | 23 | | 78 |
| Don McCauley | HB-FB | 6'1" | 211 | 31 | | 30 |
| Joe Washington | HB | 5'10" | 179 | 26 | | 24 |
| Cleveland Franklin | FB | 6'2" | 212 | 25 | | 12 |
| Ben Garry | FB | 6' | 223 | 24 | | |
| Marvin Sims | FB | 6'4" | 237 | 23 | | 12 |
| Randy Burke | WR | 6'2" | 190 | 25 | | 18 |
| Ray Butler | WR | 6'3" | 190 | 23 | | 12 |
| Roger Carr | WR | 6'3" | 193 | 28 | | 30 |
| Brian DeRoo | WR | 6'3" | 190 | 24 | | |
| Mike Siani | WR | 6'2" | 199 | 30 | | 6 |
| Mack Alston | TE | 6'2" | 232 | 33 | | |
| Ron LaPointe | TE | 6'2" | 235 | 23 | | |
| Reese McCall | TE | 6'7" | 235 | 24 | | 30 |
| Bob Raba | TE | 6'1" | 225 | 25 | | |
| Mike Bragg | K | 5'11" | 186 | 33 | | |
| Steve Mike-Mayer | K | 6' | 180 | 32 | | 79 |

Mark Bailey – Knee Injury
Ron Fernandes – Illness

**NEW YORK JETS** 4-12-0 Walt Michaels

| Scores of Each Game | | |
|---|---|---|
| 14 | BALTIMORE | 17 |
| 10 | Buffalo | 20 |
| 27 | SAN FRANCISCO | 37 |
| 21 | Baltimore | 35 |
| 11 | NEW ENGLAND | 21 |
| 14 | Atlanta | 7 |
| 17 | SEATTLE | 27 |
| 17 | MIAMI | 14 |
| 21 | New England | 34 |
| 24 | BUFFALO | 31 |
| 24 | Denver | 31 |
| 31 | HOUSTON | *28 |
| 13 | Los Angeles | 38 |
| 14 | Cleveland | 17 |
| 20 | NEW ORLEANS | 21 |
| 24 | Miami | 17 |

| Use Name | Pos. | Hgt. | Wgt. | Age | Int. | Pts. |
|---|---|---|---|---|---|---|
| Marvin Powell | OT | 6'5" | 268 | 25 | | |
| John Roman | OT | 6'4" | 260 | 28 | | |
| Chris Ward | OT | 6'3" | 270 | 24 | | |
| Dan Alexander | OG | 6'4" | 255 | 25 | | |
| Guy Bingham | OG-C | 6'3" | 255 | 22 | | |
| Eric Cunningham (from STL) | OG | 6'3" | 257 | 23 | | |
| Randy Rasmussen | OG | 6'2" | 255 | 35 | | |
| Stan Waldemore | OG-C-OT | 6'4" | 250 | 25 | | |
| Joe Fields | C | 6'2" | 253 | 26 | | |
| Mark Gastineau | DE | 6'5" | 280 | 23 | | |
| Chris Godfrey | DE-DT | 6'3" | 250 | 22 | | |
| Joe Klecko | DE | 6'3" | 265 | 26 | | |
| Wes Roberts | DE | 6'6" | 253 | 23 | | |
| Marty Lyons | DT | 6'5" | 260 | 23 | | |
| Abdul Salaam | DT | 6'3" | 265 | 27 | | |
| Bob Winkel | DT | 6'4" | 255 | 24 | | |
| Stan Blinka | LB | 6'2" | 230 | 23 | | |
| Greg Buttle | LB | 6'3" | 232 | 26 | 1 | |
| Ron Crosby | LB | 6'3" | 220 | 25 | 2 | |
| Mike McKibben | LB | 6'3" | 228 | 23 | | |
| Lance Mehl | LB | 6'3" | 230 | 22 | | |
| John Sullivan | LB | 6'1" | 225 | 23 | | |
| Steve Carpenter | DB | 6'2" | 195 | 22 | | |
| Donald Dykes | DB | 5'11" | 180 | 25 | 5 | |
| Jerry Holmes | DB | 6'2" | 175 | 22 | | |
| Bobby Jackson | DB | 5'9" | 175 | 23 | 1 | |
| Jesse Johnson | DB | 6'3" | 185 | 23 | | |
| Saladin Martin | DB | 6' | 179 | 24 | | |
| Tim Moresco | DB | 5'11" | 180 | 25 | | |
| Darrol Ray | DB | 6'1" | 200 | 22 | 6 | 12 |
| Ken Schroy | DB | 6'2" | 196 | 27 | 8 | 6 |
| Craig Penrose | QB | 6'3" | 212 | 27 | | |
| Pat Ryan | QB | 6'3" | 205 | 24 | | |
| Richard Todd | QB | 6'2" | 203 | 26 | | 30 |
| Bobby Batton | HB | 5'11" | 185 | 23 | | |
| Scott Dierking | HB | 5'10" | 215 | 25 | | 42 |
| Bruce Harper | HB | 5'8" | 177 | 25 | | 18 |
| Kenny Lewis | HB | 6' | 190 | 22 | | |
| Clark Gaines | FB | 6'1" | 215 | 26 | | 18 |
| Kevin Long | FB | 6'1" | 218 | 25 | | 36 |
| Tom Newton | FB | 6' | 213 | 26 | | |
| Gerald Carter (to TB) | WR | 6'1" | 185 | 23 | | |
| Paul Darby | WR | 5'10" | 192 | 23 | | 6 |
| Derrick Gaffney | WR | 6'1" | 180 | 25 | | 12 |
| Bobby Jones | WR | 5'11" | 180 | 25 | | |
| Johnny "Lam" Jones | WR | 5'11" | 180 | 22 | | 18 |
| Wesley Walker | WR | 6' | 175 | 25 | | 6 |
| Jerome Barkum | TE | 6'3" | 225 | 30 | | 6 |
| Mickey Shuler | TE | 6'3" | 235 | 24 | | 12 |
| Pat Leahy | K | 6' | 195 | 29 | | 78 |
| Chuck Ramsey | K | 6'2" | 189 | 28 | | |

Johnny Lynn–Knee Injury

*—Overtime

## BUFFALO BILLS

### RUSHING
| Last Name | No. | Yds. | Avg. | TD |
|---|---|---|---|---|
| Cribbs | 306 | 1185 | 3.9 | 11 |
| Brown | 153 | 559 | 3.7 | 3 |
| Leaks | 67 | 219 | 3.3 | 2 |
| Hooks | 25 | 118 | 4.7 | 1 |
| Ferguson | 31 | 65 | 2.1 | 0 |
| Miller | 12 | 35 | 2.9 | 0 |
| Manucci | 3 | 29 | 9.7 | 0 |
| Butler | 1 | 18 | 18.0 | 0 |
| Brammer | 1 | 8 | 8.0 | 0 |
| Humm | 1 | 5 | 5.0 | 0 |
| Jessie | 1 | −9 | −9.0 | 0 |
| Cater | 2 | −10 | −5.0 | 0 |

### RECEIVING
| Last Name | No. | Yds. | Avg. | TD |
|---|---|---|---|---|
| Butler | 57 | 832 | 15 | 6 |
| Cribbs | 52 | 415 | 8 | 1 |
| Lewis | 40 | 648 | 16 | 6 |
| Brown | 27 | 137 | 5 | 0 |
| Brammer | 26 | 283 | 11 | 4 |
| Hooks | 23 | 179 | 8 | 0 |
| Gant | 12 | 181 | 15 | 1 |
| Leaks | 8 | 57 | 7 | 1 |
| Piccone | 7 | 82 | 12 | 0 |
| Jessie | 4 | 56 | 14 | 1 |
| Fergerson | 3 | 41 | 14 | 0 |
| Miller | 3 | 25 | 8 | 0 |

### PUNT RETURNS
| Last Name | No. | Yds. | Avg. | TD |
|---|---|---|---|---|
| Cribbs | 29 | 154 | 5 | 0 |
| Hooks | 8 | 90 | 11 | 0 |
| Piccone | 2 | 15 | 8 | 0 |

### KICKOFF RETURNS
| Last Name | No. | Yds. | Avg. | TD |
|---|---|---|---|---|
| Miller | 16 | 303 | 19 | 0 |
| Brown | 10 | 181 | 18 | 0 |
| Owens | 8 | 157 | 20 | 0 |
| Hooks | 7 | 109 | 16 | 0 |
| Keating | 3 | 38 | 13 | 0 |
| Cribbs | 2 | 39 | 20 | 0 |
| Vogler | 1 | 0 | 0 | 0 |

### PASSING
| Last Name | Att. | Comp. | % | Yds. | Yd./Att. | TD | Int.–% | RK |
|---|---|---|---|---|---|---|---|---|
| Ferguson | 439 | 251 | 57 | 2805 | 6.4 | 20 | 18– 4 | 7 |
| Humm | 14 | 4 | 29 | 39 | 2.8 | 0 | 1– 7 | |
| Cater | 1 | 1 | 100 | 15 | 15.0 | 0 | 0– 0 | |
| Cribbs | 1 | 1 | 100 | 13 | 13.0 | 0 | 0– 0 | |
| Manucci | 6 | 5 | 83 | 64 | 10.7 | 0 | 0– 0 | |

### PUNTING
| Last Name | No. | Avg. |
|---|---|---|
| Cater | 73 | 38.7 |

### KICKING
| Last Name | XP | Att. | % | FG | Att. | % |
|---|---|---|---|---|---|---|
| Mike-Mayer | 37 | 39 | 95 | 13 | 23 | 57 |

## NEW ENGLAND PATRIOTS

### RUSHING
| Last Name | No. | Yds. | Avg. | TD |
|---|---|---|---|---|
| Ferguson | 211 | 818 | 3.9 | 2 |
| Calhoun | 200 | 787 | 3.9 | 9 |
| Grogan | 30 | 112 | 3.7 | 1 |
| Ivory | 42 | 111 | 2.6 | 2 |
| Cavanaugh | 19 | 97 | 5.1 | 0 |
| Tatupu | 33 | 97 | 2.9 | 3 |
| Foreman | 23 | 63 | 2.7 | 1 |
| Clark | 9 | 56 | 6.2 | 1 |
| Jackson | 5 | 37 | 7.4 | 0 |
| Morgan | 4 | 36 | 9.0 | 0 |
| Johnson | 11 | 26 | 2.4 | 0 |
| Hubach | 1 | 0 | 0.0 | 0 |

### RECEIVING
| Last Name | No. | Yds. | Avg. | TD |
|---|---|---|---|---|
| Morgan | 45 | 991 | 22 | 6 |
| Francis | 41 | 664 | 16 | 8 |
| Jackson | 35 | 737 | 21 | 5 |
| Calhoun | 27 | 129 | 5 | 0 |
| Johnson | 24 | 259 | 11 | 3 |
| Ferguson | 22 | 173 | 8 | 0 |
| Foreman | 14 | 99 | 7 | 0 |
| Ivory | 12 | 95 | 8 | 0 |
| Hasselbeck | 8 | 130 | 16 | 4 |
| Westbrook | 4 | 60 | 15 | 0 |
| Pennywell | 4 | 31 | 8 | 1 |
| Tatupu | 4 | 27 | 7 | 0 |

### PUNT RETURNS
| Last Name | No. | Yds. | Avg. | TD |
|---|---|---|---|---|
| James | 33 | 331 | 10 | 1 |
| Haynes | 17 | 140 | 8 | 0 |
| Brown | 10 | 42 | 4 | 0 |

### KICKOFF RETURNS
| Last Name | No. | Yds. | Avg. | TD |
|---|---|---|---|---|
| Ivory | 36 | 992 | 28 | 1 |
| Brown | 9 | 156 | 17 | 0 |
| Currier | 6 | 98 | 16 | 0 |
| Clark | 3 | 21 | 7 | 0 |
| Westbrook | 1 | 14 | 14 | 0 |
| Pennywell | 1 | 0 | 0 | 0 |

### PASSING
| Last Name | Att. | Comp. | % | Yds. | Yd./Att. | TD | Int.–% | RK |
|---|---|---|---|---|---|---|---|---|
| Grogan | 306 | 175 | 57 | 2475 | 8.1 | 18 | 22– 7 | 8 |
| Cavanaugh | 105 | 63 | 60 | 885 | 8.4 | 9 | 5– 5 | |
| Jackson | 2 | 2 | 100 | 35 | 175 | 0 | 0– 0 | |

### PUNTING
| Last Name | No. | Avg. |
|---|---|---|
| Hubach | 63 | 38.0 |

### KICKING
| Last Name | XP | Att. | % | FG | Att. | % |
|---|---|---|---|---|---|---|
| Smith | 51 | 51 | 100 | 26 | 34 | 77 |

## MIAMI DOLPHINS

### RUSHING
| Last Name | No. | Yds. | Avg. | TD |
|---|---|---|---|---|
| Williams | 187 | 671 | 3.6 | 2 |
| Nathan | 60 | 327 | 5.5 | 1 |
| Robiskie | 78 | 250 | 3.2 | 2 |
| Woodley | 55 | 214 | 3.9 | 3 |
| Howell | 60 | 206 | 3.4 | 1 |
| Bennett | 46 | 200 | 4.3 | 0 |
| Giaquinto | 5 | 16 | 3.2 | 0 |
| Testerman | 1 | 5 | 5.0 | 0 |
| Moore | 1 | 3 | 3.0 | 0 |
| Griese | 1 | 0 | 0.0 | 0 |
| Strock | 1 | −3 | −3.0 | 0 |

### RECEIVING
| Last Name | No. | Yds. | Avg. | TD |
|---|---|---|---|---|
| Nathan | 57 | 588 | 10 | 5 |
| Moore | 47 | 564 | 12 | 7 |
| Harris | 33 | 583 | 18 | 2 |
| Williams | 31 | 207 | 7 | 0 |
| Giaquinto | 24 | 192 | 8 | 1 |
| Hardy | 19 | 159 | 8 | 2 |
| Rose | 13 | 149 | 12 | 0 |
| Robiskie | 13 | 60 | 5 | 0 |
| Cefalo | 11 | 199 | 18 | 1 |
| Lee | 7 | 83 | 12 | 2 |
| Howell | 5 | 38 | 8 | 0 |
| Bailey | 4 | 105 | 26 | 0 |
| Bennett | 3 | 26 | 9 | 1 |

### PUNT RETURNS
| Last Name | No. | Yds. | Avg. | TD |
|---|---|---|---|---|
| Nathan | 23 | 178 | 8 | 0 |
| Giaquinto | 7 | 35 | 5 | 0 |
| Blackwood | 1 | 0 | 0 | 0 |
| Bessillieu | 1 | 0 | 0 | 0 |

### KICKOFF RETURNS
| Last Name | No. | Yds. | Avg. | TD |
|---|---|---|---|---|
| Bessillieu | 40 | 890 | 22 | 0 |
| Giaquinto | 9 | 146 | 16 | 0 |
| Bennett | 6 | 88 | 15 | 0 |
| Nathan | 5 | 102 | 20 | 0 |
| Harris | 5 | 89 | 18 | 0 |
| Barnett | 1 | 7 | 7 | 0 |
| Allen | 1 | 0 | 0 | 0 |

### PASSING
| Last Name | Att. | Comp. | % | Yds. | Yd./Att. | TD | Int.–% | RK |
|---|---|---|---|---|---|---|---|---|
| Woodley | 327 | 176 | 54 | 1850 | 5.7 | 14 | 17– 5 | 13 |
| Griese | 100 | 61 | 61 | 790 | 7.9 | 6 | 4– 4 | |
| Strock | 62 | 30 | 48 | 313 | 5.1 | 1 | 5– 8 | |
| Moore | 1 | 0 | 0 | 0 | 0.0 | 0 | 0– 0 | |
| Nathan | 1 | 0 | 0 | 0 | 0.0 | 0 | 0– 0 | |
| Williams | 1 | 0 | 0 | 0 | 0.0 | 0 | 0– 0 | |

### PUNTING
| Last Name | No. | Avg. |
|---|---|---|
| Roberts | 77 | 42.6 |

### KICKING
| Last Name | XP | Att. | % | FG | Att. | % |
|---|---|---|---|---|---|---|
| von Schamann | 32 | 32 | 100 | 14 | 23 | 61 |

## BALTIMORE COLTS

### RUSHING
| Last Name | No. | Yds. | Avg. | TD |
|---|---|---|---|---|
| Dickey | 176 | 800 | 4.5 | 11 |
| Washington | 144 | 502 | 3.5 | 1 |
| Franklin | 83 | 264 | 3.2 | 2 |
| Sims | 54 | 186 | 3.4 | 2 |
| B. Jones | 27 | 175 | 6.5 | 2 |
| McCauley | 35 | 133 | 3.8 | 1 |
| Landry | 7 | 26 | 3.7 | 1 |
| Carr | 1 | −8 | −8.0 | 0 |

### RECEIVING
| Last Name | No. | Yds. | Avg. | TD |
|---|---|---|---|---|
| Carr | 61 | 924 | 15 | 5 |
| Washington | 51 | 494 | 10 | 3 |
| Butler | 34 | 574 | 17 | 2 |
| McCauley | 34 | 313 | 9 | 4 |
| Dickey | 25 | 204 | 8 | 2 |
| McCall | 18 | 322 | 18 | 5 |
| Burke | 14 | 185 | 13 | 3 |
| Franklin | 14 | 112 | 8 | 0 |
| Siani | 9 | 174 | 19 | 1 |
| Sims | 9 | 64 | 7 | 0 |
| DeRoo | 2 | 34 | 17 | 0 |
| Garry | 1 | 9 | 9 | 0 |

### PUNT RETURNS
| Last Name | No. | Yds. | Avg. | TD |
|---|---|---|---|---|
| Glasgow | 23 | 187 | 8 | 0 |
| Anderson | 3 | 1 | 0 | 0 |

### KICKOFF RETURNS
| Last Name | No. | Yds. | Avg. | TD |
|---|---|---|---|---|
| Glasgow | 33 | 743 | 23 | 0 |
| Anderson | 20 | 386 | 19 | 0 |
| Dickey | 4 | 86 | 22 | 0 |
| Garry | 3 | 55 | 18 | 0 |
| Blackwood | 2 | 41 | 21 | 0 |
| LaPointe | 1 | 18 | 18 | 0 |
| McCauley | 1 | 18 | 18 | 0 |
| Hart | 1 | 17 | 17 | 0 |
| Sims | 1 | 10 | 10 | 0 |
| Foote | 1 | 9 | 9 | 0 |

### PASSING
| Last Name | Att. | Comp. | % | Yds. | Yd./Att. | TD | Int.–% | RK |
|---|---|---|---|---|---|---|---|---|
| B. Jones | 446 | 248 | 56 | 3134 | 7.0 | 23 | 21– 5 | 5 |
| Landry | 47 | 24 | 51 | 275 | 5.9 | 2 | 3– 6 | |

### PUNTING
| Last Name | No. | Avg. |
|---|---|---|
| Bragg | 82 | 39.1 |

### KICKING
| Last Name | XP | Att. | % | FG | Att. | % |
|---|---|---|---|---|---|---|
| Mike-Mayer | 43 | 46 | 93 | 12 | 23 | 57 |

## NEW YORK JETS

### RUSHING
| Last Name | No. | Yds. | Avg. | TD |
|---|---|---|---|---|
| Dierking | 156 | 567 | 3.6 | 6 |
| Long | 115 | 355 | 3.1 | 6 |
| Todd | 49 | 330 | 6.7 | 5 |
| Newton | 59 | 299 | 5.1 | 0 |
| Gaines | 36 | 174 | 4.8 | 0 |
| Harper | 45 | 126 | 2.8 | 0 |
| Darby | 1 | 15 | 15.0 | 0 |
| J. Jones | 2 | 5 | 2.5 | 0 |
| Batton | 3 | 4 | 1.3 | 0 |
| Ramsey | 1 | −15 | −15.0 | 0 |

### RECEIVING
| Last Name | No. | Yds. | Avg. | TD |
|---|---|---|---|---|
| Harper | 50 | 634 | 13 | 3 |
| Gaines | 36 | 310 | 9 | 3 |
| J. Jones | 25 | 482 | 19 | 3 |
| Gaffney | 24 | 397 | 17 | 2 |
| Shuler | 22 | 226 | 10 | 2 |
| Newton | 20 | 144 | 7 | 0 |
| Long | 20 | 137 | 7 | 0 |
| Dierking | 19 | 138 | 7 | 1 |
| Walker | 18 | 376 | 21 | 1 |
| B. Jones | 14 | 193 | 14 | 0 |
| Barkum | 13 | 244 | 19 | 1 |
| Darby | 3 | 48 | 16 | 1 |
| Lewis | 1 | 6 | 6 | 0 |

### PUNT RETURNS
| Last Name | No. | Yds. | Avg. | TD |
|---|---|---|---|---|
| Harper | 28 | 242 | 9 | 0 |
| Schroy | 4 | 27 | 7 | 0 |
| B. Jones | 1 | 0 | 0 | 0 |

### KICKOFF RETURNS
| Last Name | No. | Yds. | Avg. | TD |
|---|---|---|---|---|
| Harper | 49 | 1070 | 22 | 0 |
| Darby | 7 | 139 | 20 | 0 |
| J. Jones | 4 | 67 | 17 | 0 |
| B. Jones | 2 | 50 | 25 | 0 |
| Shuler | 2 | 25 | 13 | 0 |
| Bingham | 1 | 19 | 19 | 0 |
| Schroy | 1 | 17 | 17 | 0 |
| Carter | 1 | 12 | 12 | 0 |
| Winkel | 1 | 4 | 4 | 0 |

### PASSING
| Last Name | Att. | Comp. | % | Yds. | Yd./Att. | TD | Int.–% | RK |
|---|---|---|---|---|---|---|---|---|
| Todd | 479 | 264 | 55 | 3329 | 7.0 | 17 | 30– 6 | 14 |
| Ramsey | 2 | 1 | 50 | 6 | 3.0 | 0 | 0– 0 | |

### PUNTING
| Last Name | No. | Avg. |
|---|---|---|
| Ramsey | 73 | 42.4 |

### KICKING
| Last Name | XP | Att. | % | FG | Att. | % |
|---|---|---|---|---|---|---|
| Leahy | 36 | 36 | 100 | 14 | 22 | 64 |

## CLEVELAND BROWNS 11-5-0 — Sam Rutigliano

### Scores of Each Game

| Browns | Opponent | Opp |
|--:|---|--:|
| 17 | New England | 34 |
| 7 | HOUSTON | 16 |
| 20 | KANSAS CITY | 13 |
| 34 | Tampa Bay | 27 |
| 16 | DENVER | 19 |
| 27 | Seattle | 3 |
| 26 | GREEN BAY | 21 |
| 27 | PITTSBURGH | 26 |
| 27 | CHICAGO | 21 |
| 28 | Baltimore | 27 |
| 13 | Pittsburgh | 16 |
| 31 | CINCINNATI | 7 |
| 17 | Houston | 14 |
| 17 | N.Y. JETS | 14 |
| 23 | Minnesota | 28 |
| 27 | Cincinnati | 24 |

| Use Name | Pos. | Hgt. | Wgt. | Age | Int. | Pts. |
|---|---|---|---|---|---|---|
| Doug Dieken | OT | 6'5" | 252 | 31 | | |
| Joel Patten | OT | 6'6" | 240 | 22 | | |
| Cody Risien | OT | 6'7" | 255 | 23 | | |
| Joe DeLamielleure | OG | 6'3" | 245 | 29 | | |
| Robert Jackson | OG | 6'5" | 260 | 27 | | |
| Henry Sheppard | OG-OT | 6'6" | 263 | 27 | | |
| Tom DeLeone | C | 6'2" | 248 | 30 | | |
| Gerry Sullivan | C-OT | 6'4" | 250 | 28 | | |
| Lyle Alzado | DE | 6'3" | 250 | 31 | | |
| Cleveland Crosby | DE | 6'4" | 252 | 24 | | |
| Elvis Franks | DE | 6'4" | 238 | 23 | | |
| Marshall Harris | DE | 6'6" | 261 | 24 | | |
| Jerry Sherk | DE | 6'4" | 250 | 32 | | |
| Jerry Wilkinson (to SF) | DE | 6'9" | 260 | 24 | | |
| Henry Bradley | NT | 6'2" | 260 | 26 | | |
| Ron Crews | NT-DE | 6'3" | 256 | 23 | | |
| Dick Ambrose | LB | 6' | 228 | 27 | | |
| Bill Cowher | LB | 6'3" | 225 | 23 | | |
| Don Goode | LB | 6'2" | 231 | 29 | | |
| Charlie Hall | LB | 6'3" | 235 | 31 | 2 | |
| Robert Jackson | LB | 6'1" | 230 | 26 | 2 | |
| Clay Matthews | LB | 6'2" | 230 | 24 | 1 | |
| John Mohring (from DET) | LB | 6'3" | 240 | 24 | | |
| Cliff Odom | LB | 6'2" | 220 | 22 | | |
| Autry Beamon | DB | 6'1" | 190 | 26 | | |
| Ron Bolton | DB | 6'2" | 170 | 30 | 6 | |
| Clinton Burrell | DB | 6'2" | 192 | 23 | 5 | |
| Thom Darden | DB | 6'2" | 193 | 30 | 2 | |
| Oliver Davis | DB | 6'1" | 205 | 26 | 1 | |
| Judson Flint | DB | 6' | 201 | 23 | | |
| Lawrence Johnson | DB | 5'11" | 204 | 22 | 1 | |
| Clarence Scott | DB | 6' | 190 | 31 | 2 | |
| Johnny Evans | QB | 6'1" | 197 | 24 | | |
| Paul McDonald | QB | 6'2" | 185 | 22 | | |
| Brian Sipe | QB | 6'1" | 195 | 31 | | 6 |
| Dino Hall | HB | 5'7" | 165 | 24 | | |
| Calvin Hill | HB | 6'3" | 227 | 33 | | 36 |
| Greg Pruitt | HB | 5'10" | 190 | 29 | | 30 |
| Charles White | HB | 5'10" | 183 | 22 | | 36 |
| Cleo Miller | FB-HB | 5'11" | 214 | 27 | | 18 |
| Mike Pruitt | FB | 6' | 225 | 26 | | 36 |
| Willis Adams | WR | 6'2" | 194 | 24 | | |
| Ricky Feacher | WR | 5'10" | 174 | 26 | | 24 |
| Dave Logan | WR | 6'4" | 216 | 26 | | 24 |
| Reggie Rucker | WR | 6'2" | 190 | 32 | | 24 |
| Keith Wright | WR | 5'10" | 175 | 24 | | 18 |
| Ozzie Newsome | TE | 6'2" | 232 | 24 | | 18 |
| McDonald Oden | TE | 6'4" | 228 | 22 | | |
| Curtis Weathers | TE | 6'5" | 220 | 23 | | |
| Don Cockroft | K | 6'1" | 195 | 35 | | 87 |

Matt Miller – Knee Injury

## HOUSTON OILERS 11-5-0 — Bum Phillips

### Scores of Each Game

| Oilers | Opponent | Opp |
|--:|---|--:|
| 17 | Pittsburgh | 31 |
| 16 | Cleveland | 7 |
| 21 | BALTIMORE | 16 |
| 13 | Cincinnati | 10 |
| 7 | SEATTLE | 26 |
| 20 | Kansas City | 21 |
| 20 | TAMPA BAY | 14 |
| 23 | CINCINNATI | 3 |
| 20 | Denver | 16 |
| 38 | NEW ENGLAND | 34 |
| 10 | Chicago | 6 |
| 28 | N.Y. Jets | *31 |
| 14 | CLEVELAND | 17 |
| 6 | PITTSBURGH | 0 |
| 22 | Green Bay | 3 |
| 20 | MINNESOTA | 16 |

| Use Name | Pos. | Hgt. | Wgt. | Age | Int. | Pts. |
|---|---|---|---|---|---|---|
| Angelo Fields | OT | 6'6" | 330 | 22 | | |
| Leon Gray | OT | 6'3" | 260 | 28 | | |
| Conway Hayman | OG | 6'4" | 270 | 31 | | |
| Morris Towns | OT-OG | 6'4" | 275 | 26 | | |
| David Carter | OG-C | 6'2" | 245 | 27 | | |
| Ed Fisher | OG | 6'3" | 250 | 31 | | |
| Bob Young | OG | 6'2" | 279 | 37 | | |
| Greg Davidson | C | 6'2" | 250 | 22 | | |
| Carl Mauck | C | 6'3" | 250 | 33 | | |
| Jesse Baker | DE | 6'3" | 265 | 23 | | |
| Elvin Bethea | DE | 6'3" | 255 | 34 | | |
| Andy Dorris | DE | 6'4" | 240 | 29 | | |
| Mike Stensrud | DE-NT | 6'5" | 280 | 24 | | |
| Curley Culp (to DET) | NT-DT | 6'1" | 265 | 34 | | |
| Charlie Davis | NT | 6'1" | 275 | 28 | | |
| Ken Kennard | NT | 6'2" | 245 | 25 | | |
| Gregg Bingham | LB | 6'1" | 230 | 29 | | |
| Robert Brazile | LB | 6'4" | 238 | 27 | 2 | |
| John Corker | LB | 6'5" | 240 | 21 | | 6 |
| Sammy Green | LB | 6'2" | 230 | 25 | | |
| Tom Henderson (from SF) | LB | 6'2" | 220 | 27 | 1 | |
| Daryl Hunt | LB | 6'3" | 220 | 23 | | |
| Art Stringer | LB | 6'1" | 223 | 26 | | |
| Ted Thompson | LB | 6'1" | 220 | 27 | 4 | |
| Ted Washington | LB | 6'1" | 245 | 32 | | |
| Carter Hartwig | DB | 6' | 205 | 24 | 1 | |
| Charles Jefferson | DB | 6' | 178 | 23 | | |
| Vernon Perry | DB | 6'2" | 211 | 26 | 5 | |
| Mike Reinfeldt | DB | 6'2" | 195 | 27 | 4 | |
| Greg Stemrick | DB | 5'11" | 185 | 28 | 4 | |
| Jack Tatum | DB | 5'10" | 205 | 31 | 7 | |
| J.C. Wilson | DB | 6' | 177 | 24 | 2 | |
| Craig Bradshaw | QB | 6'5" | 215 | 23 | | |
| Gifford Nielsen | QB | 6'4" | 205 | 25 | | |
| Ken Stabler | QB | 6'3" | 210 | 34 | | |
| Earl Campbell | HB | 5'11" | 224 | 25 | | 78 |
| Ronnie Coleman | HB | 5'10" | 198 | 29 | | 6 |
| Adger Armstrong | FB | 6' | 210 | 23 | | |
| Rob Carpenter | FB-HB | 6'1" | 230 | 25 | | 18 |
| Booby Clark | FB | 6'2" | 245 | 29 | | |
| Tim Wilson | FB | 6'3" | 220 | 26 | | 12 |
| Ken Burrough | WR | 6'3" | 210 | 32 | | |
| Jeff Groth | WR | 5'10" | 172 | 23 | | |
| Billy Johnson | WR | 5'9" | 170 | 28 | | 12 |
| Guido Merkens (to NO) | WR-DB | 6'1" | 200 | 25 | | |
| Mike Renfro | WR | 6' | 184 | 25 | | 6 |
| Carl Roaches | WR | 5'8" | 165 | 26 | | |
| Tim Smith | WR | 6'2" | 192 | 23 | | |
| Mike Barber | TE | 6'3" | 225 | 27 | | 30 |
| Dave Casper (from OAK) | TE | 6'4" | 230 | 28 | | 24 |
| Rich Caster | TE | 6'5" | 230 | 31 | | 18 |
| Toni Fritsch | K | 5'7" | 180 | 35 | | 83 |
| Cliff Parsley | K | 6'1" | 211 | 25 | | |

George Reihner – Knee Injury
John Schumacher – Back Injury

## PITTSBURGH STEELERS 9-7-0 — Chuck Noll

### Scores of Each Game

| Steelers | Opponent | Opp |
|--:|---|--:|
| 31 | HOUSTON | 17 |
| 20 | Baltimore | 17 |
| 28 | Cincinnati | 30 |
| 38 | CHICAGO | 3 |
| 23 | Minnesota | 17 |
| 16 | CINCINNATI | 17 |
| 34 | OAKLAND | 45 |
| 26 | Cleveland | 27 |
| 22 | GREEN BAY | 20 |
| 24 | Tampa Bay | 21 |
| 16 | CLEVELAND | 13 |
| 13 | Buffalo | 28 |
| 23 | MIAMI | 10 |
| 0 | Houston | 6 |
| 21 | KANSAS CITY | 16 |
| 17 | San Diego | 26 |

| Use Name | Pos. | Hgt. | Wgt. | Age | Int. | Pts. |
|---|---|---|---|---|---|---|
| Larry Brown | OT | 6'4" | 265 | 31 | | |
| Jon Kolb | OT | 6'2" | 262 | 33 | | |
| Ted Petersen | OT | 6'5" | 244 | 25 | | |
| Steve Courson | OG | 6'1" | 260 | 24 | | |
| Tunch Ilkin | OG-OT | 6'3" | 253 | 22 | | |
| Tyrone McGriff | OG | 6' | 273 | 22 | | |
| Ray Pinney | OG-OT-C | 6'4" | 250 | 26 | | |
| Craig Wolfley | OG | 6'1" | 258 | 22 | | |
| Mike Webster | C | 6'1" | 255 | 28 | | |
| John Banaszak | DE | 6'3" | 244 | 30 | | |
| Tom Beasley | DE-DT | 6'5" | 253 | 26 | | |
| L.C. Greenwood | DE | 6'6" | 250 | 33 | | |
| Dwight White | DE | 6'4" | 255 | 31 | | |
| Gary Dunn | DT-DE | 6'3" | 247 | 27 | | |
| Steve Furness | DT | 6'4" | 255 | 29 | | |
| Joe Greene | DT | 6'4" | 260 | 33 | | |
| Robin Cole | LB | 6'2" | 220 | 24 | 1 | |
| Jack Ham | LB | 6'3" | 225 | 31 | 2 | |
| Jack Lambert | LB | 6'4" | 220 | 28 | 2 | |
| Loren Toews | LB | 6'3" | 222 | 28 | 2 | |
| Zack Valentine | LB | 6'2" | 225 | 23 | | |
| Dennis Winston | LB | 6' | 228 | 24 | 6 | |
| Larry Anderson | DB | 5'11" | 177 | 23 | | |
| Mel Blount | DB | 6'3" | 205 | 32 | 4 | |
| Marvin Cobb (to MINN) | DB | 6' | 188 | 27 | | |
| Ron Johnson | DB | 5'10" | 200 | 24 | 1 | |
| Tom Moriarty | DB | 6' | 180 | 27 | | |
| Donnie Shell | DB | 5'11" | 190 | 28 | 7 | |
| J.T. Thomas | DB | 6'2" | 196 | 29 | 2 | |
| Mike Wagner | DB | 6'1" | 190 | 31 | 6 | |
| Dwayne Woodruff | DB | 5'11" | 189 | 23 | 1 | |
| Terry Bradshaw | QB | 6'3" | 215 | 31 | | 12 |
| Mark Malone | QB | 6'4" | 223 | 21 | | |
| Cliff Stoudt | QB | 6'4" | 218 | 25 | | |
| Rocky Bleier | HB | 5'11" | 210 | 34 | | 12 |
| Greg Hawthorne | HB-FB | 6'2" | 225 | 23 | | 24 |
| Frank Pollard | HB | 5'10" | 210 | 23 | | |
| Sidney Thornton | HB-FB | 5'11" | 230 | 25 | | 24 |
| Russell Davis | FB | 6'1" | 215 | 24 | | 6 |
| Franco Harris | FB | 6'2" | 225 | 30 | | 36 |
| Theo Bell | WR | 5'11" | 180 | 26 | | 12 |
| Jim Smith | WR | 6'2" | 205 | 25 | | 54 |
| John Stallworth | WR | 6'2" | 183 | 28 | | 6 |
| Lynn Swann | WR | 6' | 180 | 28 | | 42 |
| Calvin Sweeney | WR | 6'2" | 185 | 25 | | 6 |
| Bennie Cunningham | TE | 6'4" | 247 | 25 | | 12 |
| Randy Grossman | TE | 6'1" | 215 | 26 | | |
| Matt Bahr | K | 5'10" | 165 | 24 | | 96 |
| Craig Colquitt | K | 6'2" | 182 | 26 | | |

Sam Davis – Knee Injury

## CINCINNATI BENGALS 6-10-0 — Forrest Gregg

### Scores of Each Game

| Bengals | Opponent | Opp |
|--:|---|--:|
| 12 | TAMPA BAY | 17 |
| 16 | Miami | 17 |
| 30 | PITTSBURGH | 28 |
| 10 | HOUSTON | 13 |
| 9 | Green Bay | 14 |
| 17 | Pittsburgh | 16 |
| 14 | MINNESOTA | 0 |
| 3 | Houston | 23 |
| 14 | SAN DIEGO | 31 |
| 17 | Oakland | 28 |
| 0 | BUFFALO | 14 |
| 7 | Cleveland | 31 |
| 20 | Kansas City | 6 |
| 34 | BALTIMORE | 33 |
| 17 | Chicago | *14 |
| 24 | CLEVELAND | 27 |

| Use Name | Pos. | Hgt. | Wgt. | Age | Int. | Pts. |
|---|---|---|---|---|---|---|
| Anthony Munoz | OT | 6'6" | 278 | 22 | | |
| Mike Wilson | OT | 6'5" | 271 | 25 | | |
| Glenn Bujnoch | OG | 6'5" | 258 | 26 | | |
| Bill Glass | OG | 6'4" | 261 | 22 | | |
| Dave Lapham | OG-OT | 6'4" | 262 | 28 | | |
| Max Montoya | OG | 6'5" | 275 | 24 | | |
| Blair Bush | C | 6'3" | 250 | 23 | | |
| Blake Moore | C | 6'5" | 260 | 22 | | |
| Ross Browner | DE | 6'3" | 261 | 26 | | |
| Gary Burley | DE | 6'3" | 270 | 27 | | |
| Eddie Edwards | DE | 6'5" | 261 | 26 | | |
| Mike St. Clair | DE | 6'5" | 250 | 26 | | |
| Mike White | DE-NT | 6'5" | 267 | 23 | | |
| Rod Horn | NT | 6'4" | 268 | 23 | | |
| Wilson Whitley | NT | 6'3" | 265 | 25 | | |
| Glenn Cameron | LB | 6'2" | 228 | 27 | 3 | |
| Tom Dinkel | LB | 6'3" | 235 | 24 | | |
| Bo Harris | LB | 6'3" | 226 | 27 | | |
| Jim LeClair | LB | 6'2" | 234 | 29 | | |
| Andrew Melontree | LB | 6'4" | 228 | 22 | | |
| Rick Razzano | LB | 5'11" | 227 | 24 | | |
| Ron Simpkins | LB | 6'1" | 235 | 22 | | |
| Reggie Williams | LB | 6'1" | 228 | 25 | 2 | 2 |
| Louis Breeden | DB | 5'11" | 185 | 26 | 7 | |
| Greg Bright | DB | 6' | 208 | 23 | 1 | |
| Jim Browner | DB | 6'1" | 207 | 24 | | |
| Ray Griffin | DB | 5'10" | 186 | 24 | 2 | 12 |
| Jo Jo Heath | DB | 5'10" | 182 | 23 | | |
| Bryan Hicks | DB | 6' | 192 | 23 | 1 | |
| Dick Jauron | DB | 6' | 190 | 29 | 1 | |
| Ken Riley | DB | 6' | 183 | 33 | 3 | |
| Shafer Suggs (from NYJ) | DB | 6'1" | 204 | 27 | | |
| Ken Anderson | QB | 6'1" | 208 | 31 | | |
| Turk Schonert | QB | 6'1" | 185 | 23 | | |
| Jack Thompson | QB | 6'3" | 217 | 24 | | 6 |
| Charles Alexander | HB-FB | 6'1" | 226 | 23 | | 12 |
| Archie Griffin | HB | 5'9" | 184 | 26 | | |
| Deacon Turner | HB | 5'11" | 210 | 25 | | 6 |
| Pete Johnson | FB | 6' | 249 | 26 | | 42 |
| Nathan Poole | FB | 5'9" | 205 | 23 | | |
| Alton Alexis | WR | 6'4" | 184 | 22 | | |
| Don Bass | WR | 6'2" | 220 | 25 | | 36 |
| Isaac Curtis | WR | 6'1" | 192 | 29 | | 18 |
| Steve Kreider | WR | 6'3" | 192 | 22 | | |
| Mike Levenseller | WR | 6'1" | 184 | 24 | | |
| Pat McInally | WR | 6'6" | 212 | 27 | | 12 |
| Cle Montgomery | WR | 5'8" | 183 | 24 | | |
| Jim Corbett | TE | 6'4" | 220 | 25 | | |
| M. L. Harris | TE | 6'5" | 238 | 26 | | |
| Dan Ross | TE | 6'4" | 235 | 23 | | 24 |
| Jim Breech | K | 5'6" | 155 | 24 | | 23 |
| Ian Sunter | K | 6'1" | 215 | 28 | | 48 |
| Sandro Vitiello | K | 6'2" | 197 | 22 | | 1 |

Howie Kurnick – Knee Injury

*—Overtime

## CLEVELAND BROWNS

### RUSHING

| Last Name | No. | Yds. | Avg. | TD |
|---|---|---|---|---|
| M. Pruitt | 249 | 1034 | 4.2 | 6 |
| White | 86 | 279 | 3.2 | 5 |
| Miller | 28 | 139 | 5.0 | 3 |
| G. Pruitt | 40 | 117 | 2.9 | 0 |
| Sipe | 20 | 55 | 2.8 | 1 |
| D. Hall | 2 | 26 | 13.0 | 0 |
| Newsome | 2 | 13 | 6.5 | 0 |
| Hill | 1 | 11 | 11.0 | 0 |
| Adams | 2 | 7 | 3.5 | 0 |
| McDonald | 3 | -2 | -0.7 | 0 |
| Evans | 3 | -6 | -2.0 | 0 |

### RECEIVING

| Last Name | No. | Yds. | Avg. | TD |
|---|---|---|---|---|
| M. Pruitt | 63 | 471 | 8 | 0 |
| Rucker | 52 | 768 | 15 | 4 |
| Logan | 51 | 822 | 16 | 4 |
| Newsome | 51 | 594 | 12 | 3 |
| G. Pruitt | 50 | 444 | 9 | 5 |
| Hill | 27 | 383 | 14 | 6 |
| White | 17 | 153 | 9 | 1 |
| Feacher | 10 | 244 | 24 | 4 |
| Adams | 8 | 165 | 21 | 0 |
| Wright | 3 | 62 | 21 | 3 |
| Oden | 3 | 18 | 6 | 0 |
| Miller | 2 | 8 | 4 | 0 |

### PUNT RETURNS

| Last Name | No. | Yds. | Avg. | TD |
|---|---|---|---|---|
| Wright | 29 | 129 | 4 | 0 |
| D. Hall | 6 | 41 | 7 | 0 |

### KICKOFF RETURNS

| Last Name | No. | Yds. | Avg. | TD |
|---|---|---|---|---|
| Wright | 25 | 576 | 23 | 0 |
| D. Hall | 32 | 691 | 22 | 0 |
| Miller | 2 | 22 | 11 | 0 |
| White | 1 | 20 | 20 | 0 |
| Flint | 1 | 0 | 0 | 0 |
| B. Jackson | 1 | 0 | 0 | 0 |
| Darden | 1 | -1 | -1 | 0 |

### PASSING – PUNTING – KICKING

| PASSING | Att. | Comp. | % | Yds. | Yd./Att. | TD | Int.–% | | RK |
|---|---|---|---|---|---|---|---|---|---|
| Sipe | 554 | 337 | 61 | 4132 | 7.5 | 30 | 14– | 3 | 1 |

| PUNTING | No. | Avg. |
|---|---|---|
| Evans | 66 | 38.3 |

| KICKING | XP | Att. | % | FG | Att. | % |
|---|---|---|---|---|---|---|
| Cockroft | 39 | 44 | 89 | 16 | 26 | 62 |

## HOUSTON OILERS

### RUSHING

| Last Name | No. | Yds. | Avg. | TD |
|---|---|---|---|---|
| Campbell | 373 | 1934 | 5.2 | 13 |
| Carpenter | 97 | 359 | 3.7 | 3 |
| T. Wilson | 66 | 257 | 3.9 | 1 |
| Coleman | 14 | 82 | 5.9 | 1 |
| Renfro | 1 | 12 | 12.0 | 0 |
| Casper | 2 | 8 | 4.0 | 0 |
| Clark | 1 | 3 | 3.0 | 0 |
| Barber | 1 | 1 | 1.0 | 0 |
| Johnson | 2 | 1 | 0.5 | 0 |
| Nielsen | 1 | 0 | 0.0 | 0 |
| Stabler | 15 | -22 | -1.5 | 0 |

### RECEIVING

| Last Name | No. | Yds. | Avg. | TD |
|---|---|---|---|---|
| Barber | 59 | 712 | 12 | 5 |
| Casper | 56 | 796 | 14 | 4 |
| Carpenter | 43 | 346 | 8 | 0 |
| Renfro | 35 | 459 | 13 | 1 |
| Johnson | 31 | 343 | 11 | 2 |
| T. Wilson | 30 | 170 | 6 | 1 |
| Caster | 27 | 341 | 13 | 3 |
| Coleman | 16 | 168 | 11 | 0 |
| Campbell | 11 | 47 | 4 | 0 |
| Burrough | 4 | 91 | 23 | 0 |
| Groth | 4 | 47 | 12 | 0 |
| Smith | 2 | 21 | 11 | 0 |

### PUNT RETURNS

| Last Name | No. | Yds. | Avg. | TD |
|---|---|---|---|---|
| Roaches | 47 | 384 | 8 | 0 |
| Groth | 1 | 0 | 0 | 0 |

### KICKOFF RETURNS

| Last Name | No. | Yds. | Avg. | TD |
|---|---|---|---|---|
| Roaches | 37 | 746 | 20 | 0 |
| Growth | 12 | 216 | 18 | 0 |
| Barber | 1 | 12 | 12 | 0 |
| Carpenter | 1 | 7 | 7 | 0 |
| Bingham | 1 | 0 | 0 | 0 |
| Smith | 1 | 0 | 0 | 0 |

### PASSING – PUNTING – KICKING

| PASSING | Att. | Comp. | % | Yds. | Yd./Att. | TD | Int.–% | | RK |
|---|---|---|---|---|---|---|---|---|---|
| Stabler | 457 | 293 | 64 | 3202 | 7.0 | 13 | 28– | 6 | 11 |
| Campbell | 2 | 1 | 50 | 57 | 28.5 | 1 | 0– | | |
| Nielsen | 4 | 2 | 50 | 12 | 3.0 | 1 | 0– | | |

| PUNTING | No. | Avg. |
|---|---|---|
| Parsley | 67 | 40.7 |

| KICKING | XP | Att. | % | FG | Att. | % |
|---|---|---|---|---|---|---|
| Fritsch | 26 | 27 | 96 | 19 | 24 | 79 |
| Thompson | 4 | 4 | 100 | | | |

## PITTSBURGH STEELERS

### RUSHING

| Last Name | No. | Yds. | Avg. | TD |
|---|---|---|---|---|
| Harris | 208 | 789 | 3.8 | 4 |
| Bleier | 78 | 340 | 4.4 | 1 |
| Thornton | 78 | 325 | 4.2 | 3 |
| Hawthorne | 63 | 226 | 3.6 | 4 |
| Davis | 33 | 132 | 4.0 | 1 |
| Bradshaw | 36 | 111 | 3.1 | 2 |
| Stoudt | 9 | 35 | 3.9 | 0 |
| Colquitt | 1 | 17 | 17.0 | 0 |
| Pollard | 4 | 16 | 4.0 | 0 |
| Smith | 1 | -1 | -1.0 | 0 |
| Swann | 1 | -4 | -4.0 | 0 |

### RECEIVING

| Last Name | No. | Yds. | Avg. | TD |
|---|---|---|---|---|
| Swann | 44 | 710 | 16 | 7 |
| Smith | 37 | 711 | 19 | 9 |
| Harris | 30 | 196 | 7 | 2 |
| Bell | 29 | 748 | 26 | 2 |
| Grossman | 23 | 293 | 13 | 0 |
| Bleier | 21 | 174 | 8 | 1 |
| Cunningham | 18 | 232 | 13 | 2 |
| Thornton | 15 | 131 | 9 | 1 |
| Sweeney | 12 | 282 | 24 | 1 |
| Hawthorne | 12 | 158 | 13 | 0 |
| Stallworth | 9 | 197 | 22 | 1 |

### PUNT RETURNS

| Last Name | No. | Yds. | Avg. | TD |
|---|---|---|---|---|
| Bell | 34 | 339 | 10 | 0 |
| Smith | 7 | 28 | 4 | 0 |
| Cobb | 3 | 19 | 6 | 0 |
| Pollard | 1 | 5 | 5 | 0 |

### KICKOFF RETURNS

| Last Name | No. | Yds. | Avg. | TD |
|---|---|---|---|---|
| Pollard | 22 | 494 | 23 | 0 |
| Anderson | 14 | 379 | 27 | 0 |
| Hawthorne | 9 | 169 | 19 | 0 |
| Davis | 9 | 160 | 18 | 0 |
| Bell | 3 | 50 | 17 | 0 |
| Sweeney | 3 | 42 | 14 | 0 |
| Cobb | 1 | 19 | 19 | 0 |
| Thornton | 1 | 15 | 15 | 0 |
| Winston | 1 | 13 | 13 | 0 |
| Blount | 1 | 9 | 9 | 0 |
| Valentine | 1 | 0 | 0 | 0 |

### PASSING – PUNTING – KICKING

| PASSING | Att. | Comp. | % | Yds. | Yd./Att. | TD | Int.–% | | RK |
|---|---|---|---|---|---|---|---|---|---|
| Bradshaw | 424 | 218 | 51 | 3339 | 7.9 | 24 | 22– | 5 | 6 |
| Stoudt | 60 | 32 | 53 | 493 | 8.2 | 2 | 2– | 3 | |

| PUNTING | No. | Avg. |
|---|---|---|
| Colquitt | 61 | 40.7 |
| Bradshaw | 5 | 34.6 |

| KICKING | XP | Att. | % | FG | Att. | % |
|---|---|---|---|---|---|---|
| Bahr | 39 | 42 | 93 | 19 | 28 | 68 |

## CINCINNATI BENGALS

### RUSHING

| Last Name | No. | Yds. | Avg. | TD |
|---|---|---|---|---|
| Johnson | 186 | 747 | 4.0 | 6 |
| Alexander | 169 | 702 | 4.2 | 2 |
| A. Griffin | 85 | 260 | 3.1 | 0 |
| Turner | 30 | 130 | 4.3 | 0 |
| Anderson | 16 | 122 | 7.6 | 0 |
| Thompson | 18 | 84 | 4.7 | 1 |
| Montgomery | 1 | 12 | 12.0 | 0 |
| Levenseller | 1 | 6 | 6.0 | 0 |
| Poole | 5 | 6 | 1.2 | 0 |
| M. Harris | 1 | 0 | 0.0 | 0 |
| McInally | 1 | 0 | 0.0 | 0 |

### RECEIVING

| Last Name | No. | Yds. | Avg. | TD |
|---|---|---|---|---|
| Ross | 56 | 724 | 13 | 4 |
| Curtis | 43 | 610 | 14 | 3 |
| Alexander | 36 | 192 | 5 | 0 |
| Bass | 32 | 409 | 13 | 6 |
| A. Griffin | 28 | 196 | 7 | 0 |
| Johnson | 21 | 172 | 8 | 1 |
| McInally | 18 | 269 | 15 | 2 |
| Kreider | 17 | 272 | 16 | 0 |
| Turner | 12 | 73 | 6 | 1 |
| M. Harris | 10 | 137 | 14 | 0 |
| Corbett | 3 | 28 | 9 | 0 |
| Levenseller | 2 | 30 | 15 | 0 |
| Poole | 2 | -4 | -2 | 0 |
| Munoz | 1 | -6 | -6 | 0 |

### PUNT RETURNS

| Last Name | No. | Yds. | Avg. | TD |
|---|---|---|---|---|
| Montgomery | 31 | 223 | 7 | 0 |
| Heath | 6 | 29 | 5 | 0 |
| Bright | 1 | 0 | 0 | 0 |
| Williams | 1 | 0 | 0 | 0 |

### KICKOFF RETURNS

| Last Name | No. | Yds. | Avg. | TD |
|---|---|---|---|---|
| Montgomery | 44 | 843 | 19 | 0 |
| Turner | 9 | 173 | 19 | 0 |
| Hicks | 5 | 87 | 17 | 0 |
| Heath | 3 | 51 | 17 | 0 |
| Simpkins | 3 | 8 | 3 | 0 |
| J. Browner | 2 | 10 | 5 | 0 |
| Kreider | 1 | 19 | 19 | 0 |
| Poole | 1 | 8 | 8 | 0 |

### PASSING – PUNTING – KICKING

| PASSING | Att. | Comp. | % | Yds. | Yd./Att. | TD | Int.–% | | RK |
|---|---|---|---|---|---|---|---|---|---|
| Anderson | 275 | 166 | 60 | 1778 | 6.5 | 6 | 13– | 5 | 12 |
| Thompson | 234 | 115 | 49 | 1324 | 5.7 | 11 | 12– | 5 | 15 |
| Kreider | 1 | 0 | 0 | 0 | 0.0 | 0 | 0– | 0 | |

| PUNTING | No. | Avg. |
|---|---|---|
| McInally | 83 | 40.8 |

| KICKING | XP | Att. | % | FG | Att. | % |
|---|---|---|---|---|---|---|
| Sunter | 15 | 15 | 100 | 11 | 20 | 55 |
| Breech | 11 | 12 | 92 | 4 | 7 | 57 |
| Vitiello | 1 | 1 | 100 | 0 | 2 | 0 |

### SAN DIEGO CHARGERS 11-5-0 Don Coryell

| Scores of Each Game | | |
|---|---|---|
| 34 | Seattle | 13 |
| 30 | OAKLAND | *24 |
| 30 | Denver | 13 |
| 24 | Kansas City | 7 |
| 24 | BUFFALO | 26 |
| 24 | Oakland | 38 |
| 44 | N.Y. GIANTS | 7 |
| 31 | Dallas | 42 |
| 31 | Cincinnati | 14 |
| 13 | DENVER | 20 |
| 20 | KANSAS CITY | 7 |
| 27 | Miami | *24 |
| 22 | PHILADELPHIA | 21 |
| 17 | Washington | 40 |
| 21 | SEATTLE | 14 |
| 26 | PITTSBURGH | 17 |

| Use Name | Pos. | Hgt. | Wgt. | Age | Int. | Pts. |
|---|---|---|---|---|---|---|
| Dan Audick | OT-OG | 6'3" | 253 | 25 | | |
| Chuck Loewen | OT-OG | 6'3" | 259 | 23 | | |
| Billy Shields | OT | 6'7" | 275 | 27 | | |
| Russ Washington | OT | 6'6" | 284 | 33 | | |
| Ralph Perretta (from NYG) | OG-C | 6'2" | 251 | 27 | | |
| Ed White | OG | 6'2" | 271 | 33 | | |
| Doug Wilkerson | OG | 6'2" | 262 | 33 | | |
| Don Macek | C | 6'3" | 253 | 26 | | |
| Bob Rush | C-OT | 6'5" | 264 | 24 | | |
| Fred Dean | DE | 6'3" | 230 | 28 | | |
| Leroy Jones | DE | 6'8" | 260 | 29 | | |
| John Lee | DE | 6'2" | 259 | 27 | | |
| Wilbur Young | DE-DT | 6'6" | 290 | 31 | | |
| Charles DeJurnett | DT | 6'4" | 260 | 28 | | |
| Gary Johnson | DT | 6'2" | 252 | 28 | | |
| Louie Kelcher | DT | 6'5" | 282 | 27 | 1 | |

| Use Name | Pos. | Hgt. | Wgt. | Age | Int. | Pts. |
|---|---|---|---|---|---|---|
| Bob Horn | LB | 6'3" | 230 | 26 | | |
| Keith King | LB | 6'4" | 230 | 25 | 2 | |
| Jim Laslavic | LB | 6'2" | 236 | 28 | | |
| Woodrow Lowe | LB | 6' | 227 | 26 | 3 | 6 |
| Carl McGee | LB | 6'3" | 228 | 24 | | |
| Ray Preston | LB | 6' | 218 | 26 | | |
| Cliff Thrift | LB | 6'2" | 232 | 24 | 1 | |
| Willie Buchanon | DB | 6' | 185 | 29 | 2 | |
| Jerome Dove | DB | 6'2" | 193 | 26 | | |
| Frank Duncan | DB | 6'1" | 188 | 23 | | |
| Glen Edwards | DB | 6' | 183 | 33 | 5 | 6 |
| Mike Fuller | DB | 5'9" | 182 | 27 | | |
| Pete Shaw | DB | 5'10" | 178 | 26 | 4 | |
| Hal Stringert | DB | 5'11" | 187 | 28 | 1 | |
| Mike Williams | DB | 5'10" | 179 | 26 | 1 | |
| Jim Nicholson – Knee Injury | | | | | | |

| Use Name | Pos. | Hgt. | Wgt. | Age | Int. | Pts. |
|---|---|---|---|---|---|---|
| Dan Fouts | QB | 6'3" | 210 | 29 | | 12 |
| James Harris | QB | 6'3" | 221 | 33 | | |
| Ed Luther | QB | 6'3" | 206 | 23 | | |
| Hank Bauer | HB | 5'10" | 200 | 26 | | 6 |
| Mike Thomas | HB | 5'11" | 190 | 27 | | 18 |
| Clarence Williams | HB | 5'9" | 195 | 25 | | 24 |
| John Cappelletti | FB | 6'1" | 225 | 28 | | 30 |
| LaRue Harrington | FB | 6' | 210 | 23 | | |
| Chuck Muncie (from NO) | FB-HB | 6'3" | 233 | 27 | | 36 |
| Booker Russell | FB | 6'2" | 235 | 24 | | |
| John Floyd | WR | 6'1" | 195 | 23 | | 6 |
| John Jefferson | WR | 6'1" | 198 | 24 | | 78 |
| Charlie Joiner | WR | 5'11" | 183 | 32 | | 24 |
| Ron Smith | WR | 6' | 185 | 23 | | |
| Greg McCrary | TE | 6'3" | 235 | 28 | | 12 |
| Kellen Winslow | TE | 6'5" | 252 | 22 | | 54 |
| Rolf Benirschke | K | 6' | 175 | 25 | | 118 |
| Rick Partridge | K | 6'1" | 175 | 23 | | |
| Mike Wood | K | 5'11" | 199 | 25 | | |

### OAKLAND RAIDERS 11-5-0 Tom Flores

| Scores of Each Game | | |
|---|---|---|
| 27 | Kansas City | 14 |
| 24 | San Diego | *30 |
| 24 | WASHINGTON | 21 |
| 7 | Buffalo | 24 |
| 17 | KANSAS CITY | 31 |
| 38 | SAN DIEGO | 24 |
| 45 | Pittsburgh | 34 |
| 33 | SEATTLE | 14 |
| 16 | MIAMI | 10 |
| 28 | CINCINNATI | 17 |
| 19 | Seattle | 17 |
| 7 | Philadelphia | 10 |
| 9 | DENVER | 3 |
| 13 | DALLAS | 19 |
| 24 | Denver | 21 |
| 33 | N.Y. Giants | 17 |

| Use Name | Pos. | Hgt. | Wgt. | Age | Int. | Pts. |
|---|---|---|---|---|---|---|
| Bruce Davis | OT-OG | 6'6" | 280 | 24 | | |
| Henry Lawrence | OT | 6'4" | 270 | 28 | | |
| Lindsey Mason | OT | 6'5" | 265 | 25 | | |
| Art Shell | OT | 6'5" | 280 | 33 | | |
| Mickey Marvin | OG | 6'4" | 270 | 24 | | |
| Steve Sylvester | OG-C-OT | 6'4" | 260 | 27 | | |
| Gene Upshaw | OG | 6'5" | 255 | 35 | | |
| Dave Dalby | C | 6'2" | 250 | 29 | | |
| Dave Browning | DE | 6'5" | 245 | 24 | | |
| Joe Campbell (from NO) | DE-MG | 6'6" | 254 | 25 | | |
| Cedrick Hardman | DE | 6'3" | 245 | 31 | | |
| Willie Jones | DE | 6'4" | 245 | 22 | | 6 |
| John Matuszak | DE | 6'8" | 280 | 29 | | |
| Reggie Kinlaw | NT | 6'2" | 240 | 23 | | |
| Alva Liles (to DET) | NT-DT | 6'3" | 255 | 24 | | |
| Dave Pear | NT | 6'2" | 250 | 27 | | |
| Mark Meseroll – Injury | | | | | | |
| Jeff Winans – Injury | | | | | | |

| Use Name | Pos. | Hgt. | Wgt. | Age | Int. | Pts. |
|---|---|---|---|---|---|---|
| Jeff Barnes | LB | 6'2" | 215 | 25 | | |
| Mario Celotto | LB | 6'3" | 225 | 24 | | |
| Ted Hendricks | LB | 6'7" | 225 | 32 | 3 | 2 |
| Rod Martin | LB | 6'2" | 210 | 26 | 2 | 6 |
| Randy McClanahan | LB | 6'5" | 225 | 25 | 1 | |
| Matt Millen | LB | 6'2" | 260 | 22 | 2 | |
| Bob Nelson | LB | 6'4" | 230 | 27 | 1 | |
| Mike Davis | DB | 6'2" | 200 | 24 | 3 | |
| Dwight Harrison | DB | 6'1" | 180 | 31 | | |
| Lester Hayes | DB | 6' | 195 | 25 | 13 | 6 |
| Monte Jackson | DB | 5'11" | 200 | 27 | 1 | |
| Odis McKinney | DB | 6'2" | 190 | 23 | 3 | |
| Keith Moody | DB | 5'10" | 175 | 27 | | |
| Dwayne O'Steen | DB | 6'1" | 195 | 25 | 3 | |
| Burgess Owens | DB | 6'2" | 200 | 29 | 3 | 6 |
| Mike Spivey (to NO) | DB | 6' | 200 | 26 | | |
| Monte Johnson – Knee Injury | | | | | | |
| Charlie Phillips – Knee Injury | | | | | | |

| Use Name | Pos. | Hgt. | Wgt. | Age | Int. | Pts. |
|---|---|---|---|---|---|---|
| Kyle Grossart | QB | 6'4" | 210 | 25 | | |
| Dan Pastorini | QB | 6'3" | 205 | 31 | | |
| Jim Plunkett | QB | 6'3" | 205 | 32 | | 12 |
| Marc Wilson | QB | 6'6" | 205 | 23 | | |
| I.M. Hipp | HB | 5'10" | 200 | 24 | | |
| Kenny King | HB | 5'11" | 205 | 23 | | 24 |
| Ira Matthews | HB-WR | 5'8" | 175 | 23 | | |
| Art Whittington | HB | 5'11" | 180 | 24 | | 24 |
| Todd Christensen | FB-TE | 6'3" | 230 | 24 | | 6 |
| Derrick Jensen | FB | 6'1" | 225 | 24 | | 6 |
| Mark van Eeghen | FB | 6'2" | 225 | 28 | | 30 |
| Morris Bradshaw | WR | 6' | 195 | 27 | | 6 |
| Cliff Branch | WR | 5'11" | 170 | 32 | | 42 |
| Bob Chandler | WR | 6' | 180 | 31 | | 60 |
| Rich Martini | WR | 6'2" | 185 | 24 | | |
| Ray Chester | TE | 6'3" | 235 | 32 | | 24 |
| Derrick Ramsey | TE | 6'5" | 225 | 23 | | |
| Chris Bahr | K | 5'9" | 175 | 27 | | 98 |
| Ray Guy | K | 6'3" | 190 | 30 | | |

### KANSAS CITY CHIEFS 8-8-0 Marv Levy

| Scores of Each Game | | |
|---|---|---|
| 14 | OAKLAND | 27 |
| 16 | SEATTLE | 17 |
| 13 | Cleveland | 20 |
| 7 | SAN DIEGO | 24 |
| 31 | Oakland | 17 |
| 21 | HOUSTON | 20 |
| 23 | Denver | 17 |
| 20 | DETROIT | 17 |
| 24 | BALTIMORE | 31 |
| 31 | Seattle | 30 |
| 7 | San Diego | 20 |
| 21 | St. Louis | 13 |
| 6 | CINCINNATI | 20 |
| 31 | DENVER | 14 |
| 16 | Pittsburgh | 21 |
| 38 | Baltimore | 28 |

| Use Name | Pos. | Hgt. | Wgt. | Age | Int. | Pts. |
|---|---|---|---|---|---|---|
| Charlie Getty | OT | 6'4" | 269 | 28 | | |
| Matt Herkenhoff | OT | 6'4" | 270 | 29 | | |
| Jim Rourke | OT-OG-C | 6'5" | 264 | 23 | | |
| Franky Smith | OT | 6'6" | 279 | 26 | | |
| Brad Budde | OG | 6'4" | 255 | 22 | | |
| Tom Condon | OG | 6'3" | 254 | 27 | | |
| Bob Simmons | OG-OT | 6'4" | 260 | 26 | | |
| Rod Walters (to MIA, DET) | OG | 6'3" | 258 | 26 | | |
| Charlie Ane | C | 6'1" | 237 | 28 | | |
| Jack Rudnay | C | 6'3" | 242 | 32 | | |
| Mike Bell | DE | 6'4" | 255 | 23 | | |
| Sylvester Hicks | DE | 6'4" | 252 | 25 | | |
| Dave Lindstrom | DE | 6'6" | 257 | 25 | | |
| Jerry Meyers | DE | 6'4" | 253 | 26 | | |
| Art Still | DE | 6'7" | 252 | 24 | | |
| Ken Kremer | NT-DE | 6'4" | 250 | 23 | | |
| Dino Mangiero | NT | 6'2" | 265 | 21 | 1 | |
| Don Parrish | NT | 6'2" | 259 | 25 | | |

| Use Name | Pos. | Hgt. | Wgt. | Age | Int. | Pts. |
|---|---|---|---|---|---|---|
| Jerry Blanton | LB | 6'1" | 225 | 24 | | |
| Tom Howard | LB | 6'2" | 208 | 26 | | 6 |
| Charles Jackson | LB | 6'2" | 220 | 25 | | |
| Kelly Kirchbaum | LB | 6'2" | 240 | 23 | | |
| Frank Manumaleuga | LB | 6'2" | 245 | 24 | 3 | 6 |
| Whitney Paul | LB | 6'3" | 220 | 26 | 1 | 6 |
| Cal Peterson | LB | 6'3" | 220 | 27 | | |
| Clarence Sanders | LB | 6'4" | 230 | 27 | | |
| Gary Spani | LB | 6'2" | 230 | 24 | 1 | 12 |
| Gary Barbaro | DB | 6'4" | 204 | 26 | 10 | |
| M.L. Carter | DB | 5'9" | 173 | 24 | | |
| Herb Christopher | DB | 5'10" | 190 | 26 | 2 | |
| Paul Dombroski | DB | 6' | 185 | 24 | 1 | |
| Gary Green | DB | 5'11" | 184 | 24 | 2 | |
| Eric Harris | DB | 6'3" | 191 | 25 | 7 | |
| Jerry Reese | DB | 6'3" | 192 | 25 | | |
| Donovan Rose | DB | 6'1" | 180 | 23 | | |
| Alois Blackwell – Injured | | | | | | |

| Use Name | Pos. | Hgt. | Wgt. | Age | Int. | Pts. |
|---|---|---|---|---|---|---|
| Tom Clements | QB | 6' | 183 | 27 | | |
| Steve Fuller | QB | 6'4" | 198 | 23 | | 24 |
| Bill Kenney | QB | 6'4" | 210 | 25 | | |
| Horace Belton | HB | 5'8" | 200 | 25 | | 12 |
| Earl Gant | HB | 6' | 207 | 23 | | |
| Tony Reed | HB | 5'11" | 197 | 25 | | 6 |
| Ken Talton | HB | 6' | 205 | 24 | | |
| Jim Hadnot | FB | 6'2" | 244 | 23 | | 12 |
| Ted McKnight | FB-HB | 6'1" | 216 | 26 | | 18 |
| Arnold Morgado | FB-HB | 6' | 205 | 27 | | 30 |
| Carlos Carson | WR | 5'10" | 172 | 21 | | |
| Bubba Garcia | WR | 5'11" | 185 | 22 | | 6 |
| Henry Marshall | WR | 6'2" | 214 | 26 | | 36 |
| Stan Rome | WR | 6'5" | 205 | 24 | | |
| J.T. Smith | WR | 6'2" | 185 | 24 | | 24 |
| Ed Beckman | TE | 6'4" | 226 | 25 | | |
| Al Dixon | TE | 6'5" | 220 | 26 | | 6 |
| Tony Samuels (to TB) | TE | 6'4" | 233 | 25 | | 12 |
| Mike Williams | TE | 6'3" | 222 | 22 | | 6 |
| Bob Grupp | K | 5'11" | 193 | 25 | | |
| Nick Lowery | K | 6'4" | 190 | 24 | | 97 |

### DENVER BRONCOS 8-8-0 Red Miller

| Scores of Each Game | | |
|---|---|---|
| 6 | Philadelphia | 27 |
| 41 | DALLAS | 20 |
| 13 | SAN DIEGO | 30 |
| 14 | New England | 23 |
| 19 | Cleveland | 16 |
| 20 | WASHINGTON | 17 |
| 17 | KANSAS CITY | 23 |
| 14 | N.Y. Giants | 9 |
| 16 | HOUSTON | 20 |
| 20 | San Diego | 13 |
| 31 | N.Y. JETS | 24 |
| 36 | SEATTLE | 20 |
| 3 | Oakland | 9 |
| 14 | Kansas City | 31 |
| 21 | OAKLAND | 24 |
| 25 | Seattle | 17 |

| Use Name | Pos. | Hgt. | Wgt. | Age | Int. | Pts. |
|---|---|---|---|---|---|---|
| Kelvin Clark | OT | 6'3" | 245 | 24 | | |
| Claudie Minor | OT | 6'4" | 275 | 29 | | |
| Dave Studdard | OT | 6'4" | 255 | 24 | | |
| Tom Glassic | OG | 6'3" | 250 | 26 | | |
| Paul Howard | OG | 6'3" | 260 | 29 | | |
| Glenn Hyde | OG | 6'3" | 252 | 29 | | |
| Arland Thompson | OG | 6'3" | 265 | 22 | | |
| Keith Bishop | C-OG | 6'3" | 260 | 23 | | |
| Bill Bryan | C | 6'2" | 244 | 25 | | |
| Greg Boyd | DE | 6'6" | 280 | 27 | | |
| Barney Chavous | DE | 6'3" | 245 | 29 | | |
| Rulon Jones | DE | 6'6" | 260 | 22 | | 2 |
| Brison Manor | DE | 6'4" | 248 | 28 | | |
| Rubin Carter | NT | 6' | 253 | 27 | | |
| Don Latimer | NT | 6'3" | 253 | 25 | 1 | 6 |
| Laval Short | NT | 6'3" | 250 | 21 | | |

| Use Name | Pos. | Hgt. | Wgt. | Age | Int. | Pts. |
|---|---|---|---|---|---|---|
| Greg Bracelin | LB | 6'1" | 218 | 23 | | |
| Larry Evans | LB | 6'2" | 220 | 27 | 1 | |
| Randy Gradishar | LB | 6'3" | 231 | 28 | 2 | 6 |
| Tom Jackson | LB | 5'11" | 228 | 29 | | |
| Rob Nairne | LB | 6'4" | 220 | 26 | 1 | |
| Joe Rizzo | LB | 6'1" | 220 | 29 | | |
| Jim Ryan | LB | 6'1" | 212 | 23 | 1 | |
| Art Smith | LB | 6'1" | 222 | 24 | | |
| Steve Foley | DB | 6'2" | 190 | 26 | 4 | |
| Mike Harden | DB | 6' | 188 | 22 | | |
| Maurice Harvey | DB | 5'10" | 190 | 24 | 1 | |
| Bernard Jackson (to SD) | DB | 6' | 180 | 30 | 1 | |
| Aaron Kyle | DB | 5'11" | 185 | 26 | | |
| Perry Smith | DB | 6'1" | 190 | 29 | 2 | |
| Bill Thompson | DB | 6'1" | 197 | 33 | 2 | 6 |
| Louis Wright | DB | 6'2" | 200 | 27 | | |
| Larry Canada – Knee Injury | | | | | | |
| Bob Swenson – Broken Arm | | | | | | |

| Use Name | Pos. | Hgt. | Wgt. | Age | Int. | Pts. |
|---|---|---|---|---|---|---|
| Jeff Knapple | QB | 6'2" | 200 | 24 | | |
| Craig Morton | QB | 6'4" | 211 | 37 | | 6 |
| Matt Robinson | QB | 6'2" | 196 | 25 | | 18 |
| Otis Armstrong | HB | 5'10" | 196 | 29 | | 24 |
| Rob Lytle | HB-FB | 6'1" | 195 | 25 | | 6 |
| Ben Norman | HB | 6' | 212 | 25 | | |
| Dave Preston | HB | 5'10" | 195 | 25 | | 24 |
| Jim Jensen | FB | 6'3" | 230 | 26 | | 18 |
| Jon Keyworth | FB | 6'3" | 230 | 29 | | 6 |
| Larry Brunson | WR | 5'11" | 180 | 31 | | |
| Emery Moorehead | WR | 6'2" | 210 | 26 | | |
| Haven Moses | WR | 6'3" | 201 | 34 | | 24 |
| Rick Upchurch | WR | 5'10" | 176 | 28 | | 18 |
| Steve Watson | WR | 6'4" | 192 | 23 | | |
| Ron Egloff | TE | 6'5" | 227 | 24 | | |
| Riley Odoms | TE | 6'4" | 230 | 30 | | 36 |
| James Wright | TE | 6'3" | 240 | 24 | | |
| Luke Prestridge | K | 6'4" | 235 | 23 | | |
| Fred Steinfort | K | 5'11" | 180 | 26 | | 110 |

### SEATTLE SEAHAWKS 4-12-0 Jack Patera

| Scores of Each Game | | |
|---|---|---|
| 13 | SAN DIEGO | 34 |
| 17 | Kansas City | 16 |
| 31 | NEW ENGLAND | 37 |
| 14 | Washington | 0 |
| 26 | Houston | 7 |
| 3 | CLEVELAND | 27 |
| 27 | N.Y. Jets | 17 |
| 14 | Oakland | 33 |
| 20 | PHILADELPHIA | 27 |
| 30 | KANSAS CITY | 31 |
| 17 | OAKLAND | 19 |
| 20 | Denver | 36 |
| 7 | Dallas | 51 |
| 21 | N.Y. GIANTS | 27 |
| 14 | San Diego | 21 |
| 17 | DENVER | 25 |

| Use Name | Pos. | Hgt. | Wgt. | Age | Int. | Pts. |
|---|---|---|---|---|---|---|
| Steve August | OT | 6'5" | 254 | 25 | | |
| Louis Bullard | OT | 6'6" | 265 | 24 | | |
| Ron Essink | OT-TE | 6'6" | 246 | 22 | | 6 |
| Andre Hines | OT | 6'6" | 275 | 22 | | |
| Tom Lynch | OG | 6'5" | 260 | 25 | | |
| Bob Newton | OG | 6'4" | 260 | 31 | | |
| Jeff Sevy | OG | 6'5" | 260 | 29 | | |
| Art Kuehn | C | 6'3" | 255 | 27 | | |
| John Yarno | C | 6'5" | 251 | 25 | | |
| Fred Anderson | DE | 6'4" | 235 | 25 | | |
| Mark Bell | DE | 6'4" | 240 | 23 | | |
| Terry Dion | DE | 6'6" | 254 | 22 | | |
| Jacob Green | DE | 6'3" | 247 | 23 | | |
| Bill Gregory | DE | 6'5" | 260 | 30 | | |
| Bill Cooke | DT | 6'5" | 250 | 29 | | |
| Robert Hardy | DT | 6'2" | 250 | 24 | | |
| Manu Tuiasosopo | DT | 6'3" | 252 | 23 | | |

| Use Name | Pos. | Hgt. | Wgt. | Age | Int. | Pts. |
|---|---|---|---|---|---|---|
| Terry Beeson | LB | 6'3" | 240 | 24 | | |
| Keith Butler | LB | 6'4" | 225 | 24 | 2 | |
| Michael Jackson | LB | 6'1" | 220 | 23 | 2 | |
| Joe Norman | LB | 6'1" | 220 | 23 | 1 | |
| Terry Rennaker | LB | 6'6" | 225 | 22 | | |
| Tim Walker | LB | 6'1" | 230 | 22 | | |
| Dave Brown | DB | 6'1" | 190 | 27 | 6 | |
| Don Dufek | DB | 6' | 195 | 26 | | |
| John Harris | DB | 6'2" | 200 | 24 | 6 | |
| Kerry Justin | DB | 5'11" | 175 | 25 | 1 | |
| Will Lewis | DB | 5'9" | 185 | 22 | | 6 |
| Vic Minor | DB | 6' | 198 | 21 | 1 | |
| Keith Simpson | DB | 6'1" | 195 | 24 | 3 | |
| Cornell Webster | DB | 6' | 180 | 25 | 1 | |
| Dennis Boyd – Broken Arm | | | | | | |
| Pete Cronan – Neck Injury | | | | | | |
| Steve Myer – Back Injury | | | | | | |
| Brian Peets – Broken Leg | | | | | | |

| Use Name | Pos. | Hgt. | Wgt. | Age | Int. | Pts. |
|---|---|---|---|---|---|---|
| Sam Adkins | QB | 6'2" | 214 | 25 | | |
| Dave Krieg | QB | 6'1" | 185 | 21 | | |
| Jim Zorn | QB | 6'2" | 200 | 27 | | 6 |
| Dan Doornink | HB-FB | 6'3" | 210 | 24 | | 30 |
| Al Hunter | HB | 5'11" | 195 | 25 | | |
| Lawrence McCutcheon (from DEN) | HB-FB | 6'1" | 205 | 30 | | 24 |
| Jeff Moore | HB | 6' | 195 | 24 | | |
| Sherman Smith | HB | 6'4" | 225 | 25 | | 6 |
| Larry Brinson | FB | 6' | 214 | 26 | | 6 |
| Jim Jodat | FB | 5'11" | 213 | 26 | | 36 |
| Jim Walsh | FB | 5'11" | 220 | 23 | | |
| Jessie Green | WR | 6'3" | 194 | 26 | | 6 |
| Steve Largent | WR | 5'11" | 184 | 25 | | 36 |
| Sam McCullum | WR | 6'2" | 190 | 27 | | 36 |
| Steve Raible | WR | 6'2" | 195 | 26 | | |
| Mark Bell | TE | 6'4" | 235 | 23 | | |
| John Sawyer | TE | 6'2" | 230 | 27 | | |
| Effren Herrera | K | 5'9" | 190 | 29 | | 93 |
| Herman Weaver | K | 6'4" | 210 | 31 | | |

*—Overtime

## SAN DIEGO CHARGERS

### Rushing

| Last Name | No. | Yds. | Avg. | TD |
|---|---|---|---|---|
| Muncie | 175 | 827 | 4.7 | 6 |
| Thomas | 118 | 484 | 4.1 | 3 |
| Cappelletti | 101 | 364 | 3.6 | 5 |
| C. Williams | 97 | 258 | 2.7 | 3 |
| Russell | 8 | 41 | 5.1 | 0 |
| Bauer | 10 | 34 | 3.4 | 1 |
| Jefferson | 1 | 16 | 16.0 | 0 |
| Fouts | 23 | 15 | 0.7 | 2 |
| Luther | 3 | 5 | 1.7 | 0 |
| Fuller | 2 | 0 | 0.0 | 0 |
| Partridge | 3 | 0 | 0.0 | 0 |
| Harrington | 4 | −7 | −1.8 | 0 |

### Receiving

| Last Name | No. | Yds. | Avg. | TD |
|---|---|---|---|---|
| Winslow | 89 | 1290 | 15 | 9 |
| Jefferson | 82 | 1340 | 16 | 13 |
| Joiner | 71 | 1132 | 16 | 4 |
| Muncie | 31 | 259 | 8 | 0 |
| Thomas | 29 | 218 | 8 | 0 |
| C. Williams | 26 | 230 | 9 | 1 |
| Cappelletti | 13 | 112 | 9 | 0 |
| McCrary | 11 | 106 | 10 | 2 |
| Smith | 4 | 48 | 12 | 0 |
| Floyd | 1 | 31 | 31 | 1 |

### Punt Returns

| Last Name | No. | Yds. | Avg. | TD |
|---|---|---|---|---|
| Fuller | 30 | 298 | 10 | 0 |
| Shaw | 5 | 20 | 4 | 0 |
| Edwards | 4 | 17 | 4 | 0 |
| Floyd | 1 | 0 | 0 | 0 |
| Horn | 1 | 0 | 0 | 0 |

### Kickoff Returns

| Last Name | No. | Yds. | Avg. | TD |
|---|---|---|---|---|
| Muncie | 16 | 344 | 22 | 0 |
| Fuller | 15 | 289 | 19 | 0 |
| Smith | 10 | 186 | 19 | 0 |
| Duncan | 5 | 85 | 17 | 0 |
| Bauer | 2 | 37 | 19 | 0 |
| Laslavac | 2 | 26 | 13 | 0 |
| Russell | 1 | 19 | 19 | 0 |
| Cappelletti | 1 | 0 | 0 | 0 |
| Jefferson | 1 | 0 | 0 | 0 |

### Passing – Punting – Kicking

| PASSING | Att. | Comp. | % | Yds. | Yd./Att. | TD | Int.–% | RK |
|---|---|---|---|---|---|---|---|---|
| Fouts | 589 | 348 | 59 | 4715 | 8.0 | 30 | 24– 4 | 2 |
| Luther | 3 | 2 | 67 | 26 | 8.7 | 0 | 1– 33 | |
| Thomas | 2 | 0 | 0 | 0 | 0 | 0 | 1– 50 | |

| PUNTING | No. | Avg. |
|---|---|---|
| Partridge | 60 | 39.1 |

| KICKING | XP | Att. | % | FG | Att. | % |
|---|---|---|---|---|---|---|
| Benirschke | 46 | 48 | 96 | 24 | 36 | 67 |

## OAKLAND RAIDERS

### Rushing

| Last Name | No. | Yds. | Avg. | TD |
|---|---|---|---|---|
| van Eeghen | 222 | 838 | 3.8 | 5 |
| King | 172 | 761 | 4.4 | 4 |
| Whittington | 91 | 299 | 3.3 | 3 |
| Plunkett | 28 | 141 | 5.0 | 2 |
| Guy | 3 | 38 | 12.7 | 0 |
| Jensen | 14 | 30 | 2.1 | 0 |
| Pastorini | 4 | 24 | 6.0 | 0 |
| Matthews | 5 | 11 | 2.2 | 0 |
| Wilson | 1 | 3 | 3.0 | 0 |
| Branch | 1 | 1 | 1.0 | 0 |

### Receiving

| Last Name | No. | Yds. | Avg. | TD |
|---|---|---|---|---|
| Chandler | 49 | 786 | 16 | 10 |
| Branch | 44 | 858 | 20 | 7 |
| van Eeghen | 29 | 259 | 9 | 0 |
| Chester | 28 | 366 | 13 | 4 |
| King | 22 | 145 | 7 | 0 |
| Whittington | 19 | 205 | 11 | 0 |
| Jensen | 7 | 87 | 12 | 0 |
| Bradshaw | 6 | 132 | 22 | 1 |
| Ramsey | 5 | 117 | 23 | 0 |
| Matthews | 3 | 33 | 11 | 0 |
| Martini | 1 | 36 | 36 | 0 |

### Punt Returns

| Last Name | No. | Yds. | Avg. | TD |
|---|---|---|---|---|
| Matthews | 48 | 421 | 9 | 0 |
| McKinney | 1 | 0 | 0 | 0 |

### Kickoff Returns

| Last Name | No. | Yds. | Avg. | TD |
|---|---|---|---|---|
| Matthews | 29 | 585 | 20 | 0 |
| Whittington | 21 | 392 | 19 | 1 |
| Moody | 8 | 150 | 19 | 0 |
| Jensen | 1 | 33 | 33 | 1 |
| Christensen | 1 | 10 | 10 | 0 |
| Ramsey | 1 | 10 | 10 | 0 |
| Hayes | 1 | 0 | 0 | 0 |

### Passing – Punting – Kicking

| PASSING | Att. | Comp. | % | Yds. | Yd./Att. | TD | Int.–% | RK |
|---|---|---|---|---|---|---|---|---|
| Plunkett | 320 | 165 | 52 | 2299 | 7.2 | 18 | 16– 5 | 9 |
| Pastorini | 130 | 66 | 51 | 932 | 7.2 | 5 | 8– 6 | |
| Guy | 1 | 1 | 100 | 32 | 32.0 | 0 | 0– 0 | |
| Wilson | 5 | 3 | 60 | 31 | 6.2 | 0 | 0– 0 | |

| PUNTING | No. | Avg. |
|---|---|---|
| Guy | 71 | 43.6 |

| KICKING | XP | Att. | % | FG | Att. | % |
|---|---|---|---|---|---|---|
| Bahr | 41 | 44 | 93 | 19 | 37 | 51 |

## KANSAS CITY CHIEFS

### Rushing

| Last Name | No. | Yds. | Avg. | TD |
|---|---|---|---|---|
| McKnight | 206 | 693 | 3.4 | 3 |
| Fuller | 60 | 274 | 4.6 | 4 |
| Belton | 68 | 273 | 4.0 | 2 |
| Hadnot | 76 | 244 | 3.2 | 2 |
| Reed | 68 | 180 | 2.6 | 0 |
| Morgado | 47 | 120 | 2.6 | 4 |
| Carson | 2 | 41 | 20.5 | 0 |
| Gant | 9 | 32 | 3.6 | 0 |
| Marshall | 3 | 22 | 7.3 | 0 |
| Kenney | 8 | 8 | 1.0 | 0 |
| Clements | 2 | 0 | 0.0 | 0 |
| Grupp | 3 | −14 | −4.7 | 0 |

### Receiving

| Last Name | No. | Yds. | Avg. | TD |
|---|---|---|---|---|
| Marshall | 47 | 799 | 17 | 6 |
| J. Smith | 46 | 655 | 14 | 2 |
| Reed | 44 | 422 | 10 | 1 |
| McKnight | 38 | 320 | 8 | 0 |
| Hadnot | 15 | 97 | 7 | 0 |
| Gant | 9 | 68 | 8 | 0 |
| Samuels | 8 | 110 | 14 | 2 |
| Dixon | 7 | 115 | 16 | 1 |
| Belton | 5 | 94 | 19 | 0 |
| Carson | 5 | 68 | 14 | 0 |
| Morgado | 5 | 27 | 5 | 1 |
| Rome | 3 | 58 | 19 | 0 |
| Garcia | 3 | 27 | 9 | 1 |
| Williams | 2 | 9 | 5 | 1 |

### Punt Returns

| Last Name | No. | Yds. | Avg. | TD |
|---|---|---|---|---|
| J. Smith | 40 | 581 | 15 | 2 |

### Kickoff Returns

| Last Name | No. | Yds. | Avg. | TD |
|---|---|---|---|---|
| Carson | 40 | 917 | 23 | 0 |
| Belton | 6 | 110 | 18 | 0 |
| Williams | 4 | 79 | 20 | 0 |
| Gant | 3 | 44 | 15 | 0 |
| Beckman | 3 | 38 | 13 | 0 |
| Budde | 3 | 28 | 9 | 0 |
| Morgado | 2 | 33 | 17 | 0 |
| Samuels | 1 | 10 | 10 | 0 |
| Dixon | 1 | 0 | 0 | 0 |

### Passing – Punting – Kicking

| PASSING | Att. | Comp. | % | Yds. | Yd./Att. | TD | Int.–% | RK |
|---|---|---|---|---|---|---|---|---|
| Fuller | 320 | 193 | 60 | 2250 | 7.0 | 10 | 12– 4 | 4 |
| Kenney | 69 | 37 | 54 | 542 | 7.9 | 5 | 2– 3 | |
| Clements | 12 | 7 | 58 | 77 | 6.4 | 0 | 0– 0 | |

| PUNTING | No. | Avg. |
|---|---|---|
| Grupp | 84 | 39.5 |

| KICKING | XP | Att. | % | FG | Att. | % |
|---|---|---|---|---|---|---|
| Lowery | 37 | 37 | 100 | 20 | 26 | 77 |

## DENVER BRONCOS

### Rushing

| Last Name | No. | Yds. | Avg. | TD |
|---|---|---|---|---|
| Jensen | 101 | 476 | 4.7 | 2 |
| Armstrong | 106 | 470 | 4.4 | 3 |
| Preston | 111 | 385 | 3.5 | 4 |
| Lytle | 57 | 223 | 3.9 | 1 |
| Keyworth | 38 | 127 | 3.3 | 1 |
| Upchurch | 5 | 49 | 9.8 | 0 |
| Robinson | 21 | 47 | 2.2 | 3 |
| Morton | 21 | 29 | 1.4 | 1 |
| Moorehead | 2 | 7 | 3.5 | 0 |
| Knapple | 6 | 0 | 0.0 | 0 |

### Receiving

| Last Name | No. | Yds. | Avg. | TD |
|---|---|---|---|---|
| Jensen | 49 | 377 | 8 | 1 |
| Upchurch | 46 | 605 | 13 | 3 |
| Odoms | 39 | 590 | 15 | 6 |
| Moses | 38 | 674 | 18 | 4 |
| Preston | 35 | 309 | 9 | 0 |
| Lytle | 18 | 177 | 10 | 0 |
| Keyworth | 15 | 87 | 6 | 0 |
| Armstrong | 7 | 23 | 3 | 0 |
| Watson | 6 | 146 | 24 | 0 |
| Egloff | 6 | 85 | 14 | 0 |
| Brunson | 1 | 15 | 15 | 0 |

### Punt Returns

| Last Name | No. | Yds. | Avg. | TD |
|---|---|---|---|---|
| Upchurch | 37 | 353 | 10 | 0 |
| Harden | 2 | 36 | 18 | 0 |
| Brunson | 2 | 12 | 6 | 0 |
| Preston | 1 | 7 | 7 | 0 |

### Kickoff Returns

| Last Name | No. | Yds. | Avg. | TD |
|---|---|---|---|---|
| Brunson | 40 | 923 | 23 | 0 |
| Harden | 12 | 214 | 18 | 0 |
| B. Jackson | 9 | 149 | 17 | 0 |
| Preston | 5 | 106 | 21 | 0 |
| Lytle | 1 | 19 | 19 | 0 |
| Moorehead | 1 | 18 | 18 | 0 |
| Jensen | 1 | 5 | 5 | 0 |
| Watson | 1 | 5 | 5 | 0 |
| Ryan | 1 | 0 | 0 | 0 |

### Passing – Punting – Kicking

| PASSING | Att. | Comp. | % | Yds. | Yd./Att. | TD | Int.–% | RK |
|---|---|---|---|---|---|---|---|---|
| Morton | 301 | 183 | 61 | 2150 | 7.1 | 12 | 13– 4 | 3 |
| Robinson | 162 | 78 | 48 | 942 | 5.8 | 2 | 12– 7 | |
| Knapple | 4 | 1 | 25 | 15 | 3.8 | 0 | 0– 0 | |

| PUNTING | No. | Avg. |
|---|---|---|
| Prestridge | 70 | 43.9 |

| KICKING | XP | Att. | % | FG | Att. | % |
|---|---|---|---|---|---|---|
| Steinfort | 32 | 33 | 97 | 26 | 34 | 77 |

## SEATTLE SEAHAWKS

### Rushing

| Last Name | No. | Yds. | Avg. | TD |
|---|---|---|---|---|
| Jodat | 155 | 632 | 4.1 | 5 |
| Doornink | 100 | 344 | 3.4 | 3 |
| McCutcheon | 52 | 254 | 4.9 | 3 |
| Zorn | 44 | 214 | 4.9 | 1 |
| Moore | 60 | 202 | 3.4 | 0 |
| Smith | 23 | 94 | 4.1 | 0 |
| Brinson | 16 | 57 | 3.6 | 1 |
| Adkins | 6 | 18 | 3.0 | 0 |
| Hunter | 9 | 14 | 1.6 | 0 |
| Walsh | 2 | 4 | 2.0 | 0 |
| Largent | 1 | 2 | 2.0 | 0 |

### Receiving

| Last Name | No. | Yds. | Avg. | TD |
|---|---|---|---|---|
| Largent | 66 | 1064 | 16 | 6 |
| McCullum | 62 | 874 | 14 | 6 |
| Sawyer | 36 | 410 | 11 | 0 |
| Doornink | 31 | 237 | 8 | 2 |
| Jodat | 26 | 190 | 7 | 1 |
| Moore | 25 | 231 | 9 | 0 |
| Raible | 16 | 232 | 15 | 0 |
| McCutcheon | 9 | 76 | 8 | 1 |
| Smith | 6 | 72 | 12 | 1 |
| Je. Green | 4 | 47 | 12 | 0 |
| Hunter | 3 | 40 | 13 | 0 |
| Bell | 1 | 13 | 13 | 0 |
| Brinson | 1 | 9 | 9 | 0 |
| Herrera | 1 | 9 | 9 | 0 |
| Essink | 1 | 2 | 2 | 1 |

### Punt Returns

| Last Name | No. | Yds. | Avg. | TD |
|---|---|---|---|---|
| Lewis | 41 | 349 | 9 | 1 |

### Kickoff Returns

| Last Name | No. | Yds. | Avg. | TD |
|---|---|---|---|---|
| Lewis | 25 | 585 | 23 | 0 |
| Webster | 21 | 406 | 19 | 0 |
| Je. Green | 15 | 274 | 18 | 0 |
| Hunter | 11 | 213 | 19 | 0 |
| Moore | 1 | 11 | 11 | 0 |

### Passing – Punting – Kicking

| PASSING | Att. | Comp. | % | Yds. | Yd./Att. | TD | Int.–% | RK |
|---|---|---|---|---|---|---|---|---|
| Zorn | 488 | 276 | 57 | 3346 | 6.9 | 17 | 20– 4 | 10 |
| Adkins | 23 | .10 | 44 | 136 | 5.9 | 1 | 3– 13 | |
| Krieg | 2 | | | | | | | |
| McCutcheon | 2 | 1 | 50 | 12 | 6.0 | 0 | 0– 0 | |
| Weaver | 2 | 0 | 0 | 0 | 0.0 | 0 | 0– 0 | |

| PUNTING | No. | Avg. |
|---|---|---|
| Weaver | 67 | 41.8 |
| Herrera | 1 | 29.0 |

| KICKING | XP | Att. | % | FG | Att. | % |
|---|---|---|---|---|---|---|
| Herrera | 33 | 33 | 100 | 20 | 31 | 65 |

## December 28 at Irving, Tex. (Attendance 64,533)

### SCORING

|  | 1 | 2 | 3 | 4 | T |
|---|---|---|---|---|---|
| LOS ANGELES | 6 | 7 | 0 | 0 | 13 |
| DALLAS | 3 | 10 | 14 | 7 | 34 |

**First Quarter**
Dal. — Septien 28 yard field goal
L.A. — Thomas, 1 yard run
PAT–Kick failed

**Second Quarter**
Dal. — Septien, 29 yard field goal
L.A. — Dennard, 21 yard pass from Ferragamo
PAT–Corral (kick)
Dal. — Dorsett, 12 yard rush
PAT–Septien (kick)

**Third Quarter**
Dal. — Dorsett, 10 yard pass from D. White
PAT–Septien (kick)
Dal. — B. Johnson, 35 yard pass from D. White
PAT–Septien (kick)

**Fourth Quarter**
Dal. — D. Pearson, 11 yard pass from D. White
PAT–Septien (kick)

### TEAM STATISTICS

| L.A. |  | DAL. |
|---|---|---|
| 15 | First Downs-Total | 29 |
| 6 | First Downs-Rushing | 19 |
| 7 | First Downs-Passing | 9 |
| 2 | First Downs-Penalty | 1 |
| 1 | Fumbles-Number | 2 |
| 0 | Fumbles-Lost Ball | 0 |
| 5 | Penalties-Number | 11 |
| 50 | Yards Penalized | 79 |
| 0 | Missed Field Goals | 0 |
| 55 | Offensive Plays | 71 |
| 260 | Net Yards | 528 |
| 4.7 | Average Gain | 7.4 |
| 3 | Giveaways | 3 |
| 3 | Takeaways | 3 |
| 0 | Difference | 0 |

### INDIVIDUAL STATISTICS

**LOS ANGELES — DALLAS**

#### RUSHING

| Player | No. | Yds. | Avg. | Player | No. | Yds. | Avg. |
|---|---|---|---|---|---|---|---|
| J. Thomas | 14 | 48 | 3.4 | Dorsett | 22 | 160 | 7.3 |
| Bryant | 10 | 44 | 4.4 | Springs | 4 | 58 | 14.5 |
|  | 24 | 92 | 3.8 | Newhouse | 11 | 46 | 4.2 |
|  |  |  |  | J. Jones | 5 | 38 | 7.6 |
|  |  |  |  | Newsome | 2 | 34 | 17.0 |
|  |  |  |  | D. White | 2 | 2 | 1.0 |
|  |  |  |  |  | 46 | 338 | 7.3 |

#### RECEIVING

| Player | No. | Yds. | Avg. | Player | No. | Yds. | Avg. |
|---|---|---|---|---|---|---|---|
| Dennard | 6 | 117 | 19.5 | D. Pearson | 4 | 60 | 15.0 |
| J. Thomas | 3 | 26 | 8.7 | Dorsett | 3 | 28 | 9.3 |
| Bryant | 2 | 7 | 3.5 | Saldi | 2 | 52 | 26.0 |
| Nelson | 1 | 12 | 12.0 | B. Johnson | 1 | 35 | 35.0 |
| Waddy | 1 | 9 | 9.0 | Hill | 1 | 8 | 8.0 |
| Guman | 1 | 5 | 5.0 | DuPree | 1 | 7 | 7.0 |
|  | 14 | 176 | 12.4 |  | 12 | 190 | 15.8 |

#### PUNTING

| Player | No. | Avg. | Player | No. | Avg. |
|---|---|---|---|---|---|
| Corral | 6 | 39.3 | D. White | 2 | 44.5 |

#### PUNT RETURNS

| Player | No. | Yds. | Avg. | Player | No. | Yds. | Avg. |
|---|---|---|---|---|---|---|---|
| Irvin | 1 | 2 | 2.0 | J. Jones | 5 | 81 | 16.2 |

#### KICKOFF RETURNS

| Player | No. | Yds. | Avg. | Player | No. | Yds. | Avg. |
|---|---|---|---|---|---|---|---|
| D. Hill | 5 | 110 | 22.0 | J. Jones | 3 | 72 | 24.0 |
| L. Smith | 1 | 10 | 10.0 |  |  |  |  |
|  | 6 | 120 | 20.0 |  |  |  |  |

#### INTERCEPTION RETURNS

| Player | No. | Yds. | Avg. | Player | No. | Yds. | Avg. |
|---|---|---|---|---|---|---|---|
| Cromwell | 1 | 44 | 44.0 | Mitchell | 1 | 12 | 12.0 |
| L. Smith | 1 | 7 | 7.0 | Wilson | 1 | 8 | 8.0 |
| Irvin | 1 | 0 | 0.0 | Clinkscale | 1 | 2 | 2.0 |
|  | 3 | 51 | 17.0 |  | 3 | 22 | 7.3 |

#### PASSING

**LOS ANGELES**

| Player | Att. | Comp. | Comp. Pct. | Yds. | Int. | Yds./Att. | Yds./Comp. |
|---|---|---|---|---|---|---|---|
| Ferragamo | 30 | 14 | 47.3 | 176 | 3 | 5.9 | 12.4 |

**DALLAS**

| Player | Att. | Comp. | Comp. Pct. | Yds. | Int. | Yds./Att. | Yds./Comp. |
|---|---|---|---|---|---|---|---|
| D. White | 25 | 12 | 48.0 | 190 | 3 | 7.6 | 15.8 |

---

## January 3, 1981 at Philadelphia (Attendance 68,434)

### SCORING

|  | 1 | 2 | 3 | 4 | T |
|---|---|---|---|---|---|
| MINNESOTA | 7 | 7 | 2 | 0 | 16 |
| PHILADELPHIA | 0 | 7 | 14 | 10 | 31 |

**First Quarter**
Min. — S. White, 30 yard pass from Kramer
PAT–Danmeier (kick)

**Second Quarter**
Min. — Brown, 1 yard rush
PAT–Danmeier (kick)
Phila. — Carmichael, 9 yard pass from Jaworski
PAT–Franklin (kick)

**Third Quarter**
Phi. — Montgomery, 8 yard rush
PAT–Franklin (kick)
Min. — Safety, Jaworski tackled in end zone
Phi. — Montgomery, 5 yard rush
PAT–Franklin (kick)

**Fourth Quarter**
Phi. — Franklin, 33 yard field goal
Phi. — Harrington, 2 yard rush
PAT–Franklin (kick)

### TEAM STATISTICS

| MIN. |  | PHI. |
|---|---|---|
| 14 | First Downs-Total | 24 |
| 3 | First Downs-Rushing | 12 |
| 10 | First Downs-Passing | 12 |
| 1 | First Downs-Penalty | 0 |
| 3 | Fumbles-Number | 1 |
| 3 | Fumbles-Lost Ball | 1 |
| 5 | Penalties-Number | 4 |
| 27 | Yards Penalized | 30 |
| 0 | Missed Field Goals | 1 |
| 55 | Offensive Plays | 82 |
| 215 | Net Yards | 305 |
| 3.9 | Average Gain | 3.7 |
| 8 | Giveaways | 3 |
| 3 | Takeaways | 8 |
| −5 | Difference | +5 |

### INDIVIDUAL STATISTICS

**MINNESOTA — PHILADELPHIA**

#### RUSHING

| Player | No. | Yds. | Avg. | Player | No. | Yds. | Avg. |
|---|---|---|---|---|---|---|---|
| Paschal | 4 | 26 | 6.5 | Montgomery | 26 | 74 | 2.8 |
| Brown | 5 | 14 | 2.8 | Harris | 7 | 27 | 3.9 |
| R. Miller | 1 | 2 | 2.0 | Parker | 1 | 12 | 12.0 |
| Young | 2 | 0 | 0.0 | Giammona | 7 | 11 | 1.6 |
| S. White | 1 | −6 | −6.0 | Harrington | 1 | 2 | 2.0 |
|  | 13 | 36 | 2.8 |  | 42 | 126 | 3.0 |

#### RECEIVING

| Player | No. | Yds. | Avg. | Player | No. | Yds. | Avg. |
|---|---|---|---|---|---|---|---|
| Young | 6 | 57 | 9.5 | Carmichael | 7 | 84 | 12.0 |
| Brown | 4 | 25 | 6.3 | Krepfle | 2 | 27 | 13.5 |
| Senser | 4 | 25 | 6.3 | Montgomery | 2 | 26 | 13.0 |
| S. White | 2 | 52 | 26.0 | Campfield | 2 | 21 | 10.5 |
| Rashad | 1 | 23 | 23.0 | Fitzkee | 2 | 19 | 9.5 |
| Paschal | 1 | 19 | 19.0 | Harris | 2 | 13 | 6.5 |
| Bruer | 1 | 8 | 8.0 |  | 17 | 190 | 11.2 |
|  | 19 | 209 | 11.0 |  |  |  |  |

#### PUNTING

| Player | No. | Avg. | Player | No. | Avg. |
|---|---|---|---|---|---|
| Coleman | 5 | 40.0 | Runager | 4 | 33.8 |

#### PUNT RETURNS

| Player | No. | Yds. | Avg. | Player | No. | Yds. | Avg. |
|---|---|---|---|---|---|---|---|
| Payton | 2 | 18 | 9.0 | Giammona | 3 | 21 | 7.0 |

#### KICKOFF RETURNS

| Player | No. | Yds. | Avg. | Player | No. | Yds. | Avg. |
|---|---|---|---|---|---|---|---|
| Payton | 6 | 102 | 17.0 | Campfield | 3 | 55 | 18.3 |
| Huffman | 1 | 15 | 15.0 |  |  |  |  |
|  | 7 | 117 | 16.7 |  |  |  |  |

#### INTERCEPTION RETURNS

| Player | No. | Yds. | Avg. | Player | No. | Yds. | Avg. |
|---|---|---|---|---|---|---|---|
| Hannon | 1 | 0 | 0.0 | Edwards | 2 | 15 | 7.5 |
| Turner | 1 | 0 | 0.0 | Young | 2 | 0 | 0.0 |
|  |  |  |  | LeMaster | 1 | 7 | 7.0 |
|  |  |  |  |  | 5 | 22 | 4.4 |

#### PASSING

**MINNESOTA**

| Player | Att. | Comp. | Comp. Pct. | Yds. | Int. | Yds./Att. | Yds./Comp. |
|---|---|---|---|---|---|---|---|
| Kramer | 39 | 19 | 48.7 | 209 | 5 | 5.4 | 11.0 |

**PHILADELPHIA**

| Player | Att. | Comp. | Comp. Pct. | Yds. | Int. | Yds./Att. | Yds./Comp. |
|---|---|---|---|---|---|---|---|
| Jaworski | 38 | 17 | 44.7 | 190 | 2 | 5.0 | 11.2 |

---

## January 4, 1981 at Atlanta (Attendance 60,022)

### SCORING

|  | 1 | 2 | 3 | 4 | T |
|---|---|---|---|---|---|
| DALLAS | 3 | 7 | 0 | 20 | 30 |
| ATLANTA | 10 | 7 | 7 | 3 | 27 |

**First Quarter**
Atl. — Mazzetti, 38 yard field goal
Atl. — Jenkins, 60 yard pass from Bartkowski
PAT–Mazzetti (kick)
Dal. — Septien, 38 yard field goal

**Second Quarter**
Dal. — DuPree, 5 yard pass from D. White
PAT–Septien (kick)
Atl. — Cain, 1 yard rush
PAT–Mazzetti (kick)

**Third Quarter**
Atl. — Andrews, 12 yard pass from Bartkowski
PAT–Mazzetti (kick)

**Fourth Quarter**
Dal. — Newhouse, 1 yard rush
PAT–Septien (kick)
Atl. — Mazzetti, 34 yard field goal
Dal. — D. Pearson, 14 yard pass from D. White
PAT–Septien (kick)
Dal. — D. Pearson, 23 yard pass from D. White
PAT–pass failed

### TEAM STATISTICS

| DAL. |  | ATL. |
|---|---|---|
| 22 | First Downs-Total | 18 |
| 5 | First Downs-Rushing | 6 |
| 16 | First Downs-Passing | 11 |
| 1 | First Downs-Penalty | 1 |
| 4 | Fumbles-Number | 1 |
| 1 | Fumbles-Lost Ball | 1 |
| 6 | Penalties-Number | 4 |
| 72 | Yards Penalized | 48 |
| 0 | Missed Field Goals | 0 |
| 65 | Offensive Plays | 64 |
| 422 | Net Yards | 349 |
| 6.5 | Average Gain | 5.5 |
| 2 | Giveaways | 2 |
| 2 | Takeaways | 2 |
| 0 | Difference | 0 |

### INDIVIDUAL STATISTICS

**DALLAS — ATLANTA**

#### RUSHING

| Player | No. | Yds. | Avg. | Player | No. | Yds. | Avg. |
|---|---|---|---|---|---|---|---|
| Dorsett | 10 | 51 | 5.1 | Andrews | 14 | 43 | 3.1 |
| Newhouse | 6 | 31 | 5.2 | Cain | 13 | 43 | 3.3 |
| P. Pearson | 1 | 11 | 11.0 |  | 27 | 86 | 3.2 |
| D. Pearson | 1 | 9 | 9.0 |  |  |  |  |
| DuPree | 1 | 5 | 5.0 |  |  |  |  |
| Newsome | 1 | 4 | 4.0 |  |  |  |  |
| D. White | 4 | 1 | 0.3 |  |  |  |  |
|  | 24 | 112 | 4.7 |  |  |  |  |

#### RECEIVING

| Player | No. | Yds. | Avg. | Player | No. | Yds. | Avg. |
|---|---|---|---|---|---|---|---|
| D. Pearson | 5 | 90 | 18.0 | Francis | 6 | 66 | 11.0 |
| Dorsett | 5 | 40 | 8.0 | Jenkins | 4 | 155 | 38.8 |
| Hill | 4 | 53 | 13.3 | Miller | 3 | 48 | 16.0 |
| P. Pearson | 4 | 51 | 12.8 | Cain | 2 | 20 | 10.0 |
| Springs | 3 | 39 | 13.0 | Andrews | 2 | 19 | 9.5 |
| DuPree | 3 | 29 | 9.7 | Jackson | 1 | 12 | 12.0 |
| Johnson | 1 | 20 | 20.0 |  | 18 | 320 | 17.8 |
|  | 25 | 322 | 12.9 |  |  |  |  |

#### PUNTING

| Player | No. | Avg. | Player | No. | Avg. |
|---|---|---|---|---|---|
| D. White | 4 | 38.8 | James | 4 | 36.0 |

#### PUNT RETURNS

| Player | No. | Yds. | Avg. | Player | No. | Yds. | Avg. |
|---|---|---|---|---|---|---|---|
| J. Jones | 2 | −4 | −2.0 | Johnson | 3 | 8 | 2.7 |

#### KICKOFF RETURNS

| Player | No. | Yds. | Avg. | Player | No. | Yds. | Avg. |
|---|---|---|---|---|---|---|---|
| J. Jones | 3 | 58 | 19.3 | M. Smith | 5 | 108 | 21.6 |
| Newsome | 3 | 46 | 15.3 |  |  |  |  |
|  | 6 | 104 | 17.3 |  |  |  |  |

#### INTERCEPTION RETURNS

| Player | No. | Yds. | Avg. | Player | No. | Yds. | Avg. |
|---|---|---|---|---|---|---|---|
| Wilson | 1 | 6 | 6.0 | Pridemore | 1 | 22 | 22.0 |

#### PASSING

**DALLAS**

| Player | Att. | Comp. | Comp. Pct. | Yds. | Int. | Yds./Att. | Yds./Comp. |
|---|---|---|---|---|---|---|---|
| D. White | 39 | 25 | 64.1 | 322 | 1 | 8.3 | 12.9 |
| Springs | 1 | 0 | 0.0 | 0 | 0 | 0.0 | 0.0 |
|  | 40 | 25 | 62.5 | 322 | 1 | 8.1 | 12.9 |

**ATLANTA**

| Player | Att. | Comp. | Comp. Pct. | Yds. | Int. | Yds./Att. | Yds./Comp. |
|---|---|---|---|---|---|---|---|
| Barkowski | 33 | 18 | 54.5 | 320 | 1 | 9.7 | 17.8 |

## December 28 at Oakland (Attendance 52,762)

### SCORING

| | | | | | |
|---|---|---|---|---|---|
| HOUSTON | 7 | 0 | 0 | 0– | 7 |
| OAKLAND | 3 | 7 | 0 | 17– | 27 |

**First Quarter**
Oak.   Bahr, 47 yard field goal
Hou.   Campbell, 1 yard rush
          PAT–Fritsch (kick)

**Second Quarter**
Oak.   Christensen, 1 yard pass
          from Plunkett
          PAT–Bahr (kick)

**Fourth Quarter**
Oak.   Whittington, 44 yard pass
          from Plunkett
          PAT–Bahr (kick)
Oak.   Bahr, 37 yard field goal
Oak.   Hayes, 20 yard intercep-
          tion return
          PAT–Bahr (kick)

### TEAM STATISTICS

| HOU. | | OAK. |
|---|---|---|
| 18 | First Downs–Total | 12 |
| 5 | First Downs–Rushing | 4 |
| 11 | First Downs–Passing | 7 |
| 2 | First Downs–Penalty | 1 |
| 1 | Fumbles–Number | 0 |
| 1 | Fumbles–Lost Ball | 0 |
| 8 | Penalties–Number | 14 |
| 64 | Yards Penalized | 91 |
| 2 | Missed Field Goals | 0 |
| 67 | Offensive Plays | 61 |
| 275 | Net Yards | 250 |
| 4.1 | Average Gain | 4.1 |
| 3 | Giveaways | 1 |
| 1 | Takeaways | 3 |
| –2 | Difference | +2 |

### INDIVIDUAL STATISTICS

**HOUSTON** / **OAKLAND**

#### RUSHING

| | No. | Yds. | Avg. | | No. | Yds. | Avg. |
|---|---|---|---|---|---|---|---|
| Campbell | 27 | 91 | 3.4 | King | 13 | 55 | 4.2 |
| Carpenter | 5 | 9 | 1.8 | Van Eeghen | 14 | 46 | 3.3 |
| T. Wilson | 1 | –3 | –3.0 | Whittington | 5 | 11 | 2.5 |
| | 33 | 97 | 2.9 | Jensen | 2 | 0 | 0.0 |
| | | | | Plunkett | 1 | –1 | –1.0 |
| | | | | | 35 | 111 | 3.2 |

#### RECEIVING

| | No. | Yds. | Avg. | | No. | Yds. | Avg. |
|---|---|---|---|---|---|---|---|
| Barber | 4 | 83 | 20.8 | Whittington | 2 | 64 | 32.0 |
| Renfro | 3 | 69 | 23.0 | Chester | 2 | 12 | 6.0 |
| Casper | 3 | 31 | 10.3 | King | 1 | 37 | 37.0 |
| Carpenter | 3 | 26 | 8.7 | Branch | 1 | 33 | 33.0 |
| Coleman | 1 | 23 | 23.0 | van Eeghen | 1 | 21 | 21.0 |
| B. Johnson | 1 | 11 | 11.0 | Christen'n | 1 | 1 | 1.0 |
| | 15 | 243 | 16.2 | | 8 | 168 | 21.0 |

#### PUNTING

| | No. | | Avg. | | No. | | Avg. |
|---|---|---|---|---|---|---|---|
| Parsley | 9 | | 44.0 | Guy | 9 | | 51.1 |

#### PUNT RETURNS

| | No. | Yds. | Avg. | | No. | Yds. | Avg. |
|---|---|---|---|---|---|---|---|
| Roaches | 7 | 84 | 12.0 | Moody | 4 | 27 | 6.8 |
| | | | | Matthews | 2 | 2 | 1.0 |
| | | | | | 6 | 29 | 4.8 |

#### KICKOFF RETURNS

| | No. | Yds. | Avg. | | No. | Yds. | Avg. |
|---|---|---|---|---|---|---|---|
| Coleman | 4 | 70 | 17.5 | Moody | 1 | 33 | 33.0 |
| Roaches | 2 | 48 | 24.0 | Matthews | 1 | 14 | 14.0 |
| | 6 | 118 | 19.7 | | 2 | 47 | 23.5 |

#### INTERCEPTION RETURNS

| | No. | Yds. | Avg. | | No. | Yds. | Avg. |
|---|---|---|---|---|---|---|---|
| Perry | 1 | 0 | 0.0 | Hayes | 2 | 26 | 13.0 |

#### PASSING

| HOUSTON | Att. | Comp. | Comp. Pct. | Yds. | Int. | Yds./ Att. | Yds./ Comp. |
|---|---|---|---|---|---|---|---|
| Stabler | 26 | 15 | 57.7 | 243 | 2 | 9.3 | 16.2 |
| Campbell | 1 | 0 | 0.0 | 0 | 0 | 0.0 | 0.0 |
| | 27 | 15 | 55.6 | 243 | 2 | 9.0 | 16.2 |

| OAKLAND | Att. | Comp. | Comp. Pct. | Yds. | Int. | Yds./ Att. | Yds./ Comp. |
|---|---|---|---|---|---|---|---|
| Plunkett | 23 | 8 | 34.8 | 168 | 1 | 7.3 | 21.0 |

---

## January 3, 1981 at San Diego (Attendance 52,028)

### SCORING

| | | | | | |
|---|---|---|---|---|---|
| BUFFALO | 0 | 14 | 0 | 0– | 14 |
| SAN DIEGO | 3 | 0 | 7 | 10– | 20 |

**First Quarter**
S.D.   Benirschke, 22 yard field
          goal

**Second Quarter**
Buf.   Leaks, 1 yard rush
          PAT–Mike-Mayer (kick)
Buf.   Lewis, 9 yard pass from
          Ferguson
          PAT–Mike-Mayer (kick)

**Third Quarter**
S.D.   Joiner, 9 yard pass from
          Fouts
          PAT–Benirschke (kick)

**Fourth Quarter**
S.D.   Benirschke, 22 yard field
          goal
S.D.   Smith, 50 yard pass from
          Fouts
          PAT–Benirschke (kick)

### TEAM STATISTICS

| BUF. | | S.D. |
|---|---|---|
| 17 | First Downs-Total | 21 |
| 6 | First Downs-Rushing | 6 |
| 9 | First Downs-Passing | 14 |
| 2 | First Downs-Penalty | 1 |
| 0 | Fumbles-Number | 3 |
| 0 | Fumbles-Lost Ball | 2 |
| 5 | Penalties-Number | 6 |
| 40 | Yards Penalized | 66 |
| 2 | Missed Field Goals | 1 |
| 66 | Offensive Plays | 64 |
| 244 | Net Yards | 397 |
| 3.7 | Average Gain | 6.2 |
| 3 | Giveaways | 3 |
| 3 | Takeaways | 3 |
| 0 | Difference | 0 |

### INDIVIDUAL STATISTICS

**BUFFALO** / **SAN DIEGO**

#### RUSHING

| | No. | Yds. | Avg. | | No. | Yds. | Avg. |
|---|---|---|---|---|---|---|---|
| Cribbs | 18 | 53 | 2.9 | Muncie | 18 | 80 | 4.4 |
| Manucci | 2 | 21 | 10.5 | Thomas | 5 | 22 | 4.4 |
| Brown | 9 | 17 | 1.9 | Fouts | 2 | –6 | –3.0 |
| Leaks | 4 | 6 | 1.5 | | 25 | 96 | 3.8 |
| | 33 | 97 | 2.9 | | | | |

#### RECEIVING

| | No. | Yds. | Avg. | | No. | Yds. | Avg. |
|---|---|---|---|---|---|---|---|
| Brammer | 4 | 62 | 15.5 | Jefferson | 7 | 102 | 14.6 |
| Cribbs | 4 | 36 | 9.0 | Muncie | 6 | 53 | 8.8 |
| Lewis | 3 | 45 | 15.0 | Joiner | 4 | 83 | 20.8 |
| Butler | 2 | 19 | 9.5 | McCrary | 2 | 19 | 9.5 |
| Leaks | 1 | 17 | 17.0 | Smith | 1 | 50 | 50.0 |
| Hooks | 1 | 1 | 1.0 | Winslow | 1 | 5 | 5.0 |
| | 15 | 180 | 12.0 | Thomas | 1 | 2 | 2.0 |
| | | | | | 22 | 314 | 14.2 |

#### PUNTING

| | No. | | Avg. | | No. | | Avg. |
|---|---|---|---|---|---|---|---|
| Cater | 6 | | 44.5 | Partridge | 3 | | 37.0 |

#### PUNT RETURNS

| | No. | Yds. | Avg. | | No. | Yds. | Avg. |
|---|---|---|---|---|---|---|---|
| Hooks | 2 | 13 | 6.5 | Fuller | 3 | 29 | 9.7 |

#### KICKOFF RETURNS

| | No. | Yds. | Avg. | | No. | Yds. | Avg. |
|---|---|---|---|---|---|---|---|
| Solomon | 5 | 84 | 16.8 | Bauer | 2 | 39 | 19.5 |
| | | | | Duncan | 1 | 11 | 11.0 |
| | | | | | 3 | 50 | 16.7 |

#### INTERCEPTION RETURNS

| | No. | Yds. | Avg. | | No. | Yds. | Avg. |
|---|---|---|---|---|---|---|---|
| Simpson | 1 | 0 | 0.0 | Edwards | 2 | 27 | 13.5 |
| | | | | Fuller | 1 | 20 | 20.0 |
| | | | | | 3 | 47 | 15.7 |

#### PASSING

| BUFFALO | Att. | Comp. | Comp. Pct. | Yds. | Int. | Yds./ Att. | Yds./ Comp. |
|---|---|---|---|---|---|---|---|
| Ferguson | 29 | 15 | 51.7 | 180 | 3 | 6.2 | 12.0 |
| Manucci | 1 | 0 | 0.0 | 0 | 0 | 0.0 | 0.0 |
| | 30 | 15 | 50.0 | 180 | 3 | 6.0 | 12.0 |

| SAN DIEGO | Att. | Comp. | Comp. Pct. | Yds. | Int. | Yds./ Att. | Yds./ Comp. |
|---|---|---|---|---|---|---|---|
| Fouts | 37 | 22 | 59.5 | 314 | 1 | 8.5 | 14.2 |

---

## January 4, 1981 at Cleveland (Attendance 77,655)

### SCORING

| | | | | | |
|---|---|---|---|---|---|
| OAKLAND | 0 | 7 | 0 | 7– | 14 |
| CLEVELAND | 0 | 6 | 6 | 0– | 12 |

**Second Quarter**
Cle.   Bolton, 42 yard intercep-
          tion return
          PAT-kick failed
Oak.   van Eeghen, 1 yard rush
          PAT–Bahr (kick)

**Third Quarter**
Cle.   Cockroft, 30 yard field goal
Cle.   Cockroft, 29 yard field goal

**Fourth Quarter**
Oak.   van Eeghen, 1 yard rush
          PAT–Bahr (kick)

### TEAM STATISTICS

| OAK. | | CLE. |
|---|---|---|
| 12 | First Downs-Total | 17 |
| 4 | First Downs-Rushing | 6 |
| 8 | First Downs-Passing | 8 |
| 0 | First Downs Penalty | 3 |
| 2 | Fumbles-Number | 6 |
| 1 | Fumbles-Lost Ball | 1 |
| 5 | Penalties-Number | 2 |
| 39 | Yards Penalized | 10 |
| 0 | Missed Field Goals | 2 |
| 70 | Offensive Plays | 69 |
| 208 | Net Yards | 254 |
| 3.0 | Average Gain | 3.7 |
| 3 | Giveaways | 4 |
| 4 | Takeaways | 3 |
| +1 | Difference | –1 |

### INDIVIDUAL STATISTICS

**OAKLAND** / **CLEVELAND**

#### RUSHING

| | No. | Yds. | Avg. | | No. | Yds. | Avg. |
|---|---|---|---|---|---|---|---|
| van Eeghen | 20 | 45 | 2.3 | M. Pruitt | 13 | 48 | 3.7 |
| King | 12 | 23 | 1.9 | Hill | 2 | 23 | 11.5 |
| Plunkett | 4 | 8 | 2.0 | Sipe | 6 | 13 | 2.2 |
| Whittington | 1 | 1 | 1.0 | G. Pruitt | 4 | 11 | 2.8 |
| Jensen | 1 | –1 | –1.0 | Miller | 1 | 1 | 1.0 |
| | 38 | 76 | 2.0 | McDonald | 1 | –11 | –11.0 |
| | | | | | 27 | 85 | 3.1 |

#### RECEIVING

| | No. | Yds. | Avg. | | No. | Yds. | Avg. |
|---|---|---|---|---|---|---|---|
| King | 4 | 14 | 3.2 | Newsome | 4 | 51 | 12.8 |
| Chester | 3 | 64 | 21.3 | G. Pruitt | 3 | 54 | 18.0 |
| van Eeghen | 3 | 23 | 7.7 | Rucker | 2 | 38 | 19.0 |
| Branch | 2 | 23 | 11.5 | Logan | 2 | 36 | 18.0 |
| Chandler | 1 | 15 | 15.0 | Hill | 2 | 4 | 2.0 |
| Whittington | 1 | 10 | 10.0 | | 13 | 183 | 14.1 |
| | 14 | 149 | 10.6 | | | | |

#### PUNTING

| | No. | | Avg. | | No. | | Avg. |
|---|---|---|---|---|---|---|---|
| Guy | 9 | | 38.3 | Evans | 6 | | 39.5 |

#### PUNT RETURNS

| | No. | Yds. | Avg. | | No. | Yds. | Avg. |
|---|---|---|---|---|---|---|---|
| Moody | 1 | 1 | 1.0 | D. Hall | 5 | 57 | 11.4 |
| | | | | Wright | 2 | 24 | 12.0 |
| | | | | | 7 | 81 | 11.6 |

#### KICKOFF RETURNS

| | No. | Yds. | Avg. | | No. | Yds. | Avg. |
|---|---|---|---|---|---|---|---|
| Whittington | 2 | 44 | 22.0 | D.Hall | 2 | 47 | 23.5 |
| Moody | 1 | 14 | 14.0 | White | 1 | 28 | 28.0 |
| Christensen | 1 | 7 | 7.0 | | 3 | 75 | 25.0 |
| | 4 | 65 | 16.3 | | | | |

#### INTERCEPTION RETURNS

| | No. | Yds. | Avg. | | No. | Yds. | Avg. |
|---|---|---|---|---|---|---|---|
| Hayes | 2 | 3 | 1.5 | Bolton | 2 | 42 | 21.0 |
| M. Davis | 1 | 0 | 0.0 | | | | |
| | 3 | 3 | 1.0 | | | | |

#### PASSING

| OAKLAND | Att. | Comp. | Comp. Pct. | Yds. | Int. | Yds./ Att. | Yds./ Comp. |
|---|---|---|---|---|---|---|---|
| Plunkett | 30 | 14 | 46.7 | 149 | 2 | 5.0 | 10.6 |

| CLEVELAND | Att. | Comp. | Comp. Pct. | Yds. | Int. | Yds./ Att. | Yds./ Comp. |
|---|---|---|---|---|---|---|---|
| Sipe | 40 | 13 | 32.5 | 183 | 3 | 4.6 | 14.1 |

# 1980 Championship Games

## SCORING

| | | | | |
|---|---|---|---|---|
| DALLAS | 0 | 7 | 0 | 0– 7 |
| PHILADELPHIA | 7 | 0 | 10 | 3–20 |

**First Quarter**
Phi.    Montgomery, 42 yard rush
        PAT–Franklin (kick)

**Second Quarter**
Dal.    Dorsett, 3 yard rush
        PAT–Septien (kick)

**Third Quarter**
Phi.    Franklin, 26 yard field goal
Phi.    Harris, 9 yard rush
        PAT–Franklin (kick)

**Fourth Quarter**
Phi.    Franklin, 20 yard field goal

## TEAM STATISTICS

| DAL | | PHIL |
|---|---|---|
| 11 | First Downs-Total | 19 |
| 5 | First Downs-Rushing | 13 |
| 6 | First Downs-Passing | 5 |
| 0 | First Downs-Penalty | 1 |
| 5 | Fumbles-Number | 4 |
| 3 | Fumbles-Lost Ball | 0 |
| 5 | Penalties-Number | 5 |
| 40 | Yards Penalized | 45 |
| 0 | Missed Field Goals | 1 |
| 55 | Offensive Plays | 71 |
| 202 | Net Yards | 340 |
| 3.7 | Average Gain | 4.8 |
| 4 | Giveaways | 2 |
| 2 | Takeaways | 4 |
| –2 | Difference | +2 |

Two clubs from the Eastern Division met in Philadelphia for a place in the Super Bowl. The Eagles had captured first place and beat Minnesota to get to this game. The Cowboys had taken a longer path, beating the Rams and Falcons as a wild-card team. The two teams had split their meetings during the season, but the Cowboys had won the most recent meeting and had plenty of big game experience.

The Eagles, however, showed no jitters. On the second play after the opening kickoff, Wilbert Montgomery bolted 42 yards for a touchdown. With the temperature hovering around zero, the quick lead steeled the Eagles' confidence. With their passing game hampered by the cold, the Eagles called on Montgomery to carry the ball repeatedly. Although the Philadelphia blockers controlled the line of scrimmage, the Eagles scored no more points in the first half. The Cowboys did drive to a touchdown in the second quarter and left the field at halftime with a 7-7 tie despite being clearly outplayed.

In the third quarter, the Eagles cashed in on Cowboy mistakes. When sacked by Carl Hairston, quarterback Danny White fumbled the ball away deep in Dallas territory. Although the Cowboy defense held, Tony Franklin put the Eagles ahead 10-7 with a field goal.

After the kickoff, Dallas drove across midfield only to lose the ball on a Tony Dorsett fumble. Jerry Robinson returned the ball to the Dallas 38 yard line, and the Eagles soon scored on a run by Leroy Harris.

Ahead 17-7 at the start of the fourth quarter, the Eagles joined with the weather in making Danny White's life miserable. The Cowboys would score no more, and a Franklin field goal made the final tally 20-7. Montgomery ran for a total of 194 yards, two yards shy of the playoff record set by Steve Van Buren in 1947.

### AFC CHAMPIONSHIP GAME

The best of the West met for the AFC title in balmy San Diego. The Raiders had played one week earlier in one-degree weather in Cleveland, beating the Browns 14-12 in a thrilling contest. The Chargers came off a 20-14 victory over Buffalo and were rated as solid favorites. The two combatants split their two games during the season, but did not meet after mid-October.

The Raiders took the field with a missionary's zeal. They drew first blood with an early 65-yard touchdown pass from Jim Plunkett to Ray Chester. The famous San Diego offense responded, with Charlie Joiner scoring on a 48-yard pass from Dan Fouts.

Now it was the Raiders' turn again. Plunkett capped a drive by running five yards for the score. Before the quarter ended, the Raiders scored again on a pass to Kenny King. Those rooting for the Chargers demanded that their team stop fooling around.

But the swarming Oakland defense smothered the San Diego fleet of receivers and stopped their runners dead. Plunkett directed another Oakland rally which led to a Mark van Eeghen touchdown. With the score now 28-7, the hometown fans began to panic. The Chargers stayed calm and cut the lead to 28-14 by halftime.

The Chargers dominated the first part of the third quarter. On a Rolf Benirschke field goal and a Chuck Muncie touchdown, they cut the lead to 28-24 and brought their fans alive. The Chargers, however, would get no closer. The Raiders began grinding the yards out on the ground, eating up the clock as they traveled. While holding Fouts in check, Oakland used two field goals to fortify their lead. With the Raider defense holding firm, Oakland triumphed 34-27 and earned the first wild-card trip to the Super Bowl.

## INDIVIDUAL STATISTICS

### RUSHING

| DALLAS | No. | Yds. | Avg. | PHILADELPHIA | No. | Yds. | Avg. |
|---|---|---|---|---|---|---|---|
| Newhouse | 7 | 44 | 6.3 | Montgomery | 26 | 194 | 7.5 |
| Dorsett | 13 | 41 | 3.2 | Harris | 10 | 60 | 6.0 |
| Johnson | 1 | 5 | 5.0 | Harrington | 1 | 4 | 4.0 |
| D. White | 1 | –4 | –4.0 | Camfield | 1 | 3 | 3.0 |
| | 22 | 86 | 3.9 | Jaworski | 2 | 2 | 1.0 |
| | | | | | 40 | 263 | 6.6 |

### RECEIVING

| | No. | Yds. | Avg. | | No. | Yds. | Avg. |
|---|---|---|---|---|---|---|---|
| Dorsett | 3 | 27 | 9.0 | Parker | 4 | 31 | 7.8 |
| P. Pearson | 2 | 32 | 16.0 | Krepfle | 2 | 22 | 11.0 |
| Johnson | 2 | 27 | 13.5 | Campfield | 1 | 17 | 17.0 |
| D. Pearson | 2 | 15 | 7.5 | Montgomery | 1 | 14 | 14.0 |
| Springs | 2 | –2 | –1.0 | Carmichael | 1 | 7 | 7.0 |
| Saldi | 1 | 28 | 28.0 | | 9 | 91 | 10.1 |
| | 12 | 127 | 10.6 | | | | |

### PUNTING

| | No. | Yds. | Avg. | | No. | Yds. | Avg. |
|---|---|---|---|---|---|---|---|
| D. White | 7 | | 33.7 | Runager | 4 | | 34.3 |

### PUNT RETURNS

| | No. | Yds. | Avg. | | No. | Yds. | Avg. |
|---|---|---|---|---|---|---|---|
| J. Jones | 3 | 4 | 1.3 | Sciarra | 6 | 69 | 11.5 |

### KICKOFF RETURNS

| | No. | Yds. | Avg. | | No. | Yds. | Avg. |
|---|---|---|---|---|---|---|---|
| J. Jones | 3 | 70 | 23.3 | Campfield | 2 | 40 | 20.0 |
| Wilson | 1 | 19 | 19.0 | | | | |
| Newsome | 1 | 15 | 15.0 | | | | |
| | 5 | 104 | 20.8 | | | | |

### INTERCEPTION RETURNS

| | No. | Yds. | Avg. | | No. | Yds. | Avg. |
|---|---|---|---|---|---|---|---|
| Dickerson | 1 | 0 | 0.0 | Young | 1 | 5 | 5.0 |
| Mitchell | 1 | 0 | 0.0 | | | | |
| | 2 | 0 | 0.0 | | | | |

### PASSING

| DALLAS | Att. | Comp. | Comp. Pct. | Yds. | Int. | Yds./ Att. | Yds./ Comp. |
|---|---|---|---|---|---|---|---|
| D. White | 31 | 12 | 38.7 | 127 | 1 | 4.1 | 10.6 |
| D. Pearson | 1 | 0 | 0.0 | 0 | 0 | 0.0 | 0.0 |
| | 32 | 12 | 37.5 | 127 | 1 | 4.0 | 10.6 |
| **PHILADELPHIA** | | | | | | | |
| Jaworski | 29 | 9 | 31.0 | 91 | 2 | 3.1 | 10.1 |

---

## SCORING

| | | | | |
|---|---|---|---|---|
| OAKLAND | 21 | 7 | 3 | 3–34 |
| SAN DIEGO | 7 | 7 | 10 | 3–27 |

**First Quarter**
Oak.    Chester, 65 yard pass from Plunkett
        PAT–Bahr (kick)
S.D.    Joiner, 48 yard pass from Fouts
        PAT–Benirschke (kick)
Oak.    Plunkett, 5 yard rush
        PAT–Bahr (kick)
Oak.    King, 21 yard pass from Plunkett
        PAT–Bahr (kick)

**Second Quarter**
Oak.    van Eeghen, 3 yard rush
        PAT–Bahr (kick)
S.D.    Joiner, 8 yard pass from Fouts
        PAT–Benirschke (kick)

**Third Quarter**
S.D.    Benirschke, 26 yard field goal
S.D.    Muncie, 6 yard rush
        PAT–Benirschke (kick)
Oak.    Bahr, 27 yard field goal

**Fourth Quarter**
Oak.    Bahr, 33 yard field goal
S.D.    Benirschke, 27 yard field goal

## TEAM STATISTICS

| OAK | | S.D. |
|---|---|---|
| 21 | First Downs-Total | 26 |
| 8 | First Downs-Rushing | 6 |
| 12 | First Downs-Passing | 17 |
| 1 | First Downs-Penalty | 3 |
| 0 | Fumbles-Number | 5 |
| 0 | Fumbles-Lost Ball | 1 |
| 7 | Penalties-Number | 6 |
| 54 | Yards Penalized | 45 |
| 0 | Missed Field Goals | 0 |
| 66 | Offensive Plays | 71 |
| 362 | Net Yards | 434 |
| 5.5 | Average Gain | 6.1 |
| 0 | Giveaways | 3 |
| 3 | Takeaways | 0 |
| +3 | Difference | –3 |

## INDIVIDUAL STATISTICS

### RUSHING

| OAKLAND | No. | Yds. | Avg. | SAN DIEGO | No. | Yds. | Avg. |
|---|---|---|---|---|---|---|---|
| van Eeghen | 20 | 85 | 4.3 | Thomas | 12 | 48 | 4.0 |
| King | 11 | 35 | 3.2 | Muncie | 9 | 34 | 3.8 |
| Jensen | 2 | 7 | 3.5 | Fouts | 1 | 2 | 2.0 |
| Plunkett | 4 | 6 | 1.5 | Smith | 1 | –1 | –1.0 |
| Whittington | 5 | 5 | 1.0 | | 23 | 83 | 3.6 |
| | 42 | 138 | 3.3 | | | | |

### RECEIVING

| | No. | Yds. | Avg. | | No. | Yds. | Avg. |
|---|---|---|---|---|---|---|---|
| Chester | 5 | 102 | 20.4 | Joiner | 6 | 130 | 21.7 |
| Branch | 3 | 78 | 26.0 | Thomas | 5 | 40 | 8.0 |
| King | 2 | 43 | 21.5 | Jefferson | 4 | 71 | 17.8 |
| Chandler | 2 | 27 | 13.5 | Smith | 3 | 76 | 25.3 |
| Whittington | 2 | 11 | 5.5 | Winslow | 3 | 42 | 14.0 |
| | 14 | 261 | 18.6 | Muncie | 2 | 5 | 2.5 |
| | | | | | 23 | 364 | 15.8 |

### PUNTING

| | No. | Yds. | Avg. | | No. | Yds. | Avg. |
|---|---|---|---|---|---|---|---|
| Guy | 4 | | 56.0 | Partridge | 2 | | 40.5 |

### PUNT RETURNS

| | No. | Yds. | Avg. | | No. | Yds. | Avg. |
|---|---|---|---|---|---|---|---|
| Matthews | 2 | 20 | 10.0 | Fuller | 2 | 41 | 20.5 |

### KICKOFF RETURNS

| | No. | Yds. | Avg. | | No. | Yds. | Avg. |
|---|---|---|---|---|---|---|---|
| Whittington | 4 | 67 | 16.8 | Bauer | 5 | 89 | 17.8 |
| Moody | 2 | 36 | 18.0 | Duncan | 1 | 10 | 10.0 |
| | 6 | 103 | 17.2 | | 6 | 99 | 16.5 |

### INTERCEPTION RETURNS

| | No. | Yds. | Avg. | | | | |
|---|---|---|---|---|---|---|---|
| Owens | 1 | 25 | 25.0 | none | | | |
| Hayes | 1 | 16 | 16.0 | | | | |
| | 2 | 41 | 20.5 | | | | |

### PASSING

| OAKLAND | Att. | Comp. | Comp. Pct. | Yds. | Int. | Yds./ Att. | Yds./ Comp. |
|---|---|---|---|---|---|---|---|
| Plunkett | 18 | 14 | 77.8 | 261 | 0 | 14.5 | 18.6 |
| **SAN DIEGO** | | | | | | | |
| Fouts | 45 | 22 | 48.9 | 336 | 2 | 7.5 | 15.3 |
| Winslow | 1 | 1 | 100.0 | 28 | 0 | 28.0 | 28.0 |
| | 46 | 23 | 50.0 | 364 | 2 | 7.9 | 15.8 |

# Super Bowl XV Davis' Bulldog Brigade

The Raiders didn't bring a pedigree to the Super Bowl, they just brought a lot of spirit. It was the spirit of the redeemed, of those who had come back from the garbage pile to smell the roses. Lightly regarded before the season, the Raiders were stocked with many players who had been cut loose by other clubs. Jim Plunkett had been released by the 49ers, Kenny King had ridden the bench for the Oilers, and John Matuszak was unwanted before Al Davis called. Other Oakland players had made similar unorthodox journeys. Davis himself was embroiled in a nasty lawsuit over whether he could move the Raiders to Los Angeles. This crew of pirates even took the hard road in the playoffs, starting out on wild-card weekend and beating the Oilers, Browns, and Chargers. The Eagles had a less colorful story but ranked as three-point favorites because of their tough defense and quick-strike offense.

The feisty mutts dominated the game. Rod Martin picked off Ron Jaworski's first pass of the day and returned it to the Philadelphia 30-yard line. Before seven minutes had elapsed, the Raiders scored a touchdown and led 7-0. The Eagles replied with a long touchdown pass to Rodney Parker, but a penalty wiped the score out. Late in the

quarter, Oakland had the ball on its own 20-yard line. Plunkett threw a pass to King near the 40-yard line, and the halfback outsprinted the napping secondary for an 80-yard touchdown. With a 14-0 lead, the confidence of the Raiders was growing as the Eagles realized that they were collectively off their best form. A Tony Franklin field goal cut the lead to 14-3 at halftime.

In need of a second-half revival, the Eagles instead sank out of the game in the third quarter. Unable to score, they fell prey to Plunkett's precision quarterbacking. A touchdown pass to Cliff Branch in the third quarter lengthened the lead to 21-3 and put the handwriting on the wall for the Eagles. Although Jaworski kept throwing and did connect with Keith Krepfle for a score in the fourth quarter, the Raiders stormed to a 27-10 victory. Plunkett won the MVP award, while Martin starred on defense with three interceptions. In the clubhouse after the game, Pete Rozelle presented the championship trophy to AL Davis in a polite ceremony which skirted the bitter feelings between the two men and which must have given Davis an extra rich taste of victory.

## LINEUPS

| OAKLAND | | PHILADELPHIA |
|---|---|---|
| | OFFENSE | |
| Branch | WR | Carmichael |
| Shell | LT | Walters |
| Upshaw | LG | Perot |
| Dalby | C | Morriss |
| Marvin | RG | Peoples |
| Lawrence | RT | Sisemore |
| Chester | TE | Krepfle |
| Chandler | WR/TE | Spagnola |
| Plunkett | QB | Jaworski |
| van Eeghen | RB | Montgomery |
| King | RB | Harris |
| | DEFENSE | |
| Matuszak | LE | Harrison |
| Kinlaw | MG | Johnson |
| Browning | RE | Hairston |
| Hendricks | LLB | Bunting |
| Miller | ILB | Bergey |
| Nelson | ILB | LeMaster |
| Martin | RLB | Robinson |
| Hayes | LCB | Young |
| O'Steen | RCB | Edwards |
| M. Davis | SS | Logan |
| Owens | FS | Wilson |

### SUBSTITUTES

**OAKLAND**

| | OFFENSE | |
|---|---|---|
| Bradshaw | Martini | Sylvester |
| Christ'sen | Mason | Whittington |
| B. Davis | Matthews | Wilson |
| Jensen | Ramsey | |
| | DEFENSE | |
| Barnes | Jackson | McKinney |
| Campbell | Jones | Moody |
| Celotto | McClan'n | Pear |
| Hardman | | |
| | KICKERS | |
| Bahr | Guy | |

**PHILADELPHIA**

| | OFFENSE | |
|---|---|---|
| Baker | Henry | Pisarcik |
| Campfield | Hertel | Slater |
| Giammona | Kenney | Smith |
| Harrington | Parker | Torrey |
| | DEFENSE | |
| Blackmore | Clarke | Phillips |
| Brown | Hender'n | Sciarra |
| Chesley | Humphrey | Wilkes |
| | KICKERS | |
| Franklin | Runager | |

## SCORING

| | | | | | |
|---|---|---|---|---|---|
| OAKLAND | 14 | 0 | 10 | 3– | 27 |
| PHILADELPHIA | 0 | 3 | 0 | 7– | 10 |

**First Quarter**
Oak.   Branch, 2 yard pass from Plunkett
  PAT–Bahr (kick)
Oak.   King, 80 yard pass from Plunkett
  PAT–Bahr (kick)

**Second Quarter**
Phi.   Franklin, 30 yard field goal

**Third Quarter**
Oak.   Branch, 29 yard pass from Plunkett
  PAT–Bahr (kick)
Oak.   Bahr, 46 yard yard field goal

**Fourth Quarter**
Phi.   Krepfle, 8 yard pass from Jaworski
  PAT–Franklin (kick)
Oak.   Bahr, 35 yard field goal

## TEAM STATISTICS

| OAK. | | PHI. |
|---|---|---|
| 17 | First Downs–Total | 19 |
| 6 | First Downs–Rushing | 3 |
| 10 | First Downs–Passing | 14 |
| 1 | First Downs–Penalty | 2 |
| 0 | Fumbles–Number | 1 |
| 0 | Fumbles–Lost Ball | 1 |
| 5 | Penalties–Number | 6 |
| 37 | Yards Penalized | 57 |
| 1 | Missed Field Goals | 1 |
| 56 | Offensive Plays | 64 |
| 377 | Net Yards | 360 |
| 6.7 | Average Gain | 5.6 |
| 0 | Giveaways | 4 |
| 4 | Takeaways | 0 |
| +4 | Difference | −4 |

## INDIVIDUAL STATISTICS

### RUSHING

| OAKLAND | No. | Yds. | Avg. | PHILADELPHIA | No. | Yds. | Avg. |
|---|---|---|---|---|---|---|---|
| van Eeghen | 19 | 80 | 4.2 | Montgomery | 16 | 44 | 2.8 |
| King | 6 | 18 | 3.0 | Harris | 7 | 14 | 2.0 |
| Jensen | 3 | 12 | 4.0 | Giammona | 1 | 7 | 7.0 |
| Plunkett | 3 | 9 | 3.0 | Harrington | 1 | 4 | 4.0 |
| Whittington | 3 | −2 | −0.7 | Jaworski | 1 | 0 | 0.0 |
| | 34 | 117 | 3.4 | | 26 | 69 | 2.4 |

### RECEIVING

| | No. | Yds. | Avg. | | No. | Yds. | Avg. |
|---|---|---|---|---|---|---|---|
| Branch | 5 | 67 | 13.4 | Montgomery | 6 | 91 | 15.2 |
| Chandler | 4 | 77 | 19.3 | Carmichael | 5 | 83 | 16.6 |
| King | 2 | 93 | 46.5 | Krepfle | 2 | 16 | 8.0 |
| Chester | 2 | 24 | 12.0 | Smith | 2 | 59 | 29.5 |
| | 13 | 261 | 20.1 | Spagnola | 1 | 22 | 22.0 |
| | | | | Parker | 1 | 19 | 19.0 |
| | | | | Harris | 1 | 1 | 1.0 |
| | | | | | 18 | 291 | 16.2 |

### PUNTING

| | No. | | Avg. | | No. | | Avg. |
|---|---|---|---|---|---|---|---|
| Guy | 3 | | 42.0 | Runager | 3 | | 36.7 |

### PUNT RETURNS

| | No. | Yds. | Avg. | | No. | Yds. | Avg. |
|---|---|---|---|---|---|---|---|
| Matthews | 2 | 1 | 0.5 | Sciarra | 2 | 18 | 9.0 |
| | | | | Henry | 1 | 2 | 2.0 |
| | | | | | 3 | 20 | 6.7 |

### KICKOFF RETURNS

| | No. | Yds. | Avg. | | No. | Yds. | Avg. |
|---|---|---|---|---|---|---|---|
| Matthews | 2 | 29 | 14.5 | Campfield | 5 | 87 | 17.4 |
| Moody | 1 | 19 | 19.0 | Harrington | 1 | 0 | 0.0 |
| | 3 | 48 | 16.0 | | 6 | 87 | 14.5 |

### INTERCEPTION RETURNS

| | No. | Yds. | Avg. | | |
|---|---|---|---|---|---|
| Martin | 3 | 44 | 14.7 | none | |

### PASSING

| OAKLAND | Att. | Comp. | Comp. Pct. | Yds. | Int. | Yds./ Att. | Yds./ Comp. | Yards Lost Tackled |
|---|---|---|---|---|---|---|---|---|
| Plunkett | 21 | 13 | 61.9 | 261 | 0 | 12.4 | 20.1 | 1-1 |
| **PHILADELPHIA** | | | | | | | | |
| Jaworski | 38 | 18 | 47.4 | 291 | 3 | 7.7 | 16.2 | 0-0 |

Waving a stack of dollars, Nelson Skalbania signed up a crew of prominent players for his newly purchased Montreal team of the Canadian Football League. He snatched three veteran players out of the NFL. Quarterback Vince Ferragamo left the Los Angeles Rams to head north, while James Scott of the Bears and Billy Johnson of the Oilers went to Montreal as Ferragamo's receivers. Skalbania also signed two college players taken in the first round of the N.F.L. draft. Defensive end Keith Gary turned down the Pittsburgh Steelers, and running back David Overstreet chose Montreal over Miami. With all this flashy talent, the Alouettes suffered through a miserable season, and by the end of the year, the club was swimming in debt and teetering on the edge of bankruptcy.

## EASTERN DIVISION

**Dallas Cowboys**—Dallas fans worried when the 49ers whipped the Cowboys 45–14 on October 11. That loss dropped the Pokes two games behind the streaking Eagles. By the end of the season, however, Cowboy excellence had worn down the other Eastern teams like water eating away rock. Some of the excellence at Tom Landry's command were the running of Tony Dorsett, the blocking of Herbert Scott and Pat Donovan, and the pass rushing of Randy White and Too Tall Jones. Landry also plugged his leaky secondary with talented rookies Everson Walls and Michael Downs. The Cowboys reclaimed a share of first place on November 1 by beating the Eagles 17–14. While the Eagles faded over the backstretch of the schedule, the Cowboys won four of their last five games, including another victory over Philadelphia. When the standings were final, the Cowboys had taken first place and their fifteenth playoff berth in 16 years.

**Philadelphia Eagles**—For two months, the Eagles looked like the N.F.L.'s next dominant team. They won their first six games and perched atop the N.F.C. East with a 7–1 record as October ended. Even the loss of Bill Bergey didn't weaken the defense, as coach Dick Vermeil had rigged up a tight unit around stars Charles Johnson, Jerry Robinson, and Roynell Young. After a defeat by Dallas on November 1, the Eagles destroyed St. Louis 52–10 and Baltimore 38–13. Then, with a first place battle on their hands, the Eagles plummeted to earth. The offense showed the effects of losing fullbacks Leroy Harris and Perry Harrington to injuries and a lack of game-breaking speed. Four weeks in a row, the Eagles scored under 14 points and lost despite good defensive work. Although their early rush had sewn up a wild-card spot for them, the Eagles looked like an error-prone loser in December. A 38–0 victory over the Cardinals on the final weekend gave Vermeil hope that his team was returning to form just in time.

**New York Giants**—Two new faces turned the Giants around with will and desire. Lawrence Taylor joined the team from North Carolina via the first round of the college draft. A linebacker with amazing speed, his endless pursuit and jarring tackles threw enemy offenses out of their normal game plans. Joining the Giants in October was fullback Rob Carpenter, a pickup from the Oilers. Carpenter ran the ball with power and persistence, enabling the Giants to control the ball on offense. Although these two led the way, other players helped them take the Giants into the playoffs for the first time since 1963. Harry Carson came back from a knee injury to star at linebacker, and Mark Haynes rebounded from a miserable rookie year to blossom into a top cornerback. Reserve quarterback Scott Brunner also came through when needed. Phil Simms went out with a separated shoulder during a 30–27 overtime loss to the Redskins on November 15. With Brunner at the helm, the Giants won four of their final five games, including a 13-10 overtime victory against the Cowboys on the final weekend.

**Washington Redskins**—Hired from Don Coryell's San Diego staff, Joe Gibbs came to Washington to install a pass-oriented offense. The players took a while to get the hang of it, as they lost their first five games. With signs of panic in the media, the Skins turned around and won eight of their final eleven games. Joe Theismann enjoyed the increased passing, but the offense profited most from the return of fullback John Riggins after his holdout and the addition of halfback Joe Washington from Baltimore. Gibbs overhauled both the offensive and defensive lines, and both units improved as the season wore on. Although the Skins harbored some wild-card playoff hopes in mid-season, the early losses were too much to make up. Nevertheless, the Redskins ended the season on the upswing, beating the Eagles 15–13, the Colts 38–14, and the Rams 30–7.

**St. Louis Cardinals**—Although they improved two games over their 1980 record, the Cardinals still finished last with the only losing record in the N.F.C. East. A feeble pass rush and a patchy secondary prevented any further improvement. Two young faces made the Cardinals an interesting bunch despite the losing record. Roy Green began the season as a kick returner and defensive back. When injuries struck the St. Louis receiving corps, Green shifted to offense and starred as a deep threat. While working as a receiver, he also played defense as a fifth back on passing downs, raising romantic memories of two-way

players. Despite Green's heroics, the Cards dropped to a 3–7 record after a 52–10 debacle with the Eagles on November 8. Coach Jim Hanifan benched veteran quarterback Jim Hart the next week and started rookie Neil Lomax. With the freshman at QB the Cards ran off four straight victories, including impressive beatings of the Bills and Saints. Although they dropped the final two games of the year, the Cardinals hoped that they had found a passing combination for the 1980s.

## CENTRAL DIVISION

**Tampa Bay Buccaneers**—For most of the year, the Bucs did not look like champions. Nevertheless, when none of the other NFC Central teams took control of the race, the brass ring was still there when the Bucs made their move. After a 24–7 loss to Denver on November 15, the Buccaneers fell to a 5–6 mark, two games behind the first place Vikings. Instead of fading, John McKay rallied his club for a late-season push. They beat Green Bay, New Orleans, and Atlanta to forge ahead into first place with two weeks to go. A last-minute 24–23 loss to the Chargers on December 13 threw the race into a tie, to be settled on the final Sunday between the Bucs and Lions in the Pontiac Silverdome. Doug Williams hit Kevin House with an 84-yard touchdown pass in the second quarter for a 10–7 halftime lead. In the second half, Lee Roy Selmon sacked Detroit's Eric Hipple, and David Logan returned the resulting fumble for a touchdown. The 20–17 victory on enemy turf put the Buccaneers in the playoffs for the second time in three years. The big changes from two years ago were the infrequent play of runner Ricky Bell and the sparkling rookie season of linebacker Hugh Green.

**Detroit Lions**—When quarterback Gary Danielson injured his wrist on September 27, visions of disaster danced before coach Monte Clark. Jeff Komlo started the next two games, but two losses dropped the Lions to a 2-4 record. Clark then turned to Eric Hipple, an untried second-year benchwarmer. In his starting debut, he led the Lions to a 48–17 victory over the Bears on a Monday night. In his first eight starts, Hipple engineered seven victories and boosted the Lions into a first-place tie. Along the way, the Lions beat Dallas 27–24 on a last-minute field goal; photographs showed that the Lions had twelve men on the field for the kick, but the win stood up in the standings. Hipple was aided greatly by the running of Billy Sims, and tackle Doug English returned from a year's retirement to shine on defense. The Lions lost to the Packers on December 6, but beat the Vikings one week later to set up a first-place showdown with the Buccaneers in the Pontiac Silverdome. The Lions had won all seven of their home games, but the Bucs broke the string and their hearts by winning the contest 20–17.

**Green Bay Packers**—Stripped of his general manager duties, Bart Starr kept a fingertip grip on his coaching job. The Packers beat the Bears on opening day but lost halfback Eddie Lee Ivery to knee surgery. Six defeats in the next seven games put the wolves at Starr's door, but then the Packers rescued him by going on a hot streak. With six victories over the back half of the schedule, the Packers charged into the race for a playoff spot. The offense learned how to use two standout receivers, James Lofton and John Jefferson. Obtained from San Diego after the start of the season, Jefferson gave quarterback Lynn Dickey a matched set of speedburners to fire away at. Just as important to Dickey was the improved offensive line, with center Larry McCarren shining brightest. The defense had its shaky moments but did profit by the return to health of linebackers Rich Wingo, George Cumby, and John Anderson. Down the stretch, the Packers beat the Vikings, Lions, and Saints to set up a do-or-die match with the Jets in New York on the final Sunday. A victory would wrap up a wild-card berth, but the Jets needed a victory just as badly and blew the Pack out 28–3.

**Minnesota Vikings**—They didn't have the best material, but Bud Grant had coaxed his Vikings into first place in mid-November. Their 7–4 record put them two games ahead of the pack in the NFC Central. The Vikes had a second-rate defense but a first-rate passing attack. Tommy Kramer unleashed the usual barrage of passes to wide receivers Ahmad Rashad and Sammy White, but he also sent a lot of footballs toward Joe Senser, the new tight end. On the way to the top, the Vikings had beaten undefeated Philadelphia and won games over Detroit and San Diego on late field goals. With Bud Grant's track record as a winner, fans were surprised to see the Vikings come apart like a cheap Coney Island shirt. That two-game lead evaporated in a five-game losing streak which ended only when the players went home for the winter. The unbalanced offense abruptly dried up, while the defense allowed Detroit to score 45 points. They key loss came at home on November 26, as the Vikes blew a 14–0 lead and were beaten 35–23 by the Packers.

**Chicago Bears**—For two months, the Bears played like dispirited, disinterested losers. With minor injuries hampering Walter Payton and with James Scott playing for Montreal in the C.F.L., the Chicago offense rarely scored more than 20 points. Despite another star season

FINAL TEAM STATISTICS

**OFFENSE**

| | ATL. | CHI. | DALL. | DET. | G.B. | L.A. | MINN. | N.O. | NY G | PHIL. | STL. | S.F. | T.B. | WASH. |
|---|---|---|---|---|---|---|---|---|---|---|---|---|---|---|
| FIRST DOWNS: | | | | | | | | | | | | | | |
| Total | 318 | 278 | 321 | 340 | 308 | 305 | **343** | 280 | 253 | 332 | 300 | 317 | 269 | 334 |
| by Rushing | 116 | 126 | 137 | **167** | 104 | 142 | 91 | 126 | 92 | 157 | 135 | 110 | 95 | 136 |
| by Passing | 176 | 126 | 158 | 150 | 174 | 134 | **217** | 124 | 140 | 150 | 141 | 183 | 159 | 173 |
| by Penalty | 26 | 26 | 26 | 23 | 30 | 29 | **35** | 30 | 21 | 25 | 24 | 24 | 15 | 25 |
| RUSHING: | | | | | | | | | | | | | | |
| Number | 495 | 608 | **630** | 596 | 478 | 559 | 391 | 546 | 481 | 559 | 519 | 560 | 458 | 532 |
| Yards | 1965 | 2171 | 2711 | **2795** | 1670 | 2236 | 1512 | 2286 | 1685 | 2509 | 2213 | 1941 | 1731 | 2157 |
| Average Yards | 4.0 | 3.6 | 4.3 | **4.7** | 3.5 | 4.0 | 3.9 | 4.2 | 3.5 | 4.5 | 4.3 | 3.5 | 3.8 | 4.1 |
| Touchdowns | 15 | 13 | 15 | **26** | 11 | 17 | 8 | 16 | 11 | 17 | 20 | 17 | 13 | 19 |
| PASSING: | | | | | | | | | | | | | | |
| Attempts | 563 | 489 | 439 | 436 | 514 | 477 | **709** | 441 | 506 | 476 | 477 | 517 | 473 | 525 |
| Completions | 311 | 222 | 241 | 228 | 286 | 235 | **382** | 238 | 251 | 258 | 253 | 328 | 239 | 307 |
| Completion Pct. | 55.2 | 45.4 | 54.9 | 52.3 | 55.6 | 49.3 | 53.9 | 54.0 | 49.6 | 54.2 | 53.0 | **63.4** | 50.5 | 58.5 |
| Passing Yards | 3986 | 2728 | 3414 | 3475 | 3576 | 3008 | **4567** | 2778 | 3009 | 3249 | 3269 | 3766 | 3565 | 3743 |
| Avg. Yds per Att. | 6.2 | 4.7 | 6.7 | 6.5 | 5.6 | 4.9 | 5.9 | 5.0 | 4.8 | 6.1 | 5.5 | 6.5 | **7.0** | 6.3 |
| Avg. Yds per Comp. | 12.8 | 12.3 | 14.2 | **15.2** | 12.5 | 12.8 | 12.0 | 11.7 | 12.0 | 12.6 | 12.9 | 11.5 | 14.9 | 12.2 |
| Times Tackled | 37 | 35 | 31 | 44 | 52 | 50 | 29 | 41 | 47 | 22 | 48 | 29 | **19** | 30 |
| Yds Lost Tackled | 287 | 266 | 245 | 337 | 387 | 451 | 234 | 359 | 368 | 205 | 405 | 223 | **136** | 277 |
| Net Yards | 3699 | 2462 | 3169 | 3138 | 3189 | 2557 | **4333** | 2419 | 2641 | 3044 | 2864 | 3543 | 2429 | 3466 |
| Touchdowns | **30** | 14 | 24 | 18 | 24 | 15 | 27 | 8 | 16 | 25 | 15 | 20 | 20 | 19 |
| Interceptions | 24 | 23 | 15 | 23 | 24 | 32 | 29 | 27 | 20 | 22 | 24 | **13** | 14 | 22 |
| Pct. Intercepted | 4.3 | 4.7 | 3.4 | 5.3 | 4.7 | 6.7 | 4.1 | 6.1 | 4.0 | 4.6 | 5.0 | **2.5** | **3.0** | 4.2 |
| PUNTS: | | | | | | | | | | | | | | |
| Number | 88 | **114** | 81 | 64 | 84 | 89 | 88 | 66 | 97 | 64 | 69 | 93 | 82 | 73 |
| Average | 40.3 | 39.7 | 40.5 | **43.5** | 39.6 | 42.0 | 41.4 | 40.5 | 43.3 | 40.3 | 41.8 | 41.5 | 41.2 | 40.0 |
| PUNT RETURNS | | | | | | | | | | | | | | |
| Number | 50 | 45 | 45 | 52 | 40 | 49 | 39 | 41 | **64** | 58 | 43 | 48 | 38 | 49 |
| Yards | 383 | 518 | 235 | 450 | 306 | **676** | 303 | 426 | 502 | 422 | 453 | 344 | 244 | 507 |
| Average Yards | 7.7 | 11.5 | 5.2 | 8.7 | 7.7 | **13.8** | 7.8 | 10.4 | 7.8 | 7.3 | 10.5 | 7.2 | 6.4 | 10.3 |
| Touchdowns | 0 | 1 | 0 | 1 | 1 | **3** | 0 | 0 | 0 | 0 | 1 | 0 | 0 | 2 |
| KICKOFF RET.: | | | | | | | | | | | | | | |
| Number | 62 | 64 | 53 | 61 | 58 | 68 | 67 | 70 | 57 | 43 | **75** | 45 | 46 | 67 |
| Yards | 1419 | 1214 | 981 | 1164 | 1066 | 1244 | 1328 | 1523 | 1120 | 832 | 1625 | 909 | 912 | **1673** |
| Average Yards | 22.9 | 19.0 | 18.5 | 19.1 | 18.4 | 18.3 | 19.8 | 21.8 | 19.6 | 19.3 | 21.7 | 20.2 | 19.8 | **25.0** |
| Touchdowns | 0 | 0 | 0 | 0 | 0 | 0 | **1** | 0 | 0 | 0 | 0 | **1** | 0 | 0 |
| INTERCEPT RET.: | | | | | | | | | | | | | | |
| Number | 25 | 18 | **37** | 24 | 30 | 17 | 16 | 17 | 17 | 26 | 21 | 27 | 32 | 24 |
| Yards | 494 | 345 | 482 | 286 | 495 | 237 | 120 | 214 | 222 | 266 | 281 | 448 | **648** | 249 |
| Average Yards | 19.8 | 19.2 | 13.0 | 11.9 | 16.5 | 13.9 | 7.5 | 12.6 | 13.1 | 10.2 | 13.4 | 16.6 | **20.3** | 10.4 |
| Touchdowns | 3 | 3 | 0 | 1 | 1 | 0 | 0 | 0 | 1 | 0 | 1 | **4** | **4** | 2 |
| PENALTIES: | | | | | | | | | | | | | | |
| Number | 90 | 121 | 103 | 111 | **84** | 117 | 109 | 109 | 108 | 113 | 106 | 92 | 89 | 98 |
| Yards | 940 | 996 | 839 | 990 | **687** | 916 | 865 | 899 | 897 | 855 | 877 | 752 | 779 | 940 |
| FUMBLES: | | | | | | | | | | | | | | |
| Number | 31 | 37 | 45 | 41 | 31 | 34 | 39 | 40 | 38 | 33 | 33 | **26** | 27 | 32 |
| Number Lost | 17 | 17 | 20 | 20 | 17 | 15 | 21 | 20 | 16 | 17 | 20 | **12** | 14 | 19 |
| POINTS: | | | | | | | | | | | | | | |
| Total | **426** | 253 | 367 | 397 | 324 | 303 | 325 | 207 | 295 | 368 | 315 | 357 | 315 | 347 |
| PAT Attempts | **52** | 31 | 40 | 46 | 37 | 36 | 37 | 24 | 32 | 44 | 37 | 43 | 38 | 42 |
| PAT Made | **51** | 29 | 40 | 46 | 36 | 36 | 34 | 24 | 31 | 42 | 36 | 42 | 36 | 38 |
| FG Attempts | 33 | 23 | 35 | 35 | 24 | 26 | 25 | 25 | **38** | 31 | 32 | 29 | 28 | 30 |
| FG Made | 21 | 12 | **27** | 25 | 22 | 17 | 21 | 13 | 24 | 20 | 19 | 19 | 17 | 19 |
| Percent FG Made | 63.6 | 52.2 | 77.1 | 71.4 | **91.7** | 65.4 | 84.0 | 52.0 | 63.2 | 64.5 | 59.4 | 65.5 | 60.7 | 63.3 |
| Safeties | 0 | 1 | **3** | 0 | 0 | 0 | **3** | 0 | 0 | 1 | 0 | 0 | 0 | 0 |

**DEFENSE**

| | ATL. | CHI. | DALL. | DET. | G.B. | L.A. | MINN. | N.O. | NY G | PHIL. | STL. | S.F. | T.B. | WASH. |
|---|---|---|---|---|---|---|---|---|---|---|---|---|---|---|
| FIRST DOWNS: | | | | | | | | | | | | | | |
| Total | 303 | 290 | 286 | 279 | 326 | 285 | 299 | 303 | 291 | **266** | 328 | 280 | 320 | 310 |
| by Rushing | 94 | 120 | 106 | **93** | 140 | 125 | 117 | 127 | 106 | 102 | 134 | 113 | 123 | 133 |
| by Passing | 172 | 144 | 162 | 158 | 168 | **128** | 163 | 161 | 156 | 137 | 171 | 144 | 174 | 152 |
| by Penalty | 37 | 26 | 18 | 28 | 18 | 32 | 19 | **15** | 29 | 27 | 23 | 23 | 23 | 25 |
| RUSHING: | | | | | | | | | | | | | | |
| Number | 459 | 521 | 468 | 469 | 546 | 585 | 540 | 504 | 553 | 476 | 509 | 464 | 551 | 532 |
| Yards | 1666 | 2146 | 2049 | **1623** | 2098 | 2397 | 2045 | 1916 | 1891 | 1751 | 2428 | 1918 | 2172 | 2161 |
| Average Yards | 3.6 | 4.1 | 4.4 | 3.5 | 3.8 | 4.1 | 3.8 | 3.8 | **3.4** | 3.7 | 4.8 | 4.1 | 3.9 | 4.1 |
| Touchdowns | **10** | 13 | 16 | 14 | 21 | 19 | 15 | 17 | **10** | 11 | 20 | **10** | 16 | 17 |
| PASSING: | | | | | | | | | | | | | | |
| Attempts | 565 | 525 | 511 | 475 | 505 | **439** | 481 | 471 | 544 | 507 | 495 | 514 | 541 | 452 |
| Completions | 322 | 233 | 236 | 261 | 284 | **204** | 265 | 287 | 294 | 248 | 282 | 273 | 317 | 214 |
| Completion Pct. | 57.0 | **44.4** | 46.2 | 54.9 | 56.2 | 46.5 | 55.1 | 60.9 | 54.0 | 48.9 | 57.0 | 53.1 | 58.6 | 47.3 |
| Passing Yards | 3927 | 3527 | 3717 | 3596 | 3353 | 3057 | 3599 | 3578 | 3318 | **3050** | 3547 | 3135 | 3297 | 3310 |
| Avg. Yds per Att. | 6.2 | 5.8 | 6.1 | 6.2 | 5.7 | 5.7 | 6.5 | 6.7 | 5.0 | **4.9** | 6.3 | 5.2 | 5.6 | 6.3 |
| Avg. Yds per Comp. | 12.2 | 15.1 | 15.8 | 13.8 | 11.8 | 15.0 | 13.6 | 12.5 | 11.3 | 12.3 | 12.6 | 11.5 | **10.4** | 15.5 |
| Times Tackled | 29 | 31 | 42 | **47** | 36 | 43 | 33 | 27 | 44 | 40 | 32 | 36 | 23 | 32 |
| Yds Lost Tackled | 239 | 279 | 347 | 373 | 266 | 330 | 271 | 241 | **284** | 354 | 252 | 290 | 157 | 265 |
| Net Yards | 3688 | 3248 | 3370 | 3223 | 3087 | 2727 | 3328 | 3337 | 2934 | **2696** | 3295 | 2845 | 3140 | 3045 |
| Touchdowns | 30 | 23 | 17 | 22 | 18 | 17 | 26 | 26 | 14 | 12 | 29 | 16 | 10 | 21 |
| Interceptions | 25 | 18 | **37** | 24 | 30 | 17 | 16 | 17 | 17 | 26 | 21 | 27 | 32 | 24 |
| Pct. Intercepted | 4.4 | 3.4 | **7.2** | 5.1 | 5.9 | 3.9 | 3.3 | 3.6 | 3.1 | 5.1 | 4.2 | 5.3 | 5.9 | 5.3 |
| PUNTS: | | | | | | | | | | | | | | |
| Number | 96 | 98 | 80 | 81 | 69 | 94 | 84 | 69 | **105** | 76 | 69 | 83 | 73 | 80 |
| Average | 42.2 | 40.7 | 41.2 | 42.9 | 39.7 | 41.0 | 40.7 | 44.1 | **39.6** | 40.7 | 41.3 | 41.4 | 41.2 | 41.7 |
| PUNT RETURNS | | | | | | | | | | | | | | |
| Number | 59 | 66 | 38 | 39 | 50 | 52 | 46 | 36 | 61 | **34** | 37 | 57 | 52 | 50 |
| Yards | 577 | 594 | **231** | 299 | 511 | 481 | 399 | 282 | 561 | 246 | 276 | 664 | 668 | 388 |
| Average Yards | 9.8 | 9.0 | **6.1** | 7.7 | 10.2 | 9.3 | 8.7 | 7.8 | 9.2 | 7.2 | 7.5 | 11.6 | 12.8 | 7.8 |
| Touchdowns | 2 | 1 | 0 | 0 | 0 | 0 | 1 | 0 | 1 | 0 | 0 | 1 | 1 | 1 |
| KICKOFF RET.: | | | | | | | | | | | | | | |
| Number | 67 | **44** | 71 | 70 | 70 | 60 | 62 | 50 | 50 | 60 | 55 | 67 | 64 | 69 |
| Yards | 1286 | **937** | 1508 | 1257 | 1183 | 1443 | 1260 | 966 | 959 | 1334 | 1163 | 1389 | 1332 | 1275 |
| Average Yards | 19.2 | 21.3 | 21.2 | 18.0 | **16.9** | 24.1 | 20.3 | 19.3 | 19.2 | 22.2 | 21.1 | 20.7 | 20.8 | 18.5 |
| Touchdowns | 0 | 0 | 0 | 0 | 0 | 2 | 0 | 0 | 0 | 0 | 0 | 0 | 0 | 0 |
| INTERCEPT RET.: | | | | | | | | | | | | | | |
| Number | 24 | 23 | 15 | 23 | 24 | 32 | 29 | 27 | 20 | 22 | 24 | **13** | 14 | 22 |
| Yards | 301 | 385 | **124** | 274 | 475 | 361 | 384 | 479 | 252 | 357 | 312 | 297 | 179 | 391 |
| Average Yards | 12.5 | 16.7 | **8.3** | 11.9 | 19.8 | 11.3 | 13.2 | 17.7 | 12.6 | 16.2 | 13.0 | 22.8 | 12.8 | 17.8 |
| Touchdowns | **0** | 2 | 1 | 1 | 3 | 1 | 3 | 1 | 2 | 2 | **0** | 2 | **0** | 1 |
| PENALTIES: | | | | | | | | | | | | | | |
| Number | 97 | **119** | 104 | 95 | 108 | 118 | 115 | 118 | 111 | 91 | 98 | 108 | 79 | 108 |
| Yards | 804 | 961 | 837 | 872 | 907 | 1018 | 991 | **1089** | 876 | 813 | 845 | 866 | 650 | 921 |
| FUMBLES: | | | | | | | | | | | | | | |
| Number | **43** | 33 | **43** | 29 | 42 | 37 | 27 | 31 | 38 | 38 | 35 | 36 | 32 | 32 |
| Number Lost | 21 | 22 | 16 | 15 | **24** | 16 | 19 | 17 | 17 | 21 | 17 | 21 | 14 | 15 |
| POINTS: | | | | | | | | | | | | | | |
| Total | 355 | 324 | 277 | 322 | 361 | 351 | 369 | 378 | 257 | **221** | 408 | 250 | 268 | 349 |
| PAT Attempts | 43 | 39 | 34 | 38 | 45 | 39 | 46 | 46 | 27 | **26** | 50 | 30 | 27 | 43 |
| PAT Made | 41 | 37 | 31 | 37 | 43 | 37 | 42 | 45 | 27 | **23** | 48 | 29 | 27 | 38 |
| FG Attempts | 29 | 29 | 29 | **22** | 24 | 33 | 27 | 25 | 33 | 28 | 26 | 23 | 33 | 24 |
| FG Made | 18 | 17 | 14 | 19 | 16 | 26 | 17 | 19 | 22 | 14 | 20 | **13** | 25 | 17 |
| Percent FG Made | 62.1 | 58.6 | **48.3** | 86.4 | 66.7 | 78.8 | 63.0 | 76.0 | 66.7 | 50.0 | 76.9 | 56.5 | 75.8 | 70.8 |
| Safeties | 1 | 1 | 0 | 0 | 0 | 1 | 0 | 0 | 1 | 0 | 0 | 1 | 2 | 1 |

from Gary Fencik, the defense also suffered periodic breakdowns. Things picked up at the end of the year. After a close loss to the Cowboys on Thanksgiving, the Bears beat the Vikings, Raiders, and Broncos to end the season on an assertive note. Also asserting himself was N.F.L. patriarch George Halas, the 86-year-old owner of the franchise from its earliest days. He took a more active role in the running of the club, taking under his scrutiny the fates of coach Neill Armstrong and general manager Jim Finks. At the conclusion of the schedule, the verdict came in; Finks stays, Armstrong goes.

## WESTERN DIVISION

**San Francisco '49ers**—They didn't look like much on paper, but Bill Walsh led the 49ers to a surprise divisional title. Two losses in the first three games promised the usual losing season. Starting on September 27, however, the 49ers won 12 of 13 games with an open offense and swarming defense. The offense used their runners only to set up an all-out passing attack. In his first full season as a starter, quarterback Joe Montana engineered the complex offense with the coolness of a surgeon. Lanky receiver Dwight Clark broke clear for lots of passes despite his limited speed. With Randy Cross leading the way, the offensive line gave Montana plenty of time to operate. The defense blended youth with two veteran pickups. Inside linebacker Jack Reynolds came from Los Angeles to inject ferocity into the heart of the unit, while end Fred Dean left San Diego in a salary dispute to give Walsh a pass-rushing maniac. The secondary combined three rookies with third-year safety Dwight Hicks. Rather than stumbling in their inexperience, the secondary terrorized quarterbacks with daring, as Hicks and cornerback Ronnie Lott feasted on errant passes. With a 4–1 record within their division, the 49ers went to the playoffs for the first time since 1972.

**Atlanta Falcons**—For every step the offense took, the defense went back one. After three straight victories to open the season, the Falcons lost three straight and never again hit their stride. The offense had aces in all departments. William Andrews plugged away for his third 1,000-yard rushing season in as many tries. Working off this running threat, Steve Bartkowski ate up yardage with his passes, with Al Jenkins burning defenses regularly. Led by tackle Mike Kenn, the offensive line supported both the ground and air attacks handsomely. While the Falcons rang up scores with passing, enemy air attacks victimized the Atlanta defense. An injury to linebacker Joel Williams cut the best pass rusher out of the lineup. With a secondary high on inexperience and low on speed, the Falcons couldn't stop enemy passers. Although the Falcons stayed in the running for a wild-card berth into December, three losses at the end of the year crushed that hope.

**Los Angeles Rams**—Things went badly for the Rams over the summer and never improved much. Salary hassles sent linebacker Jack Reynolds to San Francisco and quarterback Vince Ferragamo to Montreal of the CFL. Pat Haden brought experience to the QB position, but he did not have Ferragamo's long distance arm. To make Haden's job impossible, the offensive line broke down after years of excellence. Doug France's shoulder injury and poor seasons by Kent Hill and Jackie Slater exposed Haden to a pass rush which gave him a set of bruised ribs. To juice up the offense, coach Ray Malavasi signed Dan Pastorini in mid-season, but the ex-Oiler quarterback had no greater success than Haden. The defense suffered from the departure of Reynolds, Bob Brudzinski, and Fred Dryer. Although Nolan Cromwell starred in the secondary and Wendell Tyler rebounded from injuries to run for over 1,000 yards, the Rams had a collective off-season and lost six of their last seven games. Their losing record was the first since 1972.

**New Orleans Saints**—Although the Saints didn't win too often under Bum Phillips, they didn't feel like doormats any longer. Released by the Oilers after a string of playoff seasons, Phillips began rebuilding the Saints in the image of his old Houston club. With the number one position in the college draft, he picked workhorse runner George Rogers from South Carolina. Phillips immediately structured the offense around Rogers, forced in part by an injury to receiver Ike Harris and the trade of Wes Chandler to San Diego. When injuries slowed quarterback Archie Manning, rookie Dave Wilson got some experience at running the attack. Although he had a good rookie class, Phillips still had a long way to go in building his club up to the standards he had set in Houston. An opening day loss to Atlanta by a 27–0 score dampened some spirits, but the Saints enjoyed beating the Rams twice for the first time ever. They also beat the playoff-bound 49ers and relished a 27–24 upset over the Oilers in the Astrodome, a fine homecoming for Bum.

## DALLAS COWBOYS 12-4-0 Tom Landry

| Scores of Each Game | | |
|---|---|---|
| 26 | Washington | 10 |
| 30 | ST. LOUIS | 17 |
| 35 | New England | 21 |
| 18 | N.Y. GIANTS | 10 |
| 17 | St. Louis | 20 |
| 14 | San Francisco | 45 |
| 29 | LOS ANGELES | 17 |
| 28 | MIAMI | 27 |
| 17 | Philadelphia | 14 |
| 27 | BUFFALO | 14 |
| 24 | Detroit | 27 |
| 24 | WASHINGTON | 10 |
| 10 | CHICAGO | 9 |
| 37 | Baltimore | 13 |
| 21 | PHILADELPHIA | 10 |
| 10 | N.Y. Giants | *13 |

| Use Name | Pos. | Hgt. | Wgt. | Age | Int. | Pts. |
|---|---|---|---|---|---|---|
| Jim Cooper | OT-C | 6'5" | 260 | 25 | | |
| Pat Donovan | OT | 6'4" | 250 | 28 | | |
| Andy Frederick | OT | 6'6" | 255 | 26 | | |
| Steve Wright | OT | 6'5" | 245 | 22 | | |
| Kurt Petersen | OG | 6'4" | 250 | 24 | | |
| Howard Richards | OG-OT | 6'6" | 262 | 22 | | |
| Herbert Scott | OG | 6'2" | 252 | 28 | | |
| Glen Titensor | OG-C | 6'4" | 256 | 23 | | |
| Tom Rafferty | C-OG | 6'3" | 250 | 27 | | |
| Robert Shaw | C | 6'4" | 245 | 24 | | |
| Too Tall Jones | DE | 6'9" | 270 | 30 | | |
| Harvey Martin | DE | 6'5" | 250 | 30 | | 2 |
| Don Smerek | DE | 6'7" | 246 | 23 | | |
| Bruce Thornton | DE-DT | 6'5" | 265 | 23 | | |
| Larry Bethea | DT-DE | 6'5" | 254 | 25 | | |
| John Dutton | DT | 6'7" | 265 | 30 | | 2 |
| Randy White | DT | 6'4" | 250 | 28 | | |

| Use Name | Pos. | Hgt. | Wgt. | Age | Int. | Pts. |
|---|---|---|---|---|---|---|
| Bob Breunig | LB | 6'2" | 225 | 28 | 2 | |
| Guy Brown | LB | 6'4" | 228 | 26 | 1 | |
| Anthony Dickerson | LB | 6'2" | 215 | 24 | | |
| Mike Hegman | LB | 6'1" | 225 | 28 | | |
| Angelo King | LB | 6'1" | 220 | 23 | | |
| D.D. Lewis | LB | 6'2" | 215 | 35 | 1 | |
| Danny Spradlin | LB | 6'1" | 228 | 22 | | |
| Benny Barnes | DB | 6'1" | 195 | 30 | 1 | 6 |
| Michael Downs | DB | 6'3" | 195 | 22 | 7 | |
| Ron Fellows | DB | 6' | 173 | 22 | | |
| Dennis Thurman | DB | 5'11" | 170 | 25 | 9 | |
| Everson Walls | DB | 6'1" | 195 | 21 | 11 | |
| Charlie Waters | DB | 6'1" | 200 | 32 | 3 | |
| Steve Wilson | DB | 5'10" | 192 | 24 | 2 | |

Dextor Clinkscale – Achilles Injury
John Fitzgerald – Knee Injury
Randy Hughes – Shoulder Injury
Bill Roe – Ankle Injury

| Use Name | Pos. | Hgt. | Wgt. | Age | Int. | Pts. |
|---|---|---|---|---|---|---|
| Glenn Carano | QB | 6'3" | 202 | 25 | | |
| Gary Hogeboom | QB | 6'4" | 200 | 23 | | |
| Danny White | QB | 6'2" | 192 | 29 | | |
| Tony Dorsett | HB | 5'11" | 190 | 27 | | 36 |
| James Jones | HB | 5'10" | 200 | 22 | | 6 |
| Robert Newhouse | FB | 5'10" | 215 | 31 | | |
| Timmy Newsome | FB | 6'1" | 227 | 23 | | |
| Ron Springs | FB-HB | 6'1" | 210 | 24 | | 72 |
| Doug Donley | WR | 6' | 174 | 22 | | |
| Tony Hill | WR | 6'2" | 198 | 25 | | 24 |
| Butch Johnson | WR | 6'1" | 192 | 27 | | 30 |
| Drew Pearson | WR | 6' | 183 | 30 | | 18 |
| Doug Cosbie | TE | 6'6" | 230 | 25 | | 30 |
| Billy Joe DuPree | TE | 6'4" | 229 | 31 | | 12 |
| Jay Saldi | TE | 6'3" | 227 | 26 | | 6 |
| Rafael Septien | K | 5'9" | 171 | 27 | | 121 |

## PHILADELPHIA EAGLES 10-6-0 Dick Vermeil

| Scores of Each Game | | |
|---|---|---|
| 24 | N.Y. Giants | 10 |
| 13 | NEW ENGLAND | 3 |
| 20 | Buffalo | 14 |
| 36 | WASHINGTON | 13 |
| 16 | ATLANTA | 13 |
| 31 | New Orleans | 14 |
| 23 | Minnesota | 35 |
| 20 | TAMPA BAY | 10 |
| 14 | DALLAS | 17 |
| 52 | St. Louis | 10 |
| 38 | BALTIMORE | 13 |
| 10 | N.Y. GIANTS | 20 |
| 10 | Miami | 13 |
| 13 | Washington | 15 |
| 10 | Dallas | 21 |
| 38 | ST. LOUIS | 0 |

| Use Name | Pos. | Hgt. | Wgt. | Age | Int. | Pts. |
|---|---|---|---|---|---|---|
| Frank Giddens | OT | 6'7" | 300 | 22 | | |
| Jerry Sisemore | OT | 6'4" | 265 | 30 | | |
| Stan Walters | OT | 6'6" | 275 | 33 | | |
| Ron Baker | OG | 6'4" | 250 | 26 | | |
| Steve Kenney | OG-OT | 6'4" | 262 | 25 | | |
| Dean Miraldi | OG | 6'5" | 254 | 23 | | |
| Petey Perot | OG | 6'2" | 261 | 24 | | |
| Guy Morriss | C | 6'4" | 255 | 30 | | |
| Mark Slater | C | 6'1" | 257 | 26 | | |
| Greg Brown | DE | 6'5" | 235 | 24 | | 6 |
| Carl Hairston | DE | 6'3" | 260 | 28 | | |
| Dennis Harrison | DE | 6'8" | 275 | 25 | | |
| Claude Humphrey | DE | 6'5" | 258 | 37 | | |
| Leonard Mitchell | DE | 6'7" | 272 | 22 | | |
| Ken Clarke | NT | 6'2" | 255 | 25 | | 2 |
| Charles Johnson | NT | 6'3" | 262 | 29 | | 1 |

| Use Name | Pos. | Hgt. | Wgt. | Age | Int. | Pts. |
|---|---|---|---|---|---|---|
| John Bunting | LB | 6'1" | 220 | 31 | | |
| Al Chesley | LB | 6'3" | 240 | 24 | 2 | |
| Mike Curcio | LB | 6'1" | 237 | 24 | | |
| Frank LeMaster | LB | 6'2" | 238 | 29 | 2 | 6 |
| Ray Phillips | LB | 6'4" | 230 | 27 | 1 | |
| Jerry Robinson | LB | 6'2" | 218 | 24 | 1 | |
| Reggie Wilkes | LB | 6'4" | 230 | 25 | 2 | 1 |
| Richard Blackmore | DB | 5'10" | 174 | 25 | 2 | |
| Herman Edwards | DB | 6' | 190 | 27 | 3 | |
| Ray Ellis | DB | 6'1" | 192 | 22 | | |
| Jo Jo Heath | DB | 5'10" | 182 | 24 | | |
| Randy Logan | DB | 6'1" | 195 | 30 | 2 | |
| John Sciarra | DB | 5'11" | 185 | 27 | 1 | |
| Brenard Wilson | DB | 6' | 175 | 26 | 5 | |
| Roynell Young | DB | 6'1" | 181 | 23 | 4 | |

Bill Bergey – Knee Injury
Leroy Harris – Broken Arm
Steve Wagner – Shoulder Injury

| Use Name | Pos. | Hgt. | Wgt. | Age | Int. | Pts. |
|---|---|---|---|---|---|---|
| Ron Jaworski | QB | 6'2" | 196 | 30 | | |
| Joe Pisarcik | QB | 6'4" | 220 | 29 | | |
| Steve Atkins (from G.B.) | HB | 6' | 216 | 25 | | |
| Billy Campfield | HB-FB | 5'11" | 205 | 25 | | 24 |
| Louie Giammona | HB | 5'9" | 180 | 28 | | 12 |
| Wilbert Montgomery | HB | 5'10" | 195 | 26 | | 60 |
| Calvin Murray | HB | 5'11" | 188 | 22 | | |
| Mickey Fitzgerald (from ATL) | FB | 6'2" | 235 | 23 | | |
| Perry Harrington | FB | 5'11" | 210 | 23 | | 12 |
| Hubie Oliver | FB | 5'10" | 212 | 23 | | 6 |
| Booker Russell | FB | 6'2" | 235 | 25 | | 24 |
| Harold Carmichael | WR | 6'7" | 225 | 31 | | 36 |
| Wally Henry | WR | 5'8" | 180 | 26 | | 12 |
| Alvin Hooks | WR | 5'11" | 170 | 24 | | |
| Rodney Parker | WR | 6'1" | 190 | 28 | | 12 |
| Charlie Smith | WR | 6'1" | 185 | 31 | | 24 |
| Ron Smith (from S.D.) | WR | 6' | 185 | 24 | | 12 |
| Steve Folsom | TE | 6'4" | 230 | 23 | | |
| Keith Krepfle | TE | 6'3" | 230 | 29 | | 30 |
| John Spagnola | TE | 6'4" | 240 | 24 | | |
| Tony Franklin | K | 5'8" | 182 | 24 | | 101 |
| Max Runager | K | 6'1" | 189 | 25 | | |

## NEW YORK GIANTS 9-7-0 Ray Perkins

| Scores of Each Game | | |
|---|---|---|
| 10 | PHILADELPHIA | 24 |
| 17 | Washington | 7 |
| 20 | NEW ORLEANS | 7 |
| 10 | Dallas | 18 |
| 14 | GREEN BAY | 27 |
| 34 | ST. LOUIS | 14 |
| 32 | Seattle | 0 |
| 27 | Atlanta | *24 |
| 7 | N.Y. JETS | 26 |
| 24 | Green Bay | 26 |
| 27 | WASHINGTON | *30 |
| 20 | Philadelphia | 10 |
| 10 | San Francisco | 17 |
| 10 | LOS ANGELES | 7 |
| 20 | St. Louis | 10 |
| 13 | DALLAS | *10 |

| Use Name | Pos. | Hgt. | Wgt. | Age | Int. | Pts. |
|---|---|---|---|---|---|---|
| Brad Benson | OT | 6'3" | 258 | 25 | | |
| Gordon King | OT | 6'6" | 275 | 25 | | |
| Jeff Weston | OT | 6'5" | 250 | 24 | | |
| Billy Ard | OG | 6'3" | 250 | 22 | | |
| Roy Simmons | OG | 6'3" | 264 | 24 | | |
| J.T. Turner | OG | 6'3" | 250 | 28 | | |
| Jim Clack | C | 6'3" | 250 | 33 | | |
| Ernie Hughes | C | 6'3" | 260 | 26 | | |
| Ed McGlasson | C | 6'4" | 248 | 25 | | |
| Dee Hardison | DE | 6'4" | 269 | 25 | | |
| Gary Jeter | DE | 6'4" | 260 | 26 | | |
| George Martin | DE | 6'4" | 245 | 28 | | 12 |
| Curtis McGriff | DE | 6'5" | 270 | 23 | | |
| Phil Tabor | DE | 6'4" | 255 | 24 | | |
| Carl Barisich | NT | 6'4" | 255 | 30 | | |
| Jim Burt | NT | 6'1" | 255 | 22 | | |
| Bill Neill | NT | 6'4" | 255 | 22 | | |

| Use Name | Pos. | Hgt. | Wgt. | Age | Int. | Pts. |
|---|---|---|---|---|---|---|
| Harry Carson | LB | 6'2" | 235 | 27 | | |
| Byron Hunt | LB | 6'4" | 230 | 22 | 1 | |
| Brian Kelley | LB | 6'3" | 222 | 30 | 2 | |
| Frank Marion | LB | 6'3" | 228 | 30 | | |
| Joe McLaughlin | LB | 6'1" | 235 | 24 | | |
| Lawrence Taylor | LB | 6'3" | 237 | 22 | 1 | |
| Brad Van Pelt | LB | 6'5" | 235 | 30 | 1 | |
| Mike Whittington | LB | 6'2" | 220 | 23 | 1 | |
| Bill Currier | DB | 6' | 195 | 26 | 3 | |
| Mike Dennis | DB | 5'10" | 190 | 22 | | 6 |
| Larry Flowers | DB | 6'1" | 190 | 23 | 1 | |
| Mark Haynes | DB | 5'11" | 185 | 22 | 1 | |
| Terry Jackson | DB | 5'10" | 197 | 25 | 3 | 6 |
| Beasley Reece | DB | 6'1" | 195 | 27 | 4 | 6 |

Eric Felton – Shoulder Injury
Larry Heater – Thumb Injury
Myron Lapka – Knee Injury
Dan Lloyd – Illness
Kervin Wyatt – Injury

| Use Name | Pos. | Hgt. | Wgt. | Age | Int. | Pts. |
|---|---|---|---|---|---|---|
| Scott Brunner | QB | 6'5" | 200 | 24 | | |
| Cliff Olander | QB | 6'5" | 187 | 26 | | |
| Phil Simms | QB | 6'3" | 216 | 25 | | |
| Leon Bright | HB | 5'9" | 192 | 26 | | 12 |
| Ike Forte | HB | 6' | 211 | 27 | | |
| Alvin Garrett (to WAS) | HB-WR | 5'7" | 178 | 24 | | |
| Louis Jackson | HB | 5'11" | 195 | 23 | | 6 |
| Doug Kotar | HB | 5'11" | 205 | 30 | | 6 |
| Billy Taylor (to NYJ) | HB | 6' | 215 | 25 | | 12 |
| Rob Carpenter (from HOU) | FB-HB | 6'1" | 230 | 26 | | 36 |
| Bo Matthews (to MIA) | FB | 6'4" | 222 | 29 | | |
| Leon Perry | FB | 5'11" | 225 | 24 | | 6 |
| Mike Friede | WR | 6'3" | 205 | 23 | | 6 |
| Earnest Gray | WR | 6'3" | 195 | 24 | | 12 |
| John Mistler | WR | 6'2" | 186 | 22 | | 6 |
| Johnny Perkins | WR | 6'2" | 205 | 28 | | 36 |
| Danny Pittman | WR | 6'2" | 205 | 23 | | |
| Tom Mullady | TE | 6'3" | 232 | 24 | | 6 |
| Gary Shirk | TE | 6'1" | 220 | 31 | | 18 |
| Dave Young | TE | 6'5" | 242 | 22 | | 6 |
| Joe Danelo | K | 5'9" | 166 | 27 | | 103 |
| Dave Jennings | K | 6'4" | 205 | 29 | | |

## WASHINGTON REDSKINS 8-8-0 Jack Gibbs

| Scores of Each Game | | |
|---|---|---|
| 10 | DALLAS | 26 |
| 7 | N.Y. GIANTS | 17 |
| 30 | St. Louis | 40 |
| 13 | Philadelphia | 36 |
| 17 | SAN FRANCISCO | 30 |
| 24 | Chicago | 7 |
| 10 | Miami | 13 |
| 24 | NEW ENGLAND | 22 |
| 42 | ST. LOUIS | 21 |
| 33 | DETROIT | 31 |
| 30 | N.Y. Giants | *27 |
| 10 | Dallas | 24 |
| 14 | Buffalo | 21 |
| 15 | PHILADELPHIA | 13 |
| 38 | BALTIMORE | 14 |
| 30 | Los Angeles | 7 |

| Use Name | Pos. | Hgt. | Wgt. | Age | Int. | Pts. |
|---|---|---|---|---|---|---|
| Mike Daum | OT | 6'6" | 256 | 22 | | |
| Joe Jacoby | OT | 6'7" | 282 | 22 | | |
| Mark May | OT | 6'6" | 270 | 21 | | |
| Jerry Scanlan | OT-OG | 6'5" | 270 | 24 | | |
| George Starke | OT | 6'5" | 250 | 33 | | |
| Robert Woods | OT-OG | 6'3" | 259 | 31 | | |
| Darryl Grant | OG-C-OT | 6'1" | 230 | 21 | | |
| Russ Grimm | OG-C | 6'3" | 250 | 22 | | |
| Melvin Jones | OG | 6'2" | 260 | 25 | | |
| Ron Saul | OG | 6'2" | 254 | 33 | | |
| Jeff Bostic | C | 6'2" | 246 | 22 | | |
| Coy Bacon | DE | 6'4" | 265 | 39 | | |
| Calvin Clark | DE | 6'4" | 260 | 22 | | |
| Mike Clark | DE | 6'4" | 240 | 22 | | |
| Dallas Hickman (from BAL) | DE-LB | 6'6" | 245 | 29 | | |
| Karl Lorch | DE-DT | 6'3" | 258 | 31 | | |
| Dexter Manley | DE | 6'3" | 240 | 22 | | |
| Mat Mendenhall | DE | 6'6" | 253 | 24 | | |
| Perry Brooks | DT | 6'3" | 260 | 26 | | |
| Dave Butz | DT | 6'7" | 285 | 31 | 1 | |
| Pat Ogrin | DT | 6'5" | 265 | 23 | | |
| Wilbur Young (to S.D.) | DT | 6'6" | 290 | 32 | | |

| Use Name | Pos. | Hgt. | Wgt. | Age | Int. | Pts. |
|---|---|---|---|---|---|---|
| Monte Coleman | LB | 6'2" | 230 | 23 | 3 | 6 |
| Pete Cronan (from SEA) | LB | 6'2" | 238 | 26 | | |
| Brad Dusek | LB | 6'2" | 223 | 30 | | |
| Dave Graf | LB | 6'2" | 220 | 28 | | |
| Mel Kaufman | LB | 6'2" | 227 | 23 | 2 | |
| Quentin Lowry | LB | 6'3" | 235 | 23 | | |
| Rich Milot | LB | 6'4" | 230 | 24 | | |
| Neal Olkewicz | LB | 6' | 227 | 24 | 2 | 6 |
| Trent Bryant | DB | 5'9" | 180 | 22 | | |
| Cris Crissy | DB | 5'11" | 195 | 22 | | |
| Curtis Jordan | DB | 6'2" | 205 | 27 | | |
| Joe Lavender | DB | 6'4" | 190 | 32 | 4 | |
| LeCharls McDaniel | DB | 5'9" | 183 | 22 | | |
| Mark Murphy | DB | 6'4" | 210 | 26 | 7 | |
| Mike Nelms | DB | 6'1" | 185 | 26 | 1 | 12 |
| Lemar Parrish | DB | 5'11" | 170 | 33 | 1 | |
| Tony Peters | DB | 6'1" | 177 | 28 | 3 | |
| Jeris White | DB | 5'11" | 188 | 28 | | |

Fred Dean – Arm Injury
Dan Peiffer – Knee Injury
Ray Waddy – Leg Injury

| Use Name | Pos. | Hgt. | Wgt. | Age | Int. | Pts. |
|---|---|---|---|---|---|---|
| Tom Flick | QB | 6'3" | 190 | 23 | | |
| Mike Rae | QB | 6' | 195 | 30 | | |
| Joe Theismann | QB | 6' | 195 | 31 | | 12 |
| Rickey Claitt | HB | 5'10" | 206 | 24 | | |
| Nick Giaquinto (from MIA) | HB-FB | 5'11" | 204 | 26 | | 12 |
| Clarence Harmon | HB-FB | 5'11" | 210 | 25 | | |
| Joe Washington | HB | 5'10" | 179 | 27 | | 42 |
| Wilbur Jackson | FB | 6'1" | 219 | 29 | | |
| John Riggins | FB | 6'2" | 230 | 32 | | 78 |
| Otis Wonsley | FB | 5'10" | 205 | 24 | | |
| Terry Metcalf | WR-HB | 5'10" | 183 | 29 | | |
| Art Monk | WR | 6'3" | 210 | 23 | | 36 |
| Virgil Seay | WR | 5'8" | 170 | 23 | | 18 |
| Ricky Thompson | WR | 6' | 177 | 27 | | 24 |
| Greg McCrary | TE | 6'3" | 235 | 29 | | |
| Bob Raba | TE | 6'1" | 225 | 26 | | |
| Rick Walker | TE | 6'3" | 235 | 26 | | 6 |
| Don Warren | TE | 6'4" | 236 | 25 | | 6 |
| Mike Connell | K | 6'1" | 200 | 25 | | |
| Mark Moseley | K | 5'11" | 205 | 33 | | 95 |

## ST. LOUIS CARDINALS 7-9-0 Jim Hanifan

| Scores of Each Game | | |
|---|---|---|
| 7 | MIAMI | 20 |
| 17 | Dallas | 30 |
| 40 | WASHINGTON | 30 |
| 10 | Tampa Bay | 20 |
| 20 | DALLAS | 17 |
| 14 | N.Y. Giants | 34 |
| 20 | Atlanta | 41 |
| 30 | MINNESOTA | 17 |
| 21 | Washington | 42 |
| 10 | PHILADELPHIA | 52 |
| 24 | BUFFALO | 0 |
| 35 | Baltimore | 24 |
| 27 | New England | 20 |
| 30 | NEW ORLEANS | 3 |
| 10 | N.Y. GIANTS | 20 |
| 0 | Philadelphia | 38 |

| Use Name | Pos. | Hgt. | Wgt. | Age | Int. | Pts. |
|---|---|---|---|---|---|---|
| George Collins | OT-OG | 6'2" | 260 | 25 | | |
| Dan Dierdorf | OT | 6'4" | 288 | 32 | | |
| Dale Markham | OT | 6'8" | 280 | 24 | | |
| Art Plunkett | OT | 6'7" | 260 | 22 | | |
| Keith Wortman | OT | 6'2" | 275 | 31 | | |
| Joe Bostic | OG | 6'3" | 265 | 24 | | |
| Barney Cotton | OG | 6'5" | 265 | 24 | | |
| Terry Stieve | OG | 6'2" | 263 | 27 | | |
| Tom Brahaney | C | 6'2" | 246 | 29 | | |
| Randy Clark | C-OT | 6'3" | 254 | 24 | | |
| Rush Brown | DE | 6'2" | 257 | 27 | | |
| Kirby Criswell | DE | 6'5" | 238 | 24 | | |
| Curtis Greer | DE | 6'4" | 252 | 23 | | |
| Stafford Mays | DE | 6'2" | 240 | 23 | | |
| Bob Pollard | DE | 6'3" | 252 | 32 | | |
| Bill Acker | NT | 6'2" | 255 | 25 | | |
| Mike Dawson | NT | 6'4" | 275 | 27 | | |
| Bruce Radford | NT-DE | 6'5" | 260 | 25 | | |
| Ken Times | NT | 6'2" | 246 | 25 | | |

| Use Name | Pos. | Hgt. | Wgt. | Age | Int. | Pts. |
|---|---|---|---|---|---|---|
| Dave Ahrens | LB | 6'3" | 228 | 22 | 1 | 6 |
| Charlie Baker | LB | 6'2" | 217 | 23 | | |
| Calvin Favron | LB | 6'1" | 225 | 24 | 1 | |
| Doak Field | LB | 6'2" | 226 | 22 | | |
| John Gillen | LB | 6'3" | 227 | 22 | | |
| E.J. Junior | LB | 6'3" | 235 | 21 | 1 | |
| Tim Kearney | LB | 6'2" | 224 | 30 | | |
| Eric Williams | LB | 6'2" | 225 | 26 | 1 | |
| Carl Allen | DB | 6' | 186 | 25 | | |
| Steve Carpenter | DB | 6'2" | 195 | 23 | | |
| Tim Collier | DB | 6' | 174 | 27 | 1 | |
| Ken Greene | DB | 6'3" | 203 | 25 | 7 | |
| Jeff Griffin | DB | 6' | 185 | 23 | 1 | |
| Charles Johnson | DB | 5'10" | 180 | 25 | 1 | |
| Lee Nelson | DB | 5'10" | 185 | 27 | | |
| Don Schwartz | DB | 6'1" | 191 | 25 | | |
| Roger Wehrli | DB | 6'1" | 194 | 33 | 4 | |
| Herb Williams | DB | 6' | 198 | 23 | | |

Ron Coder – Knee Injury

| Use Name | Pos. | Hgt. | Wgt. | Age | Int. | Pts. |
|---|---|---|---|---|---|---|
| Jim Hart | QB | 6'2" | 210 | 37 | | |
| Rusty Lisch | QB | 6'3" | 215 | 24 | | |
| Neil Lomax | QB | 6'3" | 215 | 22 | | 12 |
| Ottis Anderson | HB-FB | 6'2" | 215 | 24 | | 54 |
| Will Harrell | HB | 5'9" | 182 | 28 | | 12 |
| Stump Mitchell | HB | 5'9" | 188 | 22 | | 12 |
| Randy Love | FB | 6'1" | 205 | 24 | | |
| Wayne Morris | FB | 6' | 208 | 27 | | 30 |
| Mark Bell | WR | 5'9" | 175 | 24 | | |
| Ralph Clayton | WR-FB | 6'3" | 222 | 22 | | |
| Mike Fisher | WR | 5'11" | 172 | 23 | | |
| John Floyd | WR | 6'1" | 195 | 24 | | |
| Mel Gray | WR | 5'9" | 173 | 32 | | 12 |
| Roy Green | WR-DB | 5'11" | 190 | 24 | 3 | 30 |
| Dave Stief | WR | 6'3" | 195 | 25 | | 6 |
| Pat Tilley | WR | 5'10" | 171 | 28 | | 18 |
| Chris Combs | TE-OT | 6'4" | 237 | 23 | | |
| Greg LaFleur | TE | 6'4" | 237 | 22 | | 12 |
| Doug Marsh | TE | 6'3" | 236 | 23 | | 6 |
| Carl Birdsong | K | 6' | 192 | 22 | | |
| Neil O'Donoghue | K | 6'6" | 210 | 28 | | 93 |

*—Overtime

## DALLAS COWBOYS

### Rushing

| Last Name | No. | Yds. | Avg. | TD |
|---|---|---|---|---|
| Dorsett | 342 | 1646 | 4.8 | 4 |
| Springs | 172 | 625 | 3.6 | 10 |
| J. Jones | 34 | 183 | 5.4 | 1 |
| D. White | 38 | 104 | 2.7 | 0 |
| Newsome | 13 | 38 | 2.9 | 0 |
| Cosbie | 4 | 33 | 8.3 | 0 |
| Newhouse | 14 | 33 | 2.4 | 0 |
| Pearson | 3 | 31 | 10.3 | 0 |
| DuPree | 1 | 12 | 12.0 | 0 |
| Carano | 8 | 9 | 1.1 | 0 |
| Hill | 1 | −3 | −3.0 | 0 |

### Receiving

| Last Name | No. | Yds. | Avg. | TD |
|---|---|---|---|---|
| Hill | 46 | 953 | 21 | 4 |
| Springs | 46 | 359 | 8 | 2 |
| Pearson | 38 | 614 | 16 | 3 |
| Dorsett | 32 | 325 | 10 | 2 |
| Johnson | 25 | 552 | 22 | 5 |
| DuPree | 19 | 214 | 11 | 2 |
| Cosbie | 17 | 225 | 13 | 5 |
| Saldi | 8 | 82 | 10 | 1 |
| J. Jones | 6 | 37 | 6 | 0 |
| Donley | 3 | 32 | 11 | 0 |
| Newhouse | 1 | 21 | 21 | 0 |

### Punt Returns

| Last Name | No. | Yds. | Avg. | TD |
|---|---|---|---|---|
| J. Jones | 33 | 188 | 6 | 0 |
| Fellows | 11 | 44 | 4 | 0 |
| Donley | 1 | 3 | 3 | 0 |

### Kickoff Returns

| Last Name | No. | Yds. | Avg. | TD |
|---|---|---|---|---|
| J. Jones | 27 | 517 | 19 | 0 |
| Newsome | 12 | 228 | 19 | 0 |
| Fellows | 8 | 170 | 21 | 0 |
| Newhouse | 3 | 34 | 11 | 0 |
| Wilson | 2 | 32 | 16 | 0 |
| Cosbie | 1 | 0 | 0 | 0 |

### Passing – Punting – Kicking

| PASSING | Att. | Comp. | % | Yds. | Yd./Att. | TD | Int.-% | RK |
|---|---|---|---|---|---|---|---|---|
| D. White | 391 | 223 | 57 | 3098 | 7.9 | 22 | 13- 3 | 2 |
| Carano | 45 | 16 | 36 | 235 | 5.2 | 1 | 1- 2 | |
| Pearson | 2 | 2 | 100 | 81 | 40.5 | 1 | 0- 0 | |
| Springs | 1 | 0 | 0 | 0 | 0.0 | 0 | 1-100 | |

| PUNTING | No. | Avg. |
|---|---|---|
| D. White | 79 | 40.8 |
| Septien | 2 | 31.0 |

| KICKING | XP | Att. | % | FG | Att. | % |
|---|---|---|---|---|---|---|
| Septien | 40 | 40 | 100 | 27 | 35 | 77 |

## PHILADELPHIA EAGLES

### Rushing

| Last Name | No. | Yds. | Avg. | TD |
|---|---|---|---|---|
| Montgomery | 286 | 1402 | 4.9 | 8 |
| Oliver | 75 | 329 | 4.4 | 1 |
| Harrington | 34 | 140 | 4.1 | 2 |
| Murray | 23 | 134 | 5.8 | 0 |
| Jaworski | 22 | 128 | 5.8 | 0 |
| Russell | 38 | 123 | 3.2 | 4 |
| Campfield | 31 | 115 | 3.7 | 1 |
| Giammona | 35 | 98 | 2.8 | 1 |
| Atkins | 12 | 33 | 2.8 | 0 |
| LeMaster | 1 | 7 | 7.0 | 0 |
| R. Smith | 1 | 7 | 7.0 | 0 |
| C. Smith | 2 | 5 | 2.5 | 0 |
| Carmichael | 1 | 1 | 1.0 | 0 |
| Pisarcik | 7 | 1 | 0.1 | 0 |
| Sciarra | 1 | 0 | 0.0 | 0 |
| Henry | 1 | −2 | −2.0 | 0 |

### Receiving

| Last Name | No. | Yds. | Avg. | TD |
|---|---|---|---|---|
| Carmichael | 61 | 1028 | 17 | 6 |
| Montgomery | 49 | 521 | 11 | 2 |
| C. Smith | 38 | 564 | 15 | 4 |
| Campfield | 36 | 326 | 9 | 3 |
| Krepfle | 20 | 210 | 11 | 5 |
| Oliver | 10 | 37 | 4 | 0 |
| Henry | 9 | 145 | 16 | 2 |
| Harrington | 9 | 27 | 3 | 0 |
| Parker | 8 | 168 | 21 | 2 |
| R. Smith | 7 | 168 | 24 | 2 |
| Spagnola | 6 | 83 | 14 | 0 |
| Giammona | 6 | 54 | 9 | 1 |
| Murray | 1 | 7 | 7 | 0 |
| Atkins | 1 | 2 | 2 | 0 |
| Russell | 1 | −5 | −5 | 0 |

### Punt Returns

| Last Name | No. | Yds. | Avg. | TD |
|---|---|---|---|---|
| Henry | 54 | 396 | 7 | 0 |
| Sciarra | 4 | 26 | 7 | 0 |

### Kickoff Returns

| Last Name | No. | Yds. | Avg. | TD |
|---|---|---|---|---|
| Henry | 25 | 533 | 21 | 0 |
| Campfield | 12 | 223 | 19 | 0 |
| R. Smith | 2 | 32 | 16 | 0 |
| Russell | 2 | 28 | 14 | 0 |
| Giammona | 1 | 19 | 19 | 0 |
| Atkins | 1 | 15 | 15 | 0 |
| Murray | 1 | 14 | 14 | 0 |
| Clarke | 1 | 0 | 0 | 0 |

### Passing – Punting – Kicking

| PASSING | Att. | Comp. | % | Yds. | Yd./Att. | TD | Int.-% | RK |
|---|---|---|---|---|---|---|---|---|
| Jaworski | 461 | 250 | 54 | 3095 | 6.7 | 23 | 20- 4 | 8 |
| Pisarcik | 15 | 8 | 53 | 154 | 10.3 | 2 | 2- 13 | |

| PUNTING | No. | Avg. |
|---|---|---|
| Runager | 63 | 40.7 |
| Franklin | 1 | 13.0 |

| KICKING | XP | Att. | % | FG | Att. | % |
|---|---|---|---|---|---|---|
| Franklin | 41 | 43 | 95 | 20 | 31 | 65 |

## NEW YORK GIANTS

### Rushing

| Last Name | No. | Yds. | Avg. | TD |
|---|---|---|---|---|
| Carpenter | 208 | 822 | 4.0 | 5 |
| Perry | 72 | 257 | 3.6 | 0 |
| Bright | 51 | 197 | 3.9 | 2 |
| Kotar | 46 | 154 | 3.3 | 1 |
| B. Taylor | 38 | 111 | 2.9 | 2 |
| Forte | 19 | 74 | 3.9 | 0 |
| L. Jackson | 27 | 68 | 2.5 | 1 |
| Simms | 19 | 42 | 2.2 | 0 |
| Brunner | 14 | 20 | 1.4 | 0 |
| Matthews | 4 | 14 | 3.5 | 0 |
| Garrett | 1 | 2 | 2.0 | 0 |
| Perkins | 2 | −1 | −0.5 | 0 |

### Receiving

| Last Name | No. | Yds. | Avg. | TD |
|---|---|---|---|---|
| Perkins | 51 | 858 | 17 | 6 |
| Shirk | 42 | 445 | 11 | 3 |
| Carpenter | 37 | 281 | 8 | 1 |
| Bright | 28 | 291 | 10 | 0 |
| Gray | 22 | 360 | 16 | 2 |
| Friede | 18 | 250 | 14 | 1 |
| Mullady | 14 | 136 | 10 | 1 |
| Perry | 13 | 140 | 11 | 1 |
| Kotar | 9 | 32 | 4 | 0 |
| Mistler | 8 | 119 | 15 | 1 |
| B. Taylor | 8 | 71 | 9 | 0 |
| Young | 5 | 49 | 10 | 1 |
| L. Jackson | 3 | 25 | 8 | 0 |
| Forte | 3 | 11 | 4 | 0 |
| Matthews | 2 | 13 | 7 | 0 |
| Pittman | 1 | 8 | 8 | 0 |

### Punt Returns

| Last Name | No. | Yds. | Avg. | TD |
|---|---|---|---|---|
| Bright | 52 | 410 | 8 | 0 |
| Garrett | 8 | 57 | 7 | 0 |
| T. Jackson | 2 | 22 | 11 | 0 |
| Pittman | 1 | 13 | 13 | 0 |
| Reece | 1 | 0 | 0 | 0 |

### Kickoff Returns

| Last Name | No. | Yds. | Avg. | TD |
|---|---|---|---|---|
| Garrett | 18 | 401 | 22 | 0 |
| Bright | 25 | 481 | 19 | 0 |
| Pittman | 10 | 194 | 19 | 0 |
| Dennis | 3 | 51 | 17 | 0 |
| McLaughlin | 2 | 9 | 5 | 0 |
| Reece | 1 | 24 | 24 | 0 |

### Passing – Punting – Kicking

| PASSING | Att. | Comp. | % | Yds. | Yd./Att. | TD | Int.-% | RK |
|---|---|---|---|---|---|---|---|---|
| Simms | 316 | 172 | 54 | 2031 | 6.4 | 11 | 9- 3 | 7 |
| Brunner | 190 | 79 | 42 | 978 | 5.2 | 5 | 11- 6 | |

| PUNTING | No. | Avg. |
|---|---|---|
| Jennings | 97 | 43.3 |

| KICKING | XP | Att. | % | FG | Att. | % |
|---|---|---|---|---|---|---|
| Danelo | 31 | 31 | 100 | 24 | 38 | 63 |

## WASHINGTON REDSKINS

### Rushing

| Last Name | No. | Yds. | Avg. | TD |
|---|---|---|---|---|
| Washington | 210 | 916 | 4.4 | 4 |
| Riggins | 195 | 714 | 3.7 | 13 |
| Jackson | 46 | 183 | 4.0 | 0 |
| Theismann | 36 | 177 | 4.9 | 2 |
| Giaquinto | 20 | 104 | 5.2 | 0 |
| Metcalf | 18 | 60 | 3.3 | 0 |
| Claitt | 3 | 19 | 6.3 | 0 |
| Wonsley | 3 | 11 | 3.7 | 0 |
| Walker | 1 | 5 | 5.0 | 0 |
| Harmon | 1 | 4 | 4.0 | 0 |
| Connell | 1 | 0 | 0.0 | 0 |
| Monk | 1 | −5 | −5.0 | 0 |

### Receiving

| Last Name | No. | Yds. | Avg. | TD |
|---|---|---|---|---|
| Washington | 70 | 558 | 8 | 3 |
| Monk | 56 | 894 | 16 | 6 |
| Metcalf | 48 | 595 | 12 | 0 |
| Warren | 29 | 335 | 12 | 1 |
| Thompson | 28 | 423 | 15 | 4 |
| Seay | 26 | 472 | 18 | 3 |
| Giaquinto | 12 | 93 | 8 | 2 |
| Walker | 11 | 112 | 10 | 1 |
| Harmon | 11 | 98 | 9 | 0 |
| Jackson | 7 | 51 | 7 | 0 |
| Riggins | 6 | 59 | 10 | 0 |
| McCrary | 3 | 13 | 4 | 0 |
| Wonsley | 1 | 5 | 5 | 0 |
| Bostic | 1 | −4 | −4 | 0 |

### Punt Returns

| Last Name | No. | Yds. | Avg. | TD |
|---|---|---|---|---|
| Nelms | 45 | 492 | 11 | 2 |
| Metcalf | 4 | 15 | 4 | 0 |

### Kickoff Returns

| Last Name | No. | Yds. | Avg. | TD |
|---|---|---|---|---|
| Nelms | 37 | 1099 | 30 | 0 |
| Metcalf | 14 | 283 | 20 | 0 |
| Wonsley | 6 | 124 | 21 | 0 |
| Cronan | 3 | 60 | 20 | 0 |
| Seay | 2 | 36 | 18 | 0 |
| Jackson | 2 | 34 | 17 | 0 |
| Giaquinto | 1 | 22 | 22 | 0 |
| Grant | 1 | 20 | 20 | 0 |
| Claitt | 1 | 14 | 14 | 0 |
| Peters | 1 | 5 | 5 | 0 |

### Passing – Punting – Kicking

| PASSING | Att. | Comp. | % | Yds. | Yd./Att. | TD | Int.-% | RK |
|---|---|---|---|---|---|---|---|---|
| Theismann | 496 | 293 | 59 | 3568 | 7.2 | 19 | 20- 4 | 5 |
| Flick | 27 | 13 | 48 | 143 | 5.3 | 0 | 2- 7 | |
| Washington | 2 | 1 | 50 | 32 | 16.0 | 0 | 0- 0 | |

| PUNTING | No. | Avg. |
|---|---|---|
| Connell | 73 | 40.0 |

| KICKING | XP | Att. | % | FG | Att. | % |
|---|---|---|---|---|---|---|
| Moseley | 38 | 42 | 90 | 19 | 30 | 63 |

## ST. LOUIS CARDINALS

### Rushing

| Last Name | No. | Yds. | Avg. | TD |
|---|---|---|---|---|
| Anderson | 328 | 1376 | 4.2 | 9 |
| Morris | 109 | 417 | 3.8 | 5 |
| Mitchell | 31 | 175 | 5.6 | 0 |
| Lomax | 19 | 104 | 5.5 | 2 |
| Green | 3 | 60 | 20.0 | 1 |
| Love | 3 | 11 | 3.7 | 0 |
| Stief | 1 | 8 | 8.0 | 0 |
| Harrell | 5 | 6 | 1.2 | 1 |
| Gray | 1 | 4 | 4.0 | 0 |
| Hart | 3 | 2 | 0.7 | 0 |
| Birdsong | 1 | −2 | −2.0 | 0 |

### Receiving

| Last Name | No. | Yds. | Avg. | TD |
|---|---|---|---|---|
| Tilley | 66 | 1040 | 16 | 3 |
| Anderson | 51 | 387 | 8 | 0 |
| Green | 33 | 708 | 22 | 4 |
| Gray | 27 | 310 | 12 | 2 |
| Morris | 19 | 165 | 9 | 0 |
| LaFleur | 14 | 190 | 14 | 2 |
| Harrell | 14 | 131 | 9 | 1 |
| Marsh | 6 | 80 | 13 | 1 |
| Mitchell | 6 | 35 | 6 | 1 |
| Stief | 5 | 77 | 15 | 1 |
| Combs | 5 | 54 | 11 | 0 |
| Floyd | 3 | 32 | 11 | 0 |

### Punt Returns

| Last Name | No. | Yds. | Avg. | TD |
|---|---|---|---|---|
| Mitchell | 42 | 445 | 11 | 1 |
| Harrell | 1 | 8 | 8 | 0 |

### Kickoff Returns

| Last Name | No. | Yds. | Avg. | TD |
|---|---|---|---|---|
| Mitchell | 55 | 1292 | 24 | 0 |
| Green | 8 | 135 | 17 | 0 |
| Harrell | 7 | 118 | 17 | 0 |
| Love | 3 | 46 | 15 | 0 |
| Griffin | 2 | 34 | 17 | 0 |

### Passing – Punting – Kicking

| PASSING | Att. | Comp. | % | Yds. | Yd./Att. | TD | Int.-% | RK |
|---|---|---|---|---|---|---|---|---|
| Hart | 241 | 134 | 56 | 1694 | 7.0 | 11 | 14- 6 | 11 |
| Lomax | 236 | 119 | 50 | 1575 | 6.7 | 4 | 10- 4 | 14 |

| PUNTING | No. | Avg. |
|---|---|---|
| Birdsong | 69 | 41.8 |

| KICKING | XP | Att. | % | FG | Att. | % |
|---|---|---|---|---|---|---|
| O'Donoghue | 36 | 37 | 97 | 19 | 32 | 59 |

### TAMPA BAY BUCCANEERS 9-7-0 John McKay

| Scores of Each Game | | |
|---|---|---|
| 21 | MINNESOTA | 13 |
| 10 | Kansas City | 19 |
| 17 | Chicago | 28 |
| 20 | ST. LOUIS | 10 |
| 28 | DETROIT | 10 |
| 21 | Green Bay | 10 |
| 16 | Oakland | 18 |
| 10 | Philadelphia | 20 |
| 20 | CHICAGO | 10 |
| 10 | Minnesota | 25 |
| 7 | DENVER | 24 |
| 37 | GREEN BAY | 3 |
| 31 | New Orleans | 14 |
| 24 | ATLANTA | 23 |
| 23 | SAN DIEGO | 24 |
| 20 | Detroit | 17 |

| Use Name | Pos. | Hgt. | Wgt. | Age | Int. | Pts. |
|---|---|---|---|---|---|---|
| **Charley Hannah** | OT | 6'5" | 260 | 26 | | |
| Dave Reavis | OT | 6'5" | 260 | 31 | | |
| Gene Sanders | OT | 6'3" | 260 | 24 | | |
| Greg Roberts | OG | 6'3" | 260 | 24 | | |
| Ray Snell | OG-OT | 6'3" | 255 | 23 | | |
| George Yarno | OG | 6'2" | 255 | 24 | | |
| Jim Leonard | OG-C | 6'3" | 250 | 23 | | |
| Steve Wilson | C | 6'3" | 265 | 27 | | |
| Joe Campbell (from OAK) | DE | 6'6" | 250 | 26 | | |
| Scott Hutchinson | DE | 6'4" | 245 | 25 | | |
| Bill Kollar | DE | 6'4" | 250 | 28 | | |
| **Lee Roy Selmon** | DE | 6'3" | 250 | 26 | | |
| David Stalls | DE | 6'4" | 250 | 25 | | |
| David Logan | NT | 6'2" | 250 | 24 | | 6 |
| Laval Short | NT | 6'3" | 250 | 22 | | |
| Brad White | NT | 6'2" | 250 | 23 | | |
| Scot Brantley | LB | 6'1" | 230 | 23 | 1 | |
| Hugh Green | LB | 6'2" | 225 | 22 | 2 | |
| Andy Hawkins | LB | 6'2" | 220 | 23 | | |
| Cecil Johnson | LB | 6'2" | 230 | 26 | 5 | |
| Dave Lewis | LB | 6'4" | 245 | 26 | 2 | |
| Dana Nafziger | LB | 6'1" | 220 | 27 | | |
| Richard Wood | LB | 6'2" | 230 | 28 | | |
| Cedric Brown | DB | 6'1" | 205 | 27 | 9 | 12 |
| Billy Cesare | DB | 5'11" | 190 | 26 | | |
| Neal Colzie | DB | 6'2" | 195 | 28 | 6 | 6 |
| John Holt | DB | 5'11" | 180 | 22 | 1 | |
| Aaron Mitchell | DB | 6'1" | 196 | 24 | | |
| Norris Thomas | DB | 5'11" | 185 | 27 | | |
| Mike Washington | DB | 6'3" | 200 | 28 | 6 | 6 |
| Mike Ford | QB | 6'3" | 220 | 22 | | |
| Chuck Fusina | QB | 6'1" | 195 | 24 | | |
| Doug Williams | QB | 6'4" | 215 | 26 | | 24 |
| Ricky Bell | HB-FB | 6'2" | 215 | 26 | | |
| Gary Davis (to CLE) | HB | 5'10" | 210 | 26 | | |
| Jerry Eckwood | HB-FB | 6' | 200 | 26 | | 12 |
| James Owens | HB | 5'11" | 188 | 26 | | 18 |
| Tony Davis | FB | 5'10" | 210 | 28 | | |
| James Wilder | FB | 6'2" | 220 | 23 | | 30 |
| Theo Bell | WR | 5'11" | 180 | 27 | | 12 |
| Gerald Carter | WR | 6'1" | 185 | 24 | | |
| Kevin House | WR | 6'1" | 175 | 23 | | 54 |
| Gordon Jones | WR | 6' | 190 | 24 | | 6 |
| **Jimmie Giles** | TE | 6'3" | 240 | 26 | | 36 |
| Jim Obradovich | TE | 6'2" | 230 | 28 | | 6 |
| Tom Blanchard | K | 6' | 180 | 33 | | |
| Bill Capece | K | 5'7" | 170 | 22 | | 75 |
| Larry Swider | K | 6'2" | 195 | 26 | | |
| Garo Yepremian | K | 5'8" | 175 | 37 | | 12 |

Darrell Austin – Neck Injury
Mark Cotney – Knee Injury
Randy Crowder – Knee Injury
Tony Samuels – Knee Injury
Dewey Selmon – Hamstring Injury

### DETROIT LIONS 8-8-0 Monte Clark

| Scores of Each Game | | |
|---|---|---|
| 24 | SAN FRANCISCO | 17 |
| 23 | San Diego | 28 |
| 24 | Minnesota | 26 |
| 16 | OAKLAND | 0 |
| 10 | Tampa Bay | 28 |
| 21 | Denver | 27 |
| 48 | CHICAGO | 17 |
| 31 | GREEN BAY | 27 |
| 13 | Los Angeles | 20 |
| 31 | Washington | 33 |
| 27 | DALLAS | 24 |
| 23 | Chicago | 7 |
| 27 | KANSAS CITY | 10 |
| 17 | Green Bay | 31 |
| 45 | MINNESOTA | 7 |
| 17 | TAMPA BAY | 20 |

| Use Name | Pos. | Hgt. | Wgt. | Age | Int. | Pts. |
|---|---|---|---|---|---|---|
| Karl Baldischwiler | OT | 6'5" | 265 | 25 | | |
| **Chris Dieterich** | OT | 6'3" | 269 | 23 | | |
| Keith Dorney | OT | 6'5" | 265 | 23 | | |
| Russ Bolinger | OG | 6'5" | 255 | 26 | | |
| Homer Elias | OG | 6'3" | 255 | 26 | | |
| Tommie Ginn | OG | 6'3" | 255 | 23 | | |
| Larry Lee | OG-C | 6'2" | 274 | 21 | | |
| Amos Fowler | C | 6'3" | 250 | 25 | | |
| Tom Turnure | C | 6'4" | 243 | 24 | | |
| Al Baker | DE | 6'6" | 250 | 24 | | |
| Dave Pureifory | DE | 6'1" | 255 | 32 | | |
| Curly Culp | DT | 6'1" | 265 | 35 | | |
| Joe Ehrmann | DT | 6'5" | 250 | 32 | | |
| Doug English | DT | 6'5" | 255 | 28 | | |
| Edgar Fields | DT | 6'2" | 255 | 27 | | |
| Steve Furness | DT | 6'4" | 255 | 30 | | |
| **William Gay** | DT-DE | 6'5" | 250 | 26 | | |
| Curtis Green | DT-DE | 6'3" | 256 | 24 | | |
| Garry Cobb | LB | 6'2" | 210 | 24 | 3 | |
| Ken Fantetti | LB | 6'2" | 230 | 24 | 2 | |
| James Harrell | LB | 6'1" | 215 | 24 | | |
| Terry Tautolo (from S.F.) | LB | 6'2" | 235 | 27 | | |
| Charlie Weaver (to WAS) | LB | 6'2" | 225 | 32 | | |
| Stan White | LB | 6'1" | 225 | 31 | 4 | |
| Jim Allen | DB | 6'2" | 195 | 29 | 9 | |
| Luther Bradley | DB | 6'2" | 195 | 26 | 1 | |
| Jeff Delaney (to T.B.) | DB | 6' | 195 | 24 | | |
| Hector Gray | DB | 6'1" | 197 | 24 | 1 | |
| Alvin Hall | DB | 5'10" | 193 | 23 | 1 | 6 |
| James Hunter | DB | 6'3" | 195 | 27 | 1 | |
| Ray Oldham | DB | 6' | 192 | 30 | 1 | |
| Wayne Smith | DB | 6' | 170 | 24 | | |
| Gary Danielson | QB | 6'2 | 195 | 29 | | 12 |
| Eric Hipple | QB | 6'2" | 196 | 23 | | 42 |
| Jeff Komlo | QB | 6'2" | 200 | 25 | | |
| Ken Callicutt | HB | 6' | 190 | 26 | | |
| Rick Kane | HB-FB | 5'11" | 200 | 26 | | 18 |
| Billy Sims | HB | 6' | 212 | 25 | | 90 |
| Dexter Bussey | FB | 6'1" | 210 | 29 | | |
| Horace King | FB-HB | 5'10" | 210 | 28 | | 6 |
| Vince Thompson | FB | 6' | 230 | 24 | | 6 |
| Robbie Martin | WR | 5'8" | 179 | 22 | | 6 |
| Mark Nichols | WR | 6'2" | 213 | 21 | | 6 |
| Tracy Porter | WR | 6'1" | 196 | 22 | | 6 |
| Freddie Scott | WR | 6'2" | 175 | 29 | | 30 |
| Leonard Thompson | WR | 5'10" | 190 | 29 | | 24 |
| David Hill | TE | 6'2" | 230 | 27 | | 24 |
| Bob Niziolek | TE | 6'4" | 220 | 23 | | |
| Ulysses Norris | TE | 6'4" | 225 | 24 | | |
| **Eddie Murray** | K | 5'10" | 165 | 25 | | 121 |
| Tom Skladany | K | 6' | 195 | 26 | | |

Jesse Thompson – Achilles Injury
Steve Towle – Hamstring Injury
Ray Williams – Knee Injury

### GREEN BAY PACKERS 8-8-0 Bart Starr

| Scores of Each Game | | |
|---|---|---|
| 16 | Chicago | 9 |
| 17 | ATLANTA | 31 |
| 23 | Los Angeles | 35 |
| 13 | MINNESOTA | 30 |
| 27 | N.Y. Giants | 14 |
| 10 | TAMPA BAY | 21 |
| 3 | SAN FRANCISCO | 13 |
| 27 | Detroit | 31 |
| 34 | SEATTLE | 24 |
| 26 | N.Y. GIANTS | 24 |
| 21 | CHICAGO | 17 |
| 3 | Tampa Bay | 37 |
| 35 | Minnesota | 23 |
| 31 | DETROIT | 17 |
| 35 | New Orleans | 7 |
| 3 | N.Y. Jets | 28 |

| Use Name | Pos. | Hgt. | Wgt. | Age | Int. | Pts. |
|---|---|---|---|---|---|---|
| Tim Huffman | OT-OG | 6'5" | 277 | 22 | | |
| Greg Koch | OT | 6'4" | 265 | 26 | | |
| Mark Koncar | OT | 6'5" | 268 | 28 | | |
| Tim Stokes (from NYG) | OT | 6'5" | 252 | 31 | | |
| Karl Swanke | OT-OG | 6'6" | 250 | 23 | | 6 |
| Derrel Gofourth | OG | 6'3" | 260 | 26 | | |
| Leotis Harris | OG | 6'1" | 267 | 26 | | |
| Syd Kitson | OG-OT | 6'4" | 252 | 22 | | |
| Arland Thompson | OG | 6'3" | 265 | 23 | | |
| Charlie Ane | C | 6'1" | 237 | 29 | | |
| Larry McCarren | C | 6'3" | 238 | 29 | | |
| Byron Braggs | DE | 6'4" | 290 | 21 | | |
| Mike Butler | DE | 6'5" | 265 | 27 | | |
| Ezra Johnson | DE | 6'4" | 240 | 25 | | |
| Casey Merrill | DE | 6'4" | 255 | 24 | | |
| Terry Jones | NT | 6'2" | 259 | 24 | | |
| Richard Turner | NT | 6'2" | 260 | 22 | | |
| Kurt Allerman | LB | 6'3" | 222 | 26 | | |
| John Anderson | LB | 6'3" | 221 | 25 | 3 | |
| George Cumby | LB | 6' | 215 | 25 | 3 | |
| Mike Douglass | LB | 6' | 224 | 26 | 3 | |
| Cliff Lewis | LB | 6'1" | 226 | 21 | | |
| Guy Prather | LB | 6'2" | 230 | 23 | | |
| Randy Scott | LB | 6'1" | 220 | 22 | | |
| Rich Wingo | LB | 6'1" | 230 | 25 | 1 | 1 |
| Johnnie Gray | DB | 5'11" | 185 | 27 | | |
| Maurice Harvey | DB | 5'10" | 190 | 25 | 6 | |
| Estus Hood | DB | 5'11" | 180 | 25 | 3 | 6 |
| Mark Lee | DB | 5'11" | 186 | 23 | 6 | 6 |
| Mike McCoy | DB | 5'11" | 183 | 28 | 2 | |
| Mark Murphy | DB | 6'2" | 199 | 23 | 3 | |
| David Petway | DB | 6'1" | 207 | 25 | | |
| Bill Whitaker | DB | 6' | 182 | 21 | | |
| Rich Campbell | QB | 6'4" | 224 | 22 | | |
| Lynn Dickey | QB | 6'4" | 220 | 31 | | |
| David Whitehurst | QB | 6'2" | 204 | 26 | | 6 |
| Harlan Huckleby | HB | 6'1" | 200 | 23 | | 48 |
| Eddie Lee Ivery | HB | 6'1" | 210 | 24 | | 6 |
| Terdell Middleton | HB | 6' | 195 | 26 | | 6 |
| Del Williams | HB | 6' | 200 | 30 | | |
| Gerry Ellis | FB | 5'11" | 215 | 23 | | 42 |
| Jim Jensen | FB | 6'3" | 230 | 27 | | |
| Eric Torkelson | FB-HB | 6'2" | 210 | 29 | | |
| Ron Cassidy | WR | 6' | 185 | 24 | | |
| John Jefferson | WR | 6'1" | 198 | 25 | | 24 |
| James Lofton | WR | 6'3" | 187 | 25 | | 48 |
| Fred Nixon | WR | 5'11" | 190 | 22 | | |
| Paul Coffman | TE | 6'3" | 218 | 25 | | 24 |
| Bill Larson | TE | 6'4" | 225 | 27 | | |
| Gary Lewis | TE-WR | 6'5" | 234 | 22 | | |
| John Thompson | TE | 6'3" | 228 | 24 | | |
| Ray Stachowicz | K | 5'11" | 185 | 22 | | |
| Jan Stenerud | K | 6'2" | 190 | 38 | | 10 |

Buddy Aydelette – Knee Injury
Chris Godfrey – Knee Injury
Mike Jolly – Knee Injury
Paul Rudzinski – Back Injury

### MINNESOTA VIKINGS 7-9-0 Bud Grant

| Scores of Each Game | | |
|---|---|---|
| 13 | Tampa Bay | 21 |
| 10 | OAKLAND | 36 |
| 26 | DETROIT | 24 |
| 30 | Green Bay | 13 |
| 24 | CHICAGO | 21 |
| 33 | San Diego | 31 |
| 35 | PHILADELPHIA | 23 |
| 17 | St. Louis | 30 |
| 17 | Denver | 19 |
| 25 | TAMPA BAY | 10 |
| 20 | NEW ORLEANS | 10 |
| 30 | Atlanta | 31 |
| 23 | GREEN BAY | 35 |
| 9 | Chicago | 10 |
| 7 | Detroit | 45 |
| 6 | KANSAS CITY | 10 |

| Use Name | Pos. | Hgt. | Wgt. | Age | Int. | Pts. |
|---|---|---|---|---|---|---|
| Tim Irwin | OT | 6'6" | 275 | 24 | | |
| Steve Riley | OT | 6'6" | 253 | 28 | | |
| Ron Yary | OT | 6'6" | 255 | 35 | | |
| Brent Boyd | OG | 6'3" | 260 | 24 | | |
| Wes Hamilton | OG | 6'3" | 255 | 28 | | |
| Jim Hough | OG | 6'2" | 267 | 25 | | |
| Dave Huffman | OG | 6'6" | 255 | 24 | | |
| Jim Langer | C | 6'2" | 253 | 33 | | |
| Dennis Swilley | C | 6'3" | 241 | 26 | | |
| Neil Elshire | DE | 6'6" | 256 | 23 | | |
| Randy Holloway | DE | 6'5" | 245 | 26 | | 6 |
| Doug Martin | DE | 6'3" | 258 | 24 | | |
| Mark Mullaney | DE | 6'6" | 242 | 28 | | |
| Ken Sanders | DE | 6'5" | 245 | 31 | | |
| James White | NT | 6'3" | 263 | 27 | | |
| Ray Yakavonis | NT | 6'4" | 243 | 24 | | |
| Matt Blair | LB | 6'5" | 229 | 30 | 1 | |
| Dennis Johnson | LB | 6'3" | 230 | 23 | | |
| Henry Johnson | LB | 6'1" | 235 | 23 | | |
| Fred McNeill | LB | 6'2" | 229 | 29 | 2 | |
| Robin Sendlein | LB | 6'3" | 224 | 22 | | |
| Jeff Siemon | LB | 6'2" | 237 | 31 | | |
| Scott Studwell | LB | 6'2" | 237 | 27 | | |
| Tom Hannon | DB | 5'11" | 193 | 26 | 4 | 4 |
| Kurt Knoff | DB | 6'2" | 188 | 27 | 3 | |
| Keith Nord | DB | 6' | 197 | 24 | | |
| John Swain | DB | 6'1" | 195 | 21 | 2 | |
| Willie Teal | DB | 5'10" | 195 | 23 | 4 | |
| John Turner | DB | 6' | 199 | 25 | | |
| Walt Williams | DB | 6' | 185 | 27 | | 2 |
| Steve Dils | QB | 6'1" | 190 | 25 | | |
| Tommy Kramer | QB | 6'1" | 199 | 26 | | |
| Wade Wilson | QB | 6'3" | 212 | 22 | | |
| Eddie Payton | HB | 5'8" | 179 | 30 | | 6 |
| Jarvis Redwine | HB | 5'10" | 198 | 24 | | |
| Rickey Young | HB | 6'2" | 195 | 27 | | 12 |
| Ted Brown | FB-HB | 5'10" | 198 | 24 | | 48 |
| Tony Galbreath | FB | 6' | 230 | 27 | | 12 |
| Sam Harrell | FB | 6'2" | 213 | 24 | | |
| Terry LeCount | WR | 5'10" | 172 | 25 | | 12 |
| Leo Lewis | WR | 5'8" | 170 | 24 | | |
| Mardye McDole | WR | 5'11" | 195 | 22 | | |
| Ahmad Rashad | WR | 6'2" | 200 | 31 | | 42 |
| Sammy White | WR | 5'11" | 189 | 27 | | 18 |
| **Bob Bruer** | TE | 6'5" | 235 | 28 | | 18 |
| Joe Senser | TE | 6'4" | 238 | 25 | | 48 |
| Greg Coleman | K | 6' | 178 | 26 | | |
| Rick Danmeier | K | 6' | 200 | 29 | | 97 |

Doug Paschal – Knee Injury

### CHICAGO BEARS 6-10-0 Neill Armstrong

| Scores of Each Game | | |
|---|---|---|
| 9 | GREEN BAY | 16 |
| 17 | San Francisco | 28 |
| 28 | TAMPA BAY | 17 |
| 7 | LOS ANGELES | 24 |
| 21 | Minnesota | 24 |
| 7 | WASHINGTON | 24 |
| 17 | Detroit | 48 |
| 20 | SAN DIEGO | *17 |
| 10 | Tampa Bay | 20 |
| 16 | Kansas City | *13 |
| 17 | Green Bay | 21 |
| 7 | DETROIT | 23 |
| 9 | Dallas | 10 |
| 10 | MINNESOTA | 9 |
| 23 | Oakland | 6 |
| 35 | DENVER | 24 |

| Use Name | Pos. | Hgt. | Wgt. | Age | Int. | Pts. |
|---|---|---|---|---|---|---|
| Ted Albrecht | OT-OG | 6'4" | 250 | 26 | | |
| Dan Jiggetts | OT-OG | 6'4" | 270 | 27 | | |
| Dennis Lick | OT | 6'3" | 265 | 27 | | |
| Keith Van Horne | OT | 6'6" | 265 | 23 | | |
| Noah Jackson | OG | 6'2" | 265 | 30 | | |
| Revie Sorey | OG | 6'2" | 260 | 27 | | |
| Emanuel Zanders | OG | 6'1" | 248 | 30 | | |
| Jay Hilgenberg | C | 6'3" | 250 | 22 | | |
| Dan Neal | C | 6'4" | 255 | 32 | | |
| Dan Hampton | DE-DT | 6'5" | 255 | 23 | | |
| Al Harris | DE | 6'5" | 240 | 24 | 1 | 6 |
| Mike Hartenstine | DE | 6'3" | 243 | 28 | | |
| Steve McMichael | DT | 6'1" | 245 | 23 | | |
| Jim Osborne | DT | 6'2" | 245 | 31 | | |
| Alan Page | DT | 6'5" | 225 | 36 | | |
| Brad Shearer | DT | 6'3" | 247 | 26 | | |
| Brian Cabral | LB | 6' | 224 | 25 | | |
| Gary Campbell | LB | 6'1" | 220 | 29 | | |
| Bruce Herron | LB | 6'2" | 220 | 27 | | |
| Lee Kunz | LB | 6'2" | 225 | 24 | | |
| Mike Singletary | LB | 5'11" | 230 | 22 | 1 | |
| Otis Wilson | LB | 6'2" | 222 | 23 | | |
| Todd Bell | DB | 6'1" | 207 | 22 | 1 | 6 |
| Gary Fencik | DB | 6'1" | 197 | 27 | 6 | 6 |
| Jeff Fisher | DB | 5'11" | 188 | 23 | 2 | 6 |
| **Leslie Frazier** | DB | 6' | 189 | 22 | | |
| Reuben Henderson | DB | 6'1" | 200 | 22 | 4 | |
| Doug Plank | DB | 6' | 202 | 28 | | 2 |
| Terry Schmidt | DB | 6' | 177 | 29 | 2 | |
| Len Walterscheid | DB | 5'11" | 190 | 26 | 1 | |
| Bob Avellini | QB | 6'2" | 210 | 28 | | |
| Vince Evans | QB | 6'2" | 212 | 26 | | 18 |
| Mike Phipps | QB | 6'3" | 209 | 33 | | |
| Willie McClendon | HB | 6'1" | 205 | 23 | | |
| Walter Payton | HB | 5'11" | 202 | 27 | | 48 |
| Roland Harper | FB | 6' | 210 | 28 | | 6 |
| John Skibinski | FB | 6' | 222 | 26 | | |
| Matt Suhey | FB | 5'11" | 212 | 23 | | 18 |
| Dave Williams | FB-HB | 6'2" | 217 | 27 | | 12 |
| Marcus Anderson | WR | 6' | 178 | 22 | | 12 |
| Brian Baschnagel | WR | 6' | 184 | 27 | | 18 |
| Kris Haines | WR | 5'11" | 180 | 24 | | |
| Ken Margerum | WR | 5'11" | 170 | 22 | | 6 |
| Emery Moorehead | WR | 6'2" | 210 | 27 | | |
| Rickey Watts | WR | 6'1" | 203 | 24 | | 18 |
| Mike Cobb | TE | 6'5" | 243 | 25 | | |
| Robin Earl | TE | 6'5" | 240 | 26 | | 6 |
| Robert Fisher | TE | 6'3" | 240 | 23 | | |
| Bob Parsons | TE | 6'4" | 225 | 31 | | |
| Hans Nielsen | K | 5'11" | 165 | 28 | | 8 |
| John Roveto | K | 5'11" | 175 | 23 | | 49 |
| Bob Thomas | K | 5'10" | 175 | 29 | | 8 |

Jerry Muckensturm – Shoulder Injury
Paul Tabor – Knee Injury

*—Overtime

## TAMPA BAY BUCCANEERS

### Rushing

| Last Name | No. | Yds. | Avg. | TD |
|---|---|---|---|---|
| Eckwood | 172 | 651 | 3.8 | 2 |
| Owens | 91 | 406 | 4.5 | 3 |
| Wilder | 107 | 370 | 3.5 | 4 |
| Williams | 48 | 209 | 4.4 | 4 |
| R. Bell | 30 | 80 | 2.7 | 0 |
| House | 2 | 9 | 4.5 | 0 |
| T. Bell | 1 | 7 | 7.0 | 0 |
| T. Davis | 2 | 5 | 2.5 | 0 |
| Fusina | 3 | 3 | 1.0 | 0 |
| Blanchard | 1 | 0 | 0.0 | 0 |
| Swider | 1 | −9 | −9.0 | 0 |

### Receiving

| Last Name | No. | Yds. | Avg. | TD |
|---|---|---|---|---|
| House | 56 | 1176 | 21 | 9 |
| Wilder | 48 | 507 | 11 | 1 |
| Giles | 45 | 786 | 18 | 6 |
| Eckwood | 24 | 213 | 9 | 0 |
| T. Bell | 21 | 318 | 15 | 2 |
| Jones | 20 | 276 | 14 | 1 |
| Owens | 12 | 145 | 12 | 0 |
| R. Bell | 8 | 92 | 12 | 0 |
| Obradovich | 4 | 42 | 11 | 1 |
| Carter | 1 | 10 | 10 | 0 |

### Punt Returns

| Last Name | No. | Yds. | Avg. | TD |
|---|---|---|---|---|
| T. Bell | 27 | 132 | 5 | 0 |
| Holt | 9 | 100 | 11 | 0 |
| Colzie | 2 | 12 | 6 | 0 |

### Kickoff Returns

| Last Name | No. | Yds. | Avg. | TD |
|---|---|---|---|---|
| Owens | 24 | 473 | 20 | 0 |
| Holt | 11 | 274 | 25 | 0 |
| G. Davis | 5 | 81 | 16 | 0 |
| T. Davis | 3 | 51 | 17 | 0 |
| Wilder | 1 | 19 | 19 | 0 |
| Obradovich | 1 | 14 | 14 | 0 |
| Brantley | 1 | 0 | 0 | 0 |

### Passing – Punting – Kicking

| PASSING | Att. | Comp. | % | Yds. | Yd./Att. | TD | Int.–% | RK |
|---|---|---|---|---|---|---|---|---|
| Williams | 471 | 238 | 51 | 3563 | 7.6 | 19 | 14– 3 | 6 |
| Fusina | 1 | 1 | 100 | 2 | 2.0 | 1 | 0– 0 | |
| House | 1 | 0 | 0 | 0 | 0.0 | 0 | 0– 0 | |

| PUNTING | No. | Avg. |
|---|---|---|
| Swider | 58 | 42.7 |
| Blanchard | 22 | 40.9 |

| KICKING | XP | Att. | % | FG | Att. | % |
|---|---|---|---|---|---|---|
| Capece | 30 | 32 | 93 | 15 | 24 | 63 |
| Yepremian | 6 | 6 | 100 | 2 | 4 | 50 |

## DETROIT LIONS

### Rushing

| Last Name | No. | Yds. | Avg. | TD |
|---|---|---|---|---|
| Sims | 296 | 1437 | 4.9 | 13 |
| Bussey | 105 | 446 | 4.2 | 0 |
| Kane | 77 | 332 | 4.3 | 2 |
| V. Thompson | 35 | 211 | 6.0 | 1 |
| Hipple | 41 | 168 | 4.1 | 7 |
| L. Thompson | 10 | 75 | 7.5 | 1 |
| Nichols | 3 | 50 | 16.7 | 0 |
| King | 7 | 25 | 3.6 | 0 |
| Scott | 7 | 25 | 3.6 | 0 |
| Danielson | 9 | 23 | 2.6 | 2 |
| Komlo | 6 | 3 | 0.5 | 0 |

### Receiving

| Last Name | No. | Yds. | Avg. | TD |
|---|---|---|---|---|
| Scott | 53 | 1022 | 19 | 5 |
| Hill | 33 | 462 | 14 | 4 |
| L. Thompson | 30 | 550 | 18 | 3 |
| Sims | 28 | 451 | 16 | 2 |
| King | 20 | 211 | 11 | 1 |
| Kane | 18 | 187 | 10 | 1 |
| Bussey | 18 | 92 | 5 | 0 |
| Nichols | 10 | 222 | 22 | 1 |
| Norris | 8 | 132 | 17 | 0 |
| V. Thompson | 4 | 40 | 10 | 0 |
| Porter | 3 | 63 | 21 | 1 |
| Callicutt | 2 | 24 | 12 | 0 |
| Cobb | 1 | 19 | 19 | 0 |

### Punt Returns

| Last Name | No. | Yds. | Avg. | TD |
|---|---|---|---|---|
| Martin | 52 | 450 | 9 | 1 |

### Kickoff Returns

| Last Name | No. | Yds. | Avg. | TD |
|---|---|---|---|---|
| Hall | 25 | 525 | 21 | 0 |
| Martin | 25 | 509 | 20 | 0 |
| Nichols | 4 | 74 | 19 | 0 |
| King | 3 | 33 | 11 | 0 |
| Callicutt | 2 | 23 | 12 | 0 |
| Harrell | 1 | 0 | 0 | 0 |
| Lee | 1 | 0 | 0 | 0 |

### Passing – Punting – Kicking

| PASSING | Att. | Comp. | % | Yds. | Yd./Att. | TD | Int.–% | RK |
|---|---|---|---|---|---|---|---|---|
| Hipple | 279 | 140 | 50 | 2358 | 8.5 | 14 | 15– 5 | 9 |
| Danielson | 96 | 56 | 58 | 784 | 8.2 | 3 | 5– 5 | |
| Komlo | 57 | 29 | 51 | 290 | 5.1 | 1 | 3– 5 | |
| Skladany | 3 | 3 | 100 | 43 | 14.3 | 0 | 0– 0 | |
| Scott | 1 | 0 | 0 | 0 | 0.0 | 0 | 0– 0 | |

| PUNTING | No. | Avg. |
|---|---|---|
| Skladany | 64 | 43.5 |

| KICKING | XP | Att. | % | FG | Att. | % |
|---|---|---|---|---|---|---|
| Murray | 46 | 46 | 100 | 25 | 35 | 71 |

## GREEN BAY PACKERS

### Rushing

| Last Name | No. | Yds. | Avg. | TD |
|---|---|---|---|---|
| Ellis | 196 | 860 | 4.4 | 4 |
| Huckleby | 139 | 381 | 2.7 | 5 |
| Middleton | 53 | 181 | 3.4 | 0 |
| Jensen | 27 | 79 | 2.9 | 0 |
| Ivery | 14 | 72 | 5.1 | 1 |
| Whitehurst | 15 | 51 | 3.4 | 1 |
| Jefferson | 2 | 22 | 11.0 | 0 |
| Dickey | 19 | 6 | 0.3 | 0 |
| Torkelson | 1 | 4 | 4.0 | 0 |

### Receiving

| Last Name | No. | Yds. | Avg. | TD |
|---|---|---|---|---|
| Lofton | 71 | 1294 | 18 | 8 |
| Ellis | 65 | 499 | 8 | 3 |
| Coffman | 55 | 687 | 13 | 4 |
| Jefferson | 39 | 632 | 16 | 4 |
| Huckleby | 27 | 221 | 8 | 3 |
| Middleton | 12 | 86 | 7 | 1 |
| Jensen | 5 | 49 | 10 | 0 |
| Lewis | 3 | 31 | 10 | 0 |
| Nixon | 2 | 27 | 14 | 0 |
| Ivery | 2 | 10 | 5 | 0 |
| Cassidy | 1 | 6 | 6 | 0 |
| Swanke | 1 | 2 | 2 | 1 |

### Punt Returns

| Last Name | No. | Yds. | Avg. | TD |
|---|---|---|---|---|
| Lee | 20 | 187 | 9 | 1 |
| Nixon | 15 | 118 | 8 | 0 |
| Whitaker | 2 | 1 | 1 | 0 |
| Cassidy | 2 | 0 | 0 | 0 |
| Gray | 1 | 0 | 0 | 0 |

### Kickoff Returns

| Last Name | No. | Yds. | Avg. | TD |
|---|---|---|---|---|
| Lee | 14 | 270 | 19 | 0 |
| Nixon | 12 | 222 | 19 | 0 |
| McCoy | 11 | 221 | 20 | 0 |
| Huckleby | 7 | 134 | 19 | 0 |
| Middleton | 6 | 100 | 17 | 0 |
| Coffman | 3 | 77 | 26 | 0 |
| Gray | 2 | 24 | 12 | 0 |
| Jensen | 1 | 15 | 15 | 0 |
| Jefferson | 1 | 3 | 3 | 0 |
| Braggs | 1 | 0 | 0 | 0 |

### Passing – Punting – Kicking

| PASSING | Att. | Comp. | % | Yds. | Yd./Att. | TD | Int.–% | RK |
|---|---|---|---|---|---|---|---|---|
| Dickey | 354 | 204 | 58 | 2593 | 7.3 | 17 | 15– 4 | 4 |
| Whitehurst | 128 | 66 | 52 | 792 | 6.2 | 7 | 5– 4 | |
| Campbell | 30 | 15 | 50 | 168 | 5.6 | 0 | 4– 13 | |
| Ellis | 2 | 1 | 50 | 23 | 11.5 | 0 | 0– 0 | |

| PUNTING | No. | Avg. |
|---|---|---|
| Stachowicz | 82 | 40.6 |

| KICKING | XP | Att. | % | FG | Att. | % |
|---|---|---|---|---|---|---|
| Stenerud | 35 | 36 | 97 | 22 | 24 | 92 |

## MINNESOTA VIKINGS

### Rushing

| Last Name | No. | Yds. | Avg. | TD |
|---|---|---|---|---|
| Brown | 274 | 1063 | 3.9 | 6 |
| Galbreath | 42 | 198 | 4.7 | 2 |
| Young | 47 | 129 | 2.7 | 0 |
| LeCount | 3 | 51 | 17.0 | 0 |
| Redwine | 5 | 20 | 4.0 | 0 |
| Lewis | 1 | 16 | 16.0 | 0 |
| Dils | 4 | 14 | 3.5 | 0 |
| Kramer | 10 | 13 | 1.3 | 0 |
| Harrell | 1 | 7 | 7.0 | 0 |
| Senser | 1 | 2 | 2.0 | 0 |
| Siemon | 1 | 0 | 0.0 | 0 |
| S. White | 2 | −1 | −0.5 | 0 |

### Receiving

| Last Name | No. | Yds. | Avg. | TD |
|---|---|---|---|---|
| Brown | 83 | 694 | 8 | 2 |
| Senser | 79 | 1004 | 13 | 8 |
| S. White | 66 | 1001 | 15 | 3 |
| Rashad | 58 | 884 | 15 | 7 |
| Young | 43 | 296 | 7 | 2 |
| LeCount | 24 | 425 | 18 | 2 |
| Galbreath | 18 | 144 | 8 | 0 |
| Bruer | 7 | 38 | 5 | 3 |
| Lewis | 2 | 58 | 29 | 0 |
| Harrell | 2 | 23 | 12 | 0 |

### Punt Returns

| Last Name | No. | Yds. | Avg. | TD |
|---|---|---|---|---|
| Payton | 38 | 303 | 8 | 0 |
| S. White | 1 | 0 | 0 | 0 |

### Kickoff Returns

| Last Name | No. | Yds. | Avg. | TD |
|---|---|---|---|---|
| Payton | 39 | 898 | 23 | 1 |
| Nord | 14 | 229 | 16 | 0 |
| McDole | 11 | 170 | 16 | 0 |
| Galbreath | 1 | 16 | 16 | 0 |
| Young | 1 | 15 | 15 | 0 |
| Blair | 1 | 0 | 0 | 0 |

### Passing – Punting – Kicking

| PASSING | Att. | Comp. | % | Yds. | Yd./Att. | TD | Int.–% | RK |
|---|---|---|---|---|---|---|---|---|
| Kramer | 593 | 322 | 54 | 3912 | 6.6 | 26 | 24– 4 | 10 |
| Dils | 102 | 54 | 53 | 607 | 6.0 | 1 | 2– 2 | |
| Wilson | 13 | 6 | 46 | 48 | 3.7 | 0 | 2– 15 | |
| Brown | 1 | 0 | 0 | 0 | 0.0 | 0 | 1–100 | |

| PUNTING | No. | Avg. |
|---|---|---|
| Coleman | 88 | 41.4 |

| KICKING | XP | Att. | % | FG | Att. | % |
|---|---|---|---|---|---|---|
| Danmeier | 34 | 37 | 92 | 21 | 25 | 84 |

## CHICAGO BEARS

### Rushing

| Last Name | No. | Yds. | Avg. | TD |
|---|---|---|---|---|
| Payton | 339 | 1222 | 3.6 | 6 |
| Suhey | 150 | 521 | 3.5 | 3 |
| Evans | 43 | 218 | 5.1 | 3 |
| Harper | 34 | 106 | 3.1 | 1 |
| McClendon | 30 | 74 | 2.5 | 0 |
| Williams | 2 | 19 | 9.5 | 0 |
| Margerum | 1 | 11 | 11.0 | 0 |
| Baschnagel | 1 | 10 | 10.0 | 0 |
| Avellini | 5 | 2 | 0.4 | 0 |
| Phipps | 1 | 0 | 0.0 | 0 |
| Neal | 1 | −6 | −6.0 | 0 |
| Parsons | 1 | −6 | −6.0 | 0 |

### Receiving

| Last Name | No. | Yds. | Avg. | TD |
|---|---|---|---|---|
| Payton | 41 | 379 | 9 | 2 |
| Margerum | 39 | 584 | 15 | 1 |
| Baschnagel | 34 | 554 | 16 | 3 |
| Suhey | 33 | 168 | 5 | 0 |
| Watts | 27 | 465 | 17 | 3 |
| Williams | 18 | 126 | 7 | 2 |
| Earl | 10 | 118 | 12 | 1 |
| Anderson | 9 | 243 | 27 | 2 |
| Cobb | 2 | 20 | 10 | 0 |
| Harper | 2 | 10 | 5 | 0 |
| McClendon | 2 | 4 | 2 | 0 |
| Harris | 1 | 18 | 18 | 0 |
| Zanders | 1 | 7 | 7 | 0 |

### Punt Returns

| Last Name | No. | Yds. | Avg. | TD |
|---|---|---|---|---|
| J. Fisher | 43 | 509 | 12 | 1 |
| Walterscheid | 1 | 6 | 6 | 0 |
| Plank | 1 | 3 | 3 | 0 |

### Kickoff Returns

| Last Name | No. | Yds. | Avg. | TD |
|---|---|---|---|---|
| Williams | 23 | 486 | 21 | 0 |
| Moorehead | 23 | 476 | 21 | 0 |
| J. Fisher | 7 | 108 | 15 | 0 |
| Frazier | 6 | 77 | 13 | 0 |
| Baschnagel | 2 | 34 | 17 | 0 |
| R. Fisher | 1 | 9 | 9 | 0 |
| Anderson | 1 | −5 | −5 | 0 |

### Passing – Punting – Kicking

| PASSING | Att. | Comp. | % | Yds. | Yd./Att. | TD | Int.–% | RK |
|---|---|---|---|---|---|---|---|---|
| Evans | 436 | 195 | 45 | 2354 | 5.4 | 11 | 20– 5 | 15 |
| Avellini | 32 | 15 | 47 | 185 | 5.8 | 1 | 3– 9 | |
| Phipps | 17 | 11 | 65 | 171 | 10.1 | 2 | 0– 0 | |
| Baschnagel | 1 | 1 | 100 | 18 | 18.0 | 0 | 0– 0 | |
| Parsons | 1 | 0 | 0 | 0 | 0.0 | 0 | 0– 0 | |
| Payton | 2 | 0 | 0 | 0 | 0.0 | 0 | 0– 0 | |

| PUNTING | No. | Avg. |
|---|---|---|
| Parsons | 114 | 39.7 |

| KICKING | XP | Att. | % | FG | Att. | % |
|---|---|---|---|---|---|---|
| Roveto | 19 | 20 | 95 | 10 | 18 | 56 |
| Thomas | 2 | 3 | 67 | 2 | 3 | 67 |
| Nielsen | 8 | 8 | 100 | 0 | 2 | 0 |

**SAN FRANCISCO FORTY-NINERS** 13-3-0 Bill Walsh

| Scores of Each Game | | |
|---|---|---|
| 17 | Detroit | 24 |
| 28 | CHICAGO | 17 |
| 17 | Atlanta | 34 |
| 21 | NEW ORLEANS | 14 |
| 30 | Washington | 17 |
| 45 | DALLAS | 14 |
| 13 | Green Bay | 3 |
| 20 | LOS ANGELES | 17 |
| 17 | Pittsburgh | 14 |
| 17 | ATLANTA | 14 |
| 12 | CLEVELAND | 15 |
| 33 | Los Angeles | 31 |
| 17 | N.Y. GIANTS | 10 |
| 21 | Cincinnati | 3 |
| 28 | HOUSTON | 6 |
| 21 | New Orleans | 17 |

| Use Name | Pos. | Hgt. | Wgt. | Age | Int. | Pts. |
|---|---|---|---|---|---|---|
| Dan Audick | OT | 6'3" | 253 | 26 | | |
| Keith Fahnhorst | OT | 6'6" | 263 | 29 | | |
| Allan Kennedy | OT | 6'7" | 268 | 23 | | |
| Jim Nicholson | OT | 6'6" | 275 | 31 | | |
| John Ayers | OG-OT | 6'5" | 255 | 28 | | |
| John Choma | OG-OT | 6'5" | 261 | 26 | | |
| Randy Cross | OG | 6'3" | 255 | 27 | | |
| Walt Downing | C-OG | 6'3" | 254 | 25 | | |
| Fred Quillan | C | 6'5" | 260 | 25 | | |
| Dwaine Board | DE | 6'5" | 245 | 24 | | |
| Fred Dean (from S.D.) | DE | 6'3" | 230 | 29 | | |
| Lawrence Pillers | DE | 6'3" | 260 | 28 | | |
| Jim Stuckey | DE | 6'4" | 250 | 23 | | |
| John Harty | NT | 6'4" | 253 | 22 | | |
| Pete Kugler | NT-DE | 6'4" | 255 | 22 | | |
| Archie Reese | NT | 6'3" | 262 | 25 | | |
| Dan Bunz | LB | 6'4" | 225 | 25 | | |
| Willie Harper | LB | 6'2" | 215 | 31 | | |
| Bobby Leopold | LB | 6'1" | 215 | 23 | | |
| Jim Looney | LB | 6' | 225 | 24 | | |
| Milt McColl | LB | 6'6" | 220 | 22 | 1 | |
| Craig Puki | LB | 6'1" | 230 | 24 | | |
| Jack Reynolds | LB | 6'1" | 232 | 33 | 1 | |
| Keena Turner | LB | 6'2" | 220 | 22 | 1 | |
| Ricky Churchman | DB | 6'1" | 193 | 23 | | |
| Rick Gervais | DB | 5'11" | 190 | 21 | | |
| Dwight Hicks | DB | 6'1" | 189 | 25 | 9 | 12 |
| Ronnie Lott | DB | 6' | 199 | 22 | 7 | 18 |
| Saladin Martin | DB | 6' | 180 | 25 | 1 | |
| Lynn Thomas | DB | 5'11" | 181 | 22 | | |
| Carlton Williamson | DB | 6' | 204 | 23 | 4 | |
| Eric Wright | DB | 6'1" | 180 | 22 | 3 | |
| Guy Benjamin | QB | 6'4" | 210 | 26 | | |
| Joe Montana | QB | 6'2" | 200 | 25 | | 12 |
| Lenvil Elliott | HB | 6' | 210 | 29 | | |
| Paul Hofer | HB | 6' | 195 | 29 | | 6 |
| Amos Lawrence | HB | 5'11" | 181 | 23 | | 12 |
| Ricky Patton | HB | 5'11" | 192 | 27 | | 30 |
| Bill Ring | HB-FB | 5'10" | 215 | 24 | | 6 |
| Earl Cooper | FB | 6'2" | 226 | 23 | | 6 |
| Johnny Davis | FB | 6'1" | 235 | 25 | | 42 |
| Walt Easley | FB | 6'1" | 226 | 23 | | 6 |
| Arrington Jones | FB | 6' | 225 | 21 | | |
| Matt Bouza | WR | 6'2" | 205 | 23 | | |
| Dwight Clark | WR | 6'3" | 205 | 24 | | 24 |
| Mike Shumann | WR | 6' | 175 | 25 | | |
| Freddie Solomon | WR | 5'11" | 188 | 28 | | 48 |
| Mike Wilson | WR | 6'3" | 210 | 22 | | 6 |
| Brian Peets | TE | 6'4" | 225 | 25 | | |
| Eason Ramson | TE | 6'2" | 235 | 25 | | |
| Charlie Young | TE | 6'4" | 235 | 30 | | 30 |
| Jim Miller | K | 5'11" | 185 | 24 | | |
| Ray Wersching | K | 5'11" | 222 | 31 | | 81 |

Ken Bungarda – Knee Injury
Phil Francis – Knee Injury
George Visger – Knee Injury

**ATLANTA FALCONS** 7-9-0 Leeman Bennett

| Scores of Each Game | | |
|---|---|---|
| 27 | NEW ORLEANS | 0 |
| 31 | Green Bay | 17 |
| 34 | SAN FRANCISCO | 17 |
| 17 | Cleveland | 28 |
| 13 | Philadelphia | 16 |
| 35 | LOS ANGELES | 37 |
| 41 | ST. LOUIS | 20 |
| 24 | N.Y. GIANTS | *27 |
| 41 | New Orleans | 10 |
| 14 | San Francisco | 17 |
| 20 | PITTSBURGH | 34 |
| 31 | MINNESOTA | 30 |
| 31 | Houston | 27 |
| 23 | Tampa Bay | 24 |
| 16 | Los Angeles | 21 |
| 28 | CINCINNATI | 30 |

| Use Name | Pos. | Hgt. | Wgt. | Age | Int. | Pts. |
|---|---|---|---|---|---|---|
| Warren Bryant | OT | 6'6" | 270 | 25 | | |
| Mike Kenn | OT | 6'6" | 257 | 25 | | |
| Eric Sanders | OT-C | 6'6" | 255 | 22 | | |
| Pat Howell | OG | 6'5" | 253 | 24 | | |
| Dave Scott | OG | 6'4" | 265 | 27 | | |
| R.C. Thielemann | OG | 6'4" | 247 | 26 | | |
| John Scully | C | 6'5" | 255 | 23 | | |
| Jeff Van Note | C | 6'2" | 247 | 35 | | |
| Wilson Faumuina | DE | 6'5" | 275 | 27 | | |
| Jeff Merrow | DE | 6'4" | 230 | 28 | | |
| Matthew Teague | DE | 6'5" | 240 | 22 | | |
| Jeff Yeates | DE | 6'3" | 248 | 30 | | |
| Don Smith | NT | 6'5" | 248 | 24 | | |
| Mike Zele | NT | 6'3" | 236 | 25 | | |
| Buddy Curry | LB | 6'3" | 220 | 23 | 1 | 6 |
| Paul Davis | LB | 6'2" | 214 | 23 | | |
| Tony Daykin | LB | 6'1" | 215 | 26 | | |
| Fulton Kuykendall | LB | 6'5" | 225 | 28 | 1 | 6 |
| Jim Laughlin | LB | 6' | 212 | 23 | | |
| Neal Musser | LB | 6'2" | 218 | 24 | 1 | |
| Al Richardson | LB | 6'2" | 206 | 23 | 1 | |
| Lyman White | LB | 6' | 217 | 22 | | |
| Joel Williams | LB | 6'1" | 215 | 24 | 1 | 6 |
| Bobby Butler | DB | 5'11" | 170 | 22 | 5 | |
| Blaine Gaison | DB | 6' | 185 | 23 | 1 | |
| Bob Glazebrook | DB | 6'1" | 200 | 25 | 2 | |
| Kenny Johnson | DB | 5'10" | 176 | 23 | 3 | 12 |
| Earl Jones | DB | 6' | 178 | 24 | 2 | |
| Tom Moriarty | DB | 6' | 180 | 28 | | |
| Tom Pridemore | DB | 5'10" | 186 | 25 | 7 | 6 |
| Scott Woerner | DB | 6' | 195 | 22 | | |
| Steve Bartkowski | QB | 6'4" | 213 | 28 | | |
| June Jones | QB | 6'4" | 200 | 28 | | |
| Mike Moroski | QB | 6'4" | 200 | 23 | | |
| Lynn Cain | HB | 6'1" | 205 | 25 | | 36 |
| Ray Strong | HB | 5'9" | 184 | 25 | | |
| William Andrews | FB | 6' | 200 | 25 | | 72 |
| James Mayberry | FB-HB | 5'11" | 210 | 23 | | |
| Bo Robinson | FB | 6'2" | 225 | 25 | | |
| Wallace Francis | WR | 5'11" | 190 | 29 | | 30 |
| Alfred Jackson | WR | 5'11" | 176 | 26 | | 42 |
| Al Jenkins | WR | 5'10" | 172 | 29 | | 78 |
| Reggie Smith | WR | 5'4" | 168 | 25 | | |
| Russ Mikeska | TE | 6'3" | 225 | 25 | | |
| Junior Miller | TE | 6'4" | 243 | 23 | | 18 |
| John James | K | 6'3" | 200 | 32 | | |
| Mick Luckhurst | K | 6' | 180 | 23 | | 114 |

Rolland Lawrence – Hamstring Injury

**LOS ANGELES RAMS** 6-10-0 Ray Malavasi

| Scores of Each Game | | |
|---|---|---|
| 20 | HOUSTON | 27 |
| 17 | New Orleans | 23 |
| 35 | GREEN BAY | 23 |
| 24 | Chicago | 7 |
| 27 | CLEVELAND | 16 |
| 37 | Atlanta | 35 |
| 17 | Dallas | 29 |
| 17 | San Francisco | 20 |
| 20 | DETROIT | 13 |
| 13 | NEW ORLEANS | 21 |
| 10 | Cincinnati | 24 |
| 31 | SAN FRANCISCO | 33 |
| 0 | Pittsburgh | 24 |
| 7 | N.Y. Giants | 10 |
| 21 | ATLANTA | 16 |
| 7 | WASHINGTON | 30 |

| Use Name | Pos. | Hgt. | Wgt. | Age | Int. | Pts. |
|---|---|---|---|---|---|---|
| Doug France | OT | 6'5" | 270 | 28 | | |
| Phil McKinnely | OT | 6'4" | 248 | 27 | | |
| Irv Pankey | OT | 6'4" | 270 | 23 | | |
| Jackie Slater | OT | 6'4" | 271 | 27 | | |
| Bill Bain | OG | 6'4" | 277 | 29 | | |
| Dennis Harrah | OG-C | 6'5" | 255 | 28 | | |
| Kent Hill | OG-OT | 6'5" | 260 | 24 | | |
| Doug Smith | OG-C-OT | 6'3" | 255 | 24 | | |
| Rich Saul | C | 6'3" | 245 | 33 | | |
| Bob Cobb | DE | 6'4" | 248 | 23 | | |
| Fred Dryer | DE | 6'6" | 231 | 35 | | |
| Cody Jones | DE | 6'5" | 244 | 30 | | |
| Jack Youngblood | DE | 6'4" | 244 | 31 | | |
| Larry Brooks | DT | 6'3" | 253 | 31 | | |
| Reggie Doss | DT-DE | 6'4" | 267 | 24 | | |
| Mike Fanning | DT | 6'6" | 252 | 28 | | |
| Greg Meisner | DT | 6'3" | 250 | 22 | | |
| Phil Murphy | DT | 6'5" | 300 | 23 | | |
| George Andrews | LB | 6'3" | 223 | 25 | | |
| Howard Carson | LB | 6'2" | 233 | 24 | | |
| Jim Collins | LB | 6'2" | 230 | 23 | | |
| Carl Ekern | LB | 6'3" | 223 | 27 | | |
| Joe Harris | LB | 6'1" | 224 | 28 | 1 | 6 |
| Mel Owens | LB | 6'2" | 225 | 22 | | |
| Jim Youngblood | LB | 6'3" | 231 | 31 | 1 | |
| Kirk Collins | DB | 5'11" | 179 | 23 | | |
| Nolan Cromwell | DB | 6'1" | 198 | 26 | 5 | |
| LeRoy Irvin | DB | 5'11" | 180 | 23 | 3 | 18 |
| Johnnie Johnson | DB | 6'1" | 185 | 24 | | |
| Rod Perry | DB | 5'9" | 182 | 27 | 3 | |
| Lucious Smith | DB | 5'10" | 190 | 24 | | |
| Ivory Sully | DB | 6' | 193 | 24 | | |
| Pat Thomas | DB | 5'9" | 182 | 27 | 4 | |
| Pat Haden | QB | 5'11" | 185 | 28 | | |
| Jeff Kemp | QB | 6' | 200 | 22 | | |
| Dan Pastorini | QB | 6'3" | 205 | 32 | | |
| Jeff Rutledge | QB | 6'1" | 190 | 24 | | |
| Jewerl Thomas | HB-FB | 5'10" | 235 | 23 | | |
| Wendell Tyler | HB | 5'10" | 195 | 26 | | 102 |
| Cullen Bryant | FB | 6'1" | 236 | 30 | | 6 |
| Mike Guman | FB-HB | 6'2" | 210 | 23 | | 24 |
| Jairo Penaranda | FB | 5'11" | 217 | 23 | | |
| Preston Dennard | WR | 6'1" | 183 | 25 | | 24 |
| Drew Hill | WR | 5'9" | 170 | 24 | | 18 |
| Willie Miller | WR | 5'9" | 172 | 34 | | |
| Jeff Moore | WR | 6'1" | 187 | 24 | | |
| Billy Waddy | WR | 5'11" | 188 | 27 | | |
| Walt Arnold | TE | 6'3" | 225 | 23 | | 12 |
| Ron Battle | TE | 6'3" | 220 | 22 | | |
| Henry Childs | TE | 6'2" | 231 | 30 | | 6 |
| Phil DuBois | TE | 6'2" | 230 | 24 | | |
| Lewis Gilbert | TE | 6'4" | 225 | 25 | | |
| Frank Corral | K | 6'2" | 228 | 26 | | 87 |

Victor Hicks – Achilles Injury

**NEW ORLEANS SAINTS** 4-12-0 Bum Phillips

| Scores of Each Game | | |
|---|---|---|
| 0 | Atlanta | 27 |
| 23 | LOS ANGELES | 17 |
| 7 | N.Y. Giants | 20 |
| 14 | San Francisco | 21 |
| 6 | PITTSBURGH | 20 |
| 14 | PHILADELPHIA | 31 |
| 17 | Cleveland | 20 |
| 17 | CINCINNATI | 7 |
| 10 | ATLANTA | 41 |
| 21 | Los Angeles | 13 |
| 10 | Minnesota | 20 |
| 27 | Houston | 24 |
| 14 | TAMPA BAY | 31 |
| 3 | St. Louis | 30 |
| 7 | GREEN BAY | 35 |
| 17 | SAN FRANCISCO | 21 |

| Use Name | Pos. | Hgt. | Wgt. | Age | Int. | Pts. |
|---|---|---|---|---|---|---|
| Stan Brock | OT | 6'6" | 275 | 23 | | |
| Dave Lafary | OT | 6'7" | 280 | 26 | | |
| J.T. Taylor | OT | 6'4" | 265 | 25 | | |
| Sam Adams | OG | 6'3" | 260 | 32 | | |
| Nat Hudson | OG | 6'3" | 270 | 23 | | |
| Fred Sturt | OG | 6'4" | 255 | 30 | | |
| Bob Young | OG | 6'2" | 279 | 38 | | |
| John Hill | C | 6'2" | 246 | 31 | | |
| Jim Pietrzak | C-OT | 6'5" | 260 | 28 | | |
| Paul Ryczek | C | 6'2" | 230 | 29 | | |
| Elois Grooms | DE | 6'4" | 250 | 28 | | |
| Derland Moore | DE | 6'4" | 253 | 29 | | |
| Frank Warren | DE | 6'4" | 275 | 21 | | |
| Jim Wilks | DE | 6'4" | 252 | 23 | | |
| Barry Bennett | NT | 6'4" | 257 | 25 | | |
| Monte Bennett | NT | 6'3" | 260 | 22 | | |
| Jerry Boyarsky | NT | 6'3" | 290 | 22 | | |
| Ken Bordelon | LB | 6'4" | 226 | 27 | 1 | |
| Chuck Evans | LB | 6'3" | 235 | 24 | | |
| Rickey Jackson | LB | 6'2" | 230 | 23 | | |
| Jim Kovach | LB | 6'2" | 225 | 25 | 1 | |
| Rob Nairne | LB | 6'4" | 227 | 27 | 1 | |
| Scott Pelleur | LB | 6'2" | 210 | 22 | | |
| Glen Redd | LB | 6'1" | 225 | 23 | 1 | |
| Russell Gary | DB | 5'11" | 195 | 22 | 1 | |
| Bill Hurley | DB | 5'11" | 195 | 24 | | |
| Tom Myers | DB | 5'11" | 180 | 30 | 2 | |
| Johnnie Poe | DB | 6'1" | 182 | 22 | 1 | |
| Ricky Ray (to MIA) | DB | 5'11" | 180 | 24 | 1 | |
| Mike Spivey | DB | 6' | 198 | 27 | 1 | |
| Frank Wattelet | DB | 6' | 185 | 22 | 3 | |
| Dave Waymer | DB | 6'1" | 195 | 23 | 4 | |
| Archie Manning | QB | 6'3" | 200 | 32 | | |
| Bobby Scott | QB | 6'1" | 197 | 32 | | |
| Dave Wilson | QB | 6'3" | 195 | 22 | | |
| George Rogers | HB | 6'2" | 224 | 22 | | 78 |
| Jimmy Rogers | HB | 5'10" | 190 | 26 | | |
| Scott Stauch | HB | 5'11" | 204 | 22 | | |
| Wayne Wilson | HB-FB | 6'3" | 208 | 23 | | 30 |
| Jack Holmes | FB | 5'11" | 210 | 28 | | 12 |
| Toussaint Tyler | FB | 6'2" | 220 | 22 | | |
| Gordon Banks | WR | 5'9" | 178 | 23 | | |
| Jeff Groth | WR | 5'10" | 172 | 24 | | 6 |
| Ike Harris | WR | 6'3" | 210 | 28 | | |
| Rich Martini | WR | 6'2" | 185 | 25 | | |
| Guido Merkens | WR | 6'1" | 200 | 26 | | 6 |
| Aundra Thompson (from GB, SD) | WR | 6' | 186 | 28 | | |
| Hoby Brenner | TE | 6'4" | 240 | 22 | | |
| Rich Caster (to WAS) | TE | 6'5" | 230 | 32 | | |
| Larry Hardy | TE | 6'3" | 230 | 25 | | 6 |
| Brooks Williams (to CHI) | TE | 6'4" | 226 | 26 | | |
| Russell Erxleben | K | 6'4" | 220 | 24 | | |
| Benny Ricardo | K | 5'10" | 170 | 27 | | 63 |

Rich Mauti – Broken Collarbone
Tinker Owens – Knee Injury

*—Overtime

## SAN FRANCISCO FORTY-NINERS

### RUSHING

| Last Name | No. | Yds. | Avg. | TD |
|---|---|---|---|---|
| Patton | 152 | 543 | 3.6 | 4 |
| Cooper | 98 | 330 | 3.4 | 1 |
| Davis | 94 | 297 | 3.2 | 7 |
| Easley | 76 | 224 | 2.9 | 1 |
| Hofer | 60 | 193 | 3.2 | 1 |
| Ring | 22 | 106 | 4.8 | 0 |
| Montana | 25 | 95 | 3.8 | 2 |
| Lawrence | 13 | 48 | 3.7 | 1 |
| Solomon | 9 | 43 | 4.8 | 0 |
| Clark | 3 | 32 | 10.7 | 0 |
| Elliott | 7 | 29 | 4.1 | 0 |
| Benjamin | 1 | 1 | 1.0 | 0 |

### RECEIVING

| Last Name | No. | Yds. | Avg. | TD |
|---|---|---|---|---|
| Clark | 85 | 1105 | 13 | 4 |
| Solomon | 59 | 969 | 16 | 8 |
| Cooper | 51 | 477 | 9 | 0 |
| Young | 37 | 400 | 11 | 5 |
| Hofer | 27 | 244 | 9 | 0 |
| Patton | 27 | 195 | 7 | 1 |
| Wilson | 9 | 125 | 14 | 1 |
| Easley | 9 | 62 | 7 | 0 |
| Elliott | 7 | 81 | 12 | 0 |
| Ramson | 4 | 45 | 11 | 0 |
| Ring | 3 | 28 | 9 | 1 |
| Shumann | 3 | 21 | 7 | 0 |
| Lawrence | 3 | 10 | 3 | 0 |
| Davis | 3 | −1 | 0 | 0 |
| Peets | 1 | 5 | 5 | 0 |

### PUNT RETURNS

| Last Name | No. | Yds. | Avg. | TD |
|---|---|---|---|---|
| Hicks | 19 | 171 | 9 | 0 |
| Solomon | 29 | 173 | 6 | 0 |

### KICKOFF RETURNS

| Last Name | No. | Yds. | Avg. | TD |
|---|---|---|---|---|
| Lawrence | 17 | 437 | 26 | 1 |
| Ring | 10 | 217 | 22 | 0 |
| Lott | 7 | 111 | 16 | 0 |
| Wilson | 4 | 67 | 17 | 0 |
| Jones | 3 | 43 | 14 | 0 |
| Hicks | 1 | 22 | 22 | 0 |
| Ramson | 1 | 12 | 12 | 0 |
| Davis | 1 | 0 | 0 | 0 |
| Patton | 1 | 0 | 0 | 0 |

### PASSING – PUNTING – KICKING

| PASSING | Att. | Comp. | % | Yds. | Yd./Att. | TD | Int.–% | | RK |
|---|---|---|---|---|---|---|---|---|---|
| Montana | 488 | 311 | 64 | 3565 | 7.3 | 19 | 12– | 3 | 1 |
| Benjamin | 26 | 15 | 58 | 171 | 6.6 | 1 | 1– | 4 | |
| Solomon | 1 | 1 | 100 | 25 | 25.0 | 0 | 0– | 0 | |
| Easley | 1 | 1 | 100 | 5 | 5.0 | 0 | 0– | 0 | |
| Clark | 1 | 0 | 0 | 0 | 0.0 | 0 | 0– | 0 | |

| PUNTING | No. | Avg. |
|---|---|---|
| Miller | 93 | 41.5 |

| KICKING | XP | Att. | % | FG | Att. | % |
|---|---|---|---|---|---|---|
| Wersching | 30 | 30 | 100 | 17 | 23 | 74 |

## ATLANTA FALCONS

### RUSHING

| Last Name | No. | Yds. | Avg. | TD |
|---|---|---|---|---|
| Andrews | 289 | 1301 | 4.5 | 10 |
| Cain | 156 | 542 | 3.5 | 4 |
| Mayberry | 18 | 66 | 3.7 | 0 |
| Robinson | 9 | 24 | 2.7 | 0 |
| Moroski | 3 | 17 | 5.7 | 0 |
| Francis | 1 | 8 | 8.0 | 1 |
| Strong | 3 | 6 | 2.0 | 0 |
| Jackson | 2 | 5 | 2.5 | 0 |
| Daykin | 1 | 2 | 2.0 | 0 |
| Bartkowski | 11 | 2 | 0.2 | 0 |
| J. Jones | 1 | −1 | −1.0 | 0 |
| James | 1 | −7 | −7.0 | 0 |

### RECEIVING

| Last Name | No. | Yds. | Avg. | TD |
|---|---|---|---|---|
| Andrews | 81 | 735 | 9 | 2 |
| Jenkins | 70 | 1358 | 19 | 13 |
| Cain | 55 | 421 | 8 | 2 |
| Jackson | 37 | 604 | 16 | 6 |
| Miller | 32 | 398 | 12 | 0 |
| Francis | 30 | 441 | 15 | 4 |
| Mayberry | 3 | 4 | 1 | 0 |
| Mikeska | 2 | 16 | 8 | 0 |
| Strong | 1 | 9 | 9 | 0 |

### PUNT RETURNS

| Last Name | No. | Yds. | Avg. | TD |
|---|---|---|---|---|
| Woerner | 33 | 278 | 8 | 0 |
| R. Smith | 12 | 99 | 8 | 0 |
| Johnson | 4 | 6 | 2 | 0 |
| Pridemore | 1 | 0 | 0 | 0 |

### KICKOFF RETURNS

| Last Name | No. | Yds. | Avg. | TD |
|---|---|---|---|---|
| R. Smith | 47 | 1143 | 24 | 0 |
| Woerner | 10 | 210 | 21 | 0 |
| Gaison | 3 | 43 | 14 | 0 |
| Mayberry | 2 | 23 | 12 | 0 |

### PASSING – PUNTING – KICKING

| PASSING | Att. | Comp. | % | Yds. | Yd./Att. | TD | Int.–% | | RK |
|---|---|---|---|---|---|---|---|---|---|
| Bartkowski | 533 | 297 | 56 | 3829 | 7.2 | 30 | 23– | 4 | 3 |
| Moroski | 26 | 12 | 46 | 132 | 5.1 | 0 | 1– | 4 | |
| J. Jones | 3 | 2 | 67 | 25 | 8.3 | 0 | 0– | 0 | |
| James | 1 | 0 | 0 | 0 | 0.0 | 0 | 0– | 0 | |

| PUNTING | No. | Avg. |
|---|---|---|
| James | 87 | 40.7 |

| KICKING | XP | Att. | % | FG | Att. | % |
|---|---|---|---|---|---|---|
| Luckhurst | 51 | 51 | 100 | 21 | 33 | 64 |

## LOS ANGELES RAMS

### RUSHING

| Last Name | No. | Yds. | Avg. | TD |
|---|---|---|---|---|
| Tyler | 260 | 1074 | 4.1 | 12 |
| Bryant | 109 | 436 | 4.0 | 1 |
| Guman | 115 | 433 | 3.8 | 4 |
| J. Thomas | 34 | 118 | 3.5 | 0 |
| Haden | 18 | 104 | 5.8 | 0 |
| Dennard | 6 | 29 | 4.8 | 0 |
| D. Hill | 1 | 14 | 14.0 | 0 |
| Kemp | 2 | 9 | 4.5 | 0 |
| Pastorini | 7 | 5 | 0.7 | 0 |
| Childs | 1 | 0 | 0.0 | 0 |
| Rutledge | 5 | −3 | −0.6 | 0 |

### RECEIVING

| Last Name | No. | Yds. | Avg. | TD |
|---|---|---|---|---|
| Dennard | 49 | 821 | 17 | 4 |
| Tyler | 45 | 436 | 10 | 5 |
| Waddy | 31 | 460 | 15 | 0 |
| Bryant | 22 | 160 | 7 | 0 |
| Arnold | 20 | 212 | 11 | 2 |
| Guman | 18 | 130 | 7 | 0 |
| D. Hill | 16 | 355 | 22 | 3 |
| Childs | 12 | 145 | 12 | 1 |
| Miller | 10 | 147 | 15 | 0 |
| Moore | 7 | 105 | 15 | 0 |
| J. Thomas | 5 | 37 | 7 | 0 |

### PUNT RETURNS

| Last Name | No. | Yds. | Avg. | TD |
|---|---|---|---|---|
| Irvin | 46 | 615 | 13 | 3 |
| D. Hill | 2 | 22 | 11 | 0 |
| Johnson | 1 | 39 | 39 | 0 |

### KICKOFF RETURNS

| Last Name | No. | Yds. | Avg. | TD |
|---|---|---|---|---|
| D. Hill | 60 | 1170 | 20 | 0 |
| Sully | 3 | 31 | 10 | 0 |
| Meisner | 1 | 17 | 17 | 0 |
| J. Thomas | 1 | 15 | 15 | 0 |
| Guman | 1 | 10 | 10 | 0 |
| Penaranda | 1 | 1 | 1 | 0 |
| Pankey | 1 | 0 | 0 | 0 |

### PASSING – PUNTING – KICKING

| PASSING | Att. | Comp. | % | Yds. | Yd./Att. | TD | Int.–% | | RK |
|---|---|---|---|---|---|---|---|---|---|
| Haden | 267 | 138 | 52 | 1815 | 6.8 | 9 | 13– | 5 | 12 |
| Pastorini | 152 | 64 | 42 | 719 | 4.7 | 2 | 14– | 9 | |
| Rutledge | 50 | 30 | 60 | 442 | 8.8 | 3 | 4– | 8 | |
| Kemp | 6 | 2 | 33 | 25 | 4.2 | 0 | 1– | 17 | |
| Guman | 1 | 1 | 100 | 7 | 7.0 | 1 | 0– | 0 | |
| Corral | 1 | 0 | 0 | 0 | 0.0 | 0 | 0– | 0 | |

| PUNTING | No. | Avg. |
|---|---|---|
| Corral | 89 | 42.0 |

| KICKING | XP | Att. | % | FG | Att. | % |
|---|---|---|---|---|---|---|
| Corral | 36 | 36 | 100 | 17 | 26 | 65 |

## NEW ORLEANS SAINTS

### RUSHING

| Last Name | No. | Yds. | Avg. | TD |
|---|---|---|---|---|
| G. Rogers | 378 | 1674 | 4.4 | 13 |
| Holmes | 58 | 194 | 3.3 | 2 |
| Tyler | 36 | 183 | 5.1 | 0 |
| W. Wilson | 44 | 137 | 3.1 | 1 |
| J. Rogers | 9 | 37 | 4.1 | 0 |
| Manning | 2 | 28 | 14.0 | 0 |
| Groth | 2 | 27 | 13.5 | 0 |
| Erxleben | 2 | 10 | 5.0 | 0 |
| Stauch | 2 | 6 | 3.0 | 0 |
| Thompson | 1 | 2 | 2.0 | 0 |
| D. Wilson | 5 | 1 | 0.2 | 0 |
| Merkens | 2 | −1 | −0.5 | 0 |
| Myers | 2 | −3 | −1.5 | 0 |
| Caster | 1 | −3 | −3.0 | 0 |
| Scott | 3 | −4 | −1.3 | 0 |

### RECEIVING

| Last Name | No. | Yds. | Avg. | TD |
|---|---|---|---|---|
| Holmes | 38 | 206 | 5 | 0 |
| W. Wilson | 31 | 384 | 12 | 4 |
| Merkens | 29 | 458 | 16 | 1 |
| Hardy | 23 | 275 | 12 | 1 |
| Tyler | 23 | 135 | 6 | 0 |
| Groth | 20 | 380 | 19 | 1 |
| G. Rogers | 16 | 126 | 8 | 0 |
| Caster | 12 | 185 | 15 | 0 |
| Thompson | 8 | 111 | 14 | 0 |
| Williams | 8 | 82 | 10 | 0 |
| Martini | 8 | 72 | 9 | 0 |
| Brenner | 7 | 143 | 20 | 0 |
| Harris | 2 | 33 | 17 | 0 |
| Banks | 2 | 18 | 9 | 0 |
| J. Rogers | 2 | 12 | 6 | 0 |
| Stauch | 1 | 7 | 7 | 0 |
| Lafary | 1 | 5 | 5 | 0 |

### PUNT RETURNS

| Last Name | No. | Yds. | Avg. | TD |
|---|---|---|---|---|
| Groth | 37 | 436 | 12 | 0 |
| Banks | 2 | 0 | 0 | 0 |
| Poe | 1 | 2 | 2 | 0 |
| Merkens | 1 | −12 | −12 | 0 |

### KICKOFF RETURNS

| Last Name | No. | Yds. | Avg. | TD |
|---|---|---|---|---|
| W. Wilson | 31 | 722 | 23 | 0 |
| J. Rogers | 28 | 621 | 22 | 0 |
| Stauch | 3 | 65 | 22 | 0 |
| Groth | 3 | 50 | 17 | 0 |
| Thompson | 2 | 44 | 22 | 0 |
| Merkens | 2 | 38 | 19 | 0 |
| Brock | 2 | 18 | 9 | 0 |
| Williams | 1 | 35 | 35 | 0 |
| Banks | 1 | 9 | 9 | 0 |

### PASSING – PUNTING – KICKING

| PASSING | Att. | Comp. | % | Yds. | Yd./Att. | TD | Int.–% | | RK |
|---|---|---|---|---|---|---|---|---|---|
| Manning | 232 | 134 | 58 | 1447 | 6.2 | 5 | 11– | 5 | 13 |
| D. Wilson | 159 | 82 | 52 | 1058 | 6.7 | 1 | 11– | 7 | |
| Scott | 46 | 20 | 44 | 245 | 5.3 | 1 | 5– | 11 | |
| Merkens | 2 | 1 | 50 | 20 | 10.0 | 0 | 0– | 0 | |
| Myers | 2 | 1 | 50 | 8 | 4.0 | 1 | 0– | 0 | |

| PUNTING | No. | Avg. |
|---|---|---|
| Erxleben | 66 | 40.5 |

| KICKING | XP | Att. | % | FG | Att. | % |
|---|---|---|---|---|---|---|
| Ricardo | 24 | 24 | 100 | 13 | 25 | 52 |

Pete Rozelle had a hard time with both management and labor this year. The lawsuit involving the Oakland Raiders' planned move to Los Angeles went to trial in the federal court in Los Angeles. Both Rozelle and Al Davis had exchanged bitter words and charges in the media, and they now appeared as the principal actors in a long courtroom drama. When the jury sat down to decide the case, they could not reach a unanimous decision, and the judge declared a mistrial. A new trial was scheduled for the spring of 1982, when Rozelle would again argue for the need for the rule requiring permission of the other owners before a club could be moved.

While dealing with Davis's challenge to the N.F.L. by-laws, Rozelle also took part in negotiations with Ed Garvey, the executive director of the N.F.L. Players Association. The collective bargaining agreement between the players and the league would expire in July of 1982, and negotiations moved slowly under the threat of a players' strike when the contract ran out. Garvey made strong demands for the players to share in the profits of the teams, but the owners declared that they didn't want any new partners in the players.

## EASTERN DIVISION

**Miami Dolphins**—Under Don Shula's master touch, the Dolphins made it back into the playoffs after a one-year sabbatical. They lost a prospect when first-round draft pick David Overstreet, a halfback from Oklahoma, chose to play with Montreal in the C.F.L. Shula simply fashioned the personnel at hand into a divisional champion. The gritty defensive unit gave up the fewest points in the A.F.C. despite the summer death of linebacker Rusty Chambers and the unproductive switch of Kim Bokamper from linebacker to defensive end. As usual, nose tackle Bob Baumhower stood out on an excellent unit. The offense was manned by lots of young faces, although veteran guard Ed Newman led the blocking. Second year quarterback David Woodley played well in spurts, ably assisted by relief pitcher Don Strock. Making Overstreet's absence less noticeable was halfback Tony Nathan, a kick-returning star who brought speed into the offensive backfield. In a stretch run battle with the Jets and Bills, the Dolphins ran off four straight victories at the end of the year, including a 16-6 whipping of the Bills on the final Sunday to clinch the Eastern title.

**New York Jets**—Three embarrassing losses at the start of the year pushed coach Walt Michaels to the brink of unemployment. The Jets saved his job with a 33-17 trouncing of the Oilers, teeing off for seven quarterback sacks. They then went to Miami and played an inspirational 28-28 tie with the unbeaten Dolphins. Just like that, the Jets began believing in themselves and began winning. Without any warning, they won 10 of their last 13 games to charge into the playoffs for the first time since 1969. A ferocious defense made quarterback hunting the team's signature. The front four became known as the New York Sack Exchange, with ends Joe Klecko and Mark Gastineau doing the greatest business in enemy backfields. Without much fanfare, safety Darrol Ray grew into a leader in the secondary. The stars on the offense were blockers like Marvin Powell and Joe Fields, whose efforts made high-yardage runners out of a corps of yeoman backs. The magic streak of success included intoxicating moments such as a revenge 33-14 beating of the Bills and a 16-15 victory over the Dolphins on a last-minute touchdown. A surprise loss to the Seahawks on December 6 put the playoffs in doubt, but victories over the Browns and Packers gave the Jets a wild-card ticket undreamed of three months earlier.

**Buffalo Bills**—Over the first two months of the season, the Bills didn't live up to their hopes of a dominant campaign in the AFC East. Dawdling along with a 6-5 record in mid-November, the Bills threw themselves into gear and won the next four games. They had a chance to take first place by beating Miami on the final Saturday, but the Dolphins smothered them in a 16-6 decision. Nevertheless, the Bills marched into the wild-card showdown with a solid outfit. The defense ranked with the best in the league, beginning with star nose tackle Fred Smerlas and moving through a deep platoon of talented linebackers and backs. The offense made good use of a quick front line. Joe Cribbs ran through enough holes to chalk up his second 1,000-yard season in as many years, while quarterback Joe Ferguson had enough protection to make oldster Frank Lewis one of the most productive receivers in pro football.

**Baltimore Colts**—With their hopes fueled by a classy rookie crop, the Colts beat New England 29-28 to earn a share of first place. After that, the script turned so sour that some fans called their team the Dolts by the end of the year. Simply put, the Colts fielded the worst defense in NFL history, allowing an unprecedented 533 points. Bert Jones threw bushels of passes to keep the Colts competitive, but the production of enemy offenses could not be matched. As the losses piled up, the mood of the team turned ugly. In November, quarterback Jones and halfback Curtis Dickey broke into bitter public feuding, showing to everyone that the Colts indeed were in a sorry state. On the final Sunday of the schedule, the Colts entertained the Patriots in a battle for the number-one pick in the upcoming college draft. The

Colts lost the pick by winning the game, but the victory didn't stave off the firing of head coach Mike McCormick.

**New England Patriots**—After just missing the playoffs for the last several seasons, the Patriots spared everyone the suspense by collapsing right at the start of the schedule. Although they rarely lost by huge scores, the Pats lost consistently. They lost their first four games, and they lost their last nine games. Any number of reasons could be cited. Tight end Russ Francis announced his retirement at the peak of a brilliant career. Injuries kept linebacker Steve Nelson and cornerback Mike Haynes out of action for much of the campaign. The defensive line got old in a hurry and exerted little pressure on enemy passers. But no matter how many reasons could be found, the blame ultimately landed on head coach Ron Erhardt, who was canned after the season.

## CENTRAL DIVISION

**Cincinnati Bengals**—At the start of the year, fans talked about the Bengals' new striped helmets. By the end of the year, they talked about the Bengals' fabulous rise to the top of the Central Division. Like a magical charm, the helmets turned a last-place club into champions. The magic worked slowly on quarterback Ken Anderson, who was benched in the opener and was booed lustily for most of September. For most of the year, his precision passing shredded enemy defenses and made Cincinnati the site of repeated scoring outbursts. Rookie Chris Collinsworth, a gangling and elusive receiver, assisted Anderson in reviving the Bengal air attack. Pete Johnson handled the bulk of the running chores with his massive power. On the effective front line, tackle Anthony Munoz moved into the front ranks of blockers in his second pro year. Although the 3-4 Cincinnati defense lacked any star players, it played well enough to take the Bengals to the playoffs for the first time since 1975.

**Pittsburgh Steelers**—Their fans had hoped that 1980 was merely a one-year's hiatus, but 1981 proved that the Steeler dynasty was over. Chuck Noll's crew put together bursts of championship football but could not sustain it. They lost their first two games of the season very unimpressively, but bounced back with four victories. By November 8, however, a loss to Seattle dropped them to the .500 level. Regrouping for a drive to the playoffs, the Steelers won three straight contests to climb into wild-card contention. On December 7, the Raiders edged the Steelers 30-27 and sent Terry Bradshaw to the sidelines with a broken hand. In the glorious past, the Steelers had gone on winning despite injuries to Bradshaw. This time, they lost their final two games to finish at 8-8. When Bradshaw was healthy and at his best, the attack still moved the football with force. The defense still fielded stars in Jack Lambert, Mel Blount, and Donnie Shell, but the front line launched a puny pass rush. Old pros Joe Greene and L. C. Greenwood slipped into senior status and played only in spots.

**Houston Oilers**—Ed Biles stepped into a miserable situation for a new head coach. The Oilers had canned Bum Phillips for not getting to the Super Bowl, despite a string of three playoff berths. The Oilers were styled to Phillips' particular brand of hard-nosed football, and many of the players were angry to see him replaced by the disciplinarian Biles. Just before training camp, quarterback Ken Stabler announced his retirement, only to return in time for the regular season opener when Gifford Nielsen was injured. Stabler's name then was linked to a probe of gambling which grabbed headlines. On the field, Biles tried to diversify the Houston offense. Unfortunately, with Stabler's limited passing range, Biles was forced to return to an attack which relied predominantly on Earl Campbell's power running. A midseason stretch of six losses in seven games dropped the Oilers out of the playoff picture and pointed to the need for extensive retooling.

**Cleveland Browns**—The Kardiac Kids gave their fans only heartache with a general collapse this season. The Browns had won close games galore and coaxed super seasons out of a bunch of players in 1980, but they could not repeat the charm. Brian Sipe still took the Browns up the field with his passing arm, but the high yardage was converted into fewer points. The defense never put any pressure on enemy passers and suffered from successful air attacks. On opening day, the tone was set for the year by a 44-14 drubbing at the hands of the Chargers. Although the Browns recovered to reach the .500 level in mid-season, they dropped their final six games to fall into the basement of the Central Division. A final Sunday loss to the Seahawks by a 42-21 score sent the Browns home for the summer with much to think about.

## WESTERN DIVISION

**San Diego Chargers**—The Chargers were good enough to lose both John Jefferson and Fred Dean and still repeat as divisional champions.

FINAL TEAM STATISTICS

| | BALT. | BUFF. | CIN. | CLEV. | DENV. | HOU. | K.C. | MIA. | N.E. | NY J | OAK. | PIT. | S.D. | SEA. |
|---|---|---|---|---|---|---|---|---|---|---|---|---|---|---|
| FIRST DOWNS: | | | | | | | | | | | | | | |
| Total | 274 | 315 | 361 | **364** | 306 | 241 | 315 | 306 | 306 | 318 | 296 | 318 | 379 | 295 |
| by Rushing | 95 | 127 | 124 | 131 | 91 | 103 | **160** | 123 | 124 | 122 | 108 | 137 | 127 | 103 |
| by Passing | 158 | 163 | 210 | 196 | 181 | 124 | 132 | 157 | 166 | 170 | 166 | 156 | **224** | 166 |
| by Penalty | 21 | 25 | 27 | **37** | 34 | 14 | 23 | 26 | 16 | 26 | 22 | 25 | 28 | 26 |
| RUSHING | | | | | | | | | | | | | | |
| Number | 441 | 524 | 493 | 474 | 515 | 466 | **610** | 535 | 499 | 571 | 493 | 554 | 481 | 440 |
| Yards | 1850 | 2125 | 1973 | 1929 | 1895 | 1734 | **2633** | 2173 | 2040 | 2341 | 2058 | 2372 | 2005 | 1594 |
| Average Yards | 4.2 | 4.1 | 4.0 | 4.1 | 3.7 | 3.7 | **4.3** | 4.1 | 4.1 | 4.1 | 4.2 | 4.3 | 4.2 | 3.6 |
| Touchdowns | 11 | 13 | 19 | 11 | 12 | 11 | 22 | 18 | 23 | 11 | 11 | 21 | **26** | 14 |
| PASSING: | | | | | | | | | | | | | | |
| Attempts | 479 | 503 | 550 | 624 | 485 | 441 | 410 | 498 | 482 | 507 | 545 | 461 | **629** | 524 |
| Completions | 265 | 253 | 332 | 348 | 289 | 258 | 224 | 271 | 254 | 283 | 267 | 247 | **368** | 307 |
| Completion Pct. | 55.3 | 50.3 | **60.4** | 55.8 | 59.6 | 58.5 | 54.6 | 54.4 | 52.7 | 55.8 | 49.0 | 53.6 | 58.5 | 58.6 |
| Passing Yards | 3379 | 3661 | 4200 | 4339 | 3992 | 3119 | 2917 | 3385 | 3904 | 3279 | 3356 | 3457 | **4873** | 3727 |
| Avg. Yds per Att. | 5.9 | 6.8 | 6.8 | 6.0 | 6.5 | 5.8 | 5.9 | 6.0 | 6.8 | 5.7 | 4.9 | 6.6 | **7.3** | 6.1 |
| Avg. Yds per Comp. | 12.8 | 14.5 | 12.7 | 12.5 | 13.8 | 12.1 | 13.0 | 12.5 | **15.4** | 11.6 | 12.6 | 14.0 | 13.2 | 12.1 |
| Times Tackled | 37 | **16** | 35 | 40 | 61 | 40 | 37 | 30 | 45 | 30 | 53 | 27 | 19 | 37 |
| Yds Lost Tackled | 321 | 146 | 205 | 353 | 461 | 342 | 277 | 236 | 321 | 224 | 437 | 231 | **134** | 300 |
| Net Yards | 3058 | 3515 | 3995 | 3986 | 3531 | 2777 | 2640 | 3149 | 3583 | 3055 | 2919 | 3226 | **4739** | 3427 |
| Touchdowns | 21 | 25 | 30 | 21 | 27 | 21 | 12 | 18 | 17 | 26 | 18 | 25 | **34** | 21 |
| Interceptions | 23 | 20 | **12** | 27 | 21 | 23 | 22 | 21 | 34 | 14 | 28 | 19 | 18 | 15 |
| Pct. Intercepted | 4.8 | 4.0 | **2.2** | 4.3 | 4.3 | 5.2 | 5.4 | 4.2 | 7.1 | 2.8 | 5.1 | 4.1 | 2.9 | 2.9 |
| PUNTS: | | | | | | | | | | | | | | |
| Number | 78 | **80** | 73 | 70 | 86 | 79 | 70 | 83 | 75 | 81 | **98** | 84 | 63 | 68 |
| Average | 39.4 | 39.7 | **44.8** | 41.2 | 40.4 | 39.7 | 38.5 | 40.8 | 39.3 | 40.6 | 43.2 | 43.3 | 40.3 | 39.0 |
| PUNT RETURNS: | | | | | | | | | | | | | | |
| Number | 12 | 35 | 29 | 50 | 51 | 41 | 50 | 45 | 31 | 50 | **52** | 50 | 31 | 32 |
| Yards | 56 | 292 | 205 | 369 | 441 | 325 | **528** | 458 | 199 | 337 | 380 | 412 | 378 | 293 |
| Average Yards | 4.7 | 8.3 | 7.1 | 7.4 | 8.6 | 7.9 | 10.6 | 10.2 | 6.4 | 6.7 | 7.3 | 8.2 | **12.2** | 9.2 |
| Touchdowns | 0 | 0 | 0 | 0 | 0 | 0 | 0 | **1** | 0 | 0 | **1** | 0 | 0 | 0 |
| KICKOFF RET.: | | | | | | | | | | | | | | |
| Number | **84** | 57 | 49 | 72 | 47 | 72 | 52 | 54 | 65 | 58 | 71 | 53 | 70 | 69 |
| Yards | 1651 | 1085 | 1056 | 1537 | 801 | **1722** | 1043 | 1228 | 1190 | 1151 | 1411 | 1096 | 1422 | 1278 |
| Average Yards | 19.7 | 19.0 | 21.6 | 21.3 | 17.0 | **23.9** | 20.1 | 22.7 | 18.3 | 19.8 | 19.9 | 20.7 | 20.3 | 18.5 |
| Touchdowns | 0 | 0 | 0 | 0 | 0 | **2** | 0 | 1 | 0 | 0 | 0 | 0 | 0 | 0 |
| INTERCEPT RET.: | | | | | | | | | | | | | | |
| Number | 16 | 19 | 19 | 15 | 23 | 18 | 26 | 18 | 16 | 21 | 13 | **30** | 23 | 21 |
| Yards | 210 | 352 | 318 | 165 | 342 | 330 | 406 | 254 | 195 | **432** | 97 | 376 | 224 | 397 |
| Average Yards | 13.1 | 18.5 | 16.7 | 11.0 | 10.5 | 18.3 | 15.6 | 14.1 | 12.2 | **20.6** | 7.5 | 12.5 | 9.7 | 18.9 |
| Touchdowns | 0 | 0 | 1 | 0 | 0 | 0 | 1 | 0 | 0 | 2 | 1 | 1 | 1 | **3** |
| PENALTIES: | | | | | | | | | | | | | | |
| Number | 106 | 114 | 109 | 109 | 99 | 93 | 97 | **71** | 89 | 112 | 101 | 97 | 128 | 106 |
| Yards | 913 | 1001 | 896 | 971 | 833 | 825 | 924 | **541** | 742 | 936 | 867 | 840 | 947 | 823 |
| FUMBLES: | | | | | | | | | | | | | | |
| Number | 27 | 33 | **25** | 38 | 26 | 33 | 36 | 26 | 32 | 38 | 42 | 39 | 39 | 41 |
| Number Lost | 14 | 18 | 12 | 26 | 18 | 21 | 24 | **10** | 16 | 17 | 20 | 22 | 22 | 23 |
| POINTS: | | | | | | | | | | | | | | |
| Total | 259 | 311 | 421 | 276 | 321 | 281 | 343 | 345 | 322 | 355 | 273 | 356 | **478** | 322 |
| PAT Attempts | 33 | 38 | 51 | 32 | 39 | 34 | 38 | 39 | 40 | 40 | 33 | 46 | **61** | 40 |
| PAT Made | 29 | 37 | 49 | 31 | 36 | 32 | 37 | 37 | 37 | 38 | 27 | 38 | **55** | 37 |
| FG attempts | 18 | 24 | 32 | 33 | 30 | 22 | **36** | 31 | 24 | **36** | 24 | 17 | 26 | 24 |
| FG Made | 10 | 14 | 22 | 17 | 17 | 15 | **26** | 24 | 15 | 25 | 14 | 12 | 19 | 15 |
| Percent FG Made | 55.6 | 58.3 | 68.8 | 51.5 | 56.7 | 68.2 | 72.2 | **77.9** | 62.5 | 69.4 | 58.3 | 70.6 | 73.1 | 62.5 |
| Safeties | 1 | 2 | 0 | 1 | 0 | 0 | 0 | 1 | 0 | 1 | **3** | 0 | 0 | 0 |

| | BALT. | BUFF. | CIN. | CLEV. | DENV. | HOU. | K.C. | MIA. | N.E. | NY J | OAK. | PIT. | S.D. | SEA. |
|---|---|---|---|---|---|---|---|---|---|---|---|---|---|---|
| FIRST DOWNS: | | | | | | | | | | | | | | |
| Total | 406 | 298 | 324 | 299 | **268** | 325 | 316 | 296 | 328 | 291 | 316 | 323 | 365 | 371 |
| by Rushing | 162 | 113 | 126 | 119 | **108** | 138 | 112 | 124 | 160 | 112 | 104 | 114 | 114 | 175 |
| by Passing | 214 | 154 | 167 | 157 | **142** | 162 | 177 | 160 | 148 | 155 | 178 | 181 | 216 | 173 |
| by Penalty | 30 | 31 | 31 | 23 | 23 | 25 | 27 | **12** | 20 | 24 | 34 | 28 | 35 | 23 |
| RUSHING | | | | | | | | | | | | | | |
| Number | 607 | 516 | **465** | 516 | 467 | 549 | 507 | 492 | 644 | **465** | 524 | 500 | 491 | 588 |
| Yards | 2665 | 2075 | 1881 | 2078 | 2005 | 2411 | **1747** | 2032 | 2950 | 1867 | 1832 | 1869 | 1825 | 2806 |
| Average Yards | 4.4 | 4.0 | 4.0 | 4.0 | 4.3 | 4.4 | **3.4** | 4.1 | 4.6 | 4.0 | 3.5 | 3.7 | 3.7 | 4.8 |
| Touchdowns | 30 | **7** | 12 | 14 | 17 | 16 | 17 | 10 | 20 | 19 | 15 | 10 | 25 | 20 |
| PASSING: | | | | | | | | | | | | | | |
| Attempts | 491 | 474 | 548 | 469 | 497 | 502 | 567 | 509 | 439 | 505 | 537 | 544 | 571 | 502 |
| Completions | 301 | 267 | 316 | 275 | 267 | 295 | 291 | 297 | **243** | 275 | 289 | 302 | 313 | 294 |
| Completion Pct. | 61.3 | 56.3 | 57.7 | 58.6 | 53.7 | 58.8 | **51.3** | 58.3 | 55.4 | 54.5 | 53.8 | 55.5 | 54.8 | 58.6 |
| Passing Yards | 4228 | 3243 | 3757 | 3512 | 3168 | 3554 | 3821 | 3645 | **3052** | 3522 | 4011 | 4108 | 4695 | 3394 |
| Avg. Yds per Att. | 8.2 | 5.5 | 5.8 | 6.6 | 5.4 | 6.2 | 6.1 | 6.1 | 6.3 | **5.3** | 6.2 | 6.5 | 7.0 | 5.8 |
| Avg. Yds per Comp. | 14.1 | 12.2 | 11.9 | 12.8 | 11.9 | 12.1 | 13.1 | 12.3 | 12.6 | 12.8 | 13.9 | 13.6 | 15.0 | **11.5** |
| Times Tackled | 13 | 47 | 42 | 29 | 36 | 33 | 27 | 38 | 20 | **66** | 52 | 40 | 47 | 36 |
| Yds Lost Tackled | 100 | 373 | 349 | 223 | 295 | 239 | 195 | 314 | 175 | **518** | 370 | 325 | 384 | 260 |
| Net Yards | 4128 | **2870** | 3408 | 3289 | 2873 | 3315 | 3626 | 3331 | 2877 | 3004 | 3641 | 3783 | 4311 | 3134 |
| Touchdowns | 37 | 21 | 24 | 28 | **13** | 22 | 16 | 23 | 18 | 15 | 24 | 22 | 22 | 25 |
| Interceptions | 16 | 19 | 19 | 15 | 23 | 18 | 26 | 18 | 16 | 21 | 13 | **30** | 23 | 21 |
| Pct. Intercepted | 3.3 | 4.0 | 3.5 | 3.2 | 5.8 | 5.5 | 8.2 | 6.1 | 4.9 | 7.2 | 4.1 | **9.3** | 6.3 | 5.7 |
| PUNTS: | | | | | | | | | | | | | | |
| Number | 48 | 77 | 81 | 78 | 88 | 70 | 80 | 87 | 74 | 94 | **101** | 78 | 72 | 55 |
| Average | **37.9** | 42.0 | 40.3 | 40.7 | 43.1 | 41.9 | 38.9 | 41.0 | 38.8 | 40.4 | 38.9 | 42.1 | 40.3 | 42.5 |
| PUNT RETURNS: | | | | | | | | | | | | | | |
| Number | 44 | 34 | 42 | **30** | 46 | 47 | 46 | 45 | 35 | 31 | 45 | 34 | 31 | 33 |
| Yards | 402 | 220 | 416 | 253 | 388 | 360 | 293 | 286 | 305 | **149** | 514 | 358 | 168 | 153 |
| Average Yards | 9.1 | 6.5 | 9.9 | 8.4 | 8.4 | 7.7 | 6.4 | 6.4 | 8.7 | 4.8 | 11.4 | 10.5 | 5.4 | **4.6** |
| Touchdowns | 0 | 0 | 0 | 0 | 0 | 0 | 0 | 0 | 1 | 0 | 0 | 2 | 0 | 0 |
| KICKOFF RET.: | | | | | | | | | | | | | | |
| Number | **43** | 61 | 80 | 45 | 47 | 59 | 68 | 60 | 68 | 63 | 49 | 52 | 88 | 67 |
| Yards | **864** | 1268 | 1612 | 1156 | 1007 | 1201 | 1296 | 1218 | 1326 | 1415 | 1068 | 1253 | 1528 | 1177 |
| Average Yards | 20.1 | 20.8 | 20.2 | 25.7 | 21.4 | 20.4 | 19.1 | 20.3 | 19.5 | 22.5 | 21.8 | 24.1 | **17.4** | 17.6 |
| Touchdowns | 0 | 1 | 1 | 0 | 0 | 0 | 0 | 0 | 0 | 0 | 1 | 0 | 0 | 0 |
| INTERCEPT RET.: | | | | | | | | | | | | | | |
| Number | 23 | 20 | **12** | 27 | 21 | 23 | 22 | 21 | 34 | 14 | 28 | 19 | 18 | 15 |
| Yards | 281 | 333 | **143** | 347 | 405 | 289 | 247 | 288 | 570 | 212 | 339 | 226 | 377 | 257 |
| Average Yards | 12.2 | 16.7 | 11.9 | 12.9 | 19.3 | 12.6 | **11.2** | 13.6 | 16.8 | 15.1 | 12.1 | 11.9 | 20.9 | 17.1 |
| Touchdowns | 1 | 0 | 1 | 1 | 4 | 0 | 1 | 0 | 1 | 0 | 0 | 0 | 1 | 1 |
| PENALTIES: | | | | | | | | | | | | | | |
| Number | 101 | 93 | 104 | 100 | 104 | 102 | 89 | 104 | 83 | 106 | 102 | **112** | 108 | 104 |
| Yards | 776 | 690 | 787 | 870 | 949 | 838 | 740 | 886 | 763 | 935 | 826 | **960** | 877 | 944 |
| FUMBLES: | | | | | | | | | | | | | | |
| Number | 28 | 38 | 32 | 31 | 36 | 20 | 42 | 30 | 34 | 35 | 28 | 31 | 38 | **43** |
| Number Lost | 14 | 17 | 18 | 20 | 23 | 13 | 21 | 15 | 17 | 15 | 19 | 16 | 18 | **27** |
| POINTS: | | | | | | | | | | | | | | |
| Total | 533 | 276 | 304 | 375 | 289 | 355 | 290 | **275** | 370 | 287 | 343 | 297 | 390 | 388 |
| PAT Attempts | 68 | **30** | 38 | 45 | 35 | 39 | 34 | 33 | 41 | 36 | 42 | 35 | 48 | 46 |
| PAT Made | 65 | 30 | 38 | 40 | 34 | 38 | **29** | 33 | 39 | 33 | 38 | 33 | 45 | 41 |
| FG attempts | 31 | 26 | 21 | 34 | 27 | 42 | 27 | 21 | 39 | **20** | 30 | 33 | 26 | 29 |
| FG Made | 20 | 22 | **12** | 21 | 15 | 27 | 19 | 14 | 25 | **12** | 17 | 18 | 19 | 23 |
| Percent FG Made | 64.5 | 84.6 | 57.1 | 61.8 | 55.6 | 64.3 | 70.4 | 66.7 | 64.1 | 60.0 | 56.7 | **54.5** | 73.1 | 79.3 |
| Safeties | 0 | 0 | 1 | 1 | 0 | 1 | 0 | 1 | 2 | 1 | 1 | 0 | 0 | 1 |

Bitter salary disputes prompted the trading of these two stars. Wes Chandler came from New Orleans to join Kellen Winslow and Charlie Joiner as Dan Fouts' primary targets, while Chuck Muncie handled most of the running on this explosive offense. Russ Washington recovered from his knee injury to play offensive tackle, while guard Doug Wilkerson had the best campaign of his life. The explosive attack scored 44 points on opening day and went over 40 points three more times during the year. The defense, however, broke down several times, giving up 40 or more points on three occasions. Although Louie Kelcher and Gary Johnson anchored the center of the defensive line, the absence of Dean's pass rushing was felt throughout the back ranks of the platoon. After an embarrassing 44-23 loss to Seattle on Monday night November 16, the Chargers stood two games behind the Denver Broncos. Coming down the stretch, the Chargers reeled off four victories in five games, edging the Broncos for first place on the tiebreaker calculations.

**Denver Broncos**—The new Denver ownership brought in Dan Reeves as the new head coach. Heir apparent to Tom Landry at Dallas, Reeves brought the Cowboy winning touch with him for most of the season. He kept the rugged Denver defense intact and was rewarded with low enemy scoring and star performances from Randy Gradishar and Bob Swenson. Reeves worked his biggest changes on the offense. He uncovered a fine small fullback in Rick Parros, and he gave back-up receiver Steve Watson a starting job with marvelous results. Craig Morton, a former teammate of Reeves, thrived under the new regime. He burned the Chargers for 42 points on September 27 and had the Broncos in first place by one game in mid-November. Suddenly, the defense cracked under the pressure of a playoff drive. The Bengals and Chargers both ran up scores of over 30 points in beating the Broncos and dropping them into a three-way tie for first. Victories in the next two games put them one game ahead of the Chargers going into the final weekend. The Broncos went to Chicago on Sunday and were stunned by a 35-24 loss. When the Chargers beat Oakland on Mondy night, the Chargers took first place on the tiebreaker and the Broncos went home for Christmas.

**Kansas City Chiefs**—With little attention from the national media, the Chiefs stayed in the playoff race until the late stages of the schedule. Known as a conservative offensive team, the Chiefs unveiled a flashy new weapon in rookie halfback Joe Delaney, a small speedster who ran for over 1,000 yards despite backing up Ted McKnight in the early games. A knee injury sent McKnight to the sidelines in mid-season, just as quarterback Steve Fuller was returning from a two-month layoff with his own knee injury. A bad knee also hampered star defensive end Art Still. The defense nevertheless kept the Chiefs in playoff contention, led by star backs Gary Green and Gary Barbaro. Head Coach Marv Levy had his club in a first-place tie through most of November, dropping off the pace with a Thanksgiving Day loss in Detroit. Ten days later, they traveled to Denver and were beaten 16-13. A 17-7 loss to the Dolphins at home finally sent the Kansas City playoff hopes to the deep.

**Oakland Raiders**—The Raiders made headlines this year not by winning the Super Bowl, but by going three full games without scoring a point. Not since the Brooklyn Dodgers of the World War II era had an NFL club been shutout three straight times. The radical decline in the Oakland offense dropped them out of the playoff picture and cost several players their starting jobs. Super Bowl hero Jim Plunkett went to the bench together with Ray Chester, Art Shell, Gene Upshaw, and Dave Dalby. Injuries also took Bob Chandler, and Mark van Eeghen out of the lineup for much of the schedule. The defense lost Mike Davis, Reggie Kinlaw, and Bob Nelson to injuries, but Ted Hendricks and Lester Hayes successfully kept enemy attacks in check. After the string of shutouts, the Raiders battled back to the .500 mark with lots of young players on the field, but two closing losses sealed a season of disappointment.

**Seattle Seahawks**—Even though they came in last in the West, the Seahawks shed the abject look of last year. They got off to a miserable start, dropping six of their first seven games. A lethargic 32-0 beating at the hands of the Giants on Octoger 18 humiliated the Seahawks before their hometown fans, but it also served as a turn-around point. From that week on, the Hawks won five of their remaining nine games. Theotis Brown came in a trade with St. Louis and helped the resurgence with forceful running in the league's worst ground game. One high point of the season was a 44-23 ambush of the Chargers on Monday night television on November 16. Two weeks later, they blew a 24-3 lead and lost 32-31 to Oakland, with quarterback Jim Zorn suffering a broken ankle. Unheralded Dave Krieg stepped in for Zorn and engineered a 27-23 upset over the streaking Jets. Krieg also took the Hawks to a 42-21 victory over the Browns in the season's finale, their fifth triumph of the year before the home fans.

## MIAMI DOLPHINS 11-4-1 Don Shula

| Scores of Each Game | | |
|---|---|---|
| 20 | St. Louis | 7 |
| 30 | PITTSBURGH | 10 |
| 16 | Houston | 10 |
| 31 | Baltimore | 28 |
| 28 | N.Y. JETS | *28 |
| 21 | Buffalo | 31 |
| 13 | WASHINGTON | 10 |
| 27 | Dallas | 28 |
| 27 | BALTIMORE | 10 |
| 30 | New England | *27 |
| 17 | OAKLAND | 33 |
| 15 | N.Y. Jets | 16 |
| 13 | PHILADELPHIA | 10 |
| 24 | NEW ENGLAND | 14 |
| 17 | Kansas City | 7 |
| 16 | BUFFALO | 6 |

| Use Name | Pos. | Hgt. | Wgt. | Age | Int. | Pts. |
|---|---|---|---|---|---|---|
| Jon Giesler | OT | 6'5" | 260 | 24 | | |
| Cleveland Green | OT | 6'3" | 265 | 23 | | |
| Eric Laasko | OT-OG | 6'4" | 265 | 24 | | |
| Bob Kuechenberg | OG-OT-C | 6'3" | 255 | 33 | | |
| Burton Lawless | OG | 6'4" | 255 | 27 | | |
| Ed Newman | OG | 6'2" | 255 | 30 | | |
| Jeff Toews | OG-C | 6'3" | 255 | 23 | | |
| Mark Dennard | C | 6'1" | 252 | 25 | | |
| Dwight Stephenson | C-OT | 6'2" | 255 | 23 | | |
| Bill Barnett | DE-NT | 6'4" | 255 | 25 | | |
| Doug Betters | DE | 6'7" | 260 | 25 | | |
| Kim Bokamper | DE-LB | 6'6" | 247 | 26 | | |
| Vern Den Herder | DE-NT | 6'6" | 252 | 32 | | |
| Ken Poole | DE | 6'3" | 251 | 22 | | |
| Bob Baumhower | NT | 6'5" | 260 | 26 | | |
| Bob Brudzinski | LB | 6'4" | 230 | 26 | 2 | |
| A.J. Duhe | LB | 6'4" | 252 | 25 | 1 | |
| Larry Gordon | LB | 6'4" | 230 | 28 | | 2 |
| Steve Potter | LB | 6'3" | 235 | 23 | | |
| Earnest Rhone | LB | 6'2" | 224 | 28 | 3 | |
| Steve Shull | LB | 6'1" | 218 | 23 | | |
| Don Bessillieu | DB | 6'1" | 200 | 25 | 1 | |
| Glenn Blackwood | DB | 6' | 183 | 24 | 4 | |
| Lyle Blackwood | DB | 6' | 188 | 30 | 3 | |
| Mike Kozlowski | DB | 6' | 197 | 25 | 3 | 6 |
| Don McNeal | DB | 5'11" | 192 | 23 | | |
| Gerald Small | DB | 5'11" | 192 | 25 | | |
| Ed Taylor | DB | 6' | 175 | 28 | | |
| Fulton Walker | DB | 5'10" | 193 | 23 | 1 | 6 |
| Jim Jensen | QB | 6'4" | 212 | 22 | | |
| Don Strock | QB | 6'5" | 220 | 30 | | |
| David Woodley | QB | 6'2" | 204 | 22 | | 24 |
| Eddie Hill | HB | 6'2" | 210 | 24 | | 12 |
| Tony Nathan | HB-FB | 6' | 206 | 24 | | 48 |
| Tommy Vigorito | HB | 5'10" | 197 | 21 | | 24 |
| Woody Bennett | FB | 6'2" | 222 | 26 | | |
| Andra Franklin | FB | 5'10" | 225 | 21 | | 48 |
| Steve Howell | FB | 6'2" | 230 | 24 | | |
| Terry Robiskie | FB | 6'1" | 210 | 26 | | |
| Elmer Bailey | WR | 6' | 195 | 23 | | |
| Jimmy Cefalo | WR | 5'11" | 188 | 24 | | 18 |
| Duriel Harris | WR | 5'11" | 184 | 26 | | 12 |
| Nat Moore | WR | 5'9" | 188 | 29 | | 12 |
| Bruce Hardy | TE | 6'5" | 230 | 25 | | |
| Ronnie Lee | TE | 6'3" | 235 | 24 | | 6 |
| Joe Rose | TE | 6'3" | 225 | 24 | | 12 |
| Tom Orosz | K | 6'1" | 204 | 21 | | |
| Uwe von Schamann | K | 6' | 188 | 25 | | 109 |

Tom Henderson – Broken Neck
Rusty Chambers – Killed in auto accident in July

## NEW YORK JETS 10-5-1 Walt Michaels

| Scores of Each Game | | |
|---|---|---|
| 0 | Buffalo | 31 |
| 30 | CINCINNATI | 31 |
| 10 | Pittsburgh | 38 |
| 33 | HOUSTON | 17 |
| 28 | Miami | *28 |
| 28 | NEW ENGLAND | 24 |
| 33 | BUFFALO | 14 |
| 3 | SEATTLE | 19 |
| 26 | N.Y. Giants | 7 |
| 41 | Baltimore | 14 |
| 17 | New England | 6 |
| 16 | MIAMI | 15 |
| 25 | BALTIMORE | 0 |
| 23 | Seattle | 27 |
| 14 | Cleveland | 13 |
| 28 | GREEN BAY | 3 |

| Use Name | Pos. | Hgt. | Wgt. | Age | Int. | Pts. |
|---|---|---|---|---|---|---|
| Marvin Powell | OT | 6'5" | 268 | 26 | | |
| John Roman | OT | 6'4" | 260 | 29 | | |
| Chris Ward | OT | 6'3" | 270 | 25 | | |
| Dan Alexander | OG | 6'4" | 255 | 26 | | |
| Randy Rasmussen | OG | 6'2" | 255 | 36 | | |
| Stan Waldemore | OG-C | 6'4" | 269 | 26 | | |
| Guy Bingham | C-OG-OT | 6'3" | 255 | 23 | | |
| Joe Fields | C | 6'2" | 253 | 27 | | |
| Ralph DeLoach | DE | 6'5" | 254 | 24 | | |
| Mark Gastineau | DE | 6'5" | 280 | 24 | | |
| Joe Klecko | DE | 6'3" | 265 | 27 | | |
| Kenny Neil | DE-DT | 6'4" | 244 | 22 | | |
| Marty Lyons | DT | 6'5" | 260 | 24 | | |
| Abdul Salaam | DT | 6'3" | 265 | 28 | | |
| Ben Rudolph | DT-DE | 6'5" | 271 | 24 | | |
| Stan Blinka | LB | 6'2" | 230 | 24 | 1 | |
| Greg Buttle | LB | 6'3" | 232 | 27 | 2 | 2 |
| Ron Crosby | LB | 6'3" | 222 | 26 | | |
| Lance Mehl | LB | 6'3" | 230 | 23 | 3 | |
| Al Washington | LB | 6'3" | 235 | 22 | | |
| Marty Wetzel | LB | 6'3" | 235 | 23 | | |
| John Woodring | LB | 6'2" | 230 | 22 | | |
| Donald Dykes | DB | 5'11" | 180 | 26 | | |
| Jerry Holmes | DB | 6'2" | 175 | 23 | 1 | |
| Bobby Jackson | DB | 5'9" | 175 | 24 | | |
| Jesse Johnson | DB | 6'3" | 185 | 24 | | |
| Johnny Lynn | DB | 6' | 190 | 24 | 3 | |
| Darrol Ray | DB | 6'1" | 200 | 23 | 7 | 12 |
| Ken Schroy | DB | 6'2" | 196 | 28 | 2 | |
| Kirk Springs | DB | 6' | 192 | 23 | 2 | |
| Kyle Grossart | QB | 6'4" | 210 | 26 | | |
| Pat Ryan | QB | 6'3" | 205 | 25 | | |
| Richard Todd | QB | 6'2" | 203 | 27 | | |
| Scott Dierking | HB-FB | 5'10" | 215 | 26 | | 12 |
| Bruce Harper | HB | 5'8" | 177 | 26 | | 30 |
| Kenny Lewis | HB | 6' | 190 | 23 | | |
| Freeman McNeil | HB | 5'11" | 225 | 22 | | 18 |
| Mike Augustyniak | FB | 5'11" | 220 | 25 | | 6 |
| Kevin Long | FB | 6'1" | 218 | 26 | | 30 |
| Tom Newton | FB | 6' | 213 | 27 | | 6 |
| Derrick Gaffney | WR | 6'1" | 180 | 26 | | |
| Bobby Jones | WR | 5'11" | 180 | 26 | | 12 |
| Johnny "Lam" Jones | WR | 5'11" | 180 | 23 | | 18 |
| Kurt Sohn | WR | 5'11" | 176 | 24 | | |
| Wesley Walker | WR | 6' | 175 | 26 | | 54 |
| Jerome Barkum | TE | 6'3" | 225 | 31 | | 42 |
| Mickey Shuler | TE | 6'3" | 235 | 25 | | |
| Steve Stephens | TE | 6'3" | 227 | 24 | | |
| Pat Leahy | K | 6' | 195 | 30 | | 113 |
| Chuck Ramsey | K | 6'2" | 189 | 29 | | |

Mike McKibben–Knee Injury

## BUFFALO BILLS 10-6-0 Chuck Knox

| Scores of Each Game | | |
|---|---|---|
| 31 | N.Y. JETS | 0 |
| 35 | Baltimore | 3 |
| 14 | PHILADELPHIA | 20 |
| 24 | Cincinnati | *27 |
| 23 | BALTIMORE | 17 |
| 31 | MIAMI | 21 |
| 14 | N.Y. Jets | 33 |
| 9 | DENVER | 7 |
| 22 | CLEVELAND | 13 |
| 14 | Dallas | 27 |
| 0 | St. Louis | 24 |
| 20 | NEW ENGLAND | 17 |
| 21 | WASHINGTON | 14 |
| 28 | San Diego | 27 |
| 19 | New England | 10 |
| 6 | Miami | 16 |

| Use Name | Pos. | Hgt. | Wgt. | Age | Int. | Pts. |
|---|---|---|---|---|---|---|
| Jon Borchardt | OT-OG | 6'5" | 255 | 24 | | |
| Joe Devlin | OT | 6'5" | 250 | 27 | | |
| Ken Jones | OT | 6'5" | 250 | 28 | | |
| Conrad Dobler | OG | 6'3" | 255 | 30 | | |
| Tom Lynch | OG | 6'5" | 260 | 26 | | |
| Reggie McKenzie | OG | 6'4" | 242 | 31 | | |
| Jim Ritcher | OG-C | 6'3" | 251 | 23 | | |
| Will Grant | C | 6'3" | 248 | 27 | | |
| Tim Vogler | C-OG | 6'3" | 245 | 24 | | |
| Darrell Irvin | DE | 6'4" | 255 | 24 | | |
| Ken Johnson | DE | 6'5" | 253 | 26 | | |
| Sherman White | DE | 6'5" | 250 | 32 | | |
| Ben Williams | DE | 6'3" | 245 | 27 | 1 | 2 |
| Mike Kadish | NT | 6'5" | 270 | 31 | | |
| Fred Smerlas | NT | 6'3" | 270 | 24 | | |
| Jim Haslett | LB | 6'3" | 237 | 25 | | |
| Mike Humiston | LB | 6'3" | 238 | 22 | | |
| Chris Keating | LB | 6'2" | 223 | 23 | | |
| Shane Nelson | LB | 6'1" | 232 | 26 | 1 | |
| Ervin Parker | LB | 6'4" | 240 | 23 | | |
| Isiah Robertson | LB | 6'3" | 225 | 32 | 2 | |
| Lucius Sanford | LB | 6'2" | 216 | 25 | | |
| Phil Villapiano | LB | 6'2" | 225 | 32 | | |
| Rufus Bess | DB | 5'9" | 180 | 24 | 1 | |
| Mario Clark | DB | 6'2" | 195 | 27 | 5 | |
| Steve Freeman | DB | 5'11" | 185 | 28 | | |
| Rod Kush | DB | 6' | 188 | 24 | 1 | |
| Jeff Nixon | DB | 6'3" | 190 | 24 | | |
| Charles Romes | DB | 6'1" | 190 | 27 | 4 | |
| Bill Simpson | DB | 6'1" | 191 | 29 | 4 | |
| Joe Ferguson | QB | 6'1" | 195 | 31 | | 6 |
| Matt Robinson | QB | 6'2" | 196 | 26 | | |
| Joe Cribbs | HB | 5'11" | 190 | 23 | | 60 |
| Roland Hooks | HB | 6' | 195 | 28 | | 30 |
| Robb Riddick | HB | 6' | 195 | 23 | | |
| Curtis Brown | FB | 5'10" | 203 | 26 | | 6 |
| Roosevelt Leaks | FB | 5'10" | 225 | 28 | | 36 |
| Lawrence McCutcheon | FB | 6'1" | 205 | 31 | | |
| Jerry Butler | WR | 6' | 178 | 23 | | 48 |
| Byron Franklin | WR | 6'1" | 179 | 22 | | |
| Ron Jessie | WR | 6' | 181 | 33 | | |
| Frank Lewis | WR | 6'1" | 196 | 34 | | 24 |
| Lou Piccone | WR | 5'9" | 175 | 32 | | |
| Steve Alvers | TE-C | 6'4" | 240 | 24 | | |
| Buster Barnett | TE | 6'5" | 225 | 22 | | 6 |
| Mark Brammer | TE | 6'3" | 235 | 23 | | 12 |
| Greg Cater | K | 6' | 191 | 24 | | |
| Nick Mike-Mayer | K | 5'8" | 185 | 31 | | 79 |

Sid Justin – Injury

## BALTIMORE COLTS 2-14-0 Mike McCormack

| Scores of Each Game | | |
|---|---|---|
| 29 | New England | 28 |
| 3 | BUFFALO | 35 |
| 10 | Denver | 28 |
| 28 | MIAMI | 31 |
| 17 | Buffalo | 23 |
| 19 | CINCINNATI | 41 |
| 14 | SAN DIEGO | 43 |
| 28 | Cleveland | 42 |
| 10 | Miami | 27 |
| 14 | N.Y. JETS | 41 |
| 13 | Philadelphia | 38 |
| 24 | ST. LOUIS | 35 |
| 0 | N.Y. Jets | 25 |
| 13 | DALLAS | 37 |
| 14 | Washington | 38 |
| 23 | NEW ENGLAND | 21 |

| Use Name | Pos. | Hgt. | Wgt. | Age | Int. | Pts. |
|---|---|---|---|---|---|---|
| Tim Foley | OT | 6'6" | 275 | 23 | | |
| Wade Griffin | OT | 6'5" | 270 | 27 | | |
| Jeff Hart | OT | 6'5" | 272 | 27 | | |
| Randy Van Divier | OT | 6'5" | 282 | 23 | | |
| Ken Huff | OG | 6'4" | 253 | 28 | | |
| Jimmy Moore | OG | 6'5" | 268 | 24 | | |
| Robert Pratt | OG | 6'4" | 250 | 30 | | |
| Ray Donaldson | C | 6'3" | 263 | 23 | | |
| Chris Foote | C-OG | 6'3" | 247 | 24 | | |
| Mike Ozdowski | DE | 6'5" | 243 | 25 | | |
| Hosea Taylor | DE | 6'5" | 250 | 22 | | 2 |
| Donnell Thompson | DE | 6'4" | 252 | 22 | | |
| Daryl Wilkerson | DE | 6'4" | 255 | 22 | | |
| Mike Barnes | DT | 6'6" | 264 | 30 | | |
| Mike Fultz (from MIA) | DT | 6'5" | 278 | 27 | | |
| Bubba Green | DT | 6'4" | 278 | 22 | 1 | |
| Herb Orvis | DT | 6'5" | 255 | 34 | | |
| Joe Federspiel | LB | 6'1" | 230 | 31 | | |
| Ricky Jones | LB | 6'1" | 222 | 26 | | |
| Barry Krauss | LB | 6'3" | 238 | 24 | 1 | |
| Sanders Shiver | LB | 6'2" | 230 | 26 | | |
| Ed Simonini | LB | 6' | 206 | 27 | | |
| Ed Smith | LB | 6'2" | 216 | 24 | 2 | |
| Mike Woods | LB | 6'2" | 237 | 26 | | |
| Kim Anderson | DB | 5'11" | 184 | 24 | 1 | |
| Larry Braziel | DB | 6' | 184 | 26 | 3 | |
| Nesby Glasgow | DB | 5'10" | 185 | 24 | 2 | |
| Derrick Hatchett | DB | 5'11" | 186 | 23 | 2 | |
| Steve Henry | DB | 6'2" | 190 | 24 | | |
| Bruce Laird | DB | 6' | 194 | 31 | 3 | |
| Reggie Pinkney | DB | 5'11" | 187 | 26 | 1 | |
| David Humm | QB | 6'2" | 190 | 29 | | |
| Bert Jones | QB | 6'3" | 218 | 29 | | |
| Greg Landry | QB | 6'4" | 208 | 34 | | 6 |
| Jay Venuto | QB | 6'1" | 195 | 23 | | |
| Curtis Dickey | HB | 6'1" | 205 | 24 | | 60 |
| Zachary Dixon | HB | 6' | 204 | 25 | | 6 |
| Don McCauley | HB | 6'1" | 211 | 32 | | 12 |
| Cleveland Franklin | FB | 6'2" | 220 | 26 | | 6 |
| Randy McMillan | FB | 6' | 226 | 22 | | 24 |
| Marvin Sims | FB | 6'4" | 234 | 24 | | |
| Randy Burke | WR | 6'2" | 198 | 26 | | |
| Ray Butler | WR | 6'3" | 190 | 24 | | 54 |
| Roger Carr | WR | 6'3" | 195 | 29 | | 18 |
| Brian DeRoo | WR | 6'3" | 200 | 25 | | |
| Dave Shula | WR | 5'11" | 182 | 22 | | |
| Kevin Williams | WR | 5'8" | 164 | 23 | | |
| Reese McCall | TE | 6'7" | 243 | 25 | | 12 |
| Tim Sherwin | TE | 6'5" | 239 | 23 | | |
| Mike Garrett | K | 6'1" | 184 | 24 | | |
| Mike Wood | K | 5'11" | 199 | 26 | | 59 |

## NEW ENGLAND PATRIOTS 2-14-0 Ron Erhardt

| Scores of Each Game | | |
|---|---|---|
| 28 | BALTIMORE | 29 |
| 3 | Philadelphia | 13 |
| 21 | DALLAS | 35 |
| 21 | Pittsburgh | *27 |
| 33 | KANSAS CITY | 17 |
| 24 | N.Y. Jets | 28 |
| 38 | HOUSTON | 10 |
| 22 | Washington | 24 |
| 17 | Oakland | 27 |
| 27 | MIAMI | *30 |
| 6 | N.Y. JETS | 17 |
| 17 | Buffalo | 20 |
| 20 | ST. LOUIS | 27 |
| 14 | Miami | 24 |
| 10 | BUFFALO | 19 |
| 21 | Baltimore | 23 |

*—Overtime

| Use Name | Pos. | Hgt. | Wgt. | Age | Int. | Pts. |
|---|---|---|---|---|---|---|
| Brian Holloway | OT | 6'7" | 273 | 22 | | |
| Shelby Jordan | OT | 6'7" | 260 | 29 | | |
| Dwight Wheeler | OT-C | 6'3" | 255 | 26 | | |
| Bob Cryder | OG | 6'4" | 265 | 24 | | |
| John Hannah | OG | 6'2" | 265 | 30 | | |
| Gary Puetz | OG-OT | 6'4" | 265 | 29 | | |
| Pete Brock | C | 6'5" | 260 | 27 | | |
| Bill Lenkaitis | C | 6'3" | 255 | 35 | | |
| Julius Adams | DE | 6'3" | 263 | 33 | | |
| Mark Buben | DE | 6'3" | 260 | 24 | 1 | |
| Steve Clark | DE | 6'5" | 258 | 21 | | |
| John Lee | DE | 6'2" | 259 | 28 | | |
| Tony McGee | DE | 6'4" | 250 | 32 | | |
| Richard Bishop | NT | 6'1" | 260 | 31 | | |
| Ray Hamilton | NT | 6'1" | 245 | 30 | | |
| Don Blackmon | LB | 6'3" | 235 | 23 | | |
| Bob Golic | LB | 6'2" | 240 | 23 | | |
| Mike Hawkins | LB | 6'2" | 235 | 25 | 1 | |
| Steve King | LB | 6'4" | 230 | 30 | | |
| Bill Matthews | LB | 6'2" | 235 | 25 | | |
| Steve Nelson | LB | 6'2" | 230 | 30 | | |
| Rod Shoate | LB | 6'1" | 215 | 28 | 1 | |
| John Zamberlin | LB | 6'2" | 230 | 25 | 1 | |
| Raymond Clayborn | DB | 6'1" | 190 | 26 | 2 | |
| Paul Dombroski | DB | 6' | 185 | 25 | | |
| Tim Fox | DB | 5'11" | 190 | 27 | 3 | |
| Mike Haynes | DB | 6'2" | 195 | 28 | 1 | |
| Roland James | DB | 6'2" | 189 | 23 | 2 | |
| Keith Lee | DB | 5'11" | 192 | 23 | 1 | |
| Rick Sanford | DB | 6'1" | 192 | 24 | 3 | |
| Darrell Wilson | DB | 5'11" | 180 | 23 | | |
| Matt Cavanaugh | QB | 6'1" | 210 | 24 | | 18 |
| Steve Grogan | QB | 6'4" | 208 | 28 | | 12 |
| Tom Owen | QB | 6'1" | 194 | 28 | | |
| Tony Collins | HB | 5'11" | 202 | 22 | | 42 |
| Vagas Ferguson | HB | 6'1" | 194 | 24 | | 18 |
| Andy Johnson | HB | 6' | 204 | 28 | | 6 |
| Don Calhoun | FB | 6' | 212 | 29 | | 12 |
| Sam Cunningham | FB | 6'3" | 230 | 31 | | 24 |
| Mosi Tatupu | FB | 6' | 225 | 26 | | 18 |
| Harold Jackson | WR | 5'10" | 175 | 35 | | |
| Stanley Morgan | WR | 5'11" | 180 | 26 | | 36 |
| Carlos Pennywell | WR | 6'2" | 180 | 25 | | 6 |
| Ken Toler | WR | 6'2" | 195 | 22 | | |
| Don Westbrook | WR | 5'10" | 184 | 28 | | 12 |
| Lin Dawson | TE | 6'3" | 235 | 22 | | |
| Don Hasselbeck | TE | 6'7" | 245 | 27 | | 36 |
| Rich Camarillo | K | 5'11" | 189 | 21 | | |
| Ken Hartley | K | 6'2" | 200 | 24 | | |
| Mike Hubach | K | 5'10" | 185 | 23 | | |
| John Smith | K | 6' | 185 | 31 | | 82 |

Preston Brown – Back Injury
Allan Clark – Knee Injury
Larry McGrew – Knee Injury

## MIAMI DOLPHINS

### RUSHING

| Last Name | No. | Yds. | Avg. | TD |
|---|---|---|---|---|
| Nathan | 147 | 782 | 5.3 | 5 |
| Franklin | 201 | 711 | 3.5 | 7 |
| Woodley | 63 | 272 | 4.3 | 4 |
| Hill | 37 | 146 | 3.9 | 1 |
| Vigorito | 35 | 116 | 3.3 | 1 |
| Bennett | 28 | 104 | 3.7 | 0 |
| Howell | 5 | 21 | 4.2 | 0 |
| Orosz | 1 | 13 | 13.0 | 0 |
| Moore | 1 | 3 | 3.0 | 0 |
| Strock | 14 | −26 | −1.9 | 0 |

### RECEIVING

| Last Name | No. | Yds. | Avg. | TD |
|---|---|---|---|---|
| Harris | 53 | 911 | 17 | 2 |
| Nathan | 50 | 452 | 9 | 3 |
| Vigorito | 33 | 237 | 7 | 2 |
| Cefalo | 29 | 631 | 22 | 3 |
| Moore | 26 | 452 | 17 | 2 |
| Rose | 23 | 316 | 14 | 2 |
| Hardy | 15 | 174 | 12 | 0 |
| Lee | 14 | 64 | 5 | 1 |
| Hill | 12 | 73 | 6 | 1 |
| Bennett | 4 | 22 | 6 | 0 |
| Franklin | 3 | 6 | 2 | 1 |
| Howell | 2 | 9 | 5 | 0 |

### PUNT RETURNS

| Last Name | No. | Yds. | Avg. | TD |
|---|---|---|---|---|
| Vigorito | 36 | 379 | 11 | 1 |
| Walker | 5 | 50 | 10 | 0 |
| G. Blackwood | 2 | 8 | 4 | 0 |
| Bessillieu | 1 | 12 | 12 | 0 |
| Kozlowski | 1 | 9 | 9 | 0 |

### KICKOFF RETURNS

| Last Name | No. | Yds. | Avg. | TD |
|---|---|---|---|---|
| Walker | 38 | 932 | 25 | 1 |
| Bessillieu | 7 | 114 | 16 | 0 |
| Vigorito | 4 | 84 | 21 | 0 |
| Kozlowski | 1 | 40 | 40 | 0 |
| Harris | 1 | 20 | 20 | 0 |
| Hill | 1 | 11 | 11 | 0 |
| Rose | 1 | 5 | 5 | 0 |

### PASSING – PUNTING – KICKING

| Last Name | Att. | Comp. | % | Yds. | Yd./Att. | TD | Int.-% | RK |
|---|---|---|---|---|---|---|---|---|
| Woodley | 366 | 191 | 52 | 2470 | 6.8 | 12 | 13- 4 | 9 |
| Strock | 130 | 79 | 61 | 901 | 6.9 | 6 | 8- 6 | |
| Hill | 1 | 1 | 100 | 14 | 14.0 | 0 | 0- 0 | |
| Nathan | 1 | 0 | 0 | 0 | 0 | 0 | 0- 0 | |

| Last Name | No. | Avg. |
|---|---|---|
| PUNTING Orosz | 83 | 40.8 |

| Last Name | XP | Att. | % | FG | Att. | % |
|---|---|---|---|---|---|---|
| KICKING von Schamann | 37 | 38 | 97 | 24 | 31 | 77 |

## NEW YORK JETS

### RUSHING

| Last Name | No. | Yds. | Avg. | TD |
|---|---|---|---|---|
| McNeil | 137 | 623 | 4.5 | 2 |
| Harper | 81 | 393 | 4.9 | 4 |
| Augustyniak | 85 | 339 | 4.0 | 1 |
| Dierking | 74 | 328 | 4.4 | 1 |
| Long | 73 | 269 | 3.7 | 2 |
| Newton | 73 | 244 | 3.3 | 1 |
| Todd | 32 | 131 | 4.1 | 0 |
| Lewis | 6 | 18 | 3.0 | 0 |
| J. Jones | 2 | 0 | 0.0 | 0 |
| Ramsey | 3 | 0 | 0.0 | 0 |
| Ryan | 3 | −5 | −1.7 | 0 |

### RECEIVING

| Last Name | No. | Yds. | Avg. | TD |
|---|---|---|---|---|
| Harper | 52 | 459 | 9 | 1 |
| Walker | 47 | 770 | 16 | 9 |
| Barkum | 39 | 495 | 13 | 7 |
| Dierking | 26 | 228 | 9 | 1 |
| J. Jones | 20 | 342 | 17 | 3 |
| McNeil | 18 | 171 | 10 | 1 |
| Augustyniak | 18 | 144 | 8 | 0 |
| Newton | 17 | 104 | 6 | 0 |
| B. Jones | 16 | 239 | 15 | 1 |
| Gaffney | 14 | 246 | 18 | 0 |
| Long | 13 | 66 | 5 | 3 |
| Stephens | 2 | 21 | 11 | 0 |
| Lewis | 2 | 14 | 7 | 0 |
| Rudolph | 1 | 8 | 8 | 0 |
| Todd | 1 | 1 | 1 | 0 |

### PUNT RETURNS

| Last Name | No. | Yds. | Avg. | TD |
|---|---|---|---|---|
| Harper | 35 | 265 | 8 | 0 |
| Sohn | 13 | 66 | 5 | 0 |
| Schroy | 1 | 5 | 5 | 0 |
| B. Jones | 1 | 1 | 1 | 0 |

### KICKOFF RETURNS

| Last Name | No. | Yds. | Avg. | TD |
|---|---|---|---|---|
| Harper | 23 | 480 | 21 | 0 |
| Sohn | 26 | 528 | 20 | 0 |
| Lewis | 5 | 108 | 22 | 0 |
| J. Jones | 1 | 6 | 6 | 0 |

### PASSING – PUNTING – KICKING

| Last Name | Att. | Comp. | % | Yds. | Yd./Att. | TD | Int.-% | RK |
|---|---|---|---|---|---|---|---|---|
| Todd | 497 | 279 | 56 | 3231 | 6.5 | 25 | 13- 3 | 6 |
| Ryan | 10 | 4 | 40 | 48 | 4.8 | 1 | 1- 10 | |

| Last Name | No. | Avg. |
|---|---|---|
| PUNTING Ramsey | 81 | 40.6 |

| Last Name | XP | Att. | % | FG | Att. | % |
|---|---|---|---|---|---|---|
| KICKING Leahy | 38 | 39 | 97 | 25 | 36 | 69 |

## BUFFALO BILLS

### RUSHING

| Last Name | No. | Yds. | Avg. | TD |
|---|---|---|---|---|
| Cribbs | 257 | 1097 | 4.3 | 3 |
| Leaks | 91 | 357 | 3.9 | 6 |
| Hooks | 51 | 250 | 4.9 | 3 |
| Brown | 62 | 226 | 3.6 | 0 |
| McCutcheon | 34 | 138 | 4.1 | 0 |
| Riddick | 3 | 29 | 9.7 | 0 |
| Ferguson | 20 | 29 | 1.5 | 1 |
| Brammer | 2 | 17 | 8.5 | 0 |
| Butler | 1 | 1 | 1.0 | 0 |
| Robinson | 1 | −2 | −2.0 | 0 |
| Kush | 1 | −6 | −6.0 | 0 |
| Franklin | 1 | −11 | −11.0 | 0 |

### RECEIVING

| Last Name | No. | Yds. | Avg. | TD |
|---|---|---|---|---|
| Lewis | 70 | 1244 | 18 | 4 |
| Butler | 55 | 842 | 15 | 8 |
| Cribbs | 40 | 603 | 15 | 7 |
| Brammer | 33 | 365 | 11 | 2 |
| Jessie | 15 | 200 | 13 | 0 |
| Hooks | 10 | 140 | 14 | 2 |
| Leaks | 7 | 51 | 7 | 0 |
| Brown | 7 | 46 | 7 | 1 |
| Piccone | 5 | 65 | 13 | 0 |
| McCutcheon | 5 | 40 | 8 | 0 |
| Barnett | 4 | 36 | 9 | 1 |
| Franklin | 2 | 29 | 15 | 0 |

### PUNT RETURNS

| Last Name | No. | Yds. | Avg. | TD |
|---|---|---|---|---|
| Hooks | 17 | 142 | 8 | 0 |
| Piccone | 9 | 57 | 6 | 0 |
| Franklin | 5 | 45 | 9 | 0 |
| Riddick | 4 | 48 | 12 | 0 |

### KICKOFF RETURNS

| Last Name | No. | Yds. | Avg. | TD |
|---|---|---|---|---|
| Franklin | 21 | 436 | 21 | 0 |
| Riddick | 14 | 257 | 18 | 0 |
| Hooks | 11 | 215 | 20 | 0 |
| Brown | 7 | 140 | 20 | 0 |
| Piccone | 2 | 31 | 16 | 0 |
| Bess | 1 | 6 | 6 | 0 |
| Freeman | 1 | 0 | 0 | 0 |

### PASSING – PUNTING – KICKING

| Last Name | Att. | Comp. | % | Yds. | Yd./Att. | TD | Int.-% | RK |
|---|---|---|---|---|---|---|---|---|
| Ferguson | 498 | 252 | 51 | 3652 | 7.3 | 24 | 20- 4 | 8 |
| Cribbs | 1 | 1 | 100 | 9 | 9.0 | 1 | 0- 0 | |
| Leaks | 1 | 0 | 0 | 0 | 0.0 | 0 | 0- 0 | |
| Mike-Mayer | 1 | 0 | 0 | 0 | 0.0 | 0 | 0- 0 | |
| Robinson | 2 | 0 | 0 | 0 | 0.0 | 0 | 0- 0 | |

| Last Name | No. | Avg. |
|---|---|---|
| PUNTING Cater | 80 | 39.7 |

| Last Name | XP | Att. | % | FG | Att. | % |
|---|---|---|---|---|---|---|
| KICKING Mike-Mayer | 37 | 37 | 100 | 14 | 24 | 58 |

## BALTIMORE COLTS

### RUSHING

| Last Name | No. | Yds. | Avg. | TD |
|---|---|---|---|---|
| Dickey | 164 | 779 | 4.8 | 7 |
| McMillan | 149 | 597 | 4.0 | 3 |
| Dixon | 73 | 285 | 3.9 | 0 |
| B. Jones | 20 | 85 | 4.3 | 0 |
| Franklin | 21 | 52 | 2.5 | 1 |
| McCauley | 10 | 37 | 3.7 | 0 |
| Landry | 1 | 11 | 11.0 | 0 |
| Garrett | 2 | 4 | 2.0 | 0 |
| Anderson | 1 | 0 | 0.0 | 0 |

### RECEIVING

| Last Name | No. | Yds. | Avg. | TD |
|---|---|---|---|---|
| McMillan | 50 | 466 | 9 | 1 |
| Butler | 46 | 832 | 18 | 9 |
| Carr | 38 | 584 | 15 | 3 |
| Dickey | 37 | 419 | 11 | 3 |
| McCauley | 36 | 347 | 10 | 2 |
| McCall | 21 | 314 | 15 | 2 |
| Dixon | 17 | 169 | 10 | 1 |
| Burke | 10 | 153 | 15 | 0 |
| Franklin | 6 | 39 | 7 | 0 |
| Sherwin | 2 | 19 | 10 | 0 |
| DeRoo | 1 | 38 | 38 | 0 |
| Huff | 1 | −1 | −1 | 0 |

### PUNT RETURNS

| Last Name | No. | Yds. | Avg. | TD |
|---|---|---|---|---|
| Shula | 10 | 50 | 5 | 0 |
| Anderson | 2 | 6 | 3 | 0 |

### KICKOFF RETURNS

| Last Name | No. | Yds. | Avg. | TD |
|---|---|---|---|---|
| Dixon | 36 | 737 | 21 | 0 |
| Williams | 20 | 399 | 20 | 0 |
| Anderson | 20 | 393 | 20 | 0 |
| Shula | 5 | 65 | 13 | 0 |
| Glasgow | 1 | 35 | 35 | 0 |
| Sims | 1 | 22 | 22 | 0 |
| Foote | 1 | 0 | 0 | 0 |

### PASSING – PUNTING – KICKING

| Last Name | Att. | Comp. | % | Yds. | Yd./Att. | TD | Int.-% | RK |
|---|---|---|---|---|---|---|---|---|
| B. Jones | 426 | 244 | 57 | 3094 | 7.3 | 21 | 20- 5 | 7 |
| Landry | 29 | 14 | 48 | 195 | 6.7 | 0 | 1- 3 | |
| Humm | 24 | 7 | 29 | 90 | 3.8 | 0 | 2- 8 | |

| Last Name | No. | Avg. |
|---|---|---|
| PUNTING Garrett | 78 | 39.4 |

| Last Name | XP | Att. | % | FG | Att. | % |
|---|---|---|---|---|---|---|
| KICKING Wood | 29 | 33 | 88 | 10 | 18 | 56 |

## NEW ENGLAND PATRIOTS

### RUSHING

| Last Name | No. | Yds. | Avg. | TD |
|---|---|---|---|---|
| Collins | 204 | 873 | 4.3 | 7 |
| Ferguson | 78 | 340 | 4.4 | 3 |
| Cunningham | 86 | 269 | 3.1 | 4 |
| Calhoun | 57 | 205 | 3.6 | 2 |
| Tatupu | 38 | 201 | 5.3 | 2 |
| Cavanaugh | 17 | 92 | 5.4 | 3 |
| Grogan | 12 | 49 | 4.1 | 2 |
| Morgan | 2 | 21 | 10.5 | 0 |
| Pennywell | 1 | 3 | 3.0 | 0 |
| Johnson | 2 | 1 | 0.5 | 0 |
| Jackson | 2 | −14 | −7.0 | 0 |

### RECEIVING

| Last Name | No. | Yds. | Avg. | TD |
|---|---|---|---|---|
| Hasselbeck | 46 | 808 | 18 | 6 |
| Morgan | 44 | 1029 | 23 | 6 |
| Jackson | 39 | 669 | 17 | 0 |
| Johnson | 39 | 429 | 11 | 1 |
| Collins | 26 | 232 | 9 | 0 |
| Tatupu | 12 | 132 | 11 | 1 |
| Cunningham | 12 | 92 | 8 | 0 |
| Dawson | 7 | 126 | 18 | 0 |
| Westbrook | 7 | 122 | 17 | 2 |
| Calhoun | 7 | 71 | 10 | 0 |
| Toler | 5 | 70 | 14 | 0 |
| Ferguson | 4 | 39 | 10 | 0 |
| Pennywell | 3 | 49 | 16 | 1 |
| Grogan | 2 | 27 | 14 | 0 |
| Cavanaugh | 1 | 9 | 9 | 0 |

### PUNT RETURNS

| Last Name | No. | Yds. | Avg. | TD |
|---|---|---|---|---|
| Morgan | 15 | 116 | 8 | 0 |
| James | 7 | 56 | 8 | 0 |
| Haynes | 6 | 12 | 2 | 0 |
| Collins | 3 | 15 | 5 | 0 |

### KICKOFF RETURNS

| Last Name | No. | Yds. | Avg. | TD |
|---|---|---|---|---|
| Collins | 39 | 773 | 20 | 0 |
| Toler | 9 | 148 | 16 | 0 |
| Sanford | 4 | 82 | 21 | 0 |
| Dombroski | 3 | 66 | 22 | 0 |
| Johnson | 3 | 53 | 18 | 0 |
| Calhoun | 2 | 38 | 19 | 0 |
| K. Lee | 2 | 20 | 10 | 0 |
| Hasselbeck | 1 | 7 | 7 | 0 |
| Matthews | 1 | 5 | 5 | 0 |
| Hamilton | 1 | 0 | 0 | 0 |

### PASSING – PUNTING – KICKING

| Last Name | Att. | Comp. | % | Yds. | Yd./Att. | TD | Int.-% | RK |
|---|---|---|---|---|---|---|---|---|
| Grogan | 216 | 117 | 54 | 1859 | 8.6 | 7 | 16- 7 | 13 |
| Cavanaugh | 219 | 115 | 53 | 1633 | 7.5 | 5 | 13- 6 | 14 |
| Owen | 36 | 15 | 42 | 218 | 6.1 | 1 | 4- 11 | |
| Johnson | 9 | 7 | 78 | 194 | 21.6 | 4 | 1- 11 | |
| Collins | 1 | 0 | 0 | 0 | 0.0 | 0 | 0- 0 | |
| Jackson | 1 | 0 | 0 | 0 | 0.0 | 0 | 0- 0 | |

| Last Name | No. | Avg. |
|---|---|---|
| PUNTING Camarillo | 47 | 41.7 |
| Hubach | 19 | 38.2 |
| Hartley | 9 | 29.6 |

| Last Name | XP | Att. | % | FG | Att. | % |
|---|---|---|---|---|---|---|
| KICKING Smith | 37 | 39 | 95 | 15 | 24 | 63 |

## CINCINNATI BENGALS 12-4-0 — Forrest Gregg

### Scores of Each Game

| | | |
|---|---|---|
| 27 | SEATTLE | 21 |
| 31 | N.Y. Jets | 30 |
| 17 | CLEVELAND | 20 |
| 27 | BUFFALO | *24 |
| 10 | Houston | 17 |
| 41 | Baltimore | 19 |
| 34 | PITTSBURGH | 7 |
| 7 | New Orleans | 17 |
| 34 | HOUSTON | 21 |
| 40 | San Diego | 17 |
| 24 | LOS ANGELES | 10 |
| 38 | DENVER | 21 |
| 41 | Cleveland | 21 |
| 3 | SAN FRANCISCO | 21 |
| 17 | Pittsburgh | 10 |
| 30 | Atlanta | 28 |

| Use Name | Pos. | Hgt. | Wgt. | Age | Int. | Pts. |
|---|---|---|---|---|---|---|
| Anthony Munoz | OT | 6'6" | 278 | 23 | | |
| Mike Obrovac | OT-OG | 6'6" | 275 | 25 | | |
| Mike Wilson | OT | 6'5" | 271 | 26 | | |
| Glenn Bujnoch | OG | 6'5" | 265 | 27 | | |
| Dave Lapham | OG | 6'4" | 262 | 29 | | |
| Max Montoya | OG | 6'5" | 275 | 25 | | |
| Brad Oates (to G.B.) | OG | 6'6" | 275 | 27 | | |
| Bobby Whitten | OG | 6'3" | 265 | 22 | | |
| Blair Bush | C | 6'3" | 252 | 24 | | |
| Blake Moore | C-OT-OG | 6'5" | 267 | 23 | | |
| Ross Browner | DE | 6'3" | 261 | 27 | | |
| Gary Burley | DE | 6'3" | 274 | 28 | | |
| Eddie Edwards | DE | 6'5" | 256 | 27 | | |
| Mike St. Clair | DE | 6'5" | 250 | 27 | | 6 |
| Rod Horn | NT | 6'4" | 268 | 24 | | |
| Wilson Whitley | NT | 6'3" | 265 | 26 | | |
| Glenn Cameron | LB | 6'2" | 228 | 28 | 1 | |
| Tom Dinkel | LB | 6'3" | 237 | 25 | | |
| Guy Frazier | LB | 6'2" | 215 | 22 | | |
| Bo Harris | LB | 6'3" | 226 | 28 | 2 | |
| Jim LeClair | LB | 6'2" | 234 | 30 | 1 | |
| Rick Razzano | LB | 5'11" | 227 | 25 | 1 | |
| Jeff Schuh | LB | 6'2" | 228 | 23 | | |
| Reggie Williams | LB | 6'1" | 228 | 26 | 4 | |
| Louis Breeden | DB | 5'11" | 185 | 27 | 4 | 6 |
| Greg Bright | DB | 6' | 208 | 24 | | |
| Clarence Chapman | DB | 5'10" | 182 | 27 | | |
| Oliver Davis | DB | 6'1" | 205 | 27 | | |
| Mike Fuller | DB | 5'9" | 182 | 28 | 1 | |
| Ray Griffin | DB | 5'10" | 186 | 25 | | |
| Bryan Hicks | DB | 6' | 192 | 24 | | |
| Bobby Kemp | DB | 6' | 186 | 22 | | |
| Ken Riley | DB | 6' | 183 | 34 | 5 | |
| John Simmons | DB | 5'11" | 192 | 22 | | |
| Ken Anderson | QB | 6'1" | 212 | 32 | | 6 |
| Turk Schonert | QB | 6'1" | 185 | 24 | | |
| Jack Thompson | QB | 6'3" | 217 | 25 | | |
| Charles Alexander | HB-FB | 6'1" | 221 | 24 | | 18 |
| Archie Griffin | HB | 5'9" | 184 | 27 | | 24 |
| Elvis Peacock | HB | 6'1" | 208 | 24 | | |
| Jim Hargrove | FB | 6'2" | 228 | 23 | | 6 |
| Pete Johnson | FB | 6' | 249 | 27 | | 96 |
| Don Bass | WR-TE | 6'2" | 220 | 26 | | |
| Cris Collinsworth | WR | 6'5" | 192 | 22 | | 48 |
| Isaac Curtis | WR | 6' | 192 | 30 | | 12 |
| Steve Kreider | WR | 6'3" | 192 | 24 | | 30 |
| Pat McInally | WR | 6'6" | 213 | 28 | | |
| David Verser | WR | 6'1" | 200 | 23 | | 12 |
| M.L. Harris | TE | 6'5" | 238 | 27 | | 12 |
| Dan Ross | TE | 6'4" | 235 | 24 | | 30 |
| Jim Breech | K | 5'6" | 157 | 25 | | 115 |

Dick Jauron – Knee Injury
Ron Simpklins – Hamstring Injury

## PITTSBURGH STEELERS 8-8-0 — Chuck Noll

### Scores of Each Game

| | | |
|---|---|---|
| 33 | KANSAS CITY | 37 |
| 10 | Miami | 30 |
| 38 | N.Y. JETS | 10 |
| 27 | NEW ENGLAND | *21 |
| 20 | New Orleans | 6 |
| 13 | CLEVELAND | 7 |
| 7 | Cincinnati | 34 |
| 26 | HOUSTON | 13 |
| 14 | SAN FRANCISCO | 17 |
| 21 | Seattle | 24 |
| 34 | Atlanta | 20 |
| 32 | Cleveland | 10 |
| 24 | LOS ANGELES | 0 |
| 27 | Oakland | 30 |
| 10 | CINCINNATI | 17 |
| 20 | Houston | 21 |

| Use Name | Pos. | Hgt. | Wgt. | Age | Int. | Pts. |
|---|---|---|---|---|---|---|
| Larry Brown | OT | 6'4" | 265 | 32 | | |
| Tunch Ilkin | OT-OG-C | 6'3" | 253 | 23 | | |
| Jon Kolb | OT | 6'2" | 262 | 34 | | |
| Ted Petersen | OT | 6'5" | 244 | 26 | | |
| Ray Pinney | OT-C-OG | 6'4" | 240 | 27 | 6 | |
| Steve Courson | OG | 6'1" | 260 | 25 | | |
| Tyrone McGriff | OG | 6' | 267 | 23 | | |
| Craig Wolfley | OG | 6'1" | 258 | 23 | | |
| Mike Webster | C | 6'1" | 250 | 29 | | |
| John Banaszak | DE-DT | 6'3" | 244 | 31 | | |
| John Goodman | DE-DT | 6'6" | 250 | 22 | | |
| L.C. Greenwood | DE | 6'5" | 250 | 34 | | |
| Bob Kohrs | DE | 6'3" | 245 | 22 | | |
| Tom Beasley | DT-DE | 6'5" | 253 | 27 | | |
| Gary Dunn | DT | 6'3" | 247 | 28 | | |
| Joe Greene | DT | 6'4" | 260 | 34 | | |
| Robin Cole | LB | 6'2" | 220 | 25 | 1 | |
| Jack Ham | LB | 6'3" | 225 | 32 | 1 | |
| Jack Lambert | LB | 6'4" | 220 | 29 | 6 | |
| David Little | LB | 6'1" | 220 | 22 | | |
| Loren Toews | LB | 6'3" | 222 | 29 | | |
| Zack Valentine | LB | 6'2" | 220 | 24 | | |
| Dennis Winston | LB | 6' | 228 | 25 | | |
| Larry Anderson | DB | 5'11" | 177 | 24 | | |
| Mel Blount | DB | 6'3" | 205 | 33 | 6 | 6 |
| Ron Johnson | DB | 5'10" | 200 | 25 | | |
| Donnie Shell | DB | 5'11" | 190 | 29 | 5 | |
| J.T. Thomas | DB | 6'2" | 196 | 30 | 1 | |
| Anthony Washington | DB | 6'1" | 204 | 23 | 3 | |
| Dwayne Woodruff | DB | 5'11" | 189 | 24 | 1 | |
| Terry Bradshaw | QB | 6'3" | 215 | 32 | | 12 |
| Mark Malone | QB-WR | 6'4" | 223 | 22 | | 18 |
| Cliff Stoudt | QB | 6'4" | 218 | 26 | | |
| Greg Hawthorne | HB | 6'2" | 225 | 24 | | 12 |
| Rick Moser (from K.C.) | HB | 6' | 210 | 24 | | 6 |
| Frank Pollard | HB-FB | 5'10" | 210 | 24 | | 12 |
| Sidney Thornton | HB | 5'11" | 230 | 26 | | 24 |
| Russell Davis | FB | 6'1" | 231 | 25 | | 6 |
| Franco Harris | FB | 6'2" | 225 | 31 | | 54 |
| Johnnie Dirden | WR | 6' | 184 | 29 | | |
| Jim Smith | WR | 6'2" | 205 | 26 | | 42 |
| John Stallworth | WR | 6'2" | 183 | 29 | | 30 |
| Lynn Swann | WR | 6' | 180 | 29 | | 30 |
| Calvin Sweeney | WR | 6'2" | 180 | 26 | | |
| Bennie Cunningham | TE | 6'4" | 260 | 26 | | 18 |
| Randy Grossman | TE | 6'1" | 225 | 27 | | 6 |
| Craig Colquitt | K | 6'2" | 185 | 27 | | |
| David Trout | K | 5'6" | 165 | 23 | | 74 |

Sam Davis – Knee Injury

## HOUSTON OILERS 7-9-0 — Ed Biles

### Scores of Each Game

| | | |
|---|---|---|
| 27 | Los Angeles | 20 |
| 9 | Cleveland | 3 |
| 10 | MIAMI | 16 |
| 17 | N.Y. Jets | 33 |
| 17 | CINCINNATI | 10 |
| 35 | SEATTLE | 17 |
| 10 | New England | 38 |
| 13 | Pittsburgh | 26 |
| 21 | Cincinnati | 34 |
| 17 | OAKLAND | 16 |
| 10 | Kansas City | 23 |
| 24 | NEW ORLEANS | 27 |
| 27 | ATLANTA | 31 |
| 17 | CLEVELAND | 13 |
| 6 | San Francisco | 13 |
| 21 | PITTSBURGH | 20 |

| Use Name | Pos. | Hgt. | Wgt. | Age | Int. | Pts. |
|---|---|---|---|---|---|---|
| Nick Eyre | OT | 6'5" | 274 | 22 | | |
| Angelo Fields | OT | 6'6" | 319 | 23 | | |
| Leon Gray | OT | 6'3" | 260 | 29 | | |
| Morris Towns | OT | 6'4" | 275 | 27 | | |
| David Carter | OG-C | 6'2" | 258 | 28 | | |
| Ed Fisher | OG | 6'3" | 250 | 32 | | |
| John Schuhmacher | OG | 6'3" | 275 | 25 | | |
| Greg Davidson | C | 6'2" | 250 | 23 | | |
| Carl Mauck | C | 6'3" | 250 | 34 | | |
| Jesse Baker | DE | 6'3" | 265 | 24 | | |
| Elvin Bethea | DE | 6'3" | 255 | 35 | | |
| Andy Dorris | DE | 6'4" | 240 | 30 | | |
| Mike Stensrud | DE | 6'5" | 280 | 25 | | |
| Ken Kennard | NT | 6'2" | 245 | 26 | | |
| Daryle Skaugstad | NT | 6'5" | 254 | 24 | | |
| Gregg Bingham | LB | 6'1" | 230 | 30 | 2 | |
| Robert Brazile | LB | 6'4" | 238 | 28 | 2 | |
| John Corker | LB | 6'5" | 240 | 22 | | |
| Daryl Hunt | LB | 6'3" | 220 | 24 | | |
| Avon Riley | LB | 6'3" | 211 | 22 | | |
| Art Stringer | LB | 6'1" | 223 | 27 | | |
| Ted Thompson | LB | 6'1" | 220 | 28 | | |
| Ted Washington | LB | 6'1" | 245 | 33 | 1 | |
| Carter Hartwig | DB | 6' | 205 | 25 | 3 | |
| Bill Kay | DB | 6'1" | 190 | 21 | 2 | |
| Vernon Perry | DB | 6'2" | 211 | 27 | 2 | |
| Mike Reinfeldt | DB | 6'2" | 195 | 28 | 2 | |
| Greg Stemrick | DB | 5'11" | 185 | 29 | 3 | |
| Willie Tullis | DB | 6' | 190 | 23 | 6 | |
| J.C. Wilson | DB | 6' | 177 | 25 | 1 | |
| Gifford Nielsen | QB | 6'4" | 205 | 26 | | |
| John Reaves | QB | 6'3" | 205 | 31 | | |
| Ken Stabler | QB | 6'3" | 210 | 35 | | |
| Earl Campbell | HB-FB | 5'11" | 237 | 26 | | 60 |
| Ronnie Coleman | HB | 5'10" | 198 | 30 | | 6 |
| Rich Tomaselli | HB | 6'1" | 195 | 24 | | |
| Adger Armstrong | FB | 6' | 220 | 24 | | 6 |
| Tim Wilson | FB | 6'3" | 220 | 27 | | |
| Harold Bailey | WR | 6'2" | 197 | 24 | | |
| Billy Brooks (from S.D.) | WR | 6'3" | 202 | 28 | | |
| Ken Burrough | WR | 6'4" | 210 | 33 | | 42 |
| Mike Holston | WR | 6'3" | 184 | 23 | | 12 |
| Mike Renfro | WR | 6' | 184 | 26 | | 6 |
| Carl Roaches | WR | 5'8" | 165 | 27 | | 6 |
| Tim Smith | WR | 6'2" | 192 | 24 | | |
| Mike Barber | TE | 6'3" | 233 | 28 | | 6 |
| Dave Casper | TE | 6'4" | 230 | 29 | | 48 |
| Toni Fritsch | K | 5'7" | 180 | 36 | | 77 |
| Cliff Parsley | K | 6'1" | 211 | 26 | | |

## CLEVELAND BROWNS 5-11-0 — Sam Rutigliano

### Scores of Each Game

| | | |
|---|---|---|
| 14 | SAN DIEGO | 44 |
| 3 | HOUSTON | 9 |
| 20 | Cincinnati | 17 |
| 28 | ATLANTA | 17 |
| 16 | Los Angeles | 27 |
| 7 | Pittsburgh | 13 |
| 20 | NEW ORLEANS | 17 |
| 42 | BALTIMORE | 28 |
| 13 | Buffalo | 22 |
| 20 | Denver | *23 |
| 15 | San Francisco | 12 |
| 10 | PITTSBURGH | 32 |
| 21 | CINCINNATI | 41 |
| 13 | Houston | 17 |
| 13 | N.Y. JETS | 14 |
| 21 | Seattle | 42 |

| Use Name | Pos. | Hgt. | Wgt. | Age | Int. | Pts. |
|---|---|---|---|---|---|---|
| Doug Dieken | OT | 6'5" | 252 | 32 | | |
| Matt Miller | OT-OG | 6'6" | 270 | 25 | | |
| Cody Risien | OT | 6'7" | 255 | 24 | | |
| Joe DeLamielleure | OG | 6'3" | 245 | 30 | | |
| Robert Jackson | OG-C | 6'5" | 260 | 28 | | |
| Henry Sheppard | OG-OT | 6'6" | 263 | 28 | | |
| Chuck Correal | C | 6'3" | 247 | 25 | | |
| Tom DeLeone | C | 6'2" | 248 | 31 | | |
| Gerry Sullivan | C-OG | 6'4" | 250 | 29 | | |
| Lyle Alzado | DE | 6'3" | 250 | 32 | | |
| Thomas Brown | DE-NT | 6'4" | 245 | 24 | | |
| Elvis Franks | DE | 6'4" | 238 | 24 | | |
| Marshall Harris | DE-NT | 6'6" | 261 | 25 | | |
| Mike Robinson | DE | 6'5" | 260 | 25 | | |
| Henry Bradley | NT | 6'2" | 260 | 27 | | |
| Jerry Sherk | NT-DE | 6'4" | 250 | 33 | | |
| Dick Ambrose | LB | 6' | 228 | 28 | 1 | |
| Don Goode | LB | 6'2" | 231 | 30 | 1 | |
| Bruce Huther | LB | 6'1" | 230 | 27 | | |
| Robert Jackson | LB | 6'1" | 230 | 27 | | |
| Eddie Johnson | LB | 6'1" | 210 | 22 | | |
| Clay Matthews | LB | 6'2" | 230 | 25 | 2 | |
| Curtis Weathers | LB | 6'5" | 220 | 24 | | |
| Autry Beamon | DB | 6'1" | 190 | 27 | | |
| Ron Bolton | DB | 6'2" | 170 | 31 | 1 | |
| Clinton Burrell | DB | 6'2" | 192 | 24 | | |
| Thom Darden | DB | 6'2" | 193 | 31 | 3 | |
| Hanford Dixon | DB | 5'11" | 182 | 22 | | |
| Judson Flint | DB | 6' | 201 | 24 | 2 | |
| Lawrence Johnson | DB | 5'11" | 204 | 23 | | |
| Clarence Scott | DB | 6' | 190 | 32 | 4 | |
| Paul McDonald | QB | 6'2" | 185 | 23 | | |
| Brian Sipe | QB | 6'1" | 195 | 32 | | 6 |
| Rick Trocano | QB-DB | 6'1" | 188 | 22 | | |
| Dino Hall | HB | 5'7" | 165 | 25 | | |
| Calvin Hill | HB-FB | 6'3" | 227 | 34 | | 12 |
| Cleo Miller | HB-FB | 5'11" | 214 | 29 | | 12 |
| Greg Pruitt | HB | 5'10" | 190 | 30 | | 24 |
| Charles White | HB | 5'10" | 183 | 23 | | 6 |
| Mike Pruitt | FB | 6' | 225 | 27 | | 48 |
| Willis Adams | WR | 6'2" | 194 | 25 | | |
| Ricky Feacher | WR | 5'10" | 174 | 27 | | 18 |
| Dan Fulton | WR | 6'2" | 186 | 24 | | |
| Dave Logan | WR-DB | 6'4" | 216 | 27 | 1 | 24 |
| Cle Montgomery (to OAK) | WR | 5'8" | 183 | 25 | | |
| Reggie Rucker | WR | 6'2" | 190 | 33 | | 6 |
| Ozzie Newsome | TE | 6'2" | 232 | 25 | | 36 |
| McDonald Oden | TE | 6'4" | 228 | 23 | | |
| Matt Bahr (from S.F.) | K | 5'10" | 165 | 25 | | 79 |
| Steve Cox | K | 6'4" | 195 | 23 | | |
| Dave Jacobs | K | 5'7" | 155 | 24 | | 21 |

Joel Patten–Knee Injury

*—Overtime

## CINCINNATI BENGALS

### RUSHING

| Last Name | No. | Yds. | Avg. | TD |
|---|---|---|---|---|
| Johnson | 274 | 1077 | 3.9 | 12 |
| Anderson | 46 | 320 | 7.0 | 1 |
| Alexander | 98 | 292 | 3.0 | 2 |
| A. Griffin | 47 | 163 | 3.5 | 3 |
| Hargrove | 16 | 66 | 4.1 | 1 |
| Schonert | 7 | 41 | 5.9 | 0 |
| Kreider | 1 | 21 | 21.0 | 0 |
| Verser | 2 | 11 | 5.5 | 0 |
| Bass | 1 | 9 | 9.0 | 0 |
| McInally | 1 | −27 | −27.0 | 0 |

### RECEIVING

| Last Name | No. | Yds. | Avg. | TD |
|---|---|---|---|---|
| Ross | 71 | 910 | 13 | 5 |
| Collinsworth | 67 | 1009 | 15 | 8 |
| Johnson | 46 | 320 | 7 | 4 |
| Curtis | 37 | 609 | 17 | 2 |
| Kreider | 37 | 520 | 14 | 5 |
| Alexander | 28 | 262 | 9 | 1 |
| A. Griffin | 20 | 160 | 8 | 1 |
| M. Harris | 13 | 181 | 14 | 2 |
| Verser | 6 | 161 | 27 | 2 |
| McInally | 6 | 68 | 11 | 0 |
| Hargrove | 1 | 0 | 0 | 0 |

### PUNT RETURNS

| Last Name | No. | Yds. | Avg. | TD |
|---|---|---|---|---|
| Fuller | 23 | 177 | 8 | 0 |
| Simmons | 5 | 24 | 5 | 0 |
| Hicks | 1 | 4 | 4 | 0 |

### KICKOFF RETURNS

| Last Name | No. | Yds. | Avg. | TD |
|---|---|---|---|---|
| Verser | 29 | 691 | 24 | 0 |
| Chapman | 8 | 171 | 21 | 0 |
| A. Griffin | 6 | 119 | 20 | 0 |
| R. Griffin | 2 | 31 | 16 | 0 |
| Fuller | 1 | 34 | 34 | 0 |
| Simmons | 1 | 10 | 10 | 0 |
| Dinkel | 1 | 0 | 0 | 0 |
| Kemp | 1 | 0 | 0 | 0 |

### PASSING – PUNTING – KICKING

**PASSING**

| Last Name | Att. | Comp. | % | Yds. | Yd./Att. | TD | Int.–% | RK |
|---|---|---|---|---|---|---|---|---|
| Anderson | 479 | 300 | 63 | 3754 | 7.8 | 29 | 10– | 2 | 1 |
| Thompson | 49 | 21 | 43 | 267 | 5.5 | 1 | 2– | 4 |
| Schonert | 19 | 10 | 53 | 166 | 8.7 | 0 | 0– | 0 |
| Kreider | 3 | 1 | 33 | 13 | 4.3 | 0 | 0– | 0 |

**PUNTING**

| Last Name | No. | Avg. |
|---|---|---|
| McInally | 72 | 45.4 |

**KICKING**

| Last Name | XP | Att. | % | FG | Att. | % |
|---|---|---|---|---|---|---|
| Breech | 49 | 51 | 96 | 22 | 32 | 69 |

## PITTSBURGH STEELERS

### RUSHING

| Last Name | No. | Yds. | Avg. | TD |
|---|---|---|---|---|
| Harris | 242 | 987 | 4.1 | 8 |
| Pollard | 123 | 570 | 4.6 | 2 |
| Davis | 47 | 270 | 5.7 | 1 |
| Thornton | 56 | 202 | 3.6 | 4 |
| Bradshaw | 38 | 162 | 4.3 | 2 |
| Malone | 16 | 68 | 4.3 | 2 |
| Hawthorne | 25 | 58 | 2.3 | 2 |
| Stallworth | 1 | 17 | 17.0 | 0 |
| Smith | 1 | 15 | 15.0 | 0 |
| Stoudt | 3 | 11 | 3.7 | 0 |
| Colquitt | 1 | 8 | 8.0 | 0 |
| Moser | 1 | 4 | 4.0 | 0 |

### RECEIVING

| Last Name | No. | Yds. | Avg. | TD |
|---|---|---|---|---|
| Stallworth | 63 | 1098 | 17 | 5 |
| Cunningham | 41 | 574 | 14 | 3 |
| Harris | 37 | 250 | 7 | 1 |
| Swann | 34 | 505 | 15 | 5 |
| Smith | 29 | 571 | 20 | 7 |
| Pollard | 19 | 156 | 8 | 0 |
| Thornton | 8 | 78 | 10 | 0 |
| Davis | 4 | 34 | 9 | 0 |
| Hawthorne | 4 | 23 | 6 | 0 |
| Grossman | 3 | 19 | 6 | 1 |
| Sweeney | 2 | 53 | 27 | 0 |
| Malone | 1 | 90 | 90 | 1 |
| Moser | 1 | 5 | 5 | 1 |
| Pinney | 1 | 1 | 1 | 1 |

### PUNT RETURNS

| Last Name | No. | Yds. | Avg. | TD |
|---|---|---|---|---|
| Anderson | 20 | 208 | 10 | 0 |
| Smith | 30 | 204 | 7 | 0 |

### KICKOFF RETURNS

| Last Name | No. | Yds. | Avg. | TD |
|---|---|---|---|---|
| Anderson | 37 | 825 | 22 | 0 |
| Hawthorne | 7 | 138 | 20 | 0 |
| Moser | 3 | 76 | 25 | 0 |
| Dirden | 3 | 45 | 15 | 0 |
| Davis | 1 | 8 | 8 | 0 |
| Malone | 1 | 3 | 3 | 0 |
| Thornton | 1 | 1 | 1 | 0 |

### PASSING – PUNTING – KICKING

**PASSING**

| Last Name | Att. | Comp. | % | Yds. | Yd./Att. | TD | Int.–% | RK |
|---|---|---|---|---|---|---|---|---|
| Bradshaw | 370 | 201 | 54 | 2887 | 7.8 | 22 | 14– | 4 | 4 |
| Malone | 88 | 45 | 51 | 709 | 6.3 | 3 | 5– | 6 |
| Stoudt | 3 | 1 | 33 | 17 | 5.7 | 0 | 0– | 0 |

**PUNTING**

| Last Name | No. | Avg. |
|---|---|---|
| Colquitt | 84 | 43.3 |

**KICKING**

| Last Name | XP | Att. | % | FG | Att. | % |
|---|---|---|---|---|---|---|
| Trout | 38 | 46 | 83 | 12 | 17 | 71 |

## HOUSTON OILERS

### RUSHING

| Last Name | No. | Yds. | Avg. | TD |
|---|---|---|---|---|
| Campbell | 361 | 1376 | 3.8 | 10 |
| Armstrong | 31 | 146 | 4.7 | 0 |
| Coleman | 21 | 91 | 4.3 | 1 |
| T. Wilson | 13 | 35 | 2.7 | 0 |
| Reaves | 6 | 13 | 2.2 | 0 |
| Nielsen | 6 | 2 | 0.3 | 0 |
| Stabler | 10 | −3 | −0.3 | 0 |

### RECEIVING

| Last Name | No. | Yds. | Avg. | TD |
|---|---|---|---|---|
| Burrough | 40 | 668 | 17 | 7 |
| Renfro | 39 | 451 | 12 | 1 |
| Campbell | 36 | 156 | 4 | 0 |
| Casper | 33 | 572 | 17 | 8 |
| Armstrong | 29 | 278 | 10 | 1 |
| Holston | 27 | 427 | 16 | 2 |
| Coleman | 19 | 211 | 11 | 0 |
| Barber | 13 | 190 | 15 | 1 |
| T. Wilson | 5 | 33 | 7 | 0 |
| Brooks | 3 | 37 | 12 | 0 |
| Smith | 2 | 37 | 19 | 0 |

### PUNT RETURNS

| Last Name | No. | Yds. | Avg. | TD |
|---|---|---|---|---|
| Roaches | 59 | 296 | 8 | 0 |
| Tullis | 2 | 29 | 15 | 0 |

### KICKOFF RETURNS

| Last Name | No. | Yds. | Avg. | TD |
|---|---|---|---|---|
| Roaches | 28 | 769 | 28 | 1 |
| Tullis | 32 | 779 | 24 | 1 |
| T. Wilson | 3 | 41 | 14 | 0 |
| Armstrong | 3 | 36 | 12 | 0 |
| Hunt | 3 | 19 | 6 | 0 |
| J. Wilson | 2 | 27 | 14 | 0 |
| Riley | 1 | 51 | 51 | 0 |

### PASSING – PUNTING – KICKING

**PASSING**

| Last Name | Att. | Comp. | % | Yds. | Yd./Att. | TD | Int.–% | RK |
|---|---|---|---|---|---|---|---|---|
| Stabler | 285 | 165 | 58 | 1988 | 7.0 | 14 | 18– | 6 | 10 |
| Nielsen | 93 | 60 | 65 | 709 | 7.6 | 5 | 3– | 3 |
| Reaves | 61 | 31 | 51 | 379 | 6.2 | 2 | 3– | 3 |
| Parsley | 2 | 2 | 100 | 43 | 21.5 | 0 | 0– | 0 |

**PUNTING**

| Last Name | No. | Avg. |
|---|---|---|
| Parsley | 79 | 39.7 |

**KICKING**

| Last Name | XP | Att. | % | FG | Att. | % |
|---|---|---|---|---|---|---|
| Fritsch | 32 | 34 | 94 | 15 | 22 | 68 |

## CLEVELAND BROWNS

### RUSHING

| Last Name | No. | Yds. | Avg. | TD |
|---|---|---|---|---|
| M. Pruitt | 247 | 1103 | 4.5 | 7 |
| White | 97 | 342 | 3.5 | 1 |
| C. Miller | 52 | 165 | 3.2 | 2 |
| Sipe | 38 | 153 | 4.0 | 1 |
| G. Pruitt | 31 | 124 | 4.0 | 0 |
| Hill | 4 | 23 | 5.8 | 0 |
| Newsome | 2 | 20 | 10.0 | 0 |
| McDonald | 2 | 0 | 0.0 | 0 |
| Feacher | 1 | −1 | −1.0 | 0 |

### RECEIVING

| Last Name | No. | Yds. | Avg. | TD |
|---|---|---|---|---|
| Newsome | 69 | 1002 | 15 | 6 |
| G. Pruitt | 65 | 636 | 10 | 4 |
| M. Pruitt | 63 | 442 | 7 | 1 |
| Logan | 31 | 497 | 16 | 4 |
| Feacher | 29 | 654 | 23 | 3 |
| Rucker | 27 | 532 | 20 | 1 |
| White | 27 | 219 | 8 | 0 |
| Hill | 17 | 150 | 9 | 2 |
| C. Miller | 16 | 139 | 9 | 0 |
| Fulton | 2 | 38 | 19 | 0 |
| Adams | 1 | 24 | 24 | 0 |
| Oden | 1 | 6 | 6 | 0 |

### PUNT RETURNS

| Last Name | No. | Yds. | Avg. | TD |
|---|---|---|---|---|
| Hall | 33 | 248 | 8 | 0 |
| Montgomery | 17 | 121 | 7 | 0 |

### KICKOFF RETURNS

| Last Name | No. | Yds. | Avg. | TD |
|---|---|---|---|---|
| Hall | 36 | 813 | 23 | 0 |
| Montgomery | 17 | 382 | 23 | 0 |
| White | 12 | 243 | 20 | 0 |
| G. Pruitt | 3 | 82 | 27 | 0 |
| C. Miller | 3 | 35 | 12 | 0 |
| Brown | 2 | 17 | 9 | 0 |
| E. Johnson | 1 | 7 | 7 | 0 |
| M. Miller | 1 | 6 | 6 | 0 |

### PASSING – PUNTING – KICKING

**PASSING**

| Last Name | Att. | Comp. | % | Yds. | Yd./Att. | TD | Int.–% | RK |
|---|---|---|---|---|---|---|---|---|
| Sipe | 567 | 313 | 55 | 3876 | 6.8 | 17 | 25– | 4 | 11 |
| McDonald | 57 | 35 | 61 | 463 | 8.1 | 4 | 2– | 4 |

**PUNTING**

| Last Name | No. | Avg. |
|---|---|---|
| Cox | 68 | 42.4 |

**KICKING**

| Last Name | XP | Att. | % | FG | Att. | % |
|---|---|---|---|---|---|---|
| Bahr | 34 | 34 | 100 | 15 | 26 | 58 |
| Jacobs | 9 | 10 | 90 | 4 | 12 | 33 |
| Cox | | | | 0 | 1 | 0 |

## SAN DIEGO CHARGERS 10-6-0 Don Corye II

| Scores of Each Game | | |
|---|---|---|
| 44 | Cleveland | 14 |
| 28 | DETROIT | 23 |
| 42 | Kansas City | 31 |
| 24 | Denver | 42 |
| 24 | SEATTLE | 10 |
| 31 | MINNESOTA | 33 |
| 43 | Baltimore | 14 |
| 17 | Chicago | *20 |
| 22 | KANSAS CITY | 20 |
| 17 | CINCINNATI | 40 |
| 23 | Seattle | 44 |
| 55 | Oakland | 21 |
| 34 | DENVER | 17 |
| 27 | BUFFALO | 28 |
| 24 | Tampa Bay | 23 |
| 23 | OAKLAND | 10 |

| Use Name | Pos. | Hgt. | Wgt. | Age | Int. | Pts. |
|---|---|---|---|---|---|---|
| Sammy Claphan | OT | 6′6″ | 267 | 24 | | |
| Chuck Loewen | OT-OG | 6′3″ | 259 | 24 | | |
| Billy Shields | OT | 6′7″ | 275 | 28 | | |
| Russ Washington | OT | 6′6″ | 288 | 34 | | |
| Ed White | OG | 6′2″ | 271 | 34 | | |
| Doug Wilkerson | OG | 6′2″ | 262 | 34 | | |
| Jeff Williams | OG | 6′4″ | 264 | 26 | | |
| Don Macek | C | 6′3″ | 253 | 27 | | |
| Bob Rush | C | 6′5″ | 264 | 25 | | |
| Keith Ferguson | DE | 6′5″ | 240 | 22 | | |
| Leroy Jones | DE | 6′8″ | 260 | 30 | 1 | |
| Don Reese | DE | 6′6″ | 262 | 29 | | |
| John Woodcock | DE | 6′3″ | 250 | 27 | | |
| Gary Johnson | DT | 6′2″ | 252 | 29 | 1 | 6 |
| Louie Kelcher | DT | 6′5″ | 282 | 28 | | |
| Jimmy Webb | DT | 6′5″ | 245 | 29 | | |
| Carlos Bradley | LB | 6′ | 221 | 21 | | |
| Bob Horn | LB | 6′3″ | 230 | 27 | 1 | |
| Keith King | LB | 6′4″ | 230 | 26 | 1 | |
| Jim Laslavic | LB | 6′2″ | 236 | 29 | | |
| Woodrow Lowe | LB | 6′ | 227 | 27 | 3 | |
| Ray Preston | LB | 6′ | 218 | 27 | | |
| Cliff Thrift | LB | 6′2″ | 232 | 25 | | |
| Doug Beaudoin | DB | 6′1″ | 190 | 27 | | |
| Willie Buchanon | DB | 6′ | 185 | 30 | 5 | |
| Frank Duncan | DB | 6′1″ | 188 | 24 | 1 | |
| Glen Edwards | DB | 6′ | 183 | 34 | 2 | |
| Allan Ellis | DB | 5′10″ | 177 | 30 | | |
| Bob Gregor | DB | 6′2″ | 187 | 24 | 2 | |
| Wyatt Henderson | DB | 5′10″ | 180 | 24 | | |
| Irvin Phillips | DB | 6′1″ | 192 | 21 | | |
| Pete Shaw | DB | 5′10″ | 178 | 27 | 3 | |
| Mike Williams | DB | 5′10″ | 179 | 27 | 3 | |
| Dan Fouts | QB | 6′3″ | 210 | 30 | | |
| James Harris | QB | 6′3″ | 221 | 34 | | |
| Ed Luther | QB | 6′3″ | 206 | 24 | | |
| Hank Bauer | HB-FB | 5′10″ | 200 | 27 | | 6 |
| James Brooks | HB | 5′9″ | 180 | 22 | | 36 |
| Clarence Williams | HB | 5′9″ | 195 | 26 | | 6 |
| John Cappelletti | FB | 6′1″ | 220 | 29 | | 30 |
| Chuck Muncie | FB-HB | 6′3″ | 233 | 28 | | 114 |
| Wes Chandler (from N.O.) | WR | 5′11″ | 186 | 25 | | 36 |
| Scott Fitzkee | WR | 6′ | 187 | 24 | | |
| Charlie Joiner | WR | 5′11″ | 183 | 33 | | 42 |
| Dwight Scales | WR | 6′2″ | 185 | 28 | | 6 |
| Pete Holohan | TE | 6′4″ | 226 | 22 | | |
| Eric Sievers | TE | 6′4″ | 234 | 22 | | 18 |
| Kellen Winslow | TE | 6′5″ | 252 | 23 | | 60 |
| Rolf Benirschke | K | 6′ | 175 | 26 | | 112 |
| George Roberts | K | 6′ | 186 | 26 | | |

Charles DeJurnett – Achilles Injury

## DENVER BRONCOS 10-6-0 Dan Reeves

| Scores of Each Game | | |
|---|---|---|
| 9 | OAKLAND | 7 |
| 10 | Seattle | 13 |
| 28 | BALTIMORE | 10 |
| 42 | SAN DIEGO | 24 |
| 17 | Oakland | 0 |
| 27 | DETROIT | 21 |
| 14 | Kansas City | 28 |
| 7 | Buffalo | 9 |
| 19 | MINNESOTA | 17 |
| 23 | CLEVELAND | *20 |
| 24 | Tampa Bay | 7 |
| 21 | Cincinnati | 38 |
| 17 | San Diego | 34 |
| 16 | KANSAS CITY | 13 |
| 23 | SEATTLE | 13 |
| 24 | Chicago | 35 |

| Use Name | Pos. | Hgt. | Wgt. | Age | Int. | Pts. |
|---|---|---|---|---|---|---|
| Kelvin Clark | OT | 6′3″ | 245 | 25 | | |
| Ken Lanier | OT | 6′3″ | 269 | 22 | | |
| Claudie Minor | OT | 6′4″ | 275 | 30 | | |
| Dave Studdard | OT-OG | 6′4″ | 255 | 25 | | |
| Tom Glassic | OG | 6′3″ | 250 | 27 | | |
| Paul Howard | OG | 6′3″ | 260 | 30 | | |
| Glenn Hyde | OG-C | 6′3″ | 252 | 30 | | |
| Bill Bryan | C | 6′2″ | 244 | 26 | | |
| Greg Boyd | DE | 6′6″ | 280 | 28 | | |
| Barney Chavous | DE | 6′3″ | 245 | 30 | | |
| Rulon Jones | DE | 6′6″ | 260 | 23 | | |
| Brison Manor | DE | 6′4″ | 248 | 29 | 1 | |
| Rubin Carter | NT | 6′ | 253 | 28 | | |
| Don Latimer | NT | 6′3″ | 253 | 26 | | |
| Steve Busick | LB | 6′4″ | 227 | 22 | | |
| Larry Evans | LB | 6′2″ | 220 | 28 | 1 | |
| Randy Gradishar | LB | 6′3″ | 231 | 29 | 4 | |
| Tom Jackson | LB | 5′11″ | 228 | 30 | | |
| Mark Merrill | LB | 6′4″ | 240 | 26 | | |
| Jim Ryan | LB | 6′1″ | 212 | 24 | | |
| Bob Swenson | LB | 6′3″ | 225 | 28 | 3 | |
| Steve Foley | DB | 6′2″ | 190 | 27 | 5 | |
| Mike Harden | DB | 6′ | 188 | 23 | 2 | |
| Aaron Kyle | DB | 5′11″ | 185 | 27 | 2 | |
| Dennis Smith | DB | 6′3″ | 200 | 22 | 1 | |
| Perry Smith | DB | 6′1″ | 190 | 30 | | |
| Roland Solomon | DB | 6′ | 189 | 25 | | |
| Bill Thompson | DB | 6′1″ | 197 | 34 | 4 | |
| Steve Trimble | DB | 5′10″ | 181 | 23 | | |
| Louis Wright | DB | 6′2″ | 200 | 28 | | |
| Steve DeBerg | QB | 6′2″ | 205 | 27 | | |
| Mark Herrmann | QB | 6′4″ | 184 | 22 | | |
| Craig Morton | QB | 6′4″ | 211 | 38 | | |
| Rob Lytle | HB | 6′1″ | 195 | 26 | | 30 |
| Dave Preston | HB | 5′10″ | 195 | 26 | | 18 |
| Tony Reed | HB | 5′11″ | 197 | 26 | | |
| Larry Canada | FB | 6′2″ | 226 | 26 | | 24 |
| Rick Parros | FB | 5′11″ | 200 | 23 | | 18 |
| Wade Manning | WR | 5′11″ | 190 | 26 | | |
| Haven Moses | WR | 6′3″ | 201 | 35 | | 6 |
| Rick Upchurch | WR | 5′10″ | 176 | 29 | | 18 |
| Steve Watson | WR | 6′4″ | 192 | 24 | | 78 |
| Ron Egloff | TE | 6′5″ | 227 | 25 | | 6 |
| Riley Odoms | TE | 6′4″ | 230 | 31 | | 30 |
| James Wright | TE | 6′3″ | 240 | 25 | | 6 |
| Luke Prestridge | K | 6′4″ | 235 | 24 | | |
| Fred Steinfort | K | 5′11″ | 180 | 27 | | 87 |

Keith Bishop – Foot Injury
Jim Robinson – Hamstring Injury

## KANSAS CITY CHIEFS 9-7-0 Marv Levy

| Scores of Each Game | | |
|---|---|---|
| 37 | Pittsburgh | 33 |
| 19 | TAMPA BAY | 10 |
| 31 | SAN DIEGO | 42 |
| 20 | Seattle | 14 |
| 17 | New England | 33 |
| 27 | OAKLAND | 0 |
| 28 | DENVER | 14 |
| 28 | Oakland | 17 |
| 20 | San Diego | 22 |
| 13 | CHICAGO | *16 |
| 23 | HOUSTON | 10 |
| 40 | SEATTLE | 13 |
| 10 | Detroit | 27 |
| 13 | Denver | 16 |
| 7 | MIAMI | 17 |
| 10 | Minnesota | 6 |

| Use Name | Pos. | Hgt. | Wgt. | Age | Int. | Pts. |
|---|---|---|---|---|---|---|
| Charlie Getty | OT | 6′4″ | 269 | 29 | | |
| Matt Herkenhoff | OT | 6′4″ | 270 | 30 | | |
| Roger Taylor | OT | 6′6″ | 271 | 23 | | |
| Brad Budde | OG | 6′4″ | 255 | 23 | | |
| Tom Condon | OG | 6′3″ | 272 | 28 | | |
| Jim Rourke | OG-OT-C | 6′5″ | 265 | 24 | | |
| Bob Simmons | OG | 6′4″ | 260 | 27 | | |
| Jack Rudnay | C | 6′3″ | 242 | 33 | | |
| Todd Thomas | C | 6′5″ | 262 | 21 | | |
| Mike Bell | DE | 6′4″ | 255 | 24 | | |
| Frank Case | DE | 6′4″ | 243 | 23 | | |
| Sylvester Hicks | DE | 6′4″ | 252 | 26 | | |
| Dave Lindstrom | DE | 6′6″ | 257 | 26 | | |
| Art Still | DE | 6′7″ | 252 | 25 | | |
| Ken Kremer | NT | 6′4″ | 250 | 24 | | |
| Dino Mangiero | NT-DE | 6′2″ | 265 | 22 | | |
| Don Parrish | NT | 6′2″ | 259 | 26 | | |
| Jerry Blanton | LB | 6′1″ | 225 | 25 | | |
| Phil Cancik | LB | 6′1″ | 230 | 24 | | |
| Tom Howard | LB | 6′2″ | 215 | 27 | | 6 |
| Charles Jackson | LB | 6′2″ | 220 | 26 | | |
| Dave Klug | LB | 6′4″ | 230 | 23 | | |
| Frank Manumaleuga | LB | 6′2″ | 245 | 25 | 2 | |
| John Olenchalk | LB | 6′ | 228 | 25 | | |
| Whitney Paul | LB | 6′3″ | 220 | 27 | 2 | 6 |
| Cal Peterson | LB | 6′3″ | 220 | 28 | | |
| Gary Spani | LB | 6′2″ | 230 | 25 | | 6 |
| Gary Barbaro | DB | 6′4″ | 204 | 27 | 5 | |
| Lloyd Burruss | DB | 6′ | 201 | 23 | 4 | 6 |
| M.L. Carter | DB | 5′9″ | 173 | 25 | | |
| Deron Cherry | DB | 5′11″ | 185 | 21 | 1 | |
| Herb Christopher | DB | 5′10″ | 202 | 27 | | |
| Gary Green | DB | 5′11″ | 184 | 25 | 5 | |
| Eric Harris | DB | 6′3″ | 191 | 26 | 7 | |
| Steve Fuller | QB | 6′4″ | 198 | 24 | | |
| Bob Gagliano | QB | 6′3″ | 193 | 22 | | |
| Bill Kenney | QB | 6′4″ | 210 | 26 | | 6 |
| Curtis Bledsoe | HB-FB | 5′11″ | 215 | 24 | | |
| Joe Delaney | HB | 5′10″ | 184 | 22 | | 18 |
| Clark Gaines | HB | 6′1″ | 209 | 27 | | |
| Ted McKnight | HB | 6′1″ | 216 | 27 | | 30 |
| Jim Hadnot | FB | 6′2″ | 244 | 24 | | 18 |
| Billy Jackson | FB-HB | 5′10″ | 223 | 21 | | 66 |
| Mike Williams | FB | 6′3″ | 222 | 23 | | |
| Carlos Carson | WR | 5′10″ | 172 | 22 | | 6 |
| Bubba Garcia | WR | 5′11″ | 185 | 23 | | |
| Henry Marshall | WR | 6′2″ | 214 | 27 | | 24 |
| James Murphy (from ATL) | WR | 5′10″ | 177 | 21 | | |
| Stan Rome | WR | 6′5″ | 218 | 25 | | 6 |
| J.T. Smith | WR | 6′2″ | 185 | 25 | | 12 |
| Ed Beckman | TE | 6′4″ | 226 | 26 | | |
| Al Dixon | TE | 6′5″ | 235 | 27 | | 12 |
| Marvin Harvey | TE-WR | 6′2″ | 220 | 21 | | |
| Willie Scott | TE | 6′4″ | 245 | 22 | | 6 |
| Jeff Gossett | K | 6′2″ | 195 | 24 | | |
| Bob Grupp | K | 5′11″ | 193 | 26 | | |
| Nick Lowery | K | 6′4″ | 190 | 25 | | 115 |

Horace Belton – Knee Injury

## OAKLAND RAIDERS 7-9-0 Tom Flores

| Scores of Each Game | | |
|---|---|---|
| 7 | Denver | 9 |
| 36 | Minnesota | 10 |
| 20 | SEATTLE | 10 |
| 0 | Detroit | 16 |
| 0 | DENVER | 17 |
| 0 | Kansas City | 27 |
| 18 | TAMPA BAY | 16 |
| 17 | KANSAS CITY | 28 |
| 27 | NEW ENGLAND | 17 |
| 16 | Houston | 17 |
| 33 | Miami | 17 |
| 21 | SAN DIEGO | 55 |
| 32 | Seattle | 31 |
| 30 | PITTSBURGH | 27 |
| 6 | CHICAGO | 23 |
| 10 | San Diego | 23 |

| Use Name | Pos. | Hgt. | Wgt. | Age | Int. | Pts. |
|---|---|---|---|---|---|---|
| Henry Lawrence | OT | 6′4″ | 270 | 29 | | |
| Lindsey Mason | OT | 6′5″ | 270 | 26 | | |
| Art Shell | OT | 6′5″ | 285 | 34 | | |
| Bruce Davis | OG-OT | 6′6″ | 280 | 25 | | |
| Curt Marsh | OG | 6′5″ | 275 | 22 | | |
| Mickey Marvin | OG | 6′4″ | 275 | 25 | | |
| Gene Upshaw | OG | 6′5″ | 255 | 36 | | |
| Dave Dalby | C | 6′2″ | 250 | 30 | | |
| Steve Sylvester | C-OG | 6′4″ | 260 | 28 | | |
| Dave Browning | DE | 6′5″ | 245 | 25 | 1 | |
| Cedrick Hardman | DE | 6′3″ | 245 | 32 | | 6 |
| Willie Jones | DE | 6′4″ | 245 | 23 | | 6 |
| John Matuszak | DE | 6′8″ | 285 | 30 | | |
| Reggie Kinlaw | NT | 6′2″ | 240 | 24 | | |
| Howie Long | NT-DE | 6′5″ | 265 | 21 | | |
| Johnny Robinson | NT | 6′2″ | 260 | 22 | | 2 |
| Jeff Barnes | LB | 6′2″ | 220 | 26 | | |
| Greg Bracelin | LB | 6′1″ | 218 | 24 | | |
| Mario Celotto (to BAL, LA) | LB | 6′3″ | 225 | 25 | | |
| Ted Hendricks | LB | 6′7″ | 225 | 33 | | |
| Rod Martin | LB | 6′2″ | 215 | 27 | 1 | |
| Randy McClanahan | LB | 6′5″ | 225 | 26 | | |
| Matt Millen | LB | 6′2″ | 255 | 23 | | |
| Greg Westbrooks | LB | 6′3″ | 220 | 28 | | |
| Mike Davis | DB | 6′2″ | 200 | 25 | 1 | |
| Lester Hayes | DB | 6′ | 200 | 26 | 3 | |
| Kenny Hill | DB | 6′ | 185 | 23 | | |
| Monte Jackson | DB | 5′11″ | 200 | 28 | | |
| Odis McKinney | DB | 6′2″ | 185 | 24 | 3 | |
| Dwayne O'Steen | DB | 6′1″ | 195 | 26 | 1 | |
| Burgess Owens | DB | 6′2″ | 200 | 30 | 2 | 6 |
| Ted Watts | DB | 6′ | 190 | 23 | 1 | 6 |
| Jim Plunkett | QB | 6′3″ | 210 | 33 | | 6 |
| Marc Wilson | QB | 6′6″ | 210 | 24 | | 12 |
| Kenny King | HB-FB | 5′11″ | 205 | 24 | | |
| Art Whittington | HB | 5′11″ | 180 | 25 | | 18 |
| Chester Willis | HB | 5′11″ | 195 | 23 | | 6 |
| Frank Hawkins | FB | 5′9″ | 210 | 22 | | |
| Derrick Jensen | FB | 6′1″ | 225 | 25 | | 24 |
| Mark van Eeghen | FB | 6′2″ | 225 | 29 | | 12 |
| Malcolm Barnwell | WR | 5′11″ | 180 | 23 | | 6 |
| Morris Bradshaw | WR | 6′ | 195 | 28 | | 18 |
| Cliff Branch | WR | 5′11″ | 170 | 33 | | 6 |
| Bob Chandler | WR | 6′ | 180 | 32 | | 24 |
| Ira Matthews | WR | 5′8″ | 175 | 24 | | |
| Ray Chester | TE | 6′3″ | 235 | 33 | | 6 |
| Todd Christensen | TE-FB-C | 6′3″ | 230 | 25 | | 14 |
| Derrick Ramsey | TE | 6′5″ | 230 | 24 | | 24 |
| Chris Bahr | K | 5′9″ | 175 | 28 | | 69 |
| Ray Guy | K | 6′3″ | 200 | 31 | | |

Bob Nelson – Shoulder Injury

## SEATTLE SEAHAWKS 6-10-0 Jack Patera

| Scores of Each Game | | |
|---|---|---|
| 21 | Cincinnati | 27 |
| 13 | DENVER | 10 |
| 10 | Oakland | 20 |
| 14 | KANSAS CITY | 20 |
| 10 | San Diego | 24 |
| 17 | Houston | 35 |
| 0 | N.Y. GIANTS | 32 |
| 19 | N.Y. Jets | 3 |
| 24 | Green Bay | 34 |
| 24 | PITTSBURGH | 21 |
| 44 | SAN DIEGO | 23 |
| 13 | Kansas City | 40 |
| 31 | OAKLAND | 32 |
| 27 | N.Y. JETS | 23 |
| 13 | Denver | 23 |
| 42 | CLEVELAND | 21 |

| Use Name | Pos. | Hgt. | Wgt. | Age | Int. | Pts. |
|---|---|---|---|---|---|---|
| Steve August | OT | 6′5″ | 254 | 26 | | |
| Dennis Boyd | OT-C | 6′6″ | 255 | 25 | | 6 |
| Ron Essink | OT | 6′6″ | 246 | 23 | | |
| Edwin Bailey | OG | 6′4″ | 265 | 22 | | |
| Bill Dugan | OG | 6′4″ | 271 | 22 | | |
| Bob Newton | OG | 6′4″ | 260 | 32 | | |
| Art Kuehn | C | 6′3″ | 255 | 28 | | |
| John Yarno | C | 6′5″ | 251 | 26 | | |
| Fred Anderson | DE | 6′4″ | 235 | 26 | | |
| Jacob Green | DE | 6′3″ | 247 | 24 | | |
| Mike White | DE-DT | 6′5″ | 266 | 24 | | |
| Robert Hardy | DT | 6′2″ | 250 | 25 | | |
| Doug Sutherland | DT | 6′3″ | 250 | 33 | | |
| Manu Tuiasosopo | DT-DE | 6′3″ | 252 | 24 | | |
| Terry Beeson | LB | 6′3″ | 240 | 21 | | |
| Keith Butler | LB | 6′4″ | 225 | 25 | 2 | |
| Brian Flones | LB | 6′1″ | 228 | 22 | | |
| Greg Gaines | LB | 6′3″ | 202 | 22 | | |
| Michael Jackson | LB | 6′1″ | 220 | 24 | 2 | |
| Joe Norman | LB | 6′1″ | 220 | 24 | | |
| Rodell Thomas (from MIA) | LB | 6′2″ | 227 | 23 | | 6 |
| Kevin Turner (from WAS) | LB | 6′2″ | 225 | 23 | | |
| Dave Brown | DB | 6′1″ | 190 | 28 | 2 | |
| Don Dufek | DB | 6′ | 195 | 27 | | |
| Kenny Easley | DB | 6′3″ | 206 | 22 | 3 | 6 |
| John Harris | DB | 6′2″ | 200 | 25 | 10 | 12 |
| Greggory Johnson | DB | 6′1″ | 188 | 22 | | 6 |
| Kerry Justin | DB | 5′11″ | 175 | 26 | | |
| Will Lewis | DB | 5′9″ | 185 | 23 | | |
| Vic Minor | DB | 6′ | 198 | 22 | | |
| Keith Simpson | DB | 6′1″ | 195 | 25 | 2 | |
| Sam Adkins | QB | 6′2″ | 214 | 26 | | |
| Dave Krieg | QB | 6′1″ | 185 | 22 | | 6 |
| Jim Zorn | QB | 6′2″ | 200 | 28 | | 6 |
| Theotis Brown (from STL) | HB-FB | 6′2″ | 225 | 24 | | 48 |
| Horace Ivory (from N.E.) | HB | 6′ | 198 | 27 | | |
| Eric Lane | HB | 6′ | 195 | 22 | | |
| Terry Miller | HB | 5′10″ | 196 | 25 | | |
| Jeff Moore | HB | 6′ | 195 | 25 | | |
| Sherman Smith | HB | 6′4″ | 225 | 26 | | 24 |
| Dan Doornink | FB | 6′3″ | 210 | 25 | | 30 |
| David Hughes | FB | 6′ | 220 | 22 | | 12 |
| Jim Jodat | FB | 5′11″ | 213 | 27 | | 6 |
| Paul Johns | WR | 5′11″ | 170 | 22 | | 6 |
| Steve Largent | WR | 5′11″ | 184 | 26 | | 60 |
| Sam McCullum | WR | 6′2″ | 190 | 28 | | 18 |
| Mark McGrath | WR | 5′11″ | 175 | 23 | | |
| Steve Raible | WR | 6′2″ | 195 | 27 | | |
| John Sawyer | TE | 6′2″ | 230 | 28 | | |
| Mike Tice | TE | 6′7″ | 235 | 22 | | |
| Wilson Alvarez | K | 6′ | 165 | 24 | | 23 |
| Frank Garcia | K | 6′ | 190 | 24 | | |
| Efren Herrera | K | 5′9″ | 190 | 30 | | 59 |
| Jeff West | K | 6′3″ | 210 | 28 | | |

Larry Brinson – Knee Injury
Mark Bell – Knee Injury

*—Overtime

## SAN DIEGO CHARGERS

### Rushing

| Last Name | No. | Yds. | Avg. | TD |
|---|---|---|---|---|
| Muncie | 251 | 1144 | 4.6 | 19 |
| Brooks | 109 | 525 | 4.8 | 3 |
| Cappelletti | 68 | 254 | 3.7 | 4 |
| Fouts | 22 | 56 | 2.5 | 0 |
| C. Williams | 20 | 26 | 1.3 | 0 |
| Bauer | 2 | 7 | 3.5 | 0 |
| Roberts | 1 | 2 | 2.0 | 0 |
| Chandler | 5 | −1 | −0.2 | 0 |
| Luther | 3 | −8 | −2.7 | 0 |

### Receiving

| Last Name | No. | Yds. | Avg. | TD |
|---|---|---|---|---|
| Winslow | 88 | 1075 | 12 | 10 |
| Joiner | 70 | 1188 | 17 | 7 |
| Chandler | 69 | 1142 | 17 | 6 |
| Brooks | 46 | 329 | 7 | 3 |
| Muncie | 43 | 362 | 8 | 0 |
| Sievers | 22 | 276 | 13 | 3 |
| Scales | 19 | 429 | 23 | 1 |
| C. Williams | 12 | 108 | 9 | 1 |
| Cappelletti | 10 | 126 | 13 | 1 |
| Holohan | 1 | 14 | 14 | 0 |
| Bauer | 1 | 4 | 4 | 0 |

### Punt Returns

| Last Name | No. | Yds. | Avg. | TD |
|---|---|---|---|---|
| Brooks | 22 | 290 | 13 | 0 |
| Chandler | 5 | 79 | 16 | 0 |
| Bauer | 1 | 7 | 7 | 0 |
| Edwards | 1 | 1 | 1 | 0 |
| Shaw | 1 | 1 | 1 | 0 |
| Phillips | 1 | 0 | 0 | 0 |

### Kickoff Returns

| Last Name | No. | Yds. | Avg. | TD |
|---|---|---|---|---|
| Brooks | 40 | 949 | 24 | 0 |
| Chandler | 8 | 125 | 16 | 0 |
| Shaw | 6 | 103 | 17 | 0 |
| C. Williams | 4 | 47 | 12 | 0 |
| Gregor | 3 | 47 | 16 | 0 |
| Sievers | 2 | 4 | 2 | 0 |
| Beaudoin | 1 | 31 | 31 | 0 |
| Henderson | 1 | 26 | 26 | 0 |
| Bauer | 1 | 14 | 14 | 0 |

### Passing – Punting – Kicking

**PASSING**

| Last Name | Att. | Comp. | % | Yds. | Yd./Att. | TD | Int.–% | | RK |
|---|---|---|---|---|---|---|---|---|---|
| Fouts | 609 | 360 | 59 | 4802 | 7.9 | 33 | 17– | 3 | 3 |
| Luther | 15 | 7 | 47 | 68 | 4.5 | 0 | 1– | 7 | |
| Muncie | 1 | 1 | 100 | 3 | 3.0 | 1 | 0– | 0 | |
| Chandler | 2 | 0 | 0 | 0 | 0.0 | 0 | 0– | 0 | |
| Winslow | 2 | 0 | 0 | 0 | 0.0 | 0 | 0– | 0 | |

**PUNTING**

| Last Name | No. | Avg. |
|---|---|---|
| Roberts | 62 | 41.0 |

**KICKING**

| Last Name | XP | Att. | % | FG | Att. | % |
|---|---|---|---|---|---|---|
| Benirschke | 55 | 61 | 90 | 19 | 26 | 73 |

## DENVER BRONCOS

### Rushing

| Last Name | No. | Yds. | Avg. | TD |
|---|---|---|---|---|
| Parros | 176 | 749 | 4.3 | 2 |
| Preston | 183 | 640 | 3.5 | 3 |
| Reed | 68 | 156 | 2.3 | 0 |
| Canada | 33 | 113 | 3.4 | 3 |
| Lytle | 30 | 106 | 3.5 | 4 |
| Upchurch | 5 | 56 | 11.2 | 0 |
| DeBerg | 9 | 40 | 4.4 | 0 |
| Morton | 8 | 18 | 2.3 | 0 |
| Wright | 1 | 11 | 11.0 | 0 |
| Watson | 2 | 6 | 3.0 | 0 |

### Receiving

| Last Name | No. | Yds. | Avg. | TD |
|---|---|---|---|---|
| Watson | 60 | 1244 | 21 | 13 |
| Preston | 52 | 507 | 10 | 0 |
| Odoms | 38 | 516 | 14 | 5 |
| Reed | 34 | 317 | 9 | 0 |
| Upchurch | 32 | 550 | 17 | 3 |
| Parros | 25 | 216 | 9 | 1 |
| Egloff | 17 | 231 | 14 | 1 |
| Moses | 15 | 246 | 16 | 1 |
| Lytle | 6 | 47 | 8 | 1 |
| Manning | 3 | 49 | 16 | 0 |
| Canada | 3 | 37 | 12 | 1 |
| J. Wright | 3 | 22 | 7 | 1 |
| Studdard | 1 | 10 | 10 | 0 |

### Punt Returns

| Last Name | No. | Yds. | Avg. | TD |
|---|---|---|---|---|
| Manning | 41 | 378 | 9 | 0 |
| Upchurch | 9 | 63 | 7 | 0 |
| Kyle | 1 | 0 | 0 | 0 |

### Kickoff Returns

| Last Name | No. | Yds. | Avg. | TD |
|---|---|---|---|---|
| Manning | 26 | 514 | 20 | 0 |
| Harden | 11 | 178 | 16 | 0 |
| Lytle | 5 | 80 | 16 | 0 |
| Canada | 2 | 19 | 10 | 0 |
| Egloff | 1 | 7 | 7 | 0 |
| Ryan | 1 | 2 | 2 | 0 |
| Preston | 1 | 1 | 1 | 0 |

### Passing – Punting – Kicking

**PASSING**

| Last Name | Att. | Comp. | % | Yds. | Yd./Att. | TD | Int.–% | | RK |
|---|---|---|---|---|---|---|---|---|---|
| Morton | 376 | 225 | 60 | 3195 | 8.5 | 21 | 14– | 4 | 2 |
| DeBerg | 108 | 64 | 59 | 797 | 7.4 | 6 | 6– | 6 | |
| Reed | 1 | 0 | 0 | 0 | 0.0 | 0 | 1–100 | | |

**PUNTING**

| Last Name | No. | Avg. |
|---|---|---|
| Prestridge | 86 | 40.4 |

**KICKING**

| Last Name | XP | Att. | % | FG | Att. | % |
|---|---|---|---|---|---|---|
| Steinfort | 36 | 37 | 97 | 17 | 30 | 57 |

## KANSAS CITY CHIEFS

### Rushing

| Last Name | No. | Yds. | Avg. | TD |
|---|---|---|---|---|
| Delaney | 234 | 1121 | 4.8 | 3 |
| Hadnot | 140 | 603 | 4.3 | 3 |
| B. Jackson | 111 | 398 | 3.6 | 10 |
| McKnight | 54 | 195 | 3.6 | 5 |
| Fuller | 19 | 118 | 6.2 | 0 |
| Kenny | 24 | 89 | 3.7 | 1 |
| Marshall | 3 | 69 | 23.0 | 0 |
| Bledsoe | 20 | 65 | 3.3 | 0 |
| Williams | 2 | 0 | 0.0 | 0 |
| Carson | 1 | −1 | −1.0 | 0 |
| Dixon | 1 | −5 | −5.0 | 0 |
| Grupp | 1 | −9 | −9.0 | 0 |

### Receiving

| Last Name | No. | Yds. | Avg. | TD |
|---|---|---|---|---|
| Smith | 63 | 852 | 14 | 2 |
| Marshall | 38 | 620 | 16 | 4 |
| Dixon | 29 | 356 | 12 | 2 |
| Hadnot | 23 | 215 | 9 | 0 |
| Delaney | 22 | 246 | 11 | 0 |
| Rome | 17 | 203 | 12 | 1 |
| McKnight | 8 | 77 | 10 | 0 |
| Carson | 7 | 179 | 26 | 1 |
| B. Jackson | 6 | 31 | 5 | 1 |
| Scott | 5 | 72 | 14 | 1 |
| Bledsoe | 3 | 27 | 9 | 0 |
| Murphy | 2 | 36 | 18 | 0 |
| Williams | 1 | 3 | 3 | 0 |

### Punt Returns

| Last Name | No. | Yds. | Avg. | TD |
|---|---|---|---|---|
| Smith | 50 | 528 | 11 | 0 |

### Kickoff Returns

| Last Name | No. | Yds. | Avg. | TD |
|---|---|---|---|---|
| Murphy | 20 | 457 | 23 | 0 |
| Carson | 10 | 227 | 23 | 0 |
| Bledsoe | 6 | 117 | 20 | 0 |
| Burruss | 5 | 91 | 18 | 0 |
| B. Jackson | 3 | 60 | 20 | 0 |
| Cherry | 3 | 52 | 17 | 0 |
| Rourke | 2 | 0 | 0 | 0 |
| Delaney | 1 | 11 | 11 | 0 |
| Williams | 1 | 7 | 7 | 0 |

### Passing – Punting – Kicking

**PASSING**

| Last Name | Att. | Comp. | % | Yds. | Yd./Att. | TD | Int.–% | | RK |
|---|---|---|---|---|---|---|---|---|---|
| Kenney | 274 | 147 | 54 | 1983 | 7.2 | 9 | 16– | 6 | 12 |
| Fuller | 134 | 77 | 58 | 934 | 7.0 | 3 | 4– | 3 | |
| Hadnot | 1 | 0 | 0 | 0 | 0.0 | 0 | 1–100 | | |
| Marshall | 1 | 0 | 0 | 0 | 0.0 | 0 | 0– | 0 | |

**PUNTING**

| Last Name | No. | Avg. |
|---|---|---|
| Grupp | 41 | 38.0 |
| Gossett | 29 | 39.3 |

**KICKING**

| Last Name | XP | Att. | % | FG | Att. | % |
|---|---|---|---|---|---|---|
| Lowery | 37 | 38 | 97 | 26 | 36 | 72 |

## OAKLAND RAIDERS

### Rushing

| Last Name | No. | Yds. | Avg. | TD |
|---|---|---|---|---|
| King | 170 | 828 | 4.9 | 0 |
| Jensen | 117 | 456 | 3.9 | 4 |
| Whittington | 69 | 220 | 3.2 | 1 |
| Hawkins | 40 | 165 | 4.1 | 0 |
| van Eeghen | 39 | 150 | 3.8 | 2 |
| Wilson | 30 | 147 | 4.9 | 2 |
| Willis | 16 | 54 | 3.4 | 1 |
| Plunkett | 12 | 38 | 3.2 | 1 |

### Receiving

| Last Name | No. | Yds. | Avg. | TD |
|---|---|---|---|---|
| Ramsey | 52 | 674 | 13 | 4 |
| Branch | 41 | 635 | 16 | 1 |
| Jensen | 28 | 271 | 10 | 0 |
| King | 27 | 216 | 8 | 0 |
| Chandler | 26 | 458 | 18 | 4 |
| Whittington | 23 | 213 | 9 | 2 |
| Bradshaw | 22 | 298 | 14 | 3 |
| Matthews | 15 | 92 | 6 | 0 |
| Chester | 13 | 93 | 7 | 1 |
| Hawkins | 10 | 109 | 11 | 0 |
| Barnwell | 9 | 190 | 21 | 1 |
| Christensen | 8 | 115 | 14 | 2 |
| van Eeghen | 7 | 60 | 9 | 0 |
| Willis | 1 | 24 | 24 | 0 |

### Punt Returns

| Last Name | No. | Yds. | Avg. | TD |
|---|---|---|---|---|
| Watts | 35 | 284 | 8 | 1 |
| Whittington | 2 | 4 | 2 | 0 |

### Kickoff Returns

| Last Name | No. | Yds. | Avg. | TD |
|---|---|---|---|---|
| Whittington | 25 | 563 | 23 | 0 |
| Willis | 15 | 309 | 21 | 0 |
| Barnwell | 15 | 265 | 18 | 0 |
| Matthews | 7 | 144 | 21 | 0 |
| Christensen | 4 | 54 | 14 | 0 |
| Hill | 1 | 21 | 21 | 0 |
| Hawkins | 1 | 7 | 7 | 0 |

### Passing – Punting – Kicking

**PASSING**

| Last Name | Att. | Comp. | % | Yds. | Yd./Att. | TD | Int.–% | | RK |
|---|---|---|---|---|---|---|---|---|---|
| Wilson | 366 | 173 | 47 | 2311 | 6.3 | 14 | 19– | 5 | 15 |
| Plunkett | 179 | 94 | 53 | 1045 | 5.8 | 4 | 9– | 5 | |

**PUNTING**

| Last Name | No. | Avg. |
|---|---|---|
| Guy | 96 | 43.7 |
| Bahr | 2 | 21.5 |

**KICKING**

| Last Name | XP | Att. | % | FG | Att. | % |
|---|---|---|---|---|---|---|
| Bahr | 27 | 33 | 82 | 14 | 24 | 58 |

## SEATTLE SEAHAWKS

### Rushing

| Last Name | No. | Yds. | Avg. | TD |
|---|---|---|---|---|
| J. Brown | 156 | 583 | 3.7 | 8 |
| Smith | 83 | 253 | 3.0 | 3 |
| Doornink | 65 | 194 | 3.0 | 1 |
| Zorn | 30 | 140 | 4.7 | 1 |
| Hughes | 47 | 135 | 2.9 | 0 |
| Jodat | 31 | 106 | 3.4 | 1 |
| Krieg | 11 | 56 | 5.1 | 1 |
| Largent | 6 | 47 | 7.8 | 1 |
| Ivory | 9 | 38 | 4.2 | 0 |
| Adkins | 3 | 28 | 9.3 | 0 |
| West | 3 | 25 | 8.3 | 0 |
| Lane | 8 | 22 | 2.8 | 0 |
| Moore | 1 | 15 | 15.0 | 0 |
| Miller | 2 | 4 | 4.0 | 0 |

### Receiving

| Last Name | No. | Yds. | Avg. | TD |
|---|---|---|---|---|
| Largent | 75 | 1224 | 16 | 9 |
| McCullum | 46 | 567 | 12 | 3 |
| Smith | 44 | 406 | 9 | 1 |
| Hughes | 35 | 263 | 8 | 2 |
| T. Brown | 29 | 328 | 11 | 0 |
| Doornink | 27 | 350 | 13 | 4 |
| Sawyer | 21 | 272 | 13 | 0 |
| Johns | 8 | 131 | 16 | 1 |
| Lane | 7 | 58 | 8 | 0 |
| Tice | 5 | 47 | 9 | 0 |
| Jodat | 4 | 52 | 13 | 0 |
| McGrath | 4 | 47 | 12 | 0 |
| Moore | 3 | 18 | 6 | 0 |
| Raible | 1 | 12 | 12 | 0 |
| August | 1 | 9 | 9 | 0 |
| Boyd | 1 | 3 | 3 | 0 |

### Punt Returns

| Last Name | No. | Yds. | Avg. | TD |
|---|---|---|---|---|
| Johns | 16 | 177 | 11 | 0 |
| Lewis | 15 | 100 | 7 | 0 |
| Johnson | 1 | 16 | 16 | 0 |

### Kickoff Returns

| Last Name | No. | Yds. | Avg. | TD |
|---|---|---|---|---|
| Lewis | 20 | 378 | 19 | 0 |
| Ivory | 16 | 300 | 19 | 0 |
| Johnson | 13 | 235 | 18 | 0 |
| Lane | 10 | 208 | 21 | 0 |
| Johns | 5 | 81 | 16 | 0 |
| Dufek | 3 | 45 | 15 | 0 |
| Sawyer | 1 | 8 | 8 | 0 |

### Passing – Punting – Kicking

**PASSING**

| Last Name | Att. | Comp. | % | Yds. | Yd./Att. | TD | Int.–% | | RK |
|---|---|---|---|---|---|---|---|---|---|
| Zorn | 397 | 236 | 59 | 2788 | 7.0 | 13 | 9– | 2 | 5 |
| Krieg | 112 | 64 | 57 | 843 | 7.5 | 7 | 5– | 5 | |
| Adkins | 13 | 7 | 54 | 96 | 7.4 | 1 | 1– | 8 | |
| Largent | 1 | 0 | 0 | 0 | 0.0 | 0 | 0– | 0 | |
| West | 1 | 0 | 0 | 0 | 0.0 | 0 | 0– | 0 | |

**PUNTING**

| Last Name | No. | Avg. |
|---|---|---|
| West | 66 | 39.1 |
| Garcia | 2 | 37.0 |

**KICKING**

| Last Name | XP | Att. | % | FG | Att. | % |
|---|---|---|---|---|---|---|
| Herrera | 23 | 25 | 92 | 12 | 17 | 74 |
| Alvarez | 14 | 15 | 93 | 3 | 7 | 43 |

# 1981 N.F.C. — PLAYOFFS

December 27 at Philadelphia (Attendance 71,611)

## SCORING

| | | | | | |
|---|---|---|---|---|---|
| NEW YORK | 20 | 7 | 0 | 0–27 | |
| PHILADELPHIA | 0 | 7 | 7 | 7–21 | |

**First Quarter**
N.Y.  Bright, 9 yard pass from Brunner
  PAT–Kick failed
N.Y.  Mistler, 10 yard pass from Brunner
  PAT–Danelo (kick)
N.Y.  Haynes, fumble recovery in end zone
  PAT–Danelo (kick)
**Second Quarter**
Phil.  Carmichael, 15 yard pass from Jaworski
  PAT–Franklin (kick)
N.Y.  Mullady, 22 yard pass from Brunner
  PAT–Danelo (kick)
**Third Quarter**
Phil.  Montgomery, 6 yard rush
  PAT–Franklin (kick)
**Fourth Quarter**
Phil.  Montgomery, 1 yard rush
  PAT–Franklin (kick)

## TEAM STATISTICS

| N.Y. | | PHIL. |
|---|---|---|
| 16 | First Downs-Total | 19 |
| 10 | First Downs-Rushing | 8 |
| 6 | First Downs-Passing | 8 |
| 0 | First Downs- Penalty | 3 |
| 1 | Fumbles-Number | 5 |
| 0 | Fumbles-Lost Ball | 2 |
| 5 | Penalties-Number | 4 |
| 54 | Yards Penalized | 23 |
| 1 | Missed Field Goals | 0 |
| 57 | Offensive Plays | 56 |
| 275 | Net Yards | 226 |
| 4.8 | Average Gain | 4.0 |
| 1 | Giveaways | 2 |
| 2 | Takeaways | 1 |
| +1 | Difference | −1 |

## INDIVIDUAL STATISTICS

**NEW YORK** / **PHILADELPHIA**

### RUSHING

| | No. | Yds. | Avg. | | No. | Yds. | Avg. |
|---|---|---|---|---|---|---|---|
| Carpenter | 33 | 161 | 4.9 | Montgomery | 18 | 65 | 3.6 |
| Perry | 3 | 11 | 3.7 | Oliver | 5 | 12 | 2.4 |
| Brunner | 6 | 11 | 1.8 | Campfield | 1 | 10 | 10.0 |
| | | | | Jaworski | 5 | 6 | 1.2 |
| | 42 | 183 | 4.4 | | 29 | 93 | 3.2 |

### RECEIVING

| | No. | Yds. | Avg. | | No. | Yds. | Avg. |
|---|---|---|---|---|---|---|---|
| Carpenter | 4 | 32 | 8.0 | Montgomery | 3 | 32 | 10.7 |
| Mullady | 1 | 22 | 22.0 | R. Smith | 3 | 31 | 10.3 |
| Gray | 1 | 12 | 12.0 | Carmichael | 2 | 43 | 21.5 |
| Perkins | 1 | 11 | 11.0 | C. Smith | 2 | 19 | 9.5 |
| Mistler | 1 | 10 | 10.0 | Krepfle | 1 | 18 | 18.0 |
| Bright | 1 | 9 | 9.0 | Oliver | 1 | 7 | 7.0 |
| | 9 | 96 | 10.7 | Russell | 1 | 4 | 4.0 |
| | | | | | 13 | 154 | 11.8 |

### PUNTING

| | No. | | Avg. | | No. | | Avg. |
|---|---|---|---|---|---|---|---|
| Jennings | 4 | | 44.8 | Runager | 7 | | 42.4 |

### PUNT RETURNS

| | No. | Yds. | Avg. | | No. | Yds. | Avg. |
|---|---|---|---|---|---|---|---|
| Bright | 4 | 32 | 8.0 | Sciarra | 2 | 16 | 8.0 |
| Reece | 1 | 9 | 9.0 | Henry | 1 | 0 | 0.0 |
| | 5 | 41 | 8.2 | | 3 | 16 | 5.3 |

### KICKOFF

| | No. | Yds. | Avg. | | No. | Yds. | Avg. |
|---|---|---|---|---|---|---|---|
| Reece | 3 | 64 | 21.3 | Russell | 2 | 24 | 12.0 |
| Jackson | 1 | 23 | 23.0 | Henry | 1 | 16 | 8.0 |
| | 4 | 87 | 21.8 | Campfield | 1 | 19 | 19.0 |
| | | | | | 5 | 59 | 11.8 |

### INTERCEPTION RETURNS

| | No. | Yds. | Avg. | | No. | Yds. | Avg. |
|---|---|---|---|---|---|---|---|
| none | | | | Edwards | 1 | 1 | 1.0 |

### PASSING

**NEW YORK**

| | Att. | Comp. | Comp. Pct. | Yds. | Int. | Yds./ Att. | Yds./ Comp. |
|---|---|---|---|---|---|---|---|
| Brunner | 14 | 9 | 64.2 | 96 | 1 | 6.9 | 10.7 |

**PHILADELPHIA**

| | Att. | Comp. | Comp. Pct. | Yds. | Int. | Yds./ Att. | Yds./ Comp. |
|---|---|---|---|---|---|---|---|
| Jaworski | 24 | 13 | 54.1 | 154 | 0 | 6.4 | 11.8 |

---

January 2, 1982 at Irving, Tex. (Attendance 68,848)

## SCORING

| | | | | | |
|---|---|---|---|---|---|
| TAMPA BAY | 0 | 0 | 0 | 0– 0 | |
| DALLAS | 0 | 10 | 21 | 7–38 | |

**Second Quarter**
Dal.  Hill, 9 yard pass from D. White
  PAT Septien (kick)
Dal.  Septien, 32 yard field goal
**Third Quarter**
Dal.  Springs, 1 yard rush
  PAT–Septien (kick)
Dal.  Dorsett, 5 yard rush
  PAT–Septien (kick)
Dal.  J. Jones, 5 yard rush
  PAT–Septien (kick)
**Fourth Quarter**
Dal.  Newsome, 1 yard rush
  PAT–Septien (kick)

## TEAM STATISTICS

| T.B. | | DAL. |
|---|---|---|
| 12 | First Downs-Total | 26 |
| 3 | First Downs-Rushing | 15 |
| 7 | First Downs-Passing | 10 |
| 2 | First Downs-Penalty | 1 |
| 2 | Fumbles-Number | 0 |
| 0 | Fumbles-Lost Ball | 0 |
| 10 | Penalties-Number | 5 |
| 105 | Yards Penalized | 40 |
| 0 | Missed Field Goals | 0 |
| 55 | Offensive Play | 73 |
| 222 | Net Yards | 345 |
| 4.0 | Average Gain | 4.7 |
| 4 | Giveaways | 0 |
| 0 | Takeaways | 4 |
| −4 | Difference | +4 |

## INDIVIDUAL STATISTICS

**TAMPA BAY** / **DALLAS**

### RUSHING

| | No. | Yds. | Avg. | | No. | Yds. | Avg. |
|---|---|---|---|---|---|---|---|
| Owens | 12 | 40 | 3.3 | Dorsett | 16 | 86 | 5.4 |
| Wilder | 4 | 23 | 5.8 | Springs | 15 | 70 | 4.7 |
| Williams | 2 | 9 | 4.5 | J. Jones | 9 | 32 | 3.6 |
| Eckwood | 4 | 2 | 0.5 | Newhouse | 4 | 23 | 5.8 |
| | 22 | 74 | 3.4 | Newsome | 1 | 1 | 1.0 |
| | | | | Cosbie | 1 | 0 | 0.0 |
| | | | | | 46 | 212 | 4.6 |

### RECEIVING

| | No. | Yds. | Avg. | | No. | Yds. | Avg. |
|---|---|---|---|---|---|---|---|
| T. Bell | 3 | 36 | 12.0 | Dorsett | 4 | 48 | 12.0 |
| Owens | 3 | 32 | 10.7 | DuPree | 3 | 22 | 7.3 |
| Giles | 2 | 98 | 49.0 | Pearson | 2 | 21 | 7.0 |
| Wilder | 1 | 11 | 11.0 | Hill | 2 | 18 | 9.0 |
| House | 1 | 10 | 10.0 | J. Jones | 2 | 15 | 7.5 |
| | 10 | 187 | 18.7 | Donley | 1 | 14 | 14.0 |
| | | | | Cosbie | 1 | 5 | 5.0 |
| | | | | | 15 | 143 | 9.5 |

### PUNTING

| | No. | | Avg. | | No. | | Avg. |
|---|---|---|---|---|---|---|---|
| Swider | 5 | | 38.4 | D. White | 4 | | 30.0 |

### PUNT RETURNS

| | No. | Yds. | Avg. | | No. | Yds. | Avg. |
|---|---|---|---|---|---|---|---|
| T. Bell | 1 | 1 | 1.0 | J. Johes | 3 | 53 | 17.7 |

### KICKOFF RETURNS

| | No. | Yds. | Avg. | | No. | Yds. | Avg. |
|---|---|---|---|---|---|---|---|
| Owens | 3 | 92 | 30.7 | none | | | |
| Holt | 2 | 55 | 27.5 | | | | |
| | 5 | 147 | 29.4 | | | | |

### INTERCEPTION RETURNS

| | No. | Yds. | Avg. | | No. | Yds. | Avg. |
|---|---|---|---|---|---|---|---|
| none | | | | Thurman | 2 | 50 | 25.0 |
| | | | | Downs | 1 | 21 | 21.0 |
| | | | | T. Jones | 1 | 0 | 0.0 |
| | | | | | 4 | 71 | 17.8 |

### PASSING

**TAMPA BAY**

| | Att. | Comp. | Comp. Pct. | Yds. | Int. | Yds./ Att. | Yds./ Comp. |
|---|---|---|---|---|---|---|---|
| Williams | 29 | 10 | 34.5 | 187 | 4 | 6.4 | 18.7 |

**DALLAS**

| | Att. | Comp. | Comp. Pct. | Yds. | Int. | Yds./ Att. | Yds./ Comp. |
|---|---|---|---|---|---|---|---|
| D. White | 26 | 15 | 57.7 | 143 | 0 | 5.5 | 9.5 |

---

January 3, 1982 at San Francisco (Attendance 58, 360)

## SCORING

| | | | | | |
|---|---|---|---|---|---|
| NEW YORK | 7 | 3 | 7 | 7–24 | |
| SAN FRANCISCO | 7 | 17 | 9 | 14–38 | |

**First Quarter**
S.F.  Young, 8 yard pass from Montana
  PAT–Wersching (kick)
N.Y.  Gray, 72 yard pass from Brunner
  PAT–Danelo (kick)
**Second Quarter**
S.F.  Wersching, 22 yard field goal
S.F.  Solomon, 58 yard pass from Montana
  PAT–Wersching (kick)
S.F.  Patton, 25 yard rush
  PAT–Wersching (kick)
N.Y.  Danelo, 48 yard field goal
**Third Quarter**
N.Y.  Perkins, 59 yard pass from Brunner
  PAT–Danelo (kick)
**Fourth Quarter**
S.F.  Ring, 3 yard rush
  PAT–Wersching (kick)
S.F.  Lott, 20 yard interception return
  PAT–Wersching (kick)
N.Y.  Perkins, 17 yard pass from Brunner
  PAT–Danelo (kick)

## TEAM STATISTICS

| N.Y. | | S.F. |
|---|---|---|
| 13 | First Downs-Total | 24 |
| 3 | First Downs-Rushing | 8 |
| 9 | First Downs-Passing | 13 |
| 1 | First Downs-Penalty | 3 |
| 4 | Fumbles-Number | 2 |
| 2 | Fumbles-Lost Ball | 0 |
| 9 | Penalties-Number | 14 |
| 61 | Yards Penalized | 145 |
| 1 | Missed Field Goals | 1 |
| 61 | Offensive Plays | 68 |
| 346 | Net Yards | 423 |
| 5.7 | Average Gain | 6.2 |
| 4 | Giveaways | 1 |
| 1 | Takeaways | 4 |
| −3 | Difference | +3 |

## INDIVIDUAL STATISTICS

**NEW YORK** / **SAN FRANCISCO**

### RUSHING

| | No. | Yds. | Avg. | | No. | Yds. | Avg. |
|---|---|---|---|---|---|---|---|
| Carpenter | 17 | 61 | 3.6 | Cooper | 7 | 52 | 7.4 |
| Bright | 1 | 5 | 5.0 | Patton | 7 | 32 | 4.6 |
| Perry | 2 | 1 | 0.5 | Ring | 10 | 29 | 2.9 |
| Brunner | 2 | −2 | −1.0 | Solomon | 1 | 12 | 12.0 |
| | 22 | 65 | 3.0 | Easley | 4 | 9 | 2.3 |
| | | | | Clark | 1 | 6 | 6.0 |
| | | | | Davis | 1 | 4 | 4.0 |
| | | | | Montana | 3 | −9 | −3.0 |
| | | | | | 34 | 135 | 4.0 |

### RECEIVING

| | No. | Yds. | Avg. | | No. | Yds. | Avg. |
|---|---|---|---|---|---|---|---|
| Perkins | 1 | 121 | 17.3 | Solomon | 6 | 107 | 17.8 |
| Gray | 3 | 118 | 39.3 | Clark | 5 | 104 | 20.8 |
| Carpenter | 3 | 18 | 6.0 | Patton | 2 | 38 | 19.0 |
| Young | 2 | 15 | 7.5 | Young | 2 | 22 | 11.0 |
| Mistler | 1 | 18 | 18.0 | Wilson | 2 | 21 | 10.5 |
| | 16 | 290 | 18.1 | Ramson | 1 | 11 | 11.0 |
| | | | | Elliott | 1 | 5 | 5.0 |
| | | | | Ring | 1 | −4 | −4.0 |
| | | | | | 20 | 304 | 15.2 |

### PUNTING

| | No. | | Avg. | | No. | | Avg. |
|---|---|---|---|---|---|---|---|
| Jennings | 9 | | 43.8 | Miller | 5 | | 41.2 |

### PUNT RETURNS

| | No. | Yds. | Avg. | | No. | Yds. | Avg. |
|---|---|---|---|---|---|---|---|
| Bright | 3 | 18 | 6.0 | Solomon | 1 | 22 | 22.0 |

### KICKOFF RETURNS

| | No. | Yds. | Avg. | | No. | Yds. | Avg. |
|---|---|---|---|---|---|---|---|
| Bright | 5 | 113 | 22.6 | Lawrence | 3 | 88 | 29.3 |
| McLaughlin | 1 | 15 | 15.0 | Ring | 1 | 5 | 5.0 |
| Dennis | 1 | 14 | 14.0 | Lott | 1 | 0 | 0.0 |
| | 7 | 142 | 20.3 | | 5 | 93 | 18.6 |

### INTERCEPTION RETURNS

| | No. | Yds. | Avg. | | No. | Yds. | Avg. |
|---|---|---|---|---|---|---|---|
| Currier | 1 | 2 | 2.0 | Lott | 2 | 32 | 16.0 |

### PASSING

**NEW YORK**

| | Att. | Comp. | Comp. Pct. | Yds. | Int. | Yds./ Att. | Yds./ Comp. |
|---|---|---|---|---|---|---|---|
| Brunner | 37 | 16 | 43.2 | 290 | 2 | 7.8 | 18.1 |

**SAN FRANCISCO**

| | Att. | Comp. | Comp. Pct. | Yds. | Int. | Yds./ Att. | Yds./ Comp. |
|---|---|---|---|---|---|---|---|
| Montana | 31 | 20 | 62.5 | 304 | 1 | 9.8 | 15.2 |

# 1981 A.F.C. PLAYOFFS

December 27 at New York (Attendance 57,050)

## SCORING

| | | | | | |
|---|---|---|---|---|---|
| BUFFALO | 17 | 7 | 0 | 7 | –31 |
| NEW YORK | 0 | 10 | 3 | 14 | –27 |

First Quarter
- Buf. — Romes, 26 yard fumble return PAT-Mike-Mayer (kick)
- Buf. — Lewis, 50 yard pass from Ferguson PAT-Mike-Mayer (kick)
- Buf. — Mike-Mayer 29 yard field goal

Second Quarter
- Buf. — Lewis, 26 yard pass from Ferguson PAT-Mike-Mayer (kick)
- N.Y. — Shuler, 30 yard pass from Todd PAT-Leahy (kick)
- N.Y. — Leahy, 26 yard field goal

Third Quarter
- N.Y. — Leahy, 19 yard field goal

Fourth Quarter
- Buf. — Cribbs, 45 yard rush PAT-Mike-Mayer (kick)
- N.Y. — B. Jones, 30 yard pass from Todd PAT-Leahy (kick)
- N.Y. — Long, 1 yard rush PAT-Leahy (kick)

## TEAM STATISTICS

| BUFF. | | N.Y. |
|---|---|---|
| 15 | First Downs-Total | 23 |
| 4 | First Downs-Rushing | 3 |
| 11 | First Downs-Passing | 17 |
| 0 | First Downs-Penalty | 3 |
| 1 | Fumbles-Number | 3 |
| 0 | Fumbles-Lost Ball | 1 |
| 8 | Penalties-Number | 6 |
| 62 | Yards Penalized | 55 |
| 1 | Missed Field Goals | 1 |
| 58 | Offensive Plays | 77 |
| 321 | Net Yards | 419 |
| 5.5 | Average Gain | 5.4 |
| 4 | Giveaways | 5 |
| 5 | Takeaways | 4 |
| +1 | Difference | –1 |

## INDIVIDUAL STATISTICS

| BUFFALO | No. | Yds. | Avg. | NEW YORK | No. | Yds. | Avg. |
|---|---|---|---|---|---|---|---|
| **RUSHING** | | | | | | | |
| Cribbs | 14 | 83 | 5.9 | McNeil | 12 | 32 | 2.7 |
| Leaks | 6 | 12 | 2.0 | Long | 8 | 28 | 3.5 |
| Ferguson | 2 | -4 | –2.0 | odd | 2 | 11 | 5.5 |
| | 22 | 91 | 4.1 | | 22 | 71 | 3.2 |
| **RECEIVING** | | | | | | | |
| Lewis | 7 | 158 | 22.6 | Dierking | 7 | 52 | 7.4 |
| Cribbs | 4 | 64 | 16.0 | Shuler | 6 | 116 | 19.3 |
| Leaks | 3 | 23 | 7.7 | B. Jones | 4 | 64 | 16.0 |
| Brammer | 2 | 17 | 8.5 | Gaffney | 4 | 64 | 16.0 |
| Butler | 1 | 6 | 6.0 | Walker | 3 | 24 | 8.0 |
| | | | | Barkum | 2 | 41 | 20.5 |
| | 17 | 268 | 15.8 | Newton | 1 | 12 | 12.0 |
| | | | | Harper | 1 | 4 | 4.0 |
| | | | | | 28 | 377 | 13.5 |
| **PUNTING** | | | | | | | |
| Cater | 4 | | 43.8 | Ramsey | 4 | | 33.0 |
| **PUNT RETURNS** | | | | | | | |
| Riddick | 1 | 1 | 6.0 | Harper | 3 | 31 | 10.3 |
| Piccone | 1 | 5 | 5.0 | | | | |
| | 2 | 11 | 5.5 | | | | |
| **KICKOFF RETURNS** | | | | | | | |
| Riddick | 4 | 73 | 18.3 | Harper | 4 | 82 | 20.5 |
| Brown | 1 | 27 | 27.0 | Sohn | 1 | 28 | 28.0 |
| | 5 | 100 | 20.0 | | 5 | 110 | 22.0 |
| **INTERCEPTION RETURNS** | | | | | | | |
| Simpson | 2 | 12 | 6.0 | Buttle | 2 | 40 | 20.0 |
| Bess | 1 | 49 | 49.0 | Dykes | 1 | 20 | 20.0 |
| Villipiano | 1 | 18 | 18.0 | Holmes | 1 | 0 | 0.0 |
| | 4 | 79 | 19.8 | | 4 | 60 | 15.0 |

### PASSING

| | Att. | Comp. | Comp. Pct. | Yds. | Int. | Yds./ Att. | Yds./ Comp. |
|---|---|---|---|---|---|---|---|
| **BUFFALO** | | | | | | | |
| Ferguson | 34 | 17 | 50.0 | 268 | 4 | 7.9 | 15.8 |
| **NEW YORK** | | | | | | | |
| Todd | 51 | 28 | 54.9 | 377 | 4 | 7.4 | 13.5 |

January 2, 1982 at Miami (Attendance 73,735)

## SCORING

| | | | | | | |
|---|---|---|---|---|---|---|
| SAN DIEGO | 24 | 0 | 7 | 7 | 3 | –41 |
| MIAMI | 0 | 17 | 14 | 7 | 0 | –38 |

First Quarter
- S.D. — Benirschke, 32 yard field goal
- S.D. — Chandler, 56 yard punt return PAT–Benirschke (kick)
- S.D. — Muncie, 1 yard, rush PAT–Benirschke (kick)
- S.D. — Brooks, 8 yard pass from Fouts PAT–Benirschke (kick)

Second Quarter
- Mia. — von Schaman, 34 yard field goal
- Mia. — Rose, 1 yard pass from Strock PAT–von Schamann (kick)
- Mia. — Nathan, 40 yard pass from Strock PAT–von Schamann (kick)

Third Quarter
- Mia. — Rose, 15 yard pass from Strock PAT–von Schaman (kick)
- S.D. — Winslow, 25 yard pass from Fouts PAT–Bernirschke (kick)
- Mia. — Hardy, 50 yard pass from Strock PAT–von Schaman (kick)

Fourth Quarter
- Mia. — Nathan, 12 yard rush PAT–von Schamann (kick)
- S.D. — Brooks, 9 yard pass from Fouts PAT–Benirschke (kick)

Overtime
- S.D. — Benirschke, 29 yard field goal

## TEAM STATISTICS

| S.D. | | MIAMI |
|---|---|---|
| 33 | First Downs-Total | 25 |
| 10 | First Downs-Rushing | 3 |
| 21 | First Downs-Passing | 21 |
| 2 | First Downs-Penalty | 1 |
| 3 | Fumbles-Number | 2 |
| 3 | Fumbles-Lost Ball | 1 |
| 8 | Penalties-Number | 7 |
| 45 | Yards Penalized | 44 |
| 2 | Missed Field Goals | 2 |
| 85 | Offensive Plays | 78 |
| 564 | Net Yards | 466 |
| 6.6 | Average Gain | 6.0 |
| 4 | Giveaways | 3 |
| 3 | Takeaways | 4 |
| -1 | Difference | +1 |

## INDIVIDUAL STATISTICS

| SAN DIEGO | No. | Yds. | Avg. | MIAMI | No. | Yds. | Avg. |
|---|---|---|---|---|---|---|---|
| **RUSHING** | | | | | | | |
| Muncie | 24 | 120 | 5.0 | Nathan | 14 | 48 | 3.4 |
| Brooks | 3 | 19 | 6.3 | Woodley | 1 | 10 | 10.0 |
| Fouts | 2 | 10 | 5.0 | Hill | 3 | 8 | 2.7 |
| | 29 | 149 | 5.1 | Vigorito | 1 | 6 | 6.0 |
| | | | | Franklin | 9 | 6 | 0.7 |
| | | | | | 28 | 78 | 2.8 |
| **RECEIVING** | | | | | | | |
| Winslow | 13 | 166 | 12.8 | Nathan | 8 | 108 | 13.5 |
| Joiner | 7 | 108 | 15.4 | Harris | 6 | 106 | 17.7 |
| Chandler | 6 | 106 | 17.7 | Hardy | 5 | 89 | 17.8 |
| Brooks | 4 | 31 | 7.8 | Rose | 4 | 37 | 9.3 |
| Muncie | 2 | 5 | 2.5 | Cefalo | 3 | 62 | 20.7 |
| Scales | 1 | 17 | 17.0 | Vigorito | 2 | 12 | 6.0 |
| | 33 | 433 | 13.1 | Hill | 2 | 3 | 1.5 |
| | | | | | 30 | 417 | 13.9 |
| **PUNTING** | | | | | | | |
| Roberts | 4 | | 40.3 | Orosz | 5 | | 42.0 |
| **PUNT RETURNS** | | | | | | | |
| Chandler | 1 | 56 | 56.0 | Vigorito | 1 | 12 | 12.0 |
| Brooks | 1 | 8 | 8.0 | | | | |
| | 2 | 64 | 32.0 | | | | |
| **KICKOFF RETURNS** | | | | | | | |
| Brooks | 5 | 75 | 15.0 | Vigorito | 4 | 67 | 16.8 |
| Beaudoin | 1 | 15 | 15.0 | Walker | 1 | 18 | 18.0 |
| | 6 | 90 | 15.0 | Hill | 1 | 13 | 13.0 |
| | | | | | 6 | 98 | 16.3 |
| **INTERCEPTION RETURNS** | | | | | | | |
| Edwards | 1 | 35 | 35.0 | L. Blackwood | 1 | 8 | 8.0 |
| Buchanon | 1 | 0 | 0.0 | | | | |
| | 2 | 35 | 17.5 | | | | |

### PASSING

| | Att. | Comp. | Comp. Pct. | Yds. | Int. | Yds./ Att. | Yds./ Comp. |
|---|---|---|---|---|---|---|---|
| **SAN DIEGO** | | | | | | | |
| Fouts | 53 | 33 | 62.3 | 33 | 1 | 8.2 | 13.1 |
| Muncie | 1 | 0 | 0.0 | 0 | 0 | 0.0 | 0.0 |
| | 54 | 33 | 61.1 | 433 | 1 | 8.0 | 13.1 |
| **MIAMI** | | | | | | | |
| Woodley | 5 | 2 | 40.0 | 20 | 1 | 4.0 | 10.0 |
| Strock | 42 | 28 | 66.7 | 397 | 1 | 9.5 | 14.2 |
| | 47 | 30 | 63.8 | 417 | 2 | 8.9 | 13.9 |

January 3, 1982 at Cincinnati (Attendance 55,420)

## SCORING

| | | | | | |
|---|---|---|---|---|---|
| BUFFALO | 0 | 7 | 7 | 7 | –21 |
| CINCINNATI | 14 | 0 | 7 | 7 | –28 |

First Quarter
- Cin. — Alexander, 4 yard rush PAT-Breech (kick)
- Cin. — Johnson, 1 yard rush PAT-Breech (kick)

Second Quarter
- Buf. — Cribbs, 1 yard rush PAT-Mike-Mayer (kick)

Third Quarter
- Buf. — Cribbs, 44 yard rush PAT-Mike-Mayer (kick)
- Cin. — Alexander, 20 yard rush PAT-Breech (kick)

Fourth Quarter
- Buf. — Butler, 21 yard pass from Ferguson PAT-Mike-Mayer
- Cin. — Collinsworth, 16 yard pass from Anderson PAT-Breech (kick)

## TEAM STATISTICS

| BUF. | | CIN. |
|---|---|---|
| 21 | First Downs-Total | 22 |
| 11 | First Downs-Rushing | 11 |
| 8 | First Downs-Passing | 9 |
| 2 | First Downs-Penalty | 2 |
| 0 | Fumbles-Number | 0 |
| 0 | Fumbles-Lost Ball | 0 |
| 6 | Penalties-Number | 5 |
| 56 | Yards Penalized | 44 |
| 0 | Missed Field Goals | 1 |
| 59 | Offensive Plays | 58 |
| 336 | Net Yards | 305 |
| 5.7 | Average Gain | 5.3 |
| 2 | Giveaways | 0 |
| 0 | Takeaways | 2 |
| –2 | Difference | +2 |

## INDIVIDUAL STATISTICS

| BUFFALO | No. | Yds. | Avg. | CINCINNATI | No. | Yds. | Avg. |
|---|---|---|---|---|---|---|---|
| **RUSHING** | | | | | | | |
| Cribbs | 15 | 90 | 6.0 | Alexander | 13 | 72 | 5.5 |
| Hooks | 9 | 30 | 3.3 | Johnson | 17 | 45 | 2.6 |
| Leaks | 3 | 12 | 4.0 | A. Griffin | 1 | 4 | 4.0 |
| Brown | 1 | 2 | 2.0 | Anderson | 2 | 4 | 2.0 |
| | 28 | 134 | 4.8 | | 33 | 125 | 3.8 |
| **RECEIVING** | | | | | | | |
| Butler | 4 | 98 | 24.5 | Ross | 6 | 71 | 11.8 |
| Lewis | 3 | 38 | 12.7 | Johnson | 3 | 23 | 7.7 |
| Brammer | 3 | 23 | 7.7 | Collinsworth | 2 | 24 | 12.0 |
| Leaks | 2 | 16 | 8.0 | Kreider | 1 | 42 | 42.0 |
| Hooks | 2 | 15 | 7.5 | Curtis | 1 | 22 | 22.0 |
| Jessie | 1 | 12 | 12.0 | Alexander | 1 | 10 | 10.0 |
| | 15 | 202 | 13.5 | | 14 | 192 | 13.7 |
| **PUNTING** | | | | | | | |
| Cater | 3 | | 42.0 | McInally | 4 | | 44.5 |
| **PUNT RETURNS** | | | | | | | |
| Riddick | 2 | 8 | 4.0 | Fuller | 1 | 27 | 27.0 |
| **KICKOFF RETURNS** | | | | | | | |
| Riddick | 4 | 68 | 17.0 | Verser | 4 | 94 | 23.5 |
| Brown | 1 | 14 | 14.0 | | | | |
| | 5 | 82 | 16.4 | | | | |
| **INTERCEPTION RETURNS** | | | | | | | |
| none | | | | B. Harris | 1 | 16 | 16.0 |
| | | | | Riley | 1 | 0 | 0.0 |
| | | | | | 2 | 16 | 8.0 |

### PASSING

| | Att. | Comp. | Comp. Pct. | Yds. | Int. | Yds./ Att. | Yds./ Comp. |
|---|---|---|---|---|---|---|---|
| **BUFFALO** | | | | | | | |
| Ferguson | 31 | 15 | 48.4 | 202 | 2 | 6.5 | 13.5 |
| **CINCINNATI** | | | | | | | |
| Anderson | 21 | 14 | 66.7 | 192 | 0 | 9.1 | 13.7 |

# 1981 CHAMPIONSHIP GAMES

## SCORING

| | | | | |
|---|---|---|---|---|
| DALLAS | 10 | 7 | 0 | 10—27 |
| SAN FRANCISCO | 7 | 7 | 7 | 7—28 |

**First Quarter**
S.F. — Solomon, 8 yard pass from Montana
PAT—Wersching (kick)
Dal. — Septien, 44 yard field goal
Dal. — Hill, 26 yard pass from D. White
PAT—Septien (kick)

**Second Quarter**
S.F. — Clark, 20 yard pass from Montana
PAT—Wersching (kick)
Dal. — Dorsett, 5 yard rush
PAT—Septien (kick)

**Third Quarter**
S.F. — Davis, 2 yard rush
PAT—Wersching (kick)

**Fourth Quarter**
Dal. — Septien, 22 yard field goal
Dal. — Cosbie, 21 yard pass from D. White
PAT—Septien (kick)
S.F. — Clark, 6 yard pass from Montana
PAT—Wersching (kick)

## TEAM STATISTICS

| DALLAS | | S.F. |
|---|---|---|
| 16 | First Downs–Total | 26 |
| 5 | First Downs–Rushing | 6 |
| 9 | First Downs–Passing | 17 |
| 2 | First Downs–Penalty | 3 |
| 4 | Fumbles–Number | 3 |
| 2 | Fumbles–Lost Ball | 3 |
| 5 | Penalty–Number | 7 |
| 39 | Yards Penalized | 106 |
| 0 | Missed Field Goals | 0 |
| 60 | Offensive Plays | 69 |
| 250 | Net Yards | 393 |
| 4.2 | Average Gain | 5.7 |
| 3 | Giveaways | 6 |
| 6 | Takeaways | 3 |
| –3 | Difference | –3 |

Although San Francisco had been plagued with hard rains and flooding, the playing field at Candlestick Park was in fine shape as the 49ers hosted the Dallas Cowboys. The 49ers had whipped the Cowboys 45–14 in October, but Tom Landry's crew came into this match with lots of championship experience, a commodity in short supply on the 49er roster.

But on the opening series, the 49ers showed composure and calm. They took the kickoff and drove downfield, scoring on an eight-yard pass from Joe Montana to Freddie Solomon. For the rest of the first half, the two combatants traded the lead back and forth. At the intermission, the Cowboys held a 17-14 edge.

The defensive units dominated the third quarter, with the 49er unit creating the only scoring opportunity. Bobby Leopold intercepted a pass and started a San Francisco drive which led to Johnny Davis's touchdown plunge. At the end of three quarters, the 49ers led 21–17.

Both teams rose to their fullest stature in the final period, with the young 49ers standing up to the veteran Cowboys. Raphael Septien kicked a 22-yard field goal early in the quarter to close the gap to 21-20. Midway through the period, the Cowboys launched an offensive which ended in Doug Cosbie's touchdown on a pass from Danny White. With the extra point, the Cowboys led 27–21.

With just under five minutes left on the clock, the 49ers began a do-or-die drive from their own 10-yard line. Joe Montana moved his team downfield on pinpoint passes and some hard-fought running gains, taking his team to the Dallas six-yard line. On third down, Montana rolled to the right and, eluding Larry Bethea, threw to Dwight Clark for the go-ahead touchdown. The Cowboys began moving downfield after the kickoff, but a fumble by Danny White was recovered by the 49ers, who killed off the clock and prepared for the Super Bowl.

## INDIVIDUAL STATISTICS

### RUSHING

| DALLAS | No. | Yds. | Avg. | SAN FRANCISCO | No. | Yds. | Avg. |
|---|---|---|---|---|---|---|---|
| Dorsett | 22 | 91 | 4.1 | Elliott | 10 | 48 | 4.8 |
| J. Jones | 4 | 14 | 3.5 | Cooper | 8 | 35 | 4.4 |
| Springs | 5 | 10 | 2.0 | Ring | 6 | 27 | 4.5 |
| D. White | 1 | 0 | 0.0 | Solomon | 1 | 14 | 14.0 |
| | 32 | 115 | 3.6 | Easley | 2 | 6 | 3.0 |
| | | | | Davis | 1 | 2 | 2.0 |
| | | | | Montana | 3 | –5 | –1.7 |
| | | | | | 31 | 127 | 5.0 |

### RECEIVING

| DALLAS | No. | Yds. | Avg. | SAN FRANCISCO | No. | Yds. | Avg. |
|---|---|---|---|---|---|---|---|
| J. Jones | 3 | 17 | 5.7 | Clark | 8 | 120 | 15.0 |
| DuPree | 3 | 15 | 5.0 | Solomon | 6 | 75 | 12.5 |
| Springs | 3 | 13 | 4.3 | Young | 4 | 45 | 11.3 |
| Hill | 2 | 43 | 21.5 | Cooper | 2 | 11 | 5.5 |
| Pearson | 1 | 31 | 31.0 | Elliott | 1 | 24 | 24.0 |
| Cosbie | 1 | 21 | 21.0 | Shumann | 1 | 11 | 11.0 |
| Johnson | 1 | 20 | 20.0 | | 22 | 286 | 13.0 |
| Saldi | 1 | 9 | 9.0 | | | | |
| Donley | 1 | 4 | 4.0 | | | | |
| | 16 | 173 | 10.8 | | | | |

### PUNTING

| DALLAS | No. | Yds. | Avg. | SAN FRANCISCO | No. | Yds. | Avg. |
|---|---|---|---|---|---|---|---|
| D. White | 6 | | 39.3 | Miller | 3 | | 35.7 |

### PUNT RETURNS

| DALLAS | No. | Yds. | Avg. | SAN FRANCISCO | No. | Yds. | Avg. |
|---|---|---|---|---|---|---|---|
| J. Jones | 3 | 13 | 4.3 | Hicks | 2 | 21 | 10.5 |
| | | | | Solomon | 1 | 3 | 3.0 |
| | | | | | 3 | 24 | 8.0 |

### KICKOFF RETURNS

| DALLAS | No. | Yds. | Avg. | SAN FRANCISCO | No. | Yds. | Avg. |
|---|---|---|---|---|---|---|---|
| J. Jones | 3 | 56 | 18.7 | Lawrence | 3 | 60 | 20.0 |
| Newsome | 2 | 33 | 16.5 | Ring | 3 | 47 | 15.7 |
| | 5 | 89 | 17.8 | | 6 | 107 | 17.8 |

### INTERCEPTION RETURNS

| DALLAS | No. | Yds. | Avg. | SAN FRANCISCO | No. | Yds. | Avg. |
|---|---|---|---|---|---|---|---|
| Walls | 2 | 0 | 0.0 | Leopold | 1 | 5 | 5.0 |
| R. White | 1 | 0 | 0.0 | | | | |
| | 3 | 0 | 0.0 | | | | |

### PASSING

| DALLAS | Att. | Comp. | Comp. Pct. | Yds. | Int. | Yds./ Att. | Yds./ Comp. |
|---|---|---|---|---|---|---|---|
| D. White | 24 | 16 | 66.7 | 173 | 1 | 7.2 | 10.8 |

| SAN FRANCISCO | Att. | Comp. | Comp. Pct. | Yds. | Int. | Yds./ Att. | Yds./ Comp. |
|---|---|---|---|---|---|---|---|
| Montana | 33 | 25 | 75.8 | 286 | 3 | 8.7 | 13.0 |

---

## SCORING

| | | | | |
|---|---|---|---|---|
| SAN DIEGO | 0 | 7 | 0 | 0— 7 |
| CINCINNATI | 10 | 7 | 3 | 7—27 |

**First Quarter**
Cin. — Breech, 31 yard field goal
Cin. — M. Harris, 8 yard pass from Anderson
PAT–Breech (kick)

**Second Quarter**
S.D. — Winslow, 33 yard pass from Fouts
PAT–Benirschke (kick)
Cin. — Johnson, 1 yard rush
PAT–Breech (kick)

**Third Quarter**
Cin. — Breech, 38 yard field goal

**Fourth Quarter**
Cin. — Bass, 3 yard pass from Anderson
PAT–Breech (kick)

## TEAM STATISTICS

| SAN DIEGO | | CIN. |
|---|---|---|
| 18 | First Downs–Total | 19 |
| 11 | First Downs–Rushing | 8 |
| 7 | First Downs–Passing | 11 |
| 0 | First Downs–Penalty | 0 |
| 4 | Fumbles–Number | 3 |
| 2 | Fumbles–Lost Ball | 1 |
| 2 | Penalty–Number | 3 |
| 15 | Yards Penalized | 25 |
| 2 | Missed Field Goals | 0 |
| 61 | Offensive Plays | 59 |
| 301 | Net Yards | 318 |
| 4.9 | Average Gain | 5.4 |
| 4 | Giveaways | 1 |
| 1 | Takeaways | 4 |
| –3 | Difference | –3 |

The weather was the story. At gametime in Cincinnati, the temperature was 11 below zero, with a stiff wind driving the wind chill factor down to 59 below. Pete Rozelle even considered postponing the game, but after collecting medical opinions, he ordered the game to start. 46,302 fanatics were in their seats, warmed internally and externally by a variety of devices.

Onto the Riverfront Stadium tundra charged the Bengals and Chargers, both expert practitioners of the forward pass. The Bengals were coming off a 28–21 victory over Buffalo, while the Chargers arrived here after downing Miami 41–38 in an overtime slugfest. In the extreme conditions prevailing on this day, predictions were impossible to make.

The Bengals got onto the scoreboard early, with Jim Breech booting a 31-yard field goal. On the following kickoff, James Brooks fumbled and the Bengals recovered on the 12-yard line. A short pass from Ken Anderson to M.L. Harris quickly made the score 10–0.

San Diego's Dan Fouts had trouble passing in the wind-swept freeze, but he did throw a 33-yard scoring strike to Kellen Winslow in the second quarter to cut the score to 10–7. Fouts led the Chargers deep into Cincinnati territory two other times, but threw interceptions to end the drives. With momentum up for grabs, the Bengals drove to another touchdown before the half to take a 17-7 lead into the clubhouse.

The San Diego attack remained stuck in the second half, while the Bengals adapted to the conditions to grind out ten more points. Breech kicked another field goal, and Anderson threw a touchdown pass to Don Bass. It was cold for both the teams on the field, and the Bengals played well enough in discomfort to earn a ticket to the Super Bowl.

## INDIVIDUAL STATISTICS

### RUSHING

| SAN DIEGO | No. | Yds. | Avg. | CINCINNATI | No. | Yds. | Avg. |
|---|---|---|---|---|---|---|---|
| Muncie | 23 | 94 | 4.1 | Johnson | 21 | 80 | 3.6 |
| Brooks | 6 | 23 | 3.8 | Anderson | 5 | 39 | 7.8 |
| Fouts | 1 | 6 | 6.0 | Alexander | 9 | 22 | 2.4 |
| Cappelletti | 1 | 5 | 5.0 | Collinsworth | 1 | 2 | 2.0 |
| | 31 | 128 | 4.1 | | 36 | 143 | 4.0 |

### RECEIVING

| SAN DIEGO | No. | Yds. | Avg. | CINCINNATI | No. | Yds. | Avg. |
|---|---|---|---|---|---|---|---|
| Chandler | 6 | 79 | 13.2 | Ross | 5 | 69 | 13.8 |
| Winslow | 3 | 47 | 15.7 | Alexander | 3 | 25 | 8.3 |
| Joiner | 3 | 41 | 13.7 | Collinsworth | 2 | 28 | 14.0 |
| Brooks | 2 | 5 | 2.5 | Curtis | 2 | 28 | 14.0 |
| Sievers | 1 | 13 | 13.0 | Johnson | 1 | 14 | 14.0 |
| | 15 | 185 | 12.3 | M. Harris | 1 | 8 | 8.0 |
| | | | | Bass | 1 | 3 | 3.0 |
| | | | | | 15 | 175 | 11.7 |

### PUNTING

| SAN DIEGO | No. | Yds. | Avg. | CINCINNATI | No. | Yds. | Avg. |
|---|---|---|---|---|---|---|---|
| Roberts | 2 | | 29.5 | McInally | 3 | | 30.6 |

### PUNT RETURNS

| SAN DIEGO | No. | Yds. | Avg. | CINCINNATI | No. | Yds. | Avg. |
|---|---|---|---|---|---|---|---|
| Chandler | 1 | 7 | 7.0 | none | | | |

### KICKOFF RETURNS

| SAN DIEGO | No. | Yds. | Avg. | CINCINNATI | No. | Yds. | Avg. |
|---|---|---|---|---|---|---|---|
| Brooks | 4 | 87 | 21.8 | Verser | 1 | 40 | 40.0 |
| Shaw | 1 | 7 | 7.0 | | | | |
| | 5 | 94 | 18.8 | | | | |

### INTERCEPTION RETURNS

| SAN DIEGO | No. | Yds. | Avg. | CINCINNATI | No. | Yds. | Avg. |
|---|---|---|---|---|---|---|---|
| none | | | | Kemp | 1 | 24 | 24.0 |
| | | | | Breeden | 1 | 0 | 0.0 |
| | | | | | 2 | 24 | 12.0 |

### PASSING

| SAN DIEGO | Att. | Comp. | Comp. Pct. | Yds. | Int. | Yds./ Att. | Yds./ Comp. |
|---|---|---|---|---|---|---|---|
| Fouts | 28 | 15 | 53.6 | 185 | 2 | 6.6 | 12.3 |

| CINCINNATI | Att. | Comp. | Comp. Pct. | Yds. | Int. | Yds./ Att. | Yds./ Comp. |
|---|---|---|---|---|---|---|---|
| Anderson | 22 | 14 | 63.6 | 161 | 0 | 7.3 | 11.5 |
| Thompson | 1 | 1 | 100.0 | 14 | 0 | 14.0 | 14.0 |
| | 23 | 15 | 65.2 | 175 | 0 | 7.6 | 11.7 |

# Striking Gold at the Silverdome

There was no Goliath, only two Davids who had risen up to slay all the giants in their way. Both the Bengals and the 49ers had lost regularly in recent years, and they were given little pre-season hope of any playoff appearance. Coaches Bill Walsh of San Francisco and Forrest Gregg of Cincinnati led their overachievers into the first Super Bowl staged outside the Sun Belt. While the countryside was gripped by a bitter Michigan winter, the players and fans settled in for an afternoon of football in the comfortable Pontiac Silverdome.

Cincinnati kicked off and immediately grabbed a fumble by Amos Lawrence. Stunned by the sudden change of fortune, the 49ers allowed the Bengals to drive to the five-yard line. Regaining their composure, the 49ers sacked Ken Anderson for a six-yard loss, then picked off his next pass to end the threat.

Joe Montana then led his mates to a sustained drive downfield. He completed several passes while rolling out, and he also took part in a flea-flicker play which gained 14 yards. On the eleventh play of the drive, Montana dived over for a touchdown.

In the second quarter, the Bengals moved deep into Cincinnati turf only to lose the ball on Chris Collinsworth's fumble. Starting on the eight-yard line, Montana moved his team with passes and hit Earl Cooper with a scoring strike to make the score 14–0. With 15 seconds left on the first-half clock, Ray Wersching kicked a field goal for a 17–0 lead. On the kickoff, Archie Griffin fumbled and the 49ers recovered, setting Wersching up for another chip shot and a 20-0 lead.

The Bengals returned for the second half faced with the most one-sided score in Super Bowl history. They took the kickoff and relit their spirits with an 83-yard drive for a touchdown. Along the way, they delighted fans with a razzle-dazzle play to match that of the 49ers in the first half. For the rest of the third quarter, the score stayed at 20-7. Although the Bengals upped the score to 20–14 in the fourth quarter, the 49ers recaptured the momentum by stopping the Bengals on downs on the one-yard line, shutting down powerful fullback Pete Johnson on fourth down. Two more field goals by Wersching padded the San Francisco lead and paved the road to the 26–21 triumph. Of the two Cinderella teams, the 49ers had played in their usual loose style, while the Bengals looked as if the pressure was riding their backs.

## LINEUPS

| CINCINNATI | | SAN FRANCISCO |
|---|---|---|
| | OFFENSE | |
| Collinsworth | WR | Clark |
| Munoz | LT | Audick |
| Lapham | LG | Ayers |
| Bush | C | Quillan |
| Mantoya | RG | Cross |
| Wilson | RT | Fahnhorst |
| Ross | TE | Young |
| Curtis | WR | Solomon |
| Anderson | QB | Montana |
| Alexander | HB | Patton |
| Johnson | FB | Cooper |
| | DEFENSE | |
| St. Clair | LE | Stuckey |
| Whitley | NT | Reese |
| Browner | RT | Board |
| B. Harris | LLB | Harper |
| LeClair | LLB | Reynolds |
| Cameron | RLB | Puki |
| Williams | RLB | Turner |
| Breeden | LCB | Lott |
| Riley | RCB | Wright |
| Kemp | SS | Williamson |
| Hicks | FS | Hicks |

### SUBSTITUTES

**CINCINNATI**

OFFENSE

| | | |
|---|---|---|
| Bass | Kreider | Obrovac |
| A. Griffin | McInally | Schonert |
| Hargrove | Moore | Thompson |
| M. Harris | | Verser |

DEFENSE

| | | |
|---|---|---|
| Burley | Frazier | R. Griffin |
| Davis | Fuller | Razzano |
| Dinkel | Horn | Schuh |
| Edwards | | Simmons |

KICKER

Breech

**SAN FRANCISCO**

OFFENSE

| | | |
|---|---|---|
| Benjamin | Easley | Ramson |
| Choma | Elliott | Ring |
| Davis | Kennedy | Schumann |
| Downing | Lawrence | Wilson |

DEFENSE

| | | |
|---|---|---|
| Bunz | Harty | McColl |
| Dean | Leopold | Pillers |
| Gervais | Martin | Thomas |

KICKERS

Miller          Wersching

## SCORING

| | 1 | 2 | 3 | 4 | |
|---|---|---|---|---|---|
| CINCINNATI | 0 | 0 | 7 | 14 | 21 |
| SAN FRANCISCO | 7 | 13 | 0 | 6 | 26 |

**First Quarter**
S.F.     Montana, 1 yard rush
         PAT–Wersching (kick)

**Second Quarter**
S.F.     Cooper, 11 yard pass from Montana
         PAT–Wersching (kick)
S.F.     Wersching, 22 yard field goal
S.F.     Wersching, 26 yard field goal

**Third Quarter**
Cin.     Anderson, 5 yard rush
         PAT–Breech (kick)

**Fourth Quarter**
Cin.     Ross, 4 yard pass from Anderson
         PAT–Breech (kick)
S.F.     Wersching, 40 yard field goal
S.F.     Wersching, 23 yard field goal
Cin.     Ross, 3 yard pass from Anderson
         PAT–Breech (kick)

## TEAM STATISTICS

| CIN. | | S.F. |
|---|---|---|
| 24 | First Downs–Total | 20 |
| 7 | First Downs–Rushing | 9 |
| 13 | First Downs–Passing | 9 |
| 4 | First Downs–Penalty | 2 |
| 2 | Fumbles–Number | 2 |
| 2 | Fumbles–Lost Ball | 1 |
| 8 | Penalties–Number | 8 |
| 57 | Yards Penalized | 65 |
| 0 | Missed Field Goals | 0 |
| 63 | Offensive Plays | 63 |
| 356 | Net Yards | 275 |
| 5.7 | Average Gain | 4.4 |
| 4 | Giveaways | 1 |
| 1 | Takeaways | 4 |
| – 3 | Difference | – 3 |

## INDIVIDUAL STATISTICS

### RUSHING

| CINCINNATI | No. | Yds. | Avg. | SAN FRANCISCO | No. | Yds. | Avg. |
|---|---|---|---|---|---|---|---|
| Johnson | 14 | 36 | 2.6 | Patton | 17 | 55 | 3.2 |
| Alexander | 5 | 17 | 3.4 | Cooper | 9 | 34 | 3.8 |
| Anderson | 4 | 15 | 3.8 | Montana | 6 | 18 | 3.0 |
| A. Griffin | 1 | 4 | 4.0 | Ring | 5 | 17 | 3.4 |
| | 24 | 72 | 3.0 | Davis | 2 | 5 | 2.5 |
| | | | | Clark | 1 | – 2 | – 2.0 |
| | | | | | 40 | 127 | 3.2 |

### RECEIVING

| | No. | Yds. | Avg. | | No. | Yds. | Avg. |
|---|---|---|---|---|---|---|---|
| Ross | 11 | 104 | 9.5 | Solomon | 4 | 52 | 13.0 |
| Collinsworth | 5 | 107 | 21.4 | Clark | 4 | 45 | 11.3 |
| Curtis | 3 | 42 | 14.0 | Cooper | 2 | 15 | 7.5 |
| Kreider | 2 | 36 | 18.0 | Wilson | 1 | 22 | 22.0 |
| Johnson | 2 | 8 | 4.0 | Young | 1 | 14 | 14.0 |
| Alexander | 2 | 3 | 1.5 | Patton | 1 | 6 | 6.0 |
| | 25 | 300 | 12.0 | Ring | 1 | 3 | 3.0 |
| | | | | | 14 | 157 | 11.2 |

### PUNTING

| | No. | | Avg. | | No. | | Avg. |
|---|---|---|---|---|---|---|---|
| McInally | 3 | | 43.7 | Miller | 4 | | 46.3 |

### PUNT RETURNS

| | No. | Yds. | Avg. | | No. | Yds. | Avg. |
|---|---|---|---|---|---|---|---|
| Fuller | 4 | 35 | 8.8 | Hicks | 1 | 6 | 6.0 |

### KICKOFF RETURNS

| | No. | Yds. | Avg. | | No. | Yds. | Avg. |
|---|---|---|---|---|---|---|---|
| Verser | 5 | 52 | 10.4 | Hicks | 1 | 23 | 23.0 |
| Frazier | 1 | 0 | 0.0 | Lawrence | 1 | 17 | 17.0 |
| A. Griffin | 1 | 0 | 0.0 | Clark | 1 | 0 | 0.0 |
| | 7 | 52 | 7.4 | | 3 | 40 | 13.3 |

### INTERCEPTION RETURNS

| | No. | Yds. | Avg. | | No. | Yds. | Avg. |
|---|---|---|---|---|---|---|---|
| none | | | | Hicks | 1 | 27 | 27.0 |
| | | | | Wright | 1 | 25 | 25.0 |
| | | | | | 2 | 52 | 26.0 |

### PASSING

| CINCINNATI | Att. | Comp. | Comp. Pct. | Yds. | Int. | Yds./ Att. | Yds./ Comp. | Yards Lost Tackled |
|---|---|---|---|---|---|---|---|---|
| Anderson | 34 | 25 | 73.5 | 300 | 2 | 8.8 | 12.0 | 9–16 |
| **SAN FRANCISCO** | | | | | | | | |
| Montana | 22 | 14 | 63.6 | 157 | 0 | 7.1 | 11.2 | 1–9 |

# 1982 N.F.C.    From Strike to a Long Season

The N.F.L. Players Association presented a set of demands unseen in any other pro sport. The old labor agreement expired in July, leaving the fate of the 1982 season in the hands of hard-bitten negotiators. Ed Garvey, executive director of the union, wanted the team owners to set aside 55 percent of gross revenues from all sources as a pool for player salaries; players would receive a salary determined by a formula which considered experience and playing excellence. The union did not demand more liberal free agency as its primary objective, emphasizing instead a guaranteed piece of the pie. Jack Donlan, the negotiator for the owners, scoffed at the proposal as socialistic. Although both sides compromised as they talked, the players finally went out on strike after the second week of play.

The sudden stoppage of play left a television vacuum that was filled by Canadian Football League games, the World Series and sundry other sporting events. On the first weekend of the strike, some fans held tailgate parties outside empty ballparks, and some radio stations broadcast fantasy versions of canceled games. As the strike dragged on, however, pro football stepped down in the national consciousness. The union staged all-star games in Washington on October 17 and in Los Angeles on October 18. Very few stars played, and very few fans paid or cared. Fifty-seven days after it began, the strike ended on November 16 with an agreement that left the basic structure of the game untouched. Players would still negotiate individual contracts, but the owners agreed that total player salaries for 1983-86 would total at least $1.28 billion. In addition, minimum salaries were raised, severance pay was instituted, and a fund of $60 million was set aside as a one-time bonus for the players.

Play resumed on November 21 with a revamped playoff scheme. Regular-season play was extended through the first weekend of January. The wild-card weekend and the open weekend before the Super Bowl were eliminated. Eight teams from each conference would make the playoffs and then fight through January for the N.F.L. title. Despite grumbling by fans and low attendance in some cities, the post-strike season regenerated interest, which reached its usual frenzied peak in the Super Bowl.

## EASTERN DIVISION

**Washington Redskins** — The Redskins made the fewest mistakes and had the most nicknames in the N.F.L. The improved offensive line was known as the Hogs, the corps of small receivers as the Smurfs, and the players who celebrated touchdowns with choreographed endzone high-fives as the Fun Bunch. Such nicknames sprang from the joy of Washington's first playoff berth since 1976. Strong finishers last year, the Skins won their first two games and continued their polished play after the strike. The offense prospered with Joe Theismann's high-percentage passing and John Riggins' relentless plowing behind the Hogs. Although Mike Nelms starred as a kick returner, the ace of the special teams was kicker Mark Moseley. He clicked on a miraculous 20-of-21 field-goal attempts, a performance so impressive that he won the league MVP award. The Skins lost only to the Cowboys and relished the prospect of a rematch in the playoffs.

**Dallas Cowboys** — An embarrassing 36-28 loss to the Steelers on the opening Monday night augured ill for the Cowboys. They did win their second game and then asserted their usual dominance by winning their first five games after the strike. This drive clinched a playoff spot and included a strong 24-10 victory in Washington. The defense overcame the retirements of Charlie Waters and D.D. Lewis, relying heavily on linemen Too Tall Jones, Harvey Martin and Randy White. Everson Walls capitalized on the strong pass rush to lead the N.F.C. in rushing, and Danny White ranked near the top in passing. Losses in the last two games, however, caused a little nervousness going into the playoffs.

**St. Louis Cardinals** — The Cards edged into the expanded playoffs for the first time since 1975 by winning two of their last three games. Although they didn't score points at a rapid rate, the Cards fielded good young talent in quarterback Neil Lomax, runner Ottis Anderson and receiver Roy Green. At the other end of the spectrum were receiver Mel Gray and cornerback Roger Wehrli, finishing their long careers in secondary roles.

**New York Giants** — Last year's magic faded and the Giants tumbled once again out of the playoffs. On offense, quarterback Phil Simms went out with a pre-season knee injury. Fullback Rob Carpenter joined him on the sidelines until December in a contract dispute. The defense stayed tough, showcasing stars in Lawrence Taylor, Harry Carson and Mark Haynes, and kept the Giants in the running for a playoff berth. On December 15, coach Ray Perkins announced that he would leave at the end of the season to succeed Bear Bryant at the University of Alabama. The Giants promptly dropped close games to the Redskins and Cardinals to poison their chances. They edged the Eagles in the finale but lost out on the tiebreaking formula.

**Philadelphia Eagles** — The Eagles had been flying high as recently as last November. They stumbled in the home stretch then, and they plunged to the depths this year by losing their first four games after the strike. The offense put points on the board regularly, but the defense lost its shape and crispness. It survived the loss of Bill Bergey last year, but the trade of Charles Johnson during training camp was too much to absorb. Johnson had expressed his unhappiness with the severe regime of Dick Vermeil, prompting his swap to Minnesota. The Eagles perhaps suffered a case of burnout, and Vermeil would quit after the season to seek a less-consuming job.

## CENTRAL DIVISION

**Green Bay Packers** — Last year's strong finish carried over into a stirring opening game. The Rams raced to a 23-0 halftime lead, but the embarrassed Pack stormed back to win the game 35-23. One week later, they trailed the Jets 19-7 in the third quarter, yet triumphed by a 27-19 score. They played only .500 ball after the strike, but that was good enough for a playoff berth, the first in Bart Starr's eight-year reign. The team's heart was its passing attack, with Lynn Dickey throwing to James Lofton and John Jefferson. Eddie Lee Ivery made his second comeback from knee surgery to handle the heavy running duties. Despite the hot-and-cold late season, the Pack still finished with the third-best record in the N.F.C.

**Minnesota Vikings** — Bud Grant put last year's collapse behind him and led his Vikings back into the playoffs. He programmed his offense to pass the ball about 80 percent of the time, and Tommy Kramer's strong arm made it work. Ted Brown caught a lot of passes coming out of the backfield and was the team's only effective runner. First-round draft pick Darrin Nelson never settled in as Brown's running mate. The Vikes never put together a winning streak, but they earned their post-season appearance by avoiding losing streaks.

**Tampa Bay Buccaneers** — Two pre-strike losses put the Bucs in a weak position when play resumed. With three weeks remaining, they had a 2-4 record and only slight hopes of a playoff spot. John McKay engineered a late-season drive, which earned the Bucs a place in the second season. They swept their last three games, finishing with a 26-23 overtime victory over the Bears. The offense moved primarily on Doug Williams' arm, with fullback James Wilder both the leading receiver and leading runner. The defense ranked with the N.F.L.'s best, combining mobility with hard hitting. The Bucs had stars in each defensive area; end Lee Roy Selmon rushed passers to distraction, linebacker Hugh Green swarmed the field and safety Neal Colzie policed the secondary with an iron hand.

**Detroit Lions** — The strike hurt the Lions more than anyone. They swept their first two games, then joined the rest of the league on the sidelines. Once play resumed, the Lions lost their edge and dropped their first three games. They regained their stride on December 12 by beating the Packers 30-10. Two more losses followed, reducing Detroit's record to 3-5. A 27-24 victory over the Packers in the finale salvaged a playoff spot despite the team's losing record. Monte Clark had stars in runner Billy Sims and defensive tackle Doug English, but he never got consistent work from either of his quarterbacks, Eric Hipple and Gary Danielson.

**Chicago Bears** — The Bears reached back into their glorious past by hiring Mike Ditka as their new head coach. A star on the 1963 championship team, Ditka brought a disciplined, hard-nosed attitude to the anemic Bears. Despite Ditka's changes,

FINAL TEAM STATISTICS

OFFENSE

| | ATL. | CHI. | DALL. | DET. | G.B. | L.A. | MINN. | N.O. | NY G | PHIL. | STL. | S.F. | T.B. | WASH. |
|---|---|---|---|---|---|---|---|---|---|---|---|---|---|---|
| FIRST DOWNS: | | | | | | | | | | | | | | |
| Total | 190 | 153 | 180 | 160 | 175 | 163 | 167 | 173 | 153 | 157 | 162 | 183 | 163 | 165 |
| by Rushing | 79 | 56 | 70 | 60 | 59 | 61 | 52 | 79 | 47 | 48 | 71 | 49 | 52 | 66 |
| by Passing | 92 | 83 | 99 | 83 | 97 | 90 | 107 | 76 | 96 | 100 | 81 | 121 | 105 | 87 |
| by Penalty | 19 | 14 | 11 | 17 | 19 | 12 | 8 | 18 | 10 | 9 | 10 | 13 | 6 | 12 |
| RUSHING: | | | | | | | | | | | | | | |
| Number | 310 | 276 | 296 | 283 | 283 | 251 | 245 | 331 | 244 | 211 | 307 | 219 | 268 | 315 |
| Yards | 1181 | 988 | 1313 | 1022 | 1081 | 1025 | 912 | 1257 | 842 | 829 | 1209 | 740 | 952 | 1140 |
| Average Yards | 3.8 | 3.6 | 4.4 | 3.6 | 3.8 | 4.1 | 3.7 | 3.8 | 3.5 | 3.9 | 3.9 | 3.4 | 3.6 | 3.6 |
| Touchdowns | 12 | 5 | 10 | 5 | 12 | 13 | 6 | 8 | 7 | 11 | 10 | 6 | 6 | 5 |
| PASSING: | | | | | | | | | | | | | | |
| Attempts | 275 | 262 | 258 | 285 | 267 | 297 | 334 | 248 | 298 | 288 | 240 | 348 | 308 | 253 |
| Completions | 176 | 141 | 160 | 136 | 143 | 166 | 187 | 137 | 161 | 168 | 129 | 215 | 164 | 162 |
| Completion Pct. | 64.0 | 53.8 | 62.0 | 47.7 | 53.6 | 55.9 | 56.0 | 55.2 | 54.0 | 58.3 | 53.8 | 61.8 | 53.2 | 64.0 |
| Passing Yards | 1992 | 1749 | 2150 | 1754 | 2068 | 2136 | 2105 | 1571 | 2017 | 2100 | 1576 | 2668 | 2071 | 2068 |
| Avg. Yds per Att. | 5.9 | 5.1 | 6.7 | 4.8 | 6.1 | 6.4 | 5.5 | 5.2 | 6.0 | 5.8 | 4.9 | 6.8 | 6.1 | 6.5 |
| Avg. Yds per Comp. | 11.3 | 12.4 | 13.4 | 12.9 | 14.5 | 12.9 | 11.3 | 11.5 | 12.5 | 12.5 | 12.2 | 12.4 | 12.6 | 12.8 |
| Times Tackled | 25 | 33 | 25 | 30 | 32 | 15 | 22 | 23 | 17 | 31 | 32 | 20 | 11 | 30 |
| Yds Lost Tackled | 210 | 244 | 264 | 242 | 239 | 137 | 138 | 173 | 130 | 244 | 243 | 166 | 128 | 223 |
| Net Yards | 1782 | 1505 | 1886 | 1512 | 1829 | 1999 | 1967 | 1398 | 1887 | 1856 | 1333 | 2502 | 1943 | 1845 |
| Touchdowns | 9 | 10 | 16 | 12 | 12 | 11 | 15 | 8 | 10 | 12 | 6 | 17 | 9 | 13 |
| Interceptions | 11 | 11 | 14 | 18 | 15 | 14 | 12 | 14 | 9 | 13 | 6 | 11 | 11 | 9 |
| Pct. Intercepted | 4.0 | 4.2 | 5.4 | 6.3 | 5.6 | 4.7 | 3.6 | 5.6 | 3.0 | 4.5 | 2.5 | 3.2 | 3.6 | 3.6 |
| PUNTS: | | | | | | | | | | | | | | |
| Number | 43 | 59 | 37 | 48 | 42 | 46 | 58 | 46 | 49 | 44 | 54 | 45 | 40 | 52 |
| Average | 39.3 | 41.6 | 41.7 | 40.9 | 40.2 | 42.6 | 41.1 | 43.0 | 42.8 | 40.5 | 43.8 | 37.2 | 40.5 | 37.3 |
| PUNT RETURNS | | | | | | | | | | | | | | |
| Number | 24 | 24 | 30 | 26 | 26 | 22 | 24 | 21 | 44 | 22 | 32 | 30 | 25 | 38 |
| Yards | 273 | 142 | 242 | 275 | 198 | 242 | 196 | 144 | 373 | 108 | 192 | 332 | 143 | 295 |
| Average Yards | 11.4 | 5.9 | 8.1 | 10.8 | 7.6 | 11.0 | 8.2 | 6.9 | 8.5 | 4.9 | 6.0 | 11.1 | 5.7 | 7.8 |
| Touchdowns | 0 | 0 | 0 | 0 | 0 | 1 | 0 | 0 | 0 | 0 | 0 | 1 | 0 | 0 |
| KICKOFF RET.: | | | | | | | | | | | | | | |
| Number | 29 | 34 | 33 | 36 | 34 | 45 | 37 | 26 | 39 | 39 | 35 | 36 | 33 | 30 |
| Yards | 513 | 622 | 651 | 750 | 664 | 869 | 786 | 577 | 783 | 768 | 702 | 742 | 548 | 649 |
| Average Yards | 17.7 | 18.3 | 19.7 | 20.8 | 19.5 | 19.3 | 21.2 | 22.2 | 20.1 | 19.7 | 20.1 | 20.6 | 16.6 | 21.6 |
| Touchdowns | 0 | 0 | 0 | 1 | 0 | 0 | 0 | 0 | 0 | 0 | 0 | 0 | 0 | 0 |
| INTERCEPT RET.: | | | | | | | | | | | | | | |
| Number | 10 | 13 | 15 | 18 | 12 | 11 | 12 | 9 | 12 | 15 | 6 | 9 | 11 | 11 |
| Yards | 90 | 99 | 163 | 154 | 174 | 106 | 91 | 108 | 205 | 42 | 52 | 150 | 139 | 85 |
| Average Yards | 9.0 | 7.6 | 10.9 | 8.6 | 14.5 | 9.6 | 7.6 | 12.0 | 17.1 | 2.8 | 8.7 | 16.7 | 12.6 | 7.7 |
| Touchdowns | 0 | 1 | 1 | 1 | 0 | 0 | 1 | 0 | 1 | 1 | 0 | 1 | 0 | 0 |
| PENALTIES: | | | | | | | | | | | | | | |
| Number | 77 | 58 | 42 | 58 | 42 | 63 | 62 | 63 | 47 | 38 | 56 | 45 | 38 | 46 |
| Yards | 655 | 422 | 304 | 548 | 343 | 550 | 496 | 514 | 369 | 253 | 528 | 451 | 297 | 404 |
| FUMBLES: | | | | | | | | | | | | | | |
| Number | 14 | 16 | 29 | 23 | 20 | 23 | 12 | 17 | 19 | 26 | 17 | 17 | 28 | 15 |
| Number Lost | 10 | 8 | 12 | 8 | 11 | 10 | 5 | 10 | 10 | 10 | 10 | 10 | 12 | 7 |
| POINTS: | | | | | | | | | | | | | | |
| Total | 183 | 141 | 226 | 181 | 226 | 200 | 187 | 129 | 164 | 191 | 135 | 209 | 158 | 190 |
| PAT Attempts | 22 | 16 | 28 | 19 | 27 | 25 | 23 | 16 | 18 | 25 | 16 | 25 | 15 | 19 |
| PAT Made | 21 | 16 | 28 | 19 | 25 | 23 | 23 | 15 | 18 | 23 | 15 | 23 | 14 | 16 |
| FG Attempts | 14 | 20 | 14 | 17 | 18 | 15 | 14 | 13 | 21 | 9 | 13 | 17 | 23 | 21 |
| FG Made | 10 | 9 | 10 | 16 | 13 | 9 | 8 | 6 | 12 | 6 | 8 | 12 | 18 | 20 |
| Percent FG Made | 71.4 | 45.0 | 71.4 | 94.1 | 72.2 | 60.0 | 57.1 | 46.2 | 57.1 | 66.7 | 61.5 | 70.6 | 78.3 | 95.2 |
| Safeties | 0 | 1 | 0 | 0 | 0 | 0 | 1 | 0 | 1 | 0 | 0 | 0 | 0 | 0 |

DEFENSE

| | ATL. | CHI. | DALL. | DET. | G.B. | L.A. | MINN. | N.O. | NY G | PHIL. | STL. | S.F. | T.B. | WASH. |
|---|---|---|---|---|---|---|---|---|---|---|---|---|---|---|
| FIRST DOWNS: | | | | | | | | | | | | | | |
| Total | 170 | 166 | 162 | 162 | 164 | 193 | 159 | 151 | 149 | 177 | 163 | 170 | 160 | 151 |
| by Rushing | 66 | 53 | 56 | 54 | 58 | 75 | 53 | 58 | 55 | 68 | 58 | 71 | 72 | 47 |
| by Passing | 84 | 102 | 95 | 96 | 96 | 107 | 87 | 81 | 85 | 100 | 98 | 88 | 76 | 93 |
| by Penalty | 20 | 11 | 11 | 12 | 10 | 11 | 19 | 12 | 9 | 9 | 7 | 11 | 12 | 11 |
| RUSHING: | | | | | | | | | | | | | | |
| Number | 253 | 261 | 260 | 271 | 275 | 307 | 260 | 255 | 301 | 299 | 256 | 303 | 285 | 247 |
| Yards | 1044 | 902 | 1011 | 854 | 932 | 1202 | 1020 | 974 | 1118 | 1031 | 995 | 1199 | 1058 | 946 |
| Average Yards | 4.1 | 3.5 | 3.9 | 3.2 | 3.4 | 3.9 | 3.9 | 3.8 | 3.7 | 3.4 | 3.9 | 4.0 | 3.7 | 3.8 |
| Touchdowns | 13 | 4 | 5 | 6 | 9 | 13 | 8 | 8 | 7 | 5 | 5 | 9 | 9 | 8 |
| PASSING: | | | | | | | | | | | | | | |
| Attempts | 280 | 294 | 289 | 288 | 327 | 281 | 292 | 245 | 244 | 285 | 291 | 278 | 254 | 275 |
| Completions | 157 | 164 | 152 | 155 | 177 | 175 | 157 | 149 | 148 | 168 | 174 | 158 | 145 | 146 |
| Completion Pct. | 56.1 | 55.8 | 52.6 | 53.8 | 54.1 | 62.3 | 53.8 | 60.8 | 60.7 | 58.9 | 59.8 | 56.8 | 57.1 | 53.1 |
| Passing Yards | 1945 | 2189 | 2002 | 2098 | 1950 | 2290 | 2106 | 1864 | 1810 | 2136 | 2035 | 1949 | 1608 | 1870 |
| Avg. Yds per Att. | 6.1 | 6.0 | 5.4 | 5.8 | 5.1 | 7.1 | 5.8 | 5.9 | 5.7 | 6.1 | 5.9 | 6.3 | 5.0 | 5.3 |
| Avg. Yds per Comp. | 12.4 | 13.4 | 13.2 | 13.5 | 11.0 | 13.1 | 13.4 | 12.5 | 12.2 | 12.7 | 11.7 | 12.3 | 11.1 | 12.8 |
| Times Tackled | 18 | 30 | 32 | 32 | 20 | 18 | 30 | 31 | 31 | 30 | 23 | 15 | 25 | 32 |
| Yds Lost Tackled | 141 | 240 | 260 | 230 | 175 | 159 | 231 | 231 | 244 | 229 | 182 | 113 | 224 | 256 |
| Net Yards | 1804 | 1949 | 1742 | 1868 | 1775 | 2131 | 1875 | 1633 | 1566 | 1907 | 1853 | 1836 | 1384 | 1614 |
| Touchdowns | 12 | 14 | 10 | 11 | 9 | 16 | 11 | 11 | 10 | 14 | 16 | 14 | 10 | 8 |
| Interceptions | 10 | 13 | 15 | 18 | 12 | 11 | 12 | 9 | 12 | 15 | 6 | 9 | 11 | 11 |
| Pct. Intercepted | 3.6 | 4.4 | 5.2 | 6.3 | 3.7 | 3.9 | 4.1 | 3.7 | 4.9 | 5.3 | 2.1 | 3.2 | 4.3 | 4.0 |
| PUNTS: | | | | | | | | | | | | | | |
| Number | 38 | 49 | 49 | 46 | 46 | 42 | 50 | 51 | 59 | 38 | 51 | 50 | 42 | 56 |
| Average | 41.7 | 41.6 | 42.5 | 39.8 | 41.8 | 38.1 | 41.9 | 41.1 | 41.0 | 36.8 | 41.2 | 42.7 | 43.4 | 40.1 |
| PUNT RETURNS | | | | | | | | | | | | | | |
| Number | 24 | 34 | 21 | 26 | 27 | 31 | 30 | 29 | 25 | 31 | 36 | 20 | 23 | 30 |
| Yards | 197 | 314 | 118 | 237 | 286 | 401 | 176 | 239 | 207 | 316 | 288 | 224 | 192 | 106 |
| Average Yards | 8.2 | 9.2 | 5.6 | 9.1 | 10.6 | 12.9 | 5.9 | 8.2 | 8.3 | 10.2 | 8.0 | 11.2 | 8.3 | 3.5 |
| Touchdowns | 0 | 0 | 0 | 0 | 0 | 1 | 0 | 0 | 0 | 0 | 0 | 1 | 0 | 0 |
| KICKOFF RET.: | | | | | | | | | | | | | | |
| Number | 30 | 30 | 41 | 38 | 45 | 36 | 38 | 20 | 34 | 39 | 27 | 40 | 40 | 42 |
| Yards | 678 | 537 | 936 | 755 | 875 | 844 | 663 | 388 | 616 | 885 | 558 | 857 | 870 | 726 |
| Average Yards | 22.6 | 17.9 | 22.8 | 19.9 | 19.4 | 23.4 | 17.4 | 19.4 | 18.1 | 22.7 | 20.7 | 21.4 | 21.8 | 17.3 |
| Touchdowns | 0 | 0 | 0 | 0 | 1 | 0 | 0 | 0 | 0 | 0 | 0 | 0 | 0 | 0 |
| INTERCEPT RET.: | | | | | | | | | | | | | | |
| Number | 11 | 11 | 14 | 18 | 15 | 14 | 12 | 14 | 9 | 13 | 6 | 11 | 11 | 9 |
| Yards | 58 | 195 | 125 | 248 | 146 | 98 | 337 | 79 | 29 | 118 | 37 | 130 | 114 | 68 |
| Average Yards | 5.3 | 17.7 | 8.9 | 13.8 | 9.7 | 7.0 | 28.1 | 5.6 | 3.2 | 9.1 | 6.2 | 11.8 | 10.4 | 7.6 |
| Touchdowns | 0 | 2 | 1 | 1 | 0 | 0 | 3 | 0 | 0 | 0 | 0 | 0 | 1 | 0 |
| PENALTIES: | | | | | | | | | | | | | | |
| Number | 60 | 52 | 52 | 74 | 72 | 64 | 48 | 52 | 54 | 45 | 54 | 58 | 38 | 52 |
| Yards | 549 | 451 | 431 | 605 | 629 | 531 | 399 | 459 | 417 | 341 | 420 | 542 | 325 | 419 |
| FUMBLES: | | | | | | | | | | | | | | |
| Number | 24 | 20 | 20 | 21 | 26 | 15 | 22 | 23 | 19 | 20 | 14 | 14 | 15 | 23 |
| Number Lost | 15 | 7 | 10 | 8 | 11 | 7 | 9 | 13 | 6 | 12 | 9 | 4 | 10 | 13 |
| POINTS: | | | | | | | | | | | | | | |
| Total | 199 | 174 | 145 | 176 | 169 | 250 | 198 | 160 | 160 | 195 | 170 | 206 | 178 | 128 |
| PAT Attempts | 26 | 20 | 17 | 20 | 19 | 30 | 24 | 19 | 18 | 19 | 21 | 24 | 21 | 16 |
| PAT Made | 25 | 18 | 16 | 20 | 17 | 28 | 21 | 19 | 16 | 19 | 20 | 23 | 16 | 14 |
| FG Attempts | 12 | 17 | 15 | 21 | 18 | 19 | 19 | 12 | 13 | 22 | 18 | 19 | 17 | 9 |
| FG Made | 6 | 12 | 9 | 12 | 12 | 14 | 11 | 9 | 12 | 20 | 8 | 13 | 12 | 6 |
| Percent FG Made | 50.0 | 70.6 | 60.0 | 57.1 | 66.7 | 73.7 | 57.9 | 75.0 | 92.3 | 90.9 | 44.4 | 68.4 | 70.6 | 66.7 |
| Safeties | 0 | 0 | 0 | 0 | 1 | 0 | 0 | 0 | 0 | 1 | 0 | 0 | 0 | 0 |

they dropped their pre-strike games, the second a 10-0 humbling by the Saints. They won the first game after play resumed, with rookie Jim McMahon taking over as the starting quarterback. The Chicago offense sputtered the rest of the way, but the Bears no longer had a doormat look. Walter Payton still shone as an all-purpose offensive weapon. The defense featured the pass rushing of tackle Dan Hampton.

## WESTERN DIVISION

**Atlanta Falcons** — After a year out, the Falcons returned to the playoffs with a strong offense that covered for a weak defense. William Andrews and rookie Gerald Riggs ran well behind a big offensive line, which featured all-pros Mike Kenn, R.C. Thielemann and Jeff Van Note. The same blockers kept Steve Bartkowski healthy and gave him time to pass over run-conscious defenses. The Atlanta defense failed to mount a competent pass rush despite the return to form of Joel Williams. The Falcons made their season by winning four of their first five games after the strike. With a playoff date assured, they then looked horrible in their final two matches, losing 38-7 to Green Bay and 35-6 to New Orleans.

**New Orleans Saints** — It looked like the Saints were finally going to make the playoffs. Bum Phillips had built a good defense out of an unheralded group of players. His conservative offensive philosophy found perfect expression in George Rogers and Ken Stabler. Despite news that he had spent about $10,000 last year on cocaine, Rogers was the heavy-duty tank that could control the ball. Phillips signed Stabler after the Oilers cut the old quarterback loose during the summer. Given the QB job, Stabler used his guile to take the Saints to a 3-1 record at the start of December. With a post-season position within grasp, the Saints tragically dropped four straight games, including a 35-0 thumping by the Falcons on December 12. Despite the aches of frequent sackings, Stabler engineered a 35-6 vengeance over the Falcons in the season finale. The playoff berth, however, slipped away for still another year.

**San Francisco 49ers** — Three problem areas turned the Super Bowl champs into also-rans. The pedestrian ground attack actually lost some of its bite. The pass rush fell off considerably, with Dwaine Board hobbled by a bad knee and Fred Dean reaching quarterbacks less frequently. With the pass rush diminished, the young secondary began making the errors of inexperience. The season began with a 23-17 loss to the Raiders and a 24-21 loss at the final gun to the Broncos. After the strike, Joe Montana's passing and Dwight Clark's receiving kept the Niners competitive, but their problems kept them inconsistent. Their last shot at the playoffs died with a 21-20 loss to the Rams in the finale.

**Los Angeles Rams** — Opening day was a disaster, with the Rams blowing a 23-0 halftime lead and losing to the Packers 35-23. The Rams thereafter made it a regular practice to dissipate halftime leads. They fielded an absolutely porous defense, which nullified a pretty good offense. Two veteran quarterbacks joined the team, Bert Jones from the Colts and Vince Ferragamo from his one-year sojourn in Montreal. Jones began the season as the starter but went to the bench with a neck injury. Wendell Tyler, as usual, spearheaded the attack. The Rams ended a four-game losing streak by beating San Francisco in the finale, but that wasn't enough to save the job of Ray Malavasi, a Super Bowl coach only two years ago.

**WASHINGTON REDSKINS 8-1-0 Joe Gibbs**

| Scores of Each Game | | |
|---|---|---|
| 37 | Philadelphia | 34 |
| 21 | Tampa Bay | 13 |
| 27 | N.Y.Giants | 17 |
| 13 | PHILADELPHIA | 9 |
| 10 | DALLAS | 24 |
| 12 | St.Louis | 7 |
| 15 | N.Y.GIANTS | 14 |
| 27 | New Orleans | 10 |
| 28 | ST.LOUIS | 0 |

| Use Name | Pos. | Hgt | Wgt | Age | Int | Pts |
|---|---|---|---|---|---|---|
| Joe Jacoby | OT | 6'7" | 295 | 23 | | |
| Donald Laster | OT | 6'5" | 285 | 23 | | |
| Garry Puetz | OT | 6'4" | 255 | 30 | | |
| George Starke | OT | 6'5" | 260 | 34 | | |
| Fred Dean | OG | 6'3" | 255 | 27 | | |
| Russ Grimm | OG | 6'3" | 273 | 23 | | |
| Mark May | OG | 6'6" | 288 | 22 | | |
| Jeff Bostic | C | 6'2" | 245 | 23 | | |
| Todd Liebenstein | DE | 6'6" | 245 | 22 | | |
| Dexter Manley | DE | 6'3" | 253 | 23 | 1 | |
| Tony McGee | DE | 6'4" | 250 | 33 | | |
| Mat Mandenhall | DE | 6'6" | 255 | 25 | | |
| Perry Brooks | DT | 6'3" | 265 | 27 | | |
| Dave Butz | DT | 6'7" | 295 | 32 | | |
| Darryl Grant | DT | 6'1" | 265 | 22 | | |
| Pat Ogrin | DR | 6'5" | 265 | 24 | | |
| Stuart Anderson | LB | 6'1" | 247 | 22 | | |
| Monte Coleman | LB | 6'2" | 235 | 24 | | |
| Pete Cronan | LB | 6'2" | 238 | 27 | | |
| Mel Kaufman | LB | 6'2" | 218 | 24 | | |
| Larry Kubin | LB | 6'2" | 234 | 23 | | |
| Quentin Lowry | LB | 6'3" | 225 | 24 | | |
| Rich Milot | LB | 6'4" | 237 | 25 | | |
| Neal Olkewicz | LB | 6' | 227 | 25 | | |
| Vernon Dean | DB | 5'11" | 178 | 23 | 3 | |
| Curtis Jordan | DB | 6'2" | 205 | 28 | | 6 |
| Joe Lavender | DB | 6'4" | 185 | 33 | | |
| LeCharls McDaniel | DB | 5'9" | 169 | 23 | 1 | |
| Mark Murphy | DB | 6'4" | 210 | 27 | 2 | |
| Mike Nelms | DB | 6'1" | 185 | 27 | | |
| Tony Peters | DB | 6'1" | 190 | 29 | 1 | |
| Jeris White | DB | 5'11" | 188 | 29 | 3 | |
| Greg Williams | DB | 5'11" | 185 | 23 | | |
| Bob Holly | QB | 6'2" | 205 | 22 | | |
| Tom Owen | QB | 6'1" | 194 | 30 | | |
| Joe Theismann | QB | 6' | 195 | 32 | | |
| Nick Giaquinto | HB-FB | 5'11" | 204 | 27 | | |
| Clarence Harmon | HB-FB | 5'11" | 209 | 26 | | 6 |
| Wilbur Jackson | HB | 6'1" | 219 | 30 | | |
| Joe Washington | HB | 5'10" | 179 | 28 | | 12 |
| John Riggins | FB | 6'2" | 235 | 33 | | 18 |
| Otis Wonsley | FB-HB | 5'10" | 214 | 25 | | 6 |
| Charlie Brown | WR | 5'10" | 179 | 23 | | 48 |
| Alvin Garrett | WR | 5'7" | 178 | 25 | | |
| Art Monk | WR | 6'3" | 209 | 24 | | 6 |
| Virgil Seay | WR | 5'8" | 175 | 24 | | |
| Rich Caster | TE | 6'5" | 230 | 33 | | |
| Clint Didier | TE | 6'5" | 240 | 23 | | 6 |
| Rick Walker | TE | 6'3" | 235 | 27 | | 6 |
| Don Warren | TE | 6'4" | 242 | 26 | | |
| Mike Williams | TE | 6'4" | 245 | 23 | | |
| Jeff Hayes | K | 5'11" | 175 | 23 | | |
| Mark Moseley | K | 5'11" | 205 | 34 | | 76 |

Rickey Claitt - Knee Injury
Cris Crissy - Fractured Cheeckbone

**DALLAS COWBOYS 6-3-0 Tom Landry**

| Scores of Each Game | | |
|---|---|---|
| 28 | PITTSBURGH | 36 |
| 24 | St.Louis | 7 |
| 14 | TAMPA BAY | 9 |
| 31 | CLEVELAND | 14 |
| 24 | Washington | 10 |
| 37 | Houston | 7 |
| 21 | NEW ORLEANS | 7 |
| 20 | PHILADELPHIA | 24 |
| 27 | Minnesota | 31 |

| Use Name | Pos. | Hgt | Wgt | Age | Int | Pts |
|---|---|---|---|---|---|---|
| Jim Cooper | OT | 6'5" | 263 | 26 | | |
| Pat Donovan | OT | 6'4" | 257 | 29 | | |
| Phil Pozderac | OT | 6'9" | 270 | 22 | | |
| Kurt Petersen | OG | 6'4" | 268 | 25 | | |
| Howard Richards | OG-OT | 6'6" | 258 | 23 | | |
| Herbert Scott | OG | 6'2" | 260 | 29 | | |
| Glen Titensor | OG-C | 6'4" | 260 | 24 | | |
| Steve Wright | OG-OT | 6'6" | 263 | 23 | | |
| Brian Baldinger | C-OG | 6'4" | 253 | 23 | | |
| Tom Rafferty | C-OG | 6'3" | 259 | 28 | | |
| Larry Bethea | DE-DT | 6'5" | 244 | 26 | | |
| Too Tall Jones | DE | 6'9" | 272 | 31 | 1 | |
| Harvey Martin | DE | 6'5" | 260 | 31 | | |
| John Dutton | DT | 6'7" | 275 | 31 | | |
| Don Smerek | DT-DE | 6'7" | 257 | 24 | | |
| Randy White | DT | 6'4" | 268 | 29 | | |
| Bob Breunig | LB | 6'2" | 225 | 29 | 1 | |
| Guy Brown | LB | 6'4" | 227 | 27 | | |
| Anthony Dickerson | LB | 6'2" | 222 | 25 | 1 | |
| Mike Hegman | LB | 6'1" | 228 | 29 | | |
| Angelo King | LB | 6'1" | 230 | 24 | | |
| Jeff Rohrer | LB | 6'3" | 232 | 23 | | |
| Danny Spradlin | LB | 6'1" | 241 | 23 | | |
| Benny Barnes | DB | 6'1" | 204 | 31 | | |
| Dextor Clinkscale | DB | 5'11" | 190 | 24 | 1 | |
| Micheal Downs | DB | 6'3" | 203 | 23 | 1 | 6 |
| Ron Fellows | DB | 6' | 174 | 23 | | |
| Rod Hill | DB | 6' | 182 | 23 | | |
| Monty Hunter | DB | 6' | 202 | 23 | | |
| Dennis Thurman | DB | 5'11" | 183 | 26 | 3 | 6 |
| Everson Walls | DB | 6'1" | 194 | 22 | 7 | |
| Glenn Carano | QB | 6'3" | 204 | 26 | | |
| Gary Hogeboom | QB | 6'4" | 199 | 24 | | |
| Danny White | QB | 6'2" | 196 | 30 | | |
| Brad Wright | QB | 6'2" | 209 | 23 | | |
| Tony Dorsett | HB | 5'11" | 192 | 28 | | 30 |
| James Jones | HB | 5'10" | 202 | 23 | | |
| Robert Newhouse | FB | 5'10" | 219 | 32 | | 6 |
| Timmy Newsome | FB | 6'1" | 231 | 24 | | 12 |
| George Peoples | FB | 6' | 211 | 22 | | |
| Ron Springs | FB-HB | 6'1" | 210 | 25 | | 24 |
| Doug Donley | WR | 6' | 173 | 23 | | |
| Tony Hill | WR | 6'2" | 198 | 26 | | 6 |
| Butch Johnson | WR | 6'1" | 187 | 28 | | 18 |
| Drew Pearson | WR | 6' | 193 | 31 | | 18 |
| Doug Cosbie | TE | 6'6" | 232 | 26 | | 24 |
| Billy Joe DuPree | TE | 6'4" | 223 | 32 | | 18 |
| Jay Saldi | TE | 6'3" | 230 | 27 | | |
| Rafael Septien | K | 5'10" | 180 | 28 | | 58 |

Robert Shaw - Knee Injury
Norman Wells - Knee Injury

**ST. LOUIS CARDINALS 5-4-0 Jim Hanifan**

| Scores of Each Game | | |
|---|---|---|
| 21 | New Orleans | 7 |
| 7 | DALLAS | 24 |
| 20 | SAN FRANCISCO | 31 |
| 23 | Atlanta | 20 |
| 23 | Philadelphia | 20 |
| 7 | WASHINGTON | 12 |
| 10 | Chicago | 7 |
| 24 | N.Y.GIANTS | 21 |
| 0 | Washington | 28 |

| Use Name | Pos. | Hgt | Wgt | Age | Int | Pts |
|---|---|---|---|---|---|---|
| Art Plunkett | OT | 6'7" | 270 | 23 | | |
| Tootie Robbins | OT | 6'5" | 278 | 24 | | |
| Luis Sharpe | OT | 6'4" | 260 | 22 | | |
| Joe Bostic | OT | 6'3" | 265 | 25 | | |
| George Collins | OG-OT | 6'2" | 270 | 26 | | |
| Terry Stieve | OG | 6'3" | 265 | 28 | | |
| Randy Clark | C | 6'3" | 254 | 25 | | |
| Dan Dierdorf | C | 6'4" | 290 | 33 | | |
| Curtis Greer | DE | 6'4" | 252 | 24 | | |
| Elois Grooms | DE | 6'4" | 250 | 29 | | |
| Stafford Mays | DE-DT | 6'2" | 250 | 24 | | |
| Rush Brown | DT | 6'2" | 260 | 28 | | |
| Mike Dawson | DT | 6'4" | 270 | 28 | 1 | |
| David Galloway | DT | 6'3" | 277 | 23 | | |
| Bruce Thornton | DT-DE | 6'5" | 263 | 24 | | |
| Dave Ahrens | LB | 6'3" | 228 | 23 | | |
| Kurt Allerman | LB | 6'2" | 222 | 27 | | |
| Charlie Baker | LB | 6'2" | 217 | 24 | | |
| Calvin Favron | LB | 6'1" | 227 | 25 | | |
| John Gillen | LB | 6'3" | 228 | 23 | | |
| E.J.Junior | LB | 6'3" | 235 | 22 | | |
| Craig Puki | LB | 6'1" | 231 | 25 | | |
| Craig Shaffer | LB | 6' | 230 | 23 | | |
| Carl Allen | DB | 6' | 190 | 26 | 1 | |
| Don Bessillieu | DB | 6'1" | 200 | 26 | | |
| Tim Collier (to SF) | DB | 6' | 176 | 28 | | |
| Ken Greene | DB | 6'3" | 205 | 26 | 1 | |
| Jeff Griffin | DB | 6' | 185 | 24 | 1 | |
| Lee Nelson | DB | 5'10" | 185 | 28 | 1 | |
| Benny Perrin | DB | 6'2" | 178 | 22 | 1 | |
| Dave Stief | DB | 6'3" | 195 | 26 | | |
| Roger Wehrli | DB | 6'1" | 194 | 34 | | 6 |
| Herb Williams | DB | 6' | 200 | 24 | | |
| Jim Hart | QB | 6'2" | 210 | 38 | | |
| Rusty Lisch | QB | 6'3" | 213 | 25 | | |
| Neil Lomax | QB | 6'3" | 215 | 23 | | 6 |
| Ottis Anderson | HB | 6'2" | 220 | 25 | | 18 |
| Will Harrell | HB | 5'8" | 182 | 29 | | |
| Stump Mitchell | HB | 5'9" | 188 | 23 | | 6 |
| Earl Ferrell | FB | 6' | 215 | 24 | | |
| Randy Love | FB | 6'1" | 205 | 25 | | |
| Wayne Morris | FB | 6' | 210 | 28 | | 24 |
| Mel Gray | WR | 5'9" | 175 | 33 | | |
| Roy Green | WR | 6' | 195 | 25 | | 18 |
| Mike Shumann | WR | 6' | 185 | 26 | | |
| Ken Thompson | WR | 6'1" | 178 | 23 | | |
| Ricky Thompson | WR | 6' | 177 | 28 | | |
| Pat Tilley | WR | 5'10" | 178 | 29 | | 12 |
| Greg LaFleur | TE | 6'4" | 236 | 23 | | 6 |
| Doug Marsh | TE | 6'3" | 240 | 24 | | |
| Eddie McGill | TE | 6'6" | 225 | 22 | | |
| Carl Birdsong | K | 6' | 192 | 23 | | |
| Neil O'Donoghue | K | 6'6" | 210 | 29 | | 39 |

Barney Cotton - Knee Injury

**NEW YORK GIANTS 4-5-0 Ray Perkins**

| Scores of Each Game | | |
|---|---|---|
| 14 | ATLANTA | 16 |
| 19 | GREEN BAY | 27 |
| 17 | WASHINGTON | 27 |
| 13 | Detroit | 6 |
| 17 | HOUSTON | 14 |
| 23 | PHILADELPHIA | 7 |
| 14 | Washington | 15 |
| 21 | St.Louis | 24 |
| 26 | Philadelphia | 24 |

| Use Name | Pos. | Hgt | Wgt | Age | Int | Pts |
|---|---|---|---|---|---|---|
| Rich Baldinger | OT | 6'4" | 270 | 22 | | |
| Brad Benson | OT | 6'3" | 258 | 26 | | |
| Gordon King | OT | 6'6" | 275 | 26 | | |
| Jeff Weston | OT | 6'5" | 280 | 25 | | |
| Billy Ard | OG | 6'3" | 250 | 23 | | |
| Bruce Kimball | OG | 6'2" | 260 | 26 | | |
| John Tautolo | OG | 6'3" | 260 | 23 | | |
| J.T.Turner | OG | 6'3" | 250 | 29 | | |
| Chris Foote | C | 6'3" | 250 | 25 | | |
| Ernie Hughes | C-OG | 6'3" | 265 | 27 | | |
| Rich Umphrey | C | 6'3" | 255 | 23 | | |
| Dee Hardison | DE | 6'4" | 269 | 26 | | |
| Gary Jeter | DE | 6'4" | 260 | 27 | | |
| George Martin | DE | 6'4" | 245 | 29 | | |
| Curtis McGriff | DE | 6'5" | 265 | 24 | | |
| Phil Tabor | DE | 6'4" | 255 | 25 | | |
| Jim Burt | NT | 6'1" | 255 | 23 | | |
| Bill Neill | NT | 6'4" | 255 | 23 | | |
| Jerome Sally | NT | 6'3" | 260 | 23 | | |
| Harry Carson | LB | 6'2" | 235 | 28 | 1 | |
| Byron Hunt | LB | 6'5" | 230 | 23 | | |
| Brian Kelley | LB | 6'3" | 222 | 31 | 3 | |
| Frank Marion | LB | 6'3" | 223 | 31 | | |
| Joe McLaughlin | LB | 6'1" | 235 | 25 | | |
| Lawrence Taylor | LB | 6'3" | 237 | 23 | 1 | 6 |
| Brad Van Pelt | LB | 6'5" | 235 | 31 | | |
| Mike Whittington | LB | 6'2" | 220 | 24 | | |
| Brian Carpenter | DB | 5'10" | 167 | 21 | | |
| Bill Currier | DB | 6' | 202 | 27 | 1 | |
| Mike Dennis | DB | 5'10" | 190 | 23 | | |
| Larry Flowers | DB | 6'1" | 190 | 24 | | |
| Mark Haynes | DB | 5'11" | 198 | 23 | 1 | |
| Terry Jackson | DB | 5'10" | 197 | 26 | 4 | |
| Mike Mayock | DB | 6'2" | 195 | 24 | | |
| Beasley Reece | DB | 6'1" | 195 | 28 | 1 | |
| Pete Shaw | DB | 5'10" | 183 | 28 | | |
| Scott Brunner | QB | 6'5" | 200 | 25 | | 6 |
| Mark Reed | QB | 6'3" | 195 | 23 | | |
| Jeff Rutledge | QB | 6'1" | 190 | 25 | | |
| Leon Bright | HB | 5'9" | 192 | 27 | | |
| Larry Heater | HB | 5'11" | 205 | 24 | | |
| Joe Morris | HB | 5'7" | 190 | 21 | | 6 |
| Butch Woolfolk | HB | 6'1" | 207 | 22 | | 24 |
| Rob Carpenter | FB | 6'1" | 230 | 27 | | 6 |
| Cliff Chatman | FB | 6'2" | 225 | 23 | | 12 |
| Leon Perry | FB | 5'11" | 230 | 25 | | |
| Floyd Eddings | WR | 5'11" | 177 | 24 | | |
| Earnest Gray | WR | 6'3" | 195 | 25 | | 24 |
| John Mistler | WR | 6'2" | 186 | 23 | | 12 |
| Johnny Perkins | WR | 6'2" | 205 | 29 | | 12 |
| Danny Pittman | WR | 6'2" | 205 | 24 | | |
| Steve Folson | TE | 6'4" | 230 | 24 | | |
| Tom Mullady | TE | 6'3" | 232 | 25 | | |
| Gary Shirk | TE | 6'1" | 220 | 32 | | |
| Joe Danelo | K | 5'9" | 166 | 28 | | 54 |
| Dave Jennings | K | 6'4" | 205 | 30 | | |

Bill Matthews - Knee Injury
Phil Simms - Knee Injury
Roy Simmons - Retired List

**PHILADELPHIA EAGLES 3-6-0 Dick Vermeil**

| Scores of Each Game | | |
|---|---|---|
| 34 | WASHINGTON | *37 |
| 24 | Cleveland | 21 |
| 14 | CINCINNATI | 18 |
| 9 | Washington | 13 |
| 20 | ST.LOUIS | 23 |
| 7 | N.Y.Giants | 23 |
| 35 | HOUSTON | 14 |
| 24 | Dallas | 20 |
| 24 | N.Y.GIANTS | 26 |

| Use Name | Pos. | Hgt | Wgt | Age | Int | Pts |
|---|---|---|---|---|---|---|
| Frank Giddens | OT | 6'7" | 300 | 23 | | |
| Jerry Sisemore | OT | 6'4" | 265 | 31 | | |
| Stan Walters | OT | 6'6" | 275 | 34 | | |
| Ron Baker | OG | 6'4" | 250 | 27 | | |
| Steve Kenney | OG | 6'4" | 262 | 26 | | |
| Dean Miraldi | OG | 6'5" | 254 | 24 | | |
| Petey Perot | OG | 6'2" | 261 | 25 | | |
| Guy Morriss | C | 6'4" | 255 | 31 | | |
| Mark Slater | C | 6'2" | 257 | 27 | | |
| Greg Brown | DE | 6'5" | 240 | 25 | | 6 |
| Carl Hairston | DE | 6'3" | 260 | 29 | | |
| Dennis Harrison | DE | 6'8" | 275 | 26 | | |
| Leonard Mitchell | DE | 6'7" | 272 | 23 | | |
| Harvey Armstrong | NT | 6'2" | 255 | 22 | | |
| Ken Clarke | NT | 6'2" | 255 | 26 | | |
| John Bunting | LB | 6'1" | 220 | 32 | 1 | |
| Mike Curcio (from NYG) | LB | 6'1" | 237 | 25 | | |
| Anthony Griggs | LB | 6'3" | 220 | 22 | | |
| Frank LeMaster | LB | 6'2" | 238 | 30 | | |
| Jerry Robinson | LB | 6'2" | 218 | 25 | 3 | |
| Zack Valentine | LB | 6'2" | 220 | 25 | | |
| Reggie Wilkes | LB | 6'4" | 230 | 26 | | |
| Richard Blackmore | DB | 5'10" | 174 | 26 | 1 | 6 |
| Dennis DeVaughn | DB | 5'10" | 175 | 21 | | |
| Herman Edwards | DB | 6' | 190 | 28 | 5 | |
| Ray Ellis | DB | 6'1" | 192 | 23 | | |
| Randy Logan | DB | 6'1" | 195 | 31 | | |
| Von Mansfield | DB | 5'11" | 185 | 22 | | |
| John Sciarra | DB | 5'11" | 185 | 28 | | |
| Brenard Wilson | DB | 6' | 175 | 27 | 1 | |
| Roynell Young | DB | 6'1" | 181 | 24 | 4 | |
| Ron Jaworski | QB | 6'2" | 196 | 31 | | |
| Dan Pastorini | QB | 6'3" | 205 | 33 | | |
| Joe Pisarcik | QB | 6'4" | 220 | 30 | | |
| Billy Campfield | HB | 5'11" | 205 | 26 | | 6 |
| Louie Giammona | HB | 5'9" | 180 | 29 | | 6 |
| Wilbert Montgomery | HB | 5'10" | 195 | 27 | | 54 |
| Calvin Murray | HB | 5'11" | 182 | 23 | | |
| Don Calhoun | FB | 6' | 213 | 29 | | |
| Perry Harrington | FB | 5'11" | 210 | 24 | | 6 |
| Leroy Harris | FB | 5'9" | 230 | 28 | | 12 |
| Harold Carmichael | WR | 6'7" | 225 | 32 | | 24 |
| Wally Henry | WR | 5'8" | 180 | 27 | | |
| Melvin Hoover | WR | 6' | 185 | 23 | | |
| Mike Quick | WR | 6'2" | 190 | 23 | | 6 |
| Ron Smith | WR | 6' | 185 | 25 | | 6 |
| Tony Woodruff | WR | 6' | 175 | 23 | | |
| Vyto Kab | TE | 6'5" | 255 | 22 | | 6 |
| Lawrence Sampleton | TE | 6'5" | 233 | 22 | | |
| John Spagnola | TE | 6'4" | 240 | 25 | | 12 |
| Tony Franklin | K | 5'8" | 182 | 25 | | 41 |
| Max Runager | K | 6'1" | 189 | 26 | | |

Charles Johnson - Hamstring Injury

*Overtime

## WASHINGTON REDSKINS

### RUSHING

| Last Name | No. | Yds | Avg | TD |
|---|---|---|---|---|
| Riggins | 177 | 553 | 3.1 | 3 |
| Washington | 44 | 190 | 4.3 | 1 |
| Harmon | 38 | 168 | 4.4 | 1 |
| Theismann | 31 | 150 | 4.8 | 0 |
| Wonsley | 11 | 36 | 3.3 | 0 |
| Monk | 7 | 21 | 3.0 | 0 |
| Walker | 2 | 11 | 5.5 | 0 |
| Jackson | 4 | 6 | 1.5 | 0 |
| Giaquinto | 1 | 5 | 5.0 | 0 |

### RECEIVING

| Last Name | No. | Yds | Avg | TD |
|---|---|---|---|---|
| Monk | 35 | 447 | 12.8 | 1 |
| Brown | 32 | 690 | 21.6 | 8 |
| Warren | 27 | 310 | 11.5 | 0 |
| Washington | 19 | 134 | 7.1 | 1 |
| Walker | 12 | 92 | 7.7 | 1 |
| Harmon | 11 | 86 | 7.8 | 0 |
| Riggins | 10 | 50 | 5.0 | 0 |
| Seay | 6 | 154 | 25.7 | 0 |
| M. Williams | 3 | 14 | 4.7 | 0 |
| Giaquinto | 2 | 65 | 32.5 | 0 |
| Didier | 2 | 10 | 5.0 | 1 |
| Jackson | 1 | 9 | 9.0 | 0 |
| Garrett | 1 | 6 | 6.0 | 0 |
| Wonsley | 1 | 1 | 1.0 | 1 |

### PUNT RETURNS

| Last Name | No. | Yds | Avg | TD |
|---|---|---|---|---|
| Nelms | 32 | 252 | 7.9 | 0 |
| Giaquinto | 5 | 34 | 6.8 | 0 |
| G. Williams | 1 | 9 | 9.0 | 0 |

### KICKOFF RETURNS

| Last Name | No. | Yds | Avg | TD |
|---|---|---|---|---|
| Nelms | 23 | 557 | 24.2 | 0 |
| Garrett | 2 | 35 | 17.5 | 0 |
| Giaquinto | 1 | 21 | 21.0 | 0 |
| Wonsley | 1 | 14 | 14.0 | 0 |
| Harmon | 1 | 13 | 13.0 | 0 |
| Anderson | 1 | 7 | 7.0 | 0 |
| G. Williams | 1 | 2 | 2.0 | 0 |

### PASSING — PUNTING — KICKING

PASSING

| Last Name | Att | Comp | % | Yds | Yd/Att | TD | Int- | % | RK |
|---|---|---|---|---|---|---|---|---|---|
| Theismann | 252 | 161 | 64 | 2033 | 8.06 | 13 | 9- | 4 | 1 |
| Washington | 1 | 1 | 100 | 35 | 35.00 | 0 | 0- | 0 | |

PUNTING

| Last Name | No | Avg |
|---|---|---|
| Hayes | 51 | 38.0 |

KICKING

| Last Name | XP | Att | % | FG | Att | % |
|---|---|---|---|---|---|---|
| Moseley | 16 | 19 | 84 | 20 | 21 | 95 |

## DALLAS COWBOYS

### RUSHING

| Last Name | No. | Yds | Avg | TD |
|---|---|---|---|---|
| Dorsett | 177 | 745 | 4.2 | 5 |
| Springs | 59 | 243 | 4.1 | 2 |
| Newsome | 15 | 98 | 6.5 | 1 |
| D. White | 17 | 91 | 5.4 | 0 |
| Newhouse | 14 | 79 | 5.6 | 1 |
| T. Hill | 1 | 22 | 22.0 | 0 |
| Peoples | 7 | 22 | 3.1 | 0 |
| Johnson | 1 | 9 | 9.0 | 0 |
| DuPree | 1 | 6 | 6.0 | 1 |
| Hogeboom | 3 | 0 | 0.0 | 0 |
| Cosbie | 1 | -2 | -2.0 | 0 |

### RECEIVING

| Last Name | No. | Yds | Avg | TD |
|---|---|---|---|---|
| T. Hill | 35 | 526 | 15.0 | 1 |
| Cosbie | 30 | 441 | 14.7 | 4 |
| Pearson | 26 | 382 | 14.7 | 3 |
| Dorsett | 24 | 179 | 7.5 | 0 |
| Springs | 17 | 163 | 9.6 | 2 |
| Johnson | 12 | 269 | 22.4 | 3 |
| DuPree | 7 | 41 | 5.9 | 2 |
| Newsome | 6 | 118 | 19.7 | 1 |
| Donley | 2 | 23 | 11.5 | 0 |
| Saldi | 1 | 8 | 8.0 | 0 |

### PUNT RETURNS

| Last Name | No. | Yds | Avg | TD |
|---|---|---|---|---|
| Fellows | 25 | 189 | 7.6 | 0 |
| R. Hill | 4 | 39 | 9.8 | 0 |
| Donley | 1 | 14 | 14.0 | 0 |

### KICKOFF RETURNS

| Last Name | No. | Yds | Avg | TD |
|---|---|---|---|---|
| Fellows | 16 | 359 | 22.4 | 0 |
| Donley | 8 | 151 | 18.9 | 0 |
| Newsome | 5 | 74 | 14.8 | 0 |
| J. Jones | 2 | 46 | 23.0 | 0 |
| Thurman | 1 | 17 | 17.0 | 0 |
| Cosbie | 1 | 4 | 4.0 | 0 |

### PASSING — PUNTING — KICKING

PASSING

| Last Name | Att | Comp | % | Yds | Yd/Att | TD | Int- | % | RK |
|---|---|---|---|---|---|---|---|---|---|
| D. White | 247 | 156 | 63 | 2079 | 8.42 | 16 | 12- | 5 | 2 |
| Hogeboom | 8 | 3 | 38 | 45 | 5.63 | 0 | 1- | 13 | |
| Pearson | 2 | 1 | 50 | 26 | 13.00 | 0 | 1- | 50 | |
| Dorsett | 1 | 0 | 0 | 0 | 0.00 | 0 | 0- | 0 | |

PUNTING

| Last Name | No | Avg |
|---|---|---|
| D. White | 37 | 41.7 |

KICKING

| Last Name | XP | Att | % | FG | Att | % |
|---|---|---|---|---|---|---|
| Septien | 28 | 28 | 100 | 10 | 14 | 71 |

## ST. LOUIS CARDINALS

### RUSHING

| Last Name | No. | Yds | Avg | TD |
|---|---|---|---|---|
| Anderson | 145 | 587 | 4.0 | 3 |
| Morris | 84 | 274 | 3.3 | 4 |
| Mitchell | 39 | 189 | 4.8 | 1 |
| Lomax | 28 | 119 | 4.3 | 1 |
| Wehrli | 1 | 18 | 18.0 | 1 |
| Harrell | 4 | 14 | 3.5 | 0 |
| Green | 6 | 8 | 1.2 | 0 |

### RECEIVING

| Last Name | No. | Yds | Avg | TD |
|---|---|---|---|---|
| Tilley | 36 | 465 | 14.5 | 2 |
| Green | 32 | 454 | 14.2 | 3 |
| Anderson | 14 | 106 | 7.6 | 0 |
| Mitchell | 11 | 149 | 13.5 | 0 |
| Harrell | 11 | 127 | 11.5 | 0 |
| Marsh | 5 | 83 | 16.6 | 0 |
| LaFleur | 5 | 67 | 13.4 | 1 |
| Shumann | 5 | 58 | 11.6 | 0 |
| Gray | 4 | 34 | 8.5 | 0 |
| Morris | 4 | 19 | 4.8 | 0 |
| Lomax | 1 | 10 | 10.0 | 0 |
| Thompson | 1 | 5 | 5.0 | 0 |

### PUNT RETURNS

| Last Name | No. | Yds | Avg | TD |
|---|---|---|---|---|
| Mitchell | 27 | 165 | 6.1 | 0 |
| Green | 3 | 20 | 6.7 | 0 |
| Ferrell | 1 | 6 | 6.0 | 0 |
| Harrell | 1 | 1 | 1.0 | 0 |

### KICKOFF RETURNS

| Last Name | No. | Yds | Avg | TD |
|---|---|---|---|---|
| Mitchell | 16 | 364 | 22.8 | 0 |
| Harrell | 8 | 150 | 18.8 | 0 |
| Ferrell | 4 | 88 | 22.0 | 0 |
| Love | 4 | 69 | 17.3 | 0 |
| Morris | 1 | 14 | 14.0 | 0 |
| Griffin | 1 | 12 | 12.0 | 0 |
| Ahrens | 1 | 5 | 5.0 | 0 |

### PASSING — PUNTING — KICKING

PASSING

| Last Name | Att | Comp | % | Yds | Yd/Att | TD | Int- | % | RK |
|---|---|---|---|---|---|---|---|---|---|
| Lomax | 205 | 109 | 53 | 1367 | 6.70 | 5 | 6- | 3 | 12 |
| Hart | 33 | 19 | 58 | 199 | 6.00 | 1 | 0- | 0 | |
| Harrell | 1 | 1 | 100 | 10 | 10.00 | 0 | 0- | 0 | |
| Green | 1 | 0 | 0 | 0 | 0 | 0 | 0- | 0 | |

PUNTING

| Last Name | No | Avg |
|---|---|---|
| Birdsong | 54 | 43.8 |

KICKING

| Last Name | XP | Att | % | FG | Att | % |
|---|---|---|---|---|---|---|
| O'Donoghue | 15 | 16 | 94 | 8 | 13 | 62 |

## NEW YORK GIANTS

### RUSHING

| Last Name | No. | Yds | Avg | TD |
|---|---|---|---|---|
| Woolfolk | 112 | 439 | 3.9 | 2 |
| R. Carpenter | 67 | 204 | 3.0 | 1 |
| Chatman | 22 | 80 | 3.6 | 2 |
| Morris | 15 | 48 | 3.2 | 1 |
| Brunner | 19 | 27 | 1.4 | 1 |
| Perry | 3 | 14 | 4.7 | 0 |
| Heater | 3 | 13 | 4.3 | 0 |
| Eddings | 2 | 12 | 6.0 | 0 |
| Bright | 1 | 5 | 5.0 | 0 |

### RECEIVING

| Last Name | No. | Yds | Avg | TD |
|---|---|---|---|---|
| Mullady | 27 | 287 | 10.6 | 0 |
| Perkins | 26 | 430 | 16.5 | 2 |
| Gray | 25 | 426 | 17.0 | 4 |
| Woolfolk | 23 | 224 | 9.7 | 2 |
| Mistler | 18 | 191 | 10.6 | 2 |
| Eddings | 14 | 275 | 19.6 | 0 |
| Moris | 8 | 34 | 4.3 | 0 |
| R. Carpenter | 7 | 29 | 4.1 | 0 |
| Shirk | 6 | 54 | 9.0 | 0 |
| Bright | 2 | 19 | 9.5 | 0 |
| Heater | 2 | 15 | 7.5 | 0 |
| Pittman | 1 | 21 | 21.0 | 0 |
| Chatman | 1 | 13 | 13.0 | 0 |
| Perry | 1 | -1 | -1.0 | 0 |

### PUNT RETURNS

| Last Name | No. | Yds | Avg | TD |
|---|---|---|---|---|
| Bright | 37 | 325 | 8.8 | 0 |
| Pittman | 6 | 40 | 6.7 | 0 |
| Reece | 1 | 8 | 8.0 | 0 |

### KICKOFF RETURNS

| Last Name | No. | Yds | Avg | TD |
|---|---|---|---|---|
| Woolfolk | 20 | 428 | 21.4 | 0 |
| Pittman | 5 | 117 | 23.4 | 0 |
| Heater | 5 | 84 | 16.8 | 0 |
| Bright | 4 | 72 | 18.0 | 0 |
| Dennis | 3 | 68 | 22.7 | 0 |
| McLaughlin | 1 | 14 | 14.0 | 0 |
| Shaw | 1 | 0 | 0.0 | 0 |

### PASSING — PUNTING — KICKING

PASSING

| Last Name | Att | Comp | % | Yds | Yd/Att | TD | Int- | % | RK |
|---|---|---|---|---|---|---|---|---|---|
| Brunner | 298 | 161 | 54 | 2017 | 6.77 | 10 | 9- | 3 | 10 |

PUNTING

| Last Name | No | Avg |
|---|---|---|
| Jennings | 49 | 42.8 |

KICKING

| Last Name | XP | Att | % | FG | Att | % |
|---|---|---|---|---|---|---|
| Danelo | 18 | 18 | 100 | 12 | 21 | 57 |

## PHILADELPHIA EAGLES

### RUSHING

| Last Name | No. | Yds | Avg | TD |
|---|---|---|---|---|
| Montgomery | 114 | 515 | 4.5 | 7 |
| Harrington | 56 | 231 | 4.1 | 1 |
| Harris | 17 | 39 | 2.3 | 2 |
| Giammona | 11 | 29 | 2.6 | 1 |
| Jaworski | 10 | 9 | 0.9 | 0 |
| Hoover | 1 | 5 | 5.0 | 0 |
| Campfield | 1 | 2 | 2.0 | 0 |
| LeMaster | 1 | -2 | -2.0 | 0 |

### RECEIVING

| Last Name | No. | Yds | Avg | TD |
|---|---|---|---|---|
| Carmichael | 35 | 540 | 15.4 | 4 |
| R. Smith | 34 | 475 | 14.0 | 1 |
| Spagnola | 26 | 313 | 12.0 | 2 |
| Montgomery | 20 | 258 | 12.9 | 2 |
| Campfield | 14 | 141 | 10.1 | 1 |
| Harrington | 13 | 74 | 5.7 | 0 |
| Quick | 10 | 156 | 15.6 | 1 |
| Giammona | 8 | 67 | 8.4 | 0 |
| Kab | 4 | 35 | 8.8 | 0 |
| Harris | 3 | 17 | 5.7 | 0 |
| Sampleton | 1 | 24 | 24.0 | 0 |

### PUNT RETURNS

| Last Name | No. | Yds | Avg | TD |
|---|---|---|---|---|
| Henry | 20 | 103 | 5.2 | 0 |
| Sciarra | 2 | 5 | 2.5 | 0 |
| Giammona | 0 | 0 | 0.0 | 0 |

### KICKOFF RETURNS

| Last Name | No. | Yds | Avg | TD |
|---|---|---|---|---|
| Henry | 24 | 541 | 22.5 | 0 |
| Hoover | 7 | 113 | 16.1 | 0 |
| Murray | 3 | 42 | 14.0 | 0 |
| Campfield | 2 | 30 | 15.0 | 0 |
| Slater | 2 | 30 | 15.0 | 0 |
| Montgomery | 1 | 12 | 12.0 | 0 |

### PASSING — PUNTING — KICKING

PASSING

| Last Name | Att | Comp | % | Yds | Yd/Att | TD | Int- | % | RK |
|---|---|---|---|---|---|---|---|---|---|
| Jaworski | 286 | 167 | 58 | 2076 | 7.30 | 12 | 12- | 4 | 7 |
| Pisarcik | 1 | 1 | 100 | 24 | 24.00 | 0 | 0- | 0 | |
| Giammona | 1 | 0 | 0 | 0 | 0.00 | 0 | 1- | 100 | |

PUNTING

| Last Name | No | Avg |
|---|---|---|
| Runager | 44 | 40.5 |

KICKING

| Last Name | XP | Att | % | FG | Att | % |
|---|---|---|---|---|---|---|
| Franklin | 23 | 25 | 92 | 6 | 9 | 67 |

**GREEN BAY PACKERS 5-3-1 Bart Starr**

| Scores of Each Game | | |
|---|---|---|
| 35 | L.A.RAMS | 23 |
| 27 | N.Y.Giants | 19 |
| 26 | MINNESOTA | 7 |
| 13 | N.Y.Jets | 15 |
| 33 | BUFFALO | 21 |
| 10 | DETROIT | 30 |
| 20 | Baltimore | *20 |
| 38 | Atlanta | 7 |
| 24 | Detroit | 27 |

| Use Name | Pos. | Hgt | Wgt | Age | Int | Pts |
|---|---|---|---|---|---|---|
| Greg Koch | OT | 6'4" | 265 | 27 | | |
| Tim Stokes | OT | 6'5" | 252 | 32 | | |
| Karl Swanke | OT-C | 6'6" | 251 | 24 | | |
| Derrel Gofourth | OG | 6'3" | 260 | 27 | | |
| Ron Hallstrom | OG | 6'6" | 286 | 22 | | |
| Leotis Harris | OG | 6'1" | 267 | 27 | | |
| Tim Huffman | OG | 6'5" | 277 | 23 | | |
| Larry McCarren | C | 6'3" | 238 | 30 | | |
| Larry Rubens | C | 6'1" | 253 | 23 | | |
| Byron Braggs | DE | 6'4" | 290 | 22 | | |
| Robert Brown | DE | 6'2" | 238 | 21 | | |
| Mike Butler | DE | 6'5" | 265 | 28 | | |
| Ezra Johnson | DE | 6'4" | 240 | 26 | | |
| Casey Merrill | DE | 6'4" | 255 | 25 | | |
| Terry Jones | NT | 6'2" | 259 | 25 | | |
| Richard Turner | NT | 6'2" | 260 | 23 | | |
| John Anderson | LB | 6'3" | 221 | 26 | 3 | |
| George Cumby | LB | 6' | 215 | 26 | 1 | |
| Mike Douglass | LB | 6' | 224 | 27 | 2 | |
| Jim Laslavic | LB | 6'2" | 236 | 30 | | |
| Cliff Lewis | LB | 6'1" | 226 | 22 | | |
| Mark Merrill (from DEN) | LB | 6'4" | 234 | 27 | | |
| Guy Prather | LB | 6'2" | 230 | 24 | | |
| Randy Scott | LB | 6'1" | 220 | 23 | | |
| Rich Wingo | LB | 6'1" | 230 | 26 | 1 | |
| Johnnie Gray | DB | 5'11" | 185 | 28 | 1 | |
| Maurice Harvey | DB | 5'10" | 190 | 26 | 2 | 6 |
| Estus Hood | DB | 5'11" | 180 | 26 | 1 | |
| Mike Jolly | DB | 6'3" | 185 | 23 | | |
| Mark Lee | DB | 5'11" | 187 | 24 | 1 | |
| Mike McCoy | DB | 5'11" | 183 | 29 | | |
| Mark Murphy | DB | 6'2" | 199 | 24 | | |
| Bill Whitaker | DB | 6' | 182 | 22 | | |
| Rich Campbell | QB | 6'4" | 224 | 23 | | |
| Lynn Dickey | QB | 6'4" | 220 | 32 | | |
| David Whitehurst | QB | 6'2" | 204 | 27 | | |
| Allan Clark (from BUF) | HB | 5'10" | 186 | 24 | | |
| Harlan Huckleby | HB | 6'1" | 199 | 24 | | |
| Eddie Lee Ivery | HB | 6'1" | 210 | 25 | | 60 |
| Del Rodgers | HB | 5'10" | 197 | 22 | | 18 |
| Gerry Ellis | FB | 5'11" | 216 | 24 | | 6 |
| Jim Jensen | FB | 6'3" | 235 | 28 | | 6 |
| Mike Meade | FB | 5'11" | 228 | 22 | | |
| Phillip Epps | WR | 5'10" | 165 | 23 | | 12 |
| John Jefferson | WR | 6'1" | 196 | 26 | | |
| James Lofton | WR | 6'3" | 187 | 26 | | 30 |
| Paul Coffman | TE | 6'3" | 218 | 26 | | 12 |
| Gary Lewis | TE | 6'5" | 234 | 23 | | |
| John Thompson | TE | 6'3" | 228 | 25 | | 12 |
| Ray Stachowicz | K | 5'11" | 185 | 23 | | |
| Jan Stenerud | K | 6'2" | 190 | 39 | | 64 |

Ron Cassidy - Shoulder Injury
Syd Kitson - Shoulder Injury
Fred Nixon - Knee Injury

**MINNESOTA VIKINGS 5-4-0 Bud Grant**

| Scores of Each Game | | |
|---|---|---|
| 17 | TAMPA BAY | 10 |
| 22 | Buffalo | 23 |
| 7 | Green Bay | 26 |
| 35 | CHICAGO | 7 |
| 14 | Miami | 22 |
| 13 | BALTIMORE | 10 |
| 34 | Detroit | 31 |
| 14 | N.Y.JETS | 42 |
| 31 | DALLAS | 27 |

| Use Name | Pos. | Hgt | Wgt | Age | Int | Pts |
|---|---|---|---|---|---|---|
| Tim Irwin | OT | 6'6" | 275 | 23 | | |
| Steve Riley | OT | 6'6" | 255 | 29 | | |
| Terry Tausch | OT | 6'5" | 275 | 23 | | |
| Brent Boyd | OG | 6'3" | 260 | 25 | | |
| Wes Hamilton | OG | 6'3" | 268 | 29 | | |
| Jim Hough | OG | 6'2" | 267 | 26 | | |
| David Huffman | OG-C | 6'6" | 255 | 25 | | |
| Curtis Rouse | OG | 6'3" | 290 | 22 | | |
| Dennis Swilley | C | 6'6" | 260 | 24 | | |
| Neil Elshire | DE | 6'6" | 260 | 24 | | |
| Randy Holloway | DE | 6'5" | 250 | 27 | 1 | |
| Doug Martin | DE | 6'3" | 255 | 25 | 1 | |
| Mark Mullaney | DE | 6'6" | 245 | 29 | | 2 |
| Charles Johnson | NT | 6'3" | 265 | 30 | | 6 |
| James White | NT | 6'3" | 270 | 28 | | |
| Ray Yakavonis | NT | 6'4" | 250 | 25 | | |
| Matt Blair | LB | 6'5" | 234 | 31 | | |
| Dennis Johnson | LB | 6'3" | 230 | 24 | | |
| Henry Johnson | LB | 6'1" | 235 | 24 | | |
| Fred McNeill | LB | 6'2" | 230 | 30 | | |
| Robin Sendlein | LB | 6'3" | 224 | 23 | | |
| Jeff Siemon | LB | 6'2" | 235 | 32 | | |
| Scott Studwell | LB | 6'2" | 225 | 28 | 1 | |
| Rufus Bess | DB | 5'9" | 185 | 25 | | |
| Tom Hannon | DB | 5'11" | 190 | 27 | | |
| Bryan Howard | DB | 6' | 200 | 23 | | |
| Kurt Knoff | DB | 6'2" | 190 | 28 | 1 | |
| Keith Nord | DB | 6' | 195 | 25 | | |
| John Swain | DB | 6'1" | 195 | 22 | 2 | |
| Willie Teal | DB | 5'10" | 195 | 24 | 4 | |
| John Turner | DB | 6' | 199 | 26 | 2 | 6 |
| Steve Dils | QB | 6'1" | 190 | 26 | | |
| Tommy Kramer | QB | 6'2" | 200 | 27 | | 18 |
| Wade Wilson | QB | 6'3" | 210 | 23 | | |
| Ted Brown | HB-FB | 5'10" | 210 | 25 | | 18 |
| Darrin Nelson | HB | 5'9" | 180 | 23 | | |
| Jarvis Redwine | HB | 5'10" | 205 | 25 | | |
| Rickey Young | HB | 6'2" | 200 | 28 | | 12 |
| Eddie Payton | HB | 5'8" | 179 | 31 | | |
| Tony Galbreath | FB | 6' | 230 | 28 | | 6 |
| Sam Harrell | FB | 6'2" | 225 | 25 | | |
| Harold Jackson | WR | 5'10" | 175 | 36 | | |
| Terry LeCount | WR | 5'10" | 180 | 26 | | 6 |
| Leo Lewis | WR | 5'8" | 170 | 25 | | 18 |
| Sam McCullum | WR | 6'2" | 190 | 29 | | |
| Mardye McDole | WR | 5'11" | 195 | 23 | | |
| Ahmad Rashad | WR | 6'2" | 200 | 32 | | |
| Sammy White | WR | 5'11" | 190 | 28 | | 30 |
| Bob Bruer | TE | 6'5" | 235 | 28 | | 12 |
| Steve Jordan | TE | 6'3" | 230 | 21 | | |
| Joe Senser | TE | 6'4" | 235 | 26 | | 6 |
| Greg Coleman | K | 6' | 185 | 27 | | |
| Rick Danmeier | K | 6' | 200 | 30 | | 47 |

**TAMPA BAY BUCCANEERS 5-4-0 John McKay**

| Scores of Each Game | | |
|---|---|---|
| 10 | Minnesota | 17 |
| 13 | WASHINGTON | 21 |
| 9 | Dallas | 14 |
| 23 | MIAMI | 17 |
| 13 | New Orleans | 10 |
| 17 | N.Y.Jets | 32 |
| 24 | BUFFALO | 23 |
| 23 | DETROIT | 21 |
| 26 | CHICAGO | *23 |

| Use Name | Pos. | Hgt | Wgt | Age | Int | Pts |
|---|---|---|---|---|---|---|
| Charley Hannah | OT | 6'5" | 265 | 27 | | |
| Dave Reavis | OT | 6'5" | 265 | 32 | | |
| Gene Sanders | OT | 6'3" | 270 | 25 | | |
| Sean Farrell | OG | 6'3" | 260 | 22 | | |
| Greg Roberts | OG | 6'3" | 265 | 25 | | |
| George Yarno | OG | 6'2" | 260 | 25 | | |
| Ray Snell | OG-OT | 6'4" | 265 | 24 | | |
| Jim Leonard | C-OG | 6'3" | 260 | 24 | | |
| Steve Wilson | C | 6'3" | 265 | 22 | | |
| John Cannon | DE | 6'5" | 250 | 22 | | |
| Bob Cobb | DE | 6'4" | 250 | 24 | | |
| Booker Reese | DE | 6'6" | 260 | 22 | | |
| Lee Roy Selmon | DE | 6'3" | 250 | 27 | | |
| Dave Stalls | DE | 6'5" | 250 | 26 | | |
| David Logan | NT | 6'2" | 255 | 25 | | |
| Brad White | NT | 6'2" | 250 | 24 | | |
| Scott Brantley | LB | 6'1" | 230 | 24 | | |
| Jeff Davis | LB | 6' | 225 | 22 | | |
| Hugh Green | LB | 6'2" | 225 | 23 | 1 | |
| Andy Hawkins | LB | 6'2" | 230 | 24 | | |
| Cecil Johnson | LB | 6'2" | 235 | 27 | | |
| Dana Nafziger | LB | 6'1" | 225 | 28 | | |
| Richard Wood | LB | 6'2" | 230 | 29 | | |
| Cedric Brown | DB | 6'1" | 200 | 28 | 3 | |
| Neal Colzie | DB | 6'2" | 200 | 29 | 3 | |
| Mark Cotney | DB | 6' | 200 | 30 | | |
| John Holt | DB | 5'11" | 180 | 23 | | |
| Thomas Morris | DB | 5'11" | 175 | 22 | | |
| Johnny Ray Smith | DB | 5'9" | 180 | 24 | | |
| Norris Thomas | DB | 5'11" | 185 | 28 | 1 | |
| Mike Washington | DB | 6'3" | 200 | 29 | 3 | |
| Jerry Golsteyn | QB | 6'4" | 200 | 28 | | |
| Jeff Quinn (from PIT) | QB | 6'3" | 205 | 24 | | |
| Doug Williams | QB | 6'4" | 220 | 27 | | 12 |
| Terdell Middleton | HB | 6' | 205 | 27 | | |
| Michael Morton | HB | 5'8" | 180 | 22 | | |
| James Owens | HB | 5'11" | 195 | 27 | | 6 |
| Dave Barrett | FB | 6 | 230 | 22 | | |
| Melvin Carver | FB | 5'11" | 215 | 23 | | 12 |
| James Wilder | FB | 6'3" | 225 | 24 | | 24 |
| Theo Bell | WR | 6' | 190 | 28 | | |
| Gerald Carter | WR | 6'1" | 190 | 25 | | |
| Kevin House | WR | 6'1" | 180 | 24 | | 12 |
| Gordon Jones | WR | 6' | 190 | 25 | | 6 |
| Jerry Bell | TE | 6'5" | 230 | 23 | | |
| Jim Obradovich | TE | 6'2" | 225 | 19 | | |
| Jimmie Giles | TE | 6'3" | 245 | 27 | | 18 |
| Bill Capece | K | 5'7" | 170 | 23 | | 68 |
| Brian Clark | K | 6'2" | 190 | 24 | | |
| Larry Swider | K | 6'2" | 195 | 27 | | |

Randy Crowder - Knee Injury

**DETROIT LIONS 4-5-0 Monte Clarke**

| Scores of Each Game | | |
|---|---|---|
| 17 | CHICAGO | 10 |
| 19 | L.A.Rams | 14 |
| 17 | Chicago | 20 |
| 6 | N.Y.GIANTS | 13 |
| 13 | N.Y.JETS | 28 |
| 30 | Green Bay | 10 |
| 31 | MINNESOTA | 34 |
| 21 | Tampa Bay | 23 |
| 27 | GREEN BAY | 24 |

| Use Name | Pos. | Hgt | Wgt | Age | Int | Pts |
|---|---|---|---|---|---|---|
| Karl Baldischwiler | OT | 6'5" | 260 | 26 | | |
| Chris Dieterich | OT | 6'3" | 255 | 24 | | |
| Keith Dorney | OT | 6'5" | 260 | 24 | | |
| Russ Bolinger | OG | 6'5" | 260 | 27 | | |
| Homer Elias | OG | 6'3" | 255 | 27 | | |
| Don Greco | OG | 6'3" | 255 | 23 | | |
| Larry Lee | OG-C | 6'2" | 260 | 22 | | |
| Amos Fowler | C | 6'3" | 253 | 26 | | |
| Tom Turnure | C | 6'4" | 250 | 25 | | |
| Al Baker | DE | 6'6" | 260 | 25 | | |
| Dave Pureifoy | DE | 6'1" | 255 | 33 | | |
| William Gay | DE-DT | 6'5" | 255 | 27 | 1 | |
| Curtis Green | DE-DT | 6'3" | 252 | 25 | | |
| Joe Ehrmann | DT | 6'5" | 250 | 33 | | |
| Doug English | DT | 6'5" | 258 | 29 | | |
| Martin Moss | DT | 6'4" | 252 | 23 | | |
| Roosevelt Barnes | LB | 6'2" | 220 | 24 | | |
| Garry Cobb | LB | 6'2" | 227 | 25 | 2 | |
| Steve Doig | LB | 6'2" | 240 | 22 | | |
| Ken Fantetti | LB | 6'2" | 227 | 25 | | |
| James Harrell | LB | 6'1" | 220 | 25 | | |
| Terry Tautolo | LB | 6'2" | 227 | 28 | | |
| Stan White | LB | 6'1" | 223 | 32 | 3 | |
| Jimmy Williams | LB | 6'3" | 221 | 21 | 1 | |
| Billy Cesare | DB | 5'11" | 190 | 27 | | |
| William Graham | DB | 5'11" | 191 | 22 | | |
| Hector Gray | DB | 6'1" | 190 | 25 | 1 | |
| Alvin Hall | DB | 5'10" | 184 | 24 | 1 | 6 |
| James Hunter | DB | 6'3" | 195 | 28 | 2 | |
| Al Latimer | DB | 5'11" | 177 | 24 | | |
| Bruce McNorton | DB | 5'11" | 175 | 23 | | |
| Ray Oldham | DB | 6' | 192 | 31 | 1 | 6 |
| Wayne Smith (to STL) | DB | 6' | 170 | 25 | | |
| Dan Wagoner | DB | 5'10" | 177 | 22 | | |
| Bobby Watkins | DB | 5'10" | 184 | 22 | 5 | |
| Gary Danielson | QB | 6'2" | 196 | 30 | | |
| Eric Hipple | QB | 6'2" | 196 | 24 | | |
| Mike Machurek | QB | 6'1" | 205 | 22 | | |
| Ken Callicutt | HB | 6' | 190 | 27 | | |
| Rick Kane | HB | 5'11" | 200 | 27 | | |
| Ricky Porter | HB | 5'10" | 186 | 22 | | |
| Billy Sims | HB | 6' | 212 | 26 | | 24 |
| Dexter Bussey | FB | 6'1" | 210 | 30 | | |
| Horace King | FB | 5'10" | 205 | 29 | | 6 |
| Robbie Martin | WR | 5'8" | 177 | 23 | | |
| Mark Nichols | WR | 6'2" | 213 | 22 | | 12 |
| Tracy Porter | WR | 6'1" | 196 | 23 | | |
| Freddie Scott | WR | 6'2" | 190 | 30 | | 6 |
| Leonard Thompson | WR | 5'11" | 192 | 30 | | 24 |
| David Hill | TE | 6'2" | 228 | 28 | | 24 |
| Ulysses Norris | TE | 6'4" | 232 | 25 | | |
| Rob Rubick | TE | 6'3" | 228 | 21 | | 6 |
| Eddie Murray | K | 5'10" | 170 | 26 | | 49 |
| Tom Skladany | k | 6' | 195 | 27 | | |

Tommie Ginn - Knee Injury
Vince Thompson - Abdominal Injury

**CHICAGO BEARS 3-6-0 Mike Ditka**

| Scores of Each Game | | |
|---|---|---|
| 10 | Detroit | 17 |
| 0 | New Orleans | 10 |
| 20 | DETROIT | 17 |
| 7 | Minnesota | 35 |
| 26 | NEW ENGLAND | 13 |
| 14 | Seattle | 20 |
| 7 | ST.LOUIS | 10 |
| 34 | L.A.Rams | 26 |
| 23 | Tampa Bay | *26 |

| Use Name | Pos. | Hgt | Wgt | Age | Int | Pts |
|---|---|---|---|---|---|---|
| Jerry Doerger | OT | 6'5" | 270 | 22 | | |
| Dan Jiggetts | OT | 6'4" | 270 | 28 | | |
| Dennis Lick | OT | 6'3" | 265 | 28 | | |
| Phil McKinnely | OT | 6'4" | 250 | 28 | | |
| Keith Van Horne | OT | 6'6" | 265 | 24 | | |
| Kurt Becker | OG | 6'5" | 251 | 23 | | |
| Perry Hartnett | OG | 6'5" | 275 | 22 | | |
| Noah Jackson | OG | 6'2" | 265 | 28 | | |
| Jeff Williams | OG | 6'4" | 260 | 27 | | |
| Jay Hilgenberg | C | 6'3" | 250 | 23 | | |
| Dan Neal | C | 6'4" | 255 | 33 | | |
| Al Harris | DE | 6'5" | 250 | 25 | | |
| Mike Hartenstine | DE | 6'3" | 243 | 29 | | |
| Henry Waechter | DE | 6'5" | 270 | 23 | | |
| Dan Hampton | DT | 6'5" | 255 | 24 | | |
| Steve McMichael | DT | 6'2" | 245 | 24 | | |
| Jim Osborne | DT | 6'3" | 245 | 32 | | 2 |
| Brian Cabral | LB | 6' | 224 | 26 | | |
| Gary Campbell | LB | 6'1" | 220 | 30 | | |
| Al Chesley (from PHI) | LB | 6'3" | 240 | 25 | | |
| Bruce Herron | LB | 6'2" | 220 | 28 | | |
| Bruce Huther | LB | 6'1" | 220 | 28 | | |
| Jerry Muckensturm | LB | 6'4" | 220 | 28 | | |
| Dan Rains | LB | 6'1" | 222 | 26 | | |
| Mike Singletary | LB | 5'11" | 230 | 23 | | |
| Otis Wilson | LB | 6'2" | 222 | 24 | 2 | 6 |
| Todd Bell | DB | 6'1" | 207 | 23 | | |
| Gary Fencik | DB | 6'1" | 197 | 28 | 2 | |
| Jeff Fisher | DB | 5'11" | 188 | 24 | 3 | |
| Leslie Frazier | DB | 6' | 189 | 23 | 2 | |
| Reuben Henderson | DB | 6'1" | 200 | 23 | | |
| Doug Plank | DB | 6' | 202 | 29 | | |
| Terry Schmidt | DB | 6' | 177 | 30 | 4 | |
| Len Walterscheid | DB | 5'11" | 190 | 27 | | |
| Walt Williams (from MIN) | DB | 6' | 185 | 28 | | |
| Bob Avellini | QB | 6'2" | 210 | 29 | | |
| Vince Evans | QB | 6'2" | 212 | 27 | | |
| Jim McMahon | QB | 6' | 187 | 23 | | 6 |
| Dennis Gentry | HB | 5'8" | 173 | 23 | | |
| Walter Payton | HB | 5'11" | 202 | 28 | | 6 |
| Roland Harper | FB | 6' | 210 | 29 | | |
| Willie McClendon | FB | 6'1" | 205 | 24 | | |
| Matt Suhey | FB | 5'11" | 217 | 24 | | 18 |
| Calvin Thomas | FB | 5'11" | 220 | 22 | | |
| Brian Baschnagel | WR | 6' | 184 | 28 | | 12 |
| Ken Margerum | WR | 6' | 170 | 23 | | 18 |
| James Scott | WR | 6'1" | 190 | 30 | | |
| Rickey Watts | WR | 6'1" | 203 | 25 | | |
| Robin Earl | TE | 6'5" | 240 | 27 | | |
| Emery Moorehead | TE | 6'2" | 220 | 28 | | 30 |
| Brooks Williams | TE | 6'4" | 226 | 27 | | |
| Bob Parsons | K | 6'4" | 225 | 32 | | |
| John Roveto | K | 6' | 180 | 24 | | 22 |
| Bob Thomas (from DET) | K | 5'10" | 175 | 30 | | 39 |

Ted Albrecht - Knee Injury
Revie Sorey - Larynx Injury

* Overtime

## GREEN BAY PACKERS

### RUSHING

| Last Name | No. | Yds | Avg | TD |
|---|---|---|---|---|
| Ivery | 127 | 453 | 3.6 | 9 |
| Ellis | 62 | 228 | 3.7 | 1 |
| Rodgers | 46 | 175 | 3.8 | 1 |
| Lofton | 4 | 101 | 25.3 | 1 |
| Meade | 14 | 42 | 3.0 | 0 |
| Jensen | 9 | 28 | 3.1 | 0 |
| Huckleby | 4 | 19 | 4.8 | 0 |
| Dickey | 13 | 19 | 1.5 | 0 |
| Jefferson | 2 | 16 | 8.0 | 0 |
| Stachowicz | 2 | 0 | 0.0 | 0 |

### RECEIVING

| Last Name | No. | Yds | Avg | TD |
|---|---|---|---|---|
| Lofton | 35 | 696 | 19.9 | 4 |
| Jefferson | 27 | 452 | 16.7 | 0 |
| Coffman | 23 | 287 | 12.5 | 2 |
| Ellis | 18 | 140 | 7.8 | 0 |
| Ivery | 16 | 186 | 11.6 | 1 |
| Epps | 10 | 226 | 22.6 | 2 |
| Rodgers | 3 | 23 | 7.7 | 0 |
| G. Lewis | 3 | 21 | 7.0 | 0 |
| Jensen | 3 | 18 | 6.0 | 1 |
| Meade | 3 | -5 | -1.7 | 0 |
| Thompson | 2 | 24 | 12.0 | 0 |

### PUNT RETURNS

| Last Name | No. | Yds | Avg | TD |
|---|---|---|---|---|
| Epps | 20 | 150 | 7.5 | 0 |
| Gray | 6 | 48 | 8.0 | 0 |

### KICKOFF RETURNS

| Last Name | No. | Yds | Avg | TD |
|---|---|---|---|---|
| Rodgers | 20 | 436 | 21.8 | 0 |
| Huckleby | 5 | 89 | 17.8 | 0 |
| Clark | 4 | 75 | 18.8 | 0 |
| Gray | 2 | 29 | 14.5 | 0 |
| C. Lewis | 1 | 4 | 4.0 | 0 |

### PASSING — PUNTING — KICKING

| PASSING | Att | Comp | % | Yds | Yd/Att | TD | Int- | % | RK |
|---|---|---|---|---|---|---|---|---|---|
| Dickey | 218 | 124 | 57 | 1790 | 8.21 | 12 | 14- | 6 | 9 |
| Whitehurst | 47 | 18 | 38 | 235 | 5.00 | 0 | 1- | 2 | |
| Lofton | 1 | 1 | 100 | 43 | 43.00 | 0 | 0- | 0 | |
| Ivery | 1 | 0 | 0 | 0 | 0.00 | 0 | 0- | 0 | |

| PUNTING | No | Avg |
|---|---|---|
| Stachowicz | 42 | 40.2 |

| KICKING | XP | Att | % | FG | Att | % |
|---|---|---|---|---|---|---|
| Stenerud | 25 | 27 | 93 | 13 | 18 | 72 |

## MINNESOTA VIKINGS

### RUSHING

| Last Name | No. | Yds | Avg | TD |
|---|---|---|---|---|
| Brown | 120 | 515 | 4.3 | 0 |
| Nelson | 44 | 136 | 3.1 | 0 |
| Galbreath | 39 | 116 | 3.0 | 1 |
| Kramer | 21 | 77 | 3.7 | 3 |
| Young | 16 | 49 | 3.0 | 1 |
| Coleman | 1 | 15 | 15.0 | 0 |
| Dils | 1 | 5 | 5.0 | 0 |
| Redwine | 2 | 2 | 1.0 | 0 |
| LeCount | 1 | -3 | -3.0 | 0 |

### RECEIVING

| Last Name | No. | Yds | Avg | TD |
|---|---|---|---|---|
| Brown | 31 | 207 | 6.7 | 2 |
| S. White | 29 | 503 | 17.3 | 5 |
| Senser | 29 | 261 | 9.0 | 1 |
| Rashad | 23 | 233 | 10.1 | 0 |
| Galbreath | 17 | 153 | 9.0 | 0 |
| LeCount | 14 | 179 | 12.8 | 1 |
| McCullum | 12 | 131 | 10.9 | 0 |
| Nelson | 9 | 100 | 11.1 | 0 |
| Lewis | 8 | 150 | 18.8 | 3 |
| Bruer | 8 | 102 | 12.8 | 2 |
| Young | 4 | 44 | 11.0 | 1 |
| Jordan | 3 | 42 | 14.0 | 0 |

### PUNT RETURNS

| Last Name | No. | Yds | Avg | TD |
|---|---|---|---|---|
| Payton | 22 | 179 | 8.1 | 0 |
| Bess | 2 | 17 | 8.5 | 0 |
| Hannon | 0 | 0 | 0.0 | 0 |

### KICKOFF RETURNS

| Last Name | No. | Yds | Avg | TD |
|---|---|---|---|---|
| Redwine | 12 | 286 | 23.8 | 0 |
| Payton | 12 | 271 | 22.6 | 0 |
| Nelson | 6 | 132 | 22.0 | 0 |
| Nord | 3 | 43 | 14.3 | 0 |
| Harrell | 2 | 21 | 10.5 | 0 |
| McDole | 1 | 26 | 26.0 | 0 |
| Elshire | 1 | 7 | 7.0 | 0 |

### PASSING — PUNTING — KICKING

| PASSING | Att | Comp | % | Yds | Yd/Att | TD | Int- | % | RK |
|---|---|---|---|---|---|---|---|---|---|
| Kramer | 308 | 176 | 57 | 2037 | 6.61 | 15 | 12- | 4 | 8 |
| Dils | 26 | 11 | 42 | 68 | 2.61 | 0 | 0- | 0 | |

| PUNTING | No | Avg |
|---|---|---|
| Coleman | 58 | 41.1 |

| KICKING | XP | Att | % | FG | Att | % |
|---|---|---|---|---|---|---|
| Danmeier | 23 | 23 | 100 | 8 | 14 | 57 |

## TAMPA BAY BUCCANEERS

### RUSHING

| Last Name | No. | Yds | Avg | TD |
|---|---|---|---|---|
| Wilder | 83 | 324 | 3.9 | 3 |
| Owens | 76 | 238 | 3.1 | 0 |
| Carver | 70 | 229 | 3.3 | 1 |
| Williams | 35 | 158 | 4.5 | 2 |
| Morton | 2 | 3 | 1.5 | 0 |
| Giles | 1 | 1 | 1.0 | 0 |
| House | 1 | -1 | -1.0 | 0 |

### RECEIVING

| Last Name | No. | Yds | Avg | TD |
|---|---|---|---|---|
| Wilder | 53 | 466 | 8.8 | 1 |
| Giles | 28 | 499 | 17.8 | 3 |
| House | 28 | 438 | 15.6 | 2 |
| T. Bell | 15 | 203 | 13.5 | 0 |
| Jones | 14 | 205 | 14.6 | 1 |
| Carter | 10 | 140 | 14.0 | 0 |
| Owens | 8 | 42 | 5.3 | 1 |
| Carver | 4 | 46 | 11.5 | 1 |
| Obradovich | 2 | 22 | 11.0 | 1 |
| J. Bell | 1 | 5 | 5.0 | 0 |
| Morton | 1 | 5 | 5.0 | 0 |

### PUNT RETURNS

| Last Name | No. | Yds | Avg | TD |
|---|---|---|---|---|
| Holt | 16 | 81 | 5.1 | 0 |
| T. Bell | 9 | 62 | 6.9 | 0 |

### KICKOFF RETURNS

| Last Name | No. | Yds | Avg | TD |
|---|---|---|---|---|
| Morton | 21 | 361 | 17.2 | 0 |
| Carver | 3 | 62 | 20.7 | 0 |
| Owens | 3 | 52 | 17.3 | 0 |
| J.R. Smith | 3 | 47 | 15.7 | 0 |
| Yarno | 1 | 14 | 14.0 | 0 |
| Obradovich | 1 | 12 | 12.0 | 0 |
| Davis | 1 | 0 | 0.0 | 0 |

### PASSING — PUNTING — KICKING

| PASSING | Att | Comp | % | Yds | Yd/Att | TD | Int- | % | RK |
|---|---|---|---|---|---|---|---|---|---|
| Williams | 307 | 164 | 53 | 2071 | 6.75 | 9 | 11- | 4 | 13 |
| Golsteyn | 1 | 0 | 0 | 0 | 0.00 | 0 | 0- | 0 | |

| PUNTING | No | Avg |
|---|---|---|
| Swider | 39 | 41.5 |

| KICKING | XP | Att | % | FG | Att | % |
|---|---|---|---|---|---|---|
| Capece | 14 | 14 | 100 | 18 | 23 | 78 |

## DETROIT LIONS

### RUSHING

| Last Name | No. | Yds | Avg | TD |
|---|---|---|---|---|
| Sims | 172 | 639 | 3.7 | 4 |
| Bussey | 48 | 136 | 2.8 | 0 |
| Danielson | 23 | 92 | 4.0 | 0 |
| King | 18 | 67 | 3.7 | 0 |
| Hipple | 10 | 57 | 5.7 | 0 |
| Kane | 7 | 17 | 2.4 | 0 |
| L. Thompson | 2 | 16 | 8.0 | 0 |
| Nichols | 1 | 3 | 3.0 | 0 |
| Rubick | 1 | 1 | 1.0 | 0 |
| Scott | 1 | -6 | -6.0 | 0 |

### RECEIVING

| Last Name | No. | Yds | Avg | TD |
|---|---|---|---|---|
| Sims | 34 | 342 | 10.1 | 0 |
| Hill | 22 | 252 | 11.5 | 4 |
| L. Thompson | 17 | 328 | 19.3 | 4 |
| Bussey | 16 | 138 | 8.6 | 0 |
| Scott | 13 | 231 | 17.8 | 1 |
| Porter | 9 | 124 | 13.8 | 0 |
| King | 9 | 74 | 8.2 | 1 |
| Nichols | 8 | 146 | 18.3 | 2 |
| Norris | 3 | 51 | 17.0 | 0 |
| Kane | 3 | 25 | 8.3 | 0 |
| Cobb | 1 | 25 | 25.0 | 0 |
| Martin | 1 | 18 | 18.0 | 0 |

### PUNT RETURNS

| Last Name | No. | Yds | Avg | TD |
|---|---|---|---|---|
| Martin | 26 | 275 | 10.6 | 0 |

### KICKOFF RETURNS

| Last Name | No. | Yds | Avg | TD |
|---|---|---|---|---|
| Hall | 16 | 426 | 26.6 | 0 |
| Martin | 16 | 268 | 16.8 | 0 |
| King | 2 | 23 | 11.5 | 0 |
| Kane | 1 | 19 | 19.0 | 0 |
| L. Lee | 1 | 14 | 14.0 | 0 |

### PASSING — PUNTING — KICKING

| PASSING | Att | Comp | % | Yds | Yd/Att | TD | Int- | % | RK |
|---|---|---|---|---|---|---|---|---|---|
| Danielson | 197 | 100 | 51 | 1343 | 6.82 | 10 | 14- | 7 | 14 |
| Hipple | 86 | 36 | 42 | 411 | 4.78 | 2 | 4- | 5 | |
| Porter | 1 | 0 | 0 | 0 | 0.00 | 0 | 0- | 0 | |
| Skladany | 1 | 0 | 0 | 0 | 0.00 | 0 | 0- | 0 | |

| PUNTING | No | Avg |
|---|---|---|
| Skladany | 36 | 41.2 |

| KICKING | XP | Att | % | FG | Att | % |
|---|---|---|---|---|---|---|
| Murray | 16 | 16 | 100 | 11 | 12 | 92 |

## CHICAGO BEARS

### RUSHING

| Last Name | No. | Yds | Avg | TD |
|---|---|---|---|---|
| Payton | 148 | 596 | 4.0 | 1 |
| Suhey | 70 | 206 | 2.9 | 3 |
| McMahon | 24 | 105 | 4.4 | 1 |
| McClendon | 17 | 47 | 2.8 | 0 |
| Gentry | 4 | 21 | 5.3 | 0 |
| Harper | 3 | 7 | 2.3 | 0 |
| C. Thomas | 5 | 4 | 0.8 | 0 |
| Moorehead | 2 | 3 | 1.5 | 0 |
| Evans | 2 | 0 | 0.0 | 0 |
| Watts | 1 | -1 | -1.0 | 0 |

### RECEIVING

| Last Name | No. | Yds | Avg | TD |
|---|---|---|---|---|
| Suhey | 36 | 333 | 9.3 | 0 |
| Payton | 32 | 311 | 9.7 | 0 |
| Moorehead | 30 | 363 | 12.1 | 5 |
| Margerum | 14 | 207 | 14.8 | 3 |
| Baschnagel | 12 | 194 | 16.2 | 2 |
| Watts | 8 | 217 | 27.1 | 0 |
| Earl | 4 | 56 | 14.0 | 0 |
| Scott | 2 | 44 | 22.0 | 0 |
| Gentry | 1 | 9 | 9.0 | 0 |
| Harper | 1 | 8 | 8.0 | 0 |
| McClendon | 1 | 7 | 7.0 | 0 |

### PUNT RETURNS

| Last Name | No. | Yds | Avg | TD |
|---|---|---|---|---|
| Gentry | 17 | 89 | 5.2 | 0 |
| Fisher | 7 | 53 | 7.6 | 0 |

### KICKOFF RETURNS

| Last Name | No. | Yds | Avg | TD |
|---|---|---|---|---|
| Watts | 14 | 330 | 23.6 | 0 |
| Gentry | 9 | 161 | 17.9 | 0 |
| Fisher | 7 | 102 | 14.6 | 0 |
| Harper | 2 | 10 | 5.0 | 0 |
| Bell | 1 | 14 | 14.0 | 0 |
| Muckensturm | 1 | 5 | 5.0 | 0 |

### PASSING — PUNTING — KICKING

| PASSING | Att | Comp | % | Yds | Yd/Att | TD | Int- | % | RK |
|---|---|---|---|---|---|---|---|---|---|
| McMahon | 210 | 120 | 57 | 1501 | 7.15 | 9 | 7- | 3 | 4 |
| Avellini | 20 | 8 | 40 | 84 | 4.20 | 0 | 0- | 0 | |
| Evans | 28 | 12 | 43 | 125 | 4.46 | 0 | 4- | 14 | |
| Payton | 3 | 1 | 33 | 39 | 13.00 | 0 | 0- | 0 | |
| Baschnagel | 1 | 0 | 0 | 0 | 0.00 | 0 | 0- | 0 | |

| PUNTING | No | Avg |
|---|---|---|
| Parsons | 58 | 41.3 |
| McMahon | 1 | 59.0 |

| KICKING | XP | Att | % | FG | Att | % |
|---|---|---|---|---|---|---|
| Roveto | 10 | 10 | 100 | 4 | 13 | 31 |
| Thomas | 9 | 9 | 100 | 10 | 12 | 71 |

## ATLANTA FALCONS 5-4-0 Leeman Bennett

| Scores of Each Game | | |
|---|---|---|
| 16 | N.Y.Giants | 14 |
| 14 | L.A.RAIDERS | 38 |
| 34 | L.A.RAMS | 17 |
| 20 | ST.LOUIS | 23 |
| 34 | Denver | 27 |
| 35 | NEW ORLEANS | 0 |
| 17 | San Francisco | 7 |
| 7 | GREEN BAY | 38 |
| 6 | New Orleans | 35 |

| Use Name | Pos. | Hgt | Wgt | Age | Int | Pts |
|---|---|---|---|---|---|---|
| Warren Bryant | OT | 6'6" | 270 | 26 | | |
| Mike Kenn | OT | 6'6" | 257 | 26 | | |
| Eric Sanders | OT | 6'6" | 255 | 23 | | |
| Pat Howell | OG | 6'5" | 253 | 25 | | |
| Dave Scott | OG | 6'4" | 265 | 28 | | |
| R.C. Thielemann | OG | 6'4" | 247 | 27 | | |
| John Scully | C | 6'6" | 255 | 24 | | |
| Jeff Van Note | C | 6'2" | 247 | 36 | | |
| Jeff Merrow | DE | 6'4" | 255 | 29 | | |
| Doug Rogers | DE | 6'5" | 255 | 22 | | |
| Jeff Yeates | DE | 6'3" | 248 | 31 | | |
| Mike Perko | NT | 6'4" | 235 | 25 | | |
| Don Smith | NT | 6'5" | 248 | 25 | | |
| Mike Zele | NT | 6'3" | 236 | 26 | | |

| Use Name | Pos. | Hgt | Wgt | Age | Int | Pts |
|---|---|---|---|---|---|---|
| Buddy Curry | LB | 6'3" | 221 | 24 | 1 | |
| Paul Davis | LB | 6'2" | 215 | 24 | | |
| Robert Jackson | LB | 6'1" | 230 | 28 | | |
| Fulton Kuykendall | LB | 6'5" | 225 | 29 | 2 | |
| Jim Laughlin | LB | 6' | 212 | 24 | | |
| Neal Musser | LB | 6'2" | 218 | 25 | | |
| Al Richardson | LB | 6'2" | 206 | 24 | | |
| Lyman White | LB | 6' | 217 | 23 | | |
| Joel Williams | LB | 6'1" | 215 | 25 | | |
| Bobby Butler | DB | 5'11" | 170 | 23 | 2 | |
| Biane Galson | DB | 6' | 185 | 24 | 1 | |
| Bob Glazebrook | DB | 6'1" | 200 | 26 | 1 | 6 |
| Kenny Johnson | DB | 5'10" | 176 | 24 | 2 | |
| Earl Jones | DB | 6' | 178 | 25 | | |
| Tom Pridemore | DB | 5'10" | 186 | 26 | 1 | |
| Mike Spivey | DB | 6' | 196 | 28 | | |

| Use Name | Pos. | Hgt | Wgt | Age | Int | Pts |
|---|---|---|---|---|---|---|
| Steve Bartkowski | QB | 6'4" | 213 | 29 | | 6 |
| Jeff Komlo | QB | 6'2" | 200 | 26 | | |
| Mike Moroski | QB | 6'4" | 200 | 24 | | |
| Lynn Cain | HB | 6'1" | 205 | 26 | | 12 |
| Ray Strong | HB | 5'9" | 184 | 26 | | |
| William Andrews | FB | 6' | 200 | 26 | | 42 |
| Reggie Brown | FB | 5'11" | 211 | 22 | | |
| Gerald Riggs | FB | 6'1" | 230 | 21 | | 30 |
| Bo Robinson | FB | 6'2" | 225 | 26 | | 12 |
| Stacey Bailey | WR | 6' | 162 | 22 | | 6 |
| Willie Curran | WR | 5'10" | 175 | 22 | | |
| Floyd Hodge | WR | 6' | 195 | 23 | | |
| Alfred Jackson | WR | 5'11" | 176 | 27 | | 6 |
| Alfred Jenkins | WR | 5'9" | 155 | 30 | | 6 |
| Billy Johnson | WR | 5'9" | 170 | 30 | | |
| Clay Brown | TE | 6'3" | 225 | 23 | | |
| Keith Krepfle | TE | 6'3" | 230 | 30 | | |
| Russ Mikeska | TE | 6'3" | 225 | 26 | | |
| Junior Miller | TE | 6'4" | 235 | 24 | | 6 |
| Mick Luckhurst | K | 6' | 180 | 24 | | 51 |
| Dave Smigelsky | K | 5'11" | 180 | 23 | | |
| George Roberts | K | 6' | 186 | 28 | | |

## NEW ORLEANS SAINTS 4-5-0 Bum Phillips

| Scores of Each Game | | |
|---|---|---|
| 7 | ST.LOUIS | 21 |
| 10 | Chicago | 0 |
| 27 | KANSAS CITY | 17 |
| 23 | San Francisco | 20 |
| 10 | TAMPA BAY | 13 |
| 0 | Atlanta | 35 |
| 7 | Dallas | 21 |
| 10 | WASHINGTON | 27 |
| 35 | ATLANTA | 6 |

| Use Name | Pos. | Hgt | Wgt | Age | Int | Pts |
|---|---|---|---|---|---|---|
| Stan Brock | OT | 6'6" | 285 | 24 | | |
| Leon Gray | OT | 6'3" | 258 | 30 | | |
| Dave Lafary | OT | 6'7" | 275 | 27 | | |
| Chuck Slaughter | OT | 6'5" | 260 | 23 | | |
| Kelvin Clark | OG | 6'3" | 265 | 26 | | |
| Brad Edelman | OG | 6'6" | 255 | 21 | | |
| Louis Oubre | OG | 6'4" | 262 | 24 | | |
| John Hill | C | 6'2" | 246 | 32 | | |
| Jim Pietrzak | C | 6'5" | 260 | 29 | | |
| Bruce Clark | DE | 6'3" | 250 | 24 | | |
| Reggie Lewis | DE | 6'2" | 248 | 28 | | |
| Frank Warren | DE | 6'4" | 275 | 22 | | |
| Jim Wilks | DE | 6'5" | 252 | 24 | | |
| Tony Elliott | NT | 6'2" | 247 | 23 | | |
| Derland Moore | NT | 6'4" | 253 | 30 | | |

Glen Redd - Knee Injury
Tom Myers - Knee Injury
Dave Wilson - Knee Injury

| Use Name | Pos. | Hgt | Wgt | Age | Int | Pts |
|---|---|---|---|---|---|---|
| Ken Bordelon | LB | 6'4" | 226 | 28 | | |
| Rickey Jackson | LB | 6'2" | 230 | 24 | 1 | |
| Jim Kovach | LB | 6'2" | 225 | 26 | | |
| Rob Naime | LB | 6'4" | 227 | 28 | 1 | |
| Whitney Paul | LB | 6'3" | 220 | 26 | 1 | |
| Scott Pelluer | LB | 6'2" | 215 | 23 | | |
| Ed Simonini | LB | 6' | 206 | 27 | | |
| Denis Winston | LB | 6' | 228 | 26 | 2 | |
| Russell Gary | DB | 5'11" | 195 | 23 | 2 | |
| Kevin Gray | DB | 5'11" | 179 | 24 | | |
| Bill Hurley | DB | 5'11" | 195 | 25 | 1 | 6 |
| John Krimm | DB | 6' | 190 | 22 | | |
| Rodney Lewis | DB | 5'11" | 190 | 23 | 1 | |
| Johnnie Poe | DB | 6'1" | 185 | 23 | | |
| Frank Wattelet | DB | 6' | 185 | 23 | | |
| Dave Waymer | DB | 6'1" | 195 | 24 | | |

| Use Name | Pos. | Hgt | Wgt | Age | Int | Pts |
|---|---|---|---|---|---|---|
| Guido Merkens | QB | 6'1" | 195 | 27 | | |
| Bobby Scott | QB | 6'1" | 197 | 33 | | |
| Ken Stabler | QB | 6'3" | 210 | 36 | | |
| George Rogers | HB | 6'2" | 229 | 23 | | 18 |
| Jimmy Rogers | HB | 5'10" | 190 | 27 | | 12 |
| Hokie Gajan | FB | 5'11" | 211 | 22 | | |
| Jack Holmes | FB | 5'11" | 210 | 29 | | |
| Marvin Lewis | FB | 6'3" | 208 | 22 | | |
| Toussaint Tyler | FB | 6'2" | 220 | 23 | | |
| Wayne Wilson | FB | 6'3" | 208 | 24 | | 30 |
| Kenny Duckett | WR | 6' | 187 | 22 | | 12 |
| Jeff Groth | WR | 5'10" | 172 | 25 | | 6 |
| Rich Mauti | WR | 6' | 190 | 28 | | |
| Lindsay Scott | WR | 6'1" | 190 | 21 | | |
| Aundra Thompson | WR | 6' | 186 | 29 | | 6 |
| Don Bass | TE | 6'2" | 220 | 26 | | |
| Hoby Brenner | TE | 6'4" | 240 | 23 | | |
| Larry Hardy | TE | 6'3" | 230 | 26 | | 6 |
| Morten Andersen | K | 6'2" | 190 | 22 | | 12 |
| Russell Erxleben | K | 6'4" | 219 | 25 | | 1 |
| Toni Fritsch | K | 5'7" | 201 | 37 | | 20 |

## SAN FRANCISCO 49ERS 3-6-0 Bill Walsh

| Scores of Each Game | | |
|---|---|---|
| 17 | L.A.RAIDERS | 23 |
| 21 | Denver | 24 |
| 31 | St.Louis | 20 |
| 20 | NEW ORLEANS | 23 |
| 30 | L.A.RAMS | 24 |
| 37 | SAN DIEGO | 41 |
| 7 | ATLANTA | 17 |
| 26 | Kansas City | 13 |
| 20 | L.A.RAMS | 21 |

| Use Name | Pos. | Hgt | Wgt | Age | Int | Pts |
|---|---|---|---|---|---|---|
| Keith Fahnhorst | OT | 6'6" | 273 | 30 | | |
| Lindsey Mason | OT | 6'5" | 275 | 27 | | |
| Dan Audick | OG-OT | 6'3" | 253 | 27 | | |
| John Ayers | OG | 6'5" | 265 | 29 | | |
| Randy Cross | OG | 6'3" | 265 | 28 | | |
| John Choma | OG-C | 6'6" | 261 | 27 | | |
| Walt Downing | C-OG | 6'3" | 270 | 26 | | |
| Fred Quillan | C | 6'5" | 266 | 26 | | |
| Dwaine Board | DE | 6'5" | 250 | 25 | | |
| Mike Clark | DE | 6'4" | 250 | 23 | | |
| Fred Dean | DE | 6'3" | 236 | 30 | | |
| Jeff Stover | DE | 6'5" | 275 | 24 | | |
| Jim Stuckey | DE | 6'4" | 251 | 24 | | |
| John Harty | NT | 6'4" | 263 | 23 | | |
| Pete Kugler | NT-DE | 6'4" | 255 | 23 | | |
| Lawrence Pillers | NT-DE | 6'3" | 250 | 29 | | |

Allan Kennedy - Ankle Injury

| Use Name | Pos. | Hgt | Wgt | Age | Int | Pts |
|---|---|---|---|---|---|---|
| Terry Beeson | LB | 6'3" | 233 | 26 | | |
| Dan Bunz | LB | 6'4" | 225 | 26 | | |
| Ron Ferrari | LB | 6' | 212 | 23 | | |
| Willie Harper | LB | 6'2" | 215 | 32 | 1 | |
| Bob Horn | LB | 6'3" | 230 | 28 | 1 | |
| Ed Judie | LB | 6'2" | 231 | 23 | | |
| Bobby Leopold | LB | 6'1" | 215 | 24 | | |
| Milt McColl | LB | 6'6" | 220 | 23 | | |
| Jack Reynolds | LB | 6'1" | 232 | 34 | 1 | |
| Eric Scoggins | LB | 6'2" | 235 | 23 | | |
| Keena Turner | LB | 6'2" | 219 | 23 | | |
| Rick Gervais | DB | 5'11" | 190 | 22 | | |
| Dwight Hicks | DB | 6'1" | 189 | 26 | 3 | |
| Ronnie Lott | DB | 6' | 199 | 23 | 2 | 6 |
| Dana McLemore | DB | 5'10" | 183 | 22 | | 6 |
| Lynn Thomas | DB | 5'11" | 181 | 23 | | |
| Tim Washington | DB | 5'9" | 184 | 22 | | |
| Carlton Williamson | DB | 6' | 204 | 24 | | |
| Eric Wright | DB | 6'1" | 180 | 23 | 1 | |

| Use Name | Pos. | Hgt | Wgt | Age | Int | Pts |
|---|---|---|---|---|---|---|
| Guy Benjamin | QB | 6'4" | 210 | 27 | | |
| Bryan Clark | QB | 6'2" | 196 | 22 | | |
| Joe Montana | QB | 6'2" | 200 | 26 | | 6 |
| Amos Lawrence | HB | 5'11" | 179 | 24 | | |
| Jeff Moore | HB | 6' | 196 | 26 | | 48 |
| Ricky Patton | HB | 5'11" | 192 | 28 | | |
| Bill Ring | HB | 5'10" | 215 | 25 | | 6 |
| Newton Williams | HB | 5'10" | 204 | 23 | | |
| Earl Cooper | FB | 6'2" | 227 | 24 | | 6 |
| Walt Easley | FB | 6'1" | 226 | 24 | | |
| Vince Williams | FB | 6' | 231 | 22 | | |
| Dwight Clark | WR | 6'4" | 210 | 25 | | 30 |
| Renaldo Nehemiah | WR | 6'1" | 177 | 23 | | 6 |
| Freddie Solomon | WR | 5'11" | 185 | 29 | | 18 |
| Mike Wilson | WR | 6'3" | 210 | 23 | | 6 |
| Russ Francis | TE | 6'6" | 242 | 29 | | 12 |
| Eason Ramson | TE | 6'2" | 234 | 26 | | |
| Charle Young | TE | 6'4" | 234 | 31 | | |
| Jim Miller | K | 5'11" | 183 | 25 | | |
| Ray Wersching | K | 5'11" | 210 | 32 | | 59 |

## LOS ANGELES RAMS 2-7-0 Ray Malavasi

| Scores of Each Game | | |
|---|---|---|
| 23 | Green Bay | 35 |
| 14 | DETROIT | 19 |
| 17 | Atlanta | 43 |
| 20 | KANSAS CITY | 14 |
| 24 | SAN FRANCISCO | 30 |
| 24 | DENVER | 27 |
| 31 | L.A.Raiders | 37 |
| 26 | CHICAGO | 34 |
| 21 | San Francisco | 20 |

| Use Name | Pos. | Hgt | Wgt | Age | Int | Pts |
|---|---|---|---|---|---|---|
| Wally Kersten | OT | 6'5" | 270 | 22 | | |
| Irv Pankey | OT | 6'4" | 267 | 23 | | |
| Jackie Slater | OT | 6'4" | 271 | 28 | | |
| Ron Yary | OT | 6'6" | 255 | 36 | | |
| Bill Bain | OG | 6'4" | 285 | 30 | | |
| Dennis Harrah | OG | 6'5" | 255 | 29 | | |
| Kent Hill | OG | 6'5" | 260 | 25 | | |
| George Lilja | C | 6'4" | 250 | 24 | | |
| Doug Smith | C | 6'3" | 253 | 25 | | |
| Doug Bennett | DE-C | 6'3" | 250 | 22 | | |
| Reggie Doss | DE | 6'4" | 263 | 25 | | |
| Greg Meisner | DE | 6'3" | 253 | 23 | | |
| Jack Youngblood | DE | 6'4" | 242 | 32 | | |
| Larry Brooks | DT | 6'3" | 255 | 32 | | |
| Charles DeJurnett | DT | 6'4" | 260 | 30 | | |
| Mike Fanning | DT | 6'6" | 255 | 29 | | |
| Cody Jones | DT | 6'5" | 255 | 31 | | |
| Myron Lapka | DT | 6'4" | 260 | 26 | | |

| Use Name | Pos. | Hgt | Wgt | Age | Int | Pts |
|---|---|---|---|---|---|---|
| George Andrews | LB | 6'3" | 221 | 26 | | |
| Howard Carson | LB | 6'2" | 230 | 25 | | |
| Jim Collins | LB | 6'2" | 230 | 24 | | |
| Carl Ekern | LB | 6'3" | 222 | 28 | 1 | |
| Mel Owens | LB | 6'2" | 224 | 23 | | |
| Mike Reilly | LB | 6'4" | 217 | 23 | | |
| Eric Williams | LB | 6'2" | 235 | 27 | | |
| Jim Youngblood | LB | 6'3" | 231 | 32 | | |
| Kirk Collins | DB | 5'11" | 183 | 24 | | |
| Nolan Cromwell | DB | 6'1" | 200 | 27 | 3 | 6 |
| LeRoy Irvin | DB | 5'11" | 184 | 24 | | 6 |
| Johnnie Johnson | DB | 6'1" | 183 | 25 | 1 | |
| Rod Perry | DB | 5'9" | 185 | 28 | 3 | |
| Lucious Smith | DB | 5'10" | 190 | 25 | | |
| Ivory Sully | DB | 6' | 201 | 25 | | |
| Pat Thomas | DB | 5'9" | 190 | 28 | 3 | |

| Use Name | Pos. | Hgt | Wgt | Age | Int | Pts |
|---|---|---|---|---|---|---|
| Vince Ferragamo | QB | 6'3" | 212 | 28 | | 6 |
| Bert Jones | QB | 6'3" | 209 | 30 | | |
| Jeff Kemp | QB | 6' | 201 | 23 | | |
| Robert Alexander | HB | 6' | 185 | 24 | | |
| Wendell Tyler | HB | 5'10" | 200 | 27 | | 78 |
| Barry Redden | HB-FB | 5'10" | 205 | 22 | | |
| Jewerl Thomas | HB-FB | 5'10" | 228 | 24 | | |
| Cullen Bryant | FB | 6'1" | 235 | 31 | | |
| Mike Guman | FB | 6'2" | 218 | 24 | | 12 |
| A.J. Jones | FB | 6'1" | 202 | 23 | | |
| Preston Dennard | WR | 6'1" | 183 | 26 | | 12 |
| George Farmer | WR | 5'10" | 175 | 23 | | 12 |
| Drew Hill | WR | 5'9" | 170 | 25 | | |
| Willie Miller | WR | 5'9 | 173 | 34 | | 6 |
| Billy Waddy | WR | 5'11" | 190 | 28 | | |
| Mike Barber | TE | 6'3" | 237 | 29 | | 6 |
| Ron Battle | TE | 6'3" | 225 | 23 | | 6 |
| Kerry Locklin | TE | 6'3" | 217 | 22 | | |
| Mike Lansford | K | 6' | 183 | 24 | | 50 |
| John Misko | K | 6'5" | 207 | 27 | | |

## ATLANTA FALCONS

### RUSHING

| Last Name | No. | Yds | Avg | TD |
|---|---|---|---|---|
| Andrews | 139 | 573 | 4.1 | 5 |
| Riggs | 78 | 299 | 3.8 | 5 |
| Cain | 54 | 173 | 3.2 | 1 |
| Robinson | 19 | 108 | 5.7 | 0 |
| Hodge | 2 | 11 | 5.5 | 0 |
| Strong | 4 | 9 | 2.3 | 0 |
| Jackson | 1 | 4 | 4.0 | 0 |
| Bartkowski | 13 | 4 | 0.3 | 1 |

### RECEIVING

| Last Name | No. | Yds | Avg | TD |
|---|---|---|---|---|
| Andrews | 42 | 503 | 12.0 | 2 |
| Jackson | 26 | 361 | 13.9 | 1 |
| Jenkins | 24 | 347 | 14.5 | 1 |
| Riggs | 23 | 185 | 8.0 | 0 |
| Miller | 20 | 221 | 11.1 | 1 |
| Hodge | 14 | 160 | 11.4 | 0 |
| Cain | 13 | 101 | 7.8 | 1 |
| Robinson | 7 | 55 | 7.9 | 2 |
| Bailey | 2 | 24 | 12.0 | 1 |
| Mikesla | 2 | 19 | 9.5 | 0 |
| B. Johnson | 2 | 11 | 5.5 | 0 |
| Krepile | 1 | 5 | 5.0 | 0 |

### PUNT RETURNS

| Last Name | No. | Yds | Avg | TD |
|---|---|---|---|---|
| B. Johnson | 24 | 273 | 11.4 | 0 |

### KICKOFF RETURNS

| Last Name | No. | Yds | Avg | TD |
|---|---|---|---|---|
| Brown | 24 | 466 | 19.4 | 0 |
| Galson | 2 | 14 | 7.0 | 0 |
| Hodge | 1 | 23 | 23.0 | 0 |
| Laughlin | 1 | 10 | 10.0 | 0 |
| Scully | 1 | 0 | 0.0 | 0 |

### PASSING — PUNTING — KICKING

| PASSING | Att | Comp | % | Yds | Yd/Att | TD | Int- | % | RK |
|---|---|---|---|---|---|---|---|---|---|
| Bartkowski | 262 | 166 | 63 | 1905 | 7.27 | 8 | 11- | 4 | 5 |
| Moroski | 13 | 10 | 77 | 87 | 6.69 | 1 | 0- | 0 | |
| Andrews | 0 | 0 | 0 | 0 | 0.00 | 0 | 0- | 0 | |

| PUNTING | No | Avg |
|---|---|---|
| Smigelsy | 26 | 38.5 |
| Roberts | 17 | 40.6 |

| KICKING | XP | Att | % | FG | Att | % |
|---|---|---|---|---|---|---|
| Luckhurst | 21 | 22 | 95 | 10 | 14 | 71 |

## NEW ORLEANS SAINTS

### RUSHING

| Last Name | No. | Yds | Avg | TD |
|---|---|---|---|---|
| G. Rogers | 122 | 535 | 4.4 | 3 |
| W. Wilson | 103 | 413 | 4.0 | 3 |
| J. Rogers | 60 | 178 | 3.0 | 2 |
| Gajan | 19 | 77 | 4.1 | 0 |
| Merkens | 9 | 30 | 3.3 | 0 |
| Tyler | 10 | 21 | 2.1 | 0 |
| Holmes | 2 | 8 | 4.0 | 0 |
| Thompson | 1 | 2 | 2.0 | 0 |
| Groth | 1 | 1 | 1.0 | 0 |
| Stabler | 3 | -4 | -1.3 | 0 |
| L. Scott | 1 | -4 | -4.0 | 0 |

### RECEIVING

| Last Name | No. | Yds | Avg | TD |
|---|---|---|---|---|
| Groth | 30 | 383 | 12.8 | 1 |
| W. Wilson | 25 | 175 | 7.0 | 2 |
| L. Scott | 17 | 251 | 14.8 | 0 |
| Brenner | 16 | 171 | 10.7 | 0 |
| Duckett | 12 | 196 | 16.3 | 0 |
| Thompson | 8 | 138 | 17.3 | 1 |
| Hardy | 8 | 67 | 8.4 | 0 |
| Mauti | 4 | 70 | 17.5 | 0 |
| Tyler | 4 | 31 | 7.8 | 0 |
| G. Rogers | 4 | 21 | 5.3 | 0 |
| J. Rogers | 4 | 17 | 4.3 | 0 |
| Gajan | 3 | 10 | 3.3 | 0 |
| Hurley | 1 | 39 | 39.0 | 1 |
| Holmes | 1 | 2 | 2.0 | 0 |

### PUNT RETURNS

| Last Name | No. | Yds | Avg | TD |
|---|---|---|---|---|
| Groth | 21 | 144 | 6.9 | 0 |

### KICKOFF RETURNS

| Last Name | No. | Yds | Avg | TD |
|---|---|---|---|---|
| Thompson | 10 | 211 | 21.1 | 0 |
| W. Wilson | 7 | 192 | 27.4 | 0 |
| Mauti | 5 | 93 | 18.6 | 0 |
| Duckett | 2 | 39 | 19.5 | 0 |
| J. Rogers | 1 | 24 | 24.0 | 0 |
| Gajan | 1 | 18 | 18.0 | 0 |

### PASSING — PUNTING — KICKING

| PASSING | Att | Comp | % | Yds | Yd/Att | TD | Int- | % | RK |
|---|---|---|---|---|---|---|---|---|---|
| Stabler | 189 | 117 | 62 | 1343 | 7.11 | 6 | 10- | 5 | 11 |
| Merkens | 49 | 18 | 37 | 186 | 3.80 | 1 | 2- | 4 | |
| Erxleben | 2 | 1 | 50 | 39 | 19.50 | 1 | 0- | 0 | |
| Holmes | 1 | 0 | 0 | 0 | 0.00 | 0 | 0- | 0 | |

| PUNTING | No | Avg |
|---|---|---|
| Erxleben | 46 | 43.0 |

| KICKING | XP | Att | % | FG | Att | % |
|---|---|---|---|---|---|---|
| Fritsch | 8 | 9 | 89 | 4 | 7 | 57 |
| Andersen | 6 | 6 | 100 | 2 | 5 | 40 |
| Erxleben | 1 | 1 | 100 | 1 | 0 | |

## SAN FRANCISCO 49ERS

### RUSHING

| Last Name | No. | Yds | Avg | TD |
|---|---|---|---|---|
| Moore | 85 | 281 | 3.3 | 4 |
| Ring | 48 | 183 | 3.8 | 1 |
| Montana | 30 | 118 | 3.9 | 1 |
| Cooper | 24 | 77 | 3.2 | 0 |
| V. Williams | 20 | 68 | 3.4 | 0 |
| Easley | 5 | 11 | 2.2 | 0 |
| Lawrence | 5 | 7 | 1.4 | 0 |
| Nehemiah | 1 | -1 | -1.0 | 0 |
| Solomon | 1 | -4 | -4.0 | 0 |

### RECEIVING

| Last Name | No. | Yds | Avg | TD |
|---|---|---|---|---|
| D. Clark | 60 | 913 | 15.2 | 5 |
| Moore | 37 | 405 | 10.9 | 4 |
| Francis | 23 | 278 | 12.1 | 2 |
| Young | 22 | 189 | 8.6 | 0 |
| Solomon | 19 | 323 | 17.0 | 3 |
| Cooper | 19 | 153 | 8.1 | 1 |
| Ring | 13 | 94 | 7.2 | 0 |
| Nehemiah | 8 | 161 | 20.1 | 1 |
| Wilson | 6 | 80 | 13.3 | 1 |
| V. Williams | 4 | 33 | 8.3 | 0 |
| Ramson | 2 | 27 | 13.5 | 0 |
| Lawrence | 2 | 12 | 6.0 | 0 |

### PUNT RETURNS

| Last Name | No. | Yds | Avg | TD |
|---|---|---|---|---|
| Solomon | 13 | 122 | 9.4 | 0 |
| Hicks | 10 | 54 | 5.4 | 0 |
| McLemore | 7 | 156 | 22.3 | 1 |
| Ring | 0 | 0 | 0.0 | 0 |

### KICKOFF RETURNS

| Last Name | No. | Yds | Avg | TD |
|---|---|---|---|---|
| McLemore | 16 | 353 | 22.1 | 0 |
| Lawrence | 9 | 190 | 21.1 | 0 |
| Ring | 6 | 145 | 24.2 | 0 |
| Ramson | 2 | 20 | 10.0 | 0 |
| Ferrari | 2 | 19 | 9.5 | 0 |
| Moore | 1 | 15 | 15.0 | 0 |

### PASSING — PUNTING — KICKING

| PASSING | Att | Comp | % | Yds | Yd/Att | TD | Int- | % | RK |
|---|---|---|---|---|---|---|---|---|---|
| Montana | 346 | 213 | 62 | 2613 | 7.55 | 17 | 11- | 3 | 3 |
| Francis | 1 | 1 | 100 | 45 | 45.00 | 0 | 0- | 0 | |
| Benjamin | 1 | 1 | 100 | 10 | 10.00 | 0 | 0- | 0 | |

| PUNTING | No | Avg |
|---|---|---|
| Miller | 44 | 38.1 |

| KICKING | XP | Att | % | FG | Att | % |
|---|---|---|---|---|---|---|
| Wersching | 23 | 25 | 92 | 12 | 17 | 71 |

## LOS ANGELES RAMS

### RUSHING

| Last Name | No. | Yds | Avg | TD |
|---|---|---|---|---|
| Tyler | 137 | 564 | 4.1 | 9 |
| Guman | 69 | 266 | 3.9 | 2 |
| J. Thomas | 16 | 80 | 5.0 | 0 |
| B. Jones | 11 | 73 | 6.6 | 0 |
| Redden | 8 | 24 | 3.0 | 0 |
| Cromwell | 1 | 17 | 17.0 | 1 |
| Miller | 1 | 5 | 5.0 | 0 |
| Ferragamo | 4 | 3 | 0.8 | 1 |
| Alexander | 1 | 3 | 3.0 | 0 |
| Battle | 1 | 1 | 1.0 | 0 |
| Waddy | 2 | -11 | -5.5 | 0 |

### RECEIVING

| Last Name | No. | Yds | Avg | TD |
|---|---|---|---|---|
| Tyler | 38 | 375 | 9.9 | 4 |
| Guman | 31 | 310 | 10.0 | 0 |
| Dennard | 25 | 383 | 15.3 | 2 |
| Barber | 18 | 166 | 9.2 | 1 |
| Farmer | 17 | 344 | 20.2 | 2 |
| Miller | 15 | 346 | 23.1 | 0 |
| J. Thomas | 8 | 49 | 6.1 | 0 |
| D. Hill | 7 | 92 | 13.1 | 0 |
| Redden | 4 | 16 | 4.0 | 0 |
| Battle | 2 | 62 | 31.0 | 1 |
| Alexander | 1 | -7 | -7.0 | 0 |

### PUNT RETURNS

| Last Name | No. | Yds | Avg | TD |
|---|---|---|---|---|
| Irvin | 22 | 242 | 11.0 | 1 |

### KICKOFF RETURNS

| Last Name | No. | Yds | Avg | TD |
|---|---|---|---|---|
| Redden | 22 | 502 | 22.8 | 0 |
| Alexander | 8 | 139 | 17.4 | 0 |
| Guman | 8 | 102 | 12.8 | 0 |
| Sully | 5 | 84 | 16.8 | 0 |
| D. Hill | 2 | 42 | 21.0 | 0 |

### PASSING — PUNTING — KICKING

| PASSING | Att | Comp | % | Yds | Yd/Att | TD | Int- | % | RK |
|---|---|---|---|---|---|---|---|---|---|
| Ferragamo | 209 | 118 | 57 | 1609 | 7.70 | 9 | 9- | 4 | 6 |
| B. Jones | 87 | 48 | 55 | 527 | 6.06 | 2 | 4- | 5 | |
| Guman | 1 | 0 | 0 | 0 | 0.00 | 0 | 1-100 | | |

| PUNTING | No | Avg |
|---|---|---|
| Misko | 45 | 43.6 |

| KICKING | XP | Att | % | FG | Att | % |
|---|---|---|---|---|---|---|
| Lansford | 23 | 24 | 96 | 9 | 15 | 60 |

Long victorious on the field, the Oakland Raiders triumphed in their lawsuit against the N.F.L. The jury listened to both sides, then decided that the league rule which required any franchise shift to be approved by 21 teams was a violation of federal antitrust law. With this rule declared void, Raider chief Al Davis was free to move his team to Los Angeles. The Raiders still practiced during the week in Oakland, but the home field on Sundays was the Los Angeles Coliseum, abandoned by the Rams in 1980. Further legal hurdles lay ahead for Davis. The league would appeal this decision, and Oakland's city fathers would seek to take control of the team through a court order of condemnation. Davis nevertheless figured to prevail in these court actions. The future of franchise shifts was impossible to predict, with teams free to move without league approval.

## EASTERN DIVISION

**Miami Dolphins** — Without the brilliance of any superstars, the Dolphins still played on a par with the N.F.L.'s elite. On opening day, they charged into Shea Stadium and ripped the Jets 45-28 before a shocked New York audience. After the strike, the Dolphins took awhile to regain their edge. They lost to Tampa Bay and dropped a 3-0 heartbreaker in a snowstorm in New England. In the stretch run, however, the Dolphins hit their stride and won their last three games. Of these late victories, a 20-19 triumph over the Jets was the key. The Miami offense emphasized the ground attack, with Andra Franklin the top runner and Ed Newman the star blocker. The defense hounded enemy passers and became known as the Killer Bees. The head Bee was nose tackle Bob Baumhower.

**New York Jets** — The strike actually gave the Jets a needed breather. The Dolphins trounced them on opening day, and Joe Klecko suffered a severe knee injury one week later. The New York Sack Exchange would never again reach the same heights, but Mark Gastineau still harassed quarterbacks regularly. The defense played well enough that the scintillating Jet offense won the first four games after the strike. Richard Todd engineered an offense that had stars in slashing runner Freeman McNeil, swift receiver Wesley Walker and blockers Marvin Powell and Joe Fields. On December 18, the Jets battled the Dolphins in Miami and dropped a 20-19 squeaker. After a meaningless closing loss to the Chiefs, coach Walt Michaels and his players hoped for a third meeting with the Dolphins.

**New England Patriots** — New head coach Ron Meyer brought discipline and lots of changes to the Pats. After cutting many veterans, he named Matt Cavanaugh as the starting quarterback over Steve Grogan. He also had the first player chosen in the college draft, defensive end Kenneth Sims from Texas. The experiment with Cavanaugh ended in week four when Grogan re-emerged as the starter. Sims didn't set the league on fire while learning his trade. The defense as a whole, however, shone in December, shutting out the Dolphins and Seahawks back to back. Despite the changes, the star Pats were holdovers Tony Collins, Stanley Morgan and John Hannah on offense and a healthy Mike Haynes on defense. Last year, they played on a loser; this year, they went to the playoffs.

**Buffalo Bills** — Joe Cribbs insisted that the Bills renegotiate his contract, and he held out for the first two regular-season games when the team refused. The Bills won both pre-strike games despite Cribbs' absence. When play resumed in November, Cribbs was back in uniform to aid in the playoff drive. The solid Buffalo defense reached its peak on December 12 with a 13-0 shutout of the Steelers. Fred Smerlas anchored the unit at nose tackle, but the linebacking corps was lessened by a string of injuries. With a post-season berth within grasp, the Bills blew a tire and lost their last three games. The collapse ended a five-year regime of coach Chuck Knox, who resigned to take over in Seattle.

**Baltimore Colts** — New head coach Frank Kush lived up to his reputation as an iron-willed disciplinarian. His grueling training camp saw massive personnel turnover and a major change in the Colts' identity. Veteran quarterback Bert Jones had been traded during the off-season to the Rams. In his absence, rookie Mike Pagel beat fellow freshman Art Schlichter for the starting job. The revamped roster needed time to work together, and the Colts looked outclassed in two pre-strike losses. The Jets whipped them 37-0 on November 21, and the Bills won 20-0 a week later. The Colts did gain some respect with a 20-17 loss to the Bengals on December 5 and a 20-20 tie with the Packers on December 19. There would be no victories, however, for the Colts this year.

## CENTRAL DIVISION

**Cincinnati Bengals** — No longer surprise upstarts, the Bengals stayed in the front ranks of the A.F.C. Ken Anderson passed with such precision that he set an N.F.L. single-season record with a 70.6 completion percentage. Reeling in the most passes were tall Cris Collinsworth and burly Dan Ross, a brace of all-pro receivers. When running was needed, massive fullback Pete Johnson responded with power. Anthony Munoz led the offensive line in supporting both the air and ground attacks. The Bengal defense was less impressive, getting burned by San Diego 50-34 on Monday night, December 20. Head coach Forrest Gregg aimed for a march through the playoffs for another shot at the Super Bowl ring which got away last year.

**Pittsburgh Steelers** — Bowing to the new pass-oriented rules, coach Chuck Noll installed a new 3-4 defense which replaced the fabled Steel Curtain in many situations. Veterans Joe Greene and L.C. Greenwood were gone, but Jack Lambert and Donnie Shell still carried the burden as they had in the 1970s. The season got off to a rousing start with victories over the Cowboys and Bengals. The Steelers hit a cold streak after the strike, getting shut out by the Seahawks and Bills in a three-week period. The past champions bore down at the end and won their last two games, winning a ticket to the playoffs for the first time since 1979.

**Cleveland Browns** — The Browns added two heralded linebackers in Tom Cousineau and Chip Banks. Cousineau was the first pick in the 1979 draft and returned to the United States after three seasons with Montreal of the Canadian Football League. Banks was a blue-chip rookie out of USC. Where the Browns really needed help this year was on offense. Despite the ace receiving of Ozzie Newsome, Cleveland had problems scoring. Brian Sipe couldn't spark the thrills of 1980 and lost his starting job to Paul McDonald. The left-handed McDonald started the last three games and engineered two victories, enough to inch the Browns into the expanded playoffs.

**Houston Oilers** — In the second year of Ed Biles' reign, the Oilers collapsed into the depths of the league. He cut quarterback Ken Stabler before the season and gave his job to Gifford Nielsen. One week into the schedule, Biles reconsidered and traded for Archie Manning of the Saints. The Oilers split the two pre-strike games, then nose-dived to seven straight losses after the break. Of the losses, a 35-7 drubbing at home by Dallas on Monday night was the most dispiriting. With the offensive line slumping, Earl Campbell endured his least productive season.

## WESTERN DIVISION

**Los Angeles Raiders** — The Raiders celebrated their move by returning to a dominant position in the A.F.C. Al Davis and coach Tom Flores fortified the defense with Lyle Alzado, the ace lineman of the Cleveland Browns. Alzado combined with Ted Hendricks to give the defense a pair of hard-hitting leaders. Davis and Flores equipped the offense with a marvelous new

FINAL TEAM STATISTICS

**OFFENSE**

| | BALT. | BUFF. | CIN. | CLEV. | DENV. | HOU. | K.C. | RAID. | MIA. | N.E. | NY.J. | PIT. | S.D. | SEA. |
|---|---|---|---|---|---|---|---|---|---|---|---|---|---|---|
| **FIRST DOWNS:** | | | | | | | | | | | | | | |
| Total | 152 | 180 | 207 | 176 | 170 | 138 | 163 | 175 | 165 | 146 | 193 | 171 | 233 | 159 |
| by Rushing | 62 | 83 | 63 | 64 | 52 | 52 | 71 | 65 | 84 | 74 | 87 | 69 | 72 | 51 |
| by Passing | 80 | 84 | 123 | 96 | 103 | 81 | 79 | 95 | 66 | 63 | 95 | 91 | 145 | 89 |
| by Penalty | 10 | 13 | 21 | 16 | 15 | 5 | 13 | 15 | 15 | 9 | 11 | 11 | 16 | 19 |
| **RUSHING:** | | | | | | | | | | | | | | |
| Number | 293 | 319 | 269 | 256 | 257 | 225 | 269 | 292 | 333 | 324 | 304 | 289 | 267 | 227 |
| Yards | 1044 | 1371 | 949 | 873 | 1018 | 799 | 943 | 1080 | 1344 | 1347 | 1317 | 1187 | 1121 | 795 |
| Average Yards | 3.6 | 4.3 | 3.5 | 3.4 | 4.0 | 3.6 | 3.5 | 3.7 | 4.0 | 4.2 | 4.3 | 4.1 | 4.2 | 3.5 |
| Touchdowns | 4 | 9 | 13 | 7 | 6 | 5 | 3 | 15 | 11 | 3 | 13 | 7 | 15 | 4 |
| **PASSING:** | | | | | | | | | | | | | | |
| Attempts | 283 | 273 | 310 | 334 | 311 | 287 | 264 | 267 | 238 | 187 | 279 | 275 | 338 | 326 |
| Completions | 142 | 149 | 219 | 174 | 181 | 153 | 145 | 154 | 129 | 93 | 165 | 141 | 208 | 176 |
| Completion Pct. | 50.2 | 54.6 | 70.6 | 52.1 | 58.2 | 53.3 | 54.9 | 57.7 | 54.2 | 49.7 | 59.1 | 51.3 | 61.5 | 54.0 |
| Passing Yards | 1613 | 1671 | 2501 | 2057 | 2019 | 1882 | 1864 | 2086 | 1401 | 1420 | 2107 | 1922 | 3021 | 2068 |
| Avg. Yds per Att. | 4.8 | 5.5 | 6.9 | 5.1 | 5.4 | 4.8 | 5.1 | 6.5 | 5.3 | 6.4 | 6.3 | 6.1 | 8.7 | 5.0 |
| Avg. Yds per Comp. | 11.4 | 11.2 | 11.4 | 11.8 | 11.2 | 12.3 | 12.9 | 13.6 | 10.9 | 15.3 | 12.8 | 13.6 | 14.5 | 11.6 |
| Times Tackled | 20 | 12 | 27 | 26 | 24 | 39 | 40 | 23 | 11 | 15 | 23 | 19 | 12 | 36 |
| Yds Lost Tackled | 174 | 115 | 162 | 212 | 200 | 308 | 309 | 211 | 87 | 134 | 206 | 139 | 94 | 269 |
| Net Yards | 1439 | 1556 | 2339 | 1845 | 1819 | 1574 | 1555 | 1875 | 1314 | 1286 | 1901 | 1783 | 2927 | 1799 |
| Touchdowns | 6 | 8 | 12 | 9 | 8 | 12 | 10 | 14 | 8 | 12 | 16 | 17 | 19 | 9 |
| Interceptions | 10 | 17 | 9 | 16 | 19 | 15 | 8 | 15 | 13 | 9 | 9 | 16 | 12 | 13 |
| Pct. Intercepted | 3.5 | 6.2 | 2.9 | 4.8 | 6.1 | 5.2 | 3.0 | 5.6 | 5.5 | 4.8 | 3.2 | 5.8 | 3.6 | 4.0 |
| **PUNTS:** | | | | | | | | | | | | | | |
| Number | 46 | 35 | 31 | 49 | 45 | 55 | 38 | 47 | 35 | 49 | 36 | 49 | 23 | 49 |
| Average | 44.4 | 37.9 | 38.7 | 38.3 | 45.0 | 39.7 | 40.5 | 39.1 | 38.7 | 43.7 | 37.4 | 40.4 | 37.7 | 38.6 |
| **PUNT RETURNS** | | | | | | | | | | | | | | |
| Number | 14 | 26 | 17 | 23 | 21 | 19 | 15 | 27 | 22 | 16 | 23 | 36 | 12 | 21 |
| Yards | 78 | 119 | 95 | 134 | 305 | 104 | 129 | 209 | 194 | 139 | 184 | 317 | 138 | 228 |
| Average Yards | 5.6 | 4.6 | 5.6 | 5.8 | 14.5 | 5.5 | 8.6 | 7.7 | 8.8 | 8.7 | 8.0 | 8.8 | 11.5 | 10.9 |
| Touchdowns | 0 | 0 | 0 | 0 | 2 | 0 | 0 | 0 | 1 | 0 | 0 | 0 | 0 | 0 |
| **KICKOFF RET.:** | | | | | | | | | | | | | | |
| Number | 42 | 36 | 31 | 38 | 40 | 45 | 34 | 36 | 24 | 28 | 33 | 28 | 45 | 29 |
| Yards | 753 | 792 | 643 | 754 | 818 | 905 | 723 | 754 | 507 | 646 | 667 | 569 | 890 | 544 |
| Average Yards | 17.9 | 22.0 | 20.7 | 19.8 | 20.5 | 20.1 | 21.3 | 20.9 | 21.1 | 23.1 | 20.2 | 20.3 | 19.8 | 18.8 |
| Touchdowns | 0 | 0 | 0 | 0 | 0 | 0 | 0 | 0 | 0 | 1 | 0 | 0 | 0 | 0 |
| **INTERCEPT RET.:** | | | | | | | | | | | | | | |
| Number | 5 | 13 | 14 | 17 | 12 | 3 | 12 | 18 | 19 | 12 | 17 | 17 | 12 | 13 |
| Yards | 150 | 122 | 240 | 102 | 106 | 47 | 208 | 356 | 281 | 176 | 261 | 127 | 138 | 160 |
| Average Yards | 30.0 | 9.4 | 17.1 | 6.0 | 8.8 | 15.7 | 17.3 | 19.8 | 14.8 | 14.7 | 15.4 | 7.5 | 11.5 | 12.3 |
| Touchdowns | 1 | 0 | 2 | 1 | 0 | 0 | 3 | 3 | 2 | 1 | 1 | 0 | 0 | 1 |
| **PENALTIES:** | | | | | | | | | | | | | | |
| Number | 52 | 69 | 56 | 59 | 54 | 52 | 43 | 86 | 34 | 52 | 63 | 59 | 64 | 59 |
| Yards | 433 | 582 | 475 | 461 | 516 | 424 | 372 | 840 | 240 | 412 | 533 | 459 | 530 | 523 |
| **FUMBLES:** | | | | | | | | | | | | | | |
| Number | 24 | 23 | 12 | 15 | 24 | 14 | 13 | 22 | 15 | 16 | 18 | 18 | 17 | 21 |
| Number Lost | 11 | 9 | 7 | 8 | 17 | 11 | 4 | 9 | 10 | 8 | 9 | 9 | 8 | 11 |
| **POINTS:** | | | | | | | | | | | | | | |
| Total | 113 | 150 | 232 | 140 | 148 | 136 | 176 | 260 | 198 | 143 | 245 | 204 | 288 | 127 |
| PAT Attempts | 11 | 18 | 27 | 17 | 16 | 18 | 17 | 33 | 22 | 17 | 31 | 24 | 34 | 14 |
| PAT Made | 11 | 15 | 26 | 17 | 15 | 16 | 17 | 32 | 21 | 15 | 26 | 22 | 32 | 13 |
| FG Attempts | 18 | 18 | 18 | 16 | 13 | 6 | 24 | 16 | 20 | 13 | 17 | 12 | 22 | 14 |
| FG Made | 10 | 9 | 14 | 7 | 11 | 4 | 19 | 10 | 15 | 8 | 11 | 10 | 16 | 10 |
| Percent FG Made | 55.6 | 50.0 | 77.8 | 43.8 | 84.6 | 66.7 | 79.2 | 62.5 | 75.0 | 61.5 | 64.7 | 83.3 | 72.7 | 71.4 |
| Safeties | 0 | 0 | 1 | 0 | 2 | 0 | 0 | 0 | 0 | 1 | 0 | 1 | 2 | 0 |

**DEFENSE**

| | BALT. | BUFF. | CIN. | CLEV. | DENV. | HOU. | K.C. | RAID. | MIA. | N.E. | NY.J. | PIT. | S.D. | SEA. |
|---|---|---|---|---|---|---|---|---|---|---|---|---|---|---|
| **FIRST DOWNS:** | | | | | | | | | | | | | | |
| Total | 197 | 151 | 170 | 189 | 176 | 187 | 170 | 206 | 147 | 185 | 160 | 174 | 196 | 167 |
| by Rushing | 87 | 64 | 61 | 82 | 53 | 67 | 69 | 53 | 77 | 87 | 54 | 49 | 65 | 86 |
| by Passing | 89 | 72 | 102 | 94 | 104 | 106 | 92 | 121 | 65 | 88 | 88 | 111 | 119 | 68 |
| by Penalty | 21 | 15 | 7 | 13 | 19 | 14 | 9 | 32 | 5 | 10 | 18 | 14 | 12 | 13 |
| **RUSHING:** | | | | | | | | | | | | | | |
| Number | 348 | 268 | 223 | 306 | 293 | 298 | 280 | 234 | 293 | 315 | 269 | 236 | 230 | 337 |
| Yards | 1473 | 1034 | 850 | 1292 | 935 | 1225 | 1065 | 778 | 1285 | 1289 | 983 | 762 | 961 | 1461 |
| Average Yards | 4.2 | 3.9 | 3.8 | 4.2 | 3.2 | 4.1 | 3.8 | 3.3 | 4.4 | 4.1 | 3.7 | 3.2 | 4.2 | 4.3 |
| Touchdowns | 10 | 6 | 8 | 13 | 8 | 10 | 7 | 12 | 7 | 9 | 5 | 5 | 10 | 12 |
| **PASSING:** | | | | | | | | | | | | | | |
| Attempts | 246 | 256 | 306 | 266 | 307 | 284 | 262 | 375 | 226 | 267 | 298 | 329 | 342 | 246 |
| Completions | 138 | 114 | 187 | 144 | 172 | 179 | 155 | 193 | 119 | 142 | 159 | 176 | 233 | 138 |
| Completion Pct. | 56.1 | 44.5 | 61.1 | 54.1 | 56.0 | 63.0 | 59.2 | 51.5 | 52.7 | 53.2 | 53.4 | 53.5 | 68.1 | 56.1 |
| Passing Yards | 1920 | 1382 | 2250 | 1967 | 2350 | 2453 | 1787 | 2617 | 1281 | 1691 | 1817 | 2385 | 2437 | 1468 |
| Avg. Yds per Att. | 7.1 | 4.9 | 6.2 | 6.3 | 6.9 | 7.0 | 6.0 | 5.5 | 4.0 | 5.3 | 5.2 | 5.8 | 6.4 | 5.1 |
| Avg. Yds per Comp. | 13.9 | 12.1 | 12.0 | 13.7 | 13.7 | 13.7 | 11.5 | 13.6 | 10.8 | 11.9 | 11.4 | 13.6 | 10.5 | 10.6 |
| Times Tackled | 11 | 12 | 22 | 22 | 16 | 31 | 15 | 38 | 29 | 20 | 20 | 34 | 19 | 17 |
| Yds Lost Tackled | 97 | 82 | 207 | 145 | 116 | 240 | 120 | 329 | 254 | 172 | 171 | 273 | 145 | 135 |
| Net Yards | 1823 | 1300 | 2043 | 1822 | 2234 | 2213 | 1667 | 2288 | 1027 | 1519 | 1646 | 2112 | 2292 | 1333 |
| Touchdowns | 18 | 8 | 12 | 9 | 14 | 18 | 12 | 11 | 7 | 9 | 10 | 12 | 10 | 4 |
| Interceptions | 5 | 13 | 14 | 17 | 12 | 3 | 12 | 18 | 19 | 12 | 17 | 17 | 13 | 13 |
| Pct. Intercepted | 2.0 | 5.1 | 4.6 | 6.4 | 3.9 | 1.1 | 4.6 | 4.8 | 8.4 | 4.5 | 5.7 | 5.2 | 3.8 | 5.3 |
| **PUNTS:** | | | | | | | | | | | | | | |
| Number | 41 | 44 | 37 | 40 | 42 | 38 | 37 | 49 | 40 | 43 | 42 | 53 | 27 | 50 |
| Average | 39.9 | 39.3 | 40.1 | 38.8 | 39.4 | 43.0 | 39.7 | 38.3 | 40.1 | 39.7 | 42.1 | 38.1 | 44.9 | 40.6 |
| **PUNT RETURNS** | | | | | | | | | | | | | | |
| Number | 26 | 10 | 17 | 30 | 25 | 35 | 22 | 17 | 14 | 26 | 17 | 28 | 7 | 19 |
| Yards | 226 | 30 | 68 | 216 | 227 | 293 | 338 | 71 | 77 | 191 | 153 | 182 | 86 | 69 |
| Average Yards | 8.7 | 3.0 | 4.0 | 7.2 | 9.1 | 8.4 | 15.4 | 4.2 | 5.5 | 7.3 | 9.0 | 6.5 | 12.3 | 3.6 |
| Touchdowns | 0 | 0 | 0 | 0 | 0 | 0 | 2 | 0 | 0 | 0 | 1 | 0 | 0 | 0 |
| **KICKOFF RET.:** | | | | | | | | | | | | | | |
| Number | 25 | 34 | 45 | 23 | 26 | 26 | 42 | 43 | 33 | 32 | 35 | 36 | 51 | 24 |
| Yards | 538 | 604 | 851 | 424 | 541 | 564 | 794 | 851 | 704 | 614 | 743 | 821 | 991 | 361 |
| Average Yards | 21.5 | 17.8 | 18.9 | 18.4 | 20.8 | 21.7 | 18.9 | 19.8 | 21.3 | 19.2 | 21.2 | 22.8 | 19.4 | 15.0 |
| Touchdowns | 0 | 0 | 0 | 0 | 0 | 0 | 0 | 0 | 0 | 0 | 1 | 0 | 0 | 0 |
| **INTERCEPT RET.:** | | | | | | | | | | | | | | |
| Number | 10 | 17 | 9 | 16 | 19 | 15 | 8 | 15 | 13 | 9 | 9 | 16 | 12 | 13 |
| Yards | 129 | 268 | 93 | 164 | 431 | 47 | 182 | 180 | 96 | 100 | 152 | 168 | 262 | 88 |
| Average Yards | 12.1 | 15.8 | 10.3 | 10.3 | 22.7 | 3.1 | 22.8 | 12.0 | 7.4 | 11.1 | 16.9 | 10.5 | 21.8 | 6.8 |
| Touchdowns | 0 | 0 | 1 | 0 | 3 | 1 | 1 | 1 | 0 | 0 | 3 | 0 | 3 | 1 |
| **PENALTIES:** | | | | | | | | | | | | | | |
| Number | 59 | 49 | 64 | 57 | 63 | 59 | 60 | 53 | 57 | 39 | 43 | 45 | 70 | 44 |
| Yards | 466 | 395 | 551 | 436 | 571 | 454 | 486 | 588 | 461 | 290 | 345 | 355 | 612 | 406 |
| **FUMBLES:** | | | | | | | | | | | | | | |
| Number | 11 | 14 | 19 | 20 | 17 | 20 | 23 | 18 | 17 | 19 | 20 | 17 | 19 | 18 |
| Number Lost | 6 | 8 | 6 | 11 | 7 | 14 | 10 | 11 | 8 | 11 | 9 | 8 | 12 | 9 |
| **POINTS:** | | | | | | | | | | | | | | |
| Total | 236 | 154 | 177 | 182 | 226 | 245 | 184 | 200 | 131 | 157 | 166 | 146 | 221 | 147 |
| PAT Attempts | 28 | 15 | 20 | 23 | 25 | 30 | 22 | 24 | 15 | 18 | 20 | 17 | 24 | 18 |
| PAT Made | 26 | 14 | 19 | 21 | 25 | 30 | 20 | 23 | 14 | 17 | 19 | 17 | 23 | 17 |
| FG Attempts | 19 | 20 | 12 | 11 | 24 | 18 | 14 | 14 | 15 | 15 | 15 | 14 | 19 | 15 |
| FG Made | 14 | 16 | 10 | 7 | 17 | 11 | 10 | 11 | 9 | 10 | 9 | 9 | 16 | 6 |
| Percent FG Made | 73.7 | 80.0 | 83.3 | 63.6 | 70.8 | 61.1 | 71.4 | 78.6 | 60.0 | 66.7 | 60.0 | 64.3 | 84.2 | 40.0 |
| Safeties | 0 | 1 | 1 | 1 | 0 | 1 | 1 | 0 | 0 | 1 | 0 | 0 | 0 | 2 |

weapon in halfback Marcus Allen from USC. A top-notch runner and receiver, Allen rushed for 116 yards in an opening-day victory over Super Bowl champion San Francisco. Another new offensive ace was Todd Christensen, a special-teams player who unexpectantly shone at tight end. The only blemish on the season's record was a 31-17 loss to the Bengals on November 28.

**San Diego Chargers** — En route to a fourth straight playoff berth, the Chargers scored a lot of points and allowed a lot of points. The usual cast of characters manned the Air Coryell attack. Dan Fouts tormented opponents with passes to Wes Chandler, Charlie Joiner and Kellen Winslow while Chuck Muncie and rookie James Brooks kept defenses honest with their running. The offensive line featured veterans Russ Washington and Doug Wilkerson. The defense simply could not stop enemy passers despite all-pro work from tackle Gary Johnson and newly acquired safety Tim Fox. In three weeks in December, the Chargers beat the 49ers 41-37, Bengals 50-34 and Colts 44-26, displaying their true character on both sides of the line.

**Seattle Seahawks** — Turmoil ripped the Seahawks before the season started. Wide receiver Sam McCullum was cut before the opener; many suspected that his role as union representative cost him his job. The players almost called for a strike on opening day, relenting in an atmosphere of bitterness. The Seahawks lost the two pre-strike games with young Dave Krieg at quarterback. During the strike, management fired coach Jack Patera and replaced him for the remainder of the season with Mike McCormack. Morale picked up, especially when the popular Jim Zorn was restored to the starting lineup. Fueling the second-half improvement was a talented defense led by Jacob Green, Kenny Easley and Keith Simpson.

**Kansas City Chiefs** — Things started going badly in May, with Joe Delaney undergoing eye surgery for a detached retina. The offense suffered from his reduced availability and from the shuffling of quarterbacks Steve Fuller and Bill Kenney. Neither gave coach Marv Levy any reason to choose a full-time quarterback. After the strike, the Chiefs lost their first four games, killing their playoff hopes and public interest in the team. In the season finale, they whipped the Jets 37-13 before a paltry crowd of 11,902. That was the last game for Jack Rudnay after a long career with the Chiefs. Also departing was Levy after a five-year stint that led to no post-season appearances.

**Denver Broncos** — Dan Reeves suffered through a general collapse of the Broncos in his second year as coach. The defense softened under Bill Thompson's retirement, Steve Foley's opening-day broken arm and Bob Swenson's holdout for much of the season. Turnovers plagued the offense. Craig Morton began as the starting quarterback but yielded his job to younger Steve DeBerg after the strike. The poor post-strike record was a team effort, but a few individual kudos were merited. Steve Watson continued his effective receiving, rookie Gerald Willhite ran well and Rick Upchurch carried two punt returns all the way for touchdowns.

**MIAMI DOLPHINS 7-2-0 Don Shula**

| Scores of Each Game | | |
|---|---|---|
| 45 | N.Y.Jets | 26 |
| 24 | BALTIMORE | 20 |
| 9 | Buffalo | 7 |
| 17 | Tampa Bay | 23 |
| 22 | MINNESOTA | 14 |
| 0 | New England | 3 |
| 20 | N.Y.JETS | 19 |
| 27 | BUFFALO | 10 |
| 34 | Baltimore | 7 |

| Use Name | Pos. | Hgt | Wgt | Age | Int | Pts |
|---|---|---|---|---|---|---|
| Jon Giesler | OT | 6'5" | 260 | 25 | | |
| Cleveland Green | OT | 6'3" | 262 | 24 | | |
| Erik Laakso | OT | 6'4" | 265 | 25 | | |
| Roy Foster | OG-OT | 6'4" | 275 | 22 | | |
| Bob Kuechenberg | OG | 6'3" | 255 | 34 | | |
| Ed Newman | OG | 6'2" | 255 | 31 | | |
| Jeff Toews | OG | 6'3" | 255 | 34 | | |
| Mark Dennard | C | 6'1" | 252 | 26 | | |
| Dwight Stephenson | C | 6'2" | 255 | 24 | | |
| Bill Barnett | DE | 6'4" | 260 | 26 | | |
| Doug Betters | DE | 6'7" | 260 | 26 | | |
| Kim Bokamper | DE | 6'6" | 250 | 27 | 1 | |
| Vern Den Herder | DE | 6'6" | 252 | 33 | | |
| Bob Baumhower | NT | 6'5" | 260 | 27 | | |
| Richard Bishop | NT | 6'1" | 265 | 32 | | |
| Steve Clark | NT | 6'4" | 255 | 22 | | |
| Charles Bowser | LB | 6'3" | 222 | 22 | | |
| Bob Brudzinski | LB | 6'4" | 230 | 27 | 1 | |
| A.J. Duhe | LB | 6'4" | 248 | 26 | 1 | |
| Larry Gordon | LB | 6'4" | 230 | 29 | 1 | |
| Ron Hester | LB | 6'1" | 218 | 23 | | |
| Steve Potter | LB | 6'3" | 235 | 24 | | |
| Earnest Rhone | LB | 6'2" | 224 | 29 | 1 | |
| Steve Shull | LB | 6'1" | 220 | 24 | | |
| Glenn Blackwood | DB | 6' | 186 | 25 | 2 | 6 |
| Lyle Blackwood | DB | 6' | 188 | 31 | 2 | |
| William Judson | DB | 6'1" | 181 | 23 | | |
| Mike Kozlowski | DB | 6' | 196 | 26 | 1 | |
| Paul Lankford | DB | 6'1" | 178 | 24 | | |
| Don McNeal | DB | 5'11" | 192 | 24 | 4 | 6 |
| Gerald Small | DB | 5'11" | 192 | 26 | 2 | |
| Fulton Walker | DB | 5'10" | 193 | 24 | 3 | |
| Jim Jensen | QB | 6'4" | 212 | 23 | | |
| Don Strock | QB | 6'5" | 220 | 31 | | |
| David Woodley | QB | 6'2" | 204 | 23 | | 18 |
| Eddie Hill | HB | 6'2" | 210 | 25 | | |
| Tony Nathan | HB | 6' | 206 | 25 | | 6 |
| Tommy Vigorito | HB | 5'10" | 197 | 22 | | 12 |
| Woody Bennett | FB | 6'2" | 222 | 27 | | |
| Rich Diana | FB | 5'9" | 220 | 21 | | |
| Andra Franklin | FB | 5'10" | 225 | 22 | | 42 |
| Jimmy Cefalo | WR | 5'11" | 188 | 25 | | 6 |
| Mark Duper | WR | 5'9" | 185 | 23 | | |
| Duriel Harris | WR | 5'11" | 176 | 27 | | 6 |
| Vince Heflin | WR | 6' | 185 | 23 | | |
| Nat Moore | WR | 5'9" | 186 | 30 | | 6 |
| Bruce Hardy | TE | 6'5" | 230 | 26 | | 12 |
| Ronnie Lee | TE | 6'3" | 236 | 25 | | |
| Joe Rose | TE | 6'3" | 230 | 25 | | 12 |
| Tom Orosz | K | 6'1" | 204 | 22 | | |
| Uwe von Schamann | K | 6' | 188 | 26 | | 66 |

Ken Poole - Back Injury

**NEW YORK JETS 6-3-0 Walt Michaels**

| Scores of Each Game | | |
|---|---|---|
| 28 | MIAMI | 45 |
| 31 | New England | 7 |
| 37 | BALTIMORE | 0 |
| 15 | GREEN BAY | 13 |
| 28 | Detroit | 13 |
| 32 | TAMPA BAY | 17 |
| 19 | Miami | 20 |
| 42 | Minnesota | 14 |
| 13 | Kansas City | 37 |

| Use Name | Pos. | Hgt | Wgt | Age | Int | Pts |
|---|---|---|---|---|---|---|
| Jim Luscinski | OT-OG | 6'5" | 275 | 23 | | |
| Marvin Powell | OT | 6'5" | 271 | 27 | | |
| John Roman | OT | 6'4" | 265 | 30 | | |
| Chris Ward | OT | 6'3" | 267 | 26 | | |
| Dan Alexander | OG | 6'4" | 260 | 27 | | |
| Guy Bingham | OG-C | 6'3" | 255 | 24 | | |
| Stan Waldemore | OG-C | 6'4" | 269 | 27 | | |
| Joe Fields | C-OG | 6'2" | 253 | 28 | | |
| Joe Pellegrini | C-OG | 6'4" | 252 | 25 | | |
| Mark Gastineau | DE | 6'5" | 269 | 25 | | |
| Rusty Guilbeau | DE | 6'4" | 250 | 23 | | |
| Joe Klecko | DE | 6'3" | 269 | 28 | | |
| Kenny Neil | DE-DT | 6'4" | 244 | 23 | | |
| Barry Bennett | DT-DE | 6'4" | 257 | 26 | | |
| Marty Lyons | DT | 6'5" | 269 | 25 | | |
| Ben Rudolph | DT-DE | 6'5" | 270 | 25 | | |
| Abdul Salaam | DT | 6'3" | 269 | 29 | | |
| Stan Blinka | LB | 6'2" | 230 | 24 | | |
| Greg Buttle | LB | 6'3" | 232 | 28 | 1 | |
| Bob Crable | LB | 6'3" | 228 | 22 | | |
| Ron Crosby | LB | 6'3" | 227 | 27 | | |
| Lance Mehl | LB | 6'3" | 235 | 24 | 2 | |
| John Woodring | LB | 6'2" | 232 | 23 | | |
| George Floyd | DB | 5'11" | 190 | 21 | | |
| Jerry Holmes | DB | 6'2" | 175 | 24 | 3 | |
| Bobby Jackson | DB | 5'9" | 180 | 25 | 5 | 12 |
| Jesse Johnson | DB | 6'3" | 188 | 25 | | |
| Johnny Lynn | DB | 6' | 198 | 25 | 1 | |
| Darrol Ray | DB | 6'1" | 206 | 24 | 3 | |
| Ken Schroy | DB | 6'2" | 198 | 29 | 1 | |
| Kirk Springs | DB | 6' | 192 | 24 | 1 | |
| Pat Ryan | QB | 6'3" | 210 | 26 | | |
| Richard Todd | QB | 6'2" | 206 | 28 | | 6 |
| Scott Dierking | HB | 5'10" | 220 | 27 | | 12 |
| Bruce Harper | HB | 5'8" | 177 | 27 | | 6 |
| Freeman McNeil | HB | 5'11" | 216 | 23 | | 42 |
| Mike Augustyniak | FB | 5'11" | 226 | 26 | | 24 |
| Marion Barber | FB | 6'3" | 224 | 25 | | |
| Dwayne Crutchford | FB | 6' | 235 | 22 | | 6 |
| Tom Newton | FB | 6' | 220 | 28 | | |
| Derrick Gaffney | WR | 6'1" | 182 | 27 | | 6 |
| Bobby Jones | WR | 5'11" | 185 | 27 | | |
| Johnny "Lam" Jones | WR | 5'11" | 180 | 24 | | 12 |
| Kurt Sohn | WR | 5'11" | 176 | 25 | | |
| Wesley Walker | WR | 6' | 179 | 27 | | 36 |
| Steve Alvers | TE | 6'4" | 240 | 24 | | |
| Jerome Barkum | TE | 6'4" | 227 | 32 | | 6 |
| Tom Coombs | TE | 6'3" | 236 | 23 | | |
| Mickey Shuler | TE | 6'3" | 236 | 26 | | 18 |
| Pat Leahy | K | 6' | 189 | 31 | | 59 |

**NEW ENGLAND PATRIOTS 5-4-0 Ron Meyer**

| Scores of Each Game | | |
|---|---|---|
| 24 | Baltimore | 13 |
| 7 | N.Y.Jets | 31 |
| 7 | Cleveland | 10 |
| 29 | HOUSTON | 21 |
| 13 | Chicago | 26 |
| 3 | MIAMI | 0 |
| 16 | Seattle | 0 |
| 14 | Pittsburgh | 37 |
| 30 | BUFFALO | 19 |

| Use Name | Pos. | Hgt | Wgt | Age | Int | Pts |
|---|---|---|---|---|---|---|
| Darryl Haley | OT | 6'4" | 279 | 21 | | |
| Brian Holloway | OT | 6'7" | 288 | 23 | | |
| Shelby Jordan | OT | 6'7" | 280 | 30 | | |
| Bob Cryder | OG | 6'4" | 293 | 25 | | |
| John Hannah | OG | 6'2" | 282 | 31 | | |
| Ron Wooten | OG | 6'4" | 280 | 23 | | |
| Pete Brock | C | 6'5" | 275 | 28 | | |
| Dwight Wheeler | C | 6'3" | 269 | 27 | | |
| Julius Adams | DE | 6'3" | 270 | 34 | | |
| George Crump | DE | 6'4" | 260 | 23 | | 2 |
| Kenneth Sims | DE | 6'5" | 279 | 22 | | |
| Ron Spears | DE | 6'6" | 255 | 22 | | |
| Luther Henson | NT | 6' | 275 | 23 | | |
| Dennis Owens | NT | 6'1" | 252 | 22 | | |
| Lester Williams | NT | 6'2" | 272 | 23 | | |
| Don Blackmon | LB | 6'3" | 245 | 24 | 2 | |
| Tim Golden | LB | 6'1" | 220 | 22 | | |
| Brian Ingram | LB | 6'4" | 230 | 22 | | |
| Larry McGrew | LB | 6'5" | 233 | 25 | | |
| Steve Nelson | LB | 6'2" | 230 | 31 | | |
| Andre Tippett | LB | 6'3" | 231 | 22 | | |
| Clayton Weishuhn | LB | 6'2" | 220 | 22 | | |
| John Zamberlin | LB | 6'2" | 226 | 26 | | |
| Raymond Clayborn | DB | 6'1" | 186 | 27 | 1 | |
| Paul Dombroski | DB | 6' | 185 | 26 | | |
| Mike Haynes | DB | 6'2" | 202 | 29 | 4 | |
| Roland James | DB | 6'2" | 191 | 24 | 3 | |
| Keith Lee | DB | 5'11" | 193 | 24 | | |
| Fred Marion | DB | 6'2" | 196 | 23 | | |
| Rick Sanford | DB | 6'1" | 192 | 25 | 2 | 6 |
| Ricky Smith | DB | 6' | 174 | 22 | | 6 |
| Matt Cavanaugh | QB | 6'2" | 212 | 25 | | |
| Tom Flick | QB | 6'3" | 190 | 24 | | |
| Steve Grogan | QB | 6'4" | 210 | 29 | | 6 |
| Tony Collins | HB | 5'11" | 203 | 23 | | 18 |
| Larry Cowan (from MIA) | HB | 5'11" | 194 | 22 | | |
| Vagas Ferguson | HB | 6'1" | 213 | 25 | | |
| Greg Taylor | HB | 5'8" | 175 | 23 | | |
| Mosi Tatupu | FB | 6' | 227 | 27 | | |
| Mark van Eeghen | FB | 6'2" | 220 | 30 | | 6 |
| Robert Weathers | FB | 6'2" | 217 | 21 | | 6 |
| Morris Bradshaw | WR | 6'1" | 195 | 29 | | 6 |
| Preston Brown | WR | 5'11" | 187 | 24 | | 6 |
| Cedric Jones | WR | 6' | 184 | 22 | | |
| Stanley Morgan | WR | 5'11" | 181 | 27 | | 18 |
| Ken Toler | WR | 6'2" | 191 | 23 | | 12 |
| Lin Dawson | TE | 6'3" | 240 | 23 | | 6 |
| Don Hasselbeck | TE | 6'7" | 245 | 27 | | 6 |
| Brian Williams | TE | 6'5" | 240 | 24 | | |
| Rich Camarillo | K | 5'11" | 191 | 22 | | |
| Rex Robinson | K | 5'11" | 205 | 23 | | 8 |
| John Smith | K | 6' | 185 | 32 | | 21 |

Steve Clark - Ankle Injury

**BUFFALO BILLS 4-5-0 Chuck Knox**

| Scores of Each Game | | |
|---|---|---|
| 14 | KANSAS CITY | 9 |
| 23 | MINNESOTA | 22 |
| 7 | MIAMI | 9 |
| 20 | BALTIMORE | 0 |
| 21 | Green Bay | 33 |
| 13 | PITTSBURGH | 0 |
| 23 | Tampa Bay | 24 |
| 10 | Miami | 27 |
| 19 | New England | 30 |

| Use Name | Pos. | Hgt | Wgt | Age | Int | Pts |
|---|---|---|---|---|---|---|
| Justin Cross | OT | 6'6" | 257 | 23 | | |
| Joe Devlin | OT | 6'5" | 250 | 28 | | |
| Ken Jones | OT | 6'5" | 250 | 29 | | |
| Jon Borchardt | OG | 6'5" | 255 | 25 | | |
| Tom Lynch | OG | 6'5" | 250 | 27 | | |
| Reggie McKenzie | OG | 6'4" | 242 | 32 | | |
| Jim Ritcher | OG-C | 6'3" | 251 | 24 | | |
| Will Grant | C | 6'3" | 248 | 28 | | |
| Tim Vogler | C | 6'3" | 245 | 25 | | |
| Darrell Irvin | DE | 6'4" | 255 | 25 | | |
| Ken Johnson | DE | 6'5" | 253 | 27 | | |
| Sherman White | DE | 6'5" | 250 | 33 | | |
| Ben Williams | DE | 6'3" | 245 | 28 | 1 | |
| Mark Roopenian | NT | 6'5" | 254 | 24 | | |
| Fred Smerlas | NT | 6'3" | 270 | 25 | | |
| Jim Haslett | LB | 6'3" | 232 | 26 | | |
| Chris Keating | LB | 6'2" | 223 | 24 | 1 | |
| Joey Lumpkin | LB | 6'2" | 230 | 22 | | |
| Eugene Marve | LB | 6'2" | 230 | 21 | 1 | |
| Shane Nelson | LB | 6'1" | 225 | 27 | | |
| Ervin Parker | LB | 6'4" | 240 | 24 | | |
| Isiah Robertson | LB | 6'3" | 225 | 33 | 1 | |
| Lucius Sanford | LB | 6'2" | 216 | 26 | | |
| Phil Villapiano | LB | 6'2" | 225 | 33 | | |
| Mario Clark | DB | 6'2" | 195 | 28 | | |
| Steve Freeman | DB | 5'11" | 185 | 29 | 3 | |
| Rod Kush | DB | 6' | 188 | 25 | | |
| Jeff Nixon | DB | 6'3" | 190 | 25 | | |
| Lemar Parrish | DB | 5'11" | 170 | 34 | 1 | |
| Charles Romes | DB | 6'1" | 190 | 28 | 1 | |
| Bill Simpson | DB | 6'1" | 191 | 30 | 4 | |
| Chris Williams | DB | 6' | 197 | 23 | | |
| Joe Ferguson | QB | 6'1" | 195 | 32 | | 12 |
| Matt Kofler | QB | 6'3" | 192 | 23 | | |
| Matt Robinson | QB | 6'2" | 196 | 27 | | |
| Joe Cribbs | HB | 5'11" | 190 | 24 | | 18 |
| Roland Hooks | HB | 6' | 195 | 29 | | |
| Art Whittington | HB | 5'11" | 185 | 26 | | |
| Curtis Brown | FB | 5'10" | 203 | 27 | | |
| Roosevelt Leaks | FB | 5'10" | 225 | 29 | | 30 |
| Ted McKnight | FB | 6'1" | 212 | 28 | | |
| Booker Moore | FB | 5'11" | 224 | 23 | | |
| Jerry Butler | WR | 6' | 178 | 24 | | 24 |
| Robert Holt | WR | 6'1" | 182 | 22 | | |
| Frank Lewis | WR | 6'1" | 196 | 35 | | 12 |
| Mike Mosley | WR | 6'2" | 192 | 24 | | |
| Lou Piccone | WR | 5'9" | 175 | 33 | | |
| Perry Tuttle | WR | 6' | 178 | 23 | | |
| Buster Barnett | TE | 6'5" | 225 | 23 | | |
| Mark Brammer | TE | 6'3" | 235 | 24 | | 12 |
| Greg Cater | K | 6' | 191 | 25 | | |
| Efren Herrera | K | 5'9" | 190 | 31 | | 35 |
| Nick Mike-Mayer | K | 5'8" | 185 | 32 | | 7 |

Byron Franklin - Sciatic Nerve Injury
Robb Riddick - Knee Injury

**BALTIMORE COLTS 0-8-1 Frank Kush**

| Scores of Each Game | | |
|---|---|---|
| 13 | NEW ENGLAND | 24 |
| 20 | Miami | 24 |
| 0 | N.Y.Jets | 37 |
| 0 | Buffalo | 20 |
| 17 | CINCINNATI | 20 |
| 10 | Minnesota | 13 |
| 20 | GREEN BAY | 20 |
| 26 | San Diego | 44 |
| 7 | MIAMI | 34 |

| Use Name | Pos. | Hgt | Wgt | Age | Int | Pts |
|---|---|---|---|---|---|---|
| Jeff Hart | OT | 6'5" | 272 | 28 | | |
| Greg Murtha | OT | 6'6" | 268 | 25 | | |
| John Sinnott | OT | 6'4" | 275 | 24 | | |
| Terry Crouch | OG | 6'2" | 278 | 23 | | |
| Nat Hudson | OG | 6'3" | 265 | 24 | | |
| Ken Huff | OG | 6'4" | 259 | 29 | | |
| Arland Thompson | OG | 6'3" | 265 | 24 | | |
| Ben Utt | OG | 6'4" | 255 | 23 | | |
| Ray Donaldson | C | 6'3" | 260 | 24 | | |
| Glenn Hyde | C | 6'3" | 252 | 31 | | |
| Cleveland Crosby | DE | 6'4" | 250 | 26 | | |
| Steve Durham | DE | 6'5" | 256 | 23 | | |
| Fletcher Jenkins | DE-NT | 6'2" | 258 | 22 | | |
| Harry Stanback | DE | 6'5" | 255 | 24 | | |
| Donnell Thompson | DE | 6'4" | 254 | 23 | | |
| James Hunter | NT-DE | 6'5" | 251 | 24 | | |
| Leo Wisniewski | NT | 6'1" | 263 | 22 | | |
| Greg Bracelin | LB | 6'1" | 210 | 25 | 1 | |
| Johnie Cooks | LB | 6'4" | 243 | 23 | | |
| Joe Harris | LB | 6'1" | 230 | 29 | | |
| Mike Humiston | LB | 6'3" | 238 | 23 | | |
| Ricky Jones | LB | 6'1" | 222 | 27 | | |
| Barry Krauss | LB | 6'3" | 232 | 25 | | 6 |
| Cliff Odom | LB | 6'2" | 225 | 23 | | |
| Gary Padjen | LB | 6'2" | 246 | 24 | | |
| Sanders Shiver | LB | 6'2" | 227 | 27 | | |
| Dave Simmons | LB | 6'5" | 219 | 25 | | |
| Kim Anderson | DB | 5'11" | 182 | 25 | | |
| Larry Anderson | DB | 5'11" | 188 | 25 | 2 | |
| James Burroughs | DB | 6'1" | 192 | 24 | 1 | 6 |
| Jeff Delaney | DB | 6' | 197 | 25 | | |
| Nesby Glasgow | DB | 5'10" | 180 | 25 | | |
| Derrick Hatchett | DB | 5'11" | 183 | 24 | 1 | |
| Darryl Hemphill | DB | 6' | 195 | 22 | | |
| Sid Justin | DB | 5'10" | 170 | 28 | | |
| Dwayne O'Steen (to TB for playoff game) | DB | 6'1" | 195 | 27 | | |
| David Humm | QB | 6'2" | 190 | 30 | | |
| Mike Pagel | QB | 6'2" | 201 | 21 | | 6 |
| Art Schlichter | QB | 6'2" | 210 | 22 | | |
| Curtis Dickey | HB | 6'1" | 209 | 25 | | 6 |
| Zachary Dixon | HB | 6'1" | 204 | 26 | | 6 |
| Cleveland Franklin | FB | 6'2" | 216 | 27 | | |
| Randy McMillan | FB | 6' | 220 | 23 | | 6 |
| Johnnie Wright | FB | 6'2" | 210 | 24 | | |
| Elmer Bailey | WR | 6' | 195 | 24 | | |
| Matt Bouza | WR | 6'3" | 211 | 23 | | 12 |
| Ry Butler | WR | 6'3" | 195 | 25 | | 12 |
| Bernard Henry | WR | 6' | 185 | 22 | | |
| Holden Smith | WR | 6'1" | 191 | 23 | | |
| Pat Beach | TE | 6'4" | 243 | 22 | | 6 |
| Reese McCall | TE | 6'7" | 238 | 26 | | |
| Tim Sherwin | TE | 6'6" | 237 | 24 | | 6 |
| Dan Miller (from NE) | K | 5'10" | 172 | 21 | | 27 |
| Rohn Stark | K | 6'3" | 195 | 23 | | |
| Mike Wood | K | 5'11" | 199 | 27 | | 24 |

Tim Foley - Achilles' Tendon Injury
Wade Griffin - Neck Injury
Hosea Taylor - Injury

## MIAMI DOLPHINS

### RUSHING
| Last Name | No. | Yds | Avg | TD |
|---|---|---|---|---|
| Franklin | 177 | 701 | 4.0 | 7 |
| Nathan | 66 | 233 | 3.5 | 1 |
| Woodley | 36 | 207 | 5.8 | 2 |
| Vigorito | 19 | 99 | 5.2 | 1 |
| Hill | 13 | 51 | 3.9 | 0 |
| Diana | 8 | 31 | 3.9 | 0 |
| Bennett | 9 | 15 | 1.7 | 0 |
| Harris | 1 | 13 | 13.0 | 0 |
| Strock | 3 | -9 | -3.0 | 0 |
| Cowan | 1 | 3 | 3.0 | 0 |

### RECEIVING
| Last Name | No. | Yds | Avg | TD |
|---|---|---|---|---|
| Vigorito | 24 | 186 | 7.8 | 0 |
| Harris | 22 | 331 | 15.0 | 1 |
| Cefalo | 17 | 357 | 20.9 | 1 |
| Rose | 16 | 182 | 11.4 | 2 |
| Nathan | 16 | 114 | 7.1 | 0 |
| Hardy | 12 | 66 | 5.5 | 2 |
| Moore | 8 | 82 | 10.3 | 1 |
| Hill | 6 | 33 | 5.5 | 0 |
| Franklin | 3 | 9 | 3.0 | 0 |
| Diana | 2 | 21 | 10.5 | 0 |
| Lee | 2 | 6 | 3.0 | 0 |
| Woodley | 1 | 15 | 15.0 | 1 |

### PUNT RETURNS
| Last Name | No. | Yds | Avg | TD |
|---|---|---|---|---|
| Vigorito | 20 | 192 | 9.6 | 1 |
| G. Blackwood | 2 | 2 | 1.0 | 0 |
| Kozlowski | 0 | 0 | 0.0 | 0 |

### KICKOFF RETURNS
| Last Name | No. | Yds | Avg | TD |
|---|---|---|---|---|
| Walker | 20 | 433 | 21.7 | 0 |
| Heflin | 2 | 49 | 24.5 | 0 |
| Diana | 1 | 15 | 15.0 | 0 |
| Kozlowski | 1 | 10 | 10.0 | 0 |

### PASSING
| Last Name | Att | Comp | % | Yds | Yd/Att | TD | Int- | % | RK |
|---|---|---|---|---|---|---|---|---|---|
| Woodley | 179 | 98 | 55 | 1080 | 6.03 | 5 | 8- | 4 | 10 |
| Strock | 55 | 30 | 55 | 306 | 5.56 | 2 | 5- | 9 | |
| Nathan | 2 | 1 | 50 | 15 | 7.50 | 1 | 0- | 0 | |
| Hill | 1 | 0 | 0 | 0 | 0.00 | 0 | 0- | 0 | |
| Jensen | 1 | 0 | 0 | 0 | 0.00 | 0 | 0- | 0 | |

### PUNTING
| Last Name | No. | Avg. |
|---|---|---|
| Orosz | 35 | 38.7 |

### KICKING
| Last Name | XP | Att. | % | FG | Att | % |
|---|---|---|---|---|---|---|
| von Schamann | 21 | 22 | 96 | 15 | 20 | 75 |

## NEW YORK JETS

### RUSHING
| Last Name | No. | Yds | Avg | TD |
|---|---|---|---|---|
| McNeil | 151 | 786 | 5.2 | 6 |
| Augustyniak | 50 | 178 | 3.6 | 4 |
| Dierking | 38 | 130 | 3.4 | 1 |
| Harper | 20 | 125 | 6.3 | 0 |
| Crutchfield | 22 | 78 | 3.5 | 1 |
| Barber | 8 | 24 | 3.0 | 0 |
| J. Jones | 1 | 2 | 2.0 | 0 |
| Ryan | 1 | -1 | -1.0 | 0 |
| Todd | 13 | -5 | -0.4 | 1 |

### RECEIVING
| Last Name | No. | Yds | Avg | TD |
|---|---|---|---|---|
| Walker | 39 | 620 | 15.9 | 6 |
| Augustyniak | 24 | 189 | 7.9 | 0 |
| Barkum | 19 | 182 | 9.6 | 1 |
| J. Jones | 18 | 294 | 16.3 | 2 |
| McNeil | 16 | 187 | 11.7 | 1 |
| Harper | 14 | 177 | 12.7 | 1 |
| Dierking | 12 | 80 | 6.7 | 1 |
| Gaffney | 11 | 207 | 18.8 | 1 |
| Shuler | 8 | 132 | 16.5 | 3 |
| B. Jones | 3 | 32 | 10.7 | 0 |
| Newton | 1 | 7 | 7.0 | 0 |

### PUNT RETURNS
| Last Name | No. | Yds | Avg | TD |
|---|---|---|---|---|
| Harper | 23 | 184 | 8.0 | 0 |

### KICKOFF RETURNS
| Last Name | No. | Yds | Avg | TD |
|---|---|---|---|---|
| Harper | 18 | 368 | 20.4 | 0 |
| Sohn | 15 | 299 | 19.9 | 0 |

### PASSING
| Last Name | Att | Comp | % | Yds | Yd/Att | TD | Int- | % | RK |
|---|---|---|---|---|---|---|---|---|---|
| Todd | 261 | 153 | 59 | 1961 | 7.51 | 14 | 8- | 3 | 3 |
| Ryan | 18 | 12 | 67 | 146 | 8.11 | 2 | 1- | 6 | |

### PUNTING
| Last Name | No. | Avg. |
|---|---|---|
| Ramsey | 35 | 38.5 |

### KICKING
| Last Name | XP | Att | % | FG | Att | % |
|---|---|---|---|---|---|---|
| Leahy | 26 | 31 | 84 | 11 | 17 | 65 |

## NEW ENGLAND PATRIOTS

### RUSHING
| Last Name | No. | Yds | Avg | TD |
|---|---|---|---|---|
| Collins | 164 | 632 | 3.9 | 1 |
| Van Eeghen | 82 | 386 | 4.7 | 0 |
| Tatupu | 30 | 168 | 5.6 | 0 |
| Weathers | 24 | 83 | 3.5 | 1 |
| Grogan | 9 | 42 | 4.7 | 0 |
| Cunningham | 9 | 21 | 2.3 | 0 |
| Ferguson | 1 | 5 | 5.0 | 0 |
| Toler | 1 | 4 | 4.0 | 0 |
| Cavanaugh | 2 | 3 | 1.5 | 0 |
| Morgan | 2 | 3 | 1.5 | 0 |

### RECEIVING
| Last Name | No. | Yds | Avg | TD |
|---|---|---|---|---|
| Morgan | 28 | 584 | 20.9 | 3 |
| Collins | 19 | 187 | 9.8 | 2 |
| Hasselbeck | 15 | 158 | 10.5 | 1 |
| Dawson | 13 | 160 | 12.3 | 1 |
| Bradshaw | 6 | 111 | 18.5 | 1 |
| Brown | 4 | 114 | 28.5 | 1 |
| Weathers | 3 | 24 | 8.0 | 0 |
| Toler | 2 | 63 | 31.5 | 2 |
| Van Eeghen | 2 | 14 | 7.0 | 1 |
| Jones | 1 | 5 | 5.0 | 0 |

### PUNT RETURNS
| Last Name | No. | Yds | Avg | TD |
|---|---|---|---|---|
| R. Smith | 16 | 139 | 8.7 | 0 |

### KICKOFF RETURNS
| Last Name | No. | Yds | Avg | TD |
|---|---|---|---|---|
| R. Smith | 24 | 567 | 23.6 | 1 |
| Taylor | 2 | 46 | 23.0 | 0 |
| Dombrowski | 1 | 19 | 19.0 | 0 |
| Lee | 1 | 14 | 14.0 | 0 |

### PASSING
| Last Name | Att | Comp | % | Yds | Yd/Att | TD | Int- | % | RK |
|---|---|---|---|---|---|---|---|---|---|
| Grogan | 122 | 66 | 54 | 930 | 7.62 | 7 | 4- | 3 | 4 |
| Cavanaugh | 60 | 27 | 45 | 490 | 8.17 | 5 | 5- | 8 | |
| Flick | 5 | 0 | 0 | 0 | 0.00 | 0 | 0- | 0 | |

### PUNTING
| Last Name | No | Avg |
|---|---|---|
| Camarillo | 49 | 43.7 |

### KICKING
| Last Name | XP | ATT | % | FG | ATT | % |
|---|---|---|---|---|---|---|
| J. Smith | 6 | 7 | 86 | 5 | 8 | 63 |
| Robinson | 5 | 5 | 100 | 1 | 2 | 50 |

## BUFFALO BILLS

### RUSHING
| Last Name | No. | Yds | Avg | TD |
|---|---|---|---|---|
| Cribbs | 134 | 633 | 4.7 | 3 |
| Leaks | 97 | 405 | 4.2 | 5 |
| Brown | 41 | 187 | 4.6 | 0 |
| Ferguson | 16 | 46 | 2.9 | 1 |
| Moore | 16 | 38 | 2.4 | 0 |
| Hooks | 5 | 23 | 4.6 | 0 |
| Kofler | 2 | 21 | 10.5 | 0 |
| Whitington | 7 | 15 | 2.2 | 0 |
| Holt | 1 | 3 | 3.0 | 0 |

### RECEIVING
| Last Name | No. | Yds | Avg | TD |
|---|---|---|---|---|
| Lewis | 28 | 443 | 15.8 | 2 |
| Butler | 26 | 336 | 12.9 | 4 |
| Brammer | 25 | 225 | 9.0 | 2 |
| Cribbs | 13 | 99 | 7.6 | 0 |
| Leaks | 13 | 91 | 7.0 | 0 |
| Piccone | 12 | 140 | 11.7 | 0 |
| Mosley | 9 | 96 | 10.7 | 0 |
| Tuttle | 7 | 107 | 15.3 | 0 |
| Brown | 6 | 38 | 6.3 | 0 |
| Holt | 4 | 45 | 11.3 | 0 |
| Barnett | 4 | 49 | 9.8 | 0 |
| Moore | 1 | 8 | 8.0 | 0 |
| Haslett | 1 | 4 | 4.0 | 0 |

### PUNT RETURNS
| Last Name | No. | Yds | Avg | TD |
|---|---|---|---|---|
| Mosley | 11 | 61 | 5.5 | 0 |
| Holt | 10 | 45 | 4.5 | 0 |
| Hooks | 4 | 13 | 3.3 | 0 |
| Simpson | 1 | 0 | 0.0 | 0 |
| Tuttle | 0 | 0 | 0.0 | 0 |

### KICKOFF RETURNS
| Last Name | No. | Yds | Avg | TD |
|---|---|---|---|---|
| Mosley | 18 | 487 | 27.1 | 0 |
| Holt | 7 | 156 | 22.3 | 0 |
| Piccone | 3 | 50 | 16.7 | 0 |
| McKnight | 3 | 34 | 11.3 | 0 |
| Whittington | 2 | 39 | 19.5 | 0 |
| Brown | 1 | 17 | 17.0 | 0 |
| Keating | 1 | 9 | 9.0 | 0 |
| Roopenian | 1 | 0 | 0.0 | 0 |

### PASSING
| Last Name | Att | Comp | % | Yds | Yd/Att | TD | Int- | % | RK |
|---|---|---|---|---|---|---|---|---|---|
| Ferguson | 264 | 144 | 55 | 1597 | 6.05 | 7 | 16- | 6 | 16 |
| Robinson | 8 | 5 | 63 | 74 | 9.25 | 1 | 0- | 0 | |
| Cribbs | 1 | 0 | 0 | 0 | 0.00 | 0 | 1- | 100 | |

### PUNTING
| Last Name | No | Avg |
|---|---|---|
| Cater | 35 | 37.9 |

### KICKING
| Last Name | XP | Att | % | FG | Att | % |
|---|---|---|---|---|---|---|
| Herrera | 11 | 12 | 92 | 8 | 14 | 57 |
| Mike-Mayer | 4 | 5 | 80 | 1 | 4 | 25 |

## BALTIMORE COLTS

### RUSHING
| Last Name | No. | Yds | Avg | TD |
|---|---|---|---|---|
| McMillan | 101 | 305 | 3.0 | 1 |
| Dixon | 58 | 249 | 4.3 | 1 |
| Dickey | 66 | 232 | 3.5 | 1 |
| Franklin | 43 | 152 | 3.5 | 0 |
| Pagel | 19 | 82 | 4.3 | 1 |
| Butler | 3 | 10 | 3.3 | 0 |
| Stark | 1 | 8 | 8.0 | 0 |
| Wright | 1 | 3 | 3.0 | 0 |
| Schlichter | 1 | 3 | 3.0 | 0 |

### RECEIVING
| Last Name | No. | Yds | Avg | TD |
|---|---|---|---|---|
| Bouza | 22 | 287 | 13.0 | 2 |
| Sherwin | 21 | 280 | 13.3 | 0 |
| Dickey | 21 | 228 | 10.9 | 0 |
| Dixon | 20 | 185 | 9.3 | 0 |
| Butler | 17 | 268 | 15.8 | 2 |
| McMillan | 15 | 90 | 6.0 | 0 |
| Franklin | 9 | 61 | 6.8 | 0 |
| Henry | 7 | 110 | 15.7 | 0 |
| Beach | 4 | 45 | 11.3 | 1 |
| Smith | 2 | 36 | 18.0 | 0 |
| McCall | 2 | 6 | 3.0 | 0 |
| Wright | 1 | 12 | 12.0 | 0 |
| Krauss | 1 | 5 | 5.0 | 1 |

### PUNT RETURNS
| Last Name | No. | Yds | Avg | TD |
|---|---|---|---|---|
| L. Anderson | 8 | 54 | 6.8 | 0 |
| Glasgow | 4 | 24 | 6.0 | 0 |
| Bouza | 2 | 0 | 0.0 | 0 |

### KICKOFF RETURNS
| Last Name | No. | Yds | Avg | TD |
|---|---|---|---|---|
| L. Anderson | 27 | 517 | 19.1 | 0 |
| Dixon | 11 | 197 | 17.9 | 0 |
| Bouza | 3 | 31 | 10.3 | 0 |
| Franklin | 1 | 8 | 8.0 | 0 |

### PASSING
| Last Name | Att | Comp | % | Yds | Yd/Att | TD | Int- | % | RK |
|---|---|---|---|---|---|---|---|---|---|
| Pagel | 221 | 111 | 50 | 1281 | 5.80 | 5 | 7- | 3 | 11 |
| Humm | 23 | 13 | 57 | 130 | 5.70 | 0 | 1- | 4 | |
| Schlichter | 37 | 17 | 46 | 197 | 5.30 | 0 | 2- | 5 | |
| Wood | 1 | 1 | 100 | 5 | 5.00 | 1 | 0- | 0 | |
| Stark | 1 | 0 | 0 | 0 | 0.00 | 0 | 0- | 0 | |

### PUNTING
| Last Name | No | Avg |
|---|---|---|
| Stark | 46 | 44.4 |

### KICKING
| Last Name | XP | ATT | % | FG | ATT | % |
|---|---|---|---|---|---|---|
| Wood | 6 | 6 | 100 | 6 | 10 | 60 |
| Miller | 9 | 10 | 90 | 6 | 11 | 55 |

## CINCINNATI BENGALS 7-2-0 Forrest Gregg

| Scores of Each Game | | |
|---|---|---|
| 27 | HOUSTON | 6 |
| 20 | Pittsburgh | *26 |
| 18 | Philadelphia | 14 |
| 31 | L.A.RAIDERS | 17 |
| 20 | Baltimore | 17 |
| 23 | CLEVELAND | 10 |
| 34 | San Diego | 50 |
| 24 | SEATTLE | 10 |
| 35 | Houston | 27 |

| Usa Name | Pos. | Hgt | Wgt | Age | Int | Pts |
|---|---|---|---|---|---|---|
| Anthony Munoz | OT | 6'6" | 278 | 24 | | |
| Mike Obrovac | OT | 6'6" | 275 | 26 | | |
| Ray Wagner | OT | 6'3" | 290 | 24 | | |
| Mike Wilson | OT | 6'5" | 271 | 27 | | |
| Glenn Bujnoch | OG | 6'4" | 265 | 28 | | |
| Dave Lapham | OG | 6'4" | 262 | 30 | | |
| Max Montoya | OG | 6'5" | 275 | 26 | | |
| Blair Bush | C | 6'3" | 252 | 25 | | |
| Blake Moore | C | 6'5" | 267 | 24 | | |
| Ross Browner | DE | 6'3" | 261 | 28 | 1 | |
| Gary Burley | DE | 6'3" | 274 | 29 | | |
| Glen Collins | DE | 6'6" | 260 | 23 | | |
| Eddie Edwards | DE | 6'5" | 256 | 28 | | |
| Mike St.Clair | DE | 6'5" | 254 | 28 | | |
| Jerry Boyarsky | NT | 6'3" | 290 | 23 | | |
| Emanuel Weaver | NT | 6'4" | 260 | 22 | | |
| Wilson Whitley | NT | 6'3" | 265 | 27 | | |

| Use Name | Pos. | Hgt | Wgt | Age | Int | Pts |
|---|---|---|---|---|---|---|
| Glenn Cameron | LB | 6'2" | 228 | 29 | | |
| Tom Dinkel | LB | 6'3" | 237 | 26 | | |
| Guy Frazier | LB | 6'2" | 215 | 23 | | |
| Bo Harris | LB | 6'3" | 226 | 29 | 1 | 6 |
| Jim LeClair | LB | 6'2" | 234 | 31 | 1 | |
| Rick Razzano | LB | 5'11" | 227 | 26 | | |
| Jeff Schuh | LB | 6'2" | 228 | 24 | | |
| Ron Simpkins | LB | 6'1" | 235 | 24 | | |
| Reggie Williams | LB | 6'1" | 228 | 27 | 1 | 2 |
| Louis Breeden | DB | 5'11" | 185 | 28 | 2 | |
| Oliver Davis | DB | 6'1" | 205 | 28 | | |
| Mike Fuller | DB | 5'9" | 182 | 29 | 1 | |
| Ray Griffin | DB | 5'10" | 186 | 26 | 1 | |
| Bryan Hicks | DB | 6' | 192 | 25 | | |
| Robert Jackson | DB | 5'10" | 184 | 23 | | |
| Bobby Kemp | DB | 6' | 186 | 23 | 1 | |
| Ken Riley | DB | 6' | 183 | 35 | 5 | 6 |
| John Simmons | DB | 5'11" | 192 | 23 | | |

| Use Name | Pos. | Hgt | Wgt | Age | Int | Pts |
|---|---|---|---|---|---|---|
| Ken Anderson | QB | 6'1" | 212 | 33 | | 24 |
| Turk Schonert | QB | 6'1" | 185 | 25 | | |
| Jack Thompson | QB | 6'3" | 217 | 26 | | |
| Archie Griffin | HB | 5'9" | 184 | 28 | | 6 |
| Rodney Tate | HB | 5'11" | 190 | 23 | | |
| Charles Alexander | FB | 6'1" | 221 | 25 | | 12 |
| Pete Johnson | FB | 6' | 249 | 28 | | 42 |
| Cris Collinsworth | WR | 6'5" | 192 | 23 | | 6 |
| Isaac Curtis | WR | 6' | 192 | 31 | | 6 |
| Steve Kreider | WR | 6'3" | 192 | 24 | | 7 |
| David Verser | WR | 6'1" | 200 | 24 | | 6 |
| M.L.Harris | TE | 6'5" | 238 | 28 | | 18 |
| Rodney Holman | TE | 6'3" | 230 | 22 | | 6 |
| Dan Ross | TE | 6'4" | 235 | 25 | | 18 |
| Jim Breach | K | 5'6" | 161 | 26 | | 67 |
| Pat McInally | K | 6'6" | 212 | 29 | | |

## PITTSBURGH STEELERS 6-3-0 Chuck Noll

| Scores of Each Game | | |
|---|---|---|
| 36 | Dallas | 28 |
| 26 | CINCINNATI | *20 |
| 24 | Houston | 10 |
| 0 | Seattle | 16 |
| 35 | KANSAS CITY | 14 |
| 0 | Buffalo | 13 |
| 9 | Cleveland | 10 |
| 37 | NEW ENGLAND | 14 |
| 37 | CLEVELAND | 21 |

| Usa Name | Pos. | Hgt | Wgt | Age | Int | Pts |
|---|---|---|---|---|---|---|
| Larry Brown | OT | 6'4" | 270 | 33 | | |
| Tunch Ilkin | OT | 6'3" | 253 | 24 | | |
| Ted Petersen | OT | 6'5" | 256 | 27 | | |
| Ray Pinney | OT | 6'4" | 256 | 28 | 6 | |
| Steve Courson | OG | 6'1" | 260 | 26 | | |
| Tyrone McGriff | OG | 6' | 267 | 24 | | |
| Craig Wolfley | OG | 6'1" | 265 | 24 | | |
| Emil Boures | C-OG | 6'1" | 252 | 22 | | |
| Rick Donnalley | C-OG | 6'2" | 257 | 23 | | |
| Mike Webster | C | 6'1" | 255 | 30 | | |
| Tom Beasley | DE-NT | 6'5" | 248 | 28 | | |
| John Goodman | DE | 6'6" | 250 | 23 | | |
| Keith Willis | DE | 6'1" | 251 | 23 | | |
| Gary Dunn | NT | 6'3" | 260 | 29 | | |
| Edmund Nelson | NT-DE | 6'3" | 263 | 22 | | |

| Use Name | Pos. | Hgt | Wgt | Age | Int | Pts |
|---|---|---|---|---|---|---|
| Craig Bingham | LB | 6'2" | 211 | 22 | | |
| Robin Cole | LB | 6'2" | 220 | 26 | | |
| Jack Ham | LB | 6'3" | 220 | 33 | 1 | |
| Bryan Hinkle | LB | 6'1" | 214 | 23 | | |
| Bob Kohrs | LB-DE | 6'3" | 245 | 23 | | |
| Jack Lambert | LB | 6'4" | 220 | 30 | 1 | |
| David Little | LB | 6'1" | 220 | 23 | | |
| Mike Merriweather | LB | 6'2" | 215 | 21 | | |
| Guy Ruff | LB | 6'1" | 215 | 22 | | |
| Loren Toews | LB | 6'3" | 220 | 30 | 1 | |
| Mel Blount | DB | 6'3" | 205 | 34 | 1 | |
| Fred Bohannon | DB | 6' | 201 | 24 | | |
| Ernest French | DB | 5'11" | 195 | 22 | | |
| Ron Johnson | DB | 5'10" | 200 | 26 | 2 | |
| Donnie Shell | DB | 5'11" | 190 | 30 | 5 | |
| Anthony Washington | DB | 6'1" | 204 | 24 | | |
| Sam Washington | DB | 5'8" | 180 | 22 | | |
| Dwayne Woodruff | DB | 5'11" | 198 | 25 | 5 | |
| Rick Woods | DB | 6' | 196 | 22 | 1 | |

Craig Colquitt - Achilles Tendon Injury

| Use Name | Pos. | Hgt | Wgt | Age | Int | Pts |
|---|---|---|---|---|---|---|
| Terry Bradshaw | QB | 6'3" | 210 | 33 | | |
| Mark Malone | QB | 6'4" | 223 | 23 | | |
| Cliff Stoudt | QB | 6'4" | 218 | 27 | | |
| Walter Abercrombie | HB | 5'11" | 201 | 22 | | 12 |
| Greg Hawthorne | HB-WR | 6'2" | 225 | 25 | | 18 |
| Rich Moser (to TB) | HB | 6' | 210 | 25 | | |
| Frank Pollard | HB-FB | 5'10" | 210 | 25 | | 12 |
| Russell Davis | FB | 6'1" | 231 | 26 | | |
| Franco Harris | FB | 6'2" | 225 | 32 | | 12 |
| Sidney Thornton | FB | 5'11" | 230 | 27 | | 6 |
| Jim Smith | WR | 6'2" | 205 | 27 | | 24 |
| John Stallworth | WR | 6' | 191 | 30 | | 42 |
| Lynn Swann | WR | 6' | 180 | 30 | | |
| Calvin Sweeney | WR | 6'2" | 190 | 27 | | |
| Willie Sydnor | WR | 5'11" | 170 | 23 | | |
| Bennie Cunningham | TE | 6'4" | 260 | 27 | | 12 |
| John Rodgers | TE | 6'2" | 220 | 22 | | 6 |
| Frank Wilson | TE-FB | 6'2" | 233 | 23 | | |
| Gary Anderson | K | 5'11" | 156 | 23 | | 52 |
| John Goodson | K | 6'3" | 204 | 22 | | |

## CLEVELAND BROWNS 4-5-0 Sam Rutigliano

| Scores of Each Game | | |
|---|---|---|
| 21 | Seattle | 7 |
| 21 | PHILADELPHIA | 24 |
| 10 | NEW ENGLAND | 7 |
| 14 | Dallas | 31 |
| 13 | SAN DIEGO | 30 |
| 10 | Cincinnati | 23 |
| 10 | PITTSBURGH | 9 |
| 20 | Houston | 14 |
| 21 | Pittsburgh | 37 |

| Usa Name | Pos. | Hgt | Wgt | Age | Int | Pts |
|---|---|---|---|---|---|---|
| Doug Dieken | OT | 6'5" | 252 | 33 | | |
| Andy Frederick | OT | 6'6" | 265 | 28 | | |
| Matt Miller | OT | 6'6" | 270 | 26 | | |
| Cody Risien | OT | 6'7" | 255 | 25 | | |
| Joe DeLamielleure | OG | 6'3" | 245 | 31 | | |
| Robert Jackson | OG | 6'5" | 260 | 29 | | |
| Mike Baab | C | 6'4" | 270 | 22 | | |
| Tom DeLeone | C | 6'2" | 248 | 32 | | |
| Keith Baldwin | DE | 6'4" | 245 | 21 | | |
| Elvis Franks | DE | 6'4" | 238 | 25 | | |
| Marshall Harris | DE | 6'6" | 261 | 26 | | |
| Mike Robinson | DE | 6'5" | 270 | 26 | | |
| Henry Bradley | NT | 6'2" | 260 | 28 | | |
| Mark Buben | NT | 6'3" | 260 | 25 | | |
| Bob Golic | NT | 6'2" | 248 | 24 | | |

| Use Name | Pos. | Hgt | Wgt | Age | Int | Pts |
|---|---|---|---|---|---|---|
| Dick Ambrose | LB | 6' | 228 | 29 | 1 | |
| Chip Banks | LB | 6'4" | 233 | 22 | 1 | |
| Tom Cousineau | LB | 6'3" | 225 | 25 | 1 | |
| Bill Cowher | LB | 6'3" | 225 | 25 | | |
| Eddie Johnson | LB | 6'1" | 210 | 23 | | |
| Clay Matthews | LB | 6'2" | 230 | 26 | | |
| Scott Nicolas | LB | 6'3" | 226 | 22 | | |
| Kevin Turner | LB | 6'2" | 223 | 24 | | |
| Curtis Weathers | LB | 6'5" | 220 | 25 | | |
| Ron Bolton | DB | 6'2" | 170 | 32 | 1 | |
| Larry Braziel | DB | 6' | 184 | 27 | | |
| Clinton Burrell | DB | 6'2" | 192 | 25 | 1 | 6 |
| Hanford Dixon | DB | 5'11" | 182 | 23 | 4 | |
| Judson Flint | DB | 6' | 201 | 25 | 1 | |
| Bill Jackson | DB | 6'1" | 202 | 22 | | |
| Lawrence Johnson | DB | 5'11" | 204 | 24 | 4 | |
| Mark Kafentzis | DB | 5'10" | 185 | 24 | | |
| Clarence Scott | DB | 6' | 190 | 33 | 3 | |

| Use Name | Pos. | Hgt | Wgt | Age | Int | Pts |
|---|---|---|---|---|---|---|
| Paul McDonald | QB | 6'2" | 185 | 24 | | |
| Brian Sipe | QB | 6'1" | 195 | 33 | | |
| Rick Trocano | QB-DB | 6' | 188 | 23 | | |
| David Green | HB | 5'10" | 200 | 28 | | |
| Dino Hall | HB | 5'7" | 165 | 26 | | 6 |
| Dwight Walker | HB | 5'10" | 185 | 23 | | |
| Charles White | FB | 5'10" | 183 | 24 | | 18 |
| Johnny Davis | FB | 6'1" | 235 | 26 | | 6 |
| Cleo Miller | FB | 5'11" | 214 | 29 | | |
| Mike Pruitt | FB | 6' | 225 | 28 | | 18 |
| Willis Adams | WR | 6'2" | 194 | 26 | | |
| Ricky Feacher | WR | 5'10" | 174 | 28 | | 18 |
| Dan Fulton | WR | 6'2" | 186 | 25 | | |
| Dave Logan | WR | 6'4" | 216 | 28 | | 12 |
| Mike Whitwell | WR | 6' | 175 | 23 | | |
| Ozzie Newsome | TE | 6'2" | 232 | 26 | | 18 |
| McDonald Oden | TE | 6'4" | 245 | 25 | | |
| Matt Bahr | K | 5'10" | 165 | 24 | | 38 |
| Steve Cox | K | 6'4" | 195 | 24 | | |

## HOUSTON OILERS 1-8-0 Ed Biles

| Scores of Each Game | | |
|---|---|---|
| 6 | Cincinnati | 27 |
| 23 | SEATTLE | 21 |
| 10 | PITTSBURGH | 24 |
| 21 | New England | 29 |
| 14 | N.Y. Giants | 17 |
| 7 | DALLAS | 35 |
| 14 | Philadelphia | 35 |
| 14 | CLEVELAND | 20 |
| 27 | CINCINNATI | 35 |

| Usa Name | Pos. | Hgt | Wgt | Age | Int | Pts |
|---|---|---|---|---|---|---|
| Mark Koncar | OT | 6'5" | 270 | 29 | | |
| John Schuhmacher | OT | 6'3" | 269 | 26 | | |
| Morris Towns | OT | 6'4" | 261 | 28 | | |
| Ralph Williams | OT | 6'3" | 276 | 24 | | |
| Ed Fisher | OG | 6'3" | 259 | 33 | | |
| Mike Munchak | OG | 6'3" | 263 | 22 | | |
| George Reihner | OG | 6'4" | 260 | 27 | | |
| David Carter | C | 6'2" | 262 | 29 | | |
| Greg Davidson | C | 6'2" | 254 | 24 | | |
| Jesse Baker | DE | 6'5" | 272 | 25 | | |
| Elvin Bethea | DE | 6'3" | 252 | 36 | | |
| Ken Kennard | DE | 6'2" | 258 | 27 | | |
| Malcolm Taylor | DE | 6'6" | 288 | 22 | | |
| Daryle Skaugstad | NT | 6'5" | 268 | 25 | | |
| Mike Stensrud | NT | 6'5" | 290 | 26 | | |

| Use Name | Pos. | Hgt | Wgt | Age | Int | Pts |
|---|---|---|---|---|---|---|
| Robert Abraham | LB | 6'1" | 217 | 22 | | |
| Gregg Bingham | LB | 6'1" | 225 | 31 | 1 | |
| Robert Brazile | LB | 6'4" | 245 | 29 | 1 | |
| John Corker | LB | 6'5" | 240 | 23 | | |
| Daryl Hunt | LB | 6'3" | 239 | 25 | | |
| Avon Riley | LB | 6'3" | 219 | 23 | | |
| Ted Thompson | LB | 6'1" | 229 | 29 | | |
| Ted Washington | LB | 6'1" | 248 | 34 | | |
| Carter Hartwig | DB | 6' | 205 | 26 | | |
| Bill Kay | DB | 6'1" | 190 | 22 | | |
| Vernon Perry | DB | 6'2" | 210 | 28 | 1 | |
| Tate Randle | DB | 6' | 202 | 23 | | |
| Mike Reinfeldt | DB | 6'2" | 196 | 29 | 6 | |
| Greg Stemrick | DB | 5'11" | 185 | 30 | | |
| Willie Tullis | DB | 6' | 190 | 24 | | |
| J.C. Wilson | DB | 6' | 178 | 26 | | |

Ken Burrough - Broken Ankle

| Use Name | Pos. | Hgt | Wgt | Age | Int | Pts |
|---|---|---|---|---|---|---|
| Oliver Luck | QB | 6'2" | 198 | 22 | | |
| Archie Manning (from NO) | QB | 6'3" | 211 | 33 | | |
| Gifford Nielsen | QB | 6'4" | 210 | 27 | | |
| Gary Allen | HB | 5'10" | 183 | 22 | | 6 |
| Earl Campbell | HB-FB | 5'11" | 240 | 27 | | 12 |
| Adger Armstrong | FB | 6' | 225 | 25 | | |
| Donnie Craft | FB | 6' | 209 | 22 | | 24 |
| Stan Edwards | FB | 6' | 215 | 22 | | |
| Rich Thomaselli | FB | 6'1" | 196 | 25 | | |
| Harold Bailey | WR | 6'2" | 193 | 25 | | |
| Steve Bryant | WR | 6'2" | 194 | 22 | | |
| Mike Holston | WR | 6'3" | 192 | 24 | | 6 |
| Mike Renfro | WR | 6' | 184 | 27 | | 18 |
| Carl Roaches | WR | 5'8" | 170 | 28 | | |
| Tim Smith | WR | 6'2" | 202 | 25 | | |
| Walt Arnold | TE | 6'3" | 234 | 24 | | |
| Dave Casper | TE | 6'4" | 241 | 30 | | 36 |
| Tim Wilson | TE | 6'3" | 235 | 28 | | |
| John James (from DET) | K | 6'3" | 196 | 33 | | |
| Florian Kempf | K | 5'9" | 170 | 26 | | 28 |
| Cliff Parsley | K | 6'1" | 223 | 27 | | |

* Overtime

## CINCINNATI BENGALS

### RUSHING

| Last Name | No. | Yds | Avg | TD |
|---|---|---|---|---|
| Johnson | 156 | 622 | 4.0 | 7 |
| Alexander | 64 | 207 | 3.2 | 1 |
| Anderson | 25 | 85 | 3.4 | 0 |
| A. Griffin | 12 | 39 | 3.3 | 1 |
| Curtis | 3 | 15 | 5.0 | 0 |
| Tate | 2 | 2 | 1.0 | 0 |
| Verser | 1 | 1 | 1.0 | 0 |
| M.L. Harris | 2 | -3 | -1.5 | 0 |
| Schonert | 3 | -8 | -2.7 | 0 |
| Collinsworth | 1 | -11 | -11.0 | 0 |

### RECEIVING

| Last Name | No. | Yds | Avg | TD |
|---|---|---|---|---|
| Collinsworth | 49 | 700 | 14.3 | 1 |
| Ross | 47 | 508 | 10.8 | 3 |
| Johnson | 31 | 267 | 8.6 | 0 |
| Curtis | 23 | 320 | 13.9 | 1 |
| A. Griffin | 22 | 172 | 7.9 | 1 |
| Kreider | 16 | 230 | 14.4 | 1 |
| Alexander | 14 | 85 | 6.1 | 1 |
| M.L. Harris | 10 | 103 | 10.3 | 3 |
| Verser | 4 | 98 | 24.5 | 1 |
| Holman | 3 | 18 | 6.0 | 1 |

### PUNT RETURNS

| Last Name | No. | Yds | Avg | TD |
|---|---|---|---|---|
| Fuller | 17 | 95 | 5.6 | 0 |

### KICKOFF RETURNS

| Last Name | No. | Yds | Avg | TD |
|---|---|---|---|---|
| Verser | 16 | 320 | 20.0 | 0 |
| Tate | 14 | 314 | 22.4 | 0 |
| Fuller | 1 | 9 | 9.0 | 0 |

### PASSING — PUNTING — KICKING

**PASSING**

| Last Name | Att | Comp | % | Yds | Yd/Att | TD | Int- | % | RK |
|---|---|---|---|---|---|---|---|---|---|
| Anderson | 309 | 218 | 71 | 2495 | 8.07 | 12 | 9- | 3 | 1 |
| Schonert | 1 | 1 | 100 | 6 | 6.00 | 0 | 0- | 0 | |

**PUNTING**

| Last Name | No | Avg |
|---|---|---|
| McInally | 31 | 38.7 |

**KICKING**

| Last Name | XP | Att | % | FG | Att | % |
|---|---|---|---|---|---|---|
| Breech | 25 | 26 | 96 | 14 | 18 | 78 |
| Kreider | 1 | 1 | 100 | 0 | 0 | 0 |

## PITTSBURGH STEELERS

### RUSHING

| Last Name | No. | Yds | Avg | TD |
|---|---|---|---|---|
| Harris | 140 | 604 | 4.3 | 2 |
| Pollard | 62 | 238 | 3.8 | 2 |
| Abercrombie | 21 | 100 | 4.8 | 2 |
| Davis | 24 | 72 | 3.0 | 0 |
| Hawthorne | 15 | 68 | 4.5 | 0 |
| Thornton | 6 | 33 | 5.5 | 1 |
| Stoust | 11 | 28 | 2.5 | 0 |
| Swann | 1 | 25 | 25.0 | 0 |
| Bradshaw | 8 | 10 | 1.3 | 0 |
| Stallworth | 1 | 9 | 9.0 | 0 |

### RECEIVING

| Last Name | No. | Yds | Avg | TD |
|---|---|---|---|---|
| Harris | 31 | 249 | 8.0 | 0 |
| Stallworth | 27 | 441 | 16.3 | 7 |
| Cunningham | 21 | 277 | 13.2 | 2 |
| Swann | 18 | 265 | 14.7 | 0 |
| Smith | 17 | 387 | 22.8 | 4 |
| Hawthorne | 12 | 182 | 15.2 | 3 |
| Pollard | 6 | 39 | 6.5 | 0 |
| Sweeney | 5 | 50 | 10.0 | 0 |
| Abercrombie | 1 | 14 | 14.0 | 0 |
| Davis | 1 | 11 | 11.0 | 0 |
| Thornton | 1 | 4 | 4.0 | 0 |
| Pinney | 1 | 3 | 3.0 | 0 |

### PUNT RETURNS

| Last Name | No. | Yds | Avg | TD |
|---|---|---|---|---|
| Sydnor | 22 | 172 | 7.8 | 0 |
| Woods | 13 | 142 | 10.9 | 0 |
| Merriweather | 1 | 3 | 3.0 | 0 |

### KICKOFF RETURNS

| Last Name | No. | Yds | Avg | TD |
|---|---|---|---|---|
| Bohannon | 14 | 329 | 23.5 | 0 |
| Abercrombie | 7 | 139 | 19.9 | 0 |
| French | 2 | 38 | 19.0 | 0 |
| Sydnor | 2 | 37 | 18.5 | 0 |
| Moser | 1 | 18 | 18.0 | 0 |
| Donnalley | 1 | 8 | 8.0 | 0 |
| Swann | 1 | 0 | 0.0 | 0 |

### PASSING — PUNTING — KICKING

**PASSING**

| Last Name | Att | Comp | % | Yds | Yd/Att | TD | Int- | % | RK |
|---|---|---|---|---|---|---|---|---|---|
| Bradshaw | 240 | 127 | 53 | 1768 | 7.37 | 17 | 11- | 5 | 5 |
| Stoudt | 35 | 14 | 40 | 154 | 4.40 | 0 | 5- | 14 | |

**PUNTING**

| Last Name | No | Avg |
|---|---|---|
| Goodson | 49 | 40.4 |

**KICKING**

| Last Name | XP | Att | % | FG | Att | % |
|---|---|---|---|---|---|---|
| Anderson | 22 | 23 | 96 | 10 | 12 | 83 |

## CLEVELAND BROWNS

### RUSHING

| Last Name | No. | Yds | Avg | TD |
|---|---|---|---|---|
| Pruitt | 143 | 516 | 3.6 | 3 |
| White | 69 | 259 | 3.8 | 3 |
| C. Miller | 16 | 61 | 3.8 | 0 |
| Sipe | 13 | 44 | 3.4 | 0 |
| Hall | 2 | 14 | 7.0 | 0 |
| Davis | 4 | 3 | 0.8 | 1 |
| Cox | 2 | -11 | -5.5 | 0 |
| McDonald | 7 | -13 | -1.9 | 0 |

### RECEIVING

| Last Name | No. | Yds | Avg | TD |
|---|---|---|---|---|
| Newsome | 49 | 633 | 12.9 | 3 |
| White | 34 | 283 | 8.3 | 0 |
| Feacher | 28 | 408 | 14.6 | 3 |
| Logan | 23 | 346 | 15.0 | 2 |
| Pruitt | 22 | 140 | 6.4 | 0 |
| Walker | 8 | 136 | 17.0 | 0 |
| Hall | 5 | 78 | 15.6 | 1 |
| C. Miller | 3 | 20 | 6.7 | 0 |
| Fulton | 1 | 9 | 9.0 | 0 |
| Oden | 1 | 4 | 4.0 | 0 |

### PUNT RETURNS

| Last Name | No. | Yds | Avg | TD |
|---|---|---|---|---|
| Walker | 19 | 101 | 5.3 | 0 |
| Hall | 4 | 33 | 8.3 | 0 |

### KICKOFF RETURNS

| Last Name | No. | Yds | Avg | TD |
|---|---|---|---|---|
| Hall | 22 | 430 | 19.5 | 0 |
| Walker | 13 | 295 | 22.7 | 0 |
| Nicolas | 2 | 16 | 8.0 | 0 |
| Green | 1 | 13 | 13.0 | 0 |

### PASSING — PUNTING — KICKING

**PASSING**

| Last Name | Att | Comp | % | Yds | Yd/Att | TD | Int- | % | RK |
|---|---|---|---|---|---|---|---|---|---|
| Sipe | 185 | 101 | 55 | 1064 | 5.75 | 4 | 8- | 4 | 14 |
| McDonald | 149 | 73 | 49 | 993 | 6.66 | 5 | 8- | 5 | 15 |

**PUNTING**

| Last Name | No | Avg |
|---|---|---|
| Cox | 48 | 39.1 |

**KICKING**

| Last Name | XP | Att | % | FG | Att | % |
|---|---|---|---|---|---|---|
| Bahr | 17 | 17 | 100 | 7 | 15 | 47 |
| Cox | | | | 0 | 1 | 0 |

## HOUSTON OILERS

### RUSHING

| Last Name | No. | Yds | Avg | TD |
|---|---|---|---|---|
| Campbell | 157 | 538 | 3.4 | 2 |
| Manning | 13 | 85 | 6.5 | 0 |
| Edwards | 15 | 58 | 3.9 | 0 |
| Craft | 18 | 42 | 2.3 | 0 |
| Nielsen | 9 | 37 | 4.1 | 0 |
| Armstrong | 8 | 15 | 1.9 | 0 |
| Bailey | 1 | 13 | 13.0 | 0 |
| Casper | 2 | 9 | 4.5 | 0 |
| Allen | 2 | 2 | 1.0 | 0 |

### RECEIVING

| Last Name | No. | Yds | Avg | TD |
|---|---|---|---|---|
| Casper | 36 | 573 | 15.9 | 6 |
| Bailey | 26 | 367 | 14.1 | 0 |
| Craft | 23 | 230 | 10.0 | 1 |
| Renfro | 21 | 295 | 15.0 | 3 |
| Campbell | 18 | 130 | 7.2 | 0 |
| Armstrong | 12 | 75 | 6.3 | 0 |
| Edwards | 9 | 53 | 5.9 | 0 |
| Holston | 5 | 116 | 23.2 | 1 |
| Allen | 2 | 35 | 17.5 | 1 |
| Thomaselli | 1 | 8 | 8.0 | 0 |

### PUNT RETURNS

| Last Name | No. | Yds | Avg | TD |
|---|---|---|---|---|
| Roaches | 19 | 104 | 5.5 | 0 |

### KICKOFF RETURNS

| Last Name | No. | Yds | Avg | TD |
|---|---|---|---|---|
| Roaches | 21 | 441 | 21.0 | 0 |
| Allen | 15 | 292 | 19.5 | 0 |
| Tullis | 5 | 91 | 18.2 | 0 |
| T. Wilson | 2 | 40 | 20.0 | 0 |
| Riley | 1 | 27 | 27.0 | 0 |
| Thomaselli | 1 | 7 | 7.0 | 0 |
| Smith | 0 | 7 | — | 0 |

### PASSING — PUNTING — KICKING

**PASSING**

| Last Name | Att | Cmp | % | Yds | Yd/Att | TD | Int- | % | RK |
|---|---|---|---|---|---|---|---|---|---|
| Manning | 132 | 67 | 51 | 880 | 6.67 | 6 | 8- | 6 | 13 |
| Nielson | 161 | 87 | 54 | 1005 | 6.24 | 6 | 8- | 5 | 9 |
| Campbell | 1 | 0 | 0 | 0 | 0.00 | 0 | 1-100 | | |

**PUNTING**

| Last Name | No. | Avg |
|---|---|---|
| James | 43 | 40.5 |

**KICKING**

| Last Name | XP | Att | % | FG | Att | % |
|---|---|---|---|---|---|---|
| Kempf | 16 | 18 | 89 | 4 | 6 | 67 |

# 1982 A.F.C. - Western Division

## LOS ANGELES RAIDERS 8-1-0 Tom Flores

| Scores of Each Game | | |
|---|---|---|
| 23 | San Francisco | 17 |
| 38 | Atlanta | 14 |
| 28 | SAN DIEGO | 24 |
| 17 | Cincinnati | 31 |
| 28 | SEATTLE | 23 |
| 21 | Kansas City | 16 |
| 37 | L.A.RAMS | 31 |
| 27 | DENVER | 10 |
| 41 | San Diego | 34 |

| Use Name | Pos. | Hgt | Wgt | Age | Int | Pts |
|---|---|---|---|---|---|---|
| Bruce Davis | OT | 6'6" | 280 | 26 | | |
| Henry Lawrence | OT | 6'4" | 270 | 30 | | |
| Ed Muransky | OT | 6'7" | 280 | 22 | | |
| Art Shell | OT | 6'5" | 285 | 35 | | |
| Curt Marsh | OG | 6'5" | 270 | 23 | | |
| Mickey Marvin | OG | 6'4" | 270 | 26 | | |
| Randy Van Divier | OG | 6'5" | 265 | 24 | | |
| Dave Dalby | C | 6'2" | 250 | 31 | | |
| Jim Romano | C | 6'3" | 260 | 22 | | |
| Steve Sylvester | C-OG | 6'4" | 260 | 29 | | |
| Lyle Alzado | DE | 6'3" | 250 | 33 | | |
| Dave Browning | DE | 6'5" | 245 | 26 | | |
| Howie Long | DE | 6'5" | 265 | 22 | | |
| Reggie Kinlaw | NT | 6'2" | 245 | 25 | | |
| Archie Reese | NT | 6'3" | 275 | 26 | | 6 |
| Johnny Robinson | NT | 6'2" | 260 | 23 | | |
| Ruben Vaughn | NT | 6'2" | 260 | 26 | | |
| Jeff Barnes | LB | 6'2" | 225 | 27 | | |
| Mike Hawkins | LB | 6'2" | 245 | 26 | | |
| Ted Hendricks | LB | 6'7" | 230 | 34 | | |
| Rod Martin | LB | 6'2" | 215 | 28 | 3 | 6 |
| Matt Millen | LB | 6'2" | 255 | 24 | 3 | |
| Bob Nelson | LB | 6'4" | 235 | 29 | | |
| Cal Peterson | LB | 6'3" | 225 | 29 | | |
| Jack Squirek | LB | 6'4" | 225 | 23 | | |
| James Davis | DB | 6' | 190 | 25 | 2 | 6 |
| Mike Davis | DB | 6'3" | 205 | 26 | 1 | 6 |
| Lester Hayes | DB | 6' | 200 | 27 | 2 | |
| Kenny Hill | DB | 6' | 195 | 24 | | |
| Monte Jackson | DB | 5'11" | 195 | 29 | 1 | |
| Vann McElroy | DB | 6'2" | 190 | 22 | 1 | |
| Odis McKinney | DB | 6'2" | 190 | 25 | | |
| Burgess Owens | DB | 6'2" | 200 | 31 | 4 | |
| Ted Watts | DB | 6' | 190 | 24 | 1 | |
| Jim Plunkett | QB | 6'3" | 215 | 34 | | |
| Marc Wilson | QB | 6'6" | 205 | 25 | | |
| MarcusAllen | HB | 6'2" | 205 | 22 | | 84 |
| Rick Berns | HB | 6'2" | 205 | 26 | | |
| Kenny King | HB-FB | 5'11" | 205 | 25 | | 12 |
| Cle Montgomery | HB | 5'8" | 185 | 26 | | |
| Greg Pruitt | HB | 5'10" | 190 | 31 | | 6 |
| Chester Willis | HB | 5'11" | 195 | 24 | | |
| Frank Hawkins | FB | 5'9" | 210 | 23 | | 18 |
| Derrick Jensen | FB | 6'1" | 220 | 26 | | |
| Malcolm Barnwell | WR | 5'11" | 185 | 24 | | |
| Cliff Branch | WR | 5'11" | 170 | 34 | | 24 |
| Bob Chandler | WR | 6' | 180 | 33 | | |
| Calvin Muhammad | WR | 6' | 190 | 23 | | 6 |
| Todd Christensen | TE | 6'3" | 230 | 26 | | 24 |
| Derrick Ramsey | TE | 6'5" | 235 | 25 | | |
| Chris Bahr | K | 5'10" | 175 | 29 | | 62 |
| Ray Guy | K | 6'3" | 195 | 32 | | |

Willie Jones - Knee Injury
John Matuszek - Injured Reserve
Gene Upshaw - Injured Reserve

## SAN DIEGO CHARGERS 6-3-0 Don Coryell

| Scores of Each Game | | |
|---|---|---|
| 23 | Denver | 3 |
| 12 | Kansas City | 19 |
| 24 | L.A.Raiders | 28 |
| 30 | DENVER | 20 |
| 30 | Cleveland | 13 |
| 41 | San Francisco | 37 |
| 50 | CINCINNATI | 34 |
| 44 | BALTIMORE | 26 |
| 34 | L.A.RAIDERS | 41 |

| Use Name | Pos. | Hgt | Wgt | Age | Int | Pts |
|---|---|---|---|---|---|---|
| Sam Claphan | OT | 6'6" | 267 | 25 | | |
| Andrew Gissinger | OT | 6'5" | 279 | 23 | | |
| Billy Shields | OT | 6'7" | 284 | 29 | | |
| Russ Washington | OT | 6'7" | 295 | 35 | | |
| Chuck Loewen | OG-OT | 6'3" | 264 | 25 | | |
| Ed White | OG | 6'2" | 279 | 35 | | |
| Doug Wilkerson | OG | 6'2" | 258 | 35 | | |
| Don Macek | C-OG | 6'3" | 260 | 28 | | |
| Dennis McKnight | C-OG | 6'3" | 253 | 22 | | |
| Bob Rush | C-OT | 6'5" | 270 | 27 | | |
| Keith Ferguson | DE | 6'5" | 241 | 23 | | |
| Leroy Jones | DE | 6'8" | 270 | 31 | | |
| John Woodcock | DE | 6'3" | 257 | 28 | | |
| Richard Ackerman | DT | 6'4" | 254 | 23 | | |
| Gary Johnson | DT | 6'2" | 251 | 29 | | 2 |
| Louie Kelcher | DT | 6'5" | 310 | 29 | | |
| Wilbur Young | DT | 6'6" | 285 | 33 | | |
| Carlos Bradley | LB | 6' | 226 | 22 | | |
| Linden King | LB | 6'4" | 245 | 27 | | |
| Dave Lewis | LB | 6'4" | 245 | 27 | | |
| Woodrow Lowe | LB | 6' | 226 | 28 | 1 | |
| Ray Preston | LB | 6' | 220 | 28 | | |
| Dewey Selmon | LB | 6'1" | 240 | 28 | | |
| Cliff Thrift | LB | 6'2" | 230 | 26 | 2 | |
| Jeff Allen | DB | 5'11" | 194 | 24 | 1 | |
| Willie Buchanon | DB | 6' | 185 | 31 | | |
| Donald Dykes | DB | 5'11" | 185 | 27 | | |
| Tim Fox | DB | 5'11" | 186 | 28 | 4 | |
| Bob Gregor | DB | 6'2" | 190 | 25 | 1 | |
| Bruce Laird | DB | 6' | 195 | 32 | | |
| Miles McPherson | DB | 5'11" | 175 | 22 | | |
| Mike Williams | DB | 5'10" | 186 | 28 | 2 | |
| Andre Young | DB | 6' | 203 | 21 | 2 | |
| Dan Fouts | QB | 6'3" | 205 | 31 | | 6 |
| Ed Luther | QB | 6'3" | 202 | 25 | | |
| James Brooks | HB | 5'9" | 177 | 23 | | 36 |
| Jim Jodat | HB | 5'11" | 208 | 28 | | |
| Chuck Muncie | HB | 6'3" | 228 | 29 | | 54 |
| Hank Bauer | FB-HB | 5'10" | 200 | 28 | | |
| Ricky Bell | FB | 6'2" | 216 | 27 | | |
| John Cappelletti | FB | 6'1" | 215 | 30 | | |
| Wes Chandler | WR | 6' | 183 | 26 | | 54 |
| Bobby Duckworth | WR | 6'3" | 197 | 23 | | |
| Scott Fitzkee | WR | 6' | 187 | 25 | | 6 |
| Charlie Joiner | WR | 5'11" | 180 | 34 | | |
| Dwight Scales | WR | 6'2" | 182 | 29 | | 6 |
| Pete Holohan | TE | 6'4" | 240 | 23 | | |
| Eric Sievers | TE | 6'4" | 235 | 23 | | 6 |
| Kellen Winslow | TE | 6'5" | 251 | 24 | | 36 |
| Rolf Benirschke | K | 6'1" | 179 | 27 | | 80 |
| Maury Buford | K | 6' | 185 | 22 | | |

## SEATTLE SEAHAWKS 4-5-0 Jack Patera, Mike McCormack

| Scores of Each Game | | |
|---|---|---|
| 7 | CLEVELAND | 21 |
| 21 | Houston | 23 |
| 17 | Denver | 10 |
| 16 | PITTSBURGH | 0 |
| 23 | L.A.Raiders | 28 |
| 20 | CHICAGO | 14 |
| 0 | NEW ENGLAND | 16 |
| 10 | Cincinnati | 24 |
| 13 | DENVER | 11 |

| Use Name | Pos. | Hgt | Wgt | Age | Int | Pts |
|---|---|---|---|---|---|---|
| Steve August | OT | 6'5" | 254 | 27 | | |
| Dennis Boyd | OT | 6'6" | 255 | 26 | | |
| Jack Campbell | OT | 6'5" | 277 | 23 | | |
| Ron Essink | OT | 6'6" | 254 | 24 | | |
| Edwin Bailey | OG-OT | 6'4" | 265 | 23 | | |
| Bill Dugan | OG | 6'4" | 271 | 23 | | |
| Robert Pratt | OG | 6'4" | 250 | 31 | | |
| Kani Kauahi | C-OG | 6'2" | 260 | 22 | | |
| Art Kuehn | C | 6'3" | 255 | 29 | | |
| John Yarno | C | 6'5" | 251 | 27 | | |
| Fred Anderson | DE | 6'4" | 245 | 27 | | |
| Mark Bell | DE | 6'4" | 240 | 25 | | |
| Jeff Bryant | DE | 6'5" | 260 | 22 | | |
| David Graham | DE | 6'6" | 250 | 23 | | |
| Jacob Green | DE | 6'3" | 247 | 25 | | |
| Robert Hardy | DT | 6'2" | 250 | 26 | | |
| Joe Nash | DT | 6'2" | 250 | 21 | | |
| Manu Tulasosopo | DT | 6'3" | 252 | 25 | | |
| Mike White | DT | 6'5" | 266 | 25 | | |
| Keith Butler | LB | 6'4" | 225 | 26 | | |
| Brian Flones | LB | 6'1" | 228 | 23 | | |
| Micheal Jackson | LB | 6'1" | 220 | 25 | 2 | |
| Shelton Robinson | LB | 6'2" | 233 | 21 | | |
| Bruce Scholtz | LB | 6'6" | 240 | 23 | 1 | 6 |
| Rodell Thomas | LB | 6'2" | 225 | 24 | | |
| Eugene Williams | LB | 6'1" | 220 | 22 | | |
| Dave Brown | DB | 6'1" | 190 | 29 | 1 | |
| Don Dufek | DB | 6' | 195 | 28 | 1 | |
| Kenny Easley | DB | 6'3" | 206 | 23 | 4 | |
| John Harris | DB | 6'2" | 200 | 26 | 4 | |
| Greggory Johnson | DB | 6'1" | 188 | 23 | | |
| Kerry Justin | DB | 5'11" | 175 | 27 | | |
| Ken McAlister | DB | 6'5" | 210 | 22 | | |
| Keith Simpson | DB | 6'1" | 195 | 26 | | |
| Sam Adkins | QB | 6'2" | 214 | 27 | | |
| Dave Krieg | QB | 6'1" | 185 | 23 | | |
| Jim Zorn | QB | 6'2" | 200 | 29 | | 6 |
| Theotis Brown | HB-FB | 6'2" | 225 | 25 | | 12 |
| Horace Ivory | HB | 6' | 198 | 28 | | 6 |
| Eric Lane | HB | 6' | 195 | 23 | | |
| Sherman Smith | HB | 6'4" | 225 | 27 | | |
| Dan Doornink | FB | 6'3" | 210 | 26 | | |
| David Hughes | FB | 6' | 220 | 23 | | 6 |
| Roger Carr | WR | 6'3" | 195 | 30 | | 12 |
| Paul Johns | WR | 5'11" | 170 | 23 | | 6 |
| Steve Largent | WR | 5'11" | 184 | 27 | | 18 |
| Byron Walker | WR | 6'4" | 190 | 22 | | 12 |
| Pete Metzelaars | TE | 6'7" | 240 | 22 | | |
| John Sawyer | TE | 6'2" | 230 | 29 | | |
| Mike Tice | TE | 6'7" | 250 | 23 | | |
| Norm Johnson | K | 6'2" | 193 | 22 | | 43 |
| Jeff West | K | 6'3" | 220 | 29 | | |

Greg Gaines - Knee Injury
Joe Norman - Knee Injury

## KANSAS CITY CHIEFS 3-6-0 Marv Levy

| Scores of Each Game | | |
|---|---|---|
| 9 | Buffalo | 14 |
| 19 | SAN DIEGO | 12 |
| 17 | New Orleans | 27 |
| 14 | L.A.Rams | 20 |
| 14 | Pittsburgh | 35 |
| 16 | L.A.RAIDERS | 21 |
| 37 | Denver | 16 |
| 13 | SAN FRANCISCO | 26 |
| 37 | N.Y.JETS | 13 |

| Use Name | Pos. | Hgt | Wgt | Age | Int | Pts |
|---|---|---|---|---|---|---|
| Charlie Getty | OT | 6'4" | 270 | 30 | | |
| Matt Herkenhoff | OT | 6'4" | 272 | 31 | | |
| Jim Rourke | OT-OG | 6'5" | 263 | 25 | | |
| Brad Budde | OG | 6'4" | 260 | 24 | | |
| Tom Condon | OG | 6'3" | 275 | 29 | | |
| Bob Simmons | OG | 6'4" | 255 | 28 | | |
| Al Steinfeld | C-OT | 6'4" | 256 | 23 | | |
| Jack Rudnay | C | 6'3" | 242 | 34 | | |
| Les Studdard | C | 6'4" | 260 | 23 | | |
| Mike Bell | DE | 6'4" | 260 | 25 | | |
| Dave Lindstrom | DE | 6'6" | 255 | 27 | | |
| Art Still | DE | 6'7" | 252 | 26 | | |
| Bill Acker | NT-DE | 6'3" | 255 | 25 | | |
| Dino Mangiero | NT-DE | 6'2" | 264 | 23 | | |
| Don Parrish | NT-DE | 6'2" | 255 | 27 | | |
| Ken Kremer | NT | 6'4" | 252 | 25 | | |
| Jerry Blanton | LB | 6'1" | 236 | 26 | | |
| Calvin Daniels | LB | 6'3" | 236 | 23 | | |
| Louis Haynes | LB | 6' | 227 | 22 | | |
| Tom Howard | LB | 6'2" | 215 | 28 | 2 | |
| Charles Jackson | LB | 6'2" | 222 | 27 | | |
| Dave Klug | LB | 6'4" | 230 | 24 | | 6 |
| John Olenchalk | LB-C | 6' | 225 | 26 | | |
| Gary Spani | LB | 6'2" | 228 | 26 | | |
| Gary Barbaro | DB | 6'4" | 210 | 28 | 3 | 6 |
| Trent Bryant | DB | 5'10" | 178 | 25 | | |
| Lloyd Burruss | DB | 6' | 202 | 24 | 1 | |
| Deron Cherry | DB | 5'11" | 190 | 22 | | |
| Herb Christopher | DB | 5'10" | 198 | 28 | | |
| Gary Green | DB | 5'11" | 191 | 26 | 2 | 6 |
| Eric Harris | DB | 6'3" | 202 | 27 | 3 | 6 |
| Durwood Roquemore | DB | 6'1" | 180 | 22 | 1 | |
| Steve Fuller | QB | 6'4" | 198 | 25 | | |
| Bob Gagliano | QB | 6'3" | 195 | 23 | | |
| Bill Kennedy | QB | 6'4" | 211 | 27 | | |
| Curtis Bledsoe | HB-FB | 5'11" | 215 | 25 | | |
| Joe Delaney | HB | 5'10" | 184 | 23 | | |
| Del Thompson | HB | 6' | 203 | 24 | | |
| Clark Gaines | FB | 6'1" | 214 | 28 | | |
| James Hadnot | FB | 6'2" | 245 | 25 | | |
| Billy Jackson | FB-HB | 5'10" | 215 | 22 | | 18 |
| Carlos Carson | WR | 5'10" | 174 | 23 | | 12 |
| Anthony Hancock | WR | 6' | 187 | 22 | | 6 |
| Henry Marshall | WR | 6'2" | 220 | 28 | | 18 |
| Stan Rome | WR | 6'5" | 218 | 26 | | |
| J.T. Smith | WR | 6'2" | 185 | 26 | | 6 |
| Ed Beckman | TE | 6'4" | 239 | 27 | | |
| Al Dixon | TE | 6'5" | 238 | 28 | | 12 |
| Willie Scott | TE | 6'4" | 245 | 23 | | 6 |
| Case deBruijn | K | 6'1" | 176 | 22 | | |
| Jeff Gossett | K | 6'2" | 197 | 25 | | |
| Nick Lowery | K | 6'4" | 189 | 26 | | 74 |

## DENVER BRONCOS 2-7-0 Dan Reeves

| Scores of Each Game | | |
|---|---|---|
| 3 | SAN DIEGO | 23 |
| 24 | SAN FRANCISCO | 21 |
| 10 | SEATTLE | 17 |
| 20 | San Diego | 30 |
| 27 | ATLANTA | 34 |
| 27 | L.A.Rams | 24 |
| 16 | KANSAS CITY | 37 |
| 10 | L.A.Raiders | 27 |
| 11 | Seattle | 13 |

| Use Name | Pos. | Hgt | Wgt | Age | Int | Pts |
|---|---|---|---|---|---|---|
| Brian Clark | OT | 6'6" | 260 | 21 | | |
| Ken Lanier | OT | 6'3" | 269 | 23 | | |
| Claudie Minor | OT | 6'4" | 278 | 31 | | |
| Dave Studdard | OT | 6'4" | 260 | 26 | | |
| Keith Uecker | OT | 6'5" | 260 | 22 | | |
| Tom Glassic | OG | 6'3" | 260 | 28 | | |
| Paul Howard | OG | 6'3" | 260 | 31 | | |
| Keith Bishop | C-OG | 6'3" | 260 | 25 | | |
| Bill Bryan | C | 6'2" | 258 | 27 | | |
| Greg Boyd | DE | 6'6" | 280 | 29 | | 2 |
| Barney Chavous | DE | 6'3" | 258 | 31 | | 2 |
| Rulon Jones | DE | 6'6" | 260 | 24 | | |
| Brison Manor | DE | 6'4" | 248 | 30 | | |
| Rubin Carter | NT | 6' | 256 | 29 | | |
| Don Latimer | NT | 6'3" | 253 | 27 | | |
| Steve Busick | LB | 6'4" | 227 | 23 | | |
| Darren Comeaux | LB | 6'1" | 227 | 22 | | |
| Rick Dennison | LB | 6'2" | 215 | 24 | | |
| Larry Evans | LB | 6'2" | 220 | 29 | | |
| Randy Gradishar | LB | 6'3" | 231 | 30 | | |
| Tom Jackson | LB | 5'11" | 220 | 31 | 1 | |
| Jim Ryan | LB | 6'1" | 215 | 25 | | |
| Bob Swenson | LB | 6'3" | 225 | 29 | | |
| Ken Woodard | LB | 6'1" | 218 | 22 | | |
| Steve Foley | DB | 6'2" | 190 | 28 | | |
| Mike Harden | DB | 6'1" | 192 | 24 | 2 | |
| Roger Jackson | DB | 6' | 186 | 23 | | |
| Aaron Kyle | DB | 5'11" | 185 | 28 | 2 | |
| Dennis Smith | DB | 6'3" | 200 | 23 | 1 | |
| J.T.Thomas | DB | 6'2" | 196 | 31 | 1 | |
| Steve Trimble | DB | 5'10" | 181 | 24 | | |
| Steve Wilson | DB | 5'10" | 195 | 25 | 2 | |
| Louis Wright | DB | 6'2" | 200 | 29 | 2 | |
| Steve DeBerg | QB | 6'2" | 205 | 28 | | 6 |
| Mark Herrmann | QB | 6'4" | 195 | 23 | | 6 |
| Craig Morton | QB | 6'4" | 211 | 39 | | |
| Dave Preston | HB | 5'10" | 195 | 27 | | |
| Gerald Willhite | HB | 5'10" | 200 | 23 | | 12 |
| Sammy Winder | HB | 5'11" | 203 | 23 | | 6 |
| Rob Lytle | FB | 6'1" | 195 | 27 | | |
| Rick Parros | FB | 5'11" | 200 | 24 | | 18 |
| Nathan Poole | FB | 5'9" | 212 | 25 | | |
| Wade Manning | WR | 5'11" | 190 | 27 | | |
| Orlando McDaniel | WR | 6' | 180 | 21 | | |
| Rick Upchurch | WR | 5'10" | 180 | 30 | | 30 |
| Steve Watson | WR | 6'4" | 195 | 25 | | 12 |
| Ron Egloff | TE | 6'5" | 227 | 26 | | |
| Riley Odoms | TE | 6'4" | 235 | 32 | | |
| James Wright | TE | 6'3" | 240 | 26 | | 6 |
| Rich Karlis | K | 6' | 180 | 23 | | 48 |
| Luke Prestridge | K | 6'4" | 235 | 25 | | |

## LOS ANGELES RAIDERS

### RUSHING

| Last Name | No. | Yds | Avg | TD |
|---|---|---|---|---|
| Allen | 160 | 697 | 4.4 | 11 |
| King | 69 | 264 | 3.8 | 2 |
| Hawkins | 27 | 54 | 2.0 | 2 |
| Pruitt | 4 | 22 | 5.5 | 0 |
| Barnwell | 2 | 18 | 9.0 | 0 |
| Willis | 6 | 15 | 2.5 | 0 |
| Branch | 2 | 10 | 5.0 | 0 |
| Plunkett | 15 | 6 | 0.4 | 0 |
| Taylor | 4 | 3 | 0.8 | 0 |
| Guy | 2 | -3 | -1.5 | 0 |
| Christensen | 1 | -6 | -6.0 | 0 |

### RECEIVING

| Last Name | No. | Yds | Avg | TD |
|---|---|---|---|---|
| Christensen | 42 | 510 | 12.1 | 4 |
| Allen | 38 | 401 | 10.6 | 3 |
| Branch | 30 | 575 | 19.2 | 4 |
| Barnwell | 23 | 387 | 16.8 | 0 |
| King | 9 | 57 | 6.3 | 0 |
| Hawkins | 7 | 35 | 5.0 | 1 |
| Muhammad | 3 | 92 | 30.7 | 1 |
| Pruitt | 2 | 29 | 14.5 | 1 |

### PUNT RETURNS

| Last Name | No. | Yds | Avg | TD |
|---|---|---|---|---|
| Pruitt | 27 | 209 | 7.7 | 0 |

### KICKOFF RETURNS

| Last Name | No. | Yds | Avg | TD |
|---|---|---|---|---|
| Pruitt | 14 | 371 | 26.5 | 0 |
| Montgomery | 17 | 312 | 18.4 | 0 |
| Hill | 2 | 20 | 10.0 | 0 |
| Jensen | 1 | 27 | 27.0 | 0 |
| Millen | 1 | 13 | 13.0 | 0 |
| Willis | 1 | 11 | 11.0 | 0 |

### PASSING — PUNTING — KICKING

| PASSING | Att | Comp | % | Yds | Yd/Att | TD | Int- | % | RK |
|---|---|---|---|---|---|---|---|---|---|
| Plunkett | 261 | 152 | 58 | 2035 | 7.80 | 14 | 15- | 6 | 6 |
| Allen | 4 | 1 | 25 | 47 | 11.75 | 0 | 0- | 0 | |
| Wilson | 2 | 1 | 50 | 4 | 2.00 | 0 | 0- | 0 | |

| PUNTING | No | Avg |
|---|---|---|
| Guy | 47 | 39.1 |

| KICKING | XP | Att | % | FG | Att | % |
|---|---|---|---|---|---|---|
| Bahr | 32 | 33 | 97 | 10 | 16 | 63 |

## SAN DIEGO CHARGERS

### RUSHING

| Last Name | No. | Yds | Avg | TD |
|---|---|---|---|---|
| Muncie | 138 | 569 | 4.1 | 8 |
| Brooks | 87 | 430 | 4.9 | 6 |
| Cappelletti | 22 | 82 | 3.7 | 0 |
| Chandler | 5 | 32 | 6.4 | 0 |
| Fouts | 9 | 8 | 0.9 | 1 |
| Jodat | 3 | 7 | 2.3 | 0 |
| Bell | 2 | 6 | 3.0 | 0 |
| Luther | 1 | -13 | -13.0 | 0 |

### RECEIVING

| Last Name | No. | Yds | Avg | TD |
|---|---|---|---|---|
| Winslow | 54 | 721 | 13.4 | 6 |
| Chandler | 49 | 1032 | 21.1 | 9 |
| Joiner | 36 | 545 | 15.1 | 0 |
| Muncie | 25 | 207 | 8.3 | 1 |
| Brooks | 13 | 66 | 5.1 | 0 |
| Sievers | 12 | 173 | 14.4 | 1 |
| Cappelletti | 7 | 48 | 6.9 | 0 |
| Scales | 6 | 105 | 17.5 | 1 |
| Fitzkee | 3 | 47 | 15.7 | 1 |
| Duckworth | 2 | 77 | 38.5 | 0 |
| Jodat | 1 | 0 | 0.0 | 0 |

### PUNT RETURNS

| Last Name | No. | Yds | Avg | TD |
|---|---|---|---|---|
| Brooks | 12 | 138 | 11.5 | 0 |
| Chandler | 0 | 0 | 0.0 | 0 |

### KICKOFF RETURNS

| Last Name | No. | Yds | Avg | TD |
|---|---|---|---|---|
| Brooks | 33 | 749 | 22.7 | 0 |
| A. Young | 4 | 45 | 11.3 | 0 |
| Jodat | 3 | 45 | 15.0 | 0 |
| Bauer | 2 | 24 | 12.0 | 0 |
| Sievers | 1 | 17 | 17.0 | 0 |
| Bell | 1 | 10 | 10.0 | 0 |
| Gissinger | 1 | 0 | 0.0 | 0 |

### PASSING — PUNTING — KICKING

| PASSING | Att | Comp | % | Yds | Yd/Att | TD | Int- | % | RK |
|---|---|---|---|---|---|---|---|---|---|
| Fouts | 330 | 204 | 62 | 2883 | 8.74 | 17 | 11- | 3 | 2 |
| Luther | 4 | 2 | 50 | 55 | 13.75 | 0 | 1- | 25 | |
| Muncie | 3 | 2 | 67 | 83 | 27.67 | 2 | 0- | 0 | |
| Winslow | 1 | 0 | 0 | 0 | 0.00 | 0 | 0- | 0 | |

| PUNTING | No | Avg |
|---|---|---|
| Buford | 21 | 41.3 |

| KICKING | XP | Att | % | FG | Att | % |
|---|---|---|---|---|---|---|
| Benirschke | 32 | 34 | 94 | 16 | 22 | 73 |

## SEATTLE SEAHAWKS

### RUSHING

| Last Name | No. | Yds | Avg | TD |
|---|---|---|---|---|
| Smith | 63 | 202 | 3.2 | 0 |
| Doornink | 45 | 178 | 4.0 | 0 |
| T. Brown | 53 | 141 | 2.7 | 0 |
| Zorn | 15 | 113 | 7.5 | 1 |
| Hughes | 30 | 106 | 3.5 | 0 |
| Ivory | 13 | 51 | 3.9 | 1 |
| Largent | 1 | 8 | 8.0 | 0 |
| Johns | 1 | -1 | -1.0 | 0 |
| Krieg | 6 | -3 | -0.5 | 0 |

### RECEIVING

| Last Name | No. | Yds | Avg | TD |
|---|---|---|---|---|
| Largent | 34 | 493 | 14.5 | 3 |
| Doornink | 22 | 176 | 8.0 | 0 |
| Smith | 19 | 196 | 10.3 | 0 |
| Carr | 15 | 265 | 17.7 | 2 |
| Johns | 15 | 234 | 15.6 | 1 |
| Metzelaars | 15 | 152 | 10.1 | 0 |
| T. Brown | 12 | 95 | 7.9 | 0 |
| Hughes | 11 | 98 | 8.9 | 1 |
| Walker | 10 | 156 | 15.6 | 2 |
| Tice | 9 | 46 | 5.1 | 0 |
| Sawyer | 8 | 92 | 11.5 | 0 |
| Ivory | 5 | 38 | 7.6 | 0 |
| Zorn | 1 | 27 | 27.0 | 0 |

### PUNT RETURNS

| Last Name | No. | Yds | Avg | TD |
|---|---|---|---|---|
| Johns | 19 | 210 | 11.1 | 0 |
| Easley | 1 | 15 | 15.0 | 0 |
| G. Johnson | 1 | 3 | 3.0 | 0 |

### KICKOFF RETURNS

| Last Name | No. | Yds | Avg | TD |
|---|---|---|---|---|
| Lane | 11 | 172 | 15.6 | 0 |
| Ivory | 10 | 224 | 22.4 | 0 |
| McAlister | 2 | 41 | 20.5 | 0 |
| T. Brown | 2 | 33 | 16.5 | 0 |
| Johns | 3 | 57 | 19.0 | 0 |
| Hughes | 1 | 17 | 17.0 | 0 |

### PASSING — PUNTING — KICKING

| PASSING | Att | Comp | % | Yds | Yd/Att | TD | Int- | % | RK |
|---|---|---|---|---|---|---|---|---|---|
| Zorn | 245 | 126 | 51 | 1540 | 6.29 | 7 | 11- | 5 | 12 |
| Krieg | 78 | 49 | 63 | 501 | 6.42 | 2 | 2- | 3 | |
| N. Johnson | 1 | 1 | 100 | 27 | 27.00 | 0 | 0- | 0 | |
| Smith | 1 | 0 | 0 | 0 | 0.00 | 0 | 0- | 0 | |
| Lane | 1 | 0 | 0 | 0 | 0.00 | 0 | 0- | 0 | |

| PUNTING | No | Avg |
|---|---|---|
| West | 48 | 38.2 |
| Doornink | 1 | 54.0 |

| KICKING | XP | Att | % | FG | Att | % |
|---|---|---|---|---|---|---|
| N. Johnson | 13 | 14 | 93 | 10 | 14 | 71 |

## KANSAS CITY CHIEFS

### RUSHING

| Last Name | No. | Yds | Avg | TD |
|---|---|---|---|---|
| Delaney | 95 | 380 | 4.0 | 0 |
| B. Jackson | 86 | 243 | 2.8 | 3 |
| Hadnot | 46 | 172 | 3.7 | 0 |
| Fuller | 10 | 56 | 5.6 | 0 |
| Kenney | 13 | 40 | 3.1 | 0 |
| Marshall | 3 | 25 | 8.3 | 0 |
| Bledsoe | 10 | 20 | 2.0 | 0 |
| Thompson | 4 | 7 | 1.8 | 0 |
| Gaines | 1 | 0 | 0.0 | 0 |
| Studdard | 1 | 0 | 0.0 | 0 |

### RECEIVING

| Last Name | No. | Yds | Avg | TD |
|---|---|---|---|---|
| Marshall | 40 | 549 | 13.7 | 3 |
| Carson | 27 | 494 | 18.3 | 2 |
| Dixon | 18 | 251 | 13.9 | 2 |
| Hadnot | 14 | 96 | 6.9 | 0 |
| Delaney | 11 | 53 | 4.8 | 0 |
| Smith | 10 | 168 | 16.8 | 1 |
| Scott | 8 | 49 | 6.1 | 1 |
| Hancock | 7 | 116 | 16.6 | 1 |
| B. Jackson | 5 | 41 | 8.2 | 0 |
| Rome | 2 | 25 | 12.5 | 0 |
| Gaines | 2 | 17 | 8.5 | 0 |
| Bledsoe | 1 | 5 | 5.0 | 0 |

### PUNT RETURNS

| Last Name | No. | Yds | Avg | TD |
|---|---|---|---|---|
| Hancock | 12 | 103 | 8.6 | 0 |
| Smith | 3 | 26 | 8.7 | 0 |

### KICKOFF RETURNS

| Last Name | No. | Yds | Avg | TD |
|---|---|---|---|---|
| Hancock | 27 | 609 | 22.6 | 0 |
| Thompson | 2 | 41 | 20.5 | 0 |
| Roquemore | 2 | 25 | 12.5 | 0 |
| Cherry | 1 | 39 | 39.0 | 0 |
| Mangiero | 1 | 8 | 8.0 | 0 |
| Lindstrom | 1 | 1 | 1.0 | 0 |

### PASSING — PUNTING — KICKING

| PASSING | Att | Comp | % | Yds | Yd/Att | TD | Int- | % | RK |
|---|---|---|---|---|---|---|---|---|---|
| Kenney | 169 | 95 | 56 | 1192 | 7.05 | 7 | 6- | 4 | 7 |
| Fuller | 93 | 49 | 53 | 665 | 7.15 | 3 | 2- | 2 | |
| Gagliano | 1 | 1 | 100 | 7 | 7.00 | 0 | 0- | 0 | |
| Marshall | 1 | 0 | 0 | 0 | 0.00 | 0 | 0- | 0 | |

| PUNTING | No | Avg |
|---|---|---|
| Gossett | 33 | 41.4 |
| deBruijn | 5 | 34.8 |

| KICKING | XP | Att | % | FG | Att | % |
|---|---|---|---|---|---|---|
| Lowery | 17 | 17 | 100 | 19 | 24 | 79 |

## DENVER BRONCOS

### RUSHING

| Last Name | No. | Yds | Avg | TD |
|---|---|---|---|---|
| Willhite | 70 | 347 | 5.0 | 2 |
| Parros | 77 | 277 | 3.6 | 1 |
| Winder | 67 | 259 | 3.9 | 1 |
| Preston | 19 | 81 | 4.3 | 0 |
| Poole | 7 | 36 | 5.1 | 0 |
| DeBerg | 8 | 27 | 3.4 | 1 |
| Herrmann | 3 | 7 | 2.3 | 1 |
| Lytle | 2 | 2 | 1.0 | 0 |
| Watson | 1 | -4 | -4.0 | 0 |
| Wright | 1 | -4 | -4.0 | 0 |
| Upchurch | 2 | -10 | -5.0 | 0 |

### RECEIVING

| Last Name | No. | Yds | Avg | TD |
|---|---|---|---|---|
| Parros | 37 | 259 | 7.0 | 2 |
| Watson | 36 | 555 | 15.4 | 2 |
| Upchurch | 26 | 407 | 15.7 | 3 |
| Willhite | 26 | 227 | 8.7 | 0 |
| Preston | 14 | 134 | 9.6 | 0 |
| Winder | 11 | 83 | 7.5 | 0 |
| Egloff | 10 | 96 | 9.6 | 0 |
| Wright | 9 | 120 | 13.3 | 1 |
| Odoms | 8 | 82 | 10.3 | 0 |
| Manning | 3 | 46 | 15.3 | 0 |
| Lytle | 1 | 10 | 10.0 | 0 |

### PUNT RETURNS

| Last Name | No. | Yds | Avg | TD |
|---|---|---|---|---|
| Upchurch | 15 | 242 | 16.1 | 2 |
| Willhite | 6 | 63 | 10.5 | 0 |

### KICKOFF RETURNS

| Last Name | No. | Yds | Avg | TD |
|---|---|---|---|---|
| Willhite | 17 | 337 | 19.8 | 0 |
| Manning | 15 | 346 | 23.1 | 0 |
| Wilson | 6 | 123 | 20.5 | 0 |
| Uecker | 1 | 12 | 12.0 | 0 |
| Poole | 1 | 0 | 0.0 | 0 |

### PASSING — PUNTING — KICKING

| PASSING | Att | Comp | % | Yds | Yd/Att | TD | Int- | % | RK |
|---|---|---|---|---|---|---|---|---|---|
| DeBerg | 223 | 131 | 59 | 1405 | 6.30 | 7 | 11- | 5 | 8 |
| Herrmann | 60 | 32 | 53 | 421 | 7.02 | 1 | 4- | 7 | |
| Morton | 26 | 18 | 69 | 193 | 7.42 | 0 | 3- | 11 | |
| Upchurch | 0 | 0 | 0 | 0 | 0.00 | 0 | 0- | 0 | |
| Willhite | 2 | 0 | 0 | 0 | 0.00 | 0 | 1- | 50 | |

| PUNTING | No | Avg |
|---|---|---|
| Prestridge | 45 | 45.0 |

| KICKING | XP | Att | % | FG | Att | % |
|---|---|---|---|---|---|---|
| Karlis | 15 | 16 | 94 | 11 | 13 | 85 |

January 8, 1983 at Washington (Attendance 55,045)

SCORING

| | | | | |
|---|---|---|---|---|
| DETROIT | 0 | 0 | 7 | 0- 7 |
| WASHINGTON | 10 | 14 | 7 | 0- 31 |

First Quarter
- Was. — White, 77 yard interception return; PAT—Moseley (kick)
- Was. — Moseley, 26 yard field goal

Second Quarter
- Was. — Garrett, 21 yard pass from Theismann; PAT—Moseley (kick)
- Was. — Garrett, 21 yard pass from Theismann; PAT— Moseley (kick)

Third Quarter
- Was. — Garrett, 27 yard pass from Theismann; PAT—Moseley (kick)
- Det. — Hill, 15 yard pass from Hipple; PAT—Murray (kick)

TEAM STATISTICS

| DET. | | WAS. |
|---|---|---|
| 20 | First Downs- Total | 18 |
| 6 | First Down- Rushing | 10 |
| 12 | First Downs- Passing | 8 |
| 2 | First Downs- Penalty | 0 |
| 3 | Fumbles- Number | 0 |
| 3 | Fumbles- Lost Ball | 0 |
| 5 | Penalties- Number | 4 |
| 29 | Yards Penalized | 20 |
| 1 | Missed Field Goals | 1 |
| 63 | Offensive Plays | 59 |
| 364 | Net Yards | 366 |
| 5.8 | Average Gain | 6.2 |
| 5 | Giveaways | 0 |
| 0 | Takeaways | 5 |
| -5 | Difference | +5 |

INDIVIDUAL STATISTICS

RUSHING

| DETROIT | No. | Yds. | Avg. | WASHINGTON | No. | Yds. | Avg. |
|---|---|---|---|---|---|---|---|
| Hipple | 6 | 47 | 7.8 | Riggins | 25 | 119 | 4.8 |
| Bussey | 5 | 19 | 3.8 | Jackson | 8 | 27 | 3.4 |
| Sims | 6 | 19 | 3.2 | Walker | 2 | 14 | 7.0 |
| King | 4 | 10 | 2.5 | Washington | 1 | 9 | 9.0 |
| | 21 | 95 | 4.5 | Theismann | 2 | 6 | 3.0 |
| | | | | | 38 | 175 | 4.6 |

RECEIVING

| DETROIT | No. | Yds. | Avg. | WASHINGTON | No. | Yds. | Avg. |
|---|---|---|---|---|---|---|---|
| Thompson | 7 | 150 | 21.4 | Garrett | 6 | 110 | 18.3 |
| Sims | 6 | 68 | 11.3 | Brown | 3 | 69 | 23.0 |
| Porter | 2 | 31 | 15.5 | Walker | 4 | 16 | 4.0 |
| Hill | 3 | 29 | 9.7 | Washington | 1 | 15 | 15.0 |
| Scott | 1 | 14 | 14.0 | | 14 | 210 | 15.0 |
| King | 2 | 8 | 4.0 | | | | |
| Bussey | 1 | -2 | -2.0 | | | | |
| | 22 | 298 | 13.5 | | | | |

PUNTING

| DETROIT | No. | | Avg. | WASHINGTON | No. | | Avg. |
|---|---|---|---|---|---|---|---|
| Skladany | 3 | | 38.3 | Hayes | 4 | | 31.3 |

PUNT RETURNS

| DETROIT | No. | Yds. | Avg. | WASHINGTON | No. | Yds. | Avg. |
|---|---|---|---|---|---|---|---|
| Martin | 2 | 13 | 6.5 | Nelms | 3 | 60 | 20.0 |

KICKOFF RETURNS

| DETROIT | No. | Yds. | Avg. | WASHINGTON | No. | Yds. | Avg. |
|---|---|---|---|---|---|---|---|
| Hall | 6 | 123 | 20.5 | Nelms | 2 | 37 | 18.5 |

INTERCEPTION RETURNS

| DETROIT | No. | Yds. | Avg. | WASHINGTON | No. | Yds. | Avg. |
|---|---|---|---|---|---|---|---|
| none | | | | White | 2 | 77 | 38.5 |

PASSING

| | Att. | Comp. | Comp. Pct. | Yds. | Int. | Yds./ Att. | Yds./ Comp. |
|---|---|---|---|---|---|---|---|
| **DETROIT** | | | | | | | |
| Hipple | 38 | 22 | 57.9 | 298 | 2 | 7.8 | 13.5 |
| **WASHINGTON** | | | | | | | |
| Theismann | 19 | 14 | 73.7 | 210 | 0 | 11.1 | 15.0 |

January 8, 1983 at Green Bay, Wis. (Attendance 54,282)

SCORING

| | | | | |
|---|---|---|---|---|
| ST. LOUIS | 3 | 6 | 0 | 7- 16 |
| GREEN BAY | 7 | 21 | 10 | 3- 41 |

First Quarter
- St.L. — O'Donoghue, 18 yard field goal
- G.B. — Jefferson, 60 yard pass from Dickey; PAT—Stenerud (kick)

Second Quarter
- G.B. — Lofton, 20 yard pass from Dickey; PAT—Stenerud (kick)
- G.B. — Ivery, 2 yard rush; PAT—Stenerud (kick)
- G.B. — Ivery, 4 yard pass from Dickey; PAT—Stenerud (kick)
- St.L. — Tilley, 5 yard pass from Lomax; PAT—kick failed

Third Quarter
- G.B. — Stenerud, 46 yard field goal
- G.B. — Jefferson, 7 yard pass from Dickey; PAT—Stenerud (kick)

Fourth Quarter
- G.B. — Stenerud, 34 yard field goal
- St.L. — Shumann, 18 yard pass from Lomax; PAT—O'Donoghue (kick)

TEAM STATISTICS

| ST.L. | | G.B. |
|---|---|---|
| 27 | First Downs- Total | 22 |
| 8 | First Downs- Rushing | 7 |
| 18 | First Downs- Passing | 13 |
| 1 | First Downs- Penalty | 2 |
| 3 | Fumbles- Number | 1 |
| 2 | Fumbles- Lost Ball | 1 |
| 6 | Penalties- Nuamber | 5 |
| 78 | Yards Penalized | 35 |
| 3 | Missed Field Goals | 0 |
| 79 | Offensive Plays | 57 |
| 453 | Net Yards | 394 |
| 5.7 | Average Gain | 6.9 |
| 4 | Giveaways | 1 |
| 1 | Takeaways | 4 |
| -3 | Difference | +3 |

INDIVIDUAL STATISTICS

RUSHING

| ST. LOUIS | No. | Yds. | Avg. | GREEN BAY | No. | Yds. | Avg. |
|---|---|---|---|---|---|---|---|
| Anderson | 8 | 58 | 7.3 | Ivery | 13 | 67 | 5.2 |
| Mitchell | 7 | 21 | 3.0 | Ellis | 5 | 27 | 5.4 |
| Morris | 3 | 14 | 4.7 | Rodgers | 6 | 18 | 3.0 |
| Lomax | 4 | 9 | 2.3 | Jensen | 3 | 10 | 3.3 |
| Green | 1 | 4 | 4.0 | Dickey | 1 | 0 | 0.0 |
| | 23 | 106 | 4.6 | Huckleby | 2 | -1 | -1.0 |
| | | | | Lofton | 1 | -13 | -13.0 |
| | | | | | 31 | 108 | 3.5 |

RECEIVING

| ST. LOUIS | No. | Yds. | Avg. | GREEN BAY | No. | Yds. | Avg. |
|---|---|---|---|---|---|---|---|
| Green | 9 | 113 | 12.6 | Jefferson | 6 | 148 | 24.7 |
| Shumann | 4 | 59 | 14.8 | Lofton | 3 | 52 | 17.3 |
| Mitchell | 4 | 57 | 14.3 | Coffman | 4 | 39 | 9.8 |
| Tilley | 5 | 55 | 11.0 | Ellis | 3 | 29 | 9.7 |
| Thompson | 3 | 41 | 13.7 | Rodgers | 1 | 10 | 10.0 |
| Morris | 3 | 32 | 10.7 | Ivery | 1 | 4 | 4.0 |
| Marsh | 2 | 18 | 9.0 | Jensen | 1 | 4 | 4.0 |
| Harrell | 2 | 10 | 5.0 | | 19 | 286 | 15.1 |
| | 32 | 385 | 12.0 | | | | |

PUNTING

| ST. LOUIS | No. | | Avg. | GREEN BAY | No. | | Avg. |
|---|---|---|---|---|---|---|---|
| none | | | | Stachowicz | 1 | | 28.0 |

PUNT RETURNS

| ST. LOUIS | No. | Yds. | Avg. | GREEN BAY | No. | Yds. | Avg. |
|---|---|---|---|---|---|---|---|
| none | | | | none | | | |

KICKOFF RETURNS

| ST. LOUIS | No. | Yds. | Avg. | GREEN BAY | No. | Yds. | Avg. |
|---|---|---|---|---|---|---|---|
| Mitchell | 3 | 105 | 35.0 | Rodgers | 2 | 47 | 23.5 |
| Harrell | 3 | 53 | 17.7 | Coffman | 1 | 12 | 12.0 |
| Love | 1 | 20 | 20.0 | | 3 | 59 | 19.7 |
| | 7 | 178 | 25.4 | | | | |

INTERCEPTION RETURNS

| ST. LOUIS | No. | Yds. | Avg. | GREEN BAY | No. | Yds. | Avg. |
|---|---|---|---|---|---|---|---|
| none | | | | Murphy | 1 | 22 | 22.0 |
| | | | | Hood | 1 | 0 | 0.0 |
| | | | | | 2 | 22 | 11.0 |

PASSING

| | Att. | Comp. | Comp. Pct. | Yds. | Int. | Yds./ Att. | Yds./ Comp. |
|---|---|---|---|---|---|---|---|
| **ST. LOUIS** | | | | | | | |
| Lomax | 51 | 32 | 62.7 | 385 | 2 | 7.5 | 12.0 |
| **GREEN BAY** | | | | | | | |
| Dickey | 23 | 17 | 73.9 | 260 | 0 | 11.3 | 15.3 |

January 9, 1983 at Irving, Tex. (Attendance 65,042)

SCORING

| | | | | |
|---|---|---|---|---|
| TAMPA BAY | 0 | 10 | 7 | 0- 17 |
| DALLAS | 6 | 7 | 3 | 14- 30 |

First Quarter
- Dal. — Septien, 33 yard field goal
- Dal. — Septien, 33 yard field goal

Second Quarter
- T.B. — Green, 60 yard fumble recovery return; PAT—Capece (kick)
- T.B. — Capece, 32 yard field goal
- Dal. — Springs, 6 yard pass from D. White; PAT—Septien (kick)

Third Quarter
- Dal. — Septien, 19 yard field goal
- T.B. — Jones, 49 yard pass from Williams; PAT—Capece (kick)

Fourth Quarter
- Dal. — Hunter, 19 yard interception return; PAT—Septien(kick)
- Dal. — Newsome, 10 yard pass from D. White; PAT—Septien (kick)

TEAM STATISTICS

| T.B. | | DAL. |
|---|---|---|
| 8 | First Downs- Total | 29 |
| 3 | First Downs- Rushing | 9 |
| 4 | First Downs- Passing | 19 |
| 1 | First Downs- Penalty | 1 |
| 0 | Fumbles- Number | 1 |
| 0 | Fumbles- Lost Ball | 1 |
| 4 | Penalties- Number | 6 |
| 41 | Yards Penalized | 45 |
| 0 | Missed Field Goals | 0 |
| 49 | Offensive Plays | 92 |
| 218 | Net Yards | 456 |
| 4.4 | Average Gain | 5.0 |
| 3 | Giveaways | 3 |
| 3 | Takeaways | 3 |
| 0 | Difference | 0 |

INDIVIDUAL STATISTICS

RUSHING

| TAMPA BAY | No. | Yds. | Avg. | DALLAS | No. | Yds. | Avg. |
|---|---|---|---|---|---|---|---|
| Wilder | 14 | 93 | 6.6 | Dorsett | 26 | 110 | 4.2 |
| Carver | 7 | 12 | 1.7 | Donley | 1 | 25 | 25.0 |
| | 21 | 105 | 5.0 | Springs | 7 | 24 | 3.4 |
| | | | | Newhouse | 5 | 15 | 3.0 |
| | | | | Pearson | 1 | 4 | 4.0 |
| | | | | DuPree | 1 | 1 | 1.0 |
| | | | | D. White | 1 | 0 | 0.0 |
| | | | | | 42 | 179 | 4.3 |

RECEIVING

| TAMPA BAY | No. | Yds. | Avg. | DALLAS | No. | Yds. | Avg. |
|---|---|---|---|---|---|---|---|
| House | 4 | 52 | 13.0 | Pearson | 7 | 95 | 13.6 |
| Jones | 1 | 49 | 49.0 | Johnson | 4 | 76 | 19.0 |
| Giles | 1 | 7 | 7.0 | T. Hill | 4 | 45 | 11.3 |
| Wilder | 2 | 5 | 2.5 | Cosbie | 3 | 32 | 10.7 |
| | 8 | 113 | 14.1 | Springs | 3 | 16 | 5.3 |
| | | | | Dorsett | 2 | 14 | 7.0 |
| | | | | Newsome | 2 | 14 | 7.0 |
| | | | | Newhouse | 1 | 11 | 11.0 |
| | | | | DuPree | 1 | 9 | 9.0 |
| | | | | | 27 | 312 | 11.6 |

PUNTING

| TAMPA BAY | No. | | Avg. | DALLAS | No. | | Avg. |
|---|---|---|---|---|---|---|---|
| Swider | 6 | | 43.5 | D. White | 3 | | 37.3 |

PUNT RETURNS

| TAMPA BAY | No. | Yds. | Avg. | DALLAS | No. | Yds. | Avg. |
|---|---|---|---|---|---|---|---|
| T. Bell | 1 | 8 | 8.0 | Fellows | 5 | 57 | 11.4 |

KICKOFF RETURNS

| TAMPA BAY | No. | Yds. | Avg. | DALLAS | No. | Yds. | Avg. |
|---|---|---|---|---|---|---|---|
| Owens | 5 | 110 | 22.0 | Fellows | 4 | 71 | 17.8 |

INTERCEPTION RETURNS

| TAMPA BAY | No. | Yds. | Avg. | DALLAS | No. | Yds. | Avg. |
|---|---|---|---|---|---|---|---|
| Cotney | 1 | 50 | 50.0 | Hunter | 1 | 19 | 19.0 |
| Holt | 1 | 0 | 0.0 | Clinkscale | 1 | 11 | 11.0 |
| | 2 | 50 | 25.0 | Thurman | 1 | 0 | 0.0 |
| | | | | | 3 | 30 | 10.0 |

PASSING

| | Att. | Comp. | Comp. Pct. | Yds. | Int. | Yds./ Att. | Yds./ Comp. |
|---|---|---|---|---|---|---|---|
| **TAMPA BAY** | | | | | | | |
| Williams | 28 | 8 | 28.6 | 113 | 3 | 4.0 | 14.1 |
| **DALLAS** | | | | | | | |
| D. White | 45 | 27 | 60.0 | 312 | 2 | 6.9 | 11.6 |

# 1982 N.F.C. PLAYOFFS

January 9, 1983 at Minneapolis (Attendance 60,560)

**SCORING**

| | | | | |
|---|---|---|---|---|
| ATLANTA | 7 | 0 | 14 | 3- 24 |
| MINNESOTA | 3 | 10 | 3 | 14- 30 |

First Quarter

| | |
|---|---|
| Atl. | Rogers recovered blocked punt in endzone PAT—Luckhurst (kick) |
| Min. | Danmeier, 33 yard field goal |

Second Quarter

| | |
|---|---|
| Min. | White, 36 yard pass from Kramer PAT—Danmeier (kick) |
| Min. | Danmeier, 30 yard field goal |

Third Quarter

| | |
|---|---|
| Atl. | Luckhurst, 17 yard rush PAT—Luckhurst (kick) |
| Atl. | Glazebrook, 35 yard interception return PAT—Luckhurst (kick) |
| Min. | Danmeier, 39 yard field goal |

Fourth Quarter

| | |
|---|---|
| Min. | McCullum, 11 yard pass from Kramer PAT—Danmeier (kick) |
| Atl. | Luckhurst, 41 yard field goal |
| Min. | Brown, 5 yard rush PAT—Danmeier (kick) |

**TEAM STATISTICS**

| ATL. | | MIN. |
|---|---|---|
| 14 | First Downs- Total | 24 |
| 5 | First Downs- Rushing | 8 |
| 5 | First Downs- Passing | 12 |
| 4 | First Downs- Penalty | 4 |
| 1 | Fumbles- Number | 4 |
| 0 | Fumbles- Lost Ball | 0 |
| 7 | Penalties- Number | 10 |
| 98 | Yards Penalized | 84 |
| 0 | Missed Field Goals | 0 |
| 50 | Offensive Plays | 76 |
| 235 | Net Yards | 378 |
| 4.7 | Average Gain | 5.0 |
| 2 | Giveaways | 1 |
| 1 | Takeaways | 2 |
| -1 | Difference | +1 |

**INDIVIDUAL STATISTICS**

RUSHING

| ATLANTA | No. | Yds. | Avg. | MINNESOTA | No. | Yds. | Avg. |
|---|---|---|---|---|---|---|---|
| Andrews | 11 | 48 | 4.4 | Brown | 23 | 81 | 3.5 |
| Riggs | 9 | 38 | 4.2 | Nelson | 4 | 24 | 6.0 |
| Cain | 3 | 17 | 5.7 | Kramer | 8 | 13 | 1.6 |
| Luckhurst | 1 | 17 | 17.0 | Galbreath | 6 | 10 | 1.7 |
| | 24 | 120 | 5.0 | S. White | 1 | -3 | -3.0 |
| | | | | | 42 | 125 | 3.0 |

RECEIVING

| ATLANTA | No. | Yds. | Avg. | MINNESOTA | No. | Yds. | Avg. |
|---|---|---|---|---|---|---|---|
| Jenkins | 2 | 52 | 26.0 | Senser | 6 | 81 | 13.5 |
| Hodge | 2 | 29 | 14.5 | S. White | 2 | 61 | 30.5 |
| Krepfle | 1 | 18 | 18.0 | McCullum | 4 | 51 | 12.8 |
| Riggs | 2 | 16 | 8.0 | LeCount | 2 | 24 | 12.0 |
| Cain | 1 | 14 | 14.0 | Galbreath | 3 | 14 | 4.7 |
| A. Jackson | 1 | 5 | 5.0 | Young | 2 | 13 | 6.5 |
| | 9 | 134 | 14.9 | Brown | 1 | 9 | 9.0 |
| | | | | | 20 | 253 | 12.7 |

PUNTING

| | | | | | |
|---|---|---|---|---|---|
| Roberts | 5 | 42.6 | Coleman | 4 | 40.0 |

PUNT RETURNS

| | | | | | | | |
|---|---|---|---|---|---|---|---|
| B. Johnson | 1 | 0 | 0.0 | Bess | 5 | 65 | 13.0 |

KICKOFF RETURNS

| | | | | | | | |
|---|---|---|---|---|---|---|---|
| Brown | 7 | 120 | 17.1 | Redwine | 3 | 58 | 19.3 |
| | | | | Nelson | 1 | 30 | 30.0 |
| | | | | | 7 | 165 | 23.6 |

INTERCEPTION RETURNS

| | | | | | | | |
|---|---|---|---|---|---|---|---|
| Glazebrook | 1 | 35 | 35.0 | Turner | 2 | 25 | 12.5 |

PASSING

| ATLANTA | Att. | Comp. | Comp. Pct. | Yds. | Int. | Yds./ Att. | Yds./ Comp. |
|---|---|---|---|---|---|---|---|
| Bartkowski | 23 | 9 | 39.1 | 134 | 2 | 5.8 | 14.9 |
| **MINNESOTA** | | | | | | | |
| Kramer | 34 | 20 | 58.8 | 253 | 1 | 7.4 | 12.7 |

January 15, 1983 at Washington (Attendance 54,593)

**SCORING**

| | | | | |
|---|---|---|---|---|
| MINNESOTA | 0 | 7 | 0 | 0- 7 |
| WASHINGTON | 14 | 7 | 0 | 0- 21 |

First Quarter

| | |
|---|---|
| Was. | Warren, 3 yard pass from Theismann PAT—Moseley (kick) |
| Was. | Riggins, 2 yard rush PAT—Moseley (kick) |

Second Quarter

| | |
|---|---|
| Min. | T. Brown, 18 yard rush PAT—Danmeier (kick) |
| Was. | Garrett, 18 yard pass from Theismann PAT—Moseley (kick) |

**TEAM STATISTICS**

| MIN. | | WAS. |
|---|---|---|
| 15 | First Downs- Total | 23 |
| 3 | First Downs- Rushing | 12 |
| 11 | First Downs- Passing | 11 |
| 1 | First Downs- Penalty | 0 |
| 1 | Fumbles- Number | 0 |
| 0 | Fumbles- Lost Ball | 0 |
| 5 | Penalties- Number | 3 |
| 39 | Yards Penalized | 25 |
| 1 | Missed Field Goals | 2 |
| 59 | Offensive Plays | 67 |
| 317 | Net Yards | 415 |
| 5.4 | Average Gain | 6.2 |
| 0 | Giveaways | 1 |
| 1 | Takeaways | 0 |
| +1 | Difference | -1 |

**INDIVIDUAL STATISTICS**

RUSHING

| MINNESOTA | No. | Yds. | Avg. | WASHINGTON | No. | Yds. | Avg. |
|---|---|---|---|---|---|---|---|
| Brown | 14 | 65 | 4.6 | Riggins | 37 | 185 | 5.0 |
| Young | 1 | 6 | 6.0 | Washington | 1 | 11 | 11.0 |
| Nelson | 1 | 4 | 4.0 | Garrett | 1 | 4 | 4.0 |
| Galbreath | 1 | 4 | 4.0 | Theismann | 3 | 4 | 1.3 |
| Kramer | 1 | 0 | 0.0 | | 42 | 204 | 4.9 |
| | 18 | 79 | 4.4 | | | | |

RECEIVING

| MINNESOTA | No. | Yds. | Avg. | WASHINGTON | No. | Yds. | Avg. |
|---|---|---|---|---|---|---|---|
| McCullum | 3 | 63 | 21.0 | Garrett | 3 | 75 | 25.0 |
| T. Brown | 7 | 62 | 8.9 | C. Brown | 5 | 59 | 11.8 |
| LeCount | 3 | 57 | 19.0 | Giaquinto | 2 | 39 | 19.5 |
| Senser | 1 | 32 | 32.0 | Warren | 4 | 20 | 5.0 |
| Jackson | 1 | 14 | 14.0 | Walker | 2 | 15 | 7.5 |
| S. White | 1 | 13 | 13.0 | Washington | 1 | 5 | 5.0 |
| Jordan | 2 | 11 | 5.5 | | 17 | 213 | 12.5 |
| | 18 | 252 | 14.0 | | | | |

PUNTING

| | | | | | |
|---|---|---|---|---|---|
| Coleman | 4 | 39.2 | Hayes | 2 | 30.0 |

PUNT RETURNS

| | | | | |
|---|---|---|---|---|
| none | Nelms | 1 | 9 | 9.0 |

KICKOFF RETURNS

| | | | | | | | |
|---|---|---|---|---|---|---|---|
| Redwine | 2 | 33 | 16.5 | Nelms | 1 | 22 | 22.0 |
| Nelson | 1 | 12 | 12.0 | Jackson | 1 | 18 | 18.0 |
| | 3 | 45 | 15.0 | | 2 | 40 | 20.0 |

INTERCEPTION RETURNS

| | | | | |
|---|---|---|---|---|
| none | Swain | 1 | 0 | 0.0 |

PASSING

| MINNESOTA | Att. | Comp. | Comp. Pct. | Yds. | Int. | Yds./ Att. | Yds./ Comp. |
|---|---|---|---|---|---|---|---|
| Kramer | 39 | 18 | 46.2 | 252 | 0 | 6.5 | 14.0 |
| **WASHINGTON** | | | | | | | |
| Theismann | 23 | 17 | 73.9 | 213 | 1 | 9.3 | 12.5 |

January 16, 1983 at Irving, Tex. (Attendance 63,972)

**SCORING**

| | | | | |
|---|---|---|---|---|
| GREEN BAY | 0 | 7 | 6 | 13- 26 |
| DALLAS | 6 | 14 | 3 | 14- 37 |

First Quarter

| | |
|---|---|
| Dal. | Septien, 50 yard field goal |
| Dal. | Septien, 34 yard field goal |

Second Quarter

| | |
|---|---|
| G.B. | Lofton, 6 yard pass from Dickey PAT—Stenerud (kick) |
| Dal. | Newsome, 2 yard rush PAT—Septien (kick) |
| Dal. | Thurman, 39 yard interception return PAT—Septien (kick) |

Third Quarter

| | |
|---|---|
| G.B. | Stenerud, 30 yard field goal |
| G.B. | Stenerud, 33 yard field goal |
| Dal | Septien, 24 yard field goal |

Fourth Quarter

| | |
|---|---|
| G.B. | Lofton, 71 yard rush PAT—kick failed |
| Dal. | Cosbie, 7 yard pass from D. White PAT—Septien (kick) |
| G.B. | Lee, 22 yard interception return PAT—Stenerud (kick) |
| Dal. | Newhouse, 1 yard rush PAT—Septien (kick) |

**TEAM STATISTICS**

| G.B. | | DAL. |
|---|---|---|
| 21 | First Downs- Total | 24 |
| 5 | First Downs- Rushing | 10 |
| 16 | First Downs- Passing | 13 |
| 0 | First Downs- Penalty | 1 |
| 4 | Fumbles- Number | 1 |
| 2 | Fumbles- Lost Ball | 1 |
| 3 | Penalties- Number | 5 |
| 35 | Yards Penalized | 30 |
| 0 | Missed Field Goals | 0 |
| 57 | Offensive Plays | 77 |
| 466 | Net Yards | 375 |
| 8.1 | Average Gain | 4.8 |
| 5 | Giveaways | 2 |
| 2 | Takeaways | 5 |
| -3 | Difference | +3 |

**INDIVIDUAL STATISTICS**

RUSHING

| GREEN BAY | No. | Yds. | Avg. | DALLAS | No. | Yds. | Avg. |
|---|---|---|---|---|---|---|---|
| Lofton | 1 | 71 | 71.0 | Dorsett | 27 | 99 | 3.7 |
| Rodgers | 4 | 42 | 10.5 | Newsome | 1 | 2 | 2.0 |
| Ivery | 7 | 24 | 3.4 | Newhouse | 7 | 15 | 2.1 |
| Ellis | 4 | 21 | 5.3 | D. White | 4 | -7 | -1.8 |
| Dickey | 1 | 0 | 0.0 | | 39 | 109 | 2.8 |
| | 17 | 158 | 9.3 | | | | |

RECEIVING

| GREEN BAY | No. | Yds. | Avg. | DALLAS | No. | Yds. | Avg. |
|---|---|---|---|---|---|---|---|
| Lofton | 5 | 109 | 21.8 | T. Hill | 7 | 142 | 20.3 |
| Coffman | 5 | 72 | 14.4 | Newsome | 7 | 70 | 10.0 |
| Ellis | 5 | 70 | 14.0 | Cosbie | 4 | 36 | 9.0 |
| Jefferson | 2 | 40 | 20.0 | DuPree | 2 | 14 | 7.0 |
| Ivery | 1 | 25 | 25.0 | Dorsett | 3 | 9 | 3.0 |
| Epps | 1 | 16 | 16.0 | Pearson | 1 | 3 | 3.0 |
| | 19 | 332 | 17.5 | | 24 | 274 | 11.4 |

PUNTING

| | | | | | |
|---|---|---|---|---|---|
| Stachowicz | 4 | 42.0 | D. White | 4 | 34.8 |

PUNT RETURNS

| | | | | | | | |
|---|---|---|---|---|---|---|---|
| Epps | 1 | 8 | 8.0 | R. Hill | 2 | 18 | 9.0 |
| | | | | Fellows | 1 | 5 | 5.0 |
| | | | | | 3 | 23 | 7.7 |

KICKOFF RETURNS

| | | | | | | | |
|---|---|---|---|---|---|---|---|
| Rodgers | 7 | 148 | 21.1 | R. Hill | 3 | 118 | 39.3 |
| | | | | Fellows | 2 | 37 | 18.5 |
| | | | | Donley | 1 | 18 | 18.0 |
| | | | | | 6 | 173 | 28.8 |

INTERCEPTION RETURNS

| | | | | | | | |
|---|---|---|---|---|---|---|---|
| Lee | 1 | 22 | 22.0 | Thurman | 3 | 58 | 19.3 |

PASSING

| GREEN BAY | Att. | Comp. | Comp. Pct. | Yds. | Int. | Yds./ Att. | Yds./ Comp. |
|---|---|---|---|---|---|---|---|
| Dickey | 36 | 19 | 52.8 | 332 | 3 | 9.2 | 17.5 |
| **DALLAS** | | | | | | | |
| D. White | 36 | 23 | 63.9 | 225 | 1 | 6.3 | 9.8 |
| Pearson | 1 | 1 | 100.0 | 49 | 0 | 49.0 | 49.0 |
| | 37 | 24 | 64.9 | 274 | 1 | 7.4 | 11.4 |

# 1982 A.F.C. PLAYOFFS

January 8, 1983 at Miami (Attendance 68,842)

## SCORING

| | | | | | |
|---|---|---|---|---|---|
| NEW ENGLAND | 0 | 3 | 3 | 7 | — 13 |
| MIAMI | 0 | 14 | 7 | 7 | — 28 |

Second Quarter
- N.E. — J. Smith, 23 yard field goal
- Mia. — Hardy, 2 yard pass from Woodley; PAT—von Schamann (kick)
- Mia. — Franklin, 1 yard rush; PAT—von Schamann (kick)

Third Quarter
- N.E. — J. Smith, 42 yard field goal
- Mia. — Bennett, 2 yard rush; PAT—von Schamann (kick)

Fourth Quarter
- Mia. — Hardy, 2 yard pass from Woodley; PAT—von Schamann (kick)
- N.E. — Hasselbeck, 22 yard pass from Grogan; PAT—J. Smith (kick)

## TEAM STATISTICS

| N.E. | | MIA. |
|---|---|---|
| 14 | First Downs- Total | 27 |
| 6 | First Down- Rushing | 12 |
| 8 | First Downs- Passing | 14 |
| 0 | First Downs- Penalty | 1 |
| 1 | Fumbles- Number | 3 |
| 1 | Fumbles- Lost | 3 |
| 4 | Penalties- Number | 2 |
| 27 | Yards Penalized | 15 |
| 0 | Missed Field Goals | 1 |
| 52 | Offensive Plays | 66 |
| 237 | Net Yards | 448 |
| 4.6 | Average Gain | 6.8 |
| 3 | Giveaways | 3 |
| 3 | Takeaways | 3 |
| 0 | Difference | 0 |

## INDIVIDUAL STATISTICS

### RUSHING

| NEW ENGLAND | No. | Yds. | Avg. | MIAMI | No. | Yds. | Avg. |
|---|---|---|---|---|---|---|---|
| van Eeghen | 9 | 40 | 4.4 | Franklin | 26 | 112 | 4.3 |
| Collins | 7 | 35 | 5.0 | Nathan | 12 | 71 | 5.9 |
| Tatupu | 1 | 4 | 4.0 | Woodley | 1 | 16 | 16.0 |
| Morgan | 1 | -2 | -2.0 | Bennett | 5 | 10 | 2.0 |
| | 18 | 77 | 4.3 | Vigorito | 1 | 5 | 5.0 |
| | | | | | 45 | 214 | 4.8 |

### RECEIVING

| NEW ENGLAND | No. | Yds. | Avg. | MIAMI | No. | Yds. | Avg. |
|---|---|---|---|---|---|---|---|
| Hasselbeck | 7 | 87 | 12.4 | Nathan | 5 | 68 | 13.6 |
| Dawson | 4 | 49 | 12.3 | Rose | 2 | 47 | 23.5 |
| Collins | 1 | 17 | 17.0 | Vigorito | 2 | 40 | 20.0 |
| Toler | 1 | 16 | 16.0 | Harris | 1 | 36 | 36.0 |
| Brown | 1 | 8 | 8.0 | Cefalo | 2 | 27 | 13.5 |
| Johnson | 1 | 7 | 7.0 | Hardy | 3 | 23 | 7.7 |
| van Eeghen | 1 | 5 | 5.0 | Diana | 1 | 5 | 5.0 |
| | 16 | 189 | 11.8 | | 16 | 246 | 15.4 |

### PUNTING

| NEW ENGLAND | No. | Avg. | MIAMI | No. | Avg. |
|---|---|---|---|---|---|
| Camarillo | 5 | 43.6 | Orosz | 1 | 51.0 |

### PUNT RETURNS

| NEW ENGLAND | No. | Yds. | Avg. | MIAMI | No. | Yds. | Avg. |
|---|---|---|---|---|---|---|---|
| none | | | | Vigorito | 4 | 40 | 10.0 |

### KICKOFF RETURNS

| NEW ENGLAND | No. | Yds. | Avg. | MIAMI | No. | Yds. | Avg. |
|---|---|---|---|---|---|---|---|
| R. Smith | 3 | 54 | 18.0 | Walker | 3 | 73 | 24.3 |

### INTERCEPTION RETURNS

| NEW ENGLAND | No. | Yds. | Avg. | MIAMI | No. | Yds. | Avg. |
|---|---|---|---|---|---|---|---|
| none | | | | McNeal | 1 | 16 | 16.0 |
| | | | | Small | 1 | 0 | 0.0 |
| | | | | Walker | 0 | 9 | — |
| | | | | | 2 | 25 | 12.5 |

### PASSING

| NEW ENGLAND | Att. | Comp. | Comp. Pct. | Yds. | Int. | Yds./ Att. | Yds./ Comp. |
|---|---|---|---|---|---|---|---|
| Grogan | 30 | 16 | 53.3 | 189 | 2 | 6.3 | 11.8 |
| **MIAMI** | | | | | | | |
| Woodley | 19 | 16 | 84.2 | 246 | 0 | 12.9 | 15.4 |

---

January 8, 1983 at Los Angeles (Attendance 56,555)

## SCORING

| | | | | | |
|---|---|---|---|---|---|
| CLEVELAND | 0 | 10 | 0 | 0 | — 10 |
| L.A. RAIDERS | 3 | 10 | 7 | 7 | — 27 |

First Quarter
- Raid. — C. Bahr, 27 yard field goal

Second Quarter
- Cle. — M. Bahr, 52 yard field goal
- Raid. — Allen, 2 yard rush; PAT—C. Bahr (kick)
- Cle. — Feacher, 43 yard pass from McDonald; PAT—M. Bahr (kick)
- Raid. — C. Bahr, 37 yard field goal

Third Quarter
- Raid. — Allen, 3 yard rush; PAT—C. Bahr (kick)

Fourth Quarter
- Raid. — Hawkins, 1 yard rush; PAT—C. Bahr (kick)

## TEAM STATISTICS

| CLE. | | RAID. |
|---|---|---|
| 17 | First Downs- Total | 25 |
| 1 | First Downs- Rushing | 11 |
| 11 | First Downs- Passing | 14 |
| 5 | First Downs- Penalty | 0 |
| 2 | Fumbles- Number | 2 |
| 1 | Fumbles- Lost Ball | 0 |
| 4 | Penalties- Number | 6 |
| 35 | Yards Penalized | 65 |
| 0 | Missed Field Goals | 1 |
| 61 | Offensive Plays | 75 |
| 284 | Net Yards | 510 |
| 4.7 | Average Gain | 6.8 |
| 1 | Giveaways | 2 |
| 2 | Takeaways | 1 |
| +1 | Difference | -1 |

## INDIVIDUAL STATISTICS

### RUSHING

| CLEVELAND | No. | Yds. | Avg. | L.A. RAIDERS | No. | Yds. | Avg. |
|---|---|---|---|---|---|---|---|
| White | 9 | 30 | 3.3 | Allen | 17 | 72 | 4.2 |
| Pruitt | 8 | 19 | 2.4 | King | 7 | 30 | 4.3 |
| McDonald | 1 | 7 | 7.0 | Pruitt | 3 | 15 | 5.0 |
| | 18 | 56 | 3.1 | F. Hawkins | 4 | 10 | 2.5 |
| | | | | Plunkett | 2 | 10 | 5.0 |
| | | | | Willis | 3 | 3 | 1.0 |
| | | | | | 36 | 140 | 3.9 |

### RECEIVING

| CLEVELAND | No. | Yds. | Avg. | L.A. RAIDERS | No. | Yds. | Avg. |
|---|---|---|---|---|---|---|---|
| Feacher | 4 | 124 | 31.0 | Branch | 5 | 121 | 24.2 |
| Newsome | 4 | 51 | 12.8 | Christensen | 6 | 93 | 15.5 |
| Walker | 4 | 47 | 11.8 | Allen | 6 | 75 | 12.5 |
| Logan | 1 | 27 | 27.0 | Barnwell | 2 | 38 | 19.0 |
| Pruitt | 3 | 17 | 5.7 | Ramsey | 1 | 25 | 25.0 |
| White | 2 | 15 | 7.5 | Pruitt | 2 | 14 | 7.0 |
| | 18 | 281 | 15.6 | King | 1 | 11 | 11.0 |
| | | | | F. Hawkins | 1 | 9 | 9.0 |
| | | | | | 24 | 386 | 16.1 |

### PUNTING

| CLEVELAND | No. | Avg. | L.A. RAIDERS | No. | Avg. |
|---|---|---|---|---|---|
| Cox | 6 | 48.5 | Guy | 3 | 39.0 |

### PUNT RETURNS

| CLEVELAND | No. | Yds. | Avg. | L.A. RAIDERS | No. | Yds. | Avg. |
|---|---|---|---|---|---|---|---|
| Walker | 1 | 10 | 10.0 | Pruitt | 5 | 45 | 9.0 |

### KICKOFF RETURNS

| CLEVELAND | No. | Yds. | Avg. | L.A. RAIDERS | No. | Yds. | Avg. |
|---|---|---|---|---|---|---|---|
| Hall | 4 | 86 | 21.5 | Pruitt | 2 | 57 | 28.5 |
| | | | | Montgomery | 1 | 26 | 26.0 |
| | | | | | 3 | 83 | 27.7 |

### INTERCEPTION RETURNS

| CLEVELAND | No. | Yds. | Avg. | L.A. RAIDERS | No. | Yds. | Avg. |
|---|---|---|---|---|---|---|---|
| Scott | 1 | 3 | 3.0 | none | | | |
| Dixon | 1 | 0 | 0.0 | | | | |
| | 2 | 3 | 1.5 | | | | |

### PASSING

| CLEVELAND | Att. | Comp. | Comp. Pct. | Yds. | Int. | Yds./ Att. | Yds./ Comp. |
|---|---|---|---|---|---|---|---|
| McDonald | 37 | 18 | 48.6 | 281 | 0 | 7.6 | 15.6 |
| **L.A. RAIDERS** | | | | | | | |
| Plunkett | 37 | 24 | 64.9 | 386 | 2 | 10.4 | 16.1 |

---

January 9, 1983 at Cincinnati (Attendance 57,560)

## SCORING

| | | | | | |
|---|---|---|---|---|---|
| N.Y. JETS | 3 | 17 | 3 | 21 | — 44 |
| CINCINNATI | 14 | 0 | 3 | 0 | — 17 |

First Quarter
- Cin. — Curtis, 32 yard pass from Anderson; PAT—Breech (kick)
- N.Y.J. — Leahy, 33 yard field goal
- Cin. — Ross, 2 yard pass from Anderson; PAT—Breech (kick)

Second Quarter
- N.Y.J. — Gaffney, 14 yard pass from McNeil; PAT—Leahy (kick)
- N.Y.J. — Walker, 4 yard pass from Todd; PAT—Leahy (kick)
- N.Y.J. — Leahy, 24 yard field goal

Third Quarter
- N.Y.J. — Leahy, 47 yard field goal
- Cin. — Breech, 20 yard field goal

Fourth Quarter
- N.Y.J. — McNeil, 20 yard rush; PAT—Leahy (kick)
- N.Y.J. — Ray, 98 yard interception return; PAT—Leahy (kick)
- N.Y.J. — Crutchfield, 1 yard rush; PAT—Leahy (kick)

## TEAM STATISTICS

| N.Y.J. | | CIN. |
|---|---|---|
| 27 | First Downs- Total | 23 |
| 12 | First Downs- Rushing | 3 |
| 13 | First Downs- Passing | 18 |
| 2 | First Downs- Penalty | 2 |
| 2 | Fumbles- Number | 2 |
| 1 | Fumbles- Lost Ball | 1 |
| 12 | Penalties- Number | 7 |
| 95 | Yards Penalized | 60 |
| 0 | Missed Field Goals | 1 |
| 63 | Offensive Plays | 61 |
| 517 | Net Yards | 395 |
| 8.2 | Average Gain | 6.5 |
| 2 | Giveaways | 4 |
| 4 | Takeaways | 2 |
| +2 | Difference | -2 |

## INDIVIDUAL STATISTICS

### RUSHING

| N.Y. JETS | No. | Yds. | Avg. | CINCINNATI | No. | Yds. | Avg. |
|---|---|---|---|---|---|---|---|
| McNeil | 22 | 211 | 9.6 | Johnson | 9 | 26 | 2.9 |
| Dierking | 3 | 11 | 3.7 | A. Griffin | 3 | 17 | 5.7 |
| Newton | 2 | 6 | 3.0 | Alexander | 7 | 14 | 2.0 |
| Todd | 3 | 3 | 1.0 | Anderson | 2 | 5 | 2.5 |
| Augustyniak | 2 | 2 | 1.0 | | 21 | 62 | 3.0 |
| Crutchfield | 1 | 1 | 1.0 | | | | |
| Harper | 1 | 0 | 0.0 | | | | |
| | 34 | 234 | 6.9 | | | | |

### RECEIVING

| N.Y. JETS | No. | Yds. | Avg. | CINCINNATI | No. | Yds. | Avg. |
|---|---|---|---|---|---|---|---|
| Walker | 8 | 145 | 18.1 | Collinsworth | 7 | 120 | 17.1 |
| Gaffney | 4 | 50 | 12.5 | Ross | 6 | 89 | 14.8 |
| Harper | 2 | 35 | 17.5 | Curtis | 3 | 63 | 21.0 |
| J. Jones | 2 | 22 | 11.0 | Kreider | 3 | 41 | 13.7 |
| Barkum | 1 | 9 | 9.0 | M. Harris | 1 | 20 | 20.0 |
| McNeil | 1 | 9 | 9.0 | A. Griffin | 3 | 14 | 4.7 |
| Dierking | 2 | 9 | 4.5 | Johnson | 3 | 7 | 2.3 |
| Augustyniak | 1 | 4 | 4.0 | | 26 | 354 | 13.6 |
| | 21 | 283 | 13.5 | | | | |

### PUNTING

| N.Y. JETS | No. | Avg. | CINCINNATI | No. | Avg. |
|---|---|---|---|---|---|
| none | | | McInally | 2 | 43.0 |

### PUNT RETURNS

| N.Y. JETS | No. | Yds. | Avg. | CINCINNATI | No. | Yds. | Avg. |
|---|---|---|---|---|---|---|---|
| Harper | 1 | 2 | 2.0 | none | | | |

### KICKOFF RETURNS

| N.Y. JETS | No. | Yds. | Avg. | CINCINNATI | No. | Yds. | Avg. |
|---|---|---|---|---|---|---|---|
| Sohn | 3 | 51 | 17.0 | Verser | 7 | 116 | 16.6 |
| Harper | 1 | 18 | 18.0 | Tate | 1 | 22 | 22.0 |
| | 4 | 69 | 17.3 | | 8 | 138 | 17.3 |

### INTERCEPTION RETURNS

| N.Y. JETS | No. | Yds. | Avg. | CINCINNATI | No. | Yds. | Avg. |
|---|---|---|---|---|---|---|---|
| Ray | 1 | 98 | 98.0 | Riley | 1 | 0 | 0.0 |
| Lynn | 2 | 40 | 20.0 | | | | |
| | 3 | 138 | 46.0 | | | | |

### PASSING

| N.Y. JETS | Att. | Comp. | Comp. Pct. | Yds. | Int. | Yds./ Att. | Yds./ Comp. |
|---|---|---|---|---|---|---|---|
| Todd | 28 | 20 | 71.4 | 269 | 1 | 9.6 | 13.5 |
| McNeil | 1 | 1 | 100.0 | 14 | 0 | 14.0 | 14.0 |
| | 29 | 21 | 72.4 | 283 | 1 | 9.8 | 13.5 |
| **CINCINNATI** | | | | | | | |
| Anderson | 35 | 26 | 74.3 | 354 | 3 | 10.1 | 13.6 |
| Schonert | 1 | 0 | 0.0 | 0 | 0 | 0.0 | 0.0 |
| | 36 | 26 | 72.2 | 354 | 3 | 9.8 | 13.6 |

## Game 1

January 9, 1983 at Pittsburgh (Attendance 53,546)

### SCORING

| | | | | | |
|---|---|---|---|---|---|
| SAN DIEGO | 3 | 14 | 0 | 14- | 31 |
| PITTSBURGH | 14 | 0 | 7 | 7- | 28 |

**First Quarter**
Pit.    Ruff recovered fumble in endzone
     PAT—Anderson (kick)
S.D.    Benirschke, 25 yard field goal
Pit.    Bradshaw, 1 yard rush
     PAT—Anderson (kick)

**Second Quarter**
S.D.    Brooks, 18 yard rush
     PAT—Benirschke (kick)
S.D.    Sievers, 10 yard pass from Fouts
     PAT—Benirschke (kick)

**Third Quarter**
Pit.    Cunningham, 2 yard pass from
     Bradshaw
     PAT—Anderson (kick)

**Fourth Quarter**
Pit.    Stallworth, 14 yard pass from
     Bradshaw
     PAT—Anderson (kick)
S.D.    Winslow, 8 yard pass from Fouts
     PAT—Benirschke (kick)
S.D.    Winslow, 12 yard pass from Fouts
     PAT—Benirschke (kick)

### TEAM STATISTICS

| S.D. | | PIT. |
|---|---|---|
| 29 | First Downs- Total | 26 |
| 6 | First Downs- Rushing | 6 |
| 19 | First Downs- Passing | 19 |
| 4 | First Downs- Penalty | 1 |
| 3 | Fumbles- Number | 1 |
| 2 | Fumbles- Lost Ball | 0 |
| 6 | Penalties- Number | 6 |
| 51 | Yards Penalized | 54 |
| 0 | Missed Field Goals | 0 |
| 71 | Offensive Plays | 62 |
| 479 | Net Yards | 422 |
| 6.7 | Average Gain | 6.8 |
| 2 | Giveaways | 2 |
| 2 | Takeaways | 2 |
| 0 | Difference | 0 |

### INDIVIDUAL STATISTICS

**SAN DIEGO**     **PITTSBURGH**

#### RUSHING

| SAN DIEGO | No. | Yds. | Avg. | PITTSBURGH | No. | Yds. | Avg. |
|---|---|---|---|---|---|---|---|
| Muncie | 25 | 126 | 5.0 | Pollard | 9 | 47 | 5.2 |
| Brooks | 3 | 20 | 6.7 | Harris | 10 | 35 | 3.5 |
| Cappelletti | 1 | 0 | 0.0 | Bradshaw | 2 | 12 | 6.0 |
| | 29 | 146 | 5.0 | Hawthorne | 2 | 3 | 1.5 |
| | | | | | 23 | 97 | 4.2 |

#### RECEIVING

| SAN DIEGO | No. | Yds. | Avg. | PITTSBURGH | No. | Yds. | Avg. |
|---|---|---|---|---|---|---|---|
| Chandler | 9 | 124 | 13.8 | Stallworth | 8 | 116 | 14.5 |
| Winslow | 7 | 102 | 14.6 | Harris | 11 | 71 | 6.5 |
| Joiner | 5 | 68 | 13.6 | Cunningham | 5 | 55 | 11.0 |
| Sievers | 2 | 17 | 8.5 | Smith | 1 | 40 | 40.0 |
| Muncie | 1 | 12 | 6.0 | Pollard | 2 | 29 | 14.5 |
| Fitzkee | 1 | 8 | 8.0 | Swann | 1 | 14 | 14.0 |
| Brooks | 1 | 4 | 4.0 | | 28 | 325 | 11.6 |
| Cappelletti | 1 | -2 | -2.0 | | | | |
| | 27 | 333 | 12.3 | | | | |

#### PUNTING

| | No. | | Avg. | | No. | | Avg. |
|---|---|---|---|---|---|---|---|
| Buford | 1 | | 48.0 | Goodson | 2 | | 32.5 |

#### PUNT RETURNS

| | No. | Yds. | Avg. | | No. | Yds. | Avg. |
|---|---|---|---|---|---|---|---|
| none | | | | Woods | 1 | 12 | 12.0 |

#### KICKOFF RETURNS

| | No. | Yds. | Avg. | | No. | Yds. | Avg. |
|---|---|---|---|---|---|---|---|
| Brooks | 3 | 33 | 11.0 | Abercrombie | 4 | 72 | 18.0 |
| | | | | Pollard | 1 | 18 | 18.0 |
| | | | | | 5 | 90 | 18.0 |

#### INTERCEPTION RETURNS

| | No. | Yds. | Avg. | | |
|---|---|---|---|---|---|
| Laird | 1 | 35 | 35.0 | none | |
| Allen | 1 | 8 | 8.0 | | |
| | 2 | 43 | 21.5 | | |

#### PASSING

| SAN DIEGO | Att. | Comp. | Comp. Pct. | Yds. | Int. | Yds./ Att. | Yds./ Comp. |
|---|---|---|---|---|---|---|---|
| Fouts | 42 | 27 | 64.3 | 333 | 0 | 7.9 | 12.3 |

| PITTSBURGH | Att. | Comp. | Comp. Pct. | Yds. | Int. | Yds./ Att. | Yds./ Comp. |
|---|---|---|---|---|---|---|---|
| Bradshaw | 39 | 28 | 71.8 | 325 | 2 | 8.3 | 11.6 |

## Game 2

January 15, 1983 at Los Angeles (Attendance 90,038)

### SCORING

| | | | | | |
|---|---|---|---|---|---|
| N.Y. JETS | 7 | 3 | 0 | 7- | 17 |
| L.A. RAIDERS | 0 | 0 | 14 | 0- | 14 |

**First Quarter**
N.Y.J.    Walker, 20 yard pass from Todd
     PAT—Leahy (kick)

**Second Quarter**
N.Y.J.    Leahy, 30 yard field goal

**Third Quarter**
Raid.    Allen, 3 yard rush
     PAT—Bahr (kick)
Raid.    Barnwell, 57 yard pass from Plunkett
     PAT—Bahr (kick)

**Fourth Quarter**
N.Y.J.    Dierking, 1 yard rush
     PAT—Leahy (kick)

### TEAM STATISTICS

| N.Y.J. | | RAID. |
|---|---|---|
| 21 | First Downs- Total | 19 |
| 8 | First Downs- Rushing | 7 |
| 11 | First Downs- Passing | 11 |
| 2 | First Downs- Penalty | 1 |
| 4 | Fumbles- Number | 2 |
| 3 | Fumbles- Lost Ball | 2 |
| 7 | Penalties- Number | 5 |
| 64 | Yards Penalized | 55 |
| 1 | Missed Field Goals | 1 |
| 62 | Offensive Plays | 65 |
| 391 | Net Yards | 339 |
| 6.3 | Average Gain | 5.2 |
| 5 | Giveaways | 5 |
| 5 | Takeaways | 5 |
| 0 | Difference | 0 |

### INDIVIDUAL STATISTICS

**N.Y. JETS**     **L.A. RAIDERS**

#### RUSHING

| N.Y. JETS | No. | Yds. | Avg. | L.A. RAIDERS | No. | Yds. | Avg. |
|---|---|---|---|---|---|---|---|
| McNeil | 23 | 105 | 4.6 | Allen | 15 | 36 | 2.4 |
| Augustyniak | 4 | 22 | 5.5 | Plunkett | 4 | 18 | 4.5 |
| Todd | 5 | 8 | 1.6 | King | 5 | 16 | 3.2 |
| Dierking | 2 | 4 | 2.0 | Montgomery | 1 | 11 | 11.0 |
| | 34 | 139 | 4.1 | Hawkins | 3 | 4 | 1.3 |
| | | | | Pruitt | 1 | 4 | 4.0 |
| | | | | Barnwell | 1 | 4 | 4.0 |
| | | | | | 30 | 93 | 3.1 |

#### RECEIVING

| N.Y. JETS | No. | Yds. | Avg. | L.A. RAIDERS | No. | Yds. | Avg. |
|---|---|---|---|---|---|---|---|
| Walker | 7 | 169 | 24.1 | Barnwell | 2 | 83 | 41.5 |
| J. Jones | 2 | 52 | 26.0 | Branch | 5 | 82 | 16.4 |
| Augustyniak | 2 | 18 | 9.0 | Allen | 6 | 37 | 6.2 |
| Barkum | 1 | 11 | 11.0 | Christensen | 5 | 31 | 6.2 |
| McNeil | 1 | 11 | 11.0 | Hawkins | 1 | 15 | 15.0 |
| Shuler | 1 | 9 | 9.0 | Ramsey | 1 | 14 | 14.0 |
| Dierking | 1 | 7 | 7.0 | King | 1 | 4 | 4.0 |
| | 15 | 277 | 18.5 | | 21 | 266 | 12.7 |

#### PUNTING

| | No. | | Avg. | | No. | | Avg. |
|---|---|---|---|---|---|---|---|
| Ramsey | 2 | | 31.5 | Guy | 4 | | 41.3 |

#### PUNT RETURNS

| | No. | Yds. | Avg. | | No. | Yds. | Avg. |
|---|---|---|---|---|---|---|---|
| Sohn | 1 | 4 | 4.0 | Pruitt | 1 | 0 | 0.0 |
| | | | | Squirek | 1 | 0 | 0.0 |
| | | | | | 2 | 0 | 0.0 |

#### KICKOFF RETURNS

| | No. | Yds. | Avg. | | No. | Yds. | Avg. |
|---|---|---|---|---|---|---|---|
| none | | | | Montgomery | 2 | 49 | 24.5 |

#### INTERCEPTION RETURNS

| | No. | Yds. | Avg. | | No. | Yds. | Avg. |
|---|---|---|---|---|---|---|---|
| Mehl | 2 | 20 | 10.0 | Hayes | 1 | 0 | 0.0 |
| Jackson | 1 | 10 | 10.0 | Owens | 1 | 0 | 0.0 |
| | 3 | 30 | 15.0 | | 2 | 0 | 0.0 |

#### PASSING

| N.Y. JETS | Att. | Comp. | Comp. Pct. | Yds. | Int. | Yds./ Att. | Yds./ Comp. |
|---|---|---|---|---|---|---|---|
| Todd | 24 | 15 | 62.5 | 277 | 2 | 11.5 | 18.5 |

| L.A. RAIDERS | Att. | Comp. | Comp. Pct. | Yds. | Int. | Yds./ Att. | Yds./ Comp. |
|---|---|---|---|---|---|---|---|
| Plunkett | 33 | 21 | 63.6 | 266 | 3 | 8.1 | 12.7 |

## Game 3

January 16, 1983 at Miami (Attendance 71,383)

### SCORING

| | | | | | |
|---|---|---|---|---|---|
| SAN DIEGO | 0 | 13 | 0 | 0- | 13 |
| MIAMI | 7 | 20 | 0 | 7- | 34 |

**First Quarter**
Mia.    Moore, 3 yard pass from Woodley
     PAT—von Schamann (kick)

**Second Quarter**
Mia.    Franklin, 3 yard rush
     PAT—von Schamann (kick)
Mia.    Lee, 6 yard pass from Woodley
     PAT—von Schamann (kick)
Mia.    von Schamann, 24 yard field goal
S.D.    Joiner, 28 yard pass from Fouts
     PAT—kick failed
Mia.    von Schamann, 23 yard field goal
S.D.    Muncie, 1 yard rush
     PAT—Benirschke (kick)

**Fourth Quarter**
Mia.    Woodley, 7 yard rush
     PAT—von Schamann (kick)

### TEAM STATISTICS

| S.D. | | MIA. |
|---|---|---|
| 17 | First Downs- Total | 29 |
| 5 | First Downs- Rushing | 15 |
| 9 | First Downs- Passing | 11 |
| 3 | First Downs- Penalty | 3 |
| 3 | Fumbles- Number | 2 |
| 2 | Fumbles- Lost Ball | 1 |
| 7 | Penalties- Number | 6 |
| 62 | Yards Penalized | 70 |
| 0 | Missed Field Goals | 0 |
| 54 | Offensive Plays | 80 |
| 247 | Net Yards | 413 |
| 4.6 | Average Gain | 5.2 |
| 7 | Giveaways | 2 |
| 2 | Takeaways | 7 |
| -5 | Difference | +5 |

### INDIVIDUAL STATISTICS

**SAN DIEGO**     **MIAMI**

#### RUSHING

| SAN DIEGO | No. | Yds. | Avg. | MIAMI | No. | Yds. | Avg. |
|---|---|---|---|---|---|---|---|
| Muncie | 11 | 62 | 5.6 | Franklin | 23 | 96 | 4.2 |
| Brooks | 3 | 9 | 3.0 | Nathan | 19 | 83 | 4.4 |
| Cappelletti | 1 | 5 | 5.0 | Bennett | 7 | 14 | 2.0 |
| Fouts | 2 | 3 | 1.5 | Woodley | 3 | 14 | 4.7 |
| | 17 | 79 | 4.6 | Orosz | 1 | 11 | 11.0 |
| | | | | Vigorito | 1 | 2 | 2.0 |
| | | | | Jensen | 2 | -6 | -3.0 |
| | | | | | 56 | 214 | 3.8 |

#### RECEIVING

| SAN DIEGO | No. | Yds. | Avg. | MIAMI | No. | Yds. | Avg. |
|---|---|---|---|---|---|---|---|
| Muncie | 6 | 53 | 8.8 | Cefalo | 2 | 69 | 34.5 |
| Chandler | 2 | 38 | 19.0 | Nathan | 8 | 55 | 6.9 |
| Joiner | 1 | 28 | 28.0 | Hardy | 3 | 45 | 15.0 |
| Brooks | 2 | 25 | 12.5 | Vigorito | 2 | 22 | 11.0 |
| Sievers | 2 | 21 | 10.5 | Harris | 1 | 15 | 15.0 |
| Winslow | 1 | 18 | 18.0 | Lee | 1 | 6 | 6.0 |
| Holohan | 1 | 8 | 8.0 | Moore | 1 | 3 | 3.0 |
| | 15 | 191 | 12.7 | | 18 | 215 | 11.9 |

#### PUNTING

| | No. | | Avg. | | No. | | Avg. |
|---|---|---|---|---|---|---|---|
| Buford | 4 | | 41.2 | Orosz | 3 | | 40.3 |

#### PUNT RETURNS

| | No. | Yds. | Avg. | | No. | Yds. | Avg. |
|---|---|---|---|---|---|---|---|
| Brooks | 3 | 16 | 5.3 | Vigorito | 2 | 4 | 2.0 |

#### KICKOFF RETURNS

| | No. | Yds. | Avg. | | No. | Yds. | Avg. |
|---|---|---|---|---|---|---|---|
| Brooks | 5 | 78 | 15.6 | Walker | 2 | 28 | 14.0 |
| Sievers | 1 | 15 | 15.0 | Hill | 1 | 12 | 12.0 |
| Bauer | 1 | 0 | 0.0 | | 3 | 40 | 13.3 |
| | 7 | 93 | 13.3 | | | | |

#### INTERCEPTION RETURNS

| | No. | Yds. | Avg. | | No. | Yds. | Avg. |
|---|---|---|---|---|---|---|---|
| Fox | 1 | 18 | 18.0 | McNeal | 1 | 20 | 20.0 |
| | | | | G. Blackwood | 2 | 19 | 9.5 |
| | | | | Small | 1 | 16 | 16.0 |
| | | | | L. Blackwood | 1 | -1 | -1.0 |
| | | | | | 5 | 54 | 10.8 |

#### PASSING

| SAN DIEGO | Att. | Comp. | Comp. Pct. | Yds. | Int. | Yds./ Att. | Yds./ Comp. |
|---|---|---|---|---|---|---|---|
| Fouts | 34 | 15 | 44.1 | 191 | 5 | 5.6 | 12.7 |

| MIAMI | Att. | Comp. | Comp. Pct. | Yds. | Int. | Yds./ Att. | Yds./ Comp. |
|---|---|---|---|---|---|---|---|
| Woodley | 22 | 17 | 77.3 | 195 | 1 | 8.9 | 11.5 |
| Nathan | 1 | 1 | 100.0 | 20 | 0 | 20.0 | 20.0 |
| | 23 | 18 | 78.3 | 215 | 1 | 9.3 | 11.9 |

# 1982 Championship Games

## NFC CHAMPIONSHIP GAME
### January 22, 1983 at Washington
### (Attendance 55,045)

### SCORING

| | | | | | |
|---|---|---|---|---|---|
| DALLAS | 3 | 0 | 14 | 0– | 17 |
| WASHINGTON | 7 | 7 | 7 | 10– | 31 |

**First Quarter**
Dal. Septien, 27 yard field goal
Was. Brown, 19 yard pass from Theismann
PAT—Moseley (kick)

**Second Quarter**
Was. Riggins, 1 yard rush
PAT—Moseley (kick)

**Third Quarter**
Dal. Pearson, 6 yard pass from Hogeboom
PAT—Septien (kick)
Was. Riggins, 4 yard rush
PAT—Moseley (kick)
Dal. Johnson, 23 yard pass from Hogeboom
PAT—Septien (kick)

**Fourth Quarter**
Was. Moseley, 29 yard field goal
Was. Grant, 10 yard interception return
PAT—Moseley (kick)

### TEAM STATISTICS

| DAL. | | WAS. |
|---|---|---|
| 21 | First Downs-Total | 18 |
| 2 | First Downs-Rushing | 11 |
| 19 | First Downs-Passing | 5 |
| 0 | First Downs-Penalty | 2 |
| 2 | Fumbles-Number | 1 |
| 1 | Fumbles-Lost Ball | 0 |
| 3 | Penalties-Number | 3 |
| 15 | Yards Penalized | 25 |
| 1 | Missed Field Goals | 1 |
| 65 | Offensive Plays | 63 |
| 340 | Net Yards | 260 |
| 5.2 | Average Gain | 4.1 |
| 3 | Giveaways | 0 |
| 0 | Takeaways | 3 |
| -3 | Difference | +3 |

Excellent throughout a fluky season, the Redskins won both respect and a ticket to the Super Bowl. The Cowboys had their own devils to exorcise, having lost in the NFC title game the past two years.

Dallas took the opening kickoff and drove into position for a Rafael Septien field goal. The Redskins then marched 84 yards for a touchdown. From the first series, John Riggins relentlessly plowed for yardage behind the charge of the Hogs. The Cowboys hurt themselves in the second quarter when Rod Hill fumbled a punt deep in Dallas territory. The Skins recovered on the 11-yard line, and Riggins blasted into the endzone four plays later. Just before the halftime break, Dexter Manley flattened Cowboy QB Danny White and left him groggy with a concussion.

Down 14-3, the Cowboys bounced back in the third quarter behind reserve QB Gary Hogeboom. He closed the gap to 14-10 early in the period with a TD pass to Drew Pearson. Again, the Redskins came up with a big play as Mike Nelms carried a punt 76 yards to the Dallas 20-yard line. Five plays later, Riggins plunged for the score, upping the Washington lead to 10 points. Undaunted, Hogeboom capped another scoring drive with a pass to Butch Johnson.

But the fourth quarter belonged to the Redskins. Midway through the period, Mel Kaufman intercepted a Hogeboom pass, setting up a Mark Moseley field goal. Less than a minute later, Manley tipped Hogeboom's pass into the hands of Darryl Grant, who ran 10 yards to ice the victory.

### INDIVIDUAL STATISTICS

**DALLAS**     **WASHINGTON**

#### RUSHING

| | No. | Yds. | Avg. | | No. | Yds. | Avg. |
|---|---|---|---|---|---|---|---|
| Dorsett | 15 | 57 | 3.8 | Riggins | 36 | 140 | 3.9 |
| Springs | 4 | 15 | 3.8 | Washington | 2 | 2 | 1.0 |
| Pearson | 1 | -1 | -1.0 | Garrett | 1 | -2 | -2.0 |
| T. Hill | 1 | -6 | -6.0 | Theismann | 1 | -3 | -3.0 |
| | 21 | 65 | 3.1 | | 40 | 137 | 3.4 |

#### RECEIVING

| | No. | Yds. | Avg. | | No. | Yds. | Avg. |
|---|---|---|---|---|---|---|---|
| Johnson | 5 | 73 | 14.6 | Garrett | 4 | 46 | 11.5 |
| T. Hill | 5 | 59 | 11.8 | Brown | 3 | 54 | 18.0 |
| Pearson | 5 | 55 | 11.0 | Warren | 2 | 24 | 12.0 |
| Newsome | 3 | 24 | 8.0 | Washington | 1 | 13 | 13.0 |
| Dorsett | 2 | 29 | 14.5 | Walker | 1 | 9 | 9.0 |
| Cosbie | 2 | 26 | 13.0 | Harmon | 1 | 4 | 4.0 |
| DuPree | 1 | 9 | 9.0 | | 12 | 150 | 12.5 |
| | 23 | 275 | 12.0 | | | | |

#### PUNTING

| | No. | Yds. | Avg. | | No. | Yds. | Avg. |
|---|---|---|---|---|---|---|---|
| D. White | 3 | | 31.0 | Hayes | 5 | | 40.2 |

#### PUNT RETURNS

| | No. | Yds. | Avg. | | No. | Yds. | Avg. |
|---|---|---|---|---|---|---|---|
| Donley | 2 | 10 | 5.0 | Nelms | 2 | 14 | 7.0 |
| R. Hill | 1 | 0 | 0.0 | | | | |
| | 3 | 10 | 3.3 | | | | |

#### KICKOFF RETURNS

| | No. | Yds. | Avg. | | No. | Yds. | Avg. |
|---|---|---|---|---|---|---|---|
| R. Hill | 2 | 45 | 22.5 | Nelms | 4 | 128 | 32.0 |
| Donley | 1 | 22 | 22.0 | | | | |
| Fellows | 1 | 15 | 15.0 | | | | |
| Cosbie | 1 | 12 | 12.0 | | | | |
| | 5 | 94 | 18.8 | | | | |

#### INTERCEPTION RETURNS

| | No. | Yds. | Avg. | | No. | Yds. | Avg. |
|---|---|---|---|---|---|---|---|
| none | | | | Grant | 1 | 10 | 10.0 |
| | | | | Kaufman | 1 | 2 | 2.0 |
| | | | | | 2 | 12 | 6.0 |

#### PASSING

| DALLAS | Att. | Comp. | Comp. Pct. | Yds. | Int. | Yds./ Att. | Yds./ Comp. |
|---|---|---|---|---|---|---|---|
| D. White | 15 | 9 | 60.0 | 113 | 0 | 7.5 | 12.6 |
| Hogeboom | 29 | 14 | 48.3 | 162 | 2 | 5.6 | 11.6 |
| | 44 | 23 | 52.3 | 275 | 2 | 6.3 | 12.0 |

| WASHINGTON | | | | | | | |
|---|---|---|---|---|---|---|---|
| Theismann | 20 | 12 | 60.0 | 150 | 0 | 7.5 | 12.5 |

---

## AFC CHAMPIONSHIP GAME
### January 23, 1983 at Miami
### (Attendance 67,396)

### SCORING

| | | | | | |
|---|---|---|---|---|---|
| N.Y. JETS | 0 | 0 | 0 | 0– | 0 |
| MIAMI | 0 | 0 | 7 | 7– | 14 |

**Third Quarter**
Mia. Bennett, 7 yard rush
PAT—von Schamann (kick)

**Fourth Quarter**
Mia. Duhe, 35 yard interception return
PAT—von Schamann (kick)

For the second straight year, the weather played a prominent role in the AFC title game. Rain pounded the Orange Bowl beginning the night before the game through the afternoon, turning the uncovered field into a sloppy mudpit. The Miami management had not used a tarp because it expected the turf to drain. At game time, however, the potent New York Jet offense and Miami's Killer Bee defense faced each other in a messy quagmire.

Neither team scored in the first half. Miami QB David Woodley had little success in the muck, and his runners made no headway against the Jet front four. The New York offense was stymied by a strong pass rush, double coverage on Wesley Walker and Freeman McNeil's lack of solid footing. As the half ended, each team waited for the big break in the deadlock.

Early in the third quarter, A.J. Duhe intercepted a short Jet pass that tipped off the hands of FB Mike Augustyniak. Starting 48 yards away, the Dolphins reached the endzone in seven plays. Woody Bennett's touchdown gave Miami a 7-0 lead, which loomed large in the rain.

Bothered by the wet ball and the Dolphin pass rush, Richard Todd couldn't drive the Jets to the equalizer. Early in the final quarter, Duhe grabbed his third Todd pass of the day and dashed 35 yards for the score which broke the game open.

### TEAM STATISTICS

| N.Y.J. | | MIA. |
|---|---|---|
| 10 | First Downs-Total | 13 |
| 2 | First Downs-Rushing | 7 |
| 6 | First Downs-Passing | 5 |
| 2 | First Downs-Penalty | 1 |
| 1 | Fumbles-Number | 3 |
| 0 | Fumbles-Lost Ball | 1 |
| 6 | Penalties-Number | 3 |
| 42 | Yards Penalized | 15 |
| 0 | Missed Field Goals | 0 |
| 65 | Offensive Plays | 66 |
| 139 | Net Yards | 198 |
| 2.1 | Average Gain | 3.0 |
| 5 | Giveaways | 4 |
| 4 | Takeaways | 5 |
| -1 | Difference | +1 |

### INDIVIDUAL STATISTICS

**N.Y. JETS**     **MIAMI**

#### RUSHING

| | No. | Yds. | Avg. | | No. | Yds. | Avg. |
|---|---|---|---|---|---|---|---|
| McNeil | 17 | 46 | 2.7 | Woodley | 8 | 46 | 5.8 |
| Todd | 4 | 10 | 2.5 | Franklin | 13 | 44 | 3.4 |
| Augustyniak | 2 | 5 | 2.5 | Nathan | 7 | 24 | 3.4 |
| Dierking | 1 | 1 | 1.0 | Bennett | 13 | 24 | 1.8 |
| | 24 | 62 | 2.6 | | 41 | 138 | 3.4 |

#### RECEIVING

| | No. | Yds. | Avg. | | No. | Yds. | Avg. |
|---|---|---|---|---|---|---|---|
| Harper | 4 | 14 | 3.5 | Vigorito | 3 | 29 | 9.7 |
| J. Jones | 3 | 35 | 11.7 | Harris | 2 | 28 | 14.0 |
| Barkum | 2 | 20 | 10.0 | Nathan | 2 | 4 | 2.0 |
| Augustyniak | 2 | 12 | 6.0 | Rose | 1 | 20 | 20.0 |
| McNeil | 1 | 9 | 9.0 | Lee | 1 | 6 | 6.0 |
| Gaffney | 1 | 7 | 7.0 | | 9 | 87 | 9.7 |
| Dierking | 1 | 6 | 6.0 | | | | |
| Walker | 1 | 0 | 0.0 | | | | |
| | 15 | 103 | 6.9 | | | | |

#### PUNTING

| | No. | Yds. | Avg. | | No. | Yds. | Avg. |
|---|---|---|---|---|---|---|---|
| Ramsey | 10 | | 35.7 | Orosz | 10 | | 33.3 |

#### PUNT RETURNS

| | No. | Yds. | Avg. | | No. | Yds. | Avg. |
|---|---|---|---|---|---|---|---|
| Sohn | 6 | 65 | 10.8 | Vigorito | 3 | 20 | 6.7 |

#### KICKOFF RETURNS

| | No. | Yds. | Avg. | | No. | Yds. | Avg. |
|---|---|---|---|---|---|---|---|
| Sohn | 1 | 31 | 31.0 | Walker | 1 | 20 | 20.0 |

#### INTERCEPTION RETURNS

| | No. | Yds. | Avg. | | No. | Yds. | Avg. |
|---|---|---|---|---|---|---|---|
| Schroy | 2 | 1 | 0.5 | Duhe | 3 | 36 | 12.0 |
| Buttle | 1 | 0 | 0.0 | Small | 1 | 8 | 8.0 |
| | 3 | 1 | 0.3 | G. Blackwood | 1 | 4 | 4.0 |
| | | | | | 5 | 48 | 9.6 |

#### PASSING

| N.Y. JETS | Att. | Comp. | Comp. Pct. | Yds. | Int. | Yds./ Att. | Yds./ Comp. |
|---|---|---|---|---|---|---|---|
| Todd | 37 | 15 | 40.5 | 103 | 5 | 2.8 | 6.9 |

| MIAMI | | | | | | | |
|---|---|---|---|---|---|---|---|
| Woodley | 21 | 9 | 42.9 | 87 | 3 | 4.1 | 9.7 |

# The Hogs Lead Riggins, the Smurfs and the Fun Bunch

Each team had the reputation of an underrated overachiever. The Redskins had not even figured to make the playoffs this season, and the Dolphins certainly ranked below some other A.F.C. teams in the eyes of acknowledged experts. The Redskins and Dolphins made liars of the experts. The Skins came into the game on a six-game winning streak, victorious in 14 of their last 15 matches. They had rolled over their three play-off foes behind a complex defense and the determined running of John Riggins. The Dolphins had just defused the potent San Diego and New York Jet offenses en route to this rematch of the Super Bowl that had crowned Miami's unbeaten 1972 season.

Washington's defensive plan was to stop the Miami ground game, thus forcing David Woodley to pass more than usual. Although the plan worked, Woodley burned the Skins in the first quarter with a 76-yard touchdown toss to Jimmy Cefalo. The Redskin offense, meanwhile, had success moving the ball against the Killer Bee defense but fell short in its first few series. The teams traded field goals in the second period, making the score 10-3 in favor of Miami. With its big offensive line leading the way, Washington drove 80 yards in 11 plays to score on a short pass from Joe Theismann to Alvin Garrett. With the score knotted at 10-10, Fulton Walker then took the kickoff and ran 98 yards to return Miami to a seven-point lead, 17-10 at the intermission.

What that score hid was Washington's dominance on offense and defense. The Skins came back onto the field, looking to prevent any more big plays and to keep the pressure on the Miami defense. As the second half progressed, the quick Killer Bee defense struggled to contain the physical charge of the Hogs and Riggins. The Dolphin offense could do nothing against the Washington defense, chalking up only two first downs and no completed passes in the entire half. Despite their increasing momentum, the Redskins scored only on a Mark Moseley field goal in the third quarter, cutting the Miami lead to 17-13.

Early in the final period, Washington began another drive. On fourth-and-inches at the Miami 43-yard line, coach Joe Gibbs decided to go for it. Riggins took the handoff, headed to his left, ran over cornerback Don McNeal, and dashed down the sideline in front of a shocked Miami bench. Moseley's kick made the score 20-17 in favor of the Skins with 10 minutes left. In those final minutes, the Miami attack couldn't move the ball behind either Woodley or relief quarterback Don Strock. Riggins kept churning out the yards, and a late touchdown pass from Theismann to Charlie Brown made the final score 27-17. The MVP award went to Riggins, who dominated the field and set a rushing record of 166 yards.

## LINEUPS

| MIAMI | | WASHINGTON |
|---|---|---|
| | **OFFENSE** | |
| Harris | WR | Garrett |
| Giesler | LT | Jacoby |
| Kuechenberg | LG | Grimm |
| Stephenson | C | Bostic |
| Toews | RG | Dean |
| Laakso | RT | Starke |
| Hardy | TE | Warren |
| Cefalo | WR | Brown |
| Woodley | QB | Theismann |
| Nathan | RB | Riggins |
| Franklin | RB/TE | Walker |
| | **DEFENSE** | |
| Betters | LE | Mendenhall |
| Baumhower | NT/LT | Butz |
| Bokamper | RE/RT | Grant |
| Brudzinski | LOLB/RE | Manley |
| Duhe | LILB/LLB | Kaufman |
| Rhone | RILB/MLB | Olkewicz |
| Gordon | ROLB/RLB | Milot |
| Small | LCB | White |
| McNeal | RCB | Dean |
| G. Blackwood | SS | Peters |
| L. Blackwood | FS | Murphy |

**SUBSTITUTES**

| MIAMI | | |
|---|---|---|
| | **OFFENSE** | |
| Strock | Diana | Rose |
| Jensen | Heflin | Foster |
| Hill | Moore | Green |
| Vigorito | Lee | Dennard |
| Bennett | Duper | |
| | **DEFENSE** | |
| Den Herder | Bowser | Kozlowski |
| Shull | Lankford | Bishop |
| Hester | Judson | Clark |
| Potter | Walker | |
| | **KICKERS** | |
| von Schamann | Orosz | |
| **WASHINGTON** | | |
| | **OFFENSE** | |
| Giaquinto | Didier | Owen |
| Harmon | May | Washington |
| Wonsley | Laster | Puetz |
| Jackson | Holly | Caster |
| Seay | | |
| | **DEFENSE** | |
| McGee | Coleman | McDaniel |
| Liebenstein | Cronan | Jordan |
| Brooks | Lowry | Williams |
| Kubin | Lavender | Nelms |
| | **KICKERS** | |
| Moseley | Hayes | |

## SCORING

| | | | | | |
|---|---|---|---|---|---|
| **MIAMI** | 7 | 10 | 0 | 0- | 17 |
| **WASHINGTON** | 0 | 10 | 3 | 14- | 27 |

**First Quarter**
Mia.  Cefalo, 76 yard pass from Woodley
　　　PAT—von Schamann (kick)

**Second Quarter**
Was.  Moseley, 31 yard field goal
Mia.  von Schamann, 20 yard field goal
Was.  Garrett, 4 yard pass from Theismann
　　　PAT—Moseley (kick)
Mia.  Walker, 98 yard kickoff return
　　　PAT—von Schamann (kick)

**Third Quarter**
Was.  Moseley, 20 yard field goal

**Fourth Quarter**
Was.  Riggins, 43 yard rush
　　　PAT—Moseley (kick)
Was.  Brown, 6 yard pass from Theismann
　　　PAT—Moseley (kick)

## TEAM STATISTICS

| MIA. | | WAS. |
|---|---|---|
| 9 | First Downs- Total | 24 |
| 7 | First Downs- Rushing | 14 |
| 2 | First Downs- Passing | 9 |
| 0 | First Downs- Penalty | 1 |
| 2 | Fumbles- Number | 0 |
| 1 | Fumbles- Lost Ball | 0 |
| 4 | Penalties- Number | 5 |
| 55 | Yards Penalized | 36 |
| 0 | Missed Field Goals | 0 |
| 47 | Offensive Plays | 78 |
| 176 | Net Yards | 400 |
| 3.7 | Average Gain | 5.1 |
| 2 | Giveaways | 2 |
| 2 | Takeaways | 2 |
| 0 | Difference | 0 |

## INDIVIDUAL STATISTICS

### RUSHING

| MIAMI | No. | Yds. | Avg. | WASHINGTON | No. | Yds. | Avg. |
|---|---|---|---|---|---|---|---|
| Franklin | 16 | 49 | 3.1 | Riggins | 38 | 166 | 4.4 |
| Nathan | 7 | 26 | 3.7 | Garrett | 1 | 44 | 44.0 |
| Woodley | 4 | 16 | 4.0 | Harmon | 9 | 40 | 4.4 |
| Vigorito | 1 | 4 | 4.0 | Theismann | 3 | 20 | 6.7 |
| Harris | 1 | 1 | 1.0 | Walker | 1 | 6 | 6.0 |
| | 29 | 96 | 3.3 | | 52 | 276 | 5.3 |

### RECEIVING

| MIAMI | No. | Yds. | Avg. | WASHINGTON | No. | Yds. | Avg. |
|---|---|---|---|---|---|---|---|
| Cefalo | 2 | 82 | 41.0 | Brown | 6 | 60 | 10.0 |
| Harris | 2 | 15 | 7.5 | Warren | 5 | 28 | 5.6 |
| | 4 | 97 | 24.3 | Garrett | 2 | 13 | 6.5 |
| | | | | Walker | 1 | 27 | 27.0 |
| | | | | Riggins | 1 | 15 | 15.0 |
| | | | | | 15 | 143 | 9.5 |

### PUNTING

| MIAMI | No. | Yds. | Avg. | WASHINGTON | No. | Yds. | Avg. |
|---|---|---|---|---|---|---|---|
| Orosz | 6 | | 37.8 | Hayes | 4 | | 42.0 |

### PUNT RETURNS

| MIAMI | No. | Yds. | Avg. | WASHINGTON | No. | Yds. | Avg. |
|---|---|---|---|---|---|---|---|
| Vigorito | 2 | 22 | 11.0 | Nelms | 6 | 52 | 8.7 |

### KICKOFF RETURNS

| MIAMI | No. | Yds. | Avg. | WASHINGTON | No. | Yds. | Avg. |
|---|---|---|---|---|---|---|---|
| Walker | 4 | 190 | 47.5 | Nelms | 2 | 44 | 22.0 |
| L. Blackwood | 2 | 32 | 16.0 | Wonsley | 1 | 13 | 13.0 |
| | 6 | 222 | 37.0 | | 3 | 57 | 19.0 |

### INTERCEPTION RETURNS

| MIAMI | No. | Yds. | Avg. | WASHINGTON | No. | Yds. | Avg. |
|---|---|---|---|---|---|---|---|
| Duhe | 1 | 0 | 0.0 | Murphy | 1 | 0 | 0.0 |
| L. Blackwood | 1 | 0 | 0.0 | | | | |
| | 2 | 0 | 0.0 | | | | |

### PASSING

| MIAMI | Att. | Comp. | Comp. Pct. | Yds. | Int. | Yds./ Att. | Yds./ Comp. | Yards Lost Tackled |
|---|---|---|---|---|---|---|---|---|
| Woodley | 14 | 4 | 28.6 | 97 | 1 | 6.9 | 24.3 | 1-17 |
| Strock | 3 | 0 | 0.0 | 0 | 0 | 0.0 | 0.0 | 0-0 |
| | 17 | 4 | 23.5 | 97 | 1 | 5.7 | 24.3 | 1-17 |
| **WASHINGTON** | | | | | | | | |
| Theismann | 23 | 15 | 65.2 | 143 | 2 | 6.2 | 9.5 | 3-19 |

America saw the melancholy specter of its athletic heroes dragged down by vice. Drug abuse wasted many of the nation's youth and dragged several N.F.L. players into humiliating exposures. Commissioner Pete Rozelle handed out four-game suspensions to Ross Browner and Pete Johnson of Cincinnati, E.J. Junior of St. Louis and Greg Stemrick of New Orleans for drug use. Tony Peters of Washington was docked for the entire season after a conviction for sale of cocaine. To vary the vices, Art Schlichter of Baltimore sat out the year after revelation that he was a compulsive gambler who had bet on N.F.L. games.

## EASTERN DIVISION

**Washington Redskins** — The Redskins proved they were true champions, not fluke victors in a strike-ripped season. They flopped on opening day by losing to the Cowboys 31-30 after leading 23-3 at the half. Shrugging off their disappointment, the Skins tore through the rest of the schedule, losing only a 48-47 shootout with the Packers on October 17. The Washington pass defense was vulnerable despite Mark Murphy's excellence; Tony Peters was suspended, Jeris White held out, Joe Lavender retired and Vernon Dean slumped. The brilliant offense, however, simply blew opponents away. If not handing off to John Riggins, Joe Theismann was unleashing a salvo of passes. Charlie Brown blossomed into a leading receiver in his second pro season. Supporting the entire structure were the Hogs, with Joe Jacoby, Russ Grimm and Jeff Bostic singled out for special praise. Two games sent Redskin fans into fits of delight. On October 2, the Skins scored 17 points in the final seven minutes to edge the Raiders 37-35. On December 11, the hated Cowboys were demolished 31-10 in a showdown for first place in the East.

**Dallas Cowboys** — The Cowboys had a lot of good football players in a very good system. The offense moved the ball through the air to a variety of receivers. To balance the attack, Danny White had the running skills of Tony Dorsett at his call. Of the offensive linemen, tight end Doug Cosbie developed into the star. Like the Redskins, the Cowboys could be beaten by enemy passes. Everson Walls was the leader of a shaky secondary that got some relief from the pass rushing of Randy White and Too Tall Jones. Dallas' excellence emerged in seven straight victories at the start of the schedule, including a 31-30 comeback over the Redskins. On December 11, both Washington and Dallas brought 12-2 records into Texas Stadium. Unable to run the ball, the Cowboys lost 31-10 to fall into second place. A 42-17 humbling at the hands of the 49ers then sent the Cowboys reeling into the playoffs at their lowest ebb of the year.

**St. Louis Cardinals** — While E.J. Junior sat out the first four games, the St. Louis defense was badly mauled in three losses. Beaten in five of their first six games, the Cards rebounded to win five of their next six. Although the defense never really jelled, it had solid newcomers in end Al Baker from Detroit and rookie cornerback Lionel Washington. The big offensive weapons were Roy Green and Ottis Anderson. Green burned the Seahawks on November 13 with four touchdowns in the first half. The late drive included a 44-14 whipping of the Chargers and a 34-24 victory over the Raiders after trailing 17-0. Any playoff hopes died in four losses to the Redskins and Cowboys, none closer than 17 points.

**Philadelphia Eagles** — New coach Marion Campbell revived the Eagles after their rapid fall from grace last year. Four victories in the first six games fueled hopes of a return to the playoffs after only one year away. It wasn't to be, as the Eagles lost nine of their last 10 games. Wilbert Montgomery's bad knee and Michael Haddix's poor rookie year forced the Eagles to forego the ground game for an aerial attack. Campbell unleashed a new weapon in Mike Quick, a deep receiving threat who moved into the starting lineup with flair. During their cold stretch, the Eagles lost a lot of close games, including tough matches with the Cowboys and Redskins. A 13-9 triumph over the Rams on December 4 broke the late-season gloom.

**New York Giants** — Bill Parcells moved up from defensive coordinator to head coach with terrible short-term results. After a 2-2 start, the Giants won only once in their final 12 games. The defense kept up its good work, hanging together around stars Lawrence Taylor, Harry Carson and Mark Haynes. The offense plagued Parcells with many turnovers and few points. The front line was a patchwork affair that undermined both the ground and air attacks. Injuries knocked Phil Simms and then Scott Brunner out of action, leaving third-stringer Jeff Rutledge as the only healthy quarterback by season's end. Earnest Gray hauled in 78 passes from all three of them to lead the N.F.C. in receptions. In a depressing season, the high points were a 27-3 victory over Green Bay on Monday night TV and a 23-0 shutout of the Eagles. The most alarming sign was the 51,589 no-shows for the December 4 game at Giants Stadium.

## CENTRAL DIVISION

**Detroit Lions** — After blanking Tampa Bay on opening day, the Lions lost their next four games. From that point on, the Lions were one of the N.F.L.'s best teams. The Detroit defense led the way back from the depths. Doug English starred on the front line, joined by pass-rushing William Gay, the replacement for the traded Al Baker. Bruce McNorton won a job in the secondary with his aggressive ballhawking. The offense relied on the slick running of Billy Sims, who bounced back from a broken hand suffered in the third game. The Lions shocked a national audience on Thansgiving Day by destroying the Steelers 45-3. Their next time out, they smothered Minnesota 13-2 to take first place in the division. They iced the title the final weekend by beating Tampa Bay while the Packers lost to the Bears.

**Green Bay Packers** — The Packers were regularly becoming a cold-weather San Diego Chargers. They had a marvelous passing attack and a feeble defense, which worked against each other. The defense got off to a bad start when end Mike Butler was cut after signing a contract with the U.S.F.L. By mid-season, coach Bart Starr had placed starters Casey Merrill and Maurice Harvey on waivers. On offense, Lynn Dickey had receiving riches in James Lofton, John Jefferson and Paul Coffman. The running game suffered when Eddie Lee Ivery departed in mid-season with a drug problem. The Packers reached their extremes by beating Tampa Bay 55-14, beating Washington 48-47, and losing to Atlanta 47-41. They entered the final weekend tied for first place in the Central, but fell by the wayside with a last-minute, 23-21 defeat to the Bears. That loss ended Bart Starr's nine-year reign as head coach.

**Chicago Bears** — The death of George Halas snatched away the team's founder and guiding light through years of greatness. After an inept start, the 1983 Bears recaptured some of the flair of their storied ancestors. They won five of their last six games with a solid defense and ball-control offense. They whipped Tampa Bay 27-0 on November 20, then shocked San Francisco 13-3 a week later. On the final two weekends, they eliminated the Vikings and Packers from the Central Division race. The offense was, as usual, centered around Walter Payton, but new speed arrived in the person of Willie Gault, a dangerous receiver who decided to skip the 1984 Olympics to sign with the Bears. The swarming defense had developed stars in Dan Hampton, Mike Singletary and Leslie Frazier.

**Minnesota Vikings** — The Vikings led the Pack at mid-season with a 6-2 record. Over the back leg of the schedule, however, an onslaught of injuries sent the team into a dive. Joe Senser suffered a knee injury in the pre-season and never played a down. Tommy Kramer's season ended in week three with a knee injury and Ted Brown's in week 10 with a separated shoulder. Add injuries to Mark Mullaney and Sammy White, and the Vikes were undermanned down the stretch. A 17-16 loss to the Saints on November 27 dropped them into a first-place tie with the Lions, and a showdown in the Pontiac Silverdome one week later left the Vikings 13-2 losers and playoff also-rans. After 17 years at the helm, coach Bud Grant chose this moment to retire to other pursuits.

**Tampa Bay Buccaneers** — When the Bucs lost their first nine games, fans turned their criticism on coach John McKay. With Doug Williams gone to the U.S.F.L., McKay settled on Jack Thompson and Jerry Golsteyn as his new quarterbacks. Neither man had much success behind an injury-shredded line, enduring the indignity of three shutouts. The offense relied heavily on running back James Wilder. He carried the ball a record

FINAL TEAM STATISTICS

**OFFENSE**

| | ATL. | CHI. | DALL. | DET. | G.B. | L.A. | MINN | N.O. | NY G | PHIL. | STL. | S.F. | T.B. | WASH. |
|---|---|---|---|---|---|---|---|---|---|---|---|---|---|---|
| **FIRST DOWNS:** | | | | | | | | | | | | | | |
| Total | 325 | 308 | 342 | 315 | 340 | 316 | 303 | 286 | 296 | 253 | 296 | 344 | 249 | 353 |
| by Rushing | 118 | 154 | 109 | 136 | 99 | 148 | 112 | 135 | 104 | 91 | 123 | 129 | 72 | 165 |
| by Passing | 190 | 136 | 205 | 156 | 214 | 150 | 169 | 136 | 164 | 150 | 147 | 199 | 157 | 173 |
| by Penalty | 17 | 18 | 28 | 23 | 27 | 18 | 22 | 15 | 28 | 12 | 26 | 16 | 20 | 15 |
| **RUSHING:** | | | | | | | | | | | | | | |
| Number | 492 | 583 | 519 | 513 | 439 | 511 | 470 | 595 | 506 | 402 | 525 | 511 | 428 | 629 |
| Yards | 2224 | 2727 | 2117 | 2181 | 1807 | 2253 | 1808 | 2461 | 1794 | 1417 | 2277 | 2257 | 1353 | 2625 |
| Average Yards | 4.5 | 4.7 | 4.1 | 4.3 | 4.1 | 4.4 | 3.8 | 4.1 | 3.5 | 3.5 | 4.3 | 4.4 | 3.2 | 4.2 |
| Touchdowns | 17 | 14 | 21 | 18 | 15 | 20 | 17 | 19 | 9 | 5 | 15 | 17 | 9 | 30 |
| **PASSING:** | | | | | | | | | | | | | | |
| Attempts | 507 | 447 | 554 | 503 | 526 | 489 | 555 | 425 | 575 | 486 | 460 | 528 | 528 | 463 |
| Completions | 321 | 255 | 346 | 263 | 311 | 286 | 310 | 243 | 284 | 252 | 267 | 339 | 300 | 278 |
| Completion Pct. | 63.3 | 57.0 | 62.5 | 52.3 | 59.1 | 58.5 | 55.9 | 57.2 | 49.4 | 51.9 | 58.0 | 64.2 | 56.8 | 60.0 |
| Passing Yards | 3793 | 3461 | 4156 | 3297 | 4688 | 3411 | 3514 | 2782 | 3854 | 3532 | 3309 | 4021 | 3490 | 3765 |
| Avg. Yds per Att. | 6.1 | 6.2 | 6.5 | 5.4 | 7.7 | 6.3 | 5.4 | 5.4 | 6.7 | 5.7 | 5.5 | 6.8 | 5.4 | 7.1 |
| Avg. Yds per Comp. | 11.8 | 13.6 | 12.0 | 12.5 | 15.1 | 11.9 | 11.3 | 11.5 | 13.6 | 14.0 | 12.4 | 11.9 | 11.6 | 13.5 |
| Times Tackled | 55 | 53 | 37 | 45 | 42 | 23 | 43 | 35 | 49 | 57 | 59 | 33 | 49 | 35 |
| Yds Lost Tackled | 389 | 358 | 314 | 342 | 323 | 190 | 303 | 305 | 363 | 415 | 441 | 224 | 366 | 251 |
| Net Yards | 3404 | 3103 | 3842 | 2955 | 4365 | 3221 | 3211 | 2477 | 3491 | 3117 | 2868 | 3797 | 3124 | 3514 |
| Touchdowns | 24 | 21 | 31 | 19 | 33 | 23 | 15 | 14 | 12 | 22 | 29 | 27 | 18 | 29 |
| Interceptions | 10 | 22 | 25 | 23 | 32 | 23 | 22 | 25 | 31 | 18 | 21 | 12 | 24 | 11 |
| Pct. Intercepted | 2.0 | 4.9 | 4.5 | 4.6 | 6.1 | 4.7 | 4.0 | 5.9 | 5.4 | 3.7 | 4.6 | 4.2 | 4.5 | 2.4 |
| **PUNTS:** | | | | | | | | | | | | | | |
| Number | 71 | 94 | 83 | 72 | 70 | 83 | 91 | 78 | 85 | 86 | 85 | 66 | 96 | 72 |
| Average | 39.8 | 36.2 | 39.4 | 40.4 | 41.0 | 39.8 | 41.5 | 40.7 | 39.8 | 40.9 | 41.5 | 38.7 | 41.8 | 38.8 |
| **PUNT RETURNS** | | | | | | | | | | | | | | |
| Number | 46 | 56 | 51 | 46 | 41 | 55 | 24 | 39 | 55 | 45 | 58 | 36 | 42 | 49 |
| Yards | 489 | 447 | 461 | 522 | 329 | 538 | 210 | 275 | 377 | 259 | 461 | 365 | 299 | 387 |
| Average Yards | 10.6 | 8.0 | 9.0 | 11.3 | 8.0 | 9.8 | 8.8 | 7.1 | 6.9 | 5.8 | 7.9 | 10.1 | 7.1 | 7.9 |
| Touchdowns | 1 | 1 | 1 | 1 | 1 | 1 | 0 | 0 | 0 | 0 | 0 | 1 | 0 | 0 |
| **KICKOFF RET.:** | | | | | | | | | | | | | | |
| Number | 67 | 58 | 71 | 61 | 79 | 52 | 68 | 66 | 71 | 62 | 72 | 52 | 68 | 63 |
| Yards | 1258 | 953 | 1351 | 1191 | 1339 | 946 | 1466 | 1339 | 1333 | 1168 | 1459 | 958 | 1314 | 1301 |
| Average Yards | 18.8 | 16.4 | 19.0 | 19.5 | 16.9 | 18.2 | 21.6 | 20.3 | 18.8 | 18.8 | 20.3 | 18.4 | 19.3 | 20.7 |
| Touchdowns | 0 | 0 | 0 | 0 | 0 | 0 | 0 | 0 | 0 | 0 | 0 | 0 | 0 | 0 |
| **INTERCEPT RET.:** | | | | | | | | | | | | | | |
| Number | 15 | 21 | 27 | 22 | 19 | 24 | 25 | 23 | 23 | 8 | 28 | 24 | 23 | 34 |
| Yards | 212 | 215 | 467 | 185 | 227 | 515 | 168 | 412 | 210 | 79 | 266 | 437 | 367 | 437 |
| Average Yards | 14.1 | 10.2 | 17.3 | 8.4 | 11.9 | 21.5 | 6.7 | 17.9 | 9.1 | 9.9 | 9.5 | 18.2 | 16.0 | 12.9 |
| Touchdowns | 2 | 2 | 2 | 0 | 1 | 3 | 0 | 3 | 1 | 0 | 0 | 5 | 3 | 1 |
| **PENALTIES:** | | | | | | | | | | | | | | |
| Number | 90 | 107 | 99 | 118 | 80 | 96 | 90 | 91 | 113 | 79 | 89 | 89 | 94 | 90 |
| Yards | 806 | 869 | 847 | 988 | 648 | 748 | 748 | 802 | 1020 | 637 | 770 | 695 | 832 | 776 |
| **FUMBLES:** | | | | | | | | | | | | | | |
| Number | 36 | 25 | 30 | 41 | 37 | 38 | 33 | 37 | 39 | 37 | 50 | 27 | 39 | 13 |
| Number Lost | 19 | 14 | 14 | 16 | 18 | 24 | 10 | 22 | 27 | 18 | 27 | 19 | 13 | 7 |
| **POINTS:** | | | | | | | | | | | | | | |
| Total | 370 | 311 | 479 | 347 | 429 | 361 | 316 | 319 | 267 | 233 | 374 | 432 | 241 | 541 |
| PAT Attempts | 45 | 39 | 59 | 38 | 52 | 47 | 34 | 38 | 23 | 27 | 47 | 51 | 31 | 63 |
| PAT Made | 43 | 35 | 57 | 38 | 52 | 42 | 33 | 37 | 22 | 24 | 45 | 51 | 25 | 62 |
| FG Attempts | 22 | 25 | 27 | 32 | 26 | 20 | 33 | 24 | 42 | 26 | 28 | 30 | 24 | 47 |
| FG Made | 17 | 14 | 22 | 25 | 21 | 11 | 25 | 18 | 35 | 15 | 15 | 25 | 10 | 33 |
| Percent FG Made | 77.3 | 56.0 | 81.5 | 78.1 | 80.8 | 55.0 | 75.8 | 75.0 | 83.3 | 57.7 | 53.6 | 83.3 | 41.7 | 70.2 |
| Safeties | 0 | 0 | 1 | 3 | 1 | 2 | 2 | 0 | 1 | 1 | 1 | 0 | 0 | 1 |

**DEFENSE**

| | ATL. | CHI. | DALL. | DET. | G.B. | L.A. | MINN. | N.O. | NY G | PHIL. | STL. | S.F. | T.B. | WASH. |
|---|---|---|---|---|---|---|---|---|---|---|---|---|---|---|
| **FIRST DOWNS:** | | | | | | | | | | | | | | |
| Total | 342 | 286 | 286 | 324 | 366 | 311 | 318 | 289 | 289 | 310 | 286 | 302 | 320 | 290 |
| by Rushing | 139 | 113 | 82 | 133 | 171 | 118 | 147 | 108 | 98 | 144 | 107 | 98 | 124 | 76 |
| by Passing | 187 | 154 | 181 | 161 | 187 | 179 | 150 | 159 | 167 | 149 | 161 | 181 | 172 | 196 |
| by Penalty | 16 | 19 | 23 | 30 | 8 | 14 | 21 | 22 | 24 | 17 | 18 | 23 | 24 | 18 |
| **RUSHING:** | | | | | | | | | | | | | | |
| Number | 499 | 482 | 410 | 503 | 597 | 489 | 579 | 472 | 502 | 633 | 443 | 449 | 561 | 349 |
| Yards | 2309 | 2000 | 1499 | 2104 | 2641 | 1781 | 2584 | 2000 | 1733 | 2655 | 1838 | 1936 | 2082 | 1289 |
| Average Yards | 4.6 | 4.1 | 3.7 | 4.2 | 4.4 | 3.6 | 4.5 | 4.2 | 3.5 | 4.2 | 4.1 | 4.3 | 3.7 | 3.7 |
| Touchdowns | 20 | 20 | 12 | 11 | 28 | 21 | 16 | 11 | 10 | 14 | 23 | 10 | 19 | 9 |
| **PASSING:** | | | | | | | | | | | | | | |
| Attempts | 493 | 490 | 558 | 515 | 518 | 556 | 478 | 496 | 493 | 430 | 519 | 526 | 490 | 570 |
| Completions | 313 | 249 | 299 | 297 | 300 | 319 | 263 | 271 | 283 | 247 | 290 | 322 | 300 | 301 |
| Completion Pct. | 63.5 | 50.8 | 53.6 | 57.7 | 57.9 | 57.4 | 55.0 | 54.6 | 57.4 | 57.4 | 55.9 | 61.2 | 61.2 | 52.8 |
| Passing Yards | 3734 | 3516 | 4365 | 3401 | 4033 | 3869 | 3229 | 3128 | 3584 | 3048 | 3635 | 3701 | 3624 | 4377 |
| Avg. Yds per Att. | 6.7 | 5.8 | 6.4 | 5.6 | 6.7 | 6.1 | 5.5 | 4.9 | 6.1 | 6.0 | 5.5 | 5.6 | 6.2 | 6.4 |
| Avg. Yds per Comp. | 11.9 | 14.1 | 14.6 | 11.5 | 13.4 | 12.1 | 12.3 | 11.5 | 12.7 | 12.3 | 12.5 | 11.5 | 12.1 | 14.5 |
| Times Tackled | 31 | 51 | 57 | 43 | 41 | 33 | 47 | 56 | 44 | 36 | 59 | 57 | 42 | 51 |
| Yds Lost Tackled | 217 | 384 | 437 | 289 | 271 | 258 | 326 | 437 | 323 | 256 | 468 | 448 | 309 | 402 |
| Net Yards | 3517 | 3132 | 3928 | 3112 | 3762 | 3611 | 2903 | 2691 | 3261 | 2792 | 3167 | 2253 | 3315 | 3975 |
| Touchdowns | 28 | 15 | 27 | 21 | 20 | 18 | 23 | 20 | 26 | 20 | 24 | 23 | 15 | 28 |
| Interceptions | 15 | 21 | 27 | 22 | 19 | 24 | 25 | 23 | 23 | 8 | 28 | 24 | 23 | 34 |
| Pct. Intercepted | 3.0 | 4.3 | 4.8 | 4.3 | 3.7 | 4.3 | 5.2 | 4.6 | 4.7 | 1.9 | 5.4 | 4.6 | 4.7 | 6.0 |
| **PUNTS:** | | | | | | | | | | | | | | |
| Number | 67 | 99 | 84 | 79 | 78 | 83 | 77 | 83 | 99 | 80 | 88 | 74 | 79 | 66 |
| Average | 42.0 | 38.6 | 41.8 | 40.1 | 39.1 | 41.7 | 39.3 | 41.8 | 39.2 | 37.8 | 40.3 | 40.4 | 40.7 | 41.6 |
| **PUNT RETURNS** | | | | | | | | | | | | | | |
| Number | 34 | 44 | 53 | 39 | 43 | 39 | 40 | 51 | 47 | 57 | 47 | 38 | 59 | 41 |
| Yards | 179 | 322 | 588 | 302 | 384 | 251 | 297 | 573 | 283 | 511 | 307 | 378 | 603 | 407 |
| Average Yards | 5.3 | 7.3 | 11.1 | 7.7 | 8.9 | 6.4 | 7.4 | 11.2 | 6.0 | 9.0 | 6.5 | 7.3 | 10.2 | 9.9 |
| Touchdowns | 0 | 0 | 1 | 0 | 1 | 0 | 0 | 2 | 0 | 0 | 0 | 0 | 1 | 1 |
| **KICKOFF RET.:** | | | | | | | | | | | | | | |
| Number | 60 | 66 | 78 | 71 | 78 | 71 | 70 | 44 | 67 | 45 | 66 | 78 | 50 | 91 |
| Yards | 1212 | 1229 | 1806 | 1146 | 1429 | 1325 | 1392 | 938 | 1296 | 804 | 1300 | 1675 | 1039 | 1772 |
| Average Yards | 20.2 | 18.6 | 23.2 | 16.1 | 18.3 | 18.7 | 19.9 | 21.3 | 19.3 | 17.9 | 19.7 | 21.5 | 20.8 | 19.5 |
| Touchdowns | 0 | 0 | 0 | 0 | 0 | 0 | 0 | 0 | 0 | 0 | 1 | 0 | 0 | 0 |
| **INTERCEPT RET.:** | | | | | | | | | | | | | | |
| Number | 10 | 22 | 25 | 23 | 32 | 23 | 22 | 25 | 31 | 18 | 21 | 12 | 24 | 11 |
| Yards | 94 | 291 | 358 | 241 | 337 | 303 | 308 | 424 | 436 | 155 | 385 | 168 | 316 | 90 |
| Average Yards | 9.4 | 13.2 | 14.3 | 10.5 | 10.5 | 13.2 | 14.0 | 17.0 | 14.1 | 8.6 | 18.3 | 14.0 | 13.2 | 8.2 |
| Touchdowns | 0 | 1 | 1 | 0 | 4 | 0 | 2 | 5 | 2 | 0 | 0 | 1 | 4 | 0 |
| **PENALTIES:** | | | | | | | | | | | | | | |
| Number | 81 | 86 | 100 | 117 | 110 | 89 | 92 | 96 | 114 | 94 | 102 | 91 | 105 | 80 |
| Yards | 710 | 687 | 873 | 1062 | 965 | 804 | 759 | 814 | 927 | 755 | 819 | 793 | 799 | 710 |
| **FUMBLES:** | | | | | | | | | | | | | | |
| Number | 26 | 37 | 31 | 33 | 32 | 38 | 33 | 33 | 31 | 30 | 32 | 39 | 43 | 46 |
| Number Lost | 15 | 17 | 21 | 15 | 12 | 20 | 23 | 16 | 13 | 15 | 20 | 18 | 18 | 27 |
| **POINTS:** | | | | | | | | | | | | | | |
| Total | 389 | 301 | 360 | 286 | 439 | 344 | 348 | 337 | 347 | 322 | 428 | 293 | 380 | 332 |
| PAT Attempts | 49 | 36 | 42 | 33 | 54 | 42 | 42 | 39 | 40 | 34 | 56 | 35 | 42 | 39 |
| PAT Made | 44 | 34 | 42 | 32 | 50 | 39 | 40 | 37 | 39 | 34 | 54 | 32 | 40 | 38 |
| FG Attempts | 26 | 23 | 30 | 26 | 29 | 28 | 27 | 34 | 32 | 37 | 15 | 27 | 34 | 28 |
| FG Made | 17 | 17 | 22 | 18 | 19 | 17 | 18 | 20 | 22 | 28 | 12 | 17 | 28 | 20 |
| Percent FG Made | 65.4 | 73.9 | 73.3 | 69.2 | 65.5 | 60.7 | 66.7 | 58.8 | 68.8 | 75.7 | 80.0 | 63.0 | 82.4 | 71.4 |
| Safeties | 0 | 0 | 0 | 1 | 1 | 1 | 1 | 3 | 1 | 0 | 1 | 0 | 2 | 0 |

42 times against the Steelers on October 30, gained 219 yards against the Vikings on November 6, then suffered broken ribs a week later to end his season. The defense also fell off in performance, although Lee Roy Selmon and Hugh Green still were all-pros.

## WESTERN DIVISION

**San Francisco 49ers** — The Niners proved that last year was a fluke, storming back into the playoffs with overall improvement. The intricate offense now had a welcome pair of runners in ex-Ram Wendell Tyler and rookie Roger Craig. They balanced the potent passing attack, which featured Joe Montana and Dwight Clark. The defense prospered from Fred Dean's renewed pass rushing and the return to form of Ronnie Lott and other young defensive backs. The team announced its resurgence by winning four of its first five games. A cold spell in mid-season left the Niners one game behind the Rams with three weeks left. While the Rams lost their next two games, the 49ers won twice and moved into first place. A 42-17 thrashing of the Cowboys on the final Monday night clinched the top spot and boded well for the playoffs.

**Los Angeles Rams** — Two additions turned the Rams around and led them into the playoffs. USC coach John Robinson moved into the pro ranks and rallied a demoralized team. Robinson had a superb siege gun in rookie Eric Dickerson, a magnificent runner who combined size with speed. The Los Angeles offense revived behind Dickerson's excellence and an improved front line. The defense shed its clownish look and prospered in a new 4-3 alignment. The new-look Rams dove into the playoff race and actually held first place at the start of December. Losses to the Eagles and Patriots dropped them out of first place and into a must-win situation in the season's finale against the Saints. The L.A. offense didn't score a point until the game was almost over, but Mike Lansford's 42-yard field goal with two seconds left gave the Rams a 26-24 victory and a ticket to the playoffs.

**New Orleans Saints** — It was close, but still no cigar. The Saints came within two seconds of a playoff berth before coming up empty as they had in every season of their life. One low point came on September 25 as they lost at Dallas 21-20 on a safety in the final two minutes. One week later, the Saints ambushed the Dolphins 17-7. A last-second victory at Atlanta in the next game raised New Orleans' record to 4-2. The Saints struggled on offense, with a weak passing attack negating the strong running of George Rogers and Wayne Wilson. New Orleans failed to score at all in games at San Francisco and New England. But the good young defense, featuring Rickey Jackson, Johnnie Poe and Russell Gary, kept the Saints in the running into the final weekend. Before more than 70,000 hometown fans, they took a 24-23 lead with a touchdown late in the final period, but a field goal gave the Rams a 26-24 victory and a playoff spot two seconds from the end.

**Atlanta Falcons** — Dan Henning's arrival as coach coincided with a tumble into last place in the West. Each platoon lost a key player, as linebacker Joel Williams was traded to the Eagles and receiver Alfred Jackson injured his shoulder only four games into the season. Jackson's injury came at the start of a four-game losing streak that made the playoffs a doubtful prospect. With the passing game diminished, the offense relied on William Andrews running behind linemen Mike Kenn and R.C. Thielemann. Two mid-season games lifted the team's spirits. On November 20, they beat the 49ers 28-24 as Billy Johnson grabbed a desperation pass at the final gun and lunged over the goalline. One week later, Kenny Johnson ran his second interception back for a touchdown to beat the Packers 47-41 in overtime. At the end, however, the Falcons petered out with two losses in the final three weeks. In the final two home games, attendance never topped 36,000.

## WASHINGTON REDSKINS 14-2-0 Joe Gibbs

| Scores of Each Game | | |
|---|---|---|
| 30 | DALLAS | 31 |
| 23 | Philadelphia | 13 |
| 27 | KANSAS CITY | 12 |
| 27 | Seattle | 17 |
| 37 | L.A.RAIDERS | 35 |
| 38 | St.Louis | 14 |
| 47 | Green Bay | 48 |
| 38 | DETROIT | 17 |
| 27 | San Diego | 24 |
| 45 | ST.LOUIS | 7 |
| 33 | N.Y.Giants | 17 |
| 42 | L.A.Rams | 20 |
| 28 | PHILADELPHIA | 24 |
| 37 | ATLANTA | 21 |
| 31 | Dallas | 10 |
| 31 | N.Y.GIANTS | 22 |

| Use Name | Pos. | Hgt | Wgt | Age | Int | Pts |
|---|---|---|---|---|---|---|
| Joe Jacoby | OT | 6'7" | 300 | 24 | | |
| George Starke | OT | 6'5" | 260 | 35 | | |
| Russ Grimm | OG | 6'3" | 290 | 24 | | |
| Ken Huff | OG | 6'4" | 265 | 30 | | |
| Bruce Kimball | OG | 6'2" | 260 | 27 | | |
| Mark May | OG | 6'6" | 288 | 23 | | |
| Roy Simmons | OG-OT | 6'3" | 264 | 26 | | |
| Jeff Bostic | C | 6'2" | 250 | 24 | | |
| Todd Liebenstein | DE | 6'6" | 255 | 23 | | |
| Dexter Manley | DE | 6'3" | 250 | 24 | 1 | |
| Charles Mann | DE | 6'6" | 250 | 22 | | 2 |
| Tony McGee | DE | 6'4" | 249 | 34 | | |
| Perry Brooks | DT | 6'3" | 270 | 28 | | |
| Dave Butz | DT | 6'7" | 295 | 33 | | |
| Darryl Grant | DT | 6'1" | 265 | 23 | | |

| Use Name | Pos. | Hgt | Wgt | Age | Int | Pts |
|---|---|---|---|---|---|---|
| Stuart Anderson | LB | 6'1" | 224 | 23 | | |
| Monte Coleman | LB | 6'2" | 230 | 25 | | |
| Pete Cronan | LB | 6'2" | 238 | 28 | | |
| Mel Kaufman | LB | 6'2" | 220 | 25 | 2 | 12 |
| Larry Kubin | LB | 6'2" | 234 | 24 | | |
| Rich Milot | LB | 6'4" | 237 | 26 | 2 | |
| Neal Olkewicz | LB | 6' | 233 | 26 | 1 | |
| Brian Carpenter | DB | 5'10" | 167 | 22 | 1 | |
| Ken Coffey | DB | 6' | 190 | 23 | 4 | |
| Vernon Dean | DB | 5'11" | 178 | 24 | 5 | 6 |
| Darrell Green | DB | 5'8" | 170 | 22 | 2 | |
| Curtis Jordan | DB | 6'2" | 205 | 29 | 1 | |
| Mark Murphy | DB | 6'4" | 210 | 28 | 9 | |
| Mike Nelms | DB | 6'1" | 185 | 28 | | |
| Anthony Washington | DB | 6'1" | 204 | 25 | 4 | |
| Greg Williams | DB | 5'11" | 185 | 24 | 2 | |

Donald Laster - Neck Injury
Mat Mendenhall - Non-Football Illness
Tony Peters - Suspended by N.F.L.

| Use Name | Pos. | Hgt | Wgt | Age | Int | Pts |
|---|---|---|---|---|---|---|
| Bob Holly | QB | 6'2" | 196 | 23 | | |
| Babe Laufenberg | QB | 6'2" | 195 | 23 | | |
| Joe Theismann | QB | 6' | 198 | 33 | | 6 |
| Reggie Evans | HB | 5'11" | 201 | 24 | | 24 |
| Joe Washington | HB | 5'10" | 179 | 29 | | 36 |
| Nick Giaquinto | HB-FB | 5'11" | 204 | 28 | | 6 |
| John Riggins | FB | 6'2" | 235 | 34 | | 144 |
| Otis Wonsley | FB | 5'10" | 214 | 26 | | |
| Charlie Brown | WR | 5'10" | 179 | 24 | | 48 |
| Alvin Garrett | WR | 5'7" | 185 | 26 | | 6 |
| Mark McGrath | WR | 5'11" | 175 | 25 | | |
| Art Monk | WR | 6'3" | 209 | 25 | | 30 |
| Virgil Seay | WR | 5'8" | 175 | 25 | | 6 |
| Dave Steif | WR | 6'3" | 195 | 27 | | |
| Clint Didier | TE | 6'5" | 240 | 24 | | 30 |
| Rick Walker | TE | 6'3" | 235 | 28 | | 12 |
| Don Warren | TE | 6'4" | 242 | 27 | | 12 |
| Mike Williams | TE | 6'4" | 251 | 24 | | |
| Jeff Hayes | K | 5'11" | 175 | 24 | | |
| Mark Moseley | K | 5'11" | 205 | 35 | | 161 |

## DALLAS COWBOYS 12-4-0 Tom Landry

| Scores of Each Game | | |
|---|---|---|
| 31 | Washington | 30 |
| 34 | St.Louis | 17 |
| 28 | N.Y.GIANTS | 13 |
| 21 | NEW ORLEANS | 20 |
| 37 | Minnesota | 24 |
| 27 | TAMPA BAY | *24 |
| 37 | PHILADELPHIA | 7 |
| 38 | L.A.RAIDERS | 40 |
| 38 | N.Y.Giants | 20 |
| 27 | Philadelphia | 20 |
| 23 | San Diego | 24 |
| 41 | KANSAS CITY | 21 |
| 35 | ST.LOUIS | 17 |
| 35 | Seattle | 10 |
| 10 | WASHINGTON | 31 |
| 17 | San Francisco | 42 |

| Use Name | Pos. | Hgt | Wgt | Age | Int | Pts |
|---|---|---|---|---|---|---|
| Jim Cooper | OT | 6'5" | 263 | 27 | | |
| Pat Donovan | OT | 6'4" | 257 | 30 | | |
| Phil Pozderac | OT | 6'9" | 270 | 23 | | |
| Chris Schultz | OT | 6'8" | 265 | 23 | | |
| Howard Richards | OT-OG | 6'6" | 258 | 24 | | |
| Kurt Petersen | OG | 6'4" | 268 | 26 | | |
| Herbert Scott | OG | 6'2" | 260 | 30 | | |
| Brian Baldinger | OG | 6'4" | 253 | 24 | | |
| Tom Rafferty | C | 6'3" | 259 | 29 | | |
| Glen Titensor | C | 6'4" | 260 | 25 | | |
| Jim Jeffcoat | DE | 6'5" | 264 | 22 | | |
| Too Tall Jones | DE | 6'9" | 272 | 32 | | |
| Harvey Martin | DE | 6'5" | 260 | 32 | | |
| Larry Bethea | DT | 6'5" | 244 | 27 | | |
| John Dutton | DT | 6'7" | 275 | 32 | | |
| Don Smerek | DT | 6'7" | 257 | 25 | | |
| Mark Tuinei | DT | 6'5" | 270 | 23 | | |
| Randy White | DT | 6'4" | 263 | 30 | | |

| Use Name | Pos. | Hgt | Wgt | Age | Int | Pts |
|---|---|---|---|---|---|---|
| Bob Breunig | LB | 6'2" | 225 | 30 | 1 | |
| Anthony Dickerson | LB | 6'2" | 222 | 26 | 1 | 2 |
| Mike Hegman | LB | 6'1" | 228 | 30 | | 6 |
| Bruce Huther | LB | 6'1" | 220 | 29 | | |
| Angelo King | LB | 6'1" | 230 | 25 | | |
| Scott McLean | LB | 6'4" | 233 | 22 | | |
| Jeff Rohrer | LB | 6'3" | 232 | 24 | | |
| Michael Walter | LB | 6'3" | 238 | 22 | | |
| Bill Bates | DB | 6'1" | 195 | 22 | | |
| Dextor Clinkscale | DB | 5'11" | 190 | 25 | 2 | 6 |
| Michael Downs | DB | 6'3" | 203 | 23 | 4 | 6 |
| Ron Fellows | DB | 6' | 174 | 24 | 5 | 12 |
| Rod Hill | DB | 6' | 182 | 24 | 2 | |
| Dennis Thurman | DB | 5'11" | 183 | 27 | 6 | 6 |
| Everson Walls | DB | 6'1" | 194 | 23 | 4 | |

James Jones - Knee Injury

| Use Name | Pos. | Hgt | Wgt | Age | Int | Pts |
|---|---|---|---|---|---|---|
| Glenn Carano | QB | 6'3" | 204 | 27 | | |
| Gary Hogeboom | QB | 6'4" | 199 | 25 | | |
| Danny White | QB | 6'2" | 196 | 31 | | 30 |
| Gary Allen (from HOU) | HB | 5'10" | 183 | 23 | | 6 |
| Tony Dorsett | HB | 5'11" | 192 | 29 | | 54 |
| Chuck McSwain | HB | 6' | 191 | 22 | | |
| Robert Newhouse | FB | 5'10" | 219 | 33 | | |
| Timmy Newsome | FB | 6'1" | 231 | 25 | | 36 |
| Ron Springs | FB-HB | 6'1" | 210 | 26 | | 48 |
| Doug Donley | WR | 6' | 173 | 24 | | 12 |
| Tony Hill | WR | 6'2" | 196 | 27 | | 42 |
| Butch Johnson | WR | 6'1" | 187 | 29 | | 18 |
| Drew Pearson | WR | 6' | 193 | 32 | | 30 |
| Doug Cosbie | TE | 6'6" | 232 | 27 | | 36 |
| Billy Joe DuPree | TE | 6'4" | 223 | 33 | | 6 |
| Cleo Simmons | TE | 6'2" | 225 | 21 | | |
| Jim Miller | K | 5'11" | 183 | 26 | | |
| Rafael Septien | K | 5'10" | 180 | 29 | | 123 |
| John Warren | K | 6' | 207 | 22 | | |

## ST. LOUIS CARDINALS 8-7-1 Jim Hanifan

| Scores of Each Game | | |
|---|---|---|
| 17 | New Orleans | 28 |
| 17 | DALLAS | 34 |
| 27 | SAN FRANCISCO | 42 |
| 14 | Philadelphia | 11 |
| 14 | Kansas City | 38 |
| 14 | WASHINGTON | 38 |
| 34 | Tampa Bay | 27 |
| 20 | N.Y.GIANTS | *20 |
| 41 | MINNESOTA | 31 |
| 7 | WASHINGTON | 45 |
| 33 | SEATTLE | 28 |
| 44 | SAN DIEGO | 14 |
| 17 | Dallas | 35 |
| 10 | N.Y.Giants | 6 |
| 34 | L.A.Raiders | 24 |
| 31 | PHILADELPHIA | 7 |

| Use Name | Pos. | Hgt | Wgt | Age | Int | Pts |
|---|---|---|---|---|---|---|
| Art Plunkett | OT | 6'7" | 270 | 24 | | |
| Tootie Robbins | OT | 6'5" | 278 | 25 | | |
| Luis Sharpe | OT | 6'4" | 260 | 23 | | |
| Dan Audick | OG-OT | 6'3" | 253 | 28 | | |
| Joe Bostic | OG | 6'3" | 265 | 26 | | |
| Terry Stieve | OG | 6'2" | 265 | 29 | | |
| Randy Clark | C | 6'3" | 254 | 26 | | |
| Dan Dierdorf | C | 6'4" | 290 | 34 | | |
| Carlos Scott | C | 6'4" | 300 | 23 | | |
| Al Baker | DE | 6'6" | 260 | 26 | 2 | |
| Curtis Greer | DE | 6'4" | 252 | 25 | | |
| Elois Grooms | DE | 6'4" | 250 | 30 | 1 | 6 |
| Stafford Mays | DE | 6'2" | 250 | 25 | | |
| Rush Brown | DT | 6'2" | 260 | 29 | | |
| Mark Duda | DT | 6'3" | 263 | 22 | | |
| David Galloway | DT | 6'3" | 277 | 24 | 1 | 2 |

| Use Name | Pos. | Hgt | Wgt | Age | Int | Pts |
|---|---|---|---|---|---|---|
| Dave Ahrens | LB | 6'3" | 228 | 24 | | |
| Kurt Allerman | LB | 6'2" | 222 | 28 | | |
| Charlie Baker | LB | 6'2" | 217 | 25 | | |
| Paul Davis (from NYG) | LB | 6'2" | 235 | 23 | 3 | |
| Bob Harris | LB | 6'2" | 215 | 22 | | |
| E.J. Junior | LB | 6'3" | 235 | 23 | | |
| Craig Shaffer | LB | 6' | 230 | 24 | | |
| Bill Whitaker | LB | 6' | 182 | 23 | | |
| Jeff Griffin | DB | 6' | 185 | 25 | | |
| Victor Heflin | DB | 6' | 184 | 23 | | |
| Monty Hunter | DB | 6' | 202 | 24 | | |
| Cedric Mack | DB | 6' | 190 | 22 | 3 | |
| Lee Nelson | DB | 5'10" | 185 | 29 | 1 | 6 |
| Chet Parlavecchio (from GB) | DB | 6'2" | 225 | 23 | | |
| Benny Perrin | DB | 6'2" | 178 | 23 | 4 | 6 |
| George Schmitt | DB | 5'11" | 193 | 22 | | |
| Leonard Smith | DB | 5'11" | 190 | 22 | | |
| Wayne Smith | DB | 6' | 175 | 26 | 2 | |
| Lionel Washington | DB | 6' | 184 | 22 | 8 | |

| Use Name | Pos. | Hgt | Wgt | Age | Int | Pts |
|---|---|---|---|---|---|---|
| Jim Hart | QB | 6'2" | 210 | 38 | | |
| Rusty Lisch | QB | 6'3" | 213 | 26 | | |
| Neil Lomax | QB | 6'3" | 215 | 24 | | 12 |
| Ottis Anderson | HB | 6'2" | 220 | 26 | | 36 |
| Will Harrell | HB | 5'9" | 182 | 30 | | |
| Stump Mitchell | HB | 5'9" | 188 | 24 | | 18 |
| Earl Ferrell | FB | 6' | 215 | 25 | | 6 |
| Randy Love | FB | 6'1" | 205 | 26 | | 18 |
| Wayne Morris | FB | 6' | 210 | 29 | | 12 |
| Steve Bird | WR | 5'11" | 171 | 22 | | |
| Roy Green | WR | 6' | 195 | 26 | | 84 |
| Mike Shumann | WR | 6' | 185 | 27 | | |
| Ken Thompson | WR | 6'1" | 178 | 24 | | |
| Pat Tilley | WR | 5'10" | 178 | 30 | | 30 |
| Greg LaFleur | TE | 6'4" | 236 | 24 | | |
| Doug Marsh | TE | 6'3" | 240 | 25 | | 48 |
| Eddie McGill | TE | 6'6" | 225 | 23 | | |
| Jamie Williams | TE | 6'4" | 232 | 23 | | |
| Carl Birdsong | K | 6' | 192 | 24 | | |
| Neil O'Donoghue | K | 6'6" | 210 | 30 | | 90 |

## PHILADELPHIA EAGLES 5-11-0 Marion Campbell

| Scores of Each Game | | |
|---|---|---|
| 22 | San Francisco | 17 |
| 13 | WASHINGTON | 23 |
| 13 | Denver | 10 |
| 11 | ST.LOUIS | 14 |
| 28 | ATLANTA | 24 |
| 17 | N.Y.Giants | 13 |
| 7 | Dallas | 37 |
| 6 | CHICAGO | 37 |
| 21 | BALTIMORE | 22 |
| 20 | DALLAS | 27 |
| 14 | Chicago | 17 |
| 0 | N.Y.GIANTS | 23 |
| 24 | Washington | 28 |
| 13 | L.A.RAMS | 9 |
| 17 | NEW ORLEANS | *20 |
| 7 | St.Louis | 31 |

| Use Name | Pos. | Hgt | Wgt | Age | Int | Pts |
|---|---|---|---|---|---|---|
| Jerry Sisemore | OT | 6'4" | 265 | 32 | | |
| Stan Walters | OT | 6'6" | 275 | 35 | | |
| Jim Fritzche | OT-OG | 6'8" | 265 | 22 | | |
| Dean Miraldi | OT-OG | 6'5" | 254 | 25 | | |
| Ron Baker | OG | 6'4" | 250 | 28 | | |
| Steve Kenney | OG | 6'4" | 262 | 27 | | |
| Gerry Feehery | C-OG | 6'2" | 268 | 23 | | |
| Guy Morriss | C | 6'4" | 255 | 32 | | |
| Mark Slater | C | 6'2" | 257 | 28 | | |
| Greg Brown | DE | 6'5" | 240 | 26 | | |
| Byron Darby | DE | 6'4" | 250 | 23 | | |
| Carl Hairston | DE | 6'3" | 260 | 30 | | |
| Dennis Harrison | DE | 6'8" | 275 | 27 | | |
| Leonard Mitchell | DE | 6'7" | 272 | 24 | | |
| Thomas Strauthers | DE | 6'4" | 255 | 22 | | |
| Harvey Armstrong | NT | 6'2" | 255 | 23 | | |
| Ken Clarke | NT | 6'2" | 255 | 27 | | |

| Use Name | Pos. | Hgt | Wgt | Age | Int | Pts |
|---|---|---|---|---|---|---|
| Bill Cowher | LB | 6'3" | 225 | 26 | | |
| Anthony Griggs | LB | 6'3" | 230 | 23 | 3 | |
| Rich Kraynak | LB | 6'1" | 221 | 23 | | |
| Jerry Robinson | LB | 6'2" | 225 | 26 | | |
| Jody Schulz | LB | 6'3" | 235 | 23 | | |
| Reggie Wilkes | LB | 6'4" | 230 | 27 | | |
| Joel Williams | LB | 6'1" | 220 | 26 | | |
| Dennis DeVaughn | DB | 5'10" | 175 | 22 | | |
| Herman Edwards | DB | 6' | 190 | 29 | 1 | |
| Ray Ellis | DB | 6'1" | 192 | 24 | 1 | |
| Elbert Foules | DB | 5'11" | 185 | 22 | 1 | |
| Wes Hopkins | DB | 6'1" | 205 | 21 | | |
| Randy Logan | DB | 6'1" | 195 | 32 | 1 | |
| John Sciarra | DB | 5'11" | 185 | 29 | | |
| Brenard Wilson | DB | 6' | 175 | 28 | | |
| Roynell Young | DB | 6'1" | 181 | 25 | 1 | |

Petey Perot - Shoulder Injury
John Spagnola - Back Injury
Zach Valentine - Knee Injury

| Use Name | Pos. | Hgt | Wgt | Age | Int | Pts |
|---|---|---|---|---|---|---|
| Ron Jaworski | QB | 6'2" | 196 | 32 | | 6 |
| Dan Pastorini | QB | 6'3" | 205 | 34 | | |
| Joe Pisarcik | QB | 6'4" | 220 | 31 | | |
| Wilbert Montgomery | HB | 5'10" | 195 | 28 | | |
| Major Everett | FB | 5'10" | 207 | 23 | | |
| Michael Haddix | FB | 6'2" | 225 | 21 | | 12 |
| Perry Harrington | FB | 5'11" | 210 | 25 | | 6 |
| Hubie Oliver | FB | 5'10" | 212 | 25 | | 18 |
| Michael Williams | FB | 6'2" | 217 | 22 | | |
| Harold Charmichael | WR | 6'7" | 225 | 33 | | 18 |
| Melvin Hoover | WR | 6' | 185 | 24 | | |
| Mike Quick | WR | 6'2" | 190 | 24 | | 78 |
| Ron Smith | WR | 6' | 185 | 26 | | |
| Tony Woodruff | WR | 6' | 175 | 24 | | 12 |
| Glen Young | WR | 6'2" | 205 | 22 | | 6 |
| Al Dixon | TE | 6'5" | 238 | 29 | | |
| Vyto Kab | TE | 6'5" | 240 | 23 | | 6 |
| Lawrence Sampleton | TE | 6'5" | 233 | 23 | | |
| Tony Franklin | K | 5'8" | 182 | 26 | | 69 |
| Max Runager | K | 6'1" | 189 | 27 | | |
| Tom Skladany | K | 6' | 195 | 28 | | |

## NEW YORK GIANTS 3-12-1 Bill Parcells

| Scores of Each Game | | |
|---|---|---|
| 6 | L.A.RAMS | 16 |
| 16 | Atlanta | *13 |
| 13 | Dallas | 28 |
| 27 | GREEN BAY | 3 |
| 34 | SAN DIEGO | 41 |
| 13 | PHILADELPHIA | 17 |
| 17 | Kansas City | 38 |
| 20 | St.Louis | *20 |
| 20 | DALLAS | 38 |
| 9 | Detroit | 15 |
| 17 | WASHINGTON | 33 |
| 23 | Philadelphia | 0 |
| 12 | L.A.Raiders | 27 |
| 6 | ST.LOUIS | 10 |
| 12 | SEATTLE | 17 |
| 22 | Washington | 31 |

| Use Name | Pos. | Hgt | Wgt | Age | Int | Pts |
|---|---|---|---|---|---|---|
| Brad Benson | OT | 6'3" | 258 | 27 | | |
| Gordon King | OT | 6'6" | 275 | 27 | | |
| Billy Ard | OT | 6'3" | 250 | 24 | | |
| Kevin Belcher | OG | 6'3" | 255 | 22 | | |
| John Tautolo | OG | 6'3" | 260 | 24 | | |
| J.T.Turner | OG | 6'3" | 250 | 30 | | |
| Chris Foote | C | 6'3" | 250 | 26 | | |
| Ernie Hughes | C | 6'3" | 265 | 28 | | |
| Rich Umphrey | C | 6'3" | 255 | 24 | | |
| Dee Hardison | DE | 6'4" | 269 | 27 | | |
| Leonard Marshall | DE | 6'3" | 285 | 21 | | 2 |
| George Martin | DE | 6'4" | 245 | 30 | | |
| Curtis McGriff | DE | 6'5" | 265 | 25 | | |
| Casey Merrill (from GB) | DE | 6'4" | 255 | 26 | | |
| Jim Burt | NT | 6'1" | 255 | 24 | | |
| Charles Cook | NT | 6'3" | 255 | 24 | | |
| Bill Neill | NT | 6'4" | 255 | 24 | | |
| Jerome Sally | NT | 6'3" | 260 | 24 | | |

| Use Name | Pos. | Hgt | Wgt | Age | Int | Pts |
|---|---|---|---|---|---|---|
| Harry Carson | LB | 6'2" | 235 | 29 | | |
| Andy Headen | LB | 6'5" | 230 | 23 | | |
| Byron Hunt | LB | 6'5" | 230 | 24 | | |
| Brian Kelley | LB | 6'3" | 222 | 32 | 1 | |
| Frank Marion | LB | 6'3" | 223 | 32 | | |
| Joe McLaughlin | LB | 6'1" | 235 | 26 | | |
| Lawrence Taylor | LB | 6'3" | 237 | 24 | 2 | |
| Brad Van Pelt | LB | 6'5" | 235 | 32 | 2 | |
| Mike Whittington | LB | 6'2" | 220 | 25 | | |
| Bill Currier | DB | 6' | 202 | 28 | 2 | 6 |
| Mike Dennis | DB | 5'10" | 190 | 24 | 1 | |
| Larry Flowers | DB | 6'1" | 190 | 24 | 1 | |
| Mark Haynes | DB | 5'11" | 198 | 24 | 3 | |
| Terry Jackson | DB | 5'10" | 197 | 27 | | |
| Terry Kinard | DB | 6'1" | 190 | 23 | 3 | |
| Mike Maycock | DB | 6'2" | 195 | 25 | | |
| LeCharls McDaniel | DB | 5'9" | 170 | 24 | | |
| Beasley Reese (to TB) | DB | 6'1" | 195 | 29 | 8 | |
| Pete Shaw | DB | 5'10" | 183 | 29 | | |

| Use Name | Pos. | Hgt | Wgt | Age | Int | Pts |
|---|---|---|---|---|---|---|
| Scott Brunner | QB | 6'5" | 200 | 26 | | |
| Tom Owen | QB | 6'1" | 194 | 31 | | |
| Jeff Rutledge | QB | 6'1" | 190 | 26 | | |
| Phil Simms | QB | 6'3" | 216 | 26 | | |
| Leon Bright | HB | 5'9" | 192 | 28 | | |
| Billy Campfield | HB | 5'11" | 205 | 27 | | |
| Larry Heater | HB | 5'11" | 205 | 25 | | |
| Joe Morris | HB | 5'7" | 190 | 22 | | 6 |
| Rob Carpenter | FB | 6'1" | 230 | 28 | | 36 |
| John Tuggle | FB | 6'1" | 210 | 22 | | 6 |
| Butch Woolfolk | FB | 6'1" | 207 | 23 | | 24 |
| Floyd Eddings | WR | 5'11" | 177 | 25 | | |
| Earnest Gray | WR | 6'3" | 195 | 26 | | 30 |
| Keith Hugger | WR | 5'11" | 175 | 22 | | |
| Mike Miller | WR | 6' | 182 | 23 | | |
| John Mistler | WR | 6'2" | 186 | 24 | | |
| Johnny Perkins | WR | 6'2" | 205 | 30 | | |
| Danny Pittman (to STL) | WR | 6'2" | 205 | 25 | | 6 |
| Byron Williams | WR | 6'2" | 180 | 22 | | 6 |
| Zeke Mowatt | TE | 6'3" | 238 | 22 | | 6 |
| Tom Mullady | TE | 6'3" | 232 | 26 | | |
| Malcolm Scott | TE | 6'4" | 240 | 22 | | |
| Ali Haji-Sheikh | K | 6' | 172 | 22 | | 127 |
| Dave Jennings | K | 6'4" | 205 | 31 | | |

* Overtime

## WASHINGTON REDSKINS

### RUSHING

| Last Name | No. | Yds | Avg | TD |
|---|---|---|---|---|
| Riggins | 375 | 1347 | 3.6 | 24 |
| J. Washington | 145 | 772 | 5.3 | 0 |
| Theismann | 37 | 234 | 6.3 | 1 |
| Wonsley | 25 | 88 | 3.5 | 0 |
| Hayes | 2 | 63 | 31.5 | 0 |
| Brown | 4 | 53 | 13.3 | 0 |
| Giaquinto | 14 | 53 | 3.8 | 1 |
| Holly | 4 | 13 | 3.3 | 0 |
| Evans | 16 | 11 | 0.7 | 4 |
| Walker | 2 | 10 | 5.0 | 0 |
| Garrett | 2 | 0 | 0.0 | 0 |
| Monk | 3 | -19 | -6.3 | 0 |

### RECEIVING

| Last Name | No. | Yds | Avg | TD |
|---|---|---|---|---|
| Brown | 78 | 1225 | 15.7 | 8 |
| Monk | 47 | 748 | 15.9 | 5 |
| J. Washington | 47 | 454 | 9.7 | 6 |
| Giaquinto | 27 | 372 | 13.8 | 0 |
| Garrett | 25 | 332 | 13.3 | 1 |
| Warren | 20 | 225 | 11.3 | 2 |
| Walker | 17 | 168 | 9.9 | 2 |
| Didier | 9 | 153 | 17.0 | 4 |
| Riggins | 5 | 29 | 5.8 | 0 |
| Seay | 2 | 55 | 27.5 | 1 |
| McGrath | 1 | 6 | 6.0 | 0 |

### PUNT RETURNS

| Last Name | No. | Yds | Avg | TD |
|---|---|---|---|---|
| Nelms | 38 | 289 | 7.6 | 0 |
| Seay | 5 | 57 | 11.4 | 0 |
| Green | 4 | 29 | 7.3 | 0 |
| Giaquinto | 2 | 12 | 6.0 | 0 |

### KICKOFF RETURNS

| Last Name | No. | Yds | Avg | TD |
|---|---|---|---|---|
| Nelms | 35 | 802 | 22.9 | 0 |
| Evans | 10 | 141 | 14.1 | 0 |
| Seay | 9 | 218 | 24.2 | 0 |
| Garrett | 2 | 50 | 25.0 | 0 |
| Wonsley | 2 | 36 | 18.0 | 0 |
| Cronan | 1 | 17 | 17.0 | 0 |
| Giaquinto | 1 | 0 | 0.0 | 0 |
| Sawyer | 1 | 15 | 15.0 | 0 |
| G. Williams | 1 | 6 | 6.0 | 0 |

### PASSING — PUNTING — KICKING

| PASSING | Att | Cmp | % | Yds | Yd/Att | TD | Int— | % | RK |
|---|---|---|---|---|---|---|---|---|---|
| Theismann | 459 | 276 | 60 | 3714 | 8.09 | 29 | 11— | 2 | 2 |
| Holly | 1 | 1 | 100 | 5 | 5.00 | 0 | 0— | 0 | |
| Monk | 1 | 1 | 100 | 46 | 46.00 | 0 | 0— | 0 | |
| Riggins | 1 | 0 | 0 | 0 | 0.00 | 0 | 0— | 0 | |
| J. Washington | 1 | 0 | 0 | 0 | 0.00 | 0 | 0— | 0 | |

| PUNTING | No. | Avg. |
|---|---|---|
| Hayes | 72 | 38.8 |

| KICKING | XP | Att | % | FG | Att | % |
|---|---|---|---|---|---|---|
| Moseley | 62 | 63 | 98 | 33 | 47 | 70 |

## DALLAS COWBOYS

### RUSHING

| Last Name | No. | Yds | Avg | TD |
|---|---|---|---|---|
| Dorsett | 289 | 1321 | 4.6 | 8 |
| Springs | 149 | 541 | 3.6 | 7 |
| Newsome | 44 | 185 | 4.2 | 2 |
| Newhouse | 9 | 34 | 3.8 | 0 |
| D. White | 18 | 31 | 1.7 | 4 |
| Pearson | 2 | 13 | 6.5 | 0 |
| Allen | 1 | 5 | 5.0 | 0 |
| T. Hill | 1 | 2 | 2.0 | 0 |
| Johnson | 1 | 0 | 0.0 | 0 |
| Hogeboom | 6 | -10 | -1.7 | 0 |

### RECEIVING

| Last Name | No. | Yds | Avg | TD |
|---|---|---|---|---|
| Springs | 73 | 589 | 8.1 | 1 |
| T. Hill | 49 | 801 | 16.3 | 7 |
| Pearson | 47 | 545 | 11.6 | 5 |
| Cosbie | 46 | 588 | 12.8 | 6 |
| Johnson | 41 | 561 | 13.7 | 3 |
| Dorsett | 40 | 287 | 7.2 | 1 |
| Donley | 18 | 370 | 20.6 | 2 |
| Newsome | 18 | 250 | 13.9 | 4 |
| DuPree | 12 | 142 | 11.8 | 1 |
| D. White | 1 | 15 | 15.0 | 0 |
| Rafferty | 1 | 8 | 8.0 | 0 |

### PUNT RETURNS

| Last Name | No. | Yds | Avg | TD |
|---|---|---|---|---|
| R. Hill | 30 | 232 | 7.7 | 0 |
| Fellows | 10 | 75 | 7.5 | 0 |
| Allen | 9 | 153 | 17.0 | 1 |
| Donley | 1 | 1 | 1.0 | 0 |
| Newhouse | 1 | 0 | 0.0 | 0 |

### KICKOFF RETURNS

| Last Name | No. | Yds | Avg | TD |
|---|---|---|---|---|
| Fellows | 43 | 855 | 19.9 | 0 |
| R. Hill | 14 | 243 | 17.4 | 0 |
| Allen | 8 | 178 | 22.3 | 0 |
| Cosbie | 2 | 17 | 8.5 | 0 |
| Huther | 1 | 0 | 0.0 | 0 |
| McSwain | 1 | 17 | 17.0 | 0 |
| Newsome | 1 | 28 | 28.0 | 0 |
| Springs | 1 | 13 | 13.0 | 0 |

### PASSING — PUNTING — KICKING

| PASSING | Att | Cmp | % | Yds | Yd/Att | TD | Int— | % | RK |
|---|---|---|---|---|---|---|---|---|---|
| D. White | 533 | 334 | 63 | 3980 | 7.47 | 29 | 23— | 4 | 6 |
| Hogeboom | 17 | 11 | 65 | 161 | 4.70 | 1 | 1— | 6 | |
| Springs | 2 | 1 | 50 | 15 | 15.00 | 1 | 0— | 0 | |
| Dorsett | 1 | 0 | 0 | 0 | 0.00 | 0 | 0— | 0 | |
| Pearson | 1 | 0 | 0 | 0 | 0.00 | 0 | 1—100 | | |

| PUNTING | No. | Avg. |
|---|---|---|
| Warren | 39 | 39.8 |
| D. White | 38 | 40.6 |
| Miller | 5 | 35.6 |

| KICKING | XP | Att | % | FG | Att | % |
|---|---|---|---|---|---|---|
| Septien | 57 | 59 | 97 | 22 | 27 | 82 |

## ST. LOUIS CARDINALS

### RUSHING

| Last Name | No. | Yds | Avg | TD |
|---|---|---|---|---|
| Anderson | 296 | 1270 | 4.3 | 5 |
| Mitchell | 68 | 373 | 5.5 | 3 |
| Morris | 75 | 257 | 3.4 | 2 |
| Lomax | 27 | 127 | 4.7 | 2 |
| Love | 35 | 103 | 2.9 | 2 |
| Farrell | 7 | 53 | 7.6 | 1 |
| Green | 4 | 49 | 12.3 | 0 |
| Harrell | 4 | 13 | 3.3 | 0 |
| Hart | 5 | 12 | 2.4 | 0 |
| Sharpe | 1 | 11 | 11.0 | 0 |
| Lisch | 2 | 9 | 4.5 | 0 |
| Perrin | 1 | 0 | 0.0 | 0 |

### RECEIVING

| Last Name | No. | Yds | Avg | TD |
|---|---|---|---|---|
| Green | 78 | 1227 | 15.7 | 14 |
| Anderson | 54 | 459 | 8.5 | 1 |
| Tilley | 44 | 690 | 15.7 | 5 |
| Marsh | 32 | 421 | 13.2 | 8 |
| Morris | 14 | 55 | 3.9 | 0 |
| LaFleur | 12 | 99 | 8.3 | 0 |
| Shumann | 11 | 154 | 14.0 | 0 |
| Mitchell | 7 | 54 | 7.7 | 0 |
| Love | 6 | 58 | 9.7 | 1 |
| Harrell | 3 | 25 | 8.3 | 0 |
| Thompson | 2 | 31 | 15.5 | 0 |
| McGill | 1 | 11 | 11.0 | 0 |
| Ahrens | 1 | 4 | 4.0 | 0 |

### PUNT RETURNS

| Last Name | No. | Yds | Avg | TD |
|---|---|---|---|---|
| Mitchell | 38 | 337 | 8.9 | 0 |
| Bird | 14 | 76 | 5.4 | 0 |
| Harrell | 5 | 31 | 6.2 | 0 |
| Ferrell | 1 | 17 | 17.0 | 0 |

### KICKOFF RETURNS

| Last Name | No. | Yds | Avg | TD |
|---|---|---|---|---|
| Mitchell | 36 | 778 | 21.6 | 0 |
| Ferrell | 13 | 257 | 19.8 | 0 |
| Bird | 9 | 194 | 21.6 | 0 |
| Schmitt | 4 | 41 | 10.3 | 0 |
| Harrell | 3 | 62 | 20.7 | 0 |
| Love | 3 | 71 | 23.7 | 0 |
| Allerman | 1 | 11 | 11.0 | 0 |
| Duda | 1 | 12 | 2.0 | 0 |
| Green | 1 | 14 | 14.0 | 0 |
| L. Smith | 1 | 19 | 19.0 | 0 |

### PASSING — PUNTING — KICKING

| PASSING | Att | Cmp | % | Yds | Yd/Att | TD | Int— | % | RK |
|---|---|---|---|---|---|---|---|---|---|
| Lomax | 354 | 209 | 59 | 2636 | 7.45 | 24 | 11— | 3 | 4 |
| Hart | 91 | 50 | 55 | 592 | 6.51 | 4 | 8— | 9 | |
| Lisch | 13 | 6 | 46 | 66 | 5.08 | 1 | 2— | 15 | |
| Birdsong | 1 | 1 | 100 | 11 | 11.00 | 0 | 0— | 0 | |
| Perrin | 1 | 1 | 100 | 4 | 4.00 | 0 | 0— | 0 | |

| PUNTING | No. | Avg. |
|---|---|---|
| Birdsong | 85 | 41.5 |

| KICKING | XP | Att | % | FG | Att | % |
|---|---|---|---|---|---|---|
| O'Donoghue | 45 | 47 | 96 | 15 | 28 | 54 |

## PHILADELPHIA EAGLES

### RUSHING

| Last Name | No. | Yds | Avg | TD |
|---|---|---|---|---|
| Oliver | 121 | 434 | 3.6 | 1 |
| M. Williams | 103 | 385 | 3.7 | 0 |
| Haddix | 91 | 220 | 2.4 | 0 |
| Montgomery | 29 | 139 | 4.8 | 0 |
| Jaworski | 25 | 129 | 5.2 | 1 |
| Harrington | 23 | 98 | 4.3 | 1 |
| Everett | 5 | 7 | 1.4 | 0 |
| Runager | 1 | 6 | 6.0 | 0 |
| Pastorini | 1 | 0 | 0.0 | 0 |
| Pisarcik | 3 | -1 | -0.3 | 0 |

### RECEIVING

| Last Name | No. | Yds | Avg | TD |
|---|---|---|---|---|
| Quick | 69 | 1409 | 20.4 | 13 |
| Oliver | 49 | 421 | 8.6 | 2 |
| Carmichael | 38 | 515 | 13.6 | 3 |
| Haddix | 23 | 254 | 11.0 | 0 |
| Kab | 18 | 195 | 10.8 | 1 |
| M. Williams | 17 | 142 | 8.4 | 0 |
| Hoover | 10 | 221 | 22.1 | 0 |
| Montgomery | 9 | 53 | 5.9 | 0 |
| Woodruff | 6 | 70 | 11.7 | 2 |
| Dixon | 4 | 54 | 13.5 | 0 |
| G. Young | 3 | 125 | 41.7 | 1 |
| Sampleton | 2 | 28 | 14.0 | 0 |
| Everett | 2 | 18 | 9.0 | 0 |
| Harrington | 1 | 19 | 19.0 | 0 |
| Smith | 1 | 8 | 8.0 | 0 |

### PUNT RETURNS

| Last Name | No. | Yds | Avg | TD |
|---|---|---|---|---|
| Sciarra | 22 | 115 | 5.2 | 0 |
| G. Young | 14 | 93 | 6.6 | 0 |
| Hoover | 7 | 44 | 6.3 | 0 |
| Foules | 1 | 7 | 7.0 | 0 |
| Logan | 1 | 0 | 0.0 | 0 |

### KICKOFF RETURNS

| Last Name | No. | Yds | Avg | TD |
|---|---|---|---|---|
| G. Young | 26 | 547 | 21.0 | 0 |
| Everett | 14 | 275 | 19.6 | 0 |
| Ellis | 7 | 119 | 17.0 | 0 |
| Harrington | 4 | 79 | 19.8 | 0 |
| Haddix | 3 | 51 | 17.0 | 0 |
| M. Williams | 3 | 59 | 19.7 | 0 |
| Darby | 2 | 3 | 1.5 | 0 |
| Fritzche | 2 | 17 | 8.5 | 0 |
| R. Young | 1 | 18 | 18.0 | 0 |

### PASSING — PUNTING — KICKING

| PASSING | Att | Cmp | % | Yds | Yd/Att | TD | Int— | % | RK |
|---|---|---|---|---|---|---|---|---|---|
| Jaworski | 446 | 235 | 53 | 3315 | 7.43 | 20 | 18— | 4 | 9 |
| Pisarcik | 34 | 16 | 47 | 172 | 5.06 | 1 | 4— | 0 | |
| Pastorini | 5 | 0 | 0 | 0 | 0.00 | 0 | 0— | 0 | |
| Carmichael | 1 | 1 | 100 | 45 | 45.00 | 1 | 0— | 0 | |

| PUNTING | No. | Avg. |
|---|---|---|
| Runager | 59 | 41.7 |
| Skladany | 27 | 39.3 |

| KICKING | XP | ATT | % | FG | ATT | % |
|---|---|---|---|---|---|---|
| Franklin | 24 | 27 | 89 | 15 | 26 | 58 |

## NEW YORK GIANTS

### RUSHING

| Last Name | No. | Yds | Avg | TD |
|---|---|---|---|---|
| Woolfolk | 246 | 857 | 3.5 | 4 |
| Carpenter | 170 | 624 | 3.7 | 4 |
| Morris | 35 | 145 | 4.1 | 0 |
| Brunner | 26 | 64 | 2.5 | 0 |
| Tuggle | 17 | 49 | 2.9 | 1 |
| Rutledge | 7 | 27 | 3.9 | 0 |
| Campfield | 2 | 21 | 10.5 | 0 |
| Eddings | 1 | 3 | 3.0 | 0 |
| Bright | 1 | 2 | 2.0 | 0 |
| Miller | 1 | 2 | 2.0 | 0 |

### RECEIVING

| Last Name | No. | Yds | Avg | TD |
|---|---|---|---|---|
| Gray | 78 | 1139 | 14.6 | 5 |
| Mistler | 45 | 422 | 9.4 | 0 |
| Woolfolk | 28 | 368 | 13.1 | 0 |
| Carpenter | 26 | 258 | 9.9 | 2 |
| Mowatt | 21 | 280 | 13.3 | 1 |
| B. Williams | 20 | 346 | 17.3 | 1 |
| Scott | 17 | 206 | 12.1 | 0 |
| Eddings | 14 | 231 | 16.5 | 0 |
| Mullady | 16 | 184 | 14.2 | 1 |
| Miller | 7 | 170 | 24.3 | 0 |
| Pittman | 9 | 175 | 19.4 | 1 |
| Miller | 7 | 170 | 24.3 | 0 |
| Tuggle | 3 | 50 | 16.7 | 0 |
| Bright | 2 | 33 | 16.5 | 0 |
| Morris | 2 | 1 | 0.5 | 1 |
| Campfield | 1 | 12 | 12.0 | 0 |

### PUNT RETURNS

| Last Name | No. | Yds | Avg | TD |
|---|---|---|---|---|
| Shaw | 29 | 234 | 8.1 | 0 |
| Bright | 17 | 117 | 6.9 | 0 |
| Reece | 9 | 26 | 2.9 | 0 |
| Pittman | 1 | 0 | — | 0 |

### KICKOFF RETURNS

| Last Name | No. | Yds | Avg | TD |
|---|---|---|---|---|
| Bright | 21 | 475 | 22.6 | 0 |
| Morris | 14 | 255 | 18.2 | 0 |
| Campfield | 9 | 154 | 17.1 | 0 |
| Tuggle | 9 | 156 | 17.3 | 0 |
| Pittman | 6 | 107 | 17.8 | 0 |
| Heater | 5 | 71 | 14.2 | 0 |
| Miller | 2 | 31 | 15.5 | 0 |
| Woolfolk | 2 | 13 | 6.5 | 0 |
| Dennis | 1 | 54 | 54.0 | 0 |

### PASSING — PUNTING — KICKING

| PASSING | Att | Cmp | % | Yds | Yd/Att | TD | Int— | % | RK |
|---|---|---|---|---|---|---|---|---|---|
| Brunner | 386 | 190 | 49 | 2516 | 6.52 | 9 | 22— | 6 | 14 |
| Rutledge | 174 | 87 | 50 | 1208 | 6.94 | 3 | 8— | 5 | |
| Simms | 13 | 7 | 54 | 130 | 10.00 | 0 | 1— | 7 | |
| Jennings | 1 | 0 | 0 | 0 | 0.00 | 0 | 0— | 0 | |
| Mistler | 1 | 0 | 0 | 0 | 0.00 | 0 | 0— | 0 | |

| PUNTING | No. | Avg. |
|---|---|---|
| Jennings | 84 | 40.3 |

| KICKING | XP | ATT | % | FG | Att | % |
|---|---|---|---|---|---|---|
| Haji-Sheikh | 22 | 23 | 96 | 35 | 42 | 83 |

## DETROIT LIONS 9-7-0 Monte Clark

| Scores of Each Game | | |
|---|---|---|
| 11 | Tampa Bay | 0 |
| 26 | CLEVELAND | 31 |
| 14 | ATLANTA | 30 |
| 17 | Minnesota | 20 |
| 10 | L.A.Rams | 21 |
| 38 | GREEN BAY | 14 |
| 31 | CHICAGO | 17 |
| 17 | Washington | 38 |
| 38 | Chicago | 17 |
| 15 | N.Y.Giants | 9 |
| 17 | Houston | 27 |
| 23 | Green Bay | *20 |
| 45 | PITTSBURGH | 3 |
| 13 | MINNESOTA | 2 |
| 9 | Cincinnati | 17 |
| 23 | TAMPA BAY | 20 |

| Use Name | Pos. | Hgt | Wgt | Age | Int | Pts |
|---|---|---|---|---|---|---|
| Chris Dietrich | OT | 6'3" | 255 | 25 | | |
| Keith Droney | OT | 6'5" | 265 | 25 | | |
| Rich Strenger | OT | 6'7" | 269 | 23 | | |
| Homer Elias | OG | 6'3" | 255 | 28 | | |
| Don Greco | OG | 6'3" | 255 | 24 | | |
| Larry Lee | OG-C | 6'2" | 260 | 23 | | |
| Amos Fowler | C | 6'3" | 253 | 27 | | |
| Steve Mott | C | 6'3" | 260 | 22 | | |
| Tom Turnure | C | 6'4" | 250 | 26 | | |
| Mike Cofer | DE | 6'5" | 245 | 23 | | |
| William Gay | DE | 6'3" | 255 | 28 | | |
| Curtis Green | DE | 6'3" | 252 | 26 | | |
| Mike Dawson | DT | 6'4" | 254 | 29 | | |
| Doug English | DT | 6'5" | 258 | 30 | | 4 |
| Mike Fanning | DT | 6'6" | 260 | 30 | | 2 |
| Martin Moss | DT | 6'4" | 252 | 24 | | |

| Use Name | Pos. | Hgt | Wgt | Age | Int | Pts |
|---|---|---|---|---|---|---|
| Roosevelt Barnes | LB | 6'2" | 220 | 25 | 2 | |
| Garry Cobb | LB | 6'2" | 227 | 26 | 4 | |
| August Curley | LB | 6'3" | 226 | 23 | | |
| Steve Doig | LB | 6'2" | 242 | 23 | | |
| Ken Fantetti | LB | 6'2" | 227 | 26 | 2 | |
| James Harrell | LB | 6'1" | 220 | 26 | | |
| Jimmy Williams | LB | 6'2" | 221 | 22 | | |
| James Caver | DB | 5'9" | 175 | 22 | | |
| William Graham | DB | 5'11" | 191 | 23 | | |
| Hector Gray | DB | 6'1" | 190 | 26 | | |
| Alvin Hall | DB | 5'10" | 184 | 25 | 2 | |
| Maurice Harvey (from GB) | DB | 5'10" | 187 | 27 | | |
| Demetrious Johnson | DB | 5'11" | 190 | 22 | | |
| Al Latimer | DB | 5'11" | 177 | 25 | 1 | |
| Bruce McNorton | DB | 5'11" | 175 | 24 | 7 | |
| Dan Wagoner | DB | 5'10" | 180 | 23 | | |
| Bobby Watkins | DB | 5'10" | 184 | 23 | 4 | |

| Use Name | Pos. | Hgt | Wgt | Age | Int | Pts |
|---|---|---|---|---|---|---|
| Gary Danielson | QB | 6'2" | 196 | 31 | | |
| Eric Hipple | QB | 6'2" | 196 | 25 | | 18 |
| Mike Machurek | QB | 6'1" | 205 | 23 | | |
| Ken Jenkins | HB | 5'8" | 184 | 24 | | |
| Rick Kane | HB | 5'11" | 200 | 28 | | |
| Billy Sims | HB | 6' | 212 | 27 | | 42 |
| Dexter Bussey | FB | 6'1" | 210 | 31 | | 6 |
| James Jones | FB | 6'2" | 228 | 22 | | 42 |
| Horace King | FB | 5'10" | 205 | 30 | | |
| Vince Thompson | FB | 6' | 225 | 26 | | 6 |
| Jeff Chadwick | WR | 6'3" | 185 | 22 | | 24 |
| Robbie Martin | WR | 5'8" | 177 | 23 | | 6 |
| Mark Nichols | WR | 6'2" | 208 | 23 | | 6 |
| Freddie Scott | WR | 6'2" | 190 | 31 | | 6 |
| Leonard Thompson | WR | 5'11" | 192 | 31 | | 24 |
| Reese McCall | TE | 6'7" | 232 | 27 | | |
| Ulysses Norris | TE | 6'4" | 232 | 26 | | 42 |
| Ron Rubick | TE | 6'3" | 228 | 22 | | 6 |
| Mike Black | K | 6'1" | 197 | 22 | | |
| Eddie Murray | K | 5'10" | 170 | 27 | | 113 |

## GREEN BAY PACKERS 8-8-0 Bart Starr

| Scores of Each Game | | |
|---|---|---|
| 41 | Houston | *38 |
| 21 | PITTSBURGH | 25 |
| 27 | L.A.RAMS | 24 |
| 3 | N.Y.Giants | 27 |
| 55 | TAMPA BAY | 14 |
| 14 | Detroit | 38 |
| 48 | WASHINGTON | 47 |
| 17 | MINNESOTA | *20 |
| 14 | Cincinnati | 34 |
| 35 | CLEVELAND | 21 |
| 29 | Minnesota | 21 |
| 20 | DETROIT | *23 |
| 41 | Atlanta | *47 |
| 31 | CHICAGO | 28 |
| 12 | Tampa Bay | 9 |
| 21 | Chicago | 23 |

| Use Name | Pos. | Hgt | Wgt | Age | Int | Pts |
|---|---|---|---|---|---|---|
| Charlie Getty | OT | 6'4" | 270 | 31 | | |
| Ron Hallstron | OT | 6'6" | 283 | 23 | | |
| Greg Koch | OT | 6'4" | 276 | 28 | | |
| Karl Swanke | OT-C | 6'6" | 262 | 25 | | |
| Dave Drechsler | OG | 6'3" | 264 | 23 | | |
| Leotis Harris | OG | 6'1" | 265 | 28 | | |
| Tim Huffman | OG | 6'5" | 277 | 24 | | |
| Syd Kitson | OG | 6'4" | 264 | 24 | | |
| Ron Sams | OG | 6'3" | 269 | 22 | | |
| Larry McCarren | C | 6'3" | 251 | 31 | | |
| Larry Rubens | C | 6'1" | 250 | 23 | | |
| Greg Boyd | DE | 6'6" | 280 | 29 | | |
| Byron Braggs | DE | 6'4" | 290 | 23 | | |
| Robert Brown | DE | 6'2" | 250 | 22 | | |
| Ezra Johnson | DE | 6'4" | 259 | 27 | | |
| Ron Spears (from NE) | DE | 6'6" | 255 | 23 | | |
| Charles Johnson | NT | 6'1" | 265 | 26 | | |
| Terry Jones | NT | 6'2" | 253 | 26 | | |
| Daryle Skaugstad (from SF) | NT | 6'5" | 268 | 26 | | |
| Richard Turner | NT | 6'2" | 261 | 24 | | |

| Use Name | Pos. | Hgt | Wgt | Age | Int | Pts |
|---|---|---|---|---|---|---|
| John Anderson | LB | 6'3" | 221 | 27 | 5 | 6 |
| George Cumby | LB | 6' | 225 | 27 | | |
| Mike Curcio | LB | 6'1" | 232 | 26 | | |
| Mike Douglass | LB | 6' | 214 | 28 | | 12 |
| Jim Laughlin | LB | 6' | 222 | 25 | 1 | |
| Cliff Lewis | LB | 6'1" | 226 | 23 | | |
| Guy Prather | LB | 6'2" | 229 | 25 | | |
| Randy Scott | LB | 6'1" | 220 | 24 | 1 | |
| Rich Wingo | LB | 6'1" | 227 | 27 | | |
| Johnnie Gray | DB | 5'11" | 202 | 29 | 2 | |
| Estus Hood | DB | 5'11" | 189 | 27 | | |
| Mike Jolly | DB | 6'3" | 195 | 24 | 1 | |
| Mark Lee | DB | 5'11" | 188 | 25 | 4 | |
| Tim Lewis | DB | 5'11" | 191 | 21 | 5 | |
| Mike McCoy | DB | 5'11" | 183 | 30 | | |
| Mark Murphy | DB | 6'2" | 201 | 25 | | |
| Dwayne O'Steen (from TB) | DB | 6'1" | 195 | 28 | | |

Calvin Favron - Broken Leg
Del Rodgers - Neck Injury

| Use Name | Pos. | Hgt | Wgt | Age | Int | Pts |
|---|---|---|---|---|---|---|
| Rich Campbell | QB | 6'4" | 219 | 23 | | |
| Lynn Dickey | QB | 6'4" | 210 | 32 | | 18 |
| David Whitehurst | QB | 6'2" | 204 | 28 | | |
| Harlan Huckleby | HB | 6'1" | 201 | 25 | | 24 |
| Eddie Lee Ivery | HB | 6'1" | 214 | 26 | | 10 |
| Chet Winters | HB | 5'11" | 204 | 21 | | |
| Jessie Clark | FB | 6' | 233 | 23 | | 6 |
| Gerry Ellis | FB | 5'11" | 216 | 25 | | 36 |
| Mike Meade | FB | 5'11" | 224 | 21 | | 18 |
| Ron Cassidy | WR | 6' | 180 | 26 | | |
| Phillip Epps | WR | 5'10" | 165 | 23 | | 6 |
| John Jefferson | WR | 6'1" | 204 | 27 | | 42 |
| James Lofton | WR | 6'3" | 197 | 27 | | 48 |
| Paul Coffman | TE | 6'3" | 225 | 27 | | 66 |
| Gary Lewis | TE | 6'5" | 234 | 24 | | 12 |
| Eddie Garcia | K | 5'8" | 178 | 24 | | |
| Bucky Scribner | K | 6' | 202 | 23 | | |
| Jan Stenerud | K | 6'2" | 190 | 40 | | 115 |

## CHICAGO BEARS 8-8-0 Mike Ditka

| Scores of Each Game | | |
|---|---|---|
| 17 | ATLANTA | 20 |
| 17 | TAMPA BAY | 10 |
| 31 | New Orleans | *34 |
| 19 | Baltimore | *22 |
| 31 | DENVER | 14 |
| 14 | MINNESOTA | 23 |
| 17 | Detroit | 31 |
| 7 | Philadelphia | 6 |
| 17 | DETROIT | 38 |
| 14 | L.A. Rams | 21 |
| 17 | PHILADELPHIA | 38 |
| 27 | Tampa Bay | 0 |
| 13 | SAN FRANCISCO | 3 |
| 28 | Green Bay | 31 |
| 19 | Minnesota | 13 |
| 23 | GREEN BAY | 21 |

| Use Name | Pos. | Hgt | Wgt | Age | Int | Pts |
|---|---|---|---|---|---|---|
| Jim Covert | OT | 6'4" | 283 | 23 | | |
| Andy Frederick | OT | 6'6" | 265 | 29 | | |
| John Janata | OT | 6'7" | 274 | 22 | | |
| Keith Van Horne | OT | 6'6" | 276 | 25 | | |
| Kurt Becker | OG | 6'5" | 270 | 24 | | |
| Mark Bortz | OG | 6'6" | 271 | 22 | | |
| Rob Fada | OG | 6'2" | 272 | 22 | | |
| Perry Hartnett | OG | 6'5" | 275 | 23 | | |
| Noah Jackson | OG | 6'2" | 265 | 29 | | |
| Tim Norman | OG | 6'6" | 270 | 24 | | |
| Revie Sorey | OG | 6'2" | 260 | 29 | | |
| Jay Hilgenberg | C | 6'3" | 255 | 24 | | |
| Dan Neal | C | 6'4" | 255 | 34 | | |
| Richard Dent | DE | 6'5" | 253 | 22 | | |
| Mike Hartenstine | DE | 6'3" | 253 | 30 | | 8 |
| Tyrone Keys | DE | 6'7" | 267 | 23 | | |
| Dan Hampton | DT | 6'5" | 266 | 25 | | |
| Steve McMichael | DT | 6'2" | 263 | 25 | | |
| Jim Osborne | DT | 6'3" | 259 | 33 | | |

| Use Name | Pos. | Hgt | Wgt | Age | Int | Pts |
|---|---|---|---|---|---|---|
| Kelvin Atkins | LB | 6'3" | 235 | 23 | | |
| Brian Cabral | LB | 6' | 227 | 27 | | |
| Gary Campbell | LB | 6'1" | 220 | 31 | | |
| Al Harris | LB | 6'5" | 253 | 26 | | |
| Jerry Muckensturn | LB | 6'4" | 220 | 29 | | |
| Dan Rains | LB | 6'1" | 222 | 27 | | |
| Dave Simmons | LB | 6'4" | 228 | 26 | | |
| Mike Singletary | LB | 5'11" | 228 | 24 | 1 | |
| Otis Wilson | LB | 6'2" | 231 | 25 | 1 | |
| Todd Bell | DB | 6'1" | 205 | 24 | | |
| Dave Duerson | DB | 6' | 205 | 22 | | |
| Gary Fencik | DB | 6'1" | 193 | 29 | 2 | |
| Jeff Fisher | DB | 5'11" | 190 | 25 | | |
| Leslie Frazier | DB | 6' | 189 | 24 | 7 | 6 |
| Kevin Potter | DB | 5'10" | 183 | 23 | | |
| Mike Richardson | DB | 6' | 188 | 22 | 5 | |
| Terry Schmidt | DB | 6' | 184 | 31 | 5 | 6 |
| Walt Williams | DB | 6' | 184 | 29 | | |

| Use Name | Pos. | Hgt | Wgt | Age | Int | Pts |
|---|---|---|---|---|---|---|
| Bob Avellini | QB | 6'2" | 209 | 30 | | |
| Vince Evans | QB | 6'2" | 212 | 28 | | 6 |
| Jim McMahon | QB | 6'1" | 187 | 24 | | 18 |
| Dennis Gentry | HB | 5'8" | 184 | 24 | | |
| Anthony Hutchison | HB | 5'10" | 186 | 22 | | 6 |
| Walter Payton | HB | 5'11" | 202 | 29 | | 48 |
| Matt Suhey | FB | 5'11" | 216 | 25 | | 30 |
| Calvin Thomas | FB | 5'11" | 235 | 23 | | |
| Brian Baschnagel | WR | 6' | 184 | 29 | | |
| Willie Gault | WR | 6' | 178 | 22 | | 48 |
| Ken Margerum | WR | 6' | 178 | 24 | | 12 |
| Dennis McKinnon | WR | 6'1" | 185 | 22 | | 30 |
| Rickey Watts | WR | 6'1" | 213 | 26 | | |
| Pat Dunsmore | TE | 6'3" | 237 | 23 | | |
| Emery Moorehead | TE | 6'2" | 225 | 29 | | 18 |
| Jay Saldi | TE | 6'3" | 227 | 26 | | |
| Bob Parsons | K | 6'4" | 225 | 33 | | |
| Ray Stachowicz | K | 5'11" | 192 | 24 | | |
| Bob Thomas | K | 5'10" | 177 | 31 | | 77 |

## MINNESOTA VIKINGS 8-8-0 Bud Grant

| Scores of Each Game | | |
|---|---|---|
| 27 | Cleveland | 21 |
| 17 | SAN FRANCISCO | 48 |
| 19 | Tampa Bay | *16 |
| 20 | DETROIT | 17 |
| 24 | DALLAS | 37 |
| 23 | Chicago | 14 |
| 34 | HOUSTON | 14 |
| 20 | Green Bay | *17 |
| 31 | St.Louis | 41 |
| 12 | TAMPA BAY | 17 |
| 21 | GREEN BAY | 29 |
| 17 | Pittsburgh | 14 |
| 16 | New Orleans | 17 |
| 2 | Detroit | 13 |
| 13 | CHICAGO | 19 |
| 20 | CINCINNATI | 14 |

| Use Name | Pos. | Hgt | Wgt | Age | Int | Pts |
|---|---|---|---|---|---|---|
| Tim Irwin | OT | 6'6" | 294 | 26 | | |
| Steve Riley | OT | 6'6" | 270 | 30 | | |
| Terry Tausch | OT | 6'5" | 269 | 24 | | |
| Brent Boyd | OG | 6'3" | 275 | 26 | | |
| Wes Hamilton | OG | 6'3" | 270 | 30 | | |
| Jim Hough | OG | 6'2" | 275 | 27 | | |
| Dave Huffman | OG-C | 6'6" | 255 | 26 | | 6 |
| Curtis Rouse | OG | 6'3" | 305 | 22 | | |
| Dennis Swilley | C | 6'3" | 245 | 28 | | |
| Neil Elshire | DE | 6'6" | 250 | 25 | | |
| Randy Holloway | DE | 6'5" | 255 | 28 | | |
| Doug Martin | DE-NT | 6'3" | 258 | 26 | | |
| Mark Mullaney | DE | 6'6" | 245 | 30 | | |
| Charles Johnson | NT | 6'3" | 275 | 31 | 1 | 6 |
| James White | NT | 6'3" | 270 | 29 | 1 | |

| Use Name | Pos. | Hgt | Wgt | Age | Int | Pts |
|---|---|---|---|---|---|---|
| Walker Lee Ashley | LB | 6' | 240 | 23 | | |
| Matt Blair | LB | 6'5" | 235 | 32 | 1 | |
| Dennis Johnson | LB | 6'3" | 235 | 25 | | |
| Henry Johnson | LB | 6'1" | 235 | 25 | | |
| Fred McNeill | LB | 6'2" | 230 | 21 | | |
| Robin Sendlein | LB | 6'3" | 225 | 24 | | |
| Scott Studwell | LB | 6'2" | 230 | 29 | | |
| Rufus Bess | DB | 5'9" | 185 | 27 | 3 | |
| Joey Browner | DB | 6'2" | 205 | 23 | 2 | |
| Tom Hannon | DB | 5'11" | 195 | 28 | | |
| Carl Lee | DB | 6' | 185 | 22 | 1 | |
| Keith Nord | DB | 6' | 195 | 26 | 1 | |
| John Swain | DB | 6'1" | 195 | 23 | 6 | |
| Willie Teal | DB | 5'10" | 195 | 25 | 3 | |
| John Turner | DB | 6' | 200 | 27 | 6 | |

Rick Danmeier - Back Injury
Joe Senser - Knee Injury

| Use Name | Pos. | Hgt | Wgt | Age | Int | Pts |
|---|---|---|---|---|---|---|
| Steve Dils | QB | 6'1" | 195 | 27 | | |
| Tommy Kramer | QB | 6'2" | 205 | 28 | | |
| Wade Wilson | QB | 6'3" | 210 | 24 | | |
| Rick Bell | HB | 6' | 205 | 22 | | |
| Ted Brown | HB | 5'10" | 210 | 26 | | 66 |
| Darrin Nelson | HB | 5'9" | 185 | 24 | | 6 |
| Jarvis Redwine | HB | 5'10" | 205 | 26 | | |
| Rickey Young | HB | 6'2" | 200 | 29 | | 12 |
| Tony Galbreath | FB | 6' | 228 | 29 | | 36 |
| Mike Jones | WR | 5'11" | 176 | 23 | | |
| Terry LeCount | WR | 5'10" | 185 | 27 | | 12 |
| Leo Lewis | WR | 5'8" | 170 | 26 | | |
| Mardye McDole | WR | 5'11" | 205 | 24 | | |
| Sammy White | WR | 5'11" | 195 | 29 | | 24 |
| Sam McCullum | WR | 6'2" | 195 | 30 | | 12 |
| Norris Brown | TE | 6'3" | 220 | 22 | | |
| Bob Bruer | TE | 6'5" | 240 | 29 | | 12 |
| Dave Casper (from HOU) | TE | 6'4" | 241 | 31 | | |
| Steve Jordan | TE | 6'3" | 230 | 22 | | 12 |
| Mark Mularkey | TE | 6'4" | 245 | 21 | | |
| Greg Coleman | K | 6' | 185 | 28 | | |
| Benny Ricardo | K | 5'10" | 170 | 29 | | 108 |

## TAMPA BAY BUCCANEERS 2-14-0 John McKay

| Scores of Each Game | | |
|---|---|---|
| 0 | DETROIT | 11 |
| 10 | Chicago | 17 |
| 16 | MINNESOTA | *19 |
| 17 | CINCINNATI | 23 |
| 14 | Green Bay | 55 |
| 24 | Dallas | *27 |
| 27 | St.Louis | 34 |
| 21 | NEW ORLEANS | 24 |
| 12 | Pittsburgh | 17 |
| 17 | Minnesota | 12 |
| 0 | Cleveland | 20 |
| 0 | CHICAGO | 27 |
| 33 | HOUSTON | 24 |
| 21 | San Francisco | 35 |
| 9 | GREEN BAY | *12 |
| 20 | DETROIT | 23 |

| Use Name | Pos. | Hgt | Wgt | Age | Int | Pts |
|---|---|---|---|---|---|---|
| Dave Reavis | OT | 6'5" | 263 | 33 | | |
| Gene Sanders | OT | 6'3" | 280 | 26 | | |
| Kelley Thomas | OT | 6'6" | 270 | 22 | | |
| Glenn Bujnoch | OG | 6'5" | 265 | 29 | | |
| Sean Farrell | OG | 6'3" | 260 | 23 | | |
| Randy Grimes | OG-C | 6'4" | 265 | 23 | | |
| Ray Snell | OG-OT | 6'4" | 265 | 25 | | |
| George Yarno | OG | 6'2" | 260 | 26 | | |
| Jim Leonard | C-OG | 6'3" | 260 | 25 | | |
| Steve Wilson | C | 6'3" | 270 | 29 | | |
| Hasson Arbubakrr | DE | 6'4" | 250 | 22 | | |
| John Cannon | DE | 6'5" | 260 | 23 | | |
| Booker Reese | DE | 6'6" | 260 | 23 | | 2 |
| Lee Roy Selmon | DE | 6'3" | 260 | 28 | | |
| David Logan | NT | 6'2" | 250 | 26 | | 6 |
| Brad White | NT | 6'2" | 255 | 25 | | |

| Use Name | Pos. | Hgt | Wgt | Age | Int | Pts |
|---|---|---|---|---|---|---|
| Scott Branley | LB | 6'1" | 230 | 25 | 1 | |
| Jeff Davis | LB | 6' | 230 | 23 | | |
| Hugh Green | LB | 6'2" | 225 | 24 | 2 | 12 |
| Andy Hawkins | LB | 6'2" | 230 | 25 | | |
| Cecil Johnson | LB | 6'2" | 235 | 28 | | |
| Ed Judie (from SF) | LB | 6'2" | 235 | 24 | | |
| Quentin Lowry (from WAS) | LB | 6'3" | 235 | 25 | | |
| Danny Spradlin | LB | 6'1" | 235 | 24 | | |
| Robert Thompson | LB | 6'3" | 225 | 23 | | |
| Richard Wood | LB | 6'2" | 230 | 30 | | |
| Cedric Brown | DB | 6'1" | 200 | 29 | 4 | |
| Jeremiah Castille | DB | 5'10" | 175 | 22 | 1 | 6 |
| Neal Colzie | DB | 6'2" | 205 | 30 | | |
| Mark Cotney | DB | 6' | 205 | 31 | 2 | |
| John Holt | DB | 5'11" | 175 | 24 | 3 | |
| Sandy LaBeaux | DB | 6'3" | 210 | 22 | | |
| Thomas Morris | DB | 5'11" | 175 | 23 | | |
| Johnny Ray Smith | DB | 5'9" | 185 | 25 | | |
| Norris Thomas | DB | 5'11" | 180 | 29 | | |
| Mike Washington | DB | 6'3" | 200 | 30 | 2 | |

David Barrett - Knee Injury

| Use Name | Pos. | Hgt | Wgt | Age | Int | Pts |
|---|---|---|---|---|---|---|
| Jerry Goldsteyn | QB | 6'4" | 200 | 29 | | |
| Bob Hewko | QB | 6'3" | 195 | 23 | | |
| Jeff Komlo | QB | 6'2" | 195 | 27 | | |
| Jack Thompson | QB | 6'3" | 220 | 27 | | |
| Terdell Middleton | HB | 6' | 205 | 28 | | |
| Michael Morton | HB | 5'8" | 180 | 23 | | |
| James Owens | HB | 5'11" | 195 | 28 | | 36 |
| Adger Armstrong | FB | 6' | 225 | 26 | | 12 |
| Melvin Carver | FB | 5'11" | 215 | 24 | | 6 |
| James Wilder | FB | 6'3" | 220 | 25 | | 36 |
| Theo Bell | WR | 6' | 190 | 29 | | 12 |
| Gene Branton | WR | 6'4" | 210 | 22 | | |
| Gerald Carter | WR | 6'1" | 190 | 26 | | 12 |
| Kevin House | WR | 6'1" | 175 | 25 | | 30 |
| Andre Tyler | WR | 6' | 180 | 24 | | |
| Jerry Bell | TE | 6'5" | 225 | 24 | | 6 |
| Jimmie Giles | TE | 6'3" | 245 | 28 | | 6 |
| Jim Obradovich | TE | 6'2" | 225 | 30 | | 6 |
| Mark White | TE | 6'3" | 235 | 23 | | |
| Bill Capece | K | 5'7" | 170 | 24 | | 53 |
| Frank Garcia | K | 6' | 205 | 26 | | |
| David Warnke | K | 5'11" | 185 | 23 | | 1 |

* Overtime

## DETROIT LIONS

### RUSHING
| Last Name | No. | Yds | Avg | TD |
|---|---|---|---|---|
| Sims | 220 | 1040 | 4.7 | 7 |
| Jones | 135 | 475 | 3.5 | 6 |
| Bussey | 57 | 249 | 4.4 | 0 |
| Hipple | 41 | 171 | 4.2 | 3 |
| V. Thompson | 40 | 138 | 3.5 | 1 |
| L. Thompson | 4 | 72 | 18.0 | 1 |
| Kane | 4 | 19 | 4.8 | 0 |
| Nichols | 1 | 13 | 13.0 | 0 |
| Danielson | 6 | 8 | 1.3 | 0 |
| King | 3 | 6 | 2.0 | 0 |
| Black | 2 | -10 | -5.0 | 0 |

### RECEIVING
| Last Name | No. | Yds | Avg | TD |
|---|---|---|---|---|
| Jones | 46 | 467 | 10.2 | 1 |
| Sims | 42 | 419 | 10 | 0 |
| L. Thompson | 41 | 752 | 18.3 | 3 |
| Chadwick | 40 | 617 | 15.4 | 4 |
| Nichols | 29 | 437 | 15.1 | 1 |
| Norris | 26 | 291 | 11.2 | 7 |
| Rubick | 10 | 81 | 8.1 | 1 |
| King | 9 | 76 | 8.4 | 0 |
| Bussey | 8 | 49 | 6.1 | 1 |
| Scott | 5 | 71 | 14.2 | 1 |
| V. Thompson | 4 | 16 | 4.0 | 0 |
| Kane | 2 | 15 | 7.5 | 0 |
| McCall | 1 | 6 | 6.0 | 0 |

### PUNT RETURNS
| Last Name | No. | Yds | Avg | TD |
|---|---|---|---|---|
| Jenkins | 23 | 230 | 10.0 | 0 |
| Martin | 15 | 183 | 12.2 | 1 |
| Hall | 8 | 109 | 13.6 | 0 |

### KICKOFF RETURNS
| Last Name | No. | Yds | Avg | TD |
|---|---|---|---|---|
| Hall | 23 | 492 | 21.4 | 0 |
| Jenkins | 22 | 459 | 20.9 | 0 |
| Martin | 8 | 140 | 17.5 | 0 |
| Caver | 4 | 71 | 17.8 | 0 |
| Curley | 1 | 7 | 7.0 | 0 |
| King | 1 | 11 | 11.0 | 0 |
| Lee | 1 | 11 | 11.0 | 0 |
| Norris | 1 | 0 | 0.0 | 0 |

### PASSING — PUNTING — KICKING
| PASSING | Att | Cmp | % | Yds | Yd/Att | TD | Int— | % | RK |
|---|---|---|---|---|---|---|---|---|---|
| Hipple | 387 | 204 | 53 | 2577 | 6.66 | 12 | 18— | 5 | 12 |
| Danielson | 113 | 59 | 52 | 720 | 6.37 | 7 | 4— | 4 | |
| Jones | 2 | 0 | 0 | 0 | 0.00 | 0 | 0— | 0 | |
| Black | 1 | 0 | 0 | 0 | 0.00 | 0 | 1—100 | | |

| PUNTING | No. | Avg. |
|---|---|---|
| Black | 71 | 41.0 |

| KICKING | XP | Att | % | FG | Att | % |
|---|---|---|---|---|---|---|
| Murray | 38 | 38 | 100 | 25 | 32 | 78 |

## GREEN BAY PACKERS

### RUSHING
| Last Name | No. | Yds | Avg | TD |
|---|---|---|---|---|
| Ellis | 141 | 696 | 4.9 | 4 |
| Ivery | 86 | 340 | 4.0 | 2 |
| J. Clark | 71 | 328 | 4.6 | 0 |
| Meade | 55 | 201 | 3.7 | 1 |
| Huckleby | 50 | 182 | 3.6 | 4 |
| Lofton | 9 | 36 | 4.0 | 0 |
| G. Lewis | 4 | 16 | 4.0 | 1 |
| Dickey | 21 | 12 | 0.6 | 3 |
| Whitehurst | 2 | -4 | -2.0 | 0 |

### RECEIVING
| Last Name | No. | Yds | Avg | TD |
|---|---|---|---|---|
| Lofton | 58 | 1300 | 22.4 | 8 |
| Jefferson | 57 | 830 | 14.6 | 7 |
| Coffman | 54 | 814 | 15.1 | 11 |
| Ellis | 52 | 603 | 11.6 | 2 |
| Epps | 18 | 313 | 17.4 | 0 |
| J. Clark | 18 | 279 | 15.5 | 1 |
| Ivery | 16 | 139 | 8.7 | 1 |
| Meade | 16 | 110 | 6.9 | 2 |
| G. Lewis | 11 | 204 | 18.5 | 1 |
| Huckleby | 10 | 87 | 8.7 | 0 |
| Kitson | 1 | 9 | 9.0 | 0 |

### PUNT RETURNS
| Last Name | No. | Yds | Avg | TD |
|---|---|---|---|---|
| Epps | 36 | 324 | 9.0 | 1 |
| Gray | 2 | 9 | 4.5 | 0 |
| Hood | 1 | 0 | 0.0 | 0 |
| C. Lewis | 1 | 0 | 0.0 | 0 |
| Lee | 1 | -4 | -4.0 | 0 |

### KICKOFF RETURNS
| Last Name | No. | Yds | Avg | TD |
|---|---|---|---|---|
| Huckleby | 41 | 757 | 18.5 | 0 |
| T. Lewis | 20 | 358 | 17.9 | 0 |
| Gray | 11 | 178 | 16.2 | 0 |
| Winters | 3 | 28 | 9.3 | 0 |
| Dreschler | 1 | 1 | 1.0 | 0 |
| Ivery | 1 | 17 | 17.0 | 0 |
| Kitson | 1 | 0 | 0.0 | 0 |
| Lee | 1 | 0 | 0.0 | 0 |

### PASSING — PUNTING — KICKING
| PASSING | Att | Cmp | % | Yds | Yd/Att | TD | Int— | % | RK |
|---|---|---|---|---|---|---|---|---|---|
| Dickey | 484 | 289 | 60 | 4458 | 9.21 | 32 | 29— | 6 | 5 |
| Whitehurst | 35 | 18 | 51 | 149 | 4.26 | 0 | 2— | 6 | |
| Ellis | 5 | 2 | 40 | 31 | 6.20 | 1 | 1— | 20 | |
| Ivery | 2 | 2 | 100 | 50 | 25.00 | 0 | 0— | 0 | |

| PUNTING | No. | Avg. |
|---|---|---|
| Scribner | 69 | 41.6 |

| KICKING | XP | Att | % | FG | Att | % |
|---|---|---|---|---|---|---|
| Stenerud | 52 | 52 | 100 | 21 | 26 | 81 |

## CHICAGO BEARS

### RUSHING
| Last Name | No. | Yds | Avg | TD |
|---|---|---|---|---|
| Payton | 314 | 1421 | 4.5 | 6 |
| Suhey | 149 | 681 | 4.6 | 4 |
| McMahon | 55 | 307 | 5.6 | 2 |
| Evans | 22 | 142 | 6.5 | 1 |
| Gentry | 16 | 65 | 4.1 | 0 |
| Gault | 3 | 31 | 7.8 | 0 |
| Parsons | 1 | 27 | 27.0 | 0 |
| C. Thomas | 8 | 25 | 3.1 | 0 |
| Hutchison | 6 | 13 | 2.2 | 1 |
| Margerum | 1 | 7 | 7.0 | 0 |
| Moorehead | 5 | 6 | 1.2 | 0 |
| Baschnagel | 2 | 2 | 1.0 | 0 |

### RECEIVING
| Last Name | No. | Yds | Avg | TD |
|---|---|---|---|---|
| Payton | 53 | 607 | 11.5 | 2 |
| Suhey | 49 | 429 | 8.8 | 1 |
| Moorehead | 42 | 597 | 14.2 | 3 |
| Gault | 40 | 836 | 20.9 | 8 |
| Margerum | 21 | 336 | 16.0 | 2 |
| McKinnon | 20 | 326 | 16.3 | 4 |
| Saldi | 12 | 119 | 9.9 | 0 |
| Dunsmore | 8 | 102 | 12.8 | 0 |
| Baschnagel | 5 | 70 | 14.0 | 0 |
| C. Thomas | 2 | 13 | 6.5 | 0 |
| Gentry | 2 | 8 | 4.0 | 0 |
| McMahon | 1 | 18 | 18.0 | 1 |

### PUNT RETURNS
| Last Name | No. | Yds | Avg | TD |
|---|---|---|---|---|
| McKinnon | 34 | 316 | 9.3 | 1 |
| Fisher | 13 | 71 | 5.5 | 0 |
| Gault | 9 | 60 | 6.7 | 0 |

### KICKOFF RETURNS
| Last Name | No. | Yds | Avg | TD |
|---|---|---|---|---|
| Hutchison | 17 | 259 | 15.2 | 0 |
| Gault | 13 | 276 | 21.2 | 0 |
| Gentry | 7 | 130 | 18.6 | 0 |
| Watts | 5 | 79 | 15.8 | 0 |
| Baschnagel | 3 | 42 | 14.0 | 0 |
| Duerson | 3 | 66 | 22.0 | 0 |
| Bell | 2 | 18 | 9.0 | 0 |
| Cabral | 2 | 11 | 5.5 | 0 |
| McKinnon | 2 | 42 | 21.0 | 0 |
| Rains | 2 | 11 | 5.5 | 0 |
| Janata | 1 | 2 | 2.0 | 0 |
| Richardson | 1 | 17 | 17.0 | 0 |

### PASSING — PUNTING — KICKING
| PASSING | Att | Cmp | % | Yds | Yd/Att | TD | Int— | % | RK |
|---|---|---|---|---|---|---|---|---|---|
| McMahon | 295 | 175 | 59 | 2184 | 7.40 | 12 | 13— | 4 | 7 |
| Evans | 145 | 76 | 52 | 1108 | 7.65 | 5 | 7— | 5 | |
| Payton | 6 | 3 | 50 | 95 | 15.83 | 3 | 2— | 33 | |
| Suhey | 1 | 1 | 100 | 74 | 74.00 | 1 | 0— | 0 | |

| PUNTING | No. | Avg. |
|---|---|---|
| Parsons | 79 | 36.9 |
| Stachowicz | 12 | 37.3 |
| McMahon | 1 | 36.0 |

| KICKING | XP | Att | % | FG | Att | % |
|---|---|---|---|---|---|---|
| B. Thomas | 35 | 38 | 92 | 14 | 25 | 56 |

## MINNESOTA VIKINGS

### RUSHING
| Last Name | No. | Yds | Avg | TD |
|---|---|---|---|---|
| Nelson | 154 | 642 | 4.2 | 1 |
| T. Brown | 120 | 476 | 4.0 | 10 |
| Galbreath | 113 | 474 | 4.2 | 4 |
| Young | 39 | 90 | 2.3 | 2 |
| Redwine | 10 | 48 | 4.8 | 0 |
| LeCount | 2 | 42 | 21.0 | 0 |
| Dils | 16 | 28 | 1.8 | 0 |
| Jones | 1 | 9 | 9.0 | 0 |
| S. White | 1 | 7 | 7.0 | 0 |
| Kramer | 8 | 3 | 0.4 | 0 |
| Lewis | 1 | 2 | 2.0 | 0 |
| Manning | 1 | -1 | -1.0 | 0 |
| Wilson | 3 | -3 | -1.0 | 0 |
| Coleman | 1 | -9 | -9.0 | 0 |

### RECEIVING
| Last Name | No. | Yds | Avg | TD |
|---|---|---|---|---|
| Nelson | 51 | 618 | 12.1 | 0 |
| Galbreath | 45 | 348 | 7.7 | 2 |
| T. Brown | 41 | 357 | 8.7 | 1 |
| Bruer | 31 | 315 | 10.2 | 2 |
| S. White | 29 | 412 | 14.2 | 4 |
| LeCount | 21 | 318 | 15.1 | 2 |
| McCullum | 21 | 314 | 15.0 | 2 |
| Young | 21 | 193 | 9.2 | 0 |
| Casper | 20 | 251 | 12.6 | 0 |
| Jordan | 15 | 212 | 14.1 | 2 |
| Lewis | 12 | 127 | 10.6 | 0 |
| Jones | 6 | 95 | 15.8 | 0 |
| McDole | 3 | 29 | 9.7 | 0 |
| Redwine | 1 | 4 | 4.0 | 0 |

### PUNT RETURNS
| Last Name | No. | Yds | Avg | TD |
|---|---|---|---|---|
| Bess | 21 | 158 | 7.5 | 0 |
| Lewis | 3 | 52 | 17.3 | 0 |

### KICKOFF RETURNS
| Last Name | No. | Yds | Avg | TD |
|---|---|---|---|---|
| Nelson | 18 | 445 | 24.7 | 0 |
| Redwine | 38 | 838 | 22.1 | 0 |
| Huffman | 3 | 42 | 14.0 | 0 |
| Young | 3 | 27 | 9.0 | 0 |
| Bess | 2 | 44 | 22.0 | 0 |
| Jones | 2 | 31 | 15.5 | 0 |
| Bell | 1 | 14 | 14.0 | 0 |
| Lewis | 1 | 25 | 25.0 | 0 |

### PASSING — PUNTING — KICKING
| PASSING | Att | Cmp | % | Yds | Yd/Att | TD | Int— | % | RK |
|---|---|---|---|---|---|---|---|---|---|
| Dils | 444 | 239 | 54 | 2840 | 6.40 | 11 | 16— | 4 | 11 |
| Kramer | 82 | 55 | 67 | 550 | 6.71 | 3 | 4— | 5 | |
| Wilson | 28 | 16 | 57 | 124 | 4.43 | 1 | 2— | 7 | |
| LeCount | 1 | 0 | 0.0 | 0 | 0.00 | 0 | 0— | 0 | |

| PUNTING | No. | Avg. |
|---|---|---|
| Coleman | 91 | 41.5 |

| KICKING | XP | Att | % | FG | Att | % |
|---|---|---|---|---|---|---|
| Ricardo | 33 | 34 | 97 | 25 | 33 | 76 |

## TAMPA BAY BUCCANEERS

### RUSHING
| Last Name | No. | Yds | Avg | TD |
|---|---|---|---|---|
| Wilder | 161 | 640 | 4.0 | 4 |
| Carver | 114 | 348 | 3.1 | 0 |
| Owens | 96 | 266 | 2.8 | 5 |
| Armstrong | 7 | 90 | 4.3 | 0 |
| Morton | 13 | 28 | 2.2 | 0 |
| J. Thompson | 26 | 27 | 1.0 | 0 |
| Komlo | 2 | 11 | 5.5 | 0 |
| Middleton | 2 | 4 | 2.0 | 0 |
| Golsteyn | 5 | 3 | 0.6 | 0 |
| Carter | 1 | 0 | 0.0 | 0 |
| House | 1 | -4 | -4.0 | 0 |

### RECEIVING
| Last Name | No. | Yds | Avg | TD |
|---|---|---|---|---|
| Wilder | 57 | 380 | 6.7 | 2 |
| Carter | 48 | 694 | 14.5 | 2 |
| House | 47 | 769 | 16.4 | 5 |
| Carver | 32 | 262 | 8.2 | 1 |
| T. Bell | 25 | 410 | 16.4 | 2 |
| Giles | 25 | 349 | 14.0 | 1 |
| J. Bell | 18 | 200 | 11.1 | 1 |
| Armstrong | 15 | 173 | 11.5 | 2 |
| Owens | 15 | 81 | 5.4 | 1 |
| Obradovich | 9 | 71 | 7.9 | 1 |
| Tyler | 6 | 77 | 12.8 | 0 |
| Witte | 2 | 15 | 7.5 | 0 |
| Morton | 1 | 9 | 9.0 | 0 |

### PUNT RETURNS
| Last Name | No. | Yds | Avg | TD |
|---|---|---|---|---|
| Tyler | 27 | 208 | 7.7 | 0 |
| T. Bell | 10 | 48 | 4.8 | 0 |
| Holt | 5 | 43 | 8.6 | 0 |

### KICKOFF RETURNS
| Last Name | No. | Yds | Avg | TD |
|---|---|---|---|---|
| Morton | 30 | 689 | 23.0 | 0 |
| Owens | 20 | 380 | 19.0 | 0 |
| Smith | 8 | 136 | 17.0 | 0 |
| Spradlin | 3 | 35 | 11.7 | 0 |
| Carver | 2 | 24 | 12.0 | 0 |
| O'Steen | 2 | 30 | 15.0 | 0 |
| Armstrong | 1 | 10 | 10.0 | 0 |
| Middleton | 1 | 10 | 10.0 | 0 |
| Obradovich | 1 | 0 | 0.0 | 0 |

### PASSING — PUNTING — KICKING
| PASSING | Att | Cmp | % | Yds | Yd/Att | TD | Int— | % | RK |
|---|---|---|---|---|---|---|---|---|---|
| J. Thompson | 423 | 249 | 59 | 2906 | 6.87 | 18 | 21— | 5 | 10 |
| Golsteyn | 97 | 47 | 49 | 535 | 5.51 | 2 | 2— | 2 | |
| Komlo | 8 | 4 | 50 | 49 | 6.13 | 0 | 1— | 13 | |

| PUNTING | No. | Avg. |
|---|---|---|
| Garcia | 95 | 42.2 |

| KICKING | XP | Att | % | FG | Att | % |
|---|---|---|---|---|---|---|
| Capece | 23 | 26 | 89 | 10 | 23 | 44 |
| Warnke | 1 | 2 | 50 | 0 | 1 | 0 |
| Yamo | 1 | 1 | 100 | 0 | 0 | 0 |

## SAN FRANCISCO 49ERS 10-6-0 Bill Walsh

| Scores of Each Game | | |
|---|---|---|
| 17 | PHILADELPHIA | 22 |
| 48 | Minnesota | 17 |
| 42 | St.Louis | 27 |
| 24 | ATLANTA | 20 |
| 33 | New England | 13 |
| 7 | L.A.RAMS | 10 |
| 32 | New Orleans | 13 |
| 45 | L.A.Rams | 35 |
| 13 | N.Y.JETS | 27 |
| 17 | MIAMI | 20 |
| 27 | NEW ORLEANS | 0 |
| 24 | Atlanta | 28 |
| 3 | Chicago | 13 |
| 35 | TAMPA BAY | 21 |
| 23 | Buffalo | 10 |
| 42 | DALLAS | 17 |

| Use Name | Pos. | Hgt | Wgt | Age | Int | Pts |
|---|---|---|---|---|---|---|
| Keith Fahnhorst | OT | 6'6" | 273 | 31 | | |
| Allan Kennedy | OT | 6'7" | 275 | 25 | | |
| Bubba Paris | OT | 6'6" | 295 | 22 | | |
| John Ayers | OG | 6'5" | 265 | 30 | | |
| Randy Cross | OG | 6'3" | 265 | 29 | | |
| Jesse Sapolu | OG | 6'4" | 260 | 22 | | |
| John Choma | OG-C | 6'5" | 261 | 28 | | |
| Walt Downing | C-OG | 6'3" | 270 | 27 | | |
| Fred Quillan | C | 6'5" | 266 | 27 | | |
| Dwaine Board | DE | 6'5" | 248 | 26 | | 6 |
| Fred Dean | DE | 6'3" | 236 | 31 | | |
| Jeff Stover | DE | 6'5" | 275 | 25 | | |
| Jim Stuckey | DE | 6'4" | 253 | 25 | | |
| Pete Kugler | NT-DE | 6'4" | 255 | 24 | | |
| Lawrence Pillers | NT-DE | 6'3" | 250 | 30 | 1 | |
| John Harty | NT | 6'4" | 263 | 24 | | |
| Dan Bunz | LB | 6'4" | 225 | 27 | | |
| Riki Ellison | LB | 6'2" | 225 | 27 | | |
| Ron Ferrari | LB | 6' | 212 | 24 | | |
| Willie Harper | LB | 6'2" | 215 | 33 | 1 | |
| Bob Horn | LB | 6'3" | 230 | 29 | | |
| Bobby Leopold | LB | 6'1" | 215 | 25 | 2 | |
| Ken McAlister (from SEA-DB) | LB | 6'5" | 210 | 23 | | |
| Milt McColl | LB | 6'6" | 230 | 24 | | |
| Blanchard Montgomery | LB | 6'2" | 236 | 22 | | |
| Gary Moten | LB | 6'1" | 210 | 22 | | |
| Jack Reynolds | LB | 6'1" | 232 | 35 | | |
| Keena Turner | LB | 6'2" | 219 | 24 | | |
| Richard Blackmore | DB | 5'10" | 174 | 27 | | |
| Tim Collier | DB | 6' | 176 | 29 | 3 | 6 |
| Rick Gervais | DB | 5'11" | 190 | 23 | | |
| Dwight Hicks | DB | 6'1" | 192 | 27 | 2 | 12 |
| Tom Holmoe | DB | 6'2" | 180 | 23 | | |
| Ronnie Lott | DB | 6' | 199 | 24 | 4 | |
| Dana McLemore | DB | 5'10" | 183 | 23 | | |
| Carlton Williamson | DB | 6' | 204 | 25 | 4 | |
| Eric Wright | DB | 6'1" | 180 | 24 | 7 | 12 |
| Guy Benjamin | QB | 6'4" | 210 | 28 | | |
| Matt Cavanaugh | QB | 6'2" | 212 | 26 | | |
| Joe Montana | QB | 6'2" | 195 | 27 | | 12 |
| Carl Monroe | HB | 5'8" | 166 | 23 | | |
| Jeff Moore | HB | 6' | 196 | 27 | | 6 |
| Bill Ring | HB | 5'10" | 205 | 26 | | 12 |
| Wendell Tyler | HB | 5'10" | 200 | 28 | | 36 |
| Earl Cooper | FB | 6'2" | 227 | 24 | | 18 |
| Roger Craig | FB | 6' | 222 | 23 | | 72 |
| Vince Williams | FB | 6' | 231 | 23 | | |
| Dwight Clark | WR | 6'4" | 210 | 26 | | 48 |
| Darius Durham | WR | 6'2" | 185 | 22 | | |
| Renaldo Nehemiah | WR | 6'1" | 183 | 24 | | 6 |
| Freddie Solomon | WR | 5'11" | 188 | 30 | | 24 |
| Mike Wilson | WR | 6'3" | 210 | 24 | | |
| Russ Francis | TE | 6'6" | 242 | 30 | | 24 |
| Eason Ramson | TE | 6'2" | 234 | 27 | | 6 |
| Tom Orosz | K | 6'1" | 204 | 23 | | |
| Ray Wersching | K | 5'11" | 210 | 33 | | 126 |

Bryan Clark - Separated Shoulder
Frank LeMaster - Dislocated Shoulder
Mike Wood - Injury

## LOS ANGELES RAMS 9-7-0 John Robinson

| Scores of Each Game | | |
|---|---|---|
| 16 | N.Y. Giants | 6 |
| 30 | NEW ORLEANS | 27 |
| 24 | Green Bay | 27 |
| 24 | N.Y. Jets | *27 |
| 21 | DETROIT | 10 |
| 10 | San Francisco | 45 |
| 27 | ATLANTA | 21 |
| 35 | SAN FRANCISCO | 45 |
| 14 | Miami | 30 |
| 21 | CHICAGO | 14 |
| 36 | Atlanta | 13 |
| 20 | WASHINGTON | 42 |
| 41 | BUFFALO | 17 |
| 9 | Philadelphia | 13 |
| 7 | NEW ENGLAND | 21 |
| 26 | New Orleans | 24 |

| Use Name | Pos. | Hgt | Wgt | Age | Int | Pts |
|---|---|---|---|---|---|---|
| Bill Bain | OT | 6'4" | 285 | 31 | | |
| Gary Kowalski | OT | 6'6" | 275 | 23 | | |
| Jackie Slater | OT | 6'4" | 271 | 29 | | |
| Russ Bolinger | OG | 6'5" | 255 | 28 | | |
| Dennis Harrah | OG | 6'5" | 265 | 30 | | |
| Kent Hill | OG | 6'5" | 260 | 26 | | |
| Joe Shearin | OG | 6'4" | 250 | 23 | | |
| Doug Smith | C | 6'3" | 253 | 26 | | |
| Dour Barnett | DE | 6'3" | 253 | 26 | | |
| Reggie Doss | DE | 6'4" | 263 | 26 | | |
| Gary Jeter | DE | 6'4" | 260 | 28 | | |
| Jack Youngblood | DE | 6'4" | 242 | 33 | | 2 |
| Richard Bishop | NT | 6'1" | 265 | 33 | | |
| Charles DeJurnett | NT | 6'4" | 260 | 31 | | |
| Myron Lapka | NT | 6'4" | 260 | 27 | | |
| Greg Meisner | NT | 6'3" | 253 | 24 | | |
| George Andrews | LB | 6'3" | 225 | 27 | 1 | |
| Howard Carson | LB | 6'2" | 230 | 26 | | |
| Jim Collins | LB | 6'2" | 230 | 25 | | |
| Carl Ekern | LB | 6'3" | 222 | 29 | 1 | |
| Mark Jerue | LB | 6'3" | 229 | 23 | | |
| Dave Lewis | LB | 6'4" | 245 | 28 | | |
| Mel Owens | LB | 6'2" | 224 | 24 | | |
| Mike Wilcher | LB | 6'3" | 235 | 23 | | |
| Eric Williams | LB | 6'2" | 235 | 28 | | |
| Jim Youngblood | LB | 6'3" | 231 | 33 | | |
| Kirk Collins | DB | 5'11" | 183 | 25 | 5 | |
| Nolan Cromwell | DB | 6'1" | 200 | 28 | 3 | 6 |
| Eric Harris | DB | 6'3" | 202 | 28 | 4 | |
| LeRoy Irvin | DB | 5'11" | 184 | 25 | 4 | |
| Monte Jackson | DB | 5'11" | 195 | 30 | | |
| Johnnie Johnson | DB | 6'1" | 183 | 26 | 4 | 12 |
| Vince Newsome | DB | 6'1" | 179 | 22 | | |
| Ivory Sully | DB | 6' | 200 | 26 | | |
| Henry Williams (to SD) | DB | 5'10" | 180 | 26 | | |
| Mike Williams | DB | 5'10" | 186 | 29 | | |
| Vince Ferragamo | QB | 6'3" | 212 | 29 | | |
| Steve Fuller | QB | 6'4" | 198 | 26 | | |
| Jeff Kemp | QB | 6' | 201 | 24 | | |
| Robert Alexander | HB | 6' | 185 | 25 | | |
| Barry Redden | HB-FB | 5'10" | 205 | 23 | | 12 |
| Eric Dickerson | FB | 6'3" | 220 | 22 | | 120 |
| Mike Guman | FB | 6'2" | 218 | 25 | | 24 |
| A.J. Jones | FB | 6'1" | 202 | 24 | | |
| Preston Dennard | WR | 6'1" | 183 | 27 | | 30 |
| Henry Ellard | WR | 5'11" | 170 | 22 | | 6 |
| George Farmer | WR | 5'10" | 175 | 24 | | 30 |
| Otis Grant | WR | 6'3" | 197 | 22 | | 6 |
| Gordon Jones | WR | 6' | 190 | 26 | | |
| Jeff Simmons | WR | 6'3" | 195 | 23 | | |
| Mike Barber | TE | 6'3" | 237 | 30 | | 18 |
| David Hill | TE | 6'2" | 228 | 29 | | 12 |
| James McDonald | TE | 6'5" | 230 | 22 | | 6 |
| Mike Lansford | K | 6' | 183 | 25 | | 27 |
| John Misko | K | 6'5" | 207 | 28 | | |
| Chuck Nelson | K | 6' | 175 | 23 | | 48 |

Drew Hill - Back Injury
Irv Pankey - Torn Achilles Tendon
Mike Reilly - Suspended by N.F.L.

## NEW ORLEANS SAINTS 8-8-0 Bum Phillips

| Scores of Each Game | | |
|---|---|---|
| 28 | ST. LOUIS | 17 |
| 27 | L.A. Rams | 30 |
| 34 | CHICAGO | *31 |
| 20 | Dallas | 21 |
| 17 | MIAMI | 7 |
| 19 | Atlanta | 17 |
| 13 | SAN FRANCISCO | 32 |
| 24 | Tampa Bay | 21 |
| 21 | Buffalo | 27 |
| 27 | ATLANTA | 10 |
| 0 | San Francisco | 27 |
| 28 | N.Y. JETS | 31 |
| 17 | MINNESOTA | 16 |
| 0 | New England | 7 |
| 20 | Philadelphia | *17 |
| 24 | L.A. RAMS | 26 |

| Use Name | Pos. | Hgt | Wgt | Age | Int | Pts |
|---|---|---|---|---|---|---|
| Stan Brock | OT | 6'6" | 285 | 25 | | |
| Angelo Fields | OT | 6'6" | 315 | 25 | | |
| Leon Gray | OT | 6'3" | 258 | 31 | | |
| Dave Lafary | OT | 6'7" | 280 | 28 | | |
| Kelvin Clark | OG | 6'3" | 265 | 27 | 6 | |
| Brad Edelman | OG | 6'6" | 265 | 22 | | |
| Steve Korte | OG | 6'2" | 270 | 23 | 6 | |
| Louis Oubre | OG | 6'4" | 262 | 25 | | |
| John Hill | C | 6'2" | 260 | 33 | | |
| Jim Pietrzak | C | 6'5" | 260 | 30 | | |
| Bruce Clark | DE | 6'3" | 275 | 25 | | |
| Reggie Lewis | DE | 6'2" | 260 | 29 | 1 | 6 |
| Frank Warren | DE | 6'4" | 275 | 23 | 1 | |
| Jim Wilks | DE | 6'5" | 260 | 25 | | |
| Tony Elliott | NT | 6'2" | 265 | 24 | | |
| Gary Lewis | NT | 6'3" | 260 | 22 | | |
| Derland Moore | NT | 6'4" | 270 | 31 | | |
| Rickey Jackson | LB | 6'2" | 230 | 25 | | 1 |
| Jim Kovach | LB | 6'2" | 225 | 27 | | |
| Chris Martin | LB | 6'2" | 220 | 22 | | |
| Rob Nairne | LB | 6'4" | 227 | 29 | | |
| Whitney Paul | LB | 6'3" | 220 | 27 | 2 | |
| Scott Pelluer | LB | 6'2" | 215 | 24 | | |
| Glen Redd | LB | 6'1" | 225 | 25 | | |
| Dennis Winston | LB | 6' | 230 | 27 | 3 | |
| Russell Gary | DB | 5'11" | 195 | 24 | 3 | |
| Bobby Johnson | DB | 6' | 191 | 23 | 2 | 6 |
| Rodney Lewis | DB | 5'11" | 190 | 24 | | |
| Vernon Perry | DB | 6'2" | 210 | 29 | | |
| Johnnie Poe | DB | 6'1" | 185 | 24 | 7 | 6 |
| Greg Stemrick | DB | 5'11" | 185 | 31 | 1 | |
| Frank Wattelet | DB | 6' | 185 | 24 | 2 | |
| Dave Waymer | DB | 6'1" | 195 | 25 | | |
| Guido Merkens | QB | 6'1" | 195 | 28 | | |
| Ken Stabler | QB | 6'3" | 210 | 37 | | |
| Dave Wilson | QB | 6'3" | 210 | 24 | | 6 |
| Cliff Austin | HB | 6' | 190 | 23 | | |
| George Rogers | HB | 6'2" | 229 | 24 | | 30 |
| Jimmy Rogers | HB | 5'10" | 190 | 28 | | |
| Hokie Gajan | FB | 5'11" | 220 | 23 | | 24 |
| Tim Wilson | FB | 6'3" | 235 | 29 | | |
| Wayne Wilson | FB | 6'3" | 220 | 25 | | 66 |
| Kenny Duckett | WR | 6' | 187 | 23 | | 12 |
| Eugene Goodlow | WR | 6'2" | 190 | 24 | | 12 |
| Jeff Groth | WR | 5'10" | 175 | 26 | | 6 |
| Rich Mauti | WR | 6' | 195 | 29 | | |
| Lindsay Scott | WR | 6'1" | 190 | 22 | | |
| Tyrone Young | WR | 6'6" | 190 | 23 | | 18 |
| Hoby Brenner | TE | 6'4" | 240 | 24 | | 18 |
| Larry Hardy | TE | 6'3" | 230 | 27 | | |
| Greg Knafelc | TE | 6'4" | 220 | 24 | | |
| John Tice | TE | 6'5" | 242 | 23 | | 6 |
| Morten Andersen | K | 6'2" | 200 | 23 | | 91 |
| Russell Erxleben | K | 6'4" | 221 | 26 | | |

Ken Bordelon - Achilles Tendon Injury
John Krimm - Knee Injury

## ATLANTA FALCONS 7-9-0 Dan Henning

| Scores of Each Game | | |
|---|---|---|
| 20 | Chicago | 17 |
| 13 | N.Y. GIANTS | *16 |
| 30 | Detroit | 14 |
| 20 | San Francisco | 24 |
| 24 | PHILADELPHIA | 28 |
| 17 | NEW ORLEANS | 19 |
| 21 | L.A. Rams | 27 |
| 27 | N.Y. Jets | 21 |
| 24 | NEW ENGLAND | 27 |
| 10 | New Orleans | 27 |
| 13 | L.A. RAMS | 36 |
| 28 | SAN FRANCISCO | 24 |
| 47 | GREEN BAY | *41 |
| 21 | Washington | 37 |
| 24 | Miami | 31 |
| 31 | BUFFALO | 14 |

| Use Name | Pos. | Hgt | Wgt | Age | Int | Pts |
|---|---|---|---|---|---|---|
| Warren Bryant | OT | 6'6" | 270 | 27 | | |
| Mike Kenn | OT | 6'7" | 255 | 27 | | |
| Brett Miller | OT | 6'7" | 275 | 24 | | |
| Eric Sanders | OT | 6'7" | 270 | 24 | | |
| Dan Dufour | OG | 6'5" | 280 | 22 | | |
| Ronnie Lee | OG | 6'3" | 260 | 26 | | |
| R.C. Theilemann | OG | 6'4" | 252 | 28 | | |
| John Scully | C | 6'6" | 255 | 25 | | |
| Jeff Van Note | C | 6'2" | 250 | 37 | | |
| Jeff Merrow | DE | 6'4" | 255 | 30 | | |
| Mike Pitts | DE | 6'5" | 260 | 22 | | |
| Jeff Yeates | DE | 6'3" | 252 | 32 | | |
| Dan Benish | DT | 6'5" | 265 | 21 | | |
| Andrew Provence | DT | 6'3" | 265 | 22 | | |
| Don Smith | DT | 6'5" | 260 | 26 | | |
| Mike Zele | DT | 6'3" | 250 | 27 | | |
| Buddy Curry | LB | 6'4" | 228 | 25 | | |
| Rich Dixon | LB | 6'2" | 235 | 24 | | |
| David Frye | LB | 6'2" | 213 | 22 | | |
| John Harper | LB | 6'3" | 230 | 23 | | |
| Fulton Kuykendall | LB | 6'5" | 228 | 30 | | |
| Dave Levenick | LB | 6'3" | 220 | 24 | | |
| John Rade | LB | 6'1" | 220 | 23 | | 6 |
| Al Richardson | LB | 6'2" | 206 | 25 | 1 | |
| James Britt | DB | 6' | 185 | 22 | | |
| Bobby Butler | DB | 5'11" | 175 | 23 | 4 | |
| Blane Gaison | DB | 6' | 188 | 25 | | 6 |
| Bob Glazebrook | DB | 6'1" | 200 | 27 | 3 | |
| Steve Haworth | DB | 5'11" | 190 | 21 | | |
| Kenny Johnson | DB | 5'10" | 176 | 25 | 2 | 12 |
| Earl Jones | DB | 6' | 175 | 26 | 1 | |
| Tom Pridemore | DB | 5'10" | 186 | 27 | 4 | |
| Tom Tutson | DB | 6'1" | 180 | 25 | | |
| Steve Bartkowski | QB | 6'4" | 218 | 30 | | 6 |
| Mike Moroski | QB | 6'4" | 200 | 25 | | |
| Lynn Cain | HB | 6'1" | 205 | 27 | | 6 |
| Richard Williams | HB | 6' | 205 | 23 | | |
| William Andrews | FB | 6' | 213 | 27 | | 6 |
| Reggie Brown | FB | 5'11" | 211 | 23 | | |
| Gerald Riggs | FB | 6'1" | 230 | 22 | | 48 |
| Bo Robinson | FB | 6'2" | 235 | 27 | | |
| Stacey Bailey | WR | 6' | 160 | 23 | | 36 |
| Willie Curran | WR | 5'10" | 175 | 23 | | |
| Floyd Hodge | WR | 6' | 190 | 24 | | 24 |
| Alfred Jackson | WR | 5'11" | 185 | 28 | | 18 |
| Alfred Jenkins | WR | 5'10" | 155 | 31 | | 6 |
| Billy Johnson | WR | 5'9" | 170 | 31 | | 30 |
| Arthur Cox | TE | 6'2" | 245 | 22 | | 6 |
| Allama Matthews | TE | 6'2" | 230 | 22 | | |
| Junior Miller | TE | 6'4" | 240 | 25 | | |
| Ben Young | TE | 6'4" | 225 | 23 | | 6 |
| Ralph Giacomarro | K | 6'1" | 190 | 22 | | |
| Mick Luckhurst | K | 6' | 180 | 25 | | 94 |
| Dave Smigelsky | K | 5'11" | 180 | 24 | | |

Russ Mikeska - Arch Injury
Neal Musser - Elbow Injury

* Overtime

## SAN FRANCISCO FORTY-NINERS

### RUSHING

| Last Name | No. | Yds | Avg | TD |
|---|---|---|---|---|
| Tyler | 176 | 856 | 4.9 | 4 |
| Craig | 176 | 725 | 4.1 | 8 |
| Montana | 61 | 284 | 4.7 | 2 |
| Ring | 64 | 254 | 4.0 | 2 |
| Moore | 15 | 43 | 2.9 | 1 |
| Orosz | 2 | 39 | 19.5 | 0 |
| Monroe | 10 | 23 | 2.3 | 0 |
| D. Clark | 3 | 18 | 6.0 | 0 |
| Cavanaugh | 1 | 8 | 8.0 | 0 |
| Ramson | 1 | 3 | 3.0 | 0 |
| Solomon | 1 | 3 | 3.0 | 0 |
| Benjamin | 1 | 1 | 1.0 | 0 |

### RECEIVING

| Last Name | No. | Yds | Avg | TD |
|---|---|---|---|---|
| D. Clark | 70 | 840 | 12.0 | 8 |
| Craig | 48 | 427 | 8.9 | 4 |
| Tyler | 34 | 285 | 8.4 | 2 |
| Francis | 33 | 357 | 10.8 | 4 |
| Solomon | 31 | 662 | 21.4 | 4 |
| Wilson | 30 | 433 | 14.4 | 0 |
| Ring | 23 | 182 | 7.9 | 0 |
| Moore | 19 | 206 | 10.8 | 0 |
| Nehemiah | 17 | 236 | 13.9 | 1 |
| Ramson | 17 | 125 | 7.4 | 1 |
| Cooper | 15 | 207 | 13.8 | 3 |
| Monroe | 2 | 61 | 30.5 | 0 |

### PUNT RETURNS

| Last Name | No. | Yds | Avg | TD |
|---|---|---|---|---|
| McLemore | 30 | 331 | 10.7 | 1 |
| Solomon | 5 | 34 | 6.8 | 0 |

### KICKOFF RETURNS

| Last Name | No. | Yds | Avg | TD |
|---|---|---|---|---|
| McLemore | 30 | 576 | 19.2 | 0 |
| Monroe | 8 | 152 | 19.0 | 0 |
| Moore | 7 | 117 | 16.7 | 0 |
| Ring | 4 | 68 | 17.0 | 0 |
| Cooper | 3 | 45 | 15.0 | 0 |

### PASSING — PUNTING — KICKING

**PASSING**

| Last Name | Att | Cmp | % | Yds | Yd/Att | TD | Int— | % | RK |
|---|---|---|---|---|---|---|---|---|---|
| Montana | 515 | 332 | 65 | 3910 | 7.59 | 26 | 12— | 2 | 3 |
| Benjamin | 12 | 7 | 58 | 111 | 9.25 | 1 | 0— | 0 | |
| D. Clark | 1 | 0 | 0 | 0 | 0.00 | 0 | 0— | 0 | |

**PUNTING**

| Last Name | No. | Avg. |
|---|---|---|
| Orosz | 65 | 39.3 |

**KICKING**

| Last Name | XP | Att | % | FG | Att | % |
|---|---|---|---|---|---|---|
| Wersching | 51 | 51 | 100 | 25 | 30 | 83 |

## LOS ANGELES RAMS

### RUSHING

| Last Name | No. | Yds | Avg | TD |
|---|---|---|---|---|
| Dickerson | 390 | 1808 | 4.6 | 18 |
| Redden | 75 | 372 | 5.0 | 2 |
| Guman | 7 | 42 | 6.0 | 0 |
| Alexander | 7 | 28 | 4.0 | 0 |
| Ferragamo | 22 | 17 | 0.8 | 0 |
| Ellard | 3 | 7 | 2.3 | 0 |
| Cromwell | 1 | 0 | 0.0 | 0 |
| Kemp | 3 | -2 | -0.7 | 0 |
| Farmer | 1 | -9 | -9.0 | 0 |
| Grant | 2 | -10 | -5.0 | 0 |

### RECEIVING

| Last Name | No. | Yds | Avg | TD |
|---|---|---|---|---|
| Barber | 55 | 657 | 11.9 | 3 |
| Dickerson | 51 | 404 | 7.9 | 2 |
| Farmer | 40 | 556 | 13.9 | 5 |
| Guman | 34 | 347 | 10.2 | 4 |
| Dennard | 33 | 465 | 14.1 | 5 |
| Da. Hill | 28 | 280 | 10.0 | 2 |
| Ellard | 16 | 268 | 16.8 | 0 |
| Grant | 12 | 221 | 18.4 | 1 |
| G. Jones | 11 | 172 | 15.6 | 0 |
| Redden | 4 | 30 | 7.5 | 0 |
| Alexander | 1 | 10 | 10.0 | 0 |
| McDonald | 1 | 1 | 1.0 | 1 |

### PUNT RETURNS

| Last Name | No. | Yds | Avg | TD |
|---|---|---|---|---|
| Ellard | 16 | 217 | 13.6 | 1 |
| Irvin | 25 | 212 | 8.5 | 0 |
| Johnson | 14 | 109 | 7.8 | 0 |

### KICKOFF RETURNS

| Last Name | No. | Yds | Avg | TD |
|---|---|---|---|---|
| Redden | 19 | 358 | 18.8 | 0 |
| Ellard | 15 | 314 | 20.9 | 0 |
| Alexander | 13 | 222 | 17.1 | 0 |
| Guman | 2 | 30 | 15.0 | 0 |
| Barnett | 1 | 0 | 0.0 | 0 |
| Irvin | 1 | 22 | 22.0 | 0 |

### PASSING — PUNTING — KICKING

**PASSING**

| Last Name | Att | Cmp | % | Yds | Yd/Att | TD | Int— | % | RK |
|---|---|---|---|---|---|---|---|---|---|
| Ferragamo | 464 | 274 | 59 | 3276 | 7.06 | 22 | 23— | 5 | 8 |
| Kemp | 25 | 12 | 48 | 135 | 5.40 | 1 | 0— | 0 | |

**PUNTING**

| Last Name | No. | Avg. |
|---|---|---|
| Misko | 82 | 40.3 |

**KICKING**

| Last Name | XP | Att | % | FG | Att | % |
|---|---|---|---|---|---|---|
| Nelson | 33 | 37 | 89 | 5 | 11 | 45 |
| Lansford | 9 | 9 | 100 | 6 | 9 | 67 |

## NEW ORLEANS SAINTS

### RUSHING

| Last Name | No. | Yds | Avg | TD |
|---|---|---|---|---|
| G. Rogers | 256 | 1144 | 4.5 | 5 |
| W. Wilson | 199 | 787 | 4.0 | 9 |
| Gajan | 81 | 415 | 5.1 | 4 |
| J. Rogers | 26 | 80 | 3.1 | 0 |
| T. Wilson | 8 | 21 | 2.6 | 0 |
| Austin | 4 | 16 | 4.0 | 0 |
| Merkens | 1 | 16 | 16.0 | 0 |
| Groth | 1 | 15 | 15.0 | 0 |
| Goodlow | 1 | 3 | 3.0 | 0 |
| D. Wilson | 5 | 3 | 0.6 | 0 |
| Erxleben | 2 | -9 | -4.5 | 0 |
| Stabler | 9 | -14 | -1.6 | 0 |
| Duckett | 2 | -16 | -8.0 | 0 |

### RECEIVING

| Last Name | No. | Yds | Avg | TD |
|---|---|---|---|---|
| Groth | 49 | 585 | 11.9 | 1 |
| Brenner | 41 | 574 | 14.0 | 3 |
| Goodlow | 41 | 487 | 11.9 | 2 |
| Scott | 24 | 274 | 11.4 | 0 |
| W. Wilson | 20 | 178 | 8.9 | 2 |
| Duckett | 19 | 283 | 14.9 | 2 |
| Gajan | 17 | 130 | 7.6 | 0 |
| G. Rogers | 12 | 69 | 5.8 | 0 |
| Young | 7 | 85 | 12.1 | 3 |
| Tice | 7 | 33 | 4.7 | 1 |
| Mauti | 2 | 30 | 15.0 | 0 |
| Hardy | 2 | 29 | 14.5 | 0 |
| Austin | 2 | 25 | 12.5 | 0 |

### PUNT RETURNS

| Last Name | No. | Yds | Avg | TD |
|---|---|---|---|---|
| Groth | 39 | 275 | 7.1 | 0 |

### KICKOFF RETURNS

| Last Name | No. | Yds | Avg | TD |
|---|---|---|---|---|
| Duckett | 33 | 719 | 21.8 | 0 |
| W. Wilson | 9 | 239 | 26.6 | 0 |
| Mauti | 8 | 147 | 18.4 | 0 |
| Austin | 7 | 112 | 16.0 | 0 |
| J. Rogers | 7 | 103 | 14.7 | 0 |
| Brock | 1 | 15 | 15.0 | 0 |
| Wattelet | 1 | 4 | 4.0 | 0 |

### PASSING — PUNTING — KICKING

**PASSING**

| Last Name | Att | Cmp | % | Yds | Yd/Att | TD | Int— | % | RK |
|---|---|---|---|---|---|---|---|---|---|
| Stabler | 311 | 176 | 57 | 1988 | 6.39 | 9 | 18— | 6 | 13 |
| D. Wilson | 112 | 66 | 59 | 770 | 6.88 | 5 | 7— | 6 | |
| Erxleben | 1 | 1 | 100 | 24 | 24.00 | 0 | 0— | 0 | |
| Gajan | 1 | 0 | 0 | 0 | 0.00 | 0 | 0— | 0 | |

**PUNTING**

| Last Name | No. | Avg. |
|---|---|---|
| Erxleben | 74 | 41.0 |
| Merkens | 4 | 36.0 |

**KICKING**

| Last Name | XP | Att | % | FG | Att | % |
|---|---|---|---|---|---|---|
| Andersen | 37 | 38 | 97 | 18 | 24 | 75 |

## ATLANTA FALCONS

### RUSHING

| Last Name | No. | Yds | Avg | TD |
|---|---|---|---|---|
| Andrews | 331 | 1567 | 4.7 | 7 |
| Riggs | 100 | 437 | 4.4 | 8 |
| B. Johnson | 15 | 83 | 5.5 | 0 |
| Cain | 19 | 63 | 3.3 | 1 |
| Bartkowski | 16 | 38 | 2.4 | 1 |
| Giacomarro | 2 | 13 | 6.5 | 0 |
| Moroski | 2 | 12 | 6.0 | 0 |
| Robinson | 3 | 9 | 3.0 | 0 |
| Williams | 1 | 5 | 5.0 | 5 |
| Miller | 1 | 2 | 2.0 | 0 |
| Bailey | 2 | -5 | -2.5 | 0 |

### RECEIVING

| Last Name | No. | Yds | Avg | TD |
|---|---|---|---|---|
| B. Johnson | 64 | 709 | 11.1 | 4 |
| Andrews | 59 | 609 | 10.3 | 4 |
| Bailey | 55 | 881 | 16.0 | 6 |
| Jenkins | 38 | 487 | 12.8 | 1 |
| Hodge | 25 | 280 | 11.2 | 4 |
| Riggs | 17 | 149 | 8.8 | 0 |
| Miller | 16 | 125 | 7.8 | 0 |
| Jackson | 13 | 220 | 16.9 | 3 |
| Robinson | 12 | 100 | 8.3 | 0 |
| Cox | 9 | 83 | 9.2 | 1 |
| Young | 6 | 74 | 12.3 | 1 |
| Mathews | 3 | 37 | 12.3 | 0 |
| Cain | 3 | 24 | 8.0 | 0 |
| Curran | 1 | 15 | 15.0 | 0 |

### PUNT RETURNS

| Last Name | No. | Yds | Avg | TD |
|---|---|---|---|---|
| B. Johnson | 46 | 489 | 10.6 | 1 |

### KICKOFF RETURNS

| Last Name | No. | Yds | Avg | TD |
|---|---|---|---|---|
| K. Johnson | 11 | 224 | 20.4 | 0 |
| Williams | 23 | 461 | 20.0 | 0 |
| Riggs | 17 | 330 | 19.4 | 0 |
| Cain | 11 | 200 | 18.2 | 0 |
| Butler | 1 | 17 | 17.0 | 0 |
| Curran | 2 | 26 | 13.0 | 0 |
| Glazebrook | 2 | 0 | 0.0 | 0 |

### PASSING — PUNTING — KICKING

**PASSING**

| Last Name | Att | Cmp | % | Yds | Yd/Att | TD | Int— | % | RK |
|---|---|---|---|---|---|---|---|---|---|
| Bartkowski | 432 | 274 | 63 | 3167 | 7.33 | 22 | 5— | 1 | 1 |
| Moroski | 70 | 45 | 64 | 575 | 8.12 | 2 | 4— | 6 | |
| Hodge | 2 | 1 | 50 | 28 | 14.00 | 0 | 1— | 50 | |
| Andrews | 1 | 0 | 0 | 0 | 0.00 | 0 | 0— | 0 | |
| Giacomarro | 1 | 1 | 100 | 23 | 23.00 | 0 | 0— | 0 | |
| B. Johnson | 1 | 0 | 0 | 0 | 0.00 | 0 | 0— | 0 | |

**PUNTING**

| Last Name | No. | Avg. |
|---|---|---|
| Giacomarro | 70 | 40.3 |

**KICKING**

| Last Name | XP | Att | % | FG | Att | % |
|---|---|---|---|---|---|---|
| Luckhurst | 43 | 45 | 96 | 17 | 22 | 77 |

# 1983 A.F.C.   Another New League

A new competitor with a novel idea challenged the N.F.L. for a share of the pro football market. The United States Football League broke new ground by playing from March to July, hoping to cash in on the American public's insatiable appetite for football. Aside from its scheduling novelty, the U.S.F.L. looked like any other new league with big-time aspirations. Teams took the field in Boston, New Jersey, Philadelphia, Washington, Tampa Bay, Birmingham, Michigan, Chicago, Denver, Arizona, Los Angeles and Oakland, manned mostly by anonymous rookies and N.F.L. castoffs. The league did sign a group of well-known college stars, mostly in the offensive skill positions. The most famous was Heisman Trophy winner Herschel Walker, who passed up his senior year at Georgia to carry the ball for the New Jersey Generals for $5 million over three years. Although not nearly as well-paid, Kelvin Bryant ran just as well for the Philadelphia Stars and led them into the title game against the Michigan Panthers. With quarterback Bobby Hebert, receiver Anthony Carter and linebacker John Corker in the fore, the Panthers captured their first U.S.F.L. title 24-22 before 50,906 fans in Denver. Despite a TV contract with ABC, most U.S.F.L. teams lost money and played before small crowds.

## EASTERN DIVISION

**Miami Dolphins** — The Miami offense worried coach Don Shula in the early going. Jimmy Cefalo went out with a knee injury on opening day and David Woodley had little success moving the team. On September 19, Shula sent first draft pick Dan Marino into the game in relief of Woodley. Despite Marino's two TD passes, the Dolphins lost 27-14 to the Raiders. On October 2, Marino again relieved in a 17-7 loss to the Saints. The next week, Marino started and threw three TD passes, but the Dolphins dropped to 3-3 by losing 38-35 to Buffalo in overtime. From then on, the Dolphins won nine of 10 games as Marino singed enemy defenses with his quick release. Mark Duper broke into the lineup as Marino's favorite receiver. Star linemen Ed Newman, Eric Laakso and Dwight Stephenson gave the freshman quarterback time to learn without heavy pressure. Complementing the reborn offense was the swarming Killer Bee defense. Linemen Doug Betters and Bob Baumhower starred in a unit which emphasized ensemble team play.

**New England Patriots** — A maddening inconsistency sentenced the Patriots to an early winter vacation. After losing their first two games, they then whipped the Jets and Steelers to even their mark. The Patriots played almost perfectly in beating Buffalo 31-0 on October 23. After beating the Dolphins 17-6 on November 13, they turned around and lost 30-0 to the Browns and 26-3 to the Jets. Victories over the Saints and Rams put the playoffs within grasp. New England squared off against the Seahawks on December 18 with one playoff berth available; Seattle won 24-6 and ended the Patriots' hopes. Despite Tony Collins' fine running and the sure blocking of John Hannah and Brian Holloway, the offense sputtered because of a weak passing game. Rookie QB Tony Eason started the final four games after an injury sidelined Steve Grogan. A broken leg kept defensive end Kenneth Sims under wraps for the first 11 games, but the defense nevertheless played well.

**Buffalo Bills** — The Bills went into the season with a new coach and a lame-duck star. Kay Stephenson replaced Chuck Knox at the helm and structured his offense around running back Joe Cribbs. Already signed by the U.S.F.L. for the 1984 season, Cribbs gave the Bills all-out running in his final Buffalo season. The Bills won three of their first four games and entered the stretch run at 7-4, hot in pursuit of a playoff spot. A close 27-24 loss to the Raiders was followed by a 41-17 pommeling by the Rams. After eking out a 14-9 victory at Kansas City, the Bills lost to the 49ers and Falcons to sag out of contention. While Cribbs was the offensive ace, the defense relied most heavily on nose tackle Fred Smerlas and safety Steve Freeman.

**Baltimore Colts** — First draft pick John Elway flatly refused to sign with the Colts anf forced a pre-season trade with Denver. Baltimore's anger faded when the Colts won their opener on a fumble return in overtime, then swept to victory in four of their first six games. A five-game losing streak would kill the surprise playoff bid, but the Colts still finished better than expected. Rookie guard Chris Hinton, part of the Elway trade,

starred from day one and helped rushers Curtis Dickey and Randy McMillan to impressive seasons. Rookie linebacker Vernon Maxwell gave the offense a shot of verve. Elway faced the Colts twice. He was unimpressive in a 17-10 Denver victory on September 11, but threw for three fourth-quarter touchdowns in a 21-19 victory on December 11. In eight home games, the attendance broke 40,000 only twice, with the final two games drawing crowds of under 30,000. Team owner Robert Irsay reacted with threats to take the Colts out of Baltimore.

**New York Jets** — Joe Walton stepped up to the top job when Walt Michaels resigned after last year's playoffs. The tough contenders of 1982 turned into inconsistent also-rans under Walton. After beating the Chargers on opening day, the Jets played without character and fell to a 4-7 record by late November. In a long-shot bid for a playoff berth, they swept the Saints, Patriots and Colts before collapsing in the final two losses. Blame for the offensive failure could be put on an injury to Freeman McNeil and on Richard Todd's mediocre season. Darrell Ray's slump hurt the defense. Also hurting morale was the announcement that the team would move to Giants Stadium next year, leaving the crowd at Shea Stadium in a surly mood.

## CENTRAL DIVISION

**Pittsburgh Steelers** — The old pros were getting scarce. Lynn Swann and Jack Ham had retired, John Stallworth missed 12 games with a hamstring injury, and Terry Bradshaw sat out all but 30 minutes of the season with a bad elbow. In addition, a group of veteran reserves jumped to the U.S.F.L. The mixture of new and old Steelers reeled off seven straight victories in mid-season to ensure a playoff spot. Franco Harris churned out 1,000 yards with his 33-year-old body running behind a line led by veteran Mike Webster. New faces manned the passing game with less success than the oldsters. Cliff Stoudt couldn't fill Bradshaw's shoes and became the target for jeers in Three Rivers Stadium. The defense stayed strong, with Jack Lambert in his usual leading role. The Steelers uncharacteristically stumbled late in the year, losing four of their last five games. Most embarrassing was a 45-3 loss in Detroit before a national TV audience on Thanksgiving Day.

**Cleveland Browns** — Splitting their first 10 games, the Browns launched a late bid for a wild-card playoff spot. They began with consecutive shutouts of Tampa Bay and New England, then trounced Baltimore 41-23. The momentum screeched to a halt, however, with losses to Denver and Houston. In the finale, Brian Sipe tossed four touchdown passes to beat the Steelers 30-17, not enough for a prized post-season bid. Sipe ended his Cleveland career with that game by signing a contract with the New Jersey Generals of the U.S.F.L. His chief offensive aide this year was fullback Mike Pruitt, while linebackers Chip Banks, Tom Cousineau and Clay Matthews formed the heart of the defense.

**Cincinnati Bengals** — Personnel woes savaged the team's morale from the start of training camp. The league suspended Pete Johnson and Ross Browner for the first four games for drug usage. The U.S.F.L. snatched away offensive coordinator Lindy Infante, while star receivers Cris Collinsworth and Dan Ross came to camp committed to the U.S.F.L. in the future. The Bengals lost their first three games and six of their first seven to skid completely out of the playoff picture. With Ken Anderson out for three games in mid-season, Turk Schonert quarterbacked the team to its first consecutive victories of the year. Anderson took over when healthy and engineered a 55-14 thrashing of the Oilers. The early disaster faded as the Bengals won six of their last nine games. Although the offense improved with time, the Cincinnati defense carried the team most of the year. Cornerback Ken Riley capped his long career with a terrific final season. Also leaving town would be coach Forrest Gregg, who headed north to Green Bay for 1984.

**Houston Oilers** — The bad times kept rolling for the Oilers. They lost their first 10 games, running their losing streak to 17 over two seasons. Ed Biles lost his job as head coach in the flood of losses and was replaced by assistant Chuck Studley. Things might have gone differently had the Oilers beaten Green Bay on opening day rather than losing in overtime. Three

**OFFENSE**

| | BALT. | BUFF. | CIN. | CLEV. | DENV. | HOU. | K.C. | RAID. | MIA. | N.E. | NY.J. | PIT. | S.D. | SEA. |
|---|---|---|---|---|---|---|---|---|---|---|---|---|---|---|
| FIRST DOWNS: | | | | | | | | | | | | | | |
| Total | 272 | 309 | 327 | 327 | 292 | 295 | 314 | 356 | 314 | 284 | 313 | 312 | 361 | 300 |
| by Rushing | 146 | 100 | 127 | 113 | 99 | 120 | 83 | 143 | 132 | 130 | 126 | 156 | 106 | 131 |
| by Passing | 110 | 171 | 179 | 186 | 155 | 155 | 208 | 181 | 151 | 138 | 171 | 141 | 230 | 153 |
| by Penalty | 16 | 38 | 21 | 28 | 38 | 20 | 23 | 32 | 31 | 16 | 16 | 15 | 25 | 16 |
| RUSHING: | | | | | | | | | | | | | | |
| Number | 601 | 415 | 542 | 465 | 471 | 502 | 387 | 542 | 568 | 538 | 474 | 614 | 423 | 546 |
| Yards | 2695 | 1736 | 2104 | 1922 | 1784 | 1998 | 1254 | 2240 | 2150 | 2605 | 2068 | 2610 | 1536 | 2119 |
| Average Yards | 4.5 | 4.2 | 3.9 | 4.1 | 3.8 | 4.0 | 3.2 | 4.1 | 3.8 | 4.8 | 4.4 | 4.3 | 3.6 | 3.9 |
| Touchdowns | 10 | 4 | 24 | 13 | 15 | 16 | 13 | 18 | 16 | 19 | 11 | 17 | 16 | 19 |
| PASSING: | | | | | | | | | | | | | | |
| Attempts | 377 | 571 | 454 | 567 | 499 | 482 | 641 | 504 | 442 | 412 | 559 | 409 | 635 | 449 |
| Completions | 188 | 317 | 290 | 324 | 254 | 260 | 369 | 301 | 254 | 220 | 330 | 211 | 369 | 251 |
| Completion Pct. | 49.9 | 55.5 | 63.9 | 57.1 | 50.9 | 53.9 | 57.6 | 59.7 | 57.5 | 53.3 | 59.0 | 51.6 | 58.1 | 55.9 |
| Passing Yards | 2663 | 3438 | 3492 | 3932 | 3466 | 3286 | 4684 | 3910 | 3235 | 3040 | 3742 | 2754 | 4891 | 3316 |
| Avg. Yds per Att. | 5.5 | 5.1 | 6.4 | 6.1 | 5.5 | 6.8 | 6.3 | 6.2 | 6.6 | 7.4 | 5.7 | 5.2 | 7.0 | 6.0 |
| Avg. Yds per Comp. | 14.2 | 10.9 | 12.0 | 12.1 | 13.7 | 12.6 | 12.7 | 13.0 | 12.7 | 13.8 | 11.3 | 13.1 | 13.3 | 13.2 |
| Times Tackled | 47 | 37 | 40 | 33 | 55 | 49 | 46 | 55 | 23 | 45 | 43 | 52 | 28 | 47 |
| Yds Lost Tackled | 340 | 351 | 309 | 271 | 439 | 384 | 343 | 464 | 190 | 334 | 317 | 350 | 230 | 343 |
| Net Yards | 2323 | 3087 | 3183 | 3661 | 3027 | 2902 | 4341 | 3446 | 3045 | 2706 | 3425 | 2404 | 4661 | 2973 |
| Touchdowns | 12 | 30 | 14 | 27 | 17 | 16 | 29 | 31 | 28 | 16 | 21 | 15 | 27 | 25 |
| Interceptions | 22 | 28 | 18 | 28 | 22 | 29 | 19 | 24 | 11 | 18 | 28 | 23 | 33 | 18 |
| Pct. Intercepted | 5.8 | 4.9 | 4.0 | 4.9 | 4.4 | 6.0 | 3.0 | 4.8 | 2.5 | 4.4 | 5.0 | 5.6 | 5.2 | 4.0 |
| PUNTS: | | | | | | | | | | | | | | |
| Number | 91 | 89 | 69 | 70 | 87 | 80 | 93 | 78 | 75 | 81 | 82 | 80 | 63 | 79 |
| Average | 45.3 | 39.7 | 40.6 | 40.8 | 41.6 | 39.2 | 39.9 | 42.8 | 42.5 | 44.6 | 39.2 | 41.9 | 43.9 | 39.5 |
| PUNT RETURNS | | | | | | | | | | | | | | |
| Number | 44 | 44 | 49 | 42 | 38 | 20 | 40 | 58 | 55 | 44 | 38 | 51 | 33 | 34 |
| Yards | 294 | 241 | 410 | 310 | 420 | 159 | 291 | 666 | 581 | 399 | 420 | 421 | 213 | 366 |
| Average Yards | 6.7 | 5.5 | 8.4 | 7.4 | 11.1 | 8.0 | 7.3 | 11.5 | 10.6 | 9.1 | 11.1 | 8.3 | 6.5 | 10.8 |
| Touchdowns | 0 | 0 | 0 | 0 | 1 | 0 | 0 | 1 | 1 | 0 | 1 | 0 | 0 | 1 |
| KICKOFF RET.: | | | | | | | | | | | | | | |
| Number | 62 | 64 | 54 | 63 | 56 | 83 | 54 | 61 | 47 | 57 | 66 | 59 | 74 | 71 |
| Yards | 1198 | 1363 | 1097 | 1290 | 1077 | 1676 | 929 | 1175 | 1085 | 1155 | 1375 | 1068 | 1377 | 1575 |
| Average Yards | 19.3 | 21.3 | 20.3 | 20.5 | 19.2 | 20.2 | 17.2 | 19.3 | 23.1 | 20.3 | 20.8 | 18.1 | 18.6 | 22.2 |
| Touchdowns | 0 | 0 | 0 | 0 | 0 | 2 | 0 | 0 | 0 | 0 | 0 | 0 | 0 | 1 |
| INTERCEPT RET.: | | | | | | | | | | | | | | |
| Number | 20 | 13 | 23 | 22 | 27 | 14 | 30 | 20 | 26 | 17 | 22 | 28 | 16 | 26 |
| Yards | 314 | 154 | 369 | 296 | 355 | 135 | 482 | 238 | 345 | 202 | 342 | 435 | 153 | 363 |
| Average Yards | 15.7 | 11.8 | 16.0 | 13.5 | 13.1 | 9.6 | 16.1 | 11.9 | 13.3 | 11.9 | 15.5 | 15.5 | 9.6 | 14.0 |
| Touchdowns | 1 | 1 | 4 | 2 | 0 | 0 | 2 | 2 | 3 | 1 | 3 | 4 | 1 | 2 |
| PENALTIES: | | | | | | | | | | | | | | |
| Number | 120 | 144 | 99 | 115 | 100 | 84 | 113 | 121 | 64 | 90 | 110 | 99 | 115 | 102 |
| Yards | 986 | 1094 | 837 | 991 | 804 | 784 | 911 | 992 | 567 | 815 | 1059 | 836 | 961 | 890 |
| FUMBLES: | | | | | | | | | | | | | | |
| Number | 32 | 24 | 35 | 21 | 34 | 26 | 31 | 46 | 30 | 47 | 29 | 42 | 42 | 36 |
| Number Lost | 11 | 12 | 15 | 10 | 19 | 18 | 19 | 25 | 16 | 20 | 19 | 20 | 22 | 20 |
| POINTS: | | | | | | | | | | | | | | |
| Total | 264 | 283 | 346 | 356 | 302 | 288 | 386 | 442 | 389 | 274 | 313 | 355 | 358 | 403 |
| PAT Attempts | 24 | 36 | 43 | 40 | 34 | 34 | 45 | 54 | 48 | 36 | 38 | 39 | 45 | 50 |
| PAT Made | 22 | 34 | 40 | 38 | 33 | 33 | 44 | 51 | 45 | 31 | 37 | 38 | 43 | 49 |
| FG Attempts | 35 | 26 | 23 | 25 | 25 | 21 | 30 | 27 | 27 | 22 | 24 | 31 | 24 | 25 |
| FG Made | 30 | 11 | 16 | 22 | 21 | 17 | 24 | 21 | 18 | 9 | 16 | 27 | 15 | 18 |
| Percent FG Made | 85.7 | 42.3 | 69.6 | 88.0 | 84.0 | 81.0 | 80.0 | 77.8 | 66.7 | 40.9 | 66.7 | 87.1 | 62.5 | 72.0 |
| Safeties | 1 | 0 | 0 | 0 | 1 | 0 | 0 | 2 | 1 | 0 | 0 | 1 | 0 | 0 |

**DEFENSE**

| | BALT. | BUFF. | CIN. | CLEV. | DENV. | HOU. | K.C. | RAID. | MIA. | N.E. | NY.J. | PIT. | S.D. | SEA. |
|---|---|---|---|---|---|---|---|---|---|---|---|---|---|---|
| FIRST DOWNS: | | | | | | | | | | | | | | |
| Total | 321 | 332 | 276 | 309 | 321 | 332 | 319 | 285 | 288 | 326 | 298 | 278 | 347 | 351 |
| by Rushing | 123 | 148 | 96 | 138 | 119 | 161 | 136 | 86 | 122 | 129 | 126 | 100 | 137 | 128 |
| by Passing | 166148 | 156 | 155 | 185 | 150 | 158 | 170 | 147 | 172 | 151 | 151 | 187 | 195 | |
| by Penalty | 32 | 36 | 24 | 16 | 17 | 21 | 25 | 29 | 19 | 25 | 21 | 27 | 23 | 28 |
| RUSHING: | | | | | | | | | | | | | | |
| Number | 516 | 566 | 430 | 528 | 509 | 576 | 554 | 436 | 460 | 549 | 547 | 509 | 552 | 511 |
| Yards | 2118 | 2503 | 1499 | 2065 | 1938 | 2787 | 2275 | 1586 | 2037 | 2281 | 2378 | 1833 | 2173 | 2198 |
| Average Yards | 4.1 | 4.4 | 3.5 | 3.9 | 3.8 | 4.8 | 4.1 | 3.6 | 4.4 | 4.2 | 4.3 | 3.6 | 3.9 | 4.3 |
| Touchdowns | 13 | 14 | 16 | 15 | 14 | 23 | 18 | 13 | 11 | 9 | 13 | 14 | 26 | 14 |
| PASSING: | | | | | | | | | | | | | | |
| Attempts | 488 | 480 | 502 | 469 | 552 | 424 | 500 | 531 | 480 | 514 | 463 | 447 | 544 | 521 |
| Completions | 281 | 286 | 268 | 280 | 307 | 252 | 261 | 282 | 277 | 277 | 269 | 238 | 330 | 311 |
| Completion Pct. | 57.6 | 59.6 | 57.4 | 59.7 | 55.6 | 59.4 | 52.2 | 53.1 | 57.7 | 53.9 | 58.1 | 53.2 | 60.7 | 59.7 |
| Passing Yards | 3832 | 3553 | 3163 | 3316 | 3988 | 3095 | 3361 | 3646 | 3365 | 3565 | 3301 | 3260 | 4051 | 4182 |
| Avg. Yds per Att. | 6.7 | 6.5 | 5.2 | 6.1 | 6.2 | 6.3 | 5.8 | 5.4 | 5.7 | 6.0 | 5.7 | 5.8 | 6.6 | 6.8 |
| Avg. Yds per Comp. | 13.6 | 12.4 | 11.0 | 11.8 | 13.0 | 12.3 | 12.9 | 12.9 | 12.2 | 12.9 | 12.3 | 13.7 | 12.3 | 13.5 |
| Times Tackled | 41 | 32 | 41 | 32 | 38 | 31 | 35 | 57 | 49 | 39 | 48 | 50 | 31 | 43 |
| Yds Lost Tackled | 310 | 247 | 335 | 239 | 317 | 250 | 250 | 484 | 363 | 270 | 378 | 361 | 269 | 351 |
| Net Yards | 3522 | 3306 | 2828 | 3077 | 3671 | 2845 | 3111 | 3162 | 3002 | 3295 | 2923 | 2899 | 3782 | 3831 |
| Touchdowns | 31 | 22 | 17 | 22 | 18 | 26 | 21 | 20 | 19 | 19 | 22 | 19 | 28 | 33 |
| Interceptions | 20 | 13 | 23 | 22 | 27 | 14 | 30 | 20 | 26 | 17 | 22 | 28 | 16 | 26 |
| Pct. Intercepted | 4.1 | 2.7 | 4.6 | 4.7 | 4.9 | 3.3 | 6.0 | 3.8 | 5.4 | 3.3 | 4.8 | 6.3 | 2.9 | 5.0 |
| PUNTS: | | | | | | | | | | | | | | |
| Number | 80 | 78 | 76 | 73 | 77 | 65 | 85 | 100 | 90 | 78 | 85 | 88 | 70 | 68 |
| Average | 41.6 | 42.9 | 42.3 | 40.5 | 44.2 | 39.5 | 41.2 | 40.6 | 40.8 | 42.0 | 41.1 | 41.1 | 39.7 | 40.5 |
| PUNT RETURNS | | | | | | | | | | | | | | |
| Number | 55 | 42 | 41 | 30 | 55 | 47 | 54 | 35 | 32 | 48 | 47 | 44 | 35 | 36 |
| Yards | 642 | 403 | 310 | 309 | 524 | 354 | 559 | 334 | 229 | 392 | 367 | 418 | 299 | 185 |
| Average Yards | 11.7 | 9.6 | 7.6 | 10.3 | 9.5 | 7.5 | 10.4 | 9.5 | 7.2 | 8.2 | 7.8 | 9.5 | 8.5 | 5.1 |
| Touchdowns | 1 | 0 | 0 | 0 | 0 | 0 | 1 | 2 | 0 | 0 | 1 | 1 | 0 | 0 |
| KICKOFF RET.: | | | | | | | | | | | | | | |
| Number | 61 | 53 | 68 | 61 | 46 | 61 | 75 | 68 | 54 | 55 | 50 | 65 | 70 | 59 |
| Yards | 1138 | 949 | 1299 | 1155 | 823 | 1280 | 1528 | 1227 | 1024 | 1082 | 1063 | 1507 | 1426 | 952 |
| Average Yards | 18.7 | 17.9 | 19.1 | 18.9 | 12.8 | 21.0 | 20.4 | 18.0 | 19.0 | 19.7 | 21.3 | 23.2 | 20.4 | 16.1 |
| Touchdowns | 0 | 0 | 0 | 1 | 3 | 0 | 0 | 0 | 0 | 0 | 0 | 1 | 0 | 0 |
| INTERCEPT RET.: | | | | | | | | | | | | | | |
| Number | 22 | 28 | 18 | 28 | 22 | 29 | 19 | 24 | 11 | 18 | 28 | 23 | 33 | 18 |
| Yards | 117 | 330 | 298 | 508 | 281 | 392 | 323 | 381 | 203 | 361 | 372 | 252 | 377 | 279 |
| Average Yards | 5.3 | 11.8 | 16.6 | 18.1 | 12.8 | 13.5 | 17.0 | 15.9 | 18.5 | 20.1 | 13.3 | 11.0 | 11.4 | 15.5 |
| Touchdowns | 0 | 2 | 2 | 3 | 3 | 2 | 2 | 0 | 1 | 1 | 3 | 2 | 2 | 1 |
| PENALTIES: | | | | | | | | | | | | | | |
| Number | 82 | 128 | 100 | 105 | 138 | 104 | 105 | 109 | 95 | 84 | 96 | 96 | 111 | 91 |
| Yards | 666 | 1296 | 871 | 940 | 1097 | 825 | 837 | 947 | 837 | 674 | 784 | 782 | 953 | 725 |
| FUMBLES: | | | | | | | | | | | | | | |
| Number | 29 | 32 | 35 | 30 | 46 | 34 | 35 | 31 | 38 | 30 | 29 | 34 | 26 | 44 |
| Number Lost | 16 | 18 | 16 | 10 | 20 | 15 | 21 | 16 | 17 | 19 | 14 | 17 | 17 | 28 |
| POINTS: | | | | | | | | | | | | | | |
| Total | 354 | 351 | 302 | 342 | 327 | 460 | 367 | 338 | 250 | 289 | 331 | 303 | 462 | 397 |
| PAT Attempts | 45 | 39 | 36 | 42 | 36 | 53 | 44 | 40 | 32 | 30 | 39 | 37 | 56 | 48 |
| PAT Made | 42 | 39 | 35 | 40 | 34 | 49 | 43 | 39 | 31 | 29 | 35 | 36 | 54 | 43 |
| FG Attempts | 23 | 39 | 22 | 22 | 33 | 36 | 26 | 25 | 15 | 31 | 28 | 20 | 29 | 26 |
| FG Made | 14 | 26 | 17 | 16 | 25 | 29 | 20 | 19 | 9 | 24 | 20 | 15 | 22 | 20 |
| Percent FG Made | 60.9 | 66.7 | 77.3 | 72.7 | 75.8 | 80.6 | 76.9 | 76.0 | 60.0 | 77.4 | 71.4 | 75.0 | 75.9 | 76.9 |
| Safeties | 0 | 0 | 0 | 1 | 1 | 0 | 0 | 1 | 0 | 1 | 1 | 0 | 0 | 3 |

weeks into the schedule, quarterback Archie Manning and tight end Dave Casper were traded to the Vikings for draft choices, opening the way for younger players. Gifford Nielsen started the next seven losses at quarterback, with Oliver Luck at the helm for the final six games. Luck's tenure produced six victories, aided by a good offensive line, Tim Smith's receiving and Earl Campbell's always strong rushing.

## WESTERN DIVISION

**Los Angeles Raiders** — Coach Tom Flores had top-flight players in almost all areas. Howie Long blossomed into a major force on the defensive line, backed by intense linebackers Ted Hendricks and Rod Martin. Lester Hayes and Vann McElroy ranged far in the secondary, joined by Mike Haynes after a November trade with New England. The offensive line supported Marcus Allen's running and Todd Christensen's clutch receiving. The only serious question mark was at quarterback, where Jim Plunkett started the year. The Raiders won their four September games, but had tough sledding in October. After Plunkett played poorly in a 38-36 loss at Seattle on October 16, Flores made young Marc Wilson the starter. Wilson played well in a victory over Dallas and another loss to Seattle, but he hurt his shoulder in the second half against Kansas City. Plunkett led his mates to victory over the Chiefs and played well as a starter the rest of the year. With six victories in their final seven games, the physical Raiders went into the playoffs at a fine edge.

**Seattle Seahawks** — Chuck Knox brought his winning knack to Seattle. The centerpiece of his offense was rookie Curt Warner, a heavy-duty back who led the A.F.C. in rushing. To support Warner, Knox brought in Charle Young, Reggie McKenzie and Blair Bush from other N.F.L. clubs. Already in place was the passing combination of Jim Zorn and Steve Largent. The Seahawks upset the Raiders 38-36 on October 16 despite Zorn's 4-of-16 passing mark. One week later, the Seahawks generated no offense in the first half, falling behind the Steelers 24-0. Knox put Dave Krieg into the game at quarterback and, despite some rough spots, Krieg ran the offense the rest of the way. In his first start, he took Seattle to another victory over the Raiders. Down the homestretch, the Seahawks won three of their last four, clinching their first-ever playoff berth by swamping New England on the final weekend.

**Denver Broncos** — Billed as the next great N.F.L. quarterback, John Elway needed time to learn his trade. Dan Reeves started Elway for the first five games, often relieving him with Steve DeBerg. DeBerg then started the next five games until dislocating a shoulder. Elway and fellow rookie Gary Kubiak were thrown in and swam, winning three of the final six games to ice a wild-card spot. Despite the quarterback flux, the Broncos improved greatly over last year's squad. Receiver Steve Watson and runner Sammy Winder regularly gained yardage, while the defense was led by two veterans of the old Orange Crush — Randy Gradishar and Louis Wright.

**San Diego Chargers** — The wave broke for the Chargers without ever reaching the Super Bowl. The terrific passing attack still ate up yardage, but the offense was less able to run the ball. The line underwent changes, as veteran Russ Washington was unexpectedly cut and Doug Wilkerson missed the first four games with a broken arm. A new 3-4 alignment didn't rid the Chargers of their reputation as a defensive soft touch. Four rookies started on defense, with cornerback Danny Walters the most successful. After a 3-3 start, a four-game losing streak doused the team's chances, aided by Dan Fouts' mid-season shoulder injury.

**Kansas City Chiefs** — Joe Delaney died tragically in the summer, robbing the Chiefs of an offensive ace and a valued teammate. New coach John Mackovic gave the offense a new look by turning the passing game loose. With Steve Fuller traded away, Bill Kenney played quarterback full-time and prospered. Carlos Carson received the greatest attention in the new offensive outlook. The defense lost a leader when Gary Barbaro held out and eventually signed with the U.S.F.L. New Jersey Generals. Deron Cherry replaced Barbaro admirably and joined Gary Green as a secondary star. The inconsistent play and losing record put off the public, with only 11,377 showing up for the home finale.

## MIAMI DOLPHINS 12-4-0 Don Shula

| Scores of Each Game | | |
|---|---|---|
| 12 | Buffalo | 0 |
| 34 | NEW ENGLAND | 24 |
| 14 | L.A.Raiders | 27 |
| 14 | KANSAS CITY | 6 |
| 7 | New Orleans | 17 |
| 35 | BUFFALO | *38 |
| 32 | N.Y.Jets | 14 |
| 21 | Baltimore | 7 |
| 30 | L.A.RAMS | 14 |
| 20 | San Francisco | 17 |
| 37 | New England | 17 |
| 38 | BALTIMORE | 0 |
| 38 | CINCINNATI | 14 |
| 24 | Houston | 17 |
| 31 | ATLANTA | 24 |
| 34 | N.Y.JETS | 14 |

| Use Name | Pos. | Hgt | Wgt | Age | Int | Pts |
|---|---|---|---|---|---|---|
| Jon Giesler | OT | 6'5" | 260 | 26 | | |
| Cleveland Green | OT | 6'3" | 262 | 25 | | |
| Eric Laakso | OT | 6'4" | 265 | 26 | | |
| Roy Foster | OG-OT | 6'4" | 272 | 23 | | |
| Bob Kuechenberg | OG | 6'3" | 255 | 35 | | |
| Ed Newman | OG | 6'2" | 255 | 32 | | |
| Jeff Toews | OG | 6'3" | 255 | 25 | | |
| Mark Dennard | C | 6'1" | 252 | 27 | | |
| Dwight Stephenson | C | 6'2" | 255 | 25 | | |
| Bill Barnett | DE | 6'4" | 260 | 27 | | |
| Charles Benson | DE | 6'3" | 267 | 22 | | |
| Doug Betters | DE | 6'7" | 260 | 27 | | |
| Kim Bokamper | DE | 6'6" | 250 | 28 | 2 | 6 |
| Bob Baumhower | NT | 6'5" | 265 | 28 | | |
| Mike Charles | NT | 6'4" | 283 | 20 | | 2 |
| Steve Clark | NT | 6'4" | 255 | 23 | | |

Steve Shull - Knee Injury
Larry Gordon - Died;Heart Attack

| Use Name | Pos. | Hgt | Wgt | Age | Int | Pts |
|---|---|---|---|---|---|---|
| Charles Bowser | LB | 6'3" | 232 | 23 | | |
| Mark Brown | LB | 6'2" | 218 | 22 | 1 | |
| Bob Brudzinski | LB | 6'4" | 230 | 28 | | |
| A.J.Duhe | LB | 6'4" | 248 | 27 | | |
| Earnest Rhone | LB | 6'2" | 224 | 30 | 1 | |
| Terry Tautolo | LB | 6'2" | 227 | 29 | | |
| Rodell Thomas | LB | 6'2" | 225 | 25 | | |
| Emmett Tilley | LB | 5'11" | 240 | 22 | | |
| Glenn Blackwood | DB | 6' | 186 | 26 | 3 | |
| Lyle Blackwood | DB | 6' | 195 | 32 | 4 | |
| William Judson | DB | 6'1" | 187 | 24 | | |
| Mike Kozlowski | DB | 6' | 198 | 27 | 2 | 12 |
| Paul Lankford | DB | 6'1" | 182 | 25 | 1 | |
| Gerald Small | DB | 5'11" | 192 | 27 | 5 | |
| Robert Sowell | DB | 5'11" | 175 | 22 | | |
| Fulton Walker | DB | 5'10" | 196 | 25 | 1 | |

Ron Hester - Knee Injury
Don McNeal - Achilles Tendon Injury

| Use Name | Pos. | Hgt | Wgt | Age | Int | Pts |
|---|---|---|---|---|---|---|
| Jim Jensen | QB-TE | 6'4" | 215 | 24 | | |
| Dan Marino | QB | 6'4" | 214 | 21 | | 12 |
| Don Strock | QB | 6'5" | 220 | 32 | | |
| David Woodley | QB | 6'2" | 204 | 24 | | |
| Eddie Hill | HB | 6'2" | 206 | 26 | | |
| Tony Nathan | HB | 6' | 206 | 26 | | 24 |
| Tommy Vigorito | HB | 5'10" | 190 | 23 | | |
| David Overstreet | HB-FB | 5'11" | 206 | 24 | | 18 |
| Woody Bennett | FB | 6'2" | 222 | 28 | | 12 |
| Andra Franklin | FB | 5'10" | 228 | 23 | | 48 |
| Jimmy Cefalo | WR | 5'11" | 188 | 26 | | |
| Mark Clayton | WR | 5'9" | 172 | 22 | | 12 |
| Mark Duper | WR | 5'9" | 193 | 24 | | 60 |
| Duriel Harris | WR | 5'11" | 176 | 28 | | 6 |
| Vince Heflin | WR | 6' | 185 | 24 | | |
| Nat Moore | WR | 5'9" | 188 | 31 | | 36 |
| Bruce Hardy | TE | 6'5" | 232 | 27 | | |
| Dan Johnson | TE | 6'3" | 230 | 26 | | 28 |
| Joe Rose | TE | 6'3" | 230 | 26 | | |
| Reggie Roby | K | 6'2" | 243 | 22 | | |
| Uwe Von Schamann | K | 6' | 188 | 27 | | 99 |

## NEW ENGLAND PATRIOTS 8-8-0 Ron Meyer

| Scores of Each Game | | |
|---|---|---|
| 23 | BALTIMORE | *29 |
| 24 | Miami | 34 |
| 23 | N.Y.JETS | 13 |
| 28 | Pittsburgh | 23 |
| 13 | SAN FRANCISCO | 33 |
| 7 | Baltimore | 12 |
| 37 | SAN DIEGO | 21 |
| 31 | Buffalo | 0 |
| 13 | Atlanta | 24 |
| 21 | BUFFALO | 7 |
| 17 | MIAMI | 6 |
| 0 | CLEVELAND | 30 |
| 3 | N.Y.Jets | 26 |
| 7 | NEW ORLEANS | 0 |
| 21 | L.A.Rams | 7 |
| 6 | Seattle | 24 |

| Use Name | Pos. | Hgt | Wgt | Age | Int | Pts |
|---|---|---|---|---|---|---|
| Bob Cryder | OT | 6'4" | 282 | 26 | | |
| Darryl Haley | OT | 6'4" | 265 | 22 | | |
| Brian Holloway | OT | 6'7" | 288 | 24 | | |
| Steve Moore | OT | 6'4" | 285 | 22 | | |
| John Hannah | OG | 6'2" | 265 | 32 | | |
| Ron Wooten | OG | 6'4" | 273 | 24 | | |
| Pete Brock | C | 6'5" | 270 | 29 | | |
| Art Kuehn | C | 6'3" | 255 | 30 | | |
| Dwight Wheeler | C | 6'3" | 269 | 28 | | |
| Julius Adams | DE | 6'3" | 270 | 35 | | |
| Dave Browning | DE | 6'5" | 245 | 27 | | |
| George Crump | DE | 6'4" | 260 | 24 | | |
| Marshall Harris | DE | 6'6" | 261 | 27 | | |
| Doug Rogers (from ATL) | DE | 6'5" | 260 | 23 | | |
| Kenneth Sims | DE | 6'5" | 271 | 23 | | |
| Toby Williams | DE | 6'3" | 254 | 23 | | |
| Luther Henson | NT | 6' | 275 | 24 | | |
| Dennis Owens | NT | 6'1" | 258 | 23 | | |
| Lester Williams | NT | 6'3" | 272 | 24 | | |

| Use Name | Pos. | Hgt | Wgt | Age | Int | Pts |
|---|---|---|---|---|---|---|
| Don Blackman | LB | 6'3" | 235 | 25 | 1 | |
| John Gillen | LB | 6'3" | 228 | 24 | | |
| Tim Golden | LB | 6'1" | 220 | 23 | | |
| Brian Ingram | LB | 6'4" | 235 | 23 | | |
| Larry McGrew | LB | 6'5" | 233 | 26 | 1 | |
| Steve Nelson | LB | 6'2" | 230 | 32 | 1 | |
| Johnny Rembert | LB | 6'3" | 234 | 22 | | |
| Ed Reynolds | LB | 6'5" | 230 | 21 | | |
| Andre Tippett | LB | 6'3" | 241 | 23 | | |
| Clayton Weishuhn | LB | 6'2" | 221 | 23 | | 6 |
| Raymond Clayborn | DB | 6'1" | 186 | 28 | | |
| Paul Dombroski | DB | 6' | 185 | 27 | | |
| Roland James | DB | 6'2" | 191 | 25 | 5 | |
| Keith Lee | DB | 5'11" | 193 | 25 | | |
| Ronnie Lippett | DB | 5'11" | 180 | 22 | | |
| Fred Marion | DB | 6'2" | 191 | 24 | 2 | |
| Rick Sanford | DB | 6'1" | 192 | 26 | 7 | |
| Ricky Smith | DB | 6' | 182 | 23 | | |

| Use Name | Pos. | Hgt | Wgt | Age | Int | Pts |
|---|---|---|---|---|---|---|
| Tony Eason | QB | 6'4" | 212 | 23 | | |
| Steve Grogan | QB | 6'4" | 210 | 30 | | 12 |
| Mike Kerrigan | QB | 6'3" | 205 | 23 | | |
| Tony Collins | HB | 5'11" | 203 | 24 | | 60 |
| George Peoples | HB | 6' | 215 | 23 | | |
| Mosi Tatupu | FB | 6' | 227 | 28 | | 30 |
| Mark van Eeghen | FB | 6'2" | 220 | 31 | | 6 |
| Robert Weathers | FB | 6'2" | 222 | 22 | | 6 |
| Cedric Jones | WR | 6' | 184 | 23 | | 6 |
| Stanley Morgan | WR | 5'11" | 181 | 28 | | 12 |
| Stephen Starring | WR | 5'10" | 172 | 22 | | 12 |
| Clarence Weathers | WR | 5'9" | 170 | 21 | | 18 |
| Darryal Wilson | WR | 6' | 182 | 22 | | |
| Lin Dawson | TE | 6'3" | 240 | 24 | | 6 |
| Derrick Ramsey (from RAID) | TE | 6'5" | 235 | 26 | | |
| Brooks Williams | TE | 6'4" | 226 | 28 | | |
| Rich Camarillo | K | 5'11" | 191 | 23 | | |
| John Smith | K | 6' | 185 | 33 | | 21 |
| Fred Steinfort (from BUF) | K | 5'11" | 180 | 29 | | 34 |
| Joaquin Zendejas | K | 5'11" | 176 | 23 | | 3 |

## BUFFALO BILLS 8-8-0 Kay Stephenson

| Scores of Each Game | | |
|---|---|---|
| 0 | MIAMI | 12 |
| 10 | Cincinnati | 6 |
| 28 | BALTIMORE | 23 |
| 30 | HOUSTON | 13 |
| 10 | N.Y.JETS | 34 |
| 38 | Miami | *35 |
| 30 | Baltimore | 7 |
| 0 | NEW ENGLAND | 31 |
| 27 | NEW ORLEANS | 21 |
| 7 | New England | 21 |
| 24 | N.Y.Jets | 17 |
| 24 | L.A.RAIDERS | 27 |
| 17 | L.A.RAMS | 41 |
| 14 | Kansas City | 9 |
| 10 | SAN FRANCISCO | 23 |
| 14 | Atlanta | 31 |

| Use Name | Pos. | Hgt | Wgt | Age | Int | Pts |
|---|---|---|---|---|---|---|
| Darryl Caldwell | OT | 6'5" | 245 | 23 | | |
| Justin Cross | OT | 6'6" | 265 | 24 | | |
| Ken Jones | OT | 6'5" | 256 | 30 | | |
| Jon Borchardt | OG | 6'5" | 255 | 26 | | |
| Tom Lynch | OG | 6'5" | 250 | 28 | | |
| Jim Ritcher | OG-C | 6'3" | 251 | 25 | | |
| Will Grant | C | 6'3" | 248 | 29 | | |
| Tim Vogler | C | 6'3" | 245 | 26 | | |
| Scott Hutchinson | DE | 6'4" | 255 | 27 | | |
| Ken Johnson | DE | 6'5" | 253 | 28 | | |
| Scott Virkus | DE | 6'5" | 248 | 23 | | |
| Sherman White | DE | 6'5" | 250 | 34 | | |
| Ben Williams | DE | 6'3" | 245 | 29 | | |
| Bill Acker | NT | 6'3" | 255 | 26 | | |
| Mark Roopenian | NT | 6'5" | 254 | 25 | | |
| Fred Smerlas | NT | 6'3" | 270 | 26 | | |

Joe Devlin - Broken Ankle
Robert Holt - Knee Injury
Roland Hooks - Knee Injury
Jeff Nixon - Knee Injury

| Use Name | Pos. | Hgt | Wgt | Age | Int | Pts |
|---|---|---|---|---|---|---|
| Jim Haslett | LB | 6'3" | 232 | 27 | | |
| Trey Junkin | LB | 6'2" | 221 | 22 | | |
| Chris Keating | LB | 6'2" | 223 | 25 | 2 | |
| Joey Lumpkin | LB | 6'2" | 230 | 23 | | |
| Eugene Marve | LB | 6'2" | 230 | 23 | | |
| Mark Merrill | LB | 6'4" | 234 | 28 | | |
| Ervin Parker | LB | 6'4" | 240 | 25 | | |
| Lucius Sanford | LB | 6'2" | 216 | 27 | 2 | |
| Darryl Talley | LB | 6'4" | 231 | 23 | | |
| Phil Villapiano | LB | 6'2" | 225 | 34 | | |
| Mario Clark | DB | 6'2" | 195 | 29 | | |
| Judson Flint | DB | 6' | 201 | 26 | | |
| Steve Freeman | DB | 5'11" | 185 | 30 | 3 | |
| Bill Hurley (from NO) | DB | 5'11" | 185 | 26 | | |
| Mike Kennedy | DB | 6' | 195 | 24 | 1 | 6 |
| David Kilson | DB | 6'1" | 200 | 22 | | 6 |
| Rod Kush | DB | 6' | 188 | 26 | | |
| Charles Romes | DB | 6'1" | 190 | 29 | 2 | |
| Garry Thompson | DB | 6' | 180 | 24 | | |
| Len Walterscheid | DB | 5'11" | 190 | 28 | | |
| Chris Williams | DB | 6' | 197 | 24 | 3 | |

| Use Name | Pos. | Hgt | Wgt | Age | Int | Pts |
|---|---|---|---|---|---|---|
| Joe Dufek | QB | 6'4" | 215 | 22 | | |
| Joe Ferguson | QB | 6'1" | 195 | 33 | | |
| Matt Kofler | QB | 6'3" | 192 | 24 | | |
| Joe Cribbs | HB | 5'11" | 190 | 25 | | 60 |
| Robb Riddick | HB | 6' | 195 | 26 | | |
| Van Williams | HB | 6' | 208 | 24 | | |
| Roosevelt Leaks | FB | 5'10" | 225 | 30 | | 6 |
| Booker Moore | FB | 5'11" | 224 | 24 | | 6 |
| Jerry Butler | WR | 6' | 178 | 25 | | 18 |
| Julius Dawkins | WR | 6'1" | 196 | 22 | | 6 |
| Byron Franklin | WR | 6'1" | 179 | 24 | | 24 |
| Frank Lewis | WR | 6'1" | 196 | 36 | | 18 |
| Mike Mosley | WR | 6'2" | 192 | 25 | | 18 |
| Perry Tuttle | WR | 6' | 178 | 24 | | 18 |
| Buster Barnett | TE | 6'5" | 225 | 24 | | |
| Mark Brammer | TE | 6'3" | 235 | 25 | | 12 |
| Tony Hunter | TE | 6'3" | 237 | 23 | | 18 |
| Greg Cater | K | 6' | 191 | 26 | | |
| Joe Danelo | K | 5'9" | 166 | 29 | | 63 |

## BALTIMORE COLTS 7-9-0 Frank Kush

| Scores of Each Game | | |
|---|---|---|
| 29 | New England | *23 |
| 10 | DENVER | 17 |
| 23 | Buffalo | 28 |
| 22 | CHICAGO | *19 |
| 34 | Cincinnati | 31 |
| 12 | NEW ENGLAND | 7 |
| 7 | BUFFALO | 30 |
| 7 | MIAMI | 21 |
| 22 | Philadelphia | 21 |
| 17 | N.Y.Jets | 14 |
| 13 | PITTSBURGH | 24 |
| 0 | Miami | 37 |
| 23 | Cleveland | 41 |
| 6 | N.Y.JETS | 10 |
| 19 | Denver | 21 |
| 20 | HOUSTON | 10 |

| Use Name | Pos. | Hgt | Wgt | Age | Int | Pts |
|---|---|---|---|---|---|---|
| Sid Abramowitz | OT | 6'6" | 279 | 23 | | |
| Karl Baldischwiler | OT | 6'5" | 267 | 27 | | |
| Jeff Hart | OT | 6'5" | 272 | 29 | | |
| Lindsey Mason | OT | 6'5" | 275 | 28 | | |
| Jim Mills | OT | 6'9" | 271 | 21 | | |
| Chris Hinton | OG | 6'4" | 280 | 22 | | |
| Ben Utt | OG | 6'4" | 255 | 24 | | |
| Steve Wright | OG | 6'6" | 263 | 24 | | |
| Ray Donaldson | C | 6'3" | 269 | 25 | | |
| Grant Feasel | C | 6'7" | 267 | 23 | | |
| Mark Bell | DE | 6'4" | 240 | 26 | | |
| Steve Parker | DE | 6'4" | 250 | 23 | | |
| Hosea Taylor | DE | 6'5" | 260 | 24 | | |
| Donnell Thompson | DE | 6'4" | 263 | 24 | | 2 |
| Henry Waechter | DE | 6'5" | 270 | 24 | | |
| Quinton Ballard | NT | 6'3" | 289 | 22 | | |
| Earnest Barnes | NT | 6'4" | 260 | 22 | | |
| Leo Wisniewski | NT | 6'1" | 264 | 23 | | |

| Use Name | Pos. | Hgt | Wgt | Age | Int | Pts |
|---|---|---|---|---|---|---|
| Greg Bracelin | LB | 6'1" | 210 | 26 | 2 | |
| Johnie Cooks | LB | 6'4" | 243 | 24 | 1 | 6 |
| Ricky Jones | LB | 6'1" | 234 | 28 | | |
| Barry Krauss | LB | 6'3" | 247 | 26 | | |
| Vernon Maxwell | LB | 6'2" | 219 | 22 | 1 | |
| Cliff Odom | LB | 6'2" | 233 | 24 | | |
| Gary Padjen | LB | 6'2" | 251 | 25 | | |
| Sanders Shiver | LB | 6'2" | 227 | 28 | | |
| Kim Anderson | DB | 5'11" | 189 | 26 | 2 | 6 |
| Larry Anderson | DB | 5'11" | 192 | 26 | 1 | 6 |
| James Burroughs | DB | 6'1" | 198 | 25 | 2 | |
| Jeff Delaney | DB | 6' | 197 | 26 | 2 | |
| Nesby Glasgow | DB | 5'10" | 180 | 26 | 3 | |
| Derrick Harchett (to HOU) | DB | 5'11" | 183 | 25 | 4 | |
| Mark Kefentzis | DB | 5'10" | 185 | 25 | | |
| Tate Randle (from HOU) | DB | 6' | 202 | 24 | 1 | |
| Marco Tongue | DB | 5'9" | 174 | 23 | | |
| Kendall Williams | DB | 5'9" | 189 | 24 | 1 | |

John Sinnott - Back Injury
Mike Humiston - Ankle Injury
Art Schlichter - Suspended by N.F.L.

| Use Name | Pos. | Hgt | Wgt | Age | Int | Pts |
|---|---|---|---|---|---|---|
| Mark Herrmann | QB | 6'4" | 199 | 24 | | |
| Mike Pagel | QB | 6'2" | 201 | 22 | | |
| Mark Reed | QB | 6'3" | 204 | 24 | | |
| Jim Bob Taylor | QB | 6'2" | 197 | 23 | | |
| Curtis Dickey | HB | 6'1" | 214 | 26 | | 42 |
| Alvin Moore | HB | 6' | 194 | 24 | | 6 |
| Ricky Porter | HB | 5'10" | 204 | 23 | | |
| Newton Williams | HB-FB | 5'10" | 204 | 24 | | |
| Randy McMillan | FB | 6' | 220 | 24 | | 36 |
| Matt Bouza | WR | 6'3" | 211 | 24 | | |
| Ray Butler | WR | 6'3" | 206 | 26 | | 18 |
| Bernard Henry | WR | 6' | 179 | 23 | | 24 |
| Victor Oatis | WR | 6' | 177 | 24 | | |
| Tracy Porter | WR | 6'1" | 196 | 24 | | |
| Phil Smith | WR | 6'3" | 188 | 22 | | |
| Pat Beach | TE | 6'4" | 243 | 23 | | 6 |
| Tim Sherwin | TE | 6'6" | 237 | 25 | | |
| Dave Young | TE | 6'5" | 240 | 24 | | |
| Raul Allegre | K | 5'10" | 165 | 24 | | 112 |
| Rohn Stark | K | 6'3" | 199 | 24 | | |

## NEW YORK JETS 7-9-0 Joe Walton

| Scores of Each Game | | |
|---|---|---|
| 41 | San Diego | 29 |
| 10 | SEATTLE | 17 |
| 13 | New England | 23 |
| 27 | L.A.RAMS | *24 |
| 34 | Buffalo | 10 |
| 7 | Cleveland | 10 |
| 14 | MIAMI | 32 |
| 21 | ATLANTA | 27 |
| 27 | San Francisco | 13 |
| 14 | BALTIMORE | 17 |
| 17 | BUFFALO | 24 |
| 31 | New Orleans | 28 |
| 26 | NEW ENGLAND | 3 |
| 10 | Baltimore | 6 |
| 7 | PITTSBURGH | 34 |
| 14 | Miami | 34 |

| Use Name | Pos. | Hgt | Wgt | Age | Int | Pts |
|---|---|---|---|---|---|---|
| Reggie McElroy | OT | 6'6" | 270 | 23 | | |
| Marvin Powell | OT | 6'5" | 260 | 28 | | |
| Chris Ward | OT | 6'3" | 269 | 27 | | |
| Guy Bingham | OG-OT | 6'3" | 255 | 25 | | |
| Stan Waldemore | OG-OT | 6'4" | 269 | 28 | | |
| Dan Alexander | OG | 6'4" | 252 | 28 | | |
| Joe Pellegrini | C-OG | 6'4" | 252 | 26 | | |
| Joe Fields | C | 6'2" | 253 | 29 | | |
| George Lilja | C | 6'4" | 250 | 25 | | |
| Mark Gastineau | DE | 6'5" | 265 | 26 | | 6 |
| Rusty Guilbeau | DE | 6'4" | 260 | 24 | | |
| Joe Klecko | DE | 6'3" | 263 | 29 | | |
| Kenny Neil | DE-DT | 6'4" | 244 | 24 | | |
| Barry Bennett | DT-DE | 6'4" | 257 | 27 | | |
| Ben Rudolph | DT-DE | 6'5" | 266 | 26 | | |
| Marty Lyons | DT | 6'5" | 265 | 26 | | |
| Abdul Salaam | DT | 6'3" | 269 | 30 | | |

| Use Name | Pos. | Hgt | Wgt | Age | Int | Pts |
|---|---|---|---|---|---|---|
| Stan Blinka | LB | 6'2" | 230 | 25 | | |
| Greg Buttle | LB | 6'3" | 232 | 29 | 1 | |
| Bob Crable | LB | 6'3" | 232 | 23 | 1 | |
| Ron Crosby | LB | 6'3" | 227 | 28 | | |
| Jim Eliopulos (from STL) | LB | 6'2" | 229 | 24 | | |
| Lance Mehl | LB | 6'3" | 233 | 25 | 7 | 6 |
| John Woodring | LB | 6'2" | 232 | 24 | | |
| Jerry Holmes | DB | 6'2" | 175 | 25 | 3 | 12 |
| Bobby Jackson | DB | 5'9" | 180 | 26 | 2 | |
| Jesse Johnson | DB | 6'3" | 188 | 26 | | |
| Johnny Lynn | DB | 6' | 198 | 26 | 3 | 6 |
| Davlin Mullen | DB | 6'1" | 177 | 23 | | |
| Darrol Ray | DB | 6'1" | 198 | 25 | 3 | |
| Ken Schroy | DB | 6'2" | 198 | 30 | 2 | |
| Kirk Springs | DB | 6' | 192 | 25 | | 6 |

George Floyd - Knee Injury
Jim Luscinski - Broken Vertebrae
Kurt Sohn - Knee Injury

| Use Name | Pos. | Hgt | Wgt | Age | Int | Pts |
|---|---|---|---|---|---|---|
| Ken O'Brien | QB | 6'4" | 210 | 22 | | |
| Pat Ryan | QB | 6'3" | 210 | 27 | | 1 |
| Richard Todd | QB | 6'2" | 206 | 29 | | |
| Scott Dierking | HB | 5'10" | 220 | 28 | | 18 |
| Bruce Harper | HB | 5'8" | 177 | 28 | | 18 |
| Johnny Hector | HB | 5'11" | 197 | 22 | | 6 |
| Freeman McNeil | HB | 5'11" | 218 | 24 | | 24 |
| Mike Augustyniak | FB | 5'11" | 226 | 27 | | 18 |
| Marion Barber | FB | 6'3" | 224 | 23 | | 12 |
| Dwayne Crutchfield (to HOU) | FB | 6' | 235 | 23 | | 18 |
| Rocky Klever | FB | 6'3" | 225 | 24 | | |
| Kenny Lewis | FB | 6' | 196 | 25 | | |
| Preston Brown | WR | 5'11" | 187 | 25 | | |
| Nick Bruckner | WR | 5'11" | 185 | 22 | | |
| Derrick Gaffney | WR | 6'1" | 182 | 28 | | |
| Mike Harmon | WR | 6' | 185 | 22 | | |
| Johnny "Lam" Jones | WR | 5'11" | 180 | 25 | | 24 |
| Wesley Walker | WR | 6' | 179 | 28 | | 42 |
| Jerome Barkum | TE | 6'3" | 227 | 33 | | 6 |
| Tom Coombs | TE | 6'3" | 227 | 33 | | |
| Mickey Shuler | TE | 6'3" | 231 | 27 | | 6 |
| Pat Leahy | K | 6' | 189 | 32 | | 84 |
| Chuck Ramsey | K | 6'2" | 189 | 31 | | |

* Overtime

## MIAMI DOLPHINS

### RUSHING

| Last Name | No. | Yds | Avg | TD |
|---|---|---|---|---|
| Franklin | 224 | 746 | 3.3 | 8 |
| Nathan | 151 | 685 | 4.5 | 3 |
| Overstreet | 85 | 392 | 4.6 | 1 |
| Bennett | 49 | 197 | 4.0 | 2 |
| Woodley | 19 | 78 | 4.1 | 0 |
| Marino | 28 | 45 | 1.6 | 2 |
| Hill | 2 | 12 | 6.0 | 0 |
| Clayton | 2 | 9 | 4.5 | 0 |
| Hardy | 1 | 2 | 2.0 | 0 |
| Harris | 1 | 0 | 0.0 | 0 |
| Strock | 6 | -16 | -2.7 | 0 |

### RECEIVING

| Last Name | No. | Yds | Avg | TD |
|---|---|---|---|---|
| Nathan | 52 | 461 | 8.9 | 1 |
| Duper | 51 | 1003 | 19.7 | 10 |
| Moore | 39 | 558 | 14.3 | 6 |
| Rose | 29 | 345 | 11.9 | 3 |
| Johnson | 24 | 189 | 7.9 | 4 |
| Hardy | 22 | 202 | 9.2 | 0 |
| Harris | 15 | 260 | 17.3 | 1 |
| Overstreet | 8 | 55 | 6.9 | 2 |
| Clayton | 6 | 114 | 19.0 | 1 |
| Bennett | 6 | 35 | 5.8 | 0 |
| Vigorito | 1 | 7 | 7.0 | 0 |
| Woodley | 1 | 6 | 6.0 | 0 |

### PUNT RETURNS

| Last Name | No. | Yds | Avg | TD |
|---|---|---|---|---|
| Clayton | 41 | 392 | 9.6 | 1 |
| Walker | 8 | 86 | 10.8 | 0 |
| Kozlowski | 2 | 12 | 6.0 | 0 |
| G. Blackwood | 1 | 10 | 10.0 | 0 |
| Heflin | 1 | 19 | 19.0 | 0 |
| Sowell | 1 | 0 | 0.0 | 0 |
| Vigorito | 1 | 62 | 62.0 | 0 |

### KICKOFF RETURNS

| Last Name | No. | Yds | Avg | TD |
|---|---|---|---|---|
| Walker | 36 | 962 | 26.7 | 0 |
| Kozlowski | 4 | 50 | 12.5 | 0 |
| Nathan | 3 | 15 | 5.0 | 0 |
| Bennett | 1 | 6 | 6.0 | 0 |
| Brown | 1 | 0 | 0.0 | 0 |
| Clayton | 1 | 25 | 25.0 | 0 |
| Heflin | 1 | 27 | 27.0 | 0 |

### PASSING — PUNTING — KICKING

| PASSING | Att | Cmp | % | Yds | Yd/Att | TD | Int | — | % | RK |
|---|---|---|---|---|---|---|---|---|---|---|
| Marino | 296 | 173 | 58 | 2210 | 7.47 | 20 | 6 | — | 2 | 1 |
| Woodley | 89 | 43 | 48 | 528 | 5.93 | 3 | 4 | — | 5 | |
| Strock | 52 | 34 | 65 | 403 | 7.75 | 4 | 1 | — | 2 | |
| Nathan | 4 | 3 | 75 | 46 | 11.50 | 0 | 0 | — | 0 | |
| Clayton | 1 | 1 | 100 | 48 | 48.00 | 1 | 0 | — | 0 | |

| PUNTING | No. | Avg. |
|---|---|---|
| Roby | 74 | 43.1 |

| KICKING | XP | Att. | % | FG | Att | % |
|---|---|---|---|---|---|---|
| von Schamann | 45 | 48 | 94 | 18 | 27 | 67 |

## NEW ENGLAND PATRIOTS

### RUSHING

| Last Name | No. | Yds | Avg | TD |
|---|---|---|---|---|
| Collins | 219 | 1049 | 4.8 | 10 |
| Tatupu | 106 | 578 | 5.5 | 4 |
| R. Weathers | 73 | 418 | 5.7 | 1 |
| van Eeghen | 95 | 358 | 3.8 | 2 |
| Grogan | 23 | 108 | 4.7 | 2 |
| Eason | 19 | 39 | 2.1 | 0 |
| C. Weathers | 1 | 28 | 28.0 | 0 |
| Kerrigan | 1 | 14 | 14.0 | 0 |
| Morgan | 1 | 13 | 13.0 | 0 |

### RECEIVING

| Last Name | No. | Yds | Avg | TD |
|---|---|---|---|---|
| Morgan | 58 | 863 | 14.9 | 2 |
| Collins | 27 | 257 | 9.5 | 0 |
| Ramsey | 24 | 335 | 14.0 | 6 |
| R. Weathers | 23 | 212 | 9.2 | 0 |
| Jones | 20 | 323 | 16.2 | 1 |
| C. Weathers | 19 | 379 | 19.9 | 3 |
| Starring | 17 | 389 | 22.9 | 2 |
| van Eeghen | 10 | 102 | 10.2 | 0 |
| Tatupu | 10 | 97 | 9.7 | 1 |
| Dawson | 9 | 84 | 9.3 | 1 |
| B. Williams | 1 | 0 | 0.0 | 0 |
| Grogan | 1 | -8 | -8.0 | 0 |

### PUNT RETURNS

| Last Name | No. | Yds | Avg | TD |
|---|---|---|---|---|
| R. Smith | 38 | 398 | 10.5 | 0 |
| C. Weather | 4 | 1 | 0.3 | 0 |
| Lee | 1 | 0 | 0.0 | 0 |
| Sanford | 1 | 0 | 0.0 | 0 |

### KICKOFF RETURNS

| Last Name | No. | Yds | Avg | TD |
|---|---|---|---|---|
| R. Smith | 42 | 916 | 21.8 | 0 |
| Jones | 4 | 63 | 15.8 | 0 |
| Lee | 4 | 40 | 10.0 | 0 |
| C. Weathers | 3 | 58 | 19.3 | 0 |
| R. Weathers | 3 | 68 | 22.7 | 0 |
| Golden | 1 | 10 | 10.0 | 0 |

### PASSING — PUNTING — KICKING

| PASSING | Att | Cmp | % | Yds | Yd/Att | TD | Int | — | % | RK |
|---|---|---|---|---|---|---|---|---|---|---|
| Grogan | 303 | 168 | 55 | 2411 | 7.96 | 15 | 12 | — | 4 | 6 |
| Eason | 95 | 46 | 48 | 557 | 5.86 | 1 | 5 | — | 5 | |
| Kerrigan | 14 | 6 | 43 | 72 | 5.14 | 0 | 1 | — | 7 | |

| PUNTING | No. | Avg. |
|---|---|---|
| Camarillo | 81 | 44.6 |

| KICKING | XP | Att. | % | FG | Att | % |
|---|---|---|---|---|---|---|
| Steinfort | 17 | 18 | 94 | 7 | 21 | 33 |
| J. Smith | 12 | 15 | 80 | 3 | 6 | 50 |
| Zendejas | 3 | 4 | 75 | 0 | 1 | 0 |

## BUFFALO BILLS

### RUSHING

| Last Name | No. | Yds | Avg | TD |
|---|---|---|---|---|
| Cribbs | 263 | 1131 | 4.3 | 3 |
| Moore | 60 | 275 | 4.6 | 0 |
| Leaks | 58 | 157 | 2.7 | 1 |
| Ferguson | 20 | 88 | 4.4 | 0 |
| Hunter | 2 | 28 | 14.0 | 0 |
| Kofler | 4 | 25 | 6.3 | 0 |
| Riddick | 4 | 18 | 4.5 | 0 |
| V. Williams | 3 | 11 | 3.7 | 0 |
| Franklin | 1 | 3 | 3.0 | 0 |

### RECEIVING

| Last Name | No. | Yds | Avg | TD |
|---|---|---|---|---|
| Cribbs | 57 | 524 | 9.2 | 7 |
| Lewis | 36 | 486 | 13.5 | 3 |
| Hunter | 36 | 402 | 11.2 | 0 |
| Butler | 36 | 385 | 10.7 | 3 |
| Moore | 34 | 199 | 5.9 | 1 |
| Franklin | 30 | 452 | 15.1 | 4 |
| Brammer | 25 | 215 | 8.6 | 2 |
| Tuttle | 17 | 261 | 15.4 | 3 |
| Mosley | 14 | 180 | 12.9 | 3 |
| Dawkins | 11 | 123 | 11.2 | 1 |
| Barnett | 10 | 94 | 9.4 | 0 |
| Leaks | 8 | 74 | 9.3 | 0 |
| Riddick | 3 | 43 | 14.3 | 0 |

### PUNT RETURNS

| Last Name | No. | Yds | Avg | TD |
|---|---|---|---|---|
| Riddick | 42 | 241 | 5.7 | 0 |
| Hurley | 1 | 0 | 0.0 | 0 |
| V. Williams | 1 | 0 | 0.0 | 0 |

### KICKOFF RETURNS

| Last Name | No. | Yds | Avg | TD |
|---|---|---|---|---|
| V. Williams | 22 | 494 | 22.5 | 0 |
| Riddick | 28 | 568 | 20.3 | 0 |
| Mosley | 9 | 236 | 26.2 | 0 |
| B. Williams | 3 | 56 | 18.7 | 0 |
| Talley | 2 | 9 | 4.5 | 0 |

### PASSING — PUNTING — KICKING

| PASSING | Att | Cmp | % | Yds | Yd/Att | TD | Int | — | % | RK |
|---|---|---|---|---|---|---|---|---|---|---|
| Ferguson | 508 | 281 | 55 | 2995 | 5.90 | 26 | 25 | — | 5 | 11 |
| Kofler | 61 | 35 | 57 | 440 | 7.21 | 4 | 3 | — | 5 | |
| Cribbs | 2 | 1 | 50 | 3 | 1.50 | 0 | 0 | — | 0 | |

| PUNTING | No. | Avg. |
|---|---|---|
| Cater | 89 | 39.7 |

| KICKING | XP | ATT | % | FG | ATT | % |
|---|---|---|---|---|---|---|
| Danelo | 33 | 34 | 97 | 10 | 20 | 50 |

## BALTIMORE COLTS

### RUSHING

| Last Name | No. | Yds | Avg | TD |
|---|---|---|---|---|
| Dickey | 254 | 1122 | 4.4 | 4 |
| McMillan | 198 | 802 | 4.1 | 5 |
| Pagel | 54 | 441 | 8.2 | 0 |
| Moore | 57 | 205 | 3.6 | 1 |
| N. Williams | 28 | 77 | 2.8 | 0 |
| Reed | 2 | 27 | 13.5 | 0 |
| Dixon | 5 | 14 | 28 | 0 |
| Stark | 1 | 8 | 8.0 | 0 |
| Herrmann | 1 | 0 | 0.0 | 0 |
| Krauss | 1 | -1 | -1.0 | 0 |

### RECEIVING

| Last Name | No. | Yds | Avg | TD |
|---|---|---|---|---|
| Henry | 30 | 416 | 13.9 | 4 |
| T. Porter | 28 | 384 | 13.7 | 0 |
| Bouza | 25 | 385 | 15.4 | 0 |
| Sherwin | 25 | 358 | 14.3 | 0 |
| Dickey | 24 | 483 | 20.1 | 3 |
| McMillan | 24 | 195 | 8.1 | 1 |
| Butler | 10 | 207 | 20.7 | 3 |
| Oatis | 6 | 93 | 15.5 | 0 |
| Moore | 6 | 38 | 6.3 | 0 |
| Beach | 5 | 56 | 11.2 | 1 |
| N. Williams | 4 | 46 | 11.5 | 0 |
| Dixon | 1 | 2 | 2.0 | 0 |

### PUNT RETURNS

| Last Name | No. | Yds | Avg | TD |
|---|---|---|---|---|
| L. Anderson | 20 | 138 | 6.9 | 0 |
| R. Porter | 14 | 104 | 7.4 | 0 |
| K. Williams | 9 | 43 | 4.8 | 0 |
| Glasgow | 1 | 9 | 9.0 | 0 |

### KICKOFF RETURNS

| Last Name | No. | Yds | Avg | TD |
|---|---|---|---|---|
| K. Williams | 20 | 490 | 24.5 | 0 |
| R. Porter | 18 | 340 | 18.9 | 0 |
| L. Anderson | 18 | 309 | 17.2 | 0 |
| Dixon | 2 | 23 | 11.5 | 0 |
| Moore | 2 | 40 | 20.0 | 0 |
| Beach | 1 | 0 | 0.0 | 0 |
| Bouza | 1 | -4 | -4.0 | 0 |

### PASSING — PUNTING — KICKING

| PASSING | Att | Cmp | % | Yds | Yd/Att | TD | Int | — | % | RK |
|---|---|---|---|---|---|---|---|---|---|---|
| Pagel | 328 | 163 | 50 | 2353 | 7.17 | 12 | 17 | — | 5 | 13 |
| Herrmann | 36 | 18 | 50 | 256 | 7.11 | 0 | 3 | — | 8 | |
| Reed | 10 | 6 | 60 | 34 | 3.40 | 0 | 1 | — | 10 | |
| J. Taylor | 2 | 1 | 50 | 20 | 10.00 | 0 | 1 | — | 50 | |
| Stark | 1 | 0 | 0 | 0 | 0.00 | 0 | 0 | — | 0 | |

| PUNTING | No. | Avg. |
|---|---|---|
| Stark | 91 | 45.3 |

| KICKING | XP | Att | % | FG | Att | % |
|---|---|---|---|---|---|---|
| Allegre | 22 | 24 | 92 | 30 | 35 | 86 |

## NEW YORK JETS

### RUSHING

| Last Name | No. | Yds | Avg | TD |
|---|---|---|---|---|
| McNeil | 160 | 654 | 4.1 | 1 |
| Crutchfield | 137 | 571 | 4.2 | 3 |
| Harper | 51 | 354 | 6.9 | 1 |
| Dierking | 28 | 113 | 4.0 | 3 |
| Todd | 35 | 101 | 2.9 | 0 |
| Hector | 16 | 85 | 5.3 | 0 |
| Barber | 15 | 77 | 5.1 | 1 |
| Augustyniak | 18 | 50 | 2.8 | 2 |
| Lewis | 5 | 25 | 5.0 | 0 |
| Ryan | 4 | 23 | 5.8 | 0 |
| Jones | 4 | 10 | 2.5 | 0 |
| Crosby | 1 | 5 | 5.0 | 0 |

### RECEIVING

| Last Name | No. | Yds | Avg | TD |
|---|---|---|---|---|
| Walker | 61 | 868 | 14.2 | 7 |
| Harper | 48 | 413 | 8.6 | 2 |
| Jones | 43 | 734 | 17.1 | 4 |
| Dierking | 33 | 275 | 8.3 | 0 |
| Barkum | 32 | 385 | 12.0 | 1 |
| Shuler | 26 | 272 | 10.5 | 1 |
| McNeil | 21 | 172 | 8.2 | 3 |
| Crutchfield | 19 | 133 | 7.0 | 0 |
| Gaffney | 17 | 243 | 14.3 | 0 |
| Augustyniak | 10 | 71 | 7.1 | 1 |
| Barber | 7 | 48 | 6.9 | 1 |
| Lewis | 6 | 62 | 10.3 | 0 |
| Hector | 5 | 61 | 12.2 | 1 |
| Harmon | 1 | 4 | 4.0 | 0 |

### PUNT RETURNS

| Last Name | No. | Yds | Avg | TD |
|---|---|---|---|---|
| Springs | 23 | 287 | 12.5 | 1 |
| Harmon | 12 | 109 | 9.1 | 0 |
| Mullen | 2 | 13 | 6.5 | 0 |
| Schroy | 1 | 11 | 11.0 | 0 |

### KICKOFF RETURNS

| Last Name | No. | Yds | Avg | TD |
|---|---|---|---|---|
| Springs | 16 | 364 | 22.8 | 0 |
| Brown | 29 | 645 | 22.2 | 0 |
| Hector | 14 | 274 | 19.6 | 0 |
| Mullen | 3 | 57 | 19.0 | 0 |
| Barber | 1 | 9 | 9.0 | 0 |
| Harper | 1 | 16 | 16.0 | 0 |
| McElroy | 1 | 7 | 7.0 | 0 |
| Shuler | 1 | 3 | 3.0 | 0 |

### PASSING — PUNTING — KICKING

| PASSING | Att | Cmp | % | Yds | Yd/Att | TD | Int | — | % | RK |
|---|---|---|---|---|---|---|---|---|---|---|
| Todd | 518 | 308 | 60 | 3478 | 6.71 | 18 | 26 | — | 5 | 10 |
| Ryan | 40 | 21 | 53 | 259 | 6.25 | 2 | 2 | — | 5 | |
| McNeil | 1 | 1 | 100 | 5 | 5.00 | 1 | 0 | — | 0 | |

| PUNTING | No. | Avg. |
|---|---|---|
| Ramsey | 81 | 39.7 |

| KICKING | XP | Att | % | FG | Att | % |
|---|---|---|---|---|---|---|
| Leahy | 36 | 37 | 97 | 16 | 24 | 67 |
| Ryan | 1 | 1 | 100 | 0 | 0 | 0 |

## PITTSBURGH STEELERS 10-6-0 Chunk Noll

| Scores of Each Game | | |
|---|---|---|
| 10 | DENVER | 14 |
| 25 | Green Bay | 21 |
| 40 | Houston | 28 |
| 23 | NEW ENGLAND | 28 |
| 17 | HOUSTON | 10 |
| 24 | Cincinnati | 14 |
| 44 | Cleveland | 17 |
| 27 | Seattle | 21 |
| 17 | TAMPA BAY | 12 |
| 26 | SAN DIEGO | 3 |
| 24 | Baltimore | 13 |
| 14 | MINNESOTA | 17 |
| 3 | Detroit | 45 |
| 10 | CINCINNATI | 23 |
| 34 | N.Y.Jets | 7 |
| 17 | CLEVELAND | 30 |

| Use Name | Pos. | Hgt | Wgt | Age | Int | Pts |
|---|---|---|---|---|---|---|
| Larry Brown | OT | 6'4" | 270 | 34 | | |
| Tunch Ilkin | OT | 6'3" | 255 | 25 | | |
| Ted Petersen | OT | 6'5" | 245 | 28 | | |
| Steve Courson | OG | 6'1" | 270 | 27 | | |
| Blake Wingle | OG | 6'2" | 267 | 23 | | |
| Craig Wolfley | OG | 6'1" | 265 | 25 | | |
| Emil Boures | C-OG | 6'1" | 261 | 23 | | |
| Rick Donnalley | C-OG | 6'2" | 257 | 24 | | |
| Mike Webster | C | 6'1" | 250 | 31 | | |
| Tom Beasley | DE-NT | 6'5" | 248 | 29 | | |
| John Goodman | DE | 6'6" | 250 | 24 | | |
| Keith Gary | DE | 6'3" | 255 | 23 | | |
| Keith Willis | DE-NT | 6'1" | 255 | 24 | | |
| Gary Dunn | NT | 6'3" | 260 | 30 | | |
| Edmund Nelson | NT-DE | 6'3" | 270 | 23 | | |
| Gabe Rivera | NT | 6'2" | 293 | 22 | | |
| Craig Bingham | LB | 6'2" | 211 | 23 | | |
| Robin Cole | LB | 6'2" | 220 | 27 | | |
| Bryan Hinkle | LB | 6'1" | 220 | 24 | 1 | 6 |
| Bob Kohrs | LB | 6'3" | 235 | 24 | | 2 |
| Jack Lambert | LB | 6'4" | 220 | 31 | 2 | |
| David Little | LB | 6'1" | 220 | 31 | 2 | |
| Mike Merriweather | LB | 6'2" | 215 | 22 | 3 | 6 |
| Loren Toews | LB | 6'3" | 220 | 31 | | |
| Greg Best | DB | 5'10" | 185 | 23 | | 6 |
| Mel Blount | DB | 6'3" | 205 | 35 | 4 | 6 |
| Harvey Clayton | DB | 5'9" | 170 | 22 | 1 | 6 |
| Ron Johnson | DB | 5'10" | 200 | 27 | 3 | 6 |
| Donnie Shell | DB | 5'11" | 190 | 31 | 5 | |
| Sam Washington | DB | 5'8" | 180 | 23 | 1 | |
| Eric Williams | DB | 6'1" | 183 | 23 | | |
| Dwayne Woodruff | DB | 5'11" | 196 | 26 | 3 | |
| Rick Woods | DB | 6' | 196 | 23 | 5 | 6 |
| Terry Bradshaw | QB | 6'3" | 210 | 34 | | |
| Mark Malone | QB | 6'4" | 223 | 24 | | |
| Cliff Stoudt | QB | 6'4" | 218 | 28 | | 23 |
| Walter Abercrombie | HB | 5'11" | 201 | 23 | | 42 |
| Tim Harris | HB | 5'9" | 206 | 22 | | |
| Greg Hawthorne | HB | 6'2" | 225 | 26 | | |
| Henry Odom | HB | 5'10" | 200 | 24 | | |
| Frank Pollard | HB-FB | 5'10" | 210 | 26 | | 24 |
| Russell Davis | FB | 6'1" | 231 | 27 | | |
| Franco Harris | FB | 6'2" | 225 | 33 | | 42 |
| Wayne Capers | WR | 6'2" | 193 | 22 | | 6 |
| Gregg Garrity | WR | 5'10" | 171 | 22 | | 6 |
| Paul Skanel | WR | 5'11" | 190 | 22 | | |
| John Stallworth | WR | 6'2" | 191 | 31 | | |
| Calvin Sweeney | WR | 6'2" | 190 | 28 | | 30 |
| Bennie Cunningham | TE | 6'4" | 260 | 28 | | 18 |
| Craig Dunaway | TE | 6'2" | 233 | 22 | | |
| John Rodgers | TE | 6'2" | 220 | 23 | | |
| Gary Anderson | K | 5'11" | 156 | 24 | | 119 |
| Craig Colquitt | K | 6'2" | 182 | 29 | | |

Ernest French - Knee Injury

## CLEVELAND BROWNS 9-7-0 Sam Rutigliano

| Scores of Each Game | | |
|---|---|---|
| 21 | MINNESOTA | 27 |
| 31 | Detroit | 26 |
| 17 | CINCINNATI | 7 |
| 30 | San Diego | *24 |
| 9 | SEATTLE | 24 |
| 10 | N.Y.JETS | 7 |
| 17 | PITTSBURGH | 44 |
| 21 | Cincinnati | 28 |
| 25 | HOUSTON | *19 |
| 21 | Green Bay | 35 |
| 20 | TAMPA BAY | 0 |
| 30 | New England | 0 |
| 41 | BALTIMORE | 23 |
| 6 | Denver | 27 |
| 27 | Houston | 34 |
| 30 | Pittsburgh | 17 |

| Use Name | Pos. | Hgt | Wgt | Age | Int | Pts |
|---|---|---|---|---|---|---|
| Bill Contz | OT | 6'5" | 260 | 21 | | |
| Doug Dieken | OT | 6'5" | 252 | 34 | | 6 |
| Paul Farren | OT | 6'5" | 251 | 22 | | |
| Thomas Hopkins | OT | 6'6" | 260 | 23 | | |
| Cody Risien | OT | 6'7" | 270 | 26 | | |
| Joe DeLamielleure | OG | 6'3" | 260 | 32 | | |
| Robert Jackson | OG | 6'5" | 260 | 30 | | |
| Mike Baab | C | 6'4" | 270 | 23 | | |
| Tom DeLeone | C | 6'2" | 254 | 33 | | |
| Keith Baldwin | DE | 6'4" | 250 | 22 | | |
| Thomas Brown | DE | 6'4" | 255 | 26 | | |
| Reggie Camp | DE | 6'4" | 265 | 24 | | |
| Elvis Franks | DE | 6'4" | 265 | 26 | | |
| Bob Golic | NT | 6'2" | 260 | 25 | 1 | 6 |
| Dave Puzzudi | NT | 6'3" | 260 | 22 | | |
| Dick Ambrose | LB | 6' | 228 | 30 | | |
| Chip Banks | LB | 6'4" | 233 | 23 | 3 | 6 |
| Dale Carver | LB | 6'2" | 225 | 22 | | |
| Tom Cousineau | LB | 6'3" | 225 | 26 | 4 | |
| Eddie Johnson | LB | 6'1" | 215 | 24 | | |
| Clay Matthews | LB | 6'2" | 230 | 27 | | |
| Scott Nicolas | LB | 6'3" | 226 | 23 | | |
| Curtis Weathers | LB | 6'5" | 230 | 26 | | |
| Larry Braziel | DB | 6' | 184 | 28 | | |
| Clinton Burrell | DB | 6'2" | 192 | 26 | 2 | |
| Hanford Dixon | DB | 5'11" | 182 | 24 | 3 | |
| Al Gross | DB | 6'3" | 186 | 22 | 1 | |
| Lawrence Johnson | DB | 5'11" | 204 | 25 | 2 | |
| Rod Perry | DB | 5'9" | 185 | 29 | 1 | |
| Clarence Scott | DB | 6' | 190 | 34 | 2 | |
| Mike Whitwell | DB | 6' | 175 | 24 | 3 | |
| Paul McDonald | QB | 6'2" | 190 | 25 | | |
| Brian Sipe | QB | 6'1" | 195 | 34 | | |
| Rick Trocano | QB | 6' | 188 | 24 | | |
| Dino Hall | HB | 5'7" | 165 | 27 | | |
| Dwight Walker | HB | 5'10" | 185 | 24 | | 6 |
| Johnny Davis | FB | 6'1" | 235 | 27 | | |
| Vagas Ferguson (to HOU) | FB | 6'1" | 213 | 26 | | |
| Boyce Green | FB | 5'11" | 215 | 23 | | 24 |
| Mike Pruitt | FB | 6' | 225 | 29 | | 72 |
| Willis Adams | WR | 6'2" | 194 | 27 | | 12 |
| Ricky Belk | WR | 6' | 187 | 23 | | 12 |
| Ricky Feacher | WR | 5'10" | 180 | 29 | | 18 |
| Michael Harmon | WR | 6' | 208 | 22 | | |
| Bobby Jones | WR | 5'11" | 185 | 28 | | 24 |
| Dave Logan | WR | 6'4" | 216 | 29 | | 12 |
| Harry Holt | TE | 6'4" | 230 | 25 | | 18 |
| Ozzie Newsome | TE | 6'2" | 232 | 27 | | 36 |
| Stracka | TE | 6'3" | 225 | 23 | | |
| Matt Bahr | K | 5'10" | 175 | 27 | | 101 |
| Steve Cox | K | 6'4" | 195 | 25 | | 3 |
| Gossett | K | 6'2" | 197 | 26 | | |

Charles White - Broken Ankle

## CINCINNATI BENGALS 7-9-0 Forrest Gregg

| Scores of Each Game | | |
|---|---|---|
| 10 | L.A.RAIDERS | 20 |
| 6 | BUFFALO | 10 |
| 7 | Cleveland | 17 |
| 23 | Tampa Bay | 17 |
| 31 | BALTIMORE | 34 |
| 14 | PITTSBURGH | 24 |
| 17 | Denver | 24 |
| 28 | CLEVELAND | 21 |
| 34 | GREEN BAY | 14 |
| 55 | Houston | 14 |
| 15 | Kansas City | 20 |
| 38 | HOUSTON | 10 |
| 14 | Miami | 38 |
| 23 | Pittsburgh | 10 |
| 17 | DETROIT | 9 |
| 14 | Minnesota | 20 |

| Use Name | Pos. | Hgt | Wgt | Age | Int | Pts |
|---|---|---|---|---|---|---|
| Jim Hannula | OT | 6'6" | 264 | 24 | | |
| Anthony Munoz | OT | 6'6" | 278 | 25 | | |
| Mike Wilson | OT | 6'5" | 271 | 28 | | |
| Max Montoya | OG | 6'5" | 275 | 27 | | |
| Mike Obravac | OG | 6'6" | 275 | 27 | | |
| Dave Rimington | C | 6'3" | 288 | 21 | | |
| Dave Lapham | C | 6'4" | 262 | 31 | | |
| Blake Moore | C | 6'5" | 267 | 25 | | |
| Ross Browner | DE | 6'3" | 261 | 29 | 1 | |
| Gary Burley | DE | 6'3" | 282 | 30 | | |
| Glen Collins | DE | 6'6" | 265 | 24 | | |
| Eddie Edwards | DE | 6'5" | 256 | 29 | | |
| Chris Lindstrom | DE | 6'7" | 260 | 23 | | |
| Jerry Boyarsky | NT | 6'3" | 290 | 24 | | |
| Tim Krumrie | NT | 6'2" | 262 | 23 | | |
| Glenn Cameron | LB | 6'1" | 228 | 30 | | |
| Tom Dinkel | LB | 6'3" | 237 | 27 | | |
| Guy Frazier | LB | 6'2" | 215 | 24 | | |
| Jim LeClair | LB | 6'2" | 234 | 33 | | |
| Steve Maidlow | LB | 6'2" | 228 | 25 | | |
| Rick Razzano | LB | 5'11" | 227 | 27 | | |
| Jeff Schuh | LB | 6'2" | 228 | 25 | | |
| Ron Simpkins | LB | 6'1" | 235 | 25 | | |
| Reggie Williams | LB | 6'1" | 228 | 28 | | 6 |
| Louis Breeden | DB | 5'11" | 185 | 29 | 2 | |
| James Griffin | DB | 6'2" | 197 | 21 | 1 | 6 |
| Ray Griffin | DB | 5'10" | 186 | 27 | 2 | |
| Ray Horton | DB | 5'11" | 190 | 23 | 5 | 6 |
| Robert Jackson | DB | 5'10" | 186 | 24 | 2 | |
| Bobby Kemp | DB | 6' | 186 | 24 | 3 | |
| Ken Riley | DB | 6' | 191 | 36 | 8 | 12 |
| John Simmons | DB | 5'11" | 192 | 24 | | |
| Jimmy Turner | DB | 6' | 187 | 24 | | |
| Ken Anderson | QB | 6'1" | 212 | 34 | | 6 |
| Jeff Christensen | QB | 6'3" | 202 | 23 | | |
| Turk Schonert | QB | 6'1" | 190 | 26 | | 12 |
| Rodney Tate | HB | 5'11" | 190 | 24 | | |
| Stanley Wilson | HB-FB | 5'10" | 210 | 22 | | 12 |
| Charles Alexander | FB | 6'1" | 226 | 26 | | 18 |
| Pete Johnson | FB | 6'2" | 272 | 29 | | 84 |
| Larry Kinnebrew | FB | 6'1" | 252 | 24 | | 18 |
| Cris Collinsworth | WR | 6'5" | 192 | 24 | | 30 |
| Isaac Curtis | WR | 6' | 192 | 32 | | 12 |
| Steve Kreider | WR | 6'3" | 192 | 25 | | 6 |
| Mike Martin | WR | 5'10" | 186 | 22 | | |
| David Verser | WR | 6'1" | 202 | 25 | | |
| Andy Gibler | TE | 6'4" | 234 | 22 | | |
| M.L.Harris | TE | 6'5" | 238 | 29 | | 12 |
| Rodney Holman | TE | 6'3" | 232 | 23 | | |
| Dan Ross | TE | 6'4" | 235 | 26 | | 18 |
| Jim Breech | K | 5'6" | 161 | 27 | | 87 |
| Pat McInally | K | 6'6" | 212 | 30 | | |

Bryan Hicks - Shoulder Injury
Emanuel Weaver - Knee Injury

## HOUSTON OILERS 2-14-0 Ed Biles (0-6-0), Chuck Studley (2-8-0)

| Scores of Each Game | | |
|---|---|---|
| 38 | GREEN BAY | *41 |
| 6 | L.A.Raiders | 20 |
| 28 | PITTSBURGH | 40 |
| 13 | Buffalo | 30 |
| 10 | Pittsburgh | 17 |
| 14 | DENVER | 26 |
| 10 | Minnesota | 34 |
| 10 | KANSAS CITY | *13 |
| 19 | Cleveland | *25 |
| 14 | CINCINNATI | 55 |
| 27 | DETROIT | 38 |
| 10 | Cincinnati | 38 |
| 24 | Tampa Bay | 33 |
| 17 | MIAMI | 24 |
| 34 | CLEVELAND | 27 |
| 10 | Baltimore | 20 |

| Use Name | Pos. | Hgt | Wgt | Age | Int | Pts |
|---|---|---|---|---|---|---|
| Doug France | OT | 6'5" | 266 | 30 | | |
| Harvey Salem | OT | 6'6" | 264 | 22 | | |
| Morris Towns | OT | 6'4" | 263 | 29 | | |
| Bruce Matthews | OG-OT | 6'4" | 269 | 22 | | |
| Pat Howell (from ATL) | OG | 6'5" | 260 | 26 | | |
| Mike Munchak | OG | 6'3" | 275 | 23 | | |
| John Schuhmacher | OG | 6'3" | 269 | 27 | | |
| Al Steinfeld (to NYG) | OG | 6'5" | 256 | 24 | | |
| Ralph Williams | OG | 6'3" | 276 | 25 | | |
| David Carter | C | 6'2" | 260 | 24 | | |
| Les Studdard | C | 6'4" | 260 | 24 | | |
| Jesse Baker | DE | 6'5" | 272 | 26 | | |
| Elvin Bethea | DE | 6'3" | 272 | 26 | | |
| Jerome Foster | DE | 6'2" | 252 | 37 | | |
| Bob Hamm | DE | 6'4" | 248 | 24 | | |
| Ken Kennard | DE | 6'2" | 255 | 28 | | |
| Malcolm Taylor | DE | 6'6" | 280 | 23 | | |
| Brain Sochia | NT | 6'3" | 250 | 22 | | |
| Mike Stenarud | NT | 6'5" | 285 | 27 | | |
| Robert Abraham | LB | 6'1" | 215 | 23 | 1 | |
| Gregg Bingham | LB | 6'1" | 225 | 32 | 1 | |
| Robert Brazile | LB | 6'4" | 245 | 30 | | |
| Daryl Hunt | LB | 6'3" | 235 | 26 | | |
| Tim Joiner | LB | 6'4" | 224 | 22 | | |
| Avon Riley | LB | 6'3" | 225 | 30 | 1 | |
| Ted Thompson | LB | 6'1" | 219 | 30 | | |
| Keith Bostic | DB | 6'1" | 212 | 22 | 2 | |
| Steve Brown | DB | 5'11" | 188 | 23 | 1 | 6 |
| Carter Hartwig | DB | 6' | 207 | 27 | | |
| Greg Hill | DB | 6'1" | 189 | 22 | | |
| Bill Kay | DB | 6'1" | 190 | 23 | 2 | |
| Darryl Meadows | DB | 6'1" | 199 | 22 | | |
| Vernon Perry | DB | 6'2" | 210 | 28 | | |
| Mike Reinfeldt | DB | 6'2" | 192 | 30 | 1 | |
| Willie Tullis | DB | 6' | 193 | 25 | 5 | |
| J.C.Wilson | DB | 6' | 184 | 27 | | |
| Oliver Luck | QB | 6'2" | 193 | 23 | | |
| Archie Manning (to MIN) | QB | 6'3" | 211 | 34 | | |
| Gifford Nielsen | QB | 6'4" | 210 | 28 | | |
| Brian Ransom | QB | 6'3" | 205 | 23 | | |
| Earl Campbell | HB-FB | 5'11" | 238 | 28 | | 72 |
| Curtis Brown | FB | 5'10" | 203 | 28 | | 6 |
| Donnie Craft | FB | 6' | 205 | 23 | | |
| Stan Edwards | FB | 6' | 205 | 23 | | 6 |
| Larry Moriarty | FB | 6'1" | 228 | 25 | | 18 |
| Steve Bryant | WR | 6'2" | 191 | 23 | | |
| Mike Holston | WR | 6'3" | 188 | 25 | | |
| Mike Renfro | WR | 6' | 184 | 28 | | 12 |
| Carl Roaches | WR | 5'8" | 170 | 29 | | 6 |
| Tim Smith | WR | 6'2" | 203 | 26 | | 36 |
| Herkie Walls | WR | 5'8" | 154 | 22 | | 6 |
| Walt Arnold | TE | 6'3" | 234 | 25 | | 6 |
| Chris Dressel | TE | 6'4" | 231 | 22 | | 24 |
| Mike McCloskey | TE | 6'5" | 240 | 22 | | 6 |
| John James | K | 6'3" | 196 | 34 | | |
| Florian Kempf | K | 5'9" | 170 | 27 | | 84 |

* Overtime

## PITTSBURGH STEELERS

### RUSHING

| Last Name | No. | Yds | Avg | TD |
|---|---|---|---|---|
| F. Harris | 279 | 1007 | 3.6 | 5 |
| Pollard | 135 | 608 | 4.5 | 4 |
| Stoudt | 77 | 479 | 6.2 | 4 |
| Abercrombie | 112 | 446 | 4.0 | 4 |
| Hawthrone | 5 | 47 | 9.4 | 0 |
| T. Harris | 2 | 15 | 7.5 | 0 |
| Odom | 2 | 7 | 3.5 | 0 |
| Bradshaw | 1 | 3 | 3.0 | 0 |
| Sweeney | 1 | -2 | -2.0 | 0 |

### RECEIVING

| Last Name | No. | Yds | Avg | TD |
|---|---|---|---|---|
| Sweeney | 39 | 577 | 14.8 | 5 |
| Cunningham | 35 | 442 | 12.6 | 3 |
| F. Harris | 34 | 278 | 8.2 | 2 |
| Abercrombie | 26 | 391 | 15.0 | 3 |
| Hawthorne | 19 | 300 | 15.8 | 0 |
| Garrity | 19 | 279 | 14.7 | 1 |
| Pollard | 16 | 127 | 7.9 | 0 |
| Capers | 10 | 185 | 18.5 | 1 |
| Stallworth | 8 | 100 | 12.5 | 0 |
| Skansi | 3 | 39 | 13.0 | 0 |
| Rodgers | 2 | 36 | 18.0 | 0 |

### PUNT RETURNS

| Last Name | No. | Yds | Avg | TD |
|---|---|---|---|---|
| Skansi | 43 | 363 | 8.4 | 0 |
| Woods | 5 | 46 | 9.2 | 0 |
| T. Harris | 3 | 12 | 4.0 | 0 |

### KICKOFF RETURNS

| Last Name | No. | Yds | Avg | TD |
|---|---|---|---|---|
| Odom | 39 | 756 | 19.4 | 0 |
| T. Harris | 18 | 289 | 16.1 | 0 |
| Bingham | 1 | 15 | 15.0 | 0 |
| Kohrs | 1 | 6 | 6.0 | 0 |
| Donnalley | 0 | 2 | — | 0 |

### PASSING — PUNTING — KICKING

| PASSING | Att | Cmp | % | Yds | Yd/Att | TD | Int— | % | RK |
|---|---|---|---|---|---|---|---|---|---|
| Stoudt | 381 | 197 | 52 | 2553 | 6.70 | 12 | 21— | 6 | 15 |
| Malone | 20 | 9 | 45 | 124 | 6.20 | 1 | 2— | 10 | |
| Bradshaw | 8 | 5 | 63 | 77 | 9.63 | 2 | 0— | 0 | |

| PUNTING | No. | Avg. |
|---|---|---|
| Colquitt | 80 | 41.9 |

| KICKING | XP | Att | % | FG | Att | % |
|---|---|---|---|---|---|---|
| Anderson | 38 | 39 | 97 | 27 | 31 | 87 |

## CLEVELAND BROWNS

### RUSHING

| Last Name | No. | Yds | Avg | TD |
|---|---|---|---|---|
| Pruitt | 293 | 1184 | 4.0 | 10 |
| Green | 104 | 497 | 4.8 | 4 |
| Walker | 19 | 100 | 5.3 | 0 |
| Sipe | 26 | 56 | 2.2 | 0 |
| Davis | 13 | 42 | 3.2 | 0 |
| Jones | 1 | 19 | 19.0 | 0 |
| McDonald | 3 | 17 | 5.7 | 0 |
| Holt | 3 | 8 | 2.7 | 0 |
| Adams | 1 | 2 | 2.0 | 0 |
| Hall | 1 | 2 | 2.0 | 0 |
| Belk | 1 | -5 | -5.0 | 0 |

### RECEIVING

| Last Name | No. | Yds | Avg | TD |
|---|---|---|---|---|
| Newsome | 89 | 970 | 10.9 | 6 |
| Logan | 37 | 627 | 16.9 | 2 |
| Jones | 36 | 507 | 14.1 | 4 |
| Pruitt | 30 | 157 | 5.2 | 2 |
| Holt | 29 | 420 | 14.5 | 3 |
| Walker | 29 | 273 | 9.4 | 1 |
| Green | 25 | 167 | 6.7 | 1 |
| Adams | 20 | 374 | 18.7 | 2 |
| Feacher | 13 | 217 | 16.7 | 3 |
| Belk | 5 | 141 | 28.2 | 2 |
| Davis | 5 | 20 | 4.0 | 0 |
| Hall | 4 | 33 | 8.3 | 0 |
| Dieken | 1 | 14 | 14.0 | 1 |
| Stracka | 1 | 12 | 12.0 | 0 |

### PUNT RETURNS

| Last Name | No. | Yds | Avg | TD |
|---|---|---|---|---|
| Hall | 39 | 284 | 7.3 | 0 |
| Walker | 3 | 26 | 8.7 | 0 |

### KICKOFF RETURNS

| Last Name | No. | Yds | Avg | TD |
|---|---|---|---|---|
| Walker | 29 | 627 | 21.6 | 0 |
| Green | 17 | 350 | 20.6 | 0 |
| Hall | 11 | 237 | 21.5 | 0 |
| Ferguson | 2 | 36 | 18.0 | 0 |
| Nicolas | 2 | 29 | 14.5 | 0 |
| Contz | 1 | 3 | 3.0 | 0 |
| Davis | 1 | 8 | 8.0 | 0 |

### PASSING — PUNTING — KICKING

| PASSING | Att | Cmp | % | Yds | Yd/Att | TD | Int— | % | RK |
|---|---|---|---|---|---|---|---|---|---|
| Sipe | 496 | 291 | 59 | 3566 | 7.19 | 26 | 23— | 5 | 9 |
| McDonald | 68 | 32 | 47 | 341 | 5.01 | 1 | 4— | 6 | |
| Walker | 3 | 1 | 33 | 25 | 8.33 | 0 | 1— | 33 | |

| PUNTING | No. | Avg. |
|---|---|---|
| Gossett | 70 | 40.8 |

| KICKING | XP | Att | % | FG | Att | % |
|---|---|---|---|---|---|---|
| Bahr | 38 | 40 | 95 | 21 | 24 | 88 |
| Cox | 0 | 0 | 0 | 1 | 1 | 100 |

## CINCINNATI BENGALS

### RUSHING

| Last Name | No. | Yds | Avg | TD |
|---|---|---|---|---|
| Johnson | 210 | 763 | 3.6 | 14 |
| Alexander | 153 | 523 | 3.4 | 3 |
| S. Wilson | 56 | 267 | 4.8 | 1 |
| Kinnebrew | 39 | 156 | 4.0 | 3 |
| Anderson | 22 | 147 | 6.7 | 1 |
| Schonert | 29 | 117 | 4.0 | 2 |
| Tate | 25 | 77 | 3.1 | 0 |
| Verser | 2 | 31 | 15.5 | 0 |
| Martin | 2 | 21 | 10.5 | 0 |
| Collinsworth | 2 | 2 | 1.0 | 0 |
| Kreider | 1 | 2 | 2.0 | 0 |

### RECEIVING

| Last Name | No. | Yds | Avg | TD |
|---|---|---|---|---|
| Collinsworth | 66 | 1130 | 17.1 | 5 |
| Curtis | 42 | 571 | 13.6 | 2 |
| Kreider | 42 | 554 | 13.2 | 1 |
| Ross | 42 | 483 | 11.5 | 3 |
| Alexander | 32 | 187 | 5.8 | 0 |
| Tate | 18 | 142 | 7.9 | 0 |
| Johnson | 15 | 129 | 8.6 | 0 |
| S. Wilson | 12 | 107 | 8.9 | 1 |
| Harris | 8 | 66 | 8.3 | 2 |
| Verser | 7 | 82 | 11.7 | 0 |
| Martin | 2 | 22 | 11.0 | 0 |
| Holman | 2 | 15 | 7.5 | 0 |
| Kinnebrew | 2 | 4 | 2.0 | 0 |

### PUNT RETURNS

| Last Name | No. | Yds | Avg | TD |
|---|---|---|---|---|
| Martin | 23 | 227 | 9.9 | 0 |
| Simmons | 25 | 173 | 6.9 | 0 |
| Horton | 1 | 10 | 10.0 | 0 |

### KICKOFF RETURNS

| Last Name | No. | Yds | Avg | TD |
|---|---|---|---|---|
| Simmons | 14 | 317 | 22.6 | 0 |
| Tate | 13 | 218 | 16.8 | 0 |
| Verser | 13 | 253 | 19.5 | 0 |
| S. Wilson | 7 | 161 | 23.0 | 0 |
| Horton | 5 | 128 | 25.6 | 0 |
| Dinkel | 1 | 1 | 1.0 | 0 |
| Martin | 1 | 19 | 19.0 | 0 |

### PASSING — PUNTING — KICKING

| PASSING | Att | Cmp | % | Yds | Yd/Att | TD | Int— | % | RK |
|---|---|---|---|---|---|---|---|---|---|
| Anderson | 297 | 198 | 67 | 2333 | 7.86 | 12 | 13— | 4 | 4 |
| Schonert | 156 | 92 | 59 | 1159 | 7.43 | 2 | 5— | 3 | |
| Kreider | 1 | 0 | 0 | 0 | 0.00 | 0 | 0— | 0 | |

| PUNTING | No. | Avg. |
|---|---|---|
| McInally | 67 | 41.9 |

| KICKING | XP | Att | % | FG | Att | % |
|---|---|---|---|---|---|---|
| Breech | 39 | 41 | 95 | 16 | 23 | 70 |
| Browner | 1 | 1 | 100 | 0 | 0 | 0 |

## HOUSTON OILERS

### RUSHING

| Last Name | No. | Yds | Avg | TD |
|---|---|---|---|---|
| Campbell | 322 | 1301 | 4.0 | 12 |
| Moriarty | 65 | 321 | 4.9 | 3 |
| Craft | 55 | 147 | 2.7 | 0 |
| Luck | 17 | 55 | 3.2 | 0 |
| Walls | 5 | 44 | 8.8 | 0 |
| Nielsen | 8 | 43 | 5.4 | 0 |
| Edwards | 16 | 40 | 2.5 | 0 |
| Smith | 2 | 16 | 8.0 | 0 |
| Manning | 2 | 13 | 6.5 | 0 |
| Crutchfield | 3 | 7 | 2.3 | 0 |
| Dressel | 1 | 3 | 3.0 | 0 |
| Renfro | 1 | 3 | 3.0 | 0 |
| C. Brown | 3 | 0 | 0.0 | 0 |
| James | 1 | 0 | 0.0 | 0 |

### RECEIVING

| Last Name | No. | Yds | Avg | TD |
|---|---|---|---|---|
| Smith | 83 | 1176 | 14.2 | 6 |
| Dressel | 32 | 316 | 9.9 | 4 |
| Renfro | 23 | 316 | 13.7 | 2 |
| Campbell | 19 | 216 | 11.4 | 0 |
| Bryant | 16 | 211 | 13.2 | 0 |
| McCloskey | 16 | 137 | 8.6 | 1 |
| Holston | 14 | 205 | 14.6 | 0 |
| Walls | 12 | 276 | 23.0 | 1 |
| Arnold | 12 | 137 | 11.4 | 1 |
| Craft | 12 | 99 | 8.3 | 0 |
| Edwards | 9 | 79 | 8.8 | 1 |
| Moriarty | 4 | 32 | 8.0 | 0 |
| Kempf | 1 | 7 | 7.0 | 0 |

### PUNT RETURNS

| Last Name | No. | Yds | Avg | TD |
|---|---|---|---|---|
| Roaches | 20 | 159 | 8.0 | 0 |

### KICKOFF RETURNS

| Last Name | No. | Yds | Avg | TD |
|---|---|---|---|---|
| S. Brown | 31 | 795 | 25.6 | 1 |
| Roaches | 34 | 641 | 18.9 | 1 |
| Walls | 9 | 110 | 12.2 | 0 |
| Dressel | 4 | 40 | 10.0 | 0 |
| Moriarty | 2 | 25 | 12.5 | 0 |
| Hunt | 1 | 12 | 12.0 | 0 |
| McCloskey | 1 | 11 | 11.0 | 0 |
| Tullis | 1 | 16 | 16.0 | 0 |
| Riley | 0 | 26 | — | 0 |

### PASSING — PUNTING — KICKING

| PASSING | Att | Cmp | % | Yds | Yd/Att | TD | Int— | % | RK |
|---|---|---|---|---|---|---|---|---|---|
| Luck | 217 | 124 | 57 | 1375 | 6.34 | 8 | 13— | 6 | 14 |
| Nielsen | 175 | 90 | 51 | 1125 | 6.43 | 5 | 8— | 5 | |
| Manning | 88 | 44 | 50 | 755 | 8.58 | 2 | 8— | 9 | |
| Bryant | 1 | 1 | 100 | 24 | 24.00 | 1 | 0— | 0 | |
| James | 1 | 1 | 100 | 7 | 7.00 | 0 | 0— | 0 | |

| PUNTING | No. | Avg. |
|---|---|---|
| James | 79 | 39.7 |

| KICKING | XP | Att | % | FG | Att | % |
|---|---|---|---|---|---|---|
| Kempf | 33 | 34 | 97 | 17 | 21 | 81 |

**LOS ANGELES RAIDERS** 12-4-0 Tom Flores

| Scores of Each Game | | |
|---|---|---|
| 20 | Cincinnati | 10 |
| 20 | HOUSTON | 6 |
| 27 | MIAMI | 14 |
| 22 | Denver | 7 |
| 35 | Washington | 37 |
| 21 | KANSAS CITY | 20 |
| 36 | Seattle | 38 |
| 40 | Dallas | 38 |
| 21 | SEATTLE | 34 |
| 28 | Kansas City | 20 |
| 22 | DENVER | 20 |
| 27 | Buffalo | 24 |
| 27 | N.Y.GIANTS | 12 |
| 42 | San Diego | 10 |
| 24 | ST. LOUIS | 34 |
| 30 | SAN DIEGO | 14 |

| Use Name | Pos. | Hgt | Wgt | Age | Int | Pts |
|---|---|---|---|---|---|---|
| Bruce Davis | OT | 6'6" | 280 | 27 | | |
| Shelby Jordan | OT | 6'7" | 285 | 31 | | |
| Henry Lawrence | OT | 6'4" | 270 | 31 | | |
| Don Mosebar | OT | 6'6" | 270 | 21 | | |
| Ed Muransky | OT | 6'7" | 275 | 23 | | |
| Charley Hannah | OG | 6'5" | 260 | 28 | | |
| Mickey Marvin | OG | 6'4" | 265 | 27 | | |
| Dave Dalby | C | 6'2" | 250 | 32 | | |
| Jim Romano | C | 6'3" | 255 | 30 | | |
| Steve Sylvester | C-OG | 6'4" | 260 | 30 | | |
| Lyle Alzado | DE | 6'3" | 260 | 34 | | 2 |
| Howie Long | DE | 6'5" | 270 | 23 | | |
| Bill Pickel | DE | 6'5" | 260 | 23 | | |
| Greg Townsend | DE | 6'3" | 240 | 21 | | 8 |
| Reggie Kinlaw | NT | 6'2" | 245 | 26 | | |
| Archie Reese | NT | 6'3" | 275 | 27 | | |
| Johny Robinson | NT | 6'2" | 255 | 24 | | |
| David Stalls (from TB-DE) | NT | 6'5" | 250 | 27 | | |
| Jeff Barnes | LB | 6'2" | 225 | 28 | | |
| Darryl Byrd | LB | 6'1" | 220 | 22 | | |
| Tony Caldwell | LB | 6'1" | 225 | 22 | | |
| Ted Hendricks | LB | 6'7" | 240 | 35 | | |
| Rod Martin | LB | 6'2" | 220 | 29 | 4 | 12 |
| Matt Millen | LB | 6'2" | 250 | 25 | 1 | |
| Bob Nelson | LB | 6'4" | 235 | 30 | | |
| Jack Squirek | LB | 6'4" | 225 | 24 | | |
| Don Bessillieu | DB | 6'1" | 200 | 27 | | |
| James Davis | DB | 6' | 195 | 26 | 1 | |
| Mike Davis | DB | 6'3" | 205 | 27 | 1 | |
| Lester Hayes | DB | 6' | 200 | 28 | 2 | |
| Mike Haynes | DB | 6'2" | 190 | 30 | 1 | |
| Kenny Hill | HB | 6' | 195 | 25 | | |
| Vann McElroy | DB | 6'2" | 190 | 23 | 8 | |
| Odis McKinney | DB | 6'2" | 190 | 26 | 1 | |
| Irvin Phillips | DB | 6'1" | 190 | 23 | | |
| Ted Watts | DB | 6' | 195 | 25 | 1 | |
| David Humm | QB | 6'2" | 190 | 31 | | |
| Jim Plunkett | QB | 6'3" | 215 | 35 | | |
| Marc Wilson | QB | 6'6" | 220 | 26 | | |
| Marcus Allen | HB | 6'2" | 205 | 23 | | 72 |
| Rick Berns | HB | 6'2" | 215 | 27 | | |
| Cle Montgomery | HB | 5'8" | 180 | 27 | | |
| Greg Pruitt | HB | 5'10" | 190 | 32 | | 18 |
| Chester Willis | HB | 5'11" | 195 | 25 | | |
| Kenny King | HB-FB | 5'11" | 205 | 26 | | 12 |
| Frank Hawkins | FB | 5'9" | 210 | 24 | | 48 |
| Derrick Jensen | FB | 6'1" | 220 | 27 | | 6 |
| Malcolm Barnwell | WR | 5'11" | 185 | 25 | | 6 |
| Cliff Branch | WR | 5'11" | 170 | 35 | | 30 |
| Calvin Muhammad | WR | 6' | 190 | 24 | | 12 |
| Dokie Williams | WR | 5'11" | 180 | 23 | | 18 |
| Todd Christensen | TE | 6'3" | 230 | 27 | | 72 |
| Don Hasselbeck (from NE) | TE | 6'7" | 245 | 28 | | 12 |
| Chris Bahr | K | 5'10" | 175 | 30 | | 114 |
| Ray Guy | K | 6'3" | 190 | 33 | | |

Curt Marsh - Back Injury

**SEATTLE SEAHAWKS** 9-7-0 Chuck Knox

| Scores of Each Game | | |
|---|---|---|
| 13 | Kansas City | 17 |
| 17 | N.Y.Jets | 10 |
| 34 | SAN DIEGO | 31 |
| 17 | WASHINGTON | 27 |
| 24 | Cleveland | 9 |
| 21 | San Diego | 28 |
| 38 | L.A.RAIDERS | 36 |
| 21 | PITTSBURGH | 27 |
| 34 | L.A.Raiders | 21 |
| 27 | DENVER | 19 |
| 28 | St.Louis | 33 |
| 27 | Denver | 38 |
| 51 | KANSAS CITY | *48 |
| 10 | DALLAS | 35 |
| 17 | N.Y.Giants | 12 |
| 24 | NEW ENGLAND | 6 |

| Use Name | Pos. | Hgt | Wgt | Age | Int | Pts |
|---|---|---|---|---|---|---|
| Steve August | OT | 6'5" | 258 | 28 | | |
| Ron Essink | OT | 6'6" | 260 | 25 | | |
| Matt Hernandez | OT | 6'6" | 260 | 21 | | |
| Edwin Bailey | OG | 6'4" | 265 | 24 | | |
| Bill Dugan | OG | 6'4" | 271 | 24 | | |
| Reggie McKenzie | OG | 6'4" | 255 | 33 | | |
| Robert Pratt | OG | 6'4" | 250 | 32 | | |
| Blair Bush | C | 6'3" | 252 | 26 | | |
| Kani Kauahi | C | 6'2" | 260 | 23 | | |
| Jeff Bryant | DE | 6'5" | 270 | 23 | | |
| Sam Clancy | DE | 6'6" | 244 | 25 | | |
| Jacob Green | DE | 6'3" | 255 | 26 | 1 | 6 |
| Darrell Irvin | DE | 6'4" | 270 | 26 | | |
| Joe Nash | NT | 6'2" | 250 | 22 | | |
| Manu Tulasosopo | NT | 6'3" | 252 | 26 | | |
| Jerome Boyd | LB | 6'2" | 225 | 21 | | |
| Keith Butler | LB | 6'4" | 225 | 27 | 1 | |
| Greg Gaines | LB | 6'3" | 220 | 24 | | |
| Mark Hicks | LB | 6'2" | 225 | 22 | | |
| Michael Jackson | LB | 6'1" | 220 | 26 | | |
| Sam Merriman | LB | 6'3" | 225 | 22 | | |
| Joe Norman | LB | 6'1" | 220 | 26 | | |
| Shelton Robinson | LB | 6'2" | 233 | 22 | 1 | 12 |
| Bruce Scholtz | LB | 6'6" | 240 | 24 | 1 | |
| Eugene Wiliams | LB | 6'1" | 220 | 23 | 1 | |
| Gary Wimmer | LB | 6'2" | 225 | 22 | | |
| Dave Brown | DB | 6'1" | 192 | 30 | 6 | |
| Don Dufek | DB | 6' | 195 | 29 | | |
| Kenny Easley | DB | 6'3" | 205 | 24 | 7 | |
| John Harris | DB | 6'2" | 200 | 27 | 2 | |
| Greggory Johnson | DB | 6'1" | 188 | 24 | | |
| Kerry Justin | DB | 5'11" | 175 | 28 | 1 | |
| Paul Moyer | DB | 6'1" | 201 | 22 | 1 | 6 |
| Keith Simpson | DB | 6'1" | 195 | 27 | 4 | |
| Dave King | QB | 6'1" | 185 | 24 | | 12 |
| Jim Zorn | QB | 6'2" | 200 | 30 | | 6 |
| Zachary Dixon (from BAL) | HB | 6'1" | 204 | 26 | | 6 |
| Eric Lane | HB | 6' | 195 | 24 | | |
| Curt Warner | HB | 5'11" | 205 | 22 | | 6 |
| Cullen Bryant | FB | 6'1" | 236 | 32 | | |
| Dan Doornink | FB | 6'3" | 210 | 27 | | 24 |
| David Hughes | FB | 6' | 220 | 24 | | 12 |
| Chris Castor | WR | 6' | 170 | 23 | | |
| Harold Jackson | WR | 5'10" | 175 | 37 | | 6 |
| Paul Johns | WR | 5'11" | 170 | 24 | | 30 |
| Steve Largent | WR | 5'11" | 184 | 28 | | 66 |
| Byron Walker | WR | 6'4" | 190 | 23 | | 12 |
| Pete Metzelaars | TE | 6'7" | 240 | 23 | | 6 |
| Mike Tice | TE | 6'7" | 250 | 24 | | |
| Charle Young | TE | 6'4" | 234 | 32 | | 12 |
| Norm Johnson | K | 6'2" | 193 | 23 | | 103 |
| Jeff West | K | 6'3" | 205 | 30 | | |

Brian Flones - Knee Injury
Robert Hardy - Broken Leg

**DENVER BRONCOS** 9-7-0 Dan Reeves

| Scores of Each Game | | |
|---|---|---|
| 14 | Pittsburgh | 10 |
| 17 | Baltimore | 10 |
| 10 | PHILADELPHIA | 13 |
| 7 | L.A. RAIDERS | 22 |
| 14 | Chicago | 31 |
| 26 | Houston | 14 |
| 24 | CINCINNATI | 17 |
| 14 | SAN DIEGO | 6 |
| 27 | KANSAS CITY | 24 |
| 19 | Seattle | 27 |
| 20 | L.A. Raiders | 22 |
| 38 | SEATTLE | 27 |
| 7 | San Diego | 31 |
| 27 | CLEVELAND | 6 |
| 21 | BALTIMORE | 19 |
| 17 | Kansas City | 48 |

| Use Name | Pos. | Hgt | Wgt | Age | Int | Pts |
|---|---|---|---|---|---|---|
| Mark Cooper | OT | 6'5" | 267 | 23 | | |
| Shawn Hollingsworth | OT | 6'2" | 260 | 21 | | |
| Ken Lanier | OT | 6'3" | 269 | 24 | | |
| Dave Studdard | OT | 6'4" | 260 | 27 | | |
| Keith Uecker | OT | 6'5" | 260 | 23 | | |
| Tom Glassic | OG | 6'3" | 260 | 29 | | |
| Paul Howard | OG | 6'3" | 260 | 32 | | |
| Keth Bishop | C-OG | 6'3" | 260 | 26 | | |
| Bill Bryan | C | 6'2" | 258 | 28 | | |
| Walt Bowyer | DE | 6'4" | 245 | 22 | | |
| Barney Chavous | DE | 6'3" | 258 | 32 | | 6 |
| Rulon Jones | DE | 6'6" | 260 | 25 | | 2 |
| Brison Manor | DE | 6'4" | 248 | 31 | | |
| Jerry Baker | NT | 6'2" | 297 | 23 | | |
| Rubin Carter | NT | 6' | 256 | 30 | | |
| Don Latimer | NT | 6'3" | 265 | 28 | | |
| Rich Stachowski | NT | 6'4" | 245 | 22 | | |
| Steve Busick | LB | 6'4" | 227 | 24 | | |
| Darren Comeaux | LB | 6'1" | 227 | 23 | | |
| Rick Dennison | LB | 6'2" | 215 | 25 | | |
| Randy Gradisher | LB | 6'3" | 231 | 31 | 1 | |
| Tom Jackson | LB | 5'11" | 220 | 32 | 1 | |
| Karl Mecklenburg | LB | 6'3" | 250 | 23 | | |
| Jim Ryan | LB | 6'1" | 215 | 26 | | |
| Bob Swenson | LB | 6'3" | 225 | 30 | | |
| Ken Woodard | LB | 6'1" | 218 | 23 | | |
| Myron Dupree | DB | 5'11" | 180 | 21 | | |
| Steve Foley | DB | 6'2" | 190 | 29 | 5 | |
| Mike Harden | DB | 6'1" | 192 | 25 | 4 | |
| Roger Jackson | DB | 6' - | 186 | 24 | 1 | |
| Wilbur Myers | DB | 5'11" | 195 | 22 | | |
| Dennis Smith | DB | 6'3" | 200 | 24 | 4 | |
| Steve Trimble | DB | 5'10" | 181 | 25 | | |
| Steve Wilson | DB | 5'10" | 195 | 26 | 5 | |
| Louis Wright | DB | 6'2" | 200 | 30 | 6 | |
| Steve DeBerg | QB | 6'2" | 205 | 29 | | 6 |
| John Elway | QB | 6'3" | 202 | 23 | | 6 |
| Gary Kubiak | QB | 6' | 192 | 22 | | 6 |
| Rob Lytle | HB | 6'1" | 195 | 28 | | |
| Dave Preston | HB | 5'10" | 195 | 28 | | 12 |
| Sammy Winder | HB | 5'11" | 203 | 24 | | 18 |
| Jesse Myles | HB-FB | 5'10" | 210 | 22 | | 6 |
| Rick Parros | FB | 5'11" | 200 | 25 | | 18 |
| Nathan Poole | FB | 5'9" | 212 | 26 | | 24 |
| Gerald Willhite | FB | 5'10" | 200 | 24 | | 24 |
| Clint Sampson | WR | 5'11" | 183 | 22 | | 18 |
| Zach Thomas | WR | 6' | 182 | 22 | | 6 |
| Rick Upchurch | WR | 5'10" | 180 | 31 | | 12 |
| Steve Watson | WR | 6'4" | 195 | 26 | | 30 |
| Dean Barnett | TE | 6'2" | 225 | 24 | | |
| Clay Brown | TE | 6'3" | 225 | 24 | | |
| Ron Egloff | TE | 6'5" | 227 | 27 | | 12 |
| Riley Odoms | TE | 6'4" | 235 | 33 | | |
| John Sawyer (from WAS) | TE | 6'2" | 230 | 30 | | |
| James Wright | TE | 6'3" | 240 | 27 | | |
| Rich Karlis | K | 6' | 180 | 24 | | 96 |
| Luke Prestridge | K | 6'4" | 235 | 26 | | |

**KANSAS CITY CHIEFS** 6-10-0 John Mackovic

| Scores of Each Game | | |
|---|---|---|
| 17 | SEATTLE | 13 |
| 14 | SAN DIEGO | 17 |
| 12 | Washington | 27 |
| 6 | Miami | 14 |
| 38 | ST.LOUIS | 14 |
| 20 | L.A.Raiders | 21 |
| 38 | N.Y.GIANTS | 17 |
| 13 | Houston | *10 |
| 24 | Denver | 27 |
| 20 | L.A.RAIDERS | 28 |
| 20 | CINCINNATI | 15 |
| 21 | Dallas | 41 |
| 48 | Seattle | *51 |
| 9 | BUFFALO | 14 |
| 38 | San Diego | 41 |
| 48 | DENVER | 17 |

| Use Name | Pos. | Hgt | Wgt | Age | Int | Pts |
|---|---|---|---|---|---|---|
| Matt Herkenhoff | OT | 6'4" | 272 | 32 | | |
| David Lutz | OT | 6'6" | 280 | 23 | | |
| Rich Baldinger (from NYG) | OT-OG | 6'4" | 280 | 23 | | |
| Ellis Gardner | OT-OG | 6'4" | 263 | 21 | | |
| Mark Kirchner (from PIT) | OT-OG | 6'3" | 261 | 23 | | |
| Jim Rourke | OT-OG | 6'5" | 263 | 26 | | |
| Brad Budde | OG | 6'4" | 260 | 25 | | |
| Tom Condon | OG | 6'3" | 275 | 30 | | |
| Bob Simmons | OG | 6'4" | 260 | 29 | | |
| Adam Lingner | C-OG | 6'4" | 240 | 22 | | |
| Bob Rush | C | 6'5" | 264 | 28 | | |
| Mike Bell | DE | 6'4" | 260 | 26 | | |
| Dave Lindstrom | DE | 6'6" | 255 | 28 | | |
| Dean Prater | DE | 6'4" | 245 | 24 | | |
| Art Still | DE | 6'7" | 245 | 27 | | |
| Dino Mangiero | NT | 6'2" | 264 | 24 | | |
| Ken Kremer | NT | 6'4" | 252 | 26 | | |
| Ray Yakavonis | NT | 6'4" | 250 | 26 | | |
| Jerry Blanton | LB | 6'1" | 236 | 27 | | |
| Calvin Daniels | LB | 6'3" | 236 | 24 | | |
| Louis Haynes | LB | 6' | 227 | 23 | | |
| Tom Howard | LB | 6'2" | 215 | 29 | | |
| Charles Jackson | LB | 6'2" | 222 | 28 | | 6 |
| Dave Klug | LB | 6'4" | 230 | 25 | | |
| Steve Potter | LB | 6'3" | 235 | 25 | 1 | |
| Gary Spani | LB | 6'2" | 228 | 27 | | |
| James Walker | LB | 6'1" | 250 | 23 | | |
| John Zamberlin | LB | 6'2" | 226 | 27 | | |
| Gary Barbaro | DB | 6'4" | 210 | 29 | 3 | 6 |
| Trent Bryant | DB | 5'10" | 178 | 26 | 1 | |
| Lloyd Burruss | DB | 6' | 202 | 25 | 4 | |
| Deron Cherry | DB | 5'11" | 190 | 23 | 7 | |
| Gary Green | DB | 5'11" | 191 | 27 | 6 | |
| Van Jakes | DB | 6' | 185 | 22 | | |
| Albert Lewis | DB | 6'2" | 190 | 22 | 4 | |
| Durwood Roquemore | DB | 6'1" | 180 | 23 | | |
| Lucious Smith | DB | 5'10" | 190 | 26 | 3 | 6 |
| Todd Blackledge | QB | 6'3" | 225 | 22 | | |
| Bob Gagliano | QB | 6'3" | 195 | 24 | | |
| Bill Kenney | QB | 6'4" | 211 | 28 | | 18 |
| Billy Jackson | HB | 5'10" | 215 | 23 | | 12 |
| Lawrence Ricks | HB | 5'9" | 194 | 22 | | |
| Ken Thomas | HB | 5'9" | 211 | 23 | | 6 |
| Theotis Brown (from SEA) | FB | 6'2" | 225 | 26 | | 60 |
| James Hadnot | FB | 6'2" | 245 | 26 | | |
| Jewerl Thomas | FB | 5'10" | 228 | 25 | | |
| Carlos Carson | WR | 5'11" | 174 | 24 | | 42 |
| Anthony Hancock | WR | 6' | 187 | 23 | | 6 |
| Henry Marshall | WR | 6'2" | 220 | 29 | | 36 |
| Stephone Paige | WR | 6'2" | 180 | 21 | | 36 |
| J.T.Smith | WR | 6'2" | 185 | 27 | | |
| Ed Beckman | TE | 6'4" | 239 | 28 | | |
| Willie Scott | TE | 6'4" | 245 | 24 | | 36 |
| Ron Wetzel | TE | 6'5" | 242 | 22 | | |
| Jim Arnold | K | 6'2" | 212 | 22 | | |
| Nick Lowery | K | 6'4" | 189 | 27 | | 116 |

Del Thompson - Injury

**SAN DIEGO CHARGERS** 6-10-0 Don Coryell

| Scores of Each Game | | |
|---|---|---|
| 29 | N.Y.JETS | 41 |
| 17 | Kansas City | 14 |
| 31 | Seattle | 34 |
| 24 | CLEVELAND | *30 |
| 41 | N.Y.Giants | 34 |
| 28 | SEATTLE | 21 |
| 21 | New England | 37 |
| 6 | Denver | 14 |
| 24 | WASHINGTON | 27 |
| 3 | Pittsburgh | 26 |
| 24 | DALLAS | 23 |
| 14 | St. Louis | 44 |
| 31 | DENVER | 7 |
| 10 | L.A.RAIDERS | 42 |
| 41 | KANSAS CITY | 38 |
| 14 | L.A.Raiders | 30 |

| Use Name | Pos. | Hgt | Wgt | Age | Int | Pts |
|---|---|---|---|---|---|---|
| Don Brown | OT | 6'6" | 262 | 24 | | |
| Sam Claphan | OT | 6'6" | 267 | 26 | | |
| Andrew Gissinger | OT | 6'5" | 279 | 24 | | |
| Billy Shields | OT | 6'7" | 284 | 30 | | |
| Bill Elko | OG | 6'5" | 277 | 23 | | |
| Ed White | OG | 6'2" | 279 | 36 | | |
| Doug Wilkerson | OG | 6'2" | 258 | 36 | | |
| Darrel Gofourth | OG-C | 6'3" | 260 | 28 | | |
| Don Macek | C-OG | 6'3" | 260 | 29 | | |
| Dennis McKnight | C-OG | 6'3" | 253 | 23 | | |
| Chuck Ehin | DE | 6'4" | 254 | 22 | | |
| Keith Ferguson | DE | 6'5" | 241 | 24 | | |
| Leroy Jones | DE | 6'8" | 270 | 32 | | |
| Richard Ackerman | NT | 6'4" | 254 | 22 | | |
| Gary Johnson | NT | 6'2" | 251 | 31 | | |
| Louie Kelcher | NT | 6'5" | 310 | 30 | | |
| Carlos Bradley | LB | 6' | 226 | 23 | | |
| Larry Evans | LB | 6'2" | 220 | 30 | | |
| Mike Green | LB | 6' | 226 | 22 | 1 | |
| Linden King | LB | 6'4" | 245 | 28 | 1 | |
| Woodrow Lows | LB | 6' | 226 | 29 | | |
| Derrie Nelson | LB | 6'2" | 234 | 25 | | 6 |
| Ray Preston | LB | 6' | 220 | 29 | 1 | |
| Billy Ray Smith | LB | 6'3" | 239 | 22 | | |
| Clif Thrift | LB | 6'2" | 230 | 27 | | |
| Gill Byrd | DB | 5'11" | 191 | 22 | 1 | |
| Tim Fox | DB | 5'11" | 186 | 29 | 2 | |
| Ken Greene | DB | 6'3" | 203 | 27 | | |
| Bob Gregor | DB | 6'2" | 203 | 27 | | |
| Reuben Henderson | DB | 6'1" | 188 | 24 | | |
| Bruce Laird | DB | 6' | 195 | 33 | | |
| Miles McPherson | DB | 5'11" | 183 | 23 | 1 | |
| Darrell Pattillo | DB | 5'10" | 194 | 22 | | |
| Danny Walters | DB | 6'1" | 187 | 22 | 7 | |
| Andre Young | DB | 6' | 203 | 22 | 2 | 6 |
| Dan Fouts | QB | 6'3" | 205 | 32 | | 6 |
| Ed Luther | QB | 6'3" | 210 | 26 | | |
| Bruce Mathison | QB | 6'3" | 210 | 24 | | |
| James Brooks | HB | 5'9" | 177 | 24 | | 18 |
| Earnest Jackson | HB | 5'9" | 206 | 23 | | |
| John Cappeletti | FB | 6'1" | 215 | 31 | | |
| Jim Jodat | FB | 5'11" | 213 | 29 | | |
| Chuck Muncie | FB | 6'3" | 228 | 30 | | 78 |
| Sherman Smith | FB | 6'4" | 225 | 28 | | |
| Roger Carr | WR | 6'3" | 195 | 31 | | |
| Wes Chandler | WR | 6' | 183 | 27 | | 30 |
| Bobby Duckworth | WR | 6'3" | 197 | 24 | | 30 |
| Hosea Fortune | WR | 6' | 176 | 24 | | |
| Charlie Joiner | WR | 5'11" | 180 | 35 | | 18 |
| Dwight Scales | WR | 6'2" | 182 | 30 | | |
| Pete Holohan | TE | 6'4" | 240 | 24 | | 12 |
| Eric Sievers | TE | 6'4" | 233 | 24 | | 18 |
| Kellen Winslow | TE | 6'5" | 251 | 25 | | 48 |
| Rolf Benirschke | K | 6' | 179 | 26 | | 88 |
| Maury Buford | K | 6' | 185 | 23 | | |

Chuck Loewen - Back Injury

* Overtime

# LOS ANGELES RAIDERS

**RUSHING**

| Last Name | No. | Yds | Avg | TD |
|---|---|---|---|---|
| Allen | 266 | 1014 | 3.8 | 9 |
| Hawkins | 110 | 526 | 4.8 | 6 |
| King | 82 | 294 | 3.6 | 1 |
| Pruitt | 26 | 154 | 5.9 | 2 |
| Wilson | 13 | 122 | 9.4 | 0 |
| Plunkett | 26 | 78 | 3.0 | 0 |
| Berns | 6 | 22 | 3.7 | 0 |
| Branch | 1 | 20 | 20.0 | 0 |
| Barnwell | 1 | 12 | 12.0 | 0 |
| Montgomery | 2 | 7 | 3.5 | 0 |
| Jensen | 1 | 5 | 5.0 | 0 |
| Willis | 5 | 0 | 0.0 | 0 |
| Humm | 1 | -1 | -1.0 | 0 |
| Guy | 2 | -13 | -6.5 | 0 |

**RECEIVING**

| Last Name | No. | Yds | Avg | TD |
|---|---|---|---|---|
| Christensen | 92 | 1247 | 13.6 | 12 |
| Allen | 68 | 590 | 8.7 | 2 |
| Branch | 39 | 696 | 17.8 | 5 |
| Barnwell | 35 | 513 | 14.7 | 1 |
| Hawkins | 20 | 150 | 7.5 | 2 |
| Williams | 14 | 259 | 18.5 | 3 |
| King | 14 | 149 | 10.6 | 1 |
| Muhammad | 13 | 252 | 19.4 | 2 |
| Montgomery | 2 | 29 | 14.5 | 0 |
| Hasselbeck | 3 | 24 | 8.0 | 2 |
| Pruitt | 1 | 6 | 6.0 | 0 |
| Jensen | 1 | 2 | 2.0 | 1 |

**PUNT RETURNS**

| Last Name | No. | Yds | Avg | TD |
|---|---|---|---|---|
| Pruitt | 58 | 666 | 11.5 | 1 |

**KICKOFF RETURNS**

| Last Name | No. | Yds | Avg | TD |
|---|---|---|---|---|
| Montgomery | 21 | 464 | 22.1 | 0 |
| Pruitt | 31 | 604 | 19.5 | 0 |
| Williams | 5 | 88 | 17.6 | 0 |
| Millen | 2 | 19 | 9.5 | 0 |
| Jensen | 1 | 0 | 0.0 | 0 |
| Martin | 1 | 0 | 0.0 | 0 |

**PASSING — PUNTING — KICKING**

| PASSING | Att | Cmp | % | Yds | Yd/Att | TD | Int- | % | RK |
|---|---|---|---|---|---|---|---|---|---|
| Plunkett | 379 | 230 | 60 | 2935 | 7.74 | 20 | 18— | 4 | 5 |
| Wilson | 117 | 67 | 57 | 864 | 7.38 | 8 | 6— | 5 | |
| Allen | 7 | 4 | 57 | 111 | 15.86 | 3 | 0— | 0 | |
| Pruitt | 1 | 0 | 0 | 0 | 0.00 | 0 | 0— | 0 | |

| PUNTING | No. | Avg. |
|---|---|---|
| Guy | 78 | 42.8 |

| KICKING | XP | ATT | % | FG | ATT | % |
|---|---|---|---|---|---|---|
| Bahr | 51 | 53 | 96 | 21 | 27 | 77 |

# SEATTLE SEAHAWKS

**RUSHING**

| Last Name | No. | Yds | Avg | TD |
|---|---|---|---|---|
| Warner | 335 | 1449 | 4.3 | 13 |
| Hughes | 83 | 313 | 3.8 | 1 |
| Doornink | 40 | 99 | 2.5 | 2 |
| C. Bryant | 27 | 87 | 3.2 | 0 |
| Zorn | 30 | 71 | 2.4 | 1 |
| Krieg | 16 | 55 | 3.4 | 2 |
| Dixon | 4 | 18 | 4.5 | 0 |
| T. Brown | 6 | 14 | 2.3 | 0 |
| Johns | 2 | 12 | 6.0 | 0 |
| Lane | 3 | 1 | 0.3 | 0 |

**RECEIVING**

| Last Name | No. | Yds | Avg | TD |
|---|---|---|---|---|
| Largent | 72 | 1074 | 14.9 | 11 |
| Warner | 42 | 325 | 7.7 | 1 |
| Young | 36 | 529 | 14.7 | 2 |
| Johns | 34 | 486 | 14.3 | 4 |
| Doornink | 24 | 328 | 13.7 | 2 |
| Walker | 12 | 248 | 20.7 | 2 |
| Hughes | 10 | 100 | 10.0 | 1 |
| H. Jackson | 8 | 126 | 15.8 | 0 |
| Metzelaars | 7 | 72 | 10.3 | 1 |
| C. Bryant | 3 | 8 | 2.7 | 0 |
| Lane | 2 | 9 | 4.5 | 0 |
| Krieg | 1 | 11 | 11.0 | 0 |

**PUNT RETURNS**

| Last Name | No. | Yds | Avg | TD |
|---|---|---|---|---|
| Johns | 28 | 316 | 11.3 | 1 |
| G. Johnson | 3 | 17 | 5.7 | 0 |
| Harris | 2 | 27 | 13.5 | 0 |
| Easley | 1 | 6 | 6.0 | 0 |

**KICKOFF RETURNS**

| Last Name | No. | Yds | Avg | TD |
|---|---|---|---|---|
| Dixon | 51 | 1171 | 23.0 | 1 |
| Hughes | 12 | 282 | 23.5 | 0 |
| Lane | 4 | 58 | 14.5 | 0 |
| McAlister | 3 | 59 | 19.7 | 0 |
| Tice | 2 | 28 | 14.0 | 0 |
| Metzelaars | 1 | 0 | 0.0 | 0 |

**PASSING — PUNTING — KICKING**

| PASSING | Att | Cmp | % | Yds | Yd/Att | TD | Int- | % | RK |
|---|---|---|---|---|---|---|---|---|---|
| Krieg | 243 | 147 | 61 | 2139 | 8.80 | 18 | 11— | 5 | 2 |
| Zorn | 205 | 103 | 50 | 1166 | 5.69 | 7 | 7— | 3 | 12 |
| Largent | 1 | 1 | 100 | 11 | 11.00 | 0 | 0— | 0 | |

| PUNTING | No. | Avg. |
|---|---|---|
| West | 79 | 39.5 |

| KICKING | XP | ATT | % | FG | ATT | % |
|---|---|---|---|---|---|---|
| N. Johnson | 49 | 50 | 98 | 18 | 25 | 72 |

# DENVER BRONCOS

**RUSHING**

| Last Name | No. | Yds | Avg | TD |
|---|---|---|---|---|
| Winder | 196 | 757 | 3.9 | 3 |
| Poole | 81 | 246 | 3.0 | 4 |
| Preston | 57 | 222 | 3.9 | 1 |
| Willhite | 43 | 188 | 4.4 | 3 |
| Elway | 28 | 146 | 5.2 | 1 |
| Parros | 30 | 96 | 3.2 | 1 |
| Myles | 8 | 52 | 6.5 | 0 |
| DeBerg | 13 | 28 | 2.2 | 1 |
| Upchurch | 6 | 19 | 3.2 | 0 |
| Kubiak | 4 | 17 | 4.3 | 1 |
| Watson | 3 | 17 | 5.7 | 0 |
| Prestridge | 1 | 7 | 7.0 | 0 |
| J. Wright | 1 | -11 | -11.0 | 0 |

**RECEIVING**

| Last Name | No. | Yds | Avg | TD |
|---|---|---|---|---|
| Watson | 59 | 1133 | 19.2 | 5 |
| Upchurch | 40 | 639 | 16.0 | 2 |
| Winder | 23 | 150 | 6.5 | 0 |
| Egloff | 20 | 205 | 10.3 | 2 |
| Poole | 20 | 184 | 9.2 | 0 |
| Preston | 17 | 137 | 8.1 | 1 |
| Willhite | 14 | 153 | 10.9 | 1 |
| J. Wright | 13 | 134 | 10.3 | 0 |
| Thomas | 12 | 182 | 15.2 | 0 |
| Parros | 12 | 126 | 10.5 | 2 |
| Sampson | 10 | 200 | 20.0 | 3 |
| Myles | 7 | 119 | 17.0 | 1 |
| Odoms | 4 | 62 | 15.5 | 0 |
| Sawyer | 3 | 42 | 14.0 | 0 |

**PUNT RETURNS**

| Last Name | No. | Yds | Avg | TD |
|---|---|---|---|---|
| Thomas | 33 | 368 | 11.2 | 1 |
| Upchurch | 4 | 52 | 13.0 | 0 |
| L. Wright | 1 | 0 | 0.0 | 0 |

**KICKOFF RETURNS**

| Last Name | No. | Yds | Avg | TD |
|---|---|---|---|---|
| Thomas | 28 | 573 | 20.5 | 0 |
| Wilson | 24 | 485 | 20.2 | 0 |
| Studdard | 2 | 8 | 4.0 | 0 |
| Harden | 1 | 9 | 9.0 | 0 |
| T. Jackson | 1 | 2 | 2.0 | 0 |

**PASSING — PUNTING — KICKING**

| PASSING | Att | Cmp | % | Yds | Yd/Att | TD | Int- | % | RK |
|---|---|---|---|---|---|---|---|---|---|
| DeBerg | 215 | 119 | 55 | 1617 | 7.52 | 9 | 7— | 3 | 8 |
| Elway | 259 | 123 | 47 | 1663 | 6.42 | 7 | 14— | 5 | 17 |
| Kubiak | 22 | 12 | 55 | 186 | 8.45 | 1 | 1— | 5 | |
| Upchurch | 2 | 0 | 0 | 0 | 0 | 0 | 0— | 0 | |
| Willhite | 1 | 0 | 0 | 0 | 0 | 0 | 0— | 0 | |

| PUNTING | No. | Avg. |
|---|---|---|
| Prestridge | 87 | 41.6 |

| KICKING | XP | ATT | % | FG | ATT | % |
|---|---|---|---|---|---|---|
| Karlis | 33 | 34 | 97.1 | 21 | 25 | 84 |

# KANSAS CITY CHIEFS

**RUSHING**

| Last Name | No. | Yds | Avg | TD |
|---|---|---|---|---|
| B. Jackson | 152 | 499 | 3.3 | 2 |
| Brown | 124 | 467 | 3.8 | 8 |
| J. Thomas | 44 | 115 | 2.6 | 0 |
| Kenney | 23 | 59 | 2.6 | 3 |
| K. Thomas | 15 | 55 | 3.7 | 0 |
| Ricks | 21 | 28 | 1.3 | 0 |
| Carson | 2 | 20 | 10.0 | 0 |
| Hadnot | 4 | 10 | 2.5 | 0 |
| Scott | 1 | 1 | 1.0 | 0 |
| Blackledge | 1 | 0 | 0.0 | 0 |

**RECEIVING**

| Last Name | No. | Yds | Avg | TD |
|---|---|---|---|---|
| Carson | 80 | 1351 | 16.9 | 7 |
| Marshall | 50 | 788 | 15.8 | 6 |
| Brown | 47 | 418 | 8.9 | 2 |
| Hancock | 37 | 584 | 15.8 | 1 |
| B. Jackson | 32 | 243 | 7.6 | 0 |
| Paige | 30 | 528 | 17.6 | 6 |
| Scott | 29 | 247 | 8.5 | 6 |
| K. Thomas | 28 | 236 | 8.4 | 1 |
| Beckman | 13 | 130 | 10.0 | 0 |
| J. Thomas | 10 | 51 | 5.1 | 0 |
| J. Smith | 7 | 85 | 12.1 | 0 |
| Ricks | 3 | 5 | 1.7 | 0 |
| Hadnot | 2 | 18 | 9.0 | 0 |
| Kenney | 1 | 0 | 0.0 | 0 |

**PUNT RETURNS**

| Last Name | No. | Yds | Avg | TD |
|---|---|---|---|---|
| J. Smith | 26 | 210 | 8.1 | 0 |
| Hancock | 14 | 81 | 5.8 | 0 |

**KICKOFF RETURNS**

| Last Name | No. | Yds | Avg | TD |
|---|---|---|---|---|
| Hancock | 29 | 515 | 17.8 | 0 |
| Brown | 15 | 301 | 20.1 | 0 |
| Roquemore | 3 | 36 | 12.0 | 0 |
| Cherry | 2 | 54 | 27.0 | 0 |
| Carson | 1 | 12 | 12.0 | 0 |
| Daniels | 1 | 0 | 0.0 | 0 |
| Lindstrom | 1 | 0 | 0.0 | 0 |
| J. Smith | 1 | 5 | 5.0 | 0 |
| K. Thomas | 1 | 6 | 6.0 | 0 |
| Burruss | 0 | 0 | 0.0 | 0 |

**PASSING — PUNTING — KICKING**

| PASSING | Att | Cmp | % | Yds | Yd/Att | TD | Int- | % | RK |
|---|---|---|---|---|---|---|---|---|---|
| Kenney | 603 | 346 | 57 | 4348 | 7.21 | 24 | 18— | 3 | 7 |
| Blackledge | 34 | 20 | 59 | 259 | 7.62 | 3 | 0— | 0 | |
| J. Thomas | 2 | 1 | 50 | 18 | 9.00 | 1 | 1— | 50 | |
| Brown | 1 | 1 | 100 | 11 | 11.00 | 0 | 0— | 0 | |
| Carson | 1 | 1 | 100 | 48 | 48.00 | 1 | 0— | 0 | |
| Marshall | 0 | 0 | 0 | 0 | 0 | 0 | 0— | 0 | |

| PUNTING | No. | Avg. |
|---|---|---|
| Arnold | 93 | 39.9 |

| KICKING | XP | ATT | % | FG | ATT | % |
|---|---|---|---|---|---|---|
| Lowery | 44 | 45 | 98 | 24 | 30 | 80 |

# SAN DIEGO CHARGERS

**RUSHING**

| Last Name | No. | Yds | Avg | TD |
|---|---|---|---|---|
| Muncie | 235 | 886 | 3.8 | 12 |
| Brooks | 127 | 516 | 4.1 | 3 |
| S. Smith | 24 | 91 | 3.8 | 0 |
| Jackson | 11 | 39 | 3.5 | 0 |
| Chandler | 2 | 25 | 12.5 | 0 |
| Cappelletti | 1 | 5 | 5.0 | 0 |
| Mathison | 1 | 0 | 0.0 | 0 |
| Fouts | 12 | -5 | -0.4 | 0 |
| Sievers | 1 | -7 | -7.0 | 0 |
| Luther | 9 | -14 | -1.6 | 0 |

**RECEIVING**

| Last Name | No. | Yds | Avg | TD |
|---|---|---|---|---|
| Winslow | 88 | 1172 | 13.3 | 8 |
| Joiner | 65 | 960 | 14.8 | 3 |
| Chandler | 58 | 845 | 14.6 | 5 |
| Muncie | 42 | 396 | 9.4 | 1 |
| Sievers | 33 | 452 | 13.7 | 3 |
| Brooks | 25 | 215 | 8.6 | 0 |
| Holohan | 23 | 272 | 11.8 | 2 |
| Duckworth | 20 | 422 | 21.1 | 5 |
| S. Smith | 6 | 51 | 8.5 | 0 |
| Jackson | 5 | 42 | 8.4 | 0 |
| Carr | 2 | 36 | 18.0 | 0 |
| Scales | 2 | 28 | 14.0 | 0 |

**PUNT RETURNS**

| Last Name | No. | Yds | Avg | TD |
|---|---|---|---|---|
| Brooks | 18 | 137 | 7.6 | 0 |
| Chandler | 8 | 26 | 3.3 | 0 |
| Fortune | 4 | 16 | 4.0 | 0 |
| Scales | 2 | 34 | 17.0 | 0 |
| Laird | 1 | 0 | 0.0 | 0 |

**KICKOFF RETURNS**

| Last Name | No. | Yds | Avg | TD |
|---|---|---|---|---|
| Brooks | 32 | 607 | 19.0 | 0 |
| Laird | 15 | 342 | 22.8 | 0 |
| Jackson | 11 | 201 | 18.3 | 0 |
| McPherson | 5 | 77 | 15.4 | 0 |
| Jodat | 3 | 45 | 15.0 | 0 |
| Young | 3 | 41 | 13.7 | 0 |
| S. Smith | 2 | 32 | 16.0 | 0 |
| B. Smith | 1 | 10 | 10.0 | 0 |
| Scales | 1 | 16 | 16.0 | 0 |
| Sievers | 1 | 6 | 6.0 | 0 |

**PASSING — PUNTING — KICKING**

| PASSING | Att | Cmp | % | Yds | Yd/Att | TD | Int- | % | RK |
|---|---|---|---|---|---|---|---|---|---|
| Fouts | 340 | 215 | 63 | 2975 | 8.75 | 20 | 15— | 4 | 3 |
| Luther | 287 | 151 | 53 | 1875 | 6.53 | 7 | 17— | 6 | 16 |
| Mathison | 5 | 3 | 60 | 41 | 8.20 | 0 | 1— | 20 | |
| Buford | 1 | 0 | 0 | 0 | 0.00 | 0 | 0— | 0 | |
| Holohan | 1 | 0 | 0 | 0 | 0.00 | 0 | 0— | 0 | |
| S. Smith | 1 | 0 | 0 | 0 | 0.00 | 0 | 0— | 0 | |
| Chandler | 0 | 0 | 0 | 0 | 0 | 0 | 0— | 0 | |

| PUNTING | No. | Avg. |
|---|---|---|
| Buford | 63 | 43.9 |

| KICKING | XP | ATT | % | FG | ATT | % |
|---|---|---|---|---|---|---|
| Benirschke | 43 | 45 | 96 | 15 | 24 | 63 |

# 1983 N.F.C.— PLAYOFFS

December 26, 1983 at Irving, Tx. (Attendance 43,521)

SCORING

| | | | | | |
|---|---|---|---|---|---|
| L.A. RAMS | 7 | 0 | 7 | 10- | 24 |
| DALLAS | 0 | 7 | 3 | 7- | 17 |

First Quarter
- L.A. — Da., Hill 18 yard pass from Ferragamo PAT-Lansford (kick)

Second Quarter
- Dal. — T. Hill, 14 yard pass from White PAT—Septien (kick)

Third Quarter
- Dal. — Septien, 41 yard field goal
- L.A. — Dennard, 16 yard pass from Ferragamo PAT-Lansford (kick)

Fourth Quarter
- L.A. — Farmer, 8 yard pass from Ferragamo PAT-Lansford (kick)
- L.A. — Lansford, 20 yard field goal
- Dal. — Cosbie, 2 yard pass from White PAT-Septien (kick)

TEAM STATISTICS

| L.A. | | DALL. |
|---|---|---|
| 19 | First Downs- Total | 24 |
| 5 | First Downs-Rushing | 4 |
| 11 | First Downs-Passing | 20 |
| 3 | First Downs- Penalty | 0 |
| 0 | Fumbles- Number | 2 |
| 0 | Fumbles- Lost Ball | 1 |
| 4 | Penalties- Number | 6 |
| 18 | Yards Penalized | 40 |
| 0 | Missed Field Goals | 0 |
| 63 | Offensive Plays | 76 |
| 243 | Net Yards | 363 |
| 3.5 | Average Gain | 4.8 |
| 0 | Giveaways | 4 |
| 4 | Takeaways | 0 |
| +4 | Difference | -4 |

INDIVIDUAL STATISTICS

L.A. RAMS / DALLAS

RUSHING

| L.A. RAMS | No. | Yds. | Avg. | DALLAS | No. | Yds. | Avg. |
|---|---|---|---|---|---|---|---|
| Dickerson | 23 | 99 | 4.3 | Dorsett | 17 | 59 | 3.5 |
| Redden | 3 | 5 | 1.6 | Springs | 2 | 4 | 2.0 |
| Ferragamo | 4 | -10 | -2.5 | White | 1 | 0 | 0.0 |
| | 30 | 94 | 3.1 | | 20 | 63 | 3.2 |

RECEIVING

| L.A. RAMS | No. | Yds. | Avg. | DALLAS | No. | Yds. | Avg. |
|---|---|---|---|---|---|---|---|
| Farmer | 5 | 47 | 9.4 | T. Hill | 9 | 115 | 12.8 |
| Dennard | 4 | 44 | 11.0 | Springs | 6 | 38 | 6.3 |
| Barber | 2 | 20 | 10.0 | Cosbie | 5 | 62 | 12.4 |
| Dickerson | 2 | 11 | 5.5 | Dorsett | 4 | 12 | 3.0 |
| Da. Hill | 2 | 19 | 9.5 | Johnson | 3 | 20 | 6.7 |
| Ellard | 1 | 22 | 22.0 | Pearson | 2 | 49 | 24.5 |
| | 16 | 163 | 10.2 | Newsome | 2 | 25 | 12.5 |
| | | | | DuPree | 1 | 9 | 9.0 |
| | | | | | 33 | 330 | 10.0 |

PUNTING

| L.A. RAMS | No. | Avg. | DALLAS | No. | Avg. |
|---|---|---|---|---|---|
| Misko | 6 | 37.3 | D. White | 5 | 31.4 |

PUNT RETURNS

| L.A. RAMS | No. | Yds. | Avg. | DALLAS | No. | Yds. | Avg. |
|---|---|---|---|---|---|---|---|
| Ellard | 1 | 7 | 7.0 | Allen | 4 | 16 | 4.0 |
| Johnson | 1 | 3 | 3.0 | | | | |
| | 2 | 10 | 5.0 | | | | |

KICKOFF RETURNS

| L.A. RAMS | No. | Yds. | Avg. | DALLAS | No. | Yds. | Avg. |
|---|---|---|---|---|---|---|---|
| Guman | 2 | 37 | 18.5 | Fellows | 4 | 68 | 17.0 |
| Ellard | 2 | 37 | 18.5 | Springs | 1 | 12 | 12.0 |
| | 3 | 46 | 15.3 | | 5 | 80 | 16.0 |

INTERCEPTION RETURNS

| L.A. RAMS | No. | Yds. | Avg. | DALLAS |
|---|---|---|---|---|
| Irvin | 1 | 94 | 94.0 | none |
| J. Collins | 1 | 12 | 12.0 | |
| Owens | 1 | 5 | 5.0 | |
| | 3 | 111 | 37.0 | |

PASSING

L.A. RAMS

| | Att. | Comp. | Comp. Pct. | Yds. | Int. | Yds./ Att. | Yds./ Comp. |
|---|---|---|---|---|---|---|---|
| Ferragamo | 30 | 15 | 50.0 | 162 | 0 | 5.4 | 10.8 |
| Dickerson | 1 | 1 | 100.0 | 1 | 0 | 1.0 | 1.0 |
| | 31 | 16 | 51.6 | 163 | 0 | 5.3 | 10.2 |

DALLAS

| | Att. | Comp. | Comp. Pct. | Yds. | Int. | Yds./ Att. | Yds./ Comp. |
|---|---|---|---|---|---|---|---|
| White | 53 | 32 | 60.3 | 330 | 3 | 6.2 | 10.3 |

December 31, 1983 at San Francisco (Attendance 59,979)

SCORING

| | | | | | |
|---|---|---|---|---|---|
| DETROIT | 3 | 6 | 0 | 14- | 23 |
| SAN FRAN. | 7 | 7 | 3 | 7- | 24 |

First Quarter
- Det. — Murray, 37 yard field goal
- S.F. — Craig, 1 yard rush PAT-Wersching (kick)

Second Quarter
- S.F. — Tyler, 2 yard rush PAT-Wersching (kick)
- Det. — Murray, 21 yard field goal
- Det. — Murray, 54 yard field goal

Third Quarter
- S.F. — Wersching, 19 yard field goal

Fourth Quarter
- Det. — Sims, 11 yard rush PAT-Murray (kick)
- Det. — Sims, 3 yard rush PAT-Murray (kick)
- S.F. — Solomon, 14 yard pass from Montana PAT-Wersching (kick)

TEAM STATISTICS

| DET. | | S.F. |
|---|---|---|
| 22 | First Downs- Total | 20 |
| 9 | First Downs-Rushing | 9 |
| 11 | First Downs-Passing | 10 |
| 2 | First Downs- Penalty | 1 |
| 0 | Fumbles- Number | 2 |
| 3 | Fumbles- Lost Ball | 1 |
| 7 | Penalties- Number | 5 |
| 63 | Yards Penalized | 25 |
| 2 | Missed Field Goals | 2 |
| 75 | Offensive Plays | 60 |
| 412 | Net Yards | 291 |
| 5.5 | Average Gain | 4.9 |
| 5 | Giveaways | 2 |
| 2 | Takeaways | 5 |
| -3 | Difference | +3 |

INDIVIDUAL STATISTICS

DETROIT / SAN FRANCISCO

RUSHING

| DETROIT | No. | Yds. | Avg. | SAN FRANCISCO | No. | Yds. | Avg. |
|---|---|---|---|---|---|---|---|
| Sims | 20 | 114 | 5.7 | Tyler | 17 | 74 | 4.4 |
| Jones | 10 | 33 | 3.3 | Montana | 3 | 16 | 5.3 |
| Thompson | 1 | 24 | 24.0 | Craig | 7 | 13 | 1.9 |
| Danielson | 4 | 17 | 4.3 | | 27 | 103 | 3.8 |
| | 35 | 188 | 5.4 | | | | |

RECEIVING

| DETROIT | No. | Yds. | Avg. | SAN FRANCISCO | No. | Yds. | Avg. |
|---|---|---|---|---|---|---|---|
| Thompson | 6 | 74 | 12.3 | Craig | 7 | 61 | 8.7 |
| Chadwick | 5 | 58 | 11.6 | Francis | 4 | 75 | 18.8 |
| Jones | 5 | 44 | 8.8 | Solomon | 2 | 16 | 8.0 |
| Sims | 4 | 26 | 6.5 | Tyler | 2 | 15 | 7.5 |
| Scott | 3 | 29 | 9.7 | Wilson | 1 | 26 | 26.0 |
| Norris | 1 | 5 | 5.0 | Ramson | 1 | 4 | 4.0 |
| | 24 | 217 | 9.0 | Moore | 1 | 4 | 4.0 |
| | | | | | 18 | 201 | 11.2 |

PUNTING

| DETROIT | No. | Avg. | SAN FRANCISCO | No. | Avg. |
|---|---|---|---|---|---|
| Black | 2 | 36.5 | Orosz | 5 | 35.8 |

PUNT RETURNS

| DETROIT | No. | Yds. | Avg. | SAN FRANCISCO |
|---|---|---|---|---|
| Martin | 4 | 30 | 7.5 | none |

KICKOFF RETURNS

| DETROIT | No. | Yds. | Avg. | SAN FRANCISCO | No. | Yds. | Avg. |
|---|---|---|---|---|---|---|---|
| Hall | 2 | 45 | 22.5 | Moore | 3 | 48 | 16.0 |
| Jenkins | 2 | 43 | 21.5 | McLemore | 2 | 44 | 22.0 |
| | 4 | 88 | 22.0 | | 5 | 92 | 18.4 |

INTERCEPTION RETURNS

| DETROIT | No. | Yds. | Avg. | SAN FRANCISCO | No. | Yds. | Avg. |
|---|---|---|---|---|---|---|---|
| Watkins | 1 | 24 | 24.0 | Ellison | 2 | 8 | 4.0 |
| | | | | Hicks | 1 | 22 | 22.0 |
| | | | | Turner | 1 | 11 | 11.0 |
| | | | | Lott | 1 | 0 | 0.0 |
| | | | | | 5 | 41 | 8.2 |

PASSING

DETROIT

| | Att. | Comp. | Comp. Pct. | Yds. | Int. | Yds./ Att. | Yds./ Comp. |
|---|---|---|---|---|---|---|---|
| Danielson | 38 | 24 | 63.2 | 236 | 5 | 6.2 | 9.8 |

SAN FRANCISCO

| | Att. | Comp. | Comp. Pct. | Yds. | Int. | Yds./ Att. | Yds./ Comp. |
|---|---|---|---|---|---|---|---|
| Montana | 31 | 18 | 58.1 | 201 | 1 | 6.5 | 11.2 |

January 1, 1984 at Washington, D.C. (Attendance 55,363)

SCORING

| | | | | | |
|---|---|---|---|---|---|
| L.A. RAMS | 0 | 7 | 0 | 0- | 7 |
| WASHINGTON | 17 | 21 | 6 | 7- | 51 |

First Quarter
- Wash. — Riggins, 3 yard rush return PAT-Moseley (kick)
- Wash. — Monk, 40 yard pass from Theismann PAT-Moseley (kick)
- Wash. — Moseley, 42 yard field goal

Second Quarter
- Wash. — Riggins, 1 yard rush PAT-Moseley (kick)
- L.A. — Dennard, 32 yard pass from Ferragamo PAT-Lansford (kick)
- Wash. — Monk, 21 yard pass from Theismann PAT-Moseley (kick)
- Wash. — Riggins, rush PAT-Moseley (kick)

Third Quarter
- Wash. — Moseley, 36 yard field goal
- Wash. — Moseley, 41 yard field goal

Fourth Quarter
- Wash. — Green, 72 yard interception return PAT-Moseley (kick)

TEAM STATISTICS

| L.A. RAMS | | WASH. |
|---|---|---|
| 12 | First Downs- Total | 23 |
| 2 | First Downs-Rushing | 10 |
| 9 | First Downs-Passing | 12 |
| 1 | First Downs-Penalty | 1 |
| 2 | Fumbles-Number | 2 |
| 1 | Fumbles-Lost Ball | 1 |
| 7 | Penalties- Number | 6 |
| 41 | Yards Penalized | 55 |
| 0 | Missed Field Goals | 0 |
| 62 | Offensive Plays | 65 |
| 204 | Net Yards | 445 |
| 3.3 | Average Gain | 6.8 |
| 4 | Giveaways | 1 |
| 1 | Takeaways | 4 |
| -3 | Difference | +3 |

INDIVIDUAL STATISTICS

L.A. RAMS / WASHINGTON

RUSHING

| L.A. RAMS | No. | Yds. | Avg. | WASHINGTON | No. | Yds. | Avg. |
|---|---|---|---|---|---|---|---|
| Jones | 4 | 28 | 7.0 | Riggins | 25 | 119 | 4.7 |
| Dickerson | 10 | 16 | 1.6 | Giaquinto | 4 | 9 | 2.3 |
| Redden | 2 | 7 | 3.5 | Evans | 3 | 4 | 1.3 |
| | 16 | 51 | 3.2 | Wonsley | 2 | 3 | 1.5 |
| | | | | Washington | 5 | -2 | -0.4 |
| | | | | Holly | 1 | -3 | -3.0 |
| | | | | | 40 | 130 | 3.3 |

RECEIVING

| L.A. RAMS | No. | Yds. | Avg. | WASHINGTON | No. | Yds. | Avg. |
|---|---|---|---|---|---|---|---|
| Dickerson | 6 | 9 | 1.5 | Brown | 6 | 171 | 28.5 |
| Guman | 5 | 29 | 5.8 | Monk | 4 | 60 | 15.0 |
| Barber | 3 | 42 | 14.0 | Warren | 3 | 23 | 7.7 |
| Ellard | 3 | 39 | 13.0 | Giaquinto | 2 | 17 | 8.5 |
| Dennard | 2 | 50 | 25.0 | Garrett | 2 | 13 | 6.5 |
| Johnson | 1 | 17 | 17.0 | Walker | 1 | 14 | 14.0 |
| Da. Hill | 1 | 6 | 6.0 | Washington | 1 | 10 | 10.0 |
| | 20 | 175 | 8.8 | Didier | 1 | 7 | 7.0 |
| | | | | | 20 | 315 | 15.8 |

PUNTING

| L.A. RAMS | No. | Avg. | WASHINGTON | No. | Avg. |
|---|---|---|---|---|---|
| Misko | 7 | 33.8 | Hayes | 3 | 28.0 |

PUNT RETURNS

| L.A. RAMS | No. | Yds. | Avg. | WASHINGTON | No. | Yds. | Avg. |
|---|---|---|---|---|---|---|---|
| Ellard | 1 | 4 | 4.0 | Giaquinto | 3 | 56 | 18.7 |

KICKOFF RETURNS

| L.A. RAMS | No. | Yds. | Avg. | WASHINGTON | No. | Yds. | Avg. |
|---|---|---|---|---|---|---|---|
| Ellard | 7 | 120 | 17.1 | Garrett | 2 | 47 | 23.5 |
| Redden | 2 | 22 | 11.0 | | | | |
| E. Williams | 1 | 9 | 9.0 | | | | |
| | 10 | 151 | 15.1 | | | | |

INTERCEPTION RETURNS

| L.A. RAMS | WASHINGTON | No. | Yds. | Avg. |
|---|---|---|---|---|
| none | Washington | 1 | 0 | 0.0 |
| | Coffey | 1 | 0 | 0.0 |
| | Green | 1 | 72 | 72.0 |
| | | 3 | 72 | 24.0 |

PASSING

L.A. RAMS

| | Att. | Comp. | Comp. Pct. | Yds. | Int. | Yds./ Att. | Yds./ Comp. |
|---|---|---|---|---|---|---|---|
| Ferragamo | 43 | 20 | 46.5 | 175 | 3 | 4.1 | 8.8 |

WASHINGTON

| | Att. | Comp. | Comp. Pct. | Yds. | Int. | Yds./ Att. | Yds./ Comp. |
|---|---|---|---|---|---|---|---|
| Holly | 2 | 2 | 100.0 | 13 | 0 | 6.5 | 6.5 |
| Theismann | 23 | 18 | 72.0 | 302 | 0 | 13.1 | 16.8 |
| | 25 | 20 | 80.0 | 315 | 0 | 12.6 | 15.8 |

## December 24, 1983 at Seattle (Attendance 60,752)

### SCORING

| | | | | |
|---|---|---|---|---|
| DENVER | 7 | 0 | 0 | 0- 7 |
| SEATTLE | 7 | 3 | 7 | 14- 31 |

**First Quarter**
Sea. Largent 17 pass from Krieg
PAT-N. Johnson (kick)
Den. Myles 13 pass from DeBerg
PAT-Karlis (kick)

**Second Quarter**
Sea. N. Johnson, 37 yard field goal

**Third Quarter**
Sea. Metzelaars 5 pass from Krieg
PAT-N.Johnson (kick)

**Fourth Quarter**
Sea. Johns 18 pass from Krieg
PAT-N.Johnson (kick)
Sea. Hughes 2 yard rush
PAT-N. Johnson (kick)

### TEAM STATISTICS

| DEN. | | SEA |
|---|---|---|
| 21 | First Downs- Total | 17 |
| 5 | First Downs-Rushing | 8 |
| 14 | First Downs-Passing | 9 |
| 2 | First Downs- Penalty | 0 |
| 1 | Fumbles-Number | 1 |
| 1 | Fumbles-Lost Ball | 0 |
| 5 | Penalties-Number | 3 |
| 35 | Yards Penalized | 34 |
| 0 | Missed Field Goals | 0 |
| 69 | Offensive Plays | 53 |
| 360 | Net Yards | 324 |
| 5.2 | Average Gain | 6.1 |
| 3 | Giveaways | 0 |
| 0 | Takeaways | 3 |
| -3 | Difference | +3 |

### INDIVIDUAL STATISTICS

**DENVER** / **SEATTLE**

#### RUSHING

| | No. | Yds. | Avg. | | No. | Yds. | Avg. |
|---|---|---|---|---|---|---|---|
| Winder | 16 | 59 | 3.9 | Warner | 23 | 99 | 4.3 |
| Poole | 7 | 25 | 3.6 | Hughes | 3 | 16 | 5.3 |
| Elway | 3 | 16 | 5.3 | C. Bryant | 5 | 15 | 3.0 |
| Willhite | 5 | 16 | 3.2 | Krieg | 3 | 9 | 3.0 |
| Sampson | 1 | 8 | 8.0 | Dixon | 3 | 4 | 1.3 |
| Watson | 1 | 1 | 1.0 | Zorn | 1 | 2 | 2.0 |
| | 33 | 125 | 3.8 | | 38 | 145 | 3.8 |

#### RECEIVING

| | No. | Yds. | Avg. | | No. | Yds. | Avg. |
|---|---|---|---|---|---|---|---|
| Myles | 7 | 73 | 10.4 | Largent | 4 | 76 | 19.0 |
| Watson | 4 | 51 | 12.8 | Warner | 3 | 22 | 7.3 |
| Poole | 4 | 17 | 4.3 | Johns | 2 | 59 | 29.5 |
| Sampson | 3 | 52 | 17.3 | Young | 2 | 38 | 19.0 |
| Winder | 2 | 13 | 6.5 | Metzelaars | 1 | 5 | 5.0 |
| Thomas | 1 | 19 | 19.0 | | 12 | 200 | 16.7 |
| Egloff | 1 | 16 | 16.0 | | | | |
| Wilson | 1 | 12 | 12.0 | | | | |
| Willhite | 1 | 1 | 1.0 | | | | |
| | 24 | 254 | 10.6 | | | | |

#### PUNTING

| | | | | | | |
|---|---|---|---|---|---|---|
| Prestridge | 4 | 47.8 | West | 3 | | 41.7 |

#### PUNT RETURNS

| | | | | | | |
|---|---|---|---|---|---|---|
| Thomas | 3 | 10 | 3.3 | Johns | 4 | 58 | 14.5 |

#### KICKOFF RETURNS

| | No. | Yds. | Avg. | | No. | Yds. | Avg. |
|---|---|---|---|---|---|---|---|
| Thomas | 4 | 81 | 20.3 | Dixon | 2 | 43 | 21.5 |
| Wilson | 2 | 37 | 18.5 | | | | |
| | 6 | 118 | 19.7 | | | | |

#### INTERCEPTION RETURNS

| | | | | | No. | Yds. | Avg. |
|---|---|---|---|---|---|---|---|
| none | | | | Justin | 1 | 45 | 45.0 |
| | | | | G. Johnson | 1 | 0 | 0.0 |
| | | | | | 2 | 45 | 22.5 |

#### PASSING

**DENVER**

| | Att. | Comp. | Comp. Pct. | Yds. | Int | Yds./ Att. | Yds./ Comp. |
|---|---|---|---|---|---|---|---|
| DeBerg | 19 | 14 | 73.7 | 131 | 1 | 6.9 | 9.4 |
| Elway | 15 | 10 | 66.7 | 123 | 1 | 8.2 | 12.3 |
| | 34 | 24 | 70.6 | 254 | 2 | 7.5 | 10.6 |

**SEATTLE**

| | Att. | Comp. | Comp. Pct. | Yds. | Int | Yds./ Att. | Yds./ Comp. |
|---|---|---|---|---|---|---|---|
| Krieg | 13 | 12 | 92.3 | 200 | 0 | 15.4 | 16.7 |

## December 31, 1983 at Miami (Attendance 71,032)

### SCORING

| | | | | |
|---|---|---|---|---|
| SEATTLE | 0 | 7 | 7 | 13- 27 |
| MIAMI | 0 | 13 | 0 | 7- 20 |

**Second Quarter**
MIA. D. Johnson 19 pass from Marino
PAT-kick blocked
SEA. C. Bryant 6 pass from Krieg
PAT-N. Johnson (kick)
MIA. Duper 32 pass from Marino
PAT-von Schamann (kick)

**Third Quarter**
SEA. Warner 1 yard rush
PAT—N. Johnson (kick)

**Fourth Quarter**
SEA. N. Johnson 27 yard field goal
MIA. Bennett, 2 yard rush
PAT—von Schamann (kick)
SEA. Warner 2 yard rush
PAT-N.Johnson (kick)
SEA. N. Johnson 37 yard field goal

### TEAM STATISTICS

| SEA. | | MIA. |
|---|---|---|
| 21 | First Downs- Total | 21 |
| 12 | First Downs-Rushing | 9 |
| 9 | First Downs- Passing | 11 |
| 0 | First Downs- Penalty | 1 |
| 0 | Fumbles- Number | 3 |
| 0 | Fumbles- Lost Ball | 0 |
| 2 | Penalties- Number | 5 |
| 15 | Yards Penalized | 30 |
| 1 | Missed Field Goals | 0 |
| 72 | Offensive Plays | 56 |
| 334 | Net Yards | 321 |
| 4.6 | Average Gain | 5.7 |
| 1 | Giveaways | 5 |
| 5 | Takeaways | 1 |
| -4 | Difference | -4 |

### INDIVIDUAL STATISTICS

**SEATTLE** / **MIAMI**

#### RUSHING

| | No. | Yds. | Avg. | | No. | Yds. | Avg. |
|---|---|---|---|---|---|---|---|
| Warner | 29 | 113 | 3.9 | Overstreet | 9 | 50 | 8.0 |
| C. Bryant | 5 | 22 | 4.4 | Bennett | 7 | 31 | 4.4 |
| Hughes | 4 | 21 | 5.3 | Franklin | 6 | 28 | 4.7 |
| Krieg | 4 | -5 | -1.3 | Nathan | 8 | 19 | 2.4 |
| | 42 | 151 | 3.6 | | 30 | 128 | 4.3 |

#### RECEIVING

| | No. | Yds. | Avg. | | No. | Yds. | Avg. |
|---|---|---|---|---|---|---|---|
| Warner | 4 | 25 | 6.3 | Duper | 9 | 117 | 13.0 |
| Johns | 4 | 60 | 15.0 | Johnson | 2 | 29 | 14.5 |
| Largent | 2 | 56 | 28.0 | N. Moore | 2 | 26 | 13.0 |
| Doornink | 2 | 26 | 13.0 | Nathan | 1 | 6 | 6.0 |
| C. Bryant | 2 | 12 | 6.0 | Rose | 1 | 15 | 15.0 |
| | 16 | 192 | 12.0 | | 15 | 193 | 12.9 |

#### PUNTING

| | | | | | | |
|---|---|---|---|---|---|---|
| West | 4 | | 38.0 | Roby | 4 | | 35.5 |

#### PUNT RETURNS

| | | | | | No. | Yds. | Avg. |
|---|---|---|---|---|---|---|---|
| none | | | | Clayton | 2 | 32 | 16.0 |

#### KICKOFF RETURNS

| | No. | Yds. | Avg. | | No. | Yds. | Avg. |
|---|---|---|---|---|---|---|---|
| Dixon | 2 | 86 | 43.0 | Walker | 6 | 104 | 17.3 |
| Hughes | 2 | 44 | 22.0 | | | | |
| | 4 | 130 | 32.5 | | | | |

#### INTERCEPTION RETURNS

| | No. | Yds. | Avg. | | No. | Yds. | Avg. |
|---|---|---|---|---|---|---|---|
| Harris | 1 | 0 | 0.0 | Small | 1 | 18 | 18.0 |
| Justin | 1 | 0 | 0.0 | | | | |
| | 2 | 0 | 0.0 | | | | |

#### PASSING

**SEATTLE**

| | Att. | Comp. | Comp. Pct. | Yds. | Int | Yds./ Att. | Yds./ Comp. |
|---|---|---|---|---|---|---|---|
| Krieg | 28 | 15 | 53.6 | 192 | 1 | 6.9 | 12.8 |
| Zorn | 1 | 0 | 0.0 | 0 | 0 | 0.0 | 0.0 |
| | 29 | 15 | 51.7 | 192 | 1 | 6.6 | 12.8 |

**MIAMI**

| | Att. | Comp. | Comp. Pct. | Yds. | Int | Yds./ Att. | Yds./ Comp. |
|---|---|---|---|---|---|---|---|
| Marino | 25 | 15 | 60.0 | 193 | 2 | 7.7 | 12.9 |
| Clayton | 1 | 0 | 0.0 | 0 | 0 | 0.0 | 0.0 |
| | 26 | 15 | 57.7 | 193 | 2 | 7.4 | 12.9 |

## January 1, 1984 at Los Angeles (Attendance 90,334)

### SCORING

| | | | | |
|---|---|---|---|---|
| PITTSBURGH | 3 | 0 | 7 | 0- 10 |
| L.A. RAIDERS | 7 | 10 | 21 | 0- 38 |

**First Quarter**
Pitt. Anderson 17 yard field goal
L.A. Hayes 18 yard interception return
PAT-Bahr (kick)

**Second Quarter**
L.A. Allen 4 yard rush
PAT—Bahr (kick)
L.A. Bahr 45 yard field goal

**Third Quarter**
L.A. King 9 yard rush
PAT-Bahr (kick)
L.A. Allen 49 yard rush
PAT-Bahr (kick)
Pitt. Stallworth 58 pass from Stoudt
PAT-Anderson (kick)
L.A. Hawkins 2 yard rush
PAT—Bahr (kick)

### TEAM STATISTICS

| PITT. | | L.A. |
|---|---|---|
| 17 | First Downs- Total | 24 |
| 9 | First Downs-Rushing | 13 |
| 8 | First Downs-Passing | 9 |
| 0 | First Downs-Penalty | 2 |
| 2 | Fumbles- Number | 2 |
| 1 | Fumbles-Lost Ball | 0 |
| 4 | Penalties-Number | 2 |
| 30 | Yards Penalized | 15 |
| 0 | Missed Field Goals | 0 |
| 64 | Offensive Plays | 68 |
| 331 | Net Yards | 413 |
| 5.2 | Average Gain | 6.1 |
| 2 | Giveaways | 0 |
| 0 | Takeaways | 2 |
| -2 | Difference | +2 |

### INDIVIDUAL STATISTICS

**PITTSBURGH** / **LOS ANGELES**

#### RUSHING

| | No. | Yds. | Avg. | | No. | Yds. | Avg. |
|---|---|---|---|---|---|---|---|
| Stoudt | 9 | 50 | 5.6 | Allen | 13 | 121 | 9.3 |
| Pollard | 9 | 37 | 4.1 | Plunkett | 2 | 23 | 11.5 |
| Abercrombie | 6 | 36 | 6.0 | Hawkins | 10 | 25 | 2.5 |
| F. Harris | 6 | 33 | 5.5 | King | 6 | 20 | 3.3 |
| Odom | 1 | 4 | 4.0 | Guy | 1 | 2 | 2.0 |
| T. Harris | 1 | 2 | 2.0 | Wilson | 1 | -3 | -3.0 |
| | 32 | 162 | 5.1 | | 33 | 191 | 5.8 |

#### RECEIVING

| | No. | Yds. | Avg. | | No. | Yds. | Avg. |
|---|---|---|---|---|---|---|---|
| F. Harris | 4 | 31 | 7.8 | Christensen | 7 | 88 | 12.6 |
| Capers | 2 | 54 | 37.0 | Branch | 6 | 76 | 12.7 |
| Cunningham | 2 | 32 | 16.0 | Allen | 5 | 38 | 7.6 |
| Sweeney | 2 | 24 | 12.0 | Barnwell | 3 | 30 | 10.0 |
| Stallworth | 1 | 58 | 58.0 | | 21 | 232 | 11.0 |
| Odom | 1 | 6 | 6.0 | | | | |
| Abercrombie | 1 | 4 | 4.0 | | | | |
| | 13 | 209 | 16.1 | | | | |

#### PUNTING

| | | | | | | |
|---|---|---|---|---|---|---|
| Colquitt | 8 | | 40.9 | Guy | 6 | | 41.3 |

#### PUNT RETURNS

| | No. | Yds. | Avg. | | No. | Yds. | Avg. |
|---|---|---|---|---|---|---|---|
| Woods | 3 | 21 | 7.0 | Pruitt | 5 | 47 | 9.4 |
| | | | | Montgomery | 1 | 5 | 5.0 |
| | | | | | 6 | 52 | 8.7 |

#### KICKOFF RETURNS

| | No. | Yds. | Avg. | | No. | Yds. | Avg. |
|---|---|---|---|---|---|---|---|
| Odom | 4 | 84 | 21.0 | Montgomery | 3 | 87 | 29.0 |
| T. Harris | 1 | 19 | 19.0 | | | | |
| | 5 | 103 | 20.6 | | | | |

#### INTERCEPTION RETURNS

| | | | | | No. | Yds. | Avg. |
|---|---|---|---|---|---|---|---|
| none | | | | Hayes | 1 | 18 | 18.0 |

#### PASSING

**PITTSBURGH**

| | Att. | Comp. | Comp. Pct. | Yds. | Int | Yds./ Att. | Yds./ Comp. |
|---|---|---|---|---|---|---|---|
| Stoudt | 20 | 10 | 50.0 | 187 | 1 | 9.4 | 18.7 |
| Malone | 7 | 3 | 43.0 | 22 | 0 | 3.1 | 7.3 |
| | 27 | 13 | 48.1 | 209 | 1 | 7.7 | 16.1 |

**LOS ANGELES**

| | Att. | Comp. | Comp. Pct. | Yds. | Int | Yds./ Att. | Yds./ Comp. |
|---|---|---|---|---|---|---|---|
| Plunkett | 34 | 21 | 62.0 | 232 | 0 | 6.8 | 11.0 |

## NFC CHAMPIONSHIP GAME
January 8, 1984 at Washington
(Attendance 55,363)

### SCORING

| | | | | | |
|---|---|---|---|---|---|
| SAN FRANCISCO | 0 | 0 | 0 | 21- | 21 |
| WASHINGTON | 0 | 7 | 14 | 3- | 24 |

**Second Quarter**
Wash.  Riggins, 4 yard rush
        PAT—Moseley (kick)

**Third Quarter**
Wash.  Riggins, 1 yard rush
        PAT—Moseley (kick)
Wash.  Brown, 70 yard pass from Theismann
        PAT—Moseley (kick)

**Fourth Quarter**
S.F.   Wilson, 5 yard pass from Montana
        PAT—Wersching (kick)
S.F.   Solomon, 76 yard pass from Montana
        PAT—Wersching (kick)
S.F.   Wilson, 12 yard pass from Montana
        PAT—Wersching (kick)
Wash.  Moseley, 25 yard field goal

### TEAM STATISTICS

| S.F. | | WASH. |
|---|---|---|
| 19 | First Downs-Total | 24 |
| 3 | First Downs-Rushing | 11 |
| 16 | First Downs-Passing | 10 |
| 0 | First Downs-Penalty | 3 |
| 4 | Fumbles-Number | 2 |
| 2 | Fumbles-Lost Ball | 1 |
| 6 | Penalties-Number | 4 |
| 72 | Yards Penalized | 35 |
| 2 | Missed Field Goals | 4 |
| 64 | Offensive Plays | 75 |
| 425 | Net Yards | 410 |
| 6.6 | Average Gain | 5.5 |
| 3 | Giveaways | 2 |
| 2 | Takeaways | 3 |
| -1 | Difference | +1 |

The last two Super Bowl winners faced each other before a full house at RFK Stadium in Washington.

Both the Redskins and 49ers started slowly, killing their own scoring drives with fumbles. In the second quarter, Joe Theismann hit Clint Didier with a 46-yard pass that moved the ball within the shadows of the goalposts. John Riggins soon blasted into the endzone, and Mark Moseley's kick made the score 7-0. The Redskin defense kept Joe Montana ` off stride, and Washington took its 7-0 lead into the halftime break.

The Skins kept banging away in the third quarter and apparently broke the game open. Darrell Green's clothesline tackle of Freddie Solomon caused a fumble that set up Riggins' second touchdown. Two minutes later, Theismann hit Charlie Brown with a bomb for a 70-yard score.

Ahead 21-0 after three quarters, the Redskins got the scare of their lives. San Francisco got its first touchdown early in the final period, then quickly cut the lead to 21-14 on a 76-yard scoring pass from Montana to Solomon. With seven minutes left, the Niners tied the score on a TD catch by Mike Wilson.

Staggering on the ropes, the Redskins regrouped, held the 49ers the rest of the period and drove into San Francisco territory late in the game with the benefit of controversial penalty calls against Eric Wright and Ronnie Lott. Unsuccessful in four previous tries, Moseley booted a field goal with 40 seconds left for the victory.

### INDIVIDUAL STATISTICS

**SAN FRANCISCO** / **WASHINGTON**

**RUSHING**

| | No. | Yds. | Avg. | | No. | Yds. | Avg. |
|---|---|---|---|---|---|---|---|
| Tyler | 8 | 44 | 5.5 | Riggins | 36 | 123 | 3.4 |
| Montana | 5 | 40 | 8.0 | Washington | 6 | 23 | 3.8 |
| Craig | 3 | 3 | 1.0 | Hayes | 1 | 14 | 14.0 |
| | 16 | 87 | 5.4 | Theismann | 2 | 12 | 6.0 |
| | | | | | 45 | 172 | 3.8 |

**RECEIVING**

| | No. | Yds. | Avg. | | No. | Yds. | Avg. |
|---|---|---|---|---|---|---|---|
| Wilson | 8 | 57 | 7.1 | Brown | 5 | 137 | 27.4 |
| Solomon | 4 | 106 | 26.5 | Didier | 3 | 61 | 20.3 |
| Francis | 4 | 48 | 12.0 | Monk | 3 | 35 | 11.7 |
| Ramson | 3 | 47 | 15.7 | Washington | 3 | 21 | 7.0 |
| Nehemiah | 3 | 46 | 15.3 | Walker | 1 | 11 | 11.0 |
| Craig | 3 | 15 | 5.0 | | 1 | 7 | 7.0 |
| Tyler | 1 | 17 | 17.0 | | 15 | 265 | 17.7 |
| Cooper | 1 | 11 | 11.0 | | | | |
| | 27 | 347 | 12.9 | | | | |

**PUNTING**

| | | | | | | | |
|---|---|---|---|---|---|---|---|
| Orosz | 7 | | 33.6 | Hayes | 5 | | 40.2 |

**PUNT RETURNS**

| | | | | | | | |
|---|---|---|---|---|---|---|---|
| McLemore | 2 | 7 | 3.5 | Giaquinto | 4 | 31 | 7.8 |

**KICKOFF RETURNS**

| | | | | | | | |
|---|---|---|---|---|---|---|---|
| McLemore | 5 | 98 | 19.6 | Evans | 1 | 8 | 8.0 |
| | | | | Garrett | 2 | 31 | 15.5 |
| | | | | Coleman | 1 | 9 | 9.0 |
| | | | | | 4 | 48 | 12.0 |

**INTERCEPTION RETURNS**

| | | | | | | | |
|---|---|---|---|---|---|---|---|
| Wright | 1 | 0 | 0.0 | Dean | 1 | 5 | 5.0 |

**PASSING**

| SAN FRANCISCO | Att. | Comp. | Comp. Pct. | Yds. | Int. | Yds./ Att. | Yds./ Comp. |
|---|---|---|---|---|---|---|---|
| Montana | 48 | 27 | 56.3 | 347 | 1 | 7.2 | 12.9 |

| WASHINGTON | | | | | | | |
|---|---|---|---|---|---|---|---|
| Theismann | 26 | 14 | 53.8 | 229 | 1 | 8.8 | 16.4 |
| Riggins | 1 | 1 | 100.0 | 36 | 0 | 36.0 | 36.0 |
| | 27 | 15 | 55.6 | 265 | 1 | 9.8 | 17.7 |

## AFC CHAMPIONSHIP GAME
January 8, 1984 at Los Angeles
(Attendance 88,734)

The Seahawks had beaten the Broncos and Dolphins in their first playoff action ever, enabling them to reach the AFC title game. The host Raiders, on the other hand, were seasoned veterans of post-season combat. That experience shone crystal-clear in this one-sided match.

The Raiders devoted most of their attention to stopping Curt Warner, the centerpiece of the Seattle offense. Not only was Warner shut down almost completely, but Dave Krieg also was ineffective under heavy pressure. Altogether, Seahawk quarterbacks threw five interceptions, further handicapping a lackluster attack.

While the Seahawk offense was being routed, Marcus Allen ripped the Seattle defense for big yardage. At halftime, the score was 20-0.

When Krieg threw his third interception early in the third quarter, he was yanked in favor of Jim Zorn. Although Zorn threw for two touchdowns, the second came in the final two minutes of the 30-14 Raider victory.

For the fourth time, a Chuck Knox team was knocked out of the playoffs one win shy of the Super Bowl.

### SCORING

| | | | | | |
|---|---|---|---|---|---|
| SEATTLE | 0 | 0 | 7 | 7 - | 14 |
| L.A. RAIDERS | 3 | 17 | 7 | 3 - | 30 |

**First Quarter**
Raid.  Bahr, 20 yard field goal

**Second Quarter**
Raid.  Hawkins, 1 yard rush
        PAT—Bahr (kick)
Raid.  Hawkins, 5 yard rush
        PAT—Bahr (kick)
Raid.  Bahr, 45 yard field goal

**Third Quarter**
Raid.  Allen, 3 yard pass from Plunkett
        PAT—Bahr (kick)
Sea.   Doornink, 11 pass from Zorn
        PAT—Bahr (kick)

**Fourth Quarter**
Raid.  Bahr, 35 yard field goal
Sea.   Young, 9 yard pass from Zorn
        PAT—N. Johnson (kick)

### TEAM STATISTICS

| SEA | | RAID |
|---|---|---|
| 16 | First Downs- Total | 21 |
| 4 | First Downs- Rushing | 10 |
| 10 | First Downs- Passing | 11 |
| 2 | First Downs- Penalty | 0 |
| 1 | Fumbles- Number | 3 |
| 0 | Fumbles- Lost Ball | 2 |
| 2 | Penalties- Number | 7 |
| 20 | Yards Penalized | 53 |
| 0 | Missed Field Goals | 0 |
| 58 | Offensive Plays | 72 |
| 167 | Net Yards | 401 |
| 2.9 | Average Gain | 5.6 |
| 5 | Giveaways | 4 |
| 4 | Takeaways | 5 |
| -1 | Difference | +1 |

### INDIVIDUAL STATISTICS

**SEATTLE** / **L.A. RAIDERS**

**RUSHING**

| | No. | Yds. | Avg. | | No. | Yds. | Avg. |
|---|---|---|---|---|---|---|---|
| Warner | 11 | 26 | 2.4 | Allen | 25 | 154 | 6.2 |
| Dixon | 3 | 24 | 8.0 | Plunkett | 7 | 26 | 3.7 |
| Hughes | 3 | 14 | 4.7 | Hawkins | 10 | 24 | 2.4 |
| C. Bryant | 1 | 1 | 1.0 | Pruitt | 1 | 4 | 4.0 |
| | 18 | 65 | 4.6 | King | 2 | 0 | 0.0 |
| | | | | Wilson | 1 | -3 | -3.0 |
| | | | | | 46 | 205 | 4.5 |

**RECEIVING**

| | No. | Yds. | Avg. | | No. | Yds. | Avg. |
|---|---|---|---|---|---|---|---|
| Doornink | 6 | 48 | 8.0 | Allen | 7 | 62 | 8.9 |
| Johns | 5 | 49 | 9.8 | Barnwell | 5 | 116 | 23.2 |
| Largent | 2 | 25 | 12.5 | Christensen | 3 | 14 | 4.7 |
| Warner | 2 | 10 | 5.0 | Branch | 2 | 22 | 11.0 |
| Young | 1 | 9 | 9.0 | | 17 | 220 | 12.9 |
| H. Jackson | 1 | 5 | 5.0 | | | | |
| | 17 | 146 | 8.6 | | | | |

**PUNTING**

| | | | | | | | |
|---|---|---|---|---|---|---|---|
| West | 5 | | 32.0 | Guy | 2 | | 34.0 |

**PUNT RETURNS**

| | | | | | | | |
|---|---|---|---|---|---|---|---|
| none | | | | Pruitt | 1 | 1 | 1.0 |

**KICKOFF RETURNS**

| | | | | | | | |
|---|---|---|---|---|---|---|---|
| Hughes | 2 | 60 | 30.0 | Montgomery | 2 | 46 | 23.0 |
| Dixon | 3 | 54 | 18.0 | | | | |
| Lane | 1 | 10 | 10. | | | | |
| Scholtz | 1 | 12 | 12.0 | | | | |
| | 7 | 136 | 19.4 | | | | |

**INTERCEPTION RETURNS**

| | | | | | | | |
|---|---|---|---|---|---|---|---|
| Scholtz | 1 | 8 | 8.0 | M. Davis | 2 | 2 | 1.0 |
| G. Johnson | 1 | 0 | 0.0 | Hayes | 1 | 44 | 44.0 |
| | 2 | 8 | 4.0 | Millen | 1 | 13 | 13.0 |
| | | | | McElroy | 1 | -6 | -6.0 |
| | | | | | 5 | 53 | 10.6 |

**PASSING**

| SEATTLE | Att. | Comp. | Comp. Pct. | Yds. | Int. | Yds./ Att. | Yds./ Comp. |
|---|---|---|---|---|---|---|---|
| Zorn | 27 | 14 | 51.9 | 134 | 2 | 5.0 | 9.6 |
| Krieg | 9 | 3 | 33.3 | 12 | 3 | 1.3 | 4.0 |
| | 36 | 17 | 47.2 | 146 | 5 | 4.1 | 8.6 |

| L.A. RAIDERS | | | | | | | |
|---|---|---|---|---|---|---|---|
| Plunkett | 24 | 17 | 70.8 | 214 | 2 | 8.9 | 12.6 |

# The Raider Defense Is Super

Both clubs brought an air of invincibility into this contest. The Redskins had won 27 of their last 30 games with a blend of crunching strength and surgical finesse. The Raiders were relentless winners, modeled over time by feisty owner Al Davis. Although the Skins had beaten the Raiders in October, neither team was a clear favorite as they lined up for the opening kickoff.

Five minutes into the game, lightning struck. Derrick Jensen broke through the Washington front wall, blocked Jeff Hayes' punt and covered the ball after it bounced into the endzone. With the clubs still feeling each other out, the Raiders had grabbed a 7-0 lead. The Redskins soon got a break when the Raiders fumbled back a punt, but they squandered the opportunity when Mark Moseley missed a 44-yard field-goal try.

As the second quarter progressed, the Washington offense was ineffective against the Raider defense. The heralded Hogs were being beaten by the linemen and linebackers from Los Angeles. With his blockers unable to clear a path, John Riggins had slow going on the ground. Forced to the air more than usual, Joe Theismann was thwarted by a strong pass rush and the flypaper coverage of cornerbacks Lester Hayes and Mike Haynes. With the Redskins unable to move the ball, the Raiders scored early in the second period on a three-yard drive, two of which were Jim Plunkett-to-Cliff Branch passes. Midway through the period, the Redskins launched a 13-play drive which culminated in a 24-yard field goal. Although the Raiders still led 14-3, the Redskins seemed to have stemmed the flow of momentum. With 12 seconds left on the first-half clock, Washington had the ball deep in its own territory. Rather than run the clock out or go for a deep pass, the Redskins chose to throw a short sideline pass to Joe Washington. In one stunning motion, linebacker Jack Squirek cut in front of the receiver, grabbed the ball and stepped five yards into the endzone. The play gave Los Angeles a 21-3 halftime lead and a massive psychological boost.

The Redskins came out for the second half with grim determination, cranking out a touchdown with a 70-yard drive on their first possession. When the Raiders responded with their own TD drive, the game moved more firmly into their grasp. When Marcus Allen broke away for a 74-yard gallop on the final play of the third period, the Raiders had the game won.

## LINEUPS

| WASHINGTON | | L.A. RAIDERS |
|---|---|---|
| | **OFFENSE** | |
| Brown | WR | Branch |
| Jacoby | LT | Davis |
| Grimm | LG | Hannah |
| Bostic | C | Dalby |
| May | RG | Marvin |
| Starke | RT | Lawrence |
| Warren | TE | Christensen |
| Monk | WR | Barnwell |
| Theismann | QB | Plunkett |
| Riggins | RB | Allen |
| Walker | RB | King |
| | **DEFENSE** | |
| Liebenstein | LE | Long |
| Butz | LT/NT | Kinlaw |
| Grant | RT/RE | Alzado |
| Manley | RE/LOLB | Hendricks |
| Kaufman | LLB/LILB | Millen |
| Olkewicz | MLB/RILB | Nelson |
| Milot | RLB/ROLB | Martin |
| Green | LCB | Hayes |
| Washington | RCB | Haynes |
| Coffey | SS | Davis |
| Murphy | FS | McElroy |
| | **SUBSTITUTES** | |
| **WASHINGTON** | | |
| | **OFFENSE** | |
| Evans | J. Williams | Holly |
| Giaquinto | Garrett | Laufenberg |
| Washington | Simons | McGrath |
| Wonsley | Huff | Seay |
| Didier | Kimball | |
| | **DEFENSE** | |
| Mann | Coleman | Dean |
| McGee | Cronan | C. Jordan |
| Brooks | Kubin | G. Williams |
| Anderson | Carpenter | |
| | **KICKERS** | |
| Moseley | Hayes | |
| **L.A. RAIDERS** | | |
| | **OFFENSE** | |
| Humm | Wilson | Hawkins |
| Pruitt | Willis | Hasselbeck |
| Jensen | Montgomery | Muhammad |
| D. Williams | S. Jordan | Mosebar |
| Sylvester | | |
| | **DEFENSE** | |
| Robinson | Townsend | Pickel |
| Stalls | Barnes | Davis |
| Caldwell | Squirek | Byrd |
| Watts | Hill | McKinney |
| | **KICKERS** | |
| Bahr | Guy | |

## SCORING

| | | | | | |
|---|---|---|---|---|---|
| **WASHINGTON** | 0 | 3 | 6 | 0- | 9 |
| **L.A. RAIDERS** | 7 | 14 | 14 | 3- | 38 |

**First Quarter**

Raid.   Jensen recovered blocked punt in endzone
PAT—Bahr (kick)

**Second Quarter**

Raid.   Branch, 12 yard pass from Plunkett
PAT—Bahr (kick)

Wash.   Moseley, 24 yard field goal

Raid.   Squirek, 5 yard interception return
PAT—Bahr (kick)

**Third Quarter**

Wash.   Riggins, 1 yard rush
PAT—Kick blocked

Raid.   Allen, 5 yard rush
PAT—Bahr (kick)

Raid.   Allen, 74 yard rush
PAT—Bahr (kick)

**Fourth Quarter**

Raid.   Bahr, 21 yard field goal

## TEAM STATISTICS

| WASH. | | RAID. |
|---|---|---|
| 19 | First Downs- Total | 18 |
| 7 | First Downs- Rushing | 8 |
| 10 | First Downs- Passing | 9 |
| 2 | First Downs- Penalty | 1 |
| 1 | Fumbles- Number | 3 |
| 1 | Fumbles- Lost Ball | 2 |
| 4 | Penalties- Number | 7 |
| 62 | Yards Penalized | 56 |
| 1 | Missed Field Goals | 0 |
| 73 | Offensive Plays | 60 |
| 283 | Net Yards | 385 |
| 3.9 | Average Gain | 6.4 |
| 3 | Giveaways | 2 |
| 2 | Takeaways | 3 |
| -1 | Difference | +1 |

## INDIVIDUAL STATISTICS

### WASHINGTON

| | No. | Yds. | Avg. |
|---|---|---|---|
| **RUSHING** | | | |
| Riggins | 26 | 64 | 2.5 |
| Theismann | 3 | 18 | 6.0 |
| Washington | 3 | 8 | 2.7 |
| | 32 | 90 | 2.8 |
| **RECEIVING** | | | |
| Didier | 5 | 65 | 13.0 |
| Brown | 3 | 93 | 31.0 |
| Washington | 3 | 20 | 6.7 |
| Giaquinto | 2 | 21 | 10.5 |
| Monk | 1 | 26 | 26.0 |
| Garrett | 1 | 17.0 | 17.0 |
| Riggins | 1 | 1 | 1.0 |
| | 16 | 243 | 15.2 |
| **PUNTING** | | | |
| Hayes | 7 | | 37.0 |
| **PUNT RETURNS** | | | |
| Green | 1 | 34 | 34.0 |
| Giaquinto | 1 | 1 | 1.0 |
| | 2 | 35 | 17.5 |
| **KICKOFF RETURNS** | | | |
| Garrett | 5 | 100 | 20.0 |
| Grant | 1 | 32 | 32.0 |
| Kimball | 1 | 0 | 0.0 |
| | 7 | 132 | 18.9 |
| **INTERCEPTION RETURNS** | | | |
| none | | | |

### L.A. RAIDERS

| | No. | Yds. | Avg |
|---|---|---|---|
| **RUSHING** | | | |
| Allen | 20 | 191 | 9.6 |
| Pruitt | 5 | 17 | 3.4 |
| King | 3 | 12 | 4.0 |
| Willis | 1 | 7 | 7.0 |
| Hawkins | 3 | 6 | 2.0 |
| Plunkett | 1 | -2 | -2.0 |
| | 33 | 231 | 7.0 |
| **RECEIVING** | | | |
| Branch | 6 | 94 | 15.7 |
| Christensen | 4 | 32 | 8.0 |
| Hawkins | 2 | 20 | 10.0 |
| Allen | 2 | 18 | 9.0 |
| King | 2 | 8 | 4.0 |
| | 16 | 172 | 10.8 |
| **PUNTING** | | | |
| Guy | 7 | | 42.7 |
| **PUNT RETURNS** | | | |
| Pruitt | 1 | 8 | 8.0 |
| Watts | 1 | 0 | 0.0 |
| | 2 | 8 | 4.0 |
| **KICKOFF RETURNS** | | | |
| Pruitt | 1 | 17 | 17.0 |
| **INTERCEPTION RETURNS** | | | |
| Squirek | 1 | 5 | 5.0 |
| Haynes | 1 | 0 | 0.0 |
| | 2 | 5 | 2.5 |

### PASSING

| WASHINGTON | Att. | Comp. | Comp. Pct. | Yds. | Int. | Yds./ Att. | Yds./ Comp. | Yards Lost Tackled |
|---|---|---|---|---|---|---|---|---|
| Theismann | 35 | 16 | 45.7 | 243 | 2 | 6.9 | 15.2 | 6-50 |
| **L.A. RAIDERS** | | | | | | | | |
| Plunkett | 25 | 16 | 64.0 | 172 | 0 | 6.9 | 10.8 | 2-18 |

The United States Football League completed its second season, something the late, lamented World Football League never did. To broaden its base, the U.S.F.L. expanded from 12 to 18 teams, moving into Pittsburgh, Jacksonville, Memphis, Houston, San Antonio and Oklahoma. The 1983 Boston Breakers moved to New Orleans, while the owners of the Chicago and Arizona teams swapped franchises. Some big-name talent joined the spring circuit. Doug Williams, Joe Cribbs, Brian Sipe, Dan Ross and Cliff Stoudt all jumped from the N.F.L. Among the rookies, Heisman Trophy winner Mike Rozier ran for Pittsburgh, while quarterback Jim Kelly starred for the Houston Gamblers. Another young passer, Steve Young of Brigham Young, signed a fabulous long-term contract with the Los Angeles Express. Without any famous newcomers, the Philadelphia Stars maintained a spring-long excellence. They compiled a 16-2 record behind runner Kelvin Bryant and quarterback Chuck Fusina, then beat George Allen's Arizona Wranglers for the title.

## EASTERN DIVISION

**Washington Redskins** — They didn't steamroll through their schedule, but the Redskins beat injuries and a slow start to win the Eastern Division. An opening-day loss to Miami was followed by a close loss to San Francisco. With their throne creaking, the Skins fought back to win five straight games, including a 34-14 victory over the Cowboys. The midpoint of the schedule brought a relapse, two losses to the Cardinals and Giants. With a playoff berth in doubt, the Redskins traveled to Dallas on December 9. They fell behind 21-6 at halftime, then rallied in a brilliant second half to a 30-28 victory. One week later, Mark Moseley kicked a field goal with under two minutes left to beat St. Louis 29-27 and earn another divisional title. Injuries spoiled the season for Mark Murphy and Charlie Brown, while John Riggins labored with a bad back. Art Monk stayed free of injuries and set an N.F.L. record with 106 receptions.

**New York Giants** — In his second season, coach Bill Parcells launched a major housecleaning. The offensive line was revamped, and Phil Simms was installed at quarterback. Parcells kept the strong defense intact with Lawrence Taylor, Harry Carson and Mark Haynes still functioning at all-pro levels. Hoping for respectability, the Giants jumped out to three victories in the first four games. An early autumn slump dropped them to 4-4, but the ugly duckling then blossomed into a swan. The midseason Giants charged into playoff territory with five wins in six weeks. They trounced the Redskins and Cowboys back to back and beat the Cardinals two weeks after that. Losses to the Cardinals and Saints leveled their record out, but the Giants still captured an unexpected wild-card spot.

**St. Louis Cardinals** — The Cardinals lost three September games before their defense dramatically improved. With E.J. Junior and Curtis Greer in the fore, the Cards began a four-game winning streak, including victories over the Cowboys and Redskins. St. Louis' offense spewed points from the start of the year. Ottis Anderson cranked out more than 1,100 yards on the ground, while Neil Lomax and Roy Green demoralized opposing pass defenses. Supporting the attack was a fine front line featuring Luis Sharpe. An offensive slump in November led to three straight losses and put the playoffs in question. Victories over the Eagles, Patriots and Giants set the stage for a showdown in Washington on the final weekend. With a post-season berth at stake, the Cards led the Redskins until a late field goal put Washington ahead 29-27. With time ebbing away, the Cardinals drove downfield, only to have Neil O'Donoghue's hurried kick sail wide left at the gun.

**Dallas Cowboys** — The retirements of Drew Pearson, Harvey Martin, Pat Donovan, Billy Joe DuPree and Robert Newhouse had critics relishing the downfall of the Cowboys. Tom Landry made Gary Hogeboom the starting quarterback over Danny White, a further sign of change in Dallas. After a strong 4-1 start, the Cowboys suffered a spate of injuries in the offensive line. Randy White, Everson Walls and Michael Downs led the still-tough flex defense. The Cowboys had a hard time with their Eastern rivals, losing twice to both New York and Washington and once to St. Louis. Although Danny White had recaptured the quarterback job by mid-season, the offense never clicked, falling apart in a 14-3 loss to winless Buffalo. With their nine-year

playoff run on the table, the Cowboys dropped a heartbreaker to the Redskins and faded away with a close loss to Miami on the final Monday night.

**Philadelphia Eagles** — Stuck in the N.F.C.'s toughest division, the Eagles played respectably while bringing up the rear in the East. The offense had a receiving ace in Mike Quick, but no strong running threat. After November 25, it had no first-string quarterback, as Ron Jaworski broke his leg against the Cardinals. The defense improved, with Ken Clarke and Wes Hopkins becoming major forces. The Eagles beat the Giants and Redskins along the way, but their greatest victory may have been in the decision to stay in Philadelphia despite Phoenix's strong bid to lure them away.

## CENTRAL DIVISION

**Chicago Bears** — Last year's strong finish carried over into 1984. The Bears won their first three games, including a 27-0 trouncing of the Broncos. A November 4 victory over the Raiders raised their record to 7-3 and made a playoff berth a virtual certainty. In that game, quarterback Jim McMahon suffered a lacerated kidney that ended his season. When backup Steve Fuller separated his shoulder on December 3, the Bears had severe QB problems. Rusty Lisch couldn't move the offense, Greg Landry signed as a free agent, and Walter Payton even played shotgun quarterback for six plays against Green Bay. Payton excelled in his usual role as a runner, gaining more than 1,600 yards and passing Jim Brown as the all-time rushing leader. Regardless of developments on offense, the Bears were feared for their swarming defense. Cleverly deployed and relentlessly physical, the Chicago defense had stars in linemen Dan Hampton and Richard Dent, linebackers Mike Singletary and Otis Wilson, and safeties Todd Bell and Gary Fencik. The 10-6 record put the Bears into the playoffs for the first time since 1979.

**Green Bay Packers** — Forrest Gregg returned to Green Bay to recapture the glory which eluded Bart Starr in his coaching days. An opening-day victory over St. Louis gave way to seven straight losses. In the gloom of autumn, the Packers suddenly turned around and won seven of their last eight games. The secondary led the way to improved defense, with cornerback Tim Lewis reaching all-pro heights. The offense had star receivers in James Lofton and Paul Coffman, although John Jefferson suffered through a bad season. The cold-weather surge included victories over the playoff-bound Rams and Bears.

**Tampa Bay Buccaneers** — A playoff spot was not in the cards, but the Buccaneers stepped up from their 1983 depths. Steve DeBerg came east from Denver and revived the moribund Tampa Bay passing game. The offense had a scattering of stars in receiver Kevin House, back James Wilder and guard Sean Farrell. The defense was a bigger problem this year. Although Lee Roy Selmon and David Logan excelled in the line, Hugh Green's absence after an October car crash left a hole in the unit. A gap loomed at the top, as coach John McKay announced on November 5 that he would not return in 1985 as coach. At home for their final two games, the Bucs beat Atlanta 23-6 and demolished the Jets 41-21 to give McKay a coaching bon voyage.

**Detroit Lions** — The Lions had gotten off to a rotten start in 1983 and had stormed back into the playoffs. They started badly again this year and stayed bad. They lost five of their first six games, most of them by close scores. After a brief midseason resurgence, the Lions tumbled into a spiritless home stretch. Only once did they win in their final eight games, edging Green Bay 31-28 on Thanksgiving Day. The collapse affected both offense and defense. Gary Danielson won the quarterback job in training camp, only to lose ace runner Billy Sims to a knee injury on October 21. The disappointing season cost coach Monte Clark his job after seven seasons.

**Minnesota Vikings** — Bud Grant had run the Vikings with a calm and easy manner. When Grant retired, the Vikes named 38-year-old Les Steckel to replace him. The youngest head coach in the league, Steckel brought a gung-ho approach to his job. The veteran Minnesota squad did not take well to this change in tone. The undertalented Vikings split their first four games, then nosedived into 11 losses in their remaining 12

FINAL TEAM STATISTICS

OFFENSE

| | ATL. | CHI. | DALL. | DET. | G.B. | L.A. | MINN. | N.O. | NY G | PHIL. | STL. | S.F. | T.B. | WASH. |
|---|---|---|---|---|---|---|---|---|---|---|---|---|---|---|
| FIRST DOWNS: | | | | | | | | | | | | | | |
| Total | 292 | 297 | 323 | 306 | 315 | 258 | 289 | 298 | 310 | 280 | 345 | **356** | 344 | 339 |
| by Rushing | 123 | **164** | 93 | 118 | 120 | 140 | 111 | 131 | 97 | 83 | 129 | 138 | 114 | 154 |
| by Passing | 151 | 115 | 202 | 170 | 168 | 100 | 150 | 137 | 198 | 176 | 200 | 204 | **209** | 164 |
| by Penalty | 18 | 18 | 28 | 18 | 27 | 18 | 28 | **30** | 15 | 21 | 16 | 14 | 21 | 21 |
| RUSHING: | | | | | | | | | | | | | | |
| Number | 489 | **674** | 469 | 446 | 461 | 541 | 444 | 523 | 493 | 381 | 488 | 534 | 483 | 588 |
| Yards | 1994 | **2974** | 1714 | 2017 | 2019 | 2864 | 1844 | 2171 | 1660 | 1338 | 2088 | 2465 | 1776 | 2274 |
| Average Yards | 4.1 | 4.4 | 3.7 | 4.5 | 4.4 | **5.3** | 4.2 | 4.2 | 3.4 | 3.5 | 4.3 | 4.6 | 3.7 | 3.9 |
| Touchdowns | 16 | **22** | 12 | 13 | 18 | 16 | 10 | 9 | 12 | 6 | 21 | 21 | 17 | 20 |
| PASSING: | | | | | | | | | | | | | | |
| Attempts | 478 | 390 | 604 | 531 | 506 | 358 | 533 | 476 | 535 | **606** | 566 | 496 | 563 | 485 |
| Completions | 294 | 226 | 322 | 298 | 281 | 176 | 281 | 246 | 288 | 331 | **347** | 312 | 334 | 286 |
| Completion Pct. | 61.5 | 57.9 | 53.3 | 56.1 | 55.5 | 49.2 | 52.7 | 51.7 | 53.8 | 54.6 | 61.3 | **62.9** | 59.3 | 59.0 |
| Passing Yards | 3546 | 2695 | 3995 | 3787 | 3740 | 2382 | 3337 | 3198 | 4066 | 3823 | **4634** | 4079 | 3907 | 3417 |
| Avg. Yds per Att. | 7.4 | 6.9 | 6.6 | 7.1 | 7.4 | 6.7 | 6.3 | 6.7 | 7.6 | 6.3 | 8.2 | **8.2** | 6.9 | 7.1 |
| Avg. Yds per Comp. | 12.1 | 11.9 | 12.4 | 12.7 | 13.3 | 13.5 | 11.9 | 13.0 | **14.1** | 11.6 | 13.4 | 13.1 | 11.7 | 12.0 |
| Times Tackled | **67** | 36 | 48 | 61 | 42 | 32 | 64 | 45 | 55 | 60 | 49 | 27 | 45 | 48 |
| Yds Lost Tackled | **496** | 232 | 389 | 486 | 310 | 240 | 465 | 361 | 434 | 463 | 377 | 178 | 362 | 341 |
| Net Yards | 3050 | 2463 | 3606 | 3301 | 3430 | 2142 | 2872 | 2837 | 3632 | 3360 | **4257** | 3901 | 3545 | 3076 |
| Touchdowns | 14 | 14 | 19 | 19 | 30 | 16 | 18 | 21 | 22 | 19 | 28 | **32** | 22 | 24 |
| Interceptions | 20 | 15 | 26 | 22 | **30** | 17 | 25 | 28 | 18 | 17 | 16 | 10 | 23 | 13 |
| Pct. Intercepted | 4.2 | 3.8 | 4.3 | 4.1 | **5.9** | 4.7 | 4.7 | **5.9** | 3.4 | 2.8 | 2.8 | 2.0 | 4.1 | 2.7 |
| PUNTS: | | | | | | | | | | | | | | |
| Number | 70 | 85 | **108** | 76 | 85 | 74 | 82 | 70 | 94 | 92 | 68 | 62 | 68 | 73 |
| Average | 40.8 | 39.2 | 38.2 | 41.6 | 42.3 | 38.7 | 42.4 | **43.1** | 38.3 | 42.2 | 38.1 | 40.9 | 41.9 | 38.8 |
| PUNT RETURNS | | | | | | | | | | | | | | |
| Number | 41 | **63** | 54 | 36 | 48 | 40 | 31 | 33 | 55 | 40 | 47 | 45 | 34 | 55 |
| Yards | 264 | **558** | 446 | 241 | 351 | 489 | 217 | 268 | 368 | 250 | 399 | 521 | 207 | 474 |
| Average Yards | 6.4 | 8.9 | 8.3 | 6.7 | 7.3 | **12.2** | 7.0 | 8.1 | 6.7 | 6.3 | 8.5 | 11.6 | 6.1 | 8.6 |
| Touchdowns | 0 | 0 | 0 | 0 | 0 | **2** | 0 | 0 | 0 | 0 | 0 | 1 | 0 | 0 |
| KICKOFF RET.: | | | | | | | | | | | | | | |
| Number | 70 | 49 | 63 | 74 | 67 | 58 | **86** | 72 | 61 | 59 | 74 | 47 | 68 | 60 |
| Yards | 1367 | 896 | 1199 | 1347 | 1362 | 1244 | **1775** | 1465 | 1117 | 1156 | 1563 | 1039 | 1354 | 1174 |
| Average Yards | 19.5 | 18.3 | 19.0 | 18.2 | 20.3 | 21.4 | 20.6 | 20.3 | 18.3 | 19.6 | 21.1 | **22.1** | 19.9 | 19.6 |
| Touchdowns | 0 | 0 | 0 | 0 | **1** | **1** | 0 | 0 | 0 | **1** | 0 | 0 | 0 | 0 |
| INTERCEPT RET.: | | | | | | | | | | | | | | |
| Number | 12 | 21 | **28** | 14 | 27 | 17 | 11 | 13 | 19 | 20 | 21 | 25 | 18 | 21 |
| Yards | 147 | 290 | 297 | 87 | 338 | **399** | 120 | 213 | 182 | 287 | 163 | 345 | 308 | 401 |
| Average Yards | 12.3 | 13.8 | 10.6 | 6.2 | 12.5 | **23.5** | 10.9 | 16.4 | 9.6 | 14.4 | 7.8 | 13.8 | 17.1 | 18.6 |
| Touchdowns | 1 | 1 | 2 | 0 | 2 | 3 | 1 | 3 | 0 | 0 | 1 | 2 | 1 | **4** |
| PENALTIES: | | | | | | | | | | | | | | |
| Number | 125 | 114 | 100 | **138** | 110 | 93 | 90 | 101 | 79 | 77 | 109 | 100 | 118 | 80 |
| Yards | 1011 | 851 | 947 | **1165** | 915 | 830 | 762 | 849 | 703 | 632 | 904 | 884 | 875 | 723 |
| FUMBLES: | | | | | | | | | | | | | | |
| Number | **39** | 31 | 35 | 36 | 17 | 31 | 39 | 22 | 17 | 23 | 32 | 26 | 36 | 33 |
| Number Lost | **21** | 16 | 17 | 14 | 7 | 18 | 16 | 13 | 9 | 16 | 20 | 12 | 20 | 15 |
| POINTS: | | | | | | | | | | | | | | |
| Total | 281 | 325 | 308 | 283 | 390 | 346 | 276 | 298 | 299 | 278 | 423 | **475** | 335 | 426 |
| PAT Attempts | 31 | 37 | 34 | 31 | 51 | 38 | 31 | 34 | 36 | 27 | 51 | **57** | 40 | 51 |
| PAT Made | 31 | 35 | 33 | 31 | 48 | 37 | 30 | 34 | 32 | 26 | 48 | **56** | 38 | 48 |
| FG Attempts | 27 | 28 | 29 | 27 | 21 | 33 | 23 | 27 | 33 | **37** | 35 | 35 | 26 | 31 |
| FG Made | 20 | 22 | 23 | 20 | 12 | 25 | 20 | 20 | 17 | **30** | 23 | 25 | 19 | 24 |
| Percent FG Made | 74.1 | 78.6 | 79.3 | 74.1 | 57.1 | 75.8 | **87.0** | 74.1 | 51.5 | 81.1 | 65.7 | 71.4 | 73.1 | 77.4 |
| Safeties | 2 | 1 | 1 | 0 | 0 | **3** | 0 | 0 | 0 | 0 | 0 | 1 | 0 | 0 |

DEFENSE

| | ATL. | CHI. | DALL. | DET. | G.B. | L.A. | MINN. | N.O. | NYG | PHIL. | STL. | S.F. | T.B. | WASH. |
|---|---|---|---|---|---|---|---|---|---|---|---|---|---|---|
| FIRST DOWNS: | | | | | | | | | | | | | | |
| Total | 317 | 216 | 283 | 328 | 323 | 309 | **342** | 298 | 296 | 307 | 292 | 302 | 311 | 307 |
| by Rushing | 131 | 72 | 106 | 120 | 136 | 108 | **144** | 134 | 107 | 123 | 108 | 101 | 139 | 91 |
| by Passing | 162 | 122 | 155 | 177 | 166 | 179 | 182 | 142 | 174 | 171 | 157 | 173 | 157 | **194** |
| by Penalty | 24 | 22 | 22 | **31** | 21 | 22 | 16 | 22 | 15 | 13 | 27 | 28 | 15 | 22 |
| RUSHING: | | | | | | | | | | | | | | |
| Number | 538 | 378 | 510 | 519 | 545 | 449 | 547 | 549 | 474 | **556** | 442 | 432 | 511 | 390 |
| Yards | 2153 | 1377 | 2226 | 1808 | 2145 | 1600 | **2573** | 2461 | 1818 | 2189 | 1923 | 1795 | 2233 | 1589 |
| Average Yards | 4.0 | 3.6 | 4.4 | 3.5 | 3.9 | 3.6 | **4.7** | 4.5 | 3.8 | 3.9 | 4.4 | 4.2 | 4.4 | 4.1 |
| Touchdowns | 16 | 10 | 8 | 17 | 14 | 15 | 20 | 13 | 10 | 12 | 11 | 10 | **27** | 13 |
| PASSING: | | | | | | | | | | | | | | |
| Attempts | 443 | 435 | 527 | 466 | 551 | 566 | 490 | 422 | 529 | 492 | 494 | 546 | 490 | **575** |
| Completions | 262 | 198 | 250 | 288 | 315 | **346** | 319 | 239 | 288 | 262 | 251 | 298 | 286 | 318 |
| Completion Pct. | 59.1 | 45.5 | 47.4 | 61.8 | 57.2 | 61.1 | **65.1** | 56.6 | 54.4 | 53.3 | 50.8 | 54.6 | 58.4 | 55.3 |
| Passing Yards | 3413 | 3069 | 3200 | 3782 | 3470 | 3964 | 3954 | 2873 | 3736 | 3506 | 3574 | 3744 | 3480 | **4301** |
| Avg. Yds per Att. | 7.7 | 7.1 | 6.1 | **8.1** | 6.3 | 7.0 | 8.1 | 6.8 | 7.1 | 7.1 | 7.2 | 6.9 | 7.1 | 7.5 |
| Avg. Yds per Comp. | 13.0 | **15.5** | 12.8 | 13.1 | 11.0 | 11.5 | 12.4 | 12.0 | 13.0 | 13.4 | 14.2 | 12.6 | 12.2 | 13.5 |
| Times Tackled | 38 | **72** | 57 | 37 | 44 | 43 | 25 | 55 | 48 | 60 | 55 | 51 | 32 | 66 |
| Yds Lost Tackled | 287 | **583** | 390 | 271 | 324 | 298 | 175 | 420 | 361 | 456 | 403 | 363 | 239 | 529 |
| Net Yards | 3126 | 2486 | 2810 | 3511 | 3146 | 3666 | **3779** | 2453 | 3375 | 3050 | 3171 | 3381 | 3241 | 3772 |
| Touchdowns | 27 | 14 | 23 | 27 | 16 | 18 | **35** | 23 | 20 | 22 | 26 | 14 | 20 | 25 |
| Interceptions | 12 | 21 | **28** | 14 | 27 | 17 | 11 | 13 | 19 | 20 | 21 | 25 | 18 | 21 |
| Pct. Intercepted | 2.7 | 4.8 | 5.3 | 3.0 | 4.9 | 3.0 | 2.2 | **5.9** | 3.6 | 4.1 | 4.3 | 4.6 | 3.7 | 3.7 |
| PUNTS: | | | | | | | | | | | | | | |
| Number | 60 | **100** | 99 | 73 | 89 | 71 | 68 | 84 | 92 | 89 | 81 | 80 | 68 | 78 |
| Average | 41.6 | 41.6 | 42.8 | 40.0 | 40.9 | 41.5 | 40.8 | 41.6 | 40.0 | 39.3 | **39.0** | 40.5 | 41.0 | 39.9 |
| PUNT RETURNS | | | | | | | | | | | | | | |
| Number | 42 | 41 | 55 | 49 | 46 | 35 | 49 | 47 | 50 | **58** | 27 | 30 | 36 | 38 |
| Yards | 450 | 249 | 230 | **516** | 368 | 196 | 435 | 550 | 479 | 486 | 239 | 190 | 310 | 187 |
| Average Yards | 10.7 | 6.1 | 4.2 | 10.5 | 8.0 | 5.6 | 8.9 | **11.7** | 9.6 | 8.4 | 8.9 | 6.3 | 8.6 | 4.9 |
| Touchdowns | 1 | 0 | 0 | 1 | 0 | 0 | 0 | 1 | **2** | 0 | 0 | 0 | 0 | 0 |
| KICKOFF RET.: | | | | | | | | | | | | | | |
| Number | 48 | 68 | 65 | 60 | 73 | 74 | 59 | 45 | 55 | 69 | **85** | 78 | 67 | 73 |
| Yards | 1053 | 1443 | 1310 | 1250 | 1171 | 1288 | 1281 | 916 | 1088 | 1298 | **1549** | 1499 | 1336 | 1404 |
| Average Yards | **21.9** | 21.2 | 20.2 | 20.8 | 16.0 | 17.4 | 21.7 | 20.4 | 19.8 | 18.8 | 18.2 | 19.2 | 19.9 | 19.2 |
| Touchdowns | 0 | **1** | 0 | 0 | 0 | 0 | 0 | 0 | 0 | 0 | **1** | 0 | 0 | **1** |
| INTERCEPT RET.: | | | | | | | | | | | | | | |
| Number | 20 | 15 | 26 | 22 | **30** | 17 | 25 | 28 | 18 | 17 | 16 | 10 | 23 | 13 |
| Yards | 304 | 241 | 382 | 251 | 317 | 240 | 344 | **420** | 222 | 211 | 219 | 155 | 249 | 159 |
| Average Yards | 15.2 | 16.1 | 14.7 | 11.4 | 10.6 | 14.1 | 13.8 | **16.4** | 12.3 | 12.4 | 13.7 | 15.5 | 10.8 | 12.2 |
| Touchdowns | 2 | 3 | **4** | 1 | 2 | 2 | 2 | 3 | 1 | 1 | 0 | 0 | 0 | 0 |
| PENALTIES: | | | | | | | | | | | | | | |
| Number | 93 | 86 | 95 | 107 | 145 | 115 | 113 | 119 | 93 | 96 | 75 | 91 | 136 | **84** |
| Yards | 820 | 698 | 868 | 968 | **1129** | 871 | 1047 | 1025 | 699 | 904 | 578 | 723 | 1078 | 803 |
| FUMBLES: | | | | | | | | | | | | | | |
| Number | 36 | 33 | 35 | 28 | 33 | **42** | 35 | 28 | 24 | 32 | 20 | 28 | 27 | 32 |
| Number Lost | 20 | 13 | 16 | 11 | 15 | **22** | 18 | 10 | 16 | 11 | 12 | 13 | 14 | **22** |
| POINTS: | | | | | | | | | | | | | | |
| Total | 382 | 248 | 308 | 408 | 309 | 316 | **484** | 361 | 301 | 320 | 345 | 227 | 380 | 310 |
| PAT Attempts | 48 | 29 | 36 | 48 | 34 | 36 | **59** | 41 | 35 | 36 | 39 | 24 | 46 | 39 |
| PAT Made | 46 | 26 | 35 | 48 | 33 | 32 | **58** | 41 | 34 | 36 | 36 | 24 | 44 | 37 |
| FG Attempts | 30 | 22 | 28 | 29 | 31 | 31 | 28 | 33 | 26 | 35 | **38** | 25 | 27 | 20 |
| FG Made | 16 | 16 | 19 | 24 | 24 | 22 | 24 | 24 | 17 | 22 | **25** | 19 | 18 | 13 |
| Percent FG Made | 53.3 | 72.7 | 67.9 | 82.8 | 77.4 | 71.0 | **85.7** | 72.7 | 65.4 | 62.9 | 65.8 | 76.0 | 66.7 | 65.0 |
| Safeties | 0 | 0 | 0 | 0 | 0 | 1 | 0 | 0 | **3** | 1 | 0 | 1 | 0 | 0 |

games. Three of those losses killed morale: a 45-17 debacle at Green Bay, 42-21 at Denver, and 51-7 at San Francisco. Within a week of the final game, Steckel became the league's youngest ex-coach, with Grant ending his retirement to regroup his battered charges.

## WESTERN DIVISION

**San Francisco 49ers** — The Niners were brilliant in building the N.F.L.'s best record. After edging Detroit and Washington, both offense and defense hit a fine rhythm that was jarred only by the Steelers on October 14. Joe Montana engineered the multi-dimensional attack with virtuoso skill. Wendell Tyler ran for more than 1,200 yards to balance the precise San Francisco passing game. In the front line, all-pro honors were heaped on Randy Cross, Keith Fahnhorst and Fred Quillan. The 49er defense dominated opponents despite Fred Dean's absence until mid-November in a contract dispute. Keena Turner starred among the linebackers, while the entire secondary of Ronnie Lott, Eric Wright, Carlton Williamson and Dwight Hicks went to the Pro Bowl. Bill Walsh led his team into the playoffs with a nine-game winning streak at their backs.

**Los Angeles Rams** — The Rams loved the run and hated the pass. On offense, they had Eric Dickerson running for record yardage behind an all-star line of Kent Hill, Doug Smith, Dennis Harrah, Bill Bain and Jackie Slater. The Rams passed sparingly after Vince Ferragamo broke his hand in the third game of the year. Jeff Kemp kept the offense moving by minimizing his mistakes and relying on Dickerson. The defense had a similar bias. Led by ancient Jack Youngblood and young Jim Collins, the Rams gave up running yardage only grudgingly. Opponents gained more easily through the air, as Johnnie Johnson missed part of the season on injured reserve. Before dropping their finale in San Francisco, the Rams won five of six games to ice their second straight wild-card berth.

**New Orleans Saints** — Two controversial trades spurred conversation but failed to earn the Saints their first playoff spot. In the off-season, they sent a first-round draft choice to the Jets for Richard Todd, a quarterback coming off a subpar season. In October, Bum Phillips sent another first-round choice to Houston for Earl Campbell, his battering ram when he coached the Oilers. The Saints already had George Rogers and other competent backs, so the Campbell trade cut the playing time available to each back. Todd started at quarterback, prompting Ken Stabler to retire eight games into the season. The defense was the team's backbone, with Rickey Jackson and Bruce Clark starring. Losers of three of their last four games, the Saints still had never broken the .500 barrier.

**Atlanta Falcons** — A severe pre-season knee injury sidelined William Andrews and cast a pall on the team which never lifted. Gerald Riggs stepped in and ran for 202 yards on opening day to raise spirits a bit. On October 7, Billy Johnson tore up his knee and departed for the year, triggering a nine-game losing streak, which ended only in the season's final game. Quarterback Steve Bartkowski joined Andrews and Johnson with his own season-ending knee surgery on November 18. Although Stacey Bailey emerged as a star, this season generated little optimism in Atlanta.

## WASHINGTON REDSKINS 11-5-0 Joe Gibbs

| Scores of Each Game | | |
|---|---|---|
| 17 | MIAMI | 35 |
| 31 | San Francisco | 37 |
| 30 | N.Y.GIANTS | 14 |
| 26 | New England | 10 |
| 20 | PHILADELPHIA | 0 |
| 35 | Indianapolis | 7 |
| 34 | DALLAS | 14 |
| 24 | St.Louis | 26 |
| 13 | N.Y.Giants | 37 |
| 27 | ATLANTA | 14 |
| 28 | DETROIT | 14 |
| 10 | Philadelphia | 16 |
| 41 | BUFFALO | 14 |
| 31 | Minnesota | 17 |
| 30 | Dallas | 28 |
| 29 | ST.LOUIS | 27 |

| Use Name | Pos. | Hgt | Wgt | Age | Int | Pts |
|---|---|---|---|---|---|---|
| Joe Jacoby | OT | 6'7" | 305 | 25 | | 6 |
| George Starke | OT | 6'5" | 260 | 36 | | |
| Morris Towns | OT | 6'4" | 263 | 30 | | |
| Russ Grimm | OG | 6'3" | 273 | 25 | | |
| Ken Huff | OG | 6'4" | 265 | 31 | | |
| Bruce Kimball | OG | 6'2" | 260 | 28 | | |
| Mark May | OG | 6'6" | 295 | 25 | | |
| J.T.Turner | OG | 6'3" | 265 | 31 | | |
| Rick Donnalley | C-OG | 6'2" | 257 | 25 | | |
| Jeff Bostic | C | 6'2" | 258 | 25 | | |
| Todd Liebenstein | DE | 6'6" | 255 | 24 | | |
| Dexter Manley | DE | 6'3" | 250 | 25 | | |
| Charles Mann | DE | 6'6" | 260 | 23 | | |
| Tony McGee | DE | 6'4" | 249 | 35 | | |
| Tom Beasley | DT | 6'5" | 248 | 30 | | |
| Perry Brooks | DT | 6'3" | 270 | 29 | | |
| Dave Butz | DT | 6'7" | 295 | 34 | | |
| Darryl Grant | DT | 6'1" | 275 | 24 | | 6 |
| Monte Coleman | LB | 6'2" | 230 | 26 | 16 | |
| Pete Cronan | LB | 6'2" | 238 | 29 | | |
| Trey Junkin (from BUF) | LB | 6'2" | 221 | 23 | | |
| Mel Kaufman | LB | 6'2" | 218 | 26 | | |
| Larry Kibin | LB | 6'2" | 234 | 25 | | |
| Rich Milot | LB | 6'4" | 237 | 27 | 3 | |
| Neal Olkewicz | LB | 6' | 233 | 27 | | |
| Ken Coffey | DB | 6' | 190 | 23 | 1 | |
| Vernon Dean | DB | 5'11" | 178 | 25 | 7 | 12 |
| Darrell Green | DB | 5'8" | 170 | 24 | 5 | 6 |
| Curtis Jordan | DB | 6'2" | 205 | 30 | 2 | 6 |
| Mark Murphy | DB | 6'4" | 210 | 29 | | |
| Mike Nelms | DB | 6'1" | 202 | 29 | | |
| Tony Peters | DB | 6'1" | 190 | 31 | | |
| Ricky Smith (from NE) | DB | 6' | 182 | 24 | 1 | |
| Anthony Washington | DB | 6'1" | 204 | 26 | 1 | |
| Greg Williams | DB | 5'11" | 185 | 25 | | |
| Jim Hart | QB | 6'2" | 210 | 40 | | |
| Jay Schroeder | QB | 6'4" | 215 | 23 | | |
| Joe Theismann | QB | 6' | 196 | 34 | | 6 |
| Keith Griffin | HB | 5'8" | 185 | 22 | | |
| Jeff Moore | HB | 6' | 196 | 28 | | 12 |
| Joe Washington | HB | 5'10" | 179 | 30 | | 6 |
| Rick Kane | FB-HB | 5'11" | 200 | 29 | | |
| John Riggins | FB | 6'2" | 240 | 35 | | 84 |
| Otis Wonsley | FB | 5'10" | 214 | 27 | | 24 |
| Charlie Brown | WR | 5'10" | 179 | 25 | | 18 |
| Alvin Garrett | WR | 5'7" | 178 | 27 | | |
| Rich Mauti | WR | 6' | 195 | 30 | | |
| Mark McGrath | WR | 5'11" | 175 | 26 | | 6 |
| Art Monk | WR | 6'3" | 209 | 26 | | 42 |
| Calvin Muhammad | WR | 6' | 190 | 25 | | 24 |
| Virgil Seay (to ATL) | WR | 5'8" | 180 | 26 | | 6 |
| Clint Didier | TE | 6'5" | 240 | 25 | | 3 |
| Anthony Jones | TE | 6'3" | 248 | 24 | | |
| Rick Walker | TE | 6'3" | 235 | 29 | | 6 |
| Don Warren | TE | 6'4" | 242 | 28 | | |
| Mike Williams | TE | 6'4" | 251 | 25 | | |
| Jeff Hayes | K | 5'11" | 175 | 25 | | |
| Mark Moseley | K | 5'11" | 205 | 36 | | 120 |

Babe Laufenberg - Rotor Cuff Injury

## NEW YORK GIANTS 9-7-0 Bill Parcells

| Scores of Each Game | | |
|---|---|---|
| 28 | PHILADELPHIA | 27 |
| 28 | DALLAS | 7 |
| 14 | Washington | 30 |
| 17 | TAMPA BAY | 14 |
| 12 | L.A.Rams | 33 |
| 10 | SAN FRANCISCO | 31 |
| 19 | Atlanta | 7 |
| 10 | Philadelphia | 24 |
| 37 | WASHINGTON | 13 |
| 19 | Dallas | 7 |
| 17 | Tampa Bay | 20 |
| 16 | ST.LOUIS | 10 |
| 28 | KANSAS CITY | 27 |
| 20 | N.Y.Jets | 10 |
| 21 | St.Louis | 31 |
| 3 | NEW ORLEANS | 10 |

| Use Name | Pos. | Hgt | Wgt | Age | Int | Pts |
|---|---|---|---|---|---|---|
| Brad Benson | OT | 6'3" | 270 | 28 | | |
| Chris Godfrey | OT | 6'3" | 265 | 26 | | |
| Conrad Goode | OT | 6'6" | 285 | 22 | | |
| Karl Nelson | OT | 6'6" | 285 | 24 | | |
| Bill Roberts | OT | 6'5" | 280 | 22 | | |
| Billy Ard | OG | 6'3" | 270 | 25 | | |
| Kevin Belcher | OG | 6'3" | 276 | 23 | | |
| David Jordan | OG | 6'6" | 276 | 22 | | |
| Rich Umphrey | C | 6'3" | 270 | 25 | | |
| Dee Hardison | DE | 6'4" | 274 | 28 | | |
| Leonard Marshall | DE | 6'3" | 285 | 22 | | |
| George Martin | DE | 6'4" | 255 | 31 | | |
| Curtis McGriff | DE | 6'5" | 276 | 26 | | |
| Casey Merrill | DE | 6'4" | 260 | 27 | | |
| Jim Burt | NT | 6'1" | 260 | 25 | | |
| Jerome Sally | NT | 6'3" | 270 | 25 | | |
| Carl Banks | LB | 6'4" | 235 | 22 | | |
| Harry Carson | LB | 6'2" | 240 | 30 | 1 | |
| Andy Headen | LB | 6'5" | 242 | 24 | 1 | 6 |
| Byron Hunt | LB | 6'5" | 242 | 25 | 1 | |
| Robbie Jones | LB | 6'2" | 230 | 24 | | |
| Joe McLaughlin | LB | 6'1" | 235 | 27 | | |
| Gary Reasons | LB | 6'4" | 235 | 22 | 2 | |
| Lawrence Taylor | LB | 6'3" | 243 | 25 | 1 | |
| Bill Currier | DB | 6' | 196 | 29 | 1 | |
| Kenny Daniel | DB | 5'10" | 180 | 24 | | |
| Larry Flowers | DB | 6'1" | 195 | 22 | | |
| Mark Haynes | DB | 5'11" | 195 | 25 | 7 | |
| Kenny Hill | DB | 6' | 195 | 26 | | |
| Terry Kinard | DB | 6'1" | 200 | 24 | 2 | |
| Elvis Patterson | DB | 5'11" | 190 | 23 | | |
| Pete Shaw | DB | 5'10" | 183 | 30 | | |
| Perry Williams | DB | 6'2" | 203 | 23 | 3 | |
| Jeff Hostetler | QB | 6'3" | 212 | 23 | | |
| Jeff Rutledge | QB | 6'1" | 195 | 27 | | |
| Phil Simms | QB | 6'3" | 216 | 27 | | |
| Frank Cephous | HB | 5'10" | 205 | 23 | | |
| Joe Morris | HB | 5'7" | 195 | 23 | | 24 |
| Rob Carpenter | FB | 6'1" | 226 | 29 | | 48 |
| Tony Galbreath | FB | 6' | 228 | 30 | | |
| Butch Woolfolk | FB | 6'1" | 212 | 24 | | 6 |
| Earnest Gray | WR | 6'3" | 191 | 27 | | 12 |
| Bobby Johnson | WR | 5'11" | 171 | 22 | | 42 |
| Lionel Manuel | WR | 5'11" | 175 | 22 | | 24 |
| Phil McConkey | WR | 5'10" | 170 | 27 | | 6 |
| John Mistler (to BUF) | WR | 6'2" | 186 | 25 | | |
| Byron Williams | WR | 6'2" | 183 | 23 | | 12 |
| Zeke Mowatt | TE | 6'3" | 238 | 23 | | 36 |
| Tom Mullady | TE | 6'3" | 235 | 27 | | |
| Ali Haji-Sheikh | K | 6' | 172 | 23 | | 83 |
| Dave Jennings | K | 6'4" | 200 | 32 | | |

Gordon King - Broken Arm
John Tuggle - Knee Injury

## DALLAS COWBOYS 9-7-0 Tom Landry

| Scores of Each Game | | |
|---|---|---|
| 20 | L.A.Rams | 13 |
| 7 | N.Y.Giants | 28 |
| 23 | PHILADELPHIA | 17 |
| 20 | GREEN BAY | 6 |
| 23 | Chicago | 14 |
| 20 | ST.LOUIS | 31 |
| 14 | Washington | 34 |
| 30 | NEW ORLEANS | *27 |
| 22 | INDIANAPOLIS | 3 |
| 7 | N.Y.GIANTS | 19 |
| 24 | St.Louis | 17 |
| 3 | Buffalo | 14 |
| 20 | NEW ENGLAND | 17 |
| 26 | Philadelphia | 10 |
| 28 | WASHINGTON | 30 |
| 21 | Miami | 28 |

| Use Name | Pos. | Hgt | Wgt | Age | Int | Pts |
|---|---|---|---|---|---|---|
| Jim Cooper | OT | 6'5" | 267 | 28 | | |
| John Hunt | OT | 6'4" | 254 | 21 | | |
| Phil Pozderac | OT | 6'9" | 276 | 24 | | |
| Howard Richards | OT-OG | 6'6" | 258 | 25 | | |
| Dowe Aughtman | OG | 6'2" | 258 | 23 | | |
| Kurt Petersen | OG | 6'4" | 268 | 27 | | |
| Herbert Scott | OG | 6'2" | 263 | 31 | | |
| Brian Baldinger | OG-OT | 6'4" | 258 | 25 | | |
| Tom Rafferty | C | 6'3" | 254 | 30 | | |
| Glen Titensor | C-OG | 6'4" | 264 | 26 | | |
| Jim Jeffcoat | DE | 6'5" | 264 | 23 | | 6 |
| Too Tall Jones | DE | 6'9" | 287 | 33 | | |
| John Dutton | DT | 6'7" | 267 | 33 | | 2 |
| Don Smerek | DT | 6'7" | 257 | 26 | | |
| Mark Tuinei | DT | 6'5" | 274 | 24 | | |
| Randy White | DT | 6'4" | 268 | 31 | | |
| Bob Breunig | LB | 6'2" | 225 | 31 | | |
| Billy Cannon | LB | 6'4" | 231 | 22 | | |
| Steve DeOssie | LB | 6'2" | 249 | 21 | | |
| Anthony Dickerson | LB | 6'2" | 222 | 27 | 1 | |
| Mike Hegman | LB | 6'1" | 231 | 31 | 3 | |
| Eugene Lockhart | LB | 6'2" | 231 | 23 | 1 | |
| Jeff Rohrer | LB | 6'3" | 225 | 25 | | |
| Jimmie Turner | LB | 6'2" | 220 | 22 | | |
| Vince Albritton | DB | 6'2" | 209 | 22 | | |
| Bill Bates | DB | 6'1" | 200 | 23 | 1 | |
| Dextor Clinkscale | DB | 5'11" | 190 | 26 | 3 | |
| Michael Downs | DB | 6'3" | 203 | 25 | 7 | 6 |
| Ron Fellows | DB | 6' | 174 | 25 | 3 | |
| Carl Howard | DB | 6'2" | 188 | 22 | | |
| Victor Scott | DB | 6' | 196 | 22 | 1 | |
| Dennis Thurman | DB | 5'11 | 179 | 28 | 5 | 6 |
| Everson Walls | DB | 6'1" | 194 | 24 | 3 | |
| Gary Hogeboom | QB | 6'4" | 199 | 26 | | |
| Steve Pelluer | QB | 6'4" | 208 | 22 | | |
| Danny White | QB | 6'2" | 196 | 32 | | |
| Gary Allen | HB | 5'10" | 179 | 24 | | |
| Tony Dorsett | HB | 5'11" | 185 | 30 | | 42 |
| James Jones | HB | 5'10" | 200 | 25 | | 6 |
| Chuck McSwain | HB | 6' | 191 | 23 | | |
| Norm Granger | FB | 5'9" | 221 | 22 | | |
| Timmy Newsome | FB | 6'1" | 231 | 26 | | 30 |
| Ron Springs | FB-HB | 6'1" | 224 | 27 | | 24 |
| Harold Carmichael | WR | 6'7" | 225 | 34 | | |
| Doug Donley | WR | 6' | 178 | 25 | | 12 |
| Tony Hill | WR | 6'2" | 198 | 28 | | 30 |
| Kirk Phillips | WR | 6'1" | 202 | 24 | | |
| Mike Renfro | WR | 6' | 188 | 29 | | 12 |
| Waddell Smith | WR | 6'2" | 180 | 29 | | |
| Fred Cornwell | TE | 6'6" | 238 | 23 | | 6 |
| Doug Cosbie | TE | 6'6" | 232 | 28 | | 24 |
| Brian Salonen | TE | 6'3" | 229 | 23 | | |
| Jim Miller | K | 5'11" | 183 | 27 | | |
| Rafael Septien | K | 5'10" | 180 | 30 | | 102 |
| John Warren | K | 6' | 207 | 23 | | |

Chris Schultz - Knee Injury

## ST. LOUIS CARDINALS 9-7-0 Jim Hanifan

| Scores of Each Game | | |
|---|---|---|
| 23 | Green Bay | 24 |
| 37 | BUFFALO | 7 |
| 34 | Indianapolis | 33 |
| 24 | New Orleans | 34 |
| 28 | MIAMI | 36 |
| 31 | Dallas | 20 |
| 38 | CHICAGO | 21 |
| 26 | WASHINGTON | 24 |
| 34 | Philadelphia | 14 |
| 13 | L.A.RAMS | 16 |
| 17 | DALLAS | 24 |
| 10 | N.Y.Giants | 16 |
| 17 | PHILADELPHIA | 16 |
| 33 | New England | 10 |
| 31 | N.Y.GIANTS | 21 |
| 27 | Washington | 29 |

| Use Name | Pos. | Hgt | Wgt | Age | Int | Pts |
|---|---|---|---|---|---|---|
| Art Plunkett | OT | 6'7" | 270 | 25 | | |
| Tootie Robbins | OT | 6'5" | 278 | 26 | | |
| Luis Sharpe | OT | 6'4" | 260 | 24 | | |
| Dan Audick | OG-OT | 6'3" | 253 | 29 | | |
| Ramsey Dardar | OG-OT | 6'2" | 264 | 24 | | |
| Joe Bostic | OG | 6'3" | 265 | 27 | | |
| Doug Dawson | OG | 6'3" | 267 | 22 | | |
| Terry Stieve | OG | 6'2" | 265 | 30 | | |
| Randy Clark | C | 6'3" | 254 | 27 | | |
| Carlos Scott | C | 6'4" | 300 | 24 | | |
| Al Baker | DE | 6'6" | 270 | 27 | | |
| Curtis Greer | DE | 6'4" | 258 | 26 | | |
| Elois Grooms | DE | 6'4" | 250 | 31 | | |
| Stafford Mays | DE | 6'2" | 250 | 26 | | |
| Mark Duda | DT | 6'3" | 263 | 23 | | |
| David Galloway | DT | 6'3" | 277 | 25 | | |
| Dan Ralph | DT | 6'4" | 260 | 23 | | |
| Dave Ahrens | LB | 6'3" | 228 | 25 | | |
| Kurt Allerman | LB | 6'2" | 232 | 29 | | |
| Charlie Baker | LB | 6'2" | 234 | 26 | | |
| Billy Davis | LB | 6'4" | 210 | 22 | | |
| Bob Harris | LB | 6'2" | 215 | 23 | | |
| Tom Howard | LB | 6'2" | 220 | 30 | 2 | 6 |
| E.J.Junior | LB | 6'3" | 235 | 24 | 1 | |
| Niko Noga | LB | 6'1" | 230 | 22 | | |
| Craig Shaffer | LB | 6' | 230 | 25 | | |
| Jeff Griffin | DB | 6' | 185 | 26 | 2 | |
| Victor Heflin | DB | 6' | 184 | 24 | 1 | |
| Bill Kay (to SD) | DB | 6'1" | 190 | 24 | | |
| Cedric Mack | DB-WR | 6' | 190 | 23 | | |
| Lee Nelson | DB | 5'10" | 185 | 30 | | |
| Benny Perrin | DB | 6'2" | 178 | 24 | 4 | |
| Leonard Smith | DB | 5'11" | 190 | 23 | 2 | 6 |
| Wayne Smith | DB | 6' | 175 | 27 | 4 | |
| Lionel Washington | DB | 6' | 184 | 23 | 5 | |
| Bill Whitaker | DB | 6' | 182 | 24 | | |
| Neil Lomax | QB | 6'3" | 215 | 25 | | 18 |
| Kyle Mackey | QB | 6'2" | 220 | 22 | | |
| Rick McIvor | QB | 6'4" | 210 | 23 | | |
| Ottis Anderson | HB | 6'2" | 220 | 27 | | 48 |
| Will Harrell | HB | 5'9" | 190 | 31 | | 6 |
| Stump Mitchell | HB | 5'9" | 188 | 25 | | 66 |
| Earl Ferrell | FB | 6' | 215 | 26 | | 12 |
| Perry Harrington | FB | 5'11" | 210 | 26 | | |
| Randy Love | FB | 6'1" | 205 | 27 | | 12 |
| Steve Bird (to SD) | WR | 5'11" | 171 | 23 | | |
| Clyde Duncan | WR | 6'1" | 192 | 23 | | |
| Roy Green | WR | 6' | 195 | 27 | | 72 |
| Danny Pittman | WR | 6'2" | 205 | 26 | | |
| Pat Tilley | WR | 5'10" | 178 | 31 | | 30 |
| Quentin Walker | WR | 6'1" | 200 | 23 | | |
| John Goode | TE | 6'2" | 222 | 21 | | |
| Greg LaFleur | TE | 6'4" | 236 | 25 | | |
| Doug Marsh | TE | 6'3" | 240 | 26 | | 30 |
| Carl Birdsong | K | 6' | 192 | 25 | | |
| Neil O'Donoghue | K | 6'6" | 210 | 31 | | 117 |

John Walker - Eye Injury
George Schmitt - Back Injury
Alan Bowers - Ankle Injury
Rod Clark - Knee Injury
Eddie McGill - Knee Injury

## PHILADELPHIA EAGLES 6-9-1 Marion Campbell

| Scores of Each Game | | |
|---|---|---|
| 27 | N.Y.Giants | 28 |
| 19 | MINNESOTA | 17 |
| 17 | Dallas | 23 |
| 9 | SAN FRANCISCO | 21 |
| 0 | Washington | 20 |
| 27 | Buffalo | 17 |
| 16 | INDIANAPOLIS | 7 |
| 24 | N.Y.GIANTS | 10 |
| 14 | ST.LOUIS | 34 |
| 23 | Detroit | *23 |
| 23 | Miami | 24 |
| 16 | WASHINGTON | 10 |
| 16 | St.Louis | 17 |
| 10 | DALLAS | 26 |
| 27 | NEW ENGLAND | 17 |
| 10 | Atlanta | 26 |

| Use Name | Pos. | Hgt | Wgt | Age | Int | Pts |
|---|---|---|---|---|---|---|
| Rusty Russell | OT | 6'5" | 295 | 21 | | |
| Jerry Sisemore | OT | 6'4" | 285 | 33 | | |
| Dean Miraldi | OT-OG | 6'5" | 285 | 26 | | |
| Ron Baker | OG | 6'4" | 270 | 29 | | |
| Steve Kenney | OG | 6'4" | 270 | 28 | | |
| Petey Perot | OG | 6'2" | 261 | 27 | | |
| Gerry Feehery | C-OG | 6'2" | 268 | 24 | | |
| Dave Pacella | C-OG | 6'3" | 266 | 24 | | |
| Mark Dennard | C | 6'1" | 252 | 28 | | |
| Greg Brown | DE | 6'5" | 260 | 27 | | |
| Byron Darby | DE | 6'4" | 260 | 24 | | |
| Dennis Harrison | DE | 6'8" | 280 | 28 | | |
| Leonard Mitchell | DE | 6'7" | 285 | 24 | | |
| Thomas Strauthers | DE | 6'4" | 265 | 23 | | |
| Harvey Armstrong | NT | 6'2" | 265 | 24 | | |
| Ken Clarke | NT | 6'2" | 255 | 28 | | |
| Bill Cowher | LB | 6'3" | 230 | 27 | | |
| Anthony Griggs | LB | 6'3" | 220 | 24 | | |
| Rich Kraynak | LB | 6'1" | 225 | 24 | | 6 |
| Mike Reichenbach | LB | 6'2" | 235 | 22 | | |
| Jerry Robinson | LB | 6'2" | 225 | 27 | | |
| Jody Schulz | LB | 6'3" | 235 | 24 | | |
| Reggie Wilkes | LB | 6'4" | 235 | 28 | 1 | |
| Joel Williams | LB | 6'1" | 225 | 27 | | |
| Evan Cooper | DB | 5'11" | 180 | 22 | | |
| Herman Edwards | DB | 6' | 190 | 30 | 2 | |
| Ray Ellis | DB | 6'1" | 192 | 25 | 7 | |
| Elbert Foules | DB | 5'11" | 185 | 23 | 4 | |
| Wes Hopkins | DB | 6'1" | 210 | 22 | 5 | |
| Lou Rash | DB | 5'9" | 170 | 24 | | |
| Andre Waters | DB | 5'11" | 182 | 22 | 6 | |
| Brenard Wilson | DB | 6' | 180 | 29 | 1 | |
| Roynell Young | DB | 6'1" | 181 | 26 | | |
| Jeff Christensen | QB | 6'3" | 202 | 24 | | |
| Bob Holly (to ATL) | QB | 6'2" | 205 | 24 | | |
| Ron Jaworski | QB | 6'2" | 196 | 33 | | 6 |
| Dean May | QB | 6'5" | 220 | 22 | | |
| Joe Pisarcik | QB | 6'4" | 220 | 32 | | 12 |
| Joe Hayes | HB-WR | 5'9" | 185 | 23 | | |
| Wilbert Montgomery | HB | 5'10" | 195 | 29 | | 12 |
| Major Everett | FB | 5'10" | 215 | 24 | | |
| Michael Haddix | FB | 6'2" | 225 | 22 | | 6 |
| Andre Hardy | FB | 6'1" | 233 | 22 | | |
| Hubie Oliver | FB | 5'10" | 212 | 26 | | |
| Michael Williams | FB | 6'2" | 225 | 23 | | |
| Melvin Hoover | WR | 6' | 185 | 25 | | 12 |
| Kenny Jackson | WR | 6' | 180 | 22 | | 6 |
| Mike Quick | WR | 6'2" | 190 | 25 | | 54 |
| Tony Woodruff | WR | 6' | 185 | 25 | | 18 |
| Vyto Kab | TE | 6'5" | 240 | 24 | | 18 |
| Lawrence Sampleton | TE | 6'5" | 233 | 24 | | |
| John Spagnola | TE | 6'4" | 240 | 27 | | 6 |
| Mike Horan | K | 5'11" | 190 | 25 | | |
| Paul McFadden | K | 5'11" | 155 | 22 | | 116 |

Leon Evans- Knee Injury
Tom Jelesky - Knee Injury
Sam Slater - Shoulder Injury
Todd Thomas - Back Injury

* Overtime

## WASHINGTON REDSKINS

### RUSHING
| Last Name | No. | Yds | Avg | TD |
|---|---|---|---|---|
| Riggins | 327 | 1239 | 3.8 | 14 |
| Griffin | 97 | 408 | 4.2 | 0 |
| Theismann | 62 | 314 | 5.1 | 1 |
| J. Washington | 56 | 192 | 3.4 | 1 |
| Kane | 17 | 43 | 2.5 | 0 |
| Wonsley | 18 | 38 | 2.1 | 4 |
| Monk | 2 | 18 | 9.0 | 0 |
| Hayes | 2 | 13 | 6.5 | 0 |
| Moore | 3 | 13 | 4.3 | 0 |
| Walker | 1 | 2 | 2.0 | 0 |
| Hart | 3 | -6 | -2.0 | 0 |

### RECEIVING
| Last Name | No. | Yds | Avg | TD |
|---|---|---|---|---|
| Monk | 106 | 1372 | 12.9 | 7 |
| Muhammad | 42 | 729 | 17.4 | 4 |
| Didier | 30 | 350 | 11.7 | 5 |
| Brown | 18 | 200 | 11.1 | 3 |
| Warren | 18 | 192 | 10.7 | 0 |
| Moore | 17 | 115 | 6.8 | 2 |
| J. Washington | 13 | 74 | 5.7 | 0 |
| McGrath | 10 | 118 | 11.8 | 1 |
| Seay | 9 | 111 | 12.3 | 1 |
| Griffin | 8 | 43 | 5.4 | 0 |
| Riggins | 7 | 43 | 6.1 | 0 |
| Walker | 5 | 52 | 10.4 | 1 |
| Kane | 1 | 7 | 7.0 | 0 |
| Jones | 1 | 6 | 6.0 | 0 |
| Garrett | 1 | 5 | 5.0 | 0 |

### PUNT RETURNS
| Last Name | No. | Yds | Avg | TD |
|---|---|---|---|---|
| Nelms | 49 | 428 | 8.7 | 0 |
| Green | 2 | 13 | 6.5 | 0 |
| Coffey | 1 | 6 | 6.0 | 0 |
| Mauti | 1 | 2 | 2.0 | 0 |
| Seay | 1 | -2 | -2.0 | 0 |
| G. Williams | 1 | 0 | 0.0 | 0 |
| Coleman | 0 | 27 | — | 0 |

### KICKOFF RETURNS
| Last Name | No. | Yds | Avg | TD |
|---|---|---|---|---|
| Nelms | 42 | 860 | 20.5 | 0 |
| Griffin | 9 | 164 | 18.2 | 0 |
| Kane | 3 | 43 | 14.3 | 0 |
| Seay | 3 | 53 | 17.7 | 0 |
| J. Smith | 2 | 38 | 19.0 | 0 |
| Mauti | 1 | 16 | 16.0 | 0 |
| R. Smith | 1 | 22 | 22.0 | 0 |

### PASSING — PUNTING — KICKING
| PASSING | Att | Cmp | % | Yds | Yd/Att | TD | Int- | % | RK |
|---|---|---|---|---|---|---|---|---|---|
| Theismann | 477 | 283 | 59 | 3391 | 7.1 | 24 | 13- | 3 | 5 |
| Hart | 7 | 3 | 43 | 26 | 3.7 | 0 | 0- | 0 | |
| J. Washington | 1 | 0 | 0 | 0 | 0.0 | 0 | 0- | 0 | |

| PUNTING | No | Avg |
|---|---|---|
| Hayes | 72 | 39.4 |

| KICKING | XP | Att | % | FG | Att | % |
|---|---|---|---|---|---|---|
| Moseley | 48 | 51 | 94 | 24 | 31 | 77 |

## NEW YORK GIANTS

### RUSHING
| Last Name | No. | Yds | Avg | TD |
|---|---|---|---|---|
| Carpenter | 250 | 795 | 3.2 | 7 |
| Morris | 133 | 510 | 3.8 | 4 |
| Simms | 42 | 162 | 3.9 | 0 |
| Galbreath | 22 | 97 | 4.4 | 0 |
| Woolfolk | 40 | 92 | 2.3 | 1 |
| Cephous | 3 | 2 | 0.7 | 0 |
| Manuel | 3 | 2 | 0.7 | 0 |

### RECEIVING
| Last Name | No. | Yds | Avg | TD |
|---|---|---|---|---|
| Johnson | 48 | 795 | 16.6 | 7 |
| Mowatt | 48 | 698 | 14.5 | 6 |
| Gray | 38 | 529 | 13.9 | 2 |
| Galbreath | 37 | 357 | 9.6 | 0 |
| Manuel | 33 | 619 | 18.8 | 4 |
| Carpenter | 26 | 209 | 8.0 | 1 |
| B. Williams | 24 | 471 | 19.6 | 2 |
| Morris | 12 | 124 | 10.3 | 0 |
| Woolfolk | 9 | 53 | 5.9 | 0 |
| McConkey | 8 | 154 | 19.3 | 0 |
| Mullady | 2 | 35 | 17.5 | 0 |
| Simms | 1 | 13 | 13.0 | 0 |
| Mistler | 1 | 5 | 5.0 | 0 |
| Belcher | 1 | 4 | 4.0 | 0 |

### PUNT RETURNS
| Last Name | No. | Yds | Avg | TD |
|---|---|---|---|---|
| McConkey | 46 | 306 | 6.7 | 0 |
| Manuel | 8 | 62 | 7.8 | 0 |
| Kinnard | 1 | 0 | 0.0 | 0 |

### KICKOFF RETURNS
| Last Name | No. | Yds | Avg | TD |
|---|---|---|---|---|
| McConkey | 28 | 541 | 19.3 | 0 |
| Woolfolk | 14 | 232 | 16.6 | 0 |
| Cephous | 9 | 178 | 19.8 | 0 |
| Morris | 9 | 69 | 11.5 | 0 |
| McLaughlin | 2 | 18 | 9.0 | 0 |
| Daniel | 1 | 52 | 52.0 | 0 |
| Hill | 1 | 27 | 27.0 | 0 |

### PASSING — PUNTING — KICKING
| PASSING | Att | Cmp | % | Yds | Yd/Att | TD | Int- | % | RK |
|---|---|---|---|---|---|---|---|---|---|
| Simms | 533 | 286 | 54 | 4044 | 7.6 | 22 | 18- | 3 | 10 |
| Galbreath | 1 | 1 | 100 | 13 | 13.0 | 0 | 0- | 0 | |
| Rutledge | 1 | 1 | 100 | 9 | 9.0 | 0 | 0- | 0 | |

| PUNTING | No | Avg |
|---|---|---|
| Jennings | 90 | 40.0 |

| KICKING | XP | Att | % | FG | Att | % |
|---|---|---|---|---|---|---|
| Haji-Sheikh | 32 | 35 | 91 | 17 | 33 | 52 |

## DALLAS COWBOYS

### RUSHING
| Last Name | No. | Yds | Avg | TD |
|---|---|---|---|---|
| Dorsett | 302 | 1189 | 3.9 | 6 |
| Newsome | 66 | 268 | 4.1 | 5 |
| Springs | 68 | 197 | 2.9 | 1 |
| D. White | 6 | 21 | 3.5 | 0 |
| Hogeboom | 15 | 19 | 1.3 | 0 |
| J. Jones | 8 | 13 | 1.6 | 0 |
| T. Hill | 1 | 7 | 7.0 | 0 |
| Donley | 2 | 5 | 2.5 | 0 |
| Smith | 1 | -5 | -5.0 | 0 |

### RECEIVING
| Last Name | No. | Yds | Avg | TD |
|---|---|---|---|---|
| Cosbie | 60 | 789 | 13.2 | 4 |
| T. Hill | 58 | 864 | 14.9 | 5 |
| Dorsett | 51 | 459 | 9.0 | 1 |
| Springs | 46 | 454 | 9.9 | 3 |
| Renfro | 35 | 583 | 16.7 | 2 |
| Donley | 32 | 473 | 14.8 | 2 |
| Newsome | 26 | 263 | 10.1 | 0 |
| J. Jones | 7 | 57 | 8.1 | 1 |
| Cornwell | 2 | 23 | 11.5 | 1 |
| Smith | 1 | 7 | 7.0 | 0 |
| Carmichael | 1 | 7 | 7.0 | 0 |
| Phillips | 1 | 6 | 6.0 | 0 |
| Pozderac | 1 | 1 | 1.0 | 0 |
| Harris | 1 | 9 | 9.0 | 0 |

### PUNT RETURNS
| Last Name | No. | Yds | Avg | TD |
|---|---|---|---|---|
| Allen | 54 | 446 | 8.3 | 0 |

### KICKOFF RETURNS
| Last Name | No. | Yds | Avg | TD |
|---|---|---|---|---|
| Allen | 33 | 666 | 20.2 | 0 |
| McSwain | 20 | 403 | 20.2 | 0 |
| Fellows | 6 | 94 | 15.7 | 0 |
| Salonen | 2 | 30 | 15.0 | 0 |
| Granger | 2 | 6 | 3.0 | 0 |

### PASSING — PUNTING — KICKING
| PASSING | Att | Cmp | % | Yds | Yd/Att | TD | Int- | % | RK |
|---|---|---|---|---|---|---|---|---|---|
| D. White | 233 | 126 | 54 | 1580 | 6.8 | 11 | 11- | 5 | 12 |
| Hogeboom | 367 | 195 | 53 | 2366 | 6.5 | 7 | 14- | 3.8 | 14 |
| Renfro | 2 | 1 | 50 | 49 | 24.5 | 1 | 0- | 0 | |
| Springs | 1 | 0 | 0 | 0 | 0.0 | 0 | 0- | 0 | |
| Dorsett | 1 | 0 | 0 | 0 | 0.0 | 0 | 1-100 | | |

| PUNTING | No | Avg |
|---|---|---|
| D. White | 82 | 38.4 |
| Warren | 21 | 38.0 |
| Miller | 5 | 34.6 |

| KICKING | XP | Att | % | FG | Att | % |
|---|---|---|---|---|---|---|
| Septien | 33 | 34 | 97 | 23 | 29 | 79 |

## ST. LOUIS CARDINALS

### RUSHING
| Last Name | No. | Yds | Avg | TD |
|---|---|---|---|---|
| Anderson | 289 | 1174 | 4.1 | 6 |
| Mitchell | 81 | 434 | 5.4 | 9 |
| Ferrell | 44 | 203 | 4.6 | 1 |
| Lomax | 35 | 184 | 5.3 | 3 |
| Love | 25 | 90 | 3.6 | 1 |
| Harrell | 5 | 7 | 1.4 | 1 |
| Harrington | 3 | 6 | 2.0 | 0 |
| McIvor | 3 | 5 | 1.7 | 0 |
| Marsh | 1 | -5 | -5.0 | 0 |
| Green | 1 | -10 | -10.0 | 0 |

### RECEIVING
| Last Name | No. | Yds | Avg | TD |
|---|---|---|---|---|
| Green | 78 | 1555 | 19.9 | 12 |
| Anderson | 70 | 611 | 8.7 | 2 |
| Tilley | 52 | 758 | 14.6 | 5 |
| Marsh | 39 | 608 | 15.6 | 5 |
| Mitchell | 26 | 318 | 12.2 | 2 |
| Ferrell | 26 | 218 | 8.4 | 1 |
| LaFleur | 17 | 198 | 11.6 | 0 |
| Harrell | 14 | 106 | 7.6 | 0 |
| Pittman | 10 | 145 | 14.5 | 0 |
| Love | 7 | 33 | 4.7 | 1 |
| Mack | 5 | 61 | 12.2 | 0 |
| Goode | 3 | 23 | 7.7 | 0 |

### PUNT RETURNS
| Last Name | No. | Yds | Avg | TD |
|---|---|---|---|---|
| Mitchell | 38 | 333 | 8.2 | 0 |
| Bird | 6 | 60 | 10.0 | 0 |
| Pittman | 4 | 10 | 2.5 | 0 |

### KICKOFF RETURNS
| Last Name | No. | Yds | Avg | TD |
|---|---|---|---|---|
| Mitchell | 35 | 804 | 23.0 | 0 |
| Pittman | 14 | 319 | 22.8 | 0 |
| Harrell | 13 | 231 | 17.8 | 0 |
| Bird | 11 | 205 | 18.6 | 0 |
| Green | 1 | 18 | 18.0 | 0 |
| Love | 1 | 1 | 1.0 | 0 |
| Ferrell | 1 | 0 | 0.0 | 0 |

### PASSING — PUNTING — KICKING
| PASSING | Att | Cmp | % | Yds | Yd/Att | TD | Int- | % | RK |
|---|---|---|---|---|---|---|---|---|---|
| Lomax | 560 | 345 | 62 | 4614 | 8.2 | 28 | 16- | 3 | 3 |
| McIvor | 4 | 0 | 0 | 0 | 0.0 | 0 | 0- | 0 | |
| Mitchell | 1 | 1 | 100 | 20 | 20.0 | 0 | 0- | 0 | |
| Perrin | 1 | 1 | 100 | 0 | 0.0 | 0 | 0- | 0 | |

| PUNTING | No | Avg |
|---|---|---|
| Birdsong | 67 | 38.7 |

| KICKING | XP | Att | % | FG | ATt | % |
|---|---|---|---|---|---|---|
| O'Donoghue | 48 | 51 | 94 | 23 | 35 | 66 |

## PHILADELPHIA EAGLES

### RUSHING
| Last Name | No. | Yds | Avg | TD |
|---|---|---|---|---|
| Montgomery | 201 | 789 | 3.9 | 2 |
| Oliver | 72 | 263 | 3.7 | 0 |
| Haddix | 48 | 130 | 2.7 | 1 |
| M. Williams | 33 | 83 | 2.5 | 0 |
| Hardy | 14 | 41 | 2.9 | 0 |
| Pisarcik | 7 | 19 | 2.7 | 2 |
| Jaworski | 5 | 18 | 3.6 | 1 |
| Quick | 1 | -5 | -5.0 | 0 |

### RECEIVING
| Last Name | No. | Yds | Avg | TD |
|---|---|---|---|---|
| Spagnola | 65 | 701 | 10.8 | 1 |
| Quick | 61 | 1052 | 17.2 | 9 |
| Montgomery | 60 | 501 | 8.4 | 0 |
| Haddix | 33 | 231 | 7.0 | 0 |
| Oliver | 32 | 142 | 4.4 | 0 |
| Woodruff | 30 | 484 | 16.1 | 3 |
| Jackson | 26 | 398 | 15.3 | 1 |
| Kab | 9 | 102 | 11.3 | 3 |
| M. Williams | 7 | 47 | 6.7 | 0 |
| Hoover | 6 | 143 | 23.8 | 2 |
| Hardy | 2 | 22 | 11.0 | 0 |

### PUNT RETURNS
| Last Name | No. | Yds | Avg | TD |
|---|---|---|---|---|
| Cooper | 40 | 250 | 6.3 | 0 |

### KICKOFF RETURNS
| Last Name | No. | Yds | Avg | TD |
|---|---|---|---|---|
| Hayes | 22 | 441 | 20.0 | 0 |
| Cooper | 17 | 299 | 17.6 | 0 |
| Waters | 13 | 319 | 24.5 | 1 |
| Hardy | 1 | 20 | 20.0 | 0 |
| Everett | 3 | 40 | 13.3 | 0 |
| Ellis | 2 | 25 | 12.5 | 0 |
| Strauthers | 1 | 12 | 12.0 | 0 |

### PASSING — PUNTING — KICKING
| PASSING | Att | Cmp | % | Yds | Yd/Att | TD | Int- | % | RK |
|---|---|---|---|---|---|---|---|---|---|
| Jaworski | 427 | 234 | 55 | 2754 | 6.5 | 16 | 14- | 3 | 11 |
| Pisarcik | 176 | 96 | 55 | 1036 | 5.9 | 3 | 3- | 2 | |
| Montgomery | 2 | 0 | 0 | 0 | 0.0 | 0 | 0- | 0 | |
| May | 1 | 1 | 100 | 33 | 33.0 | 0 | 0- | 0 | |

| PUNTING | No | Avg |
|---|---|---|
| Horan | 92 | 42.2 |

| KICKING | XP | Att | % | FG | Att | % |
|---|---|---|---|---|---|---|
| McFadden | 26 | 27 | 96 | 30 | 37 | 81 |

## CHICAGO BEARS 10-6-0 Mike Ditka

| Scores of Each Game | | |
|---|---|---|
| 34 | TAMPA BAY | 14 |
| 27 | DENVER | 0 |
| 9 | Green Bay | 7 |
| 9 | Seattle | 38 |
| 14 | DALLAS | 23 |
| 20 | NEW ORLEANS | 7 |
| 21 | St.Louis | 38 |
| 44 | Tampa Bay | 9 |
| 16 | MINNESOTA | 7 |
| 17 | L.A.RAIDERS | 6 |
| 13 | L.A.Rams | 29 |
| 16 | DETROIT | 14 |
| 34 | Minnesota | 3 |
| 7 | San Diego | 20 |
| 14 | GREEN BAY | 20 |
| 30 | Detroit | 13 |

| Use Name | Pos. | Hgt | Wgt | Age | Int | Pts |
|---|---|---|---|---|---|---|
| Jim Covert | OT | 6'4" | 283 | 24 | | |
| Andy Frederick | OT | 6'6" | 265 | 30 | | |
| Keith Van Horne | OT | 6'6" | 275 | 26 | | |
| Tom Andrews | OT-C | 6'4" | 261 | 22 | | |
| Kurt Becker | OG | 6'5" | 270 | 25 | | |
| Mark Bortz | OG | 6'6" | 271 | 23 | | |
| Rob Fada | OG | 6'2" | 265 | 23 | | |
| Stefan Humphries | OG | 6'3" | 265 | 22 | | |
| Jay Hilgenberg | C | 6'3" | 255 | 25 | | |
| Richard Dent | DE | 6'5" | 253 | 23 | | |
| Mike Hartenstine | DE | 6'3" | 258 | 31 | | |
| Tyrone Keys | DE | 6'7" | 267 | 24 | | |
| Dan Hampton | DT | 6'5" | 266 | 26 | | |
| Steve McMichael | DT | 6'2" | 260 | 26 | | |
| Jim Osborne | DT | 6'3" | 259 | 34 | | |

Ken Margerum - Knee Injury
Rickey Watts - Injury

| Use Name | Pos. | Hgt | Wgt | Age | Int | Pts |
|---|---|---|---|---|---|---|
| Brian Cabral | LB | 6' | 224 | 28 | | |
| Al Harris | LB | 6'5" | 250 | 27 | 1 | |
| Wilber Marshall | LB | 6'1" | 225 | 22 | | |
| Dan Rains | LB | 6'1" | 220 | 28 | | |
| Ron Rivera | LB | 6'3" | 244 | 22 | | |
| Mike Singletary | LB | 6' | 230 | 25 | 1 | |
| Otis Wilson | LB | 6'2" | 231 | 26 | | |
| Todd Bell | DB | 6'1" | 207 | 25 | 4 | 6 |
| Jack Cameron | DB | 6' | 182 | 22 | | |
| Dave Duerson | DB | 6'1" | 202 | 23 | 1 | |
| Gary Fencik | DB | 6'1" | 197 | 30 | 5 | |
| Jeff Fisher | DB | 5'11" | 195 | 25 | | |
| Leslie Frazier | DB | 6' | 189 | 25 | 5 | |
| Shaun Gayle | DB | 5'11" | 191 | 22 | 1 | |
| Kevin Potter | DB | 5'10" | 188 | 24 | | |
| Mike Richardson | DB | 6' | 188 | 23 | 2 | |
| Terry Schmidt | DB | 6' | 185 | 32 | 1 | |

| Use Name | Pos. | Hgt | Wgt | Age | Int | Pts |
|---|---|---|---|---|---|---|
| Steve Fuller | QB | 6'4" | 195 | 27 | | 6 |
| Greg Landry | QB | 6'4" | 210 | 37 | | 6 |
| Rusty Lisch | QB | 6'3" | 215 | 27 | | |
| Jim McMahon | QB | 6'1" | 187 | 25 | | 12 |
| Dennis Gentry | HB | 5'8" | 181 | 25 | | 6 |
| Anthony Hutchison | HB | 5'10" | 186 | 23 | | 6 |
| Walter Payton | HB | 5'11" | 202 | 30 | | 66 |
| Donald Jordan | FB | 6' | 210 | 22 | | |
| Matt Suhey | FB | 5'11" | 217 | 26 | | 36 |
| Calvin Thomas | FB | 5'11" | 235 | 24 | | 6 |
| Brad Anderson | WR | 6'2" | 196 | 23 | | 6 |
| Brian Baschnagel | WR | 6' | 193 | 30 | | |
| Willie Gault | WR | 6' | 178 | 23 | | 36 |
| Dennis McKinnon | WR | 6'1" | 185 | 23 | | 18 |
| Pat Dunsmore | TE | 6'3" | 237 | 24 | | 6 |
| Mitch Krenk | TE | 6'2" | 225 | 24 | | |
| Emery Moorehead | TE | 6'2" | 225 | 30 | | 6 |
| Jay Saldi | TE | 6'3" | 230 | 29 | | |
| Dave Finzer | K | 6'1" | 195 | 25 | | |
| Bob Thomas | K | 5'10" | 175 | 32 | | 101 |

## GREEN BAY PACKERS 8-8-0 Forrest Gregg

| Scores of Each Game | | |
|---|---|---|
| 24 | ST.LOUIS | 23 |
| 7 | L.A.Raiders | 28 |
| 7 | CHICAGO | 9 |
| 6 | Dallas | 20 |
| 27 | Tampa Bay | *30 |
| 28 | SAN DIEGO | 34 |
| 14 | Denver | 17 |
| 24 | SEATTLE | 30 |
| 41 | DETROIT | 9 |
| 23 | New Orleans | 13 |
| 45 | MINNESOTA | 17 |
| 31 | L.A.RAMS | 6 |
| 28 | Detroit | 31 |
| 27 | TAMPA BAY | 14 |
| 20 | Chicago | 14 |
| 38 | Minnesota | 14 |

| Use Name | Pos. | Hgt | Wgt | Age | Int | Pts |
|---|---|---|---|---|---|---|
| Ron Hallstrom | OT | 6'6" | 286 | 25 | | |
| Gary Hoffman | OT | 6'7" | 282 | 22 | | |
| Boyd Jones | OT | 6'3" | 265 | 23 | | |
| Greg Koch | OT | 6'4" | 276 | 29 | | |
| Karl Swanke | OT-C | 6'6" | 262 | 26 | | |
| Keith Uecker | OT | 6'5" | 270 | 24 | | |
| Dave Drechsler | OG | 6'3" | 264 | 24 | | |
| Tim Huffman | OG | 6'5" | 282 | 25 | | |
| Syd Kitson (to DAL) | OG | 6'4" | 264 | 25 | | |
| Mark Cannon | C | 6'3" | 258 | 22 | | |
| Larry McCarren | C | 6'3" | 248 | 32 | | |
| Blake Moore | C | 6'5" | 272 | 26 | | 6 |
| Robert Brown | DE | 6'2" | 250 | 23 | 1 | 6 |
| Alphonso Carreker | DE | 6'6" | 260 | 22 | | |
| Donnie Humphrey | DE | 6'3" | 275 | 23 | | |
| Ezra Johnson | DE | 6'4" | 259 | 28 | | |
| Charles Martin | DE | 6'4"' | 270 | 25 | | |
| Terry Jones | NT | 6'2" | 253 | 27 | | |
| Bill Neill | NT | 6'4" | 267 | 25 | | |

| Use Name | Pos. | Hgt | Wgt | Age | Int | Pts |
|---|---|---|---|---|---|---|
| John Anderson | LB | 6'3" | 228 | 28 | 3 | |
| George Cumby | LB | 6' | 224 | 28 | 1 | |
| John Dorsey | LB | 6'3" | 235 | 24 | | |
| Mike Douglass | LB | 6' | 214 | 29 | | |
| Cliff Lewis | LB | 6'1" | 224 | 24 | | |
| Guy Prather | LB | 6'2" | 230 | 26 | | |
| Randy Scott | LB | 6'1" | 220 | 25 | | |
| Rich Wingo | LB | 6'1" | 230 | 28 | | |
| Tom Flynn | DB | 6' | 195 | 22 | 9 | |
| Gary Hayes | DB | 5'10" | 180 | 27 | | |
| Estus Hood | DB | 5'11" | 189 | 28 | 1 | |
| Daryll Jones | DB | 6' | 190 | 22 | | |
| Mark Lee | DB | 5'11" | 187 | 26 | 3 | |
| Tim Lewis | DB | 5'11" | 191 | 22 | 7 | 6 |
| Mike McLeod | DB | 6' | 180 | 26 | 1 | |
| Mark Murphy | DB | 6'2" | 199 | 26 | 1 | |
| Dwayne O'Steen | DB | 6'1" | 195 | 29 | | |

Leotis Harris - Knee Injury
Mike McCoy - Leg Injury
Ken Walter - Ankle Injury
Scott Brunner - Knee Injury

| Use Name | Pos. | Hgt | Wgt | Age | Int | Pts |
|---|---|---|---|---|---|---|
| Rich Campbell | QB | 6'4" | 219 | 25 | | |
| Lynn Dickey | QB | 6'4" | 210 | 34 | | 18 |
| Randy Wright | QB | 6'2" | 194 | 23 | | |
| Harlan Huckleby | HB | 6'1" | 199 | 26 | | |
| Eddie Lee Ivery | HB | 6'1" | 210 | 27 | | 42 |
| Del Rodgers | HB | 5'10" | 202 | 24 | | 6 |
| Jessie Clark | FB | 6' | 233 | 24 | | 36 |
| Ray Crouse | FB | 5'11" | 214 | 25 | | 6 |
| Gerry Ellis | FB | 5'11" | 225 | 26 | | 36 |
| Ron Cassidy | WR | 6' | 180 | 27 | | |
| Phillip Epps | WR | 5'10" | 165 | 24 | | 18 |
| John Jefferson | WR | 6'1" | 198 | 28 | | |
| James Lofton | WR | 6'3" | 197 | 28 | | 42 |
| Lenny Taylor | WR | 5'10" | 179 | 23 | | |
| Henry Childs | TE | 6'2" | 225 | 33 | | |
| Paul Coffman | TE | 6'3" | 225 | 28 | | 54 |
| Gary Lewis | TE | 6'5" | 234 | 25 | | |
| Ed West | TE | 6'1" | 242 | 23 | | 30 |
| Al Del Greco | K | 5'10" | 190 | 22 | | 61 |
| Eddie Garcia | K | 5'8" | 178 | 25 | | 23 |
| Bucky Scribner | K | 6' | 202 | 24 | | |

## TAMPA BAY BUCCANEERS 6-10-0 John McKay

| Scores of Each Game | | |
|---|---|---|
| 14 | Chicago | 34 |
| 13 | New Orleans | 17 |
| 21 | DETROIT | 17 |
| 14 | N.Y.Giants | 17 |
| 30 | GREEN BAY | *27 |
| 35 | MINNESOTA | 31 |
| 7 | Detroit | *13 |
| 9 | CHICAGO | 44 |
| 20 | Kansas City | 24 |
| 24 | Minnesota | 27 |
| 20 | N.Y.GIANTS | 17 |
| 17 | San Francisco | 24 |
| 33 | L.A.RAMS | 34 |
| 14 | Green Bay | 27 |
| 23 | ATLANTA | 6 |
| 41 | N.Y.JETS | 21 |

| Use Name | Pos. | Hgt | Wgt | Age | Int | Pts |
|---|---|---|---|---|---|---|
| Ron Heller | OT | 6'6" | 270 | 22 | | |
| Ken Kaplan | OT | 6'4" | 270 | 24 | | |
| Gene Sanders | OT | 6'3" | 285 | 27 | | |
| Kelly Thomas | OT | 6'6" | 270 | 23 | | |
| Glenn Bujnoch | OG | 6'5" | 265 | 30 | | |
| Steve Courson | OG | 6'1" | 270 | 28 | | |
| Sean Farrell | OG | 6'3" | 260 | 24 | | |
| Randy Grimes | OG-C | 6'4" | 265 | 24 | | |
| Noah Jackson | OG | 6'2" | 265 | 33 | | |
| Steve Wilson | C | 6'3" | 270 | 30 | | |
| Byron Braggs | DE | 6'4" | 290 | 24 | | |
| John Cannon | DE | 6'5" | 260 | 24 | 1 | |
| Phil Darns | DE | 6'3" | 245 | 25 | | |
| Brison Manor (from DEN) | DE | 6'4" | 248 | 32 | | |
| Lee Roy Selmon | DE | 6'3" | 250 | 29 | | |
| David Logan | NT | 6'2" | 250 | 27 | 1 | 6 |
| Karl Morgan | NT | 6'1" | 255 | 23 | | |

Andre Tyler - Shoulder Injury
Jeff Komlo - Back Injury
Gene Branton - Hamstring Injury

| Use Name | Pos. | Hgt | Wgt | Age | Int | Pts |
|---|---|---|---|---|---|---|
| Scott Brantley | LB | 6'1" | 230 | 25 | 3 | |
| Keith Browner | LB | 6'5" | 240 | 22 | | |
| Jeff Davis | LB | 6' | 230 | 24 | 1 | |
| Hugh Green | LB | 6'2" | 225 | 25 | | |
| Cecil Johnson | LB | 6'2" | 235 | 29 | | |
| Danny Spradlin | LB | 6'1" | 235 | 25 | | |
| Robert Thompson | LB | 6'3" | 230 | 24 | | |
| Chris Washington | LB | 6'4" | 225 | 22 | | |
| Richard Wood | LB | 6'2" | 230 | 31 | | |
| Fred Acorn | DB | 5'10" | 180 | 23 | 1 | |
| Cedric Brown | DB | 6'1" | 200 | 30 | 1 | |
| Jeremiah Castille | DB | 5'10" | 175 | 23 | 3 | |
| Randy Clark | DB | 6' | 204 | 23 | | |
| Mark Cotney | DB | 6' | 205 | 32 | 5 | |
| Craig Curry | DB | 6' | 187 | 23 | | |
| Maurice Harvey | DB | 5'10" | 187 | 28 | | |
| John Holt | DB | 5'11" | 180 | 25 | 1 | |
| Beasley Reece | DB | 6'1" | 195 | 30 | 1 | |
| Norris Thomas | DB | 5'11" | 180 | 30 | | |
| Mike Washington | DB | 6'3" | 200 | 31 | | |

Don Swafford - Back Injury
Rick Mallory - Ankle Injury

| Use Name | Pos. | Hgt | Wgt | Age | Int | Pts |
|---|---|---|---|---|---|---|
| Steve DeBerg | QB | 6'2" | 205 | 30 | | 12 |
| Blair Kiel | QB | 6' | 200 | 22 | | |
| Jack Thompson | QB | 6'3" | 220 | 28 | | |
| Leon Bright | HB | 5'9" | 192 | 29 | | |
| Scott Dierking | HB-FB | 5'11" | 225 | 29 | | 6 |
| Michael Morton | HB | 5'8" | 180 | 24 | | |
| James Owens | HB | 5'11" | 200 | 29 | | 6 |
| Adger Armstrong | FB | 6' | 225 | 27 | | 30 |
| Melvin Carver | FB | 5'11" | 225 | 25 | | |
| George Peoples | FB | 6' | 215 | 24 | | |
| James Wilder | FB | 6'3" | 225 | 26 | | 78 |
| Theo Bell | WR | 6' | 195 | 30 | | |
| Gerald Carter | WR | 6'1" | 190 | 27 | | 30 |
| Dwayne Dixon | WR | 6'1" | 205 | 22 | | |
| Kevin House | WR | 6'1" | 185 | 26 | | 30 |
| Jerry Bell | TE | 6'5" | 230 | 25 | | 24 |
| Jay Carroll | TE | 6'4" | 230 | 22 | | 6 |
| Jimmie Giles | TE | 6'3" | 240 | 29 | | 12 |
| Mark Witte | TE | 6'3" | 235 | 24 | | |
| Obed Ariri | K | 5'8" | 170 | 28 | | 95 |
| Frank Garcia | K | 6' | 205 | 27 | | |

## DETROIT LIONS 4-11-1 Monte Clark

| Scores of Each Game | | |
|---|---|---|
| 27 | SAN FRANCISCO | 30 |
| 27 | Atlanta | *24 |
| 17 | Tampa Bay | 21 |
| 28 | MINNESOTA | 29 |
| 24 | San Diego | 27 |
| 7 | DENVER | 28 |
| 13 | TAMPA BAY | *7 |
| 16 | Minnesota | 14 |
| 9 | Green Bay | 41 |
| 23 | PHILADELPHIA | 23 |
| 14 | Washington | 28 |
| 14 | Chicago | 16 |
| 31 | GREEN BAY | 28 |
| 17 | Seattle | 38 |
| 3 | L.A.RAIDERS | 24 |
| 13 | CHICAGO | 30 |

| Use Name | Pos. | Hgt | Wgt | Age | Int | Pts |
|---|---|---|---|---|---|---|
| Chris Dieterich | OT-OG | 6'3" | 260 | 26 | | |
| Keith Dorney | OT | 6'5" | 260 | 26 | | |
| Donald Laster | OT | 6'5" | 278 | 25 | | |
| Rich Strenger | OT | 6'7" | 276 | 24 | | |
| Homer Elias | OG | 6'3" | 255 | 29 | | |
| Don Greco | OG | 6'3" | 265 | 25 | | |
| Larry Lee | OG-C | 6'2" | 260 | 24 | | |
| Amos Fowler | C | 6'3" | 253 | 28 | | |
| David Jones | C | 6'2" | 260 | 22 | | |
| Steve Mott | C | 6'3" | 265 | 23 | | |
| Mike Cofer | DE | 6'5" | 245 | 24 | | |
| William Gay | DE | 6'5" | 255 | 29 | | |
| Curtis Green | DE | 6'3" | 258 | 27 | | |
| Steve Baack | DT-DE | 6'4" | 260 | 23 | | |
| Doug English | DT | 6'5" | 258 | 31 | | |
| Martin Moss | DT | 6'4" | 252 | 25 | | |
| Eric Williams | DT | 6'4" | 260 | 22 | | |

| Use Name | Pos. | Hgt | Wgt | Age | Int | Pts |
|---|---|---|---|---|---|---|
| Roosevelt Barnes | LB | 6'2" | 228 | 26 | | |
| Garry Cobb | LB | 6'2" | 227 | 27 | | |
| August Curley | LB | 6'3" | 226 | 24 | | |
| Kirk Dodge | LB | 6'1" | 231 | 22 | | |
| Steve Doig | LB | 6'2" | 245 | 24 | | |
| Ken Fantetti | LB | 6'2" | 232 | 27 | 1 | |
| Angelo King | LB | 6'1" | 222 | 26 | | |
| Terry Tautolo | LB | 6'2" | 227 | 30 | | |
| Jimmy Williams | LB | 6'3" | 230 | 23 | | |
| William Frizzell | DB | 6'2" | 195 | 21 | | |
| William Graham | DB | 5'11" | 191 | 24 | 3 | |
| Alvin Hall | DB | 5'10" | 184 | 26 | 2 | |
| Demetrious Johnson | DB | 5'11" | 190 | 23 | | |
| Al Latimer | DB | 5'11" | 181 | 26 | | |
| Bruce McNorton | DB | 5'11" | 175 | 25 | 2 | |
| Bobby Watkins | DB | 5'10" | 184 | 24 | 6 | |
| Gardner Williams | DB | 6'2" | 199 | 22 | | |

| Use Name | Pos. | Hgt | Wgt | Age | Int | Pts |
|---|---|---|---|---|---|---|
| Gary Danielson | QB | 6'2" | 196 | 32 | | 24 |
| Eric Hipple | QB | 6'2" | 196 | 26 | | |
| Mike Machurek | QB | 6'1" | 205 | 24 | | |
| John Witkowski | QB | 6'1" | 200 | 22 | | |
| Ken Jenkins | HB | 5'8" | 184 | 25 | | 6 |
| Billy Sims | HB | 6' | 212 | 28 | | 30 |
| Dexter Bussey | FB | 6'1" | 210 | 32 | | |
| Dave D'Addio | FB | 6'1" | 230 | 23 | | |
| James Jones | FB | 6'2" | 228 | 23 | | 48 |
| Mike Meade | FB | 5'11" | 224 | 24 | | |
| Carl Bland | WR | 5'11" | 180 | 23 | | |
| Jeff Chadwick | WR | 6'3" | 190 | 23 | | 18 |
| Pete Mandley | WR | 5'10" | 191 | 23 | | |
| Robbie Martin | WR | 5'8" | 177 | 25 | | |
| Mark Nichols | WR | 6'2" | 208 | 24 | | 6 |
| Leonard Thompson | WR | 5'11" | 192 | 32 | | 36 |
| David Lewis | TE | 6'3" | 230 | 23 | | 18 |
| Reese McCall | TE | 6'7" | 245 | 28 | | |
| Rob Rubick | TE | 6'3" | 234 | 23 | | 6 |
| Mike Black | K | 6'1" | 197 | 23 | | |
| Eddie Murray | K | 5'10" | 175 | 28 | | 91 |

## MINNESOTA VIKINGS 3-13-0 Les Steckel

| Scores of Each Game | | |
|---|---|---|
| 13 | SAN DIEGO | 42 |
| 17 | Philadelphia | 19 |
| 27 | ATLANTA | 20 |
| 29 | Detroit | 28 |
| 12 | SEATTLE | 20 |
| 31 | Tampa Bay | 35 |
| 20 | L.A.Raiders | 23 |
| 14 | DETROIT | 16 |
| 7 | Chicago | 16 |
| 27 | TAMPA BAY | 24 |
| 17 | Green Bay | 45 |
| 21 | Denver | 42 |
| 3 | CHICAGO | 34 |
| 17 | WASHINGTON | 31 |
| 7 | San Francisco | 51 |
| 14 | GREEN BAY | 38 |

| Use Name | Pos. | Hgt | Wgt | Age | Int | Pts |
|---|---|---|---|---|---|---|
| Matt Hernandez | OT | 6'6" | 260 | 22 | | |
| Tim Irwin | OT | 6'6" | 285 | 25 | | |
| Steve Riley | OT | 6'6" | 260 | 31 | | |
| Terry Tausch | OT | 6'5" | 275 | 25 | | |
| Malcolm Carson | OG | 6'2" | 260 | 24 | | |
| Robert Cobb | OG-OT | 6'2" | 260 | 22 | | |
| Bill Dugan | OG | 6'4" | 271 | 25 | | |
| Wes Hamilton | OG | 6'3" | 268 | 31 | | |
| Jim Hough | OG | 6'2" | 267 | 28 | | |
| Curtis Rouse | OG | 6'3" | 305 | 24 | | |
| Ron Sams | OG | 6'3" | 255 | 23 | | |
| Grant Feasel (from IND) | C | 6'7" | 278 | 24 | | |
| Hasson Arbubakrr | DE | 6'4" | 250 | 23 | | |
| Neil Elshire | DE | 6'6" | 260 | 26 | | |
| Randy Holloway (to STL) | DE | 6'5" | 255 | 29 | | |
| Doug Martin | DE-NT | 6'3" | 258 | 27 | | |
| Mark Mullaney | DE | 6'6" | 242 | 31 | | |
| Ruben Vaughn | DE | 6'2" | 260 | 28 | | |
| John Haines | NT | 6'6" | 260 | 22 | | |
| Charles Johnson | NT | 6'3" | 275 | 32 | | |
| Gregory Smith | NT | 6'3" | 261 | 24 | | |
| Paul Sverchek | NT | 6'3" | 252 | 23 | | |

| Use Name | Pos. | Hgt | Wgt | Age | Int | Pts |
|---|---|---|---|---|---|---|
| Walker Lee Ashley | LB | 6' | 240 | 24 | | |
| Matt Blair | LB | 6'5" | 235 | 33 | | |
| Dennis Fowlkes | LB | 6'2" | 235 | 23 | | |
| Dennis Johnson | LB | 6'3" | 235 | 26 | | |
| Chris Martin | LB | 6'2" | 230 | 23 | | 6 |
| Fred McNeill | LB | 6'2" | 230 | 32 | 1 | |
| Robin Sendlein | LB | 6'3" | 224 | 25 | | |
| Mark Stewart | LB | 6'3" | 232 | 24 | | |
| Scott Studwell | LB | 6'2" | 230 | 30 | 1 | |
| Rufus Bess | DB | 5'9" | 185 | 28 | 3 | |
| Joey Browner | DB | 6'2" | 205 | 24 | 1 | 6 |
| Jeff Colter | DB | 5'10" | 171 | 23 | | |
| Marcellus Greene | DB | 6' | 185 | 26 | | |
| Tom Hannon | DB | 5'11" | 193 | 29 | 1 | |
| Carl Lee | DB | 6' | 185 | 23 | 1 | |
| John Swain | DB | 6'1" | 195 | 24 | 2 | |
| Willie Teal | DB | 5'10" | 195 | 26 | 1 | 6 |
| Dan Wagoner (from DET) | DB | 5'10" | 180 | 24 | | |

Brent Boyd - Knee Injury
Bob Bruer - Knee Injury
Keith Nord - Achilles Tendon Injury

| Use Name | Pos. | Hgt | Wgt | Age | Int | Pts |
|---|---|---|---|---|---|---|
| Tommy Kramer | QB | 6'2" | 205 | 29 | | 6 |
| Archie Manning | QB | 6'3" | 211 | 35 | | |
| Wade Wilson | QB | 6'3" | 210 | 25 | | |
| Ted Brown | HB | 5'10" | 208 | 27 | | 36 |
| Darrin Nelson | HB | 5'9" | 185 | 25 | | 24 |
| Maurice Turner | HB-FB | 5'11" | 200 | 23 | | |
| Alfred Anderson | FB | 6'1" | 213 | 23 | | 18 |
| David Nelson | FB | 6'2" | 230 | 23 | | |
| Allen Rice | FB | 5'10" | 198 | 22 | | 12 |
| Dwight Collins | WR | 6'1" | 208 | 23 | | |
| Mike Jones | WR | 5'11" | 180 | 24 | | 6 |
| Terry LeCount | WR | 5'10" | 180 | 28 | | |
| Leo Lewis | WR | 5'8" | 170 | 27 | | 24 |
| Billy Waddy | WR | 5'11" | 190 | 30 | | |
| Sammy White | WR | 5'11" | 195 | 30 | | 6 |
| Don Hasselbeck | TE | 6'7" | 245 | 29 | | |
| Steve Jordan | TE | 6'4" | 230 | 23 | | 18 |
| Mike Mularkey | TE | 6'4" | 245 | 22 | | 12 |
| Joe Senser | TE | 6'4" | 238 | 28 | | |
| Greg Coleman | K | 6' | 178 | 29 | | |
| Jan Stenerud | K | 6'2" | 190 | 41 | | 90 |

## CHICAGO BEARS

### RUSHING

| Last Name | No. | Yds | Avg | TD |
|---|---|---|---|---|
| Payton | 381 | 1684 | 4.4 | 11 |
| Suhey | 124 | 424 | 3.4 | 4 |
| McMahon | 39 | 276 | 7.1 | 2 |
| C. Thomas | 40 | 186 | 4.4 | 1 |
| Lisch | 18 | 121 | 6.7 | 0 |
| Fuller | 15 | 89 | 5.9 | 1 |
| Gentry | 21 | 79 | 3.8 | 1 |
| Jordan | 11 | 70 | 6.4 | 0 |
| Hutchison | 14 | 39 | 2.8 | 1 |
| McKinnon | 2 | 12 | 6.0 | 0 |
| Landry | 2 | 1 | 0.5 | 1 |
| Baschnagel | 1 | 0 | 0.0 | 0 |
| Finzer | 2 | 0 | 0.0 | 0 |
| Moorehead | 1 | -2 | -2.0 | 0 |

### RECEIVING

| Last Name | No. | Yds | Avg | TD |
|---|---|---|---|---|
| Payton | 45 | 368 | 8.2 | 0 |
| Suhey | 42 | 312 | 7.4 | 2 |
| Gault | 34 | 587 | 17.3 | 6 |
| Moorehead | 29 | 497 | 17.1 | 1 |
| McKinnon | 29 | 431 | 14.9 | 3 |
| Dunsmore | 9 | 106 | 11.8 | 1 |
| Saldi | 9 | 90 | 10.0 | 0 |
| C. Thomas | 9 | 39 | 4.3 | 0 |
| Baschnagel | 6 | 53 | 8.8 | 0 |
| Gentry | 4 | 29 | 7.3 | 0 |
| Anderson | 3 | 77 | 25.7 | 1 |
| Krenk | 2 | 31 | 15.5 | 0 |
| McMahon | 1 | 42 | 42.0 | 0 |
| Cameron | 1 | 13 | 13.0 | 0 |
| Cabral | 1 | 7 | 7.0 | 0 |
| Hutchison | 1 | 7 | 7.0 | 0 |
| Jordan | 1 | 6 | 6.0 | 0 |

### PUNT RETURNS

| Last Name | No. | Yds | Avg | TD |
|---|---|---|---|---|
| Fisher | 57 | 492 | 8.6 | 0 |
| McKinnon | 5 | 62 | 12.4 | 0 |
| Duerson | 1 | 4 | 4.0 | 0 |

### KICKOFF RETURNS

| Last Name | No. | Yds | Avg | TD |
|---|---|---|---|---|
| Cameron | 26 | 485 | 18.7 | 0 |
| Gentry | 11 | 209 | 19.0 | 0 |
| Jordan | 5 | 62 | 12.4 | 0 |
| Duerson | 4 | 95 | 23.8 | 0 |
| Bell | 2 | 33 | 16.5 | 0 |
| Gault | 1 | 12 | 12.0 | 0 |

### PASSING — PUNTING — KICKING

| PASSING | Att | Cmp | % | Yds | Yd/Att | TD | Int | % | RK |
|---|---|---|---|---|---|---|---|---|---|
| McMahon | 143 | 85 | 59 | 1146 | 8.0 | 8 | 2- | 1 | 2 |
| Lisch | 85 | 43 | 51 | 413 | 4.9 | 0 | 6- | 7 | |
| Fuller | 78 | 53 | 68 | 595 | 7.6 | 3 | 0- | 0 | |
| Landry | 20 | 11 | 55 | 199 | 10.0 | 1 | 3- | 15 | |
| Payton | 8 | 3 | 38 | 47 | 5.9 | 2 | 1- | 13 | |
| Baschnagel | 2 | 1 | 50 | 7 | 3.5 | 0 | 0- | 0 | |
| Suhey | 1 | 0 | 0 | 0 | 0.0 | 0 | 0- | 0 | |

| PUNTING | No | Avg |
|---|---|---|
| Finzer | 83 | 40.1 |

| KICKING | XP | Att | % | FG | Att | % |
|---|---|---|---|---|---|---|
| B. Thomas | 35 | 37 | 95 | 22 | 28 | 79 |

## GREEN BAY PACKERS

### RUSHING

| Last Name | No. | Yds | Avg | TD |
|---|---|---|---|---|
| Ellis | 123 | 581 | 4.7 | 4 |
| Ivery | 99 | 552 | 5.6 | 6 |
| Clark | 87 | 375 | 4.3 | 4 |
| Crouse | 53 | 169 | 3.2 | 0 |
| Huckleby | 35 | 145 | 4.1 | 0 |
| Rodgers | 25 | 94 | 3.8 | 0 |
| Lofton | 10 | 82 | 8.2 | 0 |
| Wright | 8 | 11 | 1.4 | 0 |
| Dickey | 18 | 6 | 0.3 | 3 |
| Campbell | 2 | 2 | 1.0 | 0 |
| West | 1 | 2 | 2.0 | 1 |

### RECEIVING

| Last Name | No. | Yds | Avg | TD |
|---|---|---|---|---|
| Lofton | 62 | 1361 | 22.0 | 7 |
| Coffman | 43 | 562 | 13.1 | 9 |
| Ellis | 36 | 312 | 8.7 | 2 |
| Clark | 29 | 234 | 8.1 | 2 |
| Epps | 26 | 435 | 16.7 | 3 |
| Jefferson | 26 | 339 | 13.0 | 0 |
| Ivery | 19 | 141 | 7.4 | 1 |
| Crouse | 9 | 93 | 10.3 | 1 |
| Huckleby | 8 | 65 | 8.1 | 0 |
| West | 6 | 54 | 9.0 | 4 |
| Rodgers | 5 | 56 | 11.2 | 0 |
| Childs | 4 | 32 | 8.0 | 0 |
| G. Lewis | 4 | 29 | 7.3 | 0 |
| Cassidy | 2 | 16 | 8.0 | 0 |
| Moore | 1 | 3 | 3.0 | 1 |
| Taylor | 1 | 8 | 8.0 | 0 |

### PUNT RETURNS

| Last Name | No. | Yds | Avg | TD |
|---|---|---|---|---|
| Epps | 29 | 199 | 6.9 | 0 |
| Flynn | 15 | 128 | 8.5 | 0 |
| Hayes | 4 | 24 | 6.0 | 0 |
| Murphy | 0 | 0 | — | 0 |

### KICKOFF RETURNS

| Last Name | No. | Yds | Avg | TD |
|---|---|---|---|---|
| Rodgers | 39 | 843 | 21.6 | 1 |
| Epps | 12 | 232 | 19.3 | 0 |
| Huckleby | 14 | 261 | 18.6 | 0 |
| D. Jones | 1 | 19 | 19.0 | 0 |
| Prather | 1 | 7 | 7.0 | 0 |

### PASSING — PUNTING — KICKING

| PASSING | Att | Cmp | % | Yds | Yd/Att | TD | Int | % | RK |
|---|---|---|---|---|---|---|---|---|---|
| Dickey | 401 | 237 | 59 | 3195 | 8.0 | 25 | 19- | 5 | 6 |
| Wright | 62 | 27 | 44 | 310 | 5.0 | 2 | 6- | 10 | |
| Campbell | 38 | 16 | 42 | 228 | 5.7 | 3 | 5- | 13 | |
| Ellis | 4 | 1 | 25 | 17 | 4.3 | 0 | 0- | 0 | |

| PUNTING | No | Avg |
|---|---|---|
| Scribner | 85 | 42.3 |

| KICKING | XP | Att | % | FG | Att | % |
|---|---|---|---|---|---|---|
| Del Greco | 34 | 34 | 100 | 9 | 12 | 75 |
| Garcia | 14 | 15 | 93 | 3 | 9 | 33 |

## TAMPA BAY BUCCANEERS

### RUSHING

| Last Name | No. | Yds | Avg | TD |
|---|---|---|---|---|
| Wilder | 407 | 1544 | 3.8 | 13 |
| DeBerg | 28 | 59 | 2.1 | 2 |
| Carver | 11 | 44 | 4.0 | 0 |
| J. Thompson | 5 | 35 | 7.0 | 0 |
| Armstrong | 10 | 34 | 3.4 | 2 |
| Morton | 16 | 27 | 1.7 | 0 |
| Carter | 1 | 16 | 16.0 | 0 |
| Dierking | 3 | 14 | 4.7 | 0 |
| Peoples | 1 | 2 | 2.0 | 0 |
| Owens | 1 | 1 | 1.0 | 0 |

### RECEIVING

| Last Name | No. | Yds | Avg | TD |
|---|---|---|---|---|
| Wilder | 85 | 685 | 8.1 | 0 |
| House | 76 | 1005 | 13.2 | 5 |
| Carter | 60 | 816 | 13.6 | 5 |
| J. Bell | 29 | 397 | 13.7 | 4 |
| Giles | 24 | 310 | 12.9 | 2 |
| T. Bell | 22 | 350 | 15.9 | 0 |
| Armstrong | 22 | 180 | 8.2 | 3 |
| Dixon | 5 | 69 | 13.8 | 0 |
| Carroll | 5 | 50 | 10.0 | 1 |
| Carver | 3 | 27 | 9.0 | 0 |
| Owens | 2 | 13 | 6.5 | 1 |
| Dierking | 1 | 5 | 5.0 | 0 |

### PUNT RETURNS

| Last Name | No. | Yds | Avg | TD |
|---|---|---|---|---|
| Bright | 23 | 173 | 7.5 | 0 |
| Holt | 7 | 19 | 2.7 | 0 |
| T. Bell | 3 | 8 | 2.7 | 0 |

### KICKOFF RETURNS

| Last Name | No. | Yds | Avg | TD |
|---|---|---|---|---|
| Morton | 38 | 835 | 22.0 | 0 |
| Owens | 8 | 168 | 21.0 | 0 |
| Bright | 16 | 300 | 18.8 | 0 |
| Wood | 5 | 43 | 8.6 | 0 |
| Spradlin | 1 | 5 | 5.0 | 0 |

### PASSING — PUNTING — KICKING

| PASSING | Att | Cmp | % | Yds | Yd/Att | TD | Int | % | RK |
|---|---|---|---|---|---|---|---|---|---|
| DeBerg | 509 | 308 | 61 | 3554 | 7.0 | 19 | 18- | 4 | 8 |
| Thompson | 52 | 25 | 48 | 337 | 6.5 | 2 | 5- | 10 | |
| Wilder | 1 | 1 | 100 | 16 | 16.0 | 1 | 0- | 0 | |
| Garcia | 1 | 0 | 0 | 0 | 0.0 | 0 | 0- | 0 | |

| PUNTING | No | Avg |
|---|---|---|
| Garcia | 68 | 41.9 |

| KICKING | XP | Att | % | FG | Att | % |
|---|---|---|---|---|---|---|
| Ariri | 38 | 40 | 95 | 19 | 26 | 73 |

## DETROIT LIONS

### RUSHING

| Last Name | No. | Yds | Avg | TD |
|---|---|---|---|---|
| Sims | 130 | 687 | 5.3 | 5 |
| J. Jones | 137 | 532 | 3.9 | 3 |
| Jenkins | 78 | 358 | 4.6 | 1 |
| Danielson | 41 | 218 | 5.3 | 3 |
| Bussey | 32 | 91 | 2.8 | 0 |
| D'Addio | 7 | 46 | 6.6 | 0 |
| Witkowski | 7 | 33 | 4.7 | 0 |
| Nichols | 3 | 27 | 9.0 | 0 |
| Martin | 1 | 14 | 14.0 | 0 |
| Chadwick | 1 | 12 | 12.0 | 1 |
| Machurek | 1 | 9 | 9.0 | 0 |
| Hipple | 2 | 3 | 1.5 | 0 |
| Black | 3 | -6 | -2.0 | 0 |
| Thompson | 3 | -7 | -2.3 | 0 |

### RECEIVING

| Last Name | No. | Yds | Avg | TD |
|---|---|---|---|---|
| J. Jones | 77 | 662 | 8.6 | 5 |
| L. Thompson | 50 | 773 | 15.5 | 6 |
| Chadwick | 37 | 540 | 14.6 | 2 |
| Nichols | 34 | 744 | 21.9 | 1 |
| Sims | 31 | 239 | 7.7 | 0 |
| Jenkins | 21 | 246 | 11.7 | 0 |
| Lewis | 16 | 236 | 14.8 | 3 |
| Rubick | 14 | 188 | 13.4 | 1 |
| Bussey | 9 | 63 | 7.0 | 0 |
| Mandley | 3 | 38 | 12.7 | 0 |
| McCall | 3 | 15 | 5.0 | 0 |
| Danielson | 1 | 22 | 22.0 | 1 |
| D'Addio | 1 | 12 | 12.0 | 0 |
| Martin | 1 | 9 | 9.0 | 0 |

### PUNT RETURNS

| Last Name | No. | Yds | Avg | TD |
|---|---|---|---|---|
| Martin | 25 | 210 | 8.4 | 0 |
| Hall | 7 | 30 | 4.3 | 0 |
| Jenkins | 1 | 1 | 1.0 | 0 |
| Mandley | 2 | 0 | 0.0 | 0 |
| Johnson | 1 | 0 | 0.0 | 0 |

### KICKOFF RETURNS

| Last Name | No. | Yds | Avg | TD |
|---|---|---|---|---|
| Jenkins | 18 | 396 | 22.0 | 0 |
| Hall | 19 | 385 | 20.3 | 0 |
| Mandley | 22 | 390 | 17.7 | 0 |
| Martin | 10 | 144 | 14.4 | 0 |
| Meade | 4 | 32 | 8.0 | 0 |
| D'Addio | 1 | 0 | 0.0 | 0 |

### PASSING — PUNTING — KICKING

| PASSING | Att | Cmp | % | Yds | Yd/Att | TD | Int | % | RK |
|---|---|---|---|---|---|---|---|---|---|
| Danielson | 410 | 252 | 62 | 3076 | 7.5 | 17 | 15- | 4 | 7 |
| Hipple | 38 | 16 | 42 | 246 | 6.5 | 1 | 1- | 3 | |
| Witkowski | 34 | 13 | 38 | 210 | 6.2 | 0 | 0- | 0 | |
| Machurek | 43 | 14 | 33 | 193 | 4.5 | 0 | 0- | 0 | |

| PUNTING | No | Avg |
|---|---|---|
| Black | 76 | 41.6 |

| KICKING | XP | Att | % | FG | Att | % |
|---|---|---|---|---|---|---|
| Murray | 31 | 31 | 100 | 20 | 27 | 74 |

## MINNESOTA VIKINGS

### RUSHING

| Last Name | No. | Yds | Avg | TD |
|---|---|---|---|---|
| Anderson | 201 | 773 | 3.8 | 2 |
| Brown | 98 | 442 | 4.5 | 3 |
| Dar. Nelson | 80 | 406 | 5.1 | 3 |
| Rice | 14 | 58 | 4.1 | 1 |
| Jones | 4 | 45 | 11.3 | 0 |
| Manning | 11 | 42 | 3.8 | 0 |
| Wilson | 9 | 30 | 3.3 | 0 |
| Waddy | 3 | 24 | 8.0 | 0 |
| Coleman | 2 | 11 | 5.5 | 0 |
| Lewis | 2 | 11 | 5.5 | 0 |
| Kramer | 15 | 9 | 0.6 | 0 |
| Jordan | 1 | 4 | 4.0 | 1 |
| Dav. Nelson | 1 | 3 | 3.0 | 0 |
| Collins | 3 | -14 | -4.7 | 0 |

### RECEIVING

| Last Name | No. | Yds | Avg | TD |
|---|---|---|---|---|
| Lewis | 47 | 830 | 17.7 | 4 |
| Brown | 46 | 349 | 7.6 | 3 |
| Jones | 38 | 591 | 15.6 | 1 |
| Jordan | 38 | 414 | 10.9 | 2 |
| Dar. Nelson | 27 | 162 | 6.0 | 1 |
| White | 21 | 399 | 19.0 | 1 |
| Anderson | 17 | 102 | 6.0 | 1 |
| Senser | 15 | 110 | 7.3 | 0 |
| Mularkey | 14 | 134 | 9.6 | 2 |
| Collins | 11 | 143 | 13.0 | 1 |
| Rice | 4 | 59 | 14.8 | 1 |
| Kramer | 1 | 20 | 20.0 | 1 |
| Hasselbeck | 1 | 10 | 10.0 | 0 |
| LeCount | 1 | 14 | 14.0 | 0 |

### PUNT RETURNS

| Last Name | No. | Yds | Avg | TD |
|---|---|---|---|---|
| Dar. Nelson | 23 | 180 | 7.8 | 0 |
| Lewis | 4 | 31 | 7.8 | 0 |
| Bess | 2 | 9 | 4.5 | 0 |
| Teal | 1 | 0 | 0.0 | 0 |
| Waddy | 1 | -3 | -3.0 | 0 |

### KICKOFF RETURNS

| Last Name | No. | Yds | Avg | TD |
|---|---|---|---|---|
| Dar. Nelson | 39 | 891 | 22.8 | 0 |
| Anderson | 30 | 639 | 21.3 | 0 |
| Waddy | 3 | 64 | 21.3 | 0 |
| Lewis | 1 | 31 | 31.0 | 0 |
| Bess | 3 | 47 | 15.7 | 0 |
| Smith | 2 | 26 | 13.0 | 0 |
| Rice | 3 | 34 | 11.3 | 0 |
| Rouse | 2 | 22 | 11.0 | 0 |
| Turner | 2 | 21 | 10.5 | 0 |
| Dav. Nelson | 1 | 0 | 0.0 | 0 |

### PASSING — PUNTING — KICKING

| PASSING | Att | Cmp | % | Yds | Yd/Att | TD | Int | % | RK |
|---|---|---|---|---|---|---|---|---|---|
| Kramer | 236 | 124 | 53 | 1678 | 7.1 | 9 | 10- | 4 | 13 |
| Wilson | 195 | 102 | 52 | 1019 | 5.2 | 5 | 11- | 6 | 17 |
| Manning | 94 | 52 | 55 | 545 | 5.8 | 2 | 3- | 3 | |
| Anderson | 7 | 3 | 43 | 95 | 13.6 | 2 | 1- | 14 | |
| Coleman | 1 | 0 | 0 | 0 | 0.0 | 0 | 0- | 0 | |

| PUNTING | No | Avg |
|---|---|---|
| Coleman | 82 | 42.4 |

| KICKING | XP | Att | % | FG | Att | % |
|---|---|---|---|---|---|---|
| Stenerud | 30 | 31 | 97 | 20 | 23 | 87 |

**SAN FRANCISCO 49ERS** 15-1-0 Bill Walsh

| Scores of Each Game | | |
|---|---|---|
| 30 | Detroit | 27 |
| 37 | WASHINGTON | 31 |
| 30 | NEW ORLEANS | 20 |
| 21 | Philadelphia | 9 |
| 14 | ATLANTA | 5 |
| 31 | N.Y.Giants | 10 |
| 17 | PITTSBURGH | 20 |
| 34 | Houston | 21 |
| 33 | L.A.Rams | 0 |
| 23 | CINCINNATI | 17 |
| 41 | Cleveland | 7 |
| 24 | TAMPA BAY | 17 |
| 35 | New Orleans | 3 |
| 35 | Atlanta | 17 |
| 51 | MINNESOTA | 7 |
| 19 | L.A.RAMS | 16 |

| Use Name | Pos. | Hgt | Wgt | Age | Int | Pts |
|---|---|---|---|---|---|---|
| Keith Fahnhorst | OT | 6'6" | 273 | 32 | | |
| Allan Kennedy | OT | 6'7" | 275 | 26 | | |
| Bubba Paris | OT | 6'6" | 295 | 23 | | |
| Billy Shields | OT | 6'7" | 279 | 31 | | |
| John Ayers | OG | 6'5" | 265 | 31 | | |
| Randy Cross | OG | 6'3" | 265 | 30 | | |
| Guy McIntyre | OG | 6'3" | 271 | 23 | | |
| Jesse Sapolu | OG | 6'4" | 260 | 23 | | |
| John Macauley | C | 6'3" | 254 | 25 | | |
| Fred Quillan | C | 6'5" | 266 | 28 | | |
| Dwaine Board | DE | 6'5" | 250 | 27 | | |
| Fred Dean | DE | 6'3" | 232 | 32 | | |
| Jeff Stover | DE | 6'5" | 275 | 26 | | |
| Jim Stuckey | DE | 6'4" | 251 | 26 | | |
| Michael Carter | NT | 6'2" | 281 | 23 | | |
| Gary Johnson (from SD) | NT | 6'2" | 261 | 32 | | 8 |
| Louis Kelcher | NT | 6'5" | 310 | 31 | | |
| Lawrence Pillers | NT-DE | 6'3" | 250 | 31 | | |
| Manu Tuiasosopo | NT | 6'3" | 252 | 27 | | |

Allen Fleming - Knee Injury
John Harty - Foot Injury

| Use Name | Pos. | Hgt | Wgt | Age | Int | Pts |
|---|---|---|---|---|---|---|
| Dan Bunz | LB | 6'4" | 225 | 28 | 1 | |
| Riki Ellison | LB | 6'2" | 220 | 24 | | |
| Jim Fahnhorst | LB | 6'4" | 230 | 25 | 2 | |
| Ron Ferrari | LB | 6' | 212 | 25 | | |
| Milt McColl | LB | 6'6" | 230 | 25 | | |
| Blanchard Montgomery | LB | 6'2" | 236 | 23 | | |
| Jack Reynolds | LB | 6'1" | 232 | 36 | | |
| Todd Shell | LB | 6'4" | 225 | 22 | 3. | 6 |
| Keena Turner | LB | 6'2" | 219 | 25 | 4 | |
| Michael Walter | LB | 6'3" | 238 | 23 | | |
| Mario Clark | DB | 6'2" | 195 | 30 | 1 | |
| Jeff Fuller | DB | 6'2" | 216 | 22 | 1 | |
| Dwight Hicks | DB | 6'1" | 189 | 28 | 3 | |
| Tom Holmoe | DB | 6'2" | 180 | 24 | | |
| Ronnie Lott | DB | 6' | 199 | 25 | 4 | |
| Dana McLemore | DB | 5'10" | 183 | 24 | 2 | 12 |
| Carlton Williamson | DB | 6' | 204 | 26 | 2 | |
| Eric Wright | DB | 6'1" | 180 | 25 | 2 | |

Tim Collier - Achilles Tendon Injury
Mark Bonner - Neck Injury
Danny Fulton - Shoulder Injury
Don Dow - Neck Injury

| Use Name | Pos. | Hgt | Wgt | Age | Int | Pts |
|---|---|---|---|---|---|---|
| Matt Cavanaugh | QB | 6'2" | 212 | 27 | | |
| Joe Montana | QB | 6'2" | 195 | 28 | | 12 |
| Derrick Harmon | HB | 5'10" | 202 | 21 | | 6 |
| Carl Monroe | HB | 5'8" | 166 | 24 | | 6 |
| Wendell Tyler | HB | 5'10" | 200 | 29 | | 54 |
| Roger Craig | FB | 6' | 222 | 24 | | 60 |
| Bill Ring | FB | 5'10" | 205 | 27 | | 18 |
| Dwight Clark | WR | 6'4" | 215 | 27 | | 36 |
| Renaldo Nehemiah | WR | 6'1" | 183 | 25 | | 12 |
| Freddie Solomon | WR | 5'11" | 185 | 31 | | 66 |
| Mike Wilson | WR | 6'3" | 210 | 25 | | 6 |
| Earl Cooper | TE | 6'2" | 227 | 25 | | 24 |
| Al Dixon | TE | 6'5" | 235 | 30 | | |
| Russ Francis | TE | 6'6" | 242 | 31 | | 12 |
| John Frank | TE | 6'3" | 225 | 22 | | 6 |
| Tom Orosz | K | 6'1" | 204 | 24 | | |
| Max Runager | K | 6'1" | 189 | 28 | | |
| Ray Wersching | K | 5'11" | 210 | 34 | | 131 |

**LOS ANGELES RAMS** 10-6-0 John Robinson

| Scores of Each Game | | |
|---|---|---|
| 13 | DALLAS | 20 |
| 20 | CLEVELAND | 17 |
| 14 | Pittsburgh | 24 |
| 24 | Cincinnati | 14 |
| 33 | N.Y.GIANTS | 12 |
| 28 | ATLANTA | 30 |
| 28 | New Orleans | 10 |
| 24 | Atlanta | 10 |
| 0 | SAN FRANCISCO | 33 |
| 16 | St.Louis | 13 |
| 29 | CHICAGO | 13 |
| 6 | Green Bay | 31 |
| 34 | Tampa Bay | 33 |
| 34 | NEW ORLEANS | 21 |
| 27 | HOUSTON | 16 |
| 16 | San Francisco | 19 |

| Use Name | Pos. | Hgt | Wgt | Age | Int | Pts |
|---|---|---|---|---|---|---|
| Bill Bain | OT | 6'4" | 290 | 32 | | |
| Irv Pankey | OT | 6'4" | 267 | 25 | | |
| Jackie Slater | OT | 6'4" | 271 | 30 | | |
| Russ Bolinger | OG | 6'5" | 255 | 29 | | |
| Dennis Harrah | OG | 6'5" | 265 | 31 | | |
| Kent Hill | OG | 6'5" | 260 | 27 | | |
| Joe Shearin | OG | 6'4" | 250 | 24 | | |
| Doug Smith | C | 6'3" | 253 | 27 | | |
| Reggie Doss | DE | 6'4" | 263 | 27 | | |
| Gary Jeter | DE | 6'4" | 260 | 29 | | |
| Doug Reed | DE | 6'3" | 250 | 24 | | |
| Booker Reese (from TB) | DE | 6'6" | 260 | 24 | | |
| Jack Youngblood | DE | 6'4" | 242 | 34 | | |
| Charles DeJurnett | NT | 6'4" | 260 | 32 | | |
| Greg Meisner | NT | 6'3" | 253 | 25 | | |
| Shawn Miller | NT | 6'4" | 255 | 23 | | |

Kirk Collins - Died of cancer
Doug Barnett - Knee Injury
Gary Kowalski - Knee Injury

| Use Name | Pos. | Hgt | Wgt | Age | Int | Pts |
|---|---|---|---|---|---|---|
| George Andrews | LB | 6'3" | 225 | 28 | | |
| Ed Brady | LB | 6'2" | 228 | 24 | | |
| Jim Collins | LB | 6'2" | 230 | 26 | 2 | |
| Carl Ekern | LB | 6'3" | 222 | 30 | | |
| Mark Jerue | LB | 6'3" | 229 | 24 | | |
| John Kamana | LB | 6' | 215 | 22 | | |
| Jim Laughlin | LB | 6' | 222 | 26 | | |
| Mike McDonald | LB | 6'1" | 235 | 26 | | |
| Mel Owens | LB | 6'2" | 224 | 25 | 1 | |
| Norwood Vann | LB | 6'1" | 225 | 22 | | 2 |
| Mike Wilcher | LB | 6'3" | 235 | 24 | | |
| Jim Youngblood | LB | 6'3" | 231 | 34 | | |
| Nolan Cromwell | DB | 6'1" | 200 | 29 | 3 | 6 |
| David Croudip | DB | 5'8" | 183 | 25 | | |
| Gary Green | DB | 5'11" | 191 | 28 | 3 | |
| Eric Harris | DB | 6'3" | 202 | 29 | | |
| LeRoy Irvin | DB | 5'11" | 184 | 26 | 5 | 12 |
| Johnnie Johnson | DB | 6'1" | 183 | 27 | 2 | |
| Vince Newsome | DB | 6'1" | 179 | 23 | 1 | |
| Ivory Sully | DB | 6' | 201 | 27 | | 2 |

| Use Name | Pos. | Hgt | Wgt | Age | Int | Pts |
|---|---|---|---|---|---|---|
| Steve Dils (from MIN) | QB | 6'1" | 191 | 28 | | |
| Vince Ferragamo | QB | 6'3" | 212 | 30 | | |
| Jeff Kemp | QB | 6' | 201 | 25 | | 6 |
| Eric Dickerson | HB | 6'3" | 220 | 23 | | 84 |
| A.J.Jones | HB | 6'1" | 202 | 25 | | |
| Mike Pleasant | HB | 6'1" | 195 | 26 | | |
| Barry Redden | HB-FB | 5'10" | 205 | 24 | | |
| Dwayne Crutchfield | FB | 6' | 235 | 24 | | 12 |
| Mike Guman | FB | 6'2" | 218 | 26 | | 6 |
| Ron Brown | WR | 5'11" | 181 | 23 | | 24 |
| Drew Hill | WR | 5'9" | 170 | 27 | | 24 |
| Henry Ellard | WR | 5'11" | 170 | 23 | | 48 |
| George Farmer | WR | 5'10" | 175 | 25 | | |
| Otis Grant | WR | 6'3" | 197 | 23 | | |
| Mike Barber | TE | 6'3" | 237 | 31 | | |
| Chris Faulkner | TE | 6'4" | 257 | 24 | | |
| David Hill | TE | 6'2" | 228 | 30 | | 6 |
| James McDonald | TE | 6'5" | 230 | 23 | | |
| Mike Lansford | K | 6' | 183 | 26 | | 112 |
| John Misko | K | 6'5" | 207 | 29 | | |

**NEW ORLEANS SAINTS** 7-9-0 Bum Phillips

| Scores of Each Game | | |
|---|---|---|
| 28 | ATLANTA | 36 |
| 17 | TAMPA BAY | 13 |
| 20 | San Francisco | 30 |
| 34 | ST.LOUIS | 24 |
| 27 | Houston | 10 |
| 7 | Chicago | 20 |
| 10 | L.A.RAMS | 28 |
| 27 | Dallas | *30 |
| 16 | Cleveland | 14 |
| 13 | GREEN BAY | 23 |
| 17 | Atlanta | 13 |
| 27 | PITTSBURGH | 24 |
| 3 | SAN FRANCISCO | 35 |
| 21 | L.A.Rams | 34 |
| 21 | CINCINNATI | 24 |
| 10 | N.Y.Giants | 3 |

| Use Name | Pos. | Hgt | Wgt | Age | Int | Pts |
|---|---|---|---|---|---|---|
| Stan Brock | OT | 6'6" | 285 | 26 | | |
| Angelo Fields | OT | 6'6" | 314 | 26 | | |
| Dave Lafary | OT | 6'7" | 285 | 29 | | |
| Chris Ward | OT | 6'3" | 267 | 28 | | |
| Kelvin Clark | OG | 6'3" | 273 | 28 | | |
| Brad Edelman | OG | 6'6" | 262 | 23 | | |
| Steve Korte | OG | 6'2" | 270 | 24 | | |
| Louis Oubre | OG | 6'4" | 272 | 26 | | |
| David Carter (from HOU) | OG-C | 6'2" | 275 | 30 | | |
| Joel Hilgenberg | C | 6'3" | 250 | 22 | | |
| John Hill | C | 6'2" | 260 | 34 | | |
| Jim Pietrzak | C | 6'5" | 260 | 31 | | |
| Bruce Clark | DE | 6'3" | 281 | 26 | 1 | |
| Reggie Lewis | DE | 6'2" | 248 | 30 | | |
| Frank Warren | DE | 6'4" | 275 | 24 | | |
| Jim Wilks | DE | 6'5" | 265 | 26 | | |
| Tony Elliott | NT | 6'2" | 280 | 25 | | |
| James Geathers | NT | 6'7" | 267 | 24 | | |
| Derland Moore | NT | 6'4" | 273 | 32 | | |
| Don Thorpe | NT | 6'4" | 260 | 22 | | |

| Use Name | Pos. | Hgt | Wgt | Age | Int | Pts |
|---|---|---|---|---|---|---|
| James Haynes | LB | 6'2" | 230 | 24 | | |
| Rickey Jackson | LB | 6'2" | 239 | 26 | 1 | |
| Jim Kovach | LB | 6'2" | 239 | 28 | 1 | |
| Whitney Paul | LB | 6'3" | 220 | 28 | | |
| Scott Pelluer | LB | 6'2" | 227 | 25 | | |
| Glen Redd | LB | 6'1" | 231 | 26 | | |
| Dennis Winston | LB | 6'1" | 244 | 28 | 2 | 12 |
| Jitter Fields | DB | 5'8" | 188 | 22 | | |
| Russell Gary | DB | 5'11" | 195 | 25 | | |
| Greg Harding | DB | 6'2" | 197 | 24 | | |
| Terry Hoage | DB | 6'3" | 197 | 22 | | |
| Bobby Johnson | DB | 6' | 187 | 24 | 1 | |
| Rodney Lewis | DB | 5'11" | 186 | 25 | | |
| Johnnie Poe | DB | 6'1" | 194 | 25 | 1 | |
| Frank Wattelet | DB | 6' | 185 | 25 | 2 | 12 |
| Dave Waymer | DB | 6'1" | 188 | 26 | 4 | |

Michael Dellocono - Back Injury
Gary Lewis - Non-Football Illness

| Use Name | Pos. | Hgt | Wgt | Age | Int | Pts |
|---|---|---|---|---|---|---|
| Ken Stabler | QB | 6'3" | 210 | 38 | | |
| Richard Todd | QB | 6'2" | 212 | 30 | | |
| Dave Wilson | QB | 6'3" | 210 | 25 | | |
| Tyrone Anthony | HB | 5'11" | 212 | 22 | | 6 |
| George Rogers | HB | 6'2" | 229 | 25 | | 12 |
| Jimmy Rogers | HB | 5'10" | 195 | 29 | | |
| Earl Campbell (from HOU) | FB | 5'11" | 233 | 29 | | 6 |
| Hokie Gajan | FB | 5'11" | 226 | 24 | | 42 |
| Tim Wilson | FB | 6'3" | 235 | 30 | | |
| Wayne Wilson | FB | 6'3" | 220 | 26 | | 24 |
| Kenny Duckett | WR | 6' | 179 | 24 | | |
| Eugene Goodlow | WR | 6'2" | 181 | 25 | | 18 |
| Jeff Groth | WR | 5'10" | 181 | 27 | | |
| Guido Merkens | WR-QB | 6'1" | 197 | 29 | | |
| Lindsay Scott | WR | 6'1" | 200 | 23 | | 6 |
| Tyrone Young | WR | 6'6" | 190 | 24 | | 18 |
| Hoby Brenner | TE | 6'4" | 245 | 25 | | 36 |
| Larry Hardy | TE | 6'3" | 245 | 28 | | 6 |
| Junior Miller | TE | 6'4" | 244 | 26 | | 6 |
| John Tice | TE | 6'5" | 242 | 24 | | 6 |
| Morten Andersen | K | 6'2" | 205 | 24 | | 94 |
| Brian Hansen | K | 6'3" | 218 | 23 | | |

**ATLANTA FALCONS** 4-12-0 Dan Henning

| Scores of Each Game | | |
|---|---|---|
| 36 | New Orleans | 28 |
| 24 | DETROIT | *27 |
| 20 | Minnesota | 27 |
| 42 | HOUSTON | 10 |
| 5 | San Francisco | 14 |
| 30 | L.A.Rams | 28 |
| 7 | N.Y.GIANTS | 19 |
| 10 | L.A.RAMS | 24 |
| 10 | Pittsburgh | 35 |
| 14 | Washington | 27 |
| 13 | NEW ORLEANS | 17 |
| 7 | CLEVELAND | 23 |
| 14 | Cincinnati | 35 |
| 17 | SAN FRANCISCO | 35 |
| 6 | Tampa Bay | 23 |
| 26 | PHILADELPHIA | 10 |

| Use Name | Pos. | Hgt | Wgt | Age | Int | Pts |
|---|---|---|---|---|---|---|
| Mike Kenn | OT | 6'7" | 266 | 28 | | |
| Brett Miller | OT | 6'7" | 285 | 25 | | |
| Eric Sanders | OT | 6'7" | 280 | 25 | | |
| Dan Dufour | OG | 6'5" | 280 | 23 | | |
| Joe Pellegrini | OG-C | 6'4" | 258 | 27 | | |
| R.C.Thielemann | OG | 6'4" | 262 | 29 | | |
| Mike Chapman | C-OG | 6'4" | 250 | 23 | | |
| John Scully | C | 6'6" | 255 | 26 | | |
| Jeff Van Note | C | 6'2" | 250 | 38 | | |
| Gary Burley | DE | 6'3" | 290 | 31 | | |
| Roy Harris | DE | 6'2" | 266 | 23 | | |
| Mike Pitts | DE | 6'5" | 268 | 23 | | |
| Jeff Yeates | DE | 6'3" | 257 | 33 | | |
| Dan Benish | DT | 6'5" | 265 | 22 | | |
| Rick Bryan | DT | 6'4" | 260 | 22 | | 2 |
| Andrew Provence | DT | 6'3" | 260 | 23 | | |
| Don Smith | DT | 6'5" | 270 | 27 | | |

William Andrews - Knee Injury
Stan Gay - Knee Injury

| Use Name | Pos. | Hgt | Wgt | Age | Int | Pts |
|---|---|---|---|---|---|---|
| Thomas Benson | LB | 6'2" | 235 | 22 | | |
| Buddy Curry | LB | 6'4" | 228 | 26 | | |
| David Frye | LB | 6'2" | 213 | 23 | | |
| Jeff Jackson | LB | 6'1" | 228 | 22 | 1 | 6 |
| Fulton Kuykendall | LB | 6'5" | 225 | 31 | | |
| Dave Levenick | LB | 6'3" | 220 | 25 | | |
| Rydell Malancon | LB | 6'2" | 219 | 22 | | |
| John Rade | LB | 6'1" | 225 | 24 | | |
| Al Richardson | LB | 6'2" | 222 | 26 | | |
| Johnny Taylor | LB | 6'4" | 239 | 24 | | |
| James Britt | DB | 6' | 185 | 23 | 1 | |
| Bobby Butler | DB | 5'11" | 175 | 25 | 2 | |
| Scott Case | DB | 6' | 178 | 22 | | 2 |
| Blane Gaison | DB | 6' | 185 | 26 | | |
| Steve Haworth | DB | 5'11" | 190 | 22 | | |
| Kenny Johnson | DB | 5'10" | 172 | 26 | 5 | |
| Tom Pridemore | DB | 5'10" | 186 | 28 | 2 | |
| Gerald Small | DB | 5'11" | 192 | 28 | 1 | |

| Use Name | Pos. | Hgt | Wgt | Age | Int | Pts |
|---|---|---|---|---|---|---|
| David Archer | QB | 6'2" | 206 | 22 | | |
| Steve Bartkowski | QB | 6'4" | 218 | 31 | | |
| Mike Moroski | QB | 6'4" | 200 | 26 | | |
| Cliff Austin | HB | 6' | 190 | 24 | | |
| Lynn Cain | HB | 6'1" | 205 | 28 | | 18 |
| Sylvester Stamps | HB | 5'7" | 166 | 23 | | |
| Rodney Tate | HB | 5'11" | 190 | 25 | | |
| Tim Tyrrell | HB-FB | 6'1" | 201 | 23 | | |
| Allama Matthews | FB | 6'2" | 230 | 23 | | |
| Gerald Riggs | FB | 6'1" | 230 | 23 | | 78 |
| Stacey Bailey | WR | 6' | 157 | 24 | | 36 |
| Willie Curran | WR | 5'10" | 175 | 24 | | |
| Floyd Hodge | WR | 6' | 195 | 25 | | |
| Alfred Jackson | WR | 5'11" | 190 | 29 | | 12 |
| Billy Johnson | WR | 5'9" | 177 | 32 | | 18 |
| Perry Tuttle (from TB) | WR | 6' | 178 | 25 | | |
| Cliff Benson | TE | 6'4" | 234 | 23 | | |
| Arthur Cox | TE | 6'2" | 255 | 23 | | 18 |
| Mike Landrum | TE | 6'2" | 231 | 22 | | |
| Ralph Giacomarro | K | 6'1" | 192 | 23 | | |
| Mick Luckhurst | K | 6' | 183 | 26 | | 91 |

* Overtime

## SAN FRANCISCO 49ERS

### RUSHING

| Last Name | No. | Yds | Avg | TD |
|---|---|---|---|---|
| Tyler | 246 | 1262 | 5.1 | 7 |
| Craig | 155 | 649 | 4.2 | 7 |
| D. Harmon | 39 | 192 | 4.9 | 1 |
| Ring | 38 | 162 | 4.3 | 3 |
| Montana | 39 | 118 | 3.0 | 2 |
| Solomon | 6 | 72 | 12.0 | 1 |
| Monroe | 3 | 13 | 4.3 | 0 |
| Cooper | 3 | 13 | 4.3 | 0 |
| Runager | 1 | -5 | -5.0 | 0 |
| Cavanaugh | 4 | -11 | -2.8 | 0 |

### RECEIVING

| Last Name | No. | Yds | Avg | TD |
|---|---|---|---|---|
| Craig | 71 | 675 | 9.5 | 3 |
| D. Clark | 52 | 880 | 16.9 | 6 |
| Cooper | 41 | 459 | 11.2 | 4 |
| Solomon | 40 | 737 | 18.4 | 10 |
| Tyler | 28 | 230 | 8.2 | 2 |
| Francis | 23 | 285 | 12.4 | 2 |
| Nehemiah | 18 | 357 | 19.8 | 2 |
| Wilson | 17 | 245 | 14.4 | 1 |
| Monroe | 11 | 139 | 12.6 | 1 |
| Frank | 7 | 60 | 8.6 | 1 |
| Ring | 3 | 10 | 3.3 | 0 |
| Harmon | 1 | 2 | 2.0 | 0 |

### PUNT RETURNS

| Last Name | No. | Yds | Avg | TD |
|---|---|---|---|---|
| McLemore | 45 | 521 | 11.6 | 1 |

### KICKOFF RETURNS

| Last Name | No. | Yds | Avg | TD |
|---|---|---|---|---|
| Monroe | 27 | 561 | 20.8 | 0 |
| Harmon | 13 | 357 | 27.5 | 0 |
| McLemore | 3 | 80 | 26.7 | 0 |
| Ring | 1 | 27 | 27.0 | 0 |
| Wilson | 1 | 14 | 14.0 | 0 |
| Cooper | 1 | 0 | 0.0 | 0 |
| McIntyre | 1 | 0 | 0.0 | 0 |

### PASSING — PUNTING — KICKING

#### PASSING

| Last Name | Att | Cmp | % | Yds | Yd/Att | TD | Int- | % | RK |
|---|---|---|---|---|---|---|---|---|---|
| Montana | 432 | 279 | 65 | 3630 | 8.4 | 28 | 10- | 2 | 1 |
| Cavanaugh | 61 | 33 | 54 | 449 | 7.4 | 4 | 0- | 0 | |
| Harmon | 2 | 0 | 0 | 0 | 0.0 | 0 | 0- | 0 | |
| D. Clark | 1 | 0 | 0 | 0 | 0.0 | 0 | 0- | 0 | |

#### PUNTING

| Last Name | No | Avg |
|---|---|---|
| Runager | 56 | 41.8 |
| Orosz | 5 | 39.0 |

#### KICKING

| Last Name | XP | Att | % | FG | Att | % |
|---|---|---|---|---|---|---|
| Wersching | 56 | 56 | 100 | 25 | 35 | 71 |

## LOS ANGELES RAMS

### RUSHING

| Last Name | No. | Yds | Avg | TD |
|---|---|---|---|---|
| Dickerson | 379 | 2105 | 5.6 | 14 |
| Crutchfield | 73 | 337 | 4.6 | 1 |
| Redden | 45 | 247 | 5.5 | 0 |
| Kemp | 34 | 153 | 4.5 | 1 |
| Brown | 2 | 25 | 12.5 | 0 |
| Guman | 1 | 2 | 2.0 | 0 |
| Ferragamo | 4 | 0 | 0.0 | 0 |
| Ellard | 3 | -5 | -1.7 | 0 |

### RECEIVING

| Last Name | No. | Yds | Avg | TD |
|---|---|---|---|---|
| Ellard | 34 | 622 | 18.3 | 6 |
| Da. Hill | 31 | 300 | 9.7 | 1 |
| Brown | 23 | 478 | 20.8 | 4 |
| Dickerson | 21 | 139 | 6.6 | 0 |
| Guman | 19 | 161 | 8.5 | 0 |
| Dr. Hill | 14 | 390 | 27.9 | 4 |
| Grant | 9 | 64 | 7.1 | 0 |
| Farmer | 7 | 75 | 10.7 | 0 |
| Barber | 7 | 42 | 6.0 | 0 |
| McDonald | 4 | 55 | 13.8 | 0 |
| Redden | 4 | 39 | 9.8 | 0 |
| Crutchfield | 2 | 11 | 5.5 | 1 |
| Faulkner | 1 | 6 | 6.0 | 0 |

### PUNT RETURNS

| Last Name | No. | Yds | Avg | TD |
|---|---|---|---|---|
| Ellard | 30 | 403 | 13.4 | 2 |
| Irvin | 9 | 83 | 9.2 | 0 |
| Johnson | 1 | 3 | 3.0 | 0 |

### KICKOFF RETURNS

| Last Name | No. | Yds | Avg | TD |
|---|---|---|---|---|
| Redden | 23 | 530 | 23.0 | 0 |
| Dr. Hill | 26 | 543 | 20.9 | 0 |
| Pleasant | 2 | 48 | 24.0 | 0 |
| Irvin | 2 | 33 | 16.5 | 0 |
| Ellard | 2 | 24 | 12.0 | 0 |
| Guman | 1 | 43 | 43.0 | 1 |
| Crutchfield | 1 | 20 | 20.0 | 0 |
| Sully | 1 | 3 | 3.0 | 0 |

### PASSING — PUNTING — KICKING

#### PASSING

| Last Name | Att | Cmp | % | Yds | Yd/Att | TD | Int- | % | RK |
|---|---|---|---|---|---|---|---|---|---|
| Kemp | 284 | 143 | 50 | 2021 | 7.1 | 13 | 7- | 3 | 9 |
| Ferragamo | 66 | 29 | 44 | 317 | 4.8 | 2 | 8- | 12 | |
| Dils | 7 | 4 | 57 | 44 | 6.3 | 1 | 1- | 14 | |
| Dickerson | 1 | 0 | 0 | 0 | 0.0 | 0 | 1- | 100 | |

#### PUNTING

| Last Name | No | Avg |
|---|---|---|
| Misko | 74 | 38.7 |

#### KICKING

| Last Name | XP | Att | % | FG | Att | % |
|---|---|---|---|---|---|---|
| Lansford | 37 | 38 | 97 | 25 | 33 | 76 |

## NEW ORLEANS SAINTS

### RUSHING

| Last Name | No. | Yds | Avg | TD |
|---|---|---|---|---|
| G. Rogers | 239 | 914 | 3.8 | 2 |
| Gajan | 102 | 615 | 6.0 | 5 |
| Campbell | 146 | 468 | 3.2 | 4 |
| W. Wilson | 74 | 261 | 3.5 | 1 |
| Todd | 28 | 111 | 4.0 | 0 |
| Anthony | 20 | 105 | 5.3 | 1 |
| T. Wilson | 2 | 8 | 4.0 | 0 |
| Goodlow | 1 | 5 | 5.0 | 0 |
| Stabler | 1 | -1 | -1.0 | 0 |
| Duckett | 1 | -3 | -3.0 | 0 |
| D. Wilson | 3 | -7 | -2.3 | 0 |
| Hansen | 2 | -27 | -13.5 | 0 |

### RECEIVING

| Last Name | No. | Yds | Avg | TD |
|---|---|---|---|---|
| Gajan | 35 | 288 | 8.2 | 2 |
| Groth | 33 | 487 | 14.8 | 0 |
| W. Wilson | 33 | 314 | 9.5 | 3 |
| Young | 29 | 597 | 20.6 | 3 |
| Brenner | 28 | 554 | 19.8 | 6 |
| Goodlow | 22 | 281 | 12.8 | 3 |
| Scott | 21 | 278 | 13.2 | 1 |
| Anthony | 12 | 113 | 9.4 | 0 |
| G. Rogers | 12 | 76 | 6.3 | 0 |
| Miller | 8 | 81 | 10.1 | 1 |
| Tice | 6 | 55 | 9.2 | 1 |
| Hardy | 4 | 50 | 12.5 | 1 |
| Duckett | 3 | 24 | 8.0 | 0 |
| Campbell | 3 | 27 | 9.0 | 0 |

### PUNT RETURNS

| Last Name | No. | Yds | Avg | TD |
|---|---|---|---|---|
| Fields | 27 | 236 | 8.7 | 0 |
| Groth | 6 | 32 | 5.3 | 0 |

### KICKOFF RETURNS

| Last Name | No. | Yds | Avg | TD |
|---|---|---|---|---|
| Anthony | 22 | 490 | 22.3 | 0 |
| Duckett | 29 | 580 | 20.0 | 0 |
| Fields | 19 | 356 | 18.7 | 0 |
| W. Wilson | 1 | 23 | 23.0 | 0 |
| T. Wilson | 1 | 16 | 16.0 | 0 |

### PASSING — PUNTING — KICKING

#### PASSING

| Last Name | Att | Cmp | % | Yds | Yd/Att | TD | Int- | % | RK |
|---|---|---|---|---|---|---|---|---|---|
| Todd | 312 | 161 | 52 | 2178 | 7.0 | 1 | 19- | 6 | 15 |
| D. Wilson | 93 | 51 | 55 | 647 | 7.0 | 7 | 4- | 4 | |
| Stabler | 70 | 33 | 47 | 339 | 4.8 | 2 | 5- | 7 | |
| Gajan | 1 | 1 | 100 | 34 | 34.0 | 1 | 0- | 0 | |

#### PUNTING

| Last Name | No | Avg |
|---|---|---|
| Hansen | 69 | 43.8 |

#### KICKING

| Last Name | XP | Att | % | FG | Att | % |
|---|---|---|---|---|---|---|
| Andersen | 34 | 34 | 100 | 20 | 27 | 74 |

## ATLANTA FALCONS

### RUSHING

| Last Name | No. | Yds | Avg | TD |
|---|---|---|---|---|
| Riggs | 353 | 1486 | 4.2 | 13 |
| Cain | 77 | 276 | 3.6 | 3 |
| Moroski | 21 | 98 | 4.7 | 0 |
| Archer | 6 | 38 | 6.3 | 0 |
| Bartkowski | 15 | 34 | 2.3 | 0 |
| Hodge | 2 | 17 | 8.5 | 0 |
| Stamps | 3 | 15 | 5.0 | 0 |
| C. Benson | 3 | 8 | 2.7 | 0 |
| B. Johnson | 3 | 8 | 2.7 | 0 |
| Austin | 4 | 7 | 1.8 | 0 |
| Pridemore | 1 | 7 | 7.0 | 0 |
| Giacomarro | 1 | 0 | 0.0 | 0 |

### RECEIVING

| Last Name | No. | Yds | Avg | TD |
|---|---|---|---|---|
| Bailey | 67 | 1138 | 17.0 | 6 |
| A. Jackson | 52 | 731 | 14.1 | 2 |
| Riggs | 42 | 277 | 6.6 | 0 |
| Cox | 34 | 329 | 9.7 | 3 |
| C. Benson | 26 | 244 | 9.4 | 0 |
| B. Johnson | 24 | 371 | 15.5 | 3 |
| Hodge | 24 | 234 | 9.8 | 0 |
| Cain | 12 | 87 | 7.3 | 0 |
| Landrum | 6 | 66 | 11.0 | 0 |
| Stamps | 4 | 48 | 12.0 | 0 |
| Curran | 1 | 7 | 7.0 | 0 |
| Matthews | 1 | 7 | 7.0 | 0 |
| Tuttle | 1 | 7 | 7.0 | 0 |

### PUNT RETURNS

| Last Name | No. | Yds | Avg | TD |
|---|---|---|---|---|
| B. Johnson | 15 | 152 | 10.1 | 0 |
| K. Johnson | 10 | 79 | 7.9 | 0 |
| Curran | 9 | 21 | 2.3 | 0 |

### KICKOFF RETURNS

| Last Name | No. | Yds | Avg | TD |
|---|---|---|---|---|
| Stamps | 19 | 452 | 23.8 | 0 |
| K. Johnson | 19 | 359 | 18.9 | 0 |
| Curran | 11 | 219 | 19.9 | 0 |
| Austin | 4 | 77 | 19.3 | 0 |
| B. Johnson | 2 | 39 | 19.5 | 0 |
| Tate | 9 | 148 | 16.4 | 0 |
| Gaison | 1 | 15 | 15.0 | 0 |
| Matthews | 1 | 3 | 3.0 | 0 |
| Malancon | 1 | 0 | 0.0 | 0 |
| Tyrrell | 1 | 0 | 0.0 | 0 |

### PASSING — PUNTING — KICKING

#### PASSING

| Last Name | Att | Cmp | % | Yds | Yd/Att | TD | Int- | % | RK |
|---|---|---|---|---|---|---|---|---|---|
| Bartkowski | 269 | 181 | 67 | 2158 | 8.0 | 1 | 10- | 4 | 4 |
| Moroski | 191 | 102 | 53 | 1207 | 6.3 | 4 | 9- | 5 | 16 |
| Archer | 18 | 1 | 61 | 181 | 10.1 | 1 | 1- | 6 | |

#### PUNTING

| Last Name | No | Avg |
|---|---|---|
| Giacomarro | 68 | 42.0 |

#### KICKING

| Last Name | XP | Att | % | FG | Att | % |
|---|---|---|---|---|---|---|
| Luckhurst | 31 | 31 | 100 | 20 | 27 | 74 |

Al Davis' court room success stripped the N.F.L. of its ability to govern franchise shifts. The fallout was quick in coming. Bob Irsay was wooed by Indianapolis and Phoenix and decided to move his Colts to Indiana. The move was publicly announced only after the Colts had packed their goods and driven away in the middle of a spring night in Baltimore. While Indianapolis merited an N.F.L. team, Baltimore suffered the loss of a cultural pillar, a team which traditionally had been one of the league's strongest. As the 1984 season wore down, Phoenix almost lured the Philadelphia Eagles to Arizona. Only direct intervention by government officials kept the Eagles where they had played for more than 50 years.

## EASTERN DIVISION

**Miami Dolphins** — An opening-day triumph over Washington launched the Dolphins on a season of white-hot excellence. The spotlight hugged the spectacular Miami passing game. In his second pro season, Dan Marino threw for touchdowns at a record clip. His quick delivery was matched by the quick feet of the Marks Brothers — Duper and Clayton, a brace of long-distance receivers. The offense scintillated despite David Overstreet's death in a car accident, Bob Kuechenberg's eye injury, and knee injuries to Andra Franklin and Eric Laakso. With the Killer Bee defense doing its share, the Dolphins blew away their first 11 foes before losing in overtime at San Diego. By then, Miami's fourth straight playoff trip was assured.

**New England Patriots** — Despite a 5-2 start, all was not well with the Patiots. Head coach Ron Meyer had angered his players with public criticism. The dissension came to a boil when Meyer fired defensive coordinator Rod Rust after a 44-22 loss to Miami. In the wake of the uproar, Meyer was fired and replaced by Raymond Berry. The new coach's first move was rehiring Rust. The Patriots won three of their first four games under Berry, but then dropped three straight to sabotage their playoff drive. Out of the disappointing season, the Patriots came up with a new starting quarterback in Tony Eason, an effective new runner in U.S.F.L. refugee Craig James, and a newly blossomed defensive star in Andre Tippett.

**New York Jets** — After last year's flop, the Jets unloaded players in wholesale fashion. The playoffs seemed far off in training camp with new men in key spots. The Jets shot out to a surprising 6-2 start, with veterans Freeman McNeil and Mark Gastineau leading their new mates. Pat Ryan settled comfortably into the quarterback job in the early drive. In mid-season, however, he suffered two concussions and lost his job to Ken O'Brien. At the same time, injuries decimated the secondary to a paper-thin state. The playoff hopes died in a six-game losing streak, which killed the optimism of October. A 41-21 loss at Tampa Bay ended the season on a sour note.

**Indianapolis Colts** — The Colts opened a new chapter by moving into the Hoosier Dome. Once they started playing, they looked exactly like the Baltimore Colts of recent years. The offense scored 10 points or less in half the games, with Frank Kush shuffling his quarterbacks like cards. Kush moved his best offensive lineman, Chris Hinton, from guard to tackle, then lost him to a broken leg in October. The hometown fans got a sobering view of their new team in a 50-17 defeat to the Patriots. When three straight losses followed, Kush resigned to take the coaching job of the U.S.F.L. Arizona team. Without Kush, the Colts kept their stride by losing at New England 16-10.

**Buffalo Bills** — The Bills lost games nonstop until mid-November. Sporting an 0-11 record, they welcomed the Dallas Cowboys to Rich Stadium. On the first play from scrimmage, rookie Greg Bell dashed 85 yards for a touchdown. With a quick lead in hand, the Buffalo defense stifled the Dallas offense and engineered a 14-3 upset. That victory was the high point of a brutally bad season. The offense suffered as Joe Cribbs jumped to the U.S.F.L., Frank Lewis retired, Jerry Butler injured a knee, and Joe Ferguson lost his effectiveness to ankle and arm woes. The offensive line and defensive secondary especially plagued coach Kay Stephenson.

## CENTRAL DIVISION

**Pittsburgh Steelers** — Even as the old guard departed, Chuck Noll kept the Steelers atop the Central Division. Mel Blount retired, joined by Terry Bradshaw and his dead passing arm. Franco Harris was shockingly cut in the middle of a training-camp holdout for a better contract. On opening day, Jack Lambert severely injured a toe and missed most of the season. The Steelers absorbed the changes in stride in the A.F.C.'s weakest division. Although only 6-6 in mid-November, they still held a two-game lead over Cincinnati. By winning three of their remaining four games, the Steelers earned their third straight playoff ticket. With Lambert hurt, linebackers Robin Cole and Mike Merriweather emerged as leaders on defense. Veterans John Stallworth and Mike Webster starred on offense, joined by brilliant rookie receiver Louis Lipps. David Woodley began the year at quarterback, but when he suffered two concussions and a leg injury, Mark Malone stepped in and played well.

**Cincinnati Bengals** — The Bengals took awhile getting used to new coach Sam Wyche. Before he settled into his seat, the team had lost four of its first five games. Mid-season brought relief in games against Houston and Cleveland. A 22-20 victory over the Steelers on November 11 brought the Bengals within two games of the top, but even a strong finish would not gain the playoffs. Wyche kept his offense moving despite Dan Ross' departure to the U.S.F.L. and Pete Johnson's trade to San Diego. Ken Anderson suffered back and shoulder ills, giving Turk Schonert and rookie Boomer Esiason a chance to run the attack. A 52-21 victory over Buffalo in the finale fueled hope for the future.

**Cleveland Browns** — An opening-day debacle at Seattle made Brian Sipe's absence seem fatal. As the losses piled up, rumors flew as to coach Sam Rutigliano's job security. An October 7 game against New England brought brickbats crashing into the coach. Trailing 17-16, the Browns drove deep into Patriot territory. With 23 seconds left on the clock, Rutigliano eschewed a field goal to call a pass play. The Patriots promptly intercepted Paul McDonald's pass to end the game. After two more losses, Rutigliano was fired and replaced by assistant Marty Schottenheimer. With his defense holding firm, Schottenheimer coaxed four victories out of his men in the remaining eight games.

**Houston Oilers** — The Oilers added one Campbell and subtracted another. Hugh Campbell became head coach after a long career in Canada and one season in the U.S.F.L. In October, he sent Earl Campbell to New Orleans for a first-round draft pick, parting with the team's offensive workhorse since 1978. The new offensive hub was Warren Moon, a C.F.L. quarterback lured to Texas with a rich contract. The team's new look didn't prevent 10 losses in the first 10 games, with offense and defense sharing the blame. The offense did not run well, and the defense failed to rush enemy passers. The Oilers improved and won half of their final six games. Starring on offense were guard Mike Munchak and receiver Tim Smith.

## WESTERN DIVISION

**Denver Broncos** — A 27-0 embarrassment at Chicago on September 9 was the only game the Broncos didn't win of their first dozen. The unexpected rise to the top came on the strong back of the defense. Even with Randy Gradishar retired and Bob Swenson injured, the defense created turnovers and evoked memories of the old Orange Crush defense. Veteran linebacker Tom

FINAL TEAM STATISTICS

**OFFENSE**

| | BUFF. | CIN. | CLEV. | DEN. | HOU. | IND. | K.C. | L.A. | MIA. | N.E. | NY J | PIT. | S.D. | SEA. |
|---|---|---|---|---|---|---|---|---|---|---|---|---|---|---|
| **FIRST DOWNS:** | | | | | | | | | | | | | | |
| Total | 263 | 339 | 295 | 299 | 284 | 254 | 295 | 301 | 387 | 315 | 310 | 302 | 374 | 287 |
| by Rushing | 98 | 135 | 89 | 121 | 95 | 114 | 88 | 114 | 115 | 104 | 118 | 117 | 106 | 94 |
| by Passing | 149 | 179 | 180 | 152 | 164 | 117 | 178 | 162 | 243 | 186 | 176 | 167 | 240 | 171 |
| by Penalty | 16 | 25 | 26 | 26 | 25 | 23 | 29 | 25 | 29 | 25 | 16 | 18 | 28 | 22 |
| **RUSHING:** | | | | | | | | | | | | | | |
| Number | 398 | 540 | 489 | 508 | 433 | 510 | 408 | 516 | 484 | 482 | 504 | 574 | 456 | 495 |
| Yards | 1643 | 2179 | 1696 | 2076 | 1656 | 2025 | 1527 | 1886 | 1918 | 2032 | 2189 | 2179 | 1654 | 1645 |
| Average Yards | 4.1 | 4.0 | 3.5 | 4.1 | 3.8 | 4.0 | 3.7 | 3.7 | 4.0 | 4.2 | 4.3 | 3.8 | 3.6 | 3.3 |
| Touchdowns | 9 | 18 | 10 | 12 | 13 | 13 | 12 | 19 | 18 | 15 | 17 | 13 | 18 | 10 |
| **PASSING:** | | | | | | | | | | | | | | |
| Attempts | 588 | 496 | 495 | 475 | 487 | 411 | 593 | 491 | 572 | 500 | 488 | 443 | 662 | 497 |
| Completions | 298 | 306 | 273 | 263 | 282 | 206 | 305 | 266 | 367 | 292 | 272 | 240 | 401 | 283 |
| Completion Pct. | 50.7 | 61.7 | 55.2 | 55.4 | 57.9 | 50.1 | 51.4 | 54.2 | 64.2 | 58.4 | 55.7 | 54.2 | 60.6 | 56.9 |
| Passing Yards | 3252 | 3659 | 3490 | 3116 | 3610 | 2543 | 3869 | 3718 | 5146 | 3685 | 3341 | 3519 | 4928 | 3751 |
| Avg. Yds per Att. | 5.5 | 7.4 | 7.1 | 6.6 | 7.4 | 6.2 | 6.5 | 7.6 | 9.0 | 7.4 | 6.9 | 7.9 | 7.4 | 7.6 |
| Avg. Yds per Comp. | 10.9 | 12.0 | 12.8 | 11.9 | 12.8 | 12.3 | 12.7 | 14.0 | 14.0 | 12.6 | 12.3 | 14.7 | 12.3 | 13.3 |
| Times Tackled | 60 | 45 | 55 | 35 | 49 | 58 | 33 | 54 | 14 | 66 | 52 | 35 | 36 | 42 |
| Yds Lost Tackled | 554 | 358 | 358 | 257 | 382 | 436 | 301 | 360 | 128 | 454 | 382 | 278 | 285 | 328 |
| Net Yards | 2698 | 3301 | 3132 | 2859 | 3228 | 2107 | 3568 | 3358 | 5018 | 3231 | 2959 | 3241 | 4643 | 3423 |
| Touchdowns | 18 | 17 | 14 | 22 | 14 | 13 | 21 | 21 | 49 | 26 | 20 | 25 | 25 | 32 |
| Interceptions | 30 | 22 | 23 | 17 | 15 | 22 | 22 | 28 | 18 | 14 | 21 | 25 | 21 | 26 |
| Pct. Intercepted | 5.1 | 4.4 | 4.6 | 3.6 | 3.1 | 5.4 | 3.7 | 5.7 | 3.1 | 2.8 | 4.3 | 5.6 | 3.2 | 5.2 |
| **PUNTS:** | | | | | | | | | | | | | | |
| Number | 90 | 67 | 76 | 96 | 88 | 98 | 98 | 91 | 51 | 92 | 75 | 70 | 66 | 95 |
| Average | 41.1 | 42.3 | 42.3 | 40.1 | 39.6 | 44.7 | 44.9 | 41.9 | 44.7 | 42.4 | 39.1 | 41.2 | 42.0 | 37.5 |
| **PUNT RETURNS** | | | | | | | | | | | | | | |
| Number | 33 | 38 | 40 | 41 | 26 | 38 | 42 | 67 | 39 | 48 | 35 | 61 | 33 | 44 |
| Yards | 297 | 473 | 322 | 318 | 152 | 278 | 346 | 667 | 365 | 430 | 324 | 696 | 212 | 484 |
| Average Yards | 9.0 | 12.4 | 8.1 | 7.8 | 5.8 | 7.3 | 8.2 | 10.0 | 9.4 | 9.0 | 9.3 | 11.4 | 6.4 | 11.0 |
| Touchdowns | 1 | 0 | 0 | 0 | 0 | 0 | 0 | 1 | 0 | 0 | 0 | 1 | 1 | 1 |
| **KICKOFF RET.:** | | | | | | | | | | | | | | |
| Number | 76 | 61 | 61 | 45 | 69 | 69 | 56 | 56 | 44 | 63 | 65 | 54 | 63 | 54 |
| Yards | 1422 | 1155 | 1157 | 897 | 1352 | 1331 | 1061 | 1216 | 799 | 1246 | 1498 | 1026 | 1319 | 1007 |
| Average Yards | 18.7 | 18.9 | 19.0 | 19.9 | 19.6 | 19.3 | 18.9 | 21.7 | 18.2 | 19.8 | 23.0 | 19.0 | 20.9 | 18.6 |
| Touchdowns | 0 | 0 | 0 | 0 | 0 | 1 | 0 | 0 | 0 | 0 | 1 | 0 | 0 | 0 |
| **INTERCEPT RET.:** | | | | | | | | | | | | | | |
| Number | 16 | 25 | 20 | 31 | 13 | 18 | 30 | 20 | 24 | 17 | 15 | 31 | 19 | 38 |
| Yards | 233 | 368 | 236 | 510 | 139 | 190 | 465 | 339 | 478 | 210 | 152 | 433 | 499 | 697 |
| Average Yards | 14.6 | 14.7 | 11.8 | 16.5 | 10.7 | 10.6 | 15.5 | 17.0 | 19.9 | 12.4 | 10.1 | 14.0 | 26.3 | 18.3 |
| Touchdowns | 0 | 4 | 0 | 4 | 0 | 1 | 2 | 2 | 2 | 0 | 0 | 4 | 4 | 7 |
| **PENALTIES:** | | | | | | | | | | | | | | |
| Number | 121 | 85 | 111 | 78 | 99 | 95 | 98 | 143 | 67 | 86 | 96 | 112 | 112 | 128 |
| Yards | 997 | 693 | 928 | 636 | 813 | 798 | 801 | 1209 | 527 | 674 | 779 | 948 | 1023 | 1179 |
| **FUMBLES:** | | | | | | | | | | | | | | |
| Number | 31 | 32 | 31 | 36 | 36 | 35 | 34 | 42 | 26 | 29 | 26 | 40 | 35 | 24 |
| Number Lost | 14 | 17 | 16 | 17 | 16 | 16 | 15 | 20 | 10 | 15 | 13 | 15 | 17 | 13 |
| **POINTS:** | | | | | | | | | | | | | | |
| Total | 250 | 339 | 250 | 353 | 240 | 239 | 314 | 368 | 513 | 362 | 332 | 387 | 394 | 418 |
| PAT Attempts | 31 | 37 | 25 | 42 | 28 | 28 | 35 | 44 | 70 | 42 | 40 | 45 | 47 | 51 |
| PAT Made | 31 | 37 | 25 | 38 | 27 | 27 | 35 | 40 | 66 | 42 | 39 | 45 | 46 | 50 |
| FG Attempts | 21 | 31 | 35 | 28 | 19 | 23 | 33 | 27 | 19 | 28 | 24 | 32 | 29 | 24 |
| FG Made | 11 | 22 | 25 | 21 | 15 | 14 | 23 | 20 | 9 | 22 | 17 | 24 | 20 | 20 |
| Percent FG Made | 52.4 | 71.0 | 71.4 | 75.0 | 78.9 | 60.9 | 69.7 | 74.1 | 47.4 | 78.6 | 70.8 | 75.0 | 69.0 | 83.3 |
| Safeties | 0 | 1 | 0 | 0 | 0 | 1 | 0 | 2 | 0 | 1 | 1 | 0 | 0 | 1 |

**DEFENSE**

| | BUFF. | CIN. | CLEV. | DEN. | HOU. | IND. | K.C. | L.A. | MIA. | N.E. | NY J | PIT. | S.D. | SEA. |
|---|---|---|---|---|---|---|---|---|---|---|---|---|---|---|
| **FIRST DOWNS:** | | | | | | | | | | | | | | |
| Total | 345 | 322 | 270 | 311 | 345 | 343 | 335 | 297 | 314 | 311 | 341 | 282 | 322 | 288 |
| by Rushing | 134 | 115 | 103 | 90 | 158 | 124 | 121 | 107 | 130 | 109 | 117 | 87 | 109 | 99 |
| by Passing | 186 | 191 | 145 | 206 | 168 | 194 | 192 | 147 | 172 | 182 | 198 | 167 | 189 | 160 |
| by Penalty | 25 | 16 | 22 | 15 | 19 | 25 | 22 | 43 | 12 | 20 | 26 | 28 | 24 | 29 |
| **RUSHING:** | | | | | | | | | | | | | | |
| Number | 531 | 477 | 494 | 435 | 596 | 559 | 523 | 517 | 458 | 498 | 497 | 454 | 457 | 475 |
| Yards | 2106 | 1868 | 1945 | 1664 | 2789 | 2007 | 1980 | 1892 | 2155 | 1886 | 2064 | 1617 | 1851 | 1789 |
| Average Yards | 4.0 | 3.9 | 3.9 | 3.8 | 4.7 | 3.6 | 3.8 | 3.7 | 4.7 | 3.8 | 4.2 | 3.6 | 4.1 | 3.8 |
| Touchdowns | 19 | 21 | 10 | 10 | 27 | 16 | 10 | 12 | 16 | 11 | 16 | 12 | 23 | 11 |
| **PASSING:** | | | | | | | | | | | | | | |
| Attempts | 495 | 517 | 458 | 631 | 447 | 515 | 586 | 508 | 551 | 513 | 511 | 515 | 531 | 521 |
| Completions | 300 | 302 | 261 | 346 | 271 | 298 | 332 | 254 | 310 | 283 | 312 | 299 | 323 | 265 |
| Completion Pct. | 60.6 | 58.4 | 57.0 | 54.8 | 60.6 | 57.9 | 56.7 | 50.0 | 56.3 | 55.2 | 61.1 | 58.1 | 60.8 | 50.9 |
| Passing Yards | 3667 | 3689 | 3049 | 4453 | 3446 | 3890 | 4009 | 3268 | 3604 | 3666 | 3862 | 3689 | 4303 | 3572 |
| Avg. Yds per Att. | 7.4 | 7.1 | 6.7 | 7.1 | 7.7 | 7.6 | 6.8 | 6.4 | 6.5 | 7.1 | 7.6 | 7.2 | 8.1 | 6.9 |
| Avg. Yds per Comp. | 12.2 | 12.2 | 11.7 | 12.9 | 12.7 | 13.1 | 12.1 | 12.9 | 11.6 | 13.0 | 12.4 | 12.3 | 13.3 | 13.5 |
| Times Tackled | 26 | 40 | 43 | 57 | 32 | 42 | 50 | 64 | 42 | 55 | 44 | 47 | 33 | 55 |
| Yds Lost Tackled | 191 | 298 | 353 | 430 | 267 | 320 | 364 | 516 | 339 | 452 | 360 | 390 | 218 | 398 |
| Net Yards | 3476 | 3391 | 2696 | 4023 | 3179 | 3570 | 3645 | 2752 | 3265 | 3214 | 3502 | 3299 | 4085 | 3174 |
| Touchdowns | 32 | 15 | 15 | 16 | 23 | 31 | 19 | 19 | 22 | 25 | 24 | 19 | 27 | 18 |
| Interceptions | 16 | 25 | 20 | 31 | 13 | 18 | 30 | 20 | 24 | 17 | 15 | 31 | 19 | 38 |
| Pct. Intercepted | 3.2 | 4.8 | 4.4 | 4.9 | 2.9 | 3.5 | 5.1 | 3.9 | 4.4 | 3.3 | 2.9 | 6.0 | 3.6 | 7.3 |
| **PUNTS:** | | | | | | | | | | | | | | |
| Number | 72 | 67 | 77 | 81 | 64 | 80 | 91 | 117 | 83 | 83 | 67 | 90 | 73 | 83 |
| Average | 39.1 | 41.4 | 40.6 | 41.5 | 42.2 | 42.0 | 40.0 | 43.3 | 41.9 | 40.3 | 42.6 | 42.4 | 39.6 | 40.3 |
| **PUNT RETURNS** | | | | | | | | | | | | | | |
| Number | 52 | 38 | 43 | 44 | 60 | 62 | 60 | 34 | 17 | 45 | 37 | 37 | 43 | 32 |
| Yards | 597 | 310 | 489 | 335 | 618 | 600 | 461 | 345 | 138 | 442 | 242 | 351 | 399 | 205 |
| Average Yards | 11.5 | 8.2 | 11.4 | 7.6 | 10.3 | 9.7 | 7.7 | 10.1 | 8.1 | 9.8 | 6.5 | 9.5 | 9.3 | 6.4 |
| Touchdowns | 0 | 0 | 0 | 0 | 0 | 0 | 0 | 0 | 0 | 1 | 0 | 1 | 0 | 1 |
| **KICKOFF RET.:** | | | | | | | | | | | | | | |
| Number | 44 | 69 | 52 | 55 | 51 | 42 | 64 | 61 | 66 | 73 | 48 | 61 | 72 | 67 |
| Yards | 958 | 1446 | 1159 | 1181 | 986 | 849 | 1354 | 1063 | 1368 | 1373 | 1030 | 1338 | 1437 | 1116 |
| Average Yards | 21.8 | 21.0 | 22.3 | 21.5 | 19.3 | 20.2 | 21.2 | 17.4 | 20.7 | 18.8 | 21.5 | 21.9 | 20.0 | 16.7 |
| Touchdowns | 0 | 1 | 0 | 0 | 0 | 0 | 0 | 0 | 0 | 0 | 0 | 1 | 0 | 0 |
| **INTERCEPT RET.:** | | | | | | | | | | | | | | |
| Number | 30 | 22 | 23 | 17 | 15 | 22 | 22 | 28 | 18 | 14 | 21 | 25 | 21 | 26 |
| Yards | 416 | 364 | 518 | 189 | 214 | 423 | 683 | 300 | 377 | 237 | 207 | 371 | 180 | 333 |
| Average Yards | 13.9 | 16.5 | 22.5 | 11.1 | 14.3 | 19.2 | 31.1 | 10.7 | 20.9 | 16.9 | 9.9 | 14.8 | 8.6 | 12.8 |
| Touchdowns | 4 | 2 | 3 | 0 | 2 | 2 | 7 | 2 | 1 | 3 | 0 | 1 | 0 | 3 |
| **PENALTIES:** | | | | | | | | | | | | | | |
| Number | 87 | 90 | 108 | 104 | 105 | 98 | 108 | 121 | 93 | 87 | 87 | 107 | 108 | 114 |
| Yards | 734 | 743 | 765 | 891 | 876 | 813 | 951 | 1061 | 772 | 773 | 723 | 945 | 905 | 883 |
| **FUMBLES:** | | | | | | | | | | | | | | |
| Number | 36 | 27 | 34 | 44 | 24 | 29 | 18 | 28 | 23 | 33 | 34 | 30 | 34 | 47 |
| Number Lost | 21 | 15 | 15 | 24 | 11 | 13 | 11 | 14 | 12 | 8 | 18 | 11 | 17 | 25 |
| **POINTS:** | | | | | | | | | | | | | | |
| Total | 454 | 339 | 297 | 241 | 437 | 414 | 324 | 278 | 298 | 352 | 364 | 310 | 413 | 282 |
| PAT Attempts | 56 | 39 | 30 | 26 | 53 | 50 | 38 | 33 | 38 | 42 | 41 | 35 | 51 | 34 |
| PAT Made | 56 | 37 | 30 | 26 | 51 | 47 | 37 | 29 | 37 | 37 | 40 | 34 | 50 | 34 |
| FG Attempts | 28 | 27 | 33 | 33 | 30 | 23 | 27 | 21 | 17 | 31 | 37 | 28 | 25 | 22 |
| FG Made | 20 | 22 | 29 | 19 | 22 | 21 | 19 | 17 | 9 | 21 | 26 | 22 | 19 | 14 |
| Percent FG Made | 71.4 | 81.5 | 87.9 | 57.6 | 73.3 | 91.3 | 70.4 | 81.0 | 52.9 | 67.7 | 70.3 | 78.6 | 76.0 | 63.6 |
| Safeties | 1 | 1 | 0 | 1 | 1 | 2 | 1 | 0 | 0 | 0 | 0 | 0 | 0 | 1 |

Jackson led by example while Dennis Smith achieved stardom in the secondary. The less brilliant offense showcased runner Sammy Winder and receiver Steve Watson. With Steve DeBerg gone in a trade, John Elway was secure in the quarterback job and played well. Three victories over the Raiders and Seahawks displayed a new strength of the Broncos.

**Seattle Seahawks** — A severe knee injury to Curt Warner marred a 33-0 whitewash of Cleveland on opening day. With their ace runner gone for the season, the Seattle offense appeared to be in trouble. Chuck Knox allowed no relapse and drove the Seahawks into the playoffs with a passing attack and marvelous defense. Dave Krieg threw frequently and successfully to slick Steve Largent and rookie Daryl Turner, a speedburner who perfectly complemented Largent. The defense posted three shutouts. Linemen Jacob Green, Joe Nash and Jeff Bryant starred in the 3-4 defense, as did Dave Brown and Kenny Easley in the secondary. Brown returned two interceptions for touchdowns in a 45-0 trouncing of Kansas City. Losses to the Chiefs and Broncos in December cost the Seahawks a divisional title and forced them into a wild-card berth.

**Los Angeles Raiders** — Even with Ted Hendricks retired, the Raider defense mauled enemy offenses. Howie Long and Lyle Alzado starred in the line, backed wonderfully by Rod Martin and Matt Millen. Lester Hayes, Mike Haynes and Vann McElroy earned honors in the secondary. The offense had to adjust to a new quarterback, as Jim Plunkett pulled a stomach muscle on October 7 and sat out most of the season. Marc Wilson kept Marcus Allen and Todd Christensen busy, protected by Henry lawrence and the rest of the strong blockers. After a 7-1 start, the Raiders ran into a three-game losing streak in mid-season. A late resurgence included a 45-34 victory over Miami.

**Kansas City Chiefs** — The Chiefs won their first two games and last three games and struggled in between. The glaring flaw on offense was a weak running game in which rookie Herman Heard got the most work. Coming off his best season, quarterback Bill Kenney broke his thumb in the pre-season and missed the early games. Todd Blackledge ran the offense until Kenney returned in relief in a 31-13 victory over San Diego on October 14. The defense lost Gary Green in a trade with the Rams but still had veteran stars in Art Still and Deron Cherry. Bill Maas and Kevin Ross made strong contributions as rookies. The start of November brought back-to-back humiliations, a 45-0 loss to Seattle and a 17-16 defeat to winless Houston.

**San Diego Chargers** — The Chargers beat Minnesota 42-13 on opening day, won four of their first six games, and beat the undefeated Dolphins 34-28 on November 18. Despite the high moments, the Chargers suffered through a disappointing campaign in which Chuck Muncie and Kellen Winslow contributed little. Don Coryell found Muncie's attitude objectionable and traded him to the Dolphins in September; Muncie failed a drug test in Miami, was returned to San Diego and spent the year on suspension. Winslow left the team after the opening game to force renegotiation of his contract. He returned after missing only one game, only to suffer a season-ending knee injury on October 21. The inexperienced defense was not up to carrying the wounded offense. Discovered in the offensive flux was Earnest Jackson, who stepped into Muncie's shoes and ran for more than 1,100 yards.

## MIAMI DOLPHINS 14-2-0 Don Shula

| Scores of Each Game | | |
|---|---|---|
| 35 | Washington | 17 |
| 28 | NEW ENGLAND | 7 |
| 21 | Buffalo | 17 |
| 44 | INDIANAPOLIS | 7 |
| 36 | St.Louis | 28 |
| 31 | Pittsburgh | 7 |
| 28 | HOUSTON | 10 |
| 44 | New England | 24 |
| 38 | BUFFALO | 7 |
| 31 | N.Y.Jets | 17 |
| 24 | PHILADELPHIA | 23 |
| 28 | San Diego | *34 |
| 28 | N.Y.JETS | 17 |
| 34 | L.A.RAIDERS | 45 |
| 35 | Indianapolis | 17 |
| 28 | DALLAS | 21 |

| Use Name | Pos. | Hgt | Wgt | Age | Int | Pts |
|---|---|---|---|---|---|---|
| Jon Giesler | OT | 6'5" | 260 | 27 | | |
| Cleveland Green | OT | 6'3" | 262 | 26 | | |
| Eric Laakso | OT | 6'4" | 265 | 27 | | |
| Roy Foster | OG-OT | 6'4" | 275 | 24 | | |
| Ronnie Lee | OG-OT | 6'4" | 265 | 27 | | |
| Ed Newman | OG | 6'2" | 255 | 33 | | |
| Jeff Toews | C-OG | 6'3" | 255 | 26 | | |
| Dwight Stephenson | C | 6'2" | 255 | 26 | | |
| Bill Barnett | DE | 6'4" | 260 | 28 | | |
| Charles Benson | DE | 6'3" | 267 | 23 | | |
| Doug Betters | DE | 6'7" | 265 | 28 | | |
| Kim Bokamper. | DE | 6'6" | 255 | 29 | | |
| Bob Baumhower | NT | 6'5" | 265 | 29 | | 6 |
| Mike Charles | NT | 6'4" | 283 | 21 | | |
| Steve Clark | NT | 6'4" | 255 | 24 | | |
| Charles Bowser | LB | 6'3" | 235 | 24 | | |
| Jay Brophy | LB | 6'3" | 233 | 24 | | |
| Mark Brown | LB | 6'2" | 225 | 23 | | |
| Bob Brudzinski | LB | 6'4" | 230 | 29 | 1 | |
| A.J.Duhe | LB | 6'4" | 235 | 28 | 1 | |
| Ed Judie | LB | 6'2" | 230 | 25 | | |
| Earnest Rhone | LB | 6'2" | 224 | 31 | | |
| Jackie Shipp | LB | 6'2" | 236 | 22 | | |
| Sanders Shiver | LB | 6'2" | 235 | 29 | | |
| Rodell Thomas | LB | 6'2" | 225 | 26 | | |
| Glenn Blackwood | DB | 6' | 190 | 27 | 6 | |
| Lyle Blackwood | DB | 6'1" | 190 | 33 | 3 | |
| Bud Brown | DB | 6' | 194 | 23 | 1 | |
| William Judson | DB | 6'1" | 190 | 25 | 4 | 6 |
| Mike Kozlowski | DB | 6' | 198 | 28 | 1 | |
| Paul Lankford | DB | 6'1" | 184 | 25 | 3 | |
| Don McNeal | DB | 5'11" | 192 | 26 | 3 | 6 |
| Robert Sowell | DB | 5'11" | 175 | 23 | 1 | |
| Fulton Walker | DB | 5'10" | 193 | 26 | | |
| Dan Marino | QB | 6'4" | 214 | 22 | | |
| Don Strock | QB | 6'5" | 220 | 33 | | |
| Joe Carter | HB | 5'11" | 196 | 22 | | 6 |
| Eddie Hill | HB | 6'2" | 210 | 27 | | |
| Tony Nathan | HB | 6' | 206 | 27 | | 18 |
| Woody Bennett | FB | 6'2" | 222 | 29 | | 48 |
| Andra Franklin | FB | 5'10" | 225 | 25 | | |
| Pete Johnson (from SD) | FB | 6' | 255 | 30 | | 72 |
| Jimmy Cefalo | WR | 5'11" | 188 | 27 | | 12 |
| Mark Clayton | WR | 5'9" | 172 | 23 | | 108 |
| Mark Duper | WR | 5'9" | 187 | 25 | | 48 |
| Vince Heflin | WR | 6' | 185 | 25 | | |
| Jim Jensen | WR | 6'4" | 212 | 25 | | 12 |
| Nat Moore | WR | 5'9" | 188 | 32 | | 36 |
| John Chesley | TE | 6'5" | 225 | 22 | | |
| Bruce Hardy | TE | 6'5" | 230 | 28 | | 30 |
| Dan Johnson | TE | 6'3" | 240 | 24 | | 18 |
| Joe Rose | TE | 6'3" | 230 | 27 | | 12 |
| Reggie Roby | K | 6'2" | 243 | 23 | | 12 |
| Uwe von Schamann | K | 6' | 188 | 28 | | 93 |

David Overstreet - Died in auto accident, June 24
Ron Hester - Knee Injury
Tommy Vigorito - Knee Injury
Bob Kuechenberg - Injury

## NEW ENGLAND PATRIOTS 9-7-0 Ron Meyer, Raymond Berry

| Scores of Each Game | | |
|---|---|---|
| 21 | Buffalo | 17 |
| 7 | Miami | 28 |
| 38 | SEATTLE | 23 |
| 10 | WASHINGTON | 26 |
| 28 | N.Y.Jets | 21 |
| 17 | Cleveland | 16 |
| 20 | CINCINNATI | 14 |
| 24 | MIAMI | 44 |
| 30 | N.Y.JETS | 21 |
| 19 | Denver | 26 |
| 38 | BUFFALO | 10 |
| 50 | Indianapolis | 17 |
| 17 | Dallas | 20 |
| 10 | ST.LOUIS | 33 |
| 17 | Philadelphia | 27 |
| 16 | INDIANAPOLIS | 10 |

| Use Name | Pos. | Hgt | Wgt | Age | Int | Pts |
|---|---|---|---|---|---|---|
| Darryl Haley | OT | 6'4" | 275 | 23 | | |
| Brian Holloway | OT | 6'7" | 288 | 25 | | |
| Steve Moore | OT | 6'4" | 285 | 23 | | |
| Paul Fairchild | OG | 6'4" | 270 | 23 | | |
| John Hannah | OG | 6'2" | 265 | 33 | | |
| Ron Wooten | OG | 6'4" | 273 | 25 | | |
| Pete Brock | C | 6'5" | 275 | 30 | | |
| Guy Morriss | C | 6'4" | 255 | 33 | | |
| Julius Adams | DE | 6'3" | 270 | 36 | | |
| Doug Rogers | DE | 6'5" | 270 | 24 | | |
| Kenneth Sims | DE | 6'5" | 271 | 24 | | |
| Scott Virkus(from BUF,to IND) | DE | 6'5" | 248 | 24 | | |
| Toby Williams | DE | 6'3" | 260 | 24 | | |
| Luther Henson | NT | 6' | 275 | 25 | | |
| Dennis Owens | NT | 6'1" | 258 | 24 | | |
| Lester Williams | NT | 6'3" | 272 | 25 | | |
| Don Blackmon | LB | 6'3" | 235 | 26 | 1 | |
| Tim Golden | LB | 6'1" | 220 | 24 | | |
| Brian Ingram | LB | 6'4" | 235 | 24 | | |
| Larry McGrew | LB | 6'5" | 233 | 27 | | |
| Steve Nelson | LB | 6'2" | 230 | 33 | 1 | |
| Johnny Rembert | LB | 6'3" | 234 | 23 | | |
| Ed Reynolds | LB | 6'5" | 230 | 22 | | |
| Andre Tippett | LB | 6'3" | 241 | 24 | | |
| Clayton Weishuhn | LB | 6'2" | 220 | 24 | | |
| Ed Williams | LB | 6'4" | 244 | 23 | | |
| Raymond Clayborn | DB | 6'1" | 186 | 29 | 3 | |
| Paul Dombroski | DB | 6' | 185 | 28 | 1 | |
| Ernest Gibson | DB | 5'10" | 185 | 22 | 2 | |
| Roland James | DB | 6'2" | 191 | 26 | 2 | 2 |
| Keith Lee | DB | 5'11" | 193 | 26 | | |
| Ronnie Lippett | DB | 5'11" | 180 | 23 | 3 | |
| Fred Marion | DB | 6'2" | 191 | 25 | 2 | |
| Rod McSwain | DB | 6'1" | 198 | 22 | | |
| Rick Sanford | DB | 6'1" | 192 | 27 | 2 | |
| Tony Eason | QB | 6'4" | 212 | 24 | | 30 |
| Steve Grogan | QB | 6'4" | 210 | 31 | | |
| Mike Kerrigan | QB | 6'3" | 205 | 24 | | |
| Tony Collins | HB | 5'11" | 212 | 25 | | 30 |
| Jonathan Williams | HB | 5'9" | 205 | 23 | | |
| Greg Hawthorne | FB | 6'2" | 225 | 27 | | |
| Craig James | FB | 6' | 215 | 23 | | 6 |
| Bo Robinson | FB | 6'2" | 235 | 28 | | 6 |
| Mosi Tatupu | FB | 6' | 227 | 29 | | 24 |
| Robert Weathers | FB | 6'2" | 222 | 23 | | |
| Irving Fryar | WR | 6' | 200 | 21 | | 6 |
| Cedric Jones | WR | 6' | 184 | 24 | | 18 |
| Stanley Morgan | WR | 5'11" | 181 | 29 | | 30 |
| Stephen Starring | WR | 5'10" | 172 | 23 | | 24 |
| Clarence Weathers | WR | 5'9" | 170 | 22 | | 12 |
| Lin Dawson | TE | 6'3" | 240 | 25 | | 24 |
| Derrick Ramsey | TE | 6'5" | 235 | 27 | | 42 |
| Rich Camarillo | K | 5'11" | 191 | 24 | | |
| Tony Franklin | K | 5'8" | 182 | 27 | | 108 |
| Luke Prestridge | K | 6'4" | 235 | 27 | | |

George Crump - Knee Injury
Darryal Wilson - Knee Injury

## NEW YORK JETS 7-9-0 Joe Walton

| Scores of Each Game | | |
|---|---|---|
| 23 | Indianapolis | 14 |
| 17 | PITTSBURGH | 23 |
| 43 | CINCINNATI | 23 |
| 28 | Buffalo | 26 |
| 21 | NEW ENGLAND | 28 |
| 17 | Kansas City | 16 |
| 24 | Cleveland | 20 |
| 28 | KANSAS CITY | 7 |
| 20 | New England | 30 |
| 17 | MIAMI | 31 |
| 5 | INDIANAPOLIS | 9 |
| 20 | Houston | 31 |
| 17 | Miami | 28 |
| 10 | N.Y.GIANTS | 20 |
| 21 | BUFFALO | 17 |
| 21 | Tampa Bay | 41 |

| Use Name | Pos. | Hgt | Wgt | Age | Int | Pts |
|---|---|---|---|---|---|---|
| Reggie McElroy | OT | 6'6" | 270 | 24 | | |
| Marvin Powell | OT | 6'5" | 271 | 29 | | |
| Guy Bingham | C-OG-OT | 6'3" | 255 | 26 | | |
| Stan Waldemore | OG-OT | 6'4" | 269 | 29 | | |
| Dan Alexander | OG | 6'4" | 260 | 29 | | |
| Jim Sweeney | OG-C | 6'4" | 260 | 22 | | |
| Ted Banker | OG-C | 6'2" | 255 | 23 | | |
| Joe Fields | C | 6'2" | 253 | 30 | | |
| George Lilja (to CLE) | OT-C | 6'4" | 262 | 26 | | |
| Mark Gastineau | DE | 6'5" | 265 | 27 | | 6 |
| Marty Lyons | DE-DT | 6'5" | 269 | 27 | | |
| Tom Baldwin | DT | 6'4" | 270 | 23 | | |
| Barry Bennett | DT-DE | 6'4" | 260 | 28 | | |
| Ron Faurot | DT-DE | 6'7" | 262 | 22 | | |
| Joe Klecko | DT-DE | 6'3" | 263 | 30 | | |
| Ben Rudolph | DT-DE | 6'5" | 270 | 27 | | |
| Bobby Bell | LB | 6'3" | 217 | 22 | | |
| Greg Buttle | LB | 6'3" | 232 | 30 | 2 | 6 |
| Kyle Clifton | LB | 6'4" | 233 | 22 | 1 | |
| Bob Crable | LB | 6'3" | 234 | 24 | | |
| Jim Eliopulos | LB | 6'2" | 229 | 25 | | |
| Rusty Guilbeau | LB | 6'4" | 237 | 25 | | |
| Lance Mehl | LB | 6'3" | 235 | 26 | | |
| John Woodring | LB | 6'2" | 232 | 25 | | |
| Russell Carter | DB | 6'2" | 195 | 22 | 4 | |
| Mike Dennis (from SD) | DB | 5'10" | 195 | 26 | | |
| George Floyd | DB | 5'11" | 190 | 23 | | |
| Harry Hamilton | DB | 6' | 193 | 21 | | |
| Bobby Jackson | DB | 5'9" | 180 | 27 | | |
| Skip Lane (to KC) | DB | 6'1" | 208 | 24 | | |
| Johnny Lynn | DB | 6' | 198 | 27 | 2 | |
| Davlin Mullen | DB | 6'1" | 177 | 24 | 1 | |
| Darrol Ray | DB | 6'1" | 198 | 26 | 2 | |
| Ken Schroy | DB | 6'2" | 198 | 31 | 2 | |
| Kirk Springs | DB | 6' | 192 | 26 | 1 | |
| Bob Avellini (from CHI) | QB | 6'2" | 210 | 31 | | |
| Glenn Inverso | QB | 6'1" | 199 | 26 | | |
| Ken O'Brien | QB | 6'4" | 210 | 23 | | |
| Mark Reed | QB | 6'3" | 204 | 25 | | |
| Pat Ryan | QB | 6'3" | 210 | 28 | | 1 |
| Dennis Bligen | HB | 5'11" | 215 | 22 | | |
| Bruce Harper | HB | 5'8" | 177 | 29 | | 6 |
| Johnny Hector | HB | 5'11" | 197 | 23 | | 6 |
| Freeman McNeil | HB | 5'11" | 212 | 25 | | 36 |
| Cedric Minter | HB | 5'10" | 200 | 25 | | 12 |
| Marion Barber | FB | 6'3" | 224 | 24 | | 12 |
| Tony Paige | FB | 5'10" | 230 | 21 | | 48 |
| Nick Bruckner | WR | 5'11" | 185 | 23 | | |
| Frenanza Burgess (to MIA) | WR | 6'1" | 210 | 24 | | |
| Chy Davidson | WR | 5'11" | 175 | 25 | | |
| Derrick Gaffney | WR | 6'1" | 182 | 29 | | |
| Bobby Humphrey | WR | 5'10" | 170 | 23 | | 12 |
| Johnny "Lam" Jones | WR | 5'11" | 180 | 26 | | 6 |
| Kurt Sohn | WR | 5'11" | 180 | 27 | | |
| Wesley Walker | WR | 6' | 182 | 29 | | 42 |
| Glenn Dennison | TE | 6'3" | 225 | 22 | | 6 |
| Rocky Klever | TE | 6'3" | 225 | 25 | | 6 |
| Mickey Shuler | TE | 6'3" | 231 | 28 | | 36 |
| Pat Leahy | K | 6' | 193 | 33 | | 89 |
| Chuck Ramsey | K | 6'2" | 194 | 32 | | |

Mike Augustyniak - Knee Injury

## ININAPOLIS COLTS 4-12-0 Frank Kush, Hal Hunter

| Scores of Each Game | | |
|---|---|---|
| 14 | N.Y.JETS | 23 |
| 35 | Houston | 21 |
| 33 | ST.LOUIS | 34 |
| 7 | Miami | 44 |
| 31 | BUFFALO | 17 |
| 7 | WASHINGTON | 35 |
| 7 | Philadelphia | 16 |
| 17 | PITTSBURGH | 16 |
| 3 | Dallas | 22 |
| 10 | SAN DIEGO | 38 |
| 9 | N.Y.Jets | 5 |
| 17 | NEW ENGLAND | 50 |
| 7 | L.A.Raiders | 21 |
| 15 | Buffalo | 21 |
| 17 | MIAMI | 35 |
| 10 | New England | 16 |

| Use Name | Pos. | Hgt | Wgt | Age | Int | Pts |
|---|---|---|---|---|---|---|
| Kevin Call | OT | 6'7" | 289 | 22 | | |
| Andy Ekern | OT | 6'6" | 265 | 23 | | |
| Jim Mills | OT | 6'9" | 281 | 22 | | |
| Ted Petersen (from CLE) | OT | 6'5" | 253 | 29 | | |
| Steve Wright | OT | 6'6" | 250 | 25 | | |
| Ellis Gardner | OT-OG | 6'5" | 250 | 22 | | |
| Mark Kirchner | OT-OG | 6'3" | 261 | 24 | | |
| Chris Hinton | OG | 6'4" | 283 | 23 | | |
| Ron Solt | OG | 6'3" | 275 | 22 | | |
| Ben Utt | OG | 6'5" | 280 | 25 | | |
| Don Bailey | C | 6'4" | 257 | 23 | | |
| Ray Donaldson | C | 6'3" | 273 | 26 | | |
| Steve Parker | DE | 6'4" | 262 | 24 | | |
| Chris Scott | DE | 6'5" | 253 | 22 | | |
| Byron Smith | DE | 6'5" | 264 | 21 | | |
| Donnell Thompson | DE | 6'4" | 263 | 25 | | |
| Henry Waechter (to CHI) | DE | 6'5" | 260 | 25 | | |
| Blaise Winter | DE | 6'3" | 262 | 22 | | |
| Brad White | NT | 6'2" | 260 | 26 | | |
| Leo Wisniewski | NT | 6'1" | 259 | 24 | | |
| Greg Bracelin | LB | 6'1" | 216 | 27 | | |
| Johnie Cooks | LB | 6'4" | 243 | 25 | | |
| Steve Hathaway | LB | 6'4" | 238 | 22 | | |
| Mike Humiston | LB | 6'3" | 238 | 25 | | 2 |
| Barry Krauss | LB | 6'3" | 249 | 27 | 3 | |
| Vernon Maxwell | LB | 6'2" | 238 | 23 | | |
| Cliff Odom | LB | 6'2" | 235 | 25 | | |
| Gary Padjen | LB | 6'2" | 241 | 26 | | |
| Kim Anderson | DB | 5'11" | 182 | 27 | | |
| Larry Anderson | DB | 5'11" | 194 | 27 | | |
| James Burroughs | DB | 6'1" | 187 | 26 | 3 | |
| Eugene Daniel | DB | 5'11" | 179 | 23 | 6 | |
| Preston Davis | DB | 5'11" | 180 | 22 | 1 | |
| Nesby Glasgow | DB | 5'10" | 180 | 27 | 1 | |
| Mark Kafentzis | DB | 5'10" | 200 | 26 | 1 | 6 |
| Bo Metcalf | DB | 6'2" | 193 | 23 | | |
| George Radachowsky | DB | 5'11" | 178 | 21 | | |
| Tate Randle | DB | 6' | 196 | 25 | 3 | |
| Vaughan Williams | DB | 6'2" | 193 | 22 | | |
| Mark Herrmann | QB | 6'4" | 190 | 25 | | |
| Mike Pagel | QB | 6'2" | 205 | 23 | | 6 |
| Art Schlichter | QB | 6'3" | 210 | 24 | | 6 |
| Curtis Dickey | HB | 6'1" | 222 | 27 | | 18 |
| Frank Middleton | HB | 5'11" | 201 | 23 | | 12 |
| Alvin Moore | HB | 6' | 198 | 25 | | 12 |
| George Wonsley | HB | 5'10" | 212 | 23 | | |
| Randy McMillan | FB | 6' | 212 | 25 | | 30 |
| Matt Bouza | WR | 6'3" | 211 | 25 | | |
| Ray Butler | WR | 6'3" | 195 | 28 | | 36 |
| Bernard Henry | WR | 6'1" | 179 | 24 | | 12 |
| Tracy Porter | WR | 6'1" | 202 | 25 | | 12 |
| Phil Smith | WR | 6'3" | 188 | 23 | | 6 |
| Mark Bell | TE-DE | 6'4" | 246 | 27 | | |
| Tim Sherwin | TE | 6'6" | 245 | 26 | | |
| Dave Young | TE | 6'5" | 243 | 25 | | 12 |
| Raul Allegre | K | 5'10" | 165 | 25 | | 47 |
| Dean Biasucci | K | 6' | 188 | 22 | | 22 |
| Rohn Stark | K | 6'3" | 203 | 25 | | |

Ricky Jones - Injury
Victor Oatis - Thigh Injury

Karl Baldischwiler - Neck Injury
Pat Beach - Ankle Injury
Newton Williams - Ankle Injury

## BUFFALO BILLS 2-14-0 Kay Stephenson

| Scores of Each Game | | |
|---|---|---|
| 17 | NEW ENGLAND | 21 |
| 7 | St.Louis | 37 |
| 17 | MIAMI | 21 |
| 26 | N.Y.JETS | 28 |
| 17 | Indianapolis | 31 |
| 17 | PHILADELPHIA | 27 |
| 28 | Seattle | 31 |
| 7 | DENVER | 37 |
| 7 | Miami | 38 |
| 10 | CLEVELAND | 13 |
| 10 | New England | 38 |
| 14 | DALLAS | 3 |
| 14 | Washington | 41 |
| 21 | INDIANAPOLIS | 15 |
| 17 | N.Y.Jets | 21 |
| 21 | Cincinnati | 52 |

| Use Name | Pos. | Hgt | Wgt | Age | Int | Pts |
|---|---|---|---|---|---|---|
| Justin Cross | OT | 6'6" | 265 | 25 | | |
| Joe Devlin | OT | 6'5" | 250 | 30 | | |
| Ken Jones | OT | 6'5" | 260 | 31 | | |
| Jon Borchardt | OG | 6'5" | 255 | 27 | | |
| Tom Lynch | OG | 6'5" | 250 | 29 | | |
| Jim Ritcher | OG-C | 6'3" | 251 | 26 | | |
| Will Grant | C | 6'3" | 255 | 30 | | |
| Tim Vogler | C | 6'3" | 245 | 27 | | |
| Ken Johnson | DE | 6'5" | 253 | 29 | | |
| Sean McNanie | DE | 6'5" | 252 | 22 | | |
| Dean Prater | DE | 6'4" | 245 | 25 | | |
| Ben Williams | DE | 6'3" | 260 | 30 | | |
| Bill Acker | NT | 6'3" | 255 | 27 | | |
| Fred Smerlas | NT | 6'3" | 270 | 27 | 1 | |
| Joe Azelby | LB | 6'1" | 225 | 22 | | |
| Stan David | LB | 6'3" | 210 | 22 | | 6 |
| Jim Haslett | LB | 6'3" | 232 | 27 | | |
| Chris Keating | LB | 6'2" | 233 | 26 | | 6 |
| Eugeen Marve | LB | 6'2" | 230 | 24 | | |
| Steve Potter | LB | 6'3" | 235 | 26 | | |
| Lucius Sanford | LB | 6'2" | 216 | 28 | | 6 |
| Darryl Talley | LB | 6'4" | 235 | 24 | 1 | |
| Al Wenglikowski | LB | 6'1" | 220 | 24 | | |
| Martin Bayless (from STL) | DB | 6'2" | 195 | 21 | | |
| Rodney Bellinger | DB | 5'8" | 181 | 22 | 1 | |
| Brian Carpenter (from WAS) | DB | 5'10" | 170 | 23 | 3 | |
| Steve Freeman | DB | 5'11" | 185 | 31 | 3 | |
| Rod Hill | DB | 6' | 188 | 25 | | |
| Lawrence Johnson(from CLE) | DB | 5'11" | 204 | 26 | | |
| Rod Kush | DB | 6' | 188 | 27 | 1 | |
| Charles Romes | DB | 6'1" | 190 | 29 | 5 | |
| Garry Thompson | DB | 6' | 180 | 25 | | |
| Marco Tongue | DB | 5'9" | 180 | 24 | | |
| Len Walterscheid | DB | 5'11" | 190 | 29 | | |
| Don Wilson | DB | 6'2" | 190 | 23 | | 6 |
| Joe Dufek | QB | 6'4" | 215 | 23 | | 6 |
| Joe Ferguson | QB | 6'1" | 195 | 34 | | |
| Matt Kofler | QB | 6'3" | 192 | 25 | | |
| Robb Riddick | HB | 6' | 195 | 27 | | |
| Van Williams | HB | 6' | 208 | 25 | | 6 |
| Greg Bell | FB | 5'10" | 210 | 22 | | 48 |
| Booker Moore | FB | 5'11" | 224 | 25 | | |
| Speedy Neal | FB | 6'2" | 254 | 22 | | 6 |
| Mitchell Brookins | WR | 5'11" | 196 | 23 | | 6 |
| Julius Dawkins | WR | 6'1" | 196 | 23 | | 12 |
| Preston Dennard | WR | 6'1" | 183 | 28 | | 42 |
| Byron Franklin | WR | 6'1" | 181 | 25 | | 24 |
| Mike Mosley | WR | 6'2" | 188 | 26 | | |
| Craig White | WR | 6'1" | 194 | 22 | | |
| Buster Barnett | TE | 6'5" | 235 | 25 | | |
| Mark Brammer | TE | 6'3" | 235 | 26 | | |
| Tony Hunter | TE | 6'4" | 237 | 24 | | 12 |
| Ulysses Norris | TE | 6'4" | 232 | 27 | | |
| Joe Danelo | K | 5'9" | 166 | 30 | | 41 |
| John Kidd | K | 6'3" | 201 | 23 | | |
| Chuck Nelson | K | 6' | 175 | 24 | | 23 |

Jerry Butler - Knee Injury
Jeff Nixon - Knee Injury

* Overtime

## MIAMI DOLPHINS

### RUSHING

| Last Name | No. | Yds | Avg | TD |
|---|---|---|---|---|
| Bennett | 114 | 606 | 4.2 | 7 |
| Nathan | 118 | 558 | 4.7 | 1 |
| Carter | 100 | 495 | 5.0 | 1 |
| P. Johnson | 87 | 205 | 2.4 | 12 |
| Franklin | 20 | 74 | 3.7 | 0 |
| Clayton | 3 | 35 | 11.7 | 0 |
| Moore | 1 | 3 | 3.0 | 0 |
| Strock | 2 | -5 | -2.5 | 0 |
| Marino | 28 | -7 | -0.3 | 0 |

### RECEIVING

| Last Name | No. | Yds | Avg | TD |
|---|---|---|---|---|
| Clayton | 73 | 1389 | 19.0 | 18 |
| Duper | 71 | 1306 | 18.4 | 8 |
| Nathan | 61 | 579 | 9.5 | 2 |
| Moore | 43 | 573 | 13.3 | 6 |
| D. Johnson | 28 | 426 | 12.5 | 3 |
| Hardy | 28 | 257 | 9.2 | 5 |
| Cefalo | 18 | 185 | 10.3 | 2 |
| Jensen | 13 | 139 | 10.7 | 2 |
| Rose | 12 | 195 | 16.3 | 2 |
| Carter | 8 | 53 | 6.6 | 0 |
| Bennett | 6 | 44 | 7.3 | 1 |
| P. Johnson | 2 | 7 | 3.5 | 0 |

### PUNT RETURNS

| Last Name | No. | Yds | Avg | TD |
|---|---|---|---|---|
| Walker | 21 | 169 | 8.0 | 0 |
| Clayton | 8 | 79 | 9.9 | 0 |
| Heflin | 6 | 76 | 12.7 | 0 |
| Kozlowski | 4 | 41 | 10.3 | 0 |

### KICKOFF RETURNS

| Last Name | No. | Yds | Avg | TD |
|---|---|---|---|---|
| Walker | 29 | 617 | 21.3 | 0 |
| Heflin | 9 | 130 | 14.4 | 0 |
| Clayton | 2 | 15 | 7.5 | 0 |
| Kozlowski | 2 | 23 | 11.5 | 0 |
| Duhe | 1 | 0 | 0.0 | 0 |
| Hill | 1 | 14 | 14.0 | 0 |

### PASSING — PUNTING — KICKING

| PASSING | Att | Cmp | % | Yds | Yd/Att | TD | Int- | % | RK |
|---|---|---|---|---|---|---|---|---|---|
| Marino | 564 | 362 | 64 | 5084 | 9.01 | 48 | 17- | 3 | 1 |
| Strock | 6 | 4 | 67 | 27 | 4.50 | 0 | 0- | 0 | |
| Clayton | 1 | 0 | 0 | 0 | 0 | 0 | 1-100 | | |
| Jensen | 1 | 1 | 100 | 35 | 35.0 | 1 | 0- | 0 | |

| PUNTING | No. | Avg |
|---|---|---|
| Roby | 51 | 44.7 |

| KICKING | XP | Att | % | FG | Att | % |
|---|---|---|---|---|---|---|
| von Schamann | 66 | 70 | 94 | 9 | 19 | 47 |

## NEW ENGLAND PATRIOTS

### RUSHING

| Last Name | No. | Yds | Avg | TD |
|---|---|---|---|---|
| C. James | 160 | 790 | 4.9 | 1 |
| Tatupu | 133 | 553 | 4.2 | 4 |
| Collins | 138 | 495 | 4.0 | 5 |
| Eason | 40 | 154 | 3.9 | 5 |
| Grogan | 7 | 12 | 1.7 | 0 |
| Fryar | 2 | -11 | -5.5 | 0 |
| Starring | 2 | -16 | -8.0 | 0 |

### RECEIVING

| Last Name | No. | Yds | Avg | TD |
|---|---|---|---|---|
| D. Ramsey | 66 | 792 | 12.0 | 7 |
| Starring | 46 | 657 | 14.3 | 4 |
| Dawson | 39 | 427 | 10.9 | 4 |
| Morgan | 38 | 709 | 18.7 | 5 |
| C. James | 22 | 159 | 7.2 | 0 |
| Jones | 19 | 244 | 12.8 | 2 |
| Tatupu | 16 | 159 | 9.9 | 0 |
| Collins | 16 | 100 | 6.3 | 0 |
| Fryar | 11 | 164 | 14.9 | 1 |
| C. Weathers | 8 | 115 | 14.4 | 2 |
| Hawthorne | 7 | 127 | 18.1 | 0 |
| Robinson | 4 | 32 | 8.0 | 1 |

### PUNT RETURNS

| Last Name | No. | Yds | Avg | TD |
|---|---|---|---|---|
| Fryar | 36 | 347 | 9.6 | 0 |
| Starring | 10 | 73 | 7.3 | 0 |
| C. Weathers | 1 | 7 | 7.0 | 0 |
| Gibson | 1 | 3 | 3.0 | 0 |

### KICKOFF RETURNS

| Last Name | No. | Yds | Avg | TD |
|---|---|---|---|---|
| Collins | 25 | 544 | 21.8 | 0 |
| J. Williams | 23 | 461 | 20.0 | 0 |
| Fryar | 5 | 95 | 19.0 | 0 |
| Lee | 3 | 43 | 14.3 | 0 |
| Robinson | 3 | 38 | 12.7 | 0 |
| Jones | 1 | 20 | 20.0 | 0 |
| Hawthorne | 1 | 14 | 14.0 | 0 |
| Tatupu | 1 | 9 | 9.0 | 0 |

### PASSING — PUNTING — KICKING

| PASSING | Att | Cmp | % | Yds | Yd/Att | TD | Int- | % | RK |
|---|---|---|---|---|---|---|---|---|---|
| Eason | 431 | 259 | 60 | 3228 | 7.5 | 23 | 8- | 2 | 2 |
| Grogan | 68 | 32 | 47 | 444 | 6.53 | 3 | 6- | 9 | |
| Kerrigan | 1 | 1 | 100 | 13 | 13.0 | 0 | 0- | 0 | |

| PUNTING | No. | Avg |
|---|---|---|
| Prestridge | 44 | 42.8 |

| KICKING | XP | Att | % | FG | Att | % |
|---|---|---|---|---|---|---|
| Franklin | 42 | 42 | 100 | 22 | 28 | 79 |

## NEW YORK JETS

### RUSHING

| Last Name | No. | Yds | Avg | TD |
|---|---|---|---|---|
| McNeil | 229 | 1070 | 4.7 | 5 |
| Hector | 124 | 531 | 4.3 | 1 |
| Barber | 31 | 148 | 4.8 | 2 |
| Minter | 34 | 136 | 4.0 | 1 |
| Paige | 35 | 130 | 3.7 | 7 |
| Ryan | 23 | 92 | 4.0 | 0 |
| Harper | 10 | 48 | 4.8 | 1 |
| O'Brien | 16 | 29 | 1.8 | 0 |
| Dennison | 1 | 4 | 4.0 | 0 |
| Walker | 1 | 1 | 1.0 | 0 |
| Avellini | 3 | -5 | -1.7 | 0 |

### RECEIVING

| Last Name | No. | Yds | Avg | TD |
|---|---|---|---|---|
| Shuler | 68 | 782 | 11.5 | 6 |
| Walker | 41 | 623 | 15.2 | 7 |
| Jones | 32 | 470 | 14.7 | 1 |
| McNeil | 25 | 294 | 11.8 | 1 |
| Hector | 20 | 182 | 9.1 | 0 |
| Gaffney | 19 | 285 | 15.0 | 0 |
| Dennison | 16 | 141 | 8.8 | 1 |
| Humphrey | 14 | 206 | 14.7 | 1 |
| Minter | 10 | 109 | 10.9 | 1 |
| Barber | 10 | 79 | 7.9 | 0 |
| Paige | 6 | 31 | 5.2 | 1 |
| Harper | 5 | 71 | 14.2 | 0 |
| Klever | 3 | 29 | 9.7 | 1 |
| Sohn | 2 | 28 | 14.0 | 0 |
| Bruckner | 1 | 11 | 11.0 | 0 |

### PUNT RETURNS

| Last Name | No. | Yds | Avg | TD |
|---|---|---|---|---|
| Springs | 28 | 247 | 8.8 | 0 |
| Minter | 4 | 44 | 11.0 | 0 |
| Bruckner | 2 | 25 | 12.5 | 0 |
| Mullen | 1 | 8 | 8.0 | 0 |

### KICKOFF RETURNS

| Last Name | No. | Yds | Avg | TD |
|---|---|---|---|---|
| Humphrey | 22 | 675 | 30.7 | 1 |
| Springs | 23 | 521 | 22.7 | 0 |
| Minter | 10 | 224 | 22.4 | 0 |
| Mullen | 2 | 34 | 17.0 | 0 |
| Paige | 3 | 7 | 2.3 | 0 |
| Bruckner | 1 | 17 | 17.0 | 0 |
| Davidson | 1 | 9 | 9.0 | 0 |
| Gaffney | 1 | 6 | 6.0 | 0 |
| Banker | 1 | 5 | 5.0 | 0 |
| Shuler | 1 | 0 | 0.0 | 0 |

### PASSING — PUNTING — KICKING

| PASSING | Att | Cmp | % | Yds | Yd/Att | TD | Int- | % | RK |
|---|---|---|---|---|---|---|---|---|---|
| O'Brien | 203 | 116 | 57 | 1402 | 6.91 | 6 | 7- | 3 | 11 |
| Ryan | 285 | 156 | 55 | 1939 | 6.80 | 14 | 14- | 5 | 13 |
| Avellini | 53 | 30 | 57 | 288 | 5.43 | 0 | 3- | 6 | |

| PUNTING | No. | Avg |
|---|---|---|
| Ramsey | 74 | 39.7 |

| KICKING | XP | Att | % | FG | Att | % |
|---|---|---|---|---|---|---|
| Leahy | 38 | 39 | 97 | 17 | 24 | 71 |

## INDIANAPOLIS COLTS

### RUSHING

| Last Name | No. | Yds | Avg | TD |
|---|---|---|---|---|
| McMillan | 163 | 705 | 4.3 | 5 |
| Dickey | 131 | 523 | 4.0 | 3 |
| Middleton | 92 | 275 | 3.0 | 1 |
| Moore | 38 | 127 | 3.3 | 2 |
| Wonsley | 37 | 111 | 3.0 | 0 |
| Pagel | 26 | 149 | 5.7 | 1 |
| Schlichter | 19 | 145 | 7.6 | 1 |
| P. Smith | 2 | -10 | -5.0 | 0 |
| Stark | 2 | 0 | 0.0 | 0 |

### RECEIVING

| Last Name | No. | Yds | Avg | TD |
|---|---|---|---|---|
| Butler | 43 | 664 | 15.4 | 6 |
| Porter | 39 | 590 | 15.1 | 2 |
| Bouza | 22 | 270 | 12.3 | 0 |
| McMillan | 19 | 201 | 10.6 | 0 |
| Middleton | 15 | 112 | 7.5 | 1 |
| Young | 14 | 164 | 11.7 | 2 |
| Dickey | 14 | 135 | 9.6 | 0 |
| Henry | 11 | 139 | 12.6 | 2 |
| Sherwin | 11 | 169 | 15.4 | 0 |
| Moore | 9 | 52 | 5.8 | 0 |
| Wonsley | 9 | 47 | 5.2 | 0 |

### PUNT RETURNS

| Last Name | No. | Yds | Avg | TD |
|---|---|---|---|---|
| L. Anderson | 27 | 182 | 6.7 | 0 |
| Glasgow | 7 | 79 | 11.3 | 0 |
| Bouza | 3 | 17 | 5.7 | 0 |
| Padjen | 1 | 0 | 0.0 | 0 |

### KICKOFF RETURNS

| Last Name | No. | Yds | Avg | TD |
|---|---|---|---|---|
| L. Anderson | 22 | 525 | 23.9 | 0 |
| P. Smith | 32 | 651 | 20.3 | 1 |
| Kafentzis | 5 | 69 | 13.8 | 0 |
| Wonsley | 4 | 52 | 13.0 | 0 |
| Moore | 2 | 19 | 9.5 | 0 |
| Hathaway | 1 | 2 | 2.0 | 0 |
| Radachowsky | 1 | 0 | 0.0 | 0 |
| Middleton | 1 | 11 | 11.0 | 0 |
| Sherwin | 1 | 2 | 2.0 | 0 |

### PASSING — PUNTING — KICKING

| PASSING | Att | Cmp | % | Yds | Yd/Att | TD | Int- | % | RK |
|---|---|---|---|---|---|---|---|---|---|
| Pagel | 212 | 114 | 54 | 1426 | 6.73 | 8 | 8- | 4 | 14 |
| Schlichter | 140 | 62 | 44 | 702 | 5.01 | 3 | 7- | 5 | |
| Herman | 56 | 29 | 52 | 352 | 6.30 | 1 | 6- | 11 | |
| Dickey | 1 | 1 | 100 | 63 | 63.0 | 1 | 0- | 0 | |

| PUNTING | No. | Avg |
|---|---|---|
| Stark | 98 | 44.7 |

| KICKING | XP | Att | % | FG | Att | % |
|---|---|---|---|---|---|---|
| Allegre | 14 | 14 | 100 | 11 | 18 | 61 |
| Biasucci | 13 | 14 | 93 | 3 | 5 | 60 |

## BUFFALO BILLS

### RUSHING

| Last Name | No. | Yds | Avg | TD |
|---|---|---|---|---|
| Bell | 262 | 1100 | 4.2 | 7 |
| Neal | 49 | 175 | 3.6 | 1 |
| Ferguson | 19 | 102 | 5.4 | 0 |
| Moore | 24 | 84 | 3.5 | 0 |
| Kofler | 10 | 80 | 8.0 | 0 |
| V. Williams | 18 | 51 | 2.8 | 0 |
| Brookins | 2 | 27 | 13.5 | 0 |
| Dufek | 9 | 22 | 2.4 | 1 |
| Hunter | 1 | 6 | 6.0 | 0 |
| Riddick | 3 | 3 | 1.0 | 0 |
| Franklin | 1 | -7 | -7.0 | 0 |

### RECEIVING

| Last Name | No. | Yds | Avg | TD |
|---|---|---|---|---|
| Franklin | 69 | 862 | 12.5 | 4 |
| Bell | 34 | 277 | 8.1 | 1 |
| Hunter | 33 | 331 | 10.0 | 2 |
| Moore | 33 | 172 | 5.2 | 0 |
| Dennard | 30 | 417 | 13.9 | 7 |
| Riddick | 23 | 276 | 12.0 | 0 |
| Dawkins | 21 | 295 | 14.1 | 2 |
| Brookins | 18 | 318 | 17.7 | 1 |
| Neal | 9 | 76 | 8.4 | 0 |
| Barnett | 8 | 67 | 8.4 | 0 |
| Bramer | 7 | 49 | 7.0 | 0 |
| V. Williams | 5 | 46 | 9.2 | 1 |
| White | 4 | 28 | 7.0 | 0 |
| Mosley | 4 | 38 | 9.5 | 0 |

### PUNT RETURNS

| Last Name | No. | Yds | Avg | TD |
|---|---|---|---|---|
| Wilson | 33 | 297 | 9.0 | 1 |

### KICKOFF RETURNS

| Last Name | No. | Yds | Avg | TD |
|---|---|---|---|---|
| V. Williams | 39 | 820 | 21.0 | 0 |
| Wilson | 34 | 576 | 16.9 | 0 |
| Bell | 1 | 15 | 15.0 | 0 |
| David | 1 | 6 | 6.0 | 0 |
| White | 1 | 5 | 5.0 | 0 |

### PASSING — PUNTING — KICKING

| PASSING | Att | Cmp | % | Yds | Yd/Att | TD | Int- | % | RK |
|---|---|---|---|---|---|---|---|---|---|
| Ferguson | 344 | 191 | 56 | 1991 | 5.79 | 12 | 17- | 5 | 18 |
| Dufek | 150 | 74 | 49 | 829 | 5.53 | 4 | 8- | 5 | |
| Kofler | 93 | 33 | 36 | 432 | 4.65 | 2 | 5- | 5 | |
| Mosley | 1 | 0 | 0 | 0 | 0.0 | 0 | 0- | 0 | |

| PUNTING | No. | Avg |
|---|---|---|
| Kidd | 88 | 42.0 |

| KICKING | XP | Att | % | FG | Att | % |
|---|---|---|---|---|---|---|
| Danelo | 17 | 17 | 100 | 8 | 16 | 50 |
| Nelson | 14 | 14 | 100 | 3 | 5 | 60 |

**PITTSBURGH STEELERS** 9-7-0 Chuck Noll

| Scores of Each Game | | |
|---|---|---|
| 27 | KANSAS CITY | 37 |
| 23 | N.Y.Jets | 17 |
| 24 | L.A.RAMS | 14 |
| 10 | Cleveland | 20 |
| 38 | CINCINNATI | 17 |
| 7 | MIAMI | 31 |
| 20 | San Francisco | 17 |
| 16 | Indianapolis | 17 |
| 35 | ATLANTA | 10 |
| 35 | HOUSTON | 7 |
| 20 | Cincinnati | 22 |
| 24 | New Orleans | 27 |
| 52 | SAN DIEGO | 24 |
| 20 | Houston | *23 |
| 23 | CLEVELAND | 20 |
| 13 | L.A.Raiders | 7 |

| Use Name | Pos. | Hgt | Wgt | Age | Int | Pts |
|---|---|---|---|---|---|---|
| Steve August (from SEA) | OT | 6'5" | 258 | 29 | | |
| Larry Brown | OT | 6'4" | 270 | 35 | | |
| Mark Catano | OT | 6'3" | 265 | 22 | | |
| Tunch Ilkin | OT | 6'3" | 253 | 26 | | |
| Pete Rostosky | OT | 6'4" | 255 | 23 | | |
| Terry Long | OG | 5'11" | 272 | 25 | | |
| Ray Snell | OG | 6'4" | 265 | 26 | | |
| Blake Wingle | OG | 6'2" | 267 | 24 | | |
| Craig Wolfley | OG | 6'1" | 255 | 26 | | |
| Emil Boures | C-OG | 6'1" | 261 | 24 | | |
| Randy Rasmussen | C-OG | 6'2" | 253 | 23 | | |
| Mike Webster | C | 6'1" | 250 | 32 | | |
| Keith Gary | DE | 6'3" | 260 | 24 | | |
| John Goodman | DE | 6'6" | 255 | 25 | | |
| Keith Willis | DE | 6'1" | 260 | 25 | | |
| Gary Dunn | NT | 6'3" | 265 | 31 | | |
| Edmund Nelson | NT-DE | 6'3" | 270 | 24 | | |
| Craig Bingham | LB | 6'2" | 220 | 24 | | |
| Robin Cole | LB | 6'2" | 225 | 28 | 1 | |
| Terry Echols | LB | 6' | 220 | 22 | | |
| Bryan Hinkle | LB | 6'2" | 220 | 25 | 3 | 6 |
| Bob Kohrs | LB | 6'3" | 235 | 25 | | |
| Jack Lambert | LB | 6'4" | 220 | 32 | | |
| David Little | LB | 6'1" | 230 | 25 | | |
| Mike Merriweather | LB | 6'2" | 215 | 23 | 2 | |
| Todd Seabaugh | LB | 6'4" | 225 | 23 | | |
| Chris Brown | DB | 6' | 195 | 22 | 1 | |
| Harvey Clayton | DB | 5'9" | 180 | 23 | 1 | |
| Ron Johnson | DB | 5'10" | 200 | 28 | | |
| Donnie Shell | DB | 5'11" | 190 | 32 | 7 | 6 |
| Sam Washington | DB | 5'8" | 180 | 24 | 6 | 12 |
| Eric Williams | DB | 6'1" | 183 | 24 | 3 | |
| Robert Williams | DB | 5'11" | 202 | 21 | | |
| Dwayne Woodruff | DB | 6' | 198 | 27 | 5 | 12 |
| Rick Woods | DB | 6' | 191 | 24 | 2 | |
| Scott Campbell | QB | 6' | 201 | 22 | | |
| Mark Malone | QB | 6'4" | 218 | 25 | | 18 |
| David Woodley | QB | 6'2" | 204 | 25 | | |
| Walter Abercrombie | HB | 6' | 210 | 24 | | 6 |
| Rich Erenberg | HB | 5'10" | 200 | 22 | | 18 |
| Fernandars Gillespie | HB | 5'10" | 185 | 22 | | |
| Todd Spenser | HB | 6' | 200 | 22 | | |
| Anthony Corley | FB | 6' | 210 | 24 | | |
| Frank Pollard | FB | 5'10" | 218 | 27 | | 36 |
| Elton Veals | FB | 5'11" | 230 | 23 | | |
| Wayne Capers | WR | 6'2" | 193 | 23 | | |
| Gregg Garrity (to PHI) | WR | 5'10" | 171 | 23 | | |
| Louis Lipps | WR | 5'10" | 190 | 22 | | 66 |
| John Stallworth | WR | 6'2" | 191 | 32 | | 66 |
| Calvin Sweeney | WR | 6'2" | 190 | 29 | | |
| Weegie Thompson | WR | 6'6" | 210 | 23 | | 18 |
| Bennie Cunningham | TE | 6'4" | 255 | 29 | | 6 |
| Chris Kolodziejski | TE | 6'3" | 231 | 23 | | |
| Darrell Nelson | TE | 6'2" | 235 | 22 | | |
| John Rodgers | TE | 6'2" | 238 | 24 | | |
| Gary Anderson | K | 5'11" | 170 | 25 | | 117 |
| Craig Colquitt | K | 6'2" | 182 | 30 | | |

**CINCINNATI BENGALS** 8-8-0 Sam Wyche

| Scores of Each Game | | |
|---|---|---|
| 17 | Denver | 20 |
| 22 | KANSAS CITY | 27 |
| 23 | N.Y.Jets | 43 |
| 14 | L.A.RAMS | 24 |
| 17 | Pittsburgh | 38 |
| 13 | HOUSTON | 3 |
| 14 | New England | 20 |
| 12 | CLEVELAND | 9 |
| 31 | Houston | 13 |
| 17 | San Francisco | 23 |
| 22 | PITTSBURGH | 20 |
| 6 | SEATTLE | 26 |
| 35 | ATLANTA | 14 |
| 20 | Cleveland | *17 |
| 24 | New Orleans | 21 |
| 52 | BUFFALO | 21 |

| Use Name | Pos. | Hgt | Wgt | Age | Int | Pts |
|---|---|---|---|---|---|---|
| Brain Blados | OT | 6'4" | 295 | 22 | | |
| Anthony Munoz | OT | 6'6" | 278 | 26 | | 6 |
| Bruce Reimers | OT | 6'7" | 280 | 23 | | |
| Mike Wilson | OT | 6'5" | 271 | 29 | | |
| Max Montoya | OG | 6'5" | 275 | 28 | | |
| Gary Smith | OG | 6'2" | 265 | 24 | | |
| Bruce Kozerski | C | 6'4" | 275 | 22 | | |
| Dave Rimington | C | 6'3" | 288 | 22 | | |
| Ross Browner | DE | 6'3" | 261 | 30 | | |
| Glen Collins | DE | 6'6" | 265 | 25 | | |
| Eddie Edwards | DE | 6'5" | 256 | 30 | | |
| Jerry Boyarsky | NT | 6'3" | 290 | 25 | | |
| Pete Koch | NT | 6'6" | 265 | 22 | | |
| Tim Krumrie | NT | 6'2" | 262 | 24 | | |
| Leo Barker | LB | 6'1" | 221 | 24 | | |
| Glenn Cameron | LB | 6'2" | 228 | 31 | 1 | |
| Guy Frazier | LB | 6'2" | 221 | 25 | | |
| Steve Maidlow | LB | 6'2" | 234 | 24 | | |
| Brian Pillman | LB | 5'10" | 228 | 22 | | |
| Rick Razzano | LB | 5'11" | 227 | 28 | | |
| Jeff Schuh | LB | 6'2" | 228 | 26 | 1 | |
| Ron Simpkins | LB | 6'1" | 235 | 26 | | |
| Reggie Williams | LB | 6'1" | 228 | 29 | 2 | |
| Ralph Battle | DB | 6'2" | 205 | 23 | | |
| Louis Breeden | DB | 5'11" | 185 | 30 | 4 | |
| James Griffin | DB | 6'2" | 197 | 22 | 1 | 6 |
| Ray Griffin | DB | 5'10" | 186 | 28 | 2 | |
| Ray Horton | DB | 5'11" | 190 | 24 | 3 | 6 |
| Robert Jackson | DB | 5'10" | 184 | 25 | 4 | 6 |
| Bobby Kemp | DB | 6' | 191 | 25 | 4 | |
| John Simmons | DB | 5'11" | 192 | 25 | 2 | 6 |
| Jimmy Turner | DB | 6' | 187 | 25 | 1 | |
| Ken Anderson | QB | 6'1" | 212 | 35 | | |
| Bryan Clark | QB | 6'2" | 196 | 24 | | |
| Boomer Esiason | QB | 6'4" | 220 | 23 | | 12 |
| Turk Schonert | QB | 6'1" | 190 | 27 | | 6 |
| James Brooks | HB | 5'10" | 182 | 25 | | 24 |
| John Farley | HB | 5'10" | 202 | 23 | | |
| Stanford Jennings | HB | 6'1" | 205 | 22 | | 30 |
| Stanley Wilson | HB-FB | 5'10" | 210 | 23 | | |
| Charles Alexander | FB | 6'1" | 226 | 27 | | 12 |
| Larry Kinnebrew | FB | 6'1" | 252 | 25 | | 60 |
| Cris Collinsworth | WR | 6'5" | 192 | 25 | | 36 |
| Isaac Curtis | WR | 6' | 192 | 33 | | |
| Steve Kreider | WR | 6'3" | 192 | 26 | | 6 |
| Mike Martin | WR | 5'10" | 186 | 23 | | |
| Clay Pickering | WR | 6'5" | 215 | 23 | | |
| David Verser | WR | 6'1" | 200 | 26 | | |
| Gary Williams | WR | 6'2" | 215 | 24 | | |
| M.L.Harris | TE | 6'5" | 238 | 30 | | 12 |
| Rodney Holman | TE | 6'3" | 230 | 24 | | 6 |
| Don Kern | TE | 6'4" | 225 | 22 | | |
| Jim Breech | K | 5'6" | 161 | 28 | | 103 |
| Pat McInally | K | 6'6" | 212 | 31 | | |

Mike Obrovac - Knee Injury

**CLEVELAND BROWNS** 5-11-0 Sam Rutigliano, Marty Schottenheimer

| Scores of Each Game | | |
|---|---|---|
| 0 | Seattle | 33 |
| 17 | L.A.RAMS | 20 |
| 14 | Denver | 24 |
| 20 | PITTSBURGH | 10 |
| 6 | Kansas City | 10 |
| 16 | NEW ENGLAND | 17 |
| 20 | N.Y.JETS | 24 |
| 9 | Cincinnati | 12 |
| 14 | NEW ORLEANS | 16 |
| 13 | Buffalo | 10 |
| 7 | SAN FRANCISCO | 41 |
| 23 | Atlanta | 7 |
| 27 | HOUSTON | 10 |
| 17 | CINCINNATI | 20 |
| 20 | Pittsburgh | *23 |
| 27 | Houston | 20 |

| Use Name | Pos. | Hgt | Wgt | Age | Int | Pts |
|---|---|---|---|---|---|---|
| Bill Contz | OT | 6'5" | 260 | 23 | | |
| Doug Dieken | OT | 6'5" | 252 | 35 | | |
| Paul Farren | OT | 6'5" | 260 | 23 | | |
| Robert Sikora | OT | 6'8" | 285 | 22 | | |
| Joe DeLamielleure | OG | 6'3" | 260 | 33 | | |
| Robert Jackson | OG | 6'5" | 260 | 31 | | |
| Mike Baab | C | 6'4" | 270 | 24 | | |
| Tom DeLeone | C | 6'2" | 254 | 34 | | |
| Keith Baldwin | DE | 6'4" | 270 | 23 | | |
| Reggie Camp | DE | 6'4" | 270 | 23 | | |
| Elvis Franks | DE | 6'4" | 265 | 27 | | |
| Carl Hairston | DE | 6'3" | 260 | 31 | | |
| Bob Golic | NT | 6'2" | 260 | 26 | | |
| Dave Puzzuoli | NT | 6'3" | 260 | 23 | | |
| Stuart Anderson (from WAS) | LB | 6'1" | 224 | 24 | | |
| Chip Banks | LB | 6'4" | 233 | 24 | 1 | |
| Tom Cousineau | LB | 6'3" | 225 | 27 | 2 | |
| Jim Dumont | LB | 6'1" | 224 | 23 | | |
| Eddie Johnson | LB | 6'1" | 215 | 25 | 2 | |
| David Marshall | LB | 6'3" | 220 | 23 | | |
| Clay Matthews | LB | 6'2" | 235 | 28 | | |
| Scott Nicolas | LB | 6'3" | 226 | 24 | | |
| Curtis Weathers | LB | 6'5" | 230 | 27 | | |
| Greg Best | DB | 5'10" | 185 | 24 | | |
| Larry Braziel | DB | 6' | 184 | 29 | | |
| Clinton Burrell | DB | 6'2" | 192 | 27 | | |
| Hanford Dixon | DB | 5'11" | 182 | 25 | 5 | |
| Al Gross | DB | 6'3" | 186 | 23 | 5 | |
| Frank Minnifield | DB | 5'9" | 180 | 24 | 1 | |
| Chris Rockins | DB | 6' | 195 | 22 | 1 | |
| Don Rogers | DB | 6'1" | 206 | 21 | 1 | |
| Tom Flick | QB | 6'3" | 190 | 26 | | |
| Paul McDonald | QB | 6'2" | 185 | 26 | | 6 |
| Terry Nugent | QB | 6'4" | 218 | 22 | | |
| James Black | HB | 5'11" | 198 | 22 | | |
| Dwight Walker | HB | 5'10" | 185 | 25 | | |
| Charles White | HB | 5'10" | 190 | 26 | | |
| Earnest Byner | FB | 5'10" | 215 | 21 | | 18 |
| Johnny Davis | FB | 6'1" | 235 | 28 | | 6 |
| Boyce Green | FB | 5'11" | 215 | 24 | | 6 |
| Mike Pruitt | FB | 6' | 225 | 30 | | 36 |
| Willis Adams | WR | 6'2" | 200 | 28 | | |
| Brian Brennan | WR | 5'9" | 178 | 22 | | 18 |
| Preston Brown | WR | 5'11" | 187 | 26 | | |
| Bruce Davis | WR | 5'8" | 160 | 21 | | 125 |
| Ricky Feacher | WR | 5'10" | 180 | 30 | | 6 |
| Duriel Harris (to DAL) | WR | 5'11" | 184 | 29 | | 12 |
| Glen Young | WR | 6'2" | 205 | 23 | | |
| Ricky Bolden | TE | 6'6" | 250 | 22 | | |
| Harry Holt | TE | 6'4" | 230 | 26 | | |
| Darryl Lewis | TE | 6'6" | 232 | 23 | | |
| Ozzie Newsome | TE | 6'2" | 232 | 28 | | 30 |
| Tim Stracka | TE | 6'3" | 225 | 24 | | |
| Matt Bahr | K | 5'10" | 175 | 28 | | 97 |
| Steve Cox | K | 6'4" | 195 | 26 | | 3 |

Cody Risien - Knee Injury
Mike Whitwell - Knee Injury
Dick Ambrose - Ankle Injury

**HOUSTON OILERS** 3-13-0 Hugh Campbell

| Scores of Each Game | | |
|---|---|---|
| 14 | L.A.RAIDERS | 24 |
| 21 | INDIANAPOLIS | 35 |
| 14 | San Diego | 31 |
| 10 | Atlanta | 42 |
| 10 | NEW ORLEANS | 27 |
| 3 | Cincinnati | 13 |
| 10 | Miami | 28 |
| 21 | SAN FRANCISCO | 34 |
| 13 | CINCINNATI | 31 |
| 7 | Pittsburgh | 35 |
| 17 | Kansas City | 16 |
| 31 | N.Y.JETS | 20 |
| 10 | Cleveland | 27 |
| 23 | PITTSBURGH | *20 |
| 16 | L.A.Rams | 27 |
| 20 | CLEVELAND | 27 |

| Use Name | Pos. | Hgt | Wgt | Age | Int | Pts |
|---|---|---|---|---|---|---|
| Eric Moran | OT | 6'5" | 280 | 24 | | |
| Harvey Salem | OT | 6'6" | 285 | 23 | | |
| Dean Steinkuhler | OT | 6'3" | 273 | 23 | | |
| Pat Howell | OG | 6'5" | 265 | 27 | | |
| Mike Munchak | OG | 6'3" | 286 | 24 | | |
| John Schuhmacher | OG | 6'3" | 277 | 28 | | |
| Bruce Matthews | C | 6'4" | 280 | 23 | | |
| Jim Romano (from RAID) | C | 6'3" | 255 | 24 | | |
| Jesse Baker | DE | 6'5" | 272 | 27 | | |
| Bryan Caldwell | DE | 6'4" | 248 | 24 | | |
| Jerome Foster | DE | 6'2" | 263 | 24 | | |
| Bob Hamm | DE | 6'4" | 263 | 25 | | |
| Mike Johnson | DE | 6'5" | 253 | 22 | | |
| Mark Studaway | DE | 6'3" | 269 | 23 | | |
| Brian Sochia | NT | 6'3" | 254 | 23 | | |
| Mike Stensrud | NT | 6'5" | 280 | 28 | | |
| Robert Abraham | LB | 6'1" | 230 | 24 | 1 | |
| Gregg Bingham | LB | 6'1" | 232 | 33 | | |
| Robert Brazile | LB | 6'4" | 253 | 31 | 1 | |
| John Grimsley | LB | 6'2" | 232 | 22 | | |
| Daryl Hunt | LB | 6'3" | 239 | 27 | | |
| Tim Joiner | LB | 6'4" | 248 | 23 | | |
| Robert Lyles | LB | 6'1" | 223 | 23 | | |
| Johnny Meads | LB | 6'2" | 225 | 23 | | |
| Avon Riley | LB | 6'3" | 236 | 25 | | |
| Ted Thompson | LB | 6'1" | 218 | 31 | | |
| Patrick Allen | DB | 5'10" | 173 | 23 | 1 | |
| Keith Bostic | DB | 6'1" | 212 | 23 | | 6 |
| Steve Brown | DB | 5'11" | 188 | 24 | 1 | |
| Jeff Donaldson | DB | 6' | 193 | 22 | | |
| Bo Eason | DB | 6'2" | 200 | 23 | 1 | |
| Carter Hartwig | DB | 6' | 210 | 28 | 3 | |
| Mike Kennedy | DB | 6' | 195 | 25 | | |
| Allen Lyday | DB | 5'10" | 186 | 23 | 1 | |
| Darryl Meadows | DB | 6'1" | 199 | 23 | | |
| Willie Tullis | DB | 6' | 195 | 26 | 4 | |
| Oliver Luck | QB | 6'2" | 198 | 24 | | 6 |
| Warren Moon | QB | 6'3" | 208 | 27 | | 6 |
| Brian Ransom | QB | 6'3" | 202 | 24 | | |
| Willie Joyner | HB | 5'10" | 200 | 22 | | |
| Richard Williams (from ATL) | HB | 6' | 205 | 24 | | |
| Donnie Craft | FB | 6' | 205 | 24 | | |
| Stan Edwards | FB | 6' | 210 | 24 | | 6 |
| Larry Moriarty | FB | 6'1" | 240 | 26 | | 42 |
| Steve Bryant | WR | 6'2" | 197 | 24 | | |
| Mike Holston | WR | 6'3" | 192 | 26 | | 6 |
| Eric Mullins | WR | 5'11" | 181 | 22 | | 6 |
| Carl Roaches | WR | 5'8" | 170 | 30 | | |
| Tim Smith | WR | 6'2" | 206 | 27 | | 24 |
| Herkie Walls | WR | 5'8" | 160 | 23 | | 6 |
| Chris Dressel | TE | 6'4" | 238 | 23 | | 12 |
| Mike McCloskey | TE | 6'5" | 246 | 23 | | 6 |
| Jamie Williams | TE | 6'4" | 232 | 24 | | 18 |
| Joe Cooper | K | 5'10" | 175 | 24 | | 46 |
| John James | K | 6'3" | 196 | 35 | | |
| Florian Kempf | K | 5'9" | 170 | 28 | | 26 |

Doug France - Shoulder Injury

* Overtime

## PITTSBURGH STEELERS

### RUSHING

| Last Name | No. | Yds | Avg | TD |
|---|---|---|---|---|
| Pollard | 213 | 851 | 4.0 | 6 |
| Abercrombie | 145 | 610 | 4.2 | 1 |
| Erenberg | 115 | 405 | 3.5 | 2 |
| Corley | 18 | 89 | 4.9 | 0 |
| Veals | 31 | 87 | 2.8 | 0 |
| Lipps | 3 | 71 | 23.7 | 1 |
| Malone | 25 | 42 | 1.7 | 3 |
| Gillespie | 7 | 18 | 2.6 | 0 |
| Woodley | 11 | 14 | 1.3 | 0 |
| Colquitt | 1 | 0 | 0.0 | 0 |
| Spencer | 1 | 0 | 0.0 | 0 |
| Capers | 1 | -3 | -3.0 | 0 |
| Campbell | 3 | -5 | -1.7 | 0 |

### RECEIVING

| Last Name | No. | Yds | Avg | TD |
|---|---|---|---|---|
| Stallworth | 80 | 1395 | 17.4 | 11 |
| Lipps | 45 | 860 | 19.1 | 9 |
| Erenberg | 38 | 358 | 9.4 | 1 |
| Pollard | 21 | 186 | 8.9 | 0 |
| Thompson | 17 | 291 | 17.1 | 3 |
| Abercrombie | 16 | 135 | 8.4 | 0 |
| Capers | 7 | 81 | 11.6 | 0 |
| Kolodziejski | 5 | 59 | 11.8 | 0 |
| Cunningham | 4 | 64 | 16.0 | 1 |
| D. Nelson | 2 | 31 | 15.5 | 0 |
| Sweeney | 2 | 25 | 12.5 | 0 |
| Garrity | 2 | 22 | 11.0 | 0 |
| Gillespie | 1 | 12 | 12.0 | 0 |

### PUNT RETURNS

| Last Name | No. | Yds | Avg | TD |
|---|---|---|---|---|
| Lipps | 53 | 656 | 12.4 | 1 |
| Woods | 6 | 40 | 6.7 | 0 |
| Clayton | 1 | 0 | 0.0 | 0 |
| Long | 1 | 0 | 0.0 | 0 |

### KICKOFF RETURNS

| Last Name | No. | Yds | Avg | TD |
|---|---|---|---|---|
| Spencer | 18 | 373 | 20.7 | 0 |
| Erenberg | 28 | 575 | 20.5 | 0 |
| Veals | 4 | 40 | 10.0 | 0 |
| C. Brown | 1 | 11 | 11.0 | 0 |
| Catano | 1 | 0 | 0.0 | 0 |
| Corley | 1 | 15 | 15.0 | 0 |
| Gillespie | 1 | 12 | 12.0 | 0 |

### PASSING — PUNTING — KICKING

| PASSING | Att | Cmp | % | Yds | Yd/Att | TD | Int- | % | RK |
|---|---|---|---|---|---|---|---|---|---|
| Malone | 272 | 147 | 54 | 2137 | 7.86 | 16 | 17- | 6 | 9 |
| Woodley | 156 | 85 | 55 | 1273 | 8.16 | 8 | 7- | 5 | 12 |
| Campbell | 15 | 8 | 53 | 109 | 7.27 | 1 | 1- | 7 | |

| PUNTING | No | Avg |
|---|---|---|
| Colquitt | 70 | 41.2 |

| KICKING | XP | Att | % | FG | Att | % |
|---|---|---|---|---|---|---|
| Anderson | 45 | 45 | 100 | 24 | 32 | 75 |

## CINCINNATI BENGALS

### RUSHING

| Last Name | No. | Yds | Avg | TD |
|---|---|---|---|---|
| Kinnebrew | 154 | 623 | 4.0 | 9 |
| Alexander | 132 | 479 | 3.6 | 2 |
| Brooks | 103 | 396 | 3.8 | 2 |
| Jennings | 79 | 379 | 4.8 | 2 |
| Schonert | 13 | 77 | 5.9 | 1 |
| S. Wilson | 17 | 74 | 4.4 | 0 |
| Esiason | 19 | 63 | 3.3 | 2 |
| Anderson | 11 | 64 | 5.8 | 0 |
| Farley | 7 | 11 | 1.6 | 0 |
| Collinsworth | 1 | 7 | 7.0 | 0 |
| Martin | 1 | 3 | 3.0 | 0 |
| Verser | 2 | 5 | 2.5 | 0 |
| Harris | 1 | -2 | -2.0 | 0 |

### RECEIVING

| Last Name | No. | Yds | Avg | TD |
|---|---|---|---|---|
| Collinsworth | 64 | 989 | 15.5 | 6 |
| Harris | 48 | 759 | 15.8 | 2 |
| Jennings | 35 | 346 | 9.9 | 3 |
| Brooks | 34 | 268 | 7.9 | 2 |
| Alexander | 29 | 203 | 7.0 | 0 |
| Holman | 21 | 239 | 11.4 | 1 |
| Kreider | 20 | 243 | 12.2 | 1 |
| Kinnebrew | 19 | 159 | 8.4 | 1 |
| Curtis | 12 | 135 | 11.3 | 0 |
| Martin | 11 | 164 | 14.9 | 0 |
| Kern | 2 | 14 | 7.0 | 0 |
| Verser | 6 | 113 | 18.8 | 0 |
| Farley | 2 | 11 | 5.5 | 0 |
| Wilson | 2 | 15 | 7.5 | 0 |
| Munoz | 1 | 1 | 1.0 | 1 |

### PUNT RETURNS

| Last Name | No. | Yds | Avg | TD |
|---|---|---|---|---|
| Martin | 24 | 376 | 15.7 | 0 |
| Simmons | 12 | 98 | 8.2 | 0 |
| Horton | 2 | -1 | -0.5 | 0 |

### KICKOFF RETURNS

| Last Name | No. | Yds | Avg | TD |
|---|---|---|---|---|
| Jennings | 22 | 452 | 20.5 | 0 |
| Martin | 19 | 386 | 20.3 | 0 |
| Brooks | 7 | 144 | 20.6 | 0 |
| Farley | 6 | 93 | 15.5 | 0 |
| Verser | 3 | 46 | 15.3 | 0 |
| Simmons | 1 | 15 | 15.0 | 0 |
| Kinnebrew | 1 | 7 | 7.0 | 0 |
| Harris | 1 | 12 | 12.0 | 0 |
| Williams | 1 | 0 | 0.0 | 0 |

### PASSING — PUNTING — KICKING

| PASSING | Att | Cmp | % | Yds | Yd/Att | TD | Int- | % | RK |
|---|---|---|---|---|---|---|---|---|---|
| Anderson | 275 | 175 | 64 | 2107 | 7.66 | 10 | 12- | 4 | 7 |
| Schonert | 117 | 78 | 67 | 945 | 8.08 | 4 | 7- | 6 | |
| Esiason | 102 | 51 | 50 | 530 | 5.20 | 3 | 3- | 3 | |
| McInally | 2 | 2 | 100 | 77 | 38.50 | 0 | 0- | 0 | |

| PUNTING | No | Avg |
|---|---|---|
| McInally | 67 | 42.3 |

| KICKING | XP | Att | % | FG | Att | % |
|---|---|---|---|---|---|---|
| Breech | 37 | 37 | 100 | 22 | 31 | 71 |

## CLEVELAND BROWNS

### RUSHING

| Last Name | No. | Yds | Avg | TD |
|---|---|---|---|---|
| Green | 202 | 673 | 3.3 | 0 |
| Pruitt | 163 | 506 | 3.1 | 6 |
| Byner | 72 | 426 | 5.9 | 2 |
| White | 24 | 62 | 2.6 | 0 |
| J. Davis | 3 | 15 | 5.0 | 1 |
| Holt | 1 | 12 | 12.0 | 0 |
| B. Davis | 1 | 6 | 6.0 | 0 |
| McDonald | 22 | 4 | 0.2 | 1 |
| Walker | 1 | -8 | -8.0 | 0 |

### RECEIVING

| Last Name | No. | Yds | Avg | TD |
|---|---|---|---|---|
| Newsome | 89 | 1001 | 11.2 | 5 |
| Brennan | 35 | 455 | 13.0 | 3 |
| Harris | 32 | 512 | 16.0 | 2 |
| Feacher | 22 | 382 | 17.4 | 1 |
| Adams | 21 | 261 | 12.4 | 0 |
| Holt | 20 | 261 | 13.1 | 0 |
| Green | 12 | 124 | 10.3 | 1 |
| Byner | 11 | 118 | 10.7 | 0 |
| Walker | 10 | 122 | 12.2 | 0 |
| B. Davis | 7 | 119 | 17.0 | 2 |
| White | 5 | 29 | 5.8 | 0 |
| Pruitt | 5 | 29 | 5.8 | 0 |
| Young | 1 | 47 | 47.0 | 0 |
| Bolden | 1 | 19 | 19.0 | 0 |
| Stracka | 1 | 15 | 15.0 | 0 |
| McDonald | 1 | 4 | 4.0 | 0 |

### PUNT RETURNS

| Last Name | No. | Yds | Avg | TD |
|---|---|---|---|---|
| Brennan | 29 | 199 | 8.0 | 0 |
| Harris | 9 | 73 | 8.1 | 0 |
| Walker | 6 | 50 | 8.3 | 0 |

### KICKOFF RETURNS

| Last Name | No. | Yds | Avg | TD |
|---|---|---|---|---|
| B. Davis | 18 | 369 | 20.5 | 0 |
| Byner | 22 | 415 | 18.9 | 0 |
| P. Brown | 8 | 136 | 17.0 | 0 |
| Young | 5 | 134 | 26.8 | 0 |
| White | 5 | 80 | 16.0 | 0 |
| Nicolas | 1 | 12 | 12.0 | 0 |
| Contz | 1 | 10 | 10.0 | 0 |
| Holt | 1 | 1 | 1.0 | 0 |

### PASSING — PUNTING — KICKING

| PASSING | Att | Cmp | % | Yds | Yd/Att | TD | Int- | % | RK |
|---|---|---|---|---|---|---|---|---|---|
| McDonald | 493 | 271 | 55 | 3472 | 7.0 | 14 | 23- | 5 | 17 |
| Flick | 1 | 1 | 100 | 2 | 2.0 | 0 | 0- | 0 | |
| Cox | 1 | 1 | 100 | 16 | 16.0 | 0 | 0- | 0 | |

| PUNTING | No | Avg |
|---|---|---|
| Cox | 74 | 43.4 |

| KICKING | XP | Att | % | FG | Att | % |
|---|---|---|---|---|---|---|
| Bahr | 25 | 25 | 100 | 24 | 32 | 75 |
| Cox | 0 | 0 | 0.0 | 1 | 3 | 33 |

## HOUSTON OILERS

### RUSHING

| Last Name | No. | Yds | Avg | TD |
|---|---|---|---|---|
| Moriarty | 189 | 785 | 4.2 | 6 |
| Edwards | 60 | 267 | 4.5 | 1 |
| Moon | 58 | 211 | 3.6 | 1 |
| Luck | 10 | 75 | 7.5 | 1 |
| Walls | 4 | 20 | 5.0 | 0 |
| Joyner | 14 | 22 | 1.6 | 0 |
| Mullins | 1 | 0 | 0.0 | 0 |
| Cooper | 1 | -2 | -2.0 | 0 |

### RECEIVING

| Last Name | No. | Yds | Avg | TD |
|---|---|---|---|---|
| Smith | 69 | 1141 | 16.5 | 4 |
| J. Williams | 41 | 545 | 13.3 | 3 |
| Dressel | 40 | 378 | 9.5 | 2 |
| Moriarty | 31 | 206 | 6.6 | 1 |
| Holston | 22 | 287 | 13.0 | 1 |
| Edwards | 20 | 151 | 7.6 | 0 |
| Bryant | 19 | 278 | 14.6 | 0 |
| Walls | 18 | 291 | 16.2 | 1 |
| McCloskey | 9 | 152 | 16.9 | 1 |
| Mullins | 6 | 85 | 14.2 | 1 |
| Roaches | 4 | 69 | 17.3 | 0 |

### PUNT RETURNS

| Last Name | No. | Yds | Avg | TD |
|---|---|---|---|---|
| Roaches | 26 | 152 | 5.8 | 0 |

### KICKOFF RETURNS

| Last Name | No. | Yds | Avg | TD |
|---|---|---|---|---|
| Roaches | 30 | 679 | 22.6 | 0 |
| Walls | 15 | 289 | 19.3 | 0 |
| Allen | 11 | 210 | 19.1 | 0 |
| R. Williams | 5 | 84 | 16.8 | 0 |
| Joyner | 3 | 57 | 19.0 | 0 |
| Brown | 3 | 17 | 5.7 | 0 |
| Thompson | 1 | 16 | 16.0 | 0 |
| J. Williams | 1 | 0 | 0.0 | 0 |

### PASSING — PUNTING — KICKING

| PASSING | Att | Cmp | % | Yds | Yd/Att | TD | Int- | % | RK |
|---|---|---|---|---|---|---|---|---|---|
| Moon | 450 | 259 | 58 | 3338 | 7.42 | 12 | 14- | 3 | 8 |
| Luck | 36 | 22 | 61 | 256 | 7.11 | 2 | 1- | 3 | |
| Moriarty | 1 | 1 | 100 | 16 | 16.0 | 0 | 0- | 0 | |

| PUNTING | No | Avg |
|---|---|---|
| James | 88 | 39.6 |

| KICKING | XP | Att | % | FG | Att | % |
|---|---|---|---|---|---|---|
| Cooper | 13 | 13 | 100 | 11 | 13 | 85 |
| Kempf | 14 | 14 | 100 | 4 | 6 | 67 |

## DENVER BRONCOS 13-3-0 Dan Reeves

| Scores of Each Game | | |
|---|---|---|
| 20 | CINCINNATI | 17 |
| 0 | Chicago | 27 |
| 24 | Cleveland | 14 |
| 21 | KANSAS CITY | 0 |
| 16 | L.A.RAIDERS | 13 |
| 28 | Detroit | 7 |
| 17 | GREEN BAY | 14 |
| 37 | Buffalo | 7 |
| 22 | L.A.Raiders | *19 |
| 26 | NEW ENGLAND | 19 |
| 16 | San Diego | 13 |
| 42 | MINNESOTA | 21 |
| 24 | SEATTLE | 27 |
| 13 | Kansas City | 16 |
| 16 | SAN DIEGO | 13 |
| 31 | Seattle | 14 |

| Use Name | Pos. | Hgt | Wgt | Age | Int | Pts |
|---|---|---|---|---|---|---|
| Mark Cooper | OT | 6'5" | 267 | 24 | | |
| Marsharne Graves | OT | 6'4" | 272 | 22 | | |
| Ken Lanier | OT | 6'3" | 269 | 25 | | |
| Dave Studdard | OT | 6'4" | 260 | 28 | | |
| Mike Freeman | OG | 6'3" | 256 | 22 | | |
| Winford Hood | OG | 6'3" | 262 | 22 | | |
| Paul Howard | OG | 6'3" | 260 | 33 | | |
| Keith Bishop | C-OG | 6'3" | 265 | 27 | | |
| Bill Bryan | C | 6'2" | 255 | 28 | | |
| Walt Bowyer | DE | 6'4" | 252 | 23 | | |
| Barney Chavous | DE | 6'3" | 258 | 33 | | |
| Rulon Jones | DE | 6'6" | 260 | 26 | | |
| Andre Townsend | DE-NT | 6'3" | 265 | 21 | | |
| Rubin Carter | NT | 6' | 256 | 31 | | |
| Scott Garnett | NT | 6'2" | 271 | 21 | | |

Bob Swenson - Knee Injury
Wilbur Myers - Knee Injury

| Use Name | Pos. | Hgt | Wgt | Age | Int | Pts |
|---|---|---|---|---|---|---|
| Steve Busick | LB | 6'4" | 227 | 25 | 2 | |
| Darren Comeaux | LB | 6'1" | 227 | 24 | 1 | |
| Rick Dennison | LB | 6'3" | 220 | 26 | | |
| Ricky Hunley | LB | 6'2" | 238 | 22 | | |
| Tom Jackson | LB | 5'11" | 220 | 33 | | |
| Karl Mecklenburg | LB | 6'3" | 250 | 24 | 2 | |
| Jim Ryan | LB | 6'1" | 215 | 27 | 1 | |
| Aaron Smith | LB | 6'2" | 223 | 22 | | |
| Ken Woodard | LB | 6'1" | 218 | 24 | 1 | 6 |
| Steve Foley | DB | 6'2" | 190 | 30 | 6 | 12 |
| Mike Harden | DB | 6'1" | 192 | 26 | 6 | 6 |
| Roger Jackson | DB | 6' | 186 | 25 | 1 | |
| Tony Lilly | DB | 6' | 199 | 22 | 1 | |
| Randy Robbins | DB | 6'2" | 189 | 21 | 2 | 6 |
| Dennis Smith | DB | 6'3" | 200 | 25 | 3 | 6 |
| Steve Wilson | DB | 5'10" | 195 | 27 | 4 | |
| Louis Wright | DB | 6'2" | 200 | 31 | 1 | 6 |

| Use Name | Pos. | Hgt | Wgt | Age | Int | Pts |
|---|---|---|---|---|---|---|
| John Elway | QB | 6'3" | 202 | 24 | | 6 |
| Gary Kubiak | QB | 6' | 192 | 23 | | 6 |
| Scott Stankavage | QB | 6'1" | 192 | 22 | | |
| Chris Brewer | HB | 6'1" | 193 | 22 | | |
| Gene Lang | HB | 5'10" | 196 | 22 | | 18 |
| Sammy Winder | HB | 5'11" | 203 | 25 | | 36 |
| Jesse Myles | FB-HB | 5'10" | 210 | 23 | | |
| Rick Parros | FB | 5'11" | 200 | 26 | | 12 |
| Gerald Willhite | FB | 5'10" | 200 | 25 | | 12 |
| Ray Alexander | WR | 6'4" | 195 | 22 | | 6 |
| Butch Johnson | WR | 6'1" | 187 | 30 | | 36 |
| Dave Logan | WR | 6'4" | 216 | 30 | | |
| Clint Sampson | WR | 5'11" | 183 | 23 | | 6 |
| Zach Thomas (to TB) | WR | 6' | 182 | 23 | | |
| Steve Watson | WR | 6'4" | 195 | 27 | | 42 |
| Clarence Kay | TE | 6'2" | 237 | 23 | | 18 |
| John Sawyer | TE | 6'2" | 230 | 31 | | |
| Don Summers | TE | 6'4" | 226 | 23 | | |
| James Wright | TE | 6'3" | 240 | 28 | | 6 |
| Rich Karlis | K | 6' | 180 | 25 | | 101 |
| Chris Norman | K | 6'2" | 198 | 22 | | |

## SEATTLE SEAHAWKS 12-4-0 Chuck Knox

| Scores of Each Game | | |
|---|---|---|
| 33 | CLEVELAND | 0 |
| 31 | SAN DIEGO | 17 |
| 23 | New England | 38 |
| 38 | CHICAGO | 9 |
| 20 | Minnesota | 12 |
| 14 | L.A.Raiders | 28 |
| 31 | BUFFALO | 28 |
| 30 | Green Bay | 24 |
| 24 | San Diego | 0 |
| 45 | KANSAS CITY | 0 |
| 17 | L.A.RAIDERS | 14 |
| 26 | Cincinnati | 6 |
| 27 | Denver | 24 |
| 38 | DETROIT | 17 |
| 7 | Kansas City | 34 |
| 14 | DENVER | 31 |

| Use Name | Pos. | Hgt | Wgt | Age | Int | Pts |
|---|---|---|---|---|---|---|
| Sid Abramowitz | OT-OG | 6'6" | 279 | 24 | | |
| Ron Essink | OT | 6'6" | 275 | 26 | | |
| Brian Millard | OT | 6'5" | 284 | 24 | | |
| Edwin Bailey | OG | 6'4" | 265 | 25 | | |
| Bob Cryder | OG | 6'4" | 282 | 27 | | |
| Reggie McKenzie | OG | 6'4" | 255 | 34 | | |
| Robert Pratt | OG | 6'4" | 250 | 33 | | |
| Adam Schreiber | OG | 6'4" | 280 | 22 | | |
| Blair Bush | C | 6'3" | 252 | 27 | | |
| Kani Kauahi | C | 6'2" | 260 | 24 | | |
| Jeff Bryant | DE | 6'5" | 270 | 24 | 1 | 2 |
| Jacob Green | DE | 6'3" | 255 | 27 | | |
| Randy Edwards | NT | 6'4" | 255 | 23 | | |
| Mike Fanning | NT | 6'6" | 255 | 31 | | |
| Dino Mangiero | NT | 6'2" | 270 | 25 | | |
| Joe Nash | NT | 6'2" | 250 | 23 | | 6 |

Mark Hicks - Knee Injury
Eugene Williams - Stress Fracture of Leg
Joe Norman - Knee Injury

| Use Name | Pos. | Hgt | Wgt | Age | Int | Pts |
|---|---|---|---|---|---|---|
| Chuck Butler | LB | 6' | 220 | 22 | | |
| Keith Butler | LB | 6'4" | 238 | 28 | | |
| Greg Gaines | LB | 6'3" | 220 | 25 | 1 | |
| Michael Jackson | LB | 6'1" | 220 | 27 | | |
| John Kaiser | LB | 6'3" | 221 | 22 | | |
| Sam Merriman | LB | 6'3" | 225 | 23 | | |
| Shelton Robinson | LB | 6'2" | 233 | 23 | | |
| Bruce Scholtz | LB | 6'6" | 240 | 25 | 1 | |
| Fredd Young | LB | 6'1" | 225 | 22 | | |
| Dave Brown | DB | 6'1" | 190 | 31 | 8 | 12 |
| Don Dufek | DB | 6' | 195 | 30 | | |
| Kenny Easley | DB | 6'3" | 206 | 25 | 10 | 12 |
| John Harris | DB | 6'2" | 200 | 28 | 6 | |
| Terry Jackson | DB | 5'10" | 197 | 28 | 4 | 6 |
| Paul Moyer | DB | 6'1" | 201 | 23 | | |
| Keith Simpson | DB | 6'1" | 195 | 28 | 4 | 12 |
| Terry Taylor | DB | 5'10" | 175 | 23 | 3 | |
| Ray Wilmer | DB | 6'2" | 190 | 22 | | |

| Use Name | Pos. | Hgt | Wgt | Age | Int | Pts |
|---|---|---|---|---|---|---|
| Dave Kreig | QB | 6'1" | 185 | 25 | | 18 |
| Jim Zorn | QB | 6'2" | 200 | 31 | | |
| Zachary Dixon | HB | 6'1" | 204 | 27 | | 12 |
| Eric Lane | HB | 6' | 195 | 25 | | 30 |
| Randall Morris | HB | 6' | 190 | 23 | | |
| Curt Warner | HB | 5'11" | 205 | 23 | | |
| Cullen Bryant | FB | 6'1" | 236 | 33 | | |
| Dan Doornink | FB | 6'3" | 210 | 28 | | 12 |
| Franco Harris | FB | 6'2" | 225 | 34 | | |
| David Hughes | FB | 6' | 220 | 25 | | 12 |
| Chris Castor | WR | 6' | 170 | 24 | | |
| Paul Johns | WR | 5'11" | 180 | 25 | | 12 |
| Steve Largent | WR | 5'11" | 184 | 29 | | 72 |
| Dwight Scales | WR | 6'2" | 182 | 31 | | |
| Paul Skansi | WR | 5'11" | 190 | 23 | | |
| Daryl Turner | WR | 6'3" | 198 | 22 | | 60 |
| Bryon Walker | WR | 6'4" | 190 | 24 | | 6 |
| Pete Metzelaars | TE | 6'7" | 240 | 24 | | |
| Mike Tice | TE | 6'7" | 250 | 25 | | 18 |
| Charle Young | TE | 6'4" | 234 | 33 | | 6 |
| Norm Johnson | K | 6'2" | 193 | 24 | | 110 |
| Jeff West | K | 6'3" | 205 | 31 | | |

## LOS ANGELES RAIDERS 11-5-0 Tom Flores

| Scores of Each Game | | |
|---|---|---|
| 24 | Houston | 14 |
| 28 | GREEN BAY | 7 |
| 22 | Kansas City | 20 |
| 33 | SAN DIEGO | 30 |
| 13 | Denver | 16 |
| 28 | SEATTLE | 14 |
| 23 | MINNESOTA | 20 |
| 44 | San Diego | 37 |
| 19 | DENVER | *22 |
| 6 | Chicago | 17 |
| 14 | Seattle | 17 |
| 17 | KANSAS CITY | 7 |
| 21 | INDIANAPOLIS | 7 |
| 42 | Miami | 34 |
| 24 | Detroit | 3 |
| 7 | PITTSBURGH | 13 |

| Use Name | Pos. | Hgt | Wgt | Age | Int | Pts |
|---|---|---|---|---|---|---|
| Warren Bryant (from ATL) | OT | 6'7" | 285 | 28 | | |
| Bruce Davis | OT | 6'6" | 280 | 28 | | |
| Shelby Jordan | OT | 6'7" | 280 | 32 | | |
| Henry Lawrence | OT | 6'4" | 270 | 32 | | |
| Ed Muransky | OT | 6'7" | 275 | 24 | | |
| Charley Hannah | OG | 6'5" | 260 | 29 | | |
| Curt Marsh | OG | 6'5" | 270 | 25 | | |
| Mickey Marvin | OG | 6'4" | 265 | 28 | | |
| Dave Dalby | C | 6'2" | 255 | 34 | | |
| Don Mosebar | C-OG | 6'6" | 260 | 22 | | |
| Dwight Wheeler | C | 6'3" | 274 | 29 | | |
| Lyle Alzado | DE | 6'3" | 260 | 35 | | |
| Greg Boyd (from SF) | DE | 6'6" | 280 | 31 | | |
| Sean Jones | DE | 6'7" | 265 | 21 | | |
| Howie Long | DE | 6'5" | 270 | 24 | | |
| Bill Pickel | DE-NT | 6'5" | 260 | 24 | | |
| Greg Townsend | DE-NT | 6'3" | 240 | 22 | | |
| Reggie Kinlaw | NT | 6'2" | 245 | 27 | | |

| Use Name | Pos. | Hgt | Wgt | Age | Int | Pts |
|---|---|---|---|---|---|---|
| Stanley Adams | LB | 6'2" | 215 | 24 | | |
| Jeff Barnes | LB | 6'2" | 230 | 29 | 1 | |
| Darryl Byrd | LB | 6'1" | 220 | 23 | | |
| Tony Caldwell | LB | 6'1" | 225 | 23 | | |
| Rod Martin | LB | 6'2" | 225 | 30 | 2 | 14 |
| Larry McCoy | LB | 6'2" | 240 | 23 | | |
| Mark Merrill (from BUF) | LB | 6'4" | 234 | 29 | | |
| Matt Millen | LB | 6'2" | 250 | 26 | | |
| Bob Nelson | LB | 6'4" | 235 | 31 | | |
| Jack Squirek | LB | 6'4" | 230 | 25 | | |
| Brad Van Pelt | LB | 6'5" | 235 | 33 | 1 | |
| James Davis | DB | 6' | 190 | 27 | 1 | |
| Mike Davis | DB | 6'3" | 205 | 28 | 2 | |
| Lester Hayes | DB | 6' | 200 | 29 | 1 | |
| Mike Haynes | DB | 6'2" | 190 | 31 | 6 | 6 |
| Vann McElroy | DB | 6'2" | 190 | 24 | 4 | |
| Odis McKinney | DB | 6'2" | 190 | 27 | 1 | |
| Stacey Toran | DB | 6'2" | 200 | 22 | | |
| Ted Watts | DB | 6' | 190 | 26 | 1 | |

| Use Name | Pos. | Hgt | Wgt | Age | Int | Pts |
|---|---|---|---|---|---|---|
| Jerry Goldsteyn | QB | 6'4" | 210 | 30 | | |
| David Humm | QB | 6'2" | 190 | 32 | | |
| Jim Plunkett | QB | 6'3" | 220 | 36 | | 6 |
| Marc Wilson | QB | 6'6" | 205 | 27 | | 6 |
| Marcus Allen | HB | 6'2" | 205 | 24 | | 108 |
| Joe McCall | HB-FB | 6' | 200 | 22 | | |
| Greg Pruitt | HB | 5'10" | 190 | 33 | | |
| Jimmy Smith(from WAS) | HB | 6' | 205 | 23 | | |
| Chester Willis | HB | 5'11" | 200 | 26 | | |
| Frank Hawkins | FB | 5'9" | 210 | 25 | | 18 |
| Kenny King | FB | 5'11" | 205 | 27 | | |
| Malcolm Barnwell | WR | 5'11" | 185 | 26 | | 12 |
| Cliff Branch | WR | 5'11" | 170 | 36 | | |
| Cle Montgomery | WR | 5'8" | 180 | 26 | | 6 |
| Sam Seale | WR-DB | 5'9" | 175 | 21 | | |
| Dokie Williams | WR | 5'11" | 180 | 24 | | 24 |
| Dave Casper | TE | 6'4" | 240 | 32 | | 12 |
| Todd Christensen | TE | 6'3" | 230 | 28 | | 42 |
| Derrick Jensen | TE-FB | 6'1" | 215 | 28 | | 12 |
| Andy Parker | TE | 6'5" | 240 | 22 | | |
| Chris Bahr | K | 5'10" | 170 | 31 | | 100 |
| Ray Guy | K | 6'3" | 195 | 34 | | |

## KANSAS CITY CHIEFS 8-8-0 John Mackovic

| Scores of Each Game | | |
|---|---|---|
| 37 | Pittsburgh | 27 |
| 27 | Cincinnati | 22 |
| 0 | L.A.RAIDERS | 22 |
| 0 | Denver | 21 |
| 10 | CLEVELAND | 6 |
| 16 | N.Y.JETS | 17 |
| 31 | SAN DIEGO | 13 |
| 7 | N.Y.Jets | 28 |
| 24 | TAMPA BAY | 20 |
| 0 | Seattle | 45 |
| 16 | HOUSTON | 17 |
| 7 | L.A.Raiders | 17 |
| 27 | N.Y.Giants | 28 |
| 16 | DENVER | 13 |
| 34 | SEATTLE | 7 |
| 45 | San Diego | 21 |

| Use Name | Pos. | Hgt | Wgt | Age | Int | Pts |
|---|---|---|---|---|---|---|
| John Alt | OT | 6'7" | 278 | 22 | | |
| Scott Auer | OT-OG | 6'5" | 255 | 22 | | |
| Rich Baldinger | OT-OG | 6'4" | 285 | 24 | | |
| Matt Herkenhoff | OT | 6'4" | 275 | 33 | | |
| David Lutz | OT | 6'6" | 285 | 24 | | |
| Jim Rourke | OT-OG | 6'5" | 263 | 27 | | |
| Brad Budde | OG | 6'4" | 260 | 26 | | |
| Tom Condon | OG | 6'3" | 275 | 31 | | |
| Adam Lingner | C-OG | 6'4" | 250 | 23 | | |
| Bob Rush | C | 6'5" | 264 | 29 | | |
| Mike Bell | DE | 6'4" | 250 | 27 | | |
| Eric Holle | DE | 6'5" | 250 | 23 | | |
| Dave Lindstrom | DE | 6'6" | 255 | 29 | | |
| Art Still | DE | 6'7" | 257 | 28 | | |
| Mike Dawson | NT | 6'4" | 254 | 30 | | |
| Ken Kremer | NT | 6'4" | 260 | 27 | 1 | |
| Bill Maas | NT | 6'5" | 265 | 22 | | |

Ken Thomas - Knee Injury

| Use Name | Pos. | Hgt | Wgt | Age | Int | Pts |
|---|---|---|---|---|---|---|
| Jerry Blanton | LB | 6'1" | 236 | 27 | 1 | |
| Calvin Daniels | LB | 6'3" | 236 | 25 | 2 | |
| Charles Jackson | LB | 6'2" | 222 | 29 | 1 | |
| Ken Jolly | LB | 6'2" | 220 | 22 | | |
| Ken McAlister | LB | 6'5" | 230 | 24 | 2 | |
| Jeff Paine | LB | 6'2" | 224 | 23 | | |
| Scott Radecic | LB | 6'3" | 240 | 22 | 2 | 6 |
| Gary Spani | LB | 6'2" | 228 | 28 | | |
| John Zamberlin | LB | 6'2" | 226 | 28 | | |
| Lloyd Burruss | DB | 6' | 202 | 26 | 2 | |
| Deron Cherry | DB | 5'11" | 190 | 24 | 7 | |
| Greg Hill | DB | 6'1" | 189 | 23 | 2 | |
| Van Jakes | DB | 6' | 185 | 23 | | |
| Albert Lewis | DB | 6'2" | 190 | 23 | 4 | |
| Kerry Parker | DB | 6'1" | 195 | 28 | | |
| Mark Robinson | DB | 5'11" | 206 | 21 | | |
| Kevin Ross | DB | 5'9" | 180 | 22 | 6 | 6 |

| Use Name | Pos. | Hgt | Wgt | Age | Int | Pts |
|---|---|---|---|---|---|---|
| Todd Blackledge | QB | 6'3" | 225 | 23 | | 6 |
| Bill Kenney | QB | 6'4" | 211 | 29 | | |
| Sandy Osiecki | QB | 6'5" | 202 | 24 | | |
| David Whitehurst | QB | 6'2" | 204 | 29 | | |
| Herman Heard | HB | 5'10" | 184 | 22 | | 24 |
| Billy Jackson | HB | 5'10" | 215 | 24 | | 12 |
| Lawrence Ricks | HB | 5'9" | 194 | 23 | | |
| Theotis Brown | FB | 6'2" | 225 | 27 | | 24 |
| Mike Gunter | FB | 5'11" | 206 | 23 | | |
| Ken Lacy | FB | 6' | 222 | 23 | | |
| Carlos Carson | WR | 5'11" | 180 | 25 | | 24 |
| Anthony Hancock | WR | 6' | 200 | 24 | | 6 |
| Henry Marshall | WR | 6'2" | 220 | 30 | | 24 |
| Stephone Paige | WR | 6'2" | 180 | 22 | | 24 |
| J.T.Smith | WR | 6'2" | 185 | 28 | | |
| Walt Arnold (from WAS) | TE | 6'3" | 234 | 26 | | 6 |
| Ed Beckman | TE | 6'4" | 227 | 29 | | 6 |
| Dave Little | TE | 6'2" | 239 | 23 | | |
| Willie Scott | TE | 6'4" | 245 | 25 | | 18 |
| Jim Arnold | K | 6'2" | 212 | 23 | | |
| Nick Lowery | K | 6'4" | 189 | 28 | | 104 |

## SAN DIEGO CHARGERS 7-9-0 Don Coryell

| Scores of Each Game | | |
|---|---|---|
| 42 | Minnesota | 13 |
| 17 | Seattle | 31 |
| 31 | HOUSTON | 14 |
| 30 | L.A.Raiders | 33 |
| 27 | DETROIT | 24 |
| 34 | Green Bay | 28 |
| 13 | Kansas City | 31 |
| 37 | L.A.RAIDERS | 44 |
| 0 | SEATTLE | 24 |
| 38 | Indianapolis | 10 |
| 13 | DENVER | 16 |
| 34 | MIAMI | *28 |
| 24 | Pittsburgh | 52 |
| 20 | CHICAGO | 7 |
| 13 | Denver | 16 |
| 21 | KANSAS CITY | 42 |

| Use Name | Pos. | Hgt | Wgt | Age | Int | Pts |
|---|---|---|---|---|---|---|
| Sam Claphan | OT | 6'6" | 282 | 27 | | |
| Andrew Gissinger | OT | 6'5" | 279 | 25 | | |
| Chuck Loewen | OT-OG | 6'3" | 268 | 27 | | |
| Bill Elko | OG | 6'5" | 280 | 24 | | |
| Ed White | OG | 6'2" | 284 | 37 | | |
| Doug Wilkerson | OG | 6'2" | 253 | 37 | | |
| Derrel Gofourth | OG-C | 6'3" | 250 | 29 | | |
| Don Macek | C-OG | 6'3" | 260 | 30 | | |
| Dennis McKnight | C-OG | 6'3" | 272 | 24 | | |
| Chuck Ehin | DE | 6'4" | 260 | 23 | | |
| Keith Ferguson | DE | 6'5" | 255 | 25 | | |
| Fred Robinson | DE | 6'4" | 240 | 22 | | |
| Lee Williams | DE | 6'6" | 270 | 21 | 1 | |
| Richard Ackerman (to RAID) | NT | 6'4" | 262 | 25 | | |
| Tony Chickillo | NT | 6'3" | 257 | 24 | | |
| Keith Guthrie | NT | 6'3" | 267 | 22 | | |
| Rickey Hogood | NT | 6'2" | 286 | 23 | | |

| Use Name | Pos. | Hgt | Wgt | Age | Int | Pts |
|---|---|---|---|---|---|---|
| Carlos Bradley | LB | 6' | 226 | 24 | | |
| Mike Green | LB | 6' | 239 | 23 | | |
| Linden King | LB | 6'4" | 250 | 29 | 2 | |
| Woodrow Lowe | LB | 6' | 219 | 30 | 3 | |
| Derrie Nelson | LB | 6'2" | 238 | 26 | | |
| Vince Osby | LB | 5'11" | 220 | 23 | | |
| Ray Preston | LB | 6' | 220 | 30 | | |
| Billy Ray Smith | LB | 6'3" | 231 | 23 | 3 | |
| Cliff Thrift | LB | 6'2" | 237 | 28 | | |
| Eric Williams | LB | 6'2" | 235 | 29 | | |
| Gill Byrd | DB | 5'11" | 191 | 23 | 4 | 12 |
| Scott Byers | DB | 5'11" | 170 | 23 | | |
| Tim Fox | DB | 5'11" | 186 | 30 | | |
| Ken Greene | DB | 6'3" | 196 | 28 | | |
| Bob Gregor | DB | 6'2" | 190 | 27 | | |
| Reuben Henderson | DB | 6'1" | 196 | 25 | | |
| Miles McPherson | DB | 5'11" | 191 | 24 | | |
| Lucious Smith (from BUF) | DB | 5'10" | 190 | 27 | | |
| Johnny Ray Smith | DB | 5'9" | 185 | 26 | | |
| John Turner | DB | 6' | 193 | 28 | 2 | |
| Danny Walters | DB | 6'1" | 180 | 23 | | |
| Andre Young | DB | 6' | 190 | 23 | 2 | |

| Use Name | Pos. | Hgt | Wgt | Age | Int | Pts |
|---|---|---|---|---|---|---|
| Dan Fouts | QB | 6'3" | 205 | 33 | | |
| Ed Luther | QB | 6'3" | 210 | 27 | | |
| Bruce Mathison | QB | 6'3" | 203 | 25 | | |
| Earnest Jackson | HB | 5'9" | 208 | 24 | | 54 |
| Lionel James | HB | 5'7" | 171 | 22 | | |
| Buford McGee | HB | 6' | 206 | 24 | | 36 |
| Wayne Morris | FB | 6' | 210 | 30 | | |
| Chuck Muncie | FB | 6'3" | 228 | 31 | | |
| Jewerl Thomas | FB | 5'10" | 230 | 26 | | 12 |
| Jesse Bendross | WR | 6' | 197 | 23 | | |
| Wes Chandler | WR | 6' | 183 | 28 | | 36 |
| Bobby Duckworth | WR | 6'3" | 197 | 25 | | 24 |
| Charlie Joiner | WR | 5'11" | 180 | 36 | | 36 |
| Ron Egloff | TE | 6'5" | 227 | 28 | | |
| Pete Holohan | TE | 6'4" | 249 | 25 | | |
| Bobby Micho | TE | 6'3" | 227 | 22 | | |
| Eric Sievers | TE | 6'4" | 236 | 25 | | 18 |
| Kellen Winslow | TE | 6'5" | 242 | 26 | | 12 |
| Rolf Benirschke | K | 6'1" | 184 | 29 | | 92 |
| Maury Buford | K | 6'1" | 191 | 24 | | |
| Benny Ricardo | K | 5'10" | 170 | 30 | | 14 |

* Overtime

## DENVER BRONCOS

### RUSHING

| Last Name | No. | Yds | Avg | TD |
|---|---|---|---|---|
| Winder | 296 | 1153 | 3.9 | 4 |
| Willhite | 77 | 371 | 4.8 | 2 |
| Elway | 56 | 237 | 4.2 | 1 |
| Parros | 46 | 208 | 4.5 | 2 |
| Lang | 8 | 42 | 5.3 | 2 |
| Brewer | 10 | 28 | 2.8 | 0 |
| Kubiak | 9 | 27 | 3.0 | 1 |
| Myles | 5 | 7 | 1.4 | 0 |
| Johnson | 1 | 3 | 3.0 | 0 |

### RECEIVING

| Last Name | No. | Yds | Avg | TD |
|---|---|---|---|---|
| Watson | 69 | 1170 | 17.0 | 7 |
| Winder | 44 | 288 | 6.5 | 2 |
| Johnson | 42 | 587 | 14.0 | 6 |
| Willhite | 27 | 298 | 11.0 | 0 |
| Sawyer | 17 | 122 | 7.2 | 0 |
| Kay | 16 | 136 | 8.5 | 3 |
| J. Wright | 11 | 118 | 10.7 | 1 |
| Sampson | 9 | 123 | 13.7 | 1 |
| Alexander | 8 | 132 | 16.5 | 1 |
| Parros | 6 | 25 | 4.2 | 0 |
| Lang | 4 | 24 | 6.0 | 1 |
| Summers | 3 | 32 | 10.7 | 0 |
| Myles | 2 | 22 | 11.0 | 0 |
| Brewer | 2 | 20 | 10.0 | 0 |
| Kubiak | 1 | 20 | 20.0 | 0 |
| Logan | 1 | 3 | 3.0 | 0 |
| Studdard | 1 | -4 | -4.0 | 0 |

### PUNT RETURNS

| Last Name | No. | Yds | Avg | TD |
|---|---|---|---|---|
| Thomas | 21 | 125 | 6.0 | 0 |
| Wilhite | 20 | 200 | 10.0 | 0 |
| Wilson | 1 | 0 | 0.0 | 0 |

### KICKOFF RETURNS

| Last Name | No. | Yds | Avg | TD |
|---|---|---|---|---|
| Lang | 19 | 404 | 21.3 | 0 |
| Thomas | 18 | 351 | 19.5 | 0 |
| Willhite | 4 | 109 | 27.3 | 0 |
| Dennison | 2 | 27 | 13.5 | 0 |
| Harden | 1 | 4 | 4.0 | 0 |
| A. Smith | 1 | 2 | 2.0 | 0 |

### PASSING — PUNTING — KICKING

| PASSING | Att | Cmp | % | Yds | Yd/Att | TD | Int- | % | RK |
|---|---|---|---|---|---|---|---|---|---|
| Elway | 380 | 214 | 56 | 2598 | 6.84 | 18 | 15- | 4 |
| Kubiak | 75 | 44 | 59 | 440 | 5.87 | 4 | 1- | 1 |
| Stankavage | 18 | 4 | 22 | 58 | 3.22 | 0 | 1- | 6 |
| Willhite | 2 | 1 | 50 | 20 | 10.0 | 0 | 0- | 0 |

| PUNTING | No | Avg |
|---|---|---|
| Norman | 96 | 40.1 |

| KICKING | XP | Att | % | FG | Att | % |
|---|---|---|---|---|---|---|
| Karlis | 38 | 41 | 93 | 21 | 28 | 75 |

## SEATTLE SEAHAWKS

### RUSHING

| Last Name | No. | Yds | Avg | TD |
|---|---|---|---|---|
| Hughes | 94 | 327 | 3.5 | 1 |
| Lane | 80 | 299 | 3.7 | 4 |
| Doornink | 57 | 215 | 3.8 | 0 |
| Morris | 58 | 189 | 3.3 | 0 |
| Krieg | 46 | 186 | 4.0 | 3 |
| F. Harris | 68 | 170 | 2.5 | 0 |
| Dixon | 52 | 149 | 2.9 | 2 |
| C. Bryant | 20 | 58 | 2.9 | 0 |
| Warner | 10 | 40 | 4.0 | 0 |
| Largent | 2 | 10 | 5.0 | 0 |
| C. Young | 1 | 5 | 5.0 | 0 |
| Zorn | 7 | -3 | -0.4 | 0 |

### RECEIVING

| Last Name | No. | Yds | Avg | TD |
|---|---|---|---|---|
| Largent | 74 | 1164 | 15.7 | 12 |
| Turner | 35 | 715 | 20.4 | 10 |
| C. Young | 33 | 337 | 10.2 | 1 |
| Doornink | 31 | 365 | 11.8 | 2 |
| Hughes | 22 | 121 | 5.5 | 1 |
| Johns | 17 | 207 | 12.2 | 1 |
| Walker | 13 | 236 | 18.2 | 1 |
| Lane | 11 | 101 | 9.2 | 1 |
| Morris | 9 | 61 | 6.8 | 0 |
| Tice | 8 | 90 | 11.1 | 0 |
| Castor | 8 | 89 | 11.1 | 0 |
| Skansi | 7 | 85 | 12.1 | 0 |
| Metzelaars | 5 | 80 | 16.0 | 0 |
| C. Bryant | 3 | 20 | 6.7 | 0 |
| Scales | 2 | 22 | 11.0 | 0 |
| Dixon | 2 | 6 | 3.0 | 0 |
| Pratt | 1 | 30 | 30.0 | 0 |
| Warner | 1 | 19 | 19.0 | 0 |
| F. Harris | 1 | 3 | 3.0 | 0 |

### PUNT RETURNS

| Last Name | No. | Yds | Avg | TD |
|---|---|---|---|---|
| Easley | 16 | 194 | 12.1 | 0 |
| Skansi | 16 | 145 | 9.1 | 0 |
| Johns | 11 | 140 | 12.7 | 1 |
| Dixon | 1 | 5 | 5.0 | 0 |

### KICKOFF RETURNS

| Last Name | No. | Yds | Avg | TD |
|---|---|---|---|---|
| Hughes | 17 | 348 | 20.5 | 0 |
| Dixon | 25 | 446 | 17.8 | 0 |
| Morris | 8 | 153 | 19.1 | 0 |
| C. Bryant | 3 | 53 | 17.7 | 0 |
| J. Harris | 1 | 7 | 7.0 | 0 |

### PASSING — PUNTING — KICKING

| PASSING | Att | Cmp | % | Yds | Yd/Att | TD | Int- | % | RK |
|---|---|---|---|---|---|---|---|---|---|
| Krieg | 480 | 276 | 58 | 3671 | 7.7 | 32 | 24- | 5 |
| Zorn | 17 | 7 | 41 | 80 | 4.7 | 0 | 2- | 12 |

| PUNTING | No | Avg |
|---|---|---|
| West | 95 | 37.5 |

| KICKING | XP | Att | % | FG | Att | % |
|---|---|---|---|---|---|---|
| N. Johnson | 50 | 51 | 98 | 20 | 24 | 83 |

## LOS ANGELES RAIDERS

### RUSHING

| Last Name | No. | Yds | Avg | TD |
|---|---|---|---|---|
| Allen | 275 | 1168 | 4.2 | 15 |
| Hawkins | 108 | 376 | 3.5 | 3 |
| King | 67 | 254 | 3.8 | 0 |
| Wilson | 30 | 56 | 1.9 | 1 |
| Plunkett | 16 | 14 | 0.9 | 1 |
| Humm | 2 | 7 | 3.5 | 0 |
| Willis | 5 | 4 | 0.8 | 0 |
| McCall | 1 | 3 | 3.0 | 0 |
| Jensen | 3 | 3 | 1.0 | 1 |
| Pruitt | 8 | 0 | 0.0 | 0 |
| Montgomery | 1 | 1 | 1.0 | 0 |

### RECEIVING

| Last Name | No. | Yds | Avg | TD |
|---|---|---|---|---|
| Christensen | 80 | 1007 | 12.6 | 7 |
| Allen | 64 | 758 | 11.8 | 5 |
| Barnwell | 45 | 851 | 18.9 | 2 |
| Branch | 27 | 401 | 14.9 | 0 |
| Williams | 22 | 509 | 23.1 | 4 |
| King | 14 | 99 | 7.1 | 0 |
| Hawkins | 7 | 51 | 7.3 | 0 |
| Casper | 4 | 29 | 7.3 | 2 |
| Pruitt | 2 | 12 | 6.0 | 0 |
| Jensen | 1 | 1 | 1.0 | 1 |

### PUNT RETURNS

| Last Name | No. | Yds | Avg | TD |
|---|---|---|---|---|
| Pruitt | 53 | 473 | 8.9 | 0 |
| Montgomery | 14 | 194 | 13.9 | 1 |

### KICKOFF RETURNS

| Last Name | No. | Yds | Avg | TD |
|---|---|---|---|---|
| Williams | 24 | 621 | 25.9 | 0 |
| Montgomery | 26 | 555 | 21.3 | 0 |
| Pruitt | 3 | 16 | 5.3 | 0 |
| Willis | 1 | 13 | 13.0 | 0 |
| Jensen | 1 | 11 | 11.0 | 0 |
| McKinney | 1 | 0 | 0.0 | 0 |

### PASSING — PUNTING — KICKING

| PASSING | Att | Cmp | % | Yds | Yd/Att | TD | Int- | % | RK |
|---|---|---|---|---|---|---|---|---|---|
| Plunkett | 198 | 108 | 55 | 1473 | 7.4 | 6 | 10- | 5 |
| Wilson | 282 | 153 | 54 | 2151 | 7.6 | 15 | 17- | 6 |
| Humm | 7 | 4 | 57 | 56 | 8.0 | 0 | 1- | 14 |
| Allen | 4 | 1 | 25 | 38 | 9.5 | 0 | 0- | 0 |

| PUNTING | No | Avg |
|---|---|---|
| Guy | 91 | 41.9 |

| KICKING | XP | Att | % | FG | Att | % |
|---|---|---|---|---|---|---|
| Bahr | 40 | 42 | 95 | 20 | 27 | 74 |

## KANSAS CITY CHIEFS

### RUSHING

| Last Name | No. | Yds | Avg | TD |
|---|---|---|---|---|
| Heard | 165 | 684 | 4.1 | 4 |
| Brown | 97 | 337 | 3.5 | 4 |
| B. Jackson | 50 | 225 | 4.5 | 1 |
| Lacy | 46 | 165 | 3.6 | 2 |
| Blackledge | 18 | 102 | 5.7 | 1 |
| Paige | 3 | 19 | 6.3 | 0 |
| Gunter | 15 | 12 | 0.8 | 0 |
| Ricks | 2 | 1 | 0.5 | 0 |
| J. Arnold | 1 | 0 | 0.0 | 0 |
| Osiecki | 1 | -2 | -2.0 | 0 |
| Kenney | 9 | -8 | -0.9 | 0 |
| Carson | 1 | -8 | -8.0 | 0 |

### RECEIVING

| Last Name | No. | Yds | Avg | TD |
|---|---|---|---|---|
| Marshall | 62 | 912 | 14.7 | 4 |
| Carson | 57 | 1078 | 18.9 | 4 |
| Brown | 38 | 236 | 6.2 | 0 |
| Paige | 30 | 541 | 18.0 | 4 |
| Scott | 28 | 253 | 9.0 | 3 |
| Heard | 25 | 223 | 8.9 | 0 |
| B. Jackson | 15 | 101 | 6.7 | 1 |
| Lacy | 13 | 87 | 6.7 | 2 |
| W. Arnold | 11 | 95 | 8.6 | 1 |
| Hancock | 10 | 217 | 21.7 | 1 |
| J.T. Smith | 8 | 69 | 8.6 | 0 |
| Beckman | 7 | 44 | 6.3 | 1 |
| Little | 1 | 13 | 13.0 | 0 |

### PUNT RETURNS

| Last Name | No. | Yds | Avg | TD |
|---|---|---|---|---|
| J.T. Smith | 39 | 332 | 8.5 | 0 |
| Hancock | 3 | 14 | 4.7 | 0 |

### KICKOFF RETURNS

| Last Name | No. | Yds | Avg | TD |
|---|---|---|---|---|
| J.T. Smith | 19 | 391 | 20.6 | 0 |
| Paige | 27 | 544 | 20.1 | 0 |
| Ricks | 5 | 83 | 16.6 | 0 |
| Hancock | 2 | 32 | 16.0 | 0 |
| Scott | 1 | 9 | 9.0 | 0 |
| Carson | 1 | 2 | 2.0 | 0 |
| Cherry | 1 | 0 | 0.0 | 0 |

### PASSING — PUNTING — KICKING

| PASSING | Att | Cmp | % | Yds | Yd/Att | TD | Int- | % | RK |
|---|---|---|---|---|---|---|---|---|---|
| Kenney | 282 | 151 | 54 | 2098 | 7.4 | 15 | 10- | 4 |
| Blackledge | 294 | 147 | 50 | 1707 | 5.8 | 6 | 11- | 4 |
| Osiecki | 17 | 7 | 41 | 64 | 3.8 | 0 | 1- | 6 |

| PUNTING | No | Avg |
|---|---|---|
| J. Arnold | 98 | 44.9 |

| KICKING | XP | Att | % | FG | Att | % |
|---|---|---|---|---|---|---|
| Lowery | 35 | 35 | 100 | 23 | 33 | 70 |

## SAN DIEGO CHARGERS

### RUSHING

| Last Name | No. | Yds | Avg | TD |
|---|---|---|---|---|
| Jackson | 296 | 1179 | 4.0 | 8 |
| McGee | 67 | 226 | 3.4 | 4 |
| James | 25 | 115 | 4.6 | 0 |
| Muncie | 14 | 51 | 3.6 | 0 |
| Thomas | 14 | 43 | 3.1 | 2 |
| Morris | 5 | 12 | 2.4 | 1 |
| Luther | 4 | 11 | 2.8 | 0 |
| Fouts | 12 | -29 | -2.4 | 0 |

### RECEIVING

| Last Name | No. | Yds | Avg | TD |
|---|---|---|---|---|
| Joiner | 61 | 793 | 13.0 | 6 |
| Holohan | 56 | 734 | 13.1 | 1 |
| Winslow | 55 | 663 | 12.1 | 2 |
| Chandler | 52 | 708 | 13.6 | 6 |
| Sievers | 41 | 438 | 10.7 | 3 |
| Jackson | 39 | 222 | 5.7 | 1 |
| Duckworth | 25 | 715 | 28.6 | 4 |
| James | 23 | 206 | 9.0 | 0 |
| Bendross | 16 | 213 | 13.3 | 0 |
| Egloff | 11 | 92 | 8.4 | 0 |
| McGee | 9 | 76 | 8.4 | 2 |
| Muncie | 4 | 38 | 9.5 | 0 |
| Gissinger | 1 | 3 | 3.0 | 0 |
| Fouts | 1 | 0 | 0.0 | 0 |

### PUNT RETURNS

| Last Name | No. | Yds | Avg | TD |
|---|---|---|---|---|
| James | 30 | 208 | 6.9 | 1 |
| Henderson | 1 | 0 | 0.0 | 0 |
| L. Smith | 1 | 0 | 0.0 | 0 |

### KICKOFF RETURNS

| Last Name | No. | Yds | Avg | TD |
|---|---|---|---|---|
| James | 43 | 959 | 22.3 | 0 |
| McGee | 14 | 315 | 22.5 | 0 |
| Egloff | 2 | 20 | 10.0 | 0 |
| Jackson | 1 | 10 | 10.0 | 0 |

### PASSING — PUNTING — KICKING

| PASSING | Att | Cmp | % | Yds | Yd/Att | TD | Int- | % | RK |
|---|---|---|---|---|---|---|---|---|---|
| Fouts | 507 | 317 | 63 | 3740 | 7.4 | 19 | 17- | 3 |
| Luther | 151 | 83 | 55 | 1163 | 7.7 | 5 | 3- | 2 |
| Holohan | 2 | 1 | 50 | 25 | 12.5 | 1 | 0- | 0 |
| James | 2 | 0 | 0 | 0 | 0.0 | 0 | 1- | 50 |

| PUNTING | No | Avg |
|---|---|---|
| Buford | 66 | 42.0 |

| KICKING | XP | Att | % | FG | Att | % |
|---|---|---|---|---|---|---|
| Benirschke | 41 | 41 | 100 | 17 | 26 | 65 |
| Ricardo | 5 | 6 | 83 | 3 | 3 | 100 |

# 1984 N.F.C.—PLAYOFFS

December 23, at Anaheim, Calif. (Attendance 67,037)

**SCORING**

| | | | | |
|---|---|---|---|---|
| N.Y. GIANTS | 10 | 0 | 6 | 0- 16 |
| L.A. RAMS | 0 | 3 | 7 | 3- 13 |

| | |
|---|---|
| First Quarter | |
| N.Y.G. | Haji-Sheikh, 37 yard field goal |
| N.Y.G. | Carpenter, 1 yard rush<br>PAT—Haji-Sheikh (kick) |
| Second Quarter | |
| L.A. Rams | Lansford, 38 yard field goal |
| Third Quarter | |
| N.Y.G. | Haji-Sheikh, 39 yard field goal |
| L.A. Rams | Dickerson, 14 yard rush<br>PAT—Lansford (kick) |
| N.Y.G. | Haji-Sheikh, 36 yard field goal |
| Fourth Quarter | |
| L.A. Rams | Lansford, 22 yard field goal |

**TEAM STATISTICS**

| N.Y.G. | | L.A. |
|---|---|---|
| 16 | First Downs-Total | 12 |
| 5 | First Downs-Rushing | 5 |
| 8 | First Downs-Passing | 5 |
| 3 | First Downs-Penalty | 2 |
| 3 | Fumbles-Number | 2 |
| 0 | Fumbles-Lost Ball | 2 |
| 5 | Penalty-Number | 10 |
| 81 | Yards Penalized | 75 |
| 0 | Missed Field Goals | 0 |
| 62 | Offensive Plays | 43 |
| 192 | Net Yards | 214 |
| 3.1 | Average Gain | 5.0 |
| 0 | Giveaways | 2 |
| 2 | Takeaways | 0 |
| +2 | Difference | -2 |

**INDIVIDUAL STATISTICS**

| N.Y. GIANTS | No. | Yds. | Avg. | L.A. RAMS | No. | Yds. | Avg. |
|---|---|---|---|---|---|---|---|
| | | | RUSHING | | | | |
| Morris | 10 | 21 | 2.1 | Dickerson | 23 | 107 | 4.7 |
| Carpenter | 13 | 20 | 1.5 | Kemp | 1 | 2 | 2.0 |
| Simms | 4 | -1 | -0.3 | Crutchfield | 2 | -2 | -1.0 |
| | 27 | 20 | 1.5 | | 26 | 107 | 4.1 |
| | | | RECEIVING | | | | |
| Carpenter | 7 | 23 | 3.3 | Brown | 3 | 32 | 10.7 |
| Mowatt | 7 | 73 | 10.4 | Barber | 3 | 31 | 10.3 |
| Manuel | 3 | 52 | 17.3 | Ellard | 2 | 22 | 11.0 |
| Gray | 2 | 20 | 10.0 | McDonald | 2 | 18 | 9.0 |
| Johnson | 1 | 6 | 6.0 | Da. Hill | 1 | 6 | 6.0 |
| Galbreath | 1 | 3 | 3.0 | | 11 | 109 | 9.9 |
| Morris | 1 | 2 | 2.0 | | | | |
| | 22 | 179 | 8.1 | | | | |
| | | | PUNTING | | | | |
| Jennings | 4 | | 38.8 | Misko | 4 | | 37.8 |
| | | | PUNT RETURNS | | | | |
| Manuel | 3 | 25 | 8.3 | Ellard | 2 | 17 | 8.5 |
| | | | KICKOFF RETURNS | | | | |
| Hill | 3 | 49 | 16.3 | Redden | 5 | 92 | 18.4 |
| Cephous | 1 | 20 | 20.0 | | | | |
| | 4 | 69 | 17.3 | | | | |
| | | | INTERCEPTION RETURNS | | | | |
| none | | | | none | | | |

**PASSING**

| N.Y. GIANTS | Att. | Cmp | Cmp Pct | Yds | Int | Yds./ Att | Yds./ Cmp |
|---|---|---|---|---|---|---|---|
| Simms | 31 | 22 | 71 | 179 | 0 | 5.8 | 8.1 |
| **L.A. RAMS** | | | | | | | |
| Kemp | 15 | 11 | 73 | 109 | 0 | 7.3 | 9.9 |

December 29 at San Francisco, Calif. (Attendance 60,303)

**SCORING**

| | | | | |
|---|---|---|---|---|
| N.Y. GIANTS | 0 | 10 | 0 | 0 - 10 |
| SAN FRANCISCO | 14 | 7 | 0 | 0 - 21 |

| | |
|---|---|
| First Quarter | |
| S.F. | Clark, 21 yard pass from Montana<br>PAT—Wersching (kick) |
| S.F. | Francis, 9 yard pass from Montana<br>PAT—Wersching (kick) |
| Second Quarter | |
| N.Y.G. | Haji-Sheikh, 46 yard field goal |
| N.Y.G. | Carson, 14 yard interception return |
| S.F. | Solomon, 29 yard pass from Montana<br>PAT—Wersching (kick) |

**TEAM STATISTICS**

| N.Y.G. | | S.F. |
|---|---|---|
| 18 | First Downs-Total | 22 |
| 7 | First Downs-Rushing | 5 |
| 10 | First Downs-Passing | 16 |
| 1 | First Downs-Penalty | 1 |
| 2 | Fumbles-Number | 0 |
| 1 | Fumble-Lost Ball | 0 |
| 2 | Penalties-Number | 5 |
| 25 | Yards Penalized | 29 |
| 1 | Missed Field Goals | 2 |
| 75 | Offensive Plays | 71 |
| 260 | Net Yards | 412 |
| 3.5 | Average Gain | 5.8 |
| 3 | Giveaways | 3 |
| 3 | Takeaways | 3 |
| 0 | Difference | 0 |

**INDIVIDUAL STATISTICS**

| N.Y. GIANTS | No. | Yds. | Avg. | SAN FRANCISCO | No. | Yds. | Avg. |
|---|---|---|---|---|---|---|---|
| | | | RUSHING | | | | |
| Morris | 17 | 46 | 2.7 | Montana | 3 | 63 | 21.0 |
| Galbreath | 4 | 34 | 8.5 | Tyler | 14 | 35 | 2.5 |
| Carpenter | 3 | 4 | 1.3 | Craig | 10 | 34 | 3.4 |
| Simms | 1 | 3 | 3.0 | Harmon | 1 | -1 | -1.0 |
| | 25 | 87 | 3.5 | | 28 | 131 | 4.7 |
| | | | RECEIVING | | | | |
| Mowatt | 5 | 49 | 9.8 | D. Clark | 9 | 112 | 12.4 |
| Morris | 4 | 45 | 11.3 | Solomon | 4 | 94 | 23.5 |
| Manuel | 2 | 32 | 16.0 | Wilson | 3 | 37 | 12.3 |
| Galbreath | 4 | 25 | 6.3 | Craig | 4 | 31 | 7.8 |
| Johnson | 3 | 23 | 7.7 | Tyler | 2 | 26 | 13.0 |
| Carpenter | 5 | 22 | 4.4 | Francis | 1 | 9 | 9.0 |
| Mullady | 2 | 22 | 11.0 | Cooper | 2 | 0 | 0.0 |
| | 25 | 218 | 8.7 | | 25 | 309 | 12.4 |
| | | | PUNTING | | | | |
| Jennings | 6 | | 37.7 | Runager | 5 | | 42.0 |
| | | | PUNT RETURNS | | | | |
| Manuel | 3 | 22 | 7.3 | McLemore | 2 | 7 | 3.5 |
| | | | KICKOFF RETURNS | | | | |
| Hill | 4 | 109 | 27.3 | Monroe | 2 | 26 | 13.0 |
| | | | | Harmon | 1 | 14 | 14.0 |
| | | | | | 3 | 40 | 13.3 |
| | | | INTERCEPTION RETURNS | | | | |
| Reasons | 2 | 33 | 16.5 | Lott | 1 | 38 | 38.0 |
| Carson | 1 | 14 | 14.0 | Ellison | 1 | 12 | 12.0 |
| | 3 | 47 | 15.7 | | 2 | 50 | 25.0 |

**PASSING**

| N.Y. GIANTS | Att. | Comp. | Cmp. Pct | Yds | Int | Yds/. Att. | Yds/ Comp |
|---|---|---|---|---|---|---|---|
| Simms | 44 | 25 | 57 | 218 | 2 | 5.0 | 8.7 |
| **SAN FRANCISCO** | | | | | | | |
| Montana | 39 | 25 | 64 | 309 | 3 | 7.9 | 12.4 |

December 30, at Washington, D.C. (Attendance 55,431)

**SCORING**

| | | | | |
|---|---|---|---|---|
| CHICAGO | 0 | 10 | 13 | 0- 23 |
| WASHINGTON | 3 | 0 | 14 | 2- 19 |

| | |
|---|---|
| First Quarter | |
| Wash. | Moseley, 25 yard field goal |
| Second Quarter | |
| Chicago | B. Thomas, 34 yard field goal |
| Chicago | Dunsmore, 19 yard pass from Payton<br>PAT—B. Thomas (kick) |
| Third Quarter | |
| Chicago | Gault, 75 yard pass from Fuller<br>PAT—kick failed |
| Wash. | Riggins, 1 yard rush<br>PAT—Moseley (kick) |
| Chicago | McKinnon, 16 yard pass from Fuller<br>PAT—B. Thomas (kick) |
| Wash. | Riggins, 1 yard rush<br>PAT—Moseley (kick) |
| Fourth Quarter | |
| Wash. | Safety, Finzer stepped out of endzone |

**TEAM STATISTICS**

| CHI. | | WASH. |
|---|---|---|
| 13 | First Downs-Total | 22 |
| 5 | First Downs-Rushing | 6 |
| 7 | First Downs-Passing | 14 |
| 1 | First Downs-Penalty | 2 |
| 2 | Fumbles-Number | 3 |
| 1 | Fumbles-Lost Ball | 2 |
| 6 | Penalties-Number | 7 |
| 34 | Yards Penalized | 55 |
| 0 | Missed Field Goals | 1 |
| 57 | Offensive Plays | 76 |
| 310 | Net Yards | 336 |
| 5.4 | Average Gain | 4.4 |
| 1 | Giveaways | 3 |
| 3 | Takeaways | 1 |
| +2 | Difference | -2 |

**INDIVIDUAL STATISTICS**

| CHICAGO | No. | Yds. | Avg. | WASHINGTON | No. | Yds. | Avg. |
|---|---|---|---|---|---|---|---|
| | | | RUSHING | | | | |
| Payton | 24 | 104 | 4.3 | Riggins | 21 | 50 | 2.4 |
| Suhey | 7 | 7 | 1.0 | Theismann | 5 | 38 | 7.6 |
| C. Thomas | 1 | 5 | 5.0 | J. Washington | 1 | 5 | 5.0 |
| Fuller | 2 | 5 | 2.5 | | 27 | 93 | 3.4 |
| Finzer | 1 | -7 | -7.0 | | | | |
| | 35 | 114 | 3.3 | | | | |
| | | | RECEIVING | | | | |
| McKinnon | 4 | 72 | 18.0 | Monk | 10 | 122 | 12.2 |
| Gault | 1 | 75 | 75.0 | Muhammad | 5 | 62 | 12.4 |
| Suhey | 1 | 33 | 33.0 | Didier | 4 | 85 | 21.2 |
| Dunsmore | 1 | 19 | 19.0 | Washington | 2 | 12 | 6.0 |
| C. Thomas | 1 | 13 | 13.0 | Warren | 1 | 11 | 11.0 |
| Payton | 1 | 12 | 12.0 | | 22 | 292 | 13.3 |
| Moorehead | 1 | 6 | 6.0 | | | | |
| | 10 | 230 | 23.0 | | | | |
| | | | PUNTING | | | | |
| Finzer | 5 | | 39.4 | Hayes | 5 | | 36.8 |
| | | | PUNT RETURNS | | | | |
| Fisher | 2 | 17 | 8.5 | Nelms | 3 | 29 | 9.7 |
| | | | KICKOFF RETURNS | | | | |
| Gault | 3 | 74 | 24.7 | Nelms | 4 | 77 | 19.3 |
| | | | | Kane | 1 | 10 | 10.0 |
| | | | | Griffin | 1 | 0 | 0.0 |
| | | | | Coleman | 0 | 25 | — |
| | | | | | 6 | 112 | 18.7 |
| | | | INTERCEPTION RETURNS | | | | |
| Richardson | 1 | 0 | 0.0 | none | | | |

**PASSING**

| CHICAGO | Att. | Comp. | Comp. Pct. | Yds. | Int. | Yds./ Att. | Yds./ Comp. |
|---|---|---|---|---|---|---|---|
| Fuller | 15 | 9 | 60 | 211 | 0 | 14.1 | 23.4 |
| Payton | 2 | 1 | 50 | 19 | 0 | 9.5 | 19.0 |
| | 17 | 10 | 59 | 230 | 0 | 13.5 | 23.0 |
| **WASHINGTON** | | | | | | | |
| Theismann | 42 | 22 | 52 | 292 | 1 | 7.0 | 13.3 |

## December 22, at Seattle, Wa. (Attendance 62,049)

### SCORING

| | | | | | |
|---|---|---|---|---|---|
| L.A. RAIDERS | 0 | 0 | 0 | 7- | 7 |
| SEATTLE | 0 | 7 | 3 | 3- | 13 |

**Second Quarter**
Seattle — Turner, 26 yard pass from Krieg
PAT—N. Johnson (kick)

**Third Quarter**
Seattle — N. Johnson, 35 yard field goal

**Fourth Quarter**
Seattle — N. Johnson, 44 yard field goal
L.A. Raiders — Allen, 46 yard pass from Plunkett
PAT—Bahr (kick)

### TEAM STATISTICS

| RAID. | | SEA. |
|---|---|---|
| 14 | First Downs-Total | 17 |
| 5 | First Downs-Rushing | 12 |
| 8 | First Downs-Passing | 4 |
| 1 | First Downs-Penalty | 0 |
| 2 | Fumbles-Number | 0 |
| 1 | Fumbles-Lost Ball | 0 |
| 8 | Penalty-Number | 7 |
| 68 | Yards Penalized | 55 |
| 0 | Missed Field Goals | 0 |
| 58 | Offensive Plays | 63 |
| 240 | Net Yards | 248 |
| 4.1 | Average Gain | 3.9 |
| 3 | Giveaways | 0 |
| 0 | Takeaways | 3 |
| -3 | Difference | +3 |

### INDIVIDUAL STATISTICS

**RAIDERS** — **SEATTLE**

#### RUSHING

| | No. | Yds. | Avg. | | No. | Yds. | Avg. |
|---|---|---|---|---|---|---|---|
| Allen | 17 | 61 | 3.6 | Doornink | 27 | 123 | 4.6 |
| Hawkins | 6 | 34 | 5.7 | Hughes | 14 | 54 | 3.9 |
| Pruitt | 1 | 6 | 6.0 | Lane | 4 | 17 | 4.3 |
| King | 1 | 4 | 4.0 | Krieg | 3 | 10 | 3.3 |
| | 25 | 105 | 4.2 | Largent | 1 | -2 | -2.0 |
| | | | | | 49 | 202 | 4.1 |

#### RECEIVING

| | No. | Yds. | Avg. | | No. | Yds. | Avg. |
|---|---|---|---|---|---|---|---|
| Allen | 5 | 90 | 18.0 | Turner | 1 | 26 | 26.0 |
| Hawkins | 4 | 27 | 6.8 | Tice | 1 | 20 | 20.0 |
| Barnwell | 3 | 34 | 11.3 | Doornink | 1 | 14 | 14.0 |
| Christensen | 1 | 21 | 21.0 | Hughes | 1 | 10 | 10.0 |
| King | 1 | 12 | 12.0 | | 4 | 70 | 17.5 |
| | 14 | 184 | 13.1 | | | | |

#### PUNTING

| | | | | | | |
|---|---|---|---|---|---|---|
| Guy | 8 | | 41.9 | West | 8 | | 37.8 |

#### PUNT RETURNS

| | | | | | | | |
|---|---|---|---|---|---|---|---|
| Montgomery | 3 | 5 | 1.7 | Easley | 5 | 52 | 10.4 |

#### KICKOFF RETURNS

| | | | | | | | |
|---|---|---|---|---|---|---|---|
| Pruitt | 2 | 28 | 14.0 | Hughes | 2 | 38 | 19.0 |

#### INTERCEPTION RETURNS

| | | | | | | | |
|---|---|---|---|---|---|---|---|
| none | | | | Haris | 1 | 0 | 0.0 |
| | | | | Easley | 1 | 21 | 21.0 |
| | | | | | 2 | 21 | 10.5 |

#### PASSING

| L.A. RAIDERS | Att. | Comp. | Pct. | Yds. | Int. | Yds./Att. | Yds./Comp. |
|---|---|---|---|---|---|---|---|
| Plunkett | 27 | 14 | 52 | 184 | 2 | 6.8 | 13.1 |
| **SEATTLE** | | | | | | | |
| Krieg | 10 | 4 | 40 | 70 | 0 | 7.0 | 17.5 |

---

## December 29, at Miami, Fl. Attendance 73,469

### SCORING

| | | | | | |
|---|---|---|---|---|---|
| SEATTLE | 0 | 10 | 0 | 0- | 10 |
| MIAMI | 7 | 7 | 14 | 3- | 31 |

**First Quarter**
Miami — Nathan, 14 yard rush
PAT—von Schamann (kick)

**Second Quarter**
Seattle — N. Johnson, 27 yard field goal
Miami — Cefalo, 34 yard pass from Marino
PAT—von Schamann (kick)
Seattle — Largent, 56 yard pass from Krieg
PAT—N. Johnson (kick)

**Third Quarter**
Miami — Hardy, 3 yard pass from Marino
PAT—von Schamann (kick)
Miami — Clayton, 33 yard pass from Marino
PAT—von Schamann (kick)

**Fourth Quarter**
Miami — von Schamann, 37 yard field goal

### TEAM STATISTICS

| SEA. | | MIA. |
|---|---|---|
| 8 | First Downs-Total | 22 |
| 2 | First Downs-Rushing | 8 |
| 6 | First Downs-Passing | 12 |
| 0 | First Downs-Penalty | 2 |
| 1 | Fumbles-Number | 0 |
| 1 | Fumbles-Lost Ball | 0 |
| 4 | Penalties-Number | 1 |
| 20 | Yards Penalized | 5 |
| 1 | Missed Field Goals | 2 |
| 55 | Offensive Plays | 70 |
| 267 | Net Yards | 405 |
| 4.9 | Average Gain | 5.8 |
| 1 | Giveaways | 2 |
| 2 | Takeaways | 1 |
| +1 | Difference | -1 |

### INDIVIDUAL STATISTICS

**SEATTLE** — **MIAMI**

#### RUSHING

| | No. | Yds. | Avg. | | No. | Yds. | Avg. |
|---|---|---|---|---|---|---|---|
| Doornink | 10 | 35 | 3.5 | Nathan | 18 | 76 | 4.2 |
| Hughes | 7 | 14 | 2.0 | Bennett | 11 | 41 | 3.7 |
| Krieg | 1 | 2 | 2.0 | P. Johnson | 6 | 22 | 3.7 |
| | 18 | 51 | 2.8 | Carter | 1 | 4 | 4.0 |
| | | | | | 36 | 143 | 4.0 |

#### RECEIVING

| | No. | Yds. | Avg. | | No. | Yds. | Avg. |
|---|---|---|---|---|---|---|---|
| Largent | 6 | 128 | 21.3 | Clayton | 5 | 75 | 15.0 |
| Doornink | 6 | 23 | 3.8 | Nathan | 4 | 20 | 5.0 |
| Turner | 3 | 38 | 12.7 | Hardy | 3 | 48 | 16.0 |
| Skansi | 2 | 31 | 15.5 | Duper | 3 | 32 | 10.7 |
| Hughes | 1 | 8 | 8.0 | Cefalo | 2 | 43 | 21.5 |
| C. Young | 1 | 5 | 5.0 | Moore | 2 | 11 | 5.5 |
| Krieg | 1 | 1 | 1.0 | Bennett | 1 | 20 | 20.0 |
| | 20 | 234 | 11.7 | Rose | 1 | 13 | 13.0 |
| | | | | | 21 | 262 | 12.5 |

#### PUNTING

| | | | | | | |
|---|---|---|---|---|---|---|
| West | 7 | | 37.0 | Roby | 3 | | 37.0 |

#### PUNT RETURNS

| | | | | | | | |
|---|---|---|---|---|---|---|---|
| Easley | 1 | 5 | 5.0 | Walker | 3 | 30 | 10.0 |

#### KICKOFF RETURNS

| | No. | Yds. | Avg. | | No. | Yds. | Avg. |
|---|---|---|---|---|---|---|---|
| Bryant | 2 | 43 | 21.5 | Walker | 2 | 30 | 15.0 |
| Hughes | 1 | 21 | 21.0 | Hardy | 1 | 21 | 21.0 |
| Tice | 1 | 13 | 13.0 | | 3 | 51 | 17.0 |
| | 4 | 77 | 19.3 | | | | |

#### INTERCEPTIONS RETURNS

| | | | | | | | |
|---|---|---|---|---|---|---|---|
| J. Harris | 2 | 45 | 22.5 | | | | |

#### PASSING

| SEATTLE | Att. | Comp. | Pct. | Yds. | Int. | Yds./Att. | Yds./Comp. |
|---|---|---|---|---|---|---|---|
| Krieg | 35 | 20 | 57 | 234 | 0 | 6.7 | 11.7 |
| **MIAMI** | | | | | | | |
| Marino | 34 | 21 | 62 | 262 | 2 | 7.7 | 12.5 |

---

## December 30, at Denver, Co. (Attendance 74,981)

### SCORING

| | | | | | |
|---|---|---|---|---|---|
| PITTSBURGH | 0 | 10 | 7 | 7- | 24 |
| DENVER | 7 | 0 | 10 | 0- | 17 |

**First Quarter**
Denver — Wright, 9 yard pass from Elway
PAT—Karlis (kick)

**Second Quarter**
Pitt. — Anderson, 28 yard field goal
Pitt. — Pollard, 1 yard rush
PAT—Anderson (kick)

**Third Quarter**
Denver — Karlis, 21 yard field goal
Denver — Watson, 20 yard pass from Elway
PAT—Karlis (kick)
Pitt. — Lipps, 10 yard pass from Malone
PAT—Anderson (kick)

**Fourth Quarter**
Pitt. — Pollard, 2 yard rush
PAT—Anderson (kick)

### TEAM STATISTICS

| PITT. | | DEN. |
|---|---|---|
| 25 | First Downs-Total | 15 |
| 12 | First Downs-Rushing | 4 |
| 13 | First Downs-Passing | 11 |
| 0 | First Downs-Penalty | 0 |
| 3 | Fumbles-Number | 2 |
| 2 | Fumbles-Lost Ball | 0 |
| 4 | Peanlties-Number | 1 |
| 30 | Yards Penalized | 5 |
| 3 | Missed Field Goals | 2 |
| 70 | Offensive Plays | 64 |
| 381 | Net Yards | 250 |
| 5.4 | Average Gain | 3.9 |
| 2 | Giveaways | 2 |
| 2 | Takeaways | 2 |
| 0 | Difference | 0 |

### INDIVIDUAL STATISTICS

**PITTSBURGH** — **DENVER**

#### RUSHING

| | No. | Yds. | Avg. | | No. | Yds. | Avg. |
|---|---|---|---|---|---|---|---|
| Pollard | 16 | 99 | 6.2 | Winder | 15 | 37 | 2.5 |
| Abercrombie | 17 | 75 | 4.4 | Elway | 4 | 16 | 4.0 |
| Veals | 1 | 1 | 1.0 | Willhite | 1 | 1 | 1.0 |
| Lipps | 1 | 0 | 0.0 | Parros | 1 | 0 | 0.0 |
| Malone | 5 | -6 | -1.2 | Watson | 1 | -3 | -3.0 |
| | 40 | 169 | 4.2 | | 22 | 51 | 2.3 |

#### RECEIVING

| | No. | Yds. | Avg. | | No. | Yds. | Avg. |
|---|---|---|---|---|---|---|---|
| Lipps | 5 | 86 | 17.2 | Watson | 11 | 177 | 16.1 |
| Pollard | 4 | 48 | 12.0 | Winder | 4 | 22 | 5.5 |
| Stallworth | 3 | 38 | 12.7 | Wright | 2 | 16 | 8.0 |
| Abercrombie | 3 | 18 | 6.0 | Willhite | 2 | 12 | 6.0 |
| Cunningham | 1 | 19 | 19.0 | Alexander | 1 | 9 | 9.0 |
| Thompson | 1 | 15 | 15.0 | | 20 | 236 | 11.8 |
| | 17 | 224 | 13.2 | | | | |

#### PUNTING

| | | | | | | |
|---|---|---|---|---|---|---|
| Colquitt | 3 | | 28.3 | Norman | 4 | | 42.3 |

#### PUNT RETURNS

| | | | | | | | |
|---|---|---|---|---|---|---|---|
| Lipps | 3 | 9 | 3.0 | Willhite | 2 | 17 | 8.5 |

#### KICKOFF RETURNS

| | No. | Yds. | Avg. | | No. | Yds. | Avg. |
|---|---|---|---|---|---|---|---|
| Erenberg | 1 | 29 | 29.0 | Willhite | 2 | 56 | 28.0 |
| Lipps | 3 | 73 | 24.3 | | | | |
| | 4 | 102 | 25.5 | | | | |

#### INTERCEPTIONS RETURNS

| | | | | | |
|---|---|---|---|---|---|
| E. Williams | 1 | 28 | 28.0 | none | |
| Dunn | 1 | 6 | 6.0 | | |
| | 2 | 34 | 17.0 | | |

#### PASSING

| PITTSBURGH | Att. | Comp. | Pct. | Yds. | Int. | Yds./Att. | Yds./Comp. |
|---|---|---|---|---|---|---|---|
| Malone | 28 | 17 | 61 | 224 | 0 | 8.0 | 13.2 |
| **DENVER** | | | | | | | |
| Elway | 37 | 19 | 51 | 184 | 2 | 5.0 | 9.7 |
| Willhite | 1 | 1 | 100 | 52 | 0 | 52.0 | 52.0 |
| | 38 | 20 | 53 | 236 | 2 | 6.2 | 11.8 |

## NFC CHAMPIONSHIP GAME
January 6, 1985 at San Francisco
(Attendance 61,040)

### SCORING

| | | | | | |
|---|---|---|---|---|---|
| CHICAGO | 0 | 0 | 0 | 0- | 0 |
| SAN FRANCISCO | 3 | 3 | 7 | 10- | 23 |

**First Quarter**
S.F. — Wersching, 22 yard field goal

**Second Quarter**
S.F. — Wersching, 22 yard field goal

**Third Quarter**
S.F. — Tyler, 9 yard rush
PAT—Wersching (kick)

**Fourth Quarter**
S.F. — Solomon, 10 yard pass from Montana
PAT—Wersching (kick)
S.F. — Wersching, 34 yard field goal

### TEAM STATISTICS

| CHI. | | S.F. |
|---|---|---|
| 13 | First Downs-Total | 25 |
| 9 | First Downs-Rushing | 9 |
| 3 | First Downs-Passing | 14 |
| 1 | First Downs-Penalty | 2 |
| 1 | Fumbles-Number | 1 |
| 0 | Fumbles-Lost Ball | 0 |
| 7 | Penalties-Number | 3 |
| 50 | Yards Penalized | 20 |
| 1 | Missed Field Goals | 0 |
| 63 | Offensive Plays | 67 |
| 186 | Net Yards | 387 |
| 3.0 | Average Gain | 5.8 |
| 1 | Giveaways | 2 |
| 2 | Takeaways | 1 |
| +1 | Difference | -1 |

The 49ers brimmed with confidence as they faced the Bears before a raucous San Francisco crowd. While the 49ers had talent in all sectors, the Bears got this far on the strength of their spirited defense, which overwhelmed foes with novel deployments.

Steve Fuller had returned from an injury to quarterback Chicago to an upset victory over the Redskins en route to San Francisco.

The Chicago defense played well in the first half despite three 49er penetrations into their territory. Twice they held the Niners to field goals, and once they covered a Joe Montana fumble on the two-yard line. While the Chicago defense held the 49ers to six first-half points, the San Francisco defense blanked the Bear offense.

In the second half, the Niners continued their incessant pressure on Fuller. On offense, they rigged up new blocking assignments, which gave Montana room to move. They drove to two touchdowns and a field goal for a 23-0 victory and a trip to the Super Bowl.

Although the Chicago defense had the bigger reputation, the San Francisco defense left the field with nine sacks and a shutout.

### INDIVIDUAL STATISTICS

**RUSHING**

| CHICAGO | No. | Yds. | Avg. | SAN FRANCISCO | No. | Yds. | Avg. |
|---|---|---|---|---|---|---|---|
| Payton | 22 | 92 | 4.2 | Tyler | 10 | 68 | 6.8 |
| Fuller | 6 | 39 | 6.5 | Craig | 8 | 44 | 5.5 |
| Suhey | 3 | 16 | 5.3 | Montana | 5 | 22 | 4.4 |
| C. Thomas | 1 | 2 | 2.0 | Harmon | 3 | 18 | 6.0 |
| | 32 | 149 | 4.7 | Ring | 2 | 5 | 2.5 |
| | | | | Cavanaugh | 1 | 2 | 2.0 |
| | | | | | 29 | 159 | 5.5 |

**RECEIVING**

| CHICAGO | No. | Yds. | Avg. | SAN FRANCISCO | No. | Yds. | Avg. |
|---|---|---|---|---|---|---|---|
| McKinnon | 3 | 48 | 16.0 | D. Clark | 4 | 83 | 20.8 |
| Moorehead | 2 | 14 | 7.0 | Solomon | 7 | 73 | 10.4 |
| Suhey | 4 | 11 | 2.8 | Wilson | 2 | 25 | 12.5 |
| Payton | 3 | 11 | 3.7 | Tyler | 2 | 22 | 11.0 |
| Dunsmore | 1 | 3 | 3.0 | Francis | 2 | 20 | 10.0 |
| | 13 | 87 | 6.7 | Nehemiah | 1 | 10 | 10.0 |
| | | | | Harmon | 1 | 3 | 3.0 |
| | | | | | 19 | 236 | 12.4 |

**PUNTING**

| CHICAGO | No. | Yds. | Avg. | SAN FRANCISCO | No. | Yds. | Avg. |
|---|---|---|---|---|---|---|---|
| Finzer | 7 | | 43.1 | Runager | 3 | | 39.0 |

**PUNT RETURNS**

| CHICAGO | No. | Yds. | Avg. | SAN FRANCISCO | No. | Yds. | Avg. |
|---|---|---|---|---|---|---|---|
| Fisher | 2 | 12 | 6.0 | McLemore | 4 | 69 | 17.3 |

**KICKOFF RETURNS**

| CHICAGO | No. | Yds. | Avg. | SAN FRANCISCO | No. | Yds. | Avg. |
|---|---|---|---|---|---|---|---|
| Gentry | 3 | 49 | 16.3 | Harmon | 1 | 15 | 15.0 |
| Gault | 1 | 18 | 18.0 | | | | |
| | 4 | 67 | 16.8 | | | | |

**INTERCEPTIONS RETURNS**

| CHICAGO | No. | Yds. | Avg. | SAN FRANCISCO | No. | Yds. | Avg. |
|---|---|---|---|---|---|---|---|
| Fencik | 2 | 5 | 2.5 | Hicks | 1 | 0 | 0.0 |

**PASSING**

| CHICAGO | Att. | Comp. | Comp. Pct. | Yds. | Int. | Yds./ Att. | Yds./ Comp. |
|---|---|---|---|---|---|---|---|
| Fuller | 22 | 13 | 59 | 87 | 1 | 4.0 | 6.7 |

| SAN FRANCISCO | Att. | Comp. | Comp. Pct. | Yds. | Int. | Yds./ Att. | Yds./ Comp. |
|---|---|---|---|---|---|---|---|
| Montana | 34 | 18 | 53 | 233 | 2 | 6.9 | 12.9 |
| Cavanaugh | 1 | 1 | 100 | 3 | 0 | 3.0 | 3.0 |
| | 35 | 19 | 54 | 236 | 2 | 6.7 | 12.4 |

---

## AFC CHAMPIONSHIP GAME
January 6, 1985 at Miami
(Attendance 76,029)

### SCORING

| | | | | | |
|---|---|---|---|---|---|
| PITTSBURGH | 7 | 7 | 7 | 7- | 28 |
| MIAMI | 7 | 17 | 14 | 7- | 45 |

**First Quarter**
Miami — Clayton, 40 yard pass from Marino
PAT—von Schamann (kick)
Pitt. — Erenberg, 7 yard run
PAT—Anderson (kick)

**Second Quarter**
Miami — von Schamann, 26 yard field goal
Pitt. — Stallworth, 65 yard pass from Malone
PAT—Anderson (kick)
Miami — Duper, 41 yard pass from Marino
PAT—von Schamann (kick)
Miami — Nathan, 2 yard rush
PAT—von Schamann (kick)

**Third Quarter**
Miami — Duper, 36 yard pass from Marino
PAT—von Schamann (kick)
Pitt. — Stallworth, 19 yard pass from Malone
PAT—Anderson (kick)
Miami — Bennett, 1 yard rush
PAT—von Schamann (kick)

**Fourth Quarter**
Miami — Moore, 6 yard pass from Marino
PAT—von Schamann (kick)
Pitt. — Capers, 29 yard pass from Malone
PAT—Anderson (kick)

### TEAM STATISTICS

| PITT. | | MIA. |
|---|---|---|
| 22 | First Downs-Total | 28 |
| 8 | First Downs-Rushing | 10 |
| 14 | First Downs-Passing | 18 |
| 2 | Fumbles-Number | 1 |
| 1 | Fumbles-Lost Ball | 1 |
| 3 | Penalties-Number | 3 |
| 30 | Yards Penalized | 25 |
| 1 | Missed Field Goals | 1 |
| 68 | Offensive Plays | 71 |
| 455 | Net Yards | 569 |
| 6.7 | Average Gain | 8.0 |
| 4 | Giveaways | 2 |
| 2 | Takeaways | 4 |
| -2 | Difference | +2 |

The Miami passing attack had blown all opponents away, but Pittsburgh coach Chuck Noll had a game plan to defuse it. The Steelers would rely on a grinding ground game to minimize Dan Marino's time on the field. When the Dolphins did have the ball, Pittsburgh would torment them with blitzes.

It was a good plan with limited success. The Steelers did drive downfield early in the game, only to lose the ball on a goalline interception by William Judson. Four plays later, Marino hit Mark Clayton for a 40-yard touchdown. The Steelers drove back on the ground to tie the game at the end of the second quarter, and Pittsburgh took the lead on a Mark Malone pass to John Stallworth.

Eighty-two seconds later, Mark Duper carried a Marino pass into the endzone. A Lyle Blackwood interception set up another Miami touchdown late in the first half for a 24-14 lead.

Forced to play catch-up ball in the second half, the Steelers had less success on the ground and were unable to ignite their passing game. Although the Steelers did score two second-half touchdowns, the Dolphins scored three.

The 45-28 Miami victory featured Marino's four touchdown passes, which negated Noll's best-laid plans.

### INDIVIDUAL STATISTICS

**RUSHING**

| PITTSBURGH | No. | Yds. | Avg. | MIAMI | No. | Yds. | Avg. |
|---|---|---|---|---|---|---|---|
| Abercrombie | 15 | 68 | 4.5 | Nathan | 19 | 64 | 3.4 |
| Pollard | 11 | 48 | 4.4 | Johnson | 10 | 39 | 3.9 |
| Erenberg | 6 | 27 | 4.5 | Bennett | 8 | 33 | 4.1 |
| | 32 | 143 | 4.5 | Strock | 1 | -2 | -2.0 |
| | | | | | 38 | 134 | 3.5 |

**RECEIVING**

| PITTSBURGH | No. | Yds. | Avg. | MIAMI | No. | Yds. | Avg. |
|---|---|---|---|---|---|---|---|
| Stallworth | 4 | 111 | 27.8 | Nathan | 8 | 114 | 14.3 |
| Lipps | 3 | 45 | 15.0 | Duper | 5 | 148 | 29.6 |
| Sweeney | 3 | 42 | 14.0 | Clayton | 4 | 95 | 23.8 |
| Pollard | 3 | 13 | 4.3 | Moore | 2 | 34 | 17.0 |
| Erenberg | 5 | 59 | 11.8 | Hardy | 2 | 16 | 8.0 |
| Capers | 1 | 29 | 29.0 | Rose | 1 | 28 | 28.0 |
| Abercrombie | 1 | 13 | 13.0 | | 22 | 435 | 19.8 |
| | 20 | 312 | 15.6 | | | | |

**PUNTING**

| PITTSBURGH | No. | Yds. | Avg. | MIAMI | No. | Yds. | Avg. |
|---|---|---|---|---|---|---|---|
| Colquitt | 3 | | 43.7 | Roby | 2 | | 42.5 |

**PUNT RETURNS**

| PITTSBURGH | No. | Yds. | Avg. | MIAMI | No. | Yds. | Avg. |
|---|---|---|---|---|---|---|---|
| Lipps | 1 | 7 | 7.0 | Walker | 2 | 10 | 5.0 |
| | | | | Kozlowski | 1 | 2 | 2.0 |
| | | | | | 3 | 12 | 4.0 |

**KICKOFF RETURNS**

| PITTSBURGH | No. | Yds. | Avg. | MIAMI | No. | Yds. | Avg. |
|---|---|---|---|---|---|---|---|
| Erenberg | 5 | 106 | 21.2 | Walker | 3 | 62 | 20.7 |

**INTERCEPTIONS RETURNS**

| PITTSBURGH | No. | Yds. | Avg. | MIAMI | No. | Yds. | Avg. |
|---|---|---|---|---|---|---|---|
| Shell | 1 | 18 | 18.0 | L. Blackwood | 1 | 4 | 4.0 |
| | | | | Judson | 1 | 34 | 34.0 |
| | | | | G. Blackwood | 1 | 4 | 4.0 |
| | | | | | 3 | 42 | 14.0 |

**PASSING**

| PITTSBURGH | Att. | Comp. | Comp. Pct. | Yds. | Int. | Yds./ Att. | Yds./ Comp. |
|---|---|---|---|---|---|---|---|
| Malone | 36 | 20 | 56 | 312 | 3 | 8.7 | 15.6 |

| MIAMI | Att. | Comp. | Comp. Pct. | Yds. | Int. | Yds./ Att. | Yds./ Comp. |
|---|---|---|---|---|---|---|---|
| Marino | 32 | 21 | 66 | 421 | 1 | 13.2 | 20.0 |
| Nathan | 1 | 1 | 100 | 14 | 0 | 14.0 | 14.0 |
| | 33 | 22 | 67 | 435 | 1 | 13.2 | 19.8 |

# Montana & Co. Beat the Killer Bees and Marino

The league's best two teams squared off for the championship. The Dolphins had the Killer Bee defense and a killer passing attack featuring Dan Marino and the Marks Brothers. The 49ers had a versatile offense and a mobile defense, both devised by strategic master Bill Walsh. On the same day that Ronald Reagan took his second presidential oath, Stanford Stadium rocked with the cheers of 84,059 fans.

Marino lived up to his advance notices in the first quarter. He completed 9-of-10 passes for 103 yards and a touchdown. Miami twice launched sustained drives and had a 10-7 lead after 15 minutes. The second quarter brought a shift in momentum. The 49ers adjusted their defense by using five defensive backs and playing Fred Dean in a four-man line. The new alignment blanketed Mark Duper and Mark Clayton and kept a steady pressure on Marino. With their offense stalled, the Dolphins had the misfortune of several bad punts by Reggie Roby. After a 37-yard punt, the Niners took four plays to reach the endzone. On the next Miami drive, Roby kicked a 40-yard line drive that Dana McLemore returned 28 yards to the San Francisco 45-yard line. Six plays later, Joe Montana dashed six yards for another touchdown. Another weak Roby punt set up a nine-play San Francisco drive, giving the 49ers a 28-10 lead. The Dolphins did respond with a field goal 22 seconds before halftime. On the perfunctory kickoff, San Francisco guard Guy McIntyre picked up the squib kick and promptly fumbled it away. The Dolphins rushed their field-goal team onto the field and closed the gap to 28-16 at the half.

In need of a big second half, the Dolphins couldn't keep the momentum generated by McIntyre's blunder. The 49ers gave Marino little time to throw and sacked him three times early in the third quarter. The San Francisco offense, meanwhile, continued its steady advance against the Killer Bee defense. It added a field goal and a touchdown to run the score to 38-16 by the end of the period. Neither team scored in the fourth quarter.

Kudos were due for many of the 49ers. The San Francisco defense held Miami to 25 rushing yards and sacked Marino four times. Fullback Roger Craig set a Super Bowl record by scoring three touchdowns, less with heroics than by fitting perfectly into the balanced offense. Leading that offense was Montana, the MVP of the game. He passed for a record 331 yards, threw three touchdowns and ran for 59 yards, more than double the Miami team total.

## LINEUPS

| MIAMI | | S.F. |
|---|---|---|
| **OFFENSE** | | |
| Duper | WR | Clark |
| Giesler | LT | Paris |
| Foster | LG | Ayers |
| Stephenson | C | Quillan |
| Newman | RG | Cross |
| Green | RT | Fahnhorst |
| Hardy | TE | Francis |
| Clayton | WR | Solomon |
| Marino | QB | Montana |
| Nathan | RB | Tyler |
| Bennett | FB | Craig |
| **DEFENSE** | | |
| Betters | LE | Pillers |
| Baumhower | NT | Tuiasosopo |
| Bokamper | RE | Board |
| Brudzinski | LOLB | Bunz |
| Brophy | LILB | Ellison |
| Brown | RILB | Reynolds |
| Bowser | ROLB | Turner |
| McNeal | LCB | Lott |
| Judson | RCB | Wright |
| G. Blackwood | SS | Williamson |
| L. Blackwood | FS | Hicks |
| **SUBSTITUTES** | | |

**MIAMI**

| OFFENSE | |
|---|---|
| Carter | Jensen | Rose |
| Cefalo | D. Johnson | Strock |
| Heflin | Moore | |
| **DEFENSE** | | |
| Barnett | Hill | Shipp |
| Benson | Kozlowski | Shiver |
| B. Brown | Lankford | Sowell |
| Charles | Lee | Toews |
| Clark | Rhone | Walker |
| Duhe | | |
| **KICKERS** | | |
| Roby | von Schamann | |

**SAN FRANCISCO**

| OFFENSE | |
|---|---|
| Cooper | Monroe | Ring |
| Harmon | Nehemiah | Wilson |
| **DEFENSE** | | |
| Carter | Kennedy | Shell |
| Dean | McColl | Shields |
| Fuller | McIntyre | Stover |
| Holmoe | McLemore | Stuckey |
| Johnson | Montgomery | Walter |
| Kelcher | | |
| **KICKERS** | | |
| Runager | Wersching | |

## SCORING

| | | | | | |
|---|---|---|---|---|---|
| MIAMI | 10 | 6 | 0 | 0- | 16 |
| SAN FRAN. | 7 | 21 | 10 | 0- | 38 |

**First Quarter**
Miami — von Schamann, 37 yard field goal
S.F. — Monroe, 33 yard pass from Montana
PAT—Wersching (kick)
Miami — D. Johnson, 2 yard pass from Marino
PAT—von Schamann (kick)

**Second Quarter**
S.F. — Craig, 8 yard pass from Montana
PAT—Wersching (kick)
S.F. — Montana, 6 yard run
PAT—Wersching (kick)
S.F. — Craig, 2 yard run
PAT—Wersching (kick)
Miami — von Schamann, 31 yard field goal
Miami — von Schamann, 30 yard field goal

**Third Quarter**
S.F. — Wersching, 27 yard field goal
S.F. — Craig, 16 yard pass from Montana
PAT—Wersching (kick)

## TEAM STATISTICS

| MIA | | S.F. |
|---|---|---|
| 19 | First Downs-Total | 31 |
| 2 | First Downs-Rushing | 16 |
| 17 | First Downs-Passing | 15 |
| 0 | First Downs-Penalty | 0 |
| 1 | Fumbles-Number | 2 |
| 0 | Fumbles-Lost Ball | 2 |
| 1 | Penalties-Number | 2 |
| 10 | Yards Penalized | 10 |
| 0 | Missed Field Goals | 0 |
| 63 | Offensive Plays | 76 |
| 314 | Net Yards | 537 |
| 5.0 | Average Gain | 7.1 |
| 2 | Giveaways | 2 |
| 2 | Takeaways | 2 |
| 0 | Difference | 0 |

## INDIVIDUAL STATISTICS

### RUSHING

| MIAMI | No. | Yds. | Avg. | SAN FRANCISCO | No. | Yds. | Avg. |
|---|---|---|---|---|---|---|---|
| Nathan | 5 | 18 | 3.6 | Tyler | 13 | 65 | 5.0 |
| Bennett | 3 | 7 | 2.3 | Montana | 5 | 59 | 11.8 |
| Marino | 1 | 0 | 0.0 | Craig | 15 | 58 | 3.9 |
| | 9 | 25 | 2.8 | Harmon | 5 | 20 | 4.0 |
| | | | | Solomon | 1 | 5 | 5.0 |
| | | | | Cooper | 1 | 4 | 4.0 |
| | | | | | 40 | 211 | 5.3 |

### RECEIVING

| MIAMI | No. | Yds. | Avg. | SAN FRANCISCO | No. | Yds. | Avg. |
|---|---|---|---|---|---|---|---|
| Nathan | 10 | 83 | 8.3 | Craig | 7 | 77 | 11.0 |
| Clayton | 6 | 92 | 15.3 | D. Clark | 6 | 77 | 12.8 |
| Rose | 6 | 73 | 12.2 | Francis | 5 | 60 | 12.0 |
| D. Johnson | 3 | 28 | 9.3 | Tyler | 4 | 70 | 17.5 |
| Moore | 2 | 17 | 8.5 | Monroe | 1 | 33 | 33.0 |
| Cefalo | 1 | 14 | 14.0 | Solomon | 1 | 14 | 14.0 |
| Duper | 1 | 11 | 11.0 | | 24 | 331 | 13.8 |
| | 29 | 318 | 11.0 | | | | |

### PUNTING

| MIAMI | No. | | Avg. | SAN FRANCISCO | No. | | Avg. |
|---|---|---|---|---|---|---|---|
| Roby | 6 | | 39.3 | Runager | 3 | | 32.7 |

### PUNT RETURNS

| MIAMI | No. | Yds. | Avg. | SAN FRANCISCO | No. | Yds. | Avg. |
|---|---|---|---|---|---|---|---|
| Walker | 2 | 15 | 7.5 | McLemore | 5 | 51 | 10.2 |

### KICKOFF RETURNS

| MIAMI | No. | Yds. | Avg. | SAN FRANCISCO | No. | Yds. | Avg. |
|---|---|---|---|---|---|---|---|
| Walker | 4 | 93 | 23.3 | Harmon | 2 | 24 | 12.0 |
| Hardy | 2 | 31 | 15.5 | Monroe | 1 | 16 | 16.0 |
| Hill | 1 | 16 | 16.0 | McIntyre | 1 | 0 | 0.0 |
| | 7 | 140 | 20.0 | | 4 | 40 | 10.0 |

### INTERCEPTIONS RETURNS

| MIAMI | No. | Yds. | Avg. | SAN FRANCISCO | No. | Yds. | Avg. |
|---|---|---|---|---|---|---|---|
| none | | | | Wright | 1 | 0 | 0.0 |
| | | | | Williamson | 1 | 0 | 0.0 |
| | | | | | 2 | 0 | 0.0 |

### PASSING

| MIAMI | Att. | Comp. | Comp. Pct. | Yds. | Int. | Yds./ Att. | Yds./ Comp. | Yards Lost Tackled |
|---|---|---|---|---|---|---|---|---|
| Marino | 50 | 29 | 58 | 318 | 2 | 6.4 | 11.0 | 4-29 |
| **SAN FRANCISCO** | | | | | | | | |
| Montana | 35 | 24 | 69 | 331 | 0 | 9.5 | 13.8 | 1-5 |

# 1985 N.F.C.   The Midway's New Monsters

Coach Mike Ditka's Bears were *the* pro football story of 1985 and deserved to be. They had all the elements. For those who like intrigue, there were constant rumors of friction between Ditka and defensive coordinator Buddy Ryan, architect of the Bears' much-publicized "46" defense, the league's best. For nostalgia, Walter Payton padded his all-time record rushing total with 1,551 yards and looked toward his first Super Bowl. Flaky Jim McMahon was the N.F.L.'s most inspirational leader, the N.F.C.'s second-best passer and football's most unpredictable character. For comic relief, 308-pound defensive tackle William "The Refrigerator" Perry became a national hero by moving into the backfield as a blocker on short-yardage plays and then scoring three touchdowns, one on a pass reception. Suspense was added when the Bears won their first 12 games, raising the question — answered by Miami in week 13 — of whether they could go all the way undefeated.

## EASTERN DIVISION

**Dallas Cowboys** — Although the Cowboys returned to the playoffs as N.F.C. East champs, success was catching up to them. All those years of drafting near the end of the pack had produced few stars to replace the aging nucleus of the team. Of the first draft choices from the previous eight years, only defensive end Jim Jeffcoat was a starter. Coach Tom Landry got the team away and winging with a big 44-14 win over the arch-rival Redskins in the Monday night opener, and the Cowboys stood 7-3 after 10 weeks. Then, on November 17, the Bears came to Dallas and crushed them 44-0, ending the N.F.L.'s second-longest non-shutout skein at 218 games, and showing the Cowboys had slipped badly. A later 50-24 thrashing by Cincinnati confirmed the diagnosis. Tony Dorsett, Danny White, Randy White, Too Tall Jones and several others were past 30. Of the younger players, only Jeffcoat, middle linebacker Eugene Lockhart and cornerback Everson Walls had established themselves. Walls became the N.F.L.'s first three-time interception leader with nine steals.

**New York Giants** — Clearly, the Giants were a team on the rise. For the second straight year, New York made the playoffs as a wild-card team, and only a pair of frustrating defeats by the Cowboys kept them from the N.F.C. East title. Of the team's six losses, only one was by as many as seven points. The defense, led by all-world linebacker Lawrence Taylor, had been getting raves for years. In 1985, coach Bill Parcells found an offense. Stubby running back Joe Morris emerged as one of the N.F.L.'s top threats with 1,336 yards and 21 touchdowns. Trouble loomed when tight end Zeke Mowatt went out with a knee injury, but Mark Bavaro proved a more-than-adequate replacement. Phil Simms showed continued improvement at quarterback, and — equally important — good health. His 3,829 passing yards put him into the Pro Bowl where he was MVP.

**Washington Redskins** — On Monday night, November 18, America watched the end of Joe Theismann's career, when a Lawrence Taylor sack snapped his right leg. After Theismann was carried off, a new star appeared for the Skins, who were only 5-5 going into the game. Young Jay Schroeder rallied the team to a 23-21 win over the Giants and four more victories in the last five games. In the only loss, he passed for 348 yards against San Francisco. Although Washington could not overcome its stumbling start — it lost three of its first four games — the final 10-6 record was the same as the Cowboys and Giants posted. Only a tiebreaker kept them out of the playoffs. In another changing of the guard, George Rogers replaced sorebacked John Riggins as the No. 1 runner. Some things stayed the same. Receiver Art Monk caught 91 passes, and the celebrated Hogs' offensive line continued to block no matter who was in the backfield.

**Philadelphia Eagles** — For the third straight year, the Eagles' record improved, but the progress wasn't fast enough for new owners Norman Braman and Ed Leibowitz. Coach Marion Campbell was fired with a game left on the schedule. A streak of five wins in six games at mid-season raised too many hopes for Campbell to survive the inevitable collapse. The Eagles' defense, led by Pro Bowl safety Wes Hopkins, was respectable, but the offense creaked, despite the presence of well-named wide receiver Mike Quick. A 99-yard Ron Jaworski-to-Quick pass in overtime against Atlanta produced one of Philadelphia's wins.

The main culprit was the offensive line, which was offensive only to lovers of good blocking. Somehow, new running back Earnest Jackson gained 1,028 yards and Jaworski survived.

**St. Louis Cardinals** — Big things were expected of the Big Red after a 9-7 year in '84, and three victories in the first four games did nothing to diminish confidence. Then, injuries to receiver Roy Green and back Ottis Anderson put the team into a tailspin — losing 10 of the remaining 12 games and costing Jim Hanifan, the coach since 1980, his job. Stump Mitchell did a good job as Anderson's replacement, but, without Green or Anderson in his arsenal, quarterback Neil Lomax regressed to just another thrower. In a fashion note, the team played its December 8 game with New Orleans in knee-length maroon socks. Possibly from embarrassment, but more likely because of Mitchell's 158 rushing yards, the Cardinals won their only game in the final seven weeks. The league office quickly ruled the socks out of bounds, and the much-relieved Cards went back to losing in traditional garb.

## CENTRAL DIVISION

**Chicago Bears** — The Bears reached near-perfection in mid-November as they annihilated Detroit, Dallas and Atlanta by an aggregate 104-3. When Miami finally stopped them 38-24 on a Monday night at the Orange Bowl, Chicago was already focusing on the playoffs. William Perry, Walter Payton and Jim McMahon were the media darlings, but the heart of the team was its defense. Linebackers Mike Singletary and Otis Wilson, linemen Richard Dent and Dan Hampton, and safety Dave Duerson were Pro Bowlers, but several other Bear defenders could have been equally honored. They led the league in fewest points allowed, rushing defense, overall defense, interceptions, fewest points allowed, and takeaway-giveaway ratio. Dent led the N.F.C. in sacks for the second consecutive year with 17. Although safety Gary Fencik's 118 tackles topped the team, the leader of the impregnable defense was Singletary, voted United Press International's defensive player of the year. About the only thing they couldn't defend against was media backlash. When a Bears' rock-video hit the charts, some fans were ready to cry, "Enough!"

**Green Bay Packers** — The Packers' .500 finish was their second under Forrest Gregg, third in a row and fourth in five years. The only time they missed 8-8 during that stretch was the strike-shortened '82 season. The roster, with the exception of receiver James Lofton, was mostly middling in quality. Lofton caught 69 passes for 1,153 yards, even though he was double- and triple-covered. The offensive line was less than average. QB Lynn Dickey finally tired of being sacked and asked to be benched for the fourth game. After that, Randy Wright, Jim Zorn and Dickey took turns at signal-calling. Regardless, the Packers' offense consisted of short passes to tight end Paul Coffman and bombs to Lofton.

**Minnesota Vikings** — Easygoing Bud Grant's return as coach lasted only one season, but it was enough to get the Vikings back to respectability. The encouraging 7-9 season was accomplished with much the same crew that floundered to 3-13 in '84. QB Tommy Kramer, still the model of inconsistency, threw for a bundle of yards one week and a bunch of interceptions the next. One of his best nights came in a losing effort when he zinged the Bears' all-everything defense for 436 yards and three touchdowns. Little Darrin Nelson was a versatile runner-receiver, and U.S.F.L. refugee Anthony Carter gave Kramer a consistent deep threat, but the team's bread-and-butter pass catcher was tight end Steve Jordan. With the Vikings on the right track again, Grant turned the reins over to long-time assistant Jerry Burns and retired again.

**Detroit Lions** — Had the Lions been able to play all their games at the Pontiac Silverdome, they might have challenged the Bears. Under new coach Darryl Rogers, they won their first six home games before a pair of losses dropped them to 6-2. Among the victims were Dallas, San Francisco and Miami. On the road, the Lions were a dreadful 1-7, losing to Tampa Bay and Indianapolis, among others. Eric Hipple was at quarterback most of the time, but he was adequate, at best. Billy Sims, nursing his injured knee, didn't play all year, putting the pressure on James Jones, who gained a respectable 886 yards.

FINAL TEAM STATISTICS

**OFFENSE**

| | ATL. | CHI. | DALL. | DET. | G.B. | L.A. | MINN. | N.O. | NY G | PHIL. | STL. | S.F. | T.B. | WASH. |
|---|---|---|---|---|---|---|---|---|---|---|---|---|---|---|
| **FIRST DOWNS:** | | | | | | | | | | | | | | |
| Total | 296 | 343 | 336 | 259 | 318 | 258 | 317 | 250 | 356 | 292 | 301 | 340 | 291 | 319 |
| by Rushing | 149 | 176 | 95 | 89 | 114 | 115 | 95 | 83 | 138 | 82 | 108 | 137 | 95 | 147 |
| by Passing | 132 | 145 | 208 | 150 | 172 | 131 | 189 | 148 | 192 | 188 | 171 | 179 | 162 | 157 |
| by Penalty | 15 | 22 | 33 | 20 | 32 | 12 | 33 | 19 | 26 | 22 | 22 | 24 | 34 | 15 |
| **RUSHING:** | | | | | | | | | | | | | | |
| Number | 560 | 610 | 462 | 452 | 470 | 503 | 406 | 431 | 581 | 428 | 417 | 477 | 434 | 571 |
| Yards | 2466 | 2761 | 1741 | 1538 | 2208 | 2057 | 1516 | 1683 | 2451 | 1630 | 1974 | 2232 | 1644 | 2523 |
| Average Yards | 4.4 | 4.5 | 3.8 | 3.4 | 4.7 | 4.1 | 3.7 | 3.9 | 4.2 | 3.8 | 4.7 | 4.7 | 3.8 | 4.4 |
| Touchdowns | 14 | 27 | 11 | 13 | 16 | 15 | 19 | 4 | 24 | 8 | 14 | 20 | 11 | 20 |
| **PASSING:** | | | | | | | | | | | | | | |
| Attempts | 462 | 432 | 587 | 462 | 513 | 403 | 576 | 508 | 497 | 567 | 534 | 550 | 508 | 512 |
| Completions | 254 | 237 | 344 | 254 | 267 | 234 | 311 | 260 | 275 | 290 | 296 | 331 | 269 | 280 |
| Completion Pct. | 55.0 | 54.9 | 58.6 | 55.0 | 52.0 | 58.1 | 54.0 | 51.2 | 55.3 | 51.1 | 55.4 | 60.2 | 53.0 | 54.7 |
| Passing Yards | 3025 | 3303 | 4236 | 3316 | 3552 | 2872 | 3931 | 3257 | 3829 | 4036 | 3581 | 3987 | 3423 | 3243 |
| Avg. Yds per Att. | 4.7 | 6.5 | 6.1 | 5.7 | 5.6 | 5.4 | 5.9 | 4.9 | 6.3 | 5.8 | 5.2 | 6.2 | 5.7 | 5.0 |
| Avg. Yds per Comp. | 11.9 | 13.9 | 12.3 | 13.1 | 13.3 | 12.3 | 12.6 | 12.5 | 13.9 | 13.9 | 12.1 | 12.1 | 12.7 | 11.6 |
| Times Tackled | 69 | 43 | 44 | 53 | 50 | 57 | 45 | 58 | 52 | 55 | 65 | 42 | 40 | 52 |
| Yds Lost Tackled | 531 | 227 | 375 | 378 | 389 | 409 | 296 | 461 | 396 | 450 | 469 | 299 | 301 | 428 |
| Net Yards | 2494 | 3076 | 3861 | 2938 | 3163 | 2463 | 3635 | 2796 | 3433 | 3586 | 3112 | 3688 | 3122 | 2815 |
| Touchdowns | 13 | 17 | 27 | 19 | 21 | 16 | 22 | 20 | 22 | 19 | 19 | 28 | 22 | 13 |
| Interceptions | 20 | 16 | 25 | 21 | 27 | 14 | 29 | 23 | 20 | 28 | 18 | 14 | 26 | 21 |
| Pct. Intercepted | 4.3 | 3.7 | 4.3 | 4.5 | 5.3 | 3.5 | 5.0 | 4.5 | 4.0 | 4.9 | 3.4 | 2.5 | 5.1 | 4.1 |
| **PUNTS:** | | | | | | | | | | | | | | |
| Number | 89 | 69 | 83 | 73 | 82 | 88 | 67 | 89 | 81 | 91 | 87 | 87 | 79 | 73 |
| Average | 42.2 | 41.6 | 41.4 | 41.8 | 39.8 | 42.7 | 42.8 | 42.3 | 42.9 | 41.5 | 40.7 | 39.3 | 40.9 | 40.7 |
| **PUNT RETURNS** | | | | | | | | | | | | | | |
| Number | 31 | 54 | 40 | 38 | 38 | 38 | 25 | 30 | 53 | 45 | 40 | 38 | 25 | 47 |
| Yards | 223 | 503 | 237 | 403 | 370 | 501 | 250 | 215 | 442 | 393 | 393 | 258 | 229 | 508 |
| Average Yards | 7.2 | 9.3 | 5.9 | 10.6 | 9.7 | 13.2 | 10.0 | 7.2 | 8.3 | 8.7 | 9.8 | 6.8 | 9.2 | 10.8 |
| Touchdowns | 0 | 0 | 0 | 1 | 0 | 1 | 0 | 0 | 0 | 0 | 0 | 0 | 0 | 0 |
| **KICKOFF RET.:** | | | | | | | | | | | | | | |
| Number | 72 | 43 | 62 | 68 | 67 | 56 | 68 | 71 | 50 | 56 | 78 | 58 | 80 | 60 |
| Yards | 1406 | 1089 | 1210 | 1494 | 1318 | 1394 | 1576 | 1547 | 866 | 1160 | 1421 | 1269 | 1622 | 1349 |
| Average Yards | 19.5 | 25.3 | 19.5 | 22.0 | 19.7 | 24.9 | 23.2 | 21.8 | 17.3 | 20.7 | 18.2 | 21.9 | 20.3 | 22.5 |
| Touchdowns | 1 | 2 | 0 | 0 | 0 | 3 | 0 | 0 | 0 | 0 | 0 | 1 | 0 | 0 |
| **INTERCEPT RET.:** | | | | | | | | | | | | | | |
| Number | 22 | 34 | 33 | 18 | 15 | 29 | 22 | 21 | 24 | 18 | 13 | 18 | 18 | 23 |
| Yards | 247 | 512 | 263 | 136 | 262 | 359 | 283 | 312 | 339 | 125 | 240 | 310 | 146 | 220 |
| Average Yards | 11.2 | 15.1 | 8.0 | 7.6 | 17.5 | 12.4 | 12.9 | 14.9 | 14.1 | 6.9 | 18.5 | 17.2 | 8.1 | 9.6 |
| Touchdowns | 1 | 4 | 4 | 0 | 2 | 4 | 1 | 2 | 2 | 2 | 1 | 1 | 0 | 0 |
| **PENALTIES:** | | | | | | | | | | | | | | |
| Number | 126 | 104 | 100 | 104 | 101 | 97 | 88 | 96 | 80 | 98 | 101 | 105 | 103 | 74 |
| Yards | 1149 | 912 | 759 | 741 | 798 | 730 | 690 | 805 | 781 | 736 | 816 | 868 | 751 | 596 |
| **FUMBLES:** | | | | | | | | | | | | | | |
| Number | 23 | 24 | 29 | 36 | 39 | 35 | 27 | 23 | 36 | 25 | 38 | 29 | 37 | 27 |
| Number Lost | 10 | 15 | 16 | 20 | 18 | 21 | 18 | 13 | 18 | 12 | 16 | 20 | 22 | 19 |
| **POINTS:** | | | | | | | | | | | | | | |
| Total | 282 | 456 | 357 | 307 | 337 | 340 | 346 | 294 | 399 | 286 | 278 | 411 | 294 | 297 |
| PAT Attempts | 30 | 51 | 43 | 33 | 40 | 39 | 43 | 29 | 48 | 30 | 34 | 53 | 33 | 33 |
| PAT Made | 30 | 51 | 42 | 31 | 38 | 38 | 41 | 27 | 45 | 29 | 33 | 52 | 30 | 31 |
| FG Attempts | 31 | 37 | 28 | 31 | 26 | 29 | 26 | 35 | 33 | 30 | 28 | 21 | 32 | 35 |
| FG Made | 24 | 31 | 19 | 26 | 19 | 22 | 15 | 31 | 22 | 25 | 13 | 13 | 22 | 22 |
| Percent FG Made | 77.4 | 83.8 | 67.9 | 83.9 | 73.1 | 75.9 | 57.7 | 88.6 | 66.7 | 83.3 | 46.4 | 61.9 | 68.8 | 62.9 |
| Safeties | 0 | 3 | 0 | 0 | 1 | 1 | 1 | 0 | 0 | 1 | 1 | 1 | 0 | 1 |

**DEFENSE**

| | ATL. | CHI. | DALL. | DET. | G.B. | L.A. | MINN. | N.O. | NY G | PHIL. | STL. | S.F. | T.B. | WASH. |
|---|---|---|---|---|---|---|---|---|---|---|---|---|---|---|
| **FIRST DOWNS:** | | | | | | | | | | | | | | |
| Total | 329 | 236 | 312 | 359 | 310 | 281 | 324 | 335 | 258 | 307 | 314 | 293 | 351 | 244 |
| by Rushing | 112 | 74 | 98 | 179 | 111 | 104 | 139 | 125 | 77 | 122 | 115 | 89 | 146 | 94 |
| by Passing | 181 | 141 | 193 | 156 | 178 | 155 | 163 | 188 | 163 | 160 | 169 | 183 | 185 | 134 |
| by Penalty | 36 | 21 | 21 | 24 | 21 | 22 | 22 | 22 | 18 | 25 | 30 | 21 | 20 | 16 |
| **RUSHING:** | | | | | | | | | | | | | | |
| Number | 437 | 359 | 465 | 560 | 494 | 444 | 542 | 508 | 419 | 526 | 552 | 435 | 547 | 424 |
| Yards | 2052 | 1319 | 1853 | 2685 | 2047 | 1586 | 2223 | 2162 | 1482 | 2205 | 2378 | 1683 | 2430 | 1734 |
| Average Yards | 4.7 | 3.7 | 4.0 | 4.8 | 4.1 | 3.6 | 4.1 | 4.3 | 3.5 | 4.2 | 4.3 | 3.9 | 4.4 | 4.1 |
| Touchdowns | 24 | 6 | 18 | 19 | 17 | 9 | 16 | 19 | 9 | 17 | 11 | 10 | 28 | 11 |
| **PASSING:** | | | | | | | | | | | | | | |
| Attempts | 535 | 522 | 549 | 478 | 509 | 548 | 490 | 529 | 535 | 478 | 461 | 621 | 505 | 465 |
| Completions | 289 | 249 | 279 | 283 | 295 | 296 | 280 | 306 | 278 | 251 | 253 | 346 | 318 | 239 |
| Completion Pct. | 54.0 | 47.7 | 50.8 | 59.2 | 58.0 | 54.0 | 57.1 | 57.8 | 52.0 | 52.5 | 54.9 | 55.7 | 63.0 | 51.4 |
| Passing Yards | 4129 | 3299 | 4214 | 3242 | 3509 | 3483 | 3464 | 3975 | 3377 | 3289 | 3257 | 3965 | 3955 | 3124 |
| Avg. Yds per Att. | 6.6 | 4.8 | 6.2 | 5.6 | 5.6 | 5.1 | 6.2 | 6.4 | 4.7 | 5.5 | 6.1 | 5.2 | 6.8 | 5.3 |
| Avg. Yds per Comp. | 14.3 | 13.3 | 15.1 | 11.5 | 11.9 | 11.8 | 12.4 | 13.0 | 12.2 | 13.1 | 12.9 | 11.5 | 12.4 | 13.1 |
| Times Tackled | 42 | 64 | 62 | 45 | 48 | 56 | 33 | 46 | 68 | 53 | 32 | 60 | 35 | 52 |
| Yds Lost Tackled | 331 | 483 | 459 | 336 | 383 | 421 | 223 | 322 | 539 | 359 | 254 | 457 | 277 | 378 |
| Net Yards | 3798 | 2816 | 3755 | 2906 | 3126 | 3062 | 3241 | 3653 | 2838 | 2930 | 3003 | 3508 | 3678 | 2746 |
| Touchdowns | 32 | 16 | 20 | 16 | 22 | 19 | 20 | 26 | 20 | 18 | 34 | 11 | 18 | 19 |
| Interceptions | 22 | 34 | 33 | 18 | 15 | 29 | 22 | 21 | 24 | 18 | 13 | 18 | 18 | 23 |
| Pct. Intercepted | 4.1 | 6.5 | 6.0 | 3.8 | 2.9 | 5.3 | 4.5 | 4.0 | 4.5 | 3.8 | 2.8 | 2.9 | 3.6 | 4.9 |
| **PUNTS:** | | | | | | | | | | | | | | |
| Number | 69 | 90 | 78 | 64 | 77 | 89 | 65 | 81 | 107 | 92 | 75 | 92 | 59 | 85 |
| Average | 42.0 | 40.4 | 41.3 | 40.2 | 42.7 | 42.0 | 41.4 | 42.2 | 40.8 | 42.6 | 40.9 | 39.6 | 44.4 | 43.8 |
| **PUNT RETURNS** | | | | | | | | | | | | | | |
| Number | 52 | 23 | 44 | 44 | 46 | 43 | 36 | 45 | 29 | 41 | 51 | 33 | 47 | 32 |
| Yards | 417 | 203 | 286 | 420 | 411 | 297 | 328 | 397 | 247 | 462 | 456 | 294 | 519 | 285 |
| Average Yards | 8.0 | 8.8 | 6.5 | 9.5 | 8.9 | 6.9 | 9.1 | 8.8 | 8.5 | 11.3 | 8.9 | 8.9 | 11.0 | 8.9 |
| Touchdowns | 0 | 0 | 0 | 0 | 0 | 0 | 0 | 0 | 0 | 1 | 0 | 1 | 0 | 0 |
| **KICKOFF RET.:** | | | | | | | | | | | | | | |
| Number | 62 | 78 | 68 | 60 | 71 | 66 | 68 | 43 | 79 | 65 | 56 | 72 | 51 | 53 |
| Yards | 1135 | 1827 | 1310 | 1313 | 1570 | 1253 | 1491 | 968 | 1697 | 1293 | 1150 | 1485 | 1187 | 1186 |
| Average Yards | 18.3 | 23.4 | 19.3 | 21.9 | 22.1 | 19.0 | 21.9 | 22.5 | 21.5 | 19.9 | 20.5 | 20.6 | 23.3 | 22.4 |
| Touchdowns | 0 | 0 | 0 | 1 | 2 | 0 | 0 | 1 | 0 | 0 | 0 | 1 | 0 | 2 |
| **INTERCEPT RET.:** | | | | | | | | | | | | | | |
| Number | 20 | 16 | 25 | 21 | 27 | 14 | 29 | 23 | 20 | 28 | 18 | 14 | 26 | 21 |
| Yards | 172 | 99 | 319 | 247 | 326 | 138 | 311 | 251 | 285 | 474 | 245 | 80 | 368 | 215 |
| Average Yards | 8.6 | 6.2 | 12.8 | 11.8 | 12.1 | 9.9 | 10.7 | 10.9 | 14.3 | 16.9 | 13.6 | 5.7 | 14.2 | 10.2 |
| Touchdowns | 0 | 1 | 2 | 1 | 1 | 1 | 2 | 1 | 4 | 2 | 1 | 1 | 4 | 2 |
| **PENALTIES:** | | | | | | | | | | | | | | |
| Number | 97 | 118 | 108 | 105 | 102 | 72 | 123 | 108 | 106 | 99 | 88 | 106 | 114 | 89 |
| Yards | 738 | 944 | 990 | 729 | 797 | 529 | 1000 | 837 | 821 | 834 | 742 | 778 | 945 | 699 |
| **FUMBLES:** | | | | | | | | | | | | | | |
| Number | 18 | 30 | 24 | 35 | 44 | 30 | 37 | 24 | 36 | 27 | 28 | 31 | 37 | 28 |
| Number Lost | 12 | 20 | 15 | 18 | 25 | 17 | 22 | 16 | 13 | 14 | 14 | 17 | 22 | 11 |
| **POINTS:** | | | | | | | | | | | | | | |
| Total | 452 | 198 | 333 | 366 | 355 | 277 | 359 | 401 | 283 | 310 | 414 | 263 | 448 | 312 |
| PAT Attempts | 57 | 23 | 40 | 40 | 43 | 30 | 39 | 48 | 33 | 39 | 47 | 26 | 50 | 35 |
| PAT Made | 55 | 22 | 37 | 40 | 41 | 28 | 38 | 48 | 31 | 37 | 46 | 24 | 50 | 34 |
| FG Attempts | 23 | 19 | 27 | 36 | 31 | 29 | 37 | 28 | 21 | 29 | 38 | 35 | 43 | 28 |
| FG Made | 17 | 12 | 18 | 28 | 16 | 23 | 29 | 21 | 18 | 13 | 28 | 27 | 32 | 22 |
| Percent FG Made | 73.9 | 63.2 | 66.7 | 77.8 | 51.6 | 79.3 | 78.4 | 75.0 | 85.7 | 44.8 | 73.7 | 77.1 | 74.4 | 78.6 |
| Safeties | 2 | 1 | 1 | 1 | 4 | 0 | 0 | 1 | 0 | 0 | 1 | 1 | 1 | 1 |

Some improvement in the offensive line and on the defense gave hope for the future.

**Tampa Bay Buccaneers** — The Bucs were the Central Division omega to the Bears' alpha. By mid-season, Chicago looked like it would never lose, and Tampa Bay looked like it would never win. After new coach Leeman Bennett's team topped St. Louis in the 10th week and then was stomped 62-28 the next week by the Jets, he switched from Steve DeBerg to ex-U.S.F.L. QB Steve Young. The result was an 19-16 overtime win over Detroit. Four more losses resulted in a 2-14 finish. Tight end Jimmie Giles and running back James Wilder played tough all year, and Young gave promise for the future, but the general talent level indicated several coming years of early draft positions.

## WESTERN DIVISION

**Los Angeles Rams** — The Rams signed Dieter Brock out of the Canadian Football League where he was twice MVP, hoping the 34-year-old "rookie" could finally give them some passing punch. In camp, Brock won the starting job from Jeff Kemp, but, after that, his short passes satisfied virtually no one. Eric Dickerson, the Rams' most important weapon, held out until the third game while free agent Charles White filled in admirably. Once signed, Dickerson, though inconsistent, rushed for 1,234 yards and 12 scores, a good season for anyone else. The team won its first seven games, then lost four of its next six. The lead over San Francisco was down to a game, but, on December 9, Ron Brown's TD kickoff return and Gary Green's interception runback for another score sparked a 27-20 victory over the 49ers to lock up the West title.

**San Francisco 49ers** — The defense slumped badly and quarterback Joe Montana got off to a slow start. The '84 Super Bowl champs slipped below .500 after seven games. Five victories in the next half-dozen games got them back into the race and eventually to a wild-card berth. The defense was unreliable to the end, but Montana came back to lead the N.F.C. in passing. Reliable Dwight Clark and tight end Russ Francis were steady receivers, and rookie Jerry Rice gave Montana an exciting long-ball threat. Running back Roger Craig had a gangbuster year, rushing for 1,050 yards and catching a league-leading 92 passes for another 1,106, to become the first player ever to gain a thousand yards both ways.

**New Orleans Saints** — For the 19th consecutive year, the Saints failed to finish above .500. Kicker Morten Andersen provided most of the offense with 31 field goals out of 35 attempts. In the spring, the Saints handed Earl Campbell the running back job by trading George Rogers to Washington, but Campbell showed he was past his prime. The quarterback situation was never completely settled, although ex-U.S.F.L.er Bobby Hebert showed promise. The defense had been the best thing coach Bum Phillips had going for him, but it fell apart. After the Saints upset Minnesota on November 24, Phillips resigned. His son Wade, the team's defensive coordinator, replaced him on an interim basis. The team responded with a second upset, over the Rams, and then dropped its last three games to finish 5-11.

**Atlanta Falcons** — The Falcons signed first-round draft choice Bill Fralic, a guaranteed future all-pro. Once the season opened, they dropped like a rock to the bottom of the division by losing their first six games. Quarterback David Archer replaced an injured Steve Bartkowski after five weeks, but Atlanta had little luck passing the ball. Billy "White Shoes" Johnson, at 34 years old, was the only receiver with more than 30 catches. The one-dimensional offense was almost all Gerald Riggs. He was excellent, leading the N.F.C. in rushing with 1,719 yards, but the so-so defense couldn't make up for the lack of a passing attack.

**DALLAS COWBOYS** 10-6 Tom Landry

| Scores of Each Game | | |
|---|---|---|
| 44 | WASHINGTON | 14 |
| 21 | Detroit | 26 |
| 20 | CLEVELAND | 7 |
| 17 | Houston | 10 |
| 30 | N.Y.Giants | 29 |
| 27 | PITTSBURGH | 13 |
| 14 | Philadelphia | 16 |
| 24 | ATLANTA | 10 |
| 10 | St.Louis | 21 |
| 13 | Washington | 7 |
| 0 | CHICAGO | 44 |
| 34 | PHILADELPHIA | 17 |
| 35 | ST.LOUIS | 17 |
| 24 | Cincinnati | 50 |
| 28 | N.Y.GIANTS | 21 |
| 16 | San Francisco | 31 |

| Use Name | Pos. | Hgt | Wgt | Age | Int | Pts |
|---|---|---|---|---|---|---|
| Jim Cooper | OT | 6'5" | 274 | 29 | | |
| Phil Pozderac | OT | 6'9" | 282 | 25 | | |
| Chris Schultz | OT | 6'8" | 288 | 25 | | |
| Crawford Ker | OG | 6'3" | 293 | 23 | | |
| Kurt Petersen | OG | 6'4" | 278 | 28 | | |
| Howard Richards | OG-OT | 6'6" | 262 | 26 | | |
| Broderick Thompson | OG | 6'5" | 280 | 25 | | |
| Glen Titensor | OG | 6'4" | 261 | 27 | | |
| Tom Rafferty | C | 6'3" | 264 | 31 | | |
| Mark Tuinel | C | 6'5" | 270 | 25 | | |
| Kevin Brooks | DE | 6'6" | 270 | 22 | | |
| Jim Jeffcoat | DE | 6'5" | 263 | 24 | 1 | 6 |
| Too Tall Jones | DE | 6'9" | 287 | 34 | | |
| John Dutton | DT | 6'7" | 268 | 34 | | |
| David Ponder | DT | 6'3" | 250 | 23 | | |
| Don Smerek | DT | 6'7" | 265 | 27 | | |
| Randy White | DT | 6'4" | 272 | 32 | | |
| Vince Albritton | LB | 6'2" | 213 | 23 | | |
| Steve DeOssie | LB | 6'2" | 245 | 22 | | |
| Mike Hegman | LB | 6'1" | 228 | 32 | 1 | |
| Eugene Lockhart | LB | 6'2" | 234 | 24 | 1 | 6 |
| Jesse Penn | LB | 6'3" | 217 | 22 | | 6 |
| Jeff Rohrer | LB | 6'3" | 230 | 26 | | |
| Brian Salonen | LB | 6'3" | 226 | 24 | | |
| Bill Bates | DB | 6'1" | 199 | 24 | 4 | |
| Dextor Clinkscale | DB | 5'11" | 195 | 27 | 3 | |
| Michael Downs | DB | 6'3" | 204 | 26 | 3 | |
| Ricky Easmon (to TB) | DB | 5'10" | 160 | 22 | | |
| Ron Fellows | DB | 6' | 180 | 26 | 4 | |
| Victor Scott | DB | 6' | 196 | 23 | 2 | 6 |
| Dennis Thurmna | DB | 5'11" | 179 | 29 | 5 | 6 |
| Everson Walls | DB | 6'1" | 194 | 25 | 9 | |
| Steve Pelluer | QB | 6'4" | 208 | 23 | | |
| Danny White | QB | 6'2" | 196 | 33 | | 12 |
| Gary Hogeboom | QB | 6'4" | 207 | 27 | | 6 |
| Tony Dorsett | HB | 5'11" | 185 | 31 | | 60 |
| James Jones | HB | 5'10" | 203 | 26 | | |
| Robert Lavette | HB | 5'11" | 199 | 21 | | |
| John Williams (to SEA) | HB | 5'11" | 219 | 24 | | |
| Todd Fowler | FB | 6'3" | 218 | 23 | | |
| Timmy Newsome | FB | 6'1" | 237 | 27 | | 18 |
| Gordon Banks | WR | 5'10" | 173 | 27 | | |
| Kenny Duckett (from NO) | WR | 6' | 183 | 25 | | |
| Leon Gonzales | WR | 5'10" | 162 | 21 | | |
| Tony Hill | WR | 6'2" | 202 | 29 | | 42 |
| Karl Powe | WR | 6'2" | 175 | 23 | | |
| Mike Renfro | WR | 6' | 189 | 30 | | 48 |
| Fred Cornwell | TE | 6'6" | 233 | 24 | | 6 |
| Doug Cosbie | TE | 6'6" | 245 | 29 | | 36 |
| Mike Saxon | K | 6'3" | 187 | 23 | | |
| Rafael Septien | K | 5'10" | 179 | 31 | | 99 |

Dowe Aughtman - Shoulder Injury
Brian Baldinger - Knee Injury

**NEW YORK GIANTS** 10-6 Bill Parcells

| Scores of Each Game | | |
|---|---|---|
| 21 | PHILADELPHIA | 0 |
| 20 | Green Bay | 23 |
| 27 | ST.LOUIS | 17 |
| 16 | Philadelphia | *10 |
| 29 | DALLAS | 30 |
| 30 | Cincinnati | 35 |
| 17 | WASHINGTON | 3 |
| 21 | New Orleans | 13 |
| 22 | TAMPA BAY | 20 |
| 24 | L.A.RAMS | 19 |
| 21 | Washington | 23 |
| 34 | St.Louis | 3 |
| 33 | CLEVELAND | 35 |
| 35 | Houston | 14 |
| 21 | Dallas | 28 |
| 28 | PITTSBURGH | 10 |

| Use Name | Pos. | Hgt | Wgt | Age | Int | Pts |
|---|---|---|---|---|---|---|
| Brad Benson | OT | 6'3" | 270 | 29 | | |
| Conrad Goode | OT-C | 6'6" | 285 | 23 | | |
| Gordon King | OT | 6'6" | 275 | 29 | | |
| Karl Nelson | OT | 6'6" | 285 | 25 | | |
| Billy Ard | OG | 6'3" | 270 | 26 | | |
| Chris Godfrey | OG | 6'3" | 265 | 27 | | |
| David Jordan | OG | 6'6" | 276 | 23 | | |
| Bart Oates | C | 6'3" | 265 | 26 | | |
| Dee Hardison | DE | 6'4" | 274 | 29 | | |
| Leonard Marshall | DE | 6'3" | 285 | 23 | 1 | |
| George Martin | DE | 6'4" | 255 | 32 | 1 | 6 |
| Curtis McGriff | DE | 6'5" | 276 | 27 | | |
| Casey Merrill | DE | 6'4" | 260 | 28 | | |
| Jim Burt | NT | 6'1" | 260 | 26 | | |
| Jerome Sally | NT | 6'3" | 270 | 26 | | |
| Carl Banks | LB | 6'4" | 235 | 23 | | |
| Harry Carson | LB | 6'2" | 240 | 31 | | |
| Andy Headen | LB | 6'5" | 242 | 25 | 2 | |
| Byron Hunt | LB | 6'5" | 242 | 26 | | |
| Robbie Jones | LB | 6'2" | 230 | 25 | | |
| Gary Reasons | LB | 6'4" | 234 | 23 | 1 | |
| Lawrence Taylor | LB | 6'3" | 243 | 26 | | |
| Tyrone Davis | DB | 6'1" | 190 | 23 | | |
| Bill Currier | DB | 6' | 196 | 30 | 1 | |
| Larry Flowers (to NYJ) | DB | 6'1" | 195 | 27 | | |
| Mark Haynes | DB | 5'11" | 195 | 26 | | |
| Kenny Hill | DB | 6' | 195 | 27 | 2 | |
| Terry Kinard | DB | 6'1" | 200 | 25 | 5 | |
| Elvis Patterson | DB | 5'11" | 188 | 24 | 6 | 6 |
| Ted Watts | DB | 6' | 190 | 27 | 1 | |
| Herb Welch | DB | 5'11" | 180 | 24 | 2 | |
| Perry Williams | DB | 6'2" | 203 | 24 | 2 | |
| Jeff Hostetler | QB | 6'3" | 212 | 24 | | |
| Jeff Rutledge | QB | 6'1" | 195 | 28 | | |
| Phil Simms | QB | 6'3" | 214 | 28 | | |
| Joe Morris | HB | 5'7" | 195 | 24 | | 126 |
| Lee Rouson | HB | 6'1" | 210 | 22 | | |
| George Adams | FB | 6'1" | 225 | 22 | | 24 |
| Rob Carpenter | FB | 6'1" | 226 | 30 | | |
| Maurice Carthon | FB | 6'1" | 225 | 24 | | |
| Tony Galbreath | FB | 6' | 228 | 31 | | 6 |
| Bobby Johnson | WR | 5'11" | 171 | 23 | | 48 |
| Lionel Manuel | WR | 5'11" | 175 | 23 | | 30 |
| Phil McConkey | WR | 5'10" | 170 | 28 | | 6 |
| Stacy Robinson | WR | 5'11" | 186 | 23 | | |
| Byron Williams | WR | 6'2" | 183 | 24 | | |
| Mark Bavaro | TE | 6'4" | 245 | 22 | | 24 |
| Don Jasselbeck | TE | 6'7" | 245 | 30 | | 6 |
| Vyto Kab (from PHI) | TE | 6'5" | 240 | 25 | | |
| Jess Atkinson (to STL) | K | 5'9" | 165 | 23 | | 53 |
| Ali Haji-Sheikh | K | 6' | 170 | 24 | | 11 |
| Sean Landetta | K | 6' | 200 | 23 | | |
| Eric Schubert | K | 5'8" | 193 | 23 | | 53 |

Kenny Daniel - Broken Hand
Zeke Mowatt - Knee Injury

**WASHINGTON REDSKINS** 10-6 Joe Gibbs

| Scores of Each Game | | |
|---|---|---|
| 14 | Dallas | 44 |
| 16 | HOUSTON | 13 |
| 6 | PHILADELPHIA | 19 |
| 10 | Chicago | 45 |
| 27 | ST.LOUIS | 10 |
| 24 | DETROIT | 3 |
| 3 | N.Y.Giants | 17 |
| 14 | Cleveland | 7 |
| 44 | Atlanta | 10 |
| 7 | DALLAS | 13 |
| 23 | N.Y.GIANTS | 21 |
| 30 | Pittsburgh | 23 |
| 8 | SAN FRANCISCO | 35 |
| 17 | Philadelphia | 12 |
| 27 | CINCINNATI | 24 |
| 27 | St.Louis | 16 |

| Use Name | Pos. | Hgt | Wgt | Age | Int | Pts |
|---|---|---|---|---|---|---|
| Joe Jacoby | OT | 6'7" | 305 | 26 | | |
| Mark May | OT | 6'6" | 295 | 25 | | |
| Dan McQuaid | OT | 6'7" | 278 | 24 | | |
| Russ Grimm | OG | 6'3" | 275 | 26 | | |
| Ken Huff | OG | 6'4" | 265 | 32 | | |
| Raleigh McKenzie | OG | 6'2" | 262 | 22 | | |
| R.C. Thielemann | OG | 6'4" | 262 | 30 | | |
| Jeff Bostic | C-OG | 6'2" | 260 | 26 | | |
| Rick Donnalley | C | 6'2" | 257 | 26 | | |
| Doug Barnett | DE | 6'3" | 250 | 25 | | |
| Steve Hamilton | DE | 6'4" | 255 | 23 | | |
| Todd Liebenstein | DE | 6'6" | 255 | 25 | | |
| Dexter Manley | DE | 6'3" | 250 | 26 | | |
| Charles Mann | DE | 6'6" | 260 | 24 | | |
| Tom Beasley | DT-DE | 6'5" | 248 | 31 | | |
| Dave Butz | DT | 6'7" | 295 | 35 | | |
| Darryl Grant | DT | 6'1" | 275 | 25 | | |
| Dean Hamel | DT | 6'3" | 275 | 24 | | |
| Stuart Anderson | LB | 6'1" | 255 | 25 | | |
| Monte Coleman | LB | 6'2" | 230 | 27 | | |
| Pete Cronan | LB | 6'2" | 238 | 30 | | |
| Mel Kaufman | LB | 6'2" | 218 | 27 | 3 | |
| Chris Keating | LB | 6'2" | 233 | 27 | | |
| Rich Milot | LB | 6'4" | 237 | 28 | 2 | |
| Neal Olkewicz | LB | 6' | 233 | 28 | 1 | |
| Raphel Cherry | DB | 6' | 194 | 23 | 2 | |
| Vernon Dean | DB | 5'11" | 178 | 26 | 5 | |
| Darrel Green | DB | 5'8" | 170 | 25 | 2 | |
| Curtis Jordan | DB | 6'2" | 205 | 31 | 5 | |
| Tony Peters | DB | 6'1" | 190 | 32 | 2 | |
| Barry Willburn | DB | 6'3" | 186 | 21 | 1 | |
| Greg Williams | DB | 5'11" | 185 | 26 | | |
| Kevin Williams | DB | 5'9" | 169 | 23 | | |
| Babe Laufenberg (from SD) | QB | 6'2" | 195 | 25 | | |
| Jay Schroeder | QB | 6'4" | 215 | 24 | | |
| Joe Theismann | QB | 6' | 198 | 35 | | 12 |
| Keith Griffin | HB | 5'8" | 185 | 23 | | 18 |
| Ken Jenkins | HB | 5'8" | 185 | 26 | | |
| Michael Morton | HB | 5'8" | 180 | 25 | | |
| Otis Wonsley | HB-FB | 5'10" | 214 | 28 | | |
| Reggie Branch | FB | 5'11" | 227 | 22 | | |
| John Riggins | FB | 6'2" | 240 | 36 | | 48 |
| George Rogers | FB | 6'2" | 229 | 26 | | 42 |
| Malcolm Barnwell (to NO) | WR | 5'11" | 185 | 27 | | |
| Gary Clark | WR | 5'9" | 173 | 23 | | 30 |
| Mark McGrath | WR | 5'11" | 175 | 27 | | |
| Art Monk | WR | 6'3" | 209 | 27 | | 12 |
| Calvin Muhammad | WR | 6' | 190 | 26 | | 6 |
| Joe Phillips | WR | 5'9" | 188 | 22 | | |
| Clint Didier | TE | 6'5" | 240 | 26 | | 24 |
| Anthony Jones | TE | 6'3" | 248 | 25 | | |
| Rick Walker | TE | 6'3" | 245 | 30 | | |
| Don Warren | TE | 6'4" | 242 | 29 | | 6 |
| Steve Cox | K | 6'4" | 195 | 27 | | |
| Jeff Hayes | K | 5'11" | 175 | 26 | | |
| Mark Moseley | K | 5'11" | 204 | 37 | | 97 |

Ken Coffey - Knee Injury

**PHILADELPHIA EAGLES** 7-9 Marion Campbell (6-9), Fred Bruney (1-0)

| Scores of Each Game | | |
|---|---|---|
| 0 | N.Y.Giants | 21 |
| 6 | L.A.RAMS | 17 |
| 19 | Washington | 6 |
| 10 | N.Y.GIANTS | *16 |
| 21 | New Orleans | 23 |
| 30 | ST.LOUIS | 7 |
| 16 | DALLAS | 14 |
| 21 | BUFFALO | 17 |
| 13 | San Francisco | 24 |
| 23 | ATLANTA | *17 |
| 24 | St.Louis | 14 |
| 17 | Dallas | 34 |
| 23 | MINNESOTA | 28 |
| 12 | WASHINGTON | 17 |
| 14 | San Diego | 20 |
| 37 | Minnesota | 35 |

| Use Name | Pos. | Hgt | Wgt | Age | Int | Pts |
|---|---|---|---|---|---|---|
| Kevin Allen | OT | 6'5" | 284 | 22 | | |
| Tom Jelesky | OT | 6'6" | 275 | 24 | | |
| Leonard Mitchell | OT | 6'7" | 295 | 26 | | |
| Ken Reeves | OT-OG | 6'5" | 268 | 23 | | |
| Ron Baker | OG | 6'4" | 274 | 30 | | |
| Steve Kenney | OG | 6'4" | 274 | 29 | | |
| Mark Dennard | C | 6'1" | 262 | 29 | | |
| Gerry Feehery | C | 6'2" | 270 | 25 | | |
| Greg Brown | DE | 6'5" | 265 | 28 | | |
| Smiley Creswell | DE | 6'4" | 251 | 25 | | |
| Byron Darby | DE | 6'4" | 262 | 25 | | |
| Thomas Strauthers | DE | 6'4" | 264 | 24 | | |
| Ken Clarke | DT | 6'2" | 272 | 29 | | |
| Joe Drake | DT | 6'2" | 290 | 22 | | |
| Dwaine Morris | DT | 6'2" | 255 | 22 | | |
| Reggie White | DT | 6'5" | 285 | 23 | | |
| Aaron Brown | LB | 6'2" | 235 | 29 | | |
| Garry Cobb | LB | 6'2" | 228 | 28 | | |
| Tim Golden | LB | 6'1" | 220 | 25 | | |
| Anthony Griggs | LB | 6'3" | 230 | 25 | | |
| Dwayne Jiles | LB | 6'4" | 242 | 21 | | |
| Jon Kimmel | LB | 6'4" | 240 | 25 | | |
| Rich Kraynak | LB | 6'1" | 230 | 24 | 1 | |
| Tom Polley | LB | 6'3" | 242 | 23 | | |
| Mike Reichenbach | LB | 6'2" | 238 | 23 | 1 | |
| Reggie Wilkes | LB | 6'4" | 242 | 29 | | |
| Joel Williams | LB | 6'1" | 227 | 28 | | |
| Evan Cooper | DB | 5'11" | 184 | 23 | 2 | |
| Herman Edwards | DB | 6' | 194 | 31 | 3 | 6 |
| Ray Ellis | DB | 6'1" | 196 | 26 | 4 | |
| Elbert Foules | DB | 5'11" | 185 | 24 | | |
| Wes Hopkins | DB | 6'1" | 212 | 23 | 6 | 6 |
| Andre Waters | DB | 5'11" | 185 | 23 | | |
| Brenard Wilson | DB | 6' | 185 | 30 | | |
| Roynell Young | DB | 6'1" | 185 | 27 | 1 | |
| Jeff Christensen | QB | 6'3" | 202 | 25 | | |
| Randall Cunningham | QB | 6'4" | 192 | 22 | | |
| Ron Jaworski | QB | 6'2" | 199 | 34 | | 12 |
| Herman Hunter | HB | 6'1" | 193 | 24 | | 12 |
| Earnest Jackson | HB | 5'9" | 208 | 25 | | 36 |
| Major Everett | FB | 5'10" | 218 | 25 | | |
| Michael Haddix | FB | 6'2" | 227 | 23 | | |
| Hubie Oliver | FB | 5'10" | 212 | 27 | | |
| Jairo Penaranda | FB | 5'11" | 218 | 27 | | |
| Keith Baker | WR | 5'10" | 185 | 28 | | |
| Gregg Garrity | WR | 5'10" | 169 | 24 | | |
| Kenny Jackson | WR | 6' | 177 | 23 | | 6 |
| Ron Johnson | WR | 6'3" | 186 | 26 | | |
| Mike Quick | WR | 6'2" | 190 | 26 | | 66 |
| John Goode | TE | 6'2" | 243 | 22 | | |
| Dave Little | TE | 6'2" | 232 | 24 | | 6 |
| John Spagnola | TE | 6'4" | 238 | 28 | | 30 |
| Mike Horan | K | 5'11" | 190 | 26 | | |
| Paul McFadden | K | 5'11" | 163 | 23 | | 104 |

Jody Schulz - Knee Injury

**ST. LOUIS CARDINALS** 5-11 Jim Hanifan

| Scores of Each Game | | |
|---|---|---|
| 27 | Cleveland | *24 |
| 41 | CINCINNATI | 27 |
| 17 | N.Y.Giants | 27 |
| 43 | GREEN BAY | 28 |
| 10 | Washington | 27 |
| 7 | Philadelphia | 30 |
| 10 | Pittsburgh | 23 |
| 10 | HOUSTON | 20 |
| 21 | DALLAS | 10 |
| 0 | Tampa Bay | 16 |
| 14 | PHILADELPHIA | 24 |
| 3 | N.Y.GIANTS | 34 |
| 17 | Dallas | 35 |
| 28 | NEW ORLEANS | 16 |
| 14 | L.A.Rams | 46 |
| 16 | WASHINGTON | 27 |

| Use Name | Pos. | Hgt | Wgt | Age | Int | Pts |
|---|---|---|---|---|---|---|
| Scott Bergold | OT | 6'7" | 263 | 23 | | |
| Tootie Robbins | OT | 6'5" | 302 | 27 | | |
| Carlos Scott | OT-C | 6'4" | 285 | 25 | | |
| Luis Sharpe | OT | 6'4" | 260 | 25 | | |
| Joe Bostic | OG | 6'3" | 268 | 28 | | |
| Doug Dawson | OG | 6'3" | 267 | 23 | | |
| Lance Smith | OG | 6'2" | 262 | 22 | | |
| Randy Clark | C | 6'3" | 270 | 28 | | |
| Rob Monaco | C | 6'3" | 283 | 23 | | |
| Al Baker | DE | 6'6" | 270 | 28 | | |
| Curtis Greer | DE | 6'4" | 258 | 27 | | |
| Stafford Mays | DE | 6'2" | 255 | 27 | | |
| Mark Duda | DT | 6'3" | 279 | 24 | | |
| David Galloway | DT | 6'3" | 279 | 26 | | |
| Elois Grooms | DT | 6'4" | 250 | 32 | | |
| Charlie Baker | LB | 6'2" | 234 | 27 | | |
| Bob Harris | LB | 6'2" | 223 | 24 | | |
| Tom Howard | LB | 6'2" | 220 | 31 | | |
| E.J.Junior | LB | 6'3" | 235 | 25 | 5 | |
| Niko Noga | LB | 6'1" | 235 | 23 | | |
| Freddie Joe Nunn | LB | 6'4" | 228 | 23 | | |
| Danny Spradlin | LB | 6'1" | 235 | 26 | | |
| Jeff Griffin | DB | 6' | 185 | 27 | | |
| Lifford Hobley | DB | 6' | 207 | 22 | | |
| Bobby Johnson | DB | 6' | 187 | 25 | | |
| Cedric Mack | DB | 6' | 194 | 24 | 2 | |
| Lee Nelson | DB | 5'10" | 185 | 31 | | |
| Benny Perrin | DB | 6'2" | 175 | 25 | | |
| Leonard Smith | DB | 5'11" | 202 | 24 | 2 | |
| Wayne Smith | DB | 6' | 170 | 28 | | |
| Lionel Washington | DB | 6' | 188 | 24 | 1 | 6 |
| Lonnie Young | DB | 6'1" | 182 | 22 | 3 | |
| Scott Brunner | QB | 6'5" | 215 | 28 | | |
| Neil Lomax | QB | 6'3" | 215 | 26 | | |
| Rick McIvor | QB | 6'4" | 210 | 24 | | |
| Perry Harrington | HB | 5'11" | 216 | 27 | | 6 |
| Randy Love | HB | 6'1" | 224 | 28 | | |
| Stump Mitchell | HB | 5'9" | 188 | 26 | | 60 |
| Tony Mumford | HB | 6' | 215 | 22 | | |
| Ottis Anderson | FB | 6'2" | 225 | 28 | | 24 |
| Earl Ferrell | FB | 6' | 224 | 27 | | 24 |
| Ron Wolfley | FB | 6' | 222 | 22 | | |
| Clyde Duncan | WR | 6'2" | 211 | 24 | | 6 |
| Earnest Gray | WR | 6'3" | 195 | 28 | | |
| Roy Green | WR | 6' | 195 | 28 | | 30 |
| Jay Novacek | WR | 6'4" | 217 | 22 | | |
| J.T.Smith | WR | 6'2" | 185 | 29 | | 6 |
| Pat Tilley | WR | 5'10" | 178 | 32 | | 36 |
| Greg LaFleur | TE | 6'4" | 236 | 26 | | |
| Doug Marsh | TE | 6'3" | 238 | 27 | | 6 |
| Carl Birdsong | K | 6' | 192 | 26 | | |
| Novo Bojovic | K | 5'10" | 172 | 25 | | 20 |
| Neil O'Donoghue | K | 6'6" | 210 | 32 | | 49 |

Dan Ralph - Back Injury

Quentin Walker - Wrist Injury

* Overtime

## DALLAS COWBOYS

### RUSHING

| Last Name | No. | Yds | Avg | TD |
|---|---|---|---|---|
| Dorsett | 305 | 1307 | 4.3 | 7 |
| Newsome | 88 | 252 | 2.9 | 2 |
| Hogeboom | 8 | 48 | 6.0 | 1 |
| D. White | 22 | 44 | 2.0 | 1 |
| Williams | 14 | 42 | 3.0 | 0 |
| Lavette | 13 | 34 | 2.6 | 0 |
| Fowler | 7 | 25 | 3.6 | 0 |
| J. Jones | 1 | 0 | 0.0 | 0 |
| Banks | 1 | -1 | -1.0 | 0 |
| Pelluer | 3 | -2 | -0.7 | 0 |
| Hill | 1 | -6 | -6.0 | 0 |

### RECEIVING

| Last Name | No. | Yds | Avg | TD |
|---|---|---|---|---|
| Hill | 74 | 1113 | 15.0 | 7 |
| Cosbie | 64 | 793 | 12.4 | 6 |
| Renfro | 60 | 955 | 15.9 | 8 |
| Dorsett | 46 | 449 | 9.8 | 3 |
| Newsome | 46 | 361 | 7.8 | 1 |
| J. Jones | 24 | 179 | 7.5 | 0 |
| Powe | 14 | 237 | 16.9 | 0 |
| Cornwell | 6 | 77 | 12.8 | 1 |
| Fowler | 5 | 24 | 4.8 | 0 |
| Gonzales | 3 | 28 | 9.3 | 0 |
| D. White | 1 | 12 | 12.0 | 1 |
| Lavette | 1 | 8 | 8.0 | 0 |

### PUNT RETURNS

| Last Name | No. | Yds | Avg | TD |
|---|---|---|---|---|
| Bates | 22 | 152 | 6.9 | 0 |
| Gonzales | 15 | 58 | 3.9 | 0 |
| Banks | 3 | 27 | 9.0 | 0 |

### KICKOFF RETURNS

| Last Name | No. | Yds | Avg | TD |
|---|---|---|---|---|
| Lavette | 34 | 682 | 20.1 | 0 |
| Duckett | 9 | 173 | 19.2 | 0 |
| J. Jones | 9 | 161 | 17.9 | 0 |
| Williams | 6 | 129 | 21.5 | 0 |
| Fowler | 3 | 48 | 16.0 | 0 |
| Powe | 1 | 17 | 17.0 | 0 |

### PASSING — PUNTING — KICKING

| PASSING | Att | Cmp | % | Yds | Yd/Att | TD | Int— | % | RK |
|---|---|---|---|---|---|---|---|---|---|
| D. White | 450 | 267 | 59 | 3157 | 7.0 | 21 | 17— | 4 | |
| Hogeboom | 126 | 70 | 56 | 978 | 7.8 | 5 | 7— | 6 | |
| Pelluer | 8 | 5 | 63 | 47 | 5.9 | 0 | 0— | 0 | |
| J. Jones | 2 | 1 | 50 | 12 | 6.0 | 1 | 1— | 50 | |
| Hill | 1 | 1 | 100 | 42 | 42.0 | 0 | 0— | 0 | |

| PUNTING | No | Avg |
|---|---|---|
| Saxon | 81 | 41.9 |
| D. White | 1 | 43.0 |

| KICKING | XP | Att | % | FG | Att | % |
|---|---|---|---|---|---|---|
| Septien | 42 | 43 | 98 | 19 | 28 | 68 |

## NEW YORK GIANTS

### RUSHING

| Last Name | No. | Yds | Avg | TD |
|---|---|---|---|---|
| Morris | 294 | 1336 | 4.5 | 21 |
| Adams | 128 | 498 | 3.9 | 2 |
| Carpenter | 60 | 201 | 3.4 | 0 |
| Galbreath | 29 | 187 | 6.4 | 0 |
| Sims | 37 | 132 | 3.6 | 0 |
| Carthon | 27 | 70 | 2.6 | 0 |
| B. Williams | 2 | 18 | 9.0 | 0 |
| Atkinson | 1 | 14 | 14.0 | 1 |
| Rouson | 1 | 1 | 1.0 | 0 |
| Rutledge | 2 | -6 | -3.0 | 0 |

### RECEIVING

| Last Name | No. | Yds | Avg | TD |
|---|---|---|---|---|
| Manuel | 49 | 859 | 17.5 | 5 |
| Bavaro | 37 | 511 | 13.8 | 4 |
| Johnson | 33 | 533 | 16.2 | 8 |
| Adams | 31 | 389 | 12.5 | 2 |
| Galbreath | 30 | 327 | 10.9 | 1 |
| McConkey | 25 | 404 | 16.2 | 1 |
| Morris | 22 | 212 | 9.6 | 0 |
| Carpenter | 20 | 162 | 8.1 | 0 |
| B. Williams | 15 | 280 | 18.7 | 0 |
| Carthon | 8 | 81 | 10.1 | 0 |
| Hasselbeck | 5 | 71 | 14.2 | 1 |

### PUNT RETURNS

| Last Name | No. | Yds | Avg | TD |
|---|---|---|---|---|
| McConkey | 53 | 442 | 8.3 | 0 |

### KICKOFF RETURNS

| Last Name | No. | Yds | Avg | TD |
|---|---|---|---|---|
| Adams | 14 | 241 | 17.2 | 0 |
| McConkey | 12 | 234 | 19.5 | 0 |
| Hill | 11 | 186 | 16.9 | 0 |
| Galbreath | 7 | 120 | 17.1 | 0 |
| Rouson | 2 | 35 | 17.5 | 0 |
| Morris | 2 | 25 | 12.5 | 0 |
| Hasselbeck | 1 | 21 | 21.0 | 0 |
| Sally | 1 | 4 | 4.0 | 0 |

### PASSING — PUNTING — KICKING

| PASSING | Att | Cmp | % | Yds | Yd/Att | TD | Int— | % | RK |
|---|---|---|---|---|---|---|---|---|---|
| Simms | 495 | 275 | 56 | 3829 | 7.7 | 22 | 20— | 4 | |
| Adams | 1 | 0 | 0 | 0 | 0.0 | 0 | 0— | 0 | |
| Landeta | 1 | 0 | 0 | 0 | 0.0 | 0 | 0— | 0 | |

| PUNTING | No | Avg |
|---|---|---|
| Landeta | 81 | 42.9 |

| KICKING | XP | Att | % | FG | Att | % |
|---|---|---|---|---|---|---|
| Atkinson | 14 | 15 | 93 | 10 | 15 | 67 |
| Schubert | 26 | 27 | 96 | 10 | 13 | 77 |
| Haji-Sheikh | 5 | 5 | 100 | 2 | 5 | 40 |

## WASHINGTON REDSKINS

### RUSHING

| Last Name | No. | Yds | Avg | TD |
|---|---|---|---|---|
| Rogers | 231 | 1093 | 4.7 | 7 |
| Riggins | 176 | 677 | 3.8 | 8 |
| Griffin | 102 | 473 | 4.6 | 3 |
| Theismann | 25 | 115 | 4.6 | 2 |
| Monk | 7 | 51 | 7.3 | 0 |
| Jenkins | 2 | 39 | 19.5 | 0 |
| Schroeder | 17 | 30 | 1.8 | 0 |
| Walker | 3 | 16 | 5.3 | 0 |
| Clark | 2 | 10 | 5.0 | 0 |
| Wonsley | 4 | 8 | 2.0 | 0 |
| Green | 1 | 6 | 6.0 | 0 |
| Warren | 1 | 5 | 5.0 | 0 |

### RECEIVING

| Last Name | No. | Yds | Avg | TD |
|---|---|---|---|---|
| Monk | 91 | 1226 | 13.5 | 2 |
| Clark | 72 | 926 | 12.9 | 5 |
| Didier | 41 | 433 | 10.6 | 4 |
| Griffin | 37 | 285 | 7.7 | 0 |
| Warren | 15 | 163 | 10.9 | 1 |
| Muhammad | 9 | 116 | 12.9 | 1 |
| Riggins | 6 | 18 | 3.0 | 0 |
| Rogers | 4 | 29 | 7.3 | 0 |
| Barnwell | 3 | 28 | 9.3 | 0 |
| Cherry | 1 | 11 | 11.0 | 0 |
| Walker | 1 | 8 | 8.0 | 0 |

### PUNT RETURNS

| Last Name | No. | Yds | Avg | TD |
|---|---|---|---|---|
| Jenkins | 26 | 272 | 10.5 | 0 |
| Green | 16 | 214 | 13.4 | 0 |
| Cherry | 4 | 22 | 5.5 | 0 |
| Dean | 1 | 0 | 0.0 | 0 |

### KICKOFF RETURNS

| Last Name | No. | Yds | Avg | TD |
|---|---|---|---|---|
| Jenkins | 41 | 1018 | 24.8 | 0 |
| Griffin | 7 | 142 | 20.3 | 0 |
| Morton | 6 | 131 | 21.8 | 0 |
| Wonsley | 2 | 26 | 13.0 | 0 |
| Hamel | 1 | 14 | 14.0 | 0 |
| Cherry | 1 | 9 | 9.0 | 0 |
| Keating | 1 | 9 | 9.0 | 0 |
| Jones | 1 | 0 | 0.0 | 0 |

### PASSING — PUNTING — KICKING

| PASSING | Att | Cmp | % | Yds | Yd/Att | TD | Int— | % | RK |
|---|---|---|---|---|---|---|---|---|---|
| Theismann | 301 | 167 | 56 | 1774 | 5.9 | 8 | 16— | 5 | |
| Schroeder | 209 | 112 | 54 | 1458 | 6.9 | 5 | 5— | 2 | |
| Cox | 1 | 1 | 100 | 11 | 11.0 | 0 | 0— | 0 | |
| Riggins | 1 | 0 | 0 | 0 | 0.0 | 0 | 0— | 0 | |

| PUNTING | No | Avg |
|---|---|---|
| Cox | 52 | 41.8 |
| Hayes | 16 | 41.6 |
| Schroeder | 4 | 33.0 |
| Theismann | 1 | 1.0 |

| KICKING | XP | Att. | % | FG | Att | % |
|---|---|---|---|---|---|---|
| Moseley | 31 | 33 | 94 | 22 | 34 | 65 |
| Cox | | | | 0 | 1 | 0 |

## PHILADELPHIA EAGLES

### RUSHING

| Last Name | No. | Yds | Avg | TD |
|---|---|---|---|---|
| E. Jackson | 282 | 1028 | 3.6 | 5 |
| Haddix | 67 | 213 | 3.2 | 0 |
| Cunningham | 29 | 205 | 7.1 | 0 |
| Hunter | 27 | 121 | 4.5 | 1 |
| Jaworski | 17 | 35 | 2.1 | 2 |
| Everett | 4 | 13 | 3.3 | 0 |
| Horan | 1 | 12 | 12.0 | 0 |
| Oliver | 1 | 3 | 3.0 | 0 |

### RECEIVING

| Last Name | No. | Yds | Avg | TD |
|---|---|---|---|---|
| Quick | 73 | 1247 | 17.1 | 11 |
| Spagnola | 64 | 772 | 12.1 | 5 |
| Haddix | 43 | 330 | 7.7 | 0 |
| K. Jackson | 40 | 692 | 17.3 | 1 |
| Hunter | 28 | 405 | 14.5 | 1 |
| Johnson | 11 | 186 | 16.9 | 0 |
| E. Jackson | 10 | 126 | 12.6 | 1 |
| Garrity | 7 | 142 | 20.3 | 0 |
| Little | 7 | 82 | 11.7 | 0 |
| Everett | 4 | 25 | 6.3 | 0 |
| K. Baker | 2 | 25 | 12.5 | 0 |
| Oliver | 1 | 4 | 4.0 | 0 |

### PUNT RETURNS

| Last Name | No. | Yds | Avg | TD |
|---|---|---|---|---|
| Cooper | 43 | 364 | 8.5 | 0 |
| Waters | 1 | 23 | 23.0 | 0 |
| Hunter | 1 | 6 | 6.0 | 0 |

### KICKOFF RETURNS

| Last Name | No. | Yds | Avg | TD |
|---|---|---|---|---|
| Hunter | 48 | 1047 | 21.8 | 0 |
| Waters | 4 | 74 | 18.5 | 0 |
| Cooper | 3 | 32 | 10.7 | 0 |
| Foules | 1 | 7 | 7.0 | 0 |

### PASSING — PUNTING — KICKING

| PASSING | Att | Cmp | % | Yds | Yd/Att | TD | Int— | % | RK |
|---|---|---|---|---|---|---|---|---|---|
| Jaworski | 484 | 255 | 53 | 3450 | 7.1 | 17 | 20— | 4 | |
| Cunningham | 81 | 34 | 42 | 584 | 6.8 | 1 | 8— | 10 | |
| Hunter | 2 | 1 | 50 | 38 | 19 | 1 | 0— | 0 | |

| PUNTING | No | Avg |
|---|---|---|
| Horan | 91 | 41.5 |

| KICKING | XP | Att | % | FG | Att | % |
|---|---|---|---|---|---|---|
| McFadden | 29 | 29 | 100 | 25 | 30 | 83 |

## ST. LOUIS CARDINALS

### RUSHING

| Last Name | No. | Yds | Avg | TD |
|---|---|---|---|---|
| Mitchell | 183 | 1006 | 5.5 | 7 |
| Anderson | 117 | 479 | 4.1 | 4 |
| Ferrell | 46 | 208 | 4.5 | 2 |
| Lomax | 32 | 125 | 3.9 | 0 |
| Wolfley | 24 | 64 | 2.7 | 0 |
| Harrington | 7 | 42 | 6.0 | 1 |
| J.T. Smith | 3 | 36 | 12.0 | 0 |
| Brunner | 3 | 8 | 2.7 | 0 |
| Love | 1 | 4 | 4.0 | 0 |
| Green | 1 | 2 | 2.0 | 0 |

### RECEIVING

| Last Name | No. | Yds | Avg | TD |
|---|---|---|---|---|
| Green | 50 | 693 | 13.9 | 5 |
| Tilley | 49 | 726 | 14.8 | 6 |
| Mitchell | 47 | 502 | 10.7 | 3 |
| J.T. Smith | 43 | 581 | 13.5 | 1 |
| Marsh | 37 | 355 | 9.6 | 1 |
| Ferrell | 25 | 277 | 11.1 | 2 |
| Anderson | 23 | 225 | 9.8 | 0 |
| LaFleur | 9 | 119 | 13.2 | 0 |
| Duncan | 4 | 39 | 9.8 | 1 |
| Gray | 3 | 22 | 7.3 | 0 |
| Wolfley | 2 | 18 | 9.0 | 0 |
| Love | 2 | 4 | 2.0 | 0 |
| Mack | 1 | 16 | 16.0 | 0 |
| Novacek | 1 | 4 | 4.0 | 0 |

### PUNT RETURNS

| Last Name | No. | Yds | Avg | TD |
|---|---|---|---|---|
| J.T. Smith | 26 | 283 | 10.9 | 0 |
| Mitchell | 11 | 97 | 8.8 | 0 |
| Nelson | 2 | 14 | 7.0 | 0 |
| Tilley | 1 | -1 | -1.0 | 0 |

### KICKOFF RETURNS

| Last Name | No. | Yds | Avg | TD |
|---|---|---|---|---|
| Duncan | 28 | 550 | 19.6 | 0 |
| Mitchell | 19 | 345 | 18.2 | 0 |
| Wolfley | 13 | 234 | 18.0 | 0 |
| Le. Smith | 5 | 68 | 13.6 | 0 |
| Harrington | 4 | 77 | 19.3 | 0 |
| J.T. Smith | 4 | 59 | 14.8 | 0 |
| Nelson | 3 | 49 | 16.3 | 0 |
| Novacek | 1 | 20 | 20.0 | 0 |
| Mumford | 1 | 19 | 19.0 | 0 |

### PASSING — PUNTING — KICKING

| PASSING | Att | Cmp | % | Yds | Yd/Att | TD | Int— | % | RK |
|---|---|---|---|---|---|---|---|---|---|
| Lomax | 471 | 265 | 56 | 3214 | 6.8 | 18 | 12— | 3 | |
| Brunner | 60 | 30 | 50 | 336 | 5.6 | 1 | 6— | 10 | |
| Mitchell | 2 | 1 | 50 | 31 | 15.5 | 0 | 0— | 0 | |
| Birdsong | 1 | 0 | 0 | 0 | 0.0 | 0 | 0— | 0 | |

| PUNTING | No | Avg |
|---|---|---|
| Birdsong | 85 | 41.7 |

| KICKING | XP | Att | % | FG | Att | % |
|---|---|---|---|---|---|---|
| O'Donoghue | 19 | 19 | 100 | 10 | 18 | 56 |
| Bojovic | 11 | 12 | 92 | 3 | 7 | 43 |

**CHICAGO BEARS 15-1 Mike Ditka**

| Scores of Each Game | | |
|---|---|---|
| 38 | TAMPA BAY | 28 |
| 20 | NEW ENGLAND | 7 |
| 33 | Minnesota | 24 |
| 45 | WASHINGTON | 10 |
| 27 | Tampa Bay | 19 |
| 26 | San Francisco | 10 |
| 23 | GREEN BAY | 7 |
| 27 | MINNESOTA | 9 |
| 16 | Green Bay | 10 |
| 24 | DETROIT | 3 |
| 44 | Dallas | 0 |
| 36 | ATLANTA | 0 |
| 24 | Miami | 38 |
| 17 | INDIANAPOLIS | 10 |
| 19 | N.Y.Jets | 6 |
| 37 | Detroit | 17 |

| Use Name | Pos. | Hgt | Wgt | Age | Int | Pts |
|---|---|---|---|---|---|---|
| Jim Covert | OT | 6'4" | 271 | 25 | | |
| Andy Frederick | OT | 6'6" | 265 | 31 | | |
| Keith Van Horne | OT | 6'6" | 280 | 27 | | |
| Kurt Becker | OG | 6'5" | 270 | 26 | | |
| Mark Bortz | OG | 6'6" | 269 | 24 | | |
| Stefan Humphries | OG | 6'3" | 263 | 23 | | |
| Tom Thayer | OG-C | 6'4" | 261 | 24 | | |
| Tom Andrews | C | 6'4" | 267 | 23 | | |
| Jay Hilgenberg | C | 6'3" | 258 | 26 | | |
| Richard Dent | DE | 6'5" | 263 | 24 | 2 | 6 |
| Mike Hartenstine | DE | 6'3" | 254 | 32 | | |
| Tyrone Keys | DE | 6'7" | 267 | 25 | | |
| Dan Hampton | DT | 6'5" | 267 | 27 | | |
| Steve McMichael | DT | 6'2" | 260 | 27 | | 2 |
| William Perry | DT-FB | 6'2" | 308 | 22 | | 18 |
| Henry Waechter | DT | 6'5" | 275 | 26 | | 2 |

Brian Baschnagel - Knee Injury
Pat Dunsmore - Thigh Injury
Mitch Krenk - Back Injury

| Use Name | Pos. | Hgt | Wgt | Age | Int | Pts |
|---|---|---|---|---|---|---|
| Brian Cabral | LB | 6' | 227 | 29 | | |
| Wilber Marshall | LB | 6'1" | 225 | 23 | 4 | |
| Jim Morrissey | LB | 6'3" | 215 | 22 | | |
| Ron Rivera | LB | 6'3" | 239 | 23 | 1 | 6 |
| Mike Singletary | LB | 6' | 228 | 26 | 1 | |
| Cliff Thrift | LB | 6'2" | 230 | 29 | | |
| Otis Wilson | LB | 6'2" | 232 | 27 | 3 | 8 |
| Dave Duerson | DB | 6'1" | 203 | 24 | 5 | |
| Gary Fencik | DB | 6'1" | 196 | 31 | 5 | |
| Leslie Frazier | DB | 6' | 187 | 26 | 6 | 6 |
| Shaun Gayle | DB | 5'11" | 193 | 23 | | |
| Reggie Phillips | DB | 5'10" | 170 | 24 | | |
| Mike Richardson | DB | 6' | 188 | 24 | 4 | 6 |
| Ken Taylor | DB | 6'1" | 185 | 21 | 3 | |

Todd Bell - Holdout
Al Harris - Holdout
Dan Rains - Knee Injury

| Use Name | Pos. | Hgt | Wgt | Age | Int | Pts |
|---|---|---|---|---|---|---|
| Steve Fuller | QB | 6'4" | 195 | 28 | | 30 |
| Jim McMahon | QB | 6'1" | 190 | 26 | | 24 |
| Mike Tomczak | QB | 6'1" | 195 | 22 | | |
| Dennis Gentry | HB | 5'8" | 181 | 26 | | 18 |
| Walter Payton | HB | 5'11" | 202 | 31 | | 66 |
| Thomas Sanders | FB | 5'11" | 203 | 23 | | 6 |
| Matt Suhey | FB | 5'11" | 216 | 27 | | 12 |
| Calvin Thomas | FB | 5'11" | 245 | 25 | | 24 |
| Brad Anderson | WR | 6'2" | 198 | 24 | | |
| Willie Gault | WR | 6' | 183 | 25 | | 12 |
| James Maness | WR | 6'1" | 174 | 22 | | |
| Ken Margerum | WR | 6' | 180 | 26 | | 12 |
| Dennis McKinnon | WR | 6'1" | 185 | 24 | | 42 |
| Keith Ortego | WR | 6' | 180 | 22 | | |
| Emery Moorehead | TE | 6'2" | 220 | 31 | | 6 |
| Tim Wrightman | TE | 6'3" | 237 | 25 | | 6 |
| Maury Buford | K | 6'1" | 190 | 25 | | |
| Kevin Butler | K | 6'1" | 204 | 23 | | 144 |

**GREEN BAY PACKERS 8-8 Forrest Gregg**

| Scores of Each Game | | |
|---|---|---|
| 20 | New England | 26 |
| 23 | N.Y. GIANTS | 20 |
| 3 | N.Y.JETS | 24 |
| 28 | St.Louis | 43 |
| 43 | DETROIT | 10 |
| 20 | MINNESOTA | 17 |
| 7 | Chicago | 23 |
| 10 | Indianapolis | 37 |
| 10 | CHICAGO | 16 |
| 27 | Minnesota | 17 |
| 38 | NEW ORLEANS | 14 |
| 17 | L.A.Rams | 34 |
| 21 | TAMPA BAY | 0 |
| 24 | MIAMI | 34 |
| 26 | Detroit | 23 |
| 20 | Tampa Bay | 17 |

| Use Name | Pos. | Hgt | Wgt | Age | Int | Pts |
|---|---|---|---|---|---|---|
| Tim Huffman | OT | 6'5" | 282 | 26 | | |
| Greg Koch | OT | 6'4" | 276 | 30 | | |
| Ken Ruettgers | OT | 6'5" | 267 | 23 | | |
| Karl Swanke | OT-C | 6'6" | 262 | 27 | | |
| Ron Hallstrom | OG | 6'6" | 283 | 26 | | |
| Keith Uecker | OG-OT | 6'5" | 270 | 25 | | |
| Mark Cannon | C | 6'3" | 258 | 23 | | |
| Blake Moore | C-OG | 6'5" | 272 | 27 | | 6 |
| Rich Moran | C-OG | 6'3" | 272 | 23 | | |
| Robert Brown | DE | 6'2" | 250 | 25 | | 2 |
| Mike Butler | DE | 6'5" | 269 | 31 | | |
| Alphonso Carreker | DE | 6'6" | 260 | 23 | | |
| Tony Degrate | DE | 6'3" | 280 | 23 | | |
| Donnie Humphrey | DE | 6'3" | 275 | 24 | | |
| Ezra Johnson | DE | 6'4" | 259 | 29 | | |
| Charles Martin | NT-DE | 6'4" | 270 | 26 | | |
| Mark Shumate (from NYJ) | NT | 6'5" | 265 | 25 | | |

| Use Name | Pos. | Hgt | Wgt | Age | Int | Pts |
|---|---|---|---|---|---|---|
| John Anderson | LB | 6'3" | 229 | 29 | 2 | |
| George Cumby | LB | 6' | 224 | 29 | | |
| John Dorsey | LB | 6'3" | 235 | 25 | | |
| Mike Douglass | LB | 6' | 214 | 30 | 2 | 6 |
| Brian Noble | LB | 6'3" | 237 | 23 | | |
| Guy Prather | LB | 6'2" | 229 | 27 | | |
| Randy Scott | LB | 6'1" | 222 | 26 | 2 | |
| Ronnie Burgess | DB | 5'11" | 175 | 22 | | |
| Mossy Cade | DB | 6'1" | 195 | 23 | 1 | |
| Chuck Clanton | DB | 5'11" | 192 | 23 | | |
| Tom Flynn | DB | 6' | 195 | 23 | 1 | |
| Gary Hayes | DB | 5'10" | 180 | 28 | | |
| Daryll Jones | DB | 6' | 190 | 23 | | |
| Mark Lee | DB | 5'11" | 188 | 27 | 1 | |
| Tim Lewis | DB | 5'11" | 191 | 23 | 4 | 6 |
| Mike McLeod | DB | 6' | 180 | 27 | | |
| Mark Murphy | DB | 6'2" | 201 | 27 | 2 | 6 |
| Ken Stills | DB | 5'10" | 185 | 21 | | |

| Use Name | Pos. | Hgt | Wgt | Age | Int | Pts |
|---|---|---|---|---|---|---|
| Lynn Dickey | QB | 6'4" | 203 | 35 | | 6 |
| Joe Shield | QB | 6'1" | 185 | 23 | | |
| Randy Wright | QB | 6'2" | 194 | 24 | | |
| Jim Zorn | QB | 6'2" | 200 | 32 | | |
| Harlan Huckleby | HB | 6'1" | 201 | 27 | | |
| Eddie Lee Ivery | HB | 6'1" | 214 | 28 | | 24 |
| Jessie Clark | FB | 6' | 233 | 25 | | 42 |
| Gary Ellerson | FB | 5'11" | 220 | 22 | | 12 |
| Gerry Ellis | FB | 5'11" | 225 | 27 | | 30 |
| Preston Dennard | WR | 6'1" | 183 | 29 | | 12 |
| Phillip Epps | WR | 5'10" | 165 | 25 | | 24 |
| James Lofton | WR | 6'3" | 197 | 29 | | 24 |
| Walter Stanley | WR | 5'9" | 180 | 22 | | |
| Paul Coffman | TE | 6'3" | 225 | 29 | | 36 |
| Mark Lewis | TE | 6'2" | 218 | 24 | | |
| Ed West | TE | 6'1" | 242 | 24 | | 6 |
| Don Bracken | K | 6' | 205 | 23 | | |
| Al Del Greco | K | 5'10" | 195 | 23 | | 95 |
| Joe Prokop | K | 6'3" | 225 | 25 | | |

**MINNESOTA VIKINGS 7-9 Bud Grant**

| Scores of Each Game | | |
|---|---|---|
| 28 | SAN FRANCISCO | 21 |
| 31 | Tampa Bay | 16 |
| 24 | CHICAGO | 33 |
| 27 | Buffalo | 20 |
| 10 | L.A.Rams | 13 |
| 17 | Green Bay | 20 |
| 21 | SAN DIEGO | 17 |
| 9 | Chicago | 27 |
| 16 | DETROIT | 13 |
| 17 | GREEN BAY | 27 |
| 21 | Detroit | 41 |
| 23 | NEW ORLEANS | 30 |
| 28 | Philadelphia | 23 |
| 26 | TAMPA BAY | 7 |
| 13 | Atlanta | 14 |
| 35 | PHILADELPHIA | 37 |

| Use Name | Pos. | Hgt | Wgt | Age | Int | Pts |
|---|---|---|---|---|---|---|
| Tim Irwin | OT | 6'6" | 289 | 26 | | |
| Tery Tausch | OT | 6'5" | 275 | 26 | | |
| Brent Boyd | OG | 6'3" | 276 | 28 | | |
| Jim Hough | OG | 6'2" | 276 | 29 | | |
| Dave Huffman | OG | 6'6" | 283 | 28 | | |
| Mark MacDonald | OG | 6'4" | 267 | 24 | | |
| Curtis Rouse | OG | 6'3" | 322 | 25 | | |
| Kirk Lowdermilk | C | 6'3" | 263 | 22 | | |
| Dennis Swilley | C | 6'3" | 257 | 30 | | |
| Neil Elshire | DE | 6'6" | 270 | 27 | | 2 |
| Doug Martin | DE | 6'3" | 270 | 28 | | |
| Keith Millard | DE | 6'5" | 260 | 23 | | |
| Mark Mullaney | DE | 6'6" | 246 | 32 | 1 | |
| Robert Smith | DE | 6'5" | 255 | 22 | | |
| Tim Newton | NT | 6' | 283 | 22 | 2 | |

Wes Hamilton - Back Injury

| Use Name | Pos. | Hgt | Wgt | Age | Int | Pts |
|---|---|---|---|---|---|---|
| Matt Blair | LB | 6'5" | 242 | 34 | | |
| Chris Doleman | LB | 6'5" | 250 | 23 | 1 | |
| Dennis Fowlkes | LB | 6'2" | 234 | 24 | | |
| David Howard | LB | 6'2" | 228 | 23 | | |
| Chris Martin | LB | 6'2" | 233 | 24 | | |
| Fred McNeill | LB | 6'2" | 230 | 33 | | |
| Tim Meamber | LB | 6'3" | 231 | 22 | | |
| Scott Studwell | LB | 6'2" | 228 | 31 | 2 | |
| Rufus Bess | DB | 5'9" | 187 | 29 | 2 | |
| Joey Browner | DB | 6'2" | 212 | 25 | 2 | 6 |
| Issiac Holt | DB | 6'1" | 197 | 22 | 1 | |
| Carl Lee | DB | 6' | 184 | 24 | 3 | |
| Keith Nord | DB | 6' | 192 | 28 | | |
| Ted Rosnagle | DB | 6'3" | 207 | 23 | | |
| Willie Teal | DB | 5'10" | 190 | 27 | 3 | 6 |
| John Turner | DB | 6' | 196 | 29 | 5 | |

Walker Lee Ashley - Achilles Tendon

| Use Name | Pos. | Hgt | Wgt | Age | Int | Pts |
|---|---|---|---|---|---|---|
| Steve Bono | QB | 6'4" | 216 | 23 | | |
| Tommy Kramer | QB | 6'2" | 207 | 30 | | |
| Wade Wilson | QB | 6'3" | 208 | 26 | | |
| Darrin Nelson | HB | 5'9" | 183 | 26 | | 36 |
| Allen Rice | HB | 5'10" | 203 | 23 | | 24 |
| Maurice Turner (to GB) | HB | 5'11" | 199 | 24 | | |
| Alfred Anderson | FB | 6'1" | 219 | 24 | | 30 |
| Ted Brown | FB | 5'10" | 212 | 28 | | 60 |
| Anthony Carter | WR | 5'11" | 166 | 24 | | 48 |
| Mike Jones | WR | 5'11" | 183 | 25 | | 24 |
| Leo Lewis | WR | 5'8" | 171 | 28 | | 18 |
| Buster Rhymes | WR | 6'2" | 216 | 23 | | |
| Sammy White | WR | 5'11" | 210 | 31 | | |
| Jay Carroll | TE | 6'4" | 232 | 23 | | |
| Steve Jordan | TE | 6'4" | 236 | 24 | | |
| Mike Mularkey | TE | 6'4" | 238 | 23 | | 6 |
| Greg Coleman | K | 6' | 181 | 30 | | |
| Jan Stenerud | K | 6'2" | 190 | 42 | | 86 |

**DETROIT LIONS 7-9 Darryl Rogers**

| Scores of Each Game | | |
|---|---|---|
| 28 | Atlanta | 27 |
| 26 | DALLAS | 21 |
| 6 | Indianapolis | 14 |
| 30 | TAMPA BAY | 9 |
| 10 | Green Bay | 43 |
| 3 | Washington | 24 |
| 23 | SAN FRANCISCO | 21 |
| 31 | MIAMI | 21 |
| 13 | Minnesota | 16 |
| 3 | Chicago | 24 |
| 41 | MINNESOTA | 21 |
| 16 | Tampa Bay | *19 |
| 31 | N.Y.JETS | 20 |
| 6 | New England | 23 |
| 23 | GREEN BAY | 26 |
| 17 | CHICAGO | 37 |

| Use Name | Pos. | Hgt | Wgt | Age | Int | Pts |
|---|---|---|---|---|---|---|
| Lomas Brown | OT | 6'4" | 282 | 22 | | |
| Rich Stenger | OT | 6'7" | 276 | 25 | | |
| Chris Dieterich | OG-OT | 6'3" | 260 | 27 | | |
| Keith Dorney | OG-OT | 6'5" | 270 | 27 | | |
| Don Greco | OG | 6'3" | 265 | 26 | | |
| Larry Lee (to MIA) | OG-C | 6'2" | 263 | 25 | | |
| Mark Stevenson | OG-C | 6'3" | 285 | 27 | | |
| Kevin Glover | C-OG | 6'2" | 267 | 22 | | |
| David Jones | C-OG | 6'3" | 260 | 23 | | |
| Steve Mott | C | 6'3" | 265 | 24 | | |
| Tom Turnure | C-OG | 6'4" | 253 | 28 | | |
| Leon Evans | DE | 6'5" | 282 | 23 | | |
| William Gay | DE | 6'5" | 260 | 30 | 1 | |
| Martin Moss | DE | 6'4" | 255 | 26 | | |
| Steve Baack | NT-DE | 6'4" | 265 | 24 | | |
| Doug English | NT | 6'5" | 258 | 32 | | |
| Curtis Green | NT-DE | 6'3" | 258 | 28 | | |
| Eric Williams | NT | 6'4" | 280 | 23 | | |

| Use Name | Pos. | Hgt | Wgt | Age | Int | Pts |
|---|---|---|---|---|---|---|
| Kurt Allerman | LB | 6'3" | 231 | 30 | | |
| Roosevelt Barnes | LB | 6'2" | 228 | 27 | 1 | |
| Dan Bunz | LB | 6'4" | 225 | 29 | 1 | |
| Mike Cofer | LB | 6'5" | 245 | 25 | | |
| August Curley | LB | 6'3" | 226 | 25 | | |
| Ken Fantetti | LB | 6'2" | 232 | 28 | | |
| James Harrell | LB | 6'1" | 230 | 28 | 1 | |
| June James | LB | 6'1" | 218 | 22 | | |
| Angelo King | LB | 6'1" | 222 | 27 | | |
| Vernon Maxwell | LB | 6'2" | 235 | 23 | | |
| Jimmy Williams | LB | 6'3" | 230 | 24 | | |
| John Bostic | DB | 5'10" | 178 | 22 | | |
| Arnold Brown | DB | 5'10" | 185 | 23 | | |
| Clarence Chapman | DB | 5'10" | 195 | 31 | | |
| William Frizzell | DB | 6'3" | 198 | 22 | 1 | |
| Duane Galloway | DB | 5'8" | 181 | 23 | | |
| William Graham | DB | 5'11" | 191 | 25 | 3 | |
| Alvin Hall | DB | 5'10" | 184 | 27 | | |
| Demetrious Johnson | DB | 5'11" | 190 | 24 | 3 | |
| Bruce McNorton | DB | 5'11" | 175 | 26 | 2 | |
| Bobby Watkins | DB | 5'10" | 184 | 25 | 5 | |

Kirk Dodge - Shoulder Injury

| Use Name | Pos. | Hgt | Wgt | Age | Int | Pts |
|---|---|---|---|---|---|---|
| Joe Ferguson | QB | 6'1" | 195 | 35 | | 6 |
| Eric Hipple | QB | 6'2" | 198 | 27 | | 12 |
| A.J. Jones (from LA) | HB | 6'1" | 202 | 26 | | |
| Rick Kane | HB | 5'11" | 200 | 30 | | |
| Wilbert Montgomery | HB | 5'10" | 194 | 30 | | |
| Alvin Moore | HB | 6' | 194 | 26 | | 30 |
| James Jones | FB | 6'2" | 229 | 24 | | 54 |
| Mike Meade | FB | 5'11" | 227 | 25 | | |
| Carl Bland | WR | 5'11" | 182 | 24 | | |
| Jeff Chadwick | WR | 6'3" | 190 | 24 | | 18 |
| Pat Mandley | WR | 5'10" | 191 | 24 | | 6 |
| Mark Nichols | WR | 6'2" | 208 | 25 | | 24 |
| Leonard Thompson | WR | 5'11" | 192 | 33 | | 30 |
| David Lewis | TE | 6'3" | 235 | 24 | | 18 |
| Reese McCall | TE | 6'7" | 245 | 29 | | |
| Rob Rubick | TE | 6'3" | 234 | 24 | | |
| Mike Black | K | 6'2" | 197 | 24 | | |
| Eddie Murray | K | 5'10" | 175 | 29 | | 109 |

Dave D'Addio - Ankle Injury

**TAMPA BAY BUCCANEERS 2-14 Leeman Bennett**

| Scores of Each Game | | |
|---|---|---|
| 28 | Chicago | 38 |
| 16 | MINNESOTA | 31 |
| 13 | New Orleans | 20 |
| 9 | Detroit | 30 |
| 19 | CHICAGO | 27 |
| 27 | L.A.RAMS | 31 |
| 38 | Miami | 41 |
| 14 | NEW ENGLAND | 32 |
| 20 | N.Y.Giants | 22 |
| 16 | ST.LOUIS | 0 |
| 28 | N.Y.Jets | 62 |
| 19 | DETROIT | *16 |
| 0 | Green Bay | 21 |
| 7 | Minnesota | 26 |
| 23 | INDIANAPOLIS | 31 |
| 17 | GREEN BAY | 20 |

| Use Name | Pos. | Hgt | Wgt | Age | Int | Pts |
|---|---|---|---|---|---|---|
| Ron Heller | OT | 6'6" | 280 | 23 | | |
| Ken Kaplan | OT | 6'4" | 275 | 25 | | |
| Gene Sanders | OT | 6'3" | 285 | 28 | | |
| Steve Courson | OG | 6'1" | 275 | 29 | | |
| Sean Farrell | OG | 6'3" | 260 | 25 | | |
| Rick Mallory | OG | 6'2" | 260 | 24 | | |
| Joe Shearin | OG | 6'4" | 250 | 25 | | |
| George Yarno | OG-OT | 6'2" | 265 | 28 | | |
| Steve Wilson | C | 6'3" | 270 | 31 | | |
| Randy Grimes | C | 6'4" | 270 | 25 | | |
| John Cannon | DE | 6'5" | 260 | 25 | | |
| Don Fielder | DE | 6'3" | 260 | 26 | | |
| Ron Holmes | DE | 6'4" | 255 | 22 | | |
| Chris Lindstrom | DE | 6'7" | 260 | 25 | | |
| Mark Studaway | DE | 6'4" | 275 | 24 | | |
| David Logan | NT | 6'2" | 250 | 22 | | |
| Karl Morgan | NT | 6'1" | 255 | 24 | | |

John Janata - Elbow and wrist injuries

| Use Name | Pos. | Hgt | Wgt | Age | Int | Pts |
|---|---|---|---|---|---|---|
| Scot Brantley | LB | 6'1" | 230 | 27 | | |
| Keith Browner | LB | 6'5" | 240 | 23 | 1 | |
| Jeff Davis | LB | 6' | 230 | 25 | 1 | |
| Cecil Johnson | LB | 6'2" | 235 | 30 | 1 | |
| Dennis Johnson (from MIN) | LB | 6'3" | 235 | 27 | | |
| Larry Kubin (from BUF) | LB | 6'2" | 238 | 26 | | |
| Ervin Randle | LB | 6'1" | 250 | 22 | 1 | |
| Chris Washington | LB | 6'4" | 230 | 23 | | |
| Paul Dombroski | DB | 6' | 185 | 29 | | |
| Carl Howard (to NYJ) | DB | 6'2" | 190 | 23 | | |
| Bret Clark | DB | 6'2" | 200 | 24 | | |
| Jeremiah Castille | DB | 5'10" | 175 | 24 | 7 | |
| Craig Curry | DB | 6' | 190 | 24 | | |
| David Greenwood | DB | 6'3" | 210 | 25 | 5 | |
| John Holt | DB | 5'11" | 180 | 26 | 1 | |
| Mike Prior | DB | 6' | 200 | 21 | | |
| Ivory Sully | DB | 6' | 200 | 28 | 1 | |

| Use Name | Pos. | Hgt | Wgt | Age | Int | Pts |
|---|---|---|---|---|---|---|
| Steve DeBerg | QB | 6'2" | 210 | 31 | | |
| Alan Risher | QB | 6'2" | 190 | 24 | | |
| Steve Young | QB | 6'2" | 200 | 23 | | 6 |
| Leon Bright | HB | 5'9" | 190 | 30 | | |
| Melvin Carver | HB | 5'11" | 225 | 26 | | |
| George Peoples | HB | 6' | 215 | 25 | | |
| Adger Armstrong | FB | 6' | 230 | 28 | | 6 |
| Ron Springs | FB | 6'2" | 225 | 28 | | |
| James Wilder | FB | 6'3" | 225 | 27 | | 60 |
| Theo Bell | WR | 6' | 195 | 31 | | |
| Gerald Carter | WR | 6'1" | 190 | 28 | | 18 |
| Phil Freeman | WR | 5'11" | 185 | 22 | | |
| Kevin House | WR | 6'1" | 185 | 27 | | 30 |
| David Verser | WR | 6'1" | 200 | 27 | | |
| Gene Branton | TE | 6'4" | 235 | 24 | | |
| Jerry Bell | TE | 6'5" | 230 | 26 | | 12 |
| K.D.Dunn | TE | 6'3" | 235 | 22 | | |
| Jimmie Giles | TE | 6'3" | 240 | 30 | | 48 |
| Calvin Magee | TE | 6'3" | 240 | 22 | | 18 |
| Mark Witte | TE | 6'3" | 235 | 25 | | |
| Frank Garcia | K | 6' | 210 | 28 | | |
| Donald Igwebuike | K | 5'9" | 185 | 24 | | 96 |

* Overtime

## CHICAGO BEARS

### RUSHING

| Last Name | No. | Yds | Avg | TD |
|---|---|---|---|---|
| Payton | 324 | 1551 | 4.8 | 9 |
| Suhey | 115 | 471 | 4.1 | 1 |
| McMahon | 47 | 252 | 5.4 | 3 |
| Gentry | 30 | 160 | 5.3 | 2 |
| Thomas | 31 | 125 | 4.0 | 4 |
| Sanders | 25 | 104 | 4.2 | 1 |
| Fuller | 24 | 77 | 3.2 | 5 |
| Gault | 5 | 18 | 3.6 | 0 |
| Perry | 5 | 7 | 1.4 | 2 |
| Tomczak | 2 | 3 | 1.5 | 0 |
| McKinnon | 1 | 0 | 0.0 | 0 |
| Margerum | 1 | -7 | -7.0 | 0 |

### RECEIVING

| Last Name | No. | Yds | Avg | TD |
|---|---|---|---|---|
| Payton | 49 | 483 | 9.9 | 2 |
| Moorehead | 35 | 481 | 13.7 | 1 |
| Gault | 33 | 704 | 21.3 | 1 |
| Suhey | 33 | 295 | 8.9 | 1 |
| McKinnon | 31 | 555 | 17.9 | 7 |
| Wrightman | 24 | 407 | 17.0 | 1 |
| Margerum | 17 | 190 | 11.2 | 2 |
| Gentry | 5 | 77 | 15.4 | 0 |
| Thomas | 5 | 45 | 9.0 | 0 |
| Maness | 1 | 34 | 34.0 | 0 |
| McMahon | 1 | 13 | 13.0 | 1 |
| Sanders | 1 | 9 | 9.0 | 0 |
| Anderson | 1 | 6 | 6.0 | 0 |
| Perry | 1 | 4 | 4.0 | 1 |

### PUNT RETURNS

| Last Name | No. | Yds | Avg | TD |
|---|---|---|---|---|
| Taylor | 25 | 198 | 7.9 | 0 |
| Ortego | 17 | 158 | 9.3 | 0 |
| Duerson | 6 | 47 | 7.8 | 0 |
| McKinnon | 4 | 44 | 11.0 | 0 |
| Maness | 2 | 9 | 4.5 | 0 |
| Gentry | 0 | 47 | — | 0 |

### KICKOFF RETURNS

| Last Name | No. | Yds | Avg | TD |
|---|---|---|---|---|
| Gault | 22 | 577 | 26.2 | 1 |
| Gentry | 18 | 466 | 25.9 | 1 |
| Taylor | 1 | 18 | 18.0 | 0 |
| McKinnon | 1 | 16 | 16.0 | 0 |
| Sanders | 1 | 10 | 10.0 | 0 |
| Marshall | 0 | 2 | — | 0 |

### PASSING — PUNTING — KICKING

**PASSING**

| Last Name | Att | Cmp | % | Yds | Yd/Att | TD | Int— | % | RK |
|---|---|---|---|---|---|---|---|---|---|
| McMahon | 313 | 178 | 57 | 2392 | 7.6 | 15 | 11— | | 4 |
| Fuller | 107 | 53 | 50 | 777 | 7.3 | 1 | 5— | | 5 |
| Tomczak | 6 | 2 | 33 | 33 | 5.5 | 0 | 0— | | 0 |
| Payton | 5 | 3 | 60 | 96 | 19.2 | 1 | 0— | | 0 |
| Buford | 1 | 1 | 100 | 5 | 5.0 | 0 | 0— | | 0 |

**PUNTING**

| Last Name | No | Avg |
|---|---|---|
| Buford | 68 | 42.2 |

**KICKING**

| Last Name | XP | Att | % | FG | Att | % |
|---|---|---|---|---|---|---|
| Butler | 51 | 51 | 100 | 31 | 37 | 84 |

## GREEN BAY PACKERS

### RUSHING

| Last Name | No. | Yds | Avg | TD |
|---|---|---|---|---|
| Ivery | 132 | 636 | 4.8 | 2 |
| Clark | 147 | 633 | 4.3 | 5 |
| Ellis | 104 | 571 | 5.5 | 5 |
| Ellerson | 32 | 205 | 6.4 | 2 |
| Epps | 5 | 103 | 20.6 | 1 |
| Huckleby | 8 | 41 | 5.1 | 0 |
| Lofton | 4 | 14 | 3.5 | 0 |
| Zorn | 10 | 9 | 0.9 | 0 |
| Wright | 8 | 8 | 1.0 | 0 |
| Prather | 1 | 0 | 0.0 | 0 |
| West | 1 | 0 | 0.0 | 0 |
| Dickey | 18 | -12 | -0.7 | 1 |

### RECEIVING

| Last Name | No. | Yds | Avg | TD |
|---|---|---|---|---|
| Lofton | 69 | 1153 | 16.7 | 4 |
| Coffman | 49 | 666 | 13.6 | 6 |
| Epps | 44 | 683 | 15.5 | 3 |
| Ivery | 28 | 270 | 9.6 | 2 |
| Clark | 24 | 252 | 10.5 | 2 |
| Ellis | 24 | 206 | 8.6 | 0 |
| Dennard | 13 | 182 | 14.0 | 2 |
| West | 8 | 95 | 11.9 | 1 |
| Huckleby | 5 | 27 | 5.4 | 0 |
| Ellerson | 2 | 15 | 7.5 | 0 |
| Moore | 1 | 3 | 3.0 | 1 |

### PUNT RETURNS

| Last Name | No. | Yds | Avg | TD |
|---|---|---|---|---|
| Epps | 15 | 146 | 9.7 | 0 |
| Stanley | 14 | 179 | 12.8 | 0 |
| Flynn | 7 | 41 | 5.9 | 0 |
| Murphy | 1 | 4 | 4.0 | 0 |
| Hayes | 1 | 0 | 0.0 | 0 |

### KICKOFF RETURNS

| Last Name | No. | Yds | Avg | TD |
|---|---|---|---|---|
| Ellerson | 29 | 521 | 18.0 | 0 |
| Ellis | 13 | 247 | 19.0 | 0 |
| Epps | 12 | 279 | 23.3 | 0 |
| Stanley | 9 | 212 | 23.6 | 0 |
| Flynn | 1 | 20 | 20.0 | 0 |
| Anderson | 1 | 14 | 14.0 | 0 |
| Stills | 1 | 14 | 14.0 | 0 |
| Jones | 1 | 11 | 11.0 | 0 |

### PASSING — PUNTING — KICKING

**PASSING**

| Last Name | Att | Cmp | % | Yds | Yd/Att | TD | Int— | % | RK |
|---|---|---|---|---|---|---|---|---|---|
| Dickey | 314 | 172 | 55 | 2206 | 7.0 | 15 | 17— | | 5 |
| Zorn | 123 | 56 | 46 | 794 | 6.5 | 4 | 6— | | 5 |
| Wright | 74 | 39 | 53 | 552 | 7.5 | 2 | 4— | | 5 |
| Ellis | 1 | 0 | 0 | 0 | 0.0 | 0 | 0— | | 0 |
| Ivery | 1 | 0 | 0 | 0 | 0.0 | 0 | 0— | | 0 |

**PUNTING**

| Last Name | No | Avg |
|---|---|---|
| Prokop | 56 | 39.5 |
| Bracken | 26 | 40.5 |

**KICKING**

| Last Name | XP | Att | % | FG | Att | % |
|---|---|---|---|---|---|---|
| Del Greco | 38 | 40 | 95 | 19 | 26 | 73 |

## MINNESOTA VIKINGS

### RUSHING

| Last Name | No. | Yds | Avg | TD |
|---|---|---|---|---|
| Nelson | 200 | 893 | 4.5 | 5 |
| Brown | 93 | 336 | 3.6 | 7 |
| Anderson | 50 | 121 | 2.4 | 4 |
| Rice | 31 | 104 | 3.4 | 3 |
| Kramer | 27 | 54 | 2.0 | 0 |
| Jones | 2 | 6 | 3.0 | 0 |
| Lewis | 1 | 2 | 2.0 | 0 |
| Coleman | 2 | 0 | 0.0 | 0 |

### RECEIVING

| Last Name | No. | Yds | Avg | TD |
|---|---|---|---|---|
| Jordan | 68 | 795 | 11.7 | 0 |
| Jones | 46 | 641 | 13.9 | 4 |
| Carter | 43 | 821 | 19.1 | 8 |
| Nelson | 43 | 301 | 7.0 | 1 |
| Brown | 30 | 291 | 9.7 | 3 |
| Lewis | 29 | 442 | 15.2 | 3 |
| Anderson | 16 | 175 | 10.9 | 1 |
| Mularkey | 13 | 196 | 15.1 | 1 |
| Rice | 9 | 61 | 6.8 | 1 |
| White | 8 | 76 | 9.5 | 0 |
| Rhymes | 5 | 124 | 24.8 | 0 |
| Carroll | 1 | 8 | 8.0 | 0 |

### PUNT RETURNS

| Last Name | No. | Yds | Avg | TD |
|---|---|---|---|---|
| Nelson | 16 | 133 | 8.3 | 0 |
| Carter | 9 | 117 | 13.0 | 0 |

### KICKOFF RETURNS

| Last Name | No. | Yds | Avg | TD |
|---|---|---|---|---|
| Rhymes | 53 | 1345 | 25.4 | 0 |
| Rice | 4 | 70 | 17.5 | 0 |
| M. Turner | 4 | 61 | 15.3 | 0 |
| Nelson | 3 | 51 | 17.0 | 0 |
| Bess | 2 | 33 | 16.5 | 0 |
| Brown | 1 | 7 | 7.0 | 0 |
| Browner | 1 | 0 | 0.0 | 0 |
| Mularkey | 0 | 9 | — | 0 |

### PASSING — PUNTING — KICKING

**PASSING**

| Last Name | Att | Cmp | % | Yds | Yd/Att | TD | Int— | % | RK |
|---|---|---|---|---|---|---|---|---|---|
| Kramer | 506 | 277 | 55 | 3522 | 7.0 | 19 | 26— | | 5 |
| Wilson | 60 | 33 | 55 | 404 | 6.7 | 3 | 5— | | 5 |
| Bono | 10 | 1 | 10 | 5 | 0.5 | 0 | 0— | | 0 |

**PUNTING**

| Last Name | No | Avg |
|---|---|---|
| Coleman | 67 | 42.8 |

**KICKING**

| Last Name | XP | Att | % | FG | Att | % |
|---|---|---|---|---|---|---|
| Stenerud | 41 | 43 | 95 | 15 | 26 | 58 |

## DETROIT LIONS

### RUSHING

| Last Name | No. | Yds | Avg | TD |
|---|---|---|---|---|
| J. Jones | 244 | 886 | 3.6 | 6 |
| Montgomery | 75 | 251 | 3.3 | 0 |
| Moore | 80 | 221 | 2.8 | 4 |
| Hipple | 32 | 89 | 2.8 | 2 |
| Kane | 11 | 44 | 4.0 | 0 |
| Meade | 3 | 18 | 6.0 | 0 |
| Nichols | 1 | 15 | 15.0 | 0 |
| Ferguson | 4 | 12 | 3.0 | 1 |
| A.J. Jones | 1 | 2 | 2.0 | 0 |
| Black | 1 | 0 | 0.0 | 0 |

### RECEIVING

| Last Name | No. | Yds | Avg | TD |
|---|---|---|---|---|
| Thompson | 51 | 736 | 14.4 | 5 |
| J. Jones | 45 | 334 | 7.4 | 3 |
| Nichols | 36 | 592 | 16.4 | 4 |
| Lewis | 28 | 354 | 12.6 | 3 |
| Chadwick | 25 | 478 | 19.1 | 3 |
| Moore | 19 | 154 | 8.1 | 1 |
| Mandley | 18 | 316 | 17.6 | 0 |
| Bland | 12 | 157 | 13.1 | 0 |
| Montgomery | 7 | 55 | 7.9 | 0 |
| Kane | 5 | 56 | 11.2 | 0 |
| Rubick | 2 | 33 | 16.5 | 0 |
| Meade | 2 | 21 | 10.5 | 0 |
| McCall | 1 | 7 | 7.0 | 0 |

### PUNT RETURNS

| Last Name | No. | Yds | Avg | TD |
|---|---|---|---|---|
| Mandley | 38 | 403 | 10.6 | 1 |

### KICKOFF RETURNS

| Last Name | No. | Yds | Avg | TD |
|---|---|---|---|---|
| Hall | 39 | 886 | 22.7 | 0 |
| Moore | 13 | 230 | 17.7 | 0 |
| A.J. Jones | 10 | 226 | 22.6 | 0 |
| Mandley | 6 | 152 | 25.3 | 0 |

### PASSING — PUNTING — KICKING

**PASSING**

| Last Name | Att | Cmp | % | Yds | Yd/Att | TD | Int— | % | RK |
|---|---|---|---|---|---|---|---|---|---|
| Hipple | 406 | 223 | 55 | 2952 | 7.3 | 17 | 18— | | 5 |
| J. Ferguson | 54 | 31 | 57 | 364 | 6.7 | 2 | 3— | | 6 |
| J. Jones | 1 | 0 | 0 | 0 | 0.0 | 0 | 0— | | 0 |
| Moore | 1 | 0 | 0 | 0 | 0.0 | 0 | 0— | | 0 |

**PUNTING**

| Last Name | No | Avg |
|---|---|---|
| Black | 73 | 41.8 |

**KICKING**

| Last Name | XP | Att | % | FG | Att | % |
|---|---|---|---|---|---|---|
| Murray | 31 | 33 | 94 | 26 | 31 | 84 |

## TAMPA BAY BUCCANEERS

### RUSHING

| Last Name | No. | Yds | Avg | TD |
|---|---|---|---|---|
| Wilder | 365 | 1300 | 3.6 | 10 |
| Young | 40 | 233 | 5.8 | 1 |
| Springs | 16 | 54 | 3.4 | 0 |
| DeBerg | 9 | 28 | 3.1 | 0 |
| Carter | 1 | 13 | 13.0 | 0 |
| Fisher | 1 | 10 | 10.0 | 0 |
| Armstrong | 2 | 6 | 3.0 | 0 |

### RECEIVING

| Last Name | No. | Yds | Avg | TD |
|---|---|---|---|---|
| Wilder | 53 | 341 | 6.4 | 0 |
| House | 44 | 803 | 18.3 | 5 |
| Giles | 43 | 673 | 15.7 | 8 |
| J. Bell | 43 | 496 | 11.5 | 2 |
| Carter | 40 | 557 | 13.9 | 3 |
| Magee | 26 | 288 | 11.1 | 3 |
| T. Bell | 12 | 184 | 15.8 | 0 |
| Springs | 3 | 44 | 14.7 | 0 |
| Witte | 3 | 28 | 9.3 | 0 |
| Armstrong | 2 | 4 | 2.0 | 1 |

### PUNT RETURNS

| Last Name | No. | Yds | Avg | TD |
|---|---|---|---|---|
| Prior | 13 | 105 | 8.1 | 0 |
| Bright | 12 | 124 | 10.3 | 0 |

### KICKOFF RETURNS

| Last Name | No. | Yds | Avg | TD |
|---|---|---|---|---|
| Freeman | 48 | 1085 | 22.6 | 0 |
| Bright | 11 | 213 | 19.4 | 0 |
| Prior | 10 | 131 | 13.1 | 0 |
| Springs | 5 | 112 | 22.4 | 0 |
| Verser | 4 | 61 | 15.3 | 0 |
| Magee | 2 | 20 | 10.0 | 0 |

### PASSING — PUNTING — KICKING

**PASSING**

| Last Name | Att | Cmp | % | Yds | Yd/Att | TD | Int— | % | RK |
|---|---|---|---|---|---|---|---|---|---|
| DeBerg | 370 | 197 | 53 | 2488 | 6.7 | 19 | 18— | | 6 |
| Young | 138 | 72 | 52 | 935 | 6.8 | 3 | 6— | | 6 |

**PUNTING**

| Last Name | No | Avg |
|---|---|---|
| Garcia | 77 | 42.0 |

**KICKING**

| Last Name | XP | Att | % | FG | Att | % |
|---|---|---|---|---|---|---|
| Igwebuike | 30 | 32 | 91 | 22 | 32 | 69 |

### LOS ANGELES RAMS 11-5 John Robinson

| Scores of Each Game | | |
|---|---|---|
| 20 | DENVER | 16 |
| 17 | Philadelphia | 6 |
| 35 | Seattle | 24 |
| 17 | ATLANTA | 6 |
| 13 | MINNESOTA | 10 |
| 31 | Tampa Bay | 27 |
| 16 | Kansas City | 0 |
| 14 | SAN FRANCISCO | 28 |
| 28 | NEW ORLEANS | 10 |
| 19 | N.Y.Giants | 24 |
| 14 | Atlanta | 30 |
| 34 | GREEN BAY | 17 |
| 3 | New Orleans | 29 |
| 27 | San Francisco | 20 |
| 46 | ST.LOUIS | 14 |
| 6 | L.A.RAIDERS | 16 |

| Use Name | Pos. | Hgt | Wgt | Age | Int | Pts |
|---|---|---|---|---|---|---|
| Bill Bain | OT | 6'4" | 290 | 33 | | |
| Irv Pankey | OT | 6'4" | 267 | 26 | | |
| Jackie Slater | OT | 6'4" | 271 | 31 | | |
| Russ Bolinger | OG | 6'5" | 255 | 30 | | |
| Dennis Harrah | OG | 6'5" | 265 | 32 | | |
| Kent Hill | OG | 6'5" | 260 | 28 | | |
| Duval Love | OG | 6'3" | 263 | 22 | | |
| Tony Slaton | C | 6'3" | 265 | 24 | | |
| Doug Smith | C | 6'3" | 260 | 28 | | |
| Reggie Doss | DE | 6'4" | 263 | 28 | | 2 |
| Dennis Harrison | DE | 6'8" | 280 | 29 | | |
| Gary Jester | DE | 6'4" | 260 | 30 | | |
| Doug Reed | DE | 6'3" | 262 | 25 | | |
| Booker Reese | DE | 6'6" | 260 | 25 | | |
| Charles DeJurnett | NT | 6'4" | 260 | 33 | | |
| Greg Meisner | NT | 6'3" | 253 | 26 | | |
| Shawn Miller | NT | 6'4" | 255 | 24 | | |

| Use Name | Pos. | Hgt | Wgt | Age | Int | Pts |
|---|---|---|---|---|---|---|
| Ed Brady | LB | 6'2" | 235 | 25 | | |
| Jim Collins | LB | 6'2" | 230 | 27 | 2 | |
| Carl Ekern | LB | 6'3" | 230 | 31 | 2 | 6 |
| Kevin Greene | LB | 6'3" | 238 | 23 | | |
| Mark Jerue | LB | 6'3" | 232 | 25 | | |
| Jim Laughlin | LB | 6' | 222 | 27 | | |
| Mel Owens | LB | 6'2" | 224 | 26 | | |
| Norwood Vann | LB | 6'1" | 225 | 23 | | |
| Mike Wilcher | LB | 6'3" | 240 | 25 | 1 | |
| Nolan Cromwell | DB | 6'1" | 200 | 30 | 2 | |
| Tim Fox | DB | 5'11" | 186 | 31 | 2 | |
| Jerry Gray | DB | 6' | 185 | 22 | | |
| Gary Green | DB | 5'11" | 191 | 29 | 6 | 6 |
| Eric Harris | DB | 6'3" | 202 | 30 | | |
| LeRoy Irvin | DB | 5'11" | 184 | 27 | 6 | 6 |
| Johnnie Johnson | DB | 6'1" | 183 | 28 | 5 | 6 |
| Vince Newsome | DB | 6'1" | 179 | 24 | 3 | |

George Andrews - Knee Injury
Mike Pleasant - Leg Injury

| Use Name | Pos. | Hgt | Wgt | Age | Int | Pts |
|---|---|---|---|---|---|---|
| Dieter Brock | QB | 6'1" | 195 | 34 | | |
| Steve Dils | QB | 6'1" | 191 | 29 | | |
| Jeff Kemp | QB | 6' | 201 | 26 | | |
| Lynn Cain | HB | 6'1" | 205 | 29 | | |
| Barry Redden | HB | 5'10" | 205 | 25 | | |
| Charles White | HB | 5'10" | 190 | 27 | | 18 |
| Eric Dickerson | FB | 6'3" | 220 | 24 | | 72 |
| Mike Guman | FB | 6'2" | 218 | 27 | | |
| Ron Brown | WR | 5'11" | 181 | 24 | | 36 |
| Bobby Duckworth | WR | 6'3" | 196 | 26 | | 18 |
| Henry Ellard | WR | 5'11" | 175 | 24 | | 36 |
| Michael Young | WR | 6'1" | 185 | 23 | | |
| David Hill | TE | 6'2" | 240 | 31 | | 6 |
| Tony Hunter | TE | 6'4" | 237 | 25 | | 24 |
| James McDonald (from DET) | TE | 6'5" | 230 | 24 | | |
| Dale Hatcher | K | 6'2" | 200 | 22 | | |
| Mike Lansford | K | 6' | 183 | 27 | | 104 |

### SAN FRANCISCO FORTY NINERS 10-6 Bill Walsh

| Scores of Each Game | | |
|---|---|---|
| 21 | Minnesota | 28 |
| 35 | ATLANTA | 16 |
| 34 | L.A.Raiders | 10 |
| 17 | NEW ORLEANS | 20 |
| 38 | Atlanta | 17 |
| 10 | CHICAGO | 26 |
| 21 | Detroit | 23 |
| 28 | L.A.Rams | 14 |
| 24 | PHILADELPHIA | 13 |
| 16 | Denver | 17 |
| 31 | KANSAS CITY | 3 |
| 19 | SEATTLE | 6 |
| 35 | Washington | 8 |
| 20 | L.A.RAMS | 27 |
| 31 | New Orleans | 19 |
| 31 | DALLAS | 16 |

| Use Name | Pos. | Hgt | Wgt | Age | Int | Pts |
|---|---|---|---|---|---|---|
| Bruce Collie | OT | 6'6" | 275 | 23 | | |
| Keith Fahnhorst | OT | 6'6" | 273 | 33 | | |
| Bubba Parris | OT | 6'6" | 299 | 24 | | |
| Vince Stroth | OT | 6'4" | 256 | 24 | | |
| John Ayers | OG | 6'5" | 265 | 32 | | |
| Randy Cross | OG | 6'3" | 265 | 31 | | |
| Guy McIntyre | OG | 6'3" | 264 | 24 | | 6 |
| John Hill | C | 6'2" | 260 | 34 | | |
| Jim Leonard (to SD) | C | 6'3" | 260 | 27 | | |
| Fred Quillan | C | 6'5" | 266 | 29 | | |
| Dwaine Board | DE | 6'5" | 248 | 28 | | |
| Fred Dean | DE | 6'3" | 232 | 33 | | |
| John Harty | DE | 6'4" | 260 | 26 | | 2 |
| Jeff Stover | DE | 6'5" | 275 | 27 | | |
| Jim Stuckey | DE | 6'4" | 253 | 27 | | |
| Michael Carter | NT | 6'2" | 285 | 25 | | |
| Gary Johnson | NT | 6'2" | 261 | 33 | | |
| Manu Tuiasosopo | NT | 6'3" | 262 | 28 | | |

Allan Kennedy - Knee Injury
Jesse Sapolu - Broken foot

| Use Name | Pos. | Hgt | Wgt | Age | Int | Pts |
|---|---|---|---|---|---|---|
| Riki Ellison | LB | 6'2" | 225 | 25 | | |
| Jim Fahnhorst | LB | 6'4" | 230 | 26 | | |
| Ron Ferrari | LB | 6' | 215 | 26 | | |
| Jim Kovach (from NO) | LB | 6'2" | 239 | 29 | 1 | |
| Fulton Kuykendall | LB | 6'5" | 228 | 32 | | |
| Milt McColl | LB | 6'6" | 230 | 26 | | 6 |
| Todd Shell | LB | 6'4" | 225 | 23 | 1 | |
| Keena Turner | LB | 6'2" | 222 | 26 | | 6 |
| Michael Walter | LB | 6'3" | 238 | 24 | 1 | |
| Dwight Hicks | DB | 6'1" | 192 | 29 | 4 | |
| Jeff Fuller | DB | 6'2" | 216 | 23 | 1 | |
| Ronnie Lott | DB | 6' | 200 | 26 | 6 | |
| Dana McLemore | DB | 5'10" | 183 | 25 | 1 | |
| Tory Nixon | DB | 5'11" | 186 | 23 | | |
| Carlton Williamson | DB | 6' | 204 | 27 | 3 | 6 |
| Eric Wright | DB | 6'1" | 185 | 26 | 1 | |

Tom Holmoe - Shoulder Injury

| Use Name | Pos. | Hgt | Wgt | Age | Int | Pts |
|---|---|---|---|---|---|---|
| Matt Cavanaugh | QB | 6'2" | 212 | 28 | | |
| Joe Montana | QB | 6'2" | 195 | 29 | | 18 |
| Derrick Harmon | HB | 5'10" | 202 | 22 | | |
| Carl Monroe | HB | 5'8" | 180 | 25 | | 6 |
| Bill Ring | HB | 5'10" | 205 | 28 | | 6 |
| Wendell Tyler | HB | 5'10" | 207 | 30 | | 48 |
| Roger Craig | FB | 6' | 224 | 25 | | 90 |
| Freddie Solomon | WR | 5'11" | 188 | 32 | | 6 |
| Dwight Clark | WR | 6'4" | 215 | 28 | | 60 |
| Jerry Rice | WR | 6'2" | 200 | 22 | | 24 |
| Mike Wilson | WR | 6'3" | 215 | 26 | | 12 |
| Earl Cooper | TE | 6'2" | 232 | 27 | | |
| Russ Francis | TE | 6'6" | 242 | 32 | | 18 |
| John Frank | TE | 6'3" | 225 | 23 | | 6 |
| Max Runager | K | 6'1" | 189 | 29 | | |
| Ray Wersching | K | 5'11" | 215 | 35 | | 91 |

### NEW ORLEANS SAINTS 5-11 Bum Phillips (4-8) Wade Phillips (1-3)

| Scores of Each Game | | |
|---|---|---|
| 27 | KANSAS CITY | 47 |
| 23 | Denver | 34 |
| 20 | TAMPA BAY | 13 |
| 20 | San Francisco | 17 |
| 23 | PHILADELPHIA | 21 |
| 13 | L.A.Raiders | 23 |
| 24 | Atlanta | 31 |
| 13 | N.Y.GIANTS | 21 |
| 10 | L.A.Rams | 28 |
| 3 | SEATTLE | 27 |
| 14 | Green Bay | 38 |
| 30 | Minnesota | 23 |
| 29 | L.A.RAMS | 3 |
| 16 | St.Louis | 28 |
| 19 | SAN FRANCISCO | 31 |
| 10 | ATLANTA | 16 |

| Use Name | Pos. | Hgt | Wgt | Age | Int | Pts |
|---|---|---|---|---|---|---|
| Stan Brock | OT | 6'6" | 288 | 27 | | |
| Daren Gilbert | OT | 6'6" | 285 | 21 | | |
| Dave Lafary | OT | 6'7" | 285 | 30 | | |
| Jim Rourke | OT | 6'5" | 263 | 28 | | |
| Ralph Williams | OT | 6'3" | 270 | 27 | | |
| Kelvin Clark | OG | 6'3" | 273 | 29 | | |
| Brad Edelman | OG | 6'6" | 262 | 24 | | |
| Petey Perot | OG | 6'2" | 271 | 28 | | |
| Adam Schreiber | OG | 6'4" | 270 | 23 | | |
| David Carter | C-OG | 6'2" | 275 | 31 | | |
| Joel Hilgenberg | C-OG | 6'3" | 253 | 23 | | |
| Steve Korte | C | 6'2" | 271 | 25 | | |
| Bruce Clark | DE | 6'3" | 281 | 27 | | |
| James Geathers | DE | 6'7" | 267 | 25 | | |
| Frank Warren | DE | 6'4" | 278 | 25 | | 12 |
| Jim Wilks | DE | 6'5" | 265 | 27 | | |
| Tony Elliott | NT | 6'2" | 300 | 26 | | |
| Derland Moore | NT | 6'4" | 273 | 33 | | |

| Use Name | Pos. | Hgt | Wgt | Age | Int | Pts |
|---|---|---|---|---|---|---|
| Jack Del Rio | LB | 6'4" | 235 | 22 | 2 | 6 |
| James Haynes | LB | 6'2" | 227 | 25 | | |
| Rickey Jackson | LB | 6'2" | 239 | 27 | | |
| Joe Kohlbrand | LB | 6'4" | 242 | 22 | | |
| Whitney Paul | LB | 6'3" | 218 | 29 | | |
| Scott Pelluer | LB | 6'2" | 227 | 26 | | |
| Glen Redd | LB | 6'1" | 231 | 27 | 1 | |
| Alvin Toles | LB | 6'1" | 211 | 22 | | |
| Russell Gary | DB | 5'11" | 196 | 26 | | |
| Terry Hoage | DB | 6'3" | 199 | 23 | 4 | 6 |
| Earl Johnson | DB | 6' | 190 | 21 | | |
| Brett Maxie | DB | 6'2" | 190 | 23 | | |
| Johnnie Poe | DB | 6'1" | 194 | 26 | 3 | 6 |
| David Rackley | DB | 5'9" | 172 | 24 | | |
| Willie Tullis | DB | 6' | 190 | 27 | 2 | |
| Frank Wattelet | DB | 6' | 185 | 26 | 2 | |
| Dave Waymer | DB | 6'1" | 188 | 27 | 6 | |

| Use Name | Pos. | Hgt | Wgt | Age | Int | Pts |
|---|---|---|---|---|---|---|
| Bobby Hebert | QB | 6'4" | 215 | 25 | | 6 |
| Guido Merkens | QB | 6'1" | 197 | 30 | | 6 |
| Richard Todd | QB | 6'2" | 212 | 31 | | |
| Dave Wilson | QB | 6'3" | 211 | 26 | | |
| Earl Campbell | HB | 5'11" | 233 | 30 | | 6 |
| Tyrone Anthony | FB | 5'11" | 212 | 23 | | |
| Bobby Fowler | FB | 6'2" | 230 | 24 | | |
| Hokie Gajan | FB | 5'11" | 226 | 25 | | 12 |
| Wayne Wilson | FB | 6'3" | 220 | 27 | | 18 |
| Eugene Goodlow | WR | 6'2" | 181 | 26 | | 18 |
| Jeff Groth | WR | 5'10" | 181 | 28 | | 12 |
| Eric Martin | WR | 6'1" | 195 | 23 | | 24 |
| Mike Miller | WR | 6' | 183 | 25 | | |
| Carl Roaches | WR | 5'8" | 165 | 31 | | |
| Lindsay Scott | WR | 6'1" | 200 | 24 | | |
| Hoby Brenner | TE | 6'4" | 245 | 26 | | 18 |
| Larry Hardy | TE | 6'3" | 246 | 29 | | 12 |
| John Tice | TE | 6'5" | 243 | 25 | | 12 |
| Morten Andersen | K | 6'2" | 205 | 25 | | 120 |
| Brian Hansen | K | 6'3" | 218 | 24 | | |

Tyrone Young - Knee Injury

### ATLANTA FALCONS 4-12 Dan Henning

| Scores of Each Game | | |
|---|---|---|
| 27 | DETROIT | 28 |
| 16 | San Francisco | 35 |
| 28 | DENVER | 44 |
| 6 | L.A.Rams | 17 |
| 17 | SAN FRANCISCO | 38 |
| 26 | Seattle | 30 |
| 31 | NEW ORLEANS | 24 |
| 10 | Dallas | 24 |
| 10 | WASHINGTON | 44 |
| 17 | Philadelphia | *23 |
| 30 | L.A.RAMS | 14 |
| 0 | Chicago | 36 |
| 24 | L.A.RAIDERS | 34 |
| 10 | Kansas City | 38 |
| 14 | MINNESOTA | 13 |
| 16 | New Orleans | 10 |

| Use Name | Pos. | Hgt | Wgt | Age | Int | Pts |
|---|---|---|---|---|---|---|
| Glen Howe (from PIT) | OT | 6'6" | 292 | 23 | | |
| Mike Kenn | OT | 6'7" | 277 | 29 | | |
| Brett Miller | OT | 6'7" | 290 | 26 | | |
| Eric Sanders | OT | 6'7" | 280 | 26 | | |
| Bill Fralic | OG-OT | 6'5" | 280 | 22 | | |
| Jeff Kiewel | OG | 6'4" | 265 | 24 | | |
| Joe Pellegrini | OG-C | 6'4" | 264 | 28 | | |
| John Scully | OG | 6'6" | 265 | 27 | | |
| Jeff Van Note | C | 6'2" | 264 | 39 | | |
| Wayne Tadloff | C-OG | 6'5" | 263 | 24 | | |
| Chuck Thomas | C-OG | 6'3" | 277 | 24 | | |
| Rick Bryan | DE | 6'4" | 270 | 23 | | 6 |
| Mike Gann | DE | 6'5" | 265 | 21 | | 6 |
| Andrew Provence | DE | 6'3" | 267 | 24 | | |
| Lawrence Pillers | DE | 6'3" | 257 | 32 | | |
| Dan Benish | DT | 6'5" | 280 | 23 | | |
| Willard Goff | DT | 6'3" | 265 | 23 | | |
| Mike Pitts | DT | 6'5" | 277 | 24 | 1 | |
| Roy Harris | DT | 6'2" | 266 | 24 | | |

| Use Name | Pos. | Hgt | Wgt | Age | Int | Pts |
|---|---|---|---|---|---|---|
| Thomas Benson | LB | 6'2" | 235 | 23 | | |
| Buddy Curry | LB | 6'4" | 222 | 27 | 1 | |
| David Frye | LB | 6'2" | 218 | 24 | 1 | |
| Jeff Jackson | LB | 6'1" | 228 | 23 | | |
| John Rade | LB | 6'1" | 220 | 25 | 2 | 6 |
| Al Richardson | LB | 6'2" | 222 | 27 | | |
| Johnny Taylor | LB | 6'4" | 235 | 25 | | |
| Ronnie Washington | LB | 6'1" | 236 | 22 | | |
| James Britt | DB | 6' | 185 | 24 | 1 | |
| Bobby Butler | DB | 5'11" | 170 | 26 | 5 | |
| Scott Case | DB | 6' | 178 | 23 | 4 | |
| Wendell Cason | DB | 5'11" | 183 | 22 | 3 | |
| David Croudip (from SD) | DB | 5'8" | 180 | 26 | | |
| Tiger Greene | DB | 6' | 184 | 23 | 2 | |
| Kenny Johnson | DB | 5'10" | 167 | 27 | | |
| Reggie Pleasant | DB | 5'9" | 175 | 23 | | |
| Tom Pridemore | DB | 5'10" | 186 | 29 | 2 | |
| Sean Thomas (from CIN) | DB | 5'11" | 190 | 23 | | |
| Dan Wagoner | DB | 5'10" | 180 | 25 | | |

Rydell Malancon - Knee Injury

| Use Name | Pos. | Hgt | Wgt | Age | Int | Pts |
|---|---|---|---|---|---|---|
| Dave Archer | QB | 6'2" | 203 | 23 | | 12 |
| Bob Holly | QB | 6'2" | 205 | 25 | | 6 |
| Steve Bartkowski (to WAS) | QB | 6'4" | 218 | 32 | | |
| Cliff Austin | HB | 6' | 207 | 25 | | 6 |
| Sylvester Stamps | HB | 5'7" | 166 | 24 | | |
| Tim Tyrrell | HB | 6'1" | 201 | 24 | | |
| Joe Washington | HB | 5'10" | 179 | 31 | | 12 |
| Gerald Riggs | FB | 6'1" | 232 | 24 | | 60 |
| Anthony Allen | WR | 5'11" | 182 | 26 | | 12 |
| Stacey Bailey | WR | 6' | 157 | 25 | | |
| Charlie Brown | WR | 5'10" | 184 | 26 | | 12 |
| Billy Johnson | WR | 5'9" | 170 | 33 | | 30 |
| Cliff Benson | TE | 6'4" | 238 | 24 | | |
| Arthur Cox | TE | 6'2" | 255 | 24 | | 12 |
| Allama Matthews | TE | 6'2" | 230 | 24 | | 6 |
| Ken Whisenhunt | TE | 6'2" | 233 | 23 | | |
| Rick Donnelly | K | 6' | 184 | 23 | | |
| Ralph Giacomarro | K | 6'1" | 194 | 24 | | |
| Mick Luckhurst | K | 6' | 183 | 27 | | 101 |

William Andrews - Knee Injury
Mike Landrum - Knee Injury

* Overtime

## LOS ANGELES RAMS

### RUSHING

| Last Name | No. | Yds | Avg | TD |
|---|---|---|---|---|
| Dickerson | 292 | 1234 | 4.2 | 12 |
| Redden | 87 | 380 | 4.4 | 0 |
| White | 70 | 310 | 4.4 | 3 |
| Cain | 11 | 46 | 4.2 | 0 |
| Brock | 20 | 38 | 1.9 | 0 |
| Guman | 11 | 32 | 2.9 | 0 |
| Brown | 2 | 13 | 6.5 | 0 |
| Ellard | 3 | 8 | 2.7 | 0 |
| Kemp | 5 | 0 | 0.0 | 0 |
| Dils | 2 | -4 | -2.0 | 0 |

### RECEIVING

| Last Name | No. | Yds | Avg | TD |
|---|---|---|---|---|
| Ellard | 54 | 811 | 15.0 | 5 |
| Hunter | 50 | 562 | 11.2 | 4 |
| D. Hill | 29 | 271 | 9.3 | 1 |
| Duckworth | 25 | 422 | 16.9 | 3 |
| Dickerson | 20 | 126 | 6.3 | 0 |
| Redden | 16 | 162 | 10.1 | 0 |
| Brown | 14 | 215 | 15.4 | 3 |
| Young | 14 | 157 | 11.2 | 0 |
| McDonald | 5 | 81 | 16.2 | 0 |
| Cain | 5 | 24 | 4.8 | 0 |
| Guman | 3 | 23 | 7.7 | 0 |
| White | 1 | 12 | 12.0 | 0 |

### PUNT RETURNS

| Last Name | No. | Yds | Avg | TD |
|---|---|---|---|---|
| Ellard | 37 | 501 | 13.5 | 1 |
| White | 1 | 0 | 0.0 | 0 |

### KICKOFF RETURNS

| Last Name | No. | Yds | Avg | TD |
|---|---|---|---|---|
| Brown | 28 | 918 | 32.8 | 3 |
| White | 17 | 300 | 17.6 | 0 |
| Cain | 6 | 115 | 19.2 | 0 |
| Guman | 2 | 30 | 15.0 | 0 |
| Slaton | 1 | 18 | 18.0 | 0 |
| Miller | 1 | 10 | 10.0 | 0 |
| Cromwell | 1 | 3 | 3.0 | 0 |

### PASSING — PUNTING — KICKING

**PASSING**

| Last Name | Att | Cmp | % | Yds | Yd/Att | TD | Int— | % | RK |
|---|---|---|---|---|---|---|---|---|---|
| Brock | 365 | 218 | 60 | 2658 | 7.28 | 16 | 13— | | 4 |
| Kemp | 38 | 16 | 42 | 214 | 5.63 | 0 | 1— | | 3 |

**PUNTING**

| Last Name | No | Avg |
|---|---|---|
| Hatcher | 87 | 43.2 |

**KICKING**

| Last Name | XP | Att | % | FG | Att | % |
|---|---|---|---|---|---|---|
| Lansford | 38 | 39 | 97 | 22 | 29 | 80 |

## SAN FRANCISCO FORTY NINERS

### RUSHING

| Last Name | No. | Yds | Avg | TD |
|---|---|---|---|---|
| Craig | 214 | 1050 | 4.9 | 9 |
| Tyler | 171 | 867 | 5.1 | 6 |
| Montana | 42 | 153 | 3.6 | 3 |
| Harmon | 28 | 92 | 3.3 | 0 |
| Rice | 6 | 26 | 4.3 | 1 |
| Ring | 8 | 23 | 2.9 | 1 |
| Cooper | 2 | 12 | 6.0 | 0 |
| Cavanaugh | 4 | 5 | 1.3 | 0 |
| Soloman | 2 | 4 | 2.0 | 0 |

### RECEIVING

| Last Name | No. | Yds | Avg | TD |
|---|---|---|---|---|
| Craig | 92 | 1016 | 11.0 | 6 |
| Clark | 54 | 705 | 13.1 | 10 |
| Rice | 49 | 927 | 18.9 | 3 |
| Francis | 44 | 478 | 10.9 | 3 |
| Solomon | 25 | 259 | 10.4 | 1 |
| Tyler | 20 | 154 | 7.7 | 2 |
| Harmon | 14 | 123 | 8.8 | 0 |
| Wilson | 10 | 165 | 16.5 | 2 |
| Monroe | 10 | 51 | 5.1 | 0 |
| Frank | 7 | 50 | 7.1 | 1 |
| Cooper | 4 | 45 | 11.3 | 0 |
| Ring | 2 | 14 | 7.0 | 0 |

### PUNT RETURNS

| Last Name | No. | Yds | Avg | TD |
|---|---|---|---|---|
| McLemore | 38 | 258 | 6.8 | 0 |

### KICKOFF RETURNS

| Last Name | No. | Yds | Avg | TD |
|---|---|---|---|---|
| Monroe | 28 | 717 | 25.6 | 1 |
| Harmon | 23 | 467 | 20.3 | 0 |
| McLemore | 4 | 76 | 19.0 | 0 |
| Rice | 1 | 6 | 6.0 | 0 |
| Lott | 1 | 2 | 2.0 | 0 |
| Frank | 1 | 1 | 1.0 | 0 |

### PASSING — PUNTING — KICKING

**PASSING**

| Last Name | Att | Cmp | % | Yds | Yd/Att | TD | Int— | % | RK |
|---|---|---|---|---|---|---|---|---|---|
| Montana | 494 | 303 | 61 | 3653 | 7.4 | 27 | 13— | | 3 |
| Cavanaugh | 54 | 28 | 52 | 334 | 6.2 | 1 | 1— | | 2 |
| Harmon | 1 | 0 | 0 | 0 | 0.0 | 0 | 0— | | 0 |
| Solomon | 1 | 0 | 0 | 0 | 0.0 | 0 | 0— | | 0 |

**PUNTING**

| Last Name | No | Avg |
|---|---|---|
| Runager | 86 | 39.8 |

**KICKING**

| Last Name | XP | Att | % | FG | Att | % |
|---|---|---|---|---|---|---|
| Wersching | 52 | 53 | 98 | 13 | 21 | 62 |

## NEW ORLEANS SAINTS

### RUSHING

| Last Name | No. | Yds | Avg | TD |
|---|---|---|---|---|
| W. Wilson | 168 | 645 | 3.8 | 1 |
| Campbell | 158 | 643 | 4.1 | 1 |
| Gajan | 50 | 251 | 5.0 | 2 |
| Anthony | 17 | 65 | 3.8 | 0 |
| Wattelet | 2 | 42 | 21.0 | 0 |
| Hebert | 12 | 26 | 2.2 | 0 |
| D. Wilson | 18 | 7 | 0.4 | 0 |
| Fowler | 2 | 4 | 2.0 | 0 |
| Goodlow | 1 | 3 | 3.0 | 0 |
| Martin | 2 | -1 | -0.5 | 0 |
| Merkens | 1 | -2 | -2.0 | 0 |

### RECEIVING

| Last Name | No. | Yds | Avg | TD |
|---|---|---|---|---|
| Brenner | 42 | 652 | 15.5 | 3 |
| W.Wilson | 38 | 228 | 6.0 | 2 |
| Martin | 35 | 522 | 14.9 | 4 |
| Goodlow | 32 | 603 | 18.8 | 3 |
| Anthony | 28 | 185 | 6.6 | 0 |
| Tice | 24 | 266 | 11.1 | 2 |
| Groth | 15 | 238 | 15.9 | 2 |
| Hardy | 15 | 208 | 13.9 | 2 |
| Gajan | 8 | 87 | 10.9 | 0 |
| Scott | 7 | 61 | 8.7 | 0 |
| Campbell | 6 | 88 | 14.7 | 0 |
| Fowler | 5 | 43 | 8.6 | 0 |
| Merkens | 3 | 61 | 20.3 | 1 |
| Haynes | 1 | 8 | 8.0 | 0 |
| Hebert | 1 | 7 | 7.0 | 1 |

### PUNT RETURNS

| Last Name | No. | Yds | Avg | TD |
|---|---|---|---|---|
| Tullis | 17 | 141 | 8.3 | 0 |
| Martin | 8 | 53 | 6.6 | 0 |
| Roaches | 4 | 21 | 5.3 | 0 |
| Groth | 1 | 0 | 0.0 | 0 |

### KICKOFF RETURNS

| Last Name | No. | Yds | Avg | TD |
|---|---|---|---|---|
| Anthony | 23 | 476 | 20.7 | 0 |
| Tullis | 23 | 470 | 20.4 | 0 |
| Martin | 15 | 384 | 25.6 | 0 |
| Fowler | 4 | 78 | 19.5 | 0 |
| Roaches | 4 | 76 | 19.0 | 0 |
| Rackley | 1 | 63 | 63.0 | 0 |
| Merkens | 1 | 0 | 0.0 | 0 |

### PASSING — PUNTING — KICKING

**PASSING**

| Last Name | Att | Cmp | % | Yds | Yd/Att | TD | Int— | % | RK |
|---|---|---|---|---|---|---|---|---|---|
| D. Wilson | 293 | 145 | 50 | 1843 | 6.3 | 11 | 15— | | 5 |
| Hebert | 181 | 97 | 54 | 1208 | 6.7 | 5 | 4— | | 2 |
| Todd | 32 | 16 | 50 | 191 | 6.0 | 3 | 4— | | 13 |
| Hansen | 1 | 1 | 100 | 8 | 8.0 | 0 | 0— | | 0 |
| Merkens | 1 | 1 | 100 | 7 | 7.0 | 1 | 0— | | 0 |

**PUNTING**

| Last Name | No | Avg |
|---|---|---|
| Hansen | 89 | 42.3 |

**KICKING**

| Last Name | XP | Att | % | FG | Att | % |
|---|---|---|---|---|---|---|
| Anderson | 27 | 29 | 93 | 31 | 35 | 89 |

## ATLANTA FALCONS

### RUSHING

| Last Name | No. | Yds | Avg | TD |
|---|---|---|---|---|
| Riggs | 397 | 1719 | 4.3 | 10 |
| Archer | 70 | 347 | 5.0 | 2 |
| J. Washington | 52 | 210 | 4.0 | 1 |
| Austin | 20 | 110 | 5.5 | 0 |
| Pridemore | 1 | 48 | 48.0 | 0 |
| Holly | 3 | 36 | 12.0 | 1 |
| Bartkowski | 5 | 9 | 1.8 | 0 |
| Whisenhunt | 1 | 3 | 3.0 | 0 |
| Bailey | 1 | -3 | -3.0 | 0 |
| Donnelly | 2 | -5 | -2.5 | 0 |
| B. Johnson | 8 | -8 | -1.0 | 0 |

### RECEIVING

| Last Name | No. | Yds | Avg | TD |
|---|---|---|---|---|
| B. Johnson | 62 | 830 | 13.4 | 5 |
| J. Washington | 37 | 328 | 8.9 | 1 |
| Cox | 33 | 454 | 13.8 | 2 |
| Riggs | 33 | 267 | 8.1 | 0 |
| Bailey | 30 | 364 | 12.1 | 0 |
| Brown | 24 | 412 | 17.2 | 2 |
| Allen | 14 | 207 | 14.8 | 2 |
| Benson | 10 | 37 | 3.7 | 0 |
| Matthews | 7 | 57 | 8.1 | 1 |
| Whisenhunt | 3 | 48 | 16.0 | 0 |
| Austin | 1 | 21 | 21.0 | 0 |

### PUNT RETURNS

| Last Name | No. | Yds | Avg | TD |
|---|---|---|---|---|
| Allen | 21 | 141 | 6.7 | 0 |
| B. Johnson | 10 | 82 | 8.2 | 0 |

### KICKOFF RETURNS

| Last Name | No. | Yds | Avg | TD |
|---|---|---|---|---|
| Austin | 39 | 838 | 21.5 | 1 |
| Wagoner | 13 | 262 | 20.2 | 0 |
| Allen | 8 | 140 | 17.5 | 0 |
| Stamps | 4 | 89 | 22.3 | 0 |
| Whisenhunt | 4 | 33 | 8.3 | 0 |
| K. Johnson | 1 | 20 | 20.0 | 0 |
| Tyrrell | 1 | 13 | 13.0 | 0 |
| Matthews | 1 | 11 | 11.0 | 0 |
| R. Washington | 1 | 0 | 0.0 | 0 |

### PASSING — PUNTING — KICKING

**PASSING**

| Last Name | Att | Cmp | % | Yds | Yd/Att | TD | Int— | % | RK |
|---|---|---|---|---|---|---|---|---|---|
| Archer | 312 | 161 | 52 | 1992 | 6.4 | 7 | 17— | | 5 |
| Bartkowski | 111 | 69 | 62 | 738 | 6.3 | 5 | 1— | | 1 |
| Holly | 39 | 24 | 62 | 295 | 7.6 | 1 | 2— | | 5 |

**PUNTING**

| Last Name | NO | Avg |
|---|---|---|
| Donnelly | 59 | 43.6 |
| Giacomarro | 29 | 39.9 |
| Luckhurst | 1 | 26.0 |

**KICKING**

| Last Name | XP | Att | % | FG | Att | % |
|---|---|---|---|---|---|---|
| Luckhurst | 29 | 29 | 100 | 24 | 31 | 77 |

The American Football Conference standings looked like a bowl in 1985, and not the Super variety. The Eastern Division had three strong teams in the Dolphins, Jets and Patriots. Out west, the other high points were called Raiders and Broncos. In the middle, at the bottom of the bowl, was the Central Division, once the pride of the conference. Because the Central champ automatically went to the playoffs, Denver at 11-5 stayed home to watch Cleveland at 8-8.

There was a general feeling that the A.F.C. had slipped behind the N.F.C. in quality. As evidence, only the Raiders had been able to win the Super Bowl in the '80s. Some suggested the A.F.C. teams had spent their time nurturing spectacular young quarterbacks to the detriment of the rest of their programs. That was opinion; fact was that the A.F.C. did have a multitude of spectacular young quarterbacks. Heading the list was record-breaking Dan Marino, but close on his heels were Ken O'Brien, John Elway, Boomer Esiason, Bernie Kosar and Tony Eason. Another fact: most of the really awful defenses in pro football were in the A.F.C.

## EASTERN DIVISION

**Miami Dolphins** — The Dolphins struggled early, in part due to Dan Marino's holdout through training camp and an injury that limited key wide receiver Mark "Super" Duper. With half of the Mark II receivers laid up, defenders concentrated on Mark Clayton, reducing his effectiveness. After nine games, Miami stood at only 5-4. The Killer Bee defense hadn't shown much sting and, as usual, the Miami running game was so-so, despite the estimable blocking of all-world center Dwight Stephenson. Then, while no one was looking, Shula got the act together and the Dolphins won the last seven regular-season games — including the only victory over the Bears all season — to take their third straight Eastern Division crown. Marino finished with 4,137 passing yards and 31 TD tosses — both N.F.L. highs — and it was considered an off year.

**New York Jets** — In the year Joe Namath was elected to the Pro Football Hall of Fame, the Jets finally appeared to have found his successor. Ken O'Brien, in his third season, emerged as the top quarterback while helping turn the Jets from losers to an 11-5 wild-card team. O'Brien was still criticized for holding the ball too long, contributing to a record 62 sacks, but his effective passing put him on top of the N.F.L.'s pass-rating system. Wide receivers Wesley Walker and spectacular rookie Al Toon helped a lot, as did tight end Mickey Shuler. Running back Freeman McNeil stayed healthy most of the time and rushed for 1,331 yards, but only three touchdowns. An improved defense that cut opponents' points by 100 from 1984 was as important as O'Brien and McNeil in the Jets' resurgence. Nose tackle Joe Klecko was the leader, with able assistance from end Mark Gastineau and outside linebacker Lance Mehl.

**New England Patriots** — After years of being tagged talented underachievers, the Patriots began to live up to their ability. Tony Eason began the season at quarterback and, when he went down injured, Steve Grogan stepped in to do a bang-up job. Both had the benefit of a line boasting all-pro Brian Holloway and all-universe John Hannah, excellent receivers in revitalized Stanley Morgan and meteoric Irving Fryar, and a strong running attack led by Craig James and Tony Collins. Andre Tippett keyed a tough linebacking crew, and cornerback Raymond Clayborn and free safety Fred Marion were among the A.F.C.'s better defenders. In the next-to-last game, New England had a shot at the division crown but lost to Miami for the 18th consecutive time in the Orange Bowl. A win over Cincinnati in the last game gave the Pats a wild-card berth.

**Indianapolis Colts** — When the punter is the only player on the roster selected to the Pro Bowl, your team is in trouble. The Colts actually ran the ball well for new coach Rod Dowhower, finishing first in the A.F.C. through the efforts of running back Randy McMillan and a young offensive line. The passing attack was awful. Art Schlichter opened the season at quarterback and he was cut after four games. Mike Pagel got the job by default, but did nothing to excite the fans. The defense improved slightly, but not nearly enough. Ah, but Rohn Stark's punts were fine!

**Buffalo Bills** — A team that scores fewer than 10 points in seven of its games has offensive problems. A team that gives up 49 points to the Colts has defensive troubles. A team that did both of these in '85 was Buffalo. After opening with four straight losses, coach Kay Stephenson was replaced by Hank Bullough, known for his malaprops and his defensive expertise. The Bills responded to him by handing the Colts those 49 points. The only position where help wasn't needed was running back, where young Greg Bell rushed for 883 yards. So, who came back from the U.S.F.L.? Joe Cribbs.

## CENTRAL DIVISION

**Cleveland Browns** — When the Browns won the division crown with a modest 8-8 record, critics said it showed how weak the Central had become. In Cleveland, they took it as a preview of coming attractions. Coach Marty Schottenheimer had a tough defense led by Chip Banks, one of the few linebackers mentionable in the same breath as Lawrence Taylor, and an undersized nose tackle in Bob Golic. He also had a talented but raw rookie quarterback in Bernie Kosar. Predictably, Schottenheimer chose to keep the ball on the ground all season while Kosar learned the ropes. Running backs Kevin Mack and Earnest Byner became the third tandem to each rush for more than 1,000 yards in a season. Despite the paucity of passes, Ozzie Newsome caught 62 and became the all-time top receiver among tight ends.

**Cincinnati Bengals** — The party line in Cincinnati was that another slow start under coach Sam Wyche — three straight losses — cost them the division title. But the Bengals also dropped their last two when the crown was within their grasp. A hulking offensive line, led by all-pro tackle Anthony Munoz, made it easier for lefty Boomer Esiason to blossom as a premier quarterback. Rookie receiver Eddie Brown and vet Cris Collinsworth gave him two ace targets for his passes, and the Bengals put a team-record 441 points on the scoreboard. No matter, possibly the least effective defensive unit since the Polish cavalry used horses against the Panzurs also set a team record, giving up 437 points.

**Pittsburgh Steelers** — The Steelers started off with a 45-3 win over the Colts as quarterback Mark Malone threw five touchdown passes. Then Malone got hurt, backup David Woodley showed why Miami had let him go, and third-string Scott Campbell proved he deserved to be only third-string. Receiver John Stallworth made a remarkable comeback to catch 75 passes, and Louis Lipps was a Pro Bowler at the other wideout position. Frank Pollard and Walter Abercrombie formed a strong, if unspectacular, rushing duo. Mike Merriweather was a standout at linebacker. But the team fell under .500 for the first time since 1971 and was obviously just going through the motions by the end.

**Houston Oilers** — The reason for the Oilers' inability to win was a multiple-choice quiz. The answer was: (a) coach Hugh Campbell's offense lacked inventiveness; (b) quarterback Warren Moon could not read defenses; (c) running back Mike Rozier had left his running ability in Nebraska with his Heisman Trophy; (d) all those high draft choices on the offensive line had been overrated; (e) the defense was lousy no matter what the offense did; or (f) all of the above. General manager Ladd Herzeg chose (a) and fired Campbell with two games left, replacing him with defensive coordinator Jerry Glanville.

## WESTERN DIVISION

**Los Angeles Raiders** — The Raiders take pride in doing things differently, but they were not pleased to be the only strong A.F.C. team without an impressive young quarterback. After six seasons, they'd just about given up on Marc Wilson. Ancient Jim Plunkett was reduced by age and injuries to part-

FINAL TEAM STATISTICS

| OFFENSE | BUFF. | CIN. | CLEV. | DEN. | HOU. | IND. | K.C. | L.A. | MIA. | N.E. | NY J | PIT. | S.D. | SEA. |
|---|---|---|---|---|---|---|---|---|---|---|---|---|---|---|
| **FIRST DOWNS:** | | | | | | | | | | | | | | |
| Total | 256 | 344 | 271 | 339 | 270 | 282 | 258 | 304 | 361 | 294 | 344 | 315 | 380 | 299 |
| by Rushing | 86 | 125 | 119 | 113 | 96 | 131 | 79 | 111 | 116 | 126 | 121 | 125 | 92 | 96 |
| by Passing | 151 | 191 | 128 | 192 | 149 | 130 | 158 | 167 | 218 | 153 | 201 | 165 | 259 | 179 |
| by Penalty | 19 | 28 | 24 | 34 | 25 | 21 | 21 | 26 | 27 | 15 | 22 | 25 | 29 | 24 |
| **RUSHING:** | | | | | | | | | | | | | | |
| Number | 412 | 503 | 533 | 497 | 428 | 485 | 428 | 532 | 444 | 565 | 564 | 541 | 440 | 462 |
| Yards | 1611 | 2183 | 2285 | 1851 | 1570 | 2439 | 1486 | 2262 | 1729 | 2331 | 2312 | 2177 | 1665 | 1644 |
| Average Yards | 3.9 | 4.3 | 4.3 | 3.7 | 3.7 | 5.0 | 3.5 | 4.3 | 3.9 | 4.1 | 4.1 | 4.0 | 3.8 | 3.6 |
| Touchdowns | 13 | 20 | 16 | 20 | 13 | 22 | 10 | 18 | 19 | 15 | 18 | 14 | 20 | 9 |
| **PASSING:** | | | | | | | | | | | | | | |
| Attempts | 517 | 518 | 414 | 617 | 512 | 468 | 511 | 506 | 576 | 457 | 497 | 512 | 632 | 575 |
| Completions | 263 | 302 | 222 | 329 | 277 | 235 | 267 | 269 | 343 | 255 | 303 | 254 | 386 | 304 |
| Completion Pct. | 50.9 | 58.3 | 53.6 | 53.3 | 54.1 | 50.2 | 52.3 | 53.2 | 59.5 | 55.8 | 61.0 | 49.6 | 61.1 | 52.9 |
| Passing Yards | 3331 | 4082 | 2885 | 3952 | 3523 | 2811 | 3726 | 3481 | 4278 | 3483 | 3983 | 3397 | 5175 | 3820 |
| Avg. Yds per Att. | 5.3 | 6.7 | 5.9 | 5.6 | 5.4 | 5.1 | 6.1 | 5.7 | 6.9 | 6.4 | 6.4 | 5.8 | 7.3 | 5.4 |
| Avg. Yds per Comp. | 12.7 | 13.5 | 13.0 | 12.0 | 12.8 | 12.0 | 14.0 | 12.9 | 12.5 | 13.7 | 13.2 | 13.4 | 13.4 | 12.6 |
| Times Tackled | 42 | 41 | 36 | 38 | 58 | 35 | 43 | 43 | 19 | 39 | 62 | 33 | 39 | 53 |
| Yds Lost Tackled | 347 | 365 | 249 | 307 | 441 | 244 | 335 | 335 | 164 | 315 | 399 | 224 | 305 | 457 |
| Net Yards | 2984 | 3717 | 2636 | 3645 | 3082 | 2567 | 3391 | 3146 | 4114 | 3168 | 3584 | 3173 | 4870 | 3363 |
| Touchdowns | 9 | 31 | 17 | 23 | 18 | 15 | 23 | 20 | 31 | 20 | 25 | 23 | 37 | 28 |
| Interceptions | 31 | 13 | 13 | 23 | 22 | 20 | 23 | 24 | 21 | 22 | 8 | 27 | 30 | 23 |
| Pct. Intercepted | 6.0 | 2.5 | 3.1 | 3.7 | 4.3 | 4.3 | 4.5 | 4.7 | 3.6 | 4.8 | 1.6 | 5.3 | 4.7 | 4.0 |
| **PUNTS:** | | | | | | | | | | | | | | |
| Number | 92 | 63 | 81 | 94 | 84 | 80 | 95 | 89 | 59 | 92 | 74 | 79 | 68 | 91 |
| Average | 41.5 | 40.7 | 40.3 | 40.0 | 41.5 | 44.8 | 40.3 | 40.8 | 43.7 | 43.0 | 40.2 | 39. | 42.4 | 40.3 |
| **PUNT RETURNS** | | | | | | | | | | | | | | |
| Number | 38 | 32 | 47 | 46 | 30 | 42 | 43 | 71 | 39 | 42 | 39 | 49 | 25 | 53 |
| Yards | 293 | 268 | 371 | 429 | 250 | 449 | 381 | 785 | 319 | 530 | 386 | 483 | 213 | 483 |
| Average Yards | 7.7 | 8.4 | 7.9 | 9.3 | 8.3 | 10.7 | 8.9 | 11.1 | 8.2 | 12.6 | 9.9 | 9.9 | 8.5 | 9.1 |
| Touchdowns | 0 | 0 | 1 | 0 | 0 | 1 | 0 | 0 | 0 | 2 | 0 | 2 | 0 | 0 |
| **KICKOFF RET.:** | | | | | | | | | | | | | | |
| Number | 68 | 67 | 53 | 52 | 67 | 67 | 59 | 54 | 52 | 57 | 53 | 65 | 71 | 58 |
| Yards | 1334 | 1385 | 1217 | 1203 | 1515 | 1403 | 1117 | 1132 | 1177 | 1119 | 1043 | 1337 | 1494 | 1166 |
| Average Yards | 19.6 | 20.7 | 23.0 | 23.1 | 22.6 | 20.9 | 18.9 | 21.0 | 22.6 | 19.6 | 19.7 | 20.6 | 21.0 | 20.1 |
| Touchdowns | 0 | 0 | 0 | 0 | 0 | 0 | 0 | 0 | 0 | 0 | 0 | 0 | 1 | 0 |
| **INTERCEPT RET.:** | | | | | | | | | | | | | | |
| Number | 20 | 19 | 18 | 24 | 15 | 16 | 27 | 17 | 23 | 23 | 22 | 20 | 26 | 24 |
| Yards | 225 | 283 | 254 | 290 | 144 | 75 | 298 | 235 | 265 | 427 | 127 | 211 | 461 | 272 |
| Average Yards | 11.3 | 14.9 | 14.1 | 12.1 | 9.6 | 4.7 | 11.0 | 13.8 | 11.5 | 18.6 | 5.8 | 10.6 | 17.7 | 11.3 |
| Touchdowns | 0 | 2 | 1 | 1 | 0 | 0 | 1 | 3 | 1 | 1 | 1 | 1 | 2 | 3 |
| **PENALTIES:** | | | | | | | | | | | | | | |
| Number | 132 | 110 | 99 | 85 | 127 | 87 | 87 | 116 | 77 | 114 | 119 | 85 | 100 | 102 |
| Yards | 965 | 795 | 753 | 677 | 1150 | 678 | 666 | 962 | 637 | 842 | 907 | 665 | 937 | 827 |
| **FUMBLES:** | | | | | | | | | | | | | | |
| Number | 36 | 35 | 40 | 24 | 41 | 27 | 22 | 27 | 31 | 37 | 35 | 31 | 44 | 34 |
| Number Lost | 21 | 16 | 23 | 8 | 15 | 14 | 11 | 14 | 20 | 20 | 21 | 9 | 19 | 18 |
| **POINTS:** | | | | | | | | | | | | | | |
| Total | 200 | 441 | 287 | 380 | 284 | 320 | 317 | 354 | 428 | 362 | 393 | 379 | 467 | 349 |
| PAT Attempts | 23 | 53 | 35 | 45 | 32 | 39 | 35 | 42 | 52 | 41 | 45 | 40 | 60 | 44 |
| PAT Made | 23 | 49 | 35 | 41 | 29 | 36 | 35 | 40 | 50 | 40 | 43 | 40 | 53 | 41 |
| FG Attempts | 17 | 33 | 18 | 38 | 27 | 26 | 27 | 32 | 27 | 30 | 34 | 42 | 28 | 25 |
| FG Made | 13 | 24 | 14 | 23 | 21 | 16 | 24 | 20 | 22 | 24 | 26 | 33 | 18 | 14 |
| Percent FG Made | 76.5 | 72.7 | 77.8 | 60.5 | 77.8 | 61.5 | 88.9 | 62.5 | 81.5 | 80.0 | 76.5 | 78.6 | 64.3 | 56.0 |
| Safeties | 0 | 1 | 0 | 0 | 0 | 1 | 0 | 1 | 0 | 2 | 1 | 0 | 0 | 1 |

| DEFENSE | BUFF. | CIN. | CLEV. | DEN. | HOU. | IND. | K.C. | L.A. | MIA. | N.E. | NY J | PIT. | S.D. | SEA. |
|---|---|---|---|---|---|---|---|---|---|---|---|---|---|---|
| **FIRST DOWNS:** | | | | | | | | | | | | | | |
| Total | 320 | 337 | 297 | 290 | 356 | 330 | 336 | 273 | 314 | 284 | 276 | 273 | 364 | 290 |
| by Rushing | 142 | 118 | 106 | 103 | 150 | 124 | 129 | 73 | 135 | 92 | 85 | 105 | 122 | 90 |
| by Passing | 159 | 194 | 172 | 168 | 158 | 192 | 184 | 166 | 160 | 168 | 154 | 144 | 218 | 179 |
| by Penalty | 19 | 25 | 19 | 19 | 48 | 14 | 23 | 34 | 19 | 24 | 37 | 24 | 24 | 21 |
| **RUSHING:** | | | | | | | | | | | | | | |
| Number | 569 | 461 | 497 | 475 | 588 | 539 | 513 | 461 | 509 | 466 | 433 | 470 | 470 | 473 |
| Yards | 2462 | 1999 | 1851 | 1973 | 2814 | 2145 | 2169 | 1605 | 2256 | 1655 | 1516 | 1876 | 1972 | 1837 |
| Average Yards | 4.3 | 4.3 | 3.7 | 4.2 | 4.8 | 4.0 | 4.2 | 3.5 | 4.4 | 3.6 | 3.5 | 4.0 | 4.2 | 3.9 |
| Touchdowns | 20 | 23 | 14 | 10 | 21 | 20 | 18 | 7 | 15 | 15 | 10 | 19 | 25 | 12 |
| **PASSING:** | | | | | | | | | | | | | | |
| Attempts | 477 | 518 | 509 | 547 | 462 | 504 | 576 | 511 | 487 | 525 | 507 | 484 | 595 | 496 |
| Completions | 265 | 297 | 289 | 277 | 260 | 275 | 332 | 251 | 257 | 262 | 267 | 287 | 357 | 273 |
| Completion Pct. | 55.6 | 57.3 | 56.8 | 50.6 | 56.3 | 54.6 | 57.6 | 49.1 | 52.8 | 49.9 | 52.7 | 59.3 | 60.0 | 55.0 |
| Passing Yards | 3301 | 3998 | 3460 | 3584 | 3654 | 3721 | 3752 | 3486 | 3789 | 3393 | 3626 | 3088 | 4597 | 3787 |
| Avg. Yds per Att. | 6.1 | 6.6 | 5.6 | 5.4 | 6.6 | 6.4 | 5.7 | 5.2 | 6.7 | 5.3 | 5.9 | 5.6 | 6.8 | 6.0 |
| Avg. Yds per Comp. | 12.5 | 13.5 | 12.0 | 12.9 | 14.1 | 13.5 | 11.3 | 13.9 | 14.7 | 13.0 | 13.6 | 10.8 | 12.9 | 13.9 |
| Times Tackled | 25 | 40 | 44 | 47 | 41 | 36 | 37 | 65 | 38 | 51 | 49 | 36 | 40 | 61 |
| Yds Lost Tackled | 223 | 334 | 353 | 378 | 313 | 267 | 263 | 488 | 278 | 334 | 370 | 305 | 304 | 464 |
| Net Yards | 3078 | 3664 | 3107 | 3206 | 3341 | 3454 | 3489 | 2998 | 3511 | 3059 | 3256 | 2783 | 4293 | 3323 |
| Touchdowns | 24 | 26 | 18 | 22 | 29 | 24 | 22 | 22 | 21 | 14 | 17 | 18 | 28 | 22 |
| Interceptions | 20 | 19 | 18 | 24 | 15 | 16 | 27 | 17 | 23 | 23 | 22 | 20 | 26 | 24 |
| Pct. Intercepted | 4.2 | 3.7 | 3.5 | 4.4 | 3.2 | 3.2 | 4.7 | 3.3 | 4.7 | 4.4 | 4.3 | 4.1 | 4.4 | 4.8 |
| **PUNTS:** | | | | | | | | | | | | | | |
| Number | 81 | 60 | 91 | 94 | 68 | 72 | 75 | 104 | 73 | 97 | 88 | 86 | 70 | 97 |
| Average | 40.5 | 41.3 | 42.2 | 41.1 | 39.4 | 41.4 | 41.2 | 41.9 | 40.7 | 40.5 | 41.8 | 40.9 | 38.8 | 42.1 |
| **PUNT RETURNS** | | | | | | | | | | | | | | |
| Number | 49 | 42 | 36 | 38 | 45 | 43 | 48 | 26 | 27 | 56 | 36 | 43 | 36 | 47 |
| Yards | 438 | 554 | 304 | 325 | 345 | 572 | 530 | 159 | 371 | 598 | 319 | 380 | 274 | 374 |
| Average Yards | 8.9 | 13.2 | 8.4 | 8.6 | 7.7 | 13.3 | 11.0 | 6.1 | 13.7 | 10.7 | 8.9 | 8.8 | 7.6 | 8.0 |
| Touchdowns | 1 | 1 | 0 | 0 | 0 | 1 | 1 | 0 | 1 | 0 | 1 | 0 | 0 | 0 |
| **KICKOFF RET.:** | | | | | | | | | | | | | | |
| Number | 41 | 81 | 51 | 64 | 39 | 59 | 69 | 59 | 63 | 76 | 58 | 65 | 68 | 47 |
| Yards | 798 | 1734 | 884 | 1346 | 970 | 1189 | 1626 | 1165 | 1370 | 1434 | 1135 | 1566 | 1363 | 918 |
| Average Yards | 19.5 | 21.4 | 17.3 | 21.0 | 24.9 | 20.2 | 23.6 | 19.7 | 21.7 | 18.9 | 19.6 | 24.1 | 20.0 | 19.5 |
| Touchdowns | 0 | 0 | 0 | 1 | 0 | 0 | 0 | 0 | 0 | 0 | 0 | 0 | 0 | 0 |
| **INTERCEPT RET.:** | | | | | | | | | | | | | | |
| Number | 31 | 13 | 13 | 23 | 22 | 20 | 23 | 24 | 21 | 22 | 8 | 27 | 30 | 23 |
| Yards | 418 | 199 | 217 | 332 | 267 | 232 | 251 | 365 | 100 | 243 | 101 | 409 | 268 | 389 |
| Average Yards | 13.5 | 15.3 | 16.7 | 14.4 | 12.1 | 11.6 | 10.9 | 15.2 | 4.7 | 11.0 | 12.6 | 15.1 | 8.9 | 16.9 |
| Touchdowns | 4 | 0 | 1 | 2 | 1 | 0 | 0 | 1 | 0 | 2 | 1 | 5 | 0 | 1 |
| **PENALTIES:** | | | | | | | | | | | | | | |
| Number | 107 | 84 | 102 | 91 | 121 | 90 | 89 | 109 | 112 | 83 | 113 | 89 | 86 | 106 |
| Yards | 870 | 731 | 773 | 953 | 908 | 699 | 77 | 856 | 854 | 699 | 868 | 679 | 703 | 840 |
| **FUMBLES:** | | | | | | | | | | | | | | |
| Number | 36 | 34 | 28 | 22 | 35 | 32 | 25 | 27 | 36 | 36 | 42 | 34 | 37 | 39 |
| Number Lost | 15 | 19 | 9 | 12 | 20 | 17 | 14 | 13 | 18 | 24 | 20 | 14 | 16 | 20 |
| **POINTS:** | | | | | | | | | | | | | | |
| Total | 381 | 437 | 294 | 329 | 412 | 386 | 360 | 308 | 320 | 290 | 264 | 355 | 435 | 303 |
| PAT Attempts | 50 | 51 | 34 | 36 | 51 | 45 | 41 | 34 | 38 | 32 | 30 | 43 | 55 | 35 |
| PAT Made | 45 | 51 | 33 | 35 | 49 | 41 | 39 | 32 | 35 | 30 | 30 | 40 | 51 | 31 |
| FG Attempts | 15 | 34 | 29 | 33 | 34 | 31 | 30 | 35 | 28 | 25 | 25 | 25 | 30 | 28 |
| FG Made | 12 | 26 | 19 | 26 | 19 | 25 | 25 | 24 | 19 | 22 | 18 | 19 | 18 | 20 |
| Percent FG Made | 80.0 | 76.5 | 65.5 | 78.8 | 55.9 | 80.6 | 83.3 | 68.6 | 67.9 | 88.0 | 72.0 | 76.0 | 60.0 | 71.4 |
| Safeties | 0 | 1 | 0 | 0 | 0 | 0 | 0 | 0 | 0 | 1 | 0 | 0 | 0 | 1 |

time status or less. Nevertheless, they won the Western Division title with a six-game winning streak at season's end, riding a sensational year by Marcus Allen and an intimidating defense. Allen led the N.F.L. with 1,759 rushing yards, caught 67 passes and scored 14 touchdowns. Tight end Todd Christensen took some of the pressure off Allen with 82 ball-control catches. The defense kept the pressure on with linemen Howie Long and Bill Pickel. Cornerback Mike Haynes regained his reputation as one of the best in football. The conference-leading 65 sacks was matched by a less-than-50 percent pass-completion mark for opponents.

**Denver Broncos** — Two overtime three-point losses to the Raiders within a three-week span late in the season cost the Broncos the division title and, on tie-breakers, a trip to the playoffs. Their 11-5 record was the best ever for an excluded team. John Elway took several strides toward becoming the superstar Denver bet he would. Sammy Winder was a useful all-around running back, but, with no dominant runner, the offense relied mainly on Elway throwing to Steve Watson and others. Karl Mecklenburg emerged as a defensive star without a position as he shifted among various line and linebacking spots. End Rulon Jones and cornerback Louis Wright also helped make the essentially no-name defense highly effective.

**Seattle Seahawks** — Curt Warner was back, perhaps a half step slower from knee surgery, but still good for 1,094 yards. Receiver Steve Largent caught 79 passes for a league-leading 1,287 yards, while extending his consecutive-game receiving mark to 123. The defense, boasting linemen Jacob Green, Jeff Bryant and Joe Nash, and safety Kenny Easley, was one of the best. Yet, the Seahawks slipped to .500, alternating every two wins with two losses. Most of the blame was heaped on the erratic play of quarterback Dave Krieg. His 20 interceptions helped reduce the turnover ratio from plus-24 in 1984 to plus-3 in '85. At times, he just couldn't move the team, causing a loss of confidence in him by the coaches and by himself.

**San Diego Chargers** — Nothing new this year. Once again, quarterback Dan Fouts threw a ton of passes; receivers Wes Chandler and Charlie Joiner, running back Lionel James, and others caught a high percentage of them for many yards. James caught the most of anyone in the A.F.C. with 86. Runner Earnest Jackson was traded away, so the Chargers only ran the ball when the moon was in the right phase. The offense scored lots of points. Then they turned the ball over to the other team and let them score lots of points. Another season of Air Coryell and the Little Defense That Couldn't.

**Kansas City Chiefs** — Take a seven-game losing streak out of the heart of the season, and the Chiefs had a good year. Let quarterback Bill Kenney play an entire season without injuries, and he's one of the best. Ditto for defensive end Art Still. Give this team something remotely resembling a running attack and ... get the picture? The Chiefs end almost every season with "might-have-beens." In the real world of the Chiefs, free safety Deron Cherry was all-pro and intercepted four passes in one game against Seattle. Receiver Stephone Paige broke an N.F.L. record with 309 yards on eight receptions in the season finale. And Kansas City missed post-season play for the 14th consecutive year.

## MIAMI DOLPHINS 12-4 Don Shula

| Scores of Each Game | | |
|---|---|---|
| 23 | Houston | 26 |
| 30 | INDIANAPOLIS | 13 |
| 31 | KANSAS CITY | 0 |
| 30 | Denver | 26 |
| 30 | PITTSBURGH | 20 |
| 7 | N.Y.Jets | 23 |
| 41 | TAMPA BAY | 38 |
| 21 | Detroit | 31 |
| 13 | New England | 17 |
| 21 | N.Y.JETS | 17 |
| 34 | Indianapolis | 20 |
| 23 | Buffalo | 14 |
| 38 | CHICAGO | 24 |
| 34 | Green Bay | 24 |
| 30 | NEW ENGLAND | 27 |
| 28 | BUFFALO | 0 |

| Use Name | Pos. | Hgt | Wgt | Age | Int | Pts |
|---|---|---|---|---|---|---|
| Jeff Dellenbach | OT | 6'6" | 280 | 22 | | |
| Jon Giesler | OT | 6'5" | 260 | 28 | | |
| Cleveland Green | OT | 6'3" | 262 | 27 | | |
| Steve Clark | OG | 6'4" | 255 | 25 | | |
| Roy Foster | OG | 6'4" | 275 | 25 | | |
| Ronnie Lee | OG | 6'3" | 265 | 28 | | |
| Dwight Stephenson | C | 6'2" | 255 | 27 | | |
| Jeff Toews | C-OG | 6'3" | 255 | 27 | | |
| Bill Barnett | DE-NT | 6'4" | 260 | 29 | | |
| Doug Betters | DE | 6'7" | 265 | 29 | | |
| Kim Bokamper | DE | 6'6" | 255 | 30 | | |
| Mack Moore | DE | 6'4" | 258 | 26 | | |
| Mike Charles | NT | 6'4" | 285 | 22 | | |
| George Little | NT | 6'4" | 278 | 22 | | |

Bob Baumhower - Knee Injury
Ed Newman - Knee Injury

| Use Name | Pos. | Hgt | Wgt | Age | Int | Pts |
|---|---|---|---|---|---|---|
| Charles Bowser | LB | 6'3" | 235 | 25 | | |
| Jay Brophy | LB | 6'3" | 233 | 25 | 1 | |
| Mark Brown | LB | 6'2" | 225 | 24 | 1 | |
| Bob Brudzinski | LB | 6'4" | 223 | 30 | 1 | 6 |
| Hugh Green (from TB) | LB | 6'2" | 225 | 26 | 1 | |
| Alex Moyer | LB | 6'1" | 221 | 21 | 1 | |
| Robin Sendlein | LB | 6'3" | 225 | 26 | | |
| Jackie Shipp | LB | 6'2" | 236 | 23 | 1 | |
| Sanders Shiver | LB | 6'2" | 230 | 30 | | |
| Glenn Blackwood | DB | 6' | 190 | 28 | 6- | |
| Lyle Blackwood | DB | 6' | 190 | 34 | 1 | |
| Bud Brown | DB | 6' | 194 | 24 | 2 | |
| William Judson | DB | 6'1" | 190 | 26 | 4 | 6 |
| Mike Kozlowski | DB | 6' | 198 | 29 | | |
| Paul Lankford | DB | 6'1" | 184 | 27 | 4 | |
| Don McNeal | DB | 5'11" | 192 | 27 | | |
| Mike Smith | DB | 6' | 171 | 22 | | |
| Robert Sowell | DB | 5'11" | 175 | 24 | | |

| Use Name | Pos. | Hgt | Wgt | Age | Int | Pts |
|---|---|---|---|---|---|---|
| Dan Marino | QB | 6'4" | 214 | 23 | | |
| Don Strock | QB | 6'5" | 220 | 34 | | |
| Joe Carter | HB | 5'11" | 196 | 23 | | |
| Lorenzo Hampton | HB | 6' | 212 | 23 | | 18 |
| Tony Nathan | HB | 6' | 206 | 28 | | 36 |
| Woody Bennett | FB | 6'2" | 225 | 30 | | 6 |
| Ron Davenport | FB | 6'2" | 230 | 22 | | 78 |
| Mark Clayton | WR | 5'9" | 175 | 24 | | 24 |
| Mark Duper | WR | 5'9" | 187 | 26 | | 18 |
| Duriel Harris | WR | 5'11" | 176 | 30 | | |
| Vince Heflin | WR | 6' | 185 | 26 | | 6 |
| Jim Jensen | WR | 6'4" | 215 | 26 | | 6 |
| Frank Lockett | WR | 6' | 200 | 28 | | |
| Nat Moore | WR | 5'9" | 188 | 33 | | 42 |
| Tommy Vigorito | WR | 5'10" | 190 | 25 | | |
| Bruce Hardy | TE | 6'5" | 232 | 29 | | 24 |
| Dan Johnson | TE | 6'3" | 240 | 25 | | 18 |
| Joe Rose | TE | 6'3" | 230 | 28 | | 24 |
| Fuad Reveiz | K | 5'11" | 222 | 22 | | 116 |
| Reggie Roby | K | 6'2" | 243 | 24 | | |

Joe Pisarcik - Injury

## NEW YORK JETS 11-5 Joe Walton

| Scores of Each Game | | |
|---|---|---|
| 0 | L.A.Raiders | 31 |
| 42 | BUFFALO | 3 |
| 24 | Green Bay | 3 |
| 25 | INDIANAPOLIS | 20 |
| 29 | Cincinnati | 20 |
| 23 | MIAMI | 7 |
| 13 | New England | 20 |
| 17 | SEATTLE | 14 |
| 35 | Indianapolis | 17 |
| 17 | Miami | 21 |
| 62 | TAMPA BAY | 28 |
| 16 | NEW ENGLAND | *13 |
| 20 | Detroit | 31 |
| 27 | Buffalo | 7 |
| 6 | CHICAGO | 19 |
| 37 | CLEVELAND | 10 |

| Use Name | Pos. | Hgt | Wgt | Age | Int | Pts |
|---|---|---|---|---|---|---|
| Ted Banker | OT-OG | 6'2" | 255 | 24 | | |
| Reggie McElroy | OT | 6'6" | 270 | 25 | | |
| Marvin Powell | OT | 6'5" | 270 | 30 | | |
| Billy Shields | OT | 6'8" | 284 | 32 | | |
| Sid Abramowitz | OG | 6'6" | 280 | 25 | | |
| Dan Alexander | OG | 6'4" | 260 | 30 | | |
| Guy Bingham | OG-OT | 6'3" | 255 | 27 | | |
| Jim Sweeney | OG-OT | 6'4" | 266 | 23 | | |
| Joe Fields | C | 6'2" | 253 | 31 | | |
| Barry Bennett | DE-DT | 6'4" | 260 | 29 | | |
| Mark Gastineau | DE | 6'5" | 265 | 28 | | |
| Ron Faurot | DE | 6'7" | 262 | 23 | | |
| Marty Lyons | DE-DT | 6'5" | 269 | 28 | | |
| Ben Rudolph | DE | 6'5" | 271 | 28 | | |
| Tom Baldwin | DT | 6'4" | 275 | 24 | | 6 |
| Joe Klecko | DT-DE | 6'3" | 263 | 31 | | |

Stan Waldemore - Knee Injury

| Use Name | Pos. | Hgt | Wgt | Age | Int | Pts |
|---|---|---|---|---|---|---|
| Kyle Clifton | LB | 6'4" | 233 | 23 | 3 | |
| Bob Crable | LB | 6'3" | 228 | 25 | | |
| Jim Eliopulos | LB | 6'2" | 229 | 26 | | |
| Rusty Guilbeau | LB | 6'4" | 237 | 26 | | |
| Charles Jackson | LB | 6'2" | 224 | 30 | | |
| Lance Mehl | LB | 6'3" | 233 | 27 | 3 | |
| Matt Monger | LB | 6'1" | 235 | 23 | | |
| John Woodring | LB | 6'2" | 232 | 26 | | |
| Russell Carter | DB | 6'2" | 195 | 23 | | |
| Donnie Elder | DB | 5'9" | 175 | 22 | | |
| Kerry Glenn | DB | 5'9" | 175 | 23 | 4 | 6 |
| Harry Hamilton | DB | 6' | 193 | 22 | 2 | |
| Bobby Jackson | DB | 5'9" | 180 | 28 | 4 | |
| Lester Lyles | DB | 6'3" | 209 | 22 | | |
| Johnny Lynn | DB | 6' | 198 | 28 | 1 | |
| Rich Miano | DB | 6' | 200 | 22 | 2 | |
| Davlin Mullen | DB | 6'1" | 177 | 25 | 3 | |
| Kirk Springs | DB | 6' | 197 | 27 | | |

| Use Name | Pos. | Hgt | Wgt | Age | Int | Pts |
|---|---|---|---|---|---|---|
| Ken O'Brien | QB | 6'4" | 208 | 24 | | |
| Pat Ryan | QB | 6'3" | 210 | 29 | | |
| Dennis Bligen | HB | 5'11" | 209 | 23 | | 6 |
| Johnny Hector | HB | 5'11" | 197 | 24 | | 36 |
| Freeman McNeil | HB | 5'11" | 212 | 26 | | 30 |
| Cedric Minter | HB | 5'10" | 200 | 26 | | |
| Marion Barber | FB | 6'3" | 224 | 25 | | |
| Tony Paige | FB | 5'10" | 220 | 22 | | 60 |
| Nick Bruckner | WR | 5'11" | 185 | 24 | | |
| Chy Davidson | WR | 5'11" | 175 | 26 | | |
| Bobby Humphrey | WR | 5'10" | 180 | 24 | | |
| Kurt Sohn | WR | 5'11" | 180 | 28 | | 24 |
| Al Toon | WR | 6'4" | 200 | 22 | | 18 |
| JoJo Townsell | WR | 5'9" | 180 | 24 | | |
| Wesley Walker | WR | 6' | 182 | 30 | | 32 |
| Billy Griggs | TE | 6'3" | 230 | 23 | | |
| Rocky Klever | TE | 6'3" | 225 | 26 | | 12 |
| Mickey Shuler | TE | 6'3" | 231 | 29 | | 42 |
| Dave Jennings | K | 6'4" | 200 | 33 | | |
| Pat Leahy | K | 6' | 193 | 34 | | 121 |

Glenn Dennison - Back Injury
Johnny "Lam" Jones - Finger Injury

## NEW ENGLAND PATRIOTS 11-5 Raymond Berry

| Scores of Each Game | | |
|---|---|---|
| 26 | GREEN BAY | 20 |
| 7 | Chicago | 20 |
| 17 | Buffalo | 14 |
| 20 | L.A.RAIDERS | 35 |
| 20 | Cleveland | 24 |
| 14 | BUFFALO | 3 |
| 20 | N.Y.JETS | 13 |
| 32 | Tampa Bay | 14 |
| 17 | MIAMI | 13 |
| 34 | INDIANAPOLIS | 15 |
| 20 | Seattle | 13 |
| 13 | N.Y.Jets | *16 |
| 32 | Indianapolis | 31 |
| 23 | DETROIT | 6 |
| 27 | Miami | 30 |
| 34 | CINCINNATI | 23 |

| Use Name | Pos. | Hgt | Wgt | Age | Int | Pts |
|---|---|---|---|---|---|---|
| Brian Holloway | OT | 6'7" | 288 | 26 | | |
| Art Plunkett | OT | 6'7" | 260 | 26 | | |
| Tom Condon | OG | 6'1" | 275 | 32 | | |
| Paul Fairchild | OG | 6'4" | 270 | 23 | | |
| John Hannah | OG | 6'2" | 265 | 34 | | |
| Steve Moore | OG-OT | 6'4" | 285 | 24 | | |
| Ron Wooten | OG | 6'4" | 273 | 26 | | |
| Pete Brock | C | 6'5" | 275 | 31 | | |
| Trevor Matich | C | 6'4" | 270 | 23 | | |
| Guy Morriss | C-OG | 6'4" | 255 | 34 | | |
| Julius Adams | DE | 6'3" | 265 | 37 | | |
| Kenneth Sims | DE | 6'5" | 271 | 25 | | |
| Ben Thomas | DE | 6'4" | 280 | 24 | | |
| Garin Veris | DE | 6'4" | 255 | 22 | | |
| Toby Williams | DE | 6'3" | 254 | 25 | | |
| Dennis Owens | NT | 6'1" | 258 | 25 | | |
| Lester Williams | NT | 6'3" | 272 | 26 | | |

Darryl Haley - Colitus

| Use Name | Pos. | Hgt | Wgt | Age | Int | Pts |
|---|---|---|---|---|---|---|
| Don Blackmon | LB | 6'3" | 235 | 27 | 1 | 4 |
| Brian Ingram | LB | 6'4" | 235 | 25 | | |
| Larry McGrew | LB | 6'5" | 233 | 28 | 1 | |
| Steve Nelson | LB | 6'2" | 230 | 34 | | |
| Johnny Rembert | LB | 6'3" | 234 | 24 | | 6 |
| Ed Reynolds | LB | 6'5" | 230 | 23 | | |
| Andre Tippett | LB | 6'3" | 241 | 25 | | 6 |
| Ed Williams | LB | 6'4" | 244 | 24 | | |
| Jim Bowman | DB | 6'2" | 210 | 21 | | |
| Raymond Clayborn | DB | 6'1" | 186 | 30 | 6 | 6 |
| Ernest Gibson | DB | 5'10" | 185 | 23 | | |
| Roland James | DB | 6'2" | 191 | 27 | 4 | |
| Ronnie Lippett | DB | 5'11" | 180 | 24 | 3 | |
| Fred Marion | DB | 6'2" | 191 | 26 | 7 | |
| Rod McSwain | DB | 6'1" | 198 | 23 | 1 | |

Clayton Weishuhn - Knee Injury

| Use Name | Pos. | Hgt | Wgt | Age | Int | Pts |
|---|---|---|---|---|---|---|
| Tony Eason | QB | 6'4" | 212 | 25 | | 6 |
| Steve Grogan | QB | 6'4" | 210 | 32 | | 12 |
| Tom Ramsey | QB | 6'1" | 189 | 24 | | |
| Craig James | HB | 6' | 215 | 24 | | 42 |
| Tony Collins | HB | 5'11" | 212 | 26 | | 30 |
| Mosi Tatupu | FB | 6' | 227 | 30 | | 12 |
| Robert Weathers | FB | 6'2" | 222 | 24 | | 6 |
| Irving Fryar | WR | 6' | 220 | 22 | | 60 |
| Greg Hawthorne | WR-HB | 6'2" | 225 | 28 | | 6 |
| Cedric Jones | WR | 6'1" | 184 | 25 | | 18 |
| Stanley Morgan | WR | 5'11" | 181 | 30 | | 30 |
| Stephen Starring | WR | 5'10" | 172 | 24 | | |
| Derwin Williams | WR | 6'1" | 170 | 24 | | |
| Lin Dawson | TE | 6'3" | 240 | 26 | | |
| Derrick Ramsey | TE | 6'5" | 235 | 28 | | 6 |
| Rich Camarillo | K | 5'11" | 185 | 25 | | |
| Tony Franklin | K | 5'8" | 182 | 28 | | 112 |

Eric Jordan - Jaw Injury
Bo Robinson - Groin Injury
Jon Williams - Knee Injury

## INDIANAPOLIS COLTS 5-11 Rod Dowhower

| Scores of Each Game | | |
|---|---|---|
| 3 | Pittsburgh | 45 |
| 13 | Miami | 30 |
| 14 | DETROIT | 6 |
| 20 | N.Y.Jets | 25 |
| 49 | BUFFALO | 17 |
| 10 | DENVER | 15 |
| 9 | Buffalo | 21 |
| 37 | GREEN BAY | 10 |
| 17 | N.Y.JETS | 35 |
| 15 | New England | 34 |
| 20 | MIAMI | 34 |
| 7 | Kansas City | 20 |
| 31 | NEW ENGLAND | 38 |
| 10 | Chicago | 17 |
| 31 | Tampa Bay | 23 |
| 34 | HOUSTON | 16 |

| Use Name | Pos. | Hgt | Wgt | Age | Int | Pts |
|---|---|---|---|---|---|---|
| Karl Baldischwiler | OT | 6'5" | 276 | 29 | | |
| Kevin Call | OT | 6'7" | 288 | 23 | | |
| Roger Caron | OT | 6'5" | 292 | 23 | | |
| Chris Hinton | OG | 6'4" | 285 | 24 | | |
| Ron Solt | OG | 6'3" | 283 | 23 | | |
| Ben Utt | OG | 6'5" | 281 | 26 | | |
| Don Bailey | C | 6'4" | 268 | 24 | | |
| Ray Donaldson | C | 6'3" | 281 | 27 | | |
| Charles Benson | DE | 6'3" | 267 | 24 | | |
| Willie Broughton | DE | 6'5" | 282 | 20 | | |
| Chris Scott | DE | 6'5" | 271 | 23 | | |
| Byron Smith | DE | 6'5" | 271 | 22 | | |
| Donnell Thompson | DE | 6'4" | 269 | 26 | | |
| Scott Virkus | DE | 6'5" | 283 | 25 | | |
| George Achica | NT | 6'4" | 275 | 24 | | |
| Brad White | NT | 6'2" | 261 | 27 | | |

Mark Kirchner - Injury
Jim Mills - Shoulder Injury
Blaise Winter - Shoulder Injury
Leo Wisniewski - Knee Injury

| Use Name | Pos. | Hgt | Wgt | Age | Int | Pts |
|---|---|---|---|---|---|---|
| Dave Ahrens | LB | 6'3" | 245 | 26 | | |
| Duane Bickett | LB | 6'5" | 244 | 22 | 1 | |
| Johnie Cooks | LB | 6'4" | 243 | 26 | 1 | |
| Lamonte Hunley | LB | 6'2" | 238 | 22 | | |
| Barry Krauss | LB | 6'3" | 253 | 28 | 1 | |
| Orlando Lowry | LB | 6'4" | 238 | 24 | | |
| Cliff Odom | LB | 6'2" | 241 | 26 | | |
| Don Anderson | DB | 5'10" | 197 | 22 | 1 | |
| Leonard Coleman | DB | 6'2" | 211 | 23 | | |
| Eugene Daniel | DB | 5'11" | 184 | 24 | 8 | |
| Preston Davis | DB | 5'11" | 180 | 23 | 2 | |
| Nesby Glasgow | DB | 5'10" | 191 | 28 | | |
| Keith Lee | DB | 5'11" | 200 | 27 | | |
| George Radachowsky | DB | 5'11" | 178 | 22 | | |
| Tate Randle | DB | 6' | 204 | 26 | 1 | 2 |
| Anthony Young | DB | 5'11" | 196 | 21 | 1 | 6 |

| Use Name | Pos. | Hgt | Wgt | Age | Int | Pts |
|---|---|---|---|---|---|---|
| Matt Kofler | QB | 6'3" | 203 | 26 | | 6 |
| Mike Pagel | QB | 6'2" | 211 | 24 | | 12 |
| Art Schlichter | QB | 6'3" | 210 | 25 | | |
| Albert Bentley | HB | 5'11" | 215 | 25 | | 12 |
| Frank Middleton | HB | 5'11" | 201 | 24 | | 6 |
| George Wonsley | HB | 5'10" | 221 | 24 | | 36 |
| Curtis Dickey (to CLE) | FB | 6'1" | 220 | 28 | | |
| Owen Gill | FB | 6'1" | 230 | 23 | | 12 |
| Randy McMillan | FB | 6' | 220 | 26 | | 42 |
| Matt Bouza | WR | 6'3" | 215 | 26 | | 12 |
| Ray Butler (to SEA) | WR | 6'3" | 203 | 28 | | 12 |
| Wayne Capers | WR | 6'2" | 203 | 24 | | 30 |
| Bernard Henry | WR | 6'1" | 180 | 25 | | |
| Robbie Martin | WR | 5'8" | 187 | 26 | | 6 |
| Ricky Nichols | WR | 5'10" | 176 | 23 | | |
| Oliver Williams | WR | 6'3" | 192 | 24 | | 6 |
| Pat Beach | TE | 6'4" | 244 | 25 | | 36 |
| Mark Boyer | TE | 6'4" | 232 | 22 | | |
| Keli McGregor (from DEN) | TE | 6'6" | 253 | 22 | | |
| Tim Sherwin | TE | 6'6" | 246 | 27 | | |
| Raul Allegre | K | 5'10" | 167 | 26 | | 84 |
| Rohn Stark | K | 6'3" | 212 | 26 | | |

## BUFFALO BILLS 2-14 Kay Stephenson (0-4), Hank Bullough (2-10)

| Scores of Each Game | | |
|---|---|---|
| 9 | SAN DIEGO | 14 |
| 3 | N.Y.Jets | 42 |
| 14 | NEW ENGLAND | 17 |
| 20 | MINNESOTA | 27 |
| 17 | Indianapolis | 49 |
| 3 | New England | 14 |
| 21 | INDIANAPOLIS | 9 |
| 17 | Philadelphia | 21 |
| 17 | CINCINNATI | 23 |
| 20 | HOUSTON | 0 |
| 7 | Cleveland | 17 |
| 14 | MIAMI | 23 |
| 7 | San Diego | 40 |
| 7 | N.Y.JETS | 27 |
| 24 | Pittsburgh | 30 |
| 0 | Miami | 28 |

| Use Name | Pos. | Hgt | Wgt | Age | Int | Pts |
|---|---|---|---|---|---|---|
| Justin Cross | OT | 6'6" | 265 | 26 | | |
| Joe Devlin | OT | 6'5" | 267 | 31 | | |
| Dale Hellestrae | OT | 6'5" | 261 | 23 | | |
| Ken Jones | OT | 6'5" | 279 | 32 | | |
| Greg Christy | OG | 6'4" | 279 | 23 | | |
| Joe DeLamielleure | OG | 6'3" | 260 | 34 | | |
| Jim Richer | OG | 6'3" | 258 | 27 | | |
| Mark Traynowicz | OG | 6'5" | 272 | 22 | | |
| Tim Vogler | OG | 6'3" | 267 | 28 | | |
| Will Grant | C | 6'3" | 264 | 31 | | |
| Sean McNanie | DE | 6'5" | 265 | 23 | | |
| Dean Prater | DE | 6'4" | 256 | 26 | | |
| Bruce Smith | DE | 6'4" | 279 | 22 | | |
| Ben Williams | DE | 6'3" | 266 | 31 | | |
| Fred Smerlas | NT | 6'3" | 268 | 28 | | |
| Don Smith | NT | 6'5" | 262 | 28 | | |

| Use Name | Pos. | Hgt | Wgt | Age | Int | Pts |
|---|---|---|---|---|---|---|
| Anthony Dickerson | LB | 6'2" | 222 | 28 | | |
| Guy Frazier | LB | 6'2" | 217 | 26 | 1 | |
| Hal Garner | LB | 6'4" | 220 | 23 | | |
| Jim Haslett | LB | 6'3" | 228 | 27 | 1 | |
| Steve Maidlow | LB | 6'2" | 238 | 25 | | |
| Eugene Marve | LB | 6'2" | 240 | 29 | | |
| Lucius Sanford | LB | 6'2" | 220 | 29 | | |
| Darryl Talley | LB | 6'4" | 227 | 25 | | |
| Larry Kubin | LB | 6'2" | 238 | 26 | | |
| Eric Wilson | LB | 6'1" | 247 | 23 | | |
| Martin Bayless | DB | 6'2" | 195 | 22 | 2 | |
| Rodney Bellinger | DB | 5'8" | 189 | 23 | 2 | |
| Derrick Burroughs | DB | 6'1" | 180 | 23 | 2 | |
| Steve Freeman | DB | 5'11" | 185 | 32 | | |
| Rod Hill | DB | 6' | 188 | 26 | 2 | |
| Lawrence Johnson | DB | 5'11" | 202 | 27 | 1 | |
| Jim Perryman | DB | 6' | 175 | 24 | | |
| Charles Romes | DB | 6'1" | 188 | 30 | 7 | |
| Don Wilson | DB | 6'2" | 190 | 24 | 2 | 6 |

Stan David - Torn back muscle

| Use Name | Pos. | Hgt | Wgt | Age | Int | Pts |
|---|---|---|---|---|---|---|
| Bruce Mathison | QB | 6'3" | 205 | 26 | | 6 |
| Frank Reich | QB | 6'3" | 208 | 23 | | |
| Vince Ferragamo (to GB) | QB | 6'3" | 217 | 31 | | 6 |
| Joe Cribbs | HB | 5'11" | 193 | 27 | | 6 |
| Anthony Hutchison | HB | 5'10" | 186 | 24 | | |
| Van Williams | HB | 6' | 208 | 26 | | |
| Greg Bell | FB | 5'10" | 210 | 23 | | 54 |
| Booker Moore | FB | 5'11" | 222 | 26 | | 6 |
| Anthony Steels (from SD) | FB | 5'9" | 200 | 26 | | |
| Mitchell Brookins | WR | 5'11" | 196 | 24 | | |
| Chris Burkett | WR | 6'4" | 198 | 23 | | |
| Jerry Butler | WR | 6' | 178 | 27 | | 12 |
| Andre Reed | WR | 6' | 186 | 20 | | 30 |
| Eric Richardson | WR | 6'1" | 185 | 23 | | |
| Jimmy Teal | WR | 5'10" | 170 | 23 | | |
| Pete Metzelaars | TE | 6'7" | 243 | 25 | | 6 |
| Eason Ramson | TE | 6'2" | 234 | 29 | | 6 |
| Ulysses Norris | TE | 6'4' | 232 | 28 | | |
| John Kidd | K | 6'3" | 208 | 24 | | |
| Scott Norwood | K | 6' | 205 | 25 | | 62 |

Robb Riddick - Knee Injury

* Overtime

| RUSHING | | | | |
|---|---|---|---|---|
| Last Name | No. | Yds | Avg | TD |

**MIAMI DOLPHINS**

| Last Name | No. | Yds | Avg | TD |
|---|---|---|---|---|
| Nathan | 143 | 667 | 4.7 | 5 |
| Davenport | 98 | 370 | 3.8 | 11 |
| Hampton | 105 | 369 | 3.5 | 3 |
| Bennett | 54 | 256 | 4.7 | 0 |
| Carter | 14 | 76 | 5.4 | 0 |
| N. Moore | 1 | 11 | 11.0 | 0 |
| Clayton | 1 | 10 | 10.0 | 0 |
| Strock | 2 | -6 | -3.0 | 0 |
| Marino | 26 | -24 | -0.9 | 0 |

**NEW YORK JETS**

| Last Name | No. | Yds | Avg | TD |
|---|---|---|---|---|
| McNeil | 294 | 1331 | 4.5 | 3 |
| Hector | 145 | 572 | 3.9 | 6 |
| Paige | 55 | 158 | 2.9 | 8 |
| Bilgen | 22 | 107 | 4.9 | 1 |
| O'Brien | 25 | 58 | 2.3 | 0 |
| Barber | 9 | 41 | 4.6 | 0 |
| Minter | 8 | 23 | 2.9 | 0 |
| Sohn | 1 | 12 | 12.0 | 0 |
| Humphery | 1 | 10 | 10.0 | 0 |
| Toon | 1 | 5 | 5.0 | 0 |
| Ryan | 3 | -5 | -1.7 | 0 |

**NEW ENGLAND PATRIOTS**

| Last Name | No. | Yds | Avg | TD |
|---|---|---|---|---|
| C. James | 263 | 1227 | 4.7 | 5 |
| Collins | 163 | 657 | 4.0 | 3 |
| Weathers | 41 | 174 | 4.2 | 1 |
| Tatupu | 47 | 152 | 3.2 | 2 |
| Eason | 22 | 70 | 3.2 | 1 |
| Grogan | 20 | 29 | 1.5 | 2 |
| Fryar | 7 | 27 | 3.9 | 1 |
| Morgan | 1 | 0 | 0.0 | 0 |
| Franklin | 1 | -5 | -5.0 | 0 |

**INDIANAPOLIS COLTS**

| Last Name | No. | Yds | Avg | TD |
|---|---|---|---|---|
| McMillan | 190 | 858 | 4.5 | 7 |
| Wonsley | 138 | 716 | 5.2 | 6 |
| Bentley | 54 | 288 | 5.3 | 2 |
| Gill | 45 | 262 | 5.8 | 2 |
| Pagel | 25 | 160 | 6.4 | 2 |
| Dickey | 11 | 40 | 3.6 | 0 |
| Middleton | 13 | 35 | 2.7 | 1 |
| Kofler | 4 | 33 | 8.3 | 1 |
| Martin | 1 | 23 | 23.0 | 0 |
| Capers | 3 | 18 | 6.0 | 1 |
| Schlichter | 2 | 13 | 6.5 | 0 |
| Butler | 1 | -1 | -1.0 | 0 |

**BUFFALO BILLS**

| Last Name | No. | Yds | Avg | TD |
|---|---|---|---|---|
| Bell | 223 | 883 | 4.0 | 8 |
| Cribbs | 122 | 399 | 3.3 | 1 |
| Mathison | 27 | 231 | 8.6 | 1 |
| Steels | 10 | 38 | 3.8 | 0 |
| Moore | 15 | 23 | 1.5 | 1 |
| Ferragamo | 8 | 15 | 1.9 | 1 |
| Hutchison | 2 | 11 | 5.5 | 0 |
| B. Smith | 1 | 0 | 0.0 | 0 |
| Reed | 3 | -1 | -0.3 | 1 |

---

| RECEIVING | | | | |
|---|---|---|---|---|
| Last Name | No. | Yds | Avg | TD |

**MIAMI DOLPHINS (Receiving)**

| Last Name | No. | Yds | Avg | TD |
|---|---|---|---|---|
| Nathan | 72 | 651 | 9.0 | 1 |
| Clayton | 70 | 996 | 14.2 | 4 |
| N. Moore | 51 | 701 | 13.7 | 7 |
| Hardy | 39 | 409 | 10.5 | 4 |
| Duper | 35 | 650 | 18.6 | 3 |
| Rose | 19 | 306 | 16.1 | 4 |
| Johnson | 13 | 192 | 14.8 | 3 |
| Davenport | 13 | 74 | 5.7 | 2 |
| Bennett | 10 | 101 | 10.1 | 1 |
| Hampton | 8 | 56 | 7.0 | 0 |
| Heflin | 6 | 98 | 16.3 | 1 |
| Harris | 3 | 24 | 8.0 | 0 |
| Carter | 2 | 7 | 3.5 | 0 |
| Vigorito | 1 | 9 | 9.0 | 0 |
| Jensen | 1 | 4 | 4.0 | 1 |

**NEW YORK JETS (Receiving)**

| Last Name | No. | Yds | Avg | TD |
|---|---|---|---|---|
| Shuler | 76 | 879 | 11.6 | 7 |
| Toon | 46 | 662 | 14.4 | 3 |
| Sohn | 39 | 534 | 13.7 | 4 |
| McNeil | 38 | 427 | 11.2 | 2 |
| Walker | 34 | 725 | 21.3 | 5 |
| Paige | 18 | 120 | 6.7 | 2 |
| Hector | 17 | 164 | 9.6 | 0 |
| Klever | 14 | 183 | 13.1 | 2 |
| Townsell | 12 | 187 | 15.6 | 0 |
| Bilgen | 5 | 43 | 8.6 | 0 |
| Barber | 3 | 46 | 15.3 | 0 |
| Minter | 1 | 13 | 13.0 | 0 |

**NEW ENGLAND PATRIOTS (Receiving)**

| Last Name | No. | Yds | Avg | TD |
|---|---|---|---|---|
| Collins | 52 | 549 | 10.6 | 2 |
| Morgan | 39 | 760 | 19.5 | 5 |
| Fryar | 39 | 670 | 17.2 | 7 |
| D. Ramsey | 28 | 285 | 10.2 | 1 |
| C. James | 27 | 360 | 13.3 | 2 |
| Jones | 21 | 237 | 11.3 | 2 |
| Dawson | 17 | 148 | 8.7 | 0 |
| Starring | 16 | 235 | 14.7 | 0 |
| D. Williams | 9 | 163 | 18.1 | 0 |
| Hawthorne | 3 | 42 | 14.0 | 1 |
| Weathers | 2 | 18 | 9.0 | 0 |
| Tatupu | 2 | 16 | 8.0 | 0 |

**INDIANAPOLIS COLTS (Receiving)**

| Last Name | No. | Yds | Avg | TD |
|---|---|---|---|---|
| Beach | 36 | 376 | 10.4 | 6 |
| Wonsley | 30 | 257 | 8.6 | 0 |
| Bouza | 27 | 381 | 14.1 | 2 |
| Capers | 25 | 438 | 17.5 | 4 |
| Boyer | 25 | 274 | 11.0 | 0 |
| McMillan | 22 | 115 | 5.2 | 0 |
| Butler | 19 | 345 | 18.2 | 2 |
| Bentley | 11 | 85 | 7.7 | 0 |
| Martin | 10 | 128 | 12.8 | 0 |
| Williams | 9 | 175 | 19.4 | 1 |
| Sherwin | 5 | 64 | 12.8 | 0 |
| Middleton | 5 | 54 | 10.8 | 0 |
| Gill | 5 | 52 | 10.4 | 0 |
| Dickey | 3 | 30 | 10.0 | 0 |
| Henry | 2 | 31 | 15.5 | 0 |
| Pagel | 1 | 6 | 6.0 | 0 |

**BUFFALO BILLS (Receiving)**

| Last Name | No. | Yds | Avg | TD |
|---|---|---|---|---|
| Bell | 58 | 576 | 9.9 | 1 |
| Reed | 48 | 637 | 13.3 | 4 |
| Butler | 41 | 770 | 18.8 | 2 |
| Ramson | 37 | 369 | 10.0 | 1 |
| Burkett | 21 | 371 | 17.7 | 0 |
| Cribbs | 18 | 142 | 7.9 | 0 |
| Richardson | 12 | 201 | 16.8 | 0 |
| Metzelaars | 12 | 80 | 6.7 | 1 |
| Moore | 7 | 44 | 6.3 | 0 |
| Brookins | 3 | 71 | 23.7 | 0 |
| Norris | 2 | 30 | 15.0 | 0 |
| Steels | 2 | 9 | 4.5 | 0 |
| Teal | 1 | 24 | 24.0 | 0 |
| V. Williams | 1 | 7 | 7.0 | 0 |

---

| PUNT RETURNS | | | | |
|---|---|---|---|---|
| Last Name | No. | Yds | Avg | TD |

**MIAMI DOLPHINS (Punt Returns)**

| Last Name | No. | Yds | Avg | TD |
|---|---|---|---|---|
| Vigorito | 22 | 197 | 9.0 | 0 |
| Kozlowski | 7 | 65 | 9.3 | 0 |
| Lockett | 5 | 23 | 4.6 | 0 |
| G. Blackwood | 3 | 20 | 6.7 | 0 |
| Clayton | 2 | 14 | 7.0 | 0 |

**NEW YORK JETS (Punt Returns)**

| Last Name | No. | Yds | Avg | TD |
|---|---|---|---|---|
| Sohn | 16 | 149 | 9.3 | 0 |
| Springs | 14 | 147 | 10.5 | 0 |
| Townsell | 6 | 65 | 10.8 | 0 |
| Minter | 2 | 25 | 12.5 | 0 |
| Humphery | 1 | 0 | 0.0 | 0 |

**NEW ENGLAND PATRIOTS (Punt Returns)**

| Last Name | No. | Yds | Avg | TD |
|---|---|---|---|---|
| Fryar | 37 | 520 | 14.1 | 2 |
| R. James | 2 | 13 | 6.5 | 0 |
| Starring | 2 | 0 | 0.0 | 0 |
| Bowman | 1 | -3 | -3.0 | 0 |

**INDIANAPOLIS COLTS (Punt Returns)**

| Last Name | No. | Yds | Avg | TD |
|---|---|---|---|---|
| Martin | 40 | 443 | 11.1 | 1 |
| Daniel | 1 | 6 | 6.0 | 0 |
| Lowrey | 1 | 0 | 0.0 | 0 |

**BUFFALO BILLS (Punt Returns)**

| Last Name | No. | Yds | Avg | TD |
|---|---|---|---|---|
| D. Wilson | 16 | 161 | 10.1 | 0 |
| Hill | 16 | 120 | 7.5 | 0 |
| Reed | 5 | 12 | 2.4 | 0 |
| E. Wilson | 1 | 0 | 0.0 | 0 |

---

| KICKOFF RETURNS | | | | |
|---|---|---|---|---|
| Last Name | No. | Yds | Avg | TD |

**MIAMI DOLPHINS (Kickoff Returns)**

| Last Name | No. | Yds | Avg | TD |
|---|---|---|---|---|
| Hampton | 45 | 1020 | 22.7 | 0 |
| Carter | 4 | 82 | 20.5 | 0 |
| L. Blackwood | 2 | 32 | 16.0 | 0 |
| Hardy | 1 | 11 | 11.0 | 0 |
| Kozlowski | 0 | 32 | — | 0 |

**NEW YORK JETS (Kickoff Returns)**

| Last Name | No. | Yds | Avg | TD |
|---|---|---|---|---|
| Humphery | 17 | 363 | 21.4 | 0 |
| Hector | 11 | 274 | 24.9 | 0 |
| Springs | 10 | 227 | 22.7 | 0 |
| Glenn | 5 | 71 | 14.2 | 0 |
| Elder | 3 | 42 | 14.0 | 0 |
| Sohn | 3 | 7 | 2.3 | 0 |
| Townsell | 2 | 42 | 21.0 | 0 |
| Minter | 1 | 14 | 14.0 | 0 |
| Klever | 1 | 3 | 3.0 | 0 |

**NEW ENGLAND PATRIOTS (Kickoff Returns)**

| Last Name | No. | Yds | Avg | TD |
|---|---|---|---|---|
| Starring | 48 | 1012 | 21.1 | 0 |
| Fryar | 3 | -39 | -13.0 | 0 |
| Jones | 3 | 37 | 12.3 | 0 |
| Weathers | 1 | 18 | 18.0 | 0 |
| Hawthorne | 1 | 13 | 13.0 | 0 |
| C. James | 1 | 0 | 0.0 | 0 |

**INDIANAPOLIS COLTS (Kickoff Returns)**

| Last Name | No. | Yds | Avg | TD |
|---|---|---|---|---|
| Bentley | 27 | 674 | 25.0 | 0 |
| Martin | 32 | 638 | 19.9 | 0 |
| Williams | 3 | 44 | 14.7 | 0 |
| Young | 2 | 15 | 7.5 | 0 |
| Middleton | 1 | 20 | 20.0 | 0 |
| Gill | 1 | 6 | 6.0 | 0 |
| Lee | 1 | 6 | 6.0 | 0 |

**BUFFALO BILLS (Kickoff Returns)**

| Last Name | No. | Yds | Avg | TD |
|---|---|---|---|---|
| D. Wilson | 22 | 465 | 21.1 | 0 |
| Steels | 30 | 561 | 18.7 | 0 |
| Hutchison | 12 | 239 | 19.9 | 0 |
| Brookins | 6 | 152 | 25.3 | 0 |
| Richardson | 3 | 69 | 23.0 | 0 |
| Moore | 3 | 31 | 10.3 | 0 |
| Teal | 1 | 20 | 20.0 | 0 |
| V. Williams | 1 | 20 | 20.0 | 0 |

---

**PASSING — PUNTING — KICKING**

**MIAMI DOLPHINS**

| PASSING | Att | Cmp | % | Yds | Yd/Att | TD | Int— | % | RK |
|---|---|---|---|---|---|---|---|---|---|
| Marino | 567 | 336 | 59 | 4137 | 7.3 | 30 | 21— | 4 | |
| Strock | 9 | 7 | 78 | 141 | 15.7 | 1 | 0— | 0 | |

| PUNTING | No | Avg |
|---|---|---|
| Roby | 59 | 43.7 |

| KICKING | XP | Att | % | FG | Att | % |
|---|---|---|---|---|---|---|
| Reveiz | 50 | 52 | 96 | 22 | 27 | 81 |

**NEW YORK JETS**

| PASSING | Att | Cmp | % | Yds | Yd/Att | TD | Int— | % | RK |
|---|---|---|---|---|---|---|---|---|---|
| O'Brien | 488 | 297 | 61 | 3888 | 8.0 | 25 | 8— | 2 | |
| Ryan | 9 | 6 | 67 | 95 | 10.6 | 0 | 0— | 0 | |

| PUNTING | No | Avg |
|---|---|---|
| Jennings | 74 | 40.2 |

| KICKING | XP | Att | % | FG | Att | % |
|---|---|---|---|---|---|---|
| Leahy | 43 | 45 | 96 | 26 | 34 | 77 |

**NEW ENGLAND PATRIOTS**

| PASSING | Att | Cmp | % | Yds | Yd/Att | TD | Int— | % | RK |
|---|---|---|---|---|---|---|---|---|---|
| Eason | 299 | 168 | 56 | 2156 | 7.2 | 11 | 17— | 6 | |
| Grogan | 156 | 85 | 55 | 1311 | 8.4 | 7 | 5— | 3 | |
| C. James | 2 | 2 | 100 | 16 | 8.0 | 2 | 0— | 0 | |

| PUNTING | No | Avg |
|---|---|---|
| Camarillo | 92 | 43.0 |

| KICKING | XP | Att | % | FG | Att | % |
|---|---|---|---|---|---|---|
| Franklin | 40 | 41 | 98 | 24 | 30 | 80 |

**INDIANAPOLIS COLTS**

| PASSING | Att | Cmp | % | Yds | Yd/Att | TD | Int— | % | RK |
|---|---|---|---|---|---|---|---|---|---|
| Pagel | 393 | 199 | 51 | 2414 | 6.1 | 14 | 15— | 4 | |
| Kofler | 48 | 23 | 48 | 284 | 5.9 | 1 | 3— | 6 | |
| Schlichter | 25 | 12 | 48 | 107 | 4.3 | 0 | 2— | 8 | |
| Bentley | 1 | 1 | 100 | 6 | 6.0 | 0 | 0— | 0 | |
| Stark | 1 | 0 | 0 | 0 | 0.0 | 0 | 0— | 0 | |

| PUNTING | No | Avg |
|---|---|---|
| Stark | 78 | 45.9 |

| KICKING | XP | Att | % | FG | Att | % |
|---|---|---|---|---|---|---|
| Allegre | 36 | 39 | 92 | 16 | 26 | 62 |

**BUFFALO BILLS**

| PASSING | Att | Cmp | % | Yds | Yd/Att | TD | Int— | % | RK |
|---|---|---|---|---|---|---|---|---|---|
| Ferragamo | 287 | 149 | 52 | 1677 | 5.8 | 5 | 17— | 6 | |
| Mathison | 228 | 113 | 50 | 1635 | 7.2 | 4 | 14— | 6 | |
| Reich | 1 | 1 | 100 | 19 | 19.0 | 0 | 0— | 0 | |
| Bell | 1 | 0 | 0 | 0 | 0.0 | 0 | 0— | 0 | |
| Kidd | 0 | 0 | 0 | -9 | -9.0 | 0 | 0— | 0 | |

| PUNTING | No | Avg |
|---|---|---|
| Kidd | 92 | 41.5 |

| KICKING | XP | Att | % | FG | Att | % |
|---|---|---|---|---|---|---|
| Norwood | 23 | 23 | 100 | 13 | 17 | 77 |

## CLEVELAND BROWNS 8-8 Marty Schottenheimer

| Scores of Each Game | | |
|---|---|---|
| 24 | ST.LOUIS | *27 |
| 17 | PITTSBURGH | 7 |
| 7 | Dallas | 20 |
| 21 | San Diego | 7 |
| 24 | NEW ENGLAND | 20 |
| 21 | Houston | 6 |
| 20 | L.A.RAIDERS | 21 |
| 7 | WASHINGTON | 14 |
| 9 | Pittsburgh | 10 |
| 10 | Cincinnati | 27 |
| 17 | BUFFALO | 7 |
| 24 | CINCINNATI | 6 |
| 35 | N.Y.Giants | 33 |
| 13 | Seattle | 31 |
| 28 | HOUSTON | 21 |
| 10 | N.Y.Jets | 37 |

| Use Name | Pos. | Hgt | Wgt | Age | Int | Pts |
|---|---|---|---|---|---|---|
| Scott Bolzan | OT | 6'3" | 270 | 23 | | |
| Bill Contz | OT | 6'5" | 270 | 24 | | |
| Paul Farren | OT | 6'5" | 270 | 24 | | |
| Cody Risien | OT | 6'7" | 280 | 28 | | |
| Dan Fike | OG-OT | 6'7" | 280 | 24 | | |
| George Lilja | OG-C | 6'4" | 270 | 27 | | |
| Robert Jackson | OG | 6'5" | 260 | 32 | | |
| Mike Baab | C | 6'4" | 270 | 25 | | |
| Keith Baldwin | DE | 6'4" | 270 | 24 | | |
| Reggie Camp | DE | 6'4" | 270 | 24 | | |
| Sam Clancy | DE | 6'7" | 260 | 27 | | |
| Carl Hairston | DE | 6'3" | 260 | 32 | | |
| Bob Golic | NT | 6'2" | 260 | 27 | | |
| Dave Puzzuoli | NT | 6'3" | 260 | 24 | | |
| Chip Banks | LB | 6'4" | 233 | 25 | | |
| Tom Cousineau | LB | 6'3" | 225 | 28 | 1 | |
| Eddie Johnson | LB | 6'1" | 225 | 26 | 1 | |
| Clay Matthews | LB | 6'2" | 235 | 29 | | |
| Scott Nicolas | LB | 6'3" | 226 | 25 | | |
| Curtis Weathers | LB | 6'5" | 230 | 28 | 1 | |
| Larry Braziel | DB | 6' | 184 | 30 | 2 | |
| Hanford Dixon | DB | 5'11" | 186 | 26 | 3 | |
| Al Gross | DB | 6'3" | 195 | 24 | 5 | 6 |
| D.D.Hoggard | DB | 6' | 188 | 24 | | |
| Frank Minnifield | DB | 5'9" | 180 | 25 | 1 | |
| Chris Rockins | DB | 6' | 195 | 23 | 1 | |
| Don Rogers | DB | 6'1" | 206 | 22 | 1 | |
| Harry Skipper | DB | 5'11" | 175 | 25 | | |
| Felix Wright | DB | 6'2" | 190 | 26 | 2 | |
| Gary Danielson | QB | 6'2" | 196 | 33 | | |
| Bernie Kosar | QB | 6'5" | 210 | 21 | | |
| Paul McDonald | QB | 6'2" | 185 | 27 | | |
| Greg Allen | HB | 5'11" | 200 | 22 | | |
| Herman Fontenot | HB | 6' | 206 | 21 | | |
| Boyce Green | HB | 5'11" | 215 | 25 | | |
| Kevin Mack | HB | 6' | 212 | 23 | | 60 |
| Earnest Byner | FB | 5'10" | 215 | 22 | | 60 |
| Johnny Davis | FB | 6'1" | 235 | 29 | | |
| Willie Adams | WR | 6'2" | 200 | 29 | | |
| Fred Banks | WR | 5'10" | 177 | 23 | | 12 |
| Brian Brennan | WR | 5'9" | 178 | 23 | | 6 |
| John Jefferson | WR | 6'1" | 204 | 29 | | |
| Reggie Langhorne | WR | 6'2" | 195 | 22 | | |
| Clarence Weathers | WR | 5'9" | 170 | 23 | | 18 |
| Glen Young | WR | 6'2" | 205 | 24 | | 6 |
| Harry Holt | TE | 6'4" | 230 | 27 | | 6 |
| Ozzie Newsome | TE | 6'2" | 232 | 29 | | 30 |
| Travis Tucker | TE | 6'3" | 227 | 21 | | |
| Matt Bahr | K | 5'10" | 175 | 29 | | 77 |
| Jeff Gossett | K | 6'2" | 200 | 28 | | |

## CINCINNATI BENGALS 7-9 Sam Wyche

| Scores of Each Game | | |
|---|---|---|
| 24 | SEATTLE | 28 |
| 27 | St.Louis | 41 |
| 41 | SAN DIEGO | 44 |
| 37 | Pittsburgh | 24 |
| 20 | N.Y.JETS | 29 |
| 35 | N.Y.GIANTS | 30 |
| 27 | Houston | 44 |
| 26 | PITTSBURGH | 21 |
| 23 | Buffalo | 17 |
| 27 | CLEVELAND | 10 |
| 6 | L.A.Raiders | 13 |
| 6 | Cleveland | 24 |
| 45 | HOUSTON | 27 |
| 50 | DALLAS | 24 |
| 24 | Washington | 27 |
| 23 | New England | 34 |

| Use Name | Pos. | Hgt | Wgt | Age | Int | Pts |
|---|---|---|---|---|---|---|
| Anthony Munoz | OT | 6'6" | 278 | 27 | | |
| Bruce Riemers | OT | 6'7" | 280 | 24 | | |
| Joe Walter | OT | 6'6" | 290 | 22 | | |
| Mike Wilson | OT | 6'5" | 271 | 30 | | |
| Brian Blados | OG | 6'4" | 295 | 23 | | |
| Max Montoya | OG | 6'5" | 275 | 29 | | |
| Bruce Kozerski | C | 6'4" | 275 | 23 | | |
| Dave Rimington | C | 6'3" | 288 | 23 | | |
| Ross Browner | DE | 6'3" | 265 | 31 | | 2 |
| Glen Collins | DE | 6'6" | 265 | 26 | | |
| Eddie Edwards | DE | 6'5" | 256 | 31 | | |
| Jerry Boyarsky | NT | 6'3" | 290 | 26 | | |
| Tim Krumrie | NT | 6'2" | 262 | 25 | | |
| Leo Barker | LB | 6'1" | 221 | 25 | | |
| Glenn Cameron | LB | 6'2" | 228 | 32 | | |
| Tom Dinkel | LB | 6'3" | 240 | 29 | | |
| Emanuel King | LB | 6'4" | 245 | 22 | | |
| Jeff Schuh | LB | 6'2" | 234 | 27 | | |
| Ron Simpkins | LB | 6'1" | 235 | 27 | | |
| Reggie Williams | LB | 6'1" | 228 | 30 | | |
| Carl Zander | LB | 6'2" | 235 | 22 | | |
| Louis Breeden | DB | 5'11" | 185 | 31 | 2 | |
| Lee Davis | DB | 5'11" | 198 | 22 | | |
| James Griffin | DB | 6'2" | 197 | 23 | 7 | 6 |
| Ray Horton | DB | 5'11" | 190 | 25 | 2 | |
| Robert Jackson | DB | 5'10" | 186 | 26 | 6 | 6 |
| Bobby Kemp | DB | 6' | 192 | 26 | 1 | |
| John Simmons | DB | 5'11" | 192 | 26 | | |
| Sean Thomas | DB | 6' | 190 | 23 | | |
| Jimmy Turner | DB | 6' | 187 | 26 | | 1 |
| Sam Washington (from PIT) | DB | 5'8" | 180 | 25 | | |
| Ken Anderson | QB | 6'3" | 212 | 36 | | |
| Boomer Esiason | QB | 6'4" | 220 | 24 | | 6 |
| Turk Schonert | QB | 6'1" | 190 | 28 | | |
| James Brooks | HB | 5'10" | 182 | 26 | | 72 |
| Stanford Jennings | HB | 6'1" | 205 | 23 | | 24 |
| Charles Alexander | FB | 6'1" | 226 | 28 | | 12 |
| Bill Johnson | FB | 6'2" | 230 | 24 | | |
| Larry Kinnebrew | FB | 6'1" | 255 | 26 | | 60 |
| Eddie Brown | WR | 6' | 185 | 22 | | 48 |
| Cris Collinsworth | WR | 6'5" | 192 | 26 | | 30 |
| Steve Kreider | WR | 6'3" | 192 | 27 | | 7 |
| Mike Martin | WR | 5'10" | 186 | 24 | | |
| Clay Pickering | WR | 6'5" | 215 | 24 | | |
| M.L.Harris | TE | 6'5" | 238 | 31 | | 6 |
| Rodney Holman | TE | 6'3" | 232 | 25 | | 42 |
| Don Kern | TE | 6'4" | 225 | 23 | | |
| Jim Breech | K | 5'6" | 161 | 29 | | 120 |
| Pat McInally | K | 6'6" | 212 | 32 | | |

Stanley Wilson - Suspended by N.F.L.

## PITTSBURGH STEELERS 7-9 Chuck Noll

| Scores of Each Game | | |
|---|---|---|
| 45 | INDIANAPOLIS | 3 |
| 7 | Cleveland | 17 |
| 20 | HOUSTON | 0 |
| 24 | CINCINNATI | 37 |
| 20 | Miami | 24 |
| 13 | Dallas | 27 |
| 23 | ST.LOUIS | 10 |
| 21 | Cincinnati | 26 |
| 10 | CLEVELAND | 9 |
| 36 | Kansas City | 28 |
| 30 | Houston | 7 |
| 23 | WASHINGTON | 30 |
| 23 | DENVER | 31 |
| 44 | San Diego | 54 |
| 30 | BUFFALO | 24 |
| 10 | N.Y.Giants | 28 |

| Use Name | Pos. | Hgt | Wgt | Age | Int | Pts |
|---|---|---|---|---|---|---|
| Tunch Ilkin | OT | 6'3" | 262 | 27 | | |
| Ray Pinney | OT-C | 6'4" | 262 | 31 | | |
| Pete Rostosky | OT | 6'4" | 252 | 24 | | |
| Ray Snell (to DET) | OT-OG | 6'4" | 265 | 27 | | |
| Emil Boures | OG-C | 6'1" | 260 | 25 | | |
| Terry Long | OG | 5'11" | 265 | 26 | | |
| Randy Rasmussen | OG-C | 6'2" | 254 | 24 | | |
| Blake Wingle (to GB) | OG | 6'2" | 267 | 25 | | |
| Craig Wolfley | OG | 6'1" | 265 | 27 | | |
| Dan Turk | C | 6'4" | 270 | 23 | | |
| Mike Webster | C | 6'1" | 260 | 33 | | |
| Keith Gary | DE | 6'3" | 265 | 25 | | |
| John Goodman | DE-NT | 6'6" | 258 | 26 | | |
| Edmund Nelson | DE-NT | 6'3" | 277 | 25 | | |
| Darryl Sims | DE | 6'3" | 265 | 24 | | |
| Keith Willis | DE | 6'1" | 258 | 26 | | |
| Mark Catano | DT-NT | 6'3" | 267 | 23 | | |
| Gary Dunn | NT | 6'3" | 275 | 32 | | |
| Gregg Carr | LB | 6'1" | 216 | 23 | | |
| Robin Cole | LB | 6'2" | 225 | 29 | 1 | |
| Bryan Hinkle | LB | 6'2" | 218 | 26 | | |
| Bob Kohrs | LB | 6'3" | 235 | 26 | | |
| David Little | LB | 6'1" | 238 | 26 | 2 | |
| Mike Merriweather | LB | 6'2" | 216 | 24 | 2 | 6 |
| Fred Small | LB | 5'11" | 230 | 22 | | |
| Dennis Winston (from NO) | LB | 6' | 238 | 29 | | |
| Chris Brown | DB | 6' | 205 | 23 | | |
| Harvey Clayton | DB | 5'9" | 179 | 24 | | |
| Dave Edwards | DB | 6' | 192 | 23 | | |
| Donnie Shell | DB | 5'11" | 198 | 33 | 4 | |
| John Swain (from MIA) | DB | 6'1" | 192 | 25 | 2 | |
| Anthony Tuggle | DV | 6'1" | 210 | 21 | | |
| Eric Williams | DB | 6'1" | 190 | 25 | 4 | |
| Dwayne Woodruff | DB | 6' | 198 | 28 | 5 | |
| Rick Woods | DB | 6' | 195 | 25 | | |
| Scott Campbell | QB | 6' | 194 | 23 | | |
| Mark Malone | QB | 6'4" | 220 | 26 | | 6 |
| David Woodley | QB | 6'2" | 211 | 26 | | 12 |
| Walter Abercrombie | HB | 6' | 208 | 25 | | 54 |
| Rich Erenberg | HB | 5'10" | 195 | 23 | | 18 |
| Tod Spencer | HB | 6' | 200 | 23 | | |
| Steve Morse | FB | 5'11" | 211 | 22 | | |
| Frank Pollard | FB | 5'10" | 223 | 28 | | 18 |
| Louis Lipps | WR | 5'10" | 185 | 23 | | 90 |
| Frank Pokorny | WR | 6' | 205 | 22 | | |
| John Stallworth | WR | 6'2" | 202 | 33 | | 30 |
| Calvin Sweeney | WR | 6'2" | 202 | 30 | | |
| Weegie Thompson | WR | 6'6" | 209 | 24 | | 6 |
| Bennie Cunningham | TE | 6'4" | 260 | 30 | | |
| Preston Gothard | TE | 6'4" | 237 | 23 | | |
| Darrell Nelson | TE | 6'2" | 235 | 23 | | |
| Gary Anderson | K | 5'11" | 174 | 26 | | 139 |
| Harry Newsome | K | 6' | 185 | 22 | | |

## HOUSTON OILERS 5-11 Hugh Campbell

| Scores of Each Game | | |
|---|---|---|
| 26 | MIAMI | 23 |
| 13 | Washington | 16 |
| 0 | Pittsburgh | 20 |
| 10 | DALLAS | 17 |
| 20 | Denver | 31 |
| 6 | CLEVELAND | 21 |
| 44 | CINCINNATI | 27 |
| 20 | St.Louis | 10 |
| 23 | KANSAS CITY | 20 |
| 0 | Buffalo | 20 |
| 7 | PITTSBURGH | 30 |
| 37 | SAN DIEGO | 35 |
| 27 | Cincinnati | 45 |
| 14 | N.Y.GIANTS | 35 |
| 21 | Cleveland | 28 |
| 16 | Indianapolis | 34 |

| Use Name | Pos. | Hgt | Wgt | Age | Int | Pts |
|---|---|---|---|---|---|---|
| Bruce Matthews | OT | 6'4" | 280 | 24 | | |
| Eric Moran | OT | 6'5" | 282 | 25 | | |
| Harvey Salem | OT | 6'6" | 285 | 24 | | |
| Pat Howell | OG | 6'5" | 265 | 28 | | |
| Mike Munchak | OG | 6'3" | 286 | 25 | | |
| John Schuhmacher | OG | 6'3" | 277 | 29 | | |
| Mike Kelley | C-OG | 6'5" | 266 | 23 | | |
| Jim Romano | C | 6'3" | 255 | 25 | | |
| Jesse Baker (from DAL) | DE | 6'5" | 271 | 28 | | |
| Ray Childress | DE | 6'6" | 267 | 22 | | |
| Bob Hamm | DE | 6'4" | 263 | 26 | | |
| Richard Byrd | NT | 6'3" | 255 | 23 | | |
| Doug Smith | NT | 6'5" | 285 | 26 | | |
| Brian Sochia | NT | 6'3" | 254 | 24 | | |
| Mike Stensrud | NT | 6'5" | 280 | 29 | 1 | |
| Robert Abraham | LB | 6'1" | 230 | 25 | | |
| Tom Briehl | LB | 6'3" | 247 | 22 | | |
| Frank Bush | LB | 6'1" | 218 | 22 | | |
| John Grimsley | LB | 6'2" | 232 | 23 | | |
| Robert Lyles | LB | 6'1" | 223 | 24 | | |
| Johnny Meads | LB | 6'2" | 225 | 24 | | |
| Avon Riley | LB | 6'3" | 236 | 27 | 1 | |
| Patrick Allen | DB | 5'10 | 185 | 24 | | |
| Keith Bostic | DB | 6'1" | 210 | 24 | 3 | |
| Steve Brown | DB | 5'11" | 189 | 25 | 5 | |
| Jeff Donaldson | DB | 6' | 193 | 23 | | |
| Bo Eason | DB | 6'2" | 200 | 24 | 3 | |
| Richard Johnson | DB | 6'1" | 195 | 21 | | |
| Rod Kush | DB | 6' | 195 | 28 | 2 | |
| Allen Lyday | DB | 5'10" | 186 | 24 | | |
| Audrey McMillian | DB | 6' | 190 | 23 | | |
| Oliver Luck | QB | 6'2" | 196 | 25 | | |
| Warren Moon | QB | 6'3" | 208 | 28 | | |
| Mike Moroski | QB | 6'4" | 200 | 27 | | |
| Brian Ransom | QB | 6'3" | 202 | 25 | | |
| Stan Edwards | HB | 6' | 210 | 25 | | 6 |
| Mike Rozier | HB | 5'10" | 198 | 24 | | 48 |
| Steve Tasker | HB | 5'9" | 185 | 23 | | |
| Larry Moriarty | FB | 6'1" | 240 | 27 | | 18 |
| Butch Woolfolk | FB | 6'1" | 212 | 25 | | 30 |
| Mike Akiu | WR | 5'9" | 185 | 23 | | 6 |
| Steve Bryant | WR | 6'2" | 197 | 25 | | |
| Willie Drewrey | WR | 5'7" | 158 | 22 | | |
| Drew Hill | WR | 5'9" | 170 | 28 | | 54 |
| Tim Smith | WR | 6'2" | 206 | 28 | | 12 |
| Herkie Walls | WR | 5'8" | 160 | 24 | | |
| Chris Dressel | TE | 6'4" | 238 | 24 | | 6 |
| Mike McCloskey | TE | 6'5" | 246 | 24 | | 6 |
| Jamie Williams | TE | 6'4" | 232 | 25 | | 6 |
| Lee Johnson | K | 6'2" | 204 | 23 | | |
| Tony Zendejas | K | 5'8" | 160 | 25 | | 92 |

Mike Johnson - Knee Injury
Dean Steinkuhler - Knee Injury

Dwayne Crutchfield - Knee Injury

* Overtime

## CLEVELAND BROWNS

### RUSHING

| Last Name | No. | Yds | Avg | TD |
|---|---|---|---|---|
| Mack | 222 | 1104 | 5.0 | 7 |
| Byner | 244 | 1002 | 4.1 | 8 |
| Danielson | 25 | 126 | 5.0 | 0 |
| Allen | 8 | 32 | 4.0 | 0 |
| Cl. Weathers | 1 | 18 | 18.0 | 0 |
| Davis | 4 | 9 | 2.3 | 0 |
| Baab | 1 | 0 | 0.0 | 0 |
| Kosar | 26 | -12 | -0.5 | 1 |

### RECEIVING

| Last Name | No. | Yds | Avg | TD |
|---|---|---|---|---|
| Newsome | 62 | 711 | 11.5 | 5 |
| Byner | 45 | 460 | 10.2 | 2 |
| Brennan | 32 | 487 | 15.2 | 0 |
| Mack | 29 | 297 | 10.2 | 3 |
| Cl. Weathers | 16 | 449 | 28.1 | 3 |
| Adams | 10 | 132 | 13.2 | 0 |
| Holt | 10 | 95 | 9.5 | 1 |
| Young | 5 | 111 | 22.2 | 1 |
| F. Banks | 5 | 62 | 12.4 | 2 |
| Jefferson | 3 | 30 | 10.0 | 0 |
| Tucker | 2 | 20 | 10.0 | 0 |
| Fontenot | 2 | 19 | 9.5 | 0 |
| Langhorne | 1 | 12 | 12.0 | 0 |

### PUNT RETURNS

| Last Name | No. | Yds | Avg | TD |
|---|---|---|---|---|
| Cl. Weathers | 28 | 218 | 7.8 | 0 |
| Brennan | 19 | 153 | 8.1 | 1 |

### KICKOFF RETURNS

| Last Name | No. | Yds | Avg | TD |
|---|---|---|---|---|
| Young | 35 | 898 | 25.7 | 0 |
| Fontenot | 8 | 215 | 26.9 | 0 |
| Langhorne | 3 | 46 | 15.3 | 0 |
| Green | 2 | 20 | 10.0 | 0 |
| Puzzuoli | 2 | 8 | 4.0 | 0 |
| Cl. Weathers | 1 | 17 | 17.0 | 0 |
| Nicolas | 1 | 9 | 9.0 | 0 |
| Allen | 1 | 4 | 4.0 | 0 |

### PASSING — PUNTING — KICKING Statistics

| PASSING | Att | Cmp | % | Yds | Yd/Att | TD | Int— | % | RK |
|---|---|---|---|---|---|---|---|---|---|
| Kosar | 248 | 124 | 50 | 1578 | 6.4 | 8 | 7— | 3 | |
| Danielson | 163 | 97 | 60 | 1274 | 7.8 | 8 | 6— | 4 | |
| Brennan | 1 | 1 | 100 | 33 | 33.0 | 1 | 0— | 0 | |
| Fontenot | 1 | 0 | 0 | 0 | 0.0 | 0 | 0— | 0 | |
| Gossett | 1 | 0 | 0 | 0 | 0.0 | 0 | 0— | 0 | |

| PUNTING | No | Avg |
|---|---|---|
| Gossett | 81 | 40.3 |

| KICKING | XP | Att | % | FG | Att | % |
|---|---|---|---|---|---|---|
| Bahr | 35 | 35 | 100 | 14 | 18 | 77 |

## CINCINNATI BENGALS

### RUSHING

| Last Name | No. | Yds | Avg | TD |
|---|---|---|---|---|
| Brooks | 192 | 929 | 4.8 | 7 |
| Kinnebrew | 170 | 714 | 4.2 | 9 |
| Alexander | 44 | 156 | 3.5 | 2 |
| Brown | 14 | 129 | 9.2 | 0 |
| Jennings | 31 | 92 | 3.0 | 1 |
| Esiason | 33 | 79 | 2.4 | 1 |
| Johnson | 8 | 44 | 5.5 | 0 |
| Schonert | 8 | 39 | 4.9 | 0 |
| Collinsworth | 1 | 3 | 3.0 | 0 |
| Anderson | 1 | 0 | 0.0 | 0 |
| McInally | 1 | -2 | -2.0 | 0 |

### RECEIVING

| Last Name | No. | Yds | Avg | TD |
|---|---|---|---|---|
| Collinsworth | 65 | 1125 | 17.3 | 5 |
| Brooks | 55 | 576 | 10.5 | 2 |
| Brown | 53 | 942 | 17.8 | 8 |
| Holman | 38 | 479 | 12.6 | 7 |
| Kinnebrew | 22 | 187 | 8.5 | 1 |
| Alexander | 15 | 110 | 7.3 | 0 |
| Martin | 14 | 187 | 13.4 | 0 |
| Jennings | 12 | 101 | 8.4 | 3 |
| Kreider | 10 | 184 | 18.4 | 1 |
| Harris | 10 | 123 | 12.3 | 1 |
| Blados | 1 | 4 | 4.0 | 0 |
| Munoz | 1 | 1 | 1.0 | 0 |

### PUNT RETURNS

| Last Name | No. | Yds | Avg | TD |
|---|---|---|---|---|
| Martin | 32 | 268 | 8.4 | 0 |

### KICKOFF RETURNS

| Last Name | No. | Yds | Avg | TD |
|---|---|---|---|---|
| Martin | 48 | 1104 | 23.0 | 0 |
| Jennings | 13 | 218 | 16.8 | 0 |
| Brooks | 3 | 38 | 12.7 | 0 |
| Zander | 1 | 19 | 19.0 | 0 |
| Brown | 1 | 6 | 6.0 | 0 |
| Griffin | 1 | 0 | 0.0 | 0 |

### PASSING — PUNTING — KICKING Statistics

| PASSING | Att | Cmp | % | Yds | Yd/Att | TD | Int— | % | RK |
|---|---|---|---|---|---|---|---|---|---|
| Esiason | 431 | 251 | 58 | 3443 | 8.0 | 27 | 12— | 3 | |
| Schonert | 51 | 33 | 65 | 460 | 9.0 | 1 | 0— | 0 | |
| Anderson | 32 | 16 | 50 | 170 | 5.3 | 2 | 0— | 0 | |
| Brooks | 1 | 1 | 100 | 8 | 8.0 | 1 | 0— | 0 | |
| Kreider | 1 | 1 | 100 | 1 | 1.0 | 0 | 0— | 0 | |
| Collinsworth | 1 | 0 | 0 | 0 | 0.0 | 0 | 1—100 | | |
| McInally | 1 | 0 | 0 | 0 | 0.0 | 0 | 0— | 0 | |

| PUNTING | No | Avg |
|---|---|---|
| McInally | 57 | 42.3 |
| Breech | 5 | 30.6 |

| KICKING | XP | Att | % | FG | Att | % |
|---|---|---|---|---|---|---|
| Breech | 48 | 50 | 96 | 24 | 33 | 73 |

## PITTSBURGH STEELERS

### RUSHING

| Last Name | No. | Yds | Avg | TD |
|---|---|---|---|---|
| Pollard | 233 | 991 | 4.3 | 3 |
| Abercrombie | 227 | 851 | 3.7 | 7 |
| Malone | 15 | 80 | 5.3 | 1 |
| Woodley | 17 | 71 | 4.2 | 2 |
| Erenberg | 17 | 67 | 3.9 | 0 |
| Spencer | 13 | 56 | 4.3 | 0 |
| Campbell | 9 | 28 | 3.1 | 0 |
| Morse | 8 | 17 | 2.1 | 0 |
| Lipps | 2 | 16 | 8.0 | 1 |

### RECEIVING

| Last Name | No. | Yds | Avg | TD |
|---|---|---|---|---|
| Stallworth | 75 | 937 | 12.5 | 5 |
| Lipps | 59 | 1134 | 19.2 | 12 |
| Erenberg | 33 | 326 | 9.9 | 3 |
| Pollard | 24 | 250 | 10.4 | 0 |
| Abercrombie | 24 | 209 | 8.7 | 2 |
| Sweeney | 16 | 234 | 14.6 | 0 |
| Thompson | 8 | 138 | 17.3 | 1 |
| Gothard | 6 | 83 | 13.8 | 0 |
| Cunningham | 6 | 61 | 10.2 | 0 |
| Spencer | 3 | 25 | 8.3 | 0 |

### PUNT RETURNS

| Last Name | No. | Yds | Avg | TD |
|---|---|---|---|---|
| Lipps | 36 | 437 | 12.1 | 2 |
| Woods | 13 | 46 | 3.5 | 0 |

### KICKOFF RETURNS

| Last Name | No. | Yds | Avg | TD |
|---|---|---|---|---|
| Spencer | 27 | 617 | 22.9 | 0 |
| Erenberg | 21 | 441 | 21.0 | 0 |
| Lipps | 13 | 237 | 18.2 | 0 |
| Washington | 3 | 34 | 11.3 | 0 |
| Tuggle | 1 | 8 | 8.0 | 0 |

### PASSING — PUNTING — KICKING Statistics

| PASSING | Att | Cmp | % | Yds | Yd/Att | TD | Int— | % | RK |
|---|---|---|---|---|---|---|---|---|---|
| Malone | 233 | 117 | 50 | 1428 | 6.1 | 13 | 7— | 3 | |
| Woodley | 183 | 94 | 51 | 1357 | 7.4 | 6 | 14— | 8 | |
| Campbell | 96 | 43 | 45 | 612 | 6.4 | 4 | 6— | 6 | |

| PUNTING | No | Avg |
|---|---|---|
| Newsome | 78 | 39.6 |

| KICKING | XP | Att | % | FG | Att | % |
|---|---|---|---|---|---|---|
| Anderson | 40 | 40 | 100 | 33 | 42 | 79 |

## HOUSTON OILERS

### RUSHING

| Last Name | No. | Yds | Avg | TD |
|---|---|---|---|---|
| Rozier | 133 | 462 | 3.5 | 8 |
| Woolfolk | 103 | 392 | 3.8 | 1 |
| Moriarty | 106 | 381 | 3.6 | 3 |
| Moon | 39 | 130 | 3.3 | 0 |
| Edwards | 25 | 96 | 3.8 | 1 |
| Luck | 15 | 95 | 6.3 | 0 |
| Tasker | 2 | 16 | 8.0 | 0 |
| Moroski | 2 | 2 | 1.0 | 0 |
| L. Johnson | 1 | 0 | 0.0 | 0 |
| Drewrey | 2 | -4 | -2.0 | 0 |

### RECEIVING

| Last Name | No. | Yds | Avg | TD |
|---|---|---|---|---|
| Woolfolk | 80 | 814 | 10.2 | 4 |
| Hill | 64 | 1169 | 18.3 | 9 |
| T. Smith | 46 | 660 | 14.3 | 2 |
| Williams | 39 | 444 | 11.4 | 0 |
| Moriarty | 17 | 112 | 6.6 | 0 |
| Rozier | 9 | 96 | 10.7 | 0 |
| Edwards | 7 | 71 | 10.1 | 0 |
| McCloskey | 4 | 29 | 7.3 | 1 |
| Dressel | 3 | 17 | 5.7 | 1 |
| Akiu | 2 | 32 | 16.0 | 0 |
| Drewrey | 2 | 28 | 14.0 | 0 |
| Tasker | 2 | 19 | 9.5 | 0 |
| Walls | 1 | 7 | 7.0 | 0 |

### PUNT RETURNS

| Last Name | No. | Yds | Avg | TD |
|---|---|---|---|---|
| Drewrey | 24 | 215 | 9.0 | 0 |
| Donaldson | 6 | 35 | 5.8 | 0 |

### KICKOFF RETURNS

| Last Name | No. | Yds | Avg | TD |
|---|---|---|---|---|
| Drewrey | 26 | 642 | 24.7 | 0 |
| Tasker | 17 | 447 | 26.3 | 0 |
| Walls | 12 | 234 | 19.5 | 0 |
| Donaldson | 5 | 93 | 18.6 | 0 |
| Brown | 2 | 45 | 22.5 | 0 |
| Williams | 2 | 21 | 10.5 | 0 |
| Hill | 1 | 22 | 22.0 | 0 |
| Lyday | 1 | 6 | 6.0 | 0 |
| Briehl | 1 | 5 | 5.0 | 0 |

### PASSING — PUNTING — KICKING Statistics

| PASSING | Att | Cmp | % | Yds | Yd/Att | TD | Int— | % | RK |
|---|---|---|---|---|---|---|---|---|---|
| Moon | 377 | 200 | 53 | 2709 | 7.2 | 15 | 19— | 5 | |
| Luck | 100 | 56 | 56 | 572 | 5.7 | 2 | 2— | 2 | |
| Moroski | 34 | 20 | 59 | 249 | 7.3 | 1 | 1— | 3 | |
| Zendejas | 1 | 1 | 100 | -7 | -7.0 | 0 | 0— | 0 | |

| PUNTING | No | Avg |
|---|---|---|
| L. Johnson | 83 | 41.7 |
| T. Smith | 1 | 26.0 |

| KICKING | XP | Att | % | FG | Att | % |
|---|---|---|---|---|---|---|
| Zendejas | 29 | 31 | 94 | 21 | 27 | 78 |

**LOS ANGELES RAIDERS 12-4 Tom Flores**

| Scores of Each Game | | |
|---|---|---|
| 31 | N.Y.JETS | 0 |
| 20 | Kansas City | 36 |
| 10 | SAN FRANCISCO | 34 |
| 35 | New England | 20 |
| 19 | KANSAS CITY | 10 |
| 23 | NEW ORLEANS | 13 |
| 21 | Cleveland | 20 |
| 34 | SAN DIEGO | 21 |
| 3 | Seattle | 33 |
| 34 | San Diego | *40 |
| 13 | CINCINNATI | 6 |
| 31 | DENVER | *28 |
| 34 | Atlanta | 24 |
| 17 | Denver | *14 |
| 13 | SEATTLE | 3 |
| 16 | L.A.Rams | 6 |

| Use Name | Pos. | Hgt | Wgt | Age | Int | Pts |
|---|---|---|---|---|---|---|
| Bruce Davis | OT | 6'6" | 280 | 29 | | |
| Shelby Jordan | OT | 6'7" | 280 | 33 | | |
| Henry Lawrence | OT | 6'4" | 275 | 33 | | |
| Kevin Belcher | OG | 6'5" | 285 | 23 | | |
| Charley Hannah | OG | 6'5" | 260 | 30 | | |
| Curt Marsh | OG | 6'5" | 275 | 26 | | |
| Mickey Marvin | OG | 6'4" | 265 | 29 | | |
| Dave Dalby | C | 6'2" | 250 | 34 | | |
| Don Mosebar | C | 6'6" | 270 | 23 | | |
| Lyle Alzado | DE | 6'3" | 260 | 36 | | 8 |
| Elvis Franks | DE | 6'4" | 270 | 28 | | |
| Sean Jones | DE | 6'7" | 275 | 22 | | |
| Howie Long | DE | 6'5" | 270 | 25 | | |
| Greg Townsend | DE | 6'3" | 250 | 23 | | |
| Bill Pickel | NT | 6'5" | 260 | 25 | | |
| Mitch Willis | NT | 6'7" | 275 | 23 | | |
| Dave Stalls | NT | 6'4" | 250 | 29 | | |
| Jeff Barnes | LB | 6'2" | 230 | 30 | 1 | |
| Tony Caldwell | LB | 6'1" | 220 | 24 | | |
| Rod Martin | LB | 6'2" | 225 | 31 | 1 | |
| Reggie McKenzie | LB | 6'1" | 240 | 22 | | |
| Matt Millen | LB | 6'2" | 245 | 27 | | |
| Jerry Robinson | LB | 6'2" | 225 | 28 | | |
| Jack Squirek | LB | 6'4" | 235 | 26 | 1 | |
| Brad Van Pelt | LB | 6'5" | 235 | 34 | 1 | |
| Don Bessillieu | DB | 6'1" | 190 | 29 | | |
| James Davis | DB | 6' | 200 | 28 | | |
| Mike Davis | DB | 6'3" | 205 | 29 | | |
| Lester Hayes | DB | 6' | 200 | 30 | 4 | 6 |
| Mike Haynes | DB | 6'2" | 190 | 32 | 4 | |
| Vann McElroy | DB | 6'2" | 195 | 25 | 2 | |
| Odis McKinney (from KC) | DB | 6'2" | 190 | 28 | 1 | |
| Sam Seale | DB | 5'9" | 175 | 22 | 1 | 6 |
| Stacey Toran | DB | 6'2" | 200 | 23 | 1 | 6 |
| Fulton Walker (from MIA) | DB | 5'10" | 200 | 27 | | |
| Ricky Williams | DB | 6'1" | 195 | 25 | | |
| Rusty Hilger | QB | 6'4" | 200 | 23 | | |
| Russ Jensen | QB | 6'2" | 215 | 24 | | |
| Jim Plunkett | QB | 6'3" | 225 | 37 | | |
| Marc Wilson | QB | 6'6" | 205 | 28 | | 12 |
| Marcus Allen | HB | 6'2" | 205 | 25 | | 84 |
| Frank Hawkins | HB | 5'9" | 210 | 26 | | 24 |
| Derrick Jensen | FB | 6'1" | 220 | 29 | | |
| Kenny King | FB | 5'11" | 205 | 28 | | |
| Steve Strachan | FB | 6'1" | 215 | 22 | | |
| Cliff Branch | WR | 5'11" | 170 | 37 | | |
| Jessie Hester | WR | 5'11" | 170 | 22 | | 30 |
| Tim Moffett | WR | 6'2" | 180 | 23 | | |
| Cle Montgomery | WR | 5'8" | 180 | 29 | | |
| Jim Smith | WR | 6'2" | 205 | 30 | | 6 |
| Dokie Williams | WR | 5'11" | 180 | 25 | | 30 |
| Todd Christensen | TE | 6'3" | 230 | 29 | | 36 |
| Trey Junkin | TE | 6'2" | 225 | 24 | | 6 |
| Andy Parker | TE | 6'5" | 240 | 23 | | |
| Chris Bahr | K | 5'10" | 170 | 32 | | 100 |
| Ray Guy | K | 6'3" | 200 | 35 | | |

Randy Van Divier - Injury

Bob Nelson - Knee Injury

**DENVER BRONCOS 11-5 Dan Reeves**

| Scores of Each Game | | |
|---|---|---|
| 16 | L.A.Rams | 20 |
| 34 | NEW ORLEANS | 23 |
| 44 | Atlanta | 28 |
| 26 | MIAMI | 30 |
| 31 | HOUSTON | 20 |
| 15 | Indianapolis | 10 |
| 13 | SEATTLE | *10 |
| 30 | Kansas City | 10 |
| 10 | San Diego | 30 |
| 17 | SAN FRANCISCO | 16 |
| 30 | SAN DIEGO | *24 |
| 28 | L.A.Raiders | *31 |
| 31 | Pittsburgh | 23 |
| 14 | L.A.RAIDERS | *17 |
| 14 | KANSAS CITY | 13 |
| 27 | Seattle | 24 |

| Use Name | Pos. | Hgt | Wgt | Age | Int | Pts |
|---|---|---|---|---|---|---|
| Winford Hood | OT | 6'3" | 262 | 23 | | |
| Ken Lanier | OT | 6'3" | 269 | 26 | | |
| Dean Miraldi | OT | 6'5" | 285 | 27 | | |
| Dave Studdard | OT | 6'4" | 260 | 29 | | |
| Mark Cooper | OG-OT | 6'5" | 267 | 25 | | |
| Paul Howard | OG | 6'3" | 260 | 34 | | |
| Glenn Hyde | OG-C | 6'3" | 255 | 34 | | |
| Keith Bishop | C-OG | 6'3" | 265 | 28 | | |
| Billy Bryan | C | 6'2" | 255 | 29 | | |
| Barney Chavous | DE | 6'3" | 258 | 34 | | |
| Simon Fletcher | DE | 6'5" | 240 | 23 | | |
| Rulon Jones | DE | 6'6" | 260 | 27 | | |
| Andre Townsend | DE-NT | 6'3" | 265 | 22 | | |
| Rubin Carter | NT | 6' | 256 | 32 | | |
| Greg Kragen | NT | 6'3" | 245 | 23 | | |
| Steve Busick | LB | 6'4" | 227 | 26 | | |
| Darren Comeaux | LB | 6'1 | 227 | 25 | | |
| Rick Dennison | LB | 6'3" | 220 | 27 | | |
| Ricky Hunley | LB | 6'2" | 238 | 23 | | |
| Tom Jackson | LB | 5'11" | 220 | 34 | | |
| Karl Mecklenburg | LB | 6'3" | 230 | 25 | | |
| Jim Ryan | LB | 6'1" | 218 | 28 | | |
| Ken Woodard | LB | 6'1" | 218 | 25 | 1 | |
| Steve Foley | DB | 6'2" | 190 | 31 | 3 | |
| Mike Harden | DB | 6'1" | 192 | 27 | 5 | 6 |
| Daniel Hunter | DB | 5'11" | 175 | 23 | 1 | |
| Roger Jackson | DB | 6' | 186 | 26 | | |
| Tony Lilly | DB | 6' | 199 | 23 | 2 | |
| Randy Robbins | DB | 6'2" | 189 | 22 | 1 | |
| Dennis Smith | DB | 6'3" | 200 | 26 | 3 | |
| Steve Wilson | DB | 5'10" | 195 | 28 | 3 | |
| Louis Wright | DB | 6'2" | 200 | 32 | 5 | 6 |
| John Elway | QB | 6'3" | 210 | 25 | | |
| Gary Kubiak | QB | 6' | 192 | 24 | | |
| Scott Stankavage | QB | 6'1" | 194 | 23 | | |
| Gene Lang | HB | 5'10" | 196 | 23 | | 42 |
| Gerald Willhite | HB | 5'10" | 200 | 26 | | 24 |
| Sammy Winder | HB | 5'11" | 203 | 26 | | 48 |
| Nathan Poole | FB | 5'9" | 212 | 28 | | |
| Steve Sewell | FB | 6'3" | 210 | 22 | | 30 |
| Butch Johnson | WR | 6'1" | 187 | 31 | | 18 |
| Vance Johnson | WR | 5'11" | 185 | 22 | | 18 |
| Clint Sampson | WR | 5'11" | 183 | 24 | | 24 |
| Steve Watson | WR | 6'4" | 195 | 28 | | 30 |
| Mike Barber (from LA) | TE | 6'3" | 237 | 32 | | |
| Clarence Kay | TE | 6'2" | 237 | 24 | | 18 |
| Keli McGregor | TE | 6'7" | 252 | 22 | | |
| Don Summers | TE | 6'4" | 226 | 24 | | |
| James Wright | TE | 6'3" | 240 | 29 | | 6 |
| Rich Karlis | K | 6' | 180 | 26 | | 110 |
| Chris Norman | K | 6'2" | 198 | 23 | | |

Mike Freeman - Knee Injury
Marsharne Graves - Knee Injury

Aaron Smith - Knee Injury

Al Hill - Shoulder Injury
John Sawyer - Broken hand

**SEATTLE SEAHAWKS 8-8 Chuck Knox**

| Scores of Each Game | | |
|---|---|---|
| 28 | Cincinnati | 24 |
| 49 | San Diego | 35 |
| 24 | L.A.RAMS | 35 |
| 7 | Kansas City | 28 |
| 26 | SAN DIEGO | 21 |
| 30 | ATLANTA | 26 |
| 10 | Denver | *13 |
| 14 | N.Y.Jets | 17 |
| 33 | L.A.RAIDERS | 3 |
| 27 | New Orleans | 3 |
| 13 | NEW ENGLAND | 20 |
| 6 | San Francisco | 19 |
| 24 | KANSAS CITY | 6 |
| 31 | CLEVELAND | 13 |
| 3 | L.A.Raiders | 13 |
| 24 | DENVER | 27 |

| Use Name | Pos. | Hgt | Wgt | Age | Int | Pts |
|---|---|---|---|---|---|---|
| Bob Cryder | OT | 6'4" | 286 | 28 | | |
| Ron Essink | OT | 6'6" | 279 | 27 | | |
| Edwin Bailey | OG | 6'4" | 265 | 26 | | |
| Jon Borchardt | OG | 6'5" | 270 | 28 | | |
| Bryan Millard | OG | 6'5" | 284 | 25 | | |
| Robert Pratt | OG | 6'4" | 250 | 34 | | |
| Blair Bush | C | 6'3" | 257 | 28 | | |
| Kani Kauahi | C | 6'2" | 254 | 25 | | |
| Jeff Bryant | DE | 6'5" | 270 | 25 | | |
| Randy Edwards | DE | 6'4" | 266 | 24 | | |
| Jacob Green | DE | 6'3" | 257 | 28 | 1 | 12 |
| Reggie Kinlaw | NT | 6'2" | 249 | 28 | | |
| Joe Nash | NT | 6'2" | 257 | 24 | | |
| Keith Butler | LB | 6'4" | 238 | 29 | 2 | |
| Greg Gaines | LB | 6'3" | 222 | 26 | | |
| Michael Jackson | LB | 6'1" | 228 | 28 | | |
| John Kaiser | LB | 6'3" | 227 | 23 | | |
| Sam Merriman | LB | 6'3" | 229 | 24 | | 6 |
| Shelton Robinson | LB | 6'2" | 236 | 24 | | |
| Bruce Scholtz | LB | 6'6" | 240 | 26 | | |
| Fredd Young | LB | 6'1" | 233 | 23 | | |
| Dave Brown | DB | 6'1" | 197 | 32 | 6 | 6 |
| Kenny Easley | DB | 6'3" | 206 | 26 | 2 | |
| John Harris | DB | 6'2" | 204 | 29 | 7 | |
| Terry Jackson | DB | 5'10" | 197 | 28 | | |
| Paul Moyer | DB | 6'1" | 201 | 24 | | |
| Eugene Robinson | DB | 6' | 186 | 22 | 2 | |
| Rick Sanford | DB | 6'1" | 192 | 28 | | |
| Keith Simpson | DB | 6'1" | 195 | 29 | | |
| Terry Taylor | DB | 5'10" | 188 | 24 | 4 | 12 |
| Gale Gilbert | QB | 6'3" | 206 | 23 | | |
| Dave Krieg | QB | 6'1" | 196 | 26 | | 6 |
| Eric Lane | HB | 6' | 197 | 26 | | |
| Randall Morris | HB | 6' | 199 | 24 | | |
| Rick Parros | HB | 5'11" | 202 | 27 | | |
| Curt Warner | HB | 5'11" | 205 | 24 | | 54 |
| Dan Doornink | FB | 6'3" | 210 | 29 | | |
| Andre Hardy | FB | 6'1" | 233 | 23 | | |
| David Hughes | FB | 6' | 220 | 26 | | |
| Byron Franklin | WR | 6'1" | 181 | 26 | | |
| Danny Greene | WR | 5'11" | 190 | 23 | | 6 |
| Steve Largent | WR | 5'11" | 191 | 30 | | 37 |
| Paul Skansi | WR | 5'11" | 183 | 24 | | 6 |
| Daryl Turner | WR | 6'3" | 191 | 23 | | 78 |
| Byron Walker | WR | 6'4" | 188 | 25 | | 18 |
| Dan Ross (from CIN) | TE | 6'4" | 234 | 28 | | 12 |
| Mike Tice | TE | 6'7" | 247 | 26 | | |
| Charle Young | TE | 6'4" | 234 | 34 | | 12 |
| Jimmy Colquitt | K | 6'4" | 208 | 22 | | |
| Dave Finzer | K | 6'1" | 196 | 26 | | |
| Norm Johnson | K | 6'2" | 194 | 25 | | 82 |
| Jeff West | K | 6'3" | 205 | 32 | | |

**SAN DIEGO CHARGERS 8-8 Don Coryell**

| Scores of Each Game | | |
|---|---|---|
| 14 | Buffalo | 9 |
| 35 | SEATTLE | 49 |
| 44 | Cincinnati | 41 |
| 7 | CLEVELAND | 21 |
| 21 | Seattle | 26 |
| 31 | KANSAS CITY | 20 |
| 17 | Minnesota | 21 |
| 21 | L.A.Raiders | 34 |
| 30 | DENVER | 10 |
| 40 | L.A.RAIDERS | *34 |
| 24 | Denver | *30 |
| 35 | Houston | 37 |
| 40 | BUFFALO | 7 |
| 54 | PITTSBURGH | 44 |
| 20 | PHILADELPHIA | 14 |
| 34 | Kansas City | 38 |

| Use Name | Pos. | Hgt | Wgt | Age | Int | Pts |
|---|---|---|---|---|---|---|
| Sam Claphan | OT | 6'6" | 282 | 28 | | |
| Gary Kowalski | OT | 6'6" | 290 | 25 | | |
| Jim Lachey | OT | 6'6" | 288 | 22 | | |
| Rich Umphrey | OG-C | 6'3" | 270 | 26 | | |
| Ken Dallafior | OG | 6'4" | 262 | 26 | | |
| Bill Searcey | OG | 6'1" | 281 | 26 | | |
| Ed White | OG | 6'2" | 284 | 38 | | |
| Jerry Doerger | C-OT | 6'5" | 270 | 25 | | |
| Don Macek | C | 6'3" | 260 | 31 | | |
| Dennis McKnight | C-OG | 6'3" | 273 | 25 | | |
| Keith Ferguson (to DET) | DE | 6'5" | 255 | 26 | | |
| Fred Robinson | DE | 6'4" | 242 | 23 | | |
| Tony Simmons | DE | 6'5" | 270 | 22 | | |
| Lee Williams | DE | 6'6" | 273 | 22 | 1 | |
| Earl Wilson | DE | 6'4" | 267 | 26 | | |
| Tony Chickillo | NT-OG | 6'3" | 259 | 25 | | |
| Chuck Ehin | NT | 6'4" | 265 | 24 | | |
| Scott Garnett (from SF) | NT | 6'2" | 271 | 22 | | |
| Craig Bingham | LB | 6'2" | 220 | 25 | | |
| Carlos Bradley | LB | 6' | 222 | 25 | 2 | |
| Mike Douglass | LB | 6' | 214 | 31 | | |
| Mark Fellows | LB | 6'1" | 222 | 22 | | |
| Mike Guendling | LB | 6'3" | 238 | 23 | | |
| Mike Green | LB | 6' | 239 | 24 | 2 | |
| Linden King | LB | 6'4" | 247 | 30 | 2 | |
| Woodrow Lowe | LB | 6' | 229 | 31 | 3 | |
| Derrie Nelson | LB | 6'2" | 234 | 27 | | |
| Vince Osby | LB | 5'11" | 221 | 24 | | |
| Billy Ray Smith | LB | 6'3" | 231 | 24 | 1 | |
| Gill Byrd | DB | 5'11" | 201 | 24 | 1 | |
| Jeffrey Dale | DB | 6'3" | 214 | 22 | 2 | 6 |
| Wayne Davis | DB | 5'11" | 175 | 22 | 2 | |
| John Hendy | DD | 5'10" | 196 | 22 | 4 | 6 |
| Terry Lewis | DB | 5'11" | 193 | 23 | | |
| Miles McPherson | DB | 5'11" | 186 | 25 | 1 | |
| Ronnie O'Bard | DB | 5'9" | 190 | 27 | | |
| Jim Rockford | DB | 5'10" | 180 | 23 | | |
| Lucious Smith | DB | 5'10" | 190 | 28 | | |
| Danny Walters | DB | 6'1" | 180 | 24 | 5 | |
| Joe Dufek (from BUF) | QB | 6'4" | 215 | 24 | | |
| Dan Fouts | QB | 6'3" | 205 | 34 | | |
| Mark Herrmann | QB | 6'4" | 209 | 26 | | |
| Curtis Adams | HB | 6' | 198 | 23 | | 6 |
| Gary Anderson | HB | 6'1" | 190 | 24 | | 42 |
| Anthony Corley | HB | 6' | 210 | 25 | | |
| Lionel James | HB | 5'7" | 170 | 23 | | 48 |
| Buford McGee | FB | 6' | 203 | 25 | | 18 |
| Tim Spencer | FB | 6'1" | 220 | 24 | | 60 |
| Jesse Bendross | WR | 6' | 197 | 24 | | 12 |
| Wes Chandler | WR | 6' | 182 | 29 | | 60 |
| Trumaine Johnson | WR | 6'1" | 196 | 25 | | 6 |
| Charlie Joiner | WR | 5'11" | 177 | 37 | | 42 |
| Chris Faulkner | TE | 6'4" | 250 | 25 | | |
| Pete Holohan | TE | 6'4" | 244 | 26 | | 18 |
| Eric Sievers | TE | 6'4" | 236 | 26 | | 36 |
| Kellen Winslow | TE | 6'5" | 242 | 27 | | |
| Rolf Benirschke | K | 6'1" | 183 | 30 | | 2 |
| Ralf Mojsiejenko | K | 6'3" | 198 | 22 | | |
| Bob Thomas | K | 5'10" | 177 | 33 | | 105 |

James Lockette - Knee Injury

Shane Nelson - Achillies tendon injury

Bob Micho - Foot Injury

**KANSAS CITY CHIEFS 6-10 John Mackovic**

| Scores of Each Game | | |
|---|---|---|
| 47 | New Orleans | 27 |
| 36 | L.A.RAIDERS | 20 |
| 0 | Miami | 31 |
| 28 | SEATTLE | 7 |
| 10 | L.A.Raiders | 19 |
| 20 | San Diego | 31 |
| 0 | L.A.RAMS | 16 |
| 10 | DENVER | 30 |
| 20 | Houston | 23 |
| 28 | PITTSBURGH | 36 |
| 3 | San Francisco | 31 |
| 20 | INDIANAPOLIS | 7 |
| 6 | Seattle | 24 |
| 38 | ATLANTA | 10 |
| 13 | Denver | 31 |
| 38 | SAN DIEGO | 34 |

| Use Name | Pos. | Hgt | Wgt | Age | Int | Pts |
|---|---|---|---|---|---|---|
| John Alt | OT | 6'7" | 282 | 23 | | |
| Matt Herkenhoff | OT | 6'4" | 286 | 34 | | |
| David Lutz | OT | 6'6" | 287 | 25 | | |
| Billy Shields | OT | 6'7" | 280 | 32 | | |
| Scott Auer | OG-OT | 6'5" | 255 | 23 | | |
| Rich Baldinger | OG-OT | 6'4" | 281 | 25 | | |
| Brad Budde | OG | 6'4" | 271 | 27 | | |
| Rob Fada | OG | 6'2" | 259 | 24 | | |
| Bob Olderman | OG | 6'5" | 262 | 23 | | |
| Adam Lingner | C-OG | 6'4" | 260 | 24 | | |
| Bob Rush | C | 6'5" | 270 | 30 | | |
| Mike Bell | DE | 6'4" | 259 | 28 | | |
| Bob Hamm | DE | 6'4" | 257 | 26 | | |
| Eric Holle | DE-NT | 6'5" | 258 | 24 | | |
| Pete Koch | DE | 6'6" | 265 | 23 | | |
| Dave Lindstrom | DE | 6'6" | 258 | 30 | | |
| Hal Stephens (from DET) | DE-NT | 6'4" | 252 | 24 | | |
| Art Still | DE | 6'7" | 254 | 29 | | |
| Bill Maas | NT-DE | 6'5" | 259 | 23 | | |
| Jerry Blanton | LB | 6'1" | 229 | 28 | | |
| Louis Cooper | LB | 6'2" | 235 | 22 | | |
| Calvin Daniels | LB | 6'3" | 241 | 26 | | |
| Ken Jolly | LB | 6'2" | 220 | 23 | | |
| Jeff Paine | LB | 6'2" | 224 | 24 | | |
| Scott Radecic | LB | 6'3" | 246 | 23 | 1 | |
| Gary Spani | LB | 6'2" | 229 | 29 | | |
| Lloyd Burruss | DB | 6' | 209 | 27 | 1 | |
| Deron Cherry | DB | 5'11" | 196 | 25 | 7 | 6 |
| Sherman Cocroft | DB | 6'1" | 188 | 24 | 3 | |
| Greg Hill | DB | 6'1" | 199 | 24 | 3 | |
| Garcia Lane | DB | 5'9" | 180 | 23 | | |
| Albert Lewis | DB | 6'2" | 192 | 24 | 8 | 6 |
| Mark Robinson | DB | 5'11" | 206 | 22 | 1 | |
| Kevin Ross | DB | 5'9" | 182 | 23 | 3 | |
| Todd Blackledge | QB | 6'3" | 225 | 24 | | |
| Bill Kenney | QB | 6'4" | 211 | 30 | | 6 |
| Herman Heard | HB | 5'10" | 182 | 23 | | 36 |
| E.J.Jones | HB | 5'11" | 219 | 23 | | |
| Jeff Smith | HB | 5'9" | 201 | 23 | | 12 |
| Ethan Horton | FB | 6'3" | 228 | 22 | | 24 |
| Bruce King | FB | 6'1" | 219 | 22 | | |
| Ken Lacy | FB | 6' | 222 | 24 | | |
| Mike Pruitt (from BUF) | FB | 6' | 225 | 31 | | 12 |
| Carlos Carson | WR | 5'11" | 182 | 26 | | 24 |
| Anthony Hancock | WR | 6' | 204 | 25 | | 12 |
| Mike Holston (from HOU) | WR | 6'3" | 188 | 27 | | |
| Henry Marshall | WR | 6'2" | 213 | 31 | | |
| Stephone Paige | WR | 6'2" | 191 | 23 | | 60 |
| George Shorthose | WR | 6' | 198 | 23 | | |
| Walt Arnold | TE | 6'3" | 225 | 27 | | 6 |
| Jonathan Hayes | TE | 6'5" | 234 | 23 | | 6 |
| Willie Scott | TE | 6'4" | 245 | 26 | | |
| Jim Arnold | K | 6'2" | 220 | 24 | | |
| Nick Lowery | K | 6'4" | 189 | 29 | | 107 |

Kevin McAlister - Knee Injury

* Overtime

## LOS ANGELES RAIDERS

### RUSHING

| Last Name | No. | Yds | Avg | TD |
|---|---|---|---|---|
| Allen | 380 | 1759 | 4.6 | 11 |
| Hawkins | 84 | 269 | 3.2 | 4 |
| Wilson | 24 | 98 | 4.1 | 2 |
| King | 16 | 67 | 4.2 | 0 |
| D. Jensen | 16 | 35 | 2.2 | 0 |
| Hester | 1 | 13 | 13.0 | 1 |
| Plunkett | 5 | 12 | 2.4 | 0 |
| Hilger | 3 | 8 | 2.7 | 0 |
| Strachan | 2 | 1 | 0.5 | 0 |
| Guy | 1 | 0 | 0.0 | 0 |

### RECEIVING

| Last Name | No. | Yds | Avg | TD |
|---|---|---|---|---|
| Christensen | 82 | 987 | 12.0 | 6 |
| Allen | 67 | 555 | 8.3 | 3 |
| D. Williams | 48 | 925 | 19.3 | 5 |
| Hester | 32 | 665 | 20.8 | 4 |
| Hawkins | 27 | 174 | 6.4 | 0 |
| Moffett | 5 | 90 | 18.0 | 0 |
| King | 3 | 49 | 16.3 | 0 |
| Smith | 3 | 28 | 9.3 | 1 |
| Junkin | 2 | 8 | 4.0 | 1 |

### PUNT RETURNS

| Last Name | No. | Yds | Avg | TD |
|---|---|---|---|---|
| Walker | 62 | 692 | 11.2 | 0 |
| Montgomery | 8 | 84 | 10.5 | 0 |
| Haynes | 1 | 9 | 9.0 | 0 |

### KICKOFF RETURNS

| Last Name | No. | Yds | Avg | TD |
|---|---|---|---|---|
| Walker | 21 | 467 | 22.2 | 0 |
| Seale | 23 | 482 | 21.0 | 0 |
| Montgomery | 7 | 150 | 21.4 | 0 |
| D. Williams | 1 | 19 | 19.0 | 0 |
| Hawkins | 1 | 14 | 14.0 | 0 |
| Hayes | 1 | 0 | 0.0 | 0 |

### PASSING — PUNTING — KICKING

**PASSING**

| Last Name | Att | Cmp | % | Yds | Yd/Att | TD | Int— | % | RK |
|---|---|---|---|---|---|---|---|---|---|
| Wilson | 388 | 193 | 50 | 2608 | 6.7 | 16 | 21— | | 5 |
| Plunkett | 103 | 71 | 69 | 803 | 7.8 | 3 | 3— | | 3 |
| Hilger | 13 | 4 | 31 | 54 | 4.2 | 1 | 0— | | 0 |
| Allen | 2 | 1 | 50 | 16 | 8.0 | 0 | 0— | | 0 |

**PUNTING**

| Last Name | No | Avg |
|---|---|---|
| Guy | 89 | 40.8 |

**KICKING**

| Last Name | XP | Att | % | FG | Att | % |
|---|---|---|---|---|---|---|
| Bahr | 40 | 42 | 95 | 20 | 32 | 63 |

## DENVER BRONCOS

### RUSHING

| Last Name | No. | Yds | Avg | TD |
|---|---|---|---|---|
| Winder | 199 | 714 | 3.6 | 8 |
| Lang | 84 | 318 | 3.8 | 5 |
| Sewell | 81 | 275 | 3.4 | 4 |
| Elway | 51 | 253 | 5.0 | 0 |
| Willhite | 66 | 237 | 3.6 | 3 |
| V. Johnson | 10 | 36 | 3.6 | 0 |
| Poole | 4 | 12 | 3.0 | 0 |
| Kubiak | 1 | 6 | 6.0 | 0 |
| Norman | 1 | 0 | 0.0 | 0 |

### RECEIVING

| Last Name | No. | Yds | Avg | TD |
|---|---|---|---|---|
| Watson | 61 | 915 | 15.0 | 5 |
| V. Johnson | 51 | 721 | 14.1 | 3 |
| Willhite | 35 | 297 | 8.5 | 1 |
| Winder | 31 | 197 | 6.4 | 0 |
| Kay | 29 | 339 | 11.7 | 3 |
| J. Wright | 28 | 246 | 8.8 | 1 |
| Sampson | 26 | 432 | 16.6 | 4 |
| Sewell | 24 | 224 | 9.3 | 1 |
| Lang | 23 | 180 | 7.8 | 2 |
| B. Johnson | 19 | 380 | 20.0 | 3 |
| Barber | 2 | 37 | 18.5 | 0 |
| Cooper | 1 | 13 | 13.0 | 0 |

### PUNT RETURNS

| Last Name | No. | Yds | Avg | TD |
|---|---|---|---|---|
| V. Johnson | 30 | 260 | 8.7 | 0 |
| Willhite | 16 | 169 | 10.6 | 0 |

### KICKOFF RETURNS

| Last Name | No. | Yds | Avg | TD |
|---|---|---|---|---|
| V. Johnson | 30 | 740 | 24.7 | 0 |
| Lang | 17 | 361 | 21.2 | 0 |
| Willhite | 2 | 40 | 20.0 | 0 |
| Hunter | 2 | 33 | 16.5 | 0 |
| Sewell | 1 | 29 | 29.0 | 0 |

### PASSING — PUNTING — KICKING

**PASSING**

| Last Name | Att | Cmp | % | Yds | Yd/Att | TD | Int— | % | RK |
|---|---|---|---|---|---|---|---|---|---|
| Elway | 605 | 327 | 54 | 3891 | 6.4 | 22 | 23— | | 4 |
| Kubiak | 5 | 2 | 40 | 61 | 12.2 | 1 | 0— | | 0 |
| Willhite | 3 | 0 | 0 | 0 | 0.0 | 0 | 0— | | 0 |
| V. Johnson | 1 | 0 | 0 | 0 | 0.0 | 0 | 0— | | 0 |
| Norman | 1 | 0 | 0 | 0 | 0.0 | 0 | 0— | | 0 |
| Winder | 1 | 0 | 0 | 0 | 0.0 | 0 | 0— | | 0 |
| Sewell | 1 | 0 | 0 | 0 | 0.0 | 0 | 0— | | 0 |

**PUNTING**

| Last Name | No | Avg |
|---|---|---|
| Norman | 92 | 40.9 |

**KICKING**

| Last Name | XP | Att | % | FG | Att | % |
|---|---|---|---|---|---|---|
| Karlis | 41 | 44 | 93 | 23 | 38 | 61 |

## SEATTLE SEAHAWKS

### RUSHING

| Last Name | No. | Yds | Avg | TD |
|---|---|---|---|---|
| Warner | 291 | 1094 | 3.8 | 8 |
| Morris | 55 | 236 | 4.3 | 0 |
| Hughes | 40 | 128 | 3.2 | 0 |
| Krieg | 35 | 121 | 3.5 | 1 |
| Lane | 14 | 32 | 2.3 | 0 |
| Parros | 8 | 19 | 2.4 | 0 |
| Franklin | 1 | 5 | 5.0 | 0 |
| Hardy | 5 | 5 | 1.0 | 0 |
| Gilbert | 7 | 4 | 0.6 | 0 |
| Doornink | 4 | 0 | 0.0 | 0 |
| Finzer | 1 | -2 | -2.0 | 0 |

### RECEIVING

| Last Name | No. | Yds | Avg | TD |
|---|---|---|---|---|
| Largent | 79 | 1287 | 16.3 | 6 |
| Warner | 47 | 307 | 6.5 | 1 |
| Turner | 34 | 670 | 19.7 | 13 |
| C. Young | 28 | 351 | 12.5 | 2 |
| Skansi | 21 | 269 | 12.8 | 1 |
| Walker | 19 | 285 | 15.0 | 2 |
| Hughes | 19 | 184 | 9.7 | 0 |
| Ross | 16 | 135 | 8.4 | 2 |
| Lane | 15 | 153 | 10.2 | 0 |
| Franklin | 10 | 119 | 11.9 | 0 |
| Doornink | 8 | 52 | 6.5 | 0 |
| Morris | 6 | 14 | 2.3 | 0 |
| Hardy | 3 | 7 | 2.3 | 0 |
| Tice | 2 | 13 | 6.5 | 0 |
| Greene | 2 | 10 | 5.0 | 1 |
| Parros | 1 | 27 | 27.0 | 0 |

### PUNT RETURNS

| Last Name | No. | Yds | Avg | TD |
|---|---|---|---|---|
| Skansi | 31 | 312 | 10.1 | 0 |
| Greene | 11 | 60 | 5.5 | 0 |
| Easley | 8 | 87 | 10.9 | 0 |
| Harris | 3 | 24 | 8.0 | 0 |

### KICKOFF RETURNS

| Last Name | No. | Yds | Avg | TD |
|---|---|---|---|---|
| Morris | 31 | 636 | 20.5 | 0 |
| Skansi | 19 | 358 | 18.8 | 0 |
| Greene | 5 | 144 | 28.8 | 0 |
| Tice | 1 | 17 | 17.0 | 0 |
| E. Robinson | 1 | 10 | 10.0 | 0 |
| Lane | 1 | 1 | 1.0 | 0 |

### PASSING — PUNTING — KICKING

**PASSING**

| Last Name | Att | Cmp | % | Yds | Yd/Att | TD | Int— | % | RK |
|---|---|---|---|---|---|---|---|---|---|
| Krieg | 532 | 285 | 54 | 3602 | 6.8 | 27 | 20— | | 4 |
| Gilbert | 40 | 19 | 48 | 218 | 5.5 | 1 | 2— | | 5 |
| Finzer | 1 | 0 | 0 | 0 | 0.0 | 0 | 1— | 100 | |
| Largent | 1 | 0 | 0 | 0 | 0.0 | 0 | 0— | | 0 |
| Morris | 1 | 0 | 0 | 0 | 0.0 | 0 | 0— | | 0 |

**PUNTING**

| Last Name | No | Avg |
|---|---|---|
| Finzer | 68 | 40.7 |
| Colquitt | 12 | 40.1 |
| West | 11 | 38.2 |

**KICKING**

| Last Name | XP | Att | % | FG | Att | % |
|---|---|---|---|---|---|---|
| Johnson | 40 | 41 | 93 | 14 | 25 | 56 |

## SAN DIEGO CHARGERS

### RUSHING

| Last Name | No. | Yds | Avg | TD |
|---|---|---|---|---|
| James | 105 | 516 | 4.9 | 2 |
| Spencer | 124 | 478 | 3.9 | 10 |
| Anderson | 116 | 429 | 3.7 | 4 |
| McGee | 42 | 181 | 4.3 | 3 |
| Adams | 16 | 49 | 3.1 | 1 |
| Steels | 6 | 12 | 2.0 | 0 |
| Chandler | 1 | 9 | 9.0 | 0 |
| Mojsiejenko | 1 | 0 | 0.0 | 0 |
| Fouts | 11 | -1 | -0.1 | 0 |
| Hermann | 18 | -8 | -0.4 | 0 |

### RECEIVING

| Last Name | No. | Yds | Avg | TD |
|---|---|---|---|---|
| James | 86 | 1027 | 11.9 | 6 |
| Chandler | 67 | 1199 | 17.9 | 10 |
| Joiner | 59 | 932 | 15.8 | 7 |
| Holohan | 42 | 458 | 10.9 | 3 |
| Sievers | 41 | 438 | 10.7 | 6 |
| Anderson | 35 | 422 | 12.1 | 2 |
| Winslow | 25 | 318 | 12.7 | 0 |
| Bendross | 11 | 156 | 14.2 | 2 |
| Spencer | 11 | 135 | 12.3 | 0 |
| Johnson | 4 | 51 | 12.8 | 1 |
| McGee | 3 | 15 | 5.0 | 0 |
| Adams | 1 | 12 | 12.0 | 0 |
| Faulkner | 1 | 12 | 12.0 | 0 |

### PUNT RETURNS

| Last Name | No. | Yds | Avg | TD |
|---|---|---|---|---|
| James | 25 | 213 | 8.5 | 0 |

### KICKOFF RETURNS

| Last Name | No. | Yds | Avg | TD |
|---|---|---|---|---|
| James | 36 | 779 | 21.6 | 0 |
| Anderson | 13 | 302 | 23.2 | 1 |
| McGee | 7 | 135 | 19.3 | 0 |
| Adams | 2 | 50 | 25.0 | 0 |
| Sievers | 1 | 3 | 3.0 | 0 |
| Bendross | 1 | 2 | 2.0 | 0 |
| Holohan | 1 | 0 | 0.0 | 0 |

### PASSING — PUNTING — KICKING

**PASSING**

| Last Name | Att | Cmp | % | Yds | Yd/Att | TD | Int— | % | RK |
|---|---|---|---|---|---|---|---|---|---|
| Fouts | 430 | 254 | 59 | 3638 | 8.5 | 27 | 20— | | 5 |
| Herrmann | 201 | 132 | 66 | 1537 | 7.7 | 10 | 10— | | 5 |
| Holohan | 1 | 0 | 0 | 0 | 0.0 | 0 | 0— | | 0 |

**PUNTING**

| Last Name | No | Avg |
|---|---|---|
| Mojsiejenko | 68 | 42.4 |

**KICKING**

| Last Name | XP | Att | % | FG | Att | % |
|---|---|---|---|---|---|---|
| Thomas | 51 | 55 | 93 | 18 | 28 | 64 |
| Benirschke | 2 | 2 | 100 | 0 | 0 | |

## KANSAS CITY CHIEFS

### RUSHING

| Last Name | No. | Yds | Avg | TD |
|---|---|---|---|---|
| Heard | 164 | 595 | 3.6 | 4 |
| Prui* | 112 | 390 | 3.5 | 2 |
| Horton | 48 | 146 | 3.0 | 3 |
| Smith | 30 | 118 | 3.9 | 0 |
| Blackledge | 17 | 97 | 5.7 | 0 |
| King | 28 | 83 | 3.0 | 0 |
| Carson | 3 | 25 | 8.3 | 0 |
| Lacy | 6 | 21 | 3.5 | 0 |
| Jones | 12 | 19 | 1.6 | 0 |
| Paige | 1 | 15 | 15.0 | 0 |
| Kenney | 14 | 1 | 0.1 | 1 |

### RECEIVING

| Last Name | No. | Yds | Avg | TD |
|---|---|---|---|---|
| Carson | 47 | 843 | 17.9 | 4 |
| Paige | 43 | 943 | 21.9 | 10 |
| Heard | 31 | 257 | 8.3 | 2 |
| W. Arnold | 28 | 339 | 12.1 | 1 |
| Horton | 28 | 185 | 6.6 | 1 |
| Marshall | 25 | 446 | 17.8 | 0 |
| Smith | 18 | 157 | 8.7 | 2 |
| Hancock | 15 | 286 | 19.1 | 2 |
| King | 7 | 45 | 6.4 | 0 |
| Pruitt | 7 | 43 | 6.1 | 0 |
| Holston | 6 | 76 | 12.7 | 0 |
| Scott | 5 | 61 | 12.2 | 0 |
| Hayes | 5 | 39 | 7.8 | 1 |
| Jones | 3 | 31 | 10.3 | 0 |

### PUNT RETURNS

| Last Name | No. | Yds | Avg | TD |
|---|---|---|---|---|
| Lane | 43 | 381 | 8.9 | 0 |

### KICKOFF RETURNS

| Last Name | No. | Yds | Avg | TD |
|---|---|---|---|---|
| Smith | 33 | 654 | 19.8 | 0 |
| Lane | 13 | 269 | 20.7 | 0 |
| Hancock | 6 | 125 | 20.8 | 0 |
| Paige | 2 | 36 | 18.0 | 0 |
| W. Arnold | 2 | 9 | 4.5 | 0 |
| King | 1 | 13 | 13.0 | 0 |
| Shorthose | 1 | 11 | 11.0 | 0 |
| Hayes | 1 | 0 | 0.0 | 0 |

### PASSING — PUNTING — KICKING

**PASSING**

| Last Name | Att | Cmp | % | Yds | Yd/Att | TD | Int— | % | RK |
|---|---|---|---|---|---|---|---|---|---|
| Kenney | 338 | 181 | 54 | 2536 | 7.5 | 17 | 9— | | 3 |
| Blackledge | 172 | 86 | 50 | 1190 | 6.9 | 6 | 14— | | 8 |
| Horton | 1 | 0 | 0 | 0 | 0.0 | 0 | 0— | | 0 |

**PUNTING**

| Last Name | No | Avg |
|---|---|---|
| J. Arnold | 93 | 41.2 |

**KICKING**

| Last Name | XP | Att | % | FG | Att | % |
|---|---|---|---|---|---|---|
| Lowery | 35 | 35 | 100 | 24 | 27 | 88 |

# 1985 N.F.C.— PLAYOFFS

## SCORING

| | | | | |
|---|---|---|---|---|
| SAN FRANCISCO | 0 | 3 | 0 | 0- 3 |
| N.Y. GIANTS | 3 | 7 | 7 | 0- 17 |

**First Quarter**
N.Y.G.  Schubert, 47 yard field goal

**Second Quarter**
N.Y.G.  Bavaro, 18 yard pass from Simms
  PAT—Schubert (kick)
S.F.  Wersching, 21 yard field goal

**Third Quarter**
N.Y.G.  Hasselbeck, 3 yard pass from Simms
  PAT—Schubert (kick)

### TEAM STATISTICS

| S.F. | | N.Y.G. |
|---|---|---|
| 19 | First Downs- Total | 21 |
| 6 | First Downs- Rushing | 9 |
| 10 | First Downs- Passing | 11 |
| 3 | First Downs- Penalty | 1 |
| 2 | Fumbles- Number | 0 |
| 0 | Fumbles- Lost Ball | 0 |
| 6 | Penalties- Number | 5 |
| 41 | Yards Penalized | 45 |
| 0 | Missed Field Goals | 3 |
| 74 | Offensive Plays | 72 |
| 362 | Net Yards | 355 |
| 4.9 | Average Gain | 4.9 |
| 2 | Giveaways | 1 |
| 1 | Takeaways | 2 |
| -1 | Difference | +1 |

### INDIVIDUAL STATISTICS

| SAN FRANCISCO | No. | Yds. | Avg. | NEW YORK | No. | Yds. | Avg. |
|---|---|---|---|---|---|---|---|
| **RUSHING** | | | | | | | |
| Tyler | 10 | 61 | 6.1 | Morris | 28 | 141 | 5.0 |
| Craig | 9 | 23 | 2.6 | Carpenter | 4 | 25 | 6.3 |
| Monroe | 1 | 10 | 10.0 | Adams | 4 | 13 | 3.3 |
| Harmon | 1 | 0 | 0.0 | Simms | 5 | -5 | -1.0 |
| Montana | 1 | 0 | 0.0 | | 41 | 174 | 4.2 |
| | 22 | 94 | 4.3 | | | | |
| **RECEIVING** | | | | | | | |
| Clark | 8 | 120 | 15.0 | Bavaro | 5 | 67 | 13.4 |
| Rice | 4 | 45 | 11.3 | Manuel | 3 | 56 | 18.7 |
| Francis | 4 | 39 | 9.8 | Carpenter | 3 | 36 | 12.0 |
| Frank | 3 | 25 | 8.3 | Galbreath | 1 | 9 | 9.0 |
| Craig | 2 | 18 | 9.0 | Adams | 1 | 5 | 5.0 |
| Ring | 3 | 19 | 6.3 | Morris | 1 | 5 | 5.0 |
| Harmon | 1 | 16 | 16.0 | Hasselbeck | 1 | 3 | 3.0 |
| Wilson | 1 | 14 | 14.0 | | 15 | 181 | 12.1 |
| | 26 | 296 | 11.4 | | | | |
| **PUNTING** | | | | | | | |
| Runager | 6 | | 38.0 | Landeta | 5 | | 36.5 |
| **PUNT RETURNS** | | | | | | | |
| McLemore | 1 | 5 | 5.0 | McConkey | 4 | 29 | 7.3 |
| **KICKOFF RETURNS** | | | | | | | |
| Monroe | 3 | 42 | 14.0 | Galbreath | 1 | 17 | 17.0 |
| | | | | Rouson | 1 | 18 | 18.0 |
| | | | | | 2 | 35 | 17.5 |
| **INTERCEPTION RETURNS** | | | | | | | |
| Williamson | 1 | 2 | 2.0 | Kinard | 1 | 15 | 15.0 |

#### PASSING

**SAN FRANCISCO**

| | Att. | Comp. | Comp. Pct. | Yds. | Int. | Yds./ Att. | Yds./ Comp. |
|---|---|---|---|---|---|---|---|
| Montana | 47 | 26 | 55.3 | 296 | 1 | 6.3 | 11.4 |
| Rice | 1 | 0 | 0.0 | 0 | 0 | 0.0 | 0.0 |
| | 48 | 26 | 54.2 | 296 | 1 | 6.2 | 11.4 |

**NEW YORK**

| | Att. | Comp. | Comp. Pct. | Yds. | Int. | Yds./ Att. | Yds./ Comp. |
|---|---|---|---|---|---|---|---|
| Simms | 31 | 15 | 48.4 | 181 | 1 | 5.8 | 12.1 |

---

## SCORING

| | | | | |
|---|---|---|---|---|
| DALLAS | 0 | 0 | 0 | 0- 0 |
| L.A. RAMS | 3 | 0 | 10 | 7- 20 |

**First Quarter**
L.A.  Lansford, 33 yard field goal

**Third Quarter**
L.A.  Dickerson, 55 yard rush
  PAT—Lansford (kick)
L.A.  Lansford, 34 yard field goal

**Fourth Quarter**
L.A.  Dickerson, 40 yard rush
  PAT—Lansford (kick)

### TEAM STATISTICS

| DAL. | | LA |
|---|---|---|
| 15 | First Downs- Total | 15 |
| 3 | First Downs- Rushing | 11 |
| 12 | First Downs- Passing | 3 |
| 0 | First Downs- Penalty | 1 |
| 3 | Fumbles- Number | 3 |
| 3 | Fumbles- Lost Ball | 1 |
| 5 | Penalties- Number | 4 |
| 30 | Yards Penalized | 29 |
| 0 | Missed Field Goals | 0 |
| 66 | Offensive Plays | 64 |
| 243 | Net Yards | 316 |
| 3.7 | Average Gain | 4.9 |
| 6 | Giveaways | 2 |
| 2 | Takeaways | 6 |
| -4 | Difference | +4 |

### INDIVIDUAL STATISTICS

| DALLAS | No. | Yds. | Avg. | LOS ANGELES | No. | Yds. | Avg. |
|---|---|---|---|---|---|---|---|
| **RUSHING** | | | | | | | |
| Dorsett | 17 | 58 | 3.4 | Dickerson | 34 | 248 | 7.3 |
| Newsome | 1 | 3 | 3.0 | Redden | 6 | 21 | 3.5 |
| | 18 | 61 | 3.4 | Brock | 1 | 0 | 0.0 |
| | | | | | 41 | 269 | 6.6 |
| **RECEIVING** | | | | | | | |
| Dorsett | 8 | 80 | 10.0 | Ellard | 2 | 33 | 16.5 |
| Cosbie | 6 | 61 | 10.2 | Redden | 1 | 15 | 15.0 |
| T. Hill | 5 | 41 | 8.2 | D. Hill | 1 | 3 | 3.0 |
| Newsome | 3 | 10 | 3.4 | Hunter | 1 | 3 | 3.0 |
| Powe | 1 | 19 | 19.0 | Dickerson | 1 | -4 | -4.0 |
| J. Jones | 1 | 6 | 6.0 | | 6 | 50 | 8.3 |
| | 24 | 217 | 9.0 | | | | |
| **PUNTING** | | | | | | | |
| Saxon | 7 | | 46.9 | Hatcher | 7 | | 40.7 |
| **PUNT RETURNS** | | | | | | | |
| Banks | 4 | 30 | 7.5 | Ellard | 4 | 37 | 9.3 |
| **KICKOFF RETURNS** | | | | | | | |
| Duckett | 4 | 99 | 24.8 | White | 1 | 14 | 14.0 |
| J. Jones | 1 | 11 | 11.0 | | | | |
| | 5 | 110 | 22.0 | | | | |
| **INTERCEPTION RETURNS** | | | | | | | |
| Walls | 1 | 20 | 20.0 | Irvin | 1 | 55 | 55.0 |
| | | | | Gray | 1 | 10 | 10.0 |
| | | | | Green | 1 | 1 | 1.0 |
| | | | | | 3 | 66 | 22.0 |

#### PASSING

**DALLAS**

| | Att. | Comp. | Comp. Pct. | Yds. | Int. | Yds./ Att. | Yds./ Comp. |
|---|---|---|---|---|---|---|---|
| D. White | 43 | 24 | 55.8 | 217 | 3 | 5.0 | 9.0 |

**LOS ANGELES**

| | Att. | Comp. | Comp. Pct. | Yds. | Int. | Yds./ Att. | Yds./ Comp. |
|---|---|---|---|---|---|---|---|
| Brock | 22 | 6 | 27.3 | 50 | 1 | 2.3 | 8.3 |

---

## SCORING

| | | | | |
|---|---|---|---|---|
| N.Y. GIANTS | 0 | 0 | 0 | 0- 0 |
| CHICAGO | 7 | 0 | 14 | 0- 21 |

**First Quarter**
Chi.  Gayle, 5 yard punt return
  PAT—Butler (kick)

**Third Quarter**
Chi.  McKinnon, 23 yard pass from McMahon
  PAT—Butler (kick)
Chi.  McKinnon, 20 yard pass from McMahon
  PAT—Butler (kick)

### TEAM STATISTICS

| N.Y.G. | | CHI. |
|---|---|---|
| 10 | First Downs- Total | 17 |
| 1 | First Downs- Rushing | 9 |
| 8 | First Downs- Passing | 8 |
| 1 | First Downs- Penalty | 0 |
| 3 | Fumbles- Number | 0 |
| 1 | Fumbles- Lost Ball | 0 |
| 4 | Penalties- Number | 2 |
| 25 | Yards Penalized | 20 |
| 1 | Missed Field Goals | 3 |
| 55 | Offensive Plays | 65 |
| 181 | Net Yards | 363 |
| 3.3 | Average Gain | 5.6 |
| 1 | Giveaways | 0 |
| 0 | Takeaways | 1 |
| -1 | Difference | +1 |

### INDIVIDUAL STATISTICS

| NEW YORK | No. | Yds. | Avg. | CHICAGO | No. | Yds. | Avg. |
|---|---|---|---|---|---|---|---|
| **RUSHING** | | | | | | | |
| Morris | 12 | 32 | 2.7 | Payton | 27 | 93 | 3.4 |
| Galbreath | 1 | 9 | 9.0 | Suhey | 6 | 33 | 5.5 |
| B. Williams | 1 | -9 | -9.0 | McMahon | 5 | 18 | 3.6 |
| | 14 | 32 | 2.3 | Thomas | 4 | 11 | 2.8 |
| | | | | Gentry | 1 | -1 | -1.0 |
| | | | | McKinnon | 1 | -7 | -7.0 |
| | | | | | 44 | 147 | 3.3 |
| **RECEIVING** | | | | | | | |
| Bavaro | 4 | 36 | 9.0 | Gault | 3 | 68 | 22.7 |
| Adams | 3 | 65 | 21.7 | McKinnon | 3 | 52 | 17.3 |
| Carpenter | 3 | 24 | 8.0 | Suhey | 2 | 5 | 2.5 |
| B. Williams | 1 | 33 | 33.0 | Wrightman | 1 | 46 | 46.0 |
| McConkey | 1 | 23 | 23.0 | Gentry | 1 | 41 | 41.0 |
| Johnson | 1 | 17 | 17.0 | Payton | 1 | 4 | 4.0 |
| Galbreath | 1 | 11 | 11.0 | | 11 | 216 | 19.6 |
| | 14 | 209 | 14.9 | | | | |
| **PUNTING** | | | | | | | |
| Landeta | 9 | | 38.1 | Buford | 6 | | 37.3 |
| **PUNT RETURNS** | | | | | | | |
| McConkey | 2 | 9 | 4.5 | Ortego | 5 | 22 | 4.4 |
| | | | | Gayle | 1 | 5 | 5.0 |
| | | | | | 6 | 27 | 4.5 |
| **KICKOFF RETURNS** | | | | | | | |
| Rouson | 2 | 58 | 29.0 | Gault | 1 | 21 | 21.0 |
| Hasselbeck | 1 | 20 | 20.0 | | | | |
| Galbreath | 1 | 17 | 17.0 | | | | |
| | 4 | 95 | 23.8 | | | | |
| **INTERCEPTION RETURNS** | | | | | | | |
| none | | | | none | | | |

#### PASSING

**NEW YORK**

| | Att. | Comp. | Comp. Pct. | Yds. | Int. | Yds./ Att. | Yds./ Comp. |
|---|---|---|---|---|---|---|---|
| Simms | 35 | 14 | 40.0 | 209 | 0 | 6.0 | 14.9 |

**CHICAGO**

| | Att. | Comp. | Comp. Pct. | Yds. | Int. | Yds./ Att. | Yds./ Comp. |
|---|---|---|---|---|---|---|---|
| McMahon | 21 | 11 | 52.4 | 216 | 0 | 10.3 | 19.6 |

## December 28, 1985 at East Rutherford (Attendance 75,945)

### SCORING

| | | | | | |
|---|---|---|---|---|---|
| NEW ENGLAND | 3 | 10 | 10 | 3- | 26 |
| N.Y. JETS | 0 | 7 | 7 | 0- | 14 |

**First Quarter**
N.E. — Franklin, 33 yard field goal

**Second Quarter**
N.Y.J. — Hector, 11 yard pass from O'Brien
    PAT—Leahy (kick)
N.E. — Franklin, 41 yard field goal
N.E. — Morgan, 36 yard pass from Eason
    PAT—Franklin (kick)

**Third Quarter**
N.E. — Franklin, 20 yard field goal
N.E. — Rembert, 15 yard fumble return
    PAT—Franklin (kick)
N.Y.J. — Shuler, 12 yard pass from Ryan
    PAT—Leahy (kick)

**Fourth Quarter**
N.E. — Franklin, 26 yard field goal

### TEAM STATISTICS

| N.E. | | N.Y.J. |
|---|---|---|
| 12 | First Downs- Total | 15 |
| 5 | First Downs- Rushing | 3 |
| 6 | First Downs- Passing | 12 |
| 1 | First Downs- Penalty | 0 |
| 2 | Fumbles- Number | 3 |
| 0 | Fumbles- Lost Ball | 2 |
| 1 | Penalties- Number | 6 |
| 10 | Yards Penalized | 48 |
| 1 | Missed Field Goals | 0 |
| 58 | Offensive Plays | 60 |
| 258 | Net Yards | 250 |
| 4.4 | Average Gain | 4.2 |
| 0 | Giveaways | 4 |
| 4 | Takeaways | 0 |
| +4 | Difference | -4 |

### INDIVIDUAL STATISTICS

**NEW ENGLAND**     **N.Y. Jets**

#### RUSHING

| | No. | Yds. | Avg. | | No. | Yds. | Avg. |
|---|---|---|---|---|---|---|---|
| James | 22 | 49 | 2.2 | McNeil | 16 | 41 | 2.6 |
| Collins | 11 | 36 | 3.3 | Hector | 4 | 13 | 3.3 |
| Eason | 6 | 14 | 2.3 | O'Brien | 1 | 4 | 4.0 |
| | 39 | 99 | 2.5 | | 21 | 58 | 2.8 |

#### RECEIVING

| | No. | Yds. | Avg. | | No. | Yds. | Avg. |
|---|---|---|---|---|---|---|---|
| Morgan | 4 | 62 | 15.5 | Toon | 9 | 93 | 10.3 |
| Fryar | 2 | 47 | 23.5 | Shuler | 5 | 53 | 10.6 |
| James | 2 | 36 | 18.0 | Walker | 4 | 54 | 13.5 |
| Dawson | 2 | 20 | 10.0 | McNeil | 3 | 13 | 4.3 |
| Collins | 2 | 14 | 7.0 | Hector | 1 | 11 | 11.0 |
| | 12 | 179 | 14.9 | Klever | 1 | 9 | 9.0 |
| | | | | | 23 | 233 | 10.1 |

#### PUNTING

| | | | | | | | |
|---|---|---|---|---|---|---|---|
| Camarillo | 5 | | 40.0 | Jennings | 5 | | 38.4 |

#### PUNT RETURNS

| | | | | | | | |
|---|---|---|---|---|---|---|---|
| Fryar | 4 | 12 | 3.0 | Sohn | 1 | 3 | 3.0 |

#### KICKOFF RETURNS

| | | | | | | | |
|---|---|---|---|---|---|---|---|
| Starring | 1 | 19 | 19.0 | Hector | 6 | 115 | 19.2 |
| C. Jones | 1 | 11 | 11.0 | Humphrey | 1 | 50 | 50.0 |
| | 2 | 30 | 15.0 | | 7 | 165 | 23.6 |

#### INTERCEPTION RETURNS

| | | | | |
|---|---|---|---|---|
| Marion | 1 | 28 | 28.0 | none |
| Veris | 1 | 18 | 18.0 | |
| | 2 | 46 | 23.0 | |

#### PASSING

**NEW ENGLAND**

| | Att. | Comp. | Comp. Pct. | Yds. | Int. | Yds./ Att. | Yds./ Comp. |
|---|---|---|---|---|---|---|---|
| Eason | 16 | 12 | 75 | 179 | 0 | 11.2 | 14.9 |

**NEW YORK**

| | Att. | Comp. | Comp. Pct. | Yds. | Int. | Yds./ Att. | Yds./ Comp. |
|---|---|---|---|---|---|---|---|
| O'Brien | 17 | 13 | 76 | 149 | 1 | 8.8 | 11.5 |
| Ryan | 17 | 10 | 59 | 84 | 1 | 4.9 | 8.4 |
| | 34 | 23 | 68 | 233 | 2 | 6.9 | 10.1 |

---

## January 4, 1986 at Miami (Attendance 74,667)

### SCORING

| | | | | | |
|---|---|---|---|---|---|
| CLEVELAND | 7 | 7 | 7 | 0- | 21 |
| MIAMI | 3 | 0 | 14 | 7- | 24 |

**First Quarter**
MIA. — Reveiz, 51 yard field goal
CLE. — Newsome, 16 yard pass from Kosar
    PAT—Bahr (kick)

**Second Quarter**
CLE. — Byner, 21 yard rush
    PAT—Bahr (kick)

**Third Quarter**
CLE. — Byner 66 yard rush
    PAT—Bahr (kick)]
MIA. — N. Moore, 6 yard pass from Marino
    PAT—Reveiz (kick)
MIA. — Davenport, 31 yard rush
    PAT—Reveiz (kick)

**Fourth Quarter**
MIA. — Davenport, 1 yard rush
    PAT—Reveiz (kick)

### TEAM STATISTICS

| CLE. | | MIA. |
|---|---|---|
| 17 | First Downs- Total | 20 |
| 11 | First Downs- Rushing | 6 |
| 5 | First Downs- Passing | 13 |
| 1 | First Downs- Penalty | 1 |
| 1 | Fumbles- Number | 1 |
| 0 | Fumbles- Lost Ball | 0 |
| 6 | Penalties- Number | 2 |
| 49 | Yards Penalized | 20 |
| 0 | Missed Field Goals | 1 |
| 57 | Offensive Plays | 64 |
| 313 | Net Yards | 330 |
| 5.5 | Average Gain | 5.2 |
| 1 | Giveaways | 1 |
| 1 | Takeaways | 1 |
| 0 | Difference | 0 |

### INDIVIDUAL STATISTICS

**CLEVELAND**     **MIAMI**

#### RUSHING

| | No. | Yds. | Avg. | | No. | Yds. | Avg. |
|---|---|---|---|---|---|---|---|
| Byner | 16 | 161 | 10.1 | Davenport | 6 | 48 | 8.0 |
| Mack | 13 | 56 | 4.3 | Nathan | 7 | 21 | 3.0 |
| Dickey | 6 | 28 | 4.7 | Bennett | 4 | 17 | 4.3 |
| Kosar | 2 | 6 | 3.0 | Carter | 2 | 6 | 3.0 |
| | 37 | 251 | 6.8 | | 19 | 92 | 4.8 |

#### RECEIVING

| | No. | Yds. | Avg. | | No. | Yds. | Avg. |
|---|---|---|---|---|---|---|---|
| Byner | 4 | 25 | 6.3 | Nathan | 10 | 101 | 10.1 |
| Newsome | 2 | 22 | 11.0 | Hardy | 5 | 51 | 10.2 |
| Holt | 2 | 2 | 1.0 | N. Moore | 4 | 29 | 7.3 |
| Cl. Weathers | 1 | 12 | 12.0 | Johnson | 2 | 17 | 8.5 |
| Fontenot | 1 | 5 | 5.0 | Rose | 1 | 17 | 17.0 |
| | 10 | 66 | 6.6 | Clayton | 1 | 15 | 15.0 |
| | | | | Bennett | 1 | 6 | 6.0 |
| | | | | Carter | 1 | 2 | 2.0 |
| | | | | | 25 | 238 | 9.5 |

#### PUNTING

| | | | | | | | |
|---|---|---|---|---|---|---|---|
| Gossett | 6 | | 37.2 | Roby | 5 | | 41.6 |

#### PUNT RETURNS

| | | | | | | | |
|---|---|---|---|---|---|---|---|
| Brennan | 1 | 1 | 1.0 | Vigorito | 3 | 23 | 7.7 |
| | | | | Kozlowski | 1 | 0 | 0.0 |
| | | | | | 4 | 23 | 5.8 |

#### KICKOFF RETURNS

| | | | | | | | |
|---|---|---|---|---|---|---|---|
| Young | 3 | 75 | 25.0 | Vigorito | 1 | 19 | 19.0 |
| | | | | Hampton | 3 | 70 | 23.3 |
| | | | | | 4 | 89 | 22.3 |

#### INTERCEPTION RETURNS

| | | | | | | | |
|---|---|---|---|---|---|---|---|
| Rogers | 1 | 45 | 45.0 | Lankford | 1 | 2 | 2.0 |

#### PASSING

**CLEVELAND**

| | Att. | Comp. | Comp. Pct. | Yds. | Int. | Yds./ Att. | Yds./ Comp. |
|---|---|---|---|---|---|---|---|
| Kosar | 19 | 10 | 53 | 66 | 1 | 3.5 | 6.6 |

**MIAMI**

| | Att. | Comp. | Comp. Pct. | Yds. | Int. | Yds./ Att. | Yds./ Comp. |
|---|---|---|---|---|---|---|---|
| Marino | 45 | 25 | 56 | 238 | 1 | 5.3 | 9.5 |

---

## January 5, 1986 at Los Angeles (Attendance 87,163)

### SCORING

| | | | | | |
|---|---|---|---|---|---|
| NEW ENGLAND | 7 | 10 | 10 | 0- | 27 |
| L.A. RAIDERS | 3 | 17 | 0 | 0- | 20 |

**First Quarter**
N.E. — Dawson, 13 yard pass from Eason
    PAT—Franklin (kick)
L.A. — Bahr, 29 yard field goal

**Second Quarter**
L.A. — Hester, 16 yard pass from Wilson
    PAT—Bahr (kick)
L.A. — Allen, 11 yard rush
    PAT—Bahr (kick)
N.E. — C. James, 2 yard rush
    PAT—Franklin (kick)
N.E. — Franklin, 45 yard field goal
L.A. — Bahr, 32 yard field goal

**Third Quarter**
N.E. — Franklin, 32 yard field goal
N.E. — Bowman, fumble recovery in end zone
    PAT—Franklin (kick)

### TEAM STATISTICS

| N.E. | | RAID. |
|---|---|---|
| 15 | First Downs- Total | 17 |
| 9 | First Downs- Rushing | 11 |
| 5 | First Downs- Passing | 6 |
| 1 | First Downs- Penalty | 0 |
| 3 | Fumbles- Number | 5 |
| 2 | Fumbles- Lost Ball | 3 |
| 6 | Penalties- Number | 6 |
| 45 | Yards Penalized | 53 |
| 0 | Missed Field Goals | 1 |
| 67 | Offensive Plays | 56 |
| 254 | Net Yards | 287 |
| 3.8 | Average Gain | 5.1 |
| 2 | Giveaways | 6 |
| 6 | Takeaways | 2 |
| +4 | Difference | -4 |

### INDIVIDUAL STATISTICS

**NEW ENGLAND**     **L.A. RAIDERS**

#### RUSHING

| | No. | Yds. | Avg. | | No. | Yds. | Avg. |
|---|---|---|---|---|---|---|---|
| C. James | 23 | 104 | 4.5 | Allen | 22 | 121 | 5.5 |
| Collins | 9 | 18 | 2.0 | Hawkins | 4 | 33 | 8.3 |
| Weathers | 9 | 18 | 2.0 | Wilson | 1 | 9 | 9.0 |
| Tatupu | 4 | 17 | 4.3 | | 27 | 163 | 6.0 |
| Fryar | 1 | 3 | 3.0 | | | | |
| Eason | 3 | -4 | -1.3 | | | | |
| | 49 | 156 | 3.2 | | | | |

#### RECEIVING

| | No. | Yds. | Avg. | | No. | Yds. | Avg. |
|---|---|---|---|---|---|---|---|
| C. James | 3 | 48 | 16.0 | Christensen | 4 | 78 | 19.5 |
| D. Ramsey | 2 | 34 | 17.0 | Williams | 3 | 33 | 11.0 |
| Morgan | 1 | 22 | 22.0 | Allen | 3 | 8 | 2.7 |
| Dawson | 1 | 13 | 13.0 | Hester | 1 | 16 | 16.0 |
| Collins | 1 | 8 | 8.0 | | 11 | 135 | 12.3 |
| | 8 | 125 | 15.6 | | | | |

#### PUNTING

| | | | | | | | |
|---|---|---|---|---|---|---|---|
| Camarillo | 5 | | 45.0 | Guy | 2 | | 34.0 |

#### PUNT RETURNS

| | | | | | | | |
|---|---|---|---|---|---|---|---|
| none | | | | Walker | 4 | 36 | 9.0 |

#### KICKOFF RETURNS

| | | | | | | | |
|---|---|---|---|---|---|---|---|
| Starring | 2 | 45 | 22.5 | Walker | 3 | 59 | 19.7 |
| Jones | 2 | 9 | 4.5 | Seale | 2 | 7 | 3.5 |
| | 4 | 54 | 13.5 | | 5 | 66 | 13.2 |

#### INTERCEPTION RETURNS

| | | | | |
|---|---|---|---|---|
| Marion | 1 | 22 | 22.0 | none |
| Lippett | 2 | 1 | 0.5 | |
| | 3 | 23 | 7.7 | |

#### PASSING

**NEW ENGLAND**

| | Att. | Comp. | Comp. Pct. | Yds. | Int. | Yds./ Att. | Yds./ Comp. |
|---|---|---|---|---|---|---|---|
| Eason | 14 | 7 | 50 | 117 | 0 | 8.4 | 16.7 |
| C. James | 1 | 1 | 100 | 8 | 0 | 8.0 | 8.0 |
| | 15 | 8 | 53 | 125 | 0 | 8.3 | 15.6 |

**LOS ANGELES**

| | Att. | Comp. | Comp. Pct. | Yds. | Int. | Yds./ Att. | Yds./ Comp. |
|---|---|---|---|---|---|---|---|
| Wilson | 27 | 11 | 41 | 135 | 3 | 5.0 | 12.3 |

## NFC CHAMPIONSHIP GAME
January 12, 1986 at Chicago
(Attendance 63,522)

### SCORING

| | | | | | |
|---|---|---|---|---|---|
| L.A. RAMS | 0 | 0 | 0 | 0- | 0 |
| CHICAGO | 10 | 0 | 7 | 7- | 24 |

**First Quarter**
Chi.  McMahon, 16 yard rush
PAT—Butler (kick)
Chi  Butler, 34 yard field goal

**Third Quarter**
Chi.  Gault, 22 yard pass from McMahon
PAT—Butler (kick)

**Fourth Quarter**
Chi.  Marshall, 52 yard fumble recovery return
PAT—Butler (kick)

### TEAM STATISTICS

| LA | | CHI |
|---|---|---|
| 9 | First Downs-Total | 13 |
| 5 | First Downs-Rushing | 5 |
| 3 | First Downs-Passing | 8 |
| 1 | First Downs-Penalty | 0 |
| 4 | Fumbles-Number | 3 |
| 2 | Fumbles-Lost Ball | 1 |
| 4 | Penalties-Number | 6 |
| 25 | Yards Penalized | 48 |
| 0 | Missed Field Goals | 0 |
| 60 | Offensive Plays | 61 |
| 130 | Net Yards | 232 |
| 2.2 | Average Gain | 3.8 |
| 3 | Giveaways | 1 |
| 1 | Takeaways | 3 |
| -2 | Difference | +2 |

A week after shutting out the New York Giants 21-0 in a near-perfect defensive performance, the Chicago Bears hosted the Los Angeles Rams for the NFC title in cool, gusty Soldier Field.

Excellent defenders themselves, the Rams had also posted a shutout the previous week, 20-0 over the Cowboys. But the Bears waded through Los Angeles on their first possession to score the only points they needed for victory. Bear QB Jim McMahon capped a five-play, 66-yard drive with a 16-yard scramble to make it 7-0. When the Rams couldn't move, Chicago got the ball back, and Kevin Butler kicked a 34-yard field goal, making it 10-0.

Chicago shut down Ram workhorse Eric Dickerson and harried QB Dieter Brock with a devastating pass rush led by DE Richard Dent. Late in the first half, the Rams recovered a fumble at the Bear 21 but failed to score before time ran out.

Having lost their chance to change the momentum, the Rams were flattened in the second half. Chicago built its lead to 17-0 in the third quarter on a McMahon-to-Willie Gault, 22-yard scoring pass. Then, as snow began to fall in the fourth quarter, Chicago's defense appropriately added the final points. Dent forced Brock to fumble, and LB Wilber Marshall grabbed the ball and raced 52 yards for a touchdown.

The awesome Bear defense held Dickerson to 46 yards and pressured Brock to a net gain of only 44 yards passing. Not since the Eagles in the NFL championship games of 1948 and 1949 had a team posted two consecutive shutouts in postseason play.

## INDIVIDUAL STATISTICS

### RUSHING

| L.A. RAMS | No. | Yds. | Avg. | CHICAGO | No. | Yds. | Avg. |
|---|---|---|---|---|---|---|---|
| Dickerson | 17 | 46 | 2.7 | Payton | 18 | 32 | 1.8 |
| Redden | 9 | 40 | 4.4 | McMahon | 4 | 28 | 7.0 |
| | 26 | 86 | 3.3 | Suhey | 6 | 23 | 3.8 |
| | | | | Gentry | 2 | 9 | 4.5 |
| | | | | Thomas | 3 | -1 | -0.3 |
| | | | | | 33 | 91 | 2.8 |

### RECEIVING

| | No. | Yds. | Avg. | | No. | Yds. | Avg. |
|---|---|---|---|---|---|---|---|
| Hunter | 3 | 29 | 9.7 | Payton | 7 | 48 | 6.9 |
| Dickerson | 3 | 10 | 3.3 | Gault | 4 | 56 | 14.0 |
| Brown | 2 | 14 | 7.0 | Moorehead | 2 | 28 | 14.0 |
| Duckworth | 1 | 8 | 8.0 | McKinnon | 1 | 17 | 17.0 |
| Ellard | 1 | 5 | 5.0 | Wrightman | 1 | 8 | 8.0 |
| | 10 | 66 | 6.6 | Suhey | 1 | 7 | 7.0 |
| | | | | | 16 | 164 | 10.3 |

### PUNTING

| | | | | | | |
|---|---|---|---|---|---|---|
| Hatcher | 11 | 39.2 | | Buford | 10 | 36.3 |

### PUNT RETURNS

| | No. | Yds. | Avg. | | No. | Yds. | Avg. |
|---|---|---|---|---|---|---|---|
| Johnson | 2 | 6 | 3.0 | Ortego | 4 | 21 | 5.3 |
| Ellard | 1 | 6 | 6.0 | Phillips | 1 | 0 | 0.0 |
| Irvin | 1 | 4 | 4.0 | Duerson | 0 | 0 | 0.0 |
| | 4 | 16 | 4.0 | | 5 | 21 | 4.2 |

### KICKOFF RETURNS

| | No. | Yds. | Avg. | | No. | Yds. | Avg. |
|---|---|---|---|---|---|---|---|
| Brown | 3 | 63 | 21.0 | Gentry | 1 | 22 | 22.0 |
| Redden | 1 | 13 | 13.0 | | | | |
| | 4 | 76 | 19.0 | | | | |

### INTERCEPTION RETURNS

| | | | | | No. | Yds. | Avg. |
|---|---|---|---|---|---|---|---|
| none | | | | Frazier | 1 | -3 | -3.0 |

### PASSING

| L.A. RAMS | Att. | Comp. | Comp. Pct. | Yds. | Int. | Yds./ Att. | Yds./ Comp. |
|---|---|---|---|---|---|---|---|
| Brock | 31 | 10 | 32.2 | 66 | 1 | 2.1 | 6.6 |
| **CHICAGO** | | | | | | | |
| McMahon | 25 | 16 | 64.0 | 164 | 0 | 6.6 | 10.3 |

## AFC CHAMPIONSHIP GAME
January 12, 1986 at Miami
(Attendance 74,978)

The Miami Dolphins were Eastern Division champions, whereas the New England Patriots were only wild-card qualifiers playing their third straight game on the road. Moreover, the Dolphins had never lost an AFC title game and had beaten the Patriots 18 consecutive times in the Orange Bowl.

But, on the first play from scrimmage, New England DE Garin Veris recovered Dolphin Tony Nathan's fumble to set the tone of the game. Six plays later, Tony Franklin delivered a 23-yard field goal to put the Patriots in front 3-0.

Miami took the lead on a 10-yard pass from Dan Marino to Dan Johnson, but the Patriots bounced right back with a 66-yard drive to regain the lead on a four-yard, Tony Eason-to-Tony Collins pass. Two plays after the ensuing kickoff, Marino fumbled and the Patriots recovered again. A few moments later, Eason hit Derrick Ramsey with a one-yard TD to give New England a 17-7 halftime lead.

Miami's giveaway problems continued as Lorenzo Hampton fumbled the second-half kickoff and, shortly afterward, Eason threw to Weathers for a touchdown.

Behind 24-7, Marino began throwing on every down, but the best he could do was a single 10-yard TD toss to Nathan. New England matched that with Mosi Tatupu's one-yard plunge.

### SCORING

| | | | | | |
|---|---|---|---|---|---|
| NEW ENGLAND | 3 | 14 | 7 | 7- | 31 |
| MIAMI | 0 | 7 | 0 | 7- | 14 |

**First Quarter**
N.E.  Franklin, 23 yard field goal

**Second Quarter**
Mia.  Johnson, 10 yard pass from Marino
PAT—Reveiz (kick)
N.E.  Collins, 4 yard pass from Eason
PAT—Franklin (kick)
N.E.  D. Ramsey, 1 yard pass from Eason
PAT—Franklin (kick)

**Third Quarter**
N.E.  Weathers, 2 yard pass from Eason
PAT—Franklin (kick)

**Fourth Quarter**
Mia.  Nathan, 10 yard pass from Marino
PAT—Reveiz (kick)
N.E.  Tatupu, 1 yard rush
PAT—Franklin (kick)

### TEAM STATISTICS

| NE | | MIA |
|---|---|---|
| 21 | First Downs-Total | 18 |
| 15 | First Downs-Rushing | 3 |
| 6 | First Downs-Passing | 15 |
| 0 | First Downs-Penalty | 0 |
| 2 | Fumbles-Number | 5 |
| 2 | Fumbles-Lost Ball | 4 |
| 2 | Penalties-Number | 4 |
| 15 | Yards Penalized | 35 |
| 1 | Missed Field Goals | 1 |
| 71 | Offensive Plays | 62 |
| 326 | Net Yards | 302 |
| 4.6 | Average Gain | 4.9 |
| 2 | Giveaways | 6 |
| 6 | Takeaways | 2 |
| +4 | Difference | -4 |

## INDIVIDUAL STATISTICS

### RUSHING

| NEW ENGLAND | No. | Yds. | Avg. | MIAMI | No. | Yds. | Avg. |
|---|---|---|---|---|---|---|---|
| C. James | 22 | 105 | 4.8 | Carter | 6 | 56 | 9.3 |
| Weathers | 16 | 87 | 5.4 | Davenport | 3 | 6 | 2.0 |
| Collins | 12 | 61 | 5.1 | Nathan | 2 | 4 | 2.0 |
| Tatupu | 6 | 9 | 1.5 | Bennett | 1 | 2 | 2.0 |
| Eason | 3 | -7 | -2.3 | Marino | 1 | 0 | 0.0 |
| | 59 | 255 | 4.3 | | 13 | 68 | 5.2 |

### RECEIVING

| | No. | Yds. | Avg. | | No. | Yds. | Avg. |
|---|---|---|---|---|---|---|---|
| D. Ramsey | 3 | 18 | 6.0 | Nathan | 5 | 57 | 11.4 |
| Collins | 3 | 15 | 5.0 | Hardy | 3 | 52 | 17.3 |
| Morgan | 2 | 30 | 15.0 | Duper | 3 | 45 | 15.0 |
| Tatupu | 1 | 6 | 6.0 | Clayton | 3 | 41 | 13.7 |
| Weathers | 1 | 2 | 2.0 | Davenport | 3 | 23 | 7.7 |
| | 10 | 71 | 7.1 | Johnson | 1 | 10 | 10.0 |
| | | | | Moore | 1 | 10 | 10.0 |
| | | | | Rose | 1 | 10 | 10.0 |
| | | | | | 20 | 248 | 12.4 |

### PUNTING

| | | | | | | |
|---|---|---|---|---|---|---|
| Camarillo | 5 | 40.2 | | Roby | 4 | 41.3 |

### PUNT RETURNS

| | No. | Yds. | Avg. | | No. | Yds. | Avg. |
|---|---|---|---|---|---|---|---|
| R. James | 2 | 2 | 1.0 | Vigorito | 1 | 8 | 8.0 |

### KICKOFF RETURNS

| | No. | Yds. | Avg. | | No. | Yds. | Avg. |
|---|---|---|---|---|---|---|---|
| Starring | 3 | 67 | 22.3 | Hampton | 6 | 91 | 15.2 |

### INTERCEPTION RETURNS

| | No. | Yds. | Avg. | | |
|---|---|---|---|---|---|
| Marion | 1 | 21 | 21.0 | none | |
| Clayborn | 1 | 0 | 0.0 | | |
| | 2 | 21 | 10.5 | | |

### PASSING

| NEW ENGLAND | Att. | Comp. | Comp. Pct. | Yds. | Int. | Yds./ Att. | Yds./ Comp. |
|---|---|---|---|---|---|---|---|
| Eason | 12 | 10 | 83.3 | 71 | 0 | 5.9 | 7.1 |
| **MIAMI** | | | | | | | |
| Marino | 48 | 20 | 41.7 | 248 | 2 | 5.2 | 12.4 |

# Cinderella and the 45 Bears

The 20th Super Bowl had the makings of one of the all-time David-and-Goliath stories. On one side were the Chicago Bears with a 15-1 regular-season record and fresh off two post-season shutouts to win the N.F.C. crown hands down, as just about everyone expected they would. The Bears, with their bone-crushing defense, unpredictable quarterback and ground-eating running game, were cast inevitably as Goliath. As David: the New England Patriots, a respectable 11-5 on the season but barely in the playoffs as the second wild-card team. After winning three road games against supposedly stronger opponents, the Patriots needed only a victory over the ferocious Bears to become the ultimate Cinderella team. But midnight struck early in the Louisiana Superdome. Goliath took away David's rocks and buried him in the most one-sided Super Bowl ever.

On the second play of the game, Chicago's Walter Payton fumbled, and the Patriots' Don Blackmon recovered on the Chicago 19. The Patriots had gotten to the Super Bowl by taking advantage of opponents' miscues. Three incomplete passes later, it was fourth-and-10. Tony Franklin, New England's barefoot kicker, booted a 36-yard field goal to give the Patriots a 3-0 lead, the high point of their day.

As though shocked to have someone finally score against them, the Bears roared back. Jim McMahon's 43-yard pass to Willie Gault put them in New England territory, and Matt Suhey picked up another first down on two carries. When the Patriots stiffened, Kevin Butler tied the score at 3-3 with a 28-yard field goal.

New England suddenly developed fumble-itis. Super Bowl MVP Richard Dent sacked Tony Eason, who fumbled at the 13. Butler put the Bears in front with a successful 24-yard boot. As soon as the Patriots got the ball back, Craig James fumbled and Mike Singletary recovered, again at the 13. Two plays later, when Suhey burst 11 yards for a touchdown, the game was as good as over.

The Bears tacked on 10 more points in the second quarter. McMahon's two-yard run capped a 59-yard scoring drive to make it 20-3. Eason was 0-for-6 with his passes, and coach Raymond Berry sent in veteran Steve Grogan at quarterback. It didn't help. Chicago held the ball for 11 plays on a 72-yard drive before Butler kicked his third field goal, this one from 24 yards.

In piling up a 23-3 lead, the Bears had gained 236 total yards to the Patriots' minus-14!

The second half was only slightly better statistically for the Patriots, who saw the score go to 44-3 before they finally crossed the Bear goalline. After a short drive at the opening of the third quarter, New England punted to the Bear four. On first down, McMahon trashed the Pats with a 60-yard bomb to Gault. From there, the Bears drove in, with McMahon sneaking over from the one. Three plays later, Chicago reserve cornerback Reggie Phillips stepped in front of a Grogan pass and ran it back 28 yards for another touchdown. Still another New England fumble gave the Bears the ball again. Chicago drove 30 yards to the Patriot one. William "The Refrigerator" Perry had gained national notoriety by occasionally masquerading as a roly-poly fullback, and the Bears now satisfied his fans as he took the ball into the endzone on a one-yard smash.

In the final quarter, with the game more than lost, the Patriots put on their only sustained drive of the day against the Bears' second-stringers: 76 yards to an eight-yard Grogan-to-Irving Fryar scoring pass. But the Bears had the last word. With four minutes left, Henry Waechter tackled Grogan behind the goalline for a safety.

## LINEUPS

| CHICAGO | | NEW ENGLAND |
|---|---|---|
| **OFFENSE** | | |
| Gault | WR | Morgan |
| Covert | LT | Holloway |
| Bortz | LG | Hannah |
| Hilgenberg | C | Brock |
| Thayer | RG | Wooten |
| Van Horne | RT | Moore |
| Moorehead | TE | Dawson |
| McKinnon | WR | Starring |
| McMahon | QB | Eason |
| Payton | RB | Collins |
| Suhey | RB | James |
| **DEFENSE** | | |
| Hampton | LE | Veris |
| McMichael | LT/NT | Williams |
| Perry | RT/RE | Adams |
| Dent | RE/LOLB | Tippett |
| Wilson | LLB/LILB | Nelson |
| Singletary | MLB/RILB | McGrew |
| Marshall | RLB/ROLB | Blackmon |
| Richardson | LCB | Lippett |
| Frazier | RCB | Clayborn |
| Duerson | SS | James |
| Fencik | FS | Marion |

| SUBSTITUTES | | |
|---|---|---|
| **CHICAGO** | | |
| **OFFENSE** | | |
| Andrews | Humphries | Thomas |
| Frederick | Margerum | Tomczak |
| Fuller | Ortego | Wrightman |
| Gentry | Sanders | |
| **DEFENSE** | | |
| Cabral | Keys | Rivera |
| Gayle | Morrissey | Taylor |
| Hartenstine | Phillips | Thrift |
| | **KICKERS** | |
| Buford | Butler | |
| **NEW ENGLAND** | | |
| **OFFENSE** | | |
| Fairchild | Jones | Ramsey |
| Fryar | Morriss | Tatupu |
| Grogan | Plunkett | Weathers |
| Hawthorne | | |
| **DEFENSE** | | |
| Bowman | McSwain | Reynolds |
| Creswell | Owens | Thomas |
| Gibson | Ramsey | Williams |
| Ingram | Rembert | |
| | **KICKERS** | |
| Camarillo | Franklin | |

## SCORING

| | | | | | |
|---|---|---|---|---|---|
| CHICAGO | 13 | 10 | 21 | 2- | 46 |
| NEW ENGLAND | 3 | 0 | 0 | 7- | 10 |

**First Quarter**
N.E. — Franklin, 36 yard field goal
Chi. — Butler, 28 yard field goal
Chi. — Butler, 24 yard field goal
Chi. — Suhey, 11 yard rush
　　PAT—Butler (kick)

**Second Quarter**
Chi. — McMahon, 2 yard rush
　　PAT—Butler (kick)
Chi. — Butler, 24 yard field goal

**Third Quarter**
Chi. — McMahon, 1 yard rush
　　PAT—Butler (kick)
Chi. — Phillips, 28 yard interception return
　　PAT—Butler (kick)
Chi. — Perry, 1 yard rush
　　PAT—Butler (kick)

**Fourth Quarter**
N.E. — Fryar, 8 yard pass from Grogan
　　PAT—Franklin (kick)
Chi. — Safety, Waechter tackled Grogan in end zone

## TEAM STATISTICS

| CHI | | NE |
|---|---|---|
| 23 | First Downs- Total | 12 |
| 13 | First Downs- Rushing | 1 |
| 9 | First Downs- Passing | 10 |
| 1 | First Downs- Penalty | 1 |
| 3 | Fumbles- Number | 4 |
| 2 | Fumbles- Lost Ball | 4 |
| 7 | Penalties- Number | 5 |
| 40 | Yards Penalized | 35 |
| 0 | Missed Field Goals | 0 |
| 76 | Offensive Plays | 54 |
| 408 | Net Yards | 123 |
| 5.4 | Average Gain | 2.3 |
| 2 | Giveaways | 6 |
| 6 | Takeaways | 2 |
| +4 | Difference | -4 |

## INDIVIDUAL STATISTICS

### RUSHING

| CHICAGO | No. | Yds. | Avg. | NEW ENGLAND | No. | Yds. | Avg |
|---|---|---|---|---|---|---|---|
| Payton | 22 | 61 | 2.8 | C. James | 5 | 1 | 0.2 |
| Suhey | 11 | 52 | 4.7 | Collins | 3 | 4 | 0.8 |
| McMahon | 5 | 14 | 2.8 | Grogan | 1 | 3 | 3.0 |
| Sanders | 4 | 15 | 3.8 | Weathers | 1 | 3 | 3.0 |
| Gentry | 3 | 15 | 5.0 | Hawthorne | 1 | -4 | -4.0 |
| Thomas | 2 | 8 | 4.0 | | 11 | 7 | 0.6 |
| Fuller | 1 | 1 | 1.0 | | | | |
| Perry | 1 | 1 | 1.0 | | | | |
| | 49 | 167 | 3.4 | | | | |

### RECEIVING

| CHICAGO | No. | Yds. | Avg. | NEW ENGLAND | No. | Yds. | Avg |
|---|---|---|---|---|---|---|---|
| Gault | 4 | 129 | 32.3 | Morgan | 7 | 70 | 10.0 |
| Gentry | 2 | 41 | 20.5 | Starring | 2 | 39 | 19.5 |
| Margerum | 2 | 36 | 18.0 | Fryar | 2 | 24 | 12.0 |
| Moorehead | 2 | 22 | 11.0 | Collins | 2 | 19 | 9.5 |
| Suhey | 1 | 24 | 24.0 | Ramsey | 2 | 16 | 8.0 |
| Thomas | 1 | 4 | 4.0 | C. James | 1 | 6 | 6.0 |
| | 12 | 256 | 21.3 | Weathers | 1 | 3 | 3.0 |
| | | | | | 17 | 177 | 10.4 |

### PUNTING

| | No. | | Avg. | | No. | | Avg |
|---|---|---|---|---|---|---|---|
| Buford | 4 | | 43.3 | Camarillo | 6 | | 43.8 |

### PUNT RETURNS

| | No. | Yds. | Avg. | | No. | Yds. | Avg |
|---|---|---|---|---|---|---|---|
| Ortego | 2 | 20 | 10.0 | Fryar | 2 | 22 | 11.0 |

### KICKOFF RETURNS

| | No. | Yds. | Avg. | | No. | Yds. | Avg |
|---|---|---|---|---|---|---|---|
| Gault | 4 | 49 | 12.3 | Starring | 7 | 153 | 21.9 |

### INTERCEPTION RETURNS

| | No. | Yds. | Avg. | | |
|---|---|---|---|---|---|
| Morrissey | 1 | 47 | 47.0 | none | |
| Phillips | 1 | 28 | 28.0 | | |
| | 2 | 75 | 37.5 | | |

### PASSING

| CHICAGO | Att. | Comp. | Pct. | Yds. | Yds./Int. | Yds./Att. | Comp. | Yards Lost Tackled |
|---|---|---|---|---|---|---|---|---|
| McMahon | 20 | 12 | 60.0 | 256 | 0 | 12.8 | 21.3 | 3-15 |
| Fuller | 4 | 0 | 0.0 | 0 | 0 | 0.0 | 0.0 | 0-0 |
| | 24 | 12 | 50.0 | 256 | 0 | 10.7 | 21.3 | 3-15 |
| **NEW ENGLAND** | | | | | | | | |
| Grogan | 30 | 17 | 56.7 | 177 | 2 | 5.9 | 10.4 | 4-33 |
| Eason | 6 | 0 | 0.0 | 0 | 0 | 0.0 | 0.0 | 3-28 |
| | 36 | 17 | 47.2 | 177 | 2 | 4.9 | 10.4 | 7-61 |

517

It didn't start as New York's year. Running back Joe Morris held out for contract renegotiation until four hours before the first game, and then the Giants dropped the opener to arch-rival Dallas 31-28. Top wide receiver Lionel Manuel was injured most of the time. Still, coach Bill Parcells' men won their next five before losing at Seattle. After that, they just kept on winning, rolling to the Eastern Division championship. In addition to N.F.L. foes, they had to face constant comparison with outstanding Giants' teams of the 1950s and early '60s that had not won the Big One. Much of that stopped after a December 1 meeting at San Francisco when the Giants trailed 17-0 at the half and came back to win 21-17. Quarterback Phil Simms wasn't selected to the Pro Bowl, but eight other Giants were. By season's end, one of TV's most familiar scenes was Harry Carson's ceremonial dumping of a tub full of Gatorade on Parcells after every New York victory.

## EASTERN DIVISION

**New York Giants** — Morris rushed for 1,516 yards and scored 14 touchdowns. Simms picked up 3,487 yards passing and proved he was a team leader. The offensive line was young and cohesive, and tight end Mark Bavaro blocked brilliantly and caught 66 passes for 1,001 yards. The Giants had a more-than-adequate offense. But the defense was still the key to success. Lawrence Taylor led the N.F.L. in sacks with 20 1/2 from his linebacker position and was named league MVP. Carl Banks, on the other side, was almost his equal, and Carson held his own, too. The front three also came in for recognition: end George Martin was steady and his counterpart, Leonard Marshall, had a Pro Bowl year, as did classic overachiever Jim Burt, the nose tackle.

**Washington Redskins** — Quarterback Jay Schroeder proved the promise he showed in the final five games of '85 was no fluke, throwing for a club-record 4,109 yards and pulling out six victories after his team trailed going into the fourth quarter. George Rogers rumbled for 1,203 yards and 18 touchdowns, and U.S.F.L. refugee Kelvin Bryant was an excellent all-purpose back after recovering from an early-season injury. Receivers Art Monk and Gary Clark provided a potent one-two punch with more than 70 catches and 1,000 yards apiece. Free-spirit defensive end Dexter Manley led an aggressive defense with 18 1/2 sacks, another club record. Even though nearly a third of the roster was new, the Skins would have won the division if they'd been able to beat the Giants. Two losses to New York left them second, but with a wild-card berth.

**Dallas Cowboys** — The Cowboys never recovered from a mid-season 17-14 loss to the Giants in which quarterback Danny White suffered a broken wrist. Defensive tackle Randy White and running back Tony Dorsett were also slowed by injuries, others began to show their age, and the team dropped seven of its last eight games to finish below .500 for the first time since 1965. The tailspin spoiled an impressive N.F.L. debut for Herschel Walker, about the only bright spot on coach Tom Landry's roster. Lining up at several positions, Walker topped the team in receiving, finished a close second to Dorsett in rushing, and scored 14 touchdowns.

**Philadelphia Eagles** — New coach Buddy Ryan began the season predicting a playoff berth, but the Eagles retreated from also-rans to also-staggereds. Ryan tore the '85 roster apart, cutting 20 players, including nine starters. The result was disaster. The offensive line gave up an incredible 104 sacks, shattering the league record of 70. Veteran QB Ron Jaworski was buffeted regularly and finally put out permanently in game 10. His replacement, Randall Cunningham, survived only because he was a faster runner. Wide receiver Mike Quick managed 60 catches, and defensive end Reggie White went to the Pro Bowl. Ryan went back to the drawing board.

**St. Louis Cardinals** — Injured, undermanned and inexperienced, the Cardinals were never in the race and seldom interesting, as witness their league-low attendance. The team MVP was 31-year-old journeyman receiver J.T. Smith, whose 80 catches were a pleasant surprise. Vai Sikahema had plenty of opportunity to return kicks and took two punts back for touchdowns in the final game to provide one of the team's four wins. All-time leading rusher Ottis Anderson was traded to the Giants. Quarterback Neil Lomax continued to slump and was replaced at mid-season by Cliff Stoudt for a while. Nothing helped.

## CENTRAL DIVISION

**Chicago Bears** — Quarterback Jim McMahon injured his shoulder in the opening game, was in and out of the lineup, and went out for good in week 12 after a controversial late hit. Even though coach Mike Ditka's men lost only twice, fans blamed McMahon's injury for the team's failure to blow out opponents. The Bears tried Mike Tomczak and Steve Fuller at quarterback, and ended with mid-season acquisition Doug Flutie, but none could provide McMahon's magic. The shaky quarterback situation offset a typical Walter Payton year (1,333 yards) and a record-setting performance by the defense. Mike Singletary, Wilber Marshall, Steve McMichael, et al., held opponents to just 187 points, the lowest ever for a 16-game season.

**Minnesota Vikings** — The Vikings continued to improve in '86, reaching the status of playoff contender. They would have made it to participant had they not blown fourth-quarter leads to Cleveland, the Giants and Washington. Quarterback Tommy Kramer enjoyed the best season of his 10-year career, leading the N.F.C. in passing. He credited his improved throwing to eating oysters the night before games, but most observers felt the nucleus of young talent the Vikings had stockpiled to surround him had more to do with it. Running back Darrin Nelson and receivers Anthony Carter and Steve Jordan continued to gain respect. Former U.S.F.L. offensive tackle Gary Zimmerman helped solidify the offensive line, and Keith Millard was marked a coming star at defensive tackle.

**Detroit Lions** — The Lions, who were 6-2 at home in '85, collapsed to 1-7 and were booed viciously. In a chicken-or-egg controversy, the Lions blamed the fans' booing for their poor play. The defense had an embarrassing habit of giving up big plays, especially late in the game, as happened when it blew 10- and 14-point leads in the final quarter to lose 44-40 in the nationally televised Thanksgiving Day game with Green Bay. Among the few highlights: a young and talented offensive line led by Lomas Brown, a pair of tough running backs in James Jones and Garry James, and some hope for the future in rookie quarterback Chuck Long's limited end-of-season play. The former Iowa All-American tossed a 34-yard touchdown on his first N.F.L. pass.

**Green Bay Packers** — After the Pack had finished at .500 in four of the past five years, coach Forrest Gregg decided the only way to move up was to tear the team apart and start over. He cut veterans Lynn Dickey, Paul Coffman and other regulars, and installed youngsters. Not surprisingly, the Packers were winless after six weeks. However, Gregg's drastic prescription began to look better as the season wore on. Three of the team's four victories came in the last six games. Quarterback Randy Wright, cornerback Mark Lee, kick returner Walter Stanley and a few others gave evidence that they just might make it in the N.F.L.

**Tampa Bay Buccaneers** — The Bucs spent their No. 1 pick in the '86 draft on Heisman Trophy winner Bo Jackson, but he opted to play baseball instead. The defense lost both ends to

FINAL TEAM STATISTICS

OFFENSE

| | ATL. | CHI. | DAL. | DET. | G.B. | L.A. | MINN. | N.O. | NY G | PHIL. | STL. | S.F. | T.B. | WASH. |
|---|---|---|---|---|---|---|---|---|---|---|---|---|---|---|
| FIRST DOWNS: | | | | | | | | | | | | | | |
| Total | 305 | 305 | 325 | 287 | 286 | 269 | 321 | 275 | 324 | 287 | 273 | 346 | 273 | 312 |
| by Rushing | 149 | 166 | 98 | 100 | 96 | 139 | 114 | 109 | 127 | 113 | 102 | 114 | 100 | 112 |
| by Passing | 137 | 118 | 199 | 156 | 172 | 105 | 186 | 137 | 171 | 150 | 149 | 213 | 142 | 177 |
| by Penalty | 19 | 21 | 28 | 31 | 18 | 25 | 21 | 29 | 26 | 24 | 22 | 19 | 31 | 23 |
| RUSHING: | | | | | | | | | | | | | | |
| Number | 578 | 606 | 447 | 470 | 424 | 578 | 461 | 505 | 558 | 499 | 419 | 510 | 455 | 474 |
| Yards | 2524 | 2700 | 1969 | 1771 | 1614 | 2457 | 1738 | 2074 | 2245 | 2002 | 1787 | 1986 | 1863 | 1732 |
| Average Yards | 4.4 | 4.5 | 4.4 | 3.8 | 3.8 | 4.3 | 3.8 | 4.1 | 4.0 | 4.0 | 4.3 | 3.9 | 4.1 | 3.7 |
| Touchdowns | 12 | 21 | 21 | 13 | 8 | 16 | 14 | 15 | 18 | 8 | 8 | 16 | 12 | 23 |
| PASSING: | | | | | | | | | | | | | | |
| Attempts | 452 | 415 | 547 | 500 | 565 | 403 | 519 | 425 | 472 | 514 | 516 | 582 | 459 | 542 |
| Completions | 246 | 208 | 319 | 286 | 305 | 194 | 290 | 232 | 260 | 268 | 293 | 353 | 245 | 276 |
| Completion Pct. | 54.4 | 50.1 | 58.3 | 57.2 | 54.0 | 48.1 | 55.9 | 54.6 | 55.1 | 52.1 | 56.8 | 60.7 | 53.4 | 50.9 |
| Passing Yards | 3046 | 2912 | 4003 | 3107 | 3708 | 2380 | 4185 | 2893 | 3500 | 3248 | 3140 | 4299 | 2892 | 4109 |
| Avg. Yds per Att. | 5.1 | 6.3 | 5.8 | 5.2 | 5.7 | 5.9 | 7.0 | 5.9 | 6.1 | 4.1 | 4.7 | 6.7 | 4.9 | 6.8 |
| Avg. Yds per Comp. | 12.4 | 14.0 | 12.6 | 10.9 | 12.2 | 12.3 | 14.4 | 12.5 | 13.5 | 12.1 | 10.7 | 12.2 | 11.8 | 14.9 |
| Times Tackled | 56 | 24 | 60 | 39 | 37 | 27 | 44 | 27 | 46 | 104 | 59 | 26 | 56 | 28 |
| Yds Lost Tackled | 464 | 153 | 498 | 323 | 261 | 184 | 272 | 225 | 367 | 708 | 424 | 203 | 394 | 240 |
| Net Yards | 2582 | 2759 | 3505 | 2784 | 3447 | 2196 | 3913 | 2668 | 3133 | 2540 | 2716 | 4096 | 2498 | 3869 |
| Touchdowns | 14 | 12 | 21 | 18 | 18 | 15 | 31 | 13 | 22 | 19 | 17 | 21 | 13 | 22 |
| Interceptions | 17 | 25 | 24 | 20 | 27 | 15 | 15 | 25 | 22 | 17 | 19 | 20 | 25 | 22 |
| Pct. Intercepted | 3.8 | 6.0 | 4.4 | 4.0 | 4.8 | 3.7 | 2.9 | 5.9 | 4.7 | 3.3 | 3.7 | 3.4 | 5.4 | 4.1 |
| PUNTS: | | | | | | | | | | | | | | |
| Number | 79 | 70 | 87 | 85 | 75 | 98 | 73 | 82 | 79 | 111 | 92 | 85 | 78 | 75 |
| Average | 43.3 | 40.7 | 40.2 | 39.9 | 37.7 | 38.2 | 40.0 | 42.1 | 44.8 | 41.0 | 37.1 | 40.6 | 40.2 | 43.6 |
| PUNT RETURNS | | | | | | | | | | | | | | |
| Number | 44 | 57 | 46 | 43 | 33 | 42 | 31 | 47 | 41 | 44 | 45 | 43 | 26 | 51 |
| Yards | 292 | 482 | 252 | 420 | 316 | 361 | 215 | 377 | 287 | 374 | 528 | 397 | 110 | 550 |
| Average Yards | 6.6 | 8.5 | 5.5 | 9.8 | 9.6 | 8.6 | 6.9 | 8.0 | 7.0 | 8.5 | 11.7 | 9.2 | 4.2 | 10.8 |
| Touchdowns | 0 | 0 | 0 | 1 | 1 | 0 | 0 | 0 | 0 | 1 | 2 | 1 | 0 | 0 |
| KICKOFF RET.: | | | | | | | | | | | | | | |
| Number | 54 | 50 | 59 | 67 | 76 | 59 | 56 | 55 | 50 | 53 | 70 | 42 | 75 | 60 |
| Yards | 1035 | 1115 | 1208 | 1321 | 1470 | 1160 | 1200 | 1332 | 868 | 945 | 1548 | 757 | 1302 | 1175 |
| Average Yards | 19.2 | 22.3 | 20.5 | 19.7 | 19.3 | 19.7 | 21.4 | 24.2 | 17.4 | 17.8 | 22.1 | 18.0 | 17.4 | 19.6 |
| Touchdowns | 0 | 2 | 0 | 0 | 0 | 0 | 0 | 1 | 0 | 0 | 0 | 0 | 0 | 0 |
| INTERCEPT RET.: | | | | | | | | | | | | | | |
| Number | 22 | 31 | 17 | 22 | 20 | 28 | 24 | 26 | 24 | 23 | 10 | 39 | 13 | 19 |
| Yards | 294 | 370 | 183 | 190 | 147 | 458 | 319 | 235 | 296 | 124 | 121 | 578 | 128 | 126 |
| Average Yards | 13.4 | 11.9 | 10.8 | 8.6 | 7.4 | 16.4 | 13.3 | 9.0 | 12.3 | 5.4 | 12.1 | 14.8 | 9.8 | 6.6 |
| Touchdowns | 2 | 1 | 1 | 0 | 1 | 3 | 2 | 1 | 1 | 0 | 0 | 5 | 0 | 0 |
| PENALTIES: | | | | | | | | | | | | | | |
| Number | 99 | 98 | 112 | 84 | 128 | 84 | 96 | 109 | 96 | 102 | 116 | 95 | 83 | 94 |
| Yards | 763 | 765 | 936 | 658 | 949 | 603 | 890 | 855 | 738 | 901 | 932 | 691 | 661 | 860 |
| FUMBLES: | | | | | | | | | | | | | | |
| Number | 31 | 36 | 44 | 30 | 35 | 39 | 31 | 33 | 31 | 34 | 25 | 32 | 36 | 29 |
| Number Lost | 16 | 22 | 17 | 17 | 18 | 22 | 14 | 18 | 10 | 10 | 10 | 9 | 17 | 10 |
| POINTS: | | | | | | | | | | | | | | |
| Total | 280 | 352 | 346 | 277 | 254 | 309 | 398 | 288 | 371 | 256 | 218 | 374 | 239 | 368 |
| PAT Attempts | 30 | 38 | 43 | 32 | 29 | 36 | 48 | 30 | 42 | 27 | 27 | 43 | 27 | 45 |
| PAT Made | 29 | 36 | 43 | 31 | 29 | 34 | 44 | 30 | 41 | 26 | 23 | 41 | 26 | 38 |
| FG Attempts | 36 | 41 | 21 | 25 | 27 | 24 | 28 | 30 | 37 | 31 | 24 | 35 | 24 | 32 |
| FG Made | 23 | 28 | 15 | 18 | 17 | 17 | 22 | 26 | 26 | 20 | 11 | 25 | 17 | 18 |
| Percent FG Made | 63.9 | 68.3 | 71.4 | 72.0 | 63.0 | 70.8 | 78.6 | 86.7 | 70.3 | 64.5 | 45.8 | 71.4 | 70.8 | 56.3 |
| Safeties | 1 | 2 | 0 | 0 | 0 | 1 | 0 | 0 | 0 | 1 | 0 | 0 | 0 | 0 |

DEFENSE

| | ATL. | CHI. | DAL. | DET. | G.B. | L.A. | MINN. | N.O. | NY G | PHIL. | STL. | S.F. | T.B. | WASH. |
|---|---|---|---|---|---|---|---|---|---|---|---|---|---|---|
| FIRST DOWNS: | | | | | | | | | | | | | | |
| Total | 268 | 241 | 286 | 298 | 313 | 272 | 286 | 331 | 284 | 278 | 304 | 285 | 362 | 316 |
| by Rushing | 111 | 67 | 118 | 134 | 135 | 93 | 106 | 104 | 78 | 97 | 125 | 97 | 162 | 103 |
| by Passing | 139 | 151 | 148 | 148 | 151 | 169 | 155 | 197 | 177 | 156 | 149 | 169 | 177 | 181 |
| by Penalty | 18 | 23 | 20 | 16 | 27 | 10 | 25 | 30 | 29 | 25 | 30 | 19 | 23 | 32 |
| RUSHING: | | | | | | | | | | | | | | |
| Number | 485 | 427 | 500 | 519 | 565 | 460 | 481 | 486 | 350 | 458 | 560 | 406 | 558 | 459 |
| Yards | 1916 | 1463 | 2200 | 2349 | 2095 | 1681 | 1796 | 1559 | 1284 | 1989 | 2227 | 1555 | 2648 | 1805 |
| Average Yards | 4.0 | 3.4 | 4.4 | 4.5 | 3.7 | 3.7 | 3.7 | 3.2 | 3.7 | 4.3 | 4.0 | 3.8 | 4.7 | 3.9 |
| Touchdowns | 10 | 4 | 17 | 15 | 16 | 9 | 10 | 11 | 10 | 14 | 17 | 8 | 31 | 14 |
| PASSING: | | | | | | | | | | | | | | |
| Attempts | 453 | 513 | 464 | 468 | 448 | 539 | 494 | 576 | 587 | 532 | 436 | 604 | 484 | 532 |
| Completions | 241 | 243 | 226 | 279 | 267 | 313 | 276 | 331 | 334 | 260 | 215 | 324 | 289 | 302 |
| Completion Pct. | 53.2 | 47.4 | 48.7 | 59.6 | 59.6 | 58.1 | 55.9 | 57.5 | 56.9 | 48.3 | 49.3 | 53.6 | 59.7 | 56.8 |
| Passing Yards | 3169 | 3170 | 3149 | 3090 | 3142 | 3482 | 3475 | 3886 | 3887 | 3641 | 2992 | 3773 | 3838 | 3916 |
| Avg. Yds per Att. | 6.3 | 4.6 | 5.4 | 5.5 | 6.1 | 5.5 | 6.1 | 5.7 | 5.4 | 5.5 | 5.5 | 5.1 | 7.3 | 6.0 |
| Avg. Yds per Comp. | 13.2 | 13.1 | 14.0 | 11.1 | 11.8 | 11.1 | 12.6 | 11.7 | 11.6 | 14.0 | 13.9 | 11.7 | 13.3 | 13.0 |
| Times Tackled | 26 | 62 | 53 | 41 | 28 | 39 | 38 | 47 | 59 | 53 | 41 | 51 | 19 | 55 |
| Yds Lost Tackled | 177 | 503 | 364 | 290 | 222 | 292 | 259 | 343 | 414 | 406 | 355 | 448 | 153 | 424 |
| Net Yards | 2992 | 2667 | 2785 | 2800 | 2920 | 3190 | 3216 | 3543 | 3473 | 3235 | 2637 | 3325 | 3685 | 3492 |
| Touchdowns | 19 | 12 | 21 | 14 | 31 | 17 | 16 | 21 | 15 | 21 | 21 | 18 | 23 | 21 |
| Interceptions | 22 | 31 | 17 | 22 | 20 | 28 | 24 | 26 | 24 | 23 | 10 | 39 | 13 | 19 |
| Pct. Intercepted | 4.9 | 6.0 | 3.7 | 4.7 | 4.5 | 5.2 | 4.9 | 4.5 | 4.1 | 4.3 | 2.3 | 6.5 | 2.7 | 3.6 |
| PUNTS: | | | | | | | | | | | | | | |
| Number | 83 | 100 | 87 | 68 | 70 | 96 | 75 | 78 | 89 | 97 | 83 | 91 | 59 | 95 |
| Average | 41.4 | 40.9 | 41.6 | 41.7 | 39.6 | 41.4 | 40.3 | 42.5 | 39.3 | 38.7 | 42.3 | 41.4 | 41.3 | 41.3 |
| PUNT RETURNS | | | | | | | | | | | | | | |
| Number | 47 | 23 | 41 | 39 | 44 | 47 | 40 | 37 | 41 | 63 | 44 | 49 | 39 | 36 |
| Yards | 477 | 110 | 301 | 517 | 287 | 416 | 356 | 234 | 386 | 634 | 296 | 373 | 414 | 220 |
| Average Yards | 10.1 | 4.8 | 7.3 | 13.3 | 6.5 | 8.9 | 8.9 | 6.3 | 9.4 | 10.1 | 6.7 | 7.6 | 10.6 | 6.1 |
| Touchdowns | 3 | 0 | 0 | 2 | 0 | 0 | 0 | 0 | 0 | 2 | 0 | 0 | 3 | 0 |
| KICKOFF RET.: | | | | | | | | | | | | | | |
| Number | 59 | 64 | 66 | 56 | 62 | 64 | 79 | 35 | 70 | 62 | 50 | 71 | 46 | 50 |
| Yards | 1190 | 1376 | 1358 | 1096 | 1181 | 1282 | 1532 | 662 | 1362 | 1261 | 886 | 1598 | 1009 | 1005 |
| Average Yards | 20.2 | 21.5 | 20.6 | 19.6 | 19.0 | 20.0 | 19.4 | 18.9 | 19.5 | 20.3 | 17.7 | 22.5 | 21.9 | 20.1 |
| Touchdowns | 0 | 0 | 0 | 0 | 0 | 0 | 0 | 0 | 0 | 0 | 0 | 1 | 1 | 0 |
| INTERCEPT RET.: | | | | | | | | | | | | | | |
| Number | 17 | 25 | 24 | 20 | 27 | 15 | 15 | 25 | 22 | 17 | 19 | 20 | 25 | 22 |
| Yards | 198 | 115 | 331 | 311 | 357 | 128 | 88 | 362 | 218 | 192 | 271 | 205 | 236 | 186 |
| Average Yards | 11.6 | 4.6 | 13.8 | 15.6 | 13.2 | 8.5 | 5.9 | 14.5 | 9.9 | 11.3 | 14.3 | 10.3 | 9.4 | 8.5 |
| Touchdowns | 1 | 1 | 2 | 2 | 3 | 0 | 0 | 0 | 1 | 1 | 2 | 0 | 1 | 0 |
| PENALTIES: | | | | | | | | | | | | | | |
| Number | 106 | 111 | 91 | 99 | 79 | 92 | 99 | 104 | 119 | 115 | 86 | 89 | 116 | 115 |
| Yards | 834 | 866 | 822 | 781 | 657 | 804 | 806 | 791 | 988 | 884 | 682 | 653 | 941 | 1026 |
| FUMBLES: | | | | | | | | | | | | | | |
| Number | 30 | 27 | 29 | 36 | 32 | 25 | 32 | 37 | 36 | 30 | 40 | 31 | 39 | 21 |
| Number Lost | 14 | 16 | 18 | 19 | 12 | 15 | 18 | 17 | 19 | 13 | 12 | 10 | 19 | 9 |
| POINTS: | | | | | | | | | | | | | | |
| Total | 280 | 187 | 337 | 326 | 418 | 267 | 273 | 287 | 236 | 312 | 351 | 247 | 473 | 296 |
| PAT Attempts | 34 | 20 | 41 | 36 | 52 | 27 | 27 | 34 | 26 | 39 | 40 | 29 | 58 | 35 |
| PAT Made | 31 | 19 | 39 | 36 | 48 | 27 | 24 | 32 | 26 | 37 | 37 | 28 | 56 | 35 |
| FG Attempts | 26 | 22 | 30 | 35 | 25 | 31 | 33 | 27 | 25 | 26 | 32 | 25 | 30 | 24 |
| FG Made | 15 | 16 | 16 | 24 | 18 | 24 | 27 | 17 | 18 | 13 | 24 | 15 | 21 | 17 |
| Percent FG Made | 57.7 | 72.7 | 53.3 | 68.6 | 72.0 | 77.4 | 81.8 | 63.0 | 72.0 | 50.0 | 75.0 | 60.0 | 70.0 | 70.8 |
| Safeties | 0 | 0 | 2 | 1 | 2 | 0 | 0 | 0 | 0 | 1 | 1 | 0 | 0 | 0 |

injury. At mid-season, coach Leeman Bennett cut Pro Bowl tight end Jimmie Giles and wide receiver Kevin House, his best long-distance receiver. The defense gave up 473 points and held opponents to no fewer than 20. Although quarterback Steve Young showed progress, the offense didn't and generally got worse as the season wound down. On merit, Tampa Bay won the right to pick first again in the '87 draft. This time, however, new coach Ray Perkins would make the pick, following the firing of Bennett.

## WESTERN DIVISION

**San Francisco 49ers** — Quarterback Joe Montana aggravated a chronic back injury in the opener and underwent surgery amid predictions that his season and possibly his career had ended. Although Jeff Kemp filled in well and wide receiver Jerry Rice emerged as the league's most dangerous breakaway threat, the 49ers struggled. They were only 5-3-1 when Montana, against his doctor's advice, returned to the lineup. It was a miraculous comeback. He sparked the 49ers to the top of the division in a drive that included wins over three playoff teams in the final three weeks. With all of Montana's heroics, the team lived by its defense, where free safety Ronnie Lott was an inspirational leader, topping the N.F.L. with 10 interceptions, including one he returned for a touchdown against Green Bay after he'd suffered a hairline fracture of his leg.

**Los Angeles Rams** —Last year's quarterback, Dieter Brock, was out for the year with injuries. Oft-injured Steve Bartkowski tried to get through one more season and lasted less than half. Steve Dils showed he wasn't the answer, though he did beat the Bears in November. When the Rams traded all-pro guard Kent Hill and three draft choices to Houston for the rights to highly touted Jim Everett, they hoped to have their quarterback of the future, then had to rush him into action in week 11. Everett did well behind one of football's best offensive lines. He also had a strong defense to give him the ball and Eric Dickerson to run with it. Dickerson gained more than 1,800 yards for the third time in four years. Still, the Rams dropped their last two games to let themselves be nosed out of the division crown.

**Atlanta Falcons** — After six weeks, the Falcons were 5-1 and being hailed as a playoff contender. Then the roof fell in. They went 2-7-1 the rest of the way, out of the money, including an embarrassing loss on a blocked punt in week 14 that gave the Colts their first victory. The defense, led by cornerback Scott Case and first-round nose tackle Tony Casillas, played well all season, and guard Bill Fralic was all-pro on offense. But running back Gerald Riggs was less effective than the year before, and quarterback David Archer was erratic and ultimately was injured. After the first three games, the offense averaged less than two touchdowns per game. When the season ended, coach Dan Henning was fired and replaced by his defensive coordinator, Marion Campbell, a former Falcon head man.

**New Orleans Saints** — Jim Finks, who'd built winners in Minnesota and Chicago, had become New Orleans general manager. Jim Mora, the U.S.F.L.'s most successful coach, took over on the sideline. And the Saints limped out of the starting gate at 1-4. Mora handed out fines, benched and cut starters and, in general, proved to his minions that he was in charge. Under his harsh hand, the Saints became a respectable 6-5 the rest of the way. Running back Rueben Mayes, a third-round draft choice, was the N.F.C.'s top rookie, and linebacker Rickey Jackson played back to his Pro Bowl standard. The team still had never had a winning season, but there was hope.

## NEW YORK GIANTS 14-2 Bill Parcells

| Scores of Each Game | | |
|---|---|---|
| 28 | Dallas | 31 |
| 20 | SAN DIEGO | 7 |
| 14 | L.A.Raiders | 9 |
| 20 | NEW ORLEANS | 17 |
| 13 | St.Louis | 6 |
| 35 | PHILADELPHIA | 3 |
| 12 | Seattle | 17 |
| 27 | WASHINGTON | 20 |
| 17 | DALLAS | 14 |
| 17 | Philadelphia | 14 |
| 22 | Minnesota | 20 |
| 19 | DENVER | 16 |
| 21 | San Francisco | 17 |
| 24 | Washington | 14 |
| 27 | ST.LOUIS | 7 |
| 55 | GREEN BAY | 24 |

| Use Name | Pos. | Hgt | Wgt | Age | Int | Pts |
|---|---|---|---|---|---|---|
| Brad Benson | OT | 6'3" | 270 | 30 | | |
| Damian Johnson | OT-OG | 6'5" | 290 | 23 | | |
| Karl Nelson | OT | 6'6" | 285 | 26 | | |
| William Roberts | OT | 6'5" | 280 | 24 | | |
| Billy Ard | OG | 6'3" | 270 | 27 | | |
| Chris Godfrey | OG | 6'3" | 265 | 28 | | |
| Brian Johnston | C | 6'3" | 275 | 23 | | |
| Bart Oates | C | 6'3" | 265 | 27 | | |
| Eric Dorsey | DE | 6'5" | 280 | 22 | | |
| Leonard Marshall | DE | 6'3" | 285 | 24 | | |
| George Martin | DE | 6'4" | 255 | 33 | 1 | 6 |
| John Washington | DE | 6'4" | 275 | 23 | | |
| Jim Burt | NT | 6'1" | 260 | 27 | | |
| Erik Howard | NT | 6'4" | 268 | 21 | | |
| Jerome Sally | NT | 6'3" | 270 | 27 | | |
| Carl Banks | LB | 6'4" | 235 | 24 | | |
| Harry Carson | LB | 6'2" | 240 | 32 | 1 | |
| Andy Headen | LB | 6'5" | 242 | 26 | 1 | |
| Byron Hunt | LB | 6'5" | 242 | 27 | | |
| Pepper Johnson | LB | 6'3" | 248 | 22 | 1 | |
| Robbie Jones | LB | 6'2" | 230 | 26 | | |
| Gary Reasons | LB | 6'4" | 234 | 24 | 2 | |
| Lawrence Taylor | LB | 6'3" | 243 | 27 | | |
| Mark Collins | DB | 5'10" | 190 | 22 | 1 | |
| Kenny Hill | DB | 6' | 195 | 28 | 3 | |
| Terry Kinard | DB | 6'1" | 200 | 26 | 4 | |
| Greg Lasker | DB | 6' | 200 | 21 | 1 | |
| Elvis Patterson | DB | 5'11" | 188 | 25 | 2 | |
| Herb Welch | DB | 5'11" | 180 | 25 | 2 | |
| Perry Wiliams | DB | 6'2" | 203 | 25 | 4 | |
| Jeff Hostetler | QB | 6'3" | 212 | 25 | | |
| Jeff Rutledge | QB | 6'1" | 195 | 29 | | |
| Phil Simms | QB | 6'3" | 214 | 29 | | 6 |
| Joe Morris | HB | 5'7" | 195 | 25 | | 90 |
| Lee Rouson | HB | 6'1" | 222 | 23 | | 18 |
| Maurice Carthon | FB | 6'1" | 225 | 25 | | |
| Tony Galbreath | FB | 6' | 228 | 32 | | |
| Bobby Johnson | WR | 5'11" | 171 | 24 | | 30 |
| Lionel Manuel | WR | 5'11" | 180 | 24 | | 18 |
| Phil McConkey (from GB) | WR | 5'10" | 170 | 29 | | 6 |
| Solomon Miller | WR | 6'1" | 185 | 21 | | 12 |
| Stacy Robinson | WR | 5'11" | 186 | 24 | | 12 |
| Vince Warren | WR | 6' | 180 | 23 | | |
| Mark Bavaro | TE | 6'4" | 245 | 23 | | 24 |
| Zeke Mowatt | TE | 6'3" | 240 | 25 | | 12 |
| Raul Allegre | K | 5'10" | 167 | 27 | | 105 |
| Joe Cooper | K | 5'10" | 175 | 25 | | |
| Sean Landeta | K | 6' | 200 | 24 | | |
| Bob Thomas | K | 5'10" | 175 | 34 | | 4 |

George Adams - Knee Injury
Tyrone Davis - Back Injury
David Jordan - Broken Ankle
Curtis McGriff - Leg Injury

## WASHINGTON REDSKINS 12-4 Joe Gibbs

| Scores of Each Game | | |
|---|---|---|
| 41 | PHILADELPHIA | 14 |
| 10 | L.A.RAIDERS | 6 |
| 30 | San Diego | 14 |
| 19 | SEATTLE | 14 |
| 14 | New Orleans | 6 |
| 6 | Dallas | 30 |
| 28 | ST.LOUIS | 21 |
| 20 | N.Y.Giants | 27 |
| 44 | MINNESOTA | *38 |
| 16 | Green Bay | 7 |
| 14 | SAN FRANCISCO | 6 |
| 41 | DALLAS | 14 |
| 20 | St.Louis | 17 |
| 14 | N.Y.GIANTS | 24 |
| 30 | Denver | 31 |
| 21 | Philadelphia | 14 |

| Use Name | Pos. | Hgt | Wgt | Age | Int | Pts |
|---|---|---|---|---|---|---|
| Joe Jacoby | OT | 6'7" | 305 | 27 | | |
| Mark May | OT | 6'6" | 295 | 26 | | |
| Dan McQuaid | OT | 6'7" | 278 | 25 | | |
| Russ Grimm | OG | 6'3" | 275 | 27 | | |
| Raleigh McKenzie | OG | 6'2" | 262 | 23 | | |
| R.C.Thielemann | OG | 6'4" | 262 | 31 | | |
| Ron Tilton | OG | 6'4" | 250 | 23 | | |
| Jeff Bostic | C | 6'2" | 260 | 27 | | |
| Tom Beasley | DE | 6'5" | 248 | 32 | | |
| Steve Hamilton | DE-DT | 6'4" | 255 | 24 | | |
| Markus Koch | DE | 6'5" | 275 | 23 | | |
| Dexter Manley | DE | 6'3" | 257 | 27 | | 6 |
| Charles Mann | DE | 6'6" | 270 | 25 | | |
| Dave Butz | DT | 6'7" | 295 | 36 | | |
| Darryl Grant | DT | 6'1" | 275 | 26 | | |
| Dean Hamel | DT | 6'3" | 275 | 25 | | |
| Shawn Burks | LB | 6'1" | 230 | 23 | | |
| Monte Coleman | LB | 6'2" | 230 | 28 | | |
| Calvin Daniels | LB | 6'3" | 241 | 27 | 1 | |
| Mel Kaufman | LB | 6'2" | 218 | 28 | | |
| Joe Krakowski | LB | 6'1" | 224 | 23 | | |
| Rich Milot | LB | 6'4" | 237 | 29 | 2 | |
| Neal Olkewicz | LB | 6' | 233 | 29 | 1 | |
| Jeff Paine | LB | 6'2" | 224 | 25 | | |
| Angelo Snipes (to SD) | LB | 6' | 215 | 23 | | |
| Todd Bowles | DB | 6'2" | 203 | 22 | 2 | |
| Ken Coffey | DB | 6' | 198 | 25 | 2 | |
| Vernon Dean | DB | 5'11" | 178 | 27 | 1 | |
| Darrell Green | DB | 5'8" | 170 | 26 | 5 | |
| Curtis Jordan | DB | 6'2" | 205 | 32 | 3 | |
| Tim Morrison | DB | 6'1" | 195 | 23 | | |
| Alvin Walton | DB | 6' | 180 | 22 | | |
| Barry Wilburn | DB | 6'3" | 186 | 22 | 2 | |
| Jay Schroeder | QB | 6'4" | 215 | 25 | | 6 |
| Doug Williams | QB | 6'4" | 220 | 31 | | |
| Kelvin Bryant | HB | 6'2" | 195 | 25 | | 42 |
| Dwight Garner | HB | 5'8" | 183 | 21 | | |
| Keith Griffin | HB | 5'8" | 185 | 24 | | |
| Ken Jenkins | HB | 5'8" | 185 | 27 | | |
| George Rogers | HB | 6'2" | 229 | 27 | | 108 |
| Ricky Sanders | HB | 5'11" | 180 | 24 | | 12 |
| Rick Badanjek | FB | 5'8" | 217 | 24 | | |
| Reggie Branch | FB | 5'11" | 227 | 23 | | |
| Gary Clark | WR | 5'9" | 173 | 24 | | 42 |
| Derek Holloway | WR | 5'7" | 166 | 25 | | |
| Art Monk | WR | 6'3" | 209 | 28 | | 24 |
| James Noble | WR | 6' | 193 | 23 | | |
| Clarence Verdin | WR | 5'8" | 160 | 23 | | |
| Eric Yarber | WR | 5'8" | 156 | 22 | | |
| Clint Didier | TE | 6'5" | 240 | 27 | | 24 |
| Todd Frain | TE | 6'2" | 235 | 24 | | |
| Anthony Jones | TE | 6'3" | 248 | 26 | | |
| Terry Orr | TE | 6'3" | 227 | 24 | | 6 |
| Don Warren | TE | 6'4" | 242 | 30 | | 6 |
| Jess Atkinson | K | 5'9" | 168 | 24 | | 3 |
| Steve Cox | K | 6'4" | 195 | 28 | | 9 |
| Mark Moseley (to CLE) | K | 5'11" | 204 | 38 | | 91 |
| Max Zendejas | K | 5'11" | 184 | 22 | | 50 |

## DALLAS COWBOYS 7-9 Tom Landry

| Scores of Each Game | | |
|---|---|---|
| 31 | N.Y.GIANTS | 28 |
| 31 | Detroit | 7 |
| 35 | ATLANTA | 37 |
| 31 | St.Louis | 7 |
| 14 | Denver | 29 |
| 30 | WASHINGTON | 6 |
| 17 | Philadelphia | 14 |
| 37 | ST.LOUIS | 6 |
| 14 | N.Y.Giants | 17 |
| 13 | L.A.RAIDERS | 17 |
| 24 | San Diego | 21 |
| 14 | Washington | 41 |
| 14 | SEATTLE | 31 |
| 10 | L.A.Rams | 29 |
| 21 | PHILADELPHIA | 23 |
| 10 | CHICAGO | 24 |

| Use Name | Pos. | Hgt | Wgt | Age | Int | Pts |
|---|---|---|---|---|---|---|
| Jim Cooper | OT | 6'5" | 268 | 30 | | |
| Phil Pozderac | OT | 6'9" | 283 | 26 | | |
| Howard Richards | OT | 6'6" | 269 | 27 | | |
| Brian Baldinger | OG | 6'4" | 262 | 27 | | |
| Crawford Ker | OG | 6'3" | 285 | 24 | | |
| Nate Nelson | OG | 6'3" | 317 | 24 | | |
| Glen Titensor | OG | 6'4" | 270 | 28 | | |
| Tom Rafferty | C | 6'3" | 262 | 32 | | |
| Mark Tuinei | C | 6'5" | 283 | 26 | | |
| Jesse Baker | DE | 6'5" | 271 | 29 | | |
| Kevin Brooks | DE | 6'6" | 273 | 23 | | |
| Jim Jeffcoat | DE | 6'5" | 260 | 25 | | |
| Too Tall Jones | DE | 6'9" | 273 | 25 | | |
| Bob Otto | DE | 6'6" | 251 | 23 | | |
| Kurt Ploeger (to BUF) | DE | 6'5" | 259 | 23 | | |
| John Dutton | DT | 6'7" | 261 | 35 | | |
| Don Smerek | DT | 6'7" | 262 | 28 | | |
| Randy White | DT | 6'4" | 265 | 33 | | |
| Steve DeOssie | LB | 6'2" | 245 | 23 | | |
| Mike Hegman | LB | 6'1" | 227 | 33 | | |
| Garth Jax | LB | 6'2" | 225 | 22 | | |
| Eugene Lockhart | LB | 6'2" | 235 | 25 | 1 | |
| Jesse Penn | LB | 6'3" | 218 | 23 | | |
| Jeff Rohrer | LB | 6'3" | 227 | 27 | | |
| Vince Albritton | DB | 6'2" | 210 | 24 | | |
| Bill Bates | DB | 6'1" | 204 | 25 | | |
| Michael Downs | DB | 6'3" | 204 | 27 | 6 | |
| Ron Fellows | DB | 6' | 173 | 27 | 5 | 6 |
| Cornell Gowdy | DB | 6' | 192 | 22 | | |
| Manny Hendrix | DB | 5'10" | 178 | 21 | | |
| Johnny Holloway | DB | 5'11" | 182 | 22 | 1 | |
| Victor Scott | DB | 6' | 203 | 24 | 1 | |
| Everson Walls | DB | 6'1" | 193 | 26 | 3 | |
| Reggie Collier | QB | 6'3" | 207 | 25 | | |
| Paul McDonald | QB | 6'2" | 185 | 28 | | |
| Steve Pelluer | QB | 6'4" | 208 | 24 | | 6 |
| Danny White | QB | 6'2" | 197 | 34 | | 6 |
| Darryl Clack | HB | 5'10" | 218 | 22 | | |
| Tony Dorsett | HB | 5'11" | 189 | 32 | | 36 |
| Robert Lavette | HB | 5'11" | 190 | 22 | | 6 |
| Herschel Walker | HB | 6'1" | 223 | 24 | | 84 |
| Todd Fowler | FB | 6'3" | 221 | 24 | | |
| Timmy Newsome | FB | 6'1" | 237 | 28 | | 30 |
| Gordon Banks | WR | 5'10" | 173 | 28 | | |
| Tony Hill | WR | 6'2" | 205 | 30 | | 18 |
| Karl Powe | WR | 6'2" | 178 | 24 | | |
| Mike Renfro | WR | 6' | 187 | 31 | | 18 |
| Mike Sherrard | WR | 6'2" | 187 | 23 | | 30 |
| Thornton Chandler | TE | 6'5" | 245 | 22 | | 12 |
| Doug Cosbie | TE | 6'6" | 238 | 30 | | 6 |
| Mike Saxon | K | 6'3" | 188 | 24 | | |
| Rafael Septien | K | 5'10" | 176 | 32 | | 88 |

Norm Granger - Hamstring Injury
Brian Salonen - Groin Injury
Kurt Petersen - Knee Injury

## PHILADELPHIA EAGLES 5-10-1 Buddy Ryan

| Scores of Each Game | | |
|---|---|---|
| 14 | Washington | 41 |
| 10 | Chicago | *13 |
| 7 | DENVER | 33 |
| 34 | L.A.RAMS | 20 |
| 16 | Atlanta | 0 |
| 3 | N.Y.Giants | 35 |
| 14 | DALLAS | 17 |
| 23 | SAN DIEGO | 7 |
| 10 | St.Louis | 13 |
| 14 | N.Y.GIANTS | 17 |
| 11 | DETROIT | 13 |
| 20 | Seattle | 24 |
| 33 | L.A.Raiders | *27 |
| 10 | ST.LOUIS | *10 |
| 23 | Dallas | 21 |
| 14 | WASHINGTON | 21 |

| Use Name | Pos. | Hgt | Wgt | Age | Int | Pts |
|---|---|---|---|---|---|---|
| Mike Black | OT-OG | 6'4" | 290 | 22 | | |
| Joe Conwell | OT | 6'5" | 275 | 25 | | |
| Jim Gilmore | OT | 6'5" | 262 | 23 | | |
| Tom Jelesky | OT | 6'6" | 275 | 25 | | |
| Leonard Mitchell | OT | 6'7" | 295 | 27 | | |
| Ron Baker | OG | 6'4" | 274 | 31 | | |
| Nick Haden | OG-C | 6'2" | 270 | 23 | | |
| Bob Landsee | OG-OT | 6'4" | 273 | 22 | | |
| Ken Reeves | OG-OT | 6'5" | 275 | 24 | | |
| Adam Schreiber | OG-C | 6'4" | 270 | 24 | | |
| Matt Darwin | C | 6'4" | 260 | 23 | | |
| Gerry Feehery | C | 6'2" | 270 | 26 | | |
| Greg Brown | DE | 6'5" | 265 | 29 | | 2 |
| Clyde Simmons | DE | 6'6" | 258 | 22 | | |
| Thomas Strauthers | DE | 6'4" | 264 | 25 | | |
| Jeff Tupper | DE | 6'5" | 269 | 23 | | |
| Reggie White | DE-DT | 6'5" | 285 | 24 | | |
| Ken Clarke | DT | 6'2" | 275 | 30 | | |
| Reggie Singletary | DT | 6'3" | 272 | 22 | | |
| Garry Cobb | LB | 6'2" | 230 | 29 | 1 | |
| Dwayne Jiles | LB | 6'4" | 242 | 24 | | |
| Alonzo Johnson | LB | 6'3" | 222 | 23 | 3 | |
| Seth Joyner | LB | 6'2" | 241 | 21 | 1 | |
| Rich Kraynak | LB | 6'1" | 230 | 25 | | |
| Byron Lee | LB | 6'2" | 230 | 21 | | |
| Mike Reichenbach | LB | 6'2" | 238 | 24 | | |
| Jody Schulz | LB | 6'3" | 235 | 26 | 1 | |
| Evan Cooper | DB | 5'11" | 184 | 24 | 3 | |
| Elbert Foules | DB | 5'11" | 185 | 25 | 1 | |
| William Frizzell | DB | 6'3" | 198 | 23 | | |
| Terry Hoage | DB | 6'3" | 198 | 24 | 1 | |
| Wes Hopkins | DB | 6'1" | 212 | 24 | | |
| Andre Waters | DB | 5'11" | 185 | 24 | 6 | |
| Brenard Wilson | DB | 6' | 185 | 31 | | |
| Roynell Young | DB | 6'1" | 185 | 28 | 6 | |
| Matt Cavanaugh | QB | 6'2" | 212 | 29 | | |
| Randall Cunningham | QB | 6'4" | 192 | 23 | | 30 |
| Ron Jaworski | QB | 6'2" | 199 | 35 | | |
| Kyle Mackey | QB | 6'3" | 219 | 24 | | |
| Keith Byars | HB | 6'1" | 230 | 22 | | 6 |
| Charles Crawford | HB | 6'2" | 235 | 22 | | 6 |
| Junior Tautalatasi | HB | 5'10" | 205 | 24 | | 12 |
| Michael Haddix | FB | 6'2" | 227 | 24 | | |
| Anthony Toney | FB | 6' | 227 | 23 | | 6 |
| Mike Waters | FB | 6'2" | 225 | 24 | | |
| Gregg Garrity | WR | 5'10" | 169 | 24 | | 6 |
| Kenny Jackson | WR | 6' | 180 | 24 | | 36 |
| Ron Johnson | WR | 6'3" | 186 | 27 | | 6 |
| Phil Smith | WR | 6'3" | 186 | 25 | | |
| Mike Quick | WR | 6'2" | 190 | 27 | | 54 |
| Byron Darby | TE | 6'4" | 262 | 26 | | |
| Dave Little | TE | 6'2" | 236 | 25 | | |
| John Spagnola | TE | 6'4" | 242 | 29 | | 6 |
| Paul McFadden | K | 5'11" | 163 | 24 | | 86 |
| John Teltschik | K | 6'2" | 215 | 22 | | |

## ST. LOUIS CARDINALS 4-11-1 Gene Stallings

| Scores of Each Game | | |
|---|---|---|
| 10 | L.A.RAMS | 16 |
| 13 | Atlanta | 33 |
| 10 | Buffalo | 17 |
| 7 | DALLAS | 31 |
| 6 | N.Y.GIANTS | 13 |
| 30 | Tampa Bay | 19 |
| 21 | Washington | 28 |
| 6 | Dallas | 37 |
| 13 | PHILADELPHIA | 10 |
| 17 | San Francisco | 43 |
| 7 | NEW ORLEANS | 16 |
| 23 | KANSAS CITY | 14 |
| 17 | WASHINGTON | 20 |
| 10 | Philadelphia | *10 |
| 7 | N.Y.Giants | 27 |
| 21 | TAMPA BAY | 17 |

| Use Name | Pos. | Hgt | Wgt | Age | Int | Pts |
|---|---|---|---|---|---|---|
| Ray Brown | OT-OG | 6'5" | 257 | 23 | | |
| Tootie Robbins | OT | 6'5" | 302 | 28 | | |
| Luis Sharpe | OT | 6'4" | 260 | 26 | | |
| Lance Smith | OT | 6'2" | 262 | 22 | | |
| Joe Bostic | OG | 6'3" | 268 | 29 | | |
| Doug Dawson | OG | 6'3" | 267 | 24 | | |
| Derek Kennard | OG | 6'3" | 285 | 23 | | |
| Gene Chilton | C | 6'3" | 271 | 22 | | |
| Randy Clark | C | 6'3" | 270 | 29 | | |
| Rob Monaco | C | 6'3" | 283 | 24 | | |
| Mike Ruether | C | 6'4" | 275 | 23 | | |
| Al Baker | DE | 6'6" | 270 | 29 | | |
| Bob Clasby | DE | 6'5" | 260 | 25 | | |
| Gary Dulin | DE | 6'4" | 275 | 29 | | |
| Van Hughes | DE | 6'3" | 280 | 25 | | |
| Stafford Mays | DE | 6'2" | 255 | 28 | | |
| Mark Duda | NT | 6'3" | 279 | 25 | | |
| David Galloway | NT | 6'3" | 279 | 27 | | |
| Charlie Baker | LB | 6'2" | 234 | 28 | | |
| Anthony Bell | LB | 6'3" | 231 | 22 | | |
| Rick DiBernardo | LB | 6'3" | 225 | 22 | | |
| E.J.Junior | LB | 6'3" | 235 | 26 | | |
| Ron Monaco | LB | 6'1" | 225 | 23 | | |
| Niko Noga | LB | 6'1" | 235 | 24 | | |
| Freddie Joe Nunn | LB | 6'4" | 228 | 24 | | |
| Carl Carter | DB | 5'11" | 180 | 22 | 2 | |
| Cedric Mack | DB | 6' | 194 | 25 | 4 | |
| Leonard Smith | DB | 5'11" | 202 | 25 | 1 | |
| Wayne Smith | DB | 6' | 170 | 29 | 1 | |
| Dennis Thurman | DB | 5'11" | 179 | 30 | | |
| Lionel Washington | DB | 6' | 188 | 25 | 2 | |
| Lonnie Young | DB | 6'1" | 182 | 23 | | |
| Kent Austin | QB | 6'1" | 195 | 23 | | |
| Neil Lomax | QB | 6'3" | 215 | 27 | | 6 |
| Cliff Stoudt | QB | 6'4" | 215 | 31 | | |
| Ottis Anderson (to NYG) | HB | 6'2" | 225 | 29 | | 2 |
| Stump Mitchell | HB | 5'9" | 188 | 27 | | 30 |
| Vai Sikahema | HB | 5'9 | 191 | 24 | | 18 |
| Earl Ferrell | FB | 6' | 224 | 28 | | 18 |
| Broderick Sargent | FB | 5'10" | 215 | 23 | | |
| Ron Wolfley | FB | 6' | 222 | 23 | | |
| Chas Fox | WR | 5'11" | 180 | 22 | | 6 |
| Roy Green | WR | 6' | 195 | 29 | | 36 |
| Scott Holman | WR | 6'2" | 195 | 23 | | |
| Ron Holmes | WR | 5'10" | 180 | 25 | | |
| Troy Johnson | R | 6'1" | 175 | 23 | | |
| J.T.Smith | WR | 6'2" | 185 | 30 | | 36 |
| Eric Swanson | WR | 5'11" | 186 | 23 | | |
| Pat Tilley | WR | 5'10" | 178 | 33 | | |
| Cap Boso | TE | 6'3" | 224 | 23 | | |
| Doug Marsh | TE | 6'3" | 238 | 28 | | |
| Jay Novacek | TE | 6'4" | 217 | 23 | | |
| Robert Stallings | TE | 6'6" | 250 | 22 | | |
| Evan Arapostathis | K | 5'9" | 160 | 22 | | |
| Greg Cater | K | 6' | 191 | 29 | | |
| John Lee | K | 5'11" | 182 | 22 | | 38 |
| Eric Schubert | K | 5'8" | 193 | 24 | | 18 |

Bob Harris - Ankle Injury
Scott Bergold - Back Injury
Curtis Greer - Knee Injury
Randy Love - Back Injury
Lee Nelson - Back Injury

* Overtime

## NEW YORK GIANTS

### RUSHING

| Last Name | No. | Yds | Avg | TD |
|---|---|---|---|---|
| Morris | 341 | 1516 | 4.4 | 14 |
| Carthon | 72 | 260 | 3.6 | 0 |
| Rouson | 54 | 179 | 3.3 | 2 |
| Simms | 43 | 72 | 1.7 | 1 |
| Galbreath | 16 | 61 | 3.8 | 0 |
| B. Johnson | 2 | 28 | 14.0 | 0 |
| Manuel | 1 | 25 | 25.0 | 0 |
| Rutledge | 3 | 19 | 6.3 | 0 |
| Miller | 1 | 3 | 3.0 | 0 |
| Hostetler | 1 | 1 | 1.0 | 0 |

### RECEIVING

| Last Name | No. | Yds | Avg | TD |
|---|---|---|---|---|
| Bavaro | 66 | 1001 | 15.2 | 4 |
| Galbreath | 33 | 268 | 8.1 | 0 |
| B. Johnson | 31 | 534 | 17.2 | 5 |
| Robinson | 29 | 494 | 17.0 | 2 |
| Morris | 21 | 233 | 11.1 | 1 |
| McConkey | 16 | 279 | 17.4 | 1 |
| Carthon | 16 | 67 | 4.2 | 0 |
| Manuel | 11 | 181 | 16.5 | 3 |
| Mowatt | 10 | 119 | 11.9 | 2 |
| Miller | 9 | 144 | 16.0 | 2 |
| Rouson | 8 | 121 | 15.1 | 1 |
| Carson | 1 | 13 | 13.0 | 1 |

### PUNT RETURNS

| Last Name | No. | Yds | Avg | TD |
|---|---|---|---|---|
| McConkey | 32 | 253 | 7.9 | 0 |
| Manuel | 3 | 22 | 7.3 | 0 |
| Collins | 3 | 11 | 3.7 | 0 |
| Galbreath | 3 | 1 | 0.3 | 0 |

### KICKOFF RETURNS

| Last Name | No. | Yds | Avg | TD |
|---|---|---|---|---|
| McConkey | 24 | 471 | 19.6 | 0 |
| Collins | 11 | 204 | 18.5 | 0 |
| Miller | 7 | 111 | 15.9 | 0 |
| Hill | 5 | 61 | 12.2 | 0 |
| Rouson | 2 | 21 | 10.5 | 0 |
| Lasker | 1 | 0 | 0.0 | 0 |

### PASSING — PUNTING — KICKING

| PASSING | Cmp | Att | % | Yds | Yd/Att | TD | Int— | % | Rk |
|---|---|---|---|---|---|---|---|---|---|
| Simms | 468 | 259 | 55 | 3487 | 7.45 | 21 | 22— | 5 | 3 |
| Rutledge | 3 | 1 | 33 | 13 | 4.33 | 1 | 0— | 0 | |
| Galbreath | 1 | 0 | 0 | 0 | 0.00 | 0 | 0— | 0 | |

| PUNTING | No | Avg |
|---|---|---|
| Landeta | 79 | 44.8 |

| KICKING | XP | Att | % | FG | Att | % |
|---|---|---|---|---|---|---|
| Allegre | 33 | 33 | 100 | 24 | 32 | 67 |
| Thomas | 4 | 4 | 100 | 0 | 1 | 0 |
| Cooper | 4 | 4 | 100 | 2 | 4 | 50 |

## WASHINGTON REDSKINS

### RUSHING

| Last Name | No. | Yds | Avg | TD |
|---|---|---|---|---|
| Rogers | 303 | 1203 | 4.0 | 18 |
| Bryant | 69 | 258 | 3.7 | 4 |
| Griffin | 62 | 197 | 3.2 | 0 |
| Schroeder | 36 | 47 | 1.3 | 1 |
| Monk | 4 | 27 | 6.8 | 0 |

### RECEIVING

| Last Name | No. | Yds | Avg | TD |
|---|---|---|---|---|
| Clark | 74 | 1265 | 17.1 | 7 |
| Monk | 73 | 1068 | 14.6 | 4 |
| Bryant | 43 | 449 | 10.4 | 3 |
| Didier | 34 | 691 | 20.3 | 2 |
| Warren | 20 | 164 | 8.2 | 1 |
| Sanders | 14 | 286 | 20.4 | 2 |
| Griffin | 11 | 110 | 10.0 | 0 |
| Orr | 3 | 45 | 15.0 | 1 |
| Rogers | 3 | 24 | 8.0 | 0 |
| Holloway | 1 | 7 | 7.0 | 0 |

### PUNT RETURNS

| Last Name | No. | Yds | Avg | TD |
|---|---|---|---|---|
| Jenkins | 28 | 270 | 9.6 | 0 |
| Green | 12 | 120 | 10.0 | 0 |
| Yarber | 9 | 143 | 15.9 | 0 |
| Clark | 1 | 14 | 14.0 | 0 |
| Milot | 1 | 3 | 3.0 | 0 |

### KICKOFF RETURNS

| Last Name | No. | Yds | Avg | TD |
|---|---|---|---|---|
| Jenkins | 27 | 554 | 20.5 | 0 |
| Verdin | 12 | 240 | 20.0 | 0 |
| Griffin | 8 | 156 | 19.5 | 0 |
| Garner | 7 | 142 | 20.3 | 0 |
| Holloway | 3 | 44 | 14.7 | 0 |
| Orr | 2 | 31 | 15.5 | 0 |
| Krakowski | 1 | 8 | 8.0 | 0 |

### PASSING — PUNTING — KICKING

| PASSING | Att | Cmp | % | Yds | Yd/Att | TD | Int— | % | Rk |
|---|---|---|---|---|---|---|---|---|---|
| Schroeder | 541 | 276 | 51 | 4109 | 7.60 | 22 | 22— | 4 | 4 |
| Williams | 1 | 0 | 0 | 0 | 0.00 | 0 | 0— | 0 | |

| PUNTING | No | Avg |
|---|---|---|
| Cox | 75 | 43.6 |

| KICKING | XP | ATT | % | FG | ATT | % |
|---|---|---|---|---|---|---|
| Zendejas | 23 | 28 | 82 | 9 | 14 | 64 |
| Cox | 0 | 0 | 0 | 3 | 6 | 50 |

## DALLAS COWBOYS

### RUSHING

| Last Name | No. | Yds | Avg | TD |
|---|---|---|---|---|
| Dorsett | 184 | 748 | 4.1 | 5 |
| Walker | 151 | 737 | 4.9 | 12 |
| Pelluer | 41 | 255 | 6.2 | 1 |
| Newsome | 34 | 110 | 3.2 | 2 |
| Collier | 6 | 53 | 8.8 | 0 |
| Clack | 4 | 19 | 4.8 | 0 |
| D. White | 8 | 16 | 2.0 | 1 |
| Sherrard | 2 | 11 | 5.5 | 0 |
| Cosbie | 1 | 9 | 9.0 | 0 |
| Lavette | 10 | 6 | 0.6 | 0 |
| Fowler | 6 | 5 | 0.8 | 0 |

### RECEIVING

| Last Name | No. | Yds | Avg | TD |
|---|---|---|---|---|
| Walker | 76 | 837 | 11.0 | 2 |
| Hill | 49 | 770 | 15.7 | 3 |
| Newsome | 48 | 421 | 8.8 | 3 |
| Sherrard | 41 | 744 | 18.1 | 5 |
| Cosbie | 28 | 312 | 11.1 | 1 |
| Dorsett | 25 | 267 | 10.7 | 1 |
| Renfro | 22 | 325 | 14.8 | 3 |
| Banks | 17 | 202 | 11.9 | 0 |
| Chandler | 6 | 57 | 9.5 | 2 |
| Lavette | 5 | 31 | 6.2 | 1 |
| Fowler | 1 | 19 | 19.0 | 0 |
| Clack | 1 | 18 | 18.0 | 0 |

### PUNT RETURNS

| Last Name | No. | Yds | Avg | TD |
|---|---|---|---|---|
| Banks | 27 | 160 | 5.9 | 0 |
| Lavette | 18 | 92 | 5.1 | 0 |
| Holloway | 1 | 0 | 0.0 | 0 |

### KICKOFF RETURNS

| Last Name | No. | Yds | Avg | TD |
|---|---|---|---|---|
| Lavette | 36 | 699 | 19.4 | 0 |
| Clack | 19 | 421 | 22.2 | 0 |
| Banks | 1 | 56 | 56.0 | 0 |
| Newsome | 2 | 32 | 16.0 | 0 |
| Tuinei | 1 | 0 | 0.0 | 0 |

### PASSING — PUNTING — KICKING

| PASSING | Att | Cmp | % | Yds | Yd/Att | TD | Int— | % | Rk |
|---|---|---|---|---|---|---|---|---|---|
| Pelluer | 378 | 215 | 57 | 2727 | 7.21 | 8 | 17— | 5 | 9 |
| D. White | 153 | 95 | 62 | 1157 | 7.56 | 12 | 5— | 3 | |
| Collier | 15 | 8 | 53 | 96 | 6.40 | 1 | 2— | 13 | |
| Renfro | 1 | 1 | 100 | 23 | 23.00 | 0 | 0— | 0 | |

| PUNTING | No | Avg |
|---|---|---|
| Saxon | 87 | 40.2 |

| KICKING | XP | Att | % | FG | Att | % |
|---|---|---|---|---|---|---|
| Septien | 43 | 43 | 100 | 15 | 21 | 71 |

## PHILADELPHIA EAGLES

### RUSHING

| Last Name | No. | Yds | Avg | TD |
|---|---|---|---|---|
| Byars | 177 | 577 | 3.3 | 1 |
| Cunningham | 66 | 540 | 8.2 | 5 |
| Toney | 69 | 285 | 4.1 | 1 |
| Haddix | 79 | 276 | 3.5 | 0 |
| Tautalatasi | 51 | 163 | 3.2 | 0 |
| Crawford | 28 | 88 | 3.1 | 1 |
| Jaworski | 13 | 33 | 2.5 | 0 |
| Cavanaugh | 9 | 26 | 2.9 | 0 |
| M. Waters | 5 | 8 | 1.6 | 0 |
| K. Jackson | 1 | 6 | 6.0 | 0 |
| Teltschik | 1 | 0 | 0.0 | 0 |

### RECEIVING

| Last Name | No. | Yds | Avg | TD |
|---|---|---|---|---|
| Quick | 60 | 939 | 15.7 | 9 |
| Tautalatasi | 41 | 325 | 7.9 | 2 |
| Spagnola | 39 | 397 | 10.2 | 1 |
| K.Jackson | 30 | 506 | 16.9 | 6 |
| Haddix | 26 | 150 | 5.8 | 0 |
| Little | 14 | 132 | 9.4 | 0 |
| Toney | 13 | 177 | 13.6 | 0 |
| Garrity | 12 | 227 | 18.9 | 0 |
| R.Johnson | 11 | 207 | 18.8 | 1 |
| Byars | 11 | 44 | 4.0 | 0 |
| Smith | 6 | 94 | 15.7 | 0 |
| M. Waters | 2 | 27 | 13.5 | 0 |
| Darby | 2 | 16 | 8.0 | 0 |

### PUNT RETURNS

| Last Name | No. | Yds | Avg | TD |
|---|---|---|---|---|
| Garrity | 17 | 187 | 11.0 | 1 |
| Cooper | 16 | 139 | 8.7 | 0 |
| M. Waters | 7 | 30 | 4.3 | 0 |
| Smith | 4 | 18 | 4.5 | 0 |

### KICKOFF RETURNS

| Last Name | No. | Yds | Avg | TD |
|---|---|---|---|---|
| Crawford | 27 | 497 | 18.4 | 0 |
| Tautalatasi | 18 | 344 | 19.1 | 0 |
| Byars | 2 | 47 | 23.5 | 0 |
| Cooper | 2 | 42 | 21.0 | 0 |
| Quick | 2 | 6 | 3.0 | 0 |
| Schulz | 1 | 9 | 9.0 | 0 |
| Simmons | 1 | 0 | 0.0 | 0 |

### PASSING — PUNTING — KICKING

| PASSING | Att | Cmp | % | Yds | Yd/Att | TD | Int— | % | Rk |
|---|---|---|---|---|---|---|---|---|---|
| Jaworski | 245 | 128 | 52 | 1405 | 5.73 | 8 | 6— | 2 | 8 |
| Cunningham | 209 | 111 | 53 | 1391 | 6.66 | 8 | 7— | 3 | |
| Cavanaugh | 58 | 28 | 48 | 397 | 6.84 | 2 | 4— | 7 | |
| Byars | 2 | 1 | 50 | 55 | 27.50 | 1 | 0— | 0 | |

| PUNTING | No | Avg |
|---|---|---|
| Teltschik | 109 | 41.2 |
| Cunningham | 2 | 27.0 |

| KICKING | XP | Att | % | FG | Att | % |
|---|---|---|---|---|---|---|
| McFadden | 26 | 27 | 96 | 20 | 31 | 65 |

## ST. LOUIS CARDINALS

### RUSHING

| Last Name | No. | Yds | Avg | TD |
|---|---|---|---|---|
| Mitchell | 174 | 800 | 4.6 | 5 |
| Ferrell | 124 | 548 | 4.4 | 0 |
| Anderson | 75 | 237 | 3.2 | 3 |
| Lomax | 35 | 148 | 4.2 | 1 |
| Sikahema | 16 | 62 | 3.9 | 0 |
| Stoudt | 7 | 53 | 7.6 | 0 |
| Wolfley | 8 | 19 | 2.4 | 0 |
| Marsh | 1 | 5 | 5.0 | 0 |
| Green | 2 | -4 | -2.0 | 0 |
| Austin | 1 | 0 | 0.0 | 0 |

### RECEIVING

| Last Name | No. | Yds | Avg | TD |
|---|---|---|---|---|
| J. Smith | 80 | 1014 | 12.7 | 6 |
| Ferrell | 56 | 434 | 7.8 | 3 |
| Green | 42 | 517 | 12.3 | 6 |
| Mitchell | 41 | 276 | 6.7 | 0 |
| Marsh | 25 | 313 | 12.5 | 0 |
| T. Johnson | 14 | 203 | 14.5 | 0 |
| Anderson | 19 | 137 | 7.2 | 0 |
| Fox | 5 | 59 | 11.8 | 1 |
| Sikahema | 10 | 99 | 9.9 | 1 |
| Tilley | 3 | 51 | 17.0 | 0 |
| Holman | 3 | 41 | 13.7 | 0 |
| Wolfley | 2 | 32 | 16.0 | 0 |
| Sargent | 1 | 8 | 8.0 | 0 |
| Novacek | 1 | 2 | 2.0 | 0 |

### PUNT RETURNS

| Last Name | No. | Yds | Avg | TD |
|---|---|---|---|---|
| Sikahema | 43 | 522 | 12.1 | 2 |
| J. Smith | 1 | 6 | 6.0 | 0 |
| Carter | 1 | 0 | 0.0 | 0 |

### KICKOFF RETURNS

| Last Name | No. | Yds | Avg | TD |
|---|---|---|---|---|
| Sikahema | 37 | 847 | 22.9 | 0 |
| Swanson | 10 | 206 | 20.6 | 0 |
| Mitchell | 6 | 203 | 33.8 | 0 |
| Fox | 6 | 161 | 26.8 | 0 |
| Johnson | 3 | 46 | 15.3 | 0 |
| Ferrell | 3 | 41 | 13.7 | 0 |
| Sargent | 2 | 27 | 13.5 | 0 |
| Carter | 2 | 21 | 10.5 | 0 |
| Holmes | 1 | 2 | 2.0 | 0 |
| Wolfley | 0 | -6 | -6.0 | 0 |

### PASSING — PUNTING — KICKING

| PASSING | Att | Cmp | % | Yds | Yd/Att | TD | Int— | % | Rk |
|---|---|---|---|---|---|---|---|---|---|
| Lomax | 421 | 240 | 57 | 2583 | 6.14 | 13 | 12— | 3 | 4 |
| Stoudt | 91 | 52 | 57 | 542 | 5.96 | 3 | 7— | 8 | |
| Mitchell | 3 | 1 | 33 | 15 | 5.00 | 0 | 0— | 0 | |
| Arapostathis | 1 | 0 | 0 | 0 | 0.00 | 0 | 0— | 0 | |

| PUNTING | No | Avg |
|---|---|---|
| Cater | 62 | 36.6 |
| Arapostathis | 30 | 38.0 |

| KICKING | XP | Att | % | FG | Att | % |
|---|---|---|---|---|---|---|
| Lee | 14 | 17 | 82 | 8 | 13 | 62 |
| Schubert | 9 | 10 | 90 | 3 | 11 | 27 |

## CHICAGO BEARS 14-2 Mike Ditka

| Scores of Each Game | | |
|---|---|---|
| 41 | CLEVELAND | 31 |
| 13 | PHILADELPHIA | *10 |
| 25 | Green Bay | 12 |
| 44 | Cincinnati | 7 |
| 23 | MINNESOTA | 0 |
| 20 | Houston | 7 |
| 7 | Minnesota | 23 |
| 13 | DETROIT | 7 |
| 17 | L.A.RAMS | 20 |
| 23 | Tampa Bay | 3 |
| 13 | Atlanta | 10 |
| 12 | GREEN BAY | 10 |
| 13 | PITTSBURGH | *10 |
| 48 | TAMPA BAY | 14 |
| 16 | Detroit | 13 |
| 24 | Dallas | 10 |

| Use Name | Pos. | Hgt | Wgt | Age | Int | Pts |
|---|---|---|---|---|---|---|
| Paul Blair | OT | 6'4" | 295 | 23 | | |
| Jim Covert | OT | 6'4" | 271 | 26 | | |
| Keith Van Horne | OT | 6'6" | 280 | 28 | | |
| Kurt Becker | OG | 6'5" | 267 | 27 | | |
| Mark Bortz | OG | 6'6" | 269 | 25 | | |
| Stefan Humphries | OG | 6'3" | 268 | 24 | | |
| Tom Thayer | OG-C | 6'4" | 261 | 25 | | |
| Jay Hilgenberg | C | 6'3" | 258 | 27 | | |
| Larry Rubens | C | 6'1" | 262 | 27 | | |
| Richard Dent | DE | 6'5" | 263 | 25 | | |
| Dan Hampton | DE | 6'5" | 267 | 28 | | 2 |
| Mike Hartenstine | DE | 6'3" | 254 | 33 | | |
| Steve McMichael | DT | 6'2" | 260 | 28 | 1 | 2 |
| William Perry | DT | 6'2" | 325 | 23 | | |
| Henry Waechter | DT | 6'5" | 275 | 27 | | |

| Use Name | Pos. | Hgt | Wgt | Age | Int | Pts |
|---|---|---|---|---|---|---|
| Brian Cabral | LB | 6'1" | 232 | 30 | | |
| Al Harris | LB | 6'5" | 253 | 29 | | |
| Wilber Marshall | LB | 6'1" | 225 | 24 | 5 | 12 |
| Jim Morrissey | LB | 6'3" | 215 | 23 | | |
| Dan Rains | LB | 6'1" | 232 | 30 | | |
| Ron Rivera | LB | 6'3" | 239 | 24 | | |
| Mike Singletary | LB | 6' | 228 | 27 | 1 | |
| Otis Wilson | LB | 6'2" | 232 | 28 | 2 | |
| Todd Bell | DB | 6'1" | 205 | 27 | 1 | |
| Maurice Douglass | DB | 5'11" | 200 | 22 | | |
| Dave Duerson | DB | 6'1" | 203 | 25 | 6 | |
| Gary Fencik | DB | 6'1" | 196 | 32 | 3 | |
| Shaun Gayle | DB | 5'11" | 193 | 24 | 1 | |
| Vestee Jackson | DB | 6' | 196 | 23 | 3 | |
| Reggie Phillips | DB | 5'10" | 170 | 25 | 1 | |
| Mike Richardson | DB | 6' | 188 | 25 | 7 | |

Doug Donley - Wrist Injury
Leslie Frazier - Knee Injury
Andy Frederick - Foot Injury
Dennis McKinnon - Knee Injury

| Use Name | Pos. | Hgt | Wgt | Age | Int | Pts |
|---|---|---|---|---|---|---|
| Doug Flutie | QB | 5'9" | 176 | 24 | | 6 |
| Steve Fuller | QB | 6'4" | 195 | 29 | | |
| Jim McMahon | QB | 6'1" | 190 | 27 | | 6 |
| Mike Tomczak | QB | 6'1" | 195 | 23 | | 18 |
| Neal Anderson | HB | 5'11" | 210 | 22 | | 6 |
| Dennis Gentry | HB-WR | 5'8" | 181 | 27 | | 18 |
| Walter Payton | HB | 5'11" | 202 | 32 | | 66 |
| Thomas Sanders | HB | 5'11" | 203 | 24 | | 30 |
| Matt Suhey | FB | 5'11" | 216 | 28 | | 12 |
| Calvin Thomas | FB | 5'11" | 245 | 26 | | |
| Lew Barnes | WR | 5'8" | 163 | 23 | | 6 |
| Willie Gault | WR | 6' | 183 | 25 | | 30 |
| Keith Ortego | WR | 6' | 180 | 23 | | 12 |
| Clay Pickering | WR | 6'5" | 215 | 25 | | |
| Emery Moorehead | TE | 6'2" | 220 | 32 | | 6 |
| Tim Wrightman | TE | 6'3" | 237 | 26 | | |
| Maury Buford | K | 6'1" | 196 | 26 | | |
| Kevin Butler | K | 6'1" | 195 | 24 | | 120 |

## MINNESOTA VIKINGS 9-7 Jerry Burns

| Scores of Each Game | | |
|---|---|---|
| 10 | DETROIT | 13 |
| 23 | Tampa Bay | 10 |
| 31 | PITTSBURGH | 7 |
| 42 | GREEN BAY | 7 |
| 0 | Chicago | 23 |
| 27 | San Francisco | *24 |
| 23 | CHICAGO | 7 |
| 20 | CLEVELAND | 23 |
| 38 | Washington | *44 |
| 24 | Detroit | 10 |
| 20 | N.Y.GIANTS | 22 |
| 20 | Cincinnati | 24 |
| 45 | TAMPA BAY | 13 |
| 32 | Green Bay | 6 |
| 10 | Houston | 23 |
| 33 | NEW ORLEANS | 17 |

| Use Name | Pos. | Hgt | Wgt | Age | Int | Pts |
|---|---|---|---|---|---|---|
| Dave Huffman | OT | 6'6" | 284 | 29 | | |
| Tim Irwin | OT | 6'6" | 288 | 27 | | |
| Gary Zimmerman | OT | 6'6" | 277 | 24 | | |
| Brent Boyd | OG | 6'3" | 280 | 29 | | |
| Mark MacDonald | OG | 6'4" | 267 | 25 | | |
| Curtis Rouse | OG | 6'3" | 335 | 26 | | |
| Terry Tausch | OG | 6'5" | 276 | 27 | | |
| Jim Hough | C-OG | 6'2" | 269 | 30 | | |
| Kirk Lowdermilk | C | 6'3" | 269 | 23 | | |
| Dennis Swilley | C | 6'3" | 266 | 31 | | |
| Doug Martin | DE | 6'3" | 264 | 29 | | |
| Mark Mullaney | DE | 6'6" | 248 | 33 | | |
| Gerald Robinson | DE | 6'3" | 256 | 23 | | |
| Neil Elshire | DT | 6'6" | 262 | 28 | | |
| Keith Millard | DT | 6'5" | 262 | 24 | 1 | |
| Tim Newton | DT | 6' | 287 | 23 | | |
| Joe Phillips | DT | 6'5" | 278 | 23 | | |
| Mike Stensrud | DT | 6'5" | 280 | 30 | | |

| Use Name | Pos. | Hgt | Wgt | Age | Int | Pts |
|---|---|---|---|---|---|---|
| Walker Lee Ashley | LB | 6' | 237 | 26 | | |
| Chris Doleman | LB | 6'5" | 250 | 24 | 1 | 6 |
| David Howard | LB | 6'2" | 232 | 24 | | |
| Chris Martin | LB | 6'2" | 239 | 25 | | |
| Jesse Solomon | LB | 6' | 235 | 22 | 2 | |
| Scott Studwell | LB | 6'2" | 230 | 32 | 1 | |
| Rufus Bess | DB | 5'9" | 189 | 30 | 1 | |
| Joey Browner | DB | 6'2" | 212 | 26 | 4 | 6 |
| David Evans | DB | 6' | 178 | 27 | | |
| Neal Guggemos | DB | 6'1" | 187 | 22 | | |
| John Harris | DB | 6'2" | 198 | 30 | 3 | |
| Issiac Holt | DB | 6'1" | 200 | 23 | 8 | |
| Carl Lee | DB | 6' | 187 | 25 | 3 | |
| Mike Lush (from IND) | DB | 6'1" | 195 | 28 | | |
| Kyle Morrell | DB | 6'2" | 189 | 22 | | |
| Willie Teal | DB | 5'10" | 192 | 28 | | |

| Use Name | Pos. | Hgt | Wgt | Age | Int | Pts |
|---|---|---|---|---|---|---|
| Steve Bono | QB | 6'4" | 211 | 24 | | |
| Tommy Kramer | QB | 6'2" | 205 | 31 | | 6 |
| Wade Wilson | QB | 6'3" | 213 | 27 | | 6 |
| Darrin Nelson | HB | 5'9" | 189 | 27 | | 42 |
| Allen Rice | HB | 5'10" | 204 | 24 | | 30 |
| Alfred Anderson | FB | 6'1" | 220 | 25 | | 24 |
| Ted Brown | FB-HB | 5'10" | 212 | 29 | | 24 |
| Wayne Wilson (to NO) | FB | 6'3" | 220 | 28 | | |
| Anthony Carter | WR | 5'11" | 175 | 25 | | 42 |
| Jim Gustafson | WR | 6'1" | 181 | 25 | | 12 |
| Hassan Jones | WR | 6' | 195 | 22 | | 24 |
| Leo Lewis | WR | 5'8" | 170 | 29 | | 12 |
| Buster Rhymes | WR | 6'2" | 218 | 24 | | |
| Carl Hilton | TE | 6'3" | 232 | 22 | | |
| Steve Jordan | TE | 6'4" | 239 | 25 | | 36 |
| Mike Mularkey | TE | 6'4" | 234 | 24 | | 12 |
| Greg Coleman | K | 6' | 184 | 31 | | |
| Chuck Nelson | K | 6' | 172 | 26 | | 110 |

## DETROIT LIONS 5-11 Darryl Rogers

| Scores of Each Game | | |
|---|---|---|
| 13 | Minnesota | 10 |
| 7 | DALLAS | 31 |
| 20 | TAMPA BAY | 24 |
| 21 | Cleveland | 24 |
| 24 | HOUSTON | 13 |
| 21 | Green Bay | 14 |
| 10 | L.A.Rams | 14 |
| 7 | Chicago | 13 |
| 17 | CINCINNATI | 24 |
| 10 | MINNESOTA | 24 |
| 13 | Philadelphia | 11 |
| 38 | Tampa Bay | 17 |
| 40 | GREEN BAY | 44 |
| 17 | Pittsburgh | 27 |
| 13 | CHICAGO | 16 |
| 6 | ATLANTA | 20 |

| Use Name | Pos. | Hgt | Wgt | Age | Int | Pts |
|---|---|---|---|---|---|---|
| Lomas Brown | OT | 6'4" | 282 | 23 | | |
| Harvey Salem (from HOU) | OT-OG | 6'6" | 285 | 25 | | |
| Rich Strenger | OT | 6'7" | 285 | 26 | | |
| Scott Barrows | OG-C | 6'2" | 278 | 23 | | |
| Chris Dieterich | OG-OT | 6'3" | 275 | 28 | | |
| Keith Dorney | OG-OT | 6'5" | 285 | 28 | | |
| Steve Kenney | OG | 6'4" | 262 | 30 | | |
| Kevin Glover | C-OG | 6'2" | 267 | 23 | | |
| Steve Mott | C | 6'3" | 270 | 25 | | |
| Tom Turnure | C | 6'4" | 253 | 29 | | |
| Leon Evans | DE | 6'5" | 282 | 24 | | |
| Keith Ferguson | DE | 6'5" | 260 | 27 | 1 | |
| William Gay | DE | 6'5" | 260 | 31 | | |
| Curtis Green | DE-DT | 6'3" | 265 | 29 | | |
| Steve Baack | NT-OG | 6'4" | 265 | 25 | | |
| Eric Williams | NT | 6'4" | 280 | 24 | 1 | |

| Use Name | Pos. | Hgt | Wgt | Age | Int | Pts |
|---|---|---|---|---|---|---|
| Paul Butcher | LB | 6' | 219 | 22 | | |
| Mike Cofer | LB | 6'5" | 245 | 26 | | |
| August Curley | LB | 6'3" | 226 | 26 | | |
| James Harrell | LB | 6'1" | 230 | 29 | | |
| James Johnson | LB | 6'2" | 236 | 24 | | |
| Angelo King | LB | 6'1" | 222 | 28 | | |
| Vernon Maxwell | LB | 6'2" | 235 | 24 | | |
| Shelton Robinson | LB | 6'2" | 236 | 25 | | |
| Jimmy Williams | LB | 6'3" | 230 | 25 | 2 | |
| John Bostic | DB | 5'10" | 178 | 23 | 1 | |
| Duane Galloway | DB | 5'8" | 181 | 24 | 4 | |
| William Graham | DB | 5'11" | 191 | 26 | | |
| James Griffin | DB | 6'2" | 197 | 24 | 2 | |
| Demetrious Johnson | DB | 5'11" | 190 | 25 | 2 | |
| Bruce McNorton | DB | 5'11" | 175 | 27 | 4 | |
| Devon Mitchell | DB | 6'1" | 194 | 23 | 5 | |
| Bobby Watkins | DB | 5'10" | 184 | 26 | | |

Arnold Brown - Broken Arm
Mark Nichols - Knee Injury

| Use Name | Pos. | Hgt | Wgt | Age | Int | Pts |
|---|---|---|---|---|---|---|
| Joe Fergson | QB | 6'1" | 195 | 36 | | |
| Eric Hipple | QB | 6'2" | 196 | 28 | | |
| Chuck Long | QB | 6'4" | 211 | 23 | | |
| Herman Hunter | HB | 6'1" | 193 | 25 | | 6 |
| Gary James | HB | 5'10" | 214 | 22 | | 18 |
| Alvin Moore | HB | 6' | 194 | 27 | | |
| Oscar Smith | HB | 5'9" | 203 | 23 | | |
| James Jones | FB | 6'2" | 229 | 25 | | 54 |
| Scott Williams | FB | 6'2" | 234 | 24 | | 12 |
| Carl Bland | WR | 5'11" | 182 | 25 | | 12 |
| Jeff Chadwick | WR | 6'3" | 190 | 25 | | 30 |
| Pete Mandley | WR | 5'10" | 191 | 25 | | 6 |
| Leonard Thompson | WR | 5'11" | 192 | 34 | | 30 |
| Jimmie Giles (from TB) | TE | 6'3" | 240 | 31 | | 18 |
| David Lewis | TE | 6'3" | 235 | 25 | | 6 |
| Rob Rubick | TE | 6'3" | 234 | 25 | | |
| Jim Arnold | K | 6'3" | 211 | 25 | | |
| Mike Black | K | 6'2" | 197 | 25 | | |
| Eddie Murray | K | 5'10" | 175 | 30 | | 85 |

## GREEN BAY PACKERS 4-12 Forrest Gregg

| Scores of Each Game | | |
|---|---|---|
| 3 | HOUSTON | 31 |
| 10 | New Orleans | 24 |
| 12 | CHICAGO | 25 |
| 7 | Minnesota | 42 |
| 28 | CINCINNATI | 34 |
| 14 | DETROIT | 21 |
| 17 | Cleveland | 14 |
| 17 | SAN FRANCISCO | 31 |
| 3 | Pittsburgh | 27 |
| 7 | WASHINGTON | 16 |
| 31 | TAMPA BAY | 7 |
| 10 | Chicago | 12 |
| 44 | Detroit | 40 |
| 6 | MINNESOTA | 32 |
| 21 | Tampa Bay | 7 |
| 24 | N.Y.Giants | 55 |

| Use Name | Pos. | Hgt | Wgt | Age | Int | Pts |
|---|---|---|---|---|---|---|
| Greg Feasel | OT | 6'7" | 301 | 27 | | |
| Ruben Mendoza | OT | 6'4" | 290 | 23 | | |
| Tom Neville | OT-OG | 6'5" | 306 | 24 | | |
| Ken Ruettgers | OT | 6'5" | 280 | 24 | | |
| Karl Swanke | OT-C | 6'6" | 262 | 28 | | |
| Alan Veingrad | OT-OG | 6'5" | 277 | 23 | | |
| Ron Hallstrom | OG | 6'6" | 290 | 27 | | |
| Bill Cherry | C-OG | 6'4" | 277 | 25 | | |
| Rich Moran | C-OG | 6'3" | 275 | 24 | | |
| Mark Cannon | C | 6'3" | 258 | 24 | | |
| Robert Brown | DE | 6'2" | 267 | 26 | | |
| Alphonso Carreker | DE | 6'6" | 271 | 24 | | |
| Donnie Humphrey | DE | 6'3" | 296 | 25 | | |
| Ezra Johnson | DE | 6'4" | 265 | 30 | | |
| Matt Koart | DE | 6'5" | 258 | 22 | | |
| Ben Thomas (from NE) | DE-NT | 6'4" | 275 | 25 | | |
| Charles Martin | NT | 6'4" | 280 | 27 | | |

Daryll Jones - Injury
Mark Murphy - Foot Injury
Keith Uecker - Knee Injury

| Use Name | Pos. | Hgt | Wgt | Age | Int | Pts |
|---|---|---|---|---|---|---|
| John Anderson | LB | 6'3" | 229 | 30 | 1 | |
| Burnell Dent | LB | 6'1" | 236 | 23 | | |
| John Dorsey | LB | 6'3" | 243 | 26 | | |
| Tim Harris | LB | 6'5" | 236 | 21 | | |
| Bobby Leopold | LB | 6'1" | 224 | 28 | 1 | |
| Brian Noble | LB | 6'3" | 253 | 23 | | |
| Jeff Schuh (to MIN) | LB | 6'2" | 234 | 28 | | |
| Randy Scott | LB | 6'1" | 228 | 27 | | |
| Miles Turpin | LB | 6'4" | 232 | 22 | | |
| Mike Weddington | LB | 6'4" | 245 | 25 | | |
| Ed Berry | DB | 5'10" | 183 | 22 | | |
| Mossy Cade | DB | 6'1" | 198 | 24 | 4 | |
| Tom Flynn (to NYG) | DB | 6' | 194 | 24 | 2 | |
| Tiger Greene | DB | 6' | 194 | 24 | 2 | |
| David Greenwood | DB | 6'3" | 210 | 26 | | |
| Gary Hayes | DB | 5'10" | 180 | 29 | | |
| Mark Lee | DB | 5'11" | 189 | 28 | 9 | |
| Tim Lewis | DB | 5'11" | 195 | 24 | | |
| Ken Stills | DB | 5'10" | 187 | 22 | 1 | 6 |
| Elbert Watts | DB | 6'2" | 205 | 23 | 1 | |

| Use Name | Pos. | Hgt | Wgt | Age | Int | Pts |
|---|---|---|---|---|---|---|
| Vince Ferragamo | QB | 6'3" | 217 | 32 | | |
| Chuck Fusina | QB | 6'1" | 195 | 29 | | |
| Joe Shield | QB | 6'1" | 185 | 24 | | |
| Randy Wright | QB | 6'2" | 203 | 25 | | 6 |
| Paul Ott Carruth | HB | 6'1" | 220 | 25 | | 24 |
| Kenneth Davis | HB | 5'10" | 209 | 24 | | 6 |
| Gary Ellerson | HB | 5'11" | 219 | 23 | | 18 |
| Eddie Lee Ivery | HB | 6'1" | 206 | 29 | | 6 |
| Jessie Clark | FB | 6' | 228 | 26 | | |
| Gerry Ellis | FB | 5'11" | 235 | 28 | | 12 |
| Phillip Epps | WR | 5'10" | 165 | 26 | | 24 |
| Nolan Franz | WR | 6'2" | 183 | 26 | | |
| James Lofton | WR | 6'3" | 197 | 30 | | 24 |
| Walter Stanley | WR | 5'9" | 179 | 23 | | 18 |
| Mark Lewis | TE | 6'2" | 237 | 25 | | 12 |
| Mike Moffitt | TE | 6'4" | 211 | 23 | | |
| Dan Ross | TE | 6'4" | 240 | 29 | | |
| Ed West | TE | 6'1" | 243 | 25 | | 6 |
| Al Del Greco | K | 5'10" | 191 | 24 | | 80 |
| Bill Renner | K | 6' | 198 | 27 | | |
| Don Braken | K | 6' | 211 | 24 | | |

## TAMPA BAY BUCCANEERS 2-14 Leeman Bennett

| Scores of Each Game | | |
|---|---|---|
| 7 | SAN FRANCISCO | 31 |
| 10 | MINNESOTA | 23 |
| 24 | Detroit | 20 |
| 20 | ATLANTA | *23 |
| 20 | L.A.Rams | *26 |
| 19 | ST.LOUIS | 30 |
| 7 | New Orleans | 38 |
| 20 | Kansas City | 27 |
| 34 | BUFFALO | 28 |
| 3 | CHICAGO | 23 |
| 7 | Green Bay | 31 |
| 17 | DETROIT | 38 |
| 13 | Minnesota | 45 |
| 14 | Chicago | 48 |
| 7 | GREEN BAY | 21 |
| 17 | ST. Louis | 21 |

| Use Name | Pos. | Hgt | Wgt | Age | Int | Pts |
|---|---|---|---|---|---|---|
| Ron Heller | OT | 6'6" | 280 | 24 | | 6 |
| J.D.Maarleveld | OT | 6'6" | 300 | 24 | | |
| Marvin Powell | OT | 6'5" | 270 | 31 | | |
| Greg Robinson | OT | 6'5" | 285 | 23 | | |
| Rob Taylor | OT | 6'6" | 290 | 25 | | |
| Sean Farrell | OG | 6'3" | 260 | 26 | | |
| Rick Mallory | OG | 6'2" | 265 | 25 | | |
| George Yarno | OG | 6'2" | 265 | 29 | | |
| Randy Grimes | C | 6'4" | 270 | 26 | | |
| John Cannon | DE | 6'5" | 260 | 26 | | |
| Ron Holmes | DE | 6'4" | 265 | 23 | | |
| Kevin Kellin | DE | 6'6" | 265 | 26 | | |
| Tyrone Keys | DE | 6'7" | 270 | 26 | | |
| David Logan | NT | 6'2" | 250 | 29 | | |
| Karl Morgan | NT | 6'1" | 255 | 25 | | |
| Bob Nelson | NT | 6'4" | 265 | 27 | | |

| Use Name | Pos. | Hgt | Wgt | Age | Int | Pts |
|---|---|---|---|---|---|---|
| Scot Brantley | LB | 6'1" | 230 | 28 | 2 | |
| Keith Browner | LB | 6'6" | 245 | 24 | 1 | |
| Jeff Davis | LB | 6' | 230 | 26 | 1 | |
| Kevin Murphy | LB | 6'2" | 230 | 22 | | |
| Ervin Randle | LB | 6'1" | 250 | 23 | | |
| Jackie Walker | LB | 6'5" | 245 | 23 | | |
| Chris Washington | LB | 6'4" | 230 | 24 | 1 | |
| Jeremiah Castille | DB | 5'10" | 175 | 25 | | |
| Craig Curry | DB | 6' | 190 | 25 | 2 | |
| Ricky Easmon | DB | 5'10" | 160 | 23 | | |
| Bobby Futrell | DB | 5'11" | 190 | 24 | | |
| Rod Jones | DB | 6' | 175 | 22 | 1 | |
| Vito McKeever | DB | 6' | 180 | 24 | 3 | |
| Ivory Sully | DB | 6' | 200 | 29 | | |
| Craig Swoope | DB | 6'1" | 200 | 22 | 1 | |
| Kevin Walker | DB | 5'11" | 180 | 22 | | |

Joe McCall - Knee Injury
Mike Prior - Wrist Injury
Don Fiedler - Knee Injury
Nat Hudson - Knee Injury
Ken Kaplan - Elbow Injury

| Use Name | Pos. | Hgt | Wgt | Age | Int | Pts |
|---|---|---|---|---|---|---|
| Steve DeBerg | QB | 6'2" | 210 | 32 | | |
| Steve Young | QB | 6'2" | 200 | 24 | | 30 |
| Greg Allen | HB | 5'11" | 200 | 23 | | |
| Bobby Howard | HB | 6' | 210 | 22 | | 6 |
| James Wilder | HB | 6'3" | 225 | 28 | | 18 |
| Nathan Wonsley | HB | 5'10" | 190 | 22 | | 18 |
| Mack Boatner | FB | 6' | 220 | 27 | | |
| Pat Franklin | FB | 6'1" | 230 | 23 | | 12 |
| Ron Springs | FB | 6'2" | 225 | 29 | | |
| Gerald Carter | WR | 6'1" | 190 | 29 | | 12 |
| Phil Freeman | WR | 5'11" | 185 | 23 | | 12 |
| Willie Gillespie | WR | 5'9" | 170 | 24 | | |
| Leonard Harris | WR | 5'8" | 155 | 25 | | |
| Vince Heflin | WR | 6' | 185 | 27 | | 6 |
| Kevin House (to LA) | WR | 6'1" | 185 | 28 | | 12 |
| David Williams | WR | 6'3" | 190 | 23 | | |
| Jerry Bell | TE | 6'5" | 230 | 27 | | |
| K.D. Dunn | TE | 6'3" | 235 | 23 | | |
| Calvin Magee | TE | 6'3" | 240 | 23 | | 30 |
| Jeff Spek | TE | 6'3" | 240 | 25 | | |
| Frank Garcia | K | 6' | 210 | 29 | | |
| Donald Igwebuike | K | 5'9" | 185 | 25 | | 77 |

* Overtime

## CHICAGO BEARS

### RUSHING
| Last Name | No. | Yds | Avg | TD |
|---|---|---|---|---|
| Payton | 321 | 1333 | 4.2 | 8 |
| Suhey | 84 | 270 | 3.2 | 2 |
| Sanders | 27 | 224 | 8.3 | 5 |
| Thomas | 56 | 224 | 4.0 | 0 |
| McMahon | 22 | 152 | 6.9 | 1 |
| Anderson | 35 | 146 | 4.2 | 0 |
| Tomczak | 23 | 117 | 5.1 | 3 |
| Gentry | 11 | 103 | 9.4 | 1 |
| Gault | 8 | 79 | 9.9 | 0 |
| Flutie | 9 | 36 | 4.0 | 1 |
| Fuller | 8 | 30 | 3.8 | 0 |
| Perry | 1 | -1 | -1.0 | 0 |
| Buford | 1 | -13 | -13.0 | 0 |

### RECEIVING
| Last Name | No. | Yds | Avg | TD |
|---|---|---|---|---|
| Gault | 42 | 818 | 19.5 | 5 |
| Payton | 37 | 382 | 10.3 | 3 |
| Moorehead | 26 | 390 | 15.0 | 1 |
| Suhey | 24 | 235 | 9.8 | 0 |
| Ortego | 23 | 430 | 18.7 | 2 |
| Wrightman | 22 | 241 | 11.0 | 0 |
| Gentry | 19 | 238 | 12.5 | 0 |
| Anderson | 4 | 80 | 20.0 | 1 |
| Barnes | 4 | 54 | 13.5 | 0 |
| Thomas | 4 | 18 | 4.5 | 0 |
| Sanders | 2 | 18 | 9.0 | 0 |
| Bortz | 1 | 8 | 8.0 | 0 |

### PUNT RETURNS
| Last Name | No. | Yds | Avg | TD |
|---|---|---|---|---|
| Barnes | 57 | 482 | 8.5 | 0 |

### KICKOFF RETURNS
| Last Name | No. | Yds | Avg | TD |
|---|---|---|---|---|
| Gentry | 20 | 576 | 28.8 | 1 |
| Sanders | 22 | 399 | 18.1 | 0 |
| Anderson | 4 | 26 | 6.5 | 0 |
| Barnes | 3 | 94 | 31.3 | 1 |
| Gault | 1 | 20 | 20.0 | 0 |

### PASSING — PUNTING — KICKING
| Last Name | Att | Cmp | % | Yds | Yd/Att | TD | Int— | % | Rk |
|---|---|---|---|---|---|---|---|---|---|
| **PASSING** | | | | | | | | | |
| Tomczak | 151 | 74 | 49 | 1105 | 7.32 | 2 | 10— | 3 | 7 |
| McMahon | 150 | 77 | 51 | 995 | 6.63 | 5 | 8— | 5 | |
| Fuller | 64 | 34 | 53 | 451 | 7.05 | 2 | 4— | 6 | |
| Flutie | 46 | 23 | 50 | 361 | 7.85 | 3 | 2— | 4 | |
| Payton | 4 | 0 | 0 | 0 | 0.00 | 0 | 1— | 25 | |

| Last Name | No | Avg |
|---|---|---|
| **PUNTING** | | |
| Buford | 70 | 40.7 |

| Last Name | XP | Att | % | FG | Att | % |
|---|---|---|---|---|---|---|
| **KICKING** | | | | | | |
| Butler | 37 | 37 | 97 | 28 | 41 | 68 |

## MINNESOTA VIKINGS

### RUSHING
| Last Name | No. | Yds | Avg | TD |
|---|---|---|---|---|
| D. Nelson | 191 | 793 | 4.2 | 4 |
| Anderson | 83 | 347 | 4.2 | 2 |
| Brown | 63 | 251 | 4.0 | 4 |
| Rice | 73 | 220 | 3.0 | 2 |
| Kramer | 23 | 48 | 2.1 | 1 |
| Coleman | 2 | 46 | 23.0 | 0 |
| W. Wilson | 10 | 19 | 1.9 | 0 |
| Jones | 1 | 14 | 14.0 | 0 |
| Carter | 1 | 12 | 12.0 | 0 |
| Wilson | 13 | 9 | 0.7 | 1 |
| Lewis | 3 | -16 | -5.3 | 0 |

### RECEIVING
| Last Name | No. | Yds | Avg | TD |
|---|---|---|---|---|
| Jordan | 58 | 859 | 14.8 | 6 |
| D. Nelson | 53 | 593 | 11.2 | 3 |
| Carter | 38 | 686 | 18.1 | 7 |
| Lewis | 32 | 600 | 18.8 | 2 |
| Rice | 30 | 391 | 13.0 | 3 |
| Jones | 28 | 570 | 20.4 | 4 |
| Anderson | 17 | 179 | 10.5 | 2 |
| Brown | 15 | 132 | 8.8 | 0 |
| Mularkey | 11 | 89 | 8.1 | 2 |
| Gustafson | 5 | 61 | 12.2 | 2 |
| Rhymes | 3 | 25 | 8.3 | 0 |
| W. Wilson | 1 | -3 | -3.0 | 0 |

### PUNT RETURNS
| Last Name | No. | Yds | Avg | TD |
|---|---|---|---|---|
| Bess | 23 | 162 | 7.0 | 0 |
| Lewis | 7 | 53 | 7.6 | 0 |
| Rice | 1 | 0 | 0.0 | 0 |

### KICKOFF RETURNS
| Last Name | No. | Yds | Avg | TD |
|---|---|---|---|---|
| Bess | 31 | 705 | 22.7 | 0 |
| Rhymes | 9 | 213 | 23.7 | 0 |
| Rice | 5 | 88 | 17.6 | 0 |
| D. Nelson | 3 | 105 | 35.0 | 0 |
| Anderson | 3 | 38 | 12.7 | 0 |
| W. Wilson | 2 | 33 | 16.5 | 0 |
| Brown | 2 | 18 | 9.0 | 0 |
| Irwin | 1 | 0 | 0.0 | 0 |

### PASSING — PUNTING — KICKING
| Last Name | Att | Cmp | % | Yds | Yd/Att | TD | Int— | % | Rk |
|---|---|---|---|---|---|---|---|---|---|
| **PASSING** | | | | | | | | | |
| Kramer | 372 | 208 | 56 | 3000 | 8.06 | 24 | 10— | 3 | 1 |
| Wilson | 143 | 80 | 56 | 1165 | 8.15 | 7 | 5— | 4 | |
| Anderson | 2 | 1 | 50 | 17 | 8.50 | 0 | 0— | 0 | |
| Bono | 1 | 1 | 100 | 3 | 3.00 | 0 | 0— | 0 | |
| Rice | 1 | 0 | 0 | 0 | 0.00 | 0 | 0— | 0 | |

| Last Name | No | Avg |
|---|---|---|
| **PUNTING** | | |
| Coleman | 67 | 41.4 |
| Wilson | 3 | 25.3 |
| C. Nelson | 3 | 24.0 |

| Last Name | XP | Att | % | FG | Att | % |
|---|---|---|---|---|---|---|
| **KICKING** | | | | | | |
| C. Nelson | 44 | 47 | 94 | 22 | 28 | 79 |

## DETROIT LIONS

### RUSHING
| Last Name | No. | Yds | Avg | TD |
|---|---|---|---|---|
| Jones | 252 | 903 | 3.6 | 8 |
| James | 159 | 688 | 4.3 | 3 |
| Moore | 19 | 73 | 3.8 | 0 |
| Hipple | 16 | 46 | 2.9 | 0 |
| J. Ferguson | 5 | 25 | 5.0 | 0 |
| S. Williams | 13 | 22 | 1.7 | 2 |
| Hunter | 3 | 22 | 7.3 | 0 |
| Long | 2 | 0 | 0.0 | 0 |
| Black | 1 | -8 | -8.0 | 0 |

### RECEIVING
| Last Name | No. | Yds | Avg | TD |
|---|---|---|---|---|
| Jones | 54 | 334 | 6.2 | 1 |
| Chadwick | 53 | 995 | 18.8 | 5 |
| Bland | 44 | 511 | 11.6 | 2 |
| Giles | 35 | 376 | 10.7 | 4 |
| James | 34 | 219 | 6.4 | 0 |
| Thompson | 25 | 320 | 12.8 | 5 |
| Hunter | 25 | 218 | 8.7 | 1 |
| Lewis | 10 | 88 | 8.8 | 1 |
| Moore | 8 | 47 | 5.9 | 0 |
| Mandley | 7 | 106 | 15.1 | 0 |
| Rubick | 5 | 62 | 12.4 | 0 |
| S. Williams | 2 | 9 | 4.5 | 0 |

### PUNT RETURNS
| Last Name | No. | Yds | Avg | TD |
|---|---|---|---|---|
| Mandley | 43 | 420 | 9.8 | 1 |

### KICKOFF RETURNS
| Last Name | No. | Yds | Avg | TD |
|---|---|---|---|---|
| Hunter | 48 | 1007 | 20.6 | 0 |
| Bland | 6 | 114 | 19.0 | 0 |
| Smith | 5 | 81 | 16.2 | 0 |
| Graham | 3 | 72 | 24.0 | 0 |
| Mandley | 2 | 37 | 18.5 | 0 |
| Evans | 1 | 0 | 0.0 | 0 |

### PASSING — PUNTING — KICKING
| Last Name | Att | Cmp | % | Yds | Yd/Att | TD | Int— | % | Rk |
|---|---|---|---|---|---|---|---|---|---|
| **PASSING** | | | | | | | | | |
| Hipple | 305 | 192 | 63 | 1919 | 6.29 | 9 | 11— | 4 | 4 |
| J. Ferguson | 155 | 73 | 47 | 941 | 6.07 | 7 | 7— | 5 | |
| Long | 40 | 21 | 53 | 247 | 6.18 | 2 | 2— | 5 | |

| Last Name | No | Avg |
|---|---|---|
| **PUNTING** | | |
| Black | 47 | 38.7 |
| Arnold | 37 | 41.4 |
| Murray | 1 | 37.0 |

| Last Name | XP | Att | % | FG | Att | % |
|---|---|---|---|---|---|---|
| **KICKING** | | | | | | |
| Murray | 31 | 32 | 97 | 18 | 25 | 72 |

## GREEN BAY PACKERS

### RUSHING
| Last Name | No. | Yds | Avg | TD |
|---|---|---|---|---|
| Davis | 114 | 519 | 4.6 | 0 |
| Ellis | 84 | 345 | 4.1 | 2 |
| Carruth | 81 | 308 | 3.8 | 2 |
| Ellerson | 90 | 287 | 3.2 | 3 |
| Wright | 18 | 41 | 2.3 | 1 |
| Clark | 18 | 41 | 2.3 | 0 |
| Ivery | 4 | 25 | 6.3 | 0 |
| Stanley | 1 | 19 | 19.0 | 0 |
| Epps | 4 | 18 | 4.5 | 0 |
| Fusina | 7 | 11 | 1.6 | 0 |
| Renner | 1 | 0 | 0.0 | 0 |
| Swanke | 1 | 0 | 0.0 | 0 |
| Ferragamo | 1 | 0 | 0.0 | 0 |

### RECEIVING
| Last Name | No. | Yds | Avg | TD |
|---|---|---|---|---|
| Lofton | 64 | 840 | 13.1 | 4 |
| Epps | 49 | 612 | 12.5 | 4 |
| Stanley | 35 | 723 | 20.7 | 2 |
| Ivery | 31 | 385 | 12.4 | 1 |
| Ellis | 24 | 258 | 10.8 | 0 |
| Carruth | 24 | 134 | 5.6 | 2 |
| Davis | 21 | 142 | 6.8 | 1 |
| Ross | 17 | 143 | 8.4 | 1 |
| West | 15 | 199 | 13.3 | 1 |
| Ellerson | 12 | 130 | 10.8 | 0 |
| Clark | 6 | 41 | 6.8 | 0 |
| Moffitt | 4 | 87 | 21.8 | 0 |
| M. Lewis | 2 | 7 | 3.5 | 0 |
| Franz | 1 | 7 | 7.0 | 0 |

### PUNT RETURNS
| Last Name | No. | Yds | Avg | TD |
|---|---|---|---|---|
| Stanley | 33 | 316 | 9.6 | 1 |

### KICKOFF RETURNS
| Last Name | No. | Yds | Avg | TD |
|---|---|---|---|---|
| Stanley | 28 | 559 | 20.0 | 0 |
| Watts | 12 | 239 | 19.9 | 0 |
| Davis | 12 | 231 | 19.3 | 0 |
| Stills | 10 | 209 | 20.9 | 0 |
| Ellerson | 7 | 154 | 22.0 | 0 |
| Carruth | 4 | 40 | 10.0 | 0 |
| Epps | 1 | 21 | 21.0 | 0 |
| Berry | 1 | 16 | 16.0 | 0 |
| Noble | 1 | 1 | 1.0 | 0 |

### PASSING — PUNTING — KICKING
| Last Name | Att | Cmp | % | Yds | Yd/Att | TD | Int— | % | Rk |
|---|---|---|---|---|---|---|---|---|---|
| **PASSING** | | | | | | | | | |
| Wright | 492 | 263 | 54 | 3247 | 6.60 | 17 | 23— | 5 | 10 |
| Ferragamo | 40 | 23 | 58 | 283 | 7.08 | 1 | 3— | 8 | |
| Fusina | 32 | 19 | 59 | 178 | 5.56 | 0 | 1— | 3 | |
| Lofton | 1 | 0 | 0 | 0 | 0.00 | 0 | 0— | 0 | |

| Last Name | No | Avg |
|---|---|---|
| **PUNTING** | | |
| Bracken | 57 | 38.6 |
| Renner | 18 | 34.6 |

| Last Name | XP | Att | % | FG | Att | % |
|---|---|---|---|---|---|---|
| **KICKING** | | | | | | |
| Del Greco | 29 | 29 | 100 | 17 | 27 | 63 |

## TAMPA BAY BUCCANEERS

### RUSHING
| Last Name | No. | Yds | Avg | TD |
|---|---|---|---|---|
| Wilder | 190 | 704 | 3.7 | 2 |
| Young | 74 | 425 | 5.7 | 5 |
| Wonsley | 73 | 339 | 4.6 | 3 |
| Springs | 74 | 285 | 3.9 | 0 |
| Howard | 30 | 110 | 3.7 | 1 |
| Franklin | 7 | 7 | 1.0 | 0 |
| House | 2 | 5 | 2.5 | 0 |
| DeBerg | 2 | 1 | 0.5 | 0 |
| Allen | 1 | 3 | 3.0 | 0 |
| Carter | 1 | -5 | -5.0 | 0 |
| Garcia | 1 | -11 | -11.0 | 0 |

### RECEIVING
| Last Name | No. | Yds | Avg | TD |
|---|---|---|---|---|
| Magee | 45 | 564 | 12.5 | 5 |
| Wilder | 43 | 326 | 7.6 | 1 |
| Carter | 42 | 640 | 15.2 | 2 |
| Springs | 24 | 187 | 7.8 | 0 |
| House | 18 | 384 | 21.3 | 2 |
| Freeman | 14 | 229 | 16.4 | 2 |
| Bell | 10 | 120 | 12.0 | 0 |
| Wonsley | 8 | 57 | 7.1 | 0 |
| Franklin | 7 | 29 | 4.1 | 1 |
| Williams | 6 | 91 | 15.2 | 0 |
| Howard | 5 | 60 | 12.0 | 0 |
| Dunn | 3 | 83 | 27.7 | 0 |
| Harris | 3 | 52 | 17.3 | 0 |
| Heflin | 3 | 42 | 14.0 | 0 |
| Gillespie | 1 | 18 | 18.0 | 0 |
| Mallory | 1 | 9 | 9.0 | 0 |
| Heller | 1 | 1 | 1.0 | 1 |

### PUNT RETURNS
| Last Name | No. | Yds | Avg | TD |
|---|---|---|---|---|
| Futrell | 14 | 67 | 4.8 | 0 |
| Walker | 9 | 27 | 3.0 | 0 |
| Harris | 3 | 16 | 5.3 | 0 |

### KICKOFF RETURNS
| Last Name | No. | Yds | Avg | TD |
|---|---|---|---|---|
| Freeman | 31 | 582 | 18.8 | 0 |
| Wonsley | 10 | 208 | 20.8 | 0 |
| K. Walker | 8 | 146 | 18.3 | 0 |
| Futrell | 5 | 115 | 23.0 | 0 |
| Howard | 4 | 71 | 17.8 | 0 |
| Harris | 4 | 63 | 15.8 | 0 |
| Williams | 2 | 29 | 14.5 | 0 |
| Franklin | 3 | 23 | 7.7 | 0 |
| Magee | 2 | 21 | 10.5 | 0 |
| Allen | 1 | 21 | 21.0 | 0 |
| Heflin | 1 | 15 | 15.0 | 0 |
| Curry | 1 | 6 | 6.0 | 0 |
| Boatner | 1 | 2 | 2.0 | 0 |
| Randle | 1 | 0 | 0.0 | 0 |
| Dunn | 1 | 0 | 0.0 | 0 |

### PASSING — PUNTING — KICKING
| Last Name | Att | Cmp | % | Yds | Yd/Att | TD | Int— | % | Rk |
|---|---|---|---|---|---|---|---|---|---|
| **PASSING** | | | | | | | | | |
| Young | 363 | 195 | 54 | 2382 | 6.29 | 8 | 13— | 4 | 12 |
| DeBerg | 96 | 50 | 52 | 610 | 6.35 | 5 | 12— | 13 | |

| Last Name | No | Avg |
|---|---|---|
| **PUNTING** | | |
| Garcia | 77 | 40.1 |
| Springs | 1 | 43.0 |

| Last Name | XP | Att | % | FG | Att | % |
|---|---|---|---|---|---|---|
| **KICKING** | | | | | | |
| Igwebuike | 26 | 27 | 96 | 17 | 24 | 71 |

**SAN FRANCISCO FORTY-NINERS 10-5-1 Bill Walsh**

| Scores of Each Game | | |
|---|---|---|
| 31 | Tampa Bay | 7 |
| 13 | L.A. Rams | 16 |
| 26 | NEW ORLEANS | 17 |
| 31 | Miami | 16 |
| 35 | INDIANAPOLIS | 14 |
| 24 | MINNESOTA | *27 |
| 10 | Atlanta | *10 |
| 31 | Green Bay | 17 |
| 10 | New Orleans | 23 |
| 43 | ST.LOUIS | 17 |
| 6 | Washington | 14 |
| 20 | ATLANTA | 0 |
| 17 | GIANTS | 21 |
| 24 | N.Y.JETS | 10 |
| 29 | New England | 24 |
| 24 | L.A.RAMS | 14 |

| Use Name | Pos. | Hgt | Wgt | Age | Int | Pts |
|---|---|---|---|---|---|---|
| Bruce Collie | OT-OG | 6'6" | 275 | 24 | | |
| Keith Fahnhorst | OT | 6'6" | 273 | 34 | | |
| Bubba Paris | OT | 6'6 | 299 | 25 | | |
| Steve Wallace | OT | 6'5" | 276 | 21 | | |
| John Ayers | OG | 6'5" | 265 | 33 | | |
| Randy Cross | OG | 6'3" | 265 | 32 | | |
| Michael Durrette | OG | 6'4" | 280 | 29 | | |
| Guy McIntyre | OG | 6'3" | 264 | 25 | | |
| Fred Quillan | C | 6'5" | 266 | 30 | | |
| Dwaine Board | DE | 6'5" | 248 | 29 | | |
| Charls Haley | DE | 6'5" | 230 | 22 | | |
| John Harty | DE | 6'4" | 260 | 27 | | |
| Larry Roberts | DE | 6'3" | 264 | 23 | | |
| Doug Rogers | DE | 6'5" | 280 | 26 | | |
| Jeff Stover | DE | 6'5" | 275 | 28 | | |
| Jim Stuckey | DE | 6'4" | 253 | 28 | | |
| Michael Carter | NT | 6'2" | 285 | 25 | | |
| Manu Tulasosopo | NT | 6'3" | 262 | 29 | | |
| Pete Kugler | NT-DE | 6'4" | 255 | 27 | | |

| Use Name | Pos. | Hgt | Wgt | Age | Int | Pts |
|---|---|---|---|---|---|---|
| Tom Cousineau | LB | 6'3" | 225 | 29 | 1 | |
| Riki Ellison | LB | 6'2" | 225 | 26 | | |
| Jim Fahnhorst | LB | 6'4" | 230 | 27 | 4 | |
| Ron Ferrari | LB | 6' | 215 | 27 | | |
| Milt McColl | LB | 6'6" | 230 | 27 | | |
| Todd Shell | LB | 6'4" | 225 | 24 | | |
| Keena Turner | LB | 6'2" | 222 | 27 | 1 | |
| Michael Walter | LB | 6'3" | 238 | 25 | | |
| Jeff Fuller | DB-LB | 6'2" | 216 | 24 | 4 | |
| Don Griffin | DB | 6' | 176 | 22 | 3 | |
| Tom Holmoe | DB | 6'2" | 195 | 26 | 3 | 12 |
| Ronnie Lott | DB | 6' | 200 | 27 | 10 | 6 |
| Tim McKyer | DB | 6' | 174 | 22 | 6 | 6 |
| Tory Nixon | DB | 5'11" | 186 | 24 | 2 | 6 |
| Carlton Williamson | DB | 6' | 204 | 28 | 3 | |
| Eric Wright | DB | 6'1" | 185 | 27 | | |

Wymon Henderson - Foot Injury
Jesse Sapolu - Leg Injury
Jimmy Rogers - Knee Injury

| Use Name | Pos. | Hgt | Wgt | Age | Int | Pts |
|---|---|---|---|---|---|---|
| Bob Gagliano | QB | 6'3" | 195 | 27 | | |
| Jeff Kemp | QB | 6' | 201 | 27 | | |
| Joe Montana | QB | 6'2" | 195 | 30 | | |
| Mike Moroski | QB | 6'4" | 200 | 28 | | 6 |
| Tony Cherry | HB | 5'7" | 187 | 23 | | |
| Joe Cribbs | HB | 5'11" | 193 | 28 | | 30 |
| Derrick Harmon | HB | 5'10" | 202 | 23 | | 6 |
| Carl Monroe | HB-WR | 5'8" | 180 | 26 | | |
| Wendell Tyler | HB | 5'10" | 207 | 31 | | |
| Roger Craig | FB | 6' | 224 | 26 | | 42 |
| Tom Rathman | FB | 6'1" | 232 | 23 | | 6 |
| Bill Ring | FB | 5'10 | 205 | 29 | | |
| Dwight Clark | WR | 6'4" | 215 | 29 | | 12 |
| Derrick Crawford | WR | 5'10" | 185 | 25 | | |
| Ken Margerum | WR | 6' | 180 | 27 | | |
| Jerry Rice | WR | 6'2" | 200 | 23 | | 96 |
| Mike Wilson | WR | 6'3" | 215 | 27 | | 6 |
| Russ Francis | TE | 6'6" | 242 | 33 | | 6 |
| John Frank | TE | 6'3" | 225 | 24 | | 12 |
| Max Runager | K | 6'1" | 189 | 30 | | |
| Ray Wersching | K | 5'11" | 215 | 36 | | 116 |

**LOS ANGELES RAMS 10-6 John Robinson**

| Scores of Each Game | | |
|---|---|---|
| 16 | St.Louis | 10 |
| 16 | SAN FRANCISCO | 13 |
| 24 | Indianapolis | 7 |
| 20 | Philadelphia | 34 |
| 26 | TAMPA BAY | *20 |
| 14 | Atlanta | 26 |
| 14 | DETROIT | 10 |
| 14 | ATLANTA | 7 |
| 20 | Chicago | 17 |
| 0 | New Orleans | 6 |
| 28 | NEW ENGLAND | 30 |
| 26 | NEW ORLEANS | 13 |
| 17 | N.Y.Jets | 3 |
| 29 | DALLAS | 10 |
| 31 | MIAMI | *37 |
| 14 | San Francisco | 24 |

| Use Name | Pos. | Hgt | Wgt | Age | Int | Pts |
|---|---|---|---|---|---|---|
| Irv Pankey | OT | 6'4" | 267 | 28 | | |
| Jackie Slater | OT | 6'4" | 271 | 32 | | |
| Dennis Harrah | OG | 6'5" | 265 | 33 | | |
| Kent Hill | OG | 6'5" | 260 | 29 | | |
| Duval Love | OG | 6'3" | 263 | 23 | | |
| Tom Newberry | OG | 6'2" | 279 | 23 | | 6 |
| Tony Slaton | C | 6'3" | 265 | 25 | | |
| Doug Smith | C | 6'3" | 253 | 29 | | |
| Reggie Doss | DE | 6'4" | 263 | 29 | | |
| Gary Jeter | DE | 6'4" | 260 | 31 | | 2 |
| Doug Reed | DE | 6'3" | 262 | 26 | | |
| Charles DeJurnett | NT | 6'4" | 260 | 34 | | |
| Greg Meisner | NT | 6'3" | 253 | 27 | | |
| Shawn Miller | NT | 6'4" | 255 | 25 | | |
| Alvin Wright | NT | 6'2" | 285 | 25 | | |

| Use Name | Pos. | Hgt | Wgt | Age | Int | Pts |
|---|---|---|---|---|---|---|
| Steve Busick | LB | 6'4" | 227 | 27 | | |
| Carl Ekern | LB | 6'3" | 230 | 32 | | |
| Kevin Greene | LB | 6'3" | 238 | 24 | | |
| Mark Jerue | LB | 6'3" | 232 | 26 | 2 | 6 |
| Jim Laughlin | LB | 6' | 222 | 28 | | |
| Mike McDonald | LB | 6'1" | 230 | 28 | | |
| Mel Owens | LB | 6'2" | 224 | 27 | | |
| Cliff Thrift | LB | 6'2" | 235 | 30 | | |
| Norwood Vann | LB | 6'1" | 225 | 24 | | |
| Mike Wilcher | LB | 6'3" | 240 | 26 | 1 | |
| Nolan Cromwell | DB | 6'1" | 200 | 31 | 5 | 6 |
| Herman Edwards | DB | 5'10" | 190 | 32 | | |
| Tim Fox | DB | 5'11" | 186 | 32 | | |
| Jerry Gray | DB | 6' | 185 | 23 | 8 | |
| LeRoy Irvin | DB | 5'11" | 184 | 28 | 6 | 6 |
| Johnnie Johnson | DB | 6'1" | 183 | 29 | 1 | |
| Vince Newsome | DB | 6'1" | 179 | 25 | 3 | |
| Mickey Sutton | DB | 5'8" | 165 | 26 | | |

Jim Collins - Shoulder Injury
Dieter Brock - Back Injury

| Use Name | Pos. | Hgt | Wgt | Age | Int | Pts |
|---|---|---|---|---|---|---|
| Steve Bartkowski | QB | 6'4" | 218 | 33 | | |
| Steve Dils | QB | 6'1" | 191 | 30 | | |
| Jim Everett | QB | 6'5" | 212 | 23 | | 6 |
| Eric Dickerson | HB | 6'3" | 218 | 25 | | 66 |
| Charles White | HB | 5'10" | 190 | 28 | | |
| Rob Carpenter | FB | 6'1" | 230 | 31 | | |
| Mike Guman | FB | 6'2" | 218 | 28 | | |
| Barry Redden | FB | 5'10" | 205 | 26 | | 30 |
| Tim Tyrrell (from ATL - HB) | FB | 6'1" | 201 | 25 | | |
| Ron Brown | WR | 5'11" | 181 | 25 | | 18 |
| Bobby Dickworth (to PHI) | WR | 6'3" | 196 | 27 | | |
| Henry Ellard | WR | 5'11" | 175 | 25 | | 24 |
| Chuck Scott | WR | 6'2" | 202 | 23 | | |
| Michael Young | WR | 6'1" | 185 | 24 | | |
| David Hill | TE | 6'2" | 240 | 32 | | 6 |
| Tony Hunter | TE | 6'4" | 237 | 26 | | |
| Damone Johnson | TE | 6'4" | 230 | 24 | | |
| Darren Long | TE | 6'3 | 240 | 27 | | |
| Dale Hatcher | K | 6'2" | 200 | 23 | | |
| Mike Lansford | K | 6' | 183 | 28 | | 85 |

**ATLANTA FALCONS 7-8-1 Dan Henning**

| Scores of Each Game | | |
|---|---|---|
| 31 | New Orleans | 10 |
| 33 | ST.LOUIS | 13 |
| 37 | Dallas | 35 |
| 23 | Tampa Bay | *20 |
| 0 | PHILADELPHIA | 16 |
| 26 | L.A.RAMS | 14 |
| 10 | SAN FRANCISCO | *10 |
| 7 | L.A.Rams | 14 |
| 17 | New England | 25 |
| 14 | N.Y.JETS | 28 |
| 10 | CHICAGO | 13 |
| 0 | San Francisco | 20 |
| 20 | Miami | 14 |
| 23 | INDIANAPOLIS | 28 |
| 9 | NEW ORLEANS | 14 |
| 20 | Detroit | 6 |

| Use Name | Pos. | Hgt | Wgt | Age | Int | Pts |
|---|---|---|---|---|---|---|
| Bill Fralic | OT-OG | 6'5" | 280 | 23 | | |
| Glen Howe | OT | 6'7" | 298 | 24 | | |
| Mike Kenn | OT | 6'7" | 277 | 30 | | |
| Brett Miller | OT | 6'7" | 300 | 27 | | |
| Eric Sanders (to DET) | OT-OG | 6'7" | 288 | 27 | | |
| Jamie Dukes | OG | 6'1" | 270 | 22 | | |
| Joe Pellegrini | OG-C | 6'4" | 265 | 29 | | |
| John Scully | OG | 6'6" | 270 | 28 | | |
| Wayne Radloff | C-OG | 6'5" | 277 | 25 | | |
| Jeff Van Note | C | 6'2" | 268 | 40 | | |
| Rick Bryan | DE | 6'4" | 265 | 24 | | |
| Mike Gann | DE | 6'5" | 265 | 22 | | 2 |
| Dennis Harrison (from SF) | DE | 6'8" | 280 | 30 | | |
| Mike Pitts | DE | 6'5" | 277 | 25 | | 6 |
| Andrew Provence | DE | 6'3" | 267 | 25 | | |
| Dan Benish | NT | 6'5" | 280 | 24 | | |
| Tony Casillas | NT | 6'3" | 280 | 22 | | |

Jeff Kiewel - Knee Injury
Dan Wagoner - Knee Injury

| Use Name | Pos. | Hgt | Wgt | Age | Int | Pts |
|---|---|---|---|---|---|---|
| Aaron Brown | LB | 6'2" | 238 | 30 | | |
| Joe Costello | LB | 6'3" | 250 | 26 | | |
| Buddy Curry | LB | 6'4" | 222 | 28 | 1 | |
| Tim Green | LB | 6'2" | 249 | 22 | | |
| Ray Phillips | LB | 6'3" | 245 | 22 | | |
| John Rade | LB | 6'1" | 240 | 26 | 1 | |
| Johnny Taylor (to MIA) | LB | 6'4" | 235 | 26 | | |
| Reggie Wilkes | LB | 6'4" | 242 | 30 | 2 | |
| Joel Williams | LB | 6'1" | 227 | 29 | 2 | 6 |
| James Britt | DB | 6' | 185 | 25 | | 6 |
| Bobby Butler | DB | 5'11" | 182 | 27 | 1 | 1 |
| Scott Case | DB | 6' | 178 | 24 | 4 | |
| Wendell Cason | DB | 5'11" | 197 | 23 | 1 | |
| Bret Clark | DB | 6'3" | 198 | 25 | 5 | |
| David Croudip | DB | 5'8" | 185 | 27 | 2 | |
| Herman Edwards | DB | 6' | 194 | 32 | | |
| Kenny Johnson (to HOU) | DB | 5'10" | 175 | 28 | | |
| Robert Moore | DB | 5'11" | 190 | 22 | 1 | |
| Dennis Woodberry | DB | 5'10" | 183 | 25 | 2 | |

Mike Landrum - Knee Injury
Dan Sharp - Shoulder Injury
Bobby Jackson - Hamstring Injury

| Use Name | Pos. | Hgt | Wgt | Age | Int | Pts |
|---|---|---|---|---|---|---|
| David Archer | QB | 6'2" | 208 | 24 | | |
| Turk Schonert | QB | 6'1" | 196 | 29 | | 6 |
| Tony Baker (to CLE) | HB | 5'10" | 175 | 21 | | |
| Sylvester Stamps | HB | 5'7" | 175 | 25 | | 6 |
| William Andrews | FB | 6' | 220 | 30 | | 6 |
| Cliff Austin | FB | 6' | 213 | 26 | | 6 |
| Gerald Riggs | FB | 6'1" | 232 | 25 | | 54 |
| Anthony Allen | WR | 5'11" | 182 | 27 | | 12 |
| Stacey Bailey | WR | 6' | 157 | 26 | | |
| Charlie Brown | WR | 5'10" | 184 | 27 | | 24 |
| Floyd Dixon | WR | 5'9" | 170 | 22 | | 12 |
| Billy Johnson | WR | 5'9" | 170 | 34 | | |
| Joey Jones | WR | 5'8" | 165 | 23 | | |
| Aubrey Matthews | WR | 5'7" | 165 | 23 | | |
| Keith Williams | WR-RB | 5'10" | 173 | 21 | | 6 |
| Arthur Cox | TE | 6'2" | 262 | 25 | | 6 |
| Ron Middleton | TE | 6'2" | 252 | 21 | | |
| Ken Whisenhunt | TE | 6'2" | 233 | 24 | | 18 |
| Rick Donnelly | K | 6' | 190 | 24 | | 1 |
| Ali Haji-Sheikh | K | 6' | 172 | 25 | | 34 |
| Mick Luckhurst | K | 6' | 178 | 28 | | 63 |

**NEW ORLEANS SAINTS 7-9 Jim Mora**

| Scores of Each Game | | |
|---|---|---|
| 10 | ATLANTA | 31 |
| 24 | GREEN BAY | 10 |
| 17 | San Francisco | 26 |
| 17 | N.Y.Giants | 20 |
| 6 | WASHINGTON | 14 |
| 17 | Indianapolis | 14 |
| 38 | TAMPA BAY | 7 |
| 23 | N.Y.Jets | 28 |
| 23 | SAN FRANCISCO | 10 |
| 6 | L.A.RAMS | 0 |
| 16 | St.Louis | 7 |
| 13 | L.A.Rams | 26 |
| 20 | NEW ENGLAND | 21 |
| 27 | MIAMI | 31 |
| 14 | Atlanta | 9 |
| 17 | Minnesota | 33 |

| Use Name | Pos. | Hgt | Wgt | Age | Int | Pts |
|---|---|---|---|---|---|---|
| Stan Brock | OT | 6'6" | 292 | 28 | | |
| Bill Contz (from CLE) | OT | 6'5" | 270 | 25 | | |
| Jim Dombrowski | OT | 6'5" | 298 | 22 | | |
| Daren Gilbert | OT | 6'6" | 295 | 22 | | |
| Chuck Commiskey | OG | 6'4" | 290 | 28 | | |
| Brad Edelman | OG | 6'6" | 270 | 25 | | |
| Pat Saindon | OG | 6'3" | 273 | 25 | | |
| Ralph Williams | OG | 6'3" | 298 | 28 | | |
| Joel Hilgenberg | C-OG | 6'3" | 252 | 24 | | |
| Steve Korte | C | 6'2" | 269 | 26 | | |
| Bruce Clark | DE | 6'3" | 274 | 28 | | |
| Jonathan Dumbauld | DE | 6'4" | 259 | 23 | | |
| James Geathers | DE | 6'7" | 290 | 26 | | |
| Casey Merrill | DE | 6'4" | 250 | 29 | | |
| Frank Warren | DE | 6'4" | 290 | 26 | | |
| Jim Wilks | DE | 6'5" | 266 | 28 | | |
| Sheldon Andrus | NT | 6'1" | 271 | 23 | | |
| Tony Elliott | NT | 6'2" | 285 | 27 | | |

Dave Lafary - Toe Injury

| Use Name | Pos. | Hgt | Wgt | Age | Int | Pts |
|---|---|---|---|---|---|---|
| Jack Del Rio | LB | 6'4" | 238 | 23 | | |
| James Haynes | LB | 6'2" | 233 | 26 | 1 | 6 |
| Rickey Jackson | LB | 6'2" | 243 | 28 | 1 | |
| Vaughn Johnson | LB | 6'3" | 235 | 24 | | |
| Joe Kohlbrand | LB | 6'4" | 242 | 23 | | |
| Sam Mills | LB | 5'9" | 225 | 27 | | |
| Pat Swilling | LB | 6'3" | 242 | 21 | | |
| Alvin Toles | LB | 6'1" | 227 | 23 | | |
| Russell Gary (to PHI) | DB | 5'11" | 195 | 27 | 1 | |
| Antonio Gibson | DB | 6'3" | 204 | 24 | 2 | |
| Van Jakes | DB | 6' | 190 | 25 | | |
| Bobby Johnson (from STL) | DB | 6' | 187 | 26 | | |
| Brett Maxie | DB | 6'2" | 194 | 24 | 2 | |
| Dana McLemore (from SF) | DB | 5'10" | 183 | 26 | | |
| Johnnie Poe | DB | 6'1" | 194 | 27 | 4 | |
| Willie Tullis | DB | 6' | 194 | 28 | | |
| Frank Wattelet | DB | 6' | 186 | 27 | 3 | |
| Dave Waymer | DB | 6'1" | 188 | 28 | 9 | |

Earl Johnson - Shoulder Injury
Tim Joiner - Shoulder Injury
Guido Merkens - Knee Injury

| Use Name | Pos. | Hgt | Wgt | Age | Int | Pts |
|---|---|---|---|---|---|---|
| Bobby Hebert | QB | 6'4" | 215 | 26 | | |
| Babe Laufenberg | QB | 6'2" | 196 | 26 | | |
| Dave Wilson | QB | 6'3" | 206 | 27 | | 6 |
| Mel Gray | HB | 5'9" | 166 | 25 | | 6 |
| Dalton Hilliard | HB | 5'8" | 204 | 22 | | 30 |
| Rueben Mayes | HB | 5'11" | 200 | 23 | | 48 |
| Buford Jordan | FB | 6' | 223 | 24 | | 6 |
| Wayne Wilson | FB | 6'3" | 220 | 28 | | |
| John Williams | FB | 5'11" | 213 | 25 | | |
| Kelvin Edwards | WR | 6'2" | 197 | 22 | | |
| Eugene Goodlow | WR | 6'2" | 186 | 27 | | 12 |
| Herbert Harris | WR | 6'1" | 206 | 25 | | |
| Mike Jones | WR | 5'11" | 183 | 26 | | 18 |
| Eric Martin | WR | 6'1" | 207 | 24 | | 30 |
| Hoby Brenner | TE | 6'4" | 245 | 27 | | |
| John Tice | TE | 6'5" | 249 | 26 | | 18 |
| Morten Andersen | K | 6'2" | 221 | 26 | | 108 |
| Brian Hansen | K | 6'3" | 209 | 25 | | |

Bobby Fowler - Knee Injury
Hokie Gajan - Knee Injury
Mike Miller - Achilles Tendon Injury

* Overtime

## SAN FRANCISCO FORTY-NINERS

### RUSHING

| Last Name | No. | Yds | Avg | TD |
|---|---|---|---|---|
| Craig | 204 | 830 | 4.1 | 7 |
| Cribbs | 152 | 590 | 3.9 | 5 |
| Rathman | 33 | 138 | 4.2 | 1 |
| Tyler | 31 | 127 | 4.1 | 0 |
| Harmon | 27 | 77 | 2.9 | 1 |
| Rice | 10 | 72 | 7.2 | 1 |
| Kemp | 15 | 49 | 3.3 | 0 |
| Cherry | 11 | 42 | 3.8 | 0 |
| Montana | 17 | 38 | 2.2 | 0 |
| Moroski | 6 | 22 | 3.7 | 1 |
| Ring | 3 | 4 | 1.3 | 0 |
| Frank | 1 | -3 | -3.0 | 0 |

### RECEIVING

| Last Name | No. | Yds | Avg | TD |
|---|---|---|---|---|
| Rice | 86 | 1570 | 18.3 | 15 |
| Craig | 81 | 624 | 7.7 | 0 |
| Clark | 61 | 794 | 13.0 | 2 |
| Francis | 41 | 505 | 12.3 | 1 |
| Cribbs | 35 | 346 | 9.9 | 0 |
| Rathman | 13 | 121 | 9.3 | 0 |
| Wilson | 9 | 104 | 11.6 | 1 |
| Frank | 9 | 61 | 6.8 | 2 |
| Harmon | 8 | 78 | 9.8 | 0 |
| Crawford | 5 | 70 | 14.0 | 0 |
| Margerum | 2 | 12 | 6.0 | 0 |
| Monroe | 2 | 6 | 3.0 | 0 |
| Ring | 1 | 8 | 8.0 | 0 |

### PUNT RETURNS

| Last Name | No. | Yds | Avg | TD |
|---|---|---|---|---|
| Griffin | 38 | 377 | 9.9 | 1 |
| Crawford | 4 | 15 | 3.8 | 0 |
| McKyer | 1 | 5 | 5.0 | 0 |

### KICKOFF RETURNS

| Last Name | No. | Yds | Avg | TD |
|---|---|---|---|---|
| Crawford | 15 | 280 | 18.7 | 0 |
| Monroe | 8 | 139 | 17.4 | 0 |
| Griffin | 5 | 97 | 19.4 | 0 |
| Harmon | 4 | 82 | 20.5 | 0 |
| Rathman | 3 | 66 | 22.0 | 0 |
| Cherry | 2 | 29 | 14.5 | 0 |
| Frank | 2 | 24 | 12.0 | 0 |
| McKyer | 1 | 15 | 15.0 | 0 |
| Ring | 1 | 15 | 15.0 | 0 |
| Wilson | 1 | 10 | 10.0 | 0 |

### PASSING — PUNTING — KICKING

PASSING Statistics

| Last Name | Att | Cmp | % | Yds | Yd/Att | TD | Int— | % | RK |
|---|---|---|---|---|---|---|---|---|---|
| Montana | 307 | 191 | 62 | 2236 | 7.28 | 8 | 9— | 3 | 2 |
| Kemp | 200 | 119 | 60 | 1554 | 7.77 | 11 | 8— | 4 | |
| Moroski | 73 | 42 | 58 | 493 | 6.75 | 2 | 3— | 4 | |
| Rice | 2 | 1 | 50 | 16 | 8.00 | 0 | — | 0 | |

PUNTING

| Last Name | No | Avg |
|---|---|---|
| Runager | 83 | 41.6 |

KICKING

| Last Name | XP | Att | % | FG | Att | % |
|---|---|---|---|---|---|---|
| Wersching | 41 | 42 | 98 | 25 | 35 | 72 |

## LOS ANGELES RAMS

### RUSHING

| Last Name | No. | Yds | Avg | TD |
|---|---|---|---|---|
| Dickerson | 404 | 1821 | 4.5 | 11 |
| Redden | 110 | 467 | 4.2 | 4 |
| White | 22 | 126 | 5.7 | 0 |
| Everett | 16 | 46 | 2.9 | 1 |
| Brown | 4 | 5 | 1.3 | 0 |
| Dils | 10 | 5 | 0.5 | 0 |
| Carpenter | 2 | 3 | 1.5 | 0 |
| Bartkowski | 6 | 3 | 0.5 | 0 |
| Guman | 2 | 2 | 1.0 | 0 |
| Hunter | 1 | -6 | -6.0 | 0 |
| Ellard | 1 | -15 | -15.0 | 0 |

### RECEIVING

| Last Name | No. | Yds | Avg | TD |
|---|---|---|---|---|
| Ellard | 34 | 447 | 13.1 | 4 |
| Redden | 28 | 217 | 7.8 | 1 |
| Dickerson | 26 | 205 | 7.9 | 0 |
| Brown | 25 | 396 | 15.8 | 3 |
| Hunter | 15 | 206 | 13.7 | 0 |
| Young | 15 | 181 | 12.1 | 3 |
| Hill | 14 | 202 | 14.4 | 1 |
| Duckworth | 10 | 148 | 14.8 | 1 |
| Guman | 9 | 68 | 7.6 | 0 |
| Scott | 5 | 76 | 15.2 | 0 |
| Long | 5 | 47 | 9.4 | 0 |
| Tyrrell | 1 | 9 | 9.0 | 0 |
| White | 1 | 7 | 7.0 | 0 |

### PUNT RETURNS

| Last Name | No. | Yds | Avg | TD |
|---|---|---|---|---|
| Ellard | 14 | 127 | 9.1 | 0 |
| Sutton | 28 | 234 | 8.4 | 0 |

### KICKOFF RETURNS

| Last Name | No. | Yds | Avg | TD |
|---|---|---|---|---|
| Brown | 36 | 794 | 22.1 | 0 |
| White | 12 | 216 | 18.0 | 0 |
| Sutton | 5 | 91 | 18.2 | 0 |
| Guman | 2 | 28 | 14.0 | 0 |
| Carpenter | 2 | 19 | 9.5 | 0 |
| Ellard | 1 | 18 | 18.0 | 0 |
| Love | 1 | -6 | -6.0 | 0 |

### PASSING — PUNTING — KICKING

PASSING

| Last Name | Att | Cmp | % | Yds | Yd/Att | TD | Int— | % | RK |
|---|---|---|---|---|---|---|---|---|---|
| Everett | 147 | 73 | 50 | 1018 | 6.93 | 8 | 8— | 5 | |
| Dils | 129 | 59 | 46 | 693 | 5.37 | 4 | 4— | 3 | |
| Bartkowski | 126 | 61 | 48 | 654 | 5.19 | 2 | 3— | 2 | |
| Dickerson | 1 | 1 | 100 | 15 | 15.0 | 1 | 0— | 0 | |

PUNTING

| Last Name | No | Avg |
|---|---|---|
| Hatcher | 98 | 38.2 |

KICKING

| Last Name | XP | Att | % | FG | Att | % |
|---|---|---|---|---|---|---|
| Landsford | 34 | 35 | 97 | 17 | 24 | 71 |

## ATLANTA FALCONS

### RUSHING

| Last Name | No. | Yds | Avg | TD |
|---|---|---|---|---|
| Riggs | 343 | 1327 | 3.9 | 9 |
| Archer | 52 | 398 | 5.7 | 0 |
| Austin | 62 | 280 | 4.5 | 1 |
| Stamps | 30 | 220 | 7.3 | 0 |
| Andrews | 52 | 214 | 4.1 | 1 |
| Dixon | 11 | 67 | 6.1 | 0 |
| B. Johnson | 6 | 25 | 4.2 | 0 |
| Whisenhunt | 1 | 20 | 20.0 | 0 |
| K. Williams | 3 | 18 | 6.0 | 0 |
| Matthews | 1 | 12 | 12.0 | 0 |
| Schonert | 11 | 12 | 1.1 | 0 |
| Clark | 2 | 8 | 4.0 | 0 |
| Jones | 1 | 7 | 7.0 | 0 |
| Bailey | 1 | 6 | 6.0 | 0 |
| Baker | 1 | 3 | 3.0 | 0 |

### RECEIVING

| Last Name | No. | Yds | Avg | TD |
|---|---|---|---|---|
| C. Brown | 63 | 918 | 14.6 | 4 |
| Dixon | 42 | 617 | 14.7 | 2 |
| Cox | 24 | 301 | 12.5 | 1 |
| Riggs | 24 | 136 | 5.7 | 0 |
| Stamps | 20 | 221 | 11.1 | 1 |
| Whisenhunt | 20 | 184 | 9.2 | 3 |
| K. Williams | 12 | 164 | 13.7 | 1 |
| Allen | 10 | 156 | 15.6 | 2 |
| Jones | 7 | 141 | 20.1 | 0 |
| B. Johnson | 6 | 57 | 9.5 | 0 |
| Middleton | 6 | 31 | 5.2 | 0 |
| Andrews | 5 | 35 | 7.0 | 0 |
| Bailey | 3 | 39 | 13.0 | 0 |
| Austin | 3 | 21 | 7.0 | 0 |
| Matthews | 1 | 25 | 25.0 | 0 |

### PUNT RETURNS

| Last Name | No. | Yds | Avg | TD |
|---|---|---|---|---|
| Dixon | 26 | 151 | 5.8 | 0 |
| B. Johnson | 8 | 87 | 10.9 | 0 |
| Jones | 7 | 36 | 5.1 | 0 |
| Allen | 2 | 10 | 5.0 | 0 |
| Stamps | 1 | 8 | 8.0 | 0 |

### KICKOFF RETURNS

| Last Name | No. | Yds | Avg | TD |
|---|---|---|---|---|
| Stamps | 24 | 514 | 21.4 | 0 |
| K. Williams | 14 | 255 | 18.2 | 0 |
| Austin | 7 | 120 | 17.1 | 0 |
| Andrews | 4 | 71 | 17.8 | 0 |
| Matthews | 3 | 42 | 14.0 | 0 |
| Croudip | 1 | 20 | 20.0 | 0 |
| Dixon | 1 | 13 | 13.0 | 0 |

### PASSING — PUNTING — KICKING

PASSING

| Last Name | Att | Cmp | % | Yds | Yd/Att | TD | Int— | % | RK |
|---|---|---|---|---|---|---|---|---|---|
| Archer | 294 | 150 | 51 | 2007 | 6.83 | 10 | 9— | 3 | 7 |
| Schonert | 154 | 95 | 62 | 1032 | 6.70 | 4 | 8— | 5 | |
| Riggs | 1 | 0 | 0 | 0 | 0.00 | 0 | 0— | | |

PUNTING

| Last Name | No | Avg |
|---|---|---|
| Donnelly | 79 | 43.3 |

KICKING

| Last Name | XP | Att | % | FG | Att | % |
|---|---|---|---|---|---|---|
| Luckhurst | 21 | 21 | 100 | 14 | 24 | 58 |
| Donnelly | 1 | 1 | 100 | 0 | 0 | 0 |
| Haji-Sheikh | 7 | 8 | 88 | 9 | 12 | 75 |

## NEW ORLEANS SAINTS

### RUSHING

| Last Name | No. | Yds | Avg | TD |
|---|---|---|---|---|
| Mayes | 286 | 1353 | 4.7 | 8 |
| Hilliard | 121 | 425 | 3.5 | 5 |
| Jordan | 68 | 207 | 3.0 | 1 |
| Gray | 6 | 29 | 4.8 | 0 |
| D. Wilson | 14 | 19 | 1.4 | 1 |
| Del Rio | 1 | 16 | 16.0 | 0 |
| Hebert | 5 | 14 | 2.8 | 0 |
| Edwards | 1 | 6 | 6.0 | 0 |
| Hansen | 1 | 0 | 0.0 | 0 |

### RECEIVING

| Last Name | No. | Yds | Avg | TD |
|---|---|---|---|---|
| Jones | 48 | 625 | 13.0 | 3 |
| Martin | 37 | 675 | 18.2 | 5 |
| Tice | 37 | 330 | 8.9 | 3 |
| Goodlow | 20 | 306 | 15.3 | 2 |
| Brenner | 18 | 286 | 15.9 | 0 |
| Hilliard | 17 | 107 | 6.3 | 0 |
| Mayes | 17 | 96 | 5.6 | 0 |
| Harris | 11 | 148 | 13.5 | 0 |
| Jordan | 11 | 127 | 11.5 | 0 |
| Edwards | 10 | 132 | 13.2 | 0 |
| Gray | 2 | 45 | 22.5 | 0 |
| Waymer | 1 | 13 | 13.0 | 0 |
| J. Williams | 1 | 5 | 5.0 | 0 |
| Hebert | 1 | 1 | 1.0 | 0 |

### PUNT RETURNS

| Last Name | No. | Yds | Avg | TD |
|---|---|---|---|---|
| Martin | 24 | 227 | 9.5 | 0 |
| McLemore | 10 | 67 | 6.7 | 0 |
| Poe | 8 | 71 | 8.9 | 0 |
| Edwards | 3 | 2 | 0.7 | 0 |
| Tullis | 2 | 10 | 5.0 | 0 |

### KICKOFF RETURNS

| Last Name | No. | Yds | Avg | TD |
|---|---|---|---|---|
| Gray | 31 | 866 | 27.9 | 1 |
| Mayes | 10 | 213 | 21.3 | 0 |
| Harris | 7 | 122 | 17.4 | 0 |
| Martin | 3 | 64 | 21.3 | 0 |
| McLemore | 2 | 39 | 19.5 | 0 |
| Tullis | 2 | 28 | 14.0 | 0 |

### PASSING — PUNTING — KICKING

PASSING

| Last Name | Att | Cmp | % | Yds | Yd/Att | TD | Int— | % | RK |
|---|---|---|---|---|---|---|---|---|---|
| D. Wilson | 342 | 189 | 55 | 2353 | 6.88 | 10 | 17— | 5 | 11 |
| Hebert | 79 | 41 | 52 | 498 | 6.30 | 2 | 8— | 10 | |
| Hilliard | 3 | 1 | 33 | 29 | 29.00 | 0 | 1— | 0 | |
| Wattelet | 1 | 1 | 100 | 13 | 13.00 | 0 | 0— | 0 | |

PUNTING

| Last Name | No | Avg |
|---|---|---|
| Hansen | 82 | 42.1 |

KICKING

| Last Name | XP | Att | % | FG | Att | % |
|---|---|---|---|---|---|---|
| Andersen | 30 | 30 | 100 | 26 | 30 | 87 |

The N.F.L. draft is slow but inexorable. Nothing in the league is surer than that a team drafting near the end, year after year, will eventually stock its roster with a number of athletes of lesser quality than those on teams that consistently draft near the top. It's not so certain that all teams with high draft choices every year will eventually come up winners. A team may make poor choices, key players can be injured, or luck can take a hand. But, on the other end of the scale, any team that must yearly choose its players after 20 or so others have had their picks is going to finally suffer for it. Some teams stave off the inevitable for a while with shrewd choices, clever trading or good luck, but, sooner or later, every dynasty must be rebuilt.

Several of the strongest teams of the 1970s found themselves struggling in 1986, primarily because their low draft positions had not allowed them to replace aging stars with newcomers of equal talent. The Steelers and Chargers had been crumbling for several seasons and may have hit bottom. The Dolphins and Raiders slipped to .500 ballclubs in '86, each with nearly a whole platoon in need of replacement. In the N.F.C., the Cowboys suffered their first losing season since 1965.

## EASTERN DIVISION

**New England Patriots** — The Patriots were 3-3 when they went on a seven-game winning streak to move past the Jets into first place in the East. Then, two late-season losses brought their chances down to a final game at the Orange Bowl where they'd finally broken an 18-year jinx in the 1985 A.F.C. championship game. To the surprise of any who'd questioned the Patriots' chips-down courage, the Steve Grogan-to-Stanley Morgan pass combo led them to a 34-27 win over the Dolphins. Morgan had the best season of his 10-year career, but the running game evaporated with the retirement of all-world guard John Hannah. As a team, the Patriots averaged only 2.9 yards per carry, and none of the regular runners could top that figure. Linebackers Don Blackmon and Andre Tippett and cornerbacks Ronnie Lippett and Raymond Clayborn led a generally satisfactory defense.

**New York Jets** — For the first 11 weeks, the Jets were the best team in the A.F.C. At 10-1, Ken O'Brien looked like the next great quarterback, wide receiver Al Toon was an unstoppable weapon, and the defense, led by nose tackle Joe Klecko, was strong. Then, injuries to Klecko, linebacker Lance Mehl, running back Freeman McNeil, center Joe Fields and others caught up to coach Joe Walton's club. The offense all but disappeared — O'Brien was finally replaced by Pat Ryan — and, by the end of the season, the defense had also collapsed, giving up 97 points in the last two games. But, despite closing with a five-game losing streak, the Jets still had enough wins in the till to qualify as a wild-card team.

**Miami Dolphins** — The Dolphins had half of a great team — the offense. Appropriately, they halved their schedule, going 8-8. The offense, despite a sporadic running game, was awesome as Dan Marino set N.F.L. records for pass attempts (623) and completions (392), while posting marks in yardage (4,746) and touchdowns (44) that had been exceeded only by Marino himself in 1984. His prime receivers, the Marks Brothers — Duper and Clayton — accounted for 127 catches, 2,463 yards and 21 scores between them. But, when they turned the ball over to their opponents, the Dolphins were terrible, particularly in the beginning of the season when they gave up 176 points during a 1-4 start.

**Buffalo Bills** — The much-heralded arrival of quarterback Jim Kelly from the U.S.F.L. increased home attendance by about 30,000 per game and turned the Bills into respectable losers. Besides drawing fans back to the park, Kelly gave the team two things: strong passing and on-field leadership. Despite Kelly's considerable efforts, his supporting cast doomed the Bills to another losing season. They did, however, win two more games than in 1985 and stayed close in most of the losses. Not close

enough to save coach Hank Bullough's job, however; he was replaced after nine games by Marv Levy.

**Indianapolis Colts** — The Colts were sailing along at 0-13, nearly certain of earning the first draft pick in 1987 and with an excellent chance of becoming the first team to lose 16 games in a season. Then, Ron Meyer replaced Rod Dowhower as head coach, he reinstalled Gary Hogeboom (injured in week two) at quarterback and, with the help of a last-second blocked punt, won a game. Even more surprising, the Colts won two more, losing their top draft spot but raising hopes of their fans. Until then, the play of rookie wide receiver Bill Brooks, the solid running of Randy McMillan, Rohn Stark's punting, and strong blocking from Chris Hinton and Ray Donaldson were the few bright spots.

## CENTRAL DIVISION

**Cleveland Browns** — The Browns won the Central Division title for the second straight year, but the '86 team was very different from the '85 club that sneaked in at 8-8. In 1985, Cleveland used a strong running attack and tough defense to grind out wins. The defense was back in '86, but struggled early because of the death of safety Don Rogers and the pre-season holdout of linebacker Chip Banks. Cornerback Hanford Dixon emerged as an outstanding defender. The offense changed completely under the tutelage of new coordinator Lindy Infante. Both Earnest Byner and Kevin Mack, the 1,000-yard rushers of '85, were injured at various times and played together for only eight quarters. But young Bernie Kosar became one of the A.F.C.'s most effective passers, gaining 3,854 yards through the air.

**Cincinnati Bengals** — The Bengals were consistently inconsistent, scoring a ton of points one week and yet being unable to score 10 points three times. The high-tech passing game boasted Boomer Esiason as one of football's top bombers and Cris Collinsworth and Eddie Brown as speedy targets. Back James Brooks rushed for 1,087 yards and caught 54 passes. The mountainous offensive line out-muscled everybody. Even the defense improved to nearly adequate. In week 15, the Bengals needed only a victory over the Browns to win the division, but Kosar completed a 66-yard pass on the first play of the game and Cincinnati never recovered, dropping two straight.

**Pittsburgh Steelers** — Chuck Noll's Steelers came out of the gate belly-up and were 1-6 after New England gave them a 34-0 humiliation, their worst-ever loss at Three Rivers Stadium. But waiver pick Earnest Jackson gave them a strong running attack, receivers Louis Lipps and John Stallworth and center Mike Webster got healthy, and much-maligned quarterback Mark Malone went to an effective short passing game. Pittsburgh was 5-4 down the stretch, with two of the losses in overtime to playoff teams.

**Houston Oilers** — Coach Jerry Glanville let the Oilers stumble to 1-8 before he admitted his conservative offense was not working. The team's strength was its pair of burner receivers, rookie Ernest Givins and veteran Drew Hill. Disappointing quarterback Warren Moon opened up for the remainder of the schedule and the Oilers went 4-3. The end-of-the-season spurt helped improve upon the offensive and defensive stats from 1985, but turnovers and penalties hurt them all year.

## WESTERN DIVISION

**Denver Broncos** — The Broncos' offense was almost all John Elway. The "franchise" quarterback passed for 3,485 yards and was also his team's most dangerous runner. With an under-

FINAL TEAM STATISTICS

OFFENSE

| | BUFF. | CIN. | CLEV. | DENV. | HOU. | IND. | K.C. | L.A. | MIA. | N.E. | NY J | PIT. | S.D. | SEA. |
|---|---|---|---|---|---|---|---|---|---|---|---|---|---|---|
| FIRST DOWNS: | | | | | | | | | | | | | | |
| Total | 291 | 348 | 302 | 319 | 299 | 278 | 264 | 302 | 351 | 314 | 319 | 292 | 334 | 291 |
| by Rushing | 101 | 134 | 102 | 94 | 101 | 77 | 83 | 97 | 84 | 77 | 104 | 125 | 98 | 123 |
| by Passing | 152 | 183 | 175 | 184 | 179 | 173 | 152 | 186 | 250 | 202 | 191 | 140 | 212 | 158 |
| by Penalty | 38 | 31 | 25 | 41 | 19 | 28 | 29 | 19 | 17 | 35 | 24 | 27 | 24 | 10 |
| RUSHING: | | | | | | | | | | | | | | |
| Number | 419 | 521 | 470 | 455 | 490 | 407 | 432 | 475 | 349 | 469 | 490 | 564 | 471 | 513 |
| Yards | 1654 | 2533 | 1650 | 1678 | 1700 | 1491 | 1468 | 1790 | 1545 | 1373 | 1729 | 2223 | 1576 | 2300 |
| Average Yards | 3.9 | 4.9 | 3.5 | 3.7 | 3.5 | 3.7 | 3.4 | 3.8 | 4.4 | 2.9 | 3.5 | 3.9 | 3.3 | 4.5 |
| Touchdowns | 9 | 24 | 20 | 17 | 13 | 10 | 10 | 6 | 9 | 10 | 16 | 18 | 19 | 15 |
| PASSING: | | | | | | | | | | | | | | |
| Attempts | 499 | 497 | 538 | 549 | 551 | 586 | 521 | 530 | 645 | 557 | 537 | 491 | 604 | 453 |
| Completions | 294 | 287 | 315 | 306 | 288 | 300 | 257 | 281 | 392 | 340 | 334 | 238 | 339 | 268 |
| Completion Pct. | 58.9 | 57.7 | 58.6 | 55.7 | 52.3 | 51.2 | 49.3 | 53.0 | 60.8 | 61.0 | 62.2 | 48.5 | 56.1 | 59.2 |
| Passing Yards | 3697 | 4160 | 4018 | 3811 | 3843 | 3615 | 3122 | 3973 | 4898 | 4321 | 4032 | 2747 | 4045 | 3424 |
| Avg. Yds per Att. | 6.2 | 7.5 | 6.5 | 6.0 | 5.8 | 5.0 | 4.8 | 5.9 | 7.2 | 6.6 | 6.3 | 5.1 | 5.9 | 6.3 |
| Avg. Yds per Comp. | 12.6 | 14.5 | 12.8 | 12.5 | 13.3 | 12.1 | 12.2 | 14.1 | 12.5 | 12.7 | 122.1 | 11.5 | 11.9 | 12.8 |
| Times Tackled | 45 | 28 | 39 | 38 | 48 | 53 | 50 | 64 | 17 | 47 | 45 | 20 | 32 | 39 |
| Yds Lost Tackled | 334 | 203 | 274 | 273 | 394 | 406 | 372 | 464 | 119 | 367 | 386 | 159 | 265 | 315 |
| Net Yards | 3363 | 3957 | 3744 | 3538 | 3449 | 3209 | 2750 | 3509 | 4779 | 3954 | 3646 | 2588 | 3780 | 3109 |
| Touchdowns | 22 | 25 | 18 | 22 | 14 | 16 | 23 | 27 | 46 | 29 | 27 | 16 | 21 | 24 |
| Interceptions | 19 | 20 | 11 | 16 | 31 | 24 | 18 | 25 | 23 | 13 | 21 | 20 | 33 | 14 |
| Pct. Intercepted | 3.8 | 4.0 | 2.0 | 2.9 | 5.6 | 4.1 | 3.5 | 4.7 | 3.6 | 2.3 | 3.9 | 4.1 | 5.5 | 3.1 |
| PUNTS: | | | | | | | | | | | | | | |
| Number | 75 | 59 | 83 | 86 | 89 | 81 | 99 | 90 | 56 | 92 | 85 | 89 | 79 | 79 |
| Average | 40.4 | 33.8 | 41.2 | 39.3 | 41.1 | 44.7 | 40.7 | 40.2 | 44.2 | 40.7 | 39.4 | 38.7 | 40.4 | 38.6 |
| PUNT RETURNS | | | | | | | | | | | | | | |
| Number | 32 | 29 | 41 | 48 | 43 | 35 | 35 | 56 | 40 | 42 | 39 | 36 | 37 | 39 |
| Yards | 247 | 235 | 350 | 552 | 341 | 250 | 265 | 484 | 297 | 396 | 341 | 310 | 334 | 457 |
| Average Yards | 7.7 | 8.1 | 8.5 | 11.5 | 7.9 | 7.1 | 7.6 | 8.6 | 7.4 | 9.4 | 8.7 | 8.6 | 9.0 | 11.7 |
| Touchdowns | 1 | 0 | 1 | 2 | 0 | 0 | 0 | 1 | 1 | 1 | 0 | 0 | 0 | 1 |
| KICKOFF RET.: | | | | | | | | | | | | | | |
| Number | 55 | 63 | 62 | 53 | 59 | 74 | 56 | 64 | 65 | 58 | 63 | 66 | 65 | 64 |
| Yards | 1074 | 1389 | 1213 | 1094 | 1139 | 1443 | 1117 | 1252 | 1185 | 1147 | 1189 | 1304 | 1137 | 1322 |
| Average Yards | 19.5 | 22.0 | 19.6 | 20.6 | 19.3 | 19.5 | 19.9 | 19.6 | 18.2 | 19.8 | 18.9 | 19.8 | 17.5 | 20.7 |
| Touchdowns | 0 | 0 | 1 | 0 | 0 | 0 | 1 | 0 | 0 | 0 | 2 | 0 | 0 | 0 |
| INTERCEPT RET.: | | | | | | | | | | | | | | |
| Number | 10 | 17 | 18 | 18 | 16 | 16 | 31 | 26 | 13 | 21 | 20 | 20 | 15 | 22 |
| Yards | 89 | 146 | 184 | 318 | 100 | 166 | 567 | 275 | 152 | 312 | 164 | 218 | 274 | 216 |
| Average Yards | 8.9 | 8.6 | 10.2 | 17.7 | 16.7 | 10.4 | 18.3 | 10.6 | 11.7 | 14.9 | 8.2 | 10.9 | 18.3 | 10.8 |
| Touchdowns | 0 | 1 | 0 | 2 | 0 | 0 | 4 | 1 | 0 | 1 | 0 | 1 | 1 | 1 |
| PENALTIES: | | | | | | | | | | | | | | |
| Number | 121 | 111 | 101 | 104 | 121 | 99 | 97 | 114 | 72 | 87 | 131 | 104 | 119 | 98 |
| Yards | 878 | 847 | 807 | 910 | 1018 | 880 | 829 | 951 | 609 | 672 | 981 | 853 | 977 | 813 |
| FUMBLES: | | | | | | | | | | | | | | |
| Number | 40 | 31 | 31 | 34 | 28 | 41 | 27 | 36 | 37 | 27 | 37 | 27 | 29 | 29 |
| Number Lost | 20 | 16 | 13 | 13 | 12 | 20 | 17 | 24 | 14 | 11 | 16 | 16 | 16 | 13 |
| POINTS: | | | | | | | | | | | | | | |
| Total | 287 | 409 | 391 | 378 | 274 | 229 | 358 | 323 | 430 | 412 | 364 | 307 | 335 | 366 |
| PAT Attempts | 34 | 51 | 45 | 45 | 30 | 27 | 43 | 37 | 56 | 45 | 45 | 35 | 41 | 43 |
| PAT Made | 32 | 50 | 43 | 44 | 28 | 26 | 43 | 36 | 52 | 44 | 44 | 32 | 39 | 42 |
| FG Attempts | 27 | 32 | 33 | 28 | 27 | 25 | 26 | 28 | 22 | 41 | 19 | 32 | 25 | 35 |
| FG Made | 17 | 17 | 26 | 20 | 22 | 13 | 19 | 21 | 14 | 32 | 16 | 21 | 16 | 22 |
| Percent FG Made | 63.0 | 53.1 | 78.8 | 71.4 | 81.5 | 52.0 | 73.1 | 75.0 | 63.6 | 78.0 | 84.2 | 65.6 | 64.0 | 62.9 |
| Safeties | 0 | 1 | 0 | 2 | 0 | 1 | 0 | 1 | 0 | 1 | 1 | 1 | 1 | 0 |

DEFENSE

| | BUFF. | CIN. | CLEV. | DENV. | HOU. | IND. | K.C. | L.A. | MIA. | N.E. | NY J | PIT. | S.D. | SEA. |
|---|---|---|---|---|---|---|---|---|---|---|---|---|---|---|
| FIRST DOWNS: | | | | | | | | | | | | | | |
| Total | 334 | 336 | 302 | 291 | 285 | 334 | 310 | 283 | 337 | 286 | 349 | 303 | 308 | 310 |
| by Rushing | 100 | 134 | 113 | 93 | 102 | 123 | 111 | 85 | 144 | 118 | 92 | 97 | 104 | 93 |
| by Passing | 204 | 171 | 171 | 177 | 137 | 185 | 173 | 168 | 177 | 153 | 216 | 176 | 182 | 192 |
| by Penalty | 30 | 31 | 18 | 21 | 46 | 26 | 26 | 30 | 16 | 15 | 41 | 30 | 22 | 25 |
| RUSHING: | | | | | | | | | | | | | | |
| Number | 465 | 514 | 494 | 432 | 532 | 517 | 485 | 439 | 540 | 510 | 450 | 471 | 475 | 471 |
| Yards | 1721 | 2122 | 1981 | 1681 | 2035 | 1962 | 1739 | 1728 | 2493 | 2203 | 1661 | 1872 | 1678 | 1759 |
| Average Yards | 3.7 | 4.1 | 4.0 | 3.8 | 3.8 | 3.8 | 3.6 | 3.9 | 4.6 | 4.3 | 3.7 | 4.0 | 3.5 | 3.7 |
| Touchdowns | 18 | 23 | 12 | 13 | 13 | 14 | 13 | 19 | 23 | 19 | 12 | 18 | 14 | 12 |
| PASSING: | | | | | | | | | | | | | | |
| Attempts | 570 | 495 | 518 | 545 | 490 | 510 | 569 | 501 | 485 | 473 | 603 | 536 | 509 | 535 |
| Completions | 343 | 278 | 291 | 301 | 228 | 306 | 303 | 271 | 290 | 255 | 348 | 311 | 288 | 301 |
| Completion Pct. | 60.2 | 56.2 | 56.2 | 55.2 | 46.5 | 60.0 | 53.3 | 54.1 | 59.8 | 53.9 | 57.7 | 578.0 | 56.6 | 56.3 |
| Passing Yards | 4069 | 3520 | 3546 | 3755 | 3200 | 3933 | 3555 | 3539 | 3825 | 3324 | 4567 | 3669 | 4128 | 3888 |
| Avg. Yds per Att. | 6.3 | 5.9 | 6.0 | 5.6 | 5.8 | 7.0 | 5.2 | 5.5 | 6.9 | 5.7 | 7.0 | 5.8 | 6.5 | 6.2 |
| Avg. Yds per Comp. | 11.9 | 12.7 | 12.2 | 12.5 | 14.0 | 12.9 | 11.7 | 13.1 | 13.2 | 13.0 | 13.1 | 11.8 | 14.3 | 12.9 |
| Times Tackled | 36 | 42 | 35 | 49 | 32 | 24 | 44 | 63 | 33 | 48 | 28 | 43 | 62 | 47 |
| Yds Lost Tackled | 267 | 368 | 258 | 459 | 201 | 194 | 360 | 463 | 268 | 346 | 178 | 289 | 440 | 306 |
| Net Yards | 3802 | 3152 | 3288 | 3296 | 2999 | 3739 | 3195 | 3076 | 3557 | 2978 | 4389 | 3380 | 3688 | 3582 |
| Touchdowns | 21 | 17 | 21 | 21 | 25 | 28 | 21 | 21 | 22 | 15 | 35 | 22 | 27 | 20 |
| Interceptions | 10 | 17 | 18 | 18 | 16 | 16 | 31 | 26 | 13 | 21 | 20 | 20 | 15 | 22 |
| Pct. Intercepted | 1.8 | 3.4 | 3.5 | 3.3 | 3.3 | 3.1 | 5.4 | 5.2 | 2.7 | 4.4 | 3.3 | 3.7 | 2.9 | 4.1 |
| PUNTS: | | | | | | | | | | | | | | |
| Number | 83 | 77 | 80 | 86 | 94 | 67 | 83 | 97 | 64 | 90 | 75 | 82 | 81 | 81 |
| Average | 38.1 | 39.8 | 37.9 | 42.9 | 39.5 | 40.7 | 37.0 | 42.1 | 41.4 | 39.8 | 39.7 | 39.0 | 40.8 | 40.4 |
| PUNT RETURNS | | | | | | | | | | | | | | |
| Number | 32 | 19 | 44 | 40 | 40 | 52 | 52 | 42 | 23 | 60 | 36 | 34 | 43 | 38 |
| Yards | 260 | 182 | 268 | 362 | 303 | 533 | 572 | 357 | 200 | 565 | 165 | 364 | 370 | 298 |
| Average Yards | 8.1 | 9.6 | 6.1 | 9.1 | 7.6 | 10.3 | 11.0 | 8.5 | 8.7 | 9.4 | 4.6 | 10.7 | 8.6 | 7.8 |
| Touchdowns | 0 | 0 | 0 | 0 | 0 | 1 | 1 | 1 | 0 | 0 | 0 | 0 | 1 | 0 |
| KICKOFF RET.: | | | | | | | | | | | | | | |
| Number | 56 | 80 | 78 | 65 | 32 | 43 | 71 | 63 | 53 | 81 | 62 | 56 | 60 | 59 |
| Yards | 1157 | 1611 | 1476 | 1299 | 695 | 827 | 1278 | 1064 | 997 | 1480 | 1307 | 1362 | 1088 | 1002 |
| Average Yards | 20.7 | 20.1 | 18.9 | 20.0 | 21.7 | 19.2 | 18.0 | 16.9 | 18.8 | 18.3 | 21.1 | 24.3 | 18.1 | 17.0 |
| Touchdowns | 0 | 1 | 1 | 0 | 0 | 0 | 0 | 0 | 0 | 0 | 0 | 3 | 0 | 0 |
| INTERCEPT RET.: | | | | | | | | | | | | | | |
| Number | 19 | 20 | 11 | 16 | 31 | 24 | 18 | 25 | 23 | 13 | 21 | 20 | 33 | 14 |
| Yards | 284 | 189 | 135 | 363 | 325 | 310 | 181 | 282 | 221 | 151 | 230 | 244 | 421 | 216 |
| Average Yards | 15.0 | 9.5 | 12.3 | 22.7 | 10.5 | 12.9 | 10.0 | 11.3 | 9.6 | 11.6 | 11.0 | 12.2 | 12.8 | 15.4 |
| Touchdowns | 0 | 0 | 1 | 2 | 1 | 2 | 1 | 1 | 1 | 0 | 1 | 2 | 2 | 1 |
| PENALTIES: | | | | | | | | | | | | | | |
| Number | 128 | 93 | 101 | 127 | 85 | 100 | 114 | 118 | 82 | 106 | 102 | 109 | 108 | 81 |
| Yards | 1098 | 840 | 754 | 1034 | 674 | 728 | 965 | 868 | 596 | 866 | 795 | 904 | 918 | 652 |
| FUMBLES: | | | | | | | | | | | | | | |
| Number | 19 | 30 | 36 | 32 | 31 | 41 | 26 | 33 | 32 | 38 | 48 | 31 | 42 | 26 |
| Number Lost | 8 | 11 | 19 | 17 | 16 | 19 | 18 | 12 | 14 | 19 | 18 | 13 | 22 | 14 |
| POINTS: | | | | | | | | | | | | | | |
| Total | 348 | 394 | 310 | 327 | 329 | 400 | 326 | 346 | 405 | 307 | 386 | 336 | 396 | 293 |
| PAT Attempts | 40 | 47 | 36 | 36 | 38 | 47 | 39 | 43 | 47 | 35 | 48 | 39 | 47 | 34 |
| PAT Made | 38 | 44 | 34 | 35 | 38 | 46 | 36 | 40 | 45 | 34 | 48 | 36 | 45 | 32 |
| FG Attempts | 33 | 30 | 29 | 32 | 29 | 35 | 31 | 21 | 31 | 28 | 27 | 39 | 31 | 28 |
| FG Made | 22 | 22 | 20 | 24 | 19 | 24 | 20 | 16 | 26 | 21 | 16 | 22 | 23 | 19 |
| Percent FG Made | 66.7 | 73.3 | 69.0 | 75.0 | 65.5 | 68.6 | 64.5 | 76.2 | 83.9 | 75.0 | 59.3 | 56.4 | 74.2 | 67.9 |
| Safeties | 2 | 1 | 0 | 2 | 0 | 0 | 1 | 0 | 0 | 0 | 1 | 0 | 0 | 0 |

sized offensive line that could block better for passing than running and a group of backs that was ordinary at best, Elway took over the attack with his arm and feet and led Denver to the Western Division title. They got out in front with a 6-0 start and then alternated wins and losses to hold on. The defense, bulwarked by linebackers Karl Mecklenburg and Ricky Hunley, end Rulon Jones and cornerback Louis Wright, was strong early but slumped badly at season's end.

**Kansas City Chiefs** — The Chiefs had their first winning season since 1981 and earned a playoff berth for the first time since 1971, so, naturally, they fired the coach at the end of the season. John Mackovic was blamed for the team's poor offense and general disharmony. His successor, special-teams coach Frank Gansz, had produced a unit that blocked 11 kicks (four by Albert Lewis) and had six touchdown returns. In the final game against Pittsburgh, needing a win to make the playoffs, the special teams accounted for all three touchdowns in a 24-19 win.

**Seattle Seahawks** — The Seahawks stood 5-3 after losing at Denver on October 26, but they'd been inconsistent. Coach Chuck Knox benched quarterback Dave Krieg, replacing him with Gale Gilbert, and the team became *very* inconsistent. They lost three straight with only a single touchdown in each outing. When Krieg was restored as the starter, Seattle won its final five and just missed the playoffs. During the final month, Krieg's pass rating was a sensational 138.2. Running back Curt Warner proved he was fully recovered from knee surgery by leading the A.F.C. in rushing with 1,481 yards and 13 scores. Receiver Steve Largent set an N.F.L. record after catching passes in 139 consecutive games. Defensive end Jacob Green had an outstanding year with 12 sacks, but the defense was hurt when safety Kenny Easley went out with injuries.

**Los Angeles Raiders** — The Raiders began to show their age in '86. The offensive line was blitzed for 64 sacks, which didn't help a shaky quarterback situation. By mid-season, coach Tom Flores benched Marc Wilson in favor of ancient Jim Plunkett, who played well until he was injured. Running back Marcus Allen had a terrible year, gaining only 759 yards — exactly 1,000 fewer than he gained in '85 — and fumbling at inopportune times. Even the defense, long a source of pride, showed some slippage, although cornerback Mike Haynes and nose tackle Bill Pickel were outstanding. Todd Christensen's 92 pass receptions broke his own record for tight ends.

**San Diego Chargers** — The resignation of coach Don Coryell with the team at 1-7 did not mark a great turnaround in the Chargers' fortunes, but new coach Al Saunders promised a change from the team's point-a-minute defenses of the past. Indeed, in the three games won under Saunders, the Chargers held their opponents without a touchdown. Linebacker Billy Ray Smith, with 11 sacks and 110 tackles, was the leading light in the defensive improvement. Quarterback Dan Fouts showed he could play Saunder's ball-control, short passing game but suffered a couple of concussions along the way. Running back Gary Anderson led the team in both rushing and receiving.

**NEW ENGLAND PATRIOTS** 11-5 Raymond Berry

| Scores of Each Game | | |
|---|---|---|
| 33 | INDIANAPOLIS | 3 |
| 20 | N.Y.Jets | 6 |
| 31 | SEATTLE | 38 |
| 20 | Denver | 27 |
| 34 | MIAMI | 7 |
| 24 | N.Y.JETS | 31 |
| 34 | Pittsburgh | 0 |
| 23 | Buffalo | 3 |
| 25 | ATLANTA | 17 |
| 30 | Indianapolis | 21 |
| 30 | L.A.Rams | 28 |
| 22 | BUFFALO | 19 |
| 21 | New Orleans | 20 |
| 7 | CINCINNATI | 31 |
| 24 | SAN FRANCISCO | 29 |
| 34 | Miami | 27 |

| Use Name | Pos. | Hgt | Wgt | Age | Int | Pts |
|---|---|---|---|---|---|---|
| Bill Bain (from NYJ) | OT | 6'4" | 290 | 34 | | |
| Brian Holloway | OT | 6'7" | 288 | 27 | | |
| Darryl Haley | OT-OG | 6'4" | 265 | 25 | | |
| Steve Moore | OT | 6'4" | 305 | 25 | | |
| Paul Fairchild | OG | 6'4" | 270 | 24 | | |
| Ron Wooten | OG | 6'4" | 273 | 27 | | |
| Guy Morriss | OG-C | 6'4" | 275 | 35 | | |
| Pete Brock | C | 6'5" | 275 | 32 | | |
| Trevor Matich | C | 6'4" | 270 | 24 | | |
| Milford Hodge (from NO) | DE-NT | 6'3" | 278 | 25 | | |
| Kenneth Sims | DE | 6'5" | 271 | 26 | | |
| Garin Veris | DE | 6'4" | 255 | 23 | | |
| Toby Williams | DE-NT | 6'3" | 270 | 26 | | |
| Brent Williams | DE-NT | 6'3" | 278 | 21 | | 6 |
| Dennis Owens | NT | 6'1" | 258 | 26 | | |
| Mike Ruth | NT | 6'1" | 266 | 22 | | |

Lin Dawson - Knee Injury
Art Plunkett - Knee Injury

| Use Name | Pos. | Hgt | Wgt | Age | Int | Pts |
|---|---|---|---|---|---|---|
| Mel Black | LB | 6'2" | 228 | 24 | | |
| Don Blackman | LB | 6'3" | 235 | 28 | | |
| Steve Doig | LB | 6'2" | 240 | 26 | | |
| Larry McGrew | LB | 6'5" | 233 | 29 | 2 | |
| Steve Nelson | LB | 6'2" | 230 | 25 | 2 | |
| Johnny Rembert | LB | 6'3" | 234 | 25 | 1 | 6 |
| Ed Reynolds | LB | 6'5" | 242 | 24 | | |
| Andre Tippett | LB | 6'3" | 241 | 26 | | |
| Clayton Weishuhn | LB | 6'2" | 220 | 25 | | |
| Ed Williams | LB | 6'4" | 245 | 25 | | |
| Jim Bowman | DB | 6'2" | 210 | 22 | | |
| Raymond Clayborn | DB | 6'1" | 186 | 31 | 3 | |
| Ernest Gibson | DB | 5'10" | 185 | 24 | | |
| Roland James | DB | 6'2" | 191 | 28 | 2 | |
| Ronnie Lippett | DB | 5'11" | 180 | 25 | 8 | |
| Fred Marion | DB | 6'2" | 191 | 27 | 2 | 6 |
| Rod McSwain | DB | 6'1" | 198 | 24 | 1 | 6 |
| Eugene Profit | DB | 5'10" | 165 | 21 | | |

| Use Name | Pos. | Hgt | Wgt | Age | Int | Pts |
|---|---|---|---|---|---|---|
| Tony Eason | QB | 6'4" | 212 | 26 | | |
| Steve Grogan | QB | 6'4" | 210 | 33 | | 6 |
| Tom Ramsey | QB | 6'1" | 189 | 25 | | |
| Tony Collins | HB | 5'11" | 212 | 27 | | 48 |
| Reggie Dupard | HB | 5'11" | 205 | 22 | | |
| Craig James | HB | 6' | 215 | 25 | | 24 |
| Moel Tatupu | FB | 6' | 227 | 31 | | 12 |
| Robert Weathers | FB | 6'2" | 222 | 25 | | 6 |
| Irving Fryar | WR | 6' | 200 | 23 | | 42 |
| Cedric Jones | WR | 6'1" | 184 | 26 | | 6 |
| Stanley Morgan | WR | 5'11" | 181 | 31 | | 60 |
| Stephen Starring | WR | 5'10" | 172 | 25 | | 12 |
| Derwin Williams | WR | 6'1" | 185 | 25 | | |
| Greg Baty | TE | 6'5" | 241 | 22 | | 12 |
| Greg Hawthorne | TE | 6'2" | 235 | 29 | | |
| Willie Scott | TE | 6'4" | 245 | 27 | | 18 |
| Rich Camarillo | K | 5'11" | 185 | 26 | | |
| Tony Franklin | K | 5'8" | 182 | 29 | | 140 |

**NEW YORK JETS** 10-6 Joe Walton

| Scores of Each Game | | |
|---|---|---|
| 28 | Buffalo | 24 |
| 6 | NEW ENGLAND | 20 |
| 51 | MIAMI | *45 |
| 26 | Indianapolis | 7 |
| 14 | BUFFALO | 13 |
| 31 | New England | 24 |
| 22 | DENVER | 10 |
| 28 | NEW ORLEANS | 23 |
| 38 | Seattle | 7 |
| 28 | Atlanta | 14 |
| 31 | INDIANAPOLIS | 16 |
| 3 | Miami | 45 |
| 3 | L.A.RAMS | 17 |
| 10 | San Francisco | 24 |
| 24 | PITTSBURGH | 45 |
| 21 | Cincinnati | 52 |

| Use Name | Pos. | Hgt | Wgt | Age | Int | Pts |
|---|---|---|---|---|---|---|
| Gordon King | OT-OG | 6'6" | 270 | 30 | | |
| Reggie McElroy | OT | 6'6" | 275 | 26 | | |
| Jim Sweeney | OT-OG | 6'4" | 260 | 24 | | |
| Dan Alexander | OG | 6'4" | 270 | 31 | | |
| Ted Banker | OG-OT-C | 6'2" | 265 | 25 | | |
| Mike Haight | OG-OT | 6'4" | 270 | 23 | | |
| Guy Bingham | C-OT-OG | 6'3" | 260 | 28 | | |
| Joe Fields | C | 6'2" | 253 | 32 | | |
| Barry Bennett | DE-DT | 6'4" | 260 | 30 | | |
| Mark Gastineau | DE | 6'5" | 270 | 29 | | |
| Marty Lyons | DE-DT | 6'5" | 269 | 29 | | |
| Ben Rudolph | DE | 6'5" | 271 | 29 | | |
| Tom Baldwin | DT | 6'4" | 275 | 25 | | |
| Joe Klecko | NT-DT-DE | 6'3" | 265 | 32 | | |
| Derland Moore (from NO) | NT | 6'4" | 273 | 34 | | |

Johnny "Lam" Jones - Finger Injury
Kirk Springs - Back Injury
Stan Waldemore - Knee Injury
Nick Bruckner - Shoulder Injury

| Use Name | Pos. | Hgt | Wgt | Age | Int | Pts |
|---|---|---|---|---|---|---|
| Rogers Alexander | LB | 6'3" | 220 | 22 | | |
| Troy Benson | LB | 6'2" | 235 | 23 | | |
| Kyle Clifton | LB | 6'4" | 230 | 24 | 2 | |
| Bob Crable | LB | 6'3" | 230 | 26 | 1 | |
| Rusty Guilbeau | LB | 6'4" | 235 | 27 | | |
| Charles Jackson | LB | 6'2" | 225 | 31 | | |
| Kevin McArthur | LB | 6'2" | 230 | 23 | | |
| Lance Mehl | LB | 6'3" | 233 | 28 | | |
| Matt Monger | LB | 6'1" | 238 | 24 | | |
| Russell Carter | DB | 6'2" | 195 | 24 | | |
| Robert Ducksworth | DB | 5'11" | 200 | 23 | | |
| Harry Hamilton | DB | 6' | 195 | 23 | 1 | |
| Jerry Holmes | DB | 6'2" | 175 | 28 | 6 | |
| Carl Howard | DB | 6'2" | 190 | 24 | | |
| Bobby Humphery | DB | 5'10" | 180 | 25 | | 8 |
| Kerry Glenn | DB | 5'9" | 175 | 24 | | |
| Lester Lyles | DB-LB | 6'3" | 218 | 23 | 5 | |
| Johnny Lynn | DB | 6' | 198 | 29 | 5 | |
| Rich Milano | DB | 6' | 200 | 23 | | |
| Devlin Mullen | DB | 6'1" | 177 | 26 | | |

| Use Name | Pos. | Hgt | Wgt | Age | Int | Pts |
|---|---|---|---|---|---|---|
| Ken O'Brien | QB | 6'4" | 208 | 25 | | |
| Pat Ryan | QB | 6'3" | 210 | 30 | | |
| Richard Todd | QB | 6'2" | 212 | 32 | | |
| Dennis Bilgen (to TB) | HB | 5'11" | 215 | 24 | | 6 |
| Johnny Hector | HB | 5'11" | 200 | 25 | | 48 |
| Freeman McNeil | HB | 5'11" | 214 | 27 | | 36 |
| Marlon Barber | FB | 6'3" | 228 | 26 | | |
| Nuu Faaola | FB | 5'11" | 215 | 22 | | |
| Tony Paige | FB | 5'10" | 225 | 23 | | 12 |
| Michael Harper | WR | 5'10" | 180 | 25 | | |
| Kurt Sohn | WR | 5'11" | 180 | 29 | | 12 |
| Al Toon | WR | 6'4" | 205 | 23 | | 48 |
| JoJo Townsell | WR | 5'9" | 180 | 25 | | 6 |
| Wesley Walker | WR | 6' | 182 | 31 | | 72 |
| Billy Griggs | TE | 6'3" | 230 | 24 | | |
| Rocky Klever | TE | 6'3" | 228 | 27 | | |
| Mickey Shuler | TE | 6'3" | 231 | 30 | | 24 |
| Pat Leahy | K | 6' | 200 | 35 | | 92 |
| Dave Jennings | K | 6'4" | 200 | 34 | | |

**MIAMI DOLPHINS** 8-8 Don Shula

| Scores of Each Game | | |
|---|---|---|
| 28 | San Diego | 50 |
| 30 | INDIANAPOLIS | 10 |
| 45 | N.Y.Jets | *51 |
| 16 | SAN FRANCISCO | 31 |
| 7 | New England | 34 |
| 27 | BUFFALO | 14 |
| 28 | L.A.RAIDERS | 30 |
| 17 | Indianapolis | 13 |
| 28 | HOUSTON | 7 |
| 16 | Cleveland | 26 |
| 34 | Buffalo | 24 |
| 45 | N.Y.JETS | 3 |
| 14 | ATLANTA | 20 |
| 31 | New Orleans | 27 |
| 37 | L.A.Rams | 31 |
| 27 | NEW ENGLAND | 34 |

| Use Name | Pos. | Hgt | Wgt | Age | Int | Pts |
|---|---|---|---|---|---|---|
| Jeff Dellenbach | OT | 6'6" | 280 | 23 | | |
| Jon Giesler | OT | 6'5" | 265 | 29 | | |
| Cleveland Green | OT | 6'3" | 263 | 28 | | |
| Greg Koch | OT | 6'4" | 276 | 31 | | |
| Tom Toth | OT | 6'5" | 275 | 24 | | |
| Roy Foster | OG | 6'4" | 275 | 26 | | |
| Ronnie Lee | OG | 6'3" | 265 | 29 | | |
| Larry Lee | C | 6'2" | 263 | 26 | | |
| Dwight Stephenson | C | 6'2" | 255 | 28 | | |
| Doug Betters | DE | 6'7" | 265 | 30 | | |
| Jerome Foster (to NYJ) | DE | 6'2" | 275 | 26 | | |
| George Little | DE | 6'4" | 278 | 23 | | |
| Mack Moore (to SD) | DE | 6'4" | 258 | 27 | | |
| T.J.Turner | DE | 6'4" | 265 | 23 | | |
| Bob Baumhower | NT | 6'5" | 265 | 31 | | |
| Mike Charles | NT | 6'4" | 287 | 23 | 1 | |
| Brian Sochia | NT | 6'3" | 274 | 25 | | |

Joe Rose - Leg Injury
Robin Sendlein - Knee Injury
Steve Clark - Injury
Charles Bowser - Ankle Injury

| Use Name | Pos. | Hgt | Wgt | Age | Int | Pts |
|---|---|---|---|---|---|---|
| Jay Brophy | LB | 6'3" | 233 | 26 | | |
| Mark Brown | LB | 6'2" | 230 | 25 | | |
| Bob Brudzinski | LB | 6'4" | 223 | 31 | | |
| David Frye | LB | 6'2" | 227 | 25 | | |
| Hugh Green | LB | 6'2" | 225 | 27 | | |
| Andy Hendel | LB | 6'1" | 230 | 25 | | |
| Larry Kolic | LB | 6'1" | 242 | 23 | | |
| Alex Moyer | LB | 6'1" | 221 | 22 | | |
| John Offerdahl | LB | 6'3" | 232 | 22 | 1 | |
| Jackie Shipp | LB | 6'2" | 236 | 24 | | |
| Jack Squirek | LB | 6'4" | 235 | 27 | | |
| Glenn Blackwood | DB | 6' | 190 | 29 | 2 | |
| Lyle Blackwood | DB | 6' | 190 | 35 | 1 | |
| Bud Brown | DB | 6' | 194 | 25 | 1 | |
| William Judson | DB | 6'1" | 190 | 27 | 2 | |
| Mike Kozlowski | DB | 6' | 198 | 30 | 1 | |
| Paul Lankford | DB | 6'1" | 184 | 28 | | |
| Don McNeal | DB | 5'11" | 192 | 28 | 2 | |
| Donovan Rose | DB | 6'1" | 190 | 29 | 2 | |
| Mike Smith | DB | 6' | 171 | 23 | | |
| Reyna Thompson | DB | 5'11" | 194 | 23 | | |

| Use Name | Pos. | Hgt | Wgt | Age | Int | Pts |
|---|---|---|---|---|---|---|
| Dan Marino | QB | 6'4" | 214 | 24 | | |
| Don Strock | QB | 6'5" | 225 | 35 | | |
| Joe Carter | HB | 5'11" | 198 | 24 | | |
| Craig Elis | HB | 5'11" | 180 | 25 | | |
| Lorenzo Hampton | HB | 6' | 212 | 24 | | 72 |
| Tony Nathan | HB | 6' | 206 | 29 | | 12 |
| Woody Bennett | FB | 6'2" | 225 | 30 | | |
| Ron Davenport | FB | 6'2" | 230 | 23 | | 6 |
| Mark Clayton | WR | 5'9" | 175 | 25 | | 60 |
| Mark Duper | WR | 5'9" | 187 | 27 | | 66 |
| Jim Jensen | WR | 6'4" | 215 | 27 | | 6 |
| Nat Moore | WR | 5'9" | 188 | 34 | | 42 |
| James Pruitt | WR | 6'3" | 199 | 22 | | 18 |
| Bruce Hardy | TE | 6'5" | 232 | 30 | | 30 |
| Dan Johnson | TE | 6'3" | 240 | 26 | | 24 |
| Fuad Reveiz | K | 5'11" | 222 | 23 | | 94 |
| Reggie Roby | K | 6'2" | 243 | 25 | | |

**BUFFALO BILLS** 4-12 Hank Bullough (2-7) Marv Levy (2-5)

| Scores of Each Game | | |
|---|---|---|
| 24 | N.Y.JETS | 28 |
| 33 | Cincinnati | *36 |
| 17 | ST.LOUIS | 10 |
| 17 | KANSAS CITY | 20 |
| 13 | N.Y.Jets | 14 |
| 14 | Miami | 27 |
| 24 | INDIANAPOLIS | 13 |
| 3 | NEW ENGLAND | 23 |
| 28 | Tampa Bay | 34 |
| 16 | PITTSBURGH | 12 |
| 24 | MIAMI | 34 |
| 19 | New England | 22 |
| 17 | Kansas City | 14 |
| 17 | CLEVELAND | 21 |
| 14 | Indianapolis | 24 |
| 7 | Houston | 16 |

| Use Name | Pos. | Hgt | Wgt | Age | Int | Pts |
|---|---|---|---|---|---|---|
| Justin Cross | OT | 6'6" | 265 | 27 | | |
| Joe Devlin | OT | 6'5" | 280 | 32 | | |
| Dale Hellestrae | OT | 6'5" | 275 | 24 | | |
| Ken Jones | OT | 6'5" | 285 | 34 | | |
| Will Wolford | OT | 6'5" | 276 | 22 | | |
| Jim Ritcher | OG | 6'3" | 265 | 28 | | |
| Mark Traynowicz | OG | 6'5" | 275 | 23 | | |
| Tim Vogler | OG | 6'3" | 285 | 29 | | |
| Leonard Burton | C | 6'3" | 252 | 22 | | |
| Kent Hull | C | 6'4" | 262 | 25 | | |
| Mike Hamby | DE | 6'4" | 270 | 23 | | |
| Sean McNanie | DE | 6'5" | 270 | 24 | | |
| Dean Prater | DE | 6'4" | 280 | 23 | | |
| Bruce Smith | DE | 6'4" | 280 | 23 | | |
| Jerry Boyarsky (to GB) | NT | 6'3" | 290 | 27 | | |
| Mark Catano | NT | 6'3" | 267 | 24 | | |
| Fred Smerlas | NT | 6'3" | 280 | 29 | 1 | |
| Don Smith | NT | 6'5" | 262 | 29 | | |

| Use Name | Pos. | Hgt | Wgt | Age | Int | Pts |
|---|---|---|---|---|---|---|
| Ray Bentley | LB | 6'2" | 250 | 25 | | |
| George Cumby | LB | 6' | 224 | 30 | | |
| Guy Frazier | LB | 6'2" | 217 | 27 | | |
| Tony Furjanic | LB | 6'1" | 228 | 22 | | |
| Hal Garner | LB | 6'4" | 225 | 24 | | |
| Eugene Marve | LB | 6'2" | 240 | 26 | | |
| Lucius Sanford | LB | 6'2" | 220 | 30 | | |
| Darryl Talley | LB | 6'4" | 227 | 26 | | |
| Martin Bayless | DB | 6'2" | 195 | 23 | 1 | |
| Rodney Bellinger | DB | 5'8" | 189 | 24 | 1 | 6 |
| Derrick Burroughs | DB | 6'1" | 180 | 24 | 2 | |
| Dwight Drane | DB | 6'1" | 200 | 24 | | |
| Steve Freeman | DB | 5'11" | 185 | 33 | 1 | |
| Rod Hill (to DET) | DB | 6' | 188 | 27 | | |
| Mark Kelso | DB | 5'11" | 177 | 23 | | |
| Ron Pitts | DB | 5'10" | 175 | 23 | | 6 |
| Charles Romes | DB | 6'1" | 190 | 32 | 4 | |
| Kevin Williams | DB | 5'9" | 170 | 24 | | |

Greg Christy - Neck Injury
Jim Haslett - Knee Injury
Lawrence Johnson - Leg Injury
Mitchell Brookins - Knee Injury

| Use Name | Pos. | Hgt | Wgt | Age | Int | Pts |
|---|---|---|---|---|---|---|
| Stan Gelbaugh | QB | 6'3" | 207 | 23 | | |
| Jim Kelly | QB | 6'3" | 215 | 26 | | |
| Frank Reich | QB | 6'3" | 208 | 24 | | |
| Greg Bell | HB | 5'10" | 210 | 24 | | 36 |
| Ronnie Harmon | HB | 5'11" | 192 | 22 | | 6 |
| Robb Riddick | HB | 6' | 195 | 29 | | 30 |
| Carl Byrum | FB | 6' | 232 | 23 | | 6 |
| Bruce King (from KC) | FB | 6'1" | 219 | 23 | | |
| Ricky Moore | FB | 5'11" | 230 | 23 | | 6 |
| Gary Wilkins | FB | 6'1" | 235 | 22 | | |
| Walter Broughton | WR | 5'10" | 180 | 23 | | |
| Chris Burkett | WR | 6'4" | 198 | 24 | | 24 |
| Jerry Butler | WR | 6' | 178 | 28 | | 12 |
| Andre Reed | WR | 6' | 186 | 23 | | 42 |
| Eric Richardson | WR | 6'1" | 185 | 24 | | |
| Steve Tasker (from HOU) | WR | 5'9" | 185 | 24 | | |
| Jimmy Teal | WR | 5'10" | 170 | 24 | | 6 |
| Don Kern | TE | 6'4" | 235 | 24 | | |
| Pete Metzelaars | TE | 6'7" | 243 | 26 | | 24 |
| Butch Rolle | TE | 6'3" | 242 | 22 | | |
| John Kidd | K | 6'3" | 208 | 25 | | |
| Scott Norwood | K | 6' | 207 | 26 | | 83 |

**INDIANAPOLIS COLTS** 3-13 Rod Dowhower (0-13) Ron Meyer (3-0)

| Scores of Each Game | | |
|---|---|---|
| 3 | New England | 33 |
| 10 | Miami | 30 |
| 7 | L.A.RAMS | 24 |
| 7 | N.Y.JETS | 26 |
| 14 | San Francisco | 35 |
| 14 | NEW ORLEANS | 17 |
| 13 | Buffalo | 24 |
| 13 | MIAMI | 17 |
| 9 | CLEVELAND | 24 |
| 21 | NEW ENGLAND | 30 |
| 16 | N.Y.Jets | 31 |
| 17 | Houston | 31 |
| 3 | SAN DIEGO | 17 |
| 28 | Atlanta | 23 |
| 24 | BUFFALO | 14 |
| 30 | L.A.Raiders | 24 |

| Use Name | Pos. | Hgt | Wgt | Age | Int | Pts |
|---|---|---|---|---|---|---|
| Karl Baldischwiler | OT | 6'5" | 276 | 30 | | |
| Bob Brotzki | OT | 6'5" | 269 | 23 | | |
| Kevin Call | OT | 6'7" | 293 | 24 | | |
| Roger Caron | OT | 6'5" | 272 | 24 | | |
| Chris Hinton | OT | 6'4" | 288 | 25 | | |
| Mark Kirchner | OG | 6'3" | 265 | 26 | | |
| Ron Solt | OG | 6'3" | 279 | 24 | | |
| Ben Utt | OG | 6'5" | 281 | 27 | | |
| Ray Donaldson | C | 6'3" | 282 | 28 | | |
| Willie Broughton | DE | 6'5" | 277 | 21 | | |
| Jon Hand | DE | 6'7" | 280 | 22 | 1 | |
| Donnell Thompson | DE | 6'4" | 272 | 27 | | |
| John Haines | DE-DT-NT | 6'6" | 266 | 24 | | |
| Scott Kellar | DT | 6'3" | 278 | 22 | | |
| Harvey Armstrong | NT | 6'3" | 261 | 26 | 1 | |

| Use Name | Pos. | Hgt | Wgt | Age | Int | Pts |
|---|---|---|---|---|---|---|
| Dave Ahrens | LB | 6'3" | 245 | 27 | | |
| Duane Bickett | LB | 6'5" | 241 | 23 | 2 | |
| Johnie Cooks | LB | 6'4" | 251 | 27 | 1 | |
| Lamonte Hunley | LB | 6'2" | 241 | 23 | | |
| Barry Krauss | LB | 6'3" | 253 | 29 | | |
| Jeff Leiding | LB | 6'3" | 232 | 24 | | 2 |
| Orlando Lowry | LB | 6'4" | 237 | 25 | | |
| Cliff Odom | LB | 6'2" | 241 | 28 | | |
| Glenn Redd (from NO) | LB | 6'1" | 232 | 28 | | |
| Pat Ballage | DB | 6'1" | 200 | 22 | | |
| Dexter Clinkscale | DB | 5'11" | 195 | 28 | | |
| Leonard Coleman | DB | 6'2" | 197 | 24 | 4 | |
| Eugene Daniel | DB | 5'11" | 178 | 25 | 3 | 6 |
| Kenny Daniel | DB | 5'10" | 180 | 26 | 1 | |
| Preston Davis | DB | 5'11" | 180 | 24 | | |
| Nesby Glasgow | DB | 5'10" | 186 | 29 | | |
| Dwight Hicks | DB | 6'1" | 192 | 30 | 2 | |
| John Holt | DB | 5'11" | 180 | 27 | 1 | |
| ~~Victor Jackson~~ | ~~DB~~ | ~~6'~~ | ~~205~~ | ~~26~~ | | |
| Tate Randle | DB | 6' | 204 | 27 | | |
| Tommy Sims | DB | 6' | 190 | 21 | | |

| Use Name | Pos. | Hgt | Wgt | Age | Int | Pts |
|---|---|---|---|---|---|---|
| Gary Hogeboom | QB | 6'4" | 207 | 28 | | 6 |
| Blair Kiel | QB | 6' | 200 | 24 | | |
| Ed Luther | QB | 6'3" | 210 | 29 | | |
| Jack Trudeau | QB | 6'3" | 211 | 23 | | 6 |
| Albert Bentley | HB | 5'11" | 210 | 26 | | 18 |
| George Wonsley | HB | 5'10" | 220 | 25 | | 6 |
| Owen Gill | FB | 6'1" | 230 | 24 | | 6 |
| Randy McMillan | FB | 6' | 216 | 27 | | 18 |
| Hubie Oliver (to HOU) | FB | 5'10" | 230 | 28 | | |
| Matt Bouza | WR | 6'3" | 208 | 28 | | 30 |
| Bill Brooks | WR | 5'11" | 190 | 22 | | 48 |
| Wayne Capers | WR | 6'2" | 203 | 25 | | |
| James Harbour | WR | 6'1" | 192 | 23 | | |
| Robbie Martin | WR | 5'8" | 187 | 27 | | |
| Walter Murray | WR | 6'4" | 200 | 23 | | |
| Pat Beach | TE | 6'4" | 244 | 26 | | 6 |
| Mark Boyer | TE | 6'4" | 239 | 23 | | 6 |
| Greg LaFleur (from STL) | TE | 6'4" | 236 | 27 | | |
| Tim Sherwin | TE | 6'6" | 246 | 28 | | 6 |
| Dean Biasucci | K | 6' | 198 | 24 | | 65 |
| Rohn Stark | K | 6'3" | 202 | 27 | | |

* Overtime

## NEW ENGLAND PATRIOTS

### RUSHING
| Last Name | No. | Yds | Avg | TD |
|---|---|---|---|---|
| C. James | 154 | 427 | 2.8 | 4 |
| Collins | 156 | 412 | 2.6 | 3 |
| Tatupu | 71 | 172 | 2.4 | 1 |
| Eason | 35 | 170 | 4.9 | 0 |
| Fryar | 4 | 80 | 20.0 | 0 |
| Weathers | 21 | 58 | 2.8 | 1 |
| Dupard | 15 | 39 | 2.6 | 0 |
| Grogan | 9 | 23 | 2.6 | 1 |
| Hawthorne | 1 | 5 | 5.0 | 0 |
| Starring | 1 | 0 | 0.00 | 0 |
| Ramsey | 1 | -6 | -6.0 | 0 |
| Jones | 1 | -7 | -7.0 | 0 |

### RECEIVING
| Last Name | No. | Yds | Avg | TD |
|---|---|---|---|---|
| Morgan | 84 | 1491 | 17.8 | 10 |
| Collins | 77 | 684 | 8.9 | 5 |
| Fryar | 43 | 737 | 17.1 | 6 |
| Baty | 37 | 331 | 8.9 | 2 |
| Hawthorne | 24 | 192 | 8.0 | 0 |
| C. James | 18 | 129 | 7.2 | 0 |
| Starring | 16 | 295 | 18.4 | 2 |
| Tatupu | 15 | 145 | 9.7 | 0 |
| Jones | 14 | 222 | 15.9 | 1 |
| Scott | 8 | 41 | 5.1 | 3 |
| D. Williams | 2 | 35 | 17.5 | 0 |
| Weathers | 1 | 14 | 14.0 | 0 |
| Holloway | 1 | 5 | 5.0 | 0 |

### PUNT RETURNS
| Last Name | No. | Yds | Avg | TD |
|---|---|---|---|---|
| Fryar | 35 | 366 | 10.5 | 1 |
| Starring | 6 | 18 | 3.0 | 0 |
| Marion | 1 | 12 | 12.0 | 0 |

### KICKOFF RETURNS
| Last Name | No. | Yds | Avg | TD |
|---|---|---|---|---|
| Starring | 36 | 802 | 22.3 | 0 |
| Fryar | 10 | 192 | 19.2 | 0 |
| Jones | 4 | 63 | 15.8 | 0 |
| Dupard | 3 | 50 | 16.7 | 0 |
| Rembert | 3 | 27 | 9.0 | 0 |
| Hawthorne | 2 | 13 | 6.5 | 0 |

### PASSING — PUNTING — KICKING
| PASSING | Att | Cmp | % | Yds | Yd/Att | TD | Int- | % | RK |
|---|---|---|---|---|---|---|---|---|---|
| Eason | 448 | 276 | 62 | 3328 | 7.4 | 19 | 10- | 2 | 3 |
| Grogan | 102 | 62 | 61 | 976 | 9.6 | 9 | 2- | 2 | |
| C. James | 4 | 1 | 25 | 10 | 2.5 | 1 | 1- | 25 | |
| Ramsey | 3 | 1 | 33 | 7 | 2.3 | 0 | 0- | 0 | |

| PUNTING | No | Avg |
|---|---|---|
| Camarillo | 89 | 42.1 |

| KICKING | XP | Att | % | FG | Att | % |
|---|---|---|---|---|---|---|
| Franklin | 44 | 45 | 98 | 32 | 41 | 78 |

## NEW YORK JETS

### RUSHING
| Last Name | No. | Yds | Avg | TD |
|---|---|---|---|---|
| McNeil | 214 | 856 | 4.0 | 5 |
| Hector | 164 | 605 | 3.7 | 8 |
| Paige | 47 | 109 | 2.3 | 2 |
| Bligen | 20 | 65 | 3.3 | 1 |
| O'Brien | 17 | 46 | 2.7 | 0 |
| Ryan | 8 | 28 | 3.5 | 0 |
| Barber | 11 | 27 | 2.5 | 0 |
| Faaola | 3 | 5 | 1.7 | 0 |
| Townsell | 1 | 2 | 2.0 | 0 |
| Jennings | 1 | 0 | 0.0 | 0 |
| Toon | 2 | -3 | -1.5 | 0 |
| Sohn | 2 | -11 | -5.5 | 0 |

### RECEIVING
| Last Name | No. | Yds | Avg | TD |
|---|---|---|---|---|
| Toon | 85 | 1176 | 13.8 | 8 |
| Shuler | 69 | 675 | 9.8 | 4 |
| Walker | 49 | 1016 | 20.7 | 12 |
| McNeil | 49 | 410 | 8.4 | 1 |
| Hector | 33 | 302 | 9.2 | 0 |
| Paige | 18 | 121 | 6.7 | 0 |
| Klever | 15 | 150 | 10.0 | 0 |
| Sohn | 8 | 129 | 16.1 | 2 |
| Barber | 5 | 36 | 7.2 | 0 |
| Bligen | 2 | 6 | 3.0 | 0 |
| Townsell | 1 | 11 | 11.0 | 0 |

### PUNT RETURNS
| Last Name | No. | Yds | Avg | TD |
|---|---|---|---|---|
| Sohn | 35 | 289 | 8.3 | 0 |
| Townsell | 4 | 52 | 13.0 | 0 |

### KICKOFF RETURNS
| Last Name | No. | Yds | Avg | TD |
|---|---|---|---|---|
| Humphery | 28 | 655 | 23.4 | 1 |
| Townsell | 13 | 322 | 24.8 | 0 |
| Sohn | 7 | 124 | 17.7 | 0 |
| Harper | 7 | 71 | 10.1 | 0 |
| Rudolph | 3 | 17 | 5.7 | 0 |
| Baldwin | 2 | 3 | 1.5 | 0 |
| Shuler | 2 | -3 | -1.5 | 0 |
| Lynn | 1 | 0 | 0.0 | 0 |

### PASSING — PUNTING — KICKING
| PASSING | Att | Cmp | % | Yds | Yd/Att | TD | Int- | % | RK |
|---|---|---|---|---|---|---|---|---|---|
| O'Brien | 482 | 300 | 62 | 3690 | 7.7 | 25 | 20- | 4 | 5 |
| Ryan | 55 | 34 | 62 | 342 | 6.2 | 2 | 1- | 2 | |

| PUNTING | No | Avg |
|---|---|---|
| Jennings | 85 | 39.4 |

| KICKING | XP | Att | % | FG | Att | % |
|---|---|---|---|---|---|---|
| Leahy | 44 | 44 | 100 | 16 | 19 | 84 |

## MIAMI DOLPHINS

### RUSHING
| Last Name | No. | Yds | Avg | TD |
|---|---|---|---|---|
| Hampton | 186 | 830 | 4.5 | 9 |
| Davenport | 75 | 314 | 4.2 | 0 |
| Nathan | 27 | 203 | 7.5 | 0 |
| Bennett | 36 | 162 | 4.5 | 0 |
| Clayton | 2 | 33 | 16.5 | 0 |
| Carter | 4 | 18 | 4.5 | 0 |
| Ellis | 3 | 6 | 2.0 | 0 |
| Strock | 1 | 0 | 0.0 | 0 |
| Marino | 12 | -3 | -0.3 | 0 |
| Roby | 2 | -8 | -4.0 | 0 |
| Duper | 1 | -10 | -10.0 | 0 |

### RECEIVING
| Last Name | No. | Yds | Avg | TD |
|---|---|---|---|---|
| Duper | 67 | 1313 | 19.6 | 11 |
| Hampton | 61 | 446 | 7.3 | 3 |
| Clayton | 60 | 1150 | 19.2 | 10 |
| Hardy | 54 | 430 | 8.0 | 5 |
| Nathan | 48 | 457 | 9.5 | 2 |
| N. Moore | 38 | 431 | 11.3 | 7 |
| Davenport | 20 | 177 | 8.9 | 1 |
| Johnson | 19 | 170 | 8.9 | 4 |
| Pruitt | 15 | 235 | 15.7 | 2 |
| Jensen | 5 | 50 | 10.0 | 1 |
| Bennett | 4 | 33 | 8.3 | 0 |
| Carter | 1 | 6 | 6.0 | 0 |

### PUNT RETURNS
| Last Name | No. | Yds | Avg | TD |
|---|---|---|---|---|
| Ellis | 24 | 149 | 6.2 | 0 |
| Pruitt | 11 | 150 | 13.6 | 1 |
| G. Blackwood | 1 | 0 | 0.0 | 0 |
| L. Blackwood | 1 | 0 | 0.0 | 0 |
| Clayton | 1 | 0 | 0.0 | 0 |
| Thompson | 1 | 0 | 0.0 | 0 |
| N. Moore | 1 | -2 | -2.0 | 0 |

### KICKOFF RETURNS
| Last Name | No. | Yds | Avg | TD |
|---|---|---|---|---|
| Ellis | 25 | 541 | 21.6 | 0 |
| Davenport | 16 | 285 | 17.8 | 0 |
| Hampton | 9 | 182 | 20.2 | 0 |
| Carter | 9 | 133 | 14.8 | 0 |
| Hardy | 3 | 39 | 13.0 | 0 |
| L. Lee | 1 | 5 | 5.0 | 0 |
| Johnson | 1 | 0 | 0.0 | 0 |
| Toth | 1 | 0 | 0.0 | 0 |

### PASSING — PUNTING — KICKING
| PASSING | Att | Cmp | % | Yds | Yd/Att | TD | Int- | % | RK |
|---|---|---|---|---|---|---|---|---|---|
| Marino | 623 | 378 | 61 | 4746 | 7.6 | 44 | 23- | 4 | 1 |
| Strock | 20 | 14 | 70 | 152 | 7.6 | 2 | 0- | 0 | |
| Jensen | 2 | 0 | 0 | 0 | 0.0 | 0 | 0- | 0 | |

| PUNTING | No | Avg |
|---|---|---|
| Roby | 56 | 44.2 |

| KICKING | XP | Att | % | FG | Att | % |
|---|---|---|---|---|---|---|
| Reveiz | 52 | 55 | 95 | 14 | 22 | 64 |

## BUFFALO BILLS

### RUSHING
| Last Name | No. | Yds | Avg | TD |
|---|---|---|---|---|
| Riddick | 150 | 632 | 4.2 | 4 |
| Bell | 90 | 377 | 4.2 | 4 |
| Kelly | 41 | 199 | 4.9 | 0 |
| Harmon | 54 | 172 | 3.2 | 0 |
| Byrum | 38 | 156 | 4.1 | 0 |
| Moore | 33 | 104 | 3.2 | 1 |
| Wilkins | 3 | 18 | 6.0 | 0 |
| King | 4 | 10 | 2.5 | 0 |
| Kidd | 1 | 0 | 0.0 | 0 |
| Reich | 1 | 0 | 0.0 | 0 |
| Broughton | 1 | -6 | -6.0 | 0 |
| Reed | 3 | -8 | -2.7 | 0 |

### RECEIVING
| Last Name | No. | Yds | Avg | TD |
|---|---|---|---|---|
| Reed | 53 | 739 | 13.9 | 7 |
| Metzelaars | 49 | 485 | 9.9 | 3 |
| Riddick | 49 | 468 | 9.6 | 1 |
| Burkett | 34 | 778 | 22.9 | 4 |
| Moore | 23 | 184 | 8.0 | 0 |
| Harmon | 22 | 185 | 8.4 | 1 |
| Butler | 15 | 302 | 20.1 | 2 |
| Byrum | 13 | 104 | 8.0 | 1 |
| Bell | 12 | 142 | 11.8 | 2 |
| Wilkins | 8 | 74 | 9.3 | 0 |
| Teal | 6 | 60 | 10.0 | 1 |
| Rolle | 4 | 56 | 14.0 | 0 |
| Broughton | 3 | 71 | 23.7 | 0 |
| Richardson | 3 | 49 | 16.3 | 0 |

### PUNT RETURNS
| Last Name | No. | Yds | Avg | TD |
|---|---|---|---|---|
| Pitts | 18 | 194 | 10.8 | 1 |
| Broughton | 12 | 53 | 4.4 | 0 |
| Hill | 1 | 0 | 0.0 | 0 |
| Richardson | 1 | 0 | 0.0 | 0 |

### KICKOFF RETURNS
| Last Name | No. | Yds | Avg | TD |
|---|---|---|---|---|
| Harmon | 18 | 321 | 17.8 | 0 |
| Tasker | 12 | 213 | 17.8 | 0 |
| Broughton | 11 | 243 | 22.1 | 0 |
| Riddick | 8 | 200 | 25.0 | 0 |
| Richardson | 6 | 123 | 20.5 | 0 |
| Bellinger | 2 | 32 | 16.0 | 0 |
| Pitts | 1 | 7 | 7.0 | 0 |

### PASSING — PUNTING — KICKING
| PASSING | Att | Cmp | % | Yds | Yd/Att | TD | Int- | % | RK |
|---|---|---|---|---|---|---|---|---|---|
| Kelly | 480 | 285 | 59 | 3593 | 7.5 | 22 | 17- | 4 | 7 |
| Reich | 19 | 9 | 47 | 104 | 5.5 | 0 | 2- | 11 | |

| PUNTING | No | Avg |
|---|---|---|
| Kidd | 75 | 40.4 |

| KICKING | XP | Att | % | FG | Att | % |
|---|---|---|---|---|---|---|
| Norwood | 32 | 34 | 94 | 17 | 27 | 63 |

## INDIANAPOLIS COLTS

### RUSHING
| Last Name | No. | Yds | Avg | TD |
|---|---|---|---|---|
| McMillan | 189 | 609 | 3.2 | 3 |
| Bentley | 73 | 351 | 4.8 | 3 |
| Gill | 53 | 228 | 4.3 | 1 |
| Wonsley | 60 | 214 | 3.6 | 1 |
| Trudeau | 13 | 21 | 1.6 | 1 |
| Kiel | 3 | 20 | 6.7 | 0 |
| Hogeboom | 10 | 20 | 2.0 | 1 |
| Bouza | 1 | 12 | 12.0 | 0 |
| Capers | 1 | 11 | 11.0 | 0 |
| Brooks | 4 | 5 | 1.3 | 0 |

### RECEIVING
| Last Name | No. | Yds | Avg | TD |
|---|---|---|---|---|
| Bouza | 71 | 830 | 11.7 | 5 |
| Brooks | 65 | 1131 | 17.4 | 8 |
| McMillan | 34 | 289 | 8.5 | 0 |
| Beach | 25 | 265 | 10.6 | 1 |
| Bentley | 25 | 230 | 9.2 | 0 |
| Boyer | 22 | 237 | 10.8 | 1 |
| Wonsley | 16 | 175 | 10.9 | 0 |
| Gill | 16 | 137 | 8.6 | 0 |
| Capers | 9 | 118 | 13.1 | 0 |
| LaFleur | 7 | 56 | 8.0 | 0 |
| Harbour | 4 | 46 | 11.5 | 0 |
| Sherwin | 3 | 26 | 8.7 | 1 |
| Murray | 2 | 34 | 17.0 | 0 |
| Martin | 1 | 41 | 41.0 | 0 |

### PUNT RETURNS
| Last Name | No. | Yds | Avg | TD |
|---|---|---|---|---|
| Brooks | 18 | 141 | 7.8 | 0 |
| Martin | 17 | 105 | 6.4 | 0 |

### KICKOFF RETURNS
| Last Name | No. | Yds | Avg | TD |
|---|---|---|---|---|
| Bentley | 32 | 687 | 21.5 | 0 |
| Martin | 21 | 385 | 18.3 | 0 |
| Brooks | 8 | 143 | 17.9 | 0 |
| K. Daniel | 5 | 109 | 21.8 | 0 |
| Gill | 5 | 73 | 14.6 | 0 |
| Wonsley | 2 | 31 | 15.5 | 0 |
| Williams | 1 | 15 | 15.0 | 0 |

### PASSING — PUNTING — KICKING
| PASSING | Att | Cmp | % | Yds | Yd/Att | TD | Int- | % | RK |
|---|---|---|---|---|---|---|---|---|---|
| Trudeau | 417 | 204 | 49 | 2225 | 5.3 | 8 | 18- | 4 | 15 |
| Hogeboom | 144 | 85 | 59 | 1154 | 8.0 | 6 | 6- | 4 | |
| Kiel | 25 | 11 | 44 | 236 | 9.4 | 2 | 0- | 0 | |

| PUNTING | No | Avg |
|---|---|---|
| Stark | 76 | 45.2 |
| Kiel | 5 | 38.0 |

| KICKING | XP | Att | % | FG | Att | % |
|---|---|---|---|---|---|---|
| Biasucci | 26 | 27 | 96 | 13 | 25 | 52 |

## CLEVELAND BROWNS 12-4 Marty Schottenheimer

| Scores of Each Game | | |
|---|---|---|
| 31 | Chicago | 41 |
| 23 | Houston | 20 |
| 13 | CINCINNATI | 30 |
| 24 | DETROIT | 21 |
| 27 | Pittsburgh | 24 |
| 20 | KANSAS CITY | 7 |
| 14 | GREEN BAY | 17 |
| 23 | Minnesota | 20 |
| 24 | Indianapolis | 9 |
| 26 | MIAMI | 16 |
| 14 | L.A.Raiders | 27 |
| 37 | PITTSBURGH | *31 |
| 13 | HOUSTON | *10 |
| 21 | Buffalo | 17 |
| 34 | Cincinnati | 3 |
| 47 | SAN DIEGO | 17 |

| Use Name | Pos. | Hgt | Wgt | Age | Int | Pts |
|---|---|---|---|---|---|---|
| Rickey Bolden | OT-OG | 6'6" | 280 | 24 | | |
| Bob Gruber | OT | 6'5" | 270 | 28 | | |
| Cody Risien | OT | 6'7" | 280 | 29 | | |
| Paul Farren | OG-OT | 6'5" | 280 | 25 | | |
| Dan Fike | OG-OT | 6'7" | 280 | 25 | | |
| Larry Williams | OG | 6'5" | 290 | 23 | | |
| George Lilja | OG-C | 6'4" | 270 | 28 | | |
| Jeff Wiska | OG | 6'3" | 260 | 26 | | |
| Mike Baab | C | 6'4" | 270 | 26 | | |
| Keith Baldwin | DE | 6'4" | 270 | 25 | | |
| Reggie Camp | DE | 6'4" | 280 | 25 | | |
| Sam Clancy | DE | 6'7" | 260 | 28 | | |
| Carl Hairston | DE | 6'3" | 260 | 33 | | |
| Ralph Malone | DE | 6'5" | 225 | 22 | | |
| Bob Golic | NT | 6'2" | 270 | 28 | | |
| Dave Puzzuoli | NT | 6'3" | 260 | 25 | | |
| Chip Banks | LB | 6'4" | 233 | 26 | | |
| Anthony Griggs | LB | 6'3" | 230 | 26 | | |
| Eddie Johnson | LB | 6'1" | 225 | 27 | | |
| Mike Johnson | LB | 6'1" | 228 | 23 | | |
| Clay Matthews | LB | 6'2" | 235 | 30 | 2 | |
| Scott Nicolas | LB | 6'3" | 226 | 26 | | |
| Brad Van Pelt | LB | 6'5" | 235 | 35 | | |
| Hanford Dixon | DB | 5'11" | 186 | 27 | 5 | |
| Ray Ellis | DB | 6'1" | 196 | 27 | 2 | |
| Al Gross | DB | 6'3" | 195 | 25 | | 6 |
| Mark Harper | DB | 5'9" | 174 | 24 | 1 | |
| D.D.Hoggard | DB | 6' | 188 | 25 | | |
| Frank Minnifield | DB | 5'9" | 180 | 26 | 3 | 6 |
| Chris Rockins | DB | 6' | 195 | 24 | 2 | |
| Felix Wright | DB | 6'2" | 190 | 27 | 3 | 6 |
| Gary Danielson | QB | 6'2" | 196 | 34 | | |
| Bernie Kosar | QB | 6'5" | 210 | 22 | | |
| Mike Pagel | QB | 6'2" | 200 | 25 | | |
| Earnest Byner | HB | 5'10" | 215 | 23 | | 24 |
| Curtis Dickey | HB | 6'1" | 220 | 29 | | 36 |
| Herman Fontenot | HB | 6' | 206 | 22 | | 12 |
| Johnny Davis | FB | 6'1" | 235 | 30 | | |
| Major Everett | FB | 5'10" | 218 | 26 | | |
| Kevin Mack | FB | 6' | 212 | 24 | | 60 |
| Brian Brennan | WR | 5'9" | 178 | 24 | | 42 |
| Terry Greer | WR | 6'1" | 192 | 28 | | |
| Reggie Langhorne | WR | 6'2" | 195 | 23 | | 6 |
| Gerald McNeil | WR | 5'7" | 140 | 24 | | 12 |
| Webster Slaughter | WR | 6' | 170 | 21 | | 30 |
| Clarence Weathers | WR | 5'9" | 170 | 24 | | |
| Harry Holt | TE | 6'4" | 240 | 28 | | 12 |
| Ozzie Newsome | TE | 6'2" | 232 | 30 | | 18 |
| Travis Tucker | TE | 6'3" | 240 | 22 | | |
| Matt Bahr | K | 5'10" | 175 | 30 | | 90 |
| Jeff Gossett | K | 6'2" | 200 | 29 | | |

Keith Baldwin - Knee Injury
Gary Danielson - Ankle Injury
Curtis Weathers - Knee Injury

## CINCINNATI BENGALS 10-6 Sam Wyche

| Scores of Each Game | | |
|---|---|---|
| 14 | Kansas City | 24 |
| 36 | BUFFALO | *33 |
| 30 | Cleveland | 13 |
| 7 | CHICAGO | 44 |
| 34 | Green Bay | 28 |
| 24 | PITTSBURGH | 22 |
| 31 | HOUSTON | 28 |
| 9 | Pittsburgh | 30 |
| 24 | Detroit | 17 |
| 28 | Houston | 32 |
| 34 | SEATTLE | 7 |
| 24 | MINNESOTA | 20 |
| 28 | Denver | 34 |
| 31 | New England | 7 |
| 3 | CLEVELAND | 34 |
| 52 | N.Y.JETS | 21 |

| Use Name | Pos. | Hgt | Wgt | Age | Int | Pts |
|---|---|---|---|---|---|---|
| David Douglas | OT | 6'4" | 280 | 23 | | |
| Anthony Munoz | OT | 6'6" | 278 | 28 | | 12 |
| Bruce Riemers | OT | 6'7" | 280 | 25 | | |
| Joe Walter | OT | 6'6" | 290 | 23 | | |
| Brian Blados | OG | 6'5" | 295 | 24 | | |
| Max Montoya | OG | 6'5" | 275 | 30 | | |
| Bruce Kozerski | C | 6'4" | 275 | 24 | | |
| Dave Rimington | C | 6'3" | 288 | 24 | | |
| Ross Browner | DE | 6'3" | 265 | 32 | | |
| Eddie Edwards | DE | 6'5" | 256 | 32 | | 6 |
| Mike Hammerstein | DE | 6'4" | 270 | 23 | | |
| Jim Show | DE | 6'3" | 250 | 23 | | |
| Tim Krumrie | NT | 6'2" | 262 | 26 | | |
| Leo Barker | LB | 6'2" | 227 | 26 | 2 | |
| Ed Brady | LB | 6'2" | 235 | 26 | | |
| Kiki DeAyala | LB | 6'1" | 225 | 24 | | |
| Joe Kelly | LB | 6'2" | 227 | 21 | 1 | |
| Emanuel King | LB | 6'4" | 251 | 23 | | |
| Ron Simpkins | LB | 6'1" | 235 | 28 | | |
| Leon White | LB | 6'2" | 236 | 22 | | 2 |
| Reggie Williams | LB | 6'1" | 228 | 31 | | |
| Carl Zander | LB | 6'2" | 235 | 21 | | |
| Lewis Billups | DB | 5'1" | 190 | 22 | | |
| Louis Breeden | DB | 5'11" | 185 | 32 | 7 | 6 |
| Barney Bussey | DB | 6' | 195 | 24 | 1 | |
| David Fulcher | DB | 6'3" | 228 | 21 | 4 | |
| Ray Horton | DB | 5'11" | 190 | 26 | 1 | |
| Robert Jackson | DB | 5'10" | 186 | 27 | | |
| Bobby Kemp | DB | 6' | 191 | 27 | 1 | |
| John Simmons (to GB) | DB | 5'11" | 192 | 27 | 6 | |
| Jimmy Turner (to ATL) | DB | 6' | 187 | 27 | | |
| Ken Anderson | QB | 6'3" | 212 | 37 | | |
| Boomer Esiason | QB | 6'4" | 220 | 25 | | 6 |
| Doug Gaynor | QB | 6'2" | 205 | 23 | | |
| James Brooks | HB | 5'10" | 182 | 27 | | 54 |
| Stanford Jennings | HB | 6'1" | 205 | 24 | | 6 |
| Bill Johnson | FB | 6'2" | 230 | 25 | | |
| Larry Kinnebrew | FB | 6'1" | 255 | 27 | | 54 |
| Stanley Wilson | FB | 5'10" | 210 | 25 | | 48 |
| Eddie Brown | WR | 6' | 185 | 23 | | 24 |
| Cris Collinsworth | WR | 6'5" | 192 | 27 | | 60 |
| Steve Kreider | WR | 6'3" | 192 | 28 | | |
| Mike Martin | WR | 5'10" | 186 | 25 | | |
| Tim McGee | WR | 5'10" | 175 | 22 | | 6 |
| Rodney Holman | TE | 6'3" | 238 | 26 | | 12 |
| Eric Kattus | TE | 6'5" | 235 | 23 | | 6 |
| Jim Breech | K | 5'6" | 161 | 30 | | 101 |
| Jeff Hayes | K | 5'11" | 175 | 27 | | 6 |

## PITTSBURGH STEELERS 6-10 Chuck Noll

| Scores of Each Game | | |
|---|---|---|
| 0 | Seattle | 30 |
| 10 | DENVER | 21 |
| 7 | Minnesota | 31 |
| 22 | Houston | *16 |
| 24 | CLEVELAND | 27 |
| 22 | Cincinnati | 24 |
| 0 | NEW ENGLAND | 34 |
| 30 | CINCINNATI | 9 |
| 27 | GREEN BAY | 3 |
| 12 | Buffalo | 16 |
| 21 | HOUSTON | 10 |
| 31 | Cleveland | *37 |
| 10 | Chicago | *31 |
| 27 | DETROIT | 17 |
| 45 | N.Y.Jets | 24 |
| 19 | KANSAS CITY | 24 |

| Use Name | Pos. | Hgt | Wgt | Age | Int | Pts |
|---|---|---|---|---|---|---|
| Mark Behning | OT | 6'6" | 290 | 24 | | |
| Tunch Ilkin | OT | 6'3" | 265 | 28 | | |
| Ray Pinney | OT | 6'4" | 265 | 32 | | |
| Pete Rostosky | OT | 6'4" | 270 | 25 | | |
| Terry Long | OG | 5'11" | 265 | 27 | | |
| John Rienstra | OG | 6'5" | 273 | 23 | | |
| Craig Wolfley | OG | 6'1" | 260 | 28 | | |
| Dan Turk | C | 6'4" | 265 | 24 | | |
| Mike Webster | C | 6'1" | 260 | 34 | | |
| Randy Rasmussen | C-OG | 6'2" | 254 | 26 | | |
| Keith Gary | DE | 6'3" | 265 | 26 | | |
| Edmund Nelson | DE-NT | 6'3" | 277 | 26 | | |
| Darryl Sims | DE-NT | 6'3" | 275 | 25 | | |
| Keith Willis | DE | 6'1" | 255 | 27 | | |
| Gary Dunn | NT | 6'3" | 275 | 33 | | |
| Gerald Williams | NT | 6'3" | 270 | 22 | | |
| Gregg Carr | LB | 6'2" | 220 | 24 | | |
| Robin Cole | LB | 6'2" | 225 | 30 | | |
| Anthony Henton | LB | 6'1" | 218 | 23 | | |
| Bryan Hinkle | LB | 6'2" | 220 | 27 | 3 | |
| David Little | LB | 6'1" | 240 | 27 | | |
| Mike Merriweather | LB | 6'2" | 215 | 26 | 2 | |
| Larry Station | LB | 5'11" | 227 | 22 | | |
| Dennis Winston | LB | 6' | 224 | 30 | | |
| Harvey Clayton | DB | 5'9" | 180 | 25 | 3 | |
| Dave Edwards | DB | 6' | 195 | 24 | | 2 |
| Donnie Elder (to DET) | DB | 5'9" | 175 | 23 | | |
| Lupe Sanchez | DB | 5'10" | 192 | 24 | 3 | 6 |
| Chris Sheffield | DB | 6'1" | 185 | 23 | | |
| Donnie Shell | DB | 5'11" | 198 | 34 | 3 | |
| John Swain | DB | 6'1" | 192 | 26 | | |
| Eric Williams | DB | 6'1" | 190 | 26 | 3 | |
| Rick Woods | DB | 6' | 195 | 26 | 3 | |
| Bubby Brister | QB | 6'3" | 184 | 24 | | 6 |
| Scott Campbell (to ATL) | QB | 6' | 195 | 24 | | |
| Mark Malone | QB | 6'4" | 220 | 27 | | 30 |
| Walter Abercrombie | HB | 6' | 210 | 26 | | 48 |
| Rich Erenberg | HB | 5'10" | 205 | 24 | | 24 |
| Earnest Jackson | HB | 5'9" | 208 | 26 | | 30 |
| David Hughes | FB | 6' | 220 | 27 | | |
| Frank Pollard | FB | 5'10" | 223 | 29 | | |
| Dan Reeder | FB | 5'11" | 235 | 25 | | |
| Chuck Sanders | FB | 6'1" | 233 | 22 | | |
| Jessie Britt | WR | 6'4" | 198 | 23 | | |
| Louis Lipps | WR | 5'10" | 185 | 24 | | 18 |
| John Stallworth | WR | 6'2" | 202 | 34 | | 6 |
| Calvin Sweeney | WR | 6'2" | 192 | 31 | | 6 |
| Weegie Thompson | WR | 6'6" | 210 | 25 | | 30 |
| Preston Gothard | TE | 6'4" | 240 | 24 | | 6 |
| Warren Seitz | TE | 6'4" | 223 | 23 | | |
| Gary Anderson | K | 5'11" | 170 | 27 | | 95 |
| Harry Newsome | K | 6' | 186 | 23 | | |

Dwayne Woodruff - Knee Injury

## HOUSTON OILERS 5-11 Jerry Glanville

| Scores of Each Game | | |
|---|---|---|
| 31 | Green Bay | 3 |
| 20 | CLEVELAND | 23 |
| 13 | Kansas City | 27 |
| 16 | PITTSBURGH | *22 |
| 13 | Detroit | 24 |
| 7 | CHICAGO | 20 |
| 28 | Cincinnati | 31 |
| 17 | L.A.RAIDERS | 28 |
| 7 | Miami | 28 |
| 32 | CINCINNATI | 28 |
| 10 | Pittsburgh | 21 |
| 31 | INDIANAPOLIS | 17 |
| 10 | Cleveland | *13 |
| 0 | San Diego | 27 |
| 23 | MINNESOTA | 10 |
| 16 | BUFFALO | 7 |

| Use Name | Pos. | Hgt | Wgt | Age | Int | Pts |
|---|---|---|---|---|---|---|
| Bruce Matthews | OT | 6'4" | 283 | 25 | | |
| Don Maggs | OT-OG | 6'5" | 279 | 24 | | |
| Eric Moran | OT-OG | 6'5" | 294 | 26 | | |
| Dean Steinkuhler | OT-OG | 6'3" | 275 | 25 | | |
| Doug Williams | OT-OG | 6'5" | 285 | 23 | | |
| Kent Hill | OG | 6'5" | 260 | 29 | | |
| Mike Munchak | OG | 6'3" | 286 | 26 | | 6 |
| Jay Pennison | C | 6'1" | 265 | 24 | | |
| Jim Romano | C | 6'3" | 264 | 26 | | |
| Jesse Baker | DE | 6'5" | 271 | 29 | | |
| Ray Childress | DE | 6'6" | 276 | 23 | | |
| William Fuller | DE | 6'3" | 255 | 24 | | |
| Lynn Madsen | DE | 6'4" | 260 | 26 | | |
| Malcolm Taylor | DE | 6'6" | 280 | 26 | | |
| Richard Byrd | DT | 6'3" | 264 | 24 | | |
| Mike Golic | DT | 6'5" | 272 | 23 | | |
| Karl Morgan | DT | 6'1" | 255 | 25 | | |
| Doug Smith | NT | 6'5" | 285 | 27 | | |
| Robert Abraham | LB | 6'1" | 236 | 26 | | |
| Frank Bush | LB | 6'1" | 218 | 23 | | |
| Kirk Dodge | LB | 6'1" | 232 | 24 | | |
| Eric Fairs | LB | 6'3" | 235 | 22 | | |
| John Grimsley | LB | 6'2" | 235 | 24 | | |
| Robert Lyles | LB | 6'1" | 225 | 25 | 2 | 6 |
| Johnny Meads | LB | 6'2" | 235 | 25 | | |
| Avon Riley | LB | 6'3" | 240 | 28 | | |
| Patrick Allen | DB | 5'10 | 179 | 25 | 3 | |
| Keith Bostic | DB | 6'1" | 223 | 25 | | |
| Steve Brown | DB | 5'11" | 187 | 26 | 2 | |
| Jeff Donaldson | DB | 6' | 194 | 24 | 1 | 6 |
| Bo Eason | DB | 6'2" | 200 | 25 | 2 | |
| Larry Griffin | DB | 6' | 190 | 23 | | |
| Richard Johnson | DB | 6'1" | 190 | 22 | 2 | |
| Allen Lyday | DB | 5'10" | 197 | 25 | 3 | |
| Audrey McMillian | DB | 6' | 190 | 24 | | |
| Oliver Luck | QB | 6'2" | 196 | 26 | | |
| Warren Moon | QB | 6'3" | 210 | 29 | | 12 |
| John Witkowski | QB | 6'1" | 205 | 24 | | |
| Stan Edwards | HB | 6' | 210 | 26 | | |
| Allen Pinkett | HB | 5'9" | 185 | 22 | | 18 |
| Mike Rozier | HB | 5'10" | 211 | 25 | | 24 |
| Butch Woolfolk | HB | 6'1" | 207 | 26 | | 12 |
| Chuck Banks | FB | 6'2" | 225 | 22 | | |
| Ray Wallace | FB | 6' | 221 | 22 | | 30 |
| Mike Akiu | WR | 5'9" | 182 | 24 | | |
| Willie Drewrey | WR | 5'7" | 164 | 23 | | |
| Ernest Givins | WR | 5'9" | 174 | 21 | | 24 |
| Drew Hill | WR | 5'9" | 168 | 30 | | 30 |
| Tim Smith | WR | 6'2" | 206 | 29 | | |
| Chris Dressel | TE | 6'4" | 239 | 25 | | |
| Jeff Parks | TE | 6'4" | 236 | 21 | | |
| Jamie Williams | TE | 6'4" | 245 | 26 | | 6 |
| Lee Johnson | K | 6'2" | 199 | 24 | | |
| Tony Zendejas | K | 5'8" | 165 | 26 | | 94 |

Tom Briehl - Ankle Injury
Mike Kelley - Neck Injury
Rod Kush - Knee Injury

* Overtime

## CLEVELAND BROWNS

### RUSHING

| Last Name | No. | Yds | Avg | TD |
|---|---|---|---|---|
| Mack | 174 | 665 | 3.8 | 10 |
| Dickey | 135 | 523 | 3.9 | 6 |
| Byner | 94 | 277 | 2.9 | 2 |
| Fontenot | 25 | 105 | 4.2 | 1 |
| Everett | 12 | 43 | 3.6 | 0 |
| Kosar | 24 | 19 | 0.8 | 0 |
| Holt | 1 | 16 | 16.0 | 1 |
| McNeil | 1 | 12 | 12.0 | 0 |
| Slaughter | 1 | 1 | 1.0 | 0 |
| Pagel | 2 | 0 | 0.0 | 0 |
| Langhorne | 1 | -11 | -11.0 | 0 |

### RECEIVING

| Last Name | No. | Yds | Avg | TD |
|---|---|---|---|---|
| Brennan | 55 | 838 | 15.2 | 6 |
| Fontenot | 47 | 559 | 11.9 | 1 |
| Slaughter | 40 | 577 | 14.4 | 4 |
| Langhorne | 39 | 678 | 17.4 | 1 |
| Newsome | 39 | 417 | 10.7 | 3 |
| Byner | 37 | 328 | 8.9 | 2 |
| Mack | 28 | 292 | 10.4 | 0 |
| Dickey | 10 | 78 | 7.8 | 0 |
| Weathers | 9 | 100 | 11.1 | 0 |
| Holt | 4 | 61 | 15.3 | 1 |
| Greer | 3 | 51 | 17.0 | 0 |
| Tucker | 2 | 29 | 14.5 | 0 |
| McNeil | 1 | 9 | 9.0 | 0 |
| Kosar | 1 | 1 | 1.0 | 0 |

### PUNT RETURNS

| Last Name | No. | Yds | Avg | TD |
|---|---|---|---|---|
| McNeil | 40 | 348 | 8.7 | 1 |
| Slaughter | 1 | 2 | 2.0 | 0 |

### KICKOFF RETURNS

| Last Name | No. | Yds | Avg | TD |
|---|---|---|---|---|
| McNeil | 47 | 997 | 21.2 | 1 |
| Fontenot | 7 | 99 | 14.1 | 0 |
| Langhorne | 4 | 57 | 14.3 | 0 |
| Nicolas | 3 | 28 | 9.3 | 0 |
| Puzzuoli | 1 | 32 | 32.0 | 0 |

### PASSING — PUNTING — KICKING

| PASSING | Att | Cmp | % | Yds | Yd/Att | TD | Int— | % | Rk |
|---|---|---|---|---|---|---|---|---|---|
| Kosar | 531 | 310 | 58 | 3854 | 7.3 | 17 | 10— | 2 | 6 |
| Pagel | 3 | 2 | 67 | 53 | 17.7 | 0 | 0— | 0 | |
| Gossett | 2 | 1 | 50 | 30 | 15.0 | 0 | 1— | 50 | |
| Fontenot | 1 | 1 | 100 | 46 | 46.0 | 1 | 0— | 0 | |
| Brennan | 1 | 1 | 100 | 35 | 35.0 | 0 | 0— | 0 | |

| PUNTING | Att | Avg |
|---|---|---|
| Gossett | 83 | 41.2 |

| KICKING | XP | Att | % | FG | Att | % |
|---|---|---|---|---|---|---|
| Bahr | 30 | 30 | 100 | 20 | 26 | 77 |
| Moseley | 25 | 28 | 89 | 12 | 19 | 63 |

## CINCINNATI BENGALS

### RUSHING

| Last Name | No. | Yds | Avg | TD |
|---|---|---|---|---|
| Brooks | 205 | 1087 | 5.3 | 5 |
| Kinnebrew | 131 | 519 | 4.0 | 8 |
| Wilson | 68 | 379 | 5.6 | 8 |
| Johnson | 39 | 226 | 5.8 | 0 |
| Esiason | 44 | 146 | 3.3 | 1 |
| Hayes | 3 | 92 | 30.7 | 1 |
| Jennings | 16 | 54 | 3.4 | 1 |
| Brown | 8 | 32 | 4.0 | 0 |
| McGee | 4 | 10 | 2.5 | 0 |
| Gaynor | 1 | 4 | 4.0 | 0 |
| Collinsworth | 2 | -16 | -8.0 | 0 |

### RECEIVING

| Last Name | No. | Yds | Avg | TD |
|---|---|---|---|---|
| Collinsworth | 62 | 1024 | 16.5 | 10 |
| Brown | 58 | 964 | 16.6 | 4 |
| Brooks | 54 | 686 | 12.7 | 4 |
| Holman | 40 | 570 | 14.3 | 2 |
| McGee | 16 | 276 | 17.3 | 1 |
| Johnson | 13 | 103 | 7.9 | 1 |
| Kinnebrew | 13 | 136 | 10.5 | 0 |
| Kattus | 11 | 99 | 9.0 | 1 |
| Jennings | 6 | 86 | 14.3 | 0 |
| Kreider | 5 | 96 | 19.2 | 0 |
| Wilson | 4 | 45 | 11.3 | 0 |
| Martin | 3 | 68 | 22.7 | 0 |
| Munoz | 2 | 7 | 3.5 | 2 |

### PUNT RETURNS

| Last Name | No. | Yds | Avg | TD |
|---|---|---|---|---|
| Horton | 11 | 111 | 10.1 | 0 |
| Martin | 13 | 96 | 7.4 | 0 |
| McGee | 3 | 21 | 7.0 | 0 |
| Simmons | 2 | 7 | 3.5 | 0 |

### KICKOFF RETURNS

| Last Name | No. | Yds | Avg | TD |
|---|---|---|---|---|
| McGee | 43 | 1007 | 23.4 | 0 |
| Jennings | 12 | 257 | 21.4 | 0 |
| Martin | 4 | 83 | 20.8 | 0 |
| Simpkins | 2 | 24 | 12.0 | 0 |
| Holman | 1 | 18 | 18.0 | 0 |
| Simmons | 1 | 0 | 0.0 | 0 |

### PASSING — PUNTING — KICKING

| PASSING | Att | Cmp | % | Yds | Yd/Att | TD | Int— | % | Rk |
|---|---|---|---|---|---|---|---|---|---|
| Esiason | 469 | 273 | 58 | 3959 | 8.4 | 24 | 17— | 4 | 4 |
| Anderson | 23 | 11 | 48 | 171 | 7.4 | 1 | 2— | 9 | |
| Gaynor | 3 | 3 | 100 | 30 | 10.0 | 0 | 0— | 0 | |
| Brooks | 1 | 0 | 0 | 0 | 0.0 | 0 | 0— | 0 | |
| Kreider | 1 | 0 | 0 | 0 | 0.0 | 0 | 1— | 100 | |

| PUNTING | Att | Avg |
|---|---|---|
| Hayes | 56 | 35.1 |
| Esiason | 1 | 31.0 |

| KICKING | XP | Att | % | FG | Att | % |
|---|---|---|---|---|---|---|
| Breech | 50 | 51 | 98 | 17 | 32 | 53 |

## PITTSBURGH STEELERS

### RUSHING

| Last Name | No. | Yds | Avg | TD |
|---|---|---|---|---|
| Jackson | 216 | 910 | 4.2 | 5 |
| Abercrombie | 214 | 877 | 4.1 | 6 |
| Erenberg | 42 | 170 | 4.0 | 1 |
| Malone | 31 | 107 | 3.5 | 5 |
| Pollard | 24 | 86 | 3.6 | 0 |
| Hughes | 14 | 32 | 2.3 | 0 |
| Reeder | 6 | 20 | 3.3 | 0 |
| Sanders | 4 | 12 | 3.0 | 0 |
| Brister | 6 | 10 | 1.7 | 1 |
| Campbell | 1 | 7 | 7.0 | 0 |
| Seitz | 3 | 2 | 0.7 | 0 |
| Lipps | 4 | -3 | -0.8 | 0 |

### RECEIVING

| Last Name | No. | Yds | Avg | TD |
|---|---|---|---|---|
| Abercrombie | 47 | 395 | 8.4 | 2 |
| Lipps | 38 | 590 | 15.5 | 3 |
| Stallworth | 34 | 466 | 13.7 | 1 |
| Erenberg | 27 | 217 | 8.0 | 3 |
| Sweeney | 21 | 337 | 16.0 | 1 |
| Gothard | 21 | 246 | 11.7 | 1 |
| Thompson | 17 | 191 | 11.2 | 5 |
| Jackson | 17 | 169 | 9.9 | 0 |
| Hughes | 10 | 98 | 9.8 | 0 |
| Sanders | 2 | 19 | 9.5 | 0 |
| Pollard | 2 | 15 | 7.5 | 0 |
| Reeder | 2 | 4 | 2.0 | 0 |

### PUNT RETURNS

| Last Name | No. | Yds | Avg | TD |
|---|---|---|---|---|
| Woods | 33 | 294 | 8.9 | 0 |
| Lipps | 3 | 16 | 5.3 | 0 |

### KICKOFF RETURNS

| Last Name | No. | Yds | Avg | TD |
|---|---|---|---|---|
| Sanchez | 25 | 591 | 23.6 | 0 |
| Elder | 22 | 435 | 19.8 | 0 |
| Sanders | 8 | 148 | 18.5 | 0 |
| Reeder | 4 | 52 | 13.0 | 0 |
| Hughes | 2 | 16 | 8.0 | 0 |
| Seitz | 2 | 25 | 12.5 | 0 |
| Merriweather | 1 | 27 | 27.0 | 0 |
| Rostosky | 1 | 3 | 3.0 | 0 |
| Sweeney | 1 | 0 | 0.0 | 0 |
| Woods | 1 | 17 | 17.0 | 0 |

### PASSING — PUNTING — KICKING

| PASSING | Att | Cmp | % | Yds | Yd/Att | TD | Int— | % | Rk |
|---|---|---|---|---|---|---|---|---|---|
| Malone | 425 | 216 | 51 | 2444 | 5.8 | 15 | 18— | 4 | 13 |
| Brister | 60 | 21 | 35 | 291 | 4.9 | 0 | 2— | 3 | |
| Campbell | 7 | 1 | 14 | 7 | 1.0 | 0 | 0— | 0 | |
| Newsome | 2 | 1 | 50 | 12 | 6.0 | 1 | 0— | 0 | |

| PUNTING | Att | Avg |
|---|---|---|
| Newsome | 86 | 40.1 |

| KICKING | XP | Att | % | FG | Att | % |
|---|---|---|---|---|---|---|
| Anderson | 32 | 32 | 100 | 21 | 32 | 66 |

## HOUSTON OILERS

### RUSHING

| Last Name | No. | Yds | Avg | TD |
|---|---|---|---|---|
| Rozier | 199 | 662 | 3.3 | 4 |
| Moriarty | 90 | 252 | 2.8 | 1 |
| Pinkett | 77 | 225 | 2.9 | 2 |
| Wallace | 52 | 218 | 4.2 | 3 |
| Moon | 42 | 157 | 3.7 | 2 |
| Givins | 9 | 148 | 16.4 | 1 |
| Banks | 29 | 80 | 2.8 | 0 |
| Woolfolk | 23 | 57 | 2.5 | 0 |
| Luck | 2 | 12 | 6.0 | 0 |
| Edwards | 1 | 3 | 3.0 | 0 |
| Oliver | 1 | 1 | 1.0 | 0 |

### RECEIVING

| Last Name | No. | Yds | Avg | TD |
|---|---|---|---|---|
| D. Hill | 65 | 1112 | 17.1 | 5 |
| Givins | 61 | 1062 | 17.4 | 3 |
| Pinkett | 35 | 248 | 7.1 | 1 |
| Woolfolk | 28 | 314 | 11.2 | 2 |
| Rozier | 24 | 180 | 7.5 | 0 |
| J. Williams | 22 | 227 | 10.3 | 1 |
| Drewery | 18 | 299 | 16.6 | 0 |
| Wallace | 17 | 177 | 10.4 | 2 |
| Banks | 7 | 71 | 10.1 | 0 |
| T. Smith | 4 | 72 | 18.0 | 0 |
| Akiu | 4 | 67 | 16.8 | 0 |
| Oliver | 1 | -2 | -2.0 | 0 |

### PUNT RETURNS

| Last Name | No. | Yds | Avg | TD |
|---|---|---|---|---|
| Drewery | 34 | 262 | 7.7 | 0 |
| Givins | 8 | 80 | 10.0 | 0 |
| Pinkett | 1 | -1 | -1.0 | 0 |

### KICKOFF RETURNS

| Last Name | No. | Yds | Avg | TD |
|---|---|---|---|---|
| Drewrey | 25 | 500 | 20.0 | 0 |
| Pinkett | 26 | 519 | 20.0 | 0 |
| Riley | 2 | 17 | 8.5 | 0 |
| Woolfolk | 2 | 38 | 19.0 | 0 |
| Madsen | 1 | 0 | 0.0 | 0 |

### PASSING — PUNTING — KICKING

| PASSING | Att | Cmp | % | Yds | Yd/Att | TD | Int— | % | Rk |
|---|---|---|---|---|---|---|---|---|---|
| Moon | 488 | 256 | 53 | 3489 | 7.2 | 13 | 26— | 5 | 14 |
| Luck | 60 | 31 | 52 | 341 | 5.7 | 1 | 5— | 8 | |
| Givins | 2 | 0 | 0 | 0 | 0.0 | 0 | 0— | 0 | |
| Rozier | 1 | 1 | 100 | 13 | 13.0 | 0 | 0— | 0 | |

| PUNTING | Att | Avg |
|---|---|---|
| L. Johnson | 88 | 41.2 |
| Zendejas | 1 | 36.0 |

| KICKING | XP | Att | % | FG | Att | % |
|---|---|---|---|---|---|---|
| Zendejas | 28 | 29 | 97 | 22 | 27 | 82 |

**DENVER BRONCOS 11-5 Dan Reeves**

| Scores of Each Game | | |
|---|---|---|
| 38 | L.A.RAIDERS | 36 |
| 21 | Pittsburgh | 10 |
| 33 | Philadelphia | 7 |
| 27 | NEW ENGLAND | 20 |
| 29 | DALLAS | 14 |
| 31 | San Diego | 14 |
| 10 | N.Y.Jets | 22 |
| 20 | SEATTLE | 13 |
| 21 | L.A.Raiders | 10 |
| 3 | SAN DIEGO | 9 |
| 38 | KANSAS CITY | 17 |
| 16 | N.Y.Giants | 19 |
| 34 | CINCINNATI | 28 |
| 10 | Kansas City | 37 |
| 31 | WASHINGTON | 30 |
| 16 | Seattle | 41 |

| Use Name | Pos. | Hgt | Wgt | Age | Int | Pts |
|---|---|---|---|---|---|---|
| Winford Hood | OT | 6'3" | 262 | 24 | | |
| Ken Lanier | OT | 6'3" | 269 | 27 | | |
| Dan Remsberg | OT | 6'6" | 275 | 24 | | |
| Dave Studdard | OT | 6'4" | 260 | 30 | | |
| Mark Cooper | OG | 6'5" | 267 | 26 | | |
| Mike Freeman | OG | 6'3" | 256 | 24 | | |
| Paul Howard | OG | 6'3" | 260 | 35 | | |
| Keith Bishop | C-OG | 6'3" | 265 | 29 | | |
| Billy Bryan | C | 6'2" | 255 | 30 | | |
| Simon Fletcher | DE | 6'5" | 240 | 24 | | |
| Freddie Gilbert | DE | 6'4" | 275 | 24 | | |
| Rulon Jones | DE | 6'6" | 260 | 28 | | 2 |
| Karl Mecklenburg | DE-LB | 6'3" | 230 | 26 | | |
| Andre Townsend | DE-NT | 6'3" | 265 | 23 | | 6 |
| Rubin Carter | NT | 6' | 256 | 33 | | |
| Tony Colorito | NT | 6'5" | 260 | 21 | | |
| Greg Kragen | NT | 6'3" | 245 | 24 | | |

| Use Name | Pos. | Hgt | Wgt | Age | Int | Pts |
|---|---|---|---|---|---|---|
| Darren Comeaux | LB | 6'1 | 227 | 26 | | |
| Rick Dennison | LB | 6'3" | 220 | 28 | 1 | |
| Ricky Hunley | LB | 6'2" | 238 | 24 | 1 | |
| Tom Jackson | LB | 5'11" | 220 | 35 | | |
| Jim Ryan | LB | 6'1" | 218 | 29 | | |
| Ken Woodard | LB | 6'1" | 218 | 26 | | 6 |
| Steve Foley | DB | 6'2" | 190 | 32 | 2 | |
| Mike Harden | DB | 6'1" | 192 | 28 | 6 | 18 |
| Mark Haynes | DB | 5'11" | 195 | 27 | | |
| Daniel Hunter (to SD) | DB | 5'11" | 180 | 23 | | |
| Tony Lilly | DB | 6' | 199 | 24 | 3 | |
| Randy Robbins | DB | 6'2" | 189 | 23 | | |
| Dennis Smith | DB | 6'3" | 200 | 27 | 1 | |
| Steve Wilson | DB | 5'10" | 195 | 29 | 1 | 6 |
| Louis Wright | DB | 6'2" | 200 | 33 | 3 | |

| Use Name | Pos. | Hgt | Wgt | Age | Int | Pts |
|---|---|---|---|---|---|---|
| John Elway | QB | 6'3" | 210 | 26 | | 12 |
| Gary Kubiak | QB | 6' | 192 | 25 | | |
| Ken Bell | HB | 5'10" | 190 | 21 | | |
| Tony Boddie | HB | 5'11" | 198 | 25 | | |
| Gene Lang | HB | 5'10" | 196 | 24 | | 18 |
| Gerald Willhite | HB | 5'10" | 200 | 27 | | 54 |
| Sammy Winder | HB | 5'11" | 203 | 27 | | 84 |
| Steve Sewell | FB-WR | 6'3" | 210 | 23 | | 12 |
| Mark Jackson | WR | 5'9" | 174 | 23 | | 6 |
| Vance Johnson | WR | 5'11" | 185 | 22 | | 12 |
| Clint Sampson | WR | 5'11" | 183 | 25 | | |
| Steve Watson | WR | 6'4" | 195 | 29 | | 18 |
| Joey Hackett | TE | 6'5" | 267 | 28 | | |
| Clarence Kay | TE | 6'2" | 237 | 25 | | 6 |
| Bobby Micho | TE | 6'3" | 240 | 24 | | |
| Orson Mobley | TE | 6'5" | 256 | 23 | | 6 |
| Rich Karlis | K | 6' | 180 | 27 | | 104 |
| Mike Horan | K | 5'11 | 190 | 27 | | |
| Chris Norman | K | 6'2" | 198 | 24 | | |
| Jack Weil | K | 5'11" | 175 | 24 | | |

**KANSAS CITY CHIEFS 10-6 John Mackovic**

| Scores of Each Game | | |
|---|---|---|
| 24 | CINCINNATI | 14 |
| 17 | Seattle | 23 |
| 27 | HOUSTON | 13 |
| 20 | Buffalo | 17 |
| 17 | L.A.RAIDERS | 24 |
| 7 | Cleveland | 20 |
| 42 | SAN DIEGO | 41 |
| 27 | TAMPA BAY | 20 |
| 24 | San Diego | 23 |
| 27 | SEATTLE | 7 |
| 17 | Denver | 38 |
| 14 | ST.Louis | 23 |
| 14 | BUFFALO | 17 |
| 37 | DENVER | 10 |
| 20 | L.A.Raiders | 17 |
| 24 | Pittsburgh | 19 |

| Use Name | Pos. | Hgt | Wgt | Age | Int | Pts |
|---|---|---|---|---|---|---|
| John Alt | OT | 6'7" | 282 | 24 | | |
| Irv Eastman | OT | 6'7" | 293 | 25 | | |
| Brian Jozwiak | OT | 6'5" | 308 | 23 | | |
| David Lutz | OT | 6'6" | 295 | 26 | | |
| Jim Rourke | OT | 6'5" | 263 | 29 | | |
| Rich Baldinger | OG-OT | 6'4" | 285 | 26 | | |
| Mark Adickes | OG | 6'4" | 274 | 25 | | |
| Brad Budde | OG | 6'4" | 271 | 28 | | |
| Adam Lingner | OG-C | 6'4" | 260 | 25 | | |
| Tom Baugh | C | 6'3" | 274 | 22 | | |
| Rick Donnalley | C | 6'2" | 270 | 27 | | |
| Gary Baldinger | DE-NT | 6'3" | 260 | 22 | | |
| Leonard Griffin | DE | 6'4" | 252 | 26 | | |
| Eric Holle | DE-NT | 6'5" | 265 | 25 | | |
| Pete Koch | DE | 6'6" | 275 | 24 | | |
| Kit Lathrop | DE | 6'5" | 261 | 30 | | |
| Art Still | DE | 6'7" | 255 | 30 | | |
| Bill Maas | NT | 6'5" | 268 | 24 | | |

| Use Name | Pos. | Hgt | Wgt | Age | Int | Pts |
|---|---|---|---|---|---|---|
| Tim Cofield | LB | 6'2" | 245 | 23 | | |
| Louis Cooper | LB | 6'2" | 235 | 23 | | |
| Dino Hackett | LB | 6'3" | 225 | 22 | 1 | |
| Ken McAlister | LB | 6'5" | 220 | 26 | | |
| Whitney Paul | LB | 6'3" | 219 | 32 | | |
| Aaron Pearson | LB | 6' | 183 | 23 | | |
| Scott Radecic | LB | 6'3" | 242 | 24 | 1 | |
| Gary Spani | LB | 6'2" | 229 | 30 | 1 | |
| Lloyd Burruss | DB | 6' | 209 | 28 | 5 | 24 |
| Deron Cherry | DB | 5'11" | 196 | 26 | 9 | 12 |
| Sherman Cocroft | DB | 6'1" | 195 | 25 | 3 | |
| Greg Hill | DB | 6'1" | 199 | 25 | 3 | 6 |
| Albert Lewis | DB | 6'2" | 192 | 25 | 4 | |
| J.C.Pearson | DB | 5'11" | 183 | 23 | | |
| Mark Robinson | DB | 5'11" | 206 | 23 | | |
| Kevin Ross | DB | 5'9" | 182 | 24 | 4 | 6 |

Mike Bell - Suspended by N.F.L.

| Use Name | Pos. | Hgt | Wgt | Age | Int | Pts |
|---|---|---|---|---|---|---|
| Todd Blackledge | QB | 6'3" | 223 | 25 | | |
| Bill Kenney | QB | 6'4" | 211 | 31 | | |
| Frank Seurer | QB | 6'1" | 195 | 24 | | |
| Herman Heard | HB | 5'10" | 190 | 24 | | 12 |
| Jeff Smith | HB | 5'9" | 201 | 24 | | 36 |
| Boyce Green | FB | 5'11" | 215 | 26 | | 24 |
| Larry Moriarty (from Hou) | FB | 6'1" | 237 | 28 | | 6 |
| Mike Pruitt | FB | 6' | 225 | 32 | | 12 |
| Chris Smith | FB | 6' | 222 | 23 | | |
| Carlos Carson | WR | 5'11" | 184 | 27 | | 24 |
| Anthony Hancock | WR | 6' | 224 | 26 | | |
| Emile Harry | WR | 5'11" | 175 | 23 | | 6 |
| Henry Marshall | WR | 6'2" | 216 | 32 | | 6 |
| Stephone Paige | WR | 6'2" | 183 | 24 | | 66 |
| Walt Arnold | TE | 6'3" | 224 | 28 | | 12 |
| Paul Coffman | TE | 6'3" | 225 | 30 | | 12 |
| Jonathan Hayes | TE | 6'5" | 236 | 24 | | |
| Lewis Colbert | K | 5'11" | 180 | 23 | | |
| Nick Lowery | K | 6'4" | 189 | 30 | | 100 |

**SEATTLE SEAHAWKS 10-6 Chuck Knox**

| Scores of Each Game | | |
|---|---|---|
| 30 | PITTSBURGH | 0 |
| 23 | KANSAS CITY | 17 |
| 38 | New England | 31 |
| 14 | Washington | 19 |
| 33 | SAN DIEGO | 7 |
| 10 | L.A.Raiders | 14 |
| 17 | N.Y.GIANTS | 12 |
| 13 | Denver | 20 |
| 7 | N.Y.JETS | 38 |
| 7 | Kansas City | 27 |
| 7 | Cincinnati | 34 |
| 24 | PHILADELPHIA | 20 |
| 31 | Dallas | 14 |
| 37 | L.A.RAIDERS | 0 |
| 34 | San Diego | 24 |
| 41 | DENVER | 16 |

| Use Name | Pos. | Hgt | Wgt | Age | Int | Pts |
|---|---|---|---|---|---|---|
| Bob Cryder | OT | 6'4" | 236 | 29 | | |
| Ron Mattes | OT | 6'6" | 306 | 23 | | |
| Curt Singer | OT | 6'5" | 275 | 24 | | |
| Mike Wilson | OT | 6'5" | 280 | 31 | | |
| Edwin Bailey | OG | 6'4" | 276 | 27 | | |
| Jon Borchardt | OG | 6'5" | 272 | 29 | | |
| Bryan Millard | OG | 6'5" | 284 | 25 | | |
| Blair Bush | C | 6'3" | 272 | 29 | | |
| Will Grant | C | 6'3" | 268 | 32 | | |
| Glenn Hyde | C | 6'3" | 255 | 35 | | |
| Kani Kauahi | C | 6'2" | 261 | 26 | | |
| Jeff Bryant | DE | 6'5" | 272 | 26 | | |
| Randy Edwards | DE | 6'4" | 267 | 25 | | |
| Jacob Green | DE | 6'3" | 252 | 29 | | |
| Alonzo Mitz | DE | 6'3" | 275 | 23 | | |
| Reggie Kinlaw | NT | 6'2" | 249 | 29 | | |
| Joe Nash | NT | 6'2" | 257 | 25 | | |

| Use Name | Pos. | Hgt | Wgt | Age | Int | Pts |
|---|---|---|---|---|---|---|
| Keith Butler | LB | 6'4" | 239 | 30 | | |
| Greg Gaines | LB | 6'3" | 222 | 27 | 1 | |
| Michael Jackson | LB | 6'1" | 228 | 29 | | |
| John Kaiser | LB | 6'3" | 233 | 24 | | |
| Sam Merriman | LB | 6'3" | 232 | 25 | | |
| Bruce Scholtz | LB | 6'6" | 244 | 27 | 2 | |
| Fredd Young | LB | 6'1" | 233 | 24 | | |
| Eddie Anderson | DB | 6'1" | 199 | 23 | | |
| Dave Brown | DB | 6'1" | 197 | 33 | 5 | 6 |
| Kenny Easley | DB | 6'3" | 206 | 27 | 2 | |
| Patrick Hunter | DB | 5'11" | 185 | 21 | | |
| Greggory Johnson | DB | 6'1" | 195 | 27 | | |
| Kerry Justin | DB | 5'11" | 175 | 31 | 4 | |
| Paul Moyer | DB | 6'1" | 203 | 25 | 3 | 6 |
| Eugene Robinson | DB | 6' | 186 | 23 | 3 | |
| Terry Taylor | DB | 5'10" | 191 | 25 | 2 | |

Ron Essink - Broken Arm
Danny Greene - Broken Finger

| Use Name | Pos. | Hgt | Wgt | Age | Int | Pts |
|---|---|---|---|---|---|---|
| Gale Gilbert | QB | 6'3" | 206 | 24 | | |
| Dave Krieg | QB | 6'1" | 196 | 27 | | 6 |
| Sean Salisbury | QB | 6'5" | 215 | 23 | | |
| Bobby Joe Edmonds | HB | 5'11" | 186 | 21 | | 6 |
| Randall Morris | HB | 6' | 200 | 24 | | 6 |
| Curt Warner | HB | 5'11" | 204 | 25 | | 78 |
| Eric Lane | FB | 6' | 201 | 27 | | 2 |
| John L. Williams | FB | 5'11" | 226 | 21 | | |
| Ray Butler | WR | 6'3" | 206 | 29 | | 24 |
| Byron Franklin | WR | 6'1" | 183 | 28 | | 12 |
| Steve Largent | WR | 5'11" | 191 | 31 | | 54 |
| Paul Skansi | WR | 5'11" | 183 | 25 | | |
| Daryl Turner | WR | 6'3" | 194 | 24 | | 42 |
| Byron Walker | WR | 6'4" | 188 | 26 | | |
| Gordon Hudson | TE | 6'4" | 241 | 24 | | 6 |
| Jim Laughton | TE | 6'5" | 225 | 26 | | |
| Mike Tice | TE | 6'7" | 247 | 27 | | |
| Vince Gamache | K | 5'11" | 170 | 24 | | |
| Norm Johnson | K | 6'2" | 194 | 26 | | 108 |

**LOS ANGELES RAIDERS 8-8 Tom Flores**

| Scores of Each Game | | |
|---|---|---|
| 36 | Denver | 38 |
| 6 | Washington | 10 |
| 9 | N.Y.GIANTS | 14 |
| 17 | SAN DIEGO | 13 |
| 24 | Kansas City | 17 |
| 14 | SEATTLE | 10 |
| 30 | Miami | 28 |
| 28 | Houston | 17 |
| 10 | DENVER | 21 |
| 17 | Dallas | 13 |
| 27 | CLEVELAND | 14 |
| 37 | San Diego | *31 |
| 27 | PHILADELPHIA | *33 |
| 0 | Seattle | 37 |
| 17 | KANSAS CITY | 20 |
| 24 | INDIANAPOLIS | 30 |

| Use Name | Pos. | Hgt | Wgt | Age | Int | Pts |
|---|---|---|---|---|---|---|
| Bruce Davis | OT | 6'6" | 285 | 30 | | |
| Shelby Jordan | OT | 6'7" | 285 | 34 | | |
| Henry Lawrence | OT | 6'4" | 275 | 34 | | |
| Chris Riehm | OT | 6'6" | 275 | 25 | | |
| Charley Hannah | OG | 6'5" | 265 | 31 | | |
| Curt Marsh | OG | 6'5" | 275 | 27 | | |
| Mickey Marvin | OG | 6'4" | 265 | 30 | | |
| Bill Lewis | C | 6'7" | 270 | 23 | | |
| Don Mosebar | C | 6'6" | 275 | 25 | | |
| Elvis Franks (to NYJ) | DE | 6'4" | 265 | 29 | | |
| Sean Jones | DE | 6'7" | 265 | 23 | | |
| Howie Long | DE | 6'5" | 270 | 26 | | |
| Greg Townsend | DE | 6'3" | 250 | 24 | | 6 |
| Mike Wise | DE | 6'7" | 260 | 22 | | |
| Bill Pickel | NT | 6'5" | 260 | 26 | | |
| Mitch Willis | NT | 6'8" | 275 | 24 | | |

Gene Branton - Injury
Mike Davis - Injury

| Use Name | Pos. | Hgt | Wgt | Age | Int | Pts |
|---|---|---|---|---|---|---|
| Jeff Barnes | LB | 6'2" | 230 | 31 | 2 | |
| Jamie Kimmel | LB | 6'3" | 235 | 24 | | |
| Linden King | LB | 6'4" | 250 | 31 | | |
| Rod Martin | LB | 6'2" | 225 | 32 | 1 | |
| Reggie McKenzie | LB | 6'1" | 240 | 23 | 1 | |
| Matt Millen | LB | 6'2" | 245 | 28 | | |
| Jerry Robinson | LB | 6'2" | 225 | 29 | 4 | 12 |
| Stefon Adams | DB | 5'10" | 185 | 23 | 1 | |
| James Davis | DB | 6' | 195 | 29 | | |
| Lester Hayes | DB | 6' | 200 | 31 | 2 | 6 |
| Mike Haynes | DB | 6'2" | 190 | 33 | 2 | |
| Vann McElroy | DB | 6'2" | 195 | 26 | 7 | |
| Odis McKinney | DB | 6'2" | 190 | 29 | | |
| Sam Seale | DB | 5'9" | 180 | 23 | 4 | |
| Stacey Toran | DB | 6'2" | 200 | 24 | 2 | |
| Fulton Walker | DB | 5'10" | 195 | 28 | | 6 |

| Use Name | Pos. | Hgt | Wgt | Age | Int | Pts |
|---|---|---|---|---|---|---|
| Rusty Hilger | QB | 6'4" | 205 | 24 | | |
| Jim Plunkett | QB | 6'3" | 220 | 38 | | |
| Marc Wilson | QB | 6'6" | 205 | 29 | | |
| Marcus Allen | HB | 6'2" | 205 | 26 | | 42 |
| Napoleon McCallum | HB | 6'2" | 215 | 22 | | 6 |
| Vance Mueller | HB | 6' | 205 | 22 | | |
| Steve Strachan | HB - FB | 6'1" | 220 | 23 | | |
| Frank Hawkins | FB | 5'9" | 215 | 27 | | |
| Rod Barksdale | WR | 6' | 185 | 23 | | 12 |
| Jessie Hester | WR | 5'11" | 170 | 23 | | 36 |
| Tim Moffett | WR | 6'2" | 180 | 24 | | |
| Mark Pattison (from LA) | WR | 6'2" | 190 | 24 | | |
| Dokie Williams | WR | 5'11" | 180 | 26 | | 48 |
| Todd Christensen | TE | 6'3" | 230 | 30 | | 48 |
| Earl Cooper | TE | 6'2" | 232 | 28 | | |
| Derrick Jensen | TE | 6'1" | 220 | 30 | | |
| Trey Junkin | TE | 6'2" | 225 | 25 | | |
| Andy Parker | TE | 6'5" | 240 | 24 | | 6 |
| Chris Bahr | K | 5'10" | 175 | 33 | | 99 |
| Ray Guy | K | 6'3" | 205 | 36 | | |

**SAN DIEGO CHARGERS 4-12 Don Coryell (1-7) Al Saunders (3-5)**

| Scores of Each Game | | |
|---|---|---|
| 50 | MIAMI | 28 |
| 7 | N.Y.Giants | 20 |
| 27 | WASHINGTON | 30 |
| 13 | L.A.Raiders | 17 |
| 7 | Seattle | 33 |
| 14 | DENVER | 31 |
| 41 | Kansas City | 42 |
| 7 | Philadelphia | 23 |
| 23 | KANSAS CITY | 24 |
| 9 | Denver | 3 |
| 21 | DALLAS | 24 |
| 31 | L.A.RAIDERS | *37 |
| 17 | Indianapolis | 3 |
| 27 | HOUSTON | 0 |
| 24 | SEATTLE | 34 |
| 17 | Cleveland | 47 |

| Use Name | Pos. | Hgt | Wgt | Age | Int | Pts |
|---|---|---|---|---|---|---|
| Sam Claphan | OT | 6'6" | 288 | 30 | | |
| James FitzPatrick | OT | 6'8" | 302 | 22 | | |
| Jim Lachey | OT | 6'6" | 284 | 23 | | |
| Ken Dallafior | OG | 6'4" | 277 | 27 | | |
| Curt DiGiacomo | OG | 6'4" | 275 | 22 | | |
| Gary Kowalski | OG-OT | 6'6" | 280 | 26 | | |
| Dennis McKnight | OG-C | 6'3" | 270 | 26 | | |
| Jeff Walker | OG | 6'4" | 295 | 23 | | |
| Jim Leonard | C-OG | 6'3" | 270 | 28 | | |
| Don Macek | C | 6'3" | 270 | 32 | | |
| Dee Hardison | DE | 6'4" | 274 | 30 | | |
| Leslie O'Neal | DE | 6'4" | 255 | 22 | 2 | 6 |
| Lee Williams | DE | 6'6" | 263 | 23 | | |
| Lester Williams | DE | 6'3" | 272 | 27 | | |
| Earl Wilson | DE | 6'4" | 280 | 27 | | |
| Blaise Winter | DE | 6'3" | 274 | 24 | | |
| Chuck Ehin | NT | 6'4" | 257 | 25 | | |
| Terry Unrein | NT | 6'5" | 283 | 23 | | |

Tony Simmons - Knee Injury

| Use Name | Pos. | Hgt | Wgt | Age | Int | Pts |
|---|---|---|---|---|---|---|
| Ty Allert | LB | 6'2" | 233 | 23 | | |
| Thomas Benson | LB | 6'2" | 235 | 24 | | |
| Mike Douglass | LB | 6' | 214 | 31 | | |
| Mark Fellows | LB | 6'2" | 233 | 23 | | |
| Andy Hawkins | LB | 6'2" | 230 | 28 | | |
| Woodrow Lowe | LB | 6'1" | 229 | 32 | | |
| Derrie Nelson | LB | 6'2" | 239 | 28 | | |
| Gary Plummer | LB | 6'2" | 230 | 26 | | |
| Fred Robinson (to MIA) | LB | 6'4" | 238 | 24 | | |
| Billy Ray Smith | LB | 6'3" | 236 | 25 | | |
| Donald Brown (to MIA) | DB | 5'11" | 189 | 22 | 1 | |
| Gill Byrd | DB | 5'11" | 194 | 25 | 5 | |
| Jeffrey Dale | DB | 6'3" | 213 | 23 | 4 | |
| Wayne Davis | DB | 5'11" | 175 | 23 | | |
| Vencie Green (from NE) | DB | 6' | 183 | 21 | 2 | |
| David Martin | DB | 5'9" | 187 | 27 | | |
| John Sullivan (from GB) | DB | 6'1" | 190 | 24 | | |
| Ken Taylor | DB | 6'1" | 186 | 22 | 1 | |
| Danny Walters | DB | 6'1" | 200 | 25 | | |
| Kevin Wyatt | DB | 5'10" | 190 | 22 | | |

John Hendy - Knee Injury

| Use Name | Pos. | Hgt | Wgt | Age | Int | Pts |
|---|---|---|---|---|---|---|
| Tom Flick | QB | 6'3" | 191 | 28 | | 6 |
| Dan Fouts | QB | 6'3" | 204 | 35 | | |
| Mark Herrmann | QB | 6'4" | 199 | 27 | | |
| Bruce Mathison | QB | 6'3" | 205 | 27 | | |
| Curtis Adams | HB | 6' | 194 | 24 | | 24 |
| Gary Anderson | HB-WR | 6'1" | 180 | 25 | | 54 |
| Lionel James | HB-WR | 5'7" | 170 | 24 | | |
| Buford McGee | HB | 6' | 206 | 26 | | 42 |
| Tim Spencer | FB | 6'2" | 227 | 25 | | 36 |
| Wes Chandler | WR | 6' | 188 | 30 | | 24 |
| Trumaine Johnson | WR | 6'1" | 191 | 26 | | 6 |
| Charlie Joiner | WR | 5'11" | 183 | 38 | | 12 |
| Timmie Ware | WR | 5'10" | 171 | 23 | | |
| Pete Holohan | TE | 6'4" | 232 | 27 | | 6 |
| Eric Sievers | TE | 6'4" | 235 | 27 | | |
| Kellen Winslow | TE | 6'5" | 250 | 28 | | 30 |
| Rolf Benirschke | K | 6'2" | 180 | 31 | | 87 |
| Ralf Mojsiejenko | K | 6'3" | 210 | 23 | | |

* Overtime

## DENVER BRONCOS

### RUSHING
| Last Name | No. | Yds | Avg | TD |
|---|---|---|---|---|
| Winder | 240 | 789 | 3.3 | 9 |
| Willhite | 85 | 365 | 4.3 | 5 |
| Elway | 52 | 257 | 4.9 | 1 |
| Sewell | 23 | 123 | 5.3 | 1 |
| Lang | 29 | 94 | 3.2 | 1 |
| Kubiak | 6 | 22 | 3.7 | 0 |
| Bell | 9 | 17 | 1.9 | 0 |
| Johnson | 5 | 15 | 3.0 | 0 |
| M. Jackson | 2 | 6 | 3.0 | 0 |
| Boddie | 1 | 2 | 2.0 | 0 |
| Horan | 1 | 0 | 0.0 | 0 |
| Mobley | 1 | -1 | -1.0 | 0 |
| Norman | 1 | -11 | -11.0 | 0 |

### RECEIVING
| Last Name | No. | Yds | Avg | TD |
|---|---|---|---|---|
| Willhite | 64 | 529 | 8.3 | 3 |
| Watson | 45 | 699 | 15.5 | 3 |
| M. Jackson | 38 | 738 | 19.4 | 1 |
| Johnson | 31 | 363 | 11.7 | 2 |
| Winder | 26 | 171 | 6.6 | 5 |
| Sewell | 23 | 294 | 12.8 | 1 |
| Mobley | 22 | 332 | 15.1 | 1 |
| Sampson | 21 | 259 | 12.3 | 0 |
| Kay | 15 | 195 | 13.0 | 1 |
| Lang | 13 | 105 | 8.1 | 2 |
| Hackett | 3 | 48 | 16.0 | 0 |
| Bell | 2 | 10 | 5.0 | 0 |
| Wilson | 1 | 43 | 43.0 | 1 |
| Elway | 1 | 23 | 23.0 | 1 |
| Studdard | 1 | 2 | 2.0 | 1 |

### PUNT RETURNS
| Last Name | No. | Yds | Avg | TD |
|---|---|---|---|---|
| Willhite | 42 | 468 | 11.1 | 1 |
| Johnson | 3 | 36 | 12.0 | 0 |
| M. Jackson | 2 | 7 | 3.5 | 0 |
| Harden | 1 | 41 | 41.0 | 1 |

### KICKOFF RETURNS
| Last Name | No. | Yds | Avg | TD |
|---|---|---|---|---|
| Bell | 23 | 531 | 23.1 | 0 |
| Lang | 21 | 480 | 22.9 | 0 |
| Willhite | 3 | 35 | 11.7 | 0 |
| Johnson | 2 | 21 | 10.5 | 0 |
| Hunley | 2 | 11 | 5.5 | 0 |
| M. Jackson | 1 | 16 | 16.0 | 0 |
| Ryan | 1 | 0 | 0.0 | 0 |

### PASSING — PUNTING — KICKING
| PASSING | Att | Cmp | % | Yds | Yd/Att | TD | Int- | % | RK |
|---|---|---|---|---|---|---|---|---|---|
| Norman | 1 | 1 | 100 | 43 | 43.0 | 1 | 0- | 0 | |
| Sewell | 1 | 1 | 100 | 23 | 23.0 | 1 | 0- | 0 | |
| Elway | 504 | 280 | 56 | 3485 | 6.9 | 19 | 13- | 3 | 9 |
| Kubiak | 38 | 23 | 61 | 249 | 6.6 | 1 | 3- | 8 | |
| Willhite | 4 | 1 | 25 | 11 | 2.8 | 0 | 0- | 0 | |
| Johnson | 1 | 0 | 0 | 0 | 0.0 | 0 | 0- | 0 | |

| PUNTING | No | Avg |
|---|---|---|
| Weil | 34 | 39.5 |
| Norman | 30 | 38.9 |
| Horan | 21 | 41.1 |

| KICKING | XP | Att | % | FG | Att | % |
|---|---|---|---|---|---|---|
| Karlis | 44 | 45 | 98 | 20 | 28 | 71 |

## KANSAS CITY CHIEFS

### RUSHING
| Last Name | No. | Yds | Avg | TD |
|---|---|---|---|---|
| Pruitt | 139 | 448 | 3.2 | 2 |
| Green | 90 | 314 | 3.5 | 3 |
| Heard | 71 | 295 | 4.2 | 2 |
| Smith | 54 | 238 | 4.4 | 3 |
| Blackledge | 23 | 60 | 2.6 | 0 |
| Kenney | 18 | 0 | 0.0 | 0 |
| Paige | 2 | -2 | -1.0 | 0 |

### RECEIVING
| Last Name | No. | Yds | Avg | TD |
|---|---|---|---|---|
| Paige | 52 | 829 | 15.9 | 11 |
| Marshall | 46 | 652 | 14.2 | 1 |
| Smith | 33 | 230 | 7.0 | 3 |
| Carson | 21 | 497 | 23.7 | 4 |
| Arnold | 20 | 169 | 8.5 | 1 |
| Green | 19 | 137 | 7.2 | 0 |
| Heard | 17 | 83 | 4.9 | 0 |
| Coffman | 12 | 75 | 6.3 | 2 |
| Harry | 9 | 211 | 23.4 | 1 |
| Moriarty | 9 | 67 | 7.4 | 0 |
| Hayes | 8 | 69 | 8.6 | 0 |
| Pruitt | 8 | 56 | 7.0 | 0 |
| Hancock | 4 | 63 | 15.8 | 0 |
| Kenney | 1 | 0 | 0.0 | 0 |

### PUNT RETURNS
| Last Name | No. | Yds | Avg | TD |
|---|---|---|---|---|
| Smith | 29 | 245 | 8.4 | 0 |
| Harry | 6 | 20 | 3.3 | 0 |

### KICKOFF RETURNS
| Last Name | No. | Yds | Avg | TD |
|---|---|---|---|---|
| Smith | 29 | 557 | 19.2 | 0 |
| Green | 10 | 254 | 25.4 | 1 |
| Harry | 6 | 115 | 19.2 | 0 |
| Carson | 5 | 88 | 17.6 | 0 |
| Moriarty | 4 | 80 | 20.0 | 0 |
| Cocroft | 1 | 23 | 23.0 | 0 |
| Pearson | 1 | 0 | 0.0 | 0 |

### PASSING — PUNTING — KICKING
| PASSING | Att | Cmp | % | Yds | Yd/Att | TD | Int- | % | RK |
|---|---|---|---|---|---|---|---|---|---|
| Kenney | 308 | 161 | 52 | 1922 | 6.2 | 13 | 11- | 4 | 11 |
| Blackledge | 211 | 96 | 46 | 1200 | 5.7 | 10 | 6- | 3 | |
| Green | 1 | 0 | 0 | 0 | 0.0 | 0 | 1- | 100 | |
| Marshall | 1 | 0 | 0 | 0 | 0.0 | 0 | 0- | 0 | |

| PUNTING | No | Avg |
|---|---|---|
| Colbert | 99 | 40.7 |

| KICKING | XP | Att | % | FG | Att | % |
|---|---|---|---|---|---|---|
| Lowery | 43 | 43 | 100 | 19 | 26 | 73 |

## SEATTLE SEAHAWKS

### RUSHING
| Last Name | No. | Yds | Avg | TD |
|---|---|---|---|---|
| Warner | 319 | 1481 | 4.6 | 13 |
| Williams | 129 | 538 | 4.2 | 0 |
| Morris | 19 | 149 | 7.8 | 1 |
| Krieg | 35 | 122 | 3.5 | 1 |
| Lane | 6 | 11 | 1.8 | 0 |
| Gilbert | 3 | 8 | 2.7 | 0 |
| Franklin | 1 | 2 | 2.0 | 0 |
| Edmonds | 1 | -11 | -11.0 | 0 |

### RECEIVING
| Last Name | No. | Yds | Avg | TD |
|---|---|---|---|---|
| Largent | 70 | 1070 | 15.3 | 9 |
| Warner | 41 | 342 | 8.3 | 0 |
| Franklin | 33 | 547 | 16.6 | 2 |
| Williams | 33 | 219 | 6.6 | 0 |
| Skansi | 22 | 271 | 12.3 | 0 |
| R. Butler | 19 | 351 | 18.5 | 4 |
| Turner | 18 | 334 | 18.6 | 7 |
| Tice | 15 | 150 | 10.0 | 0 |
| Hudson | 13 | 131 | 10.1 | 1 |
| Lane | 3 | 6 | 2.0 | 1 |
| Bailey | 1 | 3 | 3.0 | 0 |

### PUNT RETURNS
| Last Name | No. | Yds | Avg | TD |
|---|---|---|---|---|
| Edmonds | 34 | 419 | 12.3 | 1 |
| Skansi | 5 | 38 | 7.6 | 0 |

### KICKOFF RETURNS
| Last Name | No. | Yds | Avg | TD |
|---|---|---|---|---|
| Edmonds | 34 | 764 | 22.5 | 0 |
| Morris | 23 | 465 | 20.2 | 0 |
| Scholtz | 3 | 39 | 13.0 | 0 |
| Skansi | 1 | 21 | 21.0 | 0 |
| Tice | 1 | 17 | 17.0 | 0 |
| Edwards | 1 | 13 | 13.0 | 0 |
| Lane | 1 | 3 | 3.0 | 0 |

### PASSING — PUNTING — KICKING
| PASSING | Att | Cmp | % | Yds | Yd/Att | TD | Int- | % | RK |
|---|---|---|---|---|---|---|---|---|---|
| Krieg | 375 | 225 | 60 | 2921 | 7.8 | 21 | 11- | 3 | 2 |
| Gilbert | 76 | 42 | 55 | 485 | 6.4 | 3 | 3- | 4 | |
| Largent | 1 | 1 | 100 | 18 | 18.0 | 0 | 0- | 0 | |
| Morris | 1 | 0 | 0 | 0 | 0.0 | 0 | 0- | 0 | |

| PUNTING | No | Avg |
|---|---|---|
| Gamache | 79 | 38.6 |

| KICKING | XP | Att | % | FG | Att | % |
|---|---|---|---|---|---|---|
| N. Johnson | 42 | 42 | 100 | 22 | 35 | 63 |

## LOS ANGELES RAIDERS

### RUSHING
| Last Name | No. | Yds | Avg | TD |
|---|---|---|---|---|
| Allen | 208 | 759 | 3.6 | 5 |
| McCallum | 142 | 536 | 3.8 | 1 |
| Hawkins | 58 | 245 | 4.2 | 0 |
| Strachan | 18 | 53 | 2.9 | 0 |
| Hilger | 6 | 48 | 8.0 | 0 |
| Plunkett | 12 | 47 | 3.9 | 0 |
| Wilson | 14 | 45 | 3.2 | 0 |
| Mueller | 13 | 30 | 2.3 | 0 |
| Williams | 3 | 27 | 9.0 | 0 |
| Guy | 1 | 0 | 0.0 | 0 |

### RECEIVING
| Last Name | No. | Yds | Avg | TD |
|---|---|---|---|---|
| Christensen | 95 | 1153 | 12.1 | 8 |
| Allen | 46 | 453 | 9.8 | 2 |
| Williams | 43 | 843 | 19.6 | 8 |
| Hawkins | 25 | 166 | 6.6 | 0 |
| Hester | 23 | 632 | 27.5 | 6 |
| Barksdale | 18 | 434 | 24.1 | 2 |
| McCallum | 11 | 103 | 7.9 | 0 |
| Moffett | 6 | 77 | 12.8 | 0 |
| Mueller | 6 | 54 | 9.0 | 0 |
| Junkin | 2 | 38 | 19.0 | 0 |
| Pattison | 2 | 12 | 6.0 | 0 |
| Parker | 2 | 8 | 4.0 | 1 |

### PUNT RETURNS
| Last Name | No. | Yds | Avg | TD |
|---|---|---|---|---|
| Walker | 49 | 440 | 9.0 | 1 |
| McCallum | 7 | 44 | 6.3 | 0 |

### KICKOFF RETURNS
| Last Name | No. | Yds | Avg | TD |
|---|---|---|---|---|
| Adams | 27 | 573 | 21.2 | 0 |
| Walker | 23 | 368 | 16.0 | 0 |
| McCallum | 8 | 183 | 22.9 | 0 |
| Millen | 3 | 40 | 13.3 | 0 |
| Mueller | 2 | 73 | 36.5 | 0 |
| Hawkins | 1 | 15 | 15.0 | 0 |

### PASSING — PUNTING — KICKING
| PASSING | Att | Cmp | % | Yds | Yd/Att | TD | Int- | % | RK |
|---|---|---|---|---|---|---|---|---|---|
| Plunkett | 252 | 133 | 53 | 1986 | 7.9 | 14 | 9- | 4 | 8 |
| Wilson | 240 | 129 | 54 | 1721 | 7.2 | 12 | 15- | 6 | 11 |
| Hilger | 38 | 19 | 50 | 266 | 7.0 | 1 | 1- | 3 | |

| PUNTING | No. | Avg. |
|---|---|---|
| Guy | 90 | 3620 |

| KICKING | XP | Att | % | FG | Att | % |
|---|---|---|---|---|---|---|
| Bahr | 36 | 36 | 100 | 21 | 28 | 75 |

## SAN DIEGO CHARGERS

### RUSHING
| Last Name | No. | Yds | Avg | TD |
|---|---|---|---|---|
| Anderson | 127 | 442 | 3.5 | 1 |
| Adams | 118 | 366 | 3.1 | 4 |
| Spencer | 99 | 350 | 3.5 | 6 |
| James | 51 | 224 | 4.4 | 0 |
| McGee | 63 | 187 | 3.0 | 7 |
| Herrmann | 2 | 6 | 3.0 | 0 |
| Flick | 6 | 5 | .8 | 1 |
| Mathison | 1 | -1 | -1.0 | 0 |
| Fouts | 4 | -3 | -.8 | 0 |

### RECEIVING
| Last Name | No. | Yds | Avg | TD |
|---|---|---|---|---|
| Anderson | 80 | 871 | 10.9 | 8 |
| Winslow | 64 | 728 | 11.4 | 5 |
| Chandler | 56 | 874 | 15.6 | 4 |
| Joiner | 34 | 440 | 12.9 | 2 |
| Johnson | 30 | 399 | 13.3 | 1 |
| Holohan | 29 | 356 | 12.3 | 1 |
| James | 23 | 173 | 7.0 | 0 |
| McGee | 10 | 105 | 10.5 | 0 |
| Spencer | 6 | 48 | 8.0 | 0 |
| Adams | 4 | 26 | 6.5 | 0 |
| Sievers | 2 | 14 | 7.0 | 0 |
| Ware | 1 | 11 | 11.0 | 0 |

### PUNT RETURNS
| Last Name | No. | Yds | Avg | TD |
|---|---|---|---|---|
| Anderson | 25 | 227 | 9.1 | 0 |
| James | 9 | 94 | 10.4 | 0 |
| Chandler | 3 | 13 | 4.3 | 0 |

### KICKOFF RETURNS
| Last Name | No. | Yds | Avg | TD |
|---|---|---|---|---|
| Anderson | 24 | 482 | 20.1 | 0 |
| James | 18 | 315 | 17.5 | 0 |
| Adams | 5 | 100 | 20.0 | 0 |
| Spencer | 5 | 81 | 16.2 | 0 |
| Wyatt | 5 | 74 | 14.8 | 0 |
| Johnson | 3 | 48 | 16.0 | 0 |
| Winslow | 2 | 11 | 5.5 | 0 |
| McGee | 1 | 15 | 15.0 | 0 |
| Chandler | 1 | 11 | 11.0 | 0 |
| Plummer | 1 | 0 | 0.0 | 0 |

### PASSING — PUNTING — KICKING
| PASSING | Att | Cmp | % | Yds | Yd/Att | TD | Int- | % | RK |
|---|---|---|---|---|---|---|---|---|---|
| Fouts | 430 | 252 | 59 | 3031 | 7.1 | 16 | 22- | 5 | 10 |
| Herrmann | 97 | 51 | 53 | 627 | 6.5 | 2 | 3- | 3 | |
| Flick | 73 | 33 | 45 | 361 | 5.0 | 2 | 8- | 3 | |
| Anderson | 1 | 1 | 100 | 4 | 4.0 | 1 | 0- | 0 | |
| Holohan | 2 | 1 | 50 | 21 | 10.5 | 0 | 0- | 0 | |
| McGee | 1 | 1 | 100 | 1 | 1.0 | 0 | 0- | 0 | |

| PUNTING | No | Avg |
|---|---|---|
| Mojsiejenko | 72 | 42.0 |
| Chandler | 5 | 33.4 |

| KICKING | XP | Att | % | FG | Att | % |
|---|---|---|---|---|---|---|
| Benirschke | 39 | 41 | 95 | 16 | 25 | 64 |

December 28, 1986 at RFK Stadium (Attendance 54,180)

**SCORING**

| | | | | | |
|---|---|---|---|---|---|
| L.A. RAMS | 0 | 0 | 0 | 7- | 7 |
| WASHINGTON | 10 | 3 | 3 | 3- | 19 |

First Quarter

| | |
|---|---|
| Wash. | Atkinson, 25 yard field goal |
| Wash. | Bryant, 14 yard pass from Schroeder<br>PAT—Atkinson (kick) |

Second Quarter

| | |
|---|---|
| Wash. | Atkinson, 20 yard field goal |

Third Quarter

| | |
|---|---|
| Wash. | Atkinson, 38 yard field goal |

Fourth quarter

| | |
|---|---|
| L.A. | House, 12 yard pass from Everett<br>PAT— Lansford (kick) |
| Wash. | Atkinson, 19 yard field goal |

**TEAM STATISTICS**

| L.A. | | WASH. |
|---|---|---|
| 16 | First Downs | 15 |
| 9 | First Downs-Rushing | 9 |
| 6 | First Downs-Passing | 5 |
| 1 | First Downs-Penalty | 1 |
| 4 | Fumbles | 1 |
| 1 | Fumbles-Lost Ball | 0 |
| 8 | Penalties-Number | 6 |
| 78 | Yards Penalized | 45 |
| 1 | Missed Field Goals | 0 |
| 53 | Offensive Plays | 64 |
| 324 | Net Yards | 228 |
| 6.1 | Average Gain | 3.6 |
| 3 | Giveaways | 0 |
| 0 | Takeaways | 3 |
| -3 | Difference | +3 |

**INDIVIDUAL STATISTICS**

| L.A. RAMS | No. | Yds. | Avg. | WASHINGTON | No. | Yds. | Avg. |
|---|---|---|---|---|---|---|---|
| **RUSHING** | | | | | | | |
| Dickerson | 26 | 158 | 6.1 | Rogers | 29 | 115 | 4.0 |
| Redden | 7 | 28 | 4.0 | Bryant | 4 | 17 | 4.3 |
| Everett | 1 | 12 | 12.0 | Griffin | 5 | 8 | 1.6 |
| | 34 | 198 | 5.8 | Schroeder | 3 | -2 | -0.7 |
| | | | | | 41 | 138 | 3.4 |
| **RECEIVING** | | | | | | | |
| Ellard | 1 | 14 | 14.0 | Monk | 5 | 34 | 6.8 |
| Redden | 1 | 20 | 20.0 | Bryant | 2 | 18 | 9.0 |
| Hill | 3 | 27 | 9.0 | Didier | 1 | 4 | 4.0 |
| Long | 1 | 5 | 5.0 | Clark | 1 | 8 | 8.0 |
| House | 3 | 70 | 23.3 | Sanders | 2 | 15 | 7.5 |
| | 9 | 136 | 15.1 | Warren | 1 | 7 | 7.0 |
| | | | | Rogers | 1 | 4 | 4.0 |
| | | | | | 13 | 90 | 6.9 |
| **PUNTING** | | | | | | | |
| Hatcher | 3 | | 38.3 | Cox | 5 | | 42.2 |
| **PUNT RETURNS** | | | | | | | |
| Ellard | 2 | 23 | 11.5 | Yarber | 2 | 8 | 4.0 |
| **KICKOFF RETURNS** | | | | | | | |
| White | 3 | 42 | 14 | Garner | 2 | 27 | 13.5 |
| Sutton | 2 | 37 | 18.5 | | | | |
| McDonald | 1 | 7 | 7.0 | | | | |
| | 6 | 86 | 14.3 | | | | |
| **INTERCEPTION RETURNS** | | | | | | | |
| none | | | | Walton | 1 | 16 | 16.0 |
| | | | | Wilburn | 1 | 2 | 2.0 |
| | | | | | 2 | 18 | 9.0 |

**PASSING**

| L.A. RAMS | Att. | Comp. | Comp. Pct. | Yds. | Int. | Yds./ Att. | Yds./ Comp. |
|---|---|---|---|---|---|---|---|
| Everett | 18 | 9 | 50 | 136 | 2 | 7.6 | 15.1 |
| **WASHINGTON** | | | | | | | |
| Schroeder | 23 | 13 | 57 | 90 | 0 | 3.9 | 6.9 |

January 3, 1987 at Chicago (Attendance 65,141)

**SCORING**

| | | | | | |
|---|---|---|---|---|---|
| WASHINGTON | 7 | 0 | 7 | 13- | 27 |
| CHICAGO | 0 | 13 | 0 | 0- | 13 |

First Quarter

| | |
|---|---|
| Wash. | Monk, 28 yard pass from Schroeder<br>PAT—Atkinson (kick) |

Second Quarter

| | |
|---|---|
| Chicago | Gault, 50 yard pass from Flutie |
| Chicago | Butler, 23 yard field goal |
| Chicago | Butler, 41 yard field goal |

Third Quarter

| | |
|---|---|
| Wash. | Monk, 23 yard pass from Schroeder<br>PAT—Atkinson (kick) |

Fourth Quarter

| | |
|---|---|
| Wash. | Rogers, 1 yard run<br>PAT—Atkinson (kick) |
| Wash. | Atkinson, 35 yard field goal |
| Wash. | Atkinson, 25 yard field goal |

**TEAM STATISTICS**

| WASH. | | CHI. |
|---|---|---|
| 19 | First Downs | 14 |
| 8 | First Downs-Rushing | 8 |
| 8 | First Downs-Passing | 5 |
| 3 | First Downs-Penalty | 1 |
| 2 | Fumbles_Number | 3 |
| 0 | Fumbles-Lost | 2 |
| 8 | Penalties-Number | 4 |
| 65 | Yards Penalized | 42 |
| 1 | Missed Field Goals | 1 |
| 73 | Offensive Plays | 56 |
| 302 | Net Yards | 220 |
| 4.1 | Average Gain | 3.9 |
| 1 | Giveaways | 4 |
| 4 | Takeaways | 1 |
| +3 | Difference | -3 |

**INDIVIDUAL STATISTICS**

| WASHINGTON | No. | Yds. | Avg. | CHICAGO | No. | Yds. | Avg. |
|---|---|---|---|---|---|---|---|
| **RUSHING** | | | | | | | |
| Rogers | 28 | 72 | 2.6 | Payton | 14 | 38 | 2.7 |
| Bryant | 8 | 16 | 2.0 | Suhey | 4 | 14 | 3.5 |
| Schroeder | 3 | 16 | 5.3 | Thomas | 3 | 18 | 6.0 |
| | 39 | 104 | 2.7 | Anderson | 1 | 11 | 11.0 |
| | | | | Flutie | 2 | 12 | 6.0 |
| | | | | | 24 | 93 | 3.9 |
| **RECEIVING** | | | | | | | |
| Monk | 5 | 81 | 16.2 | Gault | 5 | 82 | 16.4 |
| Clark | 5 | 37 | 7.4 | Ortego | 2 | 36 | 18.0 |
| Bryant | 4 | 61 | 15.3 | Wrightman | 2 | 16 | 8.0 |
| Warren | 1 | 5 | 5.0 | Suhey | 1 | 2 | 2.0 |
| | 15 | 184 | 12.3 | Payton | 1 | -2 | -2.0 |
| | | | | | 11 | 134 | 12.2 |
| **PUNTING** | | | | | | | |
| Cox | 7 | | 39.3 | Buford | 5 | | 40.6 |
| **PUNT RETURNS** | | | | | | | |
| Yarber | 3 | 22 | 7.3 | Barnes | 5 | 27 | 5.4 |
| **KICKOFF RETURNS** | | | | | | | |
| Garner | 3 | 71 | 23.7 | Gentry | 3 | 127 | 42.3 |
| | | | | Thomas | 2 | 15 | 7.5 |
| | | | | Anderson | 1 | 17 | 17.0 |
| | | | | | 6 | 159 | 26.5 |
| **INTERCEPTION RETURNS** | | | | | | | |
| Dean | 1 | 16 | 16.0 | Richardson | 1 | 43 | 43.0 |
| Green | 1 | 17 | 17.0 | | | | |
| | 2 | 33 | 16.5 | | | | |

**PASSING**

| WASHINGTON | Att. | Comp. | Comp. Pct. | Yds. | Int. | Yds./ Att. | Yds./ Comp. |
|---|---|---|---|---|---|---|---|
| Schroeder | 32 | 15 | 47 | 184 | 1 | 5.8 | 12.3 |
| **CHICAGO** | | | | | | | |
| Flutie | 31 | 11 | 35 | 134 | 2 | 4.3 | 12.2 |

January 4, 1987 at East Rutherford, N.J. (Attend. 76,034)

**SCORING**

| | | | | | |
|---|---|---|---|---|---|
| SAN FRANCISCO | 3 | 0 | 0 | 0- | 3 |
| N.Y. GIANTS | 7 | 21 | 21 | 0- | 49 |

First Quarter

| | |
|---|---|
| N.Y.G. | Bavaro, 24 yard pass from Simms<br>PAT—Allegre (kick) |
| S.F. | Wersching, 26 yard field |

Second Quarter

| | |
|---|---|
| N.Y.G. | Morris, 45 yard run<br>PAT—Allegre (kick) |
| N.Y.G. | B. Johnson, 15 yard pass from Simms<br>PAT—Allegre (kick) |
| N.Y.G. | Taylor, 34 yard interception return<br>PAT—Allegre (kick) |

Third Quarter

| | |
|---|---|
| N.Y.G. | McConkey, 28 yard pass from Simms<br>PAT—Allegre (kick) |
| N.Y.G. | Mowatt, 29 yard pass from Simms<br>PAT—Allegre (kick) |
| N.Y.G. | Morris, 2 yard run<br>PAT—Allegre (kick) |

**TEAM STATISTICS**

| S.F. | | N.Y.G. |
|---|---|---|
| 9 | First Downs-Total | 21 |
| 2 | First Downs-Rushing | 12 |
| 6 | First Downs-Passing | 6 |
| 1 | First Downs-Penalty | 3 |
| 2 | Fumbles-Number | 0 |
| 1 | Fumbles-Lost Ball | 0 |
| 11 | Penalties-Number | 3 |
| 62 | Yards Penalized | 23 |
| 0 | Missed Field Goals | 0 |
| 58 | Offensive Plays | 65 |
| 184 | Net Yards | 366 |
| 3.2 | Average Gain | 5.6 |
| 4 | Giveaways | 0 |
| 0 | Takeaways | 4 |
| -4 | Difference | +4 |

**INDIVIDUAL STATISTICS**

| SAN FRANCISCO | No. | Yds. | Avg. | N.Y. GIANTS | No. | Yds. | Avg. |
|---|---|---|---|---|---|---|---|
| **RUSHING** | | | | | | | |
| Craig | 5 | 17 | 3.4 | Morris | 24 | 159 | 6.6 |
| Cribbs | 12 | 4 | 0.3 | Carthon | 6 | 17 | 2.8 |
| Rathman | 3 | 8 | 2.7 | Simms | 1 | 15 | 15.0 |
| | 20 | 29 | 1.5 | Rouson | 8 | 28 | 3.5 |
| | | | | Anderson | 4 | 2 | 0.5 |
| | | | | Manuel | 1 | -5 | -5.0 |
| | | | | | 44 | 216 | 4.9 |
| **RECEIVING** | | | | | | | |
| Rice | 3 | 48 | 16.0 | Bavaro | 2 | 47 | 23.5 |
| Clark | 3 | 52 | 17.3 | B. Johnson | 1 | 15 | 15.0 |
| Margerum | 1 | 12 | 12.0 | Galbreath | 1 | 9 | 9.0 |
| Francis | 3 | 26 | 8.7 | Mowatt | 1 | 29 | 29.0 |
| Craig | 4 | 22 | 5.5 | Carthon | 1 | 7 | 7.0 |
| Cribbs | 1 | 2 | 2.0 | Morris | 1 | 2 | 2.0 |
| | 15 | 162 | 10.8 | Rouson | 2 | 22 | 11.0 |
| | | | | McConkey | 1 | 28 | 28.0 |
| | | | | | 10 | 159 | 15.9 |
| **PUNTING** | | | | | | | |
| Runager | 10 | | 40.0 | Landeta | 7 | | 43.9 |
| **PUNT RETURNS** | | | | | | | |
| Griffin | 2 | 11 | 5.5 | McConkey | 7 | 57 | 8.1 |
| **KICKOFF RETURNS** | | | | | | | |
| Cribbs | 3 | 71 | 22.7 | Rouson | 1 | 17 | 17.0 |
| Craig | 4 | 48 | 12.0 | Hill | 1 | 15 | 15.0 |
| | 7 | 119 | 17.0 | | 2 | 32 | 16.0 |
| **INTERCEPTION RETURNS** | | | | | | | |
| none | | | | Taylor | 1 | 34 | 34.0 |
| | | | | P. Johnson | 1 | 27 | 27.0 |
| | | | | Welch | 1 | 0 | 0.0 |
| | | | | | 3 | 61 | 20.3 |

**PASSING**

| SAN FRANCISCO | Att. | Comp. | Comp. Pct. | Yds. | Int. | Yds./ Att. | Yds./ Comp. |
|---|---|---|---|---|---|---|---|
| Montana | 15 | 8 | 53 | 98 | 2 | 6.5 | 12.3 |
| Kemp | 22 | 7 | 32 | 64 | 1 | 2.9 | 9.1 |
| | 37 | 15 | 41 | 162 | 3 | 4.4 | 10.8 |
| **N.Y. GIANTS** | | | | | | | |
| Simms | 19 | 9 | 47 | 136 | 0 | 7.2 | 15.1 |
| Rutledge | 1 | 1 | 100 | 23 | 0 | 23.0 | 23.0 |
| | 20 | 10 | 50 | 159 | 0 | 7.95 | 15.9 |

# 1986 A.F.C.— PLAYOFFS

December 28, 1986 at East Rutherford (Attendance 69,307)

### SCORING

| | | | | |
|---|---|---|---|---|
| KANSAS CITY | 6 | 0 | 0 | 9- 15 |
| N.Y. JETS | 7 | 14 | 7 | 7- 35 |

First Quarter
- K.C. — J. Smith, 1 yard run; PAT—kick failed
- N.Y.J. — McNeil, 4 yard run; PAT—Leahy (kick)

Second Quarter
- N.Y.J. — McNeil, 1 yard pass from Ryan; PAT—Leahy (kick)
- N.Y.J. — Toon, 11 yard pass from Ryan; PAT—Leahy (kick)

Third Quarter
- N.Y.J. — McArthur, 21 yard interception return; PAT—Leahy (kick)

Fourth Quarter
- K.C. — Lewis, recovered blocked punt in endzone; PAT—Lowery (kick)
- N.Y.J. — Griggs, 6 yard pass from Ryan; PAT—Leahy (kick)
- K.C. — Safety, Jennings ran out of endzone

### TEAM STATISTICS

| K.C. | | N.Y.J. |
|---|---|---|
| 15 | First Downs- Total | 19 |
| 4 | First Downs- Rushing | 9 |
| 8 | First Downs-Passing | 10 |
| 3 | First Downs-Penalty | 0 |
| 2 | Fumbles- Number | 0 |
| 1 | Fumbles- Lost Ball | 0 |
| 1 | Penalties- Number | 8 |
| 5 | Yards Penalized | 54 |
| 0 | Missed Field Goals | 0 |
| 59 | Offensive Plays | 61 |
| 241 | Net Yards | 306 |
| 4.1 | Average Gain | 5.0 |
| 3 | Giveaways | 0 |
| 0 | Takeaways | 3 |
| -3 | Difference | +3 |

### INDIVIDUAL STATISTICS

| KANSAS CITY | No. | Yds. | Avg. | N.Y. JETS | No. | Yds. | Avg. |
|---|---|---|---|---|---|---|---|
| **RUSHING** | | | | | | | |
| Moriarty | 2 | 7 | 3.5 | McNeil | 31 | 135 | 4.4 |
| Green | 8 | 15 | 1.9 | Paige | 2 | 3 | 1.5 |
| Heard | 1 | 1 | 1.0 | Ryan | 2 | 30 | 15.0 |
| Smith | 4 | 12 | 3.0 | Jennings | 1 | -3 | -31.0 |
| Blackledge | 4 | 33 | 8.2 | | 36 | 165 | 4.6 |
| Paige | 1 | -2 | -2.0 | | | | |
| | 20 | 67 | 3.4 | | | | |
| **RECEIVING** | | | | | | | |
| Marshall | 6 | 72 | 12.0 | Toon | 4 | 48 | 12.0 |
| Green | 5 | 7 | 1.2 | Shuler | 4 | 28 | 7.0 |
| Coffman | 3 | 12 | 4.0 | McNeil | 3 | 16 | 5.2 |
| Carson | 2 | 43 | 21.5 | Walker | 2 | 45 | 22.5 |
| J. Smith | 2 | 12 | 6.0 | Sohn | 1 | 11 | 11.0 |
| Moriarty | 1 | 16 | 16.0 | Griggs | 1 | 7 | 7.0 |
| Heard | 1 | 15 | 15.0 | Alexander | 1 | 1 | -1.0 |
| | 20 | 174 | 8.7 | | 16 | 141 | 8.8 |
| **PUNTING** | | | | | | | |
| Colbert | 3 | | 41.3 | Jennings | 4 | | 29.0 |
| **PUNT RETURNS** | | | | | | | |
| J. Smith | 3 | 5 | 1.6 | Sohn | 1 | 4 | 4.0 |
| **KICKOFF RETURNS** | | | | | | | |
| J. Smith | 3 | 50 | 16.7 | Paige | 1 | 7 | 7.0 |
| Moriarty | 2 | 35 | 17.5 | Townsell | 1 | 13 | 13.0 |
| | 5 | 85 | 17.0 | | 2 | 20 | 10.0 |
| **INTERCEPTION RETURNS** | | | | | | | |
| none | | | | McArthur | 1 | 21 | 21.0 |
| | | | | Carter | 1 | 12 | 12.0 |
| | | | | | 2 | 23 | 11.5 |

### PASSING

**KANSAS CITY**

| | Att. | Comp. | Comp. Pct. | Yds. | Int. | Yds./ Att. | Yds./ Comp. |
|---|---|---|---|---|---|---|---|
| Kenney | 16 | 8 | 50.0 | 97 | 0 | 6.1 | 12.2 |
| Blackledge | 21 | 12 | 57.1 | 80 | 2 | 3.9 | 6.7 |
| | 37 | 20 | 54.2 | 177 | 2 | 4.8 | 8.9 |
| **N.Y. JETS** | | | | | | | |
| Ryan | 23 | 16 | 69.5 | 153 | 0 | 6.7 | 9.6 |

January 4, 1987 at Cleveland (Attendance78,106)

### SCORING

| | | | | | | | |
|---|---|---|---|---|---|---|---|
| N.Y. JETS | 7 | 3 | 3 | 7 | 0 | 0- | 17 |
| CLEVELAND | 7 | 3 | 0 | 10 | 0 | 3- | 20 |

First Quarter
- N.Y.J. — Walker, 42 yard pass from Ryan; PAT—Leahy (kick)
- Cle. — Fontenot, 37 yard pass from Kosar; PAT-Moseley (kick)

Second Quarter
- Cle. — Moseley, 38 yard field goal
- N.Y.J. — Leahy, 46 yard field goal

Third Quarter
- N.Y.J — Leahy, 37 yard field goal

Fourth Quarter
- N.Y.J. — McNeil, 25 yard run; PAT—Leahy (kick)
- Cle. — Mack, 1 yard run; PAT—Moseley (kick)
- Cle. — Moseley, 22 yard field goal

Second Overtime
- Cle. — Moseley, 27 yard field goal

### TEAM STATISTICS

| N.Y.J. | | CLE. |
|---|---|---|
| 14 | First Downs- Total | 33 |
| 6 | First Downs-Rushing | 6 |
| 8 | First Downs-Passing | 21 |
| 0 | First Downs-Penalty | 6 |
| 0 | Fumbles- Number | 2 |
| 0 | Fumbles-Lost Ball | 0 |
| 10 | Penalties- Number | 4 |
| 94 | Yards Penalized | 40 |
| 0 | Missed Field Goals | 3 |
| 71 | Offensive Plays | 96 |
| 287 | Net Yards | 558 |
| 4.0 | Average Gain | 5.8 |
| 0 | Giveaways | 2 |
| 2 | Takeaways | 0 |
| +2 | Difference | -2 |

### INDIVIDUAL STATISTICS

| N.Y. JETS | No. | Yds. | Avg. | CLEVELAND | No. | Yds. | Avg. |
|---|---|---|---|---|---|---|---|
| **RUSHING** | | | | | | | |
| McNeil | 25 | 71 | 2.9 | Mack | 20 | 63 | 3.1 |
| O'Brien | 3 | 22 | 7.1 | Fontenot | 3 | 8 | 2.6 |
| Paige | 3 | 11 | 3.8 | Dickey | 3 | 4 | 1.3 |
| | 31 | 104 | 3.4 | Kosar | 1 | 0 | 0.0 |
| | | | | | 27 | 75 | 2.8 |
| **RECEIVING** | | | | | | | |
| Toon | 5 | 93 | 18.6 | Newsome | 6 | 114 | 19.0 |
| Shuler | 4 | 43 | 10.8 | Slaughter | 6 | 86 | 14.3 |
| McNeil | 4 | 35 | 8.8 | Fontenot | 5 | 62 | 12.1 |
| Walker | 2 | 49 | 24.5 | Mack | 5 | 51 | 10.0 |
| Paige | 1 | 10 | 10.0 | Brennan | 4 | 69 | 17.3 |
| Sohn | 1 | 7 | 7.0 | Langhorne | 4 | 65 | 16.3 |
| | 17 | 237 | 13.9 | Holt | 2 | 42 | 21.0 |
| | | | | Weathers | 1 | 3 | 3.0 |
| | | | | Dickey | 1 | 2 | 2.0 |
| | | | | | 34 | 483 | 15.6 |
| **PUNTING** | | | | | | | |
| Jennings | 14 | | 37.9 | Gossett | 8 | | 38.8 |
| **PUNT RETURNS** | | | | | | | |
| Sohn | 1 | 9 | 9.0 | McNeil | 7 | 65 | 9.3 |
| McNeil | 2 | 14 | 7.0 | | | | |
| | 3 | 23 | 7.7 | | | | |
| **KICKOFF RETURNS** | | | | | | | |
| Townsell | 4 | 83 | 20.8 | McNeil | 3 | 37 | 12.3 |
| Bingham | 1 | 8 | 8.0 | Puzzuoli | 1 | 6 | 6.0 |
| | 5 | 91 | 18.2 | Nicolas | 1 | 3 | 3.0 |
| | | | | | 5 | 46 | 9.2 |
| **INTERCEPTION RETURNS** | | | | | | | |
| Carter | 1 | 0 | 0.0 | none | | | |
| Holmes | 1 | 0 | 0.0 | | | | |
| | 2 | 0 | 0.0 | | | | |

### PASSING

**N.Y. JETS**

| | Att. | Comp. | Comp. Pct. | Yds. | Int. | Yds./ Att. | Yds./ Comp. |
|---|---|---|---|---|---|---|---|
| O'Brien | 19 | 11 | 57.8 | 134 | 0 | 7.1 | 12.2 |
| Ryan | 11 | 6 | 54.5 | 103 | 0 | 9.4 | 17.2 |
| | 30 | 17 | 56.7 | 237 | 0 | 7.9 | 13.9 |
| **CLEVELAND** | | | | | | | |
| Kosar | 64 | 33 | 51.5 | 483 | 2 | 7.5 | 14.6 |

January 4,1987 at Denver (Attendance 76,105)

### SCORING

| | | | | |
|---|---|---|---|---|
| NEW ENGLAND | 0 | 10 | 7 | 0- 17 |
| DENVER | 3 | 7 | 10 | 2- 22 |

First Quarter
- Den. — Karlis, 27 yard field goal

Second Quarter
- Den. — Elway, 22 yard run; PAT—Karlis (kick)
- N.E. — Franklin, 38 yard field goal
- N.E. — Morgan, 19 pass from Eason; PAT—Franklin (kick)

Third Quarter
- Den. — Karlis, 22 yard field goal
- N.E. — Morgan, 45 yard pass from Eason; PAT—Franklin (kick)
- Den. — Johnson, 48 yard pass from Elway; PAT—Franklin (kick)

Fourth Quarter
- Den. — Safety, Eason tackled in endzone by Jones

### TEAM STATISTICS

| N.E. | | DEN. |
|---|---|---|
| 12 | First Downs- Total | 21 |
| 6 | First Downs-Rushing | 12 |
| 6 | First Downs-Passing | 9 |
| 0 | First Down-Penalty | 0 |
| 1 | Fumbles- Number | 0 |
| 0 | Fumbles- Lost Ball | 0 |
| 5 | Penalties- Number | 3 |
| 45 | Yards Penalized | 20 |
| 0 | Missed Field Goals | 0 |
| 54 | Offensive Plays | 75 |
| 271 | Net Yards | 441 |
| 5.0 | Average Gain | 5.9 |
| 0 | Giveaways | 2 |
| 2 | Takeaways | 0 |
| +2 | Difference | -2 |

### INDIVIDUAL STATISTICS

| NEW ENGLAND | No. | Yds. | Avg. | DENVER | No. | Yds. | Avg. |
|---|---|---|---|---|---|---|---|
| **RUSHING** | | | | | | | |
| C. James | 10 | 31 | 3.1 | Winder | 19 | 102 | 5.4 |
| Collins | 5 | 46 | 9.1 | Lang | 11 | 44 | 4.0 |
| Dupard | 5 | 18 | 3.6 | Elway | 5 | 18 | 3.6 |
| Eason | 2 | 23 | 11.5 | Willhite | 3 | 4 | 1.3 |
| Fryar | 1 | -2 | -2.0 | Bell | 2 | 12 | 6.0 |
| Hawthorne | 1 | 5 | 5.0 | Sewell | 2 | 8 | 4.0 |
| | 24 | 121 | 5.0 | | 42 | 188 | 4.5 |
| **RECEIVING** | | | | | | | |
| Morgan | 3 | 100 | 3.3 | Johnson | 4 | 89 | 22.3 |
| Collins | 4 | 46 | 11.5 | Sewell | 3 | 41 | 13.7 |
| Baty | 3 | 31 | 8.0 | Mobley | 2 | 69 | 34.5 |
| Hawthorne | 1 | 6 | 6.0 | Watson | 1 | 21 | 21.0 |
| Fryar | 2 | 11 | 5.5 | Winder | 1 | 16 | 16.0 |
| | 13 | 150 | 11.5 | Micho | 1 | 20 | 20.0 |
| | | | | Lang | 1 | 1 | 1.0 |
| | | | | | 13 | 253 | 19.5 |
| **PUNTING** | | | | | | | |
| Camarillo | 9 | | 50.2 | Horan | 5 | | 49.0 |
| | | | | Elway | 1 | | 31.0 |
| | | | | | 6 | | 46.0 |
| **PUNT RETURNS** | | | | | | | |
| Fryar | 2 | 13 | 6.5 | Johnson | 3 | 26 | 8.7 |
| | | | | Willhite | 1 | 9 | 9.0 |
| | | | | | 4 | 35 | 8.8 |
| **KICKOFF RETURNS** | | | | | | | |
| Starring | 2 | 13 | 6.5 | Lang | 1 | 21 | 21.0 |
| | | | | Bell | 3 | 63 | 21.0 |
| | | | | | 4 | 84 | 21.0 |
| **INTERCEPTION RETURNS** | | | | | | | |
| McSwain | 1 | 2 | 2.0 | none | | | |
| Rembert | 1 | 0 | 0.0 | | | | |
| | 2 | 2 | 1.0 | | | | |

### PASSING

**NEW ENGLAND**

| | Att. | Comp. | Comp. Pct. | Yds. | Int. | Yds./ Att. | Yds./ Comp. |
|---|---|---|---|---|---|---|---|
| Eason | 24 | 13 | 54.2 | 194 | 0 | 8.1 | 14.9 |
| **DENVER** | | | | | | | |
| Elway | 32 | 13 | 40.6 | 257 | 2 | 8.0 | 19.8 |

## SCORING

| | | | | | |
|---|---|---|---|---|---|
| WASHINGTON | 0 | 6 | 0 | 0 - | 6 |
| N.Y. GIANTS | 10 | 7 | 0 | 0 - | 17 |

**First Quarter**
N.Y.G.   Allegre, 47 yard field goal
N.Y.G.   Manuel, 11 yard pass from Simms
    PAT—Allegre (kick)

**Second Quarter**
N.Y.G.   Morris, 1 yard run
    PAT—Allegre (kick)

### TEAM STATISTICS

| WAS. | | N.Y.G. |
|---|---|---|
| 12 | First Downs-Total | 12 |
| 2 | First Downs-Rushing | 8 |
| 7 | First Downs-Passing | 3 |
| 3 | First Downs-Penalty | 1 |
| 3 | Fumbles-Number | 4 |
| 1 | Fumbles-Ball Lost | 3 |
| 3 | Penalties-Number | 6 |
| 15 | Yards Penalized | 48 |
| 0 | Missed Field Goals | 0 |
| 70 | Offensive Plays | 61 |
| 190 | Net Yards | 199 |
| 2.7 | Average Gain | 3.3 |
| 2 | Giveaways | 3 |
| 3 | Takeaways | 2 |
| +1 | Difference | -1 |

## NFC CHAMPIONSHIP GAME
### January 11, 1987 at East Rutherford, N.J.
### (Attendance 76,633)

With the wind gusting to 33 miles per hour, New York coach Bill Parcells took the wind when his team won the coin toss. It was a sound decision; the Redskins' passing game was stymied during the first period by a rugged combination of New Jersey breeze and Giant blue. Redskin QB Jay Schroeder could get only two first downs while the Giants put 10 points on the scoreboard: Raul Allegre's 47-yard field goal, to open the scoring, and a' Phil Simms-to-Lionel Manuel TD pass.

Trailing 10-0 early in the second quarter, but with the wind now at their backs, the Redskins had a chance to get back into the game. Schroeder completed a 48-yard pass to Art Monk to take his team out of a deep hole. A few moments later, the Redskins lined up for a 51-yard field-goal try by Jess Atkinson, but the snap was bad and the scoring opportunity over. Then, the Giants crushed the Skins by marching to a touchdown against the wind.

There was no scoring in the second half, as the "Big Blue Wrecking Crew" Giant defense continued to dominate and the offense ate up the clock with a conservative running game. Schroeder completed only 20-of-50 passes for an average gain of a mere 3.8 per attempt. LB Carl Banks took over as the defense's big-play man when Lawrence Taylor was forced out of action with an injury.

## INDIVIDUAL STATISTICS

| WASHINGTON | | | | N.Y. GIANTS | | |
|---|---|---|---|---|---|---|
| | No. | Yds. | Avg. | | No. | Yds. | Avg. |

**RUSHING**

| WASHINGTON | No. | Yds. | Avg. | N.Y. GIANTS | No. | Yds. | Avg. |
|---|---|---|---|---|---|---|---|
| Rogers | 9 | 15 | 1.7 | Morris | 29 | 87 | 3.0 |
| Bryant | 6 | 25 | 4.2 | Carthon | 7 | 28 | 4.0 |
| Schroeder | 1 | 0 | 0.0 | Rouson | 1 | 2 | 2.0 |
| | 16 | 40 | 2.5 | Anderson | 1 | 3 | 3.0 |
| | | | | Simms | 7 | -2 | -0.3 |
| | | | | Galbreath | 1 | -1 | -1.0 |
| | | | | | 46 | 117 | 2.5 |

**RECEIVING**

| | No. | Yds. | Avg. | | No. | Yds. | Avg. |
|---|---|---|---|---|---|---|---|
| Monk | 8 | 126 | 15.8 | Bavaro | 2 | 36 | 18.0 |
| Didier | 1 | 7 | 7.0 | Manuel | 2 | 36 | 18.0 |
| Warren | 3 | 9 | 3.0 | Carthon | 3 | 18 | 6.0 |
| Bryant | 7 | 45 | 6.4 | | 7 | 72 | 10.3 |
| Griffin | 1 | 8 | 8.0 | | | | |
| | 20 | 195 | 9.8 | | | | |

**PUNTING**

| | | | | | | |
|---|---|---|---|---|---|---|
| Cox | 9 | 35.6 | | Landeta | 6 | 42.3 |

**PUNT RETURNS**

| | | | | | | |
|---|---|---|---|---|---|---|
| Yarber | 3 | 19 | 6.3 | McConkey | 5 | 27 | 5.4 |

**KICKOFF RETURNS**

| | No. | Yds. | Avg. | | | |
|---|---|---|---|---|---|---|
| Orr | 1 | 10 | 10.0 | none | | |
| Branch | 1 | 5 | 5.0 | | | |
| | 2 | 15 | 7.5 | | | |

**INTERCEPTION RETURNS**

| | | | | | | |
|---|---|---|---|---|---|---|
| none | | | | Reasons | 1 | 15 | 15.0 |

**PASSING**

| WASHINGTON | Att. | Comp. | Comp. Pct. | Yds. | Int. | Yds./ Att. | Yds./ Comp. |
|---|---|---|---|---|---|---|---|
| Schroeder | 50 | 20 | 40.0 | 195 | 1 | 3.9 | 9.8 |
| **N.Y. GIANTS** | | | | | | | |
| Simms | 14 | 7 | 50.0 | 90 | 0 | 6.4 | 12.8 |

## SCORING

| | | | | | | |
|---|---|---|---|---|---|---|
| DENVER | 0 | 10 | 3 | 7 | 3 - | 23 |
| CLEVELAND | 7 | 3 | 0 | 10 | 0 - | 20 |

**First Quarter**
Cle.   Fontenot, 3 yard pass from Kosar
    PAT—Moseley (kick)

**Second Quarter**
Den.   Karlis, 19 yard field goal
Den.   Willhite, 1 yard run
    PAT—Moseley (kick)
Cle.   Moseley, 29 yard field goal

**Third Quarter**
Den.   Karlis, 26 yard field goal

**Fourth Quarter**
Cle.   Moseley, 24 yard field goal
Cle.   Brennan, 48 yard pass from Kosar
    PAT — Moselet (kick)
Den.   M. Jackson, 5 yard pass from Elway
    PAT — Karlis (kick)

**Overtime**
Den.   Karlis, 33 yard field goal

### TEAM STATISTICS

| DEN. | | CLE. |
|---|---|---|
| 22 | First Downs- Total | 17 |
| 6 | First Downs- Rushing | 4 |
| 13 | First Downs- Passing | 12 |
| 3 | First Downs- Penalty | 1 |
| 2 | Fumbles- Number | 3 |
| 0 | Fumbles- Lost Ball | 1 |
| 6 | Penalties- Number | 9 |
| 39 | Yards Penalized | 76 |
| 0 | Missed Field Goals | 0 |
| 77 | Offensive Plays | 66 |
| 374 | Net Yards | 356 |
| 4.9 | Average Gain | 5.4 |
| 1 | Giveaways | 3 |
| 3 | Takeaways | 1 |
| +2 | Difference | -2 |

## AFC CHAMPIONSHIP GAME
### January 11, 1987 at Cleveland
### (Attendance 79,915)

Before nearly 80,000 partisan Clevelanders, the Broncos made a remarkable comeback to win the AFC title in a see-saw overtime battle. Cleveland got off to a 7-0 lead in the first quarter with an 86-yard drive that culminated in Bernie Kosar's three-yard TD pass to Herman Fontenot. Then, turnovers stopped Cleveland through most of the remainder of the half. The Broncos were able to capitalize for a 19-yard field goal by barefoot Rich Karlis and a one-yard scoring smash by Gerald Willhite. Cleveland's Mark Moseley tied the score at 10-10 just before halftime.

Karlis' 26-yard field goal was the only score of the third quarter. Early in the fourth quarter, Moseley tied it again. With less than six minutes left, Kosar hit Brian Brennan on a 48-yard TD pass to give Cleveland a 20-13 lead. When Denver's Gene Lang mishandled the ensuing kickoff before recovering at the Denver two, the Broncos were 98 yards from a tie. Denver had been unable to sustain a long drive during the half, but John Elway patiently began moving the Broncos downfield. With 1:47 remaining, he faced a 3rd-and-18 situation at the Cleveland 48. A 20-yard toss to Mark Jackson gave the Broncos new life and, five plays later, a five-yard flip to Jackson brought the touchdown.

Cleveland received the overtime kickoff but couldn't move. Then Elway and the Broncos roared downfield. With 5:48 gone, Karlis lined up for a field goal at the Browns' 23-yard line. His kick curved dangerously toward the left upright but was good, making Denver the AFC champions.

## INDIVIDUAL STATISTICS

**RUSHING**

| DENVER | No. | Yds. | Avg. | CLEVELAND | No. | Yds. | Avg. |
|---|---|---|---|---|---|---|---|
| Winder | 26 | 83 | 3.2 | Mack | 26 | 94 | 3.6 |
| Elway | 4 | 56 | 14.0 | Kosar | 4 | 3 | 3.0 |
| Lang | 3 | 9 | 3.0 | Fontenot | 3 | 3 | 1.0 |
| Willhite | 3 | 0 | 0.0 | | 33 | 100 | 3.3 |
| Sewell | 1 | 1 | 1.0 | | | | |
| | 37 | 149 | 4.9 | | | | |

**RECEIVING**

| | No. | Yds. | Avg. | | No. | Yds. | Avg. |
|---|---|---|---|---|---|---|---|
| Johnson | 3 | 25 | 6.3 | Fontenot | 7 | 66 | 9.5 |
| Watson | 3 | 55 | 18.3 | Brennan | 4 | 72 | 18.0 |
| Sewell | 3 | 47 | 15.6 | Langhorne | 2 | 35 | 17.5 |
| Mobley | 3 | 36 | 12.0 | Mack | 2 | 20 | 10.0 |
| Kay | 2 | 23 | 11.5 | Weathers | 1 | 42 | 42.0 |
| Willhite | 2 | 20 | 10.0 | Slaughter | 1 | 20 | 20.0 |
| Winder | 2 | 2 | 1.0 | Byner | 1 | 4 | 4.0 |
| Jackson | 2 | 25 | 12.5 | | 18 | 256 | 14.2 |
| Sampson | 1 | 10 | 10.0 | | | | |
| Lang | 1 | 1 | 1.0 | | | | |
| | 22 | 225 | 10.2 | | | | |

**PUNTING**

| | No. | Yds. | Avg. | | No. | Yds. | Avg. |
|---|---|---|---|---|---|---|---|
| Horan | 6 | 40.7 | | Gossett | 6 | 43.2 | |
| Elway | 1 | 19.0 | | | | | |
| | 7 | 37.6 | | | | | |

**PUNT RETURNS**

| | | | | | | | |
|---|---|---|---|---|---|---|---|
| Willhite | 3 | 10 | 3.3 | McNeil | 3 | 37 | 12.3 |

**KICKOFF RETURNS**

| | No. | Yds. | Avg. | | No. | Yds. | Avg. |
|---|---|---|---|---|---|---|---|
| Lang | 2 | 14 | 7.0 | McNeil | 4 | 80 | 20.0 |
| Bell | 2 | 10 | 5.0 | Fontenot | 2 | 25 | 12.5 |
| Freeman | 1 | 9 | 9.0 | | | | |
| | 5 | 33 | 6.6 | | | | |

**INTERCEPTION RETURNS**

| | | | | | | | |
|---|---|---|---|---|---|---|---|
| Hunley | 1 | 14 | 14.0.0 | Harper | 1 | 0 | 0.0 |
| Ryan | 1 | 26 | 26.0 | | | | |
| | 2 | 40 | 20.0 | | | | |

**PASSING**

| DENVER | Att. | Comp. | Comp. Pct. | Yds. | Int. | Yds./ Att. | Yds./ Comp. |
|---|---|---|---|---|---|---|---|
| Elway | 38 | 22 | 57.8 | 244 | 1 | 6.4 | 11.1 |
| **CLEVELAND** | | | | | | | |
| Kosar | 32 | 18 | 56.2 | 259 | 2 | 8.1 | 14.4 |

# Two for the Price of One

Under sunny skies and with a 76-degree temperature, the Denver Broncos and New York Giants played two different Super Bowls. One game, encompassing the first half, was probably the most evenly played matchup of the 21 played. The second game, the second half, was in the tradition of the one-sided blowouts that Super Bowls too often exhibit. Indeed, it may have been the most one-sided yet, other than the Bears' win a year before. Had both teams, and all of the 101,643 in attendance at the Rose Bowl, gone home at intermission, the game would have gone down as the best. Instead, the Giants' complete dominance of the second half left only the impression of a terrible mismatch.

On the game's opening drive, Denver went 45 yards in eight plays to set up a Rich Karlis field goal, the key being a 24-yard John Elway-to-Mark Jackson pass. Karlis' barefoot boot from 48 yards matched the longest in Super Bowl history. The Giants came right back to take the lead on a 78-yard drive. Phil Simms, who was 6-for-6 on the drive, hit three crucial passes to account for most of the yardage, and his short toss to Mark Bavaro brought the score to 7-3. Back came Denver. Ken Bell returned the kickoff 28 yards to the Bronco 42. Elway passed to Orson Mobley and Sammy Winder for a total of 25 yards. Then, on a nine-yard screen pass to Winder, Giant linebacker Harry Carson was called for a late hit and, when teammate Lawrence Taylor complained too vociferously, a second penalty was tacked on to put the ball at the six. Three plays later, Elway ran up the middle on a quarterback draw to score.

The Broncos launched another drive as soon as they got the ball back. Elway's 54-yard strike to Vance Johnson was the big play as they stormed to a first-and-goal at the one. At last, the vaunted New York defense awoke. On first down, Elway was caught for a two-yard loss on a rollout. Then, Gerald Willhite gained nothing up the middle. On third down, Winder lost three around left end. On the 23-yard field-goal try, Karlis set a Super Bowl record — for the shortest miss. Most observers tagged the four-play goalline stand as the game's turning point. After a couple of first downs by the Giants, Sean Landeta punted to the Denver 15. On third-and-12, Giant defensive end Leonard Marshall sacked Elway for a safety. There was no more scoring in the first half, although Karlis missed again on a 34-yard attempt with 18 seconds left.

The Giants took the second-half kickoff and drove to their own 47 where they faced a fourth-and-1. Instead of punting, New York coach Bill Parcells sent in backup quarterback Jeff Rutledge, who ran a sneak for two yards and the first down. New York completed the 63-yard drive with a 13-yard touchdown pass from Simms to Bavaro. Before the quarter ended, the Giants had built their lead to 26-10 on a 21-yard field goal by Raul Allegre and a one-yard touchdown plunge by Joe Morris. A feature of the TD drive was a 44-yard Simms pass to Phil McConkey off a flea-flicker.

The fourth quarter saw two more New York touchdowns, the first for six yards on McConkey's catch of a deflected pass, and the other on a two-yard run by Ottis Anderson. Denver, fighting to the end, saw Karlis connect on a 28-yard field goal, and, with just over two minutes remaining, Elway hit Vance Johnson for a 47-yard TD.

Although Elway passed for 304 yards, the Broncos' running game was shut down, with Elway also the leading rusher with 27 yards. Simms was the MVP, completing 22-of-25 passes for a record 88 percent. Also standing out among the many Giant luminaries was linebacker Carl Banks, who had 10 solo tackles.

## LINEUPS

| DENVER | | N.Y. GIANTS |
|---|---|---|
| | **OFFENSE** | |
| Johnson | WR | Johnson |
| Studdard | LT | Benson |
| Bishop | LG | Ard |
| Bryan | C | Oates |
| Howard | RG | Godfrey |
| Lanier | RT | Nelson |
| Mobley | TE | Bavaro |
| Watson | WR | Robinson |
| Elway | QB | Simms |
| Winder | RB | Morris |
| Willhite | RB | Carthon |
| | **DEFENSE** | |
| Jones | LE | Martin |
| Kragen | NT | Howard |
| Townsend | RE | Marshall |
| Ryan | LOLB | Banks |
| Mecklenburg | LILB | Reasons |
| Hunley | RILB | Carson |
| Jackson | ROLB | Taylor |
| Wright | LCB | Collins |
| Harden | RCB | Williams |
| Foley | FS | Welch |
| Smith | SS | Hill |

**SUBSTITUTES**

| DENVER | | |
|---|---|---|
| | **OFFENSE** | |
| Bell | Hackett | Micho |
| Bishop | Jackson | Remsberg |
| Cooper | Kubiak | Sampson |
| Freeman | Lang | Sewell |
| | **DEFENSE** | |
| Colorito | Gilbert | Robinson |
| Comeaux | Haynes | Wilson |
| Dennison | Lilly | Woodard |
| Fletcher | | |
| | **KICKERS** | |
| Horan | Karlis | |

| NEW ENGLAND | | |
|---|---|---|
| | **OFFENSE** | |
| Anderson | Manuel | Roberts |
| Galbreath | McConkey | Rouson |
| Johnson | Miller | Rutledge |
| Johnston | Mowatt | |
| | **DEFENSE** | |
| Burt | Headen | Lasker |
| Collins | Hunt | Patterson |
| Dorsey | Johnson | Sally |
| Flynn | Jones | |
| | **KICKERS** | |
| Allegre | Landeta | |

## SCORING

| | | | | | |
|---|---|---|---|---|---|
| DENVER | 10 | 0 | 0 | 10- | 20 |
| N.Y. GIANTS | 7 | 2 | 17 | 13- | 39 |

**First Quarter**
Denver — Karlis, 48-yard field goal
N.Y.G. — Mowatt, 6 yard pass from Simms
PAT—Allegre (kick)
Denver — Elway, 4 yard run
PAT—Karlis (kick)

**Second Quarter**
N.Y.G. — Safety, Martin tackled Elway in endzone

**Third Quarter**
N.Y.G. — Bavaro, 13 yard pass from Simms
PAT—Allegre (kick)
N.Y.G. — Allegre, 21 yard field goal
N.Y.G. — Morris, 1 yard run
PAT—Allegre (kick)

**Fourth Quarter**
N.Y.G. — McConkey, 6 yard pass from Simms
PAT—Allegre (kick)
Denver — Karlis, 28 yard field goal
N.Y.G. — Anderson, 2 yard run
PAT—kick failed
Denver — V. Johnson, 47 yard pass from Elway
PAT—Karlis (kick)

## TEAM STATISTICS

| DEN | | NYG |
|---|---|---|
| 23 | First Downs-Total | 24 |
| 5 | First Downs-Rushing | 10 |
| 16 | First Downs-Passing | 13 |
| 2 | First Downs-Penalty | 1 |
| 2 | Fumbles-Number | 0 |
| 0 | Fumbles-Lost Ball | 0 |
| 4 | Penalties Number | 6 |
| 28 | Yards Penalized | 48 |
| 2 | Missed Field Goals | 0 |
| 64 | Offensive Plays | 64 |
| 372 | Net Yards | 399 |
| 5.8 | Average Gain | 6.2 |
| 1 | Giveaways | 0 |
| 0 | Takeaways | 1 |
| -1 | Difference | +1 |

## INDIVIDUAL STATISTICS

### RUSHING

| DENVER | No. | Yds. | Avg. | | N.Y. GIANTS | No. | Yds. | Avg. |
|---|---|---|---|---|---|---|---|---|
| Elway | 6 | 27 | 4.5 | | Morris | 20 | 67 | 3.3 |
| Willhite | 4 | 19 | 4.8 | | Simms | 3 | 25 | 8.3 |
| Sewell | 3 | 4 | 1.3 | | Rouson | 3 | 22 | 7.3 |
| Lang | 2 | 2 | 1.0 | | Galbreath | 4 | 17 | 4.3 |
| Winder | 4 | 0 | 0.0 | | Carthon | 3 | 4 | 1.3 |
| | 19 | 52 | 2.7 | | Anderson | 2 | 1 | 0.5 |
| | | | | | Rutledge | 3 | 0 | 0.0 |
| | | | | | | 38 | 136 | 3.6 |

### RECEIVING

| DENVER | No. | Yds. | Avg. | | N.Y. GIANTS | No. | Yds. | Avg. |
|---|---|---|---|---|---|---|---|---|
| V. Johnson | 5 | 121 | 24.2 | | Bavaro | 4 | 51 | 12.8 |
| Willhite | 5 | 39 | 7.8 | | Morris | 4 | 20 | 5.0 |
| Winder | 4 | 34 | 8.5 | | Carthon | 4 | 13 | 3.3 |
| M. Jackson | 3 | 51 | 17.0 | | Robinson | 3 | 62 | 20.7 |
| Watson | 2 | 54 | 27.0 | | Manuel | 3 | 43 | 14.3 |
| Sampson | 2 | 20 | 10.0 | | McConkey | 2 | 50 | 25.0 |
| Mobley | 2 | 17 | 8.5 | | Rouson | 1 | 23 | 23.0 |
| Sewell | 2 | 12 | 6.0 | | Mowatt | 1 | 6 | 6.0 |
| Lang | 1 | 4 | 4.0 | | | 22 | 268 | 12.2 |
| | 26 | 252 | 9.7 | | | | | |

### PUNTING

| | No. | Yds. | Avg. | | | No. | Yds. | Avg. |
|---|---|---|---|---|---|---|---|---|
| Horan | 2 | | 41.0 | | Landeta | 3 | | 46.0 |

### PUNT RETURNS

| | No. | Yds. | Avg. | | | No. | Yds. | Avg. |
|---|---|---|---|---|---|---|---|---|
| Willhite | 1 | 9 | 9.0 | | McConkey | 1 | 25 | 25.0 |

### KICKOFF RETURNS

| | No. | Yds. | Avg. | | | No. | Yds. | Avg. |
|---|---|---|---|---|---|---|---|---|
| Bell | 3 | 48 | 16.0 | | Rouson | 3 | 56 | 18.7 |
| Lang | 2 | 36 | 18.0 | | Flynn | 1 | -3 | -3.0 |
| | 5 | 84 | 16.8 | | | 4 | 53 | 13.3 |

### INTERCEPTION RETURNS

| | No. | Yds. | Avg. | | | No. | Yds. | Avg. |
|---|---|---|---|---|---|---|---|---|
| none | | | | | Patterson | 1 | -7 | -7.0 |

### PASSING

| DENVER | Att. | Comp. | Comp. Pct. | Yds. | Int. | Yds./ Att. | Yds./ Comp. | Yards Lost Tackled |
|---|---|---|---|---|---|---|---|---|
| Elway | 37 | 22 | 59.5 | 304 | 1 | 8.2 | 13.8 | 4-26 |
| Kubiak | 4 | 4 | 100.0 | 48 | 0 | 12.0 | 12.0 | 0-0 |
| | 41 | 26 | 63.4 | 352 | 1 | 8.6 | 13.5 | 4-26 |
| **N.Y. GIANTS** | | | | | | | | |
| Simms | 25 | 22 | 88 | 268 | 0 | 10.7 | 12.2 | 1-5 |

All 1987 pro football stories finished far behind the strike as news, but the N.F.C. had its share of second-page features.

On the upbeat side was the Joe Montana-to-Jerry Rice touchdown connection that kept San Francisco aglow — and winning — all season. Then there was the story in New Orleans that it was actually possible for the Saints to win more games than they lost, a revelation that took two decades to arrive.

There was Walter Payton's final season — on the whole, a graceful exit. And there was the slow and often painful progress toward stardom made by several young quarterbacks, including Tampa Bay's Vinny Testaverde, the 1986 Heisman Trophy winner and No. 1 choice in the draft.

On the downside was the utter collapse of the New York Giants, the continuing erosion of the Dallas Cowboys, strained relations among the Chicago Bears and the total ineptness of the Atlanta Falcons.

## EASTERN DIVISION

**Washington Redskins** — The Skins went through most of the season a la Rodney Dangerfield, getting little respect. They won, but seldom convincingly. Quarterback Jay Schroeder, the prodigy of '85, was erratic and twice was replaced by Doug Williams, who won in relief. Running back George Rogers nursed a toe injury in training camp and, in the regular season, ran as if he feared for the other nine toes. Age was creeping into both lines, but the Hogs were still fearsome blockers. Defensive end Charles Mann emerged as a star, and defensive end Dexter Manley, though inconsistent, was devastating much of the time. Barry Wilburn was a pleasant surprise at cornerback, but the secondary gave up more air yards than the offense gained. Fortunately, the issue was never in doubt in a division that held the Redskins and four losing teams. When the Redskins beat the Giants in Game 11, after trailing at the half, it was all over in the NFC East.

**Dallas Cowboys** — Herschel Walker was terrific, leading the league with 1,606 combined yards (891 rushing, 715 receiving) and making Tony Dorsett an unhappy benchwarmer. But he couldn't do it alone, and the Cowboys finished with another losing record. Quarterback Danny White still hadn't recovered from his '86 broken wrist, but substitute Steve Pelluer seldom looked capable of taking over. After an embarrassing 21-10 loss to Atlanta in Week 12, owner Bum Bright — in a "what have you done for me lately" move — blasted head coach Tom Landry, saying he was "horrified" at Landry's play-calling.

**St. Louis Cardinals** — Owner Bill Bidwill spent much of the season shopping for a new city for his Cardinals while a lot of St. Louis fans stayed home and voted nolo contendre. Nevertheless, the Cardinals showed signs of life on the field, as quarterback Neil Lomax made an excellent comeback that landed him in the Pro Bowl. Top receiver J.T. Smith was unaccountably absent from the Pro Bowl despite leading the league in catches (91) and accounting for 1,117 yards. Only defensive end Freddie Joe Nunn, with nine sacks, did much on defense. In March of '88, Bidwill received the NFL's permission to move the team to Phoenix after 28 years in St. Louis without a championship.

**Philadelphia Eagles** — Head coach Buddy Ryan was openly disdainful of the replacement players who lost three straight games, but his attitude may have helped build team unity among the regulars. The Eagles won three straight after the strike and were 7-5 in union games. Perhaps more important than Ryan's attitude was quarterback Randall Cunningham's improvement from a shaky question mark to a plus, passing for 2,786 yards and 23 TDs. He was less skittish in the pocket but still became the first quarterback to lead his team in rushing since Bobby Douglass in 1972. Defensive end Reggie White had 21 sacks but, overall, the defense was subpar — surprising in view of Ryan's reputation as a defensive genius.

**New York Giants** — The Giants' collapse wasn't likely to sell many of the books that so many of them authored after their '86 Super Bowl season. When offensive tackle Karl Nelson went out for the season with Hodgkin's disease in August and offensive guard Chris Godfrey was sidelined with a sprained knee the next month, the Giants lost their running game. An 0-3 replacement team and some in-house backbiting didn't help either. Without a line in front of him, Joe Morris looked like just another undersized runner. Through a long season, tight end Mark Bavaro, linebacker Carl Banks, cornerback Mark Collins and quarterback Phil Simms continued to perform as all-stars.

## CENTRAL DIVISION

**Chicago Bears** — Walter Payton's final season might have been one of appropriate sweetness, and Payton himself finished up as a gentleman. But other Bears scarred the year with bitter controversy. Head coach Mike Ditka called his striking regulars "prima donnas" and "egomaniacs." The players responded with criticism of the coach. Cracks in the once-great defense were blamed on a lack of intensity, even by some Bears themselves. But, when Ditka benched regulars Todd Bell and William Perry (who had ballooned up to 362 pounds) before the playoffs, there were more flare-ups. For once, the big Bear news wasn't quarterback Jim McMahon or his injuries.

**Minnesota Vikings** — Although quarterback Tommy Kramer didn't play a full game all season because of a recurring pinched nerve in his shoulder, Wade Wilson did a good job as a backup, and wide receiver Anthony Carter emerged as one of the top threats in the league with a 24.3-yard average per catch. Chris Doleman, a bust at linebacker, became a Pro Bowler at defensive end. Together with defensive tackle Keith Millard, he helped revive memories of the Purple People Eaters. The Vikings stumbled into the playoffs despite losing all three replacement games and three of their last four regular-season contests.

**Green Bay Packers** — No. 1 draft pick Brent Fullwood was a disappointment. When he wasn't in the training room, he was forgetting plays, missing blocks, dropping passes or making gaffes like asking Forrest Gregg, "Coach, did you ever play in this league?" On the other hand, quarterback Don Majkowski, the 255th player taken in the '87 draft, started five games and gave evidence that he could develop. Veteran cornerback Dave Brown, obtained from Seattle for next-to-nothing, made a fine comeback to anchor a surprisingly strong defense.

**Tampa Bay Buccaneers** — The Bucs started November talking playoffs with a 4-3 record. On November 8, they led the Cardinals 28-3 in the fourth quarter, yet lost 31-28, as the Cards made the biggest final-quarter comeback in NFL history. Shocked, the Bucs lost their last seven games. "If I believed in a turning point," new coach Ray Perkins admitted, "I'd say that was probably it." Still, Perkins' troops showed improvement over the abject ineptitude of '86 that had earned them the first choice in the '87 draft. All-world, $8.2 million draft choice Vinny Testaverde started at quarterback in the last four games after veteran Steve DeBerg had done an excellent job paving the way.

**Detroit Lions** — It was another long season for Detroit, which has won only one division title (1983) in the past 30 years. Quarterback Chuck Long began to develop into the player

FINAL TEAM STATISTICS

**OFFENSE**

| | ATL. | CHI. | DALL. | DET. | G.B. | L.A. | MINN. | N.O. | NY G | PHIL. | STL. | S.F. | T.B. | WASH. |
|---|---|---|---|---|---|---|---|---|---|---|---|---|---|---|
| **FIRST DOWNS:** | | | | | | | | | | | | | | |
| Total | 230 | 319 | 293 | 270 | 248 | 276 | 293 | 304 | 266 | 289 | 325 | 357 | 263 | 301 |
| by Rushing | 73 | 121 | 93 | 81 | 97 | 118 | 129 | 128 | 80 | 112 | 115 | 134 | 62 | 119 |
| by Passing | 139 | 156 | 176 | 156 | 133 | 136 | 136 | 151 | 168 | 154 | 189 | 202 | 168 | 153 |
| by Penalty | 18 | 42 | 24 | 33 | 18 | 22 | 28 | 25 | 18 | 23 | 21 | 21 | 33 | 29 |
| **RUSHING:** | | | | | | | | | | | | | | |
| Number | 333 | 485 | 465 | 398 | 464 | 512 | 482 | 569 | 440 | 509 | 462 | 524 | 394 | 500 |
| Yards | 1298 | 1954 | 1865 | 1435 | 1801 | 2097 | 1983 | 2190 | 1457 | 2027 | 1873 | 2237 | 1365 | 2102 |
| Average Yards | 3.9 | 4.0 | 4.0 | 3.6 | 3.9 | 4.1 | 4.1 | 3.8 | 3.3 | 4.0 | 4.1 | 4.3 | 3.5 | 4.2 |
| Touchdowns | 5 | 13 | 17 | 9 | 13 | 15 | 20 | 20 | 4 | 12 | 15 | 11 | 7 | 18 |
| **PASSING:** | | | | | | | | | | | | | | |
| Attempts | 501 | 493 | 500 | 509 | 455 | 420 | 446 | 411 | 499 | 520 | 529 | 501 | 517 | 478 |
| Completions | 247 | 272 | 288 | 275 | 234 | 220 | 232 | 227 | 265 | 283 | 305 | 322 | 264 | 247 |
| Completion Pct. | 49.3 | 55.2 | 57.6 | 54.0 | 51.4 | 52.4 | 52.0 | 55.2 | 53.1 | 54.4 | 57.7 | 64.3 | 51.1 | 51.7 |
| Passing Yards | 3108 | 3420 | 3594 | 3150 | 2977 | 2750 | 3185 | 2987 | 3645 | 3561 | 3850 | 3955 | 3377 | 3718 |
| Avg. Yds per Att. | 6.2 | 6.9 | 7.2 | 6.2 | 6.5 | 6.5 | 7.1 | 7.3 | 7.3 | 6.8 | 7.3 | 7.9 | 6.5 | 7.8 |
| Avg. Yds per Comp. | 12.6 | 12.6 | 12.5 | 11.5 | 12.7 | 12.5 | 13.7 | 13.2 | 13.8 | 12.6 | 12.6 | 12.3 | 12.8 | 15.1 |
| Times Tackled | 46 | 48 | 52 | 26 | 45 | 25 | 52 | 29 | 61 | 72 | 54 | 29 | 43 | 27 |
| Yds Lost Tackled | 340 | 330 | 403 | 194 | 296 | 196 | 359 | 213 | 443 | 511 | 397 | 205 | 361 | 223 |
| Net Yards | 2768 | 3090 | 3191 | 2956 | 2681 | 2554 | 2826 | 2774 | 3202 | 3050 | 3453 | 3750 | 3016 | 3495 |
| Touchdowns | 17 | 23 | 19 | 16 | 15 | 16 | 21 | 23 | 26 | 26 | 25 | 44 | 22 | 27 |
| Interceptions | 32 | 24 | 20 | 26 | 17 | 18 | 23 | 12 | 22 | 16 | 15 | 14 | 17 | 18 |
| Pct. Intercepted | 6.4 | 4.9 | 4.0 | 5.1 | 3.7 | 4.3 | 5.2 | 2.9 | 4.4 | 3.1 | 2.8 | 2.8 | 3.3 | 3.8 |
| **PUNTS:** | | | | | | | | | | | | | | |
| Number | 83 | 62 | 84 | 70 | 93 | 77 | 79 | 63 | 91 | 102 | 70 | 68 | 88 | 78 |
| Average | 40.7 | 39.3 | 39.6 | 41.8 | 39.3 | 40.8 | 38.9 | 41.1 | 39.6 | 37.0 | 38.0 | 37.4 | 39.3 | 39.1 |
| **PUNT RETURNS** | | | | | | | | | | | | | | |
| Number | 31 | 50 | 41 | 35 | 35 | 40 | 36 | 41 | 55 | 34 | 44 | 34 | 31 | 56 |
| Yards | 221 | 484 | 353 | 303 | 245 | 245 | 420 | 468 | 448 | 202 | 550 | 365 | 257 | 615 |
| Average Yards | 7.1 | 9.7 | 8.6 | 8.7 | 7.0 | 6.1 | 11.7 | 11.4 | 8.1 | 5.9 | 12.5 | 10.7 | 8.3 | 11.0 |
| Touchdowns | 0 | 2 | 0 | 0 | 0 | 0 | 1 | 0 | 0 | 0 | 1 | 1 | 0 | 0 |
| **KICKOFF RET.:** | | | | | | | | | | | | | | |
| Number | 79 | 57 | 64 | 71 | 59 | 63 | 71 | 55 | 56 | 66 | 63 | 55 | 56 | 59 |
| Yards | 1700 | 1193 | 1295 | 1428 | 1032 | 1282 | 1421 | 1149 | 1128 | 1112 | 1317 | 1144 | 1037 | 1139 |
| Average Yards | 21.5 | 20.9 | 20.2 | 20.1 | 17.5 | 20.3 | 20.0 | 20.9 | 20.1 | 16.8 | 20.9 | 20.8 | 18.5 | 19.3 |
| Touchdowns | 1 | 1 | 0 | 0 | 0 | 1 | 0 | 0 | 0 | 0 | 0 | 1 | 0 | 0 |
| **INTERCEPT RET.:** | | | | | | | | | | | | | | |
| Number | 15 | 13 | 23 | 19 | 18 | 16 | 26 | 30 | 20 | 21 | 14 | 25 | 16 | 23 |
| Yards | 182 | 69 | 208 | 290 | 220 | 305 | 303 | 280 | 263 | 197 | 167 | 205 | 248 | 329 |
| Average Yards | 12.1 | 5.3 | 9.0 | 15.3 | 12.2 | 19.1 | 11.7 | 9.3 | 13.2 | 9.4 | 11.9 | 8.2 | 15.5 | 14.3 |
| Touchdowns | 0 | 2 | 2 | 1 | 0 | 2 | 0 | 0 | 1 | 0 | 1 | 0 | 2 | 1 |
| **PENALTIES:** | | | | | | | | | | | | | | |
| Number | 98 | 103 | 131 | 86 | 135 | 91 | 96 | 107 | 100 | 116 | 101 | 88 | 115 | 82 |
| Yards | 807 | 821 | 1091 | 737 | 1103 | 677 | 814 | 994 | 835 | 919 | 797 | 792 | 894 | 691 |
| **FUMBLES:** | | | | | | | | | | | | | | |
| Number | 27 | 33 | 30 | 29 | 35 | 26 | 28 | 33 | 38 | 44 | 23 | 25 | 35 | 26 |
| Number Lost | 17 | 20 | 20 | 11 | 18 | 15 | 10 | 16 | 20 | 19 | 12 | 12 | 14 | 19 |
| **POINTS:** | | | | | | | | | | | | | | |
| Total | 205 | 356 | 340 | 269 | 255 | 317 | 336 | 422 | 280 | 337 | 362 | 459 | 286 | 379 |
| PAT Attempts | 24 | 42 | 37 | 27 | 27 | 38 | 41 | 46 | 32 | 40 | 46 | 59 | 33 | 47 |
| PAT Made | 23 | 38 | 37 | 27 | 24 | 36 | 40 | 43 | 28 | 38 | 44 | 55 | 31 | 43 |
| FG Attempts | 17 | 32 | 29 | 39 | 29 | 21 | 29 | 42 | 32 | 31 | 27 | 23 | 24 | 29 |
| FG Made | 12 | 22 | 25 | 26 | 21 | 17 | 14 | 33 | 20 | 19 | 14 | 16 | 19 | 18 |
| Percent FG Made | 70.6 | 68.8 | 86.2 | 66.7 | 72.4 | 81.0 | 48.3 | 78.6 | 62.5 | 61.3 | 51.9 | 69.6 | 79.2 | 62.1 |
| Safeties | 1 | 0 | 0 | 1 | 0 | 1 | 1 | 2 | 0 | 1 | 0 | 1 | 0 | 0 |

**DEFENSE**

| | ATL. | CHI. | DALL. | DET. | G.B. | L.A. | MINN. | N.O. | NY G | PHIL. | STL. | S.F. | T.B. | WASH. |
|---|---|---|---|---|---|---|---|---|---|---|---|---|---|---|
| **FIRST DOWNS:** | | | | | | | | | | | | | | |
| Total | 354 | 261 | 294 | 314 | 296 | 279 | 281 | 270 | 275 | 301 | 306 | 250 | 314 | 296 |
| by Rushing | 162 | 77 | 85 | 122 | 118 | 95 | 95 | 81 | 97 | 85 | 116 | 95 | 124 | 104 |
| by Passing | 164 | 158 | 175 | 162 | 152 | 162 | 159 | 155 | 148 | 186 | 168 | 132 | 163 | 177 |
| by Penalty | 28 | 26 | 34 | 30 | 26 | 22 | 27 | 34 | 30 | 30 | 22 | 23 | 27 | 15 |
| **RUSHING:** | | | | | | | | | | | | | | |
| Number | 600 | 412 | 459 | 504 | 521 | 419 | 440 | 388 | 493 | 428 | 492 | 429 | 500 | 441 |
| Yards | 2734 | 1413 | 1617 | 2070 | 1920 | 1732 | 1724 | 1550 | 1768 | 1643 | 2001 | 1611 | 2038 | 1679 |
| Average Yards | 4.6 | 3.4 | 3.5 | 4.1 | 3.7 | 4.1 | 3.9 | 4.0 | 3.6 | 3.8 | 4.1 | 3.8 | 4.1 | 3.8 |
| Touchdowns | 24 | 5 | 19 | 18 | 15 | 8 | 9 | 6 | 14 | 16 | 16 | 8 | 18 | 10 |
| **PASSING:** | | | | | | | | | | | | | | |
| Attempts | 453 | 507 | 502 | 459 | 469 | 504 | 498 | 489 | 508 | 561 | 490 | 467 | 457 | 527 |
| Completions | 243 | 255 | 269 | 259 | 279 | 281 | 278 | 246 | 292 | 305 | 276 | 224 | 271 | 276 |
| Completion Pct. | 53.6 | 50.3 | 53.6 | 56.4 | 59.5 | 55.8 | 55.8 | 50.3 | 57.5 | 54.4 | 56.3 | 48.0 | 59.3 | 52.4 |
| Passing Yards | 3291 | 3286 | 3781 | 3558 | 3200 | 3693 | 3407 | 3155 | 3272 | 4058 | 3668 | 2771 | 3255 | 3767 |
| Avg. Yds per Att. | 7.3 | 6.5 | 7.5 | 7.8 | 6.8 | 7.3 | 6.8 | 6.5 | 6.4 | 7.2 | 7.5 | 5.9 | 7.1 | 7.1 |
| Avg. Yds per Comp. | 13.5 | 12.9 | 14.1 | 13.7 | 11.5 | 13.1 | 12.3 | 12.8 | 11.2 | 13.3 | 13.3 | 12.4 | 12.0 | 13.7 |
| Times Tackled | 17 | 70 | 51 | 42 | 34 | 38 | 41 | 47 | 55 | 57 | 41 | 37 | 39 | 53 |
| Yds Lost Tackled | 118 | 484 | 337 | 355 | 197 | 304 | 307 | 355 | 382 | 452 | 285 | 287 | 306 | 424 |
| Net Yards | 3173 | 2802 | 3444 | 3203 | 3003 | 3389 | 3100 | 2800 | 2890 | 3606 | 3383 | 2484 | 2949 | 3343 |
| Touchdowns | 26 | 24 | 21 | 23 | 14 | 31 | 24 | 25 | 17 | 29 | 30 | 13 | 23 | 19 |
| Interceptions | 15 | 13 | 23 | 19 | 18 | 16 | 26 | 30 | 20 | 21 | 14 | 25 | 16 | 23 |
| Pct. Intercepted | 3.3 | 2.6 | 4.6 | 4.1 | 3.8 | 3.2 | 5.2 | 6.1 | 3.9 | 3.7 | 2.9 | 5.4 | 3.5 | 4.4 |
| **PUNTS:** | | | | | | | | | | | | | | |
| Number | 60 | 86 | 75 | 65 | 77 | 83 | 74 | 73 | 96 | 88 | 74 | 72 | 64 | 91 |
| Average | 39.7 | 39.6 | 40.6 | 37.9 | 40.1 | 37.3 | 39.9 | 37.5 | 38.1 | 37.1 | 41.2 | 39.6 | 41.2 | 39.2 |
| **PUNT RETURNS** | | | | | | | | | | | | | | |
| Number | 48 | 26 | 45 | 34 | 54 | 43 | 44 | 29 | 51 | 54 | 36 | 29 | 50 | 37 |
| Yards | 541 | 339 | 376 | 177 | 422 | 317 | 424 | 199 | 811 | 469 | 489 | 195 | 621 | 231 |
| Average Yards | 11.3 | 13.0 | 8.4 | 5.2 | 7.8 | 7.4 | 9.6 | 6.9 | 15.9 | 8.7 | 13.6 | 6.7 | 12.4 | 6.2 |
| Touchdowns | 1 | 1 | 1 | 0 | 0 | 0 | 0 | 0 | 2 | 0 | 1 | 0 | 1 | 0 |
| **KICKOFF RET.:** | | | | | | | | | | | | | | |
| Number | 44 | 58 | 65 | 56 | 61 | 57 | 64 | 55 | 68 | 59 | 59 | 76 | 61 | 63 |
| Yards | 915 | 1054 | 1281 | 1089 | 1140 | 1112 | 1173 | 1115 | 1463 | 1276 | 1063 | 1598 | 1242 | 1352 |
| Average Yards | 20.8 | 18.2 | 19.7 | 19.4 | 18.7 | 19.5 | 18.3 | 20.3 | 21.5 | 21.6 | 18.0 | 21.0 | 20.4 | 21.5 |
| Touchdowns | 1 | 0 | 0 | 0 | 0 | 0 | 0 | 0 | 0 | 0 | 0 | 1 | 0 | 1 |
| **INTERCEPT RET.:** | | | | | | | | | | | | | | |
| Number | 32 | 24 | 20 | 26 | 17 | 18 | 23 | 12 | 22 | 16 | 15 | 14 | 17 | 18 |
| Yards | 342 | 334 | 279 | 335 | 115 | 226 | 399 | 173 | 164 | 68 | 227 | 258 | 227 | 193 |
| Average Yards | 10.7 | 13.9 | 14.0 | 12.9 | 6.8 | 12.6 | 17.3 | 14.4 | 7.5 | 4.3 | 15.1 | 18.4 | 13.4 | 10.7 |
| Touchdowns | 2 | 1 | 0 | 2 | 1 | 1 | 3 | 1 | 1 | 0 | 0 | 0 | 0 | 1 |
| **PENALTIES:** | | | | | | | | | | | | | | |
| Number | 92 | 120 | 100 | 115 | 104 | 100 | 107 | 84 | 97 | 105 | 88 | 80 | 125 | 97 |
| Yards | 729 | 1108 | 851 | 907 | 852 | 888 | 964 | 685 | 802 | 830 | 718 | 660 | 926 | 801 |
| **FUMBLES:** | | | | | | | | | | | | | | |
| Number | 18 | 37 | 29 | 36 | 42 | 28 | 30 | 31 | 31 | 41 | 34 | 30 | 42 | 22 |
| Number Lost | 12 | 11 | 20 | 13 | 24 | 11 | 11 | 18 | 14 | 27 | 19 | 13 | 20 | 11 |
| **POINTS:** | | | | | | | | | | | | | | |
| Total | 436 | 282 | 348 | 384 | 300 | 361 | 335 | 283 | 312 | 380 | 368 | 253 | 360 | 285 |
| PAT Attempts | 54 | 33 | 41 | 43 | 31 | 43 | 38 | 35 | 35 | 46 | 48 | 26 | 44 | 33 |
| PAT Made | 51 | 30 | 39 | 42 | 29 | 40 | 35 | 35 | 33 | 44 | 45 | 25 | 42 | 30 |
| FG Attempts | 30 | 31 | 29 | 34 | 36 | 24 | 31 | 18 | 34 | 29 | 18 | 35 | 30 | 28 |
| FG Made | 19 | 18 | 19 | 28 | 27 | 21 | 24 | 12 | 23 | 18 | 11 | 24 | 18 | 19 |
| Percent FG Made | 63.3 | 58.1 | 65.5 | 82.4 | 75.0 | 87.5 | 77.4 | 66.7 | 67.6 | 62.1 | 61.1 | 68.6 | 60.0 | 67.9 |
| Safeties | 2 | 0 | 0 | 0 | 2 | 0 | 0 | 1 | 0 | 0 | 1 | 0 | 0 | 0 |

the Lions expected, but first-round pick, defensive end Reggie Rogers was out for 30 days in midseason for emotional counseling, and his future was in doubt. Several key players were out for various amounts of time with more visible injuries. Punter Jim Arnold was chosen for the Pro Bowl after getting plenty of opportunities to practice his specialty. Still, with a roster of young talent, the Lions considered their future to be bright.

## WESTERN DIVISION

**San Francisco 49ers** — The 49ers had the best regular-season record in the league, thanks in no small part to wide receiver Jerry Rice, who set an NFL record with 22 TD catches and was voted Player of the Year. Quarterback Joe Montana, who won the league passing title, had one of his best seasons. He seemed fully recovered from his back injury of '86, but the team had a quarterback controversy gestating, as backup Steve Young was terrific in his few opportunities. Montana, Rice, Young, running back Roger Craig and the rest helped San Francisco lead the league in total offense, despite a wave of injuries that caused wholesale shuffling of the offensive line. Nose tackle Michael Carter was a standout and free safety Ronnie Lott called signals for the NFL's top-rated defense. The only apparent weakness was age in a few key spots.

**New Orleans Saints** — Owner Tom Benson cracked, "When you're 21, you become a man!" In the 21st year of their existence, the Saints had both their first winning record and their first playoff berth. Fans went Saint-happy and Benson danced on the sideline after each victory. They were all in ecstasy during a nine-game win streak that ended the regular season. Coach of the Year Jim Mora went with underrated quarterback Bobby Hebert, who finished with the best QB rating in Saints history. Running back Rueben Mayes slumped from his rookie highs, but Dalton Hilliard picked up the slack, and Morten Andersen (121 points) remained the NFL's best kicker. Despite some soft spots in the secondary, the team's strength was its defense. Linebackers Vaughan Johnson, Rickey Jackson, Sam Mills and Pat Swilling formed one of the NFL's best units.

**Los Angeles Rams** — Running back Charles White had a magnificent season, gaining 1,324 yards rushing — only four fewer than the total for his previous six years. He got his chance after the blockbuster trade which sent contract-unhappy Eric Dickerson to Indianapolis for a trunk full of draft choices. Quarterback Jim Everett made only marginal progress toward being the passer the Rams expected, and the team really never came together after a 1-7 start. Winning five in a row put them temporarily in the playoff picture, but they lost their last two, including a 48-0 crushing by the 49ers that ended the season on a downer. For head coach John Robinson, the team's 6-9 mark was his first losing season, either college or pro. All-Pro offensive guard Dennis Harrah learned he'd been named to the Pro Bowl for the sixth time on the same day he announced his retirement.

**Atlanta Falcons** — Marion Campbell made his reputation as a defensive coach, but his Falcons gave up an NFL-high 436 points. That was compounded by the fact that they scored the fewest points (205). And, for a clean sweep of the booby prizes, they had the league's lowest attendance, in part because they played all three strike games at home. Quarterback Scott Campbell showed why he'd been unable to win a starting job in Pittsburgh. Top draft pick Chris Miller, the heir apparent at quarterback, wasn't signed until October 30 and had some rough moments once he started to play, but at least he gave some hope for the future.

**WASHINGTON REDSKINS** 11-4 Joe Gibbs

| Scores of Each Game | | |
|---|---|---|
| 34 | PHILADELPHIA | 24 |
| 20 | Atlanta | 21 |
| 28 | ST.LOUIS | 21 |
| 38 | N.Y.Giants | 12 |
| 13 | Dallas | 7 |
| 17 | N.Y.JETS | 16 |
| 27 | Buffalo | 7 |
| 27 | Philadelphia | 31 |
| 20 | DETROIT | 13 |
| 26 | L.A.RAMS | 30 |
| 23 | N.Y.GIANTS | 19 |
| 34 | St.Louis | 17 |
| 24 | DALLAS | 20 |
| 21 | Miami | 23 |
| 27 | Minnesota | *24 |

| Use Name | Pos. | Hgt | Wgt | Age | Int | Pts |
|---|---|---|---|---|---|---|
| #Mark Carlson | OT | 6'6" | 284 | 24 | | |
| Joe Jacoby | OT | 6'7" | 305 | 28 | | |
| Mark May | OT | 6'6" | 295 | 27 | | |
| Dan McQuaid | OT | 6'7" | 278 | 26 | | |
| #Willard Scissum | OT-OG | 6'3" | 275 | 24 | | |
| Ed Simmons | OT-OG | 6'5" | 275 | 23 | | |
| Darrick Britz | OG | 6'3" | 264 | 23 | | |
| #Frank Frazier | OG | 6'5" | 290 | 27 | | |
| Rick Kehr | OG | 6'3" | 285 | 28 | | |
| Raleigh McKenzie | OG-C | 6'2" | 270 | 24 | | |
| #Phil Pettey | OG | 6'4" | 274 | 25 | | |
| R.C. Thielemann | OG | 6'4" | 262 | 32 | | |
| Jeff Bostic | C | 6'2" | 260 | 28 | | |
| #John Cowne | C | 6'2" | 245 | 25 | | |
| #Eric Coyle | C | 6'3" | 260 | 23 | | |
| Russ Grimm | C-OG | 6'3" | 275 | 28 | | |
| Ray Hitchcock | C | 6'2" | 289 | 22 | | |
| #Mike Wooten | C | 6'3" | 260 | 24 | | |
| #Alec Gibson | DE | 6'4" | 270 | 23 | | |
| Steve Hamilton | DE-DT | 6'4" | 270 | 25 | | |
| Markus Koch | DE | 6'5" | 275 | 24 | | |
| #Kit Lathrop | DE | 6'5" | 261 | 31 | | |
| Dexter Manley | DE | 6'3" | 257 | 28 | | |
| Charles Mann | DE | 6'6" | 270 | 26 | | |
| #Steve Martin | DE | 6'3" | 260 | 22 | | |
| #Curtis McGriff | DE | 6'5" | 275 | 29 | | |
| #Dan Benish | DT | 6'5" | 275 | 26 | | |
| Dave Butz | DT | 6'7" | 295 | 37 | | |
| Darryl Grant | DT | 6'1" | 275 | 27 | | |
| Dean Hamel | DT | 6'3" | 290 | 26 | | |
| #Ted Karras | DT | 6'2" | 265 | 22 | | |
| #Anthony Sagnella | DT | 6'5" | 260 | 23 | | |
| #Steve Thompson | DT | 6'2" | 275 | 22 | | |
| #Henry Waechter | DT | 6'5" | 275 | 28 | | |
| #Derek Bunch | LB | 6'3" | 215 | 25 | | |
| Ravin Caldwell | LB | 6'3" | 229 | 24 | | |
| Monte Coleman | LB | 6'2" | 230 | 29 | 2 | |
| Anthony Copeland | LB | 6'2" | 250 | 24 | | |
| #Bobby Curtis | LB | 6'3" | 235 | 22 | | |
| Kurt Gouveia | LB | 6'1" | 227 | 22 | | |
| Mel Kaufman | LB | 6'2" | 218 | 29 | | |
| #Jon Kimmel | LB | 6'4" | 240 | 27 | | |
| Rich Milot | LB | 6'4" | 237 | 30 | | |
| Neal Olkewicz | LB | 6' | 233 | 30 | | |
| #Carlton Rose | LB | 6'2" | 220 | 25 | | |
| #Tony Settles | LB | 6'3" | 210 | 23 | | |
| #Eric Wilson | LB | 6'1" | 245 | 25 | | |
| #David Windham | LB | 6'2" | 240 | 26 | | |
| Todd Bowles | DB | 6'2" | 203 | 23 | 4 | |
| #Danny Burmeister | DB | 6'2" | 201 | 23 | | |
| #Joe Cofer | DB | 6' | 200 | 24 | | |
| Brian Davis | DB | 6'2" | 190 | 24 | | |
| Vernon Dean | DB | 5'11" | 178 | 28 | | |
| #David Etherly | DB | 6'1" | 190 | 24 | | |
| Steve Gage | DB | 6'3" | 210 | 23 | 1 | |
| Darrell Green | DB | 5'8" | 185 | 27 | 3 | 6 |
| #Charles Jackson | DB | 6'4" | 210 | 24 | | |
| #Garry Kimble | DB | 5'11" | 184 | 24 | | |
| #Skip Lane | DB | 6'1" | 210 | 27 | | |
| #Michael Mitchell | DB | 5'10" | 180 | 25 | 1 | |
| Tim Morrison | DB | 6'1" | 195 | 24 | | |
| Gary Thompson | DB | 6' | 180 | 28 | | |
| Clarence Vaughn | DB | 6' | 202 | 23 | | |
| Alvin Walton | DB | 6' | 180 | 23 | 3 | |
| Barry Wilburn | DB | 6'3" | 186 | 23 | 9 | 6 |
| Dennis Woodberry | DB | 5'10" | 183 | 26 | | |
| Babe Laufenberg | QB | 6'2' | 195 | 27 | | |
| #Tony Robinson | QB | 6'3" | 200 | 23 | | |
| #Ed Rubbert | QB | 6'5" | 225 | 22 | | |
| Mark Rypien | QB | 6'4" | 234 | 24 | | |
| Jay Schroeder | QB | 6'4" | 214 | 26 | | 18 |
| #Jack Stanley | QB | 6'3" | 207 | 23 | | |
| Doug Williams | QB | 6'4" | 220 | 32 | | 6 |
| Kelvin Bryant | HB | 6'2" | 195 | 26 | | 36 |
| Keith Griffin | HB | 5'8" | 185 | 25 | | 6 |
| Tim Jessie | HB | 5'11" | 190 | 24 | | 6 |
| Timmy Smith | HB | 5'11" | 216 | 23 | | |
| #Lionel Vital | HB | 5'9" | 195 | 24 | | 12 |
| Reggie Branch | FB | 5'11" | 235 | 24 | | 6 |
| #Allen Harvin | FB | 5'9" | 200 | 28 | | |
| #Walter Holman | FB | 5'10" | 208 | 27 | | |
| George Rogers | FB | 6'2" | 229 | 28 | | 36 |
| #Wayne Wilson | FB | 6'3" | 220 | 29 | | 12 |
| Anthony Allen | WR | 5'11" | 182 | 27 | | 18 |
| #Keiron Bigby | WR | 5'10" | 177 | 21 | | |
| Gary Clark | WR | 5'9" | 173 | 25 | | 42 |
| #Richard Johnson | WR | 5'7" | 178 | 25 | | |
| Art Monk | WR | 6'3" | 209 | 29 | | 36 |
| #Joe Phillips | WR | 5'9" | 188 | 24 | | |
| Ricky Sanders | WR | 5'11" | 180 | 25 | | 18 |
| #Derrick Shepard | WR | 5'10" | 183 | 23 | | |
| Clarence Verdin | WR | 5'8" | 160 | 24 | | |
| #Ted Wilson | WR | 5'9 | 170 | 23 | | 12 |
| Eric Yarber | WR | 5'8" | 156 | 23 | | |
| Joe Caravello | TE | 6'3" | 270 | 24 | | |
| Glenn Dennison | TE | 6'3" | 225 | 25 | | |
| Clint Didier | TE | 6'5" | 240 | 28 | | 6 |
| #K.D.Dunn | TE | 6'3" | 235 | 24 | | |
| Anthony Jones | TE | 6'3" | 248 | 27 | | |
| Craig McEwen | TE | 6'1" | 220 | 21 | | |
| Terry Orr | TE | 6'3" | 227 | 25 | | |
| #Dave Truitt | TE | 6'4" | 232 | 23 | | |
| Don Warren | TE | 6'4" | 242 | 31 | | |
| #Marvin Williams | TE | 6'3" | 235 | 23 | | |
| #Obed Ariri | K | 5'8" | 165 | 31 | | 15 |
| Jess Atkinson | K | 5'9" | 168 | 25 | | 4 |
| Steve Cox | K | 6'4" | 195 | 29 | | 6 |
| Ali Haji-Sheikh | K | 6' | 172 | 26 | | 68 |
| #Brendan Tolbin | K | 6' | 205 | 23 | | 4 |
| #Jack Weil | K | 5'11" | 175 | 25 | | |

**ST. LOUIS CARDINALS** 7-8 Gene Stallings

| Scores of Each Game | | |
|---|---|---|
| 24 | DALLAS | 13 |
| 24 | San Diego | 28 |
| 21 | Washington | 28 |
| 24 | NEW ORLEANS | 19 |
| 28 | San Francisco | 34 |
| 7 | N.Y.Giants | 30 |
| 23 | PHILADELPHIA | 28 |
| 31 | TAMPA BAY | 28 |
| 24 | L.A.RAMS | 27 |
| 31 | Philadelphia | 19 |
| 34 | Atlanta | 21 |
| 17 | WASHINGTON | 34 |
| 27 | N.Y.GIANTS | 24 |
| 31 | Tampa Bay | 14 |
| 16 | Dallas | 21 |

| Use Name | Pos. | Hgt | Wgt | Age | Int | Pts |
|---|---|---|---|---|---|---|
| Ray Brown | OT-OG | 6'5" | 280 | 24 | | |
| Gene Chilton | OT | 6'3" | 271 | 23 | | |
| #Victor Perry | OT | 6'5" | 278 | 23 | | |
| Tootie Robbins | OT | 6'5" | 302 | 29 | | |
| Luis Sharpe | OT | 6'4" | 260 | 27 | | |
| #Tom Welter | OT-OG | 6'5" | 280 | 23 | | |
| #Joe Bock | OG | 6'4" | 254 | 28 | | |
| Joe Bostic | OG | 6'3" | 268 | 30 | | |
| Michael Morris | OG | 6'5" | 275 | 26 | | |
| #Ron Pasquale | OG | 6'2" | 266 | 23 | | |
| Todd Peat | OG | 6'2" | 294 | 23 | | |
| Mike Ruether | OG-C | 6'4" | 275 | 24 | | |
| Lance Smith | OG-OT | 6'2" | 262 | 23 | | |
| #Charles Vatterott | OG-OT | 6'4" | 263 | 23 | | |
| Derek Kennard | C-OG | 6'3" | 285 | 24 | | |
| #Keith Radecic | C | 6'1" | 260 | 23 | | |
| #Ron Bohm | DE-DT | 6'3" | 250 | 22 | | |
| #Victor Burnett | DE | 6'5" | 250 | 24 | | |
| David Galloway | DE | 6'3" | 279 | 28 | | |
| Curtis Greer | DE | 6'4" | 258 | 29 | | |
| Freddie Joe Nunn | DE | 6'4" | 255 | 25 | | |
| Rod Saddler | DE | 6'5" | 276 | 21 | 1 | |
| Steve Alvord | DT | 6'4" | 272 | 22 | | |
| #Anthony Burke | DT | 6'3" | 262 | 22 | | |
| Bob Clasby | DT | 6'5" | 260 | 26 | | |
| Mark Duda | DT | 6'3" | 279 | 26 | | |
| #Gary Dulin | DT-DE | 6'4" | 275 | 30 | | |
| Mark Garalczyk | DT | 6'5" | 272 | 22 | | |
| Collin Scotts | DT | 6'5" | 263 | 24 | | |
| Charlie Baker | LB | 6'2" | 234 | 29 | | |
| Anthony Bell | LB | 6'3" | 231 | 23 | 1 | |
| #Tony Buford | LB | 6'2" | 222 | 23 | | |
| #Jimmie Carter | LB | 6'1" | 220 | 26 | 1 | |
| Wayne Davis | LB | 6'1" | 213 | 23 | | |
| #Phil Forney | LB | 6'2" | 230 | 23 | | |
| Ilia Jarostchuk | LB | 6'3" | 231 | 23 | | |
| E.J. Junior | LB | 6'3" | 235 | 27 | 1 | |
| Terence Mack | LB | 6'3" | 240 | 23 | | |
| Niko Noga | LB | 6'1" | 235 | 25 | | 6 |
| #Peter Noga | LB | 6' | 212 | 23 | 1 | 6 |
| #Jeff Paine | LB | 6'2" | 224 | 26 | | |
| #Dwayne Anderson | DB | 6' | 205 | 25 | | |
| #Terrence Anthony | DB | 5'10" | 183 | 22 | | |
| Carl Carter | DB | 5'11" | 180 | 23 | | |
| Travis Curtis | DB | 5'10" | 180 | 21 | 5 | |
| Johnny Holloway | DB | 5'11" | 182 | 23 | | |
| Mark Jackson | DB | 5'9" | 180 | 25 | | 6 |
| Greggory Johnson | DB | 6'1" | 195 | 28 | | |
| Cedric Mack | DB | 6' | 194 | 26 | 2 | |
| #Mark Mathis | DB | 5'9" | 178 | 22 | 1 | |
| #Tony Mayes | DB | 6' | 200 | 23 | | |
| Tim McDonald | DB | 6'2" | 207 | 22 | | |
| John Preston | DB | 6' | 207 | 25 | | |
| #Ed Scott | DB | 5'10" | 182 | 26 | | |
| #Ken Sims | DB | 5'9" | 177 | 23 | | |
| Leonard Smith | DB | 5'11" | 202 | 26 | | 6 |
| Charles Wright | DB | 5'9" | 178 | 23 | | |
| Lonnie Young | DB | 6'1" | 182 | 24 | 1 | |
| #Sammy Garza | QB | 6'1" | 184 | 21 | | 6 |
| #Shawn Halloran | QB | 6'4" | 217 | 23 | | |
| Neil Lomax | QB | 6'3" | 215 | 28 | | |
| Cliff Stoudt | QB | 6'4" | 215 | 32 | | |
| #Gregg Tipton | QB | 6'3" | 191 | 23 | | |
| Derrick McAdoo | HB | 5'10" | 198 | 22 | | 24 |
| Stump Mitchell | HB | 5'9" | 188 | 28 | | 30 |
| Val Sikahema | HB | 5'9" | 191 | 25 | | 6 |
| Earl Ferrell | FB | 6' | 224 | 29 | | 42 |
| #Don Goodman | FB | 5'11" | 214 | 28 | | |
| Broderick Sargent | FB | 5'10" | 215 | 24 | | |
| Ron Wolfley | FB | 6' | 222 | 24 | | 6 |
| Ron Brown | WR | 5'10" | 186 | 24 | | |
| #Clarence Collins | WR | 6'1" | 180 | 25 | | |
| Roy Green | WR | 6' | 190 | 30 | | 24 |
| Don Holmes | WR | 5'10" | 180 | 26 | | |
| Troy Johnson | WR | 6'1" | 175 | 24 | | 12 |
| #Adrian McBride | WR | 6' | 195 | 24 | | |
| J.T.Smith | WR | 6'2" | 185 | 31 | | 48 |
| Rob Awalt | TE | 6'5" | 248 | 23 | | 36 |
| William Harris | TE | 6'4" | 243 | 22 | | |
| #Bob Keseday | TE | 6'4" | 225 | 25 | | |
| Jay Novacek | TE | 6'4" | 235 | 24 | | 18 |
| Greg Cater | K | 6' | 205 | 30 | | |
| Jim Gallery | K | 6'1" | 190 | 25 | | 57 |
| Greg Horne (from CIN) | K | 6' | 188 | 22 | | |
| #Mark Royals (to PHI) | K | 6'5" | 216 | 24 | | |
| #Jason Staurovsky | K | 5'9" | 167 | 24 | | 9 |

**PHILADELPHIA EAGLES** 7-8 Buddy Ryan

| Scores of Each Game | | |
|---|---|---|
| 24 | Washington | 34 |
| 27 | NEW ORLEANS | 17 |
| 3 | CHICAGO | 35 |
| 22 | Dallas | 41 |
| 10 | Green Bay | *16 |
| 37 | DALLAS | 20 |
| 28 | St. Louis | 23 |
| 31 | WASHINGTON | 27 |
| 17 | N.Y.GIANTS | 20 |
| 19 | ST.LOUIS | 31 |
| 34 | New England | *31 |
| 20 | N.Y.Giants | *23 |
| 10 | MIAMI | 28 |
| 38 | N.Y.Jets | 27 |
| 17 | BUFFALO | 7 |

* Overtime

| Use Name | Pos. | Hgt | Wgt | Age | Int | Pts |
|---|---|---|---|---|---|---|
| David Alexander | OT-OG | 6'3" | 279 | 23 | | |
| Joe Conwell | OT | 6'5" | 275 | 26 | | |
| Matt Darwin | OT | 6'4" | 260 | 24 | | |
| #Mike Perrino | OT | 6'5" | 285 | 23 | | |
| Ken Reeves | OT-OG | 6'5" | 275 | 25 | | |
| #Jeff Wenzel | OT | 6'7" | 270 | 23 | | |
| #Jim Angelo | OG | 6'3" | 275 | 24 | | |
| Ron Baker | OG | 6'4" | 274 | 32 | | |
| Bob Landsee | OG | 6'4" | 273 | 29 | | |
| #Scott Leggett | OG-OT | 6'3" | 285 | 24 | | |
| #Mike Nease | OG | 6'3" | 272 | 25 | | |
| Adam Schreiber | OG | 6'4" | 270 | 25 | | |
| Reggie Singletary | OG | 6'3" | 272 | 23 | | |
| #Pete Walters | OG | 6'2" | 265 | 28 | | |
| Gerry Feehery | C | 6'2" | 270 | 27 | | |
| #Matt Long | C | 6'3" | 270 | 26 | | |
| #Paul Ryczek | C | 6'3" | 235 | 25 | | |
| Ben Tamburello | C-OG | 6'3" | 278 | 22 | | |
| #Jim Auer | DE | 6'7" | 275 | 25 | | |
| #Marvin Ayres | DE | 6'5" | 265 | 23 | | |
| Jonathan Dumbauld | DE | 6'4" | 259 | 24 | | |
| #Elois Grooms | DE-DT | 6'4" | 250 | 34 | | |
| John Klingel | DE | 6'3" | 260 | 23 | | |
| #Greg Liter | DE | 6'6" | 275 | 23 | | |
| #Tim Mooney | DE | 6'2" | 265 | 25 | | |
| #Ray Phillips | DE-LB | 6'3" | 240 | 23 | | |
| Clyde Simmons | DE-DT | 6'6" | 258 | 23 | | |
| Reggie White | DE | 6'5" | 285 | 25 | | 6 |
| #Gary Bolden | DT | 6'1" | 275 | 25 | | |
| Jerome Brown | DT | 6'2" | 292 | 22 | 2 | |
| Ken Clarke | DT | 6'2" | 275 | 31 | | |
| #Ray Conlin | DT | 6'2" | 258 | 25 | | |
| Mike Golic (from HOU) | DT-DE | 6'5" | 275 | 24 | | |
| #Skip Hamilton | DT | 6'2" | 265 | 28 | | |
| #Randall Mitchell | DT | 6'1" | 275 | 23 | | |
| Mike Pitts | DT-DE | 6'5" | 277 | 26 | | |
| Ty Allert (from SD) | LB | 6'2" | 233 | 24 | | |
| #Matt Battaglia | LB | 6'2" | 225 | 21 | | |
| #Carlos Bradley | LB | 6' | 222 | 27 | | |
| #Dave Brown | LB | 6'2" | 215 | 23 | | |
| Garry Cobb | LB | 6'2" | 230 | 30 | | |
| #George Cumby | LB | 6' | 224 | 31 | | |
| Byron Evans | LB | 6'2" | 225 | 23 | 1 | |
| #Chuck Gorecki | LB | 6'4" | 237 | 23 | | |
| Dwayne Jiles | LB | 6'4" | 242 | 25 | | |
| Alonzo Johnson | LB | 6'3" | 222 | 24 | | |
| Seth Joyner | LB | 6'2" | 241 | 22 | 2 | 6 |
| #Kelly Kirchbaum | LB | 6'2" | 240 | 30 | | |
| #Byron Lee | LB | 6'2" | 230 | 22 | | |
| Mike Reichenbach | LB | 6'2" | 238 | 25 | | |
| Jody Schulz | LB | 6'3" | 235 | 27 | | |
| #Fred Smalls | LB | 6'3" | 225 | 24 | | |
| #Victor Bellamy | DB | 6'1" | 195 | 24 | | |
| Cedrick Brown | DB | 5'10" | 178 | 22 | 1 | |
| #Thomas Caterbone | DB | 5'8" | 175 | 23 | | |
| Evan Cooper | DB | 5'11" | 184 | 25 | 2 | |
| Elbert Foules | DB | 5'11" | 185 | 26 | 4 | |
| William Frizzell | DB | 6'3" | 198 | 24 | | |
| Russell Gary | DB | 5'11" | 200 | 28 | | |
| #Chris Gerhard | DB | 5'10" | 185 | 23 | | |
| #Jeff Griffin | DB | 6' | 185 | 29 | | |
| #Greg Harding | DB | 6'2" | 197 | 27 | | |
| Terry Hoage | DB | 6'3" | 199 | 25 | 2 | |
| #Angelo James | DB | 6' | 180 | 25 | | |
| #Christopher Johnson | DB | 6'4" | 225 | 26 | | |
| #Michael Kullman | DB | 6'1" | 185 | 25 | 2 | |
| #Mike Ulmer | DB | 6' | 201 | 32 | | |
| Andre Waters | DB | 5'11" | 185 | 25 | 3 | |
| #Troy West | DB | 6'1" | 205 | 26 | 1 | |
| Roynell Young | DB | 6'1" | 185 | 29 | 1 | |
| Matt Cavanaugh | QB | 6'2" | 212 | 30 | | |
| Randall Cunningham | QB | 6'4" | 192 | 24 | | 18 |
| #Marty Horn | QB | 6'2" | 206 | 24 | | |
| #Guido Merkens | QB | 6'1" | 195 | 32 | | |
| #Scott Tinsley | QB | 6'2" | 195 | 27 | | |
| #Topper Clemons | HB | 5'11" | 205 | 23 | | 6 |
| Bobby Morse | HB | 5'10" | 201 | 21 | | |
| Alan Reid | HB | 5'8" | 190 | 26 | | |
| Junior Tautalatasi | HB | 5'10" | 205 | 25 | | |
| #Willie Turrall | HB | 5'10" | 190 | 23 | | |
| #Reggie Brown | FB | 5'11" | 211 | 27 | | |
| Keith Byars | FB | 6'1" | 230 | 23 | | 24 |
| Charles Crawford | FB | 6'2" | 235 | 23 | | |
| Michael Haddix | FB | 6'2" | 227 | 25 | | |
| #Jacque Robinson | FB | 5'11" | 215 | 25 | | |
| #Alvin Ross | FB | 5'11" | 235 | 24 | | 6 |
| Anthony Toney | FB | 6' | 227 | 24 | | 36 |
| #Jesse Bendross | WR | 6' | 196 | 25 | | |
| #Kevin Bowman | WR | 6'3" | 205 | 25 | | 6 |
| Cris Carter | WR | 6'3" | 194 | 21 | | 12 |
| Gregg Garrity | WR | 5'10" | 169 | 25 | | 12 |
| #Otis Grant | WR | 6'3" | 197 | 26 | | |
| Kenny Jackson | WR | 6' | 180 | 25 | | 18 |
| Ron Johnson | WR | 6'3" | 186 | 28 | | |
| Mike Quick | WR | 6'2" | 190 | 27 | | 66 |
| #Mike Siano | WR | 6'4" | 215 | 23 | | 6 |
| #Eric Bailey | TE | 6'5" | 240 | 25 | | |
| #Ron Fazio | TE | 6'4" | 242 | 25 | | |
| Jimmie Giles (from DET) | TE | 6'3" | 240 | 32 | | 6 |
| Dave Little | TE | 6'2" | 236 | 26 | | |
| Mike McCloskey | TE | 6'5" | 246 | 26 | | |
| #Jay Repko | TE | 6'3" | 240 | 28 | | |
| John Spagnola | TE | 6'4" | 242 | 30 | | 12 |
| #Dave Jacobs | K | 5'7" | 151 | 30 | | 11 |
| Paul McFadden | K | 5'11" | 163 | 25 | | 64 |
| John Teltschik | K | 6'2" | 215 | 23 | | |

Wes Hopkins - Knee Injury
Nick Haden - Ankle Injury

\# - on the active roster for strike replacement games only

## WASHINGTON REDSKINS

### Rushing

| Last Name | No. | Yds | Avg | TD |
|---|---|---|---|---|
| Rogers | 163 | 613 | 3.8 | 6 |
| Bryant | 77 | 406 | 5.3 | 1 |
| Vital | 80 | 346 | 4.3 | 2 |
| Griffin | 62 | 242 | 3.9 | 0 |
| Smith | 29 | 126 | 4.3 | 0 |
| Schroeder | 26 | 120 | 4.6 | 3 |
| Monk | 6 | 63 | 10.5 | 0 |
| .W. Wilson | 18 | 55 | 3.1 | 2 |
| Jessie | 10 | 37 | 3.7 | 1 |
| Rubbert | 9 | 31 | 3.4 | 0 |
| T. Wilson | 2 | 28 | 14.0 | 1 |
| Verdin | 1 | 14 | 14.0 | 0 |
| Branch | 4 | 9 | 2.3 | 0 |
| D. Williams | 7 | 9 | 1.3 | 1 |
| Holman | 2 | 7 | 3.5 | 0 |
| Clark | 1 | 0 | 0.0 | 0 |
| Robinson | 2 | 0 | 0.0 | 0 |
| Sanders | 1 | -4 | -4.0 | 0 |

### Receiving

| Last Name | No. | Yds | Avg | TD |
|---|---|---|---|---|
| Clark | 56 | 1066 | 19.0 | 7 |
| Bryant | 43 | 490 | 11.4 | 5 |
| Monk | 38 | 483 | 12.7 | 6 |
| Sanders | 37 | 630 | 17.0 | 3 |
| Allen | 13 | 337 | 25.9 | 3 |
| Didier | 13 | 178 | 13.7 | 1 |
| McEwen | 12 | 164 | 13.7 | 0 |
| Warren | 7 | 43 | 6.1 | 0 |
| T. Wilson | 5 | 112 | 22.4 | 1 |
| Rogers | 4 | 23 | 5.8 | 0 |
| Orr | 3 | 35 | 11.7 | 0 |
| Griffin | 3 | 13 | 4.3 | 1 |
| Verdin | 2 | 62 | 31.0 | 0 |
| Caravello | 2 | 29 | 14.5 | 0 |
| W. Wilson | 2 | 16 | 8.0 | 0 |
| Dennison | 2 | 8 | 4.0 | 0 |
| Vital | 1 | 13 | 13.0 | 0 |
| Jessie | 1 | 8 | 8.0 | 0 |
| Johnson | 1 | 5 | 5.0 | 0 |
| Yarber | 1 | 5 | 5.0 | 0 |
| Smith | 1 | -2 | -2.0 | 0 |

### Punt Returns

| Last Name | No. | Yds | Avg | TD |
|---|---|---|---|---|
| Yarber | 37 | 273 | 7.4 | 0 |
| T. Wilson | 8 | 143 | 17.9 | 0 |
| Shepard | 6 | 146 | 24.3 | 0 |
| Green | 5 | 53 | 10.6 | 0 |

### Kickoff Returns

| Last Name | No. | Yds | Avg | TD |
|---|---|---|---|---|
| Griffin | 25 | 478 | 19.1 | 0 |
| Verdin | 12 | 244 | 20.3 | 0 |
| Branch | 4 | 61 | 15.3 | 0 |
| Jessie | 4 | 73 | 18.3 | 0 |
| Orr | 4 | 62 | 15.5 | 0 |
| Sanders | 4 | 118 | 29.5 | 0 |
| Vital | 2 | 31 | 15.5 | 0 |
| W. Wilson | 2 | 32 | 16.0 | 0 |
| Shepard | 1 | 20 | 20.0 | 0 |
| T. Wilson | 1 | 20 | 20.0 | 0 |

### Passing — Punting — Kicking

| PASSING | Att | Cmp | % | Yds | Yd/Att | TD | Int— | % | Rk |
|---|---|---|---|---|---|---|---|---|---|
| Schroeder | 267 | 129 | 48.3 | 1878 | 7.0 | 12 | 10— | 3.7 | 21 |
| D. Williams | 143 | 81 | 56.6 | 1156 | 8.1 | 11 | 5— | 3.5 | |
| Rubbert | 49 | 26 | 53.1 | 532 | 10.9 | 4 | 1— | 2.0 | |
| Robinson | 18 | 11 | 61.1 | 152 | 8.4 | 0 | 2— | 11.1 | |
| Bryant | 1 | 0 | 0.0 | 0 | 0.0 | 0 | 0— | 0.0 | |

| PUNTING | No | Avg |
|---|---|---|
| Cox | 64 | 40.2 |
| Weil | 14 | 34.4 |

| KICKING | XP | Att | % | FG | Att | % |
|---|---|---|---|---|---|---|
| Haji-Sheikh | 29 | 32 | 94 | 13 | 19 | 68 |
| Ariri | 6 | 6 | 100 | 3 | 5 | 60 |
| Cox | 3 | 3 | 100 | 1 | 1 | 100 |
| Atkinson | 1 | 1 | 100 | 1 | 1 | 100 |
| Toibin | 4 | 4 | 100 | 0 | 2 | 0 |

## ST. LOUIS CARDINALS

### Rushing

| Last Name | No. | Yds | Avg | TD |
|---|---|---|---|---|
| Mitchell | 203 | 781 | 3.8 | 3 |
| Ferrell | 113 | 512 | 4.5 | 7 |
| McAdoo | 53 | 230 | 4.3 | 3 |
| Lomax | 29 | 107 | 3.7 | 0 |
| Sargent | 18 | 90 | 5.0 | 0 |
| Wolfley | 26 | 87 | 3.3 | 1 |
| Green | 2 | 34 | 17.0 | 0 |
| Garza | 8 | 31 | 3.9 | 1 |
| Ro. Brown | 1 | 9 | 9.0 | 0 |
| T. Johnson | 1 | 9 | 9.0 | 0 |
| Cater | 2 | 3 | 1.5 | 0 |
| Stoudt | 1 | -2 | -2.0 | 0 |
| Awalt | 2 | -9 | -4.5 | 0 |
| Halloran | 3 | -9 | -3.0 | 0 |

### Receiving

| Last Name | No. | Yds | Avg | TD |
|---|---|---|---|---|
| J. Smith | 91 | 1117 | 12.3 | 8 |
| Mitchell | 45 | 397 | 8.8 | 2 |
| Green | 43 | 731 | 17.0 | 4 |
| Awalt | 42 | 526 | 12.5 | 6 |
| Ferrell | 23 | 262 | 11.4 | 0 |
| Novacek | 20 | 254 | 12.7 | 3 |
| T. Johnson | 15 | 308 | 20.5 | 2 |
| Holmes | 11 | 132 | 12.0 | 0 |
| Wolfley | 8 | 68 | 8.5 | 0 |
| Sargent | 2 | 19 | 9.5 | 0 |
| Ro. Brown | 2 | 16 | 8.0 | 0 |
| McAdoo | 2 | 12 | 6.0 | 0 |
| Harris | 1 | 8 | 8.0 | 0 |

### Punt Returns

| Last Name | No. | Yds | Avg | TD |
|---|---|---|---|---|
| Sikahema | 44 | 550 | 12.5 | 1 |

### Kickoff Returns

| Last Name | No. | Yds | Avg | TD |
|---|---|---|---|---|
| Sikahema | 34 | 761 | 22.4 | 0 |
| McAdoo | 23 | 444 | 19.3 | 0 |
| Sargent | 3 | 37 | 12.3 | 0 |
| Ro. Brown | 1 | 40 | 40.0 | 0 |
| Ferrell | 1 | 10 | 10.0 | 0 |
| Holmes | 1 | 25 | 25.0 | 0 |

### Passing — Punting — Kicking

| PASSING | Att | Cmp | % | Yds | Yd/Att | TD | Int— | % | Rk |
|---|---|---|---|---|---|---|---|---|---|
| Lomax | 463 | 275 | 59.4 | 3387 | 7.3 | 24 | 12— | 2.6 | 5 |
| Halloran | 42 | 18 | 42.9 | 263 | 6.3 | 0 | 1— | 2.4 | |
| Garza | 20 | 11 | 55.0 | 183 | 9.2 | 1 | 2— | 10.0 | |
| Mitchell | 3 | 1 | 33.3 | 17 | 5.7 | 0 | 0— | 0.0 | |
| Stoudt | 1 | 0 | 0.0 | 0 | 0.0 | 0 | 0— | 0.0 | |

| PUNTING | No | Avg |
|---|---|---|
| Horne | 43 | 40.2 |
| Cater | 40 | 36.8 |
| Royals | 11 | 39.2 |

| KICKING | XP | Att | % | FG | Att | % |
|---|---|---|---|---|---|---|
| Gallery | 30 | 31 | 97 | 9 | 19 | 47 |
| Staurovsky | 6 | 6 | 100 | 1 | 3 | 33 |

## PHILADELPHIA EAGLES

### Rushing

| Last Name | No. | Yds | Avg | TD |
|---|---|---|---|---|
| Cunningham | 76 | 505 | 6.6 | 3 |
| Toney | 127 | 473 | 3.7 | 5 |
| Byars | 116 | 426 | 3.7 | 3 |
| Haddix | 59 | 165 | 2.8 | 0 |
| R. Brown | 39 | 136 | 3.5 | 0 |
| Robinson | 24 | 114 | 4.8 | 0 |
| Tautalatasi | 26 | 69 | 2.7 | 0 |
| Ross | 14 | 54 | 3.9 | 1 |
| Teltschik | 3 | 32 | 10.7 | 0 |
| Jackson | 6 | 27 | 4.5 | 0 |
| Grant | 1 | 20 | 20.0 | 0 |
| Morse | 6 | 14 | 2.3 | 0 |
| Tinsley | 4 | 2 | 0.5 | 0 |
| Clemons | 3 | 0 | 0.0 | 0 |
| Horn | 1 | 0 | 0.0 | 0 |
| Cavanaugh | 1 | -2 | -2.0 | 0 |
| Merkens | 3 | -8 | -2.7 | 0 |

### Receiving

| Last Name | No. | Yds | Avg | TD |
|---|---|---|---|---|
| Quick | 46 | 790 | 17.2 | 11 |
| Toney | 39 | 341 | 8.7 | 1 |
| Spagnola | 36 | 350 | 9.7 | 2 |
| Tautalatasi | 25 | 176 | 7.0 | 0 |
| Jackson | 21 | 471 | 22.4 | 3 |
| Byars | 21 | 177 | 8.4 | 1 |
| Grant | 16 | 280 | 17.5 | 0 |
| Giles | 13 | 157 | 12.1 | 1 |
| Garrity | 12 | 242 | 20.2 | 2 |
| Siano | 9 | 137 | 15.2 | 1 |
| Bailey | 8 | 69 | 8.6 | 0 |
| R. Brown | 8 | 53 | 6.6 | 0 |
| Haddix | 7 | 58 | 8.3 | 0 |
| Bowman | 6 | 127 | 21.2 | 1 |
| Carter | 5 | 84 | 16.8 | 2 |
| Repko | 5 | 46 | 9.2 | 0 |
| Ross | 5 | 41 | 8.2 | 0 |
| Robinson | 2 | 9 | 4.5 | 0 |
| Clemons | 1 | 13 | 13.0 | 1 |
| Little | 1 | 8 | 8.0 | 0 |
| Morse | 1 | 8 | 8.0 | 0 |
| Cunningham | 1 | -3 | -3.0 | 0 |
| Singletary | 1 | -11 | -11.0 | 0 |

### Punt Returns

| Last Name | No. | Yds | Avg | TD |
|---|---|---|---|---|
| Morse | 20 | 121 | 6.1 | 0 |
| Bowman | 4 | 43 | 10.8 | 0 |
| Garrity | 4 | 16 | 4.0 | 0 |
| Caterbone | 2 | 13 | 6.5 | 0 |
| Ulmer | 2 | 10 | 5.0 | 0 |
| C. Brown | 1 | -1 | -1.0 | 0 |
| A. Johnson | 1 | 0 | 0.0 | 0 |

### Kickoff Returns

| Last Name | No. | Yds | Avg | TD |
|---|---|---|---|---|
| Morse | 24 | 386 | 16.1 | 0 |
| Carter | 12 | 241 | 20.1 | 0 |
| Bowman | 7 | 153 | 21.9 | 0 |
| Cooper | 5 | 86 | 17.2 | 0 |
| Reid | 4 | 58 | 14.5 | 0 |
| Tautalatasi | 3 | 53 | 17.7 | 0 |
| Haddix | 2 | 16 | 8.0 | 0 |
| Turrall | 1 | 21 | 21.0 | 0 |
| R. Brown | 1 | 20 | 20.0 | 0 |
| C. Brown | 1 | 13 | 13.0 | 0 |
| Siano | 1 | 13 | 13.0 | 0 |
| Ulmer | 1 | 8 | 8.0 | 0 |
| Alexander | 1 | 6 | 6.0 | 0 |
| Clemons | 1 | 0 | 0.0 | 0 |
| Reeves | 0 | 1 | — | 0 |

### Passing — Punting — Kicking

| PASSING | Att | Cmp | % | Yds | Yd/Att | TD | Int— | % | Rk |
|---|---|---|---|---|---|---|---|---|---|
| Cunningham | 406 | 223 | 54.9 | 2786 | 6.9 | 23 | 12— | 3.0 | 13 |
| Tinsley | 86 | 48 | 55.8 | 637 | 7.4 | 3 | 4— | 4.7 | |
| Merkens | 14 | 7 | 50.0 | 70 | 5.0 | 0 | 0— | 0.0 | |
| Horn | 11 | 5 | 45.5 | 68 | 6.2 | 0 | 0— | 0.0 | |
| Carter | 1 | 0 | 0 | 0 | 0.0 | 0 | 0— | 0.0 | |
| Grant | 1 | 0 | 0 | 0 | 0.0 | 0 | 0— | 0.0 | |
| Toney | 1 | 0 | 0 | 0 | 0.0 | 0 | 0— | 0.0 | |

| PUNTING | No | Avg |
|---|---|---|
| Teltschik | 83 | 37.7 |
| Jacobs | 11 | 33.5 |
| Merkens | 3 | 20.3 |

| KICKING | XP | Att | % | FG | Att | % |
|---|---|---|---|---|---|---|
| McFadden | 36 | 36 | 100 | 16 | 26 | 62 |
| Jacobs | 2 | 4 | 50 | 3 | 5 | 60 |

DALLAS COWBOYS 7-8 Tom Landry

| Scores of Each Game | | |
|---|---|---|
| 13 | St. Louis | 24 |
| 16 | N.Y.Giants | 14 |
| 38 | N.Y.Jets | 24 |
| 41 | PHILADELPHIA | 22 |
| 7 | WASHINGTON | 13 |
| 20 | Philadelphia | 37 |
| 33 | N.Y.GIANTS | 24 |
| 17 | Detroit | 27 |
| 23 | New England | *17 |
| 14 | MIAMI | 20 |
| 38 | MINNESOTA | *44 |
| 10 | ATLANTA | 21 |
| 20 | Washington | 24 |
| 29 | L.A.Rams | 21 |
| 21 | ST.LOUIS | 16 |

| Use Name | Pos. | Hgt | Wgt | Age | Int | Pts |
|---|---|---|---|---|---|---|
| Brian Baldinger | OT-OG | 6'4" | 266 | 28 | | |
| #Dave Burnette | OT | 6'6" | 278 | 26 | | |
| #Steve Cisowski | OT | 6'5" | 275 | 24 | | |
| Kevin Gogan | OT | 6'7" | 310 | 22 | | |
| Phil Pozderac | OT | 6'9" | 283 | 27 | | |
| #Jon Shields | OT | 6'5" | 293 | 23 | | |
| Daryle Smith | OT | 6'5" | 278 | 23 | | |
| Mark Tuinei | OT | 6'5" | 282 | 27 | | |
| #Sal Cesario | OG | 6'4" | 255 | 24 | | |
| Crawford Ker | OG | 6'3" | 283 | 25 | | |
| Nate Newton | OG | 6'3" | 315 | 25 | | |
| #Gary Walker | OG | 6'3" | 283 | 23 | | |
| Bob White | OG | 6'5" | 270 | 24 | | |
| Jeff Zimmerman | OG | 6'3" | 310 | 22 | | |
| George Lilja | C | 6'4" | 282 | 29 | | |
| Tom Rafferty | C | 6'3" | 262 | 33 | | |
| Joe Shearin | C | 6'4" | 265 | 27 | | |
| #Mike Zentic | C | 6'3" | 255 | 23 | | |
| Jim Jeffcoat | DE | 6'5" | 263 | 26 | 1 | 6 |
| Too Tall Jones | DE | 6'9" | 275 | 36 | | |
| #Ray Perkins | DE | 6'5" | 242 | 21 | | |
| Don Smerek | DE-DT | 6'7" | 262 | 29 | | |
| Randy Watts | DE-DT | 6'6" | 275 | 24 | | |
| Kevin Brooks | DT | 6'6" | 278 | 24 | | |
| John Dutton | DT | 6'7" | 261 | 36 | | |
| #Mike Dwyer | DT | 6'3" | 280 | 24 | | |
| #Walter Johnson | DT | 6'1" | 250 | 21 | | |
| Danny Noonan | DT | 6'4" | 270 | 22 | | |
| Mark Walen | DT-DE | 6'5" | 265 | 24 | | |
| Randy White | DT | 6'4" | 263 | 34 | 1 | |
| Ron Burton | LB | 6'1" | 250 | 23 | | |
| Steve DeOssie | LB | 6'2" | 249 | 24 | | |
| #Chris Duliban | LB | 6'2" | 216 | 24 | | |
| #Harry Flaherty | LB | 6'1" | 232 | 25 | | |
| Mike Hegman | LB | 6'1" | 236 | 34 | | |
| Jeff Hurd | LB | 6'2" | 245 | 23 | | |
| Garth Jax | LB | 6'2" | 225 | 23 | | |
| #Dale Jones | LB | 6'1" | 234 | 24 | | |
| Eugene Lockhart | LB | 6'2" | 235 | 26 | 1 | |
| Jesse Penn | LB | 6'3" | 224 | 24 | 1 | |
| Jeff Rohrer | LB | 6'3" | 222 | 28 | | |
| #Victor Simmons | LB | 6'2" | 230 | 23 | | |
| #Russ Swan | LB | 6'4" | 225 | 24 | | |
| #Kirk Timmer | LB | 6'3" | 242 | 23 | | |
| #Vince Albritton | DB | 6'2" | 217 | 25 | | |
| #Jimmy Armstrong | DB | 5'8" | 165 | 25 | | |
| Bill Bates | DB | 6'1" | 204 | 26 | 3 | |
| #Anthony Coleman | DB | 6' | 185 | 23 | | |
| Michael Downs | DB | 6'3" | 212 | 28 | 4 | |
| Ron Francis | DB | 5'9" | 199 | 23 | 2 | 6 |
| #Alex Green | DB | 6'1" | 194 | 21 | 1 | |
| #Tommy Haynes | DB | 6' | 190 | 24 | 3 | |
| Manny Hendrix | DB | 5'10" | 181 | 22 | | |
| #Bill Hill | DB | 5'9" | 172 | 26 | | |
| #Bruce Livingston | DB | 5'10" | 169 | 24 | | |
| Victor Scott | DB | 6' | 203 | 25 | 1 | |
| Everson Walls | DB | 6'1" | 192 | 27 | 5 | |
| Robert Williams | DB | 5'10" | 195 | 24 | | |
| Paul McDonald | QB | 6'2" | 182 | 29 | | |
| Steve Pelluer | QB | 6'4" | 208 | 25 | | 6 |
| #Loran Snyder | QB | 6'4" | 207 | 23 | | |
| #Kevin Sweeney | QB | 6' | 191 | 23 | | |
| Danny White | QB | 6'2" | 198 | 35 | | 6 |
| #David Adams | HB | 5'6" | 170 | 23 | | 6 |
| #Alvin Blount | HB | 5'9" | 197 | 22 | | 18 |
| Tony Dorsett | HB | 5'11" | 188 | 33 | | 12 |
| Robert Lavette (to PHI) | HB | 5'11" | 190 | 23 | | |
| Herschel Walker | HB | 6'1" | 223 | 25 | | 48 |
| Darryl Clack | FB | 5'10" | 218 | 23 | | |
| Todd Fowler | FB | 6'3" | 222 | 25 | | |
| #E.J.Jones | FB | 5'11" | 212 | 25 | | |
| Timmy Newsome | FB | 6'1" | 235 | 29 | | 24 |
| #Gerald White | FB | 5'11" | 223 | 22 | | |
| Gordon Banks | WR | 5'10" | 170 | 29 | | 6 |
| Ron Barksdale | WR | 6' | 193 | 24 | | 6 |
| #Cornell Burbage | WR | 5'10" | 181 | 22 | | 12 |
| #Vince Courville | WR | 5'9" | 170 | 27 | | |
| Kelvin Edwards | WR | 6'2" | 205 | 23 | | 24 |
| Kelvin Martin | WR | 5'9" | 163 | 22 | | |
| Mike Renfro | WR | 6' | 184 | 32 | | 24 |
| #Chuck Scott | WR | 6'2" | 195 | 24 | | |
| #Sebron Spivey | WR | 5'11" | 180 | 23 | | |
| #Rich Borreson | TE | 6'5" | 252 | 23 | | |
| Thornton Chandler | TE | 6'5" | 245 | 23 | | 6 |
| Doug Cosbie | TE | 6'6" | 241 | 31 | | 18 |
| Steve Folsom | TE | 6'5" | 236 | 29 | | |
| #Tim Hendrix | TE | 6'5" | 241 | 21 | | |
| #Kerry Brady | K | 6'1" | 205 | 24 | | |
| Roger Ruzek | K | 6'1" | 190 | 26 | | 92 |
| #Buzz Sawyer | K | 6'1" | 201 | 24 | | |
| Mike Saxon | K | 6'3" | 193 | 25 | | |
| #Luis Zendejas | K | 5'9" | 160 | 25 | | 19 |

Kurt Petersen - Knee Injury
Robert Smith - Arm Injury
Glen Titensor - Knee Injury
Brian Salonen - Groin Injury
Ray Alexander - Wrist Injury
Mike Sherrard - Broken Leg

NEW YORK GIANTS 6-9 Bill Parcells

| Scores of Each Game | | |
|---|---|---|
| 19 | Chicago | 34 |
| 14 | DALLAS | 16 |
| 21 | SAN FRANCISCO | 41 |
| 12 | WASHINGTON | 38 |
| 3 | Buffalo | *6 |
| 30 | ST.LOUIS | 7 |
| 24 | Dallas | 33 |
| 17 | NEW ENGLAND | 10 |
| 20 | Philadelphia | 17 |
| 14 | New Orleans | 23 |
| 19 | Washington | 23 |
| 23 | PHILADELPHIA | *20 |
| 24 | St.Louis | 27 |
| 20 | GREEN BAY | 10 |
| 20 | N.Y.JETS | 7 |

| Use Name | Pos. | Hgt | Wgt | Age | Int | Pts |
|---|---|---|---|---|---|---|
| Brad Benson | OT | 6'3" | 270 | 31 | | |
| #Mike Black | OT | 6'4" | 280 | 23 | | |
| #Kevin Meuth | OT | 6'5" | 270 | 23 | | |
| Doug Riesenberg | OT | 6'5" | 275 | 22 | | |
| William Roberts | OT | 6'5" | 280 | 25 | | |
| #Frank Sutton | OT | 6'3" | 280 | 23 | | |
| #Gregg Swartwoudt | OT | 6'3" | 275 | 23 | | |
| Billy Ard | OG | 6'3" | 270 | 28 | | |
| #Kelvin Davis | OG | 6'2" | 260 | 24 | | |
| #Bill Dugan | OG-OT | 6'4" | 290 | 28 | | |
| Chris Godfrey | OG | 6'3" | 265 | 29 | | |
| Damian Johnson | OG | 6'5" | 290 | 24 | | |
| #Dan Morgan | OG | 6'6" | 285 | 23 | | |
| #Scott Urch | OG | 6'2" | 270 | 22 | | |
| Brian Johnston | C | 6'3" | 275 | 24 | | |
| #Chris Jones | C | 6'3" | 263 | 23 | | |
| #Russell Mitchell | C | 6'5" | 288 | 26 | | |
| Bart Oates | C | 6'3" | 265 | 28 | | |
| #Reggie Carr | DE | 6'3" | 300 | 24 | | |
| Eric Dorsey | DE | 6'5" | 280 | 23 | | |
| #Curtis Garrett | DE | 6'5" | 302 | 25 | | |
| Leonard Marshall | DE | 6'3" | 285 | 25 | | |
| George Martin | DE | 6'4" | 255 | 34 | | |
| #Brian Sisley | DE | 6'4" | 235 | 23 | | |
| #Torin Smith | DE | 6'4" | 320 | 25 | | |
| #Joe Taibi | DE | 6'5" | 265 | 24 | | |
| John Washington | DE | 6'4" | 275 | 24 | | |
| #Dennis Borcky | NT | 6'4" | 284 | 22 | | |
| Jim Burt | NT | 6'1" | 260 | 28 | | |
| #Anthony Howard | NT | 6'3" | 267 | 27 | | |
| Erik Howard | NT | 6'4" | 268 | 22 | | |
| Carl Banks | LB | 6'4" | 235 | 25 | 1 | |
| #Charlie Burgess | LB | 6' | 230 | 24 | | |
| Harry Carson | LB | 6'2" | 240 | 33 | | |
| #Chris Davis | LB | 6'1" | 225 | 24 | | |
| #Dan DeRose | LB | 6' | 230 | 25 | 1 | |
| Andy Headen | LB | 6'5" | 242 | 27 | 2 | |
| Byron Hunt | LB | 6'5" | 242 | 28 | | |
| Pepper Johnson | LB | 6'3" | 248 | 23 | | |
| Robbie Jones | LB | 6'2" | 230 | 27 | | |
| #Jerry Kimmel | LB | 6'2" | 240 | 24 | | |
| #Frank Nicholson | LB | 6'2" | 205 | 26 | | |
| Gary Reasons | LB | 6'4" | 234 | 25 | | |
| Lawrence Taylor | LB | 6'3" | 243 | 28 | 3 | |
| #Warren Thompson | LB | 6'3" | 241 | 23 | | |
| #Jeff Tootie | LB | 6'2" | 240 | 25 | | |
| #Don Brown | DB | 5'11" | 189 | 23 | 1 | |
| #Boris Byrd | DB | 6' | 210 | 25 | | |
| Harvey Clayton | DB | 5'9" | 186 | 26 | | |
| Mark Collins | DB | 5'10" | 190 | 23 | 2 | |
| Tom Flynn | DB | 6' | 195 | 25 | | 6 |
| Wayne Haddix | DB | 6'1" | 203 | 22 | | |
| Kenny Hill | DB | 6' | 195 | 29 | 1 | |
| Terry Kinard | DB | 6'1" | 200 | 27 | 5 | 6 |
| Greg Lasker | DB | 6' | 200 | 22 | | |
| #Pat Morrison | DB | 6'2" | 194 | 22 | | |
| #Jimmy Norris | DB | 5'11" | 188 | 22 | | |
| #Robert Porter | DB | 6'2" | 210 | 25 | | |
| #Steve Rehage | DB | 6'1" | 190 | 23 | 1 | |
| #Doug Smith | DB | 6' | 192 | 24 | | |
| Herb Welch | DB | 5'11" | 180 | 26 | 2 | |
| Adrian White | DB | 6' | 200 | 23 | | |
| Perry Williams | DB | 6'2" | 203 | 26 | 1 | |
| #Jim Yarbrough | DB | 6' | 195 | 23 | | |
| #Mike Busch | QB | 6'4" | 214 | 24 | | |
| #Jim Crocicchia | QB | 6'2" | 209 | 23 | | |
| Jeff Hostetler | QB | 6'3" | 212 | 26 | | |
| #Paul Kelly | QB | 6'1" | 205 | 23 | | |
| Jeff Rutledge | QB | 6'1" | 195 | 30 | | |
| Phil Simms | QB | 6'3" | 214 | 30 | | |
| Ottis Anderson | HB | 6'2" | 225 | 30 | | |
| #Earl Beecham | HB | 5'6" | 180 | 21 | | |
| #Robert DiRico | HB | 5'10" | 202 | 23 | | |
| Joe Morris | HB | 5'7" | 195 | 26 | | 18 |
| #Van Williams | HB | 6'1" | 215 | 28 | | |
| George Adams | FB | 6'1" | 225 | 24 | | 12 |
| Maurice Carthon | FB | 6'1" | 225 | 26 | | |
| #Jamie Covington | FB | 6'1" | 234 | 24 | | |
| #Fred DiRenzo | FB | 5'11" | 234 | 26 | | |
| Tony Galbreath | FB | 6' | 228 | 33 | | |
| #Kaulana Park | FB | 6'2" | 230 | 25 | | |
| Lee Rouson | FB | 6'1" | 222 | 24 | | 6 |
| #Beau Almodobar | WR | 5'9" | 180 | 24 | | |
| Stephen Baker | WR | 5'8" | 160 | 23 | | 12 |
| #Lewis Bennett | WR | 5'11" | 175 | 24 | | 6 |
| #Mack Cummings | WR | 6' | 195 | 27 | | |
| Mark Ingram | WR | 5'10" | 188 | 22 | | |
| #Edwin Lovelady | WR | 5'9" | 180 | 24 | | 12 |
| Lionel Manuel | WR | 5'11" | 180 | 25 | | 36 |
| Phil McConkey | WR | 5'10" | 170 | 30 | | |
| #Reggie McGowan | WR | 5'8" | 165 | 22 | | 6 |
| Stacy Robinson | WR | 5'11" | 186 | 25 | | 12 |
| #Warren Seitz | WR | 6'4" | 210 | 24 | | |
| Odessa Turner | WR | 6'3" | 205 | 22 | | 6 |
| Mark Bavaro | TE | 6'4" | 245 | 25 | | 48 |
| #Charles Coleman | TE | 6'4" | 222 | 23 | | |
| Zeke Mowatt | TE | 6'3" | 240 | 26 | | 6 |
| #Jeff Smith | TE | 6'4" | 230 | 24 | | |
| Raul Allegre | K | 5'10" | 167 | 28 | | 76 |
| #George Benyola | K | 5'10" | 195 | 22 | | 12 |
| Sean Landeta | K | 6' | 200 | 25 | | |
| #Jim Miller | K | 5'11" | 183 | 30 | | |
| #Dana Moore | K | 5'10" | 180 | 25 | | |

Karl Nelson - Hodgkin's disease

# Central Division

CHICAGO BEARS 11-4 Mike Ditka

| Scores of Each Game | | |
|---|---|---|
| 34 | N.Y.GIANTS | 19 |
| 20 | TAMPA BAY | 3 |
| 35 | Philadelphia | 3 |
| 27 | MINNESOTA | 7 |
| 17 | NEW ORLEANS | 19 |
| 27 | Tampa Bay | 26 |
| 31 | KANSAS CITY | 28 |
| 26 | Green Bay | 24 |
| 29 | Denver | 31 |
| 30 | DETROIT | 10 |
| 23 | GREEN BAY | 10 |
| 30 | Minnesota | 24 |
| 0 | San Francisco | 41 |
| 21 | SEATTLE | 34 |
| 6 | L.A.Raiders | 3 |

| Use Name | Pos. | Hgt | Wgt | Age | Int | Pts |
|---|---|---|---|---|---|---|
| #John Arp | OT | 6'5" | 275 | 22 | | |
| Paul Blair | OT | 6'4" | 295 | 24 | | |
| Jim Covert | OT | 6'4" | 275 | 27 | | |
| #Jack Oliver | OT | 6'3" | 281 | 25 | | |
| #Stuart Rindy | OT-OG | 6'5" | 266 | 23 | | |
| Keith Van Horne | OT | 6'6" | 285 | 29 | | |
| Kurt Becker | OG | 6'5" | 280 | 28 | | |
| Mark Bortz | OG | 6'6" | 275 | 26 | | |
| #Jon Roehik | OG | 6'2" | 257 | 26 | | |
| Tom Thayer | OG | 6'4" | 280 | 26 | | |
| John Wojciechowski | OG-OT | 6'4" | 262 | 24 | | |
| John Adickes | C | 6'3" | 264 | 23 | | |
| Jay Hilgenberg | C | 6'3" | 260 | 27 | | |
| #Brent Johnson | C | 6'2" | 255 | 24 | | |
| Mark Rodenhauser | C | 6'5" | 260 | 26 | | |
| Richard Dent | DE | 6'5" | 263 | 26 | | |
| Dan Hampton | DE-DT | 6'5" | 267 | 29 | | |
| Al Harris | DE | 6'5" | 270 | 30 | | |
| #Sean McInerney | DE | 6'3" | 255 | 26 | | |
| Jon Norris | DE-DT | 6'3" | 260 | 24 | 1 | |
| Sean Smith | DE | 6'4" | 275 | 22 | | |
| Jim Althoff | DT | 6'3" | 278 | 25 | | |
| Dick Chapura | DT | 6'3" | 280 | 23 | | |
| #Greg Fitzgerald | DT | 6'4" | 265 | 24 | | |
| Steve McMichael | DT | 6'2" | 265 | 29 | | |
| William Perry | DT | 6'2" | 315 | 24 | | |
| #Eugene Rowell | DT | 6'3" | 265 | 29 | | |
| #Guy Teafatiller | DT | 6'2" | 260 | 23 | | |
| #Bobby Bell | LB | 6'3" | 217 | 25 | | |
| #Mike January | LB | 6'1" | 234 | 23 | | |
| Will Johnson | LB | 6'4" | 242 | 23 | | |
| Wilber Marshall | LB | 6'1" | 230 | 25 | | |
| Paul Migliazzo | LB | 6'1" | 228 | 23 | | |
| #Eldridge Milton | LB | 6'1" | 235 | 25 | | |
| #Raymond Morris | LB | 5'10" | 222 | 26 | | |
| Jim Morrissey | LB | 6'3" | 222 | 24 | | |
| Jay Norvell | LB | 6'2" | 232 | 24 | | |
| Ron Rivera | LB | 6'3" | 235 | 25 | 2 | |
| #Doug Rothechild | LB | 6'2" | 231 | 22 | | |
| Mike Singletary | LB | 6' | 235 | 28 | | |
| Otis Wilson | LB | 6'2" | 227 | 29 | | |
| Egypt Allen | DB | 6' | 203 | 23 | | |
| Todd Bell | DB | 6'1" | 212 | 28 | | |
| Maurice Douglass | DB | 5'11" | 200 | 23 | 2 | |
| #George Duarte | DB | 5'9" | 172 | 23 | | |
| Dave Duerson | DB | 6'1" | 210 | 26 | 3 | |
| Gary Fencik | DB | 6'1" | 193 | 33 | | |
| Shaun Gayle | DB | 5'11" | 193 | 25 | 1 | 6 |
| #Mike Hintz | DB | 6'1" | 190 | 22 | | |
| Vestee Jackson | DB | 6' | 186 | 24 | | |
| #Eric Jeffries | DB | 5'10" | 161 | 23 | 1 | |
| #Lorenzo Lynch | DB | 5'9" | 197 | 23 | | |
| #Bruce McCray | DB | 5'9" | 181 | 24 | 1 | 6 |
| Reggie Phillips | DB | 5'10" | 170 | 26 | 2 | |
| Mike Richardson | DB | 6' | 188 | 26 | | |
| Garland Rivers | DB | 6'1" | 181 | 22 | | |
| #Mike Stoops | DB | 6'1" | 185 | 22 | | |
| #Steve Trimble | DB | 5'10" | 190 | 29 | | |
| #Steve Bradley | QB | 6'2" | 216 | 24 | | |
| Jim Harbaugh | QB | 6'3" | 202 | 23 | | |
| #Mike Hohensee | QB | 6' | 205 | 26 | | |
| Jim McMahon | QB | 6'1" | 190 | 28 | | 12 |
| #Sean Payton | QB | 5'11" | 200 | 23 | | |
| Mike Tomczak | QB | 6'1" | 195 | 24 | | 6 |
| #Darryl Clark | HB | 5'11" | 204 | 26 | | |
| #Frank Harris | HB | 6'1" | 196 | 23 | | |
| #Anthony Mosley | HB | 5'9" | 204 | 22 | | 6 |
| Walter Payton | HB | 5'11" | 205 | 33 | | 30 |
| Thomas Sanders | HB | 5'11" | 203 | 25 | | 6 |
| Neal Anderson | FB-HB | 5'11" | 210 | 23 | | 36 |
| #Chris Brewer | FB | 6'1" | 203 | 25 | | 18 |
| #Lakei Heimuli | FB | 5'11" | 219 | 22 | | 6 |
| Matt Suhey | FB | 5'11" | 216 | 29 | | |
| Calvin Thomas | FB | 5'11" | 245 | 27 | | |
| #Al Wolden | FB | 6'3" | 232 | 22 | | |
| #Todd Black | WR | 5'11" | 174 | 23 | | |
| Willie Gault | WR | 6' | 183 | 26 | | 42 |
| Dennis Gentry | WR | 5'8" | 180 | 28 | | 12 |
| #Herbert Johnson | WR | 5'11" | 182 | 23 | | |
| #Ken Knapczyk | WR | 5'11" | 190 | 24 | | |
| #Glen Kozlowski | WR | 6'1" | 190 | 24 | | 18 |
| Dennis McKinnon | WR | 6'1" | 185 | 26 | | 18 |
| Ron Morris | WR | 6'1" | 187 | 22 | | 6 |
| #Gary Mullen | WR | 5'11" | 174 | 24 | | |
| Keith Ortego | WR | 6' | 180 | 24 | | |
| #Lawrence White | WR | 6'2" | 187 | 24 | | |
| Cap Boso | TE | 6'3" | 224 | 24 | | 12 |
| #Sam Bowers | TE | 6'4" | 250 | 29 | | |
| #Brian Glasgow | TE | 6'2" | 230 | 26 | | |
| #Don Kindt | TE | 6'6" | 242 | 26 | | 6 |
| Emery Moorehead | TE | 6'2" | 225 | 33 | | 6 |
| #Kevin Brown | K | 6'2" | 178 | 24 | | |
| Kevin Butler | K | 6'1" | 204 | 25 | | 85 |
| #Tim Lashar | K | 5'9" | 160 | 22 | | 19 |
| Bryan Wagner | K | 6'2" | 195 | 25 | | |

Larry Rubens - Knee Injury
Lew Barnes - Leg Injury
Steve Fuller - Shoulder Injury
Tim Wrightman - Knee Injury

* Overtime

\# - on the active roster for replacement games only

## DALLAS COWBOYS

### RUSHING
| Last Name | No. | Yds | Avg | TD |
|---|---|---|---|---|
| Walker | 209 | 891 | 4.3 | 7 |
| Dorsett | 130 | 456 | 3.5 | 1 |
| Pelluer | 25 | 142 | 5.7 | 1 |
| Blount | 46 | 125 | 2.7 | 3 |
| Newsome | 25 | 121 | 4.8 | 2 |
| Edwards | 2 | 61 | 30.5 | 1 |
| Adams | 7 | 49 | 7.0 | 1 |
| D. White | 10 | 14 | 1.4 | 1 |
| Sweeney | 5 | 8 | 1.6 | 0 |
| E.J. Jones | 2 | 7 | 3.5 | 0 |
| Snyder | 2 | 0 | 0.0 | 0 |
| G. White | 1 | -4 | -4.0 | 0 |
| Cosbie | 1 | -5 | -5.0 | 0 |

### RECEIVING
| Last Name | No. | Yds | Avg | TD |
|---|---|---|---|---|
| Walker | 60 | 715 | 11.9 | 1 |
| Renfro | 46 | 662 | 14.4 | 4 |
| Cosbie | 36 | 421 | 11.7 | 3 |
| Edwards | 34 | 521 | 15.3 | 3 |
| Newsome | 34 | 274 | 8.1 | 2 |
| Dorsett | 19 | 177 | 9.3 | 1 |
| Banks | 15 | 231 | 15.4 | 1 |
| Barksdale | 12 | 165 | 13.8 | 1 |
| Burbage | 7 | 168 | 24.0 | 2 |
| Martin | 5 | 103 | 20.6 | 0 |
| G. White | 5 | 46 | 9.2 | 0 |
| Chandler | 5 | 25 | 5.0 | 1 |
| E.J. Jones | 3 | 16 | 5.3 | 0 |
| Spivey | 2 | 34 | 17.0 | 0 |
| C. Scott | 1 | 11 | 11.0 | 0 |
| Adams | 1 | 8 | 8.0 | 0 |
| Fowler | 1 | 6 | 6.0 | 0 |
| Lavette | 1 | 6 | 6.0 | 0 |
| Blount | 1 | 5 | 5.0 | 0 |

### PUNT RETURNS
| Last Name | No. | Yds | Avg | TD |
|---|---|---|---|---|
| Martin | 22 | 216 | 9.8 | 0 |
| Edwards | 8 | 75 | 9.4 | 0 |
| Banks | 5 | 33 | 6.6 | 0 |
| Burbage | 5 | 29 | 5.8 | 0 |
| Livingston | 1 | 0 | 0.0 | 0 |

### KICKOFF RETURNS
| Last Name | No. | Yds | Avg | TD |
|---|---|---|---|---|
| Clack | 29 | 635 | 21.9 | 0 |
| Martin | 12 | 237 | 19.8 | 0 |
| Edwards | 7 | 155 | 22.1 | 0 |
| Adams | 6 | 113 | 18.8 | 0 |
| Lavette | 6 | 109 | 18.2 | 0 |
| Spivey | 2 | 49 | 24.5 | 0 |
| Newsome | 2 | 22 | 11.0 | 0 |
| Chandler | 1 | 7 | 7.0 | 0 |
| Borresen | 1 | 5 | 5.0 | 0 |

### PASSING — PUNTING — KICKING
**PASSING**
| Last Name | Att | Cmp | % | Yds | Yd/Att | TD | Int— | % | Rk |
|---|---|---|---|---|---|---|---|---|---|
| D. White | 362 | 215 | 59.4 | 2617 | 7.2 | 12 | 17— | 4.7 | 19 |
| Pelluer | 101 | 55 | 54.5 | 642 | 6.4 | 3 | 2— | 2.0 | |
| Sweeney | 28 | 14 | 50.0 | 291 | 10.4 | 4 | 1— | 3.6 | |
| Snyder | 9 | 4 | 44.4 | 44 | 4.9 | 0 | 0— | 0.0 | |

**PUNTING**
| Last Name | No | Avg |
|---|---|---|
| Saxon | 68 | 39.5 |
| Sawyer | 16 | 39.9 |

**KICKING**
| Last Name | XP | Att | % | FG | Att | % |
|---|---|---|---|---|---|---|
| Ruzek | 26 | 26 | 100 | 22 | 25 | 88 |
| Zendejas | 10 | 10 | 100 | 3 | 4 | 75 |

## NEW YORK GIANTS

### RUSHING
| Last Name | No. | Yds | Avg | TD |
|---|---|---|---|---|
| Morris | 193 | 658 | 3.4 | 3 |
| Adams | 61 | 169 | 2.8 | 1 |
| Rouson | 41 | 155 | 3.8 | 0 |
| V. Williams | 29 | 108 | 3.7 | 0 |
| DiRico | 25 | 90 | 3.6 | 0 |
| Galbreath | 10 | 74 | 7.4 | 0 |
| Carthon | 26 | 60 | 2.3 | 0 |
| Simms | 14 | 44 | 3.1 | 0 |
| Rutledge | 15 | 31 | 2.1 | 0 |
| Beecham | 5 | 22 | 4.4 | 0 |
| Baker | 1 | 18 | 18.0 | 0 |
| Lovelady | 2 | 11 | 5.5 | 0 |
| Park | 6 | 11 | 1.8 | 0 |
| Anderson | 2 | 6 | 3.0 | 0 |
| Crocicchia | 4 | 5 | 1.3 | 0 |
| DiRenzo | 1 | 5 | 5.0 | 0 |
| Covington | 4 | 0 | 0.0 | 0 |
| Manuel | 1 | -10 | -10.0 | 0 |

### RECEIVING
| Last Name | No. | Yds | Avg | TD |
|---|---|---|---|---|
| Bavaro | 55 | 867 | 15.8 | 8 |
| Adams | 35 | 298 | 8.5 | 1 |
| Manuel | 30 | 545 | 18.2 | 6 |
| Galbreath | 26 | 248 | 9.5 | 0 |
| Baker | 15 | 277 | 18.5 | 2 |
| McConkey | 11 | 186 | 16.9 | 0 |
| Rouson | 11 | 129 | 11.7 | 1 |
| Morris | 11 | 114 | 10.4 | 0 |
| Turner | 10 | 195 | 19.5 | 1 |
| Bennett | 10 | 184 | 18.4 | 1 |
| Lovelady | 10 | 125 | 12.5 | 2 |
| Carthon | 8 | 71 | 8.9 | 0 |
| J. Smith | 6 | 72 | 12.0 | 0 |
| Robinson | 6 | 58 | 9.7 | 2 |
| V. Williams | 5 | 36 | 7.2 | 0 |
| McGowan | 4 | 111 | 27.8 | 1 |
| Mowatt | 3 | 39 | 13.0 | 1 |
| Ingram | 2 | 32 | 16.0 | 0 |
| DiRico | 2 | 22 | 11.0 | 0 |
| Anderson | 2 | 16 | 8.0 | 0 |
| Covington | 1 | 9 | 9.0 | 0 |
| Park | 1 | 6 | 6.0 | 0 |
| Coleman | 1 | 5 | 5.0 | 0 |

### PUNT RETURNS
| Last Name | No. | Yds | Avg | TD |
|---|---|---|---|---|
| McConkey | 42 | 394 | 9.4 | 0 |
| Lovelady | 10 | 38 | 3.8 | 0 |
| Baker | 3 | 16 | 5.3 | 0 |

### KICKOFF RETURNS
| Last Name | No. | Yds | Avg | TD |
|---|---|---|---|---|
| Rouson | 22 | 497 | 22.6 | 0 |
| Adams | 9 | 166 | 18.4 | 0 |
| Ingram | 6 | 114 | 19.0 | 0 |
| Byrd | 4 | 99 | 24.8 | 0 |
| Norris | 4 | 70 | 17.5 | 0 |
| Beecham | 3 | 70 | 23.3 | 0 |
| DiRico | 2 | 31 | 15.5 | 0 |
| Coleman | 1 | 20 | 20.0 | 0 |
| Bavaro | 1 | 16 | 16.0 | 0 |
| Dorsey | 1 | 13 | 13.0 | 0 |
| Urch | 1 | 13 | 13.0 | 0 |
| Cummings | 1 | 11 | 11.0 | 0 |
| McConkey | 1 | 8 | 8.0 | 0 |

### PASSING — PUNTING — KICKING
**PASSING**
| Last Name | Att | Cmp | % | Yds | Yd/Att | TD | Int— | % | Rk |
|---|---|---|---|---|---|---|---|---|---|
| Simms | 282 | 163 | 57.8 | 2230 | 7.9 | 17 | 9— | 3.2 | 3 |
| Rutledge | 155 | 79 | 51.0 | 1048 | 6.8 | 5 | 11— | 7.1 | |
| Busch | 47 | 17 | 36.2 | 278 | 5.9 | 3 | 2— | 4.3 | |
| Crocicchia | 15 | 6 | 40.0 | 89 | 5.9 | 1 | 0— | 0.0 | |

**PUNTING**
| Last Name | No | Avg |
|---|---|---|
| Landeta | 66 | 42.0 |
| Moore | 15 | 32.4 |
| Miller | 10 | 34.5 |

**KICKING**
| Last Name | XP | Att | % | FG | Att | % |
|---|---|---|---|---|---|---|
| Allegre | 25 | 26 | 96 | 17 | 27 | 63 |
| Benyola | 3 | 3 | 100 | 3 | 5 | 60 |

## CHICAGO BEARS

### RUSHING
| Last Name | No. | Yds | Avg | TD |
|---|---|---|---|---|
| Anderson | 129 | 586 | 4.5 | 3 |
| W. Payton | 146 | 533 | 3.7 | 4 |
| Heimuli | 34 | 128 | 3.8 | 0 |
| Sanders | 23 | 122 | 5.3 | 1 |
| McMahon | 22 | 88 | 4.0 | 2 |
| Thomas | 25 | 88 | 3.5 | 0 |
| Mosley | 18 | 80 | 4.4 | 0 |
| Hohensee | 9 | 56 | 6.2 | 0 |
| Brewer | 24 | 55 | 2.3 | 2 |
| Tomczak | 18 | 54 | 3.0 | 1 |
| Gentry | 6 | 41 | 6.8 | 0 |
| S. Payton | 1 | 28 | 28.0 | 0 |
| Suhey | 7 | 24 | 3.4 | 0 |
| F. Harris | 6 | 23 | 3.8 | 0 |
| Gault | 2 | 16 | 8.0 | 0 |
| Harbaugh | 4 | 15 | 3.8 | 0 |
| Clark | 5 | 11 | 2.2 | 0 |
| Wolden | 2 | 8 | 4.0 | 0 |
| Marshall | 1 | 1 | 1.0 | 0 |
| Brown | 1 | 0 | 0.0 | 0 |
| Perry | 1 | 0 | 0.0 | 0 |
| Bradley | 1 | -3 | -3.0 | 0 |

### RECEIVING
| Last Name | No. | Yds | Avg | TD |
|---|---|---|---|---|
| Anderson | 47 | 467 | 9.9 | 3 |
| Gault | 35 | 705 | 20.1 | 7 |
| W. Payton | 33 | 217 | 6.6 | 1 |
| McKinnon | 27 | 406 | 15.0 | 1 |
| Moorehead | 24 | 269 | 11.2 | 1 |
| Ro. Morris | 20 | 379 | 19.0 | 1 |
| Boso | 17 | 188 | 11.1 | 2 |
| Gentry | 17 | 183 | 10.8 | 1 |
| Kozlowski | 15 | 199 | 13.3 | 3 |
| Suhey | 7 | 54 | 7.7 | 0 |
| Brewer | 5 | 56 | 11.2 | 1 |
| Heimuli | 5 | 51 | 10.2 | 1 |
| Kindt | 5 | 34 | 6.8 | 1 |
| Knapczyk | 4 | 62 | 15.5 | 0 |
| Sanders | 3 | 53 | 17.7 | 0 |
| Mullen | 2 | 33 | 16.5 | 0 |
| Glasgow | 2 | 16 | 8.0 | 0 |
| Mosley | 2 | 16 | 8.0 | 0 |
| Wolden | 1 | 26 | 26.0 | 0 |
| Bowers | 1 | 6 | 6.0 | 0 |

### PUNT RETURNS
| Last Name | No. | Yds | Avg | TD |
|---|---|---|---|---|
| McKinnon | 40 | 405 | 10.1 | 2 |
| Duarte | 8 | 64 | 8.0 | 0 |
| Duerson | 1 | 10 | 10.0 | 0 |
| Jeffries | 1 | 5 | 5.0 | 0 |

### KICKOFF RETURNS
| Last Name | No. | Yds | Avg | TD |
|---|---|---|---|---|
| Gentry | 25 | 621 | 24.8 | 1 |
| Sanders | 20 | 349 | 17.5 | 0 |
| Kozlowski | 3 | 72 | 24.0 | 0 |
| Lynch | 3 | 66 | 22.0 | 0 |
| T. Bell | 1 | 18 | 18.0 | 0 |
| Mosley | 1 | 17 | 17.0 | 0 |
| White | 1 | 17 | 17.0 | 0 |
| Knapczyk | 1 | 14 | 14.0 | 0 |
| Milton | 1 | 10 | 10.0 | 0 |
| Suhey | 1 | 9 | 9.0 | 0 |

### PASSING — PUNTING — KICKING
**PASSING**
| Last Name | Att | Cmp | % | Yds | Yd/Att | TD | Int— | % | Rk |
|---|---|---|---|---|---|---|---|---|---|
| McMahon | 210 | 125 | 59.5 | 1639 | 7.8 | 12 | 8— | 3.8 | 7 |
| Tomczak | 178 | 97 | 54.5 | 1220 | 6.9 | 5 | 10— | 5.6 | |
| Hohensee | 52 | 28 | 53.8 | 343 | 6.6 | 4 | 1— | 1.9 | |
| S. Payton | 23 | 8 | 34.8 | 79 | 3.4 | 0 | 1— | 4.3 | |
| Bradley | 18 | 6 | 33.3 | 77 | 4.3 | 2 | 3— | 16.7 | |
| Harbaugh | 11 | 8 | 72.7 | 62 | 5.6 | 0 | 0— | 0.0 | |
| W. Payton | 1 | 0 | 0.0 | 0 | 0.0 | 0 | 1— | 100 | |

**PUNTING**
| Last Name | No | Avg |
|---|---|---|
| Wagner | 37 | 39.5 |
| Brown | 19 | 39.1 |

**KICKING**
| Last Name | XP | Att | % | FG | Att | % |
|---|---|---|---|---|---|---|
| Butler | 28 | 30 | 93 | 19 | 28 | 68 |
| Lashar | 10 | 10 | 100 | 3 | 4 | 75 |

**MINNESOTA VIKINGS 8-7 Jerry Burns**

| Scores of Each Game | | |
|---|---|---|
| 34 | DETROIT | 19 |
| 21 | L.A.Rams | 16 |
| 16 | GREEN BAY | 23 |
| 7 | Chicago | 27 |
| 10 | Tampa Bay | 20 |
| 34 | DENVER | 27 |
| 17 | Seattle | 28 |
| 31 | L.A.RAIDERS | 20 |
| 23 | TAMPA BAY | 17 |
| 24 | ATLANTA | 13 |
| 44 | Dallas | *38 |
| 24 | CHICAGO | 30 |
| 10 | Green Bay | 16 |
| 17 | Detroit | 14 |
| 24 | WASHINGTON | *27 |

| Use Name | Pos. | Hgt | Wgt | Age | Int | Pts |
|---|---|---|---|---|---|---|
| #Derek Burton | OT | 6'2" | 270 | 24 | | |
| Tim Irwin | OT | 6'6" | 290 | 28 | | |
| #John Scardina | OT | 6'4" | 265 | 29 | | |
| Gary Zimmerman | OT | 6'6" | 284 | 25 | | |
| #Mark Hanson | OG | 6'2" | 260 | 22 | | |
| Dave Huffman | OG | 6'6" | 285 | 30 | | |
| Wayne Jones | OG | 6'4" | 270 | 27 | | |
| Greg Koch (from MIA) | OG | 6'4" | 276 | 32 | | |
| Mark MacDonald | OG | 6'4" | 265 | 26 | | |
| #Mike McCurry | OG | 6'3" | 258 | 24 | | |
| #Ted Million | OG | 6'4" | 260 | 24 | | |
| #Frank Ori | OG | 6'2" | 255 | 23 | | |
| Terry Tausch | OG | 6'5" | 276 | 28 | | |
| #Mike Turner | OG | 6'3" | 255 | 27 | | |
| Chris Foote | C | 6'3" | 265 | 30 | | |
| Kirk Lowdermilk | C | 6'3" | 264 | 24 | | |
| Randy Rasmussen | C-OG | 6'2" | 254 | 26 | | |
| #Ron Selesky | C | 6'1" | 266 | 21 | | |
| Dennis Swilley | C | 6'3" | 266 | 32 | | |
| #Kevin Webster | C | 6'2" | 260 | 25 | | |
| #Daniel Coleman | DE | 6'4" | 249 | 25 | | |
| Chris Doleman | DE | 6'5" | 262 | 25 | | |
| Mike Hartenstine | DE | 6'3" | 254 | 34 | | |
| Doug Martin | DE | 6'3" | 258 | 30 | | |
| #Phil Micech | DE | 6'5" | 265 | 26 | | |
| #Tony Norman | DE | 6'5" | 270 | 32 | | |
| Gerald Robinson | DE | 6'3" | 261 | 24 | | |
| #Don Bramlett | DT | 6'2" | 270 | 24 | | |
| Stafford Mays | DT-DE | 6'2" | 264 | 29 | | |
| Keith Millard | DT | 6'5" | 264 | 25 | | |
| #Fred Molden | DT | 6'2" | 272 | 24 | | |
| Tim Newton | DT | 6' | 297 | 24 | | |
| #Kurt Ploeger | DT | 6'5" | 260 | 24 | | |
| #Joe Stepanek | DT | 6'5" | 268 | 23 | | 2 |
| Henry Thomas | DT | 6'2" | 268 | 22 | 1 | |
| #Jimmy Walker | DT | 6'2" | 265 | 30 | | |
| #Brad White | DT | 6'2" | 261 | 29 | | |

| Use Name | Pos. | Hgt | Wgt | Age | Int | Pts |
|---|---|---|---|---|---|---|
| #Steve Ache | LB | 6'3" | 229 | 25 | | |
| Sam Anno (from LA) | LB | 6'2" | 230 | 22 | | |
| Walker Lee Ashley | LB | 6' | 232 | 27 | | |
| Ray Berry | LB | 6'2" | 230 | 23 | | |
| #Tim Bryant | LB | 6'1" | 217 | 25 | | |
| #Fabray Collins | LB | 6'2" | 215 | 25 | | |
| #Jim Dick | LB | 6'1" | 230 | 23 | | |
| David Howard | LB | 6'2" | 234 | 25 | 1 | |
| Chris Martin | LB | 6'2" | 231 | 26 | | |
| Peter Najarian | LB | 6'2" | 233 | 23 | | |
| #Kelly Quinn | LB | 6'1" | 220 | 24 | | |
| #Randy Scott | LB | 6'1" | 228 | 28 | | |
| Jesse Solomon | LB | 6' | 236 | 23 | 1 | |
| Scott Studwell | LB | 6'2" | 230 | 33 | 2 | |
| #Rufus Bess | DB | 5'9" | 189 | 31 | | |
| Joey Browner | DB | 6'2" | 210 | 27 | 6 | |
| #David Evans | DB | 6' | 178 | 28 | | |
| #Jamie Fitzgerald | DB | 6' | 180 | 22 | | |
| Steve Freeman | DB | 5'11" | 185 | 34 | | |
| Neal Guggemos | DB | 6'1" | 190 | 23 | 1 | |
| John Harris | DB | 6'2" | 197 | 31 | 3 | |
| Wymon Henderson | DB | 5'10" | 186 | 25 | 4 | |
| Issiac Holt | DB | 6'2" | 199 | 24 | 2 | |
| Carl Lee | DB | 6' | 188 | 26 | 3 | |
| #Fletcher Louallen | DB | 6' | 195 | 24 | 1 | |
| #Terry Love | DB | 6'2" | 205 | 29 | | |
| #Ted Rosnagle | DB | 6'3" | 202 | 25 | | |
| Reggie Rutland | DB | 6'1" | 195 | 23 | | |
| #Mike Slaton | DB | 6'2" | 194 | 22 | | |
| Wayne Smith | DB | 6' | 170 | 30 | 1 | |
| #Timothy Starks | DB | 5'9" | 175 | 23 | | |
| John Turner | DB | 6' | 193 | 31 | | |

Mark Mullaney - Neck Injury
Buster Rhymes - Ankle Injury

| Use Name | Pos. | Hgt | Wgt | Age | Int | Pts |
|---|---|---|---|---|---|---|
| #Tony Adams | QB | 6' | 195 | 37 | | |
| #Keith Bishop | QB | 6'4" | 190 | 24 | | |
| Rich Gannon | QB | 6'3" | 197 | 21 | | |
| Tommy Kramer | QB | 6'2" | 202 | 32 | | 12 |
| #Todd Krueger | QB | 6'4" | 210 | 30 | | |
| #Larry Miller | QB | 6'4" | 220 | 25 | | |
| Wade Wilson | QB | 6'3" | 206 | 28 | | 30 |
| D.J.Dozier | HB | 6' | 198 | 21 | | 42 |
| #Phil Frye | HB | 5'11" | 180 | 26 | | |
| #Steve Harris | HB | 5'11" | 194 | 24 | | |
| Darrin Nelson | HB | 5'9" | 185 | 28 | | 12 |
| #Jimmy Smith | HB | 5'11" | 190 | 26 | | |
| #Andre Thomas | HB | 6' | 205 | 26 | | |
| #Jeff Womack | HB | 5'9" | 188 | 24 | | 6 |
| Alfred Anderson | FB | 6'1" | 217 | 26 | | 12 |
| Rick Fenney | FB | 6'1" | 240 | 22 | | 12 |
| #Sam Harrell | FB | 6'2" | 213 | 29 | | |
| #Leonard Moore | FB | 6' | 222 | 24 | | |
| Allen Rice | FB | 5'10" | 206 | 25 | | 12 |
| #Adam Walker | FB | 5'11" | 220 | 24 | | |
| #Brett Wilson | FB | 6' | 220 | 26 | | |
| #James Brim | WR | 6'3" | 187 | 24 | | 18 |
| #Larry Brown | WR | 5'11" | 180 | 23 | | |
| Anthony Carter | WR | 5'11" | 174 | 26 | | 42 |
| #Ron Daugherty | WR | 6'3" | 185 | 29 | | |
| #Steve Finch | WR | 6' | 200 | 26 | | |
| #Willie Gillespie | WR | 5'9" | 170 | 25 | | |
| Jim Gustafson | WR | 6'1" | 178 | 26 | | |
| Hassan Jones | WR | 6' | 198 | 23 | | 12 |
| #Keith Kidd | WR | 6'1" | 195 | 24 | | |
| #Terry LeCount | WR | 5'10" | 176 | 31 | | |
| Leo Lewis | WR | 5'8" | 167 | 30 | | 18 |
| #Rickey Parks | WR | 6'1" | 179 | 23 | | |
| Greg Richardson | WR | 5'7" | 172 | 22 | | |
| #Clifton Eley | TE | 6'5" | 230 | 26 | | |
| Carl Hilton | TE | 6'3" | 236 | 23 | | 12 |
| Steve Jordan | TE | 6'4" | 235 | 26 | | 12 |
| #Marc May | TE | 6'4" | 230 | 29 | | |
| Mike Mularkey | TE | 6'4" | 236 | 25 | | |
| #Ed Schenk | TE | 6'4" | 230 | 26 | | |
| #Dave Bruno | K | 6'1" | 235 | 24 | | |
| Greg Coleman | K | 6' | 185 | 32 | | |
| #Dale Dawson | K | 6' | 213 | 22 | | 7 |
| Chuck Nelson | K | 6' | 175 | 27 | | 75 |
| Bucky Scribner | K | 6' | 205 | 27 | | |

**GREEN BAY PACKERS 5-9-1 Forrest Gregg**

| Scores of Each Game | | |
|---|---|---|
| 0 | L.A.RAIDERS | 20 |
| 17 | DENVER | *17 |
| 23 | Minnesota | 16 |
| 16 | DETROIT | 19 |
| 16 | PHILADELPHIA | 10 |
| 34 | Detroit | 33 |
| 17 | TAMPA BAY | 23 |
| 24 | CHICAGO | 26 |
| 13 | Seattle | 24 |
| 23 | Kansas City | 3 |
| 10 | Chicago | 23 |
| 12 | SAN FRANCISCO | 23 |
| 16 | MINNESOTA | 10 |
| 10 | N.Y.Giants | 20 |
| 24 | New Orleans | 33 |

* Overtime

| Use Name | Pos. | Hgt | Wgt | Age | Int | Pts |
|---|---|---|---|---|---|---|
| Steve Collier | OT | 6'7" | 342 | 27 | | |
| #Bob Gruber | OT | 6'5" | 280 | 29 | | |
| #Greg Jensen | OT | 6'3" | 266 | 25 | | |
| #Ed Konopasek | OT | 6'6" | 289 | 23 | | |
| Jim Meyer | OT | 6'5" | 290 | 24 | | |
| Tom Neville | OT-OG | 6'5" | 306 | 25 | | |
| Tommy Robison | OT | 6'4" | 290 | 25 | | |
| Ken Ruettgers | OT | 6'5" | 280 | 25 | | |
| Keith Uecker | OT-OG | 6'5" | 284 | 27 | | |
| Alan Veingrad | OT-OG | 6'5" | 277 | 24 | | |
| #Mike Estep | OG | 6'4" | 265 | 23 | | |
| Ron Hallstrom | OG | 6'6" | 290 | 28 | | |
| #Perry Hartnett | OG | 6'5" | 288 | 27 | | |
| #Jim Hobbins | OG | 6'6" | 275 | 23 | | |
| #John McGarry | OG | 6'6" | 288 | 23 | | |
| Rich Moran | OG | 6'3" | 275 | 25 | | |
| #Travis Simpson | OG | 6'3" | 272 | 23 | | |
| Mark Cannon | C | 6'3" | 258 | 25 | | |
| Bill Cherry | C-OG | 6'4" | 277 | 26 | | |
| #Vince Rafferty | C-OG | 6'4" | 285 | 26 | | |
| #Warren Bone | DE | 6'4" | 260 | 22 | | |
| Robert Brown | DE | 6'2" | 267 | 27 | | |
| Alphonso Carreker | DE | 6'6" | 271 | 25 | 1 | |
| Ezra Johnson | DE | 6'4" | 265 | 31 | | |
| #Tony Leiker | DE | 6'5" | 250 | 22 | | |
| #Sylvester McGrew | DE | 6'4" | 257 | 27 | | |
| #Carl Sullivan | DE | 6'4" | 248 | 25 | | |
| #Calvin Wallace | DE | 6'3" | 230 | 22 | | |
| Jerry Boyarsky | NT | 6'3" | 290 | 28 | | |
| Ross Browner | NT-DE | 6'3" | 265 | 33 | | |
| #David Caldwell | NT | 6'1" | 261 | 22 | | |
| #Jeff Drost | NT | 6'5" | 286 | 23 | | |
| David Logan | NT | 6'2" | 250 | 30 | | |
| #Stan Mataele | NT | 6'2" | 278 | 24 | | |
| #Vince Villanucci | NT | 6'2" | 265 | 23 | | |

| Use Name | Pos. | Hgt | Wgt | Age | Int | Pts |
|---|---|---|---|---|---|---|
| #Aric Anderson | LB | 6'2" | 220 | 22 | | |
| John Anderson | LB | 6'3" | 229 | 31 | 2 | |
| #Todd Auer | LB | 6'1" | 230 | 22 | | |
| #Putt Choate | LB | 6' | 225 | 30 | | |
| Burnell Dent | LB | 6'1" | 236 | 24 | | |
| John Dorsey | LB | 6'3" | 243 | 27 | | |
| Tim Harris | LB | 6'5" | 236 | 22 | | |
| Johnny Holland | LB | 6'2" | 221 | 22 | 2 | |
| #Kenneth Jordan | LB | 6'2" | 235 | 23 | | |
| #Rydell Malancon | LB | 6'2" | 230 | 25 | | |
| #James Melka | LB | 6'1" | 235 | 25 | 1 | |
| #John Miller | LB | 6'2" | 218 | 26 | | |
| #Ron Monaco | LB | 6'2" | 240 | 24 | | |
| Brent Moore | LB | 6'5" | 242 | 24 | | |
| Brian Noble | LB | 6'3" | 252 | 24 | 1 | |
| #John Pointer | LB | 6'2" | 225 | 29 | | |
| Scott Stephen | LB | 6'2" | 232 | 23 | | |
| Mike Weddington | LB | 6'4" | 245 | 26 | | |
| Clayton Weishuhn | LB | 6'2" | 218 | 27 | | |
| Dave Brown | DB | 6'1" | 197 | 34 | 3 | |
| #Chuck Compton | DB | 5'10" | 190 | 22 | | |
| #Tony Elliott | DB | 5'10" | 195 | 23 | | |
| Tiger Greene | DB | 6' | 194 | 25 | 1 | |
| #Anthony Harrison | DB | 6'1" | 195 | 21 | 1 | |
| Norman Johnson | DB | 5'10" | 183 | 23 | 1 | |
| Kenneth Johnson | DB | 6' | 185 | 23 | 1 | |
| #David King | DB | 5'9" | 175 | 24 | | |
| #Don King | DB | 6' | 200 | 23 | | |
| Mark Lee | DB | 5'11" | 189 | 29 | 1 | |
| Chris Mandeville | DB | 6'1" | 213 | 22 | | |
| #Von Mansfield | DB | 5'11" | 183 | 27 | 1 | |
| Jim Bob Morris | DB | 6'3" | 211 | 26 | 3 | |
| Mark Murphy | DB | 6'2" | 201 | 29 | | |
| #Lou Rash | DB | 5'9" | 190 | 27 | | |
| Ken Stills | DB | 5'10" | 187 | 23 | | |
| #Chuck Washington | DB | 5'11" | 186 | 23 | | |

Mossy Cade - Prison
David Greenwood - Groin Injury
Bobby Leopold - Back Injury
Elbert Watts - Knee Injury
Ben Thomas - Knee Injury
Eddie Lee Ivery - Back Injury

| Use Name | Pos. | Hgt | Wgt | Age | Int | Pts |
|---|---|---|---|---|---|---|
| #Willie Gillus | QB | 6'4" | 215 | 24 | | |
| Don Majkowski | QB | 6'2" | 197 | 23 | | |
| #John McCarthy | QB | 6'4" | 212 | 26 | | |
| Alan Risher | QB | 6'2" | 190 | 26 | | 6 |
| Randy Wright | QB | 6'2" | 203 | 26 | | |
| Kenneth Davis | HB | 5'10" | 209 | 25 | | 18 |
| Brent Fullwood | HB | 5'11" | 209 | 23 | | 30 |
| #Larry Morris | HB | 5'7" | 207 | 25 | | |
| #John Sterling | HB | 6'2" | 203 | 22 | | |
| Lavale Thomas | HB | 6' | 205 | 23 | | 6 |
| #Kevin Willhite | HB | 5'11" | 206 | 24 | | |
| Paul Ott Carruth | FB | 6'1" | 220 | 26 | | 24 |
| Jessie Clark | FB | 6' | 228 | 27 | | 6 |
| Kelly Cook | FB | 5'11" | 225 | 25 | | |
| #Jim Hargrove | FB | 6'2" | 232 | 28 | | 6 |
| #Tony Hunter | FB | 5'9" | 215 | 24 | | |
| #Freddie Parker | FB | 5'10" | 215 | 25 | | |
| #Lee Weigel | FB | 5'11" | 220 | 23 | | |
| Phillip Epps | WR | 5'10" | 165 | 27 | | 12 |
| #Derrick Harden | WR | 6'1" | 175 | 24 | | |
| Lee Morris | WR | 5'11" | 180 | 23 | | 6 |
| Frankie Neal | WR | 6'1" | 202 | 21 | | 18 |
| Keith Paskett | WR | 5'11" | 180 | 22 | | 6 |
| #Cornelius Redick | WR | 6' | 185 | 23 | | |
| Patrick Scott | WR | 5'10" | 170 | 22 | | |
| #Wes Smith | WR | 6' | 190 | 24 | | |
| Walter Stanley | WR | 5'9" | 179 | 24 | | 18 |
| #Kevin Fitzgerald | TE | 6'3" | 235 | 23 | | |
| Joey Hackett | TE | 6'5" | 267 | 28 | | |
| #Craig Jay | TE | 6'4" | 257 | 24 | | |
| #Don Summers | TE | 6'4" | 235 | 26 | | 6 |
| Ed West | TE | 6'1" | 243 | 26 | | 6 |
| Don Bracken | K | 6' | 211 | 25 | | |
| Al Del Greco (to STL) | K | 5'10" | 191 | 25 | | 46 |
| #Bill Renner | K | 6' | 198 | 28 | | |
| Max Zendejas | K | 5'11" | 184 | 23 | | 61 |

# - on the active roster for strike replacement games only

## MINNESOTA VIKINGS

### RUSHING

| Last Name | No. | Yds | Avg | TD |
|---|---|---|---|---|
| D. Nelson | 131 | 642 | 4.9 | 2 |
| Anderson | 68 | 319 | 4.7 | 2 |
| W. Wilson | 41 | 263 | 6.4 | 5 |
| Dozier | 69 | 257 | 3.7 | 5 |
| Fenney | 42 | 174 | 4.1 | 2 |
| Rice | 51 | 131 | 2.6 | 1 |
| Kramer | 10 | 44 | 4.4 | 2 |
| Brim | 2 | 36 | 18.0 | 1 |
| Adams | 11 | 31 | 2.8 | 0 |
| A. Walker | 5 | 24 | 4.8 | 0 |
| Womack | 9 | 20 | 2.2 | 0 |
| B. Wilson | 5 | 16 | 3.3 | 0 |
| J. Smith | 7 | 13 | 1.9 | 0 |
| Moore | 4 | 11 | 2.8 | 0 |
| Harrell | 5 | 8 | 1.6 | 0 |
| Frye | 4 | 4 | 1.0 | 0 |
| A. Thomas | 6 | 4 | 0.7 | 0 |
| S. Harris | 4 | 3 | 0.8 | 0 |
| Miller | 1 | -1 | -1.0 | 0 |
| Gustafson | 1 | -2 | -2.0 | 0 |
| Lewis | 5 | -7 | -1.4 | 0 |
| Scribner | 1 | -7 | -7.0 | 0 |

### RECEIVING

| Last Name | No. | Yds | Avg | TD |
|---|---|---|---|---|
| Carter | 38 | 922 | 24.3 | 7 |
| Jordan | 35 | 490 | 14.0 | 2 |
| D. Nelson | 26 | 129 | 5.0 | 0 |
| Lewis | 24 | 383 | 16.0 | 2 |
| Rice | 19 | 201 | 10.6 | 1 |
| Brim | 18 | 282 | 15.7 | 2 |
| Dozier | 12 | 89 | 7.4 | 2 |
| H. Jones | 7 | 189 | 27.0 | 2 |
| Anderson | 7 | 69 | 9.9 | 0 |
| Fenney | 7 | 27 | 3.9 | 0 |
| Womack | 5 | 46 | 9.2 | 1 |
| Gustafson | 4 | 55 | 13.8 | 0 |
| Finch | 3 | 54 | 18.0 | 0 |
| Parks | 3 | 46 | 15.3 | 0 |
| Frye | 3 | 25 | 8.3 | 0 |
| Harrell | 3 | 20 | 6.7 | 0 |
| Gillespie | 2 | 28 | 14.0 | 0 |
| Daugherty | 2 | 21 | 10.5 | 0 |
| S. Harris | 2 | 17 | 8.5 | 0 |
| Hilton | 2 | 16 | 8.0 | 0 |
| B. Wilson | 2 | 14 | 7.0 | 0 |
| A. Thomas | 2 | 13 | 6.5 | 0 |
| A. Walker | 2 | 3 | 1.5 | 0 |
| May | 1 | 22 | 22.0 | 0 |
| Schenk | 1 | 10 | 10.0 | 0 |
| Moore | 1 | 8 | 8.0 | 0 |
| Mularkey | 1 | 6 | 6.0 | 0 |

### PUNT RETURNS

| Last Name | No. | Yds | Avg | TD |
|---|---|---|---|---|
| Lewis | 22 | 275 | 12.5 | 1 |
| Bess | 7 | 86 | 12.3 | 0 |
| Richardson | 4 | 19 | 4.8 | 0 |
| Carter | 3 | 40 | 13.3 | 0 |

### KICKOFF RETURNS

| Last Name | No. | Yds | Avg | TD |
|---|---|---|---|---|
| Guggemos | 36 | 808 | 22.4 | 0 |
| Bess | 10 | 169 | 16.9 | 0 |
| D. Nelson | 7 | 164 | 23.4 | 0 |
| Womack | 5 | 77 | 15.4 | 0 |
| Richardson | 4 | 76 | 19.0 | 0 |
| Smith | 2 | 42 | 21.0 | 0 |
| Rice | 2 | 29 | 14.5 | 0 |
| Dozier | 2 | 23 | 11.5 | 0 |
| Mularkey | 1 | 16 | 16.0 | 0 |
| Hilton | 1 | 13 | 13.0 | 0 |
| Harrell | 1 | 4 | 4.0 | 0 |

### PASSING — PUNTING — KICKING

| PASSING | Att | Cmp | % | Yds | Yd/Att | TD | Int— | % | Rk |
|---|---|---|---|---|---|---|---|---|---|
| Wade Wilson | 264 | 140 | 53.0 | 2106 | 8.0 | 14 | 13— | 4.9 | 16 |
| Adams | 89 | 49 | 55.1 | 607 | | | 5— | 5.6 | |
| Kramer | 81 | 40 | 49.4 | 452 | 5.6 | 4 | 3— | 3.7 | |
| Gannon | 6 | 2 | 33.3 | 18 | 3.0 | 0 | 1— | 16.7 | |
| Miller | 6 | 1 | 16.7 | 2 | 0.3 | 0 | 1— | 16.7 | |

| PUNTING | No | Avg |
|---|---|---|
| Coleman | 46 | 38.8 |
| Scribner | 20 | 41.3 |
| Bruno | 13 | 35.7 |

| KICKING | XP | Att | % | FG | Att | % |
|---|---|---|---|---|---|---|
| C. Nelson | 36 | 37 | 97 | 13 | 24 | 54 |
| Dawson | 4 | 4 | 100 | 1 | 5 | 20 |

## GREEN BAY PACKERS

### RUSHING

| Last Name | No. | Yds | Avg | TD |
|---|---|---|---|---|
| Davis | 109 | 413 | 3.8 | 3 |
| Fullwood | 84 | 274 | 3.3 | 5 |
| Willhite | 53 | 251 | 4.7 | 0 |
| Clark | 56 | 211 | 3.8 | 0 |
| Carruth | 64 | 192 | 3.0 | 3 |
| Majkowski | 15 | 127 | 8.5 | 0 |
| Wright | 13 | 70 | 5.4 | 0 |
| Risher | 11 | 64 | 5.8 | 1 |
| Stanley | 4 | 38 | 9.5 | 0 |
| Hargrove | 11 | 38 | 3.5 | 1 |
| Parker | 8 | 33 | 4.1 | 0 |
| Weigel | 10 | 26 | 2.6 | 0 |
| Sterling | 5 | 20 | 4.0 | 0 |
| Larry Morris | 10 | 20 | 2.0 | 0 |
| Thomas | 5 | 19 | 3.8 | 0 |
| Cook | 2 | 3 | 1.5 | 0 |
| Lee Morris | 2 | 2 | 1.0 | 0 |
| Scott | 1 | 2 | 2.0 | 0 |
| Epps | 1 | 0 | 0.0 | 0 |
| Hunter | 1 | 0 | 0.0 | 0 |
| Neal | 1 | 0 | 0.0 | 0 |

### RECEIVING

| Last Name | No. | Yds | Avg | TD |
|---|---|---|---|---|
| Stanley | 38 | 672 | 17.7 | 3 |
| Neal | 36 | 420 | 11.7 | 3 |
| Epps | 34 | 516 | 15.2 | 2 |
| Clark | 22 | 119 | 5.4 | 1 |
| West | 19 | 261 | 13.7 | 1 |
| Lee Morris | 16 | 259 | 16.2 | 1 |
| Davis | 14 | 110 | 7.9 | 0 |
| Paskett | 12 | 188 | 15.7 | 1 |
| Carruth | 10 | 78 | 7.8 | 1 |
| Scott | 8 | 79 | 9.9 | 0 |
| Summers | 7 | 83 | 11.9 | 1 |
| Willhite | 6 | 37 | 6.2 | 0 |
| Parker | 3 | 22 | 7.3 | 0 |
| Thomas | 2 | 52 | 26.0 | 1 |
| Harden | 2 | 29 | 14.5 | 0 |
| Fullwood | 2 | 11 | 5.5 | 0 |
| Redick | 1 | 18 | 18.0 | 0 |
| Weigel | 1 | 17 | 17.0 | 0 |
| Hargrove | 1 | 6 | 6.0 | 0 |

### PUNT RETURNS

| Last Name | No. | Yds | Avg | TD |
|---|---|---|---|---|
| Stanley | 28 | 173 | 6.2 | 0 |
| Scott | 6 | 71 | 11.8 | 0 |
| Lee Morris | 1 | 1 | 1.0 | 0 |

### KICKOFF RETURNS

| Last Name | No. | Yds | Avg | TD |
|---|---|---|---|---|
| Fullwood | 24 | 510 | 21.3 | 0 |
| Cook | 10 | 147 | 14.7 | 0 |
| Lee Morris | 6 | 104 | 17.3 | 0 |
| Harden | 4 | 72 | 18.0 | 0 |
| Neal | 4 | 44 | 11.0 | 0 |
| Scott | 2 | 32 | 16.0 | 0 |
| Jefferson | 2 | 30 | 15.0 | 0 |
| Carruth | 1 | 8 | 8.0 | 0 |
| Weishuhn | 1 | 1 | 1.0 | 0 |
| Sterling | 1 | 0 | 0.0 | 0 |
| Willhite | 0 | 37 | 0 | 0 |

### PASSING — PUNTING — KICKING

| PASSING | Att | Cmp | % | Yds | Yd/Att | TD | Int— | % | Rk |
|---|---|---|---|---|---|---|---|---|---|
| Wright | 247 | 132 | 53.4 | 1507 | 6.1 | 6 | 11— | 4.5 | 26 |
| Majkowski | 127 | 55 | 43.3 | 875 | 6.9 | 5 | 3— | 2.4 | |
| Risher | 74 | 44 | 59.5 | 564 | 7.6 | 3 | 3— | 4.1 | |
| Gillus | 5 | 2 | 40.0 | 28 | 5.6 | 0 | 0— | 0.0 | |
| Carruth | 1 | 1 | 100 | 3 | 3.0 | 1 | 0— | 0.0 | |
| Neal | 1 | 0 | 0 | 0 | 0.0 | 0 | 0— | 0.0 | |

| PUNTING | No | Avg |
|---|---|---|
| Bracken | 73 | 40.4 |
| Renner | 20 | 35.6 |

| KICKING | XP | Att | % | FG | Att | % |
|---|---|---|---|---|---|---|
| Zendejas | 13 | 15 | 87 | 16 | 19 | 84 |
| Del Greco | 19 | 20 | 95 | 9 | 15 | 60 |

TAMPA BAY BUCCANEERS 4-11 Ray Perkins

| Scores of Each Game | | |
|---|---|---|
| 48 | ATLANTA | 10 |
| 3 | Chicago | 20 |
| 31 | Detroit | 27 |
| 13 | SAN DIEGO | 17 |
| 20 | MINNESOTA | 10 |
| 26 | CHICAGO | 27 |
| 23 | Green Bay | 17 |
| 28 | St.Louis | 31 |
| 17 | Minnesota | 23 |
| 10 | SAN FRANCISCO | 24 |
| 3 | L.A.Rams | 35 |
| 34 | New Orleans | 44 |
| 10 | DETROIT | 20 |
| 14 | ST.LOUIS | 31 |
| 6 | Indianapolis | 24 |

| Use Name | Pos. | Hgt | Wgt | Age | Int | Pts |
|---|---|---|---|---|---|---|
| Mark Cooper (from DEN) | OT-OG | 6'5" | 270 | 27 | | |
| #Dave Heffernan | OT | 6'4" | 255 | 24 | | |
| Ron Heller | OT | 6'6" | 280 | 25 | | |
| #Hoss Johnson | OT | 6'4" | 295 | 24 | | |
| J.D. Maarleveld | OT | 6'6" | 300 | 25 | | |
| Marvin Powell | OT | 6'5" | 270 | 32 | | |
| #Donald Pumphrey | OT | 6'4" | 275 | 23 | | |
| #Reggie Smith | OT | 6'5" | 295 | 25 | | |
| Rob Taylor | OT | 6'6" | 290 | 26 | | |
| Rufus Brown | OG | 6'2" | 295 | 25 | | |
| Conrad Goode | OG-OT | 6'6" | 285 | 25 | | |
| #Jim Huddleston | OG-OT | 6'4" | 280 | 24 | | |
| #John Hunt | OG | 6'5" | 245 | 24 | | |
| David Jordan | OG | 6'6" | 270 | 25 | | |
| Rick Mallory | OG | 6'2" | 265 | 26 | | |
| #Paul O'Connor | OG | 6'3" | 270 | 24 | | |
| George Yarno | OG | 6'2" | 265 | 30 | | |
| Randy Grimes | C | 6'4" | 270 | 27 | | |
| #Charles Pitcock | C | 6'4" | 272 | 29 | | |
| Dan Turk | C-OG | 6'4" | 260 | 25 | | |
| John Cannon | DE | 6'5" | 260 | 27 | | |
| #Walter Carter | DE | 6'4" | 276 | 29 | | |
| #Mike Clark | DE | 6'4" | 268 | 28 | | |
| #Roy Harris | DE | 6'2" | 260 | 26 | | |
| Ron Holmes | DE | 6'4" | 255 | 24 | | |
| Curt Jarvis | DE-DT | 6'2" | 266 | 22 | | |
| Kevin Kellin | DE | 6'6" | 265 | 27 | | |
| Tyrone Keys | DE | 6'7" | 270 | 27 | | |
| Tom McHale | DE | 6'4" | 275 | 24 | | |
| #Jim Ramey | DE | 6'4" | 275 | 30 | | |
| #Charles Riggins | DE | 6'5" | 295 | 25 | | |
| Harry Swayne | DE | 6'5" | 268 | 22 | | |
| #Calvin Turner | DE | 6'4" | 270 | 27 | | |
| #Fred Nordgren | NT | 6' | 240 | 27 | | |
| Dan Sileo | NT | 6'2" | 282 | 23 | | |
| Mike Stensrud | NT | 6'5" | 280 | 31 | | |

| Use Name | Pos. | Hgt | Wgt | Age | Int | Pts |
|---|---|---|---|---|---|---|
| Scot Brantley | LB | 6'1" | 230 | 29 | | |
| Jeff Davis | LB | 6' | 230 | 27 | | |
| Brian Gant | LB | 6' | 235 | 21 | 1 | |
| Don Graham | LB | 6'2" | 244 | 23 | | |
| #Cam Jacobs | LB | 6'2" | 230 | 25 | | |
| #Fred McCallister | LB | 6'1' | 250 | 25 | | |
| #Sankar Montoute | LB | 6'3" | 230 | 26 | 1 | |
| Winston Moss | LB | 6'3" | 235 | 21 | | 6 |
| Kevin Murphy | LB | 6'2" | 230 | 22 | | |
| #Leon Pennington | LB | 6'1" | 225 | 23 | | |
| Ervin Randle | LB | 6'1" | 250 | 24 | | |
| #Pat Teague | LB | 6'1" | 228 | 23 | | |
| #Miles Turpin | LB | 6'4" | 232 | 23 | | |
| Jackie Walker | LB | 6'5" | 245 | 24 | | |
| Chris Washington | LB | 6'4" | 230 | 25 | | |
| Don Anderson | DB | 5'10" | 195 | 24 | | |
| #Torin Clark | DB | 6'1" | 175 | 23 | | |
| #Ivory Curry | DB | 5'11" | 185 | 26 | | |
| Bobby Futrell | DB | 5'11" | 190 | 25 | 2 | |
| #Jeff George | DB | 6'1" | 185 | 28 | | |
| Sonny Gordon | DB | 5'11" | 192 | 22 | | |
| Ray Isom | DB | 5'9" | 190 | 21 | 2 | |
| Rod Jones | DB | 6' | 175 | 23 | 2 | |
| Bobby Kemp | DB | 6' | 190 | 28 | 1 | |
| #Tim King | DB | 6'2" | 190 | 27 | | |
| Vito McKeever | DB | 6' | 180 | 25 | | |
| #Lee Paige | DB | 6' | 197 | 26 | | |
| Ricky Reynolds | DB | 5'11" | 182 | 22 | | |
| Paul Tripoli | DB | 6' | 197 | 25 | 3 | 6 |
| #Kevin Walker | DB | 5'11" | 180 | 23 | 2 | 6 |
| Rick Woods | DB | 6' | 195 | 27 | 2 | |

Ricky Easmon - Knee Injury
Quentin Walker - Achilles Tendon Injury
Nathan Wonsley - Neck Injury

| Use Name | Pos. | Hgt | Wgt | Age | Int | Pts |
|---|---|---|---|---|---|---|
| Steve DeBerg | QB | 6'2" | 210 | 33 | | |
| #Mike Hold | QB | 6' | 190 | 24 | | |
| #John Reaves | QB | 6'3" | 210 | 37 | | |
| Vinny Testaverde | QB | 6'5" | 220 | 23 | | 6 |
| #Jim Zorn | QB | 6'2" | 200 | 34 | | |
| Steve Bartalo | HB | 5'9" | 200 | 23 | | 6 |
| #Greg Boone | HB | 5'9" | 196 | 25 | | |
| #Charles Gladman | HB | 5'11" | 205 | 21 | | |
| Bobby Howard | HB | 6' | 210 | 23 | | 6 |
| #Dan Land | HB | 6' | 190 | 22 | | |
| #Harold Ricks | HB | 5'10" | 200 | 24 | | 6 |
| Cliff Austin | FB | 6' | 213 | 27 | | 6 |
| Jeff Smith | FB | 5'9" | 204 | 25 | | 24 |
| #Derrick Thomas | FB | 6' | 232 | 22 | | |
| James Wilder | FB | 6'3" | 225 | 29 | | 6 |
| #Adrian Wright | FB | 6'1" | 230 | 25 | | 6 |
| Mark Carrier | WR | 6' | 182 | 21 | | 18 |
| Gerald Carter | WR | 6'1" | 190 | 30 | | 30 |
| #Steve Carter | WR | 5'10" | 170 | 24 | | |
| #Dwayne Dixon | WR | 6'1" | 203 | 25 | | |
| Phil Freeman | WR | 5'11" | 185 | 24 | | 12 |
| Bruce Hill | WR | 6' | 175 | 23 | | 12 |
| Derek Holloway | WR | 5'7" | 188 | 26 | | |
| #David Jackson | WR | 5'8" | 175 | 22 | | |
| Solomon Miller | WR | 6'1" | 185 | 22 | | |
| #Stanley Shakespeare | WR | 5'11" | 190 | 25 | | |
| #Eric Streater | WR | 5'11" | 165 | 23 | | 12 |
| Gene Taylor | WR | 6'2" | 189 | 24 | | |
| Herkie Walls | WR | 5'8" | 160 | 26 | | |
| Ron Hall | TE | 6'4" | 238 | 23 | | 6 |
| Steve Holloway | TE | 6'3" | 235 | 23 | | |
| Calvin Magee | TE | 6'3" | 240 | 24 | | 18 |
| #Jeff Modesitt | TE | 6'5" | 245 | 23 | | |
| #Arthur Wells | TE | 6'4" | 235 | 24 | | 6 |
| #Ray Criswell | K | 6' | 189 | 24 | | |
| Frank Garcia | K | 6' | 210 | 30 | | |
| Donald Ingwebuike | K | 5'9" | 185 | 26 | | 66 |
| #Van Tiffin (to MIA) | K | 5'9" | 155 | 21 | | 22 |

DETROIT LIONS 4-11 Darryl Rogers

| Scores of Each Game | | |
|---|---|---|
| 19 | Minnesota | 34 |
| 7 | L.A.Raiders | 27 |
| 27 | TAMPA BAY | 31 |
| 19 | Green Bay | *16 |
| 14 | SEATTLE | 37 |
| 33 | GREEN BAY | 34 |
| 0 | Denver | 34 |
| 27 | DALLAS | 17 |
| 13 | Washington | 20 |
| 10 | Chicago | 30 |
| 20 | KANSAS CITY | 27 |
| 16 | L.A.RAMS | 37 |
| 20 | Tampa Bay | 10 |
| 14 | MINNESOTA | 17 |
| 30 | Atlanta | 13 |

| Use Name | Pos. | Hgt | Wgt | Age | Int | Pts |
|---|---|---|---|---|---|---|
| Lomas Brown | OT | 6'4" | 282 | 24 | | |
| #Rick Johnson | OT | 6'6" | 255 | 23 | | |
| #Jerry Quaerna | OT | 6'6" | 275 | 23 | | |
| Harvey Salem | OT-OG | 6'6" | 285 | 26 | | |
| Eric Sanders | OT-OG | 6'7" | 280 | 28 | | |
| Rich Strenger | OT | 6'7" | 285 | 27 | | |
| #Jim Warne | OT | 6'7" | 315 | 22 | | |
| Steve Baack | OG | 6'4" | 265 | 26 | | |
| Scott Barrows | OG-C | 6'2" | 278 | 24 | | |
| Keith Dorney | OG | 6'5" | 285 | 29 | | |
| #Joe Felton | OG | 6'2" | 266 | 22 | | |
| #Chris Geile | OG | 6'4" | 305 | 23 | | |
| Kevin Glover | OG-C | 6'2" | 267 | 24 | | |
| #Paul Kiser | OG | 6'4" | 270 | 23 | | |
| Joe Milinichik | OG-OT | 6'5" | 275 | 24 | | |
| #Greg Orton | OG | 6'1" | 265 | 25 | | |
| #Patrick Cain | C-OG | 6'2" | 260 | 24 | | |
| Steve Mott | C | 6'3" | 270 | 26 | | |
| #Chuck Steele | C | 6'1" | 255 | 23 | | |
| #Bob Beemer | DE | 6'5" | 231 | 24 | | |
| #Charles Benson | DE | 6'3" | 267 | 26 | 1 | |
| Keith Ferguson | DE | 6'5" | 260 | 28 | | |
| William Gay | DE | 6'5" | 260 | 32 | | |
| Curtis Green | DE-NT | 6'3" | 265 | 30 | | |
| #George McDuffie | DE | 6'6" | 270 | 24 | | |
| Reggie Rogers | DE | 6'6" | 272 | 23 | | |
| Eric M.Williams | DE-NT | 6'4" | 280 | 25 | | |
| Jerry Ball | NT | 6'1" | 283 | 22 | | |
| #Jerome Davis | NT | 6'1" | 260 | 25 | | |
| #Jeff Kacmarek | NT | 6'2" | 240 | 24 | | |
| Dan Saleaumua | NT | 6' | 285 | 21 | | |
| #Stuart Tolle | NT | 6'3" | 245 | 25 | | |

| Use Name | Pos. | Hgt | Wgt | Age | Int | Pts |
|---|---|---|---|---|---|---|
| #Ernie Adams | LB | 6'2" | 226 | 28 | | |
| #Steve Boadway | LB | 6'4" | 240 | 24 | | |
| #Thomas Boyd | LB | 6'3" | 210 | 27 | | |
| Paul Butcher | LB | 6' | 219 | 23 | | |
| #Carl Carr | LB | 6'3" | 230 | 23 | | |
| Mike Cofer | LB | 6'5" | 245 | 27 | | |
| Dennis Gibson | LB | 6'2" | 240 | 23 | 1 | |
| #Mark Hicks | LB | 6'2" | 245 | 26 | | |
| George Jamison | LB | 6'1" | 226 | 24 | | 2 |
| #Angelo King | LB | 6'1" | 222 | 29 | | 6 |
| Danny Lockett | LB | 6'2" | 228 | 23 | | |
| Vernon Maxwell | LB | 6'2" | 235 | 25 | | |
| #Anthony Office | LB | 6'2" | 250 | 27 | | |
| Shelton Robinson | LB | 6'2" | 236 | 26 | | |
| #Tom Ross | LB | 6'5" | 225 | 28 | | |
| #Robert Thompson | LB | 6'3" | 225 | 27 | | |
| Jimmy Williams | LB | 6'3" | 230 | 26 | 2 | |
| John Bostic | DB | 5'10" | 178 | 24 | | |
| Raphel Cherry | DB | 6' | 194 | 25 | 1 | |
| #Dexter Clark | DB | 6' | 190 | 23 | | |
| #Creig Federico | DB | 6'2" | 205 | 24 | | |
| #Anthony Fields | DB | 6'1" | 192 | 23 | | |
| Duane Galloway | DB | 5'8" | 181 | 25 | 3 | |
| William Graham | DB | 5'11" | 191 | 27 | | |
| James Griffin | DB | 6'2" | 197 | 25 | 6 | |
| #Alvin Hall | DB | 5'10" | 184 | 29 | 1 | |
| #Maurice Harvey | DB | 5'10" | 190 | 31 | | |
| #Ivan Hicks | DB | 6'2" | 185 | 24 | | |
| #Steve Hirsch | DB | 6' | 195 | 25 | | |
| #Bob McDonough | DB | 6'1" | 170 | 24 | | |
| Bruce McNorton | DB | 5'11" | 175 | 28 | 3 | |
| Chris Sheffield (from PIT) | DB | 6'1" | 200 | 24 | 1 | |
| Ivory Sully | DB | 6' | 201 | 30 | | |
| Bobby Watkins | DB | 5'10" | 184 | 27 | | |
| Eric T. Williams | DB | 6'1' | 190 | 27 | | |

Donnie Elder - Hamstring Injury
Devon Mitchell - Knee Injury
Bob Cryder - Knee Injury
Leon Evans - Knee Injury
Dave D'Addio - Knee Injury
Eric Hipple - Thumb Injury

| Use Name | Pos. | Hgt | Wgt | Age | Int | Pts |
|---|---|---|---|---|---|---|
| Joe Ferguson | QB | 6'1" | 195 | 37 | | |
| #Brendon Folmer | QB | 6'1" | 200 | 23 | | |
| #Todd Hons | QB | 6'1" | 195 | 25 | | |
| Chuck Long | QB | 6'4" | 211 | 24 | | |
| Karl Bernard | HB | 5'11" | 205 | 22 | | 12 |
| Garry James | HB | 5'10" | 214 | 23 | | 24 |
| #Cleve Wester | HB | 5'8" | 188 | 23 | | |
| Butch Woolfolk | HB | 6'1" | 212 | 27 | | |
| #Tony Dollinger | FB | 5'11" | 205 | 24 | | |
| #Stan Edwards | FB | 6' | 214 | 28 | | |
| Gary Ellerson | FB | 5'11" | 220 | 24 | | 24 |
| James Jones | FB | 6'2" | 229 | 26 | | |
| #Nick Kowgios | FB | 6' | 216 | 24 | | |
| Tony Paige | FB | 5'10" | 230 | 24 | | |
| Scott Williams | FB | 6'2" | 234 | 25 | | 6 |
| Carl Bland | WR | 5'11" | 182 | 26 | | 6 |
| #Danny Bradley | WR | 5'9" | 175 | 24 | | 12 |
| Jeff Chadwick | WR | 6'3" | 190 | 26 | | |
| #Darrell Grymes | WR | 6'2" | 182 | 24 | | 12 |
| #Melvin Hoover | WR | 6' | 185 | 27 | | |
| #Gilvanni Johnson | WR | 6'1" | 195 | 23 | | |
| Gary Lee | WR | 6'1" | 202 | 22 | | |
| Pete Mandley | WR | 5'10" | 191 | 26 | | 42 |
| Mark Nichols | WR | 6'2" | 208 | 27 | | |
| Ricky Smith | WR-DB | 6' | 188 | 27 | 1 | 6 |
| #Eric Truvillion | WR | 6'4" | 205 | 28 | | 6 |
| #Jerry Diorio | TE | 6'3" | 245 | 25 | | |
| Vyto Kab | TE | 6'5" | 240 | 27 | | |
| Mark Lewis (from GB) | TE | 6'2" | 250 | 26 | | |
| Derrick Ramsey | TE | 6'5" | 235 | 30 | | |
| Rob Rubick | TE | 6'3" | 234 | 26 | | 6 |
| #Mark Wheeler | TE | 6'2" | 232 | 23 | | |
| #Mark Witte | TE | 6'3" | 240 | 27 | | |
| Jim Arnold | K | 6'3" | 211 | 26 | | |
| #Mike Black | K | 6'2" | 197 | 26 | | |
| Russell Erxleben | K | 6'4" | 238 | 30 | | |
| #Matt Kinzer | K | 6'3" | 225 | 24 | | |
| #John Misko | K | 6'5" | 207 | 32 | | |
| Eddie Murray | K | 5'10" | 175 | 31 | | 81 |
| #Mike Prindle | K | 5'9" | 160 | 23 | | 24 |

## Western Division

SAN FRANCISCO 49ERS 13-2 Bill Walsh

| Scores of Each Game | | |
|---|---|---|
| 17 | Pittsburgh | 30 |
| 27 | Cincinnati | 26 |
| 41 | N.Y.Giants | 21 |
| 25 | Atlanta | 17 |
| 34 | ST.LOUIS | 28 |
| 24 | New Orleans | 22 |
| 31 | L.A.Rams | 10 |
| 27 | HOUSTON | 20 |
| 24 | NEW ORLEANS | 26 |
| 24 | Tampa Bay | 10 |
| 38 | CLEVELAND | 24 |
| 23 | Green Bay | 12 |
| 41 | CHICAGO | 0 |
| 35 | ATLANTA | 7 |
| 48 | L.A.RAMS | 0 |

* Overtime

| Use Name | Pos. | Hgt | Wgt | Age | Int | Pts |
|---|---|---|---|---|---|---|
| Harris Barton | OT | 6'3" | 280 | 23 | | |
| #Mark Cochran | OT | 6'5" | 284 | 24 | | |
| Bruce Collie | OT-OG | 6'6" | 275 | 25 | | |
| Keith Fahnhorst | OT | 6'6" | 273 | 35 | | |
| #Gary Hoffman | OT | 6'7" | 285 | 25 | | |
| Bubba Paris | OT | 6'6" | 299 | 26 | | |
| Steve Wallace | OT | 6'5" | 276 | 22 | | |
| Jeff Bregel | OG | 6'4" | 280 | 23 | | |
| #Michael Durrette | OG | 6'4" | 280 | 30 | | |
| #Tracy Franz | OG | 6'5" | 270 | 27 | | |
| Guy McIntyre | OG | 6'3" | 264 | 26 | | |
| #Limbo Parks | OG | 6'3" | 265 | 22 | | |
| #Kevin Reach | OG-C | 6'3" | 270 | 23 | | |
| Jesse Sapolu | OG-C | 6'4" | 260 | 26 | | |
| Randy Cross | C-OG | 6'3" | 265 | 33 | | |
| #Tim Long | C | 6'6" | 295 | 24 | | |
| Fred Quillan | C | 6'5" | 266 | 31 | | |
| Chuck Thomas | C-OG | 6'3" | 280 | 26 | | |
| Dwaine Board | DE | 6'5" | 248 | 30 | | |
| #Glen Collins | DE | 6'6" | 270 | 28 | | |
| Kevin Fagan | DE | 6'4" | 260 | 24 | | |
| Clyde Glover | DE | 6'6" | 280 | 27 | | |
| Pete Kugler | DE-NT | 6'4" | 255 | 28 | | |
| #Greg Liter | DE | 6'6" | 275 | 23 | | |
| #Elston Ridgle | DE | 6'6" | 260 | 24 | | |
| Larry Roberts | DE | 6'3" | 264 | 24 | | |
| Jeff Stover | DE | 6'5" | 275 | 29 | | |
| Michael Carter | NT | 6'2" | 285 | 26 | | |
| #Joe Drake | NT | 6'2" | 290 | 24 | | |
| Doug Mikolas | NT | 6'1" | 270 | 25 | | |
| #Reno Patterson | NT | 6'3" | 275 | 26 | | |

| Use Name | Pos. | Hgt | Wgt | Age | Int | Pts |
|---|---|---|---|---|---|---|
| Darren Comeaux | LB | 6'1" | 227 | 27 | | |
| George Cooper | LB | 6'2" | 225 | 28 | | |
| Tom Cousineau | LB | 6'3" | 225 | 30 | 1 | |
| Kevin Dean | LB | 6'1" | 235 | 22 | | |
| Riki Ellison | LB | 6'2" | 225 | 27 | | |
| Jim Fahnhorst | LB | 6'4" | 230 | 28 | 1 | |
| #Ron Hadley | LB | 6'2" | 240 | 23 | | |
| Charles Haley | LB-DE | 6'5" | 230 | 23 | | |
| #James Johnson (to SD) | LB | 6'2" | 235 | 25 | | |
| #Jerry Keebie | LB | 6'3" | 230 | 24 | | |
| #Carl Keever | LB | 6'2" | 236 | 26 | | |
| #Mark Korff | LB | 6'1" | 230 | 24 | | |
| Milt McColl | LB | 6'6" | 230 | 28 | 1 | |
| Todd Shell | LB | 6'4" | 225 | 25 | 1 | |
| Keena Turner | LB | 6'2" | 222 | 28 | 1 | |
| Michael Walter | LB | 6'3" | 238 | 26 | 1 | |
| #John Butler | DB | 6'1" | 200 | 22 | | |
| #Matt Courtney | DB | 5'11" | 194 | 25 | 1 | |
| #John Faylor | DB | 6'1" | 197 | 24 | | |
| Jeff Fuller | DB-LB | 6'2" | 216 | 25 | | 8 |
| Don Griffin | DB | 6' | 176 | 23 | 5 | |
| Tom Holmoe | DB | 6'2" | 195 | 27 | 1 | |
| Ronnie Lott | DB | 6' | 200 | 28 | 5 | |
| #Derrick Martin | DB | 6' | 185 | 30 | 1 | |
| Tim McKyer | DB | 6' | 174 | 23 | 2 | |
| Dana McLemore | DB | 5'10" | 183 | 27 | 2 | 1 |
| Tory Nixon | DB | 5'11" | 186 | 25 | 1 | |
| #Darryl Pollard | DB | 5'11" | 187 | 23 | | |
| #Jonathan Shelley | DB | 6' | 176 | 23 | | |
| #John Sullivan | DB | 6'1" | 190 | 25 | | |
| Carlton Williamson | DB | 6' | 204 | 29 | 1 | |
| Eric Wright | DB | 6'1" | 185 | 28 | | |

Sean Thomas - Ankle Injury
Derrick Crawford - Foot Injury

| Use Name | Pos. | Hgt | Wgt | Age | Int | Pts |
|---|---|---|---|---|---|---|
| #Ed Blount | QB | 6' | 195 | 23 | | |
| Bob Gagliano | QB | 6'3" | 195 | 28 | | |
| Joe Montana | QB | 6'2" | 195 | 31 | | 6 |
| #Mark Stevens | QB | 6'1" | 190 | 25 | | 6 |
| Steve Young | QB | 6'2" | 200 | 25 | | 6 |
| #Ray Brown | HB | 5'9" | 185 | 22 | | |
| #Tony Cherry | HB | 5'7" | 187 | 24 | | 6 |
| Joe Cribbs | HB | 5'11" | 193 | 29 | | 12 |
| Doug DuBose | HB | 5'11" | 190 | 23 | | |
| Terrence Flagler | HB | 6' | 200 | 22 | | |
| Del Rodgers | HB | 5'10" | 203 | 27 | | 6 |
| Roger Craig | FB-HB | 6' | 224 | 27 | | 24 |
| #Andre Hardy | FB | 6'1" | 230 | 25 | | |
| Tom Rathman | FB | 6'1" | 232 | 24 | | 24 |
| Harry Sydney | FB | 6' | 217 | 28 | | |
| #Mike Varajon | FB | 6'1" | 232 | 23 | | |
| Dwight Clark | WR | 6'4" | 215 | 30 | | 30 |
| #Tony Gladney | WR | 6'3" | 200 | 23 | | |
| #Terry Greer | WR | 6'1" | 192 | 29 | | 6 |
| #Thomas Henley | WR | 5'11" | 185 | 22 | | |
| Ken Margerum | WR | 6' | 180 | 28 | | |
| #Carl Monroe | WR | 5'8" | 180 | 27 | | 6 |
| Jerry Rice | WR | 6'2" | 200 | 24 | | 138 |
| John Taylor | WR | 6'1" | 185 | 25 | | 6 |
| Mike Wilson | WR | 6'3" | 215 | 28 | | 30 |
| #Chris Dressel | TE | 6'4" | 240 | 26 | | |
| Russ Francis (to NE) | TE | 6'6" | 242 | 34 | | |
| John Frank | TE | 6'3" | 225 | 25 | | 18 |
| Ron Heller | TE | 6'3" | 235 | 23 | | 18 |
| Brent Jones | TE | 6'4" | 230 | 24 | | |
| #Mike Wells | TE | 6'3" | 233 | 25 | | 6 |
| #Jim Asmus | K | 6'2" | 195 | 24 | | |
| #Jeff Brockhaus | K | 6'2" | 212 | 28 | | 20 |
| Max Runager | K | 6'1" | 189 | 31 | | |
| Ray Wersching | K | 5'11" | 215 | 37 | | 83 |

\# - on the active roster for strike replacement games only

## TAMPA BAY BUCCANEERS

### RUSHING

| Last Name | No. | Yds | Avg | TD |
|---|---|---|---|---|
| Wilder | 106 | 488 | 4.6 | 0 |
| Smith | 100 | 309 | 3.1 | 2 |
| Wright | 37 | 112 | 3.0 | 1 |
| Howard | 30 | 100 | 3.3 | 1 |
| Ricks | 24 | 76 | 3.2 | 1 |
| Hold | 7 | 69 | 9.9 | 0 |
| Testaverde | 13 | 50 | 3.8 | 1 |
| Austin | 19 | 32 | 1.7 | 1 |
| Bartalo | 9 | 30 | 3.3 | 1 |
| Gladman | 12 | 29 | 2.4 | 0 |
| Land | 9 | 20 | 2.2 | 0 |
| Streater | 1 | 5 | 5.0 | 0 |
| Zord | 4 | 4 | 1.0 | 0 |
| Hill | 3 | 3 | 3.0 | 0 |
| Boone | 1 | 2 | 2.0 | 0 |
| Thomas | 1 | 2 | 2.0 | 0 |
| Freeman | 1 | 1 | 1.0 | 0 |
| Criswell | 1 | 0 | 0.0 | 0 |
| DeBerg | 8 | -8 | -1.0 | 0 |

### RECEIVING

| Last Name | No. | Yds | Avg | TD |
|---|---|---|---|---|
| Carter | 38 | 586 | 15.4 | 5 |
| Magee | 34 | 424 | 12.5 | 3 |
| Carrier | 26 | 423 | 16.3 | 3 |
| Hill | 23 | 403 | 17.5 | 2 |
| Wilder | 40 | 328 | 8.2 | 1 |
| Smith | 20 | 197 | 9.9 | 2 |
| Hall | 16 | 169 | 10.6 | 1 |
| Freeman | 8 | 141 | 17.6 | 2 |
| Holloway | 10 | 127 | 12.7 | 0 |
| Howard | 10 | 123 | 12.3 | 0 |
| Wright | 13 | 98 | 7.5 | 1 |
| Streater | 5 | 117 | 23.4 | 2 |
| Miller | 5 | 97 | 19.4 | 0 |
| Austin | 5 | 51 | 10.2 | 0 |
| Taylor | 2 | 21 | 10.5 | 0 |
| Gladman | 2 | 8 | 4.0 | 0 |
| Dixon | 1 | 18 | 18.0 | 0 |
| Walls | 1 | 13 | 13.0 | 0 |
| Carter | 1 | 12 | 12.0 | 0 |
| Ricks | 1 | 12 | 12.0 | 0 |
| Bartalo | 1 | 5 | 5.0 | 0 |

### PUNT RETURNS

| Last Name | No. | Yds | Avg | TD |
|---|---|---|---|---|
| Futrell | 24 | 213 | 8.9 | 0 |
| Walls | 4 | 12 | 3.0 | 0 |
| Curry | 3 | 32 | 10.7 | 0 |

### KICKOFF RETURNS

| Last Name | No. | Yds | Avg | TD |
|---|---|---|---|---|
| Futrell | 31 | 609 | 19.6 | 0 |
| Walls | 6 | 136 | 22.7 | 0 |
| Smith | 5 | 84 | 16.8 | 0 |
| Miller | 3 | 68 | 22.7 | 0 |
| Curry | 3 | 53 | 17.7 | 0 |
| Ricks | 1 | 26 | 26.0 | 0 |
| Wright | 1 | 17 | 17.0 | 0 |
| Gladman | 1 | 16 | 16.0 | 0 |
| Bartalo | 1 | 15 | 15.0 | 0 |
| Hill | 1 | 8 | 8.0 | 0 |
| Howard | 1 | 5 | 5.0 | 0 |
| Carrier | 1 | 0 | 0.0 | 0 |
| Walker | 1 | 0 | 0.0 | 0 |

### PASSING — PUNTING — KICKING

**PASSING**

| Last Name | Att | Cmp | % | Yds | Yd/Att | TD | Int— | % | Rk |
|---|---|---|---|---|---|---|---|---|---|
| DeBerg | 275 | 159 | 57.8 | 1891 | 6.9 | 14 | 7— | 2.5 | 9 |
| Testaverde | 165 | 71 | 43.0 | 1081 | 6.6 | 5 | 6— | 3.6 | |
| Zom | 36 | 20 | 55.6 | 199 | 5.5 | 0 | 2— | 4.3 | |
| Hold | 24 | 1 | 4.2 | | | | 1— | 4.2 | |
| Reaves | 16 | 6 | 37.5 | 83 | 5.2 | 1 | 0— | 0.0 | |
| Bartalo | 1 | 0 | 0.0 | 0 | 0.0 | 0 | 1— | 100 | |

**PUNTING**

| Last Name | No | Avg |
|---|---|---|
| Garcia | 62 | 38.9 |
| Criswell | 26 | 40.2 |

**KICKING**

| Last Name | XP | Att | % | FG | Att | % |
|---|---|---|---|---|---|---|
| Igwebuike | 24 | 26 | 92 | 14 | 18 | 78 |
| Tiffin | 11 | 11 | 100 | 5 | 7 | 71 |

## DETROIT LIONS

### RUSHING

| Last Name | No. | Yds | Avg | TD |
|---|---|---|---|---|
| Jones | 96 | 342 | 3.6 | 0 |
| James | 82 | 270 | 3.3 | 4 |
| Ellerson | 47 | 196 | 4.2 | 3 |
| Bernard | 45 | 187 | 4.2 | 2 |
| Wester | 33 | 113 | 3.4 | 0 |
| Woolfolk | 12 | 82 | 6.8 | 0 |
| Edwards | 32 | 69 | 2.2 | 0 |
| Long | 22 | 64 | 2.9 | 1 |
| Hons | 5 | 49 | 9.8 | 0 |
| Williams | 8 | 29 | 3.6 | 1 |
| Dollinger | 8 | 22 | 2.8 | 0 |
| Paige | 4 | 13 | 3.3 | 1 |
| Mandley | 1 | 3 | 3.0 | 0 |
| Kowgios | 1 | 2 | 2.0 | 0 |
| Black | 1 | 0 | 0.0 | 0 |
| Chadwick | 1 | -6 | -6.0 | 0 |

### RECEIVING

| Last Name | No. | Yds | Avg | TD |
|---|---|---|---|---|
| Mandley | 58 | 720 | 12.4 | 7 |
| Jones | 34 | 262 | 7.7 | 0 |
| Chadwick | 30 | 416 | 13.9 | 0 |
| Lee | 19 | 308 | 16.2 | 0 |
| Woolfolk | 19 | 166 | 8.7 | 0 |
| James | 16 | 215 | 13.4 | 0 |
| Rubick | 13 | 147 | 11.3 | 1 |
| Bernard | 13 | 91 | 7.0 | 0 |
| Truvillion | 10 | 184 | 18.4 | 1 |
| Grymes | 9 | 140 | 15.6 | 2 |
| Nichols | 7 | 87 | 12.4 | 0 |
| Edwards | 7 | 82 | 11.7 | 0 |
| Ellerson | 7 | 71 | 10.1 | 1 |
| Bradley | 7 | 50 | 7.1 | 2 |
| Kab | 5 | 54 | 10.8 | 0 |
| Dollinger | 3 | 25 | 8.3 | 0 |
| Witte | 1 | 19 | 19.0 | 0 |
| Wheeler | 2 | 17 | 8.5 | 0 |
| Williams | 4 | 16 | 4.0 | 1 |
| Bland | 2 | 14 | 7.0 | 1 |
| Paige | 2 | 1 | 0.5 | 0 |
| Kowgios | 1 | 3 | 3.0 | 0 |

### PUNT RETURNS

| Last Name | No. | Yds | Avg | TD |
|---|---|---|---|---|
| Mandley | 23 | 250 | 10.9 | 0 |
| Bradley | 12 | 53 | 4.4 | 0 |

### KICKOFF RETURNS

| Last Name | No. | Yds | Avg | TD |
|---|---|---|---|---|
| Lee | 32 | 719 | 22.5 | 0 |
| Woolfolk | 11 | 219 | 19.9 | 0 |
| Bradley | 9 | 188 | 20.9 | 0 |
| Hall | 6 | 105 | 17.5 | 0 |
| Bernard | 4 | 54 | 13.5 | 0 |
| Saleaumua | 3 | 57 | 19.0 | 0 |
| Bland | 2 | 44 | 22.0 | 0 |
| Ball | 2 | 23 | 11.5 | 0 |
| Glover | 1 | 19 | 19.0 | 0 |

### PASSING — PUNTING — KICKING

**PASSING**

| Last Name | Att | Cmp | % | Yds | Yd/Att | TD | Int— | % | Rk |
|---|---|---|---|---|---|---|---|---|---|
| Long | 416 | 232 | 55.8 | 2598 | 6.3 | 11 | 20— | 4.8 | 25 |
| Hons | 92 | 43 | 46.7 | 552 | 6.0 | 5 | 5— | 5.4 | |
| Jones | 1 | 0 | 0 | 0 | 0 | 0 | 1— | 100 | |

**PUNTING**

| Last Name | No | Avg |
|---|---|---|
| Arnold | 46 | 43.6 |
| Kinzer | 7 | 34.0 |
| Black | 6 | 38.8 |
| Misko | 6 | 40.3 |
| Murray | 4 | 38.8 |
| Erxleben | 1 | 52.0 |

**KICKING**

| Last Name | XP | Att | % | FG | Att | % |
|---|---|---|---|---|---|---|
| Murray | 21 | 21 | 100 | 20 | 32 | 63 |
| Prindle | 6 | 6 | 100 | 6 | 7 | 86 |

## SAN FRANCISCO 49ers

### RUSHING

| Last Name | No. | Yds | Avg | TD |
|---|---|---|---|---|
| Craig | 215 | 815 | 3.8 | 3 |
| Cribbs | 70 | 300 | 4.3 | 1 |
| Rathman | 62 | 257 | 4.1 | 1 |
| Young | 26 | 190 | 7.3 | 1 |
| Montana | 35 | 141 | 4.0 | 1 |
| Sydney | 29 | 125 | 4.3 | 0 |
| Varajon | 18 | 82 | 4.6 | 0 |
| Cherry | 13 | 65 | 5.0 | 1 |
| Rice | 8 | 51 | 6.4 | 1 |
| Hardy | 7 | 48 | 6.9 | 0 |
| Rodgers | 11 | 46 | 4.2 | 1 |
| Stevens | 10 | 45 | 4.5 | 1 |
| DuBose | 10 | 33 | 3.3 | 0 |
| Monroe | 2 | 26 | 13.0 | 0 |
| Flagler | 6 | 11 | 1.8 | 0 |
| Frank | 1 | 2 | 2.0 | 0 |
| Blount | 1 | 0 | 0.0 | 0 |

### RECEIVING

| Last Name | No. | Yds | Avg | TD |
|---|---|---|---|---|
| Craig | 66 | 492 | 7.5 | 1 |
| Rice | 65 | 1078 | 16.6 | 22 |
| Rathman | 30 | 329 | 11.0 | 3 |
| Wilson | 29 | 450 | 15.5 | 5 |
| Frank | 26 | 296 | 11.4 | 3 |
| Clark | 24 | 290 | 12.1 | 5 |
| Francis | 22 | 202 | 9.2 | 0 |
| Heller | 12 | 165 | 13.8 | 3 |
| Taylor | 9 | 151 | 16.8 | 0 |
| Cribbs | 9 | 70 | 7.8 | 0 |
| Greer | 6 | 111 | 18.5 | 1 |
| Gladney | 4 | 60 | 15.0 | 0 |
| DuBose | 4 | 37 | 9.3 | 0 |
| Monroe | 3 | 66 | 22.0 | 1 |
| Varajon | 3 | 25 | 8.3 | 0 |
| Rodgers | 2 | 45 | 22.5 | 0 |
| Jones | 2 | 35 | 17.5 | 0 |
| Flagler | 2 | 28 | 14.0 | 0 |
| Dressel | 1 | 8 | 8.0 | 0 |
| Hardy | 1 | 7 | 7.0 | 0 |
| Margerum | 1 | 7 | 7.0 | 0 |
| Sydney | 1 | 3 | 3.0 | 0 |

### PUNT RETURNS

| Last Name | No. | Yds | Avg | TD |
|---|---|---|---|---|
| McLemore | 21 | 265 | 12.6 | 1 |
| Griffin | 9 | 79 | 8.8 | 0 |
| Martin | 2 | 12 | 6.0 | 0 |
| Taylor | 1 | 9 | 9.0 | 0 |
| Pollard | 1 | 0 | 0.0 | 0 |

### KICKOFF RETURNS

| Last Name | No. | Yds | Avg | TD |
|---|---|---|---|---|
| Rodgers | 17 | 358 | 21.1 | 0 |
| Cribbs | 13 | 327 | 25.2 | 1 |
| Sydney | 12 | 243 | 20.3 | 0 |
| Monroe | 5 | 91 | 18.2 | 0 |
| Flagler | 3 | 31 | 10.3 | 0 |
| Rathman | 2 | 37 | 18.5 | 0 |
| McLemore | 1 | 23 | 23.0 | 0 |
| Henley | 1 | 21 | 21.0 | 0 |
| Varajon | 1 | 13 | 13.0 | 0 |

### PASSING — PUNTING — KICKING

**PASSING**

| Last Name | Att | Cmp | % | Yds | Yd/Att | TD | Int— | % | Rk |
|---|---|---|---|---|---|---|---|---|---|
| Montana | 398 | 266 | 66.8 | 3054 | 7.7 | 31 | 13— | 3.3 | 1 |
| Young | 69 | 37 | 53.6 | 570 | 8.3 | 10 | 0— | 0.0 | |
| Gagliano | 29 | 16 | 55.2 | 229 | 7.9 | 1 | 1— | 3.4 | |
| Stevens | 4 | 2 | 50.0 | 52 | 13.0 | 1 | 0— | 0.0 | |
| Sydney | 1 | 1 | 100.0 | 50 | 50.0 | 1 | 0— | 0.0 | |

**PUNTING**

| Last Name | No | Avg |
|---|---|---|
| Runager | 56 | 38.5 |
| Asmus | 12 | 32.0 |

**KICKING**

| Last Name | XP | Att | % | FG | Att | % |
|---|---|---|---|---|---|---|
| Wersching | 44 | 46 | 96 | 13 | 17 | 76 |
| Brockhaus | 11 | 13 | 85 | 3 | 6 | 50 |

## NEW ORLEANS SAINTS 12-3 Jim Mora

| Scores of Each Game | | |
|---|---|---|
| 28 | CLEVELAND | 21 |
| 17 | Philadelphia | 27 |
| 37 | L.A.RAMS | 10 |
| 19 | St.Louis | 24 |
| 19 | Chicago | 17 |
| 22 | SAN FRANCISCO | 24 |
| 38 | Atlanta | 0 |
| 31 | L.A.Rams | 14 |
| 26 | San Francisco | 24 |
| 23 | N.Y.GIANTS | 14 |
| 20 | Pittsburgh | 16 |
| 44 | TAMPA BAY | 34 |
| 24 | HOUSTON | 10 |
| 41 | Cincinnati | 24 |
| 33 | GREEN BAY | 24 |

| Use Name | Pos. | Hgt | Wgt | Age | Int | Pts |
|---|---|---|---|---|---|---|
| Stan Brock | OT | 6'6" | 292 | 29 | | |
| Bill Contz | OT | 6'5" | 270 | 26 | | |
| Jim Dombrowski | OT | 6'5" | 298 | 23 | | |
| Daren Gilbert | OT | 6'6" | 295 | 23 | | |
| #Walter Housman | OT-OG | 6'5" | 285 | 24 | | |
| Ken Kaplan | OT | 6'4" | 270 | 27 | | |
| James Campen | OG-C | 6'3" | 260 | 23 | | |
| Chuck Commiskey | OG | 6'4" | 290 | 29 | | |
| Brad Edelman | OG | 6'6" | 270 | 26 | | |
| #Bill Leach | OG-OT | 6'5" | 280 | 23 | | |
| #Greg Loberg | OG-OT | 6'4" | 264 | 25 | | |
| #Henry Thomas | OG | 6'2" | 275 | 23 | | |
| Steve Trapilo | OG | 6'5" | 281 | 22 | | |
| Joel Hilgenberg | C | 6'3" | 252 | 25 | | |
| #Phillip James | C-OG | 6'2" | 265 | 22 | | |
| Steve Korte | C | 6'2" | 260 | 27 | | |
| #Robert Brannon (from CLE) | DE | 6'7" | 245 | 26 | | |
| Bruce Clark | DE | 6'3" | 275 | 29 | | 2 |
| James Geathers | DE | 6'7" | 290 | 27 | | |
| Shawn Knight | DE | 6'6" | 288 | 23 | | |
| Patrick Swoopes | DE-NT | 6'4" | 280 | 23 | | |
| Frank Warren | DE | 6'4" | 290 | 27 | | |
| Jim Wilks | DE | 6'5" | 266 | 29 | | |
| #Kevin Young | DE | 6'5" | 265 | 22 | | |
| #Sheldon Andrus | NT | 6'1" | 270 | 24 | | |
| #Ted Elliott | NT | 6'6" | 275 | 22 | | |
| Tony Elliott | NT | 6'2" | 295 | 28 | | |
| #Joe DeForest | LB | 6'1" | 240 | 22 | | |
| #Keith Fourcade | LB | 5'11" | 225 | 25 | | |
| James Haynes | LB | 6'2" | 233 | 27 | | |
| Rickey Jackson | LB | 6'2" | 243 | 29 | 2 | |
| Vaughan Johnson | LB | 6'3" | 235 | 25 | 1 | |
| Joe Kohlbrand | LB | 6'4" | 242 | 24 | | |
| #Scott Leach | LB | 6'2" | 221 | 23 | 1 | |
| #Ken Marchiol | LB | 6'2" | 248 | 22 | | |
| #Larry McCoy | LB | 6'2" | 240 | 26 | | |
| Sam Mills | LB | 5'9" | 225 | 28 | | |
| #Bill Roe | LB | 6'3" | 235 | 29 | | |
| Pat Swilling | LB | 6'3" | 242 | 22 | 1 | |
| Alvin Toles | LB | 6'1" | 227 | 24 | | 6 |
| #Ron Weissennofer | LB | 6'3" | 235 | 23 | | |
| Michael Adams | DB | 5'10" | 195 | 23 | | |
| Gene Atkins | DB | 6'1" | 200 | 23 | 3 | |
| Toi Cook | DB | 5'11" | 188 | 22 | | |
| Antonio Gibson | DB | 6'3" | 204 | 25 | 1 | |
| Van Jakes | DB | 6' | 190 | 26 | 3 | |
| Milton Mack | DB | 5'11" | 182 | 23 | 4 | |
| Brett Maxie | DB | 6'2" | 194 | 25 | 3 | 2 |
| Johnnie Poe | DB | 6'1" | 194 | 28 | 1 | 6 |
| #John Sutton | DB | 6'1" | 195 | 30 | | |
| Reggie Sutton | DB | 5'10" | 180 | 22 | 5 | 6 |
| #Derrick Taylor | DB | 5'11" | 186 | 23 | | |
| #Junior Thurman | DB | 6' | 180 | 22 | | |
| #Darrel Toussaint | DB | 6' | 175 | 28 | | |
| Dave Waymer | DB | 6'1" | 188 | 29 | 5 | |
| #Scott Woemer | DB | 6' | 185 | 28 | | |
| John Fourcade | QB | 6'1" | 208 | 26 | | |
| Bobby Hebert | QB | 6'4" | 215 | 27 | | |
| #Kevin Ingram | QB | 6' | 178 | 25 | | |
| #Tim Riordan | QB | 6'1" | 185 | 27 | | |
| Dave Wilson | QB | 6'3" | 206 | 28 | | |
| #Dwight Beverly | HB | 5'11" | 205 | 25 | | 12 |
| Mel Gray | HB | 5'9" | 166 | 26 | | 6 |
| #Nate Johnson | HB | 6'2" | 224 | 23 | | |
| Rueben Mayes | HB | 5'11" | 200 | 24 | | 30 |
| #Vincent Alexander | FB | 5'10" | 205 | 23 | | 6 |
| Dalton Hilliard | FB | 5'8" | 204 | 23 | | 48 |
| #Garland Jean-Batiste | FB | 6' | 208 | 22 | | |
| Buford Jordan | FB | 6' | 223 | 25 | | 12 |
| #Jeff Rodenberger | FB | 6'3" | 235 | 27 | | |
| Barry Word | FB | 6'2" | 220 | 23 | | 12 |
| Robert Clark | WR | 5'11" | 175 | 22 | | |
| #Stacey Dawsey | WR | 5'9" | 154 | 21 | | |
| Herbert Harris | WR | 6'1" | 206 | 26 | | |
| #Vic Harrison | WR | 5'9" | 184 | 26 | | |
| Lonzell Hill | WR | 6' | 189 | 21 | | 12 |
| Mike Jones | WR | 5'11" | 183 | 27 | | 18 |
| Eric Martin | WR | 6'1" | 207 | 25 | | 42 |
| Mark Pattison | WR | 6'2" | 190 | 25 | | |
| #Curtland Thomas | WR | 6' | 183 | 25 | | |
| #Joe Thomas | WR | 5'11" | 175 | 25 | | |
| #Dwight Walker | WR | 5'10" | 190 | 28 | | |
| Cliff Benson (from WAS) | TE | 6'4" | 240 | 26 | | |
| Hoby Brenner | TE | 6'4" | 240 | 28 | | 12 |
| #Darren Gottschalk | TE | 6'4" | 225 | 22 | | |
| #Ken O'Neal | TE | 6'3" | 240 | 25 | | 6 |
| #Malcolm Scott | TE | 6'5" | 245 | 26 | | |
| John Tice | TE | 6'5" | 249 | 27 | | 36 |
| Mike Waters | TE | 6'2" | 230 | 25 | | 6 |
| Morten Andersen | K | 6'2" | 221 | 27 | | 121 |
| Tommy Barnhardt (to CHI) | K | 6'3" | 205 | 24 | | |
| #Mike Cofer | K | 6'1" | 197 | 27 | | 8 |
| Brian Hansen | K | 6'3" | 209 | 26 | | |
| #Florian Kempf | K | 5'9" | 170 | 31 | | 13 |

Hokie Gajan - Knee Injury

## LOS ANGELES RAMS 6-9 John Robinson

| Scores of Each Game | | |
|---|---|---|
| 16 | Houston | 20 |
| 16 | MINNESOTA | 21 |
| 10 | New Orleans | 37 |
| 31 | PITTSBURGH | 21 |
| 20 | Atlanta | 24 |
| 17 | Cleveland | 30 |
| 10 | SAN FRANCISCO | 31 |
| 14 | NEW ORLEANS | 31 |
| 27 | St.Louis | 24 |
| 30 | Washington | 26 |
| 35 | TAMPA BAY | 3 |
| 37 | Detroit | 16 |
| 33 | ATLANTA | 0 |
| 21 | DALLAS | 29 |
| 0 | San Francisco | 48 |

| Use Name | Pos. | Hgt | Wgt | Age | Int | Pts |
|---|---|---|---|---|---|---|
| Robert Cox | OT | 6'5" | 258 | 23 | | |
| #Hank Goebel | OT | 6'7" | 270 | 22 | | |
| Irv Pankey | OT | 6'4" | 280 | 29 | | |
| #Greg Sinnott | OT | 6'7" | 280 | 23 | | |
| Jackie Slater | OT | 6'4" | 275 | 33 | | |
| #Kelly Thomas | OT | 6'6" | 265 | 26 | | |
| Dennis Harah | OG | 6'5" | 265 | 35 | | |
| Duval Love | OG-OT | 6'3" | 280 | 24 | | |
| #Christopher Matau | OG | 6'3" | 310 | 23 | | |
| #Joe Murray | OG | 6'4" | 265 | 26 | | |
| Tom Newberry | OG | 6'2" | 279 | 24 | | |
| #Tom Taylor | OG | 6'3" | 265 | 24 | | |
| #Tom Cox | C | 6'5" | 260 | 24 | | |
| Tony Slaton | C | 6'3" | 265 | 26 | | |
| Doug Smith | C | 6'3" | 260 | 30 | | |
| #Navy Tuiasosopo | C | 6'2" | 285 | 22 | | |
| Reggie Doss | DE | 6'4" | 263 | 30 | | |
| #Dennis Edwards | DE | 6'4" | 253 | 27 | | |
| Donald Evans | DE | 6'2" | 262 | 23 | | |
| Gary Jeter | DE | 6'4" | 260 | 32 | | |
| Shawn Miller | DE | 6'4" | 255 | 26 | | |
| #Dave Purling | DE | 6'5" | 240 | 25 | | |
| Doug Reed | DE | 6'3" | 250 | 27 | | |
| Fred Stokes | DE | 6'3" | 253 | 23 | | |
| #Marion Knight | NT | 6'2" | 265 | 23 | | |
| Greg Meisner | NT | 6'3" | 265 | 28 | | |
| #Chris Pacheco | NT | 6' | 250 | 23 | | |
| Alvin Wright | NT-DE | 6'2" | 265 | 26 | | |
| #David Aupiu | LB | 6'2" | 235 | 26 | | |
| #Kyle Borland | LB | 6'3" | 232 | 26 | | |
| Richard Brown | LB | 6'3" | 240 | 21 | | |
| #Dan Clark | LB | 6'2" | 233 | 24 | | |
| Jim Collins | LB | 6'2" | 230 | 29 | | |
| #Rick DiBernardo | LB | 6'3" | 234 | 23 | | |
| Carl Ekern | LB | 6'3" | 222 | 33 | 1 | |
| Kevin Greene | LB | 6'3" | 238 | 25 | 1 | 6 |
| #Neil Hope | LB | 6'2" | 235 | 24 | | |
| Mark Jerue | LB | 6'3" | 229 | 27 | | |
| #Jim Kalafat | LB | 6' | 235 | 22 | | |
| Larry Kelm | LB | 6'4" | 226 | 22 | | |
| Mike McDonald | LB | 6'1" | 235 | 29 | | |
| Mel Owens | LB | 6'2" | 224 | 28 | 1 | |
| Norwood Vann | LB | 6'1" | 237 | 25 | | |
| #Cary Whittingham | LB | 6'2" | 230 | 23 | | |
| #Kyle Whittingham | LB | 6' | 232 | 27 | | |
| Mike Wilcher | LB | 6'3" | 235 | 27 | 1 | 6 |
| Nolan Cromwell | DB | 6'1" | 200 | 32 | 2 | |
| Jerry Gray | DB | 6' | 185 | 24 | 2 | 6 |
| #Darryl Hall | DB | 5'11" | 185 | 27 | | |
| Clifford Hicks | DB | 5'10" | 188 | 23 | 1 | |
| LeRoy Irvin | DB | 5'11" | 184 | 29 | 2 | 6 |
| Kirby Jackson | DB | 5'9" | 177 | 22 | 1 | 6 |
| #Holbert Johnson | DB | 5'9" | 180 | 27 | 1 | |
| Johnnie Johnson | DB | 6'1" | 183 | 30 | 1 | 6 |
| Vince Newsome | DB | 6'1" | 179 | 26 | | |
| #Reggie Richardson | DB | 6' | 180 | 24 | | |
| #Craig Rutledge | DB | 6' | 190 | 23 | | |
| Michael Stewart | DB | 5'11" | 195 | 22 | | 2 |
| Mickey Sutton | DB | 5'8" | 165 | 27 | 1 | |
| Frank Wattelet (from N.O.) | DB | 6' | 190 | 28 | | |
| #Greg Williamson | DB | 5'11" | 185 | 23 | 1 | |
| #Ed Zeman | DB | 6'1" | 195 | 23 | | |
| Steve Dils | QB | 6'1" | 191 | 31 | | |
| Jim Everett | QB | 6'5" | 212 | 24 | | 6 |
| Hugh Millen | QB | 6'5" | 216 | 23 | | |
| #Bernard Quarles | QB | 6'2" | 215 | 27 | | |
| Greg Bell (from BUF) | HB | 5'10" | 210 | 25 | | 6 |
| Jon Francis | HB | 5'11" | 207 | 23 | | 12 |
| Buford McGee | HB | 6' | 206 | 27 | | 6 |
| Tim Tyrrell | HB | 6'1" | 201 | 26 | | |
| Charles White | HB | 5'10" | 190 | 29 | | 66 |
| #Alonzo Williams | HB | 5'9" | 190 | 24 | | |
| #Cullen Bryant | FB | 6'1" | 244 | 36 | | |
| Owen Gill | FB | 6'1" | 236 | 25 | | |
| Mike Guman | FB | 6'2" | 218 | 29 | | 6 |
| #Casey Tiumalu | FB | 5'8" | 206 | 26 | | |
| Ron Brown | WR | 5'11" | 181 | 26 | | 18 |
| Henry Ellard | WR | 5'11" | 175 | 26 | | 18 |
| #Bernard Henry | WR | 6' | 187 | 27 | | |
| Kevin House | WR | 6'1" | 185 | 29 | | 6 |
| #Samuel Johnson | WR | 5'11" | 180 | 22 | | |
| #Stacey Mobley | WR | 5'8" | 170 | 21 | | 6 |
| Michael Young | WR | 6'1" | 185 | 25 | | 6 |
| Jon Embree | TE | 6'2" | 230 | 21 | | |
| David Hill | TE | 6'2" | 235 | 33 | | |
| Damone Johnson | TE | 6'4" | 230 | 25 | | 12 |
| James McDonald | TE | 6'5" | 245 | 26 | | 12 |
| #Malcolm Moore | TE | 6'3" | 240 | 26 | | 6 |
| #Don Noble | TE | 6'2" | 253 | 21 | | |
| #Joe Rose | TE | 6'3" | 230 | 30 | | |
| Dale Hatcher | K | 6'2" | 200 | 24 | | |
| Mike Lansford | K | 6' | 190 | 29 | | 87 |

Jeff Walker - Knee Injury

## ATLANTA FALCONS 3-12 Marion Campbell

| Scores of Each Game | | |
|---|---|---|
| 10 | Tampa Bay | 48 |
| 21 | WASHINGTON | 20 |
| 12 | PITTSBURGH | 28 |
| 17 | SAN FRANCISCO | 25 |
| 24 | L.A.RAMS | 20 |
| 33 | Houston | 37 |
| 0 | NEW ORLEANS | 38 |
| 3 | Cleveland | 38 |
| 10 | CINCINNATI | 16 |
| 13 | Minnesota | 24 |
| 21 | ST.LOUIS | 34 |
| 21 | Dallas | 10 |
| 0 | L.A.Rams | 33 |
| 7 | San Francisco | 35 |
| 13 | DETROIT | 30 |

* Overtime

| Use Name | Pos. | Hgt | Wgt | Age | Int | Pts |
|---|---|---|---|---|---|---|
| #Randy Clark | OT | 6'3" | 270 | 30 | | |
| Mike Kenn | OT | 6'7" | 277 | 31 | | |
| #Doug Mackie | OT | 6'4" | 280 | 29 | | |
| Brett Miller | OT | 6'7" | 300 | 28 | | |
| Leonard Mitchell | OT | 6'7" | 295 | 28 | | |
| #Greg Quick | OT | 6'4" | 280 | 23 | | |
| #Don Robinson | OT | 6'5" | 280 | 21 | | |
| Jamie Dukes | OG | 6'1" | 278 | 23 | | |
| Bill Fralic | OG | 6'5" | 280 | 24 | | |
| #Lawrence Jackson | OG | 6'1" | 275 | 23 | | |
| Jeff Kiewel | OG | 6'4" | 277 | 26 | | |
| #Pat Saindon | OG | 6'3" | 273 | 26 | | |
| John Scully | OG | 6'6" | 270 | 29 | | |
| Doug Barnett | C | 6'3" | 260 | 27 | | |
| #James Hendley | C | 6'3" | 257 | 22 | | |
| Wayne Radloff | C-OG | 6'5" | 277 | 26 | | |
| #Eric Wiegand | C | 6'2" | 260 | 23 | | |
| #Dwight Bingham | DE | 6'6" | 265 | 26 | | |
| Greg Brown | DE-DT | 6'5" | 265 | 30 | | |
| Rick Bryan | DE-DT | 6'4" | 265 | 25 | | |
| Mike Gann | DE | 6'5" | 275 | 23 | | |
| Dennis Harrison | DE | 6'8" | 280 | 31 | | |
| #Buddy Moor | DE | 6'5" | 250 | 28 | | 2 |
| Mark Mraz | DE | 6'4" | 255 | 22 | | |
| Andrew Provence | DE-DT | 6'3" | 267 | 26 | | |
| #Mark Studaway | DE | 6'3" | 275 | 26 | | |
| #Leonard Wingate | DE | 6'3" | 265 | 25 | | |
| #Mitchell Young | DE | 6'4" | 260 | 26 | | |
| Tony Casillas | NT-DT | 6'3" | 280 | 23 | | |
| #Dwaine Morris | NT-DE | 6'2" | 260 | 24 | | |
| #Emanuel Weaver | NT | 6'4" | 263 | 27 | | |
| #Ken Bowen | LB | 6'1" | 220 | 24 | | |
| Aaron Brown | LB | 6'2" | 238 | 31 | | |
| Joe Costello | LB | 6'3" | 244 | 27 | | |
| Buddy Curry | LB | 6'4" | 228 | 29 | | |
| #Paul Gray | LB | 6'2" | 231 | 25 | | |
| Tim Green | LB | 6'2" | 245 | 23 | | |
| #James Hall | LB | 6'1" | 252 | 24 | | |
| Rich Kraynak | LB | 6'1" | 230 | 26 | | |
| Jim Laughlin | LB | 6' | 222 | 29 | | |
| #Art Price | LB | 6'3" | 227 | 25 | | |
| John Rade | LB | 6'1" | 240 | 27 | | |
| Michael Reid | LB | 6'2" | 226 | 23 | | |
| #Herb Spencer | LB | 6'3" | 230 | 27 | | |
| Jessie Tuggle | LB | 5'11" | 225 | 22 | | |
| Reggie Wilkes | LB | 6'4" | 242 | 31 | | |
| Joel Williams | LB | 6'1" | 227 | 30 | | |
| James Britt | DB | 6' | 185 | 26 | 1 | |
| Bobby Butler | DB | 5'11" | 175 | 28 | 4 | |
| Scott Case | DB | 6' | 178 | 25 | 1 | |
| Wendell Cason | DB | 5'11" | 192 | 24 | | |
| Bret Clark | DB | 6'3" | 198 | 26 | | |
| David Croudip | DB | 5'8" | 183 | 28 | 2 | |
| Tim Gordon | DB | 6' | 188 | 22 | 2 | |
| #Charles Huff | DB | 5'11" | 195 | 24 | 2 | |
| #Lydell Jones | DB | 5'9" | 175 | 25 | | |
| #Leander Knight | DB | 6'1" | 193 | 24 | | |
| #Mike Lush | DB | 6'1" | 195 | 29 | | |
| Robert Moore | DB | 5'11" | 190 | 23 | 2 | 6 |
| #Gary Moss | DB | 5'10" | 192 | 23 | 1 | |
| #Jerome Norris | DB | 6' | 187 | 23 | | |
| Elbert Shelley | DB | 5'11" | 180 | 22 | | |
| #Struggy Smith | DB | 6'2" | 190 | 23 | | |
| #Leon Thomasson | DB | 5'11" | 190 | 24 | | |
| Jimmy Turner | DB | 5'11" | 187 | 28 | | |
| Brenard Wilson (from PHI) | DB | 6' | 185 | 32 | | |
| David Archer | QB | 6'2" | 208 | 25 | | |
| Scott Campbell | QB | 6' | 195 | 25 | | 12 |
| #Erik Kramer | QB | 6' | 192 | 22 | | |
| Chris Miller | QB | 6'2" | 195 | 22 | | |
| #Jeff Van Raaphorst | QB | 6'1" | 210 | 23 | | |
| #Jerry Butler | HB | 5'11" | 193 | 24 | | |
| Larry Emery | HB | 5'9" | 195 | 23 | | |
| Kenny Flowers | HB | 6' | 210 | 23 | | |
| Steve L. Griffin | HB | 5'10" | 185 | 22 | | |
| #Joe McIntosh | HB | 5'10" | 192 | 24 | | 6 |
| #Darryl Oliver | HB | 5'10" | 194 | 23 | | |
| Sylvester Stamps | HB | 5'7" | 171 | 26 | | 6 |
| #Rick Badanjek | FB | 5'8" | 217 | 25 | | 6 |
| #Norm Granger | FB | 5'9" | 222 | 25 | | |
| #Shelley Poole | FB | 5'7" | 219 | 22 | | |
| Gerald Riggs | FB | 6'1" | 232 | 26 | | 12 |
| John Settle | FB | 5'9" | 207 | 22 | | |
| #Michael Williams | FB | 6'2" | 218 | 26 | | |
| Stacey Bailey | WR | 6' | 157 | 27 | | 18 |
| #Milton Barney | WR | 5'9" | 156 | 23 | | 12 |
| Charlie Brown | WR | 5'10" | 184 | 28 | | |
| Floyd Dixon | WR | 5'9" | 170 | 23 | | 30 |
| #Leon Gonzalez | WR | 5'10" | 160 | 23 | | |
| #Steve B. Griffin | WR | 5'11" | 198 | 23 | | |
| #Kwante Hampton | WR | 6'1" | 182 | 23 | | |
| Billy Johnson | WR | 5'9" | 172 | 35 | | |
| Aubrey Matthews | WR | 5'7" | 165 | 24 | | 18 |
| #James Shibest | WR | 5'10" | 187 | 22 | | |
| #Lenny Taylor | WR | 5'10" | 183 | 26 | | 6 |
| #Sylvester Byrd | TE | 6'2" | 225 | 24 | | |
| Arthur Cox | TE | 6'2" | 262 | 26 | | |
| #John Evans | TE | 6'2" | 243 | 23 | | |
| #John Kamana | TE | 6' | 230 | 26 | | 6 |
| Ron Middleton | TE | 6'2" | 252 | 22 | | |
| Dan Sharp | TE | 6'2" | 235 | 25 | | |
| Ken Whisenhunt | TE | 6'3" | 240 | 25 | | 6 |
| #Geno Zimmerlink | TE | 6'3" | 222 | 24 | | |
| #Louis Berry | K | 6' | 193 | 22 | | |
| #Greg Davis | K | 5'11" | 197 | 21 | | 15 |
| Rick Donnelly | K | 6' | 190 | 25 | | |
| Mick Luckhurst | K | 6' | 183 | 29 | | 44 |
| #John Starnes | K | 6'3" | 185 | 24 | | |

Joey Jones - Knee Injury

\# - on the active roster for strike replacement games only

## NEW ORLEANS SAINTS

### RUSHING

| Last Name | No. | Yds | Avg | TD |
|---|---|---|---|---|
| Mayes | 243 | 917 | 3.8 | 5 |
| Hilliard | 123 | 508 | 4.1 | 7 |
| Beverly | 62 | 217 | 3.5 | 2 |
| J. Fourcade | 19 | 134 | 7.1 | 0 |
| Word | 36 | 133 | 3.7 | 2 |
| Hebert | 13 | 95 | 7.3 | 0 |
| Alexander | 21 | 71 | 3.4 | 1 |
| Gray | 8 | 37 | 4.6 | 1 |
| Jordan | 12 | 36 | 3.0 | 2 |
| Rodenberger | 17 | 35 | 2.1 | 0 |
| Jean-Batiste | 8 | 18 | 2.3 | 0 |
| Ingram | 2 | 14 | 7.0 | 0 |
| Riordan | 1 | 3 | 3.0 | 0 |
| Hansen | 2 | -6 | -3.0 | 0 |
| Hill | 1 | -9 | -9.0 | 0 |
| Barnhardt | 1 | -13 | -13.0 | 0 |

### RECEIVING

| Last Name | No. | Yds | Avg | TD |
|---|---|---|---|---|
| Martin | 44 | 778 | 17.7 | 7 |
| M. Jones | 27 | 420 | 15.6 | 3 |
| Hilliard | 23 | 264 | 11.5 | 1 |
| Brenner | 20 | 280 | 14.0 | 2 |
| Hill | 19 | 322 | 16.9 | 2 |
| Tice | 16 | 181 | 11.3 | 6 |
| Mayes | 15 | 68 | 4.5 | 0 |
| Dawsey | 13 | 142 | 10.9 | 0 |
| Pattison | 9 | 132 | 14.7 | 0 |
| Word | 6 | 54 | 9.0 | 0 |
| Scott | 6 | 35 | 5.8 | 0 |
| Gray | 6 | 30 | 5.0 | 0 |
| Waters | 5 | 140 | 28 | 1 |
| Clark | 3 | 38 | 12.7 | 0 |
| O'Neal | 3 | 10 | 3.3 | 1 |
| Rodenberger | 2 | 17 | 8.5 | 0 |
| Alexander | 2 | 15 | 7.5 | 0 |
| Walker | 2 | 15 | 7.5 | 0 |
| Jordan | 2 | 13 | 6.5 | 0 |
| Benson | 2 | 11 | 5.5 | 0 |
| C. Thomas | 1 | 14 | 14.0 | 0 |
| Beverly | 1 | 8 | 8.0 | 0 |

### PUNT RETURNS

| Last Name | No. | Yds | Avg | TD |
|---|---|---|---|---|
| Gray | 24 | 352 | 14.7 | 0 |
| Martin | 14 | 88 | 6.3 | 0 |
| Jordan | 1 | 13 | 13.0 | 0 |
| Maxie | 1 | 12 | 12.0 | 0 |
| Cook | 1 | 3 | 3.0 | 0 |

### KICKOFF RETURNS

| Last Name | No. | Yds | Avg | TD |
|---|---|---|---|---|
| Gray | 30 | 636 | 21.2 | 0 |
| Hilliard | 10 | 248 | 24.8 | 0 |
| Adams | 4 | 52 | 13.0 | 0 |
| Word | 3 | 100 | 33.3 | 0 |
| Beverly | 3 | 46 | 15.3 | 0 |
| Jordan | 2 | 28 | 14.0 | 0 |
| Martin | 1 | 15 | 15.0 | 0 |
| Brock | 1 | 11 | 11.0 | 0 |
| Thomas | 1 | 11 | 11.0 | 0 |

### PASSING — PUNTING — KICKING

| PASSING | Att | Cmp | % | Yds | Yd/Att | TD | Int— | % | RK |
|---|---|---|---|---|---|---|---|---|---|
| Hebert | 294 | 164 | 55.8 | 2119 | 7.2 | 15 | 9— | 3.1 | 14 |
| J. Fourcade | 89 | 48 | 53.9 | 597 | 6.7 | 4 | — | 3.4 | |
| Wilson | 24 | 13 | 54.2 | 243 | 10.1 | 2 | 0— | 0.0 | |
| Ingram | 2 | 1 | 50.0 | 5 | 2.5 | 1 | 0— | 0.0 | |
| Hilliard | 1 | 1 | 100.0 | 23 | 23.0 | 0 | 0— | 0.0 | |
| Riordan | 1 | 0 | 0.0 | 0 | 0.0 | 0 | 0— | 0.0 | |

| PUNTING | No | Avg |
|---|---|---|
| Hansen | 52 | 40.5 |
| Barnhardt | 17 | 42.3 |

| KICKING | XP | Att | % | FG | Att | % |
|---|---|---|---|---|---|---|
| Andersen | 37 | 37 | 100 | 28 | 36 | 78 |
| Cofer | 5 | 7 | 71 | 1 | 1 | 100 |
| Kempf | 1 | 1 | 100 | 4 | 5 | 80 |

## LOS ANGELES RAMS

### RUSHING

| Last Name | No. | Yds | Avg | TD |
|---|---|---|---|---|
| White | 324 | 1374 | 4.2 | 11 |
| Francis | 35 | 138 | 3.9 | 0 |
| Guman | 36 | 98 | 2.7 | 1 |
| Bell | 22 | 86 | 3.9 | 0 |
| Everett | 18 | 83 | 4.6 | 1 |
| Tyrrell | 11 | 44 | 4.0 | 0 |
| Ro. Brown | 2 | 22 | 11.0 | 0 |
| Evans | 3 | 10 | 3.3 | 0 |
| Williams | 2 | 9 | 4.5 | 0 |
| Quarles | 1 | 8 | 8.0 | 0 |
| McGee | 3 | 6 | 2.0 | 1 |
| Ellard | 1 | 4 | 4.0 | 0 |
| Bryant | 1 | 2 | 2.0 | 0 |
| Dils | 7 | -4 | -0.6 | 0 |

### RECEIVING

| Last Name | No. | Yds | Avg | TD |
|---|---|---|---|---|
| Ellard | 51 | 799 | 15.7 | 3 |
| Ro. Brown | 26 | 521 | 20.0 | 2 |
| White | 23 | 121 | 5.3 | 0 |
| Guman | 22 | 263 | 12.0 | 0 |
| D. Johnson | 21 | 198 | 9.4 | 2 |
| Hill | 11 | 105 | 9.5 | 0 |
| Bell | 9 | 96 | 10.7 | 1 |
| Mobley | 8 | 107 | 13.4 | 1 |
| Francis | 8 | 38 | 4.8 | 2 |
| McGee | 7 | 40 | 5.7 | 0 |
| Moore | 6 | 107 | 17.8 | 1 |
| House | 6 | 63 | 10.5 | 1 |
| Tyrrell | 6 | 59 | 9.8 | 0 |
| Young | 4 | 56 | 14.0 | 1 |
| McDonald | 4 | 31 | 7.8 | 2 |
| Smith | 3 | 95 | 31.7 | 0 |
| Henry | 1 | 13 | 13.0 | 0 |

### PUNT RETURNS

| Last Name | No. | Yds | Avg | TD |
|---|---|---|---|---|
| Ellard | 15 | 107 | 7.1 | 0 |
| Hicks | 13 | 110 | 8.5 | 0 |
| S. Johnson | 4 | -4 | -1.0 | 0 |
| Rutledge | 3 | 10 | 3.3 | 0 |
| Smith | 2 | 5 | 2.5 | 0 |
| Mobley | 1 | 12 | 12.0 | 0 |
| J. Johnson | 1 | 5 | 5.0 | 0 |
| Irvin | 1 | 0 | 0.0 | 0 |

### KICKOFF RETURNS

| Last Name | No. | Yds | Avg | TD |
|---|---|---|---|---|
| Ro. Brown | 27 | 581 | 21.5 | 1 |
| Tiumalu | 8 | 158 | 19.8 | 0 |
| Tyrrell | 6 | 116 | 19.3 | 0 |
| Williams | 5 | 114 | 22.8 | 0 |
| Hicks | 4 | 119 | 29.8 | 0 |
| White | 3 | 73 | 24.3 | 0 |
| McDonald | 3 | 31 | 10.3 | 0 |
| Sutton | 2 | 37 | 18.5 | 0 |
| Guman | 2 | 18 | 9.0 | 0 |
| Ri. Brown | 1 | 15 | 15.0 | 0 |
| Cox | 1 | 12 | 12.0 | 0 |
| Ellard | 1 | 8 | 8.0 | 0 |

### PASSING — PUNTING — KICKING

| PASSING | Att | Cmp | % | Yds | Yd/Att | TD | Int— | % | RK |
|---|---|---|---|---|---|---|---|---|---|
| Everett | 302 | 162 | 53.6 | 2064 | 6.8 | 10 | 13— | 4.3 | 23 |
| Dils | 114 | 56 | 49.1 | 646 | 5.7 | 5 | 4— | 3.5 | |
| Quarles | 3 | 1 | 33.3 | 40 | 13.3 | 1 | 1— | 33.3 | |
| Millen | 1 | 1 | 100.0 | 0 | 0.0 | 0 | 0— | 0.0 | |

| PUNTING | No | Avg |
|---|---|---|
| Hatcher | 77 | 40.8 |

| KICKING | XP | Att | % | FG | Att | % |
|---|---|---|---|---|---|---|
| Lansford | 36 | 38 | 95 | 17 | 21 | 81 |

## ATLANTA FALCONS

### RUSHING

| Last Name | No. | Yds | Avg | TD |
|---|---|---|---|---|
| Riggs | 203 | 875 | 4.3 | 2 |
| Campbell | 21 | 102 | 4.9 | 2 |
| Badanjek | 29 | 87 | 3.0 | 1 |
| Settle | 19 | 72 | 3.8 | 0 |
| Flowers | 14 | 61 | 4.4 | 0 |
| M. Williams | 14 | 49 | 3.5 | 0 |
| C. Miller | 4 | 21 | 5.3 | 0 |
| Granger | 6 | 12 | 2.0 | 0 |
| McIntosh | 5 | 11 | 2.2 | 0 |
| Kramer | 2 | 10 | 5.0 | 0 |
| Archer | 2 | 8 | 4.0 | 0 |
| Stamps | 1 | 6 | 6.0 | 0 |
| Van Raaphorst | 1 | 6 | 6.0 | 0 |
| Emery | 1 | 5 | 5.0 | 0 |
| J. Butler | 1 | 1 | 1.0 | 0 |
| Oilver | 1 | 0 | 0.0 | 0 |
| Griffin | 1 | -2 | -2.0 | 0 |
| Dixon | 3 | -3 | -1.0 | 0 |
| Matthews | 1 | -4 | -4.0 | 0 |
| Donnelley | 3 | -6 | -2.0 | 0 |
| Taylor | 1 | -13 | -13.0 | 0 |

### RECEIVING

| Last Name | No. | Yds | Avg | TD |
|---|---|---|---|---|
| Dixon | 36 | 600 | 16.7 | 5 |
| Matthews | 32 | 537 | 16.8 | 3 |
| Riggs | 25 | 199 | 8.0 | 0 |
| Bailey | 20 | 325 | 16.3 | 3 |
| Whisenhunt | 17 | 145 | 8.5 | 1 |
| Taylor | 12 | 171 | 14.3 | 1 |
| Settle | 11 | 153 | 13.9 | 0 |
| Cox | 11 | 101 | 9.2 | 0 |
| Barney | 10 | 175 | 17.5 | 2 |
| M. Williams | 9 | 70 | 7.8 | 0 |
| Johnson | 8 | 84 | 10.5 | 0 |
| Byrd | 7 | 125 | 17.9 | 0 |
| Kamana | 7 | 51 | 7.3 | 1 |
| Flowers | 7 | 50 | 7.1 | 0 |
| Badanjek | 6 | 35 | 5.8 | 0 |
| C. Brown | 5 | 103 | 20.6 | 0 |
| Emery | 5 | 31 | 6.2 | 0 |
| Stamps | 4 | 40 | 10.0 | 0 |
| Gonzalez | 3 | 40 | 13.3 | 0 |
| McIntosh | 3 | 15 | 5.0 | 1 |
| Granger | 2 | 34 | 17.0 | 0 |
| J. Butler | 2 | 7 | 3.5 | 0 |
| Sharp | 2 | 6 | 3.0 | 0 |
| Evans | 1 | 8 | 8.0 | 0 |
| Oliver | 1 | 2 | 2.0 | 0 |
| Middleton | 1 | 1 | 1.0 | 0 |

### PUNT RETURNS

| Last Name | No. | Yds | Avg | TD |
|---|---|---|---|---|
| Johnson | 21 | 168 | 8.0 | 0 |
| Barney | 5 | 28 | 5.6 | 0 |
| Moss | 3 | 15 | 5.0 | 0 |
| J. Butler | 2 | 10 | 5.0 | 0 |

### KICKOFF RETURNS

| Last Name | No. | Yds | Avg | TD |
|---|---|---|---|---|
| Stamps | 24 | 660 | 27.5 | 1 |
| Emery | 21 | 440 | 21.0 | 0 |
| Settle | 10 | 158 | 15.8 | 0 |
| Oliver | 5 | 90 | 18.0 | 0 |
| Flowers | 4 | 72 | 18.0 | 0 |
| McIntosh | 3 | 108 | 36.0 | 0 |
| Babanjek | 2 | 27 | 13.5 | 0 |
| M. Williams | 2 | 15 | 7.5 | 0 |
| Moss | 1 | 23 | 23.0 | 0 |
| Griffin | 1 | 21 | 21.0 | 0 |
| Croudip | 1 | 18 | 18.0 | 0 |
| J. Butler | 1 | 13 | 13.0 | 0 |
| Cox | 1 | 11 | 11.0 | 0 |
| Sharp | 1 | 11 | 11.0 | 0 |

### PASSING — PUNTING — KICKING

| PASSING | Att | Cmp | % | Yds | Yd/Att | TD | Int— | % | RK |
|---|---|---|---|---|---|---|---|---|---|
| Campbell | 260 | 136 | 52.3 | 1728 | 6.7 | 11 | 14— | 5.4 | 24 |
| Kramer | 92 | 45 | 48.9 | 559 | 6.1 | 4 | 5— | 5.4 | |
| C. Miller | 92 | 39 | 42.4 | 552 | 6.0 | 1 | 9— | 9.8 | |
| Van Raaphorst | 34 | 18 | 52.9 | 174 | 5.1 | 1 | 2— | 5.9 | |
| Archer | 23 | 9 | 39.1 | 95 | 4.1 | 0 | 8— | 8.7 | |

| PUNTING | No | Avg |
|---|---|---|
| Donnelly | 63 | 42.7 |
| Berry | 7 | 36.9 |
| Starnes | 6 | 33.8 |
| Davis | 6 | 31.8 |
| Luckhurst | 1 | 37.0 |

| KICKING | XP | Att | % | FG | Att | % |
|---|---|---|---|---|---|---|
| Luckhurst | 17 | 17 | 100 | 9 | 13 | 69 |

The A.F.C. provided the best possible defense against fan backlash after the strike by putting on tight races in all three divisions. In the East, four of the five teams had a chance for at least a wild-card playoff berth until the last two weeks of the season. Cleveland was clearly the class of the Central Division, but Houston stayed in the race, and even Pittsburgh could have made the playoffs had they beaten the Browns in the season's final game. The West saw San Diego race to the front, only to be overtaken by Denver and Seattle. After being accused of falling behind the N.F.C. in quality for several years — underscored by one-sided Super Bowl losses — the A.F.C. improved its image by nearly splitting interconference play with 22 wins, 23 losses and one tie.

## EASTERN DIVISION

**Indianapolis Colts** — The Colt defense improved by seven points a game, largely through the efforts of linebackers Duane Bickett and Johnie Cooks and some exotic sets by defensive coordinator George Hill. Suddenly finding themselves with a chance for the playoffs, the Colts made the "deal of the century," sending unsigned No. 1 draft choice Cornelius Bennett to Buffalo and a gaggle of high draft choices to the Rams to get the unhappy running machine, Eric Dickerson. After being cheered up by a new contract, Dickerson joined the club on Halloween and did what was expected — ran for an AFC-leading 1,011 yards behind a powerful offensive line led by center Ray Donaldson. Perhaps equally important, the trade proved to the other Colt players that the front office sincerely wanted a winner. Despite another injury-plagued season for quarterback Gary Hogeboom, the Colts, who had seemed hopeless until the last three games in '86, barged into the '87 playoffs.

**Miami Dolphins** — The Dolphins had a new home, Joe Robbie Stadium, and an old problem, no defense. They finished 26th overall in that department, wasting another typical year by quarterback Dan Marino (3,245 yards and 26 touchdowns). Although wide receivers Mark Duper and Mark Clayton slumped by nearly 50 receptions from the previous year, rookie running back Troy Stradford turned out to be an excellent receiver. Stradford also put some punch in the Miami rushing attack (619 yards), but it still ranked only 23rd. Nevertheless, Marino kept the team in the playoff picture right up to the end.

**New England Patriots** — The Pats were inconsistent most of the season and missed the playoffs for the first time in head coach Raymond Berry's three-year regime. A continuing question of whether the Sullivan family would — or could — sell the team didn't help matters. None of the blame was placed on quarterback Steve Grogan, who finally received some credit for the leadership and clutch play he'd shown for years. The insertion of four rookies into the starting offense for the final three games brought some improvement to what had been a nearly invisible running attack, and the Pats finished on a high note with three straight wins.

**Buffalo Bills** — Once linebacker Cornelius Bennett was acquired from the Colts, the Bills became a surprisingly good defensive team. Defensive and Bruce Smith, with 12 sacks, was a Pro Bowler. Linebacker Shane Conlan was picked by several selectors as the top rookie defender, and Bennett, in only eight games, was being compared to the best in football. Just when it looked like Buffalo might finish with a winning record, quarterback Jim Kelly went into an unaccountable slump. The offense produced only one touchdown in the final two games — both losses.

**New York Jets** — The Jets continued the slide which they started in '86. They were suddenly old. Nose tackle Joe Klecko

played back to some of his pre-injury form but was "asked" to retire by the Jets at season's end. Jet fans asked the same of embattled coach Joe Walton all year. Walton also riled some of his players by damning them one day and praising them the next. Defensive end Mark Gastineau alienated teammates by crossing the picket line, for which he was pelted with eggs. The onetime king of sacks struggled to only 4 1/2. All told, the team managed only 29 sacks while giving up 66, the worst differential in the league.

## CENTRAL DIVISION

**Cleveland Browns** — The Browns won their third consecutive Central Division crown in Bernie Kosar's third season as quarterback. It was more than mere coincidence. Few quarterbacks look as awkward running an offense as Kosar, but even fewer could run one as well. In addition to throwing for 3,033 yards and 22 TDs while leading the A.F.C. in passing, Kosar was a master at using his running backs, Kevin Mack and Earnest Byner, to maximum effect. The Cleveland defense improved its ranking, despite trading away star linebacker Chip Banks. Most of the credit went to linebacker Clay Matthews and cornerbacks Frank Minnifield and Hanford Dixon.

**Houston Oilers** — After six years of high draft choices, the Oilers finally came through with a winning season and their first playoff berth since 1980. Key players were quarterback Warren Moon (2,806 yards and 21 TDs), running back Mike Rozier (957 rushing yards) and wide receivers Drew Hill and Ernest Givins, who combined for 102 catches, 1,922 yards and 12 TDs. The Oilers got a break when the replacement players defeated Cleveland and Denver. Despite the new-found success, attendance in the Astrodome dipped, owner Bud Adams flirted with moving the team to Jacksonville, Fla., and head coach Jerry Glanville was criticized by the local press for errors and by Steeler head coach Chuck Noll for allegedly teaching dirty play.

**Pittsburgh Steelers** — The Steelers were in the playoff picture until the final game of the season, thanks to an opportunistic defense that scored or set up 143 of the team's 285 points. Rookie defensive backs Delton Hall, Thomas Everett and Rod Woodson turned a weak secondary into a strong point, and linebacker Mike Merriweather played back to his '85 form. The offense was often dreadful. Quarterback Mark Malone, the league's lowest-rated passer, threw for only one TD and 11 interceptions in the last seven games. He got no encouragement from the fans. Malone couldn't have been more thoroughly booed at Three Rivers Stadium had he profaned motherhood and apple pie. Wide receiver Louis Lipps and running back Walter Abercrombie also disappointed, and running back Earnest Jackson was injured much of the time.

**Cincinnati Bengals** — The Bengals expected to challenge for a playoff berth but, instead, they invented new ways to lose. The worst loss came against San Francisco when the Bengals led 26-20 with six seconds to go. They chose not to punt, failed to run out the clock on a fourth-down sweep at their 30 and then allowed the 49ers to pass for the winning TD. Almost as bad, the Bengals, locked in a 20-20 tie with the Jets, attemped a late field goal which missed. But kicker Jim Breech got a second try because the whistle had blown for the two-minute warning. This time, his kick was blocked and returned for a Jet touchdown. Some improvement by the defense was more than offset by an offense that floundered, with running back James Brooks and wide receiver Cris Collinsworth injured and quarterback Boomer Esiason slumping.

## WESTERN DIVISION

**Denver Broncos** — Quarterback John Elway was the league's

**OFFENSE**

| | BUFF. | CIN. | CLEV. | DENV. | HOU. | IND. | K.C. | L.A. | MIA. | N.E. | NY J | PIT. | S.D. | SEA. |
|---|---|---|---|---|---|---|---|---|---|---|---|---|---|---|
| FIRST DOWNS: | | | | | | | | | | | | | | |
| Total | 294 | 319 | 310 | 331 | 294 | 285 | 265 | 300 | 331 | 266 | 292 | 263 | 264 | 301 |
| by Rushing | 111 | 130 | 110 | 132 | 118 | 122 | 97 | 107 | 109 | 84 | 97 | 114 | 68 | 120 |
| by Passing | 151 | 159 | 171 | 173 | 150 | 138 | 141 | 158 | 197 | 158 | 169 | 126 | 175 | 154 |
| by Penalty | 32 | 30 | 29 | 26 | 26 | 25 | 27 | 35 | 25 | 24 | 26 | 23 | 21 | 27 |
| RUSHING: | | | | | | | | | | | | | | |
| Number | 465 | 538 | 474 | 510 | 486 | 497 | 419 | 475 | 408 | 513 | 458 | 517 | 396 | 496 |
| Yards | 1840 | 2164 | 1745 | 1970 | 1923 | 2143 | 1799 | 2197 | 1662 | 1771 | 1671 | 2144 | 1308 | 2023 |
| Average Yards | 4.0 | 4.0 | 3.7 | 3.9 | 4.0 | 4.3 | 4.3 | 4.6 | 4.1 | 3.5 | 3.6 | 4.1 | 3.3 | 4.1 |
| Touchdowns | 9 | 13 | 16 | 18 | 12 | 14 | 7 | 13 | 16 | 12 | 17 | 11 | 11 | 13 |
| PASSING: | | | | | | | | | | | | | | |
| Attempts | 516 | 475 | 482 | 530 | 482 | 447 | 432 | 457 | 584 | 440 | 517 | 429 | 516 | 405 |
| Completions | 292 | 255 | 291 | 285 | 240 | 255 | 236 | 247 | 338 | 236 | 302 | 198 | 303 | 237 |
| Completion Pct. | 56.6 | 53.7 | 60.4 | 53.8 | 49.8 | 57.0 | 54.6 | 54.0 | 57.9 | 53.6 | 58.4 | 46.2 | 58.7 | 58.5 |
| Passing Yards | 3246 | 3468 | 3625 | 3874 | 3534 | 3042 | 2985 | 3429 | 3977 | 2929 | 3402 | 2464 | 3602 | 3028 |
| Avg. Yds per Att. | 6.3 | 7.3 | 7.5 | 7.3 | 7.3 | 6.8 | 6.9 | 7.5 | 6.8 | 6.7 | 6.6 | 5.7 | 7.0 | 7.5 |
| Avg. Yds per Comp. | 11.1 | 13.6 | 12.5 | 13.6 | 14.7 | 11.9 | 12.6 | 13.9 | 11.8 | 12.4 | 11.3 | 12.4 | 11.9 | 12.8 |
| Times Tackled | 37 | 32 | 29 | 30 | 30 | 24 | 48 | 53 | 13 | 33 | 66 | 27 | 39 | 36 |
| Yds Lost Tackled | 345 | 255 | 170 | 220 | 234 | 190 | 366 | 359 | 101 | 246 | 443 | 198 | 322 | 316 |
| Net Yards | 2901 | 3213 | 3455 | 3654 | 3300 | 2852 | 2619 | 3070 | 3876 | 2683 | 2959 | 2266 | 3280 | 2712 |
| Touchdowns | 21 | 17 | 27 | 24 | 24 | 16 | 17 | 19 | 29 | 22 | 18 | 13 | 13 | 31 |
| Interceptions | 19 | 20 | 12 | 19 | 23 | 16 | 17 | 18 | 20 | 18 | 15 | 25 | 23 | 21 |
| Pct. Intercepted | 3.7 | 4.2 | 2.5 | 3.6 | 4.8 | 3.6 | 3.9 | 3.9 | 3.4 | 4.1 | 2.9 | 5.8 | 4.5 | 5.2 |
| PUNTS: | | | | | | | | | | | | | | |
| Number | 83 | 73 | 57 | 65 | 75 | 78 | 69 | 71 | 63 | 89 | 82 | 82 | 84 | 61 |
| Average | 38.2 | 41.0 | 36.9 | 39.9 | 39.1 | 37.7 | 40.4 | 39.4 | 38.5 | 37.6 | 37.1 | 40.2 | 42.0 | 38.9 |
| PUNT RETURNS | | | | | | | | | | | | | | |
| Number | 31 | 34 | 44 | 48 | 37 | 38 | 32 | 44 | 37 | 25 | 42 | 36 | 45 | 32 |
| Yards | 232 | 293 | 487 | 486 | 249 | 210 | 346 | 356 | 290 | 213 | 497 | 244 | 508 | 322 |
| Average Yards | 7.5 | 8.6 | 11.1 | 10.1 | 6.7 | 5.5 | 10.8 | 8.1 | 7.8 | 8.5 | 11.8 | 6.8 | 11.3 | 10.1 |
| Touchdowns | 0 | 0 | 0 | 1 | 0 | 0 | 1 | 1 | 0 | 0 | 2 | 0 | 1 | 0 |
| KICKOFF RET.: | | | | | | | | | | | | | | |
| Number | 45 | 67 | 48 | 46 | 67 | 55 | 70 | 60 | 54 | 48 | 65 | 56 | 62 | 64 |
| Yards | 872 | 1161 | 846 | 952 | 1225 | 1115 | 1437 | 1174 | 952 | 901 | 1221 | 1060 | 1137 | 1236 |
| Average Yards | 19.4 | 17.3 | 17.6 | 20.7 | 18.3 | 20.3 | 20.5 | 19.6 | 17.6 | 18.8 | 18.8 | 18.9 | 18.3 | 19.3 |
| Touchdowns | 0 | 0 | 0 | 0 | 0 | 0 | 2 | 0 | 0 | 0 | 0 | 0 | 0 | 0 |
| INTERCEPT RET.: | | | | | | | | | | | | | | |
| Number | 17 | 14 | 23 | 28 | 23 | 20 | 11 | 13 | 16 | 21 | 18 | 27 | 13 | 17 |
| Yards | 93 | 187 | 366 | 403 | 274 | 212 | 140 | 178 | 135 | 307 | 239 | 336 | 291 | 289 |
| Average Yards | 5.5 | 13.4 | 15.9 | 14.4 | 11.9 | 10.6 | 12.7 | 13.7 | 8.4 | 14.6 | 13.3 | 12.4 | 22.4 | 17.0 |
| Touchdowns | 0 | 0 | 2 | 2 | 1 | 0 | 0 | 2 | 0 | 2 | 0 | 5 | 2 | 1 |
| PENALTIES: | | | | | | | | | | | | | | |
| Number | 94 | 99 | 100 | 95 | 114 | 90 | 108 | 114 | 76 | 64 | 135 | 105 | 98 | 79 |
| Yards | 762 | 791 | 857 | 812 | 1029 | 742 | 861 | 1048 | 634 | 506 | 1055 | 801 | 743 | 668 |
| FUMBLES: | | | | | | | | | | | | | | |
| Number | 41 | 29 | 33 | 29 | 32 | 36 | 41 | 24 | 37 | 36 | 33 | 37 | 38 | 31 |
| Number Lost | 24 | 12 | 17 | 17 | 14 | 18 | 24 | 13 | 17 | 13 | 19 | 8 | 20 | 15 |
| POINTS: | | | | | | | | | | | | | | |
| Total | 270 | 285 | 390 | 379 | 345 | 300 | 273 | 301 | 362 | 320 | 334 | 285 | 253 | 371 |
| PAT Attempts | 33 | 30 | 47 | 45 | 38 | 31 | 30 | 35 | 47 | 39 | 38 | 31 | 29 | 46 |
| PAT Made | 32 | 28 | 45 | 44 | 37 | 31 | 30 | 34 | 44 | 38 | 38 | 31 | 27 | 44 |
| FG Attempts | 20 | 32 | 31 | 29 | 32 | 32 | 25 | 30 | 16 | 28 | 26 | 29 | 28 | 22 |
| FG Made | 12 | 25 | 21 | 21 | 26 | 27 | 21 | 19 | 12 | 16 | 20 | 22 | 16 | 17 |
| Percent FG Made | 60.0 | 78.1 | 67.7 | 72.4 | 81.3 | 84.4 | 84.0 | 63.3 | 75.0 | 57.1 | 76.9 | 75.9 | 57.1 | 77.3 |
| Safeties | 2 | 1 | 0 | 1 | 1 | 1 | 0 | 0 | 0 | 0 | 1 | 1 | 2 | 0 |

**DEFENSE**

| | BUFF. | CIN. | CLEV. | DENV. | HOU. | IND. | K.C. | L.A. | MIA. | N.E. | NY J | PIT. | S.D. | SEA. |
|---|---|---|---|---|---|---|---|---|---|---|---|---|---|---|
| FIRST DOWNS: | | | | | | | | | | | | | | |
| Total | 297 | 286 | 251 | 277 | 287 | 276 | 344 | 267 | 314 | 293 | 300 | 289 | 280 | 297 |
| by Rushing | 114 | 99 | 86 | 103 | 98 | 97 | 139 | 98 | 115 | 112 | 117 | 94 | 120 | 133 |
| by Passing | 162 | 169 | 134 | 148 | 153 | 161 | 172 | 135 | 176 | 159 | 153 | 170 | 136 | 148 |
| by Penalty | 21 | 18 | 31 | 26 | 36 | 18 | 33 | 34 | 23 | 22 | 30 | 25 | 24 | 16 |
| RUSHING: | | | | | | | | | | | | | | |
| Number | 541 | 441 | 401 | 454 | 446 | 463 | 535 | 469 | 498 | 490 | 476 | 455 | 522 | 472 |
| Yards | 2052 | 1641 | 1433 | 2017 | 1848 | 1790 | 2333 | 1637 | 2198 | 1778 | 1835 | 1610 | 2171 | 2201 |
| Average Yards | 3.8 | 3.7 | 3.6 | 4.4 | 4.1 | 3.9 | 4.4 | 3.5 | 4.4 | 3.6 | 3.9 | 3.5 | 4.2 | 4.7 |
| Touchdowns | 11 | 15 | 7 | 16 | 10 | 6 | 16 | 12 | 18 | 13 | 15 | 8 | 14 | 14 |
| PASSING: | | | | | | | | | | | | | | |
| Attempts | 447 | 456 | 467 | 456 | 495 | 501 | 484 | 425 | 494 | 520 | 488 | 481 | 441 | 445 |
| Completions | 249 | 267 | 246 | 261 | 266 | 250 | 279 | 224 | 295 | 273 | 260 | 290 | 227 | 255 |
| Completion Pct. | 55.7 | 58.6 | 52.7 | 57.2 | 53.7 | 49.9 | 57.6 | 52.7 | 59.7 | 52.5 | 53.3 | 60.3 | 51.5 | 57.3 |
| Passing Yards | 3121 | 3359 | 3088 | 3040 | 3416 | 3073 | 3473 | 3088 | 3430 | 3438 | 3412 | 3506 | 3080 | 3196 |
| Avg. Yds per Att. | 7.0 | 7.4 | 6.6 | 6.7 | 6.9 | 6.1 | 7.2 | 7.3 | 6.9 | 6.6 | 7.0 | 7.3 | 7.0 | 7.2 |
| Avg. Yds per Comp. | 12.5 | 12.6 | 12.6 | 11.7 | 12.8 | 12.3 | 12.5 | 13.8 | 11.6 | 12.6 | 13.1 | 12.1 | 13.6 | 12.5 |
| Times Tackled | 34 | 40 | 34 | 31 | 35 | 39 | 26 | 44 | 21 | 43 | 29 | 26 | 45 | 37 |
| Yds Lost Tackled | 267 | 303 | 257 | 244 | 271 | 313 | 167 | 361 | 183 | 339 | 206 | 196 | 298 | 238 |
| Net Yards | 2854 | 3056 | 2831 | 2796 | 3145 | 2760 | 3306 | 2727 | 3247 | 3099 | 3206 | 3310 | 2782 | 2958 |
| Touchdowns | 25 | 24 | 15 | 15 | 25 | 19 | 25 | 18 | 21 | 17 | 27 | 22 | 19 | 20 |
| Interceptions | 17 | 14 | 23 | 28 | 23 | 20 | 11 | 13 | 16 | 21 | 18 | 27 | 13 | 17 |
| Pct. Intercepted | 3.8 | 3.1 | 4.9 | 6.1 | 4.6 | 4.0 | 2.3 | 3.1 | 3.2 | 4.0 | 3.7 | 5.6 | 2.9 | 3.8 |
| PUNTS: | | | | | | | | | | | | | | |
| Number | 88 | 75 | 81 | 75 | 77 | 82 | 56 | 78 | 71 | 77 | 80 | 70 | 89 | 63 |
| Average | 36.7 | 40.2 | 37.5 | 42.1 | 39.4 | 37.2 | 40.4 | 42.6 | 38.8 | 38.1 | 38.4 | 39.2 | 41.5 | 39.1 |
| PUNT RETURNS | | | | | | | | | | | | | | |
| Number | 35 | 42 | 17 | 34 | 43 | 39 | 43 | 34 | 26 | 41 | 33 | 46 | 43 | 32 |
| Yards | 179 | 299 | 93 | 424 | 454 | 376 | 442 | 256 | 141 | 397 | 162 | 395 | 429 | 251 |
| Average Yards | 5.1 | 7.1 | 5.5 | 12.5 | 10.6 | 9.6 | 10.3 | 7.5 | 5.4 | 9.7 | 4.9 | 8.6 | 10.0 | 7.8 |
| Touchdowns | 0 | 0 | 0 | 2 | 0 | 0 | 0 | 0 | 0 | 0 | 0 | 0 | 1 | 1 |
| KICKOFF RET.: | | | | | | | | | | | | | | |
| Number | 43 | 62 | 72 | 61 | 57 | 60 | 55 | 59 | 67 | 63 | 54 | 65 | 50 | 67 |
| Yards | 679 | 1145 | 1343 | 1168 | 1177 | 1068 | 1263 | 1136 | 1222 | 1130 | 1013 | 1083 | 985 | 1379 |
| Average Yards | 15.8 | 18.5 | 18.7 | 19.1 | 20.6 | 17.8 | 23.0 | 19.3 | 18.2 | 17.9 | 18.8 | 16.7 | 19.7 | 20.6 |
| Touchdowns | 0 | 0 | 0 | 0 | 0 | 0 | 1 | 0 | 0 | 0 | 0 | 0 | 1 | 1 |
| INTERCEPT RET.: | | | | | | | | | | | | | | |
| Number | 19 | 20 | 12 | 19 | 23 | 16 | 17 | 18 | 20 | 18 | 15 | 25 | 23 | 21 |
| Yards | 177 | 336 | 173 | 362 | 225 | 181 | 141 | 371 | 298 | 160 | 210 | 330 | 266 | 146 |
| Average Yards | 9.3 | 16.8 | 14.4 | 19.1 | 9.8 | 11.3 | 8.3 | 20.6 | 14.9 | 8.9 | 14.0 | 13.2 | 11.6 | 7.0 |
| Touchdowns | 0 | 2 | 2 | 2 | 1 | 1 | 0 | 2 | 2 | 2 | 0 | 1 | 1 | 0 |
| PENALTIES: | | | | | | | | | | | | | | |
| Number | 103 | 79 | 120 | 96 | 101 | 85 | 112 | 95 | 103 | 110 | 96 | 95 | 107 | 104 |
| Yards | 840 | 669 | 1008 | 785 | 874 | 689 | 936 | 652 | 850 | 846 | 881 | 771 | 869 | 890 |
| FUMBLES: | | | | | | | | | | | | | | |
| Number | 37 | 26 | 26 | 35 | 37 | 43 | 24 | 28 | 32 | 42 | 23 | 41 | 26 | 38 |
| Number Lost | 14 | 12 | 13 | 19 | 14 | 25 | 17 | 15 | 16 | 21 | 11 | 17 | 15 | 21 |
| POINTS: | | | | | | | | | | | | | | |
| Total | 305 | 370 | 239 | 288 | 349 | 238 | 388 | 289 | 335 | 293 | 360 | 299 | 317 | 314 |
| PAT Attempts | 37 | 43 | 26 | 35 | 37 | 28 | 45 | 33 | 41 | 33 | 43 | 34 | 37 | 36 |
| PAT Made | 36 | 43 | 26 | 32 | 35 | 25 | 44 | 31 | 41 | 33 | 42 | 31 | 36 | 35 |
| FG Attempts | 20 | 26 | 25 | 21 | 36 | 26 | 35 | 29 | 22 | 27 | 29 | 26 | 29 | 26 |
| FG Made | 15 | 23 | 17 | 14 | 30 | 15 | 24 | 20 | 14 | 18 | 20 | 20 | 19 | 21 |
| Percent FG Made | 75.0 | 88.5 | 68.0 | 66.7 | 83.3 | 57.7 | 68.6 | 69.0 | 63.6 | 66.7 | 69.0 | 76.9 | 65.5 | 80.8 |
| Safeties | 1 | 0 | 3 | 2 | 1 | 0 | 1 | 0 | 0 | 1 | 0 | 2 | 1 | 0 |

most potent weapon, and he became more dangerous when the Broncos went to the shotgun in their ninth game. It opened his view of the field and gave him greater opportunity for scrambling. Surprisingly, the running game improved out of what was considered a passing formation. Elway was aided by the "Three Amigos" — big-play wide receivers Vance Johnson, Mark Jackson and Ricky Nattiel. A spate of injuries and retirements caused a major overhaul on the defense, but linebacker Karl Mecklenburg and defensive end Rulon Jones continued their stellar play and, for the second straight year, the Broncos made it to the Super Bowl.

**Seattle Seahawks** — Although the media flocked to the "Boz" — colorful rookie linebacker Brian Bosworth — the Seahawk defense was disappointing, with only linebacker Fredd Young having a strong year. In an up-and-down season, the team won with running backs Curt Warner (985 yards) and John L. Williams (500 yards) running behind an outstanding offensive line. Quarterback Dave Krieg had nine games in which he passed for less than 200 yards, in part because of head coach Chuck Knox's decision to go with a ball-control attack. That didn't stop wide receiver Steve Largent from becoming the all-time leader in receptions with 752.

**San Diego Chargers** —With their replacement players winning three straight, the Chargers took eight of their first nine games. The defense, so often the team's Achilles' heel, was mainly patchwork, culled from other teams but generally effective. Linebacker Chip Banks helped, and linebacker Billy Ray Smith was outstanding. The team needed only two wins in its last six starts to cinch a playoff spot. Then, in a dive worthy of Greg Louganis, San Diego lost its last six to finish out of the playoffs. Longtime quarterback Dan Fouts, looking his age, could get the offense only seven touchdowns in the final eight games.

**Los Angeles Raiders** —Despite a midseason offensive transfusion from running back Bo Jackson, the Raiders were doomed by a seven-game losing streak — the team's longest since 1962. Rusty Hilger got the job at quarterback but didn't get the job done. Marc Wilson relieved him in all but two of his starts and took over permanently in November. Although Wilson had his best season for the Raiders, he was still considered a lame duck. But, when Jackson arrived after the baseball season to join Marcus Allen in the backfield, the running attack moved up to No. 1 in the league. A sprained ankle put Jackson out of the last three games, and the Raider rushing average dropped to 86.6 yards per game.

**Kansas City Chiefs** — Under new head coach Frank Gansz, the architect of the great Chief special teams of '86, Kansas City won its opening game and then plunged into a franchise-record nine-game losing streak. The defense, with the exception of nose tackle Bill Maas, was no great shakes, plummeting to 27th in the league. The offense showed some spark with running back Christian Okoye leading all rookie runners with 660 yards. Wide receiver Carlos Carson was terrific, gaining 1,044 yards on 55 catches. Quarterback Bill Kenney had an OK season after regaining his starting job.

# Eastern Division

## INDIANAPOLIS COLTS 9-6 Ron Meyer

| Scores of Each Game | | | |
|---|---|---|---|
| 21 | CINCINNATI | 23 | |
| 10 | MIAMI | 23 | |
| 47 | Buffalo | 6 | |
| 6 | N.Y.JETS | 0 | |
| 7 | Pittsburgh | 21 | |
| 30 | NEW ENGLAND | 16 | |
| 19 | N.Y.Jets | 14 | |
| 13 | SAN DIEGO | 16 | |
| 40 | Miami | 21 | |
| 0 | New England | 24 | |
| 51 | HOUSTON | 27 | |
| 9 | Cleveland | 7 | |
| 3 | BUFFALO | 27 | |
| 20 | San Diego | 7 | |
| 24 | TAMPA BAY | 6 | |

| Use Name | Pos. | Hgt | Wgt | Age | Int | Pts |
|---|---|---|---|---|---|---|
| #Sid Abramowitz | OT | 6'5" | 285 | 27 | | |
| Mark Boggs | OT | 6'5" | 301 | 23 | | |
| Bob Brotzki | OT | 6'5" | 293 | 24 | | |
| Kevin Call | OT | 6'7" | 302 | 25 | | |
| #Milt Carthens | OT | 6'4" | 305 | 26 | | |
| Randy Dixon | OT | 6'3" | 293 | 22 | | |
| #Marsharne Graves | OT | 6'4" | 265 | 25 | | |
| Chris Hinton | OT | 6'4" | 295 | 26 | | |
| Joel Patten | OT | 6'7" | 307 | 29 | | |
| Steve Knight | OG | 6'4" | 298 | 25 | | |
| #Jeff Criswell | OG | 6'7" | 265 | 24 | | |
| Ron Solt | OG | 6'3" | 285 | 25 | | |
| Ben Utt | OG | 6'5" | 286 | 28 | | |
| Ray Donaldson | C | 6'3" | 288 | 28 | | |
| Ron Plantz | C | 6'4" | 272 | 23 | | |
| Bob Hamm | DE | 6'4" | 265 | 28 | | |
| Jon Hand | DE | 6'7" | 280 | 28 | | |
| #Marcus Jackson | DE-NT | 6'5" | 260 | 30 | | |
| #Frank Mattlace | DE-NT | 6'1" | 264 | 26 | | |
| #Jim Merritts | DE-NT | 6'3" | 255 | 26 | | |
| Chris Scott | DE | 6'5" | 256 | 25 | | |
| Donnell Thompson | DE | 6'4" | 275 | 28 | | 6 |
| Don Thorpe | DE-NT | 6'4" | 260 | 25 | | |
| Harvey Armstrong | NT | 6'3" | 268 | 27 | | |
| Byron Darby | NT-DE | 6'4" | 260 | 27 | | |
| #Bill Elko | NT | 6'5" | 280 | 27 | | |
| Scott Kellar | NT | 6'3" | 285 | 23 | | |
| Jerome Sally | NT | 6'3" | 270 | 28 | | |
| Dave Ahrens | LB | 6'3" | 249 | 28 | | |
| Duane Bickett | LB | 6'5" | 243 | 25 | | |
| #Brian Bulluck | LB | 6'3" | 236 | 22 | | |
| #Ricky Chatman | LB | 6'2" | 230 | 25 | | |
| Johnie Cooks | LB | 6'4" | 252 | 22 | 1 | |
| Kevin Hancock | LB | 6'2" | 225 | 25 | | |
| June James | LB | 6'1" | 236 | 24 | | |
| Barry Krauss | LB | 6'3" | 255 | 30 | | |
| Orlando Lowry | LB | 6'4" | 236 | 26 | | |
| Cliff Odom | LB | 6'2" | 245 | 28 | | |
| #Bob Ontko | LB | 6'3" | 237 | 23 | | |
| #Gary Padjen | LB | 6'2" | 237 | 28 | | |
| #Roger Remo | LB | 6'3" | 237 | 23 | | |
| #Brad Saar | LB | 6'1" | 220 | 24 | | |
| #Pat Ballage | DB | 6'1" | 208 | 23 | | |
| Leonard Coleman | DB | 6'2" | 202 | 25 | | |
| #Craig Curry | DB | 6' | 187 | 26 | 1 | |
| Eugene Daniel | DB | 5'11" | 178 | 26 | 2 | |
| #Kenny Daniel | DB | 5'10" | 180 | 27 | | |
| #Lee Davis | DB | 5'11" | 201 | 24 | 1 | |
| Nesby Glasgow | DB | 5'10" | 187 | 30 | 1 | |
| Chris Goode | DB | 6' | 193 | 23 | | |
| John Holt | DB | 5'11" | 179 | 28 | | |
| #Bryant Jones | DB | 5'11' | 186 | 23 | 2 | 6 |
| Jim Perryman | DB | 6' | 187 | 26 | 1 | |
| Mike Prior | DB | 6' | 200 | 23 | 6 | |
| Freddie Robinson | DB | 6'1" | 191 | 23 | 2 | |
| #John Simmons | DB | 5'11" | 192 | 28 | | |
| Craig Swoope (from TB) | DB | 6'1" | 200 | 23 | | |
| Willie Tullis | DB | 6' | 195 | 29 | 3 | |
| Terry Wright | DB | 6' | 195 | 22 | | |
| Willie Broughton - Knee Injury | | | | | | |
| Randy McMillan - Knee Injury | | | | | | |
| Gary Hogeboom | QB | 6'4" | 206 | 29 | | |
| Blair Kiel | QB | 6' | 216 | 25 | | |
| Terry Nugent | QB | 6'4" | 214 | 25 | | |
| Sean Salisbury | QB | 6'5" | 215 | 24 | | |
| Jack Trudeau | QB | 6'3" | 213 | 24 | | |
| Albert Bentley | HB | 5'11" | 214 | 27 | | 54 |
| #Gordon Brown | HB | 5'11" | 220 | 24 | | 6 |
| Eric Dickerson (from LA) | HB | 6'3" | 217 | 26 | | 30 |
| George Wonsley | HB | 5'10" | 219 | 26 | | 6 |
| #Chuck Banks | FB | 6'2" | 227 | 23 | | |
| Melvin Carver | FB | 5'11" | 225 | 28 | | |
| Chris McLemore (to RAID) | FB | 6'1" | 235 | 23 | | |
| John Williams | FB | 5'11" | 205 | 26 | | |
| Roy Banks | WR | 5'10" | 190 | 23 | | |
| Mark Bellini | WR | 5'11" | 185 | 23 | | |
| Matt Bouza | WR | 6'3" | 212 | 29 | | 24 |
| Bill Brooks | WR | 6' | 197 | 23 | | 18 |
| #Steve Bryant | WR | 6'2" | 195 | 27 | | |
| #Kelley Johnson | WR | 5'8" | 168 | 25 | | |
| #Tim Kearse | WR | 5'11" | 186 | 27 | | |
| Walter Murray | WR | 6'4" | 200 | 24 | | 18 |
| #James Noble | WR | 6' | 196 | 24 | | 12 |
| Pat Beach | TE | 6'4" | 252 | 27 | | |
| Mark Boyer | TE | 6'4" | 242 | 24 | | |
| John Brandes | TE | 6'2" | 237 | 23 | | |
| #Greg Hawthorne | TE | 6'2" | 238 | 30 | | |
| Joe Jones | TE | 6'5" | 255 | 25 | | 6 |
| Keith Lester | TE | 6'5" | 235 | 25 | | |
| Tim Sherwin | TE | 6'5" | 252 | 29 | | 6 |
| Mark Walczak (from BUF) | TE | 6'6" | 246 | 25 | | |
| Dean Biasucci | K | 6' | 191 | 25 | | 96 |
| #Steve Jordan | K | 5'10" | 205 | 24 | | 16 |
| Rohn Stark | K | 6'3" | 204 | 28 | | |

## NEW ENGLAND PATRIOTS 8-7 Raymond Berry

| Scores of Each Game | | | |
|---|---|---|---|
| 28 | MIAMI | 21 | |
| 24 | N.Y.Jets | 43 | |
| 10 | CLEVELAND | 20 | |
| 14 | BUFFALO | 7 | |
| 21 | Houston | 7 | |
| 16 | Indianapolis | 30 | |
| 26 | L.A.RAIDERS | 23 | |
| 10 | N.Y.Giants | 17 | |
| 17 | DALLAS | *23 | |
| 24 | INDIANAPOLIS | 0 | |
| 31 | PHILADELPHIA | *34 | |
| 20 | Denver | 31 | |
| 42 | N.Y.JETS | 20 | |
| 13 | Buffalo | 7 | |
| 24 | Miami | 10 | |

| Use Name | Pos. | Hgt | Wgt | Age | Int | Pts |
|---|---|---|---|---|---|---|
| Bruce Armstrong | OT | 6'4" | 284 | 21 | | |
| George Colton | OT | 6'4" | 279 | 24 | | |
| Steve Moore | OT | 6'4" | 305 | 26 | | |
| Art Plunkett | OT | 6'7" | 282 | 27 | | |
| #Greg Robinson | OT | 6'5" | 275 | 24 | | |
| Danny Villa | OT | 6'5" | 305 | 22 | | |
| Sean Farrell | OG | 6'3" | 260 | 27 | | |
| #Todd Sandham | OG | 6'3" | 255 | 23 | | |
| Ron Wooten | OG | 6'4" | 273 | 28 | | |
| Pete Brock | C | 6'5" | 275 | 32 | | |
| Paul Fairchild | C-OG | 6'4" | 270 | 25 | | |
| Trevor Matich | C | 6'4" | 270 | 25 | | |
| Guy Morriss | C-OG | 6'4" | 275 | 36 | | |
| #Eric Stokes | C-OG | 6'4" | 255 | 25 | | |
| Darren Twombly | C | 6'4" | 270 | 22 | | |
| Julius Adams | DE | 6'3" | 265 | 38 | | |
| Milford Hodge | DE | 6'3" | 278 | 26 | | |
| #Ben Reed | DE | 6'5" | 265 | 24 | | |
| Kenneth Sims | DE | 6'5" | 271 | 27 | | |
| #Bill Turner | DE | 6'4" | 245 | 27 | | |
| Garin Veris | DE | 6'4" | 255 | 24 | | |
| #Steve Wilburn | DE | 6'4" | 266 | 26 | | |
| Brent Williams | DE | 6'3" | 278 | 22 | | |
| #John Guzik | NT-DE | 6'4" | 270 | 24 | | |
| #Dino Mangiero | NT | 6'2" | 270 | 28 | | |
| #Tom Porrell | NT | 6'3" | 275 | 22 | | |
| Mike Ruth | NT | 6'1" | 266 | 23 | | |
| #Murray Wichard | NT-DE | 6'2" | 260 | 23 | | |
| Toby Williams | NT | 6'3" | 270 | 27 | | |
| #Rogers Alexander | LB | 6'3" | 225 | 23 | | |
| #Mel Black | LB | 6'2" | 228 | 25 | | |
| Don Blackmon | LB | 6'3" | 235 | 29 | | |
| #Rico Corsetti | LB | 6'1" | 225 | 24 | | |
| Steve Doig | LB | 6'2" | 242 | 27 | | |
| Tim Jordan | LB | 6'3" | 226 | 23 | | |
| #Jerry McCabe | LB | 6'1" | 225 | 22 | | |
| #Joe McHale | LB | 6'2" | 227 | 23 | | |
| Larry McGrew | LB | 6'5" | 233 | 30 | | |
| #Greg Moore | LB | 6'1" | 240 | 22 | | |
| Steve Nelson | LB | 6'2" | 230 | 36 | | |
| Johnny Rembert | LB | 6'3" | 234 | 26 | 1 | |
| Ed Reynolds | LB | 6'5" | 242 | 25 | | |
| #Frank Sacco | LB | 6'4" | 240 | 23 | | |
| #Randy Sealby | LB | 6'2" | 230 | 27 | | |
| Andre Tippett | LB | 6'3" | 241 | 27 | | 6 |
| Ed Williams | LB | 6'4" | 244 | 25 | 1 | |
| #Ricky Atkinson | DB | 6' | 175 | 22 | | |
| Jim Bowman | DB | 6'2" | 210 | 23 | 2 | |
| Raymond Clayborn | DB | 6'1" | 186 | 32 | 2 | 6 |
| #Duffy Cobbs | DB | 5'11" | 178 | 23 | | |
| Ernest Gibson | DB | 5'10" | 185 | 25 | 2 | |
| #David Hendley | DB | 6' | 188 | 23 | | |
| Darryl Holmes | DB | 6'2" | 190 | 22 | 1 | |
| Roland James | DB | 6'2" | 191 | 29 | 1 | |
| Ronnie Lippett | DB | 5'11" | 180 | 26 | 3 | 12 |
| Fred Marion | DB | 6'2" | 191 | 28 | 4 | |
| Rod McSwain | DB | 6'1" | 196 | 25 | 1 | |
| #Joe Peterson | DB | 5'10" | 185 | 23 | 1 | |
| Eugene Profit | DB | 5'10" | 175 | 22 | | |
| #Jon Sawyer | DB | 5'9" | 175 | 23 | | |
| #Ron Shegog | DB | 5'11" | 190 | 24 | 1 | |
| #Perry Williams | DB | 6'1" | 200 | 23 | 1 | |
| Robert Weathers - Ankle Injury | | | | | | |
| #Bob Bleier | QB | 6'3" | 210 | 23 | | 6 |
| Tony Eason | QB | 6'4" | 212 | 27 | | |
| Doug Flutie (from CHI) | QB | 5'9" | 176 | 24 | | |
| Steve Grogan | QB | 6'4" | 210 | 34 | | 12 |
| Tom Ramsey | QB | 6'1" | 189 | 26 | | 6 |
| #Todd Whitten | QB | 6' | 185 | 22 | | |
| #Frank Bianchini | HB | 5'8" | 190 | 26 | | |
| Tony Collins | HB | 5'11" | 212 | 28 | | 36 |
| Elgin Davis | HB | 5'10" | 192 | 21 | | |
| Reggie Dupard | HB | 5'11" | 205 | 23 | | 18 |
| Michael LeBlanc | HB | 5'11" | 199 | 25 | | 6 |
| #Chuck McSwain | HB | 6' | 198 | 26 | | |
| #Carl Woods | HB | 5'11" | 200 | 22 | | 6 |
| Bruce Hansen | FB | 6'1" | 225 | 26 | | |
| Craig James | FB | 6' | 215 | 26 | | |
| Bob Perryman | FB | 6'1" | 233 | 23 | | |
| Mosi Tatupu | FB | 6' | 227 | 32 | | |
| #Brian Carey | WR | 6' | 200 | 23 | | |
| #Wayne Coffey | WR | 5'7" | 158 | 23 | | |
| Irving Fryar | WR | 6' | 200 | 24 | | 30 |
| #Dennis Gadbois | WR | 6'1" | 183 | 23 | | |
| Cedric Jones | WR | 6'1" | 184 | 27 | | 18 |
| #Larry Linne | WR | 6'1" | 185 | 25 | | 12 |
| Stanley Morgan | WR | 5'11" | 181 | 32 | | 18 |
| Stephen Starring | WR | 5'10" | 172 | 26 | | 18 |
| Darwin Williams | WR | 6'1" | 185 | 26 | | |
| Greg Baty (from LA) | TE | 6'5" | 240 | 23 | | 12 |
| Lin Dawson | TE | 6'3" | 240 | 28 | | |
| #Todd Frain | TE | 6'3" | 240 | 25 | | |
| #Arnold Franklin | TE | 6'3" | 246 | 23 | | |
| Willie Scott | TE | 6'4" | 245 | 28 | | 12 |
| Rich Camarillo | K | 5'11" | 185 | 27 | | |
| Tony Franklin | K | 5'8" | 182 | 29 | | 82 |
| #Alan Herline | K | 6' | 168 | 22 | | |
| #Eric Schubert | K | 5'8" | 193 | 25 | | 4 |

## MIAMI DOLPHINS 8-7 Don Shula

| Scores of Each Game | | | |
|---|---|---|---|
| 21 | New England | 28 | |
| 23 | Indianapolis | 10 | |
| 20 | Seattle | 24 | |
| 42 | KANSAS CITY | 0 | |
| 31 | N.Y.Jets | *37 | |
| 31 | BUFFALO | *34 | |
| 35 | PITTSBURGH | 24 | |
| 20 | Cincinnati | 14 | |
| 21 | INDIANAPOLIS | 40 | |
| 20 | Dallas | 14 | |
| 0 | Buffalo | 27 | |
| 37 | N.Y.JETS | 28 | |
| 28 | Philadelphia | 10 | |
| 23 | WASHINGTON | 21 | |
| 10 | NEW ENGLAND | 24 | |

| Use Name | Pos. | Hgt | Wgt | Age | Int | Pts |
|---|---|---|---|---|---|---|
| #Bill Bealles | OT | 6'7" | 290 | 24 | | |
| #Greg Cleveland | OT | 6'5" | 295 | 23 | | |
| Jeff Dellenbach | OT-C | 6'6" | 280 | 24 | | |
| Mark Dennis | OT | 6'6" | 291 | 22 | | |
| Jon Giesler | OT | 6'5" | 265 | 30 | | |
| #Scott Kehoe | OT | 6'4" | 282 | 22 | | |
| Ronnie Lee | OT | 6'3" | 265 | 30 | | |
| Chris Conlin | OG | 6'4" | 290 | 22 | | |
| Roy Foster | OG | 6'4" | 275 | 27 | | |
| #Jim Gilmore | OG | 6'5" | 275 | 24 | | |
| #Steve Jacobson | OG | 6'3" | 255 | 24 | | |
| Doug Marrone | OG | 6'5" | 269 | 23 | | |
| #Louis Oubre | OG | 6'4" | 274 | 29 | | |
| Tom Toth | OG | 6'5" | 275 | 25 | | |
| Jeff Wiska | OG | 6'3" | 265 | 27 | | |
| #Greg Ours | C | 6'5" | 279 | 23 | | |
| Dwight Stephenson | C | 6'2" | 258 | 29 | | |
| #Charles Bennett | DE | 6'5" | 257 | 24 | | |
| Doug Betters | DE | 6'7" | 265 | 31 | | |
| John Bosa | DE | 6'4" | 263 | 23 | | |
| George Little | DE | 6'4" | 270 | 24 | | |
| #Stanley Scott | DE | 6'3" | 255 | 23 | | |
| T.J.Turner | DE | 6'4" | 275 | 24 | | |
| #Derek Wimberly | DE | 6'4" | 270 | 23 | | |
| Jackie Cline (from PIT) | NT-DE | 6'5" | 276 | 27 | | |
| Mike Lambrecht | NT | 6'1" | 271 | 24 | | |
| #Ike Readon | NT | 6' | 273 | 24 | | |
| Brian Sochia | NT | 6'3" | 274 | 26 | | |
| Mark Brown | LB | 6'2" | 235 | 26 | | |
| Bob Brudzinski | LB | 6'4" | 223 | 32 | | |
| #Laz Chavez | LB | 6' | 220 | 23 | | |
| #Dennis Fowlkes | LB | 6'2" | 245 | 26 | | |
| David Frye | LB | 6'2" | 227 | 26 | | |
| Rick Graf | LB | 6'5" | 239 | 24 | | |
| Hugh Green | LB | 6'2" | 225 | 28 | | |
| Larry Kolic | LB | 6'1" | 238 | 24 | | |
| #Steve Lubischer | LB | 6'3" | 240 | 25 | | |
| #David Marshall | LB | 6'3" | 220 | 26 | | |
| #Victor Morris | LB | 6'1" | 243 | 23 | | |
| Scott Nicolas | LB | 6'3" | 226 | 27 | | |
| John Offerdahl | LB | 6'3" | 232 | 23 | | |
| #Tim Pidgeon | LB | 6' | 233 | 21 | | |
| #Duke Schamel | LB | 6'3" | 235 | 24 | | |
| Jackie Shipp | LB | 6'2" | 236 | 25 | | |
| #Greg Storr | LB | 6'2" | 225 | 26 | | |
| Glenn Blackwood | DB | 6' | 190 | 30 | 3 | |
| Bud Brown | DB | 6' | 194 | 26 | 1 | |
| #Marvell Burgess | DB | 6'3" | 195 | 21 | | |
| Liffort Hobley | DB | 6' | 199 | 25 | | |
| #Trell Hooper | DB | 5'11" | 182 | 25 | 2 | 6 |
| #Mark Irvin | DB | 5'10" | 190 | 22 | | |
| Demetrious Johnson | DB | 5'11" | 190 | 26 | | |
| William Judson | DB | 6'1" | 190 | 27 | 2 | |
| Paul Lankford | DB | 6'1" | 184 | 29 | 3 | |
| Don McNeal | DB | 5'11" | 192 | 29 | | |
| #Floyd Raglin | DB | 5'9" | 180 | 26 | | |
| #Tate Randle | DB | 6' | 202 | 28 | 2 | |
| Donovan Rose | DB | 6'1" | 190 | 30 | | |
| Mike Smith | DB | 6' | 175 | 24 | | |
| #Robert Sowell | DB | 5'11" | 180 | 26 | 1 | |
| #John Swain | DB | 6'2" | 200 | 27 | | |
| Reyna Thompson | DB | 5'11" | 194 | 24 | | |
| Andy Hendel - Leg Injury | | | | | | |
| Robin Sendlein - Eye Injury | | | | | | |
| Ron Jaworski | QB | 6'2" | 195 | 36 | | |
| #Kyle Mackey | QB | 6'3" | 215 | 25 | | 12 |
| Dan Marino | QB | 6'4" | 214 | 26 | | 6 |
| #Scott Stankavage | QB | 6'1" | 192 | 25 | | |
| Don Strock | QB | 6'5" | 225 | 36 | | |
| Lorenzo Hampton | HB | 5'11" | 203 | 25 | | |
| #Mark Konecny | HB | 5'11" | 197 | 24 | | |
| Tony Nathan | HB | 6' | 210 | 30 | | |
| #Ronald Scott | HB | 5'11" | 200 | 21 | | 18 |
| Troy Stradford | HB | 5'9" | 191 | 22 | | 42 |
| #John Tagliaferri | HB | 5'11" | 195 | 23 | | 6 |
| #Clarence Bailey | FB | 5'11" | 220 | 24 | | |
| Woody Bennett | FB | 6'2" | 244 | 31 | | |
| Tom Brown | FB | 6'1" | 218 | 22 | | |
| Ron Davenport | FB | 6'2" | 230 | 24 | | 12 |
| #Rickey Isom | FB | 6' | 224 | 23 | | 6 |
| #Pete Roth | FB | 5'11" | 210 | 23 | | |
| Fred Banks | WR | 5'10" | 180 | 25 | | 6 |
| #Mark Caterbone | WR | 5'11" | 175 | 25 | | |
| #Eddie Chavis | WR | 6' | 182 | 24 | | |
| Mark Clayton | WR | 5'9" | 175 | 26 | | 42 |
| #Leland Douglas | WR | 6' | 179 | 23 | | 6 |
| Mark Duper | WR | 5'9" | 187 | 28 | | 48 |
| George Farmer | WR | 5'10" | 175 | 28 | | |
| #Todd Feldman | WR | 5'10" | 184 | 25 | | |
| Jim Jensen | WR | 6'4" | 215 | 28 | | 6 |
| James Pruitt | WR | 6'3" | 199 | 23 | | 18 |
| #Dameon Reilly | WR | 5'11" | 180 | 24 | | |
| Scott Schwedes | WR | 6' | 181 | 22 | | |
| Bruce Hardy | TE | 6'5" | 234 | 31 | | 12 |
| Dan Johnson | TE | 6'3" | 245 | 27 | | 12 |
| David Lewis | TE | 6'3" | 235 | 26 | | 6 |
| #Lawrence Sampleton | TE | 6'5" | 235 | 25 | | 6 |
| #Rich Siler | TE | 6'4" | 240 | 23 | | |
| #Willie Smith | TE | 6'2" | 235 | 23 | | 6 |
| #Joel Williams | TE | 6'3" | 242 | 22 | | |
| #Willie Beecher | K | 5'10" | 170 | 24 | | 21 |
| #Stacy Gore | K | 6' | 200 | 25 | | |
| #Jeff Hayes | K | 5'11" | 175 | 28 | | |
| Fuad Reveiz | K | 5'11" | 217 | 24 | | 55 |
| Reggie Roby | K | 6'2" | 242 | 26 | | |

* Overtime

\# - on the active roster for strike replacement games only

## RUSHING

### INDIANAPOLIS COLTS

| Last Name | No. | Yds | Avg | TD |
|---|---|---|---|---|
| Dickerson | 283 | 1288 | 4.6 | 6 |
| Bentley | 142 | 631 | 4.4 | 7 |
| Banks | 50 | 245 | 4.9 | 0 |
| Brown | 19 | 85 | 4.5 | 1 |
| Wonsley | 18 | 71 | 3.9 | 1 |
| McLemore | 17 | 58 | 3.4 | 0 |
| Kiel | 4 | 30 | 7.5 | 0 |
| Trudeau | 15 | 7 | .5 | 0 |
| Carver | 2 | 3 | 1.5 | 0 |
| Hogeboom | 3 | 3 | 1.0 | 0 |
| Nugent | 2 | 1 | .5 | 0 |
| Brooks | 2 | -2 | -1.0 | 0 |

### NEW ENGLAND PATRIOTS

| Last Name | No. | Yds | Avg | TD |
|---|---|---|---|---|
| Collins | 147 | 474 | 3.2 | 3 |
| Dupard | 94 | 318 | 3.4 | 3 |
| Tatupu | 79 | 248 | 3.1 | 0 |
| Perryman | 41 | 187 | 4.6 | 0 |
| LeBlanc | 49 | 170 | 3.5 | 1 |
| Ramsey | 13 | 75 | 5.8 | 1 |
| Fryar | 9 | 52 | 5.8 | 0 |
| Hansen | 16 | 44 | 2.8 | 0 |
| Davis | 9 | 43 | 4.8 | 0 |
| Flutie | 6 | 43 | 7.2 | 0 |
| Grogan | 20 | 37 | 1.9 | 2 |
| Eason | 3 | 25 | 8.3 | 0 |
| C. McSwain | 9 | 23 | 2.6 | 0 |
| Woods | 4 | 20 | 5.0 | 0 |
| Starring | 2 | 13 | 6.5 | 0 |
| James | 4 | 10 | 2.5 | 0 |
| Camarillo | 1 | 0 | 0 | 0 |
| Bleier | 5 | -5 | -1.0 | 0 |
| Whitten | 2 | -6 | -3.0 | 0 |

### MIAMI DOLPHINS

| Last Name | No. | Yds | Avg | TD |
|---|---|---|---|---|
| Stradford | 145 | 619 | 4.3 | 6 |
| Hampton | 75 | 289 | 3.9 | 1 |
| Scott | 47 | 199 | 4.2 | 3 |
| Davenport | 32 | 114 | 3.6 | 1 |
| Bennett | 25 | 102 | 4.1 | 0 |
| Mackey | 17 | 98 | 5.8 | 2 |
| Bailey | 10 | 55 | 5.5 | 0 |
| Konecny | 6 | 46 | 7.7 | 0 |
| Tagliaferri | 13 | 45 | 3.5 | 1 |
| Isom | 9 | 41 | 4.6 | 1 |
| Nathan | 4 | 20 | 5.0 | 0 |
| Jensen | 4 | 18 | 4.5 | 0 |
| Roth | 3 | 10 | 3.3 | 0 |
| Clayton | 2 | 8 | 4.0 | 0 |
| Brown | 3 | 3 | 1.0 | 0 |
| Roby | 1 | 0 | 0.0 | 0 |

## RECEIVING

### (Indianapolis Colts)

| Last Name | No. | Yds | Avg | TD |
|---|---|---|---|---|
| Brooks | 51 | 722 | 14.2 | 3 |
| Bouza | 42 | 569 | 13.5 | 4 |
| Bentley | 34 | 447 | 13.1 | 2 |
| Beach | 28 | 239 | 8.5 | 0 |
| Murray | 20 | 339 | 17.0 | 3 |
| Dickerson | 18 | 171 | 9.5 | 0 |
| Noble | 10 | 78 | 7.8 | 2 |
| Boyer | 10 | 73 | 7.3 | 0 |
| Sherwin | 9 | 92 | 10.2 | 1 |
| Banks | 9 | 50 | 5.6 | 0 |
| Bellini | 5 | 69 | 13.8 | 0 |
| Wonsley | 5 | 48 | 9.6 | 0 |
| Brandes | 5 | 35 | 7.0 | 0 |
| Kearse | 3 | 51 | 17.0 | 0 |
| Hawthorne | 3 | 41 | 17.0 | 0 |
| Jones | 3 | 25 | 8.3 | 0 |
| McLemore | 2 | 9 | 4.5 | 0 |
| Johnson | 1 | 15 | 15.0 | 0 |
| Bryant | 1 | 12 | 12.0 | 0 |
| Utt | 1 | -4 | -4.0 | 0 |

### (New England Patriots)

| Last Name | No. | Yds | Avg | TD |
|---|---|---|---|---|
| Collins | 44 | 347 | 7.9 | 3 |
| Morgan | 40 | 672 | 16.8 | 3 |
| Fryar | 31 | 467 | 15.1 | 5 |
| Jones | 25 | 388 | 15.5 | 3 |
| Baty | 18 | 175 | 9.7 | 2 |
| Starring | 17 | 289 | 17.0 | 3 |
| Tatupu | 15 | 136 | 9.1 | 0 |
| Dawson | 12 | 81 | 6.8 | 0 |
| Linne | 11 | 158 | 14.4 | 2 |
| Scott | 5 | 35 | 7.0 | 1 |
| Coffey | 3 | 66 | 22.0 | 0 |
| Gadbois | 3 | 51 | 17.0 | 0 |
| D. Williams | 3 | 30 | 10.0 | 0 |
| Perryman | 3 | 13 | 4.3 | 0 |
| Dupard | 3 | 1 | 0.3 | 0 |
| Frain | 2 | 22 | 11.0 | 0 |
| LeBlanc | 2 | 3 | 1.5 | 0 |
| Hansen | 1 | 22 | 22.0 | 0 |
| Pickering | 1 | 10 | 10.0 | 0 |

### (Miami Dolphins)

| Last Name | No. | Yds | Avg | TD |
|---|---|---|---|---|
| Stradford | 48 | 457 | 9.5 | 1 |
| Clayton | 46 | 776 | 16.9 | 7 |
| Duper | 33 | 597 | 18.1 | 8 |
| Davenport | 27 | 249 | 9.2 | 1 |
| Pruitt | 26 | 404 | 15.5 | 3 |
| Jensen | 26 | 221 | 8.5 | 1 |
| Hampton | 23 | 223 | 9.7 | 0 |
| Tagliaferri | 12 | 117 | 9.8 | 0 |
| Nathan | 10 | 77 | 7.7 | 0 |
| Douglas | 9 | 92 | 10.2 | 1 |
| Sampleton | 8 | 64 | 8.0 | 0 |
| Chavis | 7 | 108 | 15.4 | 0 |
| Lewis | 6 | 53 | 14.5 | 1 |
| Konecny | 6 | 26 | 4.3 | 0 |
| Reilly | 5 | 70 | 14.0 | 0 |
| Bennett | 4 | 18 | 4.5 | 0 |
| Caterbone | 2 | 46 | 23.0 | 0 |
| Smith | 2 | 13 | 6.5 | 1 |
| Scott | 2 | 7 | 3.5 | 0 |
| Isom | 1 | 11 | 11.0 | 0 |
| Banks | 1 | 10 | 10.0 | 1 |
| Brown | 1 | 6 | 6.0 | 0 |

## PUNT RETURNS

### (Indianapolis Colts)

| Last Name | No. | Yds | Avg | TD |
|---|---|---|---|---|
| Brooks | 22 | 136 | 6.2 | 0 |
| Johnson | 9 | 42 | 4.7 | 0 |
| Tullis | 4 | 27 | 6.8 | 0 |
| Simmons | 2 | 5 | 2.5 | 0 |
| Ahrens | 1 | 0 | 0.0 | 0 |

### (New England Patriots)

| Last Name | No. | Yds | Avg | TD |
|---|---|---|---|---|
| Fryar | 18 | 174 | 9.7 | 0 |
| Linne | 5 | 22 | 4.4 | 0 |
| Starring | 1 | 17 | 17.0 | 0 |
| Marion | 1 | 0 | 0.0 | 0 |

### (Miami Dolphins)

| Last Name | No. | Yds | Avg | TD |
|---|---|---|---|---|
| Schwedes | 24 | 203 | 8.5 | 0 |
| Caterbone | 9 | 78 | 8.7 | 0 |
| Brown | 2 | 8 | 4.0 | 0 |
| Blackwood | 1 | 1 | 1.0 | 0 |
| Hooper | 1 | 0 | 0.0 | 0 |

## KICKOFF RETURNS

### (Indianapolis Colts)

| Last Name | No. | Yds | Avg | TD |
|---|---|---|---|---|
| Bentley | 22 | 500 | 22.7 | 0 |
| Daniel | 10 | 225 | 22.5 | 0 |
| Johnson | 6 | 98 | 16.3 | 0 |
| Prior | 3 | 47 | 15.7 | 0 |
| Noble | 2 | 35 | 17.5 | 0 |
| Wonsley | 1 | 19 | 19.0 | 0 |
| Perryman | 1 | 4 | 4.0 | 0 |

### (New England Patriots)

| Last Name | No. | Yds | Avg | TD |
|---|---|---|---|---|
| Starring | 23 | 445 | 19.3 | 0 |
| Fryar | 6 | 119 | 19.8 | 0 |
| Davis | 5 | 134 | 26.8 | 0 |
| Dupard | 4 | 61 | 15.3 | 0 |
| Perryman | 3 | 43 | 14.3 | 0 |
| C. McSwain | 2 | 32 | 16.0 | 0 |
| LeBlanc | 2 | 31 | 15.0 | 0 |
| Collins | 1 | 18 | 18.0 | 0 |
| Hansen | 1 | 14 | 14.0 | 0 |
| Alexander | 1 | 4 | 4.0 | 0 |

### (Miami Dolphins)

| Last Name | No. | Yds | Avg | TD |
|---|---|---|---|---|
| Hampton | 16 | 304 | 19.0 | 0 |
| Stradford | 14 | 258 | 18.4 | 0 |
| Schwedes | 9 | 177 | 19.7 | 0 |
| Hardy | 5 | 62 | 12.4 | 0 |
| Farmer | 3 | 56 | 18.7 | 0 |
| Roth | 2 | 49 | 24.5 | 0 |
| Johnson | 2 | 13 | 6.5 | 0 |
| Scott | 1 | 22 | 22.0 | 0 |
| Isom | 1 | 11 | 11.0 | 0 |
| Lewis | 1 | 0 | 0.0 | 0 |

## PASSING — PUNTING — KICKING

### (Indianapolis Colts)

| PASSING | Att | Cmp | % | Yds | Yd/Att | TD | Int— | % | RK |
|---|---|---|---|---|---|---|---|---|---|
| Trudeau | 229 | 128 | 56 | 1587 | 6.9 | 6 | 6— | 3 | |
| Hogeboom | 168 | 99 | 59 | 1145 | 6.8 | 9 | 5— | 3 | |
| Kiel | 33 | 17 | 52 | 195 | 5.9 | 1 | 3— | 9 | |
| Salisbury | 12 | 8 | 67 | 68 | 5.7 | 0 | 2— | 17 | |
| Nugent | 5 | 3 | 60 | 47 | 9.4 | 0 | 0— | 0 | |

| PUNTING | No | Avg |
|---|---|---|
| Stark | 63 | 38.7 |
| Kiel | 12 | 36.7 |
| Colquitt | 3 | 20.3 |

| KICKING | XP | Att | % | FG | Att | % |
|---|---|---|---|---|---|---|
| Biasucci | 24 | 24 | 100 | 24 | 27 | 89 |
| Jordan | 7 | 7 | 100 | 3 | 5 | 60 |

### (New England Patriots)

| PASSING | Att | Cmp | % | Yds | Yd/Att | TD | Int— | % | RK |
|---|---|---|---|---|---|---|---|---|---|
| Grogan | 161 | 93 | 58 | 1183 | 7.4 | 10 | 9— | 6 | |
| Ramsey | 134 | 71 | 53 | 898 | 6.7 | 6 | 6— | 5 | |
| Eason | 79 | 42 | 53 | 453 | 5.7 | 3 | 2— | 3 | |
| Bleier | 39 | 14 | 36 | 181 | 4.6 | 1 | 1— | 3 | |
| Flutie | 25 | 15 | 60 | 199 | 8.0 | 1 | 0— | 0 | |
| Tatupu | 1 | 1 | 100.0 | 15 | 15.0 | 1 | 0— | 0 | |
| Jones | 1 | 0 | 0.0 | 0 | 0.0 | 0 | 0— | 0 | |

| PUNTING | No | Avg |
|---|---|---|
| Camarillo | 63 | 39.5 |
| Hertine | 26 | 33.1 |

| KICKING | XP | Att | % | FG | Att | % |
|---|---|---|---|---|---|---|
| Franklin | 37 | 38 | 97 | 15 | 26 | 58 |
| Schubert | 1 | 1 | 100 | 1 | 2 | 50 |

### (Miami Dolphins)

| PASSING | Att | Cmp | % | Yds | Yd/Att | TD | Int— | % | RK |
|---|---|---|---|---|---|---|---|---|---|
| Marino | 444 | 263 | 59 | 3245 | 7.3 | 26 | 13— | 3 | 4 |
| Mackey | 109 | 57 | 52 | 604 | 5.5 | 3 | 5— | 5 | |
| Strock | 23 | 13 | 57 | 114 | 5.0 | 0 | 1— | 4 | |
| Stankavage | 7 | 4 | 57 | 8 | 1.1 | 0 | 1— | 14 | |
| Stradford | 1 | 1 | 100 | 6 | 6.0 | 0 | 0— | 0 | |

| PUNTING | No | Avg |
|---|---|---|
| Roby | 32 | 42.8 |
| Hayes | 8 | 34.3 |
| Gore | 14 | 35.9 |
| Strock | 9 | 30.8 |

| KICKING | XP | Att | % | FG | Att | % |
|---|---|---|---|---|---|---|
| Reveiz | 28 | 30 | 93 | 9 | 11 | 82 |
| Beecher | 12 | 12 | 100 | 3 | 4 | 75 |

### BUFFALO BILLS 7-8 Marv Levy

| Scores of Each Game | | |
|---|---|---|
| 28 | N.Y.JETS | 31 |
| 34 | HOUSTON | 30 |
| 6 | INDIANAPOLIS | 47 |
| 7 | New England | 14 |
| 6 | N.Y.GIANTS | *3 |
| 34 | Miami | *31 |
| 7 | WASHINGTON | 27 |
| 21 | DENVER | 14 |
| 21 | Cleveland | 27 |
| 17 | N.Y.Jets | 14 |
| 27 | MIAMI | 0 |
| 21 | L.A.Raiders | 34 |
| 27 | Indianapolis | 3 |
| 7 | NEW ENGLAND | 13 |
| 7 | Philadelphia | 17 |

| Use Name | Pos. | Hgt | Wgt | Age | Int | Pts |
|---|---|---|---|---|---|---|
| #Tony Brown | OT | 6'5" | 285 | 23 | | |
| Leonard Burton | OT-C | 6'3" | 275 | 23 | | |
| #Glen Campbell | OT | 6'4" | 280 | 26 | | |
| Joe Devlin | OT | 6'5" | 280 | 34 | | |
| #Don Sommer | OT | 6'4" | 290 | 23 | | |
| Will Wolford | OT | 6'5" | 276 | 23 | | |
| #Sean Dowling | OG-OT | 6'4" | 280 | 24 | | |
| #Mike Estep | OG-OT | 6'4" | 270 | 23 | | |
| Mitch Frerotte | OG | 6'3" | 280 | 22 | | |
| #Kevin Lamar | OG | 6'4" | 260 | 25 | | |
| #Rick Schulte | OG-OT | 6'2" | 270 | 24 | | |
| Jim Ritcher | OG | 6'3" | 265 | 29 | | |
| Mark Traynowicz | OG-C | 6'5" | 280 | 24 | | |
| Tim Vogler | OG | 6'3" | 280 | 30 | | |
| #Joe Bock | C | 6'4" | 254 | 28 | | |
| #Will Grant | C | 6'3" | 264 | 33 | | |
| Kent Hull | C | 6'4" | 275 | 26 | | |
| Adam Lingner | C | 6'4" | 260 | 26 | | |
| #Erik Rosenmeier | C | 6'4" | 240 | 22 | | |
| #Mark Shupe | C | 6'5" | 285 | 25 | | |
| #Joe Silipo | C | 6'3" | 295 | 28 | | |
| #Jack Bravyak | DE | 6'3" | 255 | 27 | | |
| #Arnold Campbell | DE | 6'3" | 260 | 24 | | |
| #Scott Garnett | DE-NT | 6'2" | 265 | 24 | | |
| Sean McNanie | DE | 6'5" | 270 | 25 | | 6 |
| Dean Prater | DE | 6'4" | 260 | 28 | | |
| Leon Seals | DE | 6'4" | 265 | 23 | | |
| Bruce Smith | DE | 6'4" | 285 | 24 | | |
| #Richard Tharpe | DE-NT | 6'3" | 255 | 26 | | |
| #Billy Witt | DE | 6'5" | 265 | 23 | | |
| #Ira Albright | NT-FB | 6' | 285 | 28 | | |
| #Scott Hernandez | NT | 6' | 250 | 27 | | |
| #Joe McGrail | NT | 6'3" | 280 | 23 | | |
| Bruce Mesner | NT | 6'5" | 280 | 23 | | |
| Fred Smerlas | NT | 6'3" | 280 | 30 | | |
| Cornelius Bennett | LB | 6'2" | 235 | 21 | | |
| Ray Bentley | LB | 6'2" | 245 | 26 | | |
| #Will Cokeley | LB | 6'2" | 220 | 26 | 1 | |
| Shane Conlan | LB | 6'3" | 230 | 23 | | |
| Tony Furjanic | LB | 6'1" | 228 | 23 | | |
| John Kaiser | LB | 6'3" | 227 | 25 | | |
| #Mike Jones | LB | 6'4" | 224 | 23 | | |
| #Bob LeBlanc | LB | 6'2" | 243 | 24 | | |
| #Steve Maidlow | LB | 6'2" | 240 | 27 | | |
| Eugene Marve | LB | 6'2" | 240 | 27 | | |
| Mark Pike | LB | 6'4" | 257 | 23 | | |
| Scott Radecic | LB | 6'3" | 242 | 25 | 2 | |
| #Scott Schankweiler | LB | 6' | 225 | 23 | 1 | |
| Darryl Talley | LB | 6'4" | 227 | 27 | | |
| #Craig Walls | LB | 6'1" | 215 | 29 | | |
| #Scott Waters | LB | 6'2" | 230 | 22 | | |
| #Al Wenglikowski | LB | 6'1" | 210 | 27 | | |
| #John Armstrong | DB | 5'9" | 190 | 24 | | |
| #Gerald Bess | DB | 6' | 188 | 29 | | |
| Derrick Burroughs | DB | 6'1" | 180 | 25 | 2 | |
| #Bill Callahan | DB | 6' | 200 | 23 | | |
| #Steve Clark | DB | 6'2" | 190 | 25 | 1 | |
| Wayne Davis | DB | 5'11" | 175 | 24 | | |
| Dwight Drane | DB | 6'2" | 205 | 25 | | |
| #Larry Friday | DB | 6'4" | 215 | 28 | | |
| Lawence Johnson | DB | 5'11" | 202 | 29 | | |
| Mark Kelso | DB | 5'11" | 177 | 24 | 6 | 6 |
| #John Lewis | DB | 5'10" | 175 | 25 | | |
| #David Martin | DB | 5'9" | 195 | 28 | | |
| Roland Mitchell | DB | 5'11" | 180 | 23 | | |
| #Chip Nuzzo | DB | 5'11' | 190 | 22 | | |
| Nate Odomes | DB | 5'10" | 188 | 22 | | |
| #Kerry Parker | DB | 6'1" | 188 | 31 | | |
| Ron Pitts | DB | 5'10" | 175 | 24 | 3 | |
| Durwood Roquemore | DB | 6'1" | 190 | 26 | | |
| Jim Kelly | QB | 6'3" | 218 | 27 | | |
| #Dan Manucci | QB | 6'2" | 199 | 29 | | |
| #Bran McClure | QB | 6'6" | 222 | 23 | | |
| #Mark Miller | QB | 6'2" | 210 | 24 | | |
| Frank Reich | QB | 6'3" | 208 | 25 | | |
| #Willie Totten | QB | 6'2" | 195 | 25 | | |
| #Joe Chetti | HB | 5'9" | 205 | 23 | | |
| Ronnie Harmon | HB | 5'11" | 192 | 23 | | 24 |
| #Mike Panepinto | HB | 5'11" | 202 | 21 | | |
| Kerry Porter | HB | 6'1" | 210 | 22 | | |
| Ricky Porter | HB | 5'11" | 205 | 27 | | |
| Robb Riddick | HB | 6' | 195 | 30 | | 50 |
| #Johnny Shepherd | HB | 5'10" | 185 | 30 | | |
| #Leonard Williams | HB | 6' | 205 | 23 | | |
| Carl Byrum | FB | 6' | 235 | 24 | | |
| #Bruce King | FB | 6'1" | 225 | 24 | | |
| #Warren Loving | FB | 6'1" | 230 | 25 | | |
| Jamie Mueller | FB | 6'1" | 225 | 22 | | 12 |
| #Gary Wilkins | FB | 6'1" | 235 | 23 | | |
| Walter Broughton | WR | 5'10" | 180 | 24 | | |
| #Marc Brown | WR | 6'2" | 195 | 26 | | 6 |
| Chris Burkett | WR | 6'4" | 210 | 25 | | 24 |
| #Reggie Bynum | WR | 6'1" | 185 | 23 | | |
| #Sheldon Gaines | WR | 5'9" | 155 | 23 | | |
| #Kris Haines | WR | 5'11" | 180 | 30 | | |
| Trumaine Johnson | WR | 6'1" | 196 | 27 | | |
| #Thad McFadden | WR | 6'2" | 200 | 25 | | 6 |
| Andre Reed | WR | 6' | 190 | 23 | | 30 |
| Steve Tasker | WR | 5'9" | 185 | 25 | | 2 |
| #Veno Belk | TE | 6'3" | 233 | 24 | | |
| #Keith McKeller | TE | 6'6" | 230 | 23 | | |
| Pete Metzelaars | TE | 6'7" | 243 | 27 | | |
| Butch Rolle | TE | 6'3" | 242 | 23 | | 12 |
| John Kidd | K | 6'3" | 208 | 24 | | |
| Scott Norwood | K | 6' | 207 | 27 | | 61 |
| #Rick Partridge | K | 6'1" | 175 | 30 | | |
| #Todd Schlopy | K | 5'10" | 165 | 26 | | 7 |

Mike Hamby - Hip Injury
Dale Hellestrae - Hip Injury
Clint Sampson - Knee Injury

Jerry Butler - Knee Injury
Greg Christy - Neck Injury
Chas Fox - Injury
Hal Garner - Knee Injury
Stam Gelbaugh - Elbow Injury

### NEW YORK JETS 6-9 Joe Walton

| Scores of Each Game | | |
|---|---|---|
| 31 | Buffalo | 28 |
| 43 | NEW ENGLAND | 24 |
| 24 | DALLAS | 38 |
| 0 | Indianapolis | 6 |
| 37 | MIAMI | *31 |
| 16 | Washington | 17 |
| 14 | INDIANAPOLIS | 19 |
| 30 | SEATTLE | 14 |
| 16 | Kansas City | 9 |
| 14 | BUFFALO | 17 |
| 27 | CINCINNATI | 20 |
| 28 | Miami | 37 |
| 20 | New England | 42 |
| 27 | PHILADELPHIA | 38 |
| 7 | N.Y.Giants | 20 |

| Use Name | Pos. | Hgt | Wgt | Age | Int | Pts |
|---|---|---|---|---|---|---|
| #Chris Brown | OT | 6'1" | 295 | 24 | | |
| Ken Jones | OT | 6'5" | 285 | 34 | | |
| Gordon King | OT-OG | 6'6" | 270 | 31 | | |
| Reggie McElroy | OT | 6'6" | 275 | 27 | | |
| Jim Sweeney | OT | 6'4" | 275 | 25 | | |
| #John Thomas | OT | 6'4" | 280 | 23 | | |
| Dan Alexander | OG-OT | 6'4" | 274 | 32 | | |
| Ted Banker | OG-C | 6'2" | 275 | 25 | | |
| #Anthony Corvino | OG-OT | 6'1" | 262 | 21 | | |
| Joe Fields | OG-C | 6'2" | 253 | 33 | | |
| Mike Haight | OG-OT | 6'4" | 270 | 24 | | |
| #Tom Humphrey | OG-OT | 6'3" | 280 | 24 | | |
| #Vince Jasper | OG | 6'4" | 270 | 22 | | |
| #Pete McCartney | OG | 6'6" | 260 | 25 | | |
| Guy Bingham | C-OG | 6'3" | 260 | 29 | | |
| #Martin Cornelson | C | 6'1" | 230 | 26 | | |
| #Eric Coss | C | 6'3" | 270 | 24 | | |
| Don Baldwin | DE | 6'3" | 263 | 23 | | |
| Barry Bennett | DE-DT | 6'4" | 260 | 31 | | |
| Jerome Foster | DE-DT | 6'2" | 275 | 27 | | |
| #Tony Garbarczyk | DE | 6'4" | 275 | 23 | | |
| Mark Gastineau | DE | 6'5" | 255 | 30 | | |
| Marty Lyons | DE-DT | 6'5" | 269 | 30 | | 2 |
| Scott Mersereau | DE-NT | 6'3" | 278 | 22 | | |
| Don Smith | DE | 6'5" | 262 | 30 | | |
| #Tony Chickillo | NT-DE | 6'4" | 270 | 27 | | |
| Joe Klecko | NT | 6'3" | 263 | 34 | | |
| Gerald Nichols | NT | 6'2" | 261 | 23 | | |
| #Lynwood Alford | LB | 6'3" | 220 | 24 | | |
| Troy Benson | LB | 6'2" | 235 | 24 | | |
| #Jay Brophy | LB | 6'3" | 233 | 27 | | |
| Kyle Clifton | LB | 6'4" | 236 | 25 | | |
| Bob Crable | LB | 6'3" | 230 | 27 | 1 | |
| Onzy Elam | LB | 6'2" | 225 | 23 | | |
| Alex Gordon | LB | 6'5" | 246 | 22 | | |
| #Jim Haslett | LB | 6'3" | 236 | 30 | 1 | |
| Kevin McArthur | LB | 6'2" | 245 | 24 | | |
| Lance Mehl | LB | 6'3" | 233 | 29 | | |
| Matt Monger | LB | 6'1" | 238 | 25 | | |
| Ken Rose | LB | 6'1" | 215 | 26 | 1 | |
| #Henry Walls | LB | 6'2" | 220 | 23 | | |
| #Ladell Wills | LB | 6'3" | 240 | 25 | | |
| #Mike Witteck | LB | 6'2" | 225 | 23 | | |
| Russell Carter | DB | 6'2" | 195 | 25 | | |
| #Trent Collins | DB | 6'1" | 187 | 26 | | |
| Sean Dykes | DB | 5'10" | 170 | 23 | | |
| Kerry Glenn | DB | 5'9" | 175 | 25 | | |
| Harry Hamilton | DB | 6' | 195 | 24 | 3 | |
| #Jo Jo Heath | DB | 5'10" | 178 | 30 | 1 | |
| #Marc Hogan | DB | 6' | 180 | 25 | 1 | |
| Jerry Holmes | DB | 6'2" | 175 | 29 | 1 | |
| Carl Howard | DB | 6'2" | 190 | 25 | 3 | |
| Bobby Humphrey | DB | 5'10" | 180 | 26 | | 6 |
| Sid Lewis | DB | 5'11" | 180 | 23 | | |
| Lester Lyles | DB | 6'3" | 218 | 24 | | |
| Rich Miano | DB | 6' | 200 | 24 | 3 | 6 |
| George Radachowsky | DB | 5'11" | 192 | 24 | 2 | |
| #Larry Robinson | DB | 5'9" | 194 | 25 | 1 | |
| #Treg Songy | DB | 6'2" | 200 | 25 | | |
| Mike Zordich | DB | 5'11" | 207 | 23 | | |
| #Walter Briggs | QB | 6'1" | 205 | 22 | | |
| #Tom Flick | QB | 6'3" | 190 | 28 | | |
| #David Norris | QB | 6'4" | 220 | 23 | | |
| Ken O'Brien | QB | 6'4" | 208 | 26 | | |
| Pat Ryan | QB | 6'3" | 210 | 31 | | 6 |
| Dennis Bligen | HB | 5'11" | 215 | 25 | | 6 |
| #Joe Burke | HB | 6' | 200 | 26 | | |
| Nuu Faaola | HB | 5'11" | 210 | 23 | | 12 |
| #Derrick Foster | HB | 5'11" | 205 | 23 | | |
| Johnny Hector | HB-FB | 5'11" | 200 | 26 | | 66 |
| #Eddie Hunter (to TB) | HB | 5'10" | 205 | 22 | | 12 |
| Freeman McNeil | HB | 5'11" | 214 | 28 | | 6 |
| #Maurice Turner | HB | 5'11" | 207 | 26 | | |
| Marion Barber | FB | 6'3" | 228 | 27 | | |
| #John Chirico | FB | 6' | 220 | 22 | | |
| #Tim Newman | FB | 6' | 220 | 23 | | |
| Roger Vick | FB | 6'3" | 232 | 23 | | 6 |
| #Derrick Gaffney | WR | 6'1" | 182 | 32 | | |
| #Michael Harper | WR | 5'10" | 180 | 26 | | 12 |
| #Scott Holman | WR | 6'2" | 193 | 24 | | |
| #Stan Hunter | WR | 6'2" | 184 | 23 | | 6 |
| #Tracy Martin | WR | 6'3" | 205 | 22 | | |
| Reggie Smith | WR | 5'4" | 168 | 31 | | |
| Kurt Sohn | WR | 5'11" | 180 | 30 | | 12 |
| Al Toon | WR | 6'4" | 205 | 24 | | 30 |
| JoJo Townsell | WR | 5'9" | 180 | 26 | | 6 |
| Wesley Walker | WR | 6' | 182 | 32 | | 6 |
| Billy Griggs | TE | 6'3" | 230 | 27 | | |
| Rocky Klever | TE | 6'3" | 230 | 28 | | |
| #Jamie Kurisko | TE | 6'4" | 236 | 23 | | 6 |
| #Eric Riley | TE | 6'3" | 230 | 22 | | |
| Mickey Shuler | TE | 6'3" | 231 | 31 | | 18 |
| #Tony Sweet | TE | 6'4" | 230 | 23 | | |
| Dave Jennings | K | 6'4" | 200 | 35 | | |
| Pat Leahy | K | 6' | 193 | 36 | | 85 |
| #Tom O'Connor | K | 6'1" | 190 | 24 | | |
| #Pat Ragusa | K | 5'8" | 180 | 24 | | 13 |

Tom Baldwin - Knee Injury

## Central Division

### CLEVELAND BROWNS 10-5 Marty Schottenheimer

| Scores of Each Game | | |
|---|---|---|
| 21 | New Orleans | 28 |
| 34 | PITTSBURGH | 10 |
| 20 | New England | 10 |
| 10 | HOUSTON | 15 |
| 34 | Cincinnati | 0 |
| 30 | L.A.RAMS | 17 |
| 24 | San Diego | *27 |
| 38 | ATLANTA | 3 |
| 27 | BUFFALO | 21 |
| 40 | Houston | 7 |
| 24 | San Francisco | 38 |
| 7 | INDIANAPOLIS | 9 |
| 38 | CINCINNATI | 24 |
| 24 | L.A.Raiders | 17 |
| 19 | Pittsburgh | 13 |

* Overtime

| Use Name | Pos. | Hgt | Wgt | Age | Int | Pts |
|---|---|---|---|---|---|---|
| Rickey Bolden | OT | 6'6" | 280 | 25 | | |
| #Keith Bosley | OT | 6'5" | 320 | 24 | | |
| Paul Farren | OT-OG | 6'5" | 280 | 26 | | |
| Darryl Haley | OT-OG | 6'4" | 265 | 26 | | |
| Gregg Rakoczy | OT | 6'6" | 290 | 22 | | |
| Cody Risien | OT | 6'7" | 280 | 30 | | |
| #Ralph Van Dyke | OT | 6'6" | 273 | 23 | | |
| Dan Fike | OG | 6'7" | 280 | 26 | | |
| #Mark Krerowicz | OG | 6'3" | 285 | 24 | | |
| #Dave Sparenberg | OG | 6'3" | 267 | 28 | | |
| Larry Williams | OG | 6'5" | 290 | 24 | | |
| #Blake Wingle | OG | 6'2" | 260 | 27 | | |
| Mike Baab | C | 6'4" | 270 | 27 | | |
| #Mike Katolin | C | 6'3" | 255 | 29 | | |
| #Mike Teifke | C | 6'4" | 255 | 23 | | |
| Frank Winters | C | 6'3" | 290 | 23 | | |
| Al Baker | DE | 6'6" | 270 | 30 | | |
| Reggie Camp | DE | 6'4" | 280 | 25 | | |
| #Alex Carter | DE | 6'3" | 255 | 24 | | |
| Sam Clancy | DE | 6'7" | 260 | 29 | | |
| #Scott Cooper | DE | 6'5" | 285 | 23 | | |
| Carl Hairston | DE | 6'3" | 260 | 34 | | |
| Marlon Jones | DE | 6'4" | 260 | 23 | | |
| #Aaron Moog | DE | 6'4" | 260 | 25 | | |
| Darryl Sims | DE | 6'3" | 282 | 26 | | |
| Bob Golic | NT | 6'2" | 270 | 29 | | |
| Dave Puzzuoli | NT | 6'3" | 260 | 26 | | |
| #Mike Rusinek | NT | 6'3" | 250 | 24 | | |
| #Dave Butler | LB | 6'4" | 225 | 22 | | |
| #James Capers | LB | 6'4" | 232 | 28 | | |
| #Tim Crawford | LB | 6'4" | 245 | 25 | | |
| David Grayson | LB | 6'2" | 229 | 23 | | 6 |
| Anthony Griggs | LB | 6'3" | 230 | 27 | | |
| Rusty Guilbeau | LB | 6'4" | 235 | 28 | | |
| #Cliff Hanneman | LB | 6'2" | 235 | 23 | | |
| Eddie Johnson | LB | 6'1" | 225 | 28 | 1 | |
| Mike Johnson | LB | 6'1" | 228 | 24 | 1 | |
| Mike Junkin | LB | 6'3" | 247 | 22 | | |
| #Mike Kovaleski | LB | 6'2" | 225 | 22 | | |
| Clay Matthews | LB | 6'2" | 235 | 30 | 4 | 6 |
| Nick Miller | LB | 6'2" | 238 | 23 | | |
| #Stevan Nave | LB | 6'2" | 250 | 24 | | |
| #Jerry Parker | LB | 6' | 227 | 22 | | |
| #Tom Polley | LB | 6'3" | 250 | 25 | | |
| Lucius Sanford | LB | 6'2" | 216 | 31 | | |
| #Vincent Barnett | DB | 6'1" | 200 | 22 | | |
| Stephen Braggs | DB | 5'9" | 173 | 22 | | |
| #Vince Carreker | DB | 6' | 183 | 24 | | |
| Hanford Dixon | DB | 5'11" | 186 | 28 | 3 | |
| #Brian Dudley | DB | 6'1" | 180 | 27 | | |
| Ray Ellis | DB | 6'1" | 196 | 28 | | 6 |
| Al Gross | DB | 6'3" | 195 | 26 | | |
| Mark Harper | DB | 5'9" | 174 | 25 | 2 | |
| D.D. Hoggard | DB | 6' | 188 | 22 | | |
| #Alvin Horn | DB | 5'11" | 185 | 26 | 1 | |
| #Enis Jackson | DB | 5'9" | 180 | 24 | | |
| Frank Minnifield | DB | 5'9" | 180 | 27 | 4 | |
| #Billy Robinson | DB | 6'1" | 200 | 24 | | |
| #DeJuan Robinson | DB | 5'10" | 185 | 22 | 1 | |
| Chris Rockins | DB | 6' | 195 | 25 | 2 | |
| Troy Wilson | DB | 5'10" | 170 | 21 | 1 | |
| #Felix Wright | DB | 6'2" | 190 | 26 | 4 | 6 |
| #Jeff Christensen | QB | 6'3" | 202 | 27 | | |
| Gary Danielson | QB | 6'2" | 196 | 35 | | |
| #Homer Jordan | QB | 6' | 183 | 27 | | |
| Bernie Kosar | QB | 6'5" | 210 | 23 | | 6 |
| Mike Pagel | QB | 6'2" | 206 | 27 | | |
| #Mike Crawford | HB | 5'10" | 215 | 23 | | |
| #Stacey Driver | HB | 5'7" | 190 | 23 | | |
| Major Everett (to ATL) | HB | 5'10" | 218 | 27 | | |
| #Kirk Jones | HB | 5'10" | 210 | 22 | | |
| #Larry Mason | HB | 5'11" | 205 | 26 | | |
| Earnest Byner | FB | 5'10" | 215 | 24 | | 60 |
| #Johnny Davis | FB | 6'1" | 235 | 31 | | |
| Herman Fontenot | FB | 6' | 206 | 23 | | |
| Kevin Mack | FB | 6' | 225 | 25 | | 36 |
| Tim Manoa | FB | 6'1" | 227 | 22 | | |
| George Swarn | FB | 5'10" | 205 | 23 | | |
| #Clayton Beauford | WR | 5'11" | 190 | 24 | | |
| Brian Brennan | WR | 5'9" | 178 | 25 | | 36 |
| #Perry Kemp | WR | 5'11" | 170 | 25 | | |
| Reggie Langhorne | WR | 6'2" | 195 | 24 | | 6 |
| Gerald McNeil | WR | 5'7" | 147 | 25 | | 12 |
| #Steve Pierce | WR | 5'10" | 190 | 23 | | |
| Webster Slaughter | WR | 6' | 170 | 22 | | 42 |
| #Keith Tinsley | WR | 5'9" | 184 | 22 | | |
| #David Verser | WR | 6'1" | 202 | 29 | | |
| #Louis Watson | WR | 5'11' | 175 | 24 | | |
| Remi Watson | WR | 6' | 174 | 22 | | |
| Clarence Weathers | WR | 5'9" | 170 | 25 | | 12 |
| Glen Young | WR | 6'2" | 205 | 26 | | |
| #Donnie Echols | TE | 6'3" | 240 | 29 | | |
| #Chris Kelley | TE | 6'4" | 239 | 22 | | |
| Ozzie Newsome | TE | 6'2" | 232 | 31 | | |
| Derek Tennell | TE | 6'5" | 245 | 23 | | 18 |
| Travis Tucker | TE | 6'3" | 240 | 23 | | |
| Matt Bahr | K | 5'10" | 175 | 31 | | 21 |
| #Brian Franco | K | 5'8" | 165 | 27 | | |
| Jeff Jaeger | K | 5'11" | 189 | 22 | | 75 |
| #Goran Lingmerth | K | 5'8" | 160 | 22 | | |
| Jeff Gossett (to HOU) | K | 6'2" | 200 | 30 | | |
| #Dale Walters | K | 6' | 200 | 26 | | |
| George Winslow | K | 6'4" | 205 | 24 | | |

Tony Baker - Wrist Injury
Robert Stallings - Ankle Injury

# - on the active roster for strike replacement games only

## BUFFALO BILLS

### RUSHING

| Last Name | No. | Yds | Avg | TD |
|---|---|---|---|---|
| Harmon | 116 | 485 | 4.2 | 3 |
| Mueller | 82 | 354 | 3.8 | 1 |
| Byrum | 66 | 280 | 4.2 | 0 |
| Riddick | 59 | 221 | 3.7 | 5 |
| R. Porter | 47 | 177 | 3.8 | 0 |
| Kelly | 29 | 133 | 4.6 | 0 |
| Shepherd | 12 | 42 | 3.5 | 0 |
| King | 9 | 28 | 3.1 | 0 |
| L. Williams | 9 | 25 | 2.8 | 0 |
| Partridge | 1 | 13 | 13.0 | 0 |
| Totten | 12 | 11 | 0.9 | 0 |
| Manucci | 4 | 6 | 1.5 | 0 |
| McClure | 2 | 4 | 2.0 | 0 |
| Reed | 1 | 1 | 1.0 | 0 |
| K. Porter | 2 | 0 | 0.0 | 0 |

### RECEIVING

| Last Name | No. | Yds | Avg | TD |
|---|---|---|---|---|
| Reed | 57 | 752 | 13.2 | 5 |
| Burkett | 56 | 765 | 13.7 | 4 |
| Harmon | 56 | 477 | 8.5 | 2 |
| Metzelaars | 28 | 290 | 10.4 | 0 |
| T. Johnson | 15 | 186 | 12.4 | 2 |
| Riddick | 15 | 96 | 6.4 | 3 |
| M.Brown | 9 | 120 | 13.3 | 1 |
| Gaines | 9 | 115 | 12.8 | 0 |
| McKeller | 9 | 80 | 8.9 | 0 |
| R. Porter | 9 | 70 | 7.8 | 0 |
| Broughton | 5 | 90 | 18.0 | 1 |
| McFadden | 4 | 41 | 10.3 | 1 |
| Byrum | 3 | 23 | 7.7 | 0 |
| Mueller | 3 | 13 | 4.3 | 0 |
| Bynum | 2 | 24 | 12.0 | 0 |
| Rolle | 2 | 6 | 3.0 | 2 |
| Kelly | 1 | 35 | 35.0 | 0 |
| Chetti | 1 | 9 | 9.0 | 0 |
| Belk | 1 | 7 | 7.0 | 0 |
| Williams | 1 | 5 | 5.0 | 0 |
| King | 1 | 3 | 3.0 | 0 |
| Shepherd | 1 | 2 | 2.0 | 0 |

### PUNT RETURNS

| Last Name | No. | Yds | Avg | TD |
|---|---|---|---|---|
| Pitts | 23 | 149 | 6.5 | 0 |
| McFadden | 8 | 83 | 10.4 | 0 |

### KICKOFF RETURNS

| Last Name | No. | Yds | Avg | TD |
|---|---|---|---|---|
| Tasker | 11 | 197 | 17.9 | 0 |
| R. Porter | 8 | 219 | 27.4 | 0 |
| Riddick | 7 | 151 | 21.6 | 0 |
| McFadden | 7 | 121 | 17.3 | 0 |
| Mueller | 5 | 74 | 14.8 | 0 |
| Brown | 2 | 35 | 17.5 | 0 |
| Armstrong | 2 | 25 | 12.5 | 0 |
| Harmon | 1 | 30 | 30.0 | 0 |
| Radecic | 1 | 14 | 14.0 | 0 |
| Rolle | 1 | 6 | 6.0 | 0 |

### PASSING — PUNTING — KICKING

| PASSING | Att | Cmp | % | Yds | Yd/Att | TD | Int— | % | RK |
|---|---|---|---|---|---|---|---|---|---|
| Kelly | 419 | 250 | 60 | 2798 | 6.7 | 19 | 11— | 3 | 11 |
| McClure | 38 | 20 | 53 | 181 | 4.8 | 0 | 3— | | 8 |
| Totten | 33 | 13 | 39 | 155 | 4.7 | 2 | 2— | | 6 |
| Manucci | 21 | 7 | 33 | 68 | 3.2 | | 2— | | 10 |
| Miller | 3 | 1 | 33 | 9 | 3.0 | 0 | 1— | | 33 |
| Kidd | 1 | 0 | 0 | 0 | 0.0 | 0 | 0— | | 0 |
| Riddick | 1 | 1 | 100 | 35 | 35.0 | 0 | 0— | | 0 |

| PUNTING | No | Avg |
|---|---|---|
| Kidd | 64 | 39.0 |
| Partridge | 19 | 35.7 |

| KICKING | XP | Att | % | FG | Att | % |
|---|---|---|---|---|---|---|
| Norwood | 31 | 31 | 100 | 10 | 15 | 67 |
| Schlopy | 1 | 2 | 50 | 2 | 5 | 40 |

## NEW YORK JETS

### RUSHING

| Last Name | No. | Yds | Avg | TD |
|---|---|---|---|---|
| McNeil | 121 | 530 | 4.4 | 0 |
| Hector | 111 | 435 | 3.9 | 11 |
| Vick | 77 | 257 | 3.3 | 1 |
| E. Hunter | 56 | 210 | 3.8 | 0 |
| Bligen | 31 | 128 | 4.1 | 1 |
| O'Brien | 30 | 61 | 2.0 | 0 |
| Faaola | 14 | 43 | 3.1 | 2 |
| Chirico | 12 | 22 | 1.8 | 1 |
| D. Foster | 1 | 9 | 9.0 | 0 |
| Jennings | 2 | 5 | 2.5 | 0 |
| Norrie | 5 | 5 | 1.0 | 0 |
| Ryan | 4 | 5 | 1.3 | 1 |
| Briggs | 1 | 4 | 4.0 | 0 |
| Townsell | 1 | -2 | -2.0 | 0 |

### RECEIVING

| Last Name | No. | Yds | Avg | TD |
|---|---|---|---|---|
| Toon | 68 | 976 | 14.4 | 5 |
| Shuler | 43 | 434 | 10.1 | 3 |
| Hector | 32 | 249 | 7.8 | 0 |
| McNeil | 24 | 262 | 10.9 | 1 |
| Sohn | 23 | 261 | 11.3 | 2 |
| Harper | 18 | 225 | 12.5 | 1 |
| Holman | 15 | 155 | 10.3 | 0 |
| Klever | 14 | 152 | 10.9 | 0 |
| Vick | 13 | 108 | 8.3 | 0 |
| Bligen | 11 | 81 | 7.4 | 0 |
| Walker | 9 | 190 | 21.1 | 1 |
| E. Hunter | 7 | 28 | 4.0 | 2 |
| S. Hunter | 6 | 50 | 8.3 | 1 |
| E. Riley | 4 | 42 | 10.5 | 0 |
| Townsell | 4 | 37 | 9.3 | 0 |
| Chirico | 4 | 18 | 4.5 | 0 |
| Sweet | 3 | 45 | 15.0 | 0 |
| Griggs | 2 | 17 | 8.5 | 1 |
| Dennison | 2 | 8 | 4.0 | 0 |
| Kurisko | 1 | 41 | 41.0 | 1 |
| Faaola | 1 | 16 | 16.0 | 0 |
| Gaffney | 1 | 10 | 10.0 | 0 |
| D. Foster | 1 | 9 | 9.0 | 0 |

### PUNT RETURNS

| Last Name | No. | Yds | Avg | TD |
|---|---|---|---|---|
| Townsell | 32 | 381 | 11.9 | 1 |
| Harper | 4 | 93 | 23.3 | 1 |
| D. Foster | 2 | 8 | 4.0 | 0 |
| R. Smith | 2 | 9 | 4.5 | 0 |
| Collins | 1 | 0 | 0.0 | 0 |
| Sohn | 1 | 6 | 6.0 | 0 |

### KICKOFF RETURNS

| Last Name | No. | Yds | Avg | TD |
|---|---|---|---|---|
| Humphery | 18 | 357 | 19.8 | 0 |
| Townsell | 11 | 272 | 24.7 | 0 |
| E. Hunter | 8 | 123 | 15.4 | 0 |
| Martin | 8 | 180 | 22.5 | 0 |
| Klever | 5 | 85 | 17.0 | 0 |
| Harper | 4 | 75 | 18.8 | 0 |
| R. Smith | 4 | 60 | 15.0 | 0 |
| Sohn | 3 | 47 | 15.7 | 0 |
| Barber | 2 | 5 | 2.5 | 0 |
| Faaola | 1 | 4 | 4.0 | 0 |
| Griggs | 1 | 13 | 13.0 | 0 |

### PASSING — PUNTING — KICKING

| PASSING | Att | Cmp | % | Yds | Yd/Att | TD | Int— | % | RK |
|---|---|---|---|---|---|---|---|---|---|
| O'Brien | 393 | 234 | 60 | 2696 | 6.86 | 13 | 8— | 2 | 14 |
| Norrie | 68 | 35 | 52 | 376 | 5.5 | 1 | 4— | | 6 |
| Ryan | 53 | 32 | 60 | 314 | 5.9 | 4 | 2— | | 4 |
| Briggs | 2 | 0 | 0 | 0 | 0.0 | 0 | 1— | | 50 |
| Jennings | 1 | 1 | 100 | 16 | 16.0 | 0 | 0— | | 0 |

| PUNTING | No | Avg |
|---|---|---|
| Jennings | 64 | 38.2 |
| O'Connor | 18 | 33.4 |

| KICKING | XP | Att | % | FG | Att | % |
|---|---|---|---|---|---|---|
| Leahy | 31 | 31 | 100 | 18 | 22 | 82 |
| Ragusa | 7 | 7 | 100 | 2 | 4 | 50 |

## CLEVELAND BROWNS

### RUSHING

| Last Name | No. | Yds | Avg | TD |
|---|---|---|---|---|
| Mack | 201 | 735 | 3.7 | 5 |
| Byner | 105 | 432 | 4.1 | 8 |
| Mason | 56 | 207 | 3.7 | 2 |
| Manoa | 23 | 116 | 5.0 | 0 |
| Everett | 34 | 95 | 2.8 | 0 |
| Christensen | 11 | 41 | 3.7 | 0 |
| Fontenot | 15 | 33 | 2.2 | 1 |
| Driver | 9 | 31 | 3.4 | 0 |
| Kosar | 15 | 22 | 1.5 | 1 |
| McNeil | 1 | 17 | 17.0 | 0 |
| Verser | 1 | 9 | 9.0 | 0 |
| Davis | 1 | 7 | 7.0 | 0 |
| Danielson | 1 | 0 | 0.0 | 0 |
| Katolin | 1 | 0 | 0.0 | 0 |

### RECEIVING

| Last Name | No. | Yds | Avg | TD |
|---|---|---|---|---|
| Byner | 52 | 552 | 10.6 | 2 |
| Slaughter | 47 | 806 | 17.1 | 7 |
| Brennan | 43 | 607 | 14.1 | 6 |
| Newsome | 34 | 375 | 11.0 | 0 |
| Mack | 32 | 223 | 7.0 | 1 |
| Langhorne | 20 | 288 | 14.4 | 1 |
| Kemp | 12 | 224 | 18.7 | 2 |
| Weathers | 11 | 153 | 13.9 | 2 |
| Tennell | 9 | 102 | 11.3 | 3 |
| McNeil | 8 | 120 | 15.0 | 2 |
| Everett | 8 | 41 | 5.1 | 0 |
| Mason | 5 | 26 | 5.2 | 1 |
| Fontenot | 4 | 40 | 10.0 | 0 |
| Pierce | 2 | 21 | 10.5 | 0 |
| Tinsley | 1 | 17 | 17.0 | 0 |
| R. Watson | 1 | 13 | 13.0 | 0 |
| L. Watson | 1 | 9 | 9.0 | 0 |
| Manoa | 1 | 8 | 8.0 | 0 |

### PUNT RETURNS

| Last Name | No. | Yds | Avg | TD |
|---|---|---|---|---|
| McNeil | 34 | 386 | 11.4 | 0 |
| Wilson | 10 | 101 | 10.1 | 0 |

### KICKOFF RETURNS

| Last Name | No. | Yds | Avg | TD |
|---|---|---|---|---|
| Young | 18 | 412 | 22.9 | 0 |
| McNeil | 11 | 205 | 18.6 | 0 |
| Fontenot | 9 | 130 | 14.4 | 0 |
| Everett | 2 | 33 | 16.5 | 0 |
| Tinsley | 2 | 31 | 15.5 | 0 |
| Manoa | 2 | 14 | 7.0 | 0 |
| Beauford | 1 | 22 | 22.0 | 0 |
| Driver | 1 | 16 | 16.0 | 0 |
| Langhorne | 1 | 8 | 8.0 | 0 |
| Grayson | 1 | 6 | 6.0 | 0 |
| Byner | 1 | 2 | 2.0 | 0 |
| Mason | 1 | 0 | 0.0 | 0 |

### PASSING — PUNTING — KICKING

| PASSING | Att | Cmp | % | Yds | Yd/Att | TD | Int— | % | RK |
|---|---|---|---|---|---|---|---|---|---|
| Kosar | 389 | 241 | 62.0 | 3033 | 7.80 | 22 | 9— | 2 | 2 |
| Danielson | 33 | 25 | 75.8 | 281 | 8.52 | 4 | 0— | | 0 |
| Christensen | 58 | 24 | 41.4 | 297 | 5.12 | 1 | 3— | | 5 |
| Fontenot | 1 | 1 | 100 | 14 | 14.00 | 0 | 0— | | 0 |
| Jaeger | 1 | 0 | 0.0 | 0 | 0.00 | 0 | 0— | | 0 |

| PUNTING | No | Avg |
|---|---|---|
| Gossett | 45 | 39.5 |
| Winslow | 18 | 34.2 |
| Walters | 11 | 36.4 |

| KICKING | XP | Att | % | FG | Att | % |
|---|---|---|---|---|---|---|
| Jaeger | 33 | 33 | 100 | 14 | 22 | 64 |
| Bahr | 9 | 10 | 90 | 4 | 5 | 80 |
| Franco | 2 | 2 | 100 | 3 | 4 | 75 |
| Kelley | 1 | 1 | 100 | 0 | 0 | 0 |

## HOUSTON OILERS 9-6 Jerry Glanville

| Scores of Each Game | | |
|---|---|---|
| 20 | L.A.RAMS | 16 |
| 30 | Buffalo | 34 |
| 40 | Denver | 10 |
| 15 | Cleveland | 10 |
| 7 | NEW ENGLAND | 21 |
| 37 | ATLANTA | 33 |
| 31 | Cincinnati | 29 |
| 20 | San Francisco | 27 |
| 23 | Pittsburgh | 3 |
| 7 | CLEVELAND | 40 |
| 27 | Indianapolis | 51 |
| 33 | SAN DIEGO | 18 |
| 10 | New Orleans | 24 |
| 24 | PITTSBURGH | 16 |
| 21 | CINCINNATI | 17 |

| Use Name | Pos. | Hgt | Wgt | Age | Int | Pts |
|---|---|---|---|---|---|---|
| Bruce Davis (from RAID) | OT | 6'6" | 280 | 31 | | |
| John Davis | OT-OG | 6'4" | 304 | 22 | | |
| #Jerrell Franklin | OT | 6'3" | 287 | 28 | | |
| Mike Kelley | OT-OG | 6'5" | 280 | 25 | | |
| Bruce Matthews | OT-OG | 6'4" | 280 | 26 | | |
| #Clay Miller | OT-OG | 6'4" | 273 | 24 | | |
| Barry Pettyjohn | OT-C | 6'5 | 285 | 23 | | |
| Dean Steinkuhler | OT | 6'3" | 278 | 26 | | |
| Doug Williams | OT-OG | 6'5" | 288 | 24 | | |
| #Scott Boucher | OG | 6'3" | 260 | 29 | | |
| Kent Hill | OG | 6'5" | 265 | 30 | | |
| #Doug Kellermeyer | OG-OT | 6'3" | 275 | 26 | | |
| Mike Munchak | OG | 6'3" | 280 | 27 | | |
| Vince Stroth | OG | 6'4" | 270 | 26 | | |
| #Almon Young | OG | 6'3" | 290 | 25 | | |
| Billy Kidd | C | 6'4" | 270 | 26 | | |
| Jay Pennison | C | 6'1" | 275 | 25 | | |
| #Brett Petersmark | C | 6'3" | 280 | 24 | | |
| Jesse Baker | DE | 6'5" | 260 | 30 | | 2 |
| Richard Byrd | DE | 6'4" | 265 | 25 | | |
| Ray Childress | DE | 6'6" | 276 | 24 | | |
| Rayford Cooks | DE | 6'3" | 245 | 25 | | |
| William Fuller | DE | 6'3" | 260 | 25 | | |
| #Eric Larkin | DE | 6'4" | 265 | 23 | | |
| Kenny Neil | DE | 6'4" | 249 | 28 | | |
| #Bob Otto | DE | 6'6" | 255 | 24 | | |
| Joe Dixon | NT | 6'3" | 275 | 23 | | |
| Charles Martin (from GB) | NT | 6'4" | 280 | 28 | | |
| Doug Smith | NT | 6'5" | 282 | 28 | | |
| #Dwaine Turner | NT | 6' | 290 | 23 | | |
| Robert Abraham | LB | 6'1" | 236 | 27 | | |
| #Tom Briehl | LB | 6'3" | 248 | 24 | | |
| Toby Caston | LB | 6'1" | 235 | 22 | | |
| Eric Fairs | LB | 6'3" | 240 | 23 | | |
| #Scott Fox | LB | 6'2" | 222 | 23 | | |
| John Grimsley | LB | 6'2" | 236 | 25 | | |
| #Thad Jefferson | LB | 5'11" | 225 | 23 | | |
| #Byron Johnson | LB | 6'1" | 220 | 25 | | |
| Walter Johnson | LB | 6' | 241 | 23 | | |
| Robert Lyles | LB | 6'1" | 223 | 26 | 2 | 6 |
| Johnny Meads | LB | 6'2" | 230 | 26 | | |
| Eugene Seale | LB | 5'10" | 250 | 23 | 1 | 6 |
| Al Smith | LB | 6'1" | 230 | 22 | | |
| #Larry Smith | LB | 6'1" | 210 | 22 | | |
| #Paul Vogel | LB | 6'1" | 220 | 23 | | |
| #Earl Allen | DB | 5'11" | 193 | 21 | | |
| Patrick Allen | DB | 5'10" | 180 | 26 | 1 | |
| #Craig Birdsong | DB | 6'2" | 217 | 23 | | |
| Keith Bostic | DB | 6'1" | 223 | 26 | 6 | |
| Sonny Brown | DB | 6'2" | 200 | 23 | | |
| Steve Brown | DB | 5'11' | 187 | 27 | 2 | |
| Domingo Bryant | DB | 6'4" | 175 | 23 | 4 | |
| #Charles Clinton | DB | 5'8" | 170 | 25 | | |
| Jeff Donaldson | DB | 6' | 194 | 25 | 4 | |
| Bo Eason | DB | 6'2" | 205 | 26 | | |
| Kenny Johnson | DB | 5'10" | 175 | 29 | | |
| Richard Johnson | DB | 6'1" | 190 | 23 | 1 | |
| #Larry Joyner | DB | 6' | 207 | 23 | | |
| Kurt Kafentzis | DB | 6'2" | 190 | 24 | | |
| Allen Lyday | DB | 5'10" | 192 | 26 | | |
| Audrey McMillian | DB | 6' | 190 | 23 | 1 | |
| Tony Newsom | DB | 5'8" | 175 | 22 | 1 | |
| #Donovan Small | DB | 5'11" | 190 | 23 | 1 | |
| #Emmuel Thompson | DB | 5'11' | 180 | 27 | | |
| #Robert White | DB | 6'2" | 180 | 24 | | |
| Cody Carlson | QB | 6'3" | 203 | 24 | | |
| Warren Moon | QB | 6'3" | 210 | 31 | | |
| Brent Pease | QB | 6'2" | 200 | 22 | | 6 |
| #John Witkowski | QB | 6'1" | 195 | 25 | | |
| #Eric Cobble | HB | 5'10" | 205 | 23 | | |
| #Herman Hunter | HB | 6'1" | 205 | 26 | | |
| Andrew Jackson | HB | 5'10" | 190 | 23 | | 6 |
| Allen Pinkett | HB | 5'9" | 185 | 23 | | |
| Mike Rozier | HB | 5'10" | 211 | 26 | | |
| Spencer Tillman | HB | 5'11" | 206 | 23 | | 6 |
| Ira Valentine | FB | 6' | 212 | 24 | | |
| Alonzo Highsmith | FB | 6'1" | 235 | 22 | | 18 |
| #Ricky Moore | FB | 5'11" | 230 | 24 | | |
| Ray Wallace | FB | 6' | 220 | 23 | | |
| #Chris Darrington | WR | 5'10" | 180 | 23 | | |
| Willie Drewrey | WR | 5'7" | 164 | 24 | | |
| Curtis Duncan | WR | 5'11" | 184 | 22 | | 30 |
| Ernest Givins | WR | 5'9" | 170 | 31 | | 36 |
| #Leonard Harris | WR | 5'8" | 165 | 26 | | |
| Drew Hill | WR | 5'9" | 170 | 31 | | 36 |
| Haywood Jeffires | WR | 6'2" | 198 | 22 | | |
| #Keith McDonald | WR | 5'9" | 170 | 23 | | 6 |
| Joey Walters | WR | 5'11" | 175 | 29 | | |
| #Oliver Williams | WR | 6'3" | 195 | 26 | | 6 |
| Mitch Daum | TE | 6'5" | 250 | 23 | | |
| #Scott Eccles | TE | 6'5" | 245 | 24 | | |
| Mark Gehring | TE | 6'4" | 235 | 23 | | 6 |
| #Arrike James | TE | 6'4" | 238 | 23 | | |
| Jeff Parks | TE | 6'4" | 240 | 23 | | |
| Jamie Williams | TE | 6'4" | 245 | 27 | | 18 |
| #John Diettrich | K | 6'2" | 190 | 24 | | 23 |
| Lee Johnson (to CLE) | K | 6'2" | 198 | 25 | | |
| Steve Superick | K | 5'11" | 204 | 23 | | |
| Tony Zendejas | K | 5'8" | 165 | 27 | | 92 |

## PITTSBURGH STEELERS 8-7 Chuck Noll

| Scores of Each Game | | |
|---|---|---|
| 30 | SAN FRANCISCO | 17 |
| 10 | Cleveland | 34 |
| 28 | Atlanta | 12 |
| 21 | L.A.Rams | 31 |
| 21 | INDIANAPOLIS | 7 |
| 23 | CINCINNATI | 20 |
| 24 | Miami | 35 |
| 17 | Kansas City | 16 |
| 3 | HOUSTON | 23 |
| 30 | Cincinnati | 16 |
| 16 | NEW ORLEANS | 20 |
| 13 | SEATTLE | 9 |
| 20 | San Diego | 16 |
| 16 | Houston | 24 |
| 13 | CLEVELAND | 19 |

| Use Name | Pos. | Hgt | Wgt | Age | Int | Pts |
|---|---|---|---|---|---|---|
| Buddy Aydelette | OT-C | 6'4" | 262 | 31 | | |
| #Jim Boyle | OT | 6'5" | 270 | 25 | | |
| Tunch Ilkin | OT | 6'3" | 265 | 29 | | |
| #Jeff Lucas | OT | 6'7" | 288 | 23 | | |
| Ray Pinney | OT | 6'4" | 270 | 33 | | |
| Jerry Quick | OT | 6'5" | 279 | 23 | | |
| #Robert Washington | OT | 6'4" | 251 | 24 | | |
| Brian Blankenship | OG | 6'1" | 281 | 24 | | |
| #Charlie Dickey | OG | 6'3" | 270 | 24 | | |
| #Ben Lawrence | OG | 6'1" | 325 | 23 | | |
| Terry Long | OG | 5'11" | 265 | 28 | | |
| #Ted Petersen | OG-OT | 6'5" | 235 | 32 | | |
| John Rienstra | OG | 6'5" | 275 | 23 | | |
| Craig Wolfley | OG-OT | 6'1" | 268 | 29 | | |
| #John Lott | C-OG | 6'2" | 260 | 23 | | |
| Paul Oswald | C | 6'3" | 273 | 23 | | |
| Mike Webster | C | 6'1" | 260 | 35 | | |
| #Tommy Dawkins | DE | 6'3" | 260 | 22 | | |
| Keith Gary | DE | 6'3" | 265 | 27 | | |
| Tim Johnson | DE | 6'3" | 260 | 22 | | |
| Edmund Nelson | DE-DT | 6'3" | 275 | 27 | | |
| #Brett Shugarts | DE | 6'2" | 250 | 27 | | |
| #Xavier Warren | DE | 6'1" | 250 | 23 | | |
| Gerald Williams | DE-DT | 6'3" | 270 | 23 | | |
| Keith Willis | DE | 6'1" | 263 | 28 | | |
| Gary Dunn | NT | 6'3" | 275 | 31 | | |
| Lorenzo Freeman | NT-DT | 6'5" | 270 | 23 | | |
| #Alan Huff | NT | 6'4" | 265 | 23 | | |
| #Michael Minter | NT | 6'3" | 275 | 22 | | |
| #David Opfar | NT | 6'4" | 270 | 27 | | |
| #Steve Apke | LB | 6'1" | 222 | 22 | | |
| #Craig Bingham | LB | 6'2" | 227 | 27 | | |
| Gregg Carr | LB | 6'2" | 220 | 25 | | 2 |
| Robin Cole | LB | 6'2" | 225 | 31 | 1 | |
| Bryan Hinkle | LB | 6'2" | 220 | 28 | 3 | |
| Darryl Knox | LB | 6'3" | 220 | 24 | | |
| #David Little | LB | 6'1" | 240 | 28 | | |
| Mike Merriweather | LB | 6'2" | 219 | 26 | 2 | |
| Hardy Nickerson | LB | 6'2" | 219 | 22 | | |
| #Avon Riley | LB | 6'3" | 242 | 29 | 1 | |
| Tyronne Stowe | LB | 6'1" | 235 | 22 | | |
| #Albert Williams | LB | 6'3" | 229 | 27 | | |
| #Joe Williams | LB | 6'4" | 237 | 22 | | |
| Ken Woodard | LB | 6'1" | 218 | 27 | | |
| #Dave Edwards | DB | 6' | 202 | 25 | 1 | |
| Thomas Everett | DB | 5'9" | 179 | 23 | 3 | |
| Cornell Gowdy | DB | 6'1" | 195 | 23 | 2 | 6 |
| Larry Griffin | DB | 6' | 190 | 24 | 2 | |
| Delton Hall | DB | 6'1" | 195 | 22 | 3 | 12 |
| Bruce Jones | DB | 6'1" | 197 | 22 | | |
| Kelvin Middleton | DB | 6' | 186 | 25 | | |
| #Rock Richmond | DB | 5'10" | 180 | 23 | | |
| #Cameron Riley | DB | 6'1" | 195 | 23 | | |
| Lupe Sanchez | DB | 5'10" | 192 | 25 | | |
| Donnie Shell | DB | 5'11" | 198 | 35 | 1 | 12 |
| #Anthony Tuggle | DB | 6'1" | 211 | 23 | | |
| #Ray Williams | DB | 5'11" | 198 | 21 | 1 | |
| Dwayne Woodruff | DB | 6' | 198 | 30 | 5 | 6 |
| Rod Woodson | DB | 6' | 195 | 22 | 1 | 6 |
| Steve Bono | QB | 6'4" | 216 | 25 | | 6 |
| Bubby Brister | QB | 6'3" | 200 | 25 | | |
| #Reggie Collier | QB | 6'3" | 207 | 26 | | |
| Mark Malone | QB | 6'4" | 216 | 28 | | 18 |
| Walter Abercrombie | HB | 6' | 210 | 27 | | 12 |
| Rodney Carter | HB | 6' | 222 | 22 | | 18 |
| #Spark Clark | HB | 5'7" | 182 | 22 | | |
| Earnest Jackson | HB | 5'9" | 225 | 27 | | 6 |
| Dwight Stone | HB | 6' | 188 | 23 | | |
| Frank Pollard | FB | 5'10" | 230 | 30 | | 18 |
| Merril Hoge | FB | 6'2" | 212 | 22 | | 6 |
| #Dan Reeder | FB | 5'11" | 235 | 26 | | |
| Chuck Sanders | FB | 6'1" | 233 | 23 | | 6 |
| #Lyneal Alston | WR | 6'1" | 205 | 23 | | 12 |
| Melvin Anderson | WR | 5'11" | 175 | 22 | | |
| Joey Clinkscales | WR | 6' | 199 | 23 | | 6 |
| #Moses Ford | WR | 6'2" | 220 | 23 | | |
| #Russell Hairston | WR | 6'3" | 206 | 24 | | 6 |
| Louis Lipps | WR | 5'10" | 187 | 25 | | |
| Charles Lockett | WR | 6' | 175 | 21 | | 6 |
| John Stallworth | WR | 6'2" | 206 | 35 | | 12 |
| Calvin Sweeney | WR | 6'2" | 192 | 32 | | |
| Weegie Thompson | WR | 6'6" | 210 | 26 | | 6 |
| #Ralph Britt | TE | 6'3" | 240 | 22 | | |
| Preston Gothard | TE | 6'4" | 242 | 25 | | 6 |
| Danzell Lee | TE | 6'2" | 232 | 24 | | |
| Theo Young | TE | 6'2" | 237 | 22 | | |
| Gary Anderson | K | 5'11" | 179 | 28 | | 87 |
| #John Bruno | K | 6'2" | 190 | 22 | | |
| Harry Newsome | K | 6' | 189 | 24 | | |
| #David Trout | K | 5'6" | 169 | 29 | | 10 |

Mark Behning - Achilles Tendon Injury
Rich Erenberg - Knee Injury
Anthony Henton - Knee Injury

## CINCINNATI BENGALS 4-11 Sam Wyche

| Scores of Each Game | | |
|---|---|---|
| 23 | Indianapolis | 21 |
| 26 | SAN FRANCISCO | 27 |
| 9 | SAN DIEGO | 10 |
| 17 | Seattle | 10 |
| 0 | CLEVELAND | 34 |
| 20 | Pittsburgh | 23 |
| 29 | HOUSTON | 31 |
| 14 | MIAMI | 20 |
| 16 | Atlanta | 10 |
| 16 | PITTSBURGH | 30 |
| 20 | N.Y.Jets | 27 |
| 30 | KANSAS CITY | *27 |
| 24 | Cleveland | 38 |
| 24 | NEW ORLEANS | 41 |
| 17 | Houston | 21 |

| Use Name | Pos. | Hgt | Wgt | Age | Int | Pts |
|---|---|---|---|---|---|---|
| #Keith Cupp | OT | 6'6" | 301 | 23 | | |
| Anthony Munoz | OT | 6'6" | 278 | 29 | | 6 |
| #Bob Riley | OT | 6'5" | 276 | 23 | | |
| #Tom Richey | OT | 6'4" | 274 | 26 | | |
| #Mark Tigges | OT | 6'3" | 290 | 23 | | |
| Joe Walter | OT | 6'6" | 290 | 24 | | |
| Doug Aronson | OG | 6'3" | 293 | 22 | | |
| Brian Blados | OG | 6'5" | 295 | 25 | | |
| #John Fletcher | OG | 6'3" | 293 | 22 | | |
| Bruce Kozerski | OG | 6'4" | 275 | 25 | | |
| Max Montoya | OG | 6'5" | 275 | 31 | | |
| #Bill Poe | OG | 6'3" | 280 | 23 | | |
| Bruce Reimers | OG-OT | 6'7" | 280 | 26 | | |
| #Ken Smith | OG | 6'1" | 285 | 26 | | |
| David Douglas | C-OG | 6'4" | 280 | 24 | | |
| #Sam Manos | C | 6'3" | 265 | 25 | | |
| Dave Rimington | C | 6'3" | 288 | 25 | | |
| Jason Buck | DE | 6'5" | 264 | 24 | | |
| Eddie Edwards | DE | 6'5" | 256 | 33 | | |
| #Willie Fears | DE | 6'3" | 278 | 23 | | |
| Mike Hammerstein | DE | 6'4" | 270 | 24 | | |
| Skip McClendon | DE | 6'7" | 270 | 23 | | |
| #Jeff Reinke | DE | 6'4" | 262 | 24 | | |
| Jim Skow | DE | 6'3" | 250 | 24 | | |
| #Jeff Smith | DE | 6'4" | 248 | 25 | | |
| #Bill Berthusen (to NYG) | NT | 6'5" | 290 | 23 | | |
| #James Eaddy | NT | 6'2" | 280 | 24 | | |
| Tim Krumrie | NT | 6'2" | 262 | 27 | | |
| Leo Barker | LB | 6'2" | 227 | 27 | | |
| Ed Brady | LB | 6'2" | 235 | 27 | | |
| #Toney Catchings | LB | 6'3" | 236 | 22 | | |
| Kiki DeAyala | LB | 6'1" | 225 | 25 | | |
| #Tom Flaherty | LB | 6'3" | 223 | 22 | | |
| Tim Inglis | LB | 6'3" | 232 | 23 | | |
| Joe Kelly | LB | 6'2" | 227 | 22 | | |
| Emanuel King | LB | 6'4" | 251 | 24 | | |
| #Scott Schutt | LB | 6'4" | 218 | 24 | | 2 |
| #Lance Sellers | LB | 6'1" | 230 | 24 | | |
| #David Ward | LB | 6'2" | 230 | 23 | | |
| Leon White | LB | 6'2" | 236 | 23 | | |
| Reggie Williams | LB | 6'1" | 228 | 32 | | |
| Carl Zander | LB | 6'2" | 235 | 24 | | |
| #Chris Barber | DB | 6' | 187 | 23 | | |
| Lewis Billups | DB | 5'11" | 190 | 23 | | |
| #Nate Borders | DB | 5'10" | 190 | 24 | | |
| Louis Breeden | DB | 5'11" | 185 | 34 | 2 | |
| Barney Bussey | DB | 6' | 195 | 25 | 1 | |
| David Fulcher | DB | 6'3" | 228 | 23 | 3 | |
| Ray Horton | DB | 5'11" | 190 | 27 | | |
| Gary Hunt | DB | 5'11" | 175 | 23 | | |
| Robert Jackson | DB | 5'10" | 186 | 28 | 3 | |
| #Mark Johnson | DB | 6'1" | 194 | 23 | | |
| #Aaron Manning | DB | 5'10" | 178 | 26 | | |
| #Rob Niehoff | DB | 6'2" | 205 | 23 | 1 | |
| #Daryl Smith | DB | 5'9" | 185 | 24 | 2 | |
| Eric Thomas | DB | 5'11" | 175 | 22 | 1 | |
| Solomon Wilcots | DB | 5'11" | 180 | 22 | 1 | |
| #Ben Bennett | QB | 6'1" | 200 | 25 | | |
| #Adrian Breen | QB | 6'4" | 183 | 22 | | |
| Boomer Esiason | QB | 6'4" | 220 | 26 | | |
| Mike Norseth | QB | 6'2" | 200 | 23 | | |
| Turk Schonert | QB | 6'1" | 196 | 30 | | |
| #Dave Walter | QB | 6'3" | 230 | 23 | | |
| James Brooks | HB | 5'10" | 182 | 27 | | 18 |
| Stanford Jennings | HB | 6'1" | 205 | 25 | | 18 |
| #Marc Logan | HB | 5'11" | 204 | 22 | | 6 |
| #Pat Franklin | FB | 6'1" | 230 | 24 | | |
| Bill Johnson | FB | 6'2" | 230 | 26 | | 6 |
| Larry Kinnebrew | FB | 6'1" | 258 | 28 | | 48 |
| #David McCluskey | FB | 6'1" | 227 | 23 | | 6 |
| #Dan Rice | FB | 6'1" | 241 | 23 | | |
| Dana Wright | FB | 6'1" | 219 | 24 | | |
| Eddie Brown | WR | 6' | 185 | 24 | | 18 |
| #Ken Brown | WR | 5'8" | 175 | 22 | | |
| #Tom Brown | WR | 6'4" | 190 | 23 | | |
| Cris Collinsworth | WR | 6'5" | 192 | 28 | | |
| Ira Hillary | WR | 5'11" | 190 | 24 | | |
| Mike Martin | WR | 5'10" | 186 | 26 | | 18 |
| Tim McGee | WR | 5'10" | 175 | 23 | | 6 |
| #Greg Meehan | WR | 6' | 191 | 24 | | |
| #Marquis Pleasant | WR | 6'2" | 172 | 22 | | |
| #Rodney Tweet | WR | 6'1" | 195 | 23 | | |
| Rodney Holman | TE | 6'3" | 238 | 27 | | 12 |
| #Curtis Jeffries | TE | 6'4" | 236 | 22 | | |
| Eric Kattus | TE | 6'5" | 235 | 24 | | |
| Jim Riggs | TE | 6'5" | 245 | 23 | | |
| #Dave Romasko | TE | 6'3" | 241 | 23 | | |
| #Wade Russell | TE | 6'4" | 250 | 24 | | 6 |
| #Reggie Sims | TE | 6'4" | 253 | 23 | | |
| Jim Breech | K | 5'6" | 161 | 31 | | 97 |
| Scott Fulhage | K | 5'11" | 191 | 25 | | |
| #Massimo Manca | K | 5'10" | 211 | 23 | | |

Stanley Wilson - Suspended by N.F.L.

* Overtime

# - on the active roster for strike replacement games only

## HOUSTON OILERS

### RUSHING

| Last Name | No. | Yds | Avg | TD |
|---|---|---|---|---|
| Rozier | 229 | 957 | 4.2 | 3 |
| Jackson | 60 | 232 | 3.9 | 1 |
| Pinkett | 31 | 149 | 4.8 | 2 |
| Hunter | 34 | 144 | 4.2 | 0 |
| Moon | 34 | 112 | 3.3 | 3 |
| Highsmith | 29 | 106 | 3.7 | 1 |
| Wallace | 19 | 102 | 5.4 | 0 |
| Pease | 15 | 33 | 2.2 | 1 |
| Tillman | 12 | 29 | 2.4 | 1 |
| Cobble | 9 | 23 | 2.6 | 0 |
| Moore | 7 | 22 | 3.1 | 0 |
| Valentine | 5 | 10 | 2.0 | 0 |
| Harris | 1 | 17 | 17.0 | 0 |
| Givins | 1 | -13 | -13.0 | 0 |

### RECEIVING

| Last Name | No. | Yds | Avg | TD |
|---|---|---|---|---|
| Givins | 53 | 933 | 17.6 | 6 |
| D. Hill | 49 | 989 | 20.2 | 6 |
| Rozier | 27 | 192 | 7.1 | 0 |
| Duncan | 13 | 237 | 18.2 | 5 |
| J. Williams | 13 | 158 | 12.2 | 3 |
| O. Williams | 11 | 165 | 15.0 | 0 |
| Drewrey | 11 | 148 | 13.5 | 0 |
| Harris | 10 | 164 | 16.4 | 0 |
| Jackson | 10 | 44 | 4.4 | 0 |
| Jeffires | 7 | 89 | 12.7 | 0 |
| Wallace | 7 | 34 | 4.9 | 0 |
| Walters | 5 | 99 | 19.8 | 0 |
| Gehring | 5 | 64 | 12.8 | 1 |
| McDonald | 4 | 56 | 14.0 | 1 |
| Highsmith | 4 | 55 | 13.8 | 1 |
| Moore | 3 | 21 | 7.0 | 0 |
| Hunter | 3 | 17 | 5.7 | 0 |
| Valentine | 2 | 10 | 5.0 | 0 |
| Darrington | 1 | 38 | 38.0 | 0 |
| James | 1 | 14 | 14.0 | 0 |
| Pinkett | 1 | 7 | 7.0 | 0 |

### PUNT RETURNS

| Last Name | No. | Yds | Avg | TD |
|---|---|---|---|---|
| K. Johnson | 24 | 196 | 8.2 | 0 |
| Duncan | 8 | 23 | 2.9 | 0 |
| Drewrey | 3 | 11 | 3.7 | 0 |
| Walters | 2 | 19 | 9.5 | 0 |

### KICKOFF RETURNS

| Last Name | No. | Yds | Avg | TD |
|---|---|---|---|---|
| Duncan | 28 | 546 | 19.5 | 0 |
| Pinkett | 17 | 322 | 18.9 | 0 |
| Drewrey | 8 | 136 | 17.0 | 0 |
| Hunter | 4 | 79 | 19.8 | 0 |
| Harris | 3 | 87 | 29.0 | 0 |
| K. Johnson | 2 | 24 | 12.0 | 0 |
| Walters | 1 | 18 | 18.0 | 0 |
| Valentine | 1 | 13 | 13.0 | 0 |
| J. Davis | 1 | 0 | 0.0 | 0 |
| Fuller | 1 | 0 | 0.0 | 0 |
| Tillman | 1 | 0 | 0.0 | 0 |

### PASSING — PUNTING — KICKING

**PASSING**

| Last Name | Att | Cmp | % | Yds | Yd/Att | TD | Int— | % | RK |
|---|---|---|---|---|---|---|---|---|---|
| Moon | 368 | 184 | 50 | 2806 | 7.6 | 21 | 18— | 5 | 18 |
| Pease | 113 | 56 | 50 | 728 | 6.4 | 3 | 5— | 4 | |
| D. Hill | 1 | 0 | 0 | 0 | 0.0 | 0 | 0— | 0 | |

**PUNTING**

| Last Name | No | Avg |
|---|---|---|
| Johnson | 41 | 40.3 |
| Superick | 8 | 33.6 |

**KICKING**

| Last Name | XP | Att | % | FG | Att | % |
|---|---|---|---|---|---|---|
| Zendejas | 32 | 33 | 97 | 20 | 26 | 77 |
| Diettrich | 5 | 5 | 100 | 6 | 6 | 100 |

## PITTSBURGH STEELERS

### RUSHING

| Last Name | No. | Yds | Avg | TD |
|---|---|---|---|---|
| Jackson | 180 | 696 | 3.9 | 1 |
| Pollard | 128 | 536 | 4.2 | 2 |
| Abercrombie | 123 | 459 | 3.7 | 2 |
| Malone | 34 | 162 | 4.8 | 3 |
| Stone | 17 | 135 | 7.9 | 0 |
| Sanders | 11 | 65 | 5.9 | 1 |
| Bono | 8 | 27 | 3.4 | 1 |
| Collier | 4 | 20 | 5.0 | 0 |
| Newsome | 2 | 16 | 8.0 | 0 |
| Carter | 5 | 12 | 2.4 | 0 |
| Hoge | 3 | 8 | 2.7 | 0 |
| Reeder | 2 | 8 | 4.0 | 0 |

### RECEIVING

| Last Name | No. | Yds | Avg | TD |
|---|---|---|---|---|
| Stallworth | 41 | 521 | 12.7 | 2 |
| Abercrombie | 24 | 209 | 8.7 | 0 |
| Thompson | 17 | 313 | 18.4 | 1 |
| Sweeney | 16 | 217 | 13.6 | 0 |
| Carter | 16 | 180 | 11.3 | 3 |
| Pollard | 14 | 77 | 5.5 | 0 |
| Clinkscales | 13 | 240 | 18.5 | 1 |
| Lee | 12 | 124 | 10.3 | 0 |
| Lipps | 11 | 164 | 14.9 | 0 |
| Lockett | 7 | 116 | 16.6 | 1 |
| Hoge | 7 | 97 | 13.9 | 1 |
| Jackson | 7 | 52 | 7.4 | 0 |
| Alston | 3 | 84 | 28.0 | 2 |
| Hairston | 2 | 16 | 8.0 | 1 |
| Young | 2 | 10 | 5.0 | 0 |
| Gothard | 2 | 9 | 4.5 | 1 |
| Stone | 1 | 22 | 22.0 | 0 |
| Sanders | 1 | 11 | 11.0 | 0 |
| Bono | 1 | 2 | 2.0 | 0 |
| Boyle | 1 | 0 | 0.0 | 0 |

### PUNT RETURNS

| Last Name | No. | Yds | Avg | TD |
|---|---|---|---|---|
| Woodson | 16 | 135 | 8.4 | 0 |
| Lipps | 7 | 46 | 6.6 | 0 |
| Anderson | 7 | 38 | 5.4 | 0 |
| Everett | 4 | 22 | 5.5 | 0 |
| Lockett | 2 | 3 | 1.5 | 0 |

### KICKOFF RETURNS

| Last Name | No. | Yds | Avg | TD |
|---|---|---|---|---|
| Stone | 28 | 568 | 20.3 | 0 |
| Woodson | 13 | 290 | 22.3 | 0 |
| Sanchez | 6 | 116 | 19.3 | 0 |
| Jones | 2 | 38 | 19.0 | 0 |
| Britt | 2 | 9 | 4.5 | 0 |
| Clark | 1 | 18 | 18.0 | 0 |
| Hoge | 1 | 13 | 13.0 | 0 |
| Gowdy | 1 | 0 | 0.0 | 0 |
| Riley | 1 | 0 | 0.0 | 0 |

### PASSING — PUNTING — KICKING

**PASSING**

| Last Name | Att | Cmp | % | Yds | Yd/Att | TD | Int— | % | RK |
|---|---|---|---|---|---|---|---|---|---|
| Malone | 336 | 156 | 46 | 1896 | 5.6 | 6 | 19— | 6 | 27 |
| Bono | 74 | 34 | 46 | 438 | 5.9 | 5 | 2— | 3 | |
| Brister | 12 | 4 | 33 | 20 | 1.7 | 0 | 3— | 25 | |
| Collier | 7 | 4 | 57 | 110 | 15.7 | 2 | 1— | 14 | |

**PUNTING**

| Last Name | No | Avg |
|---|---|---|
| Newsome | 65 | 41.2 |
| Bruno | 17 | 36.4 |

**KICKING**

| Last Name | XP | Att | % | FG | Att | % |
|---|---|---|---|---|---|---|
| Anderson | 21 | 21 | 100 | 22 | 27 | 82 |
| Trout | 10 | 10 | 100 | 0 | 2 | 0 |

## CINCINNATI BENGALS

### RUSHING

| Last Name | No. | Yds | Avg | TD |
|---|---|---|---|---|
| Kinnebrew | 145 | 570 | 3.9 | 8 |
| Jennings | 70 | 314 | 4.5 | 1 |
| Brooks | 94 | 290 | 3.1 | 1 |
| Esiason | 52 | 241 | 4.6 | 0 |
| B. Johnson | 39 | 205 | 5.3 | 1 |
| Logan | 37 | 203 | 5.5 | 1 |
| McCluskey | 29 | 94 | 3.2 | 1 |
| Wright | 24 | 74 | 3.1 | 0 |
| Rice | 18 | 59 | 3.3 | 0 |
| D. Walter | 16 | 70 | 4.4 | 0 |
| Meehan | 4 | 19 | 4.8 | 0 |
| Breen | 6 | 18 | 3.0 | 0 |
| Bennett | 2 | 17 | 8.5 | 0 |
| Brown | 1 | 0 | 0.0 | 0 |
| McGee | 1 | -10 | -10.0 | 0 |

### RECEIVING

| Last Name | No. | Yds | Avg | TD |
|---|---|---|---|---|
| E. Brown | 44 | 608 | 13.8 | 3 |
| Jennings | 35 | 277 | 7.9 | 2 |
| Collinsworth | 31 | 494 | 15.9 | 0 |
| Holman | 28 | 438 | 15.6 | 2 |
| McGee | 23 | 408 | 17.7 | 1 |
| Brooks | 22 | 272 | 12.4 | 2 |
| Martin | 20 | 394 | 19.7 | 3 |
| Kattus | 18 | 217 | 12.1 | 2 |
| Kinnebrew | 9 | 114 | 12.7 | 0 |
| Hillary | 5 | 65 | 13.0 | 0 |
| Wright | 4 | 28 | 7.0 | 0 |
| Meehan | 3 | 25 | 8.3 | 0 |
| B. Johnson | 3 | 19 | 6.3 | 0 |
| Logan | 3 | 14 | 4.7 | 0 |
| Pleasant | 2 | 45 | 22.5 | 0 |
| Russell | 2 | 27 | 13.5 | 1 |
| Munoz | 2 | 15 | 7.5 | 1 |
| McCluskey | 1 | 8 | 8.0 | 0 |

### PUNT RETURNS

| Last Name | No. | Yds | Avg | TD |
|---|---|---|---|---|
| Martin | 28 | 277 | 9.9 | 0 |
| K. Brown | 5 | 16 | 3.2 | 0 |
| Horton | 1 | 0 | 0.0 | 0 |

### KICKOFF RETURNS

| Last Name | No. | Yds | Avg | TD |
|---|---|---|---|---|
| Bussey | 21 | 406 | 19.3 | 0 |
| McGee | 15 | 242 | 16.1 | 0 |
| Wright | 13 | 266 | 20.5 | 0 |
| K. Brown | 3 | 45 | 15.0 | 0 |
| Logan | 3 | 31 | 10.3 | 0 |
| Martin | 3 | 51 | 17.0 | 0 |
| Brooks | 2 | 42 | 21.0 | 0 |
| Jennings | 2 | 32 | 16.0 | 0 |
| Kattus | 2 | 22 | 11.0 | 0 |
| Hillary | 1 | 15 | 15.0 | 0 |
| Meehan | 1 | 9 | 9.0 | 0 |
| Fulcher | 1 | 0 | 0.0 | 0 |

### PASSING — PUNTING — KICKING

**PASSING**

| Last Name | Att | Cmp | % | Yds | Yd/Att | TD | Int— | % | RK |
|---|---|---|---|---|---|---|---|---|---|
| Esiason | 440 | 240 | 55 | 3321 | 7.6 | 16 | 19— | 4 | 20 |
| D. Walter | 21 | 10 | 48 | 113 | 5.4 | 0 | 0— | 0 | |
| Breen | 8 | 3 | 38 | 9 | 1.1 | 1 | 0— | 0 | |
| Bennett | 6 | 2 | 33 | 25 | 4.2 | 0 | 1— | 17 | |

**PUNTING**

| Last Name | No. | Avg. |
|---|---|---|
| Fulhage | 52 | 41.7 |
| Esiason | 2 | 34.0 |

**KICKING**

| Last Name | XP | Att | % | FG | Att | % |
|---|---|---|---|---|---|---|
| Breech | 25 | 27 | 93 | 24 | 30 | 80 |
| Manca | 3 | 3 | 100 | 1 | 2 | 50 |

## Western Division

**DENVER BRONCOS** 10-4-1 Dan Reeves

| Scores of Each Game | | |
|---|---|---|
| 40 | SEATTLE | 17 |
| 17 | Green Bay | *17 |
| 10 | HOUSTON | 40 |
| 30 | L.A.RAIDERS | 14 |
| 26 | Kansas City | 17 |
| 27 | Minnesota | 34 |
| 34 | DETROIT | 0 |
| 14 | Buffalo | 21 |
| 31 | CHICAGO | 29 |
| 23 | L.A.Raiders | 17 |
| 31 | San Diego | 17 |
| 31 | NEW ENGLAND | 20 |
| 21 | Seattle | 28 |
| 20 | KANSAS CITY | 17 |
| 24 | SAN DIEGO | 0 |

| Use Name | Pos. | Hgt | Wgt | Age | Int | Pts |
|---|---|---|---|---|---|---|
| Kevin Belcher | OT | 6'5" | 310 | 25 | | |
| Archie Harris | OT | 6'6" | 270 | 22 | | |
| Keith Kartz | OT | 6'4" | 270 | 24 | | |
| Ken Lanier | OT | 6'3" | 269 | 28 | | |
| Dan Remsberg | OT | 6'6" | 275 | 25 | | |
| Dave Studdard | OT | 6'4" | 260 | 31 | | |
| John Ayers | OG | 6'5" | 265 | 34 | | |
| Keith Bishop | OG-C | 6'3" | 265 | 30 | | |
| #Winford Hood | OG | 6'3" | 265 | 25 | | |
| Stefan Humphries | OG | 6'3" | 268 | 25 | | |
| Billy Bryan | C | 6'2" | 255 | 31 | | |
| Mike Freeman | C-OG | 6'3" | 256 | 25 | | |
| David Jones | C | 6'3" | 266 | 25 | | |
| Larry Lee | C-OG | 6'2" | 263 | 27 | | |
| #Jack Peavey | C | 6'2" | 260 | 24 | | |
| Walt Bowyer | DE | 6'4" | 260 | 26 | | |
| Steve Bryan | DE-NT | 6'2" | 256 | 23 | | |
| Freddie Gilbert | DE | 6'4" | 275 | 25 | | |
| Rulon Jones | DE | 6'6" | 260 | 29 | | |
| #Bill Lobenstein | DE-NT | 6'3" | 261 | 26 | | |
| #Ron McLean | DE-NT | 6'3" | 267 | 24 | | |
| Greg Kragen | NT | 6'3" | 245 | 25 | | |
| Karl Mecklenburg | DE-LB | 6'3" | 230 | 27 | 3 | |
| Andre Townsend | DE-NT | 6'3" | 265 | 24 | | |
| Jeff Tupper | NT | 6'5" | 269 | 24 | | |
| Michael Brooks | LB | 6'1" | 235 | 22 | | |
| Rick Dennison | LB | 6'3" | 220 | 29 | 1 | |
| #Kirk Dodge | LB | 6'1" | 233 | 25 | 2 | 6 |
| Simon Fletcher | LB | 6'5" | 240 | 25 | | |
| Ricky Hunley | LB | 6'2" | 238 | 25 | 2 | 6 |
| #Tim Joiner | LB | 6'4" | 235 | 25 | | |
| Bruce Klostermann | LB | 6'4" | 225 | 24 | | |
| #Mike Knox | LB | 6'2" | 240 | 24 | | |
| Tim Lucas | LB | 6'3" | 230 | 26 | 1 | |
| #Dan MacDonald | LB | 6'2" | 230 | 23 | | |
| Marc Munford | LB | 6'2" | 231 | 22 | | |
| Jim Ryan | LB | 6'1" | 225 | 30 | 3 | |
| #Matt Smith | LB | 6'2" | 234 | 22 | | |
| #Bryant Winn | LB | 6'4" | 231 | 26 | | |
| Tyrone Braxton | DB | 5'11" | 174 | 22 | | |
| Jeremiah Castille | DB | 5'10" | 175 | 26 | | |
| Kevin Clark | DB | 5'10" | 185 | 23 | 3 | 6 |
| #Steve Fitzhugh | DB | 5'11" | 188 | 24 | | |
| Mike Harden | DB | 6'1" | 192 | 28 | 4 | |
| Mark Haynes | DB | 5'11" | 195 | 28 | 3 | 6 |
| #Roger Jackson | DB | 6' | 185 | 28 | | |
| #Earl Johnson | DB | 6' | 200 | 23 | | |
| #Darryl Jones | DB | 6' | 193 | 25 | | |
| Tony Lilly | DB | 6' | 199 | 25 | 3 | |
| #Lyle Pickens | DB | 5'10" | 175 | 22 | | |
| Bruce Plummer | DB | 6'1" | 197 | 23 | | |
| Randy Robbins | DB | 6'2" | 189 | 24 | 3 | |
| #Martin Rudolph | DB | 5'10" | 183 | 22 | | |
| #Darryl Russell | DB | 6' | 190 | 22 | | |
| Dennis Smith | DB | 6'3" | 200 | 28 | 2 | |
| Steve Wilson | DB | 5'10" | 195 | 30 | | |
| John Elway | QB | 6'3" | 210 | 26 | | 24 |
| #Ken Karcher | QB | 6'3" | 205 | 24 | | |
| Gary Kubiak | QB | 6' | 192 | 25 | | |
| #Dean May | QB | 6'5" | 220 | 25 | | |
| #Monte McGuire | QB | 6'4" | 202 | 23 | | |
| Ken Bell | HB | 5'10" | 190 | 22 | | |
| Tony Boddie | HB | 5'11" | 198 | 26 | | 6 |
| #Scott Caldwell | HB | 5'10" | 196 | 25 | | |
| #Joe Dudek | HB | 6' | 181 | 23 | | 12 |
| Gene Lang | HB | 5'10" | 196 | 25 | | 24 |
| #Nathan Poole | HB | 5'9" | 212 | 30 | | 6 |
| Gerald Willhite | HB | 5'10" | 200 | 28 | | |
| Samy Winder | HB | 5'11" | 203 | 28 | | 42 |
| Warren Marshall | FB | 6' | 216 | 23 | | |
| Bobby Micho | FB | 6'3" | 240 | 25 | | 12 |
| Steve Sewell | FB | 6'3" | 210 | 24 | | 18 |
| #Laron Brown | WR | 5'9" | 172 | 23 | | |
| Sam Graddy | WR | 5'10" | 165 | 23 | | |
| Mark Jackson | WR | 5'9" | 174 | 24 | | 12 |
| Vance Johnson | WR | 5'11" | 185 | 24 | | 42 |
| Rick Massie | WR | 6'1" | 190 | 27 | | 24 |
| Ricky Nattiel | WR | 5'9" | 180 | 21 | | 12 |
| #Shane Swanson | WR | 5'9" | 200 | 24 | | 6 |
| #Robert Thompson | WR | 5'9" | 168 | 23 | | |
| Steve Watson | WR | 6'4" | 195 | 30 | | 6 |
| Mitch Andrews | TE | 6'2" | 239 | 23 | | |
| Clarence Kay | TE | 6'2" | 237 | 26 | | |
| #Kerry Locklin | TE | 6'3" | 242 | 27 | | |
| Orson Mobley | TE | 6'5" | 256 | 24 | | 6 |
| #Russell Payne | TE | 6'1" | 240 | 22 | | |
| #Mike Clendenen | K | 5'11" | 190 | 24 | | 16 |
| #Ralph Giacomarro | K | 6'1" | 196 | 26 | | |
| Mike Horan | K | 5'11" | 180 | 27 | | |
| Rich Karlis | K | 6' | 180 | 27 | | 91 |

Tony Colorito - Knee Injury

**SEATTLE SEAHAWKS** 9-6 Chuck Knox

| Scores of Each Game | | |
|---|---|---|
| 17 | Denver | 40 |
| 43 | KANSAS CITY | 14 |
| 24 | MIAMI | 20 |
| 10 | CINCINNATI | 17 |
| 37 | Detroit | 14 |
| 35 | L.A.Raiders | 13 |
| 28 | MINNESOTA | 17 |
| 14 | N.Y.Jets | 30 |
| 24 | GREEN BAY | 13 |
| 34 | SAN DIEGO | 3 |
| 14 | L.A.RAIDERS | 37 |
| 9 | Pittsburgh | 13 |
| 28 | DENVER | 21 |
| 34 | Chicago | 21 |
| 20 | Kansas City | 41 |

| Use Name | Pos. | Hgt | Wgt | Age | Int | Pts |
|---|---|---|---|---|---|---|
| John Borchardt | OT | 6'5" | 272 | 30 | | |
| #Tim Burnham | OT | 6'5" | 280 | 24 | | |
| Ron Mattes | OT | 6'6" | 306 | 24 | | |
| #Howard Richards | OT | 6'6" | 272 | 28 | | |
| #Ron Scoggins | OT | 6'6" | 305 | 27 | | |
| Mike Wilson | OT | 6'5" | 280 | 32 | | |
| Edwin Bailey | OG | 6'4" | 276 | 28 | | |
| #Matt Hanousek | OG-OT | 6'4" | 265 | 24 | | |
| Bryan Millard | OG | 6'5" | 284 | 26 | | |
| Alvin Powell | OG | 6'5" | 291 | 27 | | |
| #Jack Sims | OG | 6'3" | 260 | 25 | | |
| #Garth Thomas | OG | 6'3" | 260 | 23 | | |
| #Tom Andrews | C-OG | 6'4" | 267 | 25 | | |
| Blair Bush | C | 6'3" | 272 | 30 | | |
| Stan Eisenhooth | C | 6'5" | 300 | 24 | | |
| Grant Feasel | C | 6'7" | 280 | 27 | | |
| Doug Hire | C | 6'2" | 245 | 22 | | |
| #Dean Perryman | C | 6'3" | 260 | 23 | | |
| Jeff Bryant | DE | 6'5" | 272 | 30 | | |
| #Dale Dorning | DE | 6'5" | 260 | 25 | | |
| Wes Dove | DE | 6'7" | 270 | 23 | | |
| Randy Edwards | DE | 6'4" | 267 | 26 | | |
| #Don Fairbanks | DE | 6'3" | 253 | 23 | | |
| Jacob Green | DE | 6'3" | 252 | 30 | | |
| #Doug Hollie | DE | 6'4" | 265 | 26 | | |
| #Van Hughes | DE | 6'3" | 280 | 26 | | |
| Alonzo Mitz | DE | 6'3" | 273 | 24 | | |
| #Greg Ramsey | DE | 6'3" | 244 | 23 | | |
| Roland Barbay | NT | 6'4" | 260 | 22 | | |
| #John Eisenhooth | NT | 6'2" | 265 | 25 | | |
| #David Graham | NT | 6'6" | 250 | 28 | | |
| Joe Nash | NT | 6'2" | 257 | 26 | | |
| #Charles Wiley | NT | 6'2" | 268 | 22 | | |
| #Lester Williams | NT | 6'3" | 290 | 28 | | |
| Brian Bosworth | LB | 6'2" | 248 | 22 | | |
| Keith Butler | LB | 6'4" | 239 | 31 | | |
| #Tony Caldwell | LB | 6'1" | 220 | 26 | 1 | |
| #Julio Cortes | LB | 6' | 226 | 26 | | |
| #Rob DeVita | LB | 6'2" | 222 | 28 | | |
| Greg Gaines | LB | 6'3" | 222 | 28 | | |
| #Joe Jackson | LB | 6'1" | 225 | 24 | | |
| M.L.Johnson | LB | 6'3" | 225 | 24 | | |
| Paul Lavine | LB | 6'2" | 207 | 25 | | |
| #John McVeigh | LB | 6'1" | 226 | 24 | | |
| Sam Merriman | LB | 6'3" | 232 | 26 | | |
| #Fred Orns | LB | 6'2" | 230 | 25 | | |
| Bruce Scholtz | LB | 6'6" | 241 | 28 | | |
| #Joe Terry | LB | 6'2" | 222 | 25 | | |
| #Rico Tipton | LB | 6'2" | 240 | 26 | | |
| Tony Woods | LB | 6'4" | 244 | 21 | | |
| David Wyman | LB | 6'2" | 231 | 23 | | |
| Fredd Young | LB | 6'1" | 233 | 25 | 1 | 6 |
| #Harvey Allen | DB | 6'3" | 215 | 22 | | |
| #Curtis Baham | DB | 5'11" | 180 | 24 | | |
| #Anthony Blue | DB | 5'9" | 185 | 22 | | |
| #Arnold Brown | DB | 5'10" | 185 | 25 | | |
| #Fred Davis | DB | 5'10" | 182 | 23 | | |
| Kenny Easley | DB | 6'3" | 198 | 28 | 4 | |
| #Charles Glaze | DB | 5'11" | 200 | 21 | 2 | |
| David Hollis | DB | 5'11" | 175 | 22 | | |
| Patrick Hunter | DB | 5'11" | 185 | 22 | 1 | |
| Melvin Jenkins | DB | 5'10" | 170 | 25 | 3 | |
| Kerry Justin | DB | 5'11" | 185 | 32 | | |
| #Kim Mack | DB | 6' | 190 | 25 | | |
| Mark Moore | DB | 6' | 194 | 22 | | |
| Paul Moyer | DB | 6'1" | 201 | 25 | 1 | |
| Eugene Robinson | DB | 6' | 186 | 24 | 3 | |
| #Dallis Smith | DB | 5'11" | 170 | 22 | | |
| Terry Taylor | DB | 5'10" | 191 | 26 | 1 | |
| #Ricky Thomas | DB | 6' | 185 | 22 | | |
| #Chris White | DB | 6'3" | 200 | 25 | | |
| #Renard Young | DB | 5'10" | 184 | 26 | | |
| Jeff Kemp | QB | 6' | 201 | 27 | | |
| Dave Krieg | QB | 6'1" | 196 | 28 | | 12 |
| #David Lindley | QB | 6' | 190 | 22 | | |
| #Bruce Mathison | QB | 6'3" | 205 | 28 | | |
| Bobby Joe Edmonds | HB | 5'11" | 186 | 22 | | |
| #Boyce Green | HB | 5'11" | 215 | 27 | | |
| #Alvin Moore | HB | 6' | 190 | 28 | | |
| Randall Morris | HB | 6' | 200 | 25 | | |
| #Michael Morton | HB | 5'8" | 175 | 27 | | |
| #Rick Parros | HB | 5'11" | 202 | 29 | | 6 |
| Curt Warner | HB | 5'11" | 205 | 26 | | 60 |
| Tony Burse | FB | 6' | 220 | 22 | | |
| #Mike Hagen | FB | 6' | 240 | 28 | | |
| Eric Lane | FB | 6' | 201 | 28 | | |
| #Chad Stark | FB | 6'1" | 220 | 22 | | |
| #James Williams | FB | 5'10" | 210 | 23 | | |
| John L.Williams | FB | 5'11" | 226 | 22 | | 24 |
| #Brent Bengen | WR | 5'8" | 172 | 23 | | |
| Ray Butler | WR | 6'3" | 206 | 23 | | |
| Louis Clark | WR | 6'1" | 193 | 23 | | |
| #Russell Evans | WR | 5'8" | 165 | 22 | | |
| Byron Franklin | WR | 6'1" | 183 | 28 | | |
| #Kevin Juma | WR | 6'2" | 195 | 25 | | |
| Steve Largent | WR | 5'11" | 191 | 32 | | 48 |
| #Curt Pardridge | WR | 5'10" | 175 | 23 | | |
| Paul Skansi | WR | 5'11" | 190 | 26 | | |
| #Donald Snell | WR | 6'2" | 177 | 22 | | |
| Jimmy Teal | WR | 5'10" | 175 | 25 | | 12 |
| Daryl Turner | WR | 6'3" | 194 | 25 | | 36 |
| #Chris Corley | TE | 6'4" | 285 | 23 | | |
| #John O'Callaghan | TE | 6'4" | 245 | 23 | | |
| #Ken Sager | TE | 6'4" | 228 | 23 | | |
| Wilbur Strozier | TE | 6'4" | 255 | 22 | | |
| Mike Tice | TE | 6'7" | 247 | 28 | | 12 |
| #Barry Bowman | K | 5'11" | 180 | 22 | | |
| #Russell Griffith | K | 5'11" | 175 | 22 | | |
| #Scott Hagler | K | 5'8" | 160 | 23 | | |
| Norm Johnson | K | 6'2" | 200 | 22 | | 85 |
| Ruben Rodriguez | K | 6'2" | 198 | 26 | | |

Gale Gilbert - Knee Injury
Curt Singer - Ankle Injury

**SAN DIEGO CHARGERS** 8-7 Al Saunders

| Scores of Each Game | | |
|---|---|---|
| 13 | Kansas City | 20 |
| 28 | ST.LOUIS | 24 |
| 10 | Cincinnati | 9 |
| 17 | Tampa Bay | 13 |
| 23 | L.A.Raiders | 17 |
| 42 | KANSAS CITY | 21 |
| 27 | CLEVELAND | *24 |
| 16 | Indianapolis | 13 |
| 16 | L.A.RAIDERS | 14 |
| 3 | Seattle | 34 |
| 17 | DENVER | 31 |
| 18 | Houston | 33 |
| 16 | PITTSBURGH | 20 |
| 7 | INDIANAPOLIS | 20 |
| 0 | Denver | 24 |

| Use Name | Pos. | Hgt | Wgt | Age | Int | Pts |
|---|---|---|---|---|---|---|
| #Greg Feasel | OT | 6'7" | 301 | 29 | | |
| Gary Kowalski | OT-OG | 6'6" | 280 | 27 | | |
| Jim Lachey | OT | 6'6" | 289 | 24 | | |
| #Emil Slovacek | OT | 6'3" | 300 | 24 | | |
| Curtis Rouse | OT-OG | 6'3" | 340 | 27 | | |
| Sam Claphan | OG-OT | 6'6" | 288 | 30 | | |
| Ken Dallafior | OG | 6'4" | 278 | 28 | | |
| James FitzPatrick | OG-OT | 6'8" | 286 | 23 | | |
| Dennis McKnight | OG-C | 6'3" | 270 | 33 | | |
| Dan Rosado | OG | 6'3" | 280 | 28 | | |
| Broderick Thompson | OG-OT | 6'5" | 290 | 27 | | |
| #David Diaz-Infante | C-OG | 6'2" | 272 | 23 | | |
| Don Macek | C | 6'3" | 270 | 33 | | |
| #John Stadnik | C | 6'4" | 275 | 27 | | |
| Keith Baldwin | DE | 6'4" | 270 | 26 | | |
| #Monte Bennett | DE | 6'3" | 270 | 28 | | |
| #Willard Goff | DE | 6'4" | 265 | 25 | | |
| Dee Hardison | DE | 6'4" | 291 | 31 | | |
| Lee Miller | DE | 6'7" | 285 | 22 | | 6 |
| #Duane Pettitt | DE | 6'4" | 265 | 22 | | |
| Joe Phillips | DE | 6'5" | 275 | 24 | | |
| Tony Simmons | DE | 6'5" | 268 | 24 | | |
| Terry Unrein | DE-NT | 6'5" | 280 | 24 | | |
| Lee Williams | DE | 6'6" | 263 | 24 | | 2 |
| Earl Wilson | DE | 6'4" | 280 | 28 | | |
| Karl Wilson | DE | 6'4" | 268 | 22 | | |
| Mike Charles | NT | 6'4" | 287 | 24 | | |
| Chuck Ehin | NT-LB | 6'4" | 266 | 25 | | 2 |
| #Blaisie Winter | NT | 6'3" | 274 | 25 | | |
| Chip Banks | LB | 6'4" | 236 | 27 | 1 | |
| Thomas Benson | LB | 6'2" | 235 | 25 | | |
| David Brandon | LB | 6'4" | 225 | 24 | | 6 |
| Steve Busick | LB | 6'4" | 227 | 27 | | |
| Andy Hawkins | LB | 6'2" | 230 | 29 | | |
| Mike Humiston | LB | 6'3" | 245 | 28 | | |
| #Brian Ingram | LB | 6'4" | 245 | 27 | | |
| Jeff Jackson | LB | 6'1" | 230 | 25 | | |
| Randy Kirk | LB | 6'2" | 235 | 22 | | |
| Gary Plummer | LB | 6'2" | 240 | 27 | 1 | |
| Billy Ray Smith | LB | 6'3" | 236 | 26 | 5 | |
| Johnny Taylor | LB | 6'4" | 237 | 27 | | |
| Anthony Anderson | DB | 6'2" | 205 | 22 | | |
| Martin Bayless | DB | 6'2" | 200 | 24 | | |
| #Ed Berry | DB | 5'10" | 183 | 24 | | |
| #Carl Brazley | DB | 6' | 180 | 30 | 1 | |
| Gill Byrd | DB | 5'11" | 195 | 26 | | |
| Vencie Glenn | DB | 6' | 187 | 22 | 4 | 6 |
| #Walter Harris | DB | 6'1" | 195 | 23 | | |
| Darrell Hopper | DB | 6'1" | 196 | 23 | | |
| Mike Hudson | DB | 6' | 202 | 23 | | |
| Daniel Hunter | DB | 5'11" | 178 | 25 | | |
| Elvis Patterson (from NYG) | DB | 5'11" | 198 | 26 | 1 | 6 |
| #Stacey Price | DB | 6'2" | 194 | 25 | | |
| Charles Romes | DB | 6'1" | 190 | 32 | | |
| #King Simmons | DB | 6'2" | 199 | 24 | | |
| Danny Walters | DB | 6'1" | 200 | 26 | | |
| Ted Watts | DB | 6' | 205 | 29 | | |
| Dan Fouts | QB | 6'3" | 210 | 35 | | 12 |
| Mark Herrmann | QB | 6'4" | 207 | 28 | | |
| #Mike Kelley | QB | 6'3" | 195 | 27 | | |
| #Rick Neuheisel | QB | 6'1" | 190 | 26 | | 7 |
| Mark Vlasic | QB | 6'3" | 206 | 23 | | |
| Curtis Adams | HB | 6' | 194 | 25 | | 6 |
| Gary Anderson | HB | 6'1" | 188 | 26 | | 30 |
| #Keyvan Jenkins | HB | 5'10" | 190 | 26 | | |
| #Frank Middleton | HB | 5'11" | 210 | 26 | | 6 |
| #Jeff Powell | HB | 5'10" | 185 | 24 | | |
| #Martin Sartin | HB | 5'10" | 202 | 24 | | 6 |
| #Todd Spencer | HB | 6' | 209 | 25 | | |
| #Anthony Steels | HB | 5'9" | 200 | 28 | | |
| Barry Redden | FB | 5'10" | 219 | 27 | | |
| Tim Spencer | FB | 6'2" | 227 | 26 | | |
| #Ken Zachary | FB | 6' | 222 | 23 | | |
| Wes Chandler | WR | 6' | 188 | 31 | | |
| Jamie Holland | WR | 6'2" | 186 | 23 | | |
| Lionel James | WR | 5'7" | 170 | 25 | | 36 |
| #Tim Moffett | WR | 6'2" | 180 | 25 | | 6 |
| #Calvin Muhammad | WR | 6' | 195 | 28 | | |
| #Tag Rome | WR | 5'9" | 175 | 25 | | |
| Timmie Ware | WR | 5'10" | 170 | 24 | | |
| #Al Williams | WR | 5'10" | 180 | 25 | | 6 |
| Rod Bernstine | TE | 6'3" | 235 | 22 | | 6 |
| #Kevin Ferguson | TE | 6'2" | 223 | 22 | | |
| Pete Holohan | TE | 6'4" | 235 | 28 | | |
| #Harry Holt | TE | 6'4" | 250 | 30 | | |
| Eric Sievers | TE | 6'4" | 230 | 28 | | |
| Kellen Winslow | TE | 6'5" | 251 | 29 | | 18 |
| Vince Abbott | K | 6' | 206 | 29 | | |
| #Jeff Gaffney | K | 6'2" | 195 | 22 | | 13 |
| Ralf Mojsiejenko | K | 6'3" | 212 | 24 | | |
| #Joe Prokop | K | 6'3" | 235 | 27 | | |

Jeffrey Dale - Back Injury
Woodrow Lowe - Knee Injury
Leslie O'Neal - Knee Injury

* Overtime

\# - on the active roster for strike replacement only

## DENVER BRONCOS

### RUSHING

| Last Name | No. | Yds | Avg | TD |
|---|---|---|---|---|
| Winder | 196 | 741 | 3.8 | 6 |
| Elway | 66 | 304 | 4.6 | 4 |
| Lang | 89 | 303 | 3.4 | 2 |
| Dudek | 35 | 154 | 4.4 | 2 |
| Willhite | 26 | 141 | 5.4 | 0 |
| Poole | 28 | 126 | 4.5 | 1 |
| Sewell | 19 | 83 | 4.4 | 2 |
| Caldwell | 16 | 53 | 3.3 | 0 |
| Bell | 13 | 43 | 3.3 | 0 |
| Nattiel | 2 | 13 | 6.5 | 0 |
| Micro | 4 | 8 | 2.0 | 0 |
| Boddie | 3 | 7 | 2.3 | 1 |
| Karcher | 9 | 3 | 0.3 | 0 |
| Kubiak | 1 | 3 | 3.0 | 0 |
| May | 2 | -4 | -2.0 | 0 |
| V. Johnson | 1 | -8 | -8.0 | 0 |

### RECEIVING

| Last Name | No. | Yds | Avg | TD |
|---|---|---|---|---|
| V. Johnson | 42 | 684 | 16.3 | 7 |
| Nattiel | 31 | 630 | 20.3 | 2 |
| Kay | 31 | 440 | 14.2 | 0 |
| Jackson | 26 | 436 | 16.8 | 2 |
| Micro | 25 | 242 | 9.7 | 2 |
| Lang | 17 | 130 | 7.6 | 2 |
| Mobley | 16 | 228 | 14.3 | 1 |
| Winder | 14 | 74 | 5.3 | 1 |
| Massie | 13 | 244 | 18.8 | 4 |
| Sewell | 13 | 209 | 16.1 | 1 |
| Watson | 11 | 167 | 15.2 | 1 |
| Boddie | 9 | 85 | 9.4 | 0 |
| Willhite | 9 | 25 | 2.8 | 0 |
| Dudek | 7 | 41 | 5.9 | 0 |
| Swanson | 6 | 87 | 14.5 | 1 |
| Andrews | 4 | 53 | 13.3 | 0 |
| Brown | 4 | 40 | 10.0 | 0 |
| Caldwell | 4 | 34 | 8.5 | 0 |
| Poole | 1 | 9 | 9.0 | 0 |
| Payne | 1 | 8 | 8.0 | 0 |
| Bell | 1 | 8 | 8.0 | |

### PUNT RETURNS

| Last Name | No. | Yds | Avg | TD |
|---|---|---|---|---|
| Clark | 18 | 233 | 12.9 | 1 |
| Nattiel | 12 | 73 | 6.1 | 0 |
| Swanson | 9 | 132 | 14.7 | 0 |
| Willhite | 4 | 22 | 5.5 | 0 |
| Harden | 2 | 11 | 5.5 | 0 |
| Lilly | 2 | 6 | 3.0 | 0 |
| V. Johnson | 1 | 9 | 9.0 | 0 |

### KICKOFF RETURNS

| Last Name | No. | Yds | Avg | TD |
|---|---|---|---|---|
| Bell | 15 | 323 | 21.5 | 0 |
| Swanson | 9 | 234 | 26.0 | 0 |
| Johnson | 7 | 140 | 20.0 | 0 |
| Lang | 4 | 78 | 19.5 | 0 |
| Nattiel | 4 | 78 | 19.5 | 0 |
| Brown | 3 | 57 | 19.0 | 0 |
| Clark | 2 | 33 | 16.5 | 0 |
| Ryan | 2 | 9 | 4.5 | 0 |

### PASSING — PUNTING — KICKING

**PASSING**

| Last Name | Att | Cmp | % | Yds | Yd/Att | TD | Int— | % | RK |
|---|---|---|---|---|---|---|---|---|---|
| Elway | 410 | 224 | 55 | 3198 | 7.8 | 19 | 12— | 3 | 12 |
| Karcher | 102 | 56 | 55 | 628 | 6.2 | 5 | 4— | 3 | |
| McGuire | 3 | 2 | 67 | 23 | 7.7 | 0 | 0— | 0 | |
| Lang | 1 | 0 | 0 | 0 | 0.0 | 0 | 0— | 0 | |
| Willhite | 1 | 0 | 0 | 0 | 0.0 | 0 | 0— | 0 | |
| V. Johnson | 1 | 0 | 0 | 0 | 0.0 | 0 | 0— | 0 | |
| Kubiak | 7 | 3 | 43 | 25 | 3.6 | 0 | 2— | 29 | |
| May | 5 | 0 | 0 | 0 | 0.0 | 0 | 1— | 20 | |

**PUNTING**

| Last Name | No | Avg |
|---|---|---|
| Horan | 46 | 39.3 |
| Giacomarro | 18 | 42.1 |
| Elway | 1 | 31.0 |

**KICKING**

| Last Name | XP | Att | % | FG | Att | % |
|---|---|---|---|---|---|---|
| Karlis | 37 | 37 | 100 | 18 | 25 | 72 |
| Clendenen | 7 | 7 | 100 | 3 | 4 | 75 |

## SEATTLE SEAHAWKS

### RUSHING

| Last Name | No. | Yds | Avg | TD |
|---|---|---|---|---|
| Warner | 234 | 985 | 4.2 | 8 |
| Williams | 113 | 500 | 4.4 | 1 |
| Krieg | 36 | 155 | 4.3 | 2 |
| B. Green | 21 | 77 | 3.7 | 0 |
| Morris | 21 | 71 | 3.4 | 0 |
| Morton | 19 | 52 | 2.7 | 1 |
| Lane | 13 | 40 | 3.1 | 0 |
| Burse | 7 | 36 | 5.1 | 0 |
| Largent | 2 | 33 | 16.5 | 0 |
| Parros | 13 | 32 | 2.5 | 1 |
| A. Moore | 3 | 15 | 5.0 | 0 |
| Mathison | 5 | 15 | 3.0 | 0 |
| Kemp | 5 | 9 | 1.8 | 0 |
| Hagen | 2 | 3 | 1.5 | 0 |
| Griffith | 1 | 0 | 0.0 | 0 |
| Rodriguez | 1 | 0 | 0.0 | 0 |

### RECEIVING

| Last Name | No. | Yds | Avg | TD |
|---|---|---|---|---|
| Largent | 58 | 912 | 15.7 | 8 |
| Jo. Williams | 38 | 420 | 11.1 | 3 |
| R. Butler | 33 | 465 | 14.1 | 5 |
| Skansi | 19 | 207 | 10.9 | 1 |
| Warner | 17 | 167 | 9.8 | 2 |
| Teal | 14 | 198 | 14.1 | 2 |
| Turner | 14 | 153 | 10.9 | 6 |
| Tice | 14 | 106 | 7.6 | 2 |
| Pardridge | 8 | 145 | 18.1 | 1 |
| Juma | 7 | 95 | 13.6 | 0 |
| Lane | 4 | 30 | 7.5 | 0 |
| Bengen | 2 | 33 | 16.5 | 0 |
| Franklin | 1 | 7 | 7.0 | 0 |
| Parros | 1 | 7 | 7.0 | 0 |
| Millard | 1 | -5 | -5.0 | 0 |

### PUNT RETURNS

| Last Name | No. | Yds | Avg | TD |
|---|---|---|---|---|
| Edmonds | 20 | 251 | 12.6 | 0 |
| Hollis | 6 | 33 | 5.5 | 0 |
| Teal | 6 | 38 | 6.3 | 0 |

### KICKOFF RETURNS

| Last Name | No. | Yds | Avg | TD |
|---|---|---|---|---|
| Edmonds | 27 | 564 | 20.9 | 0 |
| Hollis | 10 | 263 | 26.3 | 0 |
| Morris | 9 | 149 | 16.6 | 0 |
| Teal | 6 | 95 | 15.8 | 0 |
| Bengen | 2 | 47 | 23.5 | 0 |
| Lane | 2 | 34 | 17.0 | 0 |
| Pardridge | 2 | 29 | 14.5 | 0 |
| Powell | 2 | 23 | 11.5 | 0 |
| B. Green | 1 | 20 | 20.0 | 0 |
| Scholtz | 1 | 11 | 11.0 | 0 |
| Burse | 1 | 1 | 1.0 | 0 |
| Hunter | 1 | 0 | 0.0 | 0 |

### PASSING — PUNTING — KICKING

**PASSING**

| Last Name | Att | Cmp | % | Yds | Yd/Att | TD | Int— | % | RK |
|---|---|---|---|---|---|---|---|---|---|
| Krieg | 294 | 178 | 61 | 2131 | 7.3 | 23 | 15— | 5 | 6 |
| Mathison | 76 | 36 | 47 | 501 | 6.6 | 3 | 5— | 7 | |
| Kemp | 33 | 23 | 70 | 396 | 12.0 | 5 | 1— | 3 | |
| Largent | 2 | 0 | 0 | 0 | 0.0 | 0 | 0— | 0 | |

**PUNTING**

| Last Name | No | Avg |
|---|---|---|
| Rodriguez | 47 | 40.0 |
| Griffith | 11 | 35.1 |
| Bowman | 3 | 34.7 |

**KICKING**

| Last Name | XP | Att | % | FG | Att | % |
|---|---|---|---|---|---|---|
| Johnson | 40 | 40 | 100 | 15 | 20 | 75 |
| Hagler | 4 | 4 | 100 | 2 | 2 | 100 |

## SAN DIEGO CHARGERS

### RUSHING

| Last Name | No. | Yds | Avg | TD |
|---|---|---|---|---|
| Adams | 90 | 343 | 3.8 | 1 |
| Anderson | 80 | 260 | 3.3 | 3 |
| Tim Spencer | 73 | 228 | 3.1 | 0 |
| James | 27 | 102 | 3.8 | 2 |
| Jenkins | 22 | 88 | 4.0 | 0 |
| Middleton | 28 | 74 | 2.6 | 1 |
| Sartin | 19 | 52 | 2.7 | 1 |
| Neuheisel | 6 | 41 | 6.8 | 1 |
| Redden | 11 | 36 | 3.3 | 0 |
| Todd Spencer | 14 | 24 | 1.7 | 0 |
| Kelley | 4 | 17 | 4.3 | 0 |
| Holland | 1 | 17 | 17.0 | 0 |
| Bernstine | 1 | 9 | 9.0 | 0 |
| Steels | 1 | 3 | 3.0 | 0 |
| Zachary | 1 | 3 | 3.0 | 0 |
| Moffett | 1 | 1 | 1.0 | 0 |
| Fouts | 12 | 0 | 0.0 | 0 |
| Herrmann | 4 | -1 | -0.2 | 0 |

### RECEIVING

| Last Name | No. | Yds | Avg | TD |
|---|---|---|---|---|
| Winslow | 53 | 519 | 9.8 | 3 |
| Anderson | 47 | 503 | 10.7 | 3 |
| James | 41 | 593 | 14.5 | 3 |
| Chandler | 39 | 617 | 15.8 | 2 |
| Holohan | 20 | 239 | 12.0 | 0 |
| Tim Spencer | 17 | 123 | 7.2 | 0 |
| Williams | 12 | 247 | 20.6 | 1 |
| Bernstine | 10 | 76 | 7.6 | 1 |
| Middleton | 8 | 43 | 5.4 | 0 |
| Jenkins | 8 | 40 | 5.0 | 0 |
| Holt | 7 | 56 | 8.0 | 0 |
| Redden | 7 | 46 | 6.6 | 0 |
| Holland | 6 | 138 | 23.0 | 0 |
| Rome | 6 | 49 | 8.2 | 0 |
| Sartin | 6 | 19 | 3.2 | 0 |
| Moffett | 5 | 80 | 16.0 | 1 |
| Adams | 4 | 38 | 9.5 | 0 |
| Mohammad | 2 | 87 | 43.5 | 0 |
| Tom Spencer | 2 | 47 | 23.5 | 0 |
| Ware | 2 | 38 | 19.0 | 0 |
| Steels | 1 | 4 | 4.0 | 0 |

### PUNT RETURNS

| Last Name | No. | Yds | Avg | TD |
|---|---|---|---|---|
| James | 32 | 400 | 12.5 | 1 |
| Williams | 10 | 96 | 9.6 | 0 |
| Rome | 3 | 12 | 4.0 | 0 |

### KICKOFF RETURNS

| Last Name | No. | Yds | Avg | TD |
|---|---|---|---|---|
| Anderson | 22 | 433 | 19.7 | 0 |
| Holland | 19 | 410 | 21.6 | 0 |
| Sartin | 5 | 117 | 23.4 | 0 |
| Adams | 4 | 32 | 8.0 | 0 |
| Kirk | 3 | 15 | 5.0 | 0 |
| Jenkins | 2 | 46 | 23.0 | 0 |
| James | 2 | 41 | 20.5 | 0 |
| Rome | 2 | 28 | 14.0 | 0 |
| Bernstine | 1 | 13 | 13.0 | 0 |
| Zachary | 1 | 2 | 2.0 | 0 |
| Hunter | 1 | 0 | 0.0 | 0 |

### PASSING — PUNTING — KICKING

**PASSING**

| Last Name | Att | Cmp | % | Yds | Yd/Att | TD | Int— | % | RK |
|---|---|---|---|---|---|---|---|---|---|
| Fouts | 364 | 206 | 57 | 2517 | 6.9 | 10 | 15— | 4 | 22 |
| Neuheisel | 59 | 40 | 68 | 367 | 6.2 | 1 | 1— | 2 | |
| Herrmann | 57 | 37 | 65 | 405 | 7.1 | 1 | 5— | 9 | |
| Kelley | 29 | 17 | 59 | 305 | 10.5 | 1 | 0— | 0 | |
| Vlasic | 6 | 3 | 50 | 8 | 1.3 | 0 | 1— | 17 | |
| Smith | 1 | 0 | 0 | 0 | 0.0 | 0 | 1— | 100 | |

**PUNTING**

| Last Name | No | Avg |
|---|---|---|
| Mojsiejenko | 67 | 42.9 |
| Prokop | 17 | 38.5 |

**KICKING**

| Last Name | XP | Att | % | FG | Att | % |
|---|---|---|---|---|---|---|
| Abbott | 22 | 23 | 96 | 13 | 22 | 59 |
| Gaffney | 4 | 5 | 80 | 3 | 6 | 50 |

| Scores of Each Game | | Use Name | Pos. | Hgt | Wgt | Age | Int | Pts | Use Name | Pos. | Hgt | Wgt | Age | Int | Pts | Use Name | Pos. | Hgt | Wgt | Age | Int | Pts |
|---|---|---|---|---|---|---|---|---|---|---|---|---|---|---|---|---|---|---|---|---|---|---|

## LOS ANGELES RAIDERS 5-10 Tom Flores

| Score | Opponent | Opp | Use Name | Pos. | Hgt | Wgt | Age | Use Name | Pos. | Hgt | Wgt | Age | Int | Pts | Use Name | Pos. | Hgt | Wgt | Age | Pts |
|---|---|---|---|---|---|---|---|---|---|---|---|---|---|---|---|---|---|---|---|---|
| 20 | Green Bay | 0 | John Clay | OT | 6'5" | 295 | 23 | Jeff Barnes | LB | 6'2" | 230 | 32 | | | Vince Evans | QB | 6'2" | 210 | 32 | 6 |
| 27 | DETROIT | 7 | Brian Holloway | OT | 6'7" | 275 | 28 | #Keith Browner (from SF) | LB | 6'6" | 245 | 25 | | | Rusty Hilger | QB | 6'4" | 205 | 25 | |
| 35 | KANSAS CITY | 17 | #David Pyles | OT | 6'5" | 275 | 26 | #Darryl Byrd | LB | 6'1" | 225 | 26 | | | Marc Wilson | QB | 6'6" | 205 | 30 | |
| 14 | Denver | 30 | #John Tautolo | OT | 6'4" | 280 | 28 | #Joe Cormier | LB | 6'2" | 230 | 24 | | | #Scott Woolf | QB | 6'1" | 190 | 25 | |
| 17 | SAN DIEGO | 23 | Steve Wright | OT-OG | 6'6" | 280 | 28 | #Jim Ellis | LB | 6'3" | 240 | 23 | | | Marcus Allen | HB | 6'2" | 205 | 27 | 30 |
| 13 | SEATTLE | 35 | #Andy Dickerson | OG | 6'5" | 260 | 24 | #Darryl Goodlow | LB | 6'2" | 235 | 26 | | | #Rick Calhoun | HB | 5'7" | 190 | 24 | 6 |
| 23 | New England | 26 | John Gesek | OG | 6'5" | 275 | 24 | #Leonard Jackson (from CHI) | LB | 6' | 240 | 22 | | | #Craig Ellis | HB | 5'11" | 190 | 26 | 12 |
| 20 | Minnesota | 31 | Charley Hannah | OG | 6'5" | 270 | 32 | Jamie Kimmel | LB | 6'3" | 235 | 25 | | | Frank Hawkins | HB | 5'9" | 210 | 28 | |
| 14 | San Diego | 16 | Bill Lewis | OG | 6'7" | 275 | 24 | Linden King | LB | 6'4" | 250 | 32 | 1 | | Bo Jackson | HB | 6'1" | 230 | 24 | 36 |
| 17 | DENVER | 23 | Mickey Marvin | OG | 6'4" | 265 | 31 | Rod Martin | LB | 6'2" | 225 | 33 | | | Vance Mueller | HB | 6' | 210 | 23 | 6 |
| 37 | Seattle | 14 | Dean Miraldi | OG | 6'5" | 280 | 28 | Reggie McKenzie | LB | 6'1" | 235 | 23 | | | Steve Strachan | HB | 6'1" | 220 | 24 | |
| 34 | BUFFALO | 21 | Chris Riehm | OG | 6'6" | 275 | 26 | #Dan McMillen (from PHI-DE) | LB | 6'4" | 240 | 23 | | | #Jim Browne | FB | 6'1" | 215 | 25 | |
| 10 | Kansas City | 16 | Bruce Wilkerson | OG-OT | 6'5" | 280 | 23 | Matt Millen | LB | 6'2" | 245 | 29 | 1 | | #Rob Harrison | FB | 6'2" | 220 | 24 | 6 |
| 17 | CLEVELAND | 24 | #Jon Zogg | OG | 6'4" | 290 | 26 | #Mike Noble | LB | 6'4" | 220 | 23 | | | Ethan Horton | FB | 6'4" | 220 | 24 | 6 |
| 3 | CHICAGO | 6 | #Paul Dufault | C | 6'4" | 255 | 23 | Jerry Robinson | LB | 6'2" | 225 | 30 | | | Zeph Lee (from DEN) | FB | 6'3" | 215 | 24 | |
| | | | Don Mosebar | C | 6'6" | 275 | 25 | #Ronnie Washington | LB | 6'1" | 245 | 24 | | | Steve Smith | FB | 6'1" | 235 | 23 | |
| | | | #Shawn Regent | C | 6'5" | 280 | 24 | Stefon Adams | DB | 5'10" | 190 | 24 | 1 | | #Carl Aikens | WR | 6'1" | 185 | 25 | 18 |
| | | | Dwight Wheeler (to SD) | C-OG | 6'3" | 285 | 32 | Eddie Anderson | DB | 6' | 200 | 24 | 1 | | Mervyn Fernandez | WR | 6'3" | 200 | 27 | |
| | | | #Brian Belway | DE | 6'6" | 265 | 23 | #Chetti Carr | DB | 5'9" | 185 | 24 | | | Jessie Hester | WR | 5'11" | 170 | 24 | |
| | | | Bob Buczkowski | DE | 6'5" | 260 | 23 | James Davis | DB | 6' | 200 | 30 | | | #Greg Lathan | WR | 6'1" | 195 | 22 | |
| | | | #Ted Chapman | DE | 6'3" | 260 | 23 | Ron Fellows | DB | 6' | 175 | 28 | | | #Wade Lockett | WR | 6'1" | 190 | 23 | |
| | | | #Rick Goltz | DE | 6'4" | 255 | 32 | #Ron Foster | DB | 6' | 200 | 23 | | | James Lofton | WR | 6'3" | 196 | 31 | 30 |
| | | | Sean Jones | DE | 6'7" | 265 | 24 | #Lance Harkey | DB | 5'10" | 180 | 22 | | | #David Williams | WR | 6'3" | 190 | 24 | |
| | | | Howie Long | DE | 6'5" | 265 | 27 | Mike Haynes | DB | 6'2" | 190 | 34 | 2 | | Dokie Williams | WR | 5'11" | 180 | 27 | 30 |
| | | | Greg Townsend | DE | 6'3" | 250 | 25 | Rod Hill | DB | 6' | 185 | 28 | | | Chris Woods | WR | 5'11" | 190 | 25 | |
| | | | Mike Wise | DE | 6'7" | 265 | 23 | #Victor Jackson | DB | 6' | 205 | 27 | | | Todd Christensen | TE | 6'3" | 230 | 31 | 12 |
| | | | Richard Ackerman | NT-DE | 6'4" | 260 | 28 | Vann McElroy | DB | 6'2" | 195 | 27 | 4 | 6 | Trey Junkin | TE | 6'2" | 230 | 26 | |
| | | | Bill Pickel | NT | 6'5" | 260 | 28 | Sam Seale | DB | 5'9" | 185 | 24 | | | Andy Parker | TE | 6'5" | 250 | 25 | |
| | | | Mike Rodriguez | NT | 6'1" | 275 | 26 | #Willie Teal | DB | 5'10" | 180 | 29 | | | #Mario Perry | TE | 6'6" | 240 | 23 | 6 |
| | | | Malcolm Taylor | NT | 6'6" | 280 | 27 | Stacey Toran | DB | 6'2" | 200 | 25 | 3 | 6 | #Ron Wheeler | TE | 6'5" | 235 | 27 | |
| | | | Mitch Willis | NT | 6'8" | 280 | 25 | #Tony Tillmon | DB | 5'10" | 170 | 23 | | | Chris Bahr | K | 5'10" | 170 | 34 | 84 |
| | | | | | | | | Lionel Washington | DB | 6' | 185 | 26 | | | #Vince Gamache | K | 5'11" | 170 | 24 | |
| | | | | | | | | Demise Williams | DB | 6'1" | 225 | 23 | | | #David Hardy | K | 5'7" | 180 | 28 | |
| | | | | | | | | #Ricky Williams | DB | 6'1" | 200 | 27 | | | Stan Talley | K | 6'5" | 220 | 28 | |

Lester Hayes - foot injury
Shelby Jordan - triceps injury
Curt Marsh - ankle injury
Jim Plunkett - shoulder injury

## KANSAS CITY CHIEFS 4-11 Frank Gansz

| Score | Opponent | Opp | Use Name | Pos. | Hgt | Wgt | Age | Pts | Use Name | Pos. | Hgt | Wgt | Age | Int | Pts | Use Name | Pos. | Hgt | Wgt | Age | Pts |
|---|---|---|---|---|---|---|---|---|---|---|---|---|---|---|---|---|---|---|---|---|---|
| 20 | SAN DIEGO | 13 | John Alt | OT | 6'7" | 290 | 25 | | Tim Cofield | LB | 6'2" | 245 | 24 | | | Todd Blackledge | QB | 6'3" | 219 | 26 | |
| 14 | Seattle | 43 | #Dan Doubiago | OT | 6'5" | 283 | 26 | | Louis Cooper | LB | 6'2" | 240 | 24 | 1 | | #Alex Espinoza | QB | 6'1" | 193 | 23 | |
| 17 | L.A. Raiders | 35 | Irv Eatman | OT | 6'7" | 293 | 26 | | Jack Del Rio | LB | 6'4" | 238 | 24 | | | Doug Hudson | QB | 6'2" | 201 | 22 | |
| 0 | Miami | 42 | #Doug Hoppock | OT-OG | 6'4" | 280 | 27 | | #Randy Frazier | LB | 6'3" | 235 | 23 | | | Bill Kenney | QB | 6'4" | 207 | 32 | |
| 17 | DENVER | 26 | David Lutz | OT | 6'6" | 290 | 27 | | Dino Hackett | LB | 6'3" | 228 | 23 | | | Frank Seurer | QB | 6'1" | 195 | 25 | |
| 21 | San Diego | 42 | #Mark Nelson | OT | 6'4" | 270 | 23 | | James Harrell | LB | 6'1" | 240 | 30 | | | #Matt Stevens | QB | 6' | 190 | 23 | |
| 28 | Chicago | 31 | #Steve Rogers | OT | 6'5" | 260 | 28 | | #Bob Harris | LB | 6'2" | 223 | 27 | 6 | | Michael Clemens | HB | 5'5" | 166 | 22 | |
| 16 | PITTSBURGH | 17 | Mark Adickes | OG | 6'4" | 270 | 26 | 6 | #Bruce Holmes | LB | 6'2" | 235 | 22 | | | #Steve Griffin | HB | 5'10" | 205 | 23 | |
| 9 | N.Y. JETS | 16 | Rich Baldinger | OG-OT | 6'4" | 285 | 27 | | Todd Howard | LB | 6'2" | 235 | 22 | | | Herman Heard | HB | 5'10" | 182 | 25 | 18 |
| 3 | GREEN BAY | 23 | #Lee Getz | OG | 6'3" | 250 | 23 | | #Fred Jones | LB | 6'3" | 240 | 22 | | | Paul Palmer | HB | 5'9" | 184 | 22 | 12 |
| 27 | Detroit | 20 | #James Harvey | OG-OT | 6'3" | 265 | 21 | | Ken McAlister | LB | 6'5" | 220 | 27 | | | Robert Parker | HB | 6'1" | 201 | 24 | |
| 27 | Cincinnati | 30 | Byron Ingram | OG | 6'2" | 295 | 22 | | #Gary Moten | LB | 6'1" | 210 | 26 | | | James Evans | FB | 6' | 220 | 24 | |
| 16 | L.A. RAIDERS | 10 | Brian Jozwiak | OG | 6'5" | 310 | 24 | | Aaron Pearson | LB | 6' | 240 | 23 | | | #Ken Lacey | FB | 6' | 220 | 24 | |
| 17 | Denver | 20 | Arland Thompson | OG | 6'3" | 265 | 29 | | Angelo Snipes (from SD) | LB | 6' | 220 | 24 | | | Larry Moriarty | FB | 6'1" | 237 | 29 | 6 |
| 41 | SEATTLE | 20 | #Kevin Adkins | C | 6'1" | 250 | 23 | | #Gary Spann | LB | 6'1" | 218 | 24 | | | Christian Okoye | FB | 6'1" | 253 | 26 | 18 |
| | | | Tom Baugh | C | 6'3" | 274 | 23 | | #Trent Bryant | DB | 5'10" | 180 | 28 | 1 | | #Woodie Pippens | FB | 5'11" | 225 | 24 | |
| | | | Rick Donnalley | C | 6'2" | 260 | 28 | | Lloyd Burruss | DB | 6' | 209 | 30 | | | #Chris Smith | FB | 6' | 242 | 24 | |
| | | | Glenn Hyde | C | 6'3" | 252 | 36 | | Deron Cherry | DB | 5'11" | 192 | 27 | 3 | | #Ralph Stockemer | FB | 6'1" | 212 | 24 | |
| | | | #Jim Pietrzak | C | 6'5" | 263 | 34 | | Sherman Cocroft | DB | 6'1" | 192 | 26 | | | Eric Brown | WR | 6'2" | 180 | 23 | |
| | | | Gary Baldinger | DE | 6'3" | 260 | 23 | | #Jeff Colter | DB | 5'10" | 171 | 26 | | | Carlos Carson | WR | 5'11" | 185 | 29 | 42 |
| | | | Mike Bell | DE | 6'4" | 260 | 30 | | #Cornelius Dozier | DB | 6'2" | 190 | 23 | | | Darre;; Colbert | WR | 5'10" | 174 | 24 | |
| | | | James Black | DE | 6'4" | 280 | 28 | | #Jack Epps | DB | 6' | 197 | 24 | | | #Richard Estell | WR | 6'2" | 210 | 25 | |
| * Overtime | | | #Tony Holloway | DE-LB | 6'2" | 222 | 23 | | Jitter Fields (from IND) | DB | 5'8" | 180 | 25 | 6 | | #Eric Hodges | WR | 6'1" | 189 | 23 | |
| | | | #Ken Johnson | DE | 6'5" | 260 | 32 | | Greg Hill (from RAID) | DB | 6'1" | 197 | 26 | | | Henry Marshall | WR | 6'2" | 216 | 33 | |
| | | | #Chris Lindstrom | DE | 6'7" | 261 | 27 | | #Garcia Lane | DB | 5'9" | 180 | 25 | | | David Montagne | WR | 6'2" | 184 | 23 | |
| | | | #Lloyd Mumphrey | DE | 6'3" | 260 | 26 | | Albert Lewis | DB | 6'2" | 192 | 26 | 1 | | Kenny Nash | WR | 6'2" | 195 | 25 | |
| | | | Art Still | DE | 6'7" | 255 | 31 | | #Ted Nelson | DB | 5'10" | 203 | 22 | | | #Stephone Paige | WR | 6'2" | 185 | 25 | 24 |
| | | | Ray Woodard (from DEN) | DE | 6'6" | 290 | 26 | | J.C. Pearson | DB | 5'11" | 183 | 24 | | | #John Trahan | WR | 5'9" | 160 | 26 | |
| | | | #John Walker | NT-DT | 6'6" | 270 | 26 | | Mark Robinson | DB | 5'11" | 206 | 24 | 2 | | Walt Arnold | TE | 6'3" | 225 | 29 | |
| | | | #Bill Acker | DE | 6'3" | 255 | 31 | | Kevin Ross | DB | 5'9" | 182 | 25 | 3 | 6 | Paul Coffman | TE | 6'3" | 225 | 31 | 6 |
| | | | #Jeff Faulkner | NT-DE | 6'3" | 270 | 23 | | #Blane Smith | DB | 5'10" | 190 | 27 | | | Jonathan Hayes | TE | 6'5" | 240 | 23 | 12 |
| | | | Leonard Griffin | NT-DE | 6'4" | 258 | 24 | | Carlton Thomas | DB | 6' | 200 | 23 | | | #Rod Jones | TE | 6'4" | 242 | 23 | 6 |
| | | | Eric Holle | NT | 6'5" | 265 | 26 | | #Kevin Wyatt | DB | 5'10" | 208 | 23 | | | Mark Keel (from SEA) | TE | 6'4" | 228 | 25 | |
| | | | Pete Koch | NT | 6'6" | 265 | 26 | | | | | | | | | #Stein Koss | TE | 6'2" | 225 | 24 | |
| | | | Bill Maas | NT | 6'5" | 268 | 28 | 6 | Brad Budde - Stomach injury | | | | | | | #Riley Walton | TE | 6'4" | 245 | 24 | |
| | | | | | | | | | Emile Harry - Shoulder Separation | | | | | | | Lewis Colbert | K | 5'11" | 180 | 24 | |
| | | | | | | | | | Gary Spani - Knee Injury | | | | | | | Kelly Goodburn | K | 6'2" | 195 | 25 | |
| | | | | | | | | | | | | | | | | #James Hamrick | K | 5'11" | 177 | 24 | 10 |
| | | | | | | | | | | | | | | | | Nick Lowery | K | 6'4" | 189 | 31 | 83 |

# - on the active roster for strike replacement games only

## L.A. RAIDERS

### RUSHING

| Last Name | No. | Yds | Avg | TD |
|---|---|---|---|---|
| Allen | 200 | 754 | 3.8 | 5 |
| Jackson | 81 | 554 | 6.8 | 4 |
| Mueller | 37 | 175 | 4.7 | 1 |
| Evans | 11 | 144 | 13.1 | 1 |
| Strachan | 28 | 108 | 3.9 | 0 |
| Horton | 31 | 95 | 3.1 | 0 |
| Wilson | 17 | 91 | 5.4 | 0 |
| Harrison | 9 | 49 | 5.4 | 0 |
| Calhoun | 7 | 36 | 5.1 | 0 |
| Hawkins | 4 | 24 | 6.0 | 0 |
| Smith | 5 | 18 | 3.6 | 0 |
| Hilger | 8 | 8 | 1.0 | 0 |
| Aikens | 1 | 1 | 1.0 | 0 |
| Browne | 2 | 1 | 0.5 | 0 |
| Lofton | 1 | 1 | 1.0 | 0 |

### RECEIVING

| Last Name | No. | Yds | Avg | TD |
|---|---|---|---|---|
| Allen | 51 | 410 | 8.0 | 0 |
| Christensen | 47 | 663 | 14.1 | 2 |
| Lofton | 41 | 880 | 21.5 | 5 |
| Williams | 21 | 330 | 15.7 | 5 |
| Jackson | 16 | 136 | 8.5 | 2 |
| Fernandez | 14 | 236 | 16.9 | 0 |
| Mueller | 11 | 95 | 8.6 | 0 |
| Aikens | 8 | 134 | 16.8 | 3 |
| Lathan | 5 | 98 | 19.6 | 0 |
| Ellis | 5 | 39 | 7.8 | 0 |
| Williams | 4 | 106 | 26.0 | 0 |
| Strachan | 4 | 42 | 10.5 | 0 |
| Wheeler | 3 | 61 | 20.3 | 0 |
| Smith | 3 | 46 | 15.3 | 0 |
| Horton | 3 | 44 | 14.7 | 1 |
| Harrison | 2 | 18 | 9.0 | 0 |
| Junkin | 2 | 15 | 7.5 | 0 |
| Hester | 1 | 30 | 30.0 | 0 |
| Calhoun | 1 | 17 | 17.0 | 0 |
| Woods | 1 | 14 | 14.0 | 0 |
| Hawkins | 1 | 6 | 6.0 | 0 |
| Perry | 1 | 3 | 3.0 | 0 |

### PUNT RETURNS

| Last Name | No. | Yds | Avg | TD |
|---|---|---|---|---|
| Woods | 26 | 189 | 7.3 | 0 |
| Calhoun | 8 | 92 | 11.5 | 1 |
| Adams | 5 | 39 | 7.8 | 0 |
| Fellows | 2 | 19 | 9.5 | 0 |
| Harkey | 2 | 17 | 8.5 | 0 |
| Davis | 1 | 0 | 0.0 | 0 |

### KICKOFF RETURNS

| Last Name | No. | Yds | Avg | TD |
|---|---|---|---|---|
| Mueller | 27 | 588 | 21.8 | 0 |
| Williams | 14 | 221 | 15.8 | 0 |
| Calhoun | 9 | 217 | 24.1 | 0 |
| Adams | 3 | 61 | 20.3 | 0 |
| Woods | 3 | 55 | 18.3 | 0 |
| Harkey | 1 | 20 | 20.0 | 0 |
| Foster | 1 | 12 | 12.0 | 0 |
| Millen | 1 | 0 | 0.0 | 0 |
| R. Washington | 1 | 0 | 0.0 | 0 |

### PASSING — PUNTING — KICKING

#### PASSING

| Last Name | Att | Cmp | % | Yds | Yd/Att | TD | Int— | % | RK |
|---|---|---|---|---|---|---|---|---|---|
| Wilson | 266 | 152 | 57 | 2070 | 7.8 | 12 | 8— | 3 | 10 |
| Hilger | 106 | 55 | 52 | 706 | 6.7 | 2 | 6— | 6 | |
| Evans | 83 | 39 | 47 | 630 | 7.6 | 5 | 5— | 0 | |
| Allen | 2 | 1 | 50 | 23 | 11.5 | 0 | 0— | 0 | |

#### PUNTING

| Last Name | No | Avg |
|---|---|---|
| Talley | 57 | 39.9 |
| Gamache | 14 | 37.1 |

#### KICKING

| Last Name | XP | Att | % | FG | Att | % |
|---|---|---|---|---|---|---|
| C. Bahr | 27 | 28 | 96 | 19 | 29 | 66 |
| Hardy | 7 | 7 | 100 | 0 | 1 | 0 |

## KANSAS CITY CHIEFS

### RUSHING

| Last Name | No. | Yds | Avg | TD |
|---|---|---|---|---|
| Okoye | 157 | 660 | 4.2 | 3 |
| Heard | 82 | 466 | 5.7 | 3 |
| Palmer | 24 | 155 | 6.5 | 0 |
| Parker | 47 | 150 | 3.2 | 1 |
| C. Smith | 26 | 114 | 4.4 | 0 |
| Moriarty | 30 | 107 | 3.6 | 0 |
| Lacy | 14 | 49 | 3.7 | 0 |
| Seurer | 9 | 33 | 3.7 | 0 |
| Blackledge | 5 | 21 | 4.2 | 0 |
| Goodburn | 1 | 16 | 16.0 | 0 |
| Pippens | 3 | 16 | 5.3 | 0 |
| Clemons | 2 | 7 | 3.5 | 0 |
| Stevens | 3 | 7 | 2.3 | 0 |
| Espinoza | 1 | 5 | 5.0 | 0 |
| Stockemer | 1 | 2 | 2.0 | 0 |
| Hudson | 1 | 0 | 0.0 | 0 |
| Kenney | 12 | -2 | -0.2 | 0 |
| Carson | 1 | -7 | -7.0 | 0 |

### RECEIVING

| Last Name | No. | Yds | Avg | TD |
|---|---|---|---|---|
| Carson | 55 | 1044 | 19.0 | 7 |
| Paige | 43 | 707 | 16.4 | 4 |
| Okoye | 24 | 169 | 7.0 | 0 |
| Hayes | 21 | 272 | 13.3 | 2 |
| Heard | 14 | 118 | 8.4 | 0 |
| Marshall | 10 | 126 | 12.6 | 0 |
| Moriarty | 10 | 37 | 3.7 | 1 |
| Keel | 8 | 97 | 12.1 | 1 |
| R. Jones | 8 | 76 | 9.5 | 1 |
| Parker | 7 | 44 | 6.3 | 0 |
| Brown | 5 | 69 | 13.8 | 0 |
| Montagne | 5 | 47 | 9.4 | 0 |
| Coffman | 5 | 42 | 8.4 | 1 |
| Trahan | 4 | 40 | 10.0 | 0 |
| Palmer | 4 | 27 | 6.8 | 0 |
| Arnold | 3 | 26 | 8.7 | 0 |
| Estell | 3 | 24 | 8.0 | 1 |
| D. Colbert | 3 | 21 | 7.0 | 0 |
| Koss | 2 | 25 | 12.5 | 0 |
| Nash | 2 | 22 | 11.0 | 0 |
| C. Smith | 2 | 21 | 10.5 | 0 |
| Pippens | 2 | 12 | 6.0 | 0 |
| Stockemer | 1 | 4 | 4.0 | 0 |
| Adickes | 1 | 3 | 3.0 | 1 |

### PUNT RETURNS

| Last Name | No. | Yds | Avg | TD |
|---|---|---|---|---|
| Clemons | 19 | 162 | 8.5 | 0 |
| Fields | 8 | 161 | 20.1 | 1 |
| Wyatt | 2 | 4 | 2.0 | 0 |
| Cocroft | 1 | 0 | 0.0 | 0 |
| D. Colbert | 1 | 11 | 11.0 | 0 |
| Montagne | 1 | 8 | 8.0 | 0 |

### KICKOFF RETURNS

| Last Name | No. | Yds | Avg | TD |
|---|---|---|---|---|
| Palmer | 38 | 923 | 24.3 | 2 |
| Moriarty | 6 | 102 | 17.0 | 0 |
| Robinson | 5 | 97 | 19.4 | 0 |
| Wyatt | 5 | 121 | 24.2 | 0 |
| Lacy | 4 | 44 | 11.0 | 0 |
| Parker | 3 | 49 | 16.3 | 0 |
| Lane | 2 | 37 | 18.5 | 0 |
| A. Pearson | 2 | 4 | 2.0 | 0 |
| Clemons | 1 | 3 | 3.0 | 0 |
| D. Colbert | 1 | 18 | 18.0 | 0 |
| Fields | 1 | 13 | 13.0 | 0 |
| S. Griffin | 1 | 16 | 16.0 | 0 |
| B. Smith | 1 | 10 | 10.0 | 0 |

### PASSING — PUNTING — KICKING

#### PASSING

| Last Name | Att | Cmp | % | Yds | Yd/Att | TD | Int— | % | RK |
|---|---|---|---|---|---|---|---|---|---|
| Kenney | 273 | 154 | 56 | 2107 | 7.7 | 15 | 9— | 3 | 8 |
| Stevens | 57 | 32 | 56 | 315 | 5.5 | 1 | 1— | 2 | |
| Seurer | 55 | 26 | 47 | 340 | 6.2 | 0 | 4— | 7 | |
| Blackledge | 31 | 15 | 48 | 154 | 5.0 | 1 | 1— | 3 | |
| Espinoza | 14 | 9 | 64 | 69 | 4.9 | 0 | 2— | 14 | |
| Hudson | 1 | 0 | 0 | 0 | 0.0 | 0 | 0— | 0 | |
| Palmer | 1 | 0 | 0 | 0 | 0.0 | 0 | 0— | 0 | |

#### PUNTING

| Last Name | No | Avg |
|---|---|---|
| Goodburn | 59 | 40.9 |
| L. Colbert | 10 | 37.7 |

#### KICKING

| Last Name | XP | Att | % | FG | Att | % |
|---|---|---|---|---|---|---|
| Lowery | 26 | 26 | 100 | 19 | 23 | 83 |
| Hamrick | 4 | 4 | 100 | 2 | 2 | 100 |

# 1987 N.F.C.—PLAYOFFS

Jan. 3, 1988 at New Orleans (Attendance 68,127)

**SCORING**

| | | | | |
|---|---|---|---|---|
| MINNESOTA | 10 | 21 | 3 | 10-44 |
| NEW ORLEANS | 7 | 3 | 0 | 0-10 |

First quarter
- N.O. — Martin, 10 yard pass from Hebert; PAT — Andersen (kick)
- Minn. — C. Nelson, 42 yard field goal
- Minn. — Carter, 84 yard punt return; PAT — C. Nelson (kick)

Second quarter
- Minn. — Jordan, 5 yard pass from Wilson; PAT — C. Nelson (kick)
- Minn. — Carter, 10 yard pass from Rice; PAT — C. Nelson (kick)
- N.O. — Andersen, 40 yard field goal
- Minn. — Jones, 44 yard pass from Wilson; PAT — C. Nelson (kick)

Third quarter
- Minn. — C. Nelson, 42 yard field goal

Fourth quarter
- Minn. — C. Nelson, 19 yard field goal
- Minn. — Dozier, 18 yard run; PAT — C. Nelson (kick)

**TEAM STATISTICS**

| MINN. | | N.O. |
|---|---|---|
| 28 | First Downs | 9 |
| 14 | First Downs-Rushing | 0 |
| 14 | First Downs-Passing | 7 |
| 0 | First Downs-Penalty | 2 |
| 4 | Fumbles | 3 |
| 2 | Fumbles-Lost Ball | 2 |
| 5 | Penalties-Number | 4 |
| 42 | Yards Penalized | 26 |
| 0 | Missed Field Goals | 0 |
| 86 | Offensive Plays | 47 |
| 417 | Net Yards | 149 |
| 4.8 | Average Gain | 3.2 |
| 2 | Giveaways | 6 |
| 6 | Takeaways | 2 |
| +4 | Difference | -4 |

**INDIVIDUAL STATISTICS**

**RUSHING**

| MINNESOTA | No. | Yds. | Avg. | NEW ORLEANS | No. | Yds. | Avg. |
|---|---|---|---|---|---|---|---|
| D. Nelson | 17 | 73 | 4.3 | Hilliard | 8 | 39 | 4.9 |
| Anderson | 7 | 49 | 7.0 | Mayes | 3 | 11 | 3.7 |
| Dozier | 8 | 45 | 5.6 | Hebert | 2 | 2 | 1.0 |
| Fenney | 7 | 20 | 2.9 | Jordan | 1 | 1 | 1.0 |
| Rice | 4 | 10 | 2.5 | | 14 | 53 | 3.8 |
| Kramer | 2 | 5 | 2.5 | | | | |
| Wilson | 2 | 5 | 2.5 | | | | |
| Gannon | 3 | 3 | 1.0 | | | | |
| | 50 | 210 | 4.2 | | | | |

**RECEIVING**

| | | | | | | | |
|---|---|---|---|---|---|---|---|
| Carter | 6 | 79 | 13.2 | Brenner | 2 | 33 | 16.5 |
| Nelson | 2 | 50 | 25.0 | Pattison | 2 | 18 | 9.0 |
| Lewis | 2 | 27 | 13.5 | Hill | 2 | 15 | 7.5 |
| Rice | 2 | 17 | 8.5 | Hilliard | 2 | 15 | 7.5 |
| Jordan | 2 | 17 | 8.5 | Tice | 2 | 13 | 6.5 |
| H. Jones | 1 | 44 | 44.0 | Martin | 1 | 10 | 10.0 |
| Gustafson | 1 | 12 | 12.0 | | 11 | 96 | 8.7 |
| Anderson | 1 | -3 | -3.0 | | | | |
| | 17 | 207 | 12.2 | | | | |

**PUNTING**

| | | | | | | | |
|---|---|---|---|---|---|---|---|
| Scribner | 3 | | 32.0 | Hansen | 6 | | 44.2 |

**PUNT RETURNS**

| | | | | | | | |
|---|---|---|---|---|---|---|---|
| Carter | 6 | 143 | 23.8 | Gray | 1 | 0 | 0.0 |

**KICKOFF RETURNS**

| | | | | | | | |
|---|---|---|---|---|---|---|---|
| none | | | | Word | 4 | 53 | 19.2 |
| | | | | Adams | 1 | 19 | 19.0 |
| | | | | Gray | 1 | 16 | 16.0 |
| | | | | Brock | 1 | 13 | 13.0 |
| | | | | | 7 | 101 | 14.4 |

**INTERCEPTION RETURNS**

| | | | |
|---|---|---|---|
| Holt | 1 | 0 | 0.0 |
| Harris | 1 | 15 | 15.0 |
| Rutland | 1 | 0 | 0.0 |
| Freeman | 1 | 30 | 30.0 |
| | 4 | 45 | 11.3 |

**PASSING**

MINNESOTA

| | Att. | Comp. | Comp Pct. | Yds. | Int. | Yds./ Att. | Yds./ Comp. |
|---|---|---|---|---|---|---|---|
| Kramer | 9 | 5 | 56 | 50 | 0 | 5.6 | 10.0 |
| Wilson | 20 | 11 | 55 | 189 | 0 | 14.5 | 18.5 |
| Rice | 1 | 1 | 100 | 10 | 0 | 10.0 | 10.0 |
| | 30 | 17 | 57 | 249 | 0 | 8.3 | 14.6 |

NEW ORLEANS

| | Att. | Comp. | Comp Pct. | Yds. | Int. | Yds./ Att. | Yds./ Comp. |
|---|---|---|---|---|---|---|---|
| Hebert | 19 | 9 | 47 | 84 | 2 | 4.4 | 9.3 |
| Wilson | 12 | 2 | 17 | 20 | 2 | 1.7 | 10.0 |
| | 31 | 11 | 35 | 104 | 4 | 3.4 | 9.5 |

Jan. 9, 1988, at San Francisco (Attendance 62, 457)

**SCORING**

| | | | | |
|---|---|---|---|---|
| MINNESOTA | 3 | 17 | 10 | 6-36 |
| SAN FRANCISCO | 3 | 0 | 14 | 7-24 |

First Quarter
- Minn. — C. Nelson, 21 yard field goal
- S.F. — Wersching, 43 yard field goal

Second Quarter
- Minn. — Hilton, 7 yard pass from Wilson; PAT — C. Nelson (kick)
- Minn. — C. Nelson, 23 yard field goal
- Minn. — Rutland, 45 yard interception return; PAT — C. Nelson (kick)

Third Quarter
- S.F. — Fuller, 48 yard interception return; PAT—Wersching (kick)
- Minn. — H. Jones, 5 yard pass from Wilson; PAT — C. Nelson (kick)
- S.F. — Young, 5 yard run; PAT — Wersching (kick)
- Minn. — C. Nelson, 40 yard field goal

Fourth Quarter
- Minn. — C. Nelson, 40 yard field goal
- S.F. — Frank, 16 yard pass from Young; PAT — Wersching (kick)
- Minn. — C. Nelson, 23 yard field goal

**TEAM STATISTICS**

| MINN. | | S.F. |
|---|---|---|
| 22 | First Downs | 17 |
| 5 | First Downs-Rushing | 6 |
| 15 | First Down-Passing | 10 |
| 2 | First Downs-Penalty | 1 |
| 0 | Fumbes- Number | 1 |
| 0 | Fumbles-Lost | 0 |
| 2 | Penalties-Number | 8 |
| 20 | Yards Penalized | 75 |
| 0 | Missed Field Goals | 2 |
| 70 | Offensive Plays | 66 |
| 397 | Net Yards | 358 |
| 5.7 | Average Gain | 5.4 |
| 1 | Giveaways | 2 |
| 2 | Takeaways | 1 |
| +1 | Difference | -1 |

**INDIVIDUAL STATISTICS**

**RUSHING**

| MINNESOTA | No. | Yds. | Avg. | SAN FRANCISCO | No. | Yds. | Avg. |
|---|---|---|---|---|---|---|---|
| D. Nelson | 11 | 42 | 3.8 | Young | 6 | 72 | 12.0 |
| W. Wilson | 6 | 30 | 5.0 | Montana | 3 | 20 | 6.7 |
| Carter | 1 | 30 | 30.0 | Craig | 7 | 17 | 2.4 |
| Anderson | 7 | 9 | 1.3 | Rathman | 1 | 12 | 12.0 |
| Rice | 6 | 8 | 1.3 | Cribbs | 1 | -6 | -6.0 |
| Dozier | 3 | -2 | -0.7 | | 18 | 115 | 6.4 |
| | 34 | 117 | 3.4 | | | | |

**RECEIVING**

| | | | | | | | |
|---|---|---|---|---|---|---|---|
| Carter | 10 | 227 | 22.7 | Craig | 9 | 78 | 8.7 |
| Rice | 4 | 39 | 9.8 | Wilson | 5 | 50 | 10.0 |
| D. Nelson | 2 | 17 | 8.5 | Rice | 3 | 28 | 9.3 |
| Hilton | 1 | 7 | 7.0 | Taylor | 2 | 28 | 14.0 |
| H. Jones | 1 | 5 | 5.0 | Rathman | 2 | 18 | 9.0 |
| Lewis | 1 | 5 | 5.0 | Frank | 1 | 16 | 16.0 |
| Anderson | 1 | -2 | -2.0 | Clark | 1 | 13 | 13.0 |
| | 20 | 280 | 14.0 | Cribbs | 1 | 7 | 7.0 |
| | | | | Jones | 1 | 7 | 7.0 |
| | | | | Young | 0 | 2 | — |
| | | | | | 24 | 257 | 10.7 |

**PUNTING**

| | | | | | | | |
|---|---|---|---|---|---|---|---|
| Scribner | 5 | | 36.4 | Runager | 6 | | 40.8 |

**PUNT RETURNS**

| | | | | | | | |
|---|---|---|---|---|---|---|---|
| Carter | 2 | 21 | 10.5 | McLemore | 3 | 17 | 5.7 |
| Lewis | 1 | 8 | 8.0 | | | | |
| | 3 | 29 | 9.7 | | | | |

**KICKOFF RETURNS**

| | | | | | | | |
|---|---|---|---|---|---|---|---|
| D. Nelson | 2 | 56 | 28.0 | Rathman | 3 | 45 | 15.0 |
| Rice | 1 | 20 | 20.0 | Cribbs | 3 | 28 | 9.3 |
| | 3 | 76 | 25.3 | Sydney | 2 | 28 | 14.0 |
| | | | | Taylor | 0 | 29 | — |
| | | | | | 8 | 130 | 16.3 |

**INTERCEPTION RETURNS**

| | | | | | | | |
|---|---|---|---|---|---|---|---|
| Rutland | 1 | 45 | 45.0 | Fuller | 1 | 48 | 48.0 |
| Lee | 1 | -5 | -5.0 | | | | |
| | 2 | 40 | 20.0 | | | | |

**PASSING**

MINNESOTA

| | Att. | Comp. | Comp. Pct. | Yds. | Int. | Yds./ Att. | Yds./ Comp. |
|---|---|---|---|---|---|---|---|
| W. Wilson | 34 | 20 | 59 | 298 | 1 | 8.8 | 14.9 |

SAN FRANCISCO

| | Att. | Comp. | Comp. Pct. | Yds. | Int. | Yds./ Att. | Yds./ Comp. |
|---|---|---|---|---|---|---|---|
| Montana | 26 | 12 | 46 | 109 | 1 | 4.2 | 9.1 |
| Young | 17 | 12 | 71 | 158 | 1 | 9.3 | 13.2 |
| | 43 | 24 | 56 | 267 | 2 | 6.2 | 11.1 |

Jan. 10, 1988 at Chicago (Att. 58,153)

**SCORING**

| | | | | |
|---|---|---|---|---|
| WASHINGTON | 0 | 14 | 7 | 0-21 |
| CHICAGO | 7 | 7 | 3 | 0-17 |

First Quarter
- Chicago — Thomas, 2 yard run; PAT — Butler (kick)

Second Quarter
- Chicago — Morris, 14 yard pass from McMahon; PAT — Butler (kick)
- Wash. — Rogers, 3 yard run; PAT — Haji-Sheikh (kick)
- Wash. — Didier, 18 yard pass from Williams; PAT — Haji-Sheikh (kick)

Third Quarter
- Wash. — Green, 52 yard punt return; PAT—Haji-Sheikh (kick)
- Chicago — Butler, 25 yard field goal

**TEAM STATISTICS**

| WASH. | | CHI. |
|---|---|---|
| 17 | First Downs-Total | 15 |
| 4 | First Downs-Rushing | 8 |
| 11 | First Downs-Passing | 7 |
| 2 | First Downs-Penalty | 0 |
| 1 | Fumbles-Number | 1 |
| 1 | Fumbles-Lost Ball | 0 |
| 3 | Penalties-Number | 5 |
| 20 | Yards Penalized | 50 |
| 0 | Missed Field Goals | 1 |
| 59 | Offensive Plays | 64 |
| 272 | Net Yards | 280 |
| 4.6 | Average Gain | 4.4 |
| 2 | Giveaways | 3 |
| 3 | Takeaways | 2 |
| +1 | Difference | -1 |

**INDIVIDUAL STATISTICS**

**RUSHING**

| WASHINGTON | No. | Yds. | Avg. | CHICAGO | No. | Yds. | Avg. |
|---|---|---|---|---|---|---|---|
| Rogers | 6 | 13 | 2.2 | Payton | 18 | 85 | 4.7 |
| Bryant | 3 | 8 | 2.7 | Suhey | 4 | 8 | 2.0 |
| Clark | 1 | -6 | -6.0 | Thomas | 2 | 3 | 1.5 |
| Smith | 16 | 66 | 4.1 | Gentry | 2 | 5 | 2.5 |
| Schroeder | 1 | -8 | -8.0 | McMahon | 2 | 5 | 2.5 |
| Williams | 2 | -1 | -0.5 | Sanders | 2 | 4 | 2.0 |
| | 29 | 72 | 2.5 | | 30 | 110 | 3.7 |

**RECEIVING**

| | | | | | | | |
|---|---|---|---|---|---|---|---|
| Sanders | 6 | 92 | 15.3 | Gentry | 3 | 43 | 14.3 |
| Rogers | 1 | 11 | 11.0 | Boso | 3 | 19 | 6.3 |
| Clark | 4 | 56 | 14.0 | Morris | 2 | 47 | 23.5 |
| Didier | 2 | 32 | 16.0 | Suhey | 1 | 6 | 6.0 |
| Warren | 1 | 16 | 16.0 | Payton | 3 | 20 | 6.7 |
| | 14 | 207 | 14.8 | Gault | 1 | 44 | 44.0 |
| | | | | Sanders | 1 | 2 | 2.0 |
| | | | | McKinnon | 1 | 16 | 16.0 |
| | | | | | 15 | 297 | 19.8 |

**PUNTING**

| | | | | | | | |
|---|---|---|---|---|---|---|---|
| Cox | 4 | | 42.3 | Barnhardt | 4 | | 36.3 |

**PUNT RETURNS**

| | | | | | | | |
|---|---|---|---|---|---|---|---|
| Yarber | 2 | 13 | 6.5 | McKinnon | 2 | 12 | 6.0 |
| Green | 1 | 52 | 52.0 | | | | |
| | 3 | 65 | 21.7 | | | | |

**KICKOFF RETURNS**

| | | | | | | | |
|---|---|---|---|---|---|---|---|
| Sanders | 2 | 25 | 12.5 | Gentry | 2 | 74 | 37.0 |
| Smith | 1 | 19 | 19.0 | Gault | 1 | 29 | 29.0 |
| Branch | 1 | 12 | 12.0 | | 3 | 103 | 34.3 |
| | 4 | 56 | 14.0 | | | | |

**INTERCEPTION RETURNS**

| | | | | | | | |
|---|---|---|---|---|---|---|---|
| Davis | 1 | 23 | 23.0 | Richardson | 1 | 0 | 0.0 |
| Wilburn | 1 | 0 | 0.0 | | | | |
| Woodbury | 1 | 0 | 0.0 | | | | |
| | 3 | 23 | 7.7 | | | | |

**PASSING**

WASHINGTON

| | Att. | Comp. | Comp. Pct. | Yds. | Int. | Yds./ Att. | Yds./ Comp. |
|---|---|---|---|---|---|---|---|
| Williams | 29 | 14 | 48 | 207 | 1 | 7.1 | 14.8 |

CHICAGO

| | Att. | Comp. | Comp. Pct. | Yds. | Int. | Yds./ Att. | Yds./ Comp. |
|---|---|---|---|---|---|---|---|
| McMahon | 29 | 15 | 52 | 197 | 3 | 6.8 | 13.1 |

## January 3, 1988 at Houston (Attendance 49,622)

### SCORING

| | | | | | | |
|---|---|---|---|---|---|---|
| SEATTLE | 7 | 3 | 3 | 7 | 0- | 20 |
| HOUSTON | 3 | 10 | 7 | 0 | 3- | 23 |

**First Quarter**
Sea. — Largent, 20 yard pass from Krieg
    PAT-N. Johnson (kick)
Hou. — Zendejas, 47 yard field goal

**Second Quarter**
Hou. — Rozier, 1 yard rush
    PAT—Zendejas (kick)
Hou. — Zendejas, 49 yard field goal
Sea. — Johnson, 33 yard field goal

**Third Quarter**
Sea. — Johnson, 41 yard field goal
Hou. — Drewrey, 29 pass from Moon
    PAT—Zendejas (kick)

**Fourth Quarter**
Sea. — Largent, 12 yard pass from Krieg
    PAT—N. Johnson (kick)

**Overtime**
Hou. — Zendejas, 42 yard field goal

### TEAM STATISTICS

| SEA. | | HOU. |
|---|---|---|
| 11 | First Downs- Total | 27 |
| 1 | First Downs- Rushing | 9 |
| 10 | First Downs- Passing | 12 |
| 0 | First Downs- Penalty | 0 |
| 1 | Fumbles- Number | 2 |
| 1 | Fumbles- Lost Ball | 1 |
| 3 | Penalties- Number | 4 |
| 20 | Yards Penalized | 25 |
| 0 | Missed Field Goals | 2 |
| 52 | Offensive Plays | 84 |
| 250 | Net Yards | 437 |
| 4.8 | Average Gain | 5.2 |
| 1 | Giveaways | 2 |
| 2 | Takeaways | 1 |
| +1 | Difference | -1 |

### INDIVIDUAL STATISTICS

**SEATTLE**    **HOUSTON**

#### RUSHING

| SEATTLE | No. | Yds. | Avg. | HOUSTON | No. | Yds. | Avg. |
|---|---|---|---|---|---|---|---|
| J. Williams | 7 | 27 | 3.9 | Rozier | 21 | 66 | 3.1 |
| Morris | 4 | 2 | 0.5 | Highsmith | 12 | 74 | 6.2 |
| | 11 | 29 | 2.6 | Wallace | 2 | 11 | 5.5 |
| | | | | Moon | 4 | -2 | -.5 |
| | | | | Pinkett | 11 | 29 | 2.6 |
| | | | | | 50 | 178 | 3.6 |

#### RECEIVING

| SEATTLE | No. | Yds. | Avg. | HOUSTON | No. | Yds. | Avg. |
|---|---|---|---|---|---|---|---|
| Largent | 7 | 132 | 18.9 | Givins | 7 | 89 | 12.7 |
| R. Butler | 3 | 73 | 24.3 | Drewrey | 3 | 62 | 20.7 |
| Tice | 1 | 8 | 8.0 | D. Hill | 6 | 84 | 14.0 |
| Skansi | 2 | 13 | 6.5 | McNeil | 3 | 13 | 4.3 |
| Williams | 2 | 5 | 2.5 | Highsmith | 2 | 17 | 8.5 |
| Morris | 1 | 6 | 6.0 | Wallace | 1 | 11 | 11.0 |
| | 16 | 221 | 13.8 | Rozier | 1 | 7 | 7.0 |
| | | | | Pinkett | 1 | 3 | 3.0 |
| | | | | | 21 | 259 | 12.3 |

#### PUNTING

| | No. | Avg. | | No. | Avg. |
|---|---|---|---|---|---|
| Rodriguez | 7 | 44.3 | Jennings | 3 | 35.0 |

#### PUNT RETURNS

| | No. | Yds. | Avg. | | No. | Yds. | Avg. |
|---|---|---|---|---|---|---|---|
| Edmonds | 2 | 66 | 33.0 | K. Johnson | 4 | 27 | 6.8 |

#### KICKOFF RETURNS

| | No. | Yds. | Avg. | | No. | Yds. | Avg. |
|---|---|---|---|---|---|---|---|
| Edmonds | 2 | 66 | 33.0 | Pinkett | 4 | 65 | 16.8 |
| Hollis | 1 | 23 | 23.0 | | | | |
| | 3 | 89 | 26.3 | | | | |

#### INTERCEPTION RETURNS

| | No. | Yds. | Avg. | |
|---|---|---|---|---|
| Jenkins | 1 | 28 | 28.0 | none |

#### PASSING

**SEATTLE**

| | Att. | Comp. | Comp. Pct. | Yds. | Int. | Yds./ Att. | Yds./ Comp. |
|---|---|---|---|---|---|---|---|
| Krieg | 38 | 16 | 42 | 237 | 1 | 6.2 | 14.8 |
| J. Williams | 1 | 0 | 0 | 0 | 0 | 0.0 | 0.0 |
| | 39 | 16 | 41 | 237 | 1 | 6.1 | 14.8 |

**HOUSTON**

| | Att. | Comp. | Comp. Pct. | Yds. | Int. | Yds./ Att. | Yds./ Comp. |
|---|---|---|---|---|---|---|---|
| Moon | 32 | 21 | 66 | 237 | 1 | 8.5 | 13.0 |

---

## January 9, 1988 at Cleveland (Attendance 78,586)

### SCORING

| | | | | | |
|---|---|---|---|---|---|
| INDIANAPOLIS | 7 | 7 | 0 | 7- | 21 |
| CLEVELAND | 7 | 7 | 7 | 17- | 38 |

**First Quarter**
Cle. — Byner, 10 yard pass from Kosar
    PAT—Bahr (kick)
Ind. — Beach, 2 yard pass form Trudeau
    PAT—Biasucci (kick)

**Second Quarter**
Cle. — Langhorne, 39 yard pass from Kosar
    PAT—Bahr (kick)
Ind. — Dickerson, 19 yard pass from Trudeau
    PAT—Biasucci (kick)

**Third Quarter**
Cle. — Byner 2 yard rush
    PAT—Bahr (kick)]

**Fourth Quarter**
Cle. — Bahr, 22 field goal
Cle. — Brennan, 2 yard pass.from Kosar
    PAT—Bahr (kick)
Ind. — Bentley, 1 yard rush
    PAT—Biasucci (kick)
Cle. — Minnifield, 48 interception return
    PAT—Bahr (kick)

### TEAM STATISTICS

| IND. | | CLE. |
|---|---|---|
| 23 | First Downs- Total | 25 |
| 4 | First Downs- Rushing | 10 |
| 16 | First Downs- Passing | 13 |
| 3 | First Downs- Penalty | 2 |
| 1 | Fumbles- Number | 2 |
| 0 | Fumbles- Lost Ball | 0 |
| 7 | Penalties- Number | 4 |
| 75 | Yards Penalized | 20 |
| 0 | Missed Field Goals | 0 |
| 62 | Offensive Plays | 65 |
| 301 | Net Yards | 404 |
| 5.1 | Average Gain | 6.2 |
| 2 | Giveaways | 1 |
| 1 | Takeaways | 2 |
| -1 | Difference | +1 |

### INDIVIDUAL STATISTICS

**INDIANAPOLIS**    **CLEVELAND**

#### RUSHING

| INDIANAPOLIS | No. | Yds. | Avg. | CLEVELAND | No. | Yds. | Avg. |
|---|---|---|---|---|---|---|---|
| Dickerson | 15 | 50 | 3.3 | Byner | 23 | 122 | 5.3 |
| Bentley | 4 | 6 | 1.5 | Mack | 6 | 38 | 6.3 |
| Trudeau | 2 | 4 | 2.0 | Manoa | 4 | 10 | 2.5 |
| | 21 | 60 | 2.9 | | 33 | 170 | 5.2 |

#### RECEIVING

| INDIANAPOLIS | No. | Yds. | Avg. | CLEVELAND | No. | Yds. | Avg. |
|---|---|---|---|---|---|---|---|
| Dickerson | 7 | 65 | 9.3 | Newsome | 4 | 65 | 16.3 |
| Brooks | 5 | 78 | 15.6 | Byner | 4 | 36 | 9.0 |
| Bentley | 4 | 47 | 11.8 | Brennan | 3 | 25 | 8.3 |
| Bouza | 2 | 24 | 12.0 | Mack | 3 | 17 | 5.7 |
| Beach | 2 | 6 | 3.0 | Fontenot | 2 | 20 | 10.0 |
| Murray | 1 | 25 | 25.0 | Langhorne | 1 | 39 | 39.0 |
| Bellini | 1 | 21 | 21.0 | Slaughter | 1 | 14 | 14.0 |
| | 22 | 266 | 12.1 | McNeil | 1 | 8 | 8.0 |
| | | | | Weathers | 1 | 5 | 5.0 |
| | | | | | 20 | 229 | 11.5 |

#### PUNTING

| | No. | Avg. | | No. | Yds. | Avg. |
|---|---|---|---|---|---|---|
| Stark | 4 | 43.8 | L. Johnson | 1 | 37 | 37.0 |

#### PUNT RETURNS

| | | | | | No. | Yds. | Avg. |
|---|---|---|---|---|---|---|---|
| none | | | | McNeil | 3 | 32 | 10.0 |

#### KICKOFF RETURNS

| | No. | Yds. | Avg. | | No. | Yds. | Avg. |
|---|---|---|---|---|---|---|---|
| Bentley | 6 | 114 | 19.0 | Fontentot | 1 | 3 | 3.0 |
| Ahrens | 1 | 10 | 10.0 | McNeil | 1 | 18 | 18.0 |
| | | | | | 2 | 21 | 11.5 |

#### INTERCEPTION RETURNS

| | No. | Yds. | Avg. | | No. | Yds. | Avg. |
|---|---|---|---|---|---|---|---|
| Robinson | 1 | 0 | 0.0 | Minnifield | 1 | 48 | 48.0 |

#### PASSING

**INDIANAPOLIS**

| | Att. | Comp. | Comp. Pct. | Yds. | Int. | Yds./ Att. | Yds./ Comp. |
|---|---|---|---|---|---|---|---|
| Trudeau | 33 | 21 | 64 | 251 | 1 | 7.6 | 12.0 |
| Salisbury | 6 | 1 | 17 | 15 | 1 | 2.5 | 15.0 |
| | 39 | 22 | 56 | 266 | 2 | 6.8 | 12.1 |

**CLEVELAND**

| | Att. | Comp. | Comp. Pct. | Yds. | Int. | Yds./ Att. | Yds./ Comp. |
|---|---|---|---|---|---|---|---|
| Kosar | 31 | 20 | 65 | 229 | 1 | 7.4 | 11.5 |

---

## January 10, 1988 at Denver (Attendance 75,968)

### SCORING

| | | | | | |
|---|---|---|---|---|---|
| HOUSTON | 0 | 3 | 0 | 7- | 10 |
| DENVER | 14 | 10 | 3 | 7- | 34 |

**First Quarter**
Den. — Lang, 1 yard rush
    PAT—Karlis (kick)
Den. — Kay, 27 yard pass from Elway
    PAT—Karlis (kick)

**Second Quarter**
Den. — Karlis, 43 yard field goal
Hou. — Zendejas, 46 yard field goal
Den. — Kay, 1 yard pass from Elway
    PAT—Karlis (kick)

**Third Quarter**
Den. — Karlis, 23 yard field goal

**Fourth Quarter**
Hou. — Givins, 19 yard pass from Moon
    PAT—Zendejas (kick)
Den. — Elway, 3 yard rush
    PAT—Karlis (kick)

### TEAM STATISTICS

| HOU. | | DEN. |
|---|---|---|
| 20 | First Downs- Total | 19 |
| 5 | First Downs- Rushing | 9 |
| 14 | First Downs- Passing | 9 |
| 1 | First Downs- Penalty | 1 |
| 2 | Fumbles- Number | 0 |
| 1 | Fumbles- Lost Ball | 0 |
| 10 | Penalties- Number | 4 |
| 73 | Yards Penalized | 35 |
| 0 | Missed Field Goals | 0 |
| 69 | Offensive Plays | 55 |
| 337 | Net Yards | 312 |
| 4.9 | Average Gain | 5.7 |
| 3 | Giveaways | 1 |
| 1 | Takeaways | 3 |
| -2 | Difference | +2 |

### INDIVIDUAL STATISTICS

**HOUSTON**    **DENVER**

#### RUSHING

| HOUSTON | No. | Yds. | Avg. | DENVER | No. | Yds. | Avg. |
|---|---|---|---|---|---|---|---|
| Rozier | 9 | 25 | 2.8 | Winder | 13 | 46 | 3.5 |
| Pinkett | 6 | 20 | 3.3 | Sewell | 5 | 9 | 1.8 |
| Moon | 5 | 15 | 3.0 | Elway | 4 | 8 | 2.0 |
| Highsmith | 5 | 13 | 2.6 | Bell | 2 | 7 | 3.5 |
| Givins | 1 | 0 | 0.0 | Kubiak | 2 | -3 | -1.5 |
| | 26 | 73 | 2.8 | Lang | 3 | -6 | -2.0 |
| | | | | | 29 | 61 | 2.1 |

#### RECEIVING

| HOUSTON | No. | Yds. | Avg. | DENVER | No. | Yds. | Avg. |
|---|---|---|---|---|---|---|---|
| Givins | 6 | 84 | 17.0 | Johnson | 4 | 105 | 26.3 |
| D. Hill | 5 | 93 | 18.6 | Kay | 3 | 57 | 19.0 |
| Duncan | 4 | 32 | 8.0 | Sewell | 3 | 41 | 13.7 |
| Highsmith | 4 | 20 | 5.0 | Lang | 1 | 25 | 25.0 |
| Drewrey | 2 | 17 | 8.5 | Boddie | 1 | 15 | 15.0 |
| Williams | 1 | 7 | 7.0 | Mobley | 1 | 9 | 9.0 |
| Rozier | 1 | 6 | 6.0 | Nattiel | 1 | 7 | 7.0 |
| Pinkett | 1 | 5 | 5.0 | | 14 | 255 | 18.2 |
| | 24 | 264 | | | | | |

#### PUNTING

| | No. | Avg. | | No. | Avg. |
|---|---|---|---|---|---|
| Gossett | 3 | 44.7 | Horan | 2 | 46.0 |

#### PUNT RETURNS

| | | | | No. | Yds. | Avg. |
|---|---|---|---|---|---|---|
| none | | | Clark | 2 | 15 | 7.5 |

#### KICKOFF RETURNS

| | No. | Yds. | Avg. | | No. | Yds. | Avg. |
|---|---|---|---|---|---|---|---|
| Pinkett | 3 | 62 | 20.7 | Bell | 1 | 28 | 28.0 |
| | | | | Clark | 1 | 0 | 0.0 |
| | | | | | 2 | 28 | 14.0 |

#### INTERCEPTION RETURNS

| | No. | Yds. | Avg. | | No. | Yds. | Avg. |
|---|---|---|---|---|---|---|---|
| Allen | 1 | 2 | 2.0 | Mecklenburg | 1 | 18 | 18.0 |
| | | | | Haynes | 1 | 57 | 57.0 |
| | | | | | 2 | 75 | 37.5 |

#### PASSING

**HOUSTON**

| | Att. | Comp. | Comp. Pct. | Yds. | Int. | Yds./ Att. | Yds./ Comp. |
|---|---|---|---|---|---|---|---|
| Moon | 43 | 24 | 56 | 264 | 2 | 6.1 | 11.0 |

**DENVER**

| | Att. | Comp. | Comp. Pct. | Yds. | Int. | Yds./ Att. | Yds./ Comp. |
|---|---|---|---|---|---|---|---|
| Elway | 25 | 14 | 56 | 259 | 1 | 10.4 | 18.5 |

## SCORING

| | | | | | |
|---|---|---|---|---|---|
| MINNESOTA | 0 | 7 | 0 | 3- | 10 |
| WASHINGTON | 7 | 0 | 3 | 7- | 17 |

**First Quarter**
Wash.  Bryant, 42 yard pass from Williams
PAT — Haji-Sheikh (kick)

**Second Quarter**
Minn.  Lewis, 23 yard pass from Wilson
PAT—C. Nelson (kick)

**Third quarter**
Wash.  Haji-Sheikh, 28 yard field goal

**Fourth quarter**
Minn.  C. Nelson, 18 yard field goal
Wash.  Clark, 7 yard pass from Williams
PAT — Haji-Sheikh (kick)

### TEAM STATISTICS

| Minn. | | Wash. |
|---|---|---|
| 16 | First Downs-Total | 11 |
| 5 | First Downs-Rushing | 7 |
| 10 | First Downs-Passing | 4 |
| 1 | First Downs-Penalty | 0 |
| 0 | Fumbles-Number | 0 |
| 0 | Fumbles-Ball Lost | 0 |
| 2 | Penalties-Number | 3 |
| 10 | Yards Penalized | 18 |
| 0 | Missed Field Goals | 0 |
| 68 | Offensive Plays | 60 |
| 259 | Net Yards | 280 |
| 3.8 | Average Gain | 4.7 |
| 1 | Giveaways | 0 |
| 0 | Takeaways | 1 |
| -1 | Difference | +1 |

## NFC CHAMPIONSHIP GAME
### January 17, 1988 at Washington, D.C.
### (Attendance 55,212)

The Washington Redskins used a clutch defense to ruin the Minnesota Vikings' Cinderella story 17-10. The Vikes got to the title game by upsetting both New Orleans and San Francisco, the NFC teams with the best regular-season records. A Viking victory would have made them only the third wild-card team in history to reach the Super Bowl.

The Redskins drove 98 yards for a touchdown, the score coming on Doug Williams' 42-yard pass to Kelvin Bryant on a 3rd-and-10 play. The Vikings were held in check through most of the first half but drove 71 yards to score with two minutes left. Wade Wilson passed 23 yards to wide receiver Leo Lewis for the TD.

Wilson was sacked eight times on the day, one short of the title game record. But, in the fourth quarter, he led the Vikes down to the goalline. The Redskin defense stopped Minnesota on two straight shots from the one and forced the Vikings to settle for a tie score on Chuck Nelson's 18-yard field goal with 10:06 to play.

Williams completed only 9-of-26 passes for 119 yards on the day, but, following the kickoff, he took his team 70 yards for the go-ahead touchdown. His seven-yard toss to Gary Clark on an improvised play culminated the drive. Again, Minnesota drove down the field, reaching the Redskin six-yard line. And, again, Washington stopped the Vikes short of a touchdown. On fourth down, Darrin Nelson dropped Wilson's pass at the goalline.

## INDIVIDUAL STATISTICS

### MINNESOTA / WASHINGTON

#### RUSHING

| | No. | Yds. | Avg. | | No. | Yds. | Avg. |
|---|---|---|---|---|---|---|---|
| Wilson | 4 | 28 | 7.0 | Smith | 13 | 72 | 5.5 |
| Anderson | 4 | 25 | 6.3 | Rogers | 12 | 49 | 4.1 |
| D. Nelson | 8 | 15 | 1.9 | Sanders | 1 | 28 | 28.0 |
| Rice | 1 | 8 | 8.0 | Williams | 4 | 7 | 1.8 |
| Fenney | 2 | 2 | 1.0 | Clark | 1 | 5 | 5.0 |
| Dozier | 2 | -2 | -1.0 | Bryant | 3 | 3 | 1.0 |
| | 21 | 76 | 3.6 | | 34 | 161 | 4.7 |

#### RECEIVING

| | No. | Yds. | Avg. | | No. | Yds. | Avg. |
|---|---|---|---|---|---|---|---|
| Carter | 7 | 85 | 12.1 | Bryant | 4 | 47 | 11.8 |
| Lewis | 4 | 54 | 13.5 | Clark | 3 | 57 | 19.0 |
| Jordan | 3 | 56 | 18.7 | Allen | 1 | 9 | 9.0 |
| D. Nelson | 3 | 25 | 8.3 | Warren | 1 | 6 | 6.0 |
| Rice | 1 | 15 | 15.0 | | 9 | 119 | 13.2 |
| Anderson | 1 | 8 | 8.0 | | | | |
| | 19 | 243 | 12.8 | | | | |

#### PUNTING

| | | | | | | | |
|---|---|---|---|---|---|---|---|
| Scribner | 10 | 33.2 | | Cox | 8 | | 39.1 |

#### PUNT RETURNS

| | No. | Yds. | Avg. | | No. | Yds. | Avg. |
|---|---|---|---|---|---|---|---|
| Carter | 4 | 57 | 14.3 | Dean | 1 | 0 | 0.0 |
| | | | | Green | 1 | 1 | 1.0 |
| | | | | Yarber | 1 | 9 | 9.0 |
| | | | | Davis | 1 | 0 | 0.0 |
| | | | | | 4 | 10 | 2.5 |

#### KICKOFF RETURNS

| | No. | Yds. | Avg. | | No. | Yds. | Avg. |
|---|---|---|---|---|---|---|---|
| D. Nelson | 2 | 43 | 21.5 | Sanders | 2 | 30 | 15.0 |
| Rice | 1 | 15 | 15.0 | Smith | 1 | 24 | 24.0 |
| | 3 | 58 | 19.3 | | 3 | 54 | 18.0 |

#### INTERCEPTION RETURNS

| | | | | | No. | Yds. | Avg. |
|---|---|---|---|---|---|---|---|
| none | | | | Kaufman | 1 | 10 | 10.0 |

#### PASSING

| MINNESOTA | Att. | Comp. | Comp. Pct. | Yds. | Int. | Yds./Att. | Yds./Comp. |
|---|---|---|---|---|---|---|---|
| W. Wilson | 39 | 19 | 49 | 243 | 1 | 6.2 | 12.8 |

| WASHINGTON | Att. | Comp. | Comp. Pct. | Yds. | Int. | Yds./Att. | Yds./Comp. |
|---|---|---|---|---|---|---|---|
| Williams | 26 | 9 | 35 | 119 | 0 | 4.6 | 13.2 |

---

## SCORING

| | | | | | |
|---|---|---|---|---|---|
| CLEVELAND | 0 | 3 | 21 | 9- | 33 |
| DENVER | 14 | 7 | 10 | 7- | 38 |

**First Quarter**
DEN.  Nattiel, 8 yard pass from Elway
PAT—Karlis (kick)
DEN.  Sewell, 1 yard rush
PAT—Karlis (kick)

**Second Quarter**
CLE.  Bahr, 24 yard field goal
DEN.  Lang, 1 yard rush
PAT—Karlis (kick)

**Third Quarter**
CLE.  Langhorne, 18 yard pass from Kosar
PAT—Bahr (kick)
DEN.  Jackson, 80 yard pass from Elway
PAT—Karlis (kick)
CLE.  Byner, 32 yard pass from Kosar
PAT—Bahr(kick)
CLE.  Byner, 4 yard rush
PAT—Bahr (kick)

**Fourth Quarter**
CLE.  Slaughter, 4 pass from Kosar
PAT—Bahr (kick)
DEN.  Winder, 20 yard pass from Elway
PAT—Karlis (kick)
CLE.  Safety, Horan ran out of endzone

### TEAM STATISTICS

| CLE. | | DEN. |
|---|---|---|
| 25 | First Downs-Total | 24 |
| 8 | First Downs-Rushing | 10 |
| 15 | First Downs-Passing | 11 |
| 2 | First Downs-Penalty | 3 |
| 3 | Fumbles-Number | 2 |
| 3 | Fumbles-Lost Ball | 0 |
| 7 | Penalties-Number | 7 |
| 59 | Yards Penalized | 44 |
| 1 | Missed Field Goals | 1 |
| 70 | Offensive Plays | 61 |
| 444 | Net Yards | 232 |
| 6.6 | Average Gain | 3.8 |
| 4 | Giveaways | 1 |
| 1 | Takeaways | 4 |
| +3 | Difference | -3 |

## AFC CHAMPIONSHIP GAME
### January 17, 1988 at Denver
### (Attendance 75,993)

In what may have been the most exciting game played in the NFL all season, the Denver Broncos edged the Cleveland Browns 38-33 to go to the Super Bowl for the second straight year. The same two teams had waged a classic battle in the 1986 title game, but this one was even more dramatic.

The first half was Denver's. After a diving interception by DE Freddie Gilbert, Bronco QB John Elway hit WR Ricky Nattiel with an eight-yard TD pass. Cleveland CB Frank Minnifield was caught holding in the endzone on a third-down incompletion, and RB Steve Sewell went over from the one on a reverse, giving the Broncos the impetus for a 21-3 lead at the half.

Bernie Kosar brought the Browns back with ample help from RB Earnest Byner. Kosar's TD passes to Reggie Langhorne and Byner, plus Byner's TD run, cut the gap to 31-24 entering the final period.

Kosar connected with Byner on a 53-yard pass to spark an 86-yard drive. Webster Slaughter's four-yard TD catch tied the score. But Elway's 20-yard pass to Sammy Winder put Denver ahead again. Back came Cleveland on a length-of-the-field drive. But, on second down at the Denver eight, Byner burst off tackle. At the two he was stripped of the ball by Denver's Jeremiah Castille, and the Broncos recovered. As time ran out, Denver elected to take a safety rather than punt out of its own endzone, making the final score 38-33.

## INDIVIDUAL STATISTICS

### CLEVELAND / DENVER

#### RUSHING

| | No. | Yds. | Avg. | | No. | Yds. | Avg. |
|---|---|---|---|---|---|---|---|
| Byner | 15 | 67 | 4.5 | Winder | 20 | 72 | 3.6 |
| Mack | 12 | 61 | 5.1 | Elway | 11 | 36 | 3.3 |
| | 27 | 128 | 4.7 | Lang | 5 | 51 | 5.2 |
| | | | | Sewell | 1 | 1 | 1.0 |
| | | | | Boddie | 1 | 8 | 8.0 |
| | | | | Horan | 1 | -12 | -12.0 |
| | | | | | 39 | 156 | 4.0 |

#### RECEIVING

| | No. | Yds. | Avg. | | No. | Yds. | Avg. |
|---|---|---|---|---|---|---|---|
| Byner | 7 | 120 | 17.7 | Nattiel | 5 | 95 | 19.0 |
| Slaughter | 4 | 53 | 13.3 | Jackson | 4 | 134 | 33.5 |
| Brennan | 4 | 48 | 12.0 | Winder | 3 | 34 | 11.3 |
| Mack | 4 | 28 | 7.0 | Sewell | 1 | 10 | 10.0 |
| Newsome | 3 | 35 | 11.6 | Mobley | 1 | 8 | 8.0 |
| Langhorne | 2 | 48 | 24.0 | | 14 | 256 | 18.3 |
| Tennell | 1 | 5 | 5.0 | | | | |
| Weathers | 1 | 19 | 19.0 | | | | |
| | 26 | 336 | 12.9 | | | | |

#### PUNTING

| | No. | | Avg. | | No. | | Avg. |
|---|---|---|---|---|---|---|---|
| L. Johnson | 2 | | 48.0 | Horan | 2 | | 41.5 |
| | | | | Elway | 1 | | 18.0 |
| | | | | | 3 | | 33.7 |

#### PUNT RETURNS

| | No. | Yds. | Avg. | | No. | Yds. | Avg. |
|---|---|---|---|---|---|---|---|
| McNeil | 2 | 24 | 12.0 | Clark | 2 | 13 | 6.5 |

#### KICKOFF RETURNS

| | No. | Yds. | Avg. | | No. | Yds. | Avg. |
|---|---|---|---|---|---|---|---|
| McNeil | 5 | 94 | 18.8 | Bell | 3 | 43 | 14.3 |

#### INTERCEPTION RETURNS

| | No. | Yds. | Avg. | | No. | Yds. | Avg. |
|---|---|---|---|---|---|---|---|
| Wright | 1 | 13 | 13.0 | Gilbert | 1 | 0 | 0.0 |

#### PASSING

| CLEVELAND | Att | Comp | Comp Pct | Yds | Int | Yds/Att | Yds/Comp |
|---|---|---|---|---|---|---|---|
| Kosar | 41 | 26 | 63.4 | 336 | 1 | 8.2 | 12.9 |

| DENVER | Att | Comp | Comp Pct | Yds | Int | Yds/Att | Yds/Comp |
|---|---|---|---|---|---|---|---|
| Elway | 26 | 14 | 53.8 | 281 | 1 | 10.8 | 20.1 |

# Size Disadvantage Stymies Broncos Again

For the fourth consecutive year, the Super Bowl resulted in a rout of the AFC by the NFC. For the second year in a row, the victim was Denver. The consensus opinion was that Washington, a good big team, had proven superior to a fair small team with one great player — Denver's John Elway.

In spite of the 42-10 score, Super Bowl XXII had its share of drama, including the biggest single-quarter offensive explosion in Super Bowl history. The most publicized element in the two weeks prior to the game was that of Washington's Doug Williams being the first black to start a Super Bowl and inevitable comparisons of his abilities and those of Elway.

Largely because of the perceived advantage the Broncos had with Elway, Denver entered the game as a 3 1/2-point favorite. Williams, who gained the Redskins' starting job only at the end of the regular season, handled the pregame media blitz with grace, even when fielding such inane questions as, "How long have you been a black quarterback?"

The Broncos broke on top when Elway hit wide receiver Ricky Nattiel with a 56-yard touchdown bomb after only 1:57 of the first quarter. Elway looked off Redskin cornerback Barry Wilburn until the last second before turning to Nattiel. On Denver's next possession, a trick pass — Steve Sewell to Elway — helped the Broncos drive close to the Washington goalline before settling for Rich Karlis' 24-yard field goal.

Meanwhile, Washington seemed unable to muster a consistent offense. Near the end of the quarter, Williams slipped on the turf and twisted his knee, forcing him to leave the field for a play.

The Redskins entered the second quarter trailing 10-0 and with a limping quarterback. They proceeded to put together the most remarkable 15 minutes in Super Bowl history. First, Williams hit Ricky Sanders for an 80-yard TD, tying the S.B. record for the longest reception. The play, which many regarded as the turning point, was designed to go short, but, when San-

ders was bumped at the line of scrimmage, he adjusted by going long. Next, Williams threw to Gary Clark for 27 yards to put the Skins in front 14-10. Moments later, rookie running back Timmy Smith broke away for 58 yards on a counter play to widen the lead. The next possession saw the Williams-to-Sanders combination click for a 50-yard TD. Tight end Clint Didier scored the Redskins' fifth touchdown with 1:04 left in the period on an eight-yard toss from Williams.

The Redskins' 35 points in one quarter was a record for a postseason game. They totaled 356 yards on only 18 plays. Individual marks for the quarter included Smith's 122 rushing yards (on five carries), Sanders' 168 receiving yards (on five catches) and Williams' 228 passing yards (on 9-of-11 completions). His four TD passes set a record for one quarter and tied the S.B. record for a game.

The second half was anticlimactic. The Redskins kept mainly to the ground. Smith, who was not told he would start until shortly before game time, scored the only touchdown of the second half on a four-yard run at 1:51 of the fourth quarter. For the game, Smith broke Marcus Allen's S.B. record with 204 yards on 22 carries. Other S.B. records were broken by Williams (340 passing yards), Sanders (193 receiving yards) and kicker Ali Haji-Sheikh (six extra points). The Redskins' 602 net yards was also a S.B. record.

Meanwhile, Denver was held completely in check. With Elway forced to pass on most plays in a futile attempt to catch up, the Redskins sacked him five times. He completed only 14-of-38 attempts for 257 yards and had three intercepted — two by Wilburn. Williams, who completed 18-of-29, was chosen the game's Most Valuable Player, certainly the most effective answer to those who questioned the ability of a black quarterback to win a Super Bowl.

## LINEUPS

| DENVER | | WASHINGTON |
|--------|--|------------|
| | OFFENSE | |
| Jackson | WR | Clark |
| Studdard | LT | Jacoby |
| Bishop | LG | McKenzie |
| Freeman | C | Bostic |
| Humphries | RG | Thielemann |
| Lanier | RT | May |
| Kay | TE | Warren |
| Nattiel | WR | Sanders |
| Elway | QB | Williams |
| Winder | RB-TE | Didier |
| Lang | RB | Smith |
| | DEFENSE | |
| Townsend | LE | Mann |
| Kragen | NT-DLT | Butz |
| | DRT | Grant |
| Jones | DRE | Manley |
| Fletcher | LOLB | Kaufman |
| Mecklenburg | LILB | |
| | MLB | Olkewicz |
| Hunley | RILB | |
| Ryan | ROLB | Coleman |
| Haynes | LCB | Green |
| Wilson | RCB | Wilburn |
| Lilly | FS | Bowles |
| Smith | SS | Walton |
| | SUBSTITUTES | |
| DENVER | | |
| | OFFENSE | |
| Bell | Johnson | Mobley |
| Boddie | Kartz | Sewell |
| Bowyer | Kubiak | Watson |
| Braxton | Micho | |
| | DEFENSE | |
| Brooks | Fletcher | Plummer |
| Castille | Gilbert | Robbins |
| Clark | Klosterman | Woodard |
| Dennison | Lucas | |
| | KICKERS | |
| Horan | Karlis | |
| WASHINGTON | | |
| | OFFENSE | |
| Branch | Jones | Rogers |
| Bryant | Kehr | Schroeder |
| Griffin | Monk | Vaughn |
| Grimm | Orr | Yarber |
| | DEFENSE | |
| Caldwell | Gouveia | Koch |
| Davis | Hamel | Milot |
| Dean | Hamilton | Woodberry |
| | KICKERS | |
| Cox | Haji-Sheikh | |

## SCORING

| | | | | | |
|---|---|---|---|---|---|
| WASHINGTON | 0 | 35 | 0 | 7- | 42 |
| DENVER | 10 | 0 | 0 | 0- | 10 |

**First Quarter**
Denver — Nattiel, 56 yard pass from Elway
PAT — Karlis (kick)
Denver — Karlis, 24 yard field goal

**Second Quarter**
Wash. — Sanders, 80 yard pass from Williams
PAT — Haji-Sheikh (kick)
Wash. — Clark, 27 yard pass from Williams
PAT — Haji-Sheikh (kick)
Wash. — Smith, 58 yard run
PAT — Haji-Sheikh (kick)
Wash. — Sanders, 50 yard pass from Williams
PAT — Haji-Sheikh (kick)
Wash. — Didier, 8 yard pass from Williams
PAT — Haji-Sheikh (kick)

**Fourth Quarter**
Wash. — Smith, 4 yard run
PAT — Haji-Sheikh (kick)

## TEAM STATISTICS

| WASH. | | DEN |
|-------|--|-----|
| 25 | First Downs-Total | 18 |
| 13 | First Downs-Rushing | 6 |
| 11 | First Downs-Passing | 10 |
| 1 | First Downs-Penalty | 2 |
| 1 | Fumbles-Number | 0 |
| 0 | Fumbles-Lost Ball | 0 |
| 6 | Penalties Number | 5 |
| 65 | Yards Penalized | 26 |
| 0 | Missed Field Goals | 0 |
| 72 | Offensive Plays | 61 |
| 602 | Net Yards | 327 |
| 8.4 | Average Gain | 5.4 |
| 1 | Giveaways | 3 |
| 3 | Takeaways | 1 |
| +2 | Difference | -2 |

## INDIVIDUAL STATISTICS

### RUSHING

| WASHINGTON | No. | Yds. | Avg. | DENVER | No. | Yds. | Avg. |
|------------|-----|------|------|--------|-----|------|------|
| Smith | 22 | 204 | 9.3 | Lang | 5 | 38 | 7.6 |
| Bryant | 8 | 38 | 4.8 | Elway | 3 | 32 | 10.7 |
| Clark | 1 | 25 | 25.0 | Winder | 8 | 30 | 3.8 |
| Rogers | 5 | 17 | 3.4 | Sewell | 1 | -3 | -3.0 |
| Griffin | 1 | 2 | 2.0 | | 17 | 97 | 5.7 |
| Sanders | 1 | -4 | -4.0 | | | | |
| Williams | 2 | -2 | -2.0 | | | | |
| | 40 | 280 | 7.0 | | | | |

### RECEIVING

| WASHINGTON | No. | Yds. | Avg. | DENVER | No. | Yds. | Avg. |
|------------|-----|------|------|--------|-----|------|------|
| Sanders | 9 | 193 | 21.4 | Jackson | 4 | 76 | 19.0 |
| Clark | 3 | 55 | 18.3 | Sewell | 4 | 41 | 10.3 |
| Warren | 2 | 15 | 7.5 | Nattiel | 2 | 69 | 24.5 |
| Monk | 1 | 40 | 40.0 | Kay | 2 | 38 | 19.0 |
| Bryant | 1 | 20 | 20.0 | Winder | 1 | 26 | 26.0 |
| Smith | 1 | 9 | 9.0 | Elway | 1 | 23 | 23.0 |
| Didier | 1 | 8 | 8.0 | Lang | 1 | 7 | 7.0 |
| | 18 | 340 | 18.9 | | 15 | 280 | 18.7 |

### PUNTING

| WASHINGTON | No. | | Avg. | DENVER | No. | | Avg. |
|------------|-----|--|------|--------|-----|--|------|
| Cox | 4 | | 37.5 | Horan | 7 | | 36.1 |

### PUNT RETURNS

| WASHINGTON | No. | Yds. | Avg. | DENVER | No. | Yds. | Avg. |
|------------|-----|------|------|--------|-----|------|------|
| Green | 1 | 0 | 0.0 | Clark | 2 | 18 | 9.0 |

### KICKOFF RETURNS

| WASHINGTON | No. | Yds. | Avg. | DENVER | No. | Yds. | Avg. |
|------------|-----|------|------|--------|-----|------|------|
| Sanders | 3 | 46 | 15.3 | Bell | 5 | 88 | 17.6 |

### INTERCEPTION RETURNS

| WASHINGTON | No. | Yds. | Avg. | DENVER | No. | Yds. | Avg. |
|------------|-----|------|------|--------|-----|------|------|
| Wilburn | 2 | 11 | 5.5 | Castille | 1 | 0 | 0.0 |
| Davis | 1 | 0 | 0.0 | | | | |
| | 3 | 33 | 3.7 | | | | |

### PASSING

| WASHINGTON | Att. | Comp. | Comp. Pct. | Yds. | Int. | Yds./ Att. | Yds./ Comp. | Yards Lost Tackled |
|------------|------|-------|------------|------|------|------------|-------------|---------------------|
| Williams | 29 | 18 | 62 | 340 | 1 | 11.7 | 18.9 | 1-10 |
| Schroeder | 1 | 0 | 0 | 0 | 0 | 0 | 0 | 1-8 |
| | 30 | 18 | 60 | 340 | 1 | 11.3 | 18.9 | 2-18 |
| **DENVER** | | | | | | | | |
| Elway | 38 | 14 | 37 | 257 | 3 | 6.8 | 18.4 | 5-50 |
| Sewell | 1 | 1 | 100 | 23 | 0 | 23.0 | 23.0 | 0-0 |
| | 39 | 15 | 38 | 280 | 3 | 7.2 | 18.7 | 5-50 |

Charisma — that indefiniable quality that separates the stars from the merely starring — was attributed to the N.F.C. over the A.F.C. in 1988, both in a widely-quoted poll of "experts" conducted by a Houston newspaper and on television by ESPN. The Houston respondents named the Bears the most charismatic team, with the Redskins, 49ers and Cowboys also ranked high. Cumulatively, the N.F.C. teams came in ahead of the A.F.C.'s, although Atlanta finished dead last. ESPN agreed in general that the N.F.C. had the better of it in "star quality," citing the conference's recent Super Bowl successes and pointing out that the most consistently successful teams of the 1980s were in the N.F.C. Another factor, however, was that the N.F.C. had a larger share of the major television markets.

Charsima or not, the A.F.C. finished on top in interconference games for the second straight year, 30-22. In fact, the charismatic N.F.C. had come out in victories against the mundane A.F.C. only once since 1971.

## EASTERN DIVISION

**Philadelphia Eagles** — Word before the season was that coach Buddy Ryan had to get the Eagles into the playoffs — or else. He had one big weapon. QB Randall Cunningham was a unique force, leading the team in rushing for the second straight year and passing for 3,808 yards. He was the key to an offense that usually had just enough to win. The running backs were not much of a factors except as receivers, and WR Mike Quick missed half of the season with a broken ankle. Rookie TE Keith Jackson came straight from a ground-bound attack at Oklahoma to catch 81 passes for Philadelphia. Except for DE Reggie White, the Eagles' defense was ordinary only on paper, but it played tough all season. The Eagles knocked off the Giants twice — the second time on a touchdown scored after New York had blocked an overtime field-goal try. When the Giants dropped their final game to the Jets, the Eagles had the division title, and Ryan was in the playoffs.

**New York Giants** — The Giants had a soft schedule and were primed for a playoff berth. Phil Simms had another strong year, aided by healthy WR Lionel Manuel. However, TE Mark Bavaro was only so-so. RB Joe Morris gained over 1,000 yards rushing again, but most of them came in the last four games, when the offensive line finally gelled, with the play of rookies OG Eric Moore and OT John Elliott. The defense was okay, but never as dominant as it had been in the last few seasons. OLB Lawrence Taylor missed the first four games with a drug suspension, ILB Harry Carson missed the last four with an injury, and OLB Carl Banks never for rolling after holding out at the beginning of the season.

**Washington Redskins** — One quarterback controversey was defused when Jay Schroeder was traded to the Raiders after the first game, but another debate soon arose. QB Doug Williams underwent an emergency appendectomy, and unheralded Mark Rypien played so well in his stead that whichever played from then on, he was the "wrong quarterback" for most Redskins fans. The Redskins stayed close enough through two-thirds of the season, then faded. The quarterbacks both played well, but the offensive line was hurt by constant shuffling in an attempt to find a healthy, effective combination. RB Timmy Smith, the Super Bowl hero, flopped as an overweight regular, and Kelvin Bryant, who replaced Smith as the one-back, went out with a knee injury in Game 10. The secondary was also hit with injuries and the linebackers and rush line by age.

**Phoenix Cardinals** — Owner Bill Bidwell had a bonanza at Sun Devil Stadium, with team-record attendances and league-record ticket prices. The team looked like a winner, too, with a 7-4 record through Week 12. QB Neil Lomax continued the fine comeback he'd begun in 1987, RB's Earl Ferrell and Stump Mitchell provided a steady running attack, and J.T. Smith and Roy Green were among the top receivers. The defense was adequate. The the plug was pulled, and Phoenix collapsed like a — well — house of Cards, losing their last five games. Part of the problem

was a flare-up of Lomax's arthritic hip that sidelined him for a couple of games, part of it was injuries and mistakes, but most of the nose dive was simply that the other teams had more talent.

**Dallas Cowboys** — Dallas fans with long memories insisted the season was worse than 1960, when the Cowboys went through their first NFL season winless. Fans with short memories blasted coach Tom Landry, and one newsman even accused him of senility in print. More rational fans recognized an offensive line torn up by injuries, a defense longer on youth than talent, and a quarterback, in Steve Pelluer, who had fair statistics but a penchant for making the big mistake. Through the debacle that included a 10-game losing streak, Herschel Walker was terrific. He led the NFC with 1,514 rushing yards (and had 505 more on 53 pass receptions. The team was up for sale, but no one was racing to pick up the $150 milliion asked.

## CENTRAL DIVISION

**Chicago Bears** — The Bears rode their great defense to a fifth straight NFC Central championship, despite losing OLB's Wilbur Marshall to Washington through free agency and Otis Wilson to a season-ending knee injury in preseason. DE Richard Dent was having one of his best seasons (10.5 sacks) until he, too, went out with a broken ankle. Still, Mike Singletary, Dave Duerson, Steve McMichael, Dan Hampton and a host of rookies stuffed opponents for a league-low 215 points. QB Jim McMahon had his annual injury at midseason, but Mike Tomczak played well in relief. RB Neal Anderson emerged as a star in his third season. The biggest Bears' story was coach Mike Ditka's midseason heart attack. He returned to the sideline after missing only one game, promising a calmer, more patient demeanor.

**Minnesota Vikings** — The Vikings were clearly the coming power of the NFC Central. Their defense, led by DT Keith Millard, DE Chris Doleman, LB Scott Studwell, CB Carl Lee and SS Joey Browner was being compared to the Bears' — and some said it was better. QB Wade Wilson led the NFC in passing, although veteran Tommy Kramer won a couple of early-season games. Wilson caused some ripples when he complained about being benched in the second half of the final-game win over Chicago. Both quarterbacks were aided immeasurably by WR's Anthony Carter (1,225 yards) and Hassan Jones and TE Steve Jodan. The passing game had to carry the attack because none of the runners were able to gain consistently.

**Tampa Bay Buccaneers** — Vinny Testaverde was handed the quarterback job in his second season. He threw far too many interceptions (35) and his pass rating was a horrible 48.8. Nevertheless, he showed some progress, along with the other eight first- or second-year players starting on offense. Particularlty impressive were WR Bruce Hill and rookie OT Paul Gruber. When the improving defense held the last three opponents to a total of 25 points, the Bucs were able to win twice.

**Green Bay Packers** — When Forrest Gregg resigned to return to his alma mater, Southern Methodist, Lindy Infante was brought in as coach. Infante has earned an enviable reputation as an offensive coordinator, most recently with Cleveland. The young Pack had problems with the new system, and the offense lagged all season, wasting several strong efforts by a good defense. LB Tim Haris was exceptional. He, the other linebackers and a slow but cagey secondary, made up for a lack of a pass rush up front. But, with a flat offense, the Packers were set for the No. 1 draft choice in 1989 until they blew it with a victory over Phoenix in the final game.

**Detroit Lions** — The Lions were bad, slow and dull. QB Chuck Long seemed to regress and they was kayoed in the sixth game. With Eric

FINAL TEAM STATISTICS

OFFENSE

| | ATL | CHI | DAL | DET | G.B. | L.A. | MINN | N.O. | NYG | PHIL | PHX | S.F. | T.B. | WASH |
|---|---|---|---|---|---|---|---|---|---|---|---|---|---|---|
| FIRST DOWNS: | | | | | | | | | | | | | | |
| Total | 257 | 303 | 311 | 226 | 280 | 333 | 318 | 306 | 317 | 318 | **336** | 326 | 295 | 307 |
| by Rushing | 106 | 137 | 112 | 63 | 78 | 114 | 112 | 108 | 123 | 105 | 122 | **141** | 91 | 88 |
| by Passing | 136 | 134 | 175 | 141 | 175 | **203** | 187 | 179 | 168 | 179 | 195 | 167 | 173 | 202 |
| by Penalty | 15 | 32 | 24 | 22 | 27 | 16 | 19 | 19 | 26 | **34** | 19 | 18 | 31 | 17 |
| RUSHING: | | | | | | | | | | | | | | |
| Number | 478 | 555 | 469 | 391 | 385 | 507 | 501 | 512 | 493 | 464 | 480 | **527** | 452 | 437 |
| Yards | 2016 | 2319 | 1995 | 1243 | 1379 | 2003 | 1806 | 2046 | 1689 | 1945 | 2027 | **2523** | 1753 | 1543 |
| Average Yards | 4.2 | 4.2 | 4.3 | 3.2 | 3.6 | 4.0 | 3.6 | 4.0 | 3.4 | 4.2 | 4.2 | **4.8** | 3.9 | 3.5 |
| Touchdowns | 11 | **25** | 10 | 7 | 14 | 16 | 22 | 9 | 15 | 17 | 15 | 18 | 11 | 8 |
| PASSING: | | | | | | | | | | | | | | |
| Attempts | 481 | 461 | 555 | 477 | **582** | 522 | 520 | 498 | 525 | 581 | 562 | 502 | 512 | 592 |
| Completions | 250 | 248 | 307 | 213 | 319 | 312 | 294 | 286 | 290 | 309 | **322** | 293 | 253 | 327 |
| Completion Pct. | 52.0 | 53.8 | 55.3 | 44.7 | 54.8 | **59.8** | 56.5 | 57.4 | 55.2 | 53.2 | 57.3 | 58.4 | 49.4 | 55.2 |
| Passing Yards | 2914 | 3173 | 3727 | 2572 | 3609 | 4002 | 4100 | 3256 | 3716 | 3927 | 4191 | 3675 | 3608 | **4339** |
| Avg. Yds per Att. | 4.9 | 6.2 | 5.9 | 4.1 | 5.2 | **6.9** | 6.7 | 5.9 | 5.6 | 5.5 | 6.1 | 6.2 | 6.1 | 6.7 |
| Avg. Yds per Comp. | 11.7 | 12.8 | 12.1 | 12.1 | 11.3 | 12.8 | 14.0 | 11.4 | 12.8 | 12.7 | 13.0 | 12.5 | **14.3** | 13.3 |
| Times Tackled | 43 | **24** | 35 | 52 | 51 | 28 | 47 | **24** | 60 | 57 | 60 | 47 | 34 | **24** |
| Yds Lost Tackled | 348 | 175 | 239 | 410 | 324 | 197 | 311 | **171** | 450 | 442 | 411 | 298 | 300 | 203 |
| Net Yards | 2566 | 2998 | 3488 | 2162 | 3285 | 3805 | 3789 | 3085 | 3266 | 3485 | 3780 | 3377 | 3308 | **4136** |
| Touchdowns | 13 | 13 | 21 | 13 | 13 | 31 | 20 | 21 | 22 | 25 | 26 | 21 | 16 | **33** |
| Interceptions | 19 | 15 | 27 | 18 | 24 | 18 | 18 | 16 | **14** | 17 | 19 | **14** | 36 | 25 |
| Pct. Intercepted | 4.0 | 3.3 | 4.9 | 3.8 | 4.1 | 3.4 | 3.5 | 3.2 | **2.7** | 2.9 | 3.4 | 2.8 | 7.0 | 4.2 |
| PUNTS: | | | | | | | | | | | | | | |
| Number | 98 | 79 | 80 | 97 | 86 | 76 | 86 | 73 | 81 | **104** | 80 | 80 | 68 | 67 |
| Average | 40.0 | 41.5 | 40.9 | **42.4** | 38.2 | 39.5 | 39.4 | 39.9 | 39.9 | 39.7 | 40.3 | 38.7 | 36.4 | 38.2 |
| PUNT RETURNS | | | | | | | | | | | | | | |
| Number | 42 | 38 | 45 | 42 | 35 | 49 | **59** | 35 | 47 | 33 | 52 | 54 | 36 | 52 |
| Yards | 343 | 294 | 360 | 346 | 208 | 322 | 553 | 413 | 359 | 233 | 463 | **612** | 328 | 377 |
| Average Yards | 8.2 | 7.7 | 8.0 | 8.2 | 5.9 | 6.6 | 9.4 | **11.8** | 7.6 | 7.1 | 8.9 | 11.3 | 9.1 | 7.3 |
| Touchdowns | 0 | 0 | 0 | 0 | 1 | 0 | 0 | 1 | 0 | 0 | 0 | **2** | 0 | 0 |
| KICKOFF RET.: | | | | | | | | | | | | | | |
| Number | 59 | 45 | 69 | 59 | 64 | 59 | 56 | 70 | 62 | 59 | 60 | 55 | 64 | **74** |
| Yards | 1057 | 896 | **1410** | 1154 | 1181 | 1191 | 1160 | 1408 | 1154 | 1028 | 1106 | 978 | 1345 | 1355 |
| Average Yards | 17.9 | 19.9 | 20.4 | 19.6 | 18.5 | 20.2 | 20.7 | 20.1 | 18.6 | 17.4 | 18.4 | 17.8 | **21.0** | 18.3 |
| Touchdowns | 0 | 0 | 0 | 0 | 0 | 0 | 0 | 0 | 0 | 0 | 0 | 0 | 0 | 0 |
| INTERCEPT RET.: | | | | | | | | | | | | | | |
| Number | 24 | 26 | 10 | 15 | 20 | 22 | **36** | 17 | 15 | 32 | 16 | 22 | 21 | 14 |
| Yards | 185 | 237 | 67 | 247 | 224 | 281 | **589** | 295 | 292 | 371 | 88 | 88 | 283 | 193 |
| Average Yards | 7.7 | 9.1 | 6.7 | 16.5 | | 11.2 | 16.4 | 17.4 | **19.5** | 11.6 | 5.5 | 4.0 | 13.5 | 13.8 |
| Touchdowns | 1 | 0 | 1 | 2 | 0 | 1 | **5** | 0 | 2 | 0 | 0 | 0 | 1 | 0 |
| PENALTIES: | | | | | | | | | | | | | | |
| Number | **67** | 88 | 141 | 94 | 94 | 78 | 118 | 101 | 88 | 115 | 99 | 115 | 102 | 96 |
| Yards | **542** | 644 | 1148 | 804 | 785 | 587 | 998 | 821 | 660 | 907 | 790 | 986 | 816 | 817 |
| FUMBLES: | | | | | | | | | | | | | | |
| Number | 29 | 37 | **22** | 31 | 44 | 28 | **22** | 29 | 32 | 29 | 34 | 27 | 27 | 34 |
| Number Lost | 18 | 19 | 13 | 15 | 26 | 16 | 12 | 16 | 13 | **9** | 16 | 12 | 16 | 21 |
| POINTS: | | | | | | | | | | | | | | |
| Total | 244 | 312 | 265 | 220 | 240 | **407** | 406 | 312 | 359 | 379 | 344 | 369 | 261 | 345 |
| PAT Attempts | 27 | 38 | 32 | 23 | 29 | 48 | **49** | 33 | 41 | 43 | 44 | 41 | 28 | 41 |
| PAT Made | 25 | 37 | 32 | 22 | 23 | 45 | **48** | 32 | 39 | 42 | 42 | 40 | 28 | 40 |
| FG Attempts | 30 | 19 | 25 | 21 | 25 | 32 | 25 | 36 | 30 | 32 | 21 | **38** | 30 | 26 |
| FG Made | 19 | 15 | 13 | 20 | 13 | 24 | 20 | 26 | 24 | 23 | 12 | **27** | 21 | 19 |
| Percent FG Made | 63.3 | 78.9 | 52.0 | **95.2** | 52.0 | 75.0 | 80.0 | 72.2 | 80.0 | 71.9 | 57.1 | 71.1 | 70.0 | 73.1 |
| Safeties | 0 | 1 | 1 | 0 | **2** | 1 | **2** | **2** | 1 | **2** | 1 | 1 | 1 | 1 |

DEFENSE

| | ATL | CHI | DAL | DET | G.B. | L.A. | MINN | N.O. | NYG | PHIL | PHX | S.F. | T.B. | WASH |
|---|---|---|---|---|---|---|---|---|---|---|---|---|---|---|
| FIRST DOWNS: | | | | | | | | | | | | | | |
| Total | 312 | 264 | 297 | 334 | 281 | 289 | **243** | 286 | 291 | 311 | 301 | 277 | 293 | 294 |
| by Rushing | 124 | **76** | 93 | 128 | 130 | 100 | 85 | 97 | 95 | 85 | 111 | 90 | 104 | 113 |
| by Passing | 168 | 158 | 180 | 179 | 136 | 166 | **132** | 167 | 177 | 199 | 170 | 160 | 169 | 153 |
| by Penalty | 20 | 30 | 24 | 27 | **15** | 23 | 26 | 22 | 19 | 27 | 20 | 27 | 20 | 28 |
| RUSHING: | | | | | | | | | | | | | | |
| Number | 518 | **389** | 454 | 511 | 514 | 414 | 435 | 442 | 454 | 466 | 467 | 441 | 478 | 442 |
| Yards | 2319 | **1326** | 1858 | 2037 | 2110 | 1686 | 1602 | 1779 | 1759 | 1652 | 1925 | 1588 | 1551 | 1745 |
| Average Yards | 4.5 | 3.4 | 4.1 | 4.0 | 4.1 | 4.1 | 3.7 | 4.0 | 3.9 | 3.5 | 4.1 | 3.6 | **3.2** | 3.9 |
| Touchdowns | 14 | **5** | 13 | 16 | 17 | 12 | 10 | 7 | 8 | 11 | 19 | 8 | 21 | 17 |
| PASSING: | | | | | | | | | | | | | | |
| Attempts | 504 | 545 | 523 | 513 | **474** | 571 | 480 | 505 | 566 | 578 | 508 | 530 | 527 | 497 |
| Completions | 281 | 245 | 264 | 337 | 256 | 307 | **219** | 277 | 294 | 309 | 264 | 292 | 304 | 261 |
| Completion Pct. | 55.8 | **45.0** | 50.5 | 65.7 | 54.0 | 53.8 | 45.6 | 54.9 | 51.9 | 53.5 | 52.0 | 55.1 | 57.7 | 52.5 |
| Passing Yards | 3584 | 3399 | 3883 | 3672 | 2949 | 3694 | **2763** | 3579 | 3755 | 4443 | 3539 | 3284 | 3744 | 3744 |
| Avg. Yds per Att. | 6.3 | 5.2 | 6.3 | 5.9 | 5.4 | 5.3 | **4.8** | 6.2 | 5.4 | 6.7 | 5.9 | 5.2 | 6.6 | 6.4 |
| Avg. Yds per Comp. | 12.8 | 13.9 | 14.7 | **10.9** | 11.5 | 12.0 | 12.6 | 12.9 | 12.8 | 14.4 | 13.4 | 11.3 | 12.3 | 14.3 |
| Times Tackled | 30 | 43 | 46 | 47 | 30 | **56** | 37 | 31 | 52 | 42 | 39 | 42 | 20 | 43 |
| Yds Lost Tackled | 211 | 365 | 327 | 393 | 216 | 394 | 274 | 252 | **428** | 296 | 295 | 297 | 140 | 305 |
| Net Yards | 3373 | 3034 | 3556 | 3279 | **2733** | 3300 | 2489 | 3327 | 3327 | 4147 | 3244 | 2987 | 3604 | 3439 |
| Touchdowns | 17 | 18 | 30 | 17 | **12** | 17 | **12** | 19 | 23 | 23 | 30 | 25 | 19 | 24 |
| Interceptions | 24 | 26 | 10 | 15 | 20 | 22 | **36** | 17 | 15 | 32 | 16 | 22 | 21 | 14 |
| Pct. Intercepted | 4.8 | 4.8 | 1.9 | 2.9 | 4.2 | 3.9 | **7.5** | 3.4 | 2.7 | 5.5 | 3.1 | 4.2 | 4.0 | 2.8 |
| PUNTS: | | | | | | | | | | | | | | |
| Number | 73 | 90 | 86 | 74 | 76 | 93 | **96** | 70 | 93 | 85 | 83 | 86 | 77 | 79 |
| Average | 39.6 | 40.2 | 41.6 | 39.4 | 37.6 | 39.9 | **42.3** | 40.2 | 39.8 | 37.8 | 41.1 | 41.0 | 39.0 | 39.4 |
| PUNT RETURNS | | | | | | | | | | | | | | |
| Number | 51 | 40 | **37** | 57 | 39 | 43 | 39 | 39 | 38 | 47 | 41 | 47 | 38 | 39 |
| Yards | 297 | 447 | **239** | 483 | 314 | 347 | 405 | 248 | 303 | 393 | 416 | 426 | 273 | 448 |
| Average Yards | **5.8** | 11.2 | 6.5 | 8.5 | 8.1 | 8.1 | 10.4 | 6.4 | 8.0 | 8.4 | 10.1 | 9.1 | 7.2 | 11.5 |
| Touchdowns | 0 | 0 | 0 | 1 | 0 | 0 | 0 | 0 | 0 | 0 | 1 | 0 | 0 | 1 |
| KICKOFF RET.: | | | | | | | | | | | | | | |
| Number | 48 | 56 | 56 | 56 | 49 | 81 | 81 | **43** | 73 | 63 | 65 | 73 | 52 | 61 |
| Yards | 982 | 1130 | 1060 | 1076 | 966 | 1563 | 1622 | **823** | 1269 | 1266 | 1379 | 1362 | 1129 | 1111 |
| Average Yards | 20.5 | 20.2 | 18.9 | 19.2 | 19.7 | 19.3 | 20.0 | 19.1 | **17.4** | 20.1 | 21.2 | 18.7 | 21.7 | 18.2 |
| Touchdowns | 0 | 0 | 0 | 0 | 0 | 1 | 0 | 0 | 0 | 0 | 1 | 0 | 0 | 0 |
| INTERCEPT RET.: | | | | | | | | | | | | | | |
| Number | 19 | 15 | 27 | 18 | 24 | 18 | 18 | 16 | **14** | 17 | 19 | 14 | 36 | 25 |
| Yards | 214 | 175 | 314 | 159 | 386 | 138 | 212 | 226 | 116 | **98** | 264 | 185 | 486 | 271 |
| Average Yards | 11.3 | 11.7 | 11.6 | 8.8 | 16.1 | 7.7 | 11.8 | 14.1 | 8.3 | **5.8** | 13.9 | 13.2 | 13.5 | 10.8 |
| Touchdowns | 2 | 1 | **0** | **0** | 4 | 1 | 1 | 2 | **0** | **0** | **0** | 1 | 2 | **0** |
| PENALTIES: | | | | | | | | | | | | | | |
| Number | 92 | 102 | 92 | 106 | 112 | 111 | 91 | 77 | **116** | 115 | 103 | 76 | 105 | 91 |
| Yards | 761 | 804 | 772 | 869 | **903** | 937 | 753 | 628 | 902 | 897 | 770 | 603 | 872 | 711 |
| FUMBLES: | | | | | | | | | | | | | | |
| Number | 29 | 17 | 24 | 35 | 33 | **36** | **36** | 27 | **36** | 28 | 27 | 30 | 29 | 23 |
| Number Lost | 14 | 9 | 9 | **21** | **21** | 15 | 17 | 15 | 18 | 12 | 13 | 16 | 12 | 8 |
| POINTS: | | | | | | | | | | | | | | |
| Total | 315 | **215** | 381 | 313 | 315 | 293 | 233 | 283 | 304 | 319 | 398 | 294 | 350 | 387 |
| PAT Attempts | 34 | 25 | 44 | 34 | 34 | 35 | **24** | 29 | 32 | 37 | 51 | 34 | 42 | 46 |
| PAT Made | 31 | **22** | 41 | 32 | 34 | 35 | **22** | 28 | 31 | 35 | 47 | 34 | 42 | 43 |
| FG Attempts | 36 | **22** | 29 | 29 | 35 | 23 | 25 | 34 | 33 | 29 | **22** | 24 | 30 | 36 |
| FG Made | 26 | **13** | 24 | 25 | 25 | 16 | 21 | 27 | 25 | 20 | **13** | 18 | 18 | 22 |
| Percent FG Made | 72.2 | **59.1** | 82.8 | 86.2 | 71.4 | 69.6 | 84.0 | 79.4 | 75.8 | 69.0 | **59.1** | 75.0 | 60.0 | 61.1 |
| Safeties | 1 | 2 | 2 | 1 | 1 | **0** | 2 | **0** | **0** | 1 | 3 | 1 | 1 | 1 |

Hipple also out injured, Raiders' reject Rusty Hilger became the starter in his first week with the team. While the offense evaporated, the defense had some bright spots in rookies LB Chris Spielman and SS Bennie Blades and veteran LB Mike Cofer. That wasn't nearly enough to save Darryl Rogers' job. He was replaced by defensive coordinator Wayne Fontes with five games to go. The Lions won two of the remaining games.

## WESTERN DIVISION

**San Francisco 49ers** — Coach Bill Walsh lit a quarterback controversey by declaring the competition open for the No. 1 spot before training camp. Then, after Joe Montana had apparently won his job, he was kept on the bench longer than he or other observers deemed necessary when he was injured. Roger Craig had his greatest season, but Jerry Rice nursed a bad ankle through most of the schedule and the offensive line also struggled early. The 'Niners were 6-5 with five games to go. Then everything came together. San Francisco reeled off four straight victories to clinch the division title and make what might have been a showdown with the Rams academic. Down the stretch, Montana was strong, Craig kept going and the line became cohesive. The defense, led by Ronnie Lott, Michael Carter and Charles Haley, was tough all the way.

**Los Angeles Rams** — The Rams roared to a 7-2 record after nine games. The defense was on a record sack pace. Jim Everett had an All-Pro first half-season, as did Greg Bell, the runner picked up from Buffalo as part of 1987's Eric Dickerson trade. WR Henry Ellard was also enjoying his best season. Then the wheels came off the defense and Los Angeles dropped four straight to slip to third place. When the defense magically returned in Week 14, coach John Robinson's team rallied for three straight wins, including victories over the Bears and 49ers, to gain a playoff berth for the fifth time in six years.

**New Orleans Saints** — The Saints had their second consecutive winning season and only the second in their history — but 1988 was nevertheless disappointing. Saints fans were primed for a division title and a second trip to the playoffs. Instead, the Saints tripped coming down the stretch, losing three straight before winning the finale over Atlanta by a single point. Injuries cut into a squad that wasn't very deep, and one game was lost to the Giants when Morten Andersen, the nonpareil, missed a 29-yard field goal. The defense depended on the outstanding linebackers both to stop the run and rush the passer, and when opponents could neutralize Rickey Jackson, Vaughan Johnson, Sam Mills and Pat Swilling, the Saints are in trouble.

**Atlanta Falcons** — The Falcons went through another losing season in 1988, but finished up more hopeful than in recent season's past. The offense gave signs of respectability. Young quarterback Chris Miller made definite progress both in passing and leadership. When Gerald Riggs was forced out with an injury, second-year free-agent John Settle settled in for a 1,000-yard seaosn. OG Bill Fralic and OT Mike Kenn had banner seasons. The defense cut over 100 points from its largess, as Scott Case led the league in interceptions and rookie LB Aundray Bruce played like a star in the making on occasions. The Falcons also had the league's most tragic event — DB David Croudip died October 10 of an apparent drug overdose.

## PHILADELPHIA EAGLES 10-6 Buddy Ryan

| Scores of Each Game | | |
|---|---|---|
| 41 | Tampa Bay | 14 |
| 24 | CINCINNATI | 28 |
| 10 | Washington | 17 |
| 21 | Minnesota | 23 |
| 32 | HOUSTON | 23 |
| 24 | N.Y. GIANTS | 13 |
| 3 | Cleveland | 19 |
| 24 | DALLAS | 23 |
| 24 | ATLANTA | 27 |
| 30 | L.A. RAMS | 24 |
| 27 | Pittsburgh | 26 |
| 23 | N.Y. Giants | *17 |
| 31 | PHOENIX | 21 |
| 19 | WASHINGTON | 20 |
| 23 | Phoenix | 17 |
| 23 | Dallas | 7 |

| Use Name | Pos. | Hgt | Wgt | Age | Int | Pts |
|---|---|---|---|---|---|---|
| Matt Darwin | OT | 6'4" | 275 | 25 | | |
| Ron Heller | OT | 6'3" | 280 | 26 | | |
| Ken Reeves | OT-OG | 6'5" | 270 | 27 | | |
| David Alexander | OG-C | 6'3" | 275 | 23 | | |
| Ron Baker | OG | 6'4" | 274 | 34 | | |
| Reggie Singletary | OG-OT | 6'3" | 280 | 24 | | |
| Ron Solt (from IND) | OG | 6'3" | 285 | 26 | | |
| Ben Tamburello | OG-C | 6'3" | 278 | 23 | | |
| Dave Rimington | C | 6'3" | 288 | 28 | | |
| Doug Bartlett | DE-DT | 6'2" | 255 | 25 | | |
| Jonathan Dumbauld (to NO) | DE | 6'4" | 259 | 25 | | |
| Donald Evans | DE | 6'2" | 241 | 24 | | |
| John Klingel | DE | 6'3" | 267 | 24 | | |
| Clyde Simmons | DE | 6'6" | 276 | 24 | | 8 |
| Reggie White | DE-DT | 6'5" | 285 | 26 | | |
| Jerome Brown | DT | 6'2" | 288 | 23 | 1 | |
| Mike Golic | DT | 6'5" | 275 | 26 | | |
| Mike Pitts | DT | 6'5" | 277 | 28 | | |

Bob Landsee — Knee Injury

| Use Name | Pos. | Hgt | Wgt | Age | Int | Pts |
|---|---|---|---|---|---|---|
| Ty Allert | LB | 6'2" | 233 | 25 | | |
| Todd Bell | LB | 6'1" | 212 | 30 | | |
| Scott Curtis | LB | 6'1" | 230 | 24 | | |
| Byron Evans | LB | 6'2" | 225 | 24 | | |
| Dwayne Jiles | LB | 6'4" | 250 | 27 | | |
| Seth Joyner | LB | 6'2" | 248 | 24 | 4 | |
| Mike Reichenbach | LB | 6'2" | 230 | 27 | | |
| Eric Allen | DB | 5'10" | 183 | 21 | 5 | |
| Eric Everett | DB | 5'10" | 161 | 22 | 1 | |
| William Frizzell | DB | 6'3" | 205 | 26 | 3 | |
| Terry Hoage | DB | 6'3" | 201 | 26 | 8 | 6 |
| Wes Hopkins | DB | 6'1" | 212 | 27 | 5 | |
| Izel Jenkins | DB | 5'10" | 191 | 23 | | 2 |
| Andre Waters | DB | 5'11" | 195 | 26 | 3 | |
| Roynell Young | DB | 6'1" | 185 | 30 | 2 | |

| Use Name | Pos. | Hgt | Wgt | Age | Int | Pts |
|---|---|---|---|---|---|---|
| Matt Cavanaugh | QB | 6'2" | 210 | 32 | | |
| Randall Cunningham | QB | 6'4" | 203 | 25 | | 36 |
| Don McPherson | QB | 6'1" | 183 | 23 | | |
| Walter Abercrombie | HB | 6' | 210 | 29 | | |
| Keith Byars | HB | 6'1" | 238 | 25 | | 60 |
| Mark Konecny | HB | 5'11" | 200 | 25 | | |
| Junior Tautalatasi | HB-FB | 5'10" | 210 | 26 | | |
| Michael Haddix | FB | 6'2" | 227 | 27 | | |
| Anthony Toney | FB | 6' | 227 | 25 | | 30 |
| Shawn Beals | WR | 5'10" | 178 | 22 | | |
| Cris Carter | WR | 6'3" | 194 | 23 | | 42 |
| Gregg Garrity | WR | 5'10" | 169 | 26 | | 6 |
| Kenny Jackson | WR | 6' | 180 | 26 | | |
| Ron Johnson | WR | 6'3" | 186 | 30 | | 12 |
| Mike Quick | WR | 6'2" | 190 | 27 | | 24 |
| Jimmie Giles | TE | 6'3" | 240 | 34 | | 6 |
| Keith Jackson | TE | 6'2" | 250 | 23 | | 36 |
| Dave Little | TE | 6'2" | 226 | 27 | | |
| Dean Dorsey (to GB) | K | 5'11" | 195 | 31 | | 27 |
| John Teltschik | K | 6'2" | 209 | 24 | | |
| Luis Zendejas (from DAL) | K | 5'9" | 160 | 26 | | 95 |

Eric Bailey — Back Injury

## NEW YORK GIANTS 10-6 Bill Parcells

| Scores of Each Game | | |
|---|---|---|
| 27 | WASHINGTON | 20 |
| 17 | SAN FRANCISCO | 20 |
| 12 | Dallas | 10 |
| 31 | L.A. RAMS | 45 |
| 24 | Washington | 23 |
| 13 | Philadelphia | 24 |
| 30 | DETROIT | 10 |
| 23 | Atlanta | 16 |
| 13 | Detroit | *10 |
| 29 | DALLAS | 21 |
| 17 | Phoenix | 24 |
| 17 | PHILADELPHIA | *23 |
| 13 | New Orleans | 12 |
| 44 | PHOENIX | 7 |
| 28 | KANSAS CITY | 12 |
| 21 | N.Y. Jets | 27 |

| Use Name | Pos. | Hgt | Wgt | Age | Int | Pts |
|---|---|---|---|---|---|---|
| John Elliott | OT | 6'7" | 305 | 23 | | |
| Eric Moore | OT | 6'5" | 290 | 23 | | |
| Karl Nelson | OT | 6'6" | 285 | 28 | | |
| Doug Riesenberg | OT | 6'5" | 275 | 23 | | |
| Williams Roberts | OT | 6'5" | 280 | 26 | | |
| Billy Ard | OG | 6'3" | 270 | 29 | | |
| Damian Johnson | OG-OT | 6'5" | 290 | 25 | | |
| Joe Fields | C | 6'2" | 253 | 34 | | |
| Bart Oates | C | 6'3" | 265 | 29 | | |
| Eric Dorsey | DE | 6'5" | 280 | 24 | | |
| Leonard Marshall | DE | 6'3" | 285 | 26 | | |
| George Martin | DE | 6'4" | 255 | 35 | | |
| John Washington | DE | 6'4" | 275 | 25 | | |
| Robb White | DE | 6'4" | 270 | 23 | | |
| Jim Burt | NT | 6'1" | 260 | 29 | | 6 |
| Erik Howard | NT | 6'4" | 268 | 23 | | |

| Use Name | Pos. | Hgt | Wgt | Age | Int | Pts |
|---|---|---|---|---|---|---|
| Carl Banks | LB | 6'4" | 235 | 26 | 1 | 6 |
| Harry Carson | LB | 6'2" | 240 | 34 | 2 | |
| Johnie Cooks (from IND) | LB | 6'4" | 251 | 29 | | |
| Andy Headen | LB | 6'5" | 242 | 28 | | |
| Byron Hunt | LB | 6'5" | 242 | 29 | | |
| Pepper Johnson | LB | 6'3" | 248 | 24 | 1 | 6 |
| Gary Reasons | LB | 6'4" | 234 | 26 | 1 | |
| Ricky Shaw | LB | 6'4" | 240 | 23 | | |
| Lawrence Taylor | LB | 6'3" | 243 | 29 | | |
| Mark Collins | DB | 5'10" | 190 | 24 | 1 | 2 |
| Tom Flynn | DB | 6' | 195 | 26 | | 6 |
| Neal Guggemos | DB | 6'1" | 190 | 24 | | |
| Wayne Haddix | DB | 6'1" | 203 | 23 | | |
| Kenny Hill | DB | 6' | 195 | 30 | | |
| Terry Kinard | DB | 6'1" | 200 | 28 | 3 | |
| Greg Lasker (to CHI and PHX) | DB | 6' | 200 | 23 | | |
| Adrian White | DB | 6' | 200 | 24 | 1 | |
| Sheldon White | DB | 5'11" | 188 | 23 | 4 | |
| Perry Williams | DB | 6'2" | 203 | 27 | 1 | |

Herb Welch — Leg Injury

| Use Name | Pos. | Hgt | Wgt | Age | Int | Pts |
|---|---|---|---|---|---|---|
| Jeff Hostetler | QB | 6'3" | 212 | 27 | | |
| Jeff Rutledge | QB | 6'1" | 195 | 31 | | |
| Phil Simms | QB | 6'3" | 214 | 31 | | |
| Ottis Anderson | HB | 6'2" | 225 | 31 | | 48 |
| Joe Morris | HB | 5'7" | 195 | 27 | | 30 |
| George Adams | FB | 6'1" | 225 | 25 | | |
| Maurice Carthon | FB | 6'1" | 225 | 27 | | 18 |
| Lee Rouson | FB | 6'1" | 222 | 25 | | |
| Stephen Baker | WR | 5'8" | 160 | 24 | | 42 |
| Mark Ingram | WR | 5'10" | 188 | 23 | | 6 |
| Lionel Manuel | WR | 5'11" | 180 | 26 | | 24 |
| Phil McConkey | WR | 5'10" | 170 | 31 | | |
| Stacy Robinson | WR | 5'11" | 186 | 26 | | 18 |
| Odessa Turner | WR | 6'3" | 205 | 23 | | 6 |
| Mark Bavaro | TE | 6'4" | 245 | 25 | | 24 |
| Brad Beckman | TE | 6'2" | 236 | 23 | | |
| Zeke Mowatt | TE | 6'3" | 240 | 27 | | 6 |
| Tim Sherwin | TE | 6'5" | 252 | 30 | | |
| Raul Allegre | K | 5'10" | 167 | 29 | | 44 |
| Maury Buford | K | 6'1" | 195 | 28 | | |
| Sean Landeta | K | 6' | 200 | 26 | | |
| Paul McFadden | K | 5'11" | 166 | 26 | | 67 |

## WASHINGTON REDSKINS 7-9 Joe Gibbs

| Scores of Each Game | | |
|---|---|---|
| 20 | N.Y. Giants | 27 |
| 30 | PITTSBURGH | 29 |
| 17 | PHILADELPHIA | 10 |
| 21 | Phoenix | 30 |
| 23 | N.Y. GIANTS | 24 |
| 35 | Dallas | 17 |
| 33 | PHOENIX | 17 |
| 20 | Green Bay Mil.) | 17 |
| 17 | Houston | 41 |
| 27 | NEW ORLEANS | 24 |
| 14 | CHICAGO | 34 |
| 21 | San Francisco | 37 |
| 13 | CLEVELAND | 17 |
| 20 | Philadelphia | 19 |
| 17 | DALLAS | 24 |
| 17 | Cincinnati | *20 |

| Use Name | Pos. | Hgt | Wgt | Age | Int | Pts |
|---|---|---|---|---|---|---|
| Joe Jacoby | OT | 6'7" | 305 | 29 | | |
| Jim Lachey (from RAID) | OT | 6'6" | 290 | 25 | | |
| Mark May | OT-OG | 6'6" | 295 | 28 | | |
| Ed Simmons | OT | 6'5" | 280 | 24 | | |
| Russ Grimm | OG | 6'3" | 275 | 29 | | |
| Raleigh McKenzie | OG-C | 6'2" | 270 | 25 | | |
| R.C. Thielemann | OG | 6'4" | 272 | 33 | | |
| Jeff Bostic | C | 6'2" | 260 | 29 | | |
| Dave Harbour | C | 6'4" | 265 | 22 | | |
| Mike Scully | C | 6'5" | 280 | 22 | | |
| Steve Hamilton | DE-DT | 6'4" | 270 | 26 | | |
| Markus Koch | DE | 6'5" | 275 | 25 | | |
| Dexter Manley | DE | 6'3" | 257 | 29 | | |
| Charles Mann | DE | 6'6" | 270 | 27 | | |
| Dave Butz | DT | 6'7" | 295 | 39 | | |
| Darryl Grant | DT | 6'1" | 275 | 28 | | |
| Dean Hamel | DT | 6'3" | 280 | 27 | | |

Dan Benish — Knee Injury
Blake Hitchcock — Knee Injury
Rick Kehr — Knee Injury

| Use Name | Pos. | Hgt | Wgt | Age | Int | Pts |
|---|---|---|---|---|---|---|
| Ravin Caldwell | LB | 6'3" | 229 | 25 | | 2 |
| Monte Coleman | LB | 6'2" | 230 | 30 | 1 | |
| Kurt Gouveia | LB | 6'1" | 227 | 23 | | |
| Mel Kaufman | LB | 6'2" | 230 | 30 | | |
| Greg Manusky | LB | 6'1" | 242 | 22 | | |
| Wilber Marshall | LB | 6'1" | 230 | 26 | 3 | |
| Neal Olkewicz | LB | 6' | 230 | 31 | | |
| Todd Bowles | DB | 6'2" | 203 | 24 | 1 | |
| Brian Davis | DB | 6'2" | 190 | 25 | 1 | |
| Steve Gage | DB | 6'3" | 210 | 24 | | |
| Darrell Green | DB | 5'8" | 170 | 28 | 1 | |
| Johnny Thomas | DB | 5'9" | 190 | 24 | | |
| Clarence Vaughn | DB | 6' | 202 | 24 | | |
| Alvin Walton | DB | 6' | 180 | 24 | 3 | |
| Barry Wilburn | DB | 6'3" | 186 | 24 | 4 | |
| Kevin Williams | DB | 5'9" | 169 | 26 | | |
| Dennis Woodberry | DB | 5'10" | 183 | 27 | | |

Eric Yarber — Knee Injury

| Use Name | Pos. | Hgt | Wgt | Age | Int | Pts |
|---|---|---|---|---|---|---|
| David Archer | QB | 6'2" | 208 | 26 | | |
| Mark Rypien | QB | 6'4" | 234 | 25 | | 6 |
| Doug Williams | QB | 6'4" | 220 | 33 | | 6 |
| Kelvin Bryant | HB | 6'2" | 195 | 27 | | 36 |
| Keith Griffin | HB | 5'8" | 185 | 26 | | 6 |
| Jamie Morris | HB | 5'7" | 188 | 23 | | 12 |
| Mike Oliphant | HB | 5'10" | 183 | 25 | | |
| Timmy Smith | HB-FB | 5'11" | 216 | 24 | | 18 |
| Anthony Allen | WR | 5'11" | 182 | 29 | | 6 |
| Gary Clark | WR | 5'9" | 173 | 25 | | 42 |
| Billy Johnson | WR | 5'9" | 170 | 36 | | |
| Art Monk | WR | 6'3" | 209 | 30 | | 30 |
| Ricky Sanders | WR | 5'11" | 180 | 26 | | 72 |
| Derrick Shepard | WR | 5'10" | 187 | 24 | | |
| Joe Caravello | TE | 6'3" | 270 | 25 | | |
| Anrthony Jones (to SD) | TE | 6'3" | 248 | 28 | | |
| Craig McEwen | TE | 6'1" | 220 | 22 | | |
| Ron Middleton | TE | 6'2" | 252 | 23 | | |
| Terry Orr | TE | 6'3" | 227 | 26 | | 12 |
| Don Warren | TE | 6'4" | 242 | 32 | | |
| Tommy Barnhardt | K | 6'3" | 205 | 25 | | |
| Greg Coleman | K | 6' | 184 | 33 | | |
| Steve Cox | K | 6'4" | 195 | 30 | | |
| Chip Lohmiller | K | 6'3" | 213 | 22 | | 97 |

## PHOENIX CARDINALS 7-9 Gene Stallings

| Scores of Each Game | | |
|---|---|---|
| 14 | Cincinnati | 21 |
| 14 | DALLAS | 17 |
| 30 | Tampa Bay | 24 |
| 30 | WASHINGTON | 21 |
| 41 | L.A. Rams | 27 |
| 31 | PITTSBURGH | 14 |
| 17 | Washington | 33 |
| 21 | CLEVELAND | 29 |
| 16 | Dallas | 10 |
| 24 | SAN FRANCISCO | 23 |
| 24 | N.Y. GIANTS | 17 |
| 20 | Houston | 38 |
| 21 | Philadelphia | 31 |
| 7 | N.Y. Giants | 44 |
| 17 | PHILADELPHIA | 23 |
| 17 | GREEN BAY | 26 |

| Use Name | Pos. | Hgt | Wgt | Age | Int | Pts |
|---|---|---|---|---|---|---|
| Ray Brown | OT-OG | 6'5" | 280 | 25 | | |
| Tootie Robbins | OT | 6'5" | 302 | 30 | | |
| Luis Sharpe | OT | 6'4" | 260 | 28 | | |
| Joe Bostic | OG | 6'3" | 268 | 31 | | |
| Scott Dill | OG | 6'5" | 272 | 22 | | |
| Todd Peat | OG | 6'2" | 294 | 24 | | |
| Lance Smith | OG-OT | 6'2" | 262 | 24 | | |
| Mark Traynowicz (from BUF) | OG | 6'5" | 280 | 26 | | |
| Derek Kennard | C-OG | 6'3" | 285 | 25 | | |
| David Galloway | DE | 6'3" | 279 | 29 | | |
| Sean McNanie | DE | 6'5" | 270 | 26 | | |
| Freddie Joe Nunn | DE | 6'4" | 255 | 26 | | |
| Rod Saddler | DE | 6'5" | 276 | 22 | | 6 |
| Steve Alvord | DT | 6'4" | 272 | 23 | | |
| Bob Clasby | DT | 6'5" | 260 | 27 | 1 | |

Curtis Greer — Back Injury
Michael Morris — Knee Injury
Colin Scotts — Shoulder Injury

| Use Name | Pos. | Hgt | Wgt | Age | Int | Pts |
|---|---|---|---|---|---|---|
| Anthony Bell | LB | 6'3" | 231 | 24 | | |
| Wayne Davis | LB | 6'1" | 213 | 24 | | |
| Ken Harvey | LB | 6'2" | 225 | 23 | | 2 |
| Ricky Hunley | LB | 6'2" | 250 | 26 | | |
| Tyrone Jones | LB | 6'2" | 220 | 27 | | |
| E.J. Junior | LB | 6'3" | 235 | 28 | 1 | 6 |
| Niko Noga | LB | 6'1" | 235 | 26 | | |
| Michael Brim | DB | 6' | 186 | 22 | | |
| Carl Carter | DB | 5'11" | 180 | 24 | 3 | |
| Travis Curtis | DB | 5'10" | 180 | 22 | 1 | |
| Lester Lyles | DB | 6'3" | 205 | 25 | 2 | |
| Cedric Mack | DB | 6' | 194 | 27 | 3 | 6 |
| Tim McDonald | DB | 6'2" | 207 | 23 | 2 | |
| Roland Mitchell | DB | 5'11" | 180 | 24 | 1 | |
| Reggie Phillips | DB | 5'10" | 175 | 27 | | |
| Lonnie Young | DB | 6'1" | 182 | 25 | 1 | |

| Use Name | Pos. | Hgt | Wgt | Age | Int | Pts |
|---|---|---|---|---|---|---|
| Neil Lomax | QB | 6'3" | 215 | 29 | | 6 |
| Cliff Stoudt | QB | 6'4" | 215 | 33 | | |
| Tom Tupa | QB | 6'4" | 220 | 21 | | |
| Tony Jeffery | HB | 5'11" | 208 | 24 | | |
| Tony Jordan | HB | 6'2" | 220 | 23 | | 18 |
| Derrick McAdoo (from TB) | HB | 5'10" | 195 | 23 | | |
| Stump Mitchell | HB | 5'9" | 188 | 29 | | 30 |
| Vai Sikahema | HB | 5'9" | 191 | 26 | | |
| Jessie Clark (from DET) | FB | 6' | 228 | 28 | | |
| Earl Ferrell | FB | 6' | 240 | 30 | | 54 |
| Ricky Moore | FB | 5'11" | 253 | 25 | | |
| Ron Wolfley | FB | 6' | 222 | 25 | | |
| Roy Green | WR | 6' | 195 | 31 | | 42 |
| Don Holmes | WR | 5'10" | 180 | 27 | | |
| Ernie Jones | WR | 5'11" | 186 | 23 | | 18 |
| Andy Schillinger | WR | 5'11" | 179 | 23 | | |
| J.T. Smith | WR | 6'2" | 185 | 32 | | 30 |
| Rob Awalt | TE | 6'5" | 248 | 24 | | 24 |
| Greg Baty | TE | 6'5" | 242 | 24 | | |
| Jay Novacek | TE | 6'4" | 235 | 25 | | 24 |
| Mark Walczak | TE | 6'6" | 246 | 26 | | |
| Al Del Greco | K | 5'10" | 191 | 26 | | 78 |
| Greg Horne | K | 6' | 188 | 23 | | |

## DALLAS COWBOYS 3-13 Tom Landry

| Scores of Each Game | | |
|---|---|---|
| 21 | Pittsburgh | 24 |
| 17 | Phoenix | 14 |
| 10 | N.Y. GIANTS | 12 |
| 26 | ATLANTA | 20 |
| 17 | New Orleans | 20 |
| 17 | WASHINGTON | 35 |
| 7 | Chicago | 17 |
| 23 | Philadelphia | 24 |
| 10 | PHOENIX | 16 |
| 21 | N.Y. Giants | 29 |
| 3 | MINNESOTA | 43 |
| 24 | CINCINNATI | 38 |
| 17 | HOUSTON | 25 |
| 21 | Cleveland | 24 |
| 24 | Washington | 17 |
| 7 | PHILADELPHIA | 23 |

| Use Name | Pos. | Hgt | Wgt | Age | Int | Pts |
|---|---|---|---|---|---|---|
| Bob Brotzki (from IND) | OT | 6'5" | 280 | 25 | | |
| Kevin Gogan | OT | 6'7" | 306 | 23 | | |
| Daryle Smith | OT | 6'5" | 276 | 24 | | |
| Mark Tuinei | OT | 6'5" | 282 | 28 | | |
| Dave Widell | OT | 6'6" | 300 | 23 | | |
| Crawford Ker | OG | 6'3" | 290 | 26 | | |
| Nate Newton | OG | 6'3" | 314 | 26 | | |
| Glen Titensor | OG | 6'4" | 270 | 30 | | |
| Jeff Zimmerman | OG | 6'6" | 313 | 23 | | |
| Tom Rafferty | C | 6'3" | 264 | 34 | | |
| Bob White | C | 6'5" | 273 | 25 | | |
| Jim Jeffcoat | DE | 6'5" | 262 | 27 | | |
| Too Tall Jones | DE | 6'9" | 278 | 37 | | |
| Kevin Brooks | DT | 6'6" | 284 | 25 | | |
| Danny Noonan | DT | 6'4" | 266 | 23 | 1 | 8 |
| Mark Walen | DT-DE | 6'5" | 267 | 25 | | |
| Randy White | DT | 6'4" | 272 | 35 | | |

| Use Name | Pos. | Hgt | Wgt | Age | Int | Pts |
|---|---|---|---|---|---|---|
| Ron Burton | LB | 6'1" | 245 | 24 | | |
| Garry Cobb | LB | 6'2" | 233 | 31 | | |
| Steve DeOssie | LB | 6'2" | 246 | 25 | | |
| Garth Jax | LB | 6'2" | 230 | 24 | | |
| Eugene Lockhart | LB | 6'2" | 235 | 27 | | |
| Ken Norton | LB | 6'2" | 236 | 21 | | |
| Sean Scott | LB | 6'1" | 226 | 22 | | |
| Vince Albritton | DB | 6'2" | 220 | 26 | | |
| Bill Bates | DB | 6'1" | 200 | 27 | 1 | |
| Michael Downs | DB | 6'3" | 215 | 29 | 2 | |
| Ron Francis | DB | 5'9" | 201 | 24 | 1 | |
| Manny Hendrix | DB | 5'10" | 181 | 23 | 1 | |
| Billy Owens | DB | 6'1" | 207 | 22 | | |
| Victor Scott | DB | 6' | 203 | 26 | | |
| Everson Walls | DB | 6'1" | 193 | 28 | 2 | |
| Robert Williams | DB | 5'10" | 186 | 25 | 2 | |
| Charles Wright (from TB) | DB | 5'9" | 178 | 24 | | |

Jeff Hurd — Knee Injury
Jeff Rohrer — Back Injury

| Use Name | Pos. | Hgt | Wgt | Age | Int | Pts |
|---|---|---|---|---|---|---|
| Steve Pelluer | QB | 6'4" | 212 | 26 | | 12 |
| Scott Secules | QB | 6'3" | 219 | 23 | | |
| Kevin Sweeney | QB | 6' | 193 | 24 | | |
| Danny White | QB | 6'2" | 200 | 36 | | |
| Mark Higgs | HB | 5'7" | 196 | 22 | | |
| Herschel Walker | HB-FB | 6'1" | 226 | 26 | | 42 |
| Darryl Clack | FB | 5'10" | 220 | 24 | | 6 |
| Todd Fowler | FB | 6'3" | 226 | 26 | | |
| Timmy Newsome | FB | 6'1" | 236 | 30 | | 18 |
| Ray Alexander | WR | 6'4" | 193 | 26 | | 36 |
| Cornell Burbage | WR | 5'10" | 189 | 23 | | |
| Kelvin Edwards | WR | 6'2" | 204 | 24 | | |
| Everett Gay | WR | 6'2" | 209 | 23 | | 6 |
| Michael Irvin | WR | 6'2" | 202 | 22 | | 30 |
| Kelvin Martin | WR | 5'9" | 163 | 23 | | 18 |
| Thornton Chandler | TE | 6'5" | 240 | 24 | | 6 |
| Doug Cosbie | TE | 6'6" | 244 | 32 | | |
| Steve Folsom | TE | 6'5" | 240 | 30 | | 12 |
| Roger Ruzek | K | 6'1" | 195 | 27 | | 63 |
| Mike Saxon | K | 6'3" | 198 | 26 | | |

Rod Barksdale — Knee Injury
Mike Sherrard — Leg Injury

## PHILADELPHIA EAGLES

### Rushing

| Last Name | No. | Yds | Avg | TD |
|---|---|---|---|---|
| Cunningham | 93 | 624 | 6.7 | 6 |
| Byars | 152 | 517 | 3.4 | 6 |
| Toney | 139 | 502 | 3.6 | 4 |
| Haddix | 57 | 185 | 3.2 | 0 |
| Hoage | 1 | 38 | 38.0 | 1 |
| Teltschik | 2 | 36 | 18.0 | 0 |
| Tautalatasi | 14 | 28 | 2.0 | 0 |
| Abercrombie | 5 | 14 | 2.8 | 0 |
| Carter | 1 | 1 | 1.0 | 0 |

### Receiving

| Last Name | No. | Yds | Avg | TD |
|---|---|---|---|---|
| Kei. Jackson | 81 | 869 | 10.7 | 6 |
| Byars | 72 | 705 | 9.8 | 4 |
| Carter | 39 | 761 | 19.5 | 6 |
| Toney | 34 | 256 | 7.5 | 1 |
| Quick | 22 | 508 | 23.1 | 4 |
| Johnson | 19 | 417 | 21.9 | 2 |
| Garrity | 17 | 208 | 12.2 | 1 |
| Haddix | 12 | 82 | 6.8 | 0 |
| Giles | 6 | 57 | 9.5 | 1 |
| Tautalatasi | 5 | 48 | 9.6 | 0 |
| Konecny | 1 | 18 | 18.0 | 0 |
| Abercrombie | 1 | -2 | -2.0 | 0 |

### Punt Returns

| Last Name | No. | Yds | Avg | TD |
|---|---|---|---|---|
| Konecny | 33 | 233 | 7.1 | 0 |

### Kickoff Returns

| Last Name | No. | Yds | Avg | TD |
|---|---|---|---|---|
| Beals | 34 | 625 | 18.4 | 0 |
| Konecny | 17 | 276 | 16.2 | 0 |
| Abercrombie | 5 | 87 | 17.4 | 0 |
| Byars | 2 | 20 | 10.0 | 0 |
| Jenkins | 1 | 20 | 20.0 | 0 |

### Passing

| Last Name | Att | Cmp | % | Yds | Yd/Att | TD | Int— | % | RK |
|---|---|---|---|---|---|---|---|---|---|
| Cunningham | 560 | 301 | 53.8 | 3808 | 6.80 | 24 | 16— | 2.9 | 7 |
| Cavanaugh | 16 | 7 | 43.8 | 101 | 6.31 | 1 | 1— | 6.3 | |
| Teltschik | 3 | 1 | 33.3 | 18 | 6.00 | 0 | 0— | 0.0 | |
| Byars | 2 | 0 | 0.0 | 0 | 0.00 | 0 | 0— | 0.0 | |

### Punting

| Last Name | No. | Avg. |
|---|---|---|
| Teltschik | 101 | 39.2 |
| Cunningham | 3 | 55.7 |

### Kicking

| Last Name | XP | ATT | % | FG | ATT | % |
|---|---|---|---|---|---|---|
| Zendejas | 35 | 36 | 97 | 20 | 27 | 74 |
| Dorsey | 12 | 13 | 92 | 5 | 10 | 50 |

## NEW YORK GIANTS

### Rushing

| Last Name | No. | Yds | Avg | TD |
|---|---|---|---|---|
| Morris | 307 | 1083 | 3.5 | 5 |
| Anderson | 65 | 208 | 3.2 | 8 |
| Simms | 33 | 152 | 4.6 | 0 |
| Carthon | 46 | 146 | 3.2 | 2 |
| Adams | 29 | 76 | 2.6 | 0 |
| Manuel | 4 | 27 | 6.8 | 0 |
| Rouson | 1 | 1 | 1.0 | 0 |
| Rutledge | 3 | -1 | -0.3 | 0 |
| Hostetler | 5 | -3 | -0.6 | 0 |

### Receiving

| Last Name | No. | Yds | Avg | TD |
|---|---|---|---|---|
| Manuel | 65 | 1029 | 15.8 | 4 |
| Bavaro | 53 | 672 | 12.7 | 4 |
| Baker | 40 | 656 | 16.4 | 7 |
| Adams | 27 | 174 | 6.4 | 0 |
| Morris | 22 | 166 | 7.5 | 0 |
| Carthon | 19 | 194 | 10.2 | 1 |
| Mowatt | 15 | 196 | 13.1 | 1 |
| Ingram | 13 | 158 | 12.2 | 1 |
| Turner | 10 | 128 | 12.8 | 1 |
| Anderson | 9 | 57 | 6.3 | 0 |
| Robinson | 7 | 143 | 20.4 | 3 |
| McConkey | 5 | 72 | 14.4 | 0 |
| Rouson | 4 | 61 | 15.3 | 0 |
| Hostetler | 1 | 10 | 10.0 | 0 |

### Punt Returns

| Last Name | No. | Yds | Avg | TD |
|---|---|---|---|---|
| McConkey | 40 | 313 | 7.8 | 0 |
| Baker | 5 | 34 | 6.8 | 0 |
| Kinard | 1 | 8 | 8.0 | 0 |
| Flynn | 1 | 4 | 4.0 | 0 |

### Kickoff Returns

| Last Name | No. | Yds | Avg | TD |
|---|---|---|---|---|
| Guggemos | 17 | 344 | 20.2 | 0 |
| Hill | 13 | 262 | 20.2 | 0 |
| Ingram | 8 | 129 | 16.1 | 0 |
| Rouson | 8 | 130 | 16.3 | 0 |
| Haddix | 6 | 123 | 20.5 | 0 |
| Collins | 4 | 67 | 16.8 | 0 |
| S. White | 3 | 62 | 20.7 | 0 |
| McConkey | 2 | 30 | 15.0 | 0 |
| Beckman | 1 | 7 | 7.0 | 0 |

### Passing

| Last Name | Att | Cmp | % | Yds | Yd/Att | TD | Int— | % | RK |
|---|---|---|---|---|---|---|---|---|---|
| Simms | 479 | 263 | 54.9 | 3359 | 7.01 | 21 | 11— | 2.3 | 5 |
| Hostetler | 29 | 16 | 55.2 | 244 | 8.41 | 1 | 2— | 3.4 | |
| Rutledge | 17 | 11 | 64.7 | 113 | | 0 | 1— | 5.9 | |

### Punting

| Last Name | No. | Avg. |
|---|---|---|
| Buford | 75 | 40.2 |
| Landeta | 6 | 37.0 |

### Kicking

| Last Name | XP | ATT | % | FG | ATT | % |
|---|---|---|---|---|---|---|
| McFadden | 25 | 27 | 93 | 14 | 19 | 74 |
| Allegre | 14 | 14 | 100 | 10 | 11 | 91 |

## WASHINGTON REDSKINS

### Rushing

| Last Name | No. | Yds | Avg | TD |
|---|---|---|---|---|
| Bryant | 108 | 498 | 4.6 | 1 |
| Smith | 155 | 470 | 3.0 | 3 |
| Morris | 126 | 437 | 3.5 | 2 |
| Monk | 7 | 46 | 6.6 | 0 |
| Rypien | 9 | 31 | 3.4 | 1 |
| Oliphant | 8 | 30 | 3.8 | 0 |
| Griffin | 6 | 23 | 3.8 | 0 |
| Sanders | 2 | 14 | 7.0 | 0 |
| Clark | 2 | 6 | 3.0 | 0 |
| Archer | 3 | 1 | 0.3 | 0 |
| D. Williams | 9 | 0 | 0.0 | 0 |
| G. Coleman | 2 | -13 | -6.5 | 0 |

### Receiving

| Last Name | No. | Yds | Avg | TD |
|---|---|---|---|---|
| Sanders | 73 | 1148 | 15.7 | 12 |
| Monk | 72 | 946 | 13.1 | 5 |
| Clark | 59 | 892 | 15.1 | 7 |
| Bryant | 42 | 447 | 10.6 | 5 |
| McEwen | 23 | 323 | 14.0 | 0 |
| Oliphant | 15 | 111 | 7.4 | 0 |
| Warren | 12 | 112 | 9.3 | 0 |
| Orr | 11 | 222 | 20.2 | 2 |
| Smith | 8 | 53 | 6.6 | 0 |
| Allen | 5 | 48 | 9.6 | 1 |
| Jones | 3 | 21 | 7.0 | 0 |
| Caravello | 2 | 15 | 7.5 | 0 |
| Griffin | 2 | 9 | 4.5 | 1 |
| Morris | 1 | 3 | 3.0 | 0 |

### Punt Returns

| Last Name | No. | Yds | Avg | TD |
|---|---|---|---|---|
| Shepard | 12 | 104 | 8.7 | 0 |
| Allen | 10 | 62 | 6.2 | 0 |
| Green | 9 | 103 | 11.4 | 0 |
| Clark | 8 | 48 | 6.0 | 0 |
| Oliphant | 7 | 24 | 3.4 | 0 |
| Johnson | 3 | 26 | 8.7 | 0 |
| Orr | 2 | 10 | 5.0 | 0 |
| Caldwell | 1 | 0 | 0.0 | 0 |
| Gage | 0 | 0 | 0.0 | 0 |

### Kickoff Returns

| Last Name | No. | Yds | Avg | TD |
|---|---|---|---|---|
| Morris | 21 | 413 | 19.7 | 0 |
| Sanders | 19 | 362 | 19.1 | 0 |
| Shepard | 16 | 329 | 20.6 | 0 |
| Oliphant | 7 | 127 | 18.1 | 0 |
| Gage | 5 | 60 | 12.0 | 0 |
| Griffin | 3 | 45 | 15.0 | 0 |
| Jones | 1 | 13 | 13.0 | 0 |
| Hamilton | 1 | 7 | 7.0 | 0 |
| Harbour | 1 | 6 | 6.0 | 0 |
| Orr | 1 | 6 | 6.0 | 0 |

### Passing

| Last Name | Att | Cmp | % | Yds | Yd/Att | TD | Int— | % | RK |
|---|---|---|---|---|---|---|---|---|---|
| D. Williams | 380 | 213 | 56.1 | 2609 | 6.87 | 15 | 12— | 3.2 | 8 |
| Rypien | 208 | 114 | 54.8 | 1730 | 8.32 | 18 | 13— | 6.3 | |
| Archer | 2 | 0 | 0.0 | 0 | 0.00 | 0 | 0— | 0.0 | |
| G. Coleman | 1 | 0 | 0.0 | 0 | 0.00 | 0 | 0— | 0.0 | |
| Monk | 1 | 0 | 0.0 | 0 | 0.00 | 0 | 0— | 0.0 | |

### Punting

| Last Name | No. | Avg. |
|---|---|---|
| Coleman | 39 | 38.6 |
| Barnhardt | 15 | 41.9 |
| Cox | 7 | 31.6 |
| Lohmiller | 6 | 34.7 |

### Kicking

| Last Name | XP | ATT | % | FG | ATT | % |
|---|---|---|---|---|---|---|
| Lohmiller | 40 | 41 | 98 | 19 | 26 | 73 |

## PHOENIX CARDINALS

### Rushing

| Last Name | No. | Yds | Avg | TD |
|---|---|---|---|---|
| Ferrell | 202 | 924 | 4.6 | 7 |
| S. Mitchell | 164 | 726 | 4.4 | 4 |
| Jordan | 61 | 160 | 2.6 | 3 |
| Stoudt | 14 | 57 | 4.1 | 0 |
| Lomax | 17 | 55 | 3.2 | 1 |
| Wolfley | 9 | 43 | 4.8 | 0 |
| Horne | 3 | 20 | 6.7 | 0 |
| J. Smith | 1 | 15 | 15.0 | 0 |
| Novacek | 1 | 10 | 10.0 | 0 |
| Del Greco | 1 | 8 | 8.0 | 0 |
| Jeffery | 3 | 8 | 2.7 | 0 |
| Green | 4 | 1 | 0.3 | 0 |

### Receiving

| Last Name | No. | Yds | Avg | TD |
|---|---|---|---|---|
| J. Smith | 83 | 986 | 11.9 | 5 |
| Green | 68 | 1097 | 16.1 | 7 |
| Awalt | 39 | 454 | 11.6 | 4 |
| Novacek | 38 | 569 | 15.0 | 4 |
| Ferrell | 38 | 315 | 8.3 | 2 |
| S. Mitchell | 25 | 214 | 8.6 | 1 |
| Jones | 23 | 496 | 21.6 | 3 |
| Jordan | 4 | 24 | 6.0 | 0 |
| Wolfley | 2 | 11 | 5.5 | 0 |
| Moore | 1 | 15 | 15.0 | 0 |
| Holmes | 1 | 10 | 10.0 | 0 |

### Punt Returns

| Last Name | No. | Yds | Avg | TD |
|---|---|---|---|---|
| Sikahema | 33 | 341 | 10.3 | 0 |
| J. Smith | 17 | 119 | 7.0 | 0 |
| Hunley | 1 | 3 | 3.0 | 0 |
| McAdoo | 1 | 0 | 0.0 | 0 |
| McDonald | 0 | 0 | 0.0 | 0 |

### Kickoff Returns

| Last Name | No. | Yds | Avg | TD |
|---|---|---|---|---|
| Sikahema | 23 | 475 | 20.7 | 0 |
| McAdoo | 13 | 311 | 23.9 | 0 |
| Jones | 11 | 147 | 13.4 | 0 |
| S. Mitchell | 10 | 221 | 22.1 | 0 |
| Ferrell | 2 | 25 | 12.5 | 0 |
| Jeffery | 1 | 11 | 11.0 | 0 |
| Clark | 2 | 10 | 5.0 | 0 |
| Schillinger | 1 | 10 | 10.0 | 0 |
| Phillips | 1 | 4 | 4.0 | 0 |

### Passing

| Last Name | Att | Cmp | % | Yds | Yd/Att | TD | Int— | % | RK |
|---|---|---|---|---|---|---|---|---|---|
| Lomax | 443 | 255 | 57.6 | 3395 | 7.66 | 20 | 11— | 2.5 | 4 |
| Stoudt | 113 | 63 | 55.8 | 747 | 6.61 | 6 | 8— | 7.1 | |
| Tupa | 6 | 4 | 66.7 | 49 | 8.17 | 0 | 0— | 0.0 | |

### Punting

| Last Name | No. | Avg. |
|---|---|---|
| Horne | 80 | 40.4 |

### Kicking

| Last Name | XP | ATT | % | FG | ATT | % |
|---|---|---|---|---|---|---|
| Del Greco | 42 | 44 | 95 | 12 | 21 | 57 |

## DALLAS COWBOYS

### Rushing

| Last Name | No. | Yds | Avg | TD |
|---|---|---|---|---|
| Walker | 361 | 1514 | 4.2 | 5 |
| Pelluer | 51 | 314 | 6.2 | 2 |
| Newsome | 32 | 75 | 2.3 | 3 |
| Clack | 11 | 54 | 4.9 | 0 |
| Sweeney | 6 | 34 | 5.7 | 0 |
| Fowler | 3 | 6 | 2.0 | 0 |
| Irvin | 1 | 2 | 2.0 | 0 |
| Martin | 4 | -4 | -1.0 | 0 |

### Receiving

| Last Name | No. | Yds | Avg | TD |
|---|---|---|---|---|
| Alexander | 54 | 788 | 14.6 | 6 |
| Walker | 53 | 505 | 9.5 | 2 |
| Martin | 49 | 622 | 12.7 | 3 |
| Irvin | 32 | 654 | 20.4 | 5 |
| Newsome | 30 | 236 | 7.9 | 0 |
| Chandler | 18 | 186 | 10.3 | 1 |
| Clack | 17 | 126 | 7.4 | 1 |
| Gay | 15 | 205 | 13.7 | 1 |
| Cosbie | 12 | 112 | 9.3 | 0 |
| Fowler | 10 | 64 | 6.4 | 0 |
| Folsom | 9 | 84 | 9.3 | 2 |
| Edwards | 5 | 93 | 18.6 | 0 |
| Burbage | 2 | 50 | 25.0 | 0 |
| Newton | 1 | 2 | 2.0 | 0 |

### Punt Returns

| Last Name | No. | Yds | Avg | TD |
|---|---|---|---|---|
| Martin | 44 | 360 | 8.2 | 0 |
| Walls | 1 | 0 | 0.0 | 0 |

### Kickoff Returns

| Last Name | No. | Yds | Avg | TD |
|---|---|---|---|---|
| Burbage | 20 | 448 | 22.4 | 0 |
| Clack | 32 | 690 | 21.6 | 0 |
| Martin | 12 | 210 | 17.5 | 0 |
| Higgs | 2 | 31 | 15.5 | 0 |
| Smith | 2 | 24 | 12.0 | 0 |
| B. White | 1 | 7 | 7.0 | 0 |

### Passing

| Last Name | Att | Cmp | % | Yds | Yd/Att | TD | Int— | % | RK |
|---|---|---|---|---|---|---|---|---|---|
| Pelluer | 435 | 245 | 56.3 | 3139 | 7.22 | 17 | 19— | 4.4 | 9 |
| Sweeney | 78 | 33 | 42.3 | 314 | 4.03 | 3 | 5— | 6.4 | |
| D. White | 42 | 29 | 69.1 | 274 | 6.52 | 1 | 3— | 7.1 | |

### Punting

| Last Name | No. | Avg. |
|---|---|---|
| Saxon | 80 | 40.9 |

### Kicking

| Last Name | XP | ATT | % | FG | ATT | % |
|---|---|---|---|---|---|---|
| Ruzek | 27 | 27 | 100 | 12 | 22 | 55 |

## CHICAGO BEARS 12-4 Mike Ditka

| Scores of Each Game | | |
|---|---|---|
| 34 | MIAMI | 7 |
| 17 | Indianapolis | 13 |
| 17 | MINNESOTA | 31 |
| 24 | Green Bay | 6 |
| 24 | BUFFALO | 3 |
| 24 | Detroit | 7 |
| 17 | DALLAS | 7 |
| 10 | SAN FRANCISCO | 9 |
| 7 | New England | 30 |
| 28 | TAMPA BAY | 10 |
| 34 | Washington | 14 |
| 27 | Tampa Bay | 15 |
| 16 | GREEN BAY | 0 |
| 3 | L.A. Rams | 23 |
| 13 | DETROIT | 12 |
| 27 | Minnesota | 28 |

| Use Name | Pos. | Hgt | Wgt | Age | Int | Pts |
|---|---|---|---|---|---|---|
| Jim Covert | OT | 6'4" | 278 | 28 | | |
| Caesar Rentie | OT | 6'3" | 291 | 23 | | |
| Keith Van Horne | OT | 6'6" | 283 | 30 | | |
| John Wojciechowski | OT | 6'4" | 270 | 25 | | |
| Kurt Becker | OG | 6'5" | 280 | 29 | | |
| Mart Bortz | OG | 6'6" | 272 | 27 | | |
| Tom Thayer | OG | 6'4" | 270 | 27 | | |
| John Adickes | C | 6'3" | 264 | 24 | | |
| Jay Hilgenberg | C | 6'3" | 260 | 28 | | |
| Richard Dent | DE | 6'5" | 268 | 27 | | |
| Al Harris | DE | 6'5" | 270 | 31 | | |
| William Perry | DE | 6'2" | 320 | 25 | | |
| Sean Smith | DE-DT | 6'4" | 290 | 23 | | |
| Dick Chapura | DT | 6'3" | 275 | 24 | | |
| Dan Hampton | DT | 6'5" | 274 | 30 | | |
| Steve McMichael | DT | 6'2" | 268 | 30 | | 6 |
| John Shannon | DT | 6'3" | 269 | 23 | | |

Paul Blair — Knee Injury

| Use Name | Pos. | Hgt | Wgt | Age | Int | Pts |
|---|---|---|---|---|---|---|
| Greg Clark | LB | 6' | 221 | 23 | | |
| Troy Johnson | LB | 6' | 236 | 23 | | |
| Dante Jones | LB | 6'1" | 236 | 23 | | |
| Jim Morrissey | LB | 6'3" | 227 | 25 | 3 | |
| Mickey Pruitt | LB | 6'1" | 206 | 23 | | |
| Ron Rivera | LB | 6'3" | 240 | 26 | 2 | |
| Mike Singletary | LB | 6' | 230 | 29 | 1 | |
| Maurice Douglass | DB | 5'11" | 200 | 24 | 1 | |
| Dave Duerson | DB | 6'1" | 212 | 27 | 2 | |
| Shaun Gayle | DB | 5'11" | 194 | 26 | 1 | |
| Vestee Jackson | DB | 6' | 186 | 25 | 8 | |
| Todd Krumm | DB | 6' | 189 | 22 | 2 | |
| Lorenzo Lynch | DB | 5'9" | 199 | 25 | | |
| Mike Richardson | DB | 6' | 181 | 27 | 2 | |
| Lemuel Stinson | DB | 5'9" | 159 | 22 | | |
| David Tate | DB | 6' | 177 | 23 | 4 | |

Otis Wilson — Knee Injury

| Use Name | Pos. | Hgt | Wgt | Age | Int | Pts |
|---|---|---|---|---|---|---|
| Ben Bennett | QB | 6'1" | 200 | 26 | | |
| Jim Harbaugh | QB | 6'3" | 204 | 24 | | 6 |
| Jim McMahon | QB | 6'1" | 198 | 29 | | 24 |
| Mike Tomczak | QB | 6'1" | 198 | 25 | | 6 |
| Neal Anderson | HB | 5'11" | 210 | 24 | | 72 |
| Thomas Sanders | HB | 5'11" | 203 | 26 | | 18 |
| Brad Muster | FB | 6'3" | 231 | 23 | | 6 |
| Matt Suhey | FB | 5'11" | 213 | 30 | | 12 |
| Wendell Davis | WR | 5'11" | 188 | 22 | | |
| Dennis Gentry | WR-HB | 5'8" | 180 | 29 | | 24 |
| Glen Kozlowski | WR | 6'1" | 205 | 25 | | |
| Dennis McKinnon | WR | 6'1" | 177 | 27 | | 24 |
| Ron Morris | WR | 6'1' | 195 | 23 | | 24 |
| Cap Boso | TE | 6'3" | 240 | 24 | | |
| Emery Moorehead | TE | 6'2" | 230 | 34 | | 12 |
| Brent Novoselsky | TE | 6'3" | 232 | 22 | | |
| Jim Thornton | TE | 6'2" | 242 | 23 | | |
| Kevin Butler | K | 6'1" | 204 | 26 | | 82 |
| Bryan Wagner | K | 6'2" | 200 | 26 | | |

## MINNESOTA VIKINGS 11-5 Jerry Burns

| Scores of Each Game | | |
|---|---|---|
| 10 | Buffalo | 13 |
| 36 | NEW ENGLAND | 6 |
| 31 | Chicago | 7 |
| 23 | PHILADELPHIA | 21 |
| 7 | Miami | 24 |
| 14 | TAMPA BAY | 13 |
| 14 | GREEN BAY | 34 |
| 49 | Tampa Bay | 20 |
| 21 | San Francisco | 24 |
| 44 | DETROIT | 17 |
| 43 | Dallas | 3 |
| 12 | INDIANAPOLIS | 3 |
| 23 | Detroit | 0 |
| 45 | NEW ORLEANS | 3 |
| 6 | Green Bay | 18 |
| 28 | CHICAGO | 27 |

| Use Name | Pos. | Hgt | Wgt | Age | Int | Pts |
|---|---|---|---|---|---|---|
| Tim Irwin | OT | 6'6" | 285 | 29 | | |
| Gary Zimmerman | OT | 6'6" | 286 | 26 | | |
| Dave Huffman | OG-OT | 6'6" | 284 | 32 | | |
| Todd Kalis | OG | 6'5" | 284 | 23 | | |
| Mark MacDonald (to PHX) | OG | 6'4" | 265 | 27 | | |
| Randall McDaniel | OG | 6'3" | 271 | 23 | | |
| Terry Tausch | OG | 6'5" | 273 | 29 | | |
| Chris Foote | C | 6'3" | 255 | 31 | | |
| Kirk Lowdermilk | C | 6'3" | 267 | 25 | | |
| Randy Rasmussen | C-OG | 6'2" | 254 | 28 | | |
| Al Baker | DE | 6'6" | 280 | 31 | | 2 |
| Barry Bennett (from NYJ) | DE | 6'4" | 257 | 32 | | |
| Chris Doleman | DE | 6'5" | 262 | 26 | | 2 |
| William Gay | DE | 6'5" | 260 | 33 | | |
| Doug Martin | DE | 6'3" | 258 | 31 | | |
| Stafford Mays | DE | 6'2" | 264 | 30 | | |
| Keith Millard | DT | 6'5" | 262 | 26 | | |
| Tim Newton | DT | 6' | 277 | 25 | | |
| Al Noga | DT-DE | 6'1" | 261 | 22 | | |
| Henry Thomas | DT | 6'2" | 267 | 23 | 1 | 6 |

| Use Name | Pos. | Hgt | Wgt | Age | Int | Pts |
|---|---|---|---|---|---|---|
| Sam Anno | LB | 6'2" | 230 | 23 | | |
| Walker Lee Ashley | LB | 6' | 230 | 28 | 1 | 6 |
| Ray Berry | LB | 6'2" | 225 | 24 | | |
| David Howard | LB | 6'2" | 232 | 26 | 3 | |
| Chris Martin (to KC) | LB | 6'2" | 231 | 27 | | 6 |
| Jesse Solomon | LB | 6' | 232 | 24 | 4 | 6 |
| Scott Studwell | LB | 6'2" | 228 | 34 | | |
| Joey Browner | DB | 6'2" | 210 | 28 | 5 | |
| Brad Edwards | DB | 6'1" | 200 | 22 | 2 | 6 |
| Darrell Fullington | DB | 6'1" | 197 | 24 | 3 | |
| John Harris | DB | 6'2" | 199 | 32 | 3 | |
| Wymon Henderson | DB | 5'10" | 185 | 26 | 1 | |
| Issiac Holt | DB | 6'2" | 202 | 25 | 2 | 2 |
| Carl Lee | DB | 6' | 183 | 27 | 8 | 12 |
| Reggie Rutland | DB | 6'1" | 194 | 24 | 3 | |

| Use Name | Pos. | Hgt | Wgt | Age | Int | Pts |
|---|---|---|---|---|---|---|
| Rich Gannon | QB | 6'3" | 199 | 22 | | |
| Tommy Kramer | QB | 6'2" | 202 | 33 | | |
| Wade Wilson | QB | 6'3" | 208 | 29 | | 12 |
| D.J. Dozier | HB | 6' | 198 | 22 | | 12 |
| Darryl Harris | HB | 5'10" | 178 | 22 | | 6 |
| Darrin Nelson | HB | 5'9" | 184 | 28 | | 6 |
| Allen Rice | HB | 5'10" | 204 | 26 | | 36 |
| Alfred Anderson | FB | 6'1" | 223 | 26 | | 48 |
| Rick Fenney | FB | 6'1" | 232 | 23 | | 18 |
| Anthony Carter | WR | 5'11" | 177 | 27 | | 36 |
| Jim Gustafson | WR | 6'1" | 174 | 27 | | 6 |
| Hassan Jones | WR | 6' | 192 | 24 | | 30 |
| Leo Lewis | WR | 5'8" | 172 | 31 | | 6 |
| Paul Coffman | TE | 6'3" | 225 | 32 | | |
| Carl Hilton | TE | 6'3" | 230 | 24 | | 6 |
| Steve Jordan | TE | 6'4" | 239 | 27 | | 30 |
| Mike Mularkey | TE | 6'4" | 240 | 26 | | |
| Chuck Nelson | K | 6' | 172 | 28 | | 108 |
| Bucky Scribner | K | 6' | 213 | 28 | | |

## TAMPA BAY BUCCANEERS 5-11 Ray Perkins

| Scores of Each Game | | |
|---|---|---|
| 14 | PHILADELPHIA | 41 |
| 13 | Green Bay | 10 |
| 24 | PHOENIX | 30 |
| 9 | New Orleans | 13 |
| 27 | GREEN BAY | 24 |
| 13 | Minnesota | 14 |
| 31 | Indianapolis | 35 |
| 20 | MINNESOTA | 49 |
| 14 | MIAMI | 17 |
| 10 | Chicago | 28 |
| 23 | Detroit | 20 |
| 15 | CHICAGO | 27 |
| 10 | Atlanta | 17 |
| 10 | BUFFALO | 5 |
| 7 | New England | *10 |
| 21 | DETROIT | 10 |

| Use Name | Pos. | Hgt | Wgt | Age | Int | Pts |
|---|---|---|---|---|---|---|
| Mark Cooper | OT | 6'5" | 280 | 28 | | |
| Paul Gruber | OT | 6'5" | 290 | 23 | | |
| Rob Taylor | OT | 6'6" | 295 | 27 | | |
| John Bruhin | OG | 6'3" | 280 | 23 | | |
| Rick Mallory | OG | 6'2" | 265 | 27 | | |
| Tom McHale | OG | 6'4" | 275 | 25 | | |
| Dan Turk | OG | 6'4" | 260 | 26 | | |
| Randy Grimes | C | 6'4" | 275 | 28 | | |
| Kevin Thomas | C | 6'2" | 265 | 24 | | |
| John Cannon | DE-NT | 6'5" | 260 | 28 | | |
| Reuben Davis | DE | 6'4" | 290 | 23 | | |
| Robert Goff | DE | 6'3" | 270 | 22 | | |
| Ron Holmes | DE | 6'4" | 265 | 25 | | |
| Kevin Kellin | DE | 6'6" | 270 | 28 | | |
| Harry Swayne | DE | 6'5" | 270 | 23 | | |
| Curt Jarvis | NT | 6'2" | 265 | 23 | | |
| Shawn Lee | NT | 6'2" | 290 | 21 | | |

| Use Name | Pos. | Hgt | Wgt | Age | Int | Pts |
|---|---|---|---|---|---|---|
| Sidney Coleman | LB | 6'2" | 250 | 24 | | |
| Victor Jones | LB | 6'2" | 250 | 21 | | |
| Eugene Marve | LB | 6'2" | 240 | 28 | 1 | |
| Winston Moss | LB | 6'3" | 235 | 22 | | |
| Kevin Murphy | LB | 6'2" | 235 | 24 | 1 | 6 |
| Peter Najarian | LB | 6'2" | 230 | 24 | | |
| Ervin Randle | LB | 6'1" | 250 | 25 | | |
| Henry Rolling | LB | 6'2" | 225 | 22 | | |
| Jackie Walker | LB | 6'5" | 255 | 25 | | |
| Chris Washington | LB | 6'4" | 240 | 26 | | |
| Selwyn Brown | DB | 5'11" | 205 | 22 | | |
| Donnie Elder | DB | 5'9" | 175 | 24 | 3 | |
| Bobby Futrell | DB | 5'11" | 190 | 26 | 1 | |
| Harry Hamilton | DB | 6' | 195 | 25 | 6 | |
| Odie Harris | DB | 6' | 190 | 22 | 2 | |
| Ray Isom | DB | 5'9" | 190 | 22 | | |
| Rod Jones | DB | 6' | 185 | 24 | 1 | |
| Ricky Reynolds | DB | 5'11" | 190 | 23 | 4 | |
| Mark Robinson | DB | 5'11" | 200 | 25 | 2 | |

| Use Name | Pos. | Hgt | Wgt | Age | Int | Pts |
|---|---|---|---|---|---|---|
| Joe Ferguson | QB | 6'1" | 190 | 38 | | |
| Vinny Testaverde | QB | 6'5" | 215 | 24 | | 6 |
| Kerry Goode | HB | 5'11" | 200 | 22 | | 6 |
| Don Smith | HB-WR | 5'11" | 195 | 24 | | 6 |
| Jeff Smith | HB | 5'9" | 205 | 26 | | |
| Lars Tate | HB | 6'2" | 215 | 22 | | 48 |
| Bobby Howard | FB | 6' | 220 | 24 | | |
| William Howard | FB-HB | 6' | 240 | 24 | | 6 |
| James Wilder | FB-HB | 6'3" | 225 | 30 | | 6 |
| Mark Carrier | WR | 6' | 185 | 22 | | 30 |
| Bruce Hill | WR | 6' | 180 | 24 | | 54 |
| Frank Pillow | WR | 5'10" | 170 | 23 | | 6 |
| Greg Richardson | WR | 5'7" | 170 | 23 | | |
| Stephen Starring (to DET) | WR | 5'10" | 172 | 27 | | |
| Gene Taylor | WR | 6'2" | 190 | 25 | | |
| Ron Hall | TE | 6'4" | 245 | 24 | | |
| Calvin Magee | TE | 6'3" | 245 | 25 | | |
| Jeff Parks | TE | 6'4" | 240 | 23 | | |
| John Carney | K | 5'11" | 160 | 24 | | 12 |
| Ray Criswell | K | 6' | 195 | 25 | | 1 |
| Donald Igwebuike | K | 5'9" | 175 | 27 | | 78 |

## DETROIT LIONS 4-12 Darryl Rogers (2-9), Wayne Fontes (2-3)

| Scores of Each Game | | |
|---|---|---|
| 31 | ATLANTA | 17 |
| 10 | L.A. Rams | 17 |
| 14 | NEW ORLEANS | 22 |
| 10 | N.Y. JETS | 17 |
| 13 | San Francisco | 20 |
| 7 | CHICAGO | 24 |
| 10 | N.Y. Giants | 30 |
| 7 | Kansas City | 6 |
| 10 | N.Y. GIANTS | *13 |
| 17 | Minnesota | 44 |
| 20 | TAMPA BAY | 23 |
| 19 | Green Bay (Mil.) | 9 |
| 0 | MINNESOTA | 23 |
| 30 | GREEN BAY | 14 |
| 12 | Chicago | 13 |
| 10 | Tampa Bay | 21 |

| Use Name | Pos. | Hgt | Wgt | Age | Int | Pts |
|---|---|---|---|---|---|---|
| Lomas Brown | OT | 6'4" | 275 | 25 | | |
| Harvey Salem | OT | 6'6" | 285 | 27 | | |
| Eric Sanders | OT-OG | 6'7" | 280 | 29 | | |
| Curt Singer | OT | 6'5" | 279 | 26 | | |
| Eric Andolsek | OG | 6'2" | 277 | 22 | | |
| Scott Barrows | OG-C | 6'2" | 280 | 25 | | |
| Kevin Glover | OG-C | 6'2" | 275 | 25 | | |
| Joe Milinichik | OG-OT | 6'5" | 275 | 25 | | |
| Steve Mott | C | 6'3" | 265 | 27 | | |
| Keith Ferguson | DE | 6'5" | 260 | 29 | | |
| Curtis Green | DE-NT | 6'3" | 265 | 31 | | |
| Reggie Rogers | DE | 6'6" | 285 | 24 | | |
| Thomas Strauthers | DE | 6'4" | 264 | 27 | | |
| Eric Williams | DE | 6'4" | 286 | 26 | | |
| Gary Hadd | DT-NT | 6'4" | 270 | 22 | | |
| Jerry Ball | NT | 6'1" | 292 | 23 | | |
| Dan Saleaumua | NT | 6' | 285 | 22 | | |

Steve Baack — Hip Injury

| Use Name | Pos. | Hgt | Wgt | Age | Int | Pts |
|---|---|---|---|---|---|---|
| Dave Ahrens | LB | 6'3" | 245 | 29 | | |
| Paul Butcher | LB | 6' | 219 | 24 | | |
| Mike Cofer | LB | 6'5" | 245 | 28 | | |
| Dennis Gibson | LB | 6'2" | 240 | 24 | | |
| George Jamison | LB | 6'1" | 226 | 25 | 3 | 12 |
| Danny Lockett | LB | 6'2" | 250 | 24 | | |
| Shelton Robinson | LB | 6'2" | 236 | 27 | | |
| Chris Spielman | LB | 6' | 247 | 27 | | |
| Jimmy Williams | LB | 6'3" | 230 | 27 | 1 | |
| Bennie Blades | DB | 6'1" | 221 | 21 | 2 | |
| Lou Brock (from SEA) | DB | 5'10" | 175 | 24 | | |
| Raphel Cherry | DB | 6' | 190 | 26 | 2 | |
| James Griffin | DB | 6'2" | 203 | 26 | 2 | |
| Jerry Holmes | DB | 6'2" | 175 | 30 | 1 | |
| Bruce McNorton | DB | 5'11" | 175 | 29 | 1 | |
| Devon Mitchell | DB | 6'1" | 194 | 25 | 3 | 6 |
| Bobby Watkins | DB | 5'10" | 180 | 28 | | |
| William White | DB | 5'10" | 191 | 22 | | |

| Use Name | Pos. | Hgt | Wgt | Age | Int | Pts |
|---|---|---|---|---|---|---|
| Rusty Hilger | QB | 6'4" | 205 | 26 | | |
| Eric Hipple | QB | 6'2" | 198 | 30 | | |
| Chuck Long | QB | 6'4" | 221 | 25 | | |
| John Witkowski | QB | 6'1" | 205 | 26 | | |
| Garry James | HB | 5'10" | 214 | 24 | | 42 |
| Carl Painter | HB | 5'9" | 185 | 24 | | |
| Butch Woolfolk | HB | 6'1" | 212 | 28 | | |
| James Jones | FB | 6'2" | 230 | 27 | | |
| Tony Paige | FB | 5'10" | 235 | 25 | | |
| Scott Williams | FB | 6'2" | 234 | 26 | | 6 |
| Carl Bland | WR | 5'11" | 180 | 27 | | 12 |
| Jeff Chadwick | WR | 6'3" | 190 | 27 | | 18 |
| Paco Craig | WR | 5'10" | 170 | 23 | | |
| Gary Lee | WR | 6'1" | 201 | 23 | | 6 |
| Pete Mandley | WR | 5'10" | 195 | 27 | | 30 |
| Ray Roundtree | WR | 6' | 180 | 22 | | |
| Pat Carter | TE | 6'4" | 250 | 22 | | |
| Mark Lewis | TE | 6'2" | 250 | 27 | | 6 |
| Rob Rubick | TE | 6'3" | 234 | 27 | | |
| Jim Arnold | K | 6'3" | 211 | 27 | | |
| Eddie Murray | K | 5'10" | 180 | 32 | | 82 |

Karl Bernard — Knee Injury
Vyto Kab — Knee Injury

## GREEN BAY PACKERS 4-12 Lindy Infante

| Scores of Each Game | | |
|---|---|---|
| 7 | L.A. RAMS | 34 |
| 10 | TAMPA BAY | 13 |
| 17 | Miami | 24 |
| 6 | CHICAGO | 24 |
| 24 | Tampa Bay | 27 |
| 45 | NEW ENGLAND (Mil.) | 3 |
| 34 | Minnesota | 14 |
| 17 | WASHINGTON (Mil.) | 20 |
| 0 | Buffalo | 28 |
| 0 | Atlanta | 20 |
| 13 | INDIANAPOLIS | 20 |
| 9 | DETROIT (Mil.) | 19 |
| 0 | Chicago | 16 |
| 14 | Detroit | 30 |
| 18 | MINNESOTA | 6 |
| 26 | Phoenix | 17 |

| Use Name | Pos. | Hgt | Wgt | Age | Int | Pts |
|---|---|---|---|---|---|---|
| Dave Croston | OT | 6'5" | 280 | 24 | | |
| Darryl Haley | OT | 6'5" | 265 | 27 | | |
| Tom Neville | OT-OG | 6'5" | 306 | 26 | | |
| Ken Ruettgers | OT | 6'5" | 280 | 26 | | |
| Keith Uecker | OT | 6'5" | 284 | 28 | | |
| Ron Hallstrom | OG | 6'6" | 290 | 29 | | |
| Rich Moran | OG | 6'3" | 275 | 26 | | |
| Mark Cannon | C | 6'3" | 258 | 26 | | |
| Kani Kauahi | C | 6'2" | 271 | 28 | | |
| Robert Brown | DE | 6'2" | 267 | 28 | | |
| Alphonso Carreker | DE | 6'6" | 271 | 26 | | |
| Nate Hill (to MIA) | DE | 6'4" | 273 | 22 | | |
| Shawn Patterson | DE-NT | 6'5" | 261 | 23 | | |
| Blaise Winter | DE-NT | 6'3" | 275 | 26 | | |
| Jerry Boyarsky | NT | 6'3" | 290 | 29 | | |
| Bob Nelson | NT | 6'4" | 275 | 29 | | |

Tommy Robison — Groin Injury
Alan Veingrad — Hip Injury

| Use Name | Pos. | Hgt | Wgt | Age | Int | Pts |
|---|---|---|---|---|---|---|
| John Anderson | LB | 6'3" | 228 | 32 | | |
| John Corker | LB | 6'5" | 240 | 29 | | |
| Burnell Dent | LB | 6'1" | 236 | 25 | | |
| John Dorsey | LB | 6'3" | 243 | 28 | | |
| Tim Harris | LB | 6'5" | 235 | 23 | | 10 |
| Johnny Holland | LB | 6'2" | 221 | 23 | | |
| Brian Noble | LB | 6'3" | 252 | 25 | | |
| Ron Simpkins | LB | 6'1" | 234 | 30 | | |
| Scott Stephen | LB | 6'2" | 232 | 24 | | |
| Mike Weddington | LB | 6'4" | 245 | 27 | | |
| Dave Brown | DB | 6'1" | 187 | 35 | 3 | |
| Chuck Cecil | DB | 6' | 184 | 23 | 4 | |
| Tiger Greene | DB | 6' | 194 | 26 | | |
| Norman Jefferson | DB | 5'10" | 183 | 24 | | |
| Mark Lee | DB | 5'11" | 189 | 30 | 3 | |
| Mark Murphy | DB | 6'2" | 201 | 30 | 5 | |
| Ron Pitts | DB | 5'10" | 175 | 25 | 2 | 6 |
| Gary Richard | DB | 5'9" | 171 | 22 | | |
| Ken Stills | DB | 5'10" | 186 | 24 | 3 | |

Kenneth Johnson — Back Injury
Brent Moore — Knee Injury

| Use Name | Pos. | Hgt | Wgt | Age | Int | Pts |
|---|---|---|---|---|---|---|
| Blair Kiel | QB | 6' | 214 | 26 | | |
| Randy Wright | QB | 6'2" | 203 | 27 | | 12 |
| Don Majkowski | QB | 6'2" | 197 | 24 | | 6 |
| Patrick Collins | HB | 5'9" | 177 | 22 | | |
| Kenneth Davis | HB | 5'10" | 209 | 26 | | 6 |
| Lavale Thomas | HB | 6' | 205 | 24 | | |
| Keith Woodside | HB | 5'11" | 203 | 24 | | 30 |
| Paul Ott Carruth | FB | 6'1" | 220 | 27 | | |
| Brent Fullwood | FB-HB | 5'11" | 209 | 24 | | 48 |
| Larry Mason | FB | 5'11" | 205 | 27 | | 6 |
| Albert Bell | WR | 6' | 170 | 24 | | |
| Scott Bolton | WR | 6' | 188 | 23 | | |
| Phillip Epps | WR | 5'10" | 165 | 28 | | |
| Perry Kemp | WR | 5'11" | 170 | 26 | | |
| Aubrey Matthews (from ATL) | WR | 5'7" | 165 | 25 | | 12 |
| Patrick Scott | WR | 5'10" | 170 | 23 | | 6 |
| Sterling Sharpe | WR | 5'11" | 202 | 23 | | 6 |
| Walter Stanley | WR | 5'9" | 179 | 25 | | |
| Clint Didier | TE | 6'5" | 240 | 29 | | 6 |
| Joey Hackett | TE | 6'5" | 267 | 29 | | 6 |
| Ed West | TE | 6'1" | 243 | 27 | | 18 |
| Don Bracken | K | 6'1" | 211 | 26 | | |
| Curtis Burrow | K | 5'11" | 185 | 25 | | 2 |
| Dale Dawson (from PHI) | K | 6' | 213 | 23 | | 13 |
| Max Zendejas | K | 5'11" | 184 | 24 | | 44 |

## CHICAGO BEARS

**RUSHING**

| Last Name | No. | Yds | Avg | TD |
|---|---|---|---|---|
| Anderson | 249 | 1106 | 4.4 | 12 |
| Sanders | 95 | 332 | 3.5 | 3 |
| Suhey | 87 | 253 | 2.9 | 2 |
| Muster | 44 | 197 | 4.5 | 0 |
| Harbaugh | 19 | 110 | 5.8 | 1 |
| McMahon | 26 | 104 | 4.0 | 4 |
| Gentry | 7 | 86 | 12.3 | 1 |
| Morris | 3 | 40 | 13.3 | 0 |
| Tomczak | 13 | 40 | 3.1 | 1 |
| McKinnon | 3 | 25 | 8.3 | 1 |
| Davis | 1 | 3 | 3.0 | 0 |
| Kozlowski | 1 | 3 | 3.0 | 0 |
| Wagner | 2 | 0 | 0.0 | 0 |

**RECEIVING**

| Last Name | No. | Yds | Avg | TD |
|---|---|---|---|---|
| McKinnon | 45 | 704 | 15.6 | 3 |
| Anderson | 39 | 371 | 9.5 | 0 |
| Gentry | 33 | 486 | 14.7 | 3 |
| Morris | 28 | 498 | 17.8 | 4 |
| Muster | 21 | 236 | 11.2 | 1 |
| Suhey | 20 | 154 | 7.7 | 0 |
| Davis | 15 | 220 | 14.7 | 0 |
| Thornton | 15 | 135 | 9.0 | 0 |
| Moorehead | 14 | 133 | 9.5 | 2 |
| Sanders | 9 | 94 | 10.4 | 0 |
| Boso | 6 | 50 | 8.3 | 0 |
| Kozlowski | 3 | 92 | 30.7 | 0 |

**PUNT RETURNS**

| Last Name | No. | Yds | Avg | TD |
|---|---|---|---|---|
| McKinnon | 34 | 277 | 8.1 | 0 |
| Davis | 3 | 17 | 5.7 | 0 |
| Kozlowski | 1 | 0 | 0.0 | 0 |

**KICKOFF RETURNS**

| Last Name | No. | Yds | Avg | TD |
|---|---|---|---|---|
| Gentry | 27 | 578 | 21.4 | 0 |
| Sanders | 13 | 248 | 19.1 | 0 |
| Muster | 3 | 33 | 11.0 | 0 |
| Kozlowski | 2 | 37 | 18.5 | 0 |

**PASSING**

| Last Name | Att | Cmp | % | Yds | Yd/Att | TD | Int | % | RK |
|---|---|---|---|---|---|---|---|---|---|
| McMahon | 192 | 114 | 59.4 | 1346 | 7.01 | 6 | 7 | —3.6 | |
| Tomczak | 170 | 86 | 50.6 | 1310 | 7.71 | 7 | 6 | —3.5 | |
| Harbaugh | 97 | 47 | 48.5 | 514 | 5.30 | 0 | 2 | —2.1 | |
| Wagner | 1 | 1 | 100.0 | 3 | 3.00 | 0 | 0 | —0.0 | |
| Anderson | 1 | 0 | 0.0 | 0 | 0.00 | 0 | 0 | —0.0 | |

**PUNTING**

| Last Name | No. | Avg. |
|---|---|---|
| Wagner | 79 | 41.5 |

**KICKING**

| Last Name | XP | ATT | % | FG | ATT | % |
|---|---|---|---|---|---|---|
| Butler | 37 | 38 | 97 | 15 | 19 | 79 |

## MINNESOTA VIKINGS

**RUSHING**

| Last Name | No. | Yds | Avg | TD |
|---|---|---|---|---|
| D. Nelson | 112 | 380 | 3.4 | 1 |
| Rice | 110 | 322 | 2.9 | 6 |
| Anderson | 87 | 300 | 3.4 | 7 |
| Fenney | 55 | 271 | 4.9 | 3 |
| Dozier | 42 | 167 | 4.0 | 2 |
| D. Harris | 34 | 151 | 4.4 | 1 |
| Wilson | 36 | 136 | 3.8 | 2 |
| Carter | 4 | 41 | 10.3 | 0 |
| Gannon | 4 | 29 | 7.3 | 0 |
| Kramer | 14 | 8 | 0.6 | 0 |
| Jones | 1 | 7 | 7.0 | 0 |
| Scribner | 1 | 0 | 0.0 | 0 |
| Mularkey | 1 | -6 | -6.0 | 0 |

**RECEIVING**

| Last Name | No. | Yds | Avg | TD |
|---|---|---|---|---|
| Carter | 72 | 1225 | 17.0 | 6 |
| Jordan | 57 | 756 | 13.3 | 5 |
| Jones | 40 | 778 | 19.5 | 5 |
| Rice | 30 | 279 | 9.3 | 0 |
| Anderson | 23 | 242 | 10.5 | 1 |
| D. Nelson | 16 | 105 | 6.6 | 0 |
| Gustafson | 15 | 231 | 15.4 | 1 |
| Fenney | 15 | 224 | 14.9 | 0 |
| Lewis | 11 | 141 | 12.8 | 1 |
| D. Harris | 6 | 30 | 5.0 | 0 |
| Dozier | 5 | 49 | 9.8 | 0 |
| Mularkey | 3 | 39 | 13.0 | 0 |
| Hilton | 1 | 1 | 1.0 | 1 |

**PUNT RETURNS**

| Last Name | No. | Yds | Avg | TD |
|---|---|---|---|---|
| Lewis | 58 | 550 | 9.5 | 0 |
| Carter | 1 | 3 | 3.0 | 0 |

**KICKOFF RETURNS**

| Last Name | No. | Yds | Avg | TD |
|---|---|---|---|---|
| D. Harris | 39 | 833 | 21.4 | 0 |
| D. Nelson | 9 | 210 | 23.3 | 0 |
| Dozier | 5 | 105 | 21.0 | 0 |
| Lewis | 1 | 12 | 12.0 | 0 |
| Rice | 1 | 0 | 0.0 | 0 |
| Carter | 1 | 0 | 0.0 | 0 |

**PASSING**

| Last Name | Att | Cmp | % | Yds | Yd/Att | TD | Int | % | RK |
|---|---|---|---|---|---|---|---|---|---|
| Wilson | 332 | 204 | 61.4 | 2746 | 8.27 | 15 | 9 | —2.7 | 1 |
| Kramer | 173 | 83 | 48.0 | 1264 | 7.31 | 5 | 9 | —5.2 | |
| Gannon | 15 | 7 | 46.7 | 90 | 6.00 | 0 | 0 | —0.0 | |

**PUNTING**

| Last Name | No. | Avg. |
|---|---|---|
| Scribner | 86 | 39.4 |

**KICKING**

| Last Name | XP | ATT | % | FG | ATT | % |
|---|---|---|---|---|---|---|
| Nelson | 48 | 49 | 98 | 20 | 25 | 80 |

## TAMPA BAY BUCCANEERS

**RUSHING**

| Last Name | No. | Yds | Avg | TD |
|---|---|---|---|---|
| Tate | 122 | 467 | 3.8 | 7 |
| W. Howard | 115 | 452 | 3.9 | 1 |
| Wilder | 86 | 343 | 4.0 | 1 |
| Goode | 62 | 231 | 3.7 | 0 |
| Testaverde | 28 | 138 | 4.9 | 1 |
| J. Smith | 20 | 87 | 4.4 | 0 |
| D. Smith | 13 | 46 | 3.5 | 1 |
| Criswell | 2 | 0 | 0.0 | 0 |
| Ferguson | 1 | 0 | 0.0 | 0 |
| Hill | 2 | -11 | -5.5 | 0 |

**RECEIVING**

| Last Name | No. | Yds | Avg | TD |
|---|---|---|---|---|
| Hill | 58 | 1040 | 17.9 | 9 |
| Carrier | 57 | 970 | 17.0 | 5 |
| Hall | 39 | 555 | 14.2 | 0 |
| J. Smith | 16 | 134 | 8.4 | 0 |
| Pillow | 15 | 206 | 13.7 | 1 |
| Wilder | 15 | 124 | 8.3 | 0 |
| D. Smith | 12 | 138 | 11.5 | 0 |
| W. Howard | 11 | 97 | 8.8 | 0 |
| Magee | 9 | 103 | 11.4 | 0 |
| Starring | 8 | 164 | 20.5 | 0 |
| Goode | 7 | 68 | 9.7 | 0 |
| G. Taylor | 5 | 53 | 10.6 | 0 |
| Tate | 5 | 23 | 4.6 | 1 |
| Parks | 1 | 22 | 22.0 | 0 |

**PUNT RETURNS**

| Last Name | No. | Yds | Avg | TD |
|---|---|---|---|---|
| Futrell | 27 | 283 | 10.5 | 0 |
| J. Smith | 8 | 45 | 5.6 | 0 |
| Elder | 1 | 0 | 0.0 | 0 |

**KICKOFF RETURNS**

| Last Name | No. | Yds | Avg | TD |
|---|---|---|---|---|
| Elder | 34 | 772 | 22.7 | 0 |
| J. Smith | 10 | 180 | 18.0 | 0 |
| D. Smith | 9 | 188 | 20.9 | 0 |
| Starring | 8 | 130 | 16.3 | 0 |
| Pillow | 3 | 38 | 12.7 | 0 |
| Futrell | 2 | 38 | 19.0 | 0 |
| Howard | 2 | 21 | 10.5 | 0 |

**PASSING**

| Last Name | Att | Cmp | % | Yds | Yd/Att | TD | Int | % | RK |
|---|---|---|---|---|---|---|---|---|---|
| Testaverde | 466 | 222 | 47.6 | 3240 | 6.95 | 13 | 35 | —7.5 | 14 |
| Ferguson | 46 | 31 | 67.4 | 368 | 8.00 | 3 | 1 | —2.2 | |

**PUNTING**

| Last Name | No. | Avg. |
|---|---|---|
| Criswell | 68 | 36.4 |

**KICKING**

| Last Name | XP | ATT | % | FG | ATT | % |
|---|---|---|---|---|---|---|
| Igwebuike | 21 | 21 | 100 | 19 | 25 | 76 |
| Carney | 6 | 6 | 100 | 2 | 5 | 40 |
| Criswell | 1 | 1 | 100 | 0 | 0 | 0 |

## DETROIT LIONS

**RUSHING**

| Last Name | No. | Yds | Avg | TD |
|---|---|---|---|---|
| James | 182 | 552 | 3.0 | 5 |
| Jones | 96 | 314 | 3.3 | 0 |
| Paige | 52 | 207 | 4.0 | 0 |
| Mandley | 6 | 44 | 7.3 | 1 |
| Painter | 17 | 42 | 2.5 | 0 |
| Hilger | 18 | 27 | 1.5 | 0 |
| Long | 7 | 22 | 3.1 | 0 |
| S. Williams | 9 | 22 | 2.4 | 1 |
| Hipple | 1 | 5 | 5.0 | 0 |
| Woolfolk | 1 | 4 | 4.0 | 0 |
| Bland | 1 | 4 | 4.0 | 0 |
| Witkowski | 1 | 0 | 0.0 | 0 |

**RECEIVING**

| Last Name | No. | Yds | Avg | TD |
|---|---|---|---|---|
| Mandley | 44 | 617 | 14.0 | 4 |
| James | 39 | 382 | 9.8 | 2 |
| Jones | 29 | 259 | 8.9 | 0 |
| Lee | 22 | 261 | 11.9 | 1 |
| Bland | 21 | 307 | 14.6 | 2 |
| Chadwick | 20 | 304 | 15.2 | 3 |
| Carter | 13 | 145 | 11.2 | 0 |
| Paige | 11 | 100 | 9.1 | 0 |
| S. Williams | 3 | 46 | 15.3 | 0 |
| Lewis | 3 | 32 | 10.7 | 1 |
| Craig | 2 | 29 | 14.5 | 0 |
| Painter | 1 | 1 | 1.0 | 0 |

**PUNT RETURNS**

| Last Name | No. | Yds | Avg | TD |
|---|---|---|---|---|
| Mandley | 37 | 287 | 7.8 | 0 |
| Bland | 5 | 59 | 11.8 | 0 |

**KICKOFF RETURNS**

| Last Name | No. | Yds | Avg | TD |
|---|---|---|---|---|
| Lee | 18 | 355 | 19.7 | 0 |
| Painter | 17 | 347 | 20.4 | 0 |
| Bland | 8 | 179 | 22.4 | 0 |
| Woolfolk | 4 | 99 | 24.8 | 0 |
| Andolsek | 1 | 3 | 3.0 | 0 |
| Saleaumua | 1 | 0 | 0.0 | 0 |

**PASSING**

| Last Name | Att | Cmp | % | Yds | Yd/Att | TD | Int | % | RK |
|---|---|---|---|---|---|---|---|---|---|
| Hilger | 306 | 126 | 41.2 | 1558 | 5.09 | 7 | 12 | —3.9 | 13 |
| Long | 141 | 75 | 53.2 | 856 | 6.07 | 6 | 6 | —4.3 | |
| Hipple | 27 | 12 | 44.4 | 158 | 5.85 | 0 | 0 | —0.0 | |
| Arnold | 1 | 0 | 0.0 | 0 | 0.00 | 0 | 0 | —0.0 | |
| Witkowski | 1 | 0 | 0.0 | 0 | 0.00 | 0 | 0 | —0.0 | |
| Jones | 1 | 0 | 0.0 | 0 | 0.00 | 0 | 0 | —0.0 | |

**PUNTING**

| Last Name | No. | Avg. |
|---|---|---|
| Arnold | 97 | 42.4 |

**KICKING**

| Last Name | XP | ATT | % | FG | ATT | % |
|---|---|---|---|---|---|---|
| Murray | 22 | 23 | 96 | 20 | 21 | 95 |

## GREEN BAY PACKERS

**RUSHING**

| Last Name | No. | Yds | Avg | TD |
|---|---|---|---|---|
| Fullwood | 101 | 483 | 4.8 | 7 |
| Majkowski | 47 | 225 | 4.8 | 1 |
| Woodside | 83 | 195 | 2.3 | 3 |
| Mason | 48 | 194 | 4.0 | 0 |
| Davis | 39 | 121 | 3.1 | 1 |
| Carruth | 49 | 114 | 2.3 | 0 |
| Wright | 8 | 43 | 5.4 | 2 |
| Matthews | 3 | 3 | 1.0 | 0 |
| Collins | 2 | 2 | 1.0 | 0 |
| Stanley | 1 | 1 | 1.0 | 0 |
| Sharpe | 4 | -2 | -0.5 | 0 |

**RECEIVING**

| Last Name | No. | Yds | Avg | TD |
|---|---|---|---|---|
| Sharpe | 55 | 791 | 14.4 | 1 |
| Kemp | 48 | 620 | 12.9 | 0 |
| Woodside | 39 | 352 | 9.0 | 2 |
| West | 30 | 276 | 9.2 | 3 |
| Stanley | 28 | 436 | 15.6 | 0 |
| Carruth | 24 | 211 | 8.8 | 0 |
| Scott | 20 | 275 | 13.8 | 1 |
| Fullwood | 20 | 128 | 6.4 | 1 |
| matthews | 15 | 167 | 11.1 | 2 |
| Epps | 11 | 99 | 9.0 | 0 |
| Davis | 11 | 81 | 7.4 | 0 |
| Mason | 8 | 84 | 10.5 | 1 |
| Didier | 5 | 37 | 7.4 | 1 |
| Bolton | 2 | 33 | 16.5 | 0 |
| Collins | 2 | 17 | 8.5 | 0 |
| Hackett | 1 | 2 | 2.0 | 1 |

**PUNT RETURNS**

| Last Name | No. | Yds | Avg | TD |
|---|---|---|---|---|
| Pitts | 9 | 93 | 10.3 | 1 |
| Sharpe | 9 | 48 | 5.3 | 0 |
| Stanley | 12 | 52 | 4.3 | 0 |
| Jefferson | 5 | 15 | 3.0 | 0 |

**KICKOFF RETURNS**

| Last Name | No. | Yds | Avg | TD |
|---|---|---|---|---|
| Fullwood | 21 | 421 | 20.0 | 0 |
| Woodside | 19 | 343 | 18.1 | 0 |
| Scott | 12 | 207 | 17.3 | 0 |
| Jefferson | 4 | 116 | 29.0 | 0 |
| Stanley | 2 | 39 | 19.5 | 0 |
| Pitts | 1 | 17 | 17.0 | 0 |
| Sharpe | 1 | 17 | 17.0 | 0 |
| Hackett | 1 | 9 | 9.0 | 0 |
| Winter | 1 | 7 | 7.0 | 0 |
| Stills | 1 | 4 | 4.0 | 0 |
| Hill | 1 | 1 | 1.0 | 0 |

**PASSING**

| Last Name | Att | Cmp | % | Yds | Yd/Att | TD | Int | % | RK |
|---|---|---|---|---|---|---|---|---|---|
| Majkowski | 336 | 178 | 53.0 | 2119 | 6.31 | 9 | 11 | —3.3 | 10 |
| Wright | 244 | 141 | 57.8 | 1490 | 6.11 | 4 | 13 | —5.3 | 12 |
| Carruth | 2 | 0 | 0.0 | 0 | 0.00 | 0 | 0 | — 0 | |

**PUNTING**

| Last Name | No. | Avg. |
|---|---|---|
| Bracken | 86 | 38.2 |

**KICKING**

| Last Name | XP | ATT | % | FG | ATT | % |
|---|---|---|---|---|---|---|
| Zendejas | 17 | 19 | 89 | 9 | 16 | 56 |
| Dawson | 4 | 5 | 80 | 6 | | 50 |
| Burrow | 2 | 4 | 50 | 0 | 1 | 0 |

## SAN FRANCISCO 49ERS 10-6 Bill Walsh

| Scores of Each Game | | |
|---|---|---|
| 34 | New Orleans | 33 |
| 20 | N.Y. Giants | 17 |
| 17 | ATLANTA | 34 |
| 38 | Seattle | 7 |
| 20 | DETROIT | 13 |
| 13 | DENVER | * 16 |
| 24 | L.A. Rams | 21 |
| 9 | Chicago | 10 |
| 24 | MINNESOTA | 21 |
| 23 | Phoenix | 24 |
| 3 | L.A. RAIDERS | 9 |
| 37 | WASHINGTON | 21 |
| 48 | San Diego | 10 |
| 13 | Atlanta | 3 |
| 30 | NEW ORLEANS | 17 |
| 16 | L.A. RAMS | 38 |

| Use Name | Pos. | Hgt | Wgt | Age | Int | Pts |
|---|---|---|---|---|---|---|
| Harris Barton | OT | 6'4" | 280 | 24 | | |
| Bubba Paris | OT | 6'6" | 306 | 27 | | |
| Steve Wallace | OT | 6'5" | 276 | 23 | | |
| Jeff Bregel | OG | 6'4" | 280 | 24 | | |
| Bruce Collie | OG-OT | 6'6" | 275 | 26 | | |
| Guy McIntyre | OG | 6'3" | 265 | 27 | | 6 |
| Jesse Sapolu | OG-C | 6'4" | 260 | 27 | | |
| Randy Cross | C | 6'3" | 265 | 34 | | |
| Chuck Thomas | C | 6'3" | 280 | 27 | | |
| Kevin Fagan | DE | 6'4" | 265 | 25 | | |
| Pierce Holt | DE | 6'4" | 280 | 26 | | |
| Pete Kugler | DE | 6'4" | 255 | 29 | | |
| Larry Roberts | DE | 6'3" | 275 | 25 | | |
| Jeff Stover | DE | 6'5" | 275 | 30 | | |
| Danny Stubbs | DE | 6'4" | 260 | 23 | | |
| Kevin Lilly | NT-DE | 6'4" | 265 | 25 | | |
| Michael Carter | NT-DT | 6'2" | 285 | 27 | 1 | |

Mark Cochran — Knee Injury

| Use Name | Pos. | Hgt | Wgt | Age | Int | Pts |
|---|---|---|---|---|---|---|
| Riki Ellison | LB | 6'2" | 225 | 28 | | |
| Jim Fahnhorst | LB | 6'4" | 230 | 29 | | |
| Ron Hadley | LB | 6'2" | 240 | 24 | | |
| Charles Haley | LB-DE | 6'5" | 230 | 24 | | 2 |
| Sam Kennedy | LB | 6'3" | 235 | 24 | | |
| Bill Romanowski | LB | 6'4" | 231 | 22 | | |
| Keena Turner | LB | 6'2" | 222 | 29 | 1 | |
| Michael Walter | LB | 6'3" | 238 | 27 | | |
| Chet Brooks | DB | 5'11" | 191 | 22 | | |
| Greg Cox | DB | 6' | 223 | 23 | | |
| Jeff Fuller | DB | 6'2" | 216 | 26 | 4 | |
| Don Griffin | DB | 6' | 176 | 24 | | |
| Tom Holmoe | DB | 6'2" | 195 | 28 | 2 | |
| Ronnie Lott | DB | 6' | 200 | 29 | 5 | |
| Tim McKyer | DB | 6' | 174 | 24 | 7 | |
| Tory Nixon | DB | 5'11" | 186 | 26 | | |
| Darryl Pollard | DB | 5'11" | 187 | 23 | | |
| Eric Wright | DB | 6'1" | 185 | 29 | 2 | |

Todd Shell — Neck Injury
Carlton Williamson — Knee Injury

| Use Name | Pos. | Hgt | Wgt | Age | Int | Pts |
|---|---|---|---|---|---|---|
| Joe Montana | QB | 6'2" | 195 | 32 | | 18 |
| John Paye | QB | 6'3" | 205 | 23 | | |
| Todd Santos | QB | 6'2" | 207 | 24 | | |
| Steve Young | QB | 6'2" | 200 | 26 | | 6 |
| Roger Craig | HB | 6' | 224 | 28 | | 60 |
| Doug DuBose | HB | 5'11" | 190 | 24 | | 12 |
| Terrence Flagler | HB | 6' | 200 | 23 | | |
| Del Rodgers | HB | 5'10" | 203 | 28 | | |
| Steve Bartalo | FB | 5'9" | 200 | 24 | | |
| Tom Rathman | FB | 6'1" | 232 | 25 | | 12 |
| Harry Sydney | FB | 6' | 217 | 29 | | |
| Wes Chandler | WR | 6' | 188 | 32 | | |
| Terry Greer | WR | 6'1" | 192 | 30 | | |
| Calvin Nicholas | WR | 6'4" | 208 | 24 | | |
| Jerry Rice | WR | 6'2" | 200 | 25 | | 60 |
| John Taylor | WR | 6'1" | 185 | 26 | | 24 |
| Mike Wilson | WR-HB | 6'3" | 215 | 28 | | 18 |
| John Frank | TE | 6'3" | 225 | 26 | | 18 |
| Ron Heller | TE | 6'3" | 235 | 24 | | |
| Brent Jones | TE | 6'4" | 230 | 25 | | 12 |
| Mike Cofer | K | 6'1" | 190 | 24 | | 121 |
| Barry Helton | K | 6'3" | 205 | 23 | | |

Mike Sherrard — Broken Leg

## LOS ANGELES RAMS 10-6 John Robinson

| Scores of Each Game | | |
|---|---|---|
| 34 | Green Bay | 7 |
| 17 | DETROIT | 10 |
| 22 | L.A. Raiders | 17 |
| 45 | N.Y. Giants | 31 |
| 27 | PHOENIX | 41 |
| 33 | Atlanta | 0 |
| 21 | SAN FRANCISCO | 24 |
| 31 | SEATTLE | 10 |
| 12 | New Orleans | 10 |
| 24 | Philadelphia | 30 |
| 10 | NEW ORLEANS | 14 |
| 24 | SAN DIEGO | 38 |
| 24 | Denver | 35 |
| 23 | CHICAGO | 3 |
| 22 | ATLANTA | 7 |
| 38 | San Francisco | 16 |

| Use Name | Pos. | Hgt | Wgt | Age | Int | Pts |
|---|---|---|---|---|---|---|
| Robert Cox | OT | 6'5" | 270 | 24 | | |
| Irv Pankey | OT | 6'4" | 267 | 30 | | |
| Jackie Slater | OT | 6'4" | 275 | 34 | | |
| Duval Love | OG | 6'3" | 280 | 25 | | |
| Tom Newberry | OG | 6'2" | 279 | 25 | | |
| Mike Schad | OG | 6'5" | 290 | 24 | | |
| Tony Slaton | OG-C | 6'3" | 265 | 27 | | |
| Doug Smith | C | 6'3" | 260 | 31 | | |
| Gary Jeter | DE | 6'4" | 260 | 33 | | |
| Shawn Miller | DE-NT | 6'4" | 255 | 27 | | |
| Doug Reed | DE | 6'3" | 250 | 28 | | |
| Fred Stokes | DE | 6'3" | 265 | 24 | | |
| Greg Meisner | NT | 6'3" | 265 | 29 | 1 | |
| Alvin Wright | NT | 6'2" | 256 | 27 | | |

| Use Name | Pos. | Hgt | Wgt | Age | Int | Pts |
|---|---|---|---|---|---|---|
| Jim Collins | LB | 6'2" | 233 | 30 | | |
| Carl Ekern | LB | 6'3" | 222 | 34 | | |
| Brett Faryniarz | LB | 6'3" | 225 | 23 | | |
| Kevin Greene | LB | 6'3" | 238 | 26 | 1 | 2 |
| Mark Jerue | LB | 6'3" | 234 | 28 | 1 | |
| Larry Kelm | LB | 6'4" | 226 | 23 | 2 | |
| Mike McDonald | LB | 6'1" | 235 | 30 | | |
| Mel Owens | LB | 6'2" | 224 | 29 | 1 | |
| Fred Strickland | LB | 6'2" | 224 | 22 | | |
| Mike Wilcher | LB | 6'3" | 240 | 28 | | |
| Jerry Gray | DB | 6' | 185 | 25 | 3 | 6 |
| Clifford Hicks | DB | 5'10" | 188 | 24 | | |
| LeRoy Irvin | DB | 5'11" | 184 | 30 | 3 | |
| Johnnie Johnson | DB | 6'1" | 183 | 31 | 4 | |
| Anthony Newman | DB | 6' | 199 | 22 | 2 | |
| Vince Newsome | DB | 6'1" | 183 | 27 | | |
| Michael Stewart | DB | 5'11" | 195 | 23 | 2 | |
| Mickey Sutton | DB | 5'8" | 165 | 28 | 1 | |
| James Washington | DB | 6'1" | 191 | 23 | 1 | |
| Frank Wattelet | DB | 6' | 190 | 29 | | |

| Use Name | Pos. | Hgt | Wgt | Age | Int | Pts |
|---|---|---|---|---|---|---|
| Jim Everett | QB | 6'5" | 212 | 25 | | |
| Mark Herrmann | QB | 6'4" | 186 | 29 | | |
| Greg Bell | HB | 5'10" | 210 | 26 | | 108 |
| Gaston Green | HB | 5'10" | 189 | 22 | | |
| Charles White | HB | 5'10" | 193 | 30 | | |
| Robert Delpino | FB | 6' | 205 | 22 | | 12 |
| Mike Guman | FB | 6'2" | 216 | 30 | | |
| Buford McGee | FB | 6' | 206 | 28 | | 18 |
| Tim Tyrrell | FB | 6'1" | 206 | 27 | | |
| Willie Anderson | WR | 6' | 169 | 23 | | |
| Ron Brown | WR | 5'11" | 181 | 27 | | |
| Aaron Cox | WR | 5'9" | 174 | 23 | | 30 |
| Henry Ellard | WR | 5'11" | 175 | 27 | | 60 |
| Michael Young | WR | 6'1" | 183 | 26 | | |
| Jon Embree | TE | 6'2" | 237 | 23 | | |
| Pete Holohan | TE | 6'4" | 232 | 29 | | 18 |
| Damone Johnson | TE | 6'4" | 230 | 26 | | 36 |
| Rich Camarillo | K | 5'11" | 185 | 28 | | |
| Dale Hatcher | K | 6'2" | 211 | 25 | | |
| Mike Lansford | K | 6' | 183 | 30 | | 117 |

## NEW ORLEANS SAINTS 10-6 Jim Mora

| Scores of Each Game | | |
|---|---|---|
| 33 | SAN FRANCISCO | 34 |
| 29 | Atlanta | 21 |
| 22 | Detroit | 14 |
| 13 | TAMPA BAY | 9 |
| 20 | DALLAS | 17 |
| 23 | San Diego | 17 |
| 20 | Seattle | 19 |
| 20 | L.A. RAIDERS | 6 |
| 10 | L.A. RAMS | 12 |
| 24 | Washington | 27 |
| 14 | L.A. Rams | 10 |
| 42 | DENVER | 0 |
| 12 | N.Y. GIANTS | 13 |
| 3 | Minnesota | 45 |
| 17 | San Francisco | 30 |
| 10 | ATLANTA | 9 |

| Use Name | Pos. | Hgt | Wgt | Age | Int | Pts |
|---|---|---|---|---|---|---|
| Stan Brock | OT | 6'6" | 290 | 30 | | |
| Bill Contz | OT | 6'5" | 280 | 27 | | |
| Jim Dombrowski | OT | 6'5" | 298 | 25 | | |
| Daren Gilbert | OT | 6'6" | 280 | 24 | | |
| Jeff Walker | OT | 6'4" | 295 | 25 | | |
| Chuck Commiskey | OG | 6'4" | 290 | 30 | | |
| Brad Edelman | OG | 6'6" | 270 | 27 | | |
| Joel Hilgenberg | OG-C | 6'3" | 252 | 26 | | |
| Steve Trapilo | OG | 6'5" | 295 | 23 | | |
| James Campen | C-OG | 6'3" | 260 | 24 | | |
| Steve Korte | C | 6'2" | 260 | 28 | | |
| Dwaine Board (from SF) | DE | 6'5" | 248 | 31 | | |
| Bruce Clark | DE | 6'3" | 275 | 30 | | |
| James Geathers | DE | 6'7" | 290 | 28 | | |
| Frank Warren | DE | 6'4" | 290 | 28 | | |
| Jim Wilks | DE | 6'5" | 266 | 30 | | |
| Tony Elliott | NT | 6'2" | 295 | 29 | | |
| Ted Gregory | NT | 6'1" | 260 | 23 | | |

| Use Name | Pos. | Hgt | Wgt | Age | Int | Pts |
|---|---|---|---|---|---|---|
| Brian Forde | LB | 6'2" | 225 | 24 | | |
| James Haynes | LB | 6'2" | 233 | 28 | | |
| Rickey Jackson | LB | 6'2" | 243 | 30 | 1 | 2 |
| Vaughan Johnson | LB | 6'3" | 235 | 26 | 1 | |
| Joe Kohlbrand | LB | 6'4" | 242 | 25 | | |
| Sam Mills | LB | 5'9" | 225 | 29 | | |
| Pat Swilling | LB | 6'3" | 242 | 23 | | |
| Alvin Toles | LB | 6'1" | 227 | 25 | | |
| Michael Adams | DB | 5'10" | 195 | 24 | | |
| Gene Atkins | DB | 6'1" | 200 | 24 | 4 | |
| Toi Cook | DB | 5'11" | 188 | 23 | 1 | |
| Antonio Gibson | DB | 6'3" | 204 | 26 | | |
| Van Jakes | DB | 6' | 190 | 27 | 3 | |
| Milton Mack | DB | 5'11" | 182 | 24 | 1 | |
| Brett Maxie | DB | 6'2" | 194 | 26 | | |
| Reggie Sutton | DB | 5'10" | 180 | 23 | 3 | |
| Dave Waymer | DB | 6'1" | 188 | 30 | 3 | 6 |

| Use Name | Pos. | Hgt | Wgt | Age | Int | Pts |
|---|---|---|---|---|---|---|
| John Fourcade | QB | 6'1" | 208 | 27 | | |
| Bobby Hebert | QB | 6'4" | 215 | 28 | | |
| Dave Wilson | QB | 6'3" | 206 | 29 | | |
| Mel Gray | HB | 5'9" | 166 | 27 | | 6 |
| Dalton Hilliard | HB | 5'8" | 204 | 24 | | 36 |
| Rueben Mayes | HB | 5'11" | 200 | 25 | | 18 |
| Craig Heyward | FB | 5'11" | 251 | 21 | | 6 |
| Buford Jordan | FB | 6' | 223 | 26 | | 6 |
| Barry Word | FB | 6'2" | 220 | 24 | | |
| Robert Clark | WR | 5'11" | 175 | 23 | | 12 |
| Lonzell Hill | WR | 6' | 189 | 22 | | 42 |
| Eric Martin | WR | 6'1" | 207 | 26 | | 42 |
| Mark Pattison | WR | 6'2" | 198 | 26 | | |
| Brett Perriman | WR | 5'9" | 175 | 22 | | 12 |
| Cliff Benson | TE | 6'4" | 240 | 27 | | |
| Hoby Brenner | TE | 6'4" | 240 | 29 | | |
| Greg Scales | TE | 6'4" | 253 | 22 | | 6 |
| John Tice | TE | 6'5" | 249 | 28 | | 6 |
| Morten Andersen | K | 6'2" | 221 | 28 | | 110 |
| Brian Hansen | K | 6'3" | 209 | 27 | | |

Mike Waters — Back Injury

## ATLANTA FALCONS 5-11 Marion Campbell

| Scores of Each Game | | |
|---|---|---|
| 17 | Detroit | 31 |
| 21 | NEW ORLEANS | 29 |
| 34 | San Francisco | 17 |
| 20 | Dallas | 26 |
| 20 | SEATTLE | 31 |
| 0 | L.A. RAMS | 33 |
| 14 | Denver | 30 |
| 16 | N.Y. GIANTS | 23 |
| 27 | Philadelphia | 24 |
| 20 | GREEN BAY | 0 |
| 7 | SAN DIEGO | 10 |
| 12 | L.A. Raiders | 6 |
| 17 | TAMPA BAY | 10 |
| 3 | SAN FRANCISCO | 13 |
| 7 | L.A. Rams | 22 |
| 9 | New Orleans | 10 |

| Use Name | Pos. | Hgt | Wgt | Age | Int | Pts |
|---|---|---|---|---|---|---|
| Stan Clayton | OT-OG | 6'3" | 265 | 23 | | |
| Houston Hoover | OT | 6'2" | 285 | 23 | | |
| Mike Kenn | OT | 6'7" | 277 | 32 | | |
| Brett Miller | OT | 6'7" | 300 | 29 | | |
| Jamie Dukes | OG | 6'1" | 278 | 24 | | |
| Bill Fralic | OG | 6'5" | 280 | 25 | | |
| Paul Oswald (from DAL) | OG | 6'3" | 275 | 24 | | |
| John Scully | OG | 6'6" | 270 | 30 | | |
| Wayne Radloff | C | 6'5" | 277 | 27 | | |
| George Yarno | C-OG | 6'2" | 265 | 31 | | |
| Greg Brown | DE | 6'5" | 265 | 31 | | |
| Rick Bryan | DE | 6'4" | 265 | 26 | | |
| Reggie Camp | DE | 6'4" | 280 | 27 | | |
| Mike Gann | DE | 6'5" | 275 | 24 | | 6 |
| Mitch Willis (from RAID) | NT | 6'8" | 280 | 26 | | |
| Tony Casillas | NT | 6'3" | 280 | 24 | | |
| Charles Martin | NT | 6'4" | 280 | 29 | | |

| Use Name | Pos. | Hgt | Wgt | Age | Int | Pts |
|---|---|---|---|---|---|---|
| Aundray Bruce | LB | 6'5" | 245 | 22 | 2 | |
| Joe Costello | LB | 6'3" | 244 | 28 | | |
| Marcus Cotton | LB | 6'3" | 225 | 22 | | |
| Tim Green | LB | 6'2" | 245 | 24 | | |
| John Rade | LB | 6'1" | 240 | 28 | | |
| Michael Reid | LB | 6'2" | 226 | 24 | | |
| Jessie Tuggle | LB | 5'11" | 225 | 23 | | 6 |
| Joel Williams | LB | 6'1" | 227 | 31 | | |
| Vinson Smith | DB | 6' | 219 | 23 | | |
| Bobby Butler | DB | 5'11" | 175 | 29 | 1 | |
| Scott Case | DB | 6' | 178 | 26 | 10 | |
| Bret Clark | DB | 6'3" | 198 | 27 | 4 | |
| Evan Cooper | DB | 5'11" | 194 | 26 | | |
| David Croudip | DB | 5'8" | 183 | 29 | | |
| Charles Dimry | DB | 6' | 175 | 22 | | |
| Tim Gordon | DB | 6' | 188 | 23 | 2 | |
| Leander Knight | DB | 6'1" | 193 | 25 | | |
| Robert Moore | DB | 5'11" | 190 | 24 | 5 | 6 |
| Elbert Shelley | DB | 5'11" | 180 | 23 | | |

| Use Name | Pos. | Hgt | Wgt | Age | Int | Pts |
|---|---|---|---|---|---|---|
| Kerwin Bell | QB | 6'2" | 205 | 23 | | |
| Steve Dils | QB | 6'1" | 191 | 32 | | 6 |
| Hugh Millen | QB | 6'5" | 216 | 24 | | |
| Chris Miller | QB | 6'2" | 195 | 23 | | 6 |
| Gene Lang | HB | 5'10" | 206 | 26 | | 6 |
| James Primus | HB | 5'11" | 196 | 24 | | 6 |
| John Settle | HB-FB | 5'9" | 207 | 23 | | 48 |
| Sylvester Stamps | HB-WR | 5'7" | 171 | 27 | | |
| Rick Badanjek | FB-HB | 5'8" | 217 | 26 | | |
| Gerald Riggs | FB-HB | 6'1" | 232 | 27 | | 6 |
| Stacey Bailey | WR | 6' | 157 | 28 | | 12 |
| Lew Barnes | WR | 5'8" | 163 | 25 | | |
| Floyd Dixon | WR | 5'9" | 170 | 24 | | 12 |
| Michael Haynes | WR | 6' | 180 | 22 | | 24 |
| Jessie Hester | WR | 5'11" | 170 | 25 | | |
| James Milling | WR | 5'9" | 156 | 23 | | |
| Alex Higdon | TE | 6'5" | 247 | 21 | | 12 |
| Danzell Lee | TE | 6'2" | 237 | 25 | | |
| Ken Whisenhunt | TE | 6'3" | 240 | 26 | | 6 |
| Gary Wilkins | TE | 6' | 235 | 24 | | |
| Greg Davis | K | 5'11" | 197 | 22 | | 82 |
| Rick Donnelly | K | 6' | 190 | 26 | | |

Scott Campbell — Knee Injury
Kenny Flowers — Knee Injury

## SAN FRANCISCO 49ERS

### RUSHING

| Last Name | No. | Yds | Avg | TD |
|---|---|---|---|---|
| Craig | 310 | 1502 | 4.8 | 9 |
| Rathman | 102 | 427 | 4.2 | 2 |
| Young | 27 | 184 | 6.8 | 1 |
| Montana | 38 | 132 | 3.5 | 3 |
| DuBose | 24 | 116 | 4.8 | 2 |
| Rice | 13 | 107 | 8.2 | 1 |
| Sydney | 9 | 50 | 5.6 | 0 |
| Flagler | 3 | 5 | 1.7 | 0 |
| Helton | 1 | 0 | 0.0 | 0 |

### RECEIVING

| Last Name | No. | Yds | Avg | TD |
|---|---|---|---|---|
| Craig | 76 | 534 | 7.0 | 1 |
| Rice | 64 | 1306 | 20.4 | 9 |
| Rathman | 42 | 382 | 9.1 | 0 |
| Wilson | 33 | 405 | 12.3 | 3 |
| Frank | 16 | 195 | 12.2 | 3 |
| Taylor | 14 | 325 | 23.2 | 2 |
| Heller | 14 | 140 | 10.0 | 0 |
| Greer | 8 | 120 | 15.0 | 0 |
| Jones | 8 | 57 | 7.1 | 2 |
| DuBose | 6 | 57 | 9.5 | 0 |
| Flagler | 4 | 72 | 18.0 | 0 |
| Chandler | 4 | 33 | 8.3 | 0 |
| Sydney | 2 | 18 | 9.0 | 0 |
| McIntyre | 1 | 17 | 17.0 | 1 |
| Nicholas | 1 | 14 | 14.0 | 0 |

### PUNT RETURNS

| Last Name | No. | Yds | Avg | TD |
|---|---|---|---|---|
| Taylor | 44 | 556 | 12.6 | 2 |
| Chandler | 6 | 28 | 4.7 | 0 |
| Griffin | 4 | 28 | 7.0 | 0 |

### KICKOFF RETURNS

| Last Name | No. | Yds | Avg | TD |
|---|---|---|---|---|
| DuBose | 32 | 608 | 19.0 | 0 |
| Taylor | 12 | 225 | 18.8 | 0 |
| Rodgers | 6 | 98 | 16.3 | 0 |
| Craig | 2 | 32 | 16.0 | 0 |
| Sydney | 1 | 8 | 8.0 | 0 |
| Thomas | 1 | 5 | 5.0 | 0 |
| Wilson | 1 | 2 | 2.0 | 0 |

### PASSING — PUNTING — KICKING Statistics

| PASSING | Att | Cmp | % | Yds | Yd/Att | TD | Int | — | % | RK |
|---|---|---|---|---|---|---|---|---|---|---|
| Montana | 397 | 238 | 59.9 | 2981 | 7.51 | 18 | 10 | — | 2.5 | 3 |
| Young | 101 | 54 | 53.5 | 680 | 6.73 | 3 | 3 | — | 3.0 | |
| Rice | 3 | 1 | 33.3 | 14 | 4.67 | 0 | 1 | — | 33.3 | |
| Sydney | 1 | 0 | 0.0 | 0 | 0.00 | 0 | 0 | — | 0.0 | |

| PUNTING | No. | Avg. |
|---|---|---|
| Helton | 79 | 38.8 |

| KICKING | XP | ATT | % | FG | ATT | % |
|---|---|---|---|---|---|---|
| Cofer | 40 | 41 | 98 | 27 | 38 | 71 |

## LOS ANGELES RAMS

### RUSHING

| Last Name | No. | Yds | Avg | TD |
|---|---|---|---|---|
| Bell | 288 | 1212 | 4.2 | 16 |
| White | 88 | 323 | 3.7 | 0 |
| Delpino | 34 | 147 | 4.3 | 0 |
| Green | 35 | 117 | 3.3 | 0 |
| Everett | 34 | 105 | 3.1 | 0 |
| McGee | 22 | 69 | 3.1 | 0 |
| Brown | 3 | 24 | 8.0 | 0 |
| Ellard | 1 | 7 | 7.0 | 0 |
| Guman | 1 | 1 | 1.0 | 0 |
| Herrmann | 1 | -1 | -1.0 | 0 |

### RECEIVING

| Last Name | No. | Yds | Avg | TD |
|---|---|---|---|---|
| Ellard | 86 | 1414 | 16.4 | 10 |
| Holohan | 59 | 640 | 11.1 | 3 |
| D. Johnson | 42 | 350 | 8.3 | 6 |
| Delpino | 30 | 312 | 10.4 | 2 |
| Cox | 28 | 590 | 21.1 | 5 |
| Bell | 24 | 124 | 5.2 | 2 |
| McGee | 16 | 117 | 7.3 | 3 |
| Anderson | 11 | 319 | 29.0 | 0 |
| Green | 6 | 57 | 9.5 | 0 |
| White | 6 | 36 | 6.0 | 0 |
| Young | 2 | 27 | 13.5 | 0 |
| Brown | 2 | 16 | 8.0 | 0 |

### PUNT RETURNS

| Last Name | No. | Yds | Avg | TD |
|---|---|---|---|---|
| Hicks | 25 | 144 | 5.8 | 0 |
| Ellard | 17 | 119 | 7.0 | 0 |
| Sutton | 3 | 52 | 17.3 | 0 |
| J. Johnson | 2 | 4 | 2.0 | 0 |
| Irvin | 1 | 2 | 2.0 | 0 |
| Gray | 1 | 1 | 1.0 | 0 |

### KICKOFF RETURNS

| Last Name | No. | Yds | Avg | TD |
|---|---|---|---|---|
| Brown | 19 | 401 | 21.1 | 0 |
| Delpino | 14 | 333 | 23.8 | 0 |
| Green | 17 | 345 | 20.3 | 0 |
| Sutton | 2 | 41 | 20.5 | 0 |
| White | 2 | 38 | 18.5 | 0 |
| McDonald | 3 | 34 | 11.3 | 0 |
| McGee | 1 | 0 | 0.0 | 0 |
| Stewart | 1 | 0 | 0.0 | 0 |

### PASSING — PUNTING — KICKING

| PASSING | Att | Cmp | % | Yds | Yd/Att | TD | Int | — | % | RK |
|---|---|---|---|---|---|---|---|---|---|---|
| Everett | 517 | 308 | 59.6 | 3964 | 7.66 | 31 | 18 | — | 3.5 | 2 |
| Herrmann | 5 | 4 | 80.0 | 38 | 7.60 | 0 | 0 | — | 0.0 | |

| PUNTING | No. | Avg. |
|---|---|---|
| Hatcher | 36 | 39.6 |
| Camarillo | 40 | 39.5 |

| KICKING | XP | ATT | % | FG | ATT | % |
|---|---|---|---|---|---|---|
| Lansford | 45 | 48 | 94 | 24 | 32 | 75 |

## NEW ORLEANS SAINTS

### RUSHING

| Last Name | No. | Yds | Avg | TD |
|---|---|---|---|---|
| Hilliard | 204 | 823 | 4.0 | 5 |
| Mayes | 170 | 628 | 3.7 | 3 |
| Heyward | 74 | 355 | 4.8 | 1 |
| Jordan | 19 | 115 | 6.1 | 0 |
| Hebert | 37 | 79 | 2.1 | 0 |
| Perriman | 3 | 17 | 5.7 | 0 |
| Martin | 2 | 12 | 6.0 | 0 |
| Hansen | 1 | 10 | 10.0 | 0 |
| Hill | 2 | 7 | 3.5 | 0 |

### RECEIVING

| Last Name | No. | Yds | Avg | TD |
|---|---|---|---|---|
| Martin | 85 | 1083 | 12.7 | 7 |
| Hill | 66 | 703 | 10.7 | 7 |
| Hilliard | 34 | 335 | 9.9 | 1 |
| Tice | 26 | 297 | 11.4 | 1 |
| Clark | 19 | 245 | 12.9 | 2 |
| Perriman | 16 | 215 | 13.4 | 2 |
| Heyward | 13 | 105 | 8.1 | 0 |
| Mayes | 11 | 103 | 9.4 | 0 |
| Jordan | 5 | 70 | 14.0 | 0 |
| Brenner | 5 | 67 | 13.4 | 0 |
| Scales | 2 | 20 | 10.0 | 1 |
| Hebert | 2 | 0 | 0.0 | 0 |
| Pattison | 1 | 8 | 8.0 | 0 |
| Benson | 1 | 5 | 5.0 | 0 |

### PUNT RETURNS

| Last Name | No. | Yds | Avg | TD |
|---|---|---|---|---|
| Gray | 25 | 305 | 12.2 | 1 |
| Hill | 10 | 108 | 10.8 | 0 |

### KICKOFF RETURNS

| Last Name | No. | Yds | Avg | TD |
|---|---|---|---|---|
| Atkins | 20 | 424 | 21.2 | 0 |
| Gray | 32 | 670 | 20.9 | 0 |
| Mayes | 7 | 132 | 18.9 | 0 |
| Hilliard | 6 | 111 | 18.5 | 0 |
| Martin | 3 | 32 | 10.7 | 0 |
| Waymer | 2 | 39 | 19.5 | 0 |

### PASSING — PUNTING — KICKING

| PASSING | Att | Cmp | % | Yds | Yd/Att | TD | Int | — | % | RK |
|---|---|---|---|---|---|---|---|---|---|---|
| Hebert | 478 | 280 | 58.6 | 3156 | 6.60 | 20 | 15 | — | 3.1 | 6 |
| Wilson | 16 | 5 | 31.3 | 73 | 4.56 | 0 | 1 | — | 6.3 | |
| Hilliard | 2 | 1 | 50.0 | 27 | 13.50 | 1 | 0 | — | 0.0 | |
| Fourcade | 1 | 0 | 0.0 | 0 | 0.00 | 0 | 0 | — | 0.0 | |
| Hill | 1 | 0 | 0.0 | 0 | 0.00 | 0 | 0 | — | 0.0 | |

| PUNTING | No. | Avg. |
|---|---|---|
| Hansen | 73 | 39.9 |

| KICKING | XP | ATT | % | FG | ATT | % |
|---|---|---|---|---|---|---|
| Andersen | 32 | 33 | 97 | 26 | 36 | 72 |

## ATLANTA FALCONS

### RUSHING

| Last Name | No. | Yds | Avg | TD |
|---|---|---|---|---|
| Settle | 232 | 1024 | 4.4 | 7 |
| Riggs | 113 | 488 | 4.3 | 1 |
| Lang | 53 | 191 | 3.6 | 0 |
| Miller | 31 | 138 | 4.5 | 1 |
| Primus | 35 | 95 | 2.7 | 1 |
| Dixon | 7 | 69 | 9.9 | 0 |
| Millen | 1 | 7 | 7.0 | 0 |
| Hester | 1 | 3 | 3.0 | 0 |
| Dils | 2 | 1 | 0.5 | 1 |
| Stamps | 3 | 0 | 0.0 | 0 |

### RECEIVING

| Last Name | No. | Yds | Avg | TD |
|---|---|---|---|---|
| Settle | 68 | 570 | 8.4 | 1 |
| Lang | 38 | 398 | 10.8 | 1 |
| Dixon | 28 | 368 | 13.1 | 2 |
| Riggs | 22 | 171 | 7.8 | 0 |
| Bailey | 17 | 437 | 25.7 | 2 |
| Whisenhunt | 16 | 174 | 10.9 | 1 |
| Haynes | 13 | 232 | 17.8 | 4 |
| Hester | 12 | 176 | 14.7 | 0 |
| Wilkins | 11 | 134 | 12.2 | 0 |
| Primus | 8 | 42 | 5.3 | 0 |
| Milling | 5 | 66 | 13.2 | 0 |
| Stamps | 5 | 22 | 4.4 | 0 |
| Higdon | 3 | 60 | 20.0 | 2 |

### PUNT RETURNS

| Last Name | No. | Yds | Avg | TD |
|---|---|---|---|---|
| Barnes | 34 | 307 | 9.0 | 0 |
| Matthews | 6 | 26 | 4.3 | 0 |
| Cooper | 2 | 10 | 5.0 | 0 |

### KICKOFF RETURNS

| Last Name | No. | Yds | Avg | TD |
|---|---|---|---|---|
| Cooper | 16 | 331 | 20.7 | 0 |
| Gordon | 14 | 209 | 14.9 | 0 |
| Stamps | 12 | 219 | 18.3 | 0 |
| Barnes | 6 | 142 | 23.7 | 0 |
| Haynes | 6 | 113 | 18.8 | 0 |
| Dukes | 1 | 13 | 13.0 | 0 |
| Primus | 1 | 13 | 13.0 | 0 |
| Lang | 1 | 12 | 12.0 | 0 |
| Shelley | 2 | 5 | 2.5 | 0 |

### PASSING — PUNTING — KICKING

| PASSING | Att | Cmp | % | Yds | Yd/Att | TD | Int | — | % | RK |
|---|---|---|---|---|---|---|---|---|---|---|
| Miller | 351 | 184 | 52.4 | 2133 | 52.4 | 11 | 12 | — | 3.4 | 11 |
| Dils | 99 | 49 | 49.5 | 566 | 5.72 | 2 | 5 | — | 5.1 | |
| Millen | 31 | 17 | 54.8 | 215 | 6.94 | 0 | 2 | — | 6.5 | |

| PUNTING | No. | Avg. |
|---|---|---|
| Donnelly | 98 | 40.0 |

| KICKING | XP | ATT | % | FG | ATT | % |
|---|---|---|---|---|---|---|
| Davis | 25 | 27 | 93 | 19 | 30 | 63 |

# A.F.C. No. 1 In The Recovery Ward

The major NFL story through the first half of the season was the rash of quarterback injuries. Nearly every week a quarterback or two or three went on the injury list, and commentators seriously discussed what new rules might be necessary to protect what was becoming an endangered species.

The N.F.C. lost Joe Montana for a few games, Chuck Long for the last 10 weeks and, as usual, Jim McMahon for half a season. Doug Williams was temporarily kayoed by an appendectomy and Neil Lomax by an arthritic hip. The A.F.C. was hit even harder. The most extreme example was in Cleveland, where no less than four signalcallers were sidelined at one time or another. Three quarterbacks suffered serious injuries in Indianapolis. Denver lost superstar John Elway for one game with arm and ankle hurts, and he never was at the top of his game. New England had to completely retool its offense when Steve Grogan was stopped by a neck injury. Seattle's Dave Krieg missed half of the season. San Diego installed a new quarterback in Mark Vlasic in Week 10, only to lose him in Week 13. Houston's Warren Moon was knocked out for four games with a shoulder injury. Pittsburgh's Bubby Brister missed games with a broken hand.

Not surprisingly, the two A.F.C. teams with the best records — Cincinnati and Buffalo — kept their quarterbacks in good health all season.

## EASTERN DIVISION

**Buffalo Bills** — The Bills' defense was the class of the AFC. Cornelius Bennett and Shane Conlan were landslide Pro Bowlers. NT Fred Smerlas had one of his best seasons. DE Bruce Smith missed the first four games on drug suspension, but still managed 11 sacks. Veteran Art Still, picked up for a song from the Chiefs, filled in admirably in Smith's absence and played close to his old form the rest of the way. S Mark Kelso was a good ballhawk. The offense got just enough points to win most of the time. Jim Kelly was solid at quarterback. Rookie Thurman Thomas was the best of an ordinary group of runners, but the running attack by committee did the job most days. An injury to Shane Conlan precipitated a late slump, but, by then, the Bills had the division race wrapped up.

**Indianapolis Colts** — The Colts had a lot of unhappy players early in the season , and they played like it. Several linemen felt they deserved more pay to block for wealthy Eric Dickerson. When Indianapolis acquired high-priced LB Fredd Young, the other linebackers also felt underpaid. Gary Hogeboom felt under-played after being replaced at quarterback by Jack Trudeau and then rookie Chris Chandler. Coach Ron Meyer finally got everyone pulling in the same direction, and the Colts made a good, if unsuccessful, try for the playoffs in the second half of the season. One of the year's most interesting innovations was the occasional incorporation into the attack of a collegiate wishbone formation, with free-agent Ricky Turner at quarterback.

**New England Patriots** — The Patriots' ownership was settled during the season with the sale to Victor Kiam, the "I bought the company" head of Rimington. The team's on-field leadership was never finalized. Steve Grogan opened at quarterback with a wide-open attack, but after an opening win, New England lost three straight. Tom Ramsey was ineffective in Week Five against the Colts, and Doug Flutie won the starting slot with a fourth-quarter rally. The Patriots won six of eight with Flutie throwing rare rollout passes and most of the attack based on the running of super-rookie John Stephens. Then Tony Eason was given the starting job for the last two games in an effort to improve the passing attack. Instead, the New England offense hibernated, and any chance to make the playoffs was lost.

**New York Jets** — Joe Klecko was gone, but Mark Gastineau won his old defensive end spot back and by midseason led the conference in sacks. Then he suddenly retired to go to ailing girlfriend Brigitte

Nielson. Gastineau's defection left the Jets without a pass rush and the largely rookie secondary was suddenly porous, although Erik McMillan still finished as Rookie of the Year. Al Toon and Mickey Shuler were great possession receivers, but the only deep threat was Wesley Walker, who seldom saw the ball. For the third year in a row, Pat Ryan replaced Ken O'Brien at quarterback late in the season. But O'Brien was back to engineer a comeback win over the Giants in the last game. Coach Joe Walton, rumored on his way out all season, was given a new three-year contract.

**Miami Dolphins** — What had been Dan Marino, the Marks Duper and Clayton, a subpar defense and a poor running game, became Marino and Clayton — period — in 1988. Duper was off his game for most of the season and was suspended for drugs near the end. The defense, particularly against opponents' runners, was pitiful. A Miami running game simply did not exist. Coach Don Shula opted to throw two passes for every run. His strategy was sometimes spectacular and kept the Dolphins dangerous, but it produced few victories. The team was generally considered the weakest he'd ever put on the field.

## CENTRAL DIVISION

**Cincinnati Bengals** — The Bengals jumped from last to first in the division and put up one of the league's three 12-4 records. The offense deserved most of the credit. Boomer Esiason was the NFL MVP by passing judiciously but with great effectiveness to Eddie Brown, Rodney Holman and Tim McGee. James Brooks ran for 931 yards, but the new star was Ickey Woods, with 1,066 yards and 15 touchdowns. After each score, the rookie performed the "Ickey Shuffle," setting the art of the dance back to pre-minuet days. The burly offensive line, led by Anthony Munoz, Max Montoya and Joe Walter, made it all happen. The defense was less effective, although NT Tim Krumrie was exceptional and S David Fulcher was strong against the run. Coach Sam Wyche, nearly fired after the disaster of '87, was the toast of Cincinnati.

**Cleveland Browns** — The Browns went through quarterbacks like Kleenex. Bernie Kosar injured his arm in the opening quarter of the first game; backup Gary Danielson broke his leg the next week; and third-string Mike Pagel lasted to Week Six. That left 38-year-old Don Strock, signed for emergencies, as the only healthy signalcaller when the Browns beat the Eagles in Week Seven. Kosar returned, but was knocked out again in the Week 15 loss to Miami. But Strock won the finale against Houston to put the Browns into the playoffs for the fourth straight season. CB Frank Minnifield was the defensive star, as Hanford Dixon had his own injury problems. Coach Marty Schottenheimer, whose play-calling was roundly criticized, resigned after the season rather than name a new offensive coordinator.

**Houston Oilers** — Coach Jerry Glanville brought smiles all season with his joke of leaving tickets at the gate for Elvis Presley and other deceased celebrities, but his roughhouse defense and special teams were unamusing to opponents. The Astrodome was nicknamed "The House of Pain" for the bruises dealt out there. With a strong offense led by QB Warren Moon, 1,000-yard runner Mike Rozier, and two of the best receivers in the league in Drew Hill and Ernest Givins, the Oilers were one of the AFC's best teams at home. However, their inability to win on the road kept them from mounting a serious challenge to Cincinnati.

**Pittsburgh Steelers** — Bubby Brister was installed at quarterback, and his passing and fiery leadership provided most of the rare good moments for the Steelers. LB Mike Merriweather held out the entire season, DE Keith Willis went out for the year after being injured during training camp, and No. 1 draft choice Aaron Jones bombed as a pass rusher. With the Steelers putting little pressure on rival quarterbacks, the young secondary became easy pickings. Coach Chuck Noll was berated by fans

FINAL TEAM STATISTICS

| OFFENSE | BUFF | CIN | CLEV | DEN | HOU | IND | K.C. | L.A. | MIA | N.E. | NYJ | PITT | S.D. | SEA |
|---|---|---|---|---|---|---|---|---|---|---|---|---|---|---|
| FIRST DOWNS: | | | | | | | | | | | | | | |
| Total | 313 | 351 | 294 | 338 | 308 | 311 | 289 | 283 | 321 | 264 | 331 | 292 | 255 | 291 |
| by Rushing | 137 | 159 | 93 | 106 | 141 | 153 | 104 | 116 | 77 | 126 | 118 | 120 | 115 | 125 |
| by Passing | 161 | 165 | 177 | 196 | 148 | 130 | 161 | 145 | 218 | 112 | 181 | 150 | 116 | 139 |
| by Penalty | 15 | 27 | 24 | 36 | 19 | 28 | 24 | 22 | 26 | 26 | 32 | 22 | 24 | 27 |
| RUSHING: | | | | | | | | | | | | | | |
| Number | 528 | 563 | 440 | 464 | 558 | 545 | 448 | 493 | 335 | 588 | 514 | 499 | 438 | 517 |
| Yards | 2133 | 2710 | 1575 | 1815 | 2249 | 2249 | 1713 | 1852 | 1205 | 2120 | 2132 | 2228 | 2041 | 2086 |
| Average Yards | 4.0 | 4.8 | 3.6 | 3.9 | 4.0 | 4.1 | 3.8 | 3.8 | 3.6 | 3.6 | 4.1 | 4.5 | 4.7 | 4.0 |
| Touchdowns | 15 | 27 | 10 | 13 | 26 | 23 | 8 | 15 | 11 | 17 | 19 | 17 | 11 | 14 |
| PASSING: | | | | | | | | | | | | | | |
| Attempts | 454 | 392 | 537 | 581 | 428 | 403 | 528 | 496 | 621 | 389 | 538 | 489 | 468 | 437 |
| Completions | 271 | 225 | 313 | 324 | 218 | 222 | 282 | 219 | 363 | 199 | 299 | 226 | 241 | 245 |
| Completion Pct. | 59.7 | 57.4 | 58.3 | 55.8 | 50.9 | 55.1 | 53.4 | 44.2 | 58.5 | 51.2 | 55.6 | 46.2 | 51.5 | 56.1 |
| Passing Yards | 3411 | 3592 | 3686 | 3941 | 3166 | 2865 | 3484 | 3503 | 4557 | 2333 | 3374 | 3307 | 2628 | 2979 |
| Avg. Yds per Att. | 6.6 | 8.0 | 6.0 | 6.0 | 6.5 | 6.0 | 5.5 | 5.7 | 7.2 | 5.3 | 5.3 | 5.6 | 4.8 | 5.9 |
| Avg. Yds per Comp. | 12.6 | 16.0 | 11.8 | 12.2 | 14.5 | 12.9 | 12.4 | 16.0 | 12.6 | 11.7 | 11.3 | 14.6 | 10.9 | 12.2 |
| Times Tackled | 30 | 30 | 36 | 32 | 24 | 34 | 43 | 46 | 7 | 23 | 42 | 42 | 31 | 29 |
| Yds Lost Tackled | 229 | 245 | 250 | 250 | 210 | 244 | 353 | 394 | 41 | 160 | 291 | 331 | 240 | 223 |
| Net Yards | 3182 | 3347 | 3436 | 3691 | 2956 | 2621 | 3131 | 3109 | 4516 | 2173 | 3083 | 2976 | 2388 | 2756 |
| Touchdowns | 15 | 28 | 19 | 24 | 21 | 15 | 16 | 21 | 29 | 12 | 20 | 15 | 11 | 22 |
| Interceptions | 17 | 14 | 17 | 22 | 18 | 22 | 21 | 20 | 23 | 28 | 11 | 20 | 20 | 20 |
| Pct. Intercepted | 3.7 | 3.6 | 3.2 | 4.7 | 3.2 | 5.5 | 4.0 | 4.0 | 3.7 | 4.8 | 2.1 | 4.1 | 4.6 | 4.6 |
| PUNTS: | | | | | | | | | | | | | | |
| Number | 62 | 64 | 67 | 68 | 65 | 64 | 76 | 91 | 64 | 91 | 85 | 71 | 86 | 70 |
| Average | 39.5 | 36.7 | 38.5 | 43.8 | 38.8 | 43.5 | 40.3 | 41.8 | 43.0 | 38.3 | 38.9 | 41.5 | 43.5 | 40.8 |
| PUNT RETURNS | | | | | | | | | | | | | | |
| Number | 26 | 32 | 40 | 53 | 36 | 26 | 32 | 55 | 27 | 38 | 38 | 39 | 35 | 37 |
| Yards | 152 | 244 | 325 | 451 | 225 | 254 | 215 | 489 | 259 | 398 | 418 | 322 | 314 | 340 |
| Average Yards | 5.8 | 76 | 8.1 | 8.5 | 6.3 | 9.8 | 6.7 | 8.9 | 9.6 | 10.5 | 11.0 | 8.3 | 9.0 | 9.2 |
| Touchdowns | 0 | 0 | 0 | 0 | 0 | 1 | 0 | 0 | 0 | 0 | 1 | 0 | 0 | 0 |
| KICKOFF RET.: | | | | | | | | | | | | | | |
| Number | 50 | 57 | 55 | 58 | 60 | 52 | 56 | 62 | 65 | 57 | 72 | 74 | 60 | 62 |
| Yards | 935 | 1054 | 1159 | 1198 | 1232 | 1033 | 925 | 1407 | 1365 | 1248 | 1404 | 1575 | 1510 | 1352 |
| Average Yards | 18.7 | 18.5 | 21.1 | 20.7 | 20.5 | 19.9 | 16.5 | 22.7 | 21.0 | 21.9 | 19.5 | 21.3 | 25.2 | 21.8 |
| Touchdowns | 0 | 1 | 0 | 0 | 1 | 0 | 0 | 1 | 0 | 1 | 0 | 2 | 2 | 0 |
| INTERCEPT RET.: | | | | | | | | | | | | | | |
| Number | 15 | 22 | 20 | 16 | 22 | 15 | 18 | 17 | 16 | 20 | 24 | 20 | 16 | 22 |
| Yards | 244 | 181 | 319 | 200 | 302 | 189 | 166 | 278 | 219 | 244 | 228 | 381 | 179 | 280 |
| Average Yards | 16.3 | 8.2 | 16.0 | 12.5 | 13.7 | 12.6 | 9.2 | 16.3 | 13.7 | 12.2 | 9.5 | 19.1 | 11.2 | 12.7 |
| Touchdowns | 1 | 1 | 1 | 0 | 2 | 1 | 0 | 1 | 0 | 0 | 3 | 2 | 1 | 1 |
| PENALTIES: | | | | | | | | | | | | | | |
| Number | 109 | 82 | 110 | 85 | 125 | 89 | 85 | 102 | 99 | 87 | 115 | 99 | 118 | 89 |
| Yards | 824 | 647 | 875 | 717 | 1150 | 657 | 636 | 762 | 845 | 665 | 931 | 803 | 1039 | 790 |
| FUMBLES: | | | | | | | | | | | | | | |
| Number | 26 | 28 | 32 | 34 | 33 | 20 | 21 | 33 | 26 | 19 | 32 | 40 | 26 | 29 |
| Number Lost | 16 | 13 | 16 | 12 | 17 | 8 | 12 | 13 | 12 | 10 | 16 | 19 | 12 | 14 |
| POINTS: | | | | | | | | | | | | | | |
| Total | 329 | 448 | 304 | 327 | 424 | 354 | 254 | 325 | 319 | 250 | 372 | 336 | 231 | 339 |
| PAT Attempts | 33 | 59 | 33 | 37 | 51 | 40 | 24 | 39 | 41 | 31 | 43 | 36 | 27 | 39 |
| PAT Made | 33 | 56 | 32 | 36 | 48 | 39 | 23 | 37 | 37 | 25 | 43 | 34 | 27 | 39 |
| FG Attempts | 37 | 18 | 29 | 36 | 34 | 32 | 32 | 29 | 23 | 24 | 28 | 36 | 20 | 28 |
| FG Made | 32 | 12 | 24 | 23 | 22 | 25 | 27 | 18 | 12 | 13 | 23 | 28 | 14 | 22 |
| Percent FG Made | 86.5 | 66.7 | 82.8 | 63.9 | 64.7 | 78.1 | 84.4 | 62.1 | 52.2 | 54.2 | 82.1 | 77.7 | 70.0 | 78.6 |
| Safeties | 1 | 1 | 1 | 0 | 2 | 0 | 3 | 0 | 0 | 0 | 1 | 1 | 0 | 0 |

| DEFENSE | BUFF | CIN | CLEV | DEN | HOU | IND | K.C. | L.A. | MIA | N.E. | NYJ | PITT | S.D. | SEA |
|---|---|---|---|---|---|---|---|---|---|---|---|---|---|---|
| FIRST DOWNS: | | | | | | | | | | | | | | |
| Total | 299 | 322 | 301 | 316 | 304 | 315 | 318 | 310 | 359 | 272 | 310 | 319 | 335 | 321 |
| by Rushing | 114 | 126 | 114 | 140 | 94 | 109 | 162 | 124 | 155 | 119 | 123 | 110 | 135 | 134 |
| by Passing | 146 | 177 | 162 | 161 | 170 | 184 | 136 | 165 | 173 | 138 | 162 | 181 | 173 | 171 |
| by Penalty | 39 | 19 | 25 | 15 | 40 | 22 | 20 | 21 | 31 | 15 | 25 | 28 | 27 | 16 |
| RUSHING: | | | | | | | | | | | | | | |
| Number | 477 | 493 | 498 | 552 | 431 | 447 | 609 | 533 | 557 | 496 | 517 | 516 | 521 | 509 |
| Yards | 1854 | 2048 | 1920 | 2538 | 1592 | 1694 | 2592 | 2208 | 2506 | 2099 | 2124 | 1864 | 2133 | 2286 |
| Average Yards | 3.9 | 4.2 | 3.9 | 4.6 | 3.7 | 3.8 | 4.3 | 4.1 | 4.5 | 4.2 | 4.1 | 3.6 | 4.1 | 4.5 |
| Touchdowns | 14 | 18 | 13 | 21 | 20 | 14 | 23 | 17 | 22 | 20 | 15 | 20 | 15 | 14 |
| PASSING: | | | | | | | | | | | | | | |
| Attempts | 448 | 524 | 474 | 467 | 512 | 539 | 410 | 483 | 491 | 436 | 476 | 532 | 517 | 501 |
| Completions | 250 | 283 | 245 | 262 | 281 | 321 | 214 | 265 | 298 | 234 | 244 | 309 | 274 | 280 |
| Completion Pct. | 55.8 | 54.0 | 51.7 | 56.1 | 54.9 | 59.6 | 52.2 | 54.9 | 60.7 | 53.7 | 51.3 | 58.1 | 53.0 | 55.9 |
| Passing Yards | 3046 | 3508 | 3102 | 3168 | 3619 | 3803 | 2591 | 3471 | 3442 | 2801 | 3823 | 4086 | 3525 | 3618 |
| Avg. Yds per Att. | 5.5 | 5.5 | 5.6 | 5.8 | 5.9 | 6.3 | 5.6 | 6.1 | 6.4 | 5.6 | 6.7 | 7.2 | 6.0 | 6.3 |
| Avg. Yds per Comp. | 12.2 | 12.4 | 12.7 | 12.1 | 12.9 | 11.9 | 12.1 | 13.1 | 11.6 | 12.0 | 15.7 | 13.2 | 12.9 | 12.9 |
| Times Tackled | 46 | 42 | 37 | 36 | 42 | 30 | 23 | 40 | 24 | 29 | 45 | 19 | 34 | 30 |
| Yds Lost Tackled | 322 | 374 | 255 | 235 | 353 | 201 | 157 | 300 | 167 | 219 | 314 | 145 | 240 | 265 |
| Net Yards | 2724 | 3134 | 2847 | 2933 | 3266 | 3602 | 2434 | 3171 | 3275 | 2582 | 3509 | 3941 | 3285 | 3353 |
| Touchdowns | 14 | 19 | 13 | 18 | 22 | 21 | 12 | 23 | 19 | 13 | 28 | 25 | 22 | 21 |
| Interceptions | 15 | 22 | 20 | 16 | 22 | 15 | 18 | 17 | 16 | 20 | 24 | 20 | 16 | 22 |
| Pct. Intercepted | 3.3 | 4.2 | 4.2 | 3.4 | 4.3 | 2.8 | 4.4 | 3.5 | 3.3 | 4.6 | 5.0 | 3.8 | 3.1 | 4.4 |
| PUNTS: | | | | | | | | | | | | | | |
| Number | 75 | 65 | 69 | 84 | 80 | 68 | 63 | 94 | 58 | 86 | 72 | 67 | 71 | 66 |
| Average | 39.7 | 39.9 | 39.4 | 43.4 | 37.2 | 39.4 | 40.2 | 41.4 | 41.8 | 42.2 | 38.1 | 40.7 | 39.3 | 42.1 |
| PUNT RETURNS | | | | | | | | | | | | | | |
| Number | 36 | 32 | 32 | 33 | 35 | 37 | 48 | 47 | 35 | 37 | 34 | 40 | 56 | 36 |
| Yards | 222 | 280 | 304 | 364 | 206 | 418 | 473 | 397 | 318 | 217 | 201 | 418 | 558 | 202 |
| Average Yards | 6.2 | 8.8 | 9.5 | 11.0 | 5.9 | 11.3 | 9.9 | 8.4 | 9.1 | 5.9 | 5.9 | 10.5 | 10.0 | 5.6 |
| Touchdowns | 0 | 0 | 1 | 1 | 0 | 1 | 0 | 0 | 0 | 0 | 0 | 0 | 0 | 0 |
| KICKOFF RET.: | | | | | | | | | | | | | | |
| Number | 69 | 61 | 58 | 52 | 69 | 67 | 57 | 61 | 53 | 45 | 70 | 63 | 47 | 66 |
| Yards | 1117 | 1335 | 973 | 1035 | 1362 | 1480 | 1380 | 1299 | 1109 | 888 | 1491 | 1351 | 1055 | 1207 |
| Average Yards | 16.2 | 21.9 | 16.8 | 19.9 | 19.7 | 22.1 | 24.2 | 21.3 | 20.9 | 19.7 | 21.3 | 21.4 | 22.4 | 18.3 |
| Touchdowns | 0 | 0 | 0 | 0 | 1 | 1 | 2 | 0 | 0 | 0 | 0 | 1 | 1 | 0 |
| INTERCEPT RET.: | | | | | | | | | | | | | | |
| Number | 17 | 14 | 17 | 22 | 18 | 22 | 21 | 20 | 23 | 28 | 11 | 20 | 20 | 20 |
| Yards | 202 | 185 | 190 | 344 | 289 | 291 | 206 | 219 | 399 | 286 | 126 | 367 | 307 | 195 |
| Average Yards | 11.9 | 13.2 | 11.2 | 15.6 | 16.1 | 13.2 | 9.8 | 10.0 | 17.3 | 10.2 | 11.5 | 18.4 | 15.4 | 9.8 |
| Touchdowns | 1 | 0 | 2 | 1 | 1 | 1 | 1 | 0 | 4 | 0 | 0 | 1 | 0 | 1 |
| PENALTIES: | | | | | | | | | | | | | | |
| Number | 90 | 95 | 100 | 116 | 118 | 118 | 106 | 94 | 103 | 108 | 89 | 79 | 74 | 111 |
| Yards | 713 | 873 | 789 | 966 | 947 | 965 | 854 | 823 | 734 | 858 | 757 | 705 | 619 | 861 |
| FUMBLES: | | | | | | | | | | | | | | |
| Number | 28 | 28 | 23 | 23 | 33 | 32 | 30 | 31 | 31 | 29 | 35 | 35 | 25 | 31 |
| Number Lost | 17 | 14 | 11 | 13 | 20 | 20 | 13 | 17 | 15 | 15 | 16 | 13 | 10 | 18 |
| POINTS: | | | | | | | | | | | | | | |
| Total | 237 | 329 | 288 | 352 | 365 | 315 | 320 | 369 | 380 | 284 | 354 | 421 | 332 | 329 |
| PAT Attempts | 29 | 39 | 30 | 41 | 46 | 38 | 39 | 41 | 45 | 33 | 43 | 49 | 38 | 38 |
| PAT Made | 27 | 38 | 30 | 41 | 43 | 36 | 38 | 40 | 44 | 33 | 36 | 47 | 36 | 38 |
| FG Attempts | 24 | 24 | 34 | 27 | 18 | 25 | 24 | 29 | 28 | 26 | 30 | 32 | 36 | 32 |
| FG Made | 12 | 17 | 26 | 21 | 14 | 17 | 16 | 27 | 22 | 17 | 20 | 26 | 22 | 21 |
| Percent FG Made | 50.0 | 70.8 | 76.5 | 77.7 | 77.7 | 68.0 | 66.7 | 93.1 | 78.6 | 65.4 | 66.7 | 81.3 | 61.1 | 65.6 |
| Safeties | 0 | 3 | 0 | 1 | 2 | 0 | 0 | 1 | 0 | 1 | 0 | 1 | 1 | 0 |

and press with short memories.

## WESTERN DIVISION

**Seattle Seahawks** — When the Seahawks defeated the Raiders 43-37 in a see-saw finale to win their first AFC West title, coach Chuck Knox had completed a hat trick in winning division crowns for each NFL team he'd coached. FB John L. Williams became a full-fledged running and receiving star, and Curt Warner topped 1,000 yards in rushing again. The key man was QB Dave Krieg, who missed half of the season with an injury, but was sensational coming down the stretch, finishing with the AFC's second-best pass rating. The defense, led by Jacob Greene's nine sacks, was effective but small; it could be outmuscled by the league's bigger offensive lines.

**Denver Broncos** — John Elway's sore arm crippled the offense. New RB Tony Dorsett, who was past his prime, couldn't give the Broncos a viable running game to pick up the slack, and injuries among the receivers exacerbated the problems with the pass attack. But none of these hurt Denver as much as a defense that could no longer get by on quickness instead of heft. The team was especially vulnerable when star LB Karl Mecklenburg was out or playing at less than 100 percent because of a hand injury. After the season, coach Dan Reeves fired most of the defensive coaches, including coordinator Joe Collier, who'd been with the Broncos for 20 years.

**Los Angeles Raiders** — The Raiders had two new quarterbacks in rookie Steve Beuerlein and Redskins' emigree Jay Schroeder, four of the league's highest-priced receivers in Rookie of the Year Tim Brown, Canadian import Mervyn Fernandez, former Bear Willie Gault and ex-Packer James Lofton, and two Heisman Trophy runners in veteran Marcus Allen and, for half of the season, Bo Jackson. Yet, new coach Mike Shanahan's offense sputtered. The line was unsettled and the offense had too many new players in a new system and too many disappointing performances. The defense had injuries, most notably to DE Howie Long, but the major dilemma there was age.

**San Diego Chargers** — Gary Anderson rushed for 1,119 yards and a 5.0 average, but the Chargers went through three quarterbacks before settling on much-criticized Mark Malone by default. The wide receivers lacked experience, and the offensive line was made up of four free agents and a rookie. DE Lee Williams had 11 sacks, but the defense lost LB Billy Ray Smith for most of the season with injuries and LB Chip Banks for all of the season to a holdout. Still, coach Al Saunders' club won four of its last six games. It wasn' enough to save his job. He was fired the day ater the season ended.

**Kansas City Chiefs** — When Bill Kenney couldn't move the team, journeyman Steve DeBerg took over at quarterback. He passed for 2,935 yards, but had almost ne help from the runners, as Christian Okoye struggled with injuries. S Deron Cherry had an All-Pro year, but the other Pro Bowlers in the secondary, Lloyd Burrus and Albert Lewis, also had injury problems. DE Art Still was shuffled off to Buffalo at the beginning of the season, and when NT Bill Maas went out after eight games, the Chiefs lost any ability to stop opponent's runners.

## BUFFALO BILLS 12-4 Marv Levy

| Scores of Each Game | | |
|---|---|---|
| 13 | MINNESOTA | 10 |
| 9 | MIAMI | 6 |
| 16 | New England | 14 |
| 36 | PITTSBURGH | 28 |
| 3 | Chicago | 24 |
| 34 | INDIANAPOLIS | 23 |
| 37 | N.Y. Jets | 14 |
| 23 | NEW ENGLAND | 20 |
| 28 | GREEN BAY | 0 |
| 13 | Seattle | 3 |
| 31 | Miami | 6 |
| 9 | N.Y. JETS | *6 |
| 21 | Cincinnati | 35 |
| 5 | Tampa Bay | 10 |
| 37 | L.A. RAIDERS | 21 |
| 14 | Indianapolis | 17 |

| Use Name | Pos. | Hgt | Wgt | Age | Int | Pts |
|---|---|---|---|---|---|---|
| Howard Ballard | OT | 6'6" | 300 | 24 | | |
| Leonard Burton | OT | 6'3" | 275 | 24 | | |
| Joe Devlin | OT | 6'5" | 280 | 35 | | |
| Dale Hellestrae | OT | 6'5" | 280 | 26 | | |
| Will Wolford | OT-OG | 6'5" | 280 | 24 | | |
| Jim Ritcher | OG | 6'3" | 265 | 30 | | |
| Tim Vogler | OG | 6'3" | 285 | 31 | | |
| Kent Hull | C | 6'4" | 275 | 27 | | |
| Mark Pike | DE | 6'4" | 272 | 24 | | |
| Dean Prater | DE | 6'4" | 260 | 29 | | |
| Leon Seals | DE | 6'4" | 265 | 24 | | 6 |
| Bruce Smith | DE | 6'4" | 285 | 25 | | 2 |
| Art Still | DE | 6'7" | 255 | 32 | | |
| Fred Smerlas | NT | 6'3" | 280 | 31 | | |
| Jeff Wright | NT | 6'2" | 270 | 25 | | |

Rich Strenger — Knee Injury
Bruce Mesner — Knee Injury
Elston Ridgle — Ankle Injury
Tony Brown — Injury

| Use Name | Pos. | Hgt | Wgt | Age | Int | Pts |
|---|---|---|---|---|---|---|
| Carlton Bailey | LB | 6'2" | 240 | 23 | | |
| Cornelius Bennett | LB | 6'2" | 235 | 22 | 2 | |
| Ray Bentley | LB | 6'2" | 235 | 27 | 1 | |
| Shane Conlan | LB | 6'3" | 235 | 24 | 1 | |
| Tom Erlandson | LB | 6'1" | 220 | 22 | | |
| Hal Garner | LB | 6'4" | 235 | 26 | | |
| Don Graham | LB | 6'2" | 244 | 24 | | |
| Scott Radecic | LB | 6'3" | 242 | 26 | | |
| Darryl Talley | LB | 6'4" | 235 | 28 | | |
| Derrick Burroughs | DB | 6'1" | 180 | 26 | | |
| Sherman Cocroft | DB | 6'1" | 190 | 27 | 1 | |
| Wayne Davis | DB | 5'11" | 180 | 25 | 1 | |
| Dwight Drane | DB | 6'2" | 205 | 26 | | |
| John Hagy | DB | 5'11" | 190 | 22 | | |
| Kirby Jackson | DB | 5'10" | 180 | 23 | | |
| Mark Kelso | DB | 5'11" | 185 | 25 | 7 | 6 |
| Nate Odomes | DB | 5'10" | 188 | 23 | 1 | |
| Leonard Smith (from PHX) | DB | 5'11" | 202 | 27 | 2 | |
| Erroll Tucker | DB | 5'8" | 170 | 24 | | |

| Use Name | Pos. | Hgt | Wgt | Age | Int | Pts |
|---|---|---|---|---|---|---|
| Stan Gelbaugh | QB | 6'3" | 207 | 25 | | |
| Jim Kelly | QB | 6'3" | 218 | 28 | | |
| Frank Reich | QB | 6'4" | 210 | 26 | | |
| Ronnie Harmon | HB | 5'11" | 200 | 24 | | 24 |
| Robb Riddick | HB | 6' | 195 | 31 | | 84 |
| Thurman Thomas | HB | 5'10" | 198 | 22 | | 12 |
| Carl Byrum | FB | 6' | 235 | 25 | | |
| Jamie Mueller | FB | 6'1" | 225 | 23 | | |
| Walter Broughton | WR | 5'10" | 180 | 25 | | |
| Chris Burkett | WR | 6'4" | 210 | 26 | 6 | |
| Flip Johnson | WR | 5'10" | 185 | 25 | 6 | |
| Trumaine Johnson | WR | 6'1" | 196 | 28 | | |
| Andre Reed | WR | 6' | 190 | 24 | | 36 |
| Steve Tasker | WR | 5'9" | 185 | 26 | | |
| Keith McKeller | TE | 6'6" | 245 | 24 | | |
| Pete Metzelaars | TE | 6'7" | 250 | 28 | 6 | |
| Butch Rolle | TE | 6'3" | 242 | 24 | | 12 |
| John Kidd | K | 6'3" | 208 | 27 | | |
| Scott Norwood | K | 6' | 207 | 28 | | 129 |

## INDIANAPOLIS COLTS 9-7 Ron Meyer

| | | |
|---|---|---|
| 14 | HOUSTON | *17 |
| 13 | CHICAGO | 17 |
| 17 | Cleveland | 23 |
| 15 | MIAMI | 13 |
| 17 | New England | 21 |
| 23 | Buffalo | 34 |
| 35 | TAMPA BAY | 31 |
| 16 | San Diego | 0 |
| 55 | DENVER | 23 |
| 38 | N.Y. JETS | 14 |
| 20 | Green Bay | 13 |
| 3 | Minnesota | 12 |
| 24 | NEW ENGLAND | 21 |
| 31 | Miami | 28 |
| 16 | N.Y. Jets | 34 |
| 17 | BUFFALO | 14 |

| Use Name | Pos. | Hgt | Wgt | Age | Int | Pts |
|---|---|---|---|---|---|---|
| Brian Baldinger | OT | 6'4" | 268 | 29 | | |
| Kevin Call | OT | 6'7" | 302 | 26 | | |
| Chris Hinton | OT | 6'4" | 295 | 27 | | |
| Dan McQuaid (from MIN) | OT-OG | 6'7" | 278 | 27 | | |
| Joel Patten | OT | 6'7" | 301 | 30 | | |
| Randy Dixon | OG-OT | 6'3" | 290 | 23 | | |
| Ben Utt | OG | 6'5" | 286 | 29 | | |
| Ray Donaldson | C | 6'3" | 288 | 30 | | |
| Jon Hand | DE | 6'7" | 298 | 24 | | |
| Ezra Johnson | DE | 6'4" | 250 | 32 | | |
| Donnell Thompson | DE | 6'4" | 275 | 29 | | |
| Byron Darby | NT | 6'4" | 260 | 28 | | |
| Joe Klecko | NT | 6'3" | 265 | 34 | | |

Steve Knight — Knee Injury

| Use Name | Pos. | Hgt | Wgt | Age | Int | Pts |
|---|---|---|---|---|---|---|
| O'Brien Alston | LB | 6'6" | 246 | 22 | | |
| Harvey Armstrong | LB | 6'3" | 268 | 28 | | |
| Duane Bickett | LB | 6'5" | 243 | 25 | 3 | |
| Jeff Herrod | LB | 6' | 243 | 22 | | |
| Barry Krauss | LB | 6'3" | 248 | 31 | 1 | |
| Orlando Lowry | LB | 6'4" | 236 | 27 | | |
| Cliff Odom | LB | 6'2" | 245 | 30 | | |
| Fredd Young | LB | 6'1" | 233 | 26 | | |
| Michael Ball | DB | 6' | 216 | 24 | | |
| Eugene Daniel | DB | 5'11" | 178 | 27 | 2 | 6 |
| Chris Goode | DB | 6' | 193 | 24 | 2 | |
| John Holt | DB | 5'11" | 179 | 29 | | |
| Chuckie Miller | DB | 5'10" | 180 | 23 | | |
| Mike Prior | DB | 6' | 204 | 24 | 3 | |
| Freddie Robinson | DB | 6'1" | 190 | 24 | | |
| Craig Swoope | DB | 6'1" | 214 | 24 | | |
| Keith Taylor | DB | 5'11" | 193 | 23 | | |
| Willie Tullis | DB | 6' | 195 | 30 | 4 | |
| Terry Wright | DB | 6' | 195 | 23 | | |

| Use Name | Pos. | Hgt | Wgt | Age | Int | Pts |
|---|---|---|---|---|---|---|
| Chris Chandler | QB | 6'4" | 210 | 22 | | 18 |
| Bob Gagliano | QB | 6'3" | 195 | 29 | | |
| Gary Hogeboom | QB | 6'4" | 217 | 30 | | 6 |
| Bill Ransdell | QB | 6'2" | 212 | 25 | | |
| Jack Trudeau | QB | 6'3" | 214 | 25 | | |
| Ricky Turner | QB | 6' | 190 | 26 | | 12 |
| Albert Bentley | HB-FB | 5'11" | 214 | 28 | | 18 |
| Eric Dickerson | HB | 6'3" | 217 | 27 | | 90 |
| Mark Boyer | HB-TE | 6'4" | 242 | 25 | | 12 |
| George Wonsley | HB-FB | 5'10" | 219 | 27 | | 6 |
| Roy Banks | WR | 5'10" | 193 | 22 | | |
| Mark Bellini | WR | 5'11" | 182 | 24 | | |
| Matt Bouza | WR | 6'3" | 212 | 30 | | 24 |
| Bill Brooks | WR | 6' | 191 | 24 | | 18 |
| Clarence Verdin | WR | 5'8" | 163 | 25 | | 30 |
| Pat Beach | TE | 6'4" | 252 | 27 | | |
| John Brandes | TE | 6'2" | 255 | 24 | | |
| Donnie Dee | TE | 6'4" | 247 | 23 | | |
| Jess Atkinson | K | 5'9" | 168 | 26 | | |
| Dean Biasucci | K | 6' | 191 | 26 | | 114 |
| Kerry Brady | K | 6'1" | 205 | 25 | | |
| Rohn Stark | K | 6'3" | 204 | 29 | | |

## NEW ENGLAND PATRIOTS 9-7 Raymond Berry

| | | |
|---|---|---|
| 28 | N.Y. JETS | 3 |
| 6 | Minnesota | 36 |
| 14 | BUFFALO | 16 |
| 6 | Houston | 31 |
| 21 | INDIANAPOLIS | 17 |
| 3 | Green Bay (Mil.) | 45 |
| 27 | CINCINNATI | 21 |
| 20 | Buffalo | 23 |
| 30 | CHICAGO | 7 |
| 21 | MIAMI | 10 |
| 14 | N.Y. Jets | 13 |
| 6 | Miami | 3 |
| 21 | Indianapolis | 14 |
| 13 | SEATTLE | 7 |
| 10 | TAMPA BAY | *7 |
| 10 | Denver | 21 |

| Use Name | Pos. | Hgt | Wgt | Age | Int | Pts |
|---|---|---|---|---|---|---|
| Bruce Armstrong | OT | 6'4" | 284 | 22 | | |
| Tom Rehder | OT | 6'7" | 280 | 23 | | |
| Danny Villa | OT | 6'5" | 305 | 23 | | |
| Paul Fairchild | OG | 6'4" | 270 | 26 | | |
| Sean Farrell | OG | 6'3" | 260 | 28 | | |
| Ron Wooten | OG | 6'4" | 273 | 29 | | |
| Mike Baab | C | 6'4" | 270 | 28 | | |
| Trevor Matich | C | 6'4" | 270 | 26 | | |
| Milford Hodge | DE | 6'3" | 278 | 27 | | |
| Edmund Nelson | DE-DT | 6'3" | 275 | 28 | | |
| Kenneth Sims | DE | 6'5" | 271 | 28 | | |
| Verin Garis | DE | 6'4" | 255 | 25 | | |
| Tim Goad | NT | 6'3" | 280 | 22 | | |
| Brent Williams | NT-DE | 6'3" | 278 | 23 | | |
| Toby Williams | NT | 6'3" | 275 | 28 | | |

| Use Name | Pos. | Hgt | Wgt | Age | Int | Pts |
|---|---|---|---|---|---|---|
| Thomas Benson | LB | 6'2" | 245 | 26 | | |
| Vincent Brown | LB | 6'2" | 245 | 23 | | |
| Tim Jordan | LB | 6'3" | 226 | 24 | 1 | |
| Larry McGrew | LB | 6'5" | 233 | 31 | 1 | |
| Eric Naposki | LB | 6'2" | 230 | 21 | | |
| Johnny Rembert | LB | 6'3" | 234 | 27 | 2 | |
| Ed Reynolds | LB | 6'5" | 242 | 26 | | |
| Andre Tippett | LB | 6'3" | 241 | 28 | | |
| Jim Bowman | DB | 6'2" | 210 | 24 | 1 | |
| Raymond Clayborn | DB | 6'1" | 186 | 33 | 4 | |
| Ernest Gibson | DB | 5'10" | 185 | 26 | | |
| Darryl Holmes | DB | 6'2" | 190 | 23 | | |
| Roland James | DB | 6'2" | 191 | 30 | 4 | |
| Ronnie Lippett | DB | 5'11" | 180 | 27 | 1 | |
| Fred Marion | DB | 6'2" | 191 | 29 | 4 | |
| Rod McSwain | DB | 6'1" | 198 | 26 | 2 | |
| Eugene Profit | DB | 5'10" | 165 | 23 | | |

David Ward — Shoulder Injury
Ed Williams — Knee Injury

| Use Name | Pos. | Hgt | Wgt | Age | Int | Pts |
|---|---|---|---|---|---|---|
| Tony Eason | QB | 6'4" | 212 | 28 | | |
| Doug Flutie | QB | 5'9" | 175 | 25 | | 6 |
| Steve Grogan | QB | 6'4" | 210 | 35 | | 6 |
| Tom Ramsey | QB | 6'1" | 188 | 27 | | |
| Marvin Allen | HB | 5'10" | 215 | 22 | | |
| Elgin Davis | HB | 5'10" | 192 | 22 | | |
| Reggie Dupard | HB | 5'11" | 205 | 24 | | 12 |
| John Stephens | HB | 6'1" | 220 | 22 | | 30 |
| Craig James | FB | 6' | 215 | 27 | | 6 |
| Bob Perryman | FB | 6'1" | 233 | 23 | | 36 |
| Mosi Tatupu | FB | 6' | 227 | 33 | | 12 |
| Irving Fryar | WR | 6' | 200 | 25 | | 30 |
| Dennis Gadbois | WR | 6'1" | 183 | 24 | | |
| Cedric Jones | WR | 6'1" | 184 | 28 | | 6 |
| Sammy Martin | WR | 5'11" | 175 | 23 | | 6 |
| Stanley Morgan | WR | 5'11" | 181 | 33 | | 24 |
| Lin Dawson | TE | 6'3" | 240 | 29 | | 12 |
| Russ Francis | TE | 6'6" | 242 | 35 | | |
| Steve Johnson | TE | 6'6" | 245 | 23 | | |
| Willie Scott | TE | 6'4" | 245 | 29 | | |
| Jeff Feagles | K | 6' | 198 | 22 | | |
| Teddy Garcia | K | 5'10" | 190 | 24 | | 29 |
| Jason Staurovsky | K | 5'9" | 170 | 25 | | 35 |

Tony Collins — Suspended by N.F.L.

## NEW YORK JETS 8-7-1 Joe Walton

| | | |
|---|---|---|
| 3 | New England | 28 |
| 23 | Cleveland | 3 |
| 45 | HOUSTON | 3 |
| 17 | Detroit | 10 |
| 17 | KANSAS CITY | *17 |
| 19 | Cincinnati | 36 |
| 14 | BUFFALO | 37 |
| 44 | Miami | 30 |
| 24 | PITTSBURGH | 20 |
| 14 | Indianapolis | 38 |
| 13 | NEW ENGLAND | 14 |
| 6 | Buffalo | *9 |
| 38 | MIAMI | 34 |
| 34 | Kansas City | 38 |
| 34 | INDIANAPOLIS | 16 |
| 27 | N.Y. GIANTS | 21 |

| Use Name | Pos. | Hgt | Wgt | Age | Int | Pts |
|---|---|---|---|---|---|---|
| Dave Cadigan | OT | 6'4" | 285 | 23 | | |
| Jeff Criswell | OT-OG | 6'7" | 284 | 24 | | |
| Reggie McElroy | OT | 6'6" | 276 | 28 | | |
| Dan Alexander | OG | 6'4" | 274 | 33 | | |
| Ted Banker | OG-C | 6'2" | 275 | 27 | | |
| Mike Haight | OG-OT | 6'4" | 281 | 25 | | |
| Adam Schreiber (from PHI) | OG | 6'4" | 277 | 26 | | |
| Ron Tilton | OG | 6'4" | 250 | 25 | | |
| Mike Withycombe | OG-OT | 6'5" | 295 | 23 | | |
| Guy Bingham | C-OG | 6'3" | 260 | 30 | | |
| Jim Sweeney | C-OT-OG | 6'4" | 270 | 26 | | |
| Paul Frase | DE-NT | 6'5" | 273 | 23 | | |
| Mark Gastineau | DE | 6'5" | 255 | 31 | | |
| Marty Lyons | DE-NT | 6'5" | 269 | 31 | | 2 |
| Tom Baldwin | NT-DE | 6'4" | 275 | 27 | | |
| Mark Garalczyk (from PHX) | DT-DE | 6'5" | 272 | 23 | | |
| Scott Mersereau | NT | 6'3" | 273 | 23 | | |
| Gerald Nichols | NT | 6'2" | 267 | 24 | | |

Michael Mitchell — Hip Injury

| Use Name | Pos. | Hgt | Wgt | Age | Int | Pts |
|---|---|---|---|---|---|---|
| Troy Benson | LB | 6'2" | 235 | 25 | 1 | |
| Kyle Clifton | LB | 6'4" | 236 | 26 | | |
| Robin Cole | LB | 6'2" | 225 | 32 | | |
| Onzy Elam | LB | 6'2" | 225 | 23 | | |
| John Galvin | LB | 6'3" | 226 | 23 | | |
| Alex Gordon | LB | 6'5" | 246 | 23 | | |
| Steve Hammond | LB | 6'4" | 225 | 28 | | |
| Kevin McArthur | LB | 6'2" | 250 | 25 | 1 | |
| Ken Rose | LB | 6'1" | 204 | 26 | | |
| John Booty | DB | 6' | 179 | 22 | 3 | |
| James Hasty | DB | 6' | 200 | 23 | 5 | |
| Carl Howard | DB | 6'2" | 190 | 26 | 2 | |
| Bobby Humphery | DB | 5'10" | 180 | 27 | 1 | |
| Erik McMillan | DB | 6'2" | 197 | 23 | 8 | 12 |
| Rich Miano | DB | 6' | 200 | 25 | 2 | |
| George Radachowsky | DB | 5'11" | 190 | 25 | | |
| Terry Williams | DB | 5'11" | 197 | 22 | | |
| Mike Zordich | DB | 5'11" | 199 | 24 | 1 | 6 |

Bob Crable — Knee Injury
Matt Monger — Forearm Injury
Kerry Glenn — Knee Injury
Bobby Curtis — Injury

| Use Name | Pos. | Hgt | Wgt | Age | Int | Pts |
|---|---|---|---|---|---|---|
| Ken O'Brien | QB | 6'4" | 200 | 27 | | |
| Pat Ryan | QB | 6'3" | 210 | 32 | | |
| Johnny Hector | HB | 5'11" | 202 | 27 | | 60 |
| Freeman McNeil | HB | 5'11" | 209 | 29 | | 42 |
| Marion Barber | FB-TE | 6'3" | 228 | 28 | | |
| Nuu Faaola | FB | 5'11" | 220 | 24 | | |
| Roger Vick | FB | 6'3" | 228 | 24 | | 18 |
| Michael Harper | WR | 5'10" | 180 | 27 | | |
| Kurt Sohn | WR | 5'11" | 180 | 31 | | 12 |
| Al Toon | WR | 6'4" | 205 | 25 | | 30 |
| JoJo Townsell | WR | 5'9" | 180 | 27 | | 6 |
| Wesley Walker | WR | 6' | 182 | 33 | | 42 |
| K.D. Dunn | TE | 6'3" | 237 | 25 | | |
| Billy Griggs | TE | 6'3" | 234 | 26 | | |
| Keith Neubert | TE | 6'5" | 250 | 23 | | |
| Mickey Shuler | TE | 6'3" | 231 | 32 | | 30 |
| Pat Leahy | K | 6' | 196 | 37 | | 112 |
| Joe Prokop | K | 6'2" | 224 | 28 | | |

Rocky Klever — Back Injury
Jamie Kurisko — Hamstring Injury
Kyle Mackey — Shoulder Injury
Tracy Martin — Quadriceps Injury

## MIAMI DOLPHINS 6-10 Don Shula

| | | |
|---|---|---|
| 7 | Chicago | 34 |
| 6 | Buffalo | 9 |
| 24 | GREEN BAY | 17 |
| 13 | Indianapolis | 15 |
| 24 | MINNESOTA | 7 |
| 24 | L.A. Raiders | 14 |
| 31 | SAN DIEGO | 28 |
| 30 | N.Y. JETS | 44 |
| 17 | Tampa Bay | 14 |
| 10 | New England | 21 |
| 6 | BUFFALO | 31 |
| 3 | NEW ENGLAND | 6 |
| 34 | N.Y. Jets | 38 |
| 28 | INDIANAPOLIS | 31 |
| 38 | CLEVELAND | 31 |
| 24 | Pittsburgh | 40 |

| Use Name | Pos. | Hgt | Wgt | Age | Int | Pts |
|---|---|---|---|---|---|---|
| Louis Cheek | OT | 6'6" | 295 | 23 | | |
| Mark Dennis | OT | 6'6" | 290 | 23 | | |
| Jon Giesler | OT | 6'5" | 272 | 31 | | |
| Ronnie Lee | OT | 6'3" | 275 | 31 | | |
| Roy Foster | OG | 6'4" | 275 | 28 | | |
| Harry Galbreath | OG | 6'1" | 275 | 23 | | |
| Greg Johnson | OG | 6'4" | 295 | 23 | | |
| Tom Toth | OG | 6'5" | 282 | 26 | | |
| Jeff Dellenbach | C | 6'6" | 280 | 25 | | |
| John Bosa | DE | 6'4" | 273 | 24 | | |
| Jackie Cline | DE-NT | 6'5" | 280 | 28 | | |
| Jeff Cross | DE | 6'4" | 270 | 22 | | |
| T.J. Turner | DE | 6'4" | 280 | 25 | | |
| Eric Kumerow | DE-LB | 6'7" | 260 | 23 | | |
| Mike Lambrecht | NT | 6'1" | 274 | 25 | | |
| Brian Sochia | NT | 6'3" | 275 | 27 | | |

Chris Scott — Knee Injury
Dwight Stephenson — Knee Injury
Chris Conlin — Knee Injury

| Use Name | Pos. | Hgt | Wgt | Age | Int | Pts |
|---|---|---|---|---|---|---|
| Mark Brown | LB | 6'2" | 238 | 27 | 2 | |
| Bob Brudzinski | LB | 6'4" | 235 | 33 | | |
| David Frye | LB | 6'2" | 227 | 27 | | |
| Tony Furjanic | LB | 6'1" | 228 | 24 | | |
| Chris Gaines | LB | 6' | 238 | 24 | | |
| Rick Graf | LB | 6'5" | 249 | 25 | 1 | |
| Hugh Green | LB | 6'2" | 228 | 29 | | |
| Ilia Jarostchuk | LB | 6'3" | 231 | 24 | | |
| Larry Kolic | LB | 6'1" | 239 | 25 | | |
| John Offerdahl | LB | 6'3" | 237 | 24 | 2 | |
| Jackie Shipp | LB | 6'2" | 238 | 26 | | |
| Bud Brown | DB | 6' | 193 | 27 | | |
| Liffort Hobley | DB | 6' | 202 | 26 | | 6 |
| William Judson | DB | 6'1" | 192 | 29 | 4 | |
| Paul Lankford | DB | 6'1" | 190 | 30 | 1 | |
| Don McNeal | DB | 5'11" | 193 | 30 | 1 | |
| Rodney Thomas | DB | 5'10" | 190 | 22 | 1 | |
| Reyna Thompson | DB | 6' | 193 | 25 | | |
| Jarvis Williams | DB | 5'11" | 196 | 23 | 4 | |

Scott Nicholas — Knee Injury
Glenn Blackwood — Knee Injury

| Use Name | Pos. | Hgt | Wgt | Age | Int | Pts |
|---|---|---|---|---|---|---|
| Ron Jaworski | QB | 6'1" | 205 | 37 | | |
| Dan Marino | QB | 6'4" | 222 | 26 | | |
| Joe Cribbs (from IND) | HB | 5'11" | 190 | 30 | | |
| Lorenzo Hampton | HB | 6' | 208 | 26 | | 72 |
| Troy Stradford | HB | 5'9" | 192 | 23 | | 18 |
| Woody Bennett | FB | 6'2" | 244 | 33 | | |
| Ron Davenport | FB | 6'2" | 232 | 25 | | |
| Fred Banks | WR | 5'10" | 180 | 26 | | 12 |
| Mark Clayton | WR | 5'9" | 184 | 27 | | 84 |
| Mark Duper | WR | 5'9" | 190 | 29 | | 6 |
| Jim Jensen | WR-FB | 6'4" | 220 | 29 | | 30 |
| James Pruitt (to IND) | WR | 6'3" | 198 | 24 | | |
| Scott Schwedes | WR | 6' | 182 | 23 | | |
| Ferrell Edmunds | TE | 6'6" | 248 | 23 | | 18 |
| Bruce Hardy | TE | 6'5" | 234 | 32 | | |
| Brian Kinchen | TE | 6'2" | 238 | 23 | | |
| Tony Franklin | K | 5'8" | 182 | 30 | | 18 |
| Fuad Reveiz | K | 5'11" | 220 | 25 | | 55 |
| Reggie Roby | K | 6'2" | 242 | 27 | | |

Dan Johnson — Back Injury

## BUFFALO BILLS

**RUSHING**

| Last Name | No. | Yds | Avg | TD |
|---|---|---|---|---|
| Thomas | 207 | 881 | 4.3 | 2 |
| Riddick | 111 | 438 | 3.9 | 12 |
| Mueller | 81 | 296 | 3.7 | 0 |
| Harmon | 57 | 212 | 3.7 | 1 |
| Kelly | 35 | 154 | 4.4 | 0 |
| Byrum | 28 | 91 | 3.3 | 0 |
| Reed | 6 | 64 | 10.7 | 0 |
| Reich | 3 | -3 | -1.0 | 0 |

**RECEIVING**

| Last Name | No. | Yds | Avg | TD |
|---|---|---|---|---|
| Reed | 71 | 968 | 13.6 | 6 |
| T. Johnson | 37 | 514 | 13.9 | 0 |
| Harmon | 37 | 427 | 11.5 | 3 |
| Metzelaars | 33 | 438 | 13.3 | 1 |
| Burkett | 23 | 354 | 15.4 | 1 |
| Thomas | 18 | 208 | 11.6 | 0 |
| F. Johnson | 9 | 170 | 18.9 | 1 |
| Mueller | 8 | 42 | 5.3 | 0 |
| Rolle | 2 | 3 | 1.5 | 2 |
| Byrum | 2 | 0 | 0.0 | 0 |
| Kelly | 1 | 5 | 5.0 | 0 |

**PUNT RETURNS**

| Last Name | No. | Yds | Avg | TD |
|---|---|---|---|---|
| F. Johnson | 16 | 72 | 4.5 | 0 |
| Tucker | 10 | 80 | 8.0 | 0 |

**KICKOFF RETURNS**

| Last Name | No. | Yds | Avg | TD |
|---|---|---|---|---|
| Tucker | 15 | 310 | 20.7 | 0 |
| F. Johnson | 14 | 250 | 17.9 | 0 |
| Harmon | 11 | 249 | 22.6 | 0 |
| Riddick | 6 | 100 | 16.7 | 0 |
| Rolle | 1 | 12 | 12.0 | 0 |
| Byrum | 2 | 9 | 4.5 | 0 |
| Pike | 1 | 5 | 5.0 | 0 |

**PASSING — PUNTING — KICKING** — Statistics

PASSING

| Last Name | Att | Cmp | % | Yds | Yd/Att | TD | Int— | % | RK |
|---|---|---|---|---|---|---|---|---|---|
| Kelly | 452 | 269 | 59.5 | 3380 | 7.48 | 15 | 17 | 3.8 | 7 |
| Riddick | 2 | 2 | 100.0 | 31 | 15.50 | 0 | 0 | 0.0 | |

PUNTING

| Last Name | No. | Avg. |
|---|---|---|
| Kidd | 62 | 39.5 |

KICKING

| Last Name | XP | ATT | % | FG | ATT | % |
|---|---|---|---|---|---|---|
| Norwood | 33 | 33 | 100 | 32 | 37 | 86 |

## INDIANAPOLIS COLTS

**RUSHING**

| Last Name | No. | Yds | Avg | TD |
|---|---|---|---|---|
| Dickerson | 388 | 1659 | 4.3 | 14 |
| Bentley | 45 | 230 | 5.1 | 2 |
| Chandler | 46 | 139 | 3.0 | 3 |
| Verdin | 8 | 77 | 9.6 | 0 |
| Brooks | 5 | 62 | 12.4 | 0 |
| Wonsley | 26 | 48 | 1.8 | 1 |
| Turner | 16 | 42 | 2.6 | 2 |
| Hogeboom | 11 | -8 | -0.7 | 1 |

**RECEIVING**

| Last Name | No. | Yds | Avg | TD |
|---|---|---|---|---|
| Brooks | 54 | 867 | 16.1 | 3 |
| Dickerson | 36 | 377 | 10.5 | 1 |
| Boyer | 27 | 256 | 9.5 | 2 |
| Bentley | 26 | 252 | 9.7 | 1 |
| Beach | 26 | 235 | 9.0 | 0 |
| Bouza | 25 | 342 | 13.7 | 4 |
| Verdin | 20 | 437 | 21.9 | 4 |
| Bellini | 5 | 64 | 12.8 | 0 |
| Baldinger | 1 | 37 | 37.0 | 0 |
| Hinton | 1 | 1 | 1.0 | 0 |
| Donaldson | 1 | -3 | -3.0 | 0 |

**PUNT RETURNS**

| Last Name | No. | Yds | Avg | TD |
|---|---|---|---|---|
| Verdin | 22 | 239 | 10.9 | 1 |
| Brooks | 3 | 15 | 5.0 | 0 |
| Prior | 1 | 0 | 0.0 | 0 |

**KICKOFF RETURNS**

| Last Name | No. | Yds | Avg | TD |
|---|---|---|---|---|
| Bentley | 39 | 775 | 19.9 | 0 |
| Verdin | 7 | 145 | 20.7 | 0 |
| Banks | 4 | 56 | 14.0 | 0 |
| Beach | 1 | 35 | 35.0 | 0 |
| Wright | 1 | 22 | 22.0 | 0 |

PASSING

| Last Name | Att | Cmp | % | Yds | Yd/Att | TD | Int— | % | RK |
|---|---|---|---|---|---|---|---|---|---|
| Chandler | 233 | 129 | 55.4 | 1619 | 6.95 | 8 | 12 | 5.2 | 10 |
| Hogeboom | 131 | 76 | 58.0 | 996 | 7.60 | 7 | 7 | 5.3 | |
| Trudeau | 34 | 14 | 41.2 | 158 | 4.65 | 0 | 3 | 8.8 | |
| Turner | 4 | 3 | 75.0 | 92 | 23.00 | 0 | 0 | 0.0 | |
| Bentley | 1 | 0 | 0.0 | 0 | 0.00 | 0 | 0 | 0.0 | |

PUNTING

| Last Name | No. | Avg. |
|---|---|---|
| Stark | 64 | 43.5 |

KICKING

| Last Name | XP | ATT | % | FG | ATT | % |
|---|---|---|---|---|---|---|
| Biasucci | 39 | 40 | 98 | 25 | 32 | 78 |

## NEW ENGLAND PATRIOTS

**RUSHING**

| Last Name | No. | Yds | Avg | TD |
|---|---|---|---|---|
| Stephens | 297 | 1168 | 3.9 | 4 |
| Perryman | 146 | 448 | 3.1 | 6 |
| Flutie | 38 | 179 | 4.7 | 1 |
| Dupard | 52 | 151 | 2.9 | 2 |
| Tatupu | 22 | 75 | 3.4 | 2 |
| Allen | 7 | 40 | 5.7 | 0 |
| Eason | 5 | 18 | 3.6 | 0 |
| C. James | 4 | 15 | 3.8 | 1 |
| Fryar | 6 | 12 | 2.0 | 0 |
| Grogan | 6 | 12 | 2.0 | 1 |
| Ramsey | 3 | 8 | 2.7 | 0 |
| Feagles | 1 | 0 | 0.0 | 0 |
| Morgan | 1 | -6 | -6.0 | 0 |

**RECEIVING**

| Last Name | No. | Yds | Avg | TD |
|---|---|---|---|---|
| Dupard | 34 | 232 | 6.8 | 0 |
| Fryar | 33 | 490 | 14.8 | 5 |
| Morgan | 31 | 502 | 16.2 | 4 |
| Jones | 22 | 313 | 14.2 | 1 |
| Perryman | 17 | 134 | 7.9 | 0 |
| C. James | 14 | 171 | 12.2 | 0 |
| Stephens | 14 | 98 | 7.0 | 0 |
| Francis | 11 | 161 | 14.6 | 0 |
| Dawson | 8 | 106 | 13.3 | 2 |
| Tatupu | 8 | 58 | 7.3 | 0 |
| Martin | 4 | 51 | 12.8 | 0 |
| Scott | 1 | 8 | 8.0 | 0 |
| Johnson | 1 | 5 | 5.0 | 0 |
| Farrell | 1 | 4 | 4.0 | 0 |

**PUNT RETURNS**

| Last Name | No. | Yds | Avg | TD |
|---|---|---|---|---|
| Fryar | 38 | 398 | 10.5 | 0 |
| Bowman | 0 | 0 | 0.0 | 0 |

**KICKOFF RETURNS**

| Last Name | No. | Yds | Avg | TD |
|---|---|---|---|---|
| Martin | 31 | 735 | 23.7 | 1 |
| Allen | 18 | 391 | 21.7 | 0 |
| Davis | 6 | 106 | 17.7 | 0 |
| Tatupu | 1 | 13 | 13.0 | 0 |
| Fryar | 1 | 3 | 3.0 | 0 |

PASSING

| Last Name | Att | Cmp | % | Yds | Yd/Att | TD | Int— | % | RK |
|---|---|---|---|---|---|---|---|---|---|
| Flutie | 179 | 92 | 51.4 | 1150 | 6.42 | 8 | 10 | 5.6 | |
| Grogan | 140 | 67 | 47.9 | 834 | 5.96 | 4 | 13 | 9.3 | |
| Eason | 43 | 28 | 65.1 | 249 | 5.79 | 0 | 2 | 4.7 | |
| Ramsey | 27 | 12 | 44.4 | 100 | 3.70 | 0 | 3 | 11.1 | |

PUNTING

| Last Name | No. | Avg. |
|---|---|---|
| Feagles | 91 | 38.3 |

KICKING

| Last Name | XP | ATT | % | FG | ATT | % |
|---|---|---|---|---|---|---|
| Staurovsky | 14 | 15 | 93 | 7 | 11 | 63 |
| Garcia | 11 | 16 | 69 | 6 | 13 | 46 |

## NEW YORK JETS

**RUSHING**

| Last Name | No. | Yds | Avg | TD |
|---|---|---|---|---|
| McNeil | 219 | 944 | 4.3 | 6 |
| Hector | 137 | 561 | 4.1 | 10 |
| Vick | 128 | 540 | 4.2 | 3 |
| O'Brien | 21 | 25 | 1.2 | 0 |
| Ryan | 5 | 22 | 4.4 | 0 |
| Faaola | 1 | 13 | 13.0 | 0 |
| Walker | 1 | 12 | 12.0 | 0 |
| Leahy | 1 | 10 | 10.0 | 0 |
| Toon | 1 | 5 | 5.0 | 0 |

**RECEIVING**

| Last Name | No. | Yds | Avg | TD |
|---|---|---|---|---|
| Toon | 93 | 1067 | 11.5 | 5 |
| Shuler | 70 | 805 | 11.5 | 5 |
| McNeil | 34 | 288 | 8.5 | 1 |
| Walker | 26 | 551 | 21.2 | 7 |
| Hector | 26 | 237 | 9.1 | 0 |
| Vick | 19 | 120 | 6.3 | 0 |
| Griggs | 14 | 133 | 9.5 | 0 |
| Sohn | 7 | 66 | 9.4 | 2 |
| Dunn | 6 | 67 | 11.2 | 0 |
| Townsell | 4 | 40 | 10.0 | 0 |

**PUNT RETURNS**

| Last Name | No. | Yds | Avg | TD |
|---|---|---|---|---|
| Townsell | 35 | 409 | 11.7 | 1 |
| Sohn | 3 | 9 | 3.0 | 0 |

**KICKOFF RETURNS**

| Last Name | No. | Yds | Avg | TD |
|---|---|---|---|---|
| Humphery | 21 | 510 | 24.3 | 0 |
| Townsell | 31 | 601 | 19.4 | 0 |
| Sohn | 9 | 159 | 17.7 | 0 |
| Harper | 7 | 114 | 16.3 | 0 |
| Faaola | 2 | 9 | 4.5 | 0 |
| Barber | 1 | 11 | 11.0 | 0 |
| Rose | 1 | 0 | 0.0 | 0 |

PASSING

| Last Name | Att | Cmp | % | Yds | Yd/Att | TD | Int— | % | RK |
|---|---|---|---|---|---|---|---|---|---|
| O'Brien | 424 | 236 | 55.7 | 2567 | 6.05 | 15 | 7 | 1.7 | 6 |
| Ryan | 113 | 63 | 55.8 | 807 | 7.14 | 5 | 4 | 3.5 | |
| Hector | 1 | 0 | 0.0 | 0 | 0.0 | 0 | 0 | 0.0 | |

PUNTING

| Last Name | No. | Avg. |
|---|---|---|
| Prokop | 85 | 38.9 |

KICKING

| Last Name | XP | Att | % | FG | Att | % |
|---|---|---|---|---|---|---|
| Leahy | 43 | 43 | 100 | 23 | 28 | 82 |

## MIAMI DOLPHINS

**RUSHING**

| Last Name | No. | Yds | Avg | TD |
|---|---|---|---|---|
| Hampton | 117 | 414 | 3.5 | 9 |
| Stradford | 95 | 335 | 3.5 | 2 |
| Davenport | 55 | 273 | 5.0 | 0 |
| Bennett | 31 | 115 | 3.7 | 0 |
| Jensen | 10 | 68 | 6.8 | 0 |
| Cribbs | 5 | 21 | 4.2 | 0 |
| Clayton | 1 | 4 | 4.0 | 0 |
| Edmunds | 1 | -8 | -8.0 | 0 |
| Marino | 20 | -17 | -0.9 | 0 |

**RECEIVING**

| Last Name | No. | Yds | Avg | TD |
|---|---|---|---|---|
| Clayton | 86 | 1129 | 13.1 | 14 |
| Jensen | 58 | 652 | 11.2 | 5 |
| Stradford | 56 | 426 | 7.6 | 1 |
| Duper | 39 | 626 | 16.1 | 1 |
| Edmunds | 33 | 575 | 17.4 | 3 |
| Devenport | 30 | 282 | 9.4 | 0 |
| Banks | 23 | 430 | 18.7 | 2 |
| Hampton | 23 | 204 | 8.9 | 3 |
| Schwedes | 6 | 130 | 21.7 | 0 |
| Hardy | 4 | 46 | 11.5 | 0 |
| Pruitt | 2 | 38 | 19.0 | 0 |
| Bennett | 2 | 16 | 8.0 | 0 |
| Kinchen | 1 | 3 | 3.0 | 0 |

**PUNT RETURNS**

| Last Name | No. | Yds | Avg | TD |
|---|---|---|---|---|
| Schwedes | 24 | 230 | 9.6 | 0 |
| Williams | 3 | 29 | 9.7 | 0 |

**KICKOFF RETURNS**

| Last Name | No. | Yds | Avg | TD |
|---|---|---|---|---|
| Cribbs | 41 | 863 | 21.0 | 0 |
| Hampton | 9 | 216 | 24.0 | 0 |
| Williams | 8 | 159 | 19.9 | 0 |
| Schwedes | 3 | 49 | 16.3 | 0 |
| Davenport | 2 | 41 | 20.5 | 0 |
| Edmunds | 1 | 20 | 20.0 | 0 |
| Hardy | 1 | 17 | 17.0 | 0 |
| Hill | 1 | 1 | 1.0 | 0 |

PASSING

| Last Name | Att | Cmp | % | Yds | Yd/Att | TD | Int— | % | RK |
|---|---|---|---|---|---|---|---|---|---|
| Marino | 606 | 354 | 58.4 | 4434 | 7.32 | 28 | 23 | 3.8 | 5 |
| Jaworski | 14 | 9 | 64.3 | 123 | 8.79 | 1 | 0 | 0.0 | |
| Stradford | 1 | 0 | 0.0 | 0 | 0 | 0 | 0 | 0.0 | |

PUNTING

| Last Name | No. | Avg. |
|---|---|---|
| Roby | 64 | 43.0 |

KICKING

| Last Name | XP | Att. | % | FG | Att | % |
|---|---|---|---|---|---|---|
| Reveiz | 31 | 32 | 97 | 8 | 12 | 67 |
| Franklin | 6 | 7 | 86 | 4 | 11 | 36 |

1988 A.F.C. — Central Division
578

## CINCINNATI BENGALS 12-4 Sam Wyche

| Scores of Each Game | | |
|---|---|---|
| 21 | PHOENIX | 14 |
| 28 | Philadelphia | 24 |
| 17 | Pittsburgh | 12 |
| 24 | CLEVELAND | 17 |
| 45 | L.A. Raiders | 21 |
| 36 | N.Y. JETS | 19 |
| 21 | New England | 27 |
| 44 | HOUSTON | 21 |
| 16 | Cleveland | 23 |
| 42 | PITTSBURGH | 7 |
| 28 | Kansas City | 31 |
| 38 | Dallas | 24 |
| 35 | BUFFALO | 21 |
| 27 | SAN DIEGO | 10 |
| 6 | Houston | 41 |
| 20 | WASHINGTON | * 17 |

| Use Name | Pos. | Hgt | Wgt | Age | Int | Pts |
|---|---|---|---|---|---|---|
| David Douglas | OT | 6'4" | 280 | 25 | | |
| Anthony Munoz | OT | 6'6" | 278 | 30 | | |
| Dave Smith | OT | 6'7" | 290 | 23 | | |
| Joe Walter | OT | 6'6" | 290 | 25 | | |
| Brian Blados | OG | 6'5" | 295 | 26 | | |
| Max Montoya | OG | 6'5" | 275 | 32 | | |
| Bruce Reimers | OG | 6'7" | 280 | 27 | | |
| Bruce Kozerski | C-OG | 6'4" | 275 | 26 | | |
| Jason Buck | DE | 6'5" | 264 | 25 | | |
| Eddie Edwards | DE | 6'5" | 256 | 34 | | |
| Curtis Maxey | DE | 6'3" | 298 | 23 | | |
| Skip McClendon | DE | 6'7" | 275 | 24 | | |
| Jim Skow | DE | 6'3" | 255 | 25 | | |
| David Grant | NT | 6'4" | 277 | 22 | | |
| Tim Krumrie | NT | 6'2" | 268 | 28 | | |

Mike Hammerstein — Knee Injury

| Use Name | Pos. | Hgt | Wgt | Age | Int | Pts |
|---|---|---|---|---|---|---|
| Leo Barker | LB | 6'2" | 227 | 28 | | 6 |
| Ed Brady | LB | 6'2" | 235 | 28 | | |
| Tim Inglis | LB | 6'3" | 232 | 24 | | |
| Joe Kelly | LB | 6'2" | 231 | 23 | | |
| Emanuel King | LB | 6'4" | 251 | 25 | | |
| Rich Romer | LB | 6'3" | 222 | 22 | | |
| Kevin Walker | LB | 6'2" | 238 | 22 | | |
| Leon White | LB | 6'3" | 245 | 24 | | |
| Reggie Williams | LB | 6'1" | 232 | 33 | | |
| Carl Zander | LB | 6'2" | 235 | 25 | 1 | |
| Lewis Billups | DB | 5'11" | 190 | 24 | 4 | 6 |
| Barney Bussey | DB | 6' | 195 | 26 | | |
| Ellis Dillahunt | DB | 5'11" | 200 | 23 | | |
| Rickey Dixon | DB | 5'11" | 181 | 21 | 1 | |
| David Fulcher | DB | 6'3" | 228 | 26 | 5 | 6 |
| Ray Horton | DB | 5'11" | 190 | 28 | 3 | |
| Daryl Smith | DB | 5'9" | 188 | 25 | | |
| Eric Thomas | DB | 5'11" | 181 | 23 | 7 | |
| Solomon Wilcots | DB | 5'11" | 185 | 23 | 1 | |

Chris Barber — Arm Injury

| Use Name | Pos. | Hgt | Wgt | Age | Int | Pts |
|---|---|---|---|---|---|---|
| Boomer Esiason | QB | 6'4" | 225 | 27 | | 6 |
| Mike Norseth | QB | 6'2" | 200 | 24 | | |
| Turk Schonert | QB | 6'1" | 196 | 31 | | |
| James Brooks | HB | 5'10" | 182 | 29 | | 84 |
| Stanford Jennings | HB | 6'1" | 205 | 26 | | 12 |
| Marc Logan | HB | 5'11" | 207 | 23 | | |
| Stanley Wilson | FB | 5'10" | 212 | 27 | | 18 |
| Ickey Woods | FB | 6'2" | 232 | 22 | | 90 |
| Eddie Brown | WR | 6' | 185 | 25 | | 54 |
| Cris Collinsworth | WR | 6'5" | 192 | 29 | | 6 |
| Ira Hillary | WR | 5'11" | 190 | 25 | | 6 |
| Mike Martin | WR | 5'10" | 186 | 27 | | 6 |
| Tim McGee | WR | 5'10" | 175 | 24 | | 36 |
| Carl Parker | WR | 6'2" | 201 | 23 | | |
| Rodney Holman | TE | 6'3" | 238 | 28 | | 18 |
| Eric Kattus | TE | 6'5" | 235 | 25 | | |
| Jim Riggs | TE | 6'5" | 245 | 24 | | |
| Jim Breech | K | 5'6" | 161 | 32 | | 89 |
| Scott Fulhage | K | 5'11" | 191 | 23 | | |
| Lee Johnson (from CLE) | K | 6'2" | 198 | 26 | | 3 |

## CLEVELAND BROWNS 10-6 Marty Schottenheimer

| Scores of Each Game | | |
|---|---|---|
| 6 | Kansas City | 3 |
| 3 | N.Y. JETS | 23 |
| 23 | INDIANAPOLIS | 17 |
| 17 | Cincinnati | 24 |
| 23 | Pittsburgh | 9 |
| 10 | SEATTLE | 16 |
| 19 | PHILADELPHIA | 3 |
| 29 | Phoenix | 21 |
| 23 | CINCINNATI | 21 |
| 17 | Houston | 24 |
| 7 | Denver | 30 |
| 27 | PITTSBURGH | 7 |
| 17 | Washington | 13 |
| 24 | DALLAS | 21 |
| 31 | Miami | 38 |
| 28 | HOUSTON | 23 |

| Use Name | Pos. | Hgt | Wgt | Age | Int | Pts |
|---|---|---|---|---|---|---|
| Rickey Bolden | OT | 6'6" | 280 | 26 | | 6 |
| Paul Farren | OT | 6'5" | 280 | 27 | | |
| Cody Risien | OT | 6'7" | 280 | 31 | | |
| Dan Fike | OG | 6'7" | 280 | 27 | | |
| Tony Jones | OG | 6'5" | 280 | 22 | | |
| Larry Williams | OG | 6'5" | 290 | 25 | | |
| Gregg Rakoczy | C | 6'6" | 290 | 23 | | |
| Frank Winters | C | 6'3" | 280 | 24 | | |
| Charles Buchanan | DE | 6'3" | 245 | 23 | | 2 |
| Sam Clancy | DE | 6'7" | 275 | 30 | | |
| Carl Hairston | DE-LB | 6'3" | 280 | 35 | | |
| Michael Dean Perry | DE-DT | 6'1" | 285 | 23 | | |
| Darryl Sims | DE-NT | 6'3" | 290 | 27 | | |
| Marlon Jones | DT-DE | 6'4" | 260 | 24 | | |
| Bob Golic | NT-DE | 6'2" | 265 | 30 | | |

| Use Name | Pos. | Hgt | Wgt | Age | Int | Pts |
|---|---|---|---|---|---|---|
| Clifford Charlton | LB | 6'3" | 240 | 23 | | |
| Dave Grayson | LB | 6'2" | 230 | 24 | | |
| Anthony Griggs | LB | 6'3" | 230 | 28 | | |
| Eddie Johnson | LB | 6'1" | 225 | 28 | 2 | |
| Mike Johnson | LB | 6'1" | 225 | 25 | 2 | |
| Mike Junkin | LB | 6'3" | 238 | 23 | | |
| Clay Matthews | LB | 6'2" | 245 | 32 | | |
| Van Waiters | LB | 6'4" | 240 | 23 | | |
| Anthony Blaylock | DB | 5'11" | 190 | 23 | | |
| Stephen Braggs | DB | 5'10" | 180 | 23 | | |
| Hanford Dixon | DB | 5'11" | 195 | 29 | 2 | |
| Thane Gash | DB | 6' | 200 | 23 | | |
| Mark Harper | DB | 5'9" | 185 | 26 | 2 | |
| Will Hill | DB | 6' | 200 | 25 | | |
| Frank Minnifield | DB | 5'9" | 185 | 28 | 4 | 6 |
| Brian Washington | DB | 6' | 210 | 22 | 3 | 6 |
| Felix Wright | DB | 6'2" | 190 | 29 | 5 | |

| Use Name | Pos. | Hgt | Wgt | Age | Int | Pts |
|---|---|---|---|---|---|---|
| Gary Danielson | QB | 6'2" | 196 | 36 | | |
| Bernie Kosar | QB | 6'5" | 210 | 24 | | 6 |
| Mike Pagel | QB | 6'2" | 211 | 27 | | |
| Steve Slayden | QB | 6'1" | 185 | 22 | | |
| Don Strock | QB | 6'5" | 225 | 37 | | |
| Tony Baker | HB | 5'10" | 180 | 24 | | |
| Earnest Byner | HB | 5'10" | 215 | 25 | | 18 |
| Herman Fontenot | HB | 6' | 206 | 24 | | 12 |
| Kevin Mack | FB | 6' | 235 | 26 | | 18 |
| Tim Manoa | FB | 6'1" | 227 | 23 | | 12 |
| Brian Brennan | WR | 5'9" | 178 | 26 | | 6 |
| Reggie Langhorne | WR | 6'2" | 200 | 25 | | 48 |
| Gerald McNeil | WR | 5'7" | 147 | 26 | | |
| Webster Slaughter | WR | 6' | 170 | 23 | | 12 |
| Clarence Weathers | WR | 5'9" | 170 | 26 | | 6 |
| Glen Young | WR | 6'2" | 205 | 27 | | |
| Ozzie Newsome | TE | 6'2" | 232 | 32 | | 12 |
| Derek Tennell | TE | 6'5" | 245 | 24 | | 6 |
| Matt Bahr | K | 5'10" | 175 | 32 | | 100 |
| Max Runager (from SF) | K | 6'1" | 189 | 32 | | |

Jeff Jaeger — Foot Injury
Jeff Modesitt — Shoulder Injury
George Swarn — Ankle Injury

## HOUSTON OILERS 10-6 Jerry Glanville

| Scores of Each Game | | |
|---|---|---|
| 17 | Indianapolis | * 14 |
| 38 | L.A. RAIDERS | 35 |
| 3 | N.Y. Jets | 45 |
| 31 | NEW ENGLAND | 6 |
| 23 | Philadelphia | 32 |
| 7 | KANSAS CITY | 6 |
| 34 | Pittsburgh | 14 |
| 21 | Cincinnati | 44 |
| 41 | WASHINGTON | 17 |
| 24 | CLEVELAND | 17 |
| 24 | Seattle | 27 |
| 38 | PHOENIX | 20 |
| 25 | Dallas | 17 |
| 34 | PITTSBURGH | 37 |
| 41 | CINCINNATI | 6 |
| 23 | Cleveland | 28 |

| Use Name | Pos. | Hgt | Wgt | Age | Int | Pts |
|---|---|---|---|---|---|---|
| Bruce Davis | OT | 6'6" | 315 | 32 | | |
| Don Maggs | OT-OG | 6'5" | 285 | 26 | | |
| Dean Steinkuhler | OT | 6'3" | 291 | 27 | | |
| Vince Stroth | OT-TE | 6'4" | 275 | 27 | | |
| Bruce Matthews | OG | 6'4" | 293 | 27 | | |
| Mike Munchak | OG | 6'3" | 284 | 28 | | |
| John Davis | C-OT | 6'4" | 293 | 23 | | |
| Jay Pennison | C | 6'1" | 282 | 26 | | |
| Robert Banks | DE | 6'5" | 263 | 24 | | |
| Richard Byrd | DE-NT | 6'4" | 267 | 26 | 1 | |
| Ray Childress | DE | 6'6" | 270 | 25 | | |
| William Fuller | DE | 6'3" | 269 | 26 | 1 | |
| Sean Jones | DE | 6'7" | 273 | 25 | | |
| Doug Mikolas (from SF) | NT | 6'1" | 270 | 26 | | |
| Doug Smith | NT | 6'5" | 282 | 29 | 1 | |

Doug Williams — Leg Injury
Almon Young — Hand Injury

| Use Name | Pos. | Hgt | Wgt | Age | Int | Pts |
|---|---|---|---|---|---|---|
| Toby Caston | LB | 6'1" | 240 | 23 | | |
| Eric Fairs | LB | 6'3" | 240 | 24 | | 2 |
| John Grimsley | LB | 6'2" | 238 | 26 | 1 | |
| Walter Johnson | LB | 6' | 240 | 24 | | |
| Robert Lyles | LB | 6'1" | 230 | 27 | 2 | |
| Johnny Meads | LB | 6'2" | 235 | 27 | | |
| Eugene Seale | LB | 5'10" | 240 | 24 | 1 | 2 |
| Al Smith | LB | 6'1" | 236 | 23 | | |
| Patrick Allen | DB | 5'10" | 182 | 27 | 1 | |
| Keith Bostic | DB | 6'1" | 215 | 27 | 1 | |
| Steve Brown | DB | 5'11" | 192 | 28 | 2 | 6 |
| Domingo Bryant | DB | 6'4" | 178 | 24 | 3 | 6 |
| Cris Dishman | DB | 6' | 180 | 23 | | 6 |
| Jeff Donaldson | DB | 6' | 190 | 26 | 4 | |
| Kenny Johnson | DB | 5'10" | 172 | 30 | 1 | |
| Richard Johnson | DB | 6'1" | 190 | 24 | 3 | |
| Quintin Jones | DB | 5'11' | 193 | 22 | | |
| Calvin Loveall (to KC and ATL) | DB | 5'9" | 180 | 26 | | |

Audrey McMillian — Knee Injury

| Use Name | Pos. | Hgt | Wgt | Age | Int | Pts |
|---|---|---|---|---|---|---|
| Cody Carlson | QB | 6'3" | 199 | 24 | | 6 |
| Warren Moon | QB | 6'3" | 210 | 31 | | 30 |
| Brent Pease | QB | 6'2" | 204 | 23 | | 6 |
| Allen Pinkett | HB | 5'9" | 192 | 24 | | 54 |
| Mike Rozier | HB | 5'10" | 213 | 27 | | 66 |
| Lorenzo White | HB | 5'11" | 209 | 22 | | 6 |
| Alonzo Highsmith | FB | 6'1" | 234 | 23 | | 12 |
| Spencer Tillman | FB | 5'11" | 208 | 24 | | |
| Willie Drewrey | WR | 5'7" | 164 | 25 | | 6 |
| Curtis Duncan | WR | 5'11" | 185 | 23 | | 6 |
| Ernest Givins | WR | 5'9" | 172 | 23 | | 30 |
| Leonard Harris | WR | 5'8" | 162 | 27 | | |
| Drew Hill | WR | 5'9" | 175 | 31 | | 60 |
| Haywood Jeffires | WR | 6'2" | 198 | 23 | | 6 |
| Chris Verhulst | TE | 6'2" | 249 | 22 | | |
| Jamie Williams | TE | 6'4" | 255 | 28 | | |
| Greg Montgomery | K | 6'3" | 213 | 23 | | |
| Tony Zendejas | K | 5'8" | 165 | 28 | | 114 |

Ray Wallace — Ankle Injury

## PITTSBURGH STEELERS 5-11 Chuck Noll

| Scores of Each Game | | |
|---|---|---|
| 24 | DALLAS | 21 |
| 29 | Washington | 30 |
| 12 | CINCINNATI | 17 |
| 28 | Buffalo | 36 |
| 9 | CLEVELAND | 23 |
| 14 | Phoenix | 31 |
| 14 | HOUSTON | 34 |
| 39 | DENVER | 21 |
| 20 | N.Y. Jets | 24 |
| 7 | Cincinnati | 42 |
| 26 | PHILADELPHIA | 27 |
| 7 | Cleveland | 27 |
| 16 | KANSAS CITY | 10 |
| 37 | Houston | 34 |
| 14 | San Diego | 20 |
| 40 | MIAMI | 24 |

| Use Name | Pos. | Hgt | Wgt | Age | Int | Pts |
|---|---|---|---|---|---|---|
| Jim Boyle | OT | 6'5" | 275 | 26 | | |
| Tunch Ilkin | OT | 6'3" | 266 | 30 | | |
| John Jackson | OT | 6'6" | 282 | 23 | | |
| Craig Wolfley | OT-OG | 6'1" | 269 | 30 | | |
| Brian Blankenship | OG-C | 6'1" | 275 | 25 | | |
| Dermontti Dawson | OG | 6'2" | 271 | 23 | | |
| Terry Long | OG | 5'11" | 275 | 29 | | |
| John Rienstra | OG | 6'5" | 268 | 25 | | |
| Chuck Lanza | C | 6'2" | 263 | 23 | | |
| Mike Webster | C | 6'1" | 254 | 36 | | |
| Keith Gary | DE | 6'3" | 268 | 28 | | |
| Tim Johnson | DE-DT | 6'3" | 261 | 23 | | |
| Aaron Jones | DE-LB | 6'5" | 257 | 21 | | |
| Jerry Reese | DE | 6'2" | 267 | 24 | | |
| Ben Thomas | DE | 6'4" | 275 | 27 | | |
| Rollin Putzier | DT | 6'4" | 281 | 22 | | |
| Lorenzo Freeman | NT-DT | 6'5" | 298 | 24 | | |
| Gerald Williams | NT-DT | 6'3" | 262 | 24 | | |

Buddy Aydelette — Knee Injury
Keith Willis — Neck Injury

| Use Name | Pos. | Hgt | Wgt | Age | Int | Pts |
|---|---|---|---|---|---|---|
| Gregg Carr | LB | 6'2" | 222 | 26 | 1 | |
| Anthony Henton | LB | 6'1" | 230 | 25 | | |
| Bryan Hinkle | LB | 6'2" | 222 | 29 | 1 | |
| Darin Jordan | LB-DE | 6'1" | 235 | 23 | 1 | 6 |
| David Little | LB | 6'1" | 230 | 29 | 1 | |
| Greg Lloyd | LB | 6'2" | 224 | 23 | | |
| Hardy Nickerson | LB | 6'2" | 229 | 23 | 1 | |
| Tyronne Stowe | LB | 6'1" | 236 | 23 | | |
| Thomas Everett | DB | 5'9" | 179 | 23 | 3 | |
| Cornell Gowdy | DB | 6'1" | 202 | 24 | 1 | |
| Larry Griffin | DB | 6' | 200 | 25 | 2 | |
| Delton Hall | DB | 6'1" | 205 | 23 | | |
| Greg Lee | DB | 6'1" | 207 | 23 | | |
| Lupe Sanchez | DB | 5'10" | 195 | 26 | 1 | |
| Dwayne Woodruff | DB | 6' | 198 | 31 | 4 | 6 |
| Rod Woodson | DB | 6' | 199 | 23 | 4 | 6 |

Mike Merriweather — Holdout

| Use Name | Pos. | Hgt | Wgt | Age | Int | Pts |
|---|---|---|---|---|---|---|
| Todd Blackledge | QB | 6'3" | 227 | 27 | | 6 |
| Steve Bono | QB | 6'4" | 215 | 26 | | |
| Bubby Brister | QB | 6'3" | 205 | 26 | | 36 |
| Rodney Carter | HB | 6' | 216 | 23 | | 30 |
| Dwight Stone | HB | 6' | 188 | 24 | | 12 |
| Warren Williams | HB | 6' | 202 | 23 | | 6 |
| Merril Hoge | FB | 6'2" | 226 | 23 | | 36 |
| Earnest Jackson | FB-HB | 5'9" | 222 | 28 | | 18 |
| Frank Pollard | FB | 5'10" | 229 | 31 | | |
| Joey Clinkscales (to TB) | WR | 6' | 203 | 24 | | |
| Troy Johnson | WR | 6'1" | 185 | 25 | | |
| Louis Lipps | WR | 5'10" | 190 | 26 | | 36 |
| Charles Lockett | WR | 6' | 181 | 22 | | 6 |
| Weegie Thompson | WR | 6'6" | 216 | 27 | | 6 |
| Preston Gothard | TE | 6'4" | 235 | 26 | | 6 |
| Mike Hinnant | TE | 6'3" | 258 | 21 | | |
| Jeff Markland | TE | 6'3" | 245 | 22 | | |
| Gary Anderson | K | 5'11" | 175 | 29 | | 118 |
| Harry Newsome | K | 6' | 188 | 25 | | |

## CINCINNATI BENGALS

### RUSHING

| Last Name | No. | Yds | Avg | TD |
|---|---|---|---|---|
| Woods | 203 | 1066 | 5.3 | 15 |
| Brooks | 182 | 931 | 5.1 | 8 |
| Wilson | 112 | 398 | 3.6 | 2 |
| Esiason | 43 | 248 | 5.8 | 1 |
| Jennings | 17 | 47 | 2.8 | 1 |
| Logan | 2 | 10 | 5.0 | 0 |
| Schonert | 2 | 10 | 5.0 | 0 |
| Norseth | 1 | 5 | 5.0 | 0 |
| Brown | 1 | -5 | -5.0 | 0 |

### RECEIVING

| Last Name | No. | Yds | Avg | TD |
|---|---|---|---|---|
| Brown | 53 | 1273 | 24.0 | 9 |
| Holman | 39 | 527 | 13.5 | 3 |
| McGee | 36 | 686 | 19.1 | 6 |
| Brooks | 29 | 287 | 9.9 | 6 |
| Woods | 21 | 199 | 9.5 | 0 |
| Collinsworth | 13 | 227 | 17.5 | 1 |
| Wilson | 9 | 110 | 12.2 | 1 |
| Riggs | 9 | 82 | 9.1 | 0 |
| Hillary | 5 | 76 | 15.2 | 1 |
| Jennings | 5 | 75 | 15.0 | 0 |
| Martin | 2 | 22 | 11.0 | 1 |
| Logan | 2 | 20 | 10.0 | 0 |
| Kattus | 2 | 8 | 4.0 | 0 |

### PUNT RETURNS

| Last Name | No. | Yds | Avg | TD |
|---|---|---|---|---|
| Hillary | 17 | 166 | 9.8 | 0 |
| Brown | 10 | 48 | 4.8 | 0 |
| Martin | 5 | 30 | 6.0 | 0 |

### KICKOFF RETURNS

| Last Name | No. | Yds | Avg | TD |
|---|---|---|---|---|
| Jennings | 32 | 684 | 21.4 | 1 |
| Hillary | 12 | 195 | 16.3 | 0 |
| Bussey | 7 | 83 | 11.9 | 0 |
| Logan | 4 | 80 | 20.0 | 0 |
| Dixon | 1 | 18 | 18.0 | 0 |
| Brooks | 1 | -6 | -6.0 | 0 |
| Riggs | 0 | 0 | — | 0 |

### PASSING — PUNTING — KICKING

| PASSING | Att | Cmp | % | Yds | Yd/Att | TD | Int | — | % | RK |
|---|---|---|---|---|---|---|---|---|---|---|
| Esiason | 388 | 223 | 57.5 | 3572 | 9.21 | 28 | 14 | — | 3.6 | 1 |
| Schonert | 4 | 2 | 50.0 | 20 | 5.00 | 0 | 0 | — | 0.0 | |

| PUNTING | No. | Avg. |
|---|---|---|
| Johnson | 31 | 39.9 |

| KICKING | XP | Att. | % | FG | Att | % |
|---|---|---|---|---|---|---|
| Breech | 56 | 59 | 95 | 11 | 16 | 69 |
| Johnson | | | | 1 | 2 | 50 |

## CLEVELAND BROWNS

### RUSHING

| Last Name | No. | Yds | Avg | TD |
|---|---|---|---|---|
| Byner | 157 | 576 | 3.7 | 3 |
| Mack | 123 | 485 | 3.9 | 3 |
| Manoa | 99 | 389 | 3.9 | 2 |
| Fontenot | 28 | 87 | 3.1 | 0 |
| Langhorne | 2 | 26 | 13.0 | 1 |
| Baker | 3 | 19 | 6.3 | 0 |
| Danielson | 4 | 3 | 0.8 | 0 |
| Pagel | 4 | 1 | .03 | 0 |
| Runager | 1 | 0 | 0.0 | 0 |
| Kosar | 12 | -1 | -0.1 | 1 |
| Strock | 6 | -2 | -0.3 | 0 |
| Bahr | 1 | -8 | -8.0 | 0 |

### RECEIVING

| Last Name | No. | Yds | Avg | TD |
|---|---|---|---|---|
| Byner | 59 | 576 | 9.8 | 2 |
| Langhorne | 57 | 780 | 13.7 | 7 |
| Brennan | 46 | 579 | 12.6 | 1 |
| Newsome | 35 | 343 | 9.8 | 2 |
| Slaughter | 30 | 462 | 15.4 | 3 |
| Weathers | 29 | 436 | 15.0 | 1 |
| Fontenot | 19 | 170 | 8.9 | 1 |
| Mack | 11 | 87 | 7.9 | 0 |
| Manoa | 10 | 54 | 5.4 | 0 |
| Tennell | 9 | 88 | 9.8 | 1 |
| McNeil | 5 | 74 | 14.8 | 0 |
| Young | 2 | 34 | 17.0 | 0 |
| Bolden | 1 | 3 | 3.0 | 1 |

### PUNT RETURNS

| Last Name | No. | Yds | Avg | TD |
|---|---|---|---|---|
| McNeil | 38 | 315 | 8.3 | 0 |
| Weathers | 2 | 10 | 5.0 | 0 |

### KICKOFF RETURNS

| Last Name | No. | Yds | Avg | TD |
|---|---|---|---|---|
| Young | 29 | 635 | 21.9 | 0 |
| Fontenot | 45 | 879 | 19.5 | 0 |
| McNeil | 2 | 38 | 19.5 | 0 |
| Braggs | 1 | 27 | 27.0 | 0 |
| Perry | 1 | 13 | 13.0 | 0 |
| Tennell | 1 | 11 | 11.0 | 0 |

### PASSING — PUNTING — KICKING

| PASSING | Att | Cmp | % | Yds | Yd/Att | TD | Int | — | % | RK |
|---|---|---|---|---|---|---|---|---|---|---|
| Kosar | 259 | 156 | 60.2 | 1890 | 7.30 | 10 | 7 | — | 2.7 | 4 |
| Pagel | 134 | 71 | 53.0 | 736 | 5.49 | 3 | 4 | — | 3.0 | |
| Strock | 91 | 55 | 60.4 | 736 | 8.09 | 6 | 5 | — | 5.5 | |
| Danielson | 52 | 31 | 59.6 | 324 | 6.23 | 0 | 1 | — | 1.9 | |
| Fontenot | 1 | 0 | 0.0 | 0 | 0.00 | 0 | 0 | — | 0.0 | |

| PUNTING | No. | Avg. |
|---|---|---|
| Runager | 47 | 40.1 |

| KICKING | XP | Att. | % | FG | Att | % |
|---|---|---|---|---|---|---|
| Bahr | 32 | 33 | 97 | 24 | 29 | 83 |

## HOUSTON OILERS

### RUSHING

| Last Name | No. | Yds | Avg | TD |
|---|---|---|---|---|
| Rozier | 251 | 1002 | 4.0 | 10 |
| Pinkett | 122 | 513 | 4.2 | 7 |
| Highsmith | 94 | 466 | 5.0 | 2 |
| White | 31 | 115 | 3.7 | 0 |
| Moon | 33 | 88 | 2.7 | 5 |
| Carlson | 12 | 36 | 3.0 | 1 |
| Givins | 4 | 26 | 6.5 | 0 |
| Tillman | 3 | 5 | 1.7 | 0 |
| Pease | 8 | -2 | -0.3 | 1 |

### RECEIVING

| Last Name | No. | Yds | Avg | TD |
|---|---|---|---|---|
| Hill | 72 | 1141 | 15.8 | 10 |
| Givins | 60 | 976 | 16.3 | 5 |
| Duncan | 22 | 302 | 13.7 | 1 |
| Highsmith | 12 | 131 | 10.9 | 0 |
| Pinkett | 12 | 114 | 9.5 | 2 |
| Drewrey | 11 | 172 | 15.6 | 1 |
| Rozier | 11 | 99 | 9.0 | 1 |
| Harris | 10 | 136 | 13.6 | 0 |
| Williams | 6 | 46 | 7.7 | 0 |
| Jeffires | 2 | 49 | 24.5 | 0 |

### PUNT RETURNS

| Last Name | No. | Yds | Avg | TD |
|---|---|---|---|---|
| K. Johnson | 30 | 170 | 5.7 | 0 |
| Duncan | 4 | 47 | 11.8 | 0 |
| Drewrey | 2 | 8 | 4.0 | 0 |

### KICKOFF RETURNS

| Last Name | No. | Yds | Avg | TD |
|---|---|---|---|---|
| Harris | 34 | 678 | 19.9 | 0 |
| White | 8 | 196 | 24.5 | 1 |
| Pinkett | 7 | 137 | 19.6 | 0 |
| K. Johnson | 6 | 157 | 26.2 | 0 |
| Duncan | 1 | 34 | 34.0 | 0 |
| Tillman | 1 | 13 | 13.0 | 0 |
| Drewrey | 1 | 10 | 10.0 | 0 |
| Donaldson | 1 | 5 | 5.0 | 0 |
| R. Johnson | 1 | 2 | 2.0 | 0 |

### PASSING — PUNTING — KICKING

| PASSING | Att | Cmp | % | Yds | Yd/Att | TD | Int | — | % | RK |
|---|---|---|---|---|---|---|---|---|---|---|
| Moon | 294 | 160 | 54.4 | 2327 | 7.91 | 17 | 8 | — | 2.7 | 3 |
| Carlson | 112 | 52 | 46.4 | 775 | 6.92 | 4 | 6 | — | 5.4 | |
| Pease | 22 | 6 | 27.3 | 64 | 2.91 | 0 | 4 | — | 18.2 | |

| PUNTING | No. | Avg. |
|---|---|---|
| Montgomery | 65 | 38.8 |

| KICKING | XP | ATT | % | FG | ATT | % |
|---|---|---|---|---|---|---|
| Zendejas | 48 | 50 | 96 | 22 | 34 | 65 |

## PITTSBURGH STEELERS

### RUSHING

| Last Name | No. | Yds | Avg | TD |
|---|---|---|---|---|
| Hoge | 170 | 705 | 4.1 | 3 |
| W. Williams | 87 | 409 | 4.7 | 0 |
| E. Jackson | 74 | 315 | 4.3 | 3 |
| Carter | 36 | 216 | 6.0 | 3 |
| Brister | 45 | 209 | 4.6 | 6 |
| Lipps | 6 | 129 | 21.5 | 1 |
| Stone | 40 | 127 | 3.2 | 0 |
| Pollard | 31 | 93 | 3.0 | 0 |
| Blackledge | 8 | 25 | 3.1 | 1 |
| Newsome | 2 | 0 | 0.0 | 0 |

### RECEIVING

| Last Name | No. | Yds | Avg | TD |
|---|---|---|---|---|
| Lipps | 50 | 973 | 19.5 | 5 |
| Hoge | 50 | 487 | 9.7 | 3 |
| Carter | 32 | 363 | 11.3 | 2 |
| Lockett | 22 | 365 | 16.6 | 1 |
| Thompson | 16 | 370 | 23.1 | 1 |
| Gothard | 12 | 121 | 10.1 | 0 |
| Stone | 11 | 196 | 17.8 | 1 |
| W. Williams | 11 | 66 | 6.0 | 0 |
| Tr. Johnson | 10 | 237 | 23.7 | 0 |
| E. Jackson | 9 | 84 | 9.3 | 0 |
| Pollard | 2 | 22 | 11.0 | 0 |
| Hinnant | 1 | 23 | 23.0 | 0 |

### PUNT RETURNS

| Last Name | No. | Yds | Avg | TD |
|---|---|---|---|---|
| Woodson | 33 | 281 | 8.5 | 0 |
| Lipps | 4 | 30 | 7.5 | 0 |
| Sanchez | 2 | 11 | 5.5 | 0 |

### KICKOFF RETURNS

| Last Name | No. | Yds | Avg | TD |
|---|---|---|---|---|
| Woodson | 37 | 850 | 23.0 | 1 |
| Stone | 29 | 610 | 21.0 | 1 |
| Sanchez | 4 | 71 | 21.0 | 0 |
| Boyle | 1 | 19 | 19.0 | 0 |
| J. Jackson | 1 | 10 | 10.0 | 0 |
| W. Williams | 1 | 10 | 10.0 | 0 |
| Blankenship | 1 | 5 | 5.0 | 0 |

### PASSING — PUNTING — KICKING

| PASSING | Att | Cmp | % | Yds | Yd/Att | TD | Int | — | % | RK |
|---|---|---|---|---|---|---|---|---|---|---|
| Brister | 370 | 175 | 47.3 | 2634 | 7.12 | 11 | 14 | — | 3.8 | 13 |
| Blackledge | 79 | 38 | 48.1 | 494 | 6.25 | 2 | 3 | — | 3.8 | |
| Bono | 35 | 10 | 28.6 | 110 | 3.14 | 1 | 2 | — | 5.7 | |
| Carter | 3 | 2 | 66.7 | 56 | 18.67 | 0 | 0 | — | 0.0 | |
| Lipps | 2 | 1 | 50.0 | 13 | 6.50 | 1 | 1 | — | 50.0 | |

| PUNTING | No. | Avg. |
|---|---|---|
| Newsome | 71 | 41.5 |

| KICKING | XP | Att | % | FG | Att | % |
|---|---|---|---|---|---|---|
| Anderson | 34 | 35 | 97 | 28 | 36 | 78 |

# 1988 A.F.C. — Western Division

## SEATTLE SEAHAWKS 9-7 Chuck Knox

| Scores of Each Game | | |
|---|---|---|
| 21 | Denver | 14 |
| 31 | KANSAS CITY | 10 |
| 6 | San Diego | 17 |
| 7 | SAN FRANCISCO | 38 |
| 31 | Atlanta | 20 |
| 16 | Cleveland | 10 |
| 19 | NEW ORLEANS | 20 |
| 10 | L.A. Rams | 31 |
| 17 | SAN DIEGO | 14 |
| 3 | BUFFALO | 13 |
| 27 | HOUSTON | 24 |
| 24 | Kansas City | 27 |
| 35 | L.A. RAIDERS | 27 |
| 7 | New England | 13 |
| 42 | DENVER | 14 |
| 43 | L.A. Raiders | 37 |

| Use Name | Pos. | Hgt | Wgt | Age | Int | Pts |
|---|---|---|---|---|---|---|
| Ron Mattes | OT | 6'6" | 302 | 25 | | |
| Mike Wilson | OT | 6'5" | 274 | 33 | | |
| Edwin Bailey | OG | 6'4" | 270 | 29 | | |
| Tim Burnham | OG | 6'5" | 280 | 25 | | |
| Chris Godfrey | OG | 6'3" | 265 | 30 | | |
| Bryan Millard | OG-OT | 6'5" | 281 | 27 | | |
| Alvin Powell | OG | 6'5" | 296 | 28 | | |
| Blair Bush | C | 6'3" | 272 | 31 | | |
| Stan Eisenhooth | C-OT | 6'5" | 274 | 25 | | |
| Grant Feasel | C | 6'7" | 277 | 28 | | |
| Jeff Bryant | DE | 6'5" | 268 | 28 | | |
| Jacob Green | DE | 6'3" | 254 | 31 | | 6 |
| Doug Hollie | DE | 6'4" | 265 | 27 | | |
| Alonzo Mitz | DE | 6'3" | 271 | 25 | | |
| Ken Clarke | NT | 6'2" | 271 | 32 | | |
| Joe Nash | NT | 6'2" | 269 | 27 | | |
| Brian Bosworth | LB | 6'2" | 248 | 23 | | |
| Darren Comeaux | LB | 6'1" | 227 | 28 | 1 | |
| Greg Gaines | LB | 6'3" | 229 | 29 | | |
| M.L. Johnson | LB | 6'3" | 229 | 24 | | |
| Darrin Miller | LB | 6'1" | 227 | 23 | 1 | |
| Bruce Scholtz | LB | 6'6" | 241 | 29 | | |
| Tony Woods | LB | 6'4" | 244 | 22 | | |
| David Wyman | LB | 6'2" | 234 | 24 | | |
| Rufus Porter | LB | 6'1" | 207 | 23 | | |
| Vernon Dean | DB | 5'11" | 180 | 29 | 1 | 6 |
| Nesby Glasgow | DB | 5'10" | 187 | 31 | 2 | |
| Dwayne Harper | DB | 5'11" | 165 | 22 | | |
| David Hollis (to and from KC) | DB | 5'11" | 180 | 23 | 2 | |
| Patrick Hunter | DB | 5'11" | 185 | 23 | | |
| Melvin Jenkins | DB | 5'10" | 173 | 26 | 3 | |
| Paul Moyer | DB | 6'1" | 196 | 27 | 6 | |
| Eugene Robinson | DB | 6' | 183 | 25 | 1 | |
| Terry Taylor | DB | 5'10" | 191 | 27 | 5 | 6 |
| Jeff Kemp | QB | 6' | 198 | 29 | | |
| Dave Krieg | QB | 6'1" | 192 | 29 | | |
| Bruce Mathison | QB | 6'3" | 205 | 29 | | |
| Kelly Stouffer | QB | 6'3" | 210 | 24 | | |
| Bobby Joe Edmonds | HB | 5'11" | 184 | 23 | | |
| Kevin Harmon | HB | 6' | 190 | 22 | | |
| Randall Morris (to DET) | HB | 6' | 200 | 26 | | |
| Curt Warner | HB | 5'11" | 205 | 27 | | 72 |
| Tommie Agee | FB | 6' | 218 | 24 | | |
| John L. Williams | FB | 5'11" | 226 | 23 | | 42 |
| Brian Blades | WR | 5'11 | 182 | 23 | | 48 |
| Ray Butler | WR | 6'3" | 204 | 32 | | 24 |
| Louis Clark | WR | 6'1" | 193 | 24 | | 6 |
| Tommy Kane | WR | 5'11" | 180 | 24 | | |
| Steve Largent | WR | 5'11" | 191 | 33 | | 12 |
| Paul Skansi | WR | 5'11" | 184 | 27 | | 6 |
| Jimmy Teal | WR | 5'11" | 175 | 26 | | |
| John Spagnola | TE | 6'4" | 242 | 31 | | 6 |
| Mike Tice | TE | 6'7" | 244 | 29 | | |
| Norm Johnson | K | 6'2" | 197 | 28 | | 105 |
| Ruben Rodriguez | K | 6'2" | 214 | 23 | | |

Roland Barbay — Knee Injury

Sam Merriman — Knee Injury

## DENVER BRONCOS 8-8 Dan Reeves

| Scores of Each Game | | |
|---|---|---|
| 14 | SEATTLE | 21 |
| 34 | SAN DIEGO | 3 |
| 13 | Kansas City | 20 |
| 27 | L.A. RAIDERS | *30 |
| 12 | San Diego | 0 |
| 16 | San Francisco | *13 |
| 30 | ATLANTA | 14 |
| 21 | Pittsburgh | 39 |
| 23 | Indianapolis | 55 |
| 17 | KANSAS CITY | 11 |
| 30 | CLEVELAND | 7 |
| 0 | New Orleans | 42 |
| 35 | L.A. RAMS | 24 |
| 20 | L.A. Raiders | 21 |
| 14 | Seattle | 42 |
| 21 | NEW ENGLAND | 10 |

| Use Name | Pos. | Hgt | Wgt | Age | Int | Pts |
|---|---|---|---|---|---|---|
| Jim Juriga | OT-OG | 6'6" | 269 | 23 | | |
| Ken Lanier | OT | 6'3" | 269 | 29 | | |
| Gerald Perry | OT | 6'6" | 305 | 23 | | |
| Dave Studdard | OT | 6'4" | 260 | 32 | | |
| Keith Bishop | OG-C | 6'3" | 265 | 31 | | |
| Winford Hood | OG | 6'3" | 262 | 26 | | |
| Stefan Humphries | OG | 6'3" | 268 | 26 | | |
| Keith Kartz | OG-OT | 6'4" | 270 | 25 | | |
| Larry Lee | OG-C | 6'2" | 263 | 28 | | |
| Billy Bryan | C | 6'2" | 255 | 32 | | |
| Mike Ruether | C | 6'4" | 275 | 25 | | |
| Walt Bowyer | DE | 6'4" | 260 | 27 | 1 | |
| Freddie Gilbert | DE | 6'4" | 275 | 26 | | |
| Rulon Jones | DE | 6'6" | 260 | 30 | | |
| Shawn Knight | DE | 6'6" | 288 | 24 | | |
| Andre Townsend | DE-NT | 6'3" | 265 | 25 | | |
| Greg Kragen | NT | 6'3" | 260 | 26 | | |
| Michael Brooks | LB | 6'1" | 235 | 23 | | |
| Steve Bryan | LB-DE | 6'2" | 256 | 24 | | |
| Rick Dennison | LB | 6'3" | 220 | 30 | 1 | |
| Simon Fletcher | LB-DE | 6'5" | 240 | 26 | 1 | |
| Bruce Klostermann | LB | 6'4" | 232 | 25 | | |
| Tim Lucas | LB | 6'3" | 230 | 27 | | |
| Karl Mecklenburg | LB-DE | 6'3" | 230 | 28 | | |
| Marc Munford | LB | 6'2" | 231 | 23 | | |
| Jim Ryan | LB | 6'1" | 225 | 31 | | |
| Tyrone Braxton | DB | 5'11" | 174 | 23 | 2 | |
| Jeremiah Castille | DB | 5'10" | 175 | 27 | 3 | |
| Kevin Clark | DB | 5'10" | 185 | 24 | | |
| Kevin Guidry | DB | 6' | 176 | 24 | | |
| Mike Harden | DB | 6'1" | 192 | 29 | 4 | |
| Mark Haynes | DB | 5'11" | 195 | 29 | 1 | |
| Bruce Plummer (to MIA) | DB | 6'1" | 197 | 24 | | |
| Randy Robbins | DB | 6'2" | 189 | 24 | 2 | |
| Dennis Smith | DB | 6'3" | 200 | 29 | | |
| Steve Wilson | DB | 5'10" | 195 | 31 | 1 | |
| John Elway | QB | 6'3" | 210 | 28 | | 6 |
| Ken Karcher | QB | 6'3" | 205 | 25 | | |
| Gary Kubiak | QB | 6' | 192 | 27 | | |
| Ken Bell | HB | 5'10" | 190 | 23 | | |
| Tony Dorsett | HB | 5'11" | 189 | 34 | | 30 |
| Sammy Winder | HB | 5'11" | 203 | 29 | | 30 |
| Steve Sewell | FB-WR | 6'3" | 210 | 25 | | 36 |
| Calvin Thomas (from CHI) | FB | 5'11" | 245 | 28 | | |
| Gerald Willhite | FB | 5'10" | 200 | 29 | | 12 |
| Sam Graddy | WR | 5'10" | 165 | 24 | | |
| Mark Jackson | WR | 5'9" | 180 | 25 | | 36 |
| Jason Johnson | WR | 5'10" | 178 | 22 | | |
| Vance Johnson | WR | 5'11" | 185 | 25 | | 30 |
| Rick Massie | WR | 6'1" | 190 | 28 | | |
| Ricky Nattiel | WR | 5'9" | 180 | 22 | | 6 |
| Clarence Kay | TE | 6'2" | 237 | 27 | | 24 |
| Pat Kelly | TE | 6'6" | 252 | 22 | | |
| Orson Mobley | TE | 6'5" | 256 | 25 | | 12 |
| Mike Horan | K | 5'11" | 190 | 29 | | |
| Rich Karlis | K | 6' | 180 | 29 | | 105 |

Andrew Provence — Foot Injury

Steve Watson — Neck Injury

## LOS ANGELES RAIDERS 7-9 Mike Shanahan

| Scores of Each Game | | |
|---|---|---|
| 24 | SAN DIEGO | 13 |
| 35 | Houston | 38 |
| 17 | L.A. RAMS | 22 |
| 30 | Denver | *27 |
| 21 | CINCINNATI | 45 |
| 14 | MIAMI | 24 |
| 27 | Kansas City | 17 |
| 6 | New Orleans | 20 |
| 17 | KANSAS CITY | 10 |
| 13 | San Diego | 3 |
| 9 | San Francisco | 3 |
| 6 | ATLANTA | 12 |
| 27 | Seattle | 35 |
| 21 | DENVER | 20 |
| 21 | Buffalo | 37 |
| 37 | SEATTLE | 43 |

| Use Name | Pos. | Hgt | Wgt | Age | Int | Pts |
|---|---|---|---|---|---|---|
| Rory Graves | OT | 6'6" | 285 | 25 | | |
| Brian Holloway | OT-OG | 6'7" | 285 | 29 | | |
| Don Mosebar | OT | 6'6" | 280 | 26 | | |
| Steve Wright | OT | 6'6" | 280 | 29 | | |
| Charley Hannah | OG | 6'5" | 270 | 33 | | |
| Chris Riehm | OG | 6'6" | 280 | 27 | | |
| Dwight Wheeler | OG | 6'3" | 280 | 33 | | |
| Bruce Wilkerson | OG | 6'5" | 285 | 24 | | |
| Mike Freeman | C-OG | 6'3" | 265 | 26 | | |
| John Gesek | C-OG | 6'5" | 275 | 25 | | |
| Bill Lewis | C | 6'7" | 275 | 25 | | |
| Ron Brown | DE | 6'4" | 225 | 24 | | |
| Scott Davis | DE-LB | 6'7" | 270 | 23 | | |
| Howie Long | DE | 6'5" | 265 | 28 | 1 | |
| Greg Townsend | DE-NT | 6'3" | 250 | 26 | 1 | 12 |
| Mike Wise | DE | 6'7" | 280 | 24 | | |
| Malcolm Taylor | NT-DE | 6'6" | 280 | 28 | | |
| Bill Pickel | NT-DT | 6'5" | 265 | 28 | | |
| Linden King | LB | 6'4" | 245 | 33 | | |
| Rod Martin | LB | 6'2" | 225 | 34 | | |
| Milt McColl | LB | 6'6" | 230 | 29 | | |
| Reggie McKenzie | LB | 6'1" | 240 | 25 | 1 | |
| Matt Millen | LB | 6'2" | 250 | 30 | | |
| Jerry Robinson | LB | 6'2" | 230 | 31 | | |
| Norwood Vann | LB | 6'1" | 227 | 26 | | |
| Stefon Adams | DB | 5'10" | 190 | 25 | | |
| Eddie Anderson | DB | 6'1" | 195 | 25 | 2 | |
| Russell Carter | DB | 6'2" | 200 | 26 | | |
| Ron Fellows | DB | 6' | 175 | 29 | 2 | |
| David Greenwood | DB | 6'3" | 210 | 28 | | |
| Mike Haynes | DB | 6'2" | 190 | 35 | 3 | |
| Zeph Lee | DB | 6'3" | 205 | 25 | 1 | |
| Terry McDaniel | DB | 5'10" | 175 | 23 | | |
| Vann McElroy | DB | 6'2" | 195 | 28 | 3 | |
| Dennis Price | DB | 6'1" | 175 | 23 | 2 | |
| Stacey Toran | DB | 6'2" | 200 | 26 | | |
| Lionel Washington | DB | 6' | 185 | 27 | 1 | |
| Steve Beuerlein | QB | 6'2" | 205 | 23 | | |
| Vince Evans | QB | 6'2" | 205 | 33 | | |
| Jay Schroeder | QB | 6'4" | 215 | 27 | | 6 |
| Marcus Allen | HB | 6'2" | 205 | 28 | | 48 |
| Bo Jackson | HB | 6'1" | 225 | 25 | | 18 |
| Chris McLemore | FB | 6'1" | 230 | 24 | | |
| Vance Mueller | FB | 6' | 215 | 24 | | |
| Steve Smith | FB | 6'1" | 230 | 24 | | 54 |
| Steve Strachan | FB | 6'1" | 225 | 25 | | 6 |
| Tim Brown | WR | 6' | 195 | 22 | | 42 |
| Mervyn Fernandez | WR | 6'3" | 200 | 28 | | 24 |
| Willie Gault | WR | 6' | 180 | 27 | | 12 |
| James Lofton | WR | 6'3" | 190 | 32 | | |
| Chris Woods | WR | 5'11" | 190 | 26 | | |
| Todd Christensen | TE | 6'3" | 230 | 32 | | |
| Trey Junkin | TE | 6'2" | 230 | 27 | | 12 |
| Andy Parker | TE | 6'5" | 250 | 26 | | |
| Chris Bahr | K | 5'10" | 170 | 35 | | 91 |
| Jeff Gossett | K | 6'2" | 195 | 31 | | |

Jamie Kimmel — Knee Injury

## SAN DIEGO CHARGERS 6-10 Al Saunders

| Scores of Each Game | | |
|---|---|---|
| 13 | L.A. Raiders | 24 |
| 3 | Denver | 34 |
| 17 | SEATTLE | 6 |
| 24 | Kansas City | 23 |
| 0 | DENVER | 12 |
| 17 | NEW ORLEANS | 23 |
| 28 | Miami | 31 |
| 0 | INDIANAPOLIS | 16 |
| 14 | Seattle | 17 |
| 3 | L.A. RAIDERS | 13 |
| 10 | Atlanta | 7 |
| 38 | L.A. Rams | 24 |
| 10 | SAN FRANCISCO | 48 |
| 10 | Cincinnati | 27 |
| 20 | PITTSBURGH | 14 |
| 24 | KANSAS CITY | 13 |

| Use Name | Pos. | Hgt | Wgt | Age | Int | Pts |
|---|---|---|---|---|---|---|
| John Clay | OT | 6'5" | 305 | 24 | | |
| Ken Dallafior | OT-OG | 6'4" | 275 | 29 | | |
| Chris Gambol (from IND) | OT | 6'6" | 303 | 23 | | |
| Gary Kowalski | OT-OG | 6'6" | 288 | 28 | | |
| David Richards | OT | 6'5" | 310 | 22 | | |
| Darrick Brilz | OG-OT | 6'3" | 270 | 24 | | |
| James FitzPatrick | OG-OT | 6'8" | 310 | 24 | | |
| Dennis McKnight | OG-C | 6'3" | 280 | 28 | | |
| Broderick Thompson | OG-OT | 6'5" | 295 | 28 | | |
| Don Macek | C | 6'3" | 278 | 34 | | |
| Dan Rosado | C-OG | 6'3" | 280 | 29 | | |
| Keith Baldwin | DE | 6'4" | 270 | 27 | | |
| George Hinkle | DE | 6'5" | 267 | 23 | | |
| Tyrone Keys | DE | 6'7" | 291 | 27 | | |
| Les Miller | DE | 6'7" | 293 | 23 | | |
| Leslie O'Neal | DE | 6'4" | 259 | 24 | | |
| Lee Williams | DE | 6'6" | 271 | 25 | | |
| Karl Wilson | DE-LB | 6'4" | 275 | 23 | | |
| Joe Phillips | NT-DE | 6'5" | 275 | 25 | | |
| Mike Charles | NT | 6'4" | 296 | 25 | | |
| David Brandon | LB | 6'4" | 230 | 23 | | |
| Keith Browner | LB | 6'6" | 266 | 26 | 2 | 6 |
| Joe Campbell | LB | 6'4" | 245 | 21 | | |
| Chuck Faucette | LB | 6'3" | 242 | 24 | 1 | |
| Cedric Figaro | LB | 6'2" | 255 | 22 | | |
| Jeff Jackson | LB | 6'1" | 242 | 26 | | |
| Randy Kirk | LB | 6'2" | 227 | 23 | | |
| Gary Plummer | LB | 6'2" | 240 | 28 | | |
| Billy Ray Smith | LB | 6'3" | 236 | 27 | 1 | |
| Ken Woodard | LB | 6'1" | 220 | 28 | | |
| Martin Bayless | DB | 6'2" | 212 | 25 | | |
| Roy Bennett | DB | 6'2" | 195 | 27 | 1 | 6 |
| Gill Byrd | DB | 5'11" | 198 | 27 | 7 | |
| Leonard Coleman | DB | 6'2" | 202 | 26 | 2 | |
| Jeffery Dale | DB | 6'3" | 207 | 25 | | |
| Vencie Glenn | DB | 6' | 192 | 23 | 1 | |
| Pat Miller | DB | 6'1" | 206 | 24 | | |
| Elvis Patterson | DB | 5'11" | 198 | 27 | 1 | |
| Sam Seale | DB | 5'9" | 185 | 25 | | 6 |
| Steve Fuller | QB | 6'4" | 196 | 31 | | |
| Babe Laufenberg | QB | 6'3" | 205 | 28 | | |
| Mark Malone | QB | 6'4" | 222 | 29 | | 24 |
| Mark Vlasic | QB | 6'3" | 203 | 24 | | |
| Curtis Adams | HB | 6' | 207 | 26 | | 6 |
| Gary Anderson | HB-WR | 6'1" | 184 | 27 | | 18 |
| Lionel James | HB | 5'7" | 170 | 26 | | 6 |
| Kevin Scott | HB | 5'9" | 180 | 24 | | |
| Barry Redden | FB | 5'10" | 220 | 28 | | 18 |
| Tim Spencer | FB | 6'2" | 223 | 27 | | |
| Quinn Early | WR | 6' | 188 | 23 | | 24 |
| Darren Flutie | WR | 5'10" | 184 | 21 | | 12 |
| Jamie Holland | WR-HB | 6'2" | 195 | 24 | | 12 |
| Anthony Miller | WR | 5'11" | 185 | 23 | | 24 |
| Rod Bernstine | TE-FB | 6'3" | 238 | 23 | | |
| Arthur Cox | TE | 6'2" | 277 | 27 | | |
| Eric Sievers (to LA) | TE | 6'4" | 238 | 29 | | |
| Wilbur Strozier | TE | 6'4" | 255 | 23 | | |
| Vince Abbott | K | 6' | 208 | 29 | | 39 |
| Steve DeLine | K | 5'11" | 185 | 27 | | 30 |
| Ralf Mojsiejenko | K | 6'3" | 213 | 25 | | |

Demetrious Johnson — Achilles' Tendon Injury

## KANSAS CITY CHIEFS 4-11-1 Frank Gansz

| Scores of Each Game | | |
|---|---|---|
| 3 | CLEVELAND | 6 |
| 10 | Seattle | 31 |
| 20 | DENVER | 13 |
| 23 | SAN DIEGO | 24 |
| 17 | N.Y. Jets | *17 |
| 6 | Houston | 7 |
| 17 | L.A. RAIDERS | 27 |
| 6 | DETROIT | 7 |
| 10 | L.A. Raiders | 17 |
| 11 | Denver | 17 |
| 31 | CINCINNATI | 28 |
| 27 | SEATTLE | 24 |
| 10 | Pittsburgh | 16 |
| 38 | N.Y. JETS | 34 |
| 12 | N.Y. Giants | 28 |
| 13 | San Diego | 24 |

| Use Name | Pos. | Hgt | Wgt | Age | Int | Pts |
|---|---|---|---|---|---|---|
| John Alt | OT | 6'7" | 290 | 26 | | |
| Irv Eatman | OT | 6'7" | 294 | 27 | | |
| David Lutz | OT-OG | 6'6" | 290 | 28 | | |
| Mark Adickes | OG | 6'4" | 273 | 27 | | |
| Rich Baldinger | OG-OT | 6'4" | 285 | 28 | | |
| Curt DiGiacomo | OG-C | 6'4" | 265 | 23 | | |
| James Harvey | OG | 6'3" | 265 | 22 | | |
| Byron Ingram | OG | 6'2" | 295 | 23 | | |
| Brian Jozwiak | OG | 6'5" | 293 | 25 | | |
| Tom Baugh | C | 6'3" | 290 | 24 | | |
| Gerry Feehery | C | 6'2" | 270 | 28 | | |
| Adam Lingner | C | 6'4" | 265 | 27 | | |
| Gary Baldinger | DE-NT | 6'3" | 265 | 24 | | |
| Mike Bell | DE | 6'4" | 260 | 30 | | |
| Leonard Griffin | DE | 6'4" | 270 | 25 | | |
| Neil Smith | DE | 6'4" | 270 | 22 | | |
| Dee Hardison | NT | 6'4" | 291 | 32 | | |
| Bill Maas | NT | 6'5" | 268 | 26 | | 2 |
| Ron McLean | NT | 6'3" | 274 | 25 | | |
| Jerome Sally | NT | 6'3" | 270 | 29 | | |
| Mike Stensrud | DE-NT | 6'5" | 280 | 32 | 1 | |
| Don Thorp (from IND) | DE-NT | 6'4" | 260 | 26 | | |
| Tim Cofield | LB | 6'2" | 242 | 25 | 1 | |
| Louis Cooper | LB | 6'2" | 245 | 24 | | |
| Jack Del Rio | LB | 6'4" | 238 | 25 | 1 | |
| Dino Hackett | LB | 6'3" | 228 | 24 | | 2 |
| Andy Hawkins | LB | 6'2" | 244 | 30 | | |
| Todd Howard | LB | 6'2" | 244 | 23 | | |
| Jerry McCabe | LB | 6'1" | 225 | 23 | | |
| Aaron Pearson | LB | 6' | 240 | 23 | | |
| Angelo Snipes | LB | 6' | 227 | 25 | | |
| Troy Stedman | LB | 6'3" | 243 | 23 | | |
| Lloyd Burruss | DB | 6' | 205 | 30 | 2 | |
| Deron Cherry | DB | 5'11" | 203 | 28 | 7 | |
| Greg Hill | DB | 6'1" | 202 | 27 | 1 | |
| Sidney Johnson | DB | 5'9" | 175 | 23 | | |
| Albert Lewis | DB | 6'2" | 198 | 27 | 1 | 2 |
| J.C. Pearson | DB | 5'11" | 190 | 24 | 2 | |
| Kevin Porter | DB | 5'10" | 215 | 22 | | |
| Kevin Ross | DB | 5'9" | 182 | 26 | 1 | |
| Steve DeBerg | QB | 6'2" | 210 | 34 | | 6 |
| Bill Kenney | QB | 6'4" | 217 | 33 | | |
| Danny McManus | QB | 6' | 200 | 23 | | |
| Kenny Gamble | HB-DB | 5'10" | 197 | 23 | 1 | |
| Herman Heard | HB | 5'10" | 190 | 26 | | |
| Keyvan Jenkins | HB | 5'10" | 192 | 27 | | |
| Paul Palmer | HB | 5'9" | 181 | 23 | | 36 |
| Larry Moriarty | FB | 6'1" | 237 | 30 | | |
| Christian Okoye | FB | 6'1" | 253 | 27 | | 18 |
| James Saxon | FB | 5'11" | 215 | 22 | | 12 |
| Carlos Carson | WR | 5'11" | 190 | 29 | | 18 |
| Darrell Colbert | WR | 5'10" | 174 | 23 | | |
| Emile Harry | WR | 5'11" | 176 | 25 | | 6 |
| Mike Jones | WR | 5'11" | 183 | 28 | | |
| Stephone Paige | WR | 6'2" | 185 | 26 | | 42 |
| Kitrick Taylor | WR | 5'10" | 197 | 24 | | |
| Jonathan Hayes | TE | 6'5" | 239 | 25 | | 6 |
| Rod Jones | TE | 6'4" | 241 | 24 | | |
| Alfredo Roberts | TE | 6'3" | 250 | 23 | | |
| Kelly Goodburn | K | 6'2" | 198 | 26 | | |
| Nick Lowery | K | 6'4" | 189 | 32 | | 104 |

Pete Koch — Broken Wrist

## SEATTLE SEAHAWKS

### RUSHING

| Last Name | No. | Yds | Avg | TD |
|---|---|---|---|---|
| Warner | 266 | 1025 | 3.9 | 10 |
| Williams | 189 | 877 | 4.6 | 4 |
| Krieg | 24 | 64 | 2.7 | 0 |
| Kemp | 6 | 51 | 8.5 | 0 |
| Stouffer | 19 | 27 | 1.4 | 0 |
| Blades | 5 | 24 | 4.8 | 0 |
| Harmon | 2 | 13 | 6.5 | 0 |
| Morris | 3 | 6 | 2.0 | 0 |
| Agee | 1 | 2 | 2.0 | 0 |
| Rodriguez | 1 | 0 | 0.0 | 0 |
| Largent | 1 | -3 | -3.0 | 0 |

### RECEIVING

| Last Name | No. | Yds | Avg | TD |
|---|---|---|---|---|
| Williams | 58 | 651 | 11.2 | 3 |
| Blades | 40 | 682 | 17.1 | 8 |
| Largent | 39 | 645 | 16.5 | 2 |
| Tice | 29 | 244 | 8.4 | 0 |
| Skansi | 24 | 238 | 9.9 | 1 |
| Warner | 22 | 154 | 7.0 | 2 |
| Butler | 18 | 242 | 13.4 | 4 |
| Kane | 6 | 32 | 5.3 | 0 |
| Spagnola | 5 | 40 | 8.0 | 1 |
| Agee | 3 | 31 | 10.3 | 0 |
| Clark | 1 | 20 | 20.0 | 1 |

### PUNT RETURNS

| Last Name | No. | Yds | Avg | TD |
|---|---|---|---|---|
| Edmunds | 35 | 340 | 9.7 | 0 |
| Glasgow | 1 | 0 | 0.0 | 0 |
| Hunter | 1 | 0 | 0.0 | 0 |

### KICKOFF RETURNS

| Last Name | No. | Yds | Avg | TD |
|---|---|---|---|---|
| Edmonds | 40 | 900 | 22.5 | 0 |
| Hollis | 13 | 261 | 20.1 | 0 |
| Morris | 13 | 259 | 19.9 | 0 |
| Harmon | 3 | 62 | 20.7 | 0 |
| Tice | 1 | 17 | 17.0 | 0 |

### PASSING - PUNTING - KICKING

**PASSING**

| Last Name | Att | Cmp | % | Yds | Yd/Att | TD | Int | —% | RK |
|---|---|---|---|---|---|---|---|---|---|
| Krieg | 226 | 134 | 58.8 | 1741 | 7.64 | 18 | 8 | -3.5 | 2 |
| Stouffer | 173 | 98 | 56.6 | 1106 | 6.39 | 4 | 6 | -3.5 | |
| Kemp | 35 | 13 | 37.1 | 132 | 3.77 | 0 | 5 | -14.3 | |
| Agee | 1 | 0 | 0.0 | 0 | 0.00 | 0 | 1 | -100 | |

**PUNTING**

| Last Name | No. | Avg. |
|---|---|---|
| Rodriguez | 70 | 40.8 |

**KICKING**

| Last Name | XP | ATT | % | FG | ATT | % |
|---|---|---|---|---|---|---|
| N. Johnson | 39 | 39 | 100 | 22 | 28 | 79 |

## DENVER BRONCOS

### RUSHING

| Last Name | No. | Yds | Avg | TD |
|---|---|---|---|---|
| Dorset | 181 | 703 | 3.9 | 5 |
| Winder | 149 | 543 | 3.6 | 4 |
| Elway | 54 | 234 | 4.3 | 1 |
| Sewell | 32 | 135 | 4.2 | 1 |
| Kubiak | 17 | 65 | 3.8 | 0 |
| Nattiel | 5 | 51 | 10.2 | 0 |
| Willhite | 13 | 39 | 3.0 | 2 |
| Bell | 9 | 36 | 4.0 | 0 |
| Thomas | 6 | 20 | 3.3 | 0 |
| Jackson | 1 | 5 | 5.0 | 0 |
| J. Johnson | 1 | 3 | 3.0 | 0 |
| V. Johnson | 1 | 1 | 1.0 | 0 |

### RECEIVING

| Last Name | No. | Yds | Avg | TD |
|---|---|---|---|---|
| V. Johnson | 68 | 896 | 13.2 | 5 |
| Jackson | 46 | 852 | 18.5 | 6 |
| Nattiel | 46 | 574 | 12.5 | 1 |
| Sewell | 38 | 507 | 13.3 | 5 |
| Kay | 34 | 352 | 10.4 | 4 |
| Willhite | 32 | 238 | 7.4 | 0 |
| Mobley | 21 | 218 | 10.4 | 2 |
| Winder | 17 | 103 | 6.1 | 1 |
| Dorsett | 16 | 122 | 7.6 | 0 |
| Massey | 3 | 39 | 13.0 | 0 |
| Graddy | 1 | 30 | 30.0 | 0 |
| Johnson | 1 | 6 | 6.0 | 0 |
| Kelly | 1 | 4 | 4.0 | 0 |

### PUNT RETURNS

| Last Name | No. | Yds | Avg | TD |
|---|---|---|---|---|
| Nattiel | 22 | 218 | 9.9 | 0 |
| Clark | 13 | 115 | 8.8 | 0 |
| Willhite | 13 | 90 | 6.9 | 0 |
| Harden | 2 | 14 | 7.0 | 0 |
| Massey | 1 | 5 | 5.0 | 0 |
| Johnson | 1 | 5 | 5.0 | 0 |
| Bell | 1 | 4 | 4.0 | 0 |
| Johnson | 0 | 0 | 0.0 | 0 |

### KICKOFF RETURNS

| Last Name | No. | Yds | Avg | TD |
|---|---|---|---|---|
| Bell | 36 | 762 | 21.2 | 0 |
| Johnson | 14 | 285 | 20.4 | 0 |
| Nattiel | 6 | 124 | 20.7 | 0 |
| Winder | 1 | 11 | 11.0 | 0 |
| Harden | 1 | 9 | 9.0 | 0 |

### PASSING - PUNTING - KICKING

**PASSING**

| Last Name | Att | Cmp | % | Yds | Yd/Att | TD | Int | —% | RK |
|---|---|---|---|---|---|---|---|---|---|
| Elway | 496 | 274 | 55.2 | 3309 | 6.67 | 17 | 19 | -3.8 | 9 |
| Kubiak | 69 | 43 | 62.3 | 497 | 7.20 | 5 | 3 | -4.3 | |
| Karcher | 12 | 6 | 50.0 | 128 | 10.67 | 1 | 0 | -0.0 | |
| Dorsett | 2 | 1 | 50.0 | 7 | 3.50 | 0 | 0 | -0.0 | |
| Sewell | 1 | 0 | 0.0 | 0 | 0.00 | 0 | 0 | -0.0 | |
| Nattiel | 1 | 0 | 0.0 | 0 | 0.00 | 0 | 0 | -0.0 | |

**PUNTING**

| Last Name | No. | Avg. |
|---|---|---|
| Horan | 65 | 44.0 |
| Elway | 3 | 39.0 |

**KICKING**

| Last Name | XP | ATT | % | FG | ATT | % |
|---|---|---|---|---|---|---|
| Karlis | 36 | 37 | 97 | 23 | 36 | 64 |

## LOS ANGELES RAIDERS

### RUSHING

| Last Name | No. | Yds | Avg | TD |
|---|---|---|---|---|
| Allen | 223 | 831 | 3.7 | 7 |
| Jackson | 136 | 580 | 4.3 | 3 |
| Smith | 38 | 162 | 4.3 | 3 |
| Schroeder | 29 | 109 | 3.8 | 1 |
| Mueller | 17 | 60 | 3.5 | 0 |
| T. Brown | 14 | 50 | 3.6 | 1 |
| Beuerlein | 30 | 35 | 1.2 | 0 |
| Strachan | 4 | 12 | 3.0 | 0 |
| Fernandez | 1 | 9 | 9.0 | 0 |
| Gault | 1 | 4 | 4.0 | 0 |

### RECEIVING

| Last Name | No. | Yds | Avg | TD |
|---|---|---|---|---|
| T. Brown | 43 | 725 | 16.9 | 5 |
| Allen | 34 | 303 | 8.9 | 1 |
| Fernandez | 31 | 805 | 26.0 | 4 |
| Lofton | 28 | 549 | 19.6 | 0 |
| Smith | 26 | 299 | 11.5 | 6 |
| Gault | 16 | 392 | 24.5 | 2 |
| Christensen | 15 | 190 | 12.7 | 0 |
| Jackson | 9 | 79 | 8.8 | 0 |
| Mueller | 5 | 63 | 12.6 | 0 |
| Parker | 4 | 33 | 8.3 | 0 |
| Junkin | 4 | 25 | 6.3 | 2 |
| Strachan | 3 | 19 | 6.3 | 1 |
| Beuerlein | 1 | 21 | 21.0 | 0 |

### PUNT RETURNS

| Last Name | No. | Yds | Avg | TD |
|---|---|---|---|---|
| T. Brown | 49 | 444 | 9.1 | 0 |
| Adams | 6 | 45 | 7.5 | 0 |

### KICKOFF RETURNS

| Last Name | No. | Yds | Avg | TD |
|---|---|---|---|---|
| T. Brown | 41 | 1098 | 26.8 | 1 |
| Adams | 8 | 132 | 16.5 | 0 |
| Mueller | 5 | 97 | 19.4 | 0 |
| Smith | 3 | 46 | 15.3 | 0 |
| Toran | 2 | 0 | 0.0 | 0 |
| Woods | 1 | 20 | 20.0 | 0 |
| Carter | 1 | 14 | 14.0 | 0 |
| Lee | 1 | 0 | 0.0 | 0 |

### PASSING - PUNTING - KICKING

**PASSING**

| Last Name | Att | Cmp | % | Yds | Yd/Att | TD | Int | —% | RK |
|---|---|---|---|---|---|---|---|---|---|
| Schroeder | 256 | 113 | 44.1 | 1839 | 7.18 | 13 | 13 | -5.1 | 12 |
| Beuerlein | 238 | 105 | 44.1 | 1643 | 6.90 | 8 | 7 | -2.9 | 11 |
| Allen | 2 | 1 | 50.0 | 21 | 10.50 | 0 | 0 | -0.0 | |

**PUNTING**

| Last Name | No. | Avg. |
|---|---|---|
| Gossett | 91 | 41.8 |

**KICKING**

| Last Name | XP | ATT | % | FG | ATT | % |
|---|---|---|---|---|---|---|
| Bahr | 37 | 39 | 95 | 18 | 29 | 62 |

## SAN DIEGO CHARGERS

### RUSHING

| Last Name | No. | Yds | Avg | TD |
|---|---|---|---|---|
| Anderson | 225 | 1119 | 5.0 | 3 |
| Spencer | 44 | 215 | 4.9 | 0 |
| Malone | 37 | 169 | 4.6 | 4 |
| Adams | 38 | 149 | 3.9 | 1 |
| Laufenberg | 31 | 120 | 3.9 | 0 |
| James | 23 | 105 | 4.6 | 0 |
| Early | 7 | 63 | 9.0 | 0 |
| A. Miller | 7 | 45 | 6.4 | 0 |
| Redden | 19 | 30 | 1.6 | 3 |
| Holland | 3 | 19 | 6.3 | 0 |
| Bernstine | 2 | 7 | 3.5 | 0 |
| Vlasic | 2 | 0 | 0.0 | 0 |

### RECEIVING

| Last Name | No. | Yds | Avg | TD |
|---|---|---|---|---|
| Holland | 39 | 536 | 13.7 | 1 |
| A. Miller | 36 | 526 | 14.6 | 3 |
| James | 36 | 279 | 7.8 | 1 |
| Anderson | 32 | 182 | 5.7 | 0 |
| Early | 29 | 375 | 12.9 | 4 |
| Bernstine | 29 | 340 | 11.7 | 0 |
| Flutie | 18 | 208 | 11.6 | 2 |
| Cox | 18 | 144 | 8.0 | 0 |
| Spencer | 1 | 14 | 14.0 | 0 |
| Redden | 1 | 11 | 11.0 | 0 |
| Sievers | 1 | 2 | 2.0 | 0 |

### PUNT RETURNS

| Last Name | No. | Yds | Avg | TD |
|---|---|---|---|---|
| James | 28 | 278 | 9.9 | 0 |
| Flutie | 7 | 36 | 5.1 | 0 |

### KICKOFF RETURNS

| Last Name | No. | Yds | Avg | TD |
|---|---|---|---|---|
| Holland | 31 | 810 | 26.1 | 1 |
| A. Miller | 25 | 648 | 25.9 | 1 |
| Spencer | 1 | 16 | 16.0 | 0 |
| Adams | 1 | 13 | 13.0 | 0 |
| Flutie | 1 | 10 | 10.0 | 0 |

### PASSING - PUNTING - KICKING

**PASSING**

| Last Name | Att | Cmp | % | Yds | Yd/Att | TD | Int | —% | RK |
|---|---|---|---|---|---|---|---|---|---|
| Malone | 272 | 147 | 54.0 | 1580 | 5.81 | 6 | 13 | -4.8 | 14 |
| Laufenberg | 144 | 69 | 47.9 | 778 | 5.40 | 4 | 5 | -3.5 | |
| Vlasic | 52 | 25 | 48.1 | 270 | 5.19 | 1 | 2 | -3.8 | |

**PUNTING**

| Last Name | No. | Avg. |
|---|---|---|
| Mojsiejenko | 86 | 43.5 |

**KICKING**

| Last Name | XP | Att | % | FG | Att | % |
|---|---|---|---|---|---|---|
| Abbott | 15 | 15 | 100 | 8 | 12 | 67 |
| DeLine | 12 | 12 | 100 | 6 | 8 | 75 |

## KANSAS CITY CHIEFS

### RUSHING

| Last Name | No. | Yds | Avg | TD |
|---|---|---|---|---|
| Okoye | 105 | 473 | 4.5 | 3 |
| Palmer | 134 | 452 | 3.4 | 2 |
| Heard | 106 | 438 | 4.1 | 0 |
| Saxon | 60 | 236 | 3.9 | 2 |
| Moriarty | 20 | 62 | 3.1 | 0 |
| DeBerg | 18 | 30 | 1.7 | 1 |
| Goodburn | 1 | 15 | 15.0 | 0 |
| Kenney | 2 | 4 | 2.0 | 0 |
| Taylor | 1 | 2 | 2.0 | 0 |
| Carson | 1 | 1 | 1.0 | 0 |

### RECEIVING

| Last Name | No. | Yds | Avg | TD |
|---|---|---|---|---|
| Paige | 61 | 902 | 14.8 | 7 |
| Palmer | 53 | 611 | 11.5 | 4 |
| Carson | 46 | 711 | 15.5 | 3 |
| Harry | 25 | 362 | 13.9 | 1 |
| Hayes | 22 | 233 | 10.6 | 1 |
| Heard | 20 | 198 | 9.9 | 0 |
| Saxon | 19 | 177 | 9.3 | 0 |
| Roberts | 10 | 104 | 10.4 | 0 |
| Taylor | 9 | 105 | 11.7 | 0 |
| Okoye | 8 | 51 | 6.4 | 0 |
| Moriarty | 6 | 40 | 6.7 | 0 |
| Colbert | 1 | -3 | -3.0 | 0 |
| Gamble | 1 | -7 | -7.0 | 0 |

### PUNT RETURNS

| Last Name | No. | Yds | Avg | TD |
|---|---|---|---|---|
| Taylor | 29 | 187 | 6.4 | 0 |
| Hollis | 3 | 28 | 9.3 | 0 |

### KICKOFF RETURNS

| Last Name | No. | Yds | Avg | TD |
|---|---|---|---|---|
| Palmer | 23 | 364 | 15.8 | 0 |
| Gamble | 15 | 291 | 19.4 | 0 |
| Taylor | 5 | 80 | 16.0 | 0 |
| Saxon | 2 | 40 | 20.0 | 0 |
| Ingram | 2 | 16 | 8.0 | 0 |
| Jenkins | 2 | 12 | 6.0 | 0 |
| Porter | 1 | 16 | 16.0 | 0 |

### PASSING - PUNTING - KICKING

**PASSING**

| Last Name | Att | Cmp | % | Yds | Yd/Att | TD | Int | —% | RK |
|---|---|---|---|---|---|---|---|---|---|
| DeBerg | 414 | 224 | 54.1 | 2935 | 7.09 | 16 | 16 | -3.9 | 8 |
| Kenney | 114 | 58 | 50.9 | 549 | 4.82 | 0 | 5 | -4.4 | |

**PUNTING**

| Last Name | No. | Avg. |
|---|---|---|
| Goodburn | 76 | 40.3 |

**KICKING**

| Last Name | XP | Att. | % | FG | Att | % |
|---|---|---|---|---|---|---|
| Lowery | 23 | 23 | ' | 27 | 32 | 84 |

## December 26, 1988 at Minneapolis (Attendance 57,666)

### SCORING

| | | | | | |
|---|---|---|---|---|---|
| L.A. RAMS | 0 | 7 | 3 | 7 - 17 | |
| MINNESOTA | 14 | 0 | 7 | 7 - 28 | |

**First Quarter**
Minn. — Anderson, 7 yard run
   PAT—C. Nelson (kick)
Minn. — Rice, 17 yard run
   PAT—C. Nelson (kick)

**Second Quarter**
L.A. Rams — D. Johnson, 3 yard pass from Everett
   PAT—Lansford (kick)

**Third Quarter**
Minn. — Anderson, 1 yard run
   PAT—C. Nelson (kick)
L.A. Rams — Lansford, 33 yard field goal

**Fourth Quarter**
Minn. — Hilton, 5 yard pass from Wilson
   PAT—C. Nelson (kick)
L.A. Rams — Holohan, 11 yard pass from Everett
   PAT—Lansford (kick)

### TEAM STATISTICS

| L.A. RAMS | | MINN. |
|---|---|---|
| 19 | First Downs- Total | 20 |
| 4 | First Downs- Rushing | 7 |
| 15 | First Downs- Passing | 11 |
| 0 | First Downs- Penalty | 2 |
| 0 | Fumbles- Number | 1 |
| 0 | Fumbles- Lost Ball | 1 |
| 10 | Penalties- Number | 6 |
| 54 | Yards Penalized | 40 |
| 1 | Missed Field Goals | 1 |
| 70 | Offensive Plays | 66 |
| 342 | Net Yards | 310 |
| 4.9 | Average Gain | 3.7 |
| 3 | Giveaways | 0 |
| 0 | Takeaways | 3 |
| - 3 | Difference | + 3 |

### INDIVIDUAL STATISTICS

#### RUSHING

| L.A. RAMS | No. | Yds. | Avg. | MINNESOTA | No. | Yds. | Avg. |
|---|---|---|---|---|---|---|---|
| Bell | 17 | 91 | 5.4 | Rice | 17 | 79 | 4.6 |
| Delpino | 3 | 4 | 1.3 | Anderson | 6 | 9 | 1.5 |
| Everett | 2 | 4 | 2.0 | Nelson | 3 | 9 | 3.0 |
| White | 1 | 2 | 2.0 | Fenney | 2 | 5 | 2.5 |
| Ellard | 1 | 2 | 2.0 | Wilson | 5 | 1 | 0.2 |
| | 24 | 107 | 4.5 | | 33 | 103 | 3.1 |

#### RECEIVING

| L.A. RAMS | No. | Yds. | Avg. | MINNESOTA | No. | Yds. | Avg. |
|---|---|---|---|---|---|---|---|
| Ellard | 4 | 54 | 13.5 | Carter | 4 | 102 | 25.5 |
| Holohan | 3 | 44 | 14.6 | Fenney | 3 | 19 | 6.3 |
| D. Johnson | 3 | 27 | 9.0 | Gustalson | 2 | 52 | 26.0 |
| Delpino | 2 | 33 | 16.5 | Jones | 2 | 28 | 14.0 |
| W. Anderson | 2 | 29 | 14.5 | Anderson | 2 | 10 | 5.0 |
| Brown | 1 | 26 | 26.0 | Jordan | 1 | 19 | 19.0 |
| | 19 | 247 | 13.0 | Rice | 1 | 12 | 12.0 |
| | | | | Nelson | 1 | 6 | 6.0 |
| | | | | Hilton | 1 | 5 | 5.0 |
| | | | | | 17 | 253 | 14.9 |

#### PUNTING

| | No. | | Avg. | | No. | | Avg. |
|---|---|---|---|---|---|---|---|
| Hatcher | 5 | | 48.2 | Scribner | 7 | | 41.6 |

#### PUNT RETURNS

| | No. | Yds. | Avg. | | No. | Yds. | Avg. |
|---|---|---|---|---|---|---|---|
| Hicks | 4 | 46 | 11.5 | Carter | 1 | 1 | 1.0 |
| Sutton | 1 | 14 | 14.0 | Lewis | 1 | 14 | 14.0 |
| | 5 | 60 | 12.0 | | 2 | 15 | 7.5 |

#### KICKOFF RETURNS

| | No. | Yds. | Avg. | | No. | Yds. | Avg. |
|---|---|---|---|---|---|---|---|
| Brown | 4 | 71 | 17.8 | Harris | 3 | 58 | 19.3 |
| Delpino | 1 | 35 | 35.0 | | | | |
| | 5 | 106 | 21.2 | | | | |

#### INTERCEPTION RETURNS

| | No. | Yds. | Avg. |
|---|---|---|---|
| Browner | 2 | 40 | 20.0 |
| Studwell | 1 | 0 | 0.0 |
| | 3 | 40 | 13.3 |

#### PASSING

| L.A. RAMS | Att. | Comp. | Comp. Pct. | Yds. | Int. | Yds./ Att. | Yds./ Comp. |
|---|---|---|---|---|---|---|---|
| Everett | 45 | 19 | 42.2 | 247 | 3 | 5.5 | 13.0 |

| MINNESOTA | Att. | Comp. | Comp. Pct. | Yds. | Int. | Yds./ Att. | Yds./ Comp. |
|---|---|---|---|---|---|---|---|
| Wilson | 28 | 17 | 60.7 | 253 | 0 | 9.0 | 14.9 |

---

## December 31, 1988 at Chicago (Attendance 65,534)

### SCORING

| | | | | | |
|---|---|---|---|---|---|
| PHILADELPHIA | 3 | 6 | 3 | 0 - 12 | |
| CHICAGO | 7 | 10 | 0 | 3 - 20 | |

**First Quarter**
Chi. — McKinnon, 64 yard pass from Tomczak
   PAT—Butler (kick)
Phil. — Zendejas, 42 yard field goal

**Second Quarter**
Phil. — Zendejas, 29 yard field goal
Chi. — Anderson, 4 yard run
   PAT—Butler (kick)
Chi. — Butler, 46 yard field goal
Phil. — Zendejas, 30 yard field goal

**Third Quarter**
Phil. — Zendejas, 35 yard field goal

**Fourth Quarter**
Chi. — Butler, 27 yard field goal

### TEAM STATISTICS

| PHIL. | | CHI. |
|---|---|---|
| 22 | First Downs- Total | 14 |
| 1 | First Downs- Rushing | 8 |
| 21 | First Downs- Passing | 6 |
| 0 | First Downs- Penalty | 0 |
| 0 | Fumbles- Number | 1 |
| 0 | Fumbles- Lost Ball | 1 |
| 7 | Penalties- Number | 1 |
| 60 | Yards Penalized | 5 |
| 1 | Missed Field Goals | 2 |
| 75 | Offensive Plays | 57 |
| 430 | Net Yards | 341 |
| 5.7 | Average Gain | 6.0 |
| 3 | Giveaways | 4 |
| 4 | Takeaways | 3 |
| +1 | Difference | - 1 |

### INDIVIDUAL STATISTICS

#### RUSHING

| PHILADELPHIA | No. | Yds. | Avg. | CHICAGO | No. | Yds. | Avg. |
|---|---|---|---|---|---|---|---|
| Byars | 7 | 34 | 4.9 | Sanders | 8 | 94 | 11.8 |
| Toney | 5 | 3 | 0.6 | Anderson | 14 | 54 | 3.9 |
| Cunningham | 3 | 12 | 4.0 | Muster | 6 | 12 | 2.0 |
| Haddix | 1 | 3 | 3.0 | Gentry | 1 | 6 | 6.0 |
| | 16 | 52 | 3.3 | Suhey | 1 | 0 | 0.0 |
| | | | | McMahon | 2 | -2 | -1.0 |
| | | | | | 33 | 164 | 5.0 |

#### RECEIVING

| PHILADELPHIA | No. | Yds. | Avg. | CHICAGO | No. | Yds. | Avg. |
|---|---|---|---|---|---|---|---|
| Byars | 9 | 103 | 11.4 | McKinnon | 4 | 108 | 27.0 |
| Jackson | 7 | 142 | 20.2 | Boso | 2 | 9 | 4.5 |
| Quick | 5 | 82 | 16.4 | Gentry | 2 | 9 | 4.5 |
| Haddix | 2 | 23 | 11.5 | Moris | 1 | 27 | 27.0 |
| Toney | 2 | 9 | 4.5 | Davis | 1 | 11 | 11.0 |
| R. Johnson | 1 | 31 | 31.0 | Sanders | 1 | 8 | 8.0 |
| Carter | 1 | 7 | 7.0 | Anderson | 1 | 6 | 6.0 |
| | 27 | 407 | 15.1 | | 12 | 185 | 15.4 |

#### PUNTING

| | No. | | Avg. | | No. | | Avg. |
|---|---|---|---|---|---|---|---|
| Teltschik | 4 | | 32.5 | Wagner | 2 | | 43.0 |

#### PUNT RETURNS

| | No. | Yds. | Avg. | | No. | Yds. | Avg. |
|---|---|---|---|---|---|---|---|
| Garrity | 1 | 1 | 1.0 | McKinnon | 1 | 0 | 0.0 |

#### KICKOFF RETURNS

| | No. | Yds. | Avg. | | No. | Yds. | Avg. |
|---|---|---|---|---|---|---|---|
| Jenkins | 5 | 101 | 20.2 | Gentry | 4 | 63 | 15.8 |
| | | | | Kozlowski | 1 | 23 | 23.0 |
| | | | | | 5 | 86 | 17.2 |

#### INTERCEPTION RETURNS

| | No. | Yds. | Avg. | | No. | Yds. | Avg. |
|---|---|---|---|---|---|---|---|
| Hoage | 1 | 12 | 12.0 | Jackson | 1 | 51 | 51.0 |
| Joyner | 1 | 8 | 8.0 | Douglass | 1 | 47 | 47.0 |
| | 2 | 20 | 10.0 | Pruitt | 1 | 0 | 0.0 |
| | | | | | 3 | 98 | 32.7 |

#### PASSING

| PHILADELPHIA | Att. | Comp. | Comp. Pct. | Yds. | Int. | Yds./ Att. | Yds./ Comp. |
|---|---|---|---|---|---|---|---|
| Cunningham | 54 | 27 | 50.0 | 407 | 3 | 7.5 | 15.1 |
| Carter | 1 | 0 | 0.0 | 0 | 0 | 0.0 | 0.0 |

| CHICAGO | Att. | Comp. | Comp. Pct. | Yds. | Int. | Yds./ Att. | Yds./ Comp. |
|---|---|---|---|---|---|---|---|
| Tomczak | 20 | 10 | 50.0 | 172 | 3 | 8.6 | 17.2 |
| McMahon | 3 | 2 | 66.7 | 13 | 0 | 4.3 | 6.5 |

---

## January 1, 1989 at San Francisco (Attendance 61,848)

### SCORING

| | | | | | |
|---|---|---|---|---|---|
| MINNESOTA | 3 | 0 | 6 | 0 - 9 | |
| SAN FRANCISCO | 7 | 14 | 0 | 13 - 34 | |

**First Quarter**
Minn. — Nelson, 47 yard field goal
S.F. — Rice, 2 yard pass from Montana
   PAT—Cofer (kick)

**Second Quarter**
S.F. — Rice, 4 yard pass from Montana
   PAT—Cofer (kick)

**Third Quarter**
Minn. — H. Jones, 5 yard pass from Wilson
   PAT—kick failed

**Fourth Quarter**
S.F. — Craig, 4 yard run
   PAT—Cofer (kick)
S.F. — Craig, 80 yard run
   PAT—kick failed

### TEAM STATISTICS

| MINN. | | S.F. |
|---|---|---|
| 20 | First Downs- Total | 20 |
| 4 | First Downs- Rushing | 7 |
| 14 | First Downs- Passing | 11 |
| 2 | First Downs- Penalty | 2 |
| 1 | Fumbles- Number | 2 |
| 1 | Fumbles- Lost Ball | 1 |
| 9 | Penalties- Number | 6 |
| 90 | Yards Penalized | 60 |
| 0 | Missed Field Goals | 0 |
| 66 | Offensive Plays | 62 |
| 262 | Net Yards | 372 |
| 4.0 | Average Gain | 6.0 |
| 3 | Giveaways | 1 |
| 1 | Takeaways | 3 |
| - 2 | Difference | + 2 |

### INDIVIDUAL STATISTICS

#### RUSHING

| MINNESOTA | No. | Yds. | Avg. | SAN FRANCISCO | No. | Yds. | Avg. |
|---|---|---|---|---|---|---|---|
| Rice | 5 | 20 | 4.0 | Craig | 21 | 135 | 6.4 |
| Fenney | 6 | 20 | 6.3 | Rathman | 3 | 29 | 9.7 |
| Anderson | 3 | 9 | 3.0 | Rice | 1 | 21 | 21.0 |
| Nelson | 2 | 3 | 1.5 | Montana | 3 | 18 | 6.0 |
| Wilson | 3 | 2 | 0.7 | Sydney | 1 | 1 | 1.0 |
| | 19 | 54 | 2.8 | Young | 3 | 1 | 0.3 |
| | | | | Flagler | 2 | -4 | -2.0 |
| | | | | | 34 | 201 | 5.9 |

#### RECEIVING

| MINNESOTA | No. | Yds. | Avg. | SAN FRANCISCO | No. | Yds. | Avg. |
|---|---|---|---|---|---|---|---|
| Jones | 7 | 71 | 10.1 | Rice | 5 | 61 | 12.2 |
| Rice | 4 | 26 | 6.5 | Taylor | 3 | 42 | 14.0 |
| Carter | 3 | 45 | 15.0 | Craig | 3 | 26 | 8.7 |
| Jordan | 3 | 44 | 14.6 | Rathman | 2 | 20 | 10.0 |
| Anderson | 3 | 36 | 12.0 | B. Jones | 2 | 17 | 8.5 |
| Lewis | 1 | 19 | 19.0 | Wilson | 1 | 12 | 12.0 |
| Gustafson | 1 | 18 | 18.0 | Sydney | 1 | -12 | -12.0 |
| Fenney | 1 | 4 | 4.0 | | 17 | 177 | 10.4 |
| | 23 | 255 | 11.1 | | | | |

#### PUNTING

| | No. | | Avg. | | No. | | Avg. |
|---|---|---|---|---|---|---|---|
| Scribner | 7 | | 39.3 | Helton | 5 | | 36.2 |

#### PUNT RETURNS

| | No. | Yds. | Avg. | | No. | Yds. | Avg. |
|---|---|---|---|---|---|---|---|
| Carter | 2 | 15 | 7.5 | Taylor | 2 | 27 | 13.5 |
| Lewis | 1 | 12 | 12.0 | | | | |
| | 3 | 27 | 9.0 | | | | |

#### KICKOFF RETURNS

| | No. | Yds. | Avg. | | No. | Yds. | Avg. |
|---|---|---|---|---|---|---|---|
| Harris | 3 | 55 | 18.3 | Rodgers | 3 | 39 | 13.0 |
| Nelson | 2 | 37 | 18.5 | | | | |
| Jordan | 1 | 4 | 4.0 | | | | |
| | 6 | 96 | 16.0 | | | | |

#### INTERCEPTION RETURNS

| | No. | Yds. | Avg. | | No. | Yds. | Avg. |
|---|---|---|---|---|---|---|---|
| Browner | 1 | 0 | 0.0 | Lott | 2 | 10 | 5.0 |

#### PASSING

| MINNESOTA | Att. | Comp. | Comp. Pct. | Yds. | Int. | Yds./ Att. | Yds./ Comp. |
|---|---|---|---|---|---|---|---|
| Wilson | 47 | 23 | 48.9 | 255 | 2 | 5.4 | 11.1 |

| SAN FRANCISCO | Att. | Comp. | Comp. Pct. | Yds. | Int. | Yds./ Att. | Yds./ Comp. |
|---|---|---|---|---|---|---|---|
| Montana | 27 | 16 | 59.3 | 178 | 1 | 6.6 | 11.1 |
| Young | 1 | 1 | 100.0 | -1 | 0 | -1.0 | -1.0 |

## December 24, 1988 at Cleveland (Attendance 74,977)

### SCORING

| | | | | | |
|---|---|---|---|---|---|
| HOUSTON | 0 | 14 | 0 | 10 | - 24 |
| CLEVELAND | 3 | 6 | 7 | 7 | - 23 |

**First Quarter**
Clev.  Bahr, 33 yard field goal

**Second Quarter**
Hous.  Pinkett, 14 yard pass from Moon
       PAT—Zebdejas (kick)
Clev.  Bahr, 26 yard field goal
Clev.  Bahr, 28 yard field goal

**Third Quarter**
Clev.  Slaughter, 14 yard pass from Pagel
       PAT—Bahr (kick)

**Fourth Quarter**
Hous.  White, 1 yard run
       PAT—Zendejas (kick)
Hous.  Zendejas, 49 yard field goal
Clev.  Slaughter, 2 yard pass from Pagel
       PAT—Bahr (kick)

### TEAM STATISTICS

| HOUS. | | CLEV. |
|---|---|---|
| 19 | First Downs- Total | 19 |
| 7 | First Downs- Rushing | 4 |
| 12 | First Downs- Passing | 11 |
| 0 | First Downs- Penalty | 4 |
| 2 | Fumbles- Number | 1 |
| 0 | Fumbles- Lost Ball | 1 |
| 13 | Penalties- Number | 9 |
| 118 | Yards Penalized | 75 |
| 0 | Missed Field Goals | 0 |
| 62 | Offensive Plays | 54 |
| 334 | Net Yards | 260 |
| 3.8 | Average Gain | 4.5 |
| 3 | Giveaways | 2 |
| 2 | Takeaways | 3 |
| -1 | Difference | +1 |

### INDIVIDUAL STATISTICS

**HOUSTON / CLEVELAND**

#### RUSHING

| | No. | Yds. | Avg. | | No. | Yds. | Avg. |
|---|---|---|---|---|---|---|---|
| Pinkett | 14 | 82 | 5.9 | Byner | 9 | 57 | 6.3 |
| White | 12 | 30 | 2.5 | Mack | 12 | 14 | 1.2 |
| Moon | 6 | 16 | 2.7 | Strock | 1 | 0 | 0.0 |
| Highsmith | 2 | 3 | 1.5 | Pagel | 1 | -1 | -1.0 |
| Givins | 1 | -2 | -2.0 | Fontenot | 3 | -2 | -0.7 |
| | 35 | 129 | 3.7 | | 26 | 68 | 2.6 |

#### RECEIVING

| | No. | Yds. | Avg. | | No. | Yds. | Avg. |
|---|---|---|---|---|---|---|---|
| Hill | 5 | 73 | 14.6 | Langhorne | 6 | 57 | 9.5 |
| Jeffires | 3 | 52 | 17.3 | Slaughter | 5 | 58 | 1.6 |
| Duncan | 2 | 33 | 16.5 | Byner | 3 | 40 | 13.3 |
| Pinkett | 2 | 24 | 12.0 | Brennan | 2 | 34 | 17.0 |
| Williams | 1 | 14 | 14.0 | Weathers | 2 | 27 | 13.5 |
| Givins | 1 | 8 | 8.0 | Mack | 1 | 6 | 6.0 |
| Highsmith | 1 | 8 | 8.0 | | 19 | 192 | 10.1 |
| White | 1 | 1 | 1.0 | | | | |
| | 16 | 213 | 13.3 | | | | |

#### PUNTING

| | No. | Yds. | Avg. | | No. | Yds. | Avg. |
|---|---|---|---|---|---|---|---|
| Montgomery | 3 | | 37.6 | Runager | 3 | | 35.3 |

#### PUNT RETURNS

| | No. | Yds. | Avg. | | No. | Yds. | Avg. |
|---|---|---|---|---|---|---|---|
| Duncan | 0 | 0 | 0.0 | McNeil | 3 | 27 | 9.0 |

#### KICKOFF RETURNS

| | No. | Yds. | Avg. | | No. | Yds. | Avg. |
|---|---|---|---|---|---|---|---|
| White | 4 | 72 | 18.0 | Young | 2 | 58 | 29.0 |
| Pinkett | 1 | 0 | 0.0 | McNeil | 1 | 17 | 17.0 |
| | 5 | 72 | 14.4 | | 3 | 75 | 25.0 |

#### INTERCEPTION RETURNS

| | No. | Yds. | Avg. | | No. | Yds. | Avg. |
|---|---|---|---|---|---|---|---|
| R. Johnson | 1 | 0 | 0.0 | Wright | 2 | 32 | 16.0 |
| | | | | Harper | 1 | 17 | 17.0 |
| | | | | | 3 | 49 | 16.3 |

#### PASSING

**HOUSTON**

| | Att. | Comp. | Comp. Pct. | Yds. | Int. | Yds./ Att. | Yds./ Comp. |
|---|---|---|---|---|---|---|---|
| Moon | 26 | 16 | 61.5 | 213 | 3 | 8.2 | 13.3 |

**CLEVELAND**

| | Att. | Comp. | Comp. Pct. | Yds. | Int. | Yds./ Att. | Yds./ Comp. |
|---|---|---|---|---|---|---|---|
| Pagel | 25 | 17 | 68.0 | 179 | 1 | 7.2 | 10.5 |
| Strock | 3 | 2 | 67.0 | 13 | 0 | 4.3 | 6.5 |

---

## December 31, 1988 at Cincinnati (Attendance 58,560)

### SCORING

| | | | | | |
|---|---|---|---|---|---|
| SEATTLE | 0 | 0 | 13 | 13 | - 13 |
| CINCINNATI | 7 | 14 | 0 | 0 | - 21 |

**First Quarter**
Cin.  Wilson, 3 yard run
      PAT—Breech (kick)

**Second Quarter**
Cin.  Wilson, 3 yard run
      PAT—Breech (kick)
Woods.  Woods, 1 yard run
        PAT—Breech (kick)

**Fourth Quarter**
Sea.  Williams, 7 yard pass from Krieg
      PAT—N. Johnson (kick)
Sea.  Krieg, 1 yard run
      PAT—kick failed

### TEAM STATISTICS

| SEA. | | CIN. |
|---|---|---|
| 19 | First Downs- Total | 22 |
| 1 | First Downs- Rushing | 17 |
| 16 | First Downs- Passing | 5 |
| 2 | First Downs- Penalty | 0 |
| 1 | Fumbles- Number | 3 |
| 1 | Fumbles- Lost Ball | 2 |
| 5 | Penalties- Number | 2 |
| 45 | Yards Penalized | 29 |
| 0 | Missed Field Goals | 0 |
| 69 | Offensive Plays | 68 |
| 294 | Net Yards | 345 |
| 4.3 | Average Gain | 5.1 |
| 3 | Giveaways | 2 |
| 2 | Takeaways | 3 |
| -1 | Difference | +1 |

### INDIVIDUAL STATISTICS

**SEATTLE / CINCINNATI**

#### RUSHING

| | No. | Yds. | Avg. | | No. | Yds. | Avg. |
|---|---|---|---|---|---|---|---|
| Warner | 8 | 11 | 1.4 | Woods | 23 | 126 | 5.5 |
| Williams | 8 | 6 | 0.8 | Brooks | 13 | 72 | 5.5 |
| Krieg | 1 | 1 | 1.0 | Wilson | 7 | 45 | 6.4 |
| | 17 | 18 | 1.0 | Esiason | 4 | 11 | 2.8 |
| | | | | | 47 | 254 | 5.4 |

#### RECEIVING

| | No. | Yds. | Avg. | | No. | Yds. | Avg. |
|---|---|---|---|---|---|---|---|
| Williams | 11 | 137 | 12.5 | Holman | 3 | 44 | 14.7 |
| Blades | 5 | 78 | 15.6 | Collinsworth | 1 | 30 | 30.0 |
| Butler | 2 | 40 | 20.0 | Brown | 1 | 23 | 23.0 |
| Largent | 2 | 17 | 8.5 | Brooks | 1 | 9 | 9.0 |
| Skansi | 1 | 11 | 11.0 | Riggs | 1 | 2 | 2.0 |
| L. Clark | 1 | 8 | 8.0 | | 7 | 108 | 15.4 |
| Spagnola | 1 | 7 | 7.0 | | | | |
| Warner | 1 | -1 | -1.0 | | | | |
| | 24 | 297 | 12.4 | | | | |

#### PUNTING

| | No. | Yds. | Avg. | | No. | Yds. | Avg. |
|---|---|---|---|---|---|---|---|
| Rodriguez | 6 | | 44.2 | L. Johnson | 6 | | 46.0 |

#### PUNT RETURNS

| | No. | Yds. | Avg. | | No. | Yds. | Avg. |
|---|---|---|---|---|---|---|---|
| Edmonds | 5 | 30 | 6.0 | Hillary | 3 | 19 | 6.3 |

#### KICKOFF RETURNS

| | No. | Yds. | Avg. | | No. | Yds. | Avg. |
|---|---|---|---|---|---|---|---|
| Edmonds | 2 | 40 | 20.0 | Brooks | 1 | 23 | 23.0 |
| Harmon | 1 | 26 | 26.0 | Jennings | 1 | 18 | 18.0 |
| | 3 | 66 | 22.0 | Hillary | 1 | 13 | 13.0 |
| | | | | | 3 | 54 | 18.0 |

#### INTERCEPTION RETURNS

| | No. | Yds. | Avg. | | No. | Yds. | Avg. |
|---|---|---|---|---|---|---|---|
| | | | | Thomas | 1 | 0 | 0.0 |
| | | | | Wilcots | 1 | 0 | 0.0 |
| | | | | | 2 | 0 | 0.0 |

#### PASSING

**SEATTLE**

| | Att. | Comp. | Comp. Pct. | Yds. | Int. | Yds./ Att. | Yds./ Comp. |
|---|---|---|---|---|---|---|---|
| Krieg | 50 | 24 | 48.0 | 297 | 2 | 5.9 | 12.4 |

**CINCINNATI**

| | Att. | Comp. | Comp. Pct. | Yds. | Int. | Yds./ Att. | Yds./ Comp. |
|---|---|---|---|---|---|---|---|
| Esiason | 7 | 7 | 100.0 | 108 | 0 | 15.4 | 15.4 |

---

## January 1, 1989 at Orchard Park, N.Y. (Attendance 79,532)

### SCORING

| | | | | | |
|---|---|---|---|---|---|
| HOUSTON | 0 | 3 | 0 | 7 | - 10 |
| BUFFALO | 0 | 7 | 7 | 3 | - 17 |

**Second Quarter**
Buff.  Riddick, 1 yard run
       PAT—Norwood (kick)
Hous.  Zendejas, 35 yard field goal

**Third Quarter**
Buff.  Thomas, 11 yard run
       PAT—Norwood (kick)

**Fourth Quarter**
Buff.  Norwood, 27 yard field goal
Hous.  Rozier, 1 yard run
       PAT—Zendejas (kick)

### TEAM STATISTICS

| HOUS. | | BUFF. |
|---|---|---|
| 20 | First Downs- Total | 18 |
| 6 | First Downs- Rushing | 6 |
| 12 | First Downs- Passing | 9 |
| 2 | First Downs- Penalty | 3 |
| 5 | Fumbles- Number | 1 |
| 2 | Fumbles- Lost Ball | 0 |
| 8 | Penalties- Number | 8 |
| 60 | Yards Penalized | 57 |
| 2 | Missed Field Goals | 2 |
| 61 | Offensive Plays | 63 |
| 351 | Net Yards | 372 |
| 5.7 | Average Gain | 5.9 |
| 4 | Giveaways | 1 |
| 1 | Takeaways | 4 |
| -3 | Difference | +3 |

### INDIVIDUAL STATISTICS

**HOUSTON / BUFFALO**

#### RUSHING

| | No. | Yds. | Avg. | | No. | Yds. | Avg. |
|---|---|---|---|---|---|---|---|
| Highsmith | 5 | 57 | 11.4 | Thomas | 7 | 75 | 10.7 |
| Rozier | 13 | 44 | 3.4 | Mueller | 7 | 24 | 3.4 |
| Pinkett | 3 | 13 | 4.3 | Kelly | 3 | 18 | 6.0 |
| Moon | 5 | 11 | 2.2 | Riddick | 9 | 12 | 1.3 |
| | 26 | 125 | 4.9 | Harmon | 1 | 7 | 7.0 |
| | | | | Byrum | 1 | 0 | 0.0 |
| | | | | Reed | 1 | -1 | -1.0 |
| | | | | | 29 | 135 | 4.7 |

#### RECEIVING

| | No. | Yds. | Avg. | | No. | Yds. | Avg. |
|---|---|---|---|---|---|---|---|
| Jeffires | 5 | 78 | 15.6 | Reed | 6 | 91 | 15.2 |
| Hill | 4 | 64 | 16.0 | Harmon | 5 | 58 | 11.6 |
| Pinkett | 2 | 21 | 10.5 | Burkett | 3 | 55 | 18.3 |
| Harris | 2 | 44 | 22.0 | Johnson | 3 | 31 | 10.3 |
| Highsmith | 2 | 3 | 1.5 | Metzelaars | 1 | 7 | 7.0 |
| Givins | 1 | 23 | 23.0 | Mueller | 1 | 2 | 2.0 |
| Duncan | 1 | 9 | 9.0 | | 19 | 244 | 12.8 |
| | 17 | 242 | 14.2 | | | | |

#### PUNTING

| | No. | Yds. | Avg. | | No. | Yds. | Avg. |
|---|---|---|---|---|---|---|---|
| Montgomery | 6 | | 37.2 | Kidd | 4 | | 39.2 |

#### PUNT RETURNS

| | No. | Yds. | Avg. | | No. | Yds. | Avg. |
|---|---|---|---|---|---|---|---|
| Duncan | 1 | 6 | 6.0 | Tucker | 4 | 56 | 14.0 |

#### KICKOFF RETURNS

| | No. | Yds. | Avg. | | No. | Yds. | Avg. |
|---|---|---|---|---|---|---|---|
| Tillman | 2 | 31 | 15.5 | | | | |
| White | 2 | 27 | 13.5 | | | | |
| | 4 | 58 | 14.5 | | | | |

#### INTERCEPTION RETURNS

| | No. | Yds. | Avg. | | No. | Yds. | Avg. |
|---|---|---|---|---|---|---|---|
| Eaton | 1 | 0 | 0.0 | Kelso | 1 | 28 | 28.0 |

#### PASSING

**HOUSTON**

| | Att. | Comp. | Comp. Pct. | Yds. | Int. | Yds./ Att. | Yds./ Comp. |
|---|---|---|---|---|---|---|---|
| Moon | 33 | 17 | 51.5 | 240 | | 17.3 | 14.1 |

**BUFFALO**

| | Att. | Comp. | Comp. Pct. | Yds. | Int. | Yds./ Att. | Yds./ Comp. |
|---|---|---|---|---|---|---|---|
| Kelly | 33 | 19 | 57.6 | 244 | 1 | 7.4 | 12.8 |

# 1988 Championship Games

## AFC CHAMPIONSHIP GAME

January 8, 1989 at Cincinnati, Oh.

(Attendance 59,747)

### SCORING

| | | | | | |
|---|---|---|---|---|---|
| BUFFALO | 0 | 10 | 0 | 0 - | 10 |
| CINCINNATI | 7 | 7 | 0 | 7 - | 21 |

**First Quarter**
Cin.  Woods, 1 yard run
PAT—Breech (kick)

**Second Quarter**
Buff.  Reed, 9 yard pass from Kelly
PAT—Norwood (kick)
Cin.  Brooks, 10 yard pass from Esiason
PAT—Breech (kick)
Buff.  Norwood, 39 yard field goal

**Fourth Quarter**
Cin.  Woods, 1 yard run
PAT—Breech (kick)

### TEAM STATISTICS

| BUFF. | | CIN. |
|---|---|---|
| 10 | First Downs- Total | 23 |
| 2 | First Downs- Rushing | 15 |
| 8 | First Downs- Passing | 5 |
| 0 | First Downs- Penalty | 3 |
| 0 | Fumbles- Number | 2 |
| 0 | Fumbles- Lost Ball | 0 |
| 5 | Penalties- Number | 4 |
| 50 | Yards Penalized | 45 |
| 1 | Missed Field Goals | 0 |
| 50 | Offensive Plays | 73 |
| 181 | Net Yards | 249 |
| 3.6 | Average Gain | 3.4 |
| 3 | Giveaways | 2 |
| 2 | Takeaways | 3 |
| -1 | Difference | +1 |

The Cincinnati defense that received little respect all season stole the thunder from the heralded offense, as the Central Division champs humbled Buffalo at Riverfront Stadium. The Bills were held to a mere 181 total yards and were unable to convert any third-down situations. On its first three possessions in the first half and first four in the second half, Buffalo was unable to gain a first down. The defense that held Seattle to only 18 rushing yards a week before stuffed Buffalo for only 45 yards.

The Bengals stuck to a bread-and-butter diet of crunching rushes by FB Ickey Woods, who gained 102 yards on 29 carries. He scored Cincinnati's first touchdown on a one-yard plunge in the opening quarter. Buffalo came back to tie the game early in the second period on a short pass from Jim Kelly to Andre Reed. Then, after Cincinnati regained the lead on one of Boomer Esiason's infrequent passes, a 10-yarder to James Brooks, the Bills closed the gap to 14-10 on Scott Norwood's 39-yard field goal.

Despite their dominance, the Bengals were unable to put the game away until Buffalo helped them twice on a long drive midway through the second half. Facing a fourth-and-four at the Buffalo 33, Cincinnati fooled the Bills on a fake punt for the first down. Moments later, the drive seemed to stall, but Buffalo CB Derrick Burroughs was called for slugging Tim McGee in the endzone, and Cincinnati was given a first down at the Buffalo four-yard line. Two plays later, Woods crashed over for his second touchdown.

### INDIVIDUAL STATISTICS

#### RUSHING

| BUFFALO | No. | Yds. | Avg. | CINCINNATI | No. | Yds. | Avg. |
|---|---|---|---|---|---|---|---|
| Mueller | 8 | 21 | 2.6 | Woods | 29 | 102 | 3.5 |
| Kelly | 2 | 10 | 5.0 | Wilson | 5 | 29 | 5.8 |
| Thomas | 4 | 6 | 1.5 | Esiason | 7 | 26 | 3.7 |
| Riddick | 1 | 4 | 4.0 | Jennings | 2 | 12 | 6.0 |
| Byrum | 1 | 3 | 3.0 | Brooks | 7 | 6 | 0.9 |
| Harmon | 1 | 1 | 1.0 | | 50 | 175 | 3.5 |
| | 17 | 45 | 2.6 | | | | |

#### RECEIVING

| BUFFALO | No. | Yds. | Avg. | CINCINNATI | No. | Yds. | Avg. |
|---|---|---|---|---|---|---|---|
| Reed | 5 | 55 | 11.0 | Holman | 4 | 38 | 9.5 |
| Harmon | 3 | 18 | 6.0 | Riggs | 2 | 16 | 8.0 |
| Riddick | 3 | 28 | 9.3 | Brooks | 2 | 21 | 10.5 |
| T. Johnson | 2 | 48 | 24.0 | McGee | 2 | 14 | 7.0 |
| Metzelaars | 1 | 14 | 14.0 | Collinsworth | 1 | 5 | 5.0 |
| | 14 | 163 | 11.6 | | 11 | 94 | 8.5 |

#### PUNTING

| BUFFALO | No. | | Avg. | CINCINNATI | No. | | Avg. |
|---|---|---|---|---|---|---|---|
| Kidd | 6 | | 45.1 | Johnson | 6 | | 36.8 |

#### PUNT RETURNS

| BUFFALO | No. | Yds. | Avg. | CINCINNATI | No. | Yds. | Avg. |
|---|---|---|---|---|---|---|---|
| Tucker | 1 | 2 | 2.0 | Hillary | 2 | 24 | 12.0 |
| | | | | Dixon | 1 | 0 | 0.0 |
| | | | | | 3 | 24 | 8.0 |

#### KICKOFF RETURNS

| BUFFALO | No. | Yds. | Avg. | CINCINNATI | No. | Yds. | Avg. |
|---|---|---|---|---|---|---|---|
| Harmon | 2 | 45 | 22.5 | Jennings | 1 | 19 | 19.0 |
| Tucker | 1 | 12 | 12.0 | Hillary | 2 | 11 | 5.5 |
| | 3 | 57 | 19.0 | | 3 | 30 | 10.0 |

#### INTERCEPTION RETURNS

| BUFFALO | No. | Yds. | Avg. | CINCINNATI | No. | Yds. | Avg. |
|---|---|---|---|---|---|---|---|
| Kelso | 1 | 25 | 25.0 | Thomas | 1 | 26 | 26.0 |
| Bentley | 1 | 0 | 0.0 | Fulcher | 1 | 0 | 0.0 |
| | 2 | 25 | 12.5 | Billups | 1 | -3 | -3.0 |
| | | | | | 3 | 23 | 7.7 |

#### PASSING

| | Att. | Comp. | Comp. Pct. | Yds. | Int. | Yds./ Att. | Yds./ Comp. |
|---|---|---|---|---|---|---|---|
| **BUFFALO** | | | | | | | |
| Kelly | 30 | 14 | 46.7 | 163 | 3 | 5.4 | 11.6 |
| **CINCINNATI** | | | | | | | |
| Esiason | 20 | 11 | 55.0 | 94 | 2 | 4.7 | 8.5 |

---

# 1988 Championship Games

## NFC CHAMPIONSHIP GAME

January 8, 1989 at Chicago, Ill.

(Attendance 64,830)

### SCORING

| | | | | | |
|---|---|---|---|---|---|
| SAN FRANCISCO | 7 | 7 | 7 | 7 - | 28 |
| CHICAGO | 0 | 3 | 0 | 0 - | 3 |

**First Quarter**
S.F.  Rice, 61 yard pass from Montana
PAT—Cofer (kick)

**Second Quarter**
S.F.  Rice, 27 yard pass from Montana
PAT—Cofer (kick)
Chi.  Butler, 25 yard field goal

**Third Quarter**
S.F.  Frank, 5 yard pass from Montana
PAT—Cofer (kick)

**Fourth Quarter**
S.F.  Rathman, 4 yard run
PAT—Cofer (kick)

### TEAM STATISTICS

| S.F. | | CHI. |
|---|---|---|
| 21 | First Downs- Total | 15 |
| 9 | First Downs- Rushing | 8 |
| 12 | First Downs- Passing | 7 |
| 0 | First Downs- Penalty | 0 |
| 1 | Fumbles- Number | 2 |
| 1 | Fumbles- Lost Ball | 1 |
| 0 | Penalties- Number | 4 |
| 0 | Yards Penalized | 35 |
| 0 | Missed Field Goals | 0 |
| 66 | Offensive Plays | 66 |
| 406 | Net Yards | 267 |
| 6.2 | Average Gain | 4.0 |
| 1 | Giveaways | 2 |
| 2 | Takeaways | 1 |
| +1 | Difference | -1 |

The Bears' defense that was the best in the NFL proved easy pickings for Joe Montana and Jerry Rice at Soldier Field, as the 49ers moved to within a step of their third league championship in the 1980s. The temperature hovered around 17 degrees, but the Montana-to-Rice combination was red-hot. San Francisco coach Bill Walsh said of Montana, who completed 17 of 27 passes, "It may have been his greatest game under the conditions." Rice scored two TD's and had a third called back on a penalty.

With abouth three-and-a-half minutes left in the first quarter, Montana caught the Bears in single coverage on Rice and fired a short pass to him near the sideline. Rice leaped and took the ball away from Bears CB Mike Richardson, then out-raced Richardson and Vestee Jackson into the endzone. In the second quarter, Montana-to-Rice connected again. This time, Rice took a pass off his shoetops to victimize Jackson. The Bears got their only score near the end of the first half on a 25-yard field goal by Kevin Butler to make it 14-3.

San Francisco took the second-half kickoff and marched 78 yards in 13 plays to widen the lead to 21-3. Montana passed five yards to TE John Frank for the score.

Although the 49ers' defense registered no sacks, Chicago's Jim McMahon, making his first start since mid-October, was pressured all day and was unable to complete anything but short passes. He was 14 of 29, but gained only 121 yards and was replaced by Mike Tomczak. The 49ers defense held the Bears to 267 total yards on the day, and only 97 yards rushing.

In the final period, the 49ers ended the *coup de grace* on Tom Rathman's four-yard smash.

### INDIVIDUAL STATISTICS

#### RUSHING

| SAN FRANCISCO | No. | Yds. | Avg. | CHICAGO | No. | Yds. | Avg. |
|---|---|---|---|---|---|---|---|
| Craig | 18 | 68 | 3.8 | Anderson | 14 | 59 | 4.2 |
| Rathman | 10 | 36 | 3.6 | Sanders | 7 | 22 | 3.1 |
| Montana | 3 | 12 | 4.0 | McMahon | 1 | 9 | 9.0 |
| Sydney | 2 | 12 | 6.0 | Suhey | 1 | 3 | 3.0 |
| Flagler | 3 | 7 | 2.3 | Muster | 1 | 2 | 2.0 |
| Rice | 1 | 3 | 3.0 | McKinnon | 1 | -4 | -4.0 |
| | 37 | 138 | 3.7 | | 25 | 91 | 3.6 |

#### RECEIVING

| SAN FRANCISCO | No. | Yds. | Avg. | CHICAGO | No. | Yds. | Avg. |
|---|---|---|---|---|---|---|---|
| Rice | 5 | 133 | 26.6 | Anderson | 5 | 31 | 6.2 |
| Rathman | 5 | 51 | 10.2 | Thornton | 4 | 52 | 13.5 |
| Taylor | 3 | 51 | 17.0 | McKinnon | 4 | 32 | 8.0 |
| Craig | 2 | 33 | 16.5 | Morris | 2 | 25 | 12.5 |
| Frank | 2 | 20 | 10.0 | Suhey | 2 | 8 | 4.0 |
| | 17 | 288 | 16.9 | Sanders | 1 | 12 | 12.0 |
| | | | | Muster | 1 | 9 | 9.0 |
| | | | | Gentry | 1 | 7 | 7.0 |
| | | | | | 20 | 176 | 8.8 |

#### PUNTING

| SAN FRANCISCO | No. | | Avg. | CHICAGO | No. | | Avg. |
|---|---|---|---|---|---|---|---|
| Helton | 6 | | 34.5 | Wagner | 7 | | 31.4 |

#### PUNT RETURNS

| SAN FRANCISCO | No. | Yds. | Avg. | CHICAGO | No. | Yds. | Avg. |
|---|---|---|---|---|---|---|---|
| Taylor | 4 | 24 | 6.0 | McKinnon | 1 | 1 | 1.0 |

#### KICKOFF RETURNS

| SAN FRANCISCO | No. | Yds. | Avg. | CHICAGO | No. | Yds. | Avg. |
|---|---|---|---|---|---|---|---|
| Sydney | 1 | 14 | 14.0 | Sanders | 2 | 31 | 15.5 |
| Taylor | 1 | 22 | 22.0 | Muster | 1 | 21 | 21.0 |
| | 2 | 36 | 18.0 | Gentry | 1 | 19 | 19.0 |
| | | | | Stinson | 1 | 18 | 18.0 |
| | | | | | 5 | 89 | 17.8 |

#### INTERCEPTION RETURNS

| SAN FRANCISCO | No. | Yds. | Avg. | CHICAGO | No. | Yds. | Avg. |
|---|---|---|---|---|---|---|---|
| Fuller | 1 | 0 | 0.0 | | | | |

#### PASSING

| | Att. | Comp. | Comp. Pct. | Yds. | Int. | Yds./ Att. | Yds./ Comp. |
|---|---|---|---|---|---|---|---|
| **SAN FRANCISCO** | | | | | | | |
| Montana | 27 | 17 | 63.0 | 288 | 0 | 10.7 | 16.9 |
| **CHICAGO** | | | | | | | |
| McMahon | 29 | 14 | 48.3 | 121 | 1 | 4.2 | 8.6 |
| Tomczak | 12 | 6 | 50.0 | 55 | 0 | 4.2 | 9.2 |

# One Worth Watching

After several Super Bowls that were mostly hype followed by few thrills, No. 23 turned out to be better than its advance billing. During the preceding week, the traditional media overkill was somewhat upstaged by a real killing, as Miami was the scene of bloody riots precipitated by a police shooting. The tragic events put the importance of a football game — even the Super Bowl — into perspective.

Nevertheless, more than 75,000 paid $8.1 million for tickets to Joe Robbie Stadium to watch the Bengals and 49ers, and advertisers shelled out $675,000 for each 30-second chance to reach more than 100 million television fans. For once, the money may have been well spent.

The first half was a defensive struggle, punctuated by two key injuries. On the first series after the kickoff, San Francisco OT Steve Wallace was sidelined with a broken ankle, depriving the 49ers of one of their best blockers. After an exchange of punts, Cincinnati's All-Pro NT Tim Krumrie was injured on a freak play when he planted his foot and his left leg snapped in two places. The injury came on the first play of a 73-yard, 13-play San Francisco drive that culminated in Mike Cofer's 41-yard field goal. At the end of the first quarter, the 49ers started another drive from their 30 that finished at the Cincinnati two. But Cofer's attempt at a second field goal was foiled by a bad snap.

The Bengals tied the score late in the second quarter on Jim Breech's 34-yard field goal after a short drive from midfield.

The defensive battle continued into the third period. The Bengals took the kickoff and drove 61 yards, despite three penalties. Two passes from Boomer Esiason to Cris Collinsworth paced the drive. When Cincinnati stalled at the 49er 25, Breech kicked his second field goal to make the score 6-3.

San Francisco came back to tie the game late in the third quarter. Rookie LB Bill Romanowski intercepted Esiason at the 23 with 2:22 remaining. Four plays later, Cofer kicked a 32-yard field goal to knot the score again. The tie lastes until the kickoff. The Bengals' Stanford Jennings took the ball at his seven and burst 93 yards to a touchdown to put Cincinnati back in front 13-6.

Joe Montana led his team downfield in four plays from his own 15, completing a 31-yard pass to Jerry Rice and a 40-yarder to Roger Craig. From the Cincinnati 14, Montana threw into the endzone and into the hands of Bengals CB Lewis Billups, but he dropped the ball. On the next play, Montana threw left to Rice for a touchdown to tie the score again at 13-13.

Cincinnati was unable to gain and punted to San Francisco at the 49ers 18. On the first play, Montana hit Rice for 44 yards. When two running plays and a pass failed to pick up the first down, Cofer tried for a field goal from the Cincinnati 49, but his attempt was wide right. The Bengals drove to the San Francisco 22, with the key play being a 3rd-and-12 pass from Esiason to Ira Hillary. Breech kicked his third field goal, a 40-yarder, to give the Bengals a 16-13 lead with 3:20 remaining.

It was time for the drive of the game. Montana started from his own eight with short passes to John Frank and Rice. At the 35, he connected with Rice for 17 yards to move the ball into Cincinnati territory. A 13-yarder to Craig put the ball at the 35, but a penalty sent the 49ers back to the 45. With 1:15 on the clock and a 2nd-and-20 situation, Montana threw over the middle to Rice, who was finally hauled down at the Bengals' 18. A quick pass over the middle to Craig gained eight. Then Montana hit John Taylor in the endzone for the winning touchdown, completing an 11-play, 92-yard drive. Cincinnati was unable to do anything in the 34 seconds they had left, and San Francisco had its third Super Bowl victory of the 1980s.

## LINEUPS

| CIN. | | S.F |
|---|---|---|
| | **OFFENSE** | |
| McGee | WR | Taylor |
| Munoz | LT | Wallace |
| Reimers | LG | Sapolu |
| Kozerski | C | Cross |
| Montoya | RG | McIntyre |
| Blados | RT | Barton |
| Holman | TE | Frank |
| Brown | WR | Rice |
| Esiason | QB | Montana |
| Brooks | RB | Craig |
| Woods | FB | Rathman |
| | **DEFENSE** | |
| Skow | LE | Roberts |
| Krumrie | NT | Carter |
| Buck | RE | Fagan |
| White | LOLB | Haley |
| Zander | LILB | Fahnhorst |
| Kelly | RILB | Walter |
| Williams | ROLB | Turner |
| Billups | LCB | McKyer |
| Thomas | RCB | Griffin |
| Fulcher | SS | Fuller |
| Wilcots | FS | Lott |

**SUBSTITUTES**

**CINCINNATI**

| | **OFFENSE** | |
|---|---|---|
| Norseth | Schonert | Logan |
| Jennings | D. Smith | Douglas |
| Rourke | Collinsworth | Parker |
| Riggs | Hillary | |
| | **DEFENSE** | |
| Horton | Smith | Bussey |
| Dixon | Barker | Brady |
| McClendon | Eddwards | King |
| Grant | | |
| | **KICKERS** | |
| Breech | L. Johnson | |

**SAN FRANCISCO**

| | **OFFENSE** | |
|---|---|---|
| Young | Sydney | Pollard |
| Flagler | Thomas | Collie |
| Paris | Greer | B. Jones |
| Wilson | Heller | |
| | **DEFENSE** | |
| Wright | Cox | Holmoe |
| Ellison | Kennedy | Romanowski |
| Kugler | Stover | Holt |
| Stubbs | | |
| | **KICKERS** | |
| Cofer | Helton | |

## SCORING

| | 1 | 2 | 3 | 4 | | |
|---|---|---|---|---|---|---|
| CINCINNATI | 0 | 3 | 10 | 3 | - | 16 |
| SAN FRANCISCO | 3 | 0 | 3 | 14 | - | 20 |

**First Quarter**
S.F.    Cofer, 41 yard field goal

**Second Quarter**
Cin.    Breech, 34 yard field goal

**Third Quarter**
Cin.    Breech, 43 yard field goal
S.F.    Cofer, 32 yard field goal
Cin.    Jennings, 93 yard kickoff return
        PAT—Breech (kick)

**Fourth Quarter**
S.F.    Rice, 14 yard pass from Montana
        PAT—Cofer (kick)
Cin.    Breech, 40 yard field goal
S.F.    Taylor, 10 yard pass from Montana
        PAT—Cofer (kick)

## TEAM STATISTICS

| CIN. | | S.F. |
|---|---|---|
| 13 | First Downs-Total | 23 |
| 7 | First Downs-Rushing | 6 |
| 6 | First Downs-Pasing | 16 |
| 0 | First Downs-Penalty | 1 |
| 1 | Fumbles-Number | 4 |
| 0 | Fumbles-Lost Ball | 1 |
| 7 | Penaties-Number | 4 |
| 65 | Yards Penalized | 32 |
| 0 | Missed Field Goals | 2 |
| 64 | Offensive Plays | 67 |
| 229 | Net Yards | 454 |
| 3.6 | Average Gain | 6.8 |
| 1 | Giveaways | 1 |
| 1 | Takeaways | 1 |
| 0 | Difference | 0 |

## INDIVIDUAL STATISTICS

### RUSHING

**CINCINNATI**

| | No. | Yds. | Avg. |
|---|---|---|---|
| Woods | 20 | 79 | 3.9 |
| Brooks | 6 | 24 | 4.0 |
| Jennings | 1 | 3 | 3.0 |
| Esiason | 1 | 0 | 0.0 |
| | 28 | 106 | 3.8 |

**SAN FRANCISCO**

| | No. | Yds. | Avg. |
|---|---|---|---|
| Craig | 17 | 74 | 4.4 |
| Rathman | 5 | 23 | 4.6 |
| Montana | 5 | 9 | 1.8 |
| Rice | 1 | 5 | 5.0 |
| | 28 | 111 | 4.0 |

### RECEIVING

**CINCINNATI**

| | No. | Yds. | Avg. |
|---|---|---|---|
| Brown | 4 | 44 | 11.0 |
| Collinsworth | 3 | 40 | 13.3 |
| McGee | 2 | 23 | 11.5 |
| Brooks | 1 | 20 | 20.0 |
| Hillary | 1 | 17 | 17.0 |
| | 11 | 144 | 13.1 |

**SAN FRANCISCO**

| | No. | Yds. | Avg. |
|---|---|---|---|
| Rice | 11 | 215 | 19.5 |
| Craig | 8 | 101 | 12.6 |
| Frank | 2 | 15 | 7.5 |
| Rathman | 1 | 16 | 16.0 |
| Taylor | 1 | 10 | 10.0 |
| | 23 | 357 | 15.5 |

### PUNTING

**CINCINNATI**

| | No. | Yds. | Avg. |
|---|---|---|---|
| L. Johnson | 5 | | 44.6 |

**SAN FRANCISCO**

| | No. | Yds. | Avg. |
|---|---|---|---|
| Helton | 4 | | 37.0 |

### PUNT RETURNS

**CINCINNATI**

| | No. | Yds. | Avg. |
|---|---|---|---|
| Horton | 1 | 5 | 5.0 |
| Hillary | 1 | 0 | 0.0 |
| | 2 | 5 | 2.5 |

**SAN FRANCISCO**

| | No. | Yds. | Avg. |
|---|---|---|---|
| Taylor | 3 | 56 | 18.7 |

### KICKOFF RETURNS

**CINCINNATI**

| | No. | Yds. | Avg. |
|---|---|---|---|
| Jennings | 2 | 117 | 58.5 |
| Brooks | 1 | 15 | 15.0 |
| | 3 | 132 | 44.0 |

**SAN FRANCISCO**

| | No. | Yds. | Avg. |
|---|---|---|---|
| Rodgers | 3 | 53 | 17.7 |
| Taylor | 1 | 13 | 13.0 |
| Sydney | 1 | 11 | 11.0 |
| | 5 | 77 | 15.4 |

### INTERCEPTIONS RETURNS

**CINCINNATI**

**SAN FRANCISCO**

| | No. | Yds. | Avg. |
|---|---|---|---|
| Romanowski | 1 | 0 | 0.0 |

### PASSING

**CINCINNATI**

| | Att. | Comp. | Comp. Pct. | Yds. | Int. | Yds./Att. | Yds./Comp. | Yards Lost Tackled |
|---|---|---|---|---|---|---|---|---|
| Esiason | 25 | 11 | 44.0 | 144 | 1 | 5.8 | 13.9 | 5-21 |

**SAN FRANCISCO**

| | Att. | Comp. | Comp. Pct. | Yds. | Int. | Yds./Att. | Yds./Comp. | Yards Lost Tackled |
|---|---|---|---|---|---|---|---|---|
| Montana | 36 | 23 | 63.9 | 357 | 0 | 9.9 | 15.5 | 3-14 |

# 1989 N.F.C.  Who Was That Hitman?

In a year that saw the Bears' defense collapse, the Packers mount a stirring playoff drive, the Lions improve, the Saints slip, Herschel Walker traded and Joe Montana canonized, the Talk of the NFC — at least for a couple of weeks — was "bounty hunting." After Dallas lost to Philadelphia on Thanksgiving, Cowboys' coach Jimmy Johnson accused the Eagles of putting a price on the head of Luis Zendejas, the Dallas placekicker. Zendejas, an ex-Eagle kayoed by a former teammate in a kickoff collission, insisted he had proof in the form of a taped telephone conversation with a Philadelphia assistant coach. Amid charge and counter-charge, Eagle coach Buddy Ryan wondered rhetorically why anyone would want to knock a placekicker who'd been in a six-week slump out of a game.

## EASTERN DIVISION

**New York Giants** — The Giants put together their second-best won-lost record in 26 years, yet were a mere 1-4 against playoff teams, including a pair of losses to the second-place Eagles. The surprise of the season was veteran running back Ottis Anderson, who stepped in for the injured Joe Morris and produced the sixth 1,000-yard rushing season of his career (but first since 1984). Considered at the end of his days before the season, Anderson combined with a hefty young line to produce a strong power running game. Rookie Dave Meggett was another pleasant surprise, making the Pro Bowl with his jitterbug kick returning and occasional long-distance pass catching. Phil Simms was steady throughout, except for a horrible two-game stretch against the 49ers and Eagles when he committed a mind-boggling seven turnovers, six of which produced points for the opposition. Linebackers Lawrence Taylor, with 15 sacks, and Carl Banks, making a comeback after a so-so season, led an adequate defense. Banks was named the team's MVP by the players.

**Philadelphia Eagles** — Randall Cunningham led the team in rushing for the third straight year, something no quarterback has done since the T-formation became the basic pro offense in the 1940s. However, it was a subpar season for the fifth-year pro who signed an $18 million, five-year contract extension in October. After a holdout, defensive end Reggie White wasn't up to his usual standard, either, although he still made most All-Pro teams. Star receiver Mike Quick was lost in October to double-knee surgery. Nevertheless, Buddy Ryan's Eagles still won 11 games to qualify for a wild-card spot. The slack was taken up by an improved running game and the blossoming of defensive linemen Clyde Simmons and Jerome Brown, who combined for 26 sacks. Cornerback Eric Allen led the NFC with eight interceptions.

**Washington Redskins** — Coach Joe Gibbs' Redskins missed the playoffs in consecutive years for the first time in his nine years as boss. Washington hit its first season low by being the only team to lose to Dallas and its second when veteran defensive end Dexter Manley was permanently banned for drug use. Heralded trade acquisition Gerald Riggs missed most of six games with injuries. Mark Rypien, who started most of the time at quarterback, was erratic and showed an alarming tendency to fumble when he was sacked. Another rash of injuries to the offensive line didn't help either. Yet, through it all, the Redskins were improved over 1989, largely because of the stellar play of the wide receivers. Art Monk, Gary Clark and Ricky Sanders each gained more than 1,000 yards on pass receptions.

**Phoenix Cardinals** — The season began with the bad news that veteran quarterback Neil Lomax's arthritic hip would keep him from playing. He retired after the season, but by then the Cardinals had suffered through many more disasters. Injuries caused starters to miss a combined total of 77 games. Substance-abuse suspensions took care of a few others. Coach Gene Stallings somehow got the club to 5-6 with bailing wire and spit, but when he announced he would not seek a contract extension, he was fired. Under interim coach Hank Kuhlmann, Phoenix lost its last five games with seldom a whimper. Meanwhile, empty seats became the norm at Sun Devil Stadium; the club suffered an astounding 26.9 percent drop in attendance.

**Dallas Cowboys** — New owner Jerry Jones and new coach Jimmy Johnson decided on the new-book approach and swept out or aside most of the Cowboys of yore in favor of youth, even trading super-running back Herschel Walker to Minnesota for a posse of draft choices and several players. Youth must be served, but the Dallas youth was mostly served on a plate. No. 1 draft choice Troy Aikman showed promise as a quarterback and leader, but he had few tools to work with — especially after wide receiver Michael Irvin went out with a knee injury. With Aikman as the future, it was hard to figure the Dallas decision to grab quarterback Steve Walsh in the supplemental draft. It cost Dallas the first pick in the 1990 draft when the team flopped to a 1-15 record. Through the debacle, middle linebacker Eugene Lockhart performed heroically and closed 1989 with more than 200 tackles.

## CENTRAL DIVISION

**Minnesota Vikings** — Despite winning their division, the Vikings were generally disappointing, losing six of eight games away from the friendly Metrodome. The big trade that brought Herschel Walker from the Cowboys after Week Five looked like a steal wehn Walker opened his Viking career by rushing for 148 yards in his first game, but after that he performed at only an ordinary pace. The offense was also dragged down by quarterback Wade Wilson's inconsistency and nagging injuries to wide receiver Athony Carter. It was the league-leading defense that kept Minnesota afloat. Defensive end Chris Doleman topped the NFL with 21 sacks and defensive tackl﹅ Keith Millard was close behind with 18. The team sack total of 71 was only one behind the record set by the '84 Bears. An ugly early-season incident that saw some team members involved in contract disputes — one accused GM Mike Lynn of racism — didn't do anything for team morale.

**Green Bay Packers** — The Pack was back — almost. Their 10-6 mark tied Minnesota in percentage but not in the NFL's tie-breaking system. Under the expanded playoff system of 1990, Green Bay would have made postseason play. Nevertheless, it was a fine year for coach Lindy Infante, who received most of the Coach of the Year laurels. Much of the Packers' improvement was credited to the development of quarterback Don Majkowski, who went from erratic to the "Magic Man" and led several remarkable comeback victories and helped Green Bay win six games by a total of 11 points. Wide receiver Sterling Sharpe was another sensation, leading the league in receiving; he also had 12 TD's. The defense ranked in the lower echelon, but linebacker Tim Harris was an All-Pro, registering 19.5 sacks. Cornerback Dave Brown, at 36 years old, led the team with six interceptions.

**Detroit Lions** — Heisman Trophy winner Barry Sanders, coming out of college as a junior, led the NFC in rushing, but through a 1-8 start, it all seemed for naught. Then coach Wayne Fontes' troops roared down the stretch to finish a respectable 7-9. Free-agent quarterback Bob Gagliano's improvement was the big factor in the turnaround. Ironically, the Lions' new run-and-shoot offense, dubbed the "Silver Stretch," was geared to a passing attack, yet Sanders made the attack go on the ground and quarterbacks Gagliano and Rodney Peete accounted for almost as many touchdowns with their running as with their passing, nine to 11. Veteran placekicker Eddie Murray made the Pro Bowl after duplicating his '88 success on 20-of-21 field-goal attempts.

**Chicago Bears** — Jim McMahon was traded to San Diego before the season began, but the Bears still couldn't settle on a quarterback as both Mike Tomczak and Jim Harbaugh started games. Neither received much help from a crew of receivers that was, at best, ordinary. Meanwhile, Neal Anderson became a star of the first order with 1,275 rushing yards. Anderson led the team in rushing, receiving and scoring. Although the offense was undependable, it was the once-invincible Bear defense that really let them down, finishing 25th in the league and three times blowing leads in the final two minutes. Chicago started the season with four victories, but then defensive tackle Dan Hampton was lost for the year with surgery on both knees. In the absence of Hampton, opponents concentrated on stopping Richard Dent's pass rush and isolating middle linebacker Mike Singletary. Then, without a pass rush, the defensive backs became easy pickings. The Bears lost 10 of their last 12 games, including the final six.

| OFFENSE | ATL | CHI | DAL | DET | G.B. | L.A. | MINN | N.O. | NYG | PHIL | PHX | S.F. | T.B. | WASH |
|---|---|---|---|---|---|---|---|---|---|---|---|---|---|---|
| FIRST DOWNS: | | | | | | | | | | | | | | |
| Total | 261 | 302 | 246 | 274 | 342 | 321 | 326 | 304 | 298 | 321 | 262 | 350 | 288 | 338 |
| by Rushing | 75 | 136 | 78 | 117 | 114 | 107 | 126 | 108 | 118 | 120 | 83 | 124 | 84 | 101 |
| by Passing | 173 | 147 | 145 | 139 | 207 | 197 | 172 | 167 | 157 | 171 | 157 | 209 | 174 | 217 |
| by Penalty | 13 | 19 | 23 | 18 | 21 | 17 | 28 | 29 | 23 | 30 | 22 | 17 | 30 | 20 |
| RUSHING: | | | | | | | | | | | | | | |
| Number | 318 | 516 | 355 | 421 | 397 | 472 | 514 | 502 | 556 | 540 | 407 | 493 | 412 | 514 |
| Yards | 1155 | 2287 | 1409 | 2053 | 1732 | 1909 | 2066 | 1948 | 1889 | 2208 | 1361 | 1966 | 1507 | 1904 |
| Average Yards | 3.6 | 4.4 | 4.0 | 4.9 | 4.4 | 4.0 | 4.0 | 3.9 | 3.4 | 4.1 | 3.3 | 4.0 | 3.7 | 3.7 |
| Touchdowns | 11 | 22 | 7 | 23 | 13 | 19 | 12 | 19 | 17 | 14 | 10 | 14 | 10 | 14 |
| PASSING: | | | | | | | | | | | | | | |
| Attempts | 578 | 484 | 513 | 450 | 600 | 523 | 499 | 461 | 444 | 538 | 523 | 483 | 570 | 581 |
| Completions | 312 | 267 | 266 | 229 | 354 | 308 | 272 | 284 | 248 | 294 | 279 | 339 | 302 | 337 |
| Completion Pct. | 54.0 | 55.2 | 51.9 | 50.9 | 59.0 | 58.9 | 54.5 | 61.6 | 55.9 | 54.6 | 53.3 | 70.2 | 53.0 | 58.0 |
| Passing Yards | 3903 | 3262 | 3124 | 3282 | 4325 | 4369 | 3468 | 3651 | 3355 | 3455 | 3659 | 4584 | 3666 | 4476 |
| Avg. Yds per Att. | 6.0 | 6.0 | 5.3 | 5.8 | 6.3 | 7.5 | 5.9 | 6.8 | 6.3 | 5.3 | 5.7 | 8.2 | 5.4 | 7.2 |
| Avg. Yds per Comp. | 12.5 | 12.2 | 11.7 | 14.3 | 12.2 | 14.2 | 12.8 | 12.9 | 13.5 | 11.8 | 13.1 | 13.5 | 12.1 | 13.3 |
| Times Tackled | 51 | 28 | 30 | 57 | 48 | 32 | 40 | 36 | 46 | 45 | 56 | 45 | 43 | 21 |
| Yds Lost Tackled | 389 | 174 | 239 | 343 | 277 | 236 | 279 | 271 | 281 | 343 | 379 | 282 | 331 | 127 |
| Net Yards | 3514 | 3088 | 2885 | 2939 | 4048 | 4133 | 3189 | 3380 | 3074 | 3112 | 3280 | 4302 | 3335 | 4349 |
| Touchdowns | 17 | 21 | 14 | 11 | 27 | 29 | 17 | 23 | 17 | 23 | 17 | 35 | 23 | 24 |
| Interceptions | 12 | 25 | 27 | 24 | 20 | 18 | 19 | 19 | 16 | 16 | 30 | 11 | 28 | 17 |
| Pct. Intercepted | 2.1 | 5.2 | 5.3 | 5.3 | 3.3 | 3.4 | 3.8 | 4.1 | 3.6 | 3.0 | 5.7 | 2.3 | 4.9 | 2.9 |
| PUNTS: | | | | | | | | | | | | | | |
| Number | 85 | 72 | 82 | 83 | 66 | 74 | 72 | 71 | 70 | 87 | 82 | 56 | 86 | 63 |
| Average | 40.8 | 39.5 | 39.8 | 42.6 | 40.6 | 38.3 | 39.8 | 39.1 | 43.1 | 39.0 | 43.6 | 39.8 | 38.5 | 42.3 |
| PUNT RETURNS | | | | | | | | | | | | | | |
| Number | 32 | 32 | 31 | 47 | 35 | 35 | 45 | 53 | 46 | 37 | 40 | 39 | 32 | 26 |
| Yards | 341 | 220 | 197 | 572 | 289 | 332 | 448 | 428 | 582 | 331 | 469 | 429 | 296 | 226 |
| Average Yards | 10.7 | 6.9 | 6.4 | 12.2 | 8.3 | 9.5 | 10.0 | 8.1 | 12.7 | 8.9 | 11.7 | 11.0 | 9.3 | 8.7 |
| Touchdowns | 1 | 0 | 0 | 0 | 0 | 0 | 0 | 1 | 1 | 0 | 0 | 0 | 0 | 0 |
| KICKOFF RET.: | | | | | | | | | | | | | | |
| Number | 80 | 73 | 77 | 61 | 69 | 67 | 51 | 63 | 51 | 49 | 83 | 51 | 62 | 58 |
| Yards | 1509 | 1539 | 1709 | 1272 | 1239 | 1328 | 1122 | 1284 | 926 | 828 | 1650 | 954 | 1055 | 1176 |
| Average Yards | 18.9 | 21.1 | 22.2 | 20.9 | 18.0 | 19.8 | 22.0 | 20.4 | 18.2 | 16.9 | 19.9 | 18.7 | 17.0 | 20.3 |
| Touchdowns | 0 | 1 | 1 | 0 | 0 | 0 | 1 | 1 | 0 | 0 | 0 | 0 | 0 | 1 |
| INTERCEPT RET.: | | | | | | | | | | | | | | |
| Number | 20 | 26 | 7 | 16 | 25 | 21 | 18 | 21 | 22 | 30 | 16 | 21 | 21 | 27 |
| Yards | 285 | 268 | 37 | 107 | 232 | 372 | 264 | 226 | 330 | 375 | 275 | 262 | 234 | 284 |
| Average Yards | 14.3 | 10.3 | 5.3 | 6.7 | 9.3 | 17.7 | 14.7 | 10.8 | 15.0 | 12.5 | 17.2 | 12.5 | 11.1 | 10.5 |
| Touchdowns | 0 | 1 | 0 | 1 | 0 | 3 | 2 | 2 | 2 | 2 | 2 | 0 | 2 | 3 |
| PENALTIES: | | | | | | | | | | | | | | |
| Number | 82 | 95 | 100 | 121 | 81 | 102 | 119 | 90 | 83 | 114 | 113 | 109 | 104 | 105 |
| Yards | 671 | 846 | 771 | 977 | 666 | 823 | 974 | 676 | 675 | 938 | 856 | 922 | 881 | 881 |
| FUMBLES: | | | | | | | | | | | | | | |
| Number | 26 | 23 | 29 | 37 | 35 | 26 | 28 | 28 | 30 | 43 | 24 | 32 | 21 | 32 |
| Number Lost | 11 | 17 | 15 | 24 | 13 | 11 | 14 | 12 | 14 | 16 | 14 | 14 | 9 | 20 |
| POINTS: | | | | | | | | | | | | | | |
| Total | 279 | 358 | 204 | 312 | 362 | 426 | 351 | 386 | 348 | 342 | 258 | 442 | 320 | 386 |
| PAT Attempts | 30 | 45 | 25 | 36 | 42 | 51 | 36 | 46 | 37 | 40 | 29 | 51 | 36 | 42 |
| PAT Made | 30 | 43 | 24 | 36 | 42 | 51 | 35 | 44 | 35 | 40 | 28 | 49 | 34 | 41 |
| FG Attempts | 32 | 19 | 20 | 21 | 28 | 30 | 44 | 29 | 38 | 33 | 26 | 36 | 28 | 40 |
| FG Made | 23 | 15 | 10 | 20 | 22 | 23 | 32 | 20 | 29 | 20 | 18 | 29 | 22 | 29 |
| Percent FG Made | 71.9 | 78.9 | 50.0 | 95.2 | 78.6 | 76.7 | 72.7 | 69.0 | 76.3 | 60.6 | 69.2 | 80.6 | 78.6 | 72.5 |
| Safeties | 0 | 0 | 0 | 0 | 1 | 0 | 2 | 3 | 2 | 1 | 1 | 0 | 2 | 3 |

| DEFENSE | ATL | CHI | DAL | DET | G.B. | L.A. | MINN | N.O. | NYG | PHIL | PHX | S.F. | T.B. | WASH |
|---|---|---|---|---|---|---|---|---|---|---|---|---|---|---|
| FIRST DOWNS: | | | | | | | | | | | | | | |
| Total | 336 | 332 | 321 | 314 | 307 | 306 | 266 | 293 | 266 | 281 | 329 | 283 | 317 | 274 |
| by Rushing | 156 | 118 | 116 | 98 | 116 | 101 | 100 | 79 | 90 | 81 | 113 | 76 | 115 | 72 |
| by Passing | 163 | 191 | 183 | 189 | 179 | 181 | 140 | 198 | 159 | 171 | 185 | 178 | 170 | 177 |
| by Penalty | 17 | 23 | 22 | 27 | 12 | 24 | 26 | 16 | 17 | 29 | 31 | 29 | 32 | 25 |
| RUSHING: | | | | | | | | | | | | | | |
| Number | 572 | 446 | 543 | 454 | 460 | 404 | 462 | 373 | 421 | 426 | 539 | 372 | 479 | 384 |
| Yards | 2471 | 1897 | 1991 | 1621 | 2008 | 1543 | 1683 | 1326 | 1539 | 1605 | 2302 | 1383 | 2023 | 1344 |
| Average Yards | 4.3 | 4.3 | 3.7 | 3.6 | 4.4 | 38 | 3.6 | 3.6 | 3.7 | 3.8 | 4.3 | 3.7 | 4.2 | 3.5 |
| Touchdowns | 26 | 21 | 17 | 18 | 15 | 13 | 14 | 10 | 10 | 6 | 12 | 9 | 18 | 9 |
| PASSING: | | | | | | | | | | | | | | |
| Attempts | 437 | 554 | 488 | 570 | 476 | 577 | 488 | 577 | 486 | 529 | 531 | 564 | 515 | 530 |
| Completions | 259 | 307 | 301 | 370 | 302 | 345 | 252 | 320 | 273 | 258 | 286 | 316 | 301 | 277 |
| Completion Pct. | 59.3 | 55.4 | 61.7 | 64.9 | 63.4 | 59.8 | 51.6 | 55.5 | 56.2 | 48.8 | 53.9 | 56.0 | 58.4 | 52.3 |
| Passing Yards | 3737 | 4079 | 3748 | 4193 | 3553 | 4302 | 3003 | 4222 | 3427 | 3713 | 3794 | 3568 | 3659 | 3875 |
| Avg. Yds per Att. | 7.6 | 6.5 | 6.9 | 6.4 | 6.6 | 6.5 | 4.5 | 6.2 | 6.0 | 5.6 | 6.4 | 5.3 | 6.3 | 6.3 |
| Avg. Yds per Comp. | 14.4 | 13.3 | 12.5 | 11.3 | 11.8 | 12.5 | 12.0 | 13.2 | 12.6 | 14.4 | 13.3 | 11.3 | 12.2 | 14.0 |
| Times Tackled | 31 | 39 | 29 | 40 | 34 | 42 | 71 | 47 | 39 | 62 | 30 | 43 | 33 | 40 |
| Yds Lost Tackled | 183 | 247 | 183 | 277 | 214 | 278 | 502 | 362 | 302 | 424 | 219 | 333 | 222 | 304 |
| Net Yards | 3554 | 3832 | 3565 | 3916 | 3339 | 4024 | 2501 | 3860 | 3125 | 3289 | 3575 | 3235 | 3437 | 3571 |
| Touchdowns | 19 | 21 | 21 | 19 | 22 | 24 | 18 | 23 | 16 | 26 | 24 | 15 | 29 | 25 |
| Interceptions | 20 | 26 | 7 | 16 | 25 | 21 | 18 | 21 | 22 | 30 | 16 | 21 | 21 | 27 |
| Pct. Intercepted | 4.6 | 4.7 | 1.4 | 2.8 | 5.3 | 4.4 | 3.7 | 3.6 | 4.5 | 5.7 | 3.0 | 3.7 | 4.1 | 5.1 |
| PUNTS: | | | | | | | | | | | | | | |
| Number | 56 | 67 | 73 | 80 | 65 | 81 | 95 | 75 | 74 | 85 | 76 | 74 | 69 | 76 |
| Average | 41.8 | 39.6 | 39.9 | 41.2 | 40.7 | 41.5 | 40.6 | 39.4 | 40.1 | 42.0 | 41.5 | 38.9 | 40.3 | 40.1 |
| PUNT RETURNS | | | | | | | | | | | | | | |
| Number | 43 | 30 | 38 | 46 | 30 | 34 | 32 | 35 | 29 | 37 | 46 | 35 | 54 | 34 |
| Yards | 460 | 262 | 334 | 373 | 416 | 315 | 300 | 244 | 236 | 215 | 371 | 361 | 492 | 383 |
| Average Yards | 10.7 | 8.7 | 8.8 | 8.1 | 13.9 | 9.3 | 9.4 | 7.0 | 8.1 | 5.8 | 8.1 | 10.3 | 9.1 | 11.3 |
| Touchdowns | 0 | 0 | 1 | 0 | 0 | 1 | 0 | 0 | 0 | 0 | 0 | 0 | 0 | 0 |
| KICKOFF RET.: | | | | | | | | | | | | | | |
| Number | 60 | 68 | 46 | 65 | 63 | 84 | 68 | 55 | 73 | 60 | 57 | 76 | 55 | 74 |
| Yards | 1188 | 1375 | 853 | 1037 | 1389 | 1633 | 1287 | 983 | 1306 | 1307 | 1193 | 1435 | 1143 | 1532 |
| Average Yards | 19.8 | 20.2 | 18.5 | 16.0 | 22.0 | 19.4 | 18.9 | 17.9 | 17.9 | 21.8 | 20.9 | 18.9 | 20.8 | 20.7 |
| Touchdowns | 0 | 0 | 0 | 1 | 0 | 0 | 0 | 0 | 0 | 1 | 0 | 0 | 0 | 1 |
| INTERCEPT RET.: | | | | | | | | | | | | | | |
| Number | 12 | 25 | 27 | 24 | 20 | 18 | 19 | 19 | 16 | 16 | 30 | 11 | 28 | 17 |
| Yards | 85 | 182 | 396 | 447 | 321 | 207 | 138 | 265 | 240 | 147 | 327 | 140 | 240 | 229 |
| Average Yards | 7.1 | 7.3 | 14.7 | 18.6 | 16.1 | 11.5 | 7.3 | 13.9 | 15.0 | 9.2 | 10.9 | 12.7 | 8.6 | 13.5 |
| Touchdowns | 0 | 1 | 3 | 3 | 2 | 0 | 2 | 1 | 2 | 0 | 3 | 0 | 2 | 1 |
| PENALTIES: | | | | | | | | | | | | | | |
| Number | 79 | 94 | 102 | 107 | 105 | 93 | 116 | 105 | 109 | 118 | 106 | 75 | 109 | 98 |
| Yards | 682 | 802 | 723 | 993 | 851 | 798 | 903 | 850 | 800 | 956 | 916 | 581 | 869 | 796 |
| FUMBLES: | | | | | | | | | | | | | | |
| Number | 26 | 24 | 22 | 28 | 28 | 38 | 29 | 35 | 38 | 44 | 18 | 34 | 30 | 24 |
| Number Lost | 12 | 12 | 10 | 16 | 15 | 15 | 18 | 18 | 15 | 26 | 11 | 16 | 18 | 15 |
| POINTS: | | | | | | | | | | | | | | |
| Total | 437 | 377 | 393 | 364 | 356 | 344 | 275 | 301 | 252 | 274 | 377 | 253 | 419 | 308 |
| PAT Attempts | 49 | 43 | 44 | 42 | 41 | 38 | 33 | 35 | 30 | 33 | 41 | 26 | 51 | 38 |
| PAT Made | 48 | 41 | 43 | 41 | 39 | 36 | 32 | 34 | 30 | 30 | 40 | 26 | 51 | 38 |
| FG Attempts | 36 | 36 | 35 | 33 | 30 | 29 | 21 | 24 | 21 | 26 | 40 | 31 | 24 | 23 |
| FG Made | 31 | 26 | 28 | 23 | 23 | 26 | 13 | 19 | 14 | 14 | 29 | 23 | 20 | 14 |
| Percent FG Made | 86.1 | 72.2 | 80.0 | 69.7 | 76.7 | 89.7 | 61.9 | 79.2 | 66.7 | 53.8 | 72.5 | 74.2 | 83.3 | 60.9 |
| Safeties | 1 | 0 | 1 | 1 | 1 | 1 | 0 | 0 | 0 | 2 | 2 | 1 | 1 | 0 |

**Tampa Bay Buccaneers** — The Buccaneers stood 3-2 and were talking of a winning season again when apparent-patsy Detroit came to town — and left with a 17-16 victory. Tampa Bay then went into a dive, augmented by injuries, and crawled to another 5-11 season. Wide receiver Mark Carrier became one of the NFL's best, catching 86 passes for 1,422 yards and nine touchdowns. But fans were at a loss to explain why he wasn't selected to the Pro Bowl (although he made it as a replacement). Quarterback Vinny Testaverde still lacked the consistency needed to rank amont the league's elite, but he cut his interceptions to 22 and upped his touchdowns to 20. Coach Ray Perkins' Bucs had a subpar running game and a defense dinged for 419 points.

## WESTERN DIVISION

**San Francisco 49ers** — Coach Bill Walsh moved into the broadcasting booth, but the 49ers kept right on rolling under former defensive coordinator George Seifert, even improving on their 1988 record, to become everybody's choice as the "Team of the '80s." Quarterback Joe Montana had his best season ever statistically, as he set a new mark with a 112.4 pass rating. Premier receiver Jerry Rice broke the team record for TD catches in only his fifth season, and John Taylor emerged as a dangerous running mate. The offensive line survived a rash of injuries, as Roger Craig again rushed for over 1,000 yards. The defense, led by strong safety Ronnie Lott, performed admirably despite a career-ending injury to free safety Jeff Fuller.

**Los Angeles Rams** — The Rams' aerial attack brought back memories of the Van Brocklin-Waterfield days of the early 1950s, as quarterback Jim Everett passed for over 4,000 yards and a league-high 29 touchdowns. His chief targets were veteran Henry Ellard and second-year star Willie "Flipper" Anderson. Both gained over 1,000 yards, and Anderson set a single-game NFL record with 336 yards (on 15 receptions). Greg Bell topped 1,000 yards rushing with the help of of a 221-yard game against Green Bay in Week Three and a 21-yard outing in the season finale against New England. Linebacker Kevin Greene had 16.5 sacks, but the defense faltered when several other linebackers were injured. That led to a four-game losing streak after the Rams opened the season with five straight wins.

**New Orleans Saints** — Coach Jim Mora's team won one less game than in 1988 and finished out of the playoffs again, but the 9-7 mark was still a winning season, something the Saints struggled 20 years to accomplsih. Rickey Jackson's injury in an auto accident and Pat Swilling's holdout cost New Orleans its two most dominant defenders at the start of the season, and by the time the two star linebackers rounded into shape, the Saints were 1-4. Running back Dalton Hilliard was brilliant all along, rushing for 1,262 yards and scoring 18 touchdowns. But the key to the three victories in the final three games was former Arena Football League quarterback John Fourcade, who stepped in for slipping Bobby Hebert to throw seven touchdowns, run for one and ignite a dormant attack.

**Atlanta Falcons** — The Falcons hoped for improvement in the standings on the strength of the strong, end-of-the-season defense in '88. Instead, Atlanta finished dead last in the NFL in total defense. With the team at 3-8, coach Marion Campbell resigned. Interim coach Jim Hanifan couldn't pull the Falcons out of the dive, and they lost the last five games. Leading to the defensive shortcomings was a foot injury that kept cornerback Scott Case sidelined for more than half of the season and the disappointing play of young (and expensive) linebackers Aundray Bruce and Marcus Cotton. Running back John Settle also slipped form his 1988 level. But most tragic for this seemingly jinxed team was the in-season deaths of rookie offensive tackle Ralph Norwood and reserve tight end Brad Beckman in auto accidents within a month of each other. New 1990 coach Jerry Glanville took over a team with a losing heritage and a defensive back in Deion Sanders who is even better at grabbing media attention than Glanville himself.

## NEW YORK GIANTS 12-4 Bill Parcells

| Scores of Each Game | | |
|---|---|---|
| 27 | Washington | 24 |
| 24 | DETROIT | 14 |
| 35 | PHOENIX | 7 |
| 30 | Dallas | 13 |
| 19 | Philadelphia | 21 |
| 20 | WASHINGTON | 17 |
| 20 | San Diego | 13 |
| 24 | MINNESOTA | 14 |
| 20 | Phoenix | 13 |
| 10 | L.A. Rams | 31 |
| 15 | SEATTLE | 3 |
| 24 | San Francisco | 34 |
| 17 | PHILADELPHIA | 24 |
| 14 | Denver | 7 |
| 15 | DALLAS | 0 |
| 34 | L.A. RAIDERS | 17 |

| Use Name | Pos. | Hgt | Wgt | Age | Int | Pts |
|---|---|---|---|---|---|---|
| John Elliott | OT | 6'7" | 305 | 24 | | |
| Eric Moore | OT | 6'5" | 290 | 24 | | |
| Doug Riesenberg | OT | 6'5" | 275 | 24 | | |
| Bob Kratch | OG | 6'3" | 288 | 23 | | |
| Damian Johnson | OG | 6'5" | 290 | 26 | | |
| William Roberts | OG | 6'5" | 280 | 27 | | |
| Brian Williams | OG-C | 6'5" | 300 | 23 | | |
| Bart Oates | C | 6'3" | 265 | 30 | | |
| Frank Winters | C | 6'3" | 280 | 25 | | |
| Eric Dorsey | DE | 6'5" | 280 | 25 | | |
| Mark Duckens | DE | 6'4" | 270 | 24 | | |
| Leonard Marshall | DE | 6'3" | 285 | 27 | | 2 |
| John Washington | DE | 6'4" | 275 | 26 | | |
| Robb White | DE | 6'4" | 270 | 24 | | |
| Erik Howard | NT | 6'4" | 268 | 24 | | |

| Use Name | Pos. | Hgt | Wgt | Age | Int | Pts |
|---|---|---|---|---|---|---|
| Carl Banks | LB | 6'4" | 235 | 27 | 1 | 6 |
| Johnie Cooks | LB | 6'4" | 251 | 30 | | |
| Steve DeOssie | LB | 6'2" | 248 | 26 | | |
| Dwayne Jiles (from PHI) | LB | 6'4" | 245 | 27 | | |
| Pepper Johnson | LB | 6'3" | 248 | 25 | 3 | 6 |
| Gary Reasons | LB | 6'4" | 234 | 27 | 1 | 2 |
| Lawrence Taylor | LB | 6'3" | 243 | 30 | | |
| Mark Collins | DB | 5'10" | 190 | 25 | 2 | |
| Greg Cox | DB | 6' | 223 | 24 | | |
| Myron Guyton | DB | 6'1" | 205 | 22 | 2 | |
| Greg Jackson | DB | 6'1" | 200 | 23 | | |
| Terry Kinard | DB | 6'1" | 200 | 29 | 5 | 6 |
| Reyna Thompson | DB | 6' | 193 | 26 | | |
| Adrian White | DB | 6' | 200 | 25 | 2 | |
| Sheldon White | DB | 5'11" | 188 | 24 | 2 | |
| Perry Williams | DB | 6'2" | 203 | 28 | 3 | |

| Use Name | Pos. | Hgt | Wgt | Age | Int | Pts |
|---|---|---|---|---|---|---|
| Jeff Hostetler | QB | 6'3" | 212 | 28 | | |
| Jeff Rutledge | QB | 6'1" | 195 | 32 | | |
| Phil Simms | QB | 6'3" | 214 | 32 | | 6 |
| Ottis Anderson | HB | 6'2" | 225 | 32 | | 84 |
| Dave Meggett | HB | 5'7" | 180 | 23 | | 30 |
| Lewis Tillman | HB | 6' | 195 | 23 | | |
| George Adams | FB | 6'1" | 225 | 26 | | |
| Maurice Carthon | FB | 6'1" | 225 | 28 | | |
| Lee Rouson | FB | 6'1" | 222 | 26 | | |
| Stephen Baker | WR | 5'8" | 160 | 25 | | 12 |
| Mark Ingram | WR | 5'10" | 188 | 24 | | 6 |
| Lionel Manuel | WR | 5'11" | 180 | 27 | | |
| Stacy Robinson | WR | 5'11" | 186 | 27 | | |
| Odessa Turner | WR | 6'3" | 205 | 24 | | 24 |
| Mark Bavaro | TE | 6'4" | 245 | 26 | | 18 |
| Howard Cross | TE | 6'5" | 245 | 22 | | 6 |
| Zeke Mowatt | TE | 6'3" | 240 | 28 | | |
| Raul Allegre | K | 5'10" | 167 | 30 | | 83 |
| Sean Landeta | K | 6' | 200 | 27 | | |
| Bjorn Nittmo | K | 5'11" | 185 | 23 | | 39 |

Joe Morris — Foot Injury

## PHILADELPHIA EAGLES 11-5 Buddy Ryan

| Scores of Each Game | | |
|---|---|---|
| 31 | SEATTLE | 7 |
| 42 | Washington | 37 |
| 28 | SAN FRANCISCO | 38 |
| 13 | Chicago | 27 |
| 21 | N.Y. GIANTS | 19 |
| 17 | Phoenix | 5 |
| 10 | L.A. RAIDERS | 7 |
| 28 | Denver | 24 |
| 17 | San Diego | 20 |
| 3 | WASHINGTON | 10 |
| 10 | MINNESOTA | 9 |
| 27 | Dallas | 0 |
| 24 | N.Y. Giants | 17 |
| 20 | DALLAS | 10 |
| 20 | New Orleans | 30 |
| 31 | PHOENIX | 14 |

| Use Name | Pos. | Hgt | Wgt | Age | Int | Pts |
|---|---|---|---|---|---|---|
| Matt Darwin | OT | 6'4" | 275 | 26 | | |
| Ron Heller | OT | 6'3" | 280 | 27 | | |
| Ken Reeves | OT-OG | 6'5" | 270 | 28 | | |
| Mike Schad | OG | 6'5" | 290 | 25 | | |
| Reggie Singletary | OG-OT | 6'3" | 280 | 25 | | |
| Ron Solt | OG | 6'3" | 285 | 27 | | |
| Ben Tamburello | OG-C | 6'3" | 278 | 24 | | |
| David Alexander | C-OT | 6'3" | 275 | 24 | | |
| Dave Rimington | C | 6'3" | 288 | 29 | | |
| Steve Kaufusi | DE-DT | 6'4" | 274 | 25 | | |
| Clyde Simmons | DE | 6'6" | 276 | 25 | 1 | 6 |
| Reggie White | DE-DT | 6'5" | 285 | 27 | | |
| Jerome Brown | DT | 6'2" | 288 | 24 | | |
| Mike Golic | DT | 6'5" | 275 | 27 | 1 | |
| Mike Pitts | DT | 6'5" | 277 | 29 | | |

| Use Name | Pos. | Hgt | Wgt | Age | Int | Pts |
|---|---|---|---|---|---|---|
| Ty Allert | LB | 6'2" | 233 | 26 | | |
| Todd Bell | LB | 6'1" | 212 | 31 | 1 | |
| Byron Evans | LB | 6'2" | 225 | 25 | 3 | |
| Britt Hager | LB | 6'1" | 222 | 23 | | |
| Al Harris | LB | 6'5" | 265 | 32 | 2 | 2 |
| Seth Joyner | LB | 6'2" | 248 | 24 | 4 | |
| Mike Reichenbach | LB | 6'2" | 230 | 28 | | |
| Ricky Shaw (from NYG) | LB | 6'4" | 240 | 24 | | |
| Jessie Small | LB | 6'3" | 239 | 22 | | |
| Eric Allen | DB | 5'10" | 183 | 22 | 8 | |
| Alan Dial | DB | 6'1" | 188 | 24 | | |
| Eric Everett | DB | 5'10" | 161 | 23 | 4 | 6 |
| William Frizzell | DB | 6'3" | 205 | 27 | 4 | |
| Terry Hoage | DB | 6'3" | 201 | 27 | | |
| Wes Hopkins | DB | 6'1" | 212 | 28 | | |
| Izel Jenkins | DB | 5'10" | 191 | 24 | 4 | |
| Tyrone Jones | DB | 6'4" | 223 | 22 | | |
| Sammy Lilly | DB | 5'9" | 178 | 24 | | |
| Andre Waters | DB | 5'11" | 195 | 27 | 1 | 6 |

| Use Name | Pos. | Hgt | Wgt | Age | Int | Pts |
|---|---|---|---|---|---|---|
| Matt Cavanaugh | QB | 6'2" | 210 | 33 | | |
| Randall Cunningham | QB | 6'4" | 203 | 26 | | 24 |
| Don McPherson | QB | 6'1" | 183 | 24 | | |
| Keith Byars | HB | 6'1" | 238 | 26 | | 30 |
| Robert Drummond | HB | 6'1" | 205 | 22 | | 6 |
| Mark Higgs | FB | 5'7" | 200 | 23 | | |
| Heath Sherman | FB-HB | 6' | 190 | 22 | | 12 |
| Anthony Toney | FB | 6' | 227 | 26 | | 18 |
| Cris Carter | WR | 6'3" | 194 | 24 | | 66 |
| Anthony Edwards | WR | 5'11" | 195 | 23 | | |
| Gregg Garrity | WR | 5'10" | 169 | 27 | | 12 |
| Ron Johnson | WR | 6'3" | 186 | 31 | | 6 |
| Mike Quick | WR | 6'2" | 190 | 30 | | 12 |
| Henry Williams | WR | 5'6" | 185 | 27 | | |
| Jimmie Giles | TE | 6'3" | 240 | 35 | | 12 |
| Keith Jackson | TE | 6'2" | 250 | 24 | | 18 |
| Dave Little | TE | 6'2" | 226 | 28 | | 6 |
| Steve DeLine | K | 5'11" | 185 | 28 | | 12 |
| Max Runager | K | 6'1" | 189 | 33 | | |
| John Teltschik | K | 6'2" | 209 | 25 | | |
| Rick Tuten | K | 6'2" | 220 | 24 | | |
| Luis Zendejas (to DAL) | K | 5'9" | 160 | 27 | | 75 |

## WASHINGTON REDSKINS 10-6 Joe Gibbs

| Scores of Each Game | | |
|---|---|---|
| 24 | N.Y. GIANTS | 27 |
| 37 | PHILADELPHIA | 42 |
| 30 | Dallas | 7 |
| 16 | New Orleans | 14 |
| 30 | PHOENIX | 28 |
| 17 | N.Y. Giants | 20 |
| 32 | TAMPA BAY | 28 |
| 24 | L.A. Raiders | 37 |
| 3 | DALLAS | 13 |
| 10 | Philadelphia | 3 |
| 10 | DENVER | 14 |
| 38 | CHICAGO | 14 |
| 29 | Phoenix | 10 |
| 26 | SAN DIEGO | 21 |
| 31 | Atlanta | 30 |
| 29 | Seattle | 0 |

| Use Name | Pos. | Hgt | Wgt | Age | Int | Pts |
|---|---|---|---|---|---|---|
| Ray Brown | OT | 6'5" | 280 | 26 | | |
| Joe Jacoby | OT | 6'7" | 305 | 30 | | |
| Jim Lachey | OT | 6'6" | 290 | 26 | | |
| Mark May | OT-OG | 6'6" | 295 | 29 | | |
| Ed Simmons | OT | 6'5" | 280 | 25 | | |
| Russ Grimm | OG | 6'3" | 275 | 30 | | |
| Raleigh McKenzie | OG-C | 6'2" | 270 | 26 | | |
| Jeff Bostic | C | 6'2" | 260 | 30 | | |
| Dave Harbour | C | 6'4" | 265 | 23 | | |
| Mark Schlereth | C | 6'3" | 285 | 23 | | |
| Markus Koch | DE | 6'5" | 275 | 26 | | |
| Dexter Manley | DE | 6'3" | 257 | 30 | | 2 |
| Charles Mann | DE | 6'6" | 270 | 28 | | |
| Lybrant Robinson | DE | 6'4" | 250 | 25 | | |
| Fred Stokes | DE | 6'3" | 262 | 25 | | 2 |
| Darryl Grant | DT | 6'1" | 275 | 29 | 2 | |
| Tracy Rocker | DT | 6'3" | 288 | 23 | | |
| Mike Stensrud | DT | 6'5" | 280 | 33 | | |

| Use Name | Pos. | Hgt | Wgt | Age | Int | Pts |
|---|---|---|---|---|---|---|
| Brian Bonner | LB | 6'2" | 225 | 23 | | |
| Ravin Caldwell | LB | 6'3" | 229 | 26 | | |
| Monte Coleman | LB | 6'2" | 230 | 31 | 2 | 6 |
| Kurt Gouveia | LB | 6'1" | 227 | 24 | 1 | |
| Don Graham | LB | 6'2" | 245 | 25 | | |
| Greg Manusky | LB | 6'1" | 242 | 23 | | |
| Wilber Marshall | LB | 6'1" | 230 | 27 | 1 | |
| Neal Olkewicz | LB | 6' | 230 | 32 | | |
| Todd Bowles | DB | 6'2" | 203 | 25 | 3 | |
| Brian Davis | DB | 6'2" | 190 | 26 | 4 | |
| Wayne Davis (from BUF) | DB | 5'11" | 180 | 26 | 1 | |
| Darrell Green | DB | 5'8" | 170 | 29 | 2 | |
| A.J. Johnson | DB | 5'8" | 176 | 22 | 4 | 6 |
| Chris Mandeville | DB | 6'1" | 213 | 24 | | |
| Martin Mayhew | DB | 5'8" | 172 | 23 | | |
| Clarence Vaughn | DB | 6' | 202 | 25 | | |
| Alvin Walton | DB | 6' | 180 | 25 | 4 | 6 |
| Herb Welch | DB | 5'11" | 180 | 28 | | |
| Barry Wilburn | DB | 6'3" | 186 | 25 | 3 | |

Eugene Profit — Leg Injury

| Use Name | Pos. | Hgt | Wgt | Age | Int | Pts |
|---|---|---|---|---|---|---|
| Stan Humphries | QB | 6'2" | 223 | 24 | | |
| Mark Rypien | QB | 6'4" | 234 | 26 | | 6 |
| Doug Williams | QB | 6'4" | 220 | 34 | | |
| Reggie Branch | HB-FB | 5'11" | 235 | 26 | | |
| Jamie Morris | HB-FB | 5'7" | 188 | 24 | | 12 |
| Gerald Riggs | HB-FB | 6'1" | 232 | 28 | | 24 |
| Earnest Byner | FB-HB | 5'10" | 215 | 26 | | 54 |
| Joe Mickles | FB | 5'10" | 221 | 23 | | |
| Gary Clark | WR | 5'9" | 173 | 26 | | 54 |
| Carl Harry | WR | 5'9" | 168 | 23 | | |
| Joe Howard | WR | 5'8" | 170 | 26 | | 6 |
| Art Monk | WR | 6'3" | 209 | 31 | | 48 |
| Ricky Sanders | WR | 5'11" | 180 | 27 | | 24 |
| Jimmie Johnson | TE | 6'2" | 246 | 21 | | |
| Terry Orr | TE | 6'3" | 227 | 27 | | |
| Mike Tice | TE | 6'7" | 247 | 30 | | |
| Don Warren | TE | 6'4" | 242 | 33 | | 6 |
| Chip Lohmiller | K | 6'3" | 213 | 23 | | 128 |
| Ralf Mojsiejenko | K | 6'2" | 212 | 26 | | |

Kelvin Bryant — Knee Injury
Ken Whisenhunt — Leg Injury

## PHOENIX CARDINALS 5-11 Gene Stallings (5-6), Hank Kuhlmann (0-5)

| Scores of Each Game | | |
|---|---|---|
| 16 | Detroit | 13 |
| 34 | Seattle | 24 |
| 7 | N.Y. Giants | 35 |
| 13 | SAN DIEGO | 24 |
| 28 | Washington | 30 |
| 5 | PHILADELPHIA | 17 |
| 34 | ATLANTA | 20 |
| 19 | Dallas | 10 |
| 13 | N.Y. GIANTS | 20 |
| 24 | DALLAS | 20 |
| 14 | L.A. Rams | 37 |
| 13 | TAMPA BAY | 14 |
| 10 | WASHINGTON | 29 |
| 14 | L.A. Raiders | 16 |
| 0 | DENVER | 37 |
| 14 | Philadelphia | 31 |

| Use Name | Pos. | Hgt | Wgt | Age | Int | Pts |
|---|---|---|---|---|---|---|
| Tootie Robbins | OT | 6'5" | 302 | 31 | | |
| Luis Sharpe | OT | 6'4" | 260 | 29 | | |
| Scott Dill | OG | 6'5" | 272 | 23 | | |
| Todd Peat | OG | 6'2" | 294 | 25 | | |
| Lance Smith | OG | 6'2" | 262 | 25 | | |
| Mark Traynowicz | OG | 6'5" | 280 | 27 | | |
| Joe Wolf | OG-OT | 6'5" | 279 | 22 | | |
| Mike Zandofsky | OG | 6'2" | 285 | 23 | | |
| Kani Kauahi | C | 6'2" | 270 | 29 | | |
| Derek Kennard | C | 6'3" | 285 | 26 | | |
| Bob Buczkowski | DE | 6'5" | 260 | 25 | | |
| David Galloway | DE | 6'3" | 279 | 30 | | |
| Freddie Gilbert | DE | 6'4" | 275 | 27 | | |
| Shawn Knight | DE | 6'6" | 290 | 25 | | |
| Freddie Joe Nunn | DE | 6'4" | 255 | 27 | | |
| Rod Saddler | DE | 6'5" | 276 | 23 | | |
| Karl Wilson | DE | 6'4" | 275 | 24 | | 2 |
| Bob Clasby | DT | 6'5" | 260 | 28 | | |
| Gary Hadd | DT | 6'4" | 278 | 24 | | |
| Jim Wahler | DT | 6'4" | 268 | 23 | 1 | |

Joe Bostic — Knee Injury

| Use Name | Pos. | Hgt | Wgt | Age | Int | Pts |
|---|---|---|---|---|---|---|
| Anthony Bell | LB | 6'3" | 231 | 25 | | |
| Ron Burton (from DAL) | LB | 6'1" | 245 | 25 | 1 | |
| Ken Harvey | LB | 6'2" | 225 | 24 | | |
| Eric Hill | LB | 6'1" | 248 | 22 | | |
| Ilia Jarostchuk | LB | 6'3" | 231 | 25 | | |
| Garth Jax | LB | 6'2" | 229 | 25 | | |
| Randy Kirk | LB | 6'2" | 231 | 24 | | |
| Michael Adams | DB | 5'10" | 195 | 25 | | |
| Michael Downs | DB | 6'3" | 212 | 30 | 1 | |
| Carl Carter | DB | 5'11" | 180 | 25 | 1 | |
| Kevin Guidry | DB | 6' | 176 | 25 | | |
| Cedric Mack | DB | 6' | 194 | 28 | 4 | |
| Tim McDonald | DB | 6'2" | 207 | 24 | 7 | 6 |
| Roland Mitchell | DB | 5'11" | 180 | 25 | | |
| Jay Taylor | DB | 5'9" | 170 | 21 | | |
| Marcus Turner | DB | 6' | 190 | 23 | | |
| Lonnie Young | DB | 6'1" | 182 | 26 | 1 | |
| Mike Zordich | DB | 5'11" | 197 | 25 | 1 | 6 |

Reggie McKenzie — Knee Injury

| Use Name | Pos. | Hgt | Wgt | Age | Int | Pts |
|---|---|---|---|---|---|---|
| Gary Hogeboom | QB | 6'4" | 207 | 31 | | 6 |
| Timm Rosenbach | QB | 6'2" | 210 | 22 | | |
| Tom Tupa | QB-K | 6'4" | 220 | 22 | | |
| Tony Baker | HB | 5'10" | 190 | 25 | | |
| Tony Jordan | HB | 6'2" | 220 | 24 | | 12 |
| Stump Mitchell | HB | 5'9" | 188 | 30 | | |
| Vai Sikahema | HB | 5'9" | 191 | 27 | | |
| Lydell Carr | FB | 6'1" | 228 | 24 | | |
| Jessie Clark (to MIN) | FB | 6' | 233 | 29 | | |
| Earl Ferrell | FB | 6' | 240 | 31 | | 36 |
| Ron Wolfley | FB | 6' | 222 | 26 | | 6 |
| Roy Green | WR | 6' | 195 | 32 | | 42 |
| Don Holmes | WR | 5'10" | 180 | 28 | | 6 |
| Ernie Jones | WR | 5'11" | 186 | 24 | | 18 |
| Phil McConkey (to SD) | WR | 5'10" | 170 | 32 | | |
| J.T. Smith | WR | 6'2" | 185 | 33 | | 30 |
| Darryl Usher (from SD) | WR | 5'8" | 170 | 24 | | |
| Rob Awalt | TE | 6'5" | 248 | 25 | | |
| Jay Novacek | TE | 6'4" | 235 | 26 | | 6 |
| Walter Reeves | TE | 6'4" | 249 | 23 | | |
| Rich Camarillo | K | 5'11" | 193 | 28 | | |
| Al Del Greco | K | 5'10" | 191 | 27 | | 82 |

Neil Lomax — Hip Injury
Andy Schillinger — Knee Injury

## DALLAS COWBOYS 1-15 Jimmy Johnson

| Scores of Each Game | | |
|---|---|---|
| 0 | New Orleans | 28 |
| 21 | Atlanta | 27 |
| 7 | WASHINGTON | 30 |
| 13 | N.Y. GIANTS | 30 |
| 13 | Green Bay | 31 |
| 14 | SAN FRANCISCO | 31 |
| 28 | Kansas City | 36 |
| 10 | PHOENIX | 19 |
| 13 | Washington | 3 |
| 20 | Phoenix | 24 |
| 14 | MIAMI | 17 |
| 0 | PHILADELPHIA | 27 |
| 31 | L.A. RAMS | 35 |
| 10 | Philadelphia | 20 |
| 0 | N.Y. Giants | 15 |
| 10 | GREEN BAY | 20 |

| Use Name | Pos. | Hgt | Wgt | Age | Int | Pts |
|---|---|---|---|---|---|---|
| Kevin Gogan | OT | 6'7" | 309 | 24 | | |
| Mark Tuinei | OT | 6'5" | 282 | 29 | | |
| Dave Widell | OT | 6'6" | 300 | 24 | | |
| Crawford Ker | OG | 6'3" | 290 | 27 | | |
| Nate Newton | OG | 6'3" | 314 | 27 | | |
| Mark Stepnoski | OG-C | 6'2" | 269 | 22 | | |
| Jeff Zimmerman | OG | 6'6" | 313 | 24 | | |
| Tom Rafferty | C | 6'3" | 264 | 35 | | |
| Bob White | C | 6'5" | 273 | 26 | | |
| Willie Broughton | DE | 6'5" | 275 | 25 | | |
| Jim Jeffcoat | DE | 6'5" | 262 | 28 | | 6 |
| Too Tall Jones | DE | 6'9" | 278 | 38 | | |
| Tony Tolbert | DE | 6'6" | 241 | 21 | | |
| Jon Carter | DT | 6'4" | 273 | 24 | | |
| Dean Hamel | DT | 6'3" | 276 | 28 | | |
| Danny Noonan | DT | 6'4" | 266 | 24 | | |

Jeff Hurd — Knee Injury
Mark Walen — Knee Injury

| Use Name | Pos. | Hgt | Wgt | Age | Int | Pts |
|---|---|---|---|---|---|---|
| Garry Cobb | LB | 6'2" | 233 | 32 | | |
| Jack Del Rio | LB | 6'4" | 236 | 26 | | 6 |
| Onzy Elam | LB | 6'2" | 225 | 24 | | |
| David Howard (from MIN) | LB | 6'2" | 230 | 27 | | |
| Eugene Lockhart | LB | 6'2" | 235 | 28 | 2 | 6 |
| Ken Norton | LB | 6'2" | 236 | 22 | | |
| Randy Shannon | LB | 6'1" | 221 | 23 | | |
| Jesse Solomon (from MIN) | LB | 6' | 235 | 25 | | |
| Ken Tippins | LB | 6'1" | 226 | 23 | | |
| Vince Albritton | DB | 6'2" | 220 | 27 | 1 | |
| Scott Ankrom | DB | 6'1" | 194 | 23 | | |
| Bill Bates | DB | 6'1" | 200 | 28 | 1 | |
| Eric Brown | DB | 5'11" | 177 | 22 | | |
| Ron Francis | DB | 5'9" | 201 | 25 | 1 | |
| Manny Hendrix | DB | 5'10" | 181 | 24 | | |
| Issiac Holt (from MIN) | DB | 6'2" | 202 | 26 | 1 | 6 |
| Ray Horton | DB | 5'11" | 187 | 29 | 1 | |
| Tim Jackson | DB | 5'11" | 192 | 23 | | |
| Tony Lilly | DB | 6' | 199 | 27 | | |
| Everson Walls | DB | 6'1" | 193 | 29 | | |
| Robert Williams | DB | 5'10" | 186 | 26 | | |

| Use Name | Pos. | Hgt | Wgt | Age | Int | Pts |
|---|---|---|---|---|---|---|
| Troy Aikman | QB | 6'4" | 216 | 22 | | |
| Babe Laufenberg | QB | 6'3" | 205 | 29 | | |
| Steve Walsh | QB | 6'2" | 200 | 22 | | |
| Paul Palmer (from DET) | HB | 5'9" | 181 | 24 | | 12 |
| Kevin Scott | HB | 5'9" | 177 | 25 | | |
| Curtis Stewart | HB | 5'11" | 208 | 26 | | |
| Darryl Clack | FB | 5'10" | 220 | 25 | | 12 |
| Daryl Johnston | FB | 6'2" | 234 | 23 | | 18 |
| Broderick Sargent | FB | 5'10" | 220 | 26 | | 6 |
| Curtis Stewart | FB | 5'11" | 208 | 23 | | |
| Junior Tautalatasi | FB-HB | 5'11" | 208 | 27 | | |
| Ray Alexander | WR | 6'4" | 193 | 27 | | |
| Cornell Burbage | WR | 5'10" | 189 | 24 | | |
| James Dixon | WR | 5'10" | 181 | 22 | | 18 |
| Bernard Ford | WR | 5'9" | 168 | 23 | | 6 |
| Michael Irvin | WR | 6'2" | 202 | 22 | | 30 |
| Kelvin Martin | WR | 5'9" | 163 | 25 | | 12 |
| Derrick Shepard (from NO) | WR | 5'10" | 187 | 25 | | 6 |
| Thornton Chandler | TE | 6'5" | 240 | 25 | | |
| Steve Folsom | TE | 6'5" | 240 | 31 | | 12 |
| Keith Jennings | TE | 6'4" | 251 | 23 | | |
| Mike Saxon | K | 6'3" | 198 | 27 | | |
| Roger Ruzek (to PHI) | K | 6'1" | 195 | 28 | | 67 |

## NEW YORK GIANTS

### RUSHING

| Last Name | No. | Yds | Avg | TD |
|---|---|---|---|---|
| Anderson | 325 | 1023 | 3.1 | 14 |
| Tillman | 79 | 290 | 3.7 | 0 |
| Carthon | 57 | 153 | 2.7 | 0 |
| Simms | 32 | 141 | 4.4 | 1 |
| Meggett | 28 | 117 | 4.2 | 0 |
| Hostetler | 11 | 71 | 6.5 | 2 |
| Rouson | 11 | 51 | 4.6 | 0 |
| Adams | 9 | 29 | 3.2 | 0 |
| Turner | 2 | 11 | 5.5 | 0 |
| Reasons | 1 | 2 | 2.0 | 0 |
| Ingram | 1 | 1 | 1.0 | 0 |

### RECEIVING

| Last Name | No. | Yds | Avg | TD |
|---|---|---|---|---|
| Turner | 38 | 467 | 12.3 | 4 |
| Meggett | 34 | 531 | 15.6 | 4 |
| Manuel | 33 | 539 | 16.3 | 1 |
| Anderson | 28 | 268 | 9.6 | 0 |
| Mowatt | 27 | 288 | 10.7 | 0 |
| Bavaro | 22 | 278 | 12.6 | 3 |
| Ingram | 17 | 290 | 17.1 | 1 |
| Carthon | 15 | 132 | 8.8 | 0 |
| Baker | 13 | 255 | 19.6 | 2 |
| Rouson | 7 | 121 | 17.3 | 0 |
| Cross | 6 | 107 | 17.8 | 1 |
| Robinson | 4 | 41 | 10.3 | 0 |
| Adams | 2 | 7 | 3.5 | 0 |
| Banks | 1 | 22 | 22.0 | 1 |
| Tillman | 1 | 9 | 9.0 | 0 |

### PUNT RETURNS

| Last Name | No. | Yds | Avg | TD |
|---|---|---|---|---|
| Megett | 46 | 582 | 12.7 | 1 |

### KICKOFF RETURNS

| Last Name | No. | Yds | Avg | TD |
|---|---|---|---|---|
| Meggett | 27 | 577 | 21.4 | 0 |
| Ingram | 22 | 332 | 15.1 | 0 |
| Rouson | 1 | 17 | 17.0 | 0 |
| Collins | 1 | 0 | 0.0 | 0 |

### PASSING — PUNTING — KICKING Statistics

**PASSING**

| Last Name | Att | Cmp | % | Yds | Yd/Att | TD | Int | — | % | RK |
|---|---|---|---|---|---|---|---|---|---|---|
| Simms | 405 | 228 | 56.3 | 3061 | 7.56 | 14 | 14 | — | 3.5 | 6 |
| Hostetler | 39 | 20 | 51.3 | 294 | 7.54 | 3 | 2 | — | 5.1 | |

**PUNTING**

| Last Name | No. | Avg. |
|---|---|---|
| Landeta | 70 | 43.1 |

**KICKING**

| Last Name | XP | ATT | % | FG | ATT | % |
|---|---|---|---|---|---|---|
| Allegre | 23 | 24 | 96 | 20 | 26 | 77 |
| Nittmo | 12 | 13 | 92 | 9 | 12 | 75 |

## PHILADELPHIA EAGLES

### RUSHING

| Last Name | No. | Yds | Avg | TD |
|---|---|---|---|---|
| Cunningham | 104 | 621 | 6.0 | 4 |
| Toney | 172 | 582 | 3.4 | 3 |
| Byars | 133 | 452 | 3.4 | 5 |
| Higgs | 49 | 184 | 3.8 | 0 |
| Sherman | 40 | 177 | 4.4 | 2 |
| Drummond | 32 | 127 | 4.0 | 0 |
| Reichenbach | 1 | 30 | 30.0 | 0 |
| Teltschik | 1 | 23 | 23.0 | 0 |
| Carter | 2 | 16 | 8.0 | 0 |
| Runager | 2 | 5 | 2.5 | 0 |
| Johnson | 1 | 3 | 3.0 | 0 |
| Cavanaugh | 2 | -3 | -1.5 | 0 |

### RECEIVING

| Last Name | No. | Yds | Avg | TD |
|---|---|---|---|---|
| Byars | 68 | 721 | 10.6 | 0 |
| Jackson | 63 | 648 | 10.3 | 3 |
| Carter | 45 | 605 | 13.4 | 11 |
| Johnson | 20 | 295 | 14.8 | 1 |
| Toney | 19 | 124 | 6.5 | 0 |
| Drummond | 17 | 180 | 10.6 | 1 |
| Giles | 16 | 225 | 14.1 | 2 |
| Quick | 13 | 228 | 17.5 | 2 |
| Garrity | 13 | 209 | 16.1 | 2 |
| Sherman | 8 | 85 | 10.6 | 0 |
| Williams | 4 | 32 | 8.0 | 0 |
| Higgs | 3 | 9 | 3.0 | 0 |
| Edwards | 2 | 75 | 37.0 | 0 |
| Little | 2 | 8 | 4.0 | 1 |

### PUNT RETURNS

| Last Name | No. | Yds | Avg | TD |
|---|---|---|---|---|
| Williams | 30 | 267 | 8.9 | 0 |
| Edwards | 7 | 64 | 9.1 | 0 |

### KICKOFF RETURNS

| Last Name | No. | Yds | Avg | TD |
|---|---|---|---|---|
| Higgs | 16 | 293 | 18.3 | 0 |
| Williams | 14 | 249 | 17.8 | 0 |
| Sherman | 13 | 222 | 17.1 | 0 |
| Edwards | 3 | 23 | 7.7 | 0 |
| Little | 2 | 14 | 7.0 | 0 |
| Byars | 1 | 27 | 27.0 | 0 |

### PASSING — PUNTING — KICKING Statistics

**PASSING**

| Last Name | Att | Cmp | % | Yds | Yd/Att | TD | Int | — | % | RK |
|---|---|---|---|---|---|---|---|---|---|---|
| Cunningham | 532 | 290 | 54.5 | 3400 | 6.39 | 21 | 15 | — | 2.8 | 8 |
| Cavanaugh | 5 | 3 | 60.0 | 33 | 6.60 | 1 | 1 | — | 20.0 | |
| Ruzek | 1 | 1 | 100.0 | 22 | 22.00 | 1 | 0 | — | 0.0 | |

**PUNTING**

| Last Name | No. | Avg. |
|---|---|---|
| Teltschik | 57 | 39.4 |
| Cunningham | 6 | 53.2 |
| Tuten | 7 | 36.6 |
| Runager | 17 | 33.4 |

**KICKING**

| Last Name | XP | ATT | % | FG | ATT | % |
|---|---|---|---|---|---|---|
| Zendejas | 33 | 33 | 100 | 14 | 24 | 58 |
| DeLine | 3 | 3 | 100 | 3 | 7 | 43 |

## WASHINGTON REDSKINS

### RUSHING

| Last Name | No. | Yds | Avg | TD |
|---|---|---|---|---|
| Riggs | 201 | 834 | 4.1 | 4 |
| Byner | 134 | 580 | 4.3 | 7 |
| Morris | 124 | 336 | 2.7 | 2 |
| Rypien | 26 | 56 | 2.2 | 1 |
| Clark | 2 | 19 | 9.5 | 0 |
| Sanders | 4 | 19 | 4.8 | 0 |
| Humphries | 5 | 10 | 2.0 | 0 |
| Monk | 3 | 8 | 2.7 | 0 |
| Coleman | 1 | -1 | -1.0 | 0 |
| Williams | 1 | -4 | -4.0 | 0 |

### RECEIVING

| Last Name | No. | Yds | Avg | TD |
|---|---|---|---|---|
| Monk | 86 | 1186 | 13.8 | 8 |
| Sanders | 80 | 1138 | 14.2 | 4 |
| Clark | 79 | 1229 | 15.6 | 9 |
| Byner | 54 | 458 | 8.5 | 2 |
| Warren | 15 | 167 | 11.1 | 1 |
| Morris | 8 | 65 | 8.1 | 0 |
| Riggs | 7 | 67 | 9.6 | 0 |
| J. Johnson | 4 | 84 | 21.0 | 0 |
| Orr | 3 | 80 | 26.7 | 0 |
| Tice | 1 | 2 | 2.0 | 0 |

### PUNT RETURNS

| Last Name | No. | Yds | Avg | TD |
|---|---|---|---|---|
| Howard | 21 | 200 | 9.5 | 0 |
| Sanders | 2 | 12 | 6.0 | 0 |
| Green | 1 | 11 | 11.0 | 0 |
| B. Davis | 1 | 3 | 3.0 | 0 |
| Mayhew | 1 | 0 | 0.0 | 0 |

### KICKOFF RETURNS

| Last Name | No. | Yds | Avg | TD |
|---|---|---|---|---|
| Howard | 21 | 522 | 24.9 | 1 |
| A. Johnson | 24 | 504 | 21.0 | 0 |
| Sanders | 9 | 134 | 14.9 | 0 |
| Mandeville | 1 | 10 | 10.0 | 0 |
| Branch | 1 | 6 | 6.0 | 0 |
| Gouveia | 1 | 0 | 0.0 | 0 |
| Orr | 1 | 0 | 0.0 | 0 |

### PASSING — PUNTING — KICKING Statistics

**PASSING**

| Last Name | Att | Cmp | % | Yds | Yd/Att | TD | Int | — | % | RK |
|---|---|---|---|---|---|---|---|---|---|---|
| Rypien | 476 | 280 | 58.8 | 3768 | 7.92 | 22 | 13 | — | 2.7 | 3 |
| Williams | 93 | 51 | 54.8 | 585 | 6.29 | 1 | 3 | — | 3.2 | |
| Humphries | 10 | 5 | 50.0 | 91 | 9.10 | 1 | 1 | — | 10.0 | |
| Sanders | 1 | 1 | 100.0 | 32 | 32.00 | 0 | 0 | — | 0.0 | |
| Byner | 1 | 0 | 0.0 | 0 | 0.00 | 0 | 0 | — | 0.0 | |

**PUNTING**

| Last Name | No. | Avg. |
|---|---|---|
| Mojsiejenko | 63 | 42.3 |

**KICKING**

| Last Name | XP | ATT | % | FG | ATT | % |
|---|---|---|---|---|---|---|
| Lohmiller | 41 | 41 | 100 | 29 | 40 | 73 |

## PHOENIX CARDINALS

### RUSHING

| Last Name | No. | Yds | Avg | TD |
|---|---|---|---|---|
| Ferrell | 149 | 502 | 3.4 | 6 |
| Jordan | 83 | 211 | 2.5 | 2 |
| S. Mitchell | 43 | 165 | 3.8 | 0 |
| Sikahema | 38 | 145 | 3.8 | 0 |
| Clark | 20 | 99 | 5.0 | 0 |
| Hogeboom | 27 | 89 | 3.3 | 1 |
| Tupa | 15 | 75 | 5.0 | 0 |
| Wolfley | 13 | 36 | 2.8 | 1 |
| Baker | 20 | 31 | 1.6 | 0 |
| Rosenbach | 6 | 26 | 4.3 | 0 |
| J.T. Smith | 2 | 21 | 10.5 | 0 |
| Jones | 1 | 18 | 18.0 | 0 |

### RECEIVING

| Last Name | No. | Yds | Avg | TD |
|---|---|---|---|---|
| J. Smith | 62 | 778 | 12.5 | 5 |
| Jones | 45 | 838 | 18.6 | 3 |
| Green | 44 | 703 | 16.0 | 7 |
| Awalt | 33 | 360 | 10.9 | 0 |
| Sikahema | 23 | 245 | 10.7 | 0 |
| Novacek | 23 | 225 | 9.8 | 1 |
| Ferrell | 18 | 122 | 6.8 | 0 |
| Holmes | 13 | 271 | 20.8 | 1 |
| Jordan | 6 | 20 | 3.3 | 0 |
| Wolfley | 5 | 38 | 7.6 | 0 |
| Baker | 2 | 18 | 9.0 | 0 |
| McConkey | 2 | 18 | 9.0 | 0 |
| S. Mitchell | 1 | 10 | 10.0 | 0 |
| Usher | 1 | 8 | 8.0 | 0 |
| Reeves | 1 | 5 | 5.0 | 0 |

### PUNT RETURNS

| Last Name | No. | Yds | Avg | TD |
|---|---|---|---|---|
| Sikahema | 37 | 433 | 11.7 | 0 |
| McConkey | 15 | 124 | 8.3 | 0 |
| Usher | 4 | 25 | 6.3 | 0 |
| Jones | 1 | 13 | 13.0 | 0 |

### KICKOFF RETURNS

| Last Name | No. | Yds | Avg | TD |
|---|---|---|---|---|
| Sikahema | 43 | 874 | 20.3 | 0 |
| Usher | 27 | 506 | 18.7 | 0 |
| Baker | 11 | 245 | 22.3 | 0 |
| Jones | 7 | 124 | 17.7 | 0 |
| McConkey | 2 | 40 | 20.0 | 0 |
| Carr | 1 | 15 | 15.0 | 0 |
| Reeves | 1 | 5 | 5.0 | 0 |
| Clark | 2 | 6 | 3.0 | 0 |

### PASSING — PUNTING — KICKING Statistics

**PASSING**

| Last Name | Att | Cmp | % | Yds | Yd/Att | TD | Int | — | % | RK |
|---|---|---|---|---|---|---|---|---|---|---|
| Hogeboom | 364 | 204 | 56.0 | 2591 | 7.12 | 14 | 19 | — | 5.2 | 10 |
| Tupa | 134 | 65 | 48.5 | 973 | 7.26 | 3 | 9 | — | 6.7 | |
| Rosenbach | 22 | 9 | 40.9 | 95 | 4.32 | 0 | 1 | — | 4.5 | |
| Camarillo | 1 | 1 | 100.0 | 0 | 0.00 | 0 | 0 | — | 0.0 | |
| Sikahema | 1 | 1 | 100.0 | 0 | 0.00 | 0 | 0 | — | 0.0 | |
| Awalt | 1 | 0 | 0.0 | 0 | 0.00 | 0 | 1 | — | 100.0 | |

**PUNTING**

| Last Name | No. | Avg. |
|---|---|---|
| Camarillo | 76 | 43.4 |
| Tupa | 6 | 46.7 |

**KICKING**

| Last Name | XP | Att. | % | FG | Att | % |
|---|---|---|---|---|---|---|
| Del Greco | 28 | 29 | 97 | 18 | 26 | 69 |

## DALLAS COWBOYS

### RUSHING

| Last Name | No. | Yds | Avg | TD |
|---|---|---|---|---|
| Palmer | 112 | 446 | 4.0 | 2 |
| Aikman | 38 | 302 | 7.9 | 0 |
| Johnston | 67 | 212 | 3.2 | 0 |
| Sargent | 20 | 87 | 4.4 | 1 |
| Clark | 14 | 40 | 2.9 | 2 |
| Dixon | 3 | 30 | 10.0 | 0 |
| Walsh | 6 | 16 | 2.7 | 0 |
| Tautalatasi | 6 | 15 | 2.5 | 0 |
| Shepard | 3 | 12 | 4.0 | 0 |
| Irvin | 1 | 6 | 6.0 | 0 |
| Saxon | 1 | 1 | 1.0 | 0 |
| Bates | 1 | 0 | 0.0 | 0 |
| Scott | 2 | -4 | -2.0 | 0 |

### RECEIVING

| Last Name | No. | Yds | Avg | TD |
|---|---|---|---|---|
| Martin | 46 | 644 | 14.0 | 2 |
| Folsom | 28 | 265 | 9.5 | 2 |
| Irvin | 26 | 378 | 14.5 | 2 |
| Dixon | 24 | 477 | 19.9 | 2 |
| Shepard | 20 | 304 | 15.2 | 1 |
| Tautalatasi | 17 | 157 | 9.2 | 0 |
| Burbage | 17 | 134 | 7.9 | 0 |
| Palmer | 17 | 93 | 5.5 | 0 |
| Johnston | 16 | 133 | 8.3 | 3 |
| Scott | 9 | 63 | 7.0 | 0 |
| Ford | 7 | 78 | 11.1 | 1 |
| Sargent | 6 | 50 | 8.3 | 0 |
| Jennings | 6 | 47 | 7.8 | 0 |
| Clark | 4 | 69 | 17.3 | 0 |
| Alexander | 1 | 16 | 16.0 | 0 |
| Ruzek | 1 | 4 | 4.0 | 0 |
| Aikman | 1 | -13 | -13.0 | 0 |

### PUNT RETURNS

| Last Name | No. | Yds | Avg | TD |
|---|---|---|---|---|
| Shepard | 31 | 251 | 8.1 | 1 |
| Martin | 4 | 32 | 8.0 | 0 |
| Burbage | 3 | 5 | 1.7 | 0 |

### KICKOFF RETURNS

| Last Name | No. | Yds | Avg | TD |
|---|---|---|---|---|
| Dixon | 47 | 1181 | 25.1 | 1 |
| Shepard | 27 | 529 | 19.6 | 0 |
| Clark | 3 | 56 | 18.7 | 0 |
| Burbage | 3 | 55 | 18.3 | 0 |
| Ankrom | 2 | 6 | 3.0 | 0 |
| Tautalatasi | 1 | 9 | 9.0 | 0 |
| Chandler | 1 | 8 | 8.0 | 0 |
| Sargent | 1 | 0 | 0.0 | 0 |

### PASSING — PUNTING — KICKING Statistics

**PASSING**

| Last Name | Att | Cmp | % | Yds | Yd/Att | TD | Int | — | % | RK |
|---|---|---|---|---|---|---|---|---|---|---|
| Aikman | 293 | 155 | 52.9 | 1749 | 5.97 | 9 | 18 | — | 6.1 | 14 |
| Walsh | 219 | 110 | 50.2 | 1371 | 6.26 | 5 | 9 | — | 4.1 | |
| Saxon | 1 | 1 | 100.0 | 4 | 4.00 | 0 | 0 | — | 0.0 | |

**PUNTING**

| Last Name | No. | Avg. |
|---|---|---|
| Saxon | 81 | 39.9 |
| Ruzek | 1 | 28.0 |

**KICKING**

| Last Name | XP | Att. | % | FG | Att | % |
|---|---|---|---|---|---|---|
| Ruzek | 28 | 29 | 97 | 13 | 22 | 59 |

## MINNESOTA VIKINGS 10-6 Jerry Burns

| Scores of Each Game | | |
|---|---|---|
| 38 | HOUSTON | 7 |
| 7 | Chicago | 38 |
| 14 | Pittsburgh | 27 |
| 17 | TAMPA BAY | 3 |
| 24 | DETROIT | 17 |
| 26 | GREEN BAY | 14 |
| 20 | Detroit | 7 |
| 14 | N.Y. Giants | 24 |
| 23 | L.A. RAMS | * 21 |
| 24 | Tampa Bay | 10 |
| 9 | Philadelphia | 10 |
| 19 | Green Bay (Mil.) | 20 |
| 27 | CHICAGO | 16 |
| 43 | ATLANTA | 17 |
| 17 | Cleveland | * 23 |
| 29 | CINCINNATI | 21 |

| Use Name | Pos. | Hgt | Wgt | Age | Int | Pts |
|---|---|---|---|---|---|---|
| Brian Habib | OT | 6'7" | 282 | 24 | | |
| Tim Irwin | OT | 6'6" | 285 | 30 | | |
| Gary Zimmerman | OT | 6'6" | 286 | 27 | | |
| Dave Huffman | OG | 6'6" | 284 | 33 | | |
| Todd Kalis | OG | 6'5" | 284 | 24 | | |
| Randall McDaniel | OG | 6'3" | 271 | 24 | | |
| John Adickes | C | 6'3" | 264 | 25 | | |
| Chris Foote | C | 6'3" | 255 | 32 | | |
| Kirk Lowdermilk | C | 6'3" | 267 | 26 | | |
| Mark Rodenhauser | C | 6'5" | 262 | 28 | | |
| Chris Doleman | DE | 6'5" | 262 | 27 | | |
| Doug Martin | DE | 6'3" | 258 | 32 | | |
| Al Noga | DE | 6'1" | 248 | 22 | | |
| Thomas Strauthers | DE | 6'4" | 262 | 28 | | |
| Ken Clarke | DT | 6'2" | 281 | 33 | | |
| Keith Millard | DT | 6'5" | 262 | 27 | 1 | 6 |
| Tim Newton | DT | 6' | 277 | 26 | | 6 |
| Henry Thomas | DT | 6'2" | 267 | 24 | | 6 |

Randy Rasmussen — Back Injury

| Use Name | Pos. | Hgt | Wgt | Age | Int | Pts |
|---|---|---|---|---|---|---|
| Ray Berry | LB | 6'2" | 225 | 25 | | 2 |
| David Braxton | LB | 6'1" | 232 | 24 | | |
| Mark Dusbabek | LB | 6'3" | 230 | 25 | 1 | |
| John Galvin | LB | 6'3" | 226 | 24 | | |
| Mike Merriweather | LB | 6'2" | 222 | 28 | 3 | 8 |
| Scott Studwell | LB | 6'2" | 228 | 35 | 1 | |
| Michael Brim (from DET) | DB | 6' | 186 | 23 | | |
| Joey Browner | DB | 6'2" | 210 | 29 | 5 | |
| Travis Curtis | DB | 5'10" | 183 | 23 | | |
| Brad Edwards | DB | 6'1" | 200 | 23 | 1 | |
| Darrell Fullington | DB | 6'1" | 197 | 25 | 1 | |
| Ken Johnson | DB | 6'2" | 197 | 22 | | |
| Carl Lee | DB | 6' | 183 | 28 | 2 | |
| Audrey McMillian | DB | 6' | 189 | 27 | | |
| Reggie Rutland | DB | 6'1" | 194 | 25 | 2 | 6 |
| Daryl Smith | DB | 5'9" | 185 | 26 | | |

| Use Name | Pos. | Hgt | Wgt | Age | Int | Pts |
|---|---|---|---|---|---|---|
| Rich Gannon | QB | 6'3" | 199 | 23 | | |
| Tommy Kramer | QB | 6'2" | 202 | 34 | | |
| Wade Wilson | QB | 6'3" | 208 | 30 | | 6 |
| D.J. Dozier | HB | 6' | 198 | 23 | | |
| Allen Rice | HB | 5'10" | 204 | 26 | | 36 |
| Herschel Walker (from DAL) | HB-FB | 6'1" | 226 | 27 | | 60 |
| Alfred Anderson | FB-HB | 6'1" | 223 | 27 | | 12 |
| Rick Bayless | FB | 6' | 202 | 24 | | |
| Rick Fenney | FB | 6'1" | 232 | 24 | | 36 |
| Anthony Carter | WR | 5'11" | 177 | 28 | | 24 |
| Jim Gustafson | WR | 6'1" | 174 | 28 | | 12 |
| Hassan Jones | WR | 6' | 192 | 25 | | 6 |
| Leo Lewis | WR | 5'8" | 172 | 32 | | 6 |
| Carl Hilton | TE | 6'3" | 230 | 25 | | |
| Darryl Ingram | TE | 6'2" | 230 | 23 | | 6 |
| Steve Jordan | TE | 6'4" | 239 | 28 | | 18 |
| Brent Novoselsky | TE | 6'3" | 232 | 23 | | 12 |
| Teddy Garcia | K | 5'10" | 190 | 25 | | 11 |
| Rich Karlis | K | 6' | 180 | 30 | | 120 |
| Bucky Scribner | K | 6' | 213 | 29 | | |

## GREEN BAY PACKERS 10-6 Lindy Infante

| Scores of Each Game | | |
|---|---|---|
| 21 | TAMPA BAY | 23 |
| 35 | NEW ORLEANS | 34 |
| 38 | L.A. Rams | 41 |
| 23 | ATLANTA (Mil.) | 21 |
| 31 | DALLAS | 13 |
| 14 | Minnesota | 26 |
| 20 | Miami | 23 |
| 23 | DETROIT (Mil.) | * 20 |
| 14 | CHICAGO | 13 |
| 22 | Detroit | 31 |
| 21 | San Francisco | 17 |
| 20 | MINNESOTA (Mil.) | 19 |
| 17 | Tampa Bay | 16 |
| 3 | KANSAS CITY | 21 |
| 40 | Chicago | 28 |
| 20 | Dallas | 10 |

| Use Name | Pos. | Hgt | Wgt | Age | Int | Pts |
|---|---|---|---|---|---|---|
| Mike Ariey | OT | 6'5" | 285 | 25 | | |
| Tony Mandarich | OT | 6'5" | 300 | 22 | | |
| Ken Ruettgers | OT | 6'5" | 280 | 27 | | |
| Alan Veingrad | OT | 6'5" | 277 | 26 | | |
| Billy Ard | OG | 6'3" | 270 | 30 | | |
| Ron Hallstrom | OG | 6'6" | 290 | 30 | | |
| Rich Moran | OG | 6'3" | 275 | 27 | | |
| Blair Bush | C | 6'3" | 272 | 32 | | |
| James Campen | C-OG | 6'3" | 270 | 25 | | |
| Matt Brock | DE | 6'5" | 267 | 23 | | |
| Robert Brown | DE | 6'2" | 267 | 29 | | |
| Mark Hall | DE | 6'4" | 285 | 23 | | |
| Shawn Patterson | DE | 6'5" | 261 | 24 | | |
| Blaise Winter | DE-NT | 6'3" | 275 | 27 | | |
| Jerry Boyarsky | NT | 6'3" | 290 | 30 | | |
| Bob Nelson | NT | 6'4" | 275 | 30 | | |

Dave Croston — Shoulder Injury
Keith Uecker — Knee Injury

| Use Name | Pos. | Hgt | Wgt | Age | Int | Pts |
|---|---|---|---|---|---|---|
| John Anderson | LB | 6'3" | 228 | 33 | 1 | |
| Burnell Dent | LB | 6'1" | 236 | 26 | 1 | |
| Tim Harris | LB | 6'5" | 235 | 24 | | |
| Johnny Holland | LB | 6'2" | 221 | 24 | 1 | |
| Brian Noble | LB | 6'3" | 252 | 26 | | |
| Scott Stephen | LB | 6'2" | 232 | 25 | 2 | |
| Mike Weddington | LB | 6'4" | 245 | 28 | | |
| Dave Brown | DB | 6'1" | 187 | 36 | 6 | |
| Chuck Cecil | DB | 6' | 184 | 24 | 1 | |
| Tiger Greene | DB | 6' | 194 | 27 | 1 | |
| Van Jakes | DB | 6' | 190 | 28 | 1 | |
| Mark Lee | DB | 5'11" | 189 | 31 | 2 | |
| Michael McGruder | DB | 5'11" | 180 | 27 | | |
| Mark Murphy | DB | 6'2" | 201 | 31 | 3 | |
| Ron Pitts | DB | 5'10" | 175 | 26 | 1 | |
| Ken Stills | DB | 5'10" | 186 | 25 | 3 | |

John Dorsey — Knee Injury

| Use Name | Pos. | Hgt | Wgt | Age | Int | Pts |
|---|---|---|---|---|---|---|
| Anthony Dilweg | QB | 6'3" | 215 | 24 | | |
| Blair Kiel | QB | 6' | 214 | 27 | | |
| Don Majkowski | QB | 6'2" | 197 | 25 | | 30 |
| Herman Fontenot | HB | 6' | 206 | 25 | | 24 |
| Keith Woodside | HB | 5'11" | 203 | 25 | | 6 |
| Vince Workman | HB | 5'10 | 193 | 21 | | 6 |
| Michael Haddix | FB | 6'2" | 227 | 27 | | 6 |
| Brent Fullwood | FB-HB | 5'11" | 209 | 25 | | 30 |
| Carl Bland | WR | 5'11" | 182 | 27 | | 12 |
| Perry Kemp | WR | 5'11" | 170 | 27 | | 12 |
| Aubrey Matthews | WR | 5'7" | 165 | 26 | | |
| Jeff Query | WR | 6' | 165 | 22 | | 12 |
| Sterling Sharpe | WR | 5'11" | 202 | 24 | | 78 |
| Clint Didier | TE | 6'5" | 240 | 30 | | 6 |
| John Spagnola | TE | 6'4" | 242 | 32 | | |
| Ed West | TE | 6'1" | 243 | 28 | | 30 |
| Don Bracken | K | 6'1" | 211 | 27 | | |
| Chris Jacke | K | 6' | 197 | 23 | | 108 |

## DETROIT LIONS 7-9 Wayne Fontes

| Scores of Each Game | | |
|---|---|---|
| 13 | PHOENIX | 16 |
| 14 | N.Y. Giants | 24 |
| 27 | CHICAGO | 47 |
| 3 | PITTSBURGH | 23 |
| 17 | Minnesota | 24 |
| 17 | Tampa Bay | 16 |
| 7 | MINNESOTA | 20 |
| 20 | Green Bay (Mil.) | * 23 |
| 31 | Houston | 35 |
| 31 | GREEN BAY | 22 |
| 7 | Cincinnati | 42 |
| 13 | CLEVELAND | 10 |
| 21 | NEW ORLEANS | 14 |
| 27 | Chicago | 17 |
| 33 | TAMPA BAY | 7 |
| 31 | Atlanta | 24 |

| Use Name | Pos. | Hgt | Wgt | Age | Int | Pts |
|---|---|---|---|---|---|---|
| Lomas Brown | OT | 6'4" | 275 | 26 | | |
| Chris Gambol | OT | 6'6" | 303 | 24 | | |
| Harvey Salem | OT | 6'6" | 285 | 28 | | |
| Eric Sanders | OT-OG | 6'7" | 280 | 30 | | |
| Eric Andolsek | OG | 6'2" | 277 | 23 | | |
| Ken Dallafior | OG-C | 6'4" | 279 | 30 | | |
| Kevin Glover | OG-C | 6'2" | 275 | 26 | | |
| Joe Milinichik | OG-OT | 6'5" | 275 | 26 | | |
| Mike Utley | OG-OT | 6'6" | 288 | 23 | | |
| Trevor Matich | C | 6'4" | 270 | 27 | | |
| Keith Ferguson | DE | 6'5" | 260 | 30 | | |
| Curtis Green | DE-NT | 6'3" | 265 | 32 | | |
| James Cribbs | DE | 6'3" | 269 | 23 | | |
| Byron Darby | DE | 6'4" | 260 | 29 | | |
| Eric Williams | DE | 6'4" | 286 | 27 | | |
| Kevin Brooks | DT-DE | 6'6" | 278 | 26 | | |
| Jerry Ball | NT | 6'1" | 298 | 24 | | |
| Lawrence Pete | NT | 6' | 282 | 23 | | |

Steve Mott — Neck Injury

| Use Name | Pos. | Hgt | Wgt | Age | Int | Pts |
|---|---|---|---|---|---|---|
| Mark Brown | LB | 6'2" | 240 | 27 | | |
| Toby Caston | LB | 6'1" | 243 | 24 | | |
| Mike Cofer | LB | 6'5" | 245 | 29 | | |
| Dennis Gibson | LB | 6'2" | 240 | 25 | 1 | |
| George Jamison | LB | 6'1" | 226 | 26 | | |
| Victor Jones | LB | 6'2" | 240 | 22 | | |
| Keith Karpinski | LB | 6'3" | 225 | 22 | | |
| Niko Noga | LB | 6'1" | 235 | 27 | 1 | |
| Chris Spielman | LB | 6' | 247 | 28 | | |
| Jimmy Williams | LB | 6'3" | 230 | 28 | 5 | |
| Bruce Alexander | DB | 5'9" | 169 | 23 | | |
| Bennie Blades | DB | 6'1" | 221 | 22 | | |
| Ray Crockett | DB | 5'9" | 181 | 22 | 1 | |
| James Griffin | DB | 6'2" | 203 | 27 | | |
| Jerry Holmes | DB | 6'2" | 175 | 31 | 6 | 6 |
| Bruce McNorton | DB | 5'11" | 175 | 30 | | |
| John Miller | DB | 6'1" | 195 | 23 | | |
| Terry Taylor | DB | 5'10" | 191 | 28 | 1 | |
| William White | DB | 5'10" | 191 | 23 | 1 | 6 |
| Jerry Woods | DB | 5'10" | 187 | 23 | | |

| Use Name | Pos. | Hgt | Wgt | Age | Int | Pts |
|---|---|---|---|---|---|---|
| Bob Gagliano | QB | 6'3" | 196 | 30 | | 24 |
| Eric Hipple | QB | 6'2" | 198 | 31 | | 6 |
| Chuck Long | QB | 6'4" | 221 | 26 | | |
| Rodney Peete | QB | 6' | 193 | 23 | | 24 |
| Carl Painter | HB | 5'9" | 185 | 25 | | |
| Barry Sanders | HB-FB | 5'8" | 203 | 21 | | 84 |
| Tony Paige | FB | 5'10" | 235 | 26 | | |
| Robert Clark | WR | 5'11" | 173 | 24 | | 12 |
| John Ford | WR | 6'2" | 204 | 23 | | |
| Mel Gray | WR | 5'9" | 162 | 28 | | |
| Richard Johnson | WR | 5'7" | 185 | 27 | | 48 |
| Troy Johnson | WR | 6'1" | 185 | 26 | | |
| Keith McDonald | WR | 5'9" | 159 | 25 | | |
| Stacey Mobley | WR | 5'8" | 165 | 23 | | |
| Jason Phillips | WR | 5'7" | 168 | 22 | | 6 |
| Walter Stanley | WR | 5'9" | 180 | 26 | | |
| Mike Williams | WR | 5'10" | 177 | 22 | | |
| Jim Arnold | K | 6'3" | 211 | 28 | | |
| Eddie Murray | K | 5'10" | 180 | 33 | | 96 |

## CHICAGO BEARS 6-10 Mike Ditka

| Scores of Each Game | | |
|---|---|---|
| 17 | CINCINNATI | 14 |
| 38 | MINNESOTA | 7 |
| 47 | Detroit | 27 |
| 27 | PHILADELPHIA | 13 |
| 35 | Tampa Bay | 42 |
| 28 | HOUSTON | 33 |
| 7 | Cleveland | 27 |
| 20 | L.A. RAMS | 10 |
| 13 | Green Bay | 14 |
| 20 | Pittsburgh | 0 |
| 31 | TAMPA BAY | 32 |
| 14 | Washington | 38 |
| 16 | Minnesota | 27 |
| 17 | DETROIT | 27 |
| 28 | GREEN BAY | 40 |
| 0 | San Francisco | 26 |

| Use Name | Pos. | Hgt | Wgt | Age | Int | Pts |
|---|---|---|---|---|---|---|
| Jim Covert | OT | 6'4" | 278 | 29 | | |
| Chris Dyko | OT | 6'6" | 295 | 23 | | |
| Keith Van Horne | OT | 6'6" | 283 | 31 | | |
| John Wojciechowski | OT | 6'4" | 270 | 26 | | |
| Dave Zawatson | OT | 6'4" | 274 | 23 | | |
| Mark Bortz | OG | 6'6" | 272 | 28 | | |
| Jerry Fontenot | OG | 6'3" | 272 | 22 | | |
| Tom Thayer | OG | 6'4" | 270 | 28 | | |
| Jay Hilgenberg | C | 6'3" | 260 | 29 | | |
| Trace Armstrong | DE | 6'4" | 259 | 23 | | |
| Richard Dent | DE | 6'5" | 268 | 28 | 1 | |
| Tony Woods | DE-DT | 6'4" | 274 | 23 | | |
| William Perry | DT | 6'2" | 320 | 26 | | |
| Dick Chapura | DT | 6'3" | 275 | 25 | | |
| Dan Hampton | DT | 6'5" | 274 | 31 | | |
| Steve McMichael | DT | 6'2" | 268 | 31 | | |
| John Shannon | DT-DE | 6'3" | 269 | 24 | | |

| Use Name | Pos. | Hgt | Wgt | Age | Int | Pts |
|---|---|---|---|---|---|---|
| LaSalle Harper (from NYG) | LB | 6' | 226 | 22 | | |
| Steve Hyche | LB | 6'3" | 236 | 26 | | |
| Troy Johnson | LB | 6' | 236 | 24 | | |
| Dante Jones | LB | 6'1" | 236 | 24 | | |
| Jim Morrissey | LB | 6'3" | 227 | 26 | 2 | |
| Mickey Pruitt | LB | 6'1" | 206 | 24 | | |
| Ron Rivera | LB | 6'3" | 240 | 27 | 2 | |
| John Roper | LB | 6'1" | 228 | 23 | 2 | |
| Mike Singletary | LB | 6' | 230 | 30 | | |
| Maurice Douglass | DB | 5'11" | 200 | 25 | 1 | |
| Dave Duerson | DB | 6'1" | 212 | 28 | 1 | |
| Shaun Gayle | DB | 5'11" | 194 | 27 | 3 | |
| Vestee Jackson | DB | 6' | 186 | 26 | 2 | |
| Lorenzo Lynch | DB | 5'9" | 199 | 26 | 3 | |
| Markus Paul | DB | 6'2" | 199 | 23 | 1 | |
| Lemuel Stinson | DB | 5'9" | 159 | 23 | 4 | 6 |
| George Streeter | DB | 6'2" | 212 | 22 | | |
| David Tate | DB | 6' | 177 | 24 | 1 | |
| Donnell Woolford | DB | 5'9" | 187 | 23 | 3 | |

| Use Name | Pos. | Hgt | Wgt | Age | Int | Pts |
|---|---|---|---|---|---|---|
| Jim Harbaugh | QB | 6'3" | 204 | 25 | | 18 |
| Mike Tomczak | QB | 6'1" | 198 | 26 | | 6 |
| Neal Anderson | HB | 5'11" | 210 | 25 | | 90 |
| Mark Green | HB | 5'11" | 184 | 22 | | 6 |
| Thomas Sanders | HB | 5'11" | 203 | 27 | | 12 |
| Brian Taylor | HB | 5'10" | 175 | 22 | | |
| Brad Muster | FB | 6'3" | 231 | 24 | | 48 |
| Matt Suhey | FB | 5'11" | 213 | 31 | | 12 |
| Wendell Davis | WR | 5'11" | 188 | 23 | | 18 |
| Dennis Gentry | WR-HB | 5'8" | 180 | 30 | | 6 |
| Glen Kozlowski | WR | 6'1" | 205 | 26 | | |
| Dennis McKinnon | WR | 6'1" | 177 | 28 | | 18 |
| Ron Morris | WR | 6'1' | 195 | 24 | | 6 |
| Tom Waddle | WR | 6' | 181 | 22 | | |
| Cap Boso | TE | 6'3" | 240 | 25 | | 6 |
| Jim Thornton | TE | 6'2" | 242 | 24 | | 18 |
| Maury Buford | K | 6'1" | 198 | 29 | | |
| Kevin Butler | K | 6'1" | 204 | 27 | | 88 |

## TAMPA BAY BUCCANEERS 5-11 Ray Perkins

| Scores of Each Game | | |
|---|---|---|
| 23 | Green Bay | 21 |
| 16 | SAN FRANCISCO | 20 |
| 20 | NEW ORLEANS | 10 |
| 3 | Minnesota | 17 |
| 42 | CHICAGO | 35 |
| 16 | DETROIT | 17 |
| 28 | Washington | 32 |
| 23 | Cincinnati | 56 |
| 31 | CLEVELAND | 42 |
| 10 | MINNESOTA | 24 |
| 32 | Chicago | 31 |
| 14 | Phoenix | 13 |
| 16 | GREEN BAY | 17 |
| 17 | Houston | 20 |
| 7 | Detroit | 33 |
| 22 | PITTSBURGH | 31 |

| Use Name | Pos. | Hgt | Wgt | Age | Int | Pts |
|---|---|---|---|---|---|---|
| Paul Gruber | OT | 6'5" | 290 | 24 | | |
| Rob Taylor | OT | 6'6" | 295 | 28 | | |
| Harry Swayne | OT | 6'5" | 270 | 24 | | |
| Carl Bax | OG-OT | 6'4" | 290 | 23 | | |
| John Bruhin | OG | 6'3" | 280 | 24 | | |
| Sam Anno | C | 62" | 235 | 24 | | |
| Mark Cooper | OG-OT | 6'5" | 280 | 29 | | |
| Byron Ingram | OG | 6'2" | 295 | 24 | | |
| Tom McHale | OG | 6'4" | 275 | 26 | | |
| Mike Simmonds | OG | 6'4" | 285 | 25 | | |
| Dan Graham | C | 6'2" | 270 | 24 | | |
| Randy Grimes | C | 6'4" | 275 | 29 | | |
| John Cannon | DE | 6'5" | 260 | 29 | | |
| Reuben Davis | DE | 6'4" | 290 | 24 | 1 | 6 |
| Robert Goff | DE | 6'3" | 270 | 23 | | |
| Rhondy Weston | DE | 6'5" | 275 | 23 | | |
| Curt Jarvis | NT | 6'2" | 265 | 24 | | |
| Shawn Lee | NT | 6'2" | 290 | 22 | | |
| Ray Seals | NT | 6'3" | 270 | 24 | | |

| Use Name | Pos. | Hgt | Wgt | Age | Int | Pts |
|---|---|---|---|---|---|---|
| Sam Anno | LB | 6'2" | 235 | 24 | | |
| Sidney Coleman | LB | 6'2" | 250 | 25 | | |
| Eugene Marve | LB | 6'2" | 240 | 29 | | |
| Winston Moss | LB | 6'3" | 235 | 23 | | |
| Kevin Murphy | LB | 6'2" | 235 | 25 | | |
| Peter Najarian | LB | 6'2" | 230 | 25 | | |
| Ervin Randle | LB | 6'1" | 250 | 26 | | |
| Henry Rolling | LB | 6'2" | 225 | 23 | | |
| Broderick Thomas | LB-DE | 6'4" | 245 | 22 | | |
| Sherman Cocroft | DB | 6'1" | 205 | 28 | | 2 |
| Donnie Elder | DB | 5'9" | 175 | 25 | 1 | |
| Bobby Futrell | DB | 5'11" | 190 | 27 | 1 | |
| Harry Hamilton | DB | 6' | 195 | 26 | 6 | |
| Odie Harris | DB | 6' | 190 | 23 | 1 | |
| Rod Jones | DB | 6' | 185 | 25 | | |
| Ricky Reynolds | DB | 5'11" | 190 | 24 | 5 | 12 |
| Mark Robinson | DB | 5'11" | 200 | 26 | 6 | |

| Use Name | Pos. | Hgt | Wgt | Age | Int | Pts |
|---|---|---|---|---|---|---|
| Kerwin Bell | QB | 6'3" | 205 | 24 | | |
| Joe Ferguson | QB | 6'1" | 190 | 39 | | |
| Vinny Testaverde | QB | 6'5" | 215 | 25 | | |
| Don Smith | HB-WR | 5'11" | 195 | 25 | | |
| Sylvester Stamps | HB | 5'7" | 180 | 28 | | 6 |
| Lars Tate | HB | 6'2" | 215 | 23 | | 54 |
| Jamie Lawson | FB | 5'10" | 240 | 23 | | |
| Alvin Mitchell | FB | 6' | 235 | 25 | | |
| William Howard | FB-HB | 6' | 240 | 25 | | 12 |
| James Wilder | FB-HB | 6'3" | 225 | 31 | | 18 |
| Mark Carrier | WR | 6' | 185 | 23 | | 54 |
| Willie Drewrey | WR | 5'7" | 170 | 26 | | 6 |
| Everett Gay | WR | 6'2" | 209 | 24 | | |
| Bruce Hill | WR | 6' | 180 | 25 | | 30 |
| Danny Peebles | WR | 5'11" | 180 | 23 | | |
| Frank Pillow | WR | 5'10" | 170 | 24 | | |
| Ron Hall | TE | 6'4" | 245 | 25 | | 12 |
| William Harris | TE | 6'4" | 235 | 24 | | 6 |
| Jackie Walker | TE | 6'5" | 255 | 26 | | |
| John Carney | K | 5'11" | 160 | 25 | | |
| Donald Igwebuike | K | 5'9" | 175 | 28 | | 99 |
| Chris Mohr | K | 6'4" | 220 | 23 | | 1 |

## MINNESOTA VIKINGS

### RUSHING
| Last Name | No. | Yds | Avg | TD |
|---|---|---|---|---|
| Walker | 250 | 915 | 3.7 | 7 |
| Fenney | 151 | 588 | 3.9 | 4 |
| Dozier | 46 | 207 | 4.5 | 0 |
| Anderson | 52 | 189 | 3.6 | 2 |
| Wilson | 32 | 132 | 4.1 | 1 |
| Jones | 1 | 37 | 37.0 | 0 |
| Rice | 6 | 25 | 4.3 | 0 |
| Carter | 3 | 18 | 6.0 | 0 |
| Lewis | 1 | 11 | 11.0 | 0 |
| Kramer | 12 | 9 | 0.8 | 0 |

### RECEIVING
| Last Name | No. | Yds | Avg | TD |
|---|---|---|---|---|
| Carter | 65 | 1066 | 16.4 | 4 |
| Jones | 42 | 694 | 16.5 | 1 |
| Walker | 40 | 423 | 10.6 | 2 |
| Jordan | 35 | 506 | 14.5 | 3 |
| Fenney | 30 | 254 | 8.5 | 2 |
| Anderson | 20 | 193 | 9.7 | 0 |
| Dozier | 14 | 148 | 10.6 | 0 |
| Gustafson | 14 | 144 | 10.3 | 2 |
| Lewis | 12 | 148 | 12.3 | 1 |

### PUNT RETURNS
| Last Name | No. | Yds | Avg | TD |
|---|---|---|---|---|
| Lewis | 44 | 446 | 10.1 | 0 |
| Carter | 1 | 2 | 2.0 | 0 |

### KICKOFF RETURNS
| Last Name | No. | Yds | Avg | TD |
|---|---|---|---|---|
| Walker | 13 | 374 | 28.8 | 1 |
| Dozier | 12 | 258 | 21.5 | 0 |
| Anderson | 5 | 75 | 15.0 | 0 |
| Lewis | 2 | 30 | 15.0 | 0 |
| Carter | 1 | 19 | 19.0 | 0 |
| Curtis | 1 | 18 | 18.0 | 0 |
| Rice | 1 | 13 | 13.0 | 0 |
| Fenney | 1 | 12 | 12.0 | 0 |

### PASSING—PUNTING—KICKING
| Last Name | Att | Cmp | % | Yds | Yd/Att | TD | Int— | % | RK |
|---|---|---|---|---|---|---|---|---|---|
| PASSING |
| Wilson | 362 | 194 | 53.6 | 2543 | 7.02 | 9 | 12— | 3.3 | 9 |
| Kramer | 136 | 77 | 56.6 | 906 | 6.66 | 7 | 7— | 5.1 | |
| Dozier | 1 | 1 | 100.0 | 19 | 19.00 | 1 | 0— | 0.0 | |

| PUNTING | No. | Avg. |
|---|---|---|
| Scribner | 72 | 39.8 |

| KICKING | XP | ATT | % | FG | ATT | % |
|---|---|---|---|---|---|---|
| Garcia | 8 | 8 | 100 | 1 | 5 | 20 |
| Karlis | 27 | 28 | 96 | 31 | 39 | 79 |

## GREEN BAY PACKERS

### RUSHING
| Last Name | No. | Yds | Avg | TD |
|---|---|---|---|---|
| Fullwood | 204 | 821 | 4.0 | 5 |
| Majkowski | 75 | 358 | 4.8 | 5 |
| Woodside | 46 | 273 | 5.9 | 1 |
| Haddix | 44 | 135 | 3.1 | 0 |
| Fontenot | 17 | 69 | 4.1 | 1 |
| Kemp | 5 | 43 | 8.6 | 0 |
| Sharpe | 2 | 25 | 12.5 | 0 |
| Workman | 4 | 8 | 2.0 | 1 |

### RECEIVING
| Last Name | No. | Yds | Avg | TD |
|---|---|---|---|---|
| Sharpe | 90 | 1423 | 15.8 | 12 |
| Woodside | 59 | 527 | 8.9 | 0 |
| Kemp | 48 | 611 | 12.7 | 2 |
| Fontenot | 40 | 372 | 9.3 | 3 |
| Query | 23 | 350 | 15.2 | 2 |
| West | 22 | 269 | 12.2 | 5 |
| Fullwood | 19 | 214 | 11.3 | 0 |
| Matthews | 18 | 200 | 11.1 | 0 |
| Haddix | 15 | 111 | 7.4 | 1 |
| Bland | 11 | 164 | 14.9 | 1 |
| Didier | 7 | 71 | 10.1 | 1 |
| Spagnola | 2 | 13 | 6.5 | 0 |

### PUNT RETURNS
| Last Name | No. | Yds | Avg | TD |
|---|---|---|---|---|
| Query | 30 | 247 | 8.2 | 0 |

### KICKOFF RETURNS
| Last Name | No. | Yds | Avg | TD |
|---|---|---|---|---|
| Workman | 33 | 547 | 16.6 | 0 |
| Bland | 13 | 256 | 19.7 | 0 |
| Fullwood | 11 | 243 | 22.1 | 0 |
| Query | 6 | 125 | 20.8 | 0 |
| Woodside | 2 | 38 | 19.0 | 0 |
| Fontenot | 2 | 30 | 15.0 | 0 |
| Didier | 1 | 0 | 0.0 | 0 |
| Mandarich | 1 | 0 | 0.0 | 0 |

### PASSING—PUNTING—KICKING
| Last Name | Att | Cmp | % | Yds | Yd/Att | TD | Int— | % | RK |
|---|---|---|---|---|---|---|---|---|---|
| PASSING |
| Majkowski | 599 | 353 | 58.9 | 4318 | 7.21 | 27 | 20— | 3.3 | 5 |
| Dilweg | 1 | 1 | 100.0 | 7 | 7.00 | 0 | 0— | 0.0 | |

| PUNTING | No. | Avg. |
|---|---|---|
| Bracken | 66 | 40.6 |

| KICKING | XP | Att. | % | FG | Att | % |
|---|---|---|---|---|---|---|
| Jacke | 42 | 42 | 100 | 22 | 28 | 79 |

## DETROIT LIONS

### RUSHING
| Last Name | No. | Yds | Avg | TD |
|---|---|---|---|---|
| B. Sanders | 280 | 1470 | 5.3 | 14 |
| Gagliano | 41 | 192 | 4.7 | 4 |
| Peete | 33 | 148 | 4.5 | 4 |
| Paige | 3- | 105 | 3.5 | 0 |
| Painter | 15 | 64 | 4.3 | 0 |
| R. Johnson | 12 | 38 | 3.2 | 0 |
| Gray | 3 | 22 | 7.3 | 0 |
| Hipple | 2 | 11 | 5.5 | 1 |
| L. Brown | 1 | 3 | 3.0 | 0 |
| Long | 3 | 2 | 0.7 | 0 |
| McDonald | 1 | -2 | -2.0 | 0 |

### RECEIVING
| Last Name | No. | Yds | Avg | TD |
|---|---|---|---|---|
| R. Johnson | 70 | 1091 | 15.6 | 8 |
| Clark | 41 | 748 | 18.2 | 0 |
| Phillips | 30 | 352 | 11.7 | 1 |
| Stanley | 24 | 304 | 12.7 | 0 |
| B. Sanders | 24 | 282 | 11.8 | 0 |
| Mobley | 13 | 158 | 12.2 | 0 |
| McDonald | 12 | 138 | 11.5 | 0 |
| Ford | 5 | 56 | 11.2 | 0 |
| Painter | 3 | 41 | 13.7 | 0 |
| Gray | 2 | 47 | 23.5 | 0 |
| T. Johnson | 2 | 29 | 13.5 | 0 |
| Paige | 2 | 27 | 13.5 | 0 |

### PUNT RETURNS
| Last Name | No. | Yds | Avg | TD |
|---|---|---|---|---|
| Stanley | 36 | 496 | 13.8 | 0 |
| Gray | 11 | 76 | 6.9 | 0 |
| Woods | 0 | 0 | 0.0 | 0 |
| Miller | 0 | 0 | 0.0 | 0 |

### KICKOFF RETURNS
| Last Name | No. | Yds | Avg | TD |
|---|---|---|---|---|
| Gray | 24 | 640 | 26.7 | 0 |
| Palmer | 11 | 255 | 23.2 | 0 |
| Stanley | 9 | 95 | 10.6 | 0 |
| B. Sanders | 5 | 118 | 23.6 | 0 |
| Alexander | 5 | 100 | 20.0 | 0 |
| Woods | 2 | 28 | 14.0 | 0 |
| Dallafior | 2 | 13 | 6.5 | 0 |
| Painter | 1 | 14 | 14.0 | 0 |
| Crockett | 1 | 8 | 8.0 | 0 |

### PASSING—PUNTING—KICKING
| Last Name | Att | Cmp | % | Yds | Yd/Att | TD | Int— | % | RK |
|---|---|---|---|---|---|---|---|---|---|
| PASSING |
| Gagliano | 232 | 117 | 50.4 | 1671 | 7.20 | 6 | 12— | 5.2 | 13 |
| Peete | 195 | 103 | 52.8 | 1479 | 7.58 | 5 | 9— | 4.6 | |
| Hipple | 18 | 7 | 38.9 | 90 | 5.00 | 0 | 0— | 16.7 | |
| Long | 5 | 2 | 40.0 | 42 | 8.40 | 0 | 0— | 0.0 | |

| PUNTING | No. | Avg. |
|---|---|---|
| Arnold | 83 | 42.6 |

| KICKING | XP | Att. | % | FG | Att | % |
|---|---|---|---|---|---|---|
| Murray | 36 | 36 | 100 | 20 | 21 | 95 |

## CHICAGO BEARS

### RUSHING
| Last Name | No. | Yds | Avg | TD |
|---|---|---|---|---|
| Anderson | 274 | 1275 | 4.7 | 11 |
| Muster | 82 | 327 | 4.0 | 5 |
| Harbaugh | 45 | 276 | 6.1 | 3 |
| Sanders | 41 | 127 | 3.1 | 0 |
| Gentry | 17 | 106 | 6.2 | 0 |
| Tomczak | 24 | 71 | 3.0 | 1 |
| Suhey | 20 | 51 | 2.6 | 1 |
| Green | 5 | 46 | 9.2 | 0 |
| Taylor | 2 | 7 | 3.5 | 0 |
| Buford | 1 | 6 | 6.0 | 0 |
| McKinnon | 3 | 5 | 1.7 | 0 |
| Thornton | 1 | 4 | 4.0 | 0 |
| Morris | 1 | -14 | -14.0 | 0 |

### RECEIVING
| Last Name | No. | Yds | Avg | TD |
|---|---|---|---|---|
| Anderson | 50 | 434 | 8.7 | 4 |
| Gentry | 39 | 463 | 11.9 | 1 |
| Muster | 32 | 259 | 8.1 | 3 |
| Morris | 30 | 486 | 16.2 | 1 |
| McKinnon | 28 | 418 | 14.9 | 3 |
| Davis | 26 | 397 | 15.3 | 3 |
| Thornton | 24 | 392 | 16.3 | 3 |
| Boso | 17 | 182 | 10.7 | 1 |
| Suhey | 9 | 73 | 8.1 | 1 |
| Green | 5 | 48 | 9.6 | 0 |
| Kozlowski | 3 | 74 | 24.7 | 0 |
| Sanders | 3 | 28 | 9.3 | 1 |
| Waddle | 1 | 8 | 8.0 | |

### PUNT RETURNS
| Last Name | No. | Yds | Avg | TD |
|---|---|---|---|---|
| Green | 16 | 141 | 8.8 | 0 |
| McKinnon | 10 | 67 | 6.7 | 0 |
| Kozlowski | 4 | -2 | -0.5 | 0 |
| Woolford | 1 | 12 | 12.0 | 0 |
| Waddle | 1 | 2 | 2.0 | 0 |

### KICKOFF RETURNS
| Last Name | No. | Yds | Avg | TD |
|---|---|---|---|---|
| Gentry | 28 | 667 | 23.8 | 0 |
| Sanders | 23 | 491 | 21.3 | 1 |
| Green | 11 | 239 | 21.7 | 0 |
| Suhey | 6 | 93 | 15.5 | 0 |
| Pruitt | 2 | 17 | 8.5 | 0 |
| Kozlowski | 1 | 12 | 12.0 | 0 |
| Tate | 1 | 12 | 12.0 | 0 |
| Chapura | 1 | 8 | 8.0 | 0 |

### PASSING—PUNTING—KICKING
| Last Name | Att | Cmp | % | Yds | Yd/Att | TD | Int— | % | RK |
|---|---|---|---|---|---|---|---|---|---|
| PASSING |
| Tomczak | 306 | 156 | 51.0 | 2058 | 6.73 | 16 | 16— | 5.2 | 12 |
| Harbaugh | 178 | 111 | 62.4 | 1204 | 6.76 | 5 | 9— | 5.1 | |

| PUNTING | No. | Avg. |
|---|---|---|
| Buford | 72 | 39.5 |

| KICKING | XP | ATT | % | FG | ATT | % |
|---|---|---|---|---|---|---|
| Butler | 43 | 45 | 96 | 15 | 19 | 79 |

## TAMPA BAY BUCCANEERS

### RUSHING
| Last Name | No. | Yds | Avg | TD |
|---|---|---|---|---|
| Tate | 167 | 589 | 3.5 | 8 |
| Howard | 108 | 357 | 3.3 | 1 |
| Wilder | 70 | 244 | 3.5 | 0 |
| Stamps | 29 | 141 | 4.9 | 1 |
| Testaverde | 25 | 139 | 5.6 | 0 |
| D. Smith | 7 | 37 | 5.3 | 0 |
| Ferguson | 4 | 6 | 1.5 | 0 |
| Peebles | 2 | -6 | -3.0 | 0 |

### RECEIVING
| Last Name | No. | Yds | Avg | TD |
|---|---|---|---|---|
| Carrier | 86 | 1422 | 16.5 | 9 |
| Hill | 50 | 673 | 13.5 | 5 |
| Wilder | 36 | 335 | 9.3 | 3 |
| Hall | 30 | 331 | 11.0 | 2 |
| Howard | 30 | 188 | 6.3 | 1 |
| Stamps | 15 | 82 | 5.5 | 0 |
| Drewrey | 14 | 157 | 11.2 | 1 |
| Peebles | 11 | 180 | 16.4 | 0 |
| W. Harris | 11 | 102 | 9.3 | 1 |
| Tate | 11 | 75 | 6.8 | 1 |
| D. Smith | 7 | 110 | 15.7 | 0 |
| Mitchell | 1 | 11 | 11.0 | 0 |

### PUNT RETURNS
| Last Name | No. | Yds | Avg | TD |
|---|---|---|---|---|
| Drewrey | 20 | 220 | 11.0 | 0 |
| Futrell | 12 | 76 | 6.3 | 0 |

### KICKOFF RETURNS
| Last Name | No. | Yds | Avg | TD |
|---|---|---|---|---|
| Elder | 40 | 685 | 17.1 | 0 |
| Stamps | 9 | 145 | 16.1 | 0 |
| Howard | 5 | 82 | 16.4 | 0 |
| Futrell | 4 | 58 | 14.5 | 0 |
| Wilder | 2 | 42 | 21.0 | 0 |
| Drewrey | 1 | 26 | 26.0 | 0 |
| Pillow | 1 | 17 | 17.0 | 0 |

### PASSING—PUNTING—KICKING
| Last Name | Att | Cmp | % | Yds | Yd/Att | TD | Int— | % | RK |
|---|---|---|---|---|---|---|---|---|---|
| PASSING |
| Testaverde | 480 | 258 | 53.8 | 3133 | 6.53 | 20 | 22— | 4.6 | 11 |
| Ferguson | 90 | 44 | 48.9 | 533 | 5.92 | 3 | 6— | 6.7 | |

| PUNTING | No. | Avg. |
|---|---|---|
| Mohr | 86 | 38.5 |

| KICKING | XP | ATT | % | FG | ATT | % |
|---|---|---|---|---|---|---|
| Igwebuike | 33 | 35 | 94 | 22 | 28 | 79 |
| Mohr | 1 | 1 | 100 | 0 | 0 | 0 |

## SAN FRANCISCO 49ERS 14-2 George Seifert

| Scores of Each Game | | |
|---|---|---|
| 30 | Indianapolis | 24 |
| 20 | Tampa Bay | 16 |
| 38 | Philadelphia | 28 |
| 12 | L.A. RAMS | 13 |
| 24 | New Orleans | 20 |
| 31 | Dallas | 14 |
| 37 | NEW ENGLAND | 20 |
| 23 | N.Y. Jets | 10 |
| 31 | NEW ORLEANS | 13 |
| 45 | ATLANTA | 3 |
| 17 | GREEN BAY | 21 |
| 34 | N.Y. GIANTS | 24 |
| 23 | Atlanta | 10 |
| 30 | L.A. Rams | 27 |
| 21 | BUFFALO | 10 |
| 26 | CHICAGO | 0 |

| Use Name | Pos. | Hgt | Wgt | Age | Int | Pts |
|---|---|---|---|---|---|---|
| Harris Barton | OT-OG | 6'4" | 280 | 25 | | |
| Dave Cullity | OT | 6'7" | 275 | 25 | | |
| Bubba Paris | OT | 6'6" | 306 | 28 | | |
| Steve Wallace | OT | 6'5" | 276 | 24 | | |
| Jeff Bregel | OG | 6'4" | 280 | 25 | | |
| Bruce Collie | OG | 6'6" | 275 | 27 | | |
| Guy McIntyre | OG | 6'3" | 265 | 28 | | |
| Terry Tausch | OG | 6'5" | 276 | 30 | | |
| Jesse Sapolu | C | 6'4" | 260 | 28 | | |
| Chuck Thomas | C-OG | 6'3" | 280 | 28 | | |
| Kevin Fagan | DE | 6'4" | 265 | 26 | | |
| Pierce Holt | DE | 6'4" | 280 | 27 | | |
| Pete Kugler | DE | 6'4" | 255 | 30 | | |
| Larry Roberts | DE | 6'3" | 275 | 26 | | |
| Danny Stubbs | DE | 6'4" | 260 | 24 | | |
| Kevin Lilly (from DAL) | DT-DE | 6'4" | 265 | 26 | | |
| Jim Burt | NT | 6'1" | 260 | 30 | | |
| Michael Carter | NT-DT | 6'2" | 285 | 28 | | |
| Rollin Putzier | NT | 6'4" | 279 | 23 | | |

| Use Name | Pos. | Hgt | Wgt | Age | Int | Pts |
|---|---|---|---|---|---|---|
| Keith DeLong | LB | 6'2" | 235 | 22 | 1 | |
| Jim Fahnhorst | LB | 6'4" | 230 | 30 | | |
| Antonio Goss | LB | 6'4" | 228 | 23 | | |
| Charles Haley | LB-DE | 6'5" | 230 | 25 | | 6 |
| Steve Hendrickson (to DAL) | LB | 6' | 245 | 23 | | |
| Matt Millen | LB | 6'2" | 245 | 31 | 1 | |
| Bill Romanowski | LB | 6'4" | 231 | 23 | 1 | |
| Keena Turner | LB | 6'2" | 222 | 30 | 1 | |
| Michael Walter | LB | 6'3" | 238 | 28 | | |
| Chet Brooks | DB | 5'11" | 191 | 23 | 3 | |
| Jeff Fuller | DB | 6'2" | 216 | 27 | | |
| Don Griffin | DB | 6' | 176 | 25 | 2 | |
| Tom Holmoe | DB | 6'2" | 195 | 29 | 1 | |
| Johnny Jackson | DB | 6'1" | 204 | 22 | 2 | 6 |
| Ronnie Lott | DB | 6' | 200 | 30 | 5 | |
| Tim McKyer | DB | 6' | 174 | 25 | 1 | |
| Darryl Pollard | DB | 5'11" | 187 | 24 | 1 | |
| Mike Richardson | DB | 6' | 188 | 28 | | |
| Eric Wright | DB | 6'1" | 185 | 30 | 2 | |

Riki Ellison — Knee Injury
Chris Washington — Broken Leg

| Use Name | Pos. | Hgt | Wgt | Age | Int | Pts |
|---|---|---|---|---|---|---|
| Steve Bono | QB | 6'4" | 215 | 27 | | |
| Joe Montana | QB | 6'2" | 195 | 33 | | 18 |
| Steve Young | QB | 6'2" | 200 | 27 | | 12 |
| Roger Craig | HB-FB | 6' | 224 | 29 | | 42 |
| Terrence Flagler | HB | 6' | 200 | 24 | | 6 |
| Spencer Tillman | HB | 5'11" | 206 | 25 | | |
| Keith Henderson | FB | 6'1" | 220 | 23 | | 6 |
| Tom Rathman | FB | 6'1" | 232 | 26 | | 12 |
| Harry Sydney | FB | 6' | 217 | 30 | | |
| Mike Barber | WR | 5'10" | 172 | 22 | | |
| Terry Greer | WR | 6'1" | 192 | 31 | | |
| Jerry Rice | WR | 6'2" | 200 | 26 | | 102 |
| John Taylor | WR | 6'1" | 185 | 27 | | 60 |
| Mike Wilson | WR | 6'3" | 215 | 30 | | 6 |
| Brent Jones | TE | 6'4" | 230 | 26 | | 24 |
| Wesley Walls | TE | 6'5" | 246 | 23 | | 6 |
| Jamie Williams | TE | 6'4" | 245 | 29 | | |
| Mike Cofer | K | 6'1" | 190 | 25 | | 136 |
| Barry Helton | K | 6'3" | 205 | 24 | | |

Mike Sherrard — Leg Injury (played in playoffs)

## LOS ANGELES RAMS 11-5 John Robinson

| Scores of Each Game | | |
|---|---|---|
| 31 | Atlanta | 21 |
| 31 | INDIANAPOLIS | 17 |
| 41 | GREEN BAY | 38 |
| 13 | San Francisco | 12 |
| 26 | ATLANTA | 14 |
| 20 | Buffalo | 23 |
| 21 | NEW ORLEANS | 40 |
| 10 | Chicago | 20 |
| 21 | Minnesota | * 23 |
| 31 | N.Y. GIANTS | 10 |
| 37 | PHOENIX | 14 |
| 20 | New Orleans | * 17 |
| 35 | Dallas | 31 |
| 27 | SAN FRANCISCO | 30 |
| 38 | N.Y. JETS | 14 |
| 24 | New England | 20 |

| Use Name | Pos. | Hgt | Wgt | Age | Int | Pts |
|---|---|---|---|---|---|---|
| Robert Cox | OT | 6'5" | 270 | 25 | | |
| Irv Pankey | OT | 6'4" | 267 | 31 | | |
| Jackie Slater | OT | 6'4" | 275 | 35 | | |
| Kurt Becker | OG | 6'5" | 280 | 29 | | |
| Duval Love | OG | 6'3" | 280 | 26 | | |
| Tom Newberry | OG | 6'2" | 279 | 26 | | |
| Tony Slaton | C | 6'3" | 265 | 28 | | |
| Doug Smith | C | 6'3" | 260 | 32 | | |
| Shawn Miller | DT-NT-DE | 6'4" | 255 | 28 | 1 | |
| Doug Reed | DE-DT | 6'3" | 250 | 29 | | |
| Bill Hawkins | DT | 6'6" | 268 | 23 | | |
| Mark Piel | DT | 6'4" | 263 | 23 | | |
| Sean Smith (from DAL, TB) | DT-DE | 6'4" | 275 | 24 | | 2 |
| Alvin Wright | NT-DE-DT | 6'2" | 256 | 28 | | |

| Use Name | Pos. | Hgt | Wgt | Age | Int | Pts |
|---|---|---|---|---|---|---|
| George Bethune | LB | 6'4" | 240 | 22 | | |
| Richard Brown | LB | 6'3" | 240 | 23 | | |
| Brett Faryniarz | LB | 6'3" | 225 | 24 | | |
| Kevin Greene | LB-DE | 6'3" | 238 | 27 | | |
| Mark Jerue | LB | 6'3" | 234 | 29 | | |
| Larry Kelm | LB | 6'4" | 226 | 24 | | |
| Mike McDonald | LB | 6'1" | 235 | 31 | | |
| Mark Messner | LB | 6'2" | 256 | 23 | | |
| Mel Owens | LB | 6'2" | 224 | 30 | 1 | |
| Brian Smith | LB | 6'6" | 242 | 23 | | |
| Frank Stams | LB | 6'2" | 240 | 24 | 1 | |
| Fred Strickland | LB | 6'2" | 224 | 23 | 2 | |
| Mike Wilcher | LB | 6'3" | 240 | 29 | 1 | |
| Jerry Gray | DB | 6' | 185 | 26 | 6 | 6 |
| Darryl Henley | DB | 5'9" | 170 | 22 | 1 | |
| Clifford Hicks | DB | 5'10" | 188 | 25 | 2 | |
| LeRoy Irvin | DB | 5'11" | 184 | 31 | 3 | |
| Alfred Jackson | DB | 6' | 177 | 22 | | |
| Anthony Newman | DB | 6' | 199 | 23 | | |
| Vince Newsome | DB | 6'1" | 183 | 28 | 1 | 6 |
| Michael Stewart | DB | 5'11" | 195 | 24 | 2 | 6 |
| James Washington | DB | 6'1" | 191 | 24 | | |

| Use Name | Pos. | Hgt | Wgt | Age | Int | Pts |
|---|---|---|---|---|---|---|
| Steve Dils | QB | 6'1" | 191 | 33 | | |
| Jim Everett | QB | 6'5" | 212 | 26 | | 6 |
| Mark Herrmann | QB | 6'4" | 186 | 30 | | |
| Greg Bell | HB | 5'10" | 210 | 27 | | 90 |
| Cleveland Gary | HB | 6' | 226 | 23 | | 6 |
| Gaston Green | HB | 5'10" | 189 | 23 | | |
| Robert Delpino | FB | 6' | 205 | 23 | | 12 |
| Mel Farr Jr. | FB | 6' | 223 | 23 | | |
| Buford McGee | FB | 6' | 206 | 29 | | 30 |
| Willie Anderson | WR | 6' | 169 | 24 | | 30 |
| Ron Brown | WR | 5'11" | 181 | 28 | | 6 |
| Aaron Cox | WR | 5'9" | 174 | 24 | | 18 |
| Henry Ellard | WR | 5'11" | 175 | 28 | | 48 |
| Pat Carter | TE | 6'4" | 250 | 23 | | |
| Pete Holohan | TE | 6'4" | 232 | 30 | | 12 |
| Damone Johnson | TE | 6'4" | 230 | 27 | | 30 |
| Dale Hatcher | K | 6'2" | 211 | 26 | | |
| Mike Lansford | K | 6' | 183 | 31 | | 120 |

## NEW ORLEANS SAINTS 9-7 Jim Mora

| Scores of Each Game | | |
|---|---|---|
| 28 | DALLAS | 0 |
| 34 | Green Bay | 35 |
| 10 | Tampa Bay | 20 |
| 14 | WASHINGTON | 16 |
| 20 | SAN FRANCISCO | 24 |
| 29 | N.Y. JETS | 14 |
| 40 | L.A. Rams | 21 |
| 20 | ATLANTA | 13 |
| 13 | San Francisco | 31 |
| 28 | New England | 24 |
| 26 | Atlanta | 17 |
| 17 | L.A. RAMS | * 20 |
| 14 | Detroit | 21 |
| 22 | Buffalo | 19 |
| 30 | PHILADELPHIA | 20 |
| 41 | INDIANAPOLIS | 6 |

| Use Name | Pos. | Hgt | Wgt | Age | Int | Pts |
|---|---|---|---|---|---|---|
| Stan Brock | OT | 6'6" | 290 | 31 | | |
| Glenn Derby | OT | 6'6" | 290 | 25 | | |
| Jim Dombrowski | OT-OG | 6'5" | 298 | 26 | | |
| Kevin Haverdink | OT | 6'5" | 285 | 23 | | |
| Jeff Walker | OT | 6'4" | 295 | 26 | | |
| Brad Edelman | OG | 6'6" | 270 | 28 | | |
| Steve Trapilo | OG | 6'5" | 295 | 24 | | |
| Joel Hilgenberg | C-OG | 6'3" | 252 | 26 | | |
| Steve Korte | C | 6'2" | 260 | 29 | | |
| Doug Marrone | C-OT | 6'5" | 269 | 25 | | |
| James Geathers | DE | 6'7" | 290 | 29 | | |
| Wayne Martin | DE | 6'5" | 275 | 23 | | |
| Michael Simmons | DE | 6'4" | 269 | 23 | | |
| Frank Warren | DE | 6'4" | 290 | 29 | | 2 |
| Patrick Swoopes | NT | 6'4" | 280 | 25 | | |
| Jim Wilks | NT-DE | 6'5" | 266 | 31 | | |

| Use Name | Pos. | Hgt | Wgt | Age | Int | Pts |
|---|---|---|---|---|---|---|
| Brian Forde | LB | 6'2" | 225 | 25 | | 2 |
| James Haynes | LB | 6'2" | 233 | 29 | | |
| Rickey Jackson | LB | 6'2" | 243 | 31 | | |
| Vaughan Johnson | LB | 6'3" | 235 | 27 | | |
| Walter Johnson | LB | 6' | 240 | 25 | | |
| Joe Kohlbrand | LB | 6'4" | 242 | 26 | | |
| Sam Mills | LB | 5'9" | 225 | 30 | | |
| Pat Swilling | LB | 6'3" | 242 | 24 | 1 | |
| Gene Atkins | DB | 6'1" | 200 | 25 | 1 | |
| Toi Cook | DB | 5'11" | 188 | 24 | 3 | 6 |
| Antonio Gibson | DB | 6'3" | 204 | 27 | | |
| Milton Mack | DB | 5'11" | 182 | 25 | 2 | |
| Robert Massey | DB | 5'10" | 182 | 22 | 5 | |
| Brett Maxie | DB | 6'2" | 194 | 27 | 3 | 6 |
| Michael Mayes | DB | 5'10" | 182 | 23 | | |
| Calvin Nicholson | DB | 5'9" | 183 | 22 | | |
| Kim Phillips | DB | 5'9" | 188 | 21 | | |
| Bennie Thompson | DB | 6' | 200 | 26 | | |
| Dave Waymer | DB | 6'1" | 188 | 31 | 6 | |

Alvin Toles — Knee Injury

| Use Name | Pos. | Hgt | Wgt | Age | Int | Pts |
|---|---|---|---|---|---|---|
| John Fourcade | QB | 6'1" | 208 | 28 | | 6 |
| Bobby Hebert | QB | 6'4" | 215 | 29 | | |
| Dave Wilson | QB | 6'3" | 206 | 30 | | |
| Paul Frazier | HB | 5'8" | 188 | 21 | | 6 |
| Dalton Hilliard | HB | 5'8" | 204 | 25 | | 108 |
| Craig Heyward | FB | 5'11" | 260 | 22 | | 6 |
| Buford Jordan | FB | 6' | 223 | 27 | | 18 |
| Bobby Morse | FB | 5'10" | 213 | 22 | | 6 |
| Rod Harris | WR | 5'10" | 183 | 22 | | |
| Lonzell Hill | WR | 6' | 189 | 23 | | 24 |
| Undra Johnson (to ATL) | WR | 5'9" | 199 | 23 | | |
| Mike Jones | WR | 5'11" | 180 | 29 | | |
| Eric Martin | WR | 6'1" | 207 | 27 | | 48 |
| Brett Perriman | WR | 5'9" | 175 | 23 | | |
| Floyd Turner | WR | 5'11" | 188 | 23 | | 6 |
| Hoby Brenner | TE | 6'4" | 240 | 30 | | 24 |
| Greg Scales | TE | 6'4" | 253 | 23 | | 6 |
| John Tice | TE | 6'5" | 249 | 29 | | 6 |
| Morten Andersen | K | 6'2" | 221 | 29 | | 104 |
| Tommy Barnhardt | K | 6'3" | 205 | 26 | | |
| George Winslow | K | 6'4" | 201 | 26 | | |

Rueben Mayes — Achilles' Tendon Injury

## ATLANTA FALCONS 3-13 Marion Campbell (3-9), Jim Hanifan (0-4)

| Scores of Each Game | | |
|---|---|---|
| 21 | L.A. RAMS | 31 |
| 27 | DALLAS | 21 |
| 9 | Indianapolis | 13 |
| 21 | Green Bay (Mil.) | 23 |
| 14 | L.A. Rams | 26 |
| 16 | NEW ENGLAND | 15 |
| 20 | Phoenix | 34 |
| 13 | New Orleans | 20 |
| 30 | BUFFALO | 28 |
| 3 | San Francisco | 45 |
| 17 | NEW ORLEANS | 26 |
| 7 | N.Y. Jets | 27 |
| 10 | SAN FRANCISCO | 23 |
| 17 | Minnesota | 43 |
| 30 | WASHINGTON | 31 |
| 24 | DETROIT | 31 |

| Use Name | Pos. | Hgt | Wgt | Age | Int | Pts |
|---|---|---|---|---|---|---|
| Houston Hoover | OT | 6'2" | 285 | 24 | | |
| John Hunter | OT | 6'8" | 296 | 24 | | |
| Mike Kenn | OT | 6'7" | 277 | 33 | | |
| * Ralph Norwood | OT | 6'7" | 285 | 23 | | |
| Stan Clayton | OG-OT | 6'3" | 265 | 24 | | |
| Bill Fralic | OG | 6'5" | 280 | 26 | | |
| Wayne Radloff | OG | 6'5" | 277 | 28 | | |
| Tommy Robison | OG | 6'4" | 290 | 27 | | |
| Guy Bingham | C-OG | 6'3" | 260 | 31 | | |
| Jamie Dukes | C | 6'1" | 278 | 25 | | |
| Rick Bryan | DE | 6'4" | 265 | 27 | | |
| Mike Gann | DE | 6'5" | 275 | 25 | | |
| Curtis Maxey | DE-DT | 6'3" | 298 | 24 | | |
| Malcolm Taylor | DE | 6'6" | 280 | 29 | | |
| Ben Thomas | DE | 6'4" | 275 | 28 | | |
| Tony Bowick | NT | 6'2" | 265 | 22 | | |
| Tony Casillas | NT | 6'3" | 280 | 25 | | |

* died Nov. 24, 1989 in automobile accident

John Scully — Holdout

| Use Name | Pos. | Hgt | Wgt | Age | Int | Pts |
|---|---|---|---|---|---|---|
| Aundray Bruce | LB | 6'5" | 245 | 23 | 1 | |
| Marcus Cotton | LB | 6'3" | 225 | 23 | | |
| Tim Green | LB | 6'2" | 245 | 25 | | |
| John Rade | LB | 6'1" | 240 | 29 | | |
| Michael Reid | LB | 6'2" | 226 | 25 | | |
| Galand Thaxton | LB | 6'1" | 242 | 24 | | |
| Jessie Tuggle | LB | 5'11" | 225 | 24 | | |
| Joel Williams | LB | 6'1" | 227 | 32 | | |
| Bobby Butler | DB | 5'11" | 175 | 30 | | 6 |
| Scott Case | DB | 6' | 178 | 27 | 2 | |
| Evan Cooper | DB | 5'11" | 194 | 27 | 4 | |
| Charles Dimry | DB | 6' | 175 | 23 | 2 | |
| Tim Gordon | DB | 6' | 188 | 24 | 4 | |
| Brian Jordan | DB | 5'11" | 202 | 22 | | |
| Robert Moore | DB | 5'11" | 190 | 25 | | |
| Deion Sanders | DB | 6' | 187 | 22 | 5 | 6 |
| Elbert Shelley | DB | 5'11" | 180 | 24 | 1 | |
| Tony Zackery | DB | 6'2" | 195 | 22 | 1 | |

| Use Name | Pos. | Hgt | Wgt | Age | Int | Pts |
|---|---|---|---|---|---|---|
| Scott Campbell | QB | 6' | 195 | 27 | | |
| Hugh Millen | QB | 6'5" | 216 | 25 | | |
| Chris Miller | QB | 6'2" | 195 | 23 | | 3 |
| Kenny Flowers | HB | 6' | 210 | 25 | | 6 |
| Keith Jones | HB-FB | 6'1" | 210 | 23 | | 36 |
| Gene Lang | HB | 5'10" | 206 | 27 | | 12 |
| James Primus | HB | 5'11" | 196 | 25 | | |
| John Settle | HB-FB | 5'9" | 207 | 24 | | 30 |
| Greg Paterra | FB | 5'11" | 211 | 22 | | |
| Stacey Bailey | WR | 6' | 157 | 29 | | |
| Shawn Collins | WR | 6'2" | 207 | 22 | | 18 |
| Floyd Dixon | WR | 5'9" | 170 | 25 | | 12 |
| Michael Haynes | WR | 6' | 180 | 23 | | 24 |
| George Thomas | WR | 5'9" | 169 | 25 | | |
| * Brad Beckman | TE | 6'3" | 240 | 24 | | 6 |
| Ron Heller | TE | 6'3" | 238 | 25 | | 6 |
| Gary Wilkins | TE | 6'1" | 235 | 25 | | 18 |
| Scott Fulhage | K | 5'11" | 193 | 27 | | |
| Paul McFadden | K | 5'11" | 166 | 27 | | 63 |

Rick Donnelly — Back Injury
Alex Higdon — Knee Injury

* died Dec. 18, 1989 in autmobile accident

## SAN FRANCISCO 49ERS

### RUSHING

| Last Name | No. | Yds | Avg | TD |
|---|---|---|---|---|
| Craig | 271 | 1054 | 3.9 | 6 |
| Rathman | 79 | 305 | 3.9 | 1 |
| Montana | 49 | 227 | 4.6 | 3 |
| Flagler | 33 | 129 | 3.9 | 1 |
| Young | 38 | 126 | 3.3 | 2 |
| Sydney | 9 | 56 | 6.2 | 0 |
| Rice | 5 | 33 | 6.6 | 0 |
| Henderson | 7 | 30 | 4.3 | 1 |
| Taylor | 1 | 6 | 6.0 | 0 |
| Helton | 1 | 0 | 0.0 | 0 |

### RECEIVING

| Last Name | No. | Yds | Avg | TD |
|---|---|---|---|---|
| Rice | 82 | 1483 | 18.1 | 17 |
| Rathman | 73 | 616 | 8.4 | 1 |
| Taylor | 60 | 1077 | 18.0 | 10 |
| Craig | 49 | 473 | 9.7 | 1 |
| Jones | 40 | 500 | 12.5 | 4 |
| Wilson | 9 | 103 | 11.4 | 1 |
| Sydney | 9 | 71 | 7.9 | 0 |
| Flagler | 6 | 51 | 8.5 | 0 |
| Walls | 4 | 16 | 4.0 | 1 |
| Henderson | 3 | 130 | 43.3 | 0 |
| Williams | 3 | 38 | 12.7 | 0 |
| Greer | 1 | 26 | 26.0 | 0 |

### PUNT RETURNS

| Last Name | No. | Yds | Avg | TD |
|---|---|---|---|---|
| Taylor | 36 | 417 | 11.6 | 0 |
| Griffin | 1 | 9 | 9.0 | 0 |
| Greer | 1 | 3 | 3.0 | 0 |
| Romanowski | 1 | 0 | 0.0 | 0 |

### KICKOFF RETURNS

| Last Name | No. | Yds | Avg | TD |
|---|---|---|---|---|
| Flagler | 32 | 643 | 20.1 | 0 |
| Tillman | 10 | 206 | 20.6 | 0 |
| Sydney | 3 | 16 | 5.3 | 0 |
| Taylor | 2 | 51 | 25.5 | 0 |
| Henderson | 2 | 21 | 10.5 | 0 |
| Greer | 1 | 17 | 17.0 | 0 |
| Jackson | 1 | 0 | 0.0 | 0 |

### PASSING

| Last Name | Att | Cmp | % | Yds | Yd/Att | TD | Int— | % | RK |
|---|---|---|---|---|---|---|---|---|---|
| Montana | 386 | 271 | 70.2 | 3521 | 9.12 | 28 | 8— | 2.1 | 1 |
| Young | 92 | 64 | 69.6 | 1001 | 10.88 | 8 | 3— | 3.3 | |
| Bono | 5 | 4 | 80.0 | 62 | 12.40 | 1 | 0— | 0.0 | |

### PUNTING

| Last Name | No. | Avg. |
|---|---|---|
| Helton | 56 | 39.8 |

### KICKING

| Last Name | XP | ATT | % | FG | ATT | % |
|---|---|---|---|---|---|---|
| Cofer | 49 | 51 | 96 | 29 | 36 | 81 |

## LOS ANGELES RAMS

### RUSHING

| Last Name | No. | Yds | Avg | TD |
|---|---|---|---|---|
| Bell | 272 | 1137 | 4.2 | 15 |
| Delpino | 78 | 368 | 4.7 | 1 |
| Gary | 37 | 163 | 4.4 | 1 |
| McGee | 21 | 99 | 4.7 | 1 |
| Green | 26 | 73 | 2.8 | 0 |
| Everett | 25 | 31 | 1.2 | 1 |
| Ro. Brown | 6 | 27 | 4.5 | 0 |
| Ellard | 2 | 10 | 5.0 | 0 |
| Holohan | 1 | 3 | 3.0 | 0 |
| Hatcher | 1 | 0 | 0.0 | 0 |
| Anderson | 1 | -1 | -1.0 | 0 |
| Herrmann | 2 | -1 | -0.5 | 0 |

### RECEIVING

| Last Name | No. | Yds | Avg | TD |
|---|---|---|---|---|
| Ellard | 70 | 1382 | 19.7 | 8 |
| Holohan | 51 | 510 | 10.0 | 2 |
| Anderson | 44 | 1146 | 26.0 | 5 |
| McGee | 37 | 303 | 8.2 | 4 |
| Delpino | 34 | 334 | 9.8 | 1 |
| Johnson | 25 | 148 | 5.9 | 5 |
| A. Cox | 20 | 340 | 17.0 | 3 |
| Bell | 19 | 85 | 4.5 | 0 |
| Ro. Brown | 5 | 113 | 22.6 | 1 |
| Gary | 2 | 13 | 6.5 | 0 |
| Green | 1 | -5 | -5.0 | 0 |

### PUNT RETURNS

| Last Name | No. | Yds | Avg | TD |
|---|---|---|---|---|
| Henley | 29 | 273 | 9.4 | 0 |
| Hicks | 24 | 39 | 9.8 | 0 |
| Ellard | 2 | 20 | 10.0 | 0 |
| Irvin | 0 | 0 | 0.0 | 0 |

### KICKOFF RETURNS

| Last Name | No. | Yds | Avg | TD |
|---|---|---|---|---|
| Ro. Brown | 47 | 968 | 20.6 | 0 |
| Delpino | 17 | 334 | 19.6 | 0 |
| McDonald | 2 | 22 | 11.0 | 0 |
| Gary | 1 | 4 | 4.0 | 0 |

### PASSING

| Last Name | Att | Cmp | % | Yds | Yd/Att | TD | Int— | % | RK |
|---|---|---|---|---|---|---|---|---|---|
| Everett | 518 | 304 | 58.7 | 4310 | 8.32 | 29 | 17— | 3.3 | 2 |
| Herrmann | 5 | 4 | 80.0 | 59 | 11.80 | 0 | 1— | 20.0 | |

### PUNTING

| Last Name | No. | Avg. |
|---|---|---|
| Hatcher | 74 | 38.3 |

### KICKING

| Last Name | XP | ATT | % | FG | ATT | % |
|---|---|---|---|---|---|---|
| Lansford | 51 | 51 | 100 | 23 | 30 | 77 |

## NEW ORLEANS SAINTS

### RUSHING

| Last Name | No. | Yds | Avg | TD |
|---|---|---|---|---|
| Hilliard | 344 | 1262 | 3.7 | 13 |
| Heyward | 49 | 183 | 3.7 | 1 |
| Jordan | 38 | 179 | 4.7 | 3 |
| Frazier | 25 | 112 | 4.5 | 1 |
| Fourcade | 14 | 91 | 6.5 | 1 |
| Hebert | 25 | 87 | 3.5 | 0 |
| Morse | 2 | 43 | 21.5 | 0 |
| Turner | 2 | 8 | 4.0 | 0 |
| Winslow | 1 | 0 | 0.0 | 0 |
| Hill | 1 | -7 | -7.0 | 0 |
| Perriman | 1 | -10 | -10.0 | 0 |

### RECEIVING

| Last Name | No. | Yds | Avg | TD |
|---|---|---|---|---|
| Martin | 68 | 1090 | 16.0 | 8 |
| Hilliard | 52 | 514 | 9.9 | 5 |
| Hill | 48 | 636 | 13.3 | 4 |
| Brenner | 34 | 398 | 11.7 | 4 |
| Turner | 22 | 279 | 12.7 | 1 |
| Perriman | 20 | 356 | 17.8 | 0 |
| Heyward | 13 | 69 | 5.3 | 0 |
| Tice | 9 | 98 | 10.9 | 1 |
| Scales | 8 | 89 | 11.1 | 0 |
| Jordan | 4 | 53 | 13.3 | 0 |
| Shepard | 2 | 36 | 18.0 | 0 |
| Cook | 1 | 8 | 8.0 | 0 |

### PUNT RETURNS

| Last Name | No. | Yds | Avg | TD |
|---|---|---|---|---|
| Harris | 27 | 196 | 7.3 | 0 |
| Morse | 10 | 29 | 2.9 | 0 |
| Hill | 7 | 41 | 5.9 | 0 |
| Perriman | 1 | 10 | 10.0 | 0 |
| Turner | 1 | 7 | 7.0 | 0 |
| Massey | 0 | 54 | — | 0 |

### KICKOFF RETURNS

| Last Name | No. | Yds | Avg | TD |
|---|---|---|---|---|
| Harris | 19 | 378 | 19.9 | 0 |
| Atkins | 12 | 245 | 20.4 | 0 |
| Morse | 10 | 278 | 27.8 | 1 |
| Frazier | 8 | 157 | 19.6 | 0 |
| U. Johnson | 2 | 34 | 17.0 | 0 |
| Phillips | 1 | 24 | 24.0 | 0 |
| Hilliard | 1 | 20 | 20.0 | 0 |
| Hill | 1 | 13 | 13.0 | 0 |
| Scales | 1 | 0 | 0.0 | 0 |

### PASSING

| Last Name | Att | Cmp | % | Yds | Yd/Att | TD | Int— | % | RK |
|---|---|---|---|---|---|---|---|---|---|
| Hebert | 353 | 222 | 62.9 | 2686 | 7.61 | 15 | 15— | 4.2 | 4 |
| Fourcade | 107 | 61 | 57.0 | 930 | 8.69 | 7 | 4— | 3.7 | |
| Hilliard | 1 | 1 | 100.0 | 35 | 35.00 | 1 | 0— | 0.0 | |

### PUNTING

| Last Name | No. | Avg. |
|---|---|---|
| Barnhardt | 55 | 39.6 |
| Winslow | 16 | 37.2 |

### KICKING

| Last Name | XP | ATT | % | FG | ATT | % |
|---|---|---|---|---|---|---|
| Andersen | 44 | 45 | 98 | 20 | 29 | 69 |

## ATLANTA FALCONS

### RUSHING

| Last Name | No. | Yds | Avg | TD |
|---|---|---|---|---|
| Settle | 179 | 689 | 3.8 | 3 |
| Jones | 52 | 202 | 3.9 | 6 |
| Lang | 47 | 176 | 3.7 | 1 |
| Haynes | 4 | 35 | 8.8 | 0 |
| Paterra | 9 | 32 | 3.6 | 0 |
| Flowers | 13 | 24 | 1.8 | 1 |
| Miller | 10 | 20 | 2.0 | 0 |
| Fulhage | 1 | 0 | 0.0 | 0 |
| Millen | 1 | 0 | 0.0 | 0 |
| Dixon | 2 | -23 | -11.5 | 0 |

### RECEIVING

| Last Name | No. | Yds | Avg | TD |
|---|---|---|---|---|
| Collins | 58 | 862 | 14.9 | 3 |
| Jones | 41 | 396 | 9.7 | 0 |
| Haynes | 40 | 681 | 17.0 | 4 |
| Lang | 39 | 436 | 11.2 | 1 |
| Settle | 39 | 316 | 8.1 | 2 |
| Heller | 33 | 324 | 9.8 | 1 |
| Dixon | 25 | 357 | 14.3 | 2 |
| Beckman | 11 | 102 | 9.3 | 1 |
| Wilkins | 8 | 179 | 22.4 | 3 |
| Bailey | 8 | 170 | 21.3 | 0 |
| Paterra | 5 | 42 | 8.4 | 0 |
| G. Thomas | 4 | 46 | 11.5 | 0 |
| Sanders | 1 | -8 | -8.0 | 0 |

### PUNT RETURNS

| Last Name | No. | Yds | Avg | TD |
|---|---|---|---|---|
| Sanders | 28 | 307 | 11.0 | 1 |
| Jordan | 4 | 34 | 8.5 | 0 |

### KICKOFF RETURNS

| Last Name | No. | Yds | Avg | TD |
|---|---|---|---|---|
| Sanders | 35 | 725 | 20.7 | 0 |
| Jones | 23 | 440 | 19.1 | 0 |
| Paterra | 8 | 129 | 16.1 | 0 |
| G. Thomas | 7 | 142 | 20.3 | 0 |
| Jordan | 3 | 27 | 9.0 | 0 |
| Beckman | 2 | 15 | 7.5 | 0 |
| Primus | 1 | 16 | 16.0 | 0 |
| Bruce | 1 | 15 | 15.0 | 0 |

### PASSING

| Last Name | Att | Cmp | % | Yds | Yd/Att | TD | Int— | % | RK |
|---|---|---|---|---|---|---|---|---|---|
| Miller | 526 | 280 | 53.2 | 3459 | 6.58 | 16 | 10— | 1.9 | 7 |
| Millen | 50 | 31 | 62.0 | 432 | 8.64 | 1 | 2— | 4.0 | |
| Fulhage | 1 | 1 | 100.0 | 12 | 12.00 | 0 | 0— | 0.0 | |
| Jones | 1 | 0 | 0.0 | 0 | 0.00 | 0 | 0— | 0.0 | |

### PUNTING

| Last Name | No. | Avg. |
|---|---|---|
| Fulhage | 85 | 40.8 |

### KICKING

| Last Name | XP | ATT | % | FG | ATT | % |
|---|---|---|---|---|---|---|
| McFadden | 18 | 18 | 100 | 15 | 20 | 75 |
| Miller | 0 | 0 | 0 | 1 | 1 | 100 |

# 1989 A.F.C. A Question of Strength or Weakness

Although it took until the final week of the regular season for the N.F.C. to finally forge ahead of the A.F.C. in victories in games between the two conferences (for only the second time since 1970), the A.F.C. was general perceived as the weaker group of teams. Some commentators even went as far as to urge a new playoff format leading to the Super Bowl, arguing that at least five N.F.C. teams were stronger than the best A.F.C. club.

Serious analysts argued with some cause that the N.F.C. had stronger defenses, at least with its better teams. This, they said, gave the top National Conference teams a distinct advantage in "chips-down" games. Recent Super Bowls were cited as proof.

A.F.C. fans could admit their conference had not 49ers but that it didn't have the Cowboys and Falcons, either. Eleven of the 14 A.F.C. teams were in the playoff hunt up to the final week. If there were no super teams, there was a balance of power that was the very soul of parity. None of the American Conference division winners had records equal to their counterparts in the N.F.C.. But, whether this denoted strength or weakness was a matter of opinion.

## EASTERN DIVISION

**Buffalo Bills** — It was a rough season in Buffalo. All-Pro linebackers Shane Conlan and Cornelius Bennett missed time with injuries, cornerback Derrick Burroughs was diagnosed to have a career-ending spinal condition in September, and quarterback Jim Kelly was knocked out for three games. Frank Reich, a virtually unknown backup, rode to Kelly's rescue, leading the Bills to three victories, and it wasn't long before Buffalo fans were calling for him, not Kelly. But the defense wasn't up to its 1988 level. Distractions included Kelly's criticism of his teammates, the teammates criticism of Kelly, fan criticism of some of the players' attitudes, and even a fight between two assistant coaches. Almost lost in the mess were outstanding seasons by running back Thurman Thomas and wide receiver Andre Reed, and that the Bills repeated as division champs for the first time since the 1960s.

**Indianapolis Colts** — Like a bad rerun, the Colts lost their starting quarterback early in the season for the fourth straight year when Chris Chandler tore up his knee in Game Three. Jack Trudeau was OK as the replacement, but he played hurt, and having Eric Dickerson slowed all season with a hamstring injury didn't help, either. Despite his nagging injury, Dickerson became the first player to top 1,000 yards rushing in seven consecutive seasons, finishing with 1,311 yards. Bill Brooks and Andre Rison gave Trudeau a pair of dangerous receivers, but the much-balleyhooed offensive line didn't live up to expectations. DE Jon Hand, with 10 sacks, and linebackers Duane Bickett and Jeff Herrod were the strengths of an up-and-down defense.

**Miami Dolphins** — An inept running game and mediocre defense kept the Dolphins out of the playoffs for the fourth straight year, their longest dry spell since Don Shula took over as coach in 1970. No. 1 draft pick Sammie Smith showed promise as a runner but was obviously hurt by his training camp holdout and a so-so offensive line. The Dolphins finished 27th in rushing and 24th in defense to waste the usual aerial fireworks by Dan Marino. Plagued by an assortment of injuries all season, Marino still came within three yards of throwing for 4,000. Miami seemed headed for the playoffs with a 7-4 mark after 11 games, but they blew a 14-0 lead to the Steelers at home and went on to lose four of their last five games. Owner Joe Robbie died Jan. 7.

**New England Patriots** — The Patriots lost three defensive starters for the year in the final preseason game — linebacker Andre Tippett, defensive end Garin Veris and cornerback Ronnie Lippett. That crippled the defense. Wide receiver Stanely Morgan missed six games with a broken leg and Irving Fryar was out five with assorted injuries, but the offense never really jelled, as coach Raymond Berry started four different quarterbacks, with castoff Marc Wilson the apparent final choice by default. Second-year running back John Stephens didn't play up to his rookie standard, but the ineptitude of the passing game allowed opponents to concentrate on stopping his runs. Management fired Berry in February when he balked at hiring offensive and defensive coordinators.

New coach Rod Rust inherited a mending squad, but one that still lacked a proven quarterback.

**New York Jets** — The Jets fell apart in 1989; only the inept Cowboys presented a weaker aggregation to suffering fans. No single area could be blamed for the Jets' disaster because there was enough culpability for all. However, a string of holdouts, spawned by management's hardball position, got the team off and limping on the wrong foot. The young secondary was again victimized by a poor pass rush. Star wide receiver Al Toon played only six full games. And coach Joe Walton played his annual game of musical chairs at quarterback, even starting rookie Kyle Mackey at one point. Mostly, though, the Jets didn't have the horses. At the end of the season, the front office underwent a long-needed house cleaning, with Dick Steinberg being brought in from New England as GM. His first move was to fire Walton.

## CENTRAL DIVISION

**Cleveland Browns** — New coach Bud Carson brought the Browns their fifth division championship of the decade, but it took close wins over Minnesota and Houston in the final two games to do the trick. The offense never hit on all cylinders all season. Quarterback Bernie Kosar's arm wasn't sound after an early-season injury, causing much speculation as to how permanent was the condition. Fullback Kevin Mack missed the first 12 games after a drug arrest led to a suspension and prison sentence. The offensive line seldom played top quality. Rookie running back Eric Metcalf was an early sensation with his tricky, twisting runs, but even he tailed off late. A couple of new stars emerged on the defense in defensive tackle Michael Dean Perry and free safety Thane Gash. Added to linebackers Clay Matthews and Mike Johnson, cornerback Frank Minnifield and strong safety Felix Wright, they made a strong unit.

**Houston Oilers** — The Oilers were favored to win the division title going in and needed only a victory in either of their last two games to earn their first undisputed Central crown. Instead, the suffered the worst defeat in their history to Cincinnati 61-7, and then booted the finale to Cleveland with 39 seconds left. Then they were knocked out of the playoffs in overtime by the Steelers. The losses cost coach Jerry Glanville his job (although officially he resigned). Glanville was faulted for failure to settle on Alonzo Highsmith, Mike Rozier, Allen Pinkett or Lorenzo White as the main running threat, and for the team's often mindless penalties — a team record 148. But Glanville couldn't personally rush opposing passers, something his team lacked. Nor could he cover in the secondary, where the Oilers were beaten all season despite high marks for rookie Bubba McDowell. Jack Pardee left the University of Houston to replace Glanville.

**Pittsburgh Steelers** — After the Steelers lost their first two games by a combined score of 92-10, they were the league's laughing stock. Coach Chuck Noll held together a roster that was one-fourth rookies, and Pittsburgh roared down the stretch to win five of their last six games and make the playoffs. Heralded rookie Tim Worley was a long holdout and untracked slowly, but he rushed for 417 yards in the last five games. Fullback Merril Hoge was steady once he recovered from an early rib injury and the offensive line regained its health. Quarterback Bubby Brister was unspectacular in passing statistics but a major plus in leadership, and wide receiver Louis Lipps had another fine year. The strength of the team was a gritty defense that came back from the early blowouts to hang tough when it had to.

**Cincinnati Bengals** — After coming within 34 seconds of a Super Bowl victory, the Bengals had high hopes for 1989 — until fullback Ickey Woods' season ended with a knee injury in Game Two. Cincinnati got to 4-1, then blew early leads to lose two straight. They staggered home as a model of inconsistency. Veteran breakaway runner James Brooks was a sensation, posting a league-high 5.6-yard rushing average, but without Woods, the Bengals couldn't run between the tackles. Wide receiver Tim McGee joined Eddie Brown as a solid deep threat for Boomer Esiason's passes, but the team that scored 61 points against Houston was held five times under 15. Although oversized strong safety

**OFFENSE**

| | BUFF | CIN | CLEV | DEN | HOU | IND | K.C. | L.A. | MIA | N.E. | NYJ | PITT | S.D. | SEA |
|---|---|---|---|---|---|---|---|---|---|---|---|---|---|---|
| FIRST DOWNS: | | | | | | | | | | | | | | |
| Total | 334 | 348 | 285 | 308 | 327 | 273 | 304 | 259 | 310 | 335 | 292 | 244 | 267 | 290 |
| by Rushing | 136 | 136 | 101 | 125 | 112 | 118 | 120 | 93 | 88 | 114 | 91 | 106 | 95 | 86 |
| by Passing | 177 | 183 | 161 | 163 | 185 | 140 | 165 | 143 | 201 | 187 | 189 | 117 | 149 | 180 |
| by Penalty | 21 | 29 | 23 | 20 | 30 | 15 | 19 | 23 | 21 | 34 | 12 | 21 | 23 | 24 |
| RUSHING: | | | | | | | | | | | | | | |
| Number | 532 | 529 | 448 | 554 | 495 | 458 | 559 | 454 | 400 | 485 | 400 | 500 | 432 | 405 |
| Yards | 2264 | 2483 | 1609 | 2092 | 1928 | 1853 | 2227 | 2038 | 1330 | 1749 | 1596 | 1818 | 1873 | 1392 |
| Average Yards | 4.3 | 4.7 | 3.6 | 3.8 | 3.9 | 4.0 | 4.0 | 4.5 | 3.3 | 3.6 | 4.0 | 3.6 | 4.3 | 3.4 |
| Touchdowns | 15 | 17 | 14 | 15 | 16 | 11 | 18 | 9 | 10 | 12 | 11 | 17 | 13 | 5 |
| PASSING: | | | | | | | | | | | | | | |
| Attempts | 478 | 513 | 529 | 474 | 496 | 493 | 435 | 414 | 601 | 610 | 570 | 404 | 515 | 559 |
| Completions | 281 | 288 | 309 | 256 | 295 | 253 | 259 | 201 | 331 | 302 | 338 | 210 | 270 | 316 |
| Completion Pct. | 58.8 | 56.1 | 58.4 | 54.0 | 59.5 | 51.3 | 59.5 | 48.6 | 55.1 | 49.5 | 59.3 | 52.0 | 52.4 | 56.5 |
| Passing Yards | 3831 | 3950 | 3625 | 3352 | 3786 | 3134 | 3220 | 3277 | 4302 | 3972 | 3892 | 2662 | 3291 | 3583 |
| Avg. Yds per Att. | 7.0 | 6.5 | 6.1 | 5.8 | 6.6 | 5.7 | 6.6 | 6.4 | 6.9 | 7.8 | 5.4 | 4.8 | 5.5 | 5.3 |
| Avg. Yds per Comp. | 13.6 | 13.7 | 11.7 | 13.1 | 12.8 | 12.4 | 12.4 | 16.3 | 13.0 | 13.2 | 11.5 | 12.7 | 12.2 | 11.3 |
| Times Tackled | 35 | 41 | 34 | 43 | 37 | 28 | 23 | 44 | 10 | 34 | 62 | 51 | 39 | 46 |
| Yds Lost Tackled | 242 | 332 | 192 | 351 | 287 | 174 | 182 | 326 | 86 | 265 | 477 | 484 | 254 | 379 |
| Net Yards | 3586 | 3618 | 3433 | 3001 | 3499 | 2960 | 3038 | 2951 | 4216 | 3707 | 3415 | 2178 | 3037 | 3204 |
| Touchdowns | 32 | 32 | 20 | 21 | 23 | 18 | 14 | 21 | 26 | 17 | 14 | 10 | 15 | 21 |
| Interceptions | 20 | 13 | 15 | 20 | 16 | 17 | 23 | 22 | 25 | 27 | 24 | 13 | 19 | 23 |
| Pct. Intercepted | 4.2 | 2.5 | 2.8 | 4.2 | 3.2 | 3.4 | 5.3 | 5.3 | 4.2 | 4.4 | 4.2 | 3.2 | 3.7 | 4.1 |
| PUNTS: | | | | | | | | | | | | | | |
| Number | 67 | 65 | 97 | 80 | 58 | 80 | 67 | 67 | 59 | 64 | 87 | 83 | 84 | 76 |
| Average | 38.3 | 38.5 | 39.4 | 39.8 | 41.8 | 42.4 | 40.1 | 40.5 | 41.7 | 37.4 | 39.4 | 40.6 | 39.5 | 39.4 |
| PUNT RETURNS | | | | | | | | | | | | | | |
| Number | 33 | 36 | 49 | 45 | 19 | 26 | 44 | 40 | 33 | 45 | 33 | 40 | 38 | 30 |
| Yards | 301 | 209 | 496 | 344 | 122 | 322 | 331 | 378 | 338 | 379 | 299 | 278 | 272 | 251 |
| Average Yards | 9.1 | 5.8 | 10.1 | 7.6 | 6.4 | 12.4 | 7.5 | 9.5 | 10.2 | 8.4 | 9.1 | 7.0 | 7.2 | 8.4 |
| Touchdowns | 0 | 0 | 0 | 0 | 0 | 1 | 0 | 0 | 1 | 0 | 0 | 0 | 0 | 0 |
| KICKOFF RET.: | | | | | | | | | | | | | | |
| Number | 53 | 54 | 50 | 43 | 74 | 60 | 52 | 54 | 61 | 69 | 75 | 56 | 64 | 65 |
| Yards | 1058 | 941 | 932 | 876 | 1285 | 1164 | 915 | 1002 | 1153 | 1462 | 1309 | 1304 | 1235 | 1246 |
| Average Yards | 20.0 | 17.4 | 18.6 | 20.4 | 17.4 | 19.4 | 17.6 | 18.6 | 18.9 | 21.2 | 17.5 | 23.3 | 19.3 | 19.2 |
| Touchdowns | 0 | 0 | 0 | 0 | 0 | 0 | 0 | 0 | 1 | 0 | 0 | 1 | 1 | 1 |
| INTERCEPT RET.: | | | | | | | | | | | | | | |
| Number | 23 | 21 | 27 | 21 | 21 | 21 | 15 | 18 | 15 | 16 | 15 | 21 | 25 | 9 |
| Yards | 269 | 204 | 300 | 318 | 263 | 391 | 133 | 362 | 126 | 118 | 261 | 261 | 224 | 57 |
| Average Yards | 11.7 | 9.7 | 11.1 | 15.1 | 12.5 | 18.6 | 8.9 | 20.1 | 8.4 | 7.4 | 17.4 | 12.4 | 9.0 | 6.3 |
| Touchdowns | 1 | 1 | 4 | 2 | 0 | 2 | 0 | 3 | 0 | 1 | 2 | 0 | 0 | 0 |
| PENALTIES: | | | | | | | | | | | | | | |
| Number | 103 | 85 | 128 | 83 | 149 | 89 | 116 | 132 | 83 | 63 | 116 | 116 | 122 | 79 |
| Yards | 831 | 637 | 973 | 594 | 1153 | 704 | 878 | 1105 | 614 | 509 | 953 | 986 | 906 | 738 |
| FUMBLES: | | | | | | | | | | | | | | |
| Number | 30 | 29 | 23 | 26 | 39 | 33 | 32 | 28 | 30 | 26 | 32 | 32 | 24 | 43 |
| Number Lost | 21 | 19 | 15 | 12 | 17 | 10 | 18 | 12 | 16 | 12 | 17 | 18 | 17 | 14 |
| POINTS: | | | | | | | | | | | | | | |
| Total | 409 | 404 | 334 | 362 | 365 | 298 | 318 | 315 | 331 | 297 | 253 | 265 | 266 | 241 |
| PAT Attempts | 48 | 52 | 40 | 40 | 41 | 33 | 35 | 35 | 39 | 30 | 30 | 29 | 31 | 28 |
| PAT Made | 46 | 50 | 40 | 39 | 40 | 31 | 34 | 34 | 38 | 27 | 29 | 28 | 29 | 28 |
| FG Attempts | 30 | 20 | 24 | 33 | 37 | 27 | 33 | 34 | 26 | 40 | 21 | 30 | 25 | 25 |
| FG Made | 23 | 14 | 16 | 27 | 25 | 21 | 24 | 23 | 19 | 30 | 14 | 21 | 17 | 15 |
| Percent FG Made | 76.7 | 70.0 | 66.7 | 81.8 | 67.6 | 77.8 | 72.7 | 67.6 | 73.1 | 75.0 | 66.7 | 70.0 | 68.0 | 60.0 |
| Safeties | 0 | 0 | 0 | 1 | 2 | 0 | 1 | 1 | 1 | 0 | 1 | 0 | 0 | 0 |

**DEFENSE**

| | BUFF | CIN | CLEV | DEN | HOU | IND | K.C. | L.A. | MIA | N.E. | NYJ | PITT | S.D. | SEA |
|---|---|---|---|---|---|---|---|---|---|---|---|---|---|---|
| FIRST DOWNS: | | | | | | | | | | | | | | |
| Total | 299 | 280 | 276 | 246 | 314 | 336 | 252 | 308 | 337 | 297 | 328 | 323 | 295 | 293 |
| by Rushing | 117 | 114 | 93 | 90 | 119 | 126 | 92 | 121 | 139 | 110 | 127 | 112 | 102 | 119 |
| by Passing | 156 | 151 | 161 | 142 | 165 | 192 | 140 | 160 | 180 | 176 | 178 | 177 | 172 | 158 |
| by Penalty | 26 | 15 | 22 | 14 | 30 | 18 | 20 | 27 | 18 | 11 | 23 | 34 | 21 | 16 |
| RUSHING: | | | | | | | | | | | | | | |
| Number | 484 | 482 | 446 | 426 | 437 | 507 | 445 | 504 | 493 | 495 | 517 | 498 | 479 | 520 |
| Yards | 1840 | 2162 | 1670 | 1580 | 1669 | 2077 | 1766 | 1940 | 2153 | 1978 | 2136 | 2008 | 1813 | 2118 |
| Average Yards | 3.8 | 4.5 | 3.7 | 3.7 | 3.8 | 4.1 | 4.0 | 3.8 | 4.4 | 4.0 | 4.1 | 4.0 | 3.8 | 4.1 |
| Touchdowns | 15 | 9 | 8 | 10 | 20 | 10 | 9 | 15 | 19 | 19 | 16 | 16 | 13 | 11 |
| PASSING: | | | | | | | | | | | | | | |
| Attempts | 508 | 482 | 540 | 504 | 467 | 556 | 471 | 506 | 513 | 449 | 514 | 548 | 513 | 445 |
| Completions | 255 | 256 | 269 | 268 | 269 | 322 | 236 | 277 | 315 | 259 | 282 | 290 | 283 | 252 |
| Completion Pct. | 50.2 | 53.1 | 49.8 | 53.2 | 57.6 | 57.9 | 50.1 | 54.7 | 61.4 | 57.7 | 54.9 | 52.9 | 55.2 | 56.6 |
| Passing Yards | 3495 | 3383 | 3520 | 3201 | 3819 | 3918 | 2821 | 3311 | 3811 | 3905 | 4035 | 3721 | 3311 | 3332 |
| Avg. Yds per Att. | 5.9 | 6.1 | 5.4 | 5.1 | 7.0 | 5.9 | 5.0 | 5.7 | 6.4 | 7.6 | 7.1 | 6.1 | 5.2 | 6.5 |
| Avg. Yds per Comp. | 13.7 | 13.2 | 13.1 | 11.9 | 14.2 | 12.2 | 12.0 | 12.0 | 12.1 | 15.1 | 14.3 | 12.8 | 11.7 | 13.2 |
| Times Tackled | 38 | 33 | 45 | 47 | 36 | 46 | 36 | 35 | 39 | 31 | 28 | 31 | 48 | 32 |
| Yds Lost Tackled | 289 | 248 | 359 | 374 | 277 | 384 | 294 | 248 | 268 | 239 | 177 | 180 | 360 | 235 |
| Net Yards | 3206 | 3135 | 3161 | 2827 | 3542 | 3534 | 2527 | 3063 | 3543 | 3666 | 3858 | 3541 | 2951 | 3097 |
| Touchdowns | 14 | 22 | 20 | 13 | 28 | 15 | 16 | 18 | 21 | 27 | 31 | 17 | 15 | 23 |
| Interceptions | 23 | 21 | 27 | 21 | 21 | 21 | 15 | 18 | 15 | 16 | 15 | 21 | 25 | 9 |
| Pct. Intercepted | 4.5 | 4.4 | 5.0 | 4.2 | 4.5 | 3.8 | 3.2 | 3.6 | 2.9 | 3.6 | 2.9 | 3.8 | 4.9 | 2.0 |
| PUNTS: | | | | | | | | | | | | | | |
| Number | 75 | 75 | 94 | 84 | 56 | 65 | 82 | 72 | 62 | 81 | 69 | 69 | 79 | 74 |
| Average | 38.3 | 39.1 | 40.4 | 41.0 | 37.6 | 41.6 | 39.1 | 40.3 | 39.0 | 42.1 | 39.8 | 40.5 | 38.6 | 39.2 |
| PUNT RETURNS | | | | | | | | | | | | | | |
| Number | 25 | 33 | 49 | 28 | 24 | 51 | 40 | 41 | 26 | 38 | 34 | 45 | 43 | 41 |
| Yards | 227 | 323 | 418 | 370 | 191 | 558 | 325 | 301 | 256 | 346 | 257 | 361 | 451 | 334 |
| Average Yards | 9.1 | 9.8 | 8.5 | 13.2 | 8.0 | 10.9 | 8.1 | 7.3 | 9.8 | 9.1 | 7.6 | 8.0 | 10.5 | 8.1 |
| Touchdowns | 0 | 0 | 0 | 0 | 0 | 1 | 0 | 1 | 0 | 0 | 1 | 0 | 0 | 0 |
| KICKOFF RET.: | | | | | | | | | | | | | | |
| Number | 75 | 55 | 58 | 72 | 59 | 63 | 55 | 59 | 63 | 61 | 47 | 53 | 57 | 44 |
| Yards | 1187 | 1203 | 1175 | 1256 | 1024 | 1208 | 1156 | 1001 | 1215 | 1199 | 1029 | 1096 | 1249 | 814 |
| Average Yards | 15.8 | 21.9 | 20.3 | 17.4 | 17.4 | 19.2 | 21.0 | 17.0 | 19.3 | 19.7 | 21.9 | 20.7 | 21.9 | 18.5 |
| Touchdowns | 0 | 0 | 0 | 0 | 1 | 0 | 2 | 2 | 0 | 0 | 0 | 0 | 1 | 0 |
| INTERCEPT RET.: | | | | | | | | | | | | | | |
| Number | 20 | 13 | 15 | 20 | 16 | 17 | 23 | 22 | 25 | 27 | 24 | 13 | 19 | 23 |
| Yards | 364 | 42 | 306 | 194 | 171 | 345 | 269 | 298 | 335 | 338 | 282 | 103 | 179 | 248 |
| Average Yards | 18.2 | 3.2 | 20.4 | 9.7 | 10.7 | 20.3 | 11.7 | 13.5 | 13.4 | 12.5 | 11.8 | 7.9 | 9.4 | 10.8 |
| Touchdowns | 2 | 0 | 1 | 1 | 0 | 2 | 2 | 0 | 1 | 2 | 2 | 1 | 0 | 2 |
| PENALTIES: | | | | | | | | | | | | | | |
| Number | 87 | 122 | 122 | 102 | 109 | 103 | 102 | 105 | 106 | 111 | 90 | 96 | 93 | 118 |
| Yards | 616 | 1060 | 985 | 823 | 903 | 772 | 797 | 867 | 831 | 954 | 675 | 785 | 741 | 809 |
| FUMBLES: | | | | | | | | | | | | | | |
| Number | 31 | 26 | 32 | 43 | 25 | 34 | 32 | 40 | 19 | 22 | 32 | 40 | 21 | 26 |
| Number Lost | 13 | 16 | 11 | 22 | 16 | 15 | 18 | 18 | 8 | 12 | 9 | 21 | 13 | 13 |
| POINTS: | | | | | | | | | | | | | | |
| Total | 317 | 285 | 254 | 226 | 412 | 301 | 286 | 297 | 379 | 391 | 411 | 326 | 290 | 327 |
| PAT Attempts | 34 | 32 | 29 | 25 | 51 | 29 | 32 | 36 | 43 | 48 | 50 | 38 | 29 | 37 |
| PAT Made | 33 | 31 | 29 | 25 | 49 | 29 | 31 | 36 | 42 | 46 | 46 | 37 | 27 | 35 |
| FG Attempts | 37 | 27 | 28 | 27 | 21 | 43 | 26 | 21 | 33 | 26 | 31 | 27 | 41 | 32 |
| FG Made | 26 | 20 | 15 | 17 | 17 | 32 | 21 | 15 | 25 | 19 | 21 | 19 | 29 | 22 |
| Percent FG Made | 70.3 | 74.1 | 53.6 | 63.0 | 81.0 | 74.4 | 80.8 | 71.4 | 75.8 | 73.1 | 67.7 | 70.4 | 70.7 | 68.8 |
| Safeties | 1 | 1 | 0 | 0 | 0 | 1 | 0 | 0 | 2 | 0 | 1 | 2 | 1 | 2 |

David Fulcher was a terror, the otherwise undersized defense couldn't stop the run nor put up much of a pass rush.

## WESTERN DIVISION

**Denver Broncos** — After barely hitting .500 in 1988, the Broncos compiled the best record in the A.F.C. in 1989 and wrapped up the home-field playoff advantage early. The major improvement came in the revamping of the defense by coach Dan Reeves and new defensive coordinator Wade Phillips. To stalwarts such as linebackers Karl Mecklenburg and Simon Fletcher, Denver added Plan B free-agents cornerback Wymon Henderson and defensive end Alphonso Carreker and top draft pick Steve Atwater. Just as important, the Broncos installed a simpler, more aggressive scheme that allowed 126 fewer points than in '88. Quarterback John Elway had only a mediocre season, but the offense benefitted from a 1,000-yard seaosn by rookie running back Bobby Humphrey.

**Kansas City Chiefs** — The Chiefs, after making wholesale roster changes under new coach Marty Schottenheimer, staggered out of the starting gate. In the first six games, they lost eight fumbles and their quarterbacks threw 13 interceptions. Not surprisingly, they were 2-4 and far behind Denver. Once Kansas City settled down, however, they turned into one of the A.F.C.'s better teams. Fullback Christian Okoye, a 260-pound native Nigerian, led the NFL in rushing with 1,480 yards and 12 touchdowns. Veteran quarterback Steve DeBerg was twice benched early in the season but finished up strong. Rookie linebacker Derrick Thomas, with 10 sacks, keyed a defense that ranked first in the conference. Four victories in the last five games gave Kansas City only its third winning season in the last 16 years.

**Los Angeles Raiders** — When the Raiders limped off to a 1-3 start, coach Mike Shanahan was replaced by Art Shell, the Hall of Fame offensive tackle. Shell thus became the NFL's first black head coach in the modern era. The move was a popular one with the team which played better football the rest of the season. Bo Jackson took over at running back after his baseball season ended, and Steve Beuerlein won the quarterback job from costly acquisition Jay Schroeder. But the Raiders still were lacking an offense with receiver-returner Tim Brown sidelined all season and Willie Gault used mostly as a decoy. Only once in the final seven games did the Raiders score as many as three touchdowns.

**Seattle Seahawks** —The key to the Seahawks' disappointing season was a club-record 43 fumbles while intercepting a mere nine opponents' passes. The minus-15 turnover ratio was too much for Seattle's undersized defense and slumping running game to overcome — even in the AFc's weak West Division. Quarterback Dave Krieg was benched in midseason, and — as usual — he came back strong down the stretch in leading the team to three victories in its last four games. Brian Blades became the premier receiver in Steve Largent's final season. Largent retired with his consecutive-game streat intact at 177 games and the all-time records for total receptions, yardage and touchdowns.

**San Diego Chargers** —The Chargers' defense gave them hope for the future, holding all but one opponent to 20-or-less points over the last 14 games. Outstanding were pass-ruser Lee Williams, rookie Burt Grossman, linebackers Leslie O'Neal, Billy Ray Smith and Gary Plummer and cornerback Gill Bryd. Unfortunately, good efforts by the defense were more often than not offset by woeful special-teams play and a creaky offense. Breakaway star Gary Anderson was a season-long holdout, crippling the running game. Former Bears quarterback Jim McMahon was disappointing and eventually benched, and got more attention for his sometimes boorish off-the-field behavior than anything he did on the field. Wide receiver Anthony Miller emerged as the team's most potent threat. After the season, owner Alex Spanos hired former Redskins' GM Bobby Beathard to lead the Chargers back to the playoffs.

## BUFFALO BILLS 9-7 Marv Levy

| Scores of Each Game | | |
|---|---|---|
| 27 | Miami | 24 |
| 14 | DENVER | 28 |
| 47 | Houston | *41 |
| 31 | NEW ENGLAND | 10 |
| 14 | Indianapolis | 37 |
| 23 | L.A. RAMS | 20 |
| 34 | N.Y. JETS | 3 |
| 31 | MIAMI | 17 |
| 28 | Atlanta | 30 |
| 30 | INDIANAPOLIS | 7 |
| 24 | New England | 33 |
| 24 | CINCINNATI | 7 |
| 16 | Seattle | 17 |
| 19 | NEW ORLEANS | 22 |
| 10 | San Francisco | 21 |
| 37 | N.Y. Jets | 0 |

| Use Name | Pos. | Hgt | Wgt | Age | Int | Pts |
|---|---|---|---|---|---|---|
| Howard Ballard | OT | 6'6" | 300 | 25 | | |
| Leonard Burton | OT | 6'3" | 275 | 25 | | |
| John Davis | OT | 6'4" | 310 | 24 | | |
| Will Wolford | OT | 6'5" | 280 | 25 | | |
| Joe Devlin | OG | 6'5" | 280 | 36 | | |
| Jim Ritcher | OG | 6'3" | 265 | 31 | | |
| Kent Hull | C | 6'4" | 275 | 28 | | |
| Adam Lingner | C | 6'4" | 268 | 27 | | |
| Mark Pike | DE | 6'4" | 272 | 25 | | |
| Leon Seals | DE | 6'4" | 265 | 25 | | |
| Bruce Smith | DE | 6'4" | 285 | 26 | | |
| Art Still | DE | 6'7" | 255 | 33 | 1 | |
| Fred Smerlas | NT | 6'3" | 280 | 32 | | |
| Jeff Wright | NT | 6'2" | 270 | 26 | | |

Mitch Frerotte — Back Injury
Bruce Mesner — Knee Injury
Tim Vogler — Knee Injury

| Use Name | Pos. | Hgt | Wgt | Age | Int | Pts |
|---|---|---|---|---|---|---|
| Carlton Bailey | LB | 6'2" | 240 | 24 | 1 | |
| Cornelius Bennett | LB | 6'2" | 235 | 23 | 2 | |
| Ray Bentley | LB | 6'2" | 235 | 27 | | |
| Tim Cofield (from NYJ) | LB | 6'2" | 242 | 26 | | |
| Shane Conlan | LB | 6'3" | 235 | 24 | 1 | |
| Matt Monger | LB | 6'1" | 240 | 27 | | |
| Scott Radecic | LB | 6'3" | 242 | 27 | | |
| Darryl Talley | LB | 6'4" | 235 | 29 | | |
| Derrick Burroughs | DB | 6'1" | 180 | 27 | | |
| Dwight Drane | DB | 6'2" | 205 | 27 | 1 | |
| John Hagy | DB | 5'11" | 190 | 23 | | |
| Chris Hale | DB | 5'7" | 161 | 23 | | |
| Kirby Jackson | DB | 5'10" | 180 | 23 | 2 | 6 |
| Mark Kelso | DB | 5'11" | 185 | 26 | 6 | 6 |
| Nate Odomes | DB | 5'10" | 188 | 23 | 5 | |
| Leonard Smith | DB | 5'11" | 202 | 28 | 2 | |
| Mickey Sutton (from GB) | DB | 5'9" | 172 | 29 | 1 | |

Hal Garner — Suspended by N.F.L.

| Use Name | Pos. | Hgt | Wgt | Age | Int | Pts |
|---|---|---|---|---|---|---|
| Stan Gelbaugh | QB | 6'3" | 207 | 26 | | |
| Jim Kelly | QB | 6'3" | 218 | 29 | | 12 |
| Frank Reich | QB | 6'4" | 210 | 27 | | |
| Kenneth Davis | HB | 5'10" | 209 | 27 | | 18 |
| Ronnie Harmon | HB | 5'11" | 200 | 25 | | 24 |
| Thurman Thomas | HB | 5'10" | 198 | 23 | | 72 |
| Larry Kinnebrew | FB | 6'1" | 256 | 29 | | 36 |
| Jamie Mueller | FB | 6'1" | 225 | 24 | | |
| Don Beebe | WR | 5'11" | 177 | 24 | | 12 |
| Flip Johnson | WR | 5'10" | 185 | 26 | | 6 |
| James Lofton | WR | 6'3" | 190 | 33 | | 18 |
| Andre Reed | WR | 6' | 190 | 24 | | 54 |
| Steve Tasker | WR | 5'9" | 185 | 27 | | |
| Keith McKeller | TE | 6'6" | 245 | 25 | | 12 |
| Pete Metzelaars | TE | 6'7" | 250 | 29 | | 12 |
| Butch Rolle | TE | 6'3" | 242 | 24 | | 6 |
| Kerry Brady | K | 6'1" | 215 | 26 | | |
| John Kidd | K | 6'3" | 208 | 28 | | |
| Scott Norwood | K | 6' | 207 | 29 | | 115 |

Robb Riddick — Knee Injury

## MIAMI DOLPHINS 8-8 Don Shula

| Scores of Each Game | | |
|---|---|---|
| 24 | BUFFALO | 27 |
| 24 | New England | 10 |
| 33 | N.Y. JETS | 40 |
| 7 | Houston | 39 |
| 13 | CLEVELAND | 10 |
| 20 | Cincinnati | 13 |
| 23 | GREEN BAY | 20 |
| 17 | Buffalo | 31 |
| 19 | INDIANAPOLIS | 13 |
| 31 | N.Y. Jets | 23 |
| 17 | Dallas | 14 |
| 14 | PITTSBURGH | 34 |
| 21 | Kansas City | 26 |
| 31 | NEW ENGLAND | 10 |
| 13 | Indianapolis | 42 |
| 24 | KANSAS CITY | 27 |

| Use Name | Pos. | Hgt | Wgt | Age | Int | Pts |
|---|---|---|---|---|---|---|
| Louis Cheek | OT | 6'6" | 295 | 24 | | |
| Jeff Dellenbach | OT-C | 6'6" | 280 | 26 | | |
| Mark Dennis | OT | 6'6" | 290 | 24 | | |
| Ronnie Lee | OT | 6'3" | 275 | 32 | | |
| Roy Foster | OG | 6'4" | 275 | 29 | | |
| Harry Galbreath | OG | 6'1" | 275 | 24 | | |
| Alvin Powell | OG | 6'5" | 296 | 29 | | |
| Tom Toth | OG | 6'5" | 282 | 27 | | |
| Jeff Uhlenhake | C | 6'3" | 282 | 23 | | |
| John Bosa | DE | 6'4" | 273 | 25 | | |
| Jackie Cline | DE-NT | 6'5" | 280 | 29 | | |
| Jeff Cross | DE | 6'4" | 270 | 23 | | |
| T.J. Turner | DE | 6'4" | 280 | 26 | | |
| Mike Lambrecht | NT | 6'1" | 274 | 26 | | |
| Brian Sochia | NT | 6'3" | 275 | 28 | | |

Jon Giesler — Knee Injury
Greg Johnson — Knee Injury

| Use Name | Pos. | Hgt | Wgt | Age | Int | Pts |
|---|---|---|---|---|---|---|
| Dave Ahrens | LB | 6'4" | 247 | 31 | | |
| Bob Brudzinski | LB | 6'4" | 235 | 34 | | |
| Greg Clark | LB | 6'1" | 234 | 24 | | |
| David Frye | LB | 6'2" | 227 | 28 | | |
| Rick Graf | LB | 6'5" | 249 | 26 | | |
| Hugh Green | LB | 6'2" | 228 | 30 | | |
| David Griggs | LB-TE | 6'3" | 239 | 22 | | |
| E.J. Junior | LB | 6'3" | 242 | 29 | | |
| Barry Krauss | LB | 6'3" | 248 | 32 | | |
| Eric Kumerow | LB-DE | 6'7" | 268 | 24 | | |
| John Offerdahl | LB | 6'3" | 237 | 25 | | |
| J.B. Brown | DB | 6' | 192 | 23 | | |
| Ernest Gibson | DB | 5'10" | 185 | 27 | | |
| Liffort Hobley | DB | 6' | 202 | 27 | 1 | |
| William Judson | DB | 6'1" | 192 | 29 | 2 | |
| Paul Lankford | DB | 6'1" | 190 | 31 | 1 | |
| Don McNeal | DB | 5'11" | 193 | 31 | 3 | |
| Louis Oliver | DB | 6'2" | 226 | 23 | 4 | |
| Rodney Thomas | DB | 5'10" | 190 | 23 | 2 | |
| Jarvis Williams | DB | 5'11" | 196 | 24 | 2 | |

| Use Name | Pos. | Hgt | Wgt | Age | Int | Pts |
|---|---|---|---|---|---|---|
| Dan Marino | QB | 6'4" | 222 | 27 | | 12 |
| Scott Secules | QB | 6'3" | 219 | 24 | | |
| Cliff Stoudt | QB | 6'4" | 218 | 34 | | |
| Kerry Goode | HB | 5'11' | 200 | 24 | | |
| Sammie Smith | HB | 6'2" | 226 | 22 | | 36 |
| Lorenzo Hampton | HB | 6' | 208 | 27 | | 72 |
| Willard Reaves (from WAS) | HB | 5'11" | 200 | 30 | | |
| Troy Stradford | HB | 5'9" | 192 | 24 | | 6 |
| Tom Brown | FB | 6'1" | 228 | 25 | | |
| Nuu Faaola (from NYJ) | FB | 5'11" | 220 | 24 | | |
| Ron Davenport | FB | 6'2" | 232 | 26 | | 6 |
| Marc Logan | FB | 5'11" | 220 | 24 | | 12 |
| Fred Banks | WR | 5'10" | 180 | 27 | | 6 |
| Andre Brown | WR | 6'3" | 210 | 23 | | 30 |
| Mark Clayton | WR | 5'9" | 184 | 28 | | 54 |
| Mark Duper | WR | 5'9" | 190 | 30 | | 6 |
| Jim Jensen | WR-FB | 6'4" | 220 | 30 | | 36 |
| Scott Schwedes | WR | 6' | 182 | 24 | | 12 |
| Ferrell Edmunds | TE | 6'6" | 248 | 24 | | 18 |
| Bruce Hardy | TE | 6'5" | 234 | 33 | | |
| Brian Kinchen | TE | 6'2" | 238 | 24 | | |
| Pete Stoyonovich | K | 5'10" | 180 | 22 | | 95 |
| Reggie Roby | K | 6'2" | 242 | 28 | | |

## INDIANAPOLIS COLTS 8-8 Ron Meyer

| Scores of Each Game | | |
|---|---|---|
| 24 | SAN FRANCISCO | 30 |
| 17 | L.A. Rams | 31 |
| 13 | ATLANTA | 9 |
| 17 | N.Y. Jets | 10 |
| 37 | BUFFALO | 14 |
| 3 | Denver | 14 |
| 23 | Cincinnati | 12 |
| 20 | NEW ENGLAND | *23 |
| 13 | Miami | 19 |
| 7 | Buffalo | 30 |
| 27 | N.Y. JETS | 10 |
| 10 | SAN DIEGO | 6 |
| 16 | New England | 22 |
| 23 | CLEVELAND | *17 |
| 42 | MIAMI | 13 |
| 6 | New Orleans | 41 |

| Use Name | Pos. | Hgt | Wgt | Age | Int | Pts |
|---|---|---|---|---|---|---|
| Kevin Call | OT | 6'7" | 302 | 27 | | |
| Chris Hinton | OT | 6'4" | 295 | 28 | | |
| Zefross Moss | OT | 6'6" | 315 | 23 | | |
| Brian Baldinger | OG | 6'4" | 272 | 30 | | |
| Randy Dixon | OG | 6'3" | 290 | 24 | | 6 |
| Ben Utt | OG | 6'6" | 286 | 30 | | |
| Ray Donaldson | C | 6'3" | 288 | 31 | | |
| Stan Eisenhooth | C | 6'5" | 290 | 26 | | |
| Sam Clancy | DE | 6'7" | 284 | 31 | | |
| Jon Hand | DE | 6'7" | 298 | 25 | | |
| Ezra Johnson | DE | 6'4" | 250 | 33 | | |
| Donnell Thompson | DE | 6'4" | 275 | 30 | | |
| Mitchell Benson | NT | 6'3" | 302 | 22 | | |
| Harvey Armstrong | NT | 6'3" | 282 | 29 | | |

Steve Knight — Knee Injury

| Use Name | Pos. | Hgt | Wgt | Age | Int | Pts |
|---|---|---|---|---|---|---|
| O'Brien Alston | LB | 6'6" | 246 | 23 | | |
| Chip Banks | LB | 6'4" | 245 | 29 | 2 | |
| Duane Bickett | LB | 6'5" | 243 | 26 | 1 | |
| Jeff Herrod | LB | 6' | 243 | 23 | | |
| Kurt Larson | LB | 6'4" | 236 | 23 | | |
| Orlando Lowry (to NE) | LB | 6'4" | 236 | 28 | | |
| Quintus McDonald | LB | 6'3 | 240 | 22 | | |
| Dan Murray | LB | 6'1" | 240 | 22 | | |
| Eric Naposki (from NE) | LB | 6'2" | 230 | 22 | | |
| Cliff Odom | LB | 6'2" | 245 | 31 | | |
| Ronnie Washington | LB | 6'1" | 250 | 26 | | |
| Fredd Young | LB | 6'1" | 233 | 27 | 2 | |
| Michael Ball | DB | 6' | 216 | 25 | 1 | |
| John Baylor | DB | 6' | 203 | 24 | | |
| Eugene Daniel | DB | 5'11" | 178 | 28 | 1 | |
| Chris Goode | DB | 6' | 193 | 25 | | |
| Anthony Parker | DB | 5'10" | 181 | 23 | | |
| Bruce Plummer | DB | 6'1" | 203 | 25 | 1 | |
| Mike Prior | DB | 6' | 204 | 25 | 6 | 6 |
| Keith Taylor | DB | 5'11' | 193 | 24 | 7 | 6 |
| Charles Washington | DB | 6'1" | 208 | 22 | | |

| Use Name | Pos. | Hgt | Wgt | Age | Int | Pts |
|---|---|---|---|---|---|---|
| Chris Chandler | QB | 6'4" | 210 | 23 | | 6 |
| Wayne Johnson | QB | 6'4" | 221 | 23 | | |
| Tom Ramsey | QB | 6'1" | 188 | 28 | | |
| Don Strock | QB | 6'5" | 225 | 38 | | |
| Jack Trudeau | QB | 6'3" | 214 | 26 | | 12 |
| Albert Bentley | HB-FB | 5'11" | 214 | 29 | | 30 |
| Eric Dickerson | HB | 6'3" | 224 | 28 | | 48 |
| Ivy Joe Hunter | FB-HB | 6' | 237 | 22 | | |
| Matt Bouza | WR | 6'3" | 212 | 31 | | |
| Bill Brooks | WR | 6' | 191 | 25 | | 24 |
| James Pruitt | WR | 6'3" | 201 | 25 | | 6 |
| Andre Rison | WR | 5'10" | 185 | 22 | | 24 |
| Clarence Verdin | WR | 5'8" | 163 | 26 | | 12 |
| Pat Beach | TE | 6'4" | 252 | 28 | | 12 |
| Mark Boyer | TE | 6'4" | 242 | 26 | | 12 |
| John Brandes | TE | 6'2" | 255 | 25 | | |
| Dean Biasucci | K | 6' | 191 | 26 | | 94 |
| Rohn Stark | K | 6'3" | 204 | 30 | | |

## NEW ENGLAND PATRIOTS 5-11 Raymond Berry

| Scores of Each Game | | |
|---|---|---|
| 27 | N.Y. Jets | 24 |
| 10 | MIAMI | 24 |
| 3 | SEATTLE | 24 |
| 10 | Buffalo | 31 |
| 23 | HOUSTON | 13 |
| 15 | Atlanta | 16 |
| 20 | San Francisco | 37 |
| 23 | Indianapolis | 20 |
| 26 | N.Y. JETS | 27 |
| 24 | NEW ORLEANS | 28 |
| 33 | BUFFALO | 24 |
| 21 | L.A. Raiders | 24 |
| 22 | INDIANAPOLIS | 16 |
| 10 | Miami | 31 |
| 10 | Pittsburgh | 28 |
| 20 | L.A. RAMS | 24 |

| Use Name | Pos. | Hgt | Wgt | Age | Int | Pts |
|---|---|---|---|---|---|---|
| Bruce Armstrong | OT | 6'4" | 284 | 23 | | |
| Tom Rehder | OT-OG | 6'7" | 280 | 24 | | |
| David Viaene | OT | 6'5" | 300 | 24 | | |
| Danny Villa | OT | 6'5" | 305 | 24 | | |
| David Douglas | OG-OT | 6'4" | 280 | 26 | | |
| Paul Fairchild | OG | 6'4" | 270 | 27 | | |
| Sean Farrell | OG | 6'3" | 260 | 29 | | |
| Mike Baab | C | 6'4" | 270 | 29 | | |
| Mike Morris (from KC) | C-OG | 6'5" | 275 | 28 | | |
| Milford Hodge | DE | 6'3" | 278 | 28 | | |
| Gary Jeter | DE | 6'4" | 260 | 34 | | |
| Peter Shorts | DE | 6'8" | 278 | 23 | | |
| Kenneth Sims | DE | 6'5" | 271 | 29 | | |
| Tim Goad | NT | 6'3" | 280 | 23 | | |
| Emanuel McNeil | NT | 6'3" | 285 | 22 | | |
| Brent Williams | NT-DE | 6'3" | 278 | 24 | | |

Garin Veris — Knee Injury

| Use Name | Pos. | Hgt | Wgt | Age | Int | Pts |
|---|---|---|---|---|---|---|
| Vincent Brown | LB | 6'2" | 245 | 24 | 1 | |
| Terrence Cooks | LB | 6' | 230 | 22 | | |
| Tim Jordan | LB | 6'3" | 226 | 25 | | |
| Larry McGrew | LB | 6'5" | 233 | 32 | 1 | |
| Johnny Rembert | LB | 6'3" | 234 | 28 | 1 | |
| Ed Reynolds | LB | 6'5" | 242 | 27 | | |
| Bruce Scholtz | LB | 6'6" | 244 | 30 | | |
| David Ward | LB | 6'2" | 232 | 25 | | |
| Jim Bowman | DB | 6'2" | 210 | 25 | | |
| Raymond Clayborn | DB | 6'1" | 186 | 34 | 1 | |
| Eric Coleman | DB | 6' | 190 | 22 | 1 | |
| Howard Feggins | DB | 5'10" | 190 | 24 | 1 | |
| Darryl Holmes | DB | 6'2" | 190 | 24 | | |
| Maurice Hurst | DB | 5'10" | 185 | 21 | 5 | 6 |
| Roland James | DB | 6'2" | 191 | 31 | 2 | |
| Fred Marion | DB | 6'2" | 191 | 30 | 2 | |
| Rod McSwain | DB | 6'1" | 198 | 27 | 1 | |
| Rodney Rice | DB | 5'8" | 180 | 23 | | |
| Erroll Tucker (from BUF) | DB | 5'8" | 170 | 25 | | |

Andre Tippett — Shoulder Injury
Ronnie Lippett — Foot Injury
Ed Williams — Knee Injury

| Use Name | Pos. | Hgt | Wgt | Age | Int | Pts |
|---|---|---|---|---|---|---|
| Tony Eason (to NYJ) | QB | 6'4" | 212 | 28 | | |
| Doug Flutie | QB | 5'9" | 175 | 26 | | |
| Steve Grogan | QB | 6'4" | 210 | 36 | | |
| Marc Wilson | QB | 6'6" | 205 | 32 | | |
| Marvin Allen | HB | 5'10" | 215 | 23 | | 6 |
| Patrick Egu | HB | 5'11" | 205 | 22 | | 6 |
| Reggie Dupard (to WAS) | HB-TE | 5'11" | 205 | 25 | 6 | |
| John Stephens | HB | 6'1" | 220 | 23 | | 42 |
| Bob Perryman | FB | 6'1" | 233 | 24 | | 12 |
| Mosi Tatupu | FB | 6' | 227 | 34 | | |
| George Wonsley | FB | 5'10" | 219 | 28 | | |
| Glenn Antrum | WR | 5'11" | 175 | 23 | | |
| Hart Lee Dykes | WR | 6'4" | 218 | 22 | | 30 |
| Irving Fryar | WR | 6' | 200 | 26 | | 18 |
| Cedric Jones | WR | 6'1" | 184 | 29 | | 36 |
| Sammy Martin | WR | 5'11" | 175 | 24 | | |
| Stanley Morgan | WR | 5'11" | 181 | 34 | | 18 |
| Kitrick Taylor | WR | 5'11" | 190 | 25 | | |
| Michael Timpson | WR | 5'10" | 175 | 22 | | |
| Marv Cook | TE | 6'4" | 234 | 23 | | |
| Lin Dawson | TE | 6'3" | 240 | 30 | | |
| Eric Sievers | TE | 6'4" | 238 | 31 | | |
| Greg Davis (to ATL) | K | 5'11" | 197 | 23 | | 61 |
| Jeff Feagles | K | 6' | 198 | 23 | | |
| Jason Staurovsky | K | 5'9" | 170 | 26 | | 56 |

Russ Francis — Knee Injury
Tony Collins — Suspended by N.F.L.

## NEW YORK JETS 4-12 Joe Walton

| Scores of Each Game | | |
|---|---|---|
| 24 | NEW ENGLAND | 27 |
| 24 | Cleveland | 38 |
| 40 | Miami | 33 |
| 10 | INDIANAPOLIS | 17 |
| 7 | L.A. RAIDERS | 14 |
| 14 | New Orleans | 29 |
| 3 | Buffalo | 34 |
| 10 | SAN FRANCISCO | 23 |
| 27 | NEW ENGLAND | 26 |
| 23 | MIAMI | 31 |
| 10 | INDIANAPOLIS | 27 |
| 27 | ATLANTA | 7 |
| 20 | San Diego | 17 |
| 0 | PITTSBURGH | 13 |
| 14 | L.A. RAMS | 38 |
| 0 | BUFFALO | 37 |

| Use Name | Pos. | Hgt | Wgt | Age | Int | Pts |
|---|---|---|---|---|---|---|
| Dave Cadigan | OT | 6'4" | 285 | 24 | | |
| Jeff Criswell | OT-OG | 6'7" | 284 | 25 | | |
| Reggie McElroy | OT | 6'6" | 276 | 29 | | |
| Jeff Oliver | OT-OG | 6'4" | 292 | 24 | | |
| Curt Singer | OT | 6'5" | 279 | 27 | | |
| Dan Alexander | OG | 6'4" | 274 | 34 | | |
| Mike Haight | OG | 6'4" | 281 | 26 | | |
| Adam Schreiber | OG-C | 6'4" | 277 | 27 | | |
| Mike Withycombe | OG-OT | 6'5" | 295 | 24 | | |
| Jim Sweeney | C | 6'4" | 270 | 27 | | |
| Dennis Byrd | DE | 6'5" | 270 | 22 | | |
| Ron Stallworth | DE | 6'5" | 262 | 23 | | |
| Marvin Washington | DE-DT | 6'6" | 260 | 23 | | |
| Paul Frase | NT-DE | 6'5" | 273 | 24 | | |
| Marty Lyons | DE-NT | 6'5" | 269 | 32 | | |
| Gerald Nichols | DT-DE | 6'2" | 267 | 25 | | |
| Scott Mersereau | NT | 6'3" | 273 | 24 | 1 | |

| Use Name | Pos. | Hgt | Wgt | Age | Int | Pts |
|---|---|---|---|---|---|---|
| Troy Benson | LB | 6'2" | 235 | 26 | | |
| Adam Bob | LB | 6'2" | 240 | 21 | | |
| Kyle Clifton | LB | 6'4" | 236 | 27 | | |
| Alex Gordon | LB | 6'5" | 246 | 24 | 1 | |
| Jeff Lageman | LB-DE | 6'5" | 250 | 22 | | |
| Kevin McArthur | LB | 6'2" | 250 | 26 | | |
| Joe Mott | LB | 6'4" | 253 | 23 | | |
| Ken Rose | LB | 6'1" | 204 | 27 | | |
| John Booty | DB | 6' | 179 | 23 | 1 | |
| Kerry Glenn | DB | 5'9" | 175 | 27 | 1 | |
| James Hasty | DB | 6' | 200 | 24 | 5 | 6 |
| Carl Howard | DB | 6'2" | 190 | 27 | | |
| Bobby Humphery | DB | 5'10" | 180 | 28 | | |
| Leander Knight | DB | 6'1" | 196 | 26 | | |
| Erik McMillan | DB | 6'2" | 197 | 24 | 6 | 18 |
| Rich Miano | DB | 6' | 200 | 26 | | |
| Michael Mitchell | DB | 5'9" | 192 | 27 | | |
| George Radachowsky | DB | 5'11" | 190 | 26 | | 6 |
| Terry Williams | DB | 5'11" | 197 | 23 | | |

| Use Name | Pos. | Hgt | Wgt | Age | Int | Pts |
|---|---|---|---|---|---|---|
| Kyle Mackey | QB | 6'3" | 216 | 26 | | |
| Mark Malone | QB | 6'4" | 222 | 30 | | |
| Ken O'Brien | QB | 6'4" | 200 | 28 | | |
| Pat Ryan | QB | 6'3" | 210 | 33 | | |
| A.B. Brown | HB | 5'9" | 212 | 23 | | |
| Johnny Hector | HB | 5'11" | 202 | 28 | | 30 |
| Freeman McNeil | HB | 5'11" | 209 | 30 | | 18 |
| Brad Baxter | FB | 6'1" | 231 | 22 | | |
| Roger Vick | FB | 6'3" | 228 | 25 | | 42 |
| Sanjay Beach | WR | 6' | 189 | 23 | | |
| Chris Burkett (from BUF) | WR | 6'4" | 210 | 27 | | 6 |
| Titus Dixon (to IND) | WR | 5'6" | 152 | 23 | | |
| Phillip Epps | WR | 5'10" | 165 | 29 | | |
| Michael Harper | WR | 5'10" | 180 | 28 | | |
| Al Toon | WR | 6'4" | 205 | 26 | | 12 |
| JoJo Townsell | WR | 5'9" | 180 | 28 | | 30 |
| Wesley Walker | WR | 6' | 182 | 34 | | |
| K.D. Dunn | TE | 6'2" | 237 | 26 | | |
| Billy Griggs | TE | 6'3" | 234 | 27 | | |
| Keith Neubert | TE | 6'5" | 250 | 24 | | 6 |
| Mickey Shuler | TE | 6'3" | 231 | 33 | | |
| Greg Werner | TE | 6'4" | 236 | 22 | | |
| Pat Leahy | K | 6' | 196 | 38 | | 71 |
| Joe Prokop | K | 6'3" | 224 | 29 | | 6 |

Mark Konecny — Knee Injury

## BUFFALO BILLS

**RUSHING**

| Last Name | No. | Yds | Avg | TD |
|---|---|---|---|---|
| Thomas | 298 | 1244 | 4.2 | 6 |
| Kinnebrew | 131 | 533 | 4.1 | 6 |
| K. Davis | 29 | 149 | 5.1 | 1 |
| Kelly | 29 | 137 | 4.7 | 2 |
| Harmon | 17 | 99 | 5.8 | 0 |
| Mueller | 16 | 44 | 2.8 | 0 |
| Reed | 2 | 31 | 15.5 | 0 |
| Reich | 9 | 30 | 3.3 | 0 |
| Gelbaugh | 1 | -3 | -3.0 | 0 |

**RECEIVING**

| Last Name | No. | Yds | Avg | TD |
|---|---|---|---|---|
| Reed | 88 | 1312 | 14.9 | 9 |
| Thomas | 60 | 669 | 11.2 | 6 |
| Harmon | 29 | 363 | 12.5 | 4 |
| Johnson | 25 | 303 | 12.1 | 1 |
| McKeller | 20 | 341 | 17.1 | 2 |
| Metzelaars | 18 | 179 | 9.9 | 2 |
| Beebe | 17 | 317 | 18.6 | 2 |
| Lofton | 8 | 166 | 20.8 | 3 |
| K. Davis | 6 | 92 | 15.3 | 2 |
| Kinnebrew | 5 | 60 | 12.0 | 0 |
| Mueller | 1 | 8 | 8.0 | 0 |
| Rolle | 1 | 1 | 1.0 | 1 |

**PUNT RETURNS**

| Last Name | No. | Yds | Avg | TD |
|---|---|---|---|---|
| Sutton | 31 | 273 | 8.8 | 0 |
| Johnson | 1 | 7 | 7.0 | 0 |

**KICKOFF RETURNS**

| Last Name | No. | Yds | Avg | TD |
|---|---|---|---|---|
| Harmon | 18 | 409 | 22.7 | 0 |
| Beebe | 16 | 353 | 22.1 | 0 |
| K. Davis | 3 | 52 | 17.3 | 0 |
| Rolle | 2 | 20 | 10.0 | 0 |
| Tasker | 2 | 39 | 19.5 | 0 |
| Mueller | 1 | 19 | 19.0 | 0 |
| Jackson | 1 | 0 | 0.0 | 0 |

**PASSING—PUNTING—KICKING**

| PASSING | Att | Cmp | % | Yds | Yd/Att | TD | Int— | % | RK |
|---|---|---|---|---|---|---|---|---|---|
| Kelly | 391 | 228 | 58.3 | 3130 | 8.01 | 25 | 18— | 4.6 | 3 |
| Reich | 87 | 53 | 60.9 | 701 | 8.06 | 7 | 2— | 2.3 | |

| PUNTING | No. | Avg. |
|---|---|---|
| Kidd | 67 | 38.3 |

| KICKING | XP | ATT | % | FG | ATT | % |
|---|---|---|---|---|---|---|
| Norwood | 46 | 47 | 98 | 23 | 30 | 77 |

## MIAMI DOLPHINS

**RUSHING**

| Last Name | No. | Yds | Avg | TD |
|---|---|---|---|---|
| Smith | 200 | 659 | 3.3 | 6 |
| Stradford | 66 | 240 | 3.6 | 1 |
| Logan | 57 | 201 | 3.5 | 0 |
| Davenport | 14 | 56 | 4.0 | 1 |
| Jensen | 8 | 50 | 6.3 | 0 |
| Hampton | 17 | 47 | 2.8 | 0 |
| Secules | 4 | 39 | 9.8 | 0 |
| T. Brown | 13 | 26 | 2.0 | 0 |
| Faaola | 2 | 10 | 5.0 | 0 |
| Clayton | 3 | 9 | 3.0 | 0 |
| Roby | 2 | 0 | 0.0 | 0 |
| Reaves | 1 | -1 | -1.0 | 0 |
| Marino | 14 | -7 | -0.5 | 2 |

**RECEIVING**

| Last Name | No. | Yds | Avg | TD |
|---|---|---|---|---|
| Clayton | 64 | 1011 | 15.8 | 9 |
| Jensen | 61 | 557 | 9.1 | 6 |
| Duper | 49 | 717 | 14.6 | 1 |
| Edmunds | 32 | 382 | 11.9 | 3 |
| Banks | 30 | 520 | 17.3 | 1 |
| Stradford | 25 | 233 | 9.3 | 0 |
| A. Brown | 24 | 410 | 17.1 | 5 |
| T. Brown | 13 | 117 | 9.0 | 0 |
| Hampton | 8 | 25 | 3.1 | 0 |
| Schwedes | 7 | 174 | 24.9 | 1 |
| Smith | 7 | 81 | 11.6 | 0 |
| Logan | 5 | 34 | 6.8 | 0 |
| Davenport | 3 | 19 | 6.3 | 0 |
| Kinchen | 1 | 12 | 12.0 | 0 |
| Faaola | 1 | 8 | 8.0 | 0 |
| Hardy | 1 | 2 | 2.0 | 0 |

**PUNT RETURNS**

| Last Name | No. | Yds | Avg | TD |
|---|---|---|---|---|
| Schwedes | 18 | 210 | 11.7 | 1 |
| Stradford | 14 | 129 | 9.2 | 0 |
| Gibson | 1 | -1 | -1.0 | 0 |
| Williams | 0 | 0 | 0.0 | 0 |

**KICKOFF RETURNS**

| Last Name | No. | Yds | Avg | TD |
|---|---|---|---|---|
| Logan | 24 | 613 | 25.5 | 1 |
| Hampton | 17 | 303 | 17.8 | 0 |
| Reaves | 6 | 84 | 14.0 | 0 |
| Schwedes | 3 | 24 | 8.0 | 0 |
| Faaola | 2 | 30 | 15.0 | 0 |
| Kinchen | 2 | 26 | 13.0 | 0 |
| A. Brown | 2 | 9 | 4.5 | 0 |
| Williams | 1 | 21 | 21.0 | 0 |
| Davenport | 1 | 19 | 19.0 | 0 |
| Ahrens | 1 | 10 | 10.0 | 0 |
| Goode | 1 | 8 | 8.0 | 0 |
| Brudzinski | 1 | 6 | 6.0 | 0 |

**PASSING—PUNTING—KICKING**

| PASSING | Att | Cmp | % | Yds | Yd/Att | TD | Int— | % | RK |
|---|---|---|---|---|---|---|---|---|---|
| Marino | 550 | 308 | 56.0 | 3997 | 7.27 | 24 | 22— | 4.0 | 5 |
| Secules | 50 | 22 | 44.0 | 286 | 5.72 | 1 | 3— | 6.0 | |
| Jensen | 1 | 1 | 100.0 | 19 | 19.00 | 0 | 0— | 0.0 | |

| PUNTING | No. | Avg. |
|---|---|---|
| Roby | 59 | 41.7 |

| KICKING | XP | ATT | % | FG | ATT | % |
|---|---|---|---|---|---|---|
| Stoyonovich | 38 | 39 | 97 | 19 | 26 | 73 |

## INDIANAPOLIS COLTS

**RUSHING**

| Last Name | No. | Yds | Avg | TD |
|---|---|---|---|---|
| Dickerson | 314 | 1311 | 4.2 | 7 |
| Bentley | 75 | 299 | 4.0 | 1 |
| Trudeau | 35 | 91 | 2.6 | 2 |
| Chandler | 7 | 57 | 8.1 | 1 |
| Hunter | 13 | 47 | 3.6 | 0 |
| Verdin | 4 | 39 | 9.8 | 0 |
| Rison | 3 | 18 | 6.0 | 0 |
| Ramsey | 4 | 5 | 1.3 | 0 |
| Brooks | 2 | -3 | -1.5 | 0 |
| Stark | 1 | -11 | -11.0 | 0 |

**RECEIVING**

| Last Name | No. | Yds | Avg | TD |
|---|---|---|---|---|
| Brooks | 63 | 919 | 14.6 | 4 |
| Rison | 52 | 820 | 15.8 | 4 |
| Bentley | 52 | 525 | 10.1 | 3 |
| Dickerson | 30 | 211 | 7.0 | 1 |
| Verdin | 20 | 381 | 19.1 | 1 |
| Beach | 14 | 87 | 6.2 | 2 |
| Boyer | 11 | 58 | 5.3 | 2 |
| Pruitt | 5 | 71 | 14.2 | 1 |

**PUNT RETURNS**

| Last Name | No. | Yds | Avg | TD |
|---|---|---|---|---|
| Verdin | 23 | 296 | 12.9 | 1 |
| Rison | 2 | 20 | 10.0 | 0 |
| C. Washington | 1 | 6 | 6.0 | 0 |
| Prior | 0 | 0 | 0.0 | 0 |

**KICKOFF RETURNS**

| Last Name | No. | Yds | Avg | TD |
|---|---|---|---|---|
| Verdin | 19 | 371 | 19.5 | 0 |
| Bentley | 17 | 328 | 19.3 | 0 |
| Pruitt | 12 | 257 | 21.4 | 0 |
| Rison | 8 | 150 | 18.8 | 0 |
| Hunter | 4 | 58 | 14.5 | 0 |

**PASSING—PUNTING—KICKING**

| PASSING | Att | Cmp | % | Yds | Yd/Att | TD | Int— | % | RK |
|---|---|---|---|---|---|---|---|---|---|
| Trudeau | 362 | 190 | 52.5 | 2317 | 6.40 | 15 | 13— | 3.6 | 12 |
| Chandler | 80 | 39 | 48.8 | 537 | 6.71 | 2 | 3— | 3.8 | |
| Ramsey | 50 | 24 | 48.0 | 280 | 5.60 | 1 | 1— | 2.0 | |
| Bentley | 1 | 0 | 0.0 | 0 | 0.00 | 0 | 0— | 0.0 | |

| PUNTING | No. | Avg. |
|---|---|---|
| Stark | 80 | 42.4 |

| KICKING | XP | ATT | % | FG | ATT | % |
|---|---|---|---|---|---|---|
| Biasucci | 31 | 32 | 97 | 21 | 27 | 78 |

## NEW ENGLAND PATRIOTS

**RUSHING**

| Last Name | No. | Yds | Avg | TD |
|---|---|---|---|---|
| Stephens | 244 | 833 | 3.4 | 7 |
| Perryman | 150 | 562 | 3.7 | 2 |
| Dupard | 37 | 111 | 3.0 | 1 |
| Flutie | 16 | 87 | 5.4 | 0 |
| Allen | 11 | 51 | 4.6 | 1 |
| Wilson | 7 | 42 | 6.0 | 0 |
| Tatupu | 11 | 38 | 3.5 | 0 |
| Egu | 3 | 20 | 6.7 | 1 |
| Martin | 2 | 20 | 10.0 | 0 |
| Grogan | 9 | 19 | 2.1 | 0 |
| Fryar | 2 | 15 | 7.5 | 0 |
| C. Jones | 1 | 3 | 3.0 | 0 |
| Eason | 3 | -2 | -0.7 | 0 |
| Wonsley | 2 | -2 | -1.0 | 0 |

**RECEIVING**

| Last Name | No. | Yds | Avg | TD |
|---|---|---|---|---|
| Sievers | 54 | 615 | 11.4 | 0 |
| Dykes | 49 | 795 | 16.2 | 5 |
| C. Jones | 48 | 670 | 14.0 | 6 |
| Fryar | 29 | 537 | 18.5 | 3 |
| Perryman | 29 | 195 | 6.7 | 0 |
| Morgan | 28 | 486 | 17.4 | 3 |
| Stephens | 21 | 207 | 9.9 | 0 |
| Martin | 13 | 229 | 17.6 | 0 |
| Dawson | 12 | 101 | 8.4 | 0 |
| Tatupu | 10 | 54 | 5.4 | 0 |
| Dupard | 6 | 70 | 11.7 | 0 |
| Cook | 3 | 13 | 4.3 | 0 |

**PUNT RETURNS**

| Last Name | No. | Yds | Avg | TD |
|---|---|---|---|---|
| Martin | 19 | 164 | 8.6 | 0 |
| Tucker | 19 | 165 | 8.7 | 0 |
| Fryar | 12 | 107 | 8.9 | 0 |
| Hurst | 1 | 6 | 6.0 | 0 |
| Taylor | 0 | 0 | 0.0 | 0 |

**KICKOFF RETURNS**

| Last Name | No. | Yds | Avg | TD |
|---|---|---|---|---|
| Martin | 24 | 584 | 24.3 | 0 |
| Tucker | 23 | 436 | 19.0 | 0 |
| Rice | 11 | 242 | 22.0 | 0 |
| Allen | 6 | 124 | 20.7 | 0 |
| Taylor | 3 | 52 | 17.3 | 0 |
| Wonsley | 3 | 69 | 23.0 | 0 |
| Egu | 2 | 26 | 13.0 | 0 |
| Hodge | 2 | 19 | 9.5 | 0 |
| Timpson | 2 | 13 | 6.5 | 0 |
| Fryar | 1 | 47 | 47.0 | 0 |
| Rehder | 1 | 14 | 14.0 | 0 |
| Tatupu | 1 | 2 | 2.0 | 0 |

**PASSING—PUNTING—KICKING**

| PASSING | Att | Cmp | % | Yds | Yd/Att | TD | Int— | % | RK |
|---|---|---|---|---|---|---|---|---|---|
| Grogan | 261 | 133 | 51.0 | 1697 | 6.50 | 9 | 14— | 5.4 | 13 |
| Wilson | 150 | 75 | 50.0 | 1006 | 6.71 | 3 | 5— | 3.3 | |
| Eason | 141 | 79 | 56.0 | 1016 | 7.21 | 4 | 6— | 4.3 | |
| Flutie | 91 | 36 | 39.6 | 493 | 5.42 | 2 | 4— | 4.4 | |
| Feagles | 2 | 0 | 0.0 | 0 | 0.00 | 0 | 0— | 0.0 | |
| Tatupu | 1 | 1 | 100.0 | 15 | 15.00 | 0 | 0— | 0.0 | |

| PUNTING | No. | Avg. |
|---|---|---|
| Feagles | 64 | 37.4 |

| KICKING | XP | ATT | % | FG | ATT | % |
|---|---|---|---|---|---|---|
| Davis | 25 | 28 | 89 | 23 | 34 | 68 |
| Staurovsky | 14 | 14 | 100 | 14 | 17 | 82 |

## NEW YORK JETS

**RUSHING**

| Last Name | No. | Yds | Avg | TD |
|---|---|---|---|---|
| Hector | 177 | 702 | 4.0 | 3 |
| Vick | 112 | 434 | 3.9 | 5 |
| McNeil | 80 | 352 | 4.4 | 2 |
| Brown | 12 | 63 | 5.3 | 0 |
| O'Brien | 9 | 18 | 2.0 | 0 |
| Prokop | 1 | 17 | 17.0 | 1 |
| Epps | 1 | 14 | 14.0 | 0 |
| Harper | 1 | 3 | 3.0 | 0 |
| Mackey | 2 | 3 | 1.5 | 0 |
| Malone | 1 | 0 | 0.0 | 0 |
| Ryan | 1 | -1 | -1.0 | 0 |
| Burkett | 1 | -4 | -4.0 | 0 |
| Lageman | 1 | -5 | -5.0 | 0 |

**RECEIVING**

| Last Name | No. | Yds | Avg | TD |
|---|---|---|---|---|
| Toon | 63 | 693 | 11.0 | 2 |
| Townsell | 45 | 787 | 17.5 | 5 |
| Hector | 38 | 330 | 8.7 | 2 |
| Vick | 34 | 241 | 7.1 | 2 |
| McNeil | 31 | 310 | 10.0 | 1 |
| Shuler | 29 | 322 | 11.1 | 0 |
| Neubert | 28 | 302 | 10.8 | 1 |
| Burkett | 24 | 298 | 12.4 | 1 |
| Griggs | 9 | 112 | 12.4 | 0 |
| Werner | 8 | 115 | 14.4 | 0 |
| Epps | 8 | 108 | 13.5 | 0 |
| Walker | 8 | 89 | 11.1 | 0 |
| Harper | 7 | 127 | 18.1 | 0 |
| Brown | 4 | 10 | 2.5 | 0 |
| Dunn | 2 | 13 | 6.5 | 0 |

**PUNT RETURNS**

| Last Name | No. | Yds | Avg | TD |
|---|---|---|---|---|
| Townsell | 33 | 299 | 9.1 | 0 |

**KICKOFF RETURNS**

| Last Name | No. | Yds | Avg | TD |
|---|---|---|---|---|
| Townsell | 34 | 653 | 19.2 | 0 |
| Humphery | 24 | 414 | 17.3 | 0 |
| Epps | 9 | 154 | 17.1 | 0 |
| Dixon | 4 | 67 | 16.8 | 0 |
| Nichols | 2 | 9 | 4.5 | 0 |
| Washington | 1 | 11 | 11.0 | 0 |
| Byrd | 1 | 1 | 1.0 | 0 |

**PASSING—PUNTING—KICKING**

| PASSING | Att | Cmp | % | Yds | Yd/Att | TD | Int— | % | RK |
|---|---|---|---|---|---|---|---|---|---|
| O'Brien | 477 | 288 | 60.4 | 3346 | 7.01 | 12 | 18— | 3.8 | 8 |
| Ryan | 30 | 15 | 50.0 | 153 | 5.10 | 1 | 3— | 10.0 | |
| Mackey | 25 | 11 | 44.0 | 125 | 5.00 | 0 | 1— | 4.0 | |
| Malone | 2 | 2 | 100.0 | 13 | 6.50 | 0 | 0— | 0.0 | |

| PUNTING | No. | Avg. |
|---|---|---|
| Prokop | 87 | 39.4 |

| KICKING | XP | ATT | % | FG | ATT | % |
|---|---|---|---|---|---|---|
| Leahy | 29 | 30 | 97 | 14 | 21 | 67 |

## CLEVELAND BROWNS 9-6-1 Bud Carson

| Scores of Each Game | | |
|---|---|---|
| 51 | Pittsburgh | 0 |
| 38 | N.Y. JETS | 24 |
| 14 | Cincinnati | 21 |
| 16 | DENVER | 13 |
| 10 | Miami | * 13 |
| 7 | PITTSBURGH | 17 |
| 27 | CHICAGO | 7 |
| 28 | HOUSTON | 17 |
| 42 | Tampa Bay | 31 |
| 17 | Seattle | 7 |
| 10 | KANSAS CITY | * 10 |
| 10 | Detroit | 13 |
| 0 | CINCINNATI | 21 |
| 17 | Indianapolis | * 23 |
| 23 | MINNESOTA | * 17 |
| 24 | Houston | 20 |

| Use Name | Pos. | Hgt | Wgt | Age | Int | Pts |
|---|---|---|---|---|---|---|
| Rickey Bolden | OT | 6'6" | 280 | 27 | | |
| Paul Farren | OT | 6'5" | 280 | 28 | | |
| Mike Graybill | OT | 6'7" | 275 | 22 | | |
| Cody Risien | OT | 6'7" | 280 | 32 | | |
| Kevin Robbins | OT | 6'6" | 286 | 22 | | |
| Kevin Simons | OT | 6'3" | 315 | 22 | | |
| Daryle Smith | OT | 6'5" | 278 | 25 | | |
| Ted Banker | OG | 6'2" | 290 | 28 | | |
| Dan Fike | OG | 6'7" | 280 | 28 | | |
| Tony Jones | OG-OT | 6'5" | 280 | 23 | | |
| Tom Baugh | C | 6'4" | 290 | 25 | | |
| Gregg Rakoczy | C | 6'3" | 290 | 24 | | |
| Al Baker | DE | 6'6" | 280 | 32 | | |
| Robert Banks | DE | 6'5" | 255 | 25 | | |
| Tom Gibson | DE | 6'7" | 250 | 25 | | |
| Marlon Jones | DE | 6'4" | 270 | 25 | | |
| Andrew Stewart | DE | 6'5" | 265 | 23 | | |
| Carl Hairston | DT | 6'3" | 280 | 36 | | |
| Michael Dean Perry | DT | 6'1" | 285 | 24 | | |
| Chris Pike | DT | 6'8" | 290 | 25 | | |
| Clifford Charlton | LB | 6'3" | 240 | 24 | | |
| David Grayson | LB | 6'2" | 230 | 25 | 2 | 12 |
| Eddie Johnson | LB | 6'1" | 225 | 29 | | |
| Mike Johnson | LB | 6'1" | 225 | 26 | 3 | |
| Clay Matthews | LB | 6'2" | 245 | 33 | 1 | 6 |
| Van Waiters | LB | 6'4" | 240 | 24 | | 6 |
| TonyBlaylock | DB | 5'11" | 190 | 24 | | |
| Stephen Braggs | DB | 5'10" | 180 | 24 | | |
| Hanford Dixon | DB | 5'11" | 195 | 30 | 1 | |
| Thane Gash | DB | 6' | 200 | 24 | 3 | 12 |
| Mark Harper | DB | 5'9" | 185 | 27 | 3 | |
| Kyle Kramer | DB | 6'3" | 190 | 22 | 1 | |
| Robert Lyons | DB | 6'1" | 195 | 23 | 1 | |
| Frank Minnifield | DB | 5'9" | 185 | 29 | 3 | |
| Felix Wright | DB | 6'2" | 190 | 30 | 9 | 6 |
| Bernie Kosar | QB | 6'5" | 210 | 25 | | 6 |
| Mike Pagel | QB | 6'2" | 211 | 28 | | |
| Keith Jones | HB | 5'10" | 190 | 23 | | 6 |
| Eric Metcalf | HB-WR | 5'10" | 185 | 21 | | 60 |
| Mike Oliphant | HB | 5'10" | 183 | 26 | | 6 |
| Kevin Mack | FB | 6' | 235 | 27 | | 6 |
| Tim Manoa | FB | 6'1" | 227 | 24 | | 30 |
| Barry Redden | FB-HB | 5'10" | 219 | 29 | | 6 |
| Brian Brennan | WR | 5'9" | 178 | 27 | | |
| Vernon Joines | WR | 6'2" | 200 | 23 | | |
| Reggie Langhorne | WR | 6'2" | 200 | 26 | | 12 |
| Gerald McNeil | WR | 5'7" | 147 | 27 | | |
| Webster Slaughter | WR | 6' | 170 | 24 | | 36 |
| Lawyer Tillman | WR | 6'5" | 230 | 23 | | 18 |
| Ron Middleton | TE | 6'2" | 252 | 24 | | 6 |
| Ozzie Newsome | TE | 6'2" | 232 | 33 | | 6 |
| Derek Tennell | TE | 6'5" | 245 | 25 | | 6 |
| Matt Bahr | K | 5'10" | 175 | 33 | | 99 |
| Bryan Wagner | K | 6'2" | 200 | 27 | | |

Darryl Sims — Knee Injury

## HOUSTON OILERS 9-7 Jerry Glanville

| Scores of Each Game | | |
|---|---|---|
| 7 | Minnesota | 38 |
| 34 | San Diego | 27 |
| 41 | BUFFALO | * 47 |
| 39 | MIAMI | 7 |
| 13 | New England | 23 |
| 33 | Chicago | 28 |
| 27 | PITTSBURGH | 0 |
| 17 | Cleveland | 28 |
| 35 | DETROIT | 31 |
| 26 | CINCINNATI | 24 |
| 23 | L.A. RAIDERS | 7 |
| 0 | Kansas City | 34 |
| 23 | Pittsburgh | 16 |
| 20 | TAMPA BAY | 17 |
| 7 | Cincinnati | 61 |
| 20 | CLEVELAND | 24 |

| Use Name | Pos. | Hgt | Wgt | Age | Int | Pts |
|---|---|---|---|---|---|---|
| Bruce Davis | OT | 6'6" | 315 | 33 | | |
| Don Maggs | OG-OT | 6'5" | 285 | 27 | | |
| Dean Steinkuhler | OT | 6'3" | 291 | 28 | | |
| David Williams | OT | 6'5" | 292 | 23 | | |
| Bruce Matthews | OG-C | 6'4" | 293 | 28 | | |
| Mike Munchak | OG | 6'3" | 284 | 29 | | |
| Jay Pennison | C | 6'1" | 282 | 27 | | |
| George Yarno | C-OG | 6'2" | 270 | 32 | | |
| Richard Byrd | DE-NT | 6'4" | 267 | 27 | | |
| Ray Childress | DE-NT | 6'6" | 274 | 26 | | |
| William Fuller | DE | 6'3" | 269 | 27 | | |
| Sean Jones | DE | 6'7" | 273 | 26 | | |
| * Anthony Spears | DE | 6'5" | 260 | 23 | | |
| Glenn Montgomery | NT | 6' | 274 | 22 | | |
| Doug Smith | NT | 6'5" | 282 | 30 | | |
| John Brantley | LB | 6'2" | 245 | 22 | | |
| Eric Fairs | LB | 6'3" | 240 | 25 | | |
| John Grimsley | LB | 6'2" | 238 | 27 | | |
| Scott Kozak | LB | 6'3" | 226 | 23 | | |
| Robert Lyles | LB | 6'1" | 230 | 28 | 4 | |
| Johnny Meads | LB | 6'2" | 235 | 28 | | |
| Eugene Seale | LB | 5'10" | 240 | 25 | | 6 |
| Al Smith | LB | 6'1" | 236 | 24 | | |
| Billy Bell | DB | 5'10" | 170 | 28 | | |
| Patrick Allen | DB | 5'10" | 182 | 28 | | |
| Steve Brown | DB | 5'11" | 192 | 29 | 5 | |
| Cris Dishman | DB | 6' | 180 | 24 | 4 | 6 |
| Jeff Donaldson | DB | 6' | 190 | 27 | | |
| Tracey Eaton | DB | 6'1" | 195 | 24 | 3 | |
| Kenny Johnson | DB | 5'10" | 172 | 31 | | |
| Richard Johnson | DB | 6'1" | 190 | 25 | 1 | |
| Bubba McDowell | DB | 6'1" | 195 | 22 | 4 | 2 |
| Cody Carlson | QB | 6'3" | 199 | 25 | | |
| Warren Moon | QB | 6'3" | 210 | 32 | | 24 |
| Allen Pinkett | HB | 5'9" | 192 | 25 | | 12 |
| Mike Rozier | HB | 5'10" | 213 | 28 | | 12 |
| Lorenzo White | HB | 5'11" | 209 | 23 | | 30 |
| Steve Avery | FB | 6'1" | 216 | 23 | | |
| Alonzo Highsmith | FB | 6'1" | 234 | 24 | | 36 |
| Tracy Johnson | FB | 6' | 232 | 22 | | |
| Curtis Duncan | WR | 5'11" | 185 | 24 | | 30 |
| Ernest Givins | WR | 5'9" | 172 | 24 | | 18 |
| Leonard Harris | WR | 5'8" | 162 | 28 | | 12 |
| Drew Hill | WR | 5'9" | 175 | 32 | | 48 |
| Kenny Jackson | WR | 6' | 183 | 27 | | |
| Haywood Jeffires | WR | 6'2" | 198 | 24 | | 12 |
| Bob Mrosko | TE | 6'6" | 265 | 23 | | |
| Chris Verhulst | TE | 6'2" | 249 | 23 | | |
| Greg Montgomery | K | 6'3" | 213 | 24 | | |
| Tony Zendejas | K | 5'8" | 165 | 29 | | 115 |

Mark Garalczyk — Ankle Injury

* played only in playoff game

## PITTSBURGH STEELERS 9-7 Chuck Noll

| Scores of Each Game | | |
|---|---|---|
| 0 | CLEVELAND | 51 |
| 10 | Cincinnati | 41 |
| 27 | MINNESOTA | 14 |
| 23 | Detroit | 3 |
| 16 | CINCINNATI | 26 |
| 17 | Cleveland | 7 |
| 0 | Houston | 27 |
| 23 | KANSAS CITY | 17 |
| 7 | Denver | 34 |
| 0 | CHICAGO | 20 |
| 20 | SAN DIEGO | 17 |
| 34 | Miami | 14 |
| 16 | HOUSTON | 23 |
| 13 | N.Y. Jets | 0 |
| 28 | NEW ENGLAND | 10 |
| 31 | Tampa Bay | 22 |

| Use Name | Pos. | Hgt | Wgt | Age | Int | Pts |
|---|---|---|---|---|---|---|
| Tunch Ilkin | OT | 6'3" | 266 | 31 | | |
| John Jackson | OT | 6'6" | 282 | 24 | | |
| Craig Wolfley | OT-OG | 6'1" | 269 | 31 | | |
| Brian Blankenship | OG | 6'1" | 275 | 26 | | |
| Terry Long | OG | 5'11" | 275 | 30 | | |
| Tom Ricketts | OG | 6'5" | 298 | 23 | | |
| John Rienstra | OG | 6'5" | 268 | 26 | | |
| Dermontti Dawson | C | 6'2" | 271 | 24 | | |
| Chuck Lanza | C | 6'2" | 263 | 24 | | |
| Tim Johnson | DE | 6'3" | 261 | 24 | | |
| Aaron Jones | DE-LB | 6'5" | 257 | 22 | | |
| Keith Willis | DE | 6'1" | 263 | 30 | | |
| Lorenzo Freeman | NT | 6'5" | 298 | 25 | | |
| Gerald Williams | NT | 6'3" | 262 | 25 | | |
| Bryan Hinkle | LB | 6'2" | 222 | 30 | 1 | |
| A.J. Jenkins | LB-DE | 6'2" | 237 | 23 | | |
| David Little | LB | 6'1" | 230 | 30 | 3 | |
| Greg Lloyd | LB | 6'2" | 224 | 24 | 3 | |
| Hardy Nickerson | LB | 6'2" | 229 | 24 | | |
| Jerry Olsavsky | LB | 6'1" | 222 | 22 | | |
| * Tracy Simien | LB | 6'1" | 245 | 22 | | |
| Tyronne Stowe | LB | 6'1" | 236 | 24 | | |
| Jerrol Williams | LB | 6'5" | 242 | 22 | | |
| David Arnold | DB | 6'3" | 208 | 22 | | |
| Thomas Everett | DB | 5'9" | 179 | 24 | 3 | |
| Larry Griffin | DB | 6' | 200 | 26 | 1 | |
| Delton Hall | DB | 6'1" | 205 | 24 | 1 | |
| David Johnson | DB | 6' | 185 | 23 | 1 | |
| Carnell Lake | DB | 6'1" | 205 | 22 | 1 | |
| Dwayne Woodruff | DB | 6' | 198 | 32 | 4 | 6 |
| Rod Woodson | DB | 6' | 199 | 24 | 3 | 6 |
| Todd Blackledge | QB | 6'3" | 227 | 28 | | |
| Bubby Brister | QB | 6'3" | 205 | 27 | | |
| Rick Strom | QB | 6'2" | 210 | 24 | | |
| Rodney Carter | HB | 6' | 216 | 24 | | 24 |
| Dwight Stone | HB-WR | 6' | 188 | 25 | | |
| Eric Wilkerson | HB-WR | 5'9" | 185 | 22 | | |
| Warren Williams | HB | 6' | 202 | 24 | | 6 |
| Tim Worley | HB | 6'2" | 228 | 22 | | 30 |
| Merril Hoge | FB | 6'2" | 226 | 24 | | 48 |
| Tim Tyrrell | FB | 6'1" | 215 | 28 | | |
| Ray Wallace | FB | 6' | 230 | 26 | | 6 |
| Derek Hill | WR | 6'1" | 193 | 21 | | 6 |
| Jason Johnson | WR | 5'11" | 180 | 23 | | |
| Louis Lipps | WR | 5'10" | 190 | 27 | | 36 |
| Mark Stock | WR | 5'11" | 177 | 23 | | |
| Weegie Thompson | WR | 6'6" | 216 | 28 | | |
| Mike Hinnant | TE | 6'3" | 258 | 22 | | |
| Mike Mularkey | TE | 6'4" | 237 | 27 | | 6 |
| Terry O'Shea | TE | 6'4" | 236 | 22 | | |
| Gary Anderson | K | 5'11" | 175 | 30 | | 91 |
| Harry Newsome | K | 6' | 188 | 26 | | |

Vinson Smith — Foot Injury

* played only in playoff game

## CINCINNATI BENGALS 8-8 Sam Wyche

| Scores of Each Game | | |
|---|---|---|
| 14 | Chicago | 17 |
| 41 | PITTSBURGH | 10 |
| 21 | CLEVELAND | 14 |
| 21 | Kansas City | 17 |
| 26 | Pittsburgh | 16 |
| 13 | MIAMI | 20 |
| 12 | INDIANAPOLIS | 23 |
| 56 | TAMPA BAY | 23 |
| 7 | L.A. Raiders | 28 |
| 24 | Houston | 26 |
| 42 | DETROIT | 7 |
| 7 | Buffalo | 24 |
| 21 | Cleveland | 0 |
| 17 | SEATTLE | 24 |
| 61 | HOUSTON | 7 |
| 21 | Minnesota | 29 |

| Use Name | Pos. | Hgt | Wgt | Age | Int | Pts |
|---|---|---|---|---|---|---|
| Scott Jones | OT | 6'5" | 278 | 23 | | |
| Ken Moyer | OT | 6'6" | 292 | 22 | | |
| Anthony Munoz | OT | 6'6" | 278 | 31 | | |
| Joe Walter | OT | 6'6" | 290 | 26 | | |
| Paul Jetton | OG | 6'4" | 295 | 24 | | |
| Brian Blados | OG-C | 6'5" | 295 | 27 | | |
| Max Montoya | OG | 6'5" | 275 | 33 | | |
| Bruce Reimers | OG | 6'7" | 280 | 28 | | |
| Bruce Kozerski | C-OG | 6'4" | 275 | 27 | | |
| Jason Buck | DE | 6'5" | 264 | 26 | | |
| Mike Hammerstein | DE | 6'4" | 272 | 26 | | |
| Skip McClendon | DE | 6'7" | 275 | 25 | | |
| Jim Skow | DE | 6'3" | 255 | 26 | | |
| Natu Tuatagaloa | DE | 6'4" | 265 | 23 | | |
| David Grant | NT | 6'4" | 277 | 23 | | |
| Tim Krumrie | NT | 6'2" | 268 | 29 | | |
| Dana Wells | NT | 6' | 270 | 23 | | |
| Leo Barker | LB | 6'2" | 227 | 29 | | |
| Ed Brady | LB | 6'2" | 235 | 29 | | |
| Joe Kelly | LB | 6'2" | 231 | 24 | 1 | |
| Rich Romer | LB | 6'3" | 222 | 23 | | |
| Kevin Walker | LB | 6'2" | 238 | 23 | | |
| Leon White | LB | 6'3" | 245 | 25 | 1 | 6 |
| Reggie Williams | LB | 6'1" | 232 | 34 | | |
| Carl Zander | LB | 6'2" | 235 | 26 | | |
| Chris Barber | DB | 6' | 187 | 25 | | |
| Lewis Billups | DB | 5'11" | 190 | 25 | 2 | |
| Barney Bussey | DB | 6' | 195 | 27 | 1 | 6 |
| Richard Carey | DB | 5'9" | 185 | 21 | 1 | |
| Rickey Dixon | DB | 5'11" | 181 | 22 | 3 | |
| David Fulcher | DB | 6'3" | 228 | 27 | 8 | |
| Robert Jackson | DB | 5'10" | 186 | 30 | | |
| Eric Thomas | DB | 5'11" | 181 | 24 | 4 | 6 |
| Solomon Wilcots | DB | 5'11" | 185 | 24 | | |
| Boomer Esiason | QB | 6'4" | 225 | 28 | | |
| Turk Schonert | QB | 6'1" | 196 | 32 | | |
| Erik Wilhelm | QB | 6'3" | 210 | 23 | | |
| Eric Ball | HB-FB | 6'2" | 211 | 23 | | 18 |
| James Brooks | HB | 5'10" | 182 | 30 | | 54 |
| John Holifield | HB | 6' | 202 | 25 | | |
| Stanford Jennings | HB-FB | 6'1" | 205 | 27 | | 18 |
| Craig Taylor | FB | 5'11" | 224 | 23 | | 30 |
| Ickey Woods | FB | 6'2" | 232 | 23 | | 12 |
| Eddie Brown | WR | 6' | 185 | 26 | | 36 |
| John Garrett | WR | 5'11" | 180 | 24 | | |
| Kendal Smith | WR | 5'9" | 189 | 23 | | 6 |
| Ira Hillary | WR | 5'11" | 190 | 26 | | 6 |
| Mike Martin | WR | 5'10" | 186 | 28 | | 12 |
| Tim McGee | WR | 5'10" | 175 | 25 | | 48 |
| Carl Parker | WR | 6'2" | 201 | 24 | | |
| Rodney Holman | TE | 6'3" | 238 | 29 | | 54 |
| Eric Kattus | TE | 6'5" | 235 | 26 | | |
| Jim Riggs | TE | 6'5" | 245 | 25 | | |
| Jim Breech | K | 5'6" | 161 | 33 | | 73 |
| Jim Gallery | K | 6'1" | 190 | 28 | | 19 |
| Lee Johnson | K | 6'2" | 198 | 27 | | |

Stanley Wilson — Suspended by N.F.L.

## CLEVELAND BROWNS

### RUSHING

| Last Name | No. | Yds | Avg | TD |
|---|---|---|---|---|
| Metcalf | 187 | 633 | 3.4 | 6 |
| Manoa | 87 | 289 | 3.3 | 3 |
| Redden | 40 | 180 | 4.5 | 1 |
| K. Jones | 43 | 160 | 3.7 | 1 |
| Mack | 37 | 130 | 3.5 | 1 |
| Oliphant | 15 | 97 | 6.5 | 1 |
| Kosar | 30 | 70 | 2.3 | 1 |
| McNeil | 2 | 32 | 16.0 | 0 |
| Langhorne | 5 | 19 | 3.8 | 0 |
| Pagel | 2 | -1 | -0.5 | 0 |

### RECEIVING

| Last Name | No. | Yds | Avg | TD |
|---|---|---|---|---|
| Slaughter | 65 | 1236 | 19.0 | 6 |
| Langhorne | 60 | 749 | 12.5 | 2 |
| Metcalf | 54 | 397 | 7.4 | 4 |
| Newsome | 29 | 324 | 11.2 | 1 |
| Brennan | 28 | 289 | 10.3 | 0 |
| Manoa | 27 | 241 | 8.9 | 2 |
| K. Jones | 15 | 126 | 8.4 | 0 |
| McNeil | 10 | 114 | 11.4 | 0 |
| Tillman | 6 | 70 | 11.7 | 2 |
| Redden | 6 | 34 | 5.7 | 0 |
| Oliphant | 3 | 22 | 7.3 | 0 |
| Mack | 2 | 7 | 3.5 | 0 |
| Waiters | 1 | 14 | 14.0 | 1 |
| Middleton | 1 | 5 | 5.0 | 1 |
| Tennell | 1 | 4 | 4.0 | 1 |
| Kosar | 1 | -7 | -7.0 | 0 |

### PUNT RETURNS

| Last Name | No. | Yds | Avg | TD |
|---|---|---|---|---|
| McNeil | 49 | 496 | 10.1 | 0 |

### KICKOFF RETURNS

| Last Name | No. | Yds | Avg | TD |
|---|---|---|---|---|
| Metcalf | 31 | 718 | 23.2 | 0 |
| Oliphant | 5 | 69 | 13.8 | 0 |
| McNeil | 4 | 61 | 15.3 | 0 |
| K. Jones | 4 | 42 | 10.5 | 0 |
| Braggs | 2 | 20 | 10.0 | 0 |
| Redden | 2 | 2 | 1.0 | 0 |
| Joines | 1 | 12 | 12.0 | 0 |
| E. Johnson | 1 | 8 | 8.0 | 0 |

### PASSING—PUNTING—KICKING Statistics

**PASSING**

| Last Name | Att | Cmp | % | Yds | Yd/Att | TD | Int | —% | RK |
|---|---|---|---|---|---|---|---|---|---|
| Kosar | 513 | 303 | 59.1 | 3533 | 6.89 | 18 | 14 | — 2.7 | 4 |
| Pagel | 14 | 5 | 35.7 | 60 | 4.29 | 1 | 1 | — 7.1 | |
| Metcalf | 2 | 1 | 50.0 | 32 | 16.00 | 1 | 0 | — 0.0 | |

**PUNTING**

| Last Name | No. | Avg. |
|---|---|---|
| Wagner | 97 | 39.4 |

**KICKING**

| Last Name | XP | ATT | % | FG | ATT | % |
|---|---|---|---|---|---|---|
| M. Bahr | 40 | 40 | 100 | 16 | 24 | 67 |

## HOUSTON OILERS

### RUSHING

| Last Name | No. | Yds | Avg | TD |
|---|---|---|---|---|
| Highsmith | 128 | 531 | 4.1 | 4 |
| Pinkett | 94 | 449 | 4.8 | 1 |
| White | 104 | 349 | 3.4 | 5 |
| Rozier | 88 | 301 | 3.4 | 2 |
| Moon | 70 | 268 | 3.8 | 4 |
| Gr. Montgomery | 3 | 17 | 5.7 | 0 |
| T. Johnson | 4 | 16 | 4.0 | 0 |
| Duncan | 1 | 0 | 0.0 | 0 |
| Carlson | 3 | -3 | -1.0 | 0 |

### RECEIVING

| Last Name | No. | Yds | Avg | TD |
|---|---|---|---|---|
| Hill | 66 | 938 | 14.2 | 8 |
| Givins | 55 | 794 | 14.4 | 3 |
| Jeffires | 47 | 619 | 13.2 | 2 |
| Duncan | 43 | 613 | 14.3 | 5 |
| Pinkett | 31 | 239 | 7.7 | 1 |
| Highsmith | 18 | 201 | 11.2 | 2 |
| Harris | 13 | 202 | 15.5 | 2 |
| White | 6 | 37 | 6.2 | 0 |
| Verhulst | 4 | 48 | 12.0 | 0 |
| Jackson | 4 | 31 | 7.8 | 0 |
| Rozier | 4 | 28 | 7.0 | 0 |
| Mrosko | 3 | 28 | 9.3 | 0 |
| T. Johnson | 1 | 8 | 8.0 | 0 |

### PUNT RETURNS

| Last Name | No. | Yds | Avg | TD |
|---|---|---|---|---|
| K. Johnson | 19 | 122 | 6.4 | 0 |

### KICKOFF RETURNS

| Last Name | No. | Yds | Avg | TD |
|---|---|---|---|---|
| K. Johnson | 21 | 372 | 17.7 | 0 |
| White | 17 | 303 | 17.8 | 0 |
| Harris | 14 | 331 | 23.6 | 0 |
| T. Johnson | 13 | 224 | 17.2 | 0 |
| Mrosko | 3 | 46 | 15.3 | 0 |
| Williams | 2 | 8 | 4.0 | 0 |
| Fairs | 1 | 1 | 1.0 | 0 |
| Lyles | 1 | 0 | 0.0 | 0 |
| Gl. Montgomery | 1 | 0 | 0.0 | 0 |
| Verhulst | 1 | 0 | 0.0 | 0 |

### PASSING—PUNTING—KICKING Statistics

**PASSING**

| Last Name | Att | Cmp | % | Yds | Yd/Att | TD | Int | —% | RK |
|---|---|---|---|---|---|---|---|---|---|
| Moon | 464 | 280 | 60.3 | 3631 | 7.83 | 23 | 14 | — 3.0 | 2 |
| Carlson | 31 | 15 | 48.4 | 155 | 5.00 | 0 | 1 | — 3.2 | |
| Zendejas | 1 | 0 | 0.0 | 0 | 0.00 | 0 | 1 | —100.0 | |

**PUNTING**

| Last Name | No. | Avg. |
|---|---|---|
| Montgomery | 58 | 41.8 |

**KICKING**

| Last Name | XP | ATT | % | FG | ATT | % |
|---|---|---|---|---|---|---|
| Zendejas | 40 | 40 | 100 | 25 | 37 | 68 |

## PITTSBURGH STEELERS

### RUSHING

| Last Name | No. | Yds | Avg | TD |
|---|---|---|---|---|
| Worley | 195 | 770 | 3.9 | 5 |
| Hoge | 186 | 621 | 3.3 | 8 |
| Lipps | 13 | 180 | 13.8 | 1 |
| W. Williams | 37 | 131 | 3.5 | 1 |
| Stone | 10 | 53 | 5.3 | 0 |
| Brister | 27 | 25 | 0.9 | 0 |
| Blackledge | 9 | 20 | 2.2 | 0 |
| Carter | 11 | 16 | 1.5 | 1 |
| Wallace | 5 | 10 | 2.0 | 1 |
| Tyrrell | 1 | 3 | 3.0 | 0 |
| Strom | 4 | -3 | -0.8 | 0 |
| Newsome | 2 | -8 | -4.0 | 0 |

### RECEIVING

| Last Name | No. | Yds | Avg | TD |
|---|---|---|---|---|
| Lipps | 50 | 944 | 18.9 | 5 |
| Carter | 38 | 267 | 7.0 | 3 |
| Hoge | 34 | 271 | 8.0 | 0 |
| Hill | 28 | 455 | 16.3 | 1 |
| Mularkey | 22 | 326 | 14.8 | 1 |
| Worley | 15 | 113 | 7.5 | 0 |
| Stone | 7 | 92 | 13.1 | 0 |
| W. Williams | 6 | 48 | 8.0 | 0 |
| Stock | 4 | 74 | 18.5 | 0 |
| Thompson | 4 | 74 | 18.5 | 0 |
| O'Shea | 1 | 8 | 8.0 | 0 |
| Brister | 1 | -10 | 10.0 | 0 |

### PUNT RETURNS

| Last Name | No. | Yds | Avg | TD |
|---|---|---|---|---|
| Woodson | 29 | 207 | 7.1 | 0 |
| Hill | 5 | 22 | 4.4 | 0 |
| Lipps | 4 | 27 | 6.8 | 0 |
| J. Johnson | 2 | 22 | 11.0 | 0 |

### KICKOFF RETURNS

| Last Name | No. | Yds | Avg | TD |
|---|---|---|---|---|
| Woodson | 36 | 982 | 27.3 | 1 |
| Stone | 7 | 173 | 24.7 | 0 |
| Thompson | 4 | 41 | 10.3 | 0 |
| J. Williams | 4 | 31 | 7.8 | 0 |
| J. Johnson | 3 | 43 | 14.3 | 0 |
| Griffin | 1 | 21 | 21.0 | 0 |
| Hinnant | 1 | 13 | 13.0 | 0 |

### PASSING—PUNTING—KICKING Statistics

**PASSING**

| Last Name | Att | Cmp | % | Yds | Yd/Att | TD | Int | —% | RK |
|---|---|---|---|---|---|---|---|---|---|
| Brister | 342 | 187 | 54.7 | 2365 | 6.92 | 9 | 10 | — 2.9 | 11 |
| Blackledge | 60 | 22 | 36.7 | 282 | 4.70 | 1 | 3 | — 5.0 | |
| Carter | 1 | 1 | 100.0 | 15 | 15.00 | 0 | 0 | — 0.0 | |
| Strom | 1 | 0 | 0.0 | 0 | 0.00 | 0 | 0 | — 0.0 | |

**PUNTING**

| Last Name | No. | Avg. |
|---|---|---|
| Newsome | 83 | 40.6 |

**KICKING**

| Last Name | XP | ATT | % | FG | ATT | % |
|---|---|---|---|---|---|---|
| Anderson | 28 | 28 | 100 | 21 | 30 | 70 |

## CINCINNATI BENGALS

### RUSHING

| Last Name | No. | Yds | Avg | TD |
|---|---|---|---|---|
| Brooks | 221 | 1239 | 5.6 | 7 |
| Ball | 98 | 391 | 4.0 | 3 |
| Jennings | 83 | 293 | 3.5 | 2 |
| Esiason | 47 | 278 | 5.9 | 0 |
| Taylor | 30 | 111 | 3.7 | 3 |
| Woods | 29 | 94 | 3.2 | 2 |
| McGee | 2 | 36 | 18.0 | 0 |
| Wilhelm | 6 | 30 | 5.0 | 0 |
| Holifield | 11 | 20 | 1.8 | 0 |
| Hillary | 1 | -2 | -2.0 | 0 |
| Johnson | 1 | -7 | -7.0 | 0 |

### RECEIVING

| Last Name | No. | Yds | Avg | TD |
|---|---|---|---|---|
| McGee | 65 | 1211 | 18.6 | 8 |
| Brown | 52 | 814 | 15.7 | 6 |
| Holman | 50 | 736 | 14.7 | 9 |
| Brooks | 37 | 306 | 8.3 | 2 |
| Hillary | 17 | 162 | 9.5 | 1 |
| Martin | 15 | 160 | 10.7 | 2 |
| Kattus | 12 | 93 | 7.8 | 0 |
| Smith | 10 | 140 | 14.0 | 1 |
| Jennings | 10 | 119 | 11.9 | 1 |
| Ball | 6 | 44 | 7.3 | 0 |
| Riggs | 5 | 29 | 5.8 | 0 |
| Taylor | 4 | 44 | 11.0 | 2 |
| Garrett | 2 | 29 | 14.5 | 0 |
| Holifield | 2 | 18 | 9.0 | 0 |
| Parker | 1 | 45 | 45.0 | 0 |

### PUNT RETURNS

| Last Name | No. | Yds | Avg | TD |
|---|---|---|---|---|
| Martin | 15 | 107 | 7.1 | 0 |
| Smith | 12 | 54 | 4.5 | 0 |
| Hillary | 6 | 19 | 3.2 | 0 |
| Carey | 3 | 29 | 9.7 | 0 |

### KICKOFF RETURNS

| Last Name | No. | Yds | Avg | TD |
|---|---|---|---|---|
| Jennings | 26 | 525 | 20.2 | 0 |
| Hillary | 14 | 223 | 15.9 | 0 |
| Carey | 6 | 104 | 17.3 | 0 |
| Smith | 5 | 65 | 13.0 | 0 |
| Ball | 1 | 19 | 19.0 | 0 |
| Taylor | 1 | 5 | 5.0 | 0 |
| Holifield | 1 | 0 | 0.0 | 0 |

### PASSING—PUNTING—KICKING Statistics

**PASSING**

| Last Name | Att | Cmp | % | Yds | Yd/Att | TD | Int | —% | RK |
|---|---|---|---|---|---|---|---|---|---|
| Esiason | 455 | 258 | 56.7 | 3525 | 7.75 | 28 | 11 | — 2.4 | 1 |
| Wilhelm | 56 | 30 | 53.6 | 425 | 7.59 | 4 | 2 | — 3.6 | |
| Schonert | 2 | 0 | 0.0 | 0 | 0.00 | 0 | 0 | — 0.0 | |

**PUNTING**

| Last Name | No. | Avg. |
|---|---|---|
| Johnson | 63 | 38.8 |
| Breech | 2 | 29.0 |

**KICKING**

| Last Name | XP | ATT | % | FG | ATT | % |
|---|---|---|---|---|---|---|
| Breech | 37 | 38 | 97 | 12 | 14 | 81 |
| Jim Gallery | 13 | 13 | 100 | 2 | 6 | 33 |
| Johnson | 0 | 1 | 0 | 0 | 0 | — |

## DENVER BRONCOS 11-5 Dan Reeves

| Scores of Each Game | | |
|---|---|---|
| 34 | KANSAS CITY | 20 |
| 28 | Buffalo | 14 |
| 31 | L.A. RAIDERS | 21 |
| 13 | Cleveland | 16 |
| 16 | SAN DIEGO | 10 |
| 14 | INDIANAPOLIS | 3 |
| 24 | Seattle | * 21 |
| 24 | PHILADELPHIA | 28 |
| 34 | PITTSBURGH | 7 |
| 16 | Kansas City | 13 |
| 14 | Washington | 10 |
| 41 | SEATTLE | 14 |
| 13 | L.A. Raiders | * 16 |
| 7 | N.Y. GIANTS | 14 |
| 37 | Phoenix | 0 |
| 16 | San Diego | 19 |

| Use Name | Pos. | Hgt | Wgt | Age | Int | Pts |
|---|---|---|---|---|---|---|
| Jim Juriga | OT-OG | 6'6" | 269 | 24 | | |
| Ken Lanier | OT | 6'3" | 269 | 30 | | |
| Gerald Perry | OT | 6'6" | 305 | 23 | | |
| Keith Bishop | OG-C | 6'3" | 265 | 32 | | |
| Monte Smith | OG | 6'5" | 270 | 22 | | |
| Doug Widell | OG | 6'4" | 287 | 22 | | |
| Keith Kartz | C | 6'4" | 270 | 26 | | |
| Mike Ruether | C | 6'4" | 275 | 26 | | |
| Alphonso Carreker | DE | 6'6" | 272 | 27 | | |
| Brad Henke | DE-NT | 6'3" | 275 | 23 | | |
| Ron Holmes | DE | 6'4" | 265 | 26 | | |
| Jake McCullough | DE | 6'5" | 270 | 24 | | |
| Warren Powers | DE | 6'6" | 287 | 24 | | |
| Andre Townsend | DE-NT | 6'3" | 265 | 26 | | |
| Greg Kragen | NT | 6'3" | 260 | 27 | | 6 |
| Michael Brooks | LB | 6'1" | 235 | 24 | | 2 |
| Scott Curtis | LB | 6'1" | 230 | 24 | | |
| Rick Dennison | LB | 6'3" | 220 | 31 | 1 | |
| Simon Fletcher | LB-DE | 6'5" | 240 | 27 | | |
| Bruce Klostermann | LB | 6'4" | 232 | 26 | | |
| Tim Lucas | LB | 6'3" | 230 | 28 | | |
| Karl Mecklenburg | LB | 6'3" | 230 | 29 | | 6 |
| Marc Munford | LB | 6'2" | 231 | 24 | 2 | |
| Steve Atwater | DB | 6'3" | 217 | 22 | 3 | |
| Tyrone Braxton | DB | 5'11" | 174 | 24 | 6 | 6 |
| Darren Carrington | DB | 6'1" | 189 | 22 | 1 | |
| Kip Corrington | DB | 6' | 175 | 24 | 1 | |
| Mark Haynes | DB | 5'11" | 195 | 30 | | |
| Wymon Henderson | DB | 5'10" | 186 | 27 | 3 | |
| Randy Robbins | DB | 6'2" | 189 | 25 | 2 | 6 |
| Richard Shelton | DB | 5'10" | 180 | 23 | | |
| Dennis Smith | DB | 6'3" | 200 | 30 | 2 | |
| John Elway | QB | 6'3" | 210 | 29 | | 18 |
| Gary Kubiak | QB | 6' | 192 | 28 | | |
| Bobby Humphrey | HB | 6'1" | 201 | 22 | | 48 |
| Jeff Alexander | FB | 6' | 232 | 24 | | 12 |
| Melvin Bratton | FB | 6'1" | 225 | 24 | | 24 |
| Sammy Winder | FB | 5'11" | 203 | 30 | | 12 |
| Steve Sewell | FB-WR | 6'3" | 210 | 26 | | 18 |
| Ken Bell | WR | 5'10" | 190 | 24 | | |
| Mark Jackson | WR | 5'9" | 180 | 26 | | 12 |
| Vance Johnson | WR | 5'11" | 185 | 26 | | 42 |
| Ricky Nattiel | WR | 5'9" | 180 | 23 | | 6 |
| Chris Woods | WR | 5'11" | 190 | 27 | | |
| Michael Young | WR | 6'1" | 183 | 27 | | 12 |
| Clarence Kay | TE | 6'2" | 237 | 28 | | 12 |
| Pat Kelly | TE | 6'6" | 252 | 23 | | |
| Orson Mobley | TE | 6'5" | 256 | 26 | | |
| Mike Horan | K | 5'11" | 190 | 30 | | |
| David Treadwell | K | 6'1" | 175 | 22 | | 120 |

Billy Bryan — Knee Injury
Andrew Provence — Hip Injury
Tony Dorsett — Knee Injury

## KANSAS CITY CHIEFS 8-7-1 Marty Schottenheimer

| Scores of Each Game | | |
|---|---|---|
| 20 | Denver | 34 |
| 24 | L.A. RAIDERS | 19 |
| 6 | San Diego | 21 |
| 17 | CINCINNATI | 21 |
| 20 | Seattle | 16 |
| 14 | L.A. Raiders | 20 |
| 36 | DALLAS | 28 |
| 17 | Pittsburgh | 23 |
| 20 | SEATTLE | 10 |
| 13 | DENVER | 16 |
| 10 | Cleveland | * 10 |
| 34 | HOUSTON | 0 |
| 26 | MIAMI | 21 |
| 21 | Green Bay | 3 |
| 13 | SAN DIEGO | 20 |
| 27 | Miami | 24 |

| Use Name | Pos. | Hgt | Wgt | Age | Int | Pts |
|---|---|---|---|---|---|---|
| John Alt | OT | 6'7" | 290 | 27 | | |
| Irv Eatman | OT | 6'7" | 294 | 28 | | |
| David Lutz | OT-OG | 6'6" | 290 | 29 | | |
| Mark Adickes | OG | 6'4" | 273 | 28 | | |
| Rich Baldinger | OG-OT | 6'4" | 285 | 29 | | |
| Mark Cannon (from GB) | C | 6'3" | 258 | 27 | | |
| Gene Chilton | C-OG | 6'3" | 286 | 25 | | |
| Michael Harris | C-OG | 6'4" | 306 | 23 | | |
| Mike Webster | C | 6'1" | 260 | 37 | | |
| Bruce Clark | DE | 6'3" | 275 | 31 | | |
| Mike Bell | DE | 6'4" | 260 | 31 | | |
| Leonard Griffin | DE | 6'4" | 270 | 26 | | |
| Neil Smith | DE | 6'4" | 270 | 23 | | 6 |
| Greg Meisner | DE-NT | 6'3" | 271 | 30 | | |
| Bill Maas | NT | 6'5" | 268 | 27 | | 6 |
| Dan Saleaumua | NT | 6' | 289 | 23 | 1 | |
| Walker Lee Ashley | LB | 6' | 230 | 29 | 1 | |
| Louis Cooper | LB | 6'2" | 245 | 25 | | |
| Dino Hackett | LB | 6'3" | 228 | 25 | | |
| Stacy Harvey | LB | 6'4" | 245 | 24 | | |
| Mike Junkin | LB | 6'3" | 238 | 24 | | |
| Chris Martin | LB | 6'2" | 231 | 28 | | |
| Rob McGovern | LB | 6'2" | 223 | 23 | | 2 |
| Angelo Snipes | LB | 6' | 227 | 26 | 1 | |
| Derrick Thomas | LB | 6'3" | 234 | 22 | | |
| Lloyd Burruss | DB | 6' | 205 | 31 | 1 | |
| Deron Cherry | DB | 5'11" | 203 | 29 | 2 | |
| Danny Copeland | DB | 6'2" | 210 | 23 | | |
| Kenny Hill | DB | 6' | 195 | 31 | 1 | |
| Albert Lewis | DB | 6'2" | 198 | 28 | 4 | |
| J.C. Pearson | DB | 5'11" | 190 | 25 | | |
| Stan Petry | DB | 5'11" | 175 | 23 | | |
| Kevin Porter | DB | 5'10" | 215 | 23 | | |
| Kevin Ross | DB | 5'9" | 182 | 27 | | |
| Steve DeBerg | QB | 6'2" | 210 | 35 | | |
| Mike Elkins | QB | 6'3" | 225 | 23 | | |
| Ron Jaworski | QB | 6'2" | 205 | 38 | | |
| Steve Pelluer | QB | 6'4" | 212 | 27 | | 12 |
| Paul Ott Carruth | HB | 6'1" | 220 | 28 | | |
| Kenny Gamble | HB | 5'10" | 197 | 24 | | 6 |
| Herman Heard | HB | 5'10" | 190 | 27 | | 6 |
| Todd McNair | HB | 6'1" | 185 | 24 | | 6 |
| Tommie Agee | FB | 6' | 218 | 25 | | |
| Christian Okoye | FB | 6'1" | 253 | 28 | | 72 |
| James Saxon | FB-HB | 5'11" | 215 | 23 | | 18 |
| Lew Barnes | WR | 5'8" | 163 | 26 | | |
| Carlos Carson (to PHI) | WR | 5'11" | 190 | 30 | | 6 |
| Emile Harry | WR | 5'11" | 176 | 26 | | 12 |
| Pete Mandley | WR | 5'10" | 195 | 28 | | 6 |
| Stephone Paige | WR | 6'2" | 185 | 27 | | 12 |
| Robb Thomas | WR | 5'11" | 171 | 23 | | 12 |
| Clarence Weathers (from IND) | WR | 5'9" | 172 | 27 | | |
| Naz Worthen | WR | 5'8" | 177 | 23 | | |
| Chris Dressel (to NYJ) | TE | 6'4" | 245 | 27 | | 6 |
| Jonathan Hayes | TE | 6'5" | 239 | 26 | | 12 |
| Alfredo Roberts | TE | 6'3" | 250 | 24 | | 6 |
| Kelly Goodburn | K | 6'2" | 198 | 27 | | |
| Nick Lowery | K | 6'4" | 189 | 33 | | 106 |

Jerry McCabe — Broken Arm

## LOS ANGELES RAIDERS 8-8 Mike Shanahan (1-3), Art Shell (7-5)

| Scores of Each Game | | |
|---|---|---|
| 40 | SAN DIEGO | 14 |
| 19 | Kansas City | 24 |
| 21 | Denver | 31 |
| 20 | SEATTLE | 24 |
| 14 | N.Y. Jets | 7 |
| 20 | KANSAS CITY | 14 |
| 7 | Philadelphia | 10 |
| 37 | WASHINGTON | 24 |
| 28 | CINCINNATI | 7 |
| 12 | San Diego | 14 |
| 7 | Houston | 23 |
| 24 | NEW ENGLAND | 21 |
| 16 | DENVER | * 13 |
| 16 | PHOENIX | 14 |
| 17 | Seattle | 23 |
| 17 | New York Giants | 34 |

| Use Name | Pos. | Hgt | Wgt | Age | Int | Pts |
|---|---|---|---|---|---|---|
| Rory Graves | OT | 6'6" | 285 | 26 | | |
| Tim Rother | OT | 6'7" | 285 | 23 | | |
| Bruce Wilkerson | OT | 6'5" | 285 | 25 | | |
| Steve Wright | OT-OG-TE | 6'6" | 280 | 30 | | |
| John Gesek | OG | 6'5" | 275 | 26 | | |
| Steve Wisniewski | OG | 6'4" | 280 | 25 | | |
| Don Mosebar | C | 6'6" | 280 | 27 | | |
| Dan Turk | C | 6'4" | 270 | 27 | | |
| Scott Davis | DE | 6'7" | 270 | 24 | | |
| Pete Koch | DE | 6'6" | 275 | 27 | | |
| Howie Long | DE | 6'5" | 265 | 29 | | |
| Mark Mraz | DE | 6'4" | 260 | 24 | | |
| Greg Townsend | DE-LB | 6'3" | 250 | 27 | | |
| Mike Wise | DE | 6'7" | 280 | 25 | | |
| Bob Golic | NT | 6'2" | 280 | 31 | | |
| Bill Pickel | DE-NT | 6'5" | 265 | 29 | | |
| Thomas Benson | LB | 6'2" | 240 | 27 | 2 | |
| Joe Costello | LB | 6'3" | 244 | 29 | | |
| Ricky Hunley | LB | 6'2" | 250 | 28 | | |
| Emanuel King | LB | 6'4" | 251 | 26 | | |
| Linden King | LB | 6'4" | 245 | 34 | | 6 |
| Jerry Robinson | LB | 6'2" | 230 | 32 | | |
| Jackie Shipp | LB | 6'2" | 236 | 27 | | |
| Otis Wilson | LB | 6'2" | 227 | 31 | | |
| Stefon Adams | DB | 5'10" | 190 | 26 | | 2 |
| Eddie Anderson | DB | 6'1" | 195 | 26 | 5 | 12 |
| Russell Carter | DB | 6'2" | 200 | 27 | | |
| Mike Harden | DB | 6'1" | 195 | 30 | 2 | |
| Mike Haynes | DB | 6'2" | 190 | 36 | | |
| Dan Land | DB | 6' | 190 | 24 | | |
| Zeph Lee | DB | 6'3" | 205 | 26 | | |
| Terry McDaniel | DB | 5'10" | 175 | 24 | 3 | |
| Vann McElroy | DB | 6'2" | 195 | 29 | 2 | |
| Dennis Price | DB | 6'1" | 175 | 24 | | |
| Lionel Washington | DB | 6' | 185 | 28 | 3 | 12 |
| Steve Beuerlein | QB | 6'2" | 205 | 24 | | |
| Vince Evans | QB | 6'2" | 205 | 34 | | |
| Jay Schroeder | QB | 6'4" | 215 | 28 | | |
| Marcus Allen | HB | 6'2" | 205 | 29 | | 12 |
| Bobby Joe Edmonds | HB | 5'11" | 186 | 24 | | |
| Bo Jackson | HB | 6'1" | 225 | 26 | | 24 |
| Kerry Porter | HB | 6'1" | 220 | 24 | | |
| Derrick Crudup | FB | 6'2" | 225 | 24 | | |
| Vance Mueller | FB | 6' | 215 | 25 | | 24 |
| Steve Smith | FB | 6'1" | 230 | 25 | | 6 |
| Steve Strachan | FB | 6'1" | 225 | 26 | | |
| Mike Alexander | WR | 6'3" | 195 | 24 | | |
| Tim Brown | WR | 6' | 195 | 23 | | |
| Mervyn Fernandez | WR | 6'3" | 200 | 29 | | 54 |
| Willie Gault | WR | 6' | 180 | 28 | | 24 |
| Timmie Ware | WR | 5'10" | 171 | 26 | | |
| Mike Dyal | TE | 6'2" | 240 | 23 | | 12 |
| Ethan Horton | TE | 6'4" | 240 | 26 | | 6 |
| Trey Junkin | TE | 6'2" | 230 | 28 | | 12 |
| Jeff Gossett | K | 6'2" | 195 | 32 | | |
| Jeff Jaeger | K | 5'11" | 195 | 24 | | 103 |

Dale Hellestrae — Broken Leg
Sam Graddy — Knee Injury
Stacey Toran — Died in Offseason Automobile Accident

## SEATTLE SEAHAWKS 7-9 Chuck Knox

| Scores of Each Game | | |
|---|---|---|
| 7 | Philadelphia | 31 |
| 24 | PHOENIX | 34 |
| 24 | New England | 3 |
| 24 | L.A. Raiders | 20 |
| 16 | KANSAS CITY | 20 |
| 17 | San Diego | 16 |
| 21 | DENVER | * 24 |
| 10 | SAN DIEGO | 7 |
| 10 | Kansas City | 20 |
| 7 | CLEVELAND | 17 |
| 3 | N.Y. Giants | 15 |
| 14 | Denver | 41 |
| 17 | BUFFALO | 16 |
| 24 | Cincinnati | 17 |
| 23 | L.A. RAIDERS | 17 |
| 0 | WASHINGTON | 29 |

| Use Name | Pos. | Hgt | Wgt | Age | Int | Pts |
|---|---|---|---|---|---|---|
| Andy Heck | OT | 6'6" | 291 | 22 | | |
| Ron Mattes | OT | 6'6" | 302 | 26 | | |
| Mike Wilson | OT | 6'5" | 274 | 34 | | |
| Edwin Bailey | OG | 6'4" | 270 | 30 | | |
| Darrick Brilz | OG | 6'3" | 270 | 25 | | |
| Bryan Millard | OG | 6'5" | 281 | 28 | | |
| Warren Wheat | OG | 6'6" | 274 | 22 | | |
| Joe Tofflemire | C | 6'2" | 274 | 24 | | |
| Grant Feasel | C | 6'7" | 277 | 29 | | |
| Jeff Bryant | DE | 6'5" | 268 | 29 | | |
| Jethro Franklin | DE | 6'1" | 258 | 23 | | |
| Jacob Green | DE | 6'3" | 254 | 32 | | |
| Elston Ridgle (from BUF) | DE | 6'6" | 270 | 26 | | |
| Alonzo Mitz | DE-LB | 6'3" | 271 | 25 | | |
| Roy Hart | NT | 6'1" | 280 | 24 | | |
| Joe Nash | NT | 6'2" | 269 | 28 | | |
| Brian Bosworth | LB | 6'2" | 248 | 24 | | |
| Joe Cain | LB | 6'1" | 228 | 24 | | |
| Darren Comeaux | LB | 6'1" | 227 | 29 | 1 | |
| M.L. Johnson | LB | 6'3" | 229 | 25 | | |
| Vernon Maxwell | LB | 6'2" | 235 | 27 | | |
| Darrin Miller | LB | 6'1" | 227 | 24 | | |
| Rufus Porter | LB-DE | 6'1" | 207 | 24 | | |
| Rod Stephens | LB | 6'1" | 237 | 23 | | |
| Tony Woods | LB | 6'4" | 244 | 23 | | |
| David Wyman | LB | 6'2" | 234 | 25 | | |
| Nesby Glasgow | DB | 5'10" | 187 | 32 | | 6 |
| Dwayne Harper | DB | 5'11" | 165 | 23 | 2 | |
| David Hollis | DB | 5'11" | 180 | 24 | | |
| Patrick Hunter | DB | 5'11" | 185 | 24 | | |
| James Jefferson | DB | 6'1" | 199 | 25 | | 6 |
| Melvin Jenkins | DB | 5'10" | 173 | 27 | | |
| Johnnie Johnson | DB | 6'1" | 183 | 32 | 1 | |
| Thom Kaumeyer | DB | 5'11" | 187 | 22 | | |
| Paul Moyer | DB | 6'1" | 196 | 28 | | |
| Eugene Robinson | DB | 6' | 183 | 26 | 5 | |
| Jeff Kemp | QB | 6' | 198 | 30 | | |
| Dave Krieg | QB | 6'1" | 192 | 30 | | |
| Kelly Stouffer | QB | 6'3" | 210 | 25 | | |
| Derrick Fenner | HB | 6'3" | 229 | 22 | | 6 |
| Kevin Harmon | HB | 6' | 190 | 22 | | |
| Curt Warner | HB | 5'11" | 205 | 28 | | 24 |
| Elroy Harris | FB | 5'9" | 218 | 23 | | |
| James Jones | FB | 6'2" | 230 | 28 | | |
| John L. Williams | FB | 5'11" | 226 | 24 | | 42 |
| Brian Blades | WR | 5'11 | 182 | 24 | | 30 |
| Willie Bouyer | WR | 6'3" | 200 | 22 | | |
| Jeff Chadwick (from DET) | WR | 6'3" | 190 | 29 | | |
| Louis Clark | WR | 6'1" | 193 | 25 | | 6 |
| Tommy Kane | WR | 5'11" | 180 | 25 | | |
| Steve Largent | WR | 5'11" | 191 | 34 | | 19 |
| Paul Skansi | WR | 5'11" | 184 | 28 | | 30 |
| Donnie Dee (from IND) | TE | 6'4" | 247 | 24 | | |
| Rod Jones | TE | 6'5" | 245 | 25 | | |
| Harper LeBel | TE | 6'4" | 251 | 26 | | |
| Travis McNeal | TE | 6'3" | 248 | 22 | | |
| Robert Tyler | TE | 6'5" | 257 | 23 | | |
| Norm Johnson | K | 6'2" | 197 | 29 | | 72 |
| Ruben Rodriguez | K | 6'2" | 214 | 24 | | |

## SAN DIEGO CHARGERS 6-10 Dan Henning

| Scores of Each Game | | |
|---|---|---|
| 14 | L.A. Raiders | 40 |
| 27 | HOUSTON | 34 |
| 21 | KANSAS CITY | 6 |
| 24 | Phoenix | 13 |
| 10 | Denver | 16 |
| 16 | SEATTLE | 17 |
| 13 | N.Y. GIANTS | 20 |
| 7 | Seattle | 10 |
| 20 | PHILADELPHIA | 17 |
| 14 | L.A. RAIDERS | 12 |
| 17 | Pittsburgh | 20 |
| 6 | Indianapolis | 10 |
| 17 | N.Y. JETS | 20 |
| 21 | Washington | 26 |
| 20 | Kansas City | 13 |
| 19 | DENVER | 16 |

| Use Name | Pos. | Hgt | Wgt | Age | Int | Pts |
|---|---|---|---|---|---|---|
| James FitzPatrick | OT | 6'8" | 310 | 25 | | |
| Joey Howard | OT | 6'6" | 305 | 23 | | |
| Brett Miller | OT | 6'7" | 300 | 30 | | |
| Joel Patten | OT | 6'7" | 307 | 31 | | |
| David Richards | OG | 6'5" | 310 | 23 | | |
| Broderick Thompson | OG | 6'5" | 295 | 29 | | |
| Courtney Hall | C | 6'2" | 269 | 21 | | |
| Don Macek | C | 6'3" | 278 | 35 | | |
| Burt Grossman | DE | 6'6" | 270 | 22 | | |
| George Hinkle | DE | 6'5" | 267 | 24 | | |
| Les Miller | DE | 6'7" | 293 | 24 | | |
| Gerald Robinson | DE | 6'3" | 262 | 26 | | |
| Lee Williams | DE | 6'6" | 271 | 26 | | |
| Joe Phillips | NT | 6'5" | 275 | 26 | | |
| Mike Charles | NT | 6'4" | 296 | 26 | | |
| David Brandon | LB | 6'4" | 230 | 24 | | |
| Joe Campbell | LB | 6'4" | 245 | 22 | | |
| Jim Collins | LB | 6'2" | 233 | 31 | | |
| Cedric Figaro | LB | 6'2" | 255 | 23 | 1 | |
| Leslie O'Neal | LB-DE | 6'4" | 259 | 25 | | |
| Gary Plummer | LB | 6'2" | 240 | 29 | | |
| Billy Ray Smith | LB | 6'3" | 236 | 28 | 1 | 6 |
| Ken Woodard | LB | 6'1" | 220 | 29 | | |
| Martin Bayless | DB | 6'2" | 212 | 26 | 1 | |
| Roy Bennett | DB | 6'2" | 195 | 28 | 3 | |
| Michael Brooks | DB | 6' | 195 | 22 | | |
| Gill Byrd | DB | 5'11" | 198 | 28 | 7 | |
| Leonard Coleman | DB | 6'2" | 202 | 27 | | |
| Vencie Glenn | DB | 6' | 192 | 24 | 4 | 6 |
| Lester Lyles | DB | 6'3" | 200 | 26 | 2 | |
| Elvis Patterson | DB | 5'11" | 198 | 24 | 2 | |
| Sam Seale | DB | 5'9" | 185 | 25 | 4 | |
| Elliot Smith | DB | 6'2" | 192 | 22 | | |
| Johnny Thomas | DB | 5'9" | 185 | 25 | | |
| David Archer | QB | 6'2" | 208 | 27 | | |
| Jim McMahon | QB | 6'1" | 198 | 30 | | |
| Billy Joe Tolliver | QB | 6'1" | 218 | 24 | | |
| Victor Floyd | HB | 6'1" | 201 | 23 | | |
| Darrin Nelson (from MIN) | HB | 5'9" | 184 | 29 | | |
| Marion Butts | FB | 6'1" | 248 | 23 | | 54 |
| Tim Spencer | FB | 6'2" | 223 | 28 | | 18 |
| Anthony Allen | WR | 5'11" | 182 | 30 | | |
| Dana Brinson | WR | 5'9" | 167 | 24 | | |
| Quinn Early | WR | 6' | 188 | 24 | | |
| Jamie Holland | WR-HB | 6'2" | 195 | 25 | | |
| Anthony Miller | WR | 5'11" | 185 | 24 | | 66 |
| Wayne Walker | WR | 5'8" | 162 | 22 | | 6 |
| Rod Bernstine | TE-FB | 6'3" | 238 | 24 | | 12 |
| Joe Caravello | TE | 6'3" | 270 | 26 | | |
| Arthur Cox | TE | 6'2" | 277 | 28 | | 12 |
| Chris Gannon | TE | 6'6" | 265 | 23 | | |
| Craig McEwen | TE | 6'1" | 220 | 23 | | |
| Andy Parker | TE | 6'5" | 245 | 27 | | 6 |
| Mark Walczak | TE | 6'6" | 246 | 27 | | |
| Chris Bahr | K | 5'10" | 170 | 36 | | 80 |
| Lewis Colbert | K | 5'11" | 185 | 26 | | |
| Hank Ilesic | K | 6'1" | 210 | 29 | | |

Dennis McKnight — Knee Injury
Larry Williams — Shoulder Injury
Gary Anderson — Holdout
Mark Vlasic — Knee Injury

## DENVER BRONCOS

### RUSHING

| Last Name | No. | Yds | Avg | TD |
|---|---|---|---|---|
| Humphrey | 294 | 1151 | 3.9 | 7 |
| Winder | 110 | 351 | 3.2 | 2 |
| Elway | 48 | 244 | 5.1 | 3 |
| Alexander | 45 | 146 | 3.2 | 2 |
| Bratton | 30 | 108 | 3.6 | 1 |
| Sewell | 7 | 44 | 6.3 | 0 |
| Kubiak | 15 | 35 | 2.3 | 0 |
| Jackson | 5 | 13 | 2.6 | 0 |

### RECEIVING

| Last Name | No. | Yds | Avg | TD |
|---|---|---|---|---|
| V. Johnson | 76 | 1095 | 14.4 | 7 |
| Jackson | 28 | 446 | 15.9 | 2 |
| Sewell | 25 | 416 | 16.6 | 3 |
| Young | 22 | 402 | 18.3 | 2 |
| Humphrey | 22 | 156 | 7.1 | 0 |
| Kay | 21 | 197 | 9.4 | 2 |
| Mobley | 17 | 200 | 11.8 | 0 |
| Winder | 14 | 91 | 6.5 | 0 |
| Nattiel | 10 | 183 | 18.3 | 1 |
| Bratton | 10 | 69 | 6.9 | 3 |
| Alexander | 8 | 84 | 10.5 | 0 |
| Kelly | 3 | 13 | 4.3 | 0 |

### PUNT RETURNS

| Last Name | No. | Yds | Avg | TD |
|---|---|---|---|---|
| Bell | 21 | 143 | 6.8 | 0 |
| Johnson | 12 | 118 | 9.8 | 0 |
| Nattiel | 9 | 77 | 8.6 | 0 |
| Woods | 2 | 6 | 3.0 | 0 |
| Carrington | 1 | 0 | 0.0 | 0 |

### KICKOFF RETURNS

| Last Name | No. | Yds | Avg | TD |
|---|---|---|---|---|
| Bell | 30 | 602 | 20.1 | 0 |
| Carrington | 6 | 152 | 25.3 | 0 |
| Humphrey | 4 | 86 | 21.5 | 0 |
| Bratton | 2 | 19 | 9.5 | 0 |
| Woods | 1 | 17 | 17.0 | 0 |

### PASSING—PUNTING—KICKING — Statistics

| Last Name | Att | Cmp | % | Yds | Yd/Att | TD | Int— | % | RK |
|---|---|---|---|---|---|---|---|---|---|
| Elway | 416 | 223 | 53.6 | 3051 | 7.33 | 18 | 18— | 4.3 | 9 |
| Kubiak | 55 | 32 | 58.2 | 284 | 5.16 | 2 | 2— | 3.6 | |
| Humphrey | 2 | 1 | 66.7 | 17 | 8.50 | 1 | 0— | 0.0 | |
| Johnson | 1 | 0 | 0.0 | 0 | 0.00 | 0 | 0— | 0.0 | |

| PUNTING | No. | Avg. |
|---|---|---|
| Horan | 77 | 40.4 |
| Elway | 1 | 34.0 |
| Kubiak | 2 | 21.5 |

| KICKING | XP | ATT | % | FG | ATT | % |
|---|---|---|---|---|---|---|
| Treadwell | 39 | 40 | 98 | 27 | 33 | 82 |

## KANSAS CITY CHIEFS

### RUSHING

| Last Name | No. | Yds | Avg | TD |
|---|---|---|---|---|
| Okoye | 370 | 1480 | 4.0 | 12 |
| Saxon | 58 | 233 | 4.0 | 3 |
| Heard | 63 | 216 | 3.4 | 0 |
| Pelluer | 17 | 143 | 8.4 | 2 |
| McNair | 23 | 121 | 5.3 | 0 |
| Gamble | 6 | 24 | 4.0 | 1 |
| Harry | 1 | 9 | 9.0 | 0 |
| Jaworski | 4 | 5 | 1.3 | 0 |
| Agee | 1 | 3 | 3.0 | 0 |
| Mandley | 2 | 1 | 0.5 | 0 |
| DeBerg | 14 | -8 | -0.6 | 0 |
| Carson | 1 | -9 | -9.0 | 0 |

### RECEIVING

| Last Name | No. | Yds | Avg | TD |
|---|---|---|---|---|
| Paige | 44 | 759 | 17.3 | 2 |
| Mandley | 35 | 476 | 13.6 | 1 |
| McNair | 34 | 372 | 10.9 | 1 |
| Harry | 33 | 430 | 13.0 | 2 |
| Heard | 25 | 246 | 9.8 | 1 |
| Weathers | 23 | 254 | 11.0 | 0 |
| Hayes | 18 | 229 | 12.7 | 2 |
| Saxon | 11 | 86 | 7.8 | 0 |
| Dressel | 12 | 191 | 15.9 | 1 |
| R. Thomas | 8 | 58 | 7.3 | 2 |
| Roberts | 8 | 55 | 6.9 | 1 |
| Carson | 8 | 107 | 13.4 | 1 |
| Worthen | 5 | 69 | 13.8 | 0 |
| Okoye | 2 | 12 | 6.0 | 0 |
| Carruth | 1 | 3 | 3.0 | 0 |
| Gamble | 2 | 2 | 1.0 | 0 |

### PUNT RETURNS

| Last Name | No. | Yds | Avg | TD |
|---|---|---|---|---|
| Mandley | 19 | 151 | 7.9 | 0 |
| Worthen | 19 | 133 | 7.0 | 0 |
| Barnes | 2 | 41 | 20.5 | 0 |
| Harry | 2 | 6 | 3.0 | 0 |
| Ross | 2 | 0 | 0.0 | 0 |

### KICKOFF RETURNS

| Last Name | No. | Yds | Avg | TD |
|---|---|---|---|---|
| Copeland | 26 | 466 | 17.9 | 0 |
| McNair | 13 | 257 | 19.8 | 0 |
| Worthen | 5 | 113 | 22.6 | 0 |
| Gamble | 3 | 55 | 18.3 | 0 |
| Saxon | 3 | 16 | 5.3 | 0 |
| Saleaumua | 1 | 8 | 8.0 | 0 |
| Mandley | 1 | 0 | 0.0 | 0 |

### PASSING—PUNTING—KICKING — Statistics

| Last Name | Att | Cmp | % | Yds | Yd/Att | TD | Int— | % | RK |
|---|---|---|---|---|---|---|---|---|---|
| DeBerg | 324 | 196 | 2529 | 60.5 | 7.81 | 11 | 16— | 4.9 | 6 |
| Jaworski | 61 | 36 | 59.0 | 385 | 6.31 | 2 | 5— | 8.2 | |
| Pelluer | 47 | 26 | 55.3 | 301 | 6.40 | 1 | 0— | 0.0 | |
| Elkins | 2 | 1 | 50.0 | 5 | 2.50 | 0 | 1— | 50.0 | |
| Saxon | 1 | 0 | 0.0 | 0 | 0.00 | 0 | 1— | 100.0 | |

| PUNTING | No. | Avg. |
|---|---|---|
| Goodburn | 67 | 40.1 |

| KICKING | XP | ATT | % | FG | ATT | % |
|---|---|---|---|---|---|---|
| Lowery | 34 | 35 | 97 | 24 | 33 | 73 |

## LOS ANGELES RAIDERS

### RUSHING

| Last Name | No. | Yds | Avg | TD |
|---|---|---|---|---|
| Jackson | 173 | 950 | 5.5 | 4 |
| Smith | 117 | 471 | 4.0 | 1 |
| Allen | 69 | 293 | 4.2 | 2 |
| Mueller | 48 | 161 | 3.4 | 2 |
| Porter | 13 | 54 | 4.2 | 0 |
| Beuerlein | 16 | 39 | 2.4 | 0 |
| Schroeder | 15 | 38 | 2.5 | 0 |
| Evans | 1 | 16 | 16.0 | 0 |
| Fernandez | 2 | 16 | 8.0 | 0 |

### RECEIVING

| Last Name | No. | Yds | Avg | TD |
|---|---|---|---|---|
| Fernandez | 57 | 1069 | 18.8 | 9 |
| Gault | 28 | 690 | 24.6 | 4 |
| Dyal | 27 | 499 | 18.5 | 2 |
| Allen | 20 | 191 | 9.6 | 0 |
| Smith | 19 | 140 | 7.4 | 0 |
| Mueller | 18 | 240 | 7.4 | 0 |
| Alexander | 15 | 295 | 19.7 | 1 |
| Jackson | 9 | 69 | 7.7 | 0 |
| Horton | 4 | 44 | 11.0 | 1 |
| Junkin | 3 | 32 | 10.7 | 2 |
| Brown | 1 | 8 | 8.0 | 0 |

### PUNT RETURNS

| Last Name | No. | Yds | Avg | TD |
|---|---|---|---|---|
| Adams | 19 | 156 | 8.2 | 0 |
| Edmonds | 16 | 168 | 10.5 | 0 |
| Brown | 4 | 43 | 10.8 | 0 |
| Harden | 1 | 11 | 11.0 | 0 |

### KICKOFF RETURNS

| Last Name | No. | Yds | Avg | TD |
|---|---|---|---|---|
| Adams | 22 | 425 | 19.3 | 0 |
| Edmonds | 14 | 271 | 19.4 | 0 |
| Mueller | 5 | 120 | 24.0 | 0 |
| Ware | 4 | 86 | 21.5 | 0 |
| Brown | 3 | 63 | 21.0 | 0 |
| Smith | 2 | 19 | 9.5 | 0 |
| Gault | 1 | 16 | 16.0 | 0 |
| Turk | 1 | 2 | 2.0 | 0 |
| Junkin | 1 | 0 | 0.0 | 0 |
| Lee | 1 | 0 | 0.0 | 0 |

### PASSING—PUNTING—KICKING — Statistics

| Last Name | Att | Cmp | % | Yds | Yd/Att | TD | Int— | % | RK |
|---|---|---|---|---|---|---|---|---|---|
| Beuerlein | 217 | 108 | 49.8 | 1677 | 7.73 | 13 | 9— | 4.1 | |
| Schroeder | 194 | 91 | 46.9 | 1550 | 7.99 | 8 | 13— | 6.7 | |
| Evans | 2 | 2 | 100.0 | 50 | 25.00 | 0 | 0— | 0.0 | |
| Gossett | 1 | 0 | 0.0 | 0 | 0.00 | 0 | 0— | 0.0 | |

| PUNTING | No. | Avg. |
|---|---|---|
| Gossett | 67 | 40.5 |

| KICKING | XP | ATT | % | FG | ATT | % |
|---|---|---|---|---|---|---|
| Jaeger | 34 | 34 | 100 | 23 | 34 | 68 |

## SEATTLE SEAHAWKS

### RUSHING

| Last Name | No. | Yds | Avg | TD |
|---|---|---|---|---|
| Warner | 194 | 631 | 3.3 | 3 |
| Williams | 146 | 499 | 3.4 | 1 |
| Krieg | 40 | 160 | 4.0 | 0 |
| Fenner | 11 | 41 | 3.7 | 1 |
| Harmon | 1 | 24 | 24.0 | 0 |
| Harris | 8 | 23 | 2.9 | 0 |
| Stouffer | 2 | 11 | 5.5 | 0 |
| Blades | 1 | 3 | 3.0 | 0 |
| Kemp | 1 | 0 | 0.0 | 0 |
| Rodriguez | 1 | 0 | 0.0 | 0 |

### RECEIVING

| Last Name | No. | Yds | Avg | TD |
|---|---|---|---|---|
| Blades | 77 | 1063 | 13.8 | 5 |
| Williams | 76 | 657 | 8.6 | 6 |
| Skansi | 39 | 488 | 12.5 | 5 |
| Largent | 28 | 403 | 14.4 | 3 |
| Clark | 25 | 260 | 10.4 | 1 |
| Warner | 23 | 153 | 6.7 | 1 |
| Tyler | 14 | 148 | 10.6 | 0 |
| Chadwick | 9 | 104 | 11.6 | 0 |
| Kane | 7 | 94 | 13.4 | 0 |
| Harris | 3 | 26 | 8.7 | 0 |
| Fenner | 3 | 23 | 7.7 | 0 |
| Buoyer | 1 | 9 | 9.0 | 0 |
| J. Jones | 1 | 8 | 8.0 | 0 |
| Feasel | 1 | 5 | 5.0 | 0 |
| Glasgow | 1 | 4 | 4.0 | 0 |

### PUNT RETURNS

| Last Name | No. | Yds | Avg | TD |
|---|---|---|---|---|
| Hollis | 18 | 164 | 9.1 | 0 |
| Jefferson | 12 | 87 | 7.3 | 0 |

### KICKOFF RETURNS

| Last Name | No. | Yds | Avg | TD |
|---|---|---|---|---|
| Jefferson | 22 | 511 | 23.2 | 1 |
| Harris | 18 | 334 | 18.6 | 0 |
| Hollis | 15 | 247 | 16.5 | 0 |
| Harmon | 6 | 84 | 14.0 | 0 |
| Clark | 1 | 31 | 31.0 | 0 |
| McNeal | 1 | 17 | 17.0 | 0 |
| Woods | 1 | 13 | 13.0 | 0 |
| Comeaux | 1 | 9 | 9.0 | 0 |

### PASSING—PUNTING—KICKING — Statistics

| Last Name | Att | Cmp | % | Yds | Yd/Att | TD | Int— | % | RK |
|---|---|---|---|---|---|---|---|---|---|
| Krieg | 499 | 286 | 57.3 | 3309 | 6.63 | 21 | 20— | 4.0 | 7 |
| Stouffer | 59 | 29 | 49.2 | 270 | 4.58 | 0 | 3— | 5.1 | |
| Rodriguez | 1 | 1 | 100.0 | 4 | 4.00 | 0 | 0— | 0.0 | |

| PUNTING | No. | Avg. |
|---|---|---|
| Rodriguez | 76 | 39.4 |

| KICKING | XP | ATT | % | FG | ATT | % |
|---|---|---|---|---|---|---|
| N. Johnson | 27 | 27 | 100 | 15 | 25 | 60 |
| Largent | 1 | 1 | 100 | 0 | 0 | |

## SAN DIEGO CHARGERS

### RUSHING

| Last Name | No. | Yds | Avg | TD |
|---|---|---|---|---|
| Butts | 170 | 683 | 4.0 | 9 |
| Spencer | 134 | 521 | 3.9 | 3 |
| Nelson | 67 | 321 | 4.8 | 0 |
| McMahon | 29 | 141 | 4.9 | 0 |
| Bernstine | 15 | 137 | 9.1 | 1 |
| Brinson | 17 | 64 | 3.8 | 0 |
| Holland | 6 | 46 | 7.7 | 0 |
| A. Miller | 4 | 21 | 5.3 | 0 |
| Early | 1 | 19 | 19.0 | 0 |
| Floyd | 8 | 15 | 1.9 | 0 |
| Archer | 2 | 14 | 7.0 | 0 |
| Walker | 1 | 9 | 9.0 | 0 |
| Plummer | 1 | 6 | 6.0 | 0 |
| Caravello | 1 | 0 | 0.0 | 0 |
| Tolliver | 7 | 0 | 0.0 | 0 |

### RECEIVING

| Last Name | No. | Yds | Avg | TD |
|---|---|---|---|---|
| A. Miller | 75 | 1252 | 16.7 | 10 |
| Nelson | 38 | 380 | 10.0 | 0 |
| Holland | 26 | 336 | 12.9 | 0 |
| Walker | 24 | 395 | 16.5 | 1 |
| Cox | 22 | 200 | 9.1 | 2 |
| Bernstine | 21 | 222 | 10.6 | 1 |
| Spencer | 18 | 112 | 6.2 | 0 |
| Brinson | 12 | 71 | 5.9 | 0 |
| Early | 11 | 126 | 11.5 | 0 |
| Caravello | 10 | 95 | 9.5 | 0 |
| McEwen | 7 | 99 | 14.1 | 0 |
| Butts | 7 | 21 | 3.0 | 0 |
| Allen | 2 | 19 | 9.5 | 0 |
| Parker | 2 | 5 | 2.5 | 0 |
| Floyd | 1 | 6 | 6.0 | 0 |
| McMahon | 1 | 4 | 4.0 | 0 |

### PUNT RETURNS

| Last Name | No. | Yds | Avg | TD |
|---|---|---|---|---|
| Brinson | 11 | 112 | 10.2 | 0 |
| Walker | 6 | 31 | 5.2 | 0 |
| Allen | 2 | 3 | 1.5 | 0 |
| Figaro | 1 | 0 | 0.0 | 0 |
| Lyles | 1 | 0 | 0.0 | 0 |
| Byrd | 0 | 0 | 0.0 | 0 |

### KICKOFF RETURNS

| Last Name | No. | Yds | Avg | TD |
|---|---|---|---|---|
| A. Miller | 21 | 533 | 25.4 | 1 |
| Holland | 29 | 510 | 17.6 | 0 |
| Nelson | 14 | 317 | 22.6 | 0 |
| Floyd | 3 | 12 | 4.0 | 0 |
| Figaro | 1 | 21 | 21.0 | 0 |

### PASSING—PUNTING—KICKING — Statistics

| Last Name | Att | Cmp | % | Yds | Yd/Att | TD | Int— | % | RK |
|---|---|---|---|---|---|---|---|---|---|
| McMahon | 318 | 176 | 55.3 | 2132 | 6.70 | 10 | 10— | 3.1 | 10 |
| Tolliver | 185 | 89 | 48.1 | 1097 | 5.93 | 5 | 8— | 4.3 | |
| Archer | 12 | 5 | 41.7 | 62 | 5.17 | 0 | 1— | 8.3 | |

| PUNTING | No. | Avg. |
|---|---|---|
| Ilesic | 76 | 40.1 |
| Colbert | 8 | 33.3 |

| KICKING | XP | Att | % | FG | Att | % |
|---|---|---|---|---|---|---|
| C. Bahr | 29 | 30 | 97 | 17 | 25 | 68 |

# 1989 A.F.C. PLAYOFFS

## December 31, 1989 at Houston (Attendance 58,306)

### SCORING

| | | | | | | |
|---|---|---|---|---|---|---|
| PITTSBURGH | 7 | 3 | 3 | 10 | 3 | - 26 |
| HOUSTON | 0 | 6 | 3 | 14 | 0 | - 23 |

**First Quarter**
Pitt. — Worley, 9 yard run
PAT — Anderson (kick)

**Second Quarter**
Hous. — Zendejas, 26 yard field goal
Hous. — Zendejas, 35 yard field goal
Pitt. — Anderson, 25 yard field goal

**Third Quarter**
Hous. — Zendejas, 26 yard field goal
Pitt. — Anderson, 30 yard field goal

**Fourth Quarter**
Pitt. — Anderson, 40 yard field goal
Hous. — Givins, 18 yard pass from Moon
PAT — Zendejas (kick)
Hous. — Givins, 9 yard pass from Moon
PAT — Zendejas (kick)
Pitt. — Hoge, 2 yard run
PAT — Anderson (kick)

**Overtime**
Pitt. — Anderson, 50 yard field goal

### TEAM STATISTICS

| PITT. | | HOUS. |
|---|---|---|
| 17 | First Downs- Total | 22 |
| 8 | First Downs- Rushing | 2 |
| 9 | First Downs- Passing | 18 |
| 0 | First Downs- Penalty | 2 |
| 1 | Fumbles- Number | 3 |
| 1 | Fumbles- Lost Ball | 2 |
| 5 | Penalties- Number | 8 |
| 40 | Yards Penalized | 45 |
| 0 | Missed Field Goals | 1 |
| 64 | Offensive Plays | 73 |
| 289 | Net Yards | 380 |
| 4.5 | Average Gain | 5.2 |
| 1 | Giveaways | 2 |
| 2 | Takeaways | 1 |
| +1 | Difference | - 1 |

### INDIVIDUAL STATISTICS

**PITTSBURGH** / **HOUSTON**

#### RUSHING

| | No. | Yds. | Avg. | | No. | Yds. | Avg. |
|---|---|---|---|---|---|---|---|
| Hoge | 17 | 100 | 5.9 | Pinkett | 8 | 26 | 3.3 |
| Worley | 11 | 54 | 4.9 | White | 7 | 13 | 1.9 |
| Stone | 1 | 22 | 22.0 | Moon | 3 | 12 | 4.0 |
| Brister | 1 | 1 | 1.0 | Rozier | 5 | 12 | 2.4 |
| | | | | Highsmith | 2 | 2 | 1.0 |
| | 30 | 177 | 5.9 | | 25 | 65 | 2.6 |

#### RECEIVING

| | No. | Yds. | Avg. | | No. | Yds. | Avg. |
|---|---|---|---|---|---|---|---|
| Worley | 4 | 23 | 5.8 | Givins | 11 | 136 | 12.4 |
| Mularkey | 3 | 40 | 13.3 | Hill | 6 | 98 | 16.3 |
| Hoge | 3 | 26 | 8.7 | Pinkett | 3 | 24 | 8.0 |
| Lipps | 3 | 24 | 8.0 | Highsmith | 3 | 21 | 7.0 |
| Stock | 1 | 7 | 7.0 | Jeffires | 3 | 16 | 5.3 |
| Hill | 1 | 7 | 7.0 | Duncan | 2 | 15 | 7.5 |
| | | | | Rozier | 1 | 5 | 5.0 |
| | 16 | 213 | 13.3 | | 19 | 192 | 10.1 |

#### PUNTING

| | No. | | Avg. | | No. | | Avg. |
|---|---|---|---|---|---|---|---|
| Newsome | 6 | | 25.0 | Montgomery | 4 | | 33.0 |

#### PUNT RETURNS

| | No. | Yds. | Avg. | | No. | Yds. | Avg. |
|---|---|---|---|---|---|---|---|
| Woodson | 2 | 20 | 10.0 | K. Johnson | 1 | 0 | 0.0 |

#### KICKOFF RETURNS

| | No. | Yds. | Avg. | | No. | Yds. | Avg. |
|---|---|---|---|---|---|---|---|
| Woodson | 4 | 74 | 18.5 | K. Johnson | 1 | 18 | 18.0 |
| Thompson | 1 | 11 | 11.0 | L. White | 1 | 9 | 9.0 |
| Stone | 1 | 14 | 14.0 | | 2 | 27 | 13.5 |
| | 6 | 99 | 15.0 | | | | |

#### INTERCEPTION RETURNS

None / None

#### PASSING

**PITTSBURGH**

| | Att. | Comp. | Comp. Pct. | Yds. | Int. | Yds./ Att. | Yds./ Comp. |
|---|---|---|---|---|---|---|---|
| Brister | 33 | 15 | 45.5 | 127 | 0 | 3.8 | 8.5 |

**HOUSTON**

| | Att. | Comp. | Comp. Pct. | Yds. | Int. | Yds./ Att. | Yds./ Comp. |
|---|---|---|---|---|---|---|---|
| Moon | 48 | 29 | 60.4 | 315 | 0 | 6.6 | 10.9 |

---

## January 6, 1990 at Cleveland (Attendance 77,706)

### SCORING

| | | | | | |
|---|---|---|---|---|---|
| BUFFALO | 7 | 7 | 7 | 9 | - 30 |
| CLEVELAND | 3 | 14 | 14 | 3 | - 34 |

**First Quarter**
Buff. — Reed, 72 yard pass from Kelly
PAT — Norwood (kick)
Clev. — Bahr, 45 yard field goal

**Second Quarter**
Clev. — Slaughter, 52 yard pass from Kosar
PAT — Bahr (kick)
Buff. — Lofton, 33 yard pass from Kelly
PAT — Norwood (kick)
Clev. — Middleton, 3 yard pass from Kosar
PAT — Bahr (kick)

**Third Quarter**
Clev. — Slaughter 44 yard pass from Kosar
PAT — Bahr (kick)
Buff. — Thomas, 6 yard pass from Kelly
PAT — Norwood (kick)
Clev. — Metcalf, 90 yard kickoff return
PAT — Bahr (kick)

**Fourth Quarter**
Buff. — Norwood, 30 yard field goal
Clev. — Bahr, 47 yard field goal
Buff. — Thomas, 3 yard pass from Kelly
PAT — Norwood (kick)

### TEAM STATISTICS

| BUFF. | | CLEV. |
|---|---|---|
| 24 | First Downs- Total | 18 |
| 2 | First Downs- Rushing | 10 |
| 20 | First Downs- Passing | 8 |
| 2 | First Downs- Penalty | 0 |
| 2 | Fumbles- Number | 1 |
| 1 | Fumbles- Lost Ball | 1 |
| 6 | Penalties- Number | 5 |
| 35 | Yards Penalized | 30 |
| 0 | Missed Field Goals | 1 |
| 73 | Offensive Plays | 61 |
| 453 | Net Yards | 325 |
| 6.2 | Average Gain | 5.3 |
| 3 | Giveaways | 1 |
| 1 | Takeaways | 3 |
| - 2 | Difference | + 2 |

### INDIVIDUAL STATISTICS

**BUFFALO** / **CLEVELAND**

#### RUSHING

| | No. | Yds. | Avg. | | No. | Yds. | Avg. |
|---|---|---|---|---|---|---|---|
| Thomas | 10 | 27 | 2.7 | Mack | 12 | 62 | 5.2 |
| Kinnebrew | 7 | 17 | 2.4 | Redden | 6 | 13 | 2.2 |
| Kelly | 1 | 5 | 5.0 | Tillman | 1 | 8 | 8.0 |
| | 18 | 49 | 2.7 | Manoa | 3 | 6 | 2.0 |
| | | | | Metcalf | 4 | 2 | 0.5 |
| | | | | Langhorne | 1 | 0 | 0.0 |
| | | | | Kosar | 3 | -1 | -0.3 |
| | | | | | 30 | 90 | 3.0 |

#### RECEIVING

| | No. | Yds. | Avg. | | No. | Yds. | Avg. |
|---|---|---|---|---|---|---|---|
| Thomas | 13 | 150 | 11.5 | Langhorne | 6 | 48 | 8.0 |
| Reed | 6 | 115 | 19.2 | Newsome | 4 | 35 | 8.8 |
| Harmon | 4 | 50 | 12.5 | Slaughter | 3 | 114 | 38.0 |
| Lofton | 3 | 56 | 18.7 | Middleton | 3 | 12 | 4.0 |
| Beebe | 1 | 17 | 17.0 | Mack | 2 | 19 | 9.5 |
| Kinnebrew | 1 | 7 | 7.0 | Brennan | 1 | 15 | 15.0 |
| | 28 | 405 | 14.5 | Metcalf | 1 | 8 | 8.0 |
| | | | | | 20 | 251 | 12.6 |

#### PUNTING

| | No. | | Avg. | | No. | | Avg. |
|---|---|---|---|---|---|---|---|
| Kidd | 3 | | 41.3 | Wagner | 3 | | 37.7 |

#### PUNT RETURNS

| | No. | Yds. | Avg. | | No. | Yds. | Avg. |
|---|---|---|---|---|---|---|---|
| Sutton | 1 | 4 | 4.0 | McNeil | 1 | 0 | 0.0 |

#### KICKOFF RETURNS

| | No. | Yds. | Avg. | | No. | Yds. | Avg. |
|---|---|---|---|---|---|---|---|
| Harmon | 3 | 52 | 17.3 | Metcalf | 4 | 159 | 39.8 |
| Beebe | 2 | 53 | 26.5 | Oliphant | 2 | 21 | 10.5 |
| | 5 | 105 | 21.0 | | 6 | 180 | 30.0 |

#### INTERCEPTION RETURNS

| | No. | Yds. | Avg. | | No. | Yds. | Avg. |
|---|---|---|---|---|---|---|---|
| | | | | Harper | 1 | 0 | 0.0 |
| | | | | Matthews | 1 | 0 | 0.0 |
| | | | | | 2 | 0 | 0.0 |

#### PASSING

**BUFFALO**

| | Att. | Comp. | Comp. Pct. | Yds. | Int. | Yds./ Att. | Yds./ Comp. |
|---|---|---|---|---|---|---|---|
| Kelly | 54 | 28 | 51.9 | 405 | 2 | 7.5 | 14.5 |

**CLEVELAND**

| | Att. | Comp. | Comp. Pct. | Yds. | Int. | Yds./ Att. | Yds./ Comp. |
|---|---|---|---|---|---|---|---|
| Kosar | 20 | 20 | 69.0 | 251 | 0 | 8.7 | 12.6 |

---

## January 7, 1990 at Denver, Colo. (Attendance 75,868)

### SCORING

| | | | | | |
|---|---|---|---|---|---|
| PITTSBURGH | 3 | 14 | 3 | 3 | - 23 |
| DENVER | 0 | 10 | 7 | 7 | - 24 |

**First Quarter**
Pitt. — Anderson, 32 yard field goal

**Second Quarter**
Pitt. — Worley, 7 yard run
PAT — Anderson (kick)
Den. — Bratton, 1 yard run
PAT — Treadwell (kick)
Pitt. — Lipps, 9 yard pass from Brister
PAT — Anderson (kick)
Den. — Treadwell, 43 yard field goal

**Third Quarter**
Den. — V. Johnson, 37 yard pass from Elway
PAT — Treadwell (kick)
Pitt. — Anderson, 35 yard field goal

**Fourth Quarter**
Pitt. — Anderson, 32 yard field goal
Den. — Bratton, 1 yard run
PAT — Treadwell (kick)

### TEAM STATISTICS

| PITT. | | DEN. |
|---|---|---|
| 19 | First Downs- Total | 19 |
| 7 | First Downs- Rushing | 8 |
| 12 | First Downs- Passing | 9 |
| 0 | First Downs- Penalty | 2 |
| 2 | Fumbles- Number | 1 |
| 2 | Fumbles- Lost Ball | 0 |
| 8 | Penalties- Number | 2 |
| 50 | Yards Penalized | 19 |
| 0 | Missed Field Goals | 0 |
| 61 | Offensive Plays | 52 |
| 404 | Net Yards | 364 |
| 6.6 | Average Gain | 7.0 |
| 2 | Giveaways | 1 |
| 1 | Takeaways | 2 |
| - 1 | Difference | + 1 |

### INDIVIDUAL STATISTICS

**PITTSBURGH** / **DENVER**

#### RUSHING

| | No. | Yds. | Avg. | | No. | Yds. | Avg. |
|---|---|---|---|---|---|---|---|
| Hoge | 16 | 120 | 7.5 | Humphrey | 18 | 85 | 4.7 |
| Worley | 13 | 50 | 3.8 | Elway | 7 | 44 | 6.3 |
| Brister | 2 | 4 | 2.0 | Bratton | 4 | 3 | 0.8 |
| Lipps | 1 | 1 | 1.0 | Sewell | 1 | 6 | 6.0 |
| | 32 | 175 | 5.5 | Winder | 1 | 0 | 0.0 |
| | | | | | 31 | 138 | 4.5 |

#### RECEIVING

| | No. | Yds. | Avg. | | No. | Yds. | Avg. |
|---|---|---|---|---|---|---|---|
| Hoge | 8 | 60 | 7.5 | Jackson | 5 | 111 | 22.2 |
| Lipps | 3 | 29 | 9.7 | Johnson | 3 | 85 | 28.3 |
| Stone | 3 | 18 | 6.0 | Young | 2 | 22 | 11.0 |
| Mularkey | 2 | 36 | 18.0 | Nattiel | 1 | 15 | 15.0 |
| Worley | 1 | 33 | 33.0 | Humphrey | 1 | 6 | 6.0 |
| Stock | 1 | 30 | 30.0 | | 12 | 239 | 19.9 |
| Thompson | 1 | 23 | 23.0 | | | | |
| | 19 | 229 | 12.1 | | | | |

#### PUNTING

| | No. | | Avg. | | No. | | Avg. |
|---|---|---|---|---|---|---|---|
| Newsome | 2 | | 43.0 | Horan | 3 | | 44.3 |
| | | | | Elway | 1 | | 17.0 |
| | | | | | 4 | | 37.5 |

#### PUNT RETURNS

| | No. | Yds. | Avg. | | No. | Yds. | Avg. |
|---|---|---|---|---|---|---|---|
| Woodson | 1 FC | | | Johnson | 1 | 6 | 6.0 |

#### KICKOFF RETURNS

| | No. | Yds. | Avg. | | No. | Yds. | Avg. |
|---|---|---|---|---|---|---|---|
| Woodson | 2 | 33 | 16.5 | Bell | 2 | 62 | 31.0 |
| | | | | Carrington | 2 | 51 | 25.5 |
| | | | | Bratton | 1 | 6 | 6.0 |
| | | | | | 5 | 119 | 23.8 |

#### INTERCEPTION RETURNS

| | No. | Yds. | Avg. | | No. | Yds. | Avg. |
|---|---|---|---|---|---|---|---|
| Everett | 1 | 26 | 26.0 | | | | |

#### PASSING

**PITTSBURGH**

| | Att. | Comp. | Comp. Pct. | Yds. | Int. | Yds./ Att. | Yds./ Comp. |
|---|---|---|---|---|---|---|---|
| Brister | 29 | 19 | 65.5 | 229 | 0 | 7.9 | 12.1 |

**DENVER**

| | Att. | Comp. | Comp. Pct. | Yds. | Int. | Yds./ Att. | Yds./ Comp. |
|---|---|---|---|---|---|---|---|
| Elway | 20 | 12 | 60.0 | 239 | 1 | 12.0 | 19.9 |

# 1989 N.F.C. — PLAYOFFS

## December 31, 1989 at Philadelphia (Attendance 57,869)

### SCORING

| | | | | | |
|---|---|---|---|---|---|
| L.A. RAMS | 14 | 0 | 0 | 7 | - 21 |
| PHILADELPHIA | 0 | 0 | 0 | 7 | - 7 |

**First Quarter**
L.A. Rams — Ellard, 39 yard pass from Everett
　　PAT — Lansford (kick)
L.A. Rams — Johnson, 4 yard pass from Everett
　　PAT — Lansford (kick)

**Fourth Quarter**
Phil. — Toney, 1 yard run
　　PAT — Ruzek (kick)
L.A. Rams — Bell, 7 yard run
　　PAT — Lansford (kick)

### TEAM STATISTICS

| L.A. RAMS | | PHIL. |
|---|---|---|
| 19 | First Downs- Total | 14 |
| 6 | First Downs- Rushing | 6 |
| 12 | First Downs- Passing | 8 |
| 1 | First Downs- Penalty | 0 |
| 1 | Fumbles- Number | 6 |
| 1 | Fumbles- Lost Ball | 2 |
| 1 | Penalties- Number | 4 |
| 5 | Yards Penalized | 35 |
| 1 | Missed Field Goals | 1 |
| 71 | Offensive Plays | 62 |
| 409 | Net Yards | 306 |
| 5.5 | Average Gain | 4.5 |
| 3 | Giveaways | 3 |
| 3 | Takeaways | 3 |
| 0 | Difference | 0 |

### INDIVIDUAL STATISTICS

**L.A. RAMS** / **PHILADELPHIA**

RUSHING

| | No. | Yds. | Avg. | | No. | Yds. | Avg. |
|---|---|---|---|---|---|---|---|
| Bell | 27 | 124 | 4.6 | Toney | 5 | 12 | 2.4 |
| Everett | 7 | 2 | 0.3 | Cunningham | 6 | 39 | 6.5 |
| McGee | 2 | 18 | 9.0 | Sherman | 9 | 44 | 4.9 |
| | 36 | 144 | 4.0 | | 20 | 95 | 4.7 |

RECEIVING

| | No. | Yds. | Avg. | | No. | Yds. | Avg. |
|---|---|---|---|---|---|---|---|
| Delpino | 3 | 31 | 10.3 | Byars | 9 | 68 | 7.6 |
| Ellard | 4 | 87 | 21.8 | Toney | 4 | 35 | 8.8 |
| Holohan | 4 | 37 | 9.3 | Jackson | 3 | 47 | 15.7 |
| McGee | 3 | 33 | 11.0 | R. Johnson | 2 | 38 | 19.0 |
| Anderson | 2 | 77 | 38.5 | Sherman | 2 | 18 | 9.0 |
| Bell | 1 | 23 | 23.0 | Carter | 2 | 16 | 8.0 |
| D. Johnson | 1 | 4 | 4.0 | Garrity | 2 | 16 | 8.0 |
| | 18 | 281 | 15.6 | | 24 | 238 | 9.9 |

PUNTING

| | No. | | Avg. | | No. | | Avg. |
|---|---|---|---|---|---|---|---|
| Hatcher | 7 | 37.0 | | Tuten | 9 | | 36.3 |
| | | | | Cunningham | 1 | | 20.0 |
| | | | | | 10 | | 34.7 |

PUNT RETURNS

| | No. | Yds. | Avg. | | No. | Yds. | Avg. |
|---|---|---|---|---|---|---|---|
| Henley | 3 | 15 | 5.0 | Edwards | 2 | 5 | 2.5 |

KICKOFF RETURNS

| | No. | Yds. | Avg. | | No. | Yds. | Avg. |
|---|---|---|---|---|---|---|---|
| Delpino | 1 | 0 | 0.0 | Edwards | 3 | 37 | 12.3 |
| Brown | 1 | 14 | 14.0 | Higgs | 1 | 15 | 15.0 |
| | 2 | 14 | 7.0 | | 4 | 52 | 13.5 |

INTERCEPTION RETURNS

| | No. | Yds. | Avg. | | No. | Yds. | Avg. |
|---|---|---|---|---|---|---|---|
| Irvin | 1 | 0 | 0.0 | Jenkins | 1 | 33 | 33.0 |
| | | | | Joyner | 1 | 1 | 1.0 |
| | | | | | 2 | 34 | 17.0 |

PASSING

**L.A. RAMS**

| | Att. | Comp. | Comp. Pct. | Yds. | Int. | Yds./Att. | Yds./Comp. |
|---|---|---|---|---|---|---|---|
| Everett | 33 | 18 | 54.5 | 281 | 2 | 8.5 | 15.6 |

**PHILADELPHIA**

| | Att. | Comp. | Comp. Pct. | Yds. | Int. | Yds./Att. | Yds./Comp. |
|---|---|---|---|---|---|---|---|
| Cunningham | 40 | 24 | 60.0 | 238 | 1 | 6.0 | 9.9 |

---

## January 6, 1990 at San Francisco (Attendance 64,585)

### SCORING

| | | | | | |
|---|---|---|---|---|---|
| MINNESOTA | 3 | 0 | 3 | 7 | - 13 |
| SAN FRANCISCO | 7 | 20 | 0 | 14 | - 41 |

**First Quarter**
Minn. — Karlis, 38 yard field goal
S.F. — Rice, 72 yard pass from Montana
　　PAT — Cofer (kick)

**Second Quarter**
S.F. — Jones, 8 yard pass from Montana
　　PAT — Cofer (kick)
S.F. — Taylor, 8 yard pass from Montana
　　PAT — Cofer (kick)
S.F. — Rice, 13 yard pass from Montana
　　PAT — kick failed

**Third Quarter**
Minn. — Karlis, 44 yard field goal

**Fourth Quarter**
S.F. — Lott, 58 yard interception return
　　PAT — Cofer (kick)
S.F. — Craig, 4 yard run
　　PAT — Cofer (kick)
Minn. — Fenney, 3 yard run
　　PAT — Karlis (kick)

### TEAM STATISTICS

| MINN. | | S.F. |
|---|---|---|
| 25 | First Downs- Total | 22 |
| 7 | First Downs- Rushing | 10 |
| 17 | First Downs- Passing | 11 |
| 1 | First Downs- Penalty | 1 |
| 1 | Fumbles- Number | 1 |
| 1 | Fumbles- Lost Ball | 1 |
| 4 | Penalties- Number | 9 |
| 31 | Yards Penalized | 65 |
| 0 | Missed Field Goals | 2 |
| 79 | Offensive Plays | 57 |
| 385 | Net Yards | 403 |
| 4.9 | Average Gain | 7.1 |
| 5 | Giveaways | 1 |
| 1 | Takeaways | 5 |
| - 4 | Difference | + 4 |

### INDIVIDUAL STATISTICS

**MINNESOTA** / **SAN FRANCISCO**

RUSHING

| | No. | Yds. | Avg. | | No. | Yds. | Avg. |
|---|---|---|---|---|---|---|---|
| Wilson | 3 | 39 | 13.0 | Craig | 18 | 125 | 6.9 |
| Walker | 9 | 29 | 3.2 | Rathman | 7 | 24 | 3.4 |
| Fenney | 4 | 8 | 2.0 | Flagler | 5 | 13 | 2.6 |
| Gannon | 2 | 7 | 3.5 | Montana | 2 | 0 | 0.0 |
| Dozier | 3 | 13 | 4.3 | | 32 | 162 | 5.1 |
| | 21 | 86 | 4.1 | | | | |

RECEIVING

| | No. | Yds. | Avg. | | No. | Yds. | Avg. |
|---|---|---|---|---|---|---|---|
| Jordan | 9 | 149 | 16.6 | Rice | 6 | 114 | 19.0 |
| Carter | 4 | 44 | 11.0 | Taylor | 3 | 50 | 16.7 |
| Fenney | 4 | 15 | 3.8 | Rathman | 3 | 29 | 9.7 |
| Anderson | 3 | 18 | 6.0 | Jones | 3 | 24 | 8.0 |
| Dozier | 3 | 15 | 5.0 | Henderson | 2 | 24 | 12.0 |
| Gustafson | 2 | 46 | 23.0 | | 17 | 241 | 14.2 |
| Lewis | 2 | 19 | 9.5 | | | | |
| Jones | 2 | 18 | 9.0 | | | | |
| Walker | 2 | 14 | 7.0 | | | | |
| | 31 | 338 | 10.9 | | | | |

PUNTING

| | No. | | Avg. | | No. | | Avg. |
|---|---|---|---|---|---|---|---|
| Scribner | 4 | 32.0 | | Helton | 4 | | 30.8 |

PUNT RETURNS

| | No. | Yds. | Avg. | | No. | Yds. | Avg. |
|---|---|---|---|---|---|---|---|
| Lewis | 2 | 18 | 9.0 | Taylor | 2 | 6 | 3.0 |

KICKOFF RETURNS

| | No. | Yds. | Avg. | | No. | Yds. | Avg. |
|---|---|---|---|---|---|---|---|
| Walker | 5 | 97 | 19.4 | Tillman | 2 | 26 | 13.0 |
| Dozier | 1 | 19 | 19.0 | Flagler | 1 | 58 | 58.0 |
| Lewis | 1 | 14 | 14.0 | Rathman | 1 | 0 | 0.0 |
| | 7 | 130 | 18.6 | | 4 | 84 | 21.0 |

INTERCEPTION RETURNS

| | | | | | No. | Yds. | Avg. |
|---|---|---|---|---|---|---|---|
| | | | | Lott | 1 | 58 | 58.0 |
| | | | | Brooks | 1 | 28 | 28.0 |
| | | | | MyKyer | 1 | 41 | 41.0 |
| | | | | Griffin | 1 | 0 | 0.0 |
| | | | | | 4 | 127 | 31.8 |

PASSING

**MINNESOTA**

| | Att. | Comp. | Comp. Pct. | Yds. | Int. | Yds./Att. | Yds./Comp. |
|---|---|---|---|---|---|---|---|
| Wilson | 17 | 9 | 52.9 | 84 | 2 | 4.9 | 9.3 |
| Kramer | 19 | 9 | 47.4 | 110 | 1 | 5.8 | 12.2 |
| Gannon | 18 | 13 | 72.2 | 144 | 1 | 8.0 | 11.1 |
| | 54 | 31 | 57.4 | 338 | 4 | 6.3 | 10.9 |

**SAN FRANCISCO**

| | Att. | Comp. | Comp. Pct. | Yds. | Int. | Yds./Att. | Yds./Comp. |
|---|---|---|---|---|---|---|---|
| Montana | 24 | 17 | 70.8 | 241 | 0 | 10.0 | 14.2 |
| Young | 1 | 0 | 0.0 | 0 | 0 | 0.0 | 0.0 |
| | 25 | 17 | 68.0 | 241 | 0 | 9.6 | 14.2 |

---

## January 7, 1990 at East Rutherford, N.J. (Attendance 76,325)

### SCORING

| | | | | | |
|---|---|---|---|---|---|
| L.A. RAMS | 0 | 7 | 0 | 6 | 6 - 19 |
| N.Y. GIANTS | 6 | 0 | 7 | 0 | 0 - 13 |

**First Quarter**
N.Y.G. — Allegre, 35 yard field goal
N.Y.G. — Allegre, 41 yard field goal

**Second Quarter**
L.A. Rams — Anderson, 20 yard pass from Everett
　　PAT — Lansford (kick)

**Third Quarter**
N.Y.G. — Anderson, 2 yard run
　　PAT — Allegre (kick)

**Fourth Quarter**
L.A. Rams — Lansford, 31 yard field goal
L.A. Rams — Lansford, 22 yard field goal

**Overtime**
L.A. Rams — Anderson, 30 yard pass from Everett

### TEAM STATISTICS

| L.A. RAMS | | N.Y.G. |
|---|---|---|
| 26 | First Downs- Total | 20 |
| 6 | First Downs- Rushing | 11 |
| 18 | First Downs- Passing | 8 |
| 2 | First Downs- Penalty | 1 |
| 1 | Fumbles- Number | 3 |
| 1 | Fumbles- Lost Ball | 0 |
| 5 | Penalties- Number | 4 |
| 35 | Yards Penalized | 59 |
| 0 | Missed Field Goals | 0 |
| 70 | Offensive Plays | 67 |
| 448 | Net Yards | 344 |
| 5.0 | Average Gain | 5.1 |
| 2 | Giveaways | 1 |
| 1 | Takeaways | 2 |
| - 1 | Difference | + 1 |

### INDIVIDUAL STATISTICS

**L.A. RAMS** / **N.Y. GIANTS**

RUSHING

| | No. | Yds. | Avg. | | No. | Yds. | Avg. |
|---|---|---|---|---|---|---|---|
| Bell | 19 | 87 | 4.6 | O. Anderson | 24 | 120 | 5.0 |
| McGee | 3 | 34 | 11.3 | Tillman | 7 | 25 | 3.6 |
| Everett | 2 | 25 | 12.5 | Simms | 3 | 16 | 5.3 |
| | 24 | 146 | 6.1 | Meggett | 1 | 7 | 7.0 |
| | | | | Carthon | 1 | 3 | 3.0 |
| | | | | | 36 | 171 | 4.8 |

RECEIVING

| | No. | Yds. | Avg. | | No. | Yds. | Avg. |
|---|---|---|---|---|---|---|---|
| Ellard | 8 | 125 | 15.6 | Meggett | 4 | 52 | 13.0 |
| Holohan | 5 | 48 | 9.6 | Mowatt | 3 | 52 | 17.3 |
| Brown | 3 | 35 | 11.7 | Anderson | 3 | -2 | -0.7 |
| Johnson | 3 | 15 | 5.0 | Baker | 2 | 46 | 23.0 |
| Anderson | 2 | 50 | 25.0 | Manuel | 1 | 24 | 24.0 |
| McGee | 2 | 31 | 15.5 | Carthon | 1 | 8 | 8.0 |
| Bell | 2 | 11 | 5.5 | | 14 | 180 | 12.9 |
| | 25 | 315 | 12.6 | | | | |

PUNTING

| | No. | | Avg. | | No. | | Avg. |
|---|---|---|---|---|---|---|---|
| Hatcher | 4 | 30.3 | | Landeta | 5 | | 37.2 |

PUNT RETURNS

| | No. | Yds. | Avg. | | No. | Yds. | Avg. |
|---|---|---|---|---|---|---|---|
| Irvin | 1 | 3 | 3.0 | Meggett | 1 | 0 | 0.0 |
| Henley | 2 | -4 | -2.0 | | | | |
| | 3 | -1 | -0.3 | | | | |

KICKOFF RETURNS

| | No. | Yds. | Avg. | | No. | Yds. | Avg. |
|---|---|---|---|---|---|---|---|
| Delpino | 4 | 60 | 15.0 | Ingram | 2 | 41 | 20.5 |
| Brown | 1 | 38 | 38.0 | Meggett | 1 | 25 | 25.0 |
| | 5 | 98 | 19.6 | Cross | 1 | 9 | 9.0 |
| | | | | | 4 | 75 | 18.8 |

INTERCEPTION RETURNS

| | No. | Yds. | Avg. | | No. | Yds. | Avg. |
|---|---|---|---|---|---|---|---|
| Stewart | 1 | 19 | 19.0 | Collins | 1 | 0 | 0.0 |

PASSING

**L.A. RAMS**

| | Att. | Comp. | Comp. Pct. | Yds. | Int. | Yds./Att. | Yds./Comp. |
|---|---|---|---|---|---|---|---|
| Everett | 44 | 25 | 56.8 | 315 | 1 | 7.2 | 12.6 |

**N.Y. GIANTS**

| | Att. | Comp. | Comp. Pct. | Yds. | Int. | Yds./Att. | Yds./Comp. |
|---|---|---|---|---|---|---|---|
| Simms | 29 | 14 | 48.3 | 180 | 1 | 6.2 | 12.9 |
| Meggett | 1 | 0 | 0.0 | 0 | 0 | 0.0 | 0.0 |
| | 30 | 14 | 46.7 | 180 | 1 | 6.0 | 12.9 |

# 1989 Championship Games

## SCORING

| | | | | | |
|---|---|---|---|---|---|
| CLEVELAND | 0 | 0 | 21 | 0 - 21 |
| DENVER | 3 | 7 | 14 | 13 - 37 |

**First Quarter**
Den.   Treadwell, 29 yard field goal

**Second Quarter**
Den.   Young, 70 yard pass from Elway
   PAT — Treadwell (kick)

**Third Quarter**
Clev.   Brennan, 27 yard pass from Kosar
   PAT — Bahr (kick)
Den.   Mobley, 5 yard pass from Elway
   PAT — Treadwell (kick)
Den.   Winder, 7 yard run
   PAT — Treadwell (kick)
Clev.   Brennan, 10 yard pass from Kosar
   PAT — Bahr (kick)
Clev.   Manoa, 2 yard run
   PAT — Bahr (kick)

**Fourth Quarter**
Den.   Winder, 39 yard pass from Elway
   PAT — Treadwell (kick)
Den.   Treadwell, 34 yard field goal
Den.   Treadwell, 31 yard field goal

### TEAM STATISTICS

| CLEV. | | DEN. |
|---|---|---|
| 14 | First Downs- Total | 22 |
| 3 | First Downs- Rushing | 6 |
| 11 | First Downs- Passing | 14 |
| 0 | First Downs- Penalty | 2 |
| 3 | Fumbles- Number | 2 |
| 0 | Fumbles- Lost Ball | 2 |
| 8 | Penalties- Number | 1 |
| 55 | Yards Penalized | 5 |
| 0 | Missed Field Goals | 0 |
| 62 | Offensive Plays | 76 |
| 256 | Net Yards | 497 |
| 4.1 | Average Gain | 6.5 |
| 3 | Giveaways | 2 |
| 2 | Takeaways | 3 |
| -1 | Difference | +1 |

## A.F.C. CHAMPIONSHIP GAME
January 14, 1990 at Denver, Colo.
(Attendance 76,005)

The Broncos and Browns met for the A.F.C. championship for the third time in four years, but this game was not to be decided on last-minute heroics like the previous two. Denver's John Elway had, by his own admission, the game of his life. He completed 20-of-36 passes for 385 yards and three touchdowns and even led his team in rushing. Cleveland's Bernie Kosar, playing with arm miseries, was ineffective in the first half, hitting on only 7-of-23.

Denver started slowly with a 29-yard field goal by David Treadwell after safety Dennis Smith intercepted an errant Kosar pass. Early in the second quarter, Denver's arsenal was reduced when star runner Bobby Humphrey was knocked out with broken ribs, courtesy of a hit by Cleveland cornerback Frank Minnifield. But a few minutes later, Minnifield was the goat as he was burned by Michael Young for a 70-yard touchdown pass and a 10-0 Denver lead.

A little over three minutes into the third quarter, Kosar hit Brian Brennan for a 27-yard TD, but Elway answered by with an 80-yard drive capped by a five-yard scoring pass to Orson Mobley. A 60-yard drive followed, ending in Sammy Winder's seven-yard scoring scamper.

Kosar closed the gap with another touchdown pass to Brennan. Then Browns safety Felix Wright grabbed Melvin Bratton's fumble at the 26 and ran it to the one. Tim Manoa plunged over to cut the lead to 24-21. But Elway was brilliant in directing another 80-yard drive with a 39-yard pass to Sammy Winder shortly into the fourth quarter to give Denver 31-21 breathing room. Treadwell sealed the game with two field goals after interceptions of desperate Kosar passes.

### INDIVIDUAL STATISTICS

| CLEVELAND | | | | DENVER | | |
|---|---|---|---|---|---|---|
| **RUSHING** | No. | Yds. | Avg. | | No. | Yds. | Avg. |

| CLEVELAND | No. | Yds. | Avg. | DENVER | No. | Yds. | Avg. |
|---|---|---|---|---|---|---|---|
| Mack | 6 | 36 | 6.0 | Elway | 5 | 39 | 7.8 |
| Kosar | 2 | 22 | 11.0 | Winder | 21 | 37 | 1.8 |
| Manoa | 2 | 5 | 2.5 | Humphrey | 8 | 23 | 2.9 |
| Metcalf | 3 | 4 | 1.3 | Sewell | 4 | 17 | 4.3 |
| Langhorne | 1 | -1 | -1.0 | Bratton | 1 | 4 | 4.0 |
| | 14 | 66 | 4.7 | | 39 | 120 | 3.1 |

**RECEIVING**

| CLEVELAND | No. | Yds. | Avg. | DENVER | No. | Yds. | Avg. |
|---|---|---|---|---|---|---|---|
| Langhorne | 5 | 48 | 9.6 | V. Johnson | 7 | 91 | 13.0 |
| Brennan | 5 | 58 | 11.6 | Sewell | 3 | 55 | 18.3 |
| Slaughter | 3 | 36 | 12.0 | Young | 2 | 123 | 61.5 |
| Mack | 2 | 8 | 4.0 | Winder | 2 | 39 | 19.5 |
| Metcalf | 2 | 7 | 3.5 | M. Jackson | 2 | 25 | 12.5 |
| Tillman | 1 | 15 | 15.0 | Mobley | 2 | 22 | 11.0 |
| Manoa | 1 | 8 | 8.0 | Humphrey | 1 | 23 | 23.0 |
| | 19 | 210 | 11.1 | Bratton | 1 | 7 | 7.0 |
| | | | | | 20 | 385 | 19.3 |

**PUNTING**

| CLEVELAND | No. | | Avg. | DENVER | No. | | Avg. |
|---|---|---|---|---|---|---|---|
| Wagner | 8 | | 42.3 | Horan | 5 | | 46.4 |

**PUNT RETURNS**

| CLEVELAND | No. | Yds. | Avg. | DENVER | No. | Yds. | Avg. |
|---|---|---|---|---|---|---|---|
| McNeil | 1 | 7 | 7.0 | V. Johnson | 4 | 36 | 9.0 |

**KICKOFF RETURNS**

| CLEVELAND | No. | Yds. | Avg. | DENVER | | | |
|---|---|---|---|---|---|---|---|
| Metcalf | 6 | 119 | 19.8 | | | | |
| K. Jones | 1 | 12 | 12.0 | | | | |
| | 7 | 130 | 18.6 | | | | |

**INTERCEPTION RETURNS**

| | | | | DENVER | No. | Yds. | Avg. |
|---|---|---|---|---|---|---|---|
| | | | | D. Smith | 2 | 13 | 6.5 |
| | | | | Corrington | 1 | 1 | 1.0 |
| | | | | | 5 | 14 | 2.8 |

**PASSING**

| CLEVELAND | Att. | Comp. | Comp. Pct. | Yds. | Int. | Yds./Att. | Yds./Comp. |
|---|---|---|---|---|---|---|---|
| Kosar | 44 | 19 | 43.2 | 210 | 3 | 47.7 | 11.1 |
| **DENVER** | | | | | | | |
| Elway | 35 | 20 | 57.1 | 385 | 0 | 11.0 | 19.3 |

---

## SCORING

| | | | | | |
|---|---|---|---|---|---|
| L.A. RAMS | 3 | 0 | 0 | 0 - 3 |
| SAN FRANCISCO | 0 | 21 | 3 | 6 - 30 |

**First Quarter**
L.A. Rams   Lansford, 23 yard field goal

**Second Quarter**
S.F.   Jones, 20 yard pass from Montana
   PAT — Cofer (kick)
S.F.   Craig, 1 yard run
   PAT — Cofer (kick)
S.F.   Taylor, 18 yard pass from Montana
   PAT — Cofer (kick)

**Third Quarter**
S.F.   Cofer, 28 yard field goal

**Fourth Quarter**
S.F.   Cofer, 36 yard field goal
S.F.   Cofer, 25 yard field goal

### TEAM STATISTICS

| L.A. RAMS | | S.F. |
|---|---|---|
| 9 | First Downs- Total | 29 |
| 0 | First Downs- Rushing | 12 |
| 9 | First Downs- Passing | 16 |
| 0 | First Downs- Penalty | 1 |
| 1 | Fumbles- Number | 3 |
| 0 | Fumbles- Lost Ball | 2 |
| 1 | Penalties- Number | 4 |
| 10 | Yards Penalized | 40 |
| 0 | Missed Field Goals | 1 |
| 47 | Offensive Plays | 76 |
| 156 | Net Yards | 442 |
| 3.1 | Average Gain | 5.8 |
| 3 | Giveaways | 2 |
| 2 | Takeaways | 3 |
| -1 | Difference | +1 |

## N.F.C. CHAMPIONSHIP GAME
January 14, 1990 at San Francisco, Calif.
(Attendance 64,769)

The Rams beat the 49ers in October and came close in December, but it was no contest this time before a record crowd at Candlestick Park as San Francisco rolled over Los Angeles. The Rams offense, which had averaged 428 yards in two playoff victories, managed a paltry 156 against the 49ers. "Special Lark," a new defense installed by coach George Seifert to take away deep passes to Ram receivers Henry Ellard and Flipper Anderson, worked so well that Rams quarterback Jim Everett was completely befuddled. He completed only 16-of-36 passes, nine of them short tosses to his backs, for 141 yards and was intercepted three times.

Meanwhile, 49ers quarterback Joe Montana ripped through the Rams for 262 yards and two touchdowns, completing 26-of-30 passes.

The Rams had the better of the first quarter but couldn't take full advantage. After driving 44 yards on their first possession, they had to settle for Mike Lansford's 23-yard field goal. San Francisco fumbled and Everett had Anderson open for a possible touchdown, but 49ers safety Ronnie Lott batted the ball away at the last second. After that, it was all 49ers.

In the second quarter, Montana threw a 20-yard TD pass to Brent Jones, and Roger Craig plunged over for another score. With 3:10 left in the first half, the 49ers took the ball at their own 13. They drove 87 yards, with the Montana-to-John Taylor scoring pass coming with only nine seconds left. In the second half, the 49ers widened their lead on three Mike Cofer field goals, and the Rams were held to a mere 33 yards.

### INDIVIDUAL STATISTICS

| L.A. RAMS | | | | SAN FRANCISCO | | | |
|---|---|---|---|---|---|---|---|
| **RUSHING** | No. | Yds. | Avg. | | No. | Yds. | Avg. |
| Bell | 8 | 20 | 2.5 | Craig | 23 | 93 | 4.0 |
| Gary | 1 | 3 | 3.0 | Rathman | 10 | 63 | 6.3 |
| Delpino | 1 | 3 | 3.0 | Flagler | 8 | 19 | 2.4 |
| | 10 | 26 | 2.6 | Montana | 1 | 4 | 4.0 |
| | | | | Henderson | 1 | 1 | 1.0 |
| | | | | Young | 1 | -1 | -1.0 |
| | | | | | 44 | 179 | 4.1 |

**RECEIVING**

| L.A. RAMS | No. | Yds. | Avg. | SAN FRANCISCO | No. | Yds. | Avg. |
|---|---|---|---|---|---|---|---|
| McGee | 7 | 53 | 7.6 | Rice | 6 | 55 | 9.2 |
| Holohan | 3 | 26 | 8.7 | Rathman | 6 | 48 | 8.0 |
| Bell | 3 | 23 | 7.7 | Jones | 4 | 46 | 11.5 |
| Ellard | 2 | 18 | 9.0 | Taylor | 4 | 45 | 11.3 |
| Anderson | 1 | 14 | 14.0 | Craig | 3 | 40 | 13.3 |
| Johnson | 1 | 7 | 7.0 | Sherrard | 2 | 21 | 10.5 |
| | 16 | 141 | 8.8 | Wilson | 1 | 7 | 7.0 |
| | | | | Williams | 1 | 6 | 6.0 |
| | | | | | 27 | 268 | 9.9 |

**PUNTING**

| L.A. RAMS | No. | | Avg. | SAN FRANCISCO | No. | | Avg. |
|---|---|---|---|---|---|---|---|
| Hatcher | 7 | | 31.4 | Helton | 2 | | 31.0 |

**PUNT RETURNS**

| L.A. RAMS | No. | Yds. | Avg. | SAN FRANCISCO | No. | Yds. | Avg. |
|---|---|---|---|---|---|---|---|
| Irvin | 1 | 10 | 10.0 | Taylor | 1 | 4 | 4.0 |

**KICKOFF RETURNS**

| L.A. RAMS | No. | Yds. | Avg. | SAN FRANCISCO | No. | Yds. | Avg. |
|---|---|---|---|---|---|---|---|
| Delpino | 4 | 95 | 23.8 | Flagler | 1 | 19 | 19.0 |
| Brown | 2 | 51 | 25.5 | Tillman | 1 | 16 | 16.0 |
| | 6 | 146 | 24.3 | | 2 | 35 | 17.5 |

**INTERCEPTION RETURNS**

| | | | | SAN FRANCISCO | No. | Yds. | Avg. |
|---|---|---|---|---|---|---|---|
| | | | | McKyer | 1 | 27 | 27.0 |
| | | | | Turner | 1 | 15 | 15.0 |
| | | | | Lott | 1 | 14 | 14.0 |
| | | | | | 3 | 56 | 18.7 |

**PASSING**

| L.A. RAMS | Att. | Comp. | Comp. Pct. | Yds. | Int. | Yds./Att. | Yds./Comp. |
|---|---|---|---|---|---|---|---|
| Everett | 36 | 16 | 44.4 | 141 | 3 | 3.9 | 10.1 |
| **SAN FRANCISCO** | | | | | | | |
| Montana | 30 | 26 | 86.7 | 262 | 0 | 8.7 | 10.1 |
| Young | 1 | 1 | 100.0 | 6 | 0 | 6.0 | 6.0 |

# Super: Dome, Joe and the 49ers

It was possibly the best Super Bowl ever — for one team. Joe Montana and the San Francisco 49ers carved a niche in football history at the Louisiana Superdome by winning their fourth championship of the decade. Moreover, Super Bowl XXIV made them the first back-to-back winners since the Steelers of the '70s. To say they did it convincingly is the greatest understatement since Noah's weatherman predicted "possible showers." This time it was the Broncos who were deluged. San Francisco's 55-10 victory represented both the biggest margin in Super Bowl history and the most points scored by a Super Bowl team.

Meanwhile, Denver suffered its fourth loss in as many Super Bowl appearances. Ironically, a few weeks before the game, 54 percent of Denver fans responding to a survey hoped their team would *not* go to the Super Bowl and thus avoid another embarrassing defeat. The Broncos didn't listen, and apparently 100 percent of the 49ers hoped they would show up.

The Broncos, 12-point underdogs, were expected to run the ball to try to keep Montana & Co. off the field. Instead, John Elway came out throwing and the combination of the 49er pass rush and coverage, some misdirected passes and drops by receivers put Denver into a quick hole. Less than five minutes into the contest, Montana hit Jerry Rice for a 20-yard touchdown that put San Francisco ahead to stay. Denver came back to score on a 43-yard David Treadwell field goal, but the dam was about to burst. Montana's seven-yard toss to Brent Jones widened the lead with three seconds left in the first quarter.

When Tom Rathman cracked over from the one midway through the second quarter, the game was over for all purposes except counting up the score. Montana connected with Rice again for a 38-yard TD with less than a minute left in the first half to make the score 27-3, and much of

America's TV fans decided it was time to check out other channels.

If they neglected to return for the second half, they missed Rice scoring on a 28-yarder from Montana and John Taylor taking a 35-yarder for another score. The 49ers stayed on the ground in the fourth period, as Rathman and Roger Craig scored the last touchdowns. In between 49er scores, Elway directed a Bronco offense that was mostly "three downs and out," although he did run three yards for a third-quarter score that made the score "only" 41-10 at the time.

In a 55-10 game, it's difficult to find one play that makes a significant difference, however the Broncos were making a run at the 49ers midway through the first quarter when they had a first down at their own 49-yard line and trailing only 7-3. Bobby Humphrey took a handoff from Elway and attempted to run behind left tackle Gerald Perry. But 49ers defensive end Kevin Fagan wrapped up Humphrey and stripped the ball away from him. Chet Brooks recovered for San Francisco and the game was effectively over.

"The most we gave up all year was 28 points," said Denver defensive coordinator Wade Phillips, who received considerable praise for upgrading the defense (before the game). "Today they got 27 in the first half only because they missed a point (on a missed conversion), and 28 more in the second half. They have a great killer instinct. You make a mistake and they go for the big play."

Rice caught seven passes for 148 yards and three TD's, all better marks than he registered in earning MVP honors a year earlier. But the day belonged to Montana, whose 22-of-29 passing, 13 consecutive completions at one point, 297 yards and five touchdowns earned him his third Super Bowl MVP award. Amazingly, in 122 Super Bowl passes, he'd completed 68 percent and never thrown an interception.

## LINEUPS

| S.F. | | DEN. |
|---|---|---|
| | **OFFENSE** | |
| Taylor | WR | V. Johnson |
| Paris | LT | Perry |
| McIntyre | LG | Juriga |
| Sapolu | C | Kartz |
| Collie | RG | Widell |
| Barton | RT | Lanier |
| Jones | TE | Mobley |
| Rice | WR | M. Jackson |
| Montana | QB | Elway |
| Craig | RB | Humphrey |
| Rathman | FB | Sewell |
| | **DEFENSE** | |
| Holt | LE | Carreker |
| Carter | NT | Kragen |
| Fagan | RE | Holmes |
| Haley | LOLB | Brooks |
| Millen | LILB | Dennison |
| Walter | RILB | Mecklenburg |
| Turner | ROLB | Fletcher |
| Pollard | LCB | Braxton |
| Griffin | RCB | Henderson |
| Brooks | SS | Smith |
| Lott | FS | Atwater |
| **SAN FRANCISCO** | **SUBSTITUTES** | |
| | **OFFENSE** | |
| Young | Tillman | Sydney |
| Flagler | C. Thomas | Tausch |
| Wallace | J. Williams | Wilson |
| Sherrard | Walls | |
| | **DEFENSE** | |
| Wright | McKyer | J. Jackson |
| Romanowski | Hendrickson | DeLong |
| Burt | Kugler | Roberts |
| Stubbs | | |
| | **KICKERS** | |
| Cofer | Helton | |
| **DENVER** | | |
| | **OFFENSE** | |
| Kubiak | Winder | Bratton |
| Bell | Bishop | M. Smith |
| Young | Nattiel | Green |
| Kay | | |
| | **DEFENSE** | |
| Corrington | Carrington | Haynes |
| Robbins | Munford | Curtis |
| Lucas | Townsend | Henke |
| Powers | Klostermann | |
| | **KICKERS** | |
| Horan | Treadwell | |

## SCORING

| | | | | | |
|---|---|---|---|---|---|
| **SAN FRANCISCO** | 13 | 14 | 14 | 14 | - 55 |
| **DENVER** | 3 | 0 | 7 | 0 | - 10 |

**First Quarter**
S.F. — Rice, 20 yard pass from Montana
PAT — Cofer (kick)
Den. — Treadwell, 42 yard field goal
S.F. — Jones, 7 yard pass from Montana
PAT — kick failed

**Second Quarter**
S.F. — Rathman, 1 yard run
PAT — Cofer (kick)
S.F. — Rice, 38 yard pass from Montana
PAT — Cofer (kick)

**Third Quarter**
S.F. — Rice, 28 yard pass from Montana
PAT — Cofer (kick)
S.F. — Taylor, 35 yard pass from Montana
PAT — Cofer (kick)
Den. — Elway, 3 yard run
PAT — Treadwell (kick)

**Fourth Quarter**
S.F. — Rathman, 4 yard run
PAT — Cofer (kick)
S.F. — Craig, 1 yard run
PAT — Cofer (kick)

## TEAM STATISTICS

| S.F. | | DEN. |
|---|---|---|
| 28 | First Downs-Total | 12 |
| 14 | First Downs-Rushing | 5 |
| 14 | First Downs-Passing | 6 |
| 0 | First Downs-Penalty | 1 |
| 0 | Fumbles-Number | 3 |
| 0 | Fumbles-Lost Ball | 2 |
| 4 | Penalties-Number | 0 |
| 38 | Yards Penalized | 0 |
| 0 | Missed Field Goals | 0 |
| 77 | Offensive Plays | 52 |
| 461 | Net Yards | 167 |
| 6.0 | Average Gain | 3.2 |
| 0 | Giveaways | 4 |
| 4 | Takeaways | 0 |
| + 4 | Difference | - 4 |

## INDIVIDUAL STATISTICS

**SAN FRANCISCO** / **DENVER**

### RUSHING

| SAN FRANCISCO | No. | Yds. | Avg. | DENVER | No. | Yds. | Avg. |
|---|---|---|---|---|---|---|---|
| Craig | 20 | 69 | 3.5 | Humphrey | 12 | 61 | 5.1 |
| Montana | 2 | 15 | 7.5 | Elway | 4 | 8 | 2.0 |
| Rathman | 11 | 38 | 3.5 | Winder | 1 | -5 | -5.0 |
| Flagler | 6 | 14 | 2.3 | | 17 | 64 | 3.8 |
| Sydney | 1 | 2 | 2.0 | | | | |
| Young | 4 | 6 | 1.5 | | | | |
| | 44 | 144 | 3.3 | | | | |

### RECEIVING

| | No. | Yds. | Avg. | | No. | Yds. | Avg. |
|---|---|---|---|---|---|---|---|
| Rice | 7 | 148 | 21.1 | Humphrey | 3 | 38 | 12.7 |
| Craig | 5 | 34 | 6.8 | Sewell | 2 | 22 | 11.0 |
| Rathman | 4 | 43 | 10.8 | Johnson | 2 | 21 | 10.5 |
| Taylor | 3 | 49 | 16.3 | Nattiel | 1 | 28 | 28.0 |
| Sherrard | 1 | 13 | 13.0 | Bratton | 1 | 14 | 14.0 |
| Walls | 1 | 9 | 9.0 | Winder | 1 | 7 | 7.0 |
| Jones | 1 | 7 | 7.0 | Kay | 1 | 6 | 6.0 |
| Williams | 1 | 7 | 7.0 | | 11 | 136 | 12.4 |
| Sydney | 1 | 7 | 7.0 | | | | |
| | 24 | 317 | 13.2 | | | | |

### PUNTING

| | No. | | Avg. | | No. | | Avg. |
|---|---|---|---|---|---|---|---|
| Helton | 4 | | 39.5 | Horan | 6 | | 38.5 |

### PUNT RETURNS

| | No. | Yds. | Avg. | | No. | Yds. | Avg. |
|---|---|---|---|---|---|---|---|
| Taylor | 3 | 38 | 12.7 | Johnson | 2 | 11 | 5.5 |

### KICKOFF RETURNS

| | No. | Yds. | Avg. | | No. | Yds. | Avg. |
|---|---|---|---|---|---|---|---|
| Flagler | 3 | 49 | 16.3 | Carrington | 6 | 146 | 24.3 |
| | | | | Bell | 2 | 41 | 20.5 |
| | | | | Bratton | 1 | 9 | 9.0 |
| | | | | | 9 | 196 | 21.7 |

### INTERCEPTIONS RETURNS

| | No. | Yds. | Avg. | |
|---|---|---|---|---|
| Walter | 1 | 4 | 4.0 | None |
| Brooks | 1 | 38 | 38.0 | |
| | 2 | 42 | 20.5 | |

### PASSING

**SAN FRANCISCO**

| | Att. | Comp. | Comp. Pct. | Yds. | Int. | Yds./ Att. | Yds./ Comp. | Yards Lost Tackled |
|---|---|---|---|---|---|---|---|---|
| Montana | 29 | 22 | 75.9 | 297 | 0 | 10.2 | 13.5 | 0-0 |
| Young | 3 | 2 | 66.7 | 20 | 0 | 6.7 | 10.0 | 1-0 |
| | 32 | 24 | 75.0 | 317 | 0 | 9.9 | 13.2 | 1-0 |

**DENVER**

| | Att. | Comp. | Comp. Pct. | Yds. | Int. | Yds./ Att. | Yds./ Comp. | Yards Lost Tackled |
|---|---|---|---|---|---|---|---|---|
| Elway | 26 | 10 | 38.5 | 108 | 2 | 4.1 | 10.8 | 6-33 |
| Kubiak | 3 | 1 | 33.3 | 28 | 0 | 9.3 | 28.0 | 0-0 |
| | 29 | 11 | 37.9 | 136 | 2 | 4.7 | 12.4 | 6-33 |

While most critics insisted the NFC had moved ahead of the AFC in football prowess, citing the superior defense played in the former, the sad truth was that the NFC had little to offer fans in title races during the 1990 season. In the East, the Giants forged to the front early and were never in real danger of losing their lead to either Philadelphia or Washington, the only NFC teams to post winning records without wining a division title. The Central Division was a cakewalk by the Bears combined with the collapse of the Vikings and Packers. And in the West, San Francisco needed barely to work up a sweat as the Rams submerged and the Saints struggled all season to get to .500.

With the division races all but settled by midseason, interests focused on the playoffs and the 49ers' chances for a third consecutive Super Bowl championship. The game of the season was a December 3 meeting at San Francisco between the Giants and 49ers. It was widely viewed as a preview of the NFC championship game, and, indeed, it turned out to be just that. San Francisco scored the only touchdown in what NFC fans called "a great defensive battle" and AFC fans called dull. The Niners won 7-3.

## EASTERN DIVISION

**New York Giants** — Under Bill Parcells, the Giants had earned a reputation for a conservative offense over the past few years. After a few adjustments in 1990, they set an NFL record for fewest turnovers with a measly 14 — less than one per game. A 10-game winning streak from the opening of the season locked up the division title quickly. The huge offensive line, bulwarked by tackle Jumbo Elliott, opened holes for ageless Ottis Anderson, Dave Meggett and rookie Rodney Hampton all season, and the Lawrence Taylor-led defense finished first overall in the NFC. Even three defeats in the last four games and the loss of starting quarterback Phil Simms to a sprained foot and Hampton to a leg injury couldn't knock the Giants off track. Anderson continued to grind out yards, and Jeff Hostetler proved to be a capable backup for Simms.

**Philadelphia Eagles** — The Eagles bounced back from a 1-3 start to make the playoffs for the third straight year. They were criticized around the league for taunting, cheap shots, and dirty play, but coach Buddy Ryan defended his troops as merely aggressive. Whatever, it worked. The defense was spotty against the pass and the special teams weren't up to their previous efforts, but Randall Cunningham remained the league's top offensive threat. He just missed becoming the first quarterback to both run and pass for over 1,000 yards each. Although he led the Eagles in rushing for the fourth straight season, he got help from his running backs for a change, particularly Heath Sherman. Ryan was fired after the season for the team's failure to win a playoff game and for inspiring his team's ruffian reputation.

**Washington Redskins** — Coach Joe Gibbs' club never was able to put together a victory streak so they were never candidates for more than a wild-card berth in the playoffs. Gibbs complained he never knew who would show up for a game: "Elmer and the boys or a pretty good football team," he said. The most inconsistent position on the Redskins was quarterback, where Mark Rypien, Stan Humphries, and Jeff Rutledge all had excellent moments mixed with disasters and injuries. The supporting cast was strong. Wide receivers Art Monk, Gary Clark and Ricky Sanders combined for 199 receptions. Running back Gerald Riggs was hobbled with an arch injury, but Earnest Byner turned in a terrific season, rushing for 1,219 yards.

**Dallas Cowboys** — The Cowboys' season gave Jimmy Johnson NFC Coach of the Year honors. From 1-15 in '89, Dallas improved to a point where they had a shot at a .500 season and the playoffs until the last week of the season. The key to the improvement was a no-name defense that finished first in the NFC in pass defense and fourth overall. Emmitt Smith gave Dallas a running threat with a near-1,000-yard season, and Troy Aikman continued to make progress towards becoming a top pro quarterback. Aikman won seven starts before he separated his shoulder against Philadelphia in Week 15. Unfortunately for the Cowboys' playoff aspirations, the efforts of his replacement, Babe Laufenberg, were, well, lauf-able.

**Phoenix Cardinals** — Although the Cardinals fell into last place with the same 5-11 mark they'd had in 1989, the outlook was hopeful. Under new coach Joe Bugel, the Cards made progress on offense. Second-year quarterback Timm Rosenbach improved as the season went on, finishing with over 3,000 yards passing. In the final two games, he threw for 682 yards and six touchdowns. Wide receiver Ricky Proehl caught more passes than any rookie in the league, blending nicely with veterans Roy Green and Ernie Jones. Rookie running back Johnny Johnson was a revelation. And, when he was injured, second-round draft choice Anthony Thompson came on strong. Luis Sharpe and the rest of the veteran offensive line played well. But, for all the optimism generated by the offense, the defense — which gave up 50 touchdowns — still was in need of a transfusion.

## CENTRAL DIVISION

**Chicago Bears** — The famed Bears defense was back. Defensive tackle Dan Hampton returned for his 12th and final season to anchor the line with inspirational play. Richard Dent, Steve McMichael, and Mike Singletary were other strengths, and rookie free safety Mark Carrier made the Pro Bowl. His 10 interceptions broke a club record. The Bears lacked a premier wide receiver, but Jim Harbaugh took over as quarterback and played reasonably well until sidelined by a shoulder separation in the 14th game. Neal Anderson also had injury problems but still managed another 1,000-yard season. Tragedy struck when rookie defensive lineman Fred Washington was killed in an auto accident in December.

**Detroit Lions** — A leaky defense kept the Lions from taking advantage of their increasingly potent offense. Linebackers Mike Cofer and Chris Spielman and cornerback Ray Crockett were defenders of promise, but Detroit ended dead last in the NFC in defense. The line desperately needed a pass rusher. Cofer blitzed often enough to lead the team in sacks with 10. One knock on the "Silver Stretch" offense, Detroit's name for the run-and-shoot, was that it couldn't protect a lead. This was never more evident than in the November 4 game against the Redskins when the Lions piled up 38 points only to see Washington come back to tie and then win in overtime. Barry Sanders remained the NFC's top runner and Rodney Peete showed improvement at quarterback.

**Tampa Bay Buccaneers** — A 3-1 start fueled hopes for the Bucs' first winning season since 1982, but a six-game losing streak brought those dreams crashing down and cost coach Ray Perkins his job. Ironically, Perkins' ouster came after the team finally broke the loss streak. Vinny Testaverde was still inconsistent amid more and more whispers that he'd never be the franchise quarterback Tampa Bay expected when they drafted him No. 1 in 1987. Much was expected from running backs Gary Anderson and Reggie Cobb, but the ground game still sputtered. A bright spot was the play of free-agent cornerback Wayne Haddix, who ended in the Pro Bowl. Overall, the Bucs were next-to-last in offense, next-to-last in defense and dead last in disappointment.

**Green Bay Packers** — Instead of building on their 10-6 record of 1989, the Packers spun back toward the bottom of the division in 1990. The primary bugaboos were training-camp holdouts, injuries, and the complete lack of a running game. Sixteen veterans, including 13 starters, sat out a total of 302 days in various contract disputes. Quartback Don Majkowski the "Magic Man" of 1989, missed 45 days as a holdout and then, after eight starts, was knocked out for the season with a career-threatening rotator cuff tear. Backup Anthony Dilwig played well at times, badly at others, and was eventually sidelined, too. Receiver Sterling Sharpe caught 23 fewer passes than in '89 due to cracked ribs and the revolving quarterback situation. Michael Haddix, the leading Packer rusher, ranked 58th in the NFL.

**Minnesota Vikings** — The Vikings went from the penthouse to the outhouse in one season, struggling to the fourth-worst record in their history. Major factors in the plunge were injuries to quarterback Wade

**OFFENSE**

| | ATL | CHI | DAL | DET | G.B. | L.A. | MINN | N.O. | NYG | PHIL | PHX | S.F. | T.B. | WASH |
|---|---|---|---|---|---|---|---|---|---|---|---|---|---|---|
| FIRST DOWNS: | | | | | | | | | | | | | | |
| Total | 273 | 295 | 250 | 278 | 276 | 311 | 286 | 253 | 273 | 325 | 270 | 324 | 238 | 327 |
| by Rushing | 84 | 142 | 88 | 112 | 72 | 89 | 106 | 107 | 120 | 132 | 115 | 107 | 83 | 117 |
| by Passing | 168 | 134 | 135 | 152 | 183 | 191 | 164 | 133 | 135 | 170 | 135 | 201 | 142 | 193 |
| by Penalty | 21 | 19 | 27 | 14 | 21 | 31 | 18 | 13 | 18 | 23 | 20 | 16 | 13 | 17 |
| RUSHING: | | | | | | | | | | | | | | |
| Number | 420 | 551 | 393 | 366 | 350 | 422 | 455 | 464 | 541 | 540 | 452 | 454 | 410 | 515 |
| Yards | 1594 | 2436 | 1500 | 1927 | 1369 | 1612 | 1867 | 1850 | 2049 | 2556 | 1912 | 1718 | 1626 | 2083 |
| Average Yards | 3.8 | 4.4 | 3.8 | 5.3 | 3.9 | 3.8 | 4.1 | 4.0 | 3.8 | 4.7 | 4.2 | 3.8 | 4.0 | 4.0 |
| Touchdowns | 11 | 22 | 13 | 19 | 5 | 17 | 10 | 14 | 17 | 10 | 13 | 12 | 7 | 16 |
| PASSING: | | | | | | | | | | | | | | |
| Attempts | 528 | 430 | 475 | 460 | 541 | 561 | 497 | 447 | 398 | 479 | 439 | 583 | 448 | 536 |
| Completions | 293 | 229 | 254 | 242 | 302 | 310 | 265 | 226 | 231 | 281 | 238 | 360 | 245 | 301 |
| Completion Pct. | 55.5 | 53.3 | 53.5 | 52.6 | 55.8 | 55.3 | 53.3 | 50.6 | 58.0 | 58.7 | 54.2 | 61.7 | 54.7 | 56.2 |
| Passing Yards | 3726 | 2827 | 2898 | 3328 | 3696 | 4016 | 3445 | 2757 | 2898 | 3582 | 3118 | 4371 | 3282 | 3611 |
| Avg. Yds per Att. | 6.0 | 5.4 | 5.0 | 6.1 | 5.5 | 6.5 | 5.8 | 6.2 | 6.5 | 5.9 | 5.9 | 6.7 | 5.7 | 6.2 |
| Avg. Yds per Comp. | 12.7 | 12.3 | 11.4 | 13.8 | 12.2 | 13.0 | 13.0 | 12.2 | 12.6 | 12.8 | 13.1 | 12.1 | 13.4 | 12.0 |
| Times Tackled | 46 | 43 | 43 | 44 | 62 | 30 | 49 | 20 | 29 | 50 | 43 | 37 | 53 | 22 |
| Yds Lost Tackled | 265 | 283 | 317 | 278 | 390 | 198 | 278 | 131 | 142 | 438 | 285 | 194 | 433 | 132 |
| Net Yards | 3461 | 2544 | 2581 | 3050 | 3306 | 3818 | 3167 | 2626 | 2756 | 3144 | 2833 | 4177 | 2849 | 3479 |
| Touchdowns | 21 | 14 | 12 | 24 | 20 | 24 | 25 | 15 | 18 | 34 | 16 | 28 | 18 | 22 |
| Interceptions | 18 | 12 | 24 | 20 | 21 | 17 | 24 | 23 | 5 | 13 | 18 | 16 | 24 | 22 |
| Pct. Intercepted | 3.4 | 2.8 | 5.1 | 4.3 | 3.9 | 3.0 | 4.8 | 5.1 | 1.3 | 2.7 | 4.1 | 2.7 | 5.4 | 4.1 |
| PUNTS: | | | | | | | | | | | | | | |
| Number | 70 | 78 | 79 | 63 | 65 | 69 | 79 | 71 | 75 | 74 | 67 | 70 | 72 | 55 |
| Average | 41.6 | 39.4 | 43.2 | 40.6 | 37.4 | 38.6 | 41.8 | 42.1 | 44.1 | 40.9 | 42.8 | 36.2 | 40.3 | 37.5 |
| PUNT RETURNS: | | | | | | | | | | | | | | |
| Number | 35 | 36 | 39 | 35 | 32 | 35 | 33 | 45 | 43 | 40 | 40 | 48 | 23 | 48 |
| Yards | 279 | 399 | 250 | 361 | 308 | 346 | 225 | 400 | 467 | 315 | 342 | 356 | 184 | 388 |
| Average Yards | 8.0 | 11.1 | 6.4 | 10.3 | 9.6 | 9.9 | 6.8 | 8.9 | 10.9 | 7.9 | 8.6 | 7.4 | 8.0 | 8.1 |
| Touchdowns | 1 | 1 | 0 | 0 | 0 | 0 | 0 | 0 | 1 | 0 | 0 | 0 | 0 | 0 |
| KICKOFF RET.: | | | | | | | | | | | | | | |
| Number | 58 | 54 | 54 | 70 | 63 | 63 | 66 | 58 | 46 | 54 | 60 | 53 | 63 | 62 |
| Yards | 1229 | 879 | 1102 | 1466 | 1303 | 1279 | 1249 | 1205 | 884 | 965 | 1068 | 965 | 1175 | 1113 |
| Average Yards | 21.2 | 16.3 | 20.4 | 20.9 | 20.7 | 20.3 | 18.9 | 20.8 | 19.2 | 17.9 | 17.8 | 18.2 | 18.7 | 18.0 |
| Touchdowns | 1 | 0 | 1 | 0 | 1 | 1 | 0 | 0 | 0 | 0 | 0 | 0 | 0 | 0 |
| INTERCEPT RET.: | | | | | | | | | | | | | | |
| Number | 17 | 31 | 11 | 17 | 16 | 12 | 22 | 8 | 23 | 19 | 16 | 17 | 25 | 21 |
| Yards | 237 | 268 | 126 | 273 | 154 | 105 | 358 | 158 | 116 | 271 | 274 | 171 | 487 | 271 |
| Average Yards | 13.9 | 8.6 | 11.5 | 16.1 | 9.6 | 8.8 | 16.3 | 19.8 | 5.0 | 14.3 | 17.1 | 10.0 | 19.5 | 12.9 |
| Touchdowns | 3 | 1 | 1 | 1 | 1 | 1 | 2 | 1 | 2 | 3 | 2 | 0 | 3 | 2 |
| PENALTIES: | | | | | | | | | | | | | | |
| Number | 125 | 75 | 98 | 88 | 84 | 87 | 83 | 108 | 83 | 120 | 96 | 104 | 77 | 102 |
| Yards | 1004 | 615 | 729 | 711 | 669 | 632 | 565 | 829 | 655 | 981 | 883 | 828 | 651 | 824 |
| FUMBLES: | | | | | | | | | | | | | | |
| Number | 40 | 29 | 27 | 29 | 37 | 25 | 30 | 29 | 21 | 32 | 25 | 24 | 38 | 14 |
| Number Lost | 21 | 14 | 9 | 16 | 22 | 14 | 13 | 16 | 9 | 15 | 14 | 14 | 19 | 6 |
| POINTS: | | | | | | | | | | | | | | |
| Total | 348 | 348 | 244 | 373 | 271 | 345 | 351 | 274 | 335 | 396 | 268 | 353 | 264 | 381 |
| PAT Attempts | 40 | 38 | 27 | 46 | 29 | 43 | 39 | 30 | 39 | 48 | 31 | 40 | 28 | 41 |
| PAT Made | 40 | 36 | 26 | 46 | 28 | 42 | 38 | 29 | 38 | 45 | 31 | 39 | 27 | 41 |
| FG Attempts | 33 | 37 | 25 | 26 | 30 | 24 | 28 | 27 | 28 | 29 | 27 | 36 | 27 | 40 |
| FG Made | 22 | 26 | 18 | 17 | 23 | 15 | 25 | 21 | 21 | 21 | 17 | 24 | 23 | 30 |
| Percent FG Made | 66.7 | 70.3 | 72.0 | 65.4 | 76.7 | 62.5 | 89.3 | 77.8 | 75.0 | 72.4 | 63.0 | 66.7 | 85.2 | 75.0 |
| Safeties | 1 | 0 | 1 | 0 | 0 | 0 | 2 | 1 | 0 | 0 | 0 | 1 | 0 | 2 |

**DEFENSE**

| | ATL | CHI | DAL | DET | G.B. | L.A. | MINN | N.O. | NYG | PHIL | PHX | S.F. | T.B. | WASH |
|---|---|---|---|---|---|---|---|---|---|---|---|---|---|---|
| FIRST DOWNS: | | | | | | | | | | | | | | |
| Total | 300 | 256 | 280 | 334 | 286 | 286 | 257 | 279 | 245 | 251 | 306 | 250 | 313 | 267 |
| by Rushing | 79 | 91 | 109 | 142 | 113 | 93 | 107 | 91 | 90 | 59 | 140 | 77 | 129 | 77 |
| by Passing | 179 | 147 | 153 | 173 | 160 | 175 | 136 | 167 | 139 | 169 | 146 | 157 | 168 | 166 |
| by Penalty | 42 | 18 | 18 | 19 | 13 | 18 | 14 | 21 | 16 | 23 | 20 | 16 | 16 | 24 |
| RUSHING: | | | | | | | | | | | | | | |
| Number | 413 | 391 | 482 | 532 | 475 | 418 | 503 | 410 | 388 | 337 | 521 | 353 | 496 | 382 |
| Yards | 1357 | 1572 | 1976 | 2388 | 2059 | 1649 | 2074 | 1559 | 1459 | 1169 | 2318 | 1258 | 2223 | 1587 |
| Average Yards | 3.3 | 4.0 | 4.1 | 4.5 | 4.3 | 3.9 | 4.1 | 3.8 | 3.8 | 3.5 | 4.4 | 3.6 | 4.5 | 4.2 |
| Touchdowns | 11 | 10 | 18 | 22 | 16 | 17 | 12 | 8 | 9 | 9 | 20 | 7 | 20 | 8 |
| PASSING: | | | | | | | | | | | | | | |
| Attempts | 537 | 495 | 470 | 507 | 479 | 501 | 422 | 534 | 496 | 566 | 402 | 522 | 471 | 514 |
| Completions | 297 | 258 | 271 | 319 | 256 | 296 | 218 | 316 | 278 | 273 | 233 | 265 | 263 | 281 |
| Completion Pct. | 55.3 | 52.1 | 57.7 | 62.9 | 53.4 | 59.1 | 51.7 | 59.2 | 56.0 | 48.2 | 58.0 | 50.8 | 55.8 | 54.7 |
| Passing Yards | 4127 | 3220 | 2931 | 3625 | 3555 | 3942 | 2920 | 3584 | 2933 | 3771 | 3130 | 3278 | 3460 | 3483 |
| Avg. Yds per Att. | 6.9 | 5.5 | 5.2 | 6.1 | 6.7 | 7.1 | 5.6 | 5.8 | 5.2 | 5.7 | 6.6 | 5.3 | 6.5 | 5.6 |
| Avg. Yds per Comp. | 13.9 | 12.5 | 10.8 | 11.4 | 13.9 | 13.3 | 13.4 | 11.3 | 10.6 | 13.8 | 13.4 | 12.4 | 13.2 | 12.4 |
| Times Tackled | 33 | 41 | 36 | 41 | 27 | 30 | 47 | 42 | 30 | 45 | 36 | 44 | 34 | 45 |
| Yds Lost Tackled | 214 | 300 | 292 | 279 | 172 | 180 | 277 | 265 | 186 | 280 | 232 | 263 | 204 | 340 |
| Net Yards | 3913 | 2920 | 2639 | 3346 | 3383 | 3762 | 2643 | 3319 | 2747 | 3491 | 2898 | 3015 | 3256 | 3143 |
| Touchdowns | 31 | 19 | 12 | 21 | 20 | 30 | 20 | 21 | 12 | 23 | 29 | 17 | 22 | 21 |
| Interceptions | 17 | 31 | 11 | 17 | 16 | 12 | 22 | 8 | 23 | 19 | 16 | 17 | 25 | 21 |
| Pct. Intercepted | 3.2 | 6.3 | 2.3 | 3.4 | 3.3 | 2.4 | 5.2 | 1.5 | 4.6 | 3.4 | 4.0 | 3.3 | 5.3 | 4.1 |
| PUNTS: | | | | | | | | | | | | | | |
| Number | 74 | 74 | 70 | 62 | 69 | 66 | 77 | 74 | 76 | 86 | 63 | 82 | 55 | 76 |
| Average | 40.2 | 37.9 | 40.9 | 40.8 | 39.1 | 41.4 | 39.4 | 40.9 | 41.3 | 40.3 | 43.6 | 40.0 | 40.5 | 43.3 |
| PUNT RETURNS: | | | | | | | | | | | | | | |
| Number | 39 | 39 | 43 | 29 | 34 | 46 | 44 | 43 | 41 | 37 | 41 | 30 | 39 | 30 |
| Yards | 314 | 322 | 438 | 233 | 266 | 420 | 513 | 302 | 291 | 338 | 258 | 215 | 352 | 205 |
| Average Yards | 8.1 | 8.3 | 10.2 | 8.0 | 7.8 | 9.1 | 11.7 | 7.0 | 7.1 | 9.1 | 6.3 | 7.2 | 9.0 | 6.8 |
| Touchdowns | 0 | 0 | 1 | 0 | 0 | 0 | 0 | 0 | 0 | 1 | 0 | 0 | 0 | 0 |
| KICKOFF RET.: | | | | | | | | | | | | | | |
| Number | 49 | 73 | 55 | 70 | 56 | 68 | 62 | 36 | 65 | 74 | 56 | 66 | 43 | 58 |
| Yards | 814 | 1494 | 1136 | 1229 | 1125 | 1406 | 1350 | 583 | 1245 | 1408 | 1060 | 1284 | 1036 | 1008 |
| Average Yards | 16.6 | 20.5 | 20.7 | 17.6 | 20.1 | 20.7 | 21.8 | 16.2 | 19.2 | 19.0 | 18.9 | 19.5 | 24.1 | 17.4 |
| Touchdowns | 0 | 0 | 1 | 1 | 0 | 0 | 0 | 0 | 1 | 0 | 0 | 0 | 0 | 0 |
| INTERCEPT RET.: | | | | | | | | | | | | | | |
| Number | 18 | 12 | 24 | 20 | 21 | 17 | 24 | 23 | 5 | 13 | 18 | 16 | 24 | 22 |
| Yards | 368 | 164 | 353 | 346 | 293 | 204 | 260 | 283 | 54 | 88 | 201 | 176 | 346 | 271 |
| Average Yards | 7.1 | 7.3 | 14.7 | 18.6 | 16.1 | 11.5 | 7.3 | 13.9 | 15.0 | 9.2 | 10.9 | 12.7 | 8.6 | 13.5 |
| Touchdowns | 2 | 0 | 4 | 3 | 2 | 2 | 1 | 0 | 1 | 0 | 1 | 1 | 2 | 5 |
| PENALTIES: | | | | | | | | | | | | | | |
| Number | 95 | 84 | 104 | 97 | 109 | 109 | 100 | 87 | 83 | 94 | 96 | 85 | 78 | 90 |
| Yards | 811 | 676 | 911 | 788 | 854 | 968 | 787 | 655 | 569 | 706 | 834 | 641 | 617 | 712 |
| FUMBLES: | | | | | | | | | | | | | | |
| Number | 26 | 38 | 32 | 31 | 26 | 32 | 25 | 35 | 28 | 32 | 28 | 21 | 33 | 24 |
| Number Lost | 18 | 14 | 19 | 18 | 14 | 19 | 11 | 19 | 11 | 11 | 11 | 14 | 17 | 12 |
| POINTS: | | | | | | | | | | | | | | |
| Total | 365 | 280 | 308 | 413 | 347 | 412 | 326 | 275 | 211 | 299 | 396 | 239 | 367 | 301 |
| PAT Attempts | 44 | 31 | 36 | 48 | 40 | 49 | 34 | 30 | 23 | 33 | 50 | 26 | 45 | 35 |
| PAT Made | 42 | 28 | 36 | 48 | 39 | 46 | 32 | 30 | 23 | 32 | 48 | 26 | 43 | 35 |
| FG Attempts | 28 | 28 | 26 | 30 | 34 | 31 | 36 | 35 | 22 | 32 | 20 | 23 | 27 | 23 |
| FG Made | 19 | 22 | 18 | 23 | 22 | 24 | 30 | 21 | 16 | 23 | 16 | 19 | 18 | 18 |
| Percent FG Made | 67.9 | 78.6 | 69.2 | 76.7 | 64.7 | 77.4 | 83.3 | 60.0 | 72.7 | 71.9 | 80.0 | 82.6 | 66.7 | 78.3 |
| Safeties | 1 | 0 | 1 | 1 | 1 | 0 | 0 | 1 | 1 | 0 | 0 | 0 | 0 | 1 |

Wilson and defensive tackle Keith Millard that crippled both the offense and defense. The continued disappointing play of running back Herschel Walker was another element. After a 1-6 start, Minnesota won five in a row before collapsing down the stretch. Although safety Joey Browner, receiver Anthony Carter, guard Randall McDaniel and a few others continued to play well through what Wilson called "a season for hell," the general diagnosis of the flop was that the team wasn't nearly as talented as it had been given credit with being. Offensive coordinator Bob Schnelker and defensive coordinator Floyd Peters were fired after the season, but an injection of new players was called for by disappointed fans.

## WESTERN DIVISION

**San Francisco 49ers** — The 1988 and '89 champs went for a "three-peat" in '90, an their 14-2 regular-season record — the best in the NFL —indicated they were right in line. But the record was deceiving as holes began to show. Mostly it was age finally catching up with some fine players, particularly in the secondary. Safety Ronnie Lott missed five games for the second year in a row. The running attack completely disappeared as age and injuries ruined Roger Craig's season. Rookie Dexter Carter was a helpful replacement but he proved to be too small for continuous pounding. But the passing game carried all, or nearly all, through the year to give the 49ers home-field advantage for the playoffs. The Joe Montana-to-Jerry Rice connection cemented their eventual enshrinements in the Hall of Fame.

**New Orleans Saints** — The Saints spent the season trying to get to .500, a mark they finally achieved with two straight wins at the end. Quarterback Bobby Hebert spent the season holding out. New Orleans opened with John Fourcade at quarterback, but the surprise of '89 was a flop in '90. After three games, general manager Jim Finks mortgaged the future by sending three high draft picks to Dallas for Steve Walsh. Although the team had a winning record after Walsh's acquisition, his play was inconsistent. His critics derided his arm strength, while his defenders argued he needed time to learn a new offense. The strength of the team remained its defense, particularity the linebackers.

**Los Angeles Rams** — After reaching the playoffs in six of the previous seven seasons, the Rams' 1990 nosedive came as a shock. A rash of preseason injuries and holdouts got them off to a bad start. Several of the 16 second- and third-year players didn't play up to expectations. Quarterback Jim Everett threw for nearly 4,000 yards, but he was not as sharp as in previous seasons. The running game didn't help much. Cleveland Gary had fumble problems, Curt Warner was washed up, and Marcus Dupree, attempting a comeback after five years away from football, wasn't ready. The worst problem was the undersized, underachieving defense. Cornerback Jerry Gray was injured most of the year, and the defensive line was embarrassing porous. Only linebacker Kevin Greene, with 13 sacks, was a bright spot.

**Atlanta Falcons** — Under new coach Jerry Glanville the Falcons improved their record by two wins, but that was scant consolation to fans who'd hoped for a .500 season. A seven-game losing streak that began with the first game in November ruined any chance of breaking even. Chris Miller, the "franchise quarterback" prospect, never quite lived up to that billing and then was lost in the 12th game with a broken collarbone. The best that could be said was that Atlanta kept most games close and the players' morale was higher than in '89. Bright spots on an improved defense were the play of end Mike Gann and cornerback Deion Sanders. The Falcons' MVP was receiver Andre Rison, who set team records with 82 catches, 1,208 yards, and 10 touchdowns. Mike Rozier, acquired early in the season for Houston, ran for over 100 yards in each of the last two games.

## NEW YORK GIANTS 13-3 Bill Parcells

| Scores of Each Game | | |
|---|---|---|
| 27 | PHILADELPHIA | 20 |
| 28 | Dallas | 7 |
| 20 | MIAMI | 3 |
| 31 | DALLAS | 17 |
| 24 | Washington | 20 |
| 20 | PHOENIX | 19 |
| 21 | WASHINGTON | 10 |
| 24 | Indianapolis | 7 |
| 31 | L.A. Rams | 7 |
| 20 | DETROIT | 0 |
| 13 | Philadelphia | 31 |
| 3 | San Francisco | 7 |
| 23 | MINNESOTA | 15 |
| 13 | BUFFALO | 17 |
| 24 | Phoenix | 21 |
| 13 | New England | 10 |

| Use Name | Pos. | Hgt | Wgt | Age | Int | Pts |
|---|---|---|---|---|---|---|
| John Elliott | OT | 6'7" | 305 | 25 | | |
| Eric Moore | OT-OG | 6'5" | 290 | 25 | | |
| Doug Riesenberg | OT | 6'5" | 275 | 25 | | |
| Bob Kratch | OG | 6'3" | 288 | 24 | | |
| Tom Rehder | OG-OT | 6'7" | 290 | 25 | | |
| William Roberts | OG | 6'5" | 280 | 28 | | |
| Brian Williams | OG-C | 6'5" | 300 | 24 | | |
| Bart Oates | C | 6'3" | 265 | 31 | | |
| Eric Dorsey | DE | 6'5" | 280 | 26 | | |
| Mike Fox | DE | 6'6" | 275 | 23 | | |
| Leonard Marshall | DE | 6'3" | 285 | 28 | | |
| John Washington | DE | 6'4" | 275 | 27 | | |
| Erik Howard | NT | 6'4" | 268 | 25 | | |
| Kent Wells | NT | 6'4" | 295 | 25 | | |

| Use Name | Pos. | Hgt | Wgt | Age | Int | Pts |
|---|---|---|---|---|---|---|
| Bobby Abrams | LB | 6'3" | 230 | 23 | | |
| Carl Banks | LB | 6'4" | 235 | 28 | | |
| Johnie Cooks | LB | 6'4" | 251 | 31 | | |
| Steve DeOssie | LB | 6'2" | 248 | 27 | | |
| Pepper Johnson | LB | 6'3" | 248 | 26 | 1 | |
| Larry McGrew | LB | 6'5" | 250 | 33 | | |
| Gary Reasons | LB | 6'4" | 234 | 28 | 3 | |
| Lawrence Taylor | LB | 6'3" | 243 | 31 | 1 | 6 |
| Roger Brown | DB | 6' | 196 | 23 | | |
| Mark Collins | DB | 5'10" | 190 | 26 | 2 | |
| Dave Duerson | DB | 6'1" | 208 | 29 | 1 | 6 |
| Myron Guyton | DB | 6'1" | 205 | 23 | 1 | |
| Greg Jackson | DB | 6'1" | 200 | 24 | 5 | |
| Reyna Thompson | DB | 6' | 193 | 27 | | |
| Everson Walls | DB | 6'1" | 194 | 30 | 6 | 6 |
| David Whitmore | DB | 6' | 235 | 23 | | |
| Perry Williams | DB | 6'2" | 203 | 29 | 3 | |

Adrain White — Knee Injury

| Use Name | Pos. | Hgt | Wgt | Age | Int | Pts |
|---|---|---|---|---|---|---|
| Matt Cavanaugh | QB | 6'2" | 210 | 33 | | |
| Jeff Hostetler | QB | 6'3" | 212 | 29 | | 12 |
| Phil Simms | QB | 6'3" | 214 | 33 | | 6 |
| Ottis Anderson | HB | 6'2" | 225 | 33 | | 66 |
| Rodney Hampton | HB | 5'11" | 215 | 21 | | 24 |
| Dave Meggett | HB | 5'7" | 180 | 24 | | 12 |
| Lewis Tillman | HB | 6' | 195 | 24 | | 6 |
| Maurice Carthon | FB | 6'1" | 225 | 29 | | |
| Lee Rouson | FB | 6'1" | 222 | 27 | | |
| Stephen Baker | WR | 5'8" | 160 | 26 | | 24 |
| Mark Ingram | WR | 5'10" | 188 | 25 | | 30 |
| Troy Kyles | WR | 6' | 180 | 22 | | |
| Lionel Manuel | WR | 5'11" | 180 | 28 | | |
| Stacy Robinson | WR | 5'11" | 186 | 28 | | |
| Odessa Turner | WR | 6'3" | 205 | 25 | | |
| Mark Bavaro | TE | 6'4" | 245 | 27 | | |
| Howard Cross | TE | 6'5" | 245 | 23 | | |
| Bob Mrosko | TE | 6'6" | 270 | 24 | | 6 |
| Raul Allegre | K | 5'10" | 167 | 31 | | 21 |
| Matt Bahr | K | 5'10" | 175 | 34 | | 80 |
| Sean Landeta | K | 6' | 200 | 28 | | |

## PHILADELPHIA EAGLES 10-6 Buddy Ryan

| Scores of Each Game | | |
|---|---|---|
| 20 | N.Y. Giants | 27 |
| 21 | PHOENIX | 23 |
| 27 | L.A. Rams | 21 |
| 23 | INDIANAPOLIS | 24 |
| 32 | MINNESOTA | 24 |
| 7 | Washington | 13 |
| 21 | Dallas | 20 |
| 48 | NEW ENGLAND | 20 |
| 28 | WASHINGTON | 14 |
| 24 | Atlanta | 23 |
| 31 | N.Y. GIANTS | 13 |
| 23 | Buffalo | 30 |
| 20 | Miami | 23 |
| 31 | GREEN BAY | 0 |
| 17 | DALLAS | 3 |
| 23 | Phoenix | 21 |

| Use Name | Pos. | Hgt | Wgt | Age | Int | Pts |
|---|---|---|---|---|---|---|
| Matt Darwin | OT | 6'4" | 275 | 27 | | |
| Ron Heller | OT | 6'6" | 280 | 28 | | |
| Daryle Smith | OT | 6'5" | 278 | 26 | | |
| Bruce Collie | OG | 6'6" | 275 | 28 | | |
| Cecil Gray | OG-DT | 6'4" | 274 | 22 | | |
| Mike Schad | OG | 6'5" | 290 | 26 | | |
| Ron Solt | OG | 6'3" | 285 | 28 | | |
| Ben Tamburello | OG-C | 6'3" | 278 | 25 | | |
| David Alexander | C | 6'3" | 282 | 25 | | |
| David Bailey | DE | 6'4" | 240 | 24 | | |
| Steve Kaufusi | DE | 6'4" | 274 | 26 | | |
| Clyde Simmons | DE | 6'6" | 276 | 26 | | 6 |
| Reggie White | DE-DT | 6'5" | 285 | 28 | | |
| Jerome Brown | DT | 6'2" | 295 | 25 | | |
| Dick Chapura (from PHX) | DT | 6'3" | 280 | 26 | | |
| Mike Golic | DT | 6'5" | 275 | 28 | 1 | |
| Mike Pitts | DT | 6'5" | 277 | 30 | | |

| Use Name | Pos. | Hgt | Wgt | Age | Int | Pts |
|---|---|---|---|---|---|---|
| Byron Evans | LB | 6'2" | 225 | 26 | 1 | 6 |
| Britt Hager | LB | 6'1" | 222 | 24 | | |
| Al Harris | LB | 6'5" | 265 | 33 | | |
| Maurice Henry | LB | 5'11" | 220 | 23 | | |
| Seth Joyner | LB | 6'2" | 248 | 25 | | |
| Ken Rose (from CLE) | LB | 6'1" | 216 | 28 | | |
| Ricky Shaw | LB | 6'4" | 240 | 25 | | |
| Jessie Small | LB | 6'3" | 239 | 23 | | |
| Eric Allen | DB | 5'10" | 182 | 23 | 3 | 6 |
| William Frizzell | DB | 6'3" | 205 | 28 | 3 | 6 |
| Terry Hoage | DB | 6'3" | 201 | 28 | 1 | |
| Wes Hopkins | DB | 6'1" | 212 | 29 | 5 | |
| Izel Jenkins | DB | 5'10" | 191 | 25 | | |
| Sammy Lilly (to SD) | DB | 5'9" | 178 | 25 | | |
| Ben Smith | DB | 5'11" | 183 | 23 | 3 | |
| Andre Waters | DB | 5'11" | 195 | 28 | | |

| Use Name | Pos. | Hgt | Wgt | Age | Int | Pts |
|---|---|---|---|---|---|---|
| Randall Cunningham | QB | 6'4" | 203 | 27 | | 30 |
| Jim McMahon | QB | 6'1" | 190 | 31 | | |
| Keith Byars | HB | 6'1" | 238 | 27 | | 18 |
| Robert Drummond | HB | 6'1" | 205 | 23 | | 6 |
| Thomas Sanders | HB | 5'11" | 203 | 28 | | 6 |
| Heath Sherman | FB-HB | 6' | 190 | 23 | | 24 |
| Anthony Toney | FB | 6' | 227 | 27 | | 24 |
| Roger Vick | FB | 6'3" | 235 | 26 | | 6 |
| Fred Barnett | WR | 6' | 203 | 24 | | 48 |
| Mike Bellamy | WR | 6' | 195 | 24 | | |
| Anthony Edwards | WR | 5'11" | 195 | 24 | | |
| Marvin Hargrove | WR | 5'10" | 178 | 22 | | 6 |
| Kenny Jackson | WR | 6' | 180 | 28 | | |
| Mike Quick | WR | 6'2" | 190 | 31 | | 6 |
| Calvin Williams | WR | 5'11" | 181 | 23 | | 54 |
| Keith Jackson | TE | 6'2" | 250 | 25 | | 36 |
| Harper LeBel | TE | 6'4" | 251 | 27 | | |
| Mickey Shuler | TE | 6'3" | 231 | 34 | | |
| Jeff Feagles | K | 6' | 198 | 24 | | |
| Roger Ruzek | K | 6'1" | 195 | 29 | | 108 |

John Teltschik — Leg Injury
Ron Johnson — Did Not Report

## WASHINGTON REDSKINS 10-6 Joe Gibbs

| Scores of Each Game | | |
|---|---|---|
| 31 | PHOENIX | 0 |
| 13 | San Francisco | 26 |
| 19 | DALLAS | 15 |
| 38 | Phoenix | 10 |
| 20 | N.Y. GIANTS | 24 |
| 13 | PHILADELPHIA | 7 |
| 10 | N.Y. Giants | 21 |
| 41 | Detroit | 38 |
| 14 | Philadelphia | 28 |
| 31 | NEW ORLEANS | 17 |
| 17 | Dallas | 27 |
| 42 | MIAMI | 20 |
| 10 | CHICAGO | 9 |
| 25 | New England | 10 |
| 28 | Indianapolis | 35 |
| 29 | BUFFALO | 14 |

| Use Name | Pos. | Hgt | Wgt | Age | Int | Pts |
|---|---|---|---|---|---|---|
| Joe Jacoby | OT | 6'7" | 305 | 31 | | |
| Jim Lachey | OT | 6'6" | 290 | 27 | | |
| Ed Simmons | OT | 6'5" | 280 | 26 | | |
| Mark Adickes | OG | 6'4" | 275 | 29 | | |
| Russ Grimm | OG | 6'3" | 275 | 31 | | |
| Raleigh McKenzie | OG-C | 6'2" | 270 | 27 | | |
| Mark Schlereth | OG | 6'3" | 285 | 24 | | |
| Jeff Bostic | C | 6'2" | 260 | 31 | | |
| James Geathers | DT | 6'7" | 290 | 30 | | |
| Markus Koch | DE | 6'5" | 275 | 27 | | |
| Charles Mann | DE | 6'6" | 270 | 29 | | |
| Fred Stokes | DE | 6'3" | 262 | 26 | | |
| Darryl Grant | DT | 6'1" | 275 | 30 | | |
| Tim Johnson | DT | 6'3" | 261 | 25 | | |
| Tracy Rocker | DT | 6'3" | 288 | 24 | | |
| Eric Williams | DT | 6'4" | 286 | 28 | | |

Mark May — Knee Injury

| Use Name | Pos. | Hgt | Wgt | Age | Int | Pts |
|---|---|---|---|---|---|---|
| Ravin Caldwell | LB | 6'3" | 229 | 27 | | |
| Monte Coleman | LB | 6'2" | 230 | 32 | 1 | |
| Andre Collins | LB | 6'1" | 230 | 22 | | |
| Kurt Gouveia | LB | 6'1" | 227 | 25 | | 6 |
| Randy Kirk | LB | 6'2" | 235 | 25 | | |
| Greg Manusky | LB | 6'1" | 242 | 24 | | |
| Wilber Marshall | LB | 6'1" | 230 | 28 | 1 | |
| Todd Bowles | DB | 6'2" | 203 | 26 | 3 | |
| Brian Davis | DB | 6'2" | 190 | 27 | | |
| Wayne Davis | DB | 5'11" | 180 | 27 | | |
| Brad Edwards | DB | 6'1" | 196 | 24 | 2 | |
| Darrell Green | DB | 5'8" | 170 | 30 | 4 | 6 |
| A.J. Johnson | DB | 5'8" | 176 | 23 | 1 | |
| Sidney Johnson | DB | 5'9" | 175 | 25 | | |
| Martin Mayhew | DB | 5'8" | 172 | 24 | 7 | |
| Alvoid Mays | DB | 5'9" | 180 | 24 | | |
| Johnny Thomas | DB | 5'9" | 185 | 26 | | |
| Clarence Vaughn | DB | 6' | 202 | 26 | | |
| Alvin Walton | DB | 6' | 180 | 26 | 2 | 6 |

| Use Name | Pos. | Hgt | Wgt | Age | Int | Pts |
|---|---|---|---|---|---|---|
| Gary Hogeboom | QB | 6'4" | 207 | 32 | | |
| Stan Humphries | QB | 6'2" | 223 | 25 | | 12 |
| Jeff Rutledge | QB | 6'1" | 195 | 33 | | 6 |
| Mark Rypien | QB. | 6'4" | 234 | 27 | | |
| Kelvin Bryant | HB | 6'2" | 195 | 30 | | 6 |
| Reggie Dupard | HB | 5'11" | 205 | 26 | | |
| Brian Mitchell | HB | 5'10" | 195 | 22 | | 6 |
| Gerald Riggs | HB-FB | 6'1" | 232 | 29 | | 36 |
| Earnest Byner | FB-HB | 5'10" | 215 | 27 | | 42 |
| Gary Clark | WR | 5'9" | 173 | 27 | | 48 |
| Stephen Hobbs | WR | 5'11" | 195 | 24 | | 6 |
| Joe Howard | WR | 5'8" | 170 | 27 | | |
| Art Monk | WR | 6'3" | 209 | 32 | | 30 |
| Ricky Sanders | WR | 5'11" | 180 | 28 | | 18 |
| Walter Stanley | WR | 5'9" | 180 | 27 | | |
| John Brandes | TE | 6'2" | 250 | 26 | | |
| Jimmie Johnson | TE | 6'2" | 246 | 22 | | 12 |
| Ron Middleton | TE | 6'2" | 255 | 25 | | |
| Don Warren | TE | 6'4" | 242 | 34 | | 6 |
| Ken Whisenhuint | TE | 6'3" | 240 | 28 | | |
| Kelly Goodburn (from KC) | K | 6'2" | 202 | 28 | | |
| Chip Lohmiller | K | 6'3" | 213 | 24 | | 131 |
| Ralf Mojsiejenko | K | 6'3" | 212 | 27 | | |

Reggie Branch — Ankle Injury
Tom Brown — Knee Injury
Charles Lockett — Quadriceps Injury

## DALLAS COWBOYS 7-9 Jimmy Johnson

| Scores of Each Game | | |
|---|---|---|
| 17 | SAN DIEGO | 14 |
| 7 | N.Y. GIANTS | 28 |
| 15 | Washington | 19 |
| 17 | N.Y. Giants | 31 |
| 14 | TAMPA BAY | 10 |
| 3 | Phoenix | 20 |
| 17 | Tampa Bay | 13 |
| 20 | PHILADELPHIA | 21 |
| 9 | N.Y. Jets | 24 |
| 6 | SAN FRANCISCO | 24 |
| 24 | L.A. Rams | 21 |
| 27 | WASHINGTON | 17 |
| 17 | NEW ORLEANS | 13 |
| 41 | PHOENIX | 10 |
| 3 | Philadelphia | 17 |
| 7 | Atlanta | 26 |

| Use Name | Pos. | Hgt | Wgt | Age | Int | Pts |
|---|---|---|---|---|---|---|
| Louis Cheek (to PHI) | OT | 6'6" | 295 | 25 | | |
| Kevin Gogan | OT | 6'7" | 311 | 25 | | |
| Mark Tuinei | OT | 6'5" | 293 | 30 | | |
| John Gesek | OG | 6'5" | 283 | 27 | | |
| Dale Hellestrae | OG-C | 6'5" | 275 | 28 | | |
| Crawford Ker | OG | 6'3" | 283 | 28 | | |
| Nate Newton | OG | 6'3" | 322 | 28 | | |
| Tony Slaton | OG | 6'3" | 280 | 29 | | |
| Mark Stepnoski | OG | 6'2" | 266 | 23 | | |
| Jeff Zimmerman | OG | 6'6" | 332 | 25 | | |
| Lester Brinkley | DE | 6'6" | 270 | 25 | | |
| Jim Jeffcoat | DE | 6'5" | 264 | 29 | | |
| Danny Stubbs | DE | 6'4" | 264 | 25 | | |
| Tony Tolbert | DE | 6'6" | 254 | 22 | | |
| Willie Broughton | DT | 6'5" | 280 | 26 | | |
| Dean Hamel | DT | 6'3" | 271 | 29 | | |
| Jimmie Jones | DT | 6'4" | 272 | 24 | | |
| Danny Noonan | DT | 6'4" | 266 | 25 | | |
| Mitch Willis | DT | 6'8" | 285 | 28 | | |

| Use Name | Pos. | Hgt | Wgt | Age | Int | Pts |
|---|---|---|---|---|---|---|
| Willis Crockett | LB | 6'3" | 234 | 24 | | |
| Jack Del Rio | LB | 6'4" | 236 | 27 | | |
| Dave Harper | LB | 6'1" | 220 | 24 | | |
| David Howard | LB | 6'2" | 233 | 28 | | |
| Eugene Lockhart | LB | 6'2" | 235 | 29 | | |
| Ken Norton | LB | 6'2" | 236 | 23 | | |
| Randy Shannon | LB | 6'1" | 221 | 24 | | |
| Vinson Smith | LB | 6'2" | 225 | 25 | | |
| Jesse Solomon | LB | 6' | 235 | 26 | | |
| Vince Albritton | DB | 6'2" | 220 | 28 | | |
| Bill Bates | DB | 6'1" | 200 | 29 | 1 | |
| Michael Brooks (from SD) | DB | 6' | 195 | 23 | | |
| Ron Francis | DB | 5'9" | 201 | 26 | | |
| Kenneth Gant | DB | 5'11" | 181 | 23 | 1 | |
| Manny Hendrix | DB | 5'10" | 185 | 25 | 1 | |
| Issiac Holt | DB | 6'2" | 202 | 27 | 3 | 6 |
| Ray Horton | DB | 5'11" | 187 | 30 | 1 | |
| Stan Smagala | DB | 5'10" | 184 | 22 | | |
| James Washington | DB | 6'1" | 195 | 25 | 3 | |
| Robert Williams | DB | 5'10" | 186 | 27 | 1 | |

Scott Ankrum — Knee Injury

| Use Name | Pos. | Hgt | Wgt | Age | Int | Pts |
|---|---|---|---|---|---|---|
| Troy Aikman | QB | 6'4" | 216 | 23 | | 6 |
| Babe Laufenberg | QB | 6'3" | 205 | 30 | | |
| Cliff Stoudt | QB | 6'4" | 218 | 35 | | |
| James Dixon | HB-WR | 5'10" | 184 | 23 | | |
| Emmitt Smith | HB | 5'9" | 203 | 21 | | 66 |
| Timmy Smith | HB | 5'11" | 216 | 26 | | |
| Tommie Agee | FB | 6'2" | 226 | 23 | | 6 |
| Alonzo Highsmith | FB | 6'1" | 237 | 25 | | |
| Daryl Johnston | FB | 6'2" | 234 | 24 | | 12 |
| Rod Harris (to PHI) | WR | 5'10" | 183 | 23 | | |
| Michael Irvin | WR | 6'2" | 202 | 23 | | 30 |
| Kelvin Martin | WR | 5'9" | 163 | 26 | | |
| Dennis McKinnon (to MIA) | WR | 6'1" | 177 | 29 | | 6 |
| Derrick Shepard | WR | 5'10" | 181 | 26 | | |
| Alexander Wright | WR | 6' | 189 | 23 | | 6 |
| Robert Awalt | TE | 6'5" | 238 | 26 | | |
| Steve Folsom | TE | 6'5" | 240 | 32 | | |
| Jay Novacek | TE | 6'4" | 230 | 27 | | 24 |
| Mike Saxon | K | 6'3" | 200 | 28 | | |
| Ken Willis | K | 5'11" | 189 | 23 | | 80 |

Keith Jones — Knee Injury

## PHOENIX CARDINALS 5-11 Joe Bugel

| Scores of Each Game | | |
|---|---|---|
| 0 | Washington | 31 |
| 23 | Philadelphia | 21 |
| 7 | New Orleans | 28 |
| 10 | WASHINGTON | 38 |
| 20 | DALLAS | 3 |
| 19 | N.Y. Giants | 20 |
| 21 | CHICAGO | 31 |
| 3 | Miami | 23 |
| 14 | Buffalo | 45 |
| 21 | GREEN BAY | 24 |
| 34 | NEW ENGLAND | 14 |
| 20 | INDIANAPOLIS | 17 |
| 24 | Atlanta | 13 |
| 10 | Dallas | 41 |
| 21 | N.Y. GIANTS | 24 |
| 21 | PHILADELPHIA | 23 |

| Use Name | Pos. | Hgt | Wgt | Age | Int | Pts |
|---|---|---|---|---|---|---|
| Tootie Robbins | OT | 6'5" | 302 | 32 | | |
| Luis Sharpe | OT | 6'4" | 290 | 30 | | 6 |
| Joe Wolf | OT | 6'5" | 283 | 23 | | |
| Derek Kennard | OG | 6'3" | 319 | 27 | | |
| Lance Smith | OG | 6'2" | 285 | 26 | | |
| Vernice Smith | OG-OT | 6'2" | 289 | 24 | | |
| Kani Kauahi | C | 6'2" | 274 | 30 | | |
| Bill Lewis | C | 6'7" | 278 | 27 | | |
| Dexter Manley | DE | 6'3" | 257 | 32 | | |
| Freddie Joe Nunn | DE | 6'4" | 250 | 28 | | |
| Elston Ridgle | DE | 6'5" | 270 | 27 | | |
| Rod Saddler | DE | 6'5" | 280 | 24 | | |
| Carl Hairston | DT | 6'2" | 280 | 37 | | |
| Bob Clasby | DT | 6'5" | 276 | 29 | | |
| Craig Patterson | NT | 6'5" | 310 | 26 | | |
| Jim Wahler | NT-DT | 6'4" | 276 | 24 | | |

Jeff Walker — Knee Injury

| Use Name | Pos. | Hgt | Wgt | Age | Int | Pts |
|---|---|---|---|---|---|---|
| David Bavaro | LB | 6' | 236 | 23 | | |
| Anthony Bell | LB | 6'3" | 231 | 26 | 1 | |
| David Braxton (from MIN) | LB | 6'1" | 232 | 25 | | |
| Ken Harvey | LB | 6'2" | 228 | 25 | | |
| Eric Hill | LB | 6'1" | 248 | 23 | | |
| Garth Jax | LB | 6'2" | 229 | 26 | 2 | |
| Eldonta Osbourne | LB | 6' | 226 | 23 | | |
| Jeroy Robinson (from DEN) | LB | 6'1" | 241 | 22 | | |
| Chris Washington | LB | 6'4" | 240 | 28 | | |
| Stanley Blair | DB | 6' | 192 | 26 | | |
| Tracy Eaton | DB | 6'1" | 191 | 25 | | |
| Lorenzo Lynch | DB | 5'9" | 200 | 27 | | |
| Cedric Mack | DB | 6' | 194 | 29 | 2 | |
| Tim McDonald | DB | 6'2" | 207 | 25 | 4 | |
| Jay Taylor | DB | 5'9" | 170 | 22 | 4 | |
| Marcus Turner | DB | 6' | 191 | 24 | 1 | 12 |
| Lonnie Young | DB | 6'1" | 182 | 27 | 2 | |
| Mike Zordich | DB | 5'11" | 197 | 26 | 1 | |

| Use Name | Pos. | Hgt | Wgt | Age | Int | Pts |
|---|---|---|---|---|---|---|
| Timm Rosenbach | QB | 6'2" | 215 | 23 | | 18 |
| Tom Tupa | QB | 6'4" | 220 | 23 | | |
| Larry Centers | HB | 5'11" | 203 | 22 | | |
| Terrence Flagler | HB | 6' | 200 | 25 | | 12 |
| Johnny Johnson | HB | 6'2" | 216 | 22 | | 30 |
| Vai Sikahema | HB | 5'9" | 184 | 28 | | |
| Dennis Smith | HB | 6' | 230 | 23 | | |
| Anthony Thompson | HB | 5'11" | 207 | 23 | | 24 |
| Ron Wolfley | FB | 6' | 222 | 27 | | |
| Roy Green | WR | 6' | 195 | 33 | | 24 |
| Don Holmes | WR | 5'10" | 182 | 29 | | |
| John Jackson | WR | 5'10" | 175 | 23 | | |
| Ernie Jones | WR | 5'11" | 186 | 25 | | 24 |
| Ricky Proehl | WR | 5'10" | 185 | 22 | | 24 |
| J.T. Smith | WR | 6'2" | 185 | 34 | | 12 |
| Tim Jorden | TE | 6'2" | 220 | 23 | | |
| Dave Little | TE | 6'2" | 230 | 29 | | |
| Walter Reeves | TE | 6'4" | 262 | 24 | | |
| Rich Camarillo | K | 5'11" | 193 | 29 | | |
| Al Del Greco | K | 5'10" | 191 | 28 | | 82 |

Darren Flutie — Foot Injury

## NEW YORK GIANTS

### Rushing
| Last Name | No. | Yds | Avg | TD |
|---|---|---|---|---|
| Anderson | 225 | 784 | 3.5 | 11 |
| Hampton | 109 | 455 | 4.2 | 2 |
| Tillman | 84 | 231 | 2.8 | 1 |
| Hostetler | 39 | 190 | 4.9 | 2 |
| Meggett | 22 | 164 | 7.5 | 0 |
| Carthon | 36 | 143 | 4.0 | 1 |
| Simms | 21 | 61 | 2.9 | 1 |
| Rouson | 3 | 14 | 4.7 | 0 |
| Ingram | 1 | 4 | 4.0 | 0 |
| Baker | 1 | 3 | 3.0 | 0 |

### Receiving
| Last Name | No. | Yds | Avg | TD |
|---|---|---|---|---|
| Meggett | 39 | 140 | 10.5 | 1 |
| Bavaro | 33 | 393 | 11.9 | 5 |
| Hampton | 32 | 274 | 8.6 | 2 |
| Baker | 26 | 541 | 20.8 | 4 |
| Ingram | 26 | 499 | 19.2 | 5 |
| Anderson | 18 | 139 | 7.7 | 0 |
| Carthon | 14 | 151 | 10.8 | 0 |
| Manuel | 11 | 169 | 15.4 | 0 |
| Cross | 8 | 106 | 13.3 | 0 |
| Tillman | 8 | 18 | 2.3 | 0 |
| Turner | 6 | 69 | 11.5 | 0 |
| Kyles | 4 | 77 | 19.3 | 0 |
| Mrosko | 3 | 27 | 9.0 | 1 |
| Robinson | 2 | 13 | 6.5 | 0 |
| Rouson | 1 | 12 | 12.0 | 0 |

### Punt Returns
| Last Name | No. | Yds | Avg | TD |
|---|---|---|---|---|
| Megett | 43 | 467 | 10.9 | 1 |

### Kickoff Returns
| Last Name | No. | Yds | Avg | TD |
|---|---|---|---|---|
| Meggett | 21 | 492 | 23.4 | 0 |
| Hampton | 20 | 340 | 17.0 | 0 |
| Ingram | 3 | 42 | 14.0 | 0 |
| Cross | 1 | 10 | 10.0 | 0 |
| Whitmore | 1 | 0 | 0.0 | 0 |

### Passing — Punting — Kicking
| Passing | Att | Cmp | % | Yds | Yd/Att | TD | Int—% | RK |
|---|---|---|---|---|---|---|---|---|
| Simms | 311 | 184 | 59.2 | 2284 | 7.34 | 15 | 4—1.3 | 1 |
| Hostetler | 87 | 47 | 54.0 | 614 | 7.06 | 3 | 1—1.1 | |

| Punting | No. | Avg. |
|---|---|---|
| Landeta | 75 | 44.1 |

| Kicking | XP | ATT | % | FG | ATT | % |
|---|---|---|---|---|---|---|
| Allegre | 9 | 9 | 100 | 4 | 5 | 80 |
| M. Bahr | 29 | 30 | 97 | 17 | 23 | 74 |

## PHILADELPHIA EAGLES

### Rushing
| Last Name | No. | Yds | Avg | TD |
|---|---|---|---|---|
| Cunningham | 118 | 942 | 8.0 | 5 |
| Sherman | 164 | 685 | 4.2 | 1 |
| Toney | 132 | 452 | 3.4 | 1 |
| Sanders | 56 | 208 | 3.7 | 1 |
| Byars | 37 | 141 | 3.8 | 0 |
| Vick | 16 | 58 | 3.6 | 1 |
| Drummond | 8 | 33 | 4.1 | 1 |
| Williams | 2 | 20 | 10.0 | 0 |
| Barnett | 2 | 13 | 6.5 | 0 |
| Feagles | 2 | 3 | 1.5 | 0 |
| McMahon | 3 | 1 | 0.3 | 0 |

### Receiving
| Last Name | No. | Yds | Avg | TD |
|---|---|---|---|---|
| Byars | 81 | 819 | 10.1 | 3 |
| Kel. Jackson | 50 | 670 | 13.4 | 6 |
| Williams | 37 | 602 | 16.3 | 9 |
| Barnett | 36 | 721 | 20.0 | 8 |
| Sherman | 23 | 167 | 7.3 | 3 |
| Shuler | 18 | 190 | 10.6 | 0 |
| Toney | 17 | 133 | 7.8 | 3 |
| Quick | 9 | 135 | 15.0 | 1 |
| Drummond | 5 | 39 | 7.8 | 0 |
| Sanders | 2 | 20 | 10.0 | 0 |
| Ken. Jackson | 1 | 43 | 43.0 | 0 |
| Hargrove | 1 | 34 | 34.0 | 1 |
| LeBel | 1 | 9 | 9.0 | 0 |

### Punt Returns
| Last Name | No. | Yds | Avg | TD |
|---|---|---|---|---|
| Hargrove | 12 | 83 | 6.9 | 0 |
| Edwards | 8 | 60 | 7.5 | 0 |
| Bellamy | 2 | 22 | 11.0 | 0 |
| Williams | 2 | -1 | -0.5 | 0 |

### Kickoff Returns
| Last Name | No. | Yds | Avg | TD |
|---|---|---|---|---|
| Hargrove | 19 | 341 | 17.9 | 0 |
| Sanders | 15 | 299 | 19.9 | 0 |
| Ken. Jackson | 6 | 125 | 20.8 | 0 |
| Barnett | 4 | 65 | 16.3 | 0 |
| Edwards | 3 | 36 | 12.0 | 0 |
| Vick | 2 | 22 | 11.0 | 0 |
| Bellamy | 1 | 17 | 17.0 | 0 |
| Jenkins | 1 | 14 | 14.0 | 0 |
| Allen | 1 | 2 | 2.0 | 0 |
| Hager | 1 | 0 | 0.0 | 0 |

### Passing — Punting — Kicking
| Passing | Att | Cmp | % | Yds | Yd/Att | TD | Int—% | RK |
|---|---|---|---|---|---|---|---|---|
| Cunningham | 465 | 271 | 58.3 | 3466 | 7.45 | 30 | 13—2.8 | 2 |
| McMahon | 9 | 6 | 66.7 | 63 | 7.00 | 0 | 0—0.0 | |
| Byars | 4 | 4 | 100.0 | 53 | 13.25 | 4 | 0—0.0 | |
| Feagles | 1 | 0 | 0.0 | 0 | 0.00 | 0 | 0—0.0 | |

| Punting | No. | Avg. |
|---|---|---|
| Feagles | 74 | 40.9 |

| Kicking | XP | ATT | % | FG | ATT | % |
|---|---|---|---|---|---|---|
| Ruzek | 45 | 48 | 94 | 21 | 29 | 72 |

## WASHINGTON REDSKINS

### Rushing
| Last Name | No. | Yds | Avg | TD |
|---|---|---|---|---|
| Byner | 297 | 1219 | 4.1 | 6 |
| Riggs | 123 | 475 | 3.9 | 6 |
| Humphries | 23 | 106 | 4.6 | 2 |
| Dupard | 19 | 85 | 4.5 | 0 |
| Mitchell | 15 | 81 | 5.4 | 1 |
| Monk | 7 | 59 | 8.4 | 0 |
| Bryant | 6 | 24 | 4.0 | 0 |
| Sanders | 4 | 17 | 4.3 | 0 |
| Rutledge | 4 | 12 | 3.0 | 1 |
| Goodburn | 1 | 5 | 5.0 | 0 |
| Rypien | 15 | 4 | 0.3 | 0 |
| Clark | 1 | 1 | 1.0 | 0 |
| Mojsiejenko | 1 | 0 | 0.0 | 0 |

### Receiving
| Last Name | No. | Yds | Avg | TD |
|---|---|---|---|---|
| Clark | 75 | 1112 | 14.8 | 8 |
| Monk | 68 | 770 | 11.3 | 5 |
| Sanders | 56 | 727 | 13.0 | 3 |
| Byner | 31 | 279 | 9.0 | 1 |
| Bryant | 26 | 248 | 9.5 | 1 |
| J. Johnson | 15 | 218 | 14.5 | 2 |
| Warren | 15 | 123 | 8.2 | 1 |
| Riggs | 7 | 60 | 8.6 | 0 |
| Howard | 3 | 36 | 12.0 | 0 |
| Stanley | 2 | 15 | 7.5 | 0 |
| Mitchell | 2 | 5 | 2.5 | 0 |
| Hobbs | 1 | 18 | 18.0 | 1 |

### Punt Returns
| Last Name | No. | Yds | Avg | TD |
|---|---|---|---|---|
| Stanley | 24 | 176 | 7.3 | 0 |
| Mitchell | 12 | 107 | 8.9 | 0 |
| Howard | 10 | 99 | 9.9 | 0 |
| Green | 1 | 6 | 6.0 | 0 |
| Thomas | 1 | 0 | 0.0 | 0 |

### Kickoff Returns
| Last Name | No. | Yds | Avg | TD |
|---|---|---|---|---|
| Howard | 22 | 427 | 19.4 | 0 |
| Mitchell | 18 | 365 | 20.3 | 0 |
| Stanley | 9 | 177 | 19.7 | 0 |
| Hobbs | 6 | 92 | 15.3 | 0 |
| Gouveia | 2 | 23 | 11.5 | 0 |
| Sanders | 1 | 22 | 22.0 | 0 |
| Middleton | 1 | 7 | 7.0 | 0 |
| Dupard | 2 | 0 | 0.0 | 0 |
| Bowles | 1 | 0 | 0.0 | 0 |

### Passing — Punting — Kicking
| Passing | Att | Cmp | % | Yds | Yd/Att | TD | Int—% | RK |
|---|---|---|---|---|---|---|---|---|
| Rypien | 304 | 166 | 54.6 | 2070 | 6.81 | 16 | 11—3.6 | 8 |
| Humphries | 156 | 91 | 58.3 | 1015 | 6.51 | 3 | 10—6.4 | |
| Rutledge | 68 | 40 | 58.8 | 455 | 6.69 | 2 | 1—1.5 | |
| Mitchell | 6 | 3 | 50.0 | 40 | 6.67 | 0 | 0—0.0 | |
| Byner | 2 | 1 | 50.0 | 31 | 15.50 | 1 | 0—0.0 | |

| Punting | No. | Avg. |
|---|---|---|
| Mojsiejenko | 44 | 38.3 |
| Goodburn | 11 | 36.8 |

| Kicking | XP | ATT | % | FG | ATT | % |
|---|---|---|---|---|---|---|
| Lohmiller | 41 | 41 | 100 | 30 | 40 | 75 |

## DALLAS COWBOYS

### Rushing
| Last Name | No. | Yds | Avg | TD |
|---|---|---|---|---|
| E. Smith | 241 | 937 | 3.9 | 11 |
| Agee | 53 | 213 | 4.0 | 0 |
| Aikman | 40 | 172 | 4.3 | 1 |
| Highsmith | 19 | 48 | 2.5 | 0 |
| Dixon | 11 | 43 | 3.9 | 0 |
| Johnston | 10 | 35 | 3.5 | 1 |
| Wright | 3 | 26 | 8.7 | 0 |
| Saxon | 1 | 20 | 20.0 | 0 |
| Laufenberg | 2 | 6 | 3.0 | 0 |
| T. Smith | 6 | 6 | 1.0 | 0 |
| Bates | 1 | 4 | 4.0 | 0 |
| Martin | 4 | -2 | -0.5 | 0 |
| McKinnon | 1 | -8 | -8.0 | 0 |

### Receiving
| Last Name | No. | Yds | Avg | TD |
|---|---|---|---|---|
| Martin | 64 | 732 | 11.4 | 0 |
| Novacek | 59 | 657 | 11.1 | 4 |
| Agee | 30 | 272 | 9.1 | 1 |
| E. Smith | 24 | 228 | 9.5 | 0 |
| Irvin | 20 | 413 | 20.7 | 5 |
| McKinnon | 14 | 172 | 12.3 | 1 |
| Johnston | 14 | 148 | 10.6 | 1 |
| Awalt | 13 | 133 | 10.2 | 0 |
| Wright | 11 | 104 | 9.5 | 0 |
| Highsmith | 3 | 13 | 4.3 | 0 |
| Dixon | 2 | 26 | 13.0 | 0 |

### Punt Returns
| Last Name | No. | Yds | Avg | TD |
|---|---|---|---|---|
| Harris | 28 | 214 | 7.6 | 0 |
| Shepard | 20 | 121 | 6.1 | 0 |
| Martin | 5 | 46 | 9.2 | 0 |
| McKinnon | 2 | 20 | 10.0 | 0 |

### Kickoff Returns
| Last Name | No. | Yds | Avg | TD |
|---|---|---|---|---|
| Dixon | 36 | 736 | 20.4 | 0 |
| Wright | 12 | 276 | 23.0 | 1 |
| Shepard | 4 | 75 | 18.8 | 0 |
| Harris | 2 | 44 | 22.0 | 0 |
| Stepnoski | 1 | 15 | 15.0 | 0 |

### Passing — Punting — Kicking
| Passing | Att | Cmp | % | Yds | Yd/Att | TD | Int—% | RK |
|---|---|---|---|---|---|---|---|---|
| Aikman | 399 | 226 | 56.6 | 2579 | 6.46 | 11 | 18—4.5 | 14 |
| Laufenberg | 67 | 24 | 35.8 | 279 | 4.16 | 1 | 6—9.0 | |

| Punting | No. | Avg. |
|---|---|---|
| Saxon | 79 | 43.2 |

| Kicking | XP | Att. | % | FG | Att | % |
|---|---|---|---|---|---|---|
| Willis | 26 | 26 | 100 | 18 | 25 | 72 |

## PHOENIX CARDINALS

### Rushing
| Last Name | No. | Yds | Avg | TD |
|---|---|---|---|---|
| Johnson | 234 | 926 | 4.0 | 5 |
| Rosenbach | 86 | 470 | 5.5 | 3 |
| Thompson | 106 | 390 | 3.7 | 4 |
| Flagler | 13 | 85 | 6.5 | 1 |
| Jones | 4 | 33 | 8.3 | 0 |
| Sikahema | 3 | 8 | 2.7 | 0 |
| Proehl | 1 | 4 | 4.0 | 0 |
| J. Smith | 1 | 4 | 4.0 | 0 |
| Wolfley | 2 | 3 | 1.5 | 0 |
| Tupa | 1 | 0 | 0.0 | 0 |
| Camarillo | 1 | -11 | -11.0 | 0 |

### Receiving
| Last Name | No. | Yds | Avg | TD |
|---|---|---|---|---|
| Proehl | 56 | 802 | 14.3 | 4 |
| Green | 53 | 797 | 15.0 | 4 |
| Jones | 43 | 724 | 16.8 | 4 |
| Johnson | 25 | 241 | 9.6 | 0 |
| J. Smith | 18 | 225 | 12.5 | 2 |
| Reeves | 18 | 126 | 7.0 | 0 |
| Flagler | 13 | 130 | 10.0 | 1 |
| Sikahema | 7 | 51 | 7.3 | 0 |
| Thompson | 2 | 11 | 5.5 | 0 |
| Jorden | 2 | 10 | 5.0 | 0 |
| Sharpe | 1 | 1 | 1.0 | 1 |

### Punt Returns
| Last Name | No. | Yds | Avg | TD |
|---|---|---|---|---|
| Sikahema | 36 | 306 | 8.5 | 0 |
| J. Smith | 3 | 34 | 11.3 | 0 |
| Proehl | 1 | 2 | 2.0 | 0 |

### Kickoff Returns
| Last Name | No. | Yds | Avg | TD |
|---|---|---|---|---|
| Sikahema | 27 | 544 | 20.1 | 0 |
| Centers | 16 | 272 | 17.0 | 0 |
| Flagler | 10 | 167 | 16.7 | 0 |
| Proehl | 4 | 53 | 13.3 | 0 |
| Jax | 2 | 17 | 8.5 | 0 |
| Green | 1 | 15 | 15.0 | 0 |

### Passing — Punting — Kicking
| Passing | Att | Cmp | % | Yds | Yd/Att | TD | Int—% | RK |
|---|---|---|---|---|---|---|---|---|
| Rosenbach | 437 | 237 | 54.2 | 3098 | 7.09 | 16 | 17—3.9 | 11 |
| Green | 1 | 1 | 100.0 | 20 | 20.00 | 0 | 0—0.0 | |
| Johnson | 1 | 0 | 0.0 | 0 | 0.00 | 0 | 1—100.0 | |

| Punting | No. | Avg. |
|---|---|---|
| Camarillo | 67 | 42.8 |

| Kicking | XP | Att. | % | FG | Att | % |
|---|---|---|---|---|---|---|
| Del Greco | 31 | 31 | 100 | 17 | 27 | 63 |

## CHICAGO BEARS 11-5 Mike Ditka

| Scores of Each Game | | |
|---|---|---|
| 17 | SEATTLE | 0 |
| 31 | Green Bay | 13 |
| 19 | MINNESOTA | 16 |
| 10 | L.A. Raiders | 24 |
| 27 | GREEN BAY | 13 |
| 38 | L.A. RAMS | 9 |
| 31 | Phoenix | 21 |
| 26 | Tampa Bay | 6 |
| 30 | ATLANTA | 24 |
| 16 | Denver | * 13 |
| 13 | Minnesota | 41 |
| 23 | DETROIT | * 17 |
| 9 | Washington | 10 |
| 21 | Detroit | 38 |
| 27 | TAMPA BAY | 14 |
| 10 | KANSAS CITY | 21 |

| Use Name | Pos. | Hgt | Wgt | Age | Int | Pts |
|---|---|---|---|---|---|---|
| Jim Covert | OT | 6'4" | 278 | 30 | | |
| Keith Van Horne | OT | 6'6" | 283 | 32 | | |
| John Wojciechowski | OT | 6'4" | 270 | 27 | | |
| Kurt Becker | OG | 6'5" | 269 | 31 | | |
| Mark Bortz | OG | 6'6" | 272 | 28 | | |
| Jerry Fontenot | OG | 6'3" | 272 | 23 | | |
| Tom Thayer | OG | 6'4" | 270 | 29 | | |
| Jay Hilgenberg | C | 6'3" | 260 | 30 | | |
| Trace Armstrong | DE | 6'4" | 259 | 24 | | |
| Richard Dent | DE | 6'5" | 268 | 29 | 3 | 6 |
| Terry Price | DE | 6'4" | 272 | 22 | | |
| Tim Ryan | DE | 6'4" | 268 | 22 | | |
| Dan Hampton | DT | 6'5" | 274 | 32 | | |
| Steve McMichael | DT | 6'2" | 268 | 32 | | |
| William Perry | DT | 6'2" | 315 | 27 | | |
| * Fred Washington | DT | 6'2" | 277 | 23 | | |
| Ron Cox | LB | 6'2" | 242 | 22 | | |
| Dante Jones | LB | 6'1" | 236 | 25 | | |
| Jim Morrissey | LB | 6'3" | 227 | 27 | 2 | |
| Mickey Pruitt | LB | 6'1" | 206 | 25 | | |
| Ron Rivera | LB | 6'3" | 240 | 28 | 2 | |
| John Roper | LB | 6'1" | 228 | 24 | | |
| Glenell Sanders | LB | 6' | 224 | 23 | | |
| Mike Singletary | LB | 6' | 230 | 31 | | |
| Mark Carrier | DB | 6'1" | 180 | 22 | 10 | |
| Maurice Douglass | DB | 5'11" | 200 | 26 | | |
| Shaun Gayle | DB | 5'11" | 194 | 28 | 2 | |
| Vestee Jackson | DB | 6' | 186 | 27 | 1 | 6 |
| John Mangum | DB | 5'10" | 173 | 23 | | |
| Markus Paul | DB | 6'2" | 199 | 24 | 2 | |
| Lemuel Stinson | DB | 5'9" | 159 | 24 | 6 | |
| David Tate | DB | 6' | 177 | 25 | | |
| Donnell Woolford | DB | 5'9" | 187 | 24 | 3 | |
| Jim Harbaugh | QB | 6'3" | 220 | 25 | | 24 |
| Mike Tomczak | QB | 6'1" | 198 | 27 | | 12 |
| Peter Tom Willis | QB | 6'2" | 188 | 23 | | |
| Neal Anderson | HB | 5'11" | 210 | 26 | | 78 |
| Johnny Bailey | HB | 5'8" | 180 | 23 | | 6 |
| Mark Green | HB | 5'11" | 184 | 23 | | 6 |
| Lars Tate | HB | 6'2" | 215 | 24 | | |
| Brad Muster | FB | 6'3" | 231 | 25 | | 36 |
| James Rouse | FB | 6' | 220 | 23 | | |
| Wendell Davis | WR | 5'11" | 188 | 24 | | 18 |
| Dennis Gentry | WR-HB | 5'8" | 180 | 31 | | 12 |
| Glen Kozlowski | WR | 6'1" | 205 | 27 | | |
| Ron Morris | WR | 6'1' | 195 | 25 | | 18 |
| Quintin Smith | WR | 5'10" | 172 | 22 | | |
| Tom Waddle | WR | 6' | 181 | 23 | | |
| Cap Boso | TE | 6'3" | 240 | 26 | | 6 |
| James Coley | TE | 6'3" | 270 | 23 | | |
| Jim Thornton | TE | 6'2" | 242 | 25 | | 6 |
| Maury Buford | K | 6'1" | 198 | 30 | | |
| Kevin Butler | K | 6'1" | 190 | 28 | | 114 |

* died Dec. 21 in automobile accident

## TAMPA BAY BUCCANEERS 6-10 Ray Perkins (5-8), Richard Williamson (1-2)

| Scores of Each Game | | |
|---|---|---|
| 38 | Detroit | 21 |
| 14 | L.A. RAMS | 35 |
| 23 | DETROIT | 20 |
| 23 | Minnesota | * 20 |
| 10 | Dallas | 14 |
| 26 | GREEN BAY | 14 |
| 13 | DALLAS | 17 |
| 10 | San Diego | 41 |
| 6 | CHICAGO | 26 |
| 7 | New Orleans | 35 |
| 7 | San Francisco | 31 |
| 10 | Green Bay | 20 |
| 23 | ATLANTA | 17 |
| 26 | MINNESOTA | 13 |
| 14 | Chicago | 27 |
| 14 | N.Y. JETS | 16 |

| Use Name | Pos. | Hgt | Wgt | Age | Int | Pts |
|---|---|---|---|---|---|---|
| Paul Gruber | OT | 6'5" | 290 | 25 | | |
| Harry Swayne | OT | 6'5" | 270 | 25 | | |
| Rob Taylor | OT | 6'6" | 290 | 29 | | |
| Carl Bax | OG | 6'4" | 290 | 24 | | |
| Ian Beckles | OG | 6'1" | 295 | 23 | | |
| John Bruhin | OG | 6'3" | 285 | 25 | | |
| Scott Dill | OG | 6'5" | 272 | 24 | | |
| Tom McHale | OG | 6'4" | 280 | 27 | | |
| Randy Grimes | C | 6'4" | 275 | 30 | | |
| Tony Mayberry | C | 6'4" | 285 | 22 | | |
| John Cannon | DE | 6'5" | 265 | 30 | | |
| Reuben Davis | DE | 6'4" | 285 | 25 | | |
| Benji Roland | DE | 6'3" | 260 | 23 | | |
| Jim Skow | DE | 6'3" | 250 | 27 | | |
| Robb White | DE | 6'4" | 280 | 25 | | |
| Curt Jarvis | NT | 6'2" | 265 | 25 | | |
| Tim Newton | NT | 6' | 277 | 27 | | |
| Ray Seals (to IND) | NT | 6'3" | 270 | 25 | | |
| Willie Wyatt | NT | 5'11" | 275 | 22 | | |
| Sam Anno | LB | 6'2" | 235 | 25 | | |
| Sidney Coleman | LB | 6'2" | 250 | 26 | | |
| Eugene Marve | LB | 6'2" | 240 | 30 | | |
| Keith McCants | LB | 6'3" | 255 | 21 | | |
| Winston Moss | LB | 6'3" | 235 | 24 | | |
| Kevin Murphy | LB | 6'2" | 235 | 26 | | |
| Ervin Randle | LB | 6'1" | 250 | 27 | | |
| Broderick Thomas | LB | 6'4" | 245 | 23 | | |
| Eric Everett | DB | 5'10" | 170 | 24 | 4 | |
| Bobby Futrell | DB | 5'11" | 190 | 28 | | |
| Wayne Haddix | DB | 6'1" | 205 | 27 | 7 | 18 |
| Harry Hamilton | DB | 6' | 195 | 27 | 5 | |
| Odie Harris | DB | 6' | 190 | 24 | | |
| Ricky Reynolds | DB | 5'11" | 190 | 25 | 3 | |
| Rodney Rice | DB | 5'8" | 180 | 24 | 2 | |
| Mark Robinson | DB | 5'11" | 200 | 27 | 4 | |
| Jeff Carlson | QB | 6'3" | 215 | 24 | | |
| Chris Chandler | QB | 6'4" | 220 | 24 | | 6 |
| Vinny Testaverde | QB | 6'5" | 215 | 26 | | 6 |
| Gary Anderson | HB | 6' | 190 | 29 | | 30 |
| Derrick Douglas | HB | 5'10" | 205 | 22 | | |
| John Harvey | HB | 5'11" | 185 | 23 | | 6 |
| Reggie Cobb | FB | 6' | 225 | 22 | | 12 |
| Jamie Lawson (to NE) | FB | 5'10" | 240 | 24 | | |
| Bruce Perkins | FB | 6'2" | 230 | 23 | | |
| Terry Anthony | WR | 6' | 200 | 22 | | |
| Mark Carrier | WR | 6' | 185 | 24 | | 24 |
| Willie Drewrey | WR | 5'7" | 170 | 27 | | 6 |
| Chris Ford | WR | 6'1" | 185 | 23 | | |
| Bruce Hill | WR | 6' | 180 | 26 | | 30 |
| Danny Peebles | WR | 5'11" | 180 | 25 | | 6 |
| Frank Pillow | WR | 5'10" | 170 | 25 | | |
| Jesse Anderson | TE | 6'2" | 245 | 24 | | |
| Ron Hall | TE | 6'4" | 245 | 26 | | 12 |
| Ed Thomas | TE | 6'3" | 235 | 24 | | |
| Steve Christie | K | 6' | 185 | 22 | | 96 |
| Mark Royals | K | 6'5" | 215 | 26 | | |

## DETROIT LIONS 6-10 Wayne Fontes

| Scores of Each Game | | |
|---|---|---|
| 21 | TAMPA BAY | 38 |
| 21 | ATLANTA | 14 |
| 20 | Tampa Bay | 23 |
| 21 | GREEN BAY | 24 |
| 34 | Minnesota | 27 |
| 24 | Kansas City | 43 |
| 27 | New Orleans | 10 |
| 38 | WASHINGTON | * 41 |
| 7 | MINNESOTA | 17 |
| 0 | N.Y. Giants | 20 |
| 40 | DENVER | 27 |
| 17 | Chicago | * 23 |
| 31 | L.A. RAIDERS | 38 |
| 38 | CHICAGO | 21 |
| 24 | Green Bay | 17 |
| 10 | Seattle | 30 |

| Use Name | Pos. | Hgt | Wgt | Age | Int | Pts |
|---|---|---|---|---|---|---|
| Lomas Brown | OT | 6'4" | 287 | 27 | | |
| Harvey Salem | OT | 6'6" | 285 | 29 | | |
| Eric Sanders | OT-OG | 6'7" | 286 | 31 | | |
| Eric Andolsek | OG | 6'2" | 286 | 24 | | |
| Ken Dallafior | OG | 6'4" | 279 | 31 | | |
| Mike Utley | OG-OT | 6'6" | 279 | 24 | | |
| Kevin Glover | C | 6'2" | 282 | 27 | | |
| Dennis McKnight | C-OG | 6'3" | 280 | 30 | | |
| Kevin Brooks | DE | 6'6" | 278 | 27 | | |
| Jackie Cline | DE | 6'5" | 280 | 30 | | |
| Mark Duckens | DE | 6'4" | 270 | 25 | | |
| Keith Ferguson | DE | 6'5" | 260 | 31 | | |
| Jeff Hunter | DE | 6'5" | 285 | 24 | | |
| Dan Owens | DE | 6'3" | 268 | 23 | | |
| Marc Spindler | DE | 6'5" | 277 | 20 | | |
| Jerry Ball | NT | 6'1" | 298 | 25 | | |
| Lawrence Pete | NT | 6' | 282 | 24 | | |
| Mark Brown | LB | 6'2" | 240 | 28 | | |
| Toby Caston | LB | 6'1" | 243 | 25 | | |
| Mike Cofer | LB | 6'5" | 245 | 30 | 1 | |
| Dennis Gibson | LB | 6'2" | 240 | 26 | | |
| Tracy Hayworth | LB | 6'3" | 250 | 22 | | |
| George Jamison | LB | 6'1" | 226 | 27 | | |
| Victor Jones | LB | 6'2" | 240 | 23 | 1 | |
| Niko Noga | LB | 6'1" | 235 | 28 | | |
| Chris Spielman | LB | 6' | 247 | 29 | 1 | |
| Jimmy Williams (to MIN) | LB | 6'3" | 230 | 29 | | 6 |
| Bruce Alexander | DB | 5'9" | 169 | 24 | | |
| Bennie Blades | DB | 6'1" | 221 | 23 | 2 | |
| Darren Carrington | DB | 6'1" | 189 | 23 | | |
| Ray Crockett | DB | 5'9" | 181 | 23 | 3 | 6 |
| LeRoy Irvin | DB | 5'11" | 184 | 32 | 1 | |
| Bruce McNorton | DB | 5'11" | 175 | 31 | 1 | |
| John Miller | DB | 6'1" | 195 | 24 | | |
| Chris Oldham | DB | 5'9" | 183 | 21 | 1 | |
| Terry Taylor | DB | 5'10" | 191 | 29 | | |
| Herb Welch | DB | 5'11" | 180 | 29 | 1 | |
| Sheldon White | DB | 5'11" | 188 | 25 | | |
| William White | DB | 5'10" | 191 | 24 | 5 | 6 |
| Bob Gagliano | QB | 6'3" | 196 | 31 | | |
| Rodney Peete | QB | 6' | 193 | 24 | | 36 |
| Barry Sanders | HB-FB | 5'8" | 203 | 22 | | 96 |
| James Wilder (from WAS) | HB-FB | 6'2" | 225 | 32 | | 6 |
| Jeff Campbell | WR | 5'8" | 167 | 22 | | 12 |
| Robert Clark | WR | 5'11" | 173 | 25 | | 48 |
| Mike Farr | WR | 5'10" | 192 | 23 | | |
| Mel Gray | WR | 5'9" | 162 | 29 | | |
| Terry Greer | WR | 6'1" | 192 | 32 | | 18 |
| Richard Johnson | WR | 5'7" | 185 | 28 | | 36 |
| Aubrey Matthews | WR | 5'7" | 165 | 27 | | 6 |
| Jason Phillips | WR | 5'7" | 168 | 23 | | |
| Jim Arnold | K | 6'3" | 211 | 29 | | |
| Rich Karlis | K | 6' | 180 | 31 | | 24 |
| Eddie Murray | K | 5'10" | 180 | 34 | | 73 |

## GREEN BAY PACKERS 6-10 Lindy Infante

| Scores of Each Game | | |
|---|---|---|
| 36 | L.A. RAMS | 24 |
| 13 | CHICAGO | 31 |
| 3 | KANSAS CITY | 17 |
| 24 | Detroit | 21 |
| 13 | Chicago | 27 |
| 14 | Tampa Bay | 26 |
| 24 | MINNESOTA | 10 |
| 20 | SAN FRANCISCO | 24 |
| 29 | L.A. Raiders | 16 |
| 24 | Phoenix | 21 |
| 20 | TAMPA BAY | 10 |
| 7 | Minnesota | 23 |
| 14 | SEATTLE | 20 |
| 0 | Philadelphia | 31 |
| 17 | DETROIT | 24 |
| 13 | Denver | 22 |

| Use Name | Pos. | Hgt | Wgt | Age | Int | Pts |
|---|---|---|---|---|---|---|
| Tony Mandarich | OT | 6'5" | 295 | 23 | | |
| Ken Ruettgers | OT | 6'5" | 288 | 28 | | |
| Alan Veingrad | OT | 6'5" | 281 | 27 | | |
| Billy Ard | OG | 6'3" | 273 | 31 | | |
| Ron Hallstrom | OG | 6'6" | 297 | 31 | | |
| Rich Moran | OG | 6'3" | 283 | 28 | | |
| Keith Uecker | OG | 6'5" | 295 | 39 | | |
| Blair Bush | C | 6'3" | 272 | 33 | | |
| Lester Archambeau | DE | 6'4" | 274 | 23 | | |
| James Campen | C | 6'3" | 270 | 26 | | |
| Matt Brock | DE | 6'5" | 285 | 24 | | |
| Robert Brown | DE | 6'2" | 270 | 30 | | |
| Mark Hall | DE | 6'4" | 280 | 24 | | |
| Shawn Patterson | DE | 6'5" | 270 | 25 | 1 | 6 |
| Blaise Winter | DE | 6'3" | 282 | 28 | | |
| Bob Nelson | NT | 6'4" | 275 | 31 | | |
| Tony Bennett | LB | 6'2" | 233 | 23 | | |
| Burnell Dent | LB | 6'1" | 234 | 27 | | |
| Tim Harris | LB | 6'5" | 258 | 25 | | |
| Johnny Holland | LB | 6'2" | 221 | 25 | 1 | |
| Bobby Houston | LB | 6'2" | 234 | 22 | | |
| Brian Noble | LB | 6'3" | 252 | 27 | | |
| Bryce Paup | LB | 6'5" | 245 | 22 | | |
| Scott Stephen | LB | 6'2" | 232 | 26 | 2 | |
| Mike Weddington | LB | 6'4" | 245 | 29 | | |
| LeRoy Butler | DB | 6' | 192 | 22 | 3 | |
| Chuck Cecil | DB | 6' | 184 | 25 | 1 | |
| Tiger Greene | DB | 6' | 194 | 28 | | 6 |
| Jerry Holmes | DB | 6'2" | 176 | 32 | 3 | |
| Mark Lee | DB | 5'11" | 189 | 32 | 1 | |
| Mark Murphy | DB | 6'2" | 201 | 32 | 3 | |
| Ron Pitts | DB | 5'10" | 175 | 27 | 1 | |
| Jerry Woods | DB | 5'8" | 193 | 24 | | |
| Anthony Dilweg | QB | 6'3" | 215 | 25 | | |
| Blair Kiel | QB | 6' | 214 | 28 | | 6 |
| Don Majkowski | QB | 6'2" | 197 | 26 | | 6 |
| Mike Norseth | QB | 6'2" | 202 | 26 | | |
| Herman Fontenot | HB | 6' | 206 | 26 | | 6 |
| Keith Woodside | HB | 5'11" | 203 | 26 | | 6 |
| Vince Workman | HB | 5'10 | 193 | 22 | | 6 |
| Michael Haddix | FB | 6'2" | 227 | 28 | | 12 |
| Brent Fullwood (to CLE) | FB-HB | 5'11" | 209 | 26 | | 6 |
| Darrell Thompson | FB | 6' | 215 | 22 | | 12 |
| Carl Bland | WR | 5'11" | 182 | 28 | | |
| Perry Kemp | WR | 5'11" | 170 | 28 | | 12 |
| Jeff Query | WR | 6' | 165 | 23 | | 18 |
| Sterling Sharpe | WR | 5'11" | 202 | 25 | | 36 |
| Clarence Weathers | WR | 5'9" | 182 | 28 | | 6 |
| Charles Wilson | WR | 5'9" | 174 | 22 | | |
| Jackie Harris | TE | 6'3" | 240 | 22 | | |
| William Harris | TE | 6'4" | 243 | 25 | | |
| Ed West | TE | 6'1" | 243 | 29 | | 30 |
| Don Bracken | K | 6'1" | 211 | 28 | | |
| Chris Jacke | K | 6' | 197 | 24 | | 97 |

Dave Brown — Achilles' Injury

## MINNESOTA VIKINGS 6-10 Jerry Burns

| Scores of Each Game | | |
|---|---|---|
| 21 | Kansas City | 24 |
| 32 | NEW ORLEANS | 3 |
| 16 | Chicago | 19 |
| 20 | TAMPA BAY | * 23 |
| 27 | DETROIT | 34 |
| 24 | Philadelphia | 32 |
| 10 | Green Bay | 24 |
| 27 | DENVER | 22 |
| 17 | Detroit | 7 |
| 24 | Seattle | 21 |
| 41 | CHICAGO | 13 |
| 23 | GREEN BAY | 7 |
| 15 | N.Y. Giants | 23 |
| 13 | Tampa Bay | 26 |
| 24 | L.A. RAIDERS | 28 |
| 17 | SAN FRANCISCO | 20 |

| Use Name | Pos. | Hgt | Wgt | Age | Int | Pts |
|---|---|---|---|---|---|---|
| -Paul Blair | OT | 6'4" | 280 | 27 | | |
| -Brian Habib | OT | 6'7" | 288 | 25 | | |
| -Tim Irwin | OT | 6'6" | 295 | 31 | | |
| -Gary Zimmerman | OT | 6'6" | 286 | 28 | | |
| -Dave Huffman | OG | 6'6" | 284 | 34 | | |
| -Todd Kalis | OG | 6'5" | 286 | 25 | | |
| -Randall McDaniel | OG | 6'3" | 271 | 25 | | |
| -Craig Wolfley | OG | 6'1" | 277 | 32 | | |
| -Chris Foote | C | 6'3" | 266 | 33 | | |
| -Kirk Lowdermilk | C | 6'3" | 267 | 27 | | |
| -Adam Schrieber | C-OG | 6'4" | 288 | 28 | | |
| -Chris Doleman | DE | 6'5" | 262 | 28 | 1 | 2 |
| -Willie Fears | DE | 6'3" | 278 | 26 | | |
| -Al Noga | DE | 6'1" | 248 | 23 | 1 | 12 |
| -John Randle | DE | 6'1" | 248 | 22 | | |
| -Thomas Strauthers | DT-DE | 6'4" | 262 | 29 | | |
| -Ken Clarke | DT | 6'2" | 280 | 34 | | |
| -Keith Millard | DT | 6'5" | 262 | 28 | | |
| -Henry Thomas | DT | 6'2" | 267 | 25 | | |
| -Walker Lee Ashley | LB | 6' | 232 | 30 | | |
| -Ray Berry | LB | 6'2" | 226 | 26 | | |
| -David Braxton | LB | 6'1" | 230 | 25 | | 2 |
| -Mark Dusbabek | LB | 6'3" | 230 | 26 | | 2 |
| John Galvin | LB | 6'3" | 226 | 24 | | |
| -William Kirksey | LB | 6'2" | 221 | 24 | | |
| -Mike Merriweather | LB | 6'2" | 222 | 29 | 3 | 6 |
| -Scott Studwell | LB | 6'2" | 228 | 36 | | |
| -Michael Brim | DB | 6' | 186 | 24 | 2 | |
| -Joey Browner | DB | 6'2" | 210 | 30 | 7 | 6 |
| -Pat Eilers | DB | 5'11" | 195 | 23 | | |
| -Darrell Fullington | DB | 6'1" | 197 | 26 | 1 | |
| -Alonzo Hampton | DB | 5'10" | 191 | 23 | | |
| -Ken Johnson | DB | 6'2" | 197 | 23 | | |
| -Carl Lee | DB | 6' | 183 | 29 | 2 | |
| -Audrey McMillian | DB | 6' | 189 | 28 | 3 | |
| -Reggie Rutland | DB | 6'1" | 194 | 26 | 2 | |
| -Ken Stills | DB | 5'10" | 186 | 26 | | |
| Rich Gannon | QB | 6'3" | 202 | 24 | | 6 |
| Sean Salisbury | QB | 6'5" | 208 | 27 | | |
| Wade Wilson | QB | 6'3" | 208 | 31 | | |
| D.J. Dozier | HB | 6' | 198 | 24 | | |
| Allen Rice | HB | 5'10" | 204 | 27 | | |
| Herschel Walker | HB-FB | 6'1" | 226 | 28 | | 54 |
| Alfred Anderson | FB | 6'1" | 223 | 28 | | 12 |
| Jessie Clark | FB | 6' | 233 | 30 | | |
| Rick Fenney | FB | 6'1" | 232 | 25 | | 12 |
| Cedric Smith | FB | 5'10" | 223 | 22 | | |
| Anthony Carter | WR | 5'11" | 177 | 29 | | 48 |
| Cris Carter | WR | 6'3" | 200 | 24 | | 18 |
| Ira Hillary | WR | 5'11" | 190 | 27 | | |
| Hassan Jones | WR | 6' | 192 | 26 | | 42 |
| Leo Lewis (from CLE) | WR | 5'8" | 172 | 33 | | |
| Pat Newman | WR | 5'11" | 189 | 21 | | |
| Mike Jones | TE | 6'3" | 255 | 23 | | |
| Steve Jordan | TE | 6'4" | 239 | 29 | | 18 |
| Brent Novoselsky | TE | 6'3" | 232 | 24 | | |
| Jim Gallery | K | 6'1" | 190 | 28 | | |
| Donald Igwebuike | K | 5'9" | 190 | 29 | | 61 |
| Harry Newsome | K | 6' | 188 | 27 | | |
| Fuad Reveiz (from SD) | K | 5'11" | 216 | 27 | | 65 |

Jim Gustafson — Neck Injury

## CHICAGO BEARS

### RUSHING

| Last Name | No. | Yds | Avg | TD |
|---|---|---|---|---|
| Anderson | 260 | 1078 | 4.1 | 10 |
| Muster | 141 | 664 | 4.7 | 6 |
| Harbaugh | 51 | 321 | 6.3 | 4 |
| Green | 27 | 126 | 4.7 | 0 |
| Bailey | 26 | 86 | 3.3 | 0 |
| Rouse | 16 | 56 | 3.5 | 0 |
| Gentry | 11 | 43 | 3.9 | 0 |
| Tomczak | 12 | 41 | 3.4 | 2 |
| Morris | 2 | 26 | 13.0 | 0 |
| L. Tate | 3 | 5 | 1.7 | 0 |
| Perry | 1 | -1 | -1.0 | - |
| Buford | 1 | -9 | -9.0 | 0 |

### RECEIVING

| Last Name | No. | Yds | Avg | TD |
|---|---|---|---|---|
| Muster | 47 | 452 | 9.6 | 0 |
| Anderson | 42 | 484 | 11.5 | 3 |
| Davis | 39 | 572 | 14.7 | 3 |
| Morris | 31 | 437 | 14.1 | 3 |
| Gentry | 23 | 320 | 13.9 | 2 |
| Thornton | 19 | 254 | 13.4 | 1 |
| Boso | 11 | 135 | 12.3 | 1 |
| Kozlowski | 7 | 83 | 11.9 | 0 |
| Green | 4 | 26 | 6.5 | 1 |
| Waddle | 2 | 32 | 16.0 | 0 |
| Smith | 2 | 20 | 10.0 | 0 |
| Coley | 1 | 7 | 7.0 | 0 |
| Tomczak | 1 | 5 | 5.0 | 0 |

### PUNT RETURNS

| Last Name | No. | Yds | Avg | TD |
|---|---|---|---|---|
| Bailey | 36 | 399 | 11.1 | 1 |

### KICKOFF RETURNS

| Last Name | No. | Yds | Avg | TD |
|---|---|---|---|---|
| Bailey | 23 | 363 | 15.8 | 0 |
| Gentry | 18 | 388 | 21.6 | 0 |
| Green | 7 | 112 | 16.0 | 0 |
| Rouse | 3 | 17 | 5.7 | 0 |
| Roper | 1 | 0 | 0.0 | 0 |
| L. Tate | 1 | 0 | 0.0 | 0 |
| Ryan | 1 | -1 | -1.0 | 0 |

### PASSING — PUNTING — KICKING

| PASSING | Att | Cmp | % | Yds | Yd/Att | TD | Int— | % | RK |
|---|---|---|---|---|---|---|---|---|---|
| Harbaugh | 312 | 180 | 57.7 | 2178 | 6.98 | 10 | 6— | 1.9 | 4 |
| Tomczak | 104 | 39 | 37.5 | 521 | 5.01 | 3 | 5— | 4.8 | |
| Willis | 13 | 9 | 69.2 | 106 | 8.15 | 1 | 1— | 7.7 | |
| Bailey | 1 | 1 | 100.0 | 22 | 22.00 | 0 | 0— | 0.0 | |

| PUNTING | No. | Avg. |
|---|---|---|
| Buford | 78 | 39.4 |

| KICKING | XP | ATT | % | FG | ATT | % |
|---|---|---|---|---|---|---|
| Butler | 36 | 37 | 97 | 26 | 37 | 70 |

## TAMPA BAY BUCCANEERS

### RUSHING

| Last Name | No. | Yds | Avg | TD |
|---|---|---|---|---|
| G. Anderson | 166 | 646 | 3.9 | 3 |
| Cobb | 151 | 480 | 3.2 | 2 |
| Testaverde | 38 | 280 | 7.4 | 1 |
| Harvey | 27 | 113 | 4.2 | 0 |
| Chandler | 13 | 71 | 5.5 | 1 |
| Perkins | 13 | 36 | 2.8 | 0 |
| Carlson | 1 | 0 | 0.0 | 0 |
| Hill | 1 | 0 | 0.0 | 0 |

### RECEIVING

| Last Name | No. | Yds | Avg | TD |
|---|---|---|---|---|
| Carrier | 49 | 813 | 16.6 | 4 |
| Hill | 42 | 641 | 15.3 | 5 |
| Cobb | 39 | 299 | 7.7 | 0 |
| G. Anderson | 38 | 464 | 12.2 | 2 |
| Hall | 31 | 464 | 15.0 | 2 |
| Harvey | 11 | 86 | 7.8 | 1 |
| Pillow | 8 | 118 | 14.8 | 0 |
| Perkins | 8 | 85 | 10.6 | 2 |
| Drewrey | 7 | 182 | 26.0 | 1 |
| Peebles | 6 | 50 | 8.3 | 1 |
| J. Anderson | 5 | 77 | 15.4 | 0 |
| Testaverde | 1 | 3 | 3.0 | 0 |

### PUNT RETURNS

| Last Name | No. | Yds | Avg | TD |
|---|---|---|---|---|
| Drewrey | 23 | 184 | 8.0 | 0 |

### KICKOFF RETURNS

| Last Name | No. | Yds | Avg | TD |
|---|---|---|---|---|
| Peebles | 18 | 369 | 20.5 | 0 |
| Drewrey | 14 | 244 | 17.4 | 0 |
| Harvey | 12 | 207 | 17.3 | 0 |
| Cobb | 11 | 223 | 20.3 | 0 |
| G. Anderson | 6 | 123 | 20.5 | 0 |
| Coleman | 1 | 9 | 9.0 | 0 |
| Hall | 1 | 0 | 0.0 | 0 |

### PASSING — PUNTING — KICKING

| PASSING | Att | Cmp | % | Yds | Yd/Att | TD | Int— | % | RK |
|---|---|---|---|---|---|---|---|---|---|
| Testaverde | 365 | 203 | 55.6 | 2818 | 7.72 | 17 | 18— | 4.9 | 9 |
| Chandler | 83 | 42 | 50.6 | 464 | 5.59 | 1 | 6— | 7.2 | |

| PUNTING | No. | Avg. |
|---|---|---|
| Royals | 72 | 40.3 |

| KICKING | XP | ATT | % | FG | ATT | % |
|---|---|---|---|---|---|---|
| Christie | 27 | 27 | 100 | 23 | 27 | 85 |
| Team | 0 | 1 | 0 | 0 | 0 | 0 |

## DETROIT LIONS

### RUSHING

| Last Name | No. | Yds | Avg | TD |
|---|---|---|---|---|
| B. Sanders | 255 | 1304 | 5.1 | 13 |
| Peete | 48 | 365 | 7.6 | 6 |
| Gagliano | 46 | 145 | 3.2 | 0 |
| Ware | 7 | 64 | 9.1 | 0 |
| Wilder | 11 | 51 | 4.6 | 0 |

### RECEIVING

| Last Name | No. | Yds | Avg | TD |
|---|---|---|---|---|
| Johnson | 64 | 727 | 11.4 | 6 |
| Clark | 53 | 932 | 17.6 | 8 |
| B. Sanders | 35 | 462 | 13.2 | 3 |
| Matthews | 30 | 349 | 11.6 | 1 |
| Greer | 20 | 332 | 16.6 | 3 |
| Campbell | 19 | 236 | 12.4 | 2 |
| Farr | 12 | 170 | 14.2 | 0 |
| Phillips | 8 | 112 | 14.0 | 0 |
| B. Sanders | 1 | 18 | 18.0 | 0 |
| Wilder | 1 | 8 | 8.0 | 1 |

### PUNT RETURNS

| Last Name | No. | Yds | Avg | TD |
|---|---|---|---|---|
| Gray | 34 | 362 | 10.6 | 0 |
| Campbell | 1 | 0 | 0.0 | 0 |

### KICKOFF RETURNS

| Last Name | No. | Yds | Avg | TD |
|---|---|---|---|---|
| Gray | 41 | 939 | 22.9 | 0 |
| Oldham | 13 | 234 | 18.0 | 0 |
| Campbell | 12 | 238 | 19.8 | 0 |
| Phillips | 2 | 43 | 21.5 | 0 |
| Andolsek | 1 | 12 | 12.0 | 0 |
| McKnight | 1 | 0 | 0.0 | 0 |

### PASSING — PUNTING — KICKING

| PASSING | Att | Cmp | % | Yds | Yd/Att | TD | Int— | % | RK |
|---|---|---|---|---|---|---|---|---|---|
| Peete | 271 | 142 | 52.4 | 1974 | 7.28 | 13 | 8— | 3.0 | 5 |
| Gagliano | 159 | 87 | 54.7 | 1190 | 7.48 | 10 | 10— | 6.3 | |
| Ware | 30 | 13 | 43.3 | 164 | 5.47 | 1 | 2— | 6.7 | |

| PUNTING | No. | Avg. |
|---|---|---|
| Arnold | 63 | 40.6 |

| KICKING | XP | ATT | % | FG | ATT | % |
|---|---|---|---|---|---|---|
| Murray | 34 | 34 | 100 | 13 | 19 | 68 |
| Karlis | 12 | 12 | 100 | 4 | 7 | 57 |

## GREEN BAY PACKERS

### RUSHING

| Last Name | No. | Yds | Avg | TD |
|---|---|---|---|---|
| Haddix | 98 | 311 | 3.2 | 0 |
| Thompson | 76 | 264 | 3.5 | 1 |
| Majkowski | 29 | 186 | 6.4 | 1 |
| Woodside | 46 | 182 | 4.0 | 1 |
| Fullwood | 44 | 124 | 2.8 | 1 |
| Dilweg | 21 | 114 | 5.4 | 0 |
| Fontenot | 17 | 76 | 4.5 | 0 |
| Workman | 8 | 51 | 6.4 | 0 |
| Query | 3 | 39 | 13.0 | 0 |
| Sharpe | 2 | 14 | 7.0 | 0 |
| Kiel | 5 | 9 | 1.8 | 1 |
| Kemp | 1 | -1 | -1.0 | 0 |

### RECEIVING

| Last Name | No. | Yds | Avg | TD |
|---|---|---|---|---|
| Sharpe | 67 | 1105 | 16.5 | 6 |
| Kemp | 44 | 527 | 12.0 | 2 |
| Query | 34 | 458 | 13.5 | 2 |
| Weathers | 33 | 390 | 11.8 | 1 |
| Fontenot | 31 | 293 | 9.55 | 1 |
| West | 27 | 356 | 13.2 | 5 |
| Woodside | 24 | 184 | 7.7 | 0 |
| J. Harris | 12 | 157 | 13.1 | 0 |
| Wilson | 7 | 84 | 12.0 | 0 |
| Workman | 4 | 30 | 7.5 | 1 |
| Fullwood | 3 | 17 | 5.7 | 0 |
| Thompson | 3 | 1 | 0.3 | 0 |

### PUNT RETURNS

| Last Name | No. | Yds | Avg | TD |
|---|---|---|---|---|
| Query | 32 | 308 | 9.6 | 0 |
| Pitts | 0 | 0 | 0.0 | 0 |

### KICKOFF RETURNS

| Last Name | No. | Yds | Avg | TD |
|---|---|---|---|---|
| Wilson | 35 | 798 | 22.8 | 0 |
| Workman | 14 | 210 | 15.0 | 0 |
| Fullwood | 6 | 119 | 19.8 | 0 |
| Bland | 7 | 104 | 14.9 | 0 |
| Thompson | 3 | 103 | 34.3 | 1 |
| Fontenot | 3 | 88 | 29.3 | 0 |
| West | 1 | 0 | 0.0 | 0 |

### PASSING — PUNTING — KICKING

| PASSING | Att | Cmp | % | Yds | Yd/Att | TD | Int— | % | RK |
|---|---|---|---|---|---|---|---|---|---|
| Majkowski | 264 | 150 | 56.8 | 1925 | 7.29 | 10 | 12— | 4.5 | 10 |
| Dilweg | 192 | 101 | 52.6 | 1267 | 6.60 | 8 | 7— | 3.6 | |
| Kiel | 85 | 51 | 60.0 | 504 | 5.93 | 2 | 2— | 2.4 | |

| PUNTING | No. | Avg. |
|---|---|---|
| Bracken | 65 | 37.4 |

| KICKING | XP | Att. | % | FG | Att | % |
|---|---|---|---|---|---|---|
| Jacke | 28 | 29 | 97 | 23 | 30 | 77 |

## MINNESOTA VIKINGS

### RUSHING

| Last Name | No. | Yds | Avg | TD |
|---|---|---|---|---|
| Walker | 184 | 770 | 4.2 | 5 |
| Fenney | 87 | 376 | 4.3 | 2 |
| Gannon | 52 | 268 | 5.2 | 1 |
| Anderson | 59 | 207 | 3.5 | 2 |
| Wilson | 12 | 79 | 6.6 | 0 |
| Rice | 22 | 74 | 3.4 | 0 |
| Clark | 16 | 49 | 3.1 | 0 |
| Smith | 9 | 19 | 2.1 | 0 |
| A. Carter | 3 | 16 | 5.3 | 0 |
| Dozier | 6 | 12 | 2.0 | 0 |
| C. Carter | 2 | 6 | 3.0 | 0 |
| Newsome | 2 | -2 | -1.0 | 0 |
| H. Jones | 1 | -7 | -7.0 | 0 |

### RECEIVING

| Last Name | No. | Yds | Avg | TD |
|---|---|---|---|---|
| Carter | 70 | 1008 | 14.4 | 8 |
| H. Jones | 51 | 810 | 15.9 | 7 |
| Jordan | 45 | 636 | 14.1 | 3 |
| Walker | 35 | 315 | 9.0 | 4 |
| C. Carter | 27 | 413 | 15.3 | 3 |
| Fenney | 17 | 112 | 4.6 | 0 |
| Anderson | 13 | 80 | 6.2 | 0 |
| Rice | 4 | 46 | 11.5 | 0 |
| Dozier | 1 | 12 | 12.0 | 0 |
| Lewis | 1 | 9 | 9.0 | 0 |
| Clark | 1 | 4 | 4.0 | 0 |

### PUNT RETURNS

| Last Name | No. | Yds | Avg | TD |
|---|---|---|---|---|
| Lewis | 33 | 236 | 7.2 | 0 |
| Hillary | 8 | 45 | 5.6 | 0 |
| A. Carter | 0 | 0 | 0.0 | 0 |

### KICKOFF RETURNS

| Last Name | No. | Yds | Avg | TD |
|---|---|---|---|---|
| Walker | 44 | 966 | 22.0 | 0 |
| Rice | 12 | 176 | 14.7 | 0 |
| Anderson | 3 | 44 | 14.7 | 0 |
| Lewis | 3 | 39 | 13.0 | 0 |
| Smith | 1 | 16 | 16.0 | 0 |
| Hillary | 1 | 6 | 6.0 | 0 |
| Schrieber | 1 | 5 | 5.0 | 0 |
| Jordan | 1 | -3 | -3.0 | 0 |

### PASSING — PUNTING — KICKING

| PASSING | Att | Cmp | % | Yds | Yd/Att | TD | Int— | % | RK |
|---|---|---|---|---|---|---|---|---|---|
| Gannon | 349 | 182 | 52.1 | 2278 | 6.53 | 16 | 16— | 4.6 | 12 |
| Wilson | 146 | 82 | 56.2 | 1155 | 7.91 | 9 | 8— | 5.5 | |
| Walker | 2 | 1 | 50.0 | 12 | 6.00 | 0 | 0— | 0.0 | |

| PUNTING | No. | Avg. |
|---|---|---|
| Newsome | 79 | 41.8 |

| KICKING | XP | ATT | % | FG | ATT | % |
|---|---|---|---|---|---|---|
| Reveiz | 26 | 27 | 96 | 13 | 19 | 68 |
| Igwebuike | 19 | 19 | 100 | 14 | 16 | 88 |

## SAN FRANCISCO 49ERS 14-2 George Seifert

**Scores of Each Game**

| | | |
|---|---|---|
| 13 | New Orleans | 12 |
| 26 | WASHINGTON | 13 |
| 19 | ATLANTA | 13 |
| 24 | Houston | 21 |
| 45 | Atlanta | 35 |
| 27 | PITTSBURGH | 7 |
| 20 | CLEVELAND | 17 |
| 24 | Green Bay | 20 |
| 24 | Dallas | 6 |
| 31 | TAMPA BAY | 7 |
| 17 | L.A. RAMS | 28 |
| 7 | N.Y. GIANTS | 3 |
| 20 | Cincinnati | 17 |
| 26 | L.A. Rams | 10 |
| 10 | NEW ORLEANS | 13 |
| 20 | Minnesota | 17 |

| Use Name | Pos. | Hgt | Wgt | Age | Int | Pts |
|---|---|---|---|---|---|---|
| Harris Barton | OG-OT | 6'4" | 280 | 26 | | |
| Frank Pollack | OT | 6'4" | 277 | 22 | | |
| Bubba Paris | OT | 6'6" | 306 | 29 | | |
| Steve Wallace | OT-OG | 6'5" | 276 | 25 | | |
| Guy McIntyre | OG | 6'3" | 265 | 29 | | |
| Ricky Siglar | OG | 6'7" | 296 | 24 | | |
| Jesse Sapolu | C | 6'4" | 260 | 29 | | |
| Chuck Thomas | C | 6'3" | 280 | 29 | | |
| Dennis Brown | DE | 6'4" | 290 | 22 | | |
| Kevin Fagan | DE | 6'4" | 260 | 27 | | |
| Pierce Holt | DE | 6'4" | 280 | 28 | | |
| Larry Roberts | DE | 6'3" | 275 | 27 | | |
| Jim Burt | NT | 6'1" | 260 | 31 | | |
| Michael Carter | NT | 6'2" | 285 | 29 | | |
| Pete Kugler | NT-DE | 6'4" | 255 | 31 | | |
| Fred Smerlas | NT | 6'3" | 288 | 33 | | |
| Keith DeLong | LB | 6'2" | 235 | 23 | | |
| LeRoy Etienne | LB | 6'2" | 245 | 24 | | |
| Jim Fahnhorst | LB | 6'4" | 230 | 31 | | |
| Charles Haley | LB-DE | 6'5" | 230 | 26 | | |
| Martin Harrison | LB-DE | 6'5" | 240 | 22 | | |
| Matt Millen | LB | 6'2" | 245 | 32 | 1 | |
| Bill Romanowski | LB | 6'4" | 231 | 24 | | |
| Keena Turner | LB | 6'2" | 222 | 31 | 2 | |
| Michael Walter | LB | 6'3" | 238 | 29 | | |
| Chet Brooks | DB | 5'11" | 191 | 24 | | |
| Greg Cox | DB | 6' | 223 | 25 | | |
| Eric Davis | DB | 5'11" | 178 | 22 | 1 | |
| Don Griffin | DB | 6' | 176 | 26 | 3 | |
| Johnny Jackson | DB | 6'1" | 204 | 23 | | |
| Kevin Lewis | DB | 5'11" | 173 | 23 | 1 | |
| Ronnie Lott | DB | 6' | 200 | 31 | 3 | |
| Darryl Pollard | DB | 5'11" | 187 | 25 | 1 | |
| Dave Waymer | DB | 6'1" | 188 | 32 | 7 | |
| Eric Wright | DB | 6'1" | 185 | 31 | | |
| Steve Bono | QB | 6'4" | 215 | 28 | | |
| Joe Montana | QB | 6'2" | 195 | 34 | | 6 |
| Steve Young | QB | 6'2" | 200 | 28 | | |
| Dexter Carter | HB | 5'9" | 170 | 22 | | 6 |
| Roger Craig | HB | 6' | 224 | 30 | | 6 |
| Spencer Tillman | HB | 5'11" | 206 | 26 | | |
| Keith Henderson | FB | 6'1" | 220 | 24 | | |
| Tom Rathman | FB | 6'1" | 232 | 27 | | 42 |
| Harry Sydney | FB | 6' | 217 | 31 | | 18 |
| Ronald Lewis | WR | 5'11" | 173 | 22 | | |
| Jerry Rice | WR | 6'2" | 200 | 27 | | 78 |
| Mike Sherrard | WR | 6'2" | 187 | 27 | | 12 |
| John Taylor | WR | 6'1" | 185 | 28 | | 42 |
| Mike Wilson | WR | 6'3" | 215 | 31 | | |
| Brent Jones | TE | 6'4" | 230 | 27 | | 30 |
| Wesley Walls | TE | 6'5" | 246 | 24 | | |
| Jamie Williams | TE | 6'4" | 245 | 30 | | |
| Mike Cofer | K | 6'1" | 190 | 26 | | 111 |
| Barry Helton | K | 6'3" | 205 | 25 | | |

Dave Cullity — Shoulder Injury
Wayne Radloff — Knee Injury

## NEW ORLEANS SAINTS 8-8 Jim Mora

**Scores of Each Game**

| | | |
|---|---|---|
| 12 | SAN FRANCISCO | 13 |
| 3 | Minnesota | 32 |
| 28 | PHOENIX | 7 |
| 27 | Atlanta | 28 |
| 25 | CLEVELAND | 20 |
| 10 | Houston | 23 |
| 10 | DETROIT | 27 |
| 21 | Cincinnati | 7 |
| 35 | TAMPA BAY | 7 |
| 17 | Washington | 31 |
| 10 | ATLANTA | 7 |
| 13 | Dallas | 17 |
| 24 | L.A. Rams | 20 |
| 6 | PITTSBURGH | 9 |
| 13 | San Francisco | 10 |
| 20 | L.A. RAMS | 17 |

| Use Name | Pos. | Hgt | Wgt | Age | Int | Pts |
|---|---|---|---|---|---|---|
| Stan Brock | OT | 6'6" | 290 | 32 | | |
| Richard Cooper | OT | 6'4" | 285 | 25 | | |
| Glenn Derby | OT-OG | 6'6" | 290 | 26 | | |
| Kevin Haverdink | OT | 6'5" | 285 | 24 | | |
| Jim Dombrowski | OG | 6'5" | 298 | 27 | | |
| Steve Trapilo | OG | 6'5" | 281 | 25 | | |
| Joel Hilgenberg | C | 6'3" | 252 | 27 | | |
| Steve Korte | C | 6'2" | 260 | 30 | | |
| Brad Leggett | C | 6'4" | 270 | 24 | | |
| Wayne Martin | DE | 6'5" | 275 | 24 | | |
| Michael Simmons | DE | 6'4" | 269 | 24 | | |
| Joel Smeenge | DE | 6'5" | 250 | 22 | | |
| Renaldo Turnbull | DE | 6'4" | 248 | 24 | | |
| Jim Wilks | DE-NT | 6'5" | 275 | 32 | | |
| Travis Davis | NT | 6'2" | 274 | 24 | | |
| Robert Goff | NT | 6'3" | 270 | 24 | | |
| Brian Forde | LB | 6'2" | 225 | 26 | | |
| Rickey Jackson | LB | 6'2" | 243 | 32 | | |
| Vaughan Johnson | LB | 6'3" | 235 | 28 | | |
| Sam Mills | LB | 5'9" | 225 | 31 | | |
| Pat Swilling | LB | 6'3" | 242 | 25 | | |
| James Williams | LB | 6' | 230 | 21 | | |
| DeMond Winston | LB | 6'2" | 239 | 21 | | |
| Gene Atkins | DB | 6'1" | 200 | 26 | 2 | |
| Vince Buck | DB | 6' | 198 | 22 | | |
| Toi Cook | DB | 5'11" | 188 | 25 | 2 | |
| Milton Mack | DB | 5'11" | 182 | 26 | | |
| Robert Massey | DB | 5'10" | 182 | 23 | | |
| Brett Maxie | DB | 6'2" | 194 | 28 | 2 | 6 |
| Ernest Spears | DB | 5'11" | 192 | 22 | | |
| Bennie Thompson | DB | 6' | 200 | 27 | 2 | |
| Mike Buck | QB | 6'3" | 227 | 23 | | |
| John Fourcade | QB | 6'1" | 208 | 29 | | 6 |
| Tommy Kramer | QB | 6'2" | 202 | 35 | | |
| Steve Walsh | QB | 6'2" | 200 | 23 | | |
| Gill Fenerty | HB | 6' | 205 | 27 | | 12 |
| Dalton Hilliard | HB | 5'8" | 204 | 26 | | 6 |
| Rueben Mayes | HB | 5'11" | 200 | 27 | | 42 |
| Craig Heyward | FB | 5'11" | 270 | 24 | | 24 |
| Buford Jordan | FB | 6' | 223 | 28 | | |
| Bobby Morse | FB | 5'10" | 213 | 23 | | |
| Gerald Alphin | WR | 6'3" | 200 | 26 | | |
| Lonzell Hill | WR | 6' | 189 | 24 | | |
| Eric Martin | WR | 6'1" | 207 | 28 | | 30 |
| Brett Perriman | WR | 5'9" | 175 | 24 | | 12 |
| Floyd Turner | WR | 5'11" | 188 | 24 | | 24 |
| Hoby Brenner | TE | 6'4" | 240 | 31 | | 12 |
| Greg Scales | TE | 6'4" | 253 | 24 | | 6 |
| John Tice | TE | 6'5" | 249 | 30 | | |
| Morten Andersen | K | 6'2" | 221 | 30 | | 92 |
| Tommy Barnhardt | K | 6'3" | 205 | 27 | | |

Bobby Hebert — Holdout

## LOS ANGELES RAMS 5-11 John Robinson

**Scores of Each Game**

| | | |
|---|---|---|
| 24 | Green Bay | 36 |
| 35 | Tampa Bay | 14 |
| 21 | PHILADELPHIA | 27 |
| 31 | CINCINNATI | 34 |
| 9 | Chicago | 38 |
| 44 | ATLANTA | 24 |
| 10 | Pittsburgh | 41 |
| 17 | HOUSTON | 13 |
| 7 | N.Y. GIANTS | 31 |
| 21 | DALLAS | 24 |
| 28 | San Francisco | 17 |
| 38 | Cleveland | 23 |
| 20 | NEW ORLEANS | 24 |
| 10 | SAN FRANCISCO | 26 |
| 13 | Atlanta | 20 |
| 17 | New Orleans | 20 |

| Use Name | Pos. | Hgt | Wgt | Age | Int | Pts |
|---|---|---|---|---|---|---|
| Robert Cox | OT | 6'5" | 285 | 26 | | |
| Jeff Mickel | OT | 6'6" | 300 | 24 | | |
| Irv Pankey | OT | 6'4" | 267 | 32 | | |
| Jackie Slater | OT | 6'4" | 275 | 36 | | |
| Duval Love | OG | 6'3" | 287 | 27 | | |
| Joe Milinichik | OG | 6'5" | 275 | 27 | | |
| Tom Newberry | OG | 6'2" | 279 | 27 | | |
| Bern Brostek | C-OG | 6'3" | 300 | 23 | | |
| Doug Smith | C | 6'3" | 260 | 33 | | |
| Doug Reed | DE-DT | 6'3" | 250 | 30 | | |
| Bill Hawkins | DT | 6'6" | 268 | 24 | | |
| Mark Piel | DT | 6'4" | 263 | 24 | | |
| Brian Smith | DT | 6'6" | 268 | 24 | | |
| Alvin Wright | NT-DE | 6'2" | 256 | 29 | | |
| George Bethune | LB | 6'4" | 240 | 23 | | |
| Paul Butcher | LB | 6' | 230 | 26 | | |
| Greg Clark | LB | 6'1" | 232 | 25 | | |
| Brett Faryniarz | LB | 6'3" | 232 | 25 | | |
| Kevin Greene | LB-DE | 6'3" | 238 | 28 | | |
| Larry Kelm | LB | 6'4" | 226 | 25 | | |
| Bruce Klostermann | LB | 6'4" | 236 | 27 | | |
| Mike McDonald | LB | 6'1" | 235 | 32 | | |
| Frank Stams | LB | 6'2" | 240 | 24 | | |
| Fred Strickland | LB | 6'2" | 224 | 25 | | |
| Mike Wilcher | LB | 6'3" | 240 | 30 | | |
| Latin Berry | DB | 5'10" | 196 | 23 | | |
| Jerry Gray | DB | 6' | 185 | 27 | | |
| Darryl Henley | DB | 5'9" | 170 | 24 | 1 | |
| Bobby Humphery | DB | 5'10" | 180 | 29 | 4 | 6 |
| Alfred Jackson | DB | 6' | 177 | 23 | | |
| Anthony Newman | DB | 6' | 199 | 24 | 2 | |
| Vince Newsome | DB | 6'1" | 183 | 29 | 4 | |
| Michael Stewart | DB | 5'11" | 195 | 25 | | |
| Mickey Sutton | DB | 5'8" | 172 | 30 | | |
| Pat Terrell | DB | 6' | 195 | 22 | 1 | |
| Jim Everett | QB | 6'5" | 212 | 27 | | 6 |
| Chuck Long | QB | 6'4" | 221 | 27 | | |
| Marcus Dupree | HB | 6'2" | 225 | 26 | | |
| Cleveland Gary | HB | 6' | 226 | 24 | | 90 |
| Gaston Green | HB | 5'10" | 189 | 24 | | 12 |
| Curt Warner | HB | 5'11" | 205 | 29 | | 6 |
| Robert Delpino | HB | 6' | 205 | 24 | | 24 |
| Buford McGee | FB | 6' | 206 | 30 | | 30 |
| Willie Anderson | WR | 6' | 169 | 25 | | 24 |
| Aaron Cox | WR | 5'9" | 174 | 25 | | |
| Henry Ellard | WR | 5'11" | 175 | 29 | | 24 |
| Derrick Faison | WR | 6'4" | 200 | 23 | | |
| Tony Lomack | WR | 5'8" | 180 | 22 | | |
| Richard Ashe | TE | 6'4" | 260 | 23 | | |
| Pat Carter | TE | 6'4" | 250 | 24 | | |
| Pete Holohan | TE | 6'4" | 232 | 31 | | 12 |
| Damone Johnson | TE | 6'4" | 230 | 28 | | 18 |
| Keith English | K | 6'3" | 220 | 24 | | |
| Mike Lansford | K | 6' | 183 | 32 | | 87 |

Mel Owens — Back Injury

## ATLANTA FALCONS 5-11 Jerry Glanville

**Scores of Each Game**

| | | |
|---|---|---|
| 47 | HOUSTON | 27 |
| 14 | Detroit | 21 |
| 13 | San Francisco | 19 |
| 28 | NEW ORLEANS | 27 |
| 35 | SAN FRANCISCO | 45 |
| 24 | L.A. Rams | 44 |
| 38 | CINCINNATI | 17 |
| 9 | Pittsburgh | 21 |
| 24 | Chicago | 30 |
| 23 | PHILADELPHIA | 24 |
| 7 | New Orleans | 10 |
| 17 | Tampa Bay | 23 |
| 13 | PHOENIX | 24 |
| 10 | Cleveland | 13 |
| 20 | L.A. RAMS | 13 |
| 26 | DALLAS | 7 |

| Use Name | Pos. | Hgt | Wgt | Age | Int | Pts |
|---|---|---|---|---|---|---|
| Chris Hinton | OT | 6'4" | 300 | 29 | | |
| John Hunter | OT | 6'8" | 296 | 25 | | |
| Mike Kenn | OT | 6'7" | 277 | 34 | | |
| Bill Fralic | OG | 6'5" | 280 | 27 | | |
| Houston Hoover | OG-OT | 6'2" | 290 | 25 | | |
| John Scully | OG | 6'6" | 270 | 32 | | |
| Guy Bingham | C | 6'3" | 260 | 32 | | |
| Jamie Dukes | C | 6'1" | 285 | 26 | | |
| Mike Ruether | C | 6'4" | 275 | 27 | | |
| Rick Bryan | DE-NT-DT-LB | 6'4" | 265 | 28 | | |
| Mike Gann | DE | 6'5" | 270 | 24 | | |
| Oliver Barnett | DE | 6'3" | 288 | 24 | | |
| Tony Casillas | NT | 6'3" | 280 | 26 | | |
| Tory Epps | NT | 6' | 280 | 23 | | |
| Aundray Bruce | LB | 6'5" | 245 | 24 | | |
| Darion Conner | LB | 6'2" | 256 | 22 | | |
| Marcus Cotton (to CLE) | LB | 6'3" | 225 | 24 | | |
| Tim Green | LB | 6'2" | 245 | 26 | 2 | |
| Robert Lyles (from HOU) | LB | 6'1" | 230 | 29 | | |
| John Rade | LB | 6'1" | 240 | 30 | | |
| Michael Reid | LB | 6'2" | 226 | 26 | | |
| Kenny Tippins | LB | 6'1" | 230 | 24 | | |
| Jessie Tuggle | LB | 5'11" | 225 | 25 | | 6 |
| Eric Bergeson | DB | 5'11" | 192 | 24 | | |
| Bobby Butler | DB | 5'11" | 175 | 31 | 3 | 12 |
| Scott Case | DB | 6' | 178 | 28 | 3 | 6 |
| Charles Dimry | DB | 6' | 175 | 24 | 3 | |
| William Evers | DB | 5'10" | 175 | 21 | | |
| Tim Gordon | DB | 6' | 188 | 25 | | |
| Brian Jordan | DB | 5'11" | 202 | 23 | 3 | |
| Roland Mitchell | DB | 5'11" | 180 | 26 | 2 | |
| Ricky Royal | DB | 5'9" | 187 | 24 | | |
| Deion Sanders | DB | 6' | 187 | 23 | 3 | 18 |
| Elbert Shelley | DB | 5'11" | 180 | 25 | | |
| Scott Campbell | QB | 6' | 195 | 28 | | |
| Hugh Millen | QB | 6'5" | 216 | 26 | | |
| Chris Miller | QB | 6'2" | 195 | 24 | | 6 |
| Steve Broussard | HB | 5'7" | 201 | 23 | | 24 |
| Gene Lang | HB | 5'10" | 206 | 28 | | |
| Mike Pringle | HB | 5'8" | 186 | 22 | | |
| Mike Rozier (from HOU) | HB | 5'10" | 213 | 29 | | 18 |
| John Settle | FB | 5'9" | 207 | 25 | | |
| Tracy Johnson | FB | 6' | 230 | 24 | | 24 |
| Keith Jones | FB | 6'1" | 210 | 24 | | |
| Stacey Bailey | WR | 6' | 157 | 30 | | |
| Shawn Collins | WR | 6'2" | 207 | 23 | | 12 |
| Floyd Dixon | WR | 5'9" | 170 | 26 | | 24 |
| Michael Haynes | WR | 6' | 180 | 24 | | |
| James Milling | WR | 5'9" | 156 | 25 | | 6 |
| Andre Rison | WR | 6' | 191 | 23 | | 60 |
| George Thomas | WR | 5'9" | 169 | 26 | | |
| Troy Sadowski | TE | 6'5" | 265 | 24 | | |
| Gary Wilkins | TE | 6'1" | 235 | 26 | | 12 |
| Greg Davis | K | 5'11" | 197 | 24 | | 106 |
| Scott Fulhage | K | 5'11" | 193 | 28 | | |

Galand Thaxton — Ankle Injury

## SAN FRANCISCO 49ERS

### RUSHING

| Last Name | No. | Yds | Avg | TD |
|---|---|---|---|---|
| D. Carter | 114 | 460 | 4.0 | 1 |
| Craig | 141 | 439 | 3.1 | 1 |
| Rathman | 101 | 318 | 3.1 | 7 |
| Sydney | 35 | 166 | 4.7 | 2 |
| Montana | 40 | 162 | 4.1 | 1 |
| Young | 15 | 159 | 10.6 | 0 |
| Henderson | 6 | 14 | 2.3 | 0 |
| Rice | 2 | 0 | 0.0 | 0 |

### RECEIVING

| Last Name | No. | Yds | Avg | TD |
|---|---|---|---|---|
| Rice | 100 | 1502 | 15.0 | 13 |
| Jones | 56 | 747 | 13.3 | 5 |
| Taylor | 49 | 748 | 15.3 | 7 |
| Rathman | 48 | 327 | 6.8 | 0 |
| D. Carter | 25 | 217 | 8.7 | 0 |
| Craig | 25 | 201 | 8.0 | 0 |
| Sherrard | 17 | 264 | 15.5 | 2 |
| Sydney | 10 | 116 | 11.6 | 1 |
| Williams | 9 | 54 | 6.0 | 0 |
| Wilson | 7 | 89 | 12.7 | 0 |
| R. Lewis | 5 | 44 | 8.8 | 0 |
| Walls | 5 | 27 | 5.4 | 0 |
| Henderson | 4 | 35 | 8.8 | 0 |

### PUNT RETURNS

| Last Name | No. | Yds | Avg | TD |
|---|---|---|---|---|
| Taylor | 26 | 212 | 8.2 | 0 |
| Griffin | 16 | 105 | 6.6 | 0 |
| Davis | 5 | 38 | 7.6 | 0 |
| Wilson | 1 | 1 | 1.0 | 0 |

### KICKOFF RETURNS

| Last Name | No. | Yds | Avg | TD |
|---|---|---|---|---|
| D. Carter | 41 | 783 | 19.1 | 0 |
| Tillman | 6 | 111 | 18.5 | 0 |
| Sydney | 2 | 33 | 16.5 | 0 |
| Walls | 1 | 16 | 16.0 | 0 |
| Griffin | 1 | 15 | 15.0 | 0 |
| Williams | 2 | 7 | 3.5 | 0 |

### PASSING—PUNTING—KICKING

| PASSING | Att | Cmp | % | Yds | Yd/Att | TD | Int— | % | RK |
|---|---|---|---|---|---|---|---|---|---|
| Montana | 520 | 321 | 61.7 | 3944 | 7.58 | 26 | 16— | 3.1 | 3 |
| Young | 62 | 38 | 61.3 | 427 | 6.89 | 2 | 0— | 0.0 | |
| Helton | 1 | 1 | 100.0 | 0 | 0.00 | 0 | 0— | 0.0 | |

| PUNTING | No. | Avg. |
|---|---|---|
| Helton | 70 | 36.2 |

| KICKING | XP | ATT | % | FG | ATT | % |
|---|---|---|---|---|---|---|
| Cofer | 39 | 39 | 100 | 24 | 36 | 67 |

## NEW ORLEANS SAINTS

### RUSHING

| Last Name | No. | Yds | Avg | TD |
|---|---|---|---|---|
| Heyward | 129 | 599 | 4.6 | 4 |
| Mayes | 138 | 510 | 3.7 | 7 |
| Fenerty | 73 | 355 | 4.9 | 2 |
| Hilliard | 90 | 284 | 3.2 | 0 |
| Fourcade | 15 | 77 | 5.1 | 1 |
| Walsh | 20 | 25 | 1.3 | 0 |

### RECEIVING

| Last Name | No. | Yds | Avg | TD |
|---|---|---|---|---|
| E. Martin | 63 | 912 | 14.5 | 5 |
| Perriman | 36 | 382 | 10.6 | 2 |
| Turner | 21 | 396 | 18.9 | 4 |
| Fenerty | 18 | 209 | 11.6 | 0 |
| Heyward | 18 | 121 | 6.7 | 0 |
| Brenner | 17 | 213 | 12.5 | 2 |
| Hilliard | 14 | 125 | 8.9 | 1 |
| Mayes | 12 | 121 | 10.1 | 0 |
| Tice | 11 | 113 | 10.3 | 0 |
| Scales | 8 | 64 | 8.0 | 1 |
| Alphin | 4 | 57 | 14.3 | 0 |
| Hill | 3 | 35 | 11.7 | 0 |
| Hilgenberg | 1 | 9 | 9.0 | 0 |

### PUNT RETURNS

| Last Name | No. | Yds | Avg | TD |
|---|---|---|---|---|
| V. Buck | 28 | 572 | 20.4 | 0 |
| Morse | 8 | 95 | 11.9 | 0 |

### KICKOFF RETURNS

| Last Name | No. | Yds | Avg | TD |
|---|---|---|---|---|
| Fenerty | 28 | 572 | 20.4 | 0 |
| Atkins | 19 | 471 | 24.8 | 0 |
| Morse | 4 | 56 | 14.0 | 0 |
| V. Buck | 3 | 38 | 12.7 | 0 |
| Mayes | 2 | 39 | 19.5 | 0 |
| Mack | 1 | 17 | 17.0 | 0 |
| Heyward | 1 | 12 | 12.0 | 0 |

### PASSING—PUNTING—KICKING

| PASSING | Att | Cmp | % | Yds | Yd/Att | TD | Int— | % | RK |
|---|---|---|---|---|---|---|---|---|---|
| Walsh | 336 | 179 | 53.3 | 2010 | 5.98 | 12 | 13— | 3.9 | 13 |
| Fourcade | 116 | 50 | 43.1 | 785 | 6.77 | 3 | 8— | 6.9 | |
| Kramer | 3 | 1 | 33.3 | 2 | 0.67 | 0 | 1— | 33.3 | |
| Heyward | 1 | 0 | 0.0 | 0 | 0.00 | 0 | 1— | 100.0 | |

| PUNTING | No. | Avg. |
|---|---|---|
| Barnhardt | 71 | 42.1 |

| KICKING | XP | ATT | % | FG | ATT | % |
|---|---|---|---|---|---|---|
| Andersen | 29 | 29 | 100 | 21 | 27 | 78 |

## LOS ANGELES RAMS

### RUSHING

| Last Name | No. | Yds | Avg | TD |
|---|---|---|---|---|
| Gary | 204 | 808 | 4.0 | 14 |
| Green | 68 | 261 | 3.8 | 0 |
| McGee | 44 | 234 | 5.3 | 1 |
| Warner | 49 | 139 | 2.8 | 1 |
| Dupree | 19 | 72 | 3.8 | 0 |
| Delpino | 13 | 52 | 4.0 | 0 |
| Everett | 20 | 31 | 1.6 | 1 |
| Ellard | 2 | 21 | 10.5 | 0 |
| Anderson | 1 | 13 | 13.0 | 0 |
| English | 2 | -19 | -9.5 | 0 |

### RECEIVING

| Last Name | No. | Yds | Avg | TD |
|---|---|---|---|---|
| Ellard | 76 | 1294 | 17.0 | 4 |
| Anderson | 51 | 1097 | 21.5 | 4 |
| Holohan | 49 | 475 | 9.7 | 2 |
| McGee | 47 | 388 | 8.3 | 4 |
| Gary | 30 | 150 | 5.0 | 1 |
| Cox | 17 | 266 | 15.6 | 0 |
| Delpino | 15 | 172 | 11.5 | 4 |
| Johnson | 12 | 66 | 5.5 | 3 |
| Carter | 8 | 58 | 7.3 | 0 |
| Faison | 3 | 27 | 9.0 | 1 |
| Green | 2 | 23 | 11.5 | 1 |

### PUNT RETURNS

| Last Name | No. | Yds | Avg | TD |
|---|---|---|---|---|
| Henley | 19 | 195 | 10.3 | 0 |
| Sutton | 14 | 136 | 9.7 | 0 |
| Ellard | 2 | 15 | 7.5 | 0 |

### KICKOFF RETURNS

| Last Name | No. | Yds | Avg | TD |
|---|---|---|---|---|
| Green | 25 | 560 | 22.4 | 1 |
| Delpino | 20 | 389 | 19.5 | 0 |
| Berry | 17 | 315 | 18.5 | 0 |
| McDonald | 1 | 15 | 15.0 | 0 |

### PASSING—PUNTING—KICKING

| PASSING | Att | Cmp | % | Yds | Yd/Att | TD | Int— | % | RK |
|---|---|---|---|---|---|---|---|---|---|
| Everett | 554 | 307 | 55.4 | 3989 | 7.20 | 23 | 17— | 3.1 | 6 |
| Long | 5 | 1 | 20.0 | 4 | 0.80 | 0 | 0— | 0.0 | |
| McGee | 2 | 2 | 100.0 | 23 | 11.50 | 1 | 0— | 0.0 | |

| PUNTING | No. | Avg. |
|---|---|---|
| English | 68 | 39.2 |

| KICKING | XP | ATT | % | FG | ATT | % |
|---|---|---|---|---|---|---|
| Lansford | 42 | 43 | 98 | 15 | 24 | 63 |

## ATLANTA FALCONS

### RUSHING

| Last Name | No. | Yds | Avg | TD |
|---|---|---|---|---|
| Rozier | 163 | 717 | 4.4 | 3 |
| Broussard | 126 | 454 | 3.6 | 4 |
| Jones | 49 | 185 | 3.8 | 3 |
| Johnson | 30 | 106 | 3.5 | 3 |
| Miller | 26 | 99 | 3.8 | 1 |
| Campbell | 9 | 38 | 4.2 | 0 |
| Lang | 9 | 24 | 2.7 | 0 |
| Settle | 9 | 16 | 1.8 | 0 |
| Pringle | 2 | 9 | 4.5 | 0 |
| Millen | 7 | -12 | -1.7 | 0 |

### RECEIVING

| Last Name | No. | Yds | Avg | TD |
|---|---|---|---|---|
| Rison | 82 | 1208 | 14.7 | 10 |
| Dixon | 38 | 399 | 10.5 | 4 |
| Collins | 34 | 503 | 14.8 | 2 |
| Haynes | 31 | 445 | 14.4 | 0 |
| Broussard | 24 | 160 | 6.7 | 0 |
| Thomas | 18 | 383 | 21.3 | 1 |
| Milling | 18 | 161 | 8.9 | 1 |
| Rozier | 13 | 105 | 8.1 | 0 |
| Jones | 13 | 103 | 7.9 | 0 |
| Wilkins | 12 | 175 | 14.6 | 2 |
| Johnson | 10 | 79 | 7.9 | 1 |
| Bailey | 4 | 44 | 11.0 | 0 |
| Lang | 1 | 7 | 7.0 | 0 |

### PUNT RETURNS

| Last Name | No. | Yds | Avg | TD |
|---|---|---|---|---|
| Sanders | 29 | 250 | 8.6 | 1 |
| Jordan | 2 | 19 | 9.5 | 0 |
| Rison | 2 | 10 | 5.0 | 0 |
| Mitchell | 1 | 0 | 0.0 | 0 |
| Reid | 1 | 0 | 0.0 | 0 |

### KICKOFF RETURNS

| Last Name | No. | Yds | Avg | TD |
|---|---|---|---|---|
| Sanders | 39 | 851 | 21.8 | 0 |
| Jones | 8 | 236 | 29.5 | 1 |
| Broussard | 3 | 45 | 15.0 | 0 |
| Gordon | 1 | 43 | 43.0 | 0 |
| Lang | 1 | 18 | 18.0 | 0 |
| Pringle | 1 | 14 | 14.0 | 0 |
| Wilkins | 1 | 7 | 7.0 | 0 |
| Case | 1 | 13 | 13.0 | 0 |
| Johnson | 2 | 2 | 1.0 | 0 |
| Dixon | 1 | 0 | 0.0 | 0 |
| Haynes | 1 | 0 | 0.0 | 0 |

### PASSING—PUNTING—KICKING

| PASSING | Att | Cmp | % | Yds | Yd/Att | TD | Int— | % | RK |
|---|---|---|---|---|---|---|---|---|---|
| Miller | 388 | 222 | 57.2 | 2735 | 7.05 | 17 | 14— | 3.6 | 7 |
| Campbell | 76 | 36 | 47.4 | 527 | 6.93 | 3 | 4— | 5.3 | |
| Millen | 63 | 34 | 54.0 | 427 | 6.78 | 1 | 0— | 0.0 | |
| Jones | 1 | 1 | 100.0 | 37 | 37.00 | 0 | 0— | 0.0 | |

| PUNTING | No. | Avg. |
|---|---|---|
| Fulhage | 70 | 41.6 |

| KICKING | XP | ATT | % | FG | ATT | % |
|---|---|---|---|---|---|---|
| David | 40 | 40 | 100 | 22 | 33 | 67 |

# 1990 A.F.C.  A Public Black Eye

For much of the season, interest around the AFC centered on three good division races, the resurgence of the Raiders, and Buffalo's chances in the Super Bowl. But, for a couple of weeks in September, attention was focused on New England where a lockerroom incident produced one of the uglier stories of the year. According to news accounts and the NFL's subsequent investigation, *Boston Herald* reporter Lisa Olson was lewdly harassed by New England's Zeke Mowatt and several other Patriots players in the team lockerroom where she was pursuing an interview. Reportedly the players exposed themselves and made indecent remarks.

In the aftermath, team owner Victor Kiam worsened the NFL's image by suggesting that Olson had precipitated the situation. He later apologized, claiming he'd been given wrong information. Although a new debate was sparked over the rights of women reporters to have access to lockerrooms, few defended the Patriots' boorish behavior.

## EASTERN DIVISION

**Buffalo Bills** — While winning the Eastern title for the third straight year, the Bills established themselves as the AFC's most complete team. Gone were the personal problems that often disrupted the squad in the past. The defense, with end Bruce Smith and linebackers Cornelius Bennett, Shane Colan, and Darryl Talley stifled the opposition. Coach Marv Levy was criticized as "too conservative," but Buffalo put together the most potent offense in the conference. Running back Thurman Thomas ran and caught passes brilliantly, and Andre Reed established himself as perhaps the AFC's best receiver. Many felt that quarterback Jim Kelly was the NFL's Player of the Year. And, when Kelly was out with a knee injury, Frank Reich filled in capably. The season's must-win game was against Miami two days before Christmas. With Kelly on the sideline, Reich completed 15 of 21 passes for 234 yards to insure victory.

**Miami Dolphins** — Don Shula got the Dolphins turned around and came within a late-season loss to the Bills of winning the division. Foremost in Miami's improvement were a new, tougher defense and a more balanced offense. Cornerback Tim McKyer keyed the defensive upswing, bringing attitude and competence to the secondary. Linebackers John Offerdahl and Hugh Green were also factors. Although it slipped toward the end, the defense carried the Dolphins through the early season. Rookie offensive tackle Richmond Webb gave the line a big, aggressive blocker, and running back Sammie Smith supplied a ground punch that had been missing for years. With the new firepower at his command, quarterback Don Marino reestablished himself as one of the best passers in NFL history.

**Indianapolis Colts** — Eric Dickerson held out for a contract renegotiation and then was suspended for the first five games for failure to report. Albert Bentley was a workman-like replacement, but he lacked Dickerson's ability to dominate a game. Even after his return, Dickerson showed only flashes of his old running powers. Meanwhile, the offense was entrusted to expensive rookie quarterback Jeff George, who struggled early. Jack Trudeau replaced him as the starter in the fourth game. The offense perked up slightly but, after four games, he went down with his usual season-ending injury. George improved steadily upon his return, leading the Colts to five wins in the last eight games. Clearly, Indianapolis was paying the price for trading away Andre Rison, Chris Hinton, and some draft choices, but the late rally was probably enough to save coach Ron Meyer's job.

**New York Jets** — Although it was hardly a banner year for the Jets, new coach Bruce Coslett made progress in both attitude and record. The team improved its win-loss record by two and was blown out in only three of its 10 losses. Inconsistency was the stumbling point. Quarterback Ken O'Brien started well and then tailed off. Running back Blair Thomas started slowly — partly because of a protracted holdout. Receiver Al Toon was bothered by injuries, and the defense was erratic. Defensive tackle Dennis Byrd showed signs of becoming a premier pass rusher. Runner Freeman McNeil had a strong comeback season, but the team voted as its MVP veteran placekicker Pat Leahy. In the season's 11th game, with an outside shot at the playoffs, the Jets led the Colts 14-3 when safety Erik McMillan picked off an Indianapolis pass but then lost the ball on an ill-conceived lateral. The Colts scored and went on to win.

**New England Patriots** — The pitiful Patriots suffered through one of the worst seasons ever experienced by a modern NFL team. Ironically, they began well under new coach Rod Rust, losing in the final minute to Miami and trouncing Indianapolis. Then everything collapsed. The team's public relations were destroyed when the Lisa Olson incident made ugly headlines all over the country. Owner Victor Kiam further aggravated the situation by at first criticizing Olson. A few days later, receiver Irving Fryer and Hart Lee Dykes were injured in a barroom brawl. Meanwhile, a serious neck injury took quarterback Steve Grogan out of play and sank the Patriots' offense. After veteran Marc Wilson was tried and found wanting, rookie Tommy Hodson showed promise but little polish. The 181 points registered by the offense were the fewest by any team since the league went to a 16-game schedule.

## CENTRAL DIVISION

**Cincinnati Bengals** — Three straight wins got the Bengals off on the right foot, but they were 4-7 through the next 11 games before winning their final two. A porous defense and inconsistency of their own passing game were blamed for Cincinnati's lack of dominance, along with the off-field controversy coach Sam Wyche stirred up when he barred women reporters from his lockerroom in the wake of the Lisa Olson incident in New England. Quarterback Boomer Esiason threw 24 touchdown passes but also had 22 interceptions. Running back Ickey Woods came back from his 1989 injury pretty well, but James Brooks was a sensation with another 1,000-yard season. The offensive line was hurt early by the Plan B defection of guard Max Montoya and late injuries to tackle Anthony Munoz and guard Bruce Reimers.

**Houston Oilers** — Under new coach Jack Pardee, the Oilers staggered out of the starting gate with a pair of road losses. Once Houston's run-and-shoot offense began to roll, however, quarterback Warren Moon and receivers Drew Hill, Haywood Jeffires, Ernest Givins and Curtis Duncan terrorized the league. Yet, the team had an ugly habit of coming up empty against weak teams, losing to the Jets, Rams and Seahawks when the offense faltered. Moon was on a pace to set new league passing records when he dislocated his thumb in the 15th game, a blowout by the Bengals. Substitute Cody Carlson was brilliant in the season-ending, must-win victory over the Steelers that put Houston into the playoffs.

**Pittsburgh Steelers** — Joe Walton was hired as offensive coordinator to redesign the offense, but his system was so complex that the Steelers didn't scored an offensive touchdown until the fourth game. Once Walton's system was simplified, the team began to win. Quarterback Bubby Brister, although still erratic, had his best season, throwing 20 touchdowns passes. Fullback Merril Hoge was a steady running and receiving threat. Eric Green set a Steelers record for tight end with seven TD catches. Mostly the team depended on a defense that moved to the top of the league in fewest yards allowed. The secondary, led by cornerback Rod Woodson, was particularly effective. A victory in the final game would have given Pittsburgh the division title.

**Cleveland Browns** — The Browns suffered through the worst season in their history, setting team records for most losses and most points allowed. They were shut out three times. The offseason signing of 35-year-old Raymond Clayborn as a Plan B free agent caused training-camp holdouts by five starters. Frank Minnifield didn't appear until four games into the schedule. Tackle Cody Risen and guard Rickey Bolden were surprise retirements in training camp, crippling an already suspect offensive line. Quarterback Bernie Kosar was rushed and ineffective. With little offense and a fading defense, Coach John Carson lasted through nine games and seven losses. Interim coach Jim Shofner went 1-6 before escaping to the front office.

## WESTERN DIVISION

**OFFENSE**

| | BUFF | CIN | CLEV | DEN | HOU | IND | K.C. | L.A. | MIA | N.E. | NYJ | PITT | S.D. | SEA |
|---|---|---|---|---|---|---|---|---|---|---|---|---|---|---|
| FIRST DOWNS: | | | | | | | | | | | | | | |
| Total | 302 | 277 | 259 | 323 | 376 | 245 | 280 | 258 | 303 | 239 | 295 | 263 | 272 | 284 |
| by Rushing | 123 | 107 | 74 | 126 | 97 | 81 | 104 | 110 | 90 | 65 | 128 | 93 | 112 | 112 |
| by Passing | 161 | 151 | 167 | 170 | 251 | 142 | 153 | 133 | 190 | 156 | 143 | 150 | 142 | 154 |
| by Penalty | 18 | 19 | 18 | 27 | 28 | 22 | 23 | 15 | 23 | 18 | 24 | 20 | 18 | 18 |
| RUSHING: | | | | | | | | | | | | | | |
| Number | 479 | 484 | 345 | 462 | 328 | 335 | 504 | 496 | 420 | 383 | 476 | 456 | 484 | 457 |
| Yards | 2080 | 2120 | 1220 | 1872 | 1417 | 1282 | 1948 | 2028 | 1535 | 1398 | 2127 | 1880 | 2257 | 1749 |
| Average Yards | 4.3 | 4.4 | 3.5 | 4.1 | 4.3 | 3.8 | 3.9 | 4.1 | 3.7. | 3.7 | 4.5 | 4.1 | 4.7 | 3.8 |
| Touchdowns | 20 | 16 | 10 | 19 | 10 | 9 | 11 | 20 | 13 | 4 | 16 | 11 | 14 | 18 |
| PASSING: | | | | | | | | | | | | | | |
| Attempts | 425 | 425 | 573 | 527 | 639 | 488 | 449 | 336 | 539 | 514 | 451 | 408 | 472 | 448 |
| Completions | 263 | 237 | 301 | 305 | 399 | 269 | 260 | 183 | 310 | 274 | 246 | 237 | 246 | 265 |
| Completion Pct. | 61.9 | 55.8 | 52.5 | 57.9 | 62.4 | 55.1 | 57.9 | 54.5 | 57.5 | 53.3 | 54.5 | 58.1 | 52.1 | 59.2 |
| Passing Yards | 3404 | 3152 | 3407 | 3671 | 5072 | 3297 | 3458 | 2885 | 3611 | 3208 | 3059 | 2887 | 2840 | 3194 |
| Avg. Yds per Att. | 7.1 | 6.4 | 5.1 | 5.8 | 7.1 | 5.3 | 6.9 | 7.4 | 6.3 | 4.8 | 5.6 | 6.0 | 5.5 | 5.8 |
| Avg. Yds per Comp. | 12.9 | 13.3 | 11.3 | 12.0 | 12.7 | 12.3 | 13.3 | 15.8 | 11.6 | 11.7 | 12.4 | 12.2 | 11.5 | 12.1 |
| Times Tackled | 27 | 34 | 42 | 46 | 39 | 51 | 22 | 29 | 16 | 58 | 40 | 33 | 20 | 40 |
| Yds Lost Tackled | 208 | 209 | 260 | 330 | 267 | 424 | 191 | 197 | 99 | 443 | 300 | 242 | 157 | 360 |
| Net Yards | 3196 | 2943 | 3147 | 3341 | 4805 | 2873 | 3267 | 2688 | 3512 | 2765 | 2759 | 2645 | 2683 | 2834 |
| Touchdowns | 28 | 25 | 13 | 15 | 37 | 22 | 23 | 19 | 21 | 14 | 14 | 20 | 18 | 15 |
| Interceptions | 11 | 23 | 23 | 18 | 15 | 21 | 5 | 10 | 12 | 20 | 11 | 15 | 19 | 20 |
| Pct. Intercepted | 2.6 | 5.4 | 4.0 | 3.4 | 2.3 | 4.3 | 1.1 | 3.0 | 2.2 | 3.9 | 2.4 | 3.7 | 4.0 | 4.5 |
| PUNTS: | | | | | | | | | | | | | | |
| Number | 58 | 65 | 78 | 60 | 34 | 72 | 81 | 62 | 72 | 92 | 61 | 66 | 62 | 67 |
| Average | 39.3 | 42.1 | 36.9 | 43.5 | 45.0 | 42.8 | 38.7 | 37.3 | 42.0 | 40.8 | 39.3 | 37.2 | 39.4 | 40.6 |
| PUNT RETURNS | | | | | | | | | | | | | | |
| Number | 25 | 30 | 31 | 33 | 30 | 36 | 37 | 34 | 39 | 29 | 30 | 39 | 35 | 36 |
| Yards | 177 | 255 | 209 | 256 | 172 | 402 | 254 | 295 | 233 | 134 | 319 | 398 | 336 | 337 |
| Average Yards | 7.1 | 8.5 | 6.7 | 7.8 | 5.7 | 11.2 | 6.9 | 8.7 | 6.0 | 4.6 | 10.6 | 10.2 | 9.6 | 9.4 |
| Touchdowns | 0 | 1 | 0 | 0 | 0 | 0 | 0 | 0 | 0 | 0 | 1 | 1 | 2 | 0 |
| KICKOFF RET.: | | | | | | | | | | | | | | |
| Number | 51 | 62 | 71 | 66 | 47 | 65 | 46 | 64 | 43 | 77 | 61 | 50 | 55 | 50 |
| Yards | 1040 | 1266 | 1276 | 1260 | 861 | 1189 | 784 | 1237 | 780 | 1395 | 1129 | 956 | 1188 | 985 |
| Average Yards | 20.4 | 20.4 | 18.0 | 19.1 | 18.3 | 18.3 | 17.0 | 19.3 | 18.1 | 18.1 | 18.5 | 19.1 | 21.6 | 19.7 |
| Touchdowns | 0 | 0 | 2 | 0 | 0 | 0 | 0 | 0 | 0 | 0 | 0 | 0 | 0 | 0 |
| INTERCEPT RET.: | | | | | | | | | | | | | | |
| Number | 18 | 15 | 13 | 10 | 21 | 9 | 20 | 13 | 19 | 14 | 18 | 24 | 19 | 12 |
| Yards | 151 | 146 | 212 | 190 | 295 | 173 | 250 | 102 | 288 | 194 | 205 | 385 | 188 | 182 |
| Average Yards | 8.4 | 9.7 | 16.3 | 19.0 | 14.0 | 19.2 | 12.5 | 7.8 | 15.2 | 13.9 | 11.4 | 16.0 | 9.9 | 15.2 |
| Touchdowns | 2 | 1 | 1 | 1 | 1 | 1 | 1 | 1 | 2 | 0 | 0 | 1 | 0 | 0 |
| PENALTIES: | | | | | | | | | | | | | | |
| Number | 92 | 83 | 122 | 108 | 135 | 79 | 111 | 97 | 64 | 99 | 101 | 110 | 103 | 89 |
| Yards | 683 | 627 | 922 | 775 | 1009 | 590 | 886 | 682 | 486 | 744 | 848 | 928 | 886 | 746 |
| FUMBLES: | | | | | | | | | | | | | | |
| Number | 17 | 25 | 37 | 30 | 34 | 23 | 30 | 24 | 33 | 33 | 28 | 40 | 24 | 32 |
| Number Lost | 10 | 12 | 23 | 14 | 21 | 10 | 14 | 14 | 15 | 16 | 13 | 17 | 13 | 16 |
| POINTS: | | | | | | | | | | | | | | |
| Total | 428 | 360 | 228 | 331 | 405 | 281 | 369 | 337 | 336 | 181 | 295 | 292 | 315 | 306 |
| PAT Attempts | 53 | 44 | 27 | 36 | 49 | 33 | 38 | 42 | 39 | 19 | 32 | 33 | 36 | 34 |
| PAT Made | 50 | 41 | 24 | 34 | 46 | 32 | 37 | 40 | 37 | 19 | 32 | 32 | 34 | 33 |
| FG Attempts | 29 | 22 | 20 | 34 | 32 | 24 | 37 | 20 | 25 | 22 | 26 | 25 | 28 | 32 |
| FG Made | 20 | 17 | 14 | 25 | 21 | 17 | 34 | 15 | 21 | 16 | 23 | 20 | 21 | 23 |
| Percent FG Made | 69.0 | 77.3 | 70.0 | 73.5 | 65.6 | 70.8 | 91.9 | 75.0 | 84.0 | 72.7 | 88.5 | 80.0 | 75.0 | 71.9 |
| Safeties | 0 | 2 | 0 | 3 | 1 | 0 | 1 | 0 | 1 | 0 | 1 | 1 | 1 | 0 |

**DEFENSE**

| | BUFF | CIN | CLEV | DEN | HOU | IND | K.C. | L.A. | MIA | N.E. | NYJ | PITT | S.D. | SEA |
|---|---|---|---|---|---|---|---|---|---|---|---|---|---|---|
| FIRST DOWNS: | | | | | | | | | | | | | | |
| Total | 288 | 308 | 314 | 306 | 279 | 320 | 268 | 266 | 268 | 307 | 318 | 257 | 268 | 280 |
| by Rushing | 105 | 116 | 117 | 110 | 88 | 130 | 85 | 95 | 110 | 151 | 112 | 102 | 92 | 86 |
| by Passing | 159 | 180 | 169 | 181 | 160 | 176 | 164 | 152 | 145 | 139 | 186 | 130 | 152 | 171 |
| by Penalty | 24 | 12 | 28 | 15 | 31 | 14 | 19 | 19, | 13 | 17 | 20 | 25 | 24 | 23 |
| RUSHING: | | | | | | | | | | | | | | |
| Number | 483 | 442 | 511 | 456 | 392 | 513 | 373 | 439 | 461 | 565 | 423 | 446 | 424 | 413 |
| Yards | 1808 | 2085 | 2105 | 1963 | 1575 | 2212 | 1640 | 1716 | 1831 | 2676 | 2018 | 1615 | 1515 | 1605 |
| Average Yards | 3.7 | 4.7 | 4.1 | 4.3 | 4.0 | 4.3 | 4.4 | 3.9 | 4.0 | 4.7 | 4.8 | 3.6 | 3.6 | 3.9 |
| Touchdowns | 13 | 15 | 21 | 16 | 12 | 12 | 12 | 4 | 11 | 29 | 15 | 13 | 10 | 7 |
| PASSING: | | | | | | | | | | | | | | |
| Attempts | 455 | 543 | 444 | 479 | 460 | 492 | 512 | 437 | 462 | 374 | 516 | 460 | 462 | 504 |
| Completions | 254 | 300 | 253 | 284 | 267 | 301 | 267 | 246 | 257 | 218 | 311 | 236 | 254 | 300 |
| Completion Pct. | 55.8 | 55.2 | 57.0 | 59.3 | 58.0 | 61.2 | 52.1 | 56.3 | 55.6 | 58.3 | 60.3 | 51.3 | 55.0 | 59.5 |
| Passing Yards | 3125 | 3725 | 3296 | 3671 | 3332 | 3605 | 3662 | 3032 | 3064 | 3245 | 3745 | 2728 | 3255 | 3256 |
| Avg. Yds per Att. | 5.6 | 6.2 | 6.5 | 6.6 | 6.1 | 6.5 | 5.7 | 5.6 | 5.4 | 7.4 | 6.2 | 5.1 | 5.7 | 5.6 |
| Avg. Yds per Comp. | 12.3 | 12.4 | 13.0 | 12.9 | 12.5 | 12.0 | 13.7 | 12.3 | 11.9 | 14.9 | 12.0 | 11.6 | 12.8 | 10.9 |
| Times Tackled | 43 | 25 | 32 | 34 | 38 | 29 | 60 | 48 | 45 | 33 | 38 | 34 | 45 | 33 |
| Yds Lost Tackled | 326 | 205 | 211 | 289 | 272 | 203 | 421 | 335 | 348 | 224 | 308 | 228 | 345 | 252 |
| Net Yards | 2799 | 3520 | 3085 | 3382 | 3060 | 3402 | 3241 | 2697 | 2716 | 3021 | 3437 | 2500 | 2910 | 3004 |
| Touchdowns | 17 | 24 | 32 | 22 | 18 | 20 | 16 | 20 | 14 | 21 | 23 | 9 | 22 | 19 |
| Interceptions | 18 | 15 | 13 | 10 | 21 | 9 | 20 | 13 | 19 | 14 | 18 | 24 | 19 | 12 |
| Pct. Intercepted | 4.0 | 2.8 | 2.9 | 2.1 | 4.6 | 1.8 | 3.9 | 3.0 | 4.1 | 3.7 | 3.5 | 5.2 | 4.1 | 2.4 |
| PUNTS: | | | | | | | | | | | | | | |
| Number | 66 | 63 | 68 | 62 | 62 | 58 | 72 | 64 | 75 | 56 | 56 | 64 | 70 | 77 |
| Average | 38.2 | 41.8 | 38.1 | 41.4 | 38.7 | 42.0 | 37.0 | 38.2 | 40.0 | 40.8 | 41.4 | 40.9 | 41.2 | 41.9 |
| PUNT RETURNS | | | | | | | | | | | | | | |
| Number | 31 | 36 | 41 | 22 | 23 | 42 | 44 | 24 | 40 | 50 | 35 | 16 | 28 | 29 |
| Yards | 227 | 323 | 418 | 370 | 191 | 558 | 325 | 301 | 256 | 346 | 257 | 361 | 451 | 334 |
| Average Yards | 8.1 | 9.8 | 10.4 | 7.2 | 8.1 | 8.0 | 9.3 | 6.4 | 9.9 | 10.1 | 7.7 | 6.6 | 4.7 | 8.8 |
| Touchdowns | 0 | 1 | 0 | 0 | 1 | 0 | 2 | 0 | 0 | 0 | 0 | 0 | 0 | 2 |
| KICKOFF RET.: | | | | | | | | | | | | | | |
| Number | 73 | 43 | 45 | 69 | 71 | 49 | 81 | 49 | 53 | 38 | 61 | 56 | 62 | 51 |
| Yards | 1129 | 945 | 805 | 1319 | 1329 | 961 | 1391 | 1026 | 1092 | 665 | 1185 | 1245 | 1048 | 910 |
| Average Yards | 15.5 | 22.0 | 17.9 | 19.1 | 18.7 | 19.6 | 17.2 | 20.9 | 20.6 | 17.5 | 19.4 | 22.2 | 16.9 | 17.8 |
| Touchdowns | 0 | 0 | 0 | 0 | 1 | 0 | 0 | 0 | 0 | 0 | 1 | 1 | 0 | 0 |
| INTERCEPT RET.: | | | | | | | | | | | | | | |
| Number | 11 | 23 | 23 | 18 | 15 | 21 | 5 | 10 | 12 | 20 | 11 | 15 | 19 | 20 |
| Yards | 156 | 233 | 422 | 169 | 237 | 221 | 86 | 100 | 184 | 143 | 186 | 124 | 310 | 252 |
| Average Yards | 14.2 | 10.1 | 18.3 | 9.4 | 15.8 | 10.5 | 17.2 | 10.0 | 15.3 | 7.2 | 16.9 | 8.3 | 16.3 | 12.6 |
| Touchdowns | 0 | 1 | 3 | 3 | 2 | 1 | 0 | 0 | 0 | 0 | 0 | 0 | 1 | 0 |
| PENALTIES: | | | | | | | | | | | | | | |
| Number | 107 | 101 | 95 | 105 | 134 | 104 | 122 | 86 | 95 | 73 | 106 | 89 | 87 | 108 |
| Yards | 839 | 824 | 684 | 819 | 1015 | 781 | 859 | 710 | 759 | 488 | 876 | 719 | 720 | 766 |
| FUMBLES: | | | | | | | | | | | | | | |
| Number | 31 | 26 | 32 | 43 | 25 | 34 | 32 | 40 | 19 | 22 | 32 | 40 | 21 | 26 |
| Number Lost | 13 | 16 | 11 | 22 | 16 | 15 | 18 | 18 | 8 | 12 | 9 | 21 | 13 | 13 |
| POINTS: | | | | | | | | | | | | | | |
| Total | 263 | 352 | 462 | 374 | 307 | 353 | 257 | 268 | 242 | 446 | 345 | 240 | 281 | 286 |
| PAT Attempts | 30 | 41 | 59 | 43 | 37 | 36 | 30 | 26 | 26 | 52 | 39 | 26 | 33 | 32 |
| PAT Made | 29 | 40 | 56 | 38 | 34 | 35 | 29 | 25 | 26 | 51 | 35 | 26 | 33 | 32 |
| FG Attempts | 24 | 29 | 27 | 33 | 21 | 43 | 20 | 33 | 29 | 31 | 32 | 28 | 21 | 27 |
| FG Made | 18 | 22 | 16 | 26 | 17 | 32 | 16 | 29 | 20 | 27 | 24 | 18 | 16 | 20 |
| Percent FG Made | 75.0 | 75.9 | 59.3 | 78.8 | 81.0 | 74.4 | 80.0 | 87.9 | 69.0 | 87.1 | 75.0 | 64.3 | 76.2 | 74.1 |
| Safeties | 0 | 0 | 2 | 0 | 0 | 3 | 0 | 0 | 0 | 1 | 2 | 2 | 1 | 1 |

**Los Angeles Raiders** — Art Shell received several Coach of the Year honors for restoring the Raiders to a dominant position in the AFC West. His emphasis on traditional Raiders virtues — an aggressive, physical defense and long-range scoring on offense —pushed Los Angeles to the title. Quarterback Jay Schroeder showed signs of playing back to the level of his best days with the Redskins. After going 0-for-November in touchdown passes, he rallied to connect for 11 TDs down the stretch. Running back Marcus Allen put together a solid season, and, once the baseball season ended, Bo Jackson was in top form. His 88-yard run against the Bengals made everyone's highlight film.

**Kansas City Chiefs** — In his second year as coach, Marty Schottenheimer got the Chiefs to the playoffs for only the second time since 1971. Much of the success was due to an opportunistic defense that accounted for 60 sacks, six blocked punts, 25 fumble recoveries and 20 pass interceptions. Linebacker Derrick Thomas led with 20 sacks, and safety Deron Cherry made a strong comeback from injury. Quarterback Steve DeBerg had a fabulous year despite playing the last couple of games with a broken finger on his passing hand. He connected for 23 touchdowns and only four interceptions. Christian Okoye, the 1989 rushing leader, was bothered by injuries much of the season, but Barry Word came on strong to take up much of the slack.

**Seattle Seahawks** — The Seahawks started 0-3 but hung tough in enough close games to finish with a winning record and were in the playoffs until the final weekend. No fewer than six games were decided in the final play and the lead changed hands in the last three minutes of two other contests. Although it ranked as the team's strength, the defense had to survive eight serious injuries to linebackers (including the shoulder problem which caused Brian Bosworth to retire in the offseason). Fullback John L. Williams, who caught 73 passes, and halfback Derrick Fenner, who scored 14 touchdowns, formed a strong running tandem, but quarterback Dave Krieg did not have a vintage year. His 20 interceptions helped put the Seahawks at minus-6 in the giveaway column.

**San Diego Chargers** — The arrival of general manager Bobby Beathard and relatively easy schedule gave the Chargers hope for an improved record, but, when the smoke cleared, they were 6-10 once again. A solid secondary and strong pass rush from ends Lee Williams and Burt Grossman and linebacker Leslie O'Neal kept San Diego in most games, but the offense was inconsistent. Anthony Miller was the only receiving threat, and Billy Joe Tolliver never showed enough consistency to prove that he was the quarterback for the future. Twice during the season he was replaced as the starter. The season's most pleasant surprise was the blooming of fullback Marion Butts, who came from nowhere to become — until a late season injury put him on I.R. — the AFC's leading rusher.

**Denver Broncos** — After getting to the Super Bowl in three of the four previous seasons, the Broncos got busted in 1990. The season began on a worrisome note, with coach Dan Reeves undergoing surgery to clear blocked arteries. He soon returned to the sideline, but Denver's performance did little to elevate his health. The team stood 2-1 when it took a 21-9 lead into the fourth quarter at Buffalo. The Bills rallied to win by a point, and the next week Denver lost to Cleveland — again by a point. Seven of the Broncos' 11 losses were by a total of 23 points. Much of the blame fell on quarterback John Elway, who had a poor year, but the teams' problems stemmed from injuries, especially on defense . Running back Bobby Humphrey got off to a terrific start with four 100-yard games in the first five, but a sprained ankle reduced his effectiveness the rest of the way.

## BUFFALO BILLS 13-3 Marv Levy

| Scores of Each Game | | |
|---|---|---|
| 26 | INDIANAPOLIS | 10 |
| 7 | Miami | 30 |
| 30 | N.Y. Jets | 7 |
| 29 | DENVER | 28 |
| 38 | L.A. RAIDERS | 24 |
| 30 | N.Y. JETS | 27 |
| 27 | New England | 10 |
| 42 | Cleveland | 0 |
| 45 | PHOENIX | 14 |
| 14 | NEW ENGLAND | 0 |
| 24 | Houston | 27 |
| 30 | PHILADELPHIA | 23 |
| 31 | Indianapolis | 7 |
| 17 | N.Y. Giants | 13 |
| 24 | MIAMI | 14 |
| 14 | Washington | 29 |

| Use Name | Pos. | Hgt | Wgt | Age | Int | Pts |
|---|---|---|---|---|---|---|
| Howard Ballard | OT | 6'6" | 325 | 26 | | |
| Will Wolford | OT | 6'5" | 295 | 26 | | |
| John Davis | OG-OT | 6'4" | 310 | 24 | | |
| Mitch Freotte | OG | 6'3" | 285 | 25 | | |
| Glenn Parker | OG-OT | 6'5" | 304 | 24 | | |
| Jim Ritcher | OG | 6'3" | 275 | 31 | | |
| Kent Hull | C | 6'4" | 275 | 29 | | |
| Adam Lingner | C | 6'4" | 263 | 28 | | |
| Jeff Hunter | DE | 6'5" | 285 | 24 | | |
| Mike Lodish | DE | 6'3" | 270 | 23 | | |
| Mark Pike | DE | 6'4" | 272 | 26 | | |
| Leon Seals | DE | 6'4" | 270 | 26 | 1 | |
| Bruce Smith | DE | 6'4" | 275 | 27 | | |
| Gary Baldinger (from IND) | NT | 6'3" | 270 | 26 | | |
| Jeff Wright | NT | 6'2" | 270 | 26 | | |

Leonard Burton — Knee Injury

| Use Name | Pos. | Hgt | Wgt | Age | Int | Pts |
|---|---|---|---|---|---|---|
| Carlton Bailey | LB | 6'2" | 240 | 25 | | |
| Cornelius Bennett | LB | 6'2" | 235 | 24 | | 6 |
| Ray Bentley | LB | 6'2" | 235 | 28 | 1 | |
| Shane Conlan | LB | 6'3" | 235 | 25 | | |
| Hal Garner | LB | 6'4" | 238 | 28 | | |
| Matt Monger | LB | 6'1" | 235 | 28 | | |
| Marvcus Patton | LB | 6'2" | 223 | 23 | | |
| Darryl Talley | LB | 6'4" | 235 | 30 | 2 | 6 |
| Richard Carey | DB | 5'9" | 185 | 22 | | |
| Dwight Drane | DB | 6'2" | 205 | 28 | | |
| John Hagy | DB | 5'11" | 190 | 24 | 2 | |
| Chris Hale | DB | 5'7" | 161 | 24 | | |
| Clifford Hicks (from LA) | DB | 5'10" | 188 | 26 | | |
| Kirby Jackson | DB | 5'10" | 180 | 24 | 3 | |
| Mark Kelso | DB | 5'11" | 185 | 27 | 2 | |
| Nate Odomes | DB | 5'10" | 188 | 24 | 1 | 6 |
| Kim Phillips | DB | 5'9" | 188 | 22 | | |
| David Pool | DB | 5'9" | 188 | 23 | 1 | |
| Leonard Smith | DB | 5'11" | 202 | 29 | 2 | 6 |
| James Williams | DB | 5'10" | 175 | 23 | 2 | 6 |

| Use Name | Pos. | Hgt | Wgt | Age | Int | Pts |
|---|---|---|---|---|---|---|
| Gale Gilbert | QB | 6'3" | 210 | 28 | | |
| Jim Kelly | QB | 6'3" | 218 | 30 | | |
| Frank Reich | QB | 6'4" | 210 | 28 | | |
| Kenneth Davis | HB | 5'10" | 209 | 28 | | 30 |
| Thurman Thomas | HB | 5'10" | 198 | 24 | | 78 |
| Carwell Gardner | FB | 6'2" | 235 | 23 | | |
| Larry Kinnebrew | FB | 6'1" | 256 | 30 | | 6 |
| Jamie Mueller | FB | 6'1" | 225 | 25 | | 18 |
| Don Smith | FB-HB | 5'11" | 200 | 26 | | 12 |
| Don Beebe | WR | 5'11" | 177 | 25 | | 6 |
| Al Edwards | WR | 5'8" | 168 | 23 | | |
| James Lofton | WR | 6'3" | 190 | 34 | | 24 |
| Andre Reed | WR | 6' | 190 | 25 | | 48 |
| Steve Tasker | WR | 5'9" | 185 | 28 | | 12 |
| Vernon Turner | WR | 5'8" | 185 | 23 | | |
| Keith McKeller | TE | 6'6" | 245 | 26 | | 30 |
| Pete Metzelaars | TE | 6'7" | 250 | 30 | | 6 |
| Butch Rolle | TE | 6'3" | 242 | 25 | | 18 |
| John Nies | K | 6'2" | 199 | 23 | | |
| Scott Norwood | K | 6' | 207 | 30 | | 110 |
| Rick Tuten | K | 6'2" | 218 | 25 | | |

Robb Riddick — Knee Injury

## MIAMI DOLPHINS 12-4 Don Shula

| Scores of Each Game | | |
|---|---|---|
| 27 | New England | 24 |
| 30 | BUFFALO | 7 |
| 3 | N.Y. Giants | 20 |
| 28 | Pittsburgh | 6 |
| 20 | N.Y. JETS | 16 |
| 17 | NEW ENGLAND | 10 |
| 27 | Indianapolis | 7 |
| 23 | PHOENIX | 3 |
| 17 | N.Y. Jets | 3 |
| 10 | L.A. RAIDERS | 13 |
| 30 | Cleveland | 13 |
| 20 | Washington | 42 |
| 23 | PHILADELPHIA | 20 |
| 24 | SEATTLE | 17 |
| 14 | Buffalo | 24 |
| 23 | INDIANAPOLIS | 17 |

| Use Name | Pos. | Hgt | Wgt | Age | Int | Pts |
|---|---|---|---|---|---|---|
| Jeff Dellenbach | OT-C | 6'6" | 280 | 27 | | |
| Mark Dennis | OT | 6'6" | 295 | 25 | | |
| Richmond Webb | OT | 6'6" | 298 | 23 | | |
| Roy Foster | OG | 6'4" | 284 | 30 | | |
| Harry Galbreath | OG | 6'1" | 275 | 25 | | |
| Keith Sims | OG | 6'3" | 305 | 23 | | |
| Jeff Uhlenhake | C | 6'3" | 282 | 24 | | |
| Bert Weidner | C | 6'3" | 284 | 23 | | |
| Jeff Cross | DE | 6'4" | 272 | 24 | | |
| Greg Mark (to PHI) | DE-LB | 6'3" | 252 | 23 | | |
| T.J. Turner | DE | 6'4" | 280 | 27 | | |
| Karl Wilson | DE | 6'4" | 275 | 26 | | |
| Shawn Lee | NT | 6'2" | 285 | 23 | | |
| Alfred Oglesby | NT | 6'3" | 278 | 23 | | |
| Brian Sochia | NT | 6'3" | 275 | 29 | | 6 |

John Bosa — Knee Injury

| Use Name | Pos. | Hgt | Wgt | Age | Int | Pts |
|---|---|---|---|---|---|---|
| Rick Graf | LB | 6'5" | 249 | 27 | | |
| Hugh Green | LB | 6'2" | 228 | 31 | | |
| David Griggs | LB-TE | 6'3" | 239 | 23 | | |
| E.J. Junior | LB | 6'3" | 242 | 30 | | |
| Eric Kumerow | LB-DE | 6'7" | 268 | 25 | 1 | |
| Cliff Odom | LB | 6'2" | 243 | 32 | | 6 |
| John Offerdahl | LB | 6'3" | 237 | 26 | 1 | |
| Mike Reichenbach | LB | 6'2" | 240 | 28 | | |
| J.B. Brown | DB | 6' | 192 | 24 | | |
| Kerry Glenn | DB | 5'9" | 178 | 28 | 2 | 6 |
| African Grant | DB | 6' | 200 | 25 | | |
| Bobby Harden | DB | 6' | 192 | 23 | | |
| Liffort Hobley | DB | 6' | 202 | 28 | 1 | |
| Paul Lankford | DB | 6'1" | 190 | 32 | | |
| Michael McGruder | DB | 5'11" | 180 | 28 | | |
| Tim McKyer | DB | 6' | 177 | 26 | 4 | |
| Stevon Moore | DB | 5'11" | 204 | 23 | | |
| Louis Oliver | DB | 6'2" | 226 | 24 | 5 | |
| Rodney Thomas | DB | 5'10" | 190 | 24 | | |
| Jarvis Williams | DB | 5'11" | 196 | 25 | 5 | 6 |

Barry Krauss — Knee Injury

| Use Name | Pos. | Hgt | Wgt | Age | Int | Pts |
|---|---|---|---|---|---|---|
| Dan Marino | QB | 6'4" | 222 | 28 | | |
| Scott Secules | QB | 6'3" | 219 | 25 | | |
| Tony Collins | HB | 5'11" | 212 | 31 | | |
| Mark Higgs | HB | 5'7" | 196 | 24 | | 6 |
| Sammie Smith | HB | 6'2" | 226 | 23 | | 54 |
| Troy Stradford | HB | 5'9" | 192 | 25 | | 6 |
| Garrett Limbrick | FB | 6'2" | 240 | 24 | | |
| Marc Logan | FB | 5'11" | 220 | 25 | | 12 |
| Tony Paige | FB | 5'10" | 235 | 27 | | 36 |
| Fred Banks | WR | 5'10" | 180 | 28 | | |
| Andre Brown | WR | 6'3" | 210 | 24 | | |
| Mark Clayton | WR | 5'9" | 184 | 29 | | 30 |
| Mark Duper | WR | 5'9" | 190 | 31 | | 30 |
| Jim Jensen | WR-FB | 6'4" | 220 | 31 | | 6 |
| Tony Martin | WR | 6' | 180 | 24 | | 12 |
| James Pruitt | WR | 6'2" | 201 | 26 | | 18 |
| Scott Schwedes (to, from SD) | WR | 6' | 182 | 25 | | 6 |
| Greg Baty | TE | 6'5" | 240 | 26 | | |
| Ferrell Edmunds | TE | 6'6" | 248 | 25 | | 6 |
| Brian Kinchen | TE | 6'2" | 238 | 25 | | |
| Reggie Roby | K | 6'2" | 242 | 29 | | |
| Pete Stoyonovich | K | 5'10" | 180 | 23 | | 100 |

## INDIANAPOLIS COLTS 7-9 Ron Meyer

| Scores of Each Game | | |
|---|---|---|
| 10 | Buffalo | 26 |
| 14 | NEW ENGLAND | 16 |
| 10 | Houston | 24 |
| 24 | Philadelphia | 23 |
| 23 | KANSAS CITY | 19 |
| 17 | DENVER | 27 |
| 7 | MIAMI | 27 |
| 7 | N.Y. GIANTS | 24 |
| 13 | New England | 10 |
| 17 | N.Y. JETS | 14 |
| 34 | Cincinnati | 20 |
| 17 | Phoenix | 20 |
| 7 | BUFFALO | 31 |
| 29 | N.Y. Jets | 21 |
| 35 | WASHINGTON | 28 |
| 17 | Miami | 23 |

| Use Name | Pos. | Hgt | Wgt | Age | Int | Pts |
|---|---|---|---|---|---|---|
| Joey Banes | OT | 6'7" | 282 | 23 | | |
| Kevin Call | OT | 6'7" | 302 | 28 | | |
| Pat Cunningham | OT | 6'6" | 295 | 21 | | |
| Zefross Moss | OT | 6'6" | 338 | 23 | | |
| William Schultz | OT | 6'5" | 293 | 23 | | |
| Brian Baldinger | OG-OT | 6'4" | 278 | 31 | | |
| Chris Conlin | OG | 6'4" | 287 | 25 | | |
| Randy Dixon | OG | 6'3" | 302 | 25 | | |
| Pat Tomberlin | OG | 6'2" | 330 | 24 | | |
| Ray Donaldson | C | 6'3" | 300 | 32 | | |
| Sam Clancy | DE | 6'7" | 284 | 32 | | |
| Jeff Faulkner | DE | 6'3" | 280 | 26 | | |
| Jon Hand | DE | 6'7" | 301 | 26 | | |
| Ralph Jarvis | DE | 6'4" | 255 | 25 | | |
| Sean McNanie | DE | 6'5" | 270 | 28 | | |
| Donnell Thompson | DE | 6'4" | 280 | 31 | | |
| Harvey Armstrong | NT | 6'3" | 282 | 30 | | |
| Mitchell Benson | NT | 6'3" | 302 | 23 | | |
| Tony Siragusa | NT | 6'3" | 291 | 23 | | |

| Use Name | Pos. | Hgt | Wgt | Age | Int | Pts |
|---|---|---|---|---|---|---|
| Chip Banks | LB | 6'4" | 245 | 30 | | |
| Duane Bickett | LB | 6'5" | 243 | 27 | 1 | |
| Jeff Herrod | LB | 6' | 243 | 24 | 1 | |
| Kurt Larson | LB | 6'4" | 236 | 23 | | |
| Quintus McDonald | LB | 6'3 | 263 | 23 | | |
| Scott Radecic | LB | 6'3" | 236 | 28 | | |
| Matt Vanderbeek | LB | 6'3" | 258 | 23 | | |
| Tony Walker | LB | 6'3" | 235 | 22 | | |
| Fredd Young | LB | 6'1" | 233 | 27 | | |
| Michael Ball | DB | 6' | 216 | 26 | | |
| John Baylor | DB | 6' | 203 | 25 | | |
| Eugene Daniel | DB | 5'11" | 178 | 29 | | |
| Chris Goode | DB | 6' | 193 | 26 | 1 | 6 |
| Alan Grant | DB | 5'10" | 187 | 23 | 1 | 6 |
| Cornell Holloway | DB | 5'11" | 182 | 24 | | |
| Mike Prior | DB | 6' | 204 | 26 | 3 | |
| George Streeter | DB | 6'2" | 212 | 23 | | |
| Keith Taylor | DB | 5'11' | 193 | 25 | 2 | |

O'Brien Alston — Knee Injury

| Use Name | Pos. | Hgt | Wgt | Age | Int | Pts |
|---|---|---|---|---|---|---|
| Joe Ferguson | QB | 6'1" | 190 | 40 | | |
| Jeff George | QB | 6'4" | 221 | 22 | | 6 |
| Mark Herrmann | QB | 6'4" | 186 | 31 | | |
| Rusty Hilger | QB | 6'4" | 205 | 28 | | |
| Jack Trudeau | QB | 6'3" | 214 | 27 | | |
| Albert Bentley | HB-FB | 5'11" | 214 | 30 | | 36 |
| Eric Dickerson | HB | 6'3" | 224 | 29 | | 24 |
| Ken Clark | FB | 5'9" | 201 | 24 | | |
| Ivy Joe Hunter | FB-HB | 6' | 237 | 23 | | |
| Anthony Johnson | FB | 6' | 222 | 22 | | 12 |
| Bill Brooks | WR | 6' | 191 | 26 | | 30 |
| Jessie Hester | WR | 5'11" | 172 | 27 | | 36 |
| Stanley Morgan | WR | 5'11" | 185 | 35 | | 30 |
| Stacey Simmons | WR | 5'9" | 183 | 22 | | |
| Clarence Verdin | WR | 5'8" | 163 | 27 | | 6 |
| Eugene Riley | TE | 6'2" | 236 | 23 | | |
| Pat Beach | TE | 6'4" | 252 | 29 | | 6 |
| Dean Biasucci | K | 6' | 191 | 27 | | 83 |
| Rohn Stark | K | 6'3" | 204 | 31 | | |

## NEW YORK JETS 6-10 Bruce Coslet

| Scores of Each Game | | |
|---|---|---|
| 20 | Cincinnati | 25 |
| 24 | CLEVELAND | 21 |
| 7 | BUFFALO | 30 |
| 37 | New England | 13 |
| 16 | Miami | 20 |
| 3 | SAN DIEGO | 39 |
| 27 | Buffalo | 30 |
| 17 | Houston | 12 |
| 24 | DALLAS | 9 |
| 3 | MIAMI | 17 |
| 14 | Indianapolis | 17 |
| 7 | PITTSBURGH | 24 |
| 17 | San Diego | 38 |
| 21 | INDIANAPOLIS | 29 |
| 42 | NEW ENGLAND | 7 |
| 16 | Tampa Bay | 14 |

| Use Name | Pos. | Hgt | Wgt | Age | Int | Pts |
|---|---|---|---|---|---|---|
| Jeff Criswell | OT | 6'7" | 291 | 25 | | |
| Scott Jones | OT | 6'5" | 282 | 24 | | |
| Brett Miller | OT | 6'7" | 293 | 31 | | |
| Dave Cadigan | OG | 6'4" | 285 | 25 | | |
| Mike Haight | OG | 6'4" | 279 | 27 | | |
| Trevor Matich | OG-C-OT | 6'4" | 282 | 28 | | |
| Dwayne White | OG | 6'2" | 312 | 23 | | |
| Dave Zawatson | OG-OT | 6'4" | 287 | 24 | | |
| Roger Duffy | C | 6'3" | 285 | 23 | | |
| Jim Sweeney | C-OG | 6'4" | 275 | 28 | | |
| Darrell Davis | DE | 6'2" | 258 | 24 | | 6 |
| Jeff Lageman | DE | 6'5" | 255 | 23 | | |
| Ron Stallworth | DE-DT | 6'5" | 260 | 24 | | |
| Marvin Washington | DE-DT | 6'6" | 276 | 24 | | |
| Dennis Byrd | DT | 6'5" | 270 | 23 | | 2 |
| Emanuel McNeil | DT | 6'3" | 277 | 23 | | |
| Scott Mersereau | DT | 6'3" | 273 | 25 | | |
| Gerald Nichols | DT-DE | 6'2" | 260 | 26 | | |

Marty Lyons — Arm Injury
Paul Frase — Hyperthyroid Illness

| Use Name | Pos. | Hgt | Wgt | Age | Int | Pts |
|---|---|---|---|---|---|---|
| Kyle Clifton | LB | 6'4" | 236 | 28 | 3 | |
| John Galvin | LB | 6'3" | 230 | 25 | | |
| Troy Johnson | LB | 6'2" | 236 | 25 | | |
| Joe Kelly | LB | 6'2" | 235 | 25 | | |
| Joe Mott | LB | 6'4" | 253 | 24 | | |
| Dan Murray | LB | 6'1" | 240 | 23 | | |
| Mac Stephens | LB | 6'3" | 220 | 22 | | |
| John Booty | DB | 6' | 179 | 24 | | |
| Travis Curtis | DB | 5'10" | 180 | 24 | 2 | |
| James Hasty | DB | 6' | 200 | 25 | 2 | |
| Carl Howard | DB | 6'2" | 190 | 28 | | |
| Ken Johnson | DB | 6'2" | 208 | 23 | | |
| Michael Mayes | DB | 5'10" | 173 | 24 | 1 | |
| Erik McMillan | DB | 6'2" | 197 | 25 | 5 | |
| Don Odegard | DB | 6' | 180 | 23 | | |
| Tony Stargell | DB | 5'11" | 190 | 24 | 2 | |
| Brian Washington | DB | 6'1" | 220 | 24 | 3 | |

Troy Benson —Neck Injury
Dennis Price — Shoulder Injury
Terry Williams — Knee Injury

| Use Name | Pos. | Hgt | Wgt | Age | Int | Pts |
|---|---|---|---|---|---|---|
| Tony Eason | QB | 6'4" | 212 | 30 | | |
| Ken O'Brien | QB | 6'4" | 200 | 29 | | |
| Troy Taylor | QB | 6'4" | 200 | 22 | | 6 |
| A.B. Brown | HB | 5'9" | 212 | 24 | | |
| Johnny Hector | HB | 5'11" | 202 | 29 | | 12 |
| Freeman McNeil | HB | 5'11" | 209 | 31 | | 36 |
| Blair Thomas | HB | 5'10" | 195 | 22 | | 12 |
| Brad Baxter | FB | 6'1" | 231 | 23 | | |
| Chris Burkett | WR | 6'4" | 210 | 28 | | |
| Dale Dawkins | WR | 6'1" | 190 | 23 | | |
| Terance Mathis | WR | 5'10" | 170 | 23 | | 6 |
| Rob Moore | WR | 6'3" | 205 | 21 | | 36 |
| Al Toon | WR | 6'4" | 205 | 27 | | 36 |
| JoJo Townsell | WR | 5'9" | 180 | 29 | | |
| Mark Boyer | TE | 6'4" | 242 | 27 | | 6 |
| Chris Dressel | TE | 6'4" | 239 | 29 | | |
| Pat Kelly | TE | 6'6" | 252 | 24 | | |
| Doug Wellsandt | TE | 6'3" | 248 | 23 | | |
| Pat Leahy | K | 6' | 196 | 39 | | 101 |
| Joe Prokop | K | 6'3" | 224 | 30 | | |

Patrick Egu — Arm Injury

## NEW ENGLAND PATRIOTS 1-15 Rod Rust

| Scores of Each Game | | |
|---|---|---|
| 24 | MIAMI | 27 |
| 16 | Indianapolis | 14 |
| 7 | Cincinnati | 41 |
| 13 | N.Y. JETS | 37 |
| 20 | SEATTLE | 33 |
| 10 | Miami | 17 |
| 10 | BUFFALO | 27 |
| 20 | Philadelphia | 48 |
| 10 | INDIANAPOLIS | 13 |
| 0 | Buffalo | 14 |
| 14 | Phoenix | 34 |
| 7 | KANSAS CITY | 37 |
| 3 | Pittsburgh | 24 |
| 10 | WASHINGTON | 25 |
| 7 | N.Y. Jets | 42 |
| 10 | N.Y. GIANTS | 13 |

| Use Name | Pos. | Hgt | Wgt | Age | Int | Pts |
|---|---|---|---|---|---|---|
| Bruce Armstrong | OT | 6'4" | 284 | 24 | | |
| Stan Clayton | OT-OG | 6'3" | 265 | 25 | | |
| David Viaene | OT | 6'5" | 300 | 25 | | |
| Danny Villa | OT-C | 6'5" | 305 | 25 | | |
| Paul Fairchild | OG-C | 6'4" | 270 | 28 | | |
| Chris Gambol | OG-OT | 6'6" | 303 | 25 | | |
| Damian Johnson | OG | 6'5" | 290 | 27 | | |
| Gene Chilton | C | 6'3" | 286 | 26 | | |
| Elbert Crawford | C-OG | 6'3" | 280 | 24 | | |
| David Douglas | C-OG | 6'4" | 280 | 27 | | |
| Ray Agnew | DE | 6'3" | 272 | 22 | | |
| Chris Gannon | DE | 6'6" | 260 | 24 | | |
| Marion Hobby | DE | 6'4" | 277 | 23 | | |
| Sean Smith | DE | 6'4" | 280 | 23 | | |
| Garin Veris | DE | 6'4" | 255 | 27 | | |
| Fred DeRiggi | NT | 6'2" | 268 | 23 | | |
| Tim Goad | NT | 6'3" | 280 | 24 | | |
| Brent Williams | DE | 6'3" | 278 | 25 | | 6 |

Bob White — Knee Injury

| Use Name | Pos. | Hgt | Wgt | Age | Int | Pts |
|---|---|---|---|---|---|---|
| Vincent Brown | LB | 6'2" | 245 | 25 | | |
| Richard Harvey | LB | 6'1" | 227 | 23 | | |
| Ilia Jarostchuk | LB | 6'3" | 245 | 26 | | |
| Johnny Rembert | LB | 6'3" | 234 | 29 | 2 | |
| Ed Reynolds | LB | 6'5" | 242 | 28 | | |
| Chris Singleton | LB | 6'2" | 247 | 23 | | |
| Richard Tardits | LB | 6'2" | 218 | 25 | | |
| Andre Tippett | LB | 6'3" | 241 | 30 | | |
| Ed Williams | LB | 6'4" | 244 | 28 | | |
| Eric Coleman | DB | 6' | 190 | 23 | | |
| Tim Hauck | DB | 5'11" | 185 | 23 | | |
| Maurice Hurst | DB | 5'10" | 185 | 22 | 4 | |
| Brian Hutson | DB | 6'1" | 198 | 25 | | |
| Roland James | DB | 6'2" | 191 | 32 | | |
| Ronnie Lippett | DB | 5'11" | 180 | 29 | 4 | |
| Fred Marion | DB | 6'2" | 191 | 31 | 4 | |
| Rod McSwain | DB | 6'1" | 198 | 28 | | |
| Junior Robinson | DB | 5'9" | 181 | 22 | | |
| Mickey Washington | DB | 5'9" | 187 | 22 | | |
| Tony Zackery | DB | 6'2" | 195 | 23 | | |

| Use Name | Pos. | Hgt | Wgt | Age | Int | Pts |
|---|---|---|---|---|---|---|
| Steve Grogan | QB | 6'4" | 210 | 37 | | |
| Tom Hodson | QB | 6'3" | 195 | 23 | | |
| Marc Wilson | QB | 6'6" | 205 | 33 | | |
| Marvin Allen | HB | 5'10" | 215 | 24 | | 6 |
| Jamie Morris | HB | 5'7" | 188 | 25 | | |
| Don Overton | HB | 6' | 221 | 22 | | |
| John Stephens | HB | 6'1" | 220 | 24 | | 18 |
| George Adams | FB | 6'1" | 225 | 27 | | 6 |
| Bob Perryman (to DAL) | FB | 6'1" | 233 | 25 | | 6 |
| Mosi Tatupu | FB | 6' | 227 | 35 | | |
| Pat Coleman | WR | 5'7" | 173 | 23 | | |
| Hart Lee Dykes | WR | 6'4" | 218 | 23 | | 12 |
| Irving Fryar | WR | 6' | 200 | 27 | | 24 |
| Cedric Jones | WR | 6'1" | 184 | 30 | | |
| Sammy Martin | WR | 5'11" | 175 | 25 | | 6 |
| Greg McMurtry | WR | 6'2" | 207 | 22 | | |
| Michael Timpson | WR | 5'10" | 175 | 23 | | |
| Marv Cook | TE | 6'4" | 234 | 24 | | 30 |
| Lin Dawson | TE | 6'3" | 240 | 31 | | |
| Zeke Mowatt | TE | 6'3" | 240 | 29 | | |
| Eric Sievers | TE | 6'4" | 238 | 32 | | |
| Brian Hansen | K | 6'4" | 220 | 29 | | |
| Jason Staurovsky | K | 5'9" | 170 | 27 | | 67 |

## BUFFALO BILLS

### RUSHING

| Last Name | No. | Yds | Avg | TD |
|---|---|---|---|---|
| Thomas | 271 | 1297 | 4.8 | 11 |
| K. Davis | 64 | 302 | 4.7 | 4 |
| Mueller | 59 | 207 | 3.5 | 2 |
| D. Smith | 20 | 82 | 4.1 | 2 |
| Kelly | 22 | 63 | 2.9 | 0 |
| Gardner | 15 | 41 | 2.7 | 0 |
| Reich | 15 | 24 | 1.6 | 0 |
| Beebe | 1 | 23 | 23.0 | 0 |
| Reed | 3 | 23 | 7.7 | 0 |
| Kinnebrew | 9 | 18 | 2.0 | 1 |

### RECEIVING

| Last Name | No. | Yds | Avg | TD |
|---|---|---|---|---|
| Reed | 71 | 945 | 13.3 | 8 |
| Thomas | 49 | 532 | 10.9 | 2 |
| Lofton | 35 | 712 | 20.3 | 4 |
| McKeller | 34 | 464 | 13.6 | 5 |
| D. Smith | 21 | 225 | 10.7 | 0 |
| Mueller | 16 | 106 | 6.6 | 1 |
| Beebe | 11 | 221 | 20.1 | 1 |
| Metzelaars | 10 | 60 | 6.0 | 1 |
| K. Davis | 9 | 78 | 8.7 | 1 |
| Rolle | 3 | 6 | 2.0 | 3 |
| Tasker | 2 | 44 | 22.0 | 2 |
| Edwards | 2 | 11 | 5.5 | 0 |

### PUNT RETURNS

| Last Name | No. | Yds | Avg | TD |
|---|---|---|---|---|
| Edwards | 14 | 92 | 6.6 | 0 |
| Hale | 10 | 76 | 7.6 | 0 |
| Odomes | 1 | 9 | 9.0 | 0 |

### KICKOFF RETURNS

| Last Name | No. | Yds | Avg | TD |
|---|---|---|---|---|
| D. Smith | 32 | 643 | 20.1 | 0 |
| Edwards | 11 | 256 | 23.3 | 0 |
| Beebe | 6 | 119 | 19.8 | 0 |
| Rolle | 2 | 22 | 11.0 | 0 |

### PASSING — PUNTING — KICKING

| Last Name | Att | Cmp | % | Yds | Yd/Att | TD | Int— | % | RK |
|---|---|---|---|---|---|---|---|---|---|
| Kelly | 346 | 219 | 63.3 | 2829 | 8.18 | 24 | 9— | 2.6 | 1 |
| Reich | 63 | 36 | 57.1 | 469 | 7.44 | 2 | 0— | 0.0 | |
| Gilbert | 15 | 8 | 53.3 | 106 | 7.07 | 2 | 2— | 13.3 | |
| D. Smith | 1 | 0 | 0.0 | 0 | 0.00 | 0 | 0— | 0.0 | |

| PUNTING | No. | Avg. |
|---|---|---|
| Tuten | 53 | 39.8 |

| KICKING | XP | ATT | % | FG | ATT | % |
|---|---|---|---|---|---|---|
| Norwood | 50 | 52 | 96 | 20 | 29 | 69 |

## MIAMI DOLPHINS

### RUSHING

| Last Name | No. | Yds | Avg | TD |
|---|---|---|---|---|
| Smith | 226 | 831 | 3.7 | 8 |
| Logan | 79 | 317 | 4.0 | 2 |
| Stradford | 37 | 138 | 3.7 | 1 |
| Paige | 32 | 95 | 3.0 | 2 |
| Higgs | 10 | 67 | 6.7 | 0 |
| Secules | 8 | 34 | 4.3 | 0 |
| Marino | 16 | 29 | 1.8 | 0 |
| Limbrick | 5 | 14 | 2.8 | 0 |
| Martin | 1 | 8 | 8.0 | 0 |
| Jensen | 4 | 6 | 1.5 | 0 |
| Banks | 1 | 3 | 3.0 | 0 |
| Edmunds | 1 | -7 | -7.0 | 0 |

### RECEIVING

| Last Name | No. | Yds | Avg | TD |
|---|---|---|---|---|
| Duper | 52 | 810 | 15.6 | 5 |
| Jensen | 44 | 365 | 8.3 | 1 |
| Paige | 35 | 247 | 7.1 | 4 |
| Clayton | 32 | 406 | 12.7 | 3 |
| Edmunds | 31 | 446 | 14.4 | 1 |
| Stradford | 30 | 257 | 8.6 | 0 |
| Martin | 29 | 388 | 13.4 | 2 |
| Pruitt | 13 | 235 | 18.1 | 3 |
| Banks | 13 | 131 | 10.1 | 0 |
| Smith | 11 | 134 | 12.2 | 1 |
| Logan | 7 | 54 | 7.7 | 0 |
| Schwedes | 6 | 66 | 11.0 | 1 |
| Limbrick | 4 | 23 | 5.8 | 0 |
| A. Brown | 3 | 49 | 16.3 | 0 |

### PUNT RETURNS

| Last Name | No. | Yds | Avg | TD |
|---|---|---|---|---|
| Martin | 26 | 140 | 5.4 | 0 |
| Schwedes | 14 | 122 | 9.7 | 0 |
| Stradford | 3 | 4 | 1.3 | 0 |
| Williams | 1 | 5 | 5.0 | 0 |

### KICKOFF RETURNS

| Last Name | No. | Yds | Avg | TD |
|---|---|---|---|---|
| Logan | 20 | 367 | 18.4 | 0 |
| Higgs | 10 | 210 | 21.0 | 0 |
| Stradford | 3 | 56 | 18.7 | 0 |
| Collins | 2 | 30 | 15.0 | 0 |
| Schwedes | 2 | 52 | 26.0 | 0 |
| Paige | 1 | 18 | 18.0 | 0 |
| Kinchen | 1 | 16 | 16.0 | 0 |
| Sims | 1 | 9 | 9.0 | 0 |
| Graf | 1 | 6 | 6.0 | 0 |

### PASSING — PUNTING — KICKING

| Last Name | Att | Cmp | % | Yds | Yd/Att | TD | Int— | % | RK |
|---|---|---|---|---|---|---|---|---|---|
| Marino | 531 | 306 | 57.6 | 3563 | 6.71 | 21 | 11— | 2.1 | 5 |
| Secules | 7 | 3 | 42.9 | 17 | 2.43 | 0 | 1— | 14.3 | |
| Jensen | 1 | 1 | 100.0 | 31 | 31.00 | 0 | 0— | 0.0 | |

| PUNTING | No. | Avg. |
|---|---|---|
| Roby | 72 | 42.0 |

| KICKING | XP | ATT | % | FG | ATT | % |
|---|---|---|---|---|---|---|
| Stoyonovich | 37 | 37 | 100 | 21 | 25 | 84 |

## INDIANAPOLIS COLTS

### RUSHING

| Last Name | No. | Yds | Avg | TD |
|---|---|---|---|---|
| Dickerson | 166 | 677 | 4.1 | 4 |
| Bentley | 137 | 556 | 4.1 | 4 |
| Trudeau | 10 | 28 | 2.8 | 0 |
| Clark | 7 | 10 | 1.4 | 0 |
| Hester | 4 | 9 | 2.3 | 0 |
| George | 11 | 2 | 0.2 | 1 |

### RECEIVING

| Last Name | No. | Yds | Avg | TD |
|---|---|---|---|---|
| Bentley | 71 | 664 | 9.4 | 2 |
| Brooks | 62 | 823 | 13.3 | 5 |
| Hester | 54 | 924 | 17.1 | 6 |
| Morgan | 23 | 364 | 15.8 | 5 |
| Dickerson | 18 | 92 | 5.1 | 0 |
| Verdin | 14 | 178 | 12.7 | 1 |
| Beach | 12 | 124 | 10.3 | 1 |
| Johnson | 5 | 32 | 6.4 | 2 |
| Clark | 5 | 23 | 4.6 | 0 |
| Simmons | 4 | 33 | 4.6 | 0 |
| Prior | 1 | 40 | 40.0 | 0 |

### PUNT RETURNS

| Last Name | No. | Yds | Avg | TD |
|---|---|---|---|---|
| Verdin | 31 | 396 | 12.8 | 0 |
| Grant | 2 | 6 | 3.0 | 0 |
| Prior | 2 | 0 | 0.0 | 0 |
| Daniel | 1 | 0 | 0.0 | 0 |

### KICKOFF RETURNS

| Last Name | No. | Yds | Avg | TD |
|---|---|---|---|---|
| Simmons | 19 | 348 | 18.3 | 0 |
| Verdin | 18 | 350 | 19.4 | 0 |
| Grant | 15 | 280 | 18.7 | 0 |
| Bentley | 11 | 211 | 19.2 | 0 |
| Ball | 1 | 0 | 0.0 | 0 |
| Jarvis | 1 | 0 | 0.0 | 0 |

### PASSING — PUNTING — KICKING

| Last Name | Att | Cmp | % | Yds | Yd/Att | TD | Int— | % | RK |
|---|---|---|---|---|---|---|---|---|---|
| George | 334 | 181 | 54.2 | 2152 | 6.44 | 16 | 13— | 3.9 | 10 |
| Trudeau | 144 | 84 | 58.3 | 1078 | 7.49 | 6 | 6— | 4.2 | |
| Ferguson | 8 | 2 | 25.0 | 21 | 2.63 | 0 | 2— | 25.0 | |
| Herrmann | 1 | 1 | 100.0 | 6 | 6.00 | 0 | 0— | 0.0 | |
| Stark | 1 | 1 | 100.0 | 40 | 40.00 | 0 | 0— | 0.0 | |

| PUNTING | No. | Avg. |
|---|---|---|
| Stark | 72 | 42.8 |

| KICKING | XP | ATT | % | FG | ATT | % |
|---|---|---|---|---|---|---|
| Biasucci | 32 | 33 | 97 | 17 | 24 | 71 |

## NEW YORK JETS

### RUSHING

| Last Name | No. | Yds | Avg | TD |
|---|---|---|---|---|
| Thomas | 123 | 620 | 5.0 | 1 |
| Baxter | 124 | 539 | 4.3 | 6 |
| F. McNeil | 99 | 458 | 4.6 | 6 |
| Hector | 91 | 377 | 4.1 | 2 |
| O'Brien | 21 | 72 | 3.4 | 0 |
| Eason | 7 | 29 | 4.1 | 0 |
| Taylor | 2 | 20 | 10.0 | 1 |
| Mathis | 2 | 9 | 4.5 | 0 |
| Brown | 1 | 8 | 8.0 | 0 |
| Prokop | 3 | 2 | 0.7 | 0 |
| Wellsandt | 1 | -3 | -3.0 | 0 |
| Moore | 2 | -4 | -2.0 | 0 |

### RECEIVING

| Last Name | No. | Yds | Avg | TD |
|---|---|---|---|---|
| Toon | 57 | 757 | 13.3 | 6 |
| Moore | 44 | 692 | 15.7 | 6 |
| Boyer | 40 | 334 | 8.4 | 1 |
| Thomas | 20 | 204 | 10.2 | 1 |
| Mathis | 19 | 245 | 12.9 | 0 |
| F. McNeil | 16 | 230 | 14.4 | 0 |
| Burkett | 14 | 204 | 14.6 | 0 |
| Baxter | 8 | 73 | 9.1 | 0 |
| Hector | 8 | 72 | 9.0 | 0 |
| Dressel | 6 | 66 | 11.0 | 0 |
| Dawkins | 5 | 68 | 13.6 | 0 |
| Wellsandt | 5 | 57 | 11.4 | 0 |
| Townsell | 4 | 57 | 14.3 | 0 |

### PUNT RETURNS

| Last Name | No. | Yds | Avg | TD |
|---|---|---|---|---|
| Townsell | 17 | 154 | 9.1 | 0 |
| Mathis | 11 | 165 | 15.0 | 1 |
| Hasty | 1 | 0 | 0.0 | 0 |
| Odegard | 1 | 0 | 0.0 | 0 |

### KICKOFF RETURNS

| Last Name | No. | Yds | Avg | TD |
|---|---|---|---|---|
| Mathis | 43 | 787 | 18.3 | 0 |
| Townsell | 7 | 158 | 22.6 | 0 |
| Odegard | 5 | 89 | 17.8 | 0 |
| Nichols | 2 | 3 | 1.5 | 0 |
| Brown | 1 | 63 | 63.0 | 0 |
| Boyer | 1 | 14 | 14.0 | 0 |
| Duffy | 1 | 8 | 8.0 | 0 |
| Dressel | 1 | 7 | 7.0 | 0 |

### PASSING — PUNTING — KICKING

| Last Name | Att | Cmp | % | Yds | Yd/Att | TD | Int— | % | RK |
|---|---|---|---|---|---|---|---|---|---|
| O'Brien | 411 | 226 | 55.0 | 2855 | 6.95 | 13 | 10— | 2.4 | 8 |
| Eason | 28 | 13 | 46.4 | 155 | 5.54 | 0 | 1— | 3.6 | |
| Taylor | 10 | 7 | 70.0 | 49 | 4.90 | 1 | 0— | 0.0 | |
| Toon | 2 | 0 | 0.0 | 0 | 0.00 | 0 | 0— | 0.0 | |

| PUNTING | No. | Avg. |
|---|---|---|
| Prokop | 59 | 40.1 |

| KICKING | XP | ATT | % | FG | ATT | % |
|---|---|---|---|---|---|---|
| Leahy | 32 | 32 | 100 | 23 | 26 | 88 |

## NEW ENGLAND PATRIOTS

### RUSHING

| Last Name | No. | Yds | Avg | TD |
|---|---|---|---|---|
| Stephens | 212 | 808 | 3.8 | 2 |
| Allen | 63 | 237 | 3.8 | 1 |
| Adams | 28 | 111 | 4.0 | 0 |
| Perryman | 32 | 97 | 3.0 | 1 |
| Hodson | 12 | 79 | 6.6 | 0 |
| Tatupu | 16 | 56 | 3.5 | 0 |
| Overton | 5 | 8 | 1.6 | 0 |
| Wilson | 5 | 7 | 1.4 | 0 |
| Morris | 2 | 4 | 2.0 | 0 |
| Gannon | 1 | 0 | 0.0 | 0 |
| Hansen | 1 | 0 | 0.0 | 0 |
| Fryar | 2 | -4 | -2.0 | 0 |
| Grogan | 4 | -5 | -1.3 | 0 |

### RECEIVING

| Last Name | No. | Yds | Avg | TD |
|---|---|---|---|---|
| Fryar | 54 | 856 | 15.9 | 4 |
| Cook | 51 | 455 | 8.9 | 5 |
| Dykes | 34 | 549 | 16.1 | 2 |
| Stephens | 28 | 196 | 7.0 | 1 |
| McMurtry | 22 | 240 | 10.9 | 0 |
| Jones | 21 | 301 | 14.3 | 0 |
| Adams | 16 | 146 | 9.1 | 1 |
| Perryman | 15 | 88 | 5.9 | 0 |
| Sievers | 8 | 77 | 9.6 | 0 |
| Mowatt | 6 | 67 | 11.2 | 0 |
| Allen | 6 | 48 | 8.0 | 0 |
| Timpson | 5 | 91 | 18.2 | 0 |
| Martin | 4 | 65 | 16.3 | 1 |
| Overton | 2 | 19 | 9.5 | 0 |
| Tatupu | 2 | 10 | 5.0 | 0 |

### PUNT RETURNS

| Last Name | No. | Yds | Avg | TD |
|---|---|---|---|---|
| Fryar | 28 | 133 | 4.8 | 0 |
| Martin | 1 | 1 | 1.0 | 0 |

### KICKOFF RETURNS

| Last Name | No. | Yds | Avg | TD |
|---|---|---|---|---|
| Martin | 25 | 515 | 20.6 | 0 |
| Allen | 11 | 168 | 15.3 | 0 |
| Morris | 11 | 202 | 18.4 | 0 |
| Robinson | 11 | 211 | 19.2 | 0 |
| Overton | 10 | 188 | 18.8 | 0 |
| Timpson | 3 | 62 | 20.7 | 0 |
| Jones | 2 | 24 | 12.0 | 0 |
| P. Coleman | 2 | 18 | 9.0 | 0 |
| Adams | 1 | 7 | 7.0 | 0 |
| McSwain | 1 | 0 | 0.0 | 0 |

### PASSING — PUNTING — KICKING

| Last Name | Att | Cmp | % | Yds | Yd/Att | TD | Int— | % | RK |
|---|---|---|---|---|---|---|---|---|---|
| Wilson | 265 | 139 | 52.5 | 1625 | 6.13 | 6 | 11— | 4.2 | 14 |
| Hodson | 156 | 85 | 54.5 | 968 | 6.21 | 4 | 5— | 3.2 | |
| Grogan | 92 | 50 | 54.3 | 615 | 6.68 | 4 | 3— | 3.3 | |
| Stephens | 1 | 0 | 0.0 | 0 | 0.00 | 0 | 1— | 100.0 | |

| PUNTING | No. | Avg. |
|---|---|---|
| Hansen | 82 | 40.8 |

| KICKING | XP | ATT | % | FG | ATT | % |
|---|---|---|---|---|---|---|
| Staurovsky | 19 | 19 | 100 | 16 | 22 | 73 |

## CINCINNATI BENGALS 9-7 Sam Wyche

| Scores of Each Game | | |
|---|---|---|
| 25 | N.Y. JETS | 20 |
| 21 | San Diego | 16 |
| 41 | NEW ENGLAND | 7 |
| 16 | Seattle | 31 |
| 34 | L.A. Rams | * 31 |
| 17 | Houston | 48 |
| 34 | Cleveland | 13 |
| 17 | Atlanta | 38 |
| 7 | NEW ORLEANS | 21 |
| 27 | PITTSBURGH | 3 |
| 20 | INDIANAPOLIS | 34 |
| 16 | Pittsburgh | 12 |
| 17 | SAN FRANCISCO | * 20 |
| 7 | L.A. Raiders | 24 |
| 40 | HOUSTON | 20 |
| 21 | CLEVELAND | 14 |

| Use Name | Pos. | Hgt | Wgt | Age | Int | Pts |
|---|---|---|---|---|---|---|
| Mike Brennan | OT | 6'5" | 274 | 23 | | |
| Anthony Munoz | OT | 6'6" | 284 | 32 | | |
| Kirk Scrafford | OT | 6'6" | 255 | 23 | | |
| Joe Walter | OT | 6'6" | 292 | 27 | | |
| Paul Jetton | OG | 6'4" | 288 | 25 | | |
| Brian Blados | OG | 6'5" | 295 | 28 | | |
| Ken Moyer | OG | 6'6" | 297 | 23 | | |
| Bruce Reimers | OG | 6'7" | 298 | 29 | | |
| Bruce Kozerski | C | 6'4" | 287 | 28 | | |
| Jason Buck | DE-DT | 6'5" | 264 | 27 | | |
| David Grant | DE-NT | 6'4" | 278 | 24 | | |
| Mike Hammerstein | DE-DT-NT | 6'4" | 272 | 27 | | |
| Skip McClendon | DE | 6'7" | 287 | 26 | | |
| Natu Tuatagaloa | DE | 6'4" | 274 | 24 | | |
| Tim Krumrie | NT-DT | 6'2" | 274 | 30 | | |
| Leo Barker | LB | 6'2" | 227 | 30 | | |
| Ed Brady | LB | 6'2" | 235 | 30 | | |
| Bernard Clark | LB | 6'2" | 248 | 23 | | |
| James Francis | LB | 6'5" | 252 | 22 | 1 | 8 |
| Craig Ogletree | LB | 6'2" | 236 | 22 | | |
| Kevin Walker | LB | 6'2" | 238 | 24 | | |
| Leon White | LB | 6'3" | 245 | 26 | 1 | |
| Carl Zander | LB | 6'2" | 235 | 27 | | |
| Lewis Billups | DB | 5'11" | 190 | 26 | 3 | |
| Barney Bussey | DB | 6' | 195 | 28 | 4 | 6 |
| Carl Carter | DB | 5'11" | 180 | 26 | | |
| Rickey Dixon | DB | 5'11" | 181 | 23 | | |
| David Fulcher | DB | 6'3" | 228 | 28 | 4 | 2 |
| Rod Jones | DB | 6' | 185 | 26 | | |
| Mitchell Price | DB | 5'9" | 181 | 23 | 1 | 6 |
| Eric Thomas | DB | 5'11" | 181 | 25 | | |
| Solomon Wilcots | DB | 5'11" | 195 | 25 | | |
| Boomer Esiason | QB | 6'4" | 225 | 29 | | |
| Todd Philcox | QB | 6'4" | 209 | 23 | | |
| Erik Wilhelm | QB | 6'3" | 210 | 24 | | |
| Eric Ball | HB-FB | 6'2" | 211 | 24 | | 12 |
| James Brooks | HB | 5'10" | 182 | 31 | | 54 |
| Harold Green | HB | 6'2" | 222 | 22 | | 12 |
| Stanford Jennings | HB-FB | 6'1" | 205 | 28 | | 6 |
| Craig Taylor | FB | 5'11" | 224 | 24 | | 18 |
| Ickey Woods | FB | 6'2" | 232 | 24 | | 36 |
| Mike Barber | WR | 5'11" | 172 | 23 | | 6 |
| Eddie Brown | WR | 6' | 185 | 27 | | 54 |
| Lynn James | WR | 6' | 191 | 23 | | |
| Kendal Smith | WR | 5'9" | 189 | 24 | | |
| Tim McGee | WR | 5'10" | 175 | 26 | | 6 |
| Rodney Holman | TE | 6'3" | 238 | 30 | | 30 |
| Eric Kattus | TE | 6'5" | 235 | 27 | | 12 |
| Jim Riggs | TE | 6'5" | 245 | 26 | | |
| Jim Breech | K | 5'6" | 161 | 34 | | 92 |
| Lee Johnson | K | 6'2" | 198 | 28 | | |

## HOUSTON OILERS 9-7 Jack Pardee

| Scores of Each Game | | |
|---|---|---|
| 27 | Atlanta | 47 |
| 9 | Pittsburgh | 20 |
| 24 | INDIANAPOLIS | 10 |
| 17 | San Diego | 7 |
| 21 | SAN FRANCISCO | 24 |
| 48 | CINCINNATI | 17 |
| 23 | NEW ORLEANS | 10 |
| 12 | N.Y. JETS | 17 |
| 13 | L.A. Rams | 17 |
| 35 | Cleveland | 23 |
| 27 | BUFFALO | 24 |
| 10 | Seattle | * 13 |
| 58 | CLEVELAND | 14 |
| 27 | Kansas City | 10 |
| 20 | Cincinnati | 40 |
| 34 | PITTSBURGH | 14 |

| Use Name | Pos. | Hgt | Wgt | Age | Int | Pts |
|---|---|---|---|---|---|---|
| Don Maggs | OT-OG | 6'5" | 290 | 28 | | |
| Dean Steinkuhler | OT | 6'3" | 287 | 29 | | |
| David Williams | OT | 6'5" | 292 | 24 | | |
| Doug Dawson | OG-C | 6'2" | 288 | 28 | | |
| Bruce Matthews | OG-C | 6'4" | 291 | 29 | | |
| Mike Munchak | OG | 6'3" | 284 | 30 | | |
| Erik Norgard | C-OG | 6'1" | 278 | 24 | | |
| Jay Pennison | C | 6'1" | 274 | 28 | | |
| William Fuller | DE | 6'3" | 265 | 28 | | |
| Sean Jones | DE | 6'7" | 264 | 27 | | |
| Willis Peguese | DE | 6'4" | 267 | 23 | | |
| Jeff Alm | DT | 6'6" | 269 | 22 | | |
| Ray Childress | DT-DE | 6'6" | 272 | 27 | | 2 |
| Ezra Johnson | DT-DE | 6'4" | 257 | 34 | | |
| Glenn Montgomery | DT | 6' | 268 | 23 | | |
| Doug Smith | DT | 6'5" | 314 | 31 | | |
| Eric Fairs | LB | 6'3" | 244 | 26 | | |
| John Grimsley | LB | 6'2" | 238 | 28 | | |
| Scott Kozak | LB | 6'3" | 222 | 24 | | |
| Lamar Lathon | LB | 6'3" | 244 | 22 | | |
| Johnny Meads | LB | 6'2" | 226 | 29 | 1 | |
| Eugene Seale | LB | 5'10" | 253 | 26 | | |
| Al Smith | LB | 6'1" | 244 | 25 | | |
| Patrick Allen | DB | 5'10" | 182 | 29 | 1 | |
| Steve Brown | DB | 5'11" | 190 | 30 | | |
| Cris Dishman | DB | 6' | 180 | 25 | 4 | |
| Richard Johnson | DB | 6'1" | 195 | 26 | 8 | 6 |
| Quintin Jones | DB | 5'11" | 193 | 24 | | |
| Terry Kinard | DB | 6'1" | 198 | 30 | 4 | |
| Leander Knight | DB | 6'1" | 192 | 27 | 1 | |
| Bubba McDowell | DB | 6'1" | 195 | 23 | 2 | |
| Bo Orlando | DB | 5'10" | 180 | 24 | | |
| Dee Thomas | DB | 5'10" | 176 | 22 | | |
| Cody Carlson | QB | 6'3" | 199 | 26 | | |
| Warren Moon | QB | 6'3" | 210 | 33 | | 12 |
| Reggie Slack | QB | 6'1" | 221 | 22 | | |
| Victor Jones | HB-FB | 5'8" | 212 | 22 | | |
| Allen Pinkett | HB | 5'9" | 192 | 26 | | |
| Lorenzo White | HB | 5'11" | 209 | 24 | | 72 |
| Curtis Duncan | WR | 5'11" | 184 | 25 | | 6 |
| Bernard Ford | WR | 5'9" | 171 | 24 | | 6 |
| Ernest Givins | WR | 5'9" | 172 | 25 | | 54 |
| Leonard Harris | WR | 5'8" | 162 | 29 | | 18 |
| Drew Hill | WR | 5'9" | 172 | 33 | | 30 |
| Haywood Jeffires | WR | 6'2" | 201 | 25 | | 48 |
| Tony Jones | WR | 5'7" | 139 | 24 | | 36 |
| Gerald McNeil | WR | 5'7" | 142 | 28 | | |
| Teddy Garcia | K | 5'10" | 172 | 26 | | 68 |
| Greg Montgomery | K | 6'3" | 213 | 25 | | |
| Tony Zendejas | K | 5'8" | 165 | 30 | | 41 |

## PITTSBURGH STEELERS 9-7 Chuck Noll

| Scores of Each Game | | |
|---|---|---|
| 3 | Cleveland | 13 |
| 20 | HOUSTON | 9 |
| 3 | L.A. Raiders | 20 |
| 6 | MIAMI | 28 |
| 36 | SAN DIEGO | 14 |
| 34 | Denver | 17 |
| 7 | San Francisco | 27 |
| 41 | L.A. RAMS | 10 |
| 21 | ATLANTA | 9 |
| 3 | Cincinnati | 27 |
| 24 | N.Y. Jets | 7 |
| 12 | CINCINNATI | 16 |
| 24 | NEW ENGLAND | 3 |
| 9 | New Orleans | 6 |
| 35 | CLEVELAND | 0 |
| 14 | Houston | 34 |

| Use Name | Pos. | Hgt | Wgt | Age | Int | Pts |
|---|---|---|---|---|---|---|
| Tunch Ilkin | OT | 6'3" | 274 | 32 | | |
| John Jackson | OT | 6'6" | 290 | 25 | | |
| Tom Ricketts | OT-OG | 6'5" | 293 | 24 | | |
| Justin Strzelczyk | OT | 6'5" | 291 | 22 | | |
| Brian Blankenship | OG-C | 6'1" | 280 | 27 | | |
| Calton Haselrig | OG | 6'1" | 291 | 24 | | |
| Terry Long | OG | 5'11" | 278 | 31 | | |
| John Rienstra | OG | 6'5" | 272 | 27 | | |
| Dermontti Dawson | C | 6'2" | 279 | 25 | | |
| Kenny Davidson | DE | 6'5" | 272 | 23 | | |
| Donald Evans | DE | 6'2" | 265 | 26 | | |
| Aaron Jones | DE | 6'5" | 269 | 24 | 1 | |
| Keith Willis | DE | 6'1" | 263 | 31 | 1 | |
| Lorenzo Freeman | NT | 6'5" | 319 | 26 | | |
| Craig Veasey | NT-DE | 6'2" | 280 | 23 | | |
| Gerald Williams | NT | 6'3" | 291 | 26 | | |
| Bryan Hinkle | LB | 6'2" | 222 | 31 | 1 | |
| A.J. Jenkins | LB-DE | 6'2" | 237 | 24 | | |
| David Little | LB | 6'1" | 236 | 31 | 1 | |
| Greg Lloyd | LB | 6'2" | 224 | 25 | 1 | |
| Eddie Miles | B | 6'1" | 233 | 21 | | |
| Hardy Nickerson | LB | 6'2" | 229 | 25 | | |
| Jerry Olsavsky | LB | 6'1" | 222 | 23 | | |
| Tyronne Stowe | LB | 6'1" | 236 | 25 | | 2 |
| Jerrol Williams | LB | 6'5" | 242 | 22 | | |
| Thomas Everett | DB | 5'9" | 179 | 25 | 3 | |
| Larry Griffin | DB | 6' | 200 | 27 | 4 | |
| Delton Hall | DB | 6'1" | 205 | 25 | 1 | |
| David Johnson | DB | 6' | 185 | 24 | 2 | 6 |
| Gary Jones | DB | 6'1" | 203 | 22 | | |
| Carnell Lake | DB | 6'1" | 205 | 23 | 1 | |
| Richard Shelton | DB | 5'10" | 180 | 24 | | |
| Dwayne Woodruff | DB | 6' | 198 | 33 | 3 | |
| Rod Woodson | DB | 6' | 199 | 25 | 5 | 6 |
| Bubby Brister | QB | 6'3" | 208 | 28 | | |
| Neil O'Donnell | QB | 6'3" | 221 | 24 | | |
| Rick Strom | QB | 6'2" | 210 | 25 | | |
| Richard Bell | HB | 6' | 200 | 23 | | 6 |
| Barry Foster | HB | 5'10" | 223 | 21 | | 6 |
| Warren Williams | HB | 6' | 202 | 25 | | 24 |
| Tim Worley | HB | 6'2" | 228 | 23 | | |
| Merril Hoge | FB | 6'2" | 226 | 25 | | 60 |
| Chris Calloway | WR | 5'10" | 185 | 22 | | 6 |
| Lorenzo Davis | WR | 5'11" | 185 | 22 | | |
| Derek Hill | WR | 6'1" | 193 | 22 | | |
| Louis Lipps | WR | 5'10" | 190 | 28 | | 18 |
| Dwight Stone | WR-HB | 6' | 188 | 26 | | 6 |
| Eric Green | TE | 6'5" | 274 | 23 | | 42 |
| Mike Mularkey | TE | 6'4" | 237 | 28 | | 18 |
| Terry O'Shea | TE | 6'4" | 236 | 23 | | |
| Gary Anderson | K | 5'11" | 184 | 31 | | 92 |
| Dan Stryzinski | K | 6'1" | 193 | 25 | | |

Chuck Lanza — Triceps Injury

## CLEVELAND BROWNS 3-13 Bud Carson (2-7), Jim Shofner (1-6)

| Scores of Each Game | | |
|---|---|---|
| 13 | PITTSBURGH | 3 |
| 21 | N.Y. Jets | 24 |
| 14 | SAN DIEGO | 24 |
| 0 | Kansas City | 34 |
| 30 | Denver | 29 |
| 20 | New Orleans | 25 |
| 13 | CINCINNATI | 34 |
| 17 | San Francisco | 20 |
| 0 | BUFFALO | 42 |
| 23 | HOUSTON | 35 |
| 13 | MIAMI | 30 |
| 23 | L.A. RAMS | 38 |
| 14 | Houston | 58 |
| 13 | ATLANTA | 10 |
| 0 | Pittsburgh | 35 |
| 14 | Cincinnati | 21 |

| Use Name | Pos. | Hgt | Wgt | Age | Int | Pts |
|---|---|---|---|---|---|---|
| Paul Farren | OT | 6'5" | 270 | 29 | | |
| Tony Jones | OT | 6'5" | 290 | 24 | | |
| Ken Reeves | OT | 6'5" | 277 | 28 | | |
| Dan Fike | OG | 6'7" | 285 | 29 | | |
| Ben Jefferson | OG | 6'9" | 330 | 24 | | |
| Gregg Rakoczy | OG | 6'6" | 295 | 25 | | |
| Kevin Robbins | OG | 6'6" | 295 | 23 | | |
| Ralph Tamm | OG | 6'4" | 280 | 24 | | |
| Mike Baab | C | 6'4" | 275 | 30 | | |
| Michael Morris (from SEA) | C | 6'5" | 285 | 29 | | |
| Al Baker | DE | 6'6" | 260 | 33 | | |
| Robert Banks | DE | 6'5" | 255 | 26 | | |
| Rob Burnett | DE | 6'4" | 270 | 23 | | |
| Bob Buczkowski | DT | 6'5" | 260 | 26 | | |
| Tom Gibson | DT-DE | 6'7" | 270 | 26 | | |
| Anthony Pleasant | DE | 6'5" | 258 | 23 | | |
| Michael Dean Perry | DT-DE | 6'1" | 285 | 24 | | |
| Chris Pike | DT | 6'8" | 300 | 26 | | |
| David Grayson | LB | 6'2" | 230 | 26 | 1 | |
| Eddie Johnson | LB | 6'1" | 225 | 30 | | |
| Mike Johnson | LB | 6'1" | 225 | 27 | 1 | 6 |
| Jock Jones | LB | 6'2" | 230 | 22 | | |
| Clay Matthews | LB | 6'2" | 245 | 34 | | |
| Van Waiters | LB | 6'4" | 240 | 25 | 1 | |
| Stefon Adams (to MIA) | DB | 5'10" | 190 | 27 | | |
| Harlon Barnett | DB | 5'11" | 200 | 23 | | |
| Tony Blaylock | DB | 5'11" | 190 | 25 | 2 | 6 |
| Keith Bostic | DB | 6'1" | 223 | 29 | | |
| Stephen Braggs | DB | 5'10" | 180 | 25 | 2 | |
| Raymond Clayborn | DB | 6' | 190 | 35 | | |
| Thane Gash | DB | 6' | 200 | 25 | 1 | |
| Mark Harper | DB | 5'9" | 185 | 28 | | |
| Randy Hilliard | DB | 5'11" | 160 | 23 | | |
| Frank Minnifield | DB | 5'9" | 185 | 30 | 2 | |
| Felix Wright | DB | 6'2" | 190 | 31 | 3 | |
| Jeff Francis | QB | 6'4" | 225 | 24 | | |
| Bernie Kosar | QB | 6'5" | 210 | 26 | | |
| Mike Pagel | QB | 6'2" | 211 | 29 | | |
| Eric Metcalf | HB-WR | 5'10" | 185 | 22 | | 24 |
| Derrick Gainer | FB | 5'11" | 235 | 24 | | 6 |
| Leroy Hoard | FB-HB | 5'11" | 230 | 22 | | 18 |
| Kevin Mack | FB | 6' | 235 | 28 | | 42 |
| Barry Redden | FB-HB | 5'10" | 219 | 30 | | |
| Brian Brennan | WR | 5'9" | 178 | 28 | | 12 |
| Vernon Joines | WR | 6'2" | 200 | 24 | | |
| Reggie Langhorne | WR | 6'2" | 200 | 27 | | 12 |
| Eugene Rowell | WR | 6'1" | 180 | 22 | | |
| Webster Slaughter | WR | 6' | 170 | 25 | | 24 |
| Scott Galbraith | TE | 6'3" | 260 | 23 | | |
| Ozzie Newsome | TE | 6'2" | 232 | 34 | | 12 |
| John Talley | TE | 6'5" | 245 | 25 | | |
| Jerry Kauric | K | 6' | 210 | 27 | | 66 |
| Bryan Wagner | K | 6'2" | 200 | 28 | | |

Ted Banker — Knee Injury
Marlon Jones — Broken Foot
Rhony Weston — Knee Injury

Kyle Kramer — Shoulder Injury
Tom Manoa — Elbow Injury
Mike Oliphant — Hamstring Injury
Lawyer Tillman — Leg Injury

## CINCINNATI BENGALS

### RUSHING

| Last Name | No. | Yds | Avg | TD |
|---|---|---|---|---|
| Brooks | 195 | 1004 | 5.1 | 5 |
| Green | 83 | 353 | 4.3 | 1 |
| Woods | 64 | 268 | 4.2 | 6 |
| Taylor | 51 | 216 | 4.2 | 2 |
| Esiason | 50 | 157 | 3.1 | 0 |
| Ball | 22 | 72 | 3.3 | 1 |
| Jennings | 12 | 46 | 3.8 | 0 |
| James | 1 | 11 | 11.0 | 0 |
| Wilhelm | 6 | 6 | 1.0 | 0 |
| Barber | 1 | -13 | -13.0 | 0 |

### RECEIVING

| Last Name | No. | Yds | Avg | TD |
|---|---|---|---|---|
| Brown | 44 | 706 | 16.0 | 9 |
| McGee | 43 | 737 | 17.1 | 1 |
| Holman | 40 | 596 | 14.9 | 5 |
| Brooks | 26 | 269 | 10.3 | 4 |
| Woods | 20 | 162 | 8.1 | 0 |
| Barber | 14 | 196 | 14.0 | 1 |
| Green | 12 | 90 | 7.5 | 1 |
| Kattus | 11 | 145 | 13.2 | 2 |
| Riggs | 8 | 79 | 9.9 | 0 |
| Smith | 7 | 45 | 6.4 | 0 |
| Jennings | 4 | 23 | 5.8 | 0 |
| James | 3 | 36 | 12.0 | 0 |
| Taylor | 3 | 22 | 7.3 | 1 |
| Ball | 2 | 46 | 23.0 | 1 |

### PUNT RETURNS

| Last Name | No. | Yds | Avg | TD |
|---|---|---|---|---|
| Price | 29 | 251 | 8.7 | 1 |
| Smith | 1 | 4 | 4.0 | 0 |

### KICKOFF RETURNS

| Last Name | No. | Yds | Avg | TD |
|---|---|---|---|---|
| Jennings | 29 | 584 | 20.1 | 0 |
| Ball | 16 | 366 | 22.9 | 0 |
| Price | 10 | 191 | 19.1 | 0 |
| Smith | 2 | 35 | 17.5 | 0 |
| James | 1 | 43 | 43.0 | 0 |
| Taylor | 1 | 16 | 16.0 | 0 |
| Barber | 1 | 14 | 14.0 | 0 |
| Kattus | 1 | 10 | 10.0 | 0 |
| Riggs | 1 | 7 | 7.0 | 0 |

### PASSING — PUNTING — KICKING Statistics

PASSING

| Last Name | Att | Cmp | % | Yds | Yd/Att | TD | Int | — % | RK |
|---|---|---|---|---|---|---|---|---|---|
| Esiason | 402 | 224 | 55.7 | 3031 | 7.54 | 24 | 22 | -5.5 | 9 |
| Wilhelm | 19 | 12 | 63.2 | 117 | 6.16 | 0 | 0 | -0.0 | |
| Philcox | 2 | 0 | 0.0 | 0 | 0.00 | 0 | 1 | -50.0 | |
| Johnson | 1 | 1 | 100.0 | 4 | 4.00 | 1 | 0 | -0.0 | |
| James | 1 | 0 | 0.0 | 0 | 0.00 | 0 | 0 | -0.0 | |

PUNTING

| Last Name | No. | Avg. |
|---|---|---|
| Johnson | 64 | 42.3 |
| Breech | 1 | 34.0 |

KICKING

| Last Name | XP | ATT | % | FG | ATT | % |
|---|---|---|---|---|---|---|
| Breech | 41 | 44 | 93 | 17 | 21 | 81 |
| Johnson | 0 | 0 | 0 | 0 | 1 | 0 |

## HOUSTON OILERS

### RUSHING

| Last Name | No. | Yds | Avg | TD |
|---|---|---|---|---|
| L. White | 168 | 702 | 4.2 | 8 |
| Pinkett | 66 | 268 | 4.1 | 0 |
| Moon | 55 | 215 | 3.9 | 2 |
| V. Jones | 14 | 75 | 5.4 | 0 |
| Givins | 3 | 65 | 21.7 | 0 |
| Carlson | 11 | 52 | 4.7 | 0 |
| T. Jones | 1 | -2 | -2.0 | 0 |

### RECEIVING

| Last Name | No. | Yds | Avg | TD |
|---|---|---|---|---|
| Jeffires | 74 | 1048 | 14.2 | 8 |
| Hill | 74 | 1019 | 13.8 | 5 |
| Givins | 72 | 979 | 13.6 | 9 |
| Duncan | 66 | 785 | 11.9 | 1 |
| White | 39 | 368 | 9.4 | 4 |
| T. Jones | 30 | 409 | 13.6 | 6 |
| Harris | 13 | 172 | 13.2 | 3 |
| Pinkett | 11 | 85 | 7.7 | 0 |
| Ford | 10 | 98 | 9.8 | 1 |
| McNeil | 5 | 63 | 12.6 | 0 |

### PUNT RETURNS

| Last Name | No. | Yds | Avg | TD |
|---|---|---|---|---|
| McNeil | 30 | 172 | 5.7 | 0 |
| Duncan | 0 | 0 | 0.0 | 0 |

### KICKOFF RETURNS

| Last Name | No. | Yds | Avg | TD |
|---|---|---|---|---|
| McNeil | 27 | 551 | 20.4 | 0 |
| Ford | 14 | 219 | 15.6 | 0 |
| Pinkett | 4 | 91 | 22.8 | 0 |
| Norgard | 2 | 0 | 0.0 | 0 |

### PASSING — PUNTING — KICKING Statistics

PASSING

| Last Name | Att | Cmp | % | Yds | Yd/Att | TD | Int | — % | RK |
|---|---|---|---|---|---|---|---|---|---|
| Moon | 584 | 362 | 62.0 | 4689 | 8.03 | 33 | 13 | -2.2 | 2 |
| Carlson | 55 | 37 | 67.3 | 383 | 6.96 | 4 | 2 | -3.6 | |

PUNTING

| Last Name | No. | Avg. |
|---|---|---|
| Montgomery | 34 | 45.0 |

KICKING

| Last Name | XP | ATT | % | FG | ATT | % |
|---|---|---|---|---|---|---|
| Zendejas | 20 | 21 | 95 | 7 | 12 | 58 |
| Garcia | 26 | 28 | 93 | 14 | 20 | 70 |

## PITTSBURGH STEELERS

### RUSHING

| Last Name | No. | Yds | Avg | TD |
|---|---|---|---|---|
| Hoge | 203 | 772 | 3.8 | 7 |
| Worley | 109 | 418 | 3.8 | 0 |
| W. Williams | 68 | 389 | 5.7 | 3 |
| Foster | 36 | 203 | 5.6 | 1 |
| Brister | 25 | 64 | 2.6 | 0 |
| Bell | 5 | 18 | 3.6 | 0 |
| Stryzinski | 3 | 17 | 5.7 | 0 |
| Strom | 4 | 10 | 2.5 | 0 |
| Lipps | 1 | -5 | -5.0 | 0 |
| Stone | 2 | -6 | -3.0 | 0 |

### RECEIVING

| Last Name | No. | Yds | Avg | TD |
|---|---|---|---|---|
| Lipps | 50 | 682 | 13.6 | 3 |
| Hoge | 40 | 342 | 8.6 | 3 |
| Green | 34 | 387 | 11.4 | 3 |
| Mularkey | 32 | 365 | 11.4 | 3 |
| Hill | 25 | 391 | 15.6 | 0 |
| Stone | 19 | 332 | 17.5 | 1 |
| Bell | 12 | 137 | 11.4 | 1 |
| Calloway | 10 | 124 | 12.4 | 1 |
| Worley | 8 | 70 | 8.8 | 0 |
| W. Williams | 5 | 42 | 8.4 | 1 |
| O'Shea | 1 | 13 | 13.0 | 0 |
| Foster | 1 | 2 | 2.0 | 0 |

### PUNT RETURNS

| Last Name | No. | Yds | Avg | TD |
|---|---|---|---|---|
| Woodson | 38 | 398 | 10.5 | 1 |
| Hill | 1 | 0 | 0.0 | 0 |

### KICKOFF RETURNS

| Last Name | No. | Yds | Avg | TD |
|---|---|---|---|---|
| Woodson | 35 | 764 | 21.8 | 0 |
| Stone | 5 | 91 | 18.2 | 0 |
| Foster | 3 | 29 | 9.7 | 0 |
| J. Williams | 3 | 31 | 10.3 | 0 |
| Griffin | 2 | 16 | 8.0 | 0 |
| Green | 1 | 16 | 16.0 | 0 |
| Lipps | 1 | 9 | 9.0 | 0 |

### PASSING — PUNTING — KICKING Statistics

PASSING

| Last Name | Att | Cmp | % | Yds | Yd/Att | TD | Int | — % | RK |
|---|---|---|---|---|---|---|---|---|---|
| Brister | 387 | 223 | 57.6 | 2725 | 7.04 | 20 | 14 | -3.6 | 6 |
| Strom | 21 | 14 | 66.7 | 162 | 7.71 | 0 | 1 | -4.8 | |

PUNTING

| Last Name | No. | Avg. |
|---|---|---|
| Stryzinski | 66 | 37.2 |

KICKING

| Last Name | XP | ATT | % | FG | ATT | % |
|---|---|---|---|---|---|---|
| Anderson | 32 | 32 | 100 | 20 | 25 | 80 |

## CLEVELAND BROWNS

### RUSHING

| Last Name | No. | Yds | Avg | TD |
|---|---|---|---|---|
| Mack | 158 | 702 | 4.4 | 5 |
| Metcalf | 80 | 248 | 3.1 | 1 |
| Hoard | 58 | 149 | 2.6 | 3 |
| Gainer | 30 | 81 | 2.7 | 1 |
| Slaughter | 5 | 29 | 5.8 | 0 |
| Kosar | 10 | 13 | 1.3 | 0 |
| Redden | 1 | -1 | -1.0 | 0 |
| Pagel | 3 | -1 | -0.3 | 0 |

### RECEIVING

| Last Name | No. | Yds | Avg | TD |
|---|---|---|---|---|
| Slaughter | 59 | 847 | 14.4 | 4 |
| Metcalf | 57 | 452 | 7.9 | 1 |
| Langhorne | 45 | 585 | 13.0 | 2 |
| Brennan | 45 | 568 | 12.6 | 2 |
| Mack | 42 | 360 | 8.6 | 2 |
| Newsome | 23 | 240 | 10.4 | 2 |
| Hoard | 10 | 73 | 7.3 | 0 |
| Gainer | 7 | 85 | 12.1 | 0 |
| Joines | 6 | 86 | 14.3 | 0 |
| Galbraith | 4 | 62 | 15.5 | 0 |
| Talley | 2 | 28 | 14.0 | 0 |
| Kauric | 1 | 21 | 21.0 | 0 |

### PUNT RETURNS

| Last Name | No. | Yds | Avg | TD |
|---|---|---|---|---|
| Adams | 13 | 81 | 6.2 | 0 |
| Brennan | 9 | 72 | 8.0 | 0 |
| Lewis | 8 | 56 | 7.0 | 0 |
| Waiters | 1 | 0 | 0.0 | 0 |

### KICKOFF RETURNS

| Last Name | No. | Yds | Avg | TD |
|---|---|---|---|---|
| Metcalf | 52 | 1052 | 20.2 | 2 |
| Adams | 3 | 33 | 11.0 | 0 |
| Galbraith | 3 | 16 | 5.3 | 0 |
| Hoard | 2 | 18 | 9.0 | 0 |
| E. Johnson | 2 | 17 | 8.5 | 0 |
| Barnett | 1 | 15 | 15.0 | 0 |
| Talley | 1 | 6 | 6.0 | 0 |
| Gainer | 1 | 0 | 0.0 | 0 |

### PASSING — PUNTING — KICKING Statistics

PASSING

| Last Name | Att | Cmp | % | Yds | Yd/Att | TD | Int | — % | RK |
|---|---|---|---|---|---|---|---|---|---|
| Kosar | 423 | 230 | 54.4 | 2562 | 6.06 | 10 | 15 | -3.5 | 13 |
| Pagel | 148 | 69 | 46.6 | 819 | 5.53 | 3 | 8 | -5.4 | |
| Francis | 2 | 2 | 100.0 | 26 | 13.00 | 0 | 0 | -0.0 | |

PUNTING

| Last Name | No. | Avg. |
|---|---|---|
| Wagner | 78 | 36.9 |

KICKING

| Last Name | XP | ATT | % | FG | ATT | % |
|---|---|---|---|---|---|---|
| Kauric | 24 | 27 | 89 | 14 | 20 | 70 |

## LOS ANGELES RAIDERS 12-4 Art Shell

| Scores of Each Game | | |
|---|---|---|
| 14 | DENVER | 9 |
| 17 | Seattle | 13 |
| 20 | PITTSBURGH | 3 |
| 24 | CHICAGO | 10 |
| 24 | Buffalo | 38 |
| 24 | SEATTLE | 17 |
| 24 | San Diego | 9 |
| 7 | Kansas City | 9 |
| 16 | GREEN BAY | 29 |
| 13 | Miami | 10 |
| 24 | KANSAS CITY | 27 |
| 23 | Denver | 20 |
| 38 | Detroit | 31 |
| 24 | CINCINNATI | 7 |
| 28 | Minnesota | 24 |
| 17 | SAN DIEGO | 12 |

| Use Name | Pos. | Hgt | Wgt | Age | Int | Pts |
|---|---|---|---|---|---|---|
| James FitzPatrick | OT | 6'8" | 310 | 26 | | |
| Rory Graves | OT | 6'6" | 295 | 27 | | |
| Tim Rother | OT | 6'7" | 285 | 24 | | |
| Bruce Wilkerson | OT | 6'5" | 295 | 26 | | |
| Steve Wright | OT-TE | 6'6" | 280 | 31 | | |
| Max Montoya | OG | 6'5" | 290 | 34 | | |
| Todd Peat | OG | 6'2" | 315 | 26 | | |
| Steve Wisniewski | OG | 6'4" | 280 | 26 | | |
| Don Mosebar | C | 6'6" | 280 | 28 | | |
| Dan Turk | C | 6'4" | 275 | 28 | | |
| Howie Long | DE-DT | 6'5" | 270 | 30 | | |
| Greg Townsend | DE | 6'3" | 250 | 28 | 1 | 6 |
| Mike Wise | DE | 6'7" | 270 | 26 | | |
| Mike Charles | DT | 6'4" | 287 | 27 | | |
| Scott Davis | DT-DE | 6'7" | 270 | 25 | | |
| Bob Golic | DT | 6'2" | 275 | 32 | | |
| Bill Pickel | DT | 6'5" | 260 | 30 | | |
| Thomas Benson | LB | 6'2" | 240 | 28 | | |
| Ron Burton | LB | 6'1" | 245 | 26 | | |
| Riki Ellison | LB | 6'2" | 230 | 30 | 1 | |
| Alex Gordon | LB | 6'5" | 245 | 25 | | |
| Ricky Hunley | LB | 6'2" | 250 | 29 | | |
| A.J. Jimerson | LB | 6'2" | 230 | 22 | | |
| Jerry Robinson | LB | 6'2" | 230 | 33 | 1 | 6 |
| Aaron Wallace | LB | 6'3" | 230 | 23 | | |
| Eddie Anderson | DB | 6'1" | 205 | 27 | 3 | |
| Ron Brown | DB | 5'11" | 190 | 29 | | |
| Torin Dorn | DB | 6' | 190 | 22 | | |
| Mike Harden | DB | 6'1" | 195 | 31 | 3 | |
| Dan Land | DB | 6' | 190 | 25 | | |
| Garry Lewis | DB | 5'11" | 185 | 23 | | |
| Terry McDaniel | DB | 5'10" | 175 | 25 | 3 | 6 |
| Elvis Patterson | DB | 5'11" | 195 | 29 | | |
| Lionel Washington | DB | 6' | 185 | 29 | 1 | |
| Steve Beuerlein | QB | 6'2" | 205 | 25 | | |
| Vince Evans | QB | 6'2" | 205 | 35 | | |
| Jay Schroeder | QB | 6'4" | 215 | 29 | | |
| Marcus Allen | HB | 6'2' | 205 | 31 | | 78 |
| Greg Bell | HB | 5'10" | 210 | 28 | | 6 |
| Bo Jackson | HB | 6'1" | 225 | 27 | | 30 |
| Napoleon McCallum | HB | 6'2" | 220 | 26 | | |
| Vance Mueller | FB | 6' | 215 | 26 | | |
| Steve Smith | FB | 6'1" | 230 | 26 | | 30 |
| Tim Brown | WR | 6' | 195 | 24 | | 18 |
| Mervyn Fernandez | WR | 6'3" | 200 | 30 | | 30 |
| Willie Gault | WR | 6' | 180 | 29 | | 18 |
| Sam Graddy | WR | 5'10" | 175 | 26 | | 6 |
| Jamie Holland | WR | 6'2" | 195 | 26 | | |
| Rich Bartlewski | TE | 6'5" | 250 | 23 | | |
| Mike Dyal | TE | 6'2" | 240 | 24 | | |
| Ethan Horton | TE | 6'4" | 240 | 27 | | 18 |
| Andy Parker | TE | 6'5" | 245 | 28 | | |
| Jeff Gossett | K | 6'2" | 195 | 33 | | |
| Jeff Jaeger | K | 5'11" | 195 | 25 | | 85 |

Mike Alexander — Knee Injury

## KANSAS CITY CHIEFS 11-5 Marty Schottenheimer

| Scores of Each Game | | |
|---|---|---|
| 24 | MINNESOTA | 21 |
| 23 | Denver | 24 |
| 17 | Green Bay | 3 |
| 34 | CLEVELAND | 0 |
| 19 | Indianapolis | 23 |
| 43 | DETROIT | 24 |
| 7 | Seattle | 19 |
| 9 | L.A. RAIDERS | 7 |
| 16 | SEATTLE | 17 |
| 27 | SAN DIEGO | 10 |
| 27 | L.A. Raiders | 24 |
| 37 | New England | 7 |
| 31 | DENVER | 20 |
| 10 | HOUSTON | 27 |
| 24 | San Diego | 21 |
| 21 | Chicago | 10 |

| Use Name | Pos. | Hgt | Wgt | Age | Int | Pts |
|---|---|---|---|---|---|---|
| John Alt | OT | 6'7" | 296 | 28 | | |
| Rich Baldinger | OT | 6'4" | 291 | 30 | | |
| Irv Eatman | OT | 6'7" | 295 | 29 | | |
| Derrick Graham | OT | 6'4" | 306 | 23 | | |
| David Lutz | OG | 6'6" | 305 | 30 | | |
| David Szott | OG | 6'4" | 278 | 22 | | |
| Frank Winters | OG-C | 6'3" | 285 | 26 | | |
| Tim Grunhard | C | 6'2" | 302 | 22 | | |
| Mike Webster | C | 6'1" | 260 | 38 | | |
| Mike Bell | DE | 6'4" | 266 | 32 | | |
| Leonard Griffin | DE | 6'4" | 275 | 27 | | |
| Neil Smith | DE | 6'4" | 275 | 24 | | |
| Greg Meisner | DE-NT | 6'3" | 271 | 31 | | |
| Bill Maas | DE-NT | 6'5" | 270 | 28 | | 2 |
| Dan Saleaumua | NT | 6' | 285 | 24 | | 6 |
| Louis Cooper | LB | 6'2" | 245 | 26 | | |
| Dino Hackett | LB | 6'3" | 230 | 26 | | |
| Chris Martin | LB | 6'2" | 231 | 29 | | 6 |
| Rob McGovern | LB | 6'2" | 223 | 24 | | |
| Tracy Rogers | LB | 6'2" | 241 | 23 | | |
| Percy Snow | LB | 6'2" | 248 | 22 | 1 | |
| Derrick Thomas | LB | 6'3" | 244 | 23 | | |
| Lloyd Burruss | DB | 6' | 205 | 32 | 1 | |
| Deron Cherry | DB | 5'11" | 203 | 30 | 3 | |
| Danny Copeland | DB | 6'2" | 210 | 24 | | |
| Jeff Donaldson | DB | 6' | 188 | 28 | 3 | |
| Albert Lewis | DB | 6'2" | 198 | 29 | 2 | |
| J.C. Pearson | DB | 5'11" | 190 | 27 | 1 | |
| Stan Petry | DB | 5'11" | 175 | 24 | 3 | 6 |
| Kevin Porter | DB | 5'10" | 215 | 24 | 1 | |
| Kevin Ross | DB | 5'9" | 182 | 28 | 5 | 6 |
| Charles Washington | 6'1" | 210 | 23 | | | |
| Steve DeBerg | QB | 6'2" | 210 | 36 | | |
| Mike Elkins | QB | 6'3" | 225 | 24 | | |
| Steve Pelluer | QB | 6'4" | 212 | 28 | | |
| Kenny Gamble | HB | 5'10" | 197 | 25 | | |
| Bill Jones | HB | 5'11" | 228 | 23 | | 30 |
| Todd McNair | HB | 6'1" | 185 | 25 | | 12 |
| Barry Word | HB | 6'2" | 240 | 26 | | 24 |
| Christian Okoye | FB | 6'1" | 253 | 29 | | 42 |
| James Saxon | FB-HB | 5'11" | 215 | 24 | | |
| J.J. Birden | WR | 5'9" | 160 | 25 | | 18 |
| Emile Harry | WR | 5'11" | 188 | 27 | | 12 |
| Fred Jones | WR | 5'9" | 175 | 23 | | |
| Pete Mandley | WR | 5'10" | 195 | 29 | | |
| Stephone Paige | WR | 6'2" | 185 | 28 | | 30 |
| Robb Thomas | WR | 5'11" | 171 | 24 | | 24 |
| Naz Worthen | WR | 5'8" | 177 | 24 | | |
| Jonathan Hayes | TE | 6'5" | 239 | 27 | | 6 |
| Alfredo Roberts | TE | 6'3" | 250 | 25 | | |
| Danta Whitaker | TE | 6'4" | 248 | 26 | | 6 |
| Bryan Barker | K | 6'1" | 187 | 26 | | |
| Nick Lowery | K | 6'4" | 189 | 34 | | 139 |

## SEATTLE SEAHAWKS 9-7 Chuck Knox

| Scores of Each Game | | |
|---|---|---|
| 0 | Chicago | 17 |
| 13 | L.A. RAIDERS | 17 |
| 31 | Denver | * 34 |
| 31 | CINCINNATI | 16 |
| 33 | New England | 20 |
| 17 | L.A. Raiders | 24 |
| 19 | KANSAS CITY | 7 |
| 14 | SAN DIEGO | 31 |
| 17 | Kansas City | 16 |
| 21 | MINNESOTA | 24 |
| 13 | San Diego | * 10 |
| 13 | HOUSTON | * 10 |
| 20 | Green Bay | 14 |
| 17 | Miami | 24 |
| 17 | DENVER | 12 |
| 30 | DETROIT | 10 |

| Use Name | Pos. | Hgt | Wgt | Age | Int | Pts |
|---|---|---|---|---|---|---|
| Andy Heck | OT | 6'6" | 286 | 23 | | |
| Ronnie Lee | OT | 6'3" | 295 | 33 | | |
| Ron Mattes | OT | 6'6" | 302 | 27 | | |
| Edwin Bailey | OG | 6'4" | 279 | 31 | | |
| Darrick Brilz | OG | 6'3" | 281 | 26 | | |
| Bryan Millard | OG | 6'5" | 277 | 29 | | |
| Joe Tofflemire | C | 6'2" | 273 | 25 | | |
| Grant Feasel | C | 6'7" | 279 | 30 | | |
| Jeff Bryant | DT-DE | 6'5" | 281 | 30 | | |
| Jacob Green | DE | 6'3" | 256 | 33 | | |
| Eric Hayes | DT | 6'3" | 297 | 22 | | |
| Cortez Kennedy | DT | 6'3" | 293 | 22 | | |
| Joe Nash | DT | 6'2" | 278 | 29 | | |
| Dave Ahrens | LB | 6'4" | 247 | 31 | | |
| Ricky Andrews | LB | 6'2" | 236 | 24 | | |
| Ned Bolcar | LB | 6'1" | 245 | 23 | 1 | |
| Joe Cain | LB | 6'1" | 228 | 25 | | |
| Darren Comeaux | LB | 6'1" | 227 | 30 | | |
| Donald Miller | LB | 6'2" | 223 | 26 | | |
| Richard Newbill (from MIN) | LB | 6'1" | 240 | 22 | | |
| Rufus Porter | LB | 6'1" | 207 | 25 | | |
| Rod Stephens | LB | 6'1" | 237 | 24 | | |
| Terry Wooden | LB | 6'3" | 232 | 23 | | |
| Tony Woods | LB | 6'4" | 244 | 24 | | |
| David Wyman | LB | 6'2" | 234 | 26 | 1 | |
| Robert Blackmon | DB | 6' | 198 | 23 | | |
| Nesby Glasgow | DB | 5'10" | 187 | 33 | | |
| Dwayne Harper | DB | 5'11" | 165 | 24 | 3 | |
| Patrick Hunter | DB | 5'11" | 185 | 25 | 1 | |
| James Jefferson | DB | 6'1" | 199 | 26 | 1 | |
| Melvin Jenkins | DB | 5'10" | 173 | 28 | 1 | |
| Thom Kaumeyer | DB | 5'11" | 187 | 23 | | |
| Vann McElroy (from RAID) | DB | 6'2" | 190 | 30 | | |
| Eugene Robinson | DB | 6' | 183 | 27 | 3 | 6 |
| Jeff Kemp | QB | 6' | 198 | 31 | | |
| Dave Krieg | QB | 6'1" | 192 | 31 | | |
| Kelly Stouffer | QB | 6'3" | 210 | 26 | | |
| Derrick Fenner | HB | 6'3" | 228 | 23 | | 90 |
| Derek Loville | HB | 5'9" | 196 | 22 | | |
| Chris Warren | HB | 6'2" | 225 | 23 | | 6 |
| James Jones | FB | 6'2" | 230 | 29 | | |
| John L. Williams | FB | 5'11" | 226 | 25 | | 18 |
| Brian Blades | WR | 5'11 | 182 | 25 | | 18 |
| Jeff Chadwick | WR | 6'3" | 190 | 30 | | 24 |
| Louis Clark | WR | 6'1" | 193 | 26 | | |
| Tommy Kane | WR | 5'11" | 180 | 26 | | 24 |
| Paul Skansi | WR | 5'11" | 184 | 29 | | 12 |
| Ron Heller | TE | 6'3" | 242 | 26 | | 6 |
| Trey Junkin | TE | 6'2" | 240 | 29 | | |
| Travis McNeal | TE | 6'3" | 248 | 23 | | |
| Mike Tice | TE | 6'7" | 247 | 31 | | |
| Rick Donnelly | K | 6' | 209 | 28 | | |
| Norm Johnson | K | 6'2" | 197 | 30 | | 102 |

## SAN DIEGO CHARGERS 6-10 Dan Hening

| Scores of Each Game | | |
|---|---|---|
| 14 | Dallas | 17 |
| 16 | CINCINNATI | 21 |
| 24 | Cleveland | 14 |
| 7 | HOUSTON | 17 |
| 14 | Pittsburgh | 36 |
| 39 | N.Y. Jets | 3 |
| 9 | L.A. RAIDERS | 24 |
| 41 | TAMPA BAY | 10 |
| 31 | Seattle | 14 |
| 19 | DENVER | 7 |
| 10 | Kansas City | 27 |
| 10 | SEATTLE | * 13 |
| 38 | N.Y. JETS | 17 |
| 10 | Denver | 20 |
| 21 | KANSAS CITY | 24 |
| 12 | L.A. Raiders | 17 |

| Use Name | Pos. | Hgt | Wgt | Age | Int | Pts |
|---|---|---|---|---|---|---|
| Eric Floyd | OT | 6'5" | 300 | 24 | | |
| Leo Goeas | OT | 6'4" | 285 | 24 | | |
| Joel Patten | OT | 6'7" | 307 | 32 | | |
| Courtney Hall | OG-C | 6'2" | 269 | 22 | | |
| David Richards | OG | 6'5" | 310 | 24 | | |
| Broderick Thompson | OG | 6'5" | 295 | 30 | | |
| Tom Toth | OG | 6'5" | 282 | 28 | | |
| Mike Zandofsky | OG | 6'2" | 285 | 24 | | |
| Frank Cornish | C | 6'4" | 295 | 22 | | |
| Mark Rodenhauser | C | 6'5" | 263 | 29 | | |
| Burt Grossman | DE | 6'6" | 255 | 23 | | 2 |
| George Hinkle | DE-NT | 6'5" | 267 | 25 | | |
| Gerald Robinson | DE | 6'3" | 262 | 27 | | |
| Lee Williams | DE | 6'6" | 271 | 27 | | |
| Les Miller | NT | 6'7" | 300 | 25 | | 12 |
| Joe Phillips | NT | 6'5" | 300 | 27 | | |
| Tony Savage | NT | 6'3" | 300 | 23 | | |
| Richard Brown | LB | 6'3" | 240 | 24 | | |
| Steve Hendrickson | LB | 6' | 250 | 24 | | |
| Cedric Figaro | LB | 6'2" | 250 | 24 | | |
| Jeff Mills (to DEN) | LB | 6'3" | 241 | 21 | | |
| Leslie O'Neal | LB | 6'4" | 259 | 26 | | |
| Gary Plummer | LB | 6'2" | 240 | 30 | | 12 |
| Henry Rolling | LB | 6'2" | 225 | 24 | 1 | |
| Junior Seau | LB | 6'3" | 250 | 21 | | |
| Billy Ray Smith | LB | 6'3" | 236 | 29 | | |
| Martin Bayless | DB | 6'2" | 212 | 27 | 1 | |
| Gill Byrd | DB | 5'11" | 198 | 29 | 7 | |
| Donnie Elder | DB | 5'9" | 178 | 26 | 1 | |
| Donald Frank | DB | 6' | 200 | 24 | 2 | |
| Joe Fuller | DB | 5'11" | 180 | 25 | 1 | |
| Vencie Glenn | DB | 6' | 192 | 25 | 1 | |
| Lester Lyles | DB | 6'3" | 200 | 27 | 1 | |
| Sam Seale | DB | 5'9" | 185 | 27 | 2 | |
| Anthony Shelton | DB | 6'1" | 195 | 22 | | |
| John Friesz | QB | 6'4" | 209 | 23 | | |
| Billy Joe Tolliver | QB | 6'1" | 218 | 25 | | |
| Mark Vlasic | QB | 6'3" | 206 | 26 | | |
| Rod Bernstine | HB-FB | 6'3" | 238 | 25 | | 24 |
| Ronnie Harmon | HB | 5'11" | 200 | 26 | | 12 |
| Jerry Mays | HB | 5'7" | 176 | 22 | | |
| Darrin Nelson | HB | 5'9" | 184 | 30 | | |
| Marion Butts | FB | 6'1" | 248 | 24 | | 48 |
| Joe Mickles | FB | 5'10" | 221 | 24 | | |
| Tim Spencer | FB | 6'2" | 223 | 29 | | |
| Nate Lewis | WR | 5'11" | 189 | 23 | | 18 |
| Quinn Early | WR | 6' | 188 | 25 | | 6 |
| Anthony Miller | WR | 5'11" | 185 | 25 | | 42 |
| Kitrick Taylor | WR | 5'10" | 191 | 26 | | 6 |
| Walter Wilson | WR | 5'10" | 185 | 23 | | |
| Derrick Walker | TE | 6'1" | 244 | 23 | | 6 |
| Joe Caravello | TE | 6'3" | 270 | 27 | | 6 |
| Arthur Cox | TE | 6'2" | 277 | 29 | | 6 |
| Craig McEwen | TE | 6'1" | 220 | 24 | | 18 |
| Terry Orr (from WAS) | TE | 6'2" | 235 | 28 | | |
| John Carney (from LA) | K | 5'11" | 170 | 26 | | 84 |
| John Kidd | K | 6'3" | 208 | 29 | | |

Mike Simmonds — Knee Injury

David Brandon — Knee Injury

Wayne Walker — Knee Injury

## DENVER BRONCOS 5-11 Dan Reeves

| Scores of Each Game | | |
|---|---|---|
| 9 | L.A. Raiders | 14 |
| 24 | KANSAS CITY | 23 |
| 34 | SEATTLE | * 31 |
| 28 | Buffalo | 29 |
| 29 | CLEVELAND | 30 |
| 17 | PITTSBURGH | 34 |
| 27 | Indianapolis | 17 |
| 22 | Minnesota | 27 |
| 7 | San Diego | 19 |
| 13 | CHICAGO | * 16 |
| 27 | Detroit | 40 |
| 20 | L.A. RAIDERS | 23 |
| 20 | Kansas City | 31 |
| 20 | SAN DIEGO | 10 |
| 12 | Seattle | 17 |
| 22 | GREEN BAY | 13 |

| Use Name | Pos. | Hgt | Wgt | Age | Int | Pts |
|---|---|---|---|---|---|---|
| Darrell Hamilton | OT | 6'5" | 298 | 25 | | |
| Ken Lanier | OT | 6'3" | 290 | 31 | | |
| Gerald Perry | OT | 6'6" | 305 | 24 | | |
| Dave Widell | OT | 6'6" | 292 | 25 | | |
| Scott Beavers | OG | 6'4" | 277 | 23 | | |
| Jeff Davidson | OG | 6'5" | 309 | 22 | | |
| Sean Farrell | OG | 6'3" | 260 | 30 | | |
| Jim Juriga | OG | 6'6" | 275 | 25 | | |
| Doug Widell | OG | 6'4" | 287 | 23 | | |
| Keith Kartz | C | 6'4" | 270 | 27 | | |
| David Galloway | DE | 6'3" | 265 | 31 | | |
| Ron Holmes | DE | 6'4" | 265 | 27 | | |
| Jake McCullough | DE | 6'5" | 270 | 25 | | |
| Warren Powers | DE | 6'6" | 287 | 25 | | |
| Jim Szymanski | DE | 6'5" | 268 | 23 | | |
| Andre Townsend | DE-NT | 6'3" | 265 | 27 | | |
| Greg Kragen | NT | 6'3" | 265 | 28 | | |
| Ty Allert (to SEA) | LB | 6'2" | 238 | 27 | | |
| Michael Brooks | LB | 6'1" | 235 | 25 | | |
| Scott Curtis | LB | 6'1" | 230 | 25 | | |
| Rick Dennison | LB | 6'3" | 220 | 32 | | |
| Simon Fletcher | LB | 6'5" | 240 | 28 | | 2 |
| Ronnie Haliburton | LB | 6'4" | 230 | 22 | | |
| Tim Lucas | LB | 6'3" | 230 | 29 | | |
| Karl Mecklenburg | LB | 6'3" | 240 | 30 | | 8 |
| Marc Munford | LB | 6'2" | 231 | 25 | | |
| Anthony Thompson | LB | 6'1" | 227 | 23 | | |
| Steve Atwater | DB | 6'3" | 217 | 23 | 2 | |
| Tyrone Braxton | DB | 5'11" | 174 | 25 | 1 | |
| Kevin Clark | DB | 5'10" | 185 | 26 | | |
| Kip Corrington | DB | 6' | 175 | 25 | | |
| Wymon Henderson | DB | 5'10" | 186 | 28 | 2 | 6 |
| Le-Lo Lang | DB | 5'11" | 185 | 23 | 1 | |
| Alton Montgomery | DB | 6' | 195 | 22 | 2 | |
| Bruce Plummer (to SF) | DB | 6'1" | 203 | 26 | 1 | |
| Randy Robbins | DB | 6'2" | 189 | 26 | | |
| Dennis Smith | DB | 6'3" | 200 | 31 | 1 | |
| Elliott Smith | DB | 6'2" | 192 | 22 | | |
| John Elway | QB | 6'3" | 210 | 30 | | 18 |
| Gary Kubiak | QB | 6' | 192 | 29 | | |
| Blake Ezor | HB | 5'9" | 183 | 22 | | |
| Bobby Humphrey | HB | 6'1" | 201 | 23 | | 42 |
| Melvin Bratton | FB | 6'1" | 225 | 25 | | 24 |
| Kerry Porter | FB | 6'1" | 220 | 25 | | |
| Sammy Winder | FB | 5'11" | 203 | 31 | | 12 |
| Steve Sewell | FB-WR | 6'3" | 210 | 27 | | 18 |
| Mark Jackson | WR | 5'10" | 180 | 27 | | 30 |
| Vance Johnson | WR | 5'11" | 185 | 27 | | 18 |
| Ricky Nattiel | WR | 5'9" | 180 | 24 | | 12 |
| Shannon Sharpe | WR-TE | 6'2" | 225 | 22 | | 6 |
| Tim Stallworth | WR | 5'10" | 185 | 24 | | |
| Michael Young | WR | 6'1" | 183 | 28 | | 24 |
| Clarence Kay | TE | 6'2" | 237 | 29 | | |
| Orson Mobley (to IND) | TE | 6'5" | 256 | 27 | | |
| Chris Verhulst | TE | 6'2" | 249 | 24 | | |
| Mike Horan | K | 5'11" | 190 | 31 | | |
| David Treadwell | K | 6'1" | 175 | 23 | | 109 |

Alphonso Carreker — Knee Injury
Monte Smith — Foot Injury

## LOS ANGELES RAIDERS

### RUSHING

| Last Name | No. | Yds | Avg | TD |
|---|---|---|---|---|
| Jackson | 125 | 698 | 5.6 | 5 |
| Allen | 179 | 682 | 3.8 | 12 |
| Smith | 81 | 327 | 4.0 | 2 |
| Bell | 47 | 164 | 3.5 | 1 |
| Schroeder | 37 | 81 | 2.2 | 0 |
| Mueller | 13 | 43 | 3.3 | 0 |
| McCallum | 10 | 25 | 2.5 | 0 |
| Fernandez | 3 | 10 | 3.3 | 0 |
| Evans | 1 | -2 | -2.0 | 0 |

### RECEIVING

| Last Name | No. | Yds | Avg | TD |
|---|---|---|---|---|
| Fernandez | 52 | 839 | 16.1 | 5 |
| Gault | 50 | 985 | 19.7 | 3 |
| Horton | 33 | 404 | 12.2 | 3 |
| T. Brown | 18 | 265 | 14.7 | 3 |
| Allen | 15 | 189 | 12.6 | 1 |
| Jackson | 6 | 68 | 11.3 | 0 |
| Smith | 4 | 30 | 7.5 | 3 |
| Dyal | 3 | 51 | 17.0 | 0 |
| Graddy | 1 | 47 | 47.0 | 1 |
| Bell | 1 | 7 | 7.0 | 0 |

### PUNT RETURNS

| Last Name | No. | Yds | Avg | TD |
|---|---|---|---|---|
| T. Brown | 34 | 295 | 8.7 | 0 |

### KICKOFF RETURNS

| Last Name | No. | Yds | Avg | TD |
|---|---|---|---|---|
| Holland | 32 | 655 | 20.5 | 0 |
| R. Brown | 30 | 575 | 19.2 | 0 |
| McCallum | 1 | 7 | 7.0 | 0 |
| Turk | 1 | 0 | 0.0 | 0 |

### PASSING — PUNTING — KICKING

| PASSING | Att | Cmp | % | Yds | Yd/Att | TD | Int— | % | RK |
|---|---|---|---|---|---|---|---|---|---|
| Schroeder | 334 | 182 | 54.5 | 2849 | 8.53 | 19 | 9— | 2.7 | 4 |
| Evans | 1 | 1 | 100.0 | 36 | 36.00 | 0 | 0— | 0.0 | |
| Allen | 1 | 0 | 0.0 | 0 | 0.00 | 0 | 1— | 100.0 | |

| PUNTING | No. | Avg. |
|---|---|---|
| Gossett | 62 | 37.3 |

| KICKING | XP | ATT | % | FG | ATT | % |
|---|---|---|---|---|---|---|
| Jaeger | 40 | 42 | 95 | 15 | 20 | 75 |

## KANSAS CITY CHIEFS

### RUSHING

| Last Name | No. | Yds | Avg | TD |
|---|---|---|---|---|
| Word | 204 | 1015 | 5.0 | 4 |
| Okoye | 245 | 805 | 3.3 | 7 |
| McNair | 14 | 61 | 4.4 | 0 |
| B. Jones | 10 | 47 | 4.7 | 0 |
| Saxon | 3 | 15 | 5.0 | 0 |
| Pelluer | 5 | 6 | 1.2 | 0 |
| F. Jones | 1 | -1 | -1.0 | 0 |
| DeBerg | 21 | -5 | -0.2 | 0 |

### RECEIVING

| Last Name | No. | Yds | Avg | TD |
|---|---|---|---|---|
| Paige | 65 | 1021 | 15.7 | 5 |
| R. Thomas | 41 | 545 | 13.3 | 4 |
| Harry | 41 | 519 | 12.7 | 3 |
| McNair | 40 | 507 | 12.7 | 2 |
| B. Jones | 19 | 137 | 7.2 | 5 |
| Birden | 15 | 352 | 23.5 | 3 |
| Roberts | 11 | 119 | 10.8 | 0 |
| Hayes | 9 | 83 | 9.2 | 1 |
| Mandley | 7 | 97 | 13.9 | 0 |
| Word | 4 | 28 | 7.0 | 0 |
| Okoye | 4 | 23 | 5.8 | 0 |
| Whitaker | 2 | 17 | 8.5 | 1 |
| F. Jones | 1 | 5 | 5.0 | 0 |
| Saxon | 1 | 5 | 5.0 | 0 |

### PUNT RETURNS

| Last Name | No. | Yds | Avg | TD |
|---|---|---|---|---|
| Worthen | 25 | 180 | 7.2 | 0 |
| Birden | 10 | 72 | 7.2 | 0 |
| Harry | 1 | 2 | 2.0 | 0 |
| Whitaker | 1 | 0 | 0.0 | 0 |

### KICKOFF RETURNS

| Last Name | No. | Yds | Avg | TD |
|---|---|---|---|---|
| McNair | 14 | 227 | 16.2 | 0 |
| Worthen | 11 | 226 | 20.5 | 0 |
| F. Jones | 9 | 175 | 19.4 | 0 |
| Saxon | 5 | 81 | 16.2 | 0 |
| Mandley | 4 | 51 | 12.8 | 0 |
| Birden | 1 | 14 | 14.0 | 0 |
| Word | 1 | 10 | 10.0 | 0 |
| Roberts | 1 | 0 | 0.0 | 0 |

### PASSING — PUNTING — KICKING

| PASSING | Att | Cmp | % | Yds | Yd/Att | TD | Int— | % | RK |
|---|---|---|---|---|---|---|---|---|---|
| DeBerg | 444 | 258 | 58.1 | 3444 | 7.76 | 23 | 4— | 0.9 | 3 |
| Pelluer | 5 | 2 | 40.0 | 14 | 2.80 | 0 | 1— | 20.0 | |

| PUNTING | No. | Avg. |
|---|---|---|
| Barker | 64 | 38.7 |

| KICKING | XP | Att. | % | FG | Att | % |
|---|---|---|---|---|---|---|
| Lowery | 37 | 38 | 97 | 34 | 37 | 92 |

## SEATTLE SEAHAWKS

### RUSHING

| Last Name | No. | Yds | Avg | TD |
|---|---|---|---|---|
| Fenner | 215 | 859 | 4.0 | 14 |
| Williams | 187 | 714 | 3.8 | 3 |
| Krieg | 32 | 115 | 3.6 | 0 |
| Jones | 5 | 20 | 4.0 | 0 |
| Blades | 3 | 19 | 6.3 | 0 |
| Loville | 7 | 12 | 1.7 | 0 |
| Warren | 6 | 11 | 1.8 | 1 |
| McNeal | 1 | 2 | 2.0 | 0 |
| Chadwick | 1 | -3 | -3.0 | 0 |

### RECEIVING

| Last Name | No. | Yds | Avg | TD |
|---|---|---|---|---|
| Williams | 73 | 699 | 9.6 | 0 |
| Kane | 52 | 776 | 14.9 | 4 |
| Blades | 49 | 525 | 10.7 | 3 |
| Chadwick | 27 | 478 | 17.7 | 4 |
| Skansi | 22 | 257 | 11.7 | 2 |
| Fenner | 17 | 143 | 8.4 | 1 |
| Heller | 13 | 157 | 12.1 | 1 |
| McNeal | 10 | 143 | 14.3 | 0 |
| Jones | 1 | 22 | 22.0 | 0 |
| Krieg | 1 | -6 | -6.0 | 0 |

### PUNT RETURNS

| Last Name | No. | Yds | Avg | TD |
|---|---|---|---|---|
| Warren | 28 | 269 | 9.6 | 0 |
| Jefferson | 8 | 68 | 8.5 | 0 |

### KICKOFF RETURNS

| Last Name | No. | Yds | Avg | TD |
|---|---|---|---|---|
| Warren | 23 | 478 | 20.8 | 0 |
| Loville | 18 | 359 | 19.9 | 0 |
| Jefferson | 4 | 96 | 24.0 | 0 |
| McNeal | 2 | 29 | 14.5 | 0 |
| Jones | 2 | 21 | 10.5 | 0 |
| Glasgow | 1 | 2 | 2.0 | 0 |

### PASSING — PUNTING — KICKING

| PASSING | Att | Cmp | % | Yds | Yd/Att | TD | Int— | % | RK |
|---|---|---|---|---|---|---|---|---|---|
| Krieg | 448 | 265 | 59.2 | 3194 | 7.13 | 15 | 20— | 4.5 | 11 |

| PUNTING | No. | Avg. |
|---|---|---|
| Donnelley | 67 | 40.6 |

| KICKING | XP | ATT | % | FG | ATT | % |
|---|---|---|---|---|---|---|
| N. Johnson | 33 | 34 | 97 | 23 | 32 | 72 |

## SAN DIEGO CHARGERS

### RUSHING

| Last Name | No. | Yds | Avg | TD |
|---|---|---|---|---|
| Butts | 265 | 1225 | 4.6 | 8 |
| Bernstine | 124 | 589 | 4.8 | 4 |
| Harmon | 66 | 363 | 5.5 | 0 |
| Lewis | 4 | 25 | 6.3 | 1 |
| Tolliver | 14 | 22 | 1.6 | 0 |
| Nelson | 3 | 14 | 4.7 | 0 |
| A. Miller | 3 | 13 | 4.3 | 0 |
| Friesz | 1 | 3 | 3.0 | 0 |
| Plummer | 2 | 3 | 1.5 | 1 |
| Vlasic | 1 | 0 | 0.0 | 0 |
| Wilson | 1 | 0 | 0.0 | 0 |

### RECEIVING

| Last Name | No. | Yds | Avg | TD |
|---|---|---|---|---|
| A. Miller | 63 | 933 | 14.8 | 7 |
| Harmon | 46 | 511 | 11.1 | 2 |
| McEwen | 29 | 325 | 11.2 | 3 |
| Walker | 23 | 240 | 10.4 | 1 |
| Butts | 16 | 117 | 7.3 | 0 |
| Early | 15 | 238 | 15.9 | 1 |
| Lewis | 14 | 192 | 13.7 | 1 |
| Cox | 14 | 93 | 6.6 | 1 |
| Wilson | 10 | 87 | 8.7 | 0 |
| Bernstine | 8 | 40 | 5.0 | 0 |
| Nelson | 4 | 29 | 7.3 | 0 |
| Caravello | 2 | 21 | 10.5 | 1 |
| Hendrickson | 1 | 12 | 12.0 | 0 |
| Plummer | 1 | 2 | 2.0 | 1 |

### PUNT RETURNS

| Last Name | No. | Yds | Avg | TD |
|---|---|---|---|---|
| Lewis | 13 | 117 | 9.0 | 1 |
| Mays | 7 | 30 | 4.3 | 0 |
| Taylor | 6 | 112 | 18.7 | 1 |
| Nelson | 3 | 44 | 14.7 | 0 |
| Lyles | 1 | 0 | 0.0 | 0 |

### KICKOFF RETURNS

| Last Name | No. | Yds | Avg | TD |
|---|---|---|---|---|
| Elder | 24 | 571 | 23.8 | 0 |
| Lewis | 17 | 383 | 22.5 | 0 |
| Frank | 8 | 172 | 21.5 | 0 |
| Nelson | 4 | 36 | 9.0 | 0 |
| A. Miller | 1 | 13 | 13.0 | 0 |
| Orr | 1 | 13 | 13.0 | 0 |

### PASSING — PUNTING — KICKING

| PASSING | Att | Cmp | % | Yds | Yd/Att | TD | Int— | % | RK |
|---|---|---|---|---|---|---|---|---|---|
| Tolliver | 410 | 216 | 52.7 | 2574 | 6.28 | 16 | 16— | 3.09 | 12 |
| Vlasic | 40 | 19 | 47.5 | 168 | 4.20 | 1 | 2— | 5.0 | |
| Friesz | 22 | 11 | 50.0 | 98 | 4.45 | 1 | 1— | 4.5 | |

| PUNTING | No. | Avg. |
|---|---|---|
| Kidd | 62 | 39.4 |

| KICKING | XP | ATT | % | FG | ATT | % |
|---|---|---|---|---|---|---|
| Carney | 27 | 28 | 96 | 19 | 21 | 90 |

## DENVER BRONCOS

### RUSHING

| Last Name | No. | Yds | Avg | TD |
|---|---|---|---|---|
| Humphrey | 288 | 1202 | 4.2 | 7 |
| Elway | 50 | 258 | 5.2 | 3 |
| Winder | 42 | 120 | 2.9 | 2 |
| Bratton | 27 | 82 | 3.0 | 3 |
| Ezor | 23 | 81 | 3.5 | 0 |
| Kubiak | 9 | 52 | 5.8 | 0 |
| Sewell | 17 | 46 | 2.7 | 3 |
| Jackson | 5 | 28 | 5.6 | 1 |
| Porter | 1 | 3 | 3.0 | 0 |

### RECEIVING

| Last Name | No. | Yds | Avg | TD |
|---|---|---|---|---|
| Jackson | 57 | 926 | 16.2 | 4 |
| Johnson | 54 | 747 | 13.8 | 3 |
| Kay | 29 | 282 | 9.7 | 0 |
| Bratton | 29 | 276 | 9.5 | 1 |
| Young | 28 | 385 | 13.8 | 4 |
| Sewell | 26 | 268 | 10.3 | 0 |
| Humphrey | 24 | 152 | 6.3 | 0 |
| Nattiel | 18 | 297 | 16.5 | 2 |
| Winder | 17 | 145 | 8.5 | 0 |
| Mobley | 8 | 41 | 5.1 | 0 |
| Sharpe | 7 | 99 | 14.1 | 1 |
| Porter | 4 | 44 | 11.0 | 0 |
| Verhulst | 3 | 13 | 4.3 | 0 |
| Lanier | 1 | -4 | -4.0 | 0 |

### PUNT RETURNS

| Last Name | No. | Yds | Avg | TD |
|---|---|---|---|---|
| Clark | 21 | 159 | 7.6 | 0 |
| Johnson | 11 | 92 | 8.4 | 0 |
| Nattiel | 1 | 5 | 5.0 | 0 |

### KICKOFF RETURNS

| Last Name | No. | Yds | Avg | TD |
|---|---|---|---|---|
| Clark | 20 | 505 | 25.3 | 0 |
| Montgomery | 14 | 286 | 20.4 | 0 |
| Ezor | 13 | 214 | 16.5 | 0 |
| Johnson | 6 | 126 | 21.0 | 0 |
| Winder | 4 | 55 | 13.8 | 0 |
| Bratton | 3 | 37 | 12.3 | 0 |
| Jackson | 1 | 18 | 18.0 | 0 |
| Kay | 2 | 10 | 5.0 | 0 |
| Mobley | 1 | 9 | 9.0 | 0 |
| Nattiel | 1 | 0 | 0.0 | 0 |
| Atwater | 1 | 0 | 0.0 | 0 |

### PASSING — PUNTING — KICKING

| PASSING | Att | Cmp | % | Yds | Yd/Att | TD | Int— | % | RK |
|---|---|---|---|---|---|---|---|---|---|
| Elway | 502 | 294 | 58.6 | 3526 | 7.02 | 15 | 14— | 2.87 | |
| Kubiak | 22 | 11 | 50.0 | 145 | 6.59 | 0 | 4— | 18.2 | |
| Humphrey | 2 | 0 | 0.0 | 0 | 0.00 | 0 | 0— | 0.0 | |
| Sewell | 1 | 0 | 0.0 | 0 | 0.00 | 0 | 0— | 0.0 | |

| PUNTING | No. | Avg. |
|---|---|---|
| Horan | 59 | 43.6 |
| Elway | 1 | 37.0 |

| KICKING | XP | ATT | % | FG | ATT | % |
|---|---|---|---|---|---|---|
| Treadwell | 34 | 36 | 94 | 25 | 34 | 74 |

## January 5, 1991 at Miami (Attendance 67,276)

### SCORING

| | | | | | |
|---|---|---|---|---|---|
| KANSAS CITY | 3 | 7 | 6 | 0 | - 16 |
| MIAMI | 0 | 3 | 0 | 14 | - 17 |

**First Quarter**
K.C.    Lowery, 27 yard field goal

**Second Quarter**
Mia.    Stoyanovich, 58 yard field goal
K.C.    Paige, 26 yard pass from DeBerg
     PAT — Lowery (kick)

**Third Quarter**
K.C.    Lowery, 25 yard field goal
K.C.    Lowery, 38 yard field goal

**Fourth Quarter**
Mia.    Paige, 1 yard pass from Marino
     PAT — Stoyanovich (kick)
Mia.    Clayton, 12 yard pass from Marino
     PAT — Stoyanovich (kick)

### TEAM STATISTICS

| K.C. | | MIA. |
|---|---|---|
| 15 | First Downs- Total | 23 |
| 4 | First Downs- Rushing | 7 |
| 11 | First Downs- Passing | 14 |
| 1 | First Downs- Penalty | 2 |
| 0 | Fumbles- Number | 2 |
| 0 | Fumbles- Lost Ball | 2 |
| 4 | Penalties- Number | 2 |
| 35 | Yards Penalized | 22 |
| 1 | Missed Field Goals | 1 |
| 55 | Offensive Plays | 64 |
| 367 | Net Yards | 311 |
| 6.7 | Average Gain | 4.8 |
| 1 | Giveaways | 2 |
| 2 | Takeaways | 1 |
| +1 | Difference | -1 |

### INDIVIDUAL STATISTICS

**KANSAS CITY**     **MIAMI**

#### RUSHING

| | No. | Yds. | Avg. | | No. | Yds. | Avg. |
|---|---|---|---|---|---|---|---|
| Okoye | 13 | 83 | 6.4 | Smith | 20 | 82 | 4.1 |
| Word | 9 | 13 | 1.4 | Logan | 7 | 17 | 2.4 |
| McNair | 2 | 7 | 3.5 | Paige | 1 | 2 | 2.0 |
| | 24 | 103 | 4.3 | Marino | 4 | -3 | -0.8 |
| | | | | | 32 | 98 | 3.1 |

#### RECEIVING

| | No. | Yds. | Avg. | | No. | Yds. | Avg. |
|---|---|---|---|---|---|---|---|
| Paige | 8 | 142 | 17.8 | Clayton | 5 | 66 | 13.2 |
| McNair | 3 | 22 | 7.3 | Paige | 5 | 30 | 6.0 |
| Harry | 2 | 59 | 29.5 | Duper | 3 | 36 | 12.0 |
| Roberts | 2 | 26 | 13.0 | Edmunds | 2 | 49 | 24.5 |
| R. Thomas | 1 | 15 | 15.0 | Smith | 2 | 22 | 11.0 |
| Hayes | 1 | 5 | 5.0 | Jensen | 1 | 11 | 11.0 |
| | 17 | 269 | 15.8 | Martin | 1 | 7 | 7.0 |
| | | | | | 19 | 221 | 11.6 |

#### PUNTING

| | No. | Avg. | | No. | Avg. |
|---|---|---|---|---|---|
| Barker | 4 | 35.0 | Roby | 2 | 59.5 |

#### PUNT RETURNS

| | No. | Yds. | Avg. |
|---|---|---|---|
| Harry | 2 | 16 | 8.0 |

#### KICKOFF RETURNS

| | No. | Yds. | Avg. | | No. | Yds. | Avg. |
|---|---|---|---|---|---|---|---|
| F. Jones | 3 | 59 | 19.7 | Pruitt | 2 | 18 | 9.0 |
| | | | | Logan | 1 | 24 | 24.0 |
| | | | | | 3 | 42 | 14.0 |

#### INTERCEPTION RETURNS

| | No. | Yds. | Avg. |
|---|---|---|---|
| None | | | |
| Williams | 1 | 0 | 0.0 |

#### PASSING

**KANSAS CITY**

| | Att. | Comp. | Comp. Pct. | Yds. | Int. | Yds./ Att. | Yds./ Comp. |
|---|---|---|---|---|---|---|---|
| DeBerg | 30 | 17 | 56.7 | 269 | 1 | 9.0 | 15.8 |

**MIAMI**

| | Att. | Comp. | Comp. Pct. | Yds. | Int. | Yds./ Att. | Yds./ Comp. |
|---|---|---|---|---|---|---|---|
| Marino | 30 | 19 | 63.3 | 221 | 0 | 7.4 | 11.6 |

---

## January 6, 1991 at Cincinnati (Attendance 60,012)

### SCORING

| | | | | | |
|---|---|---|---|---|---|
| HOUSTON | 0 | 0 | 7 | 7 | - 14 |
| CINCINNATI | 10 | 10 | 14 | 7 | - 41 |

**First Quarter**
Cin.    Woods, 1 yard run
     PAT — Breech (kick)
Cin.    Breech, 27 yard field goal

**Second Quarter**
Cin.    Green, 2 yard pass from Esiason
     PAT — Breech (kick)
Cin.    Breech, 30 yard field goal

**Third Quarter**
Cin.    Ball, 3 yard run
     PAT — Breech (kick)
Cin.    Esiason, 10 yard run
     PAT — Breech (kick)
Hous.    Givins, 16 yard pass from Carlson
     PAT — Garcia (kick)

**Fourth Quarter**
Cin.    Kattus, 9 yard pass from Esiason
     PAT — Breech (kick)
Hous.    Givins, 5 yard pass from Carlson
     PAT — Garcia (kick)

### TEAM STATISTICS

| HOU. | | CIN. |
|---|---|---|
| 13 | First Downs- Total | 24 |
| 4 | First Downs- Rushing | 15 |
| 9 | First Downs- Passing | 7 |
| 0 | First Downs- Penalty | 2 |
| 2 | Fumbles- Number | 1 |
| 1 | Fumbles- Lost Ball | 0 |
| 5 | Penalties- Number | 4 |
| 33 | Yards Penalized | 40 |
| 0 | Missed Field Goals | 0 |
| 47 | Offensive Plays | 69 |
| 226 | Net Yards | 349 |
| 4.8 | Average Gain | 5.1 |
| 2 | Giveaways | 0 |
| 0 | Takeaways | 2 |
| -2 | Difference | +2 |

### INDIVIDUAL STATISTICS

**HOUSTON**     **CINCINNATI**

#### RUSHING

| | No. | Yds. | Avg. | | No. | Yds. | Avg. |
|---|---|---|---|---|---|---|---|
| White | 4 | 2 | 0.5 | Woods | 6 | 11 | 1.8 |
| Carlson | 4 | 22 | 5.5 | Brooks | 6 | 17 | 2.8 |
| Pinkett | 5 | 43 | 8.6 | Esiason | 5 | 57 | 11.4 |
| | 13 | 67 | 5.2 | Ball | 7 | 33 | 4.7 |
| | | | | Green | 11 | 55 | 5.0 |
| | | | | Jennings | 6 | 16 | 2.7 |
| | | | | Wilhelm | 3 | -2 | -0.7 |
| | | | | | 44 | 187 | 4.3 |

#### RECEIVING

| | No. | Yds. | Avg. | | No. | Yds. | Avg. |
|---|---|---|---|---|---|---|---|
| Givins | 6 | 60 | 10.0 | Holman | 2 | 51 | 25.5 |
| Harris | 4 | 37 | 9.3 | McGee | 2 | 23 | 11.5 |
| Jeffires | 2 | 33 | 16.5 | Kattus | 2 | 19 | 9.5 |
| Duncan | 1 | 15 | 15.0 | Jennings | 2 | 15 | 7.5 |
| Pinkett | 1 | 10 | 10.0 | Green | 2 | 15 | 7.5 |
| White | 1 | 5 | 5.0 | Brown | 2 | 14 | 7.0 |
| Hill | 1 | 5 | 5.0 | Woods | 2 | 13 | 6.5 |
| | 16 | 165 | 10.3 | Barber | 1 | 12 | 12.0 |
| | | | | | 15 | 162 | 10.8 |

#### PUNTING

| | No. | Avg. | | No. | Avg. |
|---|---|---|---|---|---|
| Montgomery | 6 | 42.6 | Johnson | 3 | 45.0 |

#### PUNT RETURNS

| | No. | Yds. | Avg. | | No. | Yds. | Avg. |
|---|---|---|---|---|---|---|---|
| McNeil | 1 | 19 | 19.0 | Price | 3 | 42 | 14.0 |

#### KICKOFF RETURNS

| | No. | Yds. | Avg. | | No. | Yds. | Avg. |
|---|---|---|---|---|---|---|---|
| Ford | 3 | 57 | 19.0 | Ball | 1 | 28 | 28.0 |
| Pinkett | 2 | 48 | 24.0 | Jennings | 1 | 18 | 18.0 |
| Norgard | 1 | 9 | 9.0 | Brown | 1 | 12 | 12.0 |
| | 6 | 114 | 19.0 | | 3 | 58 | 19.3 |

#### INTERCEPTION RETURNS

| | No. | Yds. | Avg. |
|---|---|---|---|
| None | | | |
| Fulcher | 1 | 43 | 43.0 |

#### PASSING

**HOUSTON**

| | Att. | Comp. | Comp. Pct. | Yds. | Int. | Yds./ Att. | Yds./ Comp. |
|---|---|---|---|---|---|---|---|
| Carlson | 33 | 16 | 48.5 | 165 | 1 | 5.0 | 10.3 |

**CINCINNATI**

| | Att. | Comp. | Comp. Pct. | Yds. | Int. | Yds./ Att. | Yds./ Comp. |
|---|---|---|---|---|---|---|---|
| Esiason | 20 | 14 | 70.0 | 150 | 0 | 7.5 | 10.7 |
| Wilhelm | 5 | 1 | 20.0 | 12 | 0 | 2.4 | 12.0 |
| | 25 | 15 | 60.0 | 162 | 0 | 6.5 | 10.8 |

January 5, 1991 at Philadelphia (Attendance 65,287)

### SCORING

| | | | | | | |
|---|---|---|---|---|---|---|
| WASHINGTON | 0 | 10 | 10 | 0 | - | 20 |
| PHILADELPHIA | 3 | 3 | 0 | 0 | - | 6 |

**First Quarter**
Phil. — Ruzek, 37 yard field goal

**Second Quarter**
Phil. — Ruzek, 28 yard field goal
Wash. — Monk, 16 yard pass from Rypien
PAT — Lohmiller (kick)
Wash. — Lohmiller, 20 yard field goal

**Third Quarter**
Wash. — Lohmiller, 19 yard field goal
Wash. — Clark, 3 yard pass from Rypien
PAT — Lohmiller (kick)

### TEAMSTATISTICS

| WASH. | | PHIL. |
|---|---|---|
| 15 | First Downs- Total | 16 |
| 3 | First Downs- Rushing | 6 |
| 12 | First Downs- Passing | 8 |
| 0 | First Downs- Penalty | 2 |
| 2 | Fumbles- Number | 2 |
| 1 | Fumbles- Lost Ball | 2 |
| 3 | Penalties- Number | 4 |
| 23 | Yards Penalized | 40 |
| 0 | Missed Field Goals | 0 |
| 66 | Offensive Plays | 65 |
| 299 | Net Yards | 318 |
| 4.5 | Average Gain | 4.9 |
| 2 | Giveaways | 3 |
| 3 | Takeaways | 2 |
| +1 | Difference | -1 |

### INDIVIDUALSTATISTICS

**WASHINGTON** / **PHILADELPHIA**

#### RUSHING

| | No. | Yds. | Avg. | | No. | Yds. | Avg. |
|---|---|---|---|---|---|---|---|
| Byner | 18 | 49 | 2.7 | Sherman | 17 | 53 | 3.1 |
| Riggs | 14 | 45 | 3.2 | Cunningham | 7 | 80 | 11.4 |
| Sanders | 1 | 3 | 3.0 | Toney | 2 | 3 | 1.5 |
| Rypien | 2 | -4 | -2.0 | Sanders | 2 | 12 | 6.0 |
| | 35 | 93 | 2.7 | | 28 | 148 | 5.3 |

#### RECEIVING

| | No. | Yds. | Avg. | | No. | Yds. | Avg. |
|---|---|---|---|---|---|---|---|
| Sanders | 2 | 22 | 11.0 | Kei. Jackson | 5 | 116 | 23.2 |
| Clark | 4 | 63 | 15.8 | Sherman | 2 | 15 | 7.5 |
| Monk | 2 | 44 | 22.0 | Byars | 2 | 18 | 9.0 |
| Byner | 7 | 77 | 11.0 | Williams | 1 | 9 | 9.0 |
| | 15 | 206 | 13.7 | Sanders | 5 | 47 | 9.4 |
| | | | | | 15 | 205 | 13.7 |

#### PUNTING

| | No. | | Avg. | | No. | | Avg. |
|---|---|---|---|---|---|---|---|
| Goodburn | 9 | | 36.9 | Feagles | 7 | | 39.1 |

#### PUNT RETURNS

| | No. | Yds. | Avg. | | No. | Yds. | Avg. |
|---|---|---|---|---|---|---|---|
| Howard | 0 | 0 | 0.0 | Harris | 4 | 33 | 8.3 |
| Green | 1 | 10 | 10.0 | | | | |
| Mitchell | 4 | 31 | 7.8 | | | | |
| | 5 | 41 | 8.2 | | | | |

#### KICKOFF RETURNS

| | No. | Yds. | Avg. | | No. | Yds. | Avg. |
|---|---|---|---|---|---|---|---|
| Mitchell | 1 | 17 | 17.0 | Sanders | 4 | 52 | 13.0 |
| Howard | 2 | 21 | 10.5 | | | | |
| | 3 | 38 | 12.7 | | | | |

#### INTERCEPTION RETURNS

| | No. | Yds. | Avg. | | No. | Yds. | Avg. |
|---|---|---|---|---|---|---|---|
| Green | 1 | 0 | 0.0 | Allen | 1 | 3 | 3.0 |

#### PASSING

**WASHINGTON**

| | Att. | Comp. | Comp. Pct. | Yds. | Int | Yds./ Att. | Yds./ Comp. |
|---|---|---|---|---|---|---|---|
| Rypien | 31 | 15 | 48.4 | 206 | 1 | 6.6 | 13.7 |

**PHILADELPHIA**

| | Att. | Comp. | Comp. Pct. | Yds. | Int | Yds./ Att. | Yds./ Comp. |
|---|---|---|---|---|---|---|---|
| Cunningham | 29 | 15 | 51.7 | 205 | 1 | 7.1 | 13.7 |
| McMahon | 3 | 0 | 0.0 | 0 | 0 | 0.0 | 0.0 |
| | 32 | 15 | 46.9 | 205 | 1 | 6.4 | 13.7 |

---

January 6, 1991 at Chicago (Attendance 60,767)

### SCORING

| | | | | | | |
|---|---|---|---|---|---|---|
| NEW ORLEANS | 0 | 3 | 0 | 3 | - | 6 |
| CHICAGO | 3 | 7 | 3 | 3 | - | 16 |

**First Quarter**
Chi. — Butler, 19 yard field goal

**Second Quarter**
Chi. — Thornton, 18 yard pass from Tomczak
PAT — Butler (kick)
N.O. — Andersen, 47 yard field goal

**Third Quarter**
Chi. — Butler, 22 yard field goal

**Fourth Quarter**
N.O. — Andersen, 38 yard field goal
Chi. — Butler, 21 yard field goal

### TEAMSTATISTICS

| N.O. | | CHI. |
|---|---|---|
| 11 | First Downs- Total | 18 |
| 2 | First Downs- Rushing | 9 |
| 7 | First Downs- Passing | 8 |
| 2 | First Downs- Penalty | 1 |
| 1 | Fumbles- Number | 2 |
| 0 | Fumbles- Lost Ball | 1 |
| 2 | Penalties- Number | 7 |
| 10 | Yards Penalized | 57 |
| 1 | Missed Field Goals | 1 |
| 54 | Offensive Plays | 71 |
| 193 | Net Yards | 365 |
| 3.6 | Average Gain | 5.1 |
| 3 | Giveaways | 1 |
| 1 | Takeaways | 3 |
| -2 | Difference | +2 |

### INDIVIDUALSTATISTICS

**NEW ORLEANS** / **CHICAGO**

#### RUSHING

| | No. | Yds. | Avg. | | No. | Yds. | Avg. |
|---|---|---|---|---|---|---|---|
| Heyward | 4 | 10 | 2.5 | Anderson | 27 | 102 | 3.8 |
| Fenerty | 8 | 29 | 3.6 | Muster | 12 | 71 | 5.9 |
| Fourcade | 2 | 13 | 6.5 | Tomczak | 2 | 8 | 4.0 |
| Hilliard | 4 | 13 | 3.3 | Green | 2 | 8 | 4.0 |
| | 18 | 65 | 3.6 | | 43 | 189 | 4.4 |

#### RECEIVING

| | No. | Yds. | Avg. | | No. | Yds. | Avg. |
|---|---|---|---|---|---|---|---|
| Fenerty | 4 | 22 | 5.5 | Anderson | 4 | 42 | 10.5 |
| Martin | 2 | 47 | 23.5 | Thornton | 2 | 43 | 21.5 |
| Scales | 1 | 31 | 31.0 | Gentry | 2 | 41 | 20.5 |
| Tice | 1 | 19 | 19.0 | Morris | 2 | 28 | 14.0 |
| Brenner | 1 | 17 | 17.0 | Muster | 2 | 21 | 10.5 |
| Perriman | 1 | 11 | 11.0 | Davis | 1 | 13 | 13.0 |
| Turner | 1 | 6 | 6.0 | | 13 | 175 | 13.5 |
| | 11 | 153 | 13.9 | | | | |

#### PUNTING

| | No. | | Avg. | | No. | | Avg. |
|---|---|---|---|---|---|---|---|
| Barnhardt | 3 | | 30.0 | Buford | 2 | | 27.5 |

#### PUNT RETURNS

| | No. | Yds. | Avg. | | No. | Yds. | Avg. |
|---|---|---|---|---|---|---|---|
| Buck | 1 | 2 | 2.0 | Bailey | 1 | 13 | 13.0 |
| | | | | Jackson | 1 | 0 | 0.0 |
| | | | | | 2 | 13 | 6.5 |

#### KICKOFF RETURNS

| | No. | Yds. | Avg. | | No. | Yds. | Avg. |
|---|---|---|---|---|---|---|---|
| Fenerty | 2 | 33 | 16.5 | Gentry | 1 | 39 | 39.0 |
| Hilliard | 1 | 21 | 21.0 | | | | |
| Jordan | 1 | 17 | 17.0 | | | | |
| Heyward | 1 | 14 | 14.0 | | | | |
| | 5 | 85 | 17.0 | | | | |

#### INTERCEPTION RETURNS

| | No. | Yds. | Avg. | | No. | Yds. | Avg. |
|---|---|---|---|---|---|---|---|
| None | | | | Mangum | 1 | 9 | 9.0 |
| | | | | Gayle | 1 | 27 | 27.0 |
| | | | | Carrier | 1 | 0 | 0.0 |
| | | | | | 3 | 36 | 12.0 |

#### PASSING

**NEW ORLEANS**

| | Att. | Comp. | Comp. Pct. | Yds. | Int | Yds./ Att. | Yds./ Comp. |
|---|---|---|---|---|---|---|---|
| Walsh | 16 | 6 | 37.5 | 74 | 1 | 4.6 | 12.3 |
| Fourcade | 18 | 5 | 2.8 | 79 | 2 | 4.4 | 15.8 |
| | 34 | 11 | 32.4 | 153 | 3 | 4.5 | 13.9 |

**CHICAGO**

| | Att. | Comp. | Comp. Pct. | Yds. | Int | Yds./ Att. | Yds./ Comp. |
|---|---|---|---|---|---|---|---|
| Tomczak | 25 | 12 | 48.0 | 166 | 0 | 6.4 | 13.8 |
| Anderson | 1 | 1 | 100.0 | 22 | 0 | 22.0 | 22.0 |
| | 26 | 13 | 50.0 | 188 | 0 | 7.2 | 13.8 |

January 12, 1991 at Orchard Park, N.Y. (Attendance 77,087)

## SCORING

| | | | | | |
|---|---|---|---|---|---|
| MIAMI | 3 | 14 | 3 | 14 | - 34 |
| BUFFALO | 13 | 14 | 3 | 14 | - 44 |

**First Quarter**
Buff.    Reed, 40 yard pass from Kelly
     PAT — Norwood (kick)
Mia.    Stoyanovich, 49 yard field goal
Buff.    Norwood, 40 yard field goal
Buff.    Norwood, 22 yard field goal

**Second Quarter**
Buff.    Thomas, 5 yard run
     PAT — Norwood (kick)
Mia.    Duper, 64 yard pass from Marino
     PAT — Stoyanovich (kick)
Buff.    Lofton, 13 yardd pass from Kelly
     PAT — Norwood (kick)
Mia.    Marino, 2 yard run
     PAT — Stoyanovich (kick)

**Third Quarter**
Mia.    Stoyanovich, 22 yard field goal
Buff.    Norwood, 28 yard field goal
Mia.    Foster, 2 yard pass from Marino
     PAT — Stoyanovich (kick)

**Fourth Quarter**
Buff.    Thomas, 5 yard run
     — Norwood (kick)
Buff.    Reed , 26 yard pass from Kelly
     PAT — Norwood (kick)
Mia.    Martin, 8 yard pass from Marino
     PAT — Stoyanovich (kick)

## TEAM STATISTICS

| MIA. | | BUFF. |
|---|---|---|
| 24 | First Downs- Total | 24 |
| 9 | First Downs- Rushing | 7 |
| 13 | First Downs- Passing | 16 |
| 2 | First Downs- Penalty | 1 |
| 1 | Fumbles- Number | 3 |
| 1 | Fumbles- Lost Ball | 1 |
| 4 | Penalties- Number | 4 |
| 32 | Yards Penalized | 30 |
| 0 | Missed Field Goals | 0 |
| 76 | Offensive Plays | 66 |
| 430 | Net Yards | 493 |
| 5.6 | Average Gain | 7.5 |
| 3 | Giveaways | 2 |
| 2 | Takeaways | 3 |
| -1 | Difference | +1 |

## INDIVIDUAL STATISTICS

**MIAMI**      **BUFFALO**

### RUSHING

| | No. | Yds. | Avg. | | No. | Yds. | Avg. |
|---|---|---|---|---|---|---|---|
| Smith | 21 | 99 | 4.7 | Thomas | 32 | 117 | 3.7 |
| Logan | 5 | 6 | 1.2 | Kelly | 5 | 37 | 7.4 |
| Marino | 1 | 2 | 2.0 | | 37 | 154 | 4.2 |
| | 27 | 107 | 3.9 | | | | |

### RECEIVING

| | No. | Yds. | Avg. | | No. | Yds. | Avg. |
|---|---|---|---|---|---|---|---|
| Clayton | 4 | 82 | 20.5 | Lofton | 7 | 149 | 21.3 |
| Martin | 4 | 44 | 11.0 | Reed | 4 | 123 | 30.8 |
| Jensen | 4 | 38 | 9.5 | Thomas | 3 | 38 | 12.7 |
| Duper | 3 | 113 | 37.7 | McKeller | 3 | 15 | 5.0 |
| Edmunds | 3 | 21 | 7.0 | Edwards | 1 | 12 | 12.0 |
| Logan | 2 | 8 | 4.0 | K. Davis | 1 | 3 | 3.0 |
| Smith | 1 | 9 | 9.0 | | 19 | 339 | 17.8 |
| Paige | 1 | 6 | 6.0 | | | | |
| Foster | 1 | 2 | 2.0 | | | | |
| | 23 | 323 | 14.0 | | | | |

### PUNTING

| | No. | Yds. | Avg. | | No. | Yds. | Avg. |
|---|---|---|---|---|---|---|---|
| Roby | 2 | | 40.0 | Tuten | 1 | | 47.0 |

### PUNT RETURNS

| | No. | Yds. | Avg. | | No. | Yds. | Avg. |
|---|---|---|---|---|---|---|---|
| Clayton | 1 | 3 | 3.0 | Edwards | 2 | 17 | 8.5 |

### KICKOFF RETURNS

| | No. | Yds. | Avg. | | No. | Yds. | Avg. |
|---|---|---|---|---|---|---|---|
| Logan | 8 | 138 | 17.3 | D. Smith | 3 | 51 | 17.0 |
| Adams | 1 | 13 | 13.0 | Edwards | 2 | 51 | 25.5 |
| | 9 | 151 | 16.8 | Rolle | 1 | 14 | 14.0 |
| | | | | | 6 | 116 | 19.3 |

### INTERCEPTION RETURNS

| | No. | Yds. | Avg. | | No. | Yds. | Avg. |
|---|---|---|---|---|---|---|---|
| Williams | 1 | 0 | 0.0 | Odomes | 1 | 9 | 9.0 |
| | | | | Kelso | 1 | 0 | 0.0 |
| | | | | | 2 | 9 | 4.5 |

### PASSING

**MIAMI**

| | Att. | Comp. | Comp. Pct. | Yds. | Int. | Yds./ Att. | Yds./ Comp. |
|---|---|---|---|---|---|---|---|
| Marino | 49 | 23 | 46.9 | 323 | 2 | 6.6 | 14.0 |

**BUFFALO**

| | Att. | Comp. | Comp. Pct. | Yds. | Int. | Yds./ Att. | Yds./ Comp. |
|---|---|---|---|---|---|---|---|
| Kelly | 29 | 19 | 65.5 | 339 | 1 | 11.7 | 17.8 |

---

January 13, 1991 at Los Angeles (Attendance 92,045)

## SCORING

| | | | | | |
|---|---|---|---|---|---|
| CINCINNATI | 0 | 3 | 0 | 7 | - 10 |
| L.A. RAIDERS | 0 | 7 | 3 | 10 | - 20 |

**Second Quarter**
Cin.    Breech, 27 yard field goal
L.A.    Fernandez, 13 yard pass from Schroeder
     PAT — Jaeger (kick)

**Third Quarter**
L.A.    Jaeger, 49 yard field goal

**Fourth Quarter**
Cin.    Jennings, 8 yard pass from Esiason
     PAT — Breech (kick)
L.A.    Horton, 41 yard pass from Schroeder
     PAT — Jaeger (kick)
L.A.    Jaeger, 25 yard field goal

## TEAM STATISTICS

| CIN. | | L.A. |
|---|---|---|
| 12 | First Downs- Total | 20 |
| 7 | First Downs- Rushing | 11 |
| 5 | First Downs- Passing | 9 |
| 0 | First Downs- Penalty | 0 |
| 1 | Fumbles- Number | 0 |
| 0 | Fumbles- Lost Ball | 0 |
| 1 | Penalties- Number | 0 |
| 5 | Yards Penalized | 0 |
| 0 | Missed Field Goals | 0 |
| 48 | Offensive Plays | 56 |
| 182 | Net Yards | 389 |
| 3.8 | Average Gain | 6.9 |
| 0 | Giveaways | 1 |
| 1 | Takeaways | 0 |
| +1 | Difference | -1 |

## INDIVIDUAL STATISTICS

**CINCINNATI**      **L.A. RAIDERS**

### RUSHING

| | No. | Yds. | Avg. | | No. | Yds. | Avg. |
|---|---|---|---|---|---|---|---|
| Woods | 11 | 73 | 6.6 | Allen | 21 | 140 | 6.7 |
| Brooks | 11 | 26 | 2.4 | Jackson | 6 | 77 | 12.8 |
| Ball | 5 | 14 | 2.8 | Smith | 5 | 18 | 3.6 |
| Esiason | 2 | 11 | 5.5 | | 32 | 235 | 7.3 |
| | 29 | 124 | 4.3 | | | | |

### RECEIVING

| | No. | Yds. | Avg. | | No. | Yds. | Avg. |
|---|---|---|---|---|---|---|---|
| Holman | 2 | 51 | 25.5 | Horton | 4 | 77 | 19.3 |
| Brown | 2 | 18 | 9.0 | T. Brown | 3 | 42 | 14.0 |
| Brooks | 1 | 22 | 22.0 | Fernandez | 2 | 24 | 12.0 |
| Jennings | 1 | 8 | 8.0 | Allen | 1 | 24 | 24.0 |
| Woods | 1 | 5 | 5.0 | Smith | 1 | 5 | 5.0 |
| McGee | 1 | 0 | 0.0 | | 11 | 172 | 15.6 |
| | 8 | 104 | 13.0 | | | | |

### PUNTING

| | No. | Yds. | Avg. | | No. | Yds. | Avg. |
|---|---|---|---|---|---|---|---|
| Johnson | 5 | | 51.6 | Gossett | 2 | | 39.5 |

### PUNT RETURNS

| | No. | Yds. | Avg. | | No. | Yds. | Avg. |
|---|---|---|---|---|---|---|---|
| None | | | | T. Brown | 3 | 40 | 13.3 |

### KICKOFF RETURNS

| | No. | Yds. | Avg. | | No. | Yds. | Avg. |
|---|---|---|---|---|---|---|---|
| Jennings | 3 | 68 | 22.7 | R. Brown | 1 | 18 | 18.0 |
| Ball | 1 | 14 | 14.0 | | | | |
| | 4 | 82 | 20.5 | | | | |

### INTERCEPTION RETURNS

| | No. | Yds. | Avg. | | No. | Yds. | Avg. |
|---|---|---|---|---|---|---|---|
| Fulcher | 1 | 11 | 11.0 | None | | | |

### PASSING

**BUFFALO**

| | Att. | Comp. | Comp. Pct. | Yds. | Int. | Yds./ Att. | Yds./ Comp. |
|---|---|---|---|---|---|---|---|
| Esiason | 15 | 8 | 5.3 | 104 | 0 | 6.9 | 13.0 |

**CLEVELAND**

| | Att. | Comp. | Comp. Pct. | Yds. | Int. | Yds./ Att. | Yds./ Comp. |
|---|---|---|---|---|---|---|---|
| Schroeder | 21 | 11 | 52.4 | 172 | 1 | 8.2 | 15.6 |

January 12, 1991 at San Francisco (Attendance 65,292)

## SCORING

| | | | | | | |
|---|---|---|---|---|---|---|
| WASHINGTON | 10 | 0 | 0 | 0 | - | 10 |
| SAN FRANCISCO | 7 | 14 | 0 | 7 | - | 28 |

**First Quarter**
Wash. — Monk, 31 yard pass from Rypien
    PAT — Lohmiller (kick)
S.F. — Rathman, 1 yard run
    PAT — Cofer (kick)
Wash. — Lohmiller, 44 yard field goal

**Second Quarter**
S.F. — Rice, 10 yard pass from Montana
    PAT — Cofer (kick)
S.F. — Sherrard, 8 yard pass from Montana
    PAT — Cofer (kick)

**Fourth Quarter**
S.F. — M. Carter, 61 yard interception return
    PAT — Cofer (kick)

January 13, 1991 at East Rutherford, N.J. (Attendance 77,025)

## SCORING

| | | | | | | |
|---|---|---|---|---|---|---|
| CHICAGO | 0 | 3 | 0 | 0 | - | 3 |
| N.Y. GIANTS | 10 | 7 | 7 | 7 | - | 31 |

**First Quarter**
NYG — Bahr, 46 yard field goal
NYG — Baker, 21 yard pass from Hostetler
    PAT — Bahr (kick)

**Second Quarter**
Chi. — Butler, 33 yard field goal
NYG. — Cross, 5 yard pass from Hostetler
    PAT — Bahr (kick)

**Third Quarter**
NYG — Hostetler, 3 yard run
    PAT — Bahr (kick)

**Fourth Quarter**
NYG — Carthon, 1 yard run
    PAT — Bahr (kick)

## TEAM STATISTICS

| WASH. | | S.F. |
|---|---|---|
| 25 | First Downs- Total | 20 |
| 6 | First Downs- Rushing | 3 |
| 18 | First Downs- Passing | 16 |
| 1 | First Downs- Penalty | 1 |
| 0 | Fumbles- Number | 0 |
| 0 | Fumbles- Lost Ball | 0 |
| 1 | Penalties- Number | 4 |
| 15 | Yards Penalized | 25 |
| 0 | Missed Field Goals | 0 |
| 72 | Offensive Plays | 58 |
| 441 | Net Yards | 338 |
| 6.1 | Average Gain | 5.8 |
| 3 | Giveaways | 1 |
| 1 | Takeaways | 3 |
| -2 | Difference | +2 |

## TEAM STATISTICS

| CHI. | | NYG |
|---|---|---|
| 11 | First Downs- Total | 23 |
| 0 | First Downs- Rushing | 16 |
| 11 | First Downs- Passing | 7 |
| 0 | First Downs- Penalty | 0 |
| 0 | Fumbles- Number | 1 |
| 0 | Fumbles- Lost Ball | 1 |
| 4 | Penalties- Number | 2 |
| 30 | Yards Penalized | 15 |
| 0 | Missed Field Goals | 0 |
| 52 | Offensive Plays | 68 |
| 232 | Net Yards | 288 |
| 4.5 | Average Gain | 4.2 |
| 2 | Giveaways | 1 |
| 1 | Takeaways | 2 |
| -1 | Difference | +1 |

## INDIVIDUAL STATISTICS

### WASHINGTON / SAN FRANCISCO

**RUSHING**

| | No. | Yds. | Avg. | | No. | Yds. | Avg. |
|---|---|---|---|---|---|---|---|
| Byner | 12 | 51 | 4.3 | Craig | 12 | 20 | 1.7 |
| Riggs | 10 | 18 | 1.8 | Sydney | 7 | 19 | 2.7 |
| Monk | 1 | 9 | 9.0 | Rathman | 4 | 6 | 1.5 |
| Mitchell | 1 | 2 | 2.0 | Montana | 1 | 1 | 1.0 |
| | 24 | 80 | 3.3 | | 24 | 46 | 1.9 |

**RECEIVING**

| | No. | Yds. | Avg. | | No. | Yds. | Avg. |
|---|---|---|---|---|---|---|---|
| Monk | 10 | 163 | 16.3 | Rice | 6 | 68 | 11.3 |
| Clark | 6 | 63 | 10.5 | Jones | 4 | 103 | 25.8 |
| Sanders | 4 | 78 | 19.5 | Sydney | 4 | 10 | 2.5 |
| Mitchell | 3 | 25 | 8.3 | Craig | 3 | 54 | 18.0 |
| Hobbs | 1 | 13 | 13.0 | Sherrard | 3 | 16 | 5.3 |
| Warren | 1 | 11 | 1.0 | Taylor | 2 | 38 | 19.0 |
| Riggs | 1 | 8 | 8.0 | Williams | 1 | 13 | 13.0 |
| Byner | 1 | 0 | 0.0 | | 23 | 302 | 13.1 |
| | 27 | 361 | 13.4 | | | | |

**PUNTING**

| | | | | | | |
|---|---|---|---|---|---|---|
| Goodburn | 4 | 33.0 | | Helton | 5 | 41.8 |

**PUNT RETURNS**

| | No. | Yds. | Avg. | | No. | Yds. | Avg. |
|---|---|---|---|---|---|---|---|
| Howard | 2 | 15 | 7.5 | Taylor | 1 | -4 | -4.0 |
| Green | 1 | 5 | 5.0 | | | | |
| | 3 | 20 | 6.7 | | | | |

**KICKOFF RETURNS**

| | No. | Yds. | Avg. | | No. | Yds. | Avg. |
|---|---|---|---|---|---|---|---|
| Howard | 2 | 37 | 18.5 | D. Carter | 1 | 19 | 19.0 |
| Mitchell | 2 | 37 | 18.5 | | | | |
| | 4 | 74 | 18.5 | | | | |

**INTERCEPTION RETURNS**

| | No. | Yds. | Avg. | | No. | Yds. | Avg. |
|---|---|---|---|---|---|---|---|
| Coleman | 1 | 15 | 15.0 | M. Carter | 1 | 61 | 61.0 |
| | | | | Jackson | 1 | 0 | 0.0 |
| | | | | Pollard | 1 | 0 | 0.0 |
| | | | | | 3 | 61 | 20.3 |

**PASSING**

### WASHINGTON

| | Att. | Comp. | Comp. Pct. | Yds. | Int. | Yds./ Att. | Yds./ Comp. |
|---|---|---|---|---|---|---|---|
| Rypien | 48 | 27 | 56.3 | 361 | 3 | 7.5 | 13.4 |

### SAN FRANCISCO

| | Att. | Comp. | Comp. Pct. | Yds. | Int. | Yds./ Att. | Yds./ Comp. |
|---|---|---|---|---|---|---|---|
| Montana | 31 | 22 | 71.0 | 274 | 1 | 8.8 | 12.5 |
| Sydney | 1 | 1 | 100.0 | 28 | 0 | 28.0 | 28.0 |
| | 32 | 23 | 71.9 | 302 | 1 | 9.4 | 13.1 |

## INDIVIDUAL STATISTICS

### CHICAGO / N.Y. GIANTS

**RUSHING**

| | No. | Yds. | Avg. | | No. | Yds. | Avg. |
|---|---|---|---|---|---|---|---|
| Anderson | 12 | 19 | 1.6 | O. Anderson | 21 | 80 | 3.8 |
| Muster | 4 | 8 | 2.0 | Hostetler | 6 | 43 | 7.2 |
| | 16 | 27 | 1.7 | Tillman | 9 | 31 | 3.4 |
| | | | | Carthon | 8 | 19 | 2.4 |
| | | | | Meggett | 2 | 18 | 9.0 |
| | | | | Hampton | 2 | 3 | 1.5 |
| | | | | | 48 | 194 | 4.0 |

**RECEIVING**

| | No. | Yds. | Avg. | | No. | Yds. | Avg. |
|---|---|---|---|---|---|---|---|
| Anderson | 4 | 23 | 5.8 | Baker | 3 | 58 | 19.3 |
| Davis | 3 | 76 | 25.3 | Bavaro | 3 | 25 | 8.3 |
| Thornton | 3 | 28 | 9.3 | Ingram | 1 | 12 | 12.0 |
| Muster | 3 | 21 | 7.0 | Mrosko | 1 | 6 | 6.0 |
| Gentry | 2 | 23 | 11.5 | O. Anderson | 1 | 6 | 6.0 |
| Kozlowski | 1 | 10 | 10.0 | Cross | 1 | 5 | 5.0 |
| Morris | 1 | 24 | 24.0 | Metcalf | 1 | 8 | 8.0 |
| | 17 | 205 | 12.1 | | 10 | 112 | 11.2 |

**PUNTING**

| | | | | | | |
|---|---|---|---|---|---|---|
| Buford | 2 | 42.0 | | Landeta | 3 | 40.7 |

**PUNT RETURNS**

| | No. | Yds. | Avg. | | No. | Yds. | Avg. |
|---|---|---|---|---|---|---|---|
| Bailey | 2 | 3 | 1.5 | Meggett | 1 | 13 | 13.0 |

**KICKOFF RETURNS**

| | No. | Yds. | Avg. | | No. | Yds. | Avg. |
|---|---|---|---|---|---|---|---|
| Bailey | 2 | 61 | 30.5 | Ingram | 1 | 18 | 18.0 |
| Gentry | 2 | 42 | 21.0 | | | | |
| Rouse | 1 | 9 | 9.0 | | | | |
| | 5 | 112 | 22.4 | | | | |

**INTERCEPTION RETURNS**

| | No. | Yds. | Avg. |
|---|---|---|---|
| Walls | 1 | 37 | 37.0 |
| Collins | 1 | 11 | 11.0 |
| | 2 | 48 | 24.0 |

**PASSING**

### CHICAGO

| | Att. | Comp. | Comp. Pct. | Yds. | Int. | Yds./ Att. | Yds./ Comp. |
|---|---|---|---|---|---|---|---|
| Tomczak | 36 | 17 | 47.2 | 205 | 2 | 5.7 | 12.1 |

### N.Y. GIANTS

| | Att. | Comp. | Comp. Pct. | Yds. | Int. | Yds./ Att. | Yds./ Comp. |
|---|---|---|---|---|---|---|---|
| Hostetler | 17 | 10 | 58.8 | 112 | 0 | 6.6 | 11.2 |

# 1990 Championship Games

## SCORING

| | | | | | |
|---|---|---|---|---|---|
| L.A. RAIDERS | 3 | 0 | 0 | 0 - 3 | |
| BUFFALO | 21 | 20 | 0 | 10 - 51 | |

**First Quarter**
Buf.  Lofton, 13 yard pass from Kelly
      PAT — Norwood (kick)
L.A.Rd.  Jaeger, 41 yard field goal
Buf.  Thomas, 12 yard run
      PAT — Norwood (kick)
Buf.  Talley, 27 yard interception return
      PAT — Norwood (kick)

**Second Quarter**
Buf.  K. Davis, 1 yard run
      (kick blocked)
Buf.  K. Davis, 3 yard run
      PAT — Norwood (kick)
Buf.  Lofton, 8 yard pass from Kelly
      PAT — Norwood (kick)

**Fourth Quarter**
Buf.  K. Davis, 1 yard run
      PAT — Norwood (kick)
Buf.  Norwood, 39 yard field goal

### TEAM STATISTICS

| L.A.Rd. | | BUF. |
|---|---|---|
| 21 | First Downs- Total | 30 |
| 12 | First Downs- Rushing | 14 |
| 8 | First Downs- Passing | 15 |
| 1 | First Downs- Penalty | 1 |
| 1 | Fumbles- Number | 3 |
| 1 | Fumbles- Lost Ball | 3 |
| 2 | Penalties- Number | 6 |
| 28 | Yards Penalized | 32 |
| 0 | Missed Field Goals | 1 |
| 68 | Offensive Plays | 69 |
| 320 | Net Yards | 502 |
| 4.7 | Average Gain | 7.3 |
| 7 | Giveaways | 1 |
| 1 | Takeaways | 7 |
| - 6 | Difference | + 6 |

## SCORING

| | | | | | |
|---|---|---|---|---|---|
| N.Y. GIANTS | 3 | 3 | 3 | 6 - 15 | |
| SAN FRANCISCO | 3 | 3 | 7 | 0 - 13 | |

**First Quarter**
S.F.  Cofer, 47 yard field goal
NYG  Bahr, 28 yard field goal

**Second Quarter**
NYG  Bahr, 42 yard field goal
S.F.  Cofer, 35 yard field goal

**Third Quarter**
S.F.  Taylor, 61 yard pass from Montana
      PAT — Cofer (kick)
NYG  Bahr, 46 yard field goal

**Fourth Quarter**
NYG  Bahr, 38 yard field goal
NYG  Bahr, 42 yard field goal

### TEAM STATISTICS

| NYG | | S.F. |
|---|---|---|
| 20 | First Downs- Total | 13 |
| 8 | First Downs- Rushing | 1 |
| 8 | First Downs- Passing | 11 |
| 4 | First Downs- Penalty | 1 |
| 0 | Fumbles- Number | 3 |
| 0 | Fumbles- Lost Ball | 1 |
| 5 | Penalties- Number | 9 |
| 45 | Yards Penalized | 63 |
| 1 | Missed Field Goals | 0 |
| 68 | Offensive Plays | 41 |
| 311 | Net Yards | 240 |
| 4.6 | Average Gain | 5.9 |
| 0 | Giveaways | 1 |
| 1 | Takeaways | 0 |
| +1 | Difference | - 1 |

## A.F.C. CHAMPIONSHIP GAME
### January 20, 1991 at BUFFALO, N.Y.
#### (Attendance 80,324)

The Buffalo Bills were nearly perfect in dismantling the Los Angeles Raiders for the A.F.C. title. The Bills' 41-points set a record for the biggest first-half splurge in championship game history. And, even though Buffalo concentrated on conservative, run-out-the-clock football in the second half, the 48-point margin was the second biggest ever — behind only the Bears' legendary 73-0 beating of the Redskins in 1940.

Buffalo jumped out to a 7-0 lead at 3:30 of the first quarter when Jim Kelly's 13-yard pass to Jim Lofton capped a 75-yard drive. The Raiders came right back with a 41-yard field goal by Jeff Jaeger's l. But it took the Bills only a little over a minute to score a second TD on a 12-yard run by Thurman Thomas, with a 41-yard Kelly-to-Lofton pass the key play in the 66-yard drive.

Trailing 14-3, the Raiders self-destructed. Jay Schroeder's pass was intercepted at the 27 by Darryl Talley, who raced into the end zone with Buffalo's third score of the first quarter. Schroeder was intercepted four more times.

Buffalo scored three more TD's in the second quarter, all of them on drives of more than 50 yards. Backup Kenneth Davis scored two of his three touchdowns on short runs and Lofton took another Kelly pass for the final first-half score.

The Bills stayed mainly on the ground in the second half, but at the top of the fourth quarter Davis scored his third TD to finish off a 78-yard drive. Scott Norwood ended the scoring with a 39-yard field goal a few minutes later.

## N.F.C. CHAMPIONSHIP GAME
### January 20, 1991 at San Francisco, Calif.
#### (Attendance 65,750)

The New York Giants ended the San Francisco 49ers' dreams of a third-straight Super Bowl championship in a game that had seven field goals and only one touchdown. Five of the field goals were kicked by the Giants' Matt Bahr to offset the 49ers' touchdown and pair of goals. The same two teams met a month earlier on the same field, with San Francisco collecting the only touchdown in that game, too, but holding New York to only one field goal for a 7-3 win.

With regular quarterback Phil Simms injured, the Giants used a conservative ground attack to keep the pressure off reserve Jeff Hostetler, who nevertheless hit on several key passes to help set up field-goal attempts.

San Francisco jumped off to a 3-0 lead in the first quarter with a field goal of its own, 47 yards by Mike Cofer. Bahr tied the game before the end of the period with a 28-yarder. In the second quarter, the teams again exchanged field goals, Bahr from 42 yards and Cofer from 35.

Less than five minutes into the third quarter, a 61-yard pass from Joe Montana to John Taylor gave the 49ers a 13-6 lead. Giants cornerback Everson Walls gambled on an interception on the play and was burned. Bahr hit a 46-yard field goal to narrow the gap before the period ended.

Montana was sacked and knocked from the game with a broken finger with 9:42 remaining. Trailing 13-9, the Giants surprised the 49ers with a fake punt with Gary Reasons running 30 yards to set up a 38-yard Bahr field goal to bring New York to within a point of San Francisco.

Under substitute Steve Young, the 49ers tried to control the ball on the ground as time ran down, but Roger Craig fumbled and New York's Lawrence Taylor recovered with 2:36 left. The Giants drove to within a field-goal range on a pair of Hostetler passes. Then, as time ran out, Bahr hit field goal No. 5 for the winner.

### INDIVIDUAL STATISTICS

**RUSHING**

| L.A. RAIDERS | No. | Yds. | Avg. | BUFFALO | No. | Yds. | Avg. |
|---|---|---|---|---|---|---|---|
| Bell | 5 | 36 | 7.2 | Thomas | 25 | 138 | 5.5 |
| Evans | 4 | 33 | 8.3 | Gardner | 1 | 23 | 23.0 |
| Schroeder | 4 | 33 | 8.3 | K. Davis | 10 | 21 | 2.1 |
| Allen | 10 | 26 | 2.6 | Kelly | 2 | 12 | 6.0 |
| Smith | 4 | 19 | 4.8 | Mueller | 3 | 6 | 2.0 |
| McCallum | 1 | 4 | 4.0 | D. Smith | 3 | 3 | 1.0 |
| | | | | Reich | 2 | -1 | -1.0 |
| | 28 | 151 | 5.4 | | 46 | 202 | 4.4 |

**RECEIVING**

| | No. | Yds. | Avg. | | No. | Yds. | Avg. |
|---|---|---|---|---|---|---|---|
| Fernandez | 4 | 57 | 14.3 | Lofton | 5 | 113 | 22.6 |
| Gault | 2 | 32 | 16.0 | Thomas | 5 | 61 | 12.2 |
| Horton | 3 | 23 | 7.7 | McKeller | 3 | 44 | 13.3 |
| Bell | 2 | 26 | 13.0 | Tasker | 2 | 53 | 26.5 |
| Allen | 2 | 19 | 9.5 | Reed | 2 | 29 | 14.5 |
| T. Brown | 2 | 17 | 8.5 | | 17 | 300 | 17.6 |
| | 15 | 174 | 11.7 | | | | |

**PUNTING**

| | No. | | Avg. | | No. | | Avg. |
|---|---|---|---|---|---|---|---|
| Gossett | 3 | | 40.3 | Tuten | 2 | | 37.5 |

**PUNT RETURNS**

| | No. | Yds. | Avg. | | No. | Yds. | Avg. |
|---|---|---|---|---|---|---|---|
| Patterson | 1 | 17 | 17.0 | Odomes | 1 | 18 | 18.0 |
| T. Brown | 1 | 5 | 5.0 | Edwards | 1 | 12 | 12.0 |
| | 2 | 22 | 11.0 | | 2 | 30 | 15.0 |

**KICKOFF RETURNS**

| | No. | Yds. | Avg. | | No. | Yds. | Avg. |
|---|---|---|---|---|---|---|---|
| Holland | 6 | 60 | 10.0 | D. Smith | 1 | 19 | 19.0 |
| R. Brown | 3 | 59 | 19.7 | Edwards | 1 | 11 | 11.0 |
| | 9 | 119 | 13.2 | | 2 | 30 | 15.0 |

**INTERCEPTION RETURNS**

| | No. | Yds. | Avg. | | No. | Yds. | Avg. |
|---|---|---|---|---|---|---|---|
| Lewis | 1 | 0 | 0.0 | Talley | 2 | 48 | 24.0 |
| | | | | Bentley | 1 | 32 | 32.0 |
| | | | | L. Smith | 1 | 24 | 24.0 |
| | | | | Odomes | 1 | 9 | 9.0 |
| | | | | Kelso | 1 | 0 | 0.0 |
| | | | | | 6 | 113 | 18.8 |

**PASSING**

| L.A. RAIDERS | Att. | Comp. | Comp. Pct. | Yds. | Int. | Yds./ Att. | Yds./ Comp. |
|---|---|---|---|---|---|---|---|
| Schroeder | 31 | 13 | 41.9 | 150 | 5 | 4.8 | 11.5 |
| Evans | 8 | 2 | 25.0 | 26 | 1 | 3.3 | 13.0 |
| **BUFFALO** | | | | | | | |
| Kelly | 23 | 17 | 73.9 | 300 | 1 | 13.0 | 17.6 |

### INDIVIDUAL STATISTICS

**RUSHING**

| N.Y. GIANTS | No. | Yds. | Avg. | SAN FRANCISCO | No. | Yds. | Avg. |
|---|---|---|---|---|---|---|---|
| Anderson | 20 | 67 | 3.4 | Craig | 8 | 26 | 3.3 |
| Meggett | 10 | 36 | 3.6 | Montana | 2 | 9 | 4.5 |
| Reasons | 1 | 30 | 30.0 | Rathman | 1 | 4 | 4.0 |
| Hostetler | 3 | 11 | 3.7 | | 11 | 39 | 3.5 |
| Carthon | 2 | 8 | 4.0 | | | | |
| | 36 | 152 | 4.2 | | | | |

**RECEIVING**

| | No. | Yds. | Avg. | | No. | Yds. | Avg. |
|---|---|---|---|---|---|---|---|
| Ingram | 5 | 82 | 16.4 | Taylor | 2 | 75 | 37.5 |
| Bavaro | 5 | 54 | 10.8 | Rice | 5 | 54 | 10.8 |
| Baker | 2 | 22 | 11.0 | Jones | 3 | 46 | 15.3 |
| Meggett | 2 | 15 | 7.5 | Craig | 3 | 16 | 5.3 |
| Anderson | 1 | 3 | 3.0 | Rathman | 4 | 16 | 4.0 |
| | 15 | 176 | 9.8 | Sherrard | 2 | 8 | 4.0 |
| | | | | | 19 | 215 | 11.3 |

**PUNTING**

| | No. | | Avg. | | No. | | Avg. |
|---|---|---|---|---|---|---|---|
| Landeta | 3 | | 41.3 | Helton | 5 | | 40.0 |

**PUNT RETURNS**

| | No. | Yds. | Avg. | | No. | Yds. | Avg. |
|---|---|---|---|---|---|---|---|
| Meggett | 5 | 42 | 8.4 | Taylor | 2 | 40 | 20.0 |

**KICKOFF RETURNS**

| | No. | Yds. | Avg. | | No. | Yds. | Avg. |
|---|---|---|---|---|---|---|---|
| Meggett | 2 | 36 | 18.0 | Carter | 3 | 74 | 24.7 |
| Cross | 1 | 3 | 3.0 | Tillman | 1 | 11 | 11.0 |
| | 3 | 39 | 13.0 | | 4 | 85 | 21.3 |

**INTERCEPTION RETURNS**

| | No. | Yds. | Avg. | | No. | Yds. | Avg. |
|---|---|---|---|---|---|---|---|
| | | None | | | 3 | 56 | 18.7 |

**PASSING**

| N.Y. GIANTS | Att. | Comp. | Comp. Pct. | Yds. | Int. | Yds./ Att. | Yds./ Comp. |
|---|---|---|---|---|---|---|---|
| Hostetler | 27 | 15 | 55.5 | 176 | 0 | 6.5 | 11.7 |
| Meggett | 1 | 0 | 0.0 | 0 | 0 | 0.0 | 0.0 |
| Cavanaugh | 1 | 0 | 0.0 | 0 | 0 | 0.0 | 0.0 |
| **SAN FRANCISCO** | | | | | | | |
| Montana | 26 | 18 | 69.2 | 190 | 0 | 7.3 | 10.6 |
| Young | 1 | 1 | 100.0 | 25 | 0 | 25.0 | |

# Worth Waiting For

The Silver Anniversary Super Bowl deserved no worse than a silver medal in the "best-ever" sweepstakes. Certainly it was the closest Super Bowl, with a one-point margin separating the winning New York Giants from the losing Buffalo Bills. It had the virtue of having the underdog triumph — the Bills were favored by about a touchdown, even though the AFC hadn't won a Super Bowl since XVIII. And, the decision came down to the last play of the game.

After Buffalo failed to move after the opening kickoff, New York took over on its own 31. The Giants drove to the Bills' 11 in 11 plays before settling for a 28-yard field goal by Matt Bahr. A Jeff Hostetler-to-Mark Ingram third-down pass for 16 yards was the key play of the drive.

When Buffalo got the ball back, Jim Kelly threw a 61-yard pass to James Lofton to move to the Giants' 8-yard-line, but the drive stalled. Scott Norwood tied the game with a 23-yard field goal.

Late in the first quarter, Buffalo began a drive at its own 20. In 12 plays, including passes by Kelly for 20 yards to Andre Reed and 16 yards to Thurman Thomas, the Bills drove for a touchdown. Don Smith scored on a one-yard slash.

After an exchange of punts, New York found itself in trouble when Dave Meggett elected to fair catch at the Giants' 7-yard-line. A few seconds later, Hostetler tripped over Ottis Anderson's foot while dropping back to pass and sprawled into the end zone. He scrambled to his feet but couldn't avoid Buffalo's Bruce Smith, who pulled him down for a safety. With New York kicking to them and leading 12-3, the Bills seemed about to take control, but three passes by Kelly fell incomplete. Neither team could put together a scoring drive until the Giants started from their 13 with 3:49 left in the second quarter. Hostetler mixed passes with the running of Anderson and Meggett to move the ball to the Buffalo 14, where a Hostetler-to-Stephen Baker scoring pass completed the 87-yard drive.

Trailing 12-10, the Giants began the second half with a long drive — a 75-yard, 14-play, grind-'em-out one that took 9:29 off the clock. Anderson's one-yard run put New York in front. Key plays were Hostetler's 11-yard pass to Meggett on a 3rd-and-8 and Anderson's 24-yard burst on a 3rd-and-1.

With the Giants' two long drives plus extended halftime, the Bills hadn't run anything more than a first-half-ending kneel-down in more than an hour, and it took them a while to get on-track. But, with 1:19 left in the third quarter, they started a drive from their 37 that ended in Thurman Thomas' 31-yard TD run on the first play of the fourth quarter.

Down 19-17, the Giants put together their third long, time-consuming drive of the game — 74 yards in 14 plays — with Bahr's 21-yard field goal giving New York back the lead, 20-19. Again, a clutch Hostetler pass, 16 yards to Mark Bavaro, salvaged a third-down situation.

But Buffalo wasn't finished. In the final two minutes, the Bills drove from their own 10 to the New York 29, but Norwood's attempt for a 47-yard, game-winning field goal sailed wide right.

## LINEUPS

| BUFF. | | NYG |
|---|---|---|
| | **OFFENSE** | |
| Lofton | WR | Ingram |
| Wolford | LT | Elliott |
| Ritcher | LG | Roberts |
| Hull | C | Oates |
| Davis | RG | Moore |
| Ballard | RT | Riesenberg |
| McKeller | TE | Bavaro |
| Reed | WR | Baker |
| Kelly | QB | Hostetler |
| Thomas | RB | O. Anderson |
| Mueller | FB | Carthon |
| | **DEFENSE** | |
| Seals | LE | Dorsey |
| Wright | NT | Howard |
| B. Smith | RE | Marshall |
| Bennett | LOLB | Banks |
| Conlan | LILB | DeOssie |
| Bentley | RILB | Johnson |
| Talley | ROLB | Taylor |
| Jackson | LCB | Collins |
| Odomes | RCB | Walls |
| Smith | SS | Jackson |
| Kelso | FS | Guyton |
| | **SUBSTITUTES** | |

**BUFFALO**

| | OFFENSE | |
|---|---|---|
| Reich | K. Davis | D. Smith |
| Gardner | Freotte | Lingner |
| G. Parker | Edwards | Rolle |
| Metzelaars | Tasker | G. Baldinger |
| Gilbert | | |
| | **DEFENSE** | |
| Hagy | Hicks | J. Williams |
| Drane | Bailey | Lodish |
| Pike | Garner | |
| | **KICKERS** | |
| Norwood | Tuten | |

**N.Y. GIANTS**

| | OFFENSE | |
|---|---|---|
| Rouson | Meggett | Tillman |
| B. Williams | Kratch | Mrosko |
| Robinson | Kyles | Cross |
| Cavanaugh | | |
| | **DEFENSE** | |
| Thompson | P. Williams | Duerson |
| Whitmore | R. Brown | Abrams |
| Reasons | McGrew | Washington |
| Fox | Cooks | |
| | **KICKERS** | |
| Bahr | Landeta | |

## SCORING

| | | | | | |
|---|---|---|---|---|---|
| BUFFALO | 3 | 9 | 0 | 7 | - 19 |
| N.Y. GIANTS | 3 | 7 | 7 | 3 | - 20 |

**First Quarter**
NYG — Bahr, 28 yard field goal
Buff. — Norwood, 23 yard field goal

**Second Quarter**
Buff. — D. Smith, 1 yard run
PAT — Norwood (kick)
Buff. — Hostetler, sacked by B. Smith for a safety
NYG — Baker, 14 yard pass from Hostetler
PAT — Bahr (kick)

**Third Quarter**
NYG — Anderson, 1 yard run
PAT — Bahr (kick)

**Fourth Quarter**
Buff. — Thomas, 31 yard run
PAT — Norwood (kick)
NYG — Bahr, 21 yard field goal

## TEAM STATISTICS

| BUFF. | | NYG |
|---|---|---|
| 18 | First Downs-Total | 24 |
| 8 | First Downs-Rushing | 10 |
| 9 | First Downs-Passing | 13 |
| 1 | First Downs-Penalty | 1 |
| 1 | Fumbles-Number | 0 |
| 0 | Fumbles-Lost Ball | 0 |
| 6 | Penalties-Number | 5 |
| 35 | Yards Penalized | 31 |
| 1 | Missed Field Goals | 0 |
| 56 | Offensive Plays | 73 |
| 371 | Net Yards | 386 |
| 6.6 | Average Gain | 5.3 |
| 0 | Giveaways | 0 |
| 0 | Takeaways | 0 |
| +0 | Difference | +0 |

## INDIVIDUAL STATISTICS

### BUFFALO

**RUSHING**

| | No. | Yds. | Avg. |
|---|---|---|---|
| Thomas | 15 | 135 | 9.0 |
| Kelly | 6 | 23 | 3.8 |
| Davis | 2 | 4 | 2.0 |
| Mueller | 1 | 3 | 3.0 |
| | 25 | 166 | 6.6 |

**RECEIVING**

| | No. | Yds. | Avg. |
|---|---|---|---|
| Reed | 8 | 62 | 7.8 |
| Thomas | 5 | 55 | 11.0 |
| Davis | 2 | 23 | 11.5 |
| McKeller | 2 | 11 | 5.5 |
| Lofton | 1 | 61 | 61.0 |
| | 18 | 212 | 11.8 |

**PUNTING**

| | No. | Yds. | Avg. |
|---|---|---|---|
| Tuten | 6 | | 38.8 |

**PUNT RETURNS**

| | No. | Yds. | Avg. |
|---|---|---|---|
| Edwards | 0 | 0 | 0.0 |

**KICKOFF RETURNS**

| | No. | Yds. | Avg. |
|---|---|---|---|
| D. Smith | 4 | 66 | 16.5 |
| Edwards | 2 | 48 | 24.0 |
| | 6 | 114 | 19.0 |

**INTERCEPTIONS RETURNS**

None

**PASSING**

| | Att. | Comp. | Comp. Pct. | Yds. | Int. | Yds./ Att. | Yds./ Comp. | Yards Lost Tackled |
|---|---|---|---|---|---|---|---|---|
| Kelly | 30 | 18 | 60.0 | 212 | 0 | 7.1 | 11.8 | 1-7 |

### N.Y. GIANTS

**RUSHING**

| | No. | Yds. | Avg. |
|---|---|---|---|
| Anderson | 21 | 102 | 4.9 |
| Meggett | 9 | 48 | 5.3 |
| Carthon | 3 | 12 | 4.0 |
| Hostetler | 6 | 10 | 1.7 |
| | 39 | 172 | 4.4 |

**RECEIVING**

| | No. | Yds. | Avg. |
|---|---|---|---|
| Ingram | 5 | 74 | 14.8 |
| Bavaro | 5 | 50 | 10.0 |
| Cross | 4 | 39 | 9.8 |
| Baker | 2 | 31 | 15.5 |
| Meggett | 2 | 18 | 9.0 |
| Anderson | 1 | 7 | 7.0 |
| Carthon | 1 | 3 | 3.0 |
| | 20 | 222 | 11.1 |

**PUNTING**

| | No. | Yds. | Avg. |
|---|---|---|---|
| Landeta | 4 | | 43.8 |

**PUNT RETURNS**

| | No. | Yds. | Avg. |
|---|---|---|---|
| Meggett | 3 | 37 | 18.5 |

**KICKOFF RETURNS**

| | No. | Yds. | Avg. |
|---|---|---|---|
| Meggett | 2 | 26 | 13.0 |
| Duerson | 1 | 22 | 22.0 |
| | 3 | 48 | 16.0 |

**INTERCEPTIONS RETURNS**

None

**PASSING**

| | Att. | Comp. | Comp. Pct. | Yds. | Int. | Yds./ Att. | Yds./ Comp. | Yards Lost Tackled |
|---|---|---|---|---|---|---|---|---|
| Hostetler | 32 | 20 | 62.5 | 222 | 0 | 6.9 | 11.1 | 2-8 |

# 1991 N.F.C.  Thumbs Up for Lions and Utley

The NFC won its eighth consecutive Super Bowl when the Redskins trounced the Bills in Super Bowl XXVI, which was played in Minneapolis, only the second in a northern city. But the big story of the 1991 season was the rejuvenation of the Lions coming on the heels of a tragic accident to one of their teammates. In Week 12, with Detroit's season on the line, guard Mike Utley fell forward while blocking and landed head-first on the Silverdome's artificial turf, tearing a ligament and bursting a spinal disk. Utley, 25, was paralyzed from the neck down. However, while being carried off the field on a stretcher, Utley gave his teammates the thumbs-up sign, galvanizing his teammates to five straight victories and the NFC Central Division championship.

The Lions made it all the way to the NFC championship game, where Washington knocked them back into reality. That was a lot farther than several perennial playoff teams got. The 49ers, playing without Joe Montana, missed the playoffs. So did the Eagles, who lost Randall Cunningham in the first game, and the Giants, who slumped to an 8-8 record on the heels of their Super Bowl XXV championship following a coaching change.

## EASTERN DIVISION

**Washington Redskins** — The Redskins went into the season unsure if Mark Rypien was an NFL-caliber quarterback and came out of it knowing he was the best quarterback in the league. Feeding off the team's stellar running game and throwing behind one of the league's biggest offensive lines (he was sacked only seven times all season), Rypien was able to open it up and throw long to a corps of receivers that included future Hall of Famer Art Monk, Gary Clark and Ricky Sanders. The running attack was fueled by Earnest Byner (1,048 yards), rookie Ricky Ervins (680 yards) and Gerald Riggs (11 touchdowns, and six more in the playoffs). Four Plan B free agents started on the league's second-best defense that included All-Pro's Wilber Marshall and Darrell Green. Placekicker Chip Lohmiller led the NFL with 149 points.

**Dallas Cowboys** — Two years of wheeling and dealing by owner Jerry Jones and coach Jimmy Johnson paid big dividends in 1991 as the Cowboys made the playoffs for the first time since 1985 and advanced to the second round of the playoffs. An explosive offense was led by running back Emmitt Smith, who led the NFL in rushing yards and carries (365 for 1,563) and wide receiver Michael Irvin, who caught 93 passes for a league-high 1,523 yards in his first injury-free season in the pros. Troy Aikman was the NFL's hottest quarterback over the first half of the season, and, when he went down with a sprained knee in the 12th game, the team's hopes didn't go down the tubes like they did in '90 because backup Steve Beuerlein kept the team in the playoff hunt. Defensive tackle Russell Maryland, the No. 1 pick in the 1991 draft, led an improved defense.

**Philadelphia Eagles** — Coach Rich Kotite knew his team's chances to make the the playoffs were shattered when quarterback Randall Cunningham suffered a season-ending knee injury only 18 minutes into the first game. Backup Jim McMahon battled numerous injuries and rallied the Eagles back into playoff contention. But, when he wasn't in the lineup, the Eagles were forced to start reclaimed veteran Pat Ryan and rookie Brad Goebel through a four-game losing streak and then waiver pickup Jeff Kemp for the last two games. But the big story in Philadelphia was the defense. The Eagles defense led the league in fewest total yards, fewest rushing yards and fewest passing yards — only the fifth team ever to achieve that rare triple.

**New York Giants** — When Bill Parcells resigned as head coach in May, everyone knew changes were in store for the defending Super Bowl champions. But nobody thought a .500 record and "home for the holidays" would be some of the changes. New coach Ray Handley's first decision was to decide the starting quarterback, and he chose Jeff Hostetler, who led the Giants to their victory in Super Bowl XXV. However, Hostetler was ineffective and eventually suffered a back injury and was replaced by veteran Phil Simms. Ottis Anderson was finally sent to the bench, and a star was born in the name of Rodney Hampton, who gained 1,059 yards rushing. The Giants' defense was still tough, but age was starting to show in the play of Lawrence Taylor, Carl Banks and some other veterans.

**Phoenix Cardinals** — The Cardinals got off to a quick start with victories in their first two games, but then the bottom fell out as they won only two more games in the remaining 14 contests, and the team lost its most games in franchise history. Starter Timm Rosenbach suffered a season-ending knee injury in the final preseason game, so the quarterbacking was done by Tom Tupa, Stan Gelbaugh (the Most Valuable Player in the World League of American Football) and Chris Chandler (who was cut by Tampa Bay). But, while the Phoenix defense was improved, the Cards scored no touchdowns in five games and only one in seven others. Defensive end Eric Swann, the top draft pick who didn't play college football, wasn't much help, but cornerback Aeneas Williams, a third-rounder, was one of the league's best.

## CENTRAL DIVISION

**Detroit Lions** — After years of struggling in mediocrity, the Lions broke free and did something special in 1991. They survived a 45-0 loss to Washington on Opening Day and the loss of five starters, and they rallied around a partially paralyzed teammate — guard Mike Utley — to record the best record in club history and the Central Division title. When Rodney Peete was injured in the eighth game, free-agent Erik Kramer took over and led the Lions to six straight victories to close out the season and then a thrashing of Dallas in the first round of the playoffs before the Redskins ended the season almost as it began. Detroit had gone 8-0 at home during the regular season. Barry Sanders rushed for 1,548 yards, second-most in the league, and the team's wide receivers — specifically Brett Perriman, Robert Clark and Mike Farr — blossomed.

**Chicago Bears** — Move over running game — the Bears turned into a passing team in 1991! However, Chicago lost its firm grip on the division crown by losing three of their final five games after winning five straight at midseason. Running backs Neal Anderson and Brad Muster were never 100 percent after suffering nagging injuries, and the Bears defense and special teams were inconsistent too many times. However, quarterback Jim Harbaugh did show that he could bring the team from behind, as he led them to last-minute victories over the Giants and Jets in Weeks Three and Four. Harbaugh, who set team records for passing attempts and completions, was the first Bears quarterback to start every game since 1981. And Wendell Davis had the most receptions and receiving yardage of any Bears receiver since 1970.

**Minnesota Vikings** — The Vikings had their second straight dismal season, finishing 8-8 and out of the playoffs. The quarterback situation was again the problem, as neither Wade Wilson nor Rich Gannon were effective. Running back Herschel Walker again seemed to be a disappointment, but he still rushed for 825 yards and scored 10 touchdowns. Cris Carter had the biggest year of the receivers, catching 72 passes for 962 yards and five scores. The defense, which fell apart in the second half of the season, was riddled by injuries on the line, few big plays from the linebackers and too many mistakes by the secondary men. As the season wound down, coach Jerry Burns announced his retirement.

**Green Bay Packers** — The Packers again refused to run the football, and, since neither Don Majkowski nor Mike Tomczak could spark anything at quarterback, Green Bay suffered through a 4-12 season, leading to the dismissal of head coach Lindy infante. Darrell Thompson showed some flashes at running back, but still gained only 471 yards while averaging 3.3 yards per carry. Backup Vince Workman scored 11 touchdowns but few people considered him as anything more than a role player. Run defense was the team's specialty. The Packers yielded only 96.6 yards per game, the lowest for a Green Bay team since 1940. Still, the Packers didn't have a Pro Bowl player on defense for the 13th time in 14 seasons. After the season, Ron Wolf was hired from the Jets to be Green Bay's new general manager, and Mike Holmgren came in from the 49ers as head coach.

**OFFENSE**

| | ATL | CHI | DAL | DET | G.B. | L.A. | MINN | N.O. | NYG | PHIL | PHX | S.F. | T.B. | WASH |
|---|---|---|---|---|---|---|---|---|---|---|---|---|---|---|
| FIRST DOWNS: | | | | | | | | | | | | | | |
| Total | 258 | 317 | 304 | 280 | 259 | 270 | 300 | 267 | 280 | 249 | 237 | 336 | 249 | 302 |
| by Rushing | 82 | 120 | 89 | 116 | 88 | 75 | 125 | 93 | 120 | 86 | 73 | 112 | 79 | 107 |
| by Passing | 162 | 168 | 191 | 148 | 150 | 180 | 158 | 157 | 148 | 142 | 143 | 197 | 147 | 179 |
| by Penalty | 14 | 29 | 24 | 16 | 21 | 15 | 17 | 17 | 12 | 21 | 21 | 27 | 23 | 16 |
| RUSHING: | | | | | | | | | | | | | | |
| Number | 410 | 502 | 433 | 454 | 381 | 388 | 464 | 483 | 487 | 446 | 391 | 440 | 371 | 540 |
| Yards | 1664 | 1949 | 1711 | 1930 | 1389 | 1285 | 2201 | 1709 | 2064 | 1396 | 1295 | 1861 | 1429 | 2049 |
| Average Yards | 4.1 | 3.9 | 4.0 | 4.3 | 3.6 | 3.3 | 4.7 | 3.5 | 4.2 | 3.1 | 3.3 | 4.2 | 3.9 | 3.8 |
| Touchdowns | 6 | 18 | 15 | 19 | 12 | 11 | 18 | 15 | 16 | 8 | 6 | 19 | 9 | 21 |
| PASSING: | | | | | | | | | | | | | | |
| Attempts | 500 | 497 | 500 | 459 | 514 | 518 | 477 | 506 | 428 | 513 | 492 | 522 | 495 | 447 |
| Completions | 260 | 286 | 305 | 252 | 272 | 289 | 284 | 292 | 261 | 285 | 254 | 325 | 250 | 261 |
| Completion Pct. | 52.0 | 57.5 | 61.0 | 54.9 | 52.9 | 55.8 | 59.5 | 57.7 | 61.0 | 55.6 | 51.6 | 62.3 | 50.5 | 58.4 |
| Passing Yards | 3524 | 3292 | 3663 | 2974 | 3213 | 3610 | 3016 | 3419 | 3025 | 3169 | 3039 | 4167 | 2955 | 3771 |
| Avg. Yds per Att. | 6.5 | 6.0 | 6.3 | 5.9 | 5.3 | 6.2 | 5.7 | 6.2 | 6.1 | 5.2 | 5.0 | 7.3 | 4.7 | 8.1 |
| Avg. Yds per Comp. | 14.0 | 11.5 | 12.0 | 11.8 | 11.8 | 12.5 | 10.6 | 11.7 | 11.6 | 11.1 | 12.0 | 12.8 | 11.8 | 14.5 |
| Times Tackled | 31 | 26 | 38 | 25 | 45 | 30 | 28 | 19 | 36 | 45 | 43 | 24 | 56 | 9 |
| Yds Lost Tackled | 185 | 172 | 273 | 116 | 270 | 200 | 133 | 160 | 181 | 263 | 372 | 170 | 383 | 79 |
| Net Yards | 3449 | 3120 | 3390 | 2858 | 2943 | 3410 | 2883 | 3259 | 2844 | 2906 | 2667 | 3997 | 2572 | 3692 |
| Touchdowns | 30 | 16 | 16 | 16 | 17 | 13 | 16 | 20 | 13 | 17 | 10 | 29 | 13 | 30 |
| Interceptions | 22 | 17 | 12 | 17 | 19 | 20 | 16 | 15 | 8 | 27 | 25 | 12 | 29 | 11 |
| Pct. Intercepted | 4.4 | 3.4 | 2.4 | 3.7 | 3.7 | 3.9 | 3.4 | 3.0 | 1.9 | 5.3 | 5.1 | 2.3 | 5.9 | 2.5 |
| PUNTS: | | | | | | | | | | | | | | |
| Number | 82 | 70 | 57 | 75 | 86 | 75 | 68 | 87 | 64 | 88 | 77 | 56 | 84 | 55 |
| Average | 42.6 | 40.2 | 42.6 | 41.2 | 40.4 | 38.1 | 45.5 | 43.0 | 43.3 | 41.4 | 44.7 | 39.2 | 40.3 | 37.6 |
| PUNT RETURNS | | | | | | | | | | | | | | |
| Number | 35 | 47 | 29 | 26 | 41 | 37 | 30 | 44 | 36 | 53 | 41 | 42 | 39 | 46 |
| Yards | 286 | 340 | 309 | 385 | 396 | 320 | 225 | 317 | 336 | 416 | 307 | 320 | 361 | 610 |
| Average Yards | 8.2 | 7.2 | 10.7 | 14.8 | 9.7 | 8.6 | 7.5 | 7.2 | 9.3 | 7.8 | 7.5 | 7.6 | 9.3 | 13.3 |
| Touchdowns | 0 | 0 | 1 | 1 | 0 | 0 | 0 | 0 | 1 | 0 | 0 | 0 | 0 | 2 |
| KICKOFF RET.: | | | | | | | | | | | | | | |
| Number | 52 | 45 | 52 | 57 | 60 | 59 | 44 | 50 | 50 | 47 | 52 | 50 | 60 | 49 |
| Yards | 997 | 763 | 1127 | 1170 | 1197 | 1070 | 899 | 879 | 917 | 764 | 972 | 1028 | 1047 | 926 |
| Average Yards | 19.2 | 17.0 | | 20.5 | 20.0 | 18.1 | 20.4 | 17.6 | 18.3 | 16.3 | 18.7 | 20.6 | 17.5 | 18.9 |
| Touchdowns | 1 | 0 | 1 | 0 | 1 | 0 | 0 | 0 | 0 | 0 | 0 | 1 | 0 | 0 |
| INTERCEPT RET.: | | | | | | | | | | | | | | |
| Number | 19 | 17 | 12 | 19 | 15 | 11 | 17 | 29 | 12 | 26 | 17 | 12 | 11 | 27 |
| Yards | 225 | 225 | 167 | 286 | 234 | 175 | 242 | 482 | 122 | 280 | 187 | 125 | 63 | 279 |
| Average Yards | 13.9 | 8.6 | 11.5 | 16.1 | 9.6 | 8.8 | 16.3 | 19.8 | 5.0 | 14.3 | 17.1 | 10.0 | 19.5 | 12.9 |
| Touchdowns | 1 | 1 | 2 | 2 | 0 | 1 | 2 | 2 | 0 | 1 | 1 | 0 | 0 | 3 |
| PENALTIES: | | | | | | | | | | | | | | |
| Number | 113 | 80 | 74 | 93 | 98 | 108 | 88 | 101 | 92 | 111 | 78 | 114 | 88 | 90 |
| Yards | 929 | 662 | 610 | 799 | 834 | 774 | 675 | 801 | 719 | 839 | 661 | 902 | 780 | 798 |
| FUMBLES: | | | | | | | | | | | | | | |
| Number | 19 | 25 | 23 | 25 | 41 | 32 | 21 | 24 | 33 | 34 | 31 | 33 | 30 | 26 |
| Number Lost | 14 | 16 | 12 | 13 | 17 | 20 | 10 | 15 | 15 | 16 | 14 | 19 | 18 | 12 |
| POINTS: | | | | | | | | | | | | | | |
| Total | 361 | 299 | 342 | 339 | 273 | 234 | 301 | 341 | 281 | 285 | 196 | 393 | 199 | 485 |
| PAT Attempts | 42 | 34 | 37 | 40 | 31 | 26 | 36 | 38 | 30 | 29 | 19 | 50 | 22 | 56 |
| PAT Made | 40 | 32 | 37 | 40 | 31 | 25 | 34 | 38 | 29 | 27 | 19 | 49 | 22 | 56 |
| FG Attempts | 26 | 29 | 39 | 28 | 24 | 17 | 24 | 32 | 31 | 33 | 30 | 28 | 20 | 43 |
| FG Made | 21 | 19 | 27 | 19 | 18 | 17 | 17 | 25 | 24 | 28 | 21 | 14 | 15 | 31 |
| Percent FG Made | 80.8 | 65.5 | 69.2 | 67.9 | 75.0 | 100.0 | 70.8 | 78.1 | 77.4 | 84.8 | 70.0 | 50.0 | 75.0 | 72.1 |
| Safeties | 3 | 0 | 1 | 1 | 1 | 1 | 0 | 0 | 0 | 0 | 0 | 1 | 0 | 0 |

**DEFENSE**

| | ATL | CHI | DAL | DET | G.B. | L.A. | MINN | N.O. | NYG | PHIL | PHX | S.F. | T.B. | WASH |
|---|---|---|---|---|---|---|---|---|---|---|---|---|---|---|
| FIRST DOWNS: | | | | | | | | | | | | | | |
| Total | 278 | 254 | 299 | 305 | 298 | 286 | 301 | 214 | 257 | 206 | 301 | 260 | 295 | 242 |
| by Rushing | 94 | 77 | 103 | 93 | 99 | 105 | 106 | 63 | 103 | 53 | 132 | 86 | 120 | 72 |
| by Passing | 157 | 164 | 180 | 189 | 177 | 162 | 172 | 139 | 138 | 133 | 156 | 155 | 147 | 151 |
| by Penalty | 27 | 13 | 16 | 23 | 22 | 19 | 23 | 12 | 16 | 20 | 13 | 19 | 28 | 19 |
| RUSHING: | | | | | | | | | | | | | | |
| Number | 466 | 389 | 400 | 444 | 457 | 469 | 456 | 334 | 414 | 383 | 493 | 399 | 512 | 348 |
| Yards | 1953 | 1580 | 1571 | 1760 | 1546 | 1659 | 1837 | 1213 | 1726 | 1136 | 2136 | 1512 | 2107 | 1346 |
| Average Yards | 4.2 | 4.1 | 3.9 | 4.0 | 3.4 | 3.5 | 4.0 | 3.6 | 4.2 | 3.0 | 4.3 | 3.8 | 4.1 | 3.9 |
| Touchdowns | 13 | 9 | 11 | 16 | 10 | 19 | 17 | 6 | 11 | 4 | 27 | 8 | 21 | 11 |
| PASSING: | | | | | | | | | | | | | | |
| Attempts | 481 | 513 | 540 | 534 | 531 | 434 | 499 | 491 | 440 | 467 | 447 | 499 | 438 | 549 |
| Completions | 252 | 286 | 320 | 315 | 305 | 259 | 286 | 259 | 251 | 206 | 268 | 267 | 257 | 292 |
| Completion Pct. | 52.4 | 55.8 | 59.3 | 59.0 | 57.4 | 59.7 | 57.3 | 52.7 | 57.0 | 44.1 | 60.0 | 53.5 | 58.7 | 53.2 |
| Passing Yards | 3532 | 3184 | 3646 | 3523 | 3573 | 3657 | 3396 | 3057 | 3128 | 2807 | 3069 | 3254 | 3130 | 3292 |
| Avg. Yds per Att. | 6.5 | 5.3 | 6.2 | 5.8 | 5.7 | 7.9 | 6.0 | 5.0 | 6.1 | 4.6 | 6.2 | 5.7 | 6.0 | 4.9 |
| Avg. Yds per Comp. | 14.0 | 11.1 | 11.4 | 11.2 | 11.7 | 14.1 | 11.9 | 11.8 | 12.5 | 13.6 | 11.5 | 12.2 | 12.2 | 11.3 |
| Times Tackled | 29 | 40 | 23 | 30 | 45 | 17 | 33 | 50 | 34 | 55 | 25 | 31 | 39 | 50 |
| Yds Lost Tackled | 237 | 257 | 151 | 237 | 307 | 112 | 217 | 337 | 254 | 394 | 153 | 212 | 258 | 345 |
| Net Yards | 3295 | 2927 | 3495 | 3286 | 3266 | 3545 | 3179 | 2720 | 2874 | 2413 | 2916 | 3042 | 2872 | 2947 |
| Touchdowns | 28 | 19 | 17 | 16 | 20 | 25 | 16 | 12 | 17 | 16 | 12 | 16 | 15 | 13 |
| Interceptions | 19 | 17 | 12 | 19 | 15 | 11 | 17 | 29 | 12 | 26 | 17 | 12 | 11 | 27 |
| Pct. Intercepted | 4.0 | 3.3 | 2.2 | 3.6 | 2.8 | 2.5 | 3.4 | 5.9 | 2.7 | 5.6 | 3.8 | 2.4 | 2.5 | 4.9 |
| PUNTS: | | | | | | | | | | | | | | |
| Number | 79 | 81 | 61 | 67 | 76 | 68 | 67 | 88 | 74 | 86 | 71 | 82 | 71 | 85 |
| Average | 40.3 | 41.3 | 38.8 | 39.2 | 42.1 | 41.6 | 42.7 | 42.3 | 40.5 | 42.7 | 45.2 | 41.0 | 42.9 | 41.7 |
| PUNT RETURNS | | | | | | | | | | | | | | |
| Number | 45 | 28 | 28 | 35 | 35 | 33 | 42 | 50 | 35 | 42 | 48 | 30 | 49 | 31 |
| Yards | 387 | 205 | 231 | 340 | 375 | 292 | 426 | 470 | 350 | 431 | 313 | 239 | 559 | 190 |
| Average Yards | 8.6 | 7.3 | 8.3 | 9.7 | 10.7 | 8.8 | 10.1 | 9.4 | 10.0 | 10.3 | 6.5 | 8.0 | 11.4 | 6.1 |
| Touchdowns | 0 | 0 | 0 | 1 | 1 | 0 | 0 | 0 | 1 | 1 | 0 | 0 | 1 | 0 |
| KICKOFF RET.: | | | | | | | | | | | | | | |
| Number | 67 | 58 | 69 | 63 | 47 | 39 | 43 | 35 | 55 | 60 | 42 | 66 | 32 | 66 |
| Yards | 1419 | 1134 | 1169 | 1095 | 942 | 671 | 851 | 851 | 940 | 1146 | 958 | 1288 | 720 | 1153 |
| Average Yards | 21.2 | 19.6 | 16.9 | 17.4 | 20.5 | 17.2 | 19.8 | 24.3 | 17.1 | 19.1 | 22.8 | 19.5 | 22.5 | 17.5 |
| Touchdowns | 1 | 0 | 1 | 0 | 0 | 0 | 0 | 2 | 0 | 0 | 1 | 1 | 0 | 0 |
| INTERCEPT RET.: | | | | | | | | | | | | | | |
| Number | 22 | 17 | 12 | 17 | 19 | 20 | 16 | 15 | 8 | 27 | 25 | 12 | 29 | 11 |
| Yards | 279 | 145 | 244 | 229 | 185 | 297 | 203 | 257 | 36 | 432 | 399 | 82 | 349 | 109 |
| Average Yards | 12.7 | 8.5 | 20.3 | 13.5 | 9.7 | 14.9 | 12.7 | 17.1 | 4.5 | 16.0 | 16.0 | 6.8 | 12.0 | 9.9 |
| Touchdowns | 1 | 0 | 2 | 1 | 1 | 1 | 1 | 2 | 0 | 2 | 1 | 0 | 1 | 1 |
| PENALTIES: | | | | | | | | | | | | | | |
| Number | 100 | 94 | 97 | 94 | 106 | 83 | 92 | 95 | 80 | 105 | 94 | 84 | 110 | 94 |
| Yards | 802 | 891 | 801 | 704 | 777 | 743 | 709 | 711 | 622 | 881 | 734 | 782 | 925 | 767 |
| FUMBLES: | | | | | | | | | | | | | | |
| Number | 27 | 25 | 23 | 32 | 31 | 17 | 24 | 34 | 27 | 43 | 37 | 32 | 27 | 22 |
| Number Lost | 16 | 13 | 11 | 17 | 14 | 8 | 11 | 19 | 9 | 22 | 21 | 16 | 16 | 14 |
| POINTS: | | | | | | | | | | | | | | |
| Total | 338 | 269 | 310 | 295 | 313 | 390 | 306 | 211 | 297 | 244 | 344 | 239 | 365 | 224 |
| PAT Attempts | 43 | 29 | 32 | 34 | 35 | 47 | 35 | 23 | 30 | 24 | 43 | 25 | 41 | 26 |
| PAT Made | 41 | 29 | 31 | 34 | 34 | 46 | 34 | 22 | 30 | 23 | 41 | 23 | 40 | 26 |
| FG Attempts | 26 | 30 | 39 | 28 | 31 | 28 | 29 | 21 | 30 | 33 | 23 | 25 | 35 | 18 |
| FG Made | 13 | 22 | 29 | 19 | 23 | 20 | 20 | 17 | 29 | 25 | 15 | 22 | 25 | 14 |
| Percent FG Made | 50.0 | 73.3 | 74.4 | 67.9 | 74.2 | 71.4 | 69.0 | 81.0 | 96.7 | 75.8 | 65.2 | 88.0 | 71.4 | 77.8 |
| Safeties | 0 | 0 | 0 | 0 | 0 | 1 | 1 | 0 | 0 | 1 | 0 | 0 | 2 | 0 |

**Tampa Bay Buccaneers** — The Buccaneers were just plain lousy from start to finish in 1991. The offense scored only 199 points, as quarterback Vinny Testaverde again did little to show why he was the first pick in the 1987 NFL draft. Testaverde was benched twice, but both times regained his starting job. Reggie Cobb came on in the second half of the season at running back, and rookie wide receiver Lawrence Dawsey led the Bucs in receiving. Even though the defense outperformed the offense, it had a big weakness in its inability to create turnovers and make big plays. Still, Tampa Bay is a team with talent at the skill positions and on defense, where linebacker Broderick Thomas began to shine. That's good news for new head coach Sam Wyche, who came over from Cincinnati at the end of the season to replace Richard Williamson.

## WESTERN DIVISION

**New Orleans Saints** — For the first time in their 25-year history, the Saints won a division championship with an 11-5 record. However, after that brief highlight, the team lost its third playoff game in three tries. Bobby Hebert returned from a one-year holdout and led New Orleans to a 9-2 record. However, the Saints were only 2-3 when he was injured and Steve Walsh was in the lineup. Floyd Turner blossomed into a fine wide receiver, scoring eight touchdowns. But the running attack was lethergic, with nobody gaining even 500 yards. The strength of the team was the defense, which led the NFL in fewest points allowed. Linebacker Pat Swilling led the NFL in sacks and was voted the league's Defensive Player of the Year.

**Atlanta Falcons** — For a change, the Falcons backed up their boasts in 1991, finishing 10-6 and ahead of the 49ers in the NFC West. Atlanta ranked fifth in the NFL in points scored, thanks to a potent run-and-shoot offense led by quarterback Chris Miller, who threw 26 touchdown passes. Wide receiver Michael Haynes caught only 50 passes but averaged a league-high 22.4 yards per reception and scored 12 times. Andre Rison chipped in with 11 TD's. They were the NFL's most explosive receiving duo. But, again, it was a matter of the offense outscoring the opponents, because the Atlanta defense showed some holes. Cornerbacks Deion Sanders and Tim McKyer might have been the NFL's best pair, but the Falcons couldn't stop the run.

**San Francisco 49ers** — The headlines read no Montana and no playoffs for the 49ers in 1991. For the first time in more than a decade, Joe Montana wasn't around to take the 49ers under his wing, as he missed the season after elbow surgery. Steve Young won the NFL passing title and rushed for 415 yards, but was only 5-5 as a starter and eventually was knocked out of the lineup with a sprained knee. That put journeyman Steve Bono into the lineup, and he responded with his finest showing ever and a 5-1 record. The running game again had nobody to depend on, but wide receivers Jerry Rice and John Taylor came through in typical fashion and 23 touchdowns between them. But, in the end, San Francisco missed departed veterans Ronnie Lott and Roger Craig, and it received terrible plackicking from Mike Cofer.

**Los Angeles Rams** — The Rams started off the '91 season 3-3 before losing their final nine games for a 3-13 record (and 8-24 over two seasons). Quarterback Jim Everett plummeted to mediocrity, finishing as the league's 14th-ranked passer and throwing a career-high 20 interceptions. Robert Delpino looked good at running back early in the season, but down the stretch nobody could hold down the job, and the Rams finished 27th in the NFL in rushing. And the defense didn't have enough talent to fit into coordinator Jeff Fisher's attacking schemes. Los Angeles allowed an NFC-high 390 points and finished last in the NFL with 17 sacks and 19 takeaways. When the season was over, the John Robinson era ended, giving way to the Chuck Knox era, Part Two.

### WASHINGTON REDSKINS 14-2 Joe Gibbs

| Scores of Each Game | | |
|---|---|---|
| 45 | DETROIT | 0 |
| 33 | Dallas | 31 |
| 34 | PHOENIX | 0 |
| 34 | Cincinnati | 27 |
| 23 | PHILADELPHIA | 0 |
| 20 | Chicago | 7 |
| 42 | CLEVELAND | 17 |
| 17 | N.Y. Giants | 13 |
| 16 | HOUSTON | *13 |
| 56 | ATLANTA | 17 |
| 41 | Pittsburgh | 14 |
| 21 | DALLAS | 24 |
| 27 | L.A. Rams | 6 |
| 20 | Phoenix | 14 |
| 34 | N.Y. GIANTS | 17 |
| 22 | Philadelphia | 24 |

| UseName | Pos. | Hgt. | Wgt. | Age | Int | Pts |
|---|---|---|---|---|---|---|
| Joe Jacoby | OT-OG | 6'7" | 314 | 31 | | |
| Jim Lachey | OT | 6'6" | 294 | 28 | | |
| Ed Simmons | OT | 6'5" | 300 | 27 | | |
| Mark Adickes | OG | 6'4" | 285 | 30 | | |
| Russ Grimm | OG | 6'3" | 284 | 32 | | |
| Raleigh McKenzie | OG-C | 6'2" | 279 | 28 | | |
| Mark Schlereth | OG | 6'3" | 283 | 25 | | |
| Ralph Tamm (from CLE, to CIN) | OG | 6'4" | 280 | 25 | | |
| Jeff Bostic | C | 6'2" | 278 | 32 | | |
| Jason Buck | DE | 6'4" | 265 | 28 | | |
| Markus Koch | DE | 6'5" | 275 | 28 | | |
| Charles Mann | DE | 6'6" | 272 | 30 | | |
| Fred Stokes | DE | 6'3" | 274 | 27 | 1 | |
| James Geathers | DT | 6'7" | 289 | 31 | | |
| Tim Johnson | DT | 6'3" | 283 | 26 | 1 | |
| Eric Williams | DT | 6'4" | 290 | 29 | | |
| Bobby Wilson | DT | 6'2" | 283 | 23 | | |

Ray Brown — Elbow Injury

| UseName | Pos. | Hgt. | Wgt. | Age | Int | Pts |
|---|---|---|---|---|---|---|
| Ravin Caldwell | LB | 6'3" | 240 | 28 | | |
| Monte Coleman | LB | 6'2" | 245 | 33 | 1 | |
| Andre Collins | LB | 6'1" | 233 | 23 | 2 | 6 |
| Kurt Gouveia | LB | 6'1" | 228 | 26 | 1 | |
| Wilber Marshall | LB | 6'1" | 231 | 29 | 5 | 6 |
| Matt Millen | LB | 6'2" | 245 | 33 | | |
| Danny Copeland | DB | 6'2" | 213 | 25 | 1 | |
| Travis Curtis | DB | 5'10" | 180 | 25 | | |
| Brad Edwards | DB | 6'1" | 207 | 25 | 4 | |
| Darrell Green | DB | 5'8" | 170 | 31 | 5 | |
| Terry Hoage | DB | 6'2" | 201 | 29 | | |
| A.J. Johnson | DB | 5'8" | 170 | 24 | | |
| Sidney Johnson | DB | 5'9" | 175 | 26 | 2 | |
| Martin Mayhew | DB | 5'8" | 172 | 25 | 3 | 6 |
| Alvoid Mays | DB | 5'9" | 180 | 25 | 1 | |
| Clarence Vaughn | DB | 6' | 202 | 27 | | |
| Alvin Walton | DB | 6' | 180 | 27 | | |

| UseName | Pos. | Hgt. | Wgt. | Age | Int | Pts |
|---|---|---|---|---|---|---|
| Stan Humphries | QB | 6'2" | 223 | 26 | | |
| Jeff Rutledge | QB | 6'1" | 193 | 34 | | |
| Mark Rypien | QB | 6'4" | 234 | 28 | | 6 |
| Earnest Byner | HB-FB | 5'10" | 218 | 28 | | 30 |
| Ricky Ervins | HB | 5'7" | 200 | 22 | | 24 |
| Brian Mitchell | HB | 5'10" | 209 | 23 | | 12 |
| Gerald Riggs | HB-FB | 6'1" | 240 | 30 | | 66 |
| Gary Clark | WR | 5'9" | 173 | 29 | | 60 |
| Stephen Hobbs | WR | 5'11" | 200 | 25 | | |
| Joe Johnson | WR | 5'8" | 170 | 28 | | |
| Art Monk | WR | 6'3" | 210 | 33 | | 48 |
| Ricky Sanders | WR | 5'11" | 180 | 29 | | 36 |
| John Brandes | TE | 6'2" | 249 | 27 | | |
| James Jenkins | TE | 6'2" | 234 | 24 | | |
| Jimmie Johnson | TE | 6'2" | 246 | 24 | | 12 |
| Ron Middleton | TE | 6'2" | 270 | 26 | | |
| Terry Orr | TE | 6'2" | 235 | 29 | | 24 |
| Don Warren | TE | 6'4" | 242 | 35 | | |
| Kelly Goodburn | K | 6'2" | 199 | 29 | | |
| Chip Lohmiller | K | 6'3" | 210 | 25 | | 149 |

John Settle — Rib Injury

### DALLAS COWBOYS 11-5 Jimmy Johnson

| | | |
|---|---|---|
| 26 | Cleveland | 14 |
| 31 | WASHINGTON | 33 |
| 9 | PHILADELPHIA | 24 |
| 17 | Phoenix | 9 |
| 21 | N.Y. GIANTS | 16 |
| 20 | Green Bay | 17 |
| 35 | CINCINNATI | 23 |
| 10 | Detroit | 34 |
| 27 | PHOENIX | 7 |
| 23 | Houston | *26 |
| 9 | N.Y. Giants | 22 |
| 24 | Washington | 21 |
| 20 | PITTSBURGH | 10 |
| 23 | NEW ORLEANS | 14 |
| 25 | Philadelphia | 13 |
| 31 | ATLANTA | 27 |

| UseName | Pos. | Hgt. | Wgt. | Age | Int | Pts |
|---|---|---|---|---|---|---|
| Nate Newton | OT | 6'3" | 332 | 29 | | |
| Mark Tuinei | OT | 6'5" | 299 | 31 | | |
| Erik Williams | OT | 6'6" | 319 | 22 | | |
| John Gesek | OG | 6'5" | 279 | 28 | | |
| Kevin Gogan | OG | 6'7" | 317 | 26 | | |
| Dale Hellestrae | OG-C | 6'5" | 285 | 29 | | |
| Alan Veingrad | OG-OT | 6'5" | 280 | 28 | | |
| Mark Stepnoski | C | 6'2" | 269 | 24 | | |
| Tony Hill | DE | 6'6" | 242 | 22 | | |
| Jim Jeffcoat | DE | 6'5" | 274 | 30 | | |
| Danny Stubbs (to CIN) | DE | 6'4" | 264 | 26 | | |
| Tony Tolbert | DE | 6'6" | 265 | 23 | | |
| Tony Cassillas | DT | 6'3" | 277 | 27 | | |
| Jimmie Jones | DT | 6'4" | 276 | 25 | | |
| Leon Lett | DT | 6'6" | 287 | 22 | | |
| Russell Maryland | DT-DE | 6'1" | 277 | 21 | | |
| Danny Noonan | DT | 6'4" | 275 | 26 | | |

| UseName | Pos. | Hgt. | Wgt. | Age | Int | Pts |
|---|---|---|---|---|---|---|
| Darrick Brownlow | LB | 5'10" | 237 | 22 | | |
| Reggie Cooper | LB | 6'2" | 215 | 23 | | |
| Jack Del Rio | LB | 6'4" | 240 | 28 | | |
| -Dixon Edwards | LB | 6'1" | 224 | 23 | 1 | 6 |
| Godfrey Myles | LB | 6'1" | 241 | 22 | | |
| Ken Norton | LB | 6'2" | 238 | 24 | | |
| Mickey Pruitt | LB | 6'1" | 218 | 26 | | |
| Vinson Smith | LB | 6'2" | 231 | 26 | | |
| Vince Albritton | DB | 6'2" | 216 | 29 | | |
| Bill Bates | DB | 6'1" | 205 | 30 | | |
| Larry Brown | DB | 5'11" | 182 | 21 | 2 | |
| Kenneth Gant | DB | 5'11" | 188 | 24 | 1 | |
| Manny Hendrix | DB | 5'10" | 187 | 26 | | 2 |
| Issiac Holt | DB | 6'2" | 201 | 28 | 4 | |
| Ray Horton | DB | 5'11" | 190 | 31 | 1 | 12 |
| Stan Smagala | DB | 5'10" | 184 | 23 | | |
| Donald Smith | DB | 5'11" | 189 | 23 | | |
| James Washington | DB | 6'1" | 197 | 26 | 2 | |
| Robert Williams | DB | 5'10" | 190 | 28 | 1 | 6 |

Michael Brooks — Knee Injury

| UseName | Pos. | Hgt. | Wgt. | Age | Int | Pts |
|---|---|---|---|---|---|---|
| Troy Aikman | QB | 6'4" | 222 | 24 | | 6 |
| Steve Beuerlein | QB | 6'2" | 209 | 26 | | |
| James Dixon | HB-WR | 5'10" | 184 | 24 | | |
| Curvin Richards | HB | 5'9" | 195 | 22 | | |
| Emmitt Smith | HB | 5'9" | 203 | 22 | | 78 |
| Tommie Agee | FB | 6' | 225 | 27 | | 6 |
| Ricky Blake | FB | 6'2" | 244 | 24 | | 6 |
| Daryl Johnston | FB | 6'2" | 236 | 25 | | 6 |
| Alvin Harper | WR | 6'3" | 203 | 24 | | 6 |
| Michael Irvin | WR | 6'2" | 199 | 25 | | 48 |
| Kelvin Martin | WR | 5'9" | 162 | 26 | | 6 |
| Derrick Shepard | WR | 5'10" | 183 | 27 | | |
| Alexander Wright | WR | 6' | 190 | 24 | | 6 |
| Robert Awalt | TE | 6'5" | 245 | 27 | | |
| Jay Novacek | TE | 6'4" | 231 | 28 | | 24 |
| Alfredo Roberts | TE | 6'3" | 252 | 26 | | 6 |
| Mike Saxon | K | 6'3" | 202 | 29 | | |
| Ken Willis | K | 5'11" | 185 | 24 | | 18 |

### PHILADELPHIA EAGLES 10-6 Rich Kotite

| | | |
|---|---|---|
| 20 | Green Bay | 3 |
| 10 | PHOENIX | 26 |
| 24 | Dallas | 0 |
| 23 | PITTSBURGH | 14 |
| 0 | Washington | 23 |
| 13 | Tampa Bay | 14 |
| 6 | NEW ORLEANS | 13 |
| 7 | SAN FRANCISCO | 23 |
| 30 | N.Y. GIANTS | 7 |
| 32 | Cleveland | 30 |
| 17 | CINCINNATI | 10 |
| 34 | Phoenix | 14 |
| 13 | Houston | 6 |
| 19 | N.Y. Giants | 14 |
| 13 | DALLAS | 25 |
| 24 | WASHINGTON | 22 |

| UseName | Pos. | Hgt. | Wgt. | Age | Int | Pts |
|---|---|---|---|---|---|---|
| Antone Davis | OT | 6'4" | 325 | 24 | | |
| Cecil Gray | OT-OG | 6'4" | 275 | 23 | | |
| Ron Heller | OT | 6'6" | 280 | 29 | | |
| Daryle Smith | OT | 6'5" | 276 | 27 | | |
| Bruce Collie | OG | 6'6" | 275 | 29 | | |
| John Hudson | OG-C | 6'2" | 275 | 23 | | |
| Dennis McKnight | OG-C | 6'3" | 280 | 31 | | |
| Rob Selby | OG-OT | 6'3" | 286 | 23 | | |
| Ron Solt | OG | 6'3" | 275 | 29 | | |
| David Alexander | C | 6'3" | 275 | 27 | | |
| Mike Flores | DE | 6'3" | 256 | 24 | | |
| Andy Harmon | DE | 6'4" | 265 | 22 | | |
| Clyde Simmons | DE | 6'6" | 280 | 27 | | 6 |
| Reggie White | DE-DT | 6'5" | 285 | 29 | 1 | |
| Jerome Brown | DT | 6'2" | 295 | 26 | | |
| Mike Golic | DT | 6'5" | 275 | 28 | 1 | |
| Mike Pitts | DT | 6'5" | 280 | 30 | | |

Mike Schad — Back Injury
Ben Tamburello — Knee Injury

| UseName | Pos. | Hgt. | Wgt. | Age | Int | Pts |
|---|---|---|---|---|---|---|
| Byron Evans | LB | 6'2" | 235 | 27 | 2 | |
| Britt Hager | LB | 6'1" | 225 | 25 | | |
| Seth Joyner | LB | 6'2" | 235 | 26 | 3 | 6 |
| Scott Kowalkowski | LB | 6'2" | 228 | 23 | | |
| Ken Rose | LB | 6'1" | 215 | 29 | | |
| Jessie Small | LB | 6'3" | 240 | 24 | | |
| William Thomas | LB | 6'2" | 218 | 23 | | |
| Eric Allen | DB | 5'10" | 180 | 25 | 5 | |
| John Booty | DB | 6' | 180 | 25 | | |
| Wes Hopkins | DB | 6'1" | 215 | 29 | 5 | |
| Izel Jenkins | DB | 5'10" | 190 | 27 | | |
| Rich Miano | DB | 6'1" | 200 | 28 | 3 | |
| Bruce Plummer | DB | 6' | 198 | 27 | | |
| Ben Smith | DB | 5'11" | 183 | 24 | 2 | |
| Otis Smith | DB | 5'11" | 184 | 25 | 2 | 6 |
| Andre Waters | DB | 5'11" | 200 | 29 | 1 | |

| UseName | Pos. | Hgt. | Wgt. | Age | Int | Pts |
|---|---|---|---|---|---|---|
| Randall Cunningham | QB | 6'4" | 203 | 28 | | |
| Brad Goebel | QB | 6'3" | 198 | 23 | | |
| Jim McMahon | QB | 6'1" | 195 | 32 | | 6 |
| Pat Ryan | QB | 6'3" | 210 | 35 | | |
| Keith Byars | HB | 6'1" | 238 | 27 | | 24 |
| Robert Drummond | HB | 6'1" | 205 | 24 | | 12 |
| James Joseph | HB-FB | 6' | 222 | 23 | | 18 |
| Thomas Sanders | HB | 5'11" | 203 | 29 | | 6 |
| Heath Sherman | FB-HB | 6' | 205 | 24 | | |
| Fred Barnett | WR | 6' | 199 | 25 | | 24 |
| Roy Green | WR | 6'1" | 195 | 34 | | |
| Rod Harris | WR | 5'10" | 185 | 24 | | |
| Kenny Jackson | WR | 6' | 180 | 29 | | |
| Calvin Williams | WR | 5'11" | 190 | 24 | | 18 |
| Keith Jackson | TE | 6'2" | 250 | 26 | | 30 |
| Maurice Johnson | TE | 6'2" | 243 | 24 | | 6 |
| Mickey Shuler | TE | 6'3" | 231 | 35 | | |
| Jeff Feagles | K | 6' | 205 | 25 | | |
| Roger Ruzek | K | 6'1" | 200 | 30 | | 111 |

### NEW YORK GIANTS 8-8 Ray Handley

| | | |
|---|---|---|
| 16 | SAN FRANCISCO | 14 |
| 13 | L.A. RAMS | 19 |
| 17 | Chicago | 20 |
| 13 | CLEVELAND | 10 |
| 16 | Dallas | 21 |
| 20 | PHOENIX | 9 |
| 23 | Pittsburgh | 20 |
| 13 | WASHINGTON | 17 |
| 7 | Philadelphia | 30 |
| 21 | Phoenix | 14 |
| 22 | DALLAS | 9 |
| 21 | Tampa Bay | 14 |
| 24 | Cincinnati | 27 |
| 14 | PHILADELPHIA | 19 |
| 17 | Washington | 34 |
| 24 | HOUSTON | 20 |

| UseName | Pos. | Hgt. | Wgt. | Age | Int | Pts |
|---|---|---|---|---|---|---|
| John Elliott | OT | 6'7" | 305 | 26 | | |
| Clarence Jones | OT | 6'6" | 280 | 23 | | |
| Doug Riesenberg | OT | 6'5" | 275 | 26 | | |
| Bob Kratch | OG | 6'3" | 288 | 25 | | |
| Eric Moore | OG-OT | 6'5" | 290 | 26 | | |
| William Roberts | OG | 6'5" | 280 | 29 | | |
| Brian Williams | OG-C | 6'5" | 300 | 25 | | |
| Bart Oates | C | 6'3" | 265 | 32 | | |
| Eric Dorsey | DE | 6'5" | 280 | 27 | | |
| Mike Fox | DE | 6'6" | 275 | 24 | | |
| Leonard Marshall | DE | 6'3" | 285 | 29 | | |
| Greg Meisner | DE-NT | 6'3" | 271 | 32 | | |
| Lorenzo Freeman | NT | 6'5" | 319 | 27 | | |
| Erik Howard | NT | 6'4" | 268 | 26 | | |
| John Washington | NT | 6'4" | 275 | 28 | | |

| UseName | Pos. | Hgt. | Wgt. | Age | Int | Pts |
|---|---|---|---|---|---|---|
| Bobby Abrams | LB | 6'3" | 230 | 24 | | |
| Carl Banks | LB | 6'4" | 235 | 29 | | |
| Steve DeOssie | LB | 6'2" | 248 | 28 | | |
| Pepper Johnson | LB | 6'3" | 248 | 27 | 2 | |
| Kanavis McGhee | LB | 6'4" | 257 | 22 | | |
| Corey Miller | LB | 6'2" | 225 | 22 | | |
| Gary Reasons | LB | 6'4" | 234 | 29 | | |
| Lawrence Taylor | LB | 6'3" | 243 | 32 | | |
| Roger Brown | DB | 6' | 196 | 24 | | |
| Mark Collins | DB | 5'10" | 190 | 27 | 4 | |
| A.J. Greene | DB | 5'8" | 167 | 25 | | |
| Myron Guyton | DB | 6'1" | 205 | 24 | | |
| Greg Jackson | DB | 6'1" | 200 | 25 | 1 | |
| Lamar McGriggs | DB | 6'3" | 210 | 23 | | |
| Reyna Thompson | DB | 6' | 193 | 28 | | |
| Everson Walls | DB | 6'1" | 194 | 31 | 4 | |
| Adrian White | DB | 6' | 200 | 27 | 1 | |
| Perry Williams | DB | 6'2" | 203 | 30 | | |

Thom Kaumeyer — Knee Injury

| UseName | Pos. | Hgt. | Wgt. | Age | Int | Pts |
|---|---|---|---|---|---|---|
| Matt Cavanaugh | QB | 6'2" | 210 | 34 | | |
| Jeff Hostetler | QB | 6'3" | 212 | 30 | | 12 |
| Phil Simms | QB | 6'3" | 214 | 35 | | 6 |
| Ottis Anderson | HB | 6'2" | 225 | 34 | | 6 |
| Rodney Hampton | HB | 5'11" | 215 | 22 | | 60 |
| Dave Meggett | HB | 5'7" | 180 | 25 | | 30 |
| Lewis Tillman | HB | 6' | 195 | 25 | | 6 |
| Jarrod Bunch | FB | 6'2" | 248 | 23 | | |
| Maurice Carthon | FB | 6'1" | 225 | 30 | | |
| Stephen Baker | WR | 5'8" | 160 | 27 | | 24 |
| Mark Ingram | WR | 5'10" | 188 | 26 | | 18 |
| Ed McCaffrey | WR | 6'5" | 215 | 23 | | |
| Joey Smith | WR | 5'10" | 177 | 22 | | |
| Odessa Turner | WR | 6'3" | 205 | 26 | | |
| Howard Cross | TE | 6'5" | 245 | 24 | | 12 |
| Zeke Mowatt | TE | 6'3" | 240 | 30 | | 6 |
| Raul Allegre (to NYJ) | K | 5'10" | 167 | 32 | | 22 |
| Matt Bahr | K | 5'10" | 175 | 35 | | 90 |
| Sean Landeta | K | 6' | 210 | 29 | | |

### PHOENIX CARDINALS 4-12 Joe Bugel

| | | |
|---|---|---|
| 24 | L.A. Rams | 14 |
| 26 | Philadelphia | 10 |
| 0 | Washington | 34 |
| 9 | DALLAS | 17 |
| 24 | NEW ENGLAND | 10 |
| 9 | N.Y. Giants | 20 |
| 7 | Minnesota | 34 |
| 16 | ATLANTA | 10 |
| 0 | MINNESOTA | 28 |
| 7 | Dallas | 27 |
| 14 | N.Y. GIANTS | 21 |
| 10 | San Francisco | 14 |
| 14 | PHILADELPHIA | 34 |
| 14 | WASHINGTON | 20 |
| 19 | Denver | 24 |
| 3 | NEW ORLEANS | 27 |

| UseName | Pos. | Hgt. | Wgt. | Age | Int | Pts |
|---|---|---|---|---|---|---|
| Tootie Robbins | OT | 6'5" | 310 | 33 | | |
| Luis Sharpe | OT | 6'4" | 295 | 31 | | |
| Willie Williams | OT | 6'6" | 300 | 24 | | 6 |
| Mike Brennan (from CIN, to BUF) | OG | 6'5" | 274 | 24 | | |
| Lance Smith | OG | 6'2" | 290 | 28 | | |
| Vernice Smith | OG-OT | 6'2" | 298 | 25 | | |
| Joe Wolf | OG | 6'5" | 296 | 24 | | |
| Kani Kauahi | C | 6'2" | 275 | 31 | | |
| Bill Lewis | C | 6'7" | 290 | 28 | | |
| Scott Evans | DE | 6'3" | 261 | 23 | | |
| Jeff Faulkner | DE | 6'4" | 305 | 27 | | |
| Mike Jones | DE | 6'4" | 285 | 22 | | |
| Craig Patterson | DE | 6'5" | 317 | 27 | 1 | |
| Eric Swann | DE | 6'4" | 310 | 21 | | |
| Rod Saddler (to CIN) | DE | 6'5" | 280 | 25 | | 6 |
| Jim Wahler | NT-DT | 6'4" | 275 | 25 | | |
| Chris Williams | NT | 6'3" | 304 | 22 | | |

| UseName | Pos. | Hgt. | Wgt. | Age | Int | Pts |
|---|---|---|---|---|---|---|
| David Braxton | LB | 6'1" | 230 | 26 | | |
| Sidney Coleman | LB | 6'2" | 250 | 27 | | |
| Ken Harvey | LB | 6'2" | 230 | 26 | | |
| Eric Hill | LB | 6'1" | 250 | 24 | | 6 |
| Steve Hyche | LB | 6'2" | 226 | 28 | | |
| Garth Jax | LB | 6'2" | 240 | 27 | | |
| Freddie Joe Nunn | LB-DE | 6'4" | 250 | 29 | | |
| Tyronne Stowe | LB | 6'1" | 249 | 26 | | |
| Dave Duerson | DB | 6'1" | 208 | 30 | 1 | |
| Dexter Davis | DB | 5'10" | 190 | 21 | | |
| Steve Lofton | DB | 5'9" | 180 | 22 | | |
| Lorenzo Lynch | DB | 5'9" | 200 | 28 | 3 | 6 |
| Robert Massey | DB | 5'10" | 185 | 24 | | |
| Tim McDonald | DB | 6'2" | 215 | 26 | 5 | |
| Chris Oldham | DB | 5'9" | 183 | 22 | | |
| Jay Taylor | DB | 5'9" | 175 | 23 | | |
| Marcus Turner | DB | 6' | 190 | 25 | | |
| Aeneas Williams | DB | 5'10" | 187 | 22 | 6 | |
| Mike Zordich | DB | 5'11" | 200 | 27 | 1 | |

| UseName | Pos. | Hgt. | Wgt. | Age | Int | Pts |
|---|---|---|---|---|---|---|
| Stan Gelbaugh | QB | 6'3" | 207 | 28 | | |
| Craig Kupp (to DAL) | QB | 6'4" | 215 | 24 | | |
| Tom Tupa | QB | 6'4" | 215 | 25 | | 6 |
| Larry Centers | HB | 5'11" | 200 | 23 | | |
| Terrence Flagler | HB | 6' | 200 | 26 | | |
| Johnny Johnson | HB | 6'2" | 220 | 23 | | 36 |
| Anthony Thompson | HB | 5'11" | 210 | 24 | | 6 |
| Ron Wolfley | FB | 6' | 230 | 28 | | |
| Anthony Edwards | WR | 5'9" | 190 | 25 | | |
| Amod Field | WR | 5'11" | 181 | 23 | | |
| Randal Hill | WR | 5'10" | 177 | 21 | | 6 |
| John Jackson | WR | 5'10" | 183 | 24 | | |
| Ernie Jones | WR | 5'11" | 200 | 26 | | 24 |
| Tony Lomack | WR | 5'8" | 180 | 23 | | |
| Ricky Proehl | WR | 5'10" | 190 | 23 | | 12 |
| Tim Jorden | TE | 6'2" | 235 | 24 | | |
| Walter Reeves | TE | 6'4" | 266 | 25 | | |
| Rich Camarillo | K | 5'11" | 195 | 31 | | |
| Greg Davis | K | 6' | 200 | 25 | | 82 |

Timm Rosenbach — Knee Injury

## WASHINGTON REDSKINS

### RUSHING

| Last Name | No. | Yds | Avg | TD |
|---|---|---|---|---|
| Byner | 274 | 1048 | 3.8 | 5 |
| Ervins | 145 | 680 | 4.7 | 3 |
| Riggs | 78 | 248 | 3.2 | 11 |
| Sanders | 7 | 47 | 6.7 | 1 |
| Monk | 9 | 19 | 2.1 | 0 |
| Mitchell | 3 | 14 | 4.7 | 0 |
| Rypien | 15 | 6 | 0.4 | 1 |
| Clark | 1 | 0 | 0.0 | 0 |
| Rutledge | 8 | -13 | -1.6 | 0 |

### RECEIVING

| Last Name | No. | Yds | Avg | TD |
|---|---|---|---|---|
| Monk | 71 | 1049 | 14.8 | 8 |
| Clark | 70 | 1340 | 19.1 | 10 |
| Sanders | 45 | 580 | 12.9 | 5 |
| Byner | 34 | 308 | 9.1 | 0 |
| Ervins | 16 | 181 | 11.3 | 1 |
| Orr | 10 | 201 | 20.1 | 4 |
| Warren | 5 | 51 | 10.2 | 0 |
| Middleton | 3 | 25 | 8.3 | 0 |
| Hobbs | 3 | 24 | 8.0 | 0 |
| Ji. Johnson | 3 | 7 | 2.3 | 2 |
| Riggs | 1 | 5 | 5.0 | 0 |

### PUNT RETURNS

| Last Name | No. | Yds | Avg | TD |
|---|---|---|---|---|
| Mitchell | 45 | 600 | 13.3 | 2 |
| Hobbs | 1 | 10 | 10.0 | 0 |

### KICKOFF RETURNS

| Last Name | No. | Yds | Avg | TD |
|---|---|---|---|---|
| Mitchell | 29 | 583 | 20.1 | 0 |
| Ervins | 11 | 232 | 21.1 | 0 |
| Jo. Johnson | 5 | 83 | 16.6 | 0 |
| Gouveia | 3 | 12 | 4.0 | 0 |
| Hobbs | 1 | 16 | 16.0 | 0 |

### PASSING — PUNTING — KICKING

| Last Name | Att | Cmp | % | Yds | Yd/Att | TD | Int— | % | RK |
|---|---|---|---|---|---|---|---|---|---|
| Rypien | 421 | 249 | 59.1 | 3564 | 8.47 | 28 | 11— | 2.6 | 2 |
| Rutledge | 22 | 11 | 50.0 | 189 | 8.59 | 1 | 0— | 0.0 | |
| Byner | 4 | 1 | 25.0 | 18 | 4.50 | 1 | 0— | 0.0 | |

| PUNTING | No. | Avg. |
|---|---|---|
| Goodburn | 55 | 37.6 |

| KICKING | XP | ATT | % | FG | ATT | % |
|---|---|---|---|---|---|---|
| Lohmiller | 56 | 56 | 100 | 31 | 43 | 73 |

## DALLAS COWBOYS

### RUSHING

| Last Name | No. | Yds | Avg | TD |
|---|---|---|---|---|
| E. Smith | 365 | 1563 | 4.3 | 12 |
| Blake | 15 | 80 | 5.3 | 1 |
| Johnston | 17 | 54 | 3.2 | 0 |
| Agee | 9 | 20 | 2.2 | 1 |
| Aikman | 16 | 5 | 0.3 | 1 |
| Richards | 2 | 4 | 2.0 | 0 |
| Wright | 2 | -1 | -0.5 | 0 |
| Beuerlein | 7 | -14 | -2.0 | 0 |

### RECEIVING

| Last Name | No. | Yds | Avg | TD |
|---|---|---|---|---|
| Irvin | 93 | 1523 | 16.4 | 8 |
| Novacek | 59 | 664 | 11.3 | 4 |
| E. Smith | 49 | 258 | 5.3 | 1 |
| Johnston | 28 | 244 | 8.7 | 1 |
| Harper | 20 | 326 | 16.3 | 1 |
| Martin | 16 | 243 | 15.2 | 0 |
| Roberts | 16 | 136 | 8.5 | 1 |
| Wright | 10 | 170 | 17.0 | 0 |
| Agee | 7 | 43 | 6.1 | 0 |
| Awalt | 5 | 57 | 11.4 | 0 |
| Blake | 1 | 5 | 5.0 | 0 |
| Aikman | 1 | -6 | -6.0 | 0 |

### PUNT RETURNS

| Last Name | No. | Yds | Avg | TD |
|---|---|---|---|---|
| Martin | 21 | 244 | 11.6 | 1 |
| Shepard | 6 | 57 | 9.5 | 0 |
| Horton | 1 | 8 | 8.0 | 0 |
| Brownlow | 1 | 0 | 0.0 | 0 |

### KICKOFF RETURNS

| Last Name | No. | Yds | Avg | TD |
|---|---|---|---|---|
| Wright | 21 | 514 | 24.5 | 1 |
| Dixon | 18 | 398 | 22.1 | 0 |
| Gant | 6 | 114 | 19.0 | 0 |
| Shepard | 3 | 54 | 18.0 | 0 |
| Martin | 3 | 47 | 15.7 | 0 |
| Horton | 1 | 0 | 0.0 | 0 |

### PASSING — PUNTING — KICKING

| Last Name | Att | Cmp | % | Yds | Yd/Att | TD | Int— | % | RK |
|---|---|---|---|---|---|---|---|---|---|
| Aikman | 363 | 237 | 65.3 | 2754 | 7.59 | 11 | 10— | 2.8 | 4 |
| Beuerlein | 137 | 68 | 49.6 | 909 | 6.64 | 5 | 2— | 1.5 | |

| PUNTING | No. | Avg. |
|---|---|---|
| Saxon | 57 | 42.6 |

| KICKING | XP | ATT | % | FG | ATT | % |
|---|---|---|---|---|---|---|
| Willis | 37 | 37 | 100 | 27 | 39 | 69 |

## PHILADELPHIA EAGLES

### RUSHING

| Last Name | No. | Yds | Avg | TD |
|---|---|---|---|---|
| Joseph | 135 | 440 | 3.3 | 3 |
| Byars | 94 | 383 | 4.1 | 1 |
| Sherman | 106 | 279 | 2.6 | 0 |
| Sanders | 54 | 122 | 2.3 | 1 |
| McMahon | 22 | 55 | 2.5 | 1 |
| Drummond | 12 | 27 | 2.3 | 2 |
| Ken. Jackson | 1 | 18 | 18.0 | 0 |
| Goebel | 1 | 2 | 2.0 | 0 |
| Barnett | 1 | 0 | 0.0 | 0 |
| Feagles | 3 | -1 | -0.3 | 0 |
| Ryan | 1 | -2 | -2.0 | 0 |

### RECEIVING

| Last Name | No. | Yds | Avg | TD |
|---|---|---|---|---|
| Barnett | 62 | 948 | 15.3 | 4 |
| Byars | 62 | 564 | 9.1 | 3 |
| Kei. Jackson | 48 | 569 | 11.9 | 5 |
| Williams | 33 | 326 | 9.9 | 3 |
| Green | 29 | 364 | 12.6 | 0 |
| Sherman | 14 | 59 | 4.2 | 0 |
| Joseph | 10 | 64 | 6.4 | 0 |
| Sanders | 8 | 62 | 7.8 | 0 |
| Shuler | 6 | 91 | 15.2 | 0 |
| M. Johnson | 6 | 70 | 11.7 | 2 |
| Ken. Jackson | 4 | 29 | 7.3 | 0 |
| Harris | 2 | 28 | 14.0 | 0 |
| McMahon | 1 | -5 | -5.0 | 0 |

### PUNT RETURNS

| Last Name | No. | Yds | Avg | TD |
|---|---|---|---|---|
| Harris | 53 | 416 | 7.8 | 0 |

### KICKOFF RETURNS

| Last Name | No. | Yds | Avg | TD |
|---|---|---|---|---|
| Harris | 28 | 473 | 16.9 | 0 |
| Sanders | 10 | 160 | 16.0 | 0 |
| Green | 5 | 70 | 14.0 | 0 |
| Sherman | 4 | 61 | 15.3 | 0 |

### PASSING — PUNTING — KICKING

| Last Name | Att | Cmp | % | Yds | Yd/Att | TD | Int— | % | RK |
|---|---|---|---|---|---|---|---|---|---|
| McMahon | 311 | 187 | 60.1 | 2239 | 7.20 | 12 | 11— | 3.5 | 8 |
| Goebel | 56 | 30 | 53.6 | 267 | 4.77 | 0 | 6— | 10.7 | |
| Ryan | 26 | 10 | 38.5 | 98 | 3.77 | 0 | 4— | 15.4 | |
| Cunningham | 4 | 1 | 25.0 | 19 | 4.75 | 0 | 0— | 0.0 | |
| Byars | 2 | 0 | 0.0 | 0 | 0.00 | 0 | 1— | 50.0 | |

| PUNTING | No. | Avg. |
|---|---|---|
| Feagles | 88 | 41.4 |

| KICKING | XP | ATT | % | FG | ATT | % |
|---|---|---|---|---|---|---|
| Ruzek | 27 | 29 | 93 | 28 | 33 | 85 |

## NEW YORK GIANTS

### RUSHING

| Last Name | No. | Yds | Avg | TD |
|---|---|---|---|---|
| Hampton | 256 | 1059 | 4.1 | 10 |
| Tillman | 65 | 287 | 4.4 | 1 |
| Hostetler | 42 | 273 | 6.5 | 2 |
| Meggett | 29 | 153 | 5.3 | 1 |
| Anderson | 53 | 141 | 2.7 | 1 |
| Carthon | 32 | 109 | 3.4 | 0 |
| Simms | 9 | 42 | 4.7 | 1 |
| Bunch | 1 | 0 | 0.0 | 0 |

### RECEIVING

| Last Name | No. | Yds | Avg | TD |
|---|---|---|---|---|
| Ingram | 51 | 824 | 16.2 | 3 |
| Meggett | 50 | 412 | 8.2 | 3 |
| Hampton | 43 | 283 | 6.6 | 0 |
| Baker | 30 | 525 | 17.5 | 4 |
| Turner | 21 | 356 | 17.0 | 0 |
| Cross | 20 | 283 | 14.2 | 2 |
| McCaffrey | 16 | 146 | 9.1 | 0 |
| Anderson | 11 | 41 | 3.7 | 0 |
| Carthon | 7 | 39 | 5.6 | 0 |
| Mowatt | 5 | 78 | 15.6 | 1 |
| Tillman | 5 | 30 | 6.0 | 0 |
| Bunch | 2 | 8 | 4.0 | 0 |

### PUNT RETURNS

| Last Name | No. | Yds | Avg | TD |
|---|---|---|---|---|
| Meggett | 28 | 287 | 10.3 | 1 |
| Ingram | 8 | 49 | 6.1 | 0 |

### KICKOFF RETURNS

| Last Name | No. | Yds | Avg | TD |
|---|---|---|---|---|
| Meggett | 25 | 514 | 20.6 | 0 |
| Hampton | 10 | 204 | 20.4 | 0 |
| Ingram | 8 | 125 | 15.6 | 0 |
| Smith | 3 | 34 | 11.3 | 0 |
| Tillman | 2 | 29 | 14.5 | 0 |
| Cross | 1 | 11 | 11.0 | 0 |
| Freeman | 1 | 0 | 0.0 | 0 |

### PASSING — PUNTING — KICKING

| Last Name | Att | Cmp | % | Yds | Yd/Att | TD | Int— | % | RK |
|---|---|---|---|---|---|---|---|---|---|
| Hostetler | 285 | 179 | 62.8 | 2032 | 7.13 | 5 | 4— | 1.4 | 5 |
| Simms | 141 | 82 | 58.2 | 993 | 7.04 | 8 | 4— | 2.8 | |
| Ingram | 1 | 0 | 0.0 | 0 | 0.00 | 0 | 0— | 0.0 | |
| Meggett | 1 | 0 | 0.0 | 0 | 0.00 | 0 | 0— | 0.0 | |

| PUNTING | No. | Avg. |
|---|---|---|
| Landeta | 64 | 43.3 |

| KICKING | XP | ATT | % | FG | ATT | % |
|---|---|---|---|---|---|---|
| Bahr | 24 | 25 | 96 | 22 | 29 | 76 |
| Allegre | 7 | 7 | 100 | 5 | 6 | 83 |

## PHOENIX CARDINALS

### RUSHING

| Last Name | No. | Yds | Avg | TD |
|---|---|---|---|---|
| Johnson | 196 | 666 | 3.4 | 4 |
| Thompson | 126 | 376 | 3.0 | 1 |
| Tupa | 28 | 97 | 3.5 | 1 |
| Centers | 14 | 44 | 3.1 | 0 |
| E. Jones | 5 | 24 | 4.8 | 0 |
| Gelbaugh | 9 | 23 | 2.6 | 0 |
| Proehl | 3 | 21 | 7.0 | 0 |
| Flagler | 1 | 7 | 7.0 | 0 |
| Kupp | 1 | 5 | 5.0 | 0 |

### RECEIVING

| Last Name | No. | Yds | Avg | TD |
|---|---|---|---|---|
| E. Jones | 61 | 957 | 15.7 | 4 |
| Proehl | 55 | 766 | 13.9 | 2 |
| R. Hill | 43 | 495 | 11.5 | 1 |
| Johnson | 29 | 225 | 7.8 | 2 |
| Centers | 19 | 176 | 9.3 | 0 |
| Jorden | 15 | 127 | 8.5 | 0 |
| Jackson | 8 | 108 | 13.5 | 0 |
| Flagler | 8 | 85 | 10.6 | 0 |
| Reeves | 8 | 45 | 5.6 | 0 |
| Thompson | 7 | 52 | 7.4 | 0 |
| W. Williams | 1 | 3 | 3.0 | 1 |

### PUNT RETURNS

| Last Name | No. | Yds | Avg | TD |
|---|---|---|---|---|
| Jackson | 31 | 244 | 7.9 | 0 |
| Centers | 5 | 30 | 6.0 | 0 |
| Proehl | 4 | 26 | 6.5 | 0 |
| Edwards | 1 | 7 | 7.0 | 0 |

### KICKOFF RETURNS

| Last Name | No. | Yds | Avg | TD |
|---|---|---|---|---|
| Centers | 16 | 330 | 20.6 | 0 |
| Edwards | 13 | 261 | 20.1 | 0 |
| Flagler | 12 | 208 | 17.3 | 0 |
| R. Hill | 9 | 146 | 16.2 | 0 |
| Jackson | 2 | 41 | 20.5 | 0 |
| Lomack | 1 | 19 | 19.0 | 0 |

### PASSING — PUNTING — KICKING

| Last Name | Att | Cmp | % | Yds | Yd/Att | TD | Int— | % | RK |
|---|---|---|---|---|---|---|---|---|---|
| Tupa | 315 | 165 | 52.4 | 2053 | 6.52 | 6 | 13— | 4.1 | 15 |
| Gelbaugh | 118 | 61 | 51.7 | 674 | 5.71 | 3 | 10— | 8.5 | |
| Kupp | 7 | 3 | 42.9 | 23 | 3.29 | 0 | 0— | 0.0 | |
| Camarillo | 1 | 0 | 0.0 | 0 | 0.00 | 0 | 0— | 0.0 | |
| Thompson | 1 | 0 | 0.0 | 0 | 0.00 | 0 | 0— | 0.0 | |

| PUNTING | No. | Avg. |
|---|---|---|
| Camarillo | 77 | 44.7 |

| KICKING | XP | ATT | % | FG | ATT | % |
|---|---|---|---|---|---|---|
| Davis | 19 | 19 | 100 | 21 | 30 | 70 |

## DETROIT LIONS 12-4 Wayne Fontes

| Scores of Each Game | | |
|---|---|---|
| 0 | Washington | 45 |
| 23 | GREEN BAY | 14 |
| 17 | MIAMI | 13 |
| 33 | Indianapolis | 24 |
| 31 | TAMPA BAY | 3 |
| 24 | MINNESOTA | 20 |
| 3 | San Francisco | 35 |
| 34 | DALLAS | 10 |
| 10 | Chicago | 20 |
| 21 | Tampa Bay | 30 |
| 21 | L.A. RAMS | 10 |
| 34 | Minnesota | 14 |
| 16 | CHICAGO | 6 |
| 34 | N.Y. JETS | 20 |
| 21 | Green Bay | 17 |
| 17 | Buffalo | * 14 |

| UseName | Pos. | Hgt. | Wgt. | Age | Int | Pts |
|---|---|---|---|---|---|---|
| Lomas Brown | OT | 6'4" | 287 | 28 | | |
| Roman Fortin | OT | 6'5" | 290 | 24 | | |
| Eric Sanders | OT-OG | 6'7" | 286 | 32 | | |
| Eric Andolsek | OG | 6'2" | 291 | 25 | | |
| Shawn Bouwens | OG | 6'4" | 290 | 23 | | |
| Scott Conover | OG | 6'4" | 285 | 22 | | |
| Ken Dallafior | OG-C | 6'4" | 285 | 32 | | |
| Mike Utley | OG-OT | 6'6" | 290 | 25 | | |
| Kevin Glover | C | 6'2" | 282 | 28 | | |
| Darryl Milburn | DE | 6'3" | 260 | 22 | | |
| Dan Owens | DE | 6'3" | 280 | 24 | | |
| Kelvin Pritchett | DE | 6'2" | 281 | 21 | | |
| Marc Spindler | DE | 6'5" | 290 | 21 | | |
| Jerry Ball | NT | 6'1" | 298 | 26 | | 2 |
| Lawrence Pete | NT | 6' | 295 | 25 | | |
| Anthony Bell | LB | 6'3" | 235 | 27 | | |
| Mark Brown | LB | 6'2" | 240 | 28 | | |
| Toby Caston | LB | 6'1" | 243 | 26 | | |
| Mike Cofer | LB | 6'5" | 244 | 31 | | |
| Dennis Gibson | LB | 6'2" | 243 | 27 | | |
| Tracy Hayworth | LB | 6'3" | 260 | 23 | 1 | 6 |
| George Jamison | LB | 6'1" | 228 | 28 | 3 | |
| Victor Jones | LB | 6'2" | 250 | 24 | | |
| Niko Noga | LB | 6'1" | 235 | 29 | | |
| Chris Spielman | LB | 6' | 247 | 25 | | |
| Bruce Alexander | DB | 5'9" | 169 | 25 | 1 | |
| Bennie Blades | DB | 6'1" | 221 | 24 | 1 | |
| Ray Crockett | DB | 5'9" | 181 | 24 | 6 | 6 |
| Melvin Jenkins | DB | 5'10" | 173 | 29 | | |
| Kevin Scott | DB | 5'9" | 175 | 22 | | |
| Terry Taylor | DB | 5'10" | 191 | 30 | 4 | |
| Herb Welch | DB | 5'11" | 180 | 30 | | |
| Sheldon White | DB | 5'11" | 188 | 26 | 2 | 6 |
| William White | DB | 5'10" | 191 | 25 | 1 | |
| Erik Kramer | QB | 6'1" | 195 | 26 | | 6 |
| Chuck Long | QB | 6'4" | 217 | 28 | | |
| Andre Ware | QB | 6'2" | 205 | 23 | | |
| Rodney Peete | QB | 6' | 193 | 25 | | 12 |
| D.J. Dozier | HB | 6' | 205 | 25 | | |
| Barry Sanders | HB-FB | 5'8" | 203 | 23 | | 102 |
| Cedric Jackson | FB-HB | 5'11" | 229 | 23 | | |
| Don Overton | FB-HN | 6' | 221 | 23 | | |
| Reggie Barrett | WR | 6'3" | 215 | 22 | | |
| Jeff Campbell | WR | 5'8" | 167 | 23 | | |
| Robert Clark | WR | 5'11" | 173 | 26 | | 36 |
| Mike Farr | WR | 5'10" | 192 | 24 | | 6 |
| Mel Gray | WR | 5'9" | 162 | 30 | | 6 |
| Willie Green | WR | 6'2" | 179 | 25 | | 42 |
| Aubrey Matthews | WR | 5'7" | 165 | 28 | | |
| Herman Moore | WR | 6'3" | 205 | 21 | | |
| Brett Perriman | WR | 5'9" | 180 | 25 | | 6 |
| David Little | TE | 6'2" | 226 | 30 | | |
| Eugene Riley | TE | 6'3" | 238 | 24 | | |
| Derek Tennell | TE | 6'5" | 270 | 27 | | |
| Jim Arnold | K | 6'3" | 211 | 30 | | |
| Eddie Murray | K | 5'10" | 180 | 35 | | 97 |

## CHICAGO BEARS 11-5 Mike Ditka

| Scores of Each Game | | |
|---|---|---|
| 10 | MINNESOTA | 6 |
| 21 | Tampa Bay | 20 |
| 20 | N.Y. GIANTS | 17 |
| 19 | N.Y. JETS | * 13 |
| 20 | Buffalo | 35 |
| 7 | WASHINGTON | 20 |
| 10 | Green Bay | 0 |
| 20 | New Orleans | 17 |
| 20 | DETROIT | 10 |
| 34 | Minnesota | 17 |
| 31 | Indianapolis | 17 |
| 13 | MIAMI | * 16 |
| 6 | Detroit | 16 |
| 27 | GREEN BAY | 13 |
| 27 | TAMPA BAY | 0 |
| 14 | San Francisco | 52 |

| UseName | Pos. | Hgt. | Wgt. | Age | Int | Pts |
|---|---|---|---|---|---|---|
| Ron Mattes | OT | 6'6" | 300 | 28 | | |
| Stan Thomas | OT | 6'5" | 302 | 22 | | |
| Keith Van Horne | OT | 6'6" | 283 | 33 | | |
| John Wojciechowski | OT | 6'4" | 270 | 28 | | |
| Mark Bortz | OG | 6'6" | 272 | 30 | | |
| Jerry Fontenot | OG | 6'3" | 272 | 24 | | |
| Tom Thayer | OG | 6'4" | 270 | 30 | | |
| Jay Hilgenberg | C | 6'3" | 260 | 31 | | |
| Trace Armstrong | DE | 6'4" | 259 | 25 | | |
| Richard Dent | DE | 6'5" | 268 | 30 | 1 | |
| Tim Ryan | DE-DT | 6'4" | 268 | 23 | | |
| James Williams | DE | 6'7" | 305 | 23 | | |
| Steve McMichael | DT | 6'2" | 268 | 33 | | |
| William Perry | DT | 6'2" | 350 | 28 | | |
| Chris Zorich | DT | 6'1" | 267 | 22 | | |
| Ron Cox | LB | 6'2" | 242 | 23 | | |
| Dante Jones | LB | 6'1" | 236 | 26 | | |
| Jim Morrissey | LB | 6'3" | 227 | 28 | 1 | |
| Ron Rivera | LB | 6'3" | 240 | 29 | | |
| John Roper | LB | 6'1" | 228 | 25 | | |
| Mike Singletary | LB | 6' | 230 | 32 | | |
| Mike Stonebreaker | LB | 6' | 226 | 24 | | |
| Mark Carrier | DB | 6'1" | 180 | 23 | 2 | |
| Maurice Douglass | DB | 5'11" | 200 | 27 | | |
| Shaun Gayle | DB | 5'11" | 194 | 29 | 1 | |
| John Hardy | DB | 5'10" | 166 | 23 | | |
| John Mangum | DB | 5'10" | 173 | 24 | 1 | |
| Markus Paul | DB | 6'2" | 199 | 25 | 3 | |
| Lemuel Stinson | DB | 5'9" | 159 | 25 | 4 | 6 |
| David Tate | DB | 6' | 177 | 26 | 2 | |
| Donnell Woolford | DB | 5'9" | 187 | 25 | 2 | |
| Jim Harbaugh | QB | 6'3" | 220 | 26 | | 12 |
| Peter Tom Willis | QB | 6'2" | 200 | 24 | | |
| Neal Anderson | HB | 5'11" | 210 | 27 | | 54 |
| Johnny Bailey | HB | 5'8" | 180 | 24 | | 6 |
| Mark Green | HB | 5'11" | 184 | 24 | | 18 |
| Darren Lewis | HB-FB | 5'10" | 219 | 22 | | |
| Brad Muster | FB | 6'3" | 231 | 26 | | 42 |
| James Rouse | FB | 6' | 220 | 24 | | |
| Wendell Davis | WR | 5'11" | 188 | 25 | | 36 |
| Dennis Gentry | WR-HB | 5'8" | 180 | 32 | | |
| Glen Kozlowski | WR | 6'1" | 190 | 28 | | |
| Anthony Morgan | WR | 6'1" | 195 | 23 | | 12 |
| Ron Morris | WR | 6'1' | 195 | 26 | | |
| Tom Waddle | WR | 6' | 181 | 24 | | 18 |
| Cap Boso | TE | 6'3" | 240 | 27 | | |
| Keith Jennings | TE | 6'4" | 251 | 25 | | |
| Jim Thornton | TE | 6'2" | 242 | 26 | | 6 |
| Maury Buford | K | 6'1" | 198 | 31 | | |
| Kevin Butler | K | 6'1" | 190 | 29 | | 89 |
| Chris Gardocki | K | 6'1" | 194 | 21 | | |

Jim Covert — Back Injury
Eric Kumerow — Broken Ankle

Quintin Smith — Leg Injury

## MINNESOTA VIKINGS 8-8 Jerry Burns

| Scores of Each Game | | |
|---|---|---|
| 6 | Chicago | 10 |
| 20 | Atlanta | 19 |
| 17 | SAN FRANCISCO | 14 |
| 0 | New Orleans | 26 |
| 6 | DENVER | 13 |
| 20 | Detroit | 24 |
| 34 | PHOENIX | 7 |
| 23 | New England | * 26 |
| 28 | Phoenix | 0 |
| 28 | TAMPA BAY | 13 |
| 17 | CHICAGO | 34 |
| 35 | Green Bay | 21 |
| 14 | DETROIT | 34 |
| 26 | Tampa Bay | 24 |
| 20 | L.A. RAMS | 14 |
| 7 | GREEN BAY | 27 |

| UseName | Pos. | Hgt. | Wgt. | Age | Int | Pts |
|---|---|---|---|---|---|---|
| Brian Habib | OT | 6'7" | 292 | 26 | | |
| Tim Irwin | OT | 6'6" | 301 | 32 | | |
| Gary Zimmerman | OT | 6'6" | 286 | 29 | | |
| Todd Kalis | OG | 6'5" | 285 | 26 | | |
| Randall McDaniel | OG | 6'3" | 271 | 26 | | |
| Craig Wolfley | OG | 6'1" | 265 | 33 | | |
| Chris Foote | C | 6'3" | 266 | 34 | | |
| Kirk Lowdermilk | C | 6'3" | 270 | 28 | | |
| Mike Morris | C | 6'5" | 268 | 30 | | |
| Adam Schrieber | C-OG | 6'4" | 280 | 29 | | |
| Chris Doleman | DE | 6'5" | 266 | 29 | | |
| Al Noga | DE | 6'1" | 264 | 25 | | |
| John Randle | DE | 6'1" | 264 | 23 | | |
| Thomas Strauthers | DE | 6'4" | 263 | 30 | | |
| Ken Clarke | DT | 6'2" | 279 | 35 | | |
| Mike Teeter | DT | 6'2" | 269 | 24 | | |
| Henry Thomas | DT | 6'2" | 269 | 26 | | |
| Ray Berry | LB | 6'2" | 227 | 27 | 1 | |
| Ivan Caesar | LB | 6'1" | 241 | 24 | | |
| Mark Dusbabek | LB | 6'3" | 230 | 27 | | |
| Carlos Jenkins | LB | 6'3" | 222 | 23 | | |
| Greg Manusky | LB | 6'1" | 236 | 25 | | |
| Mike Merriweather | LB | 6'2" | 226 | 30 | 1 | 6 |
| Mac Stephens | LB | 6'3" | 220 | 23 | | |
| Jimmy Williams | LB | 6'3" | 221 | 30 | | |
| Joey Browner | DB | 6'2" | 231 | 31 | 5 | |
| Pat Eilers | DB | 5'11" | 192 | 24 | | |
| Carl Lee | DB | 6' | 183 | 30 | 1 | |
| Mike Myes | DB | 5'10" | 179 | 25 | | |
| Audrey McMillian | DB | 6' | 190 | 29 | 4 | |
| Reggie Rutland | DB | 6'1" | 191 | 27 | 3 | 6 |
| Todd Scott | DB | 5'10" | 190 | 23 | | |
| Solomon Wilcots | DB | 5'11" | 200 | 26 | | |
| Felix Wright | DB | 6'2" | 197 | 32 | 2 | |
| Rich Gannon | QB | 6'3" | 203 | 25 | | 12 |
| Sean Salisbury | QB | 6'5" | 213 | 28 | | |
| Wade Wilson | QB | 6'3" | 205 | 32 | | |
| Terry Allen | HB | 5'10" | 189 | 23 | | 18 |
| Darrin Nelson | HB | 5'9" | 180 | 32 | | 12 |
| Herschel Walker | HB-FB | 6'1" | 220 | 29 | | 60 |
| Alfred Anderson | FB | 6'1" | 219 | 30 | | 6 |
| Randy Baldwin | FB | 5'10" | 210 | 24 | | |
| Rick Fenney | FB | 6'1" | 233 | 26 | | |
| Anthony Carter | WR | 5'11" | 176 | 30 | | 36 |
| Cris Carter | WR | 6'3" | 198 | 25 | | 30 |
| Hassan Jones | WR | 6' | 196 | 27 | | 6 |
| Leo Lewis | WR | 5'8" | 163 | 34 | | |
| Terry Obee | WR | 5'10" | 190 | 23 | | |
| Jake Reed | WR | 6'3" | 216 | 23 | | |
| Mike Jones | TE | 6'3" | 256 | 24 | | 12 |
| Steve Jordan | TE | 6'4" | 238 | 30 | | 12 |
| Brent Novoselsky | TE | 6'3" | 236 | 25 | | |
| Harry Newsome | K | 6' | 189 | 28 | | |
| Fuad Reveiz | K | 5'11" | 225 | 28 | | 85 |

Keith Millard — Knee Injury

## GREEN BAY PACKERS 4-12 Lindy Infante

| Scores of Each Game | | |
|---|---|---|
| 3 | PHILADELPHIA | 20 |
| 14 | Detroit | 23 |
| 15 | TAMPA BAY | 13 |
| 13 | Miami | 16 |
| 21 | L.A. Rams | 23 |
| 17 | DALLAS | 20 |
| 0 | CHICAGO | 10 |
| 27 | Tampa Bay | 0 |
| 16 | N.Y. Jets | 19 |
| 24 | BUFFALO | 34 |
| 21 | MINNESOTA | 35 |
| 14 | INDIANAPOLIS | 10 |
| 31 | Atlanta | 35 |
| 13 | Chicago | 27 |
| 17 | DETROIT | 21 |
| 27 | Minnesota | 7 |

| UseName | Pos. | Hgt. | Wgt. | Age | Int | Pts |
|---|---|---|---|---|---|---|
| Louis Cheek | OT-OG | 6'7" | 286 | 26 | | |
| Steve Gabbard | OT | 6'4" | 297 | 25 | | |
| Scott Jones | OT | 6'5" | 282 | 25 | | |
| Tony Mandarich | OT | 6'5" | 310 | 24 | | |
| Ken Ruettgers | OT | 6'5" | 286 | 29 | | |
| Billy Ard | OG | 6'3" | 273 | 32 | | |
| Ron Hallstrom | OG | 6'6" | 305 | 32 | | |
| Rich Moran | OG | 6'3" | 280 | 29 | | |
| Keith Uecker | OG | 6'5" | 299 | 31 | | |
| Blair Bush | C | 6'3" | 275 | 34 | | |
| James Campen | C | 6'3" | 277 | 27 | | |
| Lester Archambeau | DE | 6'4" | 271 | 24 | | |
| Matt Brock | DE | 6'5" | 290 | 25 | | |
| Robert Brown | DE | 6'2" | 278 | 31 | 1 | |
| Don Davey | DE | 6'4" | 273 | 23 | | |
| Shawn Patterson | DE | 6'5" | 273 | 27 | | |
| John Jurkovic | NT | 6'2" | 297 | 24 | | |
| Esera Tuaolo | NT | 6'2" | 284 | 23 | 1 | |
| Tony Bennett | LB | 6'2" | 242 | 24 | | |
| Reggie Burnette | LB | 6'2" | 240 | 22 | | |
| Burnell Dent | LB | 6'1" | 233 | 28 | | |
| Johnny Holland | LB | 6'2" | 232 | 26 | | |
| Kurt Larson | LB | 6'4" | 241 | 25 | | |
| Brian Noble | LB | 6'3" | 250 | 28 | | 6 |
| Bryce Paup | LB | 6'5" | 247 | 23 | | 2 |
| Scott Stephen | LB | 6'2" | 243 | 27 | 1 | |
| LeRoy Butler | DB | 6' | 195 | 23 | 3 | |
| Chuck Cecil | DB | 6' | 190 | 26 | 3 | |
| Vinnie Clark | DB | 6' | 194 | 22 | 2 | |
| Joe Fuller | DB | 5'11" | 186 | 26 | | |
| Tim Hauck | DB | 5'11" | 181 | 24 | | |
| Jerry Holmes | DB | 6'2" | 178 | 33 | 1 | |
| Roland Mitchell | DB | 5'11" | 198 | 27 | | |
| Mark Murphy | DB | 6'2" | 209 | 33 | 3 | |
| Blair Kiel | QB | 6' | 209 | 29 | | |
| Don Majkowski | QB | 6'2" | 206 | 27 | | 12 |
| Mike Tomczak | QB | 6'1" | 204 | 28 | | 6 |
| Vai Sikahema | HB | 5'9" | 196 | 29 | | |
| Keith Woodside | HB | 5'11" | 217 | 27 | | 6 |
| Vince Workman | HB | 5'10 | 201 | 23 | | 66 |
| Steve Avery | FB | 6'1" | 225 | 25 | | |
| Walter Dean | FB | 5'10" | 216 | 23 | | |
| Allen Rice | FB | 5'11" | 206 | 29 | | |
| Darrell Thompson | FB | 6' | 227 | 23 | | 6 |
| Chuck Webb | FB | 5'9" | 201 | 22 | | |
| Erik Affholter | WR | 6' | 187 | 25 | | |
| Perry Kemp | WR | 5'11" | 163 | 29 | | 12 |
| Jeff Query | WR | 6' | 165 | 24 | | |
| Sterling Sharpe | WR | 5'11" | 205 | 26 | | 24 |
| Clarence Weathers | WR | 5'9" | 169 | 29 | | |
| Charles Wilson | WR | 5'9" | 178 | 23 | | 12 |
| Jackie Harris | TE | 6'3" | 243 | 23 | | 18 |
| Ed West | TE | 6'1" | 244 | 30 | | 18 |
| Chris Jacke | K | 6' | 197 | 25 | | 85 |
| Paul McJulien | K | 5'10" | 190 | 26 | | |

## TAMPA BAY BUCCANEERS 3-13 Richard Williamson

| Scores of Each Game | | |
|---|---|---|
| 13 | N.Y. Jets | 16 |
| 20 | CHICAGO | 21 |
| 13 | Green Bay | 15 |
| 10 | BUFFALO | 17 |
| 3 | Detroit | 31 |
| 14 | PHILADELPHIA | 13 |
| 7 | New Orleans | 23 |
| 0 | GREEN BAY | 27 |
| 13 | Minnesota | 28 |
| 30 | DETROIT | 21 |
| 7 | Atlanta | 43 |
| 14 | N.Y. GIANTS | 21 |
| 14 | Miami | 33 |
| 24 | MINNESOTA | 26 |
| 0 | Chicago | 27 |
| 17 | INDIANAPOLIS | 3 |

| UseName | Pos. | Hgt. | Wgt. | Age | Int | Pts |
|---|---|---|---|---|---|---|
| Scott Dill | OT | 6'5" | 285 | 25 | | |
| Paul Gruber | OT | 6'5" | 290 | 26 | | |
| Charles McRae | OT | 6'7" | 290 | 22 | | |
| Rob Taylor | OT | 6'6" | 290 | 30 | | |
| Ian Beckles | OG | 6'1" | 295 | 24 | | |
| John Bruhin | OG | 6'3" | 285 | 26 | | |
| Tom McHale | OG | 6'4" | 280 | 28 | | |
| Tim Ryan | OG | 6'2" | 280 | 22 | | |
| Tony Mayberry | C | 6'4" | 285 | 23 | | |
| Al Chamblee | DE | 6'1" | 240 | 22 | | |
| Dexter Manley | DE | 6'4" | 270 | 32 | | |
| Keith McCants | DE | 6'3" | 265 | 23 | | |
| Ray Seals | DE | 6'3" | 270 | 26 | | |
| Reuben Davis | DT-DE | 6'4" | 285 | 26 | | |
| Darryl Grant | DT | 6'1" | 275 | 31 | | |
| Rhett Hall | DT | 6'2" | 260 | 22 | | |
| Tim Newton | DT | 6' | 275 | 28 | | |
| Gerald Nichols | DT | 6'2" | 260 | 27 | | |
| Sam Anno | LB | 6'2" | 235 | 26 | | |
| Eugene Marve | LB | 6'2" | 240 | 31 | 1 | |
| Kevin Murphy | LB | 6'2" | 235 | 27 | | |
| Maurice Oliver | LB | 6'3" | 235 | 24 | | |
| Jesse Solomon | LB | 6' | 235 | 27 | | |
| Broderick Thomas | LB | 6'4" | 245 | 24 | | |
| Calvin Tiggle | LB | 6'1" | 235 | 22 | | |
| Carl Carter | DB | 5'11" | 180 | 27 | 1 | |
| Marty Carter | DB | 6'1" | 200 | 21 | 1 | |
| Tony Covington | DB | 5'11" | 190 | 23 | 3 | |
| William Frizzell | DB | 6'3" | 205 | 28 | | |
| Darrell Fullington (from NE) | DB | 6'1" | 195 | 27 | 2 | |
| Harry Hamilton | DB | 6' | 195 | 28 | | |
| Alonzo Hampton | DB | 5'10" | 195 | 24 | 1 | |
| Roger Jones | DB | 5'9" | 175 | 22 | | |
| Ricky Reynolds | DB | 5'11" | 190 | 26 | 2 | |
| Glenn Rogers | DB | 6' | 185 | 22 | | |
| Jeff Carlson | QB | 6'3" | 215 | 25 | | |
| Chris Chandler (to PHX) | QB | 6'4" | 220 | 25 | | |
| Vinny Testaverde | QB | 6'5" | 215 | 27 | | |
| Gary Anderson | HB | 6' | 190 | 30 | | 6 |
| Reggie Cobb | HB-FB | 6' | 215 | 23 | | 42 |
| Robert Hardy | HB | 5'10" | 210 | 24 | | |
| Alonzo Highsmith (from DAL) | FB | 6'1" | 235 | 26 | | |
| Chuck Weatherspoon | FB | 5'7" | 230 | 23 | | |
| Robert Wilson | FB | 6' | 240 | 22 | | 12 |
| Terry Anthony | WR | 6' | 200 | 23 | | |
| Mark Carrier | WR | 6' | 185 | 25 | | 12 |
| Lawrence Dawsey | WR | 6' | 195 | 23 | | 18 |
| Willie Drewrey | WR | 5'7" | 170 | 28 | | 12 |
| Bruce Hill | WR | 6' | 180 | 27 | | 12 |
| Jesse Anderson | TE | 6'2" | 245 | 25 | | 12 |
| Ron Hall | TE | 6'4" | 245 | 27 | | |
| Ed Thomas | TE | 6'3" | 245 | 25 | | |
| Steve Christie | K | 6' | 185 | 23 | | 67 |
| Mark Royals | K | 6'5" | 215 | 27 | | |

Randy Grimes — Elbow Injury

Mark Robinson — Shoulder Injury

## DETROIT LIONS

### RUSHING
| Last Name | No. | Yds | Avg | TD |
|---|---|---|---|---|
| B. Sanders | 342 | 1548 | 4.5 | 16 |
| Peete | 25 | 125 | 5.0 | 2 |
| Overton | 14 | 59 | 4.2 | 0 |
| Jackson | 17 | 53 | 3.1 | 0 |
| Dozier | 9 | 48 | 5.3 | 0 |
| Arnold | 2 | 42 | 21.0 | 0 |
| Kramer | 34 | 21 | 0.6 | 1 |
| Gray | 2 | 11 | 5.5 | 0 |
| Perriman | 4 | 10 | 2.5 | 0 |
| Ware | 4 | 6 | 1.5 | 0 |

### RECEIVING
| Last Name | No. | Yds | Avg | TD |
|---|---|---|---|---|
| Perriman | 52 | 668 | 12.8 | 1 |
| Clark | 47 | 640 | 13.6 | 6 |
| Farr | 42 | 431 | 10.3 | 1 |
| Sanders | 41 | 307 | 7.5 | 1 |
| Green | 39 | 592 | 15.2 | 7 |
| Moore | 11 | 135 | 12.3 | 0 |
| Tennell | 4 | 43 | 10.8 | 0 |
| Overton | 4 | 38 | 9.4 | 0 |
| Gray | 3 | 42 | 14.0 | 0 |
| Matthews | 3 | 21 | 7.0 | 0 |
| Campbell | 2 | 49 | 24.5 | 0 |
| Fortin | 1 | 4 | 4.0 | 0 |
| Riley | 1 | 3 | 3.0 | 0 |
| Dozier | 1 | 3 | 3.0 | 0 |
| Jackson | 1 | -2 | -2.0 | 0 |

### PUNT RETURNS
| Last Name | No. | Yds | Avg | TD |
|---|---|---|---|---|
| Gray | 25 | 385 | 15.4 | 1 |
| Jenkins | 1 | 0 | 0.0 | 0 |

### KICKOFF RETURNS
| Last Name | No. | Yds | Avg | TD |
|---|---|---|---|---|
| Gray | 36 | 929 | 25.8 | 0 |
| Campbell | 9 | 85 | 9.4 | 0 |
| Overton | 4 | 71 | 17.8 | 0 |
| Dozier | 4 | 60 | 15.0 | 0 |
| Scott | 1 | 16 | 16.0 | 0 |
| Jackson | 1 | 9 | 9.0 | 0 |
| Clark | 1 | 0 | 0.0 | 0 |
| Bell | 1 | 0 | 0.0 | 0 |

### PASSING — PUNTING — KICKING
| PASSING | Att | Cmp | % | Yds | Yd/Att | TD | Int—% | RK |
|---|---|---|---|---|---|---|---|---|
| Kramer | 265 | 136 | 51.3 | 1635 | 6.17 | 11 | 8—3.0 | 13 |
| Peete | 194 | 116 | 59.8 | 1339 | 6.90 | 5 | 9—4.6 | |

| PUNTING | No. | Avg. |
|---|---|---|
| Arnold | 75 | 41.2 |

| KICKING | XP | Att | % | FG | Att | % |
|---|---|---|---|---|---|---|
| Murray | 40 | 40 | 100 | 19 | 28 | 68 |

## CHICAGO BEARS

### RUSHING
| Last Name | No. | Yds | Avg | TD |
|---|---|---|---|---|
| Anderson | 210 | 747 | 3.6 | 6 |
| Muster | 90 | 412 | 4.6 | 6 |
| Harbaugh | 70 | 338 | 4.8 | 2 |
| Green | 61 | 217 | 3.6 | 3 |
| Rouse | 24 | 74 | 2.7 | 0 |
| Gentry | 9 | 58 | 6.4 | 0 |
| Bailey | 15 | 43 | 2.9 | 1 |
| Lewis | 15 | 36 | 2.4 | 0 |
| Morgan | 3 | 18 | 6.0 | 0 |
| Willis | 2 | 6 | 3.0 | 0 |

### RECEIVING
| Last Name | No. | Yds | Avg | TD |
|---|---|---|---|---|
| Davis | 61 | 945 | 15.5 | 6 |
| Waddle | 55 | 599 | 10.9 | 3 |
| Anderson | 47 | 368 | 7.8 | 3 |
| Muster | 35 | 287 | 8.2 | 1 |
| Thornton | 17 | 278 | 16.4 | 1 |
| Gentry | 16 | 149 | 9.3 | 0 |
| Rouse | 15 | 93 | 6.2 | 0 |
| Morgan | 13 | 211 | 16.2 | 2 |
| Morris | 8 | 147 | 18.4 | 0 |
| Jennings | 8 | 109 | 13.6 | 0 |
| Green | 6 | 54 | 9.0 | 0 |
| Boso | 3 | 36 | 12.0 | 0 |
| Kozlowski | 2 | 16 | 8.0 | 0 |

### PUNT RETURNS
| Last Name | No. | Yds | Avg | TD |
|---|---|---|---|---|
| Bailey | 36 | 281 | 7.8 | 0 |
| Waddle | 5 | 31 | 6.2 | 0 |
| Morgan | 3 | 19 | 6.3 | 0 |
| Green | 3 | 9 | 3.0 | 0 |

### KICKOFF RETURNS
| Last Name | No. | Yds | Avg | TD |
|---|---|---|---|---|
| Bailey | 16 | 311 | 19.4 | 0 |
| Gentry | 13 | 227 | 17.5 | 0 |
| Morgan | 8 | 133 | 16.6 | 0 |
| Green | 4 | 69 | 17.3 | 0 |
| Lewis | 2 | 13 | 6.5 | 0 |
| Rouse | 2 | 10 | 5.0 | 0 |

### PASSING — PUNTING — KICKING
| PASSING | Att | Cmp | % | Yds | Yd/Att | TD | Int—% | RK |
|---|---|---|---|---|---|---|---|---|
| Harbaugh | 478 | 275 | 57.5 | 3121 | 6.53 | 15 | 16—3.3 | 11 |
| Willis | 18 | 11 | 61.1 | 171 | 9.50 | 1 | 1—5.6 | |
| Anderson | 1 | 0 | 0.0 | 0 | 0.00 | 0 | 0—0.0 | |

| PUNTING | No. | Avg. |
|---|---|---|
| Buford | 70 | 40.2 |

| KICKING | XP | ATT | % | FG | ATT | % |
|---|---|---|---|---|---|---|
| Butler | 32 | 34 | 94 | 19 | 29 | 66 |

## MINNESOTA VIKINGS

### RUSHING
| Last Name | No. | Yds | Avg | TD |
|---|---|---|---|---|
| Walker | 198 | 825 | 4.2 | 10 |
| Allen | 120 | 563 | 4.7 | 2 |
| Gannon | 43 | 236 | 5.5 | 2 |
| Nelson | 28 | 210 | 7.5 | 2 |
| Anderson | 26 | 118 | 4.5 | 1 |
| A. Carter | 13 | 117 | 9.0 | 1 |
| Fenney | 23 | 99 | 4.3 | 0 |
| Wilson | 13 | 33 | 2.5 | 0 |

### RECEIVING
| Last Name | No. | Yds | Avg | TD |
|---|---|---|---|---|
| C. Carter | 72 | 962 | 13.4 | 5 |
| Jordan | 57 | 638 | 11.2 | 2 |
| A. Carter | 51 | 553 | 10.8 | 5 |
| Walker | 33 | 204 | 6.2 | 0 |
| H. Jones | 32 | 384 | 12.0 | 1 |
| Nelson | 19 | 142 | 7.5 | 0 |
| Allen | 6 | 49 | 8.2 | 1 |
| Lewis | 4 | 36 | 9.0 | 0 |
| Novoselsky | 4 | 27 | 6.8 | 0 |
| Fenney | 2 | 11 | 5.5 | 0 |
| M. Jones | 2 | 8 | 4.0 | 2 |
| Anderson | 1 | 2 | 2.0 | 0 |
| Gannon | 1 | 0 | 0.0 | 0 |

### PUNT RETURNS
| Last Name | No. | Yds | Avg | TD |
|---|---|---|---|---|
| Lewis | 30 | 225 | 7.5 | 0 |

### KICKOFF RETURNS
| Last Name | No. | Yds | Avg | TD |
|---|---|---|---|---|
| Nelson | 31 | 682 | 22.0 | 0 |
| Eilers | 5 | 99 | 19.8 | 0 |
| Walker | 5 | 83 | 16.6 | 0 |
| Allen | 1 | 14 | 14.0 | 0 |
| Baldwin | 1 | 14 | 14.0 | 0 |
| Anderson | 1 | 7 | 7.0 | 0 |

### PASSING — PUNTING — KICKING
| PASSING | Att | Cmp | % | Yds | Yd/Att | TD | Int—% | RK |
|---|---|---|---|---|---|---|---|---|
| Gannon | 354 | 211 | 59.6 | 2166 | 6.12 | 12 | 6—1.7 | 6 |
| Wilson | 122 | 72 | 59.0 | 825 | 6.76 | 3 | 10—8.2 | |
| Nelson | 1 | 1 | 100.0 | 25 | 25.00 | 1 | 0—0.0 | |

| PUNTING | No. | Avg. |
|---|---|---|
| Newsome | 68 | 45.5 |

| KICKING | XP | ATT | % | FG | ATT | % |
|---|---|---|---|---|---|---|
| Reveiz | 34 | 35 | 97 | 17 | 24 | 71 |

## GREEN BAY PACKERS

### RUSHING
| Last Name | No. | Yds | Avg | TD |
|---|---|---|---|---|
| Thompson | 141 | 471 | 3.3 | 1 |
| Woodside | 84 | 326 | 3.9 | 1 |
| Workman | 71 | 237 | 3.3 | 7 |
| Majkowski | 25 | 108 | 4.3 | 2 |
| Rice | 30 | 100 | 3.3 | 0 |
| Tomczak | 17 | 93 | 5.5 | 1 |
| Kiel | 4 | 46 | 11.5 | 0 |
| Sharpe | 4 | 4 | 1.0 | 0 |
| Wilson | 3 | 3 | 1.0 | 0 |
| Harris | 1 | 1 | 1.0 | 0 |
| McJulien | 1 | 0 | 0.0 | 0 |

### RECEIVING
| Last Name | No. | Yds | Avg | TD |
|---|---|---|---|---|
| Sharpe | 69 | 961 | 13.9 | 4 |
| Workman | 46 | 371 | 8.1 | 4 |
| Kemp | 42 | 583 | 13.9 | 2 |
| Harris | 24 | 264 | 11.0 | 3 |
| Woodside | 22 | 185 | 8.4 | 0 |
| Wilson | 19 | 305 | 16.1 | 1 |
| West | 15 | 151 | 10.1 | 3 |
| Weathers | 12 | 150 | 12.5 | 0 |
| Query | 7 | 94 | 13.4 | 0 |
| Thompson | 7 | 71 | 10.1 | 0 |
| Affholter | 7 | 68 | 9.7 | 0 |
| Rice | 2 | 10 | 5.0 | 0 |

### PUNT RETURNS
| Last Name | No. | Yds | Avg | TD |
|---|---|---|---|---|
| Sikahema | 26 | 239 | 9.2 | 0 |
| Query | 14 | 157 | 11.2 | 0 |

### KICKOFF RETURNS
| Last Name | No. | Yds | Avg | TD |
|---|---|---|---|---|
| Wilson | 23 | 522 | 22.7 | 1 |
| Sikahema | 15 | 325 | 21.7 | 0 |
| Workman | 8 | 139 | 17.4 | 0 |
| Thompson | 7 | 127 | 18.1 | 0 |
| Rice | 3 | 36 | 12.0 | 0 |
| Webb | 2 | 40 | 20.0 | 0 |
| Davey | 1 | 8 | 8.0 | 0 |
| Dean | 1 | 0 | 0.0 | 0 |

### PASSING — PUNTING — KICKING
| PASSING | Att | Cmp | % | Yds | Yd/Att | TD | Int—% | RK |
|---|---|---|---|---|---|---|---|---|
| Tomczak | 238 | 128 | 53.8 | 1490 | 6.26 | 11 | 9—3.8 | 12 |
| Majkowski | 226 | 115 | 50.9 | 1362 | 6.03 | 3 | 8—3.5 | 16 |
| Kiel | 50 | 29 | 58.0 | 361 | 7.22 | 3 | 2—4.0 | |

| PUNTING | No. | Avg. |
|---|---|---|
| McJulien | 86 | 40.4 |

| KICKING | XP | Att. | % | FG | Att | % |
|---|---|---|---|---|---|---|
| Jacke | 31 | 31 | 100 | 18 | 24 | 75 |

## TAMPA BAY BUCCANEERS

### RUSHING
| Last Name | No. | Yds | Avg | TD |
|---|---|---|---|---|
| Cobb | 196 | 752 | 3.8 | 7 |
| G. Anderson | 72 | 263 | 3.7 | 1 |
| Wilson | 42 | 179 | 4.3 | 0 |
| Chandler | 26 | 111 | 4.3 | 0 |
| Testaverde | 32 | 101 | 3.2 | 0 |
| Carlson | 5 | 25 | 5.0 | 0 |
| Highsmith | 5 | 21 | 4.2 | 0 |

### RECEIVING
| Last Name | No. | Yds | Avg | TD |
|---|---|---|---|---|
| Dawsey | 55 | 818 | 14.9 | 3 |
| Carrier | 47 | 698 | 14.9 | 2 |
| Ro. Hall | 31 | 284 | 9.2 | 0 |
| Drewrey | 26 | 375 | 14.4 | 2 |
| G. Anderson | 25 | 184 | 7.4 | 0 |
| Wilson | 20 | 121 | 6.1 | 0 |
| Hill | 17 | 185 | 10.9 | 2 |
| Cobb | 15 | 111 | 7.4 | 0 |
| J. Anderson | 6 | 73 | 12.2 | 2 |
| E. Thomas | 4 | 55 | 13.8 | 0 |
| Anthony | 4 | 51 | 12.8 | 0 |

### PUNT RETURNS
| Last Name | No. | Yds | Avg | TD |
|---|---|---|---|---|
| Drewrey | 38 | 360 | 9.5 | 0 |
| Carter | 1 | 1 | 1.0 | 0 |

### KICKOFF RETURNS
| Last Name | No. | Yds | Avg | TD |
|---|---|---|---|---|
| G. Anderson | 34 | 643 | 18.9 | 0 |
| Drewrey | 12 | 246 | 20.5 | 0 |
| Hardy | 8 | 119 | 14.9 | 0 |
| Wilson | 2 | 19 | 9.5 | 0 |
| Cobb | 2 | 15 | 7.5 | 0 |
| Ryan | 1 | 4 | 4.0 | 0 |
| Ro. Hall | 1 | 1 | 1.0 | 0 |

### PASSING — PUNTING — KICKING
| PASSING | Att | Cmp | % | Yds | Yd/Att | TD | Int—% | RK |
|---|---|---|---|---|---|---|---|---|
| Testaverde | 326 | 166 | 50.9 | 1994 | 6.12 | 8 | 15—4.6 | 17 |
| Chandler | 154 | 78 | 50.6 | 846 | 5.49 | 5 | 10—4.0 | |

| PUNTING | No. | Avg. |
|---|---|---|
| Royals | 84 | 40.3 |

| KICKING | XP | ATT | % | FG | ATT | % |
|---|---|---|---|---|---|---|
| Christie | 22 | 22 | 100 | 15 | 20 | 75 |

## NEW ORLEANS SAINTS 11-5 Jim Mora

| Scores of Each Game | | |
|---|---|---|
| 27 | SEATTLE | 24 |
| 17 | Kansas City | 10 |
| 24 | L.A. RAMS | 7 |
| 26 | MINNESOTA | 0 |
| 27 | Atlanta | 6 |
| 13 | Philadelphia | 6 |
| 23 | TAMPA BAY | 7 |
| 17 | CHICAGO | 20 |
| 24 | L.A. Rams | 17 |
| 10 | SAN FRANCISCO | 3 |
| 21 | San Diego | 24 |
| 20 | ATLANTA | *23 |
| 24 | San Francisco | 38 |
| 14 | Dallas | 23 |
| 27 | L.A. RAIDERS | 0 |
| 27 | Phoenix | 3 |

| UseName | Pos. | Hgt. | Wgt. | Age | Int | Pts |
|---|---|---|---|---|---|---|
| Stan Brock | OT | 6'6" | 278 | 33 | | |
| Richard Cooper | OT | 6'4" | 290 | 26 | | |
| Kevin Haverdink | OT | 6'5" | 285 | 25 | | |
| Mike Keim | OT | 6'7" | 285 | 25 | | |
| Jim Dombrowski | OG | 6'5" | 298 | 27 | | |
| Derek Kennard | OG | 6'3" | 300 | 28 | | |
| Chris Port | OG | 6'5" | 290 | 23 | | |
| Larry Williams | OG-C | 6'5" | 294 | 28 | | |
| Joel Hilgenberg | C | 6'3" | 252 | 29 | | |
| Brad Leggett | C | 6'4" | 270 | 25 | | |
| Wayne Martin | DE | 6'5" | 275 | 25 | | |
| Les Miller | DE | 6'7" | 285 | 26 | | |
| Renaldo Turnbull | DE | 6'4" | 255 | 25 | | |
| Jim Wilks | NT | 6'5" | 275 | 33 | | |
| Robert Goff | NT | 6'3" | 270 | 25 | | |
| Frank Warren | DE | 6'4" | 290 | 31 | | |
| Brian Forde | LB | 6'2" | 235 | 27 | | |
| Rickey Jackson | LB | 6'2" | 243 | 33 | | |
| Vaughan Johnson | LB | 6'3" | 235 | 29 | 1 | |
| Sam Mills | LB | 5'9" | 225 | 32 | 2 | |
| Scott Ross | LB | 6'1" | 235 | 22 | | |
| Joel Smeenge | DE | 6'5" | 255 | 23 | | |
| Pat Swilling | LB | 6'3" | 242 | 26 | 1 | 6 |
| James Williams | LB | 6' | 230 | 22 | | |
| Gene Atkins | DB | 6'1" | 200 | 26 | 5 | |
| Vince Buck | DB | 6' | 198 | 23 | 5 | |
| Toi Cook | DB | 5'11" | 188 | 26 | 3 | |
| Vencie Glenn | DB | 6' | 192 | 26 | 4 | |
| Reggie Jones | DB | 6'1" | 202 | 22 | 3 | |
| Milton Mack | DB | 5'11" | 182 | 27 | | |
| Brett Maxie | DB | 6'2" | 194 | 29 | 3 | 6 |
| Calvin Nicholson | DB | 5'9" | 183 | 34 | | |
| Stan Petry (from KC) | DB | 5'11" | 180 | 25 | 1 | |
| Bennie Thompson | DB | 6' | 200 | 28 | 1 | |
| Mike Buck | QB | 6'3" | 227 | 24 | | |
| Bobby Hebert | QB | 6'4" | 215 | 31 | | |
| Steve Walsh | QB | 6'2" | 204 | 24 | | |
| Gill Fenerty | HB | 6' | 205 | 28 | | 30 |
| Dalton Hilliard | HB | 5'8" | 204 | 27 | | 30 |
| Stanford Jennings | HB | 6'1" | 212 | 29 | | |
| Fred McAfee | HB | 5'10" | 193 | 23 | | 12 |
| Craig Heyward | FB | 5'11" | 260 | 24 | | 30 |
| Buford Jordan | FB | 6' | 223 | 29 | | 18 |
| Bobby Morse | FB | 5'10" | 213 | 24 | | |
| Cedric Smith | FB | 5'10" | 223 | 23 | | |
| Gerald Alphin | WR | 6'3" | 200 | 27 | | |
| Wesley Carroll | WR | 6' | 183 | 23 | | 6 |
| Quinn Early | WR | 6' | 190 | 26 | | 12 |
| Eric Martin | WR | 6'1" | 207 | 29 | | 24 |
| Pat Newman | WR | 5'11" | 189 | 22 | | |
| Floyd Turner | WR | 5'11" | 188 | 25 | | 48 |
| Hoby Brenner | TE | 6'4" | 245 | 32 | | |
| Greg Scales | TE | 6'4" | 253 | 25 | | |
| John Tice | TE | 6'5" | 249 | 31 | | |
| Frank Wainright | TE | 6'3" | 236 | 23 | | |
| Morten Andersen | K | 6'2" | 221 | 31 | | 113 |
| Tommy Barnhardt | K | 6'3" | 207 | 28 | | |

Steve Trapilo — Knee Injury

DeMond Winston — Knee Injury

## ATLANTA FALCONS 10-6 Jerry Glanville

| Scores of Each Game | | |
|---|---|---|
| 3 | Kansas City | 14 |
| 19 | MINNESOTA | 20 |
| 13 | San Diego | 10 |
| 21 | L.A. RAIDERS | 17 |
| 6 | NEW ORLEANS | 27 |
| 39 | San Francisco | 34 |
| 10 | Phoenix | 16 |
| 31 | L.A. RAMS | 14 |
| 17 | SAN FRANCISCO | 14 |
| 17 | Washington | 56 |
| 43 | TAMPA BAY | 7 |
| 23 | New Orleans | *20 |
| 35 | GREEN BAY | 31 |
| 31 | L.A. Rams | 14 |
| 26 | SEATTLE | 13 |
| 27 | Dallas | 31 |

| UseName | Pos. | Hgt. | Wgt. | Age | Int | Pts |
|---|---|---|---|---|---|---|
| Chris Hinton | OT | 6'4" | 300 | 30 | | |
| John Hunter | OT | 6'8" | 300 | 26 | | |
| Mike Kenn | OT | 6'7" | 280 | 35 | | |
| Reggie Redding | OT | 6'3" | 290 | 22 | | |
| Joe Sims | OT | 6'3" | 294 | 22 | | |
| Bill Fralic | OG | 6'5" | 280 | 28 | | |
| Houston Hoover | OG | 6'2" | 295 | 26 | | |
| Mike Ruether | OG-C | 6'4" | 286 | 28 | | |
| Guy Bingham | C | 6'3" | 260 | 33 | | |
| Jamie Dukes | C | 6'1" | 285 | 27 | | |
| Rick Bryan | DE | 6'4" | 265 | 29 | | |
| Mike Gann | DE | 6'5" | 270 | 27 | 1 | |
| Oliver Barnett | DE | 6'3" | 285 | 25 | | 6 |
| Tim Green | DE | 6'2" | 245 | 27 | | |
| Tory Epps | NT | 6' | 270 | 24 | | |
| Moe Gardner | NT | 6'2" | 258 | 23 | | |
| Aundray Bruce | LB-TE | 6'5" | 250 | 25 | | |
| Darion Conner | LB | 6'2" | 250 | 23 | | |
| Robert Lyles | LB | 6'1" | 230 | 30 | | |
| Wes Pritchett | LB | 6'4" | 234 | 24 | | |
| John Rade | LB | 6'1" | 240 | 31 | | |
| Michael Reid | LB | 6'2" | 235 | 27 | | |
| Kenny Tippins | LB | 6'1" | 230 | 25 | 1 | 6 |
| Jessie Tuggle | LB | 5'11" | 230 | 26 | 1 | 6 |
| Bobby Butler | DB | 5'11" | 175 | 32 | | |
| Scott Case | DB | 6' | 188 | 29 | 2 | |
| Jeff Donaldson | DB | 6' | 190 | 29 | | |
| Tracey Eaton | DB | 6'1" | 195 | 26 | | |
| William Evers | DB | 5'10" | 175 | 22 | | |
| Joe Fishback | DB | 5'11" | 198 | 23 | | 6 |
| Brian Jordan | DB | 5'11" | 205 | 24 | 2 | 4 |
| Tim McKyer | DB | 6' | 174 | 27 | 6 | |
| Brian Mitchell | DB | 5'9" | 164 | 22 | | |
| Bruce Pickens | DB | 5'11" | 190 | 23 | | |
| Deion Sanders | DB | 6' | 185 | 24 | 6 | 12 |
| Elbert Shelley | DB | 5'11" | 185 | 26 | | |
| Brett Favre | QB | 6'2" | 220 | 21 | | |
| Chris Miller | QB | 6'2" | 205 | 26 | | |
| Billy Joe Tolliver | QB | 6'1" | 218 | 25 | | |
| Steve Broussard | HB | 5'7" | 201 | 24 | | 30 |
| Erric Pegram | HB | 5'9" | 188 | 22 | | 6 |
| Mike Rozier | HB | 5'10" | 213 | 30 | | |
| Pat Chaffey | FB | 6'1" | 218 | 24 | | 6 |
| Tracy Johnson | FB | 6' | 230 | 25 | | |
| Keith Jones | FB | 6'1" | 210 | 25 | | |
| Shawn Collins | WR | 6'2" | 204 | 24 | | |
| Floyd Dixon | WR | 5'9" | 170 | 27 | | 6 |
| Michael Haynes | WR | 6' | 180 | 25 | | 66 |
| Jason Phillips | WR | 5'7" | 168 | 22 | | |
| Mike Pritchard | WR | 5'11" | 180 | 21 | | 12 |
| Andre Rison | WR | 6' | 188 | 24 | | 72 |
| George Thomas | WR | 5'9" | 169 | 27 | | 12 |
| Rich Bartlewski | TE | 6'5" | 255 | 24 | | |
| Harper LeBel | TE | 6'4" | 245 | 28 | | |
| Gary Wilkins | TE | 6'1" | 248 | 27 | | 6 |
| Scott Fulhage | K | 5'11" | 193 | 29 | | |
| Norm Johnson | K | 6'2" | 203 | 31 | | 95 |

## SAN FRANCISCO 49ERS 10-6 George Seifert

| Scores of Each Game | | |
|---|---|---|
| 14 | N.Y. Giants | 16 |
| 34 | SAN DIEGO | 14 |
| 14 | Minnesota | 17 |
| 27 | L.A. RAMS | 10 |
| 6 | L.A. Raiders | 12 |
| 34 | ATLANTA | 39 |
| 35 | DETROIT | 3 |
| 23 | Philadelphia | 7 |
| 14 | Atlanta | 17 |
| 3 | New Orleans | 10 |
| 14 | PHOENIX | 10 |
| 33 | L.A. Rams | 10 |
| 38 | NEW ORLEANS | 24 |
| 24 | Seattle | 22 |
| 28 | KANSAS CITY | 14 |
| 52 | CHICAGO | 14 |

| UseName | Pos. | Hgt. | Wgt. | Age | Int | Pts |
|---|---|---|---|---|---|---|
| Harris Barton | OG-OT | 6'4" | 280 | 27 | | |
| Frank Pollack | OT-OG | 6'4" | 285 | 23 | | |
| Steve Wallace | OT | 6'5" | 276 | 26 | | |
| Roy Foster | OG | 6'4" | 290 | 31 | | |
| Guy McIntyre | OG | 6'3" | 265 | 30 | | |
| Tom Neville | OG | 6'5" | 298 | 29 | | |
| Jesse Sapolu | C | 6'4" | 260 | 30 | | |
| Chuck Thomas | C | 6'3" | 280 | 30 | | |
| Dennis Brown | DE | 6'4" | 290 | 23 | | |
| Kevin Fagan | DE | 6'4" | 260 | 28 | | |
| Pierce Holt | DE | 6'4" | 280 | 29 | | |
| Greg Joelson | DE | 6'3" | 270 | 25 | | |
| Larry Roberts | DE | 6'3" | 275 | 28 | | |
| Jim Burt | NT | 6'1" | 270 | 32 | | |
| Michael Carter | NT | 6'2" | 285 | 30 | | |
| Ted Washington | NT-DE | 6'4" | 299 | 23 | | |
| Keith DeLong | LB | 6'2" | 235 | 24 | | |
| Mitch Donahue | LB | 6'2" | 254 | 23 | | |
| Antonio Goss | LB | 6'4" | 228 | 25 | | |
| Charles Haley | LB-DE | 6'5" | 230 | 27 | | |
| Tim Harris | LB-DE | 6'6" | 258 | 26 | | |
| John Johnson | LB | 6'3" | 230 | 23 | | |
| Darin Jordan | LB | 6'2" | 245 | 26 | | 2 |
| Bill Romanowski | LB | 6'4" | 231 | 25 | 1 | |
| Michael Walter | LB | 6'3" | 238 | 30 | | |
| Todd Bowles | DB | 6'2" | 205 | 27 | 1 | |
| Greg Cox | DB | 6' | 223 | 25 | | |
| Eric Davis | DB | 5'11" | 178 | 23 | | |
| Don Griffin | DB | 6' | 176 | 27 | 1 | 6 |
| Merton Hanks | DB | 6'2" | 185 | 23 | | |
| Johnny Jackson | DB | 6'1" | 204 | 24 | 1 | |
| Mark Lee (to NO) | DB | 6' | 197 | 33 | 1 | |
| Kevin Lewis | DB | 5'11" | 173 | 24 | 2 | |
| Dave Waymer | DB | 6'1" | 188 | 33 | 4 | |
| David Whitmore | DB | 6' | 235 | 24 | | |
| Steve Bono | QB | 6'4" | 215 | 29 | | |
| Bill Musgrave | QB | 6'2" | 196 | 23 | | |
| Steve Young | QB | 6'2" | 200 | 29 | | 24 |
| Dexter Carter | HB | 5'9" | 170 | 23 | | 24 |
| Spencer Tillman | HB | 5'11" | 206 | 27 | | |
| Keith Henderson | FB | 6'1" | 220 | 25 | | 12 |
| Tom Rathman | FB | 6'1" | 232 | 28 | | 36 |
| Harry Sydney | FB | 6' | 217 | 32 | | 42 |
| Sanjay Beach | WR | 6'1" | 190 | 25 | | |
| Jerry Rice | WR | 6'2" | 200 | 28 | | 84 |
| Mike Sherrard | WR | 6'2" | 187 | 28 | | 12 |
| John Taylor | WR | 6'1" | 185 | 29 | | 54 |
| Brent Jones | TE | 6'4" | 230 | 28 | | |
| Wesley Walls | TE | 6'5" | 246 | 25 | | |
| Jamie Williams | TE | 6'4" | 245 | 31 | | 6 |
| Mike Cofer | K | 6'1" | 160 | 27 | | 91 |
| Ralf Mojsiejenko | K | 6'3" | 212 | 28 | | |
| Joe Prokop | K | 6'2" | 225 | 31 | | |

Joe Montana — Elbow Injury
Darryl Pollard — Ankle Injury
Ronald Lewis — Back Injury

## LOS ANGELES RAMS 3-13 John Robinson

| Scores of Each Game | | |
|---|---|---|
| 14 | PHOENIX | 24 |
| 19 | N.Y. Giants | 13 |
| 7 | New Orleans | 24 |
| 10 | San Francisco | 27 |
| 23 | GREEN BAY | 21 |
| 30 | SAN DIEGO | 24 |
| 17 | L.A. Raiders | 20 |
| 14 | Atlanta | 31 |
| 17 | NEW ORLEANS | 24 |
| 20 | KANSAS CITY | 27 |
| 10 | Detroit | 21 |
| 10 | SAN FRANCISCO | 33 |
| 6 | WASHINGTON | 27 |
| 14 | ATLANTA | 31 |
| 14 | Minnesota | 20 |
| 9 | Seattle | 23 |

| UseName | Pos. | Hgt. | Wgt. | Age | Int | Pts |
|---|---|---|---|---|---|---|
| Robert Jenkins | OT | 6'5" | 285 | 27 | | |
| Gerald Perry | OT | 6'6" | 305 | 26 | | |
| Jackie Slater | OT | 6'4" | 287 | 37 | | |
| Bern Brostek | OG-C | 6'3" | 300 | 24 | | |
| Duval Love | OG-OT | 6'3" | 287 | 28 | | |
| Joe Milinichik | OG | 6'5" | 290 | 28 | | |
| Jeff Pahukoa | OG-OT | 6'2" | 298 | 22 | | |
| Tom Newberry | C-OG | 6'2" | 285 | 28 | | |
| Doug Smith | C | 6'3" | 272 | 34 | | |
| Tom Gibson | DE | 6'8" | 275 | 27 | | |
| Kevin Greene | DE-LB | 6'3" | 247 | 29 | | 2 |
| Gerald Robinson | DE-DT | 6'3" | 262 | 28 | | |
| Ben Thomas | DE | 6'3" | 275 | 30 | | |
| Karl Wilson | DE | 6'4" | 275 | 27 | | |
| Mike Charles | DT | 6'4" | 305 | 28 | | |
| Bill Hawkins | DT | 6'6" | 269 | 25 | | |
| Mark Piel | DT | 6'4" | 270 | 25 | | |
| Chris Pike | DT | 6'8" | 300 | 27 | | |
| David Rocker | DT | 6'4" | 267 | 22 | | |
| Alvin Wright | DT | 6'2" | 285 | 30 | | |
| Robert Young | DT | 6'6" | 273 | 22 | | |
| Paul Butcher | LB | 6' | 230 | 27 | | |
| Terry Crews | LB | 6'2" | 244 | 23 | | |
| Brett Faryniarz | LB | 6'3" | 232 | 26 | | |
| Larry Kelm | LB | 6'4" | 240 | 26 | | |
| Mike McDonald | LB | 6'1" | 240 | 33 | | |
| Roman Phifer | LB | 6'6" | 305 | 23 | | |
| Glenell Sanders | LB | 6' | 224 | 24 | | |
| Frank Stams | LB | 6'2" | 237 | 26 | | |
| Fred Strickland | LB | 6'2" | 250 | 25 | | |
| Robert Bailey | DB | 5'9" | 176 | 22 | | |
| Jerry Gray | DB | 6' | 185 | 28 | 3 | 6 |
| Darryl Henley | DB | 5'9" | 172 | 24 | 3 | |
| Sammy Lilly | DB | 5'9" | 178 | 26 | | |
| Todd Lyght | DB | 6' | 186 | 22 | 1 | |
| Anthony Newman | DB | 6' | 199 | 25 | 1 | 6 |
| Michael Stewart | DB | 5'11" | 199 | 26 | 2 | |
| Pat Terrell | DB | 6' | 195 | 23 | 1 | |
| Rodney Thomas | DB | 5'10" | 190 | 25 | | |
| Jim Everett | QB | 6'5" | 212 | 28 | | |
| Mike Pagel | QB | 6'2" | 220 | 30 | | |
| Marcus Dupree | HB | 6'2" | 225 | 27 | | 6 |
| Cleveland Gary | HB | 6' | 226 | 25 | | 6 |
| David Lang | HB | 5'11" | 201 | 24 | | |
| Robert Delpino | FB | 6' | 205 | 25 | | 60 |
| Buford McGee | FB | 6' | 210 | 31 | | |
| Mosi Tatupu | FB | 6' | 227 | 36 | | |
| Ernie Thompson | FB | 5'11" | 230 | 21 | | 6 |
| Willie Anderson | WR | 6' | 175 | 26 | | 6 |
| Ron Brown | WR | 5'11" | 185 | 30 | | |
| Aaron Cox | WR | 5'9" | 178 | 26 | | |
| Henry Ellard | WR | 5'11" | 182 | 30 | | 18 |
| Jimmy Raye | WR | 5'9" | 165 | 22 | | |
| Vernon Turner | WR | 5'8" | 185 | 24 | | 6 |
| Pat Carter | TE | 6'4" | 255 | 25 | | 12 |
| Damone Johnson | TE | 6'4" | 250 | 29 | | 12 |
| Jim Price | TE | 6'4" | 247 | 28 | | 12 |
| Dale Hatcher | K | 6'2" | 220 | 28 | | |
| Barry Helton | K | 6'3" | 205 | 26 | | |
| Tony Zendejas | K | 5'8" | 165 | 31 | | 76 |

## NEW ORLEANS SAINTS

### RUSHING

| Last Name | No. | Yds | Avg | TD |
|---|---|---|---|---|
| McAfee | 109 | 494 | 4.5 | 2 |
| Fenerty | 139 | 477 | 3.4 | 3 |
| Heyward | 76 | 260 | 3.4 | 4 |
| Hilliard | 79 | 252 | 3.2 | 4 |
| Jordan | 47 | 150 | 3.2 | 2 |
| Hebert | 18 | 56 | 3.1 | 0 |
| Early | 3 | 13 | 4.3 | 0 |
| Morse | 3 | 7 | 2.3 | 0 |
| Barnhardt | 1 | 0 | 0.0 | 0 |
| Walsh | 8 | 0 | 0.0 | 0 |

### RECEIVING

| Last Name | No. | Yds | Avg | TD |
|---|---|---|---|---|
| E. Martin | 66 | 803 | 12.2 | 4 |
| Turner | 64 | 927 | 14.5 | 8 |
| Early | 32 | 541 | 16.9 | 2 |
| Fenerty | 26 | 235 | 9.0 | 2 |
| Tice | 22 | 230 | 10.5 | 0 |
| Hilliard | 21 | 127 | 6.0 | 1 |
| Carroll | 18 | 184 | 10.2 | 1 |
| Brenner | 16 | 179 | 11.2 | 0 |
| Jordan | 15 | 92 | 6.1 | 1 |
| Heyward | 4 | 34 | 8.5 | 1 |
| Newman | 3 | 33 | 11.0 | 0 |
| Scales | 3 | 23 | 7.7 | 0 |
| McAfee | 1 | 8 | 8.0 | 0 |
| Wainright | 1 | 3 | 3.0 | 0 |

### PUNT RETURNS

| Last Name | No. | Yds | Avg | TD |
|---|---|---|---|---|
| V. Buck | 31 | 260 | 8.4 | 0 |
| Fenerty | 12 | 55 | 4.6 | 0 |
| Morse | 1 | 2 | 2.0 | 0 |

### KICKOFF RETURNS

| Last Name | No. | Yds | Avg | TD |
|---|---|---|---|---|
| Atkins | 20 | 368 | 18.4 | 0 |
| Jennings | 12 | 213 | 17.8 | 0 |
| Early | 9 | 168 | 18.7 | 0 |
| Morse | 3 | 60 | 20.0 | 0 |
| Fenerty | 2 | 28 | 14.0 | 0 |
| Jordan | 2 | 18 | 9.0 | 0 |
| McAfee | 1 | 14 | 14.0 | 0 |
| Glenn | 1 | 10 | 10.0 | 0 |

### PASSING—PUNTING—KICKING

| PASSING | Att | Cmp | % | Yds | Yd/Att | TD | Int | — | % | RK |
|---|---|---|---|---|---|---|---|---|---|---|
| Walsh | 255 | 141 | 55.3 | 1638 | 6.42 | 11 | 6 | — | 2.4 | 9 |
| Hebert | 248 | 149 | 60.1 | 1676 | 6.76 | 9 | 8 | — | 3.2 | 10 |
| M. Buck | 2 | 1 | 50.0 | 61 | 30.50 | 0 | 1 | — | 50.0 | |
| Heyward | 1 | 1 | 100.0 | 44 | 44.00 | 0 | 0 | — | 0.0 | |

| PUNTING | No. | Avg. |
|---|---|---|
| Barnhardt | 87 | 43.0 |

| KICKING | XP | ATT | % | FG | ATT | % |
|---|---|---|---|---|---|---|
| Andersen | 38 | 38 | 100 | 25 | 32 | 78 |

## ATLANTA FALCONS

### RUSHING

| Last Name | No. | Yds | Avg | TD |
|---|---|---|---|---|
| Broussard | 99 | 449 | 4.5 | 4 |
| Rozier | 96 | 361 | 3.8 | 0 |
| Pegram | 101 | 349 | 3.5 | 1 |
| Miller | 32 | 229 | 7.2 | 0 |
| Chaffey | 29 | 127 | 4.4 | 1 |
| Jones | 35 | 126 | 3.6 | 0 |
| T. Johnson | 8 | 26 | 3.3 | 0 |
| Tolliver | 9 | 6 | 0.7 | 0 |
| Rison | 1 | -9 | -9.0 | 0 |

### RECEIVING

| Last Name | No. | Yds | Avg | TD |
|---|---|---|---|---|
| Rison | 81 | 976 | 12.0 | 12 |
| Haynes | 50 | 1122 | 22.4 | 11 |
| Pritchard | 50 | 624 | 12.5 | 2 |
| Thomas | 28 | 365 | 13.0 | 2 |
| Dixon | 12 | 146 | 12.2 | 1 |
| Broussard | 12 | 120 | 10.0 | 1 |
| Phillips | 6 | 73 | 12.2 | 0 |
| Jones | 6 | 58 | 9.7 | 0 |
| Collins | 3 | 37 | 12.3 | 0 |
| T. Johnson | 3 | 27 | 9.0 | 0 |
| Wilkins | 3 | 22 | 7.3 | 1 |
| Rozier | 2 | 15 | 7.5 | 0 |
| Ruether | 1 | 22 | 22.0 | 0 |
| Sanders | 1 | 17 | 17.0 | 0 |
| Bruce | 1 | 11 | 11.0 | 0 |
| Pegram | 1 | -1 | -1.0 | 0 |

### PUNT RETURNS

| Last Name | No. | Yds | Avg | TD |
|---|---|---|---|---|
| Sanders | 21 | 170 | 8.1 | 0 |
| Jordan | 14 | 116 | 8.3 | 0 |

### KICKOFF RETURNS

| Last Name | No. | Yds | Avg | TD |
|---|---|---|---|---|
| Sanders | 26 | 576 | 22.2 | 1 |
| Pegram | 16 | 260 | 16.3 | 0 |
| Jordan | 5 | 100 | 20.0 | 0 |
| Fishback | 3 | 29 | 9.7 | 0 |
| Pritchard | 1 | 18 | 18.0 | 0 |
| Chaffey | 1 | 14 | 14.0 | 0 |

### PASSING—PUNTING—KICKING

| PASSING | Att | Cmp | % | Yds | Yd/Att | TD | Int | — | % | RK |
|---|---|---|---|---|---|---|---|---|---|---|
| Miller | 413 | 220 | 53.3 | 3103 | 7.51 | 26 | 18 | — | 4.4 | 7 |
| Tolliver | 82 | 40 | 48.8 | 531 | 6.48 | 4 | 2 | — | 2.4 | |
| Favre | 5 | 0 | 0.0 | 0 | 0.00 | 0 | 2 | — | 40.0 | |

| PUNTING | No. | Avg. |
|---|---|---|
| Fulhage | 81 | 42.8 |

| KICKING | XP | ATT | % | FG | ATT | % |
|---|---|---|---|---|---|---|
| N. Johnson | 38 | 39 | 97 | 19 | 23 | 83 |

## SAN FRANCISCO 49ERS

### RUSHING

| Last Name | No. | Yds | Avg | TD |
|---|---|---|---|---|
| Henderson | 137 | 561 | 4.1 | 2 |
| Young | 66 | 415 | 6.3 | 4 |
| D. Carter | 85 | 379 | 4.5 | 2 |
| Sydney | 57 | 245 | 4.3 | 5 |
| Rathman | 63 | 183 | 2.9 | 6 |
| Bono | 17 | 46 | 2.7 | 0 |
| Tillman | 13 | 40 | 3.1 | 0 |
| Rice | 1 | 2 | 2.0 | 0 |
| Prokop | 1 | -10 | -10.0 | 0 |

### RECEIVING

| Last Name | No. | Yds | Avg | TD |
|---|---|---|---|---|
| Rice | 80 | 1206 | 15.1 | 14 |
| Taylor | 64 | 1011 | 15.8 | 9 |
| Rathman | 34 | 286 | 8.4 | 0 |
| Henderson | 30 | 303 | 10.1 | 0 |
| Jones | 27 | 417 | 15.4 | 0 |
| Sherrard | 24 | 296 | 12.3 | 2 |
| D. Carter | 23 | 253 | 11.0 | 1 |
| Williams | 22 | 235 | 10.7 | 1 |
| Sydney | 13 | 90 | 6.9 | 2 |
| Beach | 4 | 43 | 10.8 | 0 |
| Walls | 2 | 24 | 12.0 | 0 |
| Tillman | 2 | 3 | 1.5 | 0 |

### PUNT RETURNS

| Last Name | No. | Yds | Avg | TD |
|---|---|---|---|---|
| Taylor | 31 | 267 | 8.6 | 0 |
| Beach | 10 | 53 | 5.3 | 0 |
| K. Lewis | 1 | 0 | 0.0 | 0 |

### KICKOFF RETURNS

| Last Name | No. | Yds | Avg | TD |
|---|---|---|---|---|
| D. Carter | 37 | 839 | 22.7 | 1 |
| Tillman | 9 | 132 | 14.7 | 0 |
| Beach | 2 | 37 | 18.5 | 0 |
| Sydney | 1 | 13 | 13.0 | 0 |
| Whitmore | 1 | 7 | 7.0 | 0 |

### PASSING—PUNTING—KICKING

| PASSING | Att | Cmp | % | Yds | Yd/Att | TD | Int | — | % | RK |
|---|---|---|---|---|---|---|---|---|---|---|
| Young | 279 | 180 | 64.5 | 2517 | 9.02 | 17 | 8 | — | 2.9 | 1 |
| Bono | 237 | 141 | 59.5 | 1617 | 6.82 | 11 | 4 | — | 1.7 | 3 |
| Musgrave | 5 | 4 | 80.0 | 141 | 6.60 | 1 | 0 | — | 0.0 | |
| Sydney | 1 | 0 | 0.0 | 0 | 0.00 | 0 | 0 | — | 0.0 | |

| PUNTING | No. | Avg. |
|---|---|---|
| Mojsiejenko | 16 | 41.0 |
| Prokop | 40 | 38.5 |

| KICKING | XP | ATT | % | FG | ATT | % |
|---|---|---|---|---|---|---|
| Cofer | 49 | 50 | 98 | 14 | 28 | 50 |

## LOS ANGELES RAMS

### RUSHING

| Last Name | No. | Yds | Avg | TD |
|---|---|---|---|---|
| Delpino | 214 | 688 | 3.2 | 9 |
| Gary | 68 | 245 | 3.6 | 1 |
| Dupree | 49 | 179 | 3.7 | 1 |
| McGee | 19 | 65 | 3.4 | 0 |
| Everett | 27 | 44 | 1.6 | 0 |
| Turner | 7 | 44 | 6.3 | 0 |
| Brown | 2 | 11 | 5.5 | 0 |
| Thompson | 2 | 9 | 4.5 | 0 |

### RECEIVING

| Last Name | No. | Yds | Avg | TD |
|---|---|---|---|---|
| Ellard | 64 | 1052 | 16.4 | 3 |
| Delpino | 55 | 617 | 11.2 | 1 |
| Price | 35 | 410 | 11.7 | 2 |
| Anderson | 32 | 530 | 16.6 | 1 |
| Johnson | 32 | 253 | 7.9 | 2 |
| McGee | 20 | 160 | 8.0 | 0 |
| Cox | 15 | 216 | 14.4 | 0 |
| Gary | 13 | 110 | 8.5 | 0 |
| Carter | 8 | 69 | 8.6 | 2 |
| Dupree | 6 | 46 | 7.7 | 0 |
| Brown | 3 | 52 | 17.3 | 0 |
| Turner | 3 | 41 | 13.7 | 1 |
| Thompson | 2 | 35 | 17.5 | 1 |
| Raye | 1 | 19 | 19.0 | 0 |

### PUNT RETURNS

| Last Name | No. | Yds | Avg | TD |
|---|---|---|---|---|
| Turner | 23 | 201 | 8.7 | 0 |
| Henley | 13 | 110 | 8.5 | 0 |
| Gray | 1 | 9 | 9.0 | 0 |

### KICKOFF RETURNS

| Last Name | No. | Yds | Avg | TD |
|---|---|---|---|---|
| Turner | 24 | 457 | 19.0 | 0 |
| Brown | 12 | 256 | 21.3 | 0 |
| Lang | 12 | 194 | 16.2 | 0 |
| Delpino | 4 | 54 | 13.5 | 0 |
| McDonald | 3 | 32 | 10.7 | 0 |
| Raye | 2 | 57 | 28.5 | 0 |
| Carter | 1 | 18 | 18.0 | 0 |
| Sanders | 1 | 2 | 2.0 | 0 |

### PASSING—PUNTING—KICKING

| PASSING | Att | Cmp | % | Yds | Yd/Att | TD | Int | — | % | RK |
|---|---|---|---|---|---|---|---|---|---|---|
| Everett | 490 | 277 | 56.5 | 3438 | 7.02 | 11 | 20 | — | 4.1 | 14 |
| Pagel | 27 | 11 | 40.7 | 150 | 5.56 | 2 | 0 | — | 0.0 | |
| Helton | 1 | 1 | 100.0 | 22 | 22.00 | 0 | 0 | — | 0.0 | |

| PUNTING | No. | Avg. |
|---|---|---|
| Hatcher | 63 | 38.1 |
| Helton | 12 | 37.8 |

| KICKING | XP | ATT | % | FG | ATT | % |
|---|---|---|---|---|---|---|
| Zendejas | 25 | 26 | 96 | 17 | 17 | 100 |

# 1991 A.F.C. Coaching Carousel Continues All Season

The 1991 NFL season began in a strange way in April when Raghib "Rocket" Ismail, the Heisman Trophy winner, decided to play football in Canada. That was just a preview of things to come, as the entire rookie class produced not one impact player among the several hundred who made NFL rosters. The Rookies of the Year were New England running back Leonard Russell, who gained 959 yards but averaged only 3.6 yards per carry and scored just four touchdowns, and Denver linebacker Mike Croel, who had 10 sacks but played mostly in pass-rushing situations. Several AFC clubs started on the comeback trail, most notably New England under Dick MacPherson, the Jets with Bruce Coslet and Cleveland under Bill Belichick.

And the season ended with the league's biggest turnover among head coaches in 13 years. Nine teams changed head coaches. Indianapolis fired both Ron Meyer and interim coach Rick Venturi. Also let go were Dan Henning (San Diego), Lindy Infante (Green Bay), Richard Williamson (Tampa Bay) and Sam Wyche (Cincinnati). Resigning were Jerry Burns (Minnesota), John Robinson (Rams) and Chuck Knox (Seattle). And Pittsburgh's Chuck Noll decided he had had enough, too.

## EASTERN DIVISION

**Buffalo Bills** — The Bills went to their second straight Super Bowl before falling soundly to the Redskins 37-24 and becoming the third team to lose consecutive Super Bowls. Buffalo won 10 of its first 11 games behind a no-huddle offense that dominated the NFL. Quarterback Jim Kelly led the league with 33 touchdown passes, and running back Thurman Thomas was named the league's Most Valuable Player. He rushed for 1,407 yards, caught 61 passes for 631 yards and scored 12 touchdowns. Andre Reed led the receivers again with 81 catches and 10 TD's, and 36-year-old James Lofton chipped in with 57 receptions for 1,072 yards and eight scores. But the Bills had problems on defense. End Bruce Smith missed most of the season with a knee injury, and the team finished 27th in the NFL in yards allowed. It showed in the Super Bowl.

**New York Jets** — The Jets came a long way 1991, finishing with an 8-8 record and making the wild-card round of the playoffs. But they seemed to come up just a bit short all season, blowing at least three games they should've won(including one that was the Colts' only victory all season). Ken O'Brien had too many costly interceptions inside the opponents' 20-yard line, and running back Blair Thomas slumped in his second season, running tentatively after a costly fumble lost the Chicago game. Wide receiver Al Toon had 74 receptions but no touchdowns, and Rob Moore caught 70 passes. A bright light was fullback Brad Baxter, who scored 11 times in goal line situations.

**Miami Dolphins** — Twenty years ago, the Dolphins were famed for their "No-Name" defense. In 1991, the Dolphins had no defense. Miami ranked 25th overall and 27th against the run, allowing 21.8 points per game. Even though they salvaged an 8-8 record, they finished out of the playoffs for the fifth time in six seasons after losing their final two games (a victory in either of which would have clinched the playoffs). Quarterback Dan Marino starred again with 25 touchdown passes and 3,970 yards passing. And the Marks Brothers — Duper and Clayton — each caught 70 passes for over 1,000 yards and 17 touchdowns combined. Running back Sammie Smith was benched after fumbling twice on the goal line, and the Miami running game would have been sunk if Mark Higgs hadn't come out of nowhere to gain 905 yards rushing.

**New England Patriots** — Coach Dick MacPherson came over from Syracuse University and infused lots of spirit and motivation into a team that badly needed it. In turn, the Patriots gave MacPherson — and the NFL — a few surprises, finishing with a 6-10 record on the heels of a 1-15 season in 1990. Hugh Millen took over at quarterback after three games (all losses) and passed for 3,073 yards while leading the Patriots to a series of frantic finishes near midseason. Wide receiver Irving Fryar had his best season as a pro with 1,014 yards receiving, and tight end Marv Cook was the NFL's best with 82 receptions. Running back Leonard Russell was the NFL Offensive Rookie of the Year, as he rushed for 959 yards.

**Indianapolis Colts** — The Colts were the most inept team in the NFL in 1991. The offense scored only 143 points — the fewest ever for an NFL team in a 16-game season. A tidal wave of injuries sank the Colts from the start. The offensive line leaked like a sieve, leaving quarterback Jeff George running for his life. Running back Eric Dickerson continued to cause problems, until he was finally suspended for five games for "insubordination." On defense, Indianapolis finished last in three categories and in the bottom five in eight others. Coach Ron Meyer was fired after five games — all losses — but interim coach Rick Venturi didn't do much better, guiding the Colts to a 1-10 record. After the season, Venturi was replaced by Ted Marchibroda, who came back for his second tour of duty with the Colts.

## CENTRAL DIVISION

**Houston Oilers** — The Oilers won the Central Division title outright for the first time ever and became the only team to make the playoffs every year from 1987-91. But, for the fifth straight time they failed to get past the second round. The defense made great strides, allowing the second-fewest points in the conference, and the team put a league-high eight players in the Pro Bowl. Quarterback Warren Moon was the NFL's most prolific passer, setting league records for attempts (655) and completions (404) — but he matched a career-worst with 21 interceptions. Wide receiver Haywood Jeffires became only the fifth player in NFL history to reach 100 receptions in a season. But a 4-4 record the second half of the season and a 1-1 mark in the playoffs left fans wondering if the Oilers wouild ever get to the Super Bowl.

**Pittsburgh Steelers** — An era ended when Chuck Noll announced his retirement following the 1991 season. The only coach to win four Super Bowls called the '91 season the most disappointing of his career. The Steelers expected to make the playoffs but were out of contention by midseason, as they failed to beat winning teams for the third straight season. The biggest shock of 1991 was the fall of the defense, which was first in the league in '90. Offensively, the Steelers again failed to adapt to coordinator Joe Walton's complicated offense, and a quarterback duo began with Bubby Brister and Neil O'Donnell sharing the duties. Once again, tight end Eric Green was the team's best offensive weapon, until he was injured in Game Nine. Noll was replaced by Kansas City defensive coordinator Bill Cowher.

**Cleveland Browns** — The Browns showed signs of life under new coach Bill Belichick. They won four of their first eight games and started priming for a playoff run until injuries and a thin bench caused a 2-6 record after midseason. Quarterback Bernie Kosar had a fine comeback season, keeping the Browns in games with his gutsy performances behind a revamped offensive line that did little to help. Running back Leroy Hoard was the Browns' surprise player of the year by scoring 11 touchdowns, nine of them on receptions. He was joined in the backfield by Kevin Mack, who chipped in 10 scores and 726 yards rushing despite being hampered by injuries all season. The defense sliced its points allowed per game from 28.8 points in '90 to 18.6 in '91.

**Cincinnati Bengals** — Cincinnati lost its first eight games of the season as head coach Sam Wyche was losing his composure on the sideline. At the end of the season, Wyche lost his job and was replaced by 32-year-old Dave Shula, Don's son who became the youngest head coach in modern NFL history. Most of the Bengals had disappointing seasons, including quarterback Boomer Esiason, running backs James Brooks and Ickey Woods and wide receivers Eddie Brown and Tim McGee. The offense failed to score a touchdown in two games and scored only one in six others. And the defense finished last in total defense, pass defense and scoring defense. Second-year running back Harold Green had a promising season with 731 yards rushing.

## WESTERN DIVISION

**Denver Broncos** — After going 5-11 in 1990, the Broncos made the

**OFFENSE**

| | BUFF | CIN | CLEV | DEN | HOU | IND | K.C. | L.A. | MIA | N.E. | NYJ | PITT | S.D. | SEA |
|---|---|---|---|---|---|---|---|---|---|---|---|---|---|---|
| FIRST DOWNS: | | | | | | | | | | | | | | |
| Total | 359 | 286 | 265 | 284 | 353 | 236 | 322 | 248 | 312 | 259 | 331 | 254 | 285 | 253 |
| by Rushing | 128 | 96 | 82 | 117 | 99 | 55 | 127 | 97 | 91 | 93 | 133 | 82 | 114 | 80 |
| by Passing | 208 | 162 | 163 | 150 | 236 | 163 | 172 | 132 | 205 | 155 | 169 | 158 | 155 | 159 |
| by Penalty | 23 | 28 | 20 | 17 | 18 | 18 | 23 | 19 | 16 | 11 | 29 | 14 | 16 | 14 |
| RUSHING: | | | | | | | | | | | | | | |
| Number | 505 | 449 | 389 | 507 | 331 | 354 | 521 | 446 | 379 | 433 | 523 | 394 | 464 | 394 |
| Yards | 2381 | 1811 | 1360 | 2015 | 1366 | 1169 | 2217 | 1706 | 1352 | 1467 | 2160 | 1627 | 2248 | 1426 |
| Average Yards | 4.7 | 4.0 | 3.5 | 4.0 | 4.1 | 3.3 | 4.3 | 3.8 | 3.6 | 3.4 | 4.1 | 4.1 | 4.8 | 3.6 |
| Touchdowns | 16 | 11 | 12 | 16 | 16 | 3 | 14 | 8 | 8 | 9 | 17 | 8 | 16 | 11 |
| PASSING: | | | | | | | | | | | | | | |
| Attempts | 516 | 511 | 503 | 459 | 667 | 512 | 479 | 414 | 563 | 481 | 5023 | 476 | 511 | 488 |
| Completions | 332 | 290 | 312 | 246 | 411 | 305 | 284 | 220 | 327 | 284 | 295 | 259 | 272 | 290 |
| Completion Pct. | 64.3 | 56.8 | 62.0 | 53.6 | 61.6 | 59.6 | 59.3 | 53.1 | 58.1 | 59.0 | 58.6 | 54.4 | 53.2 | 59.4 |
| Passing Yards | 4140 | 3413 | 3547 | 3310 | 4804 | 3066 | 3281 | 2977 | 4077 | 3442 | 3429 | 3313 | 2983 | 3371 |
| Avg. Yds per Att. | 7.0 | 5.8 | 6.1 | 5.9 | 6.7 | 4.5 | 6.2 | 6.1 | 6.6 | 5.5 | 5.9 | 5.7 | 5.0 | 5.9 |
| Avg. Yds per Comp. | 12.5 | 11.8 | 11.4 | 13.5 | 11.7 | 10.1 | 11.6 | 13.5 | 12.5 | 12.1 | 11.6 | 12.8 | 11.0 | 11.6 |
| Times Tackled | 35 | 33 | 42 | 46 | 24 | 57 | 21 | 33 | 28 | 63 | 33 | 45 | 35 | 42 |
| Yds Lost Tackled | 269 | 255 | 243 | 313 | 183 | 487 | 177 | 258 | 188 | 436 | 273 | 359 | 236 | 263 |
| Net Yards | 3871 | 3158 | 3304 | 2997 | 4621 | 2579 | 3104 | 2719 | 3889 | 3006 | 3156 | 2954 | 2747 | 3108 |
| Touchdowns | 39 | 14 | 19 | 13 | 24 | 10 | 19 | 20 | 26 | 11 | 12 | 20 | 13 | 15 |
| Interceptions | 19 | 22 | 10 | 12 | 21 | 16 | 14 | 18 | 14 | 22 | 12 | 16 | 16 | 26 |
| Pct. Intercepted | 3.7 | 4.3 | 2.0 | 2.6 | 3.1 | 3.1 | 2.9 | 4.4 | 2.5 | 4.6 | 2.4 | 3.4 | 3.1 | 5.3 |
| PUNTS: | | | | | | | | | | | | | | |
| Number | 54 | 65 | 80 | 74 | 53 | 82 | 57 | 67 | 57 | 82 | 64 | 75 | 77 | 76 |
| Average | 38.6 | 43.5 | 42.5 | 41.2 | 41.7 | 42.6 | 40.4 | 44.2 | 44.8 | 39.0 | 39.4 | 39.9 | 39.8 | 40.6 |
| PUNT RETURNS | | | | | | | | | | | | | | |
| Number | 26 | 29 | 31 | 41 | 36 | 27 | 34 | 29 | 30 | 31 | 23 | 39 | 33 | 38 |
| Yards | 281 | 280 | 251 | 284 | 244 | 171 | 258 | 330 | 258 | 211 | 157 | 373 | 328 | 325 |
| Average Yards | 10.8 | 9.7 | 8.1 | 6.9 | 6.8 | 6.3 | 7.6 | 11.4 | 8.6 | 6.8 | 6.8 | 9.6 | 9.9 | 8.6 |
| Touchdowns | 0 | 1 | 0 | 0 | 0 | 0 | 0 | 1 | 0 | 0 | 0 | 1 | 0 | 1 |
| KICKOFF RET.: | | | | | | | | | | | | | | |
| Number | 52 | 69 | 55 | 37 | 46 | 55 | 48 | 52 | 50 | 56 | 58 | 67 | 55 | 60 |
| Yards | 970 | 1225 | 888 | 687 | 835 | 1061 | 978 | 928 | 890 | 1108 | 1003 | 1314 | 1171 | 1280 |
| Average Yards | 18.7 | 17.8 | 16.1 | 18.6 | 18.2 | 19.3 | 20.4 | 17.8 | 17.8 | 19.8 | 17.3 | 19.6 | 21.3 | 21.3 |
| Touchdowns | 1 | 0 | 0 | 0 | 0 | 1 | 0 | 0 | 0 | 1 | 0 | 0 | 1 | 0 |
| INTERCEPT RET.: | | | | | | | | | | | | | | |
| Number | 23 | 17 | 15 | 23 | 20 | 15 | 15 | 18 | 12 | 12 | 18 | 19 | 19 | 18 |
| Yards | 276 | 169 | 260 | 379 | 255 | 202 | 216 | 155 | 135 | 93 | 283 | 329 | 227 | 302 |
| Average Yards | 12.0 | 9.9 | 17.3 | 16.5 | 12.8 | 10.1 | 14.4 | 8.6 | 11.3 | 7.8 | 15.7 | 17.3 | 11.9 | 16.8 |
| Touchdowns | 1 | 1 | 3 | 2 | 2 | 0 | 0 | 0 | 0 | 0 | 2 | 2 | 1 | 2 |
| PENALTIES: | | | | | | | | | | | | | | |
| Number | 113 | 107 | 108 | 94 | 99 | 85 | 94 | 117 | 62 | 97 | 103 | 116 | 96 | 85 |
| Yards | 865 | 845 | 872 | 715 | 784 | 689 | 724 | 1013 | 516 | 667 | 814 | 933 | 799 | 682 |
| FUMBLES: | | | | | | | | | | | | | | |
| Number | 25 | 31 | 18 | 31 | 33 | 31 | 22 | 20 | 23 | 34 | 28 | 37 | 24 | 26 |
| Number Lost | 16 | 20 | 8 | 13 | 19 | 15 | 8 | 13 | 14 | 20 | 13 | 14 | 12 | 17 |
| POINTS: | | | | | | | | | | | | | | |
| Total | 458 | 263 | 293 | 304 | 386 | 143 | 322 | 298 | 343 | 211 | 314 | 292 | 274 | 276 |
| PAT Attempts | 58 | 27 | 34 | 32 | 46 | 14 | 35 | 30 | 35 | 21 | 32 | 31 | 31 | 29 |
| PAT Made | 56 | 27 | 33 | 31 | 41 | 14 | 35 | 29 | 34 | 19 | 32 | 31 | 31 | 27 |
| FG Attempts | 29 | 32 | 22 | 36 | 31 | 26 | 30 | 34 | 39 | 29 | 43 | 33 | 29 | 31 |
| FG Made | 18 | 24 | 16 | 27 | 23 | 15 | 25 | 29 | 33 | 20 | 30 | 23 | 19 | 25 |
| Percent FG Made | 62.1 | 75.0 | 72.7 | 75.0 | 74.2 | 57.7 | 83.3 | 85.3 | 84.6 | 69.0 | 69.8 | 69.7 | 65.6 | 80.6 |
| Safeties | 0 | 1 | 1 | 0 | 0 | 0 | 1 | 1 | 0 | 0 | 0 | 0 | 0 | 0 |

**DEFENSE**

| | BUFF | CIN | CLEV | DEN | HOU | IND | K.C. | L.A. | MIA | N.E. | NYJ | PITT | S.D. | SEA |
|---|---|---|---|---|---|---|---|---|---|---|---|---|---|---|
| FIRST DOWNS: | | | | | | | | | | | | | | |
| Total | 335 | 308 | 298 | 242 | 280 | 305 | 275 | 305 | 327 | 312 | 298 | 320 | 292 | 262 |
| by Rushing | 138 | 100 | 100 | 81 | 94 | 140 | 88 | 108 | 133 | 94 | 94 | 98 | 94 | 91 |
| by Passing | 166 | 191 | 179 | 147 | 163 | 152 | 168 | 176 | 177 | 199 | 185 | 194 | 181 | 159 |
| by Penalty | 31 | 17 | 19 | 14 | 23 | 13 | 19 | 21 | 17 | 19 | 19 | 28 | 17 | 12 |
| RUSHING: | | | | | | | | | | | | | | |
| Number | 519 | 454 | 447 | 411 | 407 | 544 | 417 | 447 | 499 | 460 | 379 | 466 | 430 | 435 |
| Yards | 2044 | 1662 | 1875 | 1794 | 1540 | 2327 | 1770 | 1889 | 2301 | 1579 | 1442 | 1582 | 1666 | 1684 |
| Average Yards | 3.9 | 3.7 | 4.2 | 4.4 | 3.8 | 4.3 | 4.2 | 4.2 | 4.6 | 3.4 | 3.8 | 3.4 | 3.9 | 3.9 |
| Touchdowns | 20 | 20 | 12 | 8 | 8 | 23 | 8 | 13 | 17 | 5 | 8 | 14 | 15 | 4 |
| PASSING: | | | | | | | | | | | | | | |
| Attempts | 536 | 505 | 522 | 476 | 532 | 388 | 471 | 513 | 485 | 565 | 540 | 535 | 503 | 517 |
| Completions | 299 | 303 | 312 | 246 | 310 | 240 | 279 | 295 | 300 | 335 | 331 | 334 | 300 | 296 |
| Completion Pct. | 55.8 | 60.0 | 59.8 | 51.7 | 58.3 | 61.9 | 59.2 | 57.5 | 61.9 | 59.3 | 61.3 | 62.4 | 59.6 | 57.3 |
| Passing Yards | 3660 | 4119 | 3445 | 3101 | 3522 | 3002 | 3532 | 3559 | 3353 | 4035 | 3765 | 3843 | 3628 | 3288 |
| Avg. Yds per Att. | 6.0 | 7.6 | 5.8 | 5.2 | 5.6 | 6.7 | 6.3 | 5.9 | 6.0 | 6.5 | 6.2 | 6.3 | 6.5 | 5.5 |
| Avg. Yds per Comp. | 12.2 | 13.6 | 11.0 | 12.6 | 11.4 | 12.5 | 12.7 | 12.1 | 11.2 | 12.0 | 11.4 | 11.5 | 12.1 | 11.1 |
| Times Tackled | 31 | 21 | 35 | 52 | 45 | 29 | 39 | 42 | 35 | 25 | 35 | 38 | 28 | 36 |
| Yds Lost Tackled | 246 | 129 | 236 | 346 | 314 | 202 | 304 | 283 | 248 | 183 | 226 | 257 | 183 | 269 |
| Net Yards | 3414 | 3990 | 3209 | 2755 | 3208 | 2800 | 3228 | 3276 | 3105 | 3852 | 3539 | 3586 | 3445 | 3019 |
| Touchdowns | 12 | 26 | 20 | 12 | 17 | 22 | 17 | 18 | 18 | 25 | 21 | 21 | 22 | 18 |
| Interceptions | 23 | 17 | 15 | 23 | 20 | 15 | 15 | 18 | 12 | 12 | 18 | 19 | 19 | 18 |
| Pct. Intercepted | 4.3 | 3.4 | 2.9 | 4.8 | 3.8 | 3.9 | 3.2 | 3.5 | 2.5 | 2.1 | 3.3 | 3.6 | 3.8 | 3.5 |
| PUNTS: | | | | | | | | | | | | | | |
| Number | 70 | 57 | 61 | 79 | 74 | 59 | 60 | 61 | 65 | 69 | 56 | 65 | 76 | 79 |
| Average | 39.1 | 42.0 | 41.3 | 44.5 | 42.1 | 41.4 | 42.5 | 38.7 | 39.8 | 42.2 | 40.6 | 41.6 | 40.3 | 39.1 |
| PUNT RETURNS | | | | | | | | | | | | | | |
| Number | 15 | 38 | 40 | 28 | 29 | 47 | 27 | 41 | 30 | 37 | 29 | 29 | 32 | 40 |
| Yards | 53 | 456 | 3988 | 170 | 192 | 516 | 190 | 341 | 332 | 303 | 164 | 210 | 267 | 289 |
| Average Yards | 3.5 | 12.0 | 9.7 | 6.1 | 6.6 | 11.0 | 7.0 | 8.3 | 11.1 | 8.2 | 5.7 | 7.2 | 8.3 | 7.2 |
| Touchdowns | 0 | 2 | 0 | 0 | 0 | 1 | 0 | 0 | 0 | 1 | 0 | 0 | 0 | 0 |
| KICKOFF RET.: | | | | | | | | | | | | | | |
| Number | 62 | 38 | 50 | 62 | 63 | 33 | 57 | 58 | 66 | 51 | 60 | 43 | 52 | 51 |
| Yards | 1266 | 741 | 1022 | 1096 | 1071 | 573 | 1171 | 1059 | 1270 | 850 | 921 | 825 | 1034 | 858 |
| Average Yards | 20.4 | 19.5 | 20.4 | 17.7 | 17.0 | 17.4 | 20.5 | 18.3 | 19.2 | 16.7 | 15.4 | 19.2 | 19.9 | 16.8 |
| Touchdowns | 0 | 0 | 0 | 0 | 0 | 0 | 0 | 1 | 0 | 0 | 1 | 0 | 0 | 0 |
| INTERCEPT RET.: | | | | | | | | | | | | | | |
| Number | 19 | 22 | 10 | 12 | 21 | 16 | 14 | 18 | 14 | 22 | 12 | 16 | 16 | 26 |
| Yards | 320 | 331 | 95 | 101 | 296 | 184 | 251 | 374 | 217 | 154 | 105 | 182 | 183 | 334 |
| Average Yards | 16.8 | 15.0 | 9.5 | 8.4 | 14.1 | 11.5 | 17.9 | 20.8 | 15.5 | 7.0 | 8.8 | 11.4 | 11.4 | 12.8 |
| Touchdowns | 2 | 3 | 1 | 0 | 0 | 1 | 2 | 2 | 2 | 0 | 0 | 2 | 1 | 2 |
| PENALTIES: | | | | | | | | | | | | | | |
| Number | 110 | 94 | 103 | 105 | 109 | 88 | 110 | 111 | 91 | 83 | 93 | 84 | 87 | 108 |
| Yards | 938 | 808 | 770 | 848 | 797 | 645 | 827 | 905 | 684 | 608 | 774 | 685 | 718 | 845 |
| FUMBLES: | | | | | | | | | | | | | | |
| Number | 26 | 23 | 33 | 26 | 27 | 21 | 27 | 24 | 19 | 32 | 38 | 27 | 22 | 34 |
| Number Lost | 14 | 14 | 18 | 10 | 18 | 13 | 18 | 13 | 9 | 19 | 19 | 11 | 9 | 21 |
| POINTS: | | | | | | | | | | | | | | |
| Total | 318 | 435 | 298 | 235 | 251 | 381 | 252 | 297 | 349 | 305 | 293 | 344 | 342 | 261 |
| PAT Attempts | 34 | 52 | 33 | 22 | 26 | 46 | 27 | 36 | 40 | 31 | 30 | 38 | 38 | 25 |
| PAT Made | 33 | 49 | 32 | 22 | 26 | 46 | 25 | 33 | 40 | 30 | 29 | 38 | 37 | 25 |
| FG Attempts | 35 | 31 | 30 | 33 | 29 | 23 | 28 | 28 | 33 | 42 | 38 | 41 | 29 | 32 |
| FG Made | 27 | 22 | 22 | 27 | 23 | 17 | 21 | 16 | 23 | 29 | 26 | 26 | 23 | 28 |
| Percent FG Made | 77.1 | 71.0 | 73.3 | 81.8 | 79.3 | 73.9 | 75.0 | 57.1 | 69.7 | 69.0 | 68.4 | 63.4 | 79.3 | 87.5 |
| Safeties | 0 | 1 | 1 | 0 | 0 | 1 | 1 | 0 | 0 | 1 | 0 | 0 | 1 | 1 |

most dramatic improvement in team history, finishing 12-4 and winning the AFC West title. The difference was a 9-3 record in games decided by a touchdown or less in 1991 as compared to a 2-7 mark the year before. The Denver defense led the AFC in virtually every category, including touchdowns allowed, points allowed, sacks, third-down conversions and passing yards allowed. With Bobby Humphrey holding out and being banished to the bench upon his return, Gaston Green went from being a bust with the Rams to a 1,000-yard rusher with the Broncos. But the team's leader once again was quarterback John Elway. Despite mediocre statistics of 13 touchdowns and 12 interceptions, he had his best season since 1987, capped off by "The Drive II" in the playoffs.

**Kansas City Chiefs** — In an up-and-down season, the Chiefs could go only as far as quarterback Steve DeBerg could take them, which was a lot farther than they thought when he was benched in Game 15. However, replacement quarterback Mark Vlasic injured himself within two quarters and DeBerg came back on to rally the Chiefs to the second round of the playoffs. The offense showed an inability to make big plays, so the Chiefs relied on their ground game. The combination of running backs Christian Okoye and Barry Word had 1,715 yards rushing and 13 touchdowns, but it was rookie Harvey Williams who drew the praise in limited playing time. The defense was strong overall, with end Neil Smith and linebacker Derrick Thomas starring in front of a secondary that hid its age well.

**Los Angeles Raiders** — Teams only one game away from the playoffs don't usually switch from a veteran quarterback to an untested rookie, but that's what the Raiders did in 1991, benching Jay Schroeder in favor of Todd Marinovich for Game 16 and the wild-card playoff. Although Marinovich won his first game and lost the playoff, he proved to be the team's future. Injuries hampered the running backs who rushed for 107 yards a game without a dominant performer. Eight players were chosen for the Pro Bowl, including Plan B pickup Ronnie Lott, who solidified the defense and led the NFL with eight interceptions. But the team was sparked by its kickers — Jeff Gossett led the NFL in punting, and Jeff Jaeger won two games with kicks and set a team record by hitting 29 of 34 field goals, usually when the offense failed near the end zone.

**Seattle Seahawks** — Seattle suffered a season of hard knocks, and then coach Chuck Knox bolted for the Rams when it ended. He was replaced by Tom Flores. In stumbling to a 7-9 record, the Seahawks saw three quarterbacks start games — none of them effectively — and four different halfbacks who could combine for only 2.9 yards per carry and 31.4 yards per game. Fullback John L. Williams led the offense with 1,240 yards rushing and receiving, and Brian Blades led the receivers with 70 catches for 1,003 yards but only two scores. But the offense averaged only 17.3 points and scored more than 24 points just twice, and an AFC-high 43 turnovers was impossible to overcome. The defense set team records for fewest points allowed (261) and was the only one in the AFC not to allow a 100-yard rusher or a 300-yard passer.

**San Diego Chargers** — The Chargers suffered through their eighth non-winning season in nine years and ninth straight out of the playoffs — the longest drought in the AFC. Coach Dan Henning was fired when it was over and replaced by Bobby Ross. The offense packed a powerful one-two punch from running backs Marion Butts (834 yards and six touchdowns) and Rod Bernstine (766 yards and eight TD's). Another back, Ronnie Harmon, led the team with 59 receptions. But quarterback John Friesz, who had one start before the '91 season, was the lowest-rated passer in the conference. His lack of experience showed in close games, and San Diego had a 2-8 record in games decided by a touchdown or less.

## BUFFALO BILLS 13-3 Marv Levy

| Scores of Each Game | | |
|---|---|---|
| 35 | MIAMI | 31 |
| 52 | PITTSBURGH | 34 |
| 23 | N.Y. Jets | 20 |
| 17 | at Tampa Bay | 10 |
| 35 | CHICAGO | 20 |
| 6 | Kansas City | 33 |
| 42 | INDIANAPOLIS | 6 |
| 35 | CINCINNATI | 16 |
| 22 | NEW ENGLAND | 17 |
| 34 | Green Bay | 24 |
| 41 | Miami | 27 |
| 13 | New England | 16 |
| 24 | N.Y. JETS | 13 |
| 30 | L.A. Raiders | * 27 |
| 35 | Indianapolis | 7 |
| 14 | DETROIT | * 17 |

| UseName | Pos. | Hgt. | Wgt. | Age | Int | Pts |
|---|---|---|---|---|---|---|
| Howard Ballard | OT | 6'6" | 325 | 27 | | |
| Joe Staysniak | OT | 6'5" | 296 | 24 | | |
| Will Wolford | OT | 6'5" | 295 | 27 | | |
| John Davis | OG | 6'4" | 310 | 26 | | |
| Mitch Frerotte | OG | 6'3" | 285 | 26 | | |
| Glenn Parker | OG-OT | 6'5" | 301 | 25 | | |
| Jim Ritcher | OG | 6'3" | 273 | 33 | | |
| Kent Hull | C | 6'4" | 275 | 30 | | |
| Adam Lingner | C | 6'4" | 263 | 30 | | |
| Phil Hansen | DE | 6'5" | 258 | 23 | | |
| Mark Pike | DE | 6'4" | 272 | 27 | | |
| Reggie Rogers | DE | 6'6" | 280 | 27 | | |
| Leon Seals | DE | 6'4" | 270 | 27 | | |
| Bruce Smith | DE | 6'4" | 275 | 28 | | |
| Gary Baldinger | NT | 6'3" | 270 | 27 | | |
| Odell Haggins | NT | 6'2" | 278 | 24 | | |
| Mike Lodish | NT-DE | 6'3" | 265 | 24 | | |
| Jeff Wright | NT | 6'2" | 270 | 28 | | |

| UseName | Pos. | Hgt. | Wgt. | Age | Int | Pts |
|---|---|---|---|---|---|---|
| Carlton Bailey | LB | 6'2" | 240 | 26 | | |
| David Bavaro | LB | 6' | 235 | 24 | | |
| Cornelius Bennett | LB | 6'2" | 236 | 26 | | 6 |
| Ray Bentley | LB | 6'2" | 235 | 30 | 1 | |
| Shane Conlan | LB | 6'3" | 235 | 27 | | |
| Hal Garner | LB | 6'4" | 235 | 29 | | |
| Marvcus Patton | LB | 6'2" | 226 | 24 | | |
| Darryl Talley | LB | 6'4" | 235 | 31 | 5 | |
| Dwight Drane | DB | 6'2" | 205 | 29 | | |
| Chris Hale | DB | 5'7" | 165 | 25 | 1 | |
| Clifford Hicks | DB | 5'10" | 188 | 27 | 1 | |
| Kirby Jackson | DB | 5'10" | 180 | 26 | 4 | |
| Henry Jones | DB | 5'11" | 197 | 23 | | |
| Mark Kelso | DB | 5'11" | 185 | 28 | 2 | |
| Nate Odomes | DB | 5'10" | 188 | 26 | 5 | 6 |
| Leonard Smith | DB | 5'11" | 202 | 30 | 3 | |
| Brian Taylor | DB | 5'10" | 195 | 24 | | |
| James Williams | DB | 5'10" | 172 | 24 | 1 | |

| UseName | Pos. | Hgt. | Wgt. | Age | Int | Pts |
|---|---|---|---|---|---|---|
| Gale Gilbert | QB | 6'3" | 210 | 29 | | |
| Jim Kelly | QB | 6'3" | 218 | 31 | | 6 |
| Frank Reich | QB | 6'4" | 210 | 29 | | |
| Kenneth Davis | HB | 5'10" | 209 | 29 | | 30 |
| Eddie Fuller | HB | 5'9" | 201 | 23 | | |
| Thurman Thomas | HB | 5'10" | 198 | 25 | | 72 |
| Carwell Gardner | FB | 6'2" | 232 | 24 | | 24 |
| Mike Alexander | WR | 6'3" | 185 | 26 | | |
| Don Beebe | WR | 5'11" | 183 | 26 | | 36 |
| Al Edwards | WR | 5'8" | 171 | 24 | | 12 |
| James Lofton | WR | 6'3" | 190 | 35 | | 48 |
| Andre Reed | WR | 6' | 190 | 27 | | 60 |
| Steve Tasker | WR | 5'9" | 183 | 29 | | 6 |
| Keith McKeller | TE | 6'6" | 245 | 27 | | 18 |
| Pete Metzelaars | TE | 6'7" | 250 | 31 | | 12 |
| Butch Rolle | TE | 6'3" | 245 | 27 | | 12 |
| Brad Daluiso | K | 6'2" | 208 | 23 | | 8 |
| Chris Mohr | K | 6'5" | 215 | 25 | | |
| Scott Norwood | K | 6' | 207 | 31 | | 110 |

Jamie Mueller— Nerve Injury

## NEW YORK JETS 8-8 Bruce Coslet

| Scores of Each Game | | |
|---|---|---|
| 16 | TAMPA BAY | 13 |
| 13 | Seattle | 20 |
| 20 | BUFFALO | 23 |
| 13 | Chicago | * 19 |
| 41 | MIAMI | 23 |
| 17 | Cleveland | 14 |
| 20 | HOUSTON | 23 |
| 17 | Indianapolis | 6 |
| 19 | GREEN BAY | * 16 |
| 27 | INDIANAPOLIS | 28 |
| 28 | New England | 21 |
| 24 | SAN DIEGO | 3 |
| 13 | Buffalo | 24 |
| 20 | Detroit | 34 |
| 3 | NEW ENGLAND | 6 |
| 23 | Miami | * 20 |

| UseName | Pos. | Hgt. | Wgt. | Age | Int | Pts |
|---|---|---|---|---|---|---|
| Jeff Criswell | OT | 6'7" | 291 | 27 | | |
| Irv Eatman | OT | 6'7" | 298 | 30 | | |
| Brett Miller | OT | 6'7" | 286 | 32 | | |
| Dave Cadigan | OG | 6'4" | 285 | 26 | | |
| Mike Haight | OG-OT | 6'4" | 291 | 28 | | |
| Trevor Matich | OG-C-OT | 6'4" | 297 | 29 | | 6 |
| Dwayne White | OG | 6'2" | 305 | 24 | | |
| Roger Duffy | C | 6'3" | 285 | 24 | | |
| Jim Sweeney | C-OG | 6'4" | 286 | 29 | | |
| Darrell Davis | DE | 6'2" | 258 | 25 | | |
| Mark Gunn | DE | 6'5" | 292 | 23 | | |
| Jeff Lageman | DE | 6'5" | 266 | 24 | | |
| Marvin Washington | DE | 6'6" | 272 | 25 | | |
| Dennis Byrd | DT | 6'5" | 266 | 24 | | |
| Paul Frase | DT-DE | 6'5" | 270 | 26 | | |
| Scott Mersereau | DT | 6'3" | 275 | 26 | 2 | |
| Bill Pickel | DT | 6'5" | 265 | 31 | | |

| UseName | Pos. | Hgt. | Wgt. | Age | Int | Pts |
|---|---|---|---|---|---|---|
| Kyle Clifton | LB | 6'4" | 236 | 29 | 1 | |
| John Galvin | LB | 6'3" | 230 | 26 | | |
| Bobby Houston | LB | 6'2" | 235 | 23 | | |
| Troy Johnson | LB | 6'2" | 236 | 26 | | |
| Joe Kelly | LB | 6'2" | 235 | 26 | 2 | |
| Mo Lewis | LB | 6'3" | 240 | 21 | | |
| Michael Brim | DB | 6' | 192 | 25 | 4 | |
| James Hasty | DB | 6' | 201 | 26 | 3 | |
| R.J. Kors | DB | 6' | 195 | 25 | 1 | |
| Erik McMillan | DB | 6'2" | 200 | 26 | 3 | 12 |
| Don Odegard | DB | 6' | 180 | 24 | | |
| Tony Stargell | DB | 5'11" | 180 | 25 | | |
| Brian Washington | DB | 6'1" | 212 | 25 | 1 | |
| Lonnie Young | DB | 6'1" | 192 | 28 | 1 | |

Joe Mott — Knee Injury
Dennis Price — Knee Injury

| UseName | Pos. | Hgt. | Wgt. | Age | Int | Pts |
|---|---|---|---|---|---|---|
| Browning Nagle | QB | 6'3" | 225 | 23 | | |
| Ken O'Brien | QB | 6'4" | 212 | 30 | | |
| Troy Taylor | QB | 6'4" | 200 | 23 | | |
| A.B. Brown | HB | 5'9" | 215 | 25 | | 6 |
| Johnny Hector | HB | 5'11" | 214 | 30 | | |
| Freeman McNeil | HB | 5'11" | 208 | 32 | | 12 |
| Blair Thomas | HB | 5'10" | 195 | 23 | | 24 |
| Brad Baxter | FB | 6'1" | 235 | 24 | | 66 |
| Chris Burkett | WR | 6'4" | 200 | 29 | | 30 |
| Dale Dawkins | WR | 6'1" | 190 | 24 | | |
| Terance Mathis | WR | 5'10" | 170 | 24 | | 6 |
| Rob Moore | WR | 6'3" | 205 | 22 | | 30 |
| Al Toon | WR | 6'4" | 205 | 28 | | |
| Mark Boyer | TE | 6'4" | 242 | 28 | | |
| Chris Dressel | TE | 6'4" | 239 | 30 | | |
| Pat Kelly | TE | 6'6" | 252 | 25 | | |
| Ken Whisenhunt | TE | 6'3" | 240 | 29 | | |
| Louis Aguiar | K | 6'2" | 200 | 25 | | |
| Pat Leahy | K | 6' | 200 | 40 | | 108 |

Patrick Egu — Knee Injury

## MIAMI DOLPHINS 8-8 Don Shula

| Scores of Each Game | | |
|---|---|---|
| 31 | Buffalo | 35 |
| 17 | INDIANAPOLIS | 6 |
| 13 | Detroit | 17 |
| 16 | GREEN BAY | 13 |
| 23 | N.Y. Jets | 41 |
| 20 | New England | 10 |
| 7 | Kansas City | 42 |
| 13 | HOUSTON | 17 |
| 10 | Indianapolis | 6 |
| 30 | NEW ENGLAND | 20 |
| 27 | BUFFALO | 41 |
| 16 | Chicago | * 13 |
| 33 | TAMPA BAY | 14 |
| 37 | CINCINNATI | 13 |
| 30 | San Diego | 38 |
| 20 | N.Y. JETS | * 23 |

| UseName | Pos. | Hgt. | Wgt. | Age | Int | Pts |
|---|---|---|---|---|---|---|
| Jeff Dellenbach | OT-C | 6'6" | 285 | 28 | | |
| Mark Dennis | OT | 6'6" | 295 | 26 | | |
| Richmond Webb | OT | 6'6" | 298 | 24 | | |
| Harry Galbreath | OG | 6'1" | 275 | 26 | | |
| Keith Sims | OG | 6'2" | 305 | 24 | | |
| Gene Williams | OG | 6'2" | 308 | 22 | | |
| Dave Zawatson | OG-OT | 6'5" | 287 | 25 | | |
| Jeff Uhlenhake | C | 6'3" | 284 | 25 | | |
| Bert Weidner | C | 6'3" | 284 | 24 | | |
| Jeff Cross | DE | 6'4" | 272 | 25 | | |
| Donnie Gardner | DE | 6'3" | 260 | 23 | | |
| Alfred Oglesby | DE-NT | 6'3" | 278 | 24 | | |
| T.J. Turner | DE-NT | 6'4" | 280 | 28 | | |
| Chuck Klingbeil | NT | 6'1" | 260 | 25 | | 6 |
| Shawn Lee | NT | 6'2" | 285 | 24 | 1 | |

Terry Price — Elbow Injury

| UseName | Pos. | Hgt. | Wgt. | Age | Int | Pts |
|---|---|---|---|---|---|---|
| Ned Bolcar | LB | 6'1" | 235 | 24 | | |
| Louis Cooper | LB | 6'2" | 238 | 28 | | |
| Bryan Cox | LB | 6'3" | 235 | 23 | | |
| Hugh Green | LB | 6'2" | 230 | 32 | | |
| David Griggs | LB-TE | 6'3" | 248 | 24 | | |
| E.J. Junior | LB | 6'3" | 242 | 31 | | |
| Cliff Odom | LB | 6'2" | 243 | 33 | 1 | |
| John Offerdahl | LB | 6'3" | 237 | 27 | | |
| Mike Reichenbach | LB | 6'2" | 240 | 29 | 1 | |
| J.B. Brown | DB | 6' | 192 | 25 | 1 | |
| Kerry Glenn | DB | 5'9" | 178 | 29 | | |
| Chris Green | DB | 5'11" | 188 | 23 | | |
| Bobby Harden | DB | 6' | 192 | 24 | 2 | |
| Mike Iaquaniello | DB | 6'3" | 208 | 23 | | |
| Vestee Jackson | DB | 6' | 186 | 28 | | |
| Paul Lankford | DB | 6'1" | 191 | 33 | | |
| Michael McGruder | DB | 5'11" | 190 | 27 | | |
| Louis Oliver | DB | 6'2" | 226 | 25 | 5 | |
| Jarvis Williams | DB | 5'11" | 196 | 26 | 1 | |

John Grimsley — Knee Injury
Bruce McNorton — Wrist Injury
Stevon Moore — Knee Injury

| UseName | Pos. | Hgt. | Wgt. | Age | Int | Pts |
|---|---|---|---|---|---|---|
| Dan Marino | QB | 6'4" | 224 | 29 | | 6 |
| Scott Mitchell | QB | 6'6" | 236 | 23 | | |
| Scott Secules | QB | 6'3" | 219 | 26 | | 6 |
| Aaron Craver | HB | 5'11" | 215 | 21 | | 6 |
| Mark Higgs | HB | 5'7" | 195 | 25 | | 24 |
| Sammie Smith | HB | 6'2" | 226 | 24 | | 6 |
| Marc Logan | FB | 5'11" | 222 | 26 | | |
| Tony Paige | FB | 5'10" | 235 | 28 | | 6 |
| Fred Banks | WR | 5'10" | 180 | 29 | | 6 |
| Mark Clayton | WR | 5'9" | 185 | 30 | | 72 |
| Mark Duper | WR | 5'9" | 192 | 32 | | 30 |
| Jim Jensen | WR-FB | 6'4" | 224 | 32 | | 12 |
| Tony Martin | WR | 6' | 180 | 25 | | 12 |
| Scott Miller | WR | 5'10" | 179 | 22 | | |
| James Pruitt | WR | 6'2" | 201 | 27 | | |
| Mike Williams | WR | 5'10" | 177 | 24 | | |
| Greg Baty | TE | 6'5" | 240 | 27 | | 6 |
| Ferrell Edmunds | TE | 6'6" | 254 | 26 | | 12 |
| Charles Henry | TE | 6'4" | 230 | 27 | | |
| Reggie Roby | K | 6'2" | 246 | 30 | | |
| Pete Stoyonovich | K | 5'10" | 185 | 24 | | 121 |

Garrett Limbrick — Shoulder Injury

## NEW ENGLAND PATRIOTS 6-10 Dick MacPherson

| Scores of Each Game | | |
|---|---|---|
| 16 | Indianapolis | 7 |
| 0 | CLEVELAND | 20 |
| 6 | Pittsburgh | 20 |
| 24 | HOUSTON | 20 |
| 10 | Phoenix | 24 |
| 10 | MIAMI | 20 |
| 26 | MINNESOTA | * 23 |
| 6 | DENVER | 9 |
| 17 | Buffalo | 22 |
| 20 | Miami | 30 |
| 21 | N.Y. JETS | 28 |
| 16 | BUFFALO | 13 |
| 3 | Denver | 20 |
| 23 | INDIANAPOLIS | * 17 |
| 6 | N.Y. Jets | 3 |
| 7 | Cincinnati | 29 |

| UseName | Pos. | Hgt. | Wgt. | Age | Int | Pts |
|---|---|---|---|---|---|---|
| Bruce Armstrong | OT | 6'4" | 284 | 25 | | |
| Fred Childress | OT | 6'4" | 333 | 23 | | 6 |
| Pat Harlow | OT | 6'6" | 290 | 22 | | |
| Jon Melander | OT | 6'7" | 280 | 24 | | |
| Danny Villa | OG-C | 6'5" | 305 | 26 | | |
| Stan Clayton | OG | 6'3" | 265 | 26 | | |
| Gene Chilton | C | 6'3" | 286 | 27 | | |
| Elbert Crawford | C-OG | 6'3" | 280 | 25 | | |
| Gregg Rakoczy | C-OG | 6'5" | 280 | 26 | | |
| Ray Agnew | DE | 6'3" | 272 | 23 | | |
| Chris Gannon | DE | 6'6" | 260 | 25 | | |
| Marion Hobby | DE | 6'4" | 277 | 24 | | |
| Sean Smith | DE | 6'4" | 280 | 24 | | |
| Garin Veris | DE | 6'4" | 255 | 28 | | |
| Brent Williams | DE | 6'3" | 275 | 26 | | |
| Tim Goad | NT | 6'3" | 280 | 25 | | |
| Fred Smerlas | NT | 6'4" | 291 | 34 | | |

David Viaene — Knee Injury

| UseName | Pos. | Hgt. | Wgt. | Age | Int | Pts |
|---|---|---|---|---|---|---|
| Vincent Brown | LB | 6'2" | 245 | 26 | | |
| Richard Harvey | LB | 6'1" | 227 | 24 | | |
| David Howard | LB | 6'1" | 230 | 29 | | |
| Eugene Lockhart | LB | 6'2" | 233 | 30 | | |
| Johnny Rembert | LB | 6'3" | 234 | 30 | | |
| Ed Reynolds | LB | 6'5" | 242 | 29 | | |
| Chris Singleton | LB | 6'2" | 247 | 24 | | |
| Richard Tardits | LB | 6'2" | 235 | 25 | | |
| Andre Tippett | LB | 6'3" | 241 | 31 | 1 | |
| Harry Colon | DB | 5'11" | 203 | 22 | | |
| Tim Gordon | DB | 6' | 188 | 26 | | |
| Jerome Henderson | DB | 5'10" | 189 | 22 | 2 | |
| Maurice Hurst | DB | 5'10" | 185 | 23 | 3 | |
| David Key | DB | 5'10" | 198 | 23 | | |
| Ronnie Lippett | DB | 5'11" | 180 | 30 | 2 | |
| Fred Marion | DB | 6'2" | 191 | 32 | 2 | |
| David Pool | DB | 5'9" | 182 | 24 | | |
| Mickey Washington | DB | 5'9" | 187 | 23 | 2 | |
| Tony Zackery | DB | 6'2" | 195 | 24 | | |

Ilia Jarostchuk — Bicep Injury

| UseName | Pos. | Hgt. | Wgt. | Age | Int | Pts |
|---|---|---|---|---|---|---|
| Tom Hodson | QB | 6'3" | 195 | 24 | | |
| Hugh Millen | QB | 6'5" | 216 | 27 | | 6 |
| Marvin Allen | HB | 5'10" | 208 | 25 | | |
| Leonard Russell | HB | 6'2" | 235 | 21 | | 24 |
| John Stephens | HB-FB | 6'1" | 215 | 25 | | 12 |
| Jon Vaughn | HB | 5'9" | 203 | 21 | | 18 |
| George Adams | FB | 6'1" | 225 | 28 | | |
| Ivy Joe Hunter | FB-HB | 6'1" | 248 | 24 | | |
| Rob Carpenter | WR | 6'2" | 215 | 23 | | |
| Irving Fryar | WR | 6' | 200 | 28 | | 18 |
| Greg McMurtry | WR | 6'2" | 207 | 23 | | 12 |
| Gene Taylor | WR | 6'2" | 289 | 28 | | |
| Michael Timpson | WR | 5'10" | 175 | 24 | | 12 |
| Ben Coates | TE | 6'4" | 245 | 22 | | 6 |
| Marv Cook | TE | 6'4" | 234 | 25 | | 18 |
| Charlie Baumann | K | 6'1" | 203 | 24 | | 42 |
| Shawn McCarthy | K | 6'6" | 227 | 23 | | |
| Jason Staurovsky | K | 5'9" | 170 | 28 | | 49 |
| Bryan Wagner | K | 6'2" | 200 | 29 | | |

Hart Lee Dykes — Knee Injury

## INDIANAPOLIS COLTS 1-15 Ron Meyer (0-5), Rick Venturi (1-10)

| Scores of Each Game | | |
|---|---|---|
| 7 | NEW ENGLAND | 16 |
| 6 | Miami | 17 |
| 0 | L.A. Raiders | 16 |
| 24 | DETROIT | 33 |
| 3 | Seattle | 31 |
| 3 | PITTSBURGH | 21 |
| 6 | Buffalo | 42 |
| 6 | N.Y. JETS | 17 |
| 6 | MIAMI | 10 |
| 28 | N.Y. Jets | 27 |
| 17 | CHICAGO | 31 |
| 10 | Green Bay | 14 |
| 0 | CLEVELAND | 31 |
| 17 | New England | * 23 |
| 7 | BUFFALO | 35 |
| 3 | Tampa Bay | 17 |

| UseName | Pos. | Hgt. | Wgt. | Age | Int | Pts |
|---|---|---|---|---|---|---|
| Kevin Call | OT | 6'7" | 308 | 29 | | |
| Jack Linn | OT | 6'5" | 295 | 24 | | |
| Zefross Moss | OT | 6'6" | 338 | 25 | | |
| Irv Pankey | OT-OG | 6'5" | 295 | 33 | | |
| Darin Shoulders | OT | 6'3" | 288 | 23 | | |
| Mark Vander Poel | OT | 6'7" | 303 | 23 | | |
| Brian Baldinger | OG-C | 6'4" | 278 | 32 | | |
| Brian Blados (from CIN) | OG | 6'5" | 296 | 29 | | |
| Chris Conlin | OG | 6'4" | 290 | 26 | | |
| Randy Dixon | OG | 6'3" | 302 | 27 | | |
| Bubba Paris (to DET) | OG-OT | 6'6" | 299 | 30 | | |
| William Schultz | OG-OT | 6'5" | 305 | 24 | | |
| Mark Cannon | C | 6'3" | 258 | 29 | | |
| Ray Donaldson | C | 6'3" | 300 | 33 | | |
| Mel Agee | DE | 6'5" | 290 | 22 | | |
| Sam Clancy | DE | 6'7" | 300 | 33 | | |
| Shane Curry | DE | 6'5" | 270 | 23 | | |
| Jon Hand | DE | 6'7" | 301 | 27 | | |
| Donnell Thompson | DE | 6'4" | 280 | 32 | | |
| Travis Davis | NT | 6'2" | 283 | 25 | | |
| Frank Giannetti | NT | 6'2" | 267 | 24 | | |
| Tony Siragusa | NT-LB | 6'3" | 303 | 24 | | |

Mark Garalczyk — Neck Injury
Pat Tomberlin — Leg Injury

| UseName | Pos. | Hgt. | Wgt. | Age | Int | Pts |
|---|---|---|---|---|---|---|
| Chip Banks | LB | 6'4" | 254 | 31 | | |
| Duane Bickett | LB | 6'5" | 251 | 28 | | |
| Jeff Herrod | LB | 6' | 246 | 25 | 1 | |
| Matt Jaworski | LB | 6'1" | 226 | 23 | | |
| Brian Jones | LB | 6'1" | 240 | 23 | | |
| Quintus McDonald | LB | 6'3 | 263 | 24 | | |
| Scott Radecic | LB | 6'3" | 236 | 29 | 1 | |
| Pat Snyder | LB | 6'1" | 225 | 28 | | |
| Matt Vanderbeek | LB | 6'3" | 258 | 24 | | |
| Tony Walker | LB | 6'3" | 235 | 23 | | |
| Michael Ball | DB | 6' | 220 | 27 | | |
| John Baylor | DB | 6' | 203 | 26 | 4 | |
| Eugene Daniel | DB | 5'11" | 188 | 30 | 3 | |
| Chris Goode | DB | 6' | 196 | 27 | 2 | |
| Alan Grant | DB | 5'10" | 187 | 24 | | |
| Cornell Holloway | DB | 5'11" | 182 | 25 | 1 | |
| Dave McCloughan | DB | 6'1" | 180 | 24 | | |
| Mike Prior | DB | 6' | 210 | 27 | 3 | |
| Keith Taylor | DB | 5'11' | 206 | 26 | | |

| UseName | Pos. | Hgt. | Wgt. | Age | Int | Pts |
|---|---|---|---|---|---|---|
| Jeff George | QB | 6'4" | 221 | 23 | | |
| Mark Herrmann | QB | 6'4" | 220 | 32 | | |
| Rusty Hilger | QB | 6'4" | 209 | 29 | | |
| Jack Trudeau | QB | 6'3" | 219 | 28 | | |
| Albert Bentley | HB-FB | 5'11" | 217 | 31 | | |
| Ken Clark | HB-FB | 5'9" | 204 | 25 | | |
| Eric Dickerson | HB | 6'3" | 224 | 30 | | 18 |
| Brian Lattimore | HB | 6'1" | 202 | 28 | | |
| Bruce Perkins | HB-FB | 6'2" | 230 | 24 | | |
| Anthony Johnson | FB | 6' | 222 | 23 | | |
| Tim Manoa | FB | 6'1" | 245 | 26 | | 6 |
| Bill Brooks | WR | 6' | 189 | 27 | | 24 |
| Jessie Hester | WR | 5'11" | 172 | 28 | | 30 |
| Darvell Huffman | WR | 5'8" | 158 | 24 | | |
| Sammy Martin (from NE) | WR | 5'11" | 175 | 26 | | |
| Reggie Thornton | WR | 5'11" | 170 | 23 | | |
| Clarence Verdin | WR | 5'8" | 162 | 28 | | 6 |
| Pat Beach | TE | 6'4" | 249 | 30 | | |
| Kerry Cash | TE | 6'4" | 247 | 22 | | |
| James Coley | TE | 6'3" | 270 | 24 | | |
| Bob Mrosko | TE | 6'5" | 260 | 25 | | |
| Dean Biasucci | K | 6' | 190 | 29 | | 59 |
| Rohn Stark | K | 6'3" | 203 | 32 | | |

## BUFFALO BILLS

### RUSHING

| Last Name | No. | Yds | Avg | TD |
|---|---|---|---|---|
| Thomas | 288 | 1407 | 4.9 | 7 |
| K. Davis | 129 | 624 | 4.8 | 4 |
| Gardner | 42 | 146 | 3.5 | 4 |
| Reed | 12 | 136 | 11.3 | 0 |
| Kelly | 20 | 45 | 2.3 | 1 |
| Edwards | 1 | 17 | 17.0 | 0 |
| Reich | 13 | 6 | 0.5 | 0 |

### RECEIVING

| Last Name | No. | Yds | Avg | TD |
|---|---|---|---|---|
| Reed | 81 | 1113 | 13.7 | 10 |
| Thomas | 62 | 631 | 10.2 | 5 |
| Lofton | 57 | 1072 | 18.8 | 8 |
| McKeller | 44 | 434 | 9.9 | 3 |
| Beebe | 32 | 414 | 12.9 | 6 |
| Edwards | 22 | 228 | 10.4 | 1 |
| K. Davis | 20 | 118 | 5.9 | 1 |
| Metzelaars | 5 | 54 | 10.8 | 2 |
| Gardner | 3 | 20 | 6.7 | 0 |
| Rolle | 3 | 10 | 3.3 | 2 |
| Tasker | 2 | 39 | 19.5 | 1 |
| Alexander | 1 | 7 | 7.0 | 0 |

### PUNT RETURNS

| Last Name | No. | Yds | Avg | TD |
|---|---|---|---|---|
| Hicks | 12 | 203 | 16.9 | 0 |
| Edwards | 13 | 69 | 5.3 | 0 |
| Odomes | 1 | 9 | 9.0 | 0 |

### KICKOFF RETURNS

| Last Name | No. | Yds | Avg | TD |
|---|---|---|---|---|
| Edwards | 31 | 623 | 20.1 | 1 |
| Fuller | 8 | 125 | 15.6 | 0 |
| Beebe | 7 | 121 | 17.3 | 0 |
| K. Davis | 4 | 73 | 18.3 | 0 |
| Taylor | 1 | 18 | 18.0 | 0 |
| Gardner | 1 | 10 | 10.0 | 0 |

### PASSING—PUNTING—KICKING Statistics

| PASSING | Att | Cmp | % | Yds | Yd/Att | TD | Int— | % | RK |
|---|---|---|---|---|---|---|---|---|---|
| Kelly | 474 | 304 | 64.1 | 3844 | 8.11 | 33 | 17— | 3.6 | 1 |
| Reich | 41 | 27 | 65.9 | 305 | 7.44 | 6 | 2— | 4.9 | |
| Mohr | 1 | 1 | 100.0 | 9 | 9.00 | 0 | 0— | 0.0 | |

| PUNTING | No. | Avg. |
|---|---|---|
| Mohr | 54 | 38.6 |

| KICKING | XP | ATT | % | FG | ATT | % |
|---|---|---|---|---|---|---|
| Norwood | 56 | 58 | 97 | 18 | 29 | 62 |

## NEW YORK JETS

### RUSHING

| Last Name | No. | Yds | Avg | TD |
|---|---|---|---|---|
| Thomas | 189 | 728 | 3.9 | 3 |
| Baxter | 184 | 666 | 3.6 | 11 |
| Hector | 62 | 345 | 5.6 | 0 |
| McNeil | 51 | 300 | 5.9 | 2 |
| O'Brien | 23 | 60 | 2.6 | 0 |
| Taylor | 7 | 23 | 3.3 | 0 |
| Mathis | 1 | 19 | 19.0 | 0 |
| Aguiar | 1 | 18 | 18.0 | 0 |
| Brown | 3 | 4 | 1.3 | 1 |
| Nagle | 1 | -1 | -1.0 | 0 |
| Burkett | 1 | -2 | -2.0 | 0 |

### RECEIVING

| Last Name | No. | Yds | Avg | TD |
|---|---|---|---|---|
| Toon | 74 | 963 | 13.0 | 0 |
| Moore | 70 | 987 | 14.1 | 5 |
| Thomas | 30 | 195 | 6.5 | 1 |
| Mathis | 28 | 329 | 11.8 | 1 |
| Burkett | 23 | 327 | 14.2 | 4 |
| Dressel | 17 | 122 | 7.2 | 0 |
| Boyer | 16 | 153 | 9.6 | 0 |
| Baxter | 12 | 124 | 10.3 | 0 |
| McNeil | 7 | 56 | 8.0 | 0 |
| Hector | 7 | 51 | 7.3 | 0 |
| Whisenhunt | 4 | 34 | 8.5 | 0 |
| Dawkins | 3 | 38 | 12.7 | 0 |
| Matich | 3 | 23 | 7.7 | 1 |
| O'Brien | 1 | 27 | 27.0 | 0 |

### PUNT RETURNS

| Last Name | No. | Yds | Avg | TD |
|---|---|---|---|---|
| Mathis | 23 | 157 | 6.8 | 0 |

### KICKOFF RETURNS

| Last Name | No. | Yds | Avg | TD |
|---|---|---|---|---|
| Mathis | 29 | 599 | 20.7 | 0 |
| Brown | 10 | 100 | 10.0 | 0 |
| Hector | 8 | 172 | 21.5 | 0 |
| Odegard | 6 | 106 | 17.7 | 0 |
| Dawkins | 2 | 22 | 11.0 | 0 |
| P. Kelly | 1 | 4 | 4.0 | 0 |
| Boyer | 1 | 0 | 0.0 | 0 |
| Dressel | 1 | 0 | 0.0 | 0 |

### PASSING—PUNTING—KICKING Statistics

| PASSING | Att | Cmp | % | Yds | Yd/Att | TD | Int— | % | RK |
|---|---|---|---|---|---|---|---|---|---|
| O'Brien | 489 | 287 | 58.7 | 3300 | 6.75 | 10 | 11— | 2.2 | 8 |
| Eason | 28 | 13 | 46.4 | 155 | 5.54 | 0 | 1— | 3.6 | |
| Taylor | 10 | 7 | 70.0 | 49 | 4.90 | 1 | 0— | 0.0 | |
| Toon | 2 | 0 | 0.0 | 0 | 0.00 | 0 | 0— | 0.0 | |

| PUNTING | No. | Avg. |
|---|---|---|
| Prokop | 59 | 40.1 |

| KICKING | XP | ATT | % | FG | ATT | % |
|---|---|---|---|---|---|---|
| Leahy | 30 | 30 | 100 | 26 | 37 | 70 |

## MIAMI DOLPHINS

### RUSHING

| Last Name | No. | Yds | Avg | TD |
|---|---|---|---|---|
| Higgs | 231 | 905 | 3.9 | 4 |
| S. Smith | 83 | 297 | 3.6 | 1 |
| Craver | 20 | 58 | 2.9 | 1 |
| Marino | 27 | 32 | 1.2 | 1 |
| Secules | 4 | 30 | 7.5 | 1 |
| Paige | 10 | 25 | 2.5 | 0 |
| Logan | 4 | 5 | 1.3 | 0 |

### RECEIVING

| Last Name | No. | Yds | Avg | TD |
|---|---|---|---|---|
| Duper | 70 | 1085 | 15.5 | 5 |
| Clayton | 70 | 1053 | 15.0 | 12 |
| Paige | 57 | 469 | 8.2 | 1 |
| Martin | 27 | 434 | 16.1 | 2 |
| Jensen | 21 | 183 | 8.7 | 2 |
| Baty | 20 | 269 | 13.5 | 1 |
| S. Smith | 14 | 95 | 6.8 | 0 |
| Edmunds | 11 | 118 | 10.7 | 2 |
| Higgs | 11 | 80 | 7.3 | 0 |
| Banks | 9 | 119 | 13.2 | 1 |
| Craver | 8 | 67 | 8.4 | 0 |
| Miller | 4 | 49 | 12.3 | 0 |
| Pruitt | 2 | 30 | 15.0 | 0 |
| Henry | 2 | 17 | 8.5 | 0 |
| Sims | 1 | 9 | 9.0 | 0 |

### PUNT RETURNS

| Last Name | No. | Yds | Avg | TD |
|---|---|---|---|---|
| Miller | 28 | 248 | 8.9 | 0 |
| Junior | 1 | 0 | 0.0 | 0 |
| Martin | 1 | 0 | 0.0 | 0 |

### KICKOFF RETURNS

| Last Name | No. | Yds | Avg | TD |
|---|---|---|---|---|
| Craver | 32 | 615 | 19.2 | 0 |
| Logan | 12 | 191 | 15.9 | 0 |
| Paige | 2 | 31 | 15.5 | 0 |
| Henry | 1 | 13 | 13.0 | 0 |
| J. Williams | 1 | 7 | 7.0 | 0 |
| Dellenbach | 1 | 0 | 0.0 | 0 |

### PASSING—PUNTING—KICKING Statistics

| PASSING | Att | Cmp | % | Yds | Yd/Att | TD | Int— | % | RK |
|---|---|---|---|---|---|---|---|---|---|
| Marino | 549 | 318 | 57.9 | 3970 | 7.23 | 25 | 13— | 2.4 | 3 |
| Secules | 13 | 8 | 61.5 | 90 | 6.92 | 1 | 1— | 7.7 | |
| Jensen | 1 | 1 | 100.0 | 17 | 17.00 | 0 | 0— | 0.0 | |

| PUNTING | No. | Avg. |
|---|---|---|
| Roby | 55 | 44.8 |

| KICKING | XP | Att. | % | FG | Att | % |
|---|---|---|---|---|---|---|
| Stoyonovich | 28 | 29 | 97 | 31 | 37 | 84 |

## NEW ENGLAND PATRIOTS

### RUSHING

| Last Name | No. | Yds | Avg | TD |
|---|---|---|---|---|
| Russell | 266 | 959 | 3.6 | 4 |
| Stephens | 63 | 163 | 2.6 | 2 |
| Vaughn | 31 | 146 | 4.7 | 2 |
| Millen | 31 | 92 | 3.0 | 1 |
| Hunter | 18 | 53 | 2.9 | 0 |
| Allen | 13 | 50 | 3.8 | 0 |
| Fryar | 2 | 11 | 5.5 | 0 |
| Adams | 2 | 3 | 1.5 | 0 |
| Chilton | 1 | 0 | 0.0 | 0 |
| Hodson | 4 | 0 | 0.0 | 0 |
| Timpson | 1 | -4 | -4.0 | 0 |
| Coates | 1 | -6 | -6.0 | 0 |

### RECEIVING

| Last Name | No. | Yds | Avg | TD |
|---|---|---|---|---|
| Cook | 82 | 808 | 9.9 | 3 |
| Fryar | 68 | 1014 | 14.9 | 3 |
| McMurtry | 41 | 614 | 15.0 | 2 |
| Timpson | 25 | 471 | 18.8 | 2 |
| Russell | 18 | 81 | 4.5 | 0 |
| Stephens | 16 | 119 | 7.4 | 0 |
| Hunter | 11 | 97 | 8.8 | 0 |
| Coates | 10 | 95 | 9.5 | 1 |
| Vaughn | 9 | 89 | 9.9 | 0 |
| Carpenter | 3 | 45 | 15.0 | 0 |
| Allen | 1 | 9 | 9.0 | 0 |

### PUNT RETURNS

| Last Name | No. | Yds | Avg | TD |
|---|---|---|---|---|
| Henderson | 27 | 201 | 7.4 | 0 |
| Fryar | 2 | 10 | 5.0 | 0 |
| Pool | 1 | 0 | 0.0 | 0 |
| Zackery | 1 | 0 | 0.0 | 0 |

### KICKOFF RETURNS

| Last Name | No. | Yds | Avg | TD |
|---|---|---|---|---|
| Vaughn | 34 | 717 | 21.1 | 1 |
| Allen | 8 | 161 | 20.1 | 0 |
| Timpson | 2 | 37 | 18.5 | 0 |
| Hobby | 2 | 0 | 0.0 | 0 |
| Rakoczy | 1 | 9 | 9.0 | 0 |
| Coates | 1 | 6 | 6.0 | 0 |

### PASSING—PUNTING—KICKING Statistics

| PASSING | Att | Cmp | % | Yds | Yd/Att | TD | Int— | % | RK |
|---|---|---|---|---|---|---|---|---|---|
| Millen | 409 | 246 | 60.1 | 3073 | 7.51 | 9 | 18— | 4.4 | 12 |
| Hodson | 68 | 36 | 52.9 | 345 | 5.07 | 1 | 4— | 5.9 | |
| Vaughn | 2 | 1 | 50.0 | 13 | 6.50 | 1 | 0— | 0.0 | |
| McCarthy | 1 | 1 | 100.0 | 11 | 11.00 | 0 | 0— | 0.0 | |
| Fryar | 1 | 0 | 0.0 | 0 | 0.00 | 0 | 0— | 0.0 | |

| PUNTING | No. | Avg. |
|---|---|---|
| McCarthy | 66 | 39.0 |

| KICKING | XP | ATT | % | FG | ATT | % |
|---|---|---|---|---|---|---|
| Staurovsky | 10 | 11 | 91 | 13 | 19 | 68 |
| Baumann | 15 | 16 | 94 | 9 | 12 | 75 |

## INDIANAPOLIS COLTS

### RUSHING

| Last Name | No. | Yds | Avg | TD |
|---|---|---|---|---|
| Dickerson | 167 | 536 | 3.2 | 2 |
| Clark | 114 | 366 | 3.2 | 0 |
| Manoa | 27 | 144 | 5.3 | 1 |
| Johnson | 22 | 94 | 4.3 | 0 |
| George | 16 | 36 | 2.3 | 0 |
| Perkins | 4 | 11 | 2.8 | 0 |
| Verdin | 1 | 4 | 4.0 | 0 |
| Herrmann | 1 | -1 | -1.0 | 0 |
| Huffman | 1 | -8 | -8.0 | 0 |
| Stark | 1 | -13 | -13.0 | 0 |

### RECEIVING

| Last Name | No. | Yds | Avg | TD |
|---|---|---|---|---|
| Brooks | 72 | 888 | 12.3 | 4 |
| Hester | 60 | 753 | 12.6 | 5 |
| Johnson | 42 | 344 | 8.2 | 0 |
| Dickerson | 41 | 269 | 6.6 | 1 |
| Clark | 33 | 245 | 7.4 | 0 |
| Verdin | 21 | 214 | 10.2 | 0 |
| Mrosko | 8 | 90 | 11.3 | 0 |
| Bentley | 7 | 42 | 6.0 | 0 |
| Martin | 5 | 79 | 15.8 | 0 |
| Beach | 5 | 56 | 11.2 | 0 |
| Huffman | 3 | 14 | 4.7 | 0 |
| Perkins | 3 | -2 | -0.7 | 0 |
| Manoa | 2 | 5 | 2.5 | 0 |
| Thornton | 1 | 38 | 38.0 | 0 |
| Cash | 1 | 18 | 18.0 | 0 |
| Coley | 1 | 13 | 13.0 | 0 |

### PUNT RETURNS

| Last Name | No. | Yds | Avg | TD |
|---|---|---|---|---|
| Verdin | 25 | 163 | 6.5 | 0 |
| Clark | 1 | 6 | 6.0 | 0 |
| Grant | 1 | 2 | 2.0 | 0 |

### KICKOFF RETURNS

| Last Name | No. | Yds | Avg | TD |
|---|---|---|---|---|
| Martin | 20 | 483 | 24.2 | 0 |
| Verdin | 36 | 689 | 19.1 | 1 |
| Grant | 3 | 20 | 6.7 | 0 |
| McCloughan | 2 | 35 | 17.5 | 0 |
| Mrosko | 1 | 9 | 9.0 | 0 |
| McDonald | 1 | 3 | 3.0 | 0 |

### PASSING—PUNTING—KICKING Statistics

| PASSING | Att | Cmp | % | Yds | Yd/Att | TD | Int— | % | RK |
|---|---|---|---|---|---|---|---|---|---|
| George | 485 | 292 | 60.2 | 2910 | 6.00 | 10 | 12— | 2.5 | 10 |
| Herrmann | 19 | 11 | 57.9 | 137 | 7.21 | 0 | 3— | 15.8 | |
| Trudeau | 7 | 2 | 28.6 | 19 | 2.71 | 0 | 1— | 14.3 | |
| Hilger | 1 | 0 | 0.0 | 0 | 0.00 | 0 | 0— | 0.0 | |

| PUNTING | No. | Avg. |
|---|---|---|
| Stark | 82 | 42.6 |

| KICKING | XP | ATT | % | FG | ATT | % |
|---|---|---|---|---|---|---|
| Biasucci | 14 | 14 | 100 | 15 | 26 | 58 |

## HOUSTON OILERS 11-5 Jack Pardee

| Scores of Each Game | | |
|---|---|---|
| 47 | L.A. RAIDERS | 17 |
| 30 | Cincinnati | 7 |
| 17 | KANSAS CITY | 7 |
| 20 | New England | 24 |
| 42 | DENVER | 14 |
| 23 | N.Y. Jets | 20 |
| 17 | Miami | 13 |
| 35 | CINCINNATI | 3 |
| 13 | Washington | * 16 |
| 26 | DALLAS | * 23 |
| 28 | CLEVELAND | 24 |
| 14 | Pittsburgh | 26 |
| 6 | PHILADELPHIA | 13 |
| 31 | PITTSBURGH | 6 |
| 17 | Cleveland | 14 |
| 20 | N.Y. Giants | 24 |

| UseName | Pos. | Hgt. | Wgt. | Age | Int | Pts |
|---|---|---|---|---|---|---|
| Kevin Donnalley | OT | 6'5" | 290 | 23 | | |
| Don Maggs | OT-OG | 6'5" | 290 | 29 | | |
| Dean Steinkuhler | OT | 6'3" | 287 | 30 | | |
| David Williams | OT | 6'5" | 292 | 25 | | |
| Doug Dawson | OG-C | 6'2" | 288 | 29 | | |
| John Flannery | OG-C | 6'3" | 304 | 22 | | |
| Mike Munchak | OG | 6'3" | 284 | 31 | | |
| Bruce Matthews | C-OG | 6'4" | 291 | 30 | | |
| William Fuller | DE | 6'3" | 274 | 29 | | |
| Sean Jones | DE | 6'7" | 264 | 28 | | |
| Willis Peguese | DE | 6'4" | 267 | 24 | | |
| Jeff Alm | DT | 6'6" | 289 | 23 | | |
| Ray Childress | DT-DE | 6'6" | 272 | 28 | | |
| Ezra Johnson | DT-DE | 6'4" | 257 | 35 | | |
| Lee Williams | DE-DT | 6'6" | 271 | 28 | | |
| Glenn Montgomery | DT | 6' | 272 | 24 | | |
| Doug Smith | DT | 6'5" | 309 | 32 | | |

Erik Norgard — Shoulder Injury

| UseName | Pos. | Hgt. | Wgt. | Age | Int | Pts |
|---|---|---|---|---|---|---|
| Eric Fairs | LB | 6'3" | 244 | 27 | | |
| Rick Graf | LB | 6'5" | 244 | 27 | | |
| Scott Kozak | LB | 6'3" | 222 | 25 | | |
| Lamar Lathon | LB | 6'3" | 250 | 23 | 1 | 6 |
| Johnny Meads | LB | 6'2" | 226 | 30 | | |
| Eugene Seale | LB | 5'10" | 253 | 27 | | |
| Al Smith | LB | 6'1" | 251 | 26 | 1 | 6 |
| Herbie Anderson | DB | 5'9" | 183 | 22 | | |
| Cris Dishman | DB | 6' | 178 | 26 | 6 | 6 |
| Mike Dumas | DB | 5'11" | 178 | 22 | 1 | 6 |
| Steve Jackson | DB | 5'8" | 182 | 22 | | |
| Richard Johnson | DB | 6'1" | 195 | 27 | | |
| Darryll Lewis | DB | 5'9" | 188 | 22 | 1 | 6 |
| Bubba McDowell | DB | 6'1" | 198 | 24 | 4 | 6 |
| Bo Orlando | DB | 5'10" | 180 | 25 | 4 | |
| Marcus Robertson | DB | 5'11" | 197 | 21 | | |

| UseName | Pos. | Hgt. | Wgt. | Age | Int | Pts |
|---|---|---|---|---|---|---|
| Cody Carlson | QB | 6'3" | 202 | 27 | | |
| Warren Moon | QB | 6'3" | 212 | 34 | | 12 |
| Gary Brown | HB-FB | 5'11" | 224 | 22 | | 6 |
| Victor Jones | HB-FB | 5'8" | 212 | 23 | | |
| Allen Pinkett | HB | 5'9" | 196 | 27 | | 60 |
| Lorenzo White | HB | 5'11" | 222 | 25 | | 24 |
| Pat Coleman | WR | 5'7" | 173 | 24 | | 6 |
| Curtis Duncan | WR | 5'11" | 184 | 26 | | 24 |
| Ernest Givins | WR | 5'9" | 172 | 26 | | 30 |
| Leonard Harris | WR | 5'8" | 162 | 30 | | |
| Drew Hill | WR | 5'9" | 172 | 34 | | 24 |
| Haywood Jeffires | WR | 6'2" | 201 | 26 | | 42 |
| Alex Johnson | WR | 5'9" | 167 | 23 | | |
| Tony Jones | WR | 5'7" | 139 | 25 | | 12 |
| Frank Miotke | WR | 6' | 175 | 25 | | |
| Al Del Greco | K | 5'10" | 200 | 29 | | 46 |
| Ian Howfield | K | 6'2" | 196 | 25 | | 64 |
| Greg Montgomery | K | 6'3" | 215 | 26 | | |
| Kent Sullivan | K | 5'10" | 197 | 27 | | |

## PITTSBURGH STEELERS 7-9 Chuck Noll

| Scores of Each Game | | |
|---|---|---|
| 26 | SAN DIEGO | 20 |
| 34 | Buffalo | 52 |
| 20 | NEW ENGLAND | 6 |
| 14 | Philadelphia | 23 |
| 21 | Indianapolis | 3 |
| 20 | N.Y. GIANTS | 23 |
| 7 | SEATTLE | 27 |
| 14 | Cleveland | 17 |
| 13 | Denver | 20 |
| 33 | Cincinnati | * 27 |
| 14 | WASHINGTON | 41 |
| 26 | HOUSTON | 14 |
| 10 | Dallas | 20 |
| 6 | Houston | 31 |
| 17 | CINCINNATI | 10 |
| 17 | CLEVELAND | 10 |

| UseName | Pos. | Hgt. | Wgt. | Age | Int | Pts |
|---|---|---|---|---|---|---|
| Tunch Ilkin | OT | 6'3" | 273 | 33 | | |
| John Jackson | OT | 6'6" | 289 | 26 | | |
| Tom Ricketts | OT-OG | 6'5" | 288 | 25 | | |
| Ariel Solomon | OT-OG | 6'5" | 271 | 23 | | |
| Justin Strzelczyk | OT | 6'5" | 297 | 23 | | |
| Brian Blankenship | OG-C | 6'1" | 280 | 28 | | |
| Dean Caliguire (from SF) | OG-C | 6'2" | 280 | 24 | | |
| Calton Haselrig | OG | 6'1" | 295 | 25 | | |
| Terry Long | OG | 5'11" | 284 | 32 | | |
| Dermontti Dawson | C | 6'2" | 275 | 26 | | |
| Kenny Davidson | DE | 6'5" | 264 | 24 | | |
| Donald Evans | DE | 6'2" | 258 | 27 | | |
| Aaron Jones | DE | 6'5" | 257 | 24 | | |
| Keith Willis | DE | 6'1" | 260 | 32 | | |
| Craig Veasey | NT-DT-DE | 6'2" | 285 | 24 | | |
| Gerald Williams | NT | 6'3" | 282 | 27 | | |

| UseName | Pos. | Hgt. | Wgt. | Age | Int | Pts |
|---|---|---|---|---|---|---|
| Jeff Brady | LB | 6'1" | 224 | 22 | | |
| Bryan Hinkle | LB | 6'2" | 224 | 32 | 2 | 6 |
| David Little | LB | 6'1" | 236 | 32 | 1 | |
| Greg Lloyd | LB | 6'2" | 223 | 26 | 1 | |
| Rob McGovern | LB | 6'2" | 223 | 24 | | |
| Hardy Nickerson | LB | 6'2" | 227 | 26 | | |
| Jerry Olsavsky | LB | 6'1" | 219 | 24 | | |
| Huey Richardson | LB-DE | 6'5" | 233 | 23 | | |
| Jerrol Williams | LB | 6'5" | 237 | 24 | | 6 |
| Thomas Everett | DB | 5'9" | 183 | 26 | 4 | |
| Larry Griffin | DB | 6' | 200 | 28 | 1 | |
| Delton Hall | DB | 6'1" | 204 | 26 | | |
| David Johnson | DB | 6' | 181 | 25 | 1 | |
| Gary Jones | DB | 6'1" | 208 | 23 | 1 | |
| Carnell Lake | DB | 6'1" | 207 | 24 | | |
| Richard Shelton | DB | 5'10" | 196 | 25 | 3 | 6 |
| Kevin Smith | DB | 5'11" | 204 | 24 | | |
| Shawn Vincent | DB | 5'10" | 180 | 23 | 2 | |
| Sammy Walker | DB | 5'11" | 197 | 22 | | |
| Rod Woodson | DB | 6' | 197 | 26 | 3 | |

| UseName | Pos. | Hgt. | Wgt. | Age | Int | Pts |
|---|---|---|---|---|---|---|
| Bubby Brister | QB | 6'3" | 217 | 29 | | |
| Neil O'Donnell | QB | 6'3" | 223 | 25 | | 6 |
| Barry Foster | HB | 5'10" | 218 | 22 | | 12 |
| Warren Williams | HB | 6' | 213 | 26 | | 24 |
| Tim Worley | HB | 6'2" | 216 | 24 | | |
| Merril Hoge | FB | 6'2" | 222 | 26 | | 18 |
| Leroy Thompson | FB | 5'10" | 215 | 22 | | |
| Chris Calloway | WR | 5'10" | 190 | 23 | | 6 |
| Jeff Graham | WR | 6'1" | 195 | 22 | | |
| Louis Lipps | WR | 5'10" | 185 | 29 | | 12 |
| Ernie Mills | WR | 5'11" | 178 | 22 | | 12 |
| Dwight Stone | WR-HB | 6' | 190 | 27 | | 30 |
| Keith Cash | TE | 6'4" | 235 | 22 | | 6 |
| Adrian Cooper | TE | 6'5" | 259 | 23 | | 12 |
| Eric Green | TE | 6'5" | 280 | 24 | | 36 |
| Mike Mularkey | TE | 6'4" | 240 | 29 | | |
| Gary Anderson | K | 5'11" | 179 | 32 | | 100 |
| Dan Stryzinski | K | 6'1" | 189 | 26 | | |

## CLEVELAND BROWNS 6-10 Bill Belichick

| Scores of Each Game | | |
|---|---|---|
| 14 | DALLAS | 26 |
| 20 | New England | 0 |
| 14 | CINCINNATI | 13 |
| 10 | N.Y. Giants | 13 |
| 14 | N.Y. JETS | 17 |
| 17 | Washington | 42 |
| 30 | San Diego | * 24 |
| 17 | PITTSBURGH | 14 |
| 21 | Cincinnati | 23 |
| 30 | PHILADELPHIA | 32 |
| 24 | Houston | 28 |
| 20 | KANSAS CITY | 15 |
| 31 | Indianapolis | 0 |
| 7 | DENVER | 17 |
| 14 | HOUSTON | 17 |
| 10 | Pittsburgh | 17 |

| UseName | Pos. | Hgt. | Wgt. | Age | Int | Pts |
|---|---|---|---|---|---|---|
| Leonard Burton | OT | 6'3" | 277 | 27 | | |
| Paul Farren | OT-OG | 6'5" | 270 | 30 | | |
| Dan Fike | OT-OG | 6'7" | 285 | 30 | | |
| Tony Jones | OT | 6'5" | 290 | 25 | | |
| Rob Woods | OT | 6'5" | 295 | 25 | | |
| Ed King | OG | 6'4" | 303 | 21 | | |
| John Rienstra | OG | 6'5" | 275 | 28 | | |
| Mike Baab | C | 6'4" | 275 | 31 | | |
| Chris Thome | C | 6'4" | 280 | 22 | | |
| Rob Burnett | DE | 6'4" | 270 | 24 | | |
| Ernie Logan | DE | 6'3" | 271 | 23 | | |
| Pio Sagapolutele | DE | 6'6" | 297 | 21 | | |
| Anthony Pleasant | DE | 6'5" | 258 | 23 | | |
| Mike Wise | DE | 6'7" | 270 | 27 | | |
| Frank Conover | DT | 6'5" | 317 | 23 | | |
| James Jones | DT-NT | 6'2" | 294 | 22 | | 8 |
| Michael Dean Perry | DT | 6'1" | 285 | 26 | | |
| John Thornton | DT | 6'3" | 303 | 22 | | |

| UseName | Pos. | Hgt. | Wgt. | Age | Int | Pts |
|---|---|---|---|---|---|---|
| David Brandon | LB | 6'4" | 230 | 26 | 2 | 6 |
| Richard Brown | LB | 6'3" | 240 | 25 | 1 | |
| Johnie Cooks | LB | 6'4" | 251 | 32 | | |
| Cedric Figaro | LB | 6'3" | 255 | 24 | 1 | |
| Mike Johnson | LB | 6'1" | 230 | 28 | 1 | |
| Jock Jones (to PHX) | LB | 6'2" | 230 | 23 | | |
| Clay Matthews | LB | 6'2" | 245 | 35 | 1 | |
| Van Waiters | LB | 6'4" | 250 | 26 | | |
| Harlon Barnett | DB | 5'11" | 200 | 24 | | |
| Latin Berry | DB | 5'10" | 196 | 24 | | |
| Anthony Blaylock (to SD) | DB | 5'11" | 190 | 26 | | |
| Stephen Braggs | DB | 5'10" | 180 | 26 | 3 | |
| Raymond Clayborn | DB | 6' | 190 | 36 | | |
| Anthony Florence | DB | 6' | 185 | 25 | | |
| Odie Harris | DB | 6' | 190 | 25 | | |
| Alfred Jackson | DB | 6' | 180 | 24 | 1 | |
| Joe King (from CIN) | DB | 6'2" | 202 | 23 | | |
| Frank Minnifield | DB | 5'9" | 180 | 31 | | |
| Vince Newsome | DB | 6'1" | 185 | 30 | 1 | 6 |
| Eric Turner | DB | 6'1" | 207 | 22 | 2 | 6 |

Thane Gash — Neck Injury
Mark Harper — Heel Injury

| UseName | Pos. | Hgt. | Wgt. | Age | Int | Pts |
|---|---|---|---|---|---|---|
| Bernie Kosar | QB | 6'5" | 215 | 27 | | |
| Todd Philcox | QB | 6'4" | 225 | 24 | | |
| Eric Metcalf | HB-WR | 5'10" | 190 | 23 | | |
| Joe Morris | HB | 5'9" | 195 | 30 | | 12 |
| Derrick Douglas | FB | 5'10" | 222 | 23 | | |
| Leroy Hoard | FB-HB | 5'11" | 230 | 23 | | 66 |
| Kevin Mack | FB | 6' | 230 | 29 | | 60 |
| Lee Rouson | FB | 6'1" | 222 | 28 | | |
| Brian Brennan | WR | 5'9" | 185 | 29 | | 6 |
| Darryl Ingram | WR | 6'3" | 240 | 25 | | |
| Michael Jackson | WR | 6'4" | 195 | 24 | | 12 |
| Lynn James | WR | 6' | 190 | 26 | | |
| Reggie Langhorne | WR | 6'2" | 205 | 28 | | 12 |
| Mike Oliphant | WR-HB | 5'9" | 171 | 28 | | |
| Danny Peebles | WR | 5'11" | 180 | 25 | | |
| Tyrone Shavers | WR | 6'3" | 210 | 23 | | |
| Webster Slaughter | WR | 6' | 170 | 26 | | 18 |
| Scott Galbraith | TE | 6'3" | 260 | 24 | | |
| Brian Kinchen | TE | 6'2" | 232 | 26 | | |
| Bruce McGonnigal | TE | 6'4" | 230 | 23 | | |
| John Talley | TE | 6'5" | 245 | 26 | | |
| Brian Hansen | K | 6'4" | 220 | 30 | | |
| Matt Stover | K | 5'11" | 178 | 23 | | 81 |

Jeff Francis — Shoulder Injury
Lawyer Tillman — Ankle Injury

## CINCINNATI BENGALS 3-13 Sam Wyche

| Scores of Each Game | | |
|---|---|---|
| 14 | Denver | 45 |
| 7 | HOUSTON | 30 |
| 13 | Cleveland | 14 |
| 27 | WASHINGTON | 34 |
| 7 | SEATTLE | 13 |
| 23 | Dallas | 35 |
| 16 | Buffalo | 35 |
| 3 | Houston | 35 |
| 23 | CLEVELAND | 21 |
| 27 | PITTSBURGH | 33 |
| 10 | Philadelphia | 17 |
| 14 | L.A. RAIDERS | 38 |
| 27 | N.Y. GIANTS | 24 |
| 13 | Miami | 37 |
| 10 | Pittsburgh | 17 |
| 29 | NEW ENGLAND | 7 |

| UseName | Pos. | Hgt. | Wgt. | Age | Int | Pts |
|---|---|---|---|---|---|---|
| Scott Jones | OT | 6'6" | 280 | 25 | | |
| Anthony Munoz | OT | 6'6" | 284 | 33 | | |
| Kirk Scrafford | OT | 6'6" | 255 | 24 | | |
| Joe Walter | OT-OG | 6'6" | 292 | 28 | | |
| Mike Withycombe | OT | 6'5" | 310 | 26 | | |
| Paul Jetton | OG | 6'4" | 288 | 26 | | |
| Ken Moyer | OG | 6'6" | 297 | 24 | | |
| Bruce Reimers | OG | 6'7" | 298 | 30 | | |
| Mike Arthur | C | 6'3" | 271 | 23 | | |
| Bruce Kozerski | C-OG | 6'4" | 287 | 29 | | |
| Jason Buck | DE-DT | 6'5" | 264 | 27 | | |
| David Grant | DE | 6'4" | 278 | 25 | 1 | |
| Alonzo Mitz | DE | 6'4" | 278 | 28 | 1 | |
| Skip McClendon (to SD) | DE | 6'7" | 287 | 27 | | |
| Lamar Rogers | DE | 6'4" | 292 | 23 | | |
| Natu Tuatagaloa | DE | 6'4" | 274 | 25 | | |
| Tim Krumrie | NT-DT | 6'2" | 274 | 31 | | |

Andrew Stewart — Knee Injury

| UseName | Pos. | Hgt. | Wgt. | Age | Int | Pts |
|---|---|---|---|---|---|---|
| Leo Barker | LB | 6'2" | 230 | 31 | 1 | |
| Ed Brady | LB | 6'2" | 236 | 31 | | |
| Bernard Clark (to, from SEA) | LB | 6'2" | 248 | 24 | | |
| James Francis | LB | 6'5" | 252 | 23 | 1 | |
| Alex Gordon | LB | 6'5" | 245 | 26 | | 2 |
| Kevin Walker | LB | 6'2" | 238 | 25 | | |
| Leon White | LB | 6'3" | 242 | 27 | | |
| Alfred Williams | LB | 6'6" | 240 | 22 | | |
| Carl Zander | LB | 6'2" | 235 | 28 | | |
| Antoine Bennett | DB | 5'11" | 185 | 23 | | |
| Lewis Billups | DB | 5'11" | 190 | 27 | | |
| Barney Bussey | DB | 6' | 210 | 29 | 2 | |
| Rickey Dixon | DB | 5'11" | 191 | 24 | 2 | |
| Richard Fain (to PHX) | DB | 5'10" | 183 | 23 | 1 | |
| David Fulcher | DB | 6'3" | 238 | 26 | 4 | 6 |
| Wayne Haddix (from TB) | DB | 6'1" | 205 | 28 | | |
| Rod Jones | DB | 6' | 185 | 27 | | |
| Mitchell Price | DB | 5'9" | 181 | 24 | 1 | 6 |
| Eric Thomas | DB | 5'11" | 181 | 26 | 3 | |
| Fernandus Vinson | DB | 5'10" | 197 | 22 | | |

| UseName | Pos. | Hgt. | Wgt. | Age | Int | Pts |
|---|---|---|---|---|---|---|
| Boomer Esiason | QB | 6'4" | 220 | 30 | | |
| Donald Hollas | QB | 6'3" | 215 | 23 | | |
| Erik Wilhelm | QB | 6'3" | 210 | 25 | | |
| Eric Ball | HB-FB | 6'2" | 211 | 25 | | 6 |
| James Brooks | HB | 5'10" | 182 | 32 | | 24 |
| Harold Green | HB | 6'2" | 222 | 23 | | 12 |
| Mike Dingle | FB | 6'2" | 240 | 22 | | 6 |
| Craig Taylor | FB | 5'11" | 228 | 25 | | 12 |
| Ickey Woods | FB | 6'2" | 232 | 25 | | 24 |
| Mike Barber | WR | 5'11" | 172 | 24 | | 6 |
| Eddie Brown | WR | 6' | 185 | 28 | | 12 |
| Shane Garrett | WR | 5'11" | 185 | 23 | | |
| Lynn James | WR | 6' | 191 | 24 | | 6 |
| Tim McGee | WR | 5'10" | 183 | 27 | | 24 |
| Reggie Rembert | WR | 6'5" | 200 | 24 | | 6 |
| Rodney Holman | TE | 6'3" | 238 | 31 | | 12 |
| Eric Kattus | TE | 6'5" | 251 | 28 | | |
| Jim Riggs | TE | 6'5" | 245 | 27 | | |
| Jim Breech | K | 5'6" | 161 | 35 | | 96 |
| Lee Johnson | K | 6'2" | 200 | 29 | | 3 |

## HOUSTON OILERS

### RUSHING
| Last Name | No. | Yds | Avg | TD |
|---|---|---|---|---|
| Pinkett | 171 | 720 | 4.2 | 9 |
| White | 110 | 465 | 4.2 | 4 |
| Brown | 8 | 85 | 10.6 | 1 |
| Moon | 33 | 68 | 2.1 | 2 |
| Givins | 4 | 30 | 7.5 | 0 |
| Hill | 1 | 1 | 1.0 | 0 |
| Carlson | 4 | -3 | -0.8 | 0 |

### RECEIVING
| Last Name | No. | Yds | Avg | TD |
|---|---|---|---|---|
| Jeffires | 100 | 1181 | 11.8 | 7 |
| Hill | 90 | 1109 | 12.3 | 4 |
| Givins | 70 | 996 | 14.2 | 5 |
| Duncan | 55 | 588 | 10.7 | 4 |
| Pinkett | 29 | 228 | 7.9 | 1 |
| White | 27 | 211 | 7.8 | 0 |
| T. Jones | 19 | 251 | 13.2 | 2 |
| Coleman | 11 | 138 | 12.5 | 1 |
| Harris | 8 | 101 | 12.6 | 0 |
| Brown | 2 | 1 | 0.5 | 0 |

### PUNT RETURNS
| Last Name | No. | Yds | Avg | TD |
|---|---|---|---|---|
| Coleman | 22 | 138 | 6.3 | 0 |
| Givins | 11 | 107 | 9.7 | 0 |
| Duncan | 1 | -1 | -1.0 | 0 |
| Jackson | 1 | 0 | 0.0 | 0 |
| Robertson | 1 | 0 | 0.0 | 0 |

### KICKOFF RETURNS
| Last Name | No. | Yds | Avg | TD |
|---|---|---|---|---|
| Pinkett | 26 | 508 | 19.5 | 0 |
| Coleman | 13 | 256 | 19.7 | 0 |
| Brown | 3 | 30 | 10.0 | 0 |
| Harris | 2 | 34 | 17.0 | 0 |
| Flannery | 1 | 0 | 0.0 | 0 |
| V. Jones | 1 | 7 | 7.0 | 0 |

### PASSING—PUNTING—KICKING

PASSING
| Last Name | Att | Cmp | % | Yds | Yd/Att | TD | Int— | % | RK |
|---|---|---|---|---|---|---|---|---|---|
| Moon | 655 | 404 | 61.7 | 4690 | 7.16 | 23 | 21— | 3.2 | 5 |
| Carlson | 12 | 7 | 58.3 | 114 | 9.50 | 1 | 0— | 0.0 | |

PUNTING
| Last Name | No. | Avg. |
|---|---|---|
| Montgomery | 50 | 42.1 |
| Sullivan | 3 | 32.3 |

KICKING
| Last Name | XP | ATT | % | FG | ATT | % |
|---|---|---|---|---|---|---|
| Howfield | 25 | 29 | 86 | 13 | 18 | 72 |
| Del Greco | 16 | 16 | 100 | 10 | 13 | 77 |

## PITTSBURGH STEELERS

### RUSHING
| Last Name | No. | Yds | Avg | TD |
|---|---|---|---|---|
| Hoge | 165 | 610 | 3.7 | 2 |
| Foster | 96 | 488 | 5.1 | 1 |
| W. Williams | 57 | 262 | 4.6 | 4 |
| Worley | 22 | 117 | 5.3 | 0 |
| O'Donnell | 18 | 82 | 4.6 | 1 |
| Thompson | 20 | 60 | 3.0 | 0 |
| Brister | 11 | 17 | 1.5 | 0 |
| Stone | 1 | 2 | 2.0 | 0 |
| Stryzinski | 4 | -11 | -2.8 | 0 |

### RECEIVING
| Last Name | No. | Yds | Avg | TD |
|---|---|---|---|---|
| Lipps | 55 | 671 | 12.2 | 2 |
| Hoge | 49 | 379 | 7.7 | 1 |
| Green | 41 | 582 | 14.2 | 5 |
| Stone | 32 | 649 | 20.3 | 5 |
| Calloway | 15 | 254 | 10.9 | 1 |
| W. Williams | 15 | 139 | 9.3 | 0 |
| Thompson | 14 | 118 | 8.4 | 0 |
| Cooper | 11 | 147 | 13.4 | 2 |
| Foster | 9 | 117 | 13.0 | 1 |
| Cash | 7 | 90 | 12.9 | 1 |
| Mularkey | 6 | 67 | 11.2 | 0 |
| Mills | 3 | 79 | 26.3 | 1 |
| Graham | 2 | 21 | 10.5 | 0 |

### PUNT RETURNS
| Last Name | No. | Yds | Avg | TD |
|---|---|---|---|---|
| Woodson | 28 | 320 | 11.4 | 0 |
| Graham | 8 | 46 | 5.8 | 0 |
| Cash | 1 | 6 | 6.0 | 0 |
| Mills | 1 | 0 | 0.0 | 0 |
| Vincent | 1 | 0 | 0.0 | 0 |

### KICKOFF RETURNS
| Last Name | No. | Yds | Avg | TD |
|---|---|---|---|---|
| Woodson | 44 | 880 | 20.0 | 0 |
| Mills | 11 | 284 | 25.8 | 0 |
| Stone | 6 | 75 | 12.5 | 0 |
| Graham | 3 | 48 | 16.0 | 0 |
| J. Williams | 1 | 19 | 19.0 | 0 |
| Thompson | 1 | 8 | 8.0 | 0 |
| McGovern | 1 | 0 | 0.0 | 0 |

### PASSING—PUNTING—KICKING

PASSING
| Last Name | Att | Cmp | % | Yds | Yd/Att | TD | Int— | % | RK |
|---|---|---|---|---|---|---|---|---|---|
| O'Donnell | 286 | 156 | 54.5 | 1963 | 6.86 | 11 | 7— | 2.4 | 7 |
| Brister | 190 | 103 | 54.2 | 1350 | 7.11 | 9 | 9— | 4.7 | |

PUNTING
| Last Name | No. | Avg. |
|---|---|---|
| Stryzinski | 75 | 39.9 |

KICKING
| Last Name | XP | ATT | % | FG | ATT | % |
|---|---|---|---|---|---|---|
| Anderson | 31 | 31 | 100 | 23 | 33 | 70 |

## CLEVELAND BROWNS

### RUSHING
| Last Name | No. | Yds | Avg | TD |
|---|---|---|---|---|
| Mack | 197 | 726 | 3.7 | 8 |
| Morris | 93 | 289 | 3.1 | 2 |
| Hoard | 37 | 154 | 4.2 | 2 |
| Metcalf | 30 | 107 | 3.6 | 0 |
| Kosar | 26 | 74 | 2.8 | 0 |
| Rouson | 3 | 14 | 4.7 | 0 |
| Philcox | 1 | -1 | -1.0 | 0 |
| Hansen | 2 | -3 | -1.5 | 0 |

### RECEIVING
| Last Name | No. | Yds | Avg | TD |
|---|---|---|---|---|
| Slaughter | 64 | 906 | 14.2 | 3 |
| Hoard | 48 | 567 | 11.8 | 9 |
| Mack | 40 | 255 | 6.4 | 2 |
| Langhorne | 39 | 505 | 12.9 | 2 |
| Brennan | 31 | 325 | 10.5 | 1 |
| Metcalf | 29 | 294 | 10.1 | 0 |
| Galbraith | 27 | 328 | 12.1 | 0 |
| Jackson | 17 | 268 | 15.8 | 2 |
| Morris | 13 | 76 | 5.8 | 0 |
| James | 7 | 103 | 14.7 | 1 |
| Rouson | 2 | 9 | 4.5 | 0 |
| Talley | 1 | 13 | 13.0 | 0 |
| Kosar | 1 | 1 | 1.0 | 0 |

### PUNT RETURNS
| Last Name | No. | Yds | Avg | TD |
|---|---|---|---|---|
| Slaughter | 17 | 112 | 6.6 | 0 |
| Metcalf | 12 | 100 | 8.3 | 0 |
| Brennan | 2 | 11 | 5.5 | 0 |
| James | 1 | 0 | 0.0 | 0 |

### KICKOFF RETURNS
| Last Name | No. | Yds | Avg | TD |
|---|---|---|---|---|
| Metcalf | 23 | 351 | 15.3 | 0 |
| Morris | 18 | 310 | 17.2 | 0 |
| Peebles | 8 | 149 | 18.6 | 0 |
| James | 8 | 143 | 17.9 | 0 |
| Galbraith | 2 | 13 | 6.5 | 0 |
| Rouson | 1 | 16 | 16.0 | 0 |

### PASSING—PUNTING—KICKING

PASSING
| Last Name | Att | Cmp | % | Yds | Yd/Att | TD | Int— | % | RK |
|---|---|---|---|---|---|---|---|---|---|
| Kosar | 494 | 307 | 62.1 | 3487 | 7.06 | 18 | 9— | 1.8 | 2 |
| Philcox | 8 | 4 | 50.0 | 49 | 6.13 | 0 | 1— | 12.5 | |
| Hansen | 1 | 1 | 100 | 11 | 11.00 | 1 | 0— | 0.0 | |

PUNTING
| Last Name | No. | Avg. |
|---|---|---|
| Hansen | 80 | 42.5 |

KICKING
| Last Name | XP | ATT | % | FG | ATT | % |
|---|---|---|---|---|---|---|
| Stover | 33 | 34 | 97 | 16 | 22 | 73 |

## CINCINNATI BENGALS

### RUSHING
| Last Name | No. | Yds | Avg | TD |
|---|---|---|---|---|
| Green | 158 | 731 | 4.6 | 2 |
| Brooks | 152 | 571 | 3.8 | 2 |
| Taylor | 33 | 153 | 4.6 | 2 |
| Woods | 36 | 97 | 2.7 | 4 |
| Dingle | 21 | 91 | 4.3 | 0 |
| Esiason | 24 | 66 | 2.8 | 0 |
| Hollas | 12 | 66 | 5.5 | 0 |
| Ball | 10 | 21 | 2.1 | 1 |
| Wilhelm | 1 | 9 | 9.0 | 0 |
| Brown | 1 | 8 | 8.0 | 0 |
| Johnson | 1 | -2 | -2.0 | 0 |

### RECEIVING
| Last Name | No. | Yds | Avg | TD |
|---|---|---|---|---|
| Brown | 59 | 827 | 14.0 | 2 |
| McGee | 51 | 802 | 15.7 | 4 |
| Brooks | 40 | 348 | 8.7 | 2 |
| Holman | 31 | 445 | 14.4 | 2 |
| Barber | 23 | 255 | 11.1 | 1 |
| Taylor | 21 | 122 | 5.8 | 0 |
| Green | 16 | 136 | 8.5 | 0 |
| Kattus | 12 | 136 | 11.3 | 0 |
| Rembert | 9 | 117 | 13.0 | 1 |
| James | 7 | 103 | 14.7 | 1 |
| Woods | 6 | 36 | 6.0 | 0 |
| Dingle | 5 | 23 | 4.6 | 1 |
| Riggs | 4 | 14 | 3.5 | 0 |
| Garrett | 3 | 32 | 10.7 | 0 |
| Ball | 3 | 17 | 5.7 | 0 |

### PUNT RETURNS
| Last Name | No. | Yds | Avg | TD |
|---|---|---|---|---|
| Price | 14 | 203 | 14.5 | 1 |
| Barber | 13 | 70 | 5.4 | 0 |
| Garrett | 1 | 7 | 7.0 | 0 |
| James | 1 | 0 | 0.0 | 0 |

### KICKOFF RETURNS
| Last Name | No. | Yds | Avg | TD |
|---|---|---|---|---|
| Ball | 13 | 262 | 20.2 | 0 |
| Garrett | 13 | 214 | 16.5 | 0 |
| Brooks | 11 | 190 | 17.3 | 0 |
| James | 8 | 143 | 17.9 | 0 |
| Dingle | 7 | 176 | 25.1 | 0 |
| Price | 5 | 91 | 18.2 | 0 |
| Green | 4 | 66 | 16.5 | 0 |
| King | 3 | 34 | 11.3 | 0 |
| Riggs | 2 | 28 | 14.0 | 0 |
| Holman | 1 | 15 | 15.0 | 0 |
| Barber | 1 | 7 | 7.0 | 0 |
| Thomas | 1 | -1 | -1.0 | 0 |

### PASSING—PUNTING—KICKING

PASSING
| Last Name | Att | Cmp | % | Yds | Yd/Att | TD | Int— | % | RK |
|---|---|---|---|---|---|---|---|---|---|
| Esiason | 413 | 233 | 56.4 | 2883 | 6.98 | 13 | 16— | 3.9 | 11 |
| Hollas | 55 | 32 | 58.2 | 310 | 5.64 | 1 | 4— | 7.3 | |
| Wilhelm | 42 | 24 | 57.1 | 217 | 5.17 | 0 | 2— | 4.8 | |
| Johnson | 1 | 1 | 100 | 3 | 3.00 | 0 | 0— | 0.0 | |

PUNTING
| Last Name | No. | Avg. |
|---|---|---|
| Johnson | 64 | 43.7 |
| Breech | 1 | 33.0 |

KICKING
| Last Name | XP | ATT | % | FG | ATT | % |
|---|---|---|---|---|---|---|
| Breech | 27 | 27 | 100 | 23 | 29 | 79 |
| Johnson | 0 | 0 | 0 | 1 | 3 | 33 |

# 1991 A.F.C. — Western Division

## DENVER BRONCOS 12-4 Dan Reeves

| Scores of Each Game | | |
|---|---|---|
| 45 | CINCINNATI | 14 |
| 13 | L.A. Raiders | 16 |
| 16 | SEATTLE | 10 |
| 27 | SAN DIEGO | 19 |
| 13 | Minnesota | 6 |
| 14 | Houston | 42 |
| 19 | KANSAS CITY | 16 |
| 9 | New England | 6 |
| 20 | PITTSBURGH | 13 |
| 16 | L.A. RAIDERS | 17 |
| 24 | Kansas City | 20 |
| 10 | Seattle | 13 |
| 20 | NEW ENGLAND | 3 |
| 17 | Cleveland | 7 |
| 24 | PHOENIX | 19 |
| 17 | San Diego | 14 |

| UseName | Pos. | Hgt. | Wgt. | Age | Int | Pts |
|---|---|---|---|---|---|---|
| Jeff Davidson | OT | 6'5" | 309 | 23 | | |
| Darrell Hamilton | OT | 6'5" | 298 | 26 | | |
| Ken Lanier | OT | 6'3" | 290 | 32 | | |
| Harvey Salem | OT | 6'6" | 289 | 30 | | |
| Nick Subis | OT-C | 6'4" | 278 | 23 | | |
| Sean Farrell | OG | 6'3" | 260 | 31 | | |
| Crawford Ker | OG | 6'3" | 285 | 29 | | |
| Dave Widell | OG | 6'6" | 292 | 26 | | |
| Doug Widell | OG | 6'4" | 287 | 24 | | |
| Keith Kartz | C | 6'4" | 270 | 28 | | |
| Alphonso Carreker | DE | 6'6" | 272 | 31 | | |
| Ron Holmes | DE | 6'4" | 265 | 28 | | |
| Warren Powers | DE | 6'6" | 287 | 26 | | 6 |
| Jim Szymanski | DE | 6'5" | 268 | 24 | | |
| Kenny Walker | DE | 6'3" | 260 | 24 | | |
| Greg Kragen | NT | 6'3" | 265 | 29 | | |
| Brian Sochia (from MIA) | NT-DE | 6'3" | 278 | 30 | | |

Jim Juriga — Back Injury

| UseName | Pos. | Hgt. | Wgt. | Age | Int | Pts |
|---|---|---|---|---|---|---|
| Michael Brooks | LB | 6'1" | 235 | 26 | 2 | |
| Mike Croel | LB | 6'3" | 231 | 22 | | |
| Simon Fletcher | LB | 6'5" | 240 | 29 | | |
| Ronnie Haliburton | LB | 6'4" | 230 | 23 | | |
| Tim Lucas | LB | 6'3" | 230 | 30 | | |
| Karl Mecklenburg | LB | 6'3" | 235 | 31 | | |
| Jeff Mills | LB | 6'3" | 238 | 22 | | |
| Mark Murray | LB | 6'2" | 240 | 23 | | |
| Keith Traylor | LB | 6'2" | 260 | 21 | | |
| Steve Atwater | DB | 6'3" | 217 | 24 | 5 | |
| Tyrone Braxton | DB | 5'11" | 185 | 26 | 4 | 6 |
| Kevin Clark | DB | 5'10" | 185 | 27 | | |
| Charles Dimry | DB | 6' | 175 | 25 | 3 | 6 |
| Wymon Henderson | DB | 5'10" | 186 | 29 | 2 | |
| Le-Lo Lang | DB | 5'11" | 185 | 24 | 1 | |
| Alton Montgomery | DB | 6' | 195 | 23 | | |
| Randy Robbins | DB | 6'2" | 189 | 28 | 1 | |
| Dennis Smith | DB | 6'3" | 200 | 32 | 5 | |

| UseName | Pos. | Hgt. | Wgt. | Age | Int | Pts |
|---|---|---|---|---|---|---|
| John Elway | QB | 6'3" | 215 | 31 | | 36 |
| Gary Kubiak | QB | 6' | 192 | 30 | | |
| Gaston Green | HB | 5'11" | 192 | 25 | | 24 |
| Bobby Humphrey | HB | 6'1" | 201 | 24 | | |
| Greg Lewis | HB-FB | 5'10" | 214 | 22 | | 24 |
| Bob Perryman | FB | 6'2" | 233 | 27 | | |
| Reggie Rivers | FB | 6'1" | 215 | 23 | | |
| Steve Sewell | FB-WR | 6'3" | 210 | 28 | | 24 |
| Mark Jackson | WR | 5'10" | 174 | 28 | | 6 |
| Barry Johnson | WR | 6'2" | 197 | 24 | | |
| Vance Johnson | WR | 5'11" | 185 | 28 | | 18 |
| Ricky Nattiel | WR | 5'9" | 180 | 25 | | 12 |
| Derek Russell | WR | 6' | 179 | 22 | | 6 |
| Michael Young | WR | 6'1" | 183 | 29 | | 6 |
| Reggie Johnson | TE | 6'2" | 256 | 23 | | 6 |
| Clarence Kay | TE | 6'2" | 237 | 30 | | |
| Shannon Sharpe | TE-WR | 6'2" | 230 | 23 | | 6 |
| Mike Horan | K | 5'11" | 190 | 32 | | |
| David Treadwell | K | 6'1" | 180 | 24 | | 112 |

## KANSAS CITY CHIEFS 10-6 Marty Schottenheimer

| Scores of Each Game | | |
|---|---|---|
| 14 | ATLANTA | 3 |
| 10 | NEW ORLEANS | 17 |
| 7 | Houston | 17 |
| 20 | SEATTLE | 13 |
| 14 | San Diego | 13 |
| 33 | BUFFALO | 6 |
| 42 | MIAMI | 7 |
| 16 | Denver | 19 |
| 24 | L.A. RAIDERS | 21 |
| 27 | L.A. Rams | 20 |
| 20 | DENVER | 24 |
| 15 | Cleveland | 20 |
| 19 | Seattle | 6 |
| 20 | SAN DIEGO | * 17 |
| 14 | San Francisco | 28 |
| 27 | L.A. Raiders | 21 |

| UseName | Pos. | Hgt. | Wgt. | Age | Int | Pts |
|---|---|---|---|---|---|---|
| John Alt | OT | 6'7" | 296 | 29 | | |
| Rich Baldinger | OT | 6'4" | 293 | 31 | | |
| Derrick Graham | OT | 6'4" | 306 | 24 | | |
| David Lutz | OG | 6'6" | 305 | 31 | | |
| David Szott | OG | 6'4" | 275 | 23 | | |
| Frank Winters | OG-C | 6'3" | 285 | 27 | | |
| Tim Grunhard | C | 6'2" | 299 | 23 | | |
| Mike Bell | DE | 6'4" | 266 | 33 | | |
| Leonard Griffin | DE | 6'4" | 278 | 28 | | |
| Neil Smith | DE | 6'4" | 275 | 25 | | |
| Bill Maas | DE-NT | 6'5" | 275 | 28 | | |
| Dan Saleaumua | NT | 6' | 295 | 26 | | 2 |
| Tom Sims | NT | 6'2" | 285 | 24 | | |
| Pat Swoopes (to MIA) | NT | 6'3" | 277 | 27 | | |

| UseName | Pos. | Hgt. | Wgt. | Age | Int | Pts |
|---|---|---|---|---|---|---|
| Dino Hackett | LB | 6'3" | 230 | 27 | | |
| Chris Martin | LB | 6'2" | 241 | 30 | 1 | 6 |
| Lonnie Marts | LB | 6'1" | 243 | 22 | | |
| Ervin Randle | LB | 6'1" | 250 | 28 | | |
| Tracy Rogers | LB | 6'2" | 241 | 24 | | |
| Tracy Simien | LB | 6'1" | 245 | 24 | | |
| Derrick Thomas | LB | 6'3" | 236 | 24 | | 6 |
| Billy Bell | DB | 5'10" | 161 | 30 | 1 | |
| Lloyd Burruss | DB | 6' | 214 | 33 | 1 | |
| Deron Cherry | DB | 5'11" | 203 | 31 | 4 | |
| Eric Everett | DB | 5'10" | 170 | 25 | | |
| Albert Lewis | DB | 6'2" | 195 | 30 | 3 | |
| Anthony Parker | DB | 5'9" | 175 | 25 | | |
| J.C. Pearson | DB | 5'11" | 186 | 28 | 3 | |
| Kevin Porter | DB | 5'10" | 214 | 25 | | |
| Kevin Ross | DB | 5'9" | 182 | 29 | 1 | |
| Charles Washington | DB | 6'1" | 210 | 23 | 1 | |

Percy Snow — Ankle Injury

| UseName | Pos. | Hgt. | Wgt. | Age | Int | Pts |
|---|---|---|---|---|---|---|
| Steve DeBerg | QB | 6'2" | 217 | 37 | | |
| Mark Vlasic | QB | 6'3" | 205 | 27 | | |
| Kimble Anders | HB | 5'11" | 219 | 24 | | |
| Bill Jones | HB | 5'11" | 227 | 24 | | 6 |
| Todd McNair | HB | 6'1" | 190 | 26 | | 6 |
| Troy Stradford | HB-WR | 5'9" | 194 | 26 | | |
| Harvey Williams | HB | 6'2" | 222 | 24 | | 18 |
| Barry Word | HB | 6'2" | 242 | 27 | | 24 |
| Christian Okoye | FB | 6'1" | 260 | 30 | | 54 |
| James Saxon | FB-HB | 5'11" | 234 | 25 | | |
| Tim Barnett | WR | 6'1" | 209 | 23 | | 30 |
| J.J. Birden | WR | 5'9" | 170 | 26 | | 12 |
| Willie Davis | WR | 6' | 170 | 23 | | |
| Emile Harry | WR | 5'11" | 186 | 28 | | 18 |
| Fred Jones | WR | 5'9" | 182 | 24 | | |
| Stephone Paige | WR | 6'2" | 188 | 29 | | |
| Robb Thomas | WR | 5'11" | 175 | 25 | | 6 |
| Jonathan Hayes | TE | 6'5" | 248 | 29 | | 12 |
| Pete Holohan | TE | 6'4" | 247 | 32 | | 12 |
| Troy Sadowski | TE | 6'5" | 258 | 25 | | |
| Bryan Barker | K | 6'1" | 187 | 27 | | |
| Nick Lowery | K | 6'4" | 205 | 35 | | 10 |

Stump Mitchell — Knee Injury

## LOS ANGELES RAIDERS 9-7 Art Shell

| Scores of Each Game | | |
|---|---|---|
| 17 | Houston | 47 |
| 16 | DENVER | 13 |
| 16 | INDIANAPOLIS | 0 |
| 17 | Atlanta | 21 |
| 12 | SAN FRANCISCO | 6 |
| 13 | SAN DIEGO | 7 |
| 23 | Seattle | * 20 |
| 20 | L.A. RAMS | 17 |
| 21 | Kansas City | 24 |
| 17 | Denver | 16 |
| 31 | SEATTLE | 7 |
| 38 | Cincinnati | 14 |
| 9 | San Diego | 7 |
| 27 | BUFFALO | * 30 |
| 0 | New Orleans | 27 |
| 21 | KANSAS CITY | 27 |

| UseName | Pos. | Hgt. | Wgt. | Age | Int | Pts |
|---|---|---|---|---|---|---|
| James FitzPatrick | OT-OG | 6'8" | 320 | 27 | | |
| Rory Graves | OT | 6'6" | 295 | 28 | | |
| Joel Patten | OT | 6'7" | 290 | 33 | | |
| Bruce Wilkerson | OT | 6'5" | 295 | 27 | | |
| Steve Wright | OT-TE | 6'6" | 280 | 32 | | |
| Reggie McElroy | OG-OT | 6'6" | 295 | 31 | | |
| Max Montoya | OG | 6'5" | 295 | 35 | | |
| Steve Wisniewski | OG | 6'4" | 285 | 24 | | |
| Don Mosebar | C | 6'6" | 285 | 29 | | |
| Dan Turk | C | 6'4" | 270 | 29 | | |
| Nolan Harrison | DE-DT | 6'5" | 290 | 22 | | |
| A.J. Jimerson | DE-LB | 6'3" | 235 | 23 | | |
| Howie Long | DE | 6'5" | 270 | 31 | | |
| Anthony Smith | DE | 6'3" | 265 | 24 | | |
| Greg Townsend | DE | 6'3" | 265 | 29 | 1 | |
| Scott Davis | DT-DE | 6'7" | 275 | 26 | | |
| Bob Golic | DT | 6'2" | 275 | 33 | | |
| Roy Hart | DT | 6' | 285 | 26 | | |

| UseName | Pos. | Hgt. | Wgt. | Age | Int | Pts |
|---|---|---|---|---|---|---|
| Thomas Benson | LB | 6'2" | 240 | 29 | 1 | |
| Riki Ellison | LB | 6'2" | 225 | 31 | | |
| Mike Jones | LB | 6'1" | 225 | 22 | | |
| Winston Moss | LB | 6'3" | 240 | 25 | | |
| Jerry Robinson | LB | 6'2" | 230 | 34 | | |
| Aaron Wallace | LB | 6'3" | 235 | 24 | | |
| Eddie Anderson | DB | 6'1" | 210 | 28 | 2 | |
| Derrick Crudup | DB | 6'2" | 220 | 26 | | |
| Torin Dorn | DB | 6' | 190 | 23 | | 2 |
| Dan Land | DB | 6' | 196 | 26 | 1 | |
| Garry Lewis | DB | 5'11" | 180 | 24 | | |
| Ronnie Lott | DB | 6' | 205 | 32 | 8 | |
| Terry McDaniel | DB | 5'10" | 180 | 26 | | |
| Elvis Patterson | DB | 5'11" | 195 | 30 | | 6 |
| Lionel Washington | DB | 6' | 185 | 30 | 5 | |

| UseName | Pos. | Hgt. | Wgt. | Age | Int | Pts |
|---|---|---|---|---|---|---|
| Vince Evans | QB | 6'2" | 210 | 36 | | |
| Todd Marinovich | QB | 6'4" | 215 | 22 | | |
| Jay Schroeder | QB | 6'4" | 210 | 30 | | |
| Marcus Allen | HB | 6'2' | 210 | 31 | | 12 |
| Nick Bell | HB | 6'2" | 255 | 23 | | 18 |
| Roger Craig | HB | 6' | 215 | 31 | | 6 |
| Napoleon McCallum | HB | 6'2" | 225 | 27 | | 6 |
| Marcus Wilson | HB | 6'1" | 200 | 23 | | |
| Doug Lloyd | FB | 6'1" | 220 | 26 | | |
| Steve Smith | FB | 6'1" | 240 | 27 | | 12 |
| Tim Brown | WR | 6' | 190 | 25 | | 36 |
| Mervyn Fernandez | WR | 6'3" | 200 | 31 | | 6 |
| Willie Gault | WR | 6' | 175 | 30 | | 24 |
| Sam Graddy | WR | 5'10" | 180 | 27 | | 6 |
| Jamie Holland | WR | 6'2" | 195 | 27 | | |
| Andrew Glover | TE | 6'6" | 245 | 24 | | 18 |
| Ethan Horton | TE | 6'4" | 240 | 28 | | 30 |
| Jeff Gossett | K | 6'2" | 195 | 34 | | |
| Jeff Jaeger | K | 5'11" | 195 | 26 | | 116 |

Vance Mueller — Knee Injury
Mike Dyal — Hamstring Injury

## SEATTLE SEAHAWKS 7-9 Chuck Knox

| Scores of Each Game | | |
|---|---|---|
| 24 | New Orleans | 27 |
| 20 | N.Y. JETS | 13 |
| 10 | Denver | 16 |
| 13 | Kansas City | 20 |
| 31 | INDIANAPOLIS | 3 |
| 13 | Cincinnati | 7 |
| 20 | L.A. RAIDERS | * 23 |
| 27 | Pittsburgh | 7 |
| 20 | SAN DIEGO | 9 |
| 14 | San Diego | 17 |
| 7 | L.A. Raiders | 31 |
| 13 | DENVER | 10 |
| 6 | KANSAS CITY | 19 |
| 22 | SAN FRANCISCO | 24 |
| 13 | Atlanta | 26 |
| 23 | L.A. RAMS | 9 |

| UseName | Pos. | Hgt. | Wgt. | Age | Int | Pts |
|---|---|---|---|---|---|---|
| Andy Heck | OT | 6'6" | 289 | 24 | | |
| Bill Hitchcock | OT | 6'6" | 291 | 24 | | |
| Ronnie Lee | OT | 6'3" | 296 | 34 | | |
| Edwin Bailey | OG | 6'4" | 284 | 32 | | |
| Darrick Brilz | OG | 6'3" | 287 | 27 | | |
| Bryan Millard | OG | 6'5" | 277 | 30 | | |
| Curt Singer | OG | 6'5" | 281 | 29 | | |
| Warren Wheat | OG | 6'6" | 286 | 24 | | |
| Grant Feasel | C | 6'7" | 283 | 31 | | |
| Jeff Bryant | DT-DE | 6'5" | 281 | 31 | | |
| Jacob Green | DE | 6'3" | 263 | 34 | 1 | |
| Jim Skow | DE | 6'3" | 250 | 28 | | |
| Tony Woods | DE | 6'4" | 269 | 25 | | |
| Eric Hayes | DT | 6'3" | 288 | 23 | | |
| Cortez Kennedy | DT | 6'3" | 293 | 23 | | |
| Joe Nash | DT | 6'2" | 278 | 30 | | |

Joe Tofflemire — Back Injury

| UseName | Pos. | Hgt. | Wgt. | Age | Int | Pts |
|---|---|---|---|---|---|---|
| Joe Cain | LB | 6'1" | 233 | 26 | 1 | |
| Darren Comeaux | LB | 6'1" | 239 | 31 | | |
| Marcus Cotton | LB | 6'3" | 233 | 25 | | |
| Richard Newbill | LB | 6'1" | 240 | 23 | | |
| Rufus Porter | LB | 6'1" | 227 | 26 | 1 | |
| Rod Stephens | LB | 6'1" | 237 | 25 | | |
| Terry Wooden | LB | 6'3" | 236 | 24 | | |
| David Wyman | LB | 6'2" | 248 | 27 | | |
| Robert Blackmon | DB | 6' | 197 | 24 | 3 | |
| Brian Davis | DB | 6'2" | 187 | 28 | 1 | 6 |
| Dedrick Dodge | DB | 6'2" | 184 | 24 | | |
| Nesby Glasgow | DB | 5'10" | 187 | 34 | 1 | |
| Dwayne Harper | DB | 5'11" | 174 | 25 | 4 | |
| Patrick Hunter | DB | 5'11" | 186 | 26 | 1 | 6 |
| James Jefferson | DB | 6'1" | 199 | 27 | | |
| Eugene Robinson | DB | 6' | 191 | 28 | 5 | |

Vann McElroy — Ankle Injury

| UseName | Pos. | Hgt. | Wgt. | Age | Int | Pts |
|---|---|---|---|---|---|---|
| Jeff Kemp (to PHIL) | QB | 6' | 198 | 32 | | |
| Dave Krieg | QB | 6'1" | 192 | 32 | | |
| Dan McGwire | QB | 6'8" | 243 | 23 | | |
| Kelly Stouffer | QB | 6'3" | 214 | 27 | | |
| Derrick Fenner | HB | 6'3" | 228 | 24 | | 24 |
| Derek Loville | HB | 5'9" | 198 | 23 | | |
| Chris Warren | HB | 6'2" | 225 | 24 | | 6 |
| James Jones | FB | 6'2" | 232 | 30 | | 18 |
| John L. Williams | FB | 5'11" | 231 | 26 | | 30 |
| Brian Blades | WR | 5'11" | 189 | 26 | | 12 |
| Jeff Chadwick | WR | 6'3" | 189 | 30 | | 18 |
| Louis Clark | WR | 6'1" | 198 | 27 | | 12 |
| David Daniels | WR | 6'1" | 190 | 21 | | |
| Tommy Kane | WR | 5'11" | 181 | 27 | | 12 |
| Paul Skansi | WR | 5'11" | 184 | 30 | | |
| Doug Thomas | WR | 5'10" | 178 | 21 | | |
| Trey Junkin | TE | 6'2" | 237 | 30 | | |
| Travis McNeal | TE | 6'3" | 244 | 24 | | 6 |
| Mike Tice | TE | 6'7" | 249 | 32 | | 24 |
| Rick Donnelly | K | 6' | 209 | 29 | | |
| John Kasay | K | 5'10" | 189 | 21 | | 102 |
| Rick Tuten | K | 6'2" | 218 | 26 | | |
| Alex Waits | K | 6'2" | 208 | 23 | | |

## SAN DIEGO CHARGERS 4-12 Dan Henning

| Scores of Each Game | | |
|---|---|---|
| 20 | Pittsburgh | 26 |
| 14 | San Francisco | 34 |
| 10 | ATLANTA | 13 |
| 19 | Denver | 27 |
| 13 | KANSAS CITY | 14 |
| 21 | L.A. Raiders | 13 |
| 24 | L.A. Rams | 30 |
| 24 | CLEVELAND | * 30 |
| 9 | Seattle | 20 |
| 17 | SEATTLE | 14 |
| 24 | NEW ORLEANS | 21 |
| 3 | N.Y. Jets | 13 |
| 7 | L.A. RAIDERS | 9 |
| 17 | Kansas City | * 20 |
| 38 | MIAMI | 30 |
| 14 | DENVER | 17 |

| UseName | Pos. | Hgt. | Wgt. | Age | Int | Pts |
|---|---|---|---|---|---|---|
| Leo Goeas | OT-OG | 6'4" | 292 | 25 | | |
| Harry Swayne | OT | 6'5" | 290 | 26 | | |
| Broderick Thompson | OT | 6'5" | 295 | 31 | | |
| Eric Floyd | OG-OT | 6'5" | 310 | 25 | | |
| Mark May | OG-OT | 6'6" | 296 | 31 | | |
| Eric Moten | OG | 6'2" | 306 | 23 | | |
| David Richards | OG | 6'5" | 310 | 25 | | |
| Mike Zandofsky | OG | 6'2" | 305 | 25 | | |
| Frank Cornish | C-OG | 6'4" | 289 | 23 | | |
| Courtney Hall | C | 6'2" | 281 | 23 | | |
| Mark Rodenhauser | C | 6'5" | 283 | 30 | | |
| Burt Grossman | DE | 6'6" | 255 | 24 | | |
| George Hinkle | DE | 6'5" | 269 | 26 | | |
| Mitchell Benson | NT-DT | 6'4" | 300 | 24 | | |
| Joe Phillips | NT | 6'5" | 315 | 28 | | |
| George Thornton | NT-DT | 6'3" | 300 | 23 | | |

| UseName | Pos. | Hgt. | Wgt. | Age | Int | Pts |
|---|---|---|---|---|---|---|
| Greg Clark (from GB) | LB | 6' | 226 | 26 | | |
| David Grayson | LB | 6'3" | 233 | 27 | | |
| Randy Kirk | LB | 6'2" | 230 | 26 | | |
| Leslie O'Neal | LB | 6'4" | 259 | 27 | | |
| Gary Plummer | LB | 6'2" | 244 | 31 | | |
| Henry Rolling | LB | 6'2" | 225 | 25 | 2 | |
| Junior Seau | LB | 6'3" | 250 | 22 | | |
| Billy Ray Smith | LB | 6'3" | 236 | 30 | 2 | |
| Galand Thaxton | LB | 6'1" | 240 | 26 | | |
| Mike Wilcher | LB | 6'3" | 245 | 31 | | |
| Martin Bayless | DB | 6'2" | 212 | 28 | 1 | |
| Gill Byrd | DB | 5'11" | 198 | 30 | 6 | |
| Darren Carrington | DB | 6'2" | 200 | 24 | 3 | |
| Donnie Elder | DB | 5'9" | 178 | 27 | 1 | |
| Floyd Fields | DB | 6' | 208 | 22 | | |
| Donald Frank | DB | 6' | 192 | 25 | 1 | 6 |
| Cedric Mack | DB | 5'11" | 190 | 30 | | |
| Stanley Richard | DB | 6'2" | 197 | 23 | 2 | |
| Sam Seale | DB | 5'9" | 185 | 28 | | |
| Anthony Shelton | DB | 6'1" | 195 | 23 | 1 | |

| UseName | Pos. | Hgt. | Wgt. | Age | Int | Pts |
|---|---|---|---|---|---|---|
| John Friesz | QB | 6'4" | 218 | 24 | | |
| Bob Gagliano | QB | 6'3" | 205 | 32 | | |
| Rod Bernstine | HB-FB | 6'3" | 238 | 26 | | 48 |
| Eric Bieniemy | HB | 5'7" | 210 | 22 | | |
| Ronnie Harmon | HB | 5'11" | 207 | 27 | | 12 |
| Chris Samuels | HB-FB | 5'10" | 202 | 22 | | |
| Marion Butts | FB-HB | 6'1" | 248 | 25 | | 42 |
| Shawn Jefferson | WR | 5'11" | 172 | 22 | | 6 |
| Nate Lewis | WR | 5'11" | 198 | 24 | | 24 |
| Anthony Miller | WR | 5'11" | 189 | 26 | | 18 |
| Kitrick Taylor | WR | 5'10" | 191 | 27 | | |
| Yancey Thigpen | WR | 6'1" | 208 | 22 | | |
| Steve Hendrickson | TE-FB | 6' | 258 | 25 | | 12 |
| Derrick Walker | TE | 6'1" | 250 | 24 | | |
| Arthur Cox (to MIA, CLE) | TE | 6'2" | 277 | 30 | | |
| Craig McEwen | TE | 6'1" | 226 | 25 | | 18 |
| Mark Walczak | TE | 6'6" | 246 | 29 | | |
| Duane Young | TE | 6'1" | 276 | 23 | | |
| John Carney | K | 5'11" | 170 | 27 | | 88 |
| John Kidd | K | 6'3" | 208 | 30 | | |

## DENVER BRONCOS

### RUSHING

| Last Name | No. | Yds | Avg | TD |
|---|---|---|---|---|
| Green | 261 | 1037 | 4.0 | 4 |
| Lewis | 99 | 376 | 3.8 | 4 |
| Elway | 54 | 258 | 4.8 | 6 |
| Sewell | 50 | 211 | 4.2 | 2 |
| Perryman | 21 | 45 | 2.1 | 0 |
| Humphrey | 11 | 33 | 3.0 | 0 |
| Jackson | 2 | 18 | 9.0 | 0 |
| Sharpe | 1 | 15 | 15.0 | 0 |
| Kubiak | 3 | 11 | 3.7 | 0 |
| Horan | 2 | 9 | 4.5 | 0 |
| Rivers | 2 | 5 | 2.5 | 0 |

### RECEIVING

| Last Name | No. | Yds | Avg | TD |
|---|---|---|---|---|
| Young | 44 | 629 | 14.3 | 2 |
| Sewell | 38 | 436 | 11.5 | 2 |
| Jackson | 33 | 603 | 18.3 | 1 |
| Sharpe | 22 | 322 | 14.6 | 1 |
| Russell | 21 | 317 | 15.1 | 1 |
| V. Johnson | 21 | 208 | 9.9 | 3 |
| Perryman | 17 | 171 | 10.1 | 0 |
| Nattiel | 16 | 288 | 18.0 | 2 |
| Green | 13 | 78 | 6.0 | 0 |
| Kay | 11 | 139 | 12.6 | 0 |
| R. Johnson | 6 | 73 | 12.2 | 1 |
| Lewis | 2 | 9 | 4.5 | 0 |
| Elway | 1 | 24 | 24.0 | 0 |
| B. Johnson | 1 | 13 | 13.0 | 0 |

### PUNT RETURNS

| Last Name | No. | Yds | Avg | TD |
|---|---|---|---|---|
| V. Johnson | 24 | 174 | 7.3 | 0 |
| Nattiel | 10 | 43 | 4.3 | 0 |
| Clark | 7 | 67 | 9.6 | 0 |

### KICKOFF RETURNS

| Last Name | No. | Yds | Avg | TD |
|---|---|---|---|---|
| Montgomery | 26 | 488 | 18.8 | 0 |
| Russell | 7 | 120 | 17.1 | 0 |
| Clark | 2 | 45 | 22.5 | 0 |
| Lewis | 1 | 20 | 20.0 | 0 |
| Sewell | 1 | 14 | 14.0 | 0 |

### PASSING—PUNTING—KICKING

| PASSING | Att | Cmp | % | Yds | Yd/Att | TD | Int— | % | RK |
|---|---|---|---|---|---|---|---|---|---|
| Elway | 451 | 242 | 53.7 | 3253 | 7.21 | 13 | 12— | 2.7 | 9 |
| Kubiak | 5 | 3 | 60.0 | 33 | 6.60 | 0 | 0— | 0.0 | |
| Sewell | 3 | 1 | 33.0 | 24 | 8.00 | 0 | 0— | 0.0 | |

| PUNTING | No. | Avg. |
|---|---|---|
| Horan | 72 | 41.3 |
| Elway | 1 | 34.0 |

| KICKING | XP | ATT | % | FG | ATT | % |
|---|---|---|---|---|---|---|
| Treadwell | 31 | 32 | 97 | 27 | 36 | 75 |

## KANSAS CITY CHIEFS

### RUSHING

| Last Name | No. | Yds | Avg | TD |
|---|---|---|---|---|
| Okoye | 225 | 1031 | 4.6 | 9 |
| Word | 160 | 684 | 4.3 | 4 |
| Williams | 97 | 447 | 4.6 | 1 |
| McNair | 10 | 51 | 5.1 | 0 |
| Saxon | 6 | 13 | 2.2 | 0 |
| Stradford | 1 | 7 | 7.0 | 0 |
| Vlasic | 1 | -1 | -1.0 | 0 |
| DeBerg | 21 | -15 | -0.7 | 0 |

### RECEIVING

| Last Name | No. | Yds | Avg | TD |
|---|---|---|---|---|
| R. Thomas | 43 | 495 | 11.5 | 1 |
| Barnett | 41 | 564 | 13.8 | 5 |
| McNair | 37 | 342 | 36 | 1 |
| Harry | 35 | 431 | 12.3 | 3 |
| Birden | 27 | 465 | 17.2 | 2 |
| Hayes | 19 | 208 | 10.9 | 2 |
| Williams | 16 | 147 | 9.2 | 2 |
| B. Jones | 14 | 97 | 6.9 | 1 |
| Holohan | 13 | 113 | 8.7 | 2 |
| Saxon | 6 | 55 | 9.2 | 0 |
| Paige | 9 | 111 | 12.3 | 0 |
| Okoye | 3 | 34 | 11.3 | 0 |
| Stradford | 9 | 91 | 10.1 | 0 |
| Anders | 2 | 30 | 15.0 | 0 |
| F. Jones | 8 | 85 | 10.6 | 0 |
| Word | 2 | 13 | 6.5 | 0 |

### PUNT RETURNS

| Last Name | No. | Yds | Avg | TD |
|---|---|---|---|---|
| Stradford | 22 | 150 | 6.8 | 0 |
| F. Jones | 12 | 108 | 9.0 | 0 |

### KICKOFF RETURNS

| Last Name | No. | Yds | Avg | TD |
|---|---|---|---|---|
| Williams | 24 | 524 | 21.8 | 0 |
| Stradford | 14 | 292 | 20.9 | 0 |
| McNair | 4 | 66 | 16.5 | 0 |
| Saxon | 4 | 56 | 14.0 | 0 |
| F. Jones | 2 | 40 | 20.0 | 0 |

### PASSING—PUNTING—KICKING

| PASSING | Att | Cmp | % | Yds | Yd/Att | TD | Int— | % | RK |
|---|---|---|---|---|---|---|---|---|---|
| DeBerg | 434 | 256 | 59.0 | 2965 | 6.83 | 17 | 14— | 3.2 | 6 |
| Vlasic | 44 | 28 | 63.6 | 316 | 7.18 | 2 | 0— | 0.0 | |
| Williams | 1 | 0 | 0.0 | 0 | 0.00 | 0 | 0— | 0.0 | |

| PUNTING | No. | Avg. |
|---|---|---|
| Barker | 57 | 40.4 |

| KICKING | XP | Att. | % | FG | Att | % |
|---|---|---|---|---|---|---|
| Lowery | 35 | 35 | 100 | 25 | 30 | 83 |

## LOS ANGELES RAIDERS

### RUSHING

| Last Name | No. | Yds | Avg | TD |
|---|---|---|---|---|
| Craig | 162 | 590 | 3.5 | 1 |
| Bell | 78 | 307 | 3.9 | 3 |
| Allen | 63 | 287 | 4.6 | 2 |
| S. Smith | 62 | 265 | 4.3 | 1 |
| McCallum | 31 | 110 | 3.5 | 1 |
| Schroeder | 28 | 76 | 2.7 | 0 |
| Wilson | 6 | 21 | 3.5 | 0 |
| Evans | 8 | 20 | 2.5 | 0 |
| Brown | 5 | 16 | 3.2 | 0 |
| Marinovich | 3 | 14 | 4.7 | 0 |

### RECEIVING

| Last Name | No. | Yds | Avg | TD |
|---|---|---|---|---|
| Horton | 53 | 650 | 12.3 | 5 |
| Fernandez | 46 | 694 | 15.1 | 1 |
| Brown | 36 | 554 | 15.4 | 5 |
| Gault | 20 | 346 | 17.3 | 4 |
| Craig | 17 | 136 | 8.0 | 0 |
| Allen | 15 | 131 | 8.7 | 0 |
| S. Smith | 15 | 130 | 8.7 | 1 |
| Graddy | 6 | 195 | 32.5 | 1 |
| Bell | 6 | 62 | 10.3 | 0 |
| Glover | 5 | 45 | 9.0 | 5 |
| Patterson | 1 | 34 | 34.0 | 0 |

### PUNT RETURNS

| Last Name | No. | Yds | Avg | TD |
|---|---|---|---|---|
| T. Brown | 29 | 330 | 11.4 | 1 |

### KICKOFF RETURNS

| Last Name | No. | Yds | Avg | TD |
|---|---|---|---|---|
| Holland | 22 | 421 | 19.1 | 0 |
| Graddy | 22 | 373 | 17.0 | 0 |
| McCallum | 5 | 105 | 21.0 | 0 |
| Brown | 1 | 29 | 29.0 | 0 |
| S. Smith | 1 | 0 | 0.0 | 0 |
| Turk | 1 | 0 | 0.0 | 0 |

### PASSING—PUNTING—KICKING

| PASSING | Att | Cmp | % | Yds | Yd/Att | TD | Int— | % | RK |
|---|---|---|---|---|---|---|---|---|---|
| Schroeder | 356 | 189 | 53.1 | 2562 | 7.20 | 15 | 16— | 4.2 | 13 |
| Marinovich | 40 | 23 | 57.5 | 243 | 6.08 | 3 | 0— | 0.0 | |
| Evans | 14 | 6 | 42.9 | 127 | 7.07 | 1 | 2— | 14.3 | |
| Allen | 2 | 1 | 50.0 | 11 | 5.50 | 1 | 0— | 0.0 | |
| Gossett | 1 | 1 | 100.0 | 34 | 34.00 | 0 | 0— | 0.0 | |

| PUNTING | No. | Avg. |
|---|---|---|
| Gossett | 67 | 44.2 |

| KICKING | XP | ATT | % | FG | ATT | % |
|---|---|---|---|---|---|---|
| Jaeger | 29 | 30 | 97 | 29 | 34 | 85 |

## SEATTLE SEAHAWKS

### RUSHING

| Last Name | No. | Yds | Avg | TD |
|---|---|---|---|---|
| Williams | 188 | 741 | 3.9 | 4 |
| Fenner | 91 | 267 | 2.9 | 4 |
| Jones | 45 | 154 | 3.4 | 3 |
| Kemp | 38 | 179 | 4.7 | 0 |
| Loville | 22 | 69 | 3.1 | 0 |
| Krieg | 13 | 59 | 4.5 | 0 |
| Blades | 2 | 17 | 8.5 | 0 |
| Warren | 11 | 13 | 1.2 | 0 |

### RECEIVING

| Last Name | No. | Yds | Avg | TD |
|---|---|---|---|---|
| Blades | 70 | 1003 | 14.3 | 2 |
| Williams | 61 | 499 | 8.2 | 1 |
| Kane | 50 | 763 | 15.3 | 2 |
| Chadwick | 22 | 255 | 11.6 | 3 |
| L. Clark | 21 | 228 | 10.9 | 2 |
| McNeal | 17 | 208 | 12.2 | 1 |
| Fenner | 11 | 72 | 6.5 | 0 |
| Jones | 10 | 103 | 10.3 | 0 |
| Tice | 10 | 70 | 7.0 | 4 |
| Skansi | 9 | 96 | 10.7 | 0 |
| Daniels | 4 | 38 | 9.5 | 0 |
| Thomas | 3 | 27 | 9.0 | 0 |
| Warren | 2 | 9 | 4.5 | 0 |

### PUNT RETURNS

| Last Name | No. | Yds | Avg | TD |
|---|---|---|---|---|
| Warren | 32 | 298 | 9.3 | 1 |
| Loville | 3 | 16 | 5.3 | 0 |
| Harper | 1 | 5 | 5.0 | 0 |
| Skansi | 1 | 5 | 5.0 | 0 |
| B. Davis | 1 | 1 | 1.0 | 0 |

### KICKOFF RETURNS

| Last Name | No. | Yds | Avg | TD |
|---|---|---|---|---|
| Warren | 35 | 792 | 22.6 | 0 |
| Loville | 18 | 412 | 22.9 | 0 |
| McNeal | 4 | 30 | 7.5 | 0 |
| Tice | 3 | 46 | 15.3 | 0 |

### PASSING—PUNTING—KICKING

| PASSING | Att | Cmp | % | Yds | Yd/Att | TD | Int— | % | RK |
|---|---|---|---|---|---|---|---|---|---|
| Krieg | 285 | 187 | 65.6 | 2080 | 7.30 | 11 | 12— | 4.2 | 4 |
| Kemp | 295 | 151 | 51.2 | 1753 | 5.94 | 9 | 17— | 5.8 | 18 |
| Stouffer | 15 | 6 | 40.0 | 57 | 3.80 | 0 | 1— | 6.7 | |
| McGwire | 7 | 3 | 42.9 | 27 | 3.86 | 0 | 1— | 14.3 | |

| PUNTING | No. | Avg. |
|---|---|---|
| Donnelley | 13 | 38.8 |
| Tuten | 49 | 43.0 |
| Waits | 14 | 33.9 |

| KICKING | XP | ATT | % | FG | ATT | % |
|---|---|---|---|---|---|---|
| Kasay | 27 | 28 | 96 | 25 | 31 | 81 |

## SAN DIEGO CHARGERS

### RUSHING

| Last Name | No. | Yds | Avg | TD |
|---|---|---|---|---|
| Butts | 193 | 834 | 4.3 | 6 |
| Bernstine | 159 | 766 | 4.8 | 8 |
| Harmon | 89 | 544 | 6.1 | 1 |
| Jefferson | 1 | 27 | 27.0 | 0 |
| Gagliano | 3 | 19 | 6.3 | 0 |
| Friesz | 10 | 18 | 1.8 | 0 |
| Bieniemy | 3 | 17 | 5.7 | 0 |
| Lewis | 3 | 10 | 3.3 | 0 |
| Samuels | 2 | 10 | 5.0 | 0 |
| Hendrickson | 1 | 3 | 3.0 | 0 |

### RECEIVING

| Last Name | No. | Yds | Avg | TD |
|---|---|---|---|---|
| Harmon | 59 | 555 | 9.4 | 1 |
| Miller | 44 | 649 | 14.8 | 3 |
| Lewis | 42 | 554 | 13.2 | 3 |
| McEwen | 37 | 399 | 10.8 | 3 |
| Taylor | 24 | 218 | 9.1 | 0 |
| Walker | 20 | 134 | 6.7 | 0 |
| Jefferson | 12 | 125 | 10.4 | 1 |
| Bernstine | 11 | 124 | 11.3 | 0 |
| Butts | 10 | 91 | 9.1 | 1 |
| Cox | 5 | 53 | 10.6 | 0 |
| Hendrickson | 4 | 36 | 9.0 | 1 |
| Samuels | 2 | 33 | 16.5 | 0 |
| Young | 2 | 12 | 6.0 | 0 |

### PUNT RETURNS

| Last Name | No. | Yds | Avg | TD |
|---|---|---|---|---|
| Taylor | 28 | 269 | 9.6 | 0 |
| Lewis | 5 | 59 | 11.8 | 0 |

### KICKOFF RETURNS

| Last Name | No. | Yds | Avg | TD |
|---|---|---|---|---|
| Lewis | 23 | 578 | 25.1 | 1 |
| Elder | 27 | 535 | 19.8 | 0 |
| Harmon | 2 | 25 | 12.5 | 0 |
| Bernstine | 1 | 7 | 7.0 | 0 |
| Benson | 1 | 2 | 2.0 | 0 |
| Butts | 1 | 0 | 0.0 | 0 |
| Carrington | 0 | 24 | — | 0 |

### PASSING—PUNTING—KICKING

| PASSING | Att | Cmp | % | Yds | Yd/Att | TD | Int— | % | RK |
|---|---|---|---|---|---|---|---|---|---|
| Friesz | 487 | 262 | 53.8 | 2896 | 5.95 | 12 | 15— | 3.1 | 14 |
| Gagliano | 23 | 9 | 39.1 | 76 | 3.30 | 1 | 1— | 4.3 | |
| Bernstine | 1 | 1 | 100.0 | 11 | 11.00 | 1 | 0— | 0.0 | |

| PUNTING | No. | Avg. |
|---|---|---|
| Kidd | 77 | 39.8 |

| KICKING | XP | Att | % | FG | Att | % |
|---|---|---|---|---|---|---|
| Carney | 31 | 31 | 100 | 19 | 29 | 66 |

December 28, 1991 at Kansas City (Attendance 75,827)

## SCORING

| | | | | | |
|---|---|---|---|---|---|
| L.A. RAIDERS | 0 | 3 | 3 | 0 - | 6 |
| KANSAS CITY | 0 | 7 | 0 | 3 - | 10 |

**Second Quarter**
K.C. — Jones, 11 yard pass from DeBerg
PAT — Lowery (kick)
L.A.Rd. — Jaeger, 32 yard field goal

**Third Quarter**
L.A.Rd. — Jaeger, 26 yard field goal

**Fourth Quarter**
K.C. — Lowery, 18 yard field goal

December 29, 1991 at Houston (Attendance 61,485)

## SCORING

| | | | | | |
|---|---|---|---|---|---|
| N.Y. JETS | 0 | 10 | 0 | 0 - | 10 |
| HOUSTON | 7 | 7 | 0 | 3 - | 17 |

**First Quarter**
Hou. — Givins, 5 yard pass from Moon
PAT — Del Greco (kick)

**Second Quarter**
NYJ — Toon, 10 yard pass from O'Brien
PAT — Allegre (kick)
Hou. — Givins, 20 yard pass from Moon
PAT — Del Greco (kick)
NYJ — Allegre, 33 yard field goal

**Fourth Quarter**
Hou. — Del Greco, 53 yard field goal

## TEAM STATISTICS

| L.A.Rd. | | K.C. |
|---|---|---|
| 16 | First Downs- Total | 16 |
| 7 | First Downs- Rushing | 10 |
| 7 | First Downs- Passing | 5 |
| 2 | First Downs- Penalty | 1 |
| 2 | Fumbles- Number | 2 |
| 2 | Fumbles- Lost Ball | 1 |
| 9 | Penalties- Number | 3 |
| 75 | Yards Penalized | 20 |
| 0 | Missed Field Goals | 2 |
| 55 | Offensive Plays | 55 |
| 276 | Net Yards | 204 |
| 5.0 | Average Gain | 3.7 |
| 6 | Giveaways | 2 |
| 2 | Takeaways | 6 |
| -4 | Difference | +4 |

## TEAM STATISTICS

| NYJ | | HOU. |
|---|---|---|
| 18 | First Downs- Total | 21 |
| 1 | First Downs- Rushing | 5 |
| 4 | First Downs- Passing | 15 |
| 3 | First Downs- Penalty | 1 |
| 0 | Fumbles- Number | 3 |
| 0 | Fumbles- Lost Ball | 1 |
| 5 | Penalties- Number | 8 |
| 45 | Yards Penalized | 55 |
| 0 | Missed Field Goals | 1 |
| 55 | Offensive Plays | 64 |
| 285 | Net Yards | 303 |
| 5.2 | Average Gain | 4.7 |
| 3 | Giveaways | 2 |
| 2 | Takeaways | 3 |
| -1 | Difference | +1 |

## INDIVIDUAL STATISTICS

### L.A. RAIDERS / KANSAS CITY

**RUSHING**

| | No. | Yds. | Avg. | | No. | Yds. | Avg. |
|---|---|---|---|---|---|---|---|
| Bell | 20 | 107 | 5.4 | Word | 33 | 130 | 3.9 |
| Allen | 7 | 39 | 5.6 | H. Williams | 2 | 4 | 2.0 |
| S. Smith | 3 | 6 | 2.0 | Okoye | 1 | 2 | 2.0 |
| | 30 | 152 | 5.1 | DeBerg | 3 | -5 | -1.7 |
| | | | | | 39 | 131 | 3.4 |

**RECEIVING**

| | No. | Yds. | Avg. | | No. | Yds. | Avg. |
|---|---|---|---|---|---|---|---|
| T. Brown | 4 | 45 | 11.3 | R. Thomas | 3 | 18 | 6.0 |
| Horton | 3 | 59 | 19.7 | B. Jones | 2 | 25 | 12.5 |
| Fernandez | 2 | 12 | 6.0 | F. Jones | 2 | 20 | 10.0 |
| Gault | 1 | 11 | 11.0 | Birden | 1 | 18 | 18.0 |
| S. Smith | 1 | 9 | 9.0 | Word | 1 | 8 | 8.0 |
| Allen | 1 | 4 | 4.0 | | 9 | 89 | 9.9 |
| | 12 | 140 | 11.7 | | | | |

**PUNTING**

| | | | | | | | |
|---|---|---|---|---|---|---|---|
| BGossett | 1 | | 20.0 | Barker | 2 | | 46.0 |

**PUNT RETURNS**

| | | | |
|---|---|---|---|
| T. Brown | 2 | 23 | 11.5 |

**KICKOFF RETURNS**

| | | | | | | | |
|---|---|---|---|---|---|---|---|
| Holland | 3 | 46 | 15.3 | Stradford | 2 | 33 | 16.5 |

**INTERCEPTION RETURNS**

| | | | | | | | |
|---|---|---|---|---|---|---|---|
| Lott | 1 | 35 | 35.0 | Cherry | 2 | 46 | 23.0 |
| | | | | Everett | 1 | 23 | 23.0 |
| | | | | Marts | 1 | 7 | 7.0 |
| | | | | | 4 | 76 | 19.0 |

**PASSING**

### L.A. RAIDERS

| | Att. | Comp. | Comp. Pct. | Yds. | Int. | Yds./Att. | Yds./Comp. |
|---|---|---|---|---|---|---|---|
| Marinovich | 23 | 12 | 52.2 | 140 | 4 | 6.1 | 11.7 |

### KANSAS CITY

| | Att. | Comp. | Comp. Pct. | Yds. | Int. | Yds./Att. | Yds./Comp. |
|---|---|---|---|---|---|---|---|
| DeBerg | 14 | 9 | 64.3 | 89 | 1 | 6.4 | 9.9 |

## INDIVIDUAL STATISTICS

### N.Y. JETS / HOUSTON

**RUSHING**

| | No. | Yds. | Avg. | | No. | Yds. | Avg. |
|---|---|---|---|---|---|---|---|
| Hector | 12 | 46 | 3.8 | White | 17 | 65 | 3.8 |
| Baxter | 5 | 14 | 2.8 | Moon | 3 | 6 | 2.0 |
| O'Brien | 2 | 10 | 5.0 | | 20 | 71 | 3.6 |
| McNeil | 4 | 1 | 0.3 | | | | |
| | 23 | 71 | 3.1 | | | | |

**RECEIVING**

| | No. | Yds. | Avg. | | No. | Yds. | Avg. |
|---|---|---|---|---|---|---|---|
| Toon | 8 | 96 | 12.0 | Hill | 9 | 77 | 8.6 |
| R. Moore | 4 | 70 | 17.5 | Givins | 6 | 83 | 13.8 |
| McNeil | 4 | 23 | 5.8 | Jeffires | 4 | 49 | 12.8 |
| Boyer | 3 | 20 | 6.7 | White | 4 | 31 | 7.8 |
| Mathis | 2 | 12 | 6.0 | Duncan | 4 | 24 | 6.0 |
| | 21 | 221 | 10.5 | Harris | 1 | 7 | 7.0 |
| | | | | | 28 | 271 | 9.7 |

**PUNTING**

| | | | | | | | |
|---|---|---|---|---|---|---|---|
| Aguiar | 2 | | 36.0 | Montgomery | 2 | 4 | 4.5 |

**PUNT RETURNS**

| | |
|---|---|
| Coleman | 2FC |

**KICKOFF RETURNS**

| | | | | | | | |
|---|---|---|---|---|---|---|---|
| Brown | 2 | 44 | 22.0 | Montgomery | 1 | 0 | 0.0 |
| Mathis | 1 | 10 | 10.0 | | | | |
| | 3 | 54 | 18.0 | | | | |

**INTERCEPTION RETURNS**

| | | | | | | | |
|---|---|---|---|---|---|---|---|
| McMillan | 1 | 0 | 0.0 | McDowell | 2 | 32 | 16.0 |
| | | | | Orlando | 1 | 0 | 1.0 |
| | | | | | 3 | 32 | 10.7 |

**PASSING**

### N.Y. JETS

| | Att. | Comp. | Comp. Pct. | Yds. | Int. | Yds./Att. | Yds./Comp. |
|---|---|---|---|---|---|---|---|
| O'Brien | 31 | 21 | 67.7 | 221 | 3 | 7.1 | 10.5 |

### HOUSTON

| | Att. | Comp. | Comp. Pct. | Yds. | Int. | Yds./Att. | Yds./Comp. |
|---|---|---|---|---|---|---|---|
| Moon | 40 | 28 | 70.0 | 271 | 1 | 6.8 | 9.7 |

December 28, 1991 at New Orleans (Attendance 68,794)

## SCORING

| | | | | | | |
|---|---|---|---|---|---|---|
| ATLANTA | 0 | 10 | 7 | 10 | - | 27 |
| NEW ORLEANS | 7 | 6 | 0 | 7 | - | 20 |

**First Quarter**
N.O.  Turner, 26 yard pass from Hebert
PAT — Andersen (kick)

**Second Quarter**
N.O.  Andersen, 45 yard field goal
Atl.  Rison, 24 yard pass from Miller
PAT — Johnson (kick)
Atl.  Johnson, 44 yard field goal
N.O.  Andersen, 35 yard field goal

**Third Quarter**
Atl.  Haynes, 20 yard pass from Miller
PAT — Johnson (kick)

**Fourth Quarter**
N.O.  Hilliard, 1 yard run
PAT — Andersen (kick)
Atl.  Johnson, 36 yard field goal
Atl.  Haynes, 61 yard pass from Miller
PAT — Johnson (kick)

December 29, 1991 at Chicago (Attendance 62,594)

## SCORING

| | | | | | | |
|---|---|---|---|---|---|---|
| DALLAS | 10 | 0 | 7 | 0 | - | 17 |
| CHICAGO | 0 | 3 | 3 | 7 | - | 13 |

**First Quarter**
Dal.  Willis, 27 yard field goal
Dal.  E. Smith, 1 yard run
PAT — Willis (kick)

**Second Quarter**
Chi.  Butler, 19 yard field goal

**Third Quarter**
Chi.  Butler, 43 yard field goal
Dal.  Novacek, 3 yard pass from Beuerlein
PAT — Willis (kick)

**Fourth Quarter**
Chi.  Waddle, 6 yard pass from Harbaugh
PAT — Butler (kick)

## TEAMSTATISTICS

| ATL | | N.O. |
|---|---|---|
| 20 | First Downs- Total | 23 |
| 6 | First Downs- Rushing | 3 |
| 13 | First Downs- Passing | 16 |
| 1 | First Downs- Penalty | 4 |
| 3 | Fumbles- Number | 2 |
| 1 | Fumbles- Lost Ball | 1 |
| 6 | Penalties- Number | 5 |
| 48 | Yards Penalized | 49 |
| 1 | Missed Field Goals | 0 |
| 57 | Offensive Plays | 67 |
| 334 | Net Yards | 330 |
| 5.9 | Average Gain | 4.9 |
| 2 | Giveaways | 3 |
| 3 | Takeaways | 2 |
| +1 | Difference | -1 |

## TEAMSTATISTICS

| DAL | | CHI. |
|---|---|---|
| 15 | First Downs- Total | 26 |
| 6 | First Downs- Rushing | 12 |
| 7 | First Downs- Passing | 14 |
| 2 | First Downs- Penalty | 0 |
| 2 | Fumbles- Number | 1 |
| 0 | Fumbles- Lost Ball | 1 |
| 2 | Penalties- Number | 4 |
| 16 | Yards Penalized | 16 |
| 2 | Missed Field Goals | 0 |
| 48 | Offensive Plays | 82 |
| 288 | Net Yards | 372 |
| 6.0 | Average Gain | 4.5 |
| 0 | Giveaways | 3 |
| 3 | Takeaways | 0 |
| +3 | Difference | -3 |

## INDIVIDUALSTATISTICS

### ATLANTA / NEW ORLEANS

**RUSHING**

| ATLANTA | No. | Yds. | Avg. | NEW ORLEANS | No. | Yds. | Avg. |
|---|---|---|---|---|---|---|---|
| Rozier | 7 | 35 | 5.0 | McAfee | 14 | 49 | 3.5 |
| Pegram | 11 | 26 | 2.4 | Hebert | 1 | 9 | 9.0 |
| Miller | 4 | 18 | 4.5 | Hilliard | 4 | 5 | 1.3 |
| | 22 | 79 | 3.6 | Jordan | 3 | 2 | 0.7 |
| | | | | | 22 | 65 | 3.0 |

**RECEIVING**

| | No. | Yds. | Avg. | | No. | Yds. | Avg. |
|---|---|---|---|---|---|---|---|
| Haynes | 6 | 144 | 24.0 | Martin | 7 | 83 | 11.9 |
| Pritchard | 5 | 63 | 12.6 | Turner | 5 | 75 | 15.0 |
| Rison | 4 | 56 | 14.0 | Early | 5 | 41 | 8.2 |
| Thomas | 1 | 19 | 19.0 | Hilliard | 5 | 33 | 6.7 |
| Pegram | 1 | 5 | 5.0 | Carroll | 2 | 23 | 11.5 |
| Dixon | 1 | 4 | 4.0 | Tice | 1 | 13 | 13.0 |
| | 18 | 291 | 16.2 | Jordan | 1 | 5 | 5.0 |
| | | | | | 26 | 273 | 10.5 |

**PUNTING**

| | No. | | Avg. | | No. | | Avg. |
|---|---|---|---|---|---|---|---|
| Fulhage | 1 | | 42.0 | Barnhardt | 3 | | 54.0 |

**PUNT RETURNS**

| | No. | Yds. | Avg. | | |
|---|---|---|---|---|---|
| Sanders | 1 | 22 | 22.0 | Fenerty | 1FC |

**KICKOFF RETURNS**

| | No. | Yds. | Avg. | | No. | Yds. | Avg. |
|---|---|---|---|---|---|---|---|
| Sanders | 2 | 32 | 16.0 | McAfee | 4 | 98 | 24.5 |
| Fishback | 1 | 0 | 0.0 | | | | |
| | 3 | 32 | 10.7 | | | | |

**INTERCEPTION RETURNS**

| | No. | Yds. | Avg. | | No. | Yds. | Avg. |
|---|---|---|---|---|---|---|---|
| Sanders | 1 | 31 | 31.0 | Glenn | 1 | 0 | 0.0 |
| McKyer | 1 | 0 | 0.0 | | | | |
| | 2 | 31 | 15.5 | | | | |

**PASSING**

| ATLANTA | Att. | Comp. | Comp. Pct. | Yds. | Int. | Yds./ Att. | Yds./ Comp. |
|---|---|---|---|---|---|---|---|
| Miller | 30 | 18 | 60.0 | 291 | 1 | 9.7 | 16.2 |

| NEW ORLEANS | Att. | Comp. | Comp. Pct. | Yds. | Int. | Yds./ Att. | Yds./ Comp. |
|---|---|---|---|---|---|---|---|
| Hebert | 44 | 26 | 59.1 | 273 | 2 | 6.2 | 10.5 |

## INDIVIDUALSTATISTICS

### DALLAS / CHICAGO

**RUSHING**

| DALLAS | No. | Yds. | Avg. | CHICAGO | No. | Yds. | Avg. |
|---|---|---|---|---|---|---|---|
| Smith | 26 | 105 | 4.0 | Lewis | 9 | 65 | 7.2 |
| Beuerlein | 4 | 3 | 0.8 | Anderson | 13 | 34 | 2.6 |
| | 30 | 108 | 3.6 | Harbaugh | 7 | 26 | 3.7 |
| | | | | Muster | 5 | 25 | 5.0 |
| | | | | | 34 | 150 | 4.4 |

**RECEIVING**

| | No. | Yds. | Avg. | | No. | Yds. | Avg. |
|---|---|---|---|---|---|---|---|
| Irvin | 4 | 83 | 20.8 | Waddle | 9 | 104 | 11.6 |
| Harper | 3 | 88 | 29.3 | Davis | 7 | 79 | 11.3 |
| Johnston | 1 | 6 | 6.0 | Anderson | 3 | 5 | 1.7 |
| Novacek | 1 | 3 | 3.0 | Lewis | 2 | 18 | 9.0 |
| | 9 | 180 | 20.0 | Rivera | 1 | 15 | 15.0 |
| | | | | Thornton | 1 | 12 | 12.0 |
| | | | | | 23 | 233 | 10.1 |

**PUNTING**

| | No. | | Avg. | | No. | | Avg. |
|---|---|---|---|---|---|---|---|
| Saxon | 3 | | 44.7 | Buford | 1 | | 0.0 |

**PUNT RETURNS**

| | | | | | No. | Yds. | Avg. |
|---|---|---|---|---|---|---|---|
| | | | | Woolford | 2 | 5 | 2.5 |

**KICKOFF RETURNS**

| | No. | Yds. | Avg. | | No. | Yds. | Avg. |
|---|---|---|---|---|---|---|---|
| Wright | 1 | 18 | 18.0 | Lewis | 3 | 44 | 13.3 |
| Gant | 1 | 16 | 16.0 | Green | 1 | 15 | 15.0 |
| | 2 | 34 | 12.0 | | 4 | 59 | 14.8 |

**INTERCEPTIONS**

| | No. | Yds. | Avg. | | | | |
|---|---|---|---|---|---|---|---|
| Bates | 1 | 7 | 7.0 | | | | |
| Brown | 1 | 0 | 0.0 | | | | |
| | 2 | 7 | 3.5 | | | | |

**PASSING**

| DALLAS | Att. | Comp. | Comp. Pct. | Yds. | Int. | Yds./ Att. | Yds./ Comp. |
|---|---|---|---|---|---|---|---|
| Beuerlein | 18 | 9 | 50.0 | 180 | 0 | 10.0 | 20.0 |

| CHICAGO | Att. | Comp. | Comp. Pct. | Yds. | Int. | Yds./ Att. | Yds./ Comp. |
|---|---|---|---|---|---|---|---|
| Harbaugh | 44 | 22 | 50.0 | 218 | 2 | 4.9 | 9.9 |
| Buford | 1 | 1 | 100.0 | 15 | 0 | 15.0 | 15.0 |
| | 45 | 23 | 51.1 | 233 | 2 | 5.2 | 10.1 |

January 4, 1992 at Denver (Attendance 75,301)

### SCORING

| | | | | | |
|---|---|---|---|---|---|
| HOUSTON | 14 | 7 | 0 | 3 - 24 | |
| DENVER | 6 | 7 | 3 | 10 - 26 | |

**First Quarter**
Hou.   Jeffries, 15 yard pass from Moon
    PAT — Del Greco (kick)
Hou.   Hill, 9 yard pass from Moon
    PAT — Del Greco (kick)
Den.   V. Johnson, 10 yard pass from Elway
    PAT — Treadwell kick failed

**Second Quarter**
Hou.   Duncan, 6 yard pass from Moon
    PAT — Del Greco (kick)
Den.   Lewis, 1 yard run
    PAT — Treadwell (kick)

**Third Quarter**
Den.   Treadwell, 49 yard field goal

**Fourth Quarter**
Hou.   Del Greco, 25 yard field goal
Den.   Lewis, 1 yard run
    PAT — Treadwell (kick)
Den.   Treadwell, 28 yard field goal

### TEAM STATISTICS

| HOU. | | DEN. |
|---|---|---|
| 23 | First Downs- Total | 26 |
| 7 | First Downs- Rushing | 13 |
| 14 | First Downs- Passing | 12 |
| 2 | First Downs- Penalty | 1 |
| 0 | Fumbles- Number | 3 |
| 0 | Fumbles- Lost Ball | 0 |
| 13 | Penalties- Number | 6 |
| 85 | Yards Penalized | 70 |
| 1 | Missed Field Goals | 0 |
| 55 | Offensive Plays | 65 |
| 422 | Net Yards | 418 |
| 7.7 | Average Gain | 6.4 |
| 1 | Giveaways | 1 |
| 1 | Takeaways | 1 |
| 0 | Difference | 0 |

### INDIVIDUAL STATISTICS

**HOUSTON**    **DENVER**

#### RUSHING

| | No. | Yds. | Avg. | | No. | Yds. | Avg. |
|---|---|---|---|---|---|---|---|
| L. White | 17 | 79 | 4.6 | Green | 17 | 59 | 3.5 |
| Moon | 2 | 18 | 9.0 | Sewell | 4 | 48 | 12.0 |
| | 19 | 97 | 5.1 | Elway | 6 | 39 | 6.5 |
| | | | | Rivers | 1 | 3 | 3.0 |
| | | | | Lewis | 3 | 2 | 0.7 |
| | | | | | 31 | 151 | 4.9 |

#### RECEIVING

| | No. | Yds. | Avg. | | No. | Yds. | Avg. |
|---|---|---|---|---|---|---|---|
| Jeffires | 7 | 99 | 14.1 | V. Johnson | 5 | 78 | 15.6 |
| Givins | 6 | 111 | 18.5 | Young | 4 | 85 | 21.3 |
| Duncan | 6 | 40 | 6.7 | Sewell | 3 | 28 | 9.3 |
| L. White | 5 | 35 | 7.0 | Sharpe | 3 | 20 | 6.7 |
| Hill | 2 | 21 | 10.5 | Nattiel | 2 | 27 | 13.5 |
| T. Jones | 1 | 19 | 19.0 | Russell | 1 | 20 | 20.0 |
| | 27 | 325 | 12.0 | Kay | 1 | 8 | 8.0 |
| | | | | Green | 1 | 1 | 1.0 |
| | | | | | 20 | 267 | 13.4 |

#### PUNTING

| | | | | | | |
|---|---|---|---|---|---|---|
| Montgomery | 1 | | 44.0 | Horan | 2 | 40.5 |

#### PUNT RETURNS

Coleman   1FC

#### KICKOFF RETURNS

| | No. | Yds. | Avg. | | No. | Yds. | Avg. |
|---|---|---|---|---|---|---|---|
| Pinkett | 3 | 46 | 15.3 | Montgomery | 4 | 88 | 22.0 |
| Coleman | 3 | 36 | 12.0 | | | | |
| | 6 | 82 | 13.7 | | | | |

#### INTERCEPTION RETURNS

| | No. | Yds. | Avg. | | No. | Yds. | Avg. |
|---|---|---|---|---|---|---|---|
| R. Johnson | 1 | 25 | 25.0 | Atwater | 1 | 0 | 0.0 |

#### PASSING

**HOUSTON**

| | Att. | Comp. | Comp. Pct. | Yds. | Int. | Yds./Att. | Yds./Comp. |
|---|---|---|---|---|---|---|---|
| Moon | 36 | 27 | 75.0 | 325 | 1 | 9.0 | 12.0 |

**DENVER**

| | Att. | Comp. | Comp. Pct. | Yds. | Int. | Yds./Att. | Yds./Comp. |
|---|---|---|---|---|---|---|---|
| Elway | 33 | 19 | 57.6 | 257 | 1 | 77.9 | 13.5 |
| Sewell | 1 | 1 | 100.0 | 10 | 0 | 10.0 | 10.0 |
| | 34 | 20 | 58.8 | 267 | 1 | 7.8 | 13.4 |

---

January 6, 1992 at Buffalo (Attendance 80,182)

### SCORING

| | | | | | |
|---|---|---|---|---|---|
| KANSAS CITY | 0 | 0 | 7 | 7 - 14 | |
| BUFFALO | 7 | 10 | 7 | 13 - 37 | |

**First Quarter**
Buff.   Reed, 25 yard pass from Kelly
    PAT — Norwood (kick)

**Second Quarter**
Buff.   Reed, 53 yard pass from Kelly
    PAT — Norwood (kick)
Buff.   Norwood, 33 yard field goal

**Third Quarter**
Buff.   Lofton, 10 yard pass from Kelly
    PAT — Norwood (kick)
K.C.   Word, 3 yard run
    PAT — Lowery (kick)

**Fourth Quarter**
Buff.   Norwood, 20 yard field goal
Buff.   Norwood, 47 yard field goal
Buff.   Davis, 5 yard run
    PAT — Norwood (kick)
K.C.   F. Jones, 20 yard pass from Vlasic
    PAT — Lowery (kick)

### TEAM STATISTICS

| K.C. | | BUFF. |
|---|---|---|
| 14 | First Downs- Total | 29 |
| 4 | First Downs- Rushing | 13 |
| 9 | First Downs- Passing | 12 |
| 1 | First Downs- Penalty | 4 |
| 3 | Fumbles- Number | 0 |
| 0 | Fumbles- Lost Ball | 0 |
| 10 | Penalties- Number | 6 |
| 59 | Yards Penalized | 40 |
| 0 | Missed Field Goals | 0 |
| 54 | Offensive Plays | 82 |
| 213 | Net Yards | 448 |
| 3.9 | Average Gain | 5.5 |
| 4 | Giveaways | 3 |
| 3 | Takeaways | 4 |
| -1 | Difference | +1 |

### INDIVIDUAL STATISTICS

**KANSAS CITY**    **BUFFALO**

#### RUSHING

| | No. | Yds. | Avg. | | No. | Yds. | Avg. |
|---|---|---|---|---|---|---|---|
| Word | 15 | 50 | 3.3 | Thomas | 22 | 100 | 4.5 |
| Williams | 8 | 24 | 3.0 | K. Davis | 19 | 75 | 3.9 |
| McNair | 1 | 3 | 3.0 | Reed | 1 | 6 | 6.0 |
| | 24 | 77 | 3.2 | Kelly | 1 | 2 | 2.0 |
| | | | | Reich | 3 | -3 | -1.0 |
| | | | | | 46 | 180 | 3.9 |

#### RECEIVING

| | No. | Yds. | Avg. | | No. | Yds. | Avg. |
|---|---|---|---|---|---|---|---|
| McNair | 5 | 52 | 10.4 | Beebe | 6 | 77 | 12.8 |
| F. Jones | 3 | 31 | 10.3 | McKeller | 5 | 34 | 6.8 |
| Birden | 2 | 19 | 9.5 | Reed | 4 | 100 | 25.0 |
| Hayes | 1 | 21 | 21.0 | Thomas | 4 | 21 | 5.3 |
| Barnett | 1 | 20 | 20.0 | Lofton | 3 | 34 | 11.3 |
| B. Jones | 1 | 2 | 2.0 | Edwards | 1 | 7 | 7.0 |
| Thomas | 1 | 1 | 1.0 | | 23 | 273 | 11.9 |
| | 14 | 146 | 10.4 | | | | |

#### PUNTING

| | | | | | | |
|---|---|---|---|---|---|---|
| Barker | 7 | | 40.3 | Mohr | 3 | 33.3 |

#### PUNT RETURNS

| | No. | Yds. | Avg. | | No. | Yds. | Avg. |
|---|---|---|---|---|---|---|---|
| Stradford | 1 | 11 | 11.0 | Hicks | 4 | 43 | 8.0 |

#### KICKOFF RETURNS

| | No. | Yds. | Avg. | | No. | Yds. | Avg. |
|---|---|---|---|---|---|---|---|
| Williams | 3 | 48 | 16.0 | Edwards | 1 | 24 | 24.0 |
| Birden | 1 | 0 | 0.0 | Beebe | 1 | 0 | 0.0 |
| | 4 | 48 | 12.0 | | 2 | 24 | 12.0 |

#### INTERCEPTION RETURNS

| | No. | Yds. | Avg. | | No. | Yds. | Avg. |
|---|---|---|---|---|---|---|---|
| Everett | 1 | 15 | 15.0 | K. Jackson | 2 | 6 | 3.0 |
| Marts | 1 | 12 | 12.0 | L. Smith | 1 | 0 | 0.0 |
| Cherry | 1 | 1 | 1.0 | Hicks | 1 | 0 | 0.0 |
| | 3 | 28 | 9.3 | | 4 | 6 | 1.5 |

#### PASSING

**KANSAS CITY**

| | Att. | Comp. | Comp. Pct. | Yds. | Int. | Yds./Att. | Yds./Comp. |
|---|---|---|---|---|---|---|---|
| DeBerg | 9 | 5 | 55.6 | 22 | 0 | 2.4 | 4.4 |
| Vlasic | 20 | 9 | 45.0 | 124 | 4 | 6.2 | 13.8 |
| | 29 | 14 | 48.3 | 146 | 4 | 5.0 | 10.4 |

**BUFFALO**

| | Att. | Comp. | Comp. Pct. | Yds. | Int. | Yds./Att. | Yds./Comp. |
|---|---|---|---|---|---|---|---|
| Kelly | 35 | 23 | 65.7 | 273 | 3 | 7.8 | 11.9 |

## January 4, 1992 at Washington (Attendance 55,181)

### SCORING

| | | | | | |
|---|---|---|---|---|---|
| ATLANTA | 0 | 7 | 0 | 0 | - 7 |
| WASHINGTON | 0 | 14 | 3 | 7 | - 24 |

**Second Quarter**
Wash.     Ervins, 17 yard run
       PAT — Lohmiller (kick)
Wash.     Riggs, 2 yard run
       PAT — Lohmiller (kick)
Atl.      T. Johnson, 1 yard run
       PAT — Johnson (kick)

**Third Quarter**
Wash.     Lohmiller, 24 yard field goal

**Fourth Quarter**
Wash.     Riggs, 1 yard run
       PAT — Lohmiller (kick)

## January 5, 1992 at Detroit (Attendance 78,290)

### SCORING

| | | | | | |
|---|---|---|---|---|---|
| DALLAS | 3 | 3 | 0 | 0 | - 6 |
| DETROIT | 7 | 10 | 14 | 7 | - 38 |

**First Quarter**
Det.      Green, 31 yard pass from Kramer
       PAT — Murray (kick)
Dall.     Willis, 28 yard field goal

**Second Quarter**
Det.      Jenkins, 41 yard interception return
       PAT — Murray (kick)
Dall.     Willis, 28 yard field goal
Det.      Murray, 36 yard field goal

**Third Quarter**
Det.      Green, 9 yard pass from Kramer
       PAT — Murray (kick)
Det.      Moore, 7 yard pass from Kramer
       PAT — Murray (kick)

**Fourth Quarter**
Det.      Sanders, 47 yard run
       PAT — Murray (kick)

### TEAM STATISTICS

| ATL. | | WASH. |
|---|---|---|
| 12 | First Downs- Total | 22 |
| 2 | First Downs- Rushing | 10 |
| 9 | First Downs- Passing | 11 |
| 1 | First Downs- Penalty | 1 |
| 3 | Fumbles- Number | 0 |
| 2 | Fumbles- Lost Ball | 0 |
| 3 | Penalties- Number | 4 |
| 19 | Yards Penalized | 23 |
| 1 | Missed Field Goals | 3 |
| 50 | Offensive Plays | 74 |
| 193 | Net Yards | 332 |
| 3.9 | Average Gain | 4.5 |
| 6 | Giveaways | 1 |
| 1 | Takeaways | 6 |
| -5 | Difference | +5 |

### TEAM STATISTICS

| DAL. | | DET. |
|---|---|---|
| 16 | First Downs- Total | 23 |
| 4 | First Downs- Rushing | 3 |
| 11 | First Downs- Passing | 19 |
| 1 | First Downs- Penalty | 1 |
| 3 | Fumbles- Number | 0 |
| 2 | Fumbles- Lost Ball | 0 |
| 3 | Penalties- Number | 4 |
| 19 | Yards Penalized | 39 |
| 0 | Missed Field Goals | 0 |
| 54 | Offensive Plays | 55 |
| 276 | Net Yards | 421 |
| 5.1 | Average Gain | 7.7 |
| 3 | Giveaways | 0 |
| 0 | Takeaways | 3 |
| -3 | Difference | +3 |

### INDIVIDUAL STATISTICS

#### ATLANTA / WASHINGTON

**RUSHING**

| ATLANTA | No. | Yds. | Avg. | WASHINGTON | No. | Yds. | Avg. |
|---|---|---|---|---|---|---|---|
| T. Johnson | 8 | 33 | 4.1 | Ervins | 23 | 104 | 4.5 |
| Chaffey | 3 | 8 | 2.7 | Byner | 14 | 57 | 4.1 |
| Pegram | 3 | 2 | 0.7 | Riggs | 4 | 7 | 1.8 |
| | 14 | 43 | 3.1 | Monk | 1 | -2 | -2.0 |
| | | | | Rypien | 3 | -4 | -0.8 |
| | | | | | 45 | 162 | 3.6 |

**RECEIVING**

| ATLANTA | No. | Yds. | Avg. | WASHINGTON | No. | Yds. | Avg. |
|---|---|---|---|---|---|---|---|
| Rison | 7 | 62 | 8.9 | Clark | 6 | 64 | 10.7 |
| Pritchard | 5 | 56 | 11.2 | Monk | 3 | 45 | 15.0 |
| Dixon | 2 | 19 | 9.5 | Ervins | 3 | 24 | 8.0 |
| Haynes | 1 | 15 | 15.0 | Sanders | 1 | 26 | 26.0 |
| Thomas | 1 | 15 | 15.0 | Byner | 1 | 11 | 11.0 |
| Phillips | 1 | 11 | 11.0 | | 14 | 170 | 12.1 |
| | 17 | 178 | 10.5 | | | | |

**PUNTING**

| ATLANTA | No. | | Avg. | WASHINGTON | No. | | Avg. |
|---|---|---|---|---|---|---|---|
| Fulhage | 4 | | 42.3 | Goodburn | 4 | | 38.8 |

**PUNT RETURNS**

| ATLANTA | No. | Yds. | Avg. | WASHINGTON | No. | Yds. | Avg. |
|---|---|---|---|---|---|---|---|
| Sanders | 2 | 11 | 5.5 | Mitchell | 3 | 28 | 9.3 |
| | | | | Green | 1FC | | |

**KICKOFF RETURNS**

| ATLANTA | No. | Yds. | Avg. | WASHINGTON | No. | Yds. | Avg. |
|---|---|---|---|---|---|---|---|
| Sanders | 4 | 92 | 23.0 | Mitchell | 2 | 51 | 25.5 |

**INTERCEPTION RETURNS**

| ATLANTA | No. | Yds. | Avg. | WASHINGTON | No. | Yds. | Avg. |
|---|---|---|---|---|---|---|---|
| Jordan | 1 | 4 | 4.0 | Copeland | 1 | 19 | 19.0 |
| | | | | Gouveia | 1 | 6 | 6.0 |
| | | | | Mayhew | 1 | 2 | 2.0 |
| | | | | Coleman | 1 | 0 | 0.0 |
| | | | | | 4 | 27 | 6.8 |

**PASSING**

| ATLANTA | Att. | Comp. | Comp. Pct. | Yds. | Int. | Yds./ Att. | Yds./ Comp. |
|---|---|---|---|---|---|---|---|
| Miller | 32 | 17 | 53.1 | 178 | 4 | 5.6 | 10.5 |

| WASHINGTON | Att. | Comp. | Comp. Pct. | Yds. | Int. | Yds./ Att. | Yds./ Comp. |
|---|---|---|---|---|---|---|---|
| Rypien | 29 | 14 | 48.3 | 170 | 1 | 5.8 | 12.1 |

### INDIVIDUAL STATISTICS

#### DALLAS / DETROIT

**RUSHING**

| DALLAS | No. | Yds. | Avg. | DETROIT | No. | Yds. | Avg. |
|---|---|---|---|---|---|---|---|
| E. Smith | 15 | 80 | 5.3 | Sanders | 12 | 69 | 5.8 |
| Agee | 3 | 12 | 4.0 | Overton | 3 | 17 | 5.7 |
| Johnston | 1 | 3 | 3.0 | Ware | 1 | -2 | -2.0 |
| Beuerlein | 1 | 2 | 2.0 | | 16 | 84 | 5.3 |
| Aikman | 2 | 0 | 0.0 | | | | |
| | 22 | 97 | 4.4 | | | | |

**RECEIVING**

| DALLAS | No. | Yds. | Avg. | DETROIT | No. | Yds. | Avg. |
|---|---|---|---|---|---|---|---|
| Irvin | 5 | 84 | 16.8 | Green | 8 | 115 | 14.4 |
| Harper | 4 | 56 | 14.0 | Moore | 6 | 87 | 14.5 |
| Novacek | 4 | 55 | 13.8 | Farr | 5 | 62 | 12.4 |
| Wright | 1 | 7 | 7.0 | Sanders | 5 | 30 | 6.0 |
| Johnston | 1 | 3 | 3.0 | Perriman | 3 | 18 | 6.0 |
| Awalt | 1 | 2 | 2.0 | Clark | 2 | 29 | 14.5 |
| E. Smith | 1 | 2 | 2.0 | | 29 | 341 | 11.8 |
| Agee | 1 | -4 | -4.0 | | | | |
| | 18 | 205 | 11.4 | | | | |

**PUNTING**

| DALLAS | No. | | Avg. | DETROIT | No. | | Avg. |
|---|---|---|---|---|---|---|---|
| Saxon | 5 | | 44.8 | Arnold | 5 | | 46.2 |

**PUNT RETURNS**

| DALLAS | No. | Yds. | Avg. | DETROIT | No. | Yds. | Avg. |
|---|---|---|---|---|---|---|---|
| Martin | 1 | 18 | 18.0 | Gray | 2 | 26 | 13.0 |

**KICKOFF RETURNS**

| DALLAS | No. | Yds. | Avg. | DETROIT | No. | Yds. | Avg. |
|---|---|---|---|---|---|---|---|
| Gant | 2 | 54 | 27.0 | Gray | 2 | 35 | 17.0 |
| Martin | 2 | 36 | 18.0 | Dozier | 1 | 14 | 14.0 |
| Wright | 1 | 12 | 12.0 | | 3 | 49 | 16.3 |
| Pruitt | 1 | 6 | 6.0 | | | | |
| | 6 | 108 | 18.0 | | | | |

**INTERCEPTION RETURNS**

| DALLAS | No. | Yds. | Avg. | DETROIT | No. | Yds. | Avg. |
|---|---|---|---|---|---|---|---|
| None | | | | Jenkins | 1 | 41 | 41.0 |
| | | | | Spielman | 1 | 0 | 0.0 |
| | | | | | 2 | 41 | 20.5 |

**PASSING**

| DALLAS | Att. | Comp. | Comp. Pct. | Yds. | Int. | Yds./ Att. | Yds./ Comp. |
|---|---|---|---|---|---|---|---|
| Beuerlein | 13 | 7 | 53.8 | 91 | 1 | 7.0 | 13.0 |
| Aikman | 16 | 11 | 68.8 | 114 | 1 | 7.1 | 10.4 |

| DETROIT | Att. | Comp. | Comp. Pct. | Yds. | Int. | Yds./ Att. | Yds./ Comp. |
|---|---|---|---|---|---|---|---|
| Kramer | 38 | 29 | 76.3 | 341 | 0 | 9.0 | 11.8 |

# 1991 Championship Games

## A.F.C. CHAMPIONSHIP GAME
### January 12, 1992 at Buffalo, N.Y.
#### (Attendance 80,272)

### SCORING

| | | | | | |
|---|---|---|---|---|---|
| DENVER | 0 | 0 | 0 | 7 | - 7 |
| BUFFALO | 0 | 0 | 7 | 3 | - 10 |

**Third Quarter**
Buff. — Bailey, 11 yard interception return
PAT — Norwood (kick)

**Fourth Quarter**
Buff. — Norwood, 44 yard field goal
Den. — Kubiak, 3 yard run
PAT — Treadwell (kick)

### TEAM STATISTICS

| DEN. | | BUFF. |
|---|---|---|
| 20 | First Downs- Total | 12 |
| 6 | First Downs- Rushing | 5 |
| 13 | First Downs- Passing | 5 |
| 1 | First Downs- Penalty | 2 |
| 4 | Fumbles- Number | 0 |
| 1 | Fumbles- Lost Ball | 0 |
| 4 | Penalties- Number | 6 |
| 20 | Yards Penalized | 35 |
| 3 | Missed Field Goals | 0 |
| 69 | Offensive Plays | 61 |
| 304 | Net Yards | 213 |
| 4.4 | Average Gain | 3.5 |
| 2 | Giveaways | 2 |
| 2 | Takeaways | 2 |
| -- | Difference | -- |

Unheralded linebacker Carlton Bailey emerged as the hero of a defensive drama in the AFC championship game with an 11-yard interception return for a touchdown that sent the Buffalo Bills to their second straight Super Bowl with a 10-7 triumph over the Denver Broncos.

Denver held the high-powered Bills without an offensive touchdown, but the Broncos' offense was shackled by the 27th-ranked defense.

Denver's hopes began to fade when quarterback John Elway suffered a bruised right thigh and limped out of the game 2:20 into the fourth quarter with his team trailing 7-0.

Gary Kubiak, who a week earlier had announced he would retire at the end of the season, replaced Elway and was able to draw the Broncos within three points with 1:28 to play.

The Broncos then recovered an onside kick and had a chance to pull out an improbable victory, but after Kubiak hit Steve Sewell inside Buffalo territory, Sewell fumbled the ball and Buffalo's Kirby Jackson recovered to clinch the victory with 1:28 to play.

After a surprising first half in which the Broncos wasted one scoring chance after another, the game seemed likely to turn on a defensive play. And it did. With the game still scoreless in the third quarter, Elway tried to throw a screen pass down the middle of the field to Sewell. But Jeff Wright tipped the ball and it went right to Bailey, who broke an attempted tackle by Elway and ran 11 yards for the breakthrough score with 9:32 to play in the period.

The Bills went up 10-0 at 4:18 of the fourth quarter on Scott Norwood's 44-yard field goal.

Kubiak scrambled three yards for Denver's only score after driving the Broncos 85 yards.

### INDIVIDUAL STATISTICS

#### RUSHING

| DENVER | No. | Yds. | Avg. | BUFFALO | No. | Yds. | Avg. |
|---|---|---|---|---|---|---|---|
| Green | 19 | 53 | 2.8 | Thomas | 26 | 72 | 2.8 |
| Kubiak | 3 | 22 | 7.3 | Reed | 1 | 16 | 16.0 |
| Elway | 4 | 10 | 2.5 | Kelly | 2 | 9 | 4.5 |
| Sewell | 4 | 3 | 0.8 | K. Davis | 6 | 7 | 1.2 |
| SV. Johnson | 2 | -7 | -3.5 | | 35 | 104 | 3.0 |
| | 32 | 81 | 2.5 | | | | |

#### RECEIVING

| DENVER | No. | Yds. | Avg. | BUFFALO | No. | Yds. | Avg. |
|---|---|---|---|---|---|---|---|
| V. Johnson | 8 | 104 | 13.0 | McKeller | 3 | 39 | 13.0 |
| Sewell | 7 | 78 | 11.1 | T. Thomas | 3 | 15 | 5.0 |
| Sharpe | 3 | 40 | 13.3 | Reed | 2 | 19 | 9.5 |
| Young | 3 | 25 | 8.3 | K. Davis | 2 | 13 | 6.5 |
| Nattiel | 1 | 10 | 10.0 | Metzelaars | 1 | 14 | 14.0 |
| | 22 | 257 | 11.7 | Lofton | 1 | 11 | 1.0 |
| | | | | Beebe | 1 | 6 | 6.0 |
| | | | | | 13 | 117 | 9.0 |

#### PUNTING

| DENVER | No. | Yds. | Avg. | BUFFALO | No. | Yds. | Avg. |
|---|---|---|---|---|---|---|---|
| Horan | 6 | | 43.7 | Mohr | 8 | | 38.0 |

#### PUNT RETURNS

| DENVER | No. | Yds. | Avg. | BUFFALO | No. | Yds. | Avg. |
|---|---|---|---|---|---|---|---|
| V. Johnson | 3 | 36 | 12.0 | Hicks | 1FC | | |

#### KICKOFF RETURNS

| DENVER | No. | Yds. | Avg. | BUFFALO | No. | Yds. | Avg. |
|---|---|---|---|---|---|---|---|
| Montgomery | 2 | 34 | 17.0 | Edwards | 1 | 24 | 24.0 |
| Russell | 1 | 15 | 15.0 | | | | |
| | 3 | 49 | 16.3 | | | | |

#### INTERCEPTION RETURNS

| DENVER | No. | Yds. | Avg. | BUFFALO | No. | Yds. | Avg. |
|---|---|---|---|---|---|---|---|
| Braxton | 1 | 5 | 5.0 | Bailey | 1 | 11 | 11.0 |
| Kragen | 1 | 0 | 0.0 | | | | |
| | 2 | 5 | 2.5 | | | | |

#### PASSING

| DENVER | Att. | Comp. | Comp. Pct. | Yds. | Int. | Yds./ Att. | Yds./ Comp. |
|---|---|---|---|---|---|---|---|
| Elway | 21 | 11 | 52.4 | 121 | 1 | 5.8 | 11.0 |
| Kubiak | 12 | 11 | 91.7 | 136 | 0 | 11.3 | 12.4 |
| | 33 | 22 | 66.7 | 257 | 1 | 7.8 | 11.7 |

| BUFFALO | Att. | Comp. | Comp. Pct. | Yds. | Int. | Yds./ Att. | Yds./ Comp. |
|---|---|---|---|---|---|---|---|
| Kelly | 25 | 13 | 52.0 | 117 | 2 | 4.7 | 9.0 |

---

## N.F.C. CHAMPIONSHIP GAME
### January 12, 1992 at Washington D.C.
#### (Attendance 55,585)

### SCORING

| | | | | | |
|---|---|---|---|---|---|
| DETROIT | 0 | 10 | 0 | 0 | - 10 |
| WASHINGTON | 10 | 7 | 10 | 14 | - 41 |

**First Quarter**
Wash. — Riggs, 2 yard run
PAT — Lohmiller (kick)
Wash. — Lohmiller, 20 yard field goal

**Second Quarter**
Det. — Green, 18 yard pass from Kramer
PAT — Murray (kick)
Wash. — Riggs, 3 yard run
PAT — Lohmiller (kick)
Det. — Murray, 30 yard field goal

**Third Quarter**
Wash. — Lohmiller, 28 yard field goal
Wash. — Clark, 45 yard pass from Rypien
PAT — Lohmiller (kick)

**Fourth Quarter**
Wash. — Monk, 21 yard pass from Rypien
PAT — Lohmiller (kick)
Wash. — Green, 32 yard interception return
PAT — Lohmiller (kick)

### TEAM STATISTICS

| DET. | | WASH. |
|---|---|---|
| 20 | First Downs- Total | 17 |
| 6 | First Downs- Rushing | 6 |
| 12 | First Downs- Passing | 10 |
| 2 | First Downs- Penalty | 1 |
| 3 | Fumbles- Number | 0 |
| 1 | Fumbles- Lost Ball | 0 |
| 7 | Penalties- Number | 6 |
| 46 | Yards Penalized | 46 |
| 1 | Missed Field Goals | 1 |
| 65 | Offensive Plays | 52 |
| 304 | Net Yards | 345 |
| 4.7 | Average Gain | 6.6 |
| 3 | Giveaways | 0 |
| 0 | Takeaways | 3 |
| - 2 | Difference | + 2 |

The Redskins turned two early turnovers into 10 points and Mark Rypien threw two long second-half touchdown passes, lifting Washington to a 41-10 rout of the Detroit Lions and into the Super Bowl for the fourth time in 10 years.

Washington jumped on two turnovers by Detroit quarterback Erik Kramer in the opening minutes as the Redskins built a seven-point halftime lead. Then Rypien threw touchdown passes of 45 yards to Gary Clark and 21 yards to Ark Monk.

The Redskins' four Super Bowl trips in the last decade have all come under the guidance of coach Joe Gibbs.

The Lions, 13-5, suffered a devastating ending to what had been a surprisingly successful season. Detroit won its last six regular-season games to capture the NFC Central title, then defeated Dallas in its first playoff game. The Lions' surge was inspired by a paralyzing injury to guard Mike Utley in a Nov. 17 game against the Los Angeles Rams.

The Redskins extended their winning streak over Detroit to 15 games and ran their record against the Lions to a perfect 16-0 in Washington. The Redskins are 11-1 in playoff games at home.

Detroit remains one of nine NFL teams never to have played in the Super Bowl.

Rypien completed 12 of 17 passes for 228 yards, completing four straight during one span in the second half for 110 yards and two touchdowns.

### INDIVIDUAL STATISTICS

#### RUSHING

| DETROIT | No. | Yds. | Avg. | WASHINGTON | No. | Yds. | Avg. |
|---|---|---|---|---|---|---|---|
| Sanders | 11 | 44 | 4.0 | Byner | 17 | 62 | 3.6 |
| Ware | 2 | 25 | 12.5 | Ervins | 13 | 53 | 4.1 |
| Kramer | 4 | 4 | 1.0 | Riggs | 2 | 5 | 2.5 |
| Long | 1 | -1 | -1.0 | Rypien | 3 | -3 | -1.0 |
| | 18 | 72 | 4.0 | | 35 | 117 | 3.3 |

#### RECEIVING

| DETROIT | No. | Yds. | Avg. | WASHINGTON | No. | Yds. | Avg. |
|---|---|---|---|---|---|---|---|
| Farr | 6 | 73 | 12.2 | Monk | 5 | 94 | 18.8 |
| Perriman | 5 | 43 | 8.6 | Clark | 4 | 77 | 19.3 |
| Moore | 4 | 69 | 17.3 | Sanders | 2 | 12 | 6.0 |
| Green | 4 | 54 | 13.5 | Orr | 1 | 45 | 45.0 |
| Sanders | 4 | 15 | 3.8 | | 12 | 228 | 19.0 |
| Overton | 2 | 10 | 5.0 | | | | |
| | 25 | 264 | 10.6 | | | | |

#### PUNTING

| DETROIT | No. | Yds. | Avg. | WASHINGTON | No. | Yds. | Avg. |
|---|---|---|---|---|---|---|---|
| Arnold | 3 | | 47.0 | Goodburn | 3 | | 35.7 |

#### PUNT RETURNS

| DETROIT | No. | Yds. | Avg. | WASHINGTON | No. | Yds. | Avg. |
|---|---|---|---|---|---|---|---|
| Gray | 3 | 13 | 4.3 | Mitchell | 1 | 13 | 13.0 |

#### KICKOFF RETURNS

| DETROIT | No. | Yds. | Avg. | WASHINGTON | No. | Yds. | Avg. |
|---|---|---|---|---|---|---|---|
| Gray | 5 | 134 | 26.8 | Ervins | 3 | 59 | 19.7 |
| Dozier | 1 | 21 | 21.0 | | | | |
| Alexander | 1 | 15 | 15.0 | | | | |
| | 7 | 170 | 24.3 | | | | |

#### INTERCEPTION RETURNS

| DETROIT | No. | Yds. | Avg. | WASHINGTON | No. | Yds. | Avg. |
|---|---|---|---|---|---|---|---|
| None | | | | Gouveia | 1 | 38 | 38.0 |
| | | | | Green | 1 | 32 | 32.0 |
| | | | | | 2 | 70 | 35.0 |

#### PASSING

| DETROIT | Att. | Comp. | Comp. Pct. | Yds. | Int. | Yds./ Att. | Yds./ Comp. |
|---|---|---|---|---|---|---|---|
| Kramer | 33 | 21 | 63.6 | 249 | 1 | 7.5 | 11.9 |
| Ware | 9 | 4 | 44.4 | 15 | 1 | 1.7 | 3.8 |
| | 42 | 25 | 59.5 | 264 | 2 | 6.3 | 10.6 |

| WASHINGTON | Att. | Comp. | Comp. Pct. | Yds. | Int. | Yds./ Att. | Yds./ Comp. |
|---|---|---|---|---|---|---|---|
| Rypien | 17 | 12 | 70.6 | 228 | 0 | 13.4 | 19.0 |

# Redskins Let 'Er Rip

Super Bowl XXVI was played like most of the last 10 or so — with the NFC champions soundly thrashing the best from the AFC. The only thing different about Washington's 37-24 victory over Buffalo was the script.

In the end, the Redskins defeated the Bills with what the losers do best — a no-huddle offense. The Redskins also stole another page from the Bills' playbook, perfecting the multiple-wide receiver offense while shutting down that of Buffalo. A little-known running back from Washington outrushed the NFL's Offensive Player of the Year from Buffalo. And a sixth-round draft pick outperformed the league's top quarterback and, in turn, was named the game's Most Valuable Player.

Still, Super Bowl XXVI was just like most of its predecessors — a super blowout that was pretty much decided by halftime. It was an embarrassment for the losers that left many of the 63,000 fans in attendance and another 120 million or so watching scross the country wondering why the Super Bowl is usually a super bore.

Redskins head coach Joe Gibbs, who became the third NFL coach to win three Super Bowls, didn't think so. "It was kind of a dream game for us," he said.

It was just the opposite for the Bills, who became the third team to lose consecutive Super Bowls. "I said before the game we need to go out and make history," said Buffalo defensive end Bruce Smith. "We did it the wrong damn way."

In the beginning of the game, it was Washington doing things the wrong way. Three times the Redskins had easy scoring chances and three times put no points on the scoreboard. And, while the Bills weren't in the game after halftime, there were four times that, if things had gone the other way, might have changed the outcome. The first turning point followed the first scoreless first quarter in 15 Super Bowls. Redskins quarterback, the game's Most Valuable Player, connected with Ricky Sanders on a 41-yard pass on the second play of the second period. Four plays later, Chip Lohmiller kicked the first of his three field goals, and Washington had the lead for good. Washington then scored on Earnest Byner's 10-yard reception and Gerald Riggs' one yard run — 17 points in a period of 5:45. Rypien completed 18 of 33 passes for 292 yards.

The Redskins intercepted Buffalo quarterback Jim Kelly four times and forced him to fumble once. Kelly's four interceptions tied the Super Bowl record, and his 58 pass attempts set a record. And Bills running back Thurman Thomas managed only 13 yards on 10 carries.

On the first play of the second half, Kelly was intercepted, and, on the next play, Riggs scored his second touchdown of the game. Buffalo then scored 10 points on its next two possessions on a one-yard run by Thomas and a field goal by Scott Norwood. But Washington responded with an 11-play, 79-yard drive that iced the game when Gary Clark caught a 30-yard touchdown pass from Rypien. Lohmiller kicked two more field goals for the Redskins. Finally, the Bills, down 37-10, scored two touchdowns in a stretch of 2:04 late in the fourth quarter, helped by the recovery of an onside kick.

## LINEUPS

| WASH. | OFFENSE | BUFF. |
|---|---|---|
| Clark | WR | Lofton |
| Middleton | TE | Metzelaars |
| Lachey | LT | Wolford |
| McKenzie | LG | Ritcher |
| Bostic | C | Hull |
| Schlereth | RG | Parker |
| Jacoby | RT | Ballard |
| Warren | TE | McKeller |
| Monk | WR | Reed |
| Rypien | QB | Kelly |
| Byner | RB | K. Davis |
| | DEFENSE | |
| Mann | LE | Seals |
| E. Williams | LT/NT | Wright |
| T. Johnson | RT/RE | B. Smith |
| Stokes | RE/LOLB | Bennett |
| Marshall | LLB/LILB | Conlan |
| Gouveia | MLB/RILB | Bailey |
| Collins | RLB/ROLB | Talley |
| Mayhew | LCB | K. Jackson |
| Green | RCB | Odomes |
| Copeland | SS | Drane |
| Edwards | FS | Kelso |

| WASHINGTON | SUBSTITUTES | |
|---|---|---|
| | OFFENSE | |
| Rutledge | B. Mitchell | Ervins |
| Riggs | Adickes | Grimm |
| Simmons | Brandes | Sanders |
| Hobbs | Jenkins | Orr |
| | DEFENSE | |
| Mays | Hoage | S. Johnson |
| A. Johnson | Caldwell | Coleman |
| B. Wilson | Geathers | Buck |
| | KICKERS | |
| Goodburn | Lohmiller | |

| BUFFALO | OFFENSE | |
|---|---|---|
| Reich | T. Thomas | Gardner |
| Frerotte | Lingner | Staysniak |
| Beebe | Edwards | Rolle |
| Tasker | | |
| | DEFENSE | |
| H. Jones | Hale | Hicks |
| J. Williams | Bentley | Patton |
| Lodish | Hansen | Pike |
| Garner | | |
| | KICKERS | |
| Daluiso | Mohr | Norwood |

## SCORING

| | 1 | 2 | 3 | 4 | | |
|---|---|---|---|---|---|---|
| WASHINGTON | 0 | 17 | 14 | 6 | - | 37 |
| BUFFALO | 0 | 0 | 10 | 14 | - | 24 |

**Second Quarter**
Wash. — Lohmiller, 34 yard field goal
Wash. — Byner, 10 yard pass from Rypien
   PAT — Lohmiller (kick)
Wash. — Riggs, 1 yard run
   PAT — Lohmiller (kick)

**Third Quarter**
Wash. — Riggs, 2 yard run
   PAT — Lohmiller (kick)
Buff. — Norwood, 21 yard field goal
Buff. — Thomas, 1 yard run
   PAT — Norwood (kick)
Wash. — Clark, 30 yard pass from Rypien
   PAT — Lohmiller (kick)

**Fourth Quarter**
Wash. — Lohmiller, 25 yard field goal
Wash. — Lohmiller, 39 yard field goal
Buff. — Metzelaars, 2 yard pass from Kelly
   PAT — Norwood (kick)
Buff. — Beebe, 4 yard pass from Kelly
   PAT — Norwood (kick)

## TEAM STATISTICS

| WASH. | | BUFF. |
|---|---|---|
| 24 | First Downs-Total | 25 |
| 10 | First Downs-Rushing | 4 |
| 12 | First Downs-Passing | 18 |
| 2 | First Downs-Penalty | 3 |
| 1 | Fumbles-Number | 6 |
| 0 | Fumbles-Lost Ball | 1 |
| 5 | Penalties-Number | 6 |
| 82 | Yards Penalized | 50 |
| 0 | Missed Field Goals | 0 |
| 73 | Offensive Plays | 82 |
| 417 | Net Yards | 283 |
| 5.7 | Average Gain | 3.5 |
| 1 | Giveaways | 5 |
| 5 | Takeaways | 1 |
| +4 | Difference | -4 |

## INDIVIDUAL STATISTICS

### WASHINGTON — RUSHING

| | No. | Yds. | Avg. |
|---|---|---|---|
| Ervins | 13 | 72 | 5.5 |
| Byner | 14 | 49 | 3.5 |
| Riggs | 5 | 7 | 1.4 |
| Sanders | 1 | 1 | 1.0 |
| Rutledge | 1 | 0 | 0.0 |
| Rypien | 6 | -4 | -0.7 |
| | 40 | 125 | 3.1 |

### BUFFALO — RUSHING

| | No. | Yds. | Avg. |
|---|---|---|---|
| K. Davis | 4 | 17 | 4.3 |
| Kelly | 3 | 16 | 5.3 |
| Thomas | 10 | 13 | 1.3 |
| Lofton | 1 | -3 | -3.0 |
| | 18 | 43 | 2.4 |

### WASHINGTON — RECEIVING

| | No. | Yds. | Avg. |
|---|---|---|---|
| Clark | 7 | 114 | 16.3 |
| Monk | 7 | 113 | 16.1 |
| Byner | 3 | 24 | 8.0 |
| Sanders | 1 | 41 | 41.0 |
| | 18 | 292 | 16.2 |

### BUFFALO — RECEIVING

| | No. | Yds. | Avg. |
|---|---|---|---|
| Lofton | 7 | 92 | 13.1 |
| Reed | 5 | 34 | 6.8 |
| Beebe | 4 | 61 | 15.3 |
| Davis | 4 | 38 | 9.5 |
| Thomas | 4 | 27 | 6.8 |
| McKeller | 2 | 29 | 14.5 |
| Edwards | 1 | 11 | 11.0 |
| Metzelaars | 1 | 2 | 2.0 |
| Kelly | 1 | -8 | -8.0 |
| | 29 | 286 | 9.9 |

### PUNTING

| | No. | | Avg. |
|---|---|---|---|
| Goodburn | 4 | | 37.5 |
| Mohr | 6 | | 35.0 |

### PUNT RETURNS

| | No. | Yds. | Avg. |
|---|---|---|---|
| Mitchell | 2FC | | |
| Hicks | 3 | 9 | 3.0 |

### KICKOFF RETURNS

| | No. | Yds. | Avg. |
|---|---|---|---|
| Mitchell | 1 | 16 | 16.0 |
| Edwards | 4 | 77 | 19.3 |

### INTERCEPTIONS RETURNS

| | No. | Yds. | Avg. |
|---|---|---|---|
| Edwards | 2 | 56 | 28.0 |
| Gouveia | 1 | 23 | 23.0 |
| Green | 1 | 0 | 0.0 |
| | 4 | 79 | 19.8 |
| Jackson | 1 | 4 | 4.0 |

### PASSING

| WASHINGTON | Att. | Comp. | Comp. Pct. | Yds. | Int. | Yds./ Att. | Yds./ Comp. | Yards Lost Tackled |
|---|---|---|---|---|---|---|---|---|
| Rypien | 33 | 18 | 54.5 | 292 | 1 | 8.8 | 16.2 | 0-0 |
| **BUFFALO** | | | | | | | | |
| Kelly | 58 | 28 | 48.3 | 275 | 4 | 47.4 | 9.8 | 5-46 |
| Reich | 1 | 1 | 100.0 | 11 | 0 | 11.0 | 11.0 | 0-0 |

# 1992 N.F.C.  A New Era Comes to Pro Football

A new era came to the National Football League in 1992 as the owners and players were forced into settling their six-year-long dispute. The owners lost the first round in September, when Federal District Judge David Doty declared four players immediate free agents.

Then, as the regular season ended in December, because of a 24-hour imposed time limit on negotiations, the two sides finally came to a settlement of all the litigation on the more than 20 suits that had been filed since the last collective bargaining agreement had expired in 1987. The players won their long sought-after free agency, and all players with five years or more in the league were given the freedom to change teams when their contracts expired. But the owners also received what they had wanted, a salary cap tied to percentage of gross revenues that guaranteed them financial stability. The draft was also shortened to eight rounds.

In the NFC, the Dallas Cowboys, the youngest team in the NFL, showed that they might have the makings of a dynasty after winning Super Bowl XXVII in a rout of the Buffalo Bills.

## EASTERN DIVISION

**Dallas Cowboys** — The Cowboys culminated one of the most remarkable comebacks in NFL history, going from 1-15 in 1989 to 13-3 and the Super Bowl championship in 1992. Dallas had several of the biggest impact players in the NFL. Troy Aikman passed for 23 TD's and was the Super Bowl MVP, Emmitt Smith led the NFL in rushing with 1,713 yards and touchdowns with 19, Michael Irvin caught 78 passes for 1,396 yards and seven scores and Jay Novacek led the league's tight ends with 68 catches. Nearly 20 players were rotated in and out of the lineup on one of the league's best defenses, although none of them made the Pro Bowl. Charles Haley and Thomas Everett, who were obtained in preseason trades, were the impact players on defense. In the end, coach Jimmy Johnson was getting doused with ice water and Jerry Jones was enjoying every second as owner of the finest team in the land.

**Philadelphia Eagles** — Keith Jackson held out and was awarded free agency, eventually signing with Miami, and by the end of the year, Reggie White, Seth Joyner and Clyde Simmons had already been declared free agents. Quarterback Randall Cunningham experienced a splendid comeback from the knee injury that caused him to miss the 1991 season, throwing 19 TD passes. Philadelphia obtained Herschel Walker in a June trade, and he responded with over 1,000 yards rushing and 10 touchdowns. The defense was again one of the league's best, but it missed tackle Jerome Brown, who was killed in a car accident before training camp began. So a season that began so promising with the Super Bowl as the goal ended with free agency destined to destroy continuity.

**Washington Redskins** — The Redskins followed up their Super Bowl season in 1991 by slipping into the playoffs, but the talk in the nation's capital was about what happened to Mark Rypien. After a long training camp holdout, the quarterback finished as the lowest-rated passer in the NFC. Art Monk became pro football's all-time leading receiver, but he had a mediocre season. Gary Clark led the team in receptions but also dropped more balls than an amateur juggler. Want more? Earnest Byner gained 1,000 yards rushing, then lost a few yards and was injured, ending with 998. The offense scored 185 fewer points than in '91, but positions on both sides of the ball were riddled with injuries. Two months after the season ended, coach Joe Gibbs surprised everyone with his retirement, leaving defensive coordinator Richie Petitbon in charge.

**New York Giants** — Maybe the highlight of the Ray Handley era was that he wasn't the first coach fired after the season. The shortest reign of any coach in New York history — 19 months — spelled the end of Handley, and some time later Dan Reeves moved east from Denver to take over. Future Hall of Famer Lawrence Taylor was planning to retire, but then he suffered a season-ending injury which caused him to re-think his plans. There was a merry-go-round at quarterback with three different starters because of injuries and a defense that aged quickly. Halfback Rodney Hampton proved to be one of the league's top runners with 1,141 yards and 14 touchdowns. Six losses in the final seven games

and a season full of turmoil meant changes in New York as 1993 approached.

**Phoenix Cardinals** — The Cardinals were probably the best once-gain last-place team in the NFL. Playing hard, stopping enemy running games and strong special-teams play were components of every Cardinals game. Phoenix defeated playoff teams Washington and San Francisco for two of its four wins. Quarterback Timm Rosenbach was injured again, and Chris Chandler took over and showed that he deserved the starting job. The defense had a couple of stars in Tim McDonald (who led the team in tackles for the fourth time in five years), Eric Swann and Freddie Joe Nunn. But with six losses in the last seven games, when the season ended coach Joe Bugel and general manager Larry Wilson were given one more year to turn things around.

## CENTRAL DIVISION

**Minnesota Vikings** — New head coach Dennis Green turned whiners into winners and captured the division title by providing tough, prove-it-or-lose-it leadership that was desperately needed. He shipped out Herschel Walker, Joey Browner, Keith Millard and Wade Wilson, But Green couldn't decide on a quarterback, flip-flopping back and forth between Rich Gannon and journeyman Sean Salisbury late in the season when the playoffs were on the line. The Vikings defense was a force all year, and it provided the team with a couple of victories with some of the eight turnovers that were returned for touchdowns. Defensive end Chris Doleman had a resurgence, and Audray McMillian and Todd Scott provided fireworks from the secondary. Terry Allen rushed for a club-record 1,102 yards and scored 15 touchdowns.

**Green Bay Packers** — Brett Favre and Sterling Sharpe were the big stories in Green Bay, as the Packers contended for a playoff spot until the final weekend of the season. In his second season after being obtained in an offseason trade with Atlanta, Favre mastered the ball-control passing game of new coach Mike Holmgren and threw for 3,227 yards and 18 touchdowns after replacing Don Majkowski. Sharpe was on the receiving end of many of Favre's passes, as he set an NFL single-season record with 108 receptions. He also led the league with 1,461 receiving yards and 13 touchdowns. Other than tight end Jackie Harris (55 catches), the Packers were devoid of stars. The Green Bay defense wasn't dominant but certainly respectable, led by safety Chuck Cecil and linebacker Tony Bennett, who had 12.5 sacks.

**Tampa Bay Buccaneers** — New head coach Sam Wyche had high hopes after the Buccaneers started out 3-1. But then they were subjected to a slow death, as they lost 10 of their last 12 games. Following a strong start, Vinny Testaverde's interception problems returned, and he did little to convince Wyche that he should be brought back for another season. Offensive bright spots were running back Reggie Cobb (1,058 yards rushing and nine touchdowns) and receiver Lawrence Dawsey (58 catches). Defensively, the Bucs had their usual problems. They finished 21st in team defense and were especially vulnerable against the pass, although cornerback Ricky Reynolds was one of the league's best. Two top rookies were linemen Santana Dotson and Mark Wheeler, while veterans Broderick Thomas and Keith McCants were disappointments.

**Chicago Bears** — Da Bears hit Da Skids with one of the biggest collapses in the team's 73-year history, losing seven of their last eight games. Coach Mike Ditka provided a steady supply of controversy all season and was fired after it ended. The biggest problems were an aging defense and an offense that had trouble generating points. Paramount to all the Bears' troubles was the lack of players on either side of the ball who could make things happen. Jim Harbaugh entered the season as the division's best quarterback, but he slumped to a point where backups Peter Tom Willis and Will Furrer got opportunities to show what they could do (and it wasn't much). Neal Anderson had another subpar year at halfback, even losing his starting job for a time to Darren Lewis.

**Detroit Lions** — The Lions slumped from division champs to the

**OFFENSE**

| | ATL | CHI | DAL | DET | G.B. | L.A. | MINN | N.O. | NYG | PHIL | PHX | S.F. | T.B. | WASH |
|---|---|---|---|---|---|---|---|---|---|---|---|---|---|---|
| **FIRST DOWNS:** | | | | | | | | | | | | | | |
| Total | 273 | 282 | 324 | 241 | 291 | 278 | 288 | 267 | 271 | 292 | 277 | 344 | 281 | 276 |
| by Rushing | 67 | 101 | 119 | 83 | 101 | 83 | 115 | 92 | 120 | 138 | 88 | 135 | 100 | 104 |
| by Passing | 194 | 157 | 183 | 133 | 171 | 174 | 157 | 155 | 119 | 138 | 161 | 192 | 165 | 160 |
| by Penalty | 12 | 24 | 22 | 25 | 19 | 21 | 16 | 20 | 32 | 16 | 28 | 17 | 16 | 12 |
| **RUSHING:** | | | | | | | | | | | | | | |
| Number | 322 | 427 | 500 | 378 | 420 | 393 | 497 | 454 | 458 | 516 | 395 | 482 | 438 | 483 |
| Yards | 1270 | 1871 | 2121 | 1644 | 1555 | 1659 | 2030 | 1628 | 2077 | 2388 | 1491 | 2315 | 1706 | 1727 |
| Average Yards | 3.9 | 4.4 | 4.2 | 4.3 | 3.7 | 4.2 | 4.1 | 3.6 | 4.5 | 4.6 | 3.8 | 4.8 | 3.9 | 3.6 |
| Touchdowns | 3 | 15 | 20 | 9 | 7 | 12 | 19 | 10 | 20 | 19 | 11 | 22 | 12 | 10 |
| **PASSING:** | | | | | | | | | | | | | | |
| Attempts | 548 | 479 | 491 | 406 | 527 | 495 | 458 | 426 | 433 | 429 | 517 | 480 | 511 | 485 |
| Completions | 336 | 266 | 314 | 231 | 340 | 289 | 258 | 251 | 232 | 255 | 298 | 319 | 299 | 272 |
| Completion Pct. | 61.3 | 55.5 | 64.0 | 56.9 | 64.5 | 58.4 | 56.3 | 58.9 | 53.6 | 59.4 | 57.6 | 66.6 | 58.5 | 56.1 |
| Passing Yards | 3892 | 3334 | 3597 | 3150 | 3498 | 3422 | 3162 | 3297 | 2628 | 3054 | 3344 | 4054 | 3399 | 3339 |
| Avg. Yds per Att. | 6.2 | 5.9 | 6.8 | 6.0 | 5.7 | 6.2 | 5.8 | 7.2 | 4.9 | 5.3 | 5.6 | 7.6 | 5.5 | 6.2 |
| Avg. Yds per Comp. | 11.6 | 12.5 | 11.5 | 13.6 | 10.3 | 11.8 | 12.3 | 13.1 | 11.3 | 12.0 | 11.2 | 12.7 | 11.4 | 12.3 |
| Times Tackled | 40 | 45 | 23 | 59 | 43 | 26 | 40 | 15 | 45 | 64 | 36 | 32 | 45 | 23 |
| Yds Lost Tackled | 259 | 264 | 112 | 354 | 268 | 204 | 293 | 119 | 283 | 462 | 258 | 174 | 334 | 176 |
| Net Yards | 3633 | 3070 | 3485 | 2796 | 3230 | 3218 | 2869 | 3178 | 2345 | 2592 | 3086 | 3880 | 3065 | 3163 |
| Touchdowns | 33 | 17 | 23 | 16 | 20 | 23 | 18 | 19 | 14 | 20 | 15 | 29 | 17 | 15 |
| Interceptions | 15 | 24 | 15 | 21 | 15 | 20 | 15 | 16 | 10 | 13 | 24 | 9 | 20 | 17 |
| Pct. Intercepted | 2.7 | 5.0 | 3.1 | 5.2 | 2.8 | 4.0 | 3.3 | 3.8 | 2.3 | 3.0 | 4.6 | 1.9 | 3.9 | 3.5 |
| **PUNTS:** | | | | | | | | | | | | | | |
| Number | 70 | 79 | 61 | 66 | 68 | 76 | 73 | 67 | 85 | 82 | 58 | 49 | 74 | 65 |
| Average | 40.8 | 42.9 | 43.0 | 43.1 | 38.4 | 41.1 | 44.4 | 44.0 | 40.6 | 42.2 | 42.8 | 39.1 | 40.7 | 39.3 |
| **PUNT RETURNS** | | | | | | | | | | | | | | |
| Number | 29 | 23 | 44 | 21 | 35 | 39 | 33 | 45 | 27 | 47 | 33 | 40 | 26 | 37 |
| Yards | 196 | 176 | 550 | 190 | 315 | 345 | 336 | 231 | 240 | 555 | 364 | 389 | 160 | 355 |
| Average Yards | 6.8 | 7.7 | 12.5 | 9.0 | 9.0 | 8.8 | 10.2 | 5.1 | 8.9 | 11.8 | 11.0 | 9.7 | 6.2 | 9.6 |
| Touchdowns | 0 | 0 | 2 | 1 | 1 | 2 | 0 | 0 | 0 | 1 | 0 | 1 | 0 | 2 |
| **KICKOFF RET.:** | | | | | | | | | | | | | | |
| Number | 64 | 56 | 37 | 59 | 54 | 63 | 45 | 42 | 56 | 48 | 51 | 42 | 50 | 48 |
| Yards | 1532 | 1143 | 699 | 1193 | 1017 | 1054 | 874 | 815 | 1098 | 987 | 1127 | 879 | 881 | 973 |
| Average Yards | 23.9 | 20.4 | 18.9 | 20.2 | 18.8 | 16.7 | 19.4 | 19.4 | 19.6 | 20.6 | 22.1 | 20.9 | 17.6 | 20.3 |
| Touchdowns | 2 | 1 | 0 | 1 | 0 | 0 | 0 | 0 | 1 | 0 | 0 | 0 | 0 | 0 |
| **INTERCEPT RET.:** | | | | | | | | | | | | | | |
| Number | 11 | 14 | 17 | 21 | 15 | 18 | 28 | 18 | 14 | 24 | 16 | 17 | 20 | 23 |
| Yards | 135 | 188 | 158 | 255 | 222 | 283 | 502 | 254 | 192 | 307 | 298 | 172 | 234 | 485 |
| Average Yards | 12.3 | 13.4 | 9.3 | 12.1 | 14.8 | 15.7 | 17.9 | 14.1 | 13.7 | 12.8 | 18.6 | 10.1 | 11.7 | 21.1 |
| Touchdowns | 0 | 0 | 1 | 0 | 1 | 1 | 6 | 3 | 1 | 2 | 3 | 1 | 1 | 2 |
| **PENALTIES:** | | | | | | | | | | | | | | |
| Number | 78 | 93 | 91 | 122 | 88 | 79 | 99 | 60 | 87 | 101 | 85 | 80 | 91 | 84 |
| Yards | 656 | 776 | 650 | 903 | 749 | 592 | 809 | 567 | 647 | 807 | 722 | 636 | 754 | 741 |
| **FUMBLES:** | | | | | | | | | | | | | | |
| Number | 30 | 23 | 16 | 26 | 41 | 30 | 29 | 27 | 25 | 25 | 26 | 29 | 19 | 18 |
| Number Lost | 14 | 10 | 9 | 15 | 21 | 17 | 17 | 13 | 13 | 15 | 18 | 13 | 9 | 7 |
| **POINTS:** | | | | | | | | | | | | | | |
| Total | 327 | 295 | 409 | 273 | 276 | 313 | 374 | 330 | 306 | 354 | 243 | 431 | 267 | 300 |
| PAT Attempts | 39 | 34 | 48 | 30 | 30 | 38 | 45 | 35 | 36 | 44 | 29 | 54 | 33 | 30 |
| PAT Made | 39 | 34 | 47 | 30 | 30 | 38 | 45 | 33 | 36 | 40 | 28 | 53 | 33 | 30 |
| FG Attempts | 22 | 26 | 35 | 26 | 29 | 20 | 25 | 34 | 23 | 25 | 26 | 27 | 22 | 40 |
| FG Made | 18 | 19 | 24 | 21 | 22 | 15 | 19 | 29 | 18 | 16 | 13 | 18 | 12 | 30 |
| Percent FG Made | 81.8 | 73.1 | 68.6 | 80.8 | 75.9 | 75.0 | 76.0 | 85.3 | 78.3 | 64.0 | 50.0 | 66.7 | 54.5 | 75.0 |
| Safeties | 0 | 0 | 1 | 0 | 0 | 1 | 1 | 0 | 0 | 1 | 1 | 0 | 0 | 0 |

**DEFENSE**

| | ATL | CHI | DAL | DET | G.B. | L.A. | MINN | N.O. | NYG | PHIL | PHX | S.F. | T.B. | WASH |
|---|---|---|---|---|---|---|---|---|---|---|---|---|---|---|
| **FIRST DOWNS:** | | | | | | | | | | | | | | |
| Total | 304 | 274 | 241 | 308 | 277 | 319 | 293 | 246 | 287 | 242 | 281 | 277 | 296 | 249 |
| by Rushing | 109 | 109 | 68 | 119 | 89 | 130 | 113 | 86 | 115 | 73 | 101 | 90 | 100 | 89 |
| by Passing | 172 | 144 | 147 | 168 | 170 | 175 | 154 | 146 | 155 | 146 | 163 | 174 | 175 | 138 |
| by Penalty | 23 | 21 | 26 | 21 | 18 | 14 | 26 | 14 | 17 | 23 | 17 | 13 | 21 | 22 |
| **RUSHING:** | | | | | | | | | | | | | | |
| Number | 464 | 468 | 345 | 460 | 406 | 467 | 438 | 381 | 458 | 387 | 436 | 351 | 441 | 406 |
| Yards | 2294 | 1948 | 1244 | 1841 | 1821 | 2230 | 1733 | 1605 | 2012 | 1481 | 1635 | 1418 | 1675 | 1696 |
| Average Yards | 4.9 | 4.2 | 3.6 | 4.0 | 4.5 | 4.8 | 4.0 | 4.2 | 4.4 | 3.8 | 3.8 | 4.0 | 3.8 | 4.2 |
| Touchdowns | 20 | 14 | 11 | 14 | 12 | 22 | 11 | 8 | 17 | 4 | 13 | 5 | 15 | 11 |
| **PASSING:** | | | | | | | | | | | | | | |
| Attempts | 439 | 442 | 484 | 487 | 483 | 507 | 508 | 511 | 440 | 517 | 452 | 551 | 508 | 466 |
| Completions | 277 | 261 | 263 | 296 | 277 | 305 | 320 | 287 | 270 | 263 | 276 | 320 | 293 | 258 |
| Completion Pct. | 63.1 | 59.0 | 54.3 | 60.8 | 57.3 | 60.2 | 63.0 | 56.2 | 61.4 | 50.9 | 61.1 | 58.1 | 57.7 | 55.4 |
| Passing Yards | 3496 | 3290 | 3034 | 3402 | 3496 | 3481 | 3124 | 2846 | 3228 | 3316 | 3687 | 3642 | 3740 | 3021 |
| Avg. Yds per Att. | 6.9 | 6.2 | 5.1 | 6.2 | 6.3 | 6.1 | 5.0 | 4.4 | 6.5 | 5.1 | 7.3 | 5.7 | 6.5 | 5.4 |
| Avg. Yds per Comp. | 12.6 | 12.6 | 11.5 | 11.5 | 12.6 | 11.4 | 9.8 | 9.9 | 12.0 | 12.6 | 13.4 | 11.4 | 12.8 | 11.7 |
| Times Tackled | 31 | 43 | 44 | 29 | 34 | 31 | 51 | 57 | 25 | 55 | 27 | 41 | 36 | 39 |
| Yds Lost Tackled | 241 | 286 | 347 | 185 | 219 | 188 | 342 | 376 | 197 | 385 | 196 | 273 | 230 | 279 |
| Net Yards | 3255 | 3004 | 2687 | 3217 | 3277 | 3293 | 2782 | 2470 | 3031 | 2931 | 3491 | 3369 | 3510 | 2742 |
| Touchdowns | 24 | 20 | 16 | 20 | 16 | 18 | 12 | 13 | 22 | 20 | 24 | 20 | 25 | 15 |
| Interceptions | 11 | 14 | 17 | 21 | 15 | 18 | 28 | 18 | 14 | 24 | 16 | 17 | 20 | 23 |
| Pct. Intercepted | 2.5 | 3.2 | 3.3 | 4.3 | 3.1 | 3.6 | 5.5 | 3.5 | 3.2 | 4.6 | 3.5 | 3.1 | 3.9 | 4.9 |
| **PUNTS:** | | | | | | | | | | | | | | |
| Number | 61 | 70 | 87 | 55 | 68 | 66 | 76 | 89 | 64 | 85 | 62 | 76 | 64 | 73 |
| Average | 41.5 | 40.6 | 42.1 | 41.1 | 43.3 | 42.1 | 41.9 | 41.2 | 38.7 | 41.5 | 42.8 | 41.2 | 41.3 | 42.8 |
| **PUNT RETURNS** | | | | | | | | | | | | | | |
| Number | 44 | 38 | 34 | 30 | 26 | 48 | 34 | 31 | 46 | 36 | 22 | 23 | 22 | 27 |
| Yards | 482 | 351 | 397 | 356 | 230 | 522 | 339 | 218 | 548 | 295 | 141 | 177 | 117 | 332 |
| Average Yards | 11.0 | 9.2 | 11.7 | 11.9 | 8.8 | 10.9 | 10.0 | 7.0 | 11.9 | 8.2 | 6.4 | 7.7 | 5.3 | 12.3 |
| Touchdowns | 4 | 1 | 0 | 0 | 1 | 1 | 1 | 0 | 2 | 0 | 0 | 0 | 0 | 1 |
| **KICKOFF RET.:** | | | | | | | | | | | | | | |
| Number | 55 | 50 | 60 | 45 | 57 | 55 | 50 | 40 | 64 | 53 | 42 | 66 | 49 | 54 |
| Yards | 1059 | 1027 | 1217 | 948 | 901 | 1128 | 925 | 923 | 1207 | 1027 | 767 | 1273 | 1236 | 1074 |
| Average Yards | 19.3 | 20.5 | 20.3 | 21.1 | 15.8 | 20.5 | 18.5 | 23.1 | 18.9 | 19.4 | 18.3 | 19.3 | 25.2 | 19.9 |
| Touchdowns | 0 | 0 | 0 | 0 | 0 | 0 | 0 | 0 | 0 | 1 | 0 | 0 | 1 | 1 |
| **INTERCEPT RET.:** | | | | | | | | | | | | | | |
| Number | 15 | 24 | 15 | 21 | 15 | 20 | 15 | 16 | 10 | 13 | 24 | 9 | 20 | 17 |
| Yards | 246 | 612 | 300 | 294 | 198 | 305 | 164 | 280 | 190 | 77 | 279 | 126 | 211 | 318 |
| Average Yards | 16.4 | 25.5 | 20.0 | 14.0 | 13.2 | 15.3 | 10.9 | 17.5 | 19.0 | 5.9 | 11.6 | 14.0 | 10.6 | 18.7 |
| Touchdowns | 3 | 6 | 0 | 1 | 1 | 1 | 1 | 2 | 2 | 0 | 1 | 2 | 1 | 2 |
| **PENALTIES:** | | | | | | | | | | | | | | |
| Number | 92 | 90 | 94 | 111 | 98 | 102 | 98 | 77 | 93 | 86 | 100 | 79 | 74 | 85 |
| Yards | 761 | 780 | 727 | 871 | 830 | 778 | 768 | 729 | 744 | 683 | 826 | 651 | 563 | 709 |
| **FUMBLES:** | | | | | | | | | | | | | | |
| Number | 24 | 34 | 25 | 25 | 32 | 26 | 23 | 37 | 27 | 27 | 25 | 23 | 19 | 23 |
| Number Lost | 16 | 13 | 11 | 17 | 14 | 8 | 11 | 19 | 9 | 22 | 21 | 16 | 16 | 14 |
| **POINTS:** | | | | | | | | | | | | | | |
| Total | 414 | 361 | 243 | 332 | 296 | 383 | 249 | 202 | 367 | 245 | 332 | 236 | 365 | 255 |
| PAT Attempts | 51 | 43 | 29 | 38 | 32 | 43 | 27 | 24 | 46 | 26 | 40 | 27 | 43 | 30 |
| PAT Made | 51 | 43 | 27 | 38 | 32 | 41 | 27 | 22 | 44 | 26 | 38 | 26 | 43 | 29 |
| FG Attempts | 31 | 25 | 17 | 35 | 27 | 34 | 25 | 17 | 21 | 32 | 28 | 20 | 30 | 21 |
| FG Made | 19 | 20 | 14 | 22 | 24 | 28 | 20 | 12 | 15 | 21 | 18 | 16 | 20 | 14 |
| Percent FG Made | 61.3 | 80.0 | 82.4 | 62.9 | 88.9 | 82.4 | 80.0 | 70.6 | 71.4 | 65.6 | 64.3 | 80.0 | 66.7 | 66.7 |
| Safeties | 0 | 0 | 0 | 0 | 0 | 0 | 0 | 0 | 1 | 0 | 0 | 0 | 2 | 2 |

cellar with tragedies, injuries and quarterback controversies all year long. The offensive line was the No. 1 headache, especially for the quarterbacks who were batted around like a beach ball. On top of Mike Utley's injury that left him paralyzed in 1991, guard Eric Andolsek was killed before the '92 season began, and two other starters were lost by midseason. Thus, running back Barry Sanders was a marked man all season, although he did overcome a slow start to become only the third player to rush for 1,000 yards in each of his first four seasons. Receivers Herman Moore and Brett Perriman and kicker Jason Hanson were solid performers, but quarterbacks Rodney Peete, Erik Kramer and Andre Ware were mostly ineffective.

## WESTERN DIVISION

**San Francisco 49ers** — Joe Montana played only 30 minutes of the season and it was a much-celebrated event in the season finale. But Steve Young is the quarterback of the present in San Francisco, and all he did was lead the NFL in passing with 25 touchdowns and only seven interceptions as well as running for 537 yards and four scores. Jerry Rice was his usual fantastic self (84 catches, 11 TD's), and the 49ers found a new star at running back in Ricky Watters, who rushed for 1,013 yards. The defense, particularly a young secondary, was ravaged in a 34-31 loss to Buffalo in Week Two, but it improved as the season progressed. In the end, Young failed to win the Super Bowl, which left many 49ers fans wondering what Montana might have done.

**New Orleans Saints** — The Saints would have won the division title, but they couldn't defeat the 49ers, dropping both games, as well as contests with the Eagles and Bills, by a total of 13 points. New Orleans sent an unprecedented four linebackers to the Pro Bowl — Rickey Jackson, Vaughan Johnson, Sam Mills and Pat Swilling — and end Wayne Martin emerged as a pass-rushing force. But the offense remained average at best. When hot, quarterback Bobby Hebert formed a dangerous combination with Eric Martin (68 catches, five touchdowns). But for the most part, coach Jim Mora's troops relied on a ground game that was anything but spectacular. Rookie Vaughn Dunbar led the team with 565 yards rushing, but he lost his starting job by midseason. Morten Andersen tied for the NFC lead with 120 points.

**Atlanta Falcons** — The team that believed it was too legit looked as if it wanted to quit by the end of a season that became what fans had learned to expect from a Jerry Glanville-coached team: respectable but hardly a Super Bowl contender. Deion Sanders played both baseball and football in the fall, sometimes both on the same day, but the Atlanta defense struggled and ranked last in the conference. The gambling style too often resulted in big scores for the opponents. Quarterback Chris Miller was second in the NFC in passing when he was injured in Week Eight and knocked out for the rest of the year. Ex-Viking Wade Wilson looked fantastic in the final three games. The Falcons didn't have a running game to speak of, but receivers Andre Rison (93 catches, 11 TD's) and Michael Haynes 48 and 10) kept the pressure on opponents.

**Los Angeles Rams** — Jim Everett began to break out of his two-year doldrums, throwing for 3,323 yards and 22 touchdowns. As expected, Chuck Knox bolstered what had been an anemic running game. Cleveland Gary returned to form, and rushed for 1,125 yards and topped the team with 52 receptions. Flipper Anderson scored seven touchdowns, and Henry Ellard caught 47 passes to lead the wideouts. Another Ram who rebounded in 1992 was Kevin Greene, who led the team in tackles and sacks after switching back to linebacker. For the most part, the Rams' defensive woes, which saw them rank next to last in the NFC, were a product of their inexperience. Two rookies, Sean Gilbert and Marc Boutte, started up front. The last game saw running back David Lang score three TD's and Todd Kinchen return two punts for scores.

## DALLAS COWBOYS 13-3 Jimmy Johnson

| Scores of Each Game | | |
|---|---|---|
| 23 | WASHINGTON | 10 |
| 34 | N.Y. Giants | 28 |
| 31 | PHOENIX | 20 |
| 7 | Philadelphia | 31 |
| 27 | SEATTLE | 0 |
| 17 | KANSAS CITY | 10 |
| 28 | L.A. Raiders | 13 |
| 20 | PHILADELPHIA | 10 |
| 37 | Detroit | 3 |
| 23 | L.A. RAMS | 27 |
| 16 | Phoenix | 10 |
| 30 | N.Y. GIANTS | 3 |
| 31 | Denver | 27 |
| 17 | Washington | 20 |
| 41 | Atlanta | 17 |
| 27 | CHICAGO | 14 |

| UseName | Pos. | Hgt. | Wgt. | Age | Int | Pts |
|---|---|---|---|---|---|---|
| Mark Tuinei | OT | 6'5" | 298 | 32 | | |
| Erik Williams | OT | 6'6" | 321 | 23 | | |
| John Gesek | OG | 6'5" | 282 | 29 | | |
| Kevin Gogan | OG-OT | 6'7" | 319 | 27 | | |
| Dale Hellestrae | OG-C | 6'5" | 283 | 30 | | |
| Nate Newton | OG | 6'3" | 303 | 30 | | |
| Alan Veingrad | OG-OT | 6'5" | 280 | 29 | | |
| Frank Cornish | C-OG | 6'4" | 285 | 24 | | |
| Mark Stepnoski | C | 6'2" | 269 | 25 | | |
| Charles Haley | DE | 6'5" | 245 | 28 | | |
| Tony Hill | DE | 6'6" | 242 | 23 | | |
| Jim Jeffcoat | DE | 6'5" | 276 | 31 | | |
| Tony Tolbert | DE | 6'6" | 265 | 24 | | |
| Tony Casillas | DT | 6'3" | 273 | 28 | | |
| Chad Hennings | DT | 6'6" | 267 | 26 | | |
| Jimmie Jones | DT | 6'4" | 276 | 26 | | |
| Leon Lett | DT | 6'6" | 292 | 23 | | |
| Russell Maryland | DT-DE | 6'1" | 275 | 22 | | 6 |
| Bobby Abrams (to CLE, NYG) | LB | 6'3" | 230 | 25 | | |
| Dixon Edwards | LB | 6'1" | 224 | 24 | | |
| Robert Jones | LB | 6'2" | 238 | 22 | | |
| Godfrey Myles | LB | 6'1" | 242 | 23 | 1 | |
| Ken Norton | LB | 6'2" | 241 | 25 | | |
| Mickey Pruitt | LB | 6'1" | 218 | 27 | | |
| Vinson Smith | LB | 6'2" | 237 | 27 | | |
| Bill Bates | DB | 6'1" | 205 | 31 | | |
| Larry Brown | DB | 5'11" | 185 | 22 | 1 | |
| Thomas Everett | DB | 5'9" | 183 | 27 | 2 | |
| Kenneth Gant | DB | 5'11" | 191 | 25 | 3 | |
| Clayton Holmes | DB | 5'10" | 181 | 23 | | |
| Issiac Holt | DB | 6'2" | 198 | 29 | 2 | 2 |
| Ray Horton | DB | 5'11" | 188 | 32 | 2 | 6 |
| Kevin Smith | DB | 5'11" | 177 | 22 | 2 | |
| James Washington | DB | 6'1" | 203 | 27 | 3 | |
| Robert Williams | DB | 5'10" | 186 | 29 | | 6 |
| Darren Woodson | DB | 6'1" | 215 | 23 | | |
| Troy Aikman | QB | 6'4" | 222 | 25 | | 6 |
| Steve Beuerlein | QB | 6'2" | 213 | 27 | | |
| Derrick Gainer (from RAID) | HB | 5'11" | 240 | 26 | | |
| Curvin Richards | HB | 5'9" | 195 | 23 | | 6 |
| Emmitt Smith | HB | 5'9" | 209 | 23 | | 114 |
| Tommie Agee | FB | 6' | 227 | 28 | | |
| Daryl Johnston | FB | 6'2" | 238 | 26 | | 12 |
| Alvin Harper | WR | 6'3" | 207 | 25 | 1 | 24 |
| Michael Irvin | WR | 6'2" | 199 | 26 | | 42 |
| Kelvin Martin | WR | 5'9" | 165 | 27 | | 30 |
| Jimmy Smith | WR | 6'1" | 205 | 23 | | |
| Jay Novacek | TE | 6'4" | 231 | 29 | | 36 |
| Alfredo Roberts | TE | 6'3" | 252 | 27 | | |
| Lin Elliott | K | 6' | 182 | 23 | | 119 |
| Mike Saxon | K | 6'3" | 200 | 30 | | |

## PHILADELPHIA EAGLES 11-5 Rich Kotite

| Scores of Each Game | | |
|---|---|---|
| 15 | NEW ORLEANS | 13 |
| 31 | Phoenix | 14 |
| 30 | DENVER | 0 |
| 31 | DALLAS | 7 |
| 17 | Kansas City | 24 |
| 12 | Washington | 16 |
| 7 | PHOENIX | 3 |
| 10 | Dallas | 20 |
| 31 | L.A. RAIDERS | 10 |
| 24 | Green Bay | 27 |
| 47 | N.Y. Giants | 34 |
| 14 | San Francisco | 20 |
| 28 | MINNESOTA | 17 |
| 20 | Seattle | * 17 |
| 17 | WASHINGTON | 13 |
| 20 | N.Y. GIANTS | 10 |

| UseName | Pos. | Hgt. | Wgt. | Age | Int | Pts |
|---|---|---|---|---|---|---|
| Brian Baldinger | OT-C | 6'4" | 278 | 32 | | |
| Antone Davis | OT | 6'4" | 325 | 25 | | |
| Ron Heller | OT | 6'6" | 280 | 30 | | |
| Daryle Smith | OT | 6'5" | 276 | 28 | | |
| Eric Floyd | OG-OT | 6'5" | 310 | 26 | | |
| John Hudson | OG-C | 6'2" | 275 | 24 | | |
| Mike Schad | OG | 6'5" | 290 | 28 | | |
| Rob Selby | OG-OT | 6'3" | 286 | 24 | | |
| David Alexander | C | 6'3" | 275 | 28 | | |
| Mike Flores | DE | 6'3" | 256 | 25 | | |
| Clyde Simmons | DE | 6'6" | 280 | 28 | | |
| Reggie White | DE | 6'5" | 305 | 30 | | |
| Mike Golic | DT | 6'5" | 275 | 29 | | |
| Andy Harmon | DT | 6'4" | 265 | 23 | | |
| Tommy Jeter | DT | 6'5" | 282 | 22 | | |
| Mike Pitts | DT | 6'5" | 280 | 31 | | |
| Leon Seals | DT | 6'5" | 270 | 28 | | |
| Ephesians Bartley | LB | 6'2" | 213 | 23 | | |
| Byron Evans | LB | 6'2" | 235 | 28 | 4 | |
| Britt Hager | LB | 6'1" | 225 | 26 | | |
| Seth Joyner | LB | 6'2" | 235 | 27 | 4 | 12 |
| Scott Kowalkowski | LB | 6'2" | 228 | 24 | | |
| Ken Rose | LB | 6'1" | 215 | 30 | | 6 |
| William Thomas | LB | 6'2" | 218 | 24 | | |
| Eric Allen | DB | 5'10" | 180 | 26 | 4 | |
| John Booty | DB | 6' | 180 | 26 | 3 | |
| William Frizzell | DB | 6'3" | 206 | 29 | | |
| Tom Gerhart | DB | 6'1" | 195 | 27 | | |
| Wes Hopkins | DB | 6'1" | 215 | 30 | 3 | |
| Izel Jenkins | DB | 5'10" | 190 | 28 | | |
| Mark McMillian | DB | 5'7" | 162 | 22 | 1 | |
| Rich Miano | DB | 6'1" | 200 | 29 | 1 | |
| Otis Smith | DB | 5'11" | 184 | 26 | 1 | |
| Andre Waters | DB | 5'11" | 200 | 30 | | |
| David Archer | QB | 6'2" | 208 | 30 | | |
| Randall Cunningham | QB | 6'4" | 205 | 29 | | 30 |
| Jim McMahon | QB | 6'1" | 195 | 33 | | |
| Tony Brooks | HB | 6' | 230 | 23 | | |
| James Joseph | HB-FB | 6' | 222 | 24 | | |
| Heath Sherman | HB-FB | 6' | 205 | 25 | | 36 |
| Siran Stacy | HB | 5'11" | 203 | 24 | | |
| Herschel Walker | HB | 6'1" | 225 | 30 | | 60 |
| Fred Barnett | WR | 6' | 199 | 26 | | 36 |
| Floyd Dixon | WR | 5'9" | 170 | 28 | | |
| Roy Green | WR | 6'1" | 195 | 35 | | |
| Vai Sikahema | WR | 5'9" | 196 | 30 | | 6 |
| Jeff Sydner | WR | 5'6" | 170 | 22 | | |
| Calvin Williams | WR | 5'11" | 190 | 25 | | 42 |
| Pat Beach | TE | 6'4" | 250 | 32 | | 12 |
| Keith Byars | TE-HB | 6'1" | 238 | 28 | | 18 |
| Maurice Johnson | TE | 6'2" | 243 | 25 | | |
| Jeff Feagles | K | 6' | 205 | 26 | | |
| Roger Ruzek | K | 6'1" | 200 | 31 | | 88 |

Jerome Brown — Died in Offseason Automobile Accident

Ben Smith — Knee Injury

## WASHINGTON REDSKINS 9-7 Joe Gibbs

| Scores of Each Game | | |
|---|---|---|
| 10 | Dallas | 23 |
| 24 | ATLANTA | 17 |
| 13 | DETROIT | 10 |
| 24 | Phoenix | 27 |
| 34 | DENVER | 3 |
| 16 | PHILADELPHIA | 12 |
| 15 | Minnesota | 13 |
| 7 | N.Y. GIANTS | 24 |
| 16 | Seattle | 3 |
| 16 | Kansas City | 35 |
| 3 | New Orleans | 20 |
| 41 | PHOENIX | 3 |
| 28 | N.Y. Giants | 10 |
| 20 | DALLAS | 17 |
| 13 | Philadelphia | 17 |
| 20 | L.A. RAIDERS | 21 |

| UseName | Pos. | Hgt. | Wgt. | Age | Int | Pts |
|---|---|---|---|---|---|---|
| Ray Brown | OT | 6'5" | 280 | 29 | | |
| Mo Elewonibi | OT | 6'4" | 310 | 27 | | |
| Mike Haight | OT | 6'4" | 291 | 29 | | |
| Joe Jacoby | OT-OG | 6'7" | 314 | 32 | | |
| Jim Lachey | OT | 6'6" | 294 | 29 | | |
| Ed Simmons | OT | 6'5" | 300 | 28 | | |
| Raleigh McKenzie | OG-C-OT | 6'2" | 279 | 29 | | |
| Tom Myslinski | OG | 6'2" | 291 | 24 | | |
| Mark Schlereth | OG | 6'3" | 283 | 26 | | |
| Guy Bingham | C | 6'3" | 260 | 34 | | |
| Jeff Bostic | C | 6'2" | 278 | 33 | | |
| Matt Elliott | C | 6'1" | 265 | 23 | | |
| Jason Buck | DE | 6'4" | 265 | 29 | | |
| Shane Collins | DE | 6'3" | 267 | 23 | | |
| Charles Mann | DE | 6'6" | 272 | 31 | | |
| Fred Stokes | DE | 6'3" | 274 | 28 | | |
| James Geathers | DT | 6'7" | 289 | 32 | | |
| Tim Johnson | DT | 6'3" | 283 | 26 | | |
| Jim Wahler (from PHX) | DT-NT | 6'4" | 275 | 26 | | |
| Eric Williams | DT | 6'4" | 290 | 30 | | |
| Bobby Wilson | DT | 6'2" | 283 | 24 | | |
| Tony Barker | LB | 6'2" | 230 | 23 | | |
| John Brantley | LB | 6'3" | 240 | 26 | | |
| Ravin Caldwell | LB | 6'3" | 240 | 29 | | |
| Monte Coleman | LB | 6'2" | 245 | 34 | | |
| Andre Collins | LB | 6'1" | 233 | 24 | 1 | |
| Kurt Gouveia | LB | 6'1" | 228 | 27 | 3 | |
| Wilber Marshall | LB | 6'1" | 231 | 30 | 2 | 6 |
| Todd Bowles | DB | 6'2" | 205 | 28 | 1 | |
| Danny Copeland | DB | 6'2" | 213 | 26 | | 6 |
| Brad Edwards | DB | 6'2" | 207 | 26 | 6 | 6 |
| Pat Eilers | DB | 5'11" | 195 | 25 | | |
| Darrell Green | DB | 5'8" | 170 | 32 | 1 | |
| David Gulledge | DB | 6'1" | 203 | 25 | | |
| A.J. Johnson | DB | 5'8" | 170 | 25 | 3 | |
| Sidney Johnson | DB | 5'9" | 175 | 27 | 1 | |
| Martin Mayhew | DB | 5'8" | 172 | 26 | 3 | |
| Alvoid Mays | DB | 5'9" | 180 | 26 | 2 | |
| Johnny Thomas | DB | 5'9" | 191 | 28 | | |
| Mickey Washington | DB | 5'9" | 187 | 24 | | |
| Cary Conklin | QB | 6'4" | 215 | 24 | | |
| Jeff Rutledge | QB | 6'1" | 193 | 35 | | |
| Mark Rypien | QB | 6'4" | 234 | 29 | | 12 |
| Earnest Byner | HB-FB | 5'10" | 218 | 29 | | 42 |
| Ricky Ervins | HB | 5'7" | 200 | 23 | | 12 |
| Robert Green | HB | 5'8" | 207 | 21 | | |
| Brian Mitchell | HB | 5'10" | 209 | 24 | | 6 |
| Gary Clark | WR | 5'9" | 173 | 30 | | 30 |
| Carl Harry | WR | 5'9" | 170 | 24 | | |
| Stephen Hobbs | WR | 5'11" | 200 | 26 | | |
| Desmond Howard | WR | 5'9" | 183 | 22 | | 6 |
| Art Monk | WR | 6'3" | 210 | 34 | | 18 |
| Ricky Sanders | WR | 5'11" | 180 | 30 | | 18 |
| James Jenkins | TE | 6'2" | 234 | 25 | | |
| Ron Middleton | TE | 6'2" | 270 | 27 | | |
| Terry Orr | TE | 6'2" | 235 | 30 | | 18 |
| Ray Rowe | TE | 6'2" | 256 | 23 | | |
| Don Warren | TE | 6'4" | 242 | 36 | | |
| Kelly Goodburn | K | 6'2" | 199 | 30 | | |
| Chip Lohmiller | K | 6'3" | 210 | 26 | | 120 |

Mark Adickes — Back Injury

Terry Hoage — Arm Injury
Clarence Vaughn — Knee Injury

John Settle — Knee Injury

## NEW YORK GIANTS 6-10 Ray Handley

| Scores of Each Game | | |
|---|---|---|
| 14 | SAN FRANCISCO | 31 |
| 28 | DALLAS | 34 |
| 27 | Chicago | 14 |
| 10 | L.A. Raiders | 13 |
| 31 | PHOENIX | 21 |
| 17 | L.A. Rams | 38 |
| 23 | SEATTLE | 10 |
| 24 | Washington | 7 |
| 27 | GREEN BAY | 7 |
| 13 | Denver | 27 |
| 34 | PHILADELPHIA | 47 |
| 3 | Dallas | 30 |
| 10 | WASHINGTON | 28 |
| 0 | Phoenix | 19 |
| 35 | KANSAS CITY | 21 |
| 10 | Philadelphia | 20 |

| UseName | Pos. | Hgt. | Wgt. | Age | Int | Pts |
|---|---|---|---|---|---|---|
| John Elliott | OT | 6'7" | 305 | 27 | | |
| Clarence Jones | OT | 6'6" | 280 | 24 | | |
| Doug Riesenberg | OT | 6'5" | 275 | 27 | | |
| Bob Kratch | OG | 6'3" | 288 | 26 | | |
| Eric Moore | OG-OT | 6'5" | 290 | 27 | | |
| William Roberts | OG | 6'5" | 280 | 30 | | |
| Bart Oates | C | 6'3" | 265 | 33 | | |
| Brian Williams | C-OG | 6'5" | 300 | 26 | | |
| Stacey Dillard | DE | 6'5" | 288 | 23 | | |
| Eric Dorsey | DE | 6'5" | 280 | 28 | | |
| Mike Fox | DE | 6'6" | 275 | 25 | | |
| Keith Hamilton | DE | 6'6" | 280 | 21 | | |
| Leonard Marshall | DE | 6'3" | 285 | 30 | | |
| Corey Widmer | DT | 6'3" | 276 | 23 | | |
| Erik Howard | NT | 6'4" | 268 | 27 | | |
| John Washington (to ATL) | NT | 6'4" | 275 | 29 | | |
| Carl Banks | LB | 6'4" | 235 | 30 | | |
| Steve DeOssie | LB | 6'2" | 248 | 29 | | |
| Pepper Johnson | LB | 6'3" | 248 | 28 | 2 | |
| Kanavis McGhee | LB | 6'4" | 257 | 23 | | |
| Corey Miller | LB | 6'2" | 225 | 23 | | |
| Ed Reynolds | LB | 6'5" | 242 | 30 | | |
| Lawrence Taylor | LB | 6'3" | 243 | 33 | | |
| Jesse Campbell | DB | 6'1" | 215 | 23 | | |
| Mark Collins | DB | 5'10" | 190 | 28 | 1 | |
| Myron Guyton | DB | 6'1" | 205 | 25 | | |
| Greg Jackson | DB | 6'1" | 200 | 26 | 4 | |
| Lamar McGriggs | DB | 6'3" | 210 | 24 | | |
| Corey Raymond | DB | 5'11" | 180 | 23 | | |
| Phillippi Sparks | DB | 5'11" | 186 | 23 | 1 | |
| Reyna Thompson | DB | 6' | 193 | 29 | 2 | 6 |
| Perry Williams | DB | 6'2" | 203 | 31 | 1 | |
| Dave Brown | QB | 6'5" | 215 | 22 | | |
| Kent Graham | QB | 6'5" | 220 | 23 | | |
| Jeff Hostetler | QB | 6'3" | 212 | 31 | | 18 |
| Phil Simms | QB | 6'3" | 214 | 36 | | |
| Ottis Anderson | HB | 6'2" | 225 | 35 | | |
| Rodney Hampton | HB | 5'11" | 215 | 23 | | 84 |
| Dave Meggett | HB | 5'7" | 180 | 26 | | 18 |
| Lewis Tillman | HB | 6' | 195 | 26 | | |
| Jarrod Bunch | FB | 6'2" | 248 | 24 | | 24 |
| Stephen Baker | WR | 5'8" | 160 | 28 | | 12 |
| Chris Calloway | WR | 5'10" | 185 | 24 | | 6 |
| Mark Ingram | WR | 5'10" | 188 | 27 | | 6 |
| Ed McCaffrey | WR | 6'5" | 215 | 24 | | 30 |
| Joey Smith | WR | 5'10" | 177 | 23 | | |
| John Brandes (from WAS) | TE | 6'2" | 249 | 28 | | |
| Derek Brown | TE | 6'6" | 252 | 22 | | |
| Howard Cross | TE | 6'5" | 245 | 25 | | 12 |
| Aaron Pierce | TE | 6'5" | 246 | 22 | | |
| Matt Bahr | K | 5'10" | 175 | 36 | | 77 |
| Sean Landeta | K | 6' | 210 | 30 | | |

Thom Kaumeyer — Knee Injury

## PHOENIX CARDINALS 4-12 Joe Bugel

| Scores of Each Game | | |
|---|---|---|
| 7 | Tampa Bay | 23 |
| 14 | PHILADELPHIA | 31 |
| 20 | Dallas | 31 |
| 27 | WASHINGTON | 24 |
| 21 | N.Y. Giants | 31 |
| 21 | NEW ORLEANS | 30 |
| 3 | Philadelphia | 7 |
| 24 | SAN FRANCISCO | 14 |
| 20 | L.A. Rams | 14 |
| 17 | Atlanta | 20 |
| 10 | DALLAS | 16 |
| 3 | Washington | 41 |
| 21 | SAN DIEGO | 27 |
| 19 | N.Y. GIANTS | 0 |
| 13 | Indianapolis | 16 |
| 3 | TAMPA BAY | 7 |

| UseName | Pos. | Hgt. | Wgt. | Age | Int | Pts |
|---|---|---|---|---|---|---|
| Rob Baxley | OT | 6'5" | 287 | 23 | | |
| Rick Cunningham | OT | 6'6" | 307 | 25 | | |
| Luis Sharpe | OT | 6'4" | 280 | 32 | | |
| Danny Villa | OT-C | 6'5" | 300 | 27 | | |
| Joe Wolf | OT | 6'5" | 296 | 25 | | |
| Mark May | OG-OT | 6'6" | 300 | 32 | | |
| Lance Smith | OG | 6'2" | 286 | 29 | | |
| Vernice Smith | OG | 6'2" | 300 | 23 | | |
| Ed Cunningham | C | 6'3" | 290 | 23 | | |
| Bill Lewis | C | 6'7" | 290 | 29 | | |
| Reuben Davis (from TB) | DE | 6'4" | 292 | 27 | | |
| Jeff Faulkner | DE | 6'4" | 290 | 28 | | |
| Mike Jones | DE | 6'4" | 287 | 23 | | |
| Eric Swann | DE | 6'4" | 299 | 22 | | 2 |
| Michael Bankston | NT | 6'2" | 290 | 22 | | |
| Keith Rucker | NT | 6'3" | 325 | 23 | | |
| David Braxton | LB | 6'1" | 240 | 27 | | |
| Ken Harvey | LB | 6'2" | 230 | 27 | | |
| Eric Hill | LB | 6'1" | 260 | 25 | | |
| Steve Hyche | LB | 6'2" | 245 | 29 | | |
| Garth Jax | LB | 6'2" | 250 | 28 | | |
| Jock Jones | LB | 6'2" | 245 | 24 | 1 | |
| Freddie Joe Nunn | LB | 6'4" | 250 | 30 | | |
| Jessie Small | LB | 6'3" | 240 | 25 | | |
| Tyronne Stowe | LB | 6'1" | 247 | 27 | | |
| Dexter Davis | DB | 5'10" | 190 | 22 | 2 | |
| Dave Duerson | DB | 6'1" | 208 | 31 | | |
| Odie Harris (from CLE) | DB | 6' | 190 | 26 | | |
| Steve Lofton | DB | 5'9" | 180 | 23 | | |
| Lorenzo Lynch | DB | 5'9" | 200 | 29 | | |
| Robert Massey | DB | 5'10" | 188 | 25 | 5 | 18 |
| Tim McDonald | DB | 6'2" | 222 | 27 | 2 | |
| Chris Oldham | DB | 5'9" | 183 | 23 | | |
| Aeneas Williams | DB | 5'10" | 192 | 23 | 3 | |
| Mike Zordich | DB | 5'11" | 200 | 28 | 3 | |
| Chris Chandler | QB | 6'4" | 220 | 26 | | 6 |
| Timm Rosenbach | QB | 6'1" | 215 | 25 | | |
| Tony Sacca | QB | 6'5" | 230 | 22 | | |
| Johnny Bailey | HB | 5'8" | 187 | 25 | | 18 |
| Eric Blount | HB | 5'9" | 190 | 21 | | |
| Ivory Lee Brown | HB-FB | 6'2" | 245 | 23 | | 12 |
| Larry Centers | HB | 5'11" | 212 | 24 | | 12 |
| Johnny Johnson | HB | 6'2" | 215 | 24 | | 36 |
| Anthony Edwards | WR | 5'9" | 188 | 26 | | 6 |
| Randal Hill | WR | 5'10" | 180 | 22 | | 18 |
| John Jackson | WR | 5'10" | 183 | 25 | | 6 |
| Ernie Jones | WR | 5'11" | 200 | 27 | | 24 |
| Ricky Proehl | WR | 5'10" | 190 | 24 | | 18 |
| Walter Reeves | TE | 6'4" | 265 | 26 | | |
| Butch Rolle | TE | 6'4" | 250 | 28 | | |
| Derek Ware | TE | 6'2" | 255 | 24 | | |
| Willie Wright | TE | 6'6" | 295 | 25 | | |
| Rich Camarillo | K | 5'11" | 195 | 32 | | |
| Greg Davis | K | 6' | 195 | 26 | | 67 |

Willie Williams — Knee Injury

Jay Taylor — Bicep Injury

## DALLAS COWBOYS

### RUSHING
| Last Name | No. | Yds | Avg | TD |
|---|---|---|---|---|
| E. Smith | 373 | 1713 | 4.6 | 18 |
| Richards | 49 | 176 | 3.6 | 1 |
| Aikman | 37 | 105 | 2.8 | 1 |
| Johnston | 17 | 61 | 3.6 | 0 |
| Agee | 16 | 54 | 3.4 | 0 |
| Harper | 1 | 15 | 15.0 | 0 |
| Martin | 2 | 13 | 6.5 | 0 |
| Beuerlein | 4 | -7 | -1.8 | 0 |
| Irvin | 1 | -9 | -9.0 | 0 |

### RECEIVING
| Last Name | No. | Yds | Avg | TD |
|---|---|---|---|---|
| Irvin | 78 | 1396 | 17.9 | 7 |
| Novacek | 68 | 630 | 9.3 | 6 |
| E. Smith | 59 | 335 | 5.7 | 1 |
| Harper | 35 | 562 | 16.1 | 4 |
| Martin | 32 | 359 | 11.2 | 3 |
| Johnston | 32 | 249 | 7.8 | 2 |
| Roberts | 3 | 36 | 12.0 | 0 |
| Agee | 3 | 18 | 6.0 | 0 |
| Richards | 3 | 8 | 2.7 | 0 |
| Gesek | 1 | 4 | 4.0 | 0 |

### PUNT RETURNS
| Last Name | No. | Yds | Avg | TD |
|---|---|---|---|---|
| Martin | 42 | 532 | 12.7 | 2 |
| K. Smith | 1 | 17 | 17.0 | 0 |
| Horton | 1 | 1 | 1.0 | 0 |

### KICKOFF RETURNS
| Last Name | No. | Yds | Avg | TD |
|---|---|---|---|---|
| Martin | 24 | 503 | 21.0 | 0 |
| Holmes | 3 | 70 | 23.3 | 0 |
| K. Smith | 1 | 9 | 9.0 | 0 |
| Edwards | 1 | 0 | 0.0 | 0 |

### PASSING
| Last Name | Att | Cmp | % | Yds | Yd/Att | TD | Int | — % | RK |
|---|---|---|---|---|---|---|---|---|---|
| Aikman | 473 | 302 | 63.8 | 3445 | 7.28 | 23 | 14 | — 3.0 | 3 |
| Beuerlein | 18 | 12 | 66.7 | 152 | 8.44 | 0 | 1 | — 5.6 | |

### PUNTING
| Last Name | No. | Avg. |
|---|---|---|
| Saxon | 61 | 43.0 |

### KICKING
| Last Name | XP | Att. | % | FG | Att | % |
|---|---|---|---|---|---|---|
| Elliott | 47 | 48 | 98 | 24 | 35 | 69 |

## PHILADELPHIA EAGLES

### RUSHING
| Last Name | No. | Yds | Avg | TD |
|---|---|---|---|---|
| Walker | 267 | 1070 | 4.0 | 8 |
| Sherman | 112 | 583 | 5.2 | 5 |
| Cunningham | 87 | 549 | 6.3 | 5 |
| Byars | 41 | 176 | 4.3 | 1 |
| McMahon | 6 | 23 | 3.8 | 0 |
| Sikahema | 2 | 2 | 1.0 | 0 |
| Barnett | 1 | -15 | -15.0 | 0 |

### RECEIVING
| Last Name | No. | Yds | Avg | TD |
|---|---|---|---|---|
| Barnett | 67 | 1083 | 16.2 | 6 |
| Byars | 56 | 502 | 9.0 | 2 |
| Williams | 42 | | 14.2 | 7 |
| Walker | 38 | 278 | 7.3 | 2 |
| Sherman | 18 | 219 | 12.2 | 1 |
| Sikahema | 13 | 142 | 10.9 | 0 |
| Green | 8 | 105 | 13.1 | 0 |
| Beach | 8 | 75 | 9.4 | 2 |
| F. Dixon | 3 | 36 | 12.0 | 0 |
| Johnson | 2 | 16 | 8.0 | 0 |

### PUNT RETURNS
| Last Name | No. | Yds | Avg | TD |
|---|---|---|---|---|
| Sikahema | 40 | 503 | 12.6 | 1 |
| Sydner | 7 | 52 | 7.4 | 0 |

### KICKOFF RETURNS
| Last Name | No. | Yds | Avg | TD |
|---|---|---|---|---|
| Sikahema | 26 | 528 | 20.3 | 0 |
| Sydner | 17 | 368 | 21.6 | 0 |
| Walker | 3 | 69 | 23.0 | 0 |
| Booty | 1 | 11 | 11.0 | 0 |
| Brooks | 1 | 11 | 11.0 | 0 |

### PASSING
| Last Name | Att | Cmp | % | Yds | Yd/Att | TD | Int | — % | RK |
|---|---|---|---|---|---|---|---|---|---|
| Cunningham | 384 | 233 | 60.7 | 2775 | 7.23 | 19 | 11 | — 2.9 | 4 |
| McMahon | 43 | 22 | 51.2 | 279 | 6.49 | 1 | 2 | — 4.7 | |
| Byars | 1 | 0 | 0.0 | 0 | 0.00 | 0 | 0 | — 0.0 | |
| Walker | 1 | 0 | 0.0 | 0 | 0.00 | 0 | 0 | — 0.0 | |

### PUNTING
| Last Name | No. | Avg. |
|---|---|---|
| Feagles | 82 | 42.2 |

### KICKING
| Last Name | XP | ATT | % | FG | ATT | % |
|---|---|---|---|---|---|---|
| Ruzek | 40 | 44 | 91 | 16 | 25 | 64 |

## WASHINGTON REDSKINS

### RUSHING
| Last Name | No. | Yds | Avg | TD |
|---|---|---|---|---|
| Byner | 262 | 998 | 3.8 | 6 |
| Ervins | 151 | 495 | 3.3 | 2 |
| Mitchell | 6 | 70 | 11.7 | 0 |
| Rypien | 36 | 50 | 1.4 | 2 |
| R. Green | 8 | 46 | 5.8 | 0 |
| Monk | 6 | 45 | 7.5 | 0 |
| Clark | 2 | 18 | 9.0 | 0 |
| Howard | 3 | 14 | 4.7 | 0 |
| Goodburn | 2 | 1 | 0.5 | 0 |
| Conklin | 3 | -4 | -1.3 | 0 |
| Sanders | 4 | -6 | -1.5 | 0 |

### RECEIVING
| Last Name | No. | Yds | Avg | TD |
|---|---|---|---|---|
| Clark | 64 | 912 | 14.3 | 5 |
| Sanders | 51 | 707 | 13.9 | 3 |
| Monk | 46 | 644 | 14.0 | 3 |
| Byner | 39 | 338 | 8.7 | 1 |
| Ervins | 32 | 252 | 7.9 | 0 |
| Orr | 22 | 356 | 16.2 | 3 |
| Middleton | 7 | 50 | 7.1 | 0 |
| Warren | 4 | 25 | 6.3 | 0 |
| Mitchell | 3 | 30 | 10.0 | 0 |
| Howard | 3 | 20 | 6.7 | 0 |
| R. Green | 1 | 5 | 5.0 | 0 |

### PUNT RETURNS
| Last Name | No. | Yds | Avg | TD |
|---|---|---|---|---|
| Mitchell | 29 | 271 | 9.3 | 1 |
| Howard | 6 | 84 | 14.0 | 1 |
| S. Johnson | 1 | 0 | 0.0 | 0 |
| Thomas | 1 | 0 | 0.0 | 0 |

### KICKOFF RETURNS
| Last Name | No. | Yds | Avg | TD |
|---|---|---|---|---|
| Mitchell | 23 | 492 | 21.4 | 0 |
| Howard | 22 | 462 | 21.0 | 0 |
| R. Green | 1 | 9 | 9.0 | 0 |
| Gouveia | 1 | 7 | 7.0 | 0 |
| Orr | 1 | 3 | 3.0 | 0 |

### PASSING
| Last Name | Att | Cmp | % | Yds | Yd/Att | TD | Int | — % | RK |
|---|---|---|---|---|---|---|---|---|---|
| Rypien | 479 | 269 | 56.2 | 3282 | 6.85 | 13 | 17 | — 3.5 | 12 |
| Byner | 3 | 1 | 33.3 | 41 | 13.67 | 1 | 0 | — 0.0 | |
| Conklin | 2 | 2 | 100.0 | 16 | 8.00 | 1 | 0 | — 0.0 | |
| Mitchell | 1 | 0 | 0.0 | 0 | 0.00 | 0 | 0 | — 0.0 | |

### PUNTING
| Last Name | No. | Avg. |
|---|---|---|
| Goodburn | 65 | 39.3 |

### KICKING
| Last Name | XP | ATT | % | FG | ATT | % |
|---|---|---|---|---|---|---|
| Lohmiller | 30 | 30 | 100 | 30 | 40 | 75 |

## NEW YORK GIANTS

### RUSHING
| Last Name | No. | Yds | Avg | TD |
|---|---|---|---|---|
| Hampton | 257 | 1141 | 4.4 | 14 |
| Bunch | 104 | 501 | 4.8 | 3 |
| Hostetler | 34 | 172 | 5.1 | 0 |
| Meggett | 32 | 167 | 5.2 | 0 |
| Graham | 6 | 36 | 6.0 | 0 |
| Anderson | 10 | 31 | 3.1 | 0 |
| Simms | 6 | 17 | 2.8 | 0 |
| Tillman | 6 | 13 | 2.2 | 0 |
| Da. Brown | 2 | -1 | -0.5 | 0 |

### RECEIVING
| Last Name | No. | Yds | Avg | TD |
|---|---|---|---|---|
| McCaffrey | 49 | 610 | 12.4 | 5 |
| Meggett | 38 | 229 | 6.0 | 2 |
| Hampton | 28 | 215 | 7.7 | 0 |
| Ingram | 27 | 408 | 15.1 | 1 |
| Cross | 27 | 357 | 13.2 | 2 |
| Calloway | 27 | 335 | 12.4 | 1 |
| Baker | 17 | 333 | 19.6 | 2 |
| Bunch | 11 | 50 | 4.5 | 1 |
| De. Brown | 4 | 31 | 7.8 | 0 |
| Smith | 3 | 45 | 15.0 | 0 |
| Tillman | 1 | 15 | 15.0 | 0 |

### PUNT RETURNS
| Last Name | No. | Yds | Avg | TD |
|---|---|---|---|---|
| Meggett | 27 | 240 | 8.9 | 0 |

### KICKOFF RETURNS
| Last Name | No. | Yds | Avg | TD |
|---|---|---|---|---|
| Meggett | 20 | 455 | 22.8 | 1 |
| Smith | 30 | 564 | 18.8 | 0 |
| Calloway | 2 | 29 | 14.5 | 0 |
| Bunch | 2 | 27 | 13.5 | 0 |
| Sparks | 2 | 23 | 11.5 | 0 |

### PASSING
| Last Name | Att | Cmp | % | Yds | Yd/Att | TD | Int | — % | RK |
|---|---|---|---|---|---|---|---|---|---|
| Hostetler | 192 | 103 | 53.6 | 1225 | 6.38 | 8 | 3 | — 1.6 | |
| Simms | 137 | 83 | 60.6 | 912 | 6.66 | 5 | 3 | — 2.2 | |
| Graham | 97 | 42 | 43.3 | 470 | 4.85 | 1 | 4 | — 4.1 | |
| Da. Brown | 7 | 4 | 57.1 | 21 | 3.00 | 0 | 0 | — 0.0 | |

### PUNTING
| Last Name | No. | Avg. |
|---|---|---|
| Landeta | 55 | 42.1 |

### KICKING
| Last Name | XP | ATT | % | FG | ATT | % |
|---|---|---|---|---|---|---|
| Bahr | 29 | 29 | 100 | 16 | 21 | 76 |

## PHOENIX CARDINALS

### RUSHING
| Last Name | No. | Yds | Avg | TD |
|---|---|---|---|---|
| Johnson | 178 | 734 | 4.1 | 6 |
| Bailey | 52 | 233 | 4.5 | 1 |
| Brown | 68 | 194 | 2.9 | 2 |
| Chandler | 36 | 149 | 4.1 | 1 |
| Centers | 37 | 139 | 3.8 | 0 |
| Proehl | 3 | 23 | 7.7 | 0 |
| Rosenbach | 9 | 11 | 1.2 | 0 |
| R. Hill | 1 | 4 | 4.0 | 0 |
| Blount | 1 | -1 | -1.0 | 0 |
| E. Jones | 2 | -3 | -1.5 | 0 |

### RECEIVING
| Last Name | No. | Yds | Avg | TD |
|---|---|---|---|---|
| Proehl | 60 | 744 | 12.4 | 3 |
| R. Hill | 58 | 861 | 14.8 | 3 |
| Centers | 50 | 417 | 8.3 | 2 |
| E. Jones | 38 | 559 | 14.7 | 4 |
| Bailey | 33 | 331 | 10.0 | 1 |
| Edwards | 14 | 147 | 10.5 | 1 |
| Johnson | 14 | 103 | 7.4 | 0 |
| Rolle | 13 | 64 | 4.9 | 0 |
| Brown | 7 | 54 | 7.7 | 0 |
| Reeves | 6 | 28 | 4.7 | 0 |
| Blount | 3 | 18 | 6.0 | 0 |
| Ware | 1 | 13 | 13.0 | 0 |
| Jackson | 1 | 5 | 5.0 | 0 |

### PUNT RETURNS
| Last Name | No. | Yds | Avg | TD |
|---|---|---|---|---|
| Bailey | 20 | 263 | 13.2 | 0 |
| Blount | 13 | 101 | 7.8 | 0 |

### KICKOFF RETURNS
| Last Name | No. | Yds | Avg | TD |
|---|---|---|---|---|
| Bailey | 28 | 690 | 24.6 | 0 |
| Blount | 11 | 251 | 22.8 | 0 |
| Edwards | 8 | 143 | 17.9 | 0 |
| L. Smith | 2 | 16 | 8.0 | 0 |
| Jackson | 1 | 17 | 17.0 | 0 |
| Rolle | 1 | 10 | 10.0 | 0 |

### PASSING
| Last Name | Att | Cmp | % | Yds | Yd/Att | TD | Int | — % | RK |
|---|---|---|---|---|---|---|---|---|---|
| Chandler | 413 | 245 | 59.3 | 2832 | 6.86 | 15 | 15 | — 3.6 | 8 |
| Rosenbach | 92 | 49 | 53.3 | 483 | 5.25 | 0 | 6 | — 6.5 | |
| Sacca | 11 | 4 | 36.4 | 29 | 2.64 | 0 | 2 | — 18.2 | |
| Proehl | 1 | 0 | 0.0 | 0 | 0.00 | 0 | 1 | — 100.0 | |

### PUNTING
| Last Name | No. | Avg. |
|---|---|---|
| Camarillo | 54 | 42.9 |
| G. Davis | 4 | 36.8 |

### KICKING
| Last Name | XP | Att. | % | FG | Att | % |
|---|---|---|---|---|---|---|
| Davis | 28 | 28 | 100 | 13 | 26 | 50z |

## MINNESOTA VIKINGS 11-5 Dennis Green

| Scores of Each Game | | |
|---|---|---|
| 23 | Green Bay | *20 |
| 17 | Detroit | 31 |
| 26 | TAMPA BAY | 20 |
| 42 | Cincinnati | 7 |
| 21 | CHICAGO | 20 |
| 31 | DETROIT | 14 |
| 13 | WASHINGTON | 15 |
| 38 | Chicago | 10 |
| 35 | Tampa Bay | 7 |
| 13 | HOUSTON | 17 |
| 17 | CLEVELAND | 13 |
| 31 | L.A. Rams | 17 |
| 17 | Philadelphia | 28 |
| 17 | SAN FRANCISCO | 20 |
| 6 | Pittsburgh | 3 |
| 27 | GREEN BAY | 7 |

| UseName | Pos. | Hgt. | Wgt. | Age | Int | Pts |
|---|---|---|---|---|---|---|
| Scott Adams | OT | 6'5" | 281 | 25 | | |
| Tim Irwin | OT | 6'6" | 297 | 33 | | |
| Gary Zimmerman | OT | 6'6" | 294 | 30 | | |
| Bernard Dafney | OG | 6'5" | 317 | 22 | | |
| Brian Habib | OG | 6'7" | 299 | 27 | | |
| Randall McDaniel | OG | 6'3" | 280 | 27 | | |
| Adam Schreiber | OG-C | 6'4" | 290 | 30 | | |
| Kirk Lowdermilk | C | 6'3" | 280 | 29 | | |
| Mike Morris | C | 6'5" | 273 | 31 | | |
| Chris Doleman | DE | 6'5" | 275 | 30 | 1 | 8 |
| Robert Harris | DE | 6'4" | 285 | 23 | | |
| Al Noga | DE | 6'1" | 269 | 26 | | |
| Roy Barker | DT | 6'4" | 292 | 23 | | |
| Brad Culpepper | DT | 6'1" | 267 | 24 | | |
| George Hinkle | DT | 6'5" | 269 | 27 | | |
| John Randle | DT | 6'1" | 270 | 24 | | |
| Henry Thomas | DT | 6'2" | 285 | 27 | | |
| Esera Tuaolo (from GB) | DT | 6'2" | 275 | 24 | | |

Lorenzo Freeman — Knee Injury
Todd Kalis — Knee Injury

| UseName | Pos. | Hgt. | Wgt. | Age | Int | Pts |
|---|---|---|---|---|---|---|
| David Bavaro | LB | 6' | 228 | 25 | | |
| Ray Berry | LB | 6'2" | 227 | 28 | | |
| Jack Del Rio | LB | 6'4" | 250 | 29 | 2 | 6 |
| Carlos Jenkins | LB | 6'3" | 222 | 24 | 1 | 12 |
| Greg Manusky | LB | 6'1" | 237 | 26 | | |
| Ed McDaniel | LB | 5'11" | 232 | 23 | | |
| Mike Merriweather | LB | 6'2" | 226 | 31 | | |
| Van Waiters | LB | 6'4" | 250 | 27 | | |
| Eric Everett | DB | 5'11" | 170 | 25 | | |
| Vencie Glenn | DB | 6' | 189 | 27 | 5 | |
| Carl Lee | DB | 6' | 182 | 31 | 2 | |
| Audrey McMillian | DB | 6' | 190 | 30 | 8 | 12 |
| Anthony Parker | DB | 5'10" | 179 | 26 | 3 | 6 |
| Todd Scott | DB | 5'10" | 191 | 24 | 5 | 6 |
| Tripp Welbourne | DB | 6' | 205 | 23 | | |
| David Wilson (from NE) | DB | 5'10" | 192 | 22 | | |
| Felix Wright | DB | 6'2" | 197 | 33 | 1 | |

Najee Mustafaa — Back Injury

| UseName | Pos. | Hgt. | Wgt. | Age | Int | Pts |
|---|---|---|---|---|---|---|
| Rich Gannon | QB | 6'3" | 208 | 26 | | |
| Sean Salisbury | QB | 6'5" | 217 | 29 | | |
| Terry Allen | HB | 5'10" | 197 | 24 | | 90 |
| Roger Craig | HB | 5'11" | 181 | 31 | | 24 |
| Keith Henderson (from SF) | HB | 6'1" | 220 | 26 | | 6 |
| Darrin Nelson | HB | 5'9" | 180 | 33 | | |
| Anthony Carter | WR | 5'11" | 181 | 31 | | 18 |
| Cris Carter | WR | 6'3" | 198 | 26 | | 36 |
| Joe Johnson | WR | 5'8" | 170 | 29 | | 6 |
| Hassan Jones | WR | 6' | 202 | 28 | | 24 |
| Jake Reed | WR | 6'3" | 216 | 24 | | |
| Ronnie West | WR | 6'1" | 215 | 24 | | |
| Steve Jordan | TE | 6'4" | 240 | 31 | | 12 |
| Brent Novoselsky | TE | 6'3" | 237 | 26 | | |
| Derek Tennell (to DAL) | TE | 6'5" | 270 | 28 | | |
| Mike Tice | TE | 6'7" | 253 | 33 | | 6 |
| Danta Whitaker | TE | 6'4" | 254 | 28 | | |
| Harry Newsome | K | 6' | 185 | 29 | | |
| Fuad Reveiz | K | 5'11" | 226 | 29 | | 102 |

## GREEN BAY PACKERS 9-7 Mike Holmgren

| Scores of Each Game | | |
|---|---|---|
| 20 | MINNESOTA | *23 |
| 3 | Tampa Bay | 31 |
| 24 | CINCINNATI | 23 |
| 17 | PITTSBURGH | 3 |
| 10 | Atlanta | 24 |
| 6 | Cleveland | 17 |
| 10 | CHICAGO | 30 |
| 27 | Detroit | 13 |
| 7 | N.Y. Giants | 27 |
| 27 | PHILADELPHIA | 24 |
| 17 | Chicago | 3 |
| 19 | TAMPA BAY | 14 |
| 38 | DETROIT | 10 |
| 16 | Houston | 14 |
| 28 | L.A. RAMS | 13 |
| 7 | Minnesota | 27 |

| UseName | Pos. | Hgt. | Wgt. | Age | Int | Pts |
|---|---|---|---|---|---|---|
| Cecil Gray | OT | 6'4" | 292 | 24 | | |
| Tootie Robbins | OT | 6'5" | 315 | 34 | | |
| Ken Ruettgers | OT | 6'5" | 286 | 30 | | |
| Harvey Salem | OT | 6'6" | 289 | 31 | | |
| Joe Sims | OT-OG | 6'3" | 294 | 23 | | |
| Ron Hallstrom | OG | 6'6" | 310 | 33 | | |
| Rich Moran | OG | 6'3" | 280 | 30 | | |
| Tom Neville | OG | 6'5" | 288 | 30 | | |
| Frank Winters | OG-C | 6'3" | 290 | 28 | | |
| David Viaene | OG-OT | 6'5" | 300 | 27 | | |
| James Campen | C | 6'3" | 280 | 28 | | |
| Lester Archambeau | DE | 6'4" | 275 | 25 | | |
| Sebastian Barrie | DE | 6'3" | 270 | 22 | | |
| Matt Brock | DE | 6'5" | 290 | 26 | | |
| Robert Brown | DE | 6'2" | 280 | 32 | | |
| Don Davey | DE | 6'4" | 280 | 24 | | |
| Keith Millard (from SEA) | DT | 6'5" | 263 | 30 | | |
| Danny Noonan (from DAL) | DT | 6'4" | 275 | 27 | | |
| John Jurkovic | NT | 6'2" | 300 | 25 | | |
| Alfred Oglesby | NT | 6'3" | 285 | 25 | | |

Tony Mandarich — Thyroid Illness
Shawn Patterson — Knee INjury

| UseName | Pos. | Hgt. | Wgt. | Age | Int | Pts |
|---|---|---|---|---|---|---|
| Tony Bennett | LB | 6'2" | 243 | 25 | | 6 |
| Jeff Brady | LB | 6'1" | 235 | 23 | | |
| Brett Collins | LB | 6'1" | 226 | 23 | | |
| Burnell Dent | LB | 6'1" | 238 | 29 | | |
| Mark D"Onofrio | LB | 6'2" | 235 | 23 | | |
| Johnny Holland | LB | 6'2" | 235 | 27 | 3 | |
| George Koonce | LB | 6'1" | 238 | 23 | | |
| Brian Noble | LB | 6'3" | 250 | 29 | | |
| Bryce Paup | LB | 6'5" | 247 | 24 | | |
| Lewis Billups | DB | 5'11" | 182 | 28 | | |
| Terrell Buckley | DB | 5'9" | 174 | 21 | 3 | 12 |
| LeRoy Butler | DB | 6' | 200 | 24 | 1 | |
| Carl Carter | DB | 5'11" | 190 | 28 | | |
| Chuck Cecil | DB | 6' | 190 | 27 | 4 | |
| Vinnie Clark | DB | 6' | 194 | 23 | 2 | |
| Tim Hauck | DB | 5'11" | 181 | 25 | | |
| Dave McCloughan | DB | 6'1" | 185 | 25 | | |
| Buford McGee | FB | | | | | |
| Roland Mitchell | DB | 5'11" | 195 | 28 | 2 | |
| Adrian White | DB | 6' | 205 | 28 | | |

| UseName | Pos. | Hgt. | Wgt. | Age | Int | Pts |
|---|---|---|---|---|---|---|
| Ty Detmer | QB | 6' | 183 | 24 | | |
| Brett Favre | QB | 6'2" | 220 | 22 | | 6 |
| Don Majkowski | QB | 6'2" | 203 | 28 | | |
| Darrell Thompson | HB | 6' | 222 | 24 | | 18 |
| Marcus Wilson | HB | 6'1" | 210 | 24 | | |
| Vince Workman | HB | 5'10 | 205 | 24 | | 12 |
| Edgar Bennett | FB | 6' | 223 | 23 | | |
| Buford McGee | FB | 6' | 210 | 32 | | |
| Dexter McNabb | FB | 6'2" | 245 | 23 | | |
| Harry Sydney | FB | 6' | 217 | 33 | | 18 |
| Sanjay Beach | WR | 6'1" | 194 | 26 | | 6 |
| Robert Brooks | WR | 6' | 171 | 22 | | 6 |
| Corey Harris (from HOU) | WR | 5'11" | 195 | 22 | | |
| Ron Lewis (from SF) | WR | 5'11" | 180 | 24 | | |
| Sterling Sharpe | WR | 5'11" | 205 | 27 | | 78 |
| Kitrick Taylor | WR | 5'11" | 189 | 28 | | 6 |
| Jackie Harris | TE | 6'3" | 243 | 24 | | 12 |
| Darryl Ingram | TE | 6'3" | 250 | 26 | | |
| Ed West | TE | 6'1" | 244 | 31 | | |
| Chris Jacke | K | 6' | 197 | 26 | | 96 |
| Paul McJulien | K | 5'10" | 190 | 27 | | |
| Bryan Wagner | K | 6'2" | 200 | 30 | | |

## TAMPA BAY BUCCANEERS 5-11 Sam Wyche

| Scores of Each Game | | |
|---|---|---|
| 23 | PHOENIX | 7 |
| 31 | GREEN BAY | 3 |
| 20 | Minnesota | 26 |
| 27 | Detroit | 23 |
| 14 | INDIANAPOLIS | 24 |
| 14 | Chicago | 31 |
| 7 | DETROIT | 38 |
| 21 | New Orleans | 23 |
| 7 | MINNESOTA | 35 |
| 20 | CHICAGO | 17 |
| 14 | San Diego | 29 |
| 14 | Green Bay | 19 |
| 27 | L.A. RAMS | 31 |
| 7 | ATLANTA | 35 |
| 14 | San Francisco | 21 |
| 7 | Phoenix | 3 |

| UseName | Pos. | Hgt. | Wgt. | Age | Int | Pts |
|---|---|---|---|---|---|---|
| Scott Dill | OT | 6'5" | 285 | 26 | | |
| Paul Gruber | OT | 6'5" | 290 | 27 | | |
| Charles McRae | OT-OG | 6'7" | 300 | 23 | | |
| Rob Taylor | OT | 6'6" | 290 | 31 | | |
| Ian Beckles | OG | 6'1" | 295 | 25 | | |
| Brian Blados | OG | 6'5" | 296 | 30 | | |
| Tom McHale | OG | 6'4" | 290 | 29 | | |
| Bruce Reimers | OG | 6'7" | 300 | 31 | | |
| Tim Ryan | OG | 6'2" | 280 | 23 | | |
| Mike Sullivan | OG | 6'3" | 290 | 24 | | |
| Randy Grimes | C | 6'4" | 275 | 32 | | |
| Tony Mayberry | C | 6'4" | 290 | 24 | | |
| Al Chamblee | DE | 6'1" | 240 | 23 | | |
| Santana Dotson | DE | 6'5" | 270 | 22 | | 6 |
| Mark Duckens | DE-DT | 6'4" | 270 | 27 | | |
| Keith McCants | DE | 6'3" | 265 | 24 | | |
| Reggie Rogers | DE | 6'6" | 280 | 28 | | |
| Ray Seals | DE | 6'3" | 270 | 27 | | |
| David Grant | DT | 6'5" | 278 | 26 | | |
| Rhett Hall | DT | 6'2" | 260 | 23 | | |
| Mark Wheeler | NT-DT | 6'2" | 280 | 22 | | |
| Corey Mayfield | NT-DT | 6'3" | 280 | 22 | | |

| UseName | Pos. | Hgt. | Wgt. | Age | Int | Pts |
|---|---|---|---|---|---|---|
| Elijah Alexander | LB | 6'2" | 230 | 22 | | |
| Ed Brady | LB | 6'2" | 235 | 30 | | |
| Darrick Brownlow | LB | 6' | 235 | 23 | | |
| Reggie Burnette | LB | 6'2" | 240 | 23 | | |
| Sidney Coleman | LB | 6'2" | 250 | 28 | | |
| Broderick Thomas | LB | 6'4" | 250 | 25 | 2 | 6 |
| Calvin Tiggle | LB | 6'1" | 235 | 23 | | |
| Jimmy Williams | LB | 6'3" | 230 | 31 | 2 | |
| Darren Anderson (from NE) | DB | 5'10" | 180 | 23 | | |
| Chris Barber | DB | 6' | 187 | 28 | | |
| Joey Browner | DB | 6'2" | 231 | 32 | | |
| Marty Carter | DB | 6'1" | 200 | 22 | 3 | |
| Tony Covington | DB | 5'11" | 190 | 24 | | |
| Darrell Fullington | DB | 6'1" | 200 | 28 | 3 | |
| Rogerick Green | DB | 5'10" | 180 | 22 | | |
| Roger Jones | DB | 5'9" | 175 | 23 | | 6 |
| Joe King | DB | 6'2" | 200 | 24 | 2 | |
| Garry Lewis | DB | 5'11" | 185 | 25 | 1 | |
| Milton Mack | DB | 5'11" | 185 | 28 | 3 | |
| Darryl Pollard | DB | 5'11" | 185 | 28 | 2 | |
| Ricky Reynolds | DB | 5'11" | 190 | 27 | 2 | 6 |

| UseName | Pos. | Hgt. | Wgt. | Age | Int | Pts |
|---|---|---|---|---|---|---|
| Steve DeBerg | QB | 6'3" | 215 | 38 | | |
| Craig Erickson | QB | 6'2" | 200 | 23 | | |
| Mike Pawlawski | QB | 6'1" | 205 | 23 | | |
| Vinny Testaverde | QB | 6'5" | 220 | 28 | | 12 |
| Gary Anderson | HB | 6' | 190 | 31 | | 6 |
| Reggie Cobb | HB-FB | 6' | 215 | 24 | | 54 |
| Stanford Jennings | HB | 6'1" | 210 | 30 | | 6 |
| Alonzo Highsmith | FB | 6'1" | 235 | 27 | | |
| Anthony McDowell | FB | 5'11" | 230 | 23 | | 12 |
| Mazio Royster | FB | 6'1" | 205 | 22 | | |
| Mike Barber | WR | 5'11" | 172 | 25 | | |
| Mark Carrier | WR | 6' | 185 | 26 | | 24 |
| Willie Culpepper | WR | 5'11" | 155 | 25 | | |
| Lawrence Dawsey | WR | 6' | 195 | 24 | | 6 |
| Willie Drewrey | WR | 5'7" | 170 | 29 | | 12 |
| Courtney Hawkins | WR | 5'9" | 180 | 22 | | 12 |
| Jeff Parker | WR | 5'10" | 185 | 23 | | |
| Charles Wilson | WR | 5'10" | 180 | 24 | | |
| Tyji Armstrong | TE | 6'4" | 255 | 21 | | 6 |
| Ron Hall | TE | 6'4" | 245 | 28 | | 24 |
| Todd Harrison | TE | 6'4" | 260 | 23 | | |
| Dave Moore (from MIA) | TE | 6'2" | 245 | 22 | | |
| Eddie Murray (from KC) | K | 5'11" | 185 | 36 | | 28 |
| Dan Stryzinski | K | 6'1" | 195 | 27 | | |
| Ken Willis (to NYG) | K | 5'11" | 190 | 25 | | 57 |

## CHICAGO BEARS 5-11 Mike Ditka

| Scores of Each Game | | |
|---|---|---|
| 27 | DETROIT | 24 |
| 6 | New Orleans | 28 |
| 14 | N.Y. GIANTS | 27 |
| 41 | ATLANTA | 31 |
| 20 | Minnesota | 21 |
| 31 | TAMPA BAY | 14 |
| 30 | Green Bay | 10 |
| 10 | MINNESOTA | 38 |
| 28 | CINCINNATI | 31 |
| 17 | Tampa Bay | 20 |
| 3 | GREEN BAY | 17 |
| 14 | Cleveland | 27 |
| 7 | Houston | 24 |
| 30 | PITTSBURGH | 6 |
| 3 | Detroit | 16 |
| 14 | Dallas | 27 |

| UseName | Pos. | Hgt. | Wgt. | Age | Int | Pts |
|---|---|---|---|---|---|---|
| Louis Age | OT | 6'7" | 350 | 22 | | |
| Troy Auzenne | OT | 6'7" | 282 | 23 | | |
| Stan Thomas | OT | 6'5" | 290 | 23 | | |
| Keith Van Horne | OT | 6'6" | 290 | 34 | | |
| Mark Bortz | OG | 6'6" | 280 | 31 | | |
| Tom Thayer | OG | 6'4" | 280 | 31 | | |
| John Wojciechowski | OG-OT | 6'4" | 280 | 29 | | |
| Jerry Fontenot | C | 6'3" | 280 | 25 | | |
| Jay Leeuwenburg | C | 6'2" | 290 | 23 | | |
| Mark Rodenhauser | C | 6'5" | 265 | 31 | | |
| Trace Armstrong | DE | 6'4" | 275 | 26 | | |
| Richard Dent | DE | 6'5" | 265 | 31 | | |
| Alonzo Spellman | DE-DT | 6'4" | 280 | 20 | | |
| Steve McMichael | DT | 6'2" | 270 | 34 | | |
| William Perry | DT | 6'2" | 320 | 29 | | |
| Tim Ryan | DT-DE | 6'4" | 270 | 24 | | |
| James Williams | DT | 6'7" | 305 | 24 | | |
| Chris Zorich | DT | 6'1" | 267 | 23 | | 6 |

| UseName | Pos. | Hgt. | Wgt. | Age | Int | Pts |
|---|---|---|---|---|---|---|
| Ron Cox | LB | 6'2" | 242 | 24 | | |
| Dante Jones | LB | 6'1" | 240 | 27 | | |
| Jim Morrissey | LB | 6'3" | 227 | 29 | 1 | |
| Ron Rivera | LB | 6'3" | 230 | 30 | | |
| John Roper | LB | 6'1" | 240 | 26 | | |
| Jim Schwantz | LB | 6'2" | 231 | 22 | | |
| Mike Singletary | LB | 6' | 240 | 33 | 1 | |
| Mark Carrier | DB | 6'1" | 192 | 24 | | |
| Maurice Douglass | DB | 5'11" | 200 | 28 | | |
| Richard Fain | DB | 5'10" | 180 | 24 | | |
| Shaun Gayle | DB | 5'11" | 202 | 30 | 2 | |
| John Mangum | DB | 5'10" | 178 | 25 | | |
| Markus Paul | DB | 6'2" | 205 | 26 | 1 | |
| Lemuel Stinson | DB | 5'9" | 170 | 26 | 2 | |
| David Tate | DB | 6' | 200 | 27 | | |
| Donnell Woolford | DB | 5'9" | 194 | 26 | 7 | |

| UseName | Pos. | Hgt. | Wgt. | Age | Int | Pts |
|---|---|---|---|---|---|---|
| Will Furrer | QB | 6'3" | 208 | 24 | | |
| Jim Harbaugh | QB | 6'3" | 215 | 27 | | 6 |
| Peter Tom Willis | QB | 6'2" | 200 | 25 | | |
| Neal Anderson | HB | 5'11" | 218 | 28 | | 66 |
| Mark Green | HB | 5'11" | 195 | 25 | | 12 |
| Darren Lewis | HB-FB | 5'10" | 225 | 23 | | 30 |
| Bob Christian | FB | 5'10" | 215 | 23 | | |
| Brad Muster | FB | 6'3" | 235 | 27 | | 30 |
| Wendell Davis | WR | 5'11" | 194 | 26 | | 12 |
| Dennis Gentry | WR-HB | 5'8" | 180 | 33 | | |
| Glen Kozlowski | WR | 6'1" | 205 | 29 | | |
| Anthony Morgan | WR | 6'1" | 195 | 24 | | 12 |
| Ron Morris | WR | 6'1' | 200 | 27 | | |
| Tom Waddle | WR | 6' | 185 | 25 | | 24 |
| Barry Wagner | WR | 6'3" | 213 | 24 | | |
| Eric Wright | WR | 6' | 196 | 23 | | |
| Kelly Blackwell | TE | 6'1" | 255 | 23 | | |
| Keith Jennings | TE | 6'4" | 265 | 26 | | 6 |
| Kevin Butler | K | 6'1" | 190 | 30 | | 91 |
| Chris Gardocki | K | 6'1" | 196 | 22 | | |

Jim Thornton — Arch Injury

## DETROIT LIONS 5-11 Wayne Fontes

| Scores of Each Game | | |
|---|---|---|
| 24 | Chicago | 27 |
| 31 | MINNESOTA | 17 |
| 10 | Washington | 13 |
| 23 | TAMPA BAY | 27 |
| 7 | NEW ORLEANS | 13 |
| 14 | Minnesota | 31 |
| 38 | Tampa Bay | 7 |
| 13 | GREEN BAY | 27 |
| 3 | DALLAS | 37 |
| 14 | Pittsburgh | 17 |
| 19 | Cincinnati | 13 |
| 21 | HOUSTON | 24 |
| 10 | Green Bay | 38 |
| 24 | CLEVELAND | 14 |
| 16 | CHICAGO | 3 |
| 6 | San Francisco | 24 |

| UseName | Pos. | Hgt. | Wgt. | Age | Int | Pts |
|---|---|---|---|---|---|---|
| Lomas Brown | OT | 6'4" | 287 | 29 | | |
| Scott Conover | OT | 6'4" | 285 | 23 | | |
| Eric Sanders | OT-OG | 6'7" | 286 | 33 | | |
| Larry Tharpe | OT | 6'4" | 299 | 21 | | |
| Shawn Bouwens | OG | 6'4" | 290 | 24 | | |
| Ken Dallafior | OG | 6'4" | 283 | 33 | | |
| Jack Linn | OG-OT | 6'5" | 285 | 25 | | |
| Dennis McKnight | OG | 6'3" | 280 | 32 | | |
| Leonard Burton | C | 6'3" | 275 | 28 | | |
| Kevin Glover | C | 6'2" | 282 | 29 | | |
| Brad Leggett | C | 6'4" | 270 | 26 | | |
| Blake Miller | C | 6'1" | 282 | 24 | | |
| Dan Owens | DE | 6'3" | 280 | 25 | | |
| Robert Porcher | DE | 6'3" | 283 | 23 | | |
| Kelvin Pritchett | DE | 6'2" | 281 | 22 | | |
| Marc Spindler | DE | 6'5" | 290 | 21 | | |
| Jerry Ball | NT | 6'1" | 298 | 27 | | 6 |
| Lawrence Pete | NT | 6' | 290 | 26 | | |

Eric Andolsek — Died in Offseason Accident

| UseName | Pos. | Hgt. | Wgt. | Age | Int | Pts |
|---|---|---|---|---|---|---|
| Toby Caston | LB | 6'1" | 243 | 27 | | |
| Mike Cofer | LB | 6'5" | 244 | 32 | | |
| John Derby | LB | 6" | 232 | 24 | | |
| Dennis Gibson | LB | 6'2" | 243 | 28 | | |
| Tracy Hayworth | LB | 6'3" | 260 | 24 | | |
| George Jamison | LB | 6'1" | 235 | 29 | | |
| Troy Johnson | LB | 6'2" | 230 | 27 | | |
| Andre Jones | LB | 6'2" | 245 | 23 | | |
| Victor Jones | LB | 6'2" | 250 | 25 | | |
| Mike McDonald | LB | 6'1" | 240 | 34 | | |
| Tracy Scroggins | LB | 6'2" | 255 | 22 | | |
| Chris Spielman | LB | 6' | 247 | 26 | | |
| Bennie Blades | DB | 6'1" | 221 | 25 | 3 | 6 |
| Willie Clay | DB | 5'9" | 184 | 21 | | |
| Harry Colon | DB | 6' | 203 | 23 | | |
| Ray Crockett | DB | 5'9" | 181 | 25 | 4 | |
| Melvin Jenkins | DB | 5'10" | 173 | 30 | 4 | 6 |
| Junior Robinson | DB | 5'9" | 181 | 24 | | |
| Kevin Scott | DB | 5'9" | 175 | 23 | 4 | |
| Sheldon White | DB | 5'11" | 188 | 27 | 2 | |
| William White | DB | 5'10" | 191 | 26 | 4 | |

| UseName | Pos. | Hgt. | Wgt. | Age | Int | Pts |
|---|---|---|---|---|---|---|
| Erik Kramer | QB | 6'1" | 199 | 27 | | |
| Rodney Peete | QB | 6' | 193 | 26 | | |
| Andre Ware | QB | 6'2" | 205 | 24 | | |
| Eric Lynch | HB | 5'10" | 224 | 22 | | |
| Barry Sanders | HB-FB | 5'8" | 203 | 24 | | 60 |
| Troy Stradford (from LA) | HB | 5'9" | 194 | 27 | | |
| Don Overton | FB-HB | 6' | 221 | 24 | | |
| Ed Tillison | FB-HB | 6' | 225 | 23 | | |
| Reggie Barrett | WR | 6'3" | 215 | 23 | | 6 |
| Jeff Campbell | WR | 5'8" | 173 | 24 | | 6 |
| Mike Farr | WR | 5'10" | 181 | 25 | | |
| Mel Gray | WR | 5'9" | 162 | 31 | | 12 |
| Willie Green | WR | 6'2" | 181 | 26 | | 30 |
| Aubrey Matthews | WR | 5'7" | 165 | 29 | | |
| Herman Moore | WR | 6'3" | 210 | 22 | | 24 |
| Brett Perriman | WR | 5'9" | 180 | 26 | | 24 |
| Mike Hinnant | TE | 6'3" | 280 | 25 | | |
| Jimmie Johnson | TE | 6'2" | 255 | 25 | | |
| Thomas McLemore | TE | 6'5" | 245 | 22 | | |
| Jim Arnold | K | 6'3" | 211 | 31 | | |
| Jason Hanson | K | 5'11" | 183 | 22 | | 93 |

Chuck Long — Shoulder Injury

## MINNESOTA VIKINGS

### RUSHING

| Last Name | No. | Yds | Avg | TD |
|---|---|---|---|---|
| Allen | 266 | 1201 | 4.5 | 13 |
| Craig | 105 | 416 | 4.0 | 4 |
| Gannon | 45 | 187 | 4.2 | 0 |
| Henderson | 44 | 150 | 3.4 | 1 |
| A. Carter | 16 | 66 | 4.1 | 1 |
| J. Johnson | 4 | 26 | 6.5 | 0 |
| C. Carter | 5 | 15 | 3.0 | 0 |
| Nelson | 10 | 5 | 0.5 | 0 |
| Jones | 1 | 1 | 1.0 | 0 |
| Salisbury | 11 | 0 | 0.0 | 0 |

### RECEIVING

| Last Name | No. | Yds | Avg | TD |
|---|---|---|---|---|
| C. Carter | 53 | 681 | 12.8 | 6 |
| Allen | 49 | 478 | 9.8 | 2 |
| A. Carter | 41 | 580 | 14.1 | 2 |
| Jordan | 28 | 394 | 14.1 | 2 |
| Jones | 22 | 308 | 14.0 | 4 |
| Craig | 22 | 164 | 7.5 | 0 |
| J. Johnson | 21 | 211 | 10.0 | 1 |
| Reed | 6 | 142 | 23.7 | 0 |
| Tice | 5 | 65 | 13.0 | 1 |
| Henderson | 5 | 64 | 12.8 | 0 |
| Novoselsky | 4 | 63 | 15.8 | 0 |
| Tennell | 2 | 12 | 6.0 | 0 |
| Whitaker | 1 | 4 | 4.0 | 0 |

### PUNT RETURNS

| Last Name | No. | Yds | Avg | TD |
|---|---|---|---|---|
| Parker | 33 | 336 | 10.2 | 0 |

### KICKOFF RETURNS

| Last Name | No. | Yds | Avg | TD |
|---|---|---|---|---|
| Nelson | 29 | 626 | 21.6 | 0 |
| Henderson | 5 | 111 | 22.2 | 0 |
| J. Johnson | 5 | 79 | 15.8 | 0 |
| Parker | 2 | 30 | 15.0 | 0 |
| West | 2 | 27 | 13.5 | 0 |
| Reed | 1 | 1 | 1.0 | 0 |
| Adams | 1 | 0 | 0.0 | 0 |

### PASSING — PUNTING — KICKING

| PASSING | Att | Cmp | % | Yds | Yd/Att | TD | Int— | % | RK |
|---|---|---|---|---|---|---|---|---|---|
| Gannon | 279 | 159 | 57.0 | 1905 | 6.83 | 12 | 13— | 4.7 | 11 |
| Salisbury | 175 | 97 | 55.4 | 1203 | 6.87 | 5 | 2— | 1.1 | |
| Henderson | 1 | 1 | 100.0 | 36 | 36.00 | 1 | 0— | 0.0 | |
| Jones | 1 | 1 | 100.0 | 18 | 18.00 | 0 | 0— | 0.0 | |
| A. Carter | 1 | 0 | 0.0 | 0 | 0.00 | 0 | 0— | 0.0 | |
| Newsome | 1 | 0 | 0.0 | 0 | 0.00 | 0 | 0— | 0.0 | |

| PUNTING | No. | Avg. |
|---|---|---|
| Newsome | 73 | 44.4 |

| KICKING | XP | ATT | % | FG | ATT | % |
|---|---|---|---|---|---|---|
| Reveiz | 45 | 45 | 100 | 19 | 25 | 76 |

## GREEN BAY PACKERS

### RUSHING

| Last Name | No. | Yds | Avg | TD |
|---|---|---|---|---|
| Workman | 159 | 631 | 4.0 | 2 |
| Thompson | 76 | 255 | 3.4 | 2 |
| E. Bennett | 61 | 214 | 3.5 | 0 |
| Favre | 47 | 198 | 4.2 | 1 |
| Sydney | 51 | 163 | 3.2 | 2 |
| Majkowski | 8 | 33 | 4.1 | 0 |
| McGee | 8 | 19 | 2.4 | 0 |
| Brooks | 2 | 14 | 7.0 | 0 |
| McNabb | 2 | 11 | 5.5 | 0 |
| C. Harris | 2 | 10 | 5.0 | 0 |
| Sharpe | 4 | 8 | 2.0 | 0 |

### RECEIVING

| Last Name | No. | Yds | Avg | TD |
|---|---|---|---|---|
| Sharpe | 108 | 1461 | 13.5 | 13 |
| J. Harris | 55 | 595 | 10.8 | 2 |
| Sydney | 49 | 384 | 7.8 | 1 |
| Workman | 47 | 290 | 6.2 | 0 |
| Beach | 17 | 122 | 7.2 | 1 |
| Lewis | 13 | 152 | 11.7 | 0 |
| Thompson | 13 | 129 | 9.9 | 1 |
| E. Bennett | 13 | 93 | 7.2 | 0 |
| Brooks | 12 | 126 | 10.5 | 1 |
| McGee | 6 | 60 | 10.0 | 0 |
| West | 4 | 30 | 7.5 | 0 |
| Taylor | 2 | 63 | 31.5 | 1 |
| Favre | 1 | -7 | -7.0 | 0 |

### PUNT RETURNS

| Last Name | No. | Yds | Avg | TD |
|---|---|---|---|---|
| Buckley | 21 | 211 | 10.0 | 1 |
| Brooks | 11 | 102 | 9.3 | 0 |
| C. Harris | 6 | 17 | 2.8 | 0 |
| Lewis | 4 | 23 | 5.8 | 0 |
| Hauck | 1 | 2 | 2.0 | 0 |
| Cecil | 1 | 0 | 0.0 | 0 |
| Clark | 1 | 0 | 0.0 | 0 |

### KICKOFF RETURNS

| Last Name | No. | Yds | Avg | TD |
|---|---|---|---|---|
| C. Harris | 33 | 691 | 20.9 | 0 |
| Brooks | 18 | 338 | 18.8 | 0 |
| E. Bennett | 5 | 104 | 20.8 | 0 |
| Jurkovic | 3 | 39 | 13.0 | 0 |
| Workman | 1 | 17 | 17.0 | 0 |
| McNabb | 1 | 15 | 15.0 | 0 |
| Sims | 1 | 11 | 11.0 | 0 |
| Davey | 1 | 8 | 8.0 | 0 |
| West | 1 | 0 | 0.0 | 0 |

### PASSING — PUNTING — KICKING

| PASSING | Att | Cmp | % | Yds | Yd/Att | TD | Int— | % | RK |
|---|---|---|---|---|---|---|---|---|---|
| Favre | 471 | 302 | 64.1 | 3227 | 6.85 | 18 | 13— | 2.8 | 5 |
| Majkowski | 55 | 38 | 69.1 | 271 | 4.93 | 2 | 2— | 3.6 | |
| McJulian | 1 | 0 | 0.0 | 0 | 0.00 | 0 | 0— | 0.0 | |

| PUNTING | No. | Avg. |
|---|---|---|
| McJulien | 38 | 36.5 |
| Wagner | 30 | 40.7 |

| KICKING | XP | Att. | % | FG | Att | % |
|---|---|---|---|---|---|---|
| Jacke | 30 | 30 | 100 | 22 | 29 | 76 |

## TAMPA BAY BUCCANEERS

### RUSHING

| Last Name | No. | Yds | Avg | TD |
|---|---|---|---|---|
| Cobb | 310 | 1171 | 3.8 | 9 |
| Testaverde | 36 | 197 | 5.5 | 2 |
| G. Anderson | 55 | 194 | 3.5 | 1 |
| McDowell | 14 | 81 | 5.8 | 0 |
| Jennings | 5 | 25 | 5.0 | 0 |
| Highsmith | 8 | 23 | 2.9 | 0 |
| Stryzinski | 1 | 7 | 7.0 | 0 |
| DeBerg | 3 | 3 | 1.0 | 0 |
| Erickson | 1 | -1 | -1.- | 0 |

### RECEIVING

| Last Name | No. | Yds | Avg | TD |
|---|---|---|---|---|
| Dawsey | 60 | 776 | 12.9 | 1 |
| Carrier | 56 | 692 | 12.4 | 4 |
| Hall | 39 | 351 | 9.0 | 4 |
| G. Anderson | 34 | 284 | 8.4 | 0 |
| McDowell | 27 | 258 | 9.6 | 2 |
| Cobb | 21 | 156 | 7.4 | 0 |
| Hawkins | 20 | 336 | 16.8 | 2 |
| Drewrey | 16 | 237 | 14.8 | 2 |
| Jennings | 9 | 69 | 7.7 | 1 |
| Armstrong | 7 | 138 | 19.7 | 1 |
| Highsmith | 5 | 28 | 5.6 | 0 |
| Barber | 1 | 32 | 32.0 | 0 |
| Parker | 1 | 12 | 12.0 | 0 |
| Fullington | 1 | 12 | 12.0 | 0 |
| Moore | 1 | 10 | 10.0 | 0 |
| Royster | 1 | 8 | 8.0 | 0 |

### PUNT RETURNS

| Last Name | No. | Yds | Avg | TD |
|---|---|---|---|---|
| Hawkins | 13 | 53 | 4.1 | 0 |
| Drewrey | 7 | 62 | 8.9 | 0 |
| Anderson | 6 | 45 | 7.5 | 0 |

### KICKOFF RETURNS

| Last Name | No. | Yds | Avg | TD |
|---|---|---|---|---|
| G. Anderson | 29 | 564 | 19.4 | 0 |
| Hawkins | 9 | 118 | 13.1 | 0 |
| Ryan | 2 | 24 | 12.0 | 0 |
| Mayfield | 2 | 22 | 11.0 | 0 |
| Wilson | 1 | 23 | 23.0 | 0 |
| Chamblee | 1 | 9 | 9.0 | 0 |

### PASSING — PUNTING — KICKING

| PASSING | Att | Cmp | % | Yds | Yd/Att | TD | Int— | % | RK |
|---|---|---|---|---|---|---|---|---|---|
| Testaverde | 358 | 206 | 57.5 | 2554 | 7.13 | 14 | 16— | 4.5 | 10 |
| DeBerg | 125 | 76 | 60.8 | 710 | 5.68 | 3 | 4— | 3.2 | |
| Erickson | 26 | 15 | 57.7 | 121 | 4.65 | 0 | 0— | 0.0 | |
| Stryzinski | 2 | 2 | 100.0 | 14 | 7.00 | 0 | 0— | 0.0 | |

| PUNTING | No. | Avg. |
|---|---|---|
| Stryzinski | 74 | 40.7 |

| KICKING | XP | ATT | % | FG | ATT | % |
|---|---|---|---|---|---|---|
| Murray | 13 | 13 | 100 | 4 | 8 | 50 |

## CHICAGO BEARS

### RUSHING

| Last Name | No. | Yds | Avg | TD |
|---|---|---|---|---|
| Anderson | 156 | 582 | 3.7 | 5 |
| Muster | 98 | 414 | 4.2 | 3 |
| Lewis | 90 | 382 | 4.2 | 4 |
| Harbaugh | 47 | 272 | 5.8 | 1 |
| Green | 23 | 107 | 4.7 | 2 |
| Morgan | 3 | 68 | 22.7 | 0 |
| Davis | 4 | 42 | 10.5 | 0 |
| Gentry | 5 | 2 | 0.4 | 0 |
| Willis | 1 | 2 | 2.0 | 0 |

### RECEIVING

| Last Name | No. | Yds | Avg | TD |
|---|---|---|---|---|
| Davis | 54 | 734 | 13.6 | 2 |
| Waddle | 46 | 674 | 14.7 | 4 |
| Anderson | 42 | 399 | 9.5 | 6 |
| Muster | 34 | 389 | 11.4 | 2 |
| Jennings | 23 | 264 | 11.5 | 1 |
| Lewis | 18 | 175 | 9.7 | 0 |
| Morgan | 14 | 323 | 23.1 | 2 |
| Gentry | 12 | 114 | 9.5 | 0 |
| Green | 7 | 85 | 12.1 | 0 |
| Wright | 5 | 56 | 11.2 | 0 |
| Blackwell | 5 | 54 | 10.8 | 0 |
| Morris | 4 | 44 | 11.0 | 0 |
| Wagner | 1 | 16 | 16.0 | 0 |
| Kozlowski | 1 | 7 | 7.0 | 0 |

### PUNT RETURNS

| Last Name | No. | Yds | Avg | TD |
|---|---|---|---|---|
| Woolford | 12 | 127 | 10.6 | 0 |
| Waddle | 8 | 28 | 3.5 | 0 |
| Morgan | 3 | 21 | 7.0 | 0 |

### KICKOFF RETURNS

| Last Name | No. | Yds | Avg | TD |
|---|---|---|---|---|
| Lewis | 23 | 511 | 22.2 | 1 |
| Gentry | 16 | 330 | 20.6 | 0 |
| Green | 11 | 224 | 20.4 | 0 |
| Morgan | 4 | 71 | 17.8 | 0 |
| Leeuwenburg | 1 | 7 | 7.0 | 0 |
| Rivera | 1 | 0 | 0.0 | 0 |

### PASSING — PUNTING — KICKING

| PASSING | Att | Cmp | % | Yds | Yd/Att | TD | Int— | % | RK |
|---|---|---|---|---|---|---|---|---|---|
| Harbaugh | 358 | 202 | 56.4 | 2486 | 6.94 | 13 | 12— | 3.4 | 7 |
| Willis | 92 | 54 | 58.7 | 716 | 7.78 | 4 | 8— | 8.7 | |
| Furrer | 25 | 9 | 36.0 | 89 | 3.56 | 0 | 3— | 12.0 | |
| Gardocki | 3 | 1 | 33.3 | 43 | 14.33 | 0 | 0— | 0.0 | |
| Muster | 1 | 0 | 0.0 | 0 | 0.00 | 0 | 0— | 100.0 | |

| PUNTING | No. | Avg. |
|---|---|---|
| Gardocki | 79 | 42.9 |

| KICKING | XP | ATT | % | FG | ATT | % |
|---|---|---|---|---|---|---|
| Butler | 34 | 34 | 100 | 19 | 26 | 73 |

## DETROIT LIONS

### RUSHING

| Last Name | No. | Yds | Avg | TD |
|---|---|---|---|---|
| B. Sanders | 312 | 1352 | 4.3 | 9 |
| Ware | 20 | 124 | 6.2 | 0 |
| Peete | 21 | 83 | 4.0 | 0 |
| Stradford | 12 | 41 | 3.4 | 0 |
| Kramer | 12 | 34 | 2.8 | 0 |
| Tillison | 4 | 22 | 5.5 | 0 |

### RECEIVING

| Last Name | No. | Yds | Avg | TD |
|---|---|---|---|---|
| Perriman | 69 | 810 | 11.7 | 4 |
| Moore | 51 | 966 | 18.9 | 4 |
| Green | 33 | 586 | 17.8 | 5 |
| Sanders | 29 | 225 | 7.8 | 1 |
| Farr | 15 | 115 | 7.7 | 0 |
| Matthews | 9 | 137 | 15.2 | 0 |
| Campbell | 8 | 155 | 19.4 | 1 |
| J. Johnson | 6 | 34 | 5.7 | 0 |
| Barrett | 4 | 67 | 16.8 | 1 |
| Hinnant | 3 | 28 | 9.3 | 0 |
| Stradford | 2 | 15 | 7.5 | 0 |
| McLemore | 2 | 12 | 6.0 | 0 |

### PUNT RETURNS

| Last Name | No. | Yds | Avg | TD |
|---|---|---|---|---|
| Gray | 18 | 175 | 9.7 | 1 |
| Campbell | 3 | 15 | 5.0 | 0 |
| Stradford | 1 | 1 | 1.0 | 0 |

### KICKOFF RETURNS

| Last Name | No. | Yds | Avg | TD |
|---|---|---|---|---|
| Gray | 42 | 1006 | 24.0 | 1 |
| Stradford | 7 | 94 | 13.4 | 0 |
| Campbell | 4 | 61 | 15.3 | 0 |
| Perriman | 4 | 59 | 14.8 | 0 |
| Scott | 3 | 5 | 1.7 | 0 |
| Tillison | 1 | 27 | 27.0 | 0 |
| J. Johnson | 1 | 0 | 0.0 | 0 |

### PASSING — PUNTING — KICKING

| PASSING | Att | Cmp | % | Yds | Yd/Att | TD | Int— | % | RK |
|---|---|---|---|---|---|---|---|---|---|
| Peete | 213 | 123 | 57.7 | 1702 | 7.99 | 9 | 9— | 4.2 | |
| Kramer | 106 | 58 | 54.7 | 771 | 7.27 | 4 | 8— | 7.5 | |
| Ware | 86 | 50 | 58.1 | 677 | 7.87 | 3 | 4— | 4.7 | |
| Sanders | 1 | 0 | 0.0 | 0 | 0.00 | 0 | 0— | 0.0 | |

| PUNTING | No. | Avg. |
|---|---|---|
| Arnold | 66 | 43.1 |

| KICKING | XP | Att | % | FG | Att | % |
|---|---|---|---|---|---|---|
| Hanson | 30 | 30 | 100 | 21 | 26 | 81 |

## SAN FRANCISCO 49ERS 14-2 George Seifert

| Scores of Each Game | | |
|---|---|---|
| 31 | N.Y. Giants | 14 |
| 31 | BUFFALO | 34 |
| 31 | N.Y. Jets | 14 |
| 16 | New Orleans | 10 |
| 27 | L.A. RAMS | 24 |
| 24 | New England | 12 |
| 56 | ATLANTA | 17 |
| 14 | Phoenix | 24 |
| 41 | Atlanta | 3 |
| 21 | NEW ORLEANS | 20 |
| 27 | L.A. Rams | 10 |
| 20 | PHILADELPHIA | 14 |
| 27 | MIAMI | 3 |
| 20 | Minnesota | 17 |
| 21 | TAMPA BAY | 14 |
| 24 | DETROIT | 6 |

| UseName | Pos. | Hgt. | Wgt. | Age | Int | Pts |
|---|---|---|---|---|---|---|
| Harris Barton | OT | 6'4" | 286 | 28 | | |
| Harry Boatswain | OT | 6'4" | 295 | 23 | | |
| Steve Wallace | OT | 6'5" | 280 | 27 | | |
| Brian Bollinger | OG | 6'5" | 285 | 23 | | |
| Roy Foster | OG | 6'4" | 290 | 32 | | |
| Guy McIntyre | OG | 6'3" | 276 | 31 | | |
| Ralph Tamm | OG-C | 6'4" | 280 | 26 | | |
| Jesse Sapolu | C | 6'4" | 278 | 31 | | |
| Chuck Thomas | C | 6'3" | 280 | 31 | | |
| Dennis Brown | DE | 6'4" | 290 | 24 | 1 | |
| Kevin Fagan | DE | 6'4" | 265 | 29 | | |
| Jacob Green | DE | 6'3" | 263 | 35 | | |
| Pierce Holt | DE | 6'4" | 280 | 30 | | |
| Larry Roberts | DE | 6'3" | 275 | 29 | 1 | |
| Garin Veris | DE | 6'4" | 255 | 29 | | |
| Michael Carter | NT-DT | 6'2" | 285 | 31 | | |
| Ted Washington | NT-DE | 6'4" | 295 | 24 | | |

| UseName | Pos. | Hgt. | Wgt. | Age | Int | Pts |
|---|---|---|---|---|---|---|
| Keith DeLong | LB | 6'2" | 250 | 25 | 1 | |
| Mitch Donahue | LB | 6'2" | 254 | 24 | | |
| Antonio Goss | LB | 6'4" | 228 | 26 | | |
| Tim Harris | LB-DE | 6'6" | 258 | 27 | | |
| Martin Harrison | LB | 6'5" | 240 | 24 | | |
| John Johnson | LB | 6'3" | 230 | 24 | 1 | 6 |
| Darin Jordan | LB | 6'2" | 245 | 27 | | |
| Reggie McKenzie | LB | 6'1" | 239 | 29 | | |
| Bill Romanowski | LB | 6'4" | 240 | 26 | | |
| Michael Walter | LB | 6'3" | 246 | 31 | | |
| David Wilkins | LB | 6'4" | 240 | 23 | | |
| Eric Davis | DB | 5'11" | 178 | 24 | 3 | |
| Thane Gash | DB | 5'11" | 198 | 26 | | |
| Alan Grant | DB | 5'10" | 187 | 25 | | |
| Don Griffin | DB | 6' | 180 | 28 | 5 | |
| Dana Hall | DB | 6'2" | 206 | 23 | 2 | |
| Merton Hanks | DB | 6'2" | 185 | 24 | 2 | 6 |
| Johnny Jackson (to GB) | DB | 6'1" | 204 | 25 | | |
| Michael McGruder | DB | 5'10" | 190 | 28 | | |
| David Whitmore | DB | 6' | 217 | 25 | 1 | |

Kevin Lewis — Neck Injury
Rodney Thomas — Knee Injury

| UseName | Pos. | Hgt. | Wgt. | Age | Int | Pts |
|---|---|---|---|---|---|---|
| Steve Bono | QB | 6'4" | 211 | 30 | | |
| Joe Montana | QB | 6'2" | 195 | 36 | | |
| Bill Musgrave | QB | 6'2" | 196 | 24 | | |
| Steve Young | QB | 6'2" | 205 | 30 | | 24 |
| Dexter Carter | HB | 5'9" | 170 | 24 | | 6 |
| Amp Lee | HB | 5'11" | 200 | 20 | | 24 |
| Marc Logan | HB | 6' | 212 | 27 | | 6 |
| Adam Walker | HB | 6'1" | 210 | 24 | | |
| Ricky Watters | HB | 6'1" | 212 | 23 | | 66 |
| Tom Rathman | FB | 6'1" | 232 | 29 | | 54 |
| Jerry Rice | WR | 6'2" | 200 | 29 | | 66 |
| Mike Sherrard | WR | 6'2" | 187 | 29 | | 6 |
| John Taylor | WR | 6'1" | 185 | 30 | | 18 |
| Odessa Turner | WR | 6'3" | 215 | 27 | | 12 |
| Chris Dressel | TE | 6'4" | 239 | 31 | | |
| Brent Jones | TE | 6'4" | 230 | 29 | | 24 |
| Jamie Williams | TE | 6'4" | 245 | 32 | | 6 |
| Mike Cofer | K | 6'1" | 190 | 28 | | 107 |
| Klaus Wilmsmeyer | K | 6'1" | 210 | 24 | | |

Wesley Walls — Shoulder Injury

## NEW ORLEANS SAINTS 12-4 Jim Mora

| Scores of Each Game | | |
|---|---|---|
| 13 | Philadelphia | 15 |
| 28 | CHICAGO | 6 |
| 10 | Atlanta | 7 |
| 10 | SAN FRANCISCO | 16 |
| 13 | Detroit | 7 |
| 13 | L.A. RAMS | 10 |
| 30 | Phoenix | 21 |
| 23 | TAMPA BAY | 21 |
| 31 | New England | 14 |
| 20 | San Francisco | 21 |
| 20 | WASHINGTON | 3 |
| 24 | MIAMI | 13 |
| 22 | ATLANTA | 14 |
| 37 | L.A. Rams | 14 |
| 16 | BUFFALO | 20 |
| 20 | N.Y. Jets | 0 |

| UseName | Pos. | Hgt. | Wgt. | Age | Int | Pts |
|---|---|---|---|---|---|---|
| Stan Brock | OT | 6'6" | 285 | 34 | | |
| Richard Cooper | OT | 6'4" | 290 | 27 | | |
| Jim Dombrowski | OG | 6'5" | 298 | 28 | | |
| Derek Kennard | OG | 6'3" | 300 | 29 | | |
| Chris Port | OG-OT | 6'5" | 290 | 24 | | |
| Steve Trapilo | OG | 6'5" | 289 | 27 | | |
| Joel Hilgenberg | C | 6'3" | 252 | 30 | | |
| Paul Jetton | C-OG | 6'4" | 288 | 27 | | |
| Gene McGuire | C | 6'2" | 284 | 22 | | |
| Wayne Martin | DE | 6'5" | 275 | 26 | | |
| Frank Warren | DE | 6'4" | 290 | 32 | | |
| Les Miller | NT-DE | 6'7" | 285 | 27 | | |
| Jim Wilks | NT | 6'5" | 275 | 33 | | |
| Robert Goff | NT-DE | 6'3" | 270 | 26 | | 12 |

Kevin Haverdink — Back Injury

| UseName | Pos. | Hgt. | Wgt. | Age | Int | Pts |
|---|---|---|---|---|---|---|
| Rickey Jackson | LB | 6'2" | 243 | 34 | | |
| Vaughan Johnson | LB | 6'3" | 235 | 30 | | |
| Sam Mills | LB | 5'9" | 225 | 33 | 1 | 6 |
| Joel Smeenge | LB | 6'5" | 255 | 24 | | |
| Pat Swilling | LB | 6'3" | 242 | 27 | | |
| Renaldo Turnbull | DE | 6'4" | 255 | 26 | | |
| James Williams | LB | 6' | 230 | 23 | | |
| DeMond Winston | LB | 6'2" | 239 | 23 | | |
| Gene Atkins | DB | 6'1" | 200 | 27 | 3 | |
| Vince Buck | DB | 6' | 198 | 24 | 2 | 6 |
| Toi Cook | DB | 5'11" | 188 | 27 | 6 | 6 |
| Antonio Gibson | DB | 6'2" | 210 | 30 | | |
| Reggie Jones | DB | 6'1" | 202 | 23 | 2 | 6 |
| Tyrone Legette | DB | 5'9" | 177 | 22 | | |
| Sean Lumpkin | DB | 6' | 206 | 22 | | |
| Cedric Mack (from KC) | DB | 5'11" | 190 | 31 | | |
| Brett Maxie | DB | 6'2" | 194 | 30 | 2 | |
| Jimmy Spencer | DB | 5'9" | 180 | 23 | | |
| Keith Taylor | DB | 5'11" | 206 | 27 | 2 | |

| UseName | Pos. | Hgt. | Wgt. | Age | Int | Pts |
|---|---|---|---|---|---|---|
| Mike Buck | QB | 6'3" | 227 | 25 | | |
| Bobby Hebert | QB | 6'4" | 215 | 32 | | |
| Steve Walsh | QB | 6'2" | 210 | 25 | | |
| Vaughn Dunbar | HB | 5'10" | 204 | 23 | | 18 |
| Dalton Hilliard | HB | 5'8" | 204 | 28 | | 42 |
| Fred McAfee | HB | 5'10" | 193 | 24 | | 6 |
| Craig Heyward | FB | 5'11" | 260 | 25 | | 18 |
| Buford Jordan | FB | 6' | 223 | 30 | | |
| Wesley Carroll | WR | 6' | 183 | 24 | | 12 |
| Marcus Dowdell | WR | 5'10" | 179 | 22 | | |
| Quinn Early | WR | 6' | 190 | 27 | | 30 |
| Louis Lipps | WR | 5'10" | 193 | 30 | | |
| Eric Martin | WR | 6'1" | 207 | 30 | | 30 |
| Pat Newman | WR | 5'11" | 189 | 23 | | |
| Torrance Small | WR | 6'3" | 201 | 21 | | 18 |
| Floyd Turner | WR | 5'11" | 188 | 26 | | |
| Hoby Brenner | TE | 6'4" | 245 | 33 | | |
| Tommie Stowers | TE | 6'3" | 240 | 25 | | |
| John Tice | TE | 6'5" | 249 | 32 | | |
| Frank Wainright | TE | 6'3" | 236 | 24 | | |
| Morten Andersen | K | 6'2" | 221 | 32 | | 120 |
| Tommy Barnhardt | K | 6'3" | 207 | 29 | | |

Allen Pinkett — Knee Injury

## ATLANTA FALCONS 6-10 Jerry Glanville

| Scores of Each Game | | |
|---|---|---|
| 20 | N.Y. JETS | 17 |
| 17 | Washington | 24 |
| 7 | NEW ORLEANS | 10 |
| 31 | Chicago | 41 |
| 24 | GREEN BAY | 10 |
| 17 | Miami | 21 |
| 17 | San Francisco | 56 |
| 30 | L.A. RAMS | 28 |
| 3 | SAN FRANCISCO | 41 |
| 20 | PHOENIX | 17 |
| 14 | Buffalo | 41 |
| 34 | NEW ENGLAND | 0 |
| 14 | New Orleans | 22 |
| 35 | Tampa Bay | 7 |
| 17 | DALLAS | 41 |
| 27 | L.A. Rams | 38 |

| UseName | Pos. | Hgt. | Wgt. | Age | Int | Pts |
|---|---|---|---|---|---|---|
| Chris Hinton | OT | 6'4" | 300 | 31 | | |
| Mike Kenn | OT | 6'7" | 280 | 36 | | |
| Bob Whitfield | OT | 6'5" | 291 | 20 | | |
| John Buddenberg | OG | 6'6" | 270 | 23 | | |
| Roman Fortin | OG | 6'5" | 285 | 25 | | |
| Bill Fralic | OG | 6'5" | 280 | 29 | | |
| Houston Hoover | OG | 6'2" | 295 | 27 | | |
| Jamie Dukes | C | 6'1" | 285 | 28 | | |
| Mike Ruether | C | 6'4" | 286 | 29 | | |
| Mike Gann | DE | 6'5" | 270 | 28 | | |
| Oliver Barnett | DE-DT | 6'3" | 288 | 26 | | |
| Tim Green | DE | 6'2" | 245 | 28 | | |
| Chuck Smith | DE | 6'2" | 242 | 22 | | |
| Tory Epps | NT | 6' | 280 | 25 | | |
| Moe Gardner | NT | 6'2" | 258 | 24 | | |
| Bill Goldberg | NT | 6'2" | 266 | 22 | | |

Rick Bryan — Neck Injury
Dave Zawatson — Elbow Injury

| UseName | Pos. | Hgt. | Wgt. | Age | Int | Pts |
|---|---|---|---|---|---|---|
| Darion Conner | LB | 6'2" | 245 | 24 | | |
| Eric Fairs | LB | 6'3" | 244 | 28 | | |
| Michael Reid | LB | 6'2" | 235 | 28 | | |
| Jesse Solomon | LB | 6' | 235 | 28 | 1 | |
| Kenny Tippins | LB | 6'1" | 230 | 26 | | |
| Jessie Tuggle | LB | 5'11" | 230 | 27 | 1 | 6 |
| Bobby Butler | DB | 5'11" | 175 | 33 | | |
| Scott Case | DB | 6' | 188 | 30 | 2 | |
| Jeff Donaldson | DB | 6' | 190 | 30 | | |
| Joe Fishback (from NYJ) | DB | 6' | 212 | 24 | | |
| Tim McKyer | DB | 6' | 174 | 28 | 1 | |
| Brian Mitchell | DB | 5'9" | 164 | 23 | 1 | |
| Bruce Pickens | DB | 5'11" | 190 | 24 | 2 | |
| Terry Ray | DB | 6'1" | 187 | 22 | | |
| Louis Riddick | DB | 6'2" | 216 | 23 | | |
| Deion Sanders | DB | 6' | 185 | 25 | 3 | 18 |
| Elbert Shelley | DB | 5'11" | 185 | 27 | | |
| Charles Washington | DB | 6'1" | 217 | 25 | | |

Brian Forde — Knee Injury
John Rade — Knee Injury
Tracey Eaton — Knee Injury

| UseName | Pos. | Hgt. | Wgt. | Age | Int | Pts |
|---|---|---|---|---|---|---|
| Chris Miller | QB | 6'2" | 205 | 27 | | |
| Billy Joe Tolliver | QB | 6'1" | 218 | 26 | | |
| Wade Wilson | QB | 6'3" | 210 | 33 | | |
| Steve Broussard | HB | 5'7" | 201 | 25 | | 12 |
| Erric Pegram | HB | 5'9" | 188 | 23 | | |
| Tony Smith | HB | 6'1" | 214 | 22 | | 12 |
| Keith Jones | FB | 6'1" | 210 | 26 | | |
| Michael Haynes | WR | 6' | 180 | 26 | | 60 |
| Drew Hill | WR | 5'9" | 172 | 35 | | 18 |
| Tony Jones | WR | 5'7" | 145 | 26 | | 6 |
| James Milling | WR | 5'9" | 160 | 27 | | |
| Jason Phillips | WR | 5'7" | 166 | 25 | | 6 |
| Mike Pritchard | WR | 5'11" | 180 | 22 | | 30 |
| Andre Rison | WR | 6' | 188 | 25 | | 66 |
| George Thomas (to TB) | WR | 5'9" | 169 | 28 | | |
| Harper LeBel | TE | 6'4" | 245 | 29 | | |
| Scott Fulhage | K | 5'11" | 193 | 30 | | |
| Norm Johnson | K | 6'2" | 203 | 32 | | 93 |

## LOS ANGELES RAMS 6-10 Chuck Knox

| Scores of Each Game | | |
|---|---|---|
| 7 | Buffalo | 40 |
| 14 | NEW ENGLAND | 0 |
| 10 | Miami | 26 |
| 18 | N.Y. JETS | 10 |
| 24 | San Francisco | 27 |
| 10 | New Orleans | 13 |
| 38 | N.Y. GIANTS | 17 |
| 28 | Atlanta | 30 |
| 14 | PHOENIX | 20 |
| 27 | Dallas | 23 |
| 10 | SAN FRANCISCO | 27 |
| 17 | MINNESOTA | 31 |
| 31 | Tampa Bay | 27 |
| 14 | NEW ORLEANS | 37 |
| 13 | Green Bay | 28 |
| 38 | ATLANTA | 27 |

| UseName | Pos. | Hgt. | Wgt. | Age | Int | Pts |
|---|---|---|---|---|---|---|
| Robert Jenkins | OT | 6'5" | 285 | 28 | | |
| Gerald Perry | OT | 6'6" | 305 | 27 | | |
| Jackie Slater | OT | 6'4" | 287 | 38 | | |
| Joe Milinichik | OG | 6'5" | 290 | 29 | | |
| Tom Newberry | OG | 6'2" | 285 | 29 | | |
| Jeff Pahukoa | OG-OT | 6'2" | 298 | 23 | | |
| Bern Brostek | C | 6'3" | 300 | 25 | | |
| Blair Bush | C | 6'3" | 275 | 35 | | |
| Bill Hawkins | DE | 6'6" | 269 | 26 | | |
| Warren Powers | DE | 6'6" | 287 | 27 | | |
| Gerald Robinson | DE | 6'3" | 262 | 29 | | |
| Jim Skow (from SD) | DE | 6'3" | 250 | 29 | | |
| Robert Young | DE | 6'6" | 277 | 23 | | |
| Marc Boutte | DT | 6'4" | 298 | 23 | | |
| Sean Gilbert | DT | 6'4" | 315 | 22 | | |
| Eric Hayes | DT | 6'3" | 288 | 24 | | |
| Mark Piel | DT | 6'4" | 270 | 26 | | |
| David Rocker | DT | 6'4" | 267 | 23 | | |

| UseName | Pos. | Hgt. | Wgt. | Age | Int | Pts |
|---|---|---|---|---|---|---|
| Paul Butcher | LB | 6' | 230 | 28 | | |
| Kevin Greene | LB | 6'3" | 247 | 30 | | 2 |
| Larry Kelm | LB | 6'4" | 240 | 27 | 1 | |
| Roman Phifer | LB | 6'2" | 230 | 24 | 1 | |
| Scott Stephen | LB | 6'3" | 243 | 28 | | |
| Fred Strickland | LB | 6'2" | 250 | 26 | | |
| Leon White | LB | 6'3" | 242 | 28 | 2 | |
| Robert Bailey | DB | 5'9" | 176 | 23 | 3 | 6 |
| Chris Crooms | DB | 6'2" | 211 | 23 | | |
| Darryl Henley | DB | 5'9" | 172 | 25 | 4 | |
| Steve Israel | DB | 5'10" | 186 | 23 | | |
| Sammy Lilly | DB | 5'9" | 178 | 27 | | |
| Todd Lyght | DB | 6' | 185 | 23 | 3 | |
| Anthony Newman | DB | 6' | 199 | 26 | 4 | |
| Michael Stewart | DB | 5'11" | 195 | 27 | | |
| Pat Terrell | DB | 6' | 195 | 24 | | |

| UseName | Pos. | Hgt. | Wgt. | Age | Int | Pts |
|---|---|---|---|---|---|---|
| Jim Everett | QB | 6'5" | 212 | 29 | | |
| Mike Pagel | QB | 6'2" | 220 | 31 | | |
| Cleveland Gary | HB | 6' | 226 | 26 | | 60 |
| David Lang | HB-FB | 5'11" | 201 | 25 | | 36 |
| Anthony Thompson (from PHX) | HB | 6' | 210 | 25 | | 6 |
| Robert Delpino | FB | 6' | 205 | 26 | | 6 |
| Tim Lester | FB | 5'9" | 215 | 24 | | |
| Willie Anderson | WR | 6' | 175 | 27 | | 42 |
| Jeff Chadwick | WR | 6'3" | 185 | 31 | | 18 |
| Aaron Cox | WR | 5'9" | 178 | 27 | | |
| Henry Ellard | WR | 5'11" | 182 | 31 | | 18 |
| Todd Kinchen | WR | 6' | 187 | 23 | | 12 |
| Vernon Turner | WR | 5'8" | 185 | 25 | | |
| Pat Carter | TE | 6'4" | 255 | 26 | | 18 |
| Damone Johnson | TE | 6'4" | 250 | 30 | | |
| Travis McNeal | TE | 6'3" | 244 | 25 | | |
| Jim Price | TE | 6'4" | 247 | 29 | | 12 |
| Don Bracken | K | 6'1" | 211 | 30 | | |
| Tony Zendejas | K | 5'8" | 165 | 32 | | 83 |

## SAN FRANCISCO 49ERS

### RUSHING

| Last Name | No. | Yds | Avg | TD |
|---|---|---|---|---|
| Watters | 206 | 1013 | 4.9 | 9 |
| Young | 76 | 537 | 7.1 | 4 |
| Lee | 91 | 362 | 4.0 | 2 |
| Rathman | 57 | 194 | 3.4 | 5 |
| Rice | 9 | 58 | 6.4 | 1 |
| Logan | 8 | 44 | 5.5 | 1 |
| Montana | 3 | 28 | 9.3 | 0 |
| Bono | 15 | 23 | 1.5 | 0 |
| Taylor | 1 | 10 | 10.0 | 0 |
| D. Carter | 4 | 9 | 2.3 | 0 |
| Wilmsmeyer | 2 | 0 | 0.0 | 0 |

### RECEIVING

| Last Name | No. | Yds | Avg | TD |
|---|---|---|---|---|
| Rice | 84 | 1201 | 14.3 | 10 |
| Jones | 45 | 628 | 14.0 | 4 |
| Rathman | 44 | 343 | 7.8 | 4 |
| Watters | 43 | 405 | 9.4 | 2 |
| Sherrard | 38 | 607 | 16.0 | 0 |
| Taylor | 25 | 428 | 17.1 | 3 |
| Lee | 20 | 102 | 5.1 | 2 |
| Turner | 9 | 200 | 22.2 | 2 |
| Williams | 7 | 76 | 10.9 | 1 |
| Logan | 2 | 17 | 8.5 | 0 |
| D. Carter | 1 | 43 | 43.0 | 1 |

### PUNT RETURNS

| Last Name | No. | Yds | Avg | TD |
|---|---|---|---|---|
| Grant | 29 | 249 | 8.6 | 0 |
| Griffin | 6 | 69 | 11.5 | 0 |
| Hanks | 1 | 48 | 48.0 | 1 |

### KICKOFF RETURNS

| Last Name | No. | Yds | Avg | TD |
|---|---|---|---|---|
| Logan | 22 | 478 | 21.7 | 0 |
| Lee | 14 | 276 | 19.7 | 0 |
| Grant | 3 | 70 | 23.3 | 0 |
| D. Carter | 2 | 55 | 27.5 | 0 |
| Turner | 1 | 0 | 0.0 | 0 |

### PASSING — PUNTING — KICKING

| PASSING | Att | Cmp | % | Yds | Yd/Att | TD | Int— % | RK |
|---|---|---|---|---|---|---|---|---|
| Young | 402 | 268 | 66.7 | 3465 | 8.62 | 25 | 7—1.7 | 1 |
| Bono | 56 | 36 | 64.3 | 463 | 8.27 | 2 | 2—3.6 | |
| Montana | 21 | 15 | 71.4 | 126 | 6.00 | 2 | 0—0.0 | |
| Watters | 1 | 0 | 0.0 | 0 | 0.00 | 0 | 0—0.0 | |

| PUNTING | No. | Avg. |
|---|---|---|
| Wilmsmeyer | 49 | 39.1 |

| KICKING | XP | ATT | % | FG | ATT | % |
|---|---|---|---|---|---|---|
| Cofer | 53 | 54 | 98 | 18 | 27 | 67 |

## NEW ORLEANS SAINTS

### RUSHING

| Last Name | No. | Yds | Avg | TD |
|---|---|---|---|---|
| Dunbar | 154 | 565 | 3.7 | 3 |
| Hilliard | 115 | 445 | 3.9 | 4 |
| Heyward | 104 | 416 | 4.0 | 3 |
| McAfee | 39 | 114 | 2.9 | 1 |
| Hebert | 32 | 95 | 3.0 | 0 |
| Early | 3 | -1 | -0.3 | 0 |
| Barnhardt | 4 | -2 | -0.5 | 0 |
| M. Buck | 3 | -4 | -1.3 | 0 |

### RECEIVING

| Last Name | No. | Yds | Avg | TD |
|---|---|---|---|---|
| E. Martin | 68 | 1041 | 15.3 | 5 |
| Hilliard | 48 | 465 | 9.7 | 4 |
| Early | 30 | 566 | 18.9 | 5 |
| Small | 23 | 278 | 12.1 | 3 |
| Heyward | 19 | 159 | 8.4 | 0 |
| Carroll | 18 | 292 | 16.2 | 2 |
| Brenner | 12 | 161 | 13.4 | 0 |
| Wainright | 9 | 143 | 15.9 | 0 |
| Dunbar | 9 | 62 | 6.9 | 0 |
| Turner | 5 | 43 | 8.6 | 0 |
| Stowers | 4 | 23 | 5.8 | 0 |
| Newman | 3 | 21 | 7.0 | 0 |
| McAfee | 1 | 16 | 16.0 | 0 |
| Dowdell | 1 | 6 | 6.0 | 0 |
| Lipps | 1 | 1 | 1.0 | 0 |
| Cooper | 0 | 20 | — | 0 |

### PUNT RETURNS

| Last Name | No. | Yds | Avg | TD |
|---|---|---|---|---|
| Newman | 23 | 158 | 6.9 | 0 |
| Dowdell | 12 | 37 | 3.1 | 0 |
| Lipps | 5 | 22 | 4.4 | 0 |
| Turner | 3 | 10 | 3.3 | 0 |
| V. Buck | 2 | 4 | 2.0 | 0 |

### KICKOFF RETURNS

| Last Name | No. | Yds | Avg | TD |
|---|---|---|---|---|
| McAfee | 19 | 393 | 20.7 | 0 |
| Dunbar | 10 | 187 | 18.7 | 0 |
| Hilliard | 7 | 130 | 18.6 | 0 |
| Newman | 3 | 62 | 20.7 | 0 |
| Jordan | 1 | 18 | 18.0 | 0 |
| Heyward | 1 | 14 | 14.0 | 0 |
| Kennard | 1 | 11 | 11.0 | 0 |

### PASSING — PUNTING — KICKING

| PASSING | Att | Cmp | % | Yds | Yd/Att | TD | Int— % | RK |
|---|---|---|---|---|---|---|---|---|
| Hebert | 422 | 249 | 59.0 | 3287 | 7.79 | 19 | 16—3.8 | 6 |
| M. Buck | 4 | 2 | 50.0 | 10 | 2.50 | 0 | 0—0.0 | |

| PUNTING | No. | Avg. |
|---|---|---|
| Barnhardt | 67 | 44.0 |

| KICKING | XP | ATT | % | FG | ATT | % |
|---|---|---|---|---|---|---|
| Andersen | 33 | 34 | 97 | 29 | 34 | 85 |

## ATLANTA FALCONS

### RUSHING

| Last Name | No. | Yds | Avg | TD |
|---|---|---|---|---|
| Broussard | 84 | 363 | 4.3 | 1 |
| T. Smith | 87 | 329 | 3.8 | 2 |
| K. Jones | 79 | 278 | 3.5 | 0 |
| Miller | 23 | 89 | 3.9 | 0 |
| Pegram | 21 | 89 | 4.2 | 0 |
| Wilson | 15 | 62 | 4.1 | 0 |
| Pritchard | 5 | 37 | 7.4 | 0 |
| Tolliver | 4 | 15 | 3.8 | 0 |
| Solomon | 2 | 12 | 6.0 | 0 |
| Fulhage | 1 | 0 | 0.0 | 0 |
| Sanders | 1 | -4 | -4.0 | 0 |

### RECEIVING

| Last Name | No. | Yds | Avg | TD |
|---|---|---|---|---|
| Rison | 93 | 1121 | 12.1 | 11 |
| Pritchard | 77 | 827 | 10.7 | 5 |
| Hill | 60 | 623 | 10.4 | 3 |
| Haynes | 48 | 808 | 16.8 | 10 |
| T. Jones | 14 | 138 | 9.9 | 1 |
| K. Jones | 12 | 94 | 7.8 | 0 |
| Broussard | 11 | 96 | 8.7 | 1 |
| Thomas | 6 | 54 | 9.0 | 0 |
| Phillips | 4 | 26 | 6.5 | 1 |
| Sanders | 3 | 45 | 15.0 | 1 |
| Milling | 3 | 25 | 8.3 | 0 |
| Pegram | 2 | 25 | 12.5 | 0 |
| T. Smith | 2 | 14 | 7.0 | 0 |
| Hinton | 1 | -2 | -2.0 | 0 |

### PUNT RETURNS

| Last Name | No. | Yds | Avg | TD |
|---|---|---|---|---|
| T. Smith | 16 | 155 | 9.7 | 0 |
| Sanders | 13 | 41 | 3.2 | 0 |

### KICKOFF RETURNS

| Last Name | No. | Yds | Avg | TD |
|---|---|---|---|---|
| Sanders | 40 | 1067 | 26.7 | 2 |
| Pegram | 9 | 161 | 17.9 | 0 |
| T. Smith | 7 | 172 | 24.6 | 0 |
| K. Jones | 6 | 114 | 19.0 | 0 |
| Barnett | 1 | 13 | 13.0 | 0 |
| Fortin | 1 | 5 | 5.0 | 0 |

### PASSING — PUNTING — KICKING

| PASSING | Att | Cmp | % | Yds | Yd/Att | TD | Int— % | RK |
|---|---|---|---|---|---|---|---|---|
| Miller | 253 | 152 | 60.1 | 1739 | 6.87 | 15 | 6—2.4 | 2 |
| Wilson | 163 | 111 | 68.1 | 1368 | 8.39 | 13 | 4—2.5 | |
| Tolliver | 131 | 73 | 55.7 | 787 | 6.01 | 5 | 5—3.8 | |
| K. Jones | 1 | 0 | 0.0 | 0 | 0.00 | 0 | 0—0.0 | |

| PUNTING | No. | Avg. |
|---|---|---|
| Fulhage | 69 | 40.8 |
| Johnson | 1 | 37.0 |

| KICKING | XP | Att | % | FG | ATT | % |
|---|---|---|---|---|---|---|
| N. Johnson | 39 | 39 | 100 | 18 | 22 | 82 |

## LOS ANGELES RAMS

### RUSHING

| Last Name | No. | Yds | Avg | TD |
|---|---|---|---|---|
| Gary | 279 | 1125 | 4.0 | 7 |
| Lang | 33 | 203 | 6.2 | 5 |
| Everett | 32 | 133 | 4.2 | 0 |
| Delpino | 32 | 115 | 3.6 | 0 |
| Thompson | 19 | 65 | 3.4 | 1 |
| Turner | 2 | 14 | 7.0 | 0 |
| Pagel | 1 | 0 | 0.0 | 0 |

### RECEIVING

| Last Name | No. | Yds | Avg | TD |
|---|---|---|---|---|
| Gary | 52 | 293 | 5.6 | 3 |
| Ellard | 47 | 727 | 15.5 | 3 |
| Anderson | 38 | 657 | 17.3 | 7 |
| Price | 34 | 324 | 9.5 | 2 |
| Chadwick | 29 | 362 | 12.5 | 3 |
| Carter | 20 | 232 | 11.6 | 3 |
| Lang | 18 | 283 | 15.7 | 1 |
| Cox | 18 | 261 | 14.5 | 0 |
| Delpino | 18 | 139 | 7.7 | 1 |
| Turner | 5 | 42 | 8.4 | 0 |
| Thompson | 5 | 11 | 2.2 | 0 |
| McNeal | 4 | 79 | 19.8 | 0 |

### PUNT RETURNS

| Last Name | No. | Yds | Avg | TD |
|---|---|---|---|---|
| Turner | 28 | 207 | 7.4 | 0 |
| Kinchen | 4 | 103 | 25.8 | 2 |

### KICKOFF RETURNS

| Last Name | No. | Yds | Avg | TD |
|---|---|---|---|---|
| Turner | 29 | 569 | 19.6 | 0 |
| Lang | 13 | 228 | 17.5 | 0 |
| Delpino | 6 | 83 | 13.8 | 0 |
| Thompson | 4 | 34 | 8.5 | 0 |
| Kinchen | 4 | 63 | 15.8 | 0 |
| Stephen | 2 | 12 | 6.0 | 0 |
| Anderson | 1 | 9 | 9.0 | 0 |
| Israel | 1 | -3 | -3.0 | 0 |

### PASSING — PUNTING — KICKING

| PASSING | Att | Cmp | % | Yds | Yd/Att | TD | Int— % | RK |
|---|---|---|---|---|---|---|---|---|
| Everett | 475 | 281 | 59.2 | 3323 | 7.00 | 22 | 18—3.8 | 7 |
| Pagel | 20 | 8 | 40.0 | 99 | 4.95 | 1 | 2—10.0 | |

| PUNTING | No. | Avg. |
|---|---|---|
| Bracken | 76 | 41.1 |

| KICKING | XP | ATT | % | FG | ATT | % |
|---|---|---|---|---|---|---|
| Zendejas | 38 | 38 | 100 | 15 | 20 | 75 |

# 1992 A.F.C.  New Coaches Are A Big Success

Beginner's luck became a part of pro football in 1992, with most of the nine new head coaches having very successful debuts. Three of them led their teams to division titles — San Diego's Bobby Ross, Pittsburgh's Bill Cowher and Minnesota's Dennis Green. Two other coaches — the Colts' Ted Marchibroda and the Packers' Mike Holmgren — had their teams in the playoff race until late in the season. Other new coaches were Cincinnati's Dave Shula, Seattle's Tom Flores, Tampa Bay's Sam Wyche and the Rams' Chuck Knox.

When the season ended, all nine of them still had their jobs, but four others had been fired — Chicago's Mike Ditka, New England's Dick MacPherson, the Giants' Ray Handley and Denver's Dan Reeves. Washington's Joe Gibbs retired after three Super Bowls.

Tragedy continued to impose upon the NFL. In the offseason, Philadelphia's Jerome Brown and Detroit's Eric Andolsek were killed in traffic accidents, and Indianapolis' Shane Curry was shot and killed by a teenager in a parking lot. During the season, the Jets' Dennis Byrd was paralyzed during a game. It was the second straight season a player has had his life changed because of a football injury.

## EASTERN DIVISION

**Miami Dolphins** — The Dolphins won their first division title since 1985. With a 6-0 start, they brought back memories of the 1972 unbeaten team. Then reality struck, as they lost five of seven games before ending with three consecutive victories. The October acquisition of free-agent Keith Jackson was a big lift for the team and gave quarterback Dan Marino another weapon in his arsenal. However, the Dolphins offense struggled late in the season, scoring only six touchdowns in the last five and a half games. The Dolphins found a defense in 1992, with new stars such as Troy Vincent, Marco Coleman and Bryan Cox. They won their first playoff game in seven years, shutting out San Diego, before falling to the eventual AFC champion Bills. Head coach Don Shula got his 300th NFL victory in Week 16, and was less than a full season away from catching George Halas on the career victories list.

**Buffalo Bills** — Three years, three Super Bowls and three super losses. The Bills joined the Broncos and Vikings as kings of the Super Bowl losers, after being demolished by Dallas in Pasadena 52-17. They even failed to win the AFC East crown in 1992, losing out to Miami to a tiebreaker. But it was still a very successful season in Buffalo. The defense, led by league interception leader Henry Jones, improved, and Thurman Thomas led the league in total yards for the fourth straight year, breaking Jim Brown's record. Quarterback Jim Kelly was red-hot for half a season, but he threw a league-high 19 interceptions before getting injured. Backup quarterback Frank Reich will always be remembered for leading the Bills to a victory over Houston in the playoffs after trailing by 32 points in the third quarter.

**Indianapolis Colts** — The Colts completed one of the best turnarounds in NFL history, going from 1-15 to 9-7 under new head coach Ted Marchibroda. They won their last five games by a total of only 20 points. It was a remarkable comeback, considering quarterback Jeff George struggled and the running game was weak. Even Steve Emtman and Quentin Coryatt, who the Colts drafted with the first two overall picks in the draft, were injured and missed the last two months of the season. Both of them, however, proved to be impact players, as did rookie halfback Rodney Culver, who scored nine touchdowns. Backup quarterback Jack Trudeau was calm in the storm when George was injured for six games.

**New York Jets** — The Jets' rebuilding took a step backward in 1992. Overconfidence after a 5-0 preseason played a major role, and they lacked an impact player on either side of the ball. But other factors were out of their control. Wide receiver Al Toon retired after suffering too many concussions, and defensive end Dennis Byrd was paralyzed in a November game after colliding with teammate Scott Mersereau. Quarterback Browning Nagle was given the starting job in training camp but failed to excite. He passed for 366 yards in the season opener, then struggled mightily the rest of the year. Defensive end Jeff Lageman was lost in Week Two with a knee injury, and running back Blair Thomas was again disappointing, even before missing half of the year.

**New England Patriots** — The Patriots were 1992's version of Team Turmoil. Too much was expected of them from the start, and they didn't have the talent to match their 6-10 mark in 1991. Coach Dick MacPherson was hospitalized with diverticulitis and missed the next seven games. The team was shut out three games and was forced to start four quarterbacks (Hugh Millen, Tommy Hodson, Scott Zolak and Jeff Carlson). The running game — especially second-year back Leonard Russell — was abysmal, with only 1,550 yards and six TD's. Receivers Irving Fryar and Marv Cook were consistent. Chief executive officer Sam Jankovich fired MacPherson after the season ended, then quit himself a day later. Bill Parcells, who led the Giants to two Super Bowl titles, was hired as the next coach, and hopes were raised immediately.

## CENTRAL DIVISION

**Pittsburgh Steelers** — New head coach Bill Cowher, only 35 years old, infused the team with new enthusiasm, and the Steelers won their first division title since 1984. It was also the Steelers' first 11-win season since 1979, when they last won a Super Bowl. But Barry Foster was the story of the year. He led the conference in rushing with 1,690 yards and 11 touchdowns. Besides breaking many of Franco Harris' team records, he tied Eric Dickerson's league record with 12 100-yard games in a season. Quarterback Neil O'Donnell was 9-3 as the starter before going out with a broken leg. Cornerback Rod Woodson was his usual All-Pro self, and solid showings were turned in by wide receiver Jeff Graham and rookie safety Darren Perry. Tight end Eric Green had his troubles and was suspended by the league for substance abuse.

**Houston Oilers** — Houston earned its NFL-best sixth straight postseason appearance during an up-and-down season. Like the Steelers, the Oilers operated down the stretch without their starting quarterback, with Cody Carlson taking over for the injured Warren Moon until the playoffs. Lorenzo White, who rushed for 1,226 yards, emerged as a star in a backfield that was far less crowded than in past years. With 90 catches, Haywood Jeffires led the AFC in receptions for the third straight year, and Ernest Givins led the AFC with 10 TD receptions. The Houston defense was again strong, ranking No. 1 in the AFC and No. 3 in the NFL. With an offense that finished second in the AFC, no other conference team could claim that kind of balance. But the season ended after Houston blew a 32-point lead against Buffalo in the playoffs.

**Cleveland Browns** — With a playoff berth at stake entering Week 15, the Browns promptly lost three straight games for their third consecutive losing season. They lacked any real explosiveness on offense, especially after quarterback Bernie Kosar went down with a broken ankle in the second game (and then again in the season finale). Todd Philcox was injured next, and then Mike Tomczak was signed for most of the rest of the season. No Cleveland players finished among the conference leaders in any major offensive category, especially the running backs who rotated all year long. Wide receiver Michael Jackson did catch seven touchdown passes. Linebacker Clay Matthews, the NFL's oldest defensive player, continued to set team marks for longevity and career sacks.

**Cincinnati Bengals** — Dave Shula took over as the youngest head coach in the league, and, even though a 2-0 start had everybody thinking he was as good as his father Don, the team finished with back-to-back 10-loss seasons for the first time in over a decade. Two five-game losing streaks were the main culprit. Boomer Esiason finished the season as the backup to rookie David Klingler, who became the team's quarterback of the present when he was surprisingly drafted early in the first round during the offseason. Another era ended when tackle Anthony Munoz announced his retirement following 13 seasons of dominating line play (though he was injured much of the season). Among the positives were running back Harold Green (who had 1,170 yards) and nose tackle Tim Krumrie, who led the defense with 97 tackles. Rookies Carl Pickens, Darryl Williams and Ricardo McDonald were impressive.

**OFFENSE**

| | BUFF | CIN | CLEV | DEN | HOU | IND | K.C. | L.A. | MIA | N.E. | NYJ | PITT | S.D. | SEA |
|---|---|---|---|---|---|---|---|---|---|---|---|---|---|---|
| FIRST DOWNS: | | | | | | | | | | | | | | |
| Total | 350 | 248 | 242 | 234 | 339 | 267 | 246 | 259 | 316 | 215 | 252 | 284 | 302 | 208 |
| by Rushing | 133 | 112 | 85 | 84 | 101 | 70 | 87 | 99 | 101 | 71 | 94 | 119 | 118 | 77 |
| by Passing | 192 | 114 | 141 | 135 | 217 | 174 | 134 | 139 | 194 | 130 | 137 | 143 | 161 | 114 |
| by Penalty | 25 | 22 | 16 | 15 | 21 | 23 | 25 | 21 | 21 | 14 | 21 | 22 | 23 | 17 |
| RUSHING: | | | | | | | | | | | | | | |
| Number | 549 | 454 | 451 | 403 | 353 | 379 | 446 | 434 | 407 | 419 | 424 | 518 | 489 | 402 |
| Yards | 2436 | 1976 | 1607 | 1500 | 1626 | 1102 | 1532 | 1794 | 1525 | 1550 | 1752 | 2156 | 1875 | 1596 |
| Average Yards | 4.4 | 4.4 | 3.6 | 3.7 | 4.6 | 2.9 | 3.4 | 4.1 | 3.7 | 3.7 | 4.1 | 4.2 | 3.8 | 4.0 |
| Touchdowns | 18 | 11 | 7 | 11 | 10 | 8 | 14 | 7 | 9 | 6 | 8 | 13 | 18 | 4 |
| PASSING: | | | | | | | | | | | | | | |
| Attempts | 509 | 435 | 398 | 473 | 573 | 546 | 413 | 471 | 563 | 444 | 495 | 431 | 496 | 476 |
| Completions | 293 | 227 | 238 | 258 | 373 | 305 | 230 | 233 | 332 | 244 | 251 | 249 | 282 | 230 |
| Completion Pct. | 57.6 | 52.2 | 59.8 | 54.5 | 65.1 | 55.9 | 55.7 | 49.5 | 59.0 | 55.0 | 50.7 | 57.8 | 56.9 | 48.3 |
| Passing Yards | 3678 | 2284 | 3102 | 3312 | 4231 | 3584 | 3115 | 2950 | 4148 | 2492 | 2962 | 3046 | 3614 | 2323 |
| Avg. Yds per Att. | 6.4 | 4.1 | 6.7 | 5.6 | 6.7 | 5.5 | 6.1 | 5.0 | 6.7 | 4.0 | 5.0 | 5.8 | 6.3 | 3.3 |
| Avg. Yds per Comp. | 12.6 | 10.1 | 13.0 | 12.8 | 11.3 | 11.8 | 13.5 | 12.7 | 12.5 | 10.2 | 11.8 | 12.2 | 12.8 | 10.1 |
| Times Tackled | 29 | 45 | 34 | 52 | 32 | 44 | 48 | 48 | 28 | 65 | 39 | 40 | 33 | 67 |
| Yds Lost Tackled | 221 | 341 | 217 | 382 | 202 | 318 | 323 | 360 | 173 | 458 | 283 | 296 | 268 | 545 |
| Net Yards | 3457 | 1943 | 2885 | 2930 | 4029 | 3266 | 2792 | 2590 | 3975 | 2034 | 2679 | 2750 | 3346 | 1778 |
| Touchdowns | 23 | 16 | 18 | 16 | 27 | 13 | 15 | 20 | 24 | 13 | 12 | 15 | 16 | 9 |
| Interceptions | 21 | 17 | 16 | 29 | 23 | 26 | 12 | 23 | 17 | 19 | 24 | 14 | 21 | 23 |
| Pct. Intercepted | 4.1 | 3.9 | 4.0 | 6.1 | 4.0 | 4.8 | 2.9 | 4.9 | 3.0 | 4.3 | 4.8 | 3.2 | 4.2 | 4.8 |
| PUNTS: | | | | | | | | | | | | | | |
| Number | 60 | 76 | 75 | 85 | 55 | 83 | 86 | 77 | 61 | 103 | 73 | 74 | 68 | 108 |
| Average | 42.2 | 42.1 | 41.1 | 43.6 | 45.2 | 44.8 | 42.2 | 42.3 | 39.7 | 41.0 | 41.0 | 42.1 | 42.6 | 44.1 |
| PUNT RETURNS | | | | | | | | | | | | | | |
| Number | 43 | 24 | 44 | 34 | 33 | 25 | 39 | 41 | 31 | 37 | 30 | 32 | 44 | 38 |
| Yards | 464 | 285 | 429 | 353 | 194 | 275 | 402 | 402 | 191 | 274 | 232 | 364 | 359 | 283 |
| Average Yards | 10.8 | 11.9 | 9.8 | 10.4 | 5.9 | 11.0 | 10.3 | 9.8 | 6.2 | 7.4 | 7.7 | 11.4 | 8.2 | 7.4 |
| Touchdowns | 0 | 1 | 1 | 0 | 0 | 2 | 2 | 0 | 0 | 0 | 0 | 1 | 0 | 0 |
| KICKOFF RET.: | | | | | | | | | | | | | | |
| Number | 41 | 59 | 43 | 51 | 46 | 51 | 39 | 43 | 44 | 64 | 54 | 48 | 45 | 50 |
| Yards | 761 | 1058 | 880 | 1028 | 885 | 1001 | 722 | 744 | 838 | 1376 | 950 | 847 | 812 | 885 |
| Average Yards | 18.6 | 17.9 | 20.5 | 20.2 | 19.2 | 19.6 | 18.5 | 17.3 | 19.0 | 21.5 | 17.6 | 17.6 | 18.0 | 17.7 |
| Touchdowns | 0 | 0 | 0 | 0 | 0 | 0 | 0 | 0 | 0 | 1 | 0 | 0 | 0 | 0 |
| INTERCEPT RET.: | | | | | | | | | | | | | | |
| Number | 23 | 16 | 13 | 15 | 20 | 20 | 24 | 12 | 18 | 14 | 21 | 22 | 25 | 20 |
| Yards | 325 | 205 | 222 | 210 | 181 | 302 | 403 | 339 | 458 | 285 | 269 | 384 | 405 | 324 |
| Average Yards | 14.1 | 12.8 | 17.1 | 14.0 | 9.1 | 15.1 | 16.8 | 28.3 | 25.4 | 20.4 | 12.8 | 17.5 | 16.2 | 16.2 |
| Touchdowns | 2 | 1 | 1 | 1 | 1 | 1 | 6 | 1 | 3 | 3 | 3 | 1 | 1 | 0 |
| PENALTIES: | | | | | | | | | | | | | | |
| Number | 103 | 98 | 104 | 98 | 111 | 122 | 82 | 113 | 86 | 111 | 107 | 106 | 91 | 111 |
| Yards | 775 | 755 | 765 | 768 | 824 | 958 | 675 | 832 | 656 | 1051 | 873 | 941 | 813 | 918 |
| FUMBLES: | | | | | | | | | | | | | | |
| Number | 31 | 32 | 19 | 29 | 28 | 24 | 28 | 25 | 31 | 43 | 28 | 28 | 26 | 37 |
| Number Lost | 17 | 10 | 12 | 14 | 12 | 11 | 9 | 15 | 17 | 26 | 15 | 18 | 12 | 18 |
| POINTS: | | | | | | | | | | | | | | |
| Total | 381 | 274 | 272 | 262 | 352 | 216 | 348 | 249 | 340 | 205 | 220 | 299 | 335 | 140 |
| PAT Attempts | 44 | 31 | 30 | 29 | 41 | 24 | 40 | 29 | 36 | 25 | 23 | 31 | 36 | 14 |
| PAT Made | 43 | 31 | 29 | 28 | 41 | 24 | 39 | 28 | 34 | 22 | 23 | 29 | 35 | 14 |
| FG Attempts | 30 | 28 | 29 | 25 | 27 | 29 | 25 | 26 | 37 | 17 | 30 | 36 | 32 | 22 |
| FG Made | 24 | 19 | 21 | 20 | 21 | 16 | 23 | 15 | 30 | 11 | 19 | 28 | 26 | 14 |
| Percent FG Made | 80.0 | 67.9 | 72.4 | 80.0 | 77.8 | 55.2 | 92.0 | 57.7 | 81.1 | 64.7 | 63.3 | 77.8 | 81.3 | 63.6 |
| Safeties | 1 | 0 | 0 | 0 | 1 | 0 | 0 | 1 | 0 | 0 | 1 | 0 | 3 | 0 |

**DEFENSE**

| | BUFF | CIN | CLEV | DEN | HOU | IND | K.C. | L.A. | MIA | N.E. | NYJ | PITT | S.D. | SEA |
|---|---|---|---|---|---|---|---|---|---|---|---|---|---|---|
| FIRST DOWNS: | | | | | | | | | | | | | | |
| Total | 278 | 319 | 281 | 283 | 254 | 314 | 256 | 264 | 273 | 292 | 276 | 266 | 250 | 247 |
| by Rushing | 77 | 126 | 86 | 105 | 93 | 129 | 97 | 104 | 92 | 112 | 110 | 99 | 80 | 96 |
| by Passing | 185 | 168 | 170 | 156 | 139 | 164 | 145 | 135 | 168 | 149 | 146 | 146 | 157 | 129 |
| by Penalty | 16 | 25 | 25 | 22 | 22 | 21 | 14 | 25 | 13 | 31 | 20 | 21 | 13 | 22 |
| RUSHING: | | | | | | | | | | | | | | |
| Number | 427 | 490 | 429 | 489 | 412 | 495 | 441 | 478 | 428 | 521 | 460 | 435 | 365 | 513 |
| Yards | 1395 | 2007 | 1605 | 1963 | 1634 | 2174 | 1787 | 1683 | 1600 | 1951 | 1919 | 1841 | 1395 | 1922 |
| Average Yards | 3.3 | 4.1 | 3.7 | 4.0 | 4.0 | 4.4 | 4.1 | 3.5 | 3.7 | 3.7 | 4.2 | 4.2 | 3.8 | 3.7 |
| Touchdowns | 8 | 15 | 5 | 10 | 6 | 16 | 12 | 17 | 9 | 15 | 13 | 6 | 10 | 14 |
| PASSING: | | | | | | | | | | | | | | |
| Attempts | 520 | 489 | 486 | 462 | 445 | 470 | 458 | 450 | 512 | 459 | 465 | 478 | 491 | 428 |
| Completions | 305 | 288 | 291 | 268 | 248 | 260 | 253 | 243 | 294 | 258 | 257 | 252 | 271 | 251 |
| Completion Pct. | 58.7 | 58.9 | 59.9 | 58.0 | 55.7 | 55.3 | 55.2 | 54.0 | 57.4 | 56.2 | 55.3 | 52.7 | 55.2 | 58.6 |
| Passing Yards | 3560 | 3620 | 3467 | 3437 | 2898 | 3236 | 2928 | 3153 | 3266 | 3211 | 3201 | 3065 | 3188 | 2978 |
| Avg. Yds per Att. | 5.7 | 6.2 | 5.9 | 6.1 | 5.2 | 5.7 | 5.0 | 5.7 | 5.4 | 6.5 | 5.9 | 5.5 | 5.2 | 5.6 |
| Avg. Yds per Comp. | 11.7 | 12.6 | 11.9 | 12.8 | 11.7 | 12.5 | 11.6 | 13.0 | 11.1 | 12.5 | 12.5 | 12.2 | 11.8 | 11.9 |
| Times Tackled | 44 | 45 | 48 | 50 | 50 | 39 | 50 | 46 | 36 | 20 | 36 | 36 | 51 | 46 |
| Yds Lost Tackled | 351 | 294 | 315 | 317 | 321 | 336 | 391 | 320 | 283 | 114 | 240 | 248 | 356 | 317 |
| Net Yards | 3209 | 3326 | 3152 | 3120 | 2577 | 2900 | 2537 | 2833 | 2983 | 3097 | 2961 | 2817 | 2832 | 2661 |
| Touchdowns | 19 | 24 | 23 | 21 | 20 | 14 | 19 | 11 | 16 | 22 | 19 | 15 | 17 | 11 |
| Interceptions | 23 | 16 | 13 | 15 | 20 | 20 | 24 | 12 | 18 | 14 | 21 | 22 | 25 | 20 |
| Pct. Intercepted | 4.4 | 3.3 | 2.7 | 3.2 | 4.5 | 4.3 | 5.2 | 2.7 | 3.5 | 3.1 | 4.5 | 4.6 | 5.1 | 4.7 |
| PUNTS: | | | | | | | | | | | | | | |
| Number | 79 | 57 | 74 | 78 | 68 | 71 | 80 | 85 | 74 | 75 | 70 | 74 | 80 | 96 |
| Average | 43.9 | 41.8 | 44.5 | 43.3 | 43.2 | 42.5 | 43.1 | 42.5 | 40.1 | 40.6 | 40.9 | 42.0 | 44.6 | 41.8 |
| PUNT RETURNS | | | | | | | | | | | | | | |
| Number | 22 | 32 | 27 | 39 | 31 | 45 | 40 | 40 | 33 | 59 | 26 | 39 | 24 | 56 |
| Yards | 185 | 284 | 234 | 382 | 255 | 313 | 328 | 385 | 382 | 499 | 189 | 308 | 244 | 416 |
| Average Yards | 8.4 | 8.9 | 8.7 | 9.8 | 8.2 | 7.0 | 8.2 | 9.6 | 11.6 | 8.5 | 7.3 | 7.9 | 10.2 | 7.4 |
| Touchdowns | 0 | 1 | 0 | 0 | 0 | 0 | 1 | 0 | 1 | 1 | 0 | 0 | 1 | 1 |
| KICKOFF RET.: | | | | | | | | | | | | | | |
| Number | 60 | 46 | 51 | 13 | 63 | 36 | 64 | 35 | 65 | 45 | 33 | 52 | 54 | 36 |
| Yards | 1215 | 1079 | 907 | 254 | 989 | 630 | 1203 | 690 | 1380 | 749 | 552 | 1052 | 962 | 685 |
| Average Yards | 20.3 | 23.5 | 17.8 | 19.5 | 15.7 | 17.5 | 18.8 | 19.7 | 21.2 | 16.6 | 16.7 | 20.2 | 17.8 | 19.0 |
| Touchdowns | 1 | 2 | 0 | 0 | 0 | 0 | 0 | 0 | 0 | 0 | 0 | 0 | 0 | 0 |
| INTERCEPT RET.: | | | | | | | | | | | | | | |
| Number | 21 | 17 | 16 | 29 | 23 | 26 | 12 | 23 | 17 | 19 | 24 | 14 | 21 | 23 |
| Yards | 423 | 127 | 213 | 567 | 367 | 461 | 162 | 345 | 446 | 232 | 347 | 235 | 241 | 231 |
| Average Yards | 20.1 | 7.5 | 13.3 | 19.6 | 16.0 | 17.7 | 13.5 | 15.0 | 26.2 | 12.2 | 14.5 | 16.8 | 11.5 | 10.0 |
| Touchdowns | 2 | 0 | 1 | 3 | 0 | 4 | 0 | 2 | 4 | 0 | 2 | 1 | 1 | 4 |
| PENALTIES: | | | | | | | | | | | | | | |
| Number | 118 | 95 | 93 | 96 | 114 | 101 | 124 | 98 | 89 | 90 | 82 | 104 | 98 | 100 |
| Yards | 933 | 797 | 764 | 715 | 886 | 836 | 959 | 755 | 679 | 673 | 808 | 814 | 798 | 776 |
| FUMBLES: | | | | | | | | | | | | | | |
| Number | 29 | 36 | 33 | 33 | 24 | 28 | 34 | 21 | 25 | 30 | 33 | 34 | 18 | 25 |
| Number Lost | 12 | 17 | 20 | 16 | 11 | 15 | 15 | 7 | 14 | 15 | 18 | 21 | 11 | 11 |
| POINTS: | | | | | | | | | | | | | | |
| Total | 283 | 364 | 275 | 329 | 258 | 302 | 282 | 281 | 281 | 363 | 315 | 225 | 241 | 312 |
| PAT Attempts | 31 | 44 | 29 | 35 | 28 | 34 | 34 | 32 | 32 | 40 | 35 | 24 | 29 | 32 |
| PAT Made | 31 | 44 | 29 | 35 | 27 | 33 | 33 | 32 | 30 | 40 | 34 | 24 | 28 | 29 |
| FG Attempts | 30 | 30 | 29 | 38 | 26 | 28 | 21 | 30 | 26 | 41 | 31 | 28 | 16 | 36 |
| FG Made | 22 | 18 | 24 | 28 | 21 | 21 | 15 | 19 | 19 | 27 | 23 | 19 | 13 | 29 |
| Percent FG Made | 73.3 | 60.0 | 82.8 | 73.7 | 80.8 | 75.0 | 71.4 | 63.3 | 73.1 | 65.9 | 74.2 | 67.9 | 81.3 | 80.6 |
| Safeties | 0 | 1 | 0 | 0 | 0 | 1 | 0 | 0 | 1 | 1 | 1 | 0 | 0 | 2 |

## WESTERN DIVISION

**San Diego Chargers** — The Chargers became the first team ever to go from 0-4 to the playoffs, and they won their first division title since 1981. After losing quarterback John Friesz in the preseason, San Diego acquired Stan Humphries in a trade with Washington. He took over as the starter in two games, and although the offense scored just 29 points in the first four games, the turnaround and eventual 11-1 finish under new head coach Bobby Ross was remarkable. Linebacker Junior Seau started to be recognized as one of the best defensive players in the game, but Leslie O'Neal, Chris Mims, Stanley Richard and others also spurred the comeback. Ronnie Harmon led NFL backs with 79 receptions, and Anthony Miller caught 72 passes for 1,060 yards and seven touchdowns.

**Kansas City Chiefs** — Quarterback Dave Krieg was supposed to be the missing piece to a Super Bowl puzzle. Instead, the Chiefs needed three defensive touchdowns in their last game to even make the playoffs. An 8-4 start evaporated into a struggle for the playoffs, and, even though they qualified for postseason play for the third straight year, the season was a disappointment. The offense was inconsistent at best, even with three solid runners in Barry Word, Christian Okoye and Harvey Williams. Each was capable of 1,000 yards, but they totaled only 1,317 yards between them. Neil Smith and Derrick Thomas, each of whom had 14.5 sacks, continued to be the center of attention on defense.

**Denver Broncos** — Dan Reeves was fired following an 8-8 season in which quarterback John Elway was injured and replaced by rotating quarterbacks in rookie Tommy Maddox and Shawn Moore. After a 7-3 start, Elway missed four starts, all losses, which killed any chances Denver had of making the playoffs. Without Elway, the offense fell apart, and the Broncos were outscored by 67 points in the 16 games. The running game, led by Gaston Green, failed to take some pressure off the passers, who were under siege when they dropped back, being sacked 52 times. Wideout Mark Jackson scored a team-high eight touchdowns, and linebacker Simon Fletcher had a team-record 16 sacks, making it 10 or more for him in four consecutive seasons. After the season, defensive coordinator Wade Phillips was promoted to head coach.

**Los Angeles Raiders** — The Raiders finished 7-9 while juggling three quarterbacks and three halfbacks, and their minus-19 turnover ratio was the worst in the league. Jay Schroeder and Todd Marinovich played most of the season, then long-time veteran Vince Evans took over in the last game. Eric Dickerson was acquired in a Draft Day trade, but he played like his best days were behind him, rushing for only 729 yards. And Marcus Allen, the wily veteran, was in Al Davis' doghouse and asked to be traded at the end of the year. The best player on offense was wide receiver Tim Brown, who led the team with 49 receptions and seven touchdowns. Veteran defensive lineman Howie Long continued to amaze, as he turned in another solid performance.

**Seattle Seahawks** — The Seahawks were clearly the worst team in the league with a horrible offense but a very good defense. The defensive players didn't mutiny against an offense that left them on the field too long, didn't take advantage of turnovers they created and yielded almost as many touchdowns (seven, plus two safeties) as it scored (13). Seattle scored only 140 points, the fewest by any team since the NFL went to a 16-game schedule in 1978. The Seahawks lost their top quarterbacks, Kelly Stouffer and Dan McGwire, to season-ending injuries. Stan Gelbaugh finished the year. A nice surprise on offense was halfback Chris Warren, who rushed for 1,017 yards. On defense, tackle Cortez Kennedy had 14 sacks and was named the league's Defensive Player of the Year.

## MIAMI DOLPHINS 11-5 Don Shula

| | Scores of Each Game | |
|---|---|---|
| 27 | Cleveland | 23 |
| 26 | L.A. RAMS | 10 |
| 19 | Seattle | 17 |
| 37 | Buffalo | 10 |
| 21 | ATLANTA | 17 |
| 38 | NEW ENGLAND | 17 |
| 20 | INDIANAPOLIS | 31 |
| 14 | at N.Y. Jets | 26 |
| 28 | Indianapolis | 0 |
| 20 | BUFFALO | 26 |
| 19 | HOUSTON | 16 |
| 13 | New Orleans | 24 |
| 3 | San Francisco | 27 |
| 20 | L.A. RAIDERS | 7 |
| 19 | N.Y. JETS | 17 |
| 16 | New England | •13 |

| Use Name | Pos. | Hgt. | Wgt. | Age | Int | Pts |
|---|---|---|---|---|---|---|
| Jeff Dellenbach | OT-C | 6'6" | 283 | 29 | | |
| Mark Dennis | OT | 6'6" | 292 | 27 | | |
| Richmond Webb | OT | 6'6" | 298 | 25 | | |
| Harry Galbreath | OG | 6'1" | 271 | 27 | | |
| Keith Sims | OG | 6'2" | 310 | 25 | | |
| Bert Weidner | OG-C | 6'3" | 284 | 26 | | |
| Gene Williams | OG | 6'2" | 308 | 23 | | |
| Jeff Uhlenhake | C | 6'3" | 284 | 26 | | |
| Marco Coleman | DE-LB | 6'3" | 259 | 22 | | |
| Jeff Cross | DE | 6'4" | 272 | 26 | | |
| Jeff Hunter (from DET) | DE | 6'5" | 293 | 26 | | |
| T.J. Turner | DE-NT | 6'4" | 280 | 29 | | |
| Larry Webster | DE | 6'5" | 285 | 23 | | |
| Chuck Klingbeil | NT | 6'1" | 265 | 26 | | |

| Use Name | Pos. | Hgt. | Wgt. | Age | Int | Pts |
|---|---|---|---|---|---|---|
| Roosevelt Collins | LB | 6'4" | 235 | 24 | | |
| Bryan Cox | LB | 6'3" | 235 | 24 | 1 | |
| David Griggs | LB | 6'3" | 248 | 25 | | |
| John Grimsley | LB | 6'2" | 236 | 30 | | |
| Dwight Hollier | LB | 6'2" | 242 | 23 | | |
| Cliff Odom | LB | 6'2" | 241 | 34 | | |
| John Offerdahl | LB | 6'3" | 237 | 28 | | |
| Mark Sander | LB | 6'2" | 232 | 24 | | |
| Bruce Alexander | DB | 5'8" | 178 | 26 | 1 | |
| Stephen Braggs | DB | 5'9" | 180 | 27 | | |
| J.B. Brown | DB | 6' | 189 | 26 | 4 | 6 |
| Kerry Glenn | DB | 5'9" | 175 | 30 | | |
| Chris Green | DB | 5'11" | 188 | 24 | | |
| Bobby Harden | DB | 6' | 192 | 25 | | |
| Liffort Hobley | DB | 6' | 207 | 30 | | |
| Vestee Jackson | DB | 6' | 186 | 29 | 3 | 6 |
| Darrell Malone (from KC) | DB | 5'10" | 177 | 24 | | |
| Louis Oliver | DB | 6'2" | 226 | 26 | 5 | 6 |
| Troy Vincent | DB | 6' | 191 | 32 | 2 | |
| Jarvis Williams | DB | 5'11" | 200 | 27 | 2 | |

Ned Bolcar — Knee Injury

| Use Name | Pos. | Hgt. | Wgt. | Age | Int | Pts |
|---|---|---|---|---|---|---|
| Dan Marino | QB | 6'4" | 224 | 30 | | |
| Scott Mitchell | QB | 6'6" | 236 | 24 | | |
| Aaron Craver | HB | 5'11" | 215 | 22 | | |
| Mark Higgs | HB | 5'7" | 195 | 26 | | 42 |
| Bobby Humphrey | HB | 6'1" | 201 | 25 | | 12 |
| Bernie Parmalee | HB | 5'11" | 190 | 24 | | |
| Tony Paige | FB | 5'10" | 235 | 29 | | 12 |
| James Saxon | FB | 5'11' | 237 | 26 | | |
| Fred Banks | WR | 5'10" | 185 | 30 | | 18 |
| Robert Clark | WR | 5'11" | 175 | 27 | | |
| Mark Clayton | WR | 5'9" | 185 | 31 | | 18 |
| Mark Duper | WR | 5'9" | 192 | 33 | | 42 |
| Jim Jensen | WR-FB | 6'4" | 224 | 33 | | |
| Tony Martin | WR | 6' | 180 | 26 | | 12 |
| Scott Miller | WR | 5'10" | 179 | 23 | | |
| Mike Williams | WR | 5'10" | 178 | 25 | | |
| Greg Baty | TE | 6'5" | 240 | 28 | | 6 |
| Ferrell Edmunds | TE | 6'6" | 254 | 27 | | 6 |
| Keith Jackson | TE | 6'2" | 250 | 27 | | 30 |
| Joe Prokop (to NYG) | K | 6'2" | 225 | 32 | | |
| Reggie Roby | K | 6'2" | 243 | 31 | | |
| Pete Stoyonovich | K | 5'10" | 181 | 25 | | 124 |

Scott Secules — Shoulder Injury

## BUFFALO BILLS 11-5 Marv Levy

| | Scores of Each Game | |
|---|---|---|
| 40 | L.A. RAMS | 7 |
| 34 | San Francisco | 31 |
| 38 | INDIANAPOLIS | 0 |
| 41 | New England | 7 |
| 10 | MIAMI | 37 |
| 3 | L.A. Raiders | 20 |
| 24 | N.Y. Jets | 20 |
| 16 | NEW ENGLAND | 7 |
| 28 | PITTSBURGH | 20 |
| 26 | Miami | 20 |
| 41 | ATLANTA | 14 |
| 13 | Indianapolis | •16 |
| 17 | N.Y. JETS | 24 |
| 27 | DENVER | 17 |
| 20 | New Orleans | 16 |
| 3 | Houston | 27 |

| Use Name | Pos. | Hgt. | Wgt. | Age | Int | Pts |
|---|---|---|---|---|---|---|
| Howard Ballard | OT | 6'6" | 325 | 28 | | |
| Jerry Crafts | OT | 6'6" | 333 | 24 | | |
| Will Wolford | OT | 6'5" | 297 | 28 | | |
| John Davis | OG | 6'4" | 311 | 27 | | |
| John Fina | OG-OT | 6'4" | 282 | 23 | | 6 |
| Mitch Frerotte | OG | 6'3" | 285 | 27 | | 12 |
| Glenn Parker | OG-OT | 6'5" | 305 | 26 | | |
| Jim Ritcher | OG | 6'3" | 273 | 34 | | |
| Kent Hull | C | 6'4" | 278 | 31 | | |
| Adam Lingner | C | 6'4" | 268 | 31 | | |
| Phil Hansen | DE | 6'5" | 275 | 24 | | |
| Mark Pike | DE | 6'4" | 272 | 28 | | |
| Bruce Smith | DE | 6'4" | 275 | 29 | | |
| Keith Willis | DE | 6'1" | 263 | 33 | | |
| Gary Baldinger | NT | 6'3" | 270 | 28 | | |
| Mike Lodish | NT | 6'3" | 272 | 25 | | 6 |
| Jeff Wright | NT | 6'2" | 270 | 29 | | |

| Use Name | Pos. | Hgt. | Wgt. | Age | Int | Pts |
|---|---|---|---|---|---|---|
| Carlton Bailey | LB | 6'2" | 235 | 27 | | |
| Cornelius Bennett | LB | 6'2" | 238 | 27 | | |
| Shane Conlan | LB | 6'3" | 230 | 28 | 1 | |
| Keith Goganious | LB | 6'2" | 237 | 23 | | |
| Richard Harvey | LB | 6'1" | 235 | 25 | | |
| Mark Maddox | LB | 6'1" | 233 | 24 | | |
| Marvcus Patton | LB | 6'2" | 225 | 25 | | |
| Darryl Talley | LB | 6'4" | 235 | 32 | | |
| Matt Darby | DB | 6'1" | 200 | 23 | | |
| Chris Hale | DB | 5'7" | 165 | 26 | | 2 |
| Cliff Hicks | DB | 5'10" | 188 | 28 | | |
| Kirby Jackson | DB | 5'10" | 180 | 27 | | |
| Henry Jones | DB | 5'11" | 197 | 24 | 8 | 12 |
| Mark Kelso | DB | 5'11" | 185 | 29 | 7 | |
| Nate Odomes | DB | 5'10" | 188 | 27 | 5 | |
| Kurt Schulz | DB | 6'1" | 206 | 23 | | |
| James Williams | DB | 5'10" | 172 | 25 | 2 | |

| Use Name | Pos. | Hgt. | Wgt. | Age | Int | Pts |
|---|---|---|---|---|---|---|
| Gale Gilbert | QB | 6'3" | 210 | 29 | | |
| Jim Kelly | QB | 6'3" | 218 | 32 | | 6 |
| Frank Reich | QB | 6'4" | 210 | 30 | | |
| Kenneth Davis | HB | 5'10" | 208 | 30 | | 36 |
| Eddie Fuller | HB | 5'9" | 201 | 24 | | |
| Thurman Thomas | HB | 5'10" | 198 | 26 | | 72 |
| Carwell Gardner | FB | 6'2" | 232 | 25 | | 12 |
| Don Beebe | WR | 5'11" | 184 | 27 | | 12 |
| Al Edwards | WR | 5'8" | 173 | 25 | | |
| Brad Lamb | WR | 5'10" | 171 | 24 | | |
| James Lofton | WR | 6'3" | 190 | 36 | | 36 |
| Andre Reed | WR | 6' | 190 | 28 | | 18 |
| Steve Tasker | WR | 5'9" | 183 | 30 | | |
| Chris Walsh | WR | 6'1" | 185 | 23 | | |
| Rob Awalt | TE | 6'5" | 238 | 32 | | |
| Keith McKeller | TE | 6'6" | 245 | 28 | | |
| Pete Metzelaars | TE | 6'7" | 250 | 32 | | 36 |
| Chris Mohr | K | 6'5" | 215 | 26 | | |
| Steve Christie | K | 6' | 185 | 24 | | 115 |

Ed Thomas — Knee Injury

## INDIANAPOLIS COLTS 9-7 Ted Marchibroda

| | Scores of Each Game | |
|---|---|---|
| 14 | CLEVELAND | 3 |
| 10 | HOUSTON | 20 |
| 0 | Buffalo | 38 |
| 24 | Tampa Bay | 14 |
| 6 | N.Y. JETS | •3 |
| 14 | SAN DIEGO | 34 |
| 31 | Miami | 20 |
| 0 | San Diego | 26 |
| 0 | MIAMI | 28 |
| 34 | NEW ENGLAND | •37 |
| 14 | Pittsburgh | 30 |
| 16 | BUFFALO | •13 |
| 6 | New England | 0 |
| 10 | N.Y. Jets | 6 |
| 16 | PHOENIX | 13 |
| 21 | Cincinnati | 17 |

| Use Name | Pos. | Hgt. | Wgt. | Age | Int | Pts |
|---|---|---|---|---|---|---|
| Kevin Call | OT | 6'7" | 308 | 30 | | |
| Ron Mattes | OT | 6'6" | 298 | 29 | | |
| Zefross Moss | OT | 6'6" | 338 | 26 | | |
| Irv Pankey | OT-OG | 6'5" | 295 | 34 | | |
| William Schultz | OT | 6'5" | 305 | 25 | | 6 |
| Mark Vander Poel | OT | 6'7" | 303 | 24 | | |
| Randy Dixon | OG | 6'3" | 305 | 28 | | |
| Trevor Matich | OG-C | 6'4" | 297 | 30 | | |
| Tom Ricketts | OG | 6'5" | 295 | 26 | | |
| Ron Solt | OG | 6'3" | 280 | 30 | | |
| Ray Donaldson | C | 6'3" | 300 | 34 | | |
| Mel Agee (to ATL) | DE | 6'5" | 290 | 22 | | |
| Sam Clancy | DE | 6'7" | 300 | 34 | | |
| Steve Emtman | DE | 6'4" | 290 | 22 | 1 | 6 |
| Jon Hand | DE | 6'7" | 301 | 28 | | |
| Skip McClendon (from MIN) | DE | 6'7" | 302 | 28 | | |
| Willis Peguese (from HOU) | DE | 6'4" | 273 | 25 | | |
| Tony McCoy | NT | 6' | 279 | 23 | | |
| Tony Siragusa | NT | 6'3" | 303 | 25 | | |

Shane Curry — Shot and Killed During Offseason

| Use Name | Pos. | Hgt. | Wgt. | Age | Int | Pts |
|---|---|---|---|---|---|---|
| Chip Banks | LB | 6'4" | 254 | 32 | 1 | |
| Duane Bickett | LB | 6'5" | 251 | 29 | 1 | |
| Quentin Coryatt | LB | 6'3" | 250 | 22 | | |
| Steve Grant | LB | 6' | 231 | 22 | | |
| Jeff Herrod | LB | 6' | 249 | 26 | 1 | |
| Scott Radecic | LB | 6'3" | 236 | 30 | 1 | |
| Matt Vanderbeek | LB | 6'3" | 258 | 25 | | |
| Tony Walker | LB | 6'3" | 246 | 24 | | |
| Ashley Ambrose | DB | 5'10" | 177 | 21 | | |
| Michael Ball | DB | 6' | 220 | 28 | | |
| John Baylor | DB | 6' | 203 | 27 | 1 | |
| Jason Belser | DB | 5'9" | 187 | 22 | 3 | |
| Eugene Daniel | DB | 5'11" | 188 | 31 | 1 | |
| Chris Goode | DB | 6' | 199 | 28 | 2 | |
| Cornell Holloway | DB | 5'11" | 182 | 26 | | |
| Mike Prior | DB | 6' | 210 | 28 | 6 | |
| Tony Stargell | DB | 5'11" | 189 | 26 | 2 | |

| Use Name | Pos. | Hgt. | Wgt. | Age | Int | Pts |
|---|---|---|---|---|---|---|
| Jeff George | QB | 6'4" | 227 | 24 | | 6 |
| Mark Herrmann | QB | 6'4" | 220 | 33 | | |
| Jack Trudeau | QB | 6'3" | 227 | 29 | | |
| Tom Tupa | QB | 6'4" | 230 | 26 | | |
| Ken Clark | HB-FB | 5'9" | 204 | 26 | | |
| Rodney Culver | HB | 5'9" | 224 | 22 | | 54 |
| Anthony Johnson | HB-FB | 6' | 222 | 24 | | 18 |
| Ed Toner | HB | 6' | 240 | 24 | | |
| Maurice Carthon | FB | 6'1" | 240 | 31 | | |
| Bill Brooks | WR | 6' | 189 | 28 | | 6 |
| Jessie Hester | WR | 5'11" | 175 | 29 | | 6 |
| Reggie Langhorne | WR | 6'2" | 207 | 29 | | 6 |
| Eddie Miller | WR | 6' | 185 | 23 | | |
| Clarence Verdin | WR | 5'8" | 162 | 29 | | 12 |
| Charles Arbuckle | TE | 6'3" | 248 | 23 | | 6 |
| Kerry Cash | TE | 6'4" | 247 | 23 | | 18 |
| Dean Biasucci | K | 6' | 190 | 30 | | 72 |
| Rohn Stark | K | 6'3" | 203 | 33 | | |

## NEW YORK JETS 4-12 Bruce Coslet

| | Scores of Each Game | |
|---|---|---|
| 17 | Atlanta | 20 |
| 10 | Pittsburgh | 27 |
| 14 | SAN FRANCISCO | 31 |
| 10 | L.A. Rams | 18 |
| 30 | NEW ENGLAND | 21 |
| 3 | Indianapolis | •6 |
| 20 | BUFFALO | 24 |
| 26 | MIAMI | 14 |
| 16 | Denver | 27 |
| 17 | CINCINNATI | 14 |
| 3 | New England | 24 |
| 7 | KANSAS CITY | 23 |
| 24 | Buffalo | 17 |
| 6 | INDIANAPOLIS | 10 |
| 17 | Miami | 19 |
| 0 | NEW ORLEANS | 20 |

| Use Name | Pos. | Hgt. | Wgt. | Age | Int | Pts |
|---|---|---|---|---|---|---|
| Jeff Criswell | OT | 6'7" | 291 | 28 | | |
| Irv Eatman | OT | 6'7" | 298 | 31 | | |
| Siupeli Malamala | OT | 6'5" | 313 | 23 | | |
| Brett Miller | OT | 6'7" | 286 | 33 | | |
| Dave Cadigan | OG | 6'4" | 285 | 27 | | |
| Dwayne White | OG | 6'2" | 305 | 25 | | |
| Cal Dixon | C | 6'4" | 284 | 22 | | |
| Roger Duffy | C | 6'3" | 285 | 24 | | |
| Jim Sweeney | C-OG | 6'4" | 286 | 30 | | |
| Dennis Byrd | DE | 6'5" | 266 | 25 | | |
| Jeff Lageman | DE | 6'5" | 266 | 25 | | |
| Marvin Washington | DE | 6'6" | 272 | 26 | | 2 |
| Karl Wilson | DE | 6'4" | 275 | 28 | | |
| Paul Frase | DT-DE | 6'5" | 270 | 27 | | |
| Mark Gunn | DT-DE | 6'5" | 285 | 24 | | |
| Mario Johnson | DT | 6'3" | 292 | 22 | | |
| Scott Mersereau | DT | 6'3" | 275 | 27 | | |
| Bill Pickel | DT | 6'5" | 265 | 32 | | |

| Use Name | Pos. | Hgt. | Wgt. | Age | Int | Pts |
|---|---|---|---|---|---|---|
| Kurt Barber | LB-DE | 6'4" | 241 | 23 | | |
| Glenn Cadrez | LB | 6'3" | 235 | 22 | | |
| Kyle Clifton | LB | 6'4" | 236 | 30 | 1 | |
| Keo Coleman | LB | 6'1" | 255 | 22 | | |
| Bobby Houston | LB | 6'2" | 235 | 24 | 1 | 6 |
| Don Jones | LB | 6' | 231 | 23 | | |
| Joe Kelly | LB | 6'2" | 235 | 27 | | |
| Mo Lewis | LB | 6'3" | 250 | 22 | 1 | |
| Huey Richardson (from WAS) | LB | 6'5" | 245 | 24 | | |
| Michael Brim | DB | 6' | 198 | 26 | 6 | 6 |
| James Hasty | DB | 6' | 201 | 27 | 2 | |
| R.J. Kors | DB | 6' | 195 | 26 | | |
| Erik McMillan | DB | 6'2" | 200 | 27 | | |
| Dennis Price | DB | 6'1" | 182 | 27 | 1 | |
| Marcus Turner | DB | 6' | 185 | 26 | | |
| Brian Washington | DB | 6'1" | 212 | 26 | 6 | 6 |
| Lonnie Young | DB | 6'1" | 196 | 29 | | |

| Use Name | Pos. | Hgt. | Wgt. | Age | Int | Pts |
|---|---|---|---|---|---|---|
| Jeff Blake | QB | 6' | 202 | 21 | | |
| Browning Nagle | QB | 6'3" | 225 | 24 | | |
| Ken O'Brien | QB | 6'4" | 212 | 31 | | |
| A.B. Brown | HB | 5'9" | 215 | 26 | | |
| Sheldon Canley | HB | 5'9" | 195 | 24 | | |
| Scottie Graham | HB | 5'9" | 220 | 23 | | |
| Johnny Hector | HB | 5'11" | 214 | 31 | | |
| Freeman McNeil | HB | 5'11" | 208 | 33 | | |
| Blair Thomas | HB | 5'10" | 202 | 24 | | |
| Brad Baxter | FB | 6'1" | 235 | 25 | | 36 |
| Pat Chaffey | FB | 6'1" | 220 | 25 | | 6 |
| Chris Burkett | WR | 6'4" | 200 | 30 | | 6 |
| Rob Carpenter | WR | 6'2" | 190 | 24 | | 6 |
| Dale Dawkins | WR | 6'1" | 190 | 25 | | |
| Terance Mathis | WR | 5'10" | 170 | 25 | | 24 |
| Rob Moore | WR | 6'3" | 205 | 23 | | 24 |
| Al Toon | WR | 6'4" | 205 | 29 | | 12 |
| Mark Boyer | TE | 6'4" | 242 | 29 | | |
| Eric Kattus | TE | 6'5" | 251 | 29 | | |
| Johnny Mitchell | TE | 6'3" | 263 | 21 | | 6 |
| Troy Sadowski | TE | 6'5" | 250 | 26 | | |
| Ken Whisenhunt | TE | 6'3" | 240 | 30 | | |
| Louis Aguiar | K | 6'2" | 215 | 26 | | |
| Cary Blanchard | K | 6'1" | 225 | 23 | | 65 |
| Jason Staurovsky | K | 5'9" | 170 | 29 | | 15 |

## NEW ENGLAND PATRIOTS 2-14 Dick MacPherson

| | Scores of Each Game | |
|---|---|---|
| 0 | L.A. Rams | 14 |
| 6 | SEATTLE | 10 |
| 7 | BUFFALO | 41 |
| 21 | N.Y. Jets | 30 |
| 12 | SAN FRANCISCO | 24 |
| 17 | Miami | 38 |
| 17 | CLEVELAND | 19 |
| 7 | Buffalo | 16 |
| 14 | NEW ORLEANS | 31 |
| 37 | Indianapolis | •34 |
| 24 | N.Y. JETS | 3 |
| 0 | Atlanta | 34 |
| 0 | INDIANAPOLIS | 6 |
| 20 | Kansas City | 27 |
| 10 | Cincinnati | 20 |
| 13 | MIAMI | •16 |

| Use Name | Pos. | Hgt. | Wgt. | Age | Int | Pts |
|---|---|---|---|---|---|---|
| Bruce Armstrong | OT | 6'4" | 284 | 26 | | |
| Pat Harlow | OT | 6'6" | 290 | 23 | | |
| Eugene Chung | OG-OT | 6'4" | 295 | 23 | | |
| Gregg Rakoczy | OG-C | 6'5" | 280 | 27 | | |
| Reggie Redding | OG-OT | 6'4" | 305 | 23 | | |
| Calvin Stephens | OG | 6'2" | 285 | 24 | | |
| Larry Williams | OG | 6'5" | 294 | 29 | | |
| Gene Chilton | C | 6'3" | 286 | 28 | | |
| Ray Agnew | DE | 6'3" | 272 | 24 | | |
| Tim Edwards | DE | 6'1" | 270 | 24 | | |
| Chris Gannon | DE | 6'6" | 260 | 26 | | |
| Marion Hobby | DE | 6'4" | 277 | 25 | | |
| Brent Williams | DE | 6'3" | 275 | 27 | | |
| Tim Goad | NT | 6'3" | 280 | 26 | | 6 |
| Fred Smerlas | NT | 6'4" | 291 | 35 | | |

| Use Name | Pos. | Hgt. | Wgt. | Age | Int | Pts |
|---|---|---|---|---|---|---|
| Vincent Brown | LB | 6'2" | 245 | 27 | 1 | 12 |
| Todd Collins | LB | 6'2" | 242 | 22 | | |
| David Howard | LB | 6'1" | 230 | 30 | 1 | |
| Eugene Lockhart | LB | 6'2" | 233 | 31 | | |
| Rob McGovern | LB | 6'2" | 234 | 25 | | |
| Johnny Rembert | LB | 6'3" | 234 | 30 | | |
| Dwayne Sabb | LB | 6'4" | 248 | 22 | | |
| Chris Singleton | LB | 6'2" | 247 | 25 | 1 | 6 |
| Richard Tardits | LB | 6'2" | 235 | 26 | | |
| Andre Tippett | LB | 6'3" | 241 | 32 | | |
| Roger Brown | DB | 6' | 196 | 25 | | |
| Tim Gordon | DB | 6' | 188 | 27 | | |
| Jerome Henderson | DB | 5'10" | 189 | 23 | 3 | |
| Maurice Hurst | DB | 5'10" | 185 | 24 | 3 | |
| Dion Lambert | DB | 6' | 185 | 23 | | |
| David Pool | DB | 5'9" | 182 | 25 | 2 | 6 |
| Randy Robbins | DB | 6'2" | 189 | 29 | 2 | |
| Rod Smith | DB | 5'11" | 187 | 22 | 1 | |

| Use Name | Pos. | Hgt. | Wgt. | Age | Int | Pts |
|---|---|---|---|---|---|---|
| Jeff Carlson | QB | 6'3" | 215 | 26 | | |
| Tom Hodson | QB | 6'3" | 195 | 25 | | |
| Hugh Millen | QB | 6'5" | 216 | 28 | | |
| Scott Zolak | QB | 6'5" | 222 | 24 | | |
| Scott Lockwood | HB | 5'10" | 196 | 24 | | |
| Leonard Russell | HB | 6'2" | 235 | 22 | | 12 |
| John Stephens | HB | 6'1" | 215 | 26 | | 12 |
| Jon Vaughn | HB | 5'9" | 203 | 22 | | 12 |
| Sam Gash | FB | 5'11" | 224 | 23 | | 6 |
| Kevin Turner | FB | 6' | 224 | 23 | | 12 |
| Irving Fryar | WR | 6' | 200 | 29 | | 24 |
| Greg McMurtry | WR | 6'2" | 207 | 24 | | 6 |
| Walter Stanley (from SD) | WR | 5'10" | 180 | 27 | | |
| Michael Timpson | WR | 5'10" | 175 | 25 | | 6 |
| Ben Coates | TE | 6'4" | 245 | 23 | | 18 |
| Marv Cook | TE | 6'4" | 234 | 26 | | 12 |
| Charlie Baumann | K | 6'1" | 203 | 25 | | 55 |
| Shawn McCarthy | K | 6'6" | 227 | 24 | | |

Ivy Joe Hunter — Knee Injury
Hart Lee Dykes — Knee Injury

## MIAMI DOLPHINS

### Rushing

| Last Name | No. | Yds | Avg | TD |
|---|---|---|---|---|
| Higgs | 256 | 915 | 3.6 | 7 |
| Humphrey | 102 | 471 | 4.6 | 1 |
| Marino | 20 | 66 | 3.3 | 0 |
| Parmalee | 6 | 38 | 6.3 | 0 |
| Paige | 7 | 11 | 1.6 | 1 |
| Mitchell | 8 | 10 | 1.3 | 0 |
| Craver | 3 | 9 | 3.0 | 0 |
| Saxon | 4 | 7 | 1.8 | 0 |
| Martin | 1 | -2 | -2.0 | 0 |

### Receiving

| Last Name | No. | Yds | Avg | TD |
|---|---|---|---|---|
| Humphrey | 54 | 507 | 9.4 | 1 |
| K. Jackson | 48 | 594 | 12.4 | 5 |
| Paige | 48 | 399 | 8.3 | 1 |
| Duper | 44 | 762 | 17.3 | 7 |
| Clayton | 43 | 619 | 14.4 | 3 |
| Martin | 33 | 553 | 16.8 | 2 |
| Banks | 22 | 319 | 14.5 | 3 |
| Higgs | 16 | 142 | 8.9 | 0 |
| Edmunds | 10 | 91 | 9.1 | 1 |
| Saxon | 5 | 41 | 8.2 | 0 |
| Clark | 3 | 59 | 19.7 | 0 |
| M. Williams | 3 | 43 | 14.3 | 0 |
| Baty | 3 | 19 | 6.3 | 1 |

### Punt Returns

| Last Name | No. | Yds | Avg | TD |
|---|---|---|---|---|
| Miller | 24 | 175 | 7.3 | 0 |
| Vincent | 5 | 16 | 3.2 | 0 |
| Martin | 1 | 0 | 0.00 | 0 |
| J. Williams | 1 | 0 | 0.00 | 0 |

### Kickoff Returns

| Last Name | No. | Yds | Avg | TD |
|---|---|---|---|---|
| M. Williams | 19 | 328 | 17.3 | 0 |
| Parmalee | 14 | 289 | 20.6 | 0 |
| Craver | 8 | 174 | 21.8 | 0 |
| Paige | 2 | 29 | 14.5 | 0 |
| Humphrey | 1 | 18 | 18.0 | 0 |

### Passing — Punting — Kicking Statistics

| PASSING | Att | Cmp | % | Yds | Yd/Att | TD | Int—% | RK |
|---|---|---|---|---|---|---|---|---|
| Marino | 554 | 330 | 59.6 | 4116 | 7.43 | 24 | 16—2.9 | 2 |
| Mitchell | 8 | 2 | 25.0 | 32 | 4.00 | 0 | 1—12.5 | |
| Martin | 1 | 0 | 0.0 | 0 | 0.00 | 0 | 0—0.0 | |

| PUNTING | No. | Avg. |
|---|---|---|
| Roby | 35 | 41.2 |
| Prokop | 32 | 37.0 |
| Stoyanovich | 2 | 45.0 |

| KICKING | XP | Att. | % | FG | Att | % |
|---|---|---|---|---|---|---|
| Stoyonovich | 34 | 36 | 94 | 30 | 37 | 81 |

## BUFFALO BILLS

### Rushing

| Last Name | No. | Yds | Avg | TD |
|---|---|---|---|---|
| Thomas | 312 | 1487 | 4.8 | 9 |
| K. Davis | 139 | 613 | 4.4 | 6 |
| Gardner | 40 | 166 | 4.2 | 2 |
| Reed | 8 | 65 | 8.1 | 0 |
| Kelly | 31 | 53 | 1.7 | 1 |
| Fuller | 6 | 39 | 6.5 | 0 |
| Mohr | 1 | 11 | 11.0 | 0 |
| Tasker | 1 | 9 | 9.0 | 0 |
| Edwards | 1 | 8 | 8.0 | 0 |
| Beebe | 1 | -6 | -6.0 | 0 |
| Reich | 9 | -9 | -1.0 | 0 |

### Receiving

| Last Name | No. | Yds | Avg | TD |
|---|---|---|---|---|
| Reed | 65 | 913 | 14.0 | 3 |
| Thomas | 58 | 626 | 10.8 | 3 |
| Lofton | 51 | 786 | 15.4 | 6 |
| Beebe | 33 | 554 | 16.8 | 2 |
| Metzelaars | 30 | 298 | 9.9 | 6 |
| K. Davis | 15 | 80 | 5.3 | 0 |
| McKeller | 14 | 110 | 7.9 | 0 |
| Lamb | 7 | 139 | 19.9 | 0 |
| Gardner | 7 | 67 | 9.6 | 0 |
| Awalt | 4 | 34 | 8.5 | 0 |
| Edwards | 2 | 25 | 12.5 | 0 |
| Tasker | 2 | 24 | 12.0 | 0 |
| Fuller | 2 | 17 | 8.5 | 0 |
| Frerotte | 2 | 4 | 2.0 | 2 |
| Fina | 1 | 1 | 1.0 | 1 |

### Punt Returns

| Last Name | No. | Yds | Avg | TD |
|---|---|---|---|---|
| Hicks | 29 | 289 | 10.0 | 0 |
| Hale | 14 | 175 | 12.5 | 0 |

### Kickoff Returns

| Last Name | No. | Yds | Avg | TD |
|---|---|---|---|---|
| K. Davis | 14 | 251 | 17.9 | 0 |
| Edwards | 12 | 274 | 22.8 | 0 |
| Fuller | 8 | 134 | 16.8 | 0 |
| Lamb | 5 | 97 | 19.4 | 0 |
| Hicks | 1 | 5 | 5.0 | 0 |
| Frerotte | 1 | 0 | 0.0 | 0 |

### Passing — Punting — Kicking

| PASSING | Att | Cmp | % | Yds | Yd/Att | TD | Int—% | RK |
|---|---|---|---|---|---|---|---|---|
| Kelly | 462 | 269 | 58.2 | 3457 | 7.48 | 23 | 19—4.1 | 4 |
| Reich | 47 | 24 | 51.1 | 221 | 4.70 | 0 | 2—4.3 | |

| PUNTING | No. | Avg. |
|---|---|---|
| Mohr | 60 | 42.2 |

| KICKING | XP | ATT | % | FG | ATT | % |
|---|---|---|---|---|---|---|
| Christie | 43 | 44 | 98 | 24 | 30 | 80 |

## INDIANAPOLIS COLTS

### Rushing

| Last Name | No. | Yds | Avg | TD |
|---|---|---|---|---|
| Johnson | 178 | 592 | 3.3 | 0 |
| Culver | 121 | 321 | 2.7 | 7 |
| Clark | 40 | 134 | 3.4 | 0 |
| George | 14 | 26 | 1.9 | 1 |
| Brooks | 2 | 14 | 7.0 | 0 |
| Carthon | 4 | 9 | 2.3 | 0 |
| Trudeau | 13 | 6 | 0.5 | 0 |
| Tupa | 3 | 9 | 3.0 | 0 |
| Herrmann | 3 | -2 | -0.7 | 0 |
| Langhorne | 1 | -7 | -7.0 | 0 |

### Receiving

| Last Name | No. | Yds | Avg | TD |
|---|---|---|---|---|
| Langhorne | 65 | 811 | 12.5 | 1 |
| Hester | 52 | 792 | 15.2 | 1 |
| Johnson | 49 | 517 | 10.6 | 3 |
| Brooks | 44 | 468 | 10.6 | 1 |
| Cash | 43 | 521 | 12.1 | 3 |
| Culver | 26 | 210 | 8.1 | 2 |
| Arbuckle | 13 | 152 | 11.7 | 1 |
| Clark | 5 | 46 | 9.2 | 0 |
| Verdin | 3 | 37 | 12.3 | 0 |
| Carthon | 3 | 10 | 3.3 | 0 |
| Prior | 1 | 17 | 17.0 | 0 |
| Schultz | 1 | 3 | 3.0 | 1 |

### Punt Returns

| Last Name | No. | Yds | Avg | TD |
|---|---|---|---|---|
| Verdin | 24 | 268 | 11.2 | 2 |
| Prior | 1 | 12 | 12.0 | 0 |

### Kickoff Returns

| Last Name | No. | Yds | Avg | TD |
|---|---|---|---|---|
| Verdin | 39 | 815 | 20.9 | 0 |
| Ambrose | 8 | 126 | 15.8 | 0 |
| Clark | 3 | 54 | 18.0 | 0 |
| Vanderbeek | 1 | 6 | 6.0 | 0 |

### Passing — Punting — Kicking

| PASSING | Att | Cmp | % | Yds | Yd/Att | TD | Int—% | RK |
|---|---|---|---|---|---|---|---|---|
| George | 306 | 167 | 54.6 | 1963 | 6.42 | 7 | 15—4.9 | 10 |
| Trudeau | 181 | 105 | 58.0 | 1271 | 7.02 | 4 | 8—4.4 | |
| Tupa | 33 | 17 | 51.5 | 156 | 4.73 | 1 | 2—6.1 | |
| Herrmann | 24 | 15 | 62.5 | 177 | 7.38 | 1 | 1—4.2 | |
| Stark | 1 | 1 | 100.0 | 17 | 17.00 | 0 | 0—0.0 | |
| Johnson | 1 | 0 | 0.0 | 0 | 0.00 | 0 | 0—0.0 | |

| PUNTING | No. | Avg. |
|---|---|---|
| Stark | 83 | 44.8 |

| KICKING | XP | ATT | % | FG | ATT | % |
|---|---|---|---|---|---|---|
| Biasucci | 24 | 24 | 100 | 16 | 29 | 55 |

## NEW YORK JETS

### Rushing

| Last Name | No. | Yds | Avg | TD |
|---|---|---|---|---|
| Baxter | 152 | 698 | 4.6 | 6 |
| Thomas | 97 | 440 | 4.5 | 0 |
| Chaffey | 27 | 186 | 6.9 | 1 |
| McNeil | 43 | 170 | 4.0 | 0 |
| Hector | 24 | 67 | 2.8 | 0 |
| Nagle | 24 | 57 | 2.4 | 0 |
| Brown | 24 | 42 | 1.8 | 0 |
| Graham | 14 | 29 | 2.1 | 0 |
| Mathis | 3 | 25 | 8.3 | 1 |
| Moore | 1 | 21 | 21.0 | 0 |
| Canley | 4 | 9 | 2.3 | 0 |
| O'Brien | 8 | 8 | 1.0 | 0 |
| Carpenter | 1 | 2 | 2.0 | 0 |
| Blake | 2 | -2 | -2.0 | 0 |

### Receiving

| Last Name | No. | Yds | Avg | TD |
|---|---|---|---|---|
| Burkett | 57 | 724 | 12.7 | 1 |
| Moore | 50 | 726 | 14.5 | 4 |
| Toon | 31 | 311 | 10.0 | 2 |
| Mathis | 22 | 316 | 14.4 | 3 |
| Boyer | 19 | 149 | 7.8 | 0 |
| Mitchell | 16 | 210 | 13.1 | 1 |
| McNeil | 16 | 154 | 9.6 | 0 |
| Carpenter | 13 | 161 | 12.4 | 1 |
| Chaffey | 7 | 56 | 8.0 | 0 |
| Thomas | 7 | 49 | 7.0 | 0 |
| Baxter | 4 | 32 | 8.0 | 0 |
| Brown | 4 | 30 | 7.5 | 0 |
| Hector | 2 | 13 | 6.5 | 0 |
| Whisenhunt | 2 | 11 | 5.5 | 0 |
| Sadowski | 1 | 20 | 20.0 | 0 |

### Punt Returns

| Last Name | No. | Yds | Avg | TD |
|---|---|---|---|---|
| Carpenter | 28 | 208 | 7.4 | 0 |
| Mathis | 2 | 24 | 12.0 | 0 |

### Kickoff Returns

| Last Name | No. | Yds | Avg | TD |
|---|---|---|---|---|
| Mathis | 28 | 492 | 17.6 | 0 |
| McMillan | 22 | 420 | 19.1 | 0 |
| Hector | 1 | 15 | 15.0 | 0 |
| Dawkins | 1 | 10 | 10.0 | 0 |
| Duffy | 1 | 7 | 7.0 | 0 |
| Dixon | 1 | 6 | 6.0 | 0 |

### Passing — Punting — Kicking

| PASSING | Att | Cmp | % | Yds | Yd/Att | TD | Int—% | RK |
|---|---|---|---|---|---|---|---|---|
| Nagle | 387 | 192 | 49.6 | 2280 | 5.89 | 7 | 17—4.4 | 12 |
| O'Brien | 98 | 55 | 56.1 | 642 | 6.55 | 5 | 6—6.1 | |
| Blake | 9 | 4 | 44.4 | 40 | 4.44 | 0 | 1—11.1 | |
| Carpenter | 1 | 0 | 0.0 | 0 | 0.00 | 0 | 0—0.0 | |

| PUNTING | No. | Avg. |
|---|---|---|
| Aguiar | 73 | 41.0 |

| KICKING | XP | ATT | % | FG | Att | % |
|---|---|---|---|---|---|---|
| Blanchard | 17 | 17 | 100 | 16 | 22 | 73 |
| Staurovsky | 6 | 6 | 100 | 3 | 8 | 38 |

## NEW ENGLAND PATRIOTS

### Rushing

| Last Name | No. | Yds | Avg | TD |
|---|---|---|---|---|
| Vaughn | 113 | 451 | 4.0 | 1 |
| Russell | 123 | 390 | 3.2 | 2 |
| J. Stephens | 75 | 277 | 3.7 | 2 |
| Lockwood | 35 | 162 | 4.6 | 0 |
| Millen | 17 | 108 | 6.4 | 0 |
| Zolak | 18 | 71 | 3.9 | 0 |
| Turner | 10 | 40 | 4.0 | 0 |
| Carlson | 11 | 32 | 2.9 | 0 |
| Hodson | 5 | 11 | 2.2 | 0 |
| Gash | 5 | 7 | 1.4 | 1 |
| Fryar | 1 | 6 | 6.0 | 0 |
| McMurtry | 2 | 3 | 1.5 | 0 |
| Coates | 1 | 2 | 2.0 | 0 |
| McCarthy | 3 | -10 | -3.3 | 0 |

### Receiving

| Last Name | No. | Yds | Avg | TD |
|---|---|---|---|---|
| Fryar | 55 | 791 | 14.4 | 4 |
| Cook | 52 | 413 | 7.9 | 2 |
| McMurtry | 35 | 424 | 12.1 | 1 |
| Timpson | 26 | 315 | 12.1 | 1 |
| J. Stephens | 21 | 161 | 7.7 | 0 |
| Coates | 20 | 171 | 8.6 | 3 |
| Vaughn | 13 | 84 | 6.5 | 0 |
| Russell | 11 | 24 | 2.2 | 0 |
| Turner | 7 | 52 | 7.4 | 2 |
| Stanley | 3 | 63 | 21.0 | 0 |
| Hodson | 1 | -6 | -6.0 | 0 |

### Punt Returns

| Last Name | No. | Yds | Avg | TD |
|---|---|---|---|---|
| Stanley | 28 | 227 | 8.1 | 0 |
| Timpson | 8 | 47 | 5.9 | 0 |
| Lambert | 1 | 0 | 0.0 | 0 |

### Kickoff Returns

| Last Name | No. | Yds | Avg | TD |
|---|---|---|---|---|
| Vaughn | 20 | 564 | 28.2 | 1 |
| Stanley | 29 | 529 | 18.2 | 0 |
| Lockwood | 11 | 233 | 21.2 | 0 |
| Timpson | 2 | 28 | 14.0 | 0 |
| Turner | 1 | 11 | 11.0 | 0 |
| Hobby | 1 | 11 | 11.0 | 0 |

### Passing — Punting — Kicking

| PASSING | Att | Cmp | % | Yds | Yd/Att | TD | Int—% | RK |
|---|---|---|---|---|---|---|---|---|
| Millen | 203 | 124 | 61.1 | 1203 | 5.93 | 8 | 10—4.9 | |
| Zolak | 100 | 52 | 52.0 | 561 | 5.61 | 2 | 4—4.0 | |
| Hodson | 91 | 50 | 54.9 | 496 | 5.45 | 2 | 2—2.2 | |
| Carlson | 49 | 18 | 36.7 | 232 | 4.73 | 1 | 3—6.1 | |
| McMurtry | 1 | 0 | 0.0 | 0 | 0.00 | 0 | 0—0.0 | |

| PUNTING | No. | Avg. |
|---|---|---|
| McCarthy | 103 | 40.9 |

| KICKING | XP | ATT | % | FG | ATT | % |
|---|---|---|---|---|---|---|
| Baumann | 22 | 24 | 92 | 11 | 17 | 65 |

## PITTSBURGH STEELERS 11-5 Bill Cowher

| Scores of Each Game | | |
|---|---|---|
| 29 | Houston | 24 |
| 27 | N.Y. JETS | 10 |
| 23 | San Diego | 6 |
| 3 | Green Bay | 17 |
| 9 | Cleveland | 17 |
| 20 | CINCINNATI | 0 |
| 27 | Kansas City | 3 |
| 21 | HOUSTON | 20 |
| 20 | Buffalo | 28 |
| 17 | DETROIT | 14 |
| 30 | INDIANAPOLIS | 14 |
| 21 | Cincinnati | 9 |
| 20 | SEATTLE | 14 |
| 6 | Chicago | 30 |
| 3 | MINNESOTA | 6 |
| 23 | CLEVELAND | 13 |

| UseName | Pos. | Hgt. | Wgt. | Age | Int | Pts |
|---|---|---|---|---|---|---|
| Tunch Ilkin | OT | 6'3" | 276 | 34 | | |
| John Jackson | OT | 6'6" | 290 | 27 | | |
| Leon Searcy | OT | 6'3" | 305 | 22 | | |
| Justin Strzelczyk | OT | 6'5" | 305 | 24 | | |
| Calton Haselrig | OG | 6'1" | 290 | 26 | | |
| Duval Love | OG | 6'3" | 291 | 29 | | |
| Dermontti Dawson | C | 6'2" | 288 | 27 | | |
| Kendall Gammon | C | 6'4" | 273 | 23 | | |
| Ariel Solomon | C-OT | 6'5" | 286 | 24 | | |
| Kenny Davidson | DE | 6'5" | 277 | 25 | | |
| Donald Evans | DE | 6'2" | 275 | 28 | | |
| Aaron Jones | DE | 6'5" | 257 | 25 | | |
| Garry Howe | NT | 6'1" | 298 | 24 | | |
| Joel Steed | NT | 6'2" | 290 | 23 | | |
| Gerald Williams | NT | 6'3" | 289 | 28 | | |

| UseName | Pos. | Hgt. | Wgt. | Age | Int | Pts |
|---|---|---|---|---|---|---|
| Darryl Ford | LB | 6'1" | 225 | 26 | | |
| Bryan Hinkle | LB | 6'2" | 229 | 33 | | |
| Levon Kirkland | LB | 6' | 247 | 23 | | |
| David Little | LB | 6'1" | 239 | 33 | 2 | |
| Greg Lloyd | LB | 6'2" | 223 | 27 | 1 | |
| Hardy Nickerson | LB | 6'2" | 233 | 27 | | |
| Jerry Olsavsky | LB | 6'1" | 222 | 25 | | |
| Elnardo Webster | LB | 6'2" | 243 | 22 | | |
| Jerrol Williams | LB | 6'5" | 237 | 25 | 1 | |
| Larry Griffin | DB | 6' | 200 | 29 | 3 | 6 |
| David Johnson | DB | 6' | 181 | 26 | 5 | |
| Carnell Lake | DB | 6'1" | 207 | 25 | | |
| Darren Perry | DB | 5'10" | 194 | 23 | 6 | |
| Richard Shelton | DB | 5'10" | 196 | 25 | | |
| Sammy Walker | DB | 5'11" | 197 | 23 | | |
| Solomon Wilcots | DB | 5'11" | 202 | 27 | | |
| Rod Woodson | DB | 6' | 197 | 27 | 4 | 6 |

Gary Jones — Knee Injury

| UseName | Pos. | Hgt. | Wgt. | Age | Int | Pts |
|---|---|---|---|---|---|---|
| Bubby Brister | QB | 6'3" | 217 | 30 | | |
| Neil O'Donnell | QB | 6'3" | 223 | 26 | | 6 |
| Rick Strom | QB | 6'2" | 205 | 27 | | |
| Albert Bentley | HB | 5'11" | 217 | 32 | | |
| Barry Foster | HB | 5'10" | 217 | 23 | | 66 |
| Warren Williams | HB | 6' | 213 | 27 | | |
| Merril Hoge | FB | 6'2" | 222 | 27 | | 6 |
| Leroy Thompson | FB | 5'10" | 215 | 23 | | 6 |
| Charles Davenport | WR | 6'3" | 210 | 23 | | 6 |
| Mark Didio | WR | 5'11" | 181 | 23 | | |
| Jeff Graham | WR | 6'1" | 195 | 23 | | 6 |
| Ernie Mills | WR | 5'11" | 186 | 23 | | 18 |
| Darrick Owens | WR | 6'2" | 195 | 21 | | |
| Dwight Stone | WR-HB | 6' | 190 | 28 | | 18 |
| Yancey Thigpen | WR | 6'1" | 203 | 23 | | |
| Jesse Anderson (from TB) | TE | 6'2" | 245 | 26 | | |
| Russ Campbell | TE | 6'5" | 259 | 23 | | |
| Adrian Cooper | TE | 6'5" | 268 | 24 | | 18 |
| Eric Green | TE | 6'5" | 284 | 25 | | 12 |
| Tim Jorden | TE | 6'3" | 239 | 25 | | 12 |
| Gary Anderson | K | 5'11" | 179 | 33 | | 113 |
| Mark Royals | K | 6'5" | 212 | 28 | | |

Tim Worley — Suspended by NFL

## HOUSTON OILERS 10-6 Jack Pardee

| Scores of Each Game | | |
|---|---|---|
| 24 | PITTSBURGH | 29 |
| 20 | Indianapolis | 10 |
| 23 | KANSAS CITY | * 20 |
| 27 | SAN DIEGO | 0 |
| 38 | Cincinnati | 24 |
| 21 | Denver | 27 |
| 26 | CINCINNATI | 10 |
| 20 | Pittsburgh | 21 |
| 14 | CLEVELAND | 24 |
| 17 | Minnesota | 13 |
| 16 | Miami | 19 |
| 24 | Detroit | 21 |
| 24 | CHICAGO | 7 |
| 14 | GREEN BAY | 16 |
| 17 | Cleveland | 14 |
| 27 | BUFFALO | 3 |

| UseName | Pos. | Hgt. | Wgt. | Age | Int | Pts |
|---|---|---|---|---|---|---|
| Kevin Donnalley | OT | 6'5" | 305 | 24 | | |
| Don Maggs | OT | 6'5" | 296 | 30 | | |
| David Williams | OT | 6'5" | 292 | 26 | | |
| Doug Dawson | OG | 6'2" | 288 | 30 | | |
| John Flannery | OG-C | 6'3" | 304 | 23 | | |
| Mike Munchak | OG | 6'3" | 284 | 32 | | |
| Bruce Matthews | C | 6'4" | 291 | 31 | | |
| Erik Norgard | C-OG | 6'1" | 282 | 26 | | |
| William Fuller | DE | 6'3" | 274 | 30 | | 6 |
| Sean Jones | DE | 6'7" | 264 | 29 | 1 | |
| Lee Williams | DE-DT | 6'6" | 271 | 29 | | |
| Jeff Alm | DT | 6'6" | 278 | 24 | | |
| Ray Childress | DT-DE | 6'6" | 272 | 29 | | 6 |
| Glenn Montgomery | DT | 6' | 272 | 25 | | |
| Tim Roberts | DT | 6'6" | 309 | 23 | | |
| Doug Smith | DT | 6'5" | 309 | 33 | | |
| Craig Veasey | DT | 6'2" | 286 | 26 | | |

| UseName | Pos. | Hgt. | Wgt. | Age | Int | Pts |
|---|---|---|---|---|---|---|
| Joe Bowden | LB | 5'11" | 227 | 22 | | |
| Rick Graf | LB | 6'5" | 244 | 28 | 1 | |
| Scott Kozak | LB | 6'3" | 222 | 26 | | |
| Lamar Lathon | LB | 6'3" | 250 | 24 | | |
| Johnny Meads (to WAS) | LB | 6'2" | 226 | 31 | | 6 |
| Eddie Robinson | LB | 6'1" | 242 | 22 | | |
| Eugene Seale | LB | 5'10" | 253 | 28 | | |
| Al Smith | LB | 6'1" | 251 | 27 | 1 | |
| Tony Brown | DB | 5'9" | 183 | 22 | | |
| Cris Dishman | DB | 6' | 178 | 27 | 3 | |
| Mike Dumas | DB | 5'11" | 178 | 23 | 1 | |
| Jerry Gray | DB | 6' | 185 | 29 | 6 | |
| Steve Jackson | DB | 5'8" | 182 | 23 | 3 | |
| Richard Johnson | DB | 6'1" | 195 | 28 | | |
| Darryll Lewis | DB | 5'9" | 188 | 23 | | |
| Bubba McDowell | DB | 6'1" | 198 | 25 | 3 | 6 |
| Bo Orlando | DB | 5'10" | 180 | 26 | | |
| Marcus Robertson | DB | 5'11" | 197 | 22 | 1 | |

| UseName | Pos. | Hgt. | Wgt. | Age | Int | Pts |
|---|---|---|---|---|---|---|
| Cody Carlson | QB | 6'3" | 202 | 28 | | 6 |
| Mike Elkins | QB | 6'3" | 225 | 26 | | |
| Warren Moon | QB | 6'3" | 212 | 35 | | 6 |
| Bucky Richardson | QB | 6'1" | 221 | 23 | | |
| Gary Brown | HB-FB | 5'11" | 229 | 23 | | 6 |
| Spencer Tillman | HB | 5'11" | 206 | 28 | | |
| Lorenzo White | HB | 5'11" | 222 | 26 | | 48 |
| Pat Coleman | WR | 5'7" | 173 | 25 | | |
| Curtis Duncan | WR | 5'11" | 184 | 27 | | 6 |
| Ernest Givins | WR | 5'9" | 172 | 27 | | 60 |
| Leonard Harris | WR | 5'8" | 162 | 31 | | 12 |
| Haywood Jeffires | WR | 6'2" | 201 | 27 | | 54 |
| Damon Mays | WR | 5'9" | 170 | 24 | | |
| Webster Slaughter | WR | 6'1" | 170 | 27 | | 24 |
| Gary Wellman | WR | 5'9" | 168 | 25 | | |
| Al Del Greco | K | 5'10" | 200 | 30 | | 104 |
| Greg Montgomery | K | 6'3" | 215 | 27 | | |

## CLEVELAND BROWNS 7-9 Bill Belichick

| Scores of Each Game | | |
|---|---|---|
| 3 | Indianapolis | 14 |
| 23 | MIAMI | 27 |
| 28 | L.A. Raiders | 16 |
| 0 | DENVER | 12 |
| 17 | PITTSBURGH | 9 |
| 17 | GREEN BAY | 6 |
| 19 | New England | 17 |
| 10 | Cincinnati | 30 |
| 24 | Houston | 14 |
| 13 | SAN DIEGO | 14 |
| 13 | Minnesota | 17 |
| 27 | CHICAGO | 14 |
| 37 | CINCINNATI | 21 |
| 14 | Detroit | 24 |
| 14 | HOUSTON | 17 |
| 13 | Pittsburgh | 23 |

| UseName | Pos. | Hgt. | Wgt. | Age | Int | Pts |
|---|---|---|---|---|---|---|
| Freddie Childress | OT | 6'4" | 330 | 25 | | |
| Bob Dahl | OT | 6'5" | 285 | 23 | | |
| Dan Fike | OT-OG | 6'7" | 285 | 31 | | |
| Tony Jones | OT | 6'5" | 290 | 26 | | |
| Ed King | OG | 6'4" | 303 | 22 | | |
| John Rienstra | OG | 6'5" | 275 | 29 | | |
| Jay Hilgenberg | C | 6'3" | 260 | 33 | | |
| Chris Thome (to NYG) | C | 6'4" | 280 | 23 | | |
| Lance Zeno | C | 6'4" | 279 | 25 | | |
| Rob Burnett | DE | 6'4" | 270 | 25 | | |
| Ernie Logan | DE | 6'3" | 271 | 24 | | |
| Pio Sagapolutele | DE | 6'6" | 297 | 22 | | |
| Anthony Pleasant | DE | 6'5" | 258 | 24 | | |
| Bill Johnson | DT | 6'4" | 305 | 23 | | |
| James Jones | DT | 6'2" | 294 | 23 | | 6 |
| Michael Dean Perry | DT | 6'1" | 285 | 27 | | |
| Alvin Wright (from LA) | DT | 6'2" | 285 | 31 | | |

Paul Farren — Back Injury
John Thornton — Leg Injury

| UseName | Pos. | Hgt. | Wgt. | Age | Int | Pts |
|---|---|---|---|---|---|---|
| David Brandon | LB | 6'4" | 230 | 27 | 2 | 12 |
| Richard Brown | LB | 6'3" | 240 | 26 | | |
| Cedric Figaro | LB | 6'3" | 255 | 25 | | |
| Mike Johnson | LB | 6'1" | 230 | 29 | 1 | 6 |
| Clay Matthews | LB | 6'2" | 245 | 36 | 1 | |
| Frank Stams | LB | 6'2" | 240 | 26 | | |
| Harlon Barnett | DB | 5'11" | 200 | 25 | | |
| Latin Berry | DB | 5'10' | 196 | 25 | | |
| Fred Foggie | DB | 6' | 188 | 23 | | |
| Alan Haller (from PIT) | DB | 5'11" | 185 | 22 | | |
| Randy Hilliard | DB | 5'11" | 160 | 25 | | |
| Alfred Jackson | DB | 6' | 180 | 25 | | |
| Frank Minnifield | DB | 5'9" | 180 | 32 | 2 | |
| Stevon Moore | DB | 5'11" | 205 | 25 | | 6 |
| Vince Newsome | DB | 6'1" | 185 | 31 | 3 | |
| Terry Taylor | DB | 5'10" | 190 | 31 | 1 | |
| Eric Turner | DB | 6'1" | 207 | 23 | 1 | |
| Everson Walls (from NYG) | DB | 6'1" | 195 | 32 | 2 | |
| Barry Wilburn | DB | 6'3" | 186 | 28 | | |

| UseName | Pos. | Hgt. | Wgt. | Age | Int | Pts |
|---|---|---|---|---|---|---|
| Jeff Francis | QB | 6'4" | 225 | 26 | | |
| Brad Goebel | QB | 6'3" | 198 | 24 | | |
| Bernie Kosar | QB | 6'5" | 215 | 28 | | |
| Todd Philcox | QB | 6'4" | 225 | 25 | | |
| Mike Tomczak | QB | 6'1" | 204 | 29 | | |
| James Brooks (to TB) | HB | 5'10" | 180 | 33 | | |
| Eric Metcalf | HB | 5'10" | 190 | 24 | | 42 |
| Ron Wolfley | HB | 6' | 230 | 29 | | 6 |
| Randy Baldwin | FB | 5'10" | 216 | 25 | | |
| Leroy Hoard | FB-HB | 5'11" | 230 | 24 | | 6 |
| Kevin Mack | FB | 6' | 225 | 30 | | 36 |
| Tommy Vardell | FB | 6'2" | 238 | 23 | | |
| Shawn Collins (from ATL) | WR | 6'2" | 204 | 25 | | |
| Jamie Holland | WR | 6'1" | 195 | 28 | | |
| Michael Jackson | WR | 6'4" | 195 | 25 | | 42 |
| Keenan McCardell | WR | 6'1" | 185 | 22 | | |
| Rico Smith | WR | 6' | 185 | 23 | | |
| Lawyer Tillman | WR | 6'5" | 230 | 26 | | |
| Mark Bavaro | TE | 6'4" | 245 | 29 | | 12 |
| Scott Galbraith | TE | 6'3" | 260 | 25 | | 6 |
| Pete Holohan | TE | 6'4" | 247 | 33 | | |
| Brian Kinchen | TE | 6'2" | 232 | 27 | | |
| Brian Hansen | K | 6'4" | 220 | 31 | | |
| Matt Stover | K | 5'11" | 178 | 24 | | 92 |

Derrick Douglas — Knee Injury

## CINCINNATI BENGALS 5-11 Dave Shula

| Scores of Each Game | | |
|---|---|---|
| 21 | Seattle | 3 |
| 24 | L.A. RAIDERS | * 21 |
| 23 | Green Bay | 24 |
| 7 | MINNESOTA | 42 |
| 24 | HOUSTON | 38 |
| 0 | Pittsburgh | 20 |
| 10 | Houston | 26 |
| 30 | CLEVELAND | 10 |
| 31 | Chicago | * 28 |
| 14 | N.Y. Jets | 17 |
| 13 | DETROIT | 19 |
| 9 | PITTSBURGH | 21 |
| 21 | Cleveland | 37 |
| 10 | San Diego | 27 |
| 20 | NEW ENGLAND | 10 |
| 17 | INDIANAPOLIS | 21 |

| UseName | Pos. | Hgt. | Wgt. | Age | Int | Pts |
|---|---|---|---|---|---|---|
| Anthony Munoz | OT | 6'6" | 284 | 34 | | |
| Tom Rayam | OT | 6'6" | 297 | 24 | | |
| Kevin Sargent | OT | 6'6" | 284 | 23 | | |
| Joe Walter | OT | 6'6" | 292 | 29 | | |
| Bruce Kozerski | OG | 6'4" | 287 | 30 | | |
| Jon Melander | OG | 6'7" | 280 | 25 | | |
| Kirk Scrafford | OG-OT | 6'6" | 255 | 25 | | |
| Mike Withycombe | OG-C | 6'5" | 297 | 27 | | |
| Mike Arthur | C | 6'3" | 280 | 24 | | |
| Mike Frier | DE | 6'5" | 299 | 23 | | |
| Alonzo Mitz | DE | 6'4" | 278 | 29 | 1 | |
| Roosevelt Nix | DE | 6'6" | 315 | 25 | | |
| Elston Ridgle | DE | 6'5" | 277 | 29 | | |
| Lamar Rogers | DE | 6'4" | 292 | 24 | | |
| Danny Stubbs | DE-LB | 6'4" | 264 | 27 | | |
| Tim Krumrie | NT | 6'2" | 274 | 32 | | |

Ken Moyer — Foot Injury

| UseName | Pos. | Hgt. | Wgt. | Age | Int | Pts |
|---|---|---|---|---|---|---|
| Ray Bentley | LB | 6'2" | 235 | 31 | | 6 |
| James Francis | LB | 6'5" | 252 | 24 | 3 | 6 |
| Alex Gordon | LB | 6'5" | 245 | 27 | | |
| Randy Kirk | LB | 6'2" | 231 | 27 | | |
| Ricardo McDonald | LB | 6'2" | 235 | 22 | 1 | |
| Gary Reasons | LB | 6'4" | 234 | 30 | | |
| Eric Shaw | LB | 6'3" | 248 | 20 | | |
| Brian Townsend | LB | 6'3" | 242 | 23 | | |
| Kevin Walker | LB | 6'2" | 238 | 26 | | |
| Alfred Williams | LB | 6'6" | 240 | 23 | | |
| Antoine Bennett | DB | 5'11" | 185 | 24 | | |
| Barney Bussey | DB | 6' | 210 | 30 | 1 | |
| Rickey Dixon | DB | 5'11" | 191 | 25 | | |
| David Fulcher | DB | 6'3" | 238 | 27 | 3 | |
| Rod Jones | DB | 6' | 185 | 28 | 2 | |
| Mitchell Price | DB | 5'9" | 181 | 25 | | |
| Eric Thomas | DB | 5'11" | 181 | 27 | | |
| Fernandus Vinson | DB | 5'10" | 197 | 23 | | 6 |
| Leonard Wheeler | DB | 5'11" | 189 | 23 | 1 | |
| Darryl Williams | DB | 6' | 191 | 22 | 4 | |

| UseName | Pos. | Hgt. | Wgt. | Age | Int | Pts |
|---|---|---|---|---|---|---|
| Boomer Esiason | QB | 6'4" | 220 | 31 | | |
| Donald Hollas | QB | 6'3" | 215 | 24 | | |
| David Klingler | QB | 6'2" | 205 | 23 | | |
| Eric Ball | HB-FB | 6'2" | 220 | 26 | | 24 |
| Harold Green | HB | 6'2" | 222 | 24 | | 12 |
| Derrick Fenner | FB-HB | 6'3" | 228 | 25 | | 48 |
| Ostell Miles | FB | 6' | 236 | 21 | | |
| Brian Brennan (to SD) | WR | 5'10" | 185 | 30 | | 6 |
| Tim McGee | WR | 5'10" | 183 | 28 | | 18 |
| Carl Pickens | WR | 6'2" | 206 | 22 | | 12 |
| Jeff Query | WR | 6' | 165 | 25 | | 18 |
| Reggie Rembert | WR | 6'5" | 200 | 25 | | |
| Milt Stegall | WR | 6' | 184 | 22 | | 6 |
| Rodney Holman | TE | 6'3" | 238 | 32 | | 12 |
| Jim Riggs | TE | 6'5" | 245 | 28 | | |
| Jeff Thomason | TE | 6'4" | 233 | 22 | | |
| Craig Thompson | TE | 6'2" | 244 | 23 | | 12 |
| Jim Breech | K | 5'6" | 161 | 36 | | 88 |
| Lee Johnson | K | 6'2" | 200 | 30 | | |

Shane Garrett — Arm Injury
Eddie Brown — Neck Injury

## RUSHING

### PITTSBURGH STEELERS

| Last Name | No. | Yds | Avg | TD |
|---|---|---|---|---|
| Foster | 390 | 1690 | 4.3 | 11 |
| Thompson | 35 | 157 | 4.5 | 1 |
| Hoge | 41 | 150 | 3.7 | 0 |
| Stone | 12 | 118 | 9.8 | 0 |
| Mills | 1 | 20 | 20.0 | 0 |
| Brister | 10 | 16 | 1.6 | 0 |
| O'Donnell | 27 | 5 | 0.2 | 1 |
| W. Williams | 2 | 0 | 0.0 | 0 |

## RECEIVING

| Last Name | No. | Yds | Avg | TD |
|---|---|---|---|---|
| Graham | 49 | 711 | 14.5 | 1 |
| Foster | 36 | 344 | 9.6 | 0 |
| Stone | 34 | 501 | 14.7 | 3 |
| Mills | 30 | 383 | 12.8 | 3 |
| Hoge | 28 | 231 | 8.3 | 1 |
| Thompson | 22 | 278 | 12.6 | 0 |
| Cooper | 16 | 197 | 12.3 | 3 |
| Green | 14 | 152 | 10.9 | 2 |
| Davenport | 9 | 136 | 15.1 | 0 |
| Jorden | 6 | 28 | 4.7 | 2 |
| Didio | 3 | 39 | 13.0 | 0 |
| W. Williams | 1 | 44 | 44.0 | 0 |
| Thigpen | 1 | 2 | 2.0 | 0 |

## PUNT RETURNS

| Last Name | No. | Yds | Avg | TD |
|---|---|---|---|---|
| Woodson | 32 | 364 | 11.4 | 1 |

## KICKOFF RETURNS

| Last Name | No. | Yds | Avg | TD |
|---|---|---|---|---|
| Woodson | 25 | 469 | 18.8 | 0 |
| Stone | 12 | 219 | 18.3 | 0 |
| Thompson | 2 | 51 | 25.5 | 0 |
| Thigpen | 2 | 44 | 22.0 | 0 |
| Hoge | 2 | 28 | 14.0 | 0 |
| Bentley | 1 | 17 | 17.0 | 0 |
| Mills | 1 | 11 | 11.0 | 0 |
| Cooper | 1 | 8 | 8.0 | 0 |
| Campbell | 1 | 0 | 0.0 | 0 |
| W. Williams | 1 | 0 | 0.0 | 0 |

## PASSING—PUNTING—KICKING

### Statistics

**PASSING**

| Last Name | Att | Cmp | % | Yds | Yd/Att | TD | Int— | % | RK |
|---|---|---|---|---|---|---|---|---|---|
| O'Donnell | 313 | 185 | 59.1 | 2283 | 7.29 | 13 | 9— | 2.9 | 3 |
| Brister | 116 | 63 | 54.3 | 719 | 6.20 | 2 | 5— | 4.3 | |
| Royals | 1 | 1 | 100.0 | 44 | 44.00 | 0 | 0— | 0.0 | |
| Foster | 1 | 0 | 0.0 | 0 | 0.00 | 0 | 0— | 0.0 | |

**PUNTING**

| | No. | Avg. |
|---|---|---|
| Royals | 74 | 42.1 |

**KICKING**

| | XP | Att | % | FG | Att | % |
|---|---|---|---|---|---|---|
| Anderson | 29 | 31 | 94 | 28 | 36 | 78 |

---

### HOUSTON OILERS

**RUSHING**

| Last Name | No. | Yds | Avg | TD |
|---|---|---|---|---|
| White | 265 | 1226 | 4.6 | 7 |
| Moon | 27 | 147 | 5.4 | 1 |
| G. Brown | 19 | 87 | 4.6 | 1 |
| Carlson | 27 | 77 | 2.9 | 1 |
| Givins | 7 | 75 | 10.7 | 0 |
| Slaughter | 3 | 20 | 6.7 | 0 |
| L. Harris | 1 | 8 | 8.0 | 0 |
| Tillman | 1 | 1 | 1.0 | 0 |
| Richardson | 1 | -1 | -1.0 | 0 |
| Gr. Montgomery | 2 | -14 | -7.0 | 0 |

**RECEIVING**

| Last Name | No. | Yds | Avg | TD |
|---|---|---|---|---|
| Jeffires | 90 | 913 | 10.1 | 9 |
| Duncan | 82 | 954 | 11.6 | 1 |
| Givins | 67 | 787 | 11.7 | 10 |
| White | 57 | 641 | 11.2 | 1 |
| Slaughter | 39 | 486 | 12.5 | 4 |
| L. Harris | 35 | 435 | 12.4 | 2 |
| Coleman | 2 | 10 | 5.0 | 0 |
| G. Brown | 1 | 5 | 5.0 | 0 |

**PUNT RETURNS**

| Last Name | No. | Yds | Avg | TD |
|---|---|---|---|---|
| Slaughter | 20 | 142 | 7.1 | 0 |
| Coleman | 7 | 35 | 5.0 | 0 |

**KICKOFF RETURNS**

| Last Name | No. | Yds | Avg | TD |
|---|---|---|---|---|
| Coleman | 14 | 290 | 20.7 | 0 |
| Tillman | 10 | 157 | 15.7 | 0 |
| Lewis | 8 | 171 | 21.4 | 0 |
| Slaughter | 1 | 21 | 21.0 | 0 |
| G. Brown | 1 | 15 | 15.0 | 0 |
| Gl. Montgomery | 1 | 13 | 13.0 | 0 |
| Flannery | 1 | 12 | 12.0 | 0 |

**PASSING**

| | Att | Cmp | % | Yds | Yd/Att | TD | Int— | % | RK |
|---|---|---|---|---|---|---|---|---|---|
| Moon | 346 | 224 | 64.7 | 2521 | 7.29 | 18 | 12— | 3.5 | 1 |
| Carlson | 227 | 149 | 65.6 | 1710 | 7.53 | 9 | 11— | 4.8 | 5 |

**PUNTING**

| | No. | Avg. |
|---|---|---|
| Montgomery | 55 | 45.2 |

**KICKING**

| | XP | ATT | % | FG | ATT | % |
|---|---|---|---|---|---|---|
| Del Greco | 41 | 41 | 100 | 21 | 27 | 78 |

---

### CLEVELAND BROWNS

**RUSHING**

| Last Name | No. | Yds | Avg | TD |
|---|---|---|---|---|
| Mack | 169 | 543 | 3.2 | 6 |
| Vardell | 99 | 369 | 3.7 | 1 |
| Metcalf | 73 | 301 | 4.1 | 1 |
| Hoard | 54 | 236 | 4.4 | 0 |
| Tomczak | 24 | 39 | 1.6 | 0 |
| Brooks | 18 | 44 | 2.4 | 0 |
| Baldwin | 10 | 31 | 3.1 | 0 |
| M. Jackson | 1 | 21 | 21.0 | 0 |
| Tillman | 2 | 15 | 7.5 | 0 |
| Kosar | 5 | 12 | 2.4 | 0 |
| Wolfley | 1 | 2 | 2.0 | 0 |

**RECEIVING**

| Last Name | No. | Yds | Avg | TD |
|---|---|---|---|---|
| M. Jackson | 47 | 755 | 16.1 | 7 |
| Metcalf | 47 | 614 | 13.1 | 5 |
| Hoard | 26 | 310 | 11.9 | 1 |
| Tillman | 25 | 498 | 19.9 | 0 |
| Bavaro | 25 | 315 | 12.6 | 2 |
| Holohan | 20 | 170 | 8.5 | 0 |
| Vardell | 13 | 128 | 9.8 | 0 |
| Mack | 13 | 81 | 6.2 | 0 |
| R. Smith | 5 | 64 | 12.8 | 0 |
| Galbraith | 4 | 63 | 15.8 | 1 |
| Collins | 3 | 31 | 10.3 | 0 |
| Baldwin | 2 | 30 | 15.0 | 0 |
| Holland | 2 | 27 | 13.5 | 0 |
| Wolfley | 2 | 8 | 4.0 | 0 |
| Brooks | 2 | -1 | -0.5 | 0 |
| McCardell | 1 | 8 | 8.0 | 0 |
| J. Jones | 1 | 1 | 1.0 | 0 |

**PUNT RETURNS**

| Last Name | No. | Yds | Avg | TD |
|---|---|---|---|---|
| Metcalf | 44 | 429 | 9.8 | 1 |
| Brooks | 3 | 49 | 16.3 | 0 |

**KICKOFF RETURNS**

| Last Name | No. | Yds | Avg | TD |
|---|---|---|---|---|
| Baldwin | 30 | 675 | 22.5 | 0 |
| Metcalf | 9 | 157 | 17.4 | 0 |
| Hoard | 2 | 34 | 17.0 | 0 |
| Vardell | 2 | 14 | 7.0 | 0 |

**PASSING**

| | Att | Cmp | % | Yds | Yd/Att | TD | Int— | % | RK |
|---|---|---|---|---|---|---|---|---|---|
| Tomczak | 211 | 120 | 56.9 | 1693 | 8.02 | 7 | 7— | 3.3 | |
| Kosar | 155 | 103 | 66.5 | 1160 | 7.48 | 8 | 7— | 4.5 | |
| Philcox | 27 | 13 | 48.1 | 217 | 8.04 | 3 | 1— | 3.7 | |
| Goebel | 3 | 2 | 66.7 | 32 | 10.67 | 0 | 0— | 0.0 | |
| Metcalf | 1 | 0 | 0.0 | 0 | 0.00 | 0 | 0— | 0.0 | |
| Stover | 1 | 0 | 0.0 | 0 | 0.00 | 0 | 1— | 100.0 | |

**PUNTING**

| | No. | Avg. |
|---|---|---|
| Hansen | 75 | 41.1 |

**KICKING**

| | XP | ATT | % | FG | ATT | % |
|---|---|---|---|---|---|---|
| Stover | 29 | 30 | 97 | 21 | 29 | 72 |

---

### CINCINNATI BENGALS

**RUSHING**

| Last Name | No. | Yds | Avg | TD |
|---|---|---|---|---|
| Green | 265 | 1170 | 4.4 | 2 |
| Fenner | 112 | 500 | 4.5 | 7 |
| Hollas | 20 | 109 | 5.5 | 0 |
| Esiason | 21 | 66 | 3.1 | 0 |
| Ball | 16 | 55 | 3.4 | 2 |
| Klingler | 11 | 53 | 4.8 | 0 |
| Miles | 8 | 22 | 2.8 | 0 |
| Query | 1 | 1 | 1.0 | 0 |

**RECEIVING**

| Last Name | No. | Yds | Avg | TD |
|---|---|---|---|---|
| Green | 41 | 214 | 5.2 | 0 |
| McGee | 35 | 408 | 11.7 | 3 |
| Pickens | 26 | 326 | 12.5 | 1 |
| Holman | 26 | 266 | 10.2 | 2 |
| Rembert | 19 | 219 | 11.5 | 0 |
| Thompson | 19 | 194 | 10.2 | 0 |
| Query | 16 | 265 | 16.6 | 3 |
| Brennan | 19 | 188 | 9.9 | 0 |
| Riggs | 11 | 70 | 6.4 | 0 |
| Fenner | 7 | 41 | 5.9 | 1 |
| Ball | 6 | 66 | 11.0 | 2 |
| Stegall | 3 | 35 | 11.7 | 1 |
| Thomason | 2 | 14 | 7.0 | 0 |

**PUNT RETURNS**

| Last Name | No. | Yds | Avg | TD |
|---|---|---|---|---|
| Pickens | 18 | 229 | 12.7 | 1 |
| Price | 6 | 41 | 6.8 | 0 |

**KICKOFF RETURNS**

| Last Name | No. | Yds | Avg | TD |
|---|---|---|---|---|
| Ball | 20 | 411 | 20.6 | 0 |
| Stegall | 25 | 430 | 17.2 | 0 |
| Miles | 8 | 128 | 16.0 | 0 |
| Fenner | 2 | 38 | 19.0 | 0 |
| Price | 2 | 20 | 10.0 | 0 |
| Bussey | 1 | 18 | 18.0 | 0 |
| Query | 1 | 13 | 13.0 | 0 |

**PASSING**

| | Att | Cmp | % | Yds | Yd/Att | TD | Int— | % | RK |
|---|---|---|---|---|---|---|---|---|---|
| Esiason | 278 | 144 | 51.8 | 1407 | 5.06 | 11 | 15— | 5.4 | 11 |
| Klingler | 98 | 47 | 48.0 | 530 | 5.41 | 3 | 2— | 2.0 | |
| Hollas | 58 | 35 | 60.3 | 335 | 5.78 | 2 | 0— | 0.0 | |
| Breech | 1 | 1 | 100.0 | 12 | 12.00 | 0 | 0— | 0.0 | |

**PUNTING**

| | | Avg. |
|---|---|---|
| Johnson | 76 | 42.1 |

**KICKING**

| | XP | ATT | % | FG | ATT | % |
|---|---|---|---|---|---|---|
| Breech | 31 | 31 | 100 | 19 | 27 | 70 |
| Johnson | 0 | 0 | 0 | 0 | 1 | 0 |

## SAN DIEGO CHARGERS 11-5 Bobby Ross

| Scores of Each Game | | |
|---|---|---|
| 10 | KANSAS CITY | 24 |
| 13 | Denver | 21 |
| 6 | PITTSBURGH | 23 |
| 0 | Houston | 27 |
| 17 | SEATTLE | 6 |
| 34 | Indianapolis | 14 |
| 24 | DENVER | 21 |
| 26 | INDIANAPOLIS | 0 |
| 14 | Kansas City | 16 |
| 14 | Cleveland | 13 |
| 29 | TAMPA BAY | 14 |
| 27 | L.A. RAIDERS | 3 |
| 27 | Phoenix | 21 |
| 27 | CINCINNATI | 10 |
| 36 | L.A. Raiders | 14 |
| 31 | Seattle | 14 |

| UseName | Pos. | Hgt. | Wgt. | Age | Int | Pts |
|---|---|---|---|---|---|---|
| Leo Goeas | OT-OG | 6'4" | 292 | 26 | | |
| Harry Swayne | OT | 6'5" | 290 | 27 | | |
| Broderick Thompson | OT | 6'5" | 295 | 32 | | |
| Eric Moten | OG | 6'2" | 306 | 24 | | |
| David Richards | OG | 6'5" | 310 | 26 | | |
| Courtney Hall | C | 6'2" | 281 | 24 | | |
| Curtis Whitley | C | 6'1" | 288 | 23 | | |
| Mike Zandofsky | C-OG | 6'2" | 305 | 26 | | |
| Burt Grossman | DE | 6'6" | 270 | 25 | | 4 |
| Shawn Lee | DE | 6'2" | 280 | 25 | | |
| Chris Mims | DE | 6'5" | 270 | 21 | | 2 |
| Leslie O'Neal | DE | 6'4" | 259 | 28 | | |
| George Thornton | DT | 6'3" | 300 | 24 | | |
| Reggie White | DT | 6'4" | 291 | 22 | | |
| Blaise Winter | DT-NT | 6'4" | 278 | 30 | | |
| Tony Savage (to CIN) | NT | 6'3" | 300 | 25 | | |
| Sam Anno | LB | 6'3" | 240 | 27 | | |
| Eugene Marve | LB | 6'2" | 240 | 32 | | |
| Kevin Murphy | LB | 6'2" | 235 | 28 | | |
| Gary Plummer | LB | 6'2" | 244 | 32 | 2 | |
| Henry Rolling | LB | 6'2" | 247 | 26 | | |
| Junior Seau | LB | 6'3" | 250 | 23 | 2 | |
| Billy Ray Smith | LB | 6'3" | 236 | 31 | | |
| Anthony Blaylock | DB | 5'10" | 185 | 27 | 2 | |
| Gill Byrd | DB | 5'11" | 198 | 31 | 4 | |
| Darren Carrington | DB | 6'2" | 200 | 25 | 6 | 6 |
| Floyd Fields | DB | 6' | 208 | 23 | 1 | |
| Donald Frank | DB | 6' | 192 | 26 | 4 | |
| Delton Hall | DB | 6'1" | 211 | 27 | | |
| Marquez Pope | DB | 5'10" | 188 | 21 | | |
| Stanley Richard | DB | 6'2" | 197 | 24 | 3 | |
| Sean Vanhorse | DB | 5'10" | 180 | 24 | | |
| Bob Gagliano | QB | 6'3" | 205 | 33 | | |
| Stan Humphries | QB | 6'2" | 223 | 27 | | 24 |
| Rod Bernstine | HB-FB-TE | 6'3" | 238 | 27 | | 24 |
| Eric Bieniemy | HB | 5'7" | 198 | 23 | | 18 |
| Ronnie Harmon | HB | 5'11" | 207 | 28 | | 24 |
| Peter Tuipulotu | HB-FB | 5'11" | 210 | 23 | | |
| Marion Butts | FB-HB | 6'1" | 248 | 26 | | 24 |
| Johnnie Barnes | WR | 6'1" | 180 | 24 | | |
| Robert Claiborne | WR | 5'10" | 175 | 25 | | |
| Shawn Jefferson | WR | 5'11" | 172 | 23 | | 12 |
| Nate Lewis | WR | 5'11" | 198 | 25 | | 24 |
| Anthony Miller | WR | 5'11" | 189 | 27 | | 48 |
| Steve Hendrickson | FB-LB | 6' | 250 | 26 | | |
| Deems May | TE | 6'4" | 250 | 23 | | |
| Alfred Pupunu | TE | 6'2" | 252 | 22 | | |
| Derrick Walker | TE | 6'1" | 244 | 25 | | 12 |
| Duane Young | TE | 6'1" | 260 | 24 | | |
| John Carney | K | 5'11" | 170 | 28 | | 113 |
| John Kidd | K | 6'3" | 208 | 31 | | |

David Grayson — Leg Injury

John Friesz — Knee Injury

## KANSAS CITY CHIEFS 10-6 Marty Schottenheimer

| Scores of Each Game | | |
|---|---|---|
| 24 | San Diego | 10 |
| 26 | SEATTLE | 7 |
| 20 | Houston | *23 |
| 27 | L.A. RAIDERS | 7 |
| 19 | Denver | 20 |
| 24 | PHILADELPHIA | 17 |
| 10 | Dallas | 17 |
| 3 | PITTSBURGH | 27 |
| 16 | SAN DIEGO | 14 |
| 35 | WASHINGTON | 16 |
| 24 | Seattle | 14 |
| 23 | N.Y. Jets | 7 |
| 7 | L.A. Raiders | 28 |
| 27 | NEW ENGLAND | 20 |
| 21 | N.Y. Giants | 35 |
| 42 | DENVER | 20 |

| UseName | Pos. | Hgt. | Wgt. | Age | Int | Pts |
|---|---|---|---|---|---|---|
| John Alt | OT | 6'7" | 303 | 30 | | |
| Rich Baldinger | OT | 6'4" | 293 | 32 | | |
| Tom Dohring | OT | 6'6" | 290 | 24 | | |
| Derrick Graham | OT | 6'4" | 306 | 25 | | |
| Joe Staysniak | OT | 6'5" | 295 | 25 | | |
| Joe Valerio | OT-C | 6'5" | 293 | 23 | | |
| David Lutz | OG | 6'6" | 305 | 32 | | |
| Dave Szott | OG | 6'4" | 290 | 24 | | |
| Mike Baab | C | 6'4" | 278 | 32 | | |
| Tim Grunhard | C | 6'2" | 299 | 24 | | |
| Kani Kauahi | C | 6'3" | 275 | 32 | | |
| Leonard Griffin | DE | 6'4" | 278 | 29 | | |
| Neil Smith | DE | 6'4" | 275 | 26 | 1 | 6 |
| Bill Maas | DE | 6'5" | 275 | 29 | | |
| Darren Mickel | DE | 6'4" | 268 | 22 | | |
| Mike Evans | DT-DE | 6'3" | 269 | 25 | | |
| Joe Phillips | DT | 6'5" | 300 | 29 | | |
| Dan Saleaumua | DT-NT | 6' | 295 | 27 | | |
| Tom Sims | DT | 6'2" | 291 | 25 | | |
| Chris Martin | LB | 6'2" | 246 | 31 | | |
| Lonnie Marts | LB | 6'1" | 243 | 23 | 1 | 6 |
| Ervin Randle | LB | 6'1" | 250 | 29 | | |
| Tracy Rogers | LB | 6'2" | 241 | 25 | | 6 |
| Tracy Simien | LB | 6'1" | 245 | 25 | 3 | |
| Percy Snow | LB | 6'2" | 250 | 24 | | |
| Derrick Thomas | LB | 6'3" | 242 | 25 | | 6 |
| Martin Bayless | DB | 6'2" | 213 | 29 | 1 | |
| Dale Carter | DB | 6'1" | 188 | 22 | 7 | 18 |
| Albert Lewis | DB | 6'2" | 195 | 31 | 1 | |
| Tahaun Lewis | DB | 5'10" | 175 | 23 | | |
| Charles Mincy | DB | 5'11" | 197 | 22 | 4 | 18 |
| J.C. Pearson | DB | 5'11" | 186 | 29 | | |
| Kevin Porter (to NYJ) | DB | 5'10" | 214 | 26 | | |
| Kevin Ross | DB | 5'9" | 185 | 30 | 1 | 6 |
| Doug Terry | DB | 5'11" | 192 | 22 | 1 | |
| Bennie Thompson | DB | 6' | 214 | 29 | | |
| Matt Blundin | QB | 6'6" | 230 | 23 | | |
| Dave Krieg | QB | 6'1" | 202 | 33 | | 12 |
| Mark Vlasic | QB | 6'3" | 205 | 28 | | |
| Kimble Anders | HB | 5'11" | 221 | 25 | | |
| Bill Jones | HB | 5'11" | 227 | 25 | | |
| Todd McNair | HB | 6'1" | 202 | 27 | | 12 |
| Harvey Williams | HB | 6'2" | 229 | 25 | | 6 |
| Barry Word | HB | 6'2" | 245 | 28 | | 24 |
| Christian Okoye | FB | 6'1" | 260 | 31 | | 36 |
| Tim Barnett | WR | 6'1" | 201 | 24 | | 24 |
| J.J. Birden | WR | 5'9" | 170 | 27 | | 18 |
| Willie Davis | WR | 6' | 170 | 24 | | 18 |
| Tony Hargain | WR | 6' | 194 | 24 | | |
| Emile Harry (to LA) | WR | 5'11" | 186 | 29 | | |
| Fred Jones | WR | 5'9" | 182 | 25 | | |
| Michael Smith | WR | 5'8" | 160 | 21 | | |
| Keith Cash | TE | 6'4" | 245 | 23 | | 12 |
| Mike Dyal | TE | 6'2" | 240 | 26 | | |
| Jonathan Hayes | TE | 6'5" | 248 | 30 | | 12 |
| Bryan Barker | K | 6'1" | 187 | 28 | | |
| Nick Lowery | K | 6'4" | 205 | 36 | | 105 |
| Kent Sullivan | K | 5'10" | 197 | 28 | | |

William Kirksey — Foot Injury
Dino Hackett — Ear Injury

## DENVER BRONCOS 8-8 Dan Reeves

| Scores of Each Game | | |
|---|---|---|
| 17 | L.A. RAIDERS | 13 |
| 21 | SAN DIEGO | 13 |
| 0 | Philadelphia | 30 |
| 12 | Cleveland | 0 |
| 20 | KANSAS CITY | 19 |
| 3 | Washington | 34 |
| 27 | HOUSTON | 21 |
| 21 | San Diego | 24 |
| 27 | N.Y. JETS | 16 |
| 27 | N.Y. GIANTS | 13 |
| 0 | L.A. Raiders | 24 |
| 13 | Seattle | *16 |
| 27 | DALLAS | 31 |
| 17 | Buffalo | 27 |
| 10 | SEATTLE | 6 |
| 20 | Kansas City | 42 |

| UseName | Pos. | Hgt. | Wgt. | Age | Int | Pts |
|---|---|---|---|---|---|---|
| Russell Freeman | OT | 6'7" | 290 | 22 | | |
| Chuck Johnson | OT | 6'5" | 275 | 23 | | |
| Ken Lanier | OT | 6'3" | 290 | 33 | | |
| Jeff Davidson | OG | 6'5" | 309 | 24 | | |
| Dave Widell | OT-C | 6'6" | 292 | 27 | | |
| Doug Widell | OG | 6'4" | 287 | 25 | | |
| Keith Kartz | C | 6'4" | 270 | 29 | | |
| Shane Dronett | DE | 6'6" | 275 | 21 | | |
| Ron Holmes | DE | 6'4" | 265 | 29 | | |
| Brian Sochia | DE | 6'3" | 278 | 31 | | |
| Kenny Walker | DE | 6'3" | 260 | 25 | | |
| Ron Geater | NT | 6'6" | 270 | 23 | | |
| Greg Kragen | NT | 6'3" | 265 | 30 | | |
| Michael Brooks | LB | 6'1" | 235 | 27 | 1 | 6 |
| Mike Croel | LB | 6'3" | 231 | 23 | | |
| Simon Fletcher | LB | 6'5" | 240 | 30 | | |
| John Kacherski | LB | 6'3" | 240 | 25 | | |
| Tim Lucas | LB | 6'3" | 230 | 31 | | |
| Karl Mecklenburg | LB | 6'3" | 235 | 32 | | |
| Jeff Mills | LB | 6'3" | 238 | 23 | | |
| John Sullins | LB | 6'1" | 225 | 22 | | |
| Keith Traylor | LB | 6'2" | 260 | 22 | | |
| Steve Atwater | DB | 6'3" | 217 | 25 | 2 | |
| Tyrone Braxton | DB | 5'11" | 185 | 27 | 2 | |
| Charles Dimry | DB | 6' | 175 | 26 | 1 | |
| John Granby | DB | 6'1" | 198 | 23 | | |
| Wymon Henderson | DB | 5'10" | 186 | 30 | 4 | 6 |
| Le-Lo Lang | DB | 5'11" | 185 | 25 | 1 | |
| Alton Montgomery | DB | 6' | 195 | 24 | | |
| Muhammad Oliver | DB | 5'11" | 170 | 23 | | |
| Frank Robinson (from CIN) | DB | 5'11" | 174 | 23 | | |
| Dennis Smith | DB | 6'3" | 200 | 33 | 4 | |
| John Elway | QB | 6'3" | 215 | 32 | | 12 |
| Tommy Maddox | QB | 6'4" | 195 | 21 | | |
| Shawn Moore | QB | 6'2" | 214 | 24 | | |
| Gaston Green | HB | 5'11" | 192 | 26 | | 12 |
| Victor Jones | HB | 5'8" | 220 | 24 | | |
| Greg Lewis | HB-FB | 5'10" | 214 | 23 | | 24 |
| Sammie Smith | DB | 6'2" | 228 | 25 | | |
| Jeff Alexander | FB | 6' | 232 | 27 | | |
| Bob Perryman | FB | 6'2" | 233 | 28 | | |
| Reggie Rivers | FB | 6'1" | 215 | 24 | | 24 |
| Mark Jackson | WR | 5'10" | 180 | 29 | | 48 |
| Vance Johnson | WR | 5'11" | 185 | 29 | | 12 |
| Arthur Marshall | WR | 5'11" | 174 | 23 | | 6 |
| Ricky Nattiel | WR | 5'9" | 180 | 26 | | |
| Derek Russell | WR | 6' | 179 | 23 | | |
| Cedric Tillman | WR | 6'2" | 204 | 22 | | 6 |
| Michael Young | WR | 6'1" | 183 | 30 | | |
| Reggie Johnson | TE | 6'2" | 256 | 24 | | 6 |
| Clarence Kay | TE | 6'2" | 237 | 31 | | |
| Shannon Sharpe | TE | 6'2" | 230 | 24 | | 12 |
| Brad Daluiso | K | 6'2" | 207 | 24 | | |
| Mike Horan | K | 5'11" | 190 | 33 | | |
| Daren Parker | K | 6' | 185 | 23 | | |
| Ruben Rodriguez | K | 6'2" | 209 | 27 | | |
| David Treadwell | K | 6'1" | 180 | 25 | | 88 |

Frank Pollack — Back Injury

Ronnie Haliburton — Neck Injury

Steve Sewell — Ankle Injury

## LOS ANGELES RAIDERS 7-9 Art Shell

| Scores of Each Game | | |
|---|---|---|
| 13 | Denver | 17 |
| 21 | Cincinnati | *24 |
| 16 | CLEVELAND | 28 |
| 7 | Kansas City | 27 |
| 13 | N.Y. GIANTS | 10 |
| 20 | BUFFALO | 3 |
| 19 | Seattle | 0 |
| 13 | DALLAS | 28 |
| 10 | Philadelphia | 31 |
| 20 | SEATTLE | 3 |
| 24 | DENVER | 0 |
| 3 | San Diego | 27 |
| 28 | KANSAS CITY | 7 |
| 7 | Miami | 20 |
| 14 | SAN DIEGO | 36 |
| 21 | Washington | 20 |

| UseName | Pos. | Hgt. | Wgt. | Age | Int | Pts |
|---|---|---|---|---|---|---|
| Greg Skrepenak | OG | 6'6" | 315 | 22 | | |
| Bruce Wilkerson | OT | 6'5" | 295 | 28 | | |
| Steve Wright | OT | 6'6" | 285 | 33 | | |
| Reggie McElroy | OT | 6'6" | 290 | 32 | | |
| Max Montoya | OG | 6'5" | 295 | 36 | | |
| Todd Peat | OG | 6'2" | 305 | 28 | | |
| Steve Wisniewski | OG | 6'4" | 290 | 25 | | |
| Don Mosebar | C | 6'6" | 305 | 30 | | |
| Dan Turk | C | 6'4" | 305 | 30 | | |
| Aundray Bruce | DE | 6'5' | 260 | 26 | | |
| Howie Long | DE | 6'5" | 275 | 32 | | |
| Anthony Smith | DE | 6'3" | 265 | 25 | | |
| Greg Townsend | DE | 6'3" | 270 | 30 | | |
| Willie Broughton | DT | 6'5" | 280 | 27 | | |
| Bob Golic | DT | 6'2" | 280 | 34 | | |
| Nolan Harrison | DT | 6'5" | 280 | 23 | | 2 |
| Chester McGlockton | DT | 6'4" | 320 | 22 | | |
| Anthony Bell | LB | 6'3" | 245 | 28 | | |
| Thomas Benson | LB | 6'2" | 240 | 30 | | |
| Riki Ellison | LB | 6'2" | 225 | 32 | | |
| Mike Jones | LB | 6'1" | 230 | 23 | | |
| Winston Moss | LB | 6'3" | 240 | 26 | | |
| Aaron Wallace | LB | 6'3" | 235 | 25 | | |
| Eddie Anderson | DB | 6'1" | 210 | 29 | 3 | 6 |
| Torin Dorn | DB | 6' | 190 | 24 | 1 | |
| Derrick Hoskins | DB | 6'2" | 200 | 21 | | |
| Dan Land | DB | 6' | 195 | 27 | 1 | |
| Ronnie Lott | DB | 6' | 205 | 33 | 1 | |
| Terry McDaniel | DB | 5'10" | 180 | 27 | 4 | |
| Elvis Patterson | DB | 5'11" | 195 | 31 | | 6 |
| Sam Seale | DB | 5'9" | 185 | 29 | | |
| Lionel Washington | DB | 6' | 190 | 31 | 2 | |
| Dave Waymer | DB | 6'1" | 205 | 34 | | |
| Vince Evans | QB | 6'2" | 210 | 37 | | |
| Todd Marinovich | QB | 6'4" | 220 | 23 | | |
| Jay Schroeder | QB | 6'4" | 210 | 31 | | |
| Marcus Allen | HB | 6'2' | 210 | 32 | | 18 |
| Nick Bell | HB | 6'2" | 255 | 24 | | 18 |
| Eric Dickerson | HB | 6'3" | 220 | 31 | | 18 |
| Napoleon McCallum | HB | 6'2" | 230 | 28 | | |
| Steve Smith | FB | 6'1" | 240 | 28 | | 6 |
| Tim Brown | WR | 6' | 195 | 26 | | 42 |
| Mervyn Fernandez | WR | 6'3" | 205 | 32 | | |
| Willie Gault | WR | 6' | 175 | 31 | | 24 |
| Sam Graddy | WR | 5'10" | 180 | 28 | | 6 |
| Alexander Wright (from DAL) | WRT | 6' | 195 | 25 | | 12 |
| Andrew Glover | TE | 6'6" | 245 | 25 | | 6 |
| Ethan Horton | TE | 6'4" | 240 | 29 | | 12 |
| David Jones | TE | 6'2" | 220 | 23 | | |
| Kevin Smith | TE | 6'4" | 255 | 23 | | |
| Jeff Gossett | K | 6'2" | 195 | 35 | | |
| Jeff Jaeger | K | 5'11" | 195 | 27 | | 73 |

James FitzPatrick — Knee Injury

## SEATTLE SEAHAWKS 2-14 Tom Flores

| Scores of Each Game | | |
|---|---|---|
| 3 | CINCINNATI | 21 |
| 7 | Kansas City | 26 |
| 10 | New England | 6 |
| 17 | MIAMI | 19 |
| 6 | San Diego | 17 |
| 0 | Dallas | 27 |
| 0 | L.A. RAIDERS | 19 |
| 10 | N.Y. Giants | 23 |
| 3 | WASHINGTON | 16 |
| 3 | L.A. Raiders | 20 |
| 14 | KANSAS CITY | 24 |
| 16 | DENVER | *13 |
| 14 | Pittsburgh | 20 |
| 17 | PHILADELPHIA | *20 |
| 6 | Denver | 10 |
| 14 | SAN DIEGO | 31 |

| UseName | Pos. | Hgt. | Wgt. | Age | Int | Pts |
|---|---|---|---|---|---|---|
| Theo Adams | OT | 6'4" | 298 | 26 | | |
| Bill Hitchcock | OT | 6'6" | 291 | 25 | | |
| Mike Keim | OT | 6'7" | 285 | 26 | | |
| Ronnie Lee | OT | 6'3" | 296 | 35 | | |
| Ray Roberts | OT | 6'6" | 304 | 23 | | |
| Darrick Brilz | OG | 6'3" | 287 | 28 | | |
| Sean Farrell | OG | 6'3" | 260 | 32 | | |
| Andy Heck | OT | 6'6" | 298 | 25 | | |
| John Hunter | OG | 6'8" | 300 | 27 | | |
| Grant Feasel | C | 6'7" | 283 | 32 | | |
| Joe Tofflemire | C | 6'3" | 273 | 27 | | |
| Jeff Bryant | DE | 6'5" | 281 | 32 | | |
| Mike Sinclair | DE | 6'4" | 255 | 24 | | |
| Natu Tuatagaloa | DE | 6'4" | 274 | 26 | 1 | |
| Tony Woods | DE | 6'4" | 269 | 26 | | |
| Cortez Kennedy | DT | 6'3" | 293 | 24 | | |
| Joe Nash | DT | 6'2" | 278 | 31 | | |
| Tyrone Rodgers | DT | 6'3" | 266 | 23 | | |
| Joe Cain | LB | 6'1" | 233 | 27 | 2 | |
| Greg Clark | LB | 6' | 226 | 27 | | |
| E.J. Junior (from TB) | LB | 6'3" | 242 | 32 | | |
| Richard Newbill | LB | 6'1" | 240 | 24 | | |
| Rufus Porter | LB | 6'1" | 227 | 27 | | |
| Bob Spitulski | LB | 6'3" | 235 | 22 | | |
| Rod Stephens | LB | 6'1" | 237 | 26 | | |
| Terry Wooden | LB | 6'3" | 236 | 25 | 1 | |
| David Wyman | LB | 6'2" | 248 | 28 | | |
| Robert Blackmon | DB | 6' | 197 | 25 | 1 | |
| Brian Davis | DB | 6'2" | 187 | 29 | 2 | |
| Dedrick Dodge | DB | 6'2" | 184 | 25 | 1 | |
| Malcolm Frank | DB | 5'8" | 182 | 23 | | |
| Nesby Glasgow | DB | 5'10" | 187 | 35 | | |
| Dwayne Harper | DB | 5'11" | 174 | 26 | 3 | 6 |
| Patrick Hunter | DB | 5'11" | 186 | 27 | 2 | |
| James Jefferson | DB | 6'1" | 199 | 28 | | |
| Eugene Robinson | DB | 6' | 191 | 29 | 7 | |
| Rafael Robinson | DB | 5'11" | 200 | 23 | | |
| Stan Gelbaugh | QB | 6'3" | 207 | 29 | | |
| Rusty Hilger | QB | 6'4" | 209 | 30 | | |
| Dan McGwire | QB | 6'8" | 243 | 24 | | |
| Kelly Stouffer | QB | 6'3" | 214 | 28 | | |
| Rueben Mayes | HB | 5'11" | 201 | 29 | | |
| Chris Warren | HB | 6'2" | 225 | 25 | | 18 |
| Tracy Johnson | FB | 6' | 230 | 25 | | |
| James Jones | FB-TE | 6'2" | 232 | 31 | | |
| John L. Williams | FB | 5'11" | 231 | 27 | | 18 |
| Brian Blades | WR | 5'11 | 189 | 27 | | 6 |
| Louis Clark | WR | 6' | 198 | 28 | | 6 |
| David Daniels | WR | 6'1" | 190 | 22 | | |
| Tommy Kane | WR | 5'11" | 181 | 28 | | 18 |
| Doug Thomas | WR | 5'10" | 178 | 22 | | |
| Robb Thomas | WR | 5'11" | 175 | 26 | | |
| Brian Treggs | WR | 5'9" | 161 | 22 | | |
| Paul Green | TE | 6'3" | 230 | 25 | | 6 |
| Ron Heller | TE | 6'3" | 242 | 28 | | |
| Mike Jones | TE | 6'3" | 255 | 25 | | |
| Trey Junkin | TE | 6'2" | 237 | 31 | | 6 |
| John Kasay | K | 5'10" | 189 | 22 | | 56 |
| Rick Tuten | K | 6'2" | 218 | 27 | | |

Bryan Millard — Back Injury

Marcus Cotton — Knee Injury
Vann McElroy — Ankle Injury

## SAN DIEGO CHARGERS

### RUSHING

| Last Name | No. | Yds | Avg | TD |
|---|---|---|---|---|
| Butts | 218 | 809 | 3.7 | 4 |
| Bernstine | 106 | 499 | 4.7 | 4 |
| Bieniemy | 74 | 264 | 3.6 | 3 |
| Harmon | 55 | 235 | 4.3 | 3 |
| Humphries | 28 | 79 | 2.8 | 4 |
| Lewis | 2 | 7 | 3.5 | 0 |
| Miller | 1 | -1 | -1.0 | 0 |
| Gagliano | 3 | -4 | -1.3 | 0 |
| Kidd | 2 | -13 | -6.5 | 0 |

### RECEIVING

| Last Name | No. | Yds | Avg | TD |
|---|---|---|---|---|
| Harmon | 79 | 914 | 11.6 | 1 |
| Miller | 72 | 1060 | 14.7 | 7 |
| Lewis | 34 | 580 | 17.1 | 4 |
| Walker | 34 | 393 | 11.6 | 2 |
| Jefferson | 29 | 377 | 13.0 | 2 |
| Bernstine | 12 | 86 | 7.2 | 0 |
| Butts | 9 | 73 | 8.1 | 0 |
| Bieniemy | 5 | 49 | 9.8 | 0 |
| Young | 4 | 45 | 11.3 | 0 |
| Claiborne | 1 | 15 | 15.0 | 0 |

### PUNT RETURNS

| Last Name | No. | Yds | Avg | TD |
|---|---|---|---|---|
| Bieniemy | 30 | 229 | 7.6 | 0 |
| Lewis | 13 | 127 | 9.8 | 0 |

### KICKOFF RETURNS

| Last Name | No. | Yds | Avg | TD |
|---|---|---|---|---|
| Lewis | 19 | 402 | 21.2 | 0 |
| Bieniemy | 15 | 257 | 17.1 | 0 |
| Harmon | 7 | 96 | 13.7 | 0 |
| Hendrickson | 2 | 14 | 7.0 | 0 |
| Miller | 1 | 33 | 33.0 | 0 |

### PASSING — PUNTING — KICKING Statistics

| PASSING | Att | Cmp | % | Yds | Yd/Att | TD | Int | — | % | RK |
|---|---|---|---|---|---|---|---|---|---|---|
| Humphries | 454 | 263 | 57.9 | 3356 | 7.39 | 16 | 18 | — | 4.0 | 7 |
| Gagliano | 42 | 19 | 45.2 | 258 | 6.14 | 0 | 3 | — | 7.1 | |

| PUNTING | No. | Avg. |
|---|---|---|
| Kidd | 68 | 42.6 |

| KICKING | XP | Att | % | FG | Att | % |
|---|---|---|---|---|---|---|
| Carney | 35 | 35 | 100 | 26 | 32 | 81 |

## KANSAS CITY CHIEFS

### RUSHING

| Last Name | No. | Yds | Avg | TD |
|---|---|---|---|---|
| Word | 163 | 607 | 3.7 | 4 |
| Okoye | 144 | 448 | 3.1 | 6 |
| Williams | 78 | 264 | 3.4 | 1 |
| McNair | 21 | 124 | 5.9 | 1 |
| Krieg | 37 | 74 | 2.0 | 2 |
| Harry | 1 | 27 | 27.0 | 0 |
| Anders | 1 | 1 | 1.0 | 0 |
| Davis | 1 | -11 | -11.0 | 0 |

### RECEIVING

| Last Name | No. | Yds | Avg | TD |
|---|---|---|---|---|
| McNair | 44 | 380 | 8.6 | 1 |
| Birden | 42 | 644 | 15.3 | 3 |
| Davis | 36 | 756 | 21.0 | 3 |
| Barnett | 24 | 442 | 18.4 | 1 |
| F. Jones | 18 | 265 | 14.7 | 0 |
| Hargain | 17 | 205 | 12.1 | 0 |
| Cash | 12 | 113 | 9.4 | 2 |
| Word | 9 | 80 | 8.9 | 0 |
| Hayes | 9 | 77 | 8.6 | 2 |
| Anders | 5 | 65 | 13.0 | 0 |
| Harry | 6 | 58 | 9.7 | 0 |
| Williams | 5 | 24 | 4.8 | 0 |
| B. Jones | 2 | 6 | 3.0 | 0 |
| Dyal | 1 | 7 | 7.0 | 0 |
| Okoye | 1 | 5 | 5.0 | 0 |

### PUNT RETURNS

| Last Name | No. | Yds | Avg | TD |
|---|---|---|---|---|
| Carter | 38 | 398 | 10.5 | 2 |
| Harry | 6 | 34 | 5.7 | 0 |
| Mincy | 1 | 1 | 1.0 | 0 |

### KICKOFF RETURNS

| Last Name | No. | Yds | Avg | TD |
|---|---|---|---|---|
| Williams | 21 | 405 | 19.3 | 0 |
| Carter | 11 | 190 | 17.3 | 0 |
| F. Jones | 3 | 51 | 17.0 | 0 |
| McNair | 2 | 20 | 10.0 | 0 |
| Cash | 1 | 36 | 36.0 | 0 |
| Anders | 1 | 20 | 20.0 | 0 |

### PASSING — PUNTING — KICKING Statistics

| PASSING | Att | Cmp | % | Yds | Yd/Att | TD | Int | — | % | RK |
|---|---|---|---|---|---|---|---|---|---|---|
| Krieg | 413 | 230 | 55.7 | 3115 | 7.54 | 15 | 12 | — | 2.9 | 6 |

| PUNTING | No. | Avg. |
|---|---|---|
| Barker | 76 | 42.7 |
| Sullivan | 6 | 41.2 |
| Lowery | 4 | 35.3 |

| KICKING | XP | Att | % | FG | Att | % |
|---|---|---|---|---|---|---|
| Lowery | 39 | 39 | 100 | 22 | 24 | 92 |

## DENVER BRONCOS

### RUSHING

| Last Name | No. | Yds | Avg | TD |
|---|---|---|---|---|
| Green | 161 | 648 | 4.0 | 2 |
| Rivers | 74 | 282 | 3.8 | 3 |
| Lewis | 73 | 268 | 3.7 | 4 |
| Elway | 34 | 94 | 2.8 | 2 |
| S. Smith | 23 | 94 | 4.1 | 0 |
| Marshall | 11 | 56 | 5.1 | 0 |
| Moore | 8 | 39 | 4.9 | 0 |
| Maddox | 9 | 20 | 2.2 | 0 |
| R. Johnson | 2 | 7 | 3.5 | 0 |
| M. Jackson | 3 | -1 | -0.3 | 0 |
| Perryman | 3 | -1 | -0.3 | 0 |
| Sharpe | 2 | -6 | -3.0 | 0 |

### RECEIVING

| Last Name | No. | Yds | Avg | TD |
|---|---|---|---|---|
| Sharpe | 53 | 640 | 12.1 | 2 |
| M. Jackson | 48 | 745 | 15.5 | 8 |
| Rivers | 45 | 449 | 10.0 | 1 |
| Marshall | 26 | 493 | 19.0 | 1 |
| V. Johnson | 24 | 294 | 12.3 | 2 |
| Tillman | 12 | 211 | 17.6 | 1 |
| Russell | 12 | 140 | 11.7 | 0 |
| R. Johnson | 10 | 139 | 13.9 | 1 |
| Green | 10 | 79 | 7.9 | 0 |
| Kay | 7 | 56 | 8.0 | 0 |
| Lewis | 4 | 30 | 7.5 | 0 |
| Jones | 3 | 17 | 5.7 | 0 |
| Perryman | 2 | 15 | 7.5 | 0 |
| Young | 1 | 11 | 11.0 | 0 |
| Do. Widell | 1 | -7 | -7.0 | 0 |

### PUNT RETURNS

| Last Name | No. | Yds | Avg | TD |
|---|---|---|---|---|
| Marshall | 33 | 349 | 10.6 | 0 |
| Dimry | 1 | 4 | 4.0 | 0 |

### KICKOFF RETURNS

| Last Name | No. | Yds | Avg | TD |
|---|---|---|---|---|
| Montgomery | 21 | 466 | 22.2 | 0 |
| Marshall | 8 | 132 | 16.5 | 0 |
| Russell | 7 | 154 | 22.0 | 0 |
| Green | 5 | 76 | 15.2 | 0 |
| Robinson | 4 | 89 | 22.3 | 0 |
| R. Johnson | 2 | 47 | 23.5 | 0 |
| S. Smith | 2 | 31 | 15.5 | 0 |
| Oliver | 1 | 20 | 20.0 | 0 |
| Traylor | 1 | 13 | 13.0 | 0 |

### PASSING — PUNTING — KICKING Statistics

| PASSING | Att | Cmp | % | Yds | Yd/Att | TD | Int | — | % | RK |
|---|---|---|---|---|---|---|---|---|---|---|
| Elway | 316 | 174 | 55.1 | 2242 | 7.09 | 10 | 17 | — | 5.4 | 8 |
| Maddox | 121 | 66 | 54.5 | 757 | 6.26 | 5 | 9 | — | 7.4 | |
| Moore | 34 | 17 | 50.0 | 232 | 6.82 | 0 | 3 | — | 8.8 | |
| Marshall | 1 | 1 | 100.0 | 81 | 81.00 | 1 | 0 | — | 0.0 | |
| Lewis | 1 | 0 | 0.0 | 0 | 0.00 | 0 | 0 | — | 0.0 | |

| PUNTING | No. | Avg. |
|---|---|---|
| Horan | 38 | 44.2 |
| Rodriguez | 47 | 40.6 |
| Parker | 12 | 40.9 |
| Daluiso | 10 | 40.7 |

| KICKING | XP | ATT | % | FG | ATT | % |
|---|---|---|---|---|---|---|
| Treadwell | 28 | 28 | 100 | 20 | 24 | 83 |

## LOS ANGELES RAIDERS

### RUSHING

| Last Name | No. | Yds | Avg | TD |
|---|---|---|---|---|
| Dickerson | 187 | 729 | 3.9 | 2 |
| N. Bell | 81 | 366 | 4.5 | 3 |
| Allen | 67 | 301 | 4.5 | 2 |
| Schroeder | 28 | 160 | 5.7 | 0 |
| S. Smith | 44 | 129 | 2.9 | 0 |
| Evans | 11 | 79 | 7.2 | 0 |
| Marinovich | 9 | 30 | 3.3 | 0 |
| Gault | 1 | 6 | 6.0 | 0 |
| Brown | 3 | -4 | -1.3 | 0 |
| Gossett | 1 | -12 | -12.0 | 0 |

### RECEIVING

| Last Name | No. | Yds | Avg | TD |
|---|---|---|---|---|
| Brown | 49 | 693 | 14.1 | 7 |
| Horton | 33 | 409 | 12.4 | 2 |
| Allen | 28 | 277 | 9.9 | 1 |
| S. Smith | 28 | 217 | 7.8 | 1 |
| Gault | 27 | 508 | 18.8 | 4 |
| Glover | 15 | 178 | 11.9 | 1 |
| Dickerson | 14 | 85 | 6.1 | 1 |
| A. Wright | 12 | 175 | 14.6 | 2 |
| Graddy | 10 | 205 | 20.5 | 1 |
| Fernandez | 9 | 121 | 13.4 | 0 |
| N. Bell | 4 | 40 | 10.0 | 0 |
| D. Jones | 2 | 29 | 14.5 | 0 |
| McCallum | 1 | 13 | 13.0 | 0 |

### PUNT RETURNS

| Last Name | No. | Yds | Avg | TD |
|---|---|---|---|---|
| T. Brown | 37 | 383 | 10.4 | 0 |
| McCallum | 4 | 19 | 4.8 | 0 |

### KICKOFF RETURNS

| Last Name | No. | Yds | Avg | TD |
|---|---|---|---|---|
| A. Wright | 26 | 442 | 17.0 | 0 |
| McCallum | 14 | 274 | 19.6 | 0 |
| Graddy | 5 | 85 | 17.0 | 0 |
| Land | 2 | 27 | 13.5 | 0 |
| Brown | 2 | 14 | 7.0 | 0 |
| N. Bell | 1 | 16 | 16.0 | 0 |
| Turk | 1 | 3 | 3.0 | 0 |

### PASSING — PUNTING — KICKING Statistics

| PASSING | Att | Cmp | % | Yds | Yd/Att | TD | Int | — | % | RK |
|---|---|---|---|---|---|---|---|---|---|---|
| Schroeder | 253 | 123 | 48.6 | 1476 | 5.83 | 11 | 11 | — | 4.3 | 9 |
| Marinovich | 165 | 81 | 49.1 | 1102 | 6.68 | 5 | 9 | — | 5.3 | |
| Evans | 53 | 29 | 54.7 | 372 | 7.02 | 4 | 3 | — | 5.7 | |

| PUNTING | No. | Avg. |
|---|---|---|
| Gossett | 77 | 42.3 |

| KICKING | XP | ATT | % | FG | ATT | % |
|---|---|---|---|---|---|---|
| Jaeger | 28 | 29 | 97 | 15 | 26 | 58 |

## SEATTLE SEAHAWKS

### RUSHING

| Last Name | No. | Yds | Avg | TD |
|---|---|---|---|---|
| Warren | 223 | 1017 | 4.6 | 3 |
| Williams | 114 | 339 | 3.0 | 1 |
| Gelbaugh | 16 | 79 | 4.9 | 0 |
| Mayes | 28 | 74 | 2.6 | 0 |
| Stouffer | 9 | 37 | 4.1 | 0 |
| Johnson | 3 | 26 | 8.7 | 0 |
| McGwire | 3 | 13 | 4.3 | 0 |
| D. Thomas | 3 | 7 | 2.3 | 0 |
| Blades | 1 | 5 | 5.0 | 0 |
| Tuten | 1 | 0 | 0.0 | 0 |
| R. Thomas | 1 | -1 | -1.0 | 0 |

### RECEIVING

| Last Name | No. | Yds | Avg | TD |
|---|---|---|---|---|
| Williams | 74 | 556 | 7.5 | 2 |
| Kane | 27 | 369 | 13.7 | 3 |
| J. Jones | 21 | 190 | 9.0 | 0 |
| L. Clark | 20 | 290 | 14.5 | 1 |
| Blades | 19 | 256 | 13.5 | 1 |
| Warren | 16 | 134 | 8.4 | 0 |
| Heller | 12 | 85 | 7.1 | 0 |
| R. Thomas | 11 | 136 | 12.4 | 0 |
| P. Green | 9 | 67 | 7.4 | 1 |
| D. Thomas | 8 | 85 | 10.6 | 0 |
| Daniels | 5 | 99 | 19.8 | 0 |
| Junkin | 3 | 25 | 8.3 | 1 |
| M. Jones | 3 | 18 | 6.0 | 0 |
| Mayes | 2 | 13 | 6.5 | 0 |

### PUNT RETURNS

| Last Name | No. | Yds | Avg | TD |
|---|---|---|---|---|
| Warren | 34 | 252 | 7.4 | 0 |
| Treggs | 4 | 31 | 7.8 | 0 |

### KICKOFF RETURNS

| Last Name | No. | Yds | Avg | TD |
|---|---|---|---|---|
| Warren | 28 | 524 | 18.7 | 0 |
| Mayes | 19 | 311 | 16.4 | 0 |
| D. Thomas | 1 | 19 | 19.0 | 0 |
| J. Jones | 1 | 16 | 16.0 | 0 |
| Johnson | 1 | 15 | 15.0 | 0 |

### PASSING — PUNTING — KICKING Statistics

| PASSING | Att | Cmp | % | Yds | Yd/Att | TD | Int | — | % | RK |
|---|---|---|---|---|---|---|---|---|---|---|
| Gelbaugh | 255 | 121 | 47.5 | 1307 | 5.13 | 6 | 11 | — | 4.3 | 13 |
| Stouffer | 190 | 92 | 48.4 | 900 | 4.74 | 3 | 9 | — | 4.7 | |
| McGwire | 30 | 17 | 56.7 | 116 | 3.87 | 0 | 3 | — | 10.0 | |
| Tuten | 1 | 0 | 0.0 | 0 | 0.00 | 0 | 0 | — | 0.0 | |

| PUNTING | No. | Avg. |
|---|---|---|
| Tuten | 108 | 44.1 |

| KICKING | XP | ATT | % | FG | ATT | % |
|---|---|---|---|---|---|---|
| Kasay | 14 | 14 | 100 | 14 | 22 | 64 |

January 2, 1993 at San Diego (Attendance 58,278)

## SCORING

| | | | | | |
|---|---|---|---|---|---|
| KANSAS CITY | 0 | 0 | 0 | 0 | - 0 |
| SAN DIEGO | 0 | 0 | 10 | 7 | - 17 |

**Third Quarter**
S.D.    Butts, 54 yard run
       PAT — Carney (kick)
S.D.    Carney, 34 yard field goal

**Fourth Quarter**
S.D.    Hendrickson, 5 yard run

## TEAM STATISTICS

| K.C. | | S.D. |
|---|---|---|
| 17 | First Downs- Total | 18 |
| 5 | First Downs- Rushing | 8 |
| 10 | First Downs- Passing | 7 |
| 2 | First Downs- Penalty | 3 |
| 2 | Fumbles- Number | 2 |
| 1 | Fumbles- Lost Ball | 1 |
| 7 | Penalties- Number | 5 |
| 62 | Yards Penalized | 44 |
| 0 | Missed Field Goals | 1 |
| 60 | Offensive Plays | 63 |
| 251 | Net Yards | 342 |
| 4.2 | Average Gain | 5.4 |
| 3 | Giveaways | 1 |
| 1 | Takeaways | 3 |
| -2 | Difference | +2 |

## INDIVIDUAL STATISTICS

**KANSAS CITY**      **SAN DIEGO**

### RUSHING

| | No. | Yds. | Avg. | | No. | Yds. | Avg. |
|---|---|---|---|---|---|---|---|
| Williams | 12 | 35 | 2.9 | Butts | 15 | 119 | 7.9 |
| McNair | 3 | 18 | 6.0 | Bieniemy | 13 | 38 | 2.9 |
| Krieg | 2 | 4 | 2.0 | Harmon | 4 | 27 | 6.8 |
| Word | 2 | 4 | 2.0 | Hendrickson | 1 | 5 | 5.0 |
| | 19 | 61 | 3.2 | Bernstine | 1 | 3 | 3.0 |
| | | | | Humphries | 1 | 0 | 0.0 |
| | | | | | 35 | 192 | 5.5 |

### RECEIVING

| | No. | Yds. | Avg. | | No. | Yds. | Avg. |
|---|---|---|---|---|---|---|---|
| Birden | 4 | 78 | 19.5 | Harmon | 4 | 21 | 5.3 |
| McNair | 4 | 35 | 8.8 | Walker | 3 | 60 | 20.0 |
| Davis | 3 | 30 | 10.0 | Miller | 2 | 58 | 29.0 |
| Hargain | 2 | 46 | 23.0 | Butts | 2 | 17 | 8.5 |
| M. Smith | 1 | 28 | 28.0 | Lewis | 1 | 39 | 39.0 |
| Williams | 1 | 11 | 11.0 | Brennan | 1 | 8 | 8.0 |
| Cash | 1 | 5 | 5.0 | Bieniemy | 1 | -4 | -4.0 |
| | 16 | 233 | 14.6 | | 14 | 199 | 14.2 |

### PUNTING

| | No. | | Avg. | | No. | | Avg. |
|---|---|---|---|---|---|---|---|
| Barker | 8 | | 45.0 | Kidd | 6 | | 44.2 |

### PUNT RETURNS

| | No. | Yds. | Avg. | | No. | Yds. | Avg. |
|---|---|---|---|---|---|---|---|
| Mincy | 1 | 4 | 4.0 | Lewis | 4 | 35 | 8.8 |
| Carter | 1 | 1 | 1.0 | Byrd | 3FC | | |
| | 2 | 5 | 2.5 | | | | |

### KICKOFF RETURNS

| | No. | Yds. | Avg. | |
|---|---|---|---|---|
| Carter | 1 | 5 | 5.0 | None |

### INTERCEPTION RETURNS

| | | No. | Yds. | Avg. |
|---|---|---|---|---|
| None | Carrington | 1 | 40 | 40.0 |
| | O'Neal | 1 | 3 | 3.0 |
| | | 2 | 43 | 21.5 |

### PASSING

**KANSAS CITY**

| | Att. | Comp. | Comp. Pct. | Yds. | Int. | Yds./ Att. | Yds./ Comp. |
|---|---|---|---|---|---|---|---|
| Krieg | 34 | 16 | 47.1 | 233 | 2 | 6.8 | 14.6 |

**SAN DIEGO**

| | Att. | Comp. | Pct. | Yds. | Int. | Att. | Comp. |
|---|---|---|---|---|---|---|---|
| Humphries | 23 | 14 | 60.9 | 199 | 0 | 8.7 | 14.2 |

---

January 3, 1993 at Orchard Park, N.Y. (Attendance 75,141)

## SCORING

| | | | | | | |
|---|---|---|---|---|---|---|
| HOUSTON | 7 | 21 | 7 | 3 | 0 | - 38 |
| BUFFALO | 3 | 0 | 28 | 7 | 3 | - 41 |

**First Quarter**
Hou.    Jeffires, 3 yard pass from Moon
       PAT — Del Greco (kick)
Buff.    Christie, 36 yard field goal

**Second Quarter**
Hou.    Slaughter, 7 yard pass from Moon
       PAT — Del Greco (kick)
Hou.    Duncan, 26 yard pass from Moon
       PAT — Del Greco (kick)
Hou.    Jeffires, 27 yard pass from Moon
       PAT — Del Greco (kick)

**Third Quarter**
Hou.    McDowell, 58 yard interception return
       PAT — Del Greco (kick)
Buff.    K. Davis, 1 yard run
       PAT — Christie (kick)
Buff.    Beebe, 38 yard pass from Reich
       PAT — Christie (kick)
Buff.    Reed, 26 yard pass from Reich
       PAT — Christie (kick)
Buff.    Reed, 18 yard pass from Reich
       PAT — Christie (kick)

**Fourth Quarter**
Buff.    Reed, 17 yard pass from Reich
       PAT — Christie (kick)
Hou.    Del Greco, 26 yard field goal

**Overtime**
Buff.    Christie, 32 yard field goal

## TEAM STATISTICS

| HOU. | | BUFF. |
|---|---|---|
| 27 | First Downs- Total | 19 |
| 6 | First Downs- Rushing | 5 |
| 18 | First Downs- Passing | 13 |
| 3 | First Downs- Penalty | 1 |
| 2 | Fumbles- Number | 0 |
| 0 | Fumbles- Lost Ball | 0 |
| 4 | Penalties- Number | 4 |
| 30 | Yards Penalized | 30 |
| 0 | Missed Field Goals | 0 |
| 76 | Offensive Plays | 63 |
| 429 | Net Yards | 366 |
| 5.6 | Average Gain | 5.8 |
| 2 | Giveaways | 1 |
| 1 | Takeaways | 2 |
| -1 | Difference | +1 |

## INDIVIDUAL STATISTICS

**HOUSTON**      **BUFFALO**

### RUSHING

| | No. | Yds. | Avg. | | No. | Yds. | Avg. |
|---|---|---|---|---|---|---|---|
| White | 19 | 75 | 3.9 | K. Davis | 13 | 68 | 5.2 |
| Moon | 2 | 7 | 3.5 | Thomas | 11 | 26 | 2.4 |
| Montgomery | 1 | 0 | 0.0 | Gardner | 1 | 5 | 5.0 |
| | 22 | 82 | 3.7 | Reich | 1 | -1 | -1.0 |
| | | | | | 26 | 98 | 3.8 |

### RECEIVING

| | No. | Yds. | Avg. | | No. | Yds. | Avg. |
|---|---|---|---|---|---|---|---|
| Givins | 9 | 117 | 13.0 | Reed | 8 | 136 | 17.0 |
| Jeffires | 8 | 98 | 12.3 | Beebe | 4 | 64 | 16.0 |
| Slaughter | 8 | 73 | 9.1 | Metzelaars | 3 | 43 | 14.3 |
| Duncan | 8 | 57 | 7.1 | K. Davis | 2 | 25 | 12.5 |
| Harris | 2 | 15 | 7.5 | Lofton | 2 | 24 | 12.0 |
| White | 1 | 11 | 11.0 | Thomas | 2 | -3 | -1.5 |
| | 36 | 371 | 10.3 | | 21 | 289 | 13.8 |

### PUNTING

| | No. | | Avg. | | No. | | Avg. |
|---|---|---|---|---|---|---|---|
| Montgomery | 2 | | 24.5 | Mohr | 2 | | 35.0 |

### PUNT RETURNS

| | No. | Yds. | Avg. | |
|---|---|---|---|---|
| Slaughter | 1 | 7 | 7.0 | None |
| Slaughter | 1FC | | | |

### KICKOFF RETURNS

| | No. | Yds. | Avg. | | No. | Yds. | Avg. |
|---|---|---|---|---|---|---|---|
| Tillman | 1 | 15 | 15.0 | K. Davis | 2 | 33 | 16.5 |
| D. Lewis | 1 | 7 | 7.0 | Lamb | 1 | 22 | 22.0 |
| Flannery | 1 | 5 | 5.0 | Schulz | 1 | 0 | 0.0 |
| T. Brown | 1 | 0 | 0.0 | Maddox | 1 | 0 | 0.0 |
| | 4 | 27 | 6.8 | | 5 | 55 | 11.0 |

### INTERCEPTION RETURNS

| | No. | Yds. | Avg. | | No. | Yds. | Avg. |
|---|---|---|---|---|---|---|---|
| McDowell | 1 | 58 | 58.0 | Jones | 1 | 15 | 15.0 |
| | | | | Odomes | 1 | 2 | 2.0 |
| | | | | | 2 | 17 | 8.5 |

### PASSING

**HOUSTON**

| | Att. | Comp. | Comp. Pct. | Yds. | Int. | Yds./ Att. | Yds./ Comp. |
|---|---|---|---|---|---|---|---|
| Moon | 50 | 36 | 72.0 | 371 | 2 | 7.4 | 10.3 |

**BUFFALO**

| | Att. | Comp. | Pct. | Yds. | Int. | Att. | Comp. |
|---|---|---|---|---|---|---|---|
| Reich | 34 | 21 | 61.8 | 289 | 1 | 8.5 | 13.8 |

# 1992 N.F.C. PLAYOFFS — FIRST ROUND

January 2, 1993 at Minneapolis (Attendance 57,353)

### SCORING

| | | | | | |
|---|---|---|---|---|---|
| WASHINGTON | 3 | 14 | 7 | 0 - 24 | |
| MINNESOTA | 7 | 0 | 0 | 0 - 7 | |

**First Quarter**
Minn.  Allen, 1 yard run
　　　PAT — Reveiz (kick)
Wash.  Lohmiller, 44 yard field goal

**Second Quarter**
Wash.  Byner, 3 yard run
　　　PAT — Lohmiller (kick)
Wash.  Mitchell, 8 yard run
　　　PAT — Lohmiller (kick)

**Third Quarter**
Wash.  Clark, 24 yard pass from Rypien
　　　PAT — Lohmiller (kick)

### TEAM STATISTICS

| WASH. | | MINN. |
|---|---|---|
| 24 | First Downs- Total | 9 |
| 12 | First Downs- Rushing | 9 |
| 9 | First Downs- Passing | 5 |
| 3 | First Downs- Penalty | 0 |
| 0 | Fumbles- Number | 1 |
| 0 | Fumbles- Lost Ball | 0 |
| 2 | Penalties- Number | 7 |
| 15 | Yards Penalized | 53 |
| 2 | Missed Field Goals | 0 |
| 73 | Offensive Plays | 41 |
| 358 | Net Yards | 148 |
| 4.9 | Average Gain | 3.6 |
| 1 | Giveaways | 2 |
| 2 | Takeaways | 1 |
| +1 | Difference | -1 |

### INDIVIDUAL STATISTICS

**WASHINGTON / MINNESOTA**

RUSHING

| | No. | Yds. | Avg. | | No. | Yds. | Avg. |
|---|---|---|---|---|---|---|---|
| Mitchell | 16 | 109 | 6.8 | Allen | 10 | 48 | 4.8 |
| Byner | 20 | 62 | 3.1 | Craig | 5 | 23 | 4.6 |
| Green | 5 | 17 | 3.4 | J. Johnson | 1 | 2 | 2.0 |
| Monk | 3 | 7 | 2.3 | Salisbury | 1 | 0 | 0.0 |
| Rypien | 3 | 1 | 0.3 | | 17 | 73 | 4.3 |
| | 47 | 196 | 4.2 | | | | |

RECEIVING

| | No. | Yds. | Avg. | | No. | Yds. | Avg. |
|---|---|---|---|---|---|---|---|
| Clark | 6 | 91 | 15.2 | Carter | 3 | 77 | 25.7 |
| Monk | 3 | 35 | 11.7 | Allen | 2 | 11 | 5.5 |
| Mitchell | 3 | 16 | 5.3 | A. Carter | 1 | 25 | 25.0 |
| Byner | 2 | 6 | 3.0 | | 6 | 113 | 18.8 |
| Middleton | 1 | 19 | 19.0 | | | | |
| Sanders | 1 | 5 | 5.0 | | | | |
| | 16 | 172 | 10.8 | | | | |

PUNTING

| | | | | | No. | | Avg. |
|---|---|---|---|---|---|---|---|
| Goodburn | 3 | | 37.0 | Newsome | 7 | | 43.1 |

PUNT RETURNS

| | No. | Yds. | Avg. | | No. | Yds. | Avg. |
|---|---|---|---|---|---|---|---|
| Mitchell | 3 | 70 | 23.3 | Parker | 1 | 13 | 13.0 |
| Mitchell | 3FC | | | Parker | 1FC | | |

KICKOFF RETURNS

| | No. | Yds. | Avg. | | No. | Yds. | Avg. |
|---|---|---|---|---|---|---|---|
| Mitchell | 1 | 14 | 14.0 | Nelson | 3 | 55 | 18.3 |
| Copeland | 1 | 6 | 6.0 | J. Johnson | 2 | 49 | 24.5 |
| | 2 | 20 | 10.0 | | 5 | 104 | 20.8 |

INTERCEPTION RETURNS

| | No. | Yds. | Avg. | | No. | Yds. | Avg. |
|---|---|---|---|---|---|---|---|
| Mayhew | 1 | 44 | 44.0 | Scott | 1 | 21 | 21.0 |
| Edwards | 1 | 6 | 6.0 | | | | |
| | 2 | 50 | 25.0 | | | | |

PASSING

**WASHINGTON**

| | Att. | Comp. | Comp. Pct. | Yds. | Int. | Yds./Att. | Yds./Comp. |
|---|---|---|---|---|---|---|---|
| Rypien | 24 | 16 | 66.7 | 172 | 1 | 7.2 | 10.8 |
| Byner | 1 | 0 | 0.0 | 0 | 0 | 0.0 | 0.0 |
| | 25 | 16 | 64.0 | 172 | 1 | 6.9 | 10.8 |

**MINNESOTA**

| | Att. | Comp. | Comp. Pct. | Yds. | Int. | Yds./Att. | Yds./Comp. |
|---|---|---|---|---|---|---|---|
| Salisbury | 20 | 6 | 30.0 | 113 | 2 | 5.7 | 18.8 |

---

January 3, 1993 at New Orleans (Attendance 68,893)

### SCORING

| | | | | | |
|---|---|---|---|---|---|
| PHILADELPHIA | 7 | 0 | 3 | 26 - 36 | |
| NEW ORLEANS | 7 | 10 | 3 | 0 - 20 | |

**First Quarter**
N.O.  Heyward, 1 yard run
　　　PAT — Andersen (kick)
Phil.  Barnett, 57 yard pass from Cunningham
　　　PAT — Ruzek (kick)

**Second Quarter**
N.O.  Andersen, 35 yard field goal
N.O.  Early, 7 yard pass from Hebert
　　　PAT — Andersen (kick)

**Third Quarter**
N.O.  Andersen, 42 yard field goal
Phil.  Ruzek, 40 yard field goal

**Fourth Quarter**
Phil.  Barnett, 35 yard pass from Cunningham
　　　PAT — Ruzek (kick)
Phil.  Sherman, 6 yard run
　　　PAT — Ruzek (kick)
Phil.  Safety, Hebert sacked by White in end zone
Phil.  Ruzek, 39 yard field goal
Phil.  Allen, 18 yard interception return
　　　PAT — Ruzek (kick)

### TEAM STATISTICS

| PHIL. | | N.O. |
|---|---|---|
| 19 | First Downs- Total | 20 |
| 10 | First Downs- Rushing | 3 |
| 8 | First Downs- Passing | 16 |
| 1 | First Downs- Penalty | 1 |
| 1 | Fumbles- Number | 1 |
| 1 | Fumbles- Lost Ball | 1 |
| 4 | Penalties- Number | 4 |
| 37 | Yards Penalized | 35 |
| 0 | Missed Field Goals | 0 |
| 64 | Offensive Plays | 60 |
| 349 | Net Yards | 360 |
| 5.5 | Average Gain | 6.0 |
| 1 | Giveaways | 4 |
| 4 | Takeaways | 1 |
| +3 | Difference | -3 |

### INDIVIDUAL STATISTICS

**PHILADELPHIA / NEW ORLEANS**

RUSHING

| | No. | Yds. | Avg. | | No. | Yds. | Avg. |
|---|---|---|---|---|---|---|---|
| Sherman | 21 | 105 | 5.0 | Dunbar | 4 | 28 | 7.0 |
| Cunningham | 2 | 19 | 9.5 | Heyward | 10 | 23 | 2.3 |
| Walker | 5 | 12 | 2.4 | Hebert | 3 | 18 | 6.0 |
| | 28 | 136 | 4.9 | Hilliard | 3 | 7 | 2.3 |
| | | | | | 34 | 150 | 4.4 |

RECEIVING

| | No. | Yds. | Avg. | | No. | Yds. | Avg. |
|---|---|---|---|---|---|---|---|
| Byars | 6 | 37 | 6.2 | Early | 7 | 93 | 13.3 |
| Barnett | 4 | 102 | 25.5 | Martin | 5 | 64 | 12.8 |
| Williams | 4 | 36 | 9.0 | Dunbar | 4 | 49 | 12.3 |
| Sherman | 3 | 29 | 9.7 | Heyward | 3 | 45 | 15.0 |
| Green | 1 | 14 | 14.0 | Brenner | 2 | 24 | 12.0 |
| Walker | 1 | 1 | 1.0 | Hilliard | 1 | 10 | 10.0 |
| | 19 | 219 | 11.5 | Small | 1 | 6 | 6.0 |
| | | | | | 23 | 291 | 12.7 |

PUNTING

| | | | | | No. | | Avg. |
|---|---|---|---|---|---|---|---|
| Feagles | 5 | | 51.2 | Barnhardt | 3 | | 45.3 |

PUNT RETURNS

| | No. | Yds. | Avg. | | No. | Yds. | Avg. |
|---|---|---|---|---|---|---|---|
| Sikahema | 2 | 8 | 4.0 | Newman | 3 | 31 | 10.3 |
| | | | | Newman | 1FC | | |

KICKOFF RETURNS

| | No. | Yds. | Avg. | | No. | Yds. | Avg. |
|---|---|---|---|---|---|---|---|
| Sikahema | 3 | 56 | 18.7 | Dunbar | 2 | 48 | 24.0 |
| | | | | Newman | 1 | 16 | 16.0 |
| | | | | | 3 | 64 | 21.3 |

INTERCEPTIONS

| | No. | Yds. | Avg. | | No. | Yds. | Avg. |
|---|---|---|---|---|---|---|---|
| Allen | 2 | 22 | 11.0 | None | | | |
| Joyner | 1 | 14 | 14.0 | | | | |
| | 3 | 36 | 12.0 | | | | |

PASSING

**PHILADELPHIA**

| | Att. | Comp. | Comp. Pct. | Yds. | Int. | Yds./Att. | Yds./Comp. |
|---|---|---|---|---|---|---|---|
| Cunningham | 35 | 19 | 54.3 | 219 | 0 | 6.3 | 11.5 |

**NEW ORLEANS**

| | Att. | Comp. | Comp. Pct. | Yds. | Int. | Yds./Att. | Yds./Comp. |
|---|---|---|---|---|---|---|---|
| Hebert | 39 | 23 | 59.0 | 291 | 3 | 7.5 | 12.7 |

January 9, 1993 at Pittsburgh (Attendance 60,407)

## SCORING

| | | | | | | |
|---|---|---|---|---|---|---|
| **BUFFALO** | 0 | 7 | 7 | 10 | - | 24 |
| **PITTSBURGH** | 3 | 0 | 0 | 0 | - | 3 |

**First Quarter**
Pit.    Anderson, 38 yard field goal

**Second Quarter**
Buff.    Frerotte, 1 yard pass from Reich
      PAT — Christie (kick)

**Third Quarter**
Buff.    Lofton, 17 yard pass from Reich
      PAT — Christie (kick)

**Fourth Quarter**
Buff.    Christie, 43 yard field goal
Buff.    Gardner, 1 yard run
      PAT — Christie (kick)

January 10, 1993 at Miami (Attendance 71,224)

## SCORING

| | | | | | | |
|---|---|---|---|---|---|---|
| **SAN DIEGO** | 0 | 0 | 0 | 0 | - | 0 |
| **MIAMI** | 0 | 21 | 0 | 10 | - | 31 |

**Second Quarter**
Mia.    Paige, 1 yard pass from Marino
      PAT — Stoyanovich (kick)
Mia.    Jackson, 9 yard pass from Marino
      PAT — Stoyanovich (kick)
Mia.    Jackson, 30 yard pass from Marino
      PAT — Stoyanovich (kick)

**Fourth Quarter**
Mia.    Stoyanovich, 22 yard field goal
Mia.    Craver, 25 yard run
      PAT — Stoyanovich (kick)

## TEAM STATISTICS

| BUFF. | | PITT. |
|---|---|---|
| 19 | First Downs- Total | 18 |
| 7 | First Downs- Rushing | 7 |
| 11 | First Downs- Passing | 10 |
| 1 | First Downs- Penalty | 1 |
| 0 | Fumbles- Number | 4 |
| 0 | Fumbles- Lost Ball | 1 |
| 4 | Penalties- Number | 2 |
| 33 | Yards Penalized | 23 |
| 0 | Missed Field Goals | 0 |
| 63 | Offensive Plays | 63 |
| 325 | Net Yards | 240 |
| 5.2 | Average Gain | 3.8 |
| 0 | Giveaways | 3 |
| 3 | Takeaways | 0 |
| +3 | Difference | -3 |

## TEAM STATISTICS

| S.D. | | MIA. |
|---|---|---|
| 10 | First Downs- Total | 18 |
| 3 | First Downs- Rushing | 9 |
| 7 | First Downs- Passing | 9 |
| 0 | First Downs- Penalty | 0 |
| 3 | Fumbles- Number | 3 |
| 1 | Fumbles- Lost Ball | 1 |
| 4 | Penalties- Number | 0 |
| 39 | Yards Penalized | 0 |
| 0 | Missed Field Goals | 0 |
| 62 | Offensive Plays | 69 |
| 202 | Net Yards | 324 |
| 3.3 | Average Gain | 4.7 |
| 5 | Giveaways | 1 |
| 1 | Takeaways | 5 |
| - 4 | Difference | +4 |

## INDIVIDUAL STATISTICS

### BUFFALO / PITTSBURGH

**RUSHING**

| | No. | Yds. | Avg. | | No. | Yds. | Avg. |
|---|---|---|---|---|---|---|---|
| K. Davis | 10 | 104 | 10.4 | Foster | 20 | 104 | 5.2 |
| Thomas | 19 | 54 | 2.8 | O'Donnell | 4 | 26 | 6.5 |
| Gardner | 7 | 22 | 3.1 | Thompson | 1 | 3 | 3.0 |
| Reich | 2 | -3 | -1.5 | Royals | 1 | 0 | 0.0 |
| Reed | 1 | -8 | -8.0 | Stone | 1 | -4 | -4.0 |
| | 39 | 169 | 4.3 | | 27 | 129 | 4.8 |

**RECEIVING**

| | No. | Yds. | Avg. | | No. | Yds. | Avg. |
|---|---|---|---|---|---|---|---|
| Beebe | 6 | 72 | 12.0 | Mills | 8 | 93 | 11.6 |
| Thomas | 3 | 25 | 8.3 | Davenport | 3 | 54 | 18.0 |
| Lofton | 2 | 29 | 14.5 | Foster | 3 | 7 | 2.3 |
| McKeller | 2 | 22 | 11.0 | Stone | 1 | 9 | 9.0 |
| Metzelaars | 2 | 11 | 5.5 | | 15 | 163 | 10.9 |
| Frerotte | 1 | 1 | 1.0 | | | | |
| | 16 | 160 | 10.0 | | | | |

**PUNTING**

| | No. | | Avg. | | No. | | Avg. |
|---|---|---|---|---|---|---|---|
| Mohr | 4 | | 42.3 | Royals | 3 | | 37.3 |

**PUNT RETURNS**

| | No. | Yds. | Avg. | | No. | Yds. | Avg. |
|---|---|---|---|---|---|---|---|
| Hicks | 1FC | | | Woodson | 2 | 14 | 7.0 |
| | | | | Thigpen | 1FC | | |

**KICKOFF RETURNS**

| | No. | Yds. | Avg. | | No. | Yds. | Avg. |
|---|---|---|---|---|---|---|---|
| Lamb | 1 | 24 | 24.0 | Stone | 3 | 65 | 21.7 |
| Davis | 1 | 18 | 18.0 | Thompson | 1 | 20 | 20.0 |
| | 2 | 42 | 21.0 | Thigpen | 1 | 14 | 14.0 |
| | | | | | 5 | 99 | 19.8 |

**INTERCEPTION RETURNS**

| | No. | Yds. | Avg. |
|---|---|---|---|
| Odomes | 1 | 1 | 1.0 |
| Williams | 1 | 0 | 0.0 |
| | 2 | 1 | 0.5 |

**PASSING**

BUFFALO

| | Att. | Comp. | Comp. Pct. | Yds. | Int. | Yds./ Att. | Yds./ Comp. |
|---|---|---|---|---|---|---|---|
| Reich | 23 | 16 | 69.6 | 160 | 0 | 7.0 | 10.0 |

PITTSBURGH

| | Att. | Comp. | Comp. Pct. | Yds. | Int. | Yds./ Att. | Yds./ Comp. |
|---|---|---|---|---|---|---|---|
| O'Donnell | 29 | 15 | 51.7 | 163 | 2 | 5.6 | 10.9 |

## INDIVIDUAL STATISTICS

### SAN DIEGO / MIAMI

**RUSHING**

| | No. | Yds. | Avg. | | No. | Yds. | Avg. |
|---|---|---|---|---|---|---|---|
| Bieniemy | 4 | 26 | 6.5 | Craver | 8 | 72 | 9.0 |
| Butts | 7 | 25 | 3.6 | Humphrey | 23 | 71 | 3.1 |
| Humphries | 1 | 10 | 10.0 | Parmalee | 5 | 18 | 3.6 |
| Harmon | 4 | 9 | 2.3 | Clayton | 1 | 0 | 0.0 |
| | 16 | 70 | 4.4 | Mitchell | 1 | -1 | -1.0 |
| | | | | Saxon | 2 | -3 | -1.5 |
| | | | | | 40 | 157 | 3.9 |

**RECEIVING**

| | No. | Yds. | Avg. | | No. | Yds. | Avg. |
|---|---|---|---|---|---|---|---|
| Harmon | 9 | 73 | 8.1 | Paige | 5 | 14 | 2.8 |
| Walker | 3 | 33 | 11.0 | Jackson | 4 | 53 | 13.3 |
| Lewis | 2 | 12 | 6.0 | Humphrey | 4 | 30 | 7.5 |
| Miller | 2 | 12 | 6.0 | Duper | 3 | 57 | 19.0 |
| Jefferson | 1 | 10 | 10.0 | Craver | 1 | 13 | 13.0 |
| Butts | 1 | 0 | 0.0 | | 17 | 167 | 9.8 |
| | 18 | 140 | 7.8 | | | | |

**PUNTING**

| | No. | | Avg. | | No. | | Avg. |
|---|---|---|---|---|---|---|---|
| Kidd | 7 | | 46.3 | Roby | 8 | | 41.0 |

**PUNT RETURNS**

| | No. | Yds. | Avg. | | No. | Yds. | Avg. |
|---|---|---|---|---|---|---|---|
| Lewis | 1 | 7 | 7.0 | Miller | 5 | 45 | 9.0 |
| Lewis | 2FC | | | | | | |

**KICKOFF RETURNS**

| | No. | Yds. | Avg. | | No. | Yds. | Avg. |
|---|---|---|---|---|---|---|---|
| Lewis | 4 | 111 | 27.8 | Craver | 1 | 18 | 18.0 |
| Bieniemy | 1 | 14 | 14.0 | | | | |
| Pupunu | 1 | 11 | 11.0 | | | | |
| | 6 | 136 | 22.7 | | | | |

**INTERCEPTION RETURNS**

| | No. | Yds. | Avg. |
|---|---|---|---|
| None | | | |
| Vincent | 2 | 2 | 1.0 |
| Oliver | 1 | 21 | 21.0 |
| Cox | 1 | 7 | 7.0 |
| | 4 | 30 | 7.5 |

**PASSING**

SAN DIEGO

| | Att. | Comp. | Comp. Pct. | Yds. | Int. | Yds./ Att. | Yds./ Comp. |
|---|---|---|---|---|---|---|---|
| Humphries | 44 | 18 | 40.9 | 140 | 4 | 3.2 | 7.8 |
| Kidd | 1 | 0 | 0.0 | 0 | 0 | 0.0 | 0.0 |
| | 29 | 14 | 48.3 | 146 | 4 | 5.0 | 10.4 |

MIAMI

| | Att. | Comp. | Comp. Pct. | Yds. | Int. | Yds./ Att. | Yds./ Comp. |
|---|---|---|---|---|---|---|---|
| Marino | 29 | 17 | 58.6 | 167 | 0 | 5.8 | 9.8 |

January 9, 1993 at San Francisco (Attendance 64,991)

### SCORING

| | | | | | |
|---|---|---|---|---|---|
| WASHINGTON | 3 | 0 | 3 | 7 | - 13 |
| SAN FRANCISCO | 7 | 10 | 0 | 3 | - 20 |

**First Quarter**
S.F. — Taylor, 5 yard pass from Young
PAT — Cofer (kick)
Wash. — Lohmiller, 19 yard field goal

**Second Quarter**
S.F. — Cofer, 23 yard field goal
S.F. — Jones, 16 yard pass from Young
PAT — Cofer (kick)

**Third Quarter**
Wash. — Lohmiller, 32 yard field goal

**Fourth Quarter**
Wash. — Rypien, 1 yard run
PAT — Lohmiller (kick)
S.F. — Cofer, 33 yard field goal

### TEAM STATISTICS

| WASH. | | S.F. |
|---|---|---|
| 20 | First Downs- Total | 22 |
| 4 | First Downs- Rushing | 10 |
| 15 | First Downs- Passing | 12 |
| 1 | First Downs- Penalty | 0 |
| 3 | Fumbles- Number | 4 |
| 2 | Fumbles- Lost Ball | 3 |
| 4 | Penalties- Number | 4 |
| 23 | Yards Penalized | 35 |
| 0 | Missed Field Goals | 0 |
| 67 | Offensive Plays | 63 |
| 323 | Net Yards | 401 |
| 4.8 | Average Gain | 6.4 |
| 4 | Giveaways | 4 |
| 4 | Takeaways | 4 |
| 0 | Difference | 0 |

### INDIVIDUAL STATISTICS

**WASHINGTON** / **SAN FRANCISCO**

#### RUSHING

| | No. | Yds. | Avg. | | No. | Yds. | Avg. |
|---|---|---|---|---|---|---|---|
| Mitchell | 8 | 38 | 4.8 | Watters | 18 | 83 | 4.6 |
| Byner | 9 | 29 | 3.2 | Young | 8 | 73 | 9.1 |
| Rypien | 3 | 3 | 1.0 | Rathman | 4 | 22 | 5.5 |
| Monk | 1 | 3 | 3.0 | Rice | 1 | 9 | 9.0 |
| | 21 | 73 | 3.5 | | 31 | 187 | 6.0 |

#### RECEIVING

| | No. | Yds. | Avg. | | No. | Yds. | Avg. |
|---|---|---|---|---|---|---|---|
| Clark | 7 | 100 | 14.3 | Rice | 6 | 88 | 14.7 |
| Byner | 3 | 45 | 15.0 | Jones | 4 | 64 | 16.0 |
| Mitchell | 3 | 39 | 13.0 | Rathman | 4 | 30 | 7.5 |
| Sanders | 3 | 33 | 11.0 | Taylor | 4 | 26 | 6.5 |
| Monk | 2 | 44 | 22.0 | Watters | 2 | 19 | 9.5 |
| Thomas | 1 | 10 | 10.0 | | 20 | 227 | 11.4 |
| Middleton | 1 | 9 | 9.0 | | | | |
| | 20 | 280 | 14.0 | | | | |

#### PUNTING

| | | | | | | |
|---|---|---|---|---|---|---|
| Goodburn | 2 | 36.0 | Wilmsmeyer | 2 | | 40.0 |

#### PUNT RETURNS

| | | | |
|---|---|---|---|
| None | | None | |

#### KICKOFF RETURNS

| | No. | Yds. | Avg. | | No. | Yds. | Avg. |
|---|---|---|---|---|---|---|---|
| Mitchell | 4 | 75 | 18.8 | Logan | 2 | 27 | 13.5 |
| Copeland | 1 | 9 | 9.0 | | | | |
| | 5 | 84 | 16.8 | | | | |

#### INTERCEPTION RETURNS

| | No. | Yds. | Avg. | | No. | Yds. | Avg. |
|---|---|---|---|---|---|---|---|
| Johnson | 1 | 0 | 0.0 | Davis | 1 | 2 | 2.0 |
| | | | | Whitmore | 1 | 2 | 2.0 |
| | | | | | 2 | 4 | 2.0 |

#### PASSING

**WASHINGTON**

| | Att. | Comp. | Comp. Pct. | Yds. | Int. | Yds./ Att. | Yds./ Comp. |
|---|---|---|---|---|---|---|---|
| Rypien | 40 | 19 | 47.5 | 270 | 2 | 6.8 | 14.2 |
| Goodburn | 1 | 1 | 100.0 | 10 | 0 | 10.0 | 10.0 |
| | 41 | 20 | 48.8 | 280 | 2 | 6.8 | 14.0 |

**SAN FRANCISCO**

| | Att. | Comp. | Comp. Pct. | Yds. | Int. | Yds./ Att. | Yds./ Comp. |
|---|---|---|---|---|---|---|---|
| Young | 30 | 20 | 66.7 | 227 | 1 | 7.6 | 11.4 |

---

January 10, 1993 at Dallas (Attendance 63,721)

### SCORING

| | | | | | |
|---|---|---|---|---|---|
| PHILADELPHIA | 3 | 0 | 0 | 7 | - 10 |
| DALLAS | 7 | 10 | 10 | 7 | - 34 |

**First Quarter**
Phil. — Ruzek, 32 yard field goal
Dall. — Tennell, 1 yard pass from Aikman
PAT — Elliott (kick)

**Second Quarter**
Dall. — Novacek, 6 yard pass from Aikman
PAT — Elliott (kick)
Dall. — Elliott, 20 yard field goal

**Third Quarter**
Dall. — Smith, 23 yard run
PAT — Elliott (kick)
Dall. — Elliott, 43 yard field goal

**Fourth Quarter**
Dall. — Gainer, 1 yard run
PAT — Elliott (kick)
Phil. — Williams, 18 yard pass from Cunningham
PAT — Ruzek (kick)

### TEAM STATISTICS

| PHIL. | | DAL. |
|---|---|---|
| 12 | First Downs- Total | 22 |
| 5 | First Downs- Rushing | 10 |
| 6 | First Downs- Passing | 11 |
| 1 | First Downs- Penalty | 1 |
| 4 | Fumbles- Number | 2 |
| 2 | Fumbles- Lost Ball | 1 |
| 6 | Penalties- Number | 5 |
| 76 | Yards Penalized | 30 |
| 0 | Missed Field Goals | 0 |
| 52 | Offensive Plays | 65 |
| 178 | Net Yards | 346 |
| 3.4 | Average Gain | 5.3 |
| 2 | Giveaways | 1 |
| 1 | Takeaways | 2 |
| -1 | Difference | +1 |

### INDIVIDUAL STATISTICS

**PHILADELPHIA** / **DALLAS**

#### RUSHING

| | No. | Yds. | Avg. | | No. | Yds. | Avg. |
|---|---|---|---|---|---|---|---|
| Walker | 6 | 29 | 4.8 | E. Smith | 25 | 114 | 4.6 |
| Cunningham | 5 | 22 | 4.4 | Gainer | 9 | 29 | 3.2 |
| Sherman | 6 | 12 | 2.0 | Aikman | 3 | 13 | 4.3 |
| | 17 | 63 | 3.7 | Johnston | 1 | 4 | 4.0 |
| | | | | | 38 | 160 | 4.2 |

#### RECEIVING

| | No. | Yds. | Avg. | | No. | Yds. | Avg. |
|---|---|---|---|---|---|---|---|
| Walker | 6 | 37 | 6.2 | Irvin | 6 | 88 | 14.7 |
| Williams | 4 | 48 | 12.0 | Novacek | 3 | 36 | 12.0 |
| Barnett | 4 | 44 | 11.0 | Martin | 3 | 27 | 9.0 |
| Byars | 3 | 31 | 10.3 | Harper | 1 | 41 | 41.0 |
| | 17 | 160 | 9.4 | Johnston | 1 | 7 | 7.0 |
| | | | | Tennell | 1 | 1 | 1.0 |
| | | | | | 15 | 200 | 13.3 |

#### PUNTING

| | | | | | | |
|---|---|---|---|---|---|---|
| Feagles | 7 | 40.9 | Saxon | 4 | | 42.8 |

#### PUNT RETURNS

| | No. | Yds. | Avg. | | No. | Yds. | Avg. |
|---|---|---|---|---|---|---|---|
| Sikahema | 4 | 24 | 6.0 | Martin | 1 | 5 | 5.0 |
| | | | | Washington 1FC | | | |

#### KICKOFF RETURNS

| | No. | Yds. | Avg. | | No. | Yds. | Avg. |
|---|---|---|---|---|---|---|---|
| Sikahema | 5 | 81 | 16.2 | Martin | 2 | 60 | 30.0 |
| Sydner | 1 | 29 | 29.0 | K. Smith | 1 | 0 | 0.0 |
| | 6 | 110 | 18.3 | | 3 | 60 | 20.0 |

#### INTERCEPTION RETURNS

| | | | |
|---|---|---|---|
| None | | None | |

#### PASSING

**PHILADELPHIA**

| | Att. | Comp. | Comp. Pct. | Yds. | Int. | Yds./ Att. | Yds./ Comp. |
|---|---|---|---|---|---|---|---|
| Cunningham | 30 | 17 | 56.7 | 160 | 0 | 5.3 | 9.4 |

**DALLAS**

| | Att. | Comp. | Comp. Pct. | Yds. | Int. | Yds./ Att. | Yds./ Comp. |
|---|---|---|---|---|---|---|---|
| Aikman | 25 | 15 | 60.0 | 200 | 0 | 8.0 | 13.3 |

# 1992 Championship Games

## A.F.C. CHAMPIONSHIP GAME
January 17, 1993 at Miami, Fla.
(Attendance 72,703)

## SCORING

| | | | | | |
|---|---|---|---|---|---|
| BUFFALO | 3 | 10 | 10 | 6 - | 29 |
| MIAMI | 3 | 0 | 0 | 7 - | 10 |

**First Quarter**
Buff.   Christie, 21 yard field goal
Mia.    Stoyanovich, 51 yard field goal

**Second Quarter**
Buff.   Thomas, 17 yard pass from Kelly
        PAT — Christie (kick)
Buff.   Christie, 33 yard field goal

**Third Quarter**
Buff.   Davis, 2 yard run
        PAT — Christie (kick)
Buff.   Christie, 21 yard field goal

**Fourth Quarter**
Buff.   Christie, 31 yard field goal
Mia.    Duper, 15 yard pass from Marino
        PAT — Stoyanovich (kick)
Buff.   Christie, 38 yard field goal

## TEAM STATISTICS

| BUFF. | | MIA. |
|---|---|---|
| 20 | First Downs- Total | 15 |
| 10 | First Downs- Rushing | 1 |
| 8 | First Downs- Passing | 14 |
| 2 | First Downs- Penalty | 0 |
| 1 | Fumbles- Number | 4 |
| 0 | Fumbles- Lost Ball | 3 |
| 3 | Penalties- Number | 5 |
| 20 | Yards Penalized | 40 |
| 1 | Missed Field Goals | 0 |
| 73 | Offensive Plays | 60 |
| 358 | Net Yards | 276 |
| 4.9 | Average Gain | 4.6 |
| 2 | Giveaways | 5 |
| 5 | Takeaways | 2 |
| +3 | Difference | -3 |

The Buffalo Bills qualified for a record-tying third straight Super Bowl with a convincing 29-10 victory over the Miami Dolphins.

The Bills became the fourth wild-card team to make it to the Super Bowl.

On defense, Buffalo end Bruce Smith played like Superman, with seven tackles, one and a half sacks, a forced fumble and a blocked pass.

On offense, Thurman Thomas, the NFL's total offense leader the last four seasons, showed why with 96 yards rushing and 70 more on five pass receptions.

And back on offense was quarterback Jim Kelly, after missing two and a half games with a knee injury. His 17-for-24 performance for 177 yards blunted any criticism of coach Marv Levy for starting him over Frank Reich, who had led the Bills to their first two playoff victories. Kelly threw a 17-yard TD pass to Thomas.

Kenneth Davis had a two-yard touchdown run and Steve Christie tied a playoff record with five field goals, from distances of 21, 33, 21, 31 and 38 yards.

The Buffalo defense was virtually inpenetrable, flustering Miami quarterback Dan Marino all game and sacking him four times.

The Dolphins, champions of the AFC East and seeking their first AFC title since 1984, hurt themselves with five turnovers. Marino was only 22 of 45 for 268 yards. He threw a 15-yard TD pass to Mark Duper.

"I think this team has really matured a lot and is ready to go out and win a Super Bowl," said Kelly.

## INDIVIDUAL STATISTICS

| BUFFALO | | | | MIAMI | | | |
|---|---|---|---|---|---|---|---|
| | No. | Yds. | Avg. | | No. | Yds. | Avg. |
| **RUSHING** | | | | | | | |
| Thomas | 20 | 96 | 4.8 | Humphrey | 8 | 22 | 2.8 |
| K. Davis | 19 | 61 | 3.2 | Craver | 2 | 13 | 6.5 |
| Lamb | 1 | 16 | 16.0 | Marino | 1 | -2 | -2.0 |
| Reed | 2 | 6 | 3.0 | | 11 | 33 | 3.0 |
| Kelly | 3 | 4 | 1.3 | | | | |
| Gardner | 3 | -1 | -0.3 | | | | |
| | 48 | 182 | 3.8 | | | | |
| **RECEIVING** | | | | | | | |
| Thomas | 5 | 70 | 14.0 | Jackson | 5 | 71 | 14.2 |
| K. Davis | 4 | 52 | 13.0 | Humphrey | 5 | 41 | 8.2 |
| Reed | 3 | 25 | 8.3 | Martin | 3 | 55 | 18.3 |
| Lofton | 2 | 19 | 9.5 | Clayton | 3 | 32 | 10.7 |
| McKeller | 1 | 11 | 11.0 | Duper | 2 | 36 | 18.0 |
| Metzelaars | 1 | 6 | 6.0 | Banks | 2 | 18 | 9.0 |
| Gardner | 1 | -6 | -6.0 | Craver | 2 | 15 | 7.5 |
| | 17 | 177 | 10.4 | | 22 | 268 | 12.2 |
| **PUNTING** | | | | | | | |
| Mohr | 2 | | 34.5 | Roby | 4 | | 37.0 |
| **PUNT RETURNS** | | | | | | | |
| Hicks | 1 | 16 | 16.0 | Miller | 1 | 14 | 14.0 |
| Hale | 1FC | | | Miller | 1FC | | |
| **KICKOFF RETURNS** | | | | | | | |
| Lamb | 1 | 36 | 36.0 | Craver | 4 | 48 | 12.0 |
| Davis | 2 | 23 | 23.0 | M. Williams | 3 | 64 | 21.3 |
| | 3 | 59 | 29.5 | | 7 | 112 | 16.0 |
| **INTERCEPTION RETURNS** | | | | | | | |
| Hicks | 1 | 31 | 31.0 | Brown | 1 | 32 | 32.0 |
| Hansen | 1 | 0 | 0.0 | Oliver | 1 | 0 | 0.0 |
| | 2 | 31 | 15.5 | | 2 | 32 | 16.0 |

**PASSING**

| BUFFALO | Att. | Comp. | Comp. Pct. | Yds. | Int. | Yds./ Att. | Yds./ Comp. |
|---|---|---|---|---|---|---|---|
| Kelly | 24 | 17 | 70.8 | 177 | 2 | 7.4 | 10.4 |
| **MIAMI** | | | | | | | |
| Marino | 45 | 22 | 48.9 | 268 | 2 | 6.0 | 12.2 |

---

## N.F.C. CHAMPIONSHIP GAME
January 17, 1993 at San Francisco, Calif.
(Attendance 64,920)

## SCORING

| | | | | | |
|---|---|---|---|---|---|
| DALLAS | 3 | 7 | 7 | 13 - | 30 |
| SAN FRANCISCO | 7 | 3 | 3 | 7 - | 20 |

**First Quarter**
Dall.   Elliott, 20 yard field goal
S.F.    Young, 1 yard run
        PAT — Cofer (kick)

**Second Quarter**
Dall.   E. Smith, 4 yard run
        PAT — Elliott (kick)
S.F.    Cofer, 28 yard field goal

**Third Quarter**
Dall.   Johnston, 3 yard run
        PAT — Elliott (kick)
S.F.    Cofer, 42 yard field goal

**Fourth Quarter**
Dall.   E. Smith, 16 yard pass from Aikman
        PAT — Elliott (kick)
S.F.    Rice, 5 yard pass from Young
        PAT — Cofer (kick)
Dall.   Martin, 6 yard pass from Aikman
        PAT — kick blocked

## TEAM STATISTICS

| DALL. | | S.F. |
|---|---|---|
| 24 | First Downs- Total | 24 |
| 7 | First Downs- Rushing | 8 |
| 16 | First Downs- Passing | 16 |
| 1 | First Downs- Penalty | 0 |
| 1 | Fumbles- Number | 2 |
| 0 | Fumbles- Lost Ball | 2 |
| 4 | Penalties- Number | 4 |
| 25 | Yards Penalized | 38 |
| 1 | Missed Field Goals | 0 |
| 68 | Offensive Plays | 59 |
| 416 | Net Yards | 415 |
| 6.1 | Average Gain | 7.0 |
| 0 | Giveaways | 4 |
| 4 | Takeaways | 0 |
| +4 | Difference | -4 |

The Dallas Cowboys capped their rise from the NFL's depths at the same spot their downfall began. The Cowboys, the NFL's youngest team, qualified for their first Super Bowl in 14 years with a 30-20 victory over the San Francisco 49ers, the team that dominated the 1980s. Dallas was just 1-15 just three years ago.

Dallas' slide from the top to bottom began 11 years earlier in San Francisco when Dwight Clark made "The Catch" that put the 49ers in the first of the four Super Bowls they won.

Dallas got to its record sixth Super Bowl thanks in large part to Troy Aikman, Emmitt Smith and two perfect second-half touchdown drives with a San Francisco field goal sandwiched in between.

Those long drives broke open a game that was tied 10-10 at halftime. Aikman was 24 of 34 for 322 yards and two touchdowns.

For the 49ers, whose 14-2 regular-season record was the league's best, it was simply a case of not being able to stop the Dallas offense and not converting their own third downs. San Francisco also lost the ball four times on two interceptions and two fumbles.

The Cowboys' two drives in the second half were 78 yards in eight plays, capped by a three-yard TD run by Daryl Johnston, and then a nine-minute march that ended in a 16-yard TD pass from Aikman to Smith.

San Francisco had several early chances to break the game open but failed, including a touchdown that was called back on its first drive.

Steve Young, who completed 25 of 35 passes for 313 yards, ran for a touchdown and threw one to Jerry Rice.

For the first time since the first Super Bowl, the visiting teams won both conference title games.

## INDIVIDUAL STATISTICS

| DALLAS | | | | SAN FRANCISCO | | | |
|---|---|---|---|---|---|---|---|
| | No. | Yds. | Avg. | | No. | Yds. | Avg. |
| **RUSHING** | | | | | | | |
| E. Smith | 24 | 114 | 4.8 | Watters | 11 | 69 | 6.3 |
| Johnston | 2 | 7 | 3.5 | Young | 8 | 33 | 4.1 |
| Harper | 1 | 3 | 3.0 | Rathman | 1 | 6 | 6.0 |
| Aikman | 3 | -3 | -3.0 | Lee | 1 | 6 | 6.0 |
| | 30 | 121 | 4.0 | | 21 | 114 | 5.4 |
| **RECEIVING** | | | | | | | |
| E. Smith | 7 | 59 | 8.4 | Rice | 8 | 123 | 15.4 |
| Irvin | 6 | 86 | 14.3 | Watters | 6 | 69 | 11.5 |
| Johnston | 4 | 26 | 6.5 | Rathman | 4 | 33 | 8.3 |
| Harper | 3 | 117 | 39.0 | Jones | 3 | 40 | 13.3 |
| Novacek | 3 | 28 | 9.3 | Taylor | 3 | 33 | 11.0 |
| K. Martin | 1 | 6 | 6.0 | Sherrard | 1 | 15 | 15.0 |
| | 24 | 322 | 13.4 | | 25 | 313 | 12.5 |
| **PUNTING** | | | | | | | |
| Saxon | 4 | | 35.8 | Wilmsmeyer | 1 | | 57.0 |
| **PUNT RETURNS** | | | | | | | |
| K. Martin | 1 | 8 | 8.0 | Grant | 3 | 30 | 10.0 |
| | | | | Grant | 1FC | | |
| **KICKOFF RETURNS** | | | | | | | |
| K. Martin | 3 | 62 | 20.7 | Logan | 3 | 79 | 26.3 |
| K. Smith | 1 | 11 | 11.0 | Grant | 2 | 35 | 17.5 |
| | 4 | 73 | 18.3 | | 5 | 114 | 22.8 |
| **INTERCEPTION RETURNS** | | | | | | | |
| Washington | 1 | 21 | 21.0 | None | | | |
| Norton | 1 | 14 | 14.0 | | | | |
| | 2 | 35 | 17.5 | | | | |

**PASSING**

| DALLAS | Att. | Comp. | Comp. Pct. | Yds. | Int. | Yds./ Att. | Yds./ Comp. |
|---|---|---|---|---|---|---|---|
| Aikman | 34 | 24 | 70.6 | 322 | 0 | 9.5 | 13.4 |
| **SAN FRANCISCO** | | | | | | | |
| Young | 35 | 25 | 71.4 | 313 | 2 | 8.9 | 12.5 |

# Another Super Blowout

If the NFC team won …

If it was a blowout that was decided by halftime …

If the quarterback was the Most Valuable Player …

Then it had to be the Super Bowl.

Which means it wasn't all that super.

The Dallas Cowboys' 52-17 win over the Buffalo Bills in Super Bowl XXVII was another in a long list of NFC victories over the AFC — nine consecutive victories dating back to Super Bowl XVIII. It might also mark the start of a dynasty for Dallas.

For the Bills, it was another tragic loss in the nation's premier sports spectacle. They lost their quarterback and lost their spirit. And they lost in a Super Bowl for the third time in a row, the first team with that ignominious record.

Super Bowl XXVII had the makings of a truly great game until just before halftime. That's when Buffalo became unglued and Dallas turned an uneasy 14-10 lead into a 28-10 rout that continued throughout the second half.

Buffalo lost the ball nine times — five fumbles and four interceptions — and they led directly to five Dallas touchdowns. The most costly turnover was a Jim Kelly interception on a fourth-down play at the Dallas one-yard line early in the second quarter.

"You turn the ball over the way we did, there's no way you're going to win the game," said Kelly, who was injured in the second quarter and sat out the rest of the game. "It's a loss. It doesn't matter if you lose by three points or 30 or 20. Nobody likes to lose."

It was another story for the Cowboys, who returned to the Super Bowl after a 13-year absence and only three seasons removed from a 1-15 record.

Troy Aikman threw four touchdown passes on 22 of 30 passing for 273 yards and no interceptions and was voted the game's MVP. He threw TD passes of 18 and 19 yards to Michael Irvin, 23 yards to Jay Novacek and 45 yards to Alvin Harper.

"Troy was definitely in a zone," said Dallas running back Emmitt Smith, who rushed for 108 yards on 22 carries and scored on a 10-yard run.

But the Dallas defense was the story of the day. Defensive end Jimmie Jones scored on a two-yard return of a Kelly fumble, and linebacker Ken Norton ended the scoring on a nine-yard return of a Frank Reich fumble. Dallas' Leon Lett almost scored on a 65-yard fumble return, but he had the ball stripped from him just before he reached the goal line.

"Any time you have nine turnovers, you don't have a chance in the world, even if you have every great player in the league on your team," said Buffalo linebacker Cornelius Bennett.

Buffalo opened the scoring on a two-yard run by Thurman Thomas, who gained only 19 yards on 11 carries. Don Beebe scored Buffalo's other touchdown on a 40-yard pass from Reich, and Steve Christie added a 21-yard field goal.

Dallas' margin of victory was the third-largest in a Super Bowl.

## LINEUPS

| BUFF. | | DALL. |
|---|---|---|
| | OFFENSE | |
| Lofton | WR | Harper |
| Wolford | LT | Tuinei |
| Ritcher | LG | Newton |
| Hull | C | Stepnoski |
| Parker | RG | Gesek |
| Ballard | RT | Williams |
| Metzelaars | TE | Novacek |
| Reed | WR | Irvin |
| Kelly | QB | Aikman |
| Thomas | RB | E. Smith |
| Beebe | WR/RB | Johnston |
| | DEFENSE | |
| Hansen | LE | Tolbert |
| Wright | NT/LT | Casillas |
| B. Smith | RE/RT | Maryland |
| Patton | LOLB/RE | Haley |
| Conlan | LILB/LLB | V. Smith |
| Bennett | RILB/MLB | R. Jones |
| Talley | ROLB/RLB | Norton |
| J. Williams | LCB | K. Smith |
| Odomes | RCB | L. Brown |
| Jones | SS | Washington |
| Kelso | FS | Everett |
| | SUBSTITUTES | |
| BUFFALO | | |
| | OFFENSE | |
| Reich | K. Davis | Gardner |
| Frerotte | Lingner | J. Davis |
| Fina | Lamb | McKeller |
| Awalt | Tasker | |
| | DEFENSE | |
| Hale | Hicks | Darby |
| K. Jackson | Bailey | Maddox |
| Lodish | Pike | Goganious |
| | KICKERS | |
| Christie | Mohr | |
| DALLAS | | |
| | OFFENSE | |
| Beuerlein | Agee | Gainer |
| Gogan | Cornish | Hellestrae |
| J. Smith | K. Martin | Tennell |
| | DEFENSE | |
| Horton | Woodson | Gant |
| Holt | Holmes | Pruitt |
| Edwards | Jeffcoat | Lett |
| Hennings | J. Jones | Myles |
| | KICKERS | |
| Elliott | Saxon | |

## SCORING

| | | | | | | |
|---|---|---|---|---|---|---|
| BUFFALO | 7 | 3 | 7 | 0 | - | 17 |
| DALLAS | 14 | 14 | 3 | 21 | - | 52 |

**First Quarter**

Buff. Thomas, 2 yard run
PAT — Christie (kick)

Dall. Novacek, 23 yard pass from Aikman
PAT — Elliott (kick)

Dall. J. Jones, 2 yard fumble return
PAT — Elliott (kick)

**Second Quarter**

Buff. Christie, 21 yard field goal

Dall. Irvin, 19 yard pass from Aikman
PAT — Elliott (kick)

Dall. Irvin, 18 yard pass from Aikman
PAT — Elliott (kick)

**Third Quarter**

Dall. Elliott, 20 yard field goal

Buff. Beebe, 40 yard pass from Reich
PAT — Christie (kick)

**Fourth Quarter**

Dall. Harper, 45 yard pass from Aikman
PAT — Elliott (kick)

Dall. E. Smith, 10 yard run
PAT — Elliott (kick)

Dall. Norton, 9 yard fumble return
PAT — Elliott (kick)

## TEAM STATISTICS

| BUFF. | | DALL. |
|---|---|---|
| 22 | First Downs-Total | 20 |
| 7 | First Downs-Rushing | 9 |
| 11 | First Downs-Passiing | 11 |
| 4 | First Downs-Penalty | 0 |
| 8 | Fumbles-Number | 4 |
| 5 | Fumbles-Lost Ball | 2 |
| 4 | Penalties-Number | 8 |
| 30 | Yards Penalized | 53 |
| 0 | Missed Field Goals | 0 |
| 71 | Offensive Plays | 60 |
| 362 | Net Yards | 408 |
| 5.1 | Average Gain | 6.8 |
| 9 | Giveaways | 2 |
| 2 | Takeaways | 9 |
| - 7 | Difference | + 7 |

## INDIVIDUAL STATISTICS

### RUSHING

| BUFFALO | No. | Yds. | Avg. | DALLAS | No. | Yds. | Avg. |
|---|---|---|---|---|---|---|---|
| K. Davis | 15 | 86 | 5.7 | E. Smith | 22 | 108 | 4.9 |
| Thomas | 11 | 19 | 1.7 | Aikman | 3 | 28 | 9.3 |
| Gardner | 1 | 3 | 3.0 | Gainer | 2 | 1 | 0.5 |
| Reich | 1 | 0 | 0.0 | Johnston | 1 | 0 | 0.0 |
| | 29 | 108 | 3.7 | Beuerlein | 1 | 0 | 0.0 |
| | | | | | 29 | 137 | 4.7 |

### RECEIVING

| BUFFALO | No. | Yds. | Avg. | DALLAS | No. | Yds. | Avg. |
|---|---|---|---|---|---|---|---|
| Reed | 8 | 152 | 19.0 | Novacek | 7 | 72 | 10.3 |
| Thomas | 4 | 10 | 2.5 | Irvin | 6 | 114 | 19.0 |
| K. Davis | 3 | 16 | 5.3 | E. Smith | 6 | 27 | 4.5 |
| Beebe | 2 | 50 | 25.0 | Johnston | 2 | 15 | 7.5 |
| Tasker | 2 | 30 | 15.0 | Harper | 1 | 45 | 45.0 |
| Metzelaars | 2 | 12 | 6.0 | | 22 | 273 | 12.4 |
| McKeller | 1 | 6 | 6.0 | | | | |
| | 22 | 276 | 12.5 | | | | |

### PUNTING

| BUFFALO | No. | Yds. | Avg. | DALLAS | No. | Yds. | Avg. |
|---|---|---|---|---|---|---|---|
| Mohr | 3 | | 45.3 | Saxon | 3 | | 43.7 |

### PUNT RETURNS

| BUFFALO | No. | Yds. | Avg. | DALLAS | No. | Yds. | Avg. |
|---|---|---|---|---|---|---|---|
| Hicks | 1 | 0 | 0.0 | Martin | 3 | 35 | 11.7 |
| Hicks | 1FC | | | | | | |

### KICKOFF RETURNS

| BUFFALO | No. | Yds. | Avg. | DALLAS | No. | Yds. | Avg. |
|---|---|---|---|---|---|---|---|
| Lamb | 2 | 49 | 24.5 | K. Martin | 4 | 79 | 19.8 |
| K. Davis | 1 | 21 | 21.0 | | | | |
| Hicks | 1 | 20 | 20.0 | | | | |
| | 4 | 90 | 22.5 | | | | |

### INTERCEPTIONS RETURNS

| BUFFALO | No. | Yds. | Avg. | DALLAS | No. | Yds. | Avg. |
|---|---|---|---|---|---|---|---|
| None | | | | Everett | 2 | 22 | 11.0 |
| | | | | Washington | 1 | 13 | 13.0 |
| | | | | Brown | 1 | 0 | 0.0 |
| | | | | | 4 | 35 | 8.8 |

### PASSING

| BUFFALO | Att. | Comp. | Comp. Pct. | Yds. | Int. | Yds./ Att. | Yds./ Comp. | Yards Lost Tackled |
|---|---|---|---|---|---|---|---|---|
| Kelly | 7 | 4 | 57.1 | 82 | 2 | 11.7 | 20.5 | 2-10 |
| Reich | 31 | 18 | 58.1 | 194 | 2 | 6.3 | 10.8 | 2-12 |
| **DALLAS** | | | | | | | | |
| Aikman | 30 | 22 | 73.3 | 273 | 0 | 9.1 | 12.4 | 1-2 |

# 1993 N.F.C. Free Agency Jolts NFL, But Cowboys Repeat

In five years of the Jerry Jones and Jimmy Johnson regime, the Cowboys have turned into the elite of the NFL, winning the last two Super Bowls and unquestionably being called the best team in the league. The Cowboys had not only the best lineup in the league, but one that was young and in little danger of reaching the salary cap that was placed on the 28 teams as the 1993 season came to an end. Jones even got Emmitt Smith to sign a new contract after the star running back missed the first two games of the season due to a holdout.

Dallas also entered the 1993 season virtually unhurt in free agency, which is why its nucleus and Smith, Troy Aikman, Michael Irvin and others were big favorites to win the Super Bowl.

Free agency was the story of 1993, as 120 players changed teams. Players with five or more years in the NFL were free to change teams when their contracts expired, and players with three or four years in the NFL could sign offer sheets that their present team had the option to match. The big names were defensive end Reggie White to Green Bay, safety Tim McDonald to San Francisco, running back Marcus Allen to Kansas City, wide receivers Mark Jackson and Mike Sherrard to the Giants and defensive tackle Pierce Holt to Atlanta. Several star players also changed teams through trades, the biggest being Eric Dickerson, who became a Falcon, and Joe Montana, who turned into a Chief.

## EASTERN DIVISION

**Dallas Cowboys** — The Cowboys became the fifth team to win back-to-back Super Bowls, mainly behind the running of Emmitt Smith, who was named the NFL's Most Valuable Player and the Super Bowl MVP. Smith, who missed the first two games of the season — both Cowboy losses — rushed for 1,486 yards to lead the NFL for the third straight year. Quarterback Troy Aikman (only six interceptions) and wide receiver Michael Irvin (88 receptions, seven touchdowns) were equally masterful, but it still wasn't an easy season for the Cowboys. Smith's holdout and injuries to Aikman, Smith, defensive end Charles Haley and linebacker Ken Norton slowed them down. But, even with Smith ailing in the playoffs, Dallas rolled over the Packers and 49ers before facing the Bills again in the Super Bowl, a 30-13 victory. The Cowboys' fifth Super Bowl victory and seventh appearance overall were both records.

**New York Giants** — The Giants were one of the surprise teams of the NFL in 1993, going 11-5 and making the playoffs under new head coach Dan Reeves, who had come over from Denver. Quarterback Phil Simms also had a fine comeback, as he completed 61.8 percent of his passes for 3,038 yards and started every game for the first time in seven years. Reeves stuck to a combination of a strong running game and a powerful defense. Rodney Hampton rushed for 1,077 yards, while two free-agent newcomers, linebackers Carlton Bailey and Michael Brooks, were the defensive mainstays. Following six straight victories, New York was tied atop the division with Dallas at 11-4 going into the final game and looking for a first-round bye in the playoffs. But the Cowboys prevailed 16-13. After the season, Lawrence Taylor announced his retirement.

**Philadelphia Eagles** — Despite numerous free-agent losses, the Eagles surprised everybody when they won their first four games of the season and took a lead in the NFC East. Then disaster hit, as quarterback Randall Cunningham suffered a broken leg. Philadelphia then lost six straight games with Ken O'Brien and Bubby Brister at quarterback. Injuries also felled wide receiver Fred Barnett, linebacker Tim Harris and several other veterans. Brister finally hit his stride late in the season. He set a team record for fewest interceptions in a season and ranked fourth in the conference in passing. The Eagles won their final three games to finish with an 8-8 record. Eric Allen tied an NFL record when he returned four of his six interceptions for touchdowns.

**Phoenix Cardinals** — Before the season, owner Bill Bidwill issued an ultimatum to head coach Joe Bugel that the team had better win nine games or else he would be fired. Phoenix started the season 2-6 amid a plethora of injuries, and Bugel seemed as good as gone. Then the Cardinals went 5-3 over the second half to finish 7-9 and possibly save Bugel's job. Bidwill waited four weeks after the season ended before he finally pulled the trigger, canning Bugel and hiring Buddy Ryan. The Cardinals were better than they had been in any of their five seasons in Phoenix. Only the 49ers and Cowboys ranked ahead of them in yards and scoring, and the defense ranked fourth in points allowed. Quarterback Steve Beuerlein, a free-agent acquisition, passed for 3,164 yards and 18 touchdowns, and rookie Ron Moore rushed for 1,018 yards after he took over for injured first-round draft choice Garrison Hearst.

**Washington Redskins** — After Joe Gibbs surprised everybody with his retirement midway through the offseason, Richie Petitbon was elevated to head coach. Washington started the season with a convincing 35-16 victory over the Cowboys, but then the bottom fell out, as the Redskins suffered through their worst season in three decades. Washington lost six straight games at one point, had their most lopsided home loss since 1940 (41-7 to the Giants) and even lost one game 3-0. There were injuries to both lines and pitiful play from quarterback Mark Rypien, who threw only four TD passes. A bright spot was registered by rookie back Reggie Brooks, who rushed for 1,063 yards and had the two longest TD runs in the league. Petitbon was fired after the season and replaced by Dallas assistant Norv Turner.

## CENTRAL DIVISION

**Detroit Lions** — Erik Kramer did it again. Two years after leading the Lions to the NFC Central Division championship and the conference title game, Kramer finally took over in December for quarterbacks Rodney Peete and Andre Ware and led Detroit to three victories in the final four games. And he did it without star running back Barry Sanders, who missed the final four games with a sprained knee. Sanders was the team MVP, as he rushed for over 1,000 yards for the fifth straight season, only the third player in NFL history to do so. Coach Wayne Fontes was under fire most of the season for his quarterback merry-go-round, until he righted the ship. The season ended quickly in the playoffs, with a loss to the Packers one week after beating them for the division title.

**Minnesota Vikings** — The Vikings were resilient in 1993, overcoming numerous injuries and free-agent losses to go 9-7 and make the playoffs. Quarterback Jim McMahon was in and out of the lineup on a frequent basis, though he was back starting by the playoffs (a 17-10 loss to the Giants). Minnesota see-sawed throughout the season with inconsistency, then, with McMahon back, won four of five games in December to squeeze into the playoffs. After top running back Terry Allen was lost for the season before it even began, Minnesota had trouble all year with its running game. Wide receiver Cris Carter was the offensive star, as he caught 86 passes for 1,071 yards and nine touchdowns. Defensively, the Vikings ranked first in the league. Defensive tackles Henry Thomas and John Randle combined for 21 sacks.

**Green Bay Packers** — The Packers had another 9-7 season, going to the playoffs for the first time since 1982 and having back-to-back winning seasons for the first time since 1966 and '67. Still, Green Bay was never a big threat in the division because it lost three of the first four games. Wide receiver Sterling Sharpe broke his own NFL record by catching 112 passes for 1,274 yards and 11 touchdowns. He had game-winning catches in three games. Defensive end Reggie White signed with Green Bay, the biggest free-agent signing in the league. White tied for the NFC lead with 13 sacks. The Green Bay defense was a pleasant surprise, as it ranked second in the NFL. Quarterback Brett Favre was the main man, however, as he threw for 19 touchdowns and 24 interceptions.

**Chicago Bears** — Unlike the top three teams in the division, who made the playoffs with late-season surges, the Bears fell apart when December rolled around. Winners of four straight games, three of them on the road, Chicago then lost its last four games to finish 7-9 and out of the playoffs for the second straight year. The Bears were improved in 1993, however, though nearly all of it was on defense. Defensive end Richard Dent, middle linebacker Dante Jones and cornerback Donnell Woolford were the defensive stars. New head coach Dave Wannstedt couldn't get much out of an offense that ranked last in passing and

**OFFENSE**

| | ATL | CHI | DAL | DET | G.B. | L.A. | MINN | N.O. | NYG | PHIL | PHX | S.F. | T.B. | WASH |
|---|---|---|---|---|---|---|---|---|---|---|---|---|---|---|
| FIRST DOWNS: | | | | | | | | | | | | | | |
| Total | 292 | 226 | 322 | 248 | 282 | 279 | 283 | 264 | 300 | 302 | 295 | 372 | 241 | 255 |
| by Rushing | 91 | 98 | 120 | 101 | 98 | 117 | 85 | 94 | 127 | 103 | 107 | 134 | 80 | 92 |
| by Passing | 185 | 113 | 172 | 139 | 166 | 147 | 182 | 158 | 153 | 184 | 173 | 212 | 141 | 143 |
| by Penalty | 16 | 15 | 30 | 8 | 18 | 15 | 16 | 12 | 20 | 15 | 15 | 26 | 20 | 20 |
| RUSHING: | | | | | | | | | | | | | | |
| Number | 395 | 477 | 490 | 456 | 448 | 449 | 447 | 414 | 560 | 456 | 452 | 463 | 402 | 396 |
| Yards | 1590 | 1677 | 2161 | 1944 | 1619 | 2014 | 1623 | 1766 | 2210 | 1761 | 1809 | 2133 | 1290 | 1726 |
| Average Yards | 4.0 | 3.5 | 4.4 | 4.3 | 3.6 | 4.5 | 3.6 | 4.3 | 3.9 | 3.9 | 4.0 | 4.6 | 3.2 | 4.4 |
| Touchdowns | 4 | 10 | 20 | 9 | 14 | 8 | 8 | 10 | 11 | 8 | 12 | 27 | 6 | 11 |
| PASSING: | | | | | | | | | | | | | | |
| Attempts | 573 | 388 | 475 | 435 | 528 | 473 | 526 | 481 | 424 | 556 | 522 | 524 | 508 | 533 |
| Completions | 334 | 230 | 317 | 264 | 322 | 247 | 315 | 274 | 257 | 328 | 310 | 354 | 262 | 287 |
| Completion Pct. | 58.3 | 59.3 | 66.7 | 60.7 | 61.0 | 52.2 | 59.9 | 57.0 | 60.6 | 59.0 | 59.4 | 67.6 | 51.6 | 53.8 |
| Passing Yards | 3787 | 2270 | 3617 | 2943 | 3330 | 3021 | 3380 | 3183 | 3180 | 3463 | 3635 | 4480 | 3295 | 2764 |
| Avg. Yds per Att. | 6.6 | 5.9 | 7.6 | 6.8 | 6.3 | 6.4 | 6.4 | 6.6 | 7.5 | 6.2 | 7.0 | 8.6 | 6.5 | 5.2 |
| Avg. Yds per Comp. | 11.3 | 9.9 | 11.4 | 11.1 | 10.3 | 12.2 | 10.7 | 11.6 | 12.4 | 10.6 | 11.7 | 12.7 | 12.6 | 9.6 |
| Times Tackled | 40 | 48 | 29 | 46 | 30 | 31 | 35 | 40 | 40 | 42 | 33 | 35 | 39 | 40 |
| Yds Lost Tackled | 267 | 230 | 163 | 229 | 199 | 231 | 181 | 242 | 245 | 302 | 231 | 178 | 274 | 219 |
| Net Yards | 3520 | 2040 | 3454 | 2714 | 3131 | 2790 | 3199 | 2941 | 2935 | 3161 | 3404 | 4302 | 3021 | 2545 |
| Touchdowns | 28 | 7 | 18 | 15 | 19 | 16 | 18 | 18 | 17 | 22 | 21 | 29 | 19 | 11 |
| Interceptions | 25 | 16 | 6 | 19 | 24 | 19 | 14 | 21 | 9 | 13 | 20 | 17 | 25 | 21 |
| Pct. Intercepted | 4.4 | 4.1 | 1.3 | 4.4 | 4.5 | 4.0 | 2.7 | 4.4 | 2.1 | 2.3 | 3.8 | 3.2 | 4.9 | 3.9 |
| PUNTS: | | | | | | | | | | | | | | |
| Number | 72 | 80 | 56 | 72 | 74 | 80 | 90 | 77 | 78 | 83 | 73 | 42 | 94 | 83 |
| Average | 43.3 | 38.5 | 41.8 | 44.5 | 42.9 | 40.9 | 42.8 | 43.6 | 41.9 | 40.0 | 43.7 | 40.9 | 40.1 | 43.9 |
| PUNT RETURNS | | | | | | | | | | | | | | |
| Number | 35 | 35 | 37 | 40 | 45 | 19 | 39 | 38 | 32 | 33 | 47 | 35 | 38 | 35 |
| Yards | 276 | 289 | 381 | 349 | 404 | 102 | 280 | 517 | 331 | 284 | 384 | 411 | 311 | 245 |
| Average Yards | 7.9 | 8.3 | 10.3 | 8.4 | 9.0 | 5.4 | 7.2 | 13.6 | 10.3 | 8.6 | 8.3 | 11.7 | 8.2 | 7.0 |
| Touchdowns | 0 | 0 | 2 | 0 | 0 | 0 | 0 | 2 | 1 | 0 | 1 | 1 | 0 | 0 |
| KICKOFF RET.: | | | | | | | | | | | | | | |
| Number | 55 | 45 | 36 | 52 | 60 | 49 | 55 | 62 | 32 | 53 | 45 | 41 | 58 | 59 |
| Yards | 1300 | 811 | 758 | 1204 | 1483 | 824 | 1086 | 1460 | 507 | 987 | 951 | 715 | 922 | 1166 |
| Average Yards | 23.6 | 18.0 | 21.0 | 23.2 | 24.7 | 16.8 | 19.7 | 23.5 | 15.8 | 18.6 | 21.1 | 17.4 | 15.9 | 19.8 |
| Touchdowns | 1 | 0 | 0 | 1 | 1 | 0 | 0 | 1 | 0 | 0 | 0 | 0 | 0 | 0 |
| INTERCEPT RET.: | | | | | | | | | | | | | | |
| Number | 13 | 18 | 14 | 19 | 18 | 11 | 24 | 10 | 18 | 20 | 9 | 19 | 9 | 17 |
| Yards | 160 | 300 | 171 | 156 | 255 | 127 | 211 | 133 | 184 | 323 | 124 | 267 | 79 | 241 |
| Average Yards | 12.3 | 16.7 | 12.2 | 8.2 | 14.2 | 11.5 | 8.8 | 13.3 | 10.2 | 16.2 | 13.8 | 14.1 | 7.9 | 14.2 |
| Touchdowns | 0 | 2 | 1 | 1 | 0 | 0 | 2 | 0 | 1 | 4 | 1 | 3 | 2 | 2 |
| PENALTIES: | | | | | | | | | | | | | | |
| Number | 111 | 68 | 94 | 93 | 85 | 71 | 109 | 81 | 90 | 101 | 77 | 95 | 89 | 90 |
| Yards | 838 | 587 | 744 | 665 | 734 | 526 | 806 | 663 | 586 | 758 | 644 | 800 | 765 | 596 |
| FUMBLES: | | | | | | | | | | | | | | |
| Number | 31 | 29 | 33 | 29 | 26 | 20 | 15 | 24 | 19 | 32 | 23 | 31 | 28 | 24 |
| Number Lost | 17 | 14 | 16 | 13 | 10 | 11 | 10 | 13 | 8 | 21 | 11 | 13 | 11 | 10 |
| POINTS: | | | | | | | | | | | | | | |
| Total | 316 | 234 | 376 | 298 | 340 | 221 | 277 | 317 | 288 | 293 | 326 | 473 | 237 | 230 |
| PAT Attempts | 34 | 22 | 41 | 28 | 36 | 25 | 28 | 33 | 30 | 33 | 37 | 61 | 27 | 26 |
| PAT Made | 34 | 21 | 40 | 28 | 35 | 23 | 27 | 33 | 28 | 30 | 37 | 59 | 27 | 24 |
| FG Attempts | 27 | 36 | 37 | 43 | 37 | 23 | 35 | 35 | 34 | 23 | 28 | 26 | 22 | 28 |
| FG Made | 26 | 27 | 30 | 34 | 31 | 16 | 26 | 28 | 26 | 16 | 21 | 16 | 16 | 16 |
| Percent FG Made | 96.2 | 75.0 | 81.1 | 79.1 | 83.8 | 69.6 | 74.3 | 80.0 | 76.5 | 69.6 | 75.0 | 61.5 | 72.7 | 57.1 |
| Safeties | 0 | 0 | 0 | 0 | 1 | 0 | 2 | 1 | 1 | 2 | 2 | 0 | 0 | 1 |

**DEFENSE**

| | ATL | CHI | DAL | DET | G.B. | L.A. | MINN | N.O. | NYG | PHIL | PHX | S.F. | T.B. | WASH |
|---|---|---|---|---|---|---|---|---|---|---|---|---|---|---|
| FIRST DOWNS: | | | | | | | | | | | | | | |
| Total | 278 | 290 | 297 | 279 | 261 | 304 | 259 | 273 | 268 | 271 | 278 | 297 | 280 | 304 |
| by Rushing | 79 | 112 | 94 | 108 | 88 | 117 | 98 | 116 | 89 | 91 | 106 | 109 | 109 | 127 |
| by Passing | 180 | 163 | 176 | 154 | 157 | 179 | 139 | 145 | 161 | 155 | 158 | 171 | 152 | 157 |
| by Penalty | 19 | 15 | 27 | 17 | 16 | 8 | 22 | 12 | 18 | 25 | 14 | 17 | 19 | 20 |
| RUSHING: | | | | | | | | | | | | | | |
| Number | 419 | 476 | 423 | 433 | 424 | 480 | 415 | 513 | 395 | 467 | 433 | 404 | 479 | 513 |
| Yards | 1784 | 1835 | 1651 | 1649 | 1582 | 1851 | 1534 | 2090 | 1547 | 2080 | 1861 | 1800 | 1994 | 2111 |
| Average Yards | 4.3 | 3.9 | 3.9 | 3.8 | 3.7 | 3.9 | 3.7 | 4.1 | 3.9 | 4.5 | 4.3 | 4.5 | 4.2 | 4.1 |
| Touchdowns | 14 | 9 | 7 | 12 | 6 | 18 | 14 | 7 | 7 | 11 | 13 | 6 | 15 | 14 |
| PASSING: | | | | | | | | | | | | | | |
| Attempts | 505 | 504 | 555 | 514 | 529 | 488 | 478 | 444 | 514 | 463 | 495 | 564 | 503 | 483 |
| Completions | 308 | 306 | 334 | 309 | 290 | 299 | 310 | 259 | 298 | 251 | 281 | 314 | 300 | 291 |
| Completion Pct. | 61.0 | 60.7 | 60.2 | 60.1 | 54.8 | 61.3 | 64.9 | 58.3 | 58.0 | 54.2 | 56.8 | 55.7 | 59.6 | 60.2 |
| Passing Yards | 3786 | 3105 | 3347 | 3273 | 3201 | 3763 | 3146 | 2924 | 3354 | 3153 | 3511 | 3513 | 3384 | 3583 |
| Avg. Yds per Att. | 7.5 | 6.2 | 6.0 | 6.4 | 6.1 | 7.7 | 6.6 | 6.6 | 6.5 | 6.8 | 7.1 | 6.2 | 6.7 | 7.4 |
| Avg. Yds per Comp. | 12.3 | 10.1 | 10.0 | 10.6 | 11.0 | 12.6 | 10.1 | 11.3 | 11.3 | 12.6 | 12.5 | 11.2 | 11.3 | 12.3 |
| Times Tackled | 27 | 46 | 34 | 43 | 46 | 35 | 45 | 51 | 41 | 36 | 34 | 44 | 29 | 31 |
| Yds Lost Tackled | 149 | 287 | 231 | 253 | 301 | 203 | 276 | 318 | 238 | 214 | 205 | 316 | 132 | 197 |
| Net Yards | 3637 | 2818 | 3116 | 3020 | 2900 | 3560 | 2870 | 2606 | 3116 | 2939 | 3306 | 3197 | 3252 | 3386 |
| Touchdowns | 27 | 12 | 14 | 19 | 16 | 17 | 11 | 22 | 13 | 22 | 14 | 23 | 22 | 24 |
| Interceptions | 13 | 18 | 14 | 19 | 18 | 11 | 24 | 10 | 18 | 20 | 9 | 19 | 9 | 17 |
| Pct. Intercepted | 2.6 | 3.6 | 2.5 | 3.7 | 3.4 | 2.3 | 5.0 | 2.3 | 3.5 | 4.3 | 1.8 | 3.4 | 1.8 | 3.5 |
| PUNTS: | | | | | | | | | | | | | | |
| Number | 74 | 78 | 78 | 81 | 79 | 58 | 78 | 80 | 80 | 75 | 78 | 68 | 76 | 73 |
| Average | 40.9 | 41.4 | 41.3 | 43.1 | 40.2 | 42.3 | 42.4 | 42.3 | 40.3 | 41.8 | 42.7 | 43.8 | 43.3 | 41.1 |
| PUNT RETURNS | | | | | | | | | | | | | | |
| Number | 41 | 22 | 32 | 45 | 38 | 43 | 46 | 36 | 44 | 35 | 30 | 16 | 53 | 34 |
| Yards | 350 | 115 | 169 | 377 | 350 | 533 | 560 | 348 | 247 | 311 | 267 | 171 | 394 | 343 |
| Average Yards | 8.5 | 5.2 | 5.3 | 8.4 | 9.1 | 12.4 | 12.2 | 9.3 | 5.6 | 8.9 | 8.9 | 10.7 | 7.4 | 10.1 |
| Touchdowns | 0 | 0 | 0 | 0 | 0 | 2 | 1 | 1 | 0 | 1 | 0 | 0 | 0 | 2 |
| KICKOFF RET.: | | | | | | | | | | | | | | |
| Number | 55 | 53 | 66 | 30 | 70 | 47 | 58 | 40 | 29 | 53 | 51 | 62 | 28 | 36 |
| Yards | 1064 | 918 | 1225 | 609 | 1407 | 984 | 1420 | 788 | 646 | 1133 | 994 | 1196 | 499 | 722 |
| Average Yards | 19.3 | 17.3 | 18.6 | 20.3 | 20.2 | 20.9 | 24.5 | 19.7 | 22.3 | 21.4 | 19.5 | 19.3 | 17.8 | 20.0 |
| Touchdowns | 0 | 0 | 1 | 0 | 0 | 0 | 1 | 0 | 0 | 0 | 0 | 0 | 0 | 0 |
| INTERCEPT RET.: | | | | | | | | | | | | | | |
| Number | 25 | 16 | 6 | 19 | 24 | 19 | 14 | 21 | 9 | 13 | 20 | 17 | 25 | 21 |
| Yards | 345 | 105 | 47 | 177 | 437 | 347 | 166 | 444 | 175 | 107 | 143 | 157 | 280 | 209 |
| Average Yards | 13.8 | 6.6 | 7.8 | 9.3 | 18.2 | 18.3 | 11.9 | 21.1 | 19.4 | 8.2 | 7.2 | 9.2 | 11.2 | 10.0 |
| Touchdowns | 2 | 1 | 0 | 1 | 3 | 2 | 3 | 6 | 1 | 0 | 0 | 0 | 1 | 2 |
| PENALTIES: | | | | | | | | | | | | | | |
| Number | 100 | 91 | 88 | 75 | 86 | 80 | 97 | 87 | 98 | 86 | 95 | 99 | 126 | 100 |
| Yards | 878 | 783 | 653 | 500 | 712 | 532 | 767 | 590 | 820 | 615 | 730 | 743 | 913 | 783 |
| FUMBLES: | | | | | | | | | | | | | | |
| Number | 25 | 24 | 22 | 34 | 33 | 26 | 24 | 30 | 27 | 33 | 27 | 20 | 27 | 25 |
| Number Lost | 11 | 12 | 14 | 16 | 15 | 9 | 10 | 20 | 10 | 15 | 17 | 11 | 13 | 14 |
| POINTS: | | | | | | | | | | | | | | |
| Total | 385 | 230 | 229 | 292 | 282 | 367 | 290 | 343 | 205 | 315 | 269 | 295 | 376 | 345 |
| PAT Attempts | 46 | 21 | 23 | 32 | 27 | 40 | 32 | 39 | 22 | 34 | 27 | 29 | 40 | 42 |
| PAT Made | 45 | 20 | 23 | 31 | 27 | 38 | 30 | 35 | 22 | 34 | 27 | 29 | 38 | 40 |
| FG Attempts | 31 | 34 | 27 | 30 | 40 | 37 | 33 | 30 | 23 | 34 | 35 | 30 | 35 | 22 |
| FG Made | 20 | 26 | 22 | 23 | 31 | 29 | 25 | 24 | 17 | 23 | 26 | 27 | 32 | 17 |
| Percent FG Made | 64.5 | 76.5 | 81.5 | 76.7 | 77.5 | 78.4 | 75.8 | 80.0 | 73.9 | 67.6 | 74.3 | 90.0 | 91.4 | 77.3 |
| Safeties | 2 | 0 | 1 | 0 | 0 | 1 | 0 | 1 | 0 | 1 | 1 | 2 | 1 | 1 |

scoring with only 14.6 points per game. Quarterback Jim Harbaugh and running backs Neal Anderson and Craig Heyward weren't much, and the receiving corps was either injured, inexperienced or ineffective.

**Tampa Bay Buccaneers** — Owning the NFL's worst record over the past 11 years, the Buccaneers had their 11th consecutive season with double-digit losses. The Bucs started the season losing seven of their first nine games by 15 or more points. Then, in the last seven outings, the Bucs won three times. There were some reasons for optimism, particularly the development of quarterback Craig Erickson and wide receiver Courtney Hawkins. And the defense, which had allowed an average of 362 yards in the first nine games, tightened to only 283 yards the final seven weeks. Erickson threw 21 interceptions but became the team's first 3,000-yard passer since 1989 and matured down the stretch. Middle linebacker Hardy Nickerson, a free-agent signee, led the Bucs with a team-record 214 tackles.

## WESTERN DIVISION

**San Francisco 49ers** — Offense was again the story of the 49ers. Quarterback Steve Young became the first player in NFL history to lead the league in passing three straight years. Running back Ricky Watters rushed for 950 yards and scored 11 touchdowns. And Jerry Rice was his usual phenomenal self, catching 98 passes for 1,503 yards and 15 TD's. The team set a club record with 6,435 yards on offense and scored 473 points (29.6 per game), just two points shy of the team record. San Francisco shook off a 3-3 start to win its 10th division title in 13 years and extended a league record of 11 seasons with 10 or more victories. Still, the 49ers lost in the NFC title game for the third time in four years.

**New Orleans Saints** — The Saints seem to have fallen into a routine of starting off quickly before slipping and seemingly falling out of the playoff race. In 1993, New Orleans won its first five games, then hit the skids with losses in six of the next eight games before a season-ending victory. That left the team with an 8-8 mark and out of the playoffs. Quarterback Wade Wilson lived up to his reputation as a streaky passer. He threw only one interception in the first five games, then 14 in the next 11. After Vaughn Dunbar was injured in preseason, a new star developed in running back Derek Brown (705 yards). But the defense started to decline because of age and injuries, finishing 22nd in points allowed. Linebacker Renaldo Turnbull tied for the NFC lead with 13 sacks.

**Atlanta Falcons** — With Deion Sanders missing, the Falcons lost their first five games. Then, with Sanders playing both offense and defense, Atlanta won six of its next eight games. Finally, with the playoffs on the line, the Falcons lost their last three games. Sanders led the NFC with seven interceptions, but the defense allowed a league-worst 385 points. Quarterback Bobby Hebert passed for 2,978 yards and 24 touchdowns, and three receivers had 70 or more receptions — Andre Rison (86 catches and 15 touchdowns), Mike Pritchard (74 catches) and Michael Haynes (72). Erric Pegram replaced Eric Dickerson and rushed for 1,185 yards. Placekicker Norm Johnson set an NFL record with 26 field goals in 27 attempts. Coach Jerry Glanville was fired after the season and replaced by offensive coordinator June Jones.

**Los Angeles Rams** — Ground Chuck returned in the name of Jerome Bettis, the NFL's Offensive Rookie of the Year, who rushed for 1,429 yards, second in the league. It was the seventh-highest total ever for an NFL rookie. Bettis was almost the entire offense, as coach Chuck Knox went back and forth at quarterback between an ineffective Jim Everett and the inexperienced T.J. Rubley. Everett finished with a career-low 49.3 completion percentage and only eight touchdowns vs. 12 interceptions. But Rubley, a second-year player, wasn't much better. On defense, tackle Sean Gilbert registered 10.5 sacks.

## DALLAS COWBOYS 12-4 Jimmy Johnson

| Scores of Each Game | | |
|---|---|---|
| 16 | Washington | 35 |
| 10 | BUFFALO | 13 |
| 17 | Phoenix | 10 |
| 36 | GREEN BAY | 14 |
| 27 | Indianapolis | 3 |
| 26 | SAN FRANCISCO | 17 |
| 23 | Philadelphia | 10 |
| 31 | N.Y. GIANTS | 9 |
| 20 | PHOENIX | 15 |
| 14 | Atlanta | 27 |
| 14 | MIAMI | 16 |
| 23 | PHILADELPHIA | 17 |
| 37 | Minnesota | 20 |
| 28 | N.Y. Jets | 7 |
| 38 | WASHINGTON | 3 |
| 16 | N.Y. Giants | *13 |

| UseName | Pos. | Hgt | Wgt | Age | Int | Pts |
|---|---|---|---|---|---|---|
| Ron Stone | OT | 6'5" | 309 | 22 | | |
| Mark Tuinei | OT | 6'5" | 305 | 23 | | |
| Erik Williams | OT | 6'6" | 324 | 24 | | |
| John Gesek | OG | 6'5" | 285 | 30 | | |
| Kevin Gogan | OG-OT | 6'7" | 328 | 28 | | |
| Dale Hellestrae | OG-C | 6'5" | 275 | 31 | | |
| Nate Newton | OG | 6'3" | 325 | 31 | | |
| Frank Cornish | C-OG | 6'4" | 287 | 25 | | |
| Mark Stepnoski | C | 6'2" | 264 | 26 | | |
| Charles Haley | DE | 6'5" | 250 | 29 | | |
| Jim Jeffcoat | DE | 6'5" | 280 | 32 | | |
| Tony Tolbert | DE | 6'6" | 263 | 25 | | |
| Tony Casillas | DT | 6'3" | 279 | 29 | | |
| Chad Hennings | DT | 6'6" | 286 | 27 | | |
| Jimmie Jones | DT | 6'4" | 284 | 27 | | |
| Leon Lett | DT-DE | 6'6" | 285 | 24 | | |
| Russell Maryland | DT | 6'1" | 279 | 24 | | |
| Bobby Abrams (to MIN) | LB | 6'3" | 230 | 26 | | |
| Dixon Edwards | LB | 6'1" | 222 | 25 | | |
| Robert Jones | LB | 6'2" | 237 | 23 | | |
| Godfrey Myles | LB | 6'1" | 242 | 24 | | |
| Ken Norton | LB | 6'2" | 240 | 26 | 1 | |
| Darrin Smith | LB | 6'1" | 227 | 23 | | |
| Matt Vanderbeek | LB-DE | 6'3" | 243 | 26 | | |
| Bill Bates | DB | 6'1" | 205 | 32 | 2 | |
| Larry Brown | DB | 5'11" | 182 | 23 | | |
| Thomas Everett | DB | 5'9" | 184 | 28 | 2 | |
| Joe Fishback | DB | 6' | 212 | 25 | | |
| Kenneth Gant | DB | 5'11" | 189 | 26 | 1 | |
| Chris Hall | DB | 6'2" | 184 | 23 | | |
| Brock Marion | DB | 5'11" | 189 | 23 | 1 | |
| Elvis Patterson (from RAID) | DB | 5'11" | 195 | 32 | | |
| Kevin Smith | DB | 5'11" | 180 | 23 | 6 | 6 |
| Dave Thomas | DB | 6'2" | 208 | 25 | | |
| James Washington | DB | 6'1" | 209 | 28 | 1 | |
| Robert Williams | DB | 5'10" | 186 | 30 | | |
| Darren Woodson | DB | 6'1" | 215 | 24 | | |
| Troy Aikman | QB | 6'4" | 228 | 26 | | |
| Jason Garrett | QB | 6'2" | 195 | 27 | | |
| Derrick Gainer | HB | 5'11" | 228 | 27 | | |
| Derrick Lassic | HB | 5'10" | 188 | 23 | | 18 |
| Emmitt Smith | HB | 5'9" | 209 | 24 | | 60 |
| Tommie Agee | FB | 6' | 235 | 29 | | |
| Lincoln Coleman | FB-HB | 6'1" | 249 | 24 | | 12 |
| Daryl Johnston | FB | 6'2" | 238 | 27 | | 24 |
| Alvin Harper | WR | 6'3" | 208 | 26 | | 30 |
| Michael Irvin | WR | 6'2" | 205 | 27 | | 42 |
| Kevin Williams | WR | 5'9" | 192 | 22 | | 36 |
| Tyrone Williams | WR | 6'5" | 220 | 23 | | |
| Kelly Blackwell | TE | 6'1" | 255 | 24 | | |
| Scott Galbraith | TE | 6'2" | 255 | 26 | | 6 |
| Joey Mickey | TE | 6'5" | 274 | 22 | | |
| Jay Novacek | TE | 6'4" | 232 | 30 | | 12 |
| Jim Price (from LA) | TE | 6'4" | 247 | 26 | | |
| Lin Elliott | K | 6' | 182 | 24 | | 8 |
| John Jett | K | 6' | 184 | 24 | | |
| Eddie Murray | K | 5'11" | 195 | 37 | | 122 |

Clayton Holmes — Knee Injury

Jimmy Smith — Appendix
Alfredo Roberts — Foot Injury

## NEW YORK GIANTS 11-5 Dan Reeves

| Scores of Each Game | | |
|---|---|---|
| 26 | Chicago | 20 |
| 23 | TAMPA BAY | 7 |
| 20 | L.A. RAMS | 10 |
| 14 | Buffalo | 17 |
| 41 | Washington | 7 |
| 21 | PHILADELPHIA | 10 |
| 6 | N.Y. JETS | 10 |
| 9 | Dallas | 31 |
| 20 | WASHINGTON | 6 |
| 7 | Philadelphia | 3 |
| 19 | PHOENIX | 17 |
| 19 | Miami | 14 |
| 20 | INDIANAPOLIS | 6 |
| 24 | New Orleans | 14 |
| 6 | Phoenix | 17 |
| 13 | DALLAS | *16 |

| UseName | Pos. | Hgt | Wgt | Age | Int | Pts |
|---|---|---|---|---|---|---|
| Greg Bishop | OT | 6'5" | 298 | 22 | | |
| John Elliott | OT | 6'7" | 305 | 28 | | |
| Clarence Jones | OT | 6'6" | 280 | 25 | | |
| Eric Moore | OT-OG | 6'5" | 290 | 28 | | |
| Doug Riesenberg | OT | 6'5" | 275 | 28 | | |
| Scott Davis | OG | 6'3" | 289 | 23 | | |
| Bob Kratch | OG | 6'3" | 288 | 27 | | |
| William Roberts | OG | 6'5" | 280 | 31 | | |
| Bart Oates | C | 6'3" | 265 | 34 | | |
| Brian Williams | C | 6'5" | 300 | 27 | | |
| Mark Flythe | DE | 6'7" | 290 | 24 | | |
| Mike Fox | DE | 6'6" | 275 | 26 | | |
| Keith Hamilton | DE | 6'6" | 280 | 22 | | 2 |
| Mike Strahan | DE | 6'4" | 275 | 21 | | |
| George Thornton | DE | 6'3" | 300 | 25 | | |
| Stacey Dillard | NT | 6'5" | 288 | 24 | | |
| Erik Howard | NT | 6'4" | 268 | 28 | | |
| Jessie Armstead | LB | 6'1" | 238 | 22 | 1 | |
| Carlton Bailey | LB | 6'3" | 235 | 28 | | |
| Michael Brooks | LB | 6'1" | 235 | 29 | | |
| Marcus Buckley | LB | 6'3" | 235 | 22 | | |
| Steve DeOssie (to NYJ) | LB | 6'2" | 248 | 30 | | |
| Kanavis McGhee | LB | 6'4" | 257 | 24 | | |
| Corey Miller | LB | 6'2" | 255 | 24 | 2 | |
| Andre Powell | LB | 6'1" | 226 | 24 | | |
| Lawrence Taylor | LB | 6'3" | 243 | 34 | | |
| Corey Widmer | DT | 6'3" | 276 | 24 | | |
| Willie Beamon | DB | 5'11" | 170 | 23 | 1 | |
| Jesse Campbell | DB | 6'1" | 215 | 24 | 1 | |
| Mark Collins | DB | 5'10" | 190 | 29 | 4 | 6 |
| Myron Guyton | DB | 6'1" | 205 | 26 | 2 | |
| Greg Jackson | DB | 6'1" | 200 | 27 | 4 | |
| Izel Jenkins (from MIN) | DB | 5'10" | 190 | 29 | | |
| Corey Raymond | DB | 5'11" | 180 | 24 | 2 | |
| Phillippi Sparks | DB | 5'11" | 186 | 24 | | |
| David Tate | DB | 6'1" | 200 | 28 | 1 | |
| Perry Williams | DB | 6'2" | 203 | 32 | | |
| Dave Brown | QB | 6'5" | 215 | 23 | | |
| Kent Graham | QB | 6'5" | 220 | 24 | | |
| Phil Simms | QB | 6'3" | 214 | 37 | | |
| Rodney Hampton | HB | 5'11" | 215 | 24 | | 30 |
| Dave Meggett | HB | 5'7" | 180 | 27 | | 6 |
| Lewis Tillman | HB | 6' | 195 | 27 | | 18 |
| Jarrod Bunch | FB | 6'2" | 248 | 25 | | 18 |
| Kenyon Rasheed | FB | 5'10" | 245 | 23 | | 6 |
| Chris Calloway | WR | 5'10" | 185 | 25 | | 18 |
| Keith Crawford | WR | 6'2" | 180 | 22 | | |
| Mark Jackson | WR | 5'9" | 180 | 30 | | 24 |
| Ed McCaffrey | WR | 6'5" | 215 | 25 | | 12 |
| Mike Sherrard | WR | 6'2" | 187 | 30 | | 12 |
| Derek Brown | TE | 6'6" | 252 | 23 | | |
| Howard Cross | TE | 6'5" | 245 | 26 | | 30 |
| Aaron Pierce | TE | 6'5" | 246 | 23 | | |
| Brad Daluiso | K | 6'2" | 207 | 25 | | 3 |
| Mike Horan | K | 5'11" | 190 | 34 | | |
| David Treadwell | K | 6'1" | 180 | 28 | | 103 |

## PHILADELPHIA EAGLES 8-8 Rich Kotite

| Scores of Each Game | | |
|---|---|---|
| 23 | PHOENIX | 17 |
| 20 | Green Bay | 17 |
| 34 | WASHINGTON | 31 |
| 35 | N.Y. Jets | 30 |
| 6 | Chicago | 17 |
| 10 | N.Y. Giants | 21 |
| 10 | DALLAS | 23 |
| 3 | Phoenix | 16 |
| 14 | MIAMI | 19 |
| 3 | N.Y. GIANTS | 7 |
| 17 | Washington | 14 |
| 17 | Dallas | 23 |
| 7 | BUFFALO | 10 |
| 20 | Indianapolis | 10 |
| 37 | NEW ORLEANS | 26 |
| 37 | San Francisco | *34 |

| UseName | Pos. | Hgt | Wgt | Age | Int | Pts |
|---|---|---|---|---|---|---|
| Brian Baldinger | OT-OG | 6'4" | 278 | 33 | | |
| Antone Davis | OT | 6'4" | 325 | 26 | | |
| Ron Heller | OT | 6'6" | 280 | 31 | | |
| Broderick Thompson | OT | 6'5" | 295 | 33 | | |
| Eric Floyd | OG | 6'5" | 310 | 27 | | |
| Lester Holmes | OG | 6'3" | 301 | 23 | | |
| John Hudson | OG-C | 6'2" | 275 | 25 | | |
| Tom McHale | OG | 6'4" | 290 | 30 | | |
| Mike Schad | OG | 6'5" | 290 | 29 | | |
| Rob Selby | OG | 6'3" | 286 | 25 | | |
| David Alexander | C | 6'3" | 275 | 29 | | |
| Mike Chalenski | DE | 6'4" | 260 | 23 | | |
| Mike Flores | DE | 6'3" | 256 | 26 | | 2 |
| Tim Harris | DE | 6'6" | 258 | 28 | | |
| Clyde Simmons | DE | 6'6" | 280 | 29 | 1 | |
| Andy Harmon | DT | 6'4" | 265 | 24 | | |
| Tommy Jeter | DT | 6'5" | 282 | 23 | | |
| Keith Millard | DT | 6'5" | 263 | 31 | | |
| Gerald Nichols (to WAS) | DT | 6'2" | 262 | 29 | | |
| William Perry (from CHI) | DT | 6'2" | 335 | 30 | | |
| Leonard Renfro | DT | 6'2" | 291 | 23 | | |
| Louis Cooper | LB | 6'1" | 243 | 30 | | |
| Byron Evans | LB | 6'2" | 235 | 29 | 1 | 6 |
| Britt Hager | LB | 6'1" | 225 | 27 | 1 | |
| Seth Joyner | LB | 6'2" | 235 | 28 | 1 | |
| Derrick Oden | LB | 5'11" | 230 | 22 | | |
| John Roper (from DAL) | LB | 6'1" | 235 | 27 | | |
| Ken Rose | LB | 6'1" | 215 | 31 | | |
| William Thomas | LB | 6'2" | 218 | 25 | 2 | |
| Eric Allen | DB | 5'10" | 180 | 27 | 6 | 24 |
| Corey Barlow | DB | 5'9" | 182 | 22 | | |
| William Frizzell | DB | 6'3" | 206 | 30 | | |
| Wes Hopkins | DB | 6'1" | 215 | 31 | 1 | |
| Erik McMillan (to CLE, KC) | DB | 6'2" | 200 | 28 | | |
| Mark McMillian | DB | 5'7" | 162 | 23 | 2 | |
| Rich Miano | DB | 6'1" | 200 | 30 | 4 | |
| Mike Reid | DB | 6'1" | 218 | 22 | | |
| Ben Smith | DB | 5'11" | 185 | 26 | | |
| Otis Smith | DB | 5'11" | 184 | 27 | 1 | |
| Andre Waters | DB | 5'11" | 200 | 31 | | |
| Bubby Brister | QB | 6'3" | 207 | 31 | | |
| Randall Cunningham | QB | 6'4" | 205 | 30 | | 6 |
| Preston Jones | QB | 6'3" | 223 | 23 | | |
| Ken O'Brien | QB | 6'4" | 212 | 32 | | |
| Vaughn Hebron | HB | 5'8" | 196 | 22 | | 18 |
| James Joseph | HB-FB | 6' | 222 | 25 | | 6 |
| Heath Sherman | HB-FB | 6' | 205 | 26 | | 12 |
| Herschel Walker | HB | 6'1" | 225 | 31 | | 24 |
| Victor Bailey | WR | 6'2" | 196 | 23 | | 6 |
| Fred Barnett | WR | 6' | 199 | 27 | | |
| Reggie Lawrence | WR | 6' | 178 | 23 | | |
| James Lofton (from LA) | WR | 6'3" | 190 | 37 | | |
| Paul Richardson | WR | 6'3" | 204 | 24 | | |
| Vai Sikahema | WR | 5'9" | 196 | 31 | | |
| Jeff Sydner | WR | 5'6" | 170 | 23 | | |
| Calvin Williams | WR | 5'11" | 190 | 26 | | 60 |
| Michael Young | WR | 6'1" | 183 | 31 | | 12 |
| Mark Bavaro | TE | 6'4" | 245 | 30 | | 36 |
| Maurice Johnson | TE | 6'2" | 243 | 26 | | |
| Matt Bahr | K | 5'10" | 175 | 37 | | 67 |
| Jeff Feagles | K | 6' | 205 | 27 | | |
| Roger Ruzek | K | 6'1" | 200 | 32 | | 37 |

Tony Brooks — Back Injury

## PHOENIX CARDINALS 7-9 Joe Bugel

| Scores of Each Game | | |
|---|---|---|
| 17 | Philadelphia | 23 |
| 17 | Washington | 10 |
| 10 | DALLAS | 17 |
| 20 | Detroit | 26 |
| 21 | NEW ENGLAND | 23 |
| 36 | WASHINGTON | 6 |
| 14 | San Francisco | 28 |
| 17 | NEW ORLEANS | 20 |
| 16 | PHILADELPHIA | 3 |
| 15 | Dallas | 20 |
| 17 | N.Y. Giants | 19 |
| 38 | L.A. RAMS | 10 |
| 14 | DETROIT | 21 |
| 30 | Seattle | *27 |
| 17 | N.Y. GIANTS | 6 |
| 27 | Atlanta | 10 |

| UseName | Pos. | Hgt | Wgt | Age | Int | Pts |
|---|---|---|---|---|---|---|
| Ben Coleman | OT | 6'6" | 335 | 22 | | |
| Rick Cunningham | OT-OG | 6'6" | 320 | 26 | | |
| Ernest Dye | OT | 6'6" | 325 | 22 | | |
| Luis Sharpe | OT | 6'4" | 280 | 33 | | |
| Mark May | OG-C | 6'6" | 305 | 33 | | |
| Lance Smith | OG | 6'2" | 285 | 30 | | |
| Joe Wolf | OG-OT | 6'6" | 296 | 26 | | |
| Ed Cunningham | C | 6'3" | 285 | 24 | | |
| Kani Kauahi | C | 6'3" | 275 | 34 | | |
| Michael Bankston | DE | 6'2" | 280 | 23 | | |
| Chad Brown | DE | 6'7" | 265 | 22 | | |
| Reuben Davis | DE-DT | 6'4" | 320 | 28 | | |
| Mike Jones | DE | 6'4" | 295 | 24 | | |
| Freddie Joe Nunn | DE-LB | 6'4" | 255 | 31 | | |
| Eric Swann | DT-DE | 6'4" | 295 | 23 | | 2 |
| Chuckie Johnson | DT | 6'4" | 310 | 24 | | |
| Keith Rucker | DT | 6'3" | 360 | 24 | | |
| David Braxton | LB | 6'1" | 240 | 28 | | |
| Ken Harvey | LB | 6'2" | 245 | 28 | | |
| Eric Hill | LB | 6'1" | 255 | 26 | | |
| Steve Hyche | LB | 6'2" | 250 | 30 | | |
| Garth Jax | LB | 6'2" | 250 | 29 | | |
| Jock Jones | LB | 6'2" | 240 | 25 | | |
| Tyronne Stowe | LB | 6'1" | 250 | 28 | | |
| Brett Wallerstedt | LB | 6'1" | 240 | 22 | | |
| John Booty | DB | 6' | 180 | 27 | 2 | |
| Chuck Cecil | DB | 6' | 185 | 28 | | |
| Dave Duerson | DB | 6'1" | 220 | 32 | | |
| Odie Harris | DB | 6' | 190 | 27 | | |
| Steve Lofton | DB | 5'9" | 185 | 24 | | |
| Lorenzo Lynch | DB | 5'9" | 200 | 30 | 3 | 6 |
| Robert Massey | DB | 5'10" | 195 | 26 | | |
| Chris Oldham | DB | 5'9" | 195 | 24 | 1 | |
| Aeneas Williams | DB | 5'10" | 190 | 25 | 2 | 12 |
| Mike Zordich | DB | 5'11" | 201 | 29 | 1 | |
| Steve Beuerlein | QB | 6'3" | 210 | 28 | | |
| Chris Chandler | QB | 6'4" | 225 | 27 | | |
| Will Furrer | QB | 6'3" | 210 | 25 | | |
| Tony Sacca | QB | 6'5" | 235 | 23 | | |
| Johnny Bailey | HB | 5'8" | 190 | 26 | | 12 |
| Eric Blount | HB | 5'9" | 200 | 22 | | 6 |
| Larry Centers | HB | 5'11" | 215 | 25 | | 18 |
| Garrison Hearst | HB | 5'11" | 215 | 22 | | 6 |
| Ron Moore | HB-FB | 5'10" | 220 | 23 | | 54 |
| Gary Clark | WR | 5'9" | 175 | 31 | | 24 |
| Anthony Edwards | WR | 5'9" | 190 | 27 | | 6 |
| Randal Hill | WR | 5'10" | 180 | 23 | | 24 |
| Ricky Proehl | WR | 5'10" | 190 | 25 | | 42 |
| Pat Beach | TE | 6'4" | 250 | 33 | | |
| Chad Fann | TE | 6'3" | 250 | 23 | | |
| Walter Reeves | TE | 6'4" | 270 | 27 | | 6 |
| Butch Rolle | TE | 6'4" | 245 | 29 | | 6 |
| Derek Ware | TE | 6'2" | 250 | 25 | | |
| Rich Camarillo | K | 5'11" | 200 | 33 | | |
| Greg Davis | K | 6' | 205 | 27 | | 100 |

Rob Baxley — Knee Injury

## WASHINGTON REDSKINS 4-12 Richie Petitbon

| Scores of Each Game | | |
|---|---|---|
| 35 | DALLAS | 16 |
| 10 | PHOENIX | 17 |
| 31 | Philadelphia | 34 |
| 10 | Miami | 17 |
| 7 | N.Y. GIANTS | 41 |
| 6 | Phoenix | 36 |
| 10 | Buffalo | 24 |
| 30 | INDIANAPOLIS | 24 |
| 6 | N.Y. Giants | 20 |
| 6 | L.A. Rams | 10 |
| 14 | PHILADELPHIA | 17 |
| 23 | Tampa Bay | 17 |
| 0 | N.Y. JETS | 3 |
| 30 | ATLANTA | 17 |
| 3 | Dallas | 38 |
| 9 | MINNESOTA | 14 |

| UseName | Pos. | Hgt | Wgt | Age | Int | Pts |
|---|---|---|---|---|---|---|
| Ray Brown | OT | 6'5" | 312 | 30 | | |
| Mo Elewonibi | OT | 6'4" | 286 | 27 | | |
| Joe Jacoby | OT | 6'7" | 314 | 33 | | |
| Ed Simmons | OT | 6'5" | 300 | 29 | | |
| Darryl Moore | OG | 6'2" | 292 | 24 | | |
| Mark Schlereth | OG | 6'3" | 278 | 27 | | |
| Guy Bingham | C | 6'3" | 260 | 35 | | |
| Jeff Bostic | C | 6'2" | 269 | 34 | | |
| Greg Huntington | C | 6'3" | 287 | 22 | | |
| Raleigh McKenzie | C-OG | 6'2" | 277 | 30 | | |
| Marc Raab | C | 6'3" | 265 | 24 | | |
| Jason Buck | DE | 6'4" | 274 | 30 | | |
| Shane Collins | DE | 6'3" | 267 | 24 | | |
| Jeff Faulkner (from NO) | DE | 6'4" | 305 | 29 | | |
| Charles Mann | DE | 6'6" | 272 | 32 | | |
| Al Noga | DE | 6'1" | 269 | 27 | | |
| Sterling Palmer | DE | 6'5" | 256 | 22 | | |
| Tim Johnson | DT | 6'3" | 275 | 27 | | |
| Jim Wahler | DT | 6'4" | 275 | 27 | | |
| Eric Williams | DT | 6'4" | 286 | 31 | | |
| Bobby Wilson | DT | 6'2" | 297 | 25 | | |
| Carl Banks | LB | 6'4" | 249 | 31 | | |
| Monte Coleman | LB | 6'2" | 242 | 35 | 2 | 6 |
| Andre Collins | LB | 6'1" | 231 | 25 | 1 | |
| Kurt Gouveia | LB | 6'1" | 233 | 28 | 1 | 6 |
| Rick Graf | LB | 6'5" | 244 | 29 | | |
| Rick Hamilton | LB | 6'2" | 241 | 23 | | |
| Lamont Hollinquest | LB | 6'3" | 245 | 22 | | |
| Todd Bowles | DB | 6'2" | 205 | 29 | | |
| Tom Carter | DB | 5'11" | 181 | 20 | 6 | |
| Danny Copeland | DB | 6'2" | 210 | 27 | 1 | |
| Brad Edwards | DB | 6'2" | 207 | 27 | 1 | |
| Pat Eilers | DB | 5'11" | 195 | 26 | | |
| Darrell Green | DB | 5'8" | 170 | 33 | 4 | 6 |
| A.J. Johnson | DB | 5'8" | 175 | 26 | 1 | 6 |
| Alvoid Mays | DB | 5'9" | 172 | 27 | | |
| Darryl Morrison | CB | 5'11" | 185 | 22 | | |
| Johnny Thomas | DB | 5'9" | 191 | 29 | | |
| Cary Conklin | QB | 6'4" | 225 | 25 | | |
| Rich Gannon | QB | 6'3" | 208 | 27 | | 6 |
| Mark Rypien | QB | 6'4" | 230 | 30 | | 18 |
| Reggie Brooks | HB | 5'8" | 202 | 22 | | 18 |
| Earnest Byner | HB-FB | 5'10" | 218 | 30 | | 6 |
| Ricky Ervins | HB | 5'7" | 195 | 24 | | |
| Brian Mitchell | HB | 5'10" | 203 | 25 | | 18 |
| Gregory Clifton | WR | 5'11" | 175 | 25 | | |
| Desmond Howard | WR | 5'9" | 180 | 23 | | |
| Tim McGee | WR | 5'10" | 174 | 29 | | 18 |
| Art Monk | WR | 6'3" | 202 | 35 | | 12 |
| Ricky Sanders | WR | 5'11" | 178 | 31 | | 24 |
| Mark Stock | WR | 6' | 180 | 27 | | |
| James Jenkins | TE | 6'2" | 241 | 26 | | |
| Ron Middleton | TE | 6'2" | 262 | 28 | | 12 |
| Terry Orr | TE | 6'2" | 235 | 31 | | |
| Jim Riggs | TE | 6'5" | 245 | 29 | | |
| Ray Rowe | TE | 6'2" | 256 | 24 | | |
| Frank Wycheck | TE | 6'3" | 235 | 21 | | |
| Kelly Goodburn | K | 6'2" | 199 | 31 | | |
| Chip Lohmiller | K | 6'3" | 215 | 27 | | 72 |
| Reggie Roby | K | 6'2" | 258 | 32 | | |

Jim Lachey — Knee Injury
Matt Elliott — Knee Injury

Stephen Hobbs — Abdomen Injury

## DALLAS COWBOYS

### RUSHING

| Last Name | No. | Yds | Avg | TD |
|---|---|---|---|---|
| E. Smith | 283 | 1486 | 5.3 | 9 |
| Lassic | 75 | 269 | 3.6 | 3 |
| Coleman | 34 | 132 | 3.9 | 2 |
| Aikman | 32 | 125 | 3.9 | 0 |
| Johnston | 24 | 74 | 3.1 | 3 |
| Gainer | 9 | 29 | 3.2 | 0 |
| K. Williams | 7 | 26 | 3.7 | 2 |
| Agee | 6 | 13 | 2.2 | 0 |
| Irvin | 2 | 6 | 3.0 | 0 |
| Novacek | 1 | 2 | 2.0 | 1 |
| J. Garrett | 8 | -8 | -1.0 | 0 |

### RECEIVING

| Last Name | No. | Yds | Avg | TD |
|---|---|---|---|---|
| Irvin | 88 | 1330 | 15.1 | 7 |
| E. Smith | 57 | 414 | 7.3 | 1 |
| Johnston | 50 | 372 | 7.4 | 1 |
| Novacek | 44 | 445 | 10.1 | 1 |
| Harper | 36 | 777 | 21.6 | 5 |
| K. Williams | 20 | 151 | 7.6 | 2 |
| Lassic | 9 | 37 | 4.1 | 0 |
| Gainer | 6 | 37 | 6.3 | 0 |
| Coleman | 4 | 24 | 6.0 | 0 |
| T. Williams | 1 | 25 | 25.0 | 0 |
| Price | 1 | 4 | 4.0 | 0 |
| Galbraith | 1 | 1 | 1.0 | 1 |

### PUNT RETURNS

| Last Name | No. | Yds | Avg | TD |
|---|---|---|---|---|
| K. Williams | 36 | 381 | 10.5 | 2 |
| Washington | 1 | 0 | 0.0 | 0 |

### KICKOFF RETURNS

| Last Name | No. | Yds | Avg | TD |
|---|---|---|---|---|
| K. Williams | 31 | 689 | 22.2 | 0 |
| K. Smith | 1 | 33 | 33.0 | 0 |
| Gant | 1 | 18 | 18.0 | 0 |
| R. Jones | 1 | 12 | 12.0 | 0 |
| Hennings | 1 | 7 | 7.0 | 0 |
| Novacek | 1 | -1 | -1.0 | 0 |
| Vanderbeek | 0 | 0 | — | 0 |

### PASSING—PUNTING—KICKING

| PASSING | Att | Cmp | % | Yds | Yd/Att | TD | Int— | % | RK |
|---|---|---|---|---|---|---|---|---|---|
| Aikman | 392 | 271 | 69.1 | 3100 | 7.91 | 15 | 6— | 1.5 | 2 |
| J. Garrett | 19 | 9 | 47.4 | 61 | 3.21 | 0 | 0— | 0.0 | |
| Harper | 1 | 1 | 100.0 | 46 | 46.00 | 0 | 0— | 0.0 | |

| PUNTING | No. | Avg. |
|---|---|---|
| Jett | 56 | 41.8 |

| KICKING | XP | Att. | % | FG | Att | % |
|---|---|---|---|---|---|---|
| Murray | 38 | 38 | 100 | 28 | 33 | 85 |
| Elliott | 2 | 3 | 67 | 2 | 4 | 50 |

## NEW YORK GIANTS

### RUSHING

| Last Name | No. | Yds | Avg | TD |
|---|---|---|---|---|
| Hampton | 292 | 1077 | 3.7 | 5 |
| Tillman | 121 | 585 | 4.8 | 3 |
| Meggett | 69 | 329 | 4.8 | 0 |
| Bunch | 33 | 128 | 3.9 | 2 |
| Rasheed | 9 | 42 | 4.7 | 1 |
| Simms | 28 | 31 | 1.1 | 0 |
| M. Jackson | 3 | 25 | 8.3 | 0 |
| Graham | 2 | -3 | -1.5 | 0 |
| Da. Brown | 3 | -4 | -1.3 | 0 |

### RECEIVING

| Last Name | No. | Yds | Avg | TD |
|---|---|---|---|---|
| M. Jackson | 58 | 708 | 12.2 | 4 |
| Meggett | 38 | 319 | 8.4 | 0 |
| Calloway | 35 | 513 | 14.7 | 3 |
| McCaffrey | 27 | 335 | 12.4 | 2 |
| Sherrard | 24 | 433 | 18.0 | 2 |
| Cross | 21 | 272 | 13.0 | 5 |
| Hampton | 18 | 210 | 11.7 | 0 |
| Bunch | 13 | 98 | 7.5 | 1 |
| Pierce | 12 | 212 | 17.7 | 0 |
| De. Brown | 7 | 56 | 8.0 | 0 |
| Tillman | 1 | 21 | 21.0 | 0 |
| Crawford | 1 | 6 | 6.0 | 0 |
| Rasheed | 1 | 3 | 3.0 | 0 |
| Simms | 1 | -6 | -6.0 | 0 |

### PUNT RETURNS

| Last Name | No. | Yds | Avg | TD |
|---|---|---|---|---|
| Meggett | 32 | 331 | 10.3 | 1 |

### KICKOFF RETURNS

| Last Name | No. | Yds | Avg | TD |
|---|---|---|---|---|
| Meggett | 24 | 403 | 16.8 | 0 |
| Calloway | 6 | 89 | 14.8 | 0 |
| Cross | 2 | 15 | 7.5 | 0 |

### PASSING—PUNTING—KICKING

| PASSING | Att | Cmp | % | Yds | Yd/Att | TD | Int— | % | RK |
|---|---|---|---|---|---|---|---|---|---|
| Simms | 400 | 247 | 61.8 | 3038 | 7.60 | 15 | 9— | 2.3 | 3 |
| Graham | 22 | 8 | 36.4 | 79 | 3.59 | 0 | 0— | 0.0 | |
| Meggett | 2 | 2 | 100.0 | 63 | 31.50 | 2 | 0— | 0.0 | |

| PUNTING | No. | Avg. |
|---|---|---|
| Horan | 44 | 42.8 |

| KICKING | XP | ATT | % | FG | ATT | % |
|---|---|---|---|---|---|---|
| Treadwell | 28 | 29 | 97 | 25 | 31 | 81 |
| Daluiso | 0 | 0 | — | 1 | 3 | 33 |

## PHILADELPHIA EAGLES

### RUSHING

| Last Name | No. | Yds | Avg | TD |
|---|---|---|---|---|
| Walker | 174 | 746 | 4.3 | 1 |
| Sherman | 115 | 406 | 3.5 | 2 |
| Hebron | 84 | 297 | 3.5 | 3 |
| Joseph | 39 | 140 | 3.6 | 0 |
| Cunningham | 18 | 110 | 6.1 | 1 |
| Brister | 20 | 39 | 2.0 | 0 |
| O'Brien | 4 | 17 | 4.3 | 0 |
| Feagles | 2 | 6 | 3.0 | 0 |

### RECEIVING

| Last Name | No. | Yds | Avg | TD |
|---|---|---|---|---|
| Walker | 75 | 610 | 8.1 | 3 |
| Williams | 60 | 725 | 12.1 | 10 |
| Bavaro | 43 | 481 | 11.2 | 6 |
| Bailey | 41 | 545 | 13.3 | 1 |
| Joseph | 29 | 291 | 10.0 | 1 |
| Barnett | 17 | 170 | 10.0 | 0 |
| Young | 14 | 186 | 13.3 | 2 |
| Lofton | 14 | 183 | 13.1 | 0 |
| Sherman | 12 | 78 | 6.5 | 0 |
| Hebron | 11 | 82 | 7.5 | 0 |
| Johnson | 10 | 81 | 8.1 | 0 |
| Sydner | 2 | 42 | 21.0 | 0 |
| Lawrence | 1 | 5 | 5.0 | 0 |

### PUNT RETURNS

| Last Name | No. | Yds | Avg | TD |
|---|---|---|---|---|
| Sikahema | 33 | 275 | 8.3 | 0 |
| O. Smith | 0 | 9 | — | 0 |

### KICKOFF RETURNS

| Last Name | No. | Yds | Avg | TD |
|---|---|---|---|---|
| Sikahema | 30 | 579 | 19.3 | 0 |
| Walker | 11 | 184 | 16.7 | 0 |
| Sydner | 9 | 158 | 17.6 | 0 |
| Hebron | 3 | 35 | 11.7 | 0 |
| Johnson | 1 | 7 | 7.0 | 0 |
| O. Smith | 0 | 24 | — | 0 |

### PASSING—PUNTING—KICKING

| PASSING | Att | Cmp | % | Yds | Yd/Att | TD | Int— | % | RK |
|---|---|---|---|---|---|---|---|---|---|
| Brister | 309 | 181 | 58.6 | 1905 | 6.17 | 14 | 5— | 1.6 | 4 |
| O'Brien | 137 | 71 | 51.8 | 708 | 5.17 | 4 | 3— | 2.2 | |
| Cunningham | 110 | 76 | 69.1 | 850 | 7.73 | 5 | 5— | 4.5 | |

| PUNTING | No. | Avg. |
|---|---|---|
| Feagles | 83 | 40.0 |

| KICKING | XP | ATT | % | FG | ATT | % |
|---|---|---|---|---|---|---|
| Bahr | 28 | 29 | 97 | 13 | 18 | 72 |
| Ruzek | 13 | 16 | 81 | 8 | 10 | 80 |

## PHOENIX CARDINALS

### RUSHING

| Last Name | No. | Yds | Avg | TD |
|---|---|---|---|---|
| Moore | 263 | 1018 | 3.9 | 9 |
| Hearst | 76 | 264 | 3.5 | 1 |
| Bailey | 49 | 253 | 5.2 | 1 |
| Centers | 25 | 152 | 6.1 | 0 |
| Proehl | 8 | 47 | 5.9 | 0 |
| Beuerlein | 22 | 45 | 2.0 | 0 |
| Blount | 5 | 28 | 5.6 | 1 |
| Chandler | 3 | 2 | 0.7 | 0 |
| Camarillo | 1 | 0 | 0.0 | 0 |

### RECEIVING

| Last Name | No. | Yds | Avg | TD |
|---|---|---|---|---|
| Centers | 66 | 603 | 9.1 | 3 |
| Proehl | 65 | 877 | 13.5 | 7 |
| Clark | 63 | 818 | 13.0 | 4 |
| R. Hill | 35 | 519 | 14.8 | 4 |
| Bailey | 32 | 243 | 7.6 | 0 |
| Edwards | 13 | 326 | 25.1 | 1 |
| Rolle | 10 | 67 | 6.7 | 1 |
| Reeves | 9 | 67 | 7.4 | 1 |
| Hearst | 6 | 18 | 3.0 | 0 |
| Blount | 5 | 36 | 7.2 | 0 |
| Ware | 3 | 45 | 15.0 | 0 |
| Moore | 3 | 16 | 5.3 | 0 |

### PUNT RETURNS

| Last Name | No. | Yds | Avg | TD |
|---|---|---|---|---|
| Bailey | 35 | 282 | 8.1 | 1 |
| Blount | 9 | 90 | 10.0 | 0 |
| Edwards | 3 | 12 | 4.0 | 0 |

### KICKOFF RETURNS

| Last Name | No. | Yds | Avg | TD |
|---|---|---|---|---|
| Bailey | 31 | 699 | 22.5 | 0 |
| Blount | 8 | 163 | 20.4 | 0 |
| Edwards | 3 | 51 | 17.0 | 0 |
| Lofton | 1 | 18 | 18.0 | 0 |
| Smith | 1 | 11 | 11.0 | 0 |
| Moore | 1 | 9 | 9.0 | 0 |

### PASSING—PUNTING—KICKING

| PASSING | Att | Cmp | % | Yds | Yd/Att | TD | Int— | % | RK |
|---|---|---|---|---|---|---|---|---|---|
| Beuerlein | 418 | 258 | 61.7 | 3164 | 7.57 | 18 | 17— | 4.1 | 6 |
| Chandler | 103 | 52 | 50.5 | 471 | 4.57 | 3 | 2— | 2.9 | |
| Hearst | 1 | 0 | 0.0 | 0 | 0.00 | 0 | 1— | 100.0 | |

| PUNTING | No. | Avg. |
|---|---|---|
| Camarillo | 73 | 43.7 |

| KICKING | XP | Att. | % | FG | Att | % |
|---|---|---|---|---|---|---|
| Davis | 37 | 37 | 100 | 21 | 28 | 75 |

## WASHINGTON REDSKINS

### RUSHING

| Last Name | No. | Yds | Avg | TD |
|---|---|---|---|---|
| Brooks | 223 | 1063 | 4.8 | 3 |
| Mitchell | 63 | 246 | 3.9 | 3 |
| Ervins | 50 | 201 | 4.0 | 0 |
| Byner | 23 | 105 | 4.6 | 1 |
| Gannon | 21 | 88 | 4.2 | 1 |
| Howard | 2 | 17 | 8.5 | 0 |
| Sanders | 1 | 7 | 7.0 | 0 |
| Rypien | 9 | 2 | 0.2 | 3 |
| Roby | 1 | 0 | 0.0 | 0 |
| Monk | 1 | -1 | -1.0 | 0 |
| Conklin | 2 | -2 | -1.0 | 0 |

### RECEIVING

| Last Name | No. | Yds | Avg | TD |
|---|---|---|---|---|
| Sanders | 58 | 638 | 11.0 | 4 |
| Monk | 41 | 398 | 9.7 | 2 |
| McGee | 39 | 500 | 12.8 | 3 |
| Byner | 27 | 194 | 7.2 | 0 |
| Middleton | 24 | 154 | 6.4 | 2 |
| Howard | 23 | 286 | 12.4 | 0 |
| Brooks | 21 | 186 | 8.9 | 0 |
| Mitchell | 20 | 157 | 7.9 | 0 |
| Ervins | 16 | 123 | 7.7 | 0 |
| Wycheck | 16 | 113 | 7.1 | 0 |
| Clifton | 2 | 15 | 7.5 | 0 |

### PUNT RETURNS

| Last Name | No. | Yds | Avg | TD |
|---|---|---|---|---|
| Mitchell | 29 | 193 | 6.7 | 0 |
| Howard | 4 | 25 | 6.3 | 0 |
| Green | 1 | 27 | 27.0 | 0 |
| Mays | 1 | 0 | 0.0 | 0 |

### KICKOFF RETURNS

| Last Name | No. | Yds | Avg | TD |
|---|---|---|---|---|
| Mitchell | 33 | 678 | 20.5 | 0 |
| Howard | 21 | 405 | 19.3 | 0 |
| Ervins | 2 | 29 | 14.5 | 0 |
| Bowles | 1 | 27 | 27.0 | 0 |
| Buck | 1 | 15 | 15.0 | 0 |
| Brooks | 1 | 12 | 12.0 | 0 |

### PASSING—PUNTING—KICKING

| PASSING | Att | Cmp | % | Yds | Yd/Att | TD | Int— | % | RK |
|---|---|---|---|---|---|---|---|---|---|
| Rypien | 319 | 166 | 52.0 | 1514 | 4.75 | 4 | 10— | 3.1 | 14 |
| Gannon | 125 | 74 | 59.2 | 704 | 5.63 | 3 | 7— | 2.4 | |
| Conklin | 87 | 46 | 52.9 | 496 | 5.70 | 4 | 3— | 3.4 | |
| Mitchell | 2 | 1 | 50.0 | 50 | 25.00 | 0 | 1— | 50.0 | |

| PUNTING | No. | Avg. |
|---|---|---|
| Roby | 78 | 44.2 |
| Goodburn | 5 | 39.4 |

| KICKING | XP | ATT | % | FG | ATT | % |
|---|---|---|---|---|---|---|
| Lohmiller | 24 | 26 | 92 | 16 | 28 | 57 |

## DETROIT LIONS 10-6 Wayne Fontes

| Scores of Each Game | | |
|---|---|---|
| 30 | ATLANTA | 13 |
| 19 | New England | *16 |
| 3 | New Orleans | 14 |
| 26 | PHOENIX | 20 |
| 10 | Tampa Bay | 27 |
| 30 | SEATTLE | 10 |
| 16 | L.A. Rams | 13 |
| 30 | Minnesota | 27 |
| 23 | TAMPA BAY | 0 |
| 17 | Green Bay | 26 |
| 6 | CHICAGO | 10 |
| 0 | MINNESOTA | 13 |
| 21 | Phoenix | 14 |
| 17 | SAN FRANCISCO | 55 |
| 20 | Chicago | 14 |
| 30 | GREEN BAY | 20 |

| Use Name | Pos. | Hgt. | Wgt. | Age | Int | Pts |
|---|---|---|---|---|---|---|
| Lomas Brown | OT | 6'4" | 287 | 30 | | |
| Scott Conover | OT | 6'4" | 285 | 24 | | |
| Jack Linn (to CIN) | OT | 6'5" | 285 | 26 | | |
| David Lutz | OT | 6'6" | 305 | 33 | | |
| Larry Tharpe | OT | 6'4" | 299 | 22 | | |
| Shawn Bouwens | OG | 6'4" | 290 | 25 | | |
| Bill Fralic | OG | 6'5" | 280 | 30 | | |
| David Richards | OG | 6'5" | 310 | 27 | | |
| Mike Compton | C-OG | 6'6" | 297 | 22 | | |
| Kevin Glover | C | 6'2" | 282 | 30 | | |
| Mark Rodenhauser | C | 6'5" | 280 | 32 | | |
| Dan Owens | DE | 6'3" | 280 | 26 | 1 | |
| Robert Porcher | DE | 6'3" | 283 | 24 | | |
| Kelvin Pritchett | DE | 6'2" | 281 | 23 | | |
| Marc Spindler | DE-NT | 6'5" | 290 | 23 | | |
| Lawrence Pete | NT | 6' | 275 | 27 | | |
| Mack Travis | NT | 6'1" | 280 | 23 | | |

| Use Name | Pos. | Hgt. | Wgt. | Age | Int | Pts |
|---|---|---|---|---|---|---|
| Toby Caston | LB | 6'1" | 243 | 28 | | |
| Darryl Ford | LB | 6'1" | 225 | 27 | | |
| Dennis Gibson | LB | 6'2" | 243 | 29 | 1 | |
| Tracy Hayworth | LB | 6'3" | 260 | 25 | | |
| George Jamison | LB | 6'1" | 235 | 30 | 2 | 6 |
| Victor Jones | LB | 6'2" | 250 | 26 | | |
| Antonio London | LB | 6'2" | 234 | 22 | | |
| Tracy Scroggins | LB | 6'2" | 255 | 23 | 1 | |
| Chris Spielman | LB | 6' | 247 | 27 | 2 | |
| Pat Swilling | LB | 6'3" | 242 | 28 | 3 | |
| Bennie Blades | DB | 6'1" | 221 | 26 | | |
| Willie Clay | DB | 5'9" | 184 | 22 | | 12 |
| Harry Colon | DB | 6' | 203 | 24 | 2 | |
| Ray Crockett | DB | 5'9" | 181 | 26 | 2 | |
| Greg Jeffries | DB | 5'9" | 184 | 21 | | |
| Tim McKyer | DB | 6' | 174 | 29 | 2 | |
| Ryan McNeil | DB | 6' | 175 | 22 | 2 | |
| Kevin Scott | DB | 5'9" | 175 | 24 | | |
| William White | DB | 5'10" | 191 | 27 | 1 | |

Mike Cofer — Knee Injury

| Use Name | Pos. | Hgt. | Wgt. | Age | Int | Pts |
|---|---|---|---|---|---|---|
| Erik Kramer | QB | 6'1" | 199 | 28 | | |
| Rodney Peete | QB | 6' | 207 | 27 | | 6 |
| Andre Ware | QB | 6'2" | 205 | 25 | | |
| Eric Lynch | HB | 5'10" | 224 | 23 | | 12 |
| Derrick Moore | HB-FB | 6'1" | 227 | 25 | | 24 |
| Curvin Richards | HB | 5'9" | 195 | 24 | | |
| Barry Sanders | HB-FB | 5'8" | 203 | 25 | | 18 |
| Reggie Barrett | WR | 6'3" | 215 | 24 | | |
| Jeff Campbell | WR | 5'8" | 173 | 25 | | |
| Mel Gray | WR | 5'9" | 172 | 32 | | 6 |
| Willie Green | WR | 6'2" | 181 | 27 | | 12 |
| Aubrey Matthews | WR | 5'7" | 165 | 30 | | |
| Herman Moore | WR | 6'3" | 210 | 23 | | 36 |
| Brett Perriman | WR | 5'9" | 180 | 27 | | 12 |
| Vernon Turner (to TB) | WR | 5'8" | 185 | 26 | | |
| Ty Hallock | TE | 6'3" | 249 | 22 | | 12 |
| Rodney Holman | TE | 6'3" | 238 | 33 | | 12 |
| Jimmie Johnson | TE | 6'2" | 255 | 26 | | |
| Marty Thompson | TE | 6'3" | 243 | 23 | | |
| Jim Arnold | K | 6'3" | 211 | 32 | | |
| Jason Hanson | K | 5'11" | 183 | 23 | | 130 |

Ed Tillison — Knee Injury

## MINNESOTA VIKINGS 9-7 Dennis Green

| Scores of Each Game | | |
|---|---|---|
| 7 | L.A. Raiders | 24 |
| 10 | CHICAGO | 7 |
| 15 | GREEN BAY | 13 |
| 19 | San Francisco | 38 |
| 15 | TAMPA BAY | 0 |
| 19 | Chicago | 12 |
| 27 | DETROIT | 30 |
| 17 | SAN DIEGO | 30 |
| 26 | Denver | 23 |
| 10 | Tampa Bay | 23 |
| 14 | NEW ORLEANS | 17 |
| 13 | Detroit | 0 |
| 20 | DALLAS | 37 |
| 21 | Green Bay | 17 |
| 30 | KANSAS CITY | 10 |
| 14 | W ashington | 9 |

| Use Name | Pos. | Hgt. | Wgt. | Age | Int | Pts |
|---|---|---|---|---|---|---|
| Scott Adams | OT | 6'5" | 293 | 26 | | |
| Bernard Dafney | OT | 6'5" | 331 | 23 | | |
| Tim Irwin | OT | 6'6" | 297 | 34 | | |
| Everett Lindsay | OT | 6'4" | 290 | 22 | | |
| John Gerak | OG | 6'3" | 285 | 23 | | |
| Todd Kalis | OG | 6'5" | 289 | 28 | | |
| Randall McDaniel | OG | 6'3" | 275 | 28 | | |
| Jeff Christy | C | 6'3" | 277 | 24 | | |
| Mike Morris | C | 6'5" | 284 | 32 | | |
| Adam Schreiber | C | 6'4" | 288 | 31 | | |
| Chris Doleman | DE | 6'5" | 274 | 31 | 1 | |
| James Harris | DE | 6'4" | 270 | 25 | | |
| Robert Harris | DE | 6'4" | 290 | 24 | | |
| Roy Barker | DT | 6'4" | 280 | 24 | | |
| Brad Culpepper | DT | 6'1" | 260 | 25 | | |
| John Randle | DT | 6'1" | 275 | 25 | | |
| Henry Thomas | DT | 6'2" | 277 | 28 | | 2 |
| Esera Tuaolo | DT | 6'2" | 275 | 25 | | |

| Use Name | Pos. | Hgt. | Wgt. | Age | Int | Pts |
|---|---|---|---|---|---|---|
| Jack Del Rio | LB | 6'4" | 243 | 30 | 4 | |
| Dave Garnett | LB | 6'2" | 219 | 22 | | |
| Bruce Holmes | LB | 6'2" | 237 | 27 | | |
| Carlos Jenkins | LB | 6'3" | 217 | 25 | 2 | |
| Greg Manusky | LB | 6'1" | 233 | 27 | | |
| Ed McDaniel | LB | 5'11" | 230 | 24 | | |
| Ashley Sheppard | LB | 6'3" | 243 | 24 | | |
| Fred Strickland | LB | 6'2" | 245 | 27 | | |
| Ron Carpenter (to CIN) | DB | 6'1" | 188 | 23 | | |
| Vencie Glenn | DB | 6' | 201 | 28 | 5 | |
| Shawn Jones | DB | 6'1" | 200 | 23 | | |
| Carl Lee | DB | 6' | 186 | 32 | 3 | |
| Lamar McGriggs | DB | 6'3" | 210 | 25 | 1 | 6 |
| Audrey McMillian | DB | 6' | 189 | 31 | 4 | 6 |
| Anthony Parker | DB | 5'10" | 181 | 27 | 1 | |
| Jayice Pearson | DB | 5'11" | 184 | 30 | 1 | |
| Todd Scott | DB | 5'10" | 207 | 25 | 2 | |

| Use Name | Pos. | Hgt. | Wgt. | Age | Int | Pts |
|---|---|---|---|---|---|---|
| Jim McMahon | QB | 6'1" | 196 | 34 | | |
| Sean Salisbury | QB | 6'5" | 218 | 30 | | |
| Gino Torretta | QB | 6'2" | 215 | 23 | | |
| Roger Craig | HB | 5'11" | 211 | 33 | | 12 |
| Chuck Evans | HB | 6'1" | 226 | 26 | | |
| Scottie Graham | HB | 5'9" | 215 | 24 | | 18 |
| Robert Smith | HB | 6' | 195 | 21 | | 12 |
| Barry Word | HB | 6'2" | 242 | 30 | | 12 |
| Anthony Carter | WR | 5'11" | 168 | 32 | | 30 |
| Cris Carter | WR | 6'3" | 198 | 27 | | 54 |
| Eric Guliford | WR | 5'8" | 165 | 23 | | |
| Qadry Ismail | WR | 6' | 192 | 22 | | 6 |
| Jake Reed | WR | 6'3" | 212 | 25 | | |
| Olanda Truitt | WR | 6' | 186 | 22 | | |
| Steve Jordan | TE | 6'4" | 242 | 32 | | 6 |
| Brent Novoselsky | TE | 6'3" | 237 | 27 | | |
| Derek Tennell | TE | 6'5" | 251 | 29 | | |
| Mike Tice | TE | 6'7" | 264 | 34 | | 6 |
| Harry Newsome | K | 6' | 193 | 30 | | |
| Fuad Reveiz | K | 5'11" | 223 | 30 | | 105 |

Terry Allen — Knee Injury
Ronnie West — Leg Injury

## GREEN BAY PACKERS 9-7 Mike Holmgren

| Scores of Each Game | | |
|---|---|---|
| 36 | L.A. RAMS | 6 |
| 17 | PHILADELPHIA | 20 |
| 13 | Minnesota | 15 |
| 14 | Dallas | 36 |
| 30 | DENVER | 27 |
| 37 | Tampa Bay | 14 |
| 17 | CHICAGO | 3 |
| 16 | Kansas City | 23 |
| 19 | New Orleans | 17 |
| 26 | DETROIT | 17 |
| 13 | TAMPA BAY | 10 |
| 17 | Chicago | 30 |
| 20 | San Diego | 13 |
| 17 | MINNESOTA | 21 |
| 28 | L.A. RAIDERS | 0 |
| 20 | Detroit | 30 |

| Use Name | Pos. | Hgt. | Wgt. | Age | Int | Pts |
|---|---|---|---|---|---|---|
| Earl Dotson | OT | 6'4" | 315 | 22 | | |
| Paul Hutchins | OT | 6'5" | 335 | 23 | | |
| Tunch Ilkin | OT | 6'3" | 272 | 35 | | |
| Tootie Robbins | OT | 6'5" | 315 | 35 | | |
| Ken Ruettgers | OT | 6'5" | 290 | 31 | | |
| Joe Sims | OT | 6'3" | 310 | 24 | | |
| Harry Galbreath | OG | 6'1" | 275 | 28 | | |
| Rich Moran | OG | 6'3" | 280 | 31 | | |
| Doug Widell | OG | 6'4" | 280 | 26 | | |
| James Campen | C | 6'3" | 280 | 29 | | |
| Frank Winters | C-OG | 6'3" | 285 | 29 | | |
| Lance Zeno (from CLE) | C | 6'4" | 279 | 26 | | |
| Matt Brock | DE | 6'5" | 280 | 27 | 1 | |
| Don Davey | DE | 6'4" | 270 | 25 | | |
| David Grant | DE | 6'4" | 275 | 27 | | |
| Shawn Patterson | DE | 6'5" | 270 | 29 | | |
| Reggie White | DE | 6'5" | 290 | 31 | | |
| Gilbert Brown | NT | 6'2" | 330 | 22 | | |
| John Jurkovic | NT | 6'2" | 285 | 26 | | |
| Bill Maas | NT | 6'5" | 295 | 31 | | |

Tom Neville — Achilles Injury

| Use Name | Pos. | Hgt. | Wgt. | Age | Int | Pts |
|---|---|---|---|---|---|---|
| Tony Bennett | LB | 6'2" | 243 | 26 | | |
| Keo Coleman | LB | 6'1" | 255 | 23 | | |
| Johnny Holland | LB | 6'2" | 235 | 28 | 2 | |
| George Koonce | LB | 6'1" | 238 | 24 | | |
| Jim Morrissey (from CHI) | LB | 6'3" | 225 | 30 | | |
| Joe Mott | LB | 6'4" | 238 | 27 | | |
| Brian Noble | LB | 6'3" | 245 | 30 | | |
| Bryce Paup | LB | 6'5" | 247 | 25 | 1 | |
| Wayne Simmons | LB | 6'3" | 240 | 23 | 2 | |
| Keith Traylor | LB | 6'2" | 260 | 23 | | |
| James Willis | LB | 6'2" | 235 | 20 | | |
| Terrell Buckley | DB | 5'9" | 174 | 22 | 2 | |
| LeRoy Butler | DB | 6' | 193 | 25 | 6 | 6 |
| Doug Evans | DB | 6'1" | 188 | 23 | 1 | |
| Corey Harris | DB-WR | 5'11" | 195 | 23 | | |
| Tim Hauck | DB | 5'11" | 185 | 26 | | |
| Roland Mitchell | DB | 5'11" | 195 | 29 | 1 | |
| Muhammad Oliver (from KC) | DB | 5'11" | 170 | 24 | | |
| Mike Prior | DB | 6' | 215 | 29 | 1 | |
| George Teague | DB | 6'1" | 187 | 22 | 1 | |
| Sammy Walker | DB | 5'11" | 203 | 24 | | |

Mark D'Onofrio — Hamstring Injury

| Use Name | Pos. | Hgt. | Wgt. | Age | Int | Pts |
|---|---|---|---|---|---|---|
| Mark Brunell | QB | 6'1" | 208 | 22 | | |
| Ty Detmer | QB | 6' | 190 | 25 | | |
| Brett Favre | QB | 6'2" | 218 | 23 | | 6 |
| Darrell Thompson | HB | 6' | 217 | 25 | | 18 |
| Kevin Williams | HB | 6' | 208 | 23 | | |
| Marcus Wilson | HB | 6'1" | 210 | 25 | | |
| Edgar Bennett | FB | 6' | 216 | 24 | | 60 |
| Dexter McNabb | FB | 6'2" | 245 | 24 | | |
| Robert Brooks | WR | 6' | 174 | 23 | | 6 |
| Mark Clayton | WR | 5'9" | 185 | 32 | | 18 |
| Shawn Collins | WR | 6'2" | 204 | 26 | | |
| Ron Lewis | WR | 5'11" | 189 | 25 | | |
| Anthony Morgan (from CHI) | WR | 6'1" | 195 | 25 | | |
| Sterling Sharpe | WR | 5'11" | 210 | 28 | | 66 |
| Mark Chmura | TE | 6'5" | 242 | 24 | | |
| Jackie Harris | TE | 6'3" | 243 | 25 | | 24 |
| Darryl Ingram | TE | 6'3" | 245 | 27 | | |
| Ed West | TE | 6'1" | 245 | 32 | | |
| Chris Jacke | K | 6' | 200 | 27 | | 128 |
| Bryan Wagner | K | 6'2" | 200 | 31 | | |

James Milling — Concussion

## CHICAGO BEARS 7-9 Dave Wannstedt

| Scores of Each Game | | |
|---|---|---|
| 20 | N.Y. GIANTS | 26 |
| 7 | Minnesota | 10 |
| 47 | TAMPA BAY | 17 |
| 6 | ATLANTA | 0 |
| 17 | Philadelphia | 6 |
| 12 | MINNESOTA | 19 |
| 3 | Green Bay | 17 |
| 14 | L.A. RAIDERS | 16 |
| 16 | San Diego | 13 |
| 19 | Kansas City | 17 |
| 10 | Detroit | 6 |
| 30 | GREEN BAY | 17 |
| 10 | Tampa Bay | 13 |
| 3 | DENVER | 13 |
| 14 | DETROIT | 20 |
| 6 | L.A. Rams | 20 |

| Use Name | Pos. | Hgt. | Wgt. | Age | Int | Pts |
|---|---|---|---|---|---|---|
| Troy Auzenne | OT | 6'7" | 290 | 24 | | |
| Jay Leeuwenburg | OT | 6'2" | 288 | 24 | | |
| Keith Van Horne | OT | 6'6" | 290 | 35 | | |
| James Williams | OT | 6'7" | 330 | 25 | | |
| Mark Bortz | OG | 6'6" | 282 | 32 | | |
| Todd Perry | OG | 6'5" | 298 | 22 | | |
| Vernice Smith (to WAS) | OG | 6'3" | 298 | 27 | | |
| John Wojciechowski | OG-OT | 6'4" | 280 | 30 | | |
| Jerry Fontenot | C | 6'3" | 287 | 26 | | |
| Mark McGuire | C | 6'2" | 286 | 23 | | |
| Trace Armstrong | DE | 6'4" | 265 | 27 | | |
| Richard Dent | DE | 6'5" | 265 | 32 | 1 | |
| Albert Fontenot | DE | 6'4" | 265 | 22 | | |
| Alonzo Spellman | DE | 6'4" | 282 | 21 | | |
| Tory Epps (from ATL) | DT | 6'1" | 280 | 26 | | |
| Steve McMichael | DT | 6'2" | 268 | 35 | 1 | |
| Tim Ryan | DT-DE | 6'4" | 265 | 25 | | |
| Carl Simpson | DT | 6'2" | 282 | 23 | | |
| Chris Zorich | DT | 6'1" | 275 | 24 | | |

| Use Name | Pos. | Hgt. | Wgt. | Age | Int | Pts |
|---|---|---|---|---|---|---|
| Myron Baker | LB | 6'1" | 228 | 22 | | 12 |
| Joe Cain | LB | 6'1" | 233 | 28 | | |
| Ron Cox | LB | 6'2" | 235 | 25 | | |
| Dante Jones | LB | 6'1" | 230 | 28 | 4 | 6 |
| Barry Minter | LB | 6'2" | 242 | 23 | | |
| Vinson Smith | LB | 6'2" | 236 | 28 | | |
| Percy Snow | LB | 6'2" | 245 | 25 | | |
| Anthony Blaylock | DB | 5'10" | 185 | 28 | 2 | |
| Mark Carrier | DB | 6'1" | 192 | 25 | 4 | 6 |
| Maurice Douglass | DB | 5'11" | 202 | 29 | | |
| Shaun Gayle | DB | 5'11" | 202 | 31 | | |
| Keshon Johnson | DB | 5'10" | 179 | 23 | | |
| Jeremy Lincoln | DB | 5'10" | 180 | 24 | 3 | 6 |
| John Mangum | DB | 5'10" | 182 | 26 | 1 | |
| Kevin Minniefield | DB | 5'9" | 178 | 23 | | |
| Markus Paul (to TB) | DB | 6'2" | 205 | 27 | | |
| Donnell Woolford | DB | 5'9" | 188 | 27 | 2 | |

| Use Name | Pos. | Hgt. | Wgt. | Age | Int | Pts |
|---|---|---|---|---|---|---|
| Jim Harbaugh | QB | 6'3" | 215 | 29 | | 24 |
| Peter Tom Willis | QB | 6'2" | 204 | 26 | | |
| Neal Anderson | HB | 5'11" | 215 | 29 | | 24 |
| Robert Green | HB | 5'8" | 209 | 22 | | |
| Darren Lewis | HB | 5'10" | 225 | 24 | | |
| Tim Worley (from PIT) | HB | 6'2" | 226 | 26 | | 12 |
| Bob Christian | FB | 5'10" | 225 | 24 | | |
| Craig Heyward | FB | 5'11" | 290 | 26 | | |
| John Ivlow | FB | 5'11" | 226 | 23 | | |
| Fred Banks (from MIA) | WR | 5'10" | 185 | 31 | | |
| Curtis Conway | WR | 6' | 185 | 22 | | 12 |
| Wendell Davis | WR | 5'11" | 194 | 27 | | |
| Terry Obee | WR | 5'10" | 180 | 25 | | 18 |
| Tom Waddle | WR | 6' | 185 | 26 | | 6 |
| Chris Gedney | TE | 6'5" | 262 | 23 | | |
| Keith Jennings | TE | 6'4" | 265 | 27 | | |
| Ryan Wetnight | TE | 6'2" | 238 | 22 | | 6 |
| Danta Whitaker | TE | 6'4" | 254 | 29 | | |
| Kevin Butler | K | 6'1" | 204 | 31 | | 102 |
| Chris Gardocki | K | 6'1" | 188 | 23 | | |

Glen Kozlowski — Knee Injury

## TAMPA BAY BUCCANEERS 5-11 Sam Wyche

| Scores of Each Game | | |
|---|---|---|
| 3 | KANSAS CITY | 27 |
| 7 | N.Y. Giants | 23 |
| 17 | Chicago | 47 |
| 27 | DETROIT | 10 |
| 0 | Minnesota | 15 |
| 14 | GREEN BAY | 37 |
| 31 | Atlanta | 24 |
| 0 | Detroit | 23 |
| 21 | SAN FRANCISCO | 45 |
| 23 | MINNESOTA | 10 |
| 10 | Green Bay | 13 |
| 17 | WASHINGTON | 23 |
| 13 | CHICAGO | 10 |
| 20 | L.A. Raiders | 27 |
| 17 | Denver | 10 |
| 17 | SAN DIEGO | 32 |

| Use Name | Pos. | Hgt. | Wgt. | Age | Int | Pts |
|---|---|---|---|---|---|---|
| Theo Adams | OT | 6'4" | 300 | 27 | | |
| Scott Dill | OT | 6'5" | 290 | 27 | | |
| Paul Gruber | OT | 6'5" | 290 | 28 | | |
| Charles McRae | OT-OG | 6'7" | 300 | 24 | | |
| Rob Taylor | OT | 6'6" | 290 | 32 | | |
| Ian Beckles | OG | 6'1" | 295 | 26 | | |
| Sean Love | OG | 6'3" | 290 | 23 | | |
| Bruce Reimers | OG | 6'7" | 300 | 32 | | |
| Tim Ryan | OG | 6'2" | 280 | 24 | | |
| Mike Sullivan | OG | 6'3" | 290 | 25 | | |
| Pat Tomberlin | OG-OT | 6'2" | 300 | 27 | | |
| Tony Mayberry | C | 6'4" | 290 | 25 | | |
| Chidi Ahanotu | DE | 6'2" | 280 | 22 | | |
| Eric Curry | DE | 6'5" | 270 | 23 | | |
| Santana Dotson | DE | 6'5" | 270 | 23 | | |
| Eric Hayes | DE-NT | 6'3" | 290 | 25 | | |
| Shawn Price | DE | 6'5" | 260 | 23 | | |
| Ray Seals | DE | 6'3" | 280 | 28 | 1 | 6 |
| Rhett Hall | DT | 6'2" | 270 | 24 | | |
| Mark Wheeler | DT-NT | 6'2" | 280 | 23 | | |
| Bernard Wilson | NT-DT | 6'2" | 295 | 23 | | |

Anthony Munoz — Shoulder Injury

| Use Name | Pos. | Hgt. | Wgt. | Age | Int | Pts |
|---|---|---|---|---|---|---|
| Ed Brady | LB | 6'2" | 235 | 31 | | |
| Darrick Brownlow | LB | 6' | 240 | 24 | | |
| Reggie Burnette | LB | 6'2" | 245 | 24 | | |
| Demetrious DuBose | LB | 6'1" | 240 | 22 | | |
| Hardy Nickerson | LB | 6'2" | 230 | 28 | 1 | |
| Broderick Thomas | LB | 6'4" | 250 | 26 | | |
| Jimmy Williams | LB | 6'3" | 220 | 32 | | |
| Darren Anderson | DB | 5'10" | 180 | 24 | 1 | |
| Curtis Buckley | DB-WR | 6' | 185 | 23 | | |
| Barney Bussey | DB | 6' | 210 | 31 | | |
| Marty Carter | DB | 6'1" | 200 | 23 | 1 | |
| Jerry Gray | DB | 6' | 185 | 30 | | |
| Roger Jones | DB | 5'9" | 175 | 24 | | |
| Joe King | DB | 6'2" | 195 | 25 | 3 | |
| John Lynch | DB | 6'2" | 220 | 21 | | |
| Milton Mack | DB | 5'11" | 195 | 29 | 1 | 6 |
| Martin Mayhew | DB | 5'8" | 175 | 27 | | |
| Ricky Reynolds | DB | 5'11" | 190 | 28 | 1 | |

Tony Covington — Back Injury
Rogerick Green — Knee Injury
Darryl Pollard — Neck Injury

| Use Name | Pos. | Hgt. | Wgt. | Age | Int | Pts |
|---|---|---|---|---|---|---|
| Craig Erickson | QB | 6'2" | 205 | 24 | | |
| Mark Vlasic | QB | 6'3" | 205 | 29 | | |
| Casey Weldon | QB | 6'1" | 200 | 24 | | |
| Gary Anderson (to DET) | HB | 6' | 190 | 32 | | 6 |
| Reggie Cobb | HB | 6' | 215 | 25 | | 24 |
| Vince Workman | HB | 5'10" | 205 | 25 | | 24 |
| Rudy Harris | FB | 6'1" | 255 | 21 | | |
| Anthony McDowell | FB | 5'11" | 235 | 24 | | 6 |
| Mazio Royster | FB | 6'1" | 200 | 23 | | 6 |
| Robert Claiborne | WR | 5'10" | 175 | 26 | | |
| Horace Copeland | WR | 6'2" | 195 | 22 | | 24 |
| Lawrence Dawsey | WR | 6' | 195 | 25 | | |
| Courtney Hawkins | WR | 5'9" | 180 | 23 | | 30 |
| Lamar Thomas | WR | 6'1" | 170 | 23 | | 12 |
| Charles Wilson | WR | 5'10" | 185 | 25 | | |
| Tyji Armstrong | TE | 6'4" | 250 | 22 | | 6 |
| Ron Hall | TE | 6'4" | 245 | 29 | | 6 |
| Dave Moore | TE | 6'2" | 245 | 23 | | 6 |
| Michael Husted | K | 6' | 190 | 23 | | 75 |
| Dan Stryzinski | K | 6'1" | 195 | 28 | | |

## DETROIT LIONS

### RUSHING
| Last Name | No. | Yds | Avg | TD |
|---|---|---|---|---|
| Sanders | 243 | 1115 | 4.6 | 3 |
| D. Moore | 88 | 405 | 4.6 | 3 |
| Lynch | 53 | 207 | 3.9 | 2 |
| Peete | 45 | 165 | 3.7 | 1 |
| Ware | 7 | 23 | 3.3 | 0 |
| Perriman | 4 | 16 | 4.0 | 0 |
| Matthews | 2 | 7 | 3.5 | 0 |
| Kramer | 10 | 5 | 0.5 | 0 |
| Richards | 4 | 1 | 0.3 | 0 |

### RECEIVING
| Last Name | No. | Yds | Avg | TD |
|---|---|---|---|---|
| H. Moore | 61 | 935 | 15.3 | 6 |
| Perriman | 49 | 496 | 10.1 | 2 |
| Sanders | 36 | 205 | 5.7 | 0 |
| Green | 28 | 462 | 16.5 | 2 |
| Holman | 25 | 244 | 9.8 | 2 |
| D. Moore | 21 | 169 | 8.0 | 1 |
| Lynch | 13 | 82 | 6.3 | 0 |
| Matthews | 11 | 171 | 15.5 | 0 |
| Hallock | 8 | 88 | 11.0 | 2 |
| Campbell | 7 | 55 | 7.9 | 0 |
| Johnson | 2 | 18 | 9.0 | 0 |
| Thompson | 1 | 15 | 15.0 | 0 |
| Turner | 1 | 7 | 7.0 | 0 |
| Fralic | 1 | -4 | -4.0 | 0 |

### PUNT RETURNS
| Last Name | No. | Yds | Avg | TD |
|---|---|---|---|---|
| Gray | 23 | 197 | 8.6 | 0 |
| Turner | 17 | 152 | 8.9 | 0 |

### KICKOFF RETURNS
| Last Name | No. | Yds | Avg | TD |
|---|---|---|---|---|
| Gray | 28 | 688 | 24.6 | 1 |
| Turner | 15 | 330 | 22.0 | 0 |
| Clay | 2 | 34 | 17.0 | 0 |
| D. Moore | 1 | 68 | 68.0 | 0 |
| Lynch | 1 | 22 | 22.0 | 0 |
| Hallock | 1 | 11 | 11.0 | 0 |
| Jamison | 1 | 0 | 0.0 | 0 |

### PASSING — PUNTING — KICKING
| PASSING | Att | Cmp | % | Yds | Yd/Att | TD | Int | — | % | RK |
|---|---|---|---|---|---|---|---|---|---|---|
| Peete | 252 | 157 | 62.3 | 1670 | 6.63 | 6 | 14 | — | 5.6 | 11 |
| Kramer | 138 | 87 | 63.0 | 1002 | 7.26 | 8 | 3 | — | 2.2 | |
| Ware | 45 | 20 | 44.4 | 271 | 6.02 | 1 | 2 | — | 4.4 | |

| PUNTING | No. | Avg. |
|---|---|---|
| Arnold | 72 | 44.8 |

| KICKING | XP | Att | % | FG | Att | % |
|---|---|---|---|---|---|---|
| Hanson | 28 | 28 | 100 | 34 | 43 | 79 |

## MINNESOTA VIKINGS

### RUSHING
| Last Name | No. | Yds | Avg | TD |
|---|---|---|---|---|
| Graham | 118 | 487 | 4.1 | 3 |
| Word | 142 | 458 | 3.2 | 2 |
| Smith | 82 | 399 | 4.9 | 2 |
| Craig | 38 | 119 | 3.1 | 1 |
| McMahon | 33 | 96 | 2.9 | 0 |
| Evans | 14 | 32 | 2.3 | 0 |
| A. Carter | 7 | 19 | 2.7 | 0 |
| Ismail | 3 | 14 | 4.7 | 0 |
| Salisbury | 10 | -1 | -0.1 | 0 |

### RECEIVING
| Last Name | No. | Yds | Avg | TD |
|---|---|---|---|---|
| C. Carter | 86 | 1071 | 12.5 | 9 |
| A. Carter | 60 | 774 | 12.9 | 5 |
| Jordan | 56 | 542 | 9.7 | 1 |
| Smith | 24 | 111 | 4.6 | 0 |
| Ismail | 19 | 212 | 11.2 | 1 |
| Craig | 19 | 169 | 8.9 | 1 |
| Tennell | 15 | 122 | 8.1 | 0 |
| Word | 9 | 105 | 11.7 | 0 |
| Graham | 7 | 46 | 6.6 | 0 |
| Tice | 6 | 39 | 6.5 | 1 |
| Reed | 5 | 65 | 13.0 | 0 |
| Evans | 4 | 39 | 9.8 | 0 |
| Truitt | 4 | 40 | 10.0 | 0 |
| Guliford | 1 | 45 | 45.0 | 0 |

### PUNT RETURNS
| Last Name | No. | Yds | Avg | TD |
|---|---|---|---|---|
| Guliford | 29 | 212 | 7.3 | 0 |
| Parker | 9 | 64 | 7.1 | 0 |
| Smith | 1 | 4 | 4.0 | 0 |

### KICKOFF RETURNS
| Last Name | No. | Yds | Avg | TD |
|---|---|---|---|---|
| Ismail | 42 | 902 | 21.5 | 0 |
| Guliford | 5 | 101 | 20.2 | 0 |
| Smith | 3 | 41 | 13.6 | 0 |
| Graham | 1 | 16 | 16.0 | 0 |
| Evans | 1 | 11 | 11.0 | 0 |
| Craig | 1 | 11 | 11.0 | 0 |
| Del Rio | 1 | 4 | 4.0 | 0 |
| McMillian | 1 | 0 | 0.0 | 0 |

### PASSING — PUNTING — KICKING
| PASSING | Att | Cmp | % | Yds | Yd/Att | TD | Int | — | % | RK |
|---|---|---|---|---|---|---|---|---|---|---|
| McMahon | 331 | 200 | 60.4 | 1967 | 5.94 | 9 | 8 | — | 2.4 | 7 |
| Salisbury | 195 | 115 | 59.0 | 1413 | 7.25 | 9 | 6 | — | 3.1 | |

| PUNTING | No. | Avg. |
|---|---|---|
| Newsome | 90 | 42.9 |

| KICKING | XP | ATT | % | FG | ATT | % |
|---|---|---|---|---|---|---|
| Reveiz | 27 | 28 | 96 | 26 | 35 | 74 |

## GREEN BAY PACKERS

### RUSHING
| Last Name | No. | Yds | Avg | TD |
|---|---|---|---|---|
| Thompson | 169 | 654 | 3.9 | 2 |
| E. Bennett | 159 | 550 | 3.5 | 9 |
| Favre | 58 | 216 | 3.7 | 1 |
| Brooks | 3 | 17 | 5.7 | 0 |
| Sharpe | 4 | 8 | 2.0 | 0 |
| Wilson | 6 | 3 | 0.5 | 0 |
| Detmer | 1 | -2 | -2.0 | 0 |

### RECEIVING
| Last Name | No. | Yds | Avg | TD |
|---|---|---|---|---|
| Sharpe | 112 | 1274 | 11.4 | 11 |
| E. Bennett | 59 | 457 | 7.7 | 1 |
| J. Harris | 42 | 604 | 14.4 | 4 |
| Clayton | 32 | 331 | 10.3 | 3 |
| West | 25 | 253 | 10.1 | 0 |
| Brooks | 20 | 180 | 9.0 | 0 |
| Thompson | 18 | 129 | 7.2 | 0 |
| Lewis | 2 | 21 | 10.5 | 0 |
| Wilson | 2 | 18 | 9.0 | 0 |
| Chmura | 2 | 13 | 6.5 | 0 |
| C. Harris | 2 | 11 | 5.5 | 0 |
| Morgan | 1 | 8 | 8.0 | 0 |

### PUNT RETURNS
| Last Name | No. | Yds | Avg | TD |
|---|---|---|---|---|
| Prior | 17 | 194 | 11.4 | 0 |
| Brooks | 16 | 135 | 8.4 | 0 |
| Buckley | 11 | 76 | 6.9 | 0 |
| Teague | 1 | -1 | -1.0 | 0 |

### KICKOFF RETURNS
| Last Name | No. | Yds | Avg | TD |
|---|---|---|---|---|
| Brooks | 23 | 611 | 26.6 | 1 |
| C. Harris | 16 | 482 | 30.1 | 0 |
| Thompson | 9 | 171 | 19.0 | 0 |
| Wilson | 9 | 197 | 21.9 | 0 |
| Jurkovic | 2 | 22 | 11.0 | 0 |
| Chmura | 1 | 0 | 0.0 | 0 |

### PASSING — PUNTING — KICKING
| PASSING | Att | Cmp | % | Yds | Yd/Att | TD | Int | — | % | RK |
|---|---|---|---|---|---|---|---|---|---|---|
| Favre | 522 | 318 | 60.9 | 3303 | 6.33 | 19 | 24 | — | 4.6 | 8 |
| Detmer | 5 | 3 | 60.0 | 26 | 5.20 | 0 | 0 | — | 0.0 | |
| Sharpe | 1 | 1 | 100.0 | 1 | 1.00 | 0 | 0 | — | 0.0 | |

| PUNTING | No. | Avg. |
|---|---|---|
| Wagner | 74 | 42.9 |

| KICKING | XP | ATT | % | FG | Att | % |
|---|---|---|---|---|---|---|
| Jacke | 35 | 35 | 100 | 31 | 37 | 84 |

## CHICAGO BEARS

### RUSHING
| Last Name | No. | Yds | Avg | TD |
|---|---|---|---|---|
| Anderson | 202 | 646 | 3.2 | 4 |
| Worley | 120 | 470 | 3.9 | 2 |
| Harbaugh | 60 | 277 | 4.6 | 4 |
| Heyward | 68 | 206 | 3.0 | 0 |
| Conway | 5 | 44 | 8.8 | 0 |
| Green | 15 | 29 | 1.9 | 0 |
| Christian | 8 | 19 | 2.4 | 0 |
| Lewis | 7 | 13 | 1.9 | 0 |
| Willis | 2 | 6 | 3.0 | 0 |

### RECEIVING
| Last Name | No. | Yds | Avg | TD |
|---|---|---|---|---|
| Waddle | 44 | 552 | 12.5 | 4 |
| Anderson | 31 | 160 | 5.2 | 0 |
| Obee | 26 | 351 | 13.5 | 3 |
| Conway | 19 | 231 | 12.2 | 2 |
| Christian | 16 | 160 | 10.0 | 0 |
| Heyward | 16 | 132 | 8.3 | 0 |
| Jennings | 14 | 150 | 10.7 | 0 |
| Green | 13 | 63 | 4.8 | 0 |
| Davis | 12 | 132 | 11.0 | 0 |
| Worley | 11 | 62 | 5.6 | 0 |
| Gedney | 10 | 98 | 9.8 | 0 |
| Wetnight | 9 | 93 | 10.3 | 1 |
| Whitaker | 6 | 53 | 8.8 | 0 |
| Lewis | 4 | 26 | 6.5 | 0 |
| Banks | 2 | 45 | 22.5 | 0 |
| Harbaugh | 1 | 1 | 1.0 | 0 |

### PUNT RETURNS
| Last Name | No. | Yds | Avg | TD |
|---|---|---|---|---|
| Obee | 35 | 289 | 8.3 | 0 |

### KICKOFF RETURNS
| Last Name | No. | Yds | Avg | TD |
|---|---|---|---|---|
| Conway | 21 | 450 | 21.4 | 0 |
| Green | 9 | 141 | 15.7 | 0 |
| Obee | 9 | 159 | 17.7 | 0 |
| Worley | 6 | 121 | 20.2 | 0 |
| Heyward | 1 | 12 | 12.0 | 0 |
| A. Fontenot | 1 | 8 | 8.0 | 0 |
| Ryan | 1 | 5 | 5.0 | 0 |
| Mangum | 1 | 0 | 0.0 | 0 |

### PASSING — PUNTING — KICKING
| PASSING | Att | Cmp | % | Yds | Yd/Att | TD | Int | — | % | RK |
|---|---|---|---|---|---|---|---|---|---|---|
| Harbaugh | 325 | 200 | 61.5 | 2002 | 6.16 | 7 | 11 | — | 3.4 | 9 |
| Willis | 60 | 30 | 50.0 | 268 | 4.47 | 0 | 5 | — | 8.3 | |
| Gardocki | 2 | 0 | 0 | 0 | 0.00 | 0 | 0 | — | 0.0 | |
| Anderson | 1 | 0 | 0.0 | 0 | 0.00 | 0 | 0 | — | 0.0 | |

| PUNTING | No. | Avg. |
|---|---|---|
| Gardocki | 80 | 38.5 |

| KICKING | XP | ATT | % | FG | ATT | % |
|---|---|---|---|---|---|---|
| Butler | 21 | 22 | 95 | 27 | 36 | 75 |

## TAMPA BAY BUCCANEERS

### RUSHING
| Last Name | No. | Yds | Avg | TD |
|---|---|---|---|---|
| Cobb | 221 | 658 | 3.0 | 3 |
| Workman | 78 | 284 | 3.6 | 2 |
| Royster | 33 | 115 | 3.5 | 1 |
| Erickson | 26 | 96 | 3.7 | 0 |
| G. Anderson | 28 | 56 | 2.0 | 0 |
| Copeland | 3 | 34 | 11.3 | 0 |
| Harris | 7 | 29 | 4.1 | 0 |
| C. Wilson | 2 | 7 | 3.5 | 0 |
| McDowell | 2 | 6 | 3.0 | 0 |
| Armstrong | 2 | 5 | 2.5 | 0 |

### RECEIVING
| Last Name | No. | Yds | Avg | TD |
|---|---|---|---|---|
| Hawkins | 62 | 933 | 15.0 | 5 |
| Workman | 54 | 411 | 7.6 | 2 |
| Copeland | 30 | 633 | 21.1 | 4 |
| Hall | 23 | 268 | 11.7 | 1 |
| C. Wilson | 15 | 225 | 15.0 | 0 |
| Dawsey | 15 | 203 | 13.5 | 0 |
| G. Anderson | 11 | 89 | 8.1 | 1 |
| Armstrong | 9 | 86 | 9.6 | 1 |
| Cobb | 9 | 61 | 6.8 | 1 |
| L. Thomas | 8 | 186 | 23.3 | 2 |
| McDowell | 8 | 26 | 3.3 | 1 |
| Claiborne | 5 | 61 | 12.2 | 0 |
| Royster | 5 | 18 | 3.6 | 0 |
| Harris | 4 | 48 | 12.0 | 0 |
| Moore | 4 | 47 | 11.8 | 1 |

### PUNT RETURNS
| Last Name | No. | Yds | Avg | TD |
|---|---|---|---|---|
| G. Anderson | 17 | 113 | 6.6 | 0 |
| Hawkins | 15 | 166 | 11.1 | 0 |
| Claiborne | 6 | 32 | 5.3 | 0 |

### KICKOFF RETURNS
| Last Name | No. | Yds | Avg | TD |
|---|---|---|---|---|
| C. Wilson | 23 | 454 | 19.7 | 0 |
| G. Anderson | 12 | 181 | 15.1 | 0 |
| Royster | 8 | 102 | 12.8 | 0 |
| Turner | 6 | 61 | 10.2 | 0 |
| Workman | 5 | 67 | 13.4 | 0 |
| Claiborne | 4 | 57 | 14.3 | 0 |

### PASSING — PUNTING — KICKING
| PASSING | Att | Cmp | % | Yds | Yd/Att | TD | Int | — | % | RK |
|---|---|---|---|---|---|---|---|---|---|---|
| Erickson | 457 | 233 | 51.0 | 3054 | 6.68 | 18 | 21 | — | 4.6 | 12 |
| Weldon | 11 | 6 | 54.5 | 55 | 5.00 | 0 | 1 | — | 9.1 | |
| Moore | 1 | 0 | 0.0 | 0 | 0.00 | 0 | 0 | — | 0.0 | |

| PUNTING | No. | Avg. |
|---|---|---|
| Stryzinski | 94 | 40.1 |

| KICKING | XP | ATT | % | FG | ATT | % |
|---|---|---|---|---|---|---|
| Husted | 27 | 27 | 100 | 16 | 22 | 73 |

## SAN FRANCISCO 49ERS 10-6 George Seifert

| Scores of Each Game | | |
|---|---|---|
| 24 | Pittsburgh | 13 |
| 13 | Cleveland | 23 |
| 37 | ATLANTA | 30 |
| 13 | New Orleans | 16 |
| 38 | MINNESOTA | 19 |
| 17 | Dallas | 26 |
| 28 | PHOENIX | 14 |
| 40 | L.A. RAMS | 17 |
| 45 | Tampa Bay | 21 |
| 42 | NEW ORLEANS | 7 |
| 35 | L.A. Rams | 10 |
| 21 | CINCINNATI | 8 |
| 24 | Atlanta | 27 |
| 55 | Detroit | 17 |
| 7 | HOUSTON | 10 |
| 34 | PHILADELPHIA | *37 |

| Use Name | Pos. | Hgt. | Wgt. | Age | Int | Pts |
|---|---|---|---|---|---|---|
| Harris Barton | OT | 6'4" | 286 | 29 | | |
| Harry Boatswain | OT | 6'4" | 295 | 24 | | |
| James Parrish | OT | 6'6" | 315 | 25 | | |
| Steve Wallace | OT | 6'5" | 280 | 28 | | |
| Brian Bollinger | OG | 6'5" | 285 | 24 | | |
| Chris Dalman | OG-C | 6'3" | 285 | 23 | | |
| Roy Foster | OG | 6'4" | 290 | 33 | | |
| Guy McIntyre | OG | 6'3" | 276 | 32 | | |
| Ralph Tamm | OG | 6'4" | 280 | 27 | | 6 |
| Jesse Sapolu | C | 6'4" | 278 | 32 | | |
| Dennis Brown | DE | 6'4" | 290 | 25 | | |
| Kevin Fagan | DE | 6'4" | 265 | 30 | | |
| Martin Harrison | DE | 6'5" | 256 | 25 | | |
| Todd Kelly | DE | 6'2" | 259 | 22 | | |
| Matt LaBounty | DE | 6'4" | 254 | 24 | | |
| Larry Roberts | DE | 6'3" | 275 | 30 | | |
| Artie Smith | DE | 6'4" | 303 | 23 | | |
| Mark Thomas | DE | 6'5" | 273 | 24 | | |
| Troy Wilson | DE | 6'4" | 235 | 22 | | |
| Karl Wilson (from MIA) | DE | 6'5" | 277 | 28 | | |
| Dana Stubblefield | DT-NT | 6'2" | 302 | 22 | | |
| Ted Washington | DT-NT-DE | 6'4" | 295 | 25 | | |

| Use Name | Pos. | Hgt. | Wgt. | Age | Int | Pts |
|---|---|---|---|---|---|---|
| Keith DeLong | LB | 6'2" | 250 | 26 | | |
| Brett Faryniarz | LB | 6'3" | 230 | 28 | | |
| Antonio Goss | LB | 6'4" | 228 | 27 | | |
| John Johnson | LB | 6'3" | 230 | 25 | 1 | |
| Darin Jordan | LB | 6'2" | 245 | 28 | | |
| Larry Kelm | LB | 6'4" | 240 | 28 | | |
| Bill Romanowski | LB | 6'4" | 240 | 27 | | |
| Michael Walter | LB | 6'3" | 246 | 32 | | |
| Eric Davis | DB | 5'11" | 178 | 25 | 4 | 12 |
| Don Griffin | DB | 6' | 180 | 29 | 3 | |
| Dana Hall | DB | 6'2" | 206 | 24 | | |
| Merton Hanks | DB | 6'2" | 185 | 25 | 3 | 6 |
| Adrian Hardy | DB | 5'11" | 194 | 23 | | |
| Terry Hoage (to HOU) | DB | 6'2" | 201 | 31 | | |
| Tim McDonald | DB | 6'2" | 215 | 28 | 3 | |
| Michael McGruder | DB | 5'10" | 190 | 29 | 5 | 6 |
| Damien Russell | DB | 6'1" | 204 | 23 | | |

Thane Gash — Knee Injury
Brian Taylor — Knee Injury
Dave Waymer — Died in offseason

| Use Name | Pos. | Hgt. | Wgt. | Age | Int | Pts |
|---|---|---|---|---|---|---|
| Steve Bono | QB | 6'4" | 211 | 31 | | 6 |
| Bill Musgrave | QB | 6'2" | 205 | 25 | | |
| Steve Young | QB | 6'2" | 205 | 31 | | 12 |
| Dexter Carter | HB | 5'9" | 174 | 25 | | 12 |
| Amp Lee | HB | 5'11" | 200 | 21 | | 18 |
| Ricky Watters | HB | 6'1" | 212 | 24 | | 66 |
| Marc Logan | FB | 6' | 212 | 28 | | 42 |
| Tom Rathman | FB | 6'1" | 232 | 30 | | 18 |
| Adam Walker | FB | 6'1" | 210 | 25 | | |
| Sanjay Beach | WR | 6'1" | 194 | 27 | | 6 |
| Jerry Rice | WR | 6'2" | 200 | 30 | | 96 |
| Nate Singleton | WR | 5'11" | 190 | 25 | | 6 |
| John Taylor | WR | 6'1" | 185 | 31 | | 30 |
| Odessa Turner | WR | 6'3" | 215 | 28 | | |
| John Brandes | TE | 6'2" | 249 | 29 | | |
| Brent Jones | TE | 6'4" | 230 | 30 | | 18 |
| Wesley Walls | TE | 6'5" | 254 | 27 | | |
| Jamie Williams | TE | 6'4" | 245 | 33 | | 6 |
| Mike Cofer | K | 6'1" | 190 | 29 | | 107 |
| Klaus Wilmsmeyer | K | 6'1" | 210 | 25 | | |

## NEW ORLEANS SAINTS 8-8 Jim Mora

| Scores of Each Game | | |
|---|---|---|
| 33 | HOUSTON | 21 |
| 34 | Atlanta | 31 |
| 14 | DETROIT | 3 |
| 16 | SAN FRANCISCO | 13 |
| 37 | L.A. Rams | 6 |
| 14 | Pittsburgh | 37 |
| 15 | ATLANTA | 26 |
| 20 | Phoenix | 17 |
| 17 | GREEN BAY | 19 |
| 7 | San Francisco | 42 |
| 17 | Minnesota | 14 |
| 13 | Cleveland | 17 |
| 20 | L.A. RAMS | 23 |
| 14 | N.Y. GIANTS | 24 |
| 26 | Philadelphia | 37 |
| 20 | CINCINNATI | 13 |

| Use Name | Pos. | Hgt. | Wgt. | Age | Int | Pts |
|---|---|---|---|---|---|---|
| Richard Cooper | OT | 6'4" | 290 | 28 | | |
| Willie Roaf | OT | 6'4" | 299 | 23 | | |
| Jim Dombrowski | OG-OT | 6'5" | 298 | 29 | | |
| Derek Kennard | OG-C | 6'3" | 300 | 30 | | |
| Chris Port | OG | 6'5" | 290 | 25 | | |
| Jay Hilgenberg | C | 6'3" | 270 | 34 | | |
| Joel Hilgenberg | C | 6'3" | 252 | 31 | | |
| Karl Dunbar | DE | 6'4" | 275 | 26 | | |
| Robert Goff | DE-NT | 6'3" | 270 | 27 | | |
| Wayne Martin | DE | 6'5" | 275 | 27 | | |
| Frank Warren | DE | 6'4" | 290 | 33 | | 6 |
| Ronnie Dixon | NT | 6'2" | 292 | 22 | | |
| Les Miller | NT-DE | 6'7" | 285 | 28 | | |
| Jim Wilks | NT-DE | 6'5" | 275 | 35 | | |

| Use Name | Pos. | Hgt. | Wgt. | Age | Int | Pts |
|---|---|---|---|---|---|---|
| Reggie Freeman | LB | 6'1" | 233 | 23 | | |
| Rickey Jackson | LB | 6'2" | 243 | 35 | | |
| Vaughan Johnson | LB | 6'3" | 240 | 31 | | |
| Sam Mills | LB | 5'9" | 225 | 34 | | 6 |
| Joel Smeenge | LB | 6'5" | 250 | 25 | | |
| Renaldo Turnbull | DE | 6'4" | 250 | 27 | 1 | |
| James Williams | LB | 6' | 230 | 24 | | |
| DeMond Winston | LB | 6'2" | 239 | 24 | | |
| Gene Atkins | DB | 6'1" | 200 | 28 | 3 | |
| Vince Buck | DB | 6' | 198 | 25 | 2 | |
| Toi Cook | DB | 5'11" | 188 | 28 | 1 | |
| Othello Henderson | DB | 6' | 192 | 31 | | |
| Tyrone Hughes | DB | 5'9" | 175 | 23 | | 18 |
| Reggie Jones | DB | 6'1" | 202 | 24 | 1 | |
| Tyrone Legette | DB | 5'9" | 177 | 23 | | |
| Sean Lumpkin | DB | 6' | 206 | 23 | | |
| Cedric Mack | DB | 5'11" | 190 | 32 | | |
| Brett Maxie | DB | 6'2" | 194 | 31 | | |
| Jimmy Spencer | DB | 5'9" | 180 | 24 | | |
| Keith Taylor | DB | 5'11" | 206 | 28 | 2 | |

| Use Name | Pos. | Hgt. | Wgt. | Age | Int | Pts |
|---|---|---|---|---|---|---|
| Mike Buck | QB | 6'3" | 227 | 26 | | |
| Steve Walsh | QB | 6'2" | 204 | 26 | | |
| Wade Wilson | QB | 6'3" | 206 | 34 | | |
| Derek Brown | HB | 5'9" | 186 | 22 | | 18 |
| Dalton Hilliard | HB | 5'8" | 204 | 29 | | 18 |
| Fred McAfee | HB | 5'10" | 195 | 25 | | 6 |
| Brad Muster | FB | 6'4" | 235 | 28 | | 18 |
| Lorenzo Neal | FB | 5'10" | 228 | 22 | | 6 |
| Derrick Ned | FB | 6'1" | 210 | 24 | | 6 |
| Marcus Dowdell | WR | 5'10" | 179 | 23 | | 6 |
| Quinn Early | WR | 6' | 190 | 28 | | 36 |
| Eric Martin | WR | 6'1" | 207 | 31 | | 18 |
| Pat Newman | WR | 5'11" | 189 | 24 | | 6 |
| Torrance Small | WR | 6'3" | 201 | 22 | | 6 |
| Floyd Turner | WR | 5'11" | 188 | 27 | | 6 |
| Jesse Anderson | TE | 6'2" | 245 | 27 | | |
| Hoby Brenner | TE | 6'4" | 245 | 34 | | 6 |
| Irv Smith | TE | 6'3" | 246 | 21 | | 12 |
| Tommie Stowers | TE | 6'3" | 240 | 26 | | 2 |
| Frank Wainright | TE | 6'3" | 245 | 25 | | |
| Morten Andersen | K | 6'2" | 221 | 33 | | 117 |
| Tommy Barnhardt | K | 6'3" | 207 | 30 | | |

Vaughn Dunbar — Knee Injury

## ATLANTA FALCONS 6-10 Jerry Glanville

| Scores of Each Game | | |
|---|---|---|
| 13 | Detroit | 30 |
| 31 | NEW ORLEANS | 34 |
| 30 | San Francisco | 37 |
| 17 | PITTSBURGH | 45 |
| 0 | Chicago | 6 |
| 30 | L.A. RAMS | 24 |
| 26 | New Orleans | 15 |
| 24 | TAMPA BAY | 31 |
| 13 | L.A. Rams | 0 |
| 27 | DALLAS | 14 |
| 17 | CLEVELAND | 14 |
| 17 | Houston | 33 |
| 27 | SAN FRANCISCO | 24 |
| 17 | Washington | 30 |
| 17 | Cincinnati | 21 |
| 10 | PHOENIX | 27 |

| Use Name | Pos. | Hgt. | Wgt. | Age | Int | Pts |
|---|---|---|---|---|---|---|
| Mike Kenn | OT | 6'7" | 286 | 37 | | |
| Bob Whitfield | OT | 6'5" | 308 | 21 | | |
| Keith Alex | OG | 6'4" | 307 | 24 | | |
| Roman Fortin | OG-C | 6'5" | 295 | 26 | | |
| Chris Hinton | OG | 6'4" | 305 | 32 | | |
| Lincoln Kennedy | OG | 6'6" | 335 | 22 | | |
| Jamie Dukes | C | 6'1" | 292 | 29 | | |
| Mike Ruether | C-OG | 6'4" | 286 | 30 | | |
| Mel Agee | DE | 6'5" | 298 | 24 | | |
| Lester Archambeau | DE | 6'5" | 275 | 26 | | |
| Rick Bryan | DE | 6'4" | 270 | 31 | | |
| Mike Gann | DE | 6'5" | 270 | 29 | | |
| Tim Green | DE | 6'2" | 249 | 29 | | |
| Ernie Logan | DE | 6'3" | 285 | 25 | | |
| Chuck Smith | DE-LB | 6'2" | 254 | 23 | | |
| Moe Gardner | DT | 6'2" | 258 | 24 | | |
| James Geathers | DT | 6'7" | 290 | 33 | | |
| Bill Goldberg | DT-DE | 6'2" | 266 | 23 | | |
| Pierce Holt | DT | 6'4" | 275 | 31 | | |

| Use Name | Pos. | Hgt. | Wgt. | Age | Int | Pts |
|---|---|---|---|---|---|---|
| Darion Conner | LB | 6'2" | 245 | 25 | | |
| Howard Dinkins | LB | 6'1" | 230 | 24 | | |
| Ron George | LB | 6'2" | 225 | 23 | | |
| Dwayne Gordon | LB | 6'1" | 231 | 23 | | |
| Jesse Solomon | LB | 6' | 240 | 29 | | |
| Kenny Tippins | LB | 6'1" | 235 | 27 | | |
| Jessie Tuggle | LB | 5'11" | 230 | 28 | | |
| Scott Case | DB | 6' | 188 | 31 | | |
| Vinnie Clark | DB | 6' | 194 | 24 | 2 | 6 |
| Jeff Donaldson | DB | 6' | 190 | 31 | | |
| Tracey Eaton | DB | 6'1" | 195 | 28 | 1 | |
| Roger Harper | DB | 6'2" | 223 | 22 | | |
| Melvin Jenkins (to DET) | DB | 5'10" | 173 | 31 | | |
| Brian Mitchell | DB | 5'9" | 175 | 24 | | |
| Alton Montgomery | DB | 6' | 202 | 25 | | |
| Deion Sanders | DB | 6' | 185 | 26 | 7 | 6 |
| Elbert Shelley | DB | 5'11" | 185 | 28 | | |
| Darnell Walker | DB | 5'8" | 164 | 23 | | |
| Charles Washington | DB | 6'1" | 217 | 26 | | |

| Use Name | Pos. | Hgt. | Wgt. | Age | Int | Pts |
|---|---|---|---|---|---|---|
| Bob Gagliano | QB | 6'3" | 205 | 34 | | |
| Bobby Hebert | QB | 6'4" | 215 | 33 | | |
| Chris Miller | QB | 6'2" | 212 | 28 | | |
| Billy Joe Tolliver | QB | 6'1" | 218 | 27 | | |
| Steve Broussard | HB-WR | 5'7" | 201 | 26 | | 6 |
| Eric Dickerson | HB | 6'3" | 220 | 32 | | |
| Erric Pegram | HB | 5'9" | 188 | 24 | | 18 |
| Tony Smith | HB | 6'1" | 224 | 23 | | 6 |
| Michael Haynes | WR | 6' | 184 | 27 | | 24 |
| Drew Hill | WR | 5'9" | 172 | 36 | | |
| David Mims | WR | 5'8" | 191 | 23 | | 6 |
| Jason Phillips | WR | 5'7" | 166 | 26 | | |
| Mike Pritchard | WR | 5'11" | 186 | 23 | | 42 |
| Andre Rison | WR | 6' | 188 | 26 | | 90 |
| Harper LeBel | TE | 6'4" | 248 | 30 | | |
| Mitch Lyons | TE | 6'4" | 255 | 23 | | |
| Harold Alexander | K | 6'2" | 224 | 22 | | |
| Norm Johnson | K | 6'2" | 203 | 33 | | 112 |

## LOS ANGELES RAMS 5-11 Chuck Knox

| Scores of Each Game | | |
|---|---|---|
| 6 | Green Bay | 36 |
| 27 | PITTSBURGH | 0 |
| 10 | N.Y. Giants | 20 |
| 28 | Houston | 13 |
| 6 | NEW ORLEANS | 37 |
| 24 | Atlanta | 30 |
| 13 | DETROIT | 16 |
| 17 | San Francisco | 40 |
| 0 | ATLANTA | 13 |
| 10 | WASHINGTON | 6 |
| 10 | SAN FRANCISCO | 35 |
| 10 | Phoenix | 38 |
| 23 | New Orleans | 20 |
| 3 | Cincinnati | 15 |
| 14 | CLEVELAND | 42 |
| 20 | CHICAGO | 6 |

| Use Name | Pos. | Hgt. | Wgt. | Age | Int | Pts |
|---|---|---|---|---|---|---|
| Darryl Ashmore | OT | 6'7" | 300 | 23 | | |
| Irv Eatman | OT | 6'7" | 300 | 32 | | |
| Robert Jenkins | OT | 6'5" | 285 | 29 | | |
| Kevin Robbins | OT | 6'4" | 286 | 25 | | |
| Jackie Slater | OT | 6'4" | 285 | 39 | | |
| Leo Goeas | OG | 6'4" | 292 | 27 | | |
| Keith Loneker | OG | 6'3" | 330 | 22 | | |
| Tom Newberry | OG | 6'2" | 285 | 30 | | |
| Jeff Pahukoa | OG-OT | 6'2" | 298 | 24 | | |
| Bern Brostek | C | 6'3" | 300 | 26 | | |
| Blair Bush | C | 6'3" | 275 | 36 | | |
| Gerald Robinson | DE | 6'3" | 262 | 30 | | |
| Fred Stokes | DE | 6'3" | 274 | 29 | | |
| Tony Woods | DE | 6'4" | 269 | 27 | | |
| Robert Young | DE | 6'6" | 273 | 24 | | |
| Marc Boutte | DT | 6'4" | 298 | 24 | | |
| Sean Gilbert | DT | 6'4" | 315 | 23 | | |
| David Rocker | DT | 6'4" | 267 | 24 | | |

| Use Name | Pos. | Hgt. | Wgt. | Age | Int | Pts |
|---|---|---|---|---|---|---|
| Jeff Brady (to SD) | LB | 6'1" | 235 | 24 | | |
| Brett Collins (from GB) | LB | 6'1" | 234 | 24 | | |
| Shane Conlan | LB | 6'3" | 235 | 29 | 1 | |
| Thomas Homco | LB | 6' | 245 | 23 | 1 | |
| Chris Martin | LB | 6'2" | 241 | 32 | | |
| Roman Phifer | LB | 6'2" | 230 | 25 | | |
| Henry Rolling | LB | 6'2" | 225 | 27 | 2 | |
| Leon White | LB | 6'3" | 242 | 29 | | |
| Robert Bailey | DB | 5'9" | 176 | 24 | 2 | |
| Deral Boykin | DB | 5'11" | 196 | 22 | | 6 |
| Dexter Davis (from PHX) | DB | 5'10" | 185 | 23 | | |
| Courtney Griffin | DB | 5'10" | 180 | 26 | | |
| Wymon Henderson | DB | 5'10" | 188 | 31 | | |
| Darryl Henley | DB | 5'9" | 172 | 26 | | |
| Steve Israel | DB | 5'10" | 186 | 24 | | |
| Todd Lyght | DB | 6' | 186 | 24 | 2 | |
| Anthony Newman | DB | 6' | 199 | 27 | | |
| Mitchell Price (from CIN) | DB | 5'9" | 181 | 26 | | |
| Sam Seale | DB | 5'9" | 185 | 30 | | |
| Michael Stewart | DB | 5'11" | 195 | 28 | 1 | |
| Pat Terrell | DB | 6' | 195 | 25 | 2 | |

| Use Name | Pos. | Hgt. | Wgt. | Age | Int | Pts |
|---|---|---|---|---|---|---|
| Jim Everett | QB | 6'5" | 212 | 30 | | |
| Mike Pagel | QB | 6'2" | 220 | 32 | | |
| T.J. Rubley | QB | 6'3" | 205 | 24 | | |
| Jerome Bettis | HB-FB | 5'11" | 243 | 21 | | 42 |
| Cleveland Gary | HB | 6' | 226 | 27 | | 12 |
| Howard Griffith | HB | 6' | 226 | 25 | | |
| David Lang | HB-FB | 5'11" | 213 | 25 | | |
| Russell White | HB | 5'11" | 186 | 22 | | |
| Tim Lester | FB | 5'9" | 215 | 25 | | |
| Willie Anderson | WR | 6' | 172 | 28 | | 24 |
| Richard Buchanan | WR | 5'10" | 178 | 24 | | |
| Henry Ellard | WR | 5'11" | 182 | 32 | | 12 |
| Ernie Jones | WR | 6' | 200 | 28 | | 12 |
| Todd Kinchen | WR | 6' | 187 | 24 | | 6 |
| Sean LaChapelle | WR | 6'3" | 205 | 23 | | |
| Pat Carter | TE | 6'4" | 250 | 27 | | 6 |
| Troy Drayton | TE | 6'3" | 255 | 23 | | 24 |
| Travis McNeal | TE | 6'3" | 244 | 26 | | 6 |
| Don Bracken | K | 6'1" | 211 | 31 | | |
| Sean Landeta (from NYG) | K | 6' | 210 | 31 | | |
| Paul McJulien | K | 5'10" | 190 | 28 | | |
| Tony Zendejas | K | 5'8" | 165 | 33 | | 71 |

## SAN FRANCISCO 49ERS

### RUSHING

| Last Name | No. | Yds | Avg | TD |
|---|---|---|---|---|
| Watters | 208 | 950 | 4.6 | 10 |
| Young | 69 | 407 | 5.9 | 2 |
| Logan | 58 | 280 | 4.8 | 7 |
| Lee | 72 | 230 | 3.2 | 1 |
| Rathman | 19 | 80 | 4.2 | 3 |
| Carter | 10 | 72 | 7.2 | 1 |
| Rice | 3 | 69 | 23.0 | 1 |
| J. Taylor | 2 | 17 | 8.5 | 0 |
| Walker | 5 | 17 | 3.4 | 0 |
| Bono | 12 | 14 | 1.2 | 1 |
| Wilmsmeyer | 2 | 0 | 0.0 | 0 |
| Musgrave | 3 | -3 | -1.0 | 0 |

### RECEIVING

| Last Name | No. | Yds | Avg | TD |
|---|---|---|---|---|
| Rice | 98 | 1503 | 15.3 | 15 |
| Jones | 68 | 735 | 10.8 | 3 |
| J. Taylor | 56 | 940 | 16.8 | 5 |
| Logan | 37 | 348 | 9.4 | 0 |
| Watters | 31 | 326 | 10.5 | 1 |
| Williams | 16 | 132 | 8.3 | 1 |
| Lee | 16 | 115 | 7.2 | 2 |
| Rathman | 10 | 86 | 8.6 | 0 |
| Singleton | 8 | 126 | 15.8 | 1 |
| Beach | 5 | 59 | 11.8 | 1 |
| Turner | 3 | 64 | 21.3 | 0 |
| Carter | 3 | 40 | 13.3 | 0 |
| Young | 2 | 2 | 1.0 | 0 |
| Walker | 1 | 4 | 4.0 | 0 |

### PUNT RETURNS

| Last Name | No. | Yds | Avg | TD |
|---|---|---|---|---|
| Carter | 34 | 411 | 12.1 | 1 |
| Kelm | 1 | 0 | 0.0 | 0 |

### KICKOFF RETURNS

| Last Name | No. | Yds | Avg | TD |
|---|---|---|---|---|
| Carter | 25 | 494 | 19.8 | 0 |
| Lee | 10 | 160 | 16.0 | 0 |
| Walker | 3 | 51 | 17.0 | 0 |
| Brandes | 1 | 10 | 10.0 | 0 |
| Kelm | 1 | 0 | 0.0 | 0 |
| Walls | 0 | 0 | — | 0 |
| Williams | 0 | 0 | — | 0 |

### PASSING

| Last Name | Att | Cmp | % | Yds | Yd/Att | TD | Int—% | RK |
|---|---|---|---|---|---|---|---|---|
| Young | 462 | 314 | 68.0 | 4023 | 8.71 | 29 | 16—3.5 | 1 |
| Bono | 61 | 39 | 63.9 | 416 | 6.82 | 0 | 1—1.6 | |
| J. Taylor | 1 | 1 | 100.0 | 41 | 41.00 | 0 | 0—0.0 | |

### PUNTING

| Last Name | No. | Avg. |
|---|---|---|
| Wilmsmeyer | 42 | 40.9 |

### KICKING

| Last Name | XP | ATT | % | FG | ATT | % |
|---|---|---|---|---|---|---|
| Cofer | 59 | 61 | 97 | 16 | 26 | 62 |

## NEW ORLEANS SAINTS

### RUSHING

| Last Name | No. | Yds | Avg | TD |
|---|---|---|---|---|
| Brown | 180 | 705 | 3.9 | 2 |
| Wilson | 31 | 230 | 7.4 | 0 |
| Muster | 64 | 214 | 3.3 | 3 |
| Neal | 21 | 175 | 8.3 | 0 |
| Hilliard | 50 | 165 | 3.3 | 2 |
| McAfee | 51 | 160 | 3.1 | 1 |
| Ned | 9 | 71 | 7.9 | 1 |
| Early | 2 | 32 | 16.0 | 0 |
| Barnhardt | 1 | 18 | 18.0 | 0 |
| M. Buck | 1 | 0 | 0.0 | 0 |
| Walsh | 4 | -4 | -1.0 | 0 |

### RECEIVING

| Last Name | No. | Yds | Avg | TD |
|---|---|---|---|---|
| E. Martin | 66 | 950 | 14.4 | 3 |
| Early | 45 | 670 | 14.9 | 6 |
| Hilliard | 40 | 296 | 7.4 | 1 |
| Muster | 23 | 195 | 8.5 | 0 |
| Brown | 21 | 170 | 8.1 | 1 |
| Smith | 16 | 180 | 11.3 | 2 |
| Small | 16 | 164 | 10.3 | 1 |
| Turner | 12 | 163 | 13.6 | 0 |
| Brenner | 11 | 171 | 15.5 | 1 |
| Ned | 9 | 54 | 6.0 | 0 |
| Newman | 8 | 121 | 15.1 | 1 |
| Dowdell | 6 | 46 | 7.7 | 1 |
| McAfee | 1 | 3 | 3.0 | 0 |

### PUNT RETURNS

| Last Name | No. | Yds | Avg | TD |
|---|---|---|---|---|
| Hughes | 37 | 503 | 13.6 | 2 |
| Newman | 1 | 14 | 14.0 | 0 |

### KICKOFF RETURNS

| Last Name | No. | Yds | Avg | TD |
|---|---|---|---|---|
| Hughes | 30 | 753 | 25.1 | 1 |
| McAfee | 28 | 580 | 20.7 | 0 |
| Brown | 3 | 58 | 19.3 | 0 |
| Hilliard | 1 | 17 | 17.0 | 0 |
| Dowdell | 0 | 52 | — | 0 |

### PASSING

| Last Name | Att | Cmp | % | Yds | Yd/Att | TD | Int—% | RK |
|---|---|---|---|---|---|---|---|---|
| Wilson | 388 | 221 | 57.0 | 2457 | 6.33 | 12 | 15—3.9 | 10 |
| M. Buck | 54 | 32 | 59.3 | 448 | 8.30 | 4 | 3—5.6 | |
| Walsh | 38 | 20 | 52.6 | 271 | 7.13 | 2 | 3—7.9 | |
| Barnhardt | 1 | 1 | 100.0 | 7 | 7.00 | 0 | 0—0.0 | |

### PUNTING

| Last Name | No. | Avg. |
|---|---|---|
| Barnhardt | 77 | 43.6 |

### KICKING

| Last Name | XP | ATT | % | FG | ATT | % |
|---|---|---|---|---|---|---|
| Andersen | 33 | 33 | 100 | 28 | 35 | 80 |

## ATLANTA FALCONS

### RUSHING

| Last Name | No. | Yds | Avg | TD |
|---|---|---|---|---|
| Pegram | 292 | 1185 | 4.1 | 3 |
| Broussard | 39 | 206 | 5.3 | 1 |
| Dickerson | 26 | 91 | 3.5 | 0 |
| Hebert | 24 | 49 | 2.0 | 0 |
| Tolliver | 7 | 48 | 6.9 | 0 |
| Miller | 2 | 11 | 5.5 | 0 |
| Pritchard | 2 | 4 | 2.0 | 0 |
| Mims | 1 | 3 | 3.0 | 0 |
| Alexander | 2 | -7 | -3.5 | 0 |

### RECEIVING

| Last Name | No. | Yds | Avg | TD |
|---|---|---|---|---|
| Rison | 86 | 1242 | 14.4 | 15 |
| Pritchard | 74 | 736 | 9.9 | 7 |
| Haynes | 72 | 778 | 10.8 | 4 |
| Hill | 34 | 384 | 11.3 | 0 |
| Pegram | 33 | 302 | 9.2 | 0 |
| Mims | 12 | 107 | 8.9 | 1 |
| Lyons | 8 | 63 | 7.9 | 0 |
| Sanders | 6 | 106 | 17.7 | 1 |
| Dickerson | 6 | 58 | 9.7 | 0 |
| Phillips | 1 | 15 | 15.0 | 0 |
| Broussard | 1 | 4 | 4.0 | 0 |
| Hinton | 1 | -8 | -8.0 | 0 |

### PUNT RETURNS

| Last Name | No. | Yds | Avg | TD |
|---|---|---|---|---|
| T. Smith | 32 | 255 | 8.0 | 0 |
| Sanders | 2 | 21 | 10.5 | 0 |
| Clark | 1 | 0 | 0.0 | 0 |

### KICKOFF RETURNS

| Last Name | No. | Yds | Avg | TD |
|---|---|---|---|---|
| T. Smith | 38 | 948 | 24.9 | 1 |
| Sanders | 7 | 169 | 24.1 | 0 |
| Pegram | 4 | 63 | 15.8 | 0 |
| Montgomery | 2 | 53 | 26.5 | 0 |
| Phillips | 2 | 38 | 19.0 | 0 |
| Mims | 1 | 22 | 22.0 | 0 |
| Ruether | 1 | 7 | 7.0 | 0 |

### PASSING

| Last Name | Att | Cmp | % | Yds | Yd/Att | TD | Int—% | RK |
|---|---|---|---|---|---|---|---|---|
| Hebert | 430 | 263 | 61.2 | 2978 | 6.93 | 24 | 17—4.0 | 5 |
| Tolliver | 76 | 39 | 51.3 | 464 | 6.11 | 3 | 5—6.6 | |
| Miller | 66 | 32 | 48.5 | 345 | 5.23 | 1 | 3—4.5 | |
| Sanders | 1 | 0 | 0.0 | 0 | 0.00 | 0 | 0—0.0 | |

### PUNTING

| Last Name | No. | Avg. |
|---|---|---|
| Alexander | 72 | 43.3 |

### KICKING

| Last Name | XP | ATT | % | FG | ATT | % |
|---|---|---|---|---|---|---|
| N. Johnson | 34 | 34 | 100 | 26 | 27 | 96 |

## LOS ANGELES RAMS

### RUSHING

| Last Name | No. | Yds | Avg | TD |
|---|---|---|---|---|
| Bettis | 294 | 1429 | 4.9 | 7 |
| Gary | 79 | 293 | 3.7 | 1 |
| Rubley | 29 | 102 | 3.5 | 0 |
| Lester | 11 | 74 | 6.7 | 0 |
| Everett | 19 | 38 | 2.0 | 0 |
| Lang | 9 | 29 | 3.2 | 0 |
| Ellard | 2 | 18 | 9.0 | 0 |
| R. White | 2 | 10 | 5.0 | 0 |
| Kinchen | 2 | 10 | 5.0 | 0 |
| Drayton | 1 | 7 | 7.0 | 0 |
| Jones | 1 | 4 | 4.0 | 0 |

### RECEIVING

| Last Name | No. | Yds | Avg | TD |
|---|---|---|---|---|
| Ellard | 61 | 945 | 15.5 | 2 |
| Anderson | 37 | 552 | 14.9 | 4 |
| Gary | 36 | 289 | 8.0 | 1 |
| Drayton | 27 | 319 | 11.8 | 4 |
| Bettis | 26 | 244 | 9.4 | 0 |
| Lester | 18 | 154 | 8.6 | 0 |
| Carter | 14 | 166 | 11.9 | 1 |
| Kinchen | 8 | 137 | 17.1 | 1 |
| McNeal | 8 | 75 | 9.4 | 1 |
| Jones | 5 | 56 | 11.2 | 2 |
| Lang | 4 | 45 | 11.3 | 0 |
| LaChapelle | 2 | 23 | 11.5 | 0 |

### PUNT RETURNS

| Last Name | No. | Yds | Avg | TD |
|---|---|---|---|---|
| Buchanan | 8 | 41 | 5.1 | 0 |
| Kinchen | 7 | 32 | 4.6 | 0 |
| Ellard | 2 | 18 | 9.0 | 0 |
| Henley | 1 | 8 | 8.0 | 0 |
| Price | 1 | 3 | 3.0 | 0 |

### KICKOFF RETURNS

| Last Name | No. | Yds | Avg | TD |
|---|---|---|---|---|
| Boykin | 13 | 216 | 16.6 | 0 |
| Griffith | 8 | 169 | 21.1 | 0 |
| Price | 8 | 144 | 16.0 | 0 |
| R. White | 8 | 122 | 15.3 | 0 |
| Kinchen | 6 | 96 | 16.0 | 0 |
| Israel | 5 | 92 | 18.4 | 0 |
| Drayton | 1 | -15 | -15.0 | 0 |

### PASSING

| Last Name | Att | Cmp | % | Yds | Yd/Att | TD | Int—% | RK |
|---|---|---|---|---|---|---|---|---|
| Rubley | 189 | 108 | 57.1 | 1338 | 7.08 | 8 | 6—3.2 | |
| Everett | 274 | 135 | 49.3 | 1652 | 6.03 | 8 | 12—4.4 | 13 |
| Pagel | 9 | 3 | 33.3 | 23 | 2.56 | 0 | 1—11.1 | |
| Gary | 1 | 1 | 100.0 | 8 | 8.00 | 0 | 0—0.0 | |

### PUNTING

| Last Name | No. | Avg. |
|---|---|---|
| Landeta | 76 | 42.3 |
| McJulien | 21 | 37.9 |
| Bracken | 17 | 38.3 |

### KICKING

| Last Name | XP | ATT | % | FG | ATT | % |
|---|---|---|---|---|---|---|
| Zendejas | 23 | 25 | 92 | 16 | 23 | 70 |

# 1993 A.F.C.  Shula Passes Halas as All-Time Winningest Coach

When Don Shula coached his first game in 1963, John F. Kennedy was still the president, three NFL head coaches were still in grade school and gasoline cost about a quarter a gallon. Times have changed, but Shula hasn't — he's still a winner. Shula got his 325th victory on November 14 to break George Halas' once-seemingly unbreakable record of 324 wins. The record victory was over the Eagles, with Doug Pederson at quarterback in place of Scott Mitchell who was in place of Dan Marino.

But after that memorable milestone, Shula's Dolphins won only two more games before losing their final five and failing to make the playoffs. In other words, a tremendous achievement for Shula came in a season of disappointment.

In the AFC, the Bills became the first team in professional sports history to get to the championship game for four consecutive years without winning at least once. In the AFC championship game, they faced the Chiefs, who were led by quarterback Joe Montana, who was trying to make it to his fifth Super Bowl. Montana and Marcus Allen, another Kansas City acquisition in the offseason, were two of the biggest surprises in the conference — old veterans who still had it.

## EASTERN DIVISION

**Buffalo Bills** — The fourth time wasn't a charm for the Bills, who, despite playing in the AFC championship game for a record-fourth straight year, lost for their fourth straight Super Bowl. Still, it was a very good year for the Bills, who improved on defense. Defensive end Bruce Smith was the NFL's Defensive Player of the Year and tied for the league lead with 13.5 sacks. But, on offense, the once-powerful, no-huddle machine seemed to have its problems. The Bills struggled to put points on the board early in the season and only a four-game winning streak in the final month gave them the home-field advantage in the playoffs. Quarterback Jim Kelly passed for 3,382 yards and 18 TD's, and running back Thurman Thomas led the AFC with 1,315 yards rushing.

**Miami Dolphins** — Don Shula began the season saying he wanted the coaching record for most victories to come in a season in which the Dolphins achieved success. It didn't happen. With a 9-2 record on Thanksgiving Day, the Dolphins had the best record in the NFL. Then they lost their final five games of the season to miss the playoffs again. Quarterback Dan Marino, who hadn't missed a game in eight years, suffered a torn Achilles tendon in the fifth game and was gone. Unproven Scott Mitchell took over and was the NFL's Player of the Month of October. Then he, too, was injured, leaving first-year pro Doug Pederson and pickup Steve DeBerg in charge until Mitchell returned. Rookie running back Terry Kirby led the team with 75 receptions, and free-agent wide receiver Irving Fryar caught 64 passes for 1,010 yards.

**New York Jets** — Quarterback Boomer Esiason was traded to the Jets during the offseason, and he quickly proved that he had a lot left by leading the team to a 7-4 mark. Esiason passed for 3,421 yards and 16 TD's, but losses in the final three games left the Jets out of the playoffs. Safety Ronnie Lott and running back Johnny Johnson (821 yards rushing and 67 catches) were other new faces on the Jets, who made strides to rebuild the team. They were vastly improved from their 4-12 mark in 1992, but missed opportunities all year eventually cost head coach Bruce Coslet his job. He was fired a few days after the end of the season and replaced by defensive coordinator Pete Carroll. Carroll's defense had improved to eighth overall in the league and allowed just 247 points.

**New England Patriots** — Bill Parcells returned to coaching and righted the Patriots sinking ship before it moved out of town. New England owned the first pick in the 1993 draft and chose quarterback Drew Bledsoe, who was quickly named the starter. The Patriots lost their first four games, won one and then lost seven more, though many of them were close. Then Parcells, Bledsoe and the Patriots got things into gear, and New England closed out the season with four consecutive victories. Bledsoe passed for 2,494 yards and 15 touchdowns, and Leonard Russell turned into a Parcells-type of dominating runner by rushing for 1,088 yards and seven scores. After the season, the team was sold by James Busch Orthwein to Robert Kraft, the owner of Foxboro Stadium.

**Indianapolis Colts** — Big things were expected from the Colts in 1993, but the season didn't go according to plan. First, quarterback Jeff George held out and asked to be traded and then was booed lustfully when he made his first appearance in the third game of the season. Defensive lineman Steve Emtman suffered another serious knee injury in the sixth game and was lost for the season. All year long the offense was unproductive and the defense was unable to play well in clutch situations. The result was a last-place, 4-12 finish. George did pass for 2,526 yards but with only eight TD passes. Wide receiver Reggie Langhorne led the AFC in receptions with 85 for 1,038 yards and three scores. And placekicker Dean Biasucci was again at the top of his game, with 26 field goals in 31 attempts to give the Colts 93 of their 189 points.

## CENTRAL DIVISION

**Houston Oilers** — The Oilers made the playoffs again in 1993, but it was a season in which all anyone will remember is the punch defensive coordinator Buddy Ryan threw at offensive coordinator Kevin Gilbride during a nationally televised Sunday night game against the Jets. Ryan and Gilbride had feuded all season, and head coach Jack Pardee was unable to stop it. "Team Turmoil" started out 1-4, and Pardee's job was on the line. Then the Oilers reeled off 11 straight victories to win the AFC Central. It was the longest winning streak in the NFL since 1972. Ryan's defense was the league's best against the run and second in takeaways. Running back Gary Brown, who replaced an injured Lorenzo White, rushed for 1,002 yards in the last eight games, and helped quarterback Warren Moon, who had an off-year with 24 interceptions. Jeff Alm, a defensive tackle, committed suicide on December 14.

**Pittsburgh Steelers** — In their second year under head coach Bill Cowher, the Steelers again made the playoffs. But numerous mistakes by the NFL's worst special teams cost the Steelers at least two victories, and the 9-8 record (including postseason) really wasn't much better than .500. Running back Barry Foster suffered a season-ending ankle injury in the ninth game after rushing for 711 yards and scoring eight touchdowns. With Foster's big-play ability out of the lineup, the Steelers scored only eight touchdowns in the final seven games. Tight end Eric Green caught 63 passes for 942 yards, but the wide receivers might have been the league's worst, dropping far too many balls. Quarterback Neil O'Donnell fought season-long tendinitis in his throwing elbow but still broke Terry Bradshaw's team record for attempts and completions.

**Cleveland Browns** — November 8, 1993 is a day that will live in infamy for fans of the Browns. That's the day coach Bill Belichick cut quarterback and home-town favorite Bernie Kosar. Cleveland won its first three games of 1993 and had a 5-3 record — and first place in the AFC Central — under Kosar. But that wasn't good enough for Belichick, who cut Kosar, citing "diminishing skills" as the motive for the change. Because Vinny Testaverde was out injured, the offense was turned over temporarily to third-stringer Todd Philcox. Cleveland lost three straight and six of the final eight to finish 7-9 and third in the division. When he returned, Testaverde did play better than he had in past years in Tampa Bay, throwing more touchdowns than interceptions for the first time in his career. Running back Eric Metcalf helped, with a league-high 1,923 all-purpose yards and two punt-return touchdowns. And Kosar? He ended up on the Super Bowl champion Cowboys.

**Cincinnati Bengals** — One thing is for sure: Dave Shula is no Don Shula. The second-year head coach of the Bengals saw his team lose its first 10 games of 1993, though the team did win three of the final six. Still, the Bengals tied a team mark for the worst record — 3-13. Cincinnati got rid of most of its high-priced veterans before the start of the season, which left it inexperienced and lacking talent. The Bengals were abysmal on offense, scoring only 14 touchdowns the entire season and none in six games. Their 16-game total of 187 points was a record-low for the franchise. The main problem was one of the league's worst offensive lines and a woefully weak running game. That all meant second-year quarterback David Klingler was in a hole from the start, though he showed improvement, too, in the final six games.

OFFENSE

| | BUFF | CIN | CLEV | DEN | HOU | IND | K.C. | L.A. | MIA | N.E. | NYJ | PITT | S.D. | SEA |
|---|---|---|---|---|---|---|---|---|---|---|---|---|---|---|
| FIRST DOWNS: | | | | | | | | | | | | | | |
| Total | 316 | 239 | 264 | 327 | 330 | 269 | 300 | 292 | 309 | 315 | 304 | 307 | 313 | 279 |
| by Rushing | 117 | 89 | 91 | 105 | 101 | 71 | 94 | 95 | 85 | 116 | 106 | 116 | 120 | 114 |
| by Passing | 176 | 133 | 152 | 187 | 208 | 180 | 180 | 168 | 207 | 169 | 173 | 180 | 171 | 144 |
| by Penalty | 23 | 17 | 21 | 35 | 21 | 18 | 26 | 29 | 17 | 30 | 25 | 11 | 22 | 21 |
| RUSHING: | | | | | | | | | | | | | | |
| Number | 551 | 423 | 425 | 486 | 409 | 365 | 445 | 433 | 419 | 502 | 521 | 491 | 455 | 473 |
| Yards | 1943 | 1511 | 1701 | 1693 | 1792 | 1288 | 1655 | 1425 | 1459 | 1780 | 1880 | 2003 | 1824 | 2015 |
| Average Yards | 3.5 | 3.6 | 4.0 | 3.6 | 4.4 | 3.5 | 3.7 | 3.3 | 3.5 | 3.5 | 3.6 | 4.1 | 4.0 | 4.3 |
| Touchdowns | 12 | 3 | 8 | 13 | 11 | 4 | 14 | 10 | 10 | 9 | 14 | 13 | 14 | 13 |
| PASSING: | | | | | | | | | | | | | | |
| Attempts | 497 | 510 | 478 | 553 | 614 | 594 | 490 | 495 | 581 | 566 | 489 | 540 | 563 | 498 |
| Completions | 304 | 272 | 262 | 350 | 357 | 332 | 287 | 281 | 342 | 289 | 294 | 299 | 301 | 280 |
| Completion Pct. | 61.2 | 53.3 | 54.8 | 63.3 | 58.1 | 55.9 | 58.6 | 56.8 | 58.9 | 51.1 | 60.1 | 55.4 | 53.5 | 56.2 |
| Passing Yards | 3535 | 2830 | 3328 | 4061 | 4145 | 3623 | 3384 | 3882 | 4564 | 3412 | 3492 | 3606 | 3383 | 2896 |
| Avg. Yds per Att. | 7.1 | 5.6 | 7.0 | 7.3 | 6.8 | 6.1 | 6.9 | 7.8 | 7.9 | 6.0 | 7.1 | 6.7 | 6.0 | 5.8 |
| Avg. Yds per Comp. | 11.6 | 10.4 | 12.7 | 11.6 | 11.6 | 10.9 | 11.8 | 13.8 | 13.3 | 11.8 | 11.9 | 12.1 | 11.2 | 10.3 |
| Times Tackled | 31 | 53 | 45 | 39 | 43 | 29 | 35 | 50 | 30 | 23 | 21 | 48 | 32 | 48 |
| Yds Lost Tackled | 218 | 289 | 289 | 293 | 279 | 206 | 204 | 293 | 211 | 127 | 160 | 374 | 240 | 242 |
| Net Yards | 3317 | 2541 | 3039 | 3768 | 3866 | 3417 | 3180 | 3589 | 4353 | 3285 | 3332 | 3232 | 3143 | 2654 |
| Touchdowns | 20 | 11 | 23 | 27 | 23 | 10 | 20 | 17 | 27 | 17 | 16 | 16 | 18 | 13 |
| Interceptions | 18 | 11 | 19 | 10 | 25 | 15 | 10 | 14 | 18 | 24 | 12 | 12 | 14 | 18 |
| Pct. Intercepted | 3.6 | 2.2 | 4.0 | 1.8 | 4.1 | 2.5 | 2.0 | 2.8 | 3.1 | 4.2 | 2.5 | 2.2 | 2.5 | 3.6 |
| PUNTS: | | | | | | | | | | | | | | |
| Number | 74 | 90 | 84 | 68 | 56 | 83 | 77 | 71 | 58 | 76 | 73 | 89 | 74 | 91 |
| Average | 40.4 | 43.4 | 43.2 | 44.4 | 45.4 | 43.3 | 42.1 | 41.8 | 39.7 | 40.7 | 38.4 | 42.5 | 42.3 | 44.0 |
| PUNT RETURNS | | | | | | | | | | | | | | |
| Number | 33 | 48 | 42 | 41 | 41 | 30 | 37 | 40 | 28 | 51 | 31 | 46 | 34 | 33 |
| Yards | 277 | 321 | 563 | 425 | 275 | 173 | 348 | 465 | 326 | 462 | 256 | 353 | 412 | 280 |
| Average Yards | 8.4 | 6.7 | 13.4 | 10.4 | 6.7 | 5.8 | 9.4 | 11.6 | 11.6 | 9.2 | 8.3 | 7.7 | 12.1 | 8.5 |
| Touchdowns | 1 | 0 | 3 | 0 | 0 | 0 | 0 | 1 | 2 | 0 | 0 | 0 | 0 | 0 |
| KICKOFF RET.: | | | | | | | | | | | | | | |
| Number | 45 | 61 | 58 | 38 | 31 | 57 | 45 | 52 | 49 | 47 | 46 | 52 | 47 | 50 |
| Yards | 746 | 1211 | 1119 | 717 | 589 | 1124 | 875 | 1061 | 1068 | 819 | 675 | 878 | 901 | 931 |
| Average Yards | 16.6 | 19.9 | 19.1 | 18.9 | 18.9 | 19.7 | 19.4 | 20.7 | 21.8 | 17.4 | 14.7 | 16.9 | 19.2 | 18.6 |
| Touchdowns | 0 | 0 | 0 | 0 | 0 | 0 | 0 | 0 | 0 | 0 | 0 | 0 | 0 | 0 |
| INTERCEPT RET.: | | | | | | | | | | | | | | |
| Number | 23 | 12 | 13 | 18 | 26 | 10 | 21 | 14 | 13 | 13 | 19 | 24 | 22 | 22 |
| Yards | 306 | 272 | 208 | 236 | 412 | 116 | 225 | 199 | 175 | 122 | 233 | 386 | 319 | 196 |
| Average Yards | 13.3 | 22.7 | 16.0 | 13.1 | 15.8 | 11.6 | 10.7 | 14.2 | 13.5 | 9.4 | 12.3 | 16.1 | 14.5 | 8.9 |
| Touchdowns | 3 | 2 | 1 | 1 | 3 | 0 | 0 | 1 | 1 | 0 | 1 | 1 | 1 | 1 |
| PENALTIES: | | | | | | | | | | | | | | |
| Number | 95 | 105 | 121 | 112 | 132 | 94 | 121 | 148 | 81 | 64 | 86 | 100 | 87 | 99 |
| Yards | 630 | 773 | 842 | 822 | 1005 | 685 | 969 | 1181 | 663 | 468 | 555 | 861 | 699 | 745 |
| FUMBLES: | | | | | | | | | | | | | | |
| Number | 26 | 24 | 27 | 29 | 37 | 34 | 28 | 23 | 30 | 30 | 38 | 27 | 13 | 25 |
| Number Lost | 17 | 9 | 17 | 18 | 20 | 20 | 18 | 11 | 14 | 10 | 16 | 15 | 5 | 13 |
| POINTS: | | | | | | | | | | | | | | |
| Total | 329 | 187 | 304 | 373 | 368 | 189 | 328 | 306 | 349 | 238 | 270 | 308 | 322 | 280 |
| PAT Attempts | 37 | 16 | 36 | 42 | 40 | 16 | 37 | 29 | 37 | 25 | 31 | 32 | 36 | 29 |
| PAT Made | 36 | 13 | 36 | 41 | 39 | 15 | 37 | 27 | 37 | 25 | 31 | 32 | 31 | 29 |
| FG Attempts | 32 | 31 | 22 | 35 | 34 | 31 | 29 | 44 | 32 | 31 | 26 | 30 | 40 | 28 |
| FG Made | 23 | 24 | 16 | 26 | 29 | 26 | 23 | 35 | 24 | 19 | 17 | 28 | 31 | 23 |
| Percent FG Made | 71.9 | 77.4 | 72.7 | 74.3 | 85.3 | 83.9 | 79.3 | 79.5 | 75.0 | 61.3 | 65.4 | 93.3 | 77.5 | 82.1 |
| Safeties | 1 | 3 | 2 | 1 | 1 | 0 | 0 | 0 | 0 | 0 | 1 | 0 | 0 | 4 |

DEFENSE

| | BUFF | CIN | CLEV | DEN | HOU | IND | K.C. | L.A. | MIA | N.E. | NYJ | PITT | S.D. | SEA |
|---|---|---|---|---|---|---|---|---|---|---|---|---|---|---|
| FIRST DOWNS: | | | | | | | | | | | | | | |
| Total | 331 | 306 | 290 | 280 | 289 | 334 | 300 | 302 | 332 | 269 | 266 | 267 | 299 | 322 |
| by Rushing | 114 | 134 | 94 | 86 | 73 | 151 | 103 | 111 | 103 | 97 | 93 | 74 | 86 | 106 |
| by Passing | 199 | 159 | 170 | 181 | 184 | 166 | 161 | 154 | 205 | 161 | 161 | 163 | 192 | 193 |
| by Penalty | 18 | 13 | 26 | 13 | 32 | 17 | 36 | 37 | 24 | 11 | 12 | 30 | 21 | 23 |
| RUSHING: | | | | | | | | | | | | | | |
| Number | 500 | 521 | 451 | 397 | 369 | 575 | 453 | 494 | 460 | 505 | 420 | 399 | 414 | 452 |
| Yards | 1921 | 2220 | 1654 | 1418 | 1273 | 2521 | 1620 | 1865 | 1665 | 1951 | 1473 | 1368 | 1314 | 1660 |
| Average Yards | 3.8 | 4.3 | 3.7 | 3.6 | 3.4 | 4.4 | 3.6 | 3.8 | 3.6 | 3.9 | 3.5 | 3.4 | 3.2 | 3.7 |
| Touchdowns | 7 | 15 | 9 | 6 | 9 | 20 | 11 | 17 | 12 | 9 | 8 | 6 | 10 | 12 |
| PASSING: | | | | | | | | | | | | | | |
| Attempts | 582 | 457 | 541 | 562 | 582 | 454 | 525 | 457 | 572 | 474 | 497 | 521 | 556 | 595 |
| Completions | 323 | 251 | 306 | 314 | 302 | 270 | 312 | 258 | 350 | 280 | 296 | 277 | 329 | 333 |
| Completion Pct. | 55.5 | 54.9 | 56.6 | 55.9 | 51.9 | 59.5 | 59.4 | 56.5 | 61.2 | 59.1 | 59.6 | 53.2 | 59.2 | 56.0 |
| Passing Yards | 3889 | 2952 | 3466 | 3969 | 3914 | 3238 | 3379 | 3141 | 3682 | 3087 | 3434 | 3440 | 3958 | 3897 |
| Avg. Yds per Att. | 6.7 | 6.5 | 6.4 | 7.1 | 6.7 | 7.1 | 6.4 | 6.9 | 6.4 | 6.5 | 6.9 | 6.6 | 7.1 | 6.6 |
| Avg. Yds per Comp. | 12.0 | 11.8 | 11.3 | 12.6 | 12.5 | 12.0 | 10.8 | 12.2 | 10.5 | 11.0 | 11.6 | 12.4 | 12.0 | 11.7 |
| Times Tackled | 37 | 22 | 48 | 46 | 52 | 21 | 35 | 45 | 29 | 34 | 32 | 42 | 32 | 38 |
| Yds Lost Tackled | 256 | 154 | 342 | 238 | 313 | 121 | 228 | 283 | 197 | 242 | 195 | 277 | 206 | 244 |
| Net Yards | 3633 | 2798 | 3124 | 3731 | 3601 | 3117 | 3151 | 2858 | 3485 | 2845 | 3239 | 3163 | 3752 | 3653 |
| Touchdowns | 18 | 20 | 19 | 21 | 16 | 22 | 18 | 17 | 26 | 20 | 15 | 16 | 17 | 16 |
| Interceptions | 23 | 12 | 13 | 18 | 26 | 10 | 21 | 14 | 13 | 13 | 19 | 24 | 22 | 22 |
| Pct. Intercepted | 4.0 | 2.6 | 2.4 | 3.2 | 4.5 | 2.2 | 4.0 | 3.1 | 2.3 | 2.7 | 3.8 | 4.6 | 4.0 | 3.7 |
| PUNTS: | | | | | | | | | | | | | | |
| Number | 65 | 74 | 85 | 81 | 78 | 71 | 68 | 80 | 76 | 90 | 66 | 82 | 72 | 73 |
| Average | 41.8 | 42.2 | 42.4 | 43.7 | 43.7 | 40.2 | 44.6 | 42.1 | 41.3 | 41.2 | 43.3 | 44.0 | 42.1 | 42.4 |
| PUNT RETURNS | | | | | | | | | | | | | | |
| Number | 29 | 47 | 48 | 33 | 28 | 41 | 43 | 35 | 32 | 34 | 26 | 50 | 36 | 47 |
| Yards | 247 | 416 | 438 | 337 | 249 | 352 | 352 | 301 | 359 | 313 | 156 | 678 | 292 | 475 |
| Average Yards | 8.5 | 8.9 | 9.1 | 10.2 | 8.9 | 8.6 | 8.2 | 8.6 | 11.2 | 9.2 | 6.0 | 13.7 | 8.2 | 10.2 |
| Touchdowns | 0 | 0 | 0 | 0 | 0 | 1 | 0 | 0 | 1 | 1 | 0 | 3 | 0 | 1 |
| KICKOFF RET.: | | | | | | | | | | | | | | |
| Number | 43 | 38 | 46 | 63 | 60 | 37 | 49 | 45 | 62 | 44 | 47 | 54 | 64 | 52 |
| Yards | 850 | 831 | 814 | 1119 | 1062 | 551 | 1007 | 783 | 1239 | 921 | 911 | 1165 | 1063 | 967 |
| Average Yards | 19.8 | 21.9 | 17.7 | 18.0 | 17.7 | 14.9 | 20.6 | 17.4 | 20.0 | 20.9 | 19.4 | 21.4 | 16.6 | 18.6 |
| Touchdowns | 0 | 0 | 0 | 0 | 0 | 0 | 0 | 0 | 0 | 0 | 0 | 1 | 0 | 1 |
| INTERCEPT RET.: | | | | | | | | | | | | | | |
| Number | 18 | 11 | 19 | 10 | 25 | 15 | 10 | 14 | 18 | 24 | 12 | 12 | 14 | 18 |
| Yards | 174 | 49 | 246 | 79 | 309 | 247 | 111 | 289 | 329 | 201 | 310 | 216 | 271 | 159 |
| Average Yards | 9.7 | 4.5 | 12.9 | 7.9 | 12.4 | 16.5 | 8.2 | 20,.5 | 18.3 | 8.4 | 25.8 | 18.0 | 19.4 | 8.8 |
| Touchdowns | 0 | 0 | 0 | 0 | 0 | 1 | 0 | 2 | 2 | 1 | 3 | 2 | 2 | 0 |
| PENALTIES: | | | | | | | | | | | | | | |
| Number | 102 | 74 | 106 | 128 | 104 | 91 | 129 | 104 | 93 | 112 | 88 | 76 | 95 | 110 |
| Yards | 681 | 560 | 831 | 1019 | 786 | 610 | 1008 | 803 | 650 | 808 | 654 | 647 | 724 | 818 |
| FUMBLES: | | | | | | | | | | | | | | |
| Number | 35 | 22 | 28 | 27 | 31 | 25 | 30 | 23 | 31 | 20 | 30 | 37 | 19 | 23 |
| Number Lost | 24 | 14 | 9 | 13 | 17 | 11 | 17 | 9 | 14 | 9 | 18 | 14 | 12 | 15 |
| POINTS: | | | | | | | | | | | | | | |
| Total | 242 | 319 | 307 | 284 | 238 | 378 | 291 | 326 | 351 | 286 | 247 | 281 | 290 | 314 |
| PAT Attempts | 24 | 37 | 30 | 29 | 26 | 45 | 29 | 37 | 42 | 32 | 26 | 30 | 30 | 30 |
| PAT Made | 23 | 37 | 30 | 27 | 25 | 43 | 27 | 37 | 40 | 32 | 26 | 29 | 30 | 29 |
| FG Attempts | 35 | 28 | 38 | 36 | 28 | 30 | 32 | 33 | 27 | 24 | 26 | 29 | 33 | 39 |
| FG Made | 23 | 20 | 31 | 31 | 19 | 21 | 28 | 21 | 17 | 20 | 21 | 24 | 26 | 29 |
| Percent FG Made | 65.7 | 71.4 | 81.6 | 86.1 | 67.9 | 70.0 | 87.5 | 63.6 | 63.0 | 83.3 | 80.8 | 82.8 | 78.8 | 74.3 |
| Safeties | 0 | 0 | 2 | 1 | 0 | 1 | 0 | 2 | 1 | 0 | 1 | 0 | 1 | 2 |

## WESTERN DIVISION

**Kansas City Chiefs** — The Chiefs advanced to the AFC championship game in 1993, further than at any time since 1969, when they won their only Super Bowl. After finishing 25th on offense in 1992, the Chiefs made wholesale changes for '93, bringing in offensive coordinator Paul Hackett, quarterback Joe Montana and running back Marcus Allen. Because of injuries, Montana missed five games and played in only 38 of 64 quarters, but he was the AFC's second-ranked passer. Allen was the NFL's Comeback Player of the Year, as he rushed for 764 yards and tied for a league-high 15 touchdowns. On the other side of the ball, defensive end Neil Smith recorded an NFL-best 15 sacks and had two blocked field goals in a three-point win over San Diego.

**Los Angeles Raiders** — The Raiders aren't what they used to be, but getting to the AFC divisional-playoff round in 1993 at least gave them their second postseason victory since 1983. They turned the corner by rebuilding through the free-agent market and the draft. Quarterback Jeff Hostetler was the best of the newcomers, as he added much-needed leadership and stability. He passed for 3,242 yards and 14 touchdowns and ran for another five TD's himself. Back Greg Robinson, an eighth-round draft pick, ran for a team-high 591 yards, despite being injured in early December. And undrafted rookie James Jett added to the Raiders' corps of speed receivers. Tim Brown caught 80 passes for an AFC-high 1,180 yards and seven touchdowns. Placekicker Jeff Jaeger tied a league record with 35 field goals for the season.

**Denver Broncos** — John Elway proved in 1993 how good he could really be if his talents were unleashed. With Dan Reeves gone and Wade Phillips in charge, Elway passed for a career-high 4,030 yards and 25 touchdowns. But the Broncos finished with a 9-7 record and a first-round playoff loss. Denver was the highest-scoring team in the conference, but the defense too often failed to hold onto leads and allowed too many big plays. The secondary ranked 27th in passing yards allowed. Shannon Sharpe, the brother of Green Bay's Sterling, had a sensational season with 81 catches for 995 yards and an AFC-best nine receiving touchdowns. Linebacker Simon Fletcher led the Broncos in sacks for the sixth straight season.

**San Diego Chargers** — Injuries were the story of the season for the Chargers in 1992. Quarterback Stan Humphries suffered a shoulder injury during the preseason and was replaced by John Friesz, who led the team to a 2-4 mark that kept people from thinking about the playoffs. Pro Bowl cornerback Gill Byrd missed the entire year, and guard Eric Moten, tight end Derrick Walker, defensive end Burt Grossman and linebacker Jerrol Williams missed large portions of it. The Chargers climbed back to 4-4, then lost two home games and eventually had to be satisfied with an 8-8 mark. There were some highlights, however. Placekicker John Carney set an NFL record by kicking 29 consecutive field goals over two seasons and 31 in 1993, and wide receiver Anthony Miller caught 84 passes for 1,162 yards and seven TD's.

**Seattle Seahawks** — A 6-10 record and last-place finish in the AFC West may not sound like reason for celebration in Seattle. But for the Seahawks they were cause for optimism. Rookie quarterback Rick Mirer, the No. 2 pick in the 1993 draft, completed 274 of 486 passes for 2,833 yards — all record numbers for a rookie. After scoring only 140 points in 1992, the Seahawks upped that total to 280 in '93, with Mirer providing a bright glimpse into the future. Back Chris Warren had his second consecutive 1,000-yard season, and having wide receiver Brian Blades (80 receptions for 945 yards) for an entire season helped. But the defense plummeted from top 10 the previous three seasons to No. 23 in 1993.

## BUFFALO BILLS 12-4 Marv Levy

| Scores of Each Game | | |
|---|---|---|
| 38 | NEW ENGLAND | 14 |
| 13 | Dallas | 10 |
| 13 | MIAMI | 22 |
| 17 | N.Y. GIANTS | 14 |
| 35 | HOUSTON | 7 |
| 19 | N.Y. Jets | 10 |
| 24 | WASHINGTON | 10 |
| 13 | New England | *10 |
| 0 | Pittsburgh | 23 |
| 23 | INDIANAPOLIS | 9 |
| 7 | Kansas City | 23 |
| 24 | L.A. RAIDERS | 25 |
| 10 | Philadelphia | 7 |
| 47 | Miami | 34 |
| 16 | N.Y. JETS | 14 |
| 30 | Indianapolis | 10 |

| UseName | Pos. | Hgt | Wgt | Age | Int | Pts |
|---|---|---|---|---|---|---|
| Howard Ballard | OT | 6'6" | 330 | 29 | | |
| Jerry Crafts | OT | 6'6" | 351 | 25 | | |
| John Fina | OT | 6'4" | 285 | 24 | | |
| John Davis | OG-C | 6'4" | 310 | 28 | | |
| Tom Myslinski (to CHI) | OG | 6'2" | 293 | 24 | | |
| Glenn Parker | OG-OT | 6'5" | 305 | 27 | | |
| Jim Ritcher | OG | 6'3" | 273 | 35 | | |
| Mike Devlin | C | 6'1" | 293 | 23 | | |
| Kent Hull | C | 6'4" | 284 | 32 | | |
| Adam Lingner | C | 6'4" | 268 | 32 | | |
| Oliver Barnett | DE | 6'3" | 292 | 27 | | |
| Phil Hansen | DE | 6'5" | 278 | 25 | | |
| John Parrella | DE | 6'3" | 296 | 23 | | |
| Mark Pike | DE | 6'4" | 272 | 29 | | |
| Bruce Smith | DE | 6'4" | 273 | 30 | 1 | |
| Mike Lodish | NT | 6'3" | 280 | 26 | | |
| James Patton | NT | 6'3" | 287 | 23 | | |
| Jeff Wright | NT | 6'2" | 274 | 30 | | |

| UseName | Pos. | Hgt | Wgt | Age | Int | Pts |
|---|---|---|---|---|---|---|
| Cornelius Bennett | LB | 6'2" | 238 | 28 | 1 | |
| Monty Brown | LB | 6' | 228 | 23 | | |
| Keith Goganious | LB | 6'2" | 239 | 24 | | |
| Richard Harvey | LB | 6'1" | 242 | 26 | | |
| Mark Maddox | LB | 6'1" | 233 | 25 | | |
| Marvcus Patton | LB | 6'2" | 243 | 26 | 2 | |
| Darryl Talley | LB | 6'4" | 235 | 33 | 3 | 6 |
| Matt Darby | DB | 6'1" | 200 | 24 | 2 | |
| Jerome Henderson (from NE) | DB | 5'10" | 189 | 24 | | |
| Henry Jones | DB | 5'11" | 197 | 25 | 2 | 8 |
| Mark Kelso | DB | 5'11" | 180 | 30 | | |
| Nate Odomes | DB | 5'10" | 188 | 28 | 9 | 6 |
| David Pool | DB | 5'9" | 182 | 26 | | |
| Kurt Schulz | DB | 6'1" | 208 | 22 | | |
| Thomas Smith | DB | 5'11" | 188 | 22 | | |
| Mickey Washington | DB | 5'9" | 191 | 25 | 1 | 6 |
| James Williams | DB | 5'10" | 186 | 26 | 2 | |

Kirby Jackson — Knee Injury

| UseName | Pos. | Hgt | Wgt | Age | Int | Pts |
|---|---|---|---|---|---|---|
| Gale Gilbert | QB | 6'3" | 210 | 31 | | |
| Jim Kelly | QB | 6'3" | 226 | 33 | | |
| Frank Reich | QB | 6'4" | 205 | 31 | | |
| Kenneth Davis | HB | 5'10" | 208 | 31 | | 36 |
| Eddie Fuller | HB | 5'9" | 198 | 25 | | |
| Thurman Thomas | HB | 5'10" | 198 | 27 | | 36 |
| Carwell Gardner | FB | 6'2" | 244 | 26 | | 6 |
| Nate Turner | FB | 6'1" | 255 | 24 | | |
| Don Beebe | WR | 5'11" | 184 | 28 | | 18 |
| Bill Brooks | WR | 6' | 189 | 29 | | 30 |
| Russell Copeland | WR | 6' | 200 | 22 | | 6 |
| Brad Lamb | WR | 5'10" | 177 | 25 | | |
| Andre Reed | WR | 6' | 190 | 29 | | 36 |
| Steve Tasker | WR | 5'9" | 181 | 31 | | |
| Chris Walsh | WR | 6'1" | 185 | 24 | | |
| Rob Awalt | TE | 6'5" | 242 | 29 | | |
| Keith McKeller | TE | 6'6" | 242 | 29 | | 6 |
| Pete Metzelaars | TE | 6'7" | 254 | 33 | | 24 |
| Chris Mohr | K | 6'5" | 215 | 27 | | |
| Steve Christie | K | 6' | 185 | 25 | | 105 |

Al Edwards — Shoulder Injury

## MIAMI DOLPHINS 9-7 Don Shula

| Scores of Each Game | | |
|---|---|---|
| 24 | Indianapolis | 20 |
| 14 | N.Y. JETS | 24 |
| 22 | Buffalo | 13 |
| 17 | WASHINGTON | 10 |
| 24 | Cleveland | 14 |
| 41 | INDIANAPOLIS | 27 |
| 30 | KANSAS CITY | 10 |
| 10 | N.Y. Jets | 27 |
| 19 | Philadelphia | 14 |
| 17 | NEW ENGLAND | 13 |
| 16 | Dallas | 14 |
| 14 | N.Y. GIANTS | 19 |
| 20 | PITTSBURGH | 21 |
| 34 | BUFFALO | 47 |
| 20 | San Diego | 45 |
| 27 | New England | *33 |

| UseName | Pos. | Hgt | Wgt | Age | Int | Pts |
|---|---|---|---|---|---|---|
| Mark Dennis | OT | 6'6" | 298 | 28 | | |
| Chris Gray | OT | 6'4" | 286 | 23 | | |
| Ron Heller | OT | 6'6" | 293 | 31 | | |
| Richmond Webb | OT | 6'6" | 298 | 26 | | |
| Keith Sims | OG | 6'2" | 310 | 26 | | |
| Tom Thayer | OG | 6'4" | 284 | 32 | | |
| Bert Weidner | OG-C | 6'3" | 290 | 27 | | |
| Jeff Dellenbach | C-OG | 6'6" | 297 | 30 | | |
| Jeff Uhlenhake | C | 6'3" | 284 | 27 | | |
| Marco Coleman | DE | 6'3" | 263 | 23 | | |
| Jeff Cross | DE | 6'4" | 274 | 27 | | |
| Jeff Hunter | DE | 6'5" | 291 | 27 | | |
| Mike Golic | DT | 6'5" | 275 | 30 | | |
| Chuck Klingbeil | DT | 6'1" | 295 | 27 | | |
| Craig Veasey (from HOU) | DT | 6'2" | 300 | 26 | | |
| Larry Webster | DT | 6'5" | 293 | 24 | | |

| UseName | Pos. | Hgt | Wgt | Age | Int | Pts |
|---|---|---|---|---|---|---|
| Chuck Bullough | LB | 6'1" | 238 | 24 | | |
| Bryan Cox | LB | 6'3" | 241 | 25 | 1 | |
| David Griggs | LB | 6'3" | 250 | 26 | | |
| John Grimsley | LB | 6'2" | 236 | 31 | | |
| Dwight Hollier | LB | 6'2" | 245 | 24 | | |
| David Merritt (to PHX) | LB | 6'1" | 237 | 21 | | |
| Cliff Odom | LB | 6'2" | 236 | 35 | | |
| John Offerdahl | LB | 6'3" | 238 | 29 | | |
| Chris Singleton (from NE) | LB | 6'2" | 247 | 26 | | |
| Bruce Alexander | DB | 5'8" | 178 | 27 | | |
| Stephen Braggs | DB | 5'9" | 177 | 28 | | |
| J.B. Brown | DB | 6' | 192 | 26 | 5 | |
| Chris Green | DB | 5'11" | 189 | 25 | 2 | |
| Bobby Harden | DB | 6' | 205 | 26 | | |
| Liffort Hobley | DB | 6' | 207 | 31 | 1 | |
| Vestee Jackson | DB | 6' | 186 | 30 | | |
| Darrell Malone | DB | 5'10" | 182 | 25 | | |
| Louis Oliver | DB | 6'2" | 224 | 27 | 2 | 6 |
| Frankie Smith | DB | 5'9" | 186 | 24 | | |
| Troy Vincent | DB | 6' | 191 | 33 | 2 | |
| Jarvis Williams | DB | 5'11" | 200 | 28 | | |

| UseName | Pos. | Hgt | Wgt | Age | Int | Pts |
|---|---|---|---|---|---|---|
| Steve DeBerg (from TB) | QB | 6'2" | 220 | 39 | | |
| Dan Marino | QB | 6'4" | 224 | 31 | | 6 |
| Scott Mitchell | QB | 6'6" | 230 | 25 | | |
| Doug Pederson | QB | 6'3" | 209 | 25 | | |
| Mark Higgs | HB | 5'7" | 198 | 27 | | 18 |
| Terry Kirby | HB | 6'1" | 221 | 23 | | 36 |
| Bernie Parmalee | HB | 5'11" | 201 | 25 | | |
| Keith Byars | FB | 6'1" | 255 | 29 | | 36 |
| James Saxon | FB | 5'11' | 237 | 27 | | |
| Irving Fryar | WR | 6' | 200 | 30 | | 30 |
| Mark Ingram | WR | 5'11" | 188 | 28 | | 36 |
| Tony Martin | WR | 6' | 181 | 27 | | 18 |
| O.J. McDuffie | WR | 5'10" | 191 | 22 | | 12 |
| Scott Miller | WR | 5'10" | 179 | 24 | | |
| Mike Williams | WR | 5'10" | 178 | 26 | | |
| Greg Baty | TE | 6'5" | 240 | 29 | | 6 |
| Keith Jackson | TE | 6'2" | 249 | 28 | | 36 |
| Ronnie Williams | TE | 6'3" | 259 | 27 | | |
| Dale Hatcher | K | 6'2" | 223 | 30 | | |
| Pete Stoyonovich | K | 5'10" | 181 | 26 | | 109 |

Aaron Craver — Knee Injury

## NEW YORK JETS 8-8 Bruce Coslet

| Scores of Each Game | | |
|---|---|---|
| 20 | DENVER | 26 |
| 24 | Miami | 14 |
| 45 | NEW ENGLAND | 7 |
| 30 | PHILADELPHIA | 35 |
| 20 | L.A. Raiders | 24 |
| 10 | BUFFALO | 19 |
| 10 | N.Y. Giants | 6 |
| 27 | MIAMI | 10 |
| 31 | Indianapolis | 17 |
| 17 | Cincinnati | 12 |
| 6 | New England | 0 |
| 6 | INDIANAPOLIS | 9 |
| 3 | Washington | 0 |
| 7 | DALLAS | 28 |
| 14 | Buffalo | 16 |
| 0 | Houston | 24 |

| UseName | Pos. | Hgt | Wgt | Age | Int | Pts |
|---|---|---|---|---|---|---|
| James Brown | OT | 6'6" | 231 | 23 | | |
| Jeff Criswell | OT | 6'7" | 291 | 29 | | |
| Siupeli Malamala | OT | 6'5" | 308 | 24 | | |
| Matt Willig | OT | 6'8" | 305 | 24 | | |
| Dave Cadigan | OG | 6'4" | 285 | 28 | | |
| Dwayne White | OG | 6'2" | 315 | 26 | | |
| Cal Dixon | C | 6'4" | 284 | 23 | | |
| Roger Duffy | C-OG | 6'3" | 285 | 26 | | |
| Jim Sweeney | C-OG | 6'4" | 286 | 31 | | |
| Jeff Lageman | DE | 6'5" | 266 | 26 | 1 | |
| Coleman Rudolph | DE-DT | 6'4" | 270 | 22 | | |
| Marvin Washington | DE | 6'6" | 272 | 27 | | |
| Keith Willis (from WAS) | DE | 6'1" | 263 | 34 | | |
| Paul Frase | DT-DE | 6'5" | 270 | 28 | | |
| Mark Gunn | DT-DE | 6'5" | 279 | 25 | | |
| Leonard Marshall | DT | 6'4" | 288 | 31 | | |
| Scott Mersereau | DT | 6'3" | 275 | 28 | | |
| Bill Pickel | DT | 6'5" | 265 | 33 | | |
| Karl Wilson (to MIA, SF) | DT-DE | 6'5" | 277 | 28 | | |

| UseName | Pos. | Hgt | Wgt | Age | Int | Pts |
|---|---|---|---|---|---|---|
| Kurt Barber | LB | 6'4" | 241 | 24 | | |
| Glenn Cadrez | LB | 6'3" | 240 | 23 | | |
| Kyle Clifton | LB | 6'4" | 236 | 31 | 1 | |
| Bobby Houston | LB | 6'2" | 239 | 25 | 1 | |
| Don Jones | LB | 6' | 231 | 24 | | |
| Marvin Jones | LB | 6'2" | 240 | 21 | | |
| Mo Lewis | LB | 6'3" | 250 | 23 | 2 | |
| Mike Merriweather | LB | 6'2" | 224 | 32 | | |
| Victor Green | DB | 5'9" | 195 | 22 | | |
| James Hasty | DB | 6' | 201 | 28 | 2 | |
| Cliff Hicks | DB | 5'10" | 195 | 29 | | |
| Ronnie Lott | DB | 6'1" | 203 | 34 | 3 | |
| Damon Pieri | DB | 6' | 186 | 22 | | |
| Anthony Prior | DB | 5'11" | 185 | 23 | | |
| Eric Thomas | DB | 5'11" | 184 | 28 | 2 | |
| Marcus Turner | DB | 6' | 190 | 27 | | |
| Brian Washington | DB | 6'1" | 206 | 27 | 6 | 6 |
| Lonnie Young | DB | 6'1" | 196 | 30 | 1 | |

Kevin Porter — Knee Injury

| UseName | Pos. | Hgt | Wgt | Age | Int | Pts |
|---|---|---|---|---|---|---|
| Boomer Esiason | QB | 6'5" | 220 | 32 | | 6 |
| Browning Nagle | QB | 6'3" | 225 | 25 | | |
| Johnny Johnson | HB | 6'3" | 220 | 25 | | 24 |
| Adrian Murrell | HB | 5'11" | 205 | 22 | | 6 |
| Blair Thomas | HB | 5'10" | 202 | 25 | | 6 |
| Richie Anderson | FB-HB | 6'2" | 215 | 21 | | |
| Brad Baxter | FB | 6'1" | 235 | 26 | | 42 |
| Pat Chaffey | FB | 6'1" | 220 | 26 | | 6 |
| Chris Burkett | WR | 6'4" | 200 | 31 | | 24 |
| Rob Carpenter | WR | 6'2" | 190 | 25 | | |
| Dale Dawkins | WR | 6'1" | 190 | 26 | | |
| Terance Mathis | WR | 5'10" | 177 | 26 | | 6 |
| Rob Moore | WR | 6'3" | 205 | 24 | | 6 |
| Fred Baxter | TE | 6'3" | 250 | 22 | | 6 |
| Johnny Mitchell | TE | 6'3" | 237 | 22 | | 36 |
| Troy Sadowski | TE | 6'5" | 250 | 27 | | |
| James Thornton | TE | 6'2" | 242 | 28 | | 12 |
| Louis Aguiar | K | 6'2" | 215 | 27 | | |
| Cary Blanchard | K | 6'1" | 225 | 24 | | 82 |

## NEW ENGLAND PATRIOTS 5-11 Bill Parcells

| Scores of Each Game | | |
|---|---|---|
| 14 | Buffalo | 38 |
| 16 | DETROIT | *19 |
| 14 | SEATTLE | 17 |
| 7 | N.Y. Jets | 45 |
| 23 | Phoenix | 21 |
| 14 | HOUSTON | 28 |
| 9 | Seattle | 10 |
| 6 | Indianapolis | 9 |
| 10 | BUFFALO | *13 |
| 13 | Miami | 17 |
| 0 | N.Y. JETS | 6 |
| 14 | Pittsburgh | 17 |
| 7 | CINCINNATI | 2 |
| 20 | Cleveland | 17 |
| 38 | INDIANAPOLIS | 0 |
| 33 | MIAMI | *27 |

| UseName | Pos. | Hgt | Wgt | Age | Int | Pts |
|---|---|---|---|---|---|---|
| Bruce Armstrong | OT | 6'4" | 284 | 27 | | |
| Pat Harlow | OT | 6'6" | 290 | 24 | | |
| Todd Jones | OT | 6'3" | 295 | 23 | | |
| Brandon Moore | OT | 6'6" | 290 | 23 | | |
| Rich Baldinger | OG | 6'4" | 293 | 33 | | |
| Eugene Chung | OG | 6'4" | 295 | 24 | | |
| Mike Gisler | OG | 6'4" | 300 | 24 | | |
| Todd Rucci | OG | 6'5" | 291 | 23 | | |
| Mike Arthur | C | 6'3" | 280 | 25 | | |
| Bill Lewis | C | 6'6" | 290 | 30 | | |
| Ray Agnew | DE | 6'3" | 272 | 25 | | |
| Aaron Jones | DE | 6'5" | 267 | 26 | | |
| Chris Gannon | DE | 6'6" | 260 | 27 | | |
| -Mike Pitts | DE | 6'5" | 277 | 32 | | |
| ohn Washington | DE | 6'4" | 290 | 30 | | |
| Brent Williams | DE | 6'3" | 275 | 28 | | |
| Tim Goad | NT | 6'3" | 280 | 27 | | |
| Mario Johnson | NT | 6'3" | 288 | 23 | | |

| UseName | Pos. | Hgt | Wgt | Age | Int | Pts |
|---|---|---|---|---|---|---|
| David Bavaro | LB | 6' | 228 | 26 | | |
| Vincent Brown | LB | 6'2" | 245 | 28 | 1 | |
| Jason Carthen | LB | 6'3" | 255 | 23 | | |
| Todd Collins | LB | 6'2" | 242 | 23 | 1 | |
| Dwayne Sabb | LB | 6'4" | 248 | 23 | | |
| Chris Slade | LB | 6'4" | 232 | 22 | | |
| Andre Tippett | LB | 6'3" | 241 | 33 | | |
| David White | LB | 6'2" | 235 | 23 | | |
| Harlon Barnett | DB | 5'11" | 200 | 26 | 1 | |
| Corwin Brown | DB | 6' | 192 | 23 | | |
| Maurice Hurst | DB | 5'10" | 185 | 25 | 4 | |
| Dion Lambert | DB | 6' | 185 | 24 | 1 | |
| Vernon Lewis | DB | 5'10" | 192 | 22 | | |
| Terry Ray | DB | 6'1" | 205 | 23 | 1 | |
| Rod Smith | DB | 5'11" | 187 | 23 | | |
| Reyna Thompson | DB | 6' | 193 | 30 | 1 | |
| Adrian White | DB | 6' | 205 | 29 | | |
| Darryl Wren | DB | 6' | 188 | 26 | 3 | |

| UseName | Pos. | Hgt | Wgt | Age | Int | Pts |
|---|---|---|---|---|---|---|
| Drew Bledsoe | QB | 6'5" | 233 | 21 | | |
| Scott Secules | QB | 6'3" | 223 | 28 | | |
| Scott Zolak | QB | 6'5" | 222 | 25 | | |
| Corey Croom | HB | 5'11" | 212 | 22 | | |
| Scott Lockwood | HB | 5'10" | 196 | 25 | | |
| Leonard Russell | HB | 6'2" | 235 | 23 | | 42 |
| Sam Gash | FB | 5'11" | 224 | 24 | | 6 |
| Burnie Legette | FB | 6' | 243 | 22 | | |
| Kevin Turner | FB | 6' | 224 | 24 | | 12 |
| Vincent Brisby | WR | 6'1" | 186 | 22 | | 12 |
| Troy Brown | WR | 5'9" | 183 | 22 | | |
| Ray Crittenden | WR | 6' | 188 | 23 | | 6 |
| Ronnie Harris | WR | 5'10" | 170 | 23 | | |
| Greg McMurtry | WR | 6'2" | 207 | 25 | | 6 |
| Michael Timpson | WR | 5'10" | 175 | 26 | | 12 |
| Ben Coates | TE | 6'4" | 245 | 24 | | 48 |
| Marv Cook | TE | 6'4" | 234 | 27 | | |
| Richard Griffith | TE | 6'5" | 256 | 24 | | |
| Mike Saxon | K | 6'3" | 202 | 31 | | |
| Scott Sisson | K | 6' | 197 | 22 | | 57 |

## INDIANAPOLIS COLTS 4-12 Ted Marchibroda

| Scores of Each Game | | |
|---|---|---|
| 20 | MIAMI | 24 |
| 9 | Cincinnati | 6 |
| 23 | CLEVELAND | 10 |
| 13 | Denver | 35 |
| 3 | DALLAS | 27 |
| 27 | Miami | 41 |
| 9 | NEW ENGLAND | 6 |
| 24 | Washington | 30 |
| 17 | N.Y. JETS | 31 |
| 9 | Buffalo | 23 |
| 0 | SAN DIEGO | 31 |
| 9 | N.Y. Jets | 6 |
| 6 | N.Y. Giants | 20 |
| 10 | PHILADELPHIA | 20 |
| 0 | New England | 38 |
| 10 | BUFFALO | 30 |

| UseName | Pos. | Hgt | Wgt | Age | Int | Pts |
|---|---|---|---|---|---|---|
| Kevin Call | OT | 6'7" | 308 | 31 | | |
| Cecil Gray | OT | 6'4" | 292 | 25 | | |
| Trevor Matich | OT-C | 6'4" | 297 | 31 | | |
| Zefross Moss | OT | 6'6" | 338 | 27 | | |
| John Ray | OT | 6'8" | 350 | 24 | | |
| Will Wolford | OT | 6'5" | 300 | 29 | | |
| Randy Dixon | OG | 6'3" | 305 | 28 | | |
| William Schultz | OG | 6'5" | 305 | 26 | | |
| Joe Staysniak | OG-OT | 6'4" | 296 | 26 | | |
| Kirk Lowdermilk | C | 6'4" | 280 | 30 | | |
| Michael Brandon | DE | 6'4" | 290 | 25 | | |
| Jon Hand | DE | 6'7" | 301 | 29 | | |
| Skip McClendon | DE | 6'7" | 302 | 29 | | |
| Willis Peguese | DE-DT | 6'4" | 273 | 26 | | |
| Steve Emtman | DT | 6'4" | 300 | 23 | | |
| Tom Sims | DT | 6'2" | 291 | 26 | | |
| Tony McCoy | DT-NT | 6' | 279 | 24 | | |
| Tony Siragusa | DT-NT | 6'3" | 303 | 26 | | |

Mark Vander Poel — Pectoral Injury
Ron Solt — Shoulder

| UseName | Pos. | Hgt | Wgt | Age | Int | Pts |
|---|---|---|---|---|---|---|
| Duane Bickett | LB | 6'5" | 251 | 30 | | |
| Paul Butcher | LB | 6' | 230 | 29 | | |
| Quentin Coryatt | LB | 6'3" | 250 | 23 | | |
| Steve Grant | LB | 6' | 231 | 23 | | |
| Jeff Herrod | LB | 6' | 249 | 27 | 1 | 6 |
| Devon McDonald | LB | 6'4" | 240 | 23 | | |
| Scott Radecic | LB | 6'3" | 240 | 31 | | |
| Ashley Ambrose | DB | 5'10" | 177 | 22 | | |
| Michael Ball | DB | 6' | 220 | 29 | | |
| John Baylor | DB | 6' | 208 | 28 | 3 | |
| Jason Belser | DB | 5'9" | 187 | 23 | 1 | |
| Ray Buchanan | DB | 5'9" | 193 | 21 | 4 | |
| Eugene Daniel | DB | 5'11" | 188 | 32 | 1 | |
| Chris Goode | DB | 6' | 199 | 29 | | |
| Derwin Gray | DB | 5'10" | 190 | 22 | | |
| Tony Stargell | DB | 5'11" | 189 | 27 | | |

Chip Banks — Shoulder Injury

| UseName | Pos. | Hgt | Wgt | Age | Int | Pts |
|---|---|---|---|---|---|---|
| Jeff George | QB | 6'4" | 218 | 25 | | |
| Don Majkowski | QB | 6'3" | 203 | 29 | | |
| Jack Trudeau | QB | 6'3" | 218 | 30 | | |
| Rodney Culver | HB | 5'9" | 224 | 23 | | 30 |
| Anthony Johnson | HB-FB | 6' | 222 | 25 | | 6 |
| Ed Toner | HB | 6' | 240 | 25 | | |
| Warren Williams | HB | 6' | 218 | 28 | | |
| Roosevelt Potts | FB-HB | 6' | 258 | 22 | | |
| Aaron Cox | WR | 5'10" | 178 | 28 | | |
| Sean Dawkins | WR | 6'4" | 213 | 22 | | 6 |
| Jessie Hester | WR | 5'11" | 175 | 30 | | 6 |
| Reggie Langhorne | WR | 6'2" | 209 | 30 | | 18 |
| Eddie Miller | WR | 6' | 185 | 24 | | |
| Clarence Verdin | WR | 5'8" | 162 | 30 | | 6 |
| Charles Arbuckle | TE | 6'3" | 248 | 24 | | |
| Kerry Cash | TE | 6'4" | 252 | 24 | | 18 |
| Dean Biasucci | K | 6' | 190 | 31 | | 93 |
| Rohn Stark | K | 6'3" | 203 | 34 | | |

## BUFFALO BILLS

### RUSHING

| Last Name | No. | Yds | Avg | TD |
|---|---|---|---|---|
| Thomas | 355 | 1315 | 3.7 | 6 |
| K. Davis | 109 | 391 | 3.6 | 6 |
| Kelly | 36 | 102 | 2.8 | 0 |
| Gardner | 20 | 56 | 2.8 | 0 |
| Turner | 11 | 36 | 3.3 | 0 |
| Brooks | 3 | 30 | 10.0 | 0 |
| Reed | 9 | 21 | 2.3 | 0 |
| Fina | 1 | -2 | -2.0 | 0 |
| Reich | 6 | -6 | -1.0 | 0 |

### RECEIVING

| Last Name | No. | Yds | Avg | TD |
|---|---|---|---|---|
| Metzelaars | 68 | 609 | 9.0 | 4 |
| Brooks | 60 | 714 | 11.9 | 5 |
| Reed | 52 | 854 | 16.4 | 6 |
| Thomas | 48 | 387 | 8.1 | 0 |
| Beebe | 31 | 504 | 16.3 | 3 |
| K. Davis | 21 | 95 | 4.5 | 0 |
| Copeland | 13 | 242 | 18.6 | 0 |
| Gardner | 4 | 50 | 12.5 | 1 |
| McKeller | 3 | 35 | 11.7 | 1 |
| Tasker | 2 | 26 | 13.0 | 0 |
| Awalt | 2 | 19 | 9.5 | 0 |

### PUNT RETURNS

| Last Name | No. | Yds | Avg | TD |
|---|---|---|---|---|
| Copeland | 31 | 274 | 8.8 | 1 |
| Brooks | 1 | 3 | 3.0 | 0 |
| Tasker | 1 | 0 | 0.0 | 0 |

### KICKOFF RETURNS

| Last Name | No. | Yds | Avg | TD |
|---|---|---|---|---|
| Copeland | 24 | 436 | 18.2 | 0 |
| Beebe | 10 | 160 | 16.0 | 0 |
| K. Davis | 8 | 100 | 12.5 | 0 |
| Lamb | 2 | 40 | 20.0 | 0 |
| Turner | 1 | 10 | 10.0 | 0 |

### PASSING

| Last Name | Att | Cmp | % | Yds | Yd/Att | TD | Int | — % | RK |
|---|---|---|---|---|---|---|---|---|---|
| Kelly | 470 | 288 | 61.3 | 3382 | 7.20 | 18 | 18 | —3.8 | 7 |
| Reich | 26 | 16 | 61.5 | 153 | 5.88 | 2 | 0 | —0.0 | |
| Thomas | 1 | 0 | 0.0 | 0 | 0.00 | 0 | 0 | —0.0 | |

### PUNTING

| Last Name | No. | Avg. |
|---|---|---|
| Mohr | 74 | 40.4 |

### KICKING

| Last Name | XP | ATT | % | FG | ATT | % |
|---|---|---|---|---|---|---|
| Christie | 36 | 37 | 97 | 23 | 32 | 72 |

## MIAMI DOLPHINS

### RUSHING

| Last Name | No. | Yds | Avg | TD |
|---|---|---|---|---|
| Higgs | 186 | 693 | 3.7 | 3 |
| Kirby | 119 | 390 | 3.3 | 3 |
| Byars | 64 | 269 | 4.2 | 3 |
| Mitchell | 21 | 89 | 4.2 | 0 |
| Parmalee | 4 | 16 | 4.0 | 0 |
| Saxon | 5 | 13 | 2.6 | 0 |
| Martin | 1 | 6 | 6.0 | 0 |
| Pederson | 2 | -1 | -0.5 | 0 |
| DeBerg | 4 | -4 | -1.0 | 0 |
| Fryar | 3 | -4 | -1.3 | 0 |
| Marino | 9 | -4 | -0.4 | 1 |
| McDuffie | 1 | -4 | -4.0 | 0 |

### RECEIVING

| Last Name | No. | Yds | Avg | TD |
|---|---|---|---|---|
| Kirby | 75 | 874 | 11.7 | 3 |
| Fryar | 64 | 1010 | 15.8 | 5 |
| Byars | 61 | 613 | 10.0 | 3 |
| Ingram | 44 | 707 | 16.1 | 6 |
| K. Jackson | 39 | 613 | 15.7 | 6 |
| Martin | 20 | 347 | 17.4 | 3 |
| McDuffie | 19 | 197 | 10.4 | 0 |
| Higgs | 10 | 72 | 7.2 | 0 |
| Baty | 5 | 78 | 15.6 | 1 |
| Miller | 2 | 15 | 7.5 | 0 |
| M. Williams | 1 | 11 | 11.0 | 0 |
| Parmalee | 1 | 1 | 1.0 | 0 |

### PUNT RETURNS

| Last Name | No. | Yds | Avg | TD |
|---|---|---|---|---|
| McDuffie | 28 | 317 | 11.3 | 2 |
| Vincent | 0 | 9 | — | 0 |

### KICKOFF RETURNS

| Last Name | No. | Yds | Avg | TD |
|---|---|---|---|---|
| McDuffie | 32 | 755 | 23.6 | 0 |
| M. Williams | 8 | 180 | 22.5 | 0 |
| Kirby | 4 | 85 | 21.3 | 0 |
| Miller | 2 | 22 | 11.0 | 0 |
| Fryar | 1 | 10 | 10.0 | 0 |
| Baty | 1 | 7 | 7.0 | 0 |
| Saxon | 1 | 7 | 7.0 | 0 |
| Vincent | 0 | 2 | — | 0 |

### PASSING

| Last Name | Att | Cmp | % | Yds | Yd/Att | TD | Int | — % | RK |
|---|---|---|---|---|---|---|---|---|---|
| Mitchell | 233 | 133 | 57.1 | 1773 | 7.61 | 12 | 8 | —3.4 | 5 |
| DeBerg | 227 | 136 | 59.9 | 1707 | 7.52 | 7 | 10 | —4.4 | 10 |
| Marino | 150 | 91 | 60.7 | 1218 | 8.12 | 8 | 3 | —2.0 | |
| Pederson | 8 | 4 | 50.0 | 41 | 5.13 | 0 | 0 | —0.0 | |
| Byars | 2 | 1 | 50.0 | 11 | 5.50 | 1 | 0 | —0.0 | |

### PUNTING

| Last Name | No. | Avg. |
|---|---|---|
| Hatcher | 58 | 39.7 |

### KICKING

| Last Name | XP | Att. | % | FG | Att | % |
|---|---|---|---|---|---|---|
| Stoyonovich | 37 | 37 | 100 | 24 | 32 | 75 |

## NEW YORK JETS

### RUSHING

| Last Name | No. | Yds | Avg | TD |
|---|---|---|---|---|
| J. Johnson | 198 | 821 | 4.1 | 3 |
| B. Baxter | 174 | 559 | 3.2 | 7 |
| B. Thomas | 59 | 221 | 3.7 | 1 |
| Murrell | 34 | 157 | 4.6 | 1 |
| Esiason | 45 | 118 | 2.6 | 1 |
| Mathis | 2 | 20 | 10.0 | 1 |
| Chaffey | 5 | 17 | 3.4 | 0 |
| Moore | 1 | -6 | -6.0 | 0 |
| Aguiar | 3 | -27 | -9.0 | 0 |

### RECEIVING

| Last Name | No. | Yds | Avg | TD |
|---|---|---|---|---|
| J. Johnson | 67 | 641 | 9.6 | 1 |
| Moore | 64 | 843 | 13.2 | 1 |
| Burkett | 40 | 531 | 13.3 | 4 |
| Mitchell | 39 | 630 | 16.2 | 6 |
| Mathis | 24 | 352 | 14.7 | 0 |
| B. Baxter | 20 | 158 | 7.9 | 0 |
| Thornton | 12 | 108 | 9.0 | 2 |
| B. Thomas | 7 | 25 | 3.6 | 0 |
| Carpenter | 6 | 83 | 13.8 | 0 |
| Murrell | 5 | 12 | 2.4 | 0 |
| Chaffey | 4 | 55 | 13.8 | 1 |
| F. Baxter | 3 | 48 | 16.0 | 1 |
| Sadowski | 2 | 14 | 7.0 | 0 |
| Esiason | 1 | -8 | -8.0 | 0 |

### PUNT RETURNS

| Last Name | No. | Yds | Avg | TD |
|---|---|---|---|---|
| Hicks | 17 | 157 | 9.2 | 0 |
| Mathis | 14 | 99 | 7.1 | 0 |

### KICKOFF RETURNS

| Last Name | No. | Yds | Avg | TD |
|---|---|---|---|---|
| Murrell | 23 | 342 | 14.9 | 0 |
| Prior | 9 | 126 | 14.0 | 0 |
| Mathis | 7 | 102 | 14.6 | 0 |
| R. Anderson | 4 | 66 | 16.5 | 0 |
| B. Thomas | 2 | 39 | 19.5 | 0 |
| Sadowski | 1 | 0 | 0.0 | 0 |

### PASSING

| Last Name | Att | Cmp | % | Yds | Yd/Att | TD | Int | — % | RK |
|---|---|---|---|---|---|---|---|---|---|
| Esiason | 473 | 288 | 60.9 | 3421 | 7.23 | 16 | 11 | —2.3 | 4 |
| Nagle | 14 | 6 | 42.9 | 71 | 5.07 | 0 | 0 | —0.0 | |
| Aguiar | 2 | 0 | 0.0 | 0 | 0.00 | 0 | 1 | —50.0 | |

### PUNTING

| Last Name | No. | Avg. |
|---|---|---|
| Aguiar | 73 | 38.4 |

### KICKING

| Last Name | XP | Att. | % | FG | Att | % |
|---|---|---|---|---|---|---|
| Blanchard | 31 | 31 | 100 | 17 | 26 | 65 |

## NEW ENGLAND PATRIOTS

### RUSHING

| Last Name | No. | Yds | Avg | TD |
|---|---|---|---|---|
| Russell | 300 | 1088 | 3.6 | 7 |
| Turner | 50 | 231 | 4.6 | 0 |
| Croom | 60 | 198 | 3.3 | 1 |
| Gash | 48 | 149 | 3.1 | 1 |
| Bledsoe | 32 | 82 | 2.6 | 0 |
| Secules | 8 | 33 | 4.1 | 0 |
| Saxon | 2 | 2 | 1.0 | 0 |
| Zolak | 1 | 0 | 0.0 | 0 |
| Crittenden | 1 | -3 | -3.0 | 0 |

### RECEIVING

| Last Name | No. | Yds | Avg | TD |
|---|---|---|---|---|
| Coates | 53 | 659 | 12.4 | 8 |
| Brisby | 45 | 626 | 13.9 | 2 |
| Timpson | 42 | 654 | 15.6 | 2 |
| Turner | 39 | 333 | 8.5 | 2 |
| Russell | 26 | 245 | 9.4 | 0 |
| McMurtry | 22 | 241 | 11.0 | 1 |
| Cook | 22 | 154 | 7.0 | 1 |
| Crittenden | 16 | 293 | 18.3 | 1 |
| Gash | 14 | 93 | 6.6 | 0 |
| Croom | 8 | 92 | 11.5 | 0 |
| T. Brown | 2 | 22 | 11.0 | 0 |

### PUNT RETURNS

| Last Name | No. | Yds | Avg | TD |
|---|---|---|---|---|
| T. Brown | 25 | 224 | 9.0 | 0 |
| Harris | 23 | 201 | 8.7 | 0 |
| Crittenden | 2 | 37 | 18.5 | 0 |
| Smith | 1 | 0 | 0.0 | 0 |

### KICKOFF RETURNS

| Last Name | No. | Yds | Avg | TD |
|---|---|---|---|---|
| Crittenden | 23 | 478 | 20.8 | 0 |
| T. Brown | 15 | 243 | 16.2 | 0 |
| Harris | 6 | 90 | 15.0 | 0 |
| Sabb | 2 | 0 | 0.0 | 0 |
| Cook | 1 | 8 | 8.0 | 0 |
| Coates | 0 | 0 | — | 0 |

### PASSING

| Last Name | Att | Cmp | % | Yds | Yd/Att | TD | Int | — % | RK |
|---|---|---|---|---|---|---|---|---|---|
| Bledsoe | 429 | 214 | 49.9 | 2494 | 5.81 | 15 | 15 | —3.5 | 16 |
| Secules | 134 | 75 | 56.0 | 918 | 6.85 | 2 | 9 | —6.7 | |
| Zolak | 2 | 0 | 0.0 | 0 | 0.00 | 0 | 0 | —0.0 | |
| Turner | 1 | 0 | 0.0 | 0 | 0.00 | 0 | 0 | —0.0 | |

### PUNTING

| Last Name | No. | Avg. |
|---|---|---|
| Saxon | 76 | 40.7 |

### KICKING

| Last Name | XP | ATT | % | FG | ATT | % |
|---|---|---|---|---|---|---|
| Sisson | 15 | 15 | 100 | 14 | 26 | 54 |

## INDIANAPOLIS COLTS

### RUSHING

| Last Name | No. | Yds | Avg | TD |
|---|---|---|---|---|
| Potts | 179 | 711 | 4.0 | 0 |
| Johnson | 95 | 331 | 3.5 | 1 |
| Culver | 65 | 150 | 2.3 | 3 |
| George | 13 | 39 | 3.0 | 0 |
| Verdin | 3 | 33 | 11.0 | 0 |
| Stark | 1 | 11 | 11.0 | 0 |
| Toner | 2 | 6 | 3.0 | 0 |
| Majkowski | 2 | 4 | 2.0 | 0 |
| Trudeau | 2 | 4 | 2.0 | 0 |

### RECEIVING

| Last Name | No. | Yds | Avg | TD |
|---|---|---|---|---|
| Langhorne | 85 | 1038 | 12.2 | 3 |
| Hester | 64 | 835 | 13.0 | 1 |
| Johnson | 55 | 443 | 8.1 | 0 |
| Cash | 43 | 402 | 9.3 | 3 |
| Dawkins | 26 | 430 | 16.5 | 1 |
| Potts | 26 | 189 | 7.3 | 0 |
| Arbuckle | 15 | 90 | 6.0 | 0 |
| Culver | 11 | 112 | 10.2 | 1 |
| Cox | 4 | 59 | 14.8 | 0 |
| Verdin | 2 | 20 | 10.0 | 1 |
| Toner | 1 | 5 | 5.0 | 0 |

### PUNT RETURNS

| Last Name | No. | Yds | Avg | TD |
|---|---|---|---|---|
| Verdin | 30 | 173 | 5.8 | 0 |

### KICKOFF RETURNS

| Last Name | No. | Yds | Avg | TD |
|---|---|---|---|---|
| Verdin | 50 | 1050 | 21.0 | 0 |
| Culver | 3 | 51 | 17.0 | 0 |
| Butcher | 2 | 2 | 1.0 | 0 |
| Cash | 1 | 11 | 11.0 | 0 |
| Radecic | 1 | 10 | 10.0 | 0 |

### PASSING

| Last Name | Att | Cmp | % | Yds | Yd/Att | TD | Int | — % | RK |
|---|---|---|---|---|---|---|---|---|---|
| George | 407 | 234 | 57.5 | 2526 | 6.21 | 8 | 6 | —1.5 | 9 |
| Trudeau | 162 | 85 | 52.5 | 992 | 5.12 | 2 | 7 | —4.3 | |
| Majkowski | 24 | 13 | 54.2 | 105 | 4.38 | 0 | 1 | —4.2 | |
| Johnson | 1 | 0 | 0.0 | 0 | 0.00 | 0 | 1 | —100.0 | |

### PUNTING

| Last Name | No. | Avg. |
|---|---|---|
| Stark | 83 | 43.3 |

### KICKING

| Last Name | XP | ATT | % | FG | ATT | % |
|---|---|---|---|---|---|---|
| Biasucci | 15 | 16 | 94 | 26 | 31 | 84 |

## HOUSTON OILERS 12-4 Jack Pardee

| Scores of Each Game | | |
|---|---|---|
| 21 | New Orleans | 33 |
| 30 | KANSAS CITY | 0 |
| 17 | San Diego | 18 |
| 13 | L.A. RAMS | 28 |
| 7 | Buffalo | 35 |
| 28 | New England | 14 |
| 28 | CINCINNATI | 12 |
| 24 | SEATTLE | 14 |
| 38 | Cincinnati | 3 |
| 27 | Cleveland | 20 |
| 23 | PITTSBURGH | 3 |
| 33 | ATLANTA | 17 |
| 19 | CLEVELAND | 17 |
| 26 | Pittsburgh | 17 |
| 10 | San Francisco | 7 |
| 24 | N.Y. JETS | 0 |

| Use Name | Pos. | Hgt. | Wgt. | Age | Int | Pts |
|---|---|---|---|---|---|---|
| Kevin Donnalley | OT | 6'5" | 305 | 25 | | |
| Brad Hopkins | OT | 6'3" | 306 | 22 | | |
| Stan Thomas | OT | 6'5" | 295 | 24 | | |
| David Williams | OT | 6'5" | 292 | 27 | | |
| Doug Dawson | OG | 6'2" | 288 | 31 | | |
| Mike Munchak | OG | 6'3" | 284 | 33 | | |
| Erik Norgard | OG-C | 6'1" | 282 | 27 | | |
| Bruce Matthews | C | 6'4" | 291 | 31 | | |
| William Fuller | DE | 6'3" | 274 | 31 | | |
| Sean Jones | DE | 6'7" | 268 | 30 | | |
| Mike Teeter | DE | 6'2" | 260 | 25 | | |
| Ray Childress | DT-DE | 6'6" | 272 | 30 | | 6 |
| Glenn Montgomery | DT | 6' | 282 | 26 | | |
| Tim Roberts | DT | 6'6" | 318 | 24 | | |
| Lee Williams | DT-DE | 6'6" | 275 | 30 | | |

John Flannery — Knee Injury
Jeff Alm — Committed Suicide in November 1993

| Use Name | Pos. | Hgt. | Wgt. | Age | Int | Pts |
|---|---|---|---|---|---|---|
| Micheal Barrow | LB | 6'1" | 236 | 23 | | |
| Joe Bowden | LB | 5'11" | 230 | 23 | | |
| Scott Kozak | LB | 6'3" | 222 | 27 | | |
| Lamar Lathon | LB | 6'3" | 252 | 25 | | |
| Wilber Marshall | LB | 6'1" | 240 | 31 | | |
| Keith McCants | LB | 6'3" | 265 | 25 | | |
| Eddie Robinson | LB | 6'1" | 245 | 23 | | |
| Al Smith | LB | 6'1" | 244 | 28 | | |
| Melvin Aldridge | DB | 6'2" | 195 | 23 | | |
| Blaine Bishop | DB | 5'8" | 197 | 23 | 1 | |
| Tony Brown | DB | 5'9" | 183 | 23 | | |
| Cris Dishman | DB | 6' | 188 | 28 | 6 | 6 |
| Steve Jackson | DB | 5'8" | 182 | 24 | 5 | 6 |
| Darryll Lewis | DB | 5'9" | 188 | 24 | 1 | 6 |
| Emanuel Martin | DB | 5'11" | 184 | 24 | | |
| Bubba McDowell | DB | 6'1" | 198 | 26 | 3 | |
| Bo Orlando | DB | 5'10" | 180 | 27 | 3 | 6 |
| Marcus Robertson | DB | 5'11" | 197 | 23 | 7 | 6 |

Mike Dumas — Foot Injury

| Use Name | Pos. | Hgt. | Wgt. | Age | Int | Pts |
|---|---|---|---|---|---|---|
| Cody Carlson | QB | 6'3" | 202 | 29 | | 12 |
| Warren Moon | QB | 6'3" | 212 | 36 | | 6 |
| Bucky Richardson | QB | 6'1" | 228 | 24 | | |
| Gary Brown | HB | 5'11" | 233 | 24 | | 48 |
| Le'Shai Maston | HB | 6'1" | 215 | 22 | | |
| Spencer Tillman | HB | 5'11" | 206 | 29 | | 6 |
| Lorenzo White | HB | 5'11" | 222 | 27 | | 12 |
| Reggie Brown | WR | 6'1" | 195 | 23 | | |
| Pat Coleman | WR | 5'7" | 176 | 26 | | |
| Willie Drewrey | WR | 5'7" | 164 | 30 | | |
| Curtis Duncan | WR | 5'11" | 184 | 28 | | 18 |
| Ernest Givins | WR | 5'9" | 178 | 28 | | 24 |
| Travis Hannah | WR | 5'7" | 161 | 23 | | |
| Leonard Harris | WR | 5'8" | 162 | 32 | | 6 |
| Haywood Jeffires | WR | 6'2" | 201 | 28 | | 36 |
| Tony Jones | WR | 5'7" | 148 | 27 | | |
| Webster Slaughter | WR | 6'1" | 170 | 28 | | 30 |
| Gary Wellman | WR | 5'9" | 173 | 26 | | 6 |
| John Henry Mills | TE | 6' | 222 | 22 | | |
| Al Del Greco | K | 5'10" | 202 | 31 | | 126 |
| Greg Montgomery | K | 6'3" | 210 | 28 | | |

## PITTSBURGH STEELERS 9-7 Bill Cowher

| Scores of Each Game | | |
|---|---|---|
| 13 | SAN FRANCISCO | 24 |
| 0 | L.A. Rams | 27 |
| 34 | CINCINNATI | 7 |
| 45 | Atlanta | 17 |
| 16 | SAN DIEGO | 3 |
| 37 | NEW ORLEANS | 14 |
| 23 | Cleveland | 28 |
| 24 | Cincinnati | 16 |
| 23 | BUFFALO | 0 |
| 13 | Denver | 37 |
| 3 | Houston | 23 |
| 17 | NEW ENGLAND | 14 |
| 21 | Miami | 20 |
| 17 | HOUSTON | 26 |
| 6 | Seattle | 16 |
| 16 | CLEVELAND | 9 |

| Use Name | Pos. | Hgt. | Wgt. | Age | Int | Pts |
|---|---|---|---|---|---|---|
| John Jackson | OT | 6'6" | 297 | 28 | | |
| Leon Searcy | OT | 6'3" | 304 | 23 | | |
| Dan Fike | OG-OT | 6'7" | 285 | 32 | | |
| Calton Haselrig | OG | 6'1" | 295 | 27 | | |
| Duval Love | OG | 6'3" | 288 | 30 | | |
| Lonnie Palelei | OG | 6'3" | 311 | 22 | | |
| Justin Strzelczyk | OG-OT | 6'5" | 295 | 25 | | |
| Dermontti Dawson | C | 6'2" | 286 | 28 | | |
| Kendall Gammon | C | 6'4" | 286 | 24 | | |
| Ariel Solomon | C-OT | 6'5" | 290 | 25 | | |
| Kenny Davidson | DE | 6'5" | 275 | 26 | 1 | 6 |
| Donald Evans | DE-DT | 6'2" | 277 | 29 | | |
| Kevin Henry | DE | 6'4" | 275 | 24 | 1 | |
| Ricky Sutton | DE | 6'2" | 281 | 22 | | |
| Jeff Zgonina | DT | 6'1" | 284 | 23 | | |
| Joel Steed | NT | 6'2" | 295 | 24 | | |
| Gerald Williams | NT | 6'3" | 288 | 29 | | |

| Use Name | Pos. | Hgt. | Wgt. | Age | Int | Pts |
|---|---|---|---|---|---|---|
| Reggie Barnes | LB | 6'1" | 235 | 23 | | |
| Chad Brown | LB | 6'2" | 240 | 23 | | |
| Kevin Greene | LB | 6'3" | 247 | 31 | | |
| Bryan Hinkle | LB | 6'2" | 229 | 34 | | |
| Dave Hoffmann | LB | 6'2" | 233 | 23 | | |
| Levon Kirkland | LB | 6' | 252 | 24 | | 6 |
| Greg Lloyd | LB | 6'2" | 226 | 28 | | |
| Rico Mack | LB | 6'4" | 239 | 22 | | |
| Jerry Olsavsky | LB | 6'1" | 224 | 26 | | |
| Deon Figures | DB | 6' | 200 | 23 | 1 | |
| Larry Griffin | DB | 6' | 202 | 30 | | |
| Alan Haller | DB | 5'11" | 185 | 23 | | |
| David Johnson | DB | 6' | 187 | 27 | 3 | |
| Gary Jones | DB | 6'2" | 214 | 25 | 2 | |
| Carnell Lake | DB | 6'1" | 210 | 26 | 4 | |
| Darren Perry | DB | 5'10" | 196 | 24 | 4 | |
| Richard Shelton | DB | 5'10" | 202 | 27 | | |
| Willie Williams | DB | 5'9" | 188 | 22 | | |
| Rod Woodson | DB | 6' | 200 | 28 | 8 | 6 |

| Use Name | Pos. | Hgt. | Wgt. | Age | Int | Pts |
|---|---|---|---|---|---|---|
| Neil O'Donnell | QB | 6'3" | 230 | 27 | | |
| Rick Strom | QB | 6'2" | 205 | 28 | | |
| Mike Tomczak | QB | 6'1" | 195 | 30 | | |
| Barry Foster | HB | 5'10" | 218 | 24 | | 54 |
| Randy Cuthbert | FB | 6'2" | 225 | 23 | | |
| Merril Hoge | FB | 6'2" | 230 | 28 | | 30 |
| Victor Jones | FB | 5'8" | 215 | 25 | | |
| Leroy Thompson | FB | 5'10" | 217 | 24 | | 18 |
| Charles Davenport | WR | 6'3" | 210 | 24 | | |
| Jeff Graham | WR | 6'1" | 196 | 24 | | |
| Andre Hastings | WR | 6' | 188 | 22 | | |
| Ernie Mills | WR | 5'11" | 192 | 24 | | 6 |
| Dwight Stone | WR-HB | 6' | 180 | 29 | | 18 |
| Yancey Thigpen | WR | 6'1" | 207 | 24 | | 18 |
| Adrian Cooper | TE | 6'5" | 270 | 25 | | |
| Eric Green | TE | 6'5" | 280 | 26 | | 30 |
| Tim Jorden | TE | 6'3" | 240 | 26 | | |
| Craig Keith | TE | 6'3" | 262 | 22 | | |
| Gary Anderson | K | 5'11" | 179 | 34 | | 116 |
| Mark Royals | K | 6'5" | 215 | 29 | | |

## CLEVELAND BROWNS 7-9 Bill Belichick

| Scores of Each Game | | |
|---|---|---|
| 27 | CINCINNATI | 14 |
| 23 | SAN FRANCISCO | 13 |
| 19 | L.A. Raiders | 16 |
| 10 | Indianapolis | 23 |
| 14 | MIAMI | 24 |
| 28 | Cincinnati | 17 |
| 28 | PITTSBURGH | 23 |
| 14 | DENVER | 29 |
| 5 | Seattle | 22 |
| 20 | HOUSTON | 27 |
| 14 | Atlanta | 17 |
| 17 | NEW ORLEANS | 13 |
| 17 | Houston | 19 |
| 17 | NEW ENGLAND | 20 |
| 42 | L.A. Rams | 14 |
| 9 | Pittsburgh | 16 |

| Use Name | Pos. | Hgt. | Wgt. | Age | Int | Pts |
|---|---|---|---|---|---|---|
| Herman Arvie | OT | 6'4" | 320 | 22 | | |
| Tony Jones | OT | 6'5" | 295 | 27 | | |
| Gene Williams | OT | 6'2" | 305 | 24 | | |
| Bob Dahl | OG-OT | 6'5" | 300 | 24 | | |
| Houston Hoover | OG | 6'2" | 300 | 28 | | |
| Ed King | OG | 6'4" | 300 | 23 | | |
| Steve Everitt | C | 6'5" | 292 | 23 | | |
| Wally Williams | C | 6'2" | 300 | 22 | | |
| Rob Burnett | DE | 6'4" | 280 | 26 | | |
| Dan Footmann | DE | 6'5" | 285 | 24 | | |
| Pio Sagapolutele | DE | 6'6" | 297 | 23 | | |
| Anthony Pleasant | DE | 6'5" | 273 | 25 | | 2 |
| Jerry Ball | DT | 6'1" | 315 | 28 | | |
| Bill Johnson | DT-DE | 6'4" | 305 | 24 | | |
| James Jones | DT | 6'2" | 290 | 24 | | 6 |
| Michael Dean Perry | DT | 6'1" | 285 | 28 | | |

| Use Name | Pos. | Hgt. | Wgt. | Age | Int | Pts |
|---|---|---|---|---|---|---|
| Mike Caldwell | LB | 6'2" | 222 | 22 | | |
| Gerald Dixon | LB | 6'3" | 252 | 24 | | |
| Mike Johnson | LB | 6'1" | 230 | 30 | 1 | |
| Pepper Johnson | LB | 6'3" | 248 | 29 | | |
| Clay Matthews | LB | 6'2" | 245 | 37 | 1 | |
| Frank Stams | LB | 6'2" | 240 | 27 | | |
| Eddie Sutter | LB | 6'3" | 240 | 23 | | |
| Stacey Hairston | DB | 5'9" | 180 | 26 | | |
| Randy Hilliard | DB | 5'11" | 160 | 26 | 1 | |
| Tim Jacobs | DB | 5'10" | 185 | 23 | | |
| Selwyn Jones | DB | 6' | 185 | 23 | 3 | |
| Stevon Moore | DB | 5'11" | 205 | 26 | | 6 |
| Najee Mustafaa | DB | 6'1" | 190 | 29 | 1 | 6 |
| Louis Riddick | DB | 6'2" | 216 | 24 | | 2 |
| Del Speer | DB | 6' | 196 | 23 | 1 | |
| Terry Taylor | DB | 5'10" | 190 | 32 | | |
| Eric Turner | DB | 6'1" | 207 | 24 | 5 | |
| Everson Walls | DB | 6'1" | 195 | 33 | | |

Richard Brown — Knee Injury
Thane Gash — Knee Injury

| Use Name | Pos. | Hgt. | Wgt. | Age | Int | Pts |
|---|---|---|---|---|---|---|
| Brad Goebel | QB | 6'3" | 198 | 25 | | |
| Bernie Kosar (to DAL) | QB | 6'5" | 215 | 29 | | |
| Todd Philcox | QB | 6'4" | 225 | 26 | | 6 |
| Vinny Testaverde | QB | 6'5" | 215 | 29 | | |
| Eric Metcalf | HB | 5'10" | 190 | 25 | | 30 |
| Ron Wolfley | HB | 6' | 230 | 30 | | 6 |
| Randy Baldwin | FB | 5'10" | 216 | 26 | | 6 |
| Leroy Hoard | FB-HB | 5'11" | 230 | 26 | | |
| Kevin Mack | FB | 6' | 225 | 31 | | 6 |
| Tommy Vardell | FB | 6'2" | 233 | 24 | | 24 |
| Clarence Williams | FB-TE | 6'2" | 240 | 24 | | |
| Mark Carrier | WR | 6' | 185 | 27 | | 30 |
| Michael Jackson | WR | 6'4" | 195 | 24 | | 48 |
| Keenan McCardell | WR | 6'1" | 175 | 23 | | 24 |
| Patrick Rowe | WR | 6'1" | 195 | 24 | | |
| Rico Smith | WR | 6' | 185 | 24 | | |
| Lawyer Tillman | WR | 6'5" | 230 | 27 | | 6 |
| Brian Kinchen | TE | 6'2" | 232 | 28 | | 12 |
| Thomas McLemore | TE | 6'5" | 230 | 23 | | |
| Brian Hansen | K | 6'4" | 215 | 32 | | |
| Matt Stover | K | 5'11" | 178 | 25 | | 84 |

## CINCINNATI BENGALS 3-13 Dave Shula

| Scores of Each Game | | |
|---|---|---|
| 14 | Cleveland | 27 |
| 6 | INDIANAPOLIS | 9 |
| 7 | Pittsburgh | 34 |
| 10 | SEATTLE | 19 |
| 15 | Kansas City | 17 |
| 17 | CLEVELAND | 28 |
| 12 | Houston | 28 |
| 16 | PITTSBURGH | 24 |
| 3 | HOUSTON | 38 |
| 12 | N.Y. Jets | 17 |
| 16 | L.A. RAIDERS | 10 |
| 8 | San Francisco | 21 |
| 2 | New England | 7 |
| 15 | L.A. RAMS | 3 |
| 21 | ATLANTA | 17 |
| 13 | New Orleans | 20 |

| Use Name | Pos. | Hgt. | Wgt. | Age | Int | Pts |
|---|---|---|---|---|---|---|
| Chuck Bradley | OT | 6'5" | 296 | 23 | | |
| Donnell Johnson | OT | 6'7" | 310 | 23 | | |
| Dan Jones | OT | 6'7" | 304 | 23 | | |
| Tom Rayam | OT | 6'6" | 297 | 25 | | |
| Kevin Sargent | OT | 6'6" | 284 | 24 | | |
| Tom Scott | OT-OG | 6'6" | 330 | 23 | | |
| Joe Walter | OT | 6'6" | 292 | 30 | | |
| Scott Brumfield | OG-OT | 6'8" | 320 | 23 | | |
| Ken Moyer | OG-OT | 6'7" | 297 | 26 | | |
| Bruce Kozerski | C | 6'4" | 287 | 31 | | |
| Mike Frier | DE | 6'5" | 299 | 24 | | |
| George Hinkle | DE | 6'5" | 288 | 28 | | |
| Roosevelt Nix | DE | 6'6" | 315 | 26 | | |
| Danny Stubbs | DE-LB | 6'4" | 264 | 8 | | |
| John Copeland | DT | 6'3" | 286 | 22 | | |
| Ty Parten | DT | 6'4" | 272 | 23 | | |
| Garry Howe | NT | 6'1" | 298 | 25 | | |
| Tim Krumrie | NT | 6'2" | 274 | 33 | | |

| Use Name | Pos. | Hgt. | Wgt. | Age | Int | Pts |
|---|---|---|---|---|---|---|
| James Francis | LB | 6'5" | 252 | 25 | 2 | |
| Alex Gordon | LB | 6'5" | 245 | 28 | | |
| Randy Kirk | LB | 6'2" | 231 | 28 | | |
| Ricardo McDonald | LB | 6'2" | 235 | 23 | | |
| Karmeeleyah McGill | LB | 6'3" | 224 | 22 | | |
| Eric Shaw | LB | 6'3" | 248 | 21 | | |
| Brad Smith | LB | 6'2" | 228 | 22 | | |
| Steve Tovar | LB | 6'3" | 244 | 23 | 1 | |
| Alfred Williams | LB | 6'6" | 240 | 24 | | 2 |
| Michael Brim | DB | 6' | 192 | 27 | 3 | 6 |
| Alan Grant (from SF) | DB | 5'10" | 187 | 26 | 1 | |
| Lance Gunn | DB | 6'3" | 222 | 23 | | |
| Rod Jones | DB | 6' | 185 | 29 | 1 | |
| R.J. Kors | DB | 6' | 200 | 27 | | |
| Marcello Simmons | DB | 6'1" | 180 | 22 | | |
| Fernandus Vinson | DB | 5'10" | 197 | 24 | | |
| Leonard Wheeler | DB | 5'11" | 189 | 24 | | |
| Sheldon White | DB | 5'11" | 188 | 28 | 2 | |
| Darryl Williams | DB | 6' | 191 | 23 | 2 | 6 |

| Use Name | Pos. | Hgt. | Wgt. | Age | Int | Pts |
|---|---|---|---|---|---|---|
| David Klingler | QB | 6'2" | 205 | 24 | | |
| Jay Schroeder | QB | 6'4" | 215 | 32 | | |
| Erik Wilhelm | QB | 6'3" | 217 | 27 | | |
| Eric Ball | HB-FB | 6'2" | 220 | 27 | | 6 |
| Ryan Benjamin | HB | 5'7" | 183 | 23 | | |
| Harold Green | HB | 6'2" | 222 | 25 | | |
| Derrick Fenner | FB-HB | 6'3" | 228 | 26 | | 6 |
| Ostell Miles | FB | 6' | 236 | 22 | | 6 |
| Wesley Carroll | WR | 6' | 183 | 25 | | |
| Allen Degraffenreid | WR | 6'3" | 200 | 23 | | |
| Carl Pickens | WR | 6'2" | 206 | 23 | | 36 |
| Jeff Query | WR | 6' | 165 | 26 | | 24 |
| Reggie Rembert | WR | 6'5" | 200 | 26 | | |
| Patrick Robinson | WR | 5'8" | 176 | 23 | | |
| Milt Stegall | WR | 6' | 184 | 23 | | |
| Reggie Thornton | WR | 5'11" | 173 | 25 | | |
| David Frisch | TE | 6'7" | 260 | 23 | | |
| Tony McGee | TE | 6'3" | 246 | 22 | | |
| Jeff Thomason | TE | 6'4" | 233 | 23 | | |
| Craig Thompson | TE | 6'2" | 244 | 24 | | 6 |
| Lee Johnson | K | 6'2" | 200 | 31 | | |
| Doug Pelfrey | K | 5'11" | 185 | 22 | | 85 |

## HOUSTON OILERS

### RUSHING

| Last Name | No. | Yds | Avg | TD |
|---|---|---|---|---|
| G. Brown | 195 | 1002 | 5.1 | 6 |
| White | 131 | 465 | 3.5 | 2 |
| Moon | 48 | 145 | 3.0 | 1 |
| Tillman | 9 | 94 | 10.4 | 2 |
| Carlson | 14 | 41 | 2.9 | 2 |
| Givins | 6 | 19 | 3.2 | 0 |
| Maston | 1 | 10 | 10.0 | 0 |
| Richardson | 2 | 9 | 4.5 | 0 |
| Wellman | 2 | 6 | 3.0 | 0 |
| Coleman | 1 | 1 | 1.0 | 0 |

### RECEIVING

| Last Name | No. | Yds | Avg | TD |
|---|---|---|---|---|
| Slaughter | 77 | 904 | 11.7 | 5 |
| Givins | 68 | 887 | 13.0 | 4 |
| Jeffires | 66 | 753 | 11.4 | 6 |
| Duncan | 41 | 456 | 11.1 | 3 |
| White | 34 | 229 | 6.7 | 0 |
| Wellman | 31 | 430 | 13.9 | 1 |
| G. Brown | 21 | 240 | 11.4 | 2 |
| Coleman | 9 | 129 | 14.3 | 0 |
| Harris | 4 | 53 | 13.3 | 1 |
| R. Brown | 2 | 30 | 15.0 | 0 |
| Maston | 1 | 14 | 14.0 | 0 |
| Norgard | 1 | 13 | 13.0 | 0 |
| Tillman | 1 | 4 | 4.0 | 0 |
| Drewrey | 1 | 3 | 3.0 | 0 |

### PUNT RETURNS

| Last Name | No. | Yds | Avg | TD |
|---|---|---|---|---|
| Drewrey | 41 | 275 | 6.7 | |

### KICKOFF RETURNS

| Last Name | No. | Yds | Avg | TD |
|---|---|---|---|---|
| Drewrey | 15 | 293 | 19.5 | 0 |
| Mills | 11 | 230 | 20.9 | 0 |
| Coleman | 3 | 37 | 12.3 | 0 |
| G. Brown | 2 | 29 | 14.5 | 0 |

### PASSING

| Last Name | Att | Cmp | % | Yds | Yd/Att | TD | Int— | % | RK |
|---|---|---|---|---|---|---|---|---|---|
| Moon | 520 | 303 | 58.3 | 3485 | 6.70 | 21 | 21— | 4.0 | 11 |
| Carlson | 90 | 51 | 56.7 | 605 | 6.72 | 2 | 4— | 4.4 | |
| Richardson | 4 | 3 | 75.0 | 55 | 13.75 | 0 | 0— | 0.0 | |

### PUNTING

| Last Name | No. | Avg. |
|---|---|---|
| Montgomery | 54 | 45.6 |

### KICKING

| Last Name | XP | ATT | % | FG | ATT | % |
|---|---|---|---|---|---|---|
| Del Greco | 39 | 40 | 98 | 29 | 34 | 85 |

## PITTSBURGH STEELERS

### RUSHING

| Last Name | No. | Yds | Avg | TD |
|---|---|---|---|---|
| Thompson | 205 | 763 | 3.7 | 3 |
| Foster | 177 | 711 | 4.0 | 8 |
| Hoge | 51 | 249 | 4.9 | 1 |
| Stone | 12 | 121 | 10.1 | 1 |
| O'Donnell | 26 | 111 | 4.3 | 0 |
| Mills | 3 | 12 | 4.0 | 0 |
| Cuthbert | 1 | 7 | 7.0 | 0 |
| Woodson | 1 | 0 | 0.0 | 0 |
| Tomczak | 5 | -4 | -0.8 | 0 |

### RECEIVING

| Last Name | No. | Yds | Avg | TD |
|---|---|---|---|---|
| Green | 63 | 942 | 15.0 | 5 |
| Stone | 41 | 587 | 14.3 | 2 |
| Graham | 38 | 579 | 15.2 | 0 |
| Thompson | 38 | 259 | 6.8 | 0 |
| Hoge | 33 | 247 | 7.5 | 4 |
| Mills | 29 | 386 | 13.3 | 1 |
| Foster | 27 | 217 | 8.0 | 1 |
| Thigpen | 9 | 154 | 17.1 | 3 |
| Cooper | 9 | 112 | 12.4 | 0 |
| Davenport | 4 | 51 | 12.8 | 0 |
| Hastings | 3 | 44 | 14.7 | 0 |
| Jorden | 1 | 12 | 12.0 | 0 |
| Cuthbert | 1 | 3 | 3.0 | 0 |

### PUNT RETURNS

| Last Name | No. | Yds | Avg | TD |
|---|---|---|---|---|
| Woodson | 41 | 338 | 8.2 | 0 |
| Figures | 5 | 15 | 3.0 | 0 |

### KICKOFF RETURNS

| Last Name | No. | Yds | Avg | TD |
|---|---|---|---|---|
| Woodson | 15 | 294 | 19.6 | 0 |
| Hastings | 12 | 177 | 14.8 | 0 |
| Stone | 11 | 168 | 15.3 | 0 |
| Thompson | 4 | 77 | 19.3 | 0 |
| Hoge | 3 | 33 | 11.0 | 0 |
| Thigpen | 1 | 23 | 23.0 | 0 |
| W. Williams | 1 | 19 | 19.0 | 0 |
| Cooper | 1 | 2 | 2.0 | 0 |

### PASSING

| Last Name | Att | Cmp | % | Yds | Yd/Att | TD | Int— | % | RK |
|---|---|---|---|---|---|---|---|---|---|
| O'Donnell | 486 | 270 | 55.6 | 3208 | 6.60 | 14 | 7— | 1.4 | 8 |
| Tomczak | 54 | 29 | 53.7 | 398 | 7.37 | 2 | 5— | 9.3 | |

### PUNTING

| Last Name | No. | Avg. |
|---|---|---|
| Royals | 89 | 42.5 |

### KICKING

| Last Name | XP | ATT | % | FG | ATT | % |
|---|---|---|---|---|---|---|
| Anderson | 32 | 32 | 100 | 28 | 30 | 93 |

## CLEVELAND BROWNS

### RUSHING

| Last Name | No. | Yds | Avg | TD |
|---|---|---|---|---|
| Vardell | 171 | 644 | 3.8 | 3 |
| Metcalf | 129 | 611 | 4.7 | 1 |
| Hoard | 56 | 227 | 4.1 | 0 |
| Testaverde | 18 | 74 | 4.1 | 0 |
| Baldwin | 18 | 61 | 3.4 | 0 |
| Mack | 10 | 33 | 3.3 | 1 |
| Carrier | 4 | 26 | 6.5 | 1 |
| Kosar | 23 | 26 | 1.1 | 0 |
| Philcox | 2 | 3 | 1.5 | 1 |
| J. Jones | 2 | 2 | 1.0 | 1 |
| Jackson | 1 | 1 | 1.0 | 0 |

### RECEIVING

| Last Name | No. | Yds | Avg | TD |
|---|---|---|---|---|
| Metcalf | 63 | 539 | 8.6 | 2 |
| Carrier | 43 | 746 | 17.3 | 3 |
| Jackson | 41 | 756 | 18.4 | 8 |
| Hoard | 35 | 351 | 10.0 | 0 |
| Kinchen | 29 | 347 | 12.0 | 2 |
| Vardell | 19 | 151 | 7.9 | 1 |
| McCardell | 13 | 234 | 18.0 | 4 |
| Tillman | 5 | 68 | 13.6 | 1 |
| Wolfley | 5 | 25 | 5.0 | 1 |
| Smith | 4 | 55 | 13.8 | 0 |
| Rowe | 3 | 37 | 12.3 | 0 |
| C. Williams | 1 | 14 | 14.0 | 0 |
| Baldwin | 1 | 5 | 5.0 | 1 |

### PUNT RETURNS

| Last Name | No. | Yds | Avg | TD |
|---|---|---|---|---|
| Metcalf | 36 | 464 | 12.9 | 2 |
| Carrier | 6 | 92 | 15.3 | 1 |
| Turner | 0 | 7 | — | |

### KICKOFF RETURNS

| Last Name | No. | Yds | Avg | TD |
|---|---|---|---|---|
| Baldwin | 24 | 444 | 18.5 | 0 |
| Metcalf | 15 | 318 | 21.2 | 0 |
| Hoard | 13 | 286 | 22.0 | 0 |
| Vardell | 4 | 58 | 14.5 | 0 |
| R. Smith | 1 | 13 | 13.0 | 0 |
| Kinchen | 1 | 0 | 0.0 | 0 |

### PASSING

| Last Name | Att | Cmp | % | Yds | Yd/Att | TD | Int— | % | RK |
|---|---|---|---|---|---|---|---|---|---|
| Testaverde | 230 | 130 | 56.5 | 1797 | 7.81 | 14 | 9— | 3.9 | 3 |
| Kosar | 201 | 115 | 57.2 | 1217 | 6.05 | 8 | 3— | 1.5 | |
| Philcox | 108 | 52 | 48.1 | 699 | 6.47 | 4 | 7— | 6.5 | |
| Jackson | 1 | 1 | 100.0 | 25 | 25.00 | 0 | 0— | 0.0 | |
| Hoard | 1 | 0 | 0.0 | 0 | 0.00 | 0 | 0— | 0.0 | |

### PUNTING

| Last Name | No. | Avg. |
|---|---|---|
| Hansen | 84 | 43.2 |
| Team | 2 | 0.0 |

### KICKING

| Last Name | XP | ATT | % | FG | ATT | % |
|---|---|---|---|---|---|---|
| Stover | 36 | 36 | 100 | 16 | 22 | 73 |

## CINCINNATI BENGALS

### RUSHING

| Last Name | No. | Yds | Avg | TD |
|---|---|---|---|---|
| Green | 215 | 589 | 2.7 | 0 |
| Fenner | 121 | 482 | 4.0 | 1 |
| Klingler | 41 | 282 | 6.9 | 0 |
| Miles | 22 | 56 | 2.5 | 1 |
| Schroeder | 10 | 41 | 4.1 | 0 |
| Ball | 8 | 37 | 4.6 | 1 |
| Query | 2 | 13 | 6.5 | 0 |
| Robinson | 1 | 6 | 6.0 | 0 |
| Benjamin | 3 | 5 | 1.7 | 0 |

### RECEIVING

| Last Name | No. | Yds | Avg | TD |
|---|---|---|---|---|
| Query | 56 | 654 | 11.7 | 4 |
| Fenner | 48 | 427 | 8.9 | 0 |
| McGee | 44 | 525 | 11.9 | 0 |
| Pickens | 43 | 565 | 13.1 | 6 |
| Green | 22 | 115 | 5.2 | 0 |
| Thompson | 17 | 87 | 5.1 | 1 |
| Rembert | 8 | 101 | 12.6 | 0 |
| Robinson | 8 | 72 | 9.0 | 0 |
| Miles | 6 | 89 | 14.8 | 0 |
| Carroll | 6 | 81 | 13.5 | 0 |
| Frisch | 6 | 43 | 7.2 | 0 |
| Ball | 4 | 39 | 9.8 | 0 |
| Thomason | 2 | 8 | 4.0 | 0 |
| Benjamin | 1 | 16 | 16.0 | 0 |
| Stegall | 1 | 8 | 8.0 | 0 |

### PUNT RETURNS

| Last Name | No. | Yds | Avg | TD |
|---|---|---|---|---|
| Robinson | 43 | 305 | 7.1 | 0 |
| Pickens | 4 | 16 | 4.0 | 0 |
| Simmons | 1 | 0 | 0.0 | 0 |

### KICKOFF RETURNS

| Last Name | No. | Yds | Avg | TD |
|---|---|---|---|---|
| Robinson | 30 | 567 | 18.9 | 0 |
| Ball | 23 | 501 | 21.8 | 0 |
| Benjamin | 4 | 78 | 19.5 | 0 |
| Miles | 4 | 65 | 16.3 | 0 |
| Shaw | 0 | 0 | — | 0 |

### PASSING

| Last Name | Att | Cmp | % | Yds | Yd/Att | TD | Int— | % | RK |
|---|---|---|---|---|---|---|---|---|---|
| Klingler | 343 | 190 | 55.4 | 1935 | 5.64 | 6 | 9— | 2.6 | 15 |
| Schroeder | 159 | 78 | 49.1 | 832 | 5.23 | 5 | 2— | 1.3 | |
| Wilhelm | 6 | 4 | 66.7 | 63 | 10.50 | 0 | 0— | 0.0 | |
| L. Johnson | 1 | 0 | 0.0 | 0 | 0.00 | 0 | 0— | 0.0 | |
| Pickens | 1 | 0 | 0.0 | 0 | 0.00 | 0 | 0— | 0.0 | |

### PUNTING

| Last Name | No. | Avg. |
|---|---|---|
| Johnson | 90 | 43.9 |

### KICKING

| Last Name | XP | ATT | % | FG | ATT | % |
|---|---|---|---|---|---|---|
| Pelfrey | 13 | 16 | 81 | 24 | 31 | 77 |

## KANSAS CITY CHIEFS 11-5 Marty Schottenheimer

| Scores of Each Game | | |
|---|---|---|
| 27 | Tampa Bay | 3 |
| 0 | Houston | 30 |
| 15 | DENVER | 7 |
| 24 | L.A. RAIDERS | 9 |
| 17 | CINCINNATI | 15 |
| 17 | San Diego | 14 |
| 10 | Miami | 30 |
| 23 | GREENBAY | 16 |
| 31 | L.A. Raiders | 20 |
| 17 | CHICAGO | 19 |
| 23 | BUFFALO | 7 |
| 31 | Seattle | 16 |
| 21 | Denver | 27 |
| 28 | SAN DIEGO | 24 |
| 10 | Minnesota | 30 |
| 34 | SEATTLE | 24 |

| UseName | Pos. | Hgt | Wgt | Age | Int | Pts |
|---|---|---|---|---|---|---|
| John Alt | OT | 6'7" | 307 | 31 | | |
| Derrick Graham | OT | 6'4" | 306 | 26 | | |
| Reggie McElroy | OT-OG | 6'6" | 290 | 33 | | |
| Ricky Siglar | OT | 6'7" | 304 | 27 | | |
| Joe Valerio | OT-C | 6'5" | 295 | 24 | | 6 |
| Tom Ricketts | OG | 6'5" | 305 | 27 | | |
| Will Shields | OG | 6'2" | 296 | 21 | | |
| Dave Szott | OG | 6'4" | 290 | 25 | | |
| Danny Villa | OG | 6'5" | 300 | 28 | | |
| Tim Grunhard | C | 6'2" | 299 | 25 | | |
| Leonard Griffin | DE | 6'4" | 278 | 30 | | |
| Pellom McDaniels | DE | 6'3" | 278 | 25 | | |
| Neil Smith | DE | 6'4" | 273 | 27 | 1 | |
| Darren Mickel | DT | 6'4" | 280 | 23 | | |
| Tim Newton | DT | 6' | 269 | 30 | | |
| Joe Phillips | DT-NT | 6'5" | 300 | 30 | | |
| Dan Saleaumua | DT-DE | 6' | 300 | 28 | 1 | 6 |
| Erick Anderson | LB | 6'1" | 235 | 24 | | |
| Jaime Fields | LB | 5'11" | 230 | 23 | | |
| Lonnie Marts | LB | 6'1" | 230 | 24 | 1 | |
| Tracy Rogers | LB | 6'2" | 241 | 26 | | |
| Tracy Simien | LB | 6'1" | 250 | 26 | | |
| Santo Stephens | LB | 6'4" | 232 | 24 | | |
| Derrick Thomas | LB-DE | 6'3" | 242 | 26 | | 6 |
| Martin Bayless | DB | 6'2" | 219 | 30 | 2 | |
| Dale Carter | DB | 6'1" | 188 | 23 | 1 | |
| Albert Lewis | DB | 6'2" | 195 | 32 | 6 | 6 |
| Garry Lewis | DB | 5'11" | 185 | 26 | | |
| Charles Mincy | DB | 5'11" | 197 | 23 | 5 | |
| Bruce Pickens (from ATL, GB) | DB | 5'11" | 190 | 25 | | |
| Kevin Ross | DB | 5'9" | 185 | 31 | 2 | |
| Jay Taylor | DB | 5'10" | 170 | 25 | 1 | |
| Doug Terry | DB | 5'11" | 192 | 23 | 1 | |
| Bennie Thompson | DB | 6' | 216 | 30 | | |
| Tim Watson | DB | 6'1" | 213 | 23 | | |
| David Whitmore | DB | 6' | 217 | 26 | | |
| Matt Blundin | QB | 6'6" | 233 | 24 | | |
| Dave Krieg | QB | 6'1" | 202 | 34 | | |
| Joe Montana | QB | 6'2" | 205 | 37 | | |
| Marcus Allen | HB | 6'2" | 210 | 33 | | 90 |
| Ron Dickerson | HB-WR | 6' | 211 | 23 | | |
| Todd McNair | HB | 6'1" | 197 | 27 | | 12 |
| John Stephens (from GB) | HB | 6'1" | 215 | 27 | | 6 |
| Harvey Williams | HB | 6'2" | 215 | 26 | | |
| Kimble Anders | FB | 5'11" | 221 | 26 | | 6 |
| Ernie Thompson | FB | 5'11" | 257 | 23 | | |
| Tim Barnett | WR | 6'1" | 200 | 25 | | 6 |
| J.J. Birden | WR | 5'9" | 165 | 28 | | 12 |
| Willie Davis | WR | 6' | 172 | 25 | | 42 |
| Danan Hughes | WR | 6'1" | 201 | 22 | | |
| Fred Jones | WR | 5'9" | 180 | 26 | | |
| Hassan Jones | WR | 6' | 202 | 29 | | |
| Mike Bartrum | TE | 6'4" | 234 | 23 | | |
| Keith Cash | TE | 6'4" | 240 | 24 | | 24 |
| Mike Dyal (to SD) | TE | 6'2" | 240 | 27 | | |
| Jonathan Hayes | TE | 6'5" | 252 | 31 | | 6 |
| Bryan Barker | K | 6'1" | 187 | 29 | | |
| Nick Lowery | K | 6'4" | 207 | 37 | | 106 |

## LOS ANGELES RAIDERS 10-6 Art Shell

| Scores of Each Game | | |
|---|---|---|
| 24 | MINNESOTA | 7 |
| 17 | Seattle | 13 |
| 16 | CLEVELAND | 19 |
| 9 | Kansas City | 24 |
| 24 | N.Y. JETS | 20 |
| 23 | Denver | 20 |
| 23 | SAN DIEGO | 30 |
| 16 | Chicago | 14 |
| 20 | Kansas City | 31 |
| 12 | San Diego | 7 |
| 10 | Cincinnati | 16 |
| 25 | Buffalo | 24 |
| 27 | SEATTLE | 23 |
| 27 | TAMPA BAY | 20 |
| 0 | Green Bay | 28 |
| 33 | DENVER | *30 |

| UseName | Pos. | Hgt | Wgt | Age | Int | Pts |
|---|---|---|---|---|---|---|
| Ken Lanier | OT | 6'3" | 290 | 34 | | |
| Gerald Perry | OT | 6'6" | 300 | 28 | | |
| Rich Stephens | OT-OG | 6'7" | 300 | 27 | | |
| Bruce Wilkerson | OT | 6'5" | 295 | 29 | | |
| Max Montoya | OG | 6'5" | 295 | 37 | | |
| Todd Peat | OG | 6'2" | 305 | 29 | | |
| Steve Wisniewski | OG | 6'4" | 285 | 26 | | |
| Don Mosebar | C | 6'6" | 300 | 31 | | |
| Dan Turk | C | 6'4" | 290 | 31 | | |
| Aundray Bruce | DE | 6'5" | 260 | 27 | | |
| Howie Long | DE | 6'5" | 275 | 33 | | |
| Anthony Smith | DE | 6'3" | 260 | 26 | | |
| Greg Townsend | DE | 6'3" | 270 | 31 | | |
| Willie Broughton | DT | 6'5" | 285 | 28 | | |
| Nolan Harrison | DT | 6'5" | 285 | 24 | | |
| Chester McGlockton | DT | 6'4" | 315 | 23 | 1 | |
| Greg Biekert | LB | 6'2" | 235 | 24 | | |
| Mike Jones | LB | 6'1" | 230 | 24 | | |
| Joe Kelly | LB | 6'2" | 230 | 28 | | |
| Winston Moss | LB | 6'3" | 240 | 27 | | |
| Aaron Wallace | LB | 6'3" | 240 | 26 | | |
| Eddie Anderson | DB | 6'1" | 210 | 30 | 2 | |
| Patrick Bates | DB | 6'3" | 220 | 22 | 1 | |
| Rickey Dixon | DB | 5'11" | 185 | 26 | | |
| Torin Dorn | DB | 6' | 190 | 25 | | |
| David Fulcher | DB | 6'3" | 245 | 28 | | |
| Derrick Hoskins | DB | 6'2" | 205 | 23 | 2 | |
| Dan Land | DB | 6' | 195 | 28 | | |
| Terry McDaniel | DB | 5'10" | 180 | 28 | 5 | 6 |
| James Trapp | DB | 6' | 180 | 23 | 1 | |
| Lionel Washington | DB | 6' | 185 | 32 | 2 | |
| Vince Evans | QB | 6'2" | 215 | 38 | | |
| Billy Joe Hobert | QB | 6'3" | 225 | 11 | | |
| Jeff Hostetler | QB | 6'3" | 220 | 32 | | 30 |
| Nick Bell | HB | 6'2" | 250 | 25 | | 6 |
| Randy Jordan | HB | 5'10" | 205 | 23 | | |
| Napoleon McCallum | HB | 6'2" | 225 | 29 | | 18 |
| Tyrone Montgomery | HB | 6' | 190 | 23 | | |
| Greg Robinson | HB | 5'10" | 200 | 24 | | 6 |
| Steve Smith | FB | 6'1" | 240 | 29 | | |
| Tim Brown | WR | 6' | 195 | 27 | | 48 |
| Willie Gault | WR | 6' | 175 | 32 | | |
| Daryl Hobbs | WR | 6'2" | 180 | 25 | | |
| Raghib Ismail | WR | 5'10" | 180 | 23 | | 6 |
| James Jett | WR | 5'10" | 165 | 22 | | 18 |
| Alexander Wright | WR | 6' | 190 | 26 | | 24 |
| John Duff | TE | 6'7" | 250 | 26 | | |
| Andrew Glover | TE | 6'6" | 245 | 26 | | 6 |
| Ethan Horton | TE | 6'4" | 240 | 30 | | 6 |
| Kevin Smith | TE | 6'4" | 255 | 24 | | |
| Jeff Gossett | K | 6'2" | 195 | 36 | | |
| Jeff Jaeger | K | 5'11" | 190 | 28 | | 132 |

Greg Skrepenak — Ankle Injury
Steve Wright — Knee Injury

Dave Waymer — Died in Offseason

## DENVER BRONCOS 9-7 Wade Phillips

| Scores of Each Game | | |
|---|---|---|
| 26 | N.Y. Jets | 20 |
| 34 | SAN DIEGO | 17 |
| 7 | Kansas City | 15 |
| 35 | INDIANAPOLIS | 13 |
| 27 | Green Bay | 30 |
| 20 | L.A. RAIDERS | 23 |
| 28 | SEATTLE | 17 |
| 29 | Cleveland | 14 |
| 23 | MINNESOTA | 26 |
| 37 | PITTSBURGH | 13 |
| 17 | Seattle | 9 |
| 10 | San Diego | 13 |
| 27 | KANSAS CITY | 21 |
| 13 | Chicago | 3 |
| 10 | TAMPA BAY | 17 |
| 30 | L.A. Raiders | *33 |

| UseName | Pos. | Hgt | Wgt | Age | Int | Pts |
|---|---|---|---|---|---|---|
| Russell Freeman | OT | 6'7" | 290 | 23 | | |
| Don Maggs | OT | 6'5" | 290 | 31 | | |
| Kirk Scrafford | OT | 6'6" | 265 | 26 | | |
| Gary Zimmerman | OT | 6'6" | 294 | 31 | | |
| Brian Habib | OG | 6'7" | 299 | 28 | | |
| Jon Melander | OG-OT | 6'7" | 280 | 26 | | |
| Dave Widell | OG-C | 6'6" | 292 | 28 | | |
| Keith Kartz | C | 6'4" | 270 | 30 | | |
| Bob Meeks | C | 6'2" | 279 | 24 | | |
| Shane Dronett | DE | 6'6" | 275 | 22 | 2 | |
| Willie Oshodin | DE | 6'4" | 265 | 23 | | |
| Jeff Robinson | DE | 6'4" | 265 | 23 | | |
| Dan Williams | DE | 6'4" | 290 | 23 | | |
| Alphonso Taylor | DT | 6'3" | 350 | 23 | | |
| Darren Drozdov | NT | 6'3" | 280 | 23 | | |
| Greg Kragen | NT | 6'3" | 265 | 31 | | |
| Elijah Alexander | LB | 6'2" | 230 | 23 | | |
| Mike Croel | LB | 6'3" | 231 | 24 | 1 | 6 |
| Mitch Donahue | LB | 6'2" | 254 | 25 | | |
| Simon Fletcher | LB | 6'5" | 240 | 31 | | |
| Tim Lucas | LB | 6'3" | 230 | 32 | | |
| Karl Mecklenburg | LB | 6'3" | 235 | 33 | | |
| Jeff Mills | LB | 6'3" | 250 | 24 | | |
| Dave Wyman | LB | 6'2" | 248 | 29 | 1 | 6 |
| Steve Atwater | DB | 6'3" | 217 | 26 | 2 | |
| Ronnie Bradford | DB | 5'10" | 188 | 22 | 1 | |
| Tyrone Braxton | DB | 5'11" | 185 | 28 | 3 | |
| Charles Dimry | DB | 6' | 175 | 27 | 1 | |
| Darryl Hall | DB | 6'2" | 210 | 27 | 1 | |
| Rondell Jones | DB | 6'2" | 210 | 22 | | |
| Le-Lo Lang | DB | 5'11" | 185 | 26 | 2 | |
| Frank Robinson | DB | 5'11" | 174 | 24 | 1 | |
| Dennis Smith | DB | 6'3" | 200 | 34 | 3 | |
| John Elway | QB | 6'3" | 215 | 33 | | |
| Tommy Maddox | QB | 6'4" | 205 | 21 | | |
| Shawn Moore | QB | 6'2" | 214 | 24 | | |
| Rod Bernstine | HB-FB | 6'3" | 238 | 28 | | 24 |
| Robert Delpino | HB | 6' | 205 | 27 | | 48 |
| Glyn Milburn | HB | 5'8" | 177 | 22 | | 18 |
| Anthony Lynn | FB | 6'3" | 230 | 24 | | |
| Reggie Rivers | FB | 6'1" | 215 | 25 | | 14 |
| Melvin Bonner | WR | 6'3" | 207 | 23 | | |
| Vance Johnson | WR | 5'11" | 185 | 30 | | 30 |
| Tony Kimbrough | WR | 6'2" | 192 | 22 | | |
| Arthur Marshall | WR | 5'11" | 174 | 24 | | 12 |
| Barry Rose | WR | 6' | 185 | 25 | | |
| Derek Russell | WR | 6' | 195 | 24 | | 24 |
| Kitrick Taylor | WR | 5'11" | 189 | 29 | | |
| Cedric Tillman | WR | 6'2" | 204 | 23 | | 12 |
| Jerry Evans | TE | 6'4" | 250 | 24 | | |
| Reggie Johnson | TE | 6'2" | 256 | 25 | | 6 |
| Shannon Sharpe | TE | 6'2" | 230 | 25 | | 54 |
| Jason Elam | K | 5'11" | 192 | 23 | | 119 |
| Tom Rouen | K | 6'3" | 215 | 25 | | |

## SAN DIEGO CHARGERS 8-8 Bobby Ross

| Scores of Each Game | | |
|---|---|---|
| 18 | SEATTLE | 12 |
| 17 | Denver | 34 |
| 18 | HOUSTON | 17 |
| 14 | Seattle | 31 |
| 3 | Pittsburgh | 16 |
| 14 | KANSAS CITY | 17 |
| 30 | L.A. Raiders | 23 |
| 30 | Minnesota | 17 |
| 13 | CHICAGO | 16 |
| 7 | L.A. RAIDERS | 12 |
| 31 | Indianapolis | 0 |
| 13 | DENVER | 10 |
| 13 | GREEN BAY | 20 |
| 24 | Kansas City | 28 |
| 45 | MIAMI | 20 |
| 32 | Tampa Bay | 17 |

| UseName | Pos. | Hgt | Wgt | Age | Int | Pts |
|---|---|---|---|---|---|---|
| Stan Brock | OT | 6'6" | 295 | 35 | | |
| Eric Jonassen | OT | 6'5" | 310 | 25 | | |
| Mike Mooney | OT | 6'6" | 320 | 24 | | |
| Harry Swayne | OT | 6'5" | 295 | 28 | | |
| Joe Cocozzo | OG | 6'4" | 300 | 23 | | |
| Joe Milinichik | OG | 6'5" | 300 | 30 | | |
| Eric Moten | OG | 6'2" | 306 | 25 | | |
| Raymond Smoot | OG-OT | 6'4" | 300 | 23 | | |
| Mike Zandofsky | OG | 6'2" | 305 | 27 | | |
| Courtney Hall | C | 6'2" | 281 | 25 | | |
| Curtis Whitley | C | 6'1" | 285 | 24 | | |
| Burt Grossman | DE | 6'6" | 270 | 26 | | |
| Raylee Johnson | DE | 6'3" | 245 | 23 | | |
| Chris Mims | DE-DT | 6'5" | 290 | 22 | | |
| Leslie O'Neal | DE | 6'4" | 265 | 29 | | |
| Shawn Lee | DT | 6'2" | 300 | 26 | | |
| Reggie White | DT | 6'4" | 300 | 23 | | |
| Blaise Winter | DT | 6'4" | 295 | 31 | | |
| Sam Anno | LB | 6'3" | 240 | 28 | | |
| Lewis Bush | LB | 6'2" | 245 | 23 | | |
| Terry Crews | LB | 6'2" | 245 | 25 | | |
| Doug Miller | LB | 6'3" | 232 | 23 | | |
| Gary Plummer | LB | 6'2" | 247 | 33 | 2 | |
| Junior Seau | LB | 6'3" | 250 | 24 | 2 | |
| Jerrol Williams | LB | 6'4" | 240 | 26 | | |
| Darren Carrington | DB | 6'2" | 200 | 26 | 7 | |
| Eric Castle | DB | 6'3" | 212 | 23 | | |
| Brian Davis | DB | 6'2" | 190 | 30 | 1 | |
| Floyd Fields | DB | 6' | 208 | 24 | | |
| Donald Frank | DB | 6' | 192 | 27 | 3 | 6 |
| James Fuller | DB | 6' | 208 | 24 | | |
| Darrien Gordon | DB | 5'11" | 182 | 22 | 1 | |
| Marquez Pope | DB | 5'10" | 193 | 22 | 2 | |
| Stanley Richard | DB | 6'2" | 197 | 25 | 1 | |
| Sean Vanhorse | DB | 5'10" | 180 | 25 | 2 | |
| John Friesz | QB | 6'4" | 218 | 26 | | |
| Stan Humphries | QB | 6'2" | 223 | 28 | | |
| Eric Bieniemy | HB | 5'7" | 198 | 24 | | 6 |
| Ronnie Harmon | HB | 5'11" | 207 | 29 | | 12 |
| Marion Butts | FB-HB | 6'1" | 248 | 27 | | 24 |
| Natrone Means | FB-HB | 5'10" | 245 | 21 | | 48 |
| Johnnie Barnes | WR | 6'1" | 180 | 25 | | |
| Shawn Jefferson | WR | 5'11" | 172 | 24 | | 12 |
| Nate Lewis | WR | 5'11" | 198 | 26 | | 24 |
| Anthony Miller | WR | 5'11" | 189 | 28 | | 42 |
| Mark Seay | WR | 6' | 175 | 26 | | |
| Steve Hendrickson | FB-LB | 6' | 250 | 27 | 1 | |
| Deems May | TE | 6'4" | 263 | 24 | | |
| Alfred Pupunu | TE | 6'2" | 255 | 23 | | |
| Derrick Walker | TE | 6'1" | 250 | 26 | | 6 |
| Duane Young | TE | 6'1" | 270 | 25 | | 12 |
| John Carney | K | 5'11" | 170 | 29 | | 124 |
| John Kidd | K | 6'3" | 208 | 32 | | 6 |
| Kent Sullivan (to HOU) | K | 5'10" | 197 | 29 | | |

Gill Byrd — Knee Injury

## SEATTLE SEAHAWKS 6-10 Tom Flores

| Scores of Each Game | | |
|---|---|---|
| 12 | San Diego | 18 |
| 13 | L.A. RAIDERS | 17 |
| 17 | New England | 14 |
| 19 | Cincinnati | 10 |
| 31 | SAN DIEGO | 14 |
| 10 | Detroit | 30 |
| 10 | NEW ENGLAND | 9 |
| 17 | Denver | 28 |
| 14 | Houston | 24 |
| 22 | CLEVELAND | 5 |
| 9 | DENVER | 17 |
| 16 | KANSAS CITY | 31 |
| 23 | L.A. Raiders | 27 |
| 27 | PHOENIX | *30 |
| 16 | PITTSBURGH | 6 |
| 24 | Kansas City | 34 |

| UseName | Pos. | Hgt | Wgt | Age | Int | Pts |
|---|---|---|---|---|---|---|
| Jason Childs | OT | 6'4" | 285 | 24 | | |
| Andy Heck | OT | 6'6" | 298 | 26 | | |
| Mike Keim | OT | 6'7" | 301 | 27 | | |
| Ray Roberts | OT | 6'6" | 304 | 24 | | |
| Rickie Shaw | OT | 6'4" | 294 | 23 | | |
| Jeff Blackshear | OG | 6'6" | 325 | 24 | | |
| Darrick Brilz | OG | 6'3" | 287 | 29 | | |
| Bill Hitchcock | OT | 6'6" | 291 | 28 | | |
| Ray Donaldson | C | 6'3" | 300 | 35 | | |
| Joe Tofflemire | C | 6'3" | 273 | 28 | | |
| Jeff Bryant | DE | 6'5" | 281 | 33 | | |
| Antonio Edwards | DE | 6'3" | 270 | 23 | | 2 |
| Michael McCrary | DE | 6'4" | 250 | 23 | | |
| Mike Sinclair | DE | 6'4" | 271 | 25 | | |
| Natu Tuatagaloa | DE | 6'4" | 274 | 27 | | |
| Cortez Kennedy | DT | 6'3" | 293 | 25 | | |
| Joe Nash | DT | 6'2" | 278 | 32 | 1 | 6 |
| Tyrone Rodgers | DT | 6'3" | 266 | 24 | | |
| Ray Berry | LB | 6'2" | 230 | 29 | | |
| David Brandon (from CLE) | LB | 6'4" | 230 | 28 | | |
| Anthony Davis | LB | 6' | 231 | 24 | | |
| Dino Hackett | LB | 6'3" | 230 | 29 | | |
| E.J. Junior | LB | 6'3" | 242 | 33 | | |
| Kevin Murphy | LB | 6'2" | 235 | 29 | | |
| Rufus Porter | LB | 6'1" | 227 | 28 | 1 | |
| Bob Spitulski | LB | 6'3" | 235 | 23 | | |
| Rod Stephens | LB | 6'1" | 237 | 27 | | 10 |
| Dean Wells | LB | 6'3" | 238 | 23 | | |
| Terry Wooden | LB | 6'3" | 239 | 26 | | |
| Brian Allred | DB | 5'10" | 175 | 24 | | |
| Robert Blackmon | DB | 6' | 197 | 26 | 2 | 6 |
| Carlton Gray | DB | 6' | 191 | 22 | 3 | |
| Dwayne Harper | DB | 5'11" | 174 | 27 | 1 | |
| Patrick Hunter | DB | 5'11" | 186 | 28 | 4 | |
| James Jefferson | DB | 6'1" | 199 | 29 | 1 | |
| Dave McCloughan | DB | 6'1" | 185 | 26 | | |
| Eugene Robinson | DB | 6' | 191 | 30 | 9 | |
| Rafael Robinson | DB | 5'11" | 200 | 24 | | |
| Stan Gelbaugh | QB | 6'3" | 207 | 30 | | |
| Dan McGwire | QB | 6'8" | 239 | 25 | | |
| Rick Mirer | QB | 6'2" | 216 | 23 | | 18 |
| Rueben Mayes | HB | 5'11" | 201 | 30 | | |
| Jon Vaughn | HB | 5'9" | 203 | 23 | | |
| Chris Warren | HB | 6'2" | 225 | 26 | | 42 |
| Tracy Johnson | FB | 6' | 230 | 26 | | 6 |
| John L. Williams | FB | 5'11" | 231 | 28 | | 24 |
| Michael Bates | WR | 5'10" | 189 | 23 | | |
| Brian Blades | WR | 5'11 | 189 | 27 | | 18 |
| Kelvin Martin | WR | 5'9" | 162 | 28 | | 30 |
| Doug Thomas | WR | 5'10" | 178 | 23 | | |
| Robb Thomas | WR | 5'11" | 175 | 27 | | |
| Terrence Warren | WR | 6'1" | 200 | 24 | | |
| Ferrell Edmunds | TE | 6'6" | 254 | 28 | | 12 |
| Paul Green | TE | 6'3" | 230 | 26 | | 6 |
| Trey Junkin | TE | 6'2" | 237 | 32 | | |
| John Kasay | K | 5'10" | 189 | 23 | | 98 |
| Rick Tuten | K | 6'2" | 218 | 28 | | |

Mitch Frerotte — Neck Injury
Grant Feasel — Knee Injury

## KANSAS CITY CHIEFS

### RUSHING

| Last Name | No. | Yds | Avg | TD |
|---|---|---|---|---|
| Allen | 206 | 764 | 3.7 | 12 |
| Anders | 75 | 291 | 3.9 | 0 |
| McNair | 51 | 278 | 5.5 | 2 |
| Stephens | 54 | 191 | 3.5 | 1 |
| H. Williams | 42 | 149 | 3.5 | 0 |
| Montana | 25 | 64 | 2.6 | 0 |
| F. Jones | 5 | 34 | 6.8 | 0 |
| E. Thompson | 11 | 28 | 2.5 | 0 |
| Krieg | 21 | 24 | 1.1 | 0 |
| Barnett | 1 | 3 | 3.0 | 0 |
| Carter | 1 | 2 | 2.0 | 0 |
| Cash | 1 | 0 | 0.0 | 0 |

### RECEIVING

| Last Name | No. | Yds | Avg | TD |
|---|---|---|---|---|
| Davis | 52 | 909 | 17.5 | 7 |
| Birden | 51 | 721 | 14.1 | 2 |
| Anders | 40 | 326 | 8.2 | 1 |
| Hayes | 24 | 331 | 13.8 | 1 |
| Cash | 24 | 242 | 10.1 | 4 |
| Barnett | 17 | 182 | 10.7 | 1 |
| McNair | 10 | 74 | 7.4 | 0 |
| F. Jones | 9 | 111 | 12.3 | 0 |
| H. Jones | 7 | 91 | 13.0 | 0 |
| Dyal | 7 | 83 | 11.9 | 0 |
| H. Williams | 7 | 42 | 6.0 | 0 |
| Stephens | 5 | 31 | 6.2 | 0 |
| E. Thompson | 4 | 33 | 8.3 | 0 |
| Valerio | 1 | 1 | 1.0 | 1 |

### PUNT RETURNS

| Last Name | No. | Yds | Avg | TD |
|---|---|---|---|---|
| Carter | 27 | 247 | 9.1 | 0 |
| Birden | 5 | 43 | 8.6 | 0 |
| Hughes | 3 | 49 | 16.3 | 0 |
| Mincy | 2 | 9 | 4.5 | 0 |

### KICKOFF RETURNS

| Last Name | No. | Yds | Avg | TD |
|---|---|---|---|---|
| Hughes | 14 | 266 | 19.0 | 0 |
| Dickerson | 11 | 237 | 21.5 | 0 |
| F. Jones | 9 | 156 | 17.3 | 0 |
| Stephens | 5 | 88 | 17.6 | 0 |
| H. Williams | 3 | 53 | 17.7 | 0 |
| Anders | 1 | 47 | 47.0 | 0 |
| McNair | 1 | 28 | 28.0 | 0 |
| Marts | 1 | 0 | 0.0 | 0 |
| Birden | 0 | 0 | — | 0 |

### PASSING — PUNTING — KICKING Statistics

| PASSING | Att | Cmp | % | Yds | Yd/Att | TD | Int | — % | RK |
|---|---|---|---|---|---|---|---|---|---|
| Montana | 298 | 181 | 60.7 | 2144 | 7.19 | 13 | 7 | —2.3 | 2 |
| Krieg | 189 | 105 | 55.6 | 1238 | 6.55 | 7 | 3 | —1.6 | |
| Blundin | 3 | 1 | 33.3 | 2 | 0.67 | 0 | 0 | —0.0 | |
| Anders | 0 | 0 | 0.0 | 0 | 0.00 | 0 | 0 | —0.0 | |

| PUNTING | No. | Avg. |
|---|---|---|
| Barker | 77 | 42.1 |

| KICKING | XP | Att. | % | FG | Att | % |
|---|---|---|---|---|---|---|
| Lowery | 37 | 37 | 100 | 23 | 29 | 79 |

## LOS ANGELES RAIDERS

### RUSHING

| Last Name | No. | Yds | Avg | TD |
|---|---|---|---|---|
| Robinson | 156 | 591 | 3.8 | 1 |
| Hostetler | 55 | 202 | 3.7 | 5 |
| Bell | 67 | 180 | 2.7 | 1 |
| S. Smith | 47 | 156 | 3.3 | 0 |
| McCallum | 37 | 114 | 3.1 | 3 |
| Montgomery | 37 | 106 | 2.9 | 0 |
| Evans | 15 | 51 | 3.6 | 0 |
| Jordan | 12 | 33 | 2.8 | 0 |
| Brown | 2 | 7 | 3.5 | 0 |
| Jett | 1 | 0 | 0.0 | 0 |
| Ismail | 4 | -5 | -1.3 | 0 |
| Gossett | 1 | -10 | -10.0 | 0 |

### RECEIVING

| Last Name | No. | Yds | Avg | TD |
|---|---|---|---|---|
| Brown | 80 | 1180 | 14.8 | 7 |
| Horton | 43 | 467 | 10.9 | 1 |
| Jett | 33 | 771 | 23.4 | 3 |
| Wright | 27 | 462 | 17.1 | 4 |
| Ismail | 26 | 353 | 13.6 | 1 |
| S. Smith | 18 | 187 | 10.4 | 0 |
| Robinson | 15 | 142 | 9.5 | 0 |
| Bell | 11 | 111 | 10.1 | 0 |
| Montgomery | 10 | 43 | 4.3 | 0 |
| Gault | 8 | 64 | 8.0 | 0 |
| Glover | 4 | 55 | 13.8 | 1 |
| Jordan | 4 | 42 | 10.5 | 0 |
| McCallum | 2 | 5 | 2.5 | 0 |

### PUNT RETURNS

| Last Name | No. | Yds | Avg | TD |
|---|---|---|---|---|
| T. Brown | 40 | 465 | 11.6 | 1 |

### KICKOFF RETURNS

| Last Name | No. | Yds | Avg | TD |
|---|---|---|---|---|
| Ismail | 25 | 605 | 24.2 | 0 |
| Wright | 10 | 167 | 16.7 | 0 |
| Gault | 7 | 187 | 26.7 | 0 |
| Robinson | 4 | 57 | 14.3 | 0 |
| Peat | 2 | 18 | 9.0 | 0 |
| K. Smith | 2 | 15 | 7.5 | 0 |
| McCallum | 1 | 12 | 12.0 | 0 |
| Turk | 1 | 0 | 0.0 | 0 |

### PASSING — PUNTING — KICKING

| PASSING | Att | Cmp | % | Yds | Yd/Att | TD | Int | — % | RK |
|---|---|---|---|---|---|---|---|---|---|
| Hostetler | 419 | 236 | 56.2 | 3242 | 7.71 | 14 | 10 | —2.4 | 6 |
| Evans | 76 | 45 | 59.2 | 640 | 8.42 | 3 | 4 | —5.3 | |

| PUNTING | No. | Avg. |
|---|---|---|
| Gossett | 71 | 41.8 |

| KICKING | XP | ATT | % | FG | ATT | % |
|---|---|---|---|---|---|---|
| Jaeger | 27 | 29 | 93 | 35 | 44 | 80 |

## DENVER BRONCOS

### RUSHING

| Last Name | No. | Yds | Avg | TD |
|---|---|---|---|---|
| Bernstine | 223 | 816 | 3.7 | 4 |
| Delpino | 131 | 445 | 3.4 | 8 |
| Milburn | 52 | 231 | 4.4 | 0 |
| Elway | 44 | 153 | 3.5 | 0 |
| Rivers | 15 | 50 | 3.3 | 1 |
| Rouen | 1 | 0 | 0.0 | 0 |
| Maddox | 2 | -2 | -1.0 | 0 |

### RECEIVING

| Last Name | No. | Yds | Avg | TD |
|---|---|---|---|---|
| Sharpe | 81 | 995 | 12.3 | 9 |
| Russell | 44 | 719 | 16.3 | 3 |
| Bernstine | 44 | 372 | 8.5 | 0 |
| Milburn | 38 | 300 | 7.9 | 3 |
| V. Johnson | 36 | 517 | 14.4 | 5 |
| Marshall | 28 | 360 | 12.9 | 2 |
| Delpino | 26 | 195 | 7.5 | 0 |
| R. Johnson | 20 | 243 | 12.2 | 1 |
| Tillman | 17 | 193 | 11.4 | 2 |
| Kimbrough | 8 | 79 | 9.9 | 0 |
| Rivers | 6 | 59 | 9.8 | 1 |
| K. Taylor | 1 | 28 | 28.0 | 0 |
| Wyman | 1 | 1 | 1.0 | 1 |

### PUNT RETURNS

| Last Name | No. | Yds | Avg | TD |
|---|---|---|---|---|
| Milburn | 40 | 425 | 10.6 | 0 |
| Bradford | 1 | 0 | 0.0 | 0 |

### KICKOFF RETURNS

| Last Name | No. | Yds | Avg | TD |
|---|---|---|---|---|
| Russell | 18 | 374 | 20.8 | 0 |
| Milburn | 12 | 188 | 15.7 | 0 |
| Delpino | 7 | 146 | 20.9 | 0 |
| Meeks | 1 | 9 | 9.0 | 0 |
| Sharpe | 1 | 0 | 0.0 | 0 |

### PASSING — PUNTING — KICKING

| PASSING | Att | Cmp | % | Yds | Yd/Att | TD | Int | — % | RK |
|---|---|---|---|---|---|---|---|---|---|
| Elway | 551 | 348 | 63.2 | 4030 | 7.31 | 25 | 10 | —1.8 | 1 |
| Maddox | 1 | 1 | 100.0 | 1 | 1.00 | 1 | 0 | —0.0 | |
| Marshall | 1 | 1 | 100.0 | 30 | 30.00 | 1 | 0 | —0.0 | |

| PUNTING | No. | Avg. |
|---|---|---|
| Rouen | 68 | 44.4 |

| KICKING | XP | ATT | % | FG | ATT | % |
|---|---|---|---|---|---|---|
| Elam | 41 | 42 | 98 | 26 | 35 | 74 |

## SAN DIEGO CHARGERS

### RUSHING

| Last Name | No. | Yds | Avg | TD |
|---|---|---|---|---|
| Butts | 185 | 746 | 4.0 | 4 |
| Means | 160 | 645 | 4.0 | 8 |
| Harmon | 46 | 216 | 4.7 | 0 |
| Bieniemy | 33 | 135 | 4.1 | 1 |
| Jefferson | 5 | 53 | 10.6 | 0 |
| Humphries | 8 | 37 | 4.6 | 0 |
| Friesz | 10 | 3 | 0.3 | 0 |
| Lewis | 3 | 2 | 0.7 | 0 |
| Hendrickson | 1 | 0 | 0.0 | 0 |
| Miller | 1 | 0 | 0.0 | 0 |
| Kidd | 3 | -13 | -4.3 | 1 |

### RECEIVING

| Last Name | No. | Yds | Avg | TD |
|---|---|---|---|---|
| A. Miller | 84 | 1162 | 13.8 | 7 |
| Harmon | 73 | 671 | 9.2 | 2 |
| Lewis | 38 | 463 | 12.2 | 4 |
| Jefferson | 30 | 391 | 13.0 | 2 |
| Walker | 21 | 212 | 10.1 | 1 |
| Butts | 15 | 105 | 7.0 | 0 |
| Pupunu | 13 | 142 | 10.9 | 0 |
| Barnes | 10 | 137 | 13.7 | 0 |
| Means | 10 | 59 | 5.9 | 0 |
| Young | 6 | 41 | 6.8 | 2 |
| Bieniemy | 1 | 0 | 0.0 | 0 |

### PUNT RETURNS

| Last Name | No. | Yds | Avg | TD |
|---|---|---|---|---|
| Gordon | 31 | 395 | 12.7 | 0 |
| Lewis | 3 | 17 | 5.7 | 0 |

### KICKOFF RETURNS

| Last Name | No. | Yds | Avg | TD |
|---|---|---|---|---|
| Lewis | 33 | 684 | 20.7 | 0 |
| Bieniemy | 7 | 110 | 15.7 | 0 |
| A. Miller | 2 | 42 | 21.0 | 0 |
| Hendrickson | 2 | 25 | 12.5 | 0 |
| Means | 2 | 22 | 11.0 | 0 |
| Harmon | 1 | 18 | 18.0 | 0 |

### PASSING — PUNTING — KICKING

| PASSING | Att | Cmp | % | Yds | Yd/Att | TD | Int | — % | RK |
|---|---|---|---|---|---|---|---|---|---|
| Humphries | 324 | 173 | 53.4 | 1981 | 6.11 | 12 | 10 | —3.1 | 13 |
| Friesz | 238 | 128 | 53.8 | 1402 | 5.89 | 6 | 4 | —2.5 | 12 |
| Means | 1 | 0 | 0.0 | 0 | 0.00 | 0 | 0 | —0.0 | |

| PUNTING | No. | Avg. |
|---|---|---|
| Kidd | 57 | 42.6 |
| Sullivan | 15 | 40.9 |
| Carney | 4 | 38.8 |

| KICKING | XP | Att | % | FG | Att | % |
|---|---|---|---|---|---|---|
| Carney | 31 | 33 | 94 | 31 | 40 | 78 |

## SEATTLE SEAHAWKS

### RUSHING

| Last Name | No. | Yds | Avg | TD |
|---|---|---|---|---|
| C. Warren | 273 | 1072 | 3.9 | 7 |
| Williams | 82 | 371 | 4.5 | 3 |
| Mirer | 68 | 343 | 5.0 | 3 |
| Vaughn | 36 | 153 | 4.3 | 0 |
| Blades | 5 | 52 | 10.4 | 0 |
| Bates | 2 | 12 | 6.0 | 0 |
| Johnson | 2 | 8 | 4.0 | 0 |
| D. Thomas | 1 | 4 | 4.0 | 0 |
| Mayes | 1 | 2 | 2.0 | 0 |
| Martin | 1 | 0 | 0.0 | 0 |
| Gelbaugh | 1 | -1 | -1.0 | 0 |
| McGwire | 1 | -1 | -1.0 | 0 |

### RECEIVING

| Last Name | No. | Yds | Avg | TD |
|---|---|---|---|---|
| Blades | 80 | 945 | 11.8 | 3 |
| Williams | 58 | 450 | 7.8 | 1 |
| Martin | 57 | 798 | 14.0 | 5 |
| Edmunds | 24 | 239 | 10.0 | 2 |
| Green | 23 | 178 | 7.7 | 1 |
| C. Warren | 15 | 99 | 6.6 | 0 |
| D. Thomas | 11 | 95 | 8.6 | 0 |
| R. Thomas | 7 | 67 | 9.6 | 0 |
| Johnson | 3 | 15 | 5.0 | 1 |
| Bates | 1 | 6 | 6.0 | 0 |
| Roberts | 1 | 4 | 4.0 | 0 |

### PUNT RETURNS

| Last Name | No. | Yds | Avg | TD |
|---|---|---|---|---|
| Martin | 32 | 270 | 8.4 | 0 |
| McCloughan | 1 | 10 | 10.0 | 0 |

### KICKOFF RETURNS

| Last Name | No. | Yds | Avg | TD |
|---|---|---|---|---|
| Bates | 30 | 603 | 20.1 | 0 |
| Vaughn | 16 | 280 | 17.5 | 0 |
| Martin | 3 | 38 | 12.7 | 0 |
| Tuatagaloa | 1 | 10 | 10.0 | 0 |

### PASSING — PUNTING — KICKING

| PASSING | Att | Cmp | % | Yds | Yd/Att | TD | Int | — % | RK |
|---|---|---|---|---|---|---|---|---|---|
| Mirer | 486 | 274 | 56.4 | 2833 | 5.83 | 12 | 17 | —3.5 | 14 |
| McGwire | 5 | 3 | 60.0 | 24 | 4.80 | 1 | 0 | —0.0 | |
| Gelbaugh | 5 | 3 | 60.0 | 39 | 7.80 | 0 | 1 | —20.0 | |
| Tuten | 1 | 0 | 0.0 | 0 | 0.00 | 0 | 0 | —0.0 | |
| Williams | 1 | 0 | 0.0 | 0 | 0.00 | 0 | 0 | —0.0 | |

| PUNTING | No. | Avg. |
|---|---|---|
| Tuten | 91 | 44.0 |

| KICKING | XP | ATT | % | FG | ATT | % |
|---|---|---|---|---|---|---|
| Kasay | 29 | 29 | 100 | 23 | 28 | 82 |

# 1993 A.F.C. — WILD-CARD PLAYOFFS

## January 8, 1994 at Kansas City, Mo. (Attendance 74,515)

### SCORING

| | | | | | | |
|---|---|---|---|---|---|---|
| PITTSBURGH | 7 | 10 | 0 | 7 | 0 - 24 |
| KANSAS CITY | 7 | 0 | 3 | 14 | 3 - 27 |

**First Quarter**
Pitt.  Cooper, 10 yard pass from O'Donnell
PAT — Anderson (kick)
K.C.  Birden, 23 yard pass from Krieg
PAT — Lowery (kick)

**Second Quarter**
Pitt.  Anderson, 30 yard field goal
Pitt.  Mills, 26 yard pass from O'Donnell
PAT — Anderson (kick)

**Third Quarter**
K.C.  Lowery, 23 yard field goal

**Fourth Quarter**
K.C.  Allen, 2 yard run
PAT — Lowery (kick)
Pitt.  Green, 22 yard pass from O'Donnell
PAT — Anderson (kick)
K.C.  Barnett, 7 yard pass from Montana
PAT — Lowery (kick)

**Overtime**
K.C.  Lowery, 32 yard field goal

### TEAM STATISTICS

| PITT. | | K.C. |
|---|---|---|
| 21 | First Downs- Total | 28 |
| 5 | First Downs- Rushing | 7 |
| 15 | First Downs- Passing | 19 |
| 1 | First Downs- Penalty | 2 |
| 1 | Fumbles- Number | 0 |
| 0 | Fumbles- Lost Ball | 0 |
| 5 | Penalties- Number | 5 |
| 40 | Yards Penalized | 25 |
| 0 | Missed Field Goals | 0 |
| 80 | Offensive Plays | 81 |
| 369 | Net Yards | 401 |
| 4.6 | Average Gain | 5.0 |
| 0 | Giveaways | 0 |
| 0 | Takeaways | 0 |
| 0 | Difference | 0 |

### INDIVIDUAL STATISTICS

**PITTSBURGH** / **KANSAS CITY**

#### RUSHING

| | No. | Yds. | Avg. | | No. | Yds. | Avg. |
|---|---|---|---|---|---|---|---|
| Thompson | 25 | 60 | 2.4 | Allen | 21 | 67 | 3.2 |
| Hoge | 6 | 27 | 4.5 | Anders | 5 | 27 | 5.4 |
| Stone | 3 | 11 | 3.7 | Montana | 4 | 13 | 3.3 |
| O'Donnell | 1 | -1 | -1.0 | McNair | 2 | 9 | 4.5 |
| | 35 | 97 | 2.8 | F. Jones | 1 | 9 | 9.0 |
| | | | | | 33 | 125 | 3.8 |

#### RECEIVING

| | No. | Yds. | Avg. | | No. | Yds. | Avg. |
|---|---|---|---|---|---|---|---|
| Graham | 7 | 96 | 13.7 | Cash | 7 | 56 | 8.0 |
| Mills | 4 | 60 | 15.0 | Birden | 6 | 72 | 12.0 |
| Hoge | 3 | 43 | 14.3 | Allen | 4 | 29 | 7.3 |
| Stone | 3 | 36 | 12.0 | Anders | 3 | 30 | 10.0 |
| Thompson | 3 | 4 | 1.3 | Barnett | 3 | 30 | 10.0 |
| Green | 2 | 37 | 18.5 | W. Davis | 2 | 47 | 23.5 |
| Cooper | 1 | 10 | 10.0 | Hayes | 2 | 11 | 5.5 |
| | 23 | 286 | 11.4 | Hughes | 1 | 15 | 15.0 |
| | | | | McNair | 1 | 9 | 9.0 |
| | | | | | 29 | 299 | 10.3 |

#### PUNTING

| | | | | | | | |
|---|---|---|---|---|---|---|---|
| Royals | 6 | | 44.7 | Barker | 6 | | 44.8 |

#### PUNT RETURNS

| | No. | Yds. | Avg. | | No. | Yds. | Avg. |
|---|---|---|---|---|---|---|---|
| Woodson | 3 | 18 | 6.0 | Hughes | 3 | 31 | 10.3 |
| | | | | Birden | 1 | 5 | 5.0 |
| | | | | | 4 | 36 | 9.0 |

#### KICKOFF RETURNS

| | No. | Yds. | Avg. | | No. | Yds. | Avg. |
|---|---|---|---|---|---|---|---|
| Woodson | 3 | 66 | 22.0 | Stephens | 3 | 72 | 24.0 |
| Stone | 1 | 18 | 18.0 | Hughes | 2 | 42 | 21.0 |
| Cuthbert | 1 | 13 | 13.0 | McNair | 1 | 13 | 13.0 |
| | 5 | 97 | 19.4 | | 6 | 127 | 21.2 |

#### INTERCEPTION RETURNS

None / None

#### PASSING

**PITTSBURGH**

| | Att. | Comp. | Comp. Pct. | Yds. | Int. | Yds./ Att. | Yds./ Comp. |
|---|---|---|---|---|---|---|---|
| O'Donnell | 42 | 23 | 54.8 | 286 | 0 | 6.8 | 12.4 |

**KANSAS CITY**

| | Att. | Comp. | Comp. Pct. | Yds. | Int. | Yds./ Att. | Yds./ Comp. |
|---|---|---|---|---|---|---|---|
| Montana | 43 | 28 | 65.1 | 276 | 0 | 6.4 | 12.4 |
| Krieg | 1 | 1 | 100.0 | 23 | 0 | 23.0 | 23.0 |
| | 44 | 29 | 65.9 | 299 | 0 | 6.8 | 10.3 |

---

## January 9, 1994 at Los Angeles (Attendance 65,314)

### SCORING

| | | | | | |
|---|---|---|---|---|---|
| DENVER | 7 | 14 | 0 | 3 - 24 |
| L.A. RAIDERS | 14 | 7 | 14 | 7 - 42 |

**First Quarter**
L.A.Rd.  Horton, 9 yard pass from Hostetler
PAT — Jaeger (kick)
Den.  Sharpe, 23 yard pass from Elway
PAT — Elam (kick)
L.A.Rd.  T. Brown, 65 yard pass from Hostetler
PAT — Jaeger (kick)

**Second Quarter**
Den.  R. Johnson, 16 yard pass from Elway
PAT — Elam (kick)
L.A.Rd.  Jett, 54 yard pass from Hostetler
PAT — Jaeger (kick)
Den.  Russell, 6 yard pass from Elway
PAT — Elway (kick)

**Third Quarter**
L.A.Rd.  McCallum, 26 yard run
PAT — Jaeger (kick)
L.A.Rd.  McCallum, 2 yard run
PAT — Jaeger (kick)

**Fourth Quarter**
Den.  Elam, 33 yard field goal
L.A.Rd.  McCallum, 1 yard run
PAT — Jaeger (kick)

### TEAM STATISTICS

| DEN. | | L.A.Rd. |
|---|---|---|
| 26 | First Downs- Total | 19 |
| 4 | First Downs- Rushing | 6 |
| 18 | First Downs- Passing | 10 |
| 4 | First Downs- Penalty | 3 |
| 2 | Fumbles- Number | 0 |
| 0 | Fumbles- Lost Ball | 0 |
| 10 | Penalties- Number | 17 |
| 97 | Yards Penalized | 130 |
| 0 | Missed Field Goals | 0 |
| 73 | Offensive Plays | 53 |
| 387 | Net Yards | 427 |
| 5.3 | Average Gain | 8.1 |
| 1 | Giveaways | 0 |
| 0 | Takeaways | 1 |
| -1 | Difference | + 1 |

### INDIVIDUAL STATISTICS

**DENVER** / **L.A. RAIDERS**

#### RUSHING

| | No. | Yds. | Avg. | | No. | Yds. | Avg. |
|---|---|---|---|---|---|---|---|
| Delpino | 9 | 32 | 3.6 | McCallum | 13 | 81 | 6.2 |
| Elway | 5 | 23 | 4.6 | Montgomery | 15 | 50 | 3.3 |
| Rivers | 1 | 2 | 2.0 | Hostetler | 4 | 5 | 1.3 |
| Maddox | 1 | 1 | 1.0 | | 32 | 136 | 4.3 |
| Milburn | 2 | -2 | -1.0 | | | | |
| | 18 | 56 | 3.1 | | | | |

#### RECEIVING

| | No. | Yds. | Avg. | | No. | Yds. | Avg. |
|---|---|---|---|---|---|---|---|
| Sharpe | 13 | 156 | 12.0 | Jett | 3 | 111 | 37.0 |
| Marshall | 5 | 69 | 13.8 | T. Brown | 3 | 86 | 28.7 |
| Milburn | 5 | 8 | 1.6 | Horton | 3 | 45 | 15.0 |
| Russell | 2 | 31 | 15.5 | Montgomery | 3 | 29 | 9.7 |
| Tillman | 2 | 25 | 12.5 | Wright | 1 | 23 | 23.0 |
| R. Johnson | 2 | 19 | 9.5 | | 13 | 294 | 22.6 |
| Taylor | 1 | 13 | 13.0 | | | | |
| Rivers | 1 | 8 | 8.0 | | | | |
| Evans | 1 | 7 | 7.0 | | | | |
| | 32 | 336 | 10.5 | | | | |

#### PUNTING

| | | | | | | | |
|---|---|---|---|---|---|---|---|
| Rouen | 4 | | 33.8 | Gossett | 4 | | 42.5 |

#### PUNT RETURNS

| | No. | Yds. | Avg. | | |
|---|---|---|---|---|---|
| Milburn | 3 | 38 | 12.7 | None | |

#### KICKOFF RETURNS

| | No. | Yds. | Avg. | | No. | Yds. | Avg. |
|---|---|---|---|---|---|---|---|
| Milburn | 6 | 85 | 14.2 | Gault | 4 | 55 | 13.8 |

#### INTERCEPTION RETURNS

| | | | | | No. | Yds. | Avg. |
|---|---|---|---|---|---|---|---|
| None | | | | Dorn | 1 | 1 | 1.0 |

#### PASSING

**DENVER**

| | Att. | Comp. | Comp. Pct. | Yds. | Int. | Yds./ Att. | Yds./ Comp. |
|---|---|---|---|---|---|---|---|
| Elway | 47 | 29 | 61.7 | 302 | 1 | 6.4 | 10.4 |
| Maddox | 7 | 3 | 42.9 | 34 | 0 | 4.9 | 11.3 |

**L.A. RAIDERS**

| | Att. | Comp. | Comp. Pct. | Yds. | Int. | Yds./ Att. | Yds./ Comp. |
|---|---|---|---|---|---|---|---|
| Hostetler | 19 | 13 | 68.4 | 294 | 0 | 15.5 | 22.6 |

January 8, 1994 at Pontiac, Mich. (Attendance 68,479)

## SCORING

| | | | | | |
|---|---|---|---|---|---|
| **GREEN BAY** | 0 | 7 | 14 | 7 | - 28 |
| **DETROIT** | 3 | 7 | 7 | 7 | - 24 |

**First Quarter**
Det.  Lohmiller, 47 yard field goal

**Second Quarter**
G.B.  Sharpe, 12 yard pass from Favre
PAT — Jacke (kick)
Det.  Perriman, 1 yard pass from Kramer
PAT — Hanson (kick)

**Third Quarter**
Det.  Jenkins, 15 yard interception return
PAT — Hanson (kick)
G.B.  Sharpe, 28 yard pass from Favre
PAT — Jacke (kick)
G.B.  Teague, 101 yard interception return
PAT — Jacke (kick)

**Fourth Quarter**
Det.  D. Moore, 5 yard run
PAT — Hanson (kick)
G.B.  Sharpe, 40 yard pass from Favre
PAT — Jacke (kick)

## TEAM STATISTICS

| G.B. | | DET. |
|---|---|---|
| 16 | First Downs- Total | 25 |
| 6 | First Downs- Rushing | 9 |
| 10 | First Downs- Passing | 14 |
| 0 | First Downs- Penalty | 2 |
| 2 | Fumbles- Number | 2 |
| 0 | Fumbles- Lost Ball | 0 |
| 6 | Penalties- Number | 5 |
| 49 | Yards Penalized | 35 |
| 0 | Missed Field Goals | 0 |
| 51 | Offensive Plays | 64 |
| 293 | Net Yards | 410 |
| 5.7 | Average Gain | 6.4 |
| 1 | Giveaways | 2 |
| 2 | Takeaways | 1 |
| + 1 | Difference | - 1 |

## INDIVIDUAL STATISTICS

### GREEN BAY / DETROIT

#### RUSHING

| GREEN BAY | No. | Yds. | Avg. | DETROIT | No. | Yds. | Avg. |
|---|---|---|---|---|---|---|---|
| Thompson | 12 | 41 | 3.4 | Sanders | 27 | 169 | 6.3 |
| Bennett | 9 | 30 | 3.3 | D. Moore | 1 | 5 | 5.0 |
| Favre | 4 | 18 | 4.5 | E. Kramer | 1 | 1 | 1.0 |
| | 25 | 89 | 3.6 | | 29 | 175 | 6.0 |

#### RECEIVING

| GREEN BAY | No. | Yds. | Avg. | DETROIT | No. | Yds. | Avg. |
|---|---|---|---|---|---|---|---|
| Sharpe | 5 | 101 | 20.2 | Perriman | 10 | 150 | 15.0 |
| West | 3 | 40 | 13.3 | D. Moore | 4 | 14 | 3.5 |
| Thompson | 3 | 32 | 10.7 | Holman | 3 | 31 | 10.3 |
| Bennett | 2 | 21 | 10.5 | Green | 2 | 33 | 16.5 |
| Clayton | 1 | 9 | 9.0 | Sanders | 2 | 0 | 0.0 |
| Brooks | 1 | 1 | 1.0 | H. Moore | 1 | 20 | 20.0 |
| | 15 | 204 | 13.6 | | 22 | 248 | 11.3 |

#### PUNTING

| | No. | | Avg. | | No. | | Avg. |
|---|---|---|---|---|---|---|---|
| Wagner | 4 | | 40.3 | Arnold | 3 | | 48.3 |

#### PUNT RETURNS

| | No. | Yds. | Avg. | | No. | Yds. | Avg. |
|---|---|---|---|---|---|---|---|
| Brooks | 2 | 43 | 21.5 | Gray | 1 | 22 | 22.0 |

#### KICKOFF RETURNS

| | No. | Yds. | Avg. | | No. | Yds. | Avg. |
|---|---|---|---|---|---|---|---|
| C. Harris | 3 | 89 | 29.7 | Gray | 4 | 44 | 11.0 |
| | | | | D. Moore | 1 | 20 | 20.0 |
| | | | | | 5 | 64 | 12.8 |

#### INTERCEPTION RETURNS

| | No. | Yds. | Avg. | | No. | Yds. | Avg. |
|---|---|---|---|---|---|---|---|
| Teague | 1 | 101 | 101.0 | Jenkins | 1 | 15 | 15.0 |
| Buckley | 1 | 0 | 0.0 | | | | |
| | 2 | 101 | 50.5 | | | | |

#### PASSING

| GREEN BAY | Att. | Comp. | Comp. Pct. | Yds. | Int. | Yds./ Att. | Yds./ Comp. |
|---|---|---|---|---|---|---|---|
| Favre | 26 | 15 | 57.7 | 204 | 1 | 7.8 | 7.8 |

| DETROIT | Att. | Comp. | Comp. Pct. | Yds. | Int. | Yds./ Att. | Yds./ Comp. |
|---|---|---|---|---|---|---|---|
| Kramer | 31 | 22 | 71.0 | 248 | 2 | 8.0 | 11.3 |

---

January 9, 1994 at East Rutherford, N.J. (Attendance 77,328)

## SCORING

| | | | | | |
|---|---|---|---|---|---|
| **MINNESOTA** | 0 | 10 | 0 | 0 | - 10 |
| **N.Y. GIANTS** | 3 | 0 | 14 | 0 | - 17 |

**First Quarter**
N.Y.G.  Treadwell, 26 yard field goal

**Second Quarter**
Minn.  C. Carter, 40 yard pass from McMahon
PAT — Reveiz (kick)
Minn.  Reveiz, 52 yard field goal

**Third Quarter**
N.Y.G.  Hampton, 51 yard run
PAT — Treadwell (kick)
N.Y.G.  Hampton, 2 yard run
PAT — Treadwell (kick)

## TEAM STATISTICS

| MINN. | | N.Y.G. |
|---|---|---|
| 11 | First Downs- Total | 17 |
| 4 | First Downs- Rushing | 10 |
| 6 | First Downs- Passing | 6 |
| 1 | First Downs- Penalty | 1 |
| 2 | Fumbles- Number | 0 |
| 1 | Fumbles- Lost Ball | 0 |
| 6 | Penalties- Number | 2 |
| 28 | Yards Penalized | 20 |
| 0 | Missed Field Goals | 1 |
| 59 | Offensive Plays | 67 |
| 260 | Net Yards | 270 |
| 4.4 | Average Gain | 4.0 |
| 1 | Giveaways | 0 |
| 0 | Takeaways | 1 |
| - 1 | Difference | + 1 |

## INDIVIDUAL STATISTICS

### MINNESOTA / NEW YORK GIANTS

#### RUSHING

| MINNESOTA | No. | Yds. | Avg. | NEW YORK GIANTS | No. | Yds. | Avg. |
|---|---|---|---|---|---|---|---|
| Graham | 19 | 69 | 3.6 | Hampton | 33 | 161 | 4.9 |
| McMahon | 1 | 5 | 5.0 | Simms | 4 | 14 | 3.5 |
| A. Carter | 1 | 4 | 4.0 | Bunch | 1 | 1 | 1.0 |
| Craig | 1 | 1 | 1.0 | M. Jackson | 1 | 1 | 1.0 |
| | 22 | 79 | 3.6 | Tillman | 2 | -1 | -0.5 |
| | | | | | 41 | 176 | 4.3 |

#### RECEIVING

| MINNESOTA | No. | Yds. | Avg. | NEW YORK GIANTS | No. | Yds. | Avg. |
|---|---|---|---|---|---|---|---|
| C. Carter | 4 | 83 | 20.8 | Hampton | 6 | 24 | 4.0 |
| Jordan | 4 | 31 | 7.8 | Meggett | 4 | 12 | 3.0 |
| A. Carter | 2 | 37 | 18.5 | Calloway | 2 | 30 | 15.0 |
| Graham | 2 | 19 | 9.5 | Cross | 2 | 11 | 5.5 |
| Reed | 2 | 16 | 8.0 | M. Jackson | 2 | 9 | 4.5 |
| Ismail | 1 | 6 | 6.0 | Pierce | 1 | 8 | 8.0 |
| | 15 | 192 | 12.1 | | 17 | 94 | 5.5 |

#### PUNTING

| | No. | | Avg. | | No. | | Avg. |
|---|---|---|---|---|---|---|---|
| Newsome | 8 | | 37.8 | Horan | 7 | | 32.0 |

#### PUNT RETURNS

| | No. | Yds. | Avg. | | No. | Yds. | Avg. |
|---|---|---|---|---|---|---|---|
| A. Carter | 2 | 22 | 11.0 | Meggett | 2 | 5 | 2.5 |
| A. Parker | 2FC | | | | | | |

#### KICKOFF RETURNS

| | No. | Yds. | Avg. | | No. | Yds. | Avg. |
|---|---|---|---|---|---|---|---|
| Ismail | 4 | 47 | 11.8 | Calloway | 1 | 12 | 12.0 |
| | | | | Meggett | 1 | 0 | 0.0 |
| | | | | | 2 | 12 | 6.0 |

#### INTERCEPTIONS

| MINNESOTA | NEW YORK GIANTS |
|---|---|
| None | None |

#### PASSING

| MINNESOTA | Att. | Comp. | Comp. Pct. | Yds. | Int. | Yds./ Att. | Yds./ Comp. |
|---|---|---|---|---|---|---|---|
| McMahon | 25 | 12 | 48.0 | 145 | 0 | 5.8 | 12.1 |
| Salisbury | 9 | 3 | 33.3 | 47 | 0 | 5.2 | 15.7 |
| | 34 | 15 | 44.1 | 192 | 0 | 5.6 | 12.8 |

| NEW YORK GIANTS | Att. | Comp. | Comp. Pct. | Yds. | Int. | Yds./ Att. | Yds./ Comp. |
|---|---|---|---|---|---|---|---|
| Simms | 26 | 17 | 65.4 | 94 | 0 | 3.6 | 5.5 |

January 15, 1994 at Orchard Park, N.Y. (Attendance 61,923)

### SCORING

| | | | | | |
|---|---|---|---|---|---|
| L.A. RAIDERS | 0 | 17 | 6 | 0 | - 23 |
| BUFFALO | 0 | 13 | 9 | 7 | - 29 |

**Second Quarter**
L.A.Rd.   Jaeger, 30 yard field goal
Buff.   Davis, 1 yard run
    PAT — Christie (kick)
L.A.Rd.   McCallum, 1 yard run
    PAT — Jaeger (kick)
L.A. Rd.   McCallum, 1 yard run
    PAT — Jaeger (kick)
Buff.   Thomas, 8 yard run
    PAT — Christie (kick)

**Third Quarter**
Buff.   Brooks, 25 yard pass from Kelly
    PAT — Christie kick blocked
Buff.   Christie, 29 yard field goal
L.A. Rd.   T. Brown, 86 yard pass from Hostetler
    PAT — Jaeger kick no good

**Fourth Quarter**
Buff.   Brooks, 22 yard pass from Kelly
    PAT — Christie (kick)

### TEAM STATISTICS

| L.A.Rd. | | BUFF. |
|---|---|---|
| 15 | First Downs- Total | 25 |
| 9 | First Downs- Rushing | 7 |
| 6 | First Downs- Passing | 14 |
| 0 | First Downs- Penalty | 4 |
| 2 | Fumbles- Number | 3 |
| 1 | Fumbles- Lost Ball | 1 |
| 9 | Penalties- Number | 2 |
| 77 | Yards Penalized | 15 |
| 1 | Missed Field Goals | 1 |
| 57 | Offensive Plays | 70 |
| 325 | Net Yards | 355 |
| 5.7 | Average Gain | 5.1 |
| 1 | Giveaways | 1 |
| 1 | Takeaways | 1 |
| 0 | Difference | 0 |

### INDIVIDUAL STATISTICS

**L.A. RAIDERS**     **BUFFALO**

#### RUSHING

| | No. | Yds. | Avg. | | No. | Yds. | Avg. |
|---|---|---|---|---|---|---|---|
| Montgomery | 9 | 22 | 2.4 | Thomas | 14 | 44 | 3.1 |
| Hostetler | 5 | 29 | 5.8 | K. Davis | 11 | 36 | 3.3 |
| McCallum | 19 | 56 | 2.9 | Kelly | 5 | -5 | -1.0 |
| Bell | 2 | 3 | 1.5 | | 30 | 75 | 2.5 |
| | 35 | 110 | 3.1 | | | | |

#### RECEIVING

| | No. | Yds. | Avg. | | No. | Yds. | Avg. |
|---|---|---|---|---|---|---|---|
| T. Brown | 5 | 127 | 25.4 | Brooks | 6 | 96 | 16.0 |
| Montgomery | 3 | 26 | 8.7 | Thomas | 6 | 48 | 8.0 |
| Horton | 2 | 42 | 21.0 | Metzelaars | 5 | 43 | 8.6 |
| McCallum | 1 | 15 | 15.0 | Reed | 4 | 53 | 13.3 |
| Bell | 1 | 12 | 12.0 | McKeller | 3 | 21 | 7.0 |
| Duff | 1 | 5 | 5.0 | K. Davis | 1 | 16 | 16.0 |
| Jett | 1 | 3 | 3.0 | Beebe | 1 | 9 | 9.0 |
| | 14 | 230 | 16.4 | Gardner | 1 | 1 | 1.0 |
| | | | | | 27 | 287 | 10.6 |

#### PUNTING

| | No. | Yds. | Avg. | | No. | Yds. | Avg. |
|---|---|---|---|---|---|---|---|
| Gossett | 6 | | 37.0 | Mohr | 3 | | 36.3 |

#### PUNT RETURNS

| | No. | Yds. | Avg. | | No. | Yds. | Avg. |
|---|---|---|---|---|---|---|---|
| T. Brown | 3 | 7 | 2.3 | Copeland | 3 | 7 | 2.3 |

#### KICKOFF RETURNS

| | No. | Yds. | Avg. | | No. | Yds. | Avg. |
|---|---|---|---|---|---|---|---|
| Ismail | 3 | 51 | 17.0 | Tasker | 1 | 67 | 67.0 |
| Gault | 2 | 22 | 11.0 | Copeland | 2 | 35 | 17.5 |
| Turk | 1 | 10 | 10.0 | Beebe | 1 | 9 | 9.0 |
| | 6 | 83 | 13.8 | | 4 | 111 | 27.8 |

#### INTERCEPTION RETURNS

None        None

#### PASSING

**L.A. RAIDERS**

| | Att. | Comp. | Comp. Pct. | Yds. | Int. | Yds./ Att. | Yds./ Comp. |
|---|---|---|---|---|---|---|---|
| Hostetler | 20 | 14 | 70.0 | 230 | 0 | 5.6 | 10.9 |

**BUFFALO**

| | Att. | Comp. | Comp. Pct. | Yds. | Int. | Yds./ Att. | Yds./ Comp. |
|---|---|---|---|---|---|---|---|
| Kelly | 37 | 27 | 73.0 | 287 | 0 | 7.8 | 10.6 |

---

January 16, 1994 at Houston (Attendance 64,011)

### SCORING

| | | | | | |
|---|---|---|---|---|---|
| KANSAS CITY | 0 | 0 | 7 | 21 | - 28 |
| HOUSTON | 10 | 0 | 0 | 10 | - 20 |

**First Quarter**
Hou.   Del Greco, 49 yard field goal
Hou.   G. Brown, 2 yard run
    PAT — Del Greco (kick)

**Third Quarter**
K.C.   K. Cash, 7 yard pass from Montana
    PAT — Lowery (kick)

**Fourth Quarter**
Hou.   Del Greco, 43 yard field goal
K.C.   Birden, 11 yard pass from Montana
    PAT — Lowery (kick)
K.C.   W. Davis, 18 yard pass from Montana
    PAT — Lowery (kick)
Hou.   Givins, 7 yard pass from Moon
    PAT — Del Greco (kick)
K.C.   Allen, 21 yard run
    PAT — Lowery (kick)

### TEAM STATISTICS

| K.C. | | HOU. |
|---|---|---|
| 18 | First Downs- Total | 19 |
| 3 | First Downs- Rushing | 4 |
| 14 | First Downs- Passing | 14 |
| 1 | First Downs- Penalty | 1 |
| 0 | Fumbles- Number | 7 |
| 0 | Fumbles- Lost Ball | 2 |
| 7 | Penalties- Number | 3 |
| 51 | Yards Penalized | 63 |
| 0 | Missed Field Goals | 0 |
| 58 | Offensive Plays | 66 |
| 354 | Net Yards | 277 |
| 6.1 | Average Gain | 4.2 |
| 2 | Giveaways | 3 |
| 3 | Takeaways | 2 |
| + 1 | Difference | - 1 |

### INDIVIDUAL STATISTICS

**KANSAS CITY**     **HOUSTON**

#### RUSHING

| | No. | Yds. | Avg. | | No. | Yds. | Avg. |
|---|---|---|---|---|---|---|---|
| Allen | 14 | 74 | 5.3 | Moon | 3 | 22 | 7.3 |
| Anders | 1 | 0 | 0.0 | G. Brown | 11 | 17 | 1.5 |
| Montana | 1 | -1 | -1.0 | | 14 | 39 | 2.8 |
| Krieg | 2 | -2 | -1.0 | | | | |
| | 18 | 71 | 3.9 | | | | |

#### RECEIVING

| | No. | Yds. | Avg. | | No. | Yds. | Avg. |
|---|---|---|---|---|---|---|---|
| Birden | 6 | 60 | 10.0 | Jeffires | 9 | 88 | 9.8 |
| W. Davis | 5 | 96 | 19.2 | Givins | 7 | 63 | 9.0 |
| K. Cash | 4 | 80 | 20.0 | Wellman | 6 | 80 | 13.3 |
| Barnett | 2 | 24 | 12.0 | Duncan | 6 | 49 | 8.2 |
| McNair | 2 | 9 | 4.5 | G. Brown | 4 | 26 | 6.5 |
| Allen | 1 | 12 | 12.0 | | 32 | 306 | 9.6 |
| Hayes | 1 | 9 | 9.0 | | | | |
| F. Jones | 1 | 9 | 9.0 | | | | |
| | 22 | 299 | 13.6 | | | | |

#### PUNTING

| | No. | Yds. | Avg. | | No. | Yds. | Avg. |
|---|---|---|---|---|---|---|---|
| Barker | 5 | | 45.0 | Montgomery | 5 | | 48.6 |

#### PUNT RETURNS

| | No. | Yds. | Avg. | | No. | Yds. | Avg. |
|---|---|---|---|---|---|---|---|
| Hughes | 3 | 42 | 14.0 | Drewrey | 1 | 12 | 12.0 |
| Birden | 1 | 2 | 2.0 | | | | |
| | 4 | 44 | 11.0 | | | | |

#### KICKOFF RETURNS

| | No. | Yds. | Avg. | | No. | Yds. | Avg. |
|---|---|---|---|---|---|---|---|
| Stephens | 2 | 38 | 19.0 | Drewrey | 2 | 39 | 19.5 |
| | | | | Hannah | 1 | 11 | 11.0 |
| | | | | | 3 | 50 | 16.7 |

#### INTERCEPTION RETURNS

| | No. | Yds. | Avg. | | No. | Yds. | Avg. |
|---|---|---|---|---|---|---|---|
| Mincy | 1 | 12 | 12.0 | S. Jackson | 1 | 14 | 14.0 |
| | | | | Hoage | 1 | 0 | 0.0 |
| | | | | | 2 | 14 | 7.0 |

#### PASSING

**KANSAS CITY**

| | Att. | Comp. | Comp. Pct. | Yds. | Int. | Yds./ Att. | Yds./ Comp. |
|---|---|---|---|---|---|---|---|
| Montana | 38 | 22 | 57.9 | 299 | 2 | 7.9 | 13.6 |

**HOUSTON**

| | Att. | Comp. | Comp. Pct. | Yds. | Int. | Yds./ Att. | Yds./ Comp. |
|---|---|---|---|---|---|---|---|
| Moon | 43 | 32 | 74.4 | 306 | 1 | 7.1 | 9.6 |

January 15, 1994 at San Francisco (Attendance 67,143)

## SCORING

| | | | | | | |
|---|---|---|---|---|---|---|
| N.Y. GIANTS | 0 | 3 | 0 | 0 | - | 3 |
| SAN FRANCISCO | 9 | 14 | 14 | 7 | - | 44 |

**First Quarter**
S.F. — Watters, 1 yard run
    PAT — Cofer kick failed
S.F. — Cofer, 29 yard field goal

**Second Quarter**
S.F. — Watters, 1 yard run
    PAT — Cofer (kick)
S.F. — Watters, 2 yard run
    PAT — Cofer (kick)
N.Y.G. — Treadwell, 25 yard field goal

**Third Quarter**
S.F. — Watters, 6 yard run
    PAT — Cofer (kick)
S.F. — Watters, 2 yard run
    PAT — Cofer (kick)

**Fourth Quarter**
S.F. — Logan, 2 yard run
    PAT — Cofer (kick)

## TEAM STATISTICS

| N.Y.G. | | S.F. |
|---|---|---|
| 12 | First Downs- Total | 25 |
| 3 | First Downs- Rushing | 13 |
| 6 | First Downs- Passing | 11 |
| 3 | First Downs- Penalty | 1 |
| 0 | Fumbles- Number | 2 |
| 0 | Fumbles- Lost Ball | 1 |
| 4 | Penalties- Number | 6 |
| 24 | Yards Penalized | 50 |
| 0 | Missed Field Goals | 0 |
| 58 | Offensive Plays | 65 |
| 194 | Net Yards | 413 |
| 3.4 | Average Gain | 6.4 |
| 3 | Giveaways | 1 |
| 1 | Takeaways | 3 |
| -2 | Difference | +2 |

## INDIVIDUAL STATISTICS

### N.Y. GIANTS / SAN FRANCISCO

#### RUSHING

| | No. | Yds. | Avg. | | No. | Yds. | Avg. |
|---|---|---|---|---|---|---|---|
| Hampton | 7 | 12 | 1.7 | Watters | 24 | 118 | 4.9 |
| Brown | 1 | 8 | 8.0 | Logan | 9 | 40 | 4.4 |
| Tillman | 4 | 8 | 2.0 | Young | 3 | 17 | 5.7 |
| Bunch | 2 | 5 | 2.5 | Rathman | 2 | 7 | 3.5 |
| Meggett | 2 | 5 | 2.5 | Lee | 1 | 5 | 5.0 |
| Simms | 2 | 3 | 1.5 | Rice | 1 | -9 | -9.0 |
| Jackson | 1 | 0 | 0.0 | | 40 | 178 | 4.5 |
| | 19 | 41 | 2.2 | | | | |

#### RECEIVING

| | No. | Yds. | Avg. | | No. | Yds. | Avg. |
|---|---|---|---|---|---|---|---|
| McCaffrey | 5 | 59 | 11.8 | Watters | 5 | 46 | 9.2 |
| Meggett | 3 | 17 | 5.7 | Jones | 4 | 39 | 9.8 |
| Cross | 2 | 32 | 16.0 | Rice | 3 | 43 | 14.3 |
| Calloway | 2 | 24 | 12.0 | Taylor | 2 | 74 | 37.0 |
| Jackson | 2 | 16 | 8.0 | Rathman | 2 | 16 | 8.0 |
| Hampton | 2 | 11 | 5.5 | Lee | 2 | 15 | 7.5 |
| Tillman | 1 | 14 | 14.0 | Logan | 1 | 8 | 8.0 |
| Pierce | 1 | 7 | 7.0 | | 19 | 241 | 12.7 |
| | 18 | 180 | 10.0 | | | | |

#### PUNTING

| | No. | | Avg. | | No. | | Avg. |
|---|---|---|---|---|---|---|---|
| Horan | 5 | | 39.8 | Wilmsmeyer | 3 | | 44.7 |

#### PUNT RETURNS

| | No. | Yds. | Avg. | | No. | Yds. | Avg. |
|---|---|---|---|---|---|---|---|
| Meggett | 1 | 3 | 3.0 | Carter | 2 | 39 | 19.5 |

#### KICKOFF RETURNS

| | No. | Yds. | Avg. | | |
|---|---|---|---|---|---|
| Meggett | 4 | 80 | 20.0 | None | |
| Calloway | 1 | 25 | 25.0 | | |
| | 5 | 105 | 21.0 | | |

#### INTERCEPTION RETURNS

| | | | | | No. | Yds. | Avg. |
|---|---|---|---|---|---|---|---|
| None | | | | Caldwell | 1 | 13 | 13.0 |
| | | | | Davis | 1 | 4 | 4.0 |
| | | | | McDonald | 1 | 4 | 4.0 |
| | | | | | 3 | 21 | 7.0 |

#### PASSING

**N.Y. GIANTS**

| | Att. | Comp. | Comp. Pct. | Yds. | Int. | Yds./ Att. | Yds./ Comp. |
|---|---|---|---|---|---|---|---|
| Simms | 25 | 12 | 48.0 | 124 | 2 | 5.0 | 10.3 |
| Brown | 10 | 6 | 60.0 | 56 | 1 | 5.6 | 9.2 |
| | 35 | 18 | 51.4 | 180 | 3 | 5.1 | 10.0 |

**SAN FRANCISCO**

| | Att. | Comp. | Comp. Pct. | Yds. | Int. | Yds./ Att. | Yds./ Comp. |
|---|---|---|---|---|---|---|---|
| Young | 22 | 17 | 77.3 | 226 | 0 | 10.3 | 13.3 |
| Bono | 2 | 2 | 100.0 | 15 | 0 | 7.5 | 7.5 |
| | 24 | 19 | 79.2 | 241 | 0 | 10.0 | 12.7 |

---

January 16, 1994 at Dallas (Attendance 64,790)

## SCORING

| | | | | | | |
|---|---|---|---|---|---|---|
| GREEN BAY | 3 | 0 | 7 | 7 | - | 17 |
| DALLAS | 0 | 17 | 7 | 3 | - | 27 |

**First Quarter**
G.B. — Jacke, 30 yard field goal

**Second Quarter**
Dal. — Harper, 25 yard pass from Aikman
    PAT — Murray (kick)
Dal. — Murray, 41 yard field goal
Dal. — Novacek, 6 yard pass from Aikman
    PAT — Murray (kick)

**Third Quarter**
Dal. — Irvin, 19 yard pass from Aikman
    PAT — Murray (kick)
G.B. — Brooks, 13 yard pass from Favre
    PAT — Jacke (kick)

**Fourth Quarter**
Dal. — Murray, 38 yard field goal
G.B. — Sharpe, 29 yard pass from Favre
    PAT — Jacke (kick)

## TEAM STATISTICS

| G.B. | | DAL. |
|---|---|---|
| 19 | First Downs- Total | 23 |
| 2 | First Downs- Rushing | 6 |
| 17 | First Downs- Passing | 16 |
| 0 | First Downs- Penalty | 1 |
| 3 | Fumbles- Number | 2 |
| 2 | Fumbles- Lost Ball | 1 |
| 4 | Penalties- Number | 5 |
| 30 | Yards Penalized | 39 |
| 1 | Missed Field Goals | 0 |
| 60 | Offensive Plays | 68 |
| 358 | Net Yards | 381 |
| 6.0 | Average Gain | 5.6 |
| 4 | Giveaways | 3 |
| 3 | Takeaways | 4 |
| -1 | Difference | +1 |

## INDIVIDUAL STATISTICS

### GREEN BAY / DALLAS

#### RUSHING

| | No. | Yds. | Avg. | | No. | Yds. | Avg. |
|---|---|---|---|---|---|---|---|
| Thompson | 7 | 28 | 4.0 | E. Smith | 13 | 60 | 4.6 |
| Bennett | 6 | 3 | 0.5 | Coleman | 5 | 19 | 3.8 |
| | 13 | 31 | 2.4 | Johnston | 3 | 12 | 4.0 |
| | | | | Lassic | 2 | 6 | 3.0 |
| | | | | Aikman | 3 | 0 | 0.0 |
| | | | | Bates | 1 | 0 | 0.0 |
| | | | | | 27 | 97 | 3.6 |

#### RECEIVING

| | No. | Yds. | Avg. | | No. | Yds. | Avg. |
|---|---|---|---|---|---|---|---|
| Bennett | 9 | 53 | 5.9 | Irvin | 9 | 126 | 14.0 |
| Sharpe | 6 | 128 | 21.3 | Novacek | 6 | 59 | 9.8 |
| West | 4 | 41 | 10.3 | Johnston | 6 | 43 | 7.2 |
| Thompson | 3 | 54 | 18.0 | Harper | 2 | 33 | 16.5 |
| Brooks | 3 | 39 | 13.0 | E. Smith | 2 | 27 | 13.5 |
| Ingram | 2 | 9 | 4.5 | Coleman | 2 | 6 | 3.0 |
| Lewis | 1 | 7 | 7.0 | Lassic | 1 | 8 | 8.0 |
| | 28 | 331 | 11.8 | | 28 | 302 | 10.8 |

#### PUNTING

| | No. | | Avg. | | No. | | Avg. |
|---|---|---|---|---|---|---|---|
| Wagner | 3 | | 39.0 | Jett | 3 | | 43.7 |

#### PUNT RETURNS

| | No. | Yds. | Avg. | | No. | Yds. | Avg. |
|---|---|---|---|---|---|---|---|
| Brooks | 2 | 59 | 29.5 | K. Williams | 2 | 14 | 7.0 |

#### KICKOFF RETURNS

| | No. | Yds. | Avg. | | No. | Yds. | Avg. |
|---|---|---|---|---|---|---|---|
| Brooks | 2 | 36 | 18.0 | K. Williams | 1 | 20 | 20.0 |
| C. Harris | 2 | 15 | 7.5 | Marion | 1 | 14 | 14.0 |
| Wilson | 1 | 17 | 17.0 | Novacek | 0 | 0 | 0.0 |
| Jurkovic | 1 | 2 | 2.0 | | 2 | 34 | 17.0 |
| | 6 | 70 | 11.7 | | | | |

#### INTERCEPTION RETURNS

| | No. | Yds. | Avg. | | No. | Yds. | Avg. |
|---|---|---|---|---|---|---|---|
| Butler | 1 | 14 | 14.0 | Woodson | 1 | 5 | 5.0 |
| Buckley | 1 | 0 | 0.0 | Haley | 1 | 0 | 0.0 |
| | 2 | 14 | 7.0 | | 2 | 5 | 2.5 |

#### PASSING

**GREEN BAY**

| | Att. | Comp. | Comp. Pct. | Yds. | Int. | Yds./ Att. | Yds./ Comp. |
|---|---|---|---|---|---|---|---|
| Favre | 45 | 28 | 62.2 | 331 | 2 | 7.4 | 11.8 |

**DALLAS**

| | Att. | Comp. | Comp. Pct. | Yds. | Int. | Yds./ Att. | Yds./ Comp. |
|---|---|---|---|---|---|---|---|
| Aikman | 37 | 28 | 75.7 | 302 | 2 | 8.2 | 10.8 |

## SCORING

| | | | | | |
|---|---|---|---|---|---|
| KANSAS CITY | 6 | 0 | 7 | 0 | - 13 |
| BUFFALO | 7 | 13 | 0 | 10 | - 30 |

**First Quarter**
Buff.    Thomas, 12 yard run
    PAT — Christie (kick)
K.C.    Lowery, 31 yard field goal
K.C.    Lowery, 31 yard field goal

**Second Quarter**
Buff.    Thomas, 3 yard run
    PAT — Christie (kick)
Buff.    Christie, 23 yard field goal
Buff.    Christie, 25 yard field goal

**Third Quarter**
K.C.    Allen, 1 yard run
    PAT — Lowery (kick)

**Fourth Quarter**
Buff.    Christie, 18 yard field goal
Buff.    Thomas, 3 yard run
    PAT — Christie (kick)

### TEAM STATISTICS

| K.C. | | BUFF. |
|---|---|---|
| 22 | First Downs- Total | 30 |
| 3 | First Downs- Rushing | 17 |
| 18 | First Downs- Passing | 9 |
| 1 | First Downs- Penalty | 4 |
| 1 | Fumbles- Number | 1 |
| 0 | Fumbles- Lost Ball | 1 |
| 6 | Penalties- Number | 2 |
| 29 | Yards Penalized | 10 |
| 0 | Missed Field Goals | 0 |
| 77 | Offensive Plays | 73 |
| 338 | Net Yards | 389 |
| 4.4 | Average Gain | 5.3 |
| 2 | Giveaways | 1 |
| 1 | Takeaways | 2 |
| +1 | Difference | -1 |

## SCORING

| | | | | | |
|---|---|---|---|---|---|
| SAN FRANCISCO | 0 | 7 | 7 | 7 | - 21 |
| DALLAS | 7 | 21 | 7 | 3 | - 38 |

**First Quarter**
Dall.    Smith, 5 yard run
    PAT — Murray (kick)

**Second Quarter**
S.F.    Rathman, 7 yard pass from Young
    PAT — Cofer (kick)
Dall.    Johnston, 4 yard run
    PAT — Murray (kick)
Dall.    Smith, 11 yard pass from Aikman
    PAT — Murray (kick)
Dall.    Novacek, 19 yard pass from Aikman
    PAT — Murray (kick)

**Third Quarter**
S.F.    Watters, 4 yard run
    PAT — Cofer (kick)
Dall.    Harper, 42 yard pass from Aikman
    PAT — Murray (kick)

**Fourth Quarter**
Dall.    Murray, 50 yard field goal
S.F.    Young, 1 yard run
    PAT — Cofer (kick)

### TEAM STATISTICS

| S.F. | | DALL. |
|---|---|---|
| 24 | First Downs- Total | 24 |
| 5 | First Downs- Rushing | 9 |
| 15 | First Downs- Passing | 15 |
| 4 | First Downs- Penalty | 0 |
| 2 | Fumbles- Number | 0 |
| 0 | Fumbles- Lost Ball | 0 |
| 6 | Penalties- Number | 4 |
| 46 | Yards Penalized | 29 |
| 0 | Missed Field Goals | 0 |
| 70 | Offensive Plays | 63 |
| 359 | Net Yards | 377 |
| 5.1 | Average Gain | 6.0 |
| 1 | Giveaways | 0 |
| 0 | Takeaways | 1 |
| - 1 | Difference | + 1 |

# 1993 Championship Games

## A.F.C. CHAMPIONSHIP GAME
January 23, 1994 at Orchard Park, N.Y.
(Attendance 76,642)

Thurman Thomas may not be much in the Super Bowl, but he does just about everything to see that the Bills get there every year.

With most of the nation rooting against Buffalo and for Joe Montana to lead the Chiefs to the Super Bowl, Thomas almost single-handedly led the Bills to a 30-10 victory over Kansas City. Thomas carried the ball 33 times for 186 yards and three touchdowns, as the Bills earned their fourth consecutive Super Bowl trip.

Over and over, Buffalo quarterback Jim Kelly kept sticking the ball in Thomas' stomach while shouting, "Go!"

"He must have said that 15-16 times today," Thomas said. He knows that on certain plays I'm going to get a lot of yardage."

A Kansas City defense that had held Thomas to 44 yards eight weeks earlier was at a loss to explain how he quadrupled his total when it counted most.

"From where I was watching the game, it looked like everything Thurman tried worked, and almost nothing we tried worked," said Chiefs defensive tackle Joe Phillips. "We didn't stop him, and the final score shows it."

Montana was unable to work his magic, as he completed only 9 of 23 passes for 125 yards. He was knocked out of the game in the third quarter with a concussion, and backup Dave Krieg, while passing for 198 yards, could manage only one touchdown for the Chiefs.

The Chiefs also gained only 52 yards on the ground, a big difference from what Thomas was doing to them.

## N.F.C. CHAMPIONSHIP GAME
January 23, 1994 at Dallas, Texas
(Attendance 64,902)

Football coaches don't like it when one of their players guarantees victories before games. But, in this instance, it was Dallas coach Jimmy Johnson who guaranteed victory over San Francisco ... and he was right.

The Cowboys decisively beat the 49ers 38-21, as Emmitt Smith, who was playing with a separated shoulder, gained 88 yards on the ground while catching seven passes for 85 more yards. He scored two touchdowns.

"I thought Jimmy Johnson's comment was insane," said 49ers wide receiver Jerry Rice. "But I guess it was accurate."

Dallas scored touchdowns on four of its first five possessions and jumped out to a 28-7 lead. The 49ers gained only 74 yards in the first half.

San Francisco managed a slight comeback in the second half after Dallas quarterback Troy Aikman was hospitalized with a concussion, narrowing the lead to 28-14. However, Cowboys backup quarterback Bernie Kosar then threw a 42-yard TD pass to Alvin Harper and the game was no longer in much doubt.

Quarterback Steve Young again failed to advance the 49ers to the Super Bowl, as they lost in the conference championship game for the third time in four years. Young was sacked four times. "I never believed we'd be beaten by this score," he said.

The closest San Francisco came was when it tied the game 7-7 in the second quarter. After that, Dallas scored three touchdowns before halftime.

"The defense played a great game," said Cowboys defensive coordinator Butch Davis, "but the key was Emmitt. He controlled the ball and kept us off the field. That's what you have to have if you have a great defense."

## INDIVIDUAL STATISTICS

**KANSAS CITY**      **BUFFALO**

### RUSHING

| | No. | Yds. | Avg. | | No. | Yds. | Avg. |
|---|---|---|---|---|---|---|---|
| Allen | 18 | 50 | 2.8 | Thomas | 33 | 186 | 5.6 |
| Anders | 2 | 1 | 0.5 | K. Davis | 10 | 32 | 3.2 |
| Montana | 1 | 1 | 1.0 | Kelly | 2 | 3 | 1.5 |
| | 21 | 52 | 2.5 | Reed | 1 | 8 | 8.0 |
| | | | | | 46 | 229 | 5.0 |

### RECEIVING

| | No. | Yds. | Avg. | | No. | Yds. | Avg. |
|---|---|---|---|---|---|---|---|
| K. Cash | 6 | 87 | 14.5 | Reed | 4 | 49 | 12.3 |
| Davis | 5 | 57 | 11.4 | Brooks | 4 | 34 | 8.5 |
| Birden | 4 | 60 | 15.0 | Metzelaars | 4 | 29 | 7.3 |
| Allen | 2 | 36 | 18.0 | Thomas | 2 | 22 | 11.0 |
| McNair | 2 | 33 | 16.5 | Beebe | 2 | 19 | 9.5 |
| Hayes | 2 | 14 | 7.0 | McKeller | 1 | 7 | 7.0 |
| Thompson | 1 | 12 | 12.0 | | 17 | 160 | 9.4 |
| Hughes | 1 | 11 | 11.0 | | | | |
| Anders | 1 | 7 | 7.0 | | | | |
| Szott | 1 | 6 | 6.0 | | | | |
| | 25 | 323 | 12.9 | | | | |

### PUNTING

| | | | | | | | |
|---|---|---|---|---|---|---|---|
| Barker | 6 | | 40.8 | Mohr | 4 | | 33.3 |

### PUNT RETURNS

| | | | | | | | |
|---|---|---|---|---|---|---|---|
| Hughes | 1 | 11 | 11.0 | Copeland | 5 | 70 | 14.0 |
| Hughes | 1FC | | | | | | |

### KICKOFF RETURNS

| | | | | | | | |
|---|---|---|---|---|---|---|---|
| Stephens | 5 | 89 | 17.8 | Copeland | 4 | 68 | 17.0 |

### INTERCEPTION RETURNS

| | | | | | | | |
|---|---|---|---|---|---|---|---|
| | | | | Jones | 1 | 15 | 15.0 |
| | | | | Williams | 1 | 0 | 0.0 |
| | | | | | 2 | 15 | 7.5 |

### PASSING

**KANSAS CITY**

| | Att. | Comp. | Comp. Pct. | Yds. | Int. | Yds./ Att. | Yds./ Comp. |
|---|---|---|---|---|---|---|---|
| Montana | 23 | 9 | 39.1 | 125 | 1 | 5.4 | 13.9 |
| Krieg | 29 | 16 | 55.2 | 198 | 1 | 6.8 | 12.4 |
| | 52 | 25 | 48.1 | 323 | 2 | 6.2 | 12.9 |

**BUFFALO**

| | Att. | Comp. | Comp. Pct. | Yds. | Int. | Yds./ Att. | Yds./ Comp. |
|---|---|---|---|---|---|---|---|
| Kelly | 27 | 17 | 63.0 | 160 | 0 | 5.9 | 9.4 |

## INDIVIDUAL STATISTICS

**SAN FRANCISCO**      **DALLAS**

### RUSHING

| | No. | Yds. | Avg. | | No. | Yds. | Avg. |
|---|---|---|---|---|---|---|---|
| Young | 7 | 38 | 5.4 | Smith | 23 | 88 | 3.8 |
| Watters | 12 | 37 | 3.1 | Aikman | 3 | 25 | 8.3 |
| Rathman | 2 | 9 | 4.5 | Johnston | 4 | 13 | 3.3 |
| | 21 | 84 | 4.0 | Lassic | 1 | 1 | 1.0 |
| | | | | Kosar | 2 | -3 | -1.5 |
| | | | | | 33 | 124 | 3.8 |

### RECEIVING

| | No. | Yds. | Avg. | | No. | Yds. | Avg. |
|---|---|---|---|---|---|---|---|
| Watters | 7 | 33 | 4.7 | Smith | 7 | 85 | 12.1 |
| Rice | 6 | 83 | 13.8 | Harper | 4 | 78 | 19.5 |
| Taylor | 3 | 61 | 20.3 | Novacek | 4 | 57 | 14.3 |
| Williams | 3 | 44 | 14.7 | Irvin | 2 | 23 | 11.5 |
| Jones | 3 | 26 | 8.7 | Johnston | 2 | 17 | 8.5 |
| Logan | 3 | 21 | 7.0 | | 19 | 260 | 13.7 |
| Turner | 1 | 12 | 12.0 | | | | |
| Rathman | 1 | 7 | 7.0 | | | | |
| | 27 | 287 | 10.6 | | | | |

### PUNTING

| | | | | | | | |
|---|---|---|---|---|---|---|---|
| Wilmsmeyer | 4 | | 45.5 | Jett | 4 | | 41.0 |

### PUNT RETURNS

| | | | | | | | |
|---|---|---|---|---|---|---|---|
| Carter | 1 | 9 | 9.0 | K. Williams | 1 | 6 | 6.0 |
| Carter | 1FC | | | K. Williams | 2FC | | |

### KICKOFF RETURNS

| | | | | | | | |
|---|---|---|---|---|---|---|---|
| Carter | 4 | 66 | 16.5 | Marion | 1 | 15 | 15.0 |
| Logan | 2 | 20 | 10.0 | K. Williams | 1 | 14 | 14.0 |
| | 4 | 73 | 18.3 | Novacek | 0 | 0 | 0.0 |
| | | | | | 2 | 29 | 14.5 |

### INTERCEPTION RETURNS

| | | | | | | | |
|---|---|---|---|---|---|---|---|
| | | | | Everett | 1 | 14 | 14.0 |

### PASSING

**SAN FRANCISCO**

| | Att. | Comp. | Comp. Pct. | Yds. | Int. | Yds./ Att. | Yds./ Comp. |
|---|---|---|---|---|---|---|---|
| Young | 45 | 27 | 60.0 | 287 | 1 | 6.4 | 10.6 |

**DALLAS**

| | Att. | Comp. | Comp. Pct. | Yds. | Int. | Yds./ Att. | Yds./ Comp. |
|---|---|---|---|---|---|---|---|
| Aikman | 18 | 14 | 77.8 | 177 | 0 | 9.8 | 12.6 |
| Kosar | 9 | 5 | 55.6 | 83 | 0 | 9.2 | 16.6 |
| Harper | 1 | 0 | 0.0 | 0 | 0 | 0.0 | 0.0 |
| | 28 | 19 | 67.9 | 260 | 0 | 9.3 | 13.7 |

# Cowboys and Bills Do It Again

Dallas repeated and Buffalo four-peated. And, for a change, the Super Bowl wasn't a blowout. At least this one was close as the third quarter began. That's when the Cowboys went ahead and pulled away for a 30-13 victory over the Bills in Super Bowl XXVIII.

Emmitt Smith was the Most Valuable Player. The Dallas star running back rushed for 132 yards on 30 carries and scored two touchdowns.

But Dallas had a star on defense, too. James Washington, a backup safety who started in a nickel defense because Buffalo started three wide receivers, was responsible for three turnovers and one touchdown.

The Bills led 13-6 after two quarters. "At halftime, guys were looking at each other, saying, 'Damn, these boys came to play,' " Dallas wide receiver Michael Irvin said of the Bills, who had already lost three straight Super Bowls. "If they had taken the second-half kickoff and gone down and scored (to make it 20-6), we would have said, 'Man, this one's slipping away.' "

That's when Washington made the play of the game. Dallas defensive tackle Leon Lett stripped the ball from Buffalo running back Thurman Thomas, and Washington scooped it up and ran 46 yards for the tying touchdown.

"I don't think I've ever seen a play in any football game that ignited an attitude among a team like that play," said Cowboys defensive coordinator Butch Davis. "It set the tempo for the second half."

Earlier, Washington had forced a fumble that set up the Cowboys' second field goal. And, in the fourth quarter with Buffalo threatening to tie the game, Washington intercepted a Jim Kelly pass.

Following Washington's touchdown, Smith took over when Dallas got the ball back. He carried the ball seven out of eight plays and scored on a 15-yard run. In the fourth quarter, Smith scored from one yard out. Eddie Murray kicked three field goals for the Cowboys.

The Dallas defense limited the Bills to 87 yards on the ground and 5-of-17 efficiency on third downs. Thomas had his third straight miserable Super Bowl performance. He gained only 37 yards on 16 carries and fumbled twice. Later he admitted that his second fumble lost the game for the Bills. Kelly put the ball into the air 50 times, completing 31 of them, but he was unable to lead Buffalo to a score in the second half.

The Bills did look good in the first half, when Thomas scored on a four-yard run and Steve Christie kicked two field goals.

Again, I am disappointed that we lost the ballgame," said Bills defensive end Bruce Smith. "As far as embarassing, I think at any point and time that you sustain a loss, you have to hold your head up, especially if you gave it all you could. I think that is what we did today."

Emmitt Smith played with a separated shoulder. "The offensive line did a great job," he said. "They opened up holes for me to run the football. They controlled the whole line of scrimmage in the second half."

The Dallas victory was its fourth in a Super Bowl, tying a record held by Pittsburgh and San Francisco. The Cowboys have also played in a record seven Super Bowls. For Buffalo, the Super Bowl records are all negative ones. But at least they keep getting there.

## LINEUPS

| DALL. | | BUFF. |
|---|---|---|
| | **OFFENSE** | |
| Harper | WR | Beebe |
| Tuinei | LT | Fina |
| Newton | LG | Parker |
| Gesek | C | Hull |
| Gogan | RG | Davis |
| E. Williams | RT | Ballard |
| Novacek | TE | Metzelaars |
| Irvin | WR | Reed |
| Aikman | QB | Kelly |
| E. Smith | RB | Thomas |
| D. Johnston | RB-WR | Brooks |
| | **DEFENSE** | |
| Tolbert | LE | Hansen |
| Casillas | LT/NT | Wright |
| Lett | RT/RE | B. Smith |
| Haley | RE/LOLB | Patton |
| Norton | MLB/LILB | Bennett |
| D. Smith | RLB/RILB | Maddox |
| Woodson | DB/ROLB | Talley |
| K. Smith | LCB | M. Washington |
| Brown | RCB | Odomes |
| Everett | SS | Jones |
| J. Washington | FS | Kelso |

| DALLAS | | |
|---|---|---|
| | **SUBSTITUTES** | |
| | **OFFENSE** | |
| Kosar | Gainer | Coleman |
| Cornish | Hellestrae | K. Williams |
| Galbraith | | |
| | **DEFENSE** | |
| Gant | Bates | D. Thomas |
| Patterson | Fishback | R. Jones |
| Edwards | Maryland | Jeffcoat |
| Vanderbeek | Hennings | Jones |
| Myles | | |
| | **KICKERS** | |
| Murray | Jett | |

| BUFFALO | | |
|---|---|---|
| | **OFFENSE** | |
| Reich | Davis | Gardner |
| Ritcher | Devlin | Lingner |
| Crafts | McKeller | Copeland |
| Tasker | | |
| | **DEFENSE** | |
| Schulz | T. Smith | Henderson |
| Darby | Goganious | Harvey |
| Lodish | Barnett | Pike |
| M. Brown | | |
| | **KICKERS** | |
| Christie | Mohr | |

## SCORING

| | | | | | | |
|---|---|---|---|---|---|---|
| DALLAS | 6 | 0 | 14 | 10 | - | 30 |
| BUFFALO | 3 | 10 | 0 | 0 | - | 13 |

**First Quarter**
Dall. — Murray, 41 yard field goal
Buff. — Christie, 54 yard field goal
Dall. — Murray, 24 yard field goal

**Second Quarter**
Buff. — Thomas, 4 yard run
PAT — Christie (kick)
Buff. — Christie, 28 yard field goal

**Third Quarter**
Dall. — J. Washington, 46 yard fumble return
PAT — Murray (kick)
Dall. — E. Smith, 15 yard run
PAT — Murray (kick)

**Fourth Quarter**
Dall. — E. Smith, 1 yard run
PAT — Murray (kick)
Dall. — Murray, 20 yard run

## TEAM STATISTICS

| DALL. | | BUFF. |
|---|---|---|
| 20 | First Downs-Total | 22 |
| 6 | First Downs-Rushing | 6 |
| 14 | First Downs-Passing | 15 |
| 0 | First Downs-Penalty | 1 |
| 0 | Fumbles-Number | 3 |
| 0 | Fumbles-Lost Ball | 2 |
| 6 | Penalties-Number | 1 |
| 50 | Yards Penalized | 10 |
| 0 | Missed Field Goals | 0 |
| 64 | Offensive Plays | 80 |
| 341 | Net Yards | 314 |
| 5.3 | Average Gain | 3.9 |
| 1 | Giveaways | 3 |
| 3 | Takeaways | 1 |
| + 2 | Difference | - 2 |

## INDIVIDUAL STATISTICS

### RUSHING

| DALLAS | No. | Yds. | Avg. | BUFFALO | No. | Yds. | Avg. |
|---|---|---|---|---|---|---|---|
| E. Smith | 30 | 132 | 4.4 | K. Davis | 9 | 38 | 4.2 |
| K. Williams | 1 | 6 | 6.0 | Thomas | 16 | 37 | 2.3 |
| Aikman | 1 | 3 | 3.0 | Kelly | 2 | 12 | 6.0 |
| Johnston | 1 | 0 | 0.0 | | 27 | 87 | 3.2 |
| Kosar | 1 | -1 | -1.0 | | | | |
| Coleman | 1 | -3 | -3.0 | | | | |
| | 35 | 137 | 3.9 | | | | |

### RECEIVING

| | No. | Yds. | Avg. | | No. | Yds. | Avg. |
|---|---|---|---|---|---|---|---|
| Irvin | 5 | 66 | 13.2 | Brooks | 7 | 63 | 9.0 |
| Novacek | 5 | 26 | 5.2 | Thomas | 7 | 52 | 7.4 |
| E. Smith | 4 | 26 | 6.5 | Reed | 6 | 75 | 12.5 |
| Harper | 3 | 75 | 25.0 | Beebe | 6 | 60 | 10.0 |
| Johnston | 2 | 14 | 7.0 | K. Davis | 3 | -5 | -1.7 |
| | 19 | 207 | 10.9 | Metzelaars | 1 | 8 | 8.0 |
| | | | | McKeller | 1 | 7 | 7.0 |
| | | | | | 31 | 260 | 8.4 |

### PUNTING

| | No. | | Avg. | | No. | | Avg. |
|---|---|---|---|---|---|---|---|
| Jett | 4 | | 43.8 | Mohr | 5 | | 37.6 |

### PUNT RETURNS

| | No. | Yds. | Avg. | | No. | Yds. | Avg. |
|---|---|---|---|---|---|---|---|
| K. Williams | 1 | 5 | 5.0 | Copeland | 1 | 5 | 5.0 |
| K. Williams | 1FC | | | Copeland | 1FC | | |

### KICKOFF RETURNS

| | No. | Yds. | Avg. | | No. | Yds. | Avg. |
|---|---|---|---|---|---|---|---|
| K. Williams | 1 | 50 | 50.0 | Copeland | 4 | 82 | 20.5 |
| Gant | 1 | 22 | 22.0 | Beebe | 2 | 62 | 31.0 |
| | 2 | 72 | 36.0 | | 6 | 144 | 24.0 |

### INTERCEPTION RETURNS

| | No. | Yds. | Avg. | | No. | Yds. | Avg. |
|---|---|---|---|---|---|---|---|
| J. Washington | 1 | 12 | 12.0 | Odomes | 1 | 41 | 41.0 |

### PASSING

| DALLAS | Att. | Comp. | Comp. Pct. | Yds. | Int. | Yds./ Att. | Yds./ Comp. | Yards Lost Tackled |
|---|---|---|---|---|---|---|---|---|
| Aikman | 27 | 19 | 70.4 | 207 | 1 | 7.7 | 10.9 | 3 |
| **BUFFALO** | | | | | | | | |
| Kelly | 50 | 31 | 62.0 | 260 | 1 | 5.1 | 8.4 | 33 |

The NFL celebrated its 75th season in fine fashion, with throwback uniforms and rule changes that increased scoring. But one fact was constant: The San Francisco 49ers remained the finest organization in the league. The 49ers won their fifth Super Bowl — the first franchise to do so — by defeating the defending champion Dallas Cowboys once during the regular season and again in the NFC championship game, and then by knocking off the San Diego Chargers in Super Bowl XXIX.

A new salary cap limited the amount teams could spend on players to $34.6 million, and the 49ers worked wonders with the cap when they added new players such as defensive stars Deion Sanders, Rickey Jackson and Richard Dent.

The Cowboys spent the season amid a little turmoil after head coach Jimmy Johnson was fired — or did he quit? — and replaced by Barry Switzer, who last coached at the University of Oklahoma in 1988. Dallas went 12-4 but couldn't beat San Francisco.

The Fox Network began broadcasting NFC games and did a good job, the Rams threatened to move to St. Louis, the Buccaneers were sold to Malcolm Glazer and once again realignment of the divisions went nowhere.

But perhaps the biggest story that pertained to the football world in 1994 was the double-murder case against Hall of Famer O.J. Simpson that captivated the country. Simpson's trial began the week of the Super Bowl.

## EASTERN DIVISION

**Dallas Cowboys —** The Cowboys won their third-straight division title, this time with Barry Switzer as head coach. Switzer, who had not coached in six years, replaced Jimmy Johnson during the offseason. Dallas lost several players to free agency, but the team's three superstars — quarterback Troy Aikman, running back Emmitt Smith and wide receiver Michael Irvin — were still around. Smith scored 22 touchdowns and rushed for 1,484 yards, although he was slowed late in the season by a pulled hamstring. Aikman missed several games, too, but he still passed for 2,676 yards and 13 TD's. And Irvin caught 79 passes for 1,241 yards and six TD's. The defense was the NFL's best, and was led by three Pro Bowlers — Charles Haley, Leon Lett and Darren Woodson.

**New York Giants —** The Giants certainly had a streaky season in 1994. They won their first three games, then lost seven in a row, and then rebounded to win their final six games. Quarterback Dave Brown replaced long-time starter Phil Simms, who was cut in a cost-cutting measure, and improved down the stretch. Brown threw for 2,536 yards and 12 touchdowns. Running back Rodney Hampton rushed for 1,075 yards and became the first Giants player to gain 1,000 yards in four consecutive seasons. Wide receiver Mike Sherrard played in all 16 games, catching 53 passes and scoring six touchdowns. But the defense allowed 305 points, exactly 100 more than its 1993 league-leading total, and the kicking game wasn't very good until Brad Daluiso replaced David Treadwell on field goals with three games to go.

**Arizona Cardinals —** Promises, promises. That's what Buddy Ryan made when he became the Cardinals' head coach during the 1994 offseason. But Ryan failed to come through, as the Cardinals finished 8-8 and out of the playoffs. Understandably, Ryan's team played excellent defense, ranking third in yards allowed. But Ryan's offense was pitiful, ranking 27th in points scored. Ryan benched quarterback Steve Beuerlein twice, but his replacement, Jay Schroeder, wasn't any better, throwing only four touchdowns. Wideouts Ricky Proehl and Gary Clark both topped 50 catches, but neither was much of a threat. Running back Ronald Moore rushed for 780 yards but late in the season was running behind Garrison Hearst. Larry Centers was the best back, catching 77 passes and scoring seven touchdowns.

**Philadelphia Eagles —** While jumping out to a 7-2 start — including a 40-8 victory over the 49ers — the Eagles looked like a definite playoff team. But Philadelphia then fell apart, losing its final seven games and costing head coach Rich Kotite his job. Quarterback Randall Cunningham had 14 TD's in the first nine games and only two the rest of the way

before he was replaced by Bubby Brister. Rookie back Charlie Garner rushed for more than 100 yards in each of his first two games, but then he disappeared. So the running attack was left to the ageless Herschel Walker, who scored eight touchdowns and had 1,609 all-purpose yards. Walker also became the first player ever to record runs of 90-plus yards on a rush, pass reception and a kick return in the same season.

**Washington Redskins —** For the second straight season, a new head coach failed to guide the Redskins to many victories. Norv Turner, the former offensive coordinator for the Cowboys, saw Washington win only three games. Turner had two rookie quarterbacks in Heath Shuler and Gus Frerotte and a journeyman in John Friesz, and all started several games. But, other than wide receiver Henry Ellard, who caught 74 passes for 1,397 yards and six touchdowns, the passing game was mostly ineffective. So was the running game, as Reggie Brooks and Ricky Ervins didn't do much to help the 24th-ranked running offense. There was hope for the future, as Shuler, Washington's first-round draft pick, showed progress in December. Linebacker Ken Harvey paced the defense with 13.5 sacks.

## CENTRAL DIVISION

**Minnesota Vikings —** Midway through the 1994 season, Minnesota looked like it might be able to contend with Dallas and San Francisco for the NFC title. But, after a 7-2 start, the Vikings finished 3-5, including a first-round playoff loss to Chicago, a team it had beaten twice during the regular season. Quarterback Warren Moon was obtained from Houston in a trade, and he passed 601 times for 4,264 yards and 18 touchdowns. The main beneficiaries were Cris Carter, who set an NFL record with 122 receptions, and Jake Reed, who finally stayed healthy to catch 85 passes. The defense was once again solid, ranking third in yards allowed, but a talented and deep running attacked ranked only 18th. Placekicker Fuad Reveiz was successful on 28 straight field goals at the end of the season. He scored 132 points.

**Green Bay Packers —** For the second straight season, the Packers finished 9-7 and defeated Detroit in the wild-card round of the playoffs only to get knocked out by Dallas in the second round. Quarterback Brett Favre finally reached his potential, cutting down on his interceptions and throwing 33 touchdown passes. Wide receiver Sterling Sharpe caught 18 of those TD's — the second-highest NFL total ever — but he suffered a neck injury in the final regular-season game. That forced him to miss the playoffs and might end his career. For the first time since the AFL-NFL merger, Green Bay had single-digit rankings in both offense (ninth) and defense (sixth) in the same season. Green Bay also tied for third in turnover ratio.

**Detroit Lions —** Barry Sanders had a tremendous season for Detroit, rushing for 1,883 yards, flirting with the 2,000-yard mark most of the season and finishing with the fourth-best single-season total in NFL history. The Lions had the biggest free-agent signing of the year, when it lured quarterback Scott Mitchell with $11.1 million. But Mitchell struggled as a starter and the Lions fared better after he was sidelined with a broken hand in the ninth game. That's when journeyman Dave Krieg took over. Krieg passed for 14 TD's and only three interceptions and led Detroit to a playoff berth. Herman Moore turned into one of the NFL's best receivers, when he caught 72 passes for 1,173 yards and 11 TD's. Linebacker Chris Spielman set a team record with 195 tackles.

**Chicago Bears —** Although largely overmatched in terms of talent, the Bears were one of the NFL's surprise teams, thanks to excellent coaching, a sturdy defense, great play from their special teams and a bit of luck. Two new quarterbacks, Erik Kramer and Steve Walsh, took over in Chicago, but it wasn't until Walsh took over for Kramer that the Bears began to win. Walsh mastered the Bears' dink-and-dunk passing game and went 8-3 as the starter, and then led the team to an upset over Minnesota in the playoffs. Running back Lewis Tillman, another free-agent acquisition, gained 899 yards, but wide receiver Jeff Graham, who came to Chicago in a trade, was the top offensive player, catching 68

## FINAL TEAM STATISTICS

**OFFENSE**

| | ARIZ | ATL | CHI | DAL | DET | G.B. | L.A. | MINN | N.O. | NYG | PHIL | S.F. | T.B. | WASH |
|---|---|---|---|---|---|---|---|---|---|---|---|---|---|---|
| **FIRST DOWNS:** | | | | | | | | | | | | | | |
| Total | 287 | 302 | 274 | 322 | 280 | 314 | 274 | 325 | 308 | 263 | 293 | 362 | 276 | 269 |
| by Rushing | 90 | 63 | 88 | 136 | 94 | 88 | 80 | 92 | 78 | 103 | 103 | 122 | 104 | 79 |
| by Passing | 169 | 218 | 165 | 160 | 164 | 205 | 163 | 215 | 203 | 136 | 168 | 210 | 149 | 166 |
| by Penalty | 28 | 21 | 21 | 26 | 22 | 21 | 31 | 18 | 27 | 24 | 22 | 30 | 23 | 24 |
| **RUSHING:** | | | | | | | | | | | | | | |
| Number | 480 | 330 | 487 | 550 | 406 | 417 | 397 | 419 | 373 | 525 | 432 | 491 | 430 | 407 |
| Yards | 1560 | 1249 | 1588 | 1953 | 2080 | 1543 | 1389 | 1524 | 1336 | 1754 | 1761 | 1897 | 1489 | 1415 |
| Average Yards | 3.3 | 3.8 | 3.3 | 3.6 | 5.1 | 3.7 | 3.5 | 3.6 | 3.6 | 3.3 | 4.1 | 3.9 | 3.5 | 3.5 |
| Touchdowns | 12 | 8 | 10 | 26 | 12 | 11 | 6 | 11 | 11 | 12 | 14 | 23 | 8 | 5 |
| **PASSING:** | | | | | | | | | | | | | | |
| Attempts | 538 | 629 | 502 | 448 | 459 | 609 | 512 | 673 | 569 | 405 | 566 | 511 | 491 | 546 |
| Completions | 287 | 374 | 308 | 282 | 250 | 375 | 291 | 409 | 366 | 226 | 316 | 359 | 271 | 271 |
| Completion Pct. | 53.3 | 59.5 | 61.4 | 62.9 | 54.5 | 61.6 | 56.8 | 60.8 | 64.3 | 55.8 | 55.8 | 70.3 | 55.2 | 49.6 |
| Passing Yards | 3284 | 4344 | 3230 | 3461 | 3085 | 3977 | 3597 | 4570 | 4027 | 2847 | 3736 | 4362 | 3436 | 3524 |
| Avg. Yds per Att. | 6.10 | 6.91 | 6.43 | 7.73 | 6.72 | 6.53 | 7.03 | 6.79 | 7.08 | 7.03 | 6.60 | 8.54 | 7.00 | 6.45 |
| Avg. Yds per Comp. | 11.44 | 11.61 | 10.48 | 12.27 | 12.34 | 10.60 | 12.36 | 11.17 | 11.00 | 12.60 | 11.82 | 12.15 | 12.68 | 13.00 |
| Times Tackled | 34 | 37 | 25 | 20 | 26 | 33 | 35 | 31 | 24 | 46 | 48 | 35 | 30 | 21 |
| Yds Lost Tackled | 237 | 232 | 139 | 93 | 163 | 204 | 239 | 246 | 181 | 285 | 372 | 199 | 171 | 146 |
| Net Yards | 3047 | 4112 | 3091 | 3368 | 2922 | 3773 | 3358 | 4324 | 3846 | 2562 | 3364 | 4163 | 3265 | 3378 |
| Touchdowns | 11 | 25 | 19 | 19 | 24 | 33 | 23 | 18 | 22 | 16 | 18 | 37 | 17 | 25 |
| Interceptions | 19 | 25 | 16 | 14 | 14 | 14 | 18 | 20 | 18 | 18 | 14 | 11 | 16 | 27 |
| Pct. Intercepted | 3.5 | 4.0 | 3.2 | 3.1 | 3.1 | 2.3 | 3.5 | 3.0 | 3.2 | 4.4 | 2.5 | 2.2 | 3.3 | 4.9 |
| **PUNTS:** | | | | | | | | | | | | | | |
| Number | 98 | 79 | 76 | 70 | 64 | 81 | 78 | 77 | 67 | 89 | 92 | 54 | 74 | 82 |
| Average | 40.8 | 39.5 | 37.8 | 41.9 | 43.5 | 41.4 | 44.8 | 42.8 | 43.6 | 40.2 | 40.5 | 41.4 | 38.6 | 44.4 |
| **PUNT RETURNS** | | | | | | | | | | | | | | |
| Number | 42 | 31 | 27 | 44 | 25 | 49 | 40 | 39 | 25 | 32 | 41 | 40 | 28 | 32 |
| Yards | 286 | 188 | 218 | 404 | 256 | 414 | 461 | 238 | 152 | 388 | 381 | 334 | 248 | 452 |
| Average Yards | 6.5 | 6.1 | 8.1 | 9.2 | 10.2 | 8.4 | 11.4 | 6.1 | 6.1 | 12.1 | 9.3 | 8.4 | 8.9 | 14.1 |
| Touchdowns | 0 | 0 | 1 | 1 | 0 | 1 | 1 | 0 | 0 | 2 | 0 | 0 | 1 | 2 |
| **KICKOFF RET.:** | | | | | | | | | | | | | | |
| Number | 57 | 75 | 66 | 50 | 71 | 56 | 71 | 60 | 82 | 73 | 67 | 58 | 70 | 71 |
| Yards | 1079 | 1627 | 1402 | 1284 | 1675 | 1168 | 1605 | 1296 | 1840 | 1328 | 1441 | 1244 | 1422 | 1685 |
| Average Yards | 18.9 | 21.7 | 21.2 | 25.7 | 23.6 | 20.9 | 22.6 | 21.6 | 22.4 | 18.2 | 21.5 | 21.4 | 20.3 | 23.7 |
| Touchdowns | 0 | 0 | 0 | 1 | 4 | 1 | 0 | 0 | 2 | 0 | 1 | 1 | 0 | 0 |
| **INTERCEPT RET.:** | | | | | | | | | | | | | | |
| Number | 23 | 22 | 12 | 22 | 12 | 21 | 14 | 18 | 17 | 16 | 21 | 23 | 9 | 17 |
| Yards | 297 | 322 | 127 | 297 | 144 | 232 | 211 | 338 | 197 | 128 | 209 | 508 | 77 | 326 |
| Average Yards | 12.9 | 14.6 | 10.6 | 13.5 | 12.0 | 11.0 | 15.1 | 18.8 | 11.6 | 8.0 | 10.0 | 22.1 | 8.6 | 19.2 |
| Touchdowns | 1 | 2 | 0 | 3 | 2 | 1 | 1 | 4 | 1 | 0 | 2 | 4 | 0 | 3 |
| **PENALTIES:** | | | | | | | | | | | | | | |
| Number | 128 | 119 | 66 | 100 | 109 | 85 | 112 | 112 | 88 | 92 | 138 | 109 | 93 | 88 |
| Yards | 1090 | 934 | 503 | 895 | 781 | 760 | 922 | 880 | 678 | 818 | 1107 | 890 | 805 | 730 |
| **FUMBLES:** | | | | | | | | | | | | | | |
| Number | 25 | 28 | 21 | 22 | 26 | 25 | 26 | 32 | 22 | 28 | 23 | 25 | 18 | 21 |
| Number Lost | 10 | 11 | 10 | 10 | 10 | 8 | 13 | 14 | 14 | 7 | 12 | 13 | 7 | 13 |
| **POINTS:** | | | | | | | | | | | | | | |
| Total | 235 | 317 | 271 | 414 | 357 | 382 | 286 | 356 | 348 | 279 | 308 | 505 | 251 | 320 |
| 1-PT PAT/ATT. | 21/21 | 32/32 | 24/24 | 48/48 | 39/40 | 41/43 | 28/28 | 30/30 | 32/32 | 27/28 | 33/33 | 60/62 | 20/20 | 30/32 |
| 2-PT PAT/Att. | 1/3 | 3/4 | 2/6 | 0/2 | 2/3 | 1/4 | 2/5 | 4/5 | 2/6 | 1/2 | 0/2 | 2/4 | 3/6 | 3/5 |
| FG Attempts | 30 | 25 | 29 | 29 | 27 | 26 | 23 | 39 | 39 | 28 | 25 | 20 | 35 | 28 |
| FG Made | 22 | 21 | 21 | 22 | 18 | 19 | 18 | 34 | 28 | 22 | 21 | 15 | 23 | 20 |
| Percent FG Made | 73.3 | 84.0 | 72.4 | 75.9 | 66.7 | 73.1 | 78.3 | 87.1 | 71.8 | 78.6 | 84.0 | 75.0 | 65.7 | 71.4 |
| Safeties | 1 | 0 | 0 | 0 | 1 | 0 | 1 | 0 | 0 | 2 | 1 | 0 | 0 | 1 |

**DEFENSE**

| | ARIZ | ATL | CHI | DAL | DET | G.B. | L.A. | MINN | N.O. | NYG | PHIL | S.F. | T.B. | WASH |
|---|---|---|---|---|---|---|---|---|---|---|---|---|---|---|
| **FIRST DOWNS:** | | | | | | | | | | | | | | |
| Total | 245 | 330 | 275 | 273 | 326 | 281 | 333 | 287 | 337 | 280 | 275 | 285 | 298 | 331 |
| by Rushing | 71 | 107 | 100 | 86 | 131 | 82 | 103 | 65 | 106 | 92 | 94 | 82 | 100 | 129 |
| by Passing | 144 | 201 | 163 | 157 | 169 | 182 | 198 | 195 | 208 | 166 | 151 | 182 | 179 | 182 |
| by Penalty | 30 | 22 | 12 | 30 | 26 | 17 | 32 | 27 | 23 | 22 | 30 | 21 | 19 | 20 |
| **RUSHING:** | | | | | | | | | | | | | | |
| Number | 409 | 426 | 432 | 437 | 512 | 381 | 496 | 355 | 458 | 447 | 449 | 375 | 468 | 556 |
| Yards | 1370 | 1693 | 1922 | 1561 | 1859 | 1363 | 1781 | 1090 | 1758 | 1728 | 1616 | 1338 | 1964 | 1975 |
| Average Yards | 3.3 | 4.0 | 4.4 | 3.6 | 3.6 | 3.6 | 3.6 | 3.1 | 3.8 | 3.9 | 3.6 | 3.6 | 4.2 | 3.6 |
| Touchdowns | 7 | 16 | 10 | 8 | 15 | 9 | 12 | 9 | 10 | 11 | 11 | 16 | 13 | 24 |
| **PASSING:** | | | | | | | | | | | | | | |
| Attempts | 465 | 580 | 522 | 522 | 547 | 605 | 541 | 597 | 559 | 500 | 490 | 583 | 498 | 496 |
| Completions | 234 | 364 | 295 | 269 | 370 | 337 | 320 | 368 | 353 | 289 | 251 | 329 | 303 | 300 |
| Completion Pct. | 50.3 | 62.8 | 56.5 | 51.5 | 67.6 | 55.7 | 59.1 | 61.6 | 63.1 | 57.8 | 51.2 | 56.4 | 60.8 | 60.5 |
| Passing Yards | 3310 | 4365 | 3262 | 3051 | 3745 | 3677 | 3548 | 3902 | 4007 | 3391 | 3359 | 3756 | 3486 | 3799 |
| Avg. Yds per Att. | 7.12 | 7.53 | 6.25 | 5.84 | 6.85 | 6.08 | 6.56 | 6.54 | 7.17 | 6.78 | 6.86 | 6.44 | 7.00 | 7.66 |
| Avg. Yds per Comp. | 14.14 | 11.99 | 11.06 | 11.34 | 10.12 | 10.91 | 11.09 | 10.60 | 11.35 | 11.73 | 13.38 | 11.41 | 11.50 | 12.66 |
| Times Tackled | 35 | 32 | 28 | 47 | 27 | 37 | 26 | 36 | 36 | 26 | 42 | 38 | 20 | 28 |
| Yds Lost Tackled | 272 | 229 | 175 | 299 | 199 | 276 | 159 | 250 | 196 | 169 | 265 | 255 | 114 | 165 |
| Net Yards | 3038 | 4136 | 3087 | 2752 | 3546 | 3401 | 3389 | 3652 | 3811 | 3222 | 3094 | 3501 | 3372 | 3634 |
| Touchdowns | 27 | 12 | 14 | 19 | 16 | 17 | 11 | 22 | 13 | 22 | 14 | 23 | 22 | 24 |
| Interceptions | 23 | 22 | 12 | 22 | 12 | 21 | 14 | 18 | 17 | 16 | 21 | 23 | 9 | 17 |
| Pct. Intercepted | 4.9 | 3.8 | 2.3 | 4.2 | 2.2 | 3.5 | 2.6 | 3.0 | 3.0 | 3.2 | 4.3 | 3.9 | 1.8 | 3.4 |
| **PUNTS:** | | | | | | | | | | | | | | |
| Number | 90 | 62 | 72 | 84 | 66 | 88 | 74 | 86 | 60 | 69 | 90 | 77 | 68 | 87 |
| Average | 40.9 | 42.9 | 39.0 | 43.3 | 45.2 | 39.7 | 42.0 | 40.6 | 42.6 | 40.5 | 39.7 | 42.5 | 42.6 | 40.3 |
| **PUNT RETURNS** | | | | | | | | | | | | | | |
| Number | 40 | 31 | 26 | 36 | 36 | 36 | 47 | 44 | 40 | 39 | 47 | 28 | 19 | 45 |
| Yards | 270 | 273 | 225 | 378 | 431 | 272 | 637 | 410 | 495 | 307 | 286 | 242 | 103 | 441 |
| Average Yards | 6.8 | 8.8 | 8.7 | 10.5 | 12.0 | 7.6 | 13.6 | 9.3 | 12.2 | 7.9 | 6.1 | 8.4 | 5.4 | 9.8 |
| Touchdowns | 0 | 0 | 0 | 0 | 2 | 0 | 3 | 1 | 2 | 0 | 1 | 0 | 0 | 1 |
| **KICKOFF RET.:** | | | | | | | | | | | | | | |
| Number | 53 | 66 | 65 | 82 | 65 | 75 | 63 | 83 | 63 | 44 | 64 | 89 | 44 | 62 |
| Yards | 1214 | 1328 | 1271 | 1709 | 1572 | 1380 | 1446 | 1843 | 1493 | 923 | 1425 | 1912 | 941 | 1389 |
| Average Yards | 22.9 | 20.1 | 19.6 | 20.8 | 24.2 | 18.4 | 23.0 | 22.2 | 23.7 | 21.0 | 22.3 | 21.5 | 21.4 | 22.4 |
| Touchdowns | 1 | 0 | 1 | 0 | 1 | 1 | 2 | 1 | 0 | 0 | 0 | 0 | 0 | 1 |
| **INTERCEPT RET.:** | | | | | | | | | | | | | | |
| Number | 19 | 25 | 16 | 14 | 14 | 14 | 18 | 20 | 18 | 18 | 14 | 11 | 16 | 27 |
| Yards | 262 | 419 | 335 | 180 | 154 | 193 | 213 | 292 | 386 | 299 | 206 | 107 | 323 | 482 |
| Average Yards | 13.8 | 16.8 | 20.9 | 12.9 | 11.0 | 13.8 | 11.8 | 14.6 | 21.4 | 16.6 | 14.7 | 9.7 | 20.2 | 17.9 |
| Touchdowns | 2 | 1 | 0 | 1 | 3 | 2 | 3 | 6 | 1 | 0 | 0 | 0 | 1 | 2 |
| **PENALTIES:** | | | | | | | | | | | | | | |
| Number | 106 | 112 | 80 | 101 | 130 | 82 | 115 | 83 | 106 | 130 | 99 | 108 | 94 | 98 |
| Yards | 790 | 853 | 645 | 817 | 1031 | 661 | 1015 | 614 | 926 | 1122 | 849 | 921 | 690 | 839 |
| **FUMBLES:** | | | | | | | | | | | | | | |
| Number | 28 | 20 | 29 | 15 | 34 | 32 | 15 | 25 | 28 | 25 | 29 | 25 | 21 | 21 |
| Number Lost | 13 | 11 | 10 | 9 | 11 | 12 | 6 | 16 | 14 | 16 | 14 | 12 | 12 | 6 |
| **POINTS:** | | | | | | | | | | | | | | |
| Total | 267 | 385 | 307 | 248 | 342 | 287 | 365 | 314 | 407 | 305 | 308 | 296 | 351 | 412 |
| 1-PT PAT/ATT. | 27/28 | 39/40 | 25/26 | 24/24 | 38/38 | 24/24 | 38/38 | 31/31 | 41/41 | 30/30 | 27/28 | 23/23 | 38/38 | 46/46 |
| 2-PT PAT/Att. | 1/2 | 1/4 | 3/4 | 0/2 | 1/2 | 3/8 | 3/3 | 2/5 | 3/4 | 0/1 | 4/5 | 7/12 | 2/2 | 1/4 |
| FG Attempts | 24 | 33 | 41 | 25 | 28 | 25 | 29 | 30 | 37 | 34 | 26 | 21 | 26 | 28 |
| FG Made | 15 | 26 | 30 | 20 | 21 | 21 | 23 | 19 | 30 | 29 | 25 | 15 | 23 | 17 |
| Percent FG Made | 62.5 | 78.8 | 73.2 | 80.0 | 75.0 | 84.0 | 79.3 | 63.3 | 81.1 | 70.6 | 96.2 | 71.4 | 88.5 | 60.7 |
| Safeties | 3 | 1 | 0 | 1 | 0 | 1 | 0 | 0 | 0 | 1 | 0 | 2 | 0 | 0 |

passes for 944 yards and four touchdowns.

**Tampa Bay Buccaneers** — The Buccaneers had a chance to avoid losing 10 or more games for the 12th consecutive season. But, after four straight victories, as one might have expected, they lost their season finale and finished with a 6-10 record. Tampa Bay drafted quarterback Trent Dilfer with the fifth pick in the draft, but he was unimpressive when he got his chances, and Craig Erickson held onto the job. Erickson passed for 2,919 yards and 16 touchdowns. The best offensive player was rookie running back Errict Rhett, who came on with a late rush and gained 1,011 yards. The defense floundered, the kicking game wasn't very good and head coach Sam Wyche was in danger of being fired much of the season.

### WESTERN DIVISION

**San Francisco 49ers** — Credit team president Carmen Policy with mastering the new salary cap and being the main reason why the 49ers won their fifth Super Bowl. San Francisco signed several key free agents, and superstars Steve Young and Jerry Rice had their usual excellent seasons to lead the 49ers. Young won his fourth consecutive passing title and completed 70.3 percent of his passes while throwing 35 TD's, and Rice caught 112 passes for 1,499 yards and 13 touchdowns. Running back Ricky Watters, wide receiver John Taylor and tight end Brent Jones were also effective weapons on an offense that scored 505 points. Deion Sanders came over from Atlanta to spark a defense that was solid if not spectacular, and he even scored three touchdowns on interception returns. San Francisco rolled through the playoffs and emerged as the NFL's best team once again.

**New Orleans Saints** — The Saints missed the playoffs for the second straight season, and only victories in three of the final four games gave them a somewhat respectable 7-9 record. The Saints signed quarterback Jim Everett away from the Rams during the offseason, and he rebounded with an excellent season — 3,855 yards passing and 22 TD's. Rookie back Mario Bates was the best runner, finishing with 579 yards on the ground, and wide receivers Quinn Early and Michael Haynes combined for 159 receptions, the most ever by a New Orleans tandem. Likewise, tight ends Wesley Walls and Irv Smith combined for seven touchdowns. New Orleans' problem was a defense that ranked 25th in yards allowed.

**Atlanta Falcons** — In June Jones' first season as head coach, the Falcons improved slightly to 7-9 and might have made the playoffs if they could have won a few more close games (four losses were by four points or less). Atlanta did find some pleasant surprises. Quarterback Jeff George was signed away from Indianapolis, and he passed for 3,734 yards and 23 touchdowns. Also in his first season in Atlanta, wide receiver Terance Mathis caught 111 passes for 1,342 yards and 11 TD's. And Craig Heyward, another free-agent pickup, bounced back with 779 yards and seven touchdowns. Andre Rison chipped in with 81 catches and eight TD's. But the defense ranked 27th in yards allowed, and let up 92 points in two games against the 49ers.

**Los Angeles Rams** — The Rams fell apart in 1994, losing their final seven games, and Chuck Knox was fired after it ended. With a career record of 186-147-1, Knox was the sixth-winningest coach in NFL history. The Rams had quarterbacking problems all season, as Chris Miller and Chris Chandler both suffered numerous injuries. And running back Jerome Bettis, who was so good as a rookie in 1993, was so average in 1994. Bettis carried the ball 319 times but averaged only 3.2 yards for 1,025 total yards. The leading receiver was a backup running back, Johnny Bailey, who had 58 catches. The defensive line failed to provide much of a pass rush. And the Rams allowed 28 points a game over the final six weeks of the season.

## DALLAS COWBOYS 12-4 Barry Switzer

| Scores of Each Game | | |
|---|---|---|
| 29 | Pittsburgh | 9 |
| 20 | HOUSTON | 17 |
| 17 | DETROIT | *20 |
| 34 | Washington | 7 |
| 38 | ARIZONA | 3 |
| 24 | PHILADELPHIA | 13 |
| 28 | Arizona | 21 |
| 23 | Cincinnati | 20 |
| 38 | N.Y. GIANTS | 10 |
| 14 | San Francisco | 21 |
| 31 | WASHINGTON | 7 |
| 42 | GREEN BAY | 31 |
| 31 | Philadelphia | 19 |
| 14 | CLEVELAND | 19 |
| 24 | New Orleans | 16 |
| 10 | N.Y. Giants | 15 |

| Use Name | Pos. | Hgt. | Wgt. | Age | Int | Pts |
|---|---|---|---|---|---|---|
| Larry Allen | OT | 6'3" | 325 | 22 | | |
| George Hegamin | OT | 6'7" | 338 | 21 | | |
| Ron Stone | OT-OG | 6'5" | 309 | 23 | | |
| Mark Tuinei | OT | 6'5" | 305 | 24 | | |
| Erik Williams | OT | 6'6" | 322 | 25 | | |
| Dale Hellestrae | OG-C | 6'5" | 288 | 32 | | |
| Derek Kennard | OG | 6'3" | 333 | 31 | | |
| Nate Newton | OG | 6'3" | 320 | 32 | | |
| Mark Stepnoski | C | 6'2" | 262 | 27 | | |
| Shante Carver | DE | 6'5" | 242 | 23 | | |
| Charles Haley | DE | 6'5" | 255 | 30 | 1 | |
| Jim Jeffcoat | DE | 6'5" | 280 | 33 | | |
| Tony Tolbert | DE | 6'6" | 263 | 26 | 1 | 6 |
| Chad Hennings | DT | 6'6" | 288 | 28 | | |
| Leon Lett | DT | 6'6" | 288 | 25 | | |
| Russell Maryland | DT | 6'1" | 279 | 25 | | |
| Hurvin McCormack | DT | 6'5" | 274 | 22 | | |
| Darrick Brownlow | LB | 6' | 241 | 25 | | |
| Dixon Edwards | LB | 6'1" | 225 | 26 | | |
| Robert Jones | LB | 6'2" | 237 | 24 | | |
| Godfrey Myles | LB | 6'1" | 242 | 25 | | |
| Jim Schwantz | LB | 6'2" | 232 | 24 | | |
| Darrin Smith | LB | 6'1" | 230 | 24 | 2 | 6 |
| Matt Vanderbeek | LB | 6'3" | 243 | 27 | | |
| Bill Bates | DB | 6'1" | 210 | 33 | | |
| Larry Brown | DB | 5'11" | 186 | 24 | 4 | |
| Joe Fishback | DB | 6' | 212 | 26 | | |
| Kenneth Gant | DB | 5'11" | 196 | 27 | 1 | |
| Clayton Holmes | DB | 5'10" | 181 | 25 | | |
| Brock Marion | DB | 5'11" | 189 | 24 | 1 | |
| Kevin Smith | DB | 5'11" | 184 | 24 | 2 | |
| Darren Studstill | DB | 6'1" | 186 | 24 | | |
| Dave Thomas | DB | 6'2" | 213 | 26 | | |
| James Washington | DB | 6'1" | 209 | 29 | 5 | |
| Darren Woodson | DB | 6'1" | 215 | 25 | 5 | 6 |
| Troy Aikman | QB | 6'4" | 228 | 27 | | 6 |
| Jason Garrett | QB | 6'2" | 195 | 28 | | |
| Rodney Peete | QB | 6' | 215 | 28 | | |
| Lincoln Coleman | HB | 6'1" | 239 | 25 | | 6 |
| Emmitt Smith | HB | 5'9" | 209 | 25 | | 132 |
| Blair Thomas (from NE) | HB | 5'10" | 202 | 27 | | 12 |
| Tommie Agee | FB | 6' | 235 | 30 | | |
| Daryl Johnston | FB | 6'2" | 228 | 28 | | 24 |
| Cory Fleming | WR | 6'1" | 216 | 23 | | |
| Alvin Harper | WR | 6'3" | 214 | 27 | | 48 |
| Michael Irvin | WR | 6'2" | 205 | 28 | | 36 |
| Kevin Williams | WR | 5'9" | 195 | 23 | | 12 |
| Scott Galbraith | TE | 6'2" | 255 | 27 | | |
| Jay Novacek | TE | 6'4" | 234 | 31 | | 12 |
| Chris Boniol | K | 5'11" | 159 | 22 | | 114 |
| John Jett | K | 6' | 194 | 25 | | |

Derrick Lassic — Knee injury

## NEW YORK GIANTS 9-7 Dan Reeves

| Scores of Each Game | | |
|---|---|---|
| 28 | PHILADELPHIA | 23 |
| 20 | Arizona | 17 |
| 31 | WASHINGTON | 23 |
| 22 | New Orleans | 27 |
| 10 | MINNESOTA | 27 |
| 10 | L.A. Rams | 17 |
| 6 | PITTSBURGH | 10 |
| 25 | DETROIT | *28 |
| 10 | Dallas | 38 |
| 9 | ARIZONA | 10 |
| 13 | Houston | 10 |
| 21 | Washington | 19 |
| 16 | Cleveland | 13 |
| 27 | CINCINNATI | 20 |
| 16 | Philadelphia | 13 |
| 15 | DALLAS | 10 |

| Use Name | Pos. | Hgt. | Wgt. | Age | Int | Pts |
|---|---|---|---|---|---|---|
| Greg Bishop | OT | 6'5" | 295 | 23 | | |
| John Elliott | OT | 6'7" | 308 | 29 | | |
| Doug Riesenberg | OT | 6'5" | 280 | 29 | | |
| Scott Davis | OG | 6'3" | 289 | 24 | | |
| William Roberts | OG | 6'5" | 292 | 32 | | |
| Lance Smith | OG | 6'3" | 290 | 31 | | |
| Adam Schrieber | C | 6'4" | 290 | 32 | | |
| Brian Williams | C | 6'5" | 300 | 28 | | |
| Chad Bratzke | DE | 6'4" | 262 | 22 | | |
| Keith Hamilton | DE | 6'6" | 290 | 23 | | |
| Coleman Rudolph | DE | 6'4" | 270 | 23 | | |
| Mike Strahan | DE | 6'4" | 270 | 22 | | |
| Stacey Dillard | DT | 6'5" | 292 | 25 | | |
| Mike Fox | DT-DE | 6'6" | 288 | 27 | | |
| Erik Howard | DT | 6'4" | 275 | 29 | | |
| Chirs Maumalanga | DT | 6'2" | 288 | 22 | | |
| Jessie Armstead | LB | 6'1" | 228 | 23 | 1 | |
| Carlton Bailey | LB | 6'3" | 235 | 29 | | |
| Michael Brooks | LB | 6'1" | 235 | 30 | 1 | |
| Marcus Buckley | LB | 6'3" | 235 | 23 | | |
| Corey Miller | LB | 6'2" | 255 | 25 | 2 | |
| Andre Powell | LB | 6'1" | 235 | 25 | | |
| Pete Shufelt | LB | 6'3" | 240 | 24 | | |
| Corey Widmer | LB | 6'3" | 250 | 25 | | |
| Willie Beamon | DB | 5'11" | 175 | 24 | | |
| John Booty | DB | 6' | 180 | 28 | 3 | |
| Jesse Campbell | DB | 6'1" | 215 | 25 | 2 | |
| Thomas Randolph | DB | 5'9" | 176 | 23 | 1 | |
| Corey Raymond | DB | 5'11" | 185 | 25 | 1 | |
| Jason Sehorn | DB | 6'2" | 212 | 23 | | |
| Phillippi Sparks | DB | 5'11" | 190 | 25 | 3 | |
| Jarvis Williams | DB | 5'11" | 200 | 29 | 2 | |
| Tito Wooten | DB | 6' | 181 | 22 | | |
| Dave Brown | QB | 6'5" | 225 | 24 | | 12 |
| Kent Graham | QB | 6'5" | 236 | 25 | | |
| Stan White | QB | 6'2" | 202 | 23 | | |
| Keith Elias | HB | 5'9" | 191 | 22 | | |
| Rodney Hampton | HB | 5'11" | 230 | 25 | | 38 |
| Dave Meggett | HB | 5'7" | 195 | 28 | | 36 |
| Gary Downs | FB | 6' | 212 | 23 | | |
| Kenyon Rasheed | FB | 5'10" | 235 | 24 | | |
| Chris Calloway | WR | 5'10" | 185 | 26 | | 12 |
| Omar Douglas | WR | 5'10" | 170 | 22 | | |
| Thomas Lewis | WR | 6'1" | 185 | 22 | | |
| Arthur Marshall | WR | 5'11" | 178 | 25 | | |
| Mike Sherrard | WR | 6'2" | 187 | 31 | | 36 |
| Derek Brown | TE | 6'6" | 260 | 24 | | |
| Howard Cross | TE | 6'5" | 258 | 27 | | 24 |
| Brian Kozlowski | TE | 6'3" | 250 | 23 | | |
| Aaron Pierce | TE | 6'5" | 248 | 25 | | 24 |
| Brad Daluiso | K | 6'2" | 215 | 26 | | 38 |
| Mike Horan | K | 5'11" | 188 | 35 | | |
| David Treadwell | K | 6'1" | 185 | 29 | | 55 |

## ARIZONA CARDINALS 8-8 Buddy Ryan

| Scores of Each Game | | |
|---|---|---|
| 12 | L.A. Rams | 14 |
| 17 | N.Y. GIANTS | 20 |
| 0 | Cleveland | 32 |
| 17 | MINNESOTA | 7 |
| 3 | Dallas | 38 |
| 19 | Washington | *16 |
| 21 | DALLAS | 28 |
| 20 | PITTSBURGH | *17 |
| 7 | Philadelphia | 17 |
| 10 | N.Y. Giants | 9 |
| 12 | PHILADELPHIA | 6 |
| 16 | CHICAGO | *19 |
| 30 | Houston | 12 |
| 17 | WASHINGTON | 15 |
| 28 | CINCINNATI | 7 |
| 6 | Atlanta | 10 |

| Use Name | Pos. | Hgt. | Wgt. | Age | Int | Pts |
|---|---|---|---|---|---|---|
| Ben Coleman | OT-OG | 6'6" | 335 | 23 | | |
| Rick Cunningham | OT-OG | 6'6" | 320 | 27 | | |
| Luis Sharpe | OT | 6'4" | 280 | 34 | | |
| Mark Vander Poel | OT | 6'7" | 303 | 26 | | |
| Ernest Dye | OG | 6'6" | 325 | 23 | | |
| Anthony Redmon | OG | 6'4" | 308 | 23 | | |
| Mark Tucker | OG | 6'3" | 290 | 26 | | |
| Joe Wolf | OG | 6'6" | 296 | 27 | | |
| Ed Cunningham | C | 6'3" | 285 | 25 | | |
| Michael Bankston | DE-DT | 6'2" | 280 | 24 | | |
| Michael Brandon | DE | 6'4" | 290 | 26 | | |
| Chad Brown | DE | 6'7" | 265 | 23 | | |
| Karl Dunbar | DE | 6'4" | 275 | 27 | | |
| Eric England | DE | 6'2" | 283 | 23 | | |
| Keith McCants (from HOU) | DE | 6'3" | 265 | 26 | 1 | 6 |
| Clyde Simmons | DE | 6'6" | 280 | 30 | | |
| Sebastian Barrie | DT | 6'2" | 280 | 24 | | |
| Eric Swann | DT | 6'4" | 295 | 24 | 1 | 2 |
| Bernard Wilson | DT | 6'2" | 295 | 24 | | |
| Eric Hill | LB | 6'1" | 255 | 27 | | |
| Terry Irving | B | 6' | 224 | 23 | | |
| Garth Jax | LB | 6'2" | 250 | 30 | | |
| Seth Joyner | LB | 6'2" | 235 | 29 | 3 | |
| Randy Kirk | LB | 6'2" | 231 | 29 | | |
| Wilber Marshall | LB | 6'1" | 231 | 32 | | |
| David Merritt | LB | 6'1" | 237 | 22 | | |
| Jamir Miller | LB | 6'4" | 242 | 20 | | |
| Brent Alexander | DB | 5'10" | 184 | 23 | | |
| Herschel Currie | DB | | | | | |
| Odie Harris | DB | 6' | 190 | 28 | | |
| Terry Hoage | DB | 6'2" | 201 | 32 | 3 | |
| Lorenzo Lynch | DB | 5'9" | 200 | 31 | 2 | |
| Chris Oldham | DB | 5'9" | 195 | 25 | | |
| Andre Waters | DB | 5'11" | 200 | 32 | | |
| Aeneas Williams | DB | 5'10" | 190 | 26 | 9 | |
| James Williams | DB | 5'10" | 185 | 27 | 4 | |
| Steve Beuerlein | QB | 6'3" | 210 | 29 | | |
| Jim McMahon | QB | 6'1" | 195 | 35 | | |
| Jay Schroeder | QB | 6'4" | 215 | 33 | | |
| Larry Centers | HB | 5'11" | 215 | 26 | | 42 |
| Garrison Hearst | HB | 5'11" | 215 | 23 | | 6 |
| Mark Higgs (from MIA) | HB | 5'7" | 199 | 28 | | |
| Chuck Levy | HB-WR | 6' | 197 | 22 | | |
| Fred McAfee (to PIT) | HB | 5'10" | 195 | 26 | | 12 |
| Ronald Moore | HB-FB | 5'10" | 220 | 23 | | 32 |
| Barry Word | HB | 6'2" | 245 | 30 | | |
| Frank Harvey | FB | 6' | 245 | 23 | | |
| Brian Henesey | FB | 5'10" | 215 | 24 | | |
| Gary Clark | WR | 5'9" | 175 | 32 | | 6 |
| Randal Hill | WR | 5'10" | 180 | 24 | | |
| Kevin Knox | WR | 6'3" | 195 | 23 | | |
| Ricky Proehl | WR | 5'10" | 190 | 26 | | 30 |
| Bryan Reeves | WR | 5'11" | 195 | 24 | | 6 |
| Patrick Robinson | WR | 5'8" | 176 | 24 | | |
| Chad Fann | TE | 6'3" | 250 | 24 | | |
| Terry Samuels | TE | 6'2" | 254 | 23 | | |
| Derek Ware (to CIN) | TE | 6'2" | 250 | 26 | | 6 |
| Greg Davis | K | 6' | 205 | 28 | | 77 |
| Jeff Feagles | K | 6'1" | 205 | 28 | | |
| Todd Peterson | K | 5'10" | 176 | 24 | | 10 |

Anthony Edwards — Knee injury

## PHILADELPHIA EAGLES 7-9 Rich Kotite

| Scores of Each Game | | |
|---|---|---|
| 23 | N.Y. Giants | 28 |
| 30 | CHICAGO | 22 |
| 13 | GREEN BAY | 7 |
| 40 | San Francisco | 8 |
| 21 | WASHINGTON | 17 |
| 13 | Dallas | 24 |
| 21 | HOUSTON | 6 |
| 31 | Washington | 29 |
| 17 | ARIZONA | 7 |
| 7 | CLEVELAND | 26 |
| 6 | Arizona | 12 |
| 21 | Atlanta | 28 |
| 19 | DALLAS | 31 |
| 3 | Pittsburgh | 14 |
| 13 | N.Y. GIANTS | 16 |
| 30 | Cincinnati | 33 |

| Use Name | Pos. | Hgt. | Wgt. | Age | Int | Pts |
|---|---|---|---|---|---|---|
| Antone Davis | OT | 6'4" | 325 | 27 | | |
| Tom McHale | OT | 6'4" | 290 | 31 | | |
| Broderick Thompson | OT | 6'5" | 295 | 34 | | |
| Bernard Williams | OT | 6'8" | 317 | 22 | | |
| Lester Holmes | OG | 6'3" | 301 | 24 | | |
| John Hudson | OG-C | 6'2" | 275 | 26 | | |
| Joe Panos | OG-C | 6'2" | 296 | 23 | | |
| Rob Selby | OG | 6'3" | 286 | 26 | | |
| David Alexander | C | 6'3" | 275 | 30 | | |
| Mike Flores | DE | 6'3" | 256 | 27 | | |
| William Fuller | DE | 6'3" | 274 | 32 | | 2 |
| Burt Grossman | DE | 6'4" | 275 | 27 | | |
| Greg Townsend | DE | 6'3" | 275 | 32 | | |
| Andy Harmon | DT | 6'4" | 265 | 25 | 1 | |
| Tommy Jeter | DT | 6'5" | 282 | 24 | | |
| William Perry | DT | 6'2" | 335 | 31 | | |
| Leonard Renfro | DT | 6'2" | 291 | 24 | | |
| Byron Evans | LB | 6'2" | 235 | 30 | 1 | |
| Britt Hager | LB | 6'1" | 225 | 28 | 1 | |
| Vaughan Johnson | LB | 6'3" | 240 | 32 | | |
| Derrick Oden | LB | 5'11" | 230 | 23 | | |
| Bill Romanowski | LB | 6'4" | 231 | 28 | 2 | |
| Ken Rose | LB | 6'1" | 215 | 32 | | |
| William Thomas | LB | 6'2" | 218 | 26 | 1 | |
| Marc Woodard | LB | 6' | 234 | 24 | | |
| Eric Allen | DB | 5'10" | 180 | 28 | 3 | |
| Derrick Frazier | DB | 5'10" | 178 | 24 | | |
| Al Jackson | DB | 6' | 182 | 22 | | |
| Greg Jackson | DB | 6'1" | 210 | 28 | 6 | 6 |
| Mark McMillian | DB | 5'7" | 162 | 24 | 2 | |
| Rich Miano | DB | 6'1" | 200 | 31 | | |
| Mike Reid | DB | 6'1" | 218 | 23 | | |
| Otis Smith | DB | 5'11" | 184 | 28 | | |
| Eric Zomalt | DB | 5'11" | 197 | 22 | | |
| Mike Zordich | DB | 6'1" | 201 | 30 | 4 | 6 |
| Bubby Brister | QB | 6'3" | 207 | 32 | | |
| Randall Cunningham | QB | 6'4" | 205 | 31 | | 18 |
| Charlie Garner | HB | 5'9" | 181 | 22 | | 18 |
| Vaughn Hebron | HB | 5'8" | 196 | 23 | | 12 |
| James Joseph | HB-FB | 6' | 222 | 26 | | 18 |
| Herschel Walker | HB | 6'1" | 225 | 32 | | 48 |
| Brian O'Neal | FB | 6' | 233 | 24 | | |
| Victor Bailey | WR | 6'2" | 196 | 24 | | 6 |
| Fred Barnett | WR | 6' | 199 | 28 | | 30 |
| Jeff Sydner | WR | 5'6" | 170 | 24 | | |
| Calvin Williams | WR | 5'11" | 190 | 27 | | 18 |
| Mark Bavaro | TE | 6'4" | 245 | 31 | | 18 |
| Maurice Johnson | TE | 6'2" | 243 | 27 | | 12 |
| Bryan Barker | K | 6'1" | 187 | 30 | | |
| Mitch Berger | K | 6'2" | 231 | 22 | | |
| Eddie Murray | K | 5'11" | 195 | 38 | | 96 |
| Jeff Wilkins | K | 6'1" | 180 | 22 | | |

Mike Chalenski — Knee injury

Corey Barlow — Knee injury

## WASHINGTON REDSKINS 3-13 Norv Turner

| Scores of Each Game | | |
|---|---|---|
| 35 | DALLAS | 16 |
| 10 | PHOENIX | 17 |
| 31 | Philadelphia | 34 |
| 10 | Miami | 17 |
| 7 | N.Y. GIANTS | 41 |
| 6 | Phoenix | 36 |
| 10 | Buffalo | 24 |
| 30 | INDIANAPOLIS | 24 |
| 6 | N.Y. Giants | 20 |
| 6 | L.A. Rams | 10 |
| 14 | PHILADELPHIA | 17 |
| 23 | Tampa Bay | 17 |
| 0 | N.Y. JETS | 3 |
| 30 | ATLANTA | 17 |
| 3 | Dallas | 38 |
| 9 | MINNESOTA | 14 |

| Use Name | Pos. | Hgt. | Wgt. | Age | Int | Pts |
|---|---|---|---|---|---|---|
| Tré Johnson | OT | 6'2" | 315 | 23 | | |
| Jim Lachey | OT | 6'6" | 294 | 31 | | |
| Ed Simmons | OT | 6'5" | 300 | 30 | | |
| Ray Brown | OT | 6'5" | 312 | 31 | | |
| Joe Patton | OG | 6'5" | 288 | 22 | | |
| Mark Schlereth | OG | 6'3" | 278 | 28 | | |
| Vernice Smith | OG | 6'3" | 298 | 28 | | |
| John Gesek | C | 6'5" | 282 | 31 | | |
| Trevor Match | C | 6'4" | 297 | 32 | | |
| Raleigh McKenzie | C-OG | 6'2" | 277 | 31 | | |
| Shane Collins | DE | 6'3" | 267 | 25 | | |
| Leonard Marshall | DE | 6'3" | 288 | 32 | | |
| Dexter Nottage | DE | 6'4" | 273 | 23 | | |
| Sterling Palmer | DE | 6'5" | 256 | 23 | | |
| Tony Woods | DE | 6'4" | 269 | 28 | | |
| Mark Boutte | DT | 6'4" | 296 | 25 | | |
| Tim Johnson | DT | 6'3" | 275 | 29 | | |
| Lamar Mills | DT | 6'5" | 270 | 23 | | |
| Bobby Wilson | DT | 6'2" | 297 | 26 | | |
| Erick Anderson | LB | 6'1" | 240 | 25 | | |
| Monte Coleman | LB | 6'2" | 242 | 36 | | |
| Andre Collins | LB | 6'1" | 231 | 26 | 4 | 12 |
| Kurt Gouveia | LB | 6'1" | 233 | 29 | 1 | |
| Ken Harvey | LB | 6'2" | 245 | 29 | | |
| Lamont Hollinquest | LB | 6'3" | 245 | 23 | 1 | |
| Tyronne Stowe | LB | 6'2" | 250 | 29 | 1 | |
| Martin Bayless | DB | 6'2" | 213 | 31 | 3 | 6 |
| Deral Boykin | DB | 5'11" | 196 | 23 | | |
| Tom Carter | DB | 5'11" | 181 | 21 | 3 | |
| Pat Eilers | DB | 5'11" | 197 | 27 | | |
| Alan Grant | DB | 5'11" | 187 | 27 | 1 | |
| Darrell Green | DB | 5'8" | 170 | 34 | 3 | 6 |
| A.J. Johnson | DB | 5'8" | 175 | 27 | | |
| Alvoid Mays | DB | 5'9" | 172 | 28 | | |
| Darryl Morrison | CB | 5'11" | 185 | 23 | | 6 |
| Sebastian Savage | DB | 5'10" | 187 | 24 | | |
| Keith Taylor | DB | 5'11" | 206 | 29 | | |
| Johnny Thomas | DB | 5'9" | 191 | 30 | | |
| Gus Frerotte | QB | 6'2" | 221 | 23 | | |
| John Friesz | QB | 6'4" | 218 | 27 | | |
| Heath Shuler | QB | 6'2" | 221 | 22 | | |
| William Bell | HB | 5'11" | 203 | 23 | | |
| Reggie Brooks | HB | 5'8" | 202 | 23 | | 12 |
| Ricky Ervins | HB | 5'7" | 195 | 25 | | 24 |
| Tyrone Rush | HB | 5'11" | 196 | 23 | | |
| Brian Mitchell | FB-HB | 5'10" | 203 | 26 | | 20 |
| Cedric Smith | FB | 5'10" | 222 | 26 | | 6 |
| Frank Wycheck | FB | 6'3" | 235 | 22 | | 6 |
| Henry Ellard | WR | 5'11" | 182 | 33 | | 36 |
| Desmond Howard | WR | 5'9" | 180 | 24 | | 32 |
| Leslie Shepherd | WR | 5'11" | 189 | 24 | | |
| Olanda Truitt | WR | 6' | 186 | 23 | | 6 |
| Tydus Winans | WR | 5'11" | 180 | 22 | | 14 |
| Kurt Haws | TE | 6'5" | 248 | 24 | | |
| Ethan Horton | TE | 6'4" | 240 | 31 | | 18 |
| James Jenkins | TE | 6'2" | 241 | 27 | | 24 |
| Chip Lohmiller | K | 6'3" | 215 | 28 | | 90 |
| Reggie Roby | K | 6'2" | 258 | 33 | | |

Mark Stock — Knee

## DALLAS COWBOYS

### RUSHING
| Last Name | No. | Yds | Avg | TD |
|---|---|---|---|---|
| E. Smith | 368 | 1484 | 4.0 | 21 |
| Coleman | 64 | 180 | 2.8 | 1 |
| Johnston | 40 | 138 | 3.5 | 2 |
| B. Thomas | 43 | 137 | 3.2 | 2 |
| Aikman | 30 | 62 | 2.1 | 1 |
| K. Williams | 6 | 20 | 3.3 | 0 |
| Agee | 5 | 4 | 0.8 | 0 |
| Wilson | 1 | -1 | -1.0 | 0 |
| Peete | 9 | -2 | -0.2 | 0 |
| Garrett | 3 | -2 | -0.7 | 0 |

### RECEIVING
| Last Name | No. | Yds | Avg | TD |
|---|---|---|---|---|
| Irvin | 79 | 1241 | 15.7 | 6 |
| E. Smith | 50 | 341 | 6.8 | 1 |
| Novacek | 47 | 475 | 10.1 | 2 |
| Johnston | 44 | 325 | 7.4 | 2 |
| Harper | 33 | 821 | 24.9 | 8 |
| K. Williams | 13 | 181 | 13.9 | 0 |
| Coleman | 8 | 46 | 5.8 | 0 |
| Galbraith | 4 | 31 | 7.8 | 0 |
| B. Thomas | 4 | 16 | 4.0 | 0 |
| Agee | 1 | 2 | 2.0 | 0 |
| Kennard | 1 | -3 | -3.0 | 0 |

### PUNT RETURNS
| Last Name | No. | Yds | Avg | TD |
|---|---|---|---|---|
| K. Williams | 39 | 349 | 8.9 | 1 |
| Holmes | 5 | 55 | 11.0 | 0 |

### KICKOFF RETURNS
| Last Name | No. | Yds | Avg | TD |
|---|---|---|---|---|
| K. Williams | 43 | 1148 | 26.7 | 1 |
| Holmes | 4 | 89 | 22.3 | 0 |
| B. Thomas | 3 | 40 | 13.3 | 0 |
| Marion | 2 | 39 | 19.5 | 0 |
| R. Jones | 1 | 8 | 8.0 | 0 |

### PASSING — PUNTING — KICKING
| PASSING | Att | Cmp | % | Yds | Yd/Att | TD | Int— | % | RK |
|---|---|---|---|---|---|---|---|---|---|
| Aikman | 361 | 233 | 64.5 | 2676 | 7.41 | 13 | 12— | 3.3 | 4 |
| Peete | 56 | 33 | 58.9 | 470 | 8.39 | 4 | 1— | 1.8 | |
| Garrett | 31 | 16 | 51.6 | 315 | 10.16 | 2 | 1— | 3.2 | |

| PUNTING | No. | Avg. |
|---|---|---|
| Jett | 70 | 41.9 |

| KICKING | XP | ATT | % | FG | ATT | % |
|---|---|---|---|---|---|---|
| Boniol | 48 | 48 | 100 | 22 | 29 | 76 |

2 POINT XP: None

## NEW YORK GIANTS

### RUSHING
| Last Name | No. | Yds | Avg | TD |
|---|---|---|---|---|
| Hampton | 327 | 1075 | 3.3 | 6 |
| Meggett | 91 | 298 | 3.3 | 4 |
| Da. Brown | 60 | 196 | 3.3 | 2 |
| Calloway | 8 | 77 | 9.6 | 0 |
| Downs | 15 | 51 | 3.4 | 0 |
| Rasheed | 17 | 44 | 2.6 | 0 |
| Graham | 2 | 11 | 5.5 | 0 |
| Marshall | 2 | 8 | 4.0 | 0 |
| Elias | 2 | 4 | 2.0 | 0 |
| Sherrard | 1 | -10 | -10.0 | 0 |

### RECEIVING
| Last Name | No. | Yds | Avg | TD |
|---|---|---|---|---|
| Sherrard | 53 | 825 | 15.6 | 6 |
| Calloway | 43 | 666 | 15.5 | 2 |
| Meggett | 32 | 293 | 9.2 | 0 |
| Cross | 31 | 364 | 11.7 | 4 |
| Pierce | 20 | 214 | 10.7 | 4 |
| Marshall | 16 | 219 | 13.7 | 0 |
| Hampton | 14 | 103 | 7.4 | 0 |
| Rasheed | 10 | 97 | 9.7 | 0 |
| Lewis | 4 | 46 | 11.5 | 0 |
| Downs | 2 | 15 | 7.5 | 0 |
| Kozlowski | 1 | 5 | 5.0 | 0 |

### PUNT RETURNS
| Last Name | No. | Yds | Avg | TD |
|---|---|---|---|---|
| Meggett | 26 | 323 | 12.4 | 2 |
| Lewis | 5 | 64 | 12.8 | 0 |
| Marshall | 1 | 1 | 1.0 | 0 |

### KICKOFF RETURNS
| Last Name | No. | Yds | Avg | TD |
|---|---|---|---|---|
| Meggett | 29 | 548 | 18.9 | 0 |
| Lewis | 26 | 509 | 19.6 | 0 |
| Marshall | 15 | 249 | 16.6 | 0 |
| Kozlowski | 2 | 21 | 10.5 | 0 |
| De. Brown | 1 | 1 | 1.0 | 0 |

### PASSING — PUNTING — KICKING
| PASSING | Att | Cmp | % | Yds | Yd/Att | TD | Int— | % | RK |
|---|---|---|---|---|---|---|---|---|---|
| Da. Brown | 350 | 201 | 57.4 | 2536 | 7.25 | 12 | 16— | 4.6 | 11 |
| Graham | 53 | 24 | 45.3 | 295 | 5.57 | 3 | 2— | 3.8 | |
| Meggett | 2 | 1 | 50.0 | 16 | 8.00 | 1 | 0— | 0.0 | |

| PUNTING | No. | Avg. |
|---|---|---|
| Horan | 87 | 40.5 |
| Da. Brown | 2 | 28.5 |

| KICKING | XP | ATT | % | FG | ATT | % |
|---|---|---|---|---|---|---|
| Treadwell | 22 | 23 | 96 | 11 | 17 | 65 |
| Daluiso | 5 | 5 | 100 | 11 | 11 | 100 |

2 POINT XP: Hampton (1)

## ARIZONA CARDINALS

### RUSHING
| Last Name | No. | Yds | Avg | TD |
|---|---|---|---|---|
| Moore | 232 | 780 | 3.4 | 4 |
| Centers | 115 | 336 | 2.9 | 5 |
| Higgs | 62 | 195 | 3.1 | 0 |
| Hearst | 37 | 169 | 4.6 | 1 |
| Schroeder | 16 | 59 | 3.7 | 0 |
| McAfee | 18 | 51 | 2.8 | 2 |
| Beuerlein | 22 | 39 | 1.8 | 1 |
| McMahon | 6 | 32 | 5.3 | 0 |
| Levy | 3 | 15 | 5.0 | 0 |
| Feagles | 2 | 8 | 4.0 | 0 |
| Samuels | 1 | 1 | 1.0 | 0 |
| Reeves | 1 | -1 | -1.0 | 0 |

### RECEIVING
| Last Name | No. | Yds | Avg | TD |
|---|---|---|---|---|
| Centers | 77 | 647 | 8.4 | 2 |
| Proehl | 51 | 651 | 12.8 | 5 |
| Clark | 50 | 771 | 15.4 | 1 |
| R. Hill | 38 | 544 | 14.3 | 0 |
| Ware | 17 | 171 | 10.1 | 1 |
| Reeves | 14 | 202 | 14.4 | 1 |
| Fann | 12 | 96 | 8.0 | 0 |
| Samuels | 8 | 57 | 7.1 | 0 |
| R. Moore | 8 | 52 | 6.5 | 1 |
| Hearst | 6 | 49 | 8.2 | 0 |
| Levy | 4 | 35 | 8.8 | 0 |
| Robinson | 1 | 5 | 5.0 | 0 |
| McAfee | 1 | 4 | 4.0 | 0 |

### PUNT RETURNS
| Last Name | No. | Yds | Avg | TD |
|---|---|---|---|---|
| Robinson | 41 | 285 | 7.0 | 0 |
| Reeves | 1 | 1 | 1.0 | 0 |

### KICKOFF RETURNS
| Last Name | No. | Yds | Avg | TD |
|---|---|---|---|---|
| Levy | 26 | 513 | 19.7 | 0 |
| Robinson | 12 | 231 | 19.3 | 0 |
| McAfee | 7 | 113 | 16.1 | 0 |
| Henesey | 6 | 108 | 18.0 | 0 |
| Reeves | 3 | 83 | 27.7 | 0 |
| Higgs | 2 | 25 | 12.5 | 0 |
| Samuels | 1 | 6 | 6.0 | 0 |

### PASSING — PUNTING — KICKING
| PASSING | Att | Cmp | % | Yds | Yd/Att | TD | Int— | % | RK |
|---|---|---|---|---|---|---|---|---|---|
| Beuerlein | 255 | 130 | 51.0 | 1545 | 6.06 | 5 | 9— | 3.5 | 14 |
| Schroeder | 238 | 133 | 55.9 | 1510 | 6.34 | 4 | 7— | 2.9 | 12 |
| McMahon | 43 | 23 | 53.5 | 219 | 5.09 | 1 | 3— | 7.0 | |
| Hearst | 1 | 1 | 100.0 | 10 | 10.00 | 1 | 0— | 0.0 | |
| R. Moore | 1 | 0 | 0.0 | 0 | 0.00 | 0 | 0— | 0.0 | |

| PUNTING | No. | Avg. |
|---|---|---|
| Feagles | 98 | 40.8 |

| KICKING | XP | ATT | % | FG | ATT | % |
|---|---|---|---|---|---|---|
| Davis | 17 | 17 | 100 | 20 | 26 | 77 |
| Peterson | 4 | 4 | 100 | 2 | 4 | 50 |

2 POINT XP: R. Moore (1)

## PHILADELPHIA EAGLES

### RUSHING
| Last Name | No. | Yds | Avg | TD |
|---|---|---|---|---|
| Walker | 113 | 528 | 4.7 | 5 |
| Garner | 109 | 399 | 3.7 | 3 |
| Hebron | 82 | 325 | 4.0 | 2 |
| Cunningham | 65 | 288 | 4.4 | 3 |
| Joseph | 60 | 203 | 3.4 | 1 |
| C. Williams | 2 | 11 | 5.5 | 0 |
| Brister | 1 | 7 | 7.0 | 0 |

### RECEIVING
| Last Name | No. | Yds | Avg | TD |
|---|---|---|---|---|
| Barnett | 78 | 1127 | 14.4 | 5 |
| C. Williams | 58 | 813 | 14.0 | 3 |
| Walker | 50 | 500 | 10.0 | 2 |
| Joseph | 43 | 344 | 8.0 | 2 |
| M. Johnson | 21 | 204 | 9.7 | 2 |
| Bailey | 20 | 311 | 15.6 | 1 |
| Hebron | 18 | 137 | 7.6 | 0 |
| Bavaro | 17 | 215 | 12.6 | 3 |
| Garner | 8 | 74 | 9.3 | 0 |
| Alexander | 2 | 1 | 0.5 | 0 |
| Sydner | 1 | 10 | 10.0 | 0 |

### PUNT RETURNS
| Last Name | No. | Yds | Avg | TD |
|---|---|---|---|---|
| Sydner | 40 | 381 | 9.5 | 0 |
| O'Neal | 1 | 0 | 0.0 | 0 |

### KICKOFF RETURNS
| Last Name | No. | Yds | Avg | TD |
|---|---|---|---|---|
| Walker | 21 | 581 | 27.7 | 1 |
| Hebron | 21 | 443 | 21.1 | 0 |
| Sydner | 20 | 392 | 19.6 | 0 |
| Smith | 1 | 14 | 14.0 | 0 |
| Joseph | 1 | 11 | 11.0 | 0 |
| M. Johnson | 1 | 0 | 0.0 | 0 |
| O'Neal | 1 | 0 | 0.0 | 0 |
| Zordich | 1 | 0 | 0.0 | 0 |

### PASSING — PUNTING — KICKING
| PASSING | Att | Cmp | % | Yds | Yd/Att | TD | Int— | % | RK |
|---|---|---|---|---|---|---|---|---|---|
| Cunningham | 490 | 265 | 54.1 | 3229 | 6.59 | 16 | 13— | 2.7 | 9 |
| Brister | 76 | 51 | 67.1 | 507 | 6.67 | 2 | 1— | 1.3 | |

| PUNTING | No. | Avg. |
|---|---|---|
| Barker | 66 | 40.8 |
| Berger | 25 | 38.0 |
| Cunningham | 1 | 80.0 |

| KICKING | XP | ATT | % | FG | ATT | % |
|---|---|---|---|---|---|---|
| Murray | 33 | 33 | 100 | 21 | 25 | 84 |

2 POINT XP: None

## WASHINGTON REDSKINS

### RUSHING
| Last Name | No. | Yds | Avg | TD |
|---|---|---|---|---|
| Ervins | 185 | 650 | 3.5 | 3 |
| Mitchell | 78 | 311 | 4.0 | 0 |
| Brooks | 100 | 297 | 3.0 | 2 |
| Shuler | 26 | 103 | 4.0 | 0 |
| C. Smith | 10 | 48 | 4.8 | 0 |
| Winans | 1 | 5 | 5.0 | 0 |
| Howard | 1 | 4 | 4.0 | 0 |
| Frerotte | 4 | 1 | 0.3 | 0 |
| Friesz | 1 | 1 | 1.0 | 0 |
| Ellard | 1 | -5 | -5.0 | 0 |

### RECEIVING
| Last Name | No. | Yds | Avg | TD |
|---|---|---|---|---|
| Ellard | 74 | 1397 | 18.9 | 6 |
| Ervins | 51 | 293 | 5.7 | 1 |
| Howard | 40 | 727 | 18.2 | 5 |
| Mitchell | 26 | 236 | 9.1 | 1 |
| Winans | 19 | 344 | 18.1 | 2 |
| Horton | 15 | 157 | 10.5 | 3 |
| C. Smith | 15 | 118 | 7.9 | 0 |
| Brooks | 13 | 68 | 5.2 | 0 |
| Jenkins | 8 | 32 | 4.0 | 4 |
| Wycheck | 7 | 55 | 7.9 | 1 |
| Truitt | 2 | 89 | 44.5 | 1 |
| Shepherd | 1 | 8 | 8.0 | 0 |

### PUNT RETURNS
| Last Name | No. | Yds | Avg | TD |
|---|---|---|---|---|
| Mitchell | 32 | 452 | 14.1 | 2 |

### KICKOFF RETURNS
| Last Name | No. | Yds | Avg | TD |
|---|---|---|---|---|
| Mitchell | 58 | 1478 | 25.5 | 0 |
| Wycheck | 4 | 84 | 21.0 | 0 |
| Rush | 3 | 45 | 15.0 | 0 |
| W. Bell | 2 | 43 | 21.5 | 0 |
| Ervins | 1 | 17 | 17.0 | 0 |
| Haws | 1 | 10 | 10.0 | 0 |
| Jenkins | 1 | 4 | 4.0 | 0 |
| A. Collins | 1 | 0 | 0.0 | 0 |
| T. Johnson | 0 | 4 | — | 0 |

### PASSING — PUNTING — KICKING
| PASSING | Att | Cmp | % | Yds | Yd/Att | TD | Int— | % | RK |
|---|---|---|---|---|---|---|---|---|---|
| Shuler | 265 | 120 | 45.3 | 1658 | 6.26 | 10 | 12— | 4.5 | |
| Friesz | 180 | 105 | 58.3 | 1266 | 7.03 | 10 | 9— | 5.0 | |
| Frerotte | 100 | 46 | 46.0 | 600 | 6.00 | 5 | 5— | 5.0 | |
| Mitchell | 1 | 0 | 0.0 | 0 | 0.00 | 0 | 0— | 100.0 | |

| PUNTING | No. | Avg. |
|---|---|---|
| Roby | 82 | 44.4 |

| KICKING | XP | ATT | % | FG | ATT | % |
|---|---|---|---|---|---|---|
| Lohmiller | 30 | 32 | 94 | 20 | 28 | 71 |

2 POINT XP: Howard (1), Mitchell (1), Winans (1)

**MINNESOTA VIKINGS** 10-6 Dennis Green

| Scores of Each Game | | |
|---|---|---|
| 10 | Green Bay | 16 |
| 10 | DETROIT | 3 |
| 42 | Chicago | 14 |
| 38 | MIAMI | 35 |
| 7 | Arizona | 17 |
| 27 | N.Y. Giants | 10 |
| 13 | GREEN BAY | 10 |
| 36 | Tampa Bay | 13 |
| 21 | NEW ORLEANS | 20 |
| 20 | New England | 26 |
| 21 | N.Y. JETS | 31 |
| 17 | TAMPA BAY | 20 |
| 33 | CHICAGO | *27 |
| 21 | Buffalo | 17 |
| 19 | Detroit | 41 |
| 21 | SAN FRANCISCO | 14 |

| Use Name | Pos. | Hgt. | Wgt. | Age | Int | Pts |
|---|---|---|---|---|---|---|
| Chris Hinton | OT | 6'4" | 300 | 33 | | |
| Reggie McElroy | OT | 6'6" | 298 | 34 | | |
| Todd Steussie | OT | 6'6" | 304 | 23 | | |
| Bernard Dafney | OG | 6'5" | 329 | 24 | | |
| David Dixon | OG | 6'5" | 354 | 25 | | |
| John Gerak | OG | 6'3" | 284 | 24 | | |
| Randall McDaniel | OG | 6'3" | 274 | 29 | | |
| Jeff Christy | C | 6'3" | 290 | 25 | | |
| Frank Cornish | C | 6'4" | 287 | 26 | | |
| Mike Morris | C | 6'5" | 277 | 33 | | |
| Roy Barker | DT | 6'4" | 285 | 25 | | |
| James Harris | DE | 6'4" | 255 | 26 | 1 | 6 |
| Robert Harris | DE | 6'4" | 279 | 25 | | |
| Martin Harrison | DE | 6'5" | 240 | 26 | | |
| Roosevelt Nix | DE | 6'6" | 307 | 27 | | |
| Fernando Smith | DE | 6'6" | 276 | 23 | | |
| John Randle | DT | 6'1" | 272 | 26 | | |
| Henry Thomas | DT | 6'2" | 276 | 29 | | |
| Esera Tuaolo | DT | 6'2" | 263 | 26 | | |

Everett Lindsay — Shoulder injury

| Use Name | Pos. | Hgt. | Wgt. | Age | Int | Pts |
|---|---|---|---|---|---|---|
| Bobby Abrams | LB | 6'3" | 240 | 27 | | |
| Richard Brown | LB | 6'3" | 240 | 28 | | |
| Jack Del Rio | LB | 6'4" | 246 | 31 | 3 | |
| Dave Garnett | LB | 6'2" | 214 | 23 | | |
| Carlos Jenkins | LB | 6'3" | 215 | 26 | | |
| Ed McDaniel | LB | 5'11" | 231 | 25 | 1 | |
| Ashley Sheppard | LB | 6'3" | 240 | 25 | | |
| William Sims | LB | 6'3" | 258 | 23 | | |
| Malik Boyd | DB | 5'10" | 176 | 23 | 1 | |
| Brian Davis | DB | 6'2" | 187 | 31 | | |
| Vencie Glenn | DB | 6' | 195 | 29 | 4 | |
| Robert Griffith | DB | 5'11" | 189 | 23 | | |
| Lamar McGriggs | DB | 6'3" | 218 | 26 | 1 | |
| Anthony Parker | DB | 5'10" | 177 | 28 | 4 | 18 |
| Todd Scott | DB | 5'10" | 203 | 26 | | |
| Dewayne Washington | DB | 5'11" | 189 | 21 | 3 | 18 |

Don Jones — Knee injury

| Use Name | Pos. | Hgt. | Wgt. | Age | Int | Pts |
|---|---|---|---|---|---|---|
| Brad Johnson | QB | 6'5" | 220 | 25 | | |
| Warren Moon | QB | 6'3" | 219 | 37 | | |
| Sean Salisbury | QB | 6'5" | 217 | 31 | | |
| Terry Allen | HB | 5'10" | 207 | 26 | | 50 |
| Chuck Evans | HB | 6'1" | 232 | 27 | | |
| Scottie Graham | HB | 5'9" | 217 | 25 | | 12 |
| Amp Lee | HB | 5'11" | 198 | 22 | | 12 |
| David Palmer | HB | 5'8" | 167 | 21 | | |
| Robert Smith | HB | 6' | 197 | 22 | | 6 |
| Cris Carter | WR | 6'3" | 202 | 28 | | 46 |
| Eric Guliford | WR | 5'8" | 169 | 24 | | |
| Qadry Ismail | WR | 6' | 191 | 23 | | 30 |
| Jake Reed | WR | 6'3" | 217 | 26 | | 24 |
| Chris Walsh | WR | 6'1" | 193 | 25 | | |
| Adrian Cooper | TE | 6'5" | 268 | 26 | | |
| Andrew Jordan | TE | 6'4" | 262 | 22 | | 2 |
| Steve Jordan | TE | 6'4" | 240 | 33 | | |
| Brent Novoselsky | TE | 6'3" | 237 | 28 | | |
| Fuad Reveiz | K | 5'11" | 227 | 31 | | 132 |
| Mike Saxon | K | 6'3" | 205 | 32 | | |

**GREEN BAY PACKERS** 9-7 Mike Holmgren

| Scores of Each Game | | |
|---|---|---|
| 16 | MINNESOTA | 10 |
| 14 | MIAMI | 24 |
| 7 | Philadelphia | 13 |
| 30 | TAMPA BAY | 3 |
| 16 | New England | 17 |
| 24 | L.A. RAMS | 17 |
| 10 | Minnesota | *13 |
| 33 | Chicago | 6 |
| 38 | DETROIT | 30 |
| 17 | N.Y. JETS | 10 |
| 20 | Buffalo | 29 |
| 31 | Dallas | 42 |
| 31 | Detroit | 34 |
| 40 | CHICAGO | 3 |
| 21 | ATLANTA | 17 |
| 34 | Tampa Bay | 19 |

| Use Name | Pos. | Hgt. | Wgt. | Age | Int | Pts |
|---|---|---|---|---|---|---|
| Gary Brown | OT | 6'4" | 290 | 23 | | |
| Earl Dotson | OT | 6'4" | 310 | 23 | | |
| Paul Hutchins | OT | 6'5" | 335 | 24 | | |
| Ken Ruettgers | OT | 6'5" | 290 | 32 | | |
| Joe Sims | OT-OG | 6'3" | 310 | 25 | | |
| Harry Galbreath | OG | 6'1" | 285 | 29 | | |
| Charles Hope | OG-C | 6'3" | 303 | 24 | | |
| Guy McIntyre | OG | 6'3" | 275 | 33 | | |
| Jamie Dukes | C | 6'2" | 295 | 30 | | |
| Frank Winters | C-OG | 6'3" | 290 | 30 | | |
| Matt Brock | DE | 6'5" | 280 | 28 | | |
| Don Davey | DE-NT | 6'4" | 270 | 26 | | |
| Sean Jones | DE | 6'7" | 275 | 31 | | |
| Reggie White | DE | 6'5" | 295 | 32 | | |
| Gabe Wilkins | DE | 6'5" | 300 | 23 | | |
| Gilbert Brown | DT | 6'2" | 330 | 23 | | |
| John Jurkovic | DT | 6'2" | 290 | 27 | | |
| Steve McMichael | DT | 6'2" | 270 | 36 | | |

Matt LaBounty — Back injury
Aaron Taylor — Knee injury

| Use Name | Pos. | Hgt. | Wgt. | Age | Int | Pts |
|---|---|---|---|---|---|---|
| Ruffin Hamilton | LB | 6'1" | 230 | 23 | | |
| George Koonce | LB | 6'1" | 240 | 25 | | |
| Bryce Paup | LB | 6'5" | 247 | 26 | 3 | 6 |
| Wayne Simmons | LB | 6'3" | 245 | 24 | | |
| Fred Strickland | LB | 6'2" | 250 | 28 | 1 | |
| Mark Williams | LB | 6'3" | 240 | 23 | | |
| James Willis | LB | 6'2" | 238 | 21 | 2 | |
| Terrell Buckley | DB | 5'9" | 176 | 23 | 5 | |
| LeRoy Butler | DB | 6' | 197 | 26 | 3 | |
| Forey Duckett (from CIN, to SEA) | DB | 6'3" | 195 | 24 | | |
| Doug Evans | DB | 6'1" | 188 | 24 | 1 | |
| Corey Harris | DB | 5'11" | 195 | 24 | | |
| Tim Hauck | DB | 5'11" | 187 | 27 | | |
| Keshon Johnson (from CHI) | DB | 5'10" | 185 | 24 | 1 | |
| Lenny McGill | DB | 6'2" | 194 | 23 | 2 | |
| Roland Mitchell | DB | 5'11" | 195 | 30 | | |
| Mike Prior | DB | 6' | 215 | 30 | | |
| George Teague | DB | 6'1" | 190 | 23 | 3 | |
| Ray Wilson (from NO) | DB | 6'1" | 204 | 23 | | |

Sammy Walker — Elbow injury

| Use Name | Pos. | Hgt. | Wgt. | Age | Int | Pts |
|---|---|---|---|---|---|---|
| Mark Brunell | QB | 6'1" | 208 | 23 | | 6 |
| Ty Detmer | QB | 6' | 186 | 26 | | |
| Brett Favre | QB | 6'2" | 222 | 24 | | 12 |
| Reggie Cobb | HB | 6' | 215 | 26 | | 24 |
| LeShon Johnson | HB | 5'11" | 200 | 23 | | |
| Dorsey Levens | HB-FB | 6'1" | 235 | 24 | | |
| Darrell Thompson | HB | 6' | 217 | 26 | | |
| Marcus Wilson | HB | 6'1" | 215 | 26 | | |
| Edgar Bennett | FB | 6' | 224 | 25 | | 54 |
| Robert Brooks | WR | 6' | 175 | 24 | | 36 |
| Charles Jordan | WR | 5'10" | 175 | 24 | | |
| Ron Lewis | WR | 5'11" | 189 | 26 | | |
| Terry Mickens | WR | 6'1" | 200 | 23 | | |
| Anthony Morgan | WR | 6'1" | 195 | 26 | | 24 |
| Sterling Sharpe | WR | 5'11" | 207 | 29 | | 108 |
| Mark Chmura | TE | 6'5" | 245 | 25 | | |
| Reggie Johnson | TE | 6'2" | 256 | 26 | | |
| Ed West | TE | 6'1" | 250 | 33 | | 14 |
| Jeff Wilner | TE | 6'5" | 250 | 22 | | |
| Craig Hentrich | K | 6'3" | 200 | 23 | | |
| Chris Jacke | K | 6' | 200 | 28 | | 98 |

**DETROIT LIONS** 9-7 Wayne Fontes

| Scores of Each Game | | |
|---|---|---|
| 31 | ATLANTA | *28 |
| 3 | Minnesota | 10 |
| 20 | Dallas | 17 |
| 17 | NEW ENGLAND | 23 |
| 14 | Tampa Bay | 24 |
| 21 | SAN FRANCISCO | 27 |
| 21 | CHICAGO | 16 |
| 28 | N.Y. Giants | *25 |
| 30 | Green Bay | 38 |
| 14 | TAMPA BAY | 9 |
| 10 | Chicago | 20 |
| 35 | BUFFALO | 21 |
| 34 | GREEN BAY | 31 |
| 18 | N.Y. Jets | 7 |
| 41 | MINNESOTA | 19 |
| 20 | Miami | 27 |

| Use Name | Pos. | Hgt. | Wgt. | Age | Int | Pts |
|---|---|---|---|---|---|---|
| Lomas Brown | OT | 6'4" | 275 | 31 | | |
| Scott Conover | OT | 6'4" | 285 | 25 | | 6 |
| David Lutz | OT | 6'6" | 305 | 34 | | |
| Larry Tharpe | OT | 6'4" | 299 | 23 | | |
| Shawn Bouwens | OG | 6'4" | 290 | 26 | | |
| Doug Widell | OG | 6'4" | 280 | 27 | | |
| Mike Compton | C-OG | 6'6" | 297 | 23 | | |
| Kevin Glover | C | 6'2" | 282 | 31 | | |
| Mark Rodenhauser | C | 6'5" | 280 | 33 | | |
| Shane Bonham | DE | 6'4" | 260 | 23 | | |
| Robert Porcher | DE | 6'3" | 283 | 25 | | |
| Kelvin Pritchett | DE | 6'2" | 281 | 24 | | |
| Mike Wells | DE | 6'3" | 287 | 23 | | |
| Dan Owens | NT | 6'3" | 280 | 27 | | |
| Marc Spindler | NT | 6'5" | 290 | 24 | | |
| Team | | | | | | 2 |

| Use Name | Pos. | Hgt. | Wgt. | Age | Int | Pts |
|---|---|---|---|---|---|---|
| Tom Beer | LB | 6'1" | 237 | 25 | | |
| Tracy Hayworth | LB | 6'3" | 260 | 26 | | |
| Mike Johnson | LB | 6'1" | 230 | 31 | 1 | 6 |
| Victor Jones | LB | 6'2" | 250 | 27 | | |
| Scott Kowalkowski | LB | 6'2" | 228 | 26 | | |
| Antonio London | LB | 6'2" | 234 | 23 | | |
| Tracy Scroggins | LB | 6'2" | 255 | 24 | | |
| Chris Spielman | LB | 6' | 247 | 28 | | 6 |
| Pat Swilling | LB | 6'3" | 242 | 29 | | |
| Broderick Thomas | LB | 6'4" | 242 | 27 | | |
| Bennie Blades | DB | 6'1" | 221 | 27 | 1 | |
| Jocelyn Borgella | DB | 5'10" | 180 | 23 | | |
| Willie Clay | DB | 5'9" | 184 | 23 | 3 | 6 |
| Harry Colon | DB | 6' | 203 | 25 | 1 | |
| Greg Jeffries | DB | 5'9" | 184 | 22 | | |
| Milton Mack | DB | 5'11" | 195 | 30 | 1 | |
| Van Malone | DB | 5'11" | 186 | 24 | | |
| Robert Massey | DB | 5'11" | 195 | 27 | 4 | |
| Ryan McNeil | DB | 6' | 192 | 23 | 1 | |

Kevin Scott — Knee injury

| Use Name | Pos. | Hgt. | Wgt. | Age | Int | Pts |
|---|---|---|---|---|---|---|
| Dave Krieg | QB | 6'1" | 202 | 35 | | |
| Chuck Long | QB | 6'4" | 217 | 31 | | |
| Scott Mitchell | QB | 6'6" | 230 | 26 | | 6 |
| Geoff Torretta | QB | 6'2" | 215 | 24 | | |
| Eric Lynch | HB | 5'10" | 224 | 24 | | |
| Derrick Moore | HB-FB | 6'1" | 227 | 26 | | 24 |
| Barry Sanders | HB-FB | 5'8" | 203 | 26 | | 48 |
| Anthony Carter | WR | 5'11" | 181 | 33 | | 18 |
| Mel Gray | WR | 5'9" | 171 | 33 | | 18 |
| Aubrey Matthews | WR | 5'7" | 165 | 31 | | 18 |
| Herman Moore | WR | 6'3" | 210 | 24 | | 66 |
| Johnnie Morton | WR | 6' | 190 | 22 | | 12 |
| Brett Perriman | WR | 5'9" | 180 | 28 | | 28 |
| Ron Hall | TE | 6'4" | 245 | 30 | | |
| Ty Hallock | TE | 6'3" | 249 | 23 | | |
| Rodney Holman | TE | 6'3" | 238 | 34 | | |
| Jason Hanson | K | 5'11" | 183 | 24 | | 93 |
| Greg Montgomery | K | 6'4" | 215 | 29 | | |

**CHICAGO BEARS** 9-7 Dave Wannstedt

| Scores of Each Game | | |
|---|---|---|
| 21 | TAMPA BAY | 9 |
| 22 | Philadelphia | 30 |
| 14 | MINNESOTA | 42 |
| 19 | N.Y. Jets | 7 |
| 20 | BUFFALO | 13 |
| 17 | NEW ORLEANS | 7 |
| 16 | Detroit | 21 |
| 6 | GREEN BAY | 33 |
| 20 | Tampa Bay | 6 |
| 17 | Miami | 14 |
| 20 | DETROIT | 10 |
| 19 | Arizona | *16 |
| 27 | Minnesota | *33 |
| 3 | Green Bay | 40 |
| 27 | L.A. RAMS | 13 |
| 3 | NEW ENGLAND | 13 |

| Use Name | Pos. | Hgt. | Wgt. | Age | Int | Pts |
|---|---|---|---|---|---|---|
| Troy Auzenne | OT | 6'7" | 300 | 25 | | |
| Andy Heck | OT | 6'6" | 296 | 27 | | |
| James Williams | OT | 6'7" | 335 | 26 | | |
| Mark Bortz | OG | 6'6" | 290 | 33 | | |
| Todd Burger | OG | 6'3" | 296 | 24 | | |
| Jay Leeuwenburg | OG | 6'2" | 290 | 25 | | |
| Tom Myslinski | OG | 6'2" | 289 | 25 | | |
| Todd Perry | OG | 6'5" | 310 | 23 | | |
| Jerry Fontenot | C | 6'3" | 285 | 27 | | |
| Trace Armstrong | DE | 6'4" | 260 | 28 | | |
| Albert Fontenot | DE | 6'4" | 272 | 23 | | |
| Alonzo Spellman | DE | 6'4" | 285 | 22 | 1 | |
| John Thierry | DE | 6'4" | 260 | 22 | | |
| Tory Epps | DT | 6'1" | 280 | 27 | | |
| Jim Flanigan | DT | 6'2" | 280 | 23 | | |
| Carl Simpson | DT | 6'2" | 285 | 24 | | |
| Chris Zorich | DT | 6'1" | 277 | 25 | | |

| Use Name | Pos. | Hgt. | Wgt. | Age | Int | Pts |
|---|---|---|---|---|---|---|
| Myron Baker | LB | 6'1" | 228 | 23 | | |
| Joe Cain | LB | 6'1" | 237 | 29 | | |
| Ron Cox | LB | 6'2" | 235 | 26 | | |
| Darwin Ireland | LB | 5'11" | 240 | 23 | | |
| Dante Jones | LB | 6'1" | 235 | 29 | | |
| Barry Minter | LB | 6'2" | 239 | 24 | | |
| Vinson Smith | LB | 6'2" | 247 | 29 | | |
| James Burton | DB | 5'9" | 181 | 23 | | |
| Mark Carrier | DB | 6'1" | 190 | 26 | 2 | |
| Maurice Douglass | DB | 5'11" | 203 | 30 | 1 | |
| Shaun Gayle | DB | 5'11" | 202 | 32 | 2 | |
| Jeremy Lincoln | DB | 5'10" | 180 | 25 | 1 | |
| John Mangum | DB | 5'10" | 192 | 27 | | |
| Anthony Marshall | DB | 6'1" | 205 | 23 | | |
| Kevin Miniefield | DB | 5'9" | 180 | 24 | | |
| Donnell Woolford | DB | 5'9" | 188 | 28 | 5 | |

| Use Name | Pos. | Hgt. | Wgt. | Age | Int | Pts |
|---|---|---|---|---|---|---|
| Erik Kramer | QB | 6'1" | 200 | 29 | | |
| Shane Matthews | QB | 6'3" | 196 | 24 | | |
| Steve Walsh | QB | 6'3" | 200 | 27 | | 6 |
| Trevor Cobb | HB | 5'9" | 209 | 23 | | |
| Robert Green | HB | 5'8" | 212 | 23 | | 12 |
| Lewis Tillman | HB | 6' | 204 | 28 | | 42 |
| Tim Worley | HB | 6'2" | 228 | 27 | | 6 |
| Tony Carter | FB | 5'11" | 216 | 22 | | |
| Bob Christian | FB | 5'10" | 225 | 25 | | |
| Raymont Harris | FB | 6' | 225 | 23 | | 6 |
| Merril Hoge | FB | 6'2" | 230 | 29 | | |
| Curtis Conway | WR | 6' | 193 | 23 | | 14 |
| Jeff Graham | WR | 6'2" | 196 | 25 | | 32 |
| Nate Lewis | WR | 5'11" | 198 | 27 | | 6 |
| Greg McMurtry | WR | 6'2" | 210 | 26 | | 6 |
| Greg Primus | WR | 5'11" | 190 | 23 | | |
| Tom Waddle | WR | 6' | 190 | 27 | | 6 |
| Marv Cook | TE | 6'4" | 234 | 28 | | 6 |
| Chris Gedney | TE | 6'5" | 265 | 24 | | 18 |
| Keith Jennings | TE | 6'4" | 270 | 28 | | 18 |
| Ryan Wetnight | TE | 6'2" | 235 | 23 | | 6 |
| Kevin Butler | K | 6'1" | 205 | 32 | | 87 |
| Chris Gardocki | K | 6'1" | 196 | 24 | | |

Terry Obee — Broken ankle

**TAMPA BAY BUCCANEERS** 6-10 Sam Wyche

| Scores of Each Game | | |
|---|---|---|
| 9 | Chicago | 21 |
| 24 | INDIANAPOLIS | 10 |
| 7 | NEW ORLEANS | 9 |
| 3 | Green Bay | 30 |
| 24 | DETROIT | 14 |
| 13 | Atlanta | 34 |
| 16 | San Francisco | 41 |
| 13 | MINNESOTA | 36 |
| 6 | CHICAGO | 20 |
| 9 | Detroit | 14 |
| 21 | Seattle | 22 |
| 20 | Minnesota | *17 |
| 26 | WASHINGTON | 21 |
| 24 | L.A. RAMS | 14 |
| 17 | Washington | 14 |
| 19 | GREEN BAY | 34 |

| Use Name | Pos. | Hgt. | Wgt. | Age | Int | Pts |
|---|---|---|---|---|---|---|
| Scott Dill | OT-OG | 6'5" | 295 | 28 | | |
| Paul Gruber | OT | 6'5" | 296 | 29 | | |
| Ian Beckles | OG | 6'1" | 304 | 27 | | |
| Sean Love | OG | 6'3" | 300 | 25 | | |
| Charles McRae | OG-OT | 6'7" | 306 | 25 | | |
| Mike Sullivan | OG-OT | 6'3" | 292 | 26 | | |
| Tony Mayberry | C | 6'4" | 292 | 26 | | |
| Chidi Ahanotu | DE-DT | 6'2" | 288 | 23 | | |
| Eric Curry | DE | 6'5" | 270 | 24 | | |
| Jeff Hunter | DE | 6'5" | 291 | 28 | | |
| Keith Powe | DE | 6'3" | 265 | 25 | | |
| Shawn Price | DE | 6'5" | 274 | 24 | | |
| Karl Wilson | DE-DT | 6'5" | 274 | 29 | | |
| Brad Culpepper | DT | 6'1" | 270 | 26 | | |
| Santana Dotson | DT-DE | 6'5" | 276 | 24 | | |
| Toddrick McIntosh | DT-DE | 6'3" | 277 | 22 | | |
| Mark Wheeler | DT-NT | 6'2" | 285 | 24 | | |

| Use Name | Pos. | Hgt. | Wgt. | Age | Int | Pts |
|---|---|---|---|---|---|---|
| Ed Brady | LB | 6'2" | 238 | 32 | | |
| Jeff Brady | LB | 6'1" | 238 | 25 | | |
| Demetrious DuBose | LB | 6'1" | 240 | 23 | | |
| Lonnie Marts | LB | 6'1" | 236 | 25 | | |
| Hardy Nickerson | LB | 6'2" | 228 | 29 | 2 | |
| Curtis Buckley | DB | 6' | 191 | 23 | | |
| Barney Bussey | DB-LB | 6' | 215 | 32 | | |
| Marty Carter | DB | 6'1" | 205 | 24 | | |
| Tony Covington | DB | 5'11" | 193 | 26 | 1 | |
| Charles Dimry | DB | 6' | 176 | 28 | 1 | |
| Thomas Everett | DB | 5'9" | 190 | 29 | 1 | |
| Rogerick Green | DB | 6' | 184 | 24 | | |
| John Lynch | DB | 6'2" | 216 | 22 | | |
| Martin Mayhew | DB | 5'8" | 178 | 28 | 2 | |
| Michael McGruder | DB | 5'10" | 182 | 29 | 1 | |
| Tony Stargell | DB | 5'11" | 186 | 28 | 1 | |

| Use Name | Pos. | Hgt. | Wgt. | Age | Int | Pts |
|---|---|---|---|---|---|---|
| Trent Dilfer | QB | 6'4" | 235 | 22 | | |
| Craig Erickson | QB | 6'2" | 212 | 25 | | 6 |
| Casey Weldon | QB | 6'1" | 206 | 25 | | |
| Errict Rhett | HB | 5'11" | 211 | 23 | | 44 |
| Vernon Turner | HB | 5'8" | 180 | 27 | | 6 |
| Vince Workman | HB | 5'10" | 205 | 26 | | |
| Rudy Harris | FB | 6'1" | 257 | 22 | | |
| Anthony McDowell | FB | 5'11" | 240 | 25 | | 6 |
| Mazio Royster | FB | 6'1" | 200 | 24 | | |
| Horace Copeland | WR | 6'2" | 198 | 23 | | 2 |
| Lawrence Dawsey | WR | 6' | 192 | 26 | | 6 |
| Willie Green | WR | 6'2" | 181 | 28 | | |
| Courtney Hawkins | WR | 5'9" | 180 | 23 | | 30 |
| Lamar Thomas | WR | 6'1" | 163 | 24 | | |
| Charles Wilson | WR | 5'10" | 185 | 26 | | 36 |
| Tyji Armstrong | TE | 6'4" | 262 | 23 | | 6 |
| Harold Bishop | TE | 6'4" | 254 | 24 | | |
| Jackie Harris | TE | 6'4" | 248 | 26 | | 20 |
| Dave Moore | TE | 6'2" | 248 | 24 | | |
| Michael Husted | K | 6' | 188 | 24 | | 89 |
| Dan Stryzinski | K | 6'1" | 197 | 29 | | |

## MINNESOTA VIKINGS

### RUSHING

| Last Name | No. | Yds | Avg | TD |
|---|---|---|---|---|
| Allen | 255 | 1031 | 4.0 | 8 |
| Graham | 64 | 207 | 3.2 | 2 |
| Smith | 31 | 106 | 3.4 | 1 |
| Lee | 29 | 104 | 3.6 | 0 |
| Moon | 27 | 55 | 2.0 | 0 |
| Evans | 6 | 20 | 3.3 | 0 |
| Salisbury | 3 | 2 | 0.7 | 0 |
| Palmer | 1 | 1 | 1.0 | 0 |
| Saxon | 1 | 0 | 0.0 | 0 |
| Johnson | 2 | -2 | -1.0 | 0 |

### RECEIVING

| Last Name | No. | Yds | Avg | TD |
|---|---|---|---|---|
| C. Carter | 122 | 1256 | 10.3 | 7 |
| Reed | 85 | 1175 | 13.8 | 4 |
| Ismail | 45 | 696 | 15.5 | 5 |
| Lee | 45 | 368 | 8.2 | 0 |
| A. Jordan | 35 | 336 | 9.6 | 0 |
| Cooper | 32 | 363 | 11.3 | 0 |
| Allen | 17 | 148 | 8.7 | 0 |
| Smith | 15 | 105 | 7.0 | 0 |
| Palmer | 5 | 82 | 16.4 | 0 |
| S. Jordan | 3 | 23 | 7.7 | 0 |
| Novoselsky | 2 | 7 | 3.5 | 0 |
| Evans | 1 | 2 | 2.0 | 0 |
| Graham | 1 | 1 | 1.0 | 0 |

### PUNT RETURNS

| Last Name | No. | Yds | Avg | TD |
|---|---|---|---|---|
| Palmer | 30 | 193 | 6.4 | 0 |
| Guliford | 5 | 14 | 2.8 | 0 |
| Parker | 4 | 31 | 7.8 | 0 |

### KICKOFF RETURNS

| Last Name | No. | Yds | Avg | TD |
|---|---|---|---|---|
| Ismail | 35 | 807 | 23.1 | 0 |
| Smith | 16 | 419 | 26.2 | 0 |
| Lee | 3 | 42 | 14.0 | 0 |
| Novoselsky | 2 | 10 | 5.0 | 0 |
| A. Jordan | 1 | 8 | 8.0 | 0 |
| Walsh | 1 | 6 | 6.0 | 0 |
| Evans | 1 | 4 | 4.0 | 0 |
| Garnett | 1 | 0 | 0.0 | 0 |

### PASSING — PUNTING — KICKING

**PASSING**

| Last Name | Att | Cmp | % | Yds | Yd/Att | TD | Int— | % | RK |
|---|---|---|---|---|---|---|---|---|---|
| Moon | 601 | 371 | 61.7 | 4264 | 7.09 | 18 | 19— | 3.2 | 7 |
| Johnson | 37 | 22 | 59.5 | 150 | 4.05 | 0 | 0— | 2.9 | |
| Salisbury | 34 | 16 | 47.1 | 156 | 4.59 | 0 | 1— | 2.9 | |
| Saxon | 1 | 0 | 0.0 | 0 | 0.00 | 0 | 0— | 0.0 | |

**PUNTING**

| Last Name | No. | Avg. |
|---|---|---|
| Saxon | 77 | 42.9 |

**KICKING**

| Last Name | XP | ATT | % | FG | ATT | % |
|---|---|---|---|---|---|---|
| Reveiz | 30 | 30 | 100 | 34 | 39 | 87 |

**2 POINT XP**
C. Carter (2)
Allen (1)
A. Jordan (1)

## GREEN BAY PACKERS

### RUSHING

| Last Name | No. | Yds | Avg | TD |
|---|---|---|---|---|
| E. Bennett | 178 | 623 | 3.5 | 5 |
| Cobb | 153 | 579 | 3.8 | 3 |
| Favre | 42 | 202 | 4.8 | 2 |
| L. Johnson | 26 | 99 | 3.8 | 0 |
| Levens | 5 | 15 | 3.0 | 0 |
| Sharpe | 3 | 15 | 5.0 | 0 |
| Brunell | 6 | 7 | 1.2 | 1 |
| Jordan | 1 | 5 | 5.0 | 0 |
| Brooks | 1 | 0 | 0.0 | 0 |
| Thompson | 2 | -2 | -1.0 | 0 |

### RECEIVING

| Last Name | No. | Yds | Avg | TD |
|---|---|---|---|---|
| Sharpe | 94 | 1119 | 11.9 | 18 |
| Bennett | 78 | 546 | 7.0 | 4 |
| Brooks | 58 | 648 | 11.2 | 4 |
| Cobb | 35 | 299 | 8.5 | 1 |
| West | 31 | 377 | 12.2 | 2 |
| Morgan | 28 | 397 | 14.2 | 4 |
| Chmura | 14 | 165 | 11.8 | 0 |
| L. Johnson | 13 | 168 | 12.9 | 0 |
| Lewis | 7 | 108 | 15.4 | 0 |
| R. Johnson | 7 | 79 | 11.3 | 0 |
| Wilner | 5 | 31 | 6.2 | 0 |
| Mickens | 4 | 31 | 7.8 | 0 |
| Levens | 1 | 9 | 9.0 | 0 |

### PUNT RETURNS

| Last Name | No. | Yds | Avg | TD |
|---|---|---|---|---|
| Brooks | 40 | 352 | 8.8 | 1 |
| Prior | 8 | 62 | 7.8 | 0 |
| Jordan | 1 | 0 | 0.0 | 0 |

### KICKOFF RETURNS

| Last Name | No. | Yds | Avg | TD |
|---|---|---|---|---|
| Harris | 29 | 618 | 21.3 | 0 |
| Brooks | 9 | 260 | 28.9 | 1 |
| Jordan | 5 | 115 | 23.0 | 0 |
| Jurkovic | 4 | 57 | 14.3 | 0 |
| Thompson | 4 | 67 | 16.8 | 0 |
| Levens | 2 | 31 | 15.5 | 0 |
| M. Wilson | 2 | 14 | 7.0 | 0 |
| Davey | 1 | 6 | 6.0 | 0 |

### PASSING — PUNTING — KICKING

**PASSING**

| Last Name | Att | Cmp | % | Yds | Yd/Att | TD | Int— | % | RK |
|---|---|---|---|---|---|---|---|---|---|
| Favre | 582 | 363 | 62.4 | 3882 | 6.67 | 33 | 14— | 2.4 | 2 |
| Brunell | 27 | 12 | 44.4 | 95 | 3.52 | 0 | 0— | 0.0 | |

**PUNTING**

| Last Name | No. | Avg. |
|---|---|---|
| Hentrich | 81 | 41.4 |

**KICKING**

| Last Name | XP | ATT | % | FG | ATT | % |
|---|---|---|---|---|---|---|
| Jacke | 41 | 43 | 95 | 19 | 26 | 73 |

**2 POINT XP**
West (1)

## DETROIT LIONS

### RUSHING

| Last Name | No. | Yds | Avg | TD |
|---|---|---|---|---|
| Sanders | 331 | 1883 | 5.7 | 7 |
| Perriman | 9 | 86 | 9.6 | 0 |
| D. Moore | 27 | 52 | 1.9 | 4 |
| Krieg | 23 | 35 | 1.5 | 0 |
| Mitchell | 15 | 24 | 1.6 | 1 |
| Lynch | 1 | 0 | 0.0 | 0 |

### RECEIVING

| Last Name | No. | Yds | Avg | TD |
|---|---|---|---|---|
| H. Moore | 72 | 1173 | 16.3 | 11 |
| Perriman | 56 | 761 | 13.6 | 4 |
| Sanders | 44 | 283 | 6.4 | 1 |
| Matthews | 29 | 359 | 12.4 | 3 |
| Holman | 17 | 163 | 9.6 | 0 |
| Hall | 10 | 106 | 10.6 | 0 |
| A. Carter | 8 | 97 | 12.1 | 3 |
| Hallock | 7 | 75 | 10.7 | 0 |
| Morton | 3 | 39 | 13.0 | 1 |
| Lynch | 2 | 18 | 9.0 | 0 |
| D. Moore | 1 | 10 | 10.0 | 0 |
| Conover | 1 | 1 | 1.0 | 1 |

### PUNT RETURNS

| Last Name | No. | Yds | Avg | TD |
|---|---|---|---|---|
| Gray | 21 | 233 | 11.1 | 0 |
| Clay | 3 | 20 | 6.7 | 0 |
| Massey | 1 | 3 | 3.0 | 0 |

### KICKOFF RETURNS

| Last Name | No. | Yds | Avg | TD |
|---|---|---|---|---|
| Gray | 45 | 1276 | 28.4 | 3 |
| D. Moore | 10 | 113 | 11.3 | 0 |
| Lynch | 9 | 105 | 11.7 | 0 |
| Morton | 3 | 143 | 47.7 | 1 |
| Malone | 3 | 38 | 12.7 | 0 |

### PASSING — PUNTING — KICKING

**PASSING**

| Last Name | Att | Cmp | % | Yds | Yd/Att | TD | Int— | % | RK |
|---|---|---|---|---|---|---|---|---|---|
| Mitchell | 246 | 119 | 48.4 | 1456 | 5.92 | 10 | 11— | 4.5 | 13 |
| Krieg | 212 | 131 | 61.8 | 1629 | 7.68 | 14 | 3— | 6.6 | |
| Perriman | 1 | 0 | 0.0 | 0 | 0.00 | 0 | 0— | 0.0 | |

**PUNTING**

| Last Name | No. | Avg. |
|---|---|---|
| Montgomery | 64 | 43.5 |

**KICKING**

| Last Name | XP | ATT | % | FG | ATT | % |
|---|---|---|---|---|---|---|
| Hanson | 39 | 40 | 98 | 18 | 27 | 67 |

**2 POINT XP**
Perriman (2)

## CHICAGO BEARS

### RUSHING

| Last Name | No. | Yds | Avg | TD |
|---|---|---|---|---|
| Tillman | 275 | 899 | 3.3 | 7 |
| Harris | 123 | 464 | 3.8 | 1 |
| Green | 25 | 122 | 4.9 | 0 |
| Conway | 6 | 31 | 5.2 | 0 |
| Christian | 7 | 29 | 4.1 | 0 |
| Hoge | 6 | 24 | 4.0 | 0 |
| Worley | 9 | 17 | 1.9 | 1 |
| Walsh | 30 | 4 | 0.1 | 0 |
| Kramer | 6 | -2 | -0.3 | 0 |

### RECEIVING

| Last Name | No. | Yds | Avg | TD |
|---|---|---|---|---|
| Graham | 68 | 944 | 13.9 | 4 |
| Conway | 39 | 546 | 14.0 | 2 |
| Harris | 39 | 236 | 6.1 | 0 |
| Tillman | 27 | 222 | 8.2 | 0 |
| Waddle | 25 | 244 | 9.8 | 1 |
| Green | 24 | 199 | 8.3 | 2 |
| Cook | 21 | 212 | 10.1 | 1 |
| Gedney | 13 | 157 | 12.1 | 3 |
| Hoge | 13 | 79 | 6.1 | 0 |
| Wetnight | 11 | 104 | 9.5 | 1 |
| Jennings | 11 | 75 | 6.8 | 3 |
| McMurtry | 8 | 112 | 14.0 | 1 |
| Primus | 3 | 25 | 8.3 | 0 |
| Christian | 2 | 30 | 15.0 | 0 |
| Lewis | 2 | 13 | 6.5 | 1 |
| Carter | 1 | 24 | 24.0 | 0 |
| Worley | 1 | 8 | 8.0 | 0 |

### PUNT RETURNS

| Last Name | No. | Yds | Avg | TD |
|---|---|---|---|---|
| Graham | 15 | 140 | 9.3 | 1 |
| Conway | 8 | 63 | 7.9 | 0 |
| Waddle | 3 | 8 | 2.7 | 0 |
| Lewis | 1 | 7 | 7.0 | 0 |

### KICKOFF RETURNS

| Last Name | No. | Yds | Avg | TD |
|---|---|---|---|---|
| Lewis | 35 | 874 | 25.0 | 0 |
| Conway | 10 | 228 | 22.8 | 0 |
| Carter | 6 | 99 | 16.5 | 0 |
| Green | 6 | 77 | 12.8 | 0 |
| Worley | 4 | 52 | 13.0 | 0 |
| Flanigan | 2 | 26 | 13.0 | 0 |
| Woolford | 1 | 28 | 28.0 | 0 |
| Harris | 1 | 18 | 18.0 | 0 |
| Thierry | 1 | 0 | 0.0 | 0 |

### PASSING — PUNTING — KICKING

**PASSING**

| Last Name | Att | Cmp | % | Yds | Yd/Att | TD | Int— | % | RK |
|---|---|---|---|---|---|---|---|---|---|
| Walsh | 343 | 208 | 60.6 | 2078 | 6.06 | 10 | 8— | 2.3 | 8 |
| Kramer | 158 | 99 | 62.7 | 1129 | 7.15 | 8 | 8— | 5.1 | |
| Conway | 1 | 1 | 100.0 | 23 | 23.00 | 1 | 0— | 0.0 | |

**PUNTING**

| Last Name | No. | Avg. |
|---|---|---|
| Gardocki | 76 | 37.8 |

**KICKING**

| Last Name | XP | ATT | % | FG | ATT | % |
|---|---|---|---|---|---|---|
| Butler | 24 | 24 | 100 | 21 | 29 | 72 |

**2 POINT XP**
Conway (1)
Graham (1)

## TAMPA BAY BUCCANEERS

### RUSHING

| Last Name | No. | Yds | Avg | TD |
|---|---|---|---|---|
| Rhett | 284 | 1011 | 3.6 | 7 |
| Workman | 79 | 291 | 3.7 | 0 |
| Erickson | 26 | 68 | 2.6 | 1 |
| McDowell | 21 | 58 | 2.8 | 0 |
| Dilfer | 2 | 27 | 13.5 | 0 |
| C. Wilson | 2 | 15 | 7.5 | 0 |
| Turner | 4 | 13 | 3.3 | 0 |
| Royster | 9 | 7 | 0.8 | 0 |
| R. Harris | 2 | 0 | 0.0 | 0 |
| Armstrong | 1 | -1 | -1.0 | 0 |

### RECEIVING

| Last Name | No. | Yds | Avg | TD |
|---|---|---|---|---|
| Dawsey | 46 | 673 | 14.6 | 1 |
| Hawkins | 37 | 438 | 11.8 | 5 |
| C. Wilson | 31 | 652 | 21.0 | 6 |
| McDowell | 29 | 193 | 6.7 | 1 |
| J. Harris | 26 | 337 | 13.0 | 3 |
| Armstrong | 22 | 265 | 12.0 | 1 |
| Rhett | 22 | 119 | 5.4 | 0 |
| Copeland | 17 | 308 | 18.1 | 0 |
| Workman | 11 | 82 | 7.5 | 0 |
| W. Green | 9 | 150 | 16.7 | 0 |
| Thomas | 7 | 94 | 13.4 | 0 |
| Royster | 7 | 36 | 5.1 | 0 |
| Moore | 4 | 57 | 14.3 | 0 |
| R. Harris | 2 | 11 | 5.5 | 0 |
| Carter | 1 | 21 | 21.0 | 0 |

### PUNT RETURNS

| Last Name | No. | Yds | Avg | TD |
|---|---|---|---|---|
| Turner | 21 | 218 | 10.4 | 1 |
| Hawkins | 5 | 28 | 5.6 | 0 |
| Everett | 2 | 2 | 1.0 | 0 |

### KICKOFF RETURNS

| Last Name | No. | Yds | Avg | TD |
|---|---|---|---|---|
| Turner | 43 | 886 | 20.6 | 0 |
| C. Wilson | 10 | 251 | 25.1 | 0 |
| Buckley | 8 | 177 | 22.1 | 0 |
| R. Green | 2 | 33 | 16.5 | 0 |
| Culpepper | 2 | 30 | 15.0 | 0 |
| Moore | 2 | 27 | 13.5 | 0 |
| R. Harris | 1 | 12 | 12.0 | 0 |
| Armstrong | 1 | 6 | 6.0 | 0 |
| Carter | 1 | 0 | 0.0 | 0 |

### PASSING — PUNTING — KICKING

**PASSING**

| Last Name | Att | Cmp | % | Yds | Yd/Att | TD | Int— | % | RK |
|---|---|---|---|---|---|---|---|---|---|
| Erickson | 399 | 225 | 56.4 | 2919 | 7.32 | 16 | 10— | 2.5 | 6 |
| Dilfer | 82 | 38 | 46.3 | 433 | 5.28 | 1 | 6— | 7.3 | |
| Weldon | 9 | 7 | 77.8 | 63 | 7.00 | 0 | 0— | 0.0 | |
| Stryzinski | 1 | 1 | 100.0 | 21 | 21.00 | 0 | 0— | 0.0 | |

**PUNTING**

| Last Name | No. | Avg. |
|---|---|---|
| Stryzinski | 72 | 38.9 |
| Husted | 2 | 26.5 |

**KICKING**

| Last Name | XP | ATT | % | FG | ATT | % |
|---|---|---|---|---|---|---|
| Husted | 20 | 20 | 100 | 23 | 35 | 66 |

**2 POINT XP**
Rhett (1)
J. Harris (1)
Copeland (1)

## SAN FRANCISCO 49ERS 13-3 George Seifert

| Scores of Each Game | | |
|---|---|---|
| 44 | L.A. RAIDERS | 14 |
| 17 | Kansas City | 24 |
| 34 | L.A. Rams | 19 |
| 24 | NEW ORLEANS | 13 |
| 8 | PHILADELPHIA | 40 |
| 27 | Detroit | 21 |
| 42 | Atlanta | 3 |
| 41 | TAMPA BAY | 16 |
| 37 | Washington | 22 |
| 21 | DALLAS | 14 |
| 31 | L.A. RAMS | 27 |
| 35 | New Orleans | 14 |
| 50 | ATLANTA | 14 |
| 38 | San Diego | 15 |
| 42 | DENVER | 19 |
| 14 | Minnesota | 21 |

| Use Name | Pos. | Hgt. | Wgt. | Age | Int | Pts |
|---|---|---|---|---|---|---|
| Harris Barton | OT | 6'4" | 286 | 30 | | |
| Harry Boatswain | OT | 6'4" | 295 | 25 | | |
| Frank Pollack | OT | 6'5" | 285 | 26 | | |
| Steve Wallace | OT | 6'5" | 280 | 29 | | |
| Brian Bollinger | OG | 6'5" | 285 | 25 | | |
| Chris Dalman | OG-C | 6'3" | 285 | 24 | | |
| Derrick Deese | OG | 6'3" | 270 | 24 | | |
| Rod Milstead | OG | 6'2" | 290 | 24 | | |
| Jesse Sapolu | OG | 6'4" | 278 | 33 | | |
| Ralph Tamm | OG | 6'4" | 280 | 28 | | |
| Bart Oates | C | 6'3" | 278 | 35 | | |
| Dennis Brown | DE | 6'4" | 290 | 26 | 1 | |
| Richard Dent | DE | 6'4" | 265 | 33 | | |
| Tim Harris | DE | 6'6" | 265 | 29 | | |
| Rickey Jackson | DE-LB | 6'2" | 245 | 36 | | |
| Todd Kelly | DE | 6'2" | 259 | 23 | | |
| Charles Mann | DE | 6'6" | 272 | 33 | | |
| Mark Thomas | DE | 6'5" | 273 | 25 | | |
| Troy Wilson | DE | 6'4" | 235 | 23 | | |
| Rhett Hall | DT | 6'2" | 260 | 25 | | |
| Dana Stubblefield | DT | 6'2" | 302 | 23 | | |
| Bryant Young | DT | 6'2" | 276 | 22 | | |
| Antonio Goss | LB | 6'4" | 228 | 28 | | |
| Kevin Mitchell | LB | 6'1" | 260 | 23 | | |
| Ken Norton | LB | 6'2" | 241 | 27 | 1 | |
| Anthony Peterson | LB | 6' | 223 | 22 | | |
| Gary Plummer | LB | 6'2" | 247 | 34 | 1 | |
| Lee Woodall | LB | 6' | 220 | 24 | | |
| Toi Cook | DB | 5'11" | 188 | 29 | 1 | |
| Eric Davis | DB | 5'11" | 178 | 26 | 1 | |
| Dedrick Dodge | DB | 6'2" | 184 | 27 | | |
| Tyronne Drakeford | DB | 5'9" | 185 | 23 | 1 | |
| Dana Hall | DB | 6'2" | 206 | 25 | 2 | |
| Merton Hanks | DB | 6'2" | 185 | 26 | 7 | |
| Tim McDonald | DB | 6'2" | 215 | 29 | 2 | 12 |
| Deion Sanders | DB | 6' | 185 | 27 | 6 | 18 |
| Elvis Grbac | QB | 6'5" | 232 | 24 | | |
| Bill Musgrave | QB | 6'2" | 205 | 26 | | |
| Steve Young | QB | 6'2" | 205 | 32 | | 42 |
| Dexter Carter | HB | 5'9" | 174 | 26 | | 6 |
| Derek Loville | HB | 5'10" | 205 | 26 | | |
| Adam Walker | HB | 6'1" | 210 | 26 | | 6 |
| Ricky Watters | HB | 6'1" | 212 | 25 | | 66 |
| William Floyd | FB | 6'1" | 242 | 22 | | 36 |
| Marc Logan | FB | 6' | 212 | 29 | | 12 |
| Ed McCaffrey | WR | 6'5" | 215 | 26 | | 12 |
| Jerry Rice | WR | 6'2" | 200 | 31 | | 92 |
| Nate Singleton | WR | 5'11" | 190 | 26 | | 12 |
| John Taylor | WR | 6'1" | 185 | 32 | | 30 |
| Brett Carolan | TE | 6'3" | 241 | 23 | | |
| Brent Jones | TE | 6'4" | 230 | 31 | | 56 |
| Ted Popson | LB | 6'4" | 250 | 27 | | |
| Doug Brien | K | 5'11" | 177 | 23 | | 105 |
| Klaus Wilmsmeyer | K | 6'1" | 210 | 26 | | |

## NEW ORLEANS SAINTS 7-9 Jim Mora

| Scores of Each Game | | |
|---|---|---|
| 17 | KANSAS CITY | 30 |
| 24 | WASHINGTON | 38 |
| 9 | Tampa Bay | 7 |
| 13 | San Francisco | 24 |
| 27 | N.Y. GIANTS | 22 |
| 7 | Chicago | 17 |
| 22 | SAN DIEGO | 36 |
| 37 | L.A. RAMS | 34 |
| 20 | Minnesota | 21 |
| 33 | ATLANTA | 32 |
| 19 | L.A. Raiders | 24 |
| 14 | SAN FRANCISCO | 35 |
| 31 | L.A. Rams | 15 |
| 29 | Atlanta | 20 |
| 16 | DALLAS | 24 |
| 30 | Denver | 28 |

| Use Name | Pos. | Hgt. | Wgt. | Age | Int | Pts |
|---|---|---|---|---|---|---|
| Richard Cooper | OT | 6'4" | 290 | 29 | | |
| Willie Roaf | OT | 6'4" | 300 | 24 | | |
| Willie Williams | OT | 6'6" | 295 | 27 | | |
| Scott Adams | OG-OT | 6'5" | 295 | 27 | | |
| Jim Dombrowski | OG | 6'5" | 300 | 30 | | |
| Chris Port | OG-OT | 6'5" | 295 | 26 | | |
| Craig Novitsky | C-OT | 6'5" | 295 | 23 | | |
| Jeff Uhlenhake | C | 6'3" | 284 | 28 | | |
| Herman Carroll | DE | 6'4" | 265 | 23 | | |
| Robert Goff | DE-NT | 6'3" | 280 | 28 | | |
| Joe Johnson | DE | 6'4" | 285 | 22 | | |
| Wayne Martin | DE | 6'5" | 275 | 28 | | |
| Frank Warren | DE-NT | 6'4" | 290 | 34 | | |
| Jim Hanna | NT | 6'4" | 255 | 23 | | |
| Les Miller (to PIT) | NT-DE | 6'7" | 285 | 29 | | |
| Darion Conner | LB | 6'2" | 245 | 26 | 1 | |
| Ernest Dixon | LB | 6'1" | 250 | 22 | | |
| Sam Mills | LB | 5'9" | 225 | 35 | 1 | |
| Joel Smeenge | LB | 6'5" | 250 | 26 | | |
| Mike Stonebreaker | LB | 6' | 235 | 27 | | |
| Winfred Tubbs | LB | 6'4" | 250 | 23 | 1 | |
| Renaldo Turnbull | DE | 6'4" | 250 | 28 | | |
| James Williams | LB | 6' | 230 | 25 | 2 | 6 |
| DeMond Winston | LB | 6'2" | 239 | 25 | | |
| Vince Buck | DB | 6' | 198 | 26 | 1 | |
| Israel Byrd | DB | 5'11" | 184 | 23 | | |
| Othello Henderson | DB | 6' | 195 | 22 | | |
| Tyrone Hughes | DB | 5'9" | 175 | 24 | 2 | 24 |
| Tyrone Johnson | DB | 5'11" | 171 | 22 | | |
| Reggie Jones | DB | 6'1" | 202 | 25 | | |
| Selwyn Jones | DB | 6' | 185 | 24 | | |
| Carl Lee | DB | 5'11" | 185 | 33 | 2 | |
| Tyrone Legette | DB | 5'9" | 177 | 24 | | |
| Sean Lumpkin | DB | 6' | 206 | 24 | 1 | |
| J.J. McCleskey | DB | 5'7" | 177 | 24 | | |
| Jimmy Spencer | DB | 5'9" | 180 | 25 | 5 | |
| Jim Everett | QB | 6'5" | 212 | 31 | | |
| Doug Nussmeier | QB | 6'3" | 211 | 23 | | |
| Wade Wilson | QB | 6'3" | 206 | 35 | | |
| Mario Bates | HB | 6'1" | 217 | 21 | | 36 |
| Derek Brown | HB | 5'9" | 197 | 23 | | 24 |
| Vaughn Dunbar | HB | 5'10" | 204 | 25 | | |
| Brad Muster | FB | 6'4" | 235 | 29 | | 6 |
| Lorenzo Neal | FB | 5'10" | 240 | 23 | | 6 |
| Derrick Ned | FB | 6'1" | 220 | 25 | | |
| Quinn Early | WR | 6' | 190 | 29 | | 24 |
| Michael Haynes | WR | 6' | 184 | 28 | | 30 |
| Derrell Mitchell | WR | 5'9" | 190 | 22 | | |
| Steve Rhem | WR | 6'2" | 212 | 22 | | |
| Torrance Small | WR | 6'3" | 201 | 23 | | 32 |
| Kirk Botkin | TE | 6'3" | 245 | 23 | | |
| Irv Smith | TE | 6'3" | 246 | 22 | | 18 |
| Wesley Walls | TE | 6'5" | 250 | 28 | | 26 |
| Morten Andersen | K | 6'2" | 221 | 34 | | 116 |
| Tommy Barnhardt | K | 6'3" | 207 | 31 | | |

Jeff Davidson — Shoulder injury

Frank Wainright — Toe injury

## ATLANTA FALCONS 7-9 June Jones

| Scores of Each Game | | |
|---|---|---|
| 28 | Detroit | *31 |
| 31 | L.A. RAMS | 13 |
| 10 | KANSAS CITY | 30 |
| 27 | Washington | 20 |
| 8 | L.A. Rams | 5 |
| 34 | TAMPA BAY | 13 |
| 3 | SAN FRANCISCO | 42 |
| 17 | L.A. Raiders | 30 |
| 10 | SAN DIEGO | 9 |
| 32 | New Orleans | 33 |
| 28 | Denver | 32 |
| 28 | PHILADELPHIA | 21 |
| 14 | San Francisco | 50 |
| 20 | NEW ORLEANS | 29 |
| 17 | Green Bay | 21 |
| 10 | ARIZONA | 6 |

| Use Name | Pos. | Hgt. | Wgt. | Age | Int | Pts |
|---|---|---|---|---|---|---|
| Irv Eatman | OT | 6'7" | 305 | 33 | | |
| Mike Kenn | OT | 6'7" | 286 | 38 | | |
| Bob Whitfield | OT | 6'5" | 300 | 22 | | |
| Lincoln Kennedy | OG-OT | 6'6" | 350 | 23 | | |
| David Richards | OG | 6'5" | 310 | 26 | | |
| Jim Ritcher | OG | 6'3" | 273 | 36 | | |
| Roman Fortin | C | 6'5" | 295 | 27 | | |
| Robbie Tobeck | C | 6'4" | 287 | 24 | | |
| Mike Zandofsky | C-OG | 6'2" | 305 | 28 | | |
| Dunstan Anderson | DE | 6'4" | 254 | 23 | | |
| Lester Archambeau | DE | 6'5" | 275 | 27 | | |
| Chris Doleman | DE | 6'5" | 275 | 32 | 1 | |
| James Geathers | DE | 6'7" | 290 | 34 | | |
| Chuck Smith | DE | 6'2" | 257 | 24 | 1 | 6 |
| Mel Agee | DT | 6'5" | 295 | 25 | | |
| Bill Goldberg | DT | 6'2" | 280 | 27 | | |
| Pierce Holt | DT | 6'4" | 275 | 32 | | |
| Moe Gardner | NT | 6'2" | 265 | 26 | | |
| Darryl Ford | LB | 6'1" | 230 | 28 | | |
| Ron George | LB | 6'2" | 225 | 24 | | |
| Dwayne Gordon | LB | 6'1" | 240 | 24 | | |
| Clay Matthews | LB | 6'2" | 245 | 38 | | |
| Kenny Tippins | LB | 6'1" | 235 | 28 | | |
| Jessie Tuggle | LB | 5'11" | 230 | 29 | 1 | |
| Scott Case | DB | 6' | 194 | 32 | 2 | |
| Vinnie Clark (to ATL) | DB | 6' | 194 | 25 | 5 | |
| Brad Edwards | DB | 6'2" | 207 | 27 | | |
| Roger Harper | DB | 6'2" | 223 | 23 | 1 | |
| Eric Jack | DB | 5'10" | 177 | 22 | | 6 |
| D.J. Johnson | DB | 6' | 190 | 28 | 5 | |
| Brett Maxie | DB | 6'2" | 194 | 32 | | |
| Alton Montgomery | DB | 6' | 202 | 26 | | |
| Anthony Phillips | DB | 6'2" | 207 | 23 | 1 | |
| Kevin Ross | DB | 5'9" | 185 | 32 | 3 | |
| Elbert Shelley | DB | 5'11" | 190 | 29 | | |
| Darnell Walker | DB | 5'8" | 168 | 24 | 3 | 6 |
| Charles Washington | DB | 6'1" | 214 | 27 | | |
| Jeff George | QB | 6'4" | 210 | 26 | | |
| Bobby Hebert | QB | 6'4" | 215 | 34 | | |
| Perry Klerin | QB | 6'2" | 218 | 23 | | |
| Jamal Anderson | HB-FB | 5'10" | 240 | 22 | | |
| Craig Heyward | HB-FB | 5'11" | 265 | 27 | | 48 |
| Erric Pegram | HB | 5'9" | 195 | 25 | | 6 |
| Tony Smith | HB | 6'1" | 224 | 24 | | |
| Bert Emanuel | WR | 5'10" | 175 | 23 | | 24 |
| Leonard Harris | WR | 5'8" | 162 | 33 | | |
| Terance Mathis | WR | 5'10" | 175 | 27 | | 70 |
| David Mims | WR | 5'8" | 191 | 24 | | |
| Andre Rison | WR | 6' | 188 | 27 | | 50 |
| Ricky Sanders | WR | 5'11" | 180 | 32 | | 6 |
| Darryl Spencer | WR | 5'8" | 172 | 24 | | |
| Clarence Verdin | WR | 5'9" | 162 | 31 | | |
| Harper LeBel | TE | 6'4" | 255 | 31 | | |
| Mitch Lyons | TE | 6'4" | 265 | 24 | | |
| Harold Alexander | K | 6'2" | 220 | 23 | | |
| Norm Johnson | K | 6'2" | 203 | 34 | | 95 |
| Scott Tyner | K | 6'1" | 189 | 22 | | |

## LOS ANGELES RAMS 4-12 Chuck Knox

| Scores of Each Game | | |
|---|---|---|
| 14 | ARIZONA | 12 |
| 13 | Atlanta | 31 |
| 19 | SAN FRANCISCO | 34 |
| 16 | Kansas City | 0 |
| 5 | ATLANTA | 8 |
| 17 | Green Bay | 24 |
| 17 | N.Y. GIANTS | 10 |
| 34 | New Orleans | 37 |
| 27 | DENVER | 21 |
| 17 | L.A. RAIDERS | 20 |
| 27 | San Francisco | 31 |
| 17 | San Diego | 31 |
| 15 | NEW ORLEANS | 31 |
| 14 | Tampa Bay | 24 |
| 13 | Chicago | 27 |
| 21 | WASHINGTON | 24 |

| Use Name | Pos. | Hgt. | Wgt. | Age | Int | Pts |
|---|---|---|---|---|---|---|
| Darryl Ashmore | OT | 6'7" | 300 | 24 | | |
| Wayne Gandy | OT | 6'4" | 289 | 23 | | |
| Clarence Jones | OT | 6'6" | 280 | 26 | | |
| Jackie Slater | OT | 6'4" | 285 | 40 | | |
| Chuck Belin | OG | 6'2" | 312 | 23 | | |
| Leo Goeas | OG-OT | 6'4" | 300 | 28 | | |
| Keith Loneker | OG | 6'3" | 330 | 23 | | |
| Tom Newberry | OG | 6'2" | 285 | 31 | | |
| Bern Brostek | C | 6'3" | 300 | 27 | | |
| Blair Bush | C | 6'3" | 275 | 37 | | |
| Brad Fichtel | C | 6'2" | 285 | 24 | | |
| Brad Ottis | DE | 6'4" | 272 | 22 | | |
| Gerald Robinson | DE | 6'3" | 280 | 31 | | |
| Fred Stokes | DE | 6'3" | 274 | 30 | | |
| Robert Young | DE | 6'6" | 273 | 25 | | |
| D'Marco Farr | DT | 6'1" | 270 | 23 | | |
| Sean Gilbert | DT | 6'4" | 315 | 24 | | 2 |
| Jimmie Jones | DT | 6'4" | 276 | 18 | | |
| David Rocker | DT | 6'4" | 267 | 25 | | |
| Shane Conlan | LB | 6'3" | 235 | 30 | | |
| Thomas Homco | LB | 6' | 245 | 24 | | |
| Joe Kelly | LB | 6'2" | 235 | 29 | 1 | |
| Chris Martin | LB | 6'2" | 241 | 33 | | |
| Roman Phifer | LB | 6'2" | 230 | 26 | 2 | |
| Henry Rolling | DE | 6'2" | 225 | 28 | | |
| Robert Bailey | DB | 5'9" | 176 | 25 | | 6 |
| Dexter Davis | DB | 5'10" | 184 | 24 | | |
| Wymon Henderson | DB | 5'10" | 188 | 32 | | |
| Darryl Henley | DB | 5'9" | 172 | 27 | 3 | |
| Steve Israel | DB | 5'10" | 186 | 25 | | |
| Todd Lyght | DB | 6' | 186 | 25 | 1 | 6 |
| Keith Lyle | DB | 6'2" | 204 | 22 | 2 | |
| Anthony Newman | DB | 6' | 199 | 28 | 2 | 6 |
| Marquez Pope | DB | 5'10" | 193 | 23 | 3 | |
| Toby Wright | DB | 5'11" | 203 | 23 | | 6 |
| Chris Chandler | QB | 6'4" | 225 | 28 | | 6 |
| Tommy Maddox | QB | 6'4" | 205 | 22 | | |
| Jamie Martin | QB | 6'2" | 215 | 24 | | |
| Chris Miller | QB | 6'2" | 212 | 23 | | |
| Johnny Bailey | HB | 5'8" | 180 | 27 | | 6 |
| Jerome Bettis | HB-FB | 5'11" | 243 | 22 | | 28 |
| Howard Griffith | HB | 6' | 226 | 26 | | 6 |
| David Lang | HB-FB | 5'11" | 213 | 26 | | |
| Tim Lester | FB | 5'9" | 215 | 26 | | |
| Willie Anderson | WR | 6' | 172 | 29 | | 30 |
| Chris Brantley | WR | 5'10" | 180 | 23 | | |
| Isaac Bruce | WR | 6' | 178 | 21 | | 18 |
| Richard Buchanan | WR | 5'10" | 178 | 25 | | |
| Jessie Hester | WR | 5'11" | 175 | 31 | | 18 |
| Todd Kinchen | WR | 6' | 187 | 25 | | 24 |
| Jermaine Ross | WR | 5'11" | 192 | 23 | | 6 |
| Rickey Brady | TE | 6'4" | 246 | 23 | | |
| Troy Drayton | TE | 6'3" | 255 | 24 | | 36 |
| Ron Middleton | TE | 6'2" | 262 | 29 | | |
| Sean Landeta | K | 6' | 210 | 32 | | |
| Tony Zendejas | K | 5'8" | 165 | 34 | | 82 |

## SAN FRANCISCO 49ERS

### RUSHING

| Last Name | No. | Yds | Avg | TD |
|---|---|---|---|---|
| Watters | 239 | 877 | 3.7 | 6 |
| Floyd | 87 | 305 | 3.5 | 6 |
| S. Young | 58 | 293 | 5.1 | 7 |
| Logan | 33 | 143 | 4.3 | 1 |
| Loville | 31 | 99 | 3.2 | 0 |
| Rice | 7 | 93 | 13.3 | 2 |
| Walker | 13 | 54 | 4.2 | 1 |
| Carter | 8 | 34 | 4.3 | 0 |
| Grbac | 13 | 1 | 0.1 | 0 |
| Taylor | 2 | -2 | -1.0 | 0 |

### RECEIVING

| Last Name | No. | Yds | Avg | TD |
|---|---|---|---|---|
| Rice | 112 | 1499 | 13.4 | 13 |
| Watters | 66 | 719 | 10.9 | 5 |
| Jones | 49 | 670 | 13.7 | 9 |
| Taylor | 41 | 531 | 13.0 | 5 |
| Singleton | 21 | 294 | 14.0 | 2 |
| Floyd | 19 | 145 | 7.6 | 0 |
| Logan | 16 | 97 | 6.1 | 1 |
| Popson | 13 | 141 | 10.8 | 0 |
| McCaffrey | 11 | 131 | 11.9 | 2 |
| Carter | 7 | 99 | 14.1 | 0 |
| Loville | 2 | 26 | 13.0 | 0 |
| Carolan | 2 | 10 | 5.0 | 0 |

### PUNT RETURNS

| Last Name | No. | Yds | Avg | TD |
|---|---|---|---|---|
| Carter | 338 | 321 | 8.4 | 0 |
| Singleton | 2 | 13 | 6.5 | 0 |

### KICKOFF RETURNS

| Last Name | No. | Yds | Avg | TD |
|---|---|---|---|---|
| Carter | 48 | 1105 | 23.0 | 1 |
| Walker | 6 | 82 | 13.7 | 0 |
| Loville | 2 | 34 | 17.0 | 0 |
| Singleton | 2 | 23 | 11.5 | 0 |

### PASSING — PUNTING — KICKING

| PASSING | Att | Cmp | % | Yds | Yd/Att | TD | Int— | % | RK |
|---|---|---|---|---|---|---|---|---|---|
| Young | 461 | 324 | 70.3 | 3969 | 8.61 | 35 | 10— | 2.2 | 1 |
| Grbac | 50 | 35 | 70.0 | 393 | 7.86 | 2 | 1— | 2.0 | |

| PUNTING | No. | Avg. |
|---|---|---|
| Wilmsmeyer | 54 | 41.4 |

| KICKING | XP | ATT | % | FG | ATT | % |
|---|---|---|---|---|---|---|
| Brien | 60 | 62 | 97 | 15 | 20 | 75 |

**2 POINT XP**
Jones (1)
Rice (1)

## NEW ORLEANS SAINTS

### RUSHING

| Last Name | No. | Yds | Avg | TD |
|---|---|---|---|---|
| Bates | 151 | 579 | 3.8 | 6 |
| Brown | 146 | 489 | 3.3 | 3 |
| Neal | 30 | 90 | 3.0 | 1 |
| Haynes | 4 | 43 | 10.8 | 0 |
| Ned | 11 | 36 | 3.3 | 0 |
| Everett | 15 | 35 | 2.3 | 0 |
| Barnhardt | 1 | 21 | 21.0 | 0 |
| W. Wilson | 7 | 15 | 2.1 | 0 |
| Early | 2 | 10 | 5.0 | 0 |
| Dunbar | 3 | 9 | 3.0 | 0 |
| Hughes | 2 | 6 | 3.0 | 0 |
| Muster | 1 | 3 | 3.0 | 1 |

### RECEIVING

| Last Name | No. | Yds | Avg | TD |
|---|---|---|---|---|
| Early | 82 | 894 | 10.9 | 4 |
| Haynes | 77 | 985 | 12.8 | 5 |
| Small | 49 | 719 | 14.7 | 5 |
| Brown | 44 | 428 | 9.7 | 1 |
| Smith | 41 | 330 | 8.0 | 3 |
| Walls | 38 | 406 | 10.7 | 4 |
| Ned | 13 | 86 | 6.6 | 0 |
| Muster | 10 | 88 | 8.8 | 0 |
| Bates | 8 | 62 | 7.8 | 0 |
| Neal | 2 | 9 | 4.5 | 0 |
| Mitchell | 1 | 13 | 13.0 | 0 |
| W. Williams | 1 | 7 | 7.0 | 0 |

### PUNT RETURNS

| Last Name | No. | Yds | Avg | TD |
|---|---|---|---|---|
| Hughes | 21 | 143 | 6.8 | 0 |
| Mitchell | 3 | 9 | 3.0 | 0 |
| Legette | 1 | 0 | 0.0 | 0 |

### KICKOFF RETURNS

| Last Name | No. | Yds | Avg | TD |
|---|---|---|---|---|
| Hughes | 63 | 1556 | 24.7 | 2 |
| Ned | 7 | 77 | 11.0 | 0 |
| Mitchell | 6 | 129 | 21.5 | 0 |
| Smith | 2 | 10 | 5.0 | 0 |
| Dunbar | 1 | 28 | 28.0 | 0 |
| Bates | 1 | 20 | 20.0 | 0 |
| Neal | 1 | 17 | 17.0 | 0 |
| Brown | 1 | 3 | 3.0 | 0 |

### PASSING — PUNTING — KICKING

| PASSING | Att | Cmp | % | Yds | Yd/Att | TD | Int— | % | RK |
|---|---|---|---|---|---|---|---|---|---|
| Everett | 540 | 346 | 64.1 | 3855 | 7.14 | 22 | 18— | 3.3 | 3 |
| W. Wilson | 28 | 20 | 71.4 | 172 | 6.14 | 0 | 0— | 0.0 | |
| Barnhardt | 1 | 0 | 0.0 | 0 | 0.00 | 0 | 0— | 0.0 | |

| PUNTING | No. | Avg. |
|---|---|---|
| Barnhardt | 67 | 43.6 |

| KICKING | XP | ATT | % | FG | ATT | % |
|---|---|---|---|---|---|---|
| Andersen | 32 | 32 | 100 | 28 | 39 | 72 |

**2 POINT XP**
Small (1)
Walls (1)

## ATLANTA FALCONS

### RUSHING

| Last Name | No. | Yds | Avg | TD |
|---|---|---|---|---|
| Heyward | 183 | 779 | 4.3 | 7 |
| Pegram | 103 | 358 | 3.5 | 1 |
| George | 30 | 66 | 2.2 | 0 |
| Hebert | 9 | 43 | 4.8 | 0 |
| Emanuel | 2 | 4 | 2.0 | 0 |
| Alexander | 1 | 0 | 0.0 | 0 |
| J. Anderson | 2 | -1 | -0.5 | 0 |

### RECEIVING

| Last Name | No. | Yds | Avg | TD |
|---|---|---|---|---|
| Mathis | 111 | 1342 | 12.1 | 11 |
| Rison | 81 | 1088 | 13.4 | 8 |
| Sanders | 67 | 599 | 8.9 | 1 |
| Emanuel | 46 | 649 | 14.1 | 4 |
| Heyward | 32 | 335 | 10.5 | 1 |
| Pegram | 16 | 99 | 6.2 | 0 |
| Harris | 9 | 113 | 12.6 | 0 |
| Lyons | 7 | 54 | 7.7 | 0 |
| Mims | 3 | 14 | 4.7 | 0 |
| Spencer | 2 | 51 | 25.5 | 0 |

### PUNT RETURNS

| Last Name | No. | Yds | Avg | TD |
|---|---|---|---|---|
| Verdin | 23 | 113 | 4.9 | 0 |
| T. Smith | 8 | 75 | 9.4 | 0 |

### KICKOFF RETURNS

| Last Name | No. | Yds | Avg | TD |
|---|---|---|---|---|
| Verdin | 44 | 1026 | 23.3 | 0 |
| T. Smith | 16 | 333 | 20.8 | 0 |
| Pegram | 9 | 145 | 16.1 | 0 |
| Montgomery | 2 | 58 | 29.0 | 0 |
| Harris | 2 | 47 | 23.5 | 0 |
| J. Anderson | 1 | 11 | 11.0 | 0 |
| Heyward | 1 | 7 | 7.0 | 0 |

### PASSING — PUNTING — KICKING

| PASSING | Att | Cmp | % | Yds | Yd/Att | TD | Int— | % | RK |
|---|---|---|---|---|---|---|---|---|---|
| George | 524 | 322 | 61.5 | 3734 | 7.13 | 23 | 18— | 3.4 | 5 |
| Hebert | 103 | 52 | 50.5 | 610 | 5.92 | 2 | 6— | 5.8 | |
| Emanuel | 1 | 0 | 0.0 | 0 | 0.00 | 0 | 1— | 100.0 | |
| Klein | 1 | 0 | 0.0 | 0 | 0.00 | 0 | 0— | 0.0 | |

| PUNTING | No. | Avg. |
|---|---|---|
| Alexander | 71 | 39.9 |
| Tyner | 8 | 35.6 |

| KICKING | XP | ATT | % | FG | ATT | % |
|---|---|---|---|---|---|---|
| N. Johnson | 32 | 32 | 100 | 21 | 25 | 84 |

**2 POINT XP**
Mathis (2)
Rison (1)

## LOS ANGELES RAMS

### RUSHING

| Last Name | No. | Yds | Avg | TD |
|---|---|---|---|---|
| Bettis | 319 | 1025 | 3.2 | 3 |
| Miller | 20 | 100 | 5.0 | 0 |
| Chandler | 18 | 61 | 3.4 | 1 |
| Kinchen | 1 | 44 | 44.0 | 1 |
| Bailey | 11 | 35 | 3.2 | 1 |
| Lang | 6 | 34 | 5.7 | 0 |
| Griffith | 9 | 30 | 3.3 | 0 |
| Hester | 2 | 28 | 14.0 | 0 |
| Lester | 7 | 14 | 2.0 | 0 |
| Anderson | 1 | 11 | 11.0 | 0 |
| Drayton | 1 | 4 | 4.0 | 0 |
| Bruce | 1 | 2 | 2.0 | 0 |
| Maddox | 1 | 1 | 1.0 | 0 |

### RECEIVING

| Last Name | No. | Yds | Avg | TD |
|---|---|---|---|---|
| Bailey | 58 | 516 | 8.9 | 0 |
| Anderson | 46 | 945 | 20.5 | 5 |
| Hester | 45 | 644 | 14.3 | 3 |
| Drayton | 32 | 276 | 8.6 | 6 |
| Bettis | 31 | 293 | 9.5 | 1 |
| Kinchen | 23 | 352 | 15.3 | 3 |
| Bruce | 21 | 272 | 13.0 | 3 |
| Griffith | 16 | 113 | 7.1 | 1 |
| Lang | 8 | 60 | 7.5 | 0 |
| Buchanan | 5 | 60 | 12.0 | 0 |
| Brantley | 4 | 29 | 7.3 | 0 |
| Ross | 1 | 36 | 36.0 | 1 |
| Lester | 1 | 1 | 1.0 | 0 |

### PUNT RETURNS

| Last Name | No. | Yds | Avg | TD |
|---|---|---|---|---|
| Bailey | 19 | 153 | 8.1 | 0 |
| Kinchen | 16 | 158 | 9.9 | 0 |
| Brantley | 3 | 18 | 6.0 | 0 |
| Bailey | 1 | 103 | 103.0 | 1 |
| Lyght | 1 | 29 | 29.0 | 0 |

### KICKOFF RETURNS

| Last Name | No. | Yds | Avg | TD |
|---|---|---|---|---|
| Lang | 27 | 626 | 23.2 | 0 |
| Kinchen | 21 | 510 | 24.3 | 0 |
| Bailey | 12 | 260 | 21.7 | 0 |
| Brantley | 7 | 150 | 21.4 | 0 |
| Griffith | 2 | 35 | 17.5 | 0 |
| Farr | 1 | 16 | 16.0 | 0 |
| Lester | 1 | 8 | 8.0 | 0 |

### PASSING — PUNTING — KICKING

| PASSING | Att | Cmp | % | Yds | Yd/Att | TD | Int— | % | RK |
|---|---|---|---|---|---|---|---|---|---|
| Miller | 317 | 173 | 54.6 | 2104 | 6.64 | 16 | 14— | 4.4 | 10 |
| Chandler | 176 | 108 | 61.4 | 1352 | 7.68 | 7 | 2— | 1.1 | |
| Maddox | 19 | 10 | 52.6 | 141 | 7.42 | 0 | 2— | 10.5 | |

| PUNTING | No. | Avg. |
|---|---|---|
| Landeta | 78 | 44.8 |

| KICKING | XP | ATT | % | FG | ATT | % |
|---|---|---|---|---|---|---|
| Zendejas | 28 | 28 | 100 | 18 | 23 | 78 |

**2 POINT XP**
Bettis (2)

# 1994 A.F.C. Broken Records and Two-Point Conversions

The 1994 season was one in which records were broken at a record pace. Jerry Rice broke Jim Brown's NFL mark for career touchdowns, finishing the season with 131. Rice also caught 3 TD's in the Super Bowl, giving him a total of seven in NFL title games, another record. In Week 15, Art Monk broke Steve Largent's record by catching at least one pass in 178 consecutive games (Monk's streak went to 180 games at the end of the year). Minnesota's Cris Carter broke Sterling Sharpe's record by catching 122 passes, and New England's Ben Coates had 96 receptions, the most ever for a tight end. And, finally, Steve Young's passer rating of 112.8 broke the previous best, set by Joe Montana, and also made Young the highest-rated career passer ever, again ahead of Montana. Young also threw six touchdown passes in the Super Bowl, breaking yet another Montana mark.

The two-point conversion made its NFL debut in 1994 and wound up playing a larger role than initially expected. During the regular season, teams tried for two points 111 times and were successful on 61 of those attempts. Kickoffs were moved back to the 30-yard line, which helped both Tyrone Hughes and Brian Mitchell break the single-season record for kickoff return yards. And Mel Gray returned three kickoffs for touchdowns, giving him six for his career.

In the AFC, as Buffalo slid out of the playoffs with a 7-9 record, Pittsburgh and San Diego were surprise division winners. They met in the AFC championship game, with the Chargers winning and advancing to their first-ever Super Bowl.

## EASTERN DIVISION

**Miami Dolphins** — Although Miami won the division title, a season that started with such high hopes with a 7-2 mark, ended in disappointment, a crushing, last-minute loss to San Diego in the divisional playoffs. The Dolphins survived season-ending injuries to the two starting running backs, Terry Kirby and Keith Byars, because Bernie Parmalee came out of nowhere to rush for 868 yards. Dan Marino, now 33, came back from a 1993 injury to lead the AFC in passing. Marino threw for 4,453 yards and 30 touchdowns. Miami did find an enforcer in defensive tackle Tim Bowens, the first-round draft pick who was voted Defensive Rookie of the Year. The regular season finished on a strange note, with head coach Don Shula sitting on a golf cart after he suffered a knee injury of his own.

**New England Patriots** — The Patriots certainly didn't seem like a team that was coached by Bill Parcells in 1994, because they threw the ball a lot, didn't run it very well and played just average defense. Quarterback Drew Bledsoe, in only his second season, set an NFL record with 691 pass attempts. Bledsoe completed 400 of them for 4,555 yards and 25 touchdowns, and five players had 52 or more receptions, a league record. Ben Coates also set an NFL record for tight ends with 96 receptions. But the running game was abysmal, as the Patriots averaged only 2.8 yards per carry as a team. Marion Butts gained 703 yards and scored eight touchdowns but was benched for the playoff loss. New England won its final seven regular-season games and had its first winning season and playoff berth since 1986.

**Indianapolis Colts** — The Colts rode rookie running back Marshall Faulk to an 8-8 record. Faulk, the No. 2 overall pick in the 1994 draft, rushed for 1,282 yards — a team total topped only by Eric Dickerson in 1988 and '89 — and caught 52 passes for another 522 yards. He scored 12 touchdowns. But Indianapolis had quarterback problems, with neither Jim Harbaugh, Don Majkowski nor Browning Nagle able to lead the team consistently. The Colts scored 307 points, their most since 1988, with special teams and the defense combining to set a team record with seven TD's on returns. The defense made great strides, especially after Ray Buchanan was moved from safety to cornerback. Buchanan intercepted eight passes, returning three of them for touchdowns. Defenders Steve Emtman and Trev Alberts missed most of the season with injuries.

**Buffalo Bills** — What goes up must come down. The Bills fell apart in 1994, losing their final two games with the playoffs on the line to finish 7-9 and in fourth place. At least they didn't have to worry about losing

another Super Bowl. Veterans such as quarterback Jim Kelly (3,114 yards, 22 touchdowns before being injured in Game 14), running back Thurman Thomas (1,093 yards, seven touchdowns) and wide receiver Andre Reed (90 receptions for 1,303 yards and eight TD's) had excellent seasons. But four losses were by a touchdown or less and the Bills allowed 356 points, more than 100 more than in 1993. Still, they beat division-winner Miami twice and still had enough good players left to make another run late in the 1994 season.

**New York Jets** — Big things were expected from the Jets in 1993 when Pete Carroll took over as head coach, but New York fell to 6-10 and Carroll was fired after the season. He was replaced by Rich Kotite, who was fired by Philadelphia. The Jets lost their final five games, the first of which was a crusher to Miami after leading 24-6. Quarterback Boomer Esiason ranked eighth in the AFC in passing but was only as good as his supporting cast. And, while running back Johnny Johnson had a career-high 931 rushing yards, he was slowed by injuries down the stretch. Wide receiver Rob Moore became the first Jet to be voted to the Pro Bowl. He caught 78 passes for 1,010 yards and six TD's.

## CENTRAL DIVISION

**Pittsburgh Steelers** — Strong defense and the NFL's top running game led Pittsburgh to the division title. The Steelers beat division-rival Cleveland twice during the regular season and again in the playoffs behind a defense that ranked No. 2 in the NFL, just 13 yards behind Dallas. Pittsburgh, which earned the nickname "Blitzburgh," led the league in sacks. Kevin Greene paced the league with 14 sacks, and Greg Lloyd had 10. The running game was led by veteran Barry Foster and rookie Bam Morris, who had 851 and 836 yards rushing, respectively. The offense had its troubles, once going 13 quarters and two overtime periods without scoring a touchdown. Quarterback Neil O'Donnell ranked seventh in the AFC in passing and threw only nine interceptions.

**Cleveland Browns** — The Browns had their best season since 1986 but couldn't beat Pittsburgh (they lost to the Steelers twice). The Cleveland defense led the NFL by allowing only 204 points, including holding six opponents to fewer than 10 points. Safety Eric Turner led the league with nine interceptions, and former Giants Pepper Johnson and Carl Banks made their presence felt. But, for all the defensive success, the offense was not nearly as good. Vinny Testaverde threw 16 touchdowns and 18 interceptions and ranked only 11th in the AFC. Wide receivers Michael Jackson and Mark Carrier were hampered by hamstring injuries, so rookie Derrick Alexander had a team-high 48 catches. Fullback Tommy Vardell was lost early in the season, but Leroy Hoard rushed for 890 yards and scored a team-high nine touchdowns.

**Cincinnati Bengals** — The Bengals didn't finish in last place again, but their 3-13 record still wasn't very good. Cincinnati did develop a new star in wide receiver Carl Pickens, who caught 71 passes for 1,127 yards and an AFC-high 11 touchdowns. At quarterback, David Klingler was replaced after seven games by Jeff Blake, who was untested. But Blake led the Bengals to all three of their victories, and he averaged 13.8 yards per completion and threw only nine interceptions in his nine games. Rookie receiver Darnay Scott scored five touchdowns on 46 receptions for 866 yards. But the offense had an NFL-high 41 turnovers. The defense was improved, especially against the run with defensive tackle Dan Wilkinson, the No. 1 overall pick in the 1994 draft.

**Houston Oilers** — The Oilers had the worst one-season turnaround in NFL history — going from 12-4 in 1993 to 2-14 in '94. Head coach Jack Pardee was fired after 10 games and replaced by defensive coordinator Jeff Fisher, who led the team to a 1-5 record. Houston started the season without quarterback Warren Moon and defensive ends Sean Jones and William Fuller because of salary cap considerations. At quarterback, Cody Carlson, Billy Joe Tolliver and Bucky Richardson couldn't do much to help the 25th-ranked passing offense, and the Oilers scored the fewest points in the league. And running back Gary Brown didn't show the same magic that he did in 1993 and was replaced by

**OFFENSE**

| | BUFF | CIN | CLEV | DEN | HOU | IND | K.C. | L.A. | MIA | N.E. | NYJ | PITT | S.D. | SEA |
|---|---|---|---|---|---|---|---|---|---|---|---|---|---|---|
| **FIRST DOWNS:** | | | | | | | | | | | | | | |
| Total | 319 | 267 | 273 | 346 | 278 | 252 | 322 | 267 | 344 | 348 | 265 | 307 | 311 | 285 |
| by Rushing | 107 | 84 | 80 | 101 | 97 | 108 | 97 | 87 | 109 | 83 | 90 | 138 | 102 | 114 |
| by Passing | 181 | 158 | 161 | 202 | 158 | 126 | 211 | 158 | 220 | 243 | 164 | 148 | 181 | 143 |
| by Penalty | 31 | 25 | 32 | 43 | 23 | 18 | 14 | 22 | 15 | 22 | 11 | 21 | 28 | 28 |
| **RUSHING:** | | | | | | | | | | | | | | |
| Number | 483 | 404 | 449 | 431 | 417 | 495 | 464 | 428 | 434 | 478 | 416 | 546 | 482 | 480 |
| Yards | 1831 | 1556 | 1657 | 1470 | 1682 | 2060 | 1732 | 1512 | 1658 | 1332 | 1566 | 2180 | 1852 | 2084 |
| Average Yards | 3.8 | 3.9 | 3.7 | 3.4 | 4.0 | 4.2 | 3.7 | 3.5 | 3.8 | 2.8 | 3.8 | 4.0 | 3.8 | 4.3 |
| Touchdowns | 14 | 5 | 12 | 19 | 10 | 15 | 12 | 7 | 13 | 12 | 8 | 15 | 13 | 16 |
| **PASSING:** | | | | | | | | | | | | | | |
| Attempts | 542 | 542 | 507 | 626 | 554 | 376 | 615 | 487 | 627 | 699 | 539 | 463 | 522 | 498 |
| Completions | 342 | 289 | 266 | 388 | 274 | 217 | 366 | 281 | 392 | 405 | 310 | 266 | 305 | 253 |
| Completion Pct. | 63.1 | 53.3 | 52.5 | 62.0 | 49.5 | 57.7 | 59.5 | 57.7 | 62.5 | 57.9 | 57.5 | 57.5 | 58.4 | 50.8 |
| Passing Yards | 3714 | 3541 | 3269 | 4383 | 3216 | 2519 | 4092 | 3556 | 4533 | 4583 | 3323 | 3247 | 3619 | 2809 |
| Avg. Yds per Att. | 6.85 | 6.53 | 6.45 | 7.00 | 5.81 | 6.70 | 6.65 | 7.30 | 7.23 | 6.56 | 6.17 | 7.01 | 6.93 | 5.64 |
| Avg. Yds per Comp. | 10.86 | 12.25 | 12.29 | 11.30 | 11.74 | 11.61 | 11.18 | 12.65 | 11.56 | 11.32 | 10.72 | 12.21 | 11.87 | 11.10 |
| Times Tackled | 41 | 44 | 14 | 55 | 65 | 28 | 19 | 50 | 17 | 22 | 28 | 39 | 29 | 40 |
| Yds Lost Tackled | 301 | 305 | 94 | 366 | 417 | 166 | 132 | 289 | 113 | 139 | 186 | 289 | 251 | 241 |
| Net Yards | 3413 | 3236 | 3175 | 4017 | 2799 | 2353 | 3960 | 3267 | 4420 | 4444 | 3137 | 2964 | 3368 | 2568 |
| Touchdowns | 23 | 21 | 20 | 18 | 13 | 15 | 20 | 22 | 31 | 25 | 18 | 17 | 20 | 13 |
| Interceptions | 21 | 19 | 21 | 13 | 17 | 14 | 14 | 16 | 18 | 27 | 18 | 9 | 14 | 9 |
| Pct. Intercepted | 3.9 | 3.5 | 4.1 | 2.1 | 3.1 | 3.7 | 2.3 | 3.3 | 2.9 | 3.9 | 3.3 | 1.9 | 2.7 | 1.8 |
| **PUNTS:** | | | | | | | | | | | | | | |
| Number | 67 | 80 | 80 | 76 | 96 | 74 | 85 | 77 | 60 | 69 | 84 | 97 | 72 | 91 |
| Average | 41.8 | 43.3 | 40.1 | 42.9 | 42.9 | 41.8 | 42.2 | 43.8 | 40.2 | 41.2 | 42.1 | 39.7 | 41.0 | 42.9 |
| **PUNT RETURNS** | | | | | | | | | | | | | | |
| Number | 33 | 37 | 46 | 41 | 50 | 42 | 43 | 40 | 33 | 46 | 39 | 56 | 36 | 37 |
| Yards | 343 | 373 | 462 | 379 | 281 | 339 | 316 | 487 | 241 | 383 | 345 | 424 | 475 | 337 |
| Average Yards | 10.4 | 10.1 | 10.0 | 9.2 | 5.8 | 8.1 | 7.4 | 12.1 | 7.3 | 8.3 | 8.8 | 7.6 | 13.2 | 9.1 |
| Touchdowns | 0 | 1 | 2 | 0 | 1 | 1 | 0 | 0 | 0 | 0 | 0 | 0 | 2 | 0 |
| **KICKOFF RET.:** | | | | | | | | | | | | | | |
| Number | 72 | 86 | 42 | 75 | 74 | 60 | 59 | 62 | 66 | 63 | 66 | 55 | 68 | 67 |
| Yards | 1345 | 1810 | 1031 | 1523 | 1436 | 1254 | 1300 | 1358 | 1294 | 1123 | 1282 | 1141 | 1636 | 1467 |
| Average Yards | 18.7 | 21.1 | 24.5 | 20.3 | 19.4 | 20.9 | 22.0 | 21.9 | 19.6 | 17.8 | 19.4 | 20.7 | 24.1 | 21.9 |
| Touchdowns | 0 | 0 | 1 | 0 | 0 | 1 | 1 | 0 | 0 | 0 | 0 | 0 | 2 | 1 |
| **INTERCEPT RET.:** | | | | | | | | | | | | | | |
| Number | 16 | 10 | 18 | 12 | 14 | 18 | 12 | 12 | 23 | 22 | 17 | 17 | 17 | 19 |
| Yards | 175 | 167 | 223 | 55 | 242 | 360 | 218 | 187 | 276 | 209 | 355 | 240 | 402 | 284 |
| Average Yards | 10.9 | 16.7 | 12.4 | 4.6 | 17.3 | 20.0 | 18.2 | 15.6 | 12.0 | 9.5 | 20.9 | 14.1 | 23.6 | 14.9 |
| Touchdowns | 0 | 0 | 1 | 0 | 1 | 3 | 1 | 3 | 1 | 1 | 3 | 2 | 3 | 2 |
| **PENALTIES:** | | | | | | | | | | | | | | |
| Number | 92 | 90 | 113 | 101 | 115 | 82 | 127 | 156 | 92 | 78 | 95 | 119 | 96 | 114 |
| Yards | 631 | 618 | 969 | 865 | 959 | 658 | 911 | 1186 | 747 | 597 | 754 | 974 | 875 | 898 |
| **FUMBLES:** | | | | | | | | | | | | | | |
| Number | 30 | 31 | 26 | 27 | 42 | 30 | 21 | 22 | 28 | 28 | 28 | 18 | 19 | 31 |
| Number Lost | 13 | 22 | 14 | 18 | 25 | 17 | 12 | 14 | 14 | 11 | 10 | 8 | 9 | 19 |
| **POINTS:** | | | | | | | | | | | | | | |
| Total | 340 | 276 | 340 | 347 | 226 | 307 | 319 | 303 | 389 | 351 | 264 | 316 | 381 | 287 |
| 1-PT PAT/ATT. | 38/38 | 24/25 | 32/32 | 28/29 | 18/18 | 37/37 | 30/30 | 31/31 | 35/35 | 36/36 | 26/26 | 32/32 | 33/33 | 25/26 |
| 2-PT PAT/Att. | 0/0 | 2/2 | 4/5 | 3/8 | 4/7 | 0/0 | 3/4 | 1/3 | 6/10 | 0/2 | 2/2 | 1/3 | 3/7 | 4/6 |
| FG Attempts | 28 | 33 | 28 | 37 | 20 | 24 | 30 | 28 | 31 | 35 | 23 | 29 | 38 | 24 |
| FG Made | 24 | 28 | 26 | 30 | 16 | 16 | 25 | 22 | 24 | 27 | 20 | 24 | 34 | 20 |
| Percent FG Made | 85.7 | 84.8 | 92.9 | 81.1 | 80.0 | 66.7 | 83.3 | 78.6 | 77.4 | 77.1 | 87.0 | 82.8 | 89.5 | 83.3 |
| Safeties | 1 | 1 | 0 | 0 | 1 | 0 | 2 | 0 | 0 | 0 | 0 | 0 | 0 | 1 |

**DEFENSE**

| | BUFF | CIN | CLEV | DEN | HOU | IND | K.C. | L.A. | MIA | N.E. | NYJ | PITT | S.D. | SEA |
|---|---|---|---|---|---|---|---|---|---|---|---|---|---|---|
| **FIRST DOWNS:** | | | | | | | | | | | | | | |
| Total | 294 | 310 | 304 | 303 | 275 | 311 | 289 | 303 | 305 | 280 | 315 | 262 | 308 | 318 |
| by Rushing | 82 | 126 | 98 | 103 | 112 | 98 | 93 | 94 | 85 | 86 | 105 | 76 | 89 | 122 |
| by Passing | 199 | 168 | 173 | 182 | 132 | 192 | 164 | 176 | 195 | 173 | 189 | 156 | 191 | 178 |
| by Penalty | 13 | 16 | 33 | 18 | 31 | 21 | 32 | 33 | 25 | 21 | 21 | 30 | 28 | 18 |
| **RUSHING:** | | | | | | | | | | | | | | |
| Number | 447 | 517 | 465 | 432 | 540 | 463 | 446 | 444 | 394 | 422 | 463 | 421 | 385 | 511 |
| Yards | 1515 | 1906 | 1669 | 1752 | 2120 | 1646 | 1734 | 1543 | 1430 | 1760 | 1809 | 1452 | 1404 | 1952 |
| Average Yards | 3.4 | 3.7 | 3.6 | 4.1 | 3.9 | 3.6 | 3.9 | 3.5 | 3.6 | 4.2 | 3.9 | 3.4 | 3.6 | 3.8 |
| Touchdowns | 10 | 16 | 9 | 12 | 17 | 8 | 11 | 11 | 14 | 11 | 17 | 7 | 11 | 15 |
| **PASSING:** | | | | | | | | | | | | | | |
| Attempts | 535 | 505 | 587 | 568 | 399 | 598 | 504 | 564 | 577 | 545 | 522 | 532 | 577 | 537 |
| Completions | 314 | 294 | 325 | 322 | 221 | 354 | 300 | 306 | 334 | 298 | 333 | 280 | 363 | 313 |
| Completion Pct. | 58.7 | 58.2 | 55.4 | 56.7 | 55.4 | 59.2 | 59.5 | 54.3 | 57.9 | 54.7 | 63.8 | 52.6 | 62.9 | 58.3 |
| Passing Yards | 3812 | 3458 | 3425 | 4296 | 2963 | 3897 | 3500 | 3684 | 3954 | 3737 | 3730 | 3256 | 3911 | 3603 |
| Avg. Yds per Att. | 7.13 | 6.85 | 5.83 | 7.56 | 7.41 | 6.52 | 6.94 | 6.53 | 6.85 | 6.86 | 7.15 | 6.12 | 6.78 | 6.71 |
| Avg. Yds per Comp. | 12.14 | 11.76 | 10.54 | 13.34 | 13.41 | 11.01 | 11.67 | 12.03 | 11.84 | 12.54 | 11.20 | 11.63 | 10.77 | 11.51 |
| Times Tackled | 25 | 31 | 38 | 23 | 31 | 29 | 39 | 38 | 29 | 39 | 29 | 55 | 43 | 29 |
| Yds Lost Tackled | 152 | 210 | 268 | 141 | 168 | 218 | 234 | 284 | 160 | 290 | 201 | 382 | 253 | 206 |
| Net Yards | 3660 | 3248 | 3157 | 4155 | 2795 | 3679 | 3266 | 3400 | 3794 | 3447 | 3529 | 2874 | 3658 | 3397 |
| Touchdowns | 26 | 22 | 13 | 28 | 18 | 24 | 23 | 24 | 23 | 21 | 19 | 12 | 20 | 15 |
| Interceptions | 16 | 10 | 18 | 12 | 14 | 18 | 12 | 12 | 23 | 22 | 17 | 17 | 17 | 19 |
| Pct. Intercepted | 3.0 | 2.0 | 3.1 | 2.1 | 3.5 | 3.0 | 2.4 | 2.1 | 4.0 | 4.0 | 3.3 | 3.2 | 2.9 | 3.5 |
| **PUNTS:** | | | | | | | | | | | | | | |
| Number | 69 | 87 | 97 | 76 | 82 | 72 | 85 | 84 | 68 | 83 | 62 | 97 | 76 | 78 |
| Average | 42.3 | 40.6 | 39.9 | 43.5 | 42.0 | 42.2 | 45.0 | 40.6 | 41.7 | 40.2 | 43.1 | 42.2 | 43.3 | 40.9 |
| **PUNT RETURNS** | | | | | | | | | | | | | | |
| Number | 38 | 43 | 38 | 39 | 50 | 40 | 50 | 38 | 32 | 34 | 38 | 39 | 38 | 43 |
| Yards | 324 | 459 | 220 | 275 | 438 | 366 | 506 | 366 | 324 | 260 | 260 | 263 | 348 | 426 |
| Average Yards | 8.5 | 10.4 | 5.8 | 7.1 | 8.8 | 9.2 | 10.1 | 9.7 | 10.2 | 7.6 | 6.8 | 6.7 | 9.2 | 9.9 |
| Touchdowns | 0 | 2 | 0 | 0 | 1 | 0 | 0 | 1 | 1 | 0 | 0 | 0 | 0 | 1 |
| **KICKOFF RET.:** | | | | | | | | | | | | | | |
| Number | 72 | 61 | 71 | 70 | 48 | 65 | 66 | 65 | 74 | 63 | 61 | 68 | 79 | 61 |
| Yards | 1455 | 1408 | 1372 | 1396 | 832 | 1316 | 1447 | 1406 | 1549 | 1375 | 1195 | 1530 | 1740 | 1229 |
| Average Yards | 20.2 | 23.1 | 19.3 | 19.9 | 17.3 | 20.2 | 21.9 | 21.6 | 20.9 | 21.8 | 19.6 | 22.5 | 22.0 | 20.1 |
| Touchdowns | 0 | 2 | 0 | 0 | 0 | 0 | 0 | 0 | 2 | 1 | 0 | 2 | 1 | 0 |
| **INTERCEPT RET.:** | | | | | | | | | | | | | | |
| Number | 21 | 19 | 21 | 13 | 17 | 14 | 14 | 16 | 18 | 27 | 18 | 9 | 14 | 9 |
| Yards | 262 | 176 | 225 | 288 | 188 | 174 | 217 | 202 | 190 | 252 | 232 | 106 | 233 | 210 |
| Average Yards | 12.5 | 9.3 | 10.7 | 22.2 | 11.1 | 12.4 | 15.5 | 12.6 | 10.6 | 9.3 | 12.9 | 11.8 | 16.6 | 23.3 |
| Touchdowns | 2 | 2 | 0 | 3 | 0 | 2 | 1 | 1 | 1 | 2 | 1 | 1 | 2 | 2 |
| **PENALTIES:** | | | | | | | | | | | | | | |
| Number | 101 | 98 | 129 | 135 | 102 | 111 | 120 | 113 | 82 | 111 | 63 | 92 | 110 | 103 |
| Yards | 769 | 851 | 1138 | 1036 | 802 | 809 | 924 | 813 | 653 | 794 | 489 | 764 | 984 | 764 |
| **FUMBLES:** | | | | | | | | | | | | | | |
| Number | 23 | 26 | 26 | 24 | 20 | 21 | 36 | 26 | 29 | 34 | 30 | 31 | 29 | 21 |
| Number Lost | 12 | 8 | 13 | 14 | 12 | 10 | 26 | 13 | 9 | 18 | 21 | 14 | 15 | 11 |
| **POINTS:** | | | | | | | | | | | | | | |
| Total | 356 | 406 | 204 | 396 | 352 | 320 | 298 | 327 | 327 | 312 | 320 | 234 | 306 | 323 |
| 1-PT PAT/ATT. | 34/36 | 41/41 | 19/19 | 35/35 | 34/35 | 29/29 | 29/29 | 34/34 | 40/40 | 32/34 | 31/32 | 22/22 | 30/30 | 28/28 |
| 2-PT PAT/Att. | 2/4 | 1/4 | 1/3 | 5/8 | 2/2 | 2/5 | 2/5 | 0/3 | 1/2 | 2/2 | 2/5 | 1/1 | 3/4 | 4/5 |
| FG Attempts | 30 | 35 | 26 | 37 | 31 | 34 | 23 | 29 | 18 | 25 | 27 | 29 | 27 | 33 |
| FG Made | 26 | 31 | 17 | 31 | 30 | 27 | 18 | 21 | 11 | 20 | 21 | 24 | 22 | 27 |
| Percent FG Made | 86.7 | 88.6 | 65.4 | 83.8 | 96.8 | 79.4 | 78.3 | 72.4 | 61.1 | 80.0 | 77.8 | 82.8 | 81.5 | 81.8 |
| Safeties | 0 | 0 | 0 | 0 | 1 | 1 | 0 | 1 | 0 | 0 | 0 | 0 | 0 | 1 |

Lorenzo White.

## WESTERN DIVISION

**San Diego Chargers** — Predicted by many to finish in last place, the Chargers bolted to a 6-0 start, survived a midseason slump and then rolled through the playoffs until getting stopped in Super Bowl XXIX by San Francisco. A roster that featured many new faces was led by quarterback Stan Humphries and running back Natrone Means. Humphries passed for 3,209 yards and Means pounded away between the tackles to rush for a team-record 1,350 yards and score 12 touchdowns. The receivers weren't spectacular, but Mark Seay, Tony Martin and Shawn Jefferson made a lot of big plays. Linebacker Junior Seau led the defense with 155 tackles and 5.5 sacks, both career highs. San Diego was an 18.5-point underdog and was soundly defeated in the Super Bowl.

**Kansas City Chiefs** — The only team to make a playoff appearance in every season in the 1990s, Kansas City was disappointed with its 9-7 record and wild-card loss. In the second year of the Joe Montana plan, the Chiefs scored fewer points than they had in 1993, even though Montana did play in 14 games. With 16 touchdowns and only nine interceptions, Montana was OK by most standards, but not by the mark he set for himself. Marcus Allen rushed for 709 yards and seven touchdowns but showed some age, and backup Greg Hill wasn't able to take over. On defense, Neil Smith (11.5 sacks) and Derrick Thomas (11 sacks) played well, but the rest of the unit was subpar. The run defense fell to 21st in the league and the pass defense was only 15th.

**Los Angeles Raiders** — The Raiders missed the playoffs in 1994 after losing their final regular-season game, a winner-makes-the-playoffs contest against Kansas City. The Raiders set one NFL record, but it wasn't one they wanted — 156 penalties. After the season, head coach Art Shell was fired by team owner Al Davis and replaced by Mike White. Wide receiver Tim Brown established career highs for catches (89), yards (1,309) and TD's (nine) and continued to be one of the league's best punt returners (12.2-yard average). Other highlights were running back Harvey Williams, who came off the Kansas City scrap heap to rush for a personal-best 983 yards, and defensive tackle Chester McGlockton, who was named All-Pro.

**Denver Broncos** — The Broncos took a step back in 1994, as injuries robbed them of running back Rod Bernstine and wide receiver Mike Pritchard for nearly all of the year, and tight end Shannon Sharpe and quarterback John Elway for part of it. An 0-4 start was followed by a 7-3 streak before Denver was embarrassed in its final three games and knocked out of the playoff race. The defense ranked last in the NFL in yards allowed, and veterans Karl Mecklenburg and Dennis Smith had to be called out of retirement. Sharpe caught 87 passes for 1,010 yards and four touchdowns, and free-agent acquisition Anthony Miller hauled in 60 passes for 1,107 yards and five TD's.

**Seattle Seahawks** — The Seahawks' 1994 season started out badly before it even began, when cornerbacks Nate Odomes and Kirby Jackson — both free-agent signees — were sidelined. Then the team was forced to play its first three home games at the University of Washington's Husky Stadium because of fallen ceiling tiles at the Kingdome. The top player was running back Chris Warren, who rushed for a team-record 1,545 yards and scored a career-best 11 TD's. Second-year quarterback Rick Mirer didn't progress much, and he finished the season injured. Still, Mirer threw only seven interceptions in 381 attempts. Wideout Brian Blades caught 81 passes, one more than his club record.

## MIAMI DOLPHINS 10-6 Don Shula

| Scores of Each Game | | |
|---|---|---|
| 39 | NEW ENGLAND | 35 |
| 24 | Green Bay | 14 |
| 28 | N.Y. JETS | 14 |
| 35 | Minnesota | 38 |
| 23 | Cincinnati | 7 |
| 11 | Buffalo | 21 |
| 20 | L.A. RAIDERS | *17 |
| 23 | New England | 3 |
| 22 | INDIANAPOLIS | 21 |
| 14 | CHICAGO | 17 |
| 13 | Pittsburgh | *16 |
| 28 | N.Y. Jets | 24 |
| 31 | BUFFALO | 42 |
| 45 | KANSAS CITY | 28 |
| 6 | Indianapolis | 10 |
| 27 | DETROIT | 20 |

| Use Name | Pos. | Hgt. | Wgt. | Age | Int | Pts |
|---|---|---|---|---|---|---|
| Ron Heller | OT | 6'6" | 293 | 32 | | |
| Richmond Webb | OT | 6'6" | 302 | 27 | | |
| Chris Gray | OG-OT | 6'4" | 294 | 24 | | |
| Houston Hoover | OG | 6'2" | 300 | 29 | | |
| Jeff Novak | OG-OT | 6'5" | 295 | 27 | | |
| Keith Sims | OG | 6'2" | 303 | 27 | | |
| Bert Weidner | OG-C | 6'3" | 299 | 28 | | |
| Jeff Dellenbach | C | 6'6" | 300 | 31 | | |
| Tim Ruddy | C | 6'3" | 286 | 22 | | |
| Marco Coleman | DE | 6'3" | 267 | 24 | | |
| Jeff Cross | DE | 6'4" | 281 | 28 | 1 | |
| Tyoka Jackson | DE | 6'1" | 266 | 22 | | |
| Tim Bowens | DT | 6'4" | 317 | 21 | | |
| William Gaines | DT | 6'5" | 306 | 23 | | |
| Chuck Klingbeil | DT | 6'1" | 301 | 28 | | |
| Craig Veasey | DT-NT | 6'2" | 285 | 27 | 1 | |
| Larry Webster | DT-DE | 6'5" | 296 | 25 | | |

| Use Name | Pos. | Hgt. | Wgt. | Age | Int | Pts |
|---|---|---|---|---|---|---|
| Aubrey Beavers | LB | 6'3" | 233 | 23 | 2 | |
| Brant Boyer | LB | 6' | 237 | 23 | | |
| Chuck Bullough | LB | 6'1" | 238 | 25 | | |
| Bryan Cox | LB | 6'3" | 249 | 26 | | |
| Dion Foxx | LB | 6'3" | 254 | 23 | | |
| Dwight Hollier | LB | 6'2" | 257 | 25 | 1 | |
| Chris Singleton | LB | 6'2" | 247 | 27 | | |
| Jesse Solomon | LB | 6' | 235 | 30 | | |
| Gene Atkins | DB | 5'11" | 200 | 29 | 3 | |
| Tyrone Braxton | DB | 5'10" | 185 | 29 | 2 | |
| J.B. Brown | DB | 6' | 193 | 27 | 3 | |
| Chris Green | DB | 5'11" | 198 | 26 | | |
| Sean Hill | DB | 5'10" | 176 | 23 | | |
| Calvin Jackson | DB | 5'10" | 179 | 21 | | |
| Darrell Malone | DB | 5'10" | 182 | 26 | 1 | |
| Muhammad Oliver | DB | 5'11" | 185 | 25 | 1 | |
| David Pool | DB | 5'9" | 182 | 27 | | |
| Frankie Smith | DB | 5'9" | 191 | 25 | | |
| Michael Stewart | DB | 5'11" | 203 | 29 | 3 | |
| Troy Vincent | DB | 6' | 197 | 24 | 5 | 6 |

| Use Name | Pos. | Hgt. | Wgt. | Age | Int | Pts |
|---|---|---|---|---|---|---|
| Bernie Kosar | QB | 6'5" | 215 | 30 | | |
| Dan Marino | QB | 6'4" | 224 | 32 | | 6 |
| Doug Pederson | QB | 6'3" | 212 | 26 | | |
| Aaron Craver | HB | 6' | 220 | 25 | | 2 |
| Cleveland Gary | HB | 6' | 226 | 28 | | |
| Terry Kirby | HB | 6'1" | 221 | 24 | | 14 |
| Bernie Parmalee | HB | 5'11" | 205 | 26 | | 44 |
| Irving Spikes | HB | 5'8" | 215 | 23 | | 12 |
| Keith Byars | FB | 6'1" | 255 | 30 | | 42 |
| James Saxon | FB | 5'11' | 239 | 28 | | |
| Robert Wilson (from DAL) | FB | 6' | 258 | 25 | | |
| Irving Fryar | WR | 6' | 200 | 31 | | 46 |
| Mark Ingram | WR | 5'11" | 194 | 29 | | 36 |
| O.J. McDuffie | WR | 5'10" | 191 | 24 | | 18 |
| Scott Miller | WR | 5'10" | 184 | 25 | | 6 |
| Mike Williams | WR | 5'10" | 190 | 27 | | |
| Greg Baty | TE | 6'5" | 240 | 30 | | 6 |
| Keith Jackson | TE | 6'2" | 258 | 29 | | 44 |
| Ronnie Williams | TE | 6'3" | 266 | 28 | | |
| Jim Arnold | K | 6'3" | 211 | 33 | | |
| John Kidd (from SD) | K | 6'3" | 213 | 33 | | |
| Pete Stoyonovich | K | 5'10" | 195 | 27 | | 107 |

## NEW ENGLAND PATRIOTS 10-6 Bill Parcells

| Scores of Each Game | | |
|---|---|---|
| 35 | Miami | 39 |
| 35 | BUFFALO | 38 |
| 31 | Cincinnati | 28 |
| 23 | Detroit | 17 |
| 17 | GREEN BAY | 16 |
| 17 | L.A. RAIDERS | 21 |
| 17 | N.Y. Jets | 24 |
| 3 | MIAMI | 23 |
| 6 | Cleveland | 13 |
| 26 | MINNESOTA | *20 |
| 23 | SAN DIEGO | 17 |
| 12 | Indianapolis | 10 |
| 24 | N.Y. JETS | 13 |
| 28 | INDIANAPOLIS | 18 |
| 41 | Buffalo | 17 |
| 13 | Chicago | 3 |

| Use Name | Pos. | Hgt. | Wgt. | Age | Int | Pts |
|---|---|---|---|---|---|---|
| Bruce Armstrong | OT | 6'4" | 284 | 28 | | |
| Pat Harlow | OT | 6'6" | 290 | 25 | | |
| Max Lane | OT | 6'6" | 295 | 23 | | |
| Brandon Moore | OT | 6'6" | 295 | 24 | | |
| Eugene Chung | OG | 6'4" | 295 | 25 | | |
| Bob Kratch | OG | 6'3" | 288 | 28 | | |
| Todd Rucci | OG | 6'5" | 291 | 24 | | |
| Doug Skene | OG | 6'6" | 295 | 24 | | |
| Mike Arthur | C | 6'3" | 280 | 26 | | |
| Mike Gisler | C-OG | 6'4" | 300 | 25 | | |
| Ray Agnew | DE | 6'3" | 272 | 26 | | |
| Troy Barnett | DE | 6'4" | 280 | 23 | | |
| Aaron Jones | DE | 6'5" | 267 | 27 | | |
| Mike Jones | DE | 6'4" | 295 | 25 | | |
| Mike Pitts | DE | 6'5" | 277 | 33 | | |
| Tim Goad | NT | 6'3" | 280 | 28 | | |
| Sylvester Stanley | NT | 6'2" | 286 | 24 | | |

| Use Name | Pos. | Hgt. | Wgt. | Age | Int | Pts |
|---|---|---|---|---|---|---|
| David Bavaro | LB | 6' | 238 | 27 | | |
| Vincent Brown | LB | 6'2" | 245 | 29 | 3 | |
| Jason Carthen | LB | 6'3" | 255 | 24 | | |
| Todd Collins | LB | 6'2" | 242 | 24 | | |
| Steve DeOssie | LB | 6'2" | 248 | 31 | | |
| Willie McGinest | LB | 6'5" | 252 | 22 | | |
| Marty Moore | LB | 6'1" | 244 | 23 | | |
| Dwayne Sabb | LB | 6'4" | 248 | 24 | 2 | |
| Chris Slade | LB | 6'4" | 232 | 23 | | |
| Harlon Barnett | DB | 5'11" | 200 | 27 | 3 | |
| Corwin Brown | DB | 6' | 200 | 24 | | |
| Myron Guyton | DB | 6'1" | 205 | 27 | 2 | |
| Maurice Hurst | DB | 5'10" | 185 | 26 | 7 | |
| Vernon Lewis | DB | 5'10" | 192 | 23 | | |
| Terry Ray | DB | 6'1" | 205 | 24 | 1 | |
| Ricky Reynolds | DB | 5'11" | 190 | 29 | 1 | 12 |
| Rod Smith | DB | 5'11" | 188 | 24 | 2 | |
| Larry Whigham | DB | 6'2" | 202 | 22 | 1 | |
| Darryl Wren | DB | 6' | 188 | 27 | | |

| Use Name | Pos. | Hgt. | Wgt. | Age | Int | Pts |
|---|---|---|---|---|---|---|
| Drew Bledsoe | QB | 6'5" | 233 | 22 | | |
| Jay Walker | QB | 6'3" | 232 | 22 | | |
| Scott Zolak | QB | 6'5" | 222 | 26 | | |
| Marion Butts | HB | 6'1" | 248 | 28 | | 48 |
| Corey Croom | HB | 5'11" | 208 | 23 | | |
| Leroy Thompson | HB | 5'11" | 216 | 26 | | 42 |
| Sam Gash | FB | 5'11" | 224 | 25 | | |
| Burnie Legette | FB | 6' | 243 | 23 | | |
| Kevin Turner | FB | 6' | 230 | 25 | | 18 |
| Vincent Brisby | WR | 6'1" | 188 | 23 | | 30 |
| Troy Brown | WR | 5'9" | 190 | 23 | | |
| Ray Crittenden | WR | 6' | 188 | 24 | | 18 |
| Steve Hawkins | WR | 6'5" | 210 | 23 | | |
| Michael Timpson | WR | 5'10" | 180 | 27 | | 18 |
| John Burke | TE | 6'2" | 255 | 22 | | |
| Ben Coates | TE | 6'4" | 245 | 25 | | 42 |
| Matt Bahr | K | 5'10" | 175 | 38 | | 117 |
| Pat O'Neill | K | 6'1" | 200 | 23 | | |

## INDIANAPOLIS COLTS 8-8 Ted Marchibroda

| Scores of Each Game | | |
|---|---|---|
| 45 | HOUSTON | 21 |
| 10 | Tampa Bay | 24 |
| 21 | Pittsburgh | 31 |
| 14 | CLEVELAND | 21 |
| 17 | SEATTLE | 15 |
| 6 | N.Y. Jets | 16 |
| 27 | Buffalo | 17 |
| 27 | WASHINGTON | 41 |
| 28 | N.Y. JETS | 25 |
| 21 | Miami | 22 |
| 17 | Cincinnati | 13 |
| 10 | NEW ENGLAND | 12 |
| 31 | Seattle | 19 |
| 13 | New England | 28 |
| 10 | MIAMI | 6 |
| 10 | BUFFALO | 9 |

| Use Name | Pos. | Hgt. | Wgt. | Age | Int | Pts |
|---|---|---|---|---|---|---|
| Cecil Gray | OT | 6'4" | 305 | 26 | | |
| Jason Mathews | OT | 6'5" | 284 | 23 | | |
| Zefross Moss | OT | 6'6" | 324 | 28 | | |
| Will Wolford | OT | 6'5" | 300 | 30 | | |
| Randy Dixon | OG | 6'3" | 305 | 29 | | |
| Eric Mahlum | OG | 6'4" | 285 | 23 | | |
| Joe Staysniak | OG | 6'4" | 302 | 27 | | |
| Kirk Lowdermilk | C | 6'4" | 280 | 31 | | |
| Jon Hand | DE | 6'7" | 310 | 30 | | |
| Al Noga | DE | 6'1" | 269 | 28 | | |
| Freddie Joe Nunn | DE | 6'5" | 255 | 32 | | |
| Lance Teichelman | DE-DT | 6'4" | 274 | 23 | | |
| Bernard Whittington | DE | 6'6" | 257 | 23 | | |
| Steve Emtman | DT | 6'4" | 300 | 24 | | |
| Garry Howe | DT | 6'1" | 298 | 26 | | |
| Tom Sims | DT | 6'2" | 308 | 27 | | |
| Tony McCoy | DT-NT | 6' | 279 | 25 | | |
| Tony Siragusa | DT-NT | 6'3" | 315 | 27 | | |

| Use Name | Pos. | Hgt. | Wgt. | Age | Int | Pts |
|---|---|---|---|---|---|---|
| Trev Alberts | LB | 6'4" | 243 | 24 | | |
| Tony Bennett | LB | 6'2" | 243 | 27 | | 6 |
| Paul Butcher | LB | 6' | 240 | 30 | | |
| Quentin Coryatt | LB | 6'3" | 250 | 24 | | 6 |
| Steve Grant | LB | 6' | 242 | 24 | | |
| Jeff Herrod | LB | 6' | 249 | 28 | | |
| Devon McDonald | LB | 6'4" | 248 | 24 | | |
| Scott Radecic | LB | 6'3" | 240 | 32 | | |
| Brian Ratigan | LB | 6'4" | 241 | 23 | | |
| Ashley Ambrose | DB | 5'10" | 185 | 23 | 2 | |
| Jason Belser | DB | 5'9" | 187 | 24 | 1 | |
| Ray Buchanan | DB | 5'9" | 193 | 22 | 8 | 18 |
| John Covington | DB | 6' | 198 | 22 | | |
| Eugene Daniel | DB | 5'11" | 188 | 33 | 2 | |
| Derwin Gray | DB | 5'10" | 198 | 23 | | |
| Leonard Humphries | DB | 5'9" | 180 | 24 | 1 | |
| Robert O'Neal | DB | 6'1" | 194 | 23 | | |
| David Tate | DB | 6'1" | 200 | 29 | 3 | |
| Damon Watts | DB | 5'10" | 173 | 22 | 1 | |

| Use Name | Pos. | Hgt. | Wgt. | Age | Int | Pts |
|---|---|---|---|---|---|---|
| Jim Harbaugh | QB | 6'3" | 215 | 30 | | |
| Don Majkowski | QB | 6'3" | 203 | 30 | | 18 |
| Browning Nagle | QB | 6'3" | 225 | 26 | | |
| Paul Justin | QB | 6'4" | 202 | 26 | | |
| Dewell Brewer | HB | 5'8" | 199 | 24 | | 6 |
| Marshall Faulk | HB | 5'10" | 200 | 21 | | 72 |
| Ronald Humphrey | HB | 5'10" | 211 | 25 | | 6 |
| Ed Toner | HB | 6' | 240 | 26 | | |
| Lamont Warren | HB | 5'11" | 194 | 21 | | |
| Roosevelt Potts | FB-HB | 6' | 245 | 23 | | 12 |
| Aaron Bailey | WR | 5'10" | 184 | 22 | | |
| Shannon Baker | WR | 5'9" | 185 | 23 | | |
| Sean Dawkins | WR | 6'4" | 210 | 23 | | 30 |
| Mark Jackson (from NYG) | WR | 5'9" | 180 | 31 | | 6 |
| Floyd Turner | WR | 5'11" | 198 | 28 | | 36 |
| Charles Arbuckle | TE | 6'3" | 248 | 25 | | |
| Bradford Banta | TE | 6'6" | 255 | 23 | | |
| Kerry Cash | TE | 6'4" | 252 | 25 | | 6 |
| Carlos Etheredge | TE | 6'5" | 236 | 24 | | |
| Dean Biasucci | K | 6' | 190 | 32 | | 85 |
| Rohn Stark | K | 6'3" | 203 | 35 | | |

## BUFFALO BILLS 7-9 Marv Levy

| Scores of Each Game | | |
|---|---|---|
| 3 | N.Y. JETS | 23 |
| 38 | New England | 35 |
| 15 | Houston | 7 |
| 27 | DENVER | 20 |
| 13 | Chicago | 20 |
| 21 | MIAMI | 11 |
| 17 | INDIANAPOLIS | 27 |
| 44 | KANSAS CITY | 10 |
| 17 | N.Y. Jets | 22 |
| 10 | Pittsburgh | 23 |
| 29 | GREEN BAY | 20 |
| 21 | Detroit | 35 |
| 42 | Miami | 31 |
| 17 | MINNESOTA | 21 |
| 17 | NEW ENGLAND | 41 |
| 9 | Indianapolis | 10 |

| Use Name | Pos. | Hgt. | Wgt. | Age | Int | Pts |
|---|---|---|---|---|---|---|
| Jerry Crafts | OT-OG | 6'6" | 351 | 26 | | |
| John Fina | OT | 6'4" | 285 | 25 | | |
| Steve Hoyem | OT | 6'7" | 287 | 23 | | |
| Corey Louchiey | OT | 6'7" | 305 | 22 | | |
| Glenn Parker | OT-OG | 6'5" | 305 | 28 | | |
| John Davis | OG-C | 6'4" | 310 | 29 | | |
| Corbin Lacina | OG | 6'4" | 297 | 23 | | |
| Jerry Ostroski | OG | 6'2" | 310 | 24 | | |
| Mike Devlin | C-OG | 6'1" | 293 | 24 | | |
| Kent Hull | C | 6'4" | 284 | 33 | | |
| Adam Lingner | C | 6'4" | 268 | 33 | | |
| Oliver Barnett | DE | 6'3" | 292 | 28 | | |
| Phil Hansen | DE | 6'5" | 278 | 26 | | |
| Mark Pike | DE | 6'4" | 272 | 30 | | |
| Bruce Smith | DE | 6'4" | 273 | 31 | 1 | |
| Ed Philion | DT | 6'2" | 273 | 24 | | |
| Mike Lodish | NT | 6'3" | 280 | 27 | | 6 |
| Jeff Wright | NT | 6'2" | 274 | 31 | | |

| Use Name | Pos. | Hgt. | Wgt. | Age | Int | Pts |
|---|---|---|---|---|---|---|
| Cornelius Bennett | LB | 6'2" | 238 | 29 | | |
| Monty Brown | LB | 6' | 228 | 24 | | |
| Keith Goganious | LB | 6'2" | 239 | 25 | | |
| Mark Maddox | LB | 6'1" | 233 | 26 | 1 | |
| Marvcus Patton | LB | 6'2" | 243 | 27 | 2 | |
| Mario Perry | LB | 6'4" | 250 | 22 | | |
| Sam Rogers | LB | 6'3" | 245 | 24 | | |
| Darryl Talley | LB | 6'4" | 235 | 34 | | |
| Jeff Burris | DB | 6' | 204 | 22 | 2 | |
| Matt Darby | DB | 6'1" | 200 | 25 | 4 | |
| Mike Dumas | DB | 5'11" | 181 | 25 | | |
| Jerome Henderson | DB | 5'10" | 189 | 25 | | |
| Henry Jones | DB | 5'11" | 197 | 26 | 2 | |
| Kurt Schulz | DB | 6'1" | 208 | 25 | | |
| Thomas Smith | DB | 5'11" | 188 | 23 | 1 | |
| Mickey Washington | DB | 5'9" | 191 | 26 | 3 | |

| Use Name | Pos. | Hgt. | Wgt. | Age | Int | Pts |
|---|---|---|---|---|---|---|
| Jim Kelly | QB | 6'3" | 226 | 34 | | 6 |
| Frank Reich | QB | 6'4" | 205 | 32 | | |
| Rick Strom | QB | 6'2" | 197 | 29 | | |
| Kenneth Davis | HB | 5'10" | 208 | 32 | | 12 |
| Yonel Jourdain | HB | 5'11" | 204 | 23 | | |
| Thurman Thomas | HB | 5'10" | 198 | 28 | | 54 |
| Carwell Gardner | FB | 6'2" | 244 | 27 | | 24 |
| Nate Turner | FB | 6'1" | 255 | 25 | | 6 |
| Don Beebe | WR | 5'11" | 180 | 29 | | 24 |
| Bucky Brooks | WR | 6' | 190 | 23 | | |
| Bill Brooks | WR | 6' | 189 | 30 | | 12 |
| Russell Copeland | WR | 6' | 200 | 22 | | 6 |
| Andre Reed | WR | 6' | 190 | 30 | | 48 |
| Steve Tasker | WR | 5'9" | 181 | 32 | | |
| Damon Thomas | WR | 6'2" | 215 | 23 | | |
| Lonnie Johnson | TE | 6'3" | 230 | 23 | | |
| Vince Marrow | TE | 6'3" | 251 | 26 | | |
| Pete Metzelaars | TE | 6'7" | 254 | 34 | | 30 |
| Steve Christie | K | 6' | 185 | 26 | | 110 |
| Chris Mohr | K | 6'5" | 215 | 28 | | |

## NEW YORK JETS 6-10 Pete Carroll

| Scores of Each Game | | |
|---|---|---|
| 23 | Buffalo | 3 |
| 25 | DENVER | *22 |
| 14 | Miami | 28 |
| 7 | CHICAGO | 19 |
| 7 | Cleveland | 27 |
| 16 | INDIANAPOLIS | 6 |
| 24 | NEW ENGLAND | 17 |
| 25 | Indianapolis | 28 |
| 22 | BUFFALO | 17 |
| 10 | Green Bay | 17 |
| 31 | Minnesota | 21 |
| 24 | MIAMI | 28 |
| 13 | New England | 24 |
| 7 | DETROIT | 18 |
| 6 | SAN DIEGO | 21 |
| 10 | Houston | 24 |

| Use Name | Pos. | Hgt. | Wgt. | Age | Int | Pts |
|---|---|---|---|---|---|---|
| James Brown | OT | 6'6" | 321 | 24 | | |
| Jeff Criswell | OT | 6'7" | 291 | 30 | | |
| Siupeli Malamala | OT | 6'5" | 315 | 25 | | |
| Matt Willig | OT | 6'8" | 305 | 25 | | |
| Roger Duffy | OG-C | 6'3" | 294 | 27 | | |
| Everett McIver | OG | 6'6" | 315 | 24 | | |
| Dwayne White | OG | 6'2" | 315 | 27 | | |
| Cal Dixon | C-OG | 6'4" | 292 | 24 | | |
| Jim Sweeney | C | 6'4" | 292 | 32 | | |
| Jeff Lageman | DE | 6'5" | 266 | 27 | | |
| Marvin Washington | DE | 6'6" | 272 | 28 | 1 | |
| Paul Frase | DT-DE | 6'5" | 270 | 29 | | |
| Mark Gunn | DT-DE | 6'5" | 279 | 26 | | |
| Lou Benfatti | DT | 6'4" | 278 | 23 | | |
| Tony Casillas | DT | 6'3" | 278 | 30 | | |
| Donald Evans | DT-DE | 6'2" | 282 | 30 | | |
| Alfred Oglesby | DT | 6'4" | 276 | 27 | | |
| Bill Pickel | DT | 6'5" | 265 | 34 | | |

| Use Name | Pos. | Hgt. | Wgt. | Age | Int | Pts |
|---|---|---|---|---|---|---|
| Tuineau Alipate | LB | 6'1" | 245 | 27 | | |
| Kurt Barber | LB | 6'4" | 249 | 25 | | |
| Glenn Cadrez | LB | 6'3" | 245 | 24 | | |
| Kyle Clifton | LB | 6'4" | 236 | 32 | | |
| Bobby Houston | LB | 6'2" | 245 | 26 | | |
| Marvin Jones | LB | 6'2" | 249 | 32 | | |
| Mo Lewis | LB | 6'3" | 250 | 24 | 4 | 12 |
| Aaron Glenn | DB | 5'9" | 185 | 22 | | |
| Victor Green | DB | 5'9" | 195 | 24 | | |
| James Hasty | DB | 6' | 201 | 29 | 5 | |
| Cliff Hicks | DB | 5'10" | 195 | 30 | | |
| Ronnie Lott | DB | 6'1" | 203 | 35 | | |
| Anthony Prior | DB | 5'11" | 185 | 24 | | |
| Pat Terrell | DB | 6'2" | 210 | 26 | | |
| Eric Thomas | DB | 5'11" | 184 | 29 | | |
| Marcus Turner | DB | 6' | 190 | 28 | 5 | 6 |
| Brian Washington | DB | 6'1" | 210 | 28 | 2 | |

Troy Johnson — Back injury

| Use Name | Pos. | Hgt. | Wgt. | Age | Int | Pts |
|---|---|---|---|---|---|---|
| Boomer Esiason | QB | 6'5" | 224 | 33 | | |
| Glenn Foley | QB | 6'2" | 205 | 23 | | |
| Jack Trudeau | QB | 6'3" | 222 | 31 | | |
| Anthony Johnson | HB | 6' | 222 | 26 | | |
| Johnny Johnson | HB | 6'3" | 220 | 26 | | 30 |
| Adrian Murrell | HB | 5'11" | 212 | 23 | | |
| Richie Anderson | FB-HB | 6'2" | 225 | 22 | | 12 |
| Brad Baxter | FB | 6'1" | 235 | 27 | | 24 |
| Steve Anderson | WR | 6'5" | 215 | 24 | | |
| Rob Carpenter | WR | 6'2" | 190 | 26 | | |
| Art Monk | WR | 6'3" | 210 | 36 | | 18 |
| Rob Moore | WR | 6'3" | 205 | 25 | | 40 |
| Orlando Parker | WR | 5'11" | 190 | 22 | | |
| Ryan Yarborough | WR | 6'2" | 190 | 23 | | 6 |
| Fred Baxter | TE | 6'3" | 260 | 23 | | 6 |
| Johnny Mitchell | TE | 6'3" | 241 | 23 | | 24 |
| James Thornton | TE | 6'2" | 252 | 29 | | |
| Brian Hansen | K | 6'4" | 215 | 33 | | |
| Nick Lowery | K | 6'4" | 205 | 38 | | 86 |

## MIAMI DOLPHINS

### RUSHING

| Last Name | No. | Yds | Avg | TD |
|---|---|---|---|---|
| Parmalee | 216 | 868 | 4.0 | 6 |
| Spikes | 70 | 312 | 4.5 | 2 |
| Kirby | 60 | 233 | 3.9 | 2 |
| Byars | 19 | 64 | 3.4 | 2 |
| Craver | 6 | 43 | 7.2 | 0 |
| McDuffie | 5 | 32 | 6.4 | 0 |
| Kosar | 1 | 17 | 17.0 | 0 |
| Saxon | 8 | 16 | 2.0 | 0 |
| Gary | 7 | 11 | 1.6 | 0 |
| Wilson | 1 | -1 | -1.0 | 0 |
| Marino | 23 | -6 | -0.3 | 0 |

### RECEIVING

| Last Name | No. | Yds | Avg | TD |
|---|---|---|---|---|
| Fryar | 73 | 1270 | 17.4 | 7 |
| K. Jackson | 59 | 673 | 11.4 | 7 |
| Byars | 49 | 418 | 8.5 | 5 |
| Ingram | 44 | 506 | 11.5 | 6 |
| McDuffie | 37 | 488 | 13.2 | 3 |
| Parmalee | 34 | 249 | 7.3 | 1 |
| Saxon | 27 | 151 | 5.6 | 0 |
| Craver | 24 | 237 | 9.9 | 0 |
| M. Williams | 15 | 221 | 14.7 | 0 |
| Kirby | 14 | 154 | 11.0 | 0 |
| Miller | 6 | 94 | 15.7 | 1 |
| Spikes | 4 | 16 | 4.0 | 0 |
| R. Williams | 2 | 26 | 13.0 | 0 |
| Gary | 2 | 19 | 9.5 | 0 |
| Baty | 2 | 11 | 5.5 | 0 |

### PUNT RETURNS

| Last Name | No. | Yds | Avg | TD |
|---|---|---|---|---|
| McDuffie | 232 | 228 | 7.1 | 0 |
| Miller | 1 | 13 | 13.0 | 0 |

### KICKOFF RETURNS

| Last Name | No. | Yds | Avg | TD |
|---|---|---|---|---|
| McDuffie | 36 | 767 | 21.3 | 0 |
| Spikes | 19 | 434 | 22.8 | 0 |
| R. Williams | 2 | 25 | 12.5 | 0 |
| M. Williams | 2 | 9 | 4.5 | 0 |
| Parmalee | 2 | 0 | 0.0 | 0 |
| Braxton | 1 | 34 | 34.0 | 0 |
| Miller | 1 | 13 | 13.0 | 0 |
| Saxon | 1 | 12 | 12.0 | 0 |
| Baty | 1 | 0 | 0.0 | 0 |
| Ingram | 1 | 0 | 0.0 | 0 |

### PASSING — PUNTING — KICKING Statistics

**PASSING**

| Last Name | Att | Cmp | % | Yds | Yd/Att | TD | Int— | % | RK |
|---|---|---|---|---|---|---|---|---|---|
| Marino | 615 | 385 | 62.6 | 4453 | 7.24 | 30 | 17— | 2.8 | 1 |
| Kosar | 12 | 7 | 58.3 | 80 | 6.67 | 1 | 1— | 8.3 | |

**PUNTING**

| Last Name | No. | Avg. |
|---|---|---|
| Arnold | 46 | 39.3 |
| Kidd | 21 | 40.4 |

**KICKING**

| Last Name | XP | ATT | % | FG | ATT | % |
|---|---|---|---|---|---|---|
| Stoyonovich | 35 | 35 | 100 | 24 | 31 | 77 |

**2 POINT XP**
Fryar (2)
Craver (1)
K. Jackson (1)
Kirby (1)
Parmalee (1)

## NEW ENGLAND PATRIOTS

### RUSHING

| Last Name | No. | Yds | Avg | TD |
|---|---|---|---|---|
| Butts | 243 | 703 | 2.9 | 8 |
| Thompson | 102 | 312 | 3.1 | 2 |
| Turner | 36 | 111 | 3.1 | 1 |
| Gash | 30 | 86 | 2.9 | 0 |
| Bledsoe | 44 | 40 | 0.9 | 0 |
| Timpson | 2 | 14 | 7.0 | 0 |
| Coates | 1 | 0 | 0.0 | 0 |
| Zolak | 1 | -1 | -1.0 | 0 |

### RECEIVING

| Last Name | No. | Yds | Avg | TD |
|---|---|---|---|---|
| Coates | 96 | 1174 | 12.2 | 7 |
| Timpson | 74 | 941 | 12.7 | 3 |
| Thompson | 65 | 465 | 7.2 | 5 |
| Brisby | 58 | 904 | 15.6 | 5 |
| Turner | 52 | 471 | 9.1 | 2 |
| Crittenden | 28 | 379 | 13.5 | 3 |
| Burke | 9 | 86 | 9.6 | 0 |
| Gash | 9 | 61 | 6.8 | 0 |
| Butts | 9 | 54 | 6.0 | 0 |
| Hawkins | 2 | 22 | 11.0 | 0 |
| Harris | 1 | 11 | 11.0 | 0 |

### PUNT RETURNS

| Last Name | No. | Yds | Avg | TD |
|---|---|---|---|---|
| T. Brown | 24 | 202 | 8.4 | 0 |
| Crittenden | 19 | 155 | 8.2 | 0 |
| Harris | 3 | 26 | 8.7 | 0 |

### KICKOFF RETURNS

| Last Name | No. | Yds | Avg | TD |
|---|---|---|---|---|
| Crittenden | 24 | 460 | 19.2 | 0 |
| Thompson | 18 | 376 | 20.9 | 0 |
| Croom | 10 | 172 | 17.2 | 0 |
| Burke | 3 | 11 | 3.7 | 0 |
| Timpson | 1 | 28 | 28.0 | 0 |
| T. Brown | 1 | 14 | 14.0 | 0 |
| DeOssie | 1 | 14 | 14.0 | 0 |
| Gash | 1 | 9 | 9.0 | 0 |
| Guyton | 1 | -1 | -1.0 | 0 |

### PASSING — PUNTING — KICKING

**PASSING**

| Last Name | Att | Cmp | % | Yds | Yd/Att | TD | Int— | % | RK |
|---|---|---|---|---|---|---|---|---|---|
| Bledsoe | 691 | 400 | 57.9 | 4555 | 6.59 | 25 | 27— | 3.9 | 10 |
| Zolak | 8 | 5 | 62.5 | 28 | 3.50 | 0 | 0— | 0.0 | |

**PUNTING**

| Last Name | No. | Avg. |
|---|---|---|
| O'Neill | 69 | 41.2 |

**KICKING**

| Last Name | XP | ATT | % | FG | ATT | % |
|---|---|---|---|---|---|---|
| Bahr | 36 | 36 | 100 | 27 | 34 | 79 |

**2 POINT XP**
None

## INDIANAPOLIS COLTS

### RUSHING

| Last Name | No. | Yds | Avg | TD |
|---|---|---|---|---|
| Faulk | 314 | 1282 | 4.1 | 11 |
| Potts | 77 | 336 | 4.4 | 1 |
| Harbaugh | 39 | 223 | 5.7 | 0 |
| Humphrey | 18 | 85 | 4.7 | 0 |
| Warren | 18 | 80 | 4.4 | 0 |
| Majkowski | 24 | 34 | 1.4 | 3 |
| Nagle | 1 | 12 | 12.0 | 0 |
| Toner | 1 | 11 | 11.0 | 0 |
| Turner | 3 | -3 | -1.0 | 0 |

### RECEIVING

| Last Name | No. | Yds | Avg | TD |
|---|---|---|---|---|
| Turner | 52 | 593 | 11.4 | 6 |
| Faulk | 52 | 522 | 10.0 | 1 |
| Dawkins | 51 | 742 | 14.5 | 5 |
| Potts | 26 | 251 | 9.7 | 1 |
| Cash | 16 | 190 | 11.9 | 1 |
| Jackson | 8 | 97 | 12.1 | 1 |
| Warren | 3 | 47 | 15.7 | 0 |
| Humphrey | 3 | 19 | 6.3 | 0 |
| Bailey | 2 | 30 | 15.0 | 0 |
| Baker | 2 | 15 | 7.5 | 0 |
| Arbuckle | 1 | 7 | 7.0 | 0 |
| Etheredge | 1 | 6 | 6.0 | 0 |

### PUNT RETURNS

| Last Name | No. | Yds | Avg | TD |
|---|---|---|---|---|
| Brewer | 42 | 339 | 8.1 | 1 |

### KICKOFF RETURNS

| Last Name | No. | Yds | Avg | TD |
|---|---|---|---|---|
| Humphrey | 35 | 783 | 22.4 | 1 |
| Brewer | 18 | 358 | 19.9 | 0 |
| Warren | 2 | 56 | 28.0 | 0 |
| Etheredge | 2 | 23 | 11.5 | 0 |
| Radecic | 1 | 17 | 17.0 | 0 |
| Toner | 1 | 8 | 8.0 | 0 |
| Jackson | 1 | 5 | 5.0 | 0 |
| Gray | 0 | 4 | — | 0 |

### PASSING — PUNTING — KICKING

**PASSING**

| Last Name | Att | Cmp | % | Yds | Yd/Att | TD | Int— | % | RK |
|---|---|---|---|---|---|---|---|---|---|
| Harbaugh | 202 | 125 | 61.9 | 1440 | 7.13 | 9 | 6— | 3.0 | |
| Majkowski | 152 | 84 | 55.3 | 1010 | 6.64 | 6 | 7— | 4.6 | |
| Nagle | 21 | 8 | 38.1 | 69 | 3.29 | 0 | 1— | 4.8 | |
| Warren | 0 | 0 | 0 | 0 | 0.00 | 0 | 0— | 0.0 | |

**PUNTING**

| Last Name | No. | Avg. |
|---|---|---|
| Stark | 74 | 41.8 |

**KICKING**

| Last Name | XP | ATT | % | FG | ATT | % |
|---|---|---|---|---|---|---|
| Biasucci | 37 | 37 | 100 | 16 | 24 | 67 |

**2 POINT XP**
None

## BUFFALO BILLS

### RUSHING

| Last Name | No. | Yds | Avg | TD |
|---|---|---|---|---|
| Thomas | 287 | 1093 | 3.8 | 7 |
| K. Davis | 91 | 381 | 4.2 | 2 |
| Gardner | 41 | 135 | 3.3 | 4 |
| Reed | 10 | 87 | 8.7 | 0 |
| Kelly | 25 | 77 | 3.1 | 1 |
| Jourdain | 17 | 56 | 3.3 | 0 |
| Beebe | 2 | 11 | 5.5 | 0 |
| Turner | 2 | 4 | 2.0 | 0 |
| Reich | 6 | 3 | 0.5 | 0 |
| Copeland | 1 | -7 | -7.0 | 0 |
| Mohr | 1 | -9 | -9.0 | 0 |

### RECEIVING

| Last Name | No. | Yds | Avg | TD |
|---|---|---|---|---|
| Reed | 90 | 1303 | 14.5 | 8 |
| Thomas | 50 | 349 | 7.0 | 2 |
| Metzelaars | 49 | 428 | 8.7 | 5 |
| Bi. Brooks | 42 | 482 | 11.5 | 2 |
| Beebe | 40 | 527 | 13.2 | 4 |
| Copeland | 21 | 255 | 12.1 | 1 |
| K. Davis | 18 | 82 | 4.6 | 0 |
| Gardner | 11 | 89 | 8.1 | 0 |
| Jourdain | 10 | 56 | 5.6 | 0 |
| Marrow | 5 | 44 | 8.8 | 0 |
| L. Johnson | 3 | 42 | 14.0 | 0 |
| D. Thomas | 2 | 31 | 15.5 | 0 |
| Turner | 1 | 26 | 26.0 | 0 |

### PUNT RETURNS

| Last Name | No. | Yds | Avg | TD |
|---|---|---|---|---|
| Burris | 32 | 332 | 10.4 | 0 |
| Copeland | 1 | 11 | 11.0 | 0 |

### KICKOFF RETURNS

| Last Name | No. | Yds | Avg | TD |
|---|---|---|---|---|
| Jourdain | 27 | 601 | 22.3 | 0 |
| Beebe | 12 | 230 | 19.2 | 0 |
| Copeland | 12 | 232 | 19.3 | 0 |
| Bu. Brooks | 9 | 162 | 18.0 | 0 |
| Turner | 6 | 102 | 17.0 | 0 |
| Pike | 2 | 9 | 4.5 | 0 |
| Gardner | 1 | 6 | 6.0 | 0 |
| Tasker | 1 | 2 | 2.0 | 0 |
| Patton | 1 | 1 | 1.0 | 0 |
| K. Davis | 1 | 0 | 0.0 | 0 |

### PASSING — PUNTING — KICKING

**PASSING**

| Last Name | Att | Cmp | % | Yds | Yd/Att | TD | Int— | % | RK |
|---|---|---|---|---|---|---|---|---|---|
| Kelly | 448 | 285 | 63.6 | 3114 | 6.95 | 22 | 17— | 3.8 | 3 |
| Reich | 93 | 56 | 60.2 | 568 | 6.11 | 1 | 4— | 4.3 | |
| Reed | 1 | 1 | 100.0 | 32 | 32.00 | 0 | 0— | 0.0 | |

**PUNTING**

| Last Name | No. | Avg. |
|---|---|---|
| Mohr | 67 | 41.8 |

**KICKING**

| Last Name | XP | ATT | % | FG | ATT | % |
|---|---|---|---|---|---|---|
| Christie | 38 | 38 | 100 | 24 | 28 | 86 |

**2 POINT XP**
None

## NEW YORK JETS

### RUSHING

| Last Name | No. | Yds | Avg | TD |
|---|---|---|---|---|
| J. Johnson | 240 | 931 | 3.9 | 3 |
| R. Anderson | 43 | 207 | 4.8 | 1 |
| B. Baxter | 60 | 170 | 2.8 | 4 |
| Murrell | 33 | 160 | 4.8 | 0 |
| Esiason | 28 | 59 | 2.1 | 0 |
| Trudeau | 6 | 30 | 5.0 | 0 |
| A. Johnson | 5 | 12 | 2.4 | 0 |
| Moore | 1 | -3 | -3.0 | 0 |

### RECEIVING

| Last Name | No. | Yds | Avg | TD |
|---|---|---|---|---|
| Moore | 78 | 1010 | 12.9 | 6 |
| Mitchell | 58 | 749 | 12.9 | 4 |
| Monk | 46 | 581 | 12.6 | 3 |
| J. Johnson | 42 | 303 | 7.2 | 2 |
| R. Anderson | 25 | 212 | 8.5 | 1 |
| Thornton | 20 | 171 | 8.6 | 0 |
| B. Baxter | 10 | 40 | 4.0 | 0 |
| S. Anderson | 9 | 90 | 10.0 | 0 |
| Murrell | 7 | 76 | 10.9 | 0 |
| Yarborough | 6 | 42 | 7.0 | 1 |
| A. Johnson | 5 | 31 | 6.2 | 0 |
| F. Baxter | 3 | 11 | 3.7 | 1 |
| Parker | 1 | 7 | 7.0 | 0 |

### PUNT RETURNS

| Last Name | No. | Yds | Avg | TD |
|---|---|---|---|---|
| Hicks | 38 | 342 | 9.0 | 0 |
| A. Johnson | 1 | 3 | 3.0 | 0 |

### KICKOFF RETURNS

| Last Name | No. | Yds | Avg | TD |
|---|---|---|---|---|
| Glenn | 27 | 582 | 21.6 | 0 |
| Prior | 16 | 316 | 19.8 | 0 |
| Murrell | 14 | 268 | 19.1 | 0 |
| R. Anderson | 3 | 43 | 14.3 | 0 |
| Hicks | 2 | 30 | 15.0 | 0 |
| F. Baxter | 1 | 20 | 20.0 | 0 |
| Cadrez | 1 | 10 | 10.0 | 0 |
| Clifton | 1 | 13 | 13.0 | 0 |
| Thornton | 1 | 0 | 0.0 | 0 |

### PASSING — PUNTING — KICKING

**PASSING**

| Last Name | Att | Cmp | % | Yds | Yd/Att | TD | Int— | % | RK |
|---|---|---|---|---|---|---|---|---|---|
| Esiason | 440 | 255 | 58.0 | 2782 | 6.32 | 17 | 13— | 3.0 | 8 |
| Trudeau | 91 | 50 | 54.9 | 496 | 5.45 | 1 | 4— | 4.4 | |
| Foley | 8 | 5 | 62.5 | 45 | 5.63 | 0 | 1— | 12.5 | |

**PUNTING**

| Last Name | No. | Avg. |
|---|---|---|
| Hansen | 84 | 42.1 |

**KICKING**

| Last Name | XP | ATT | % | FG | ATT | % |
|---|---|---|---|---|---|---|
| Lowery | 26 | 27 | 96 | 20 | 23 | 87 |

**2 POINT XP**
Moore (2)

## PITTSBURGH STEELERS 12-4 Bill Cowher

| Scores of Each Game | | |
|---|---|---|
| 9 | DALLAS | 26 |
| 17 | Cleveland | 10 |
| 31 | INDIANAPOLIS | 21 |
| 13 | Seattle | 30 |
| 30 | HOUSTON | 14 |
| 14 | CINCINNATI | 10 |
| 10 | N.Y. Giants | 6 |
| 17 | Arizona | *20 |
| 12 | Houston | *9 |
| 23 | BUFFALO | 10 |
| 16 | MIAMI | *13 |
| 21 | L.A. Raiders | 3 |
| 38 | Cincinnati | 15 |
| 14 | PHILADELPHIA | 3 |
| 17 | CLEVELAND | 7 |
| 34 | San Diego | 37 |

| Use Name | Pos. | Hgt. | Wgt. | Age | Int | Pts |
|---|---|---|---|---|---|---|
| John Jackson | OT | 6'6" | 297 | 29 | | |
| Leon Searcy | OT | 6'3" | 304 | 24 | | |
| Todd Kalis | OG | 6'6" | 296 | 29 | | |
| Duval Love | OG | 6'3" | 288 | 31 | | |
| Tim Simpson | OG-C | 6'2" | 284 | 25 | | |
| Justin Strzelczyk | OG-OT | 6'5" | 295 | 26 | | |
| Dermontti Dawson | C | 6'2" | 286 | 29 | | |
| Kendall Gammon | C | 6'4" | 288 | 25 | | |
| Ariel Solomon | C-OT | 6'5" | 290 | 26 | | |
| Brentson Buckner | DE | 6'2" | 305 | 22 | | |
| Taase Faumui | DE | 6'3" | 278 | 23 | | |
| Kevin Henry | DE | 6'4" | 270 | 25 | | |
| Ray Seals | DE | 6'3" | 309 | 29 | | |
| Gerald Williams | DE | 6'3" | 288 | 30 | | 6 |
| Jeff Zgonina | DT | 6'1" | 287 | 24 | | |
| Joel Steed | NT | 6'2" | 295 | 25 | | |
| Chad Brown | LB | 6'2" | 236 | 24 | 1 | |
| Reggie Clark | LB | 6'2" | 238 | 26 | | |
| Jason Gildon | LB | 6'3" | 237 | 22 | | |
| Kevin Greene | LB | 6'3" | 247 | 32 | | |
| Levon Kirkland | LB | 6' | 252 | 25 | 2 | |
| Greg Lloyd | LB | 6'2" | 226 | 29 | 1 | |
| Jerry Olsavsky | LB | 6'1" | 221 | 27 | | |
| Eric Ravotti | LB | 6'3" | 254 | 23 | | |
| Ed Robinson | LB | 6' | 228 | 23 | | |
| Myron Bell | DB | 5'11" | 203 | 22 | | |
| Deon Figures | DB | 6' | 203 | 24 | | |
| Fred Foggie | DB | 6' | 212 | 25 | | |
| Gary Jones | DB | 6'2" | 214 | 26 | 1 | |
| Carnell Lake | DB | 6'1" | 210 | 27 | 1 | |
| Tim McKyer | DB | 6' | 178 | 30 | | |
| Darren Perry | DB | 5'10" | 196 | 25 | 7 | |
| Willie Williams | DB | 5'9" | 185 | 23 | | |
| Rod Woodson | DB | 6' | 200 | 29 | 4 | 12 |
| Jim Miller | QB | 6'2" | 226 | 23 | | |
| Neil O'Donnell | QB | 6'3" | 230 | 28 | | 6 |
| Mike Tomczak | QB | 6'1" | 207 | 31 | | |
| Barry Foster | HB | 5'10" | 218 | 25 | | 30 |
| Bam Morris | HB | 6' | 235 | 22 | | 42 |
| Steve Avery | FB | 6'2" | 233 | 28 | | |
| Randy Cuthbert | FB | 6'2" | 225 | 24 | | |
| Anthony Daigle | FB | 5'10" | 203 | 24 | | |
| Victor Jones (to KC) | FB | 5'8" | 215 | 26 | | |
| John L. Williams | FB | 5'11" | 231 | 29 | | 18 |
| Charles Davenport | WR | 6'3" | 210 | 25 | | |
| Andre Hastings | WR | 6' | 190 | 23 | | 12 |
| Charles Johnson | WR | 6' | 189 | 22 | | 18 |
| Ernie Mills | WR | 5'11" | 192 | 25 | | 6 |
| Dwight Stone | WR-HB | 6' | 180 | 30 | | 2 |
| Yancey Thigpen | WR | 6'1" | 208 | 25 | | 24 |
| Eric Green | TE | 6'5" | 280 | 27 | | 24 |
| Jonathan Hayes | TE | 6'5" | 248 | 32 | | 6 |
| Craig Keith | TE | 6'3" | 264 | 23 | | |
| Walter Rasby | TE | 6'3" | 247 | 21 | | |
| Gary Anderson | K | 5'11" | 179 | 35 | | 104 |
| Mark Royals | K | 6'5" | 215 | 29 | | |

Rico Mack — Ankle injury

## CLEVELAND BROWNS 11-5 Bill Belichick

| Scores of Each Game | | |
|---|---|---|
| 28 | Cincinnati | 20 |
| 10 | PITTSBURGH | 17 |
| 32 | ARIZONA | 0 |
| 21 | Indianapolis | 14 |
| 27 | N.Y. JETS | 7 |
| 11 | Houston | 8 |
| 37 | CINCINNATI | 13 |
| 14 | Denver | 26 |
| 13 | NEW ENGLAND | 6 |
| 26 | Philadelphia | 7 |
| 13 | Kansas City | 20 |
| 34 | HOUSTON | 10 |
| 13 | N.Y. GIANTS | 16 |
| 19 | Dallas | 14 |
| 7 | Pittsburgh | 17 |
| 35 | SEATTLE | 9 |

| Use Name | Pos. | Hgt. | Wgt. | Age | Int | Pts |
|---|---|---|---|---|---|---|
| Herman Arvie | OT | 6'4" | 305 | 23 | | |
| Orlando Brown | OT | 6'7" | 325 | 23 | | |
| Tony Jones | OT | 6'5" | 295 | 28 | | |
| Gene Williams | OT-OG | 6'2" | 305 | 25 | | |
| Bob Dahl | OG-OT | 6'5" | 310 | 25 | | |
| Doug Dawson | OG | 6'3" | 288 | 32 | | |
| Steve Everitt | C | 6'5" | 290 | 24 | | |
| Wally Williams | C | 6'2" | 300 | 23 | | |
| Rob Burnett | DE | 6'4" | 280 | 27 | | |
| Dan Footmann | DE | 6'5" | 290 | 25 | | |
| Rick Lyle | DE | 6'5" | 275 | 23 | | |
| Anthony Pleasant | DE | 6'5" | 280 | 26 | | |
| Bill Johnson | DT-DE | 6'4" | 290 | 25 | | |
| James Jones | DT | 6'2" | 290 | 25 | | |
| Michael Dean Perry | DT | 6'1" | 285 | 29 | | |
| Pio Sagapolutele | DT | 6'6" | 297 | 24 | | |
| Carl Banks | LB | 6'4" | 235 | 32 | | |
| Mike Caldwell | LB | 6'2" | 235 | 22 | 1 | |
| Gerald Dixon | LB | 6'3" | 250 | 25 | | |
| Travis Hill | LB | 6'2" | 240 | 24 | | 6 |
| Pepper Johnson | LB | 6'3" | 248 | 30 | | |
| Frank Stams | LB | 6'2" | 230 | 28 | 1 | |
| Eddie Sutter | LB | 6'3" | 235 | 24 | | |
| Isaac Booth | DB | 6'3" | 190 | 23 | 1 | |
| Don Griffin | DB | 6' | 176 | 30 | 2 | |
| Stacey Hairston | DB | 5'9" | 185 | 27 | | |
| Tim Jacobs | DB | 5'10" | 185 | 24 | 2 | |
| Antonio Langham | DB | 6' | 180 | 22 | 2 | |
| Stevon Moore | DB | 5'11" | 210 | 27 | | |
| Louis Riddick | DB | 6'2" | 215 | 25 | | |
| Del Speer (to SEA) | DB | 6' | 196 | 24 | | |
| Bennie Thompson | DB | 6' | 214 | 31 | | |
| Eric Turner | DB | 6'1" | 207 | 25 | **9** | 6 |
| Brad Goebel | QB | 6'3" | 214 | 26 | | |
| Mark Rypien | QB | 6'4" | 234 | 31 | | |
| Vinny Testaverde | QB | 6'5" | 215 | 30 | | 12 |
| Randy Baldwin | HB | 5'10" | 216 | 27 | | 6 |
| Earnest Byner | HB | 5'10" | 215 | 31 | | 12 |
| Eric Metcalf | HB | 5'10" | 190 | 26 | | 42 |
| Leroy Hoard | FB-HB | 5'11" | 225 | 26 | | 54 |
| Tommy Vardell | FB | 6'2" | 230 | 25 | | 6 |
| Derrick Alexander | WR | 6'2" | 195 | 22 | | 14 |
| Mark Carrier | WR | 6' | 185 | 28 | | 36 |
| Michael Jackson | WR | 6'4" | 195 | 25 | | 12 |
| Keenan McCardell | WR | 6'1" | 175 | 24 | | |
| Pat Newman | WR | 5'11" | 189 | 25 | | |
| Rico Smith | WR | 6' | 185 | 25 | | |
| Frank Hartley | TE | 6'2" | 268 | 26 | | 6 |
| Brian Kinchen | TE | 6'2" | 240 | 29 | | 6 |
| Thomas McLemore | TE | 6'5" | 250 | 24 | | |
| Walter Reeves | TE | 6'4" | 270 | 28 | | 6 |
| Matt Stover | K | 5'11" | 178 | 26 | | 110 |
| Tom Tupa | K | 6'4" | 230 | 28 | | 6 |

Mike Schad — Biceps injury

## CINCINNATI BENGALS 3-13 Dave Shula

| Scores of Each Game | | |
|---|---|---|
| 20 | CLEVELAND | 28 |
| 10 | San Diego | 27 |
| 28 | NEW ENGLAND | 31 |
| 13 | Houston | 20 |
| 7 | MIAMI | 23 |
| 10 | Pittsburgh | 14 |
| 13 | Cleveland | 37 |
| 20 | DALLAS | 23 |
| 20 | Seattle | *17 |
| 34 | HOUSTON | 31 |
| 13 | INDIANAPOLIS | 17 |
| 13 | Denver | 15 |
| 15 | PITTSBURGH | 38 |
| 20 | N.Y. Giants | 27 |
| 7 | Arizona | 28 |
| 33 | PHILADELPHIA | 30 |

| Use Name | Pos. | Hgt. | Wgt. | Age | Int | Pts |
|---|---|---|---|---|---|---|
| Rich Braham | OT | 6'4" | 290 | 23 | | |
| Scott Brumfield | OT | 6'8" | 320 | 24 | | |
| Mark Dennis | OT | 6'6" | 296 | 29 | | |
| Dan Jones | OT | 6'7" | 298 | 24 | | |
| Eric Moore | OT | 6'5" | 290 | 29 | | |
| Trent Pollard | OT | 6'4" | 304 | 21 | | |
| Kevin Sargent | OT | 6'6" | 284 | 25 | | |
| Dave Cadigan | OG | 6'4" | 285 | 29 | | |
| Bruce Kozerski | OG-OT | 6'4" | 287 | 31 | | |
| Ken Moyer | OG-C | 6'7" | 297 | 27 | | |
| Darrick Brilz | C | 6'3" | 287 | 30 | | |
| Greg Truitt | C | 6' | 235 | 28 | | |
| John Copeland | DE | 6'3" | 286 | 23 | | |
| Ty Parten | DE | 6'4" | 272 | 24 | | |
| Artie Smith (from SF) | DE | 6'4" | 285 | 24 | | |
| Ramondo Stallings | DE | 6'7" | 285 | 22 | | |
| Tim Krumrie | DT | 6'2" | 274 | 34 | | |
| Keith Rucker | DT | 6'4" | 340 | 25 | | |
| Kimo Von Oelhoffen | DT | 6'4" | 300 | 23 | | |
| Dan Wilkinson | DT | 6'5" | 313 | 21 | | |
| David Braxton | LB | 6'2" | 240 | 29 | | |
| James Francis | LB | 6'5" | 252 | 26 | | |
| Kevin Jefferson | LB | 6'2" | 232 | 30 | | |
| John Johnson | LB | 6'3" | 230 | 26 | | |
| Ricardo McDonald | LB | 6'2" | 235 | 24 | | |
| Kanavis McGhee | LB | 6'4" | 257 | 25 | | |
| Eric Shaw | LB | 6'3" | 248 | 22 | | |
| Santo Stephens | LB | 6'4" | 232 | 25 | | |
| Steve Tovar | LB | 6'3" | 244 | 24 | 1 | |
| Brett Wallerstedt | LB | 6'1" | 240 | 23 | | |
| Alfred Williams | LB | 6'6" | 265 | 25 | | 2 |
| Michael Brim | DB | 6' | 192 | 28 | 2 | |
| Adrian Hardy (from SF) | DB | 5'11" | 194 | 24 | | |
| Rod Jones | DB | 6' | 185 | 30 | | |
| Roger Jones | DB | 5'9" | 175 | 25 | | |
| Louis Oliver | DB | 6'2" | 224 | 28 | 3 | |
| Corey Sawyer | DB | 5'11" | 171 | 22 | 2 | 6 |
| Fernandus Vinson | DB | 5'10" | 197 | 25 | | |
| Bracey Walker (from KC) | DB | 5'10" | 200 | 23 | | |
| Darryl Williams | DB | 6' | 191 | 24 | 2 | |
| Jeff Blake | QB | 6' | 202 | 23 | | 8 |
| Donald Hollas | QB | 6'3" | 215 | 26 | | |
| David Klingler | QB | 6'2" | 205 | 25 | | |
| Todd Philcox | QB | 6'4" | 225 | 27 | | |
| Erik Wilhelm | QB | 6'3" | 217 | 28 | | |
| Eric Ball | HB-FB | 6'2" | 220 | 28 | | |
| Steve Broussard | HB | 5'7" | 201 | 27 | | 14 |
| Harold Green | HB | 6'2" | 222 | 26 | | 12 |
| Jeff Cothran | FB | 6'1" | 249 | 23 | | 6 |
| Derrick Fenner | FB-HB | 6'3" | 228 | 27 | | 12 |
| Jeff Hill | WR | 5'11" | 178 | 21 | | |
| Tim McGee | WR | 5'10" | 183 | 30 | | 6 |
| Carl Pickens | WR | 6'2" | 206 | 24 | | 66 |
| Jeff Query | WR | 6' | 165 | 27 | | |
| Darnay Scott | WR | 6'1" | 180 | 22 | | 30 |
| Milt Stegall | WR | 6' | 184 | 24 | | |
| David Frisch | TE | 6'7" | 260 | 24 | | |
| Tony McGee | TE | 6'3" | 246 | 23 | | 6 |
| Troy Sadowski | TE | 6'5" | 250 | 28 | | |
| Lee Johnson | K | 6'2" | 200 | 32 | | |
| Doug Pelfrey | K | 5'11" | 185 | 23 | | 108 |

Joe Walter — Knee injury

Leonard Wheeler — Wrist injury

## HOUSTON OILERS 2-14 Jack Pardee (1-9), Jeff Fisher (1-5)

| Scores of Each Game | | |
|---|---|---|
| 21 | Indianapolis | 45 |
| 17 | Dallas | 20 |
| 7 | BUFFALO | 15 |
| 20 | CINCINNATI | 13 |
| 14 | Pittsburgh | 30 |
| 8 | CLEVELAND | 11 |
| 6 | Philadelphia | 21 |
| 14 | L.A. Raiders | 17 |
| 9 | PITTSBURGH | *12 |
| 31 | Cincinnati | 34 |
| 10 | N.Y. GIANTS | 13 |
| 10 | Cleveland | 34 |
| 12 | ARIZONA | 30 |
| 14 | SEATTLE | 16 |
| 9 | Kansas City | 31 |
| 24 | N.Y. JETS | 10 |

| Use Name | Pos. | Hgt. | Wgt. | Age | Int | Pts |
|---|---|---|---|---|---|---|
| Brad Hopkins | OT | 6'3" | 306 | 23 | | |
| Stan Thomas | OT | 6'5" | 295 | 25 | | |
| David Williams | OT | 6'5" | 292 | 28 | | |
| Kevin Donnalley | OG | 6'5" | 305 | 26 | | |
| John Flannery | OG | 6'3" | 304 | 26 | | |
| Bill Schultz | OG | 6'5" | 305 | 27 | | |
| Erik Norgard | OG-C | 6'1" | 282 | 28 | | |
| Bruce Matthews | C-OT | 6'4" | 299 | 33 | | |
| Kenny Davidson | DE | 6'5" | 288 | 27 | | |
| Henry Ford | DE | 6'3" | 284 | 22 | | |
| Lamar Lathon | DE-LB | 6'3" | 262 | 26 | | 2 |
| Jeremy Nunley | DE | 6'5" | 278 | 22 | | |
| Mike Teeter | DE-DT | 6'2" | 272 | 26 | | |
| Ray Childress | DT | 6'6" | 272 | 31 | | |
| Glenn Montgomery | DT | 6' | 282 | 27 | | |
| Tim Roberts | DT | 6'6" | 318 | 25 | | |
| Micheal Barrow | LB | 6'1" | 236 | 24 | | |
| Joe Bowden | LB | 5'11" | 230 | 24 | | |
| Brett Faryniarz | LB | 6'3" | 230 | 29 | | |
| Eddie Robinson | LB | 6'1" | 245 | 24 | | |
| Al Smith | LB | 6'1" | 244 | 29 | | |
| Baron Wortham | LB | 5'11" | 244 | 24 | | |
| Tomur Barnes | DB | 5'10" | 188 | 23 | | |
| Blaine Bishop | DB | 5'8" | 197 | 24 | 1 | |
| Michael Davis | DB | 6'1" | 192 | 22 | | |
| Cris Dishman | DB | 6' | 188 | 29 | 4 | 6 |
| Steve Jackson | DB | 5'8" | 182 | 25 | 1 | |
| Darryll Lewis | DB | 5'9" | 183 | 25 | 5 | |
| Bubba McDowell | DB | 6'1" | 198 | 27 | | |
| Bo Orlando | DB | 5'10" | 180 | 28 | | |
| Marcus Robertson | DB | 5'11" | 197 | 24 | 3 | |
| Cody Carlson | QB | 6'3" | 202 | 30 | | |
| Bucky Richardson | QB | 6'1" | 228 | 25 | | 6 |
| Billy Joe Tolliver | QB | 6'1" | 218 | 28 | | 12 |
| Gary Brown | HB | 5'11" | 233 | 25 | | 30 |
| Todd McNair | HB | 6'1" | 202 | 28 | | |
| Spencer Tillman | HB | 5'11" | 206 | 30 | | |
| Lorenzo White | HB | 5'11" | 222 | 28 | | 24 |
| Le'Shai Maston | FB | 6'1" | 232 | 23 | | |
| Reggie Brown | WR | 6'1" | 195 | 24 | | 2 |
| Pat Coleman | WR | 5'7" | 176 | 27 | | 6 |
| Ernest Givins | WR | 5'9" | 178 | 29 | | 12 |
| Travis Hannah | WR | 5'7" | 161 | 24 | | |
| Haywood Jeffires | WR | 6'2" | 201 | 29 | | 42 |
| Malcolm Seabron | WR | 6' | 194 | 21 | | |
| Webster Slaughter | WR | 6'1" | 175 | 29 | | 12 |
| Gary Wellman | WR | 5'9" | 173 | 27 | | |
| Pat Carter | TE | 6'4" | 258 | 28 | | 6 |
| Roderick Lewis | TE | 6'5" | 254 | 23 | | |
| John Henry Mills | TE | 6' | 222 | 24 | | |
| Rich Camarillo | K | 5'11" | 202 | 34 | | |
| Al Del Greco | K | 5'10" | 200 | 32 | | 66 |

## PITTSBURGH STEELERS

### RUSHING

| Last Name | No. | Yds | Avg | TD |
|---|---|---|---|---|
| Foster | 216 | 851 | 3.9 | 5 |
| Morris | 198 | 836 | 4.2 | 7 |
| J.L. Williams | 68 | 317 | 4.7 | 2 |
| O'Donnell | 31 | 80 | 2.6 | 1 |
| Tomczak | 4 | 22 | 5.5 | 0 |
| Mills | 3 | 18 | 6.0 | 0 |
| Stone | 2 | 7 | 3.5 | 0 |
| Avery | 2 | 4 | 2.0 | 0 |
| Anderson | 1 | 3 | 3.0 | 0 |
| Johnson | 4 | -1 | -0.3 | 0 |
| Royals | 1 | -13 | -13.0 | 0 |

### RECEIVING

| Last Name | No. | Yds | Avg | TD |
|---|---|---|---|---|
| J.L. Williams | 51 | 378 | 7.4 | 2 |
| Green | 46 | 618 | 13.4 | 4 |
| Johnson | 38 | 577 | 15.2 | 3 |
| Thigpen | 36 | 546 | 15.2 | 4 |
| Morris | 22 | 204 | 9.3 | 0 |
| Hastings | 20 | 281 | 14.1 | 2 |
| Foster | 20 | 124 | 6.2 | 0 |
| Mills | 19 | 384 | 20.2 | 1 |
| Stone | 7 | 81 | 11.6 | 0 |
| Hayes | 5 | 50 | 10.0 | 1 |
| Avery | 1 | 2 | 2.0 | 0 |
| Keith | 1 | 2 | 2.0 | 0 |

### PUNT RETURNS

| Last Name | No. | Yds | Avg | TD |
|---|---|---|---|---|
| Woodson | 39 | 319 | 8.2 | 0 |
| Johnson | 15 | 90 | 6.0 | 0 |
| Hastings | 2 | 15 | 7.5 | 0 |

### KICKOFF RETURNS

| Last Name | No. | Yds | Avg | TD |
|---|---|---|---|---|
| Johnson | 16 | 345 | 21.6 | 0 |
| Woodson | 15 | 365 | 24.3 | 0 |
| Stone | 11 | 182 | 16.5 | 0 |
| Thigpen | 5 | 121 | 24.2 | 0 |
| Morris | 4 | 114 | 28.5 | 0 |
| Zgonina | 2 | 8 | 4.0 | 0 |
| Mills | 2 | 6 | 3.0 | 0 |

### PASSING — PUNTING — KICKING Statistics

| PASSING | Att | Cmp | % | Yds | Yd/Att | TD | Int | — | % | RK |
|---|---|---|---|---|---|---|---|---|---|---|
| O'Donnell | 370 | 212 | 57.3 | 2443 | 6.60 | 13 | 9 | — | 2.4 | 7 |
| Tomczak | 93 | 54 | 58.1 | 804 | 8.65 | 4 | 0 | — | 0.0 | |

| PUNTING | No. | Avg. |
|---|---|---|
| Royals | 97 | 39.7 |

| KICKING | XP | ATT | % | FG | ATT | % |
|---|---|---|---|---|---|---|
| Anderson | 32 | 32 | 100 | 24 | 29 | 83 |

2 POINT XP
Stone (1)

## CLEVELAND BROWNS

### RUSHING

| Last Name | No. | Yds | Avg | TD |
|---|---|---|---|---|
| Hoard | 209 | 890 | 4.3 | 5 |
| Metcalf | 93 | 329 | 3.5 | 2 |
| Byner | 75 | 219 | 2.9 | 2 |
| Baldwin | 23 | 78 | 3.4 | 0 |
| Vardell | 15 | 48 | 3.2 | 0 |
| Alexander | 4 | 38 | 9.5 | 0 |
| Testaverde | 21 | 37 | 1.8 | 2 |
| Carrier | 1 | 14 | 14.0 | 1 |
| Rypien | 7 | 4 | 0.6 | 0 |
| J. Jones | 1 | 0 | 0.0 | 0 |

### RECEIVING

| Last Name | No. | Yds | Avg | TD |
|---|---|---|---|---|
| Alexander | 48 | 828 | 17.3 | 2 |
| Metcalf | 47 | 436 | 9.3 | 3 |
| Hoard | 45 | 445 | 9.9 | 4 |
| Carrier | 29 | 452 | 15.6 | 5 |
| Kinchen | 24 | 232 | 9.7 | 1 |
| Jackson | 21 | 304 | 14.5 | 2 |
| Vardell | 16 | 137 | 8.6 | 1 |
| Byner | 11 | 102 | 9.3 | 0 |
| McCardell | 10 | 182 | 18.2 | 0 |
| Reeves | 6 | 61 | 10.2 | 1 |
| Baldwin | 3 | 15 | 5.0 | 0 |
| Hartley | 3 | 13 | 4.3 | 1 |
| Smith | 2 | 61 | 30.5 | 0 |
| J. Jones | 1 | 1 | 1.0 | 0 |

### PUNT RETURNS

| Last Name | No. | Yds | Avg | TD |
|---|---|---|---|---|
| Metcalf | 35 | 348 | 9.9 | 2 |
| Carrier | 9 | 112 | 12.4 | 0 |
| Caldwell | 1 | 2 | 2.0 | 0 |
| Turner | 1 | 0 | 0.0 | 0 |

### KICKOFF RETURNS

| Last Name | No. | Yds | Avg | TD |
|---|---|---|---|---|
| Baldwin | 28 | 753 | 26.9 | 1 |
| Metcalf | 9 | 210 | 23.3 | 0 |
| Kinchen | 3 | 38 | 12.7 | 0 |
| Hoard | 2 | 30 | 15.0 | 0 |

### PASSING — PUNTING — KICKING

| PASSING | Att | Cmp | % | Yds | Yd/Att | TD | Int | — | % | RK |
|---|---|---|---|---|---|---|---|---|---|---|
| Testaverde | 376 | 207 | 55.1 | 2575 | 6.85 | 16 | 18 | — | 4.8 | 11 |
| Rypien | 128 | 59 | 46.1 | 694 | 5.42 | 4 | 3 | — | 2.3 | |
| Jackson | 2 | 0 | 0.0 | 0 | 0.00 | 0 | 0 | — | 0.0 | |
| Metcalf | 1 | 0 | 0.0 | 0 | 0.00 | 0 | 0 | — | 0.0 | |

| PUNTING | No. | Avg. |
|---|---|---|
| Tupa | 80 | 40.1 |

| KICKING | XP | ATT | % | FG | ATT | % |
|---|---|---|---|---|---|---|
| Stover | 32 | 32 | 100 | 26 | 28 | 93 |

2 POINT XP
Tupa (3)
Alexander (1)

## CINCINNATI BENGALS

### RUSHING

| Last Name | No. | Yds | Avg | TD |
|---|---|---|---|---|
| Fenner | 141 | 468 | 3.3 | 1 |
| Broussard | 94 | 403 | 4.3 | 2 |
| Green | 76 | 223 | 2.9 | 1 |
| Blake | 37 | 204 | 5.5 | 1 |
| Scott | 10 | 106 | 10.6 | 0 |
| Cothran | 26 | 85 | 3.3 | 0 |
| Klingler | 17 | 85 | 5.0 | 0 |
| Ball | 2 | 0 | 0.0 | 0 |
| Ti. McGee | 1 | -18 | -18.0 | 0 |

### RECEIVING

| Last Name | No. | Yds | Avg | TD |
|---|---|---|---|---|
| Pickens | 71 | 1127 | 15.9 | 11 |
| Scott | 46 | 866 | 18.8 | 5 |
| To. McGee | 40 | 492 | 12.3 | 1 |
| Fenner | 36 | 276 | 7.7 | 1 |
| Broussard | 34 | 218 | 6.4 | 0 |
| Green | 27 | 267 | 9.9 | 1 |
| Ti. McGee | 13 | 175 | 13.5 | 1 |
| Sadowski | 11 | 54 | 4.9 | 0 |
| Query | 5 | 44 | 8.8 | 0 |
| Cothran | 4 | 24 | 6.0 | 1 |
| Ball | 1 | 4 | 4.0 | 0 |
| Klingler | 1 | -6 | -6.0 | 0 |

### PUNT RETURNS

| Last Name | No. | Yds | Avg | TD |
|---|---|---|---|---|
| Sawyer | 26 | 307 | 11.8 | 1 |
| Pickens | 9 | 62 | 6.9 | 0 |
| D. Williams | 1 | 4 | 4.0 | 0 |
| Rog. Jones | 1 | 0 | 0.0 | 0 |

### KICKOFF RETURNS

| Last Name | No. | Yds | Avg | TD |
|---|---|---|---|---|
| Ball | 42 | 915 | 21.8 | 0 |
| Scott | 15 | 342 | 22.8 | 0 |
| Hardy | 8 | 185 | 23.1 | 0 |
| Broussard | 7 | 115 | 16.4 | 0 |
| Green | 5 | 113 | 22.6 | 0 |
| Hill | 4 | 97 | 24.3 | 0 |
| Stegall | 1 | 16 | 16.0 | 0 |
| Sawyer | 1 | 14 | 14.0 | 0 |
| Tovar | 1 | 8 | 8.0 | 0 |
| To. McGee | 1 | 4 | 4.0 | 0 |
| Shaw | 1 | 1 | 1.0 | 0 |

### PASSING — PUNTING — KICKING

| PASSING | Att | Cmp | % | Yds | Yd/Att | TD | Int | — | % | RK |
|---|---|---|---|---|---|---|---|---|---|---|
| Blake | 306 | 156 | 51.0 | 2154 | 7.04 | 14 | 9 | — | 2.9 | 9 |
| Klingler | 231 | 131 | 56.7 | 1327 | 5.74 | 6 | 9 | — | 3.9 | 13 |
| Hollas | 2 | 0 | 0.0 | 0 | 0.00 | 0 | 1 | — | 50.0 | |
| Broussard | 1 | 0 | 0.0 | 0 | 0.00 | 0 | 0 | — | 0.0 | |
| L. Johnson | 1 | 1 | 100.0 | 7 | 7.00 | 1 | 0 | — | 0.0 | |

| PUNTING | No. | Avg. |
|---|---|---|
| Johnson | 80 | 43.3 |

| KICKING | XP | ATT | % | FG | ATT | % |
|---|---|---|---|---|---|---|
| Pelfrey | 24 | 25 | 96 | 28 | 33 | 85 |

2 POINT XP
Blake (1)
Broussard (1)

## HOUSTON OILERS

### RUSHING

| Last Name | No. | Yds | Avg | TD |
|---|---|---|---|---|
| White | 191 | 757 | 4.0 | 3 |
| G. Brown | 169 | 648 | 3.8 | 4 |
| Richardson | 30 | 217 | 7.2 | 1 |
| Tolliver | 12 | 37 | 3.1 | 2 |
| Carlson | 10 | 17 | 1.7 | 0 |
| Tillman | 2 | 12 | 6.0 | 0 |
| Coleman | 1 | 2 | 2.0 | 0 |
| Wellman | 1 | -3 | -3.0 | 0 |
| Givins | 1 | -5 | -5.0 | 0 |

### RECEIVING

| Last Name | No. | Yds | Avg | TD |
|---|---|---|---|---|
| Slaughter | 68 | 846 | 12.4 | 2 |
| Jeffires | 68 | 783 | 11.5 | 6 |
| Givins | 36 | 521 | 14.5 | 1 |
| White | 21 | 188 | 9.0 | 1 |
| Coleman | 20 | 298 | 14.9 | 1 |
| G. Brown | 18 | 194 | 10.8 | 1 |
| Carter | 11 | 74 | 6.7 | 1 |
| McNair | 8 | 78 | 9.8 | 0 |
| R. Lewis | 4 | 48 | 12.0 | 0 |
| R. Brown | 4 | 34 | 8.5 | 0 |
| Hannah | 3 | 24 | 8.0 | 0 |
| Maston | 2 | 12 | 6.0 | 0 |
| Mills | 1 | 4 | 4.0 | 0 |

### PUNT RETURNS

| Last Name | No. | Yds | Avg | TD |
|---|---|---|---|---|
| Givins | 37 | 210 | 5.7 | 1 |
| Hannah | 9 | 58 | 6.4 | 0 |
| Coleman | 2 | 13 | 6.5 | 0 |
| Dishman | 1 | 0 | 0.0 | 0 |
| Robertson | 1 | 0 | 0.0 | 0 |

### KICKOFF RETURNS

| Last Name | No. | Yds | Avg | TD |
|---|---|---|---|---|
| McNair | 23 | 481 | 20.9 | 0 |
| Mills | 15 | 282 | 18.8 | 0 |
| St. Jackson | 14 | 285 | 20.4 | 0 |
| White | 8 | 167 | 20.9 | 0 |
| Hannah | 5 | 116 | 23.2 | 0 |
| Tillman | 4 | 51 | 12.8 | 0 |
| Bishop | 2 | 18 | 9.0 | 0 |
| Teeter | 2 | 9 | 4.5 | 0 |
| Givins | 1 | 27 | 27.0 | 0 |

### PASSING — PUNTING — KICKING

| PASSING | Att | Cmp | % | Yds | Yd/Att | TD | Int | — | % | RK |
|---|---|---|---|---|---|---|---|---|---|---|
| Tolliver | 240 | 121 | 50.4 | 1287 | 5.36 | 6 | 7 | — | 2.9 | 14 |
| Richardson | 181 | 94 | 51.9 | 1202 | 6.64 | 6 | 6 | — | 3.3 | |
| Carlson | 132 | 59 | 44.7 | 727 | 5.51 | 1 | 4 | — | 3.0 | |
| Camarillo | 1 | 0 | 0.0 | 0 | 0.00 | 0 | 0 | — | 0.0 | |

| PUNTING | No. | Avg. |
|---|---|---|
| Camarillo | 96 | 42.9 |

| KICKING | XP | ATT | % | FG | ATT | % |
|---|---|---|---|---|---|---|
| Del Greco | 18 | 18 | 100 | 16 | 20 | 80 |

2 POINT XP
Jeffires (3)
R. Brown (2)

## SAN DIEGO CHARGERS 11-5 Bobby Ross

| Scores of Each Game | | |
|---|---|---|
| 37 | Denver | 34 |
| 27 | CINCINNATI | 10 |
| 24 | Seattle | 10 |
| 26 | L.A. Raiders | 24 |
| 20 | KANSAS CITY | 6 |
| 36 | New Orleans | 22 |
| 15 | DENVER | 20 |
| 35 | SEATTLE | 15 |
| 9 | Atlanta | 10 |
| 14 | Kansas City | 13 |
| 17 | New England | 23 |
| 31 | L.A. RAMS | 17 |
| 17 | L.A. RAIDERS | 24 |
| 15 | SAN FRANCISCO | 38 |
| 21 | N.Y. Jets | 6 |
| 37 | PITTSBURGH | 34 |

| Use Name | Pos. | Hgt. | Wgt. | Age | Int | Pts |
|---|---|---|---|---|---|---|
| Stan Brock | OT | 6'6" | 295 | 36 | | |
| Eric Jonassen | OT | 6'5" | 310 | 26 | | |
| Vaughn Parker | OT | 6'3" | 296 | 23 | | |
| Harry Swayne | OT | 6'5" | 295 | 29 | | |
| Joe Cocozzo | OG | 6'4" | 300 | 24 | | |
| Isaac Davis | OG | 6'3" | 320 | 22 | | |
| Joe Milinichik | OG | 6'5" | 300 | 31 | | |
| Courtney Hall | C | 6'2" | 281 | 26 | | |
| Curtis Whitley | C-OG | 6'1" | 285 | 25 | | |
| Raylee Johnson | DE-DT | 6'3" | 265 | 24 | | |
| Chris Mims | DE | 6'5" | 290 | 23 | | |
| Leslie O'Neal | DE | 6'4" | 265 | 30 | | |
| Reuben Davis | DT | 6'5" | 320 | 29 | | |
| Shawn Lee | DT | 6'2" | 300 | 27 | | |
| John Parrella | DT | 6'3" | 290 | 24 | | |
| Reggie White | DT | 6'4" | 300 | 24 | | |
| Blaise Winter | DT | 6'4" | 290 | 32 | | |

Eric Moten — Knee injury

| Use Name | Pos. | Hgt. | Wgt. | Age | Int | Pts |
|---|---|---|---|---|---|---|
| Lewis Bush | LB | 6'2" | 245 | 24 | | |
| Dennis Gibson | LB | 6'2" | 240 | 30 | | |
| David Griggs | LB | 6'3" | 250 | 27 | 1 | |
| Doug Miller | LB | 6'3" | 245 | 24 | | |
| Junior Seau | LB | 6'3" | 250 | 25 | | |
| Darren Carrington | DB | 6'2" | 200 | 27 | 3 | |
| Eric Castle | DB | 6'3" | 212 | 24 | | |
| Willie Clark | DB | 5'10" | 186 | 22 | | |
| Darrien Gordon | DB | 5'11" | 182 | 23 | 4 | 12 |
| Dwayne Harper | DB | 5'11" | 175 | 28 | 3 | |
| Rodney Harrison | DB | 6' | 201 | 21 | | |
| Stanley Richard | DB | 6'2" | 201 | 26 | 4 | 12 |
| Sean Vanhorse | DB | 5'10" | 180 | 26 | 2 | 6 |
| Lonnie Young | DB | 6'1" | 196 | 31 | | |

| Use Name | Pos. | Hgt. | Wgt. | Age | Int | Pts |
|---|---|---|---|---|---|---|
| Jeff Brohm | DB | 6'1" | 200 | 23 | | |
| Gale Gilbert | QB | 6'3" | 209 | 32 | | |
| Stan Humphries | QB | 6'2" | 223 | 29 | | |
| Eric Bieniemy | HB | 5'7" | 205 | 25 | | |
| Rodney Culver | HB | 5'9" | 224 | 24 | | |
| Ronnie Harmon | HB | 5'11" | 207 | 30 | | 18 |
| Natrone Means | HB-FB | 5'10" | 245 | 22 | | 72 |
| Steve Hendrickson | FB-LB | 6' | 250 | 28 | | |
| Johnnie Barnes | WR | 6'1" | 180 | 26 | | |
| Andre Coleman | WR | 5'9" | 165 | 23 | | 12 |
| Shawn Jefferson | WR | 5'11" | 180 | 25 | | 18 |
| Tony Martin | WR | 6' | 181 | 29 | | 42 |
| Mark Seay | WR | 6' | 175 | 27 | | 36 |
| David Binn | TE | 6'3" | 240 | 22 | | |
| Aaron Laing | TE | 6'3" | 264 | 23 | | |
| Deems May | TE | 6'4" | 263 | 25 | | |
| Shannon Mitchell | TE | 6'2" | 245 | 22 | | |
| Alfred Pupunu | TE | 6'2" | 265 | 24 | | 12 |
| Duane Young | TE | 6'1" | 270 | 26 | | 6 |
| John Carney | K | 5'11" | 170 | 30 | | 135 |
| Bryan Wagner | K | 6'2" | 200 | 32 | | |

## KANSAS CITY CHIEFS 9-7 Marty Schottenheimer

| Scores of Each Game | | |
|---|---|---|
| 30 | New Orleans | 17 |
| 24 | SAN FRANCISCO | 17 |
| 30 | Atlanta | 10 |
| 0 | L.A. RAMS | 16 |
| 6 | San Diego | 20 |
| 31 | Denver | 28 |
| 38 | SEATTLE | 23 |
| 10 | Buffalo | 44 |
| 13 | L.A. RAIDERS | 3 |
| 13 | SAN DIEGO | 14 |
| 20 | CLEVELAND | 13 |
| 9 | Seattle | 10 |
| 17 | DENVER | *20 |
| 28 | Miami | 45 |
| 31 | HOUSTON | 9 |
| 19 | L.A. Raiders | 9 |

| Use Name | Pos. | Hgt. | Wgt. | Age | Int | Pts |
|---|---|---|---|---|---|---|
| John Alt | OT | 6'7" | 307 | 32 | | |
| Derrick Graham | OT | 6'4" | 310 | 27 | | |
| Ricky Siglar | OT | 6'7" | 307 | 28 | | |
| Lindsay Knapp | OG-OT | 6'6" | 290 | 24 | | |
| Will Shields | OG | 6'2" | 300 | 22 | | |
| Dave Szott | OG | 6'4" | 290 | 26 | | |
| Joe Valerio | OG-C | 6'5" | 295 | 25 | | 12 |
| Danny Villa | OG | 6'5" | 308 | 29 | | |
| Tim Grunhard | C | 6'2" | 299 | 26 | | |
| Vaughn Booker | DE | 6'5" | 283 | 26 | | |
| Pellom McDaniels | DE | 6'3" | 275 | 26 | | |
| Neil Smith | DE | 6'4" | 273 | 28 | 2 | |
| Greg Kragen | DT | 6'3" | 265 | 32 | | |
| Darren Mickell | DE | 6'4" | 284 | 24 | | |
| Joe Phillips | DT-NT | 6'5" | 300 | 31 | | |
| Dan Saleaumua | DT | 6' | 300 | 29 | | |
| Rob Waldrop | DT | 6'1" | 276 | 22 | | |

Tim Newton — Neck injury

| Use Name | Pos. | Hgt. | Wgt. | Age | Int | Pts |
|---|---|---|---|---|---|---|
| Arnold Ale | LB | 6'3" | 234 | 24 | | |
| Anthony Davis | LB | 6' | 231 | 25 | | |
| Jaime Fields | LB | 5'11" | 236 | 24 | | |
| Rick Hamilton (from WASH) | LB | 6'2" | 241 | 24 | | |
| George Jamison | LB | 6'1" | 235 | 31 | | |
| Greg Manusky | LB | 6'1" | 233 | 28 | | |
| Tracy Rogers | LB | 6'2" | 241 | 27 | | |
| Tracy Simien | LB | 6'1" | 250 | 27 | | |
| Derrick Thomas | LB-DE | 6'3" | 247 | 27 | | 2 |
| Jerrol Williams | LB | 6'4" | 240 | 27 | | |
| Darren Anderson | DB | 5'10" | 180 | 25 | | |
| Dale Carter | DB | 6'1" | 188 | 24 | 2 | |
| Mark Collins | DB | 5'10" | 196 | 30 | 2 | 6 |
| Matt Gay | DB | 6' | 197 | 24 | | |
| Monty Grow | DB | 6'3" | 214 | 22 | 1 | |
| Charles Mincy | DB | 5'11" | 197 | 24 | 3 | |
| Jay Taylor | DB | 5'10" | 170 | 26 | 1 | |
| Doug Terry | DB | 5'11" | 204 | 24 | | |
| Tim Watson | DB | 6'1" | 215 | 24 | | |
| William White | DB | 5'10" | 200 | 28 | 2 | |
| David Whitmore | DB | 6' | 222 | 27 | | |

| Use Name | Pos. | Hgt. | Wgt. | Age | Int | Pts |
|---|---|---|---|---|---|---|
| Matt Blundin | QB | 6'6" | 233 | 25 | | |
| Steve Bono | QB | 6'4" | 215 | 32 | | |
| Joe Montana | QB | 6'2" | 205 | 38 | | |
| Marcus Allen | HB | 6'2" | 210 | 34 | | 44 |
| Ron Dickerson | HB | 6' | 225 | 23 | | |
| Greg Hill | HB | 5'11" | 205 | 22 | | 6 |
| Kimble Anders | FB | 5'11" | 230 | 27 | | 18 |
| Donnell Bennett | FB | 6' | 241 | 21 | | 12 |
| J.J. Birden | WR | 5'9" | 165 | 29 | | 26 |
| Willie Davis | WR | 6' | 181 | 26 | | 32 |
| Lake Dawson | WR | 6'1" | 204 | 22 | | 12 |
| Danan Hughes | WR | 6'1" | 206 | 23 | | |
| Eric Martin | WR | 6'1" | 207 | 32 | | 6 |
| Chris Penn | WR | 6' | 198 | 23 | | |
| Michael Young | WR | 6'1" | 183 | 32 | | |
| Keith Cash | TE | 6'4" | 248 | 25 | | 12 |
| Tracy Greene | TE | 6'5" | 282 | 21 | | 6 |
| Jimmie Johnson | TE | 6'2" | 260 | 27 | | |
| Tommie Stowers | TE | 6'3" | 240 | 27 | | |
| Derrick Walker | TE | 6' | 244 | 27 | | 12 |
| Louie Aguiar | K | 6'2" | 222 | 27 | | |
| Lin Elliott | K | 6' | 182 | 25 | | 105 |

## LOS ANGELES RAIDERS 9-7 Art Shell

| Scores of Each Game | | |
|---|---|---|
| 14 | San Francisco | 44 |
| 9 | SEATTLE | 38 |
| 48 | Denver | 16 |
| 24 | SAN DIEGO | 26 |
| 21 | New England | 17 |
| 17 | Miami | *20 |
| 30 | ATLANTA | 17 |
| 17 | HOUSTON | 14 |
| 3 | Kansas City | 13 |
| 20 | L.A. Rams | 17 |
| 24 | NEW ORLEANS | 19 |
| 3 | PITTSBURGH | 21 |
| 24 | San Diego | 17 |
| 23 | DENVER | 13 |
| 17 | Seattle | 16 |
| 9 | KANSAS CITY | 19 |

| Use Name | Pos. | Hgt. | Wgt. | Age | Int | Pts |
|---|---|---|---|---|---|---|
| Robert Jenkins | OT | 6'5" | 295 | 30 | | |
| Gerald Perry | OT | 6'6" | 290 | 29 | | |
| Greg Skrepenak | OT | 6'6" | 300 | 24 | | |
| Bruce Wilkerson | OT | 6'5" | 295 | 30 | | |
| Kevin Gogan | OG | 6'7" | 315 | 29 | | |
| Max Montoya | OG | 6'5" | 295 | 38 | | |
| Steve Wisniewski | OG | 6'4" | 285 | 27 | | |
| Don Mosebar | C | 6'6" | 295 | 32 | | |
| Dan Turk | C | 6'4" | 290 | 32 | | |
| Aundray Bruce | DE | 6'5' | 260 | 28 | | |
| Scott Davis | DE | 6'7" | 285 | 29 | | |
| Nolan Harrison | DE-DT | 6'5" | 285 | 25 | | |
| Anthony Smith | DE | 6'3" | 260 | 27 | | 6 |
| Alberto White | DE | 6'3" | 245 | 23 | | |
| Jerry Ball | DT | 6'1" | 315 | 29 | | |
| Chester McGlockton | DT | 6'4" | 310 | 24 | | |
| Austin Robbins | DT | 6'6" | 290 | 23 | | |

| Use Name | Pos. | Hgt. | Wgt. | Age | Int | Pts |
|---|---|---|---|---|---|---|
| Greg Biekert | LB | 6'2" | 235 | 25 | 1 | |
| James Folston | LB | 6'3" | 235 | 23 | | |
| Rob Fredrickson | LB | 6'4" | 240 | 23 | | |
| Rob Holmberg | LB | 6'3" | 225 | 23 | | |
| Mike Jones | LB | 6'1" | 230 | 25 | | |
| Winston Moss | LB | 6'3" | 235 | 28 | | |
| Aaron Wallace | LB | 6'3" | 235 | 27 | | |
| Eddie Anderson | DB | 6'1" | 210 | 31 | | |
| Patrick Bates | DB | 6'3" | 215 | 23 | | |
| Cary Brabham | DB | 6' | 195 | 24 | | |
| Donald Frank | DB | 6' | 195 | 28 | 1 | |
| Derrick Hoskins | DB | 6'2" | 200 | 23 | | |
| Dan Land | DB | 6' | 195 | 29 | | |
| Albert Lewis | DB | 6'2" | 195 | 29 | | |
| Terry McDaniel | DB | 5'10" | 180 | 29 | 7 | 18 |
| James Trapp | DB | 6' | 180 | 24 | | |
| Lionel Washington | DB | 6' | 185 | 33 | 3 | 6 |

| Use Name | Pos. | Hgt. | Wgt. | Age | Int | Pts |
|---|---|---|---|---|---|---|
| Vince Evans | QB | 6'2" | 215 | 39 | | |
| Billy Joe Hobert | QB | 6'3" | 225 | 23 | | |
| Jeff Hostetler | QB | 6'3" | 215 | 33 | | 12 |
| Calvin Jones | HB | 5'11" | 205 | 23 | | |
| Napoleon McCallum | HB | 6'2" | 225 | 30 | | 6 |
| Tyrone Montgomery | HB | 6' | 190 | 24 | | 6 |
| Harvey Williams | HB | 6'2" | 210 | 27 | | 44 |
| Wes Bender | FB | 5'10" | 235 | 24 | | |
| Jarrod Bunch | FB | 6'2" | 248 | 26 | | |
| Tom Rathman | FB | 6'1" | 230 | 31 | | |
| Tim Brown | WR | 6' | 195 | 28 | | 54 |
| Daryl Hobbs | WR | 6'2" | 175 | 26 | | |
| Raghib Ismail | WR | 5'10" | 175 | 24 | | 30 |
| James Jett | WR | 5'10" | 165 | 23 | | |
| Alexander Wright | WR | 6' | 195 | 27 | | 12 |
| John Duff | TE | 6'7" | 250 | 27 | | |
| Andrew Glover | TE | 6'6" | 245 | 27 | | 12 |
| Kevin Smith | TE | 6'4" | 255 | 25 | | |
| Jamie Williams | TE | 6'4" | 250 | 34 | | |
| Jeff Gossett | K | 6'2" | 190 | 37 | | |
| Jeff Jaeger | K | 5'11" | 190 | 29 | | 97 |

Greg Robinson — Knee injury

## DENVER BRONCOS 7-9 Wade Phillips

| Scores of Each Game | | |
|---|---|---|
| 34 | SAN DIEGO | 37 |
| 22 | N.Y. Jets | *25 |
| 16 | L.A. RAIDERS | 48 |
| 20 | Buffalo | 27 |
| 16 | Seattle | 9 |
| 28 | KANSAS CITY | 31 |
| 20 | San Diego | 15 |
| 26 | CLEVELAND | 14 |
| 21 | L.A. Rams | 27 |
| 17 | SEATTLE | 10 |
| 32 | ATLANTA | 28 |
| 15 | CINCINNATI | 13 |
| 20 | Kansas City | *17 |
| 13 | L.A. Raiders | 23 |
| 19 | San Francisco | 42 |
| 28 | NEW ORLEANS | 30 |

| Use Name | Pos. | Hgt. | Wgt. | Age | Int | Pts |
|---|---|---|---|---|---|---|
| Russell Freeman | OT | 6'7" | 290 | 24 | | |
| Ken Lanier | OT | 6'3" | 290 | 35 | | |
| Don Maggs | OT | 6'5" | 290 | 32 | | |
| Kirk Scrafford | OT | 6'6" | 265 | 27 | | |
| Gary Zimmerman | OT | 6'6" | 294 | 32 | | |
| Brian Habib | OG | 6'7" | 299 | 29 | | |
| Jon Melander | OG | 6'7" | 280 | 27 | | |
| Tom Nalen | C-OG | 6'2" | 280 | 23 | | |
| Dave Widell | C-OG | 6'6" | 292 | 29 | | |
| Shane Dronett | DE | 6'6" | 275 | 23 | | |
| Simon Fletcher | DE | 6'5" | 240 | 32 | 1 | |
| Harald Hasselbach | DE | 6'6" | 280 | 26 | | |
| Willie Oshodin | DE | 6'4" | 265 | 24 | | |
| Jeff Robinson | DE | 6'4" | 265 | 24 | | |
| Ted Washington | DT | 6'4" | 295 | 26 | 1 | |
| Dan Williams | DT | 6'4" | 290 | 24 | 1 | |

Keith Kartz — Knee injury
Bob Meeks — Neck injury
Darren Drozdov — Leg injury

| Use Name | Pos. | Hgt. | Wgt. | Age | Int | Pts |
|---|---|---|---|---|---|---|
| Allen Aldridge | LB | 6'1" | 245 | 22 | | |
| Elijah Alexander | LB | 6'2" | 230 | 24 | 1 | |
| Keith Burns | LB | 6'2" | 245 | 22 | | |
| Mike Croel | LB | 6'3" | 231 | 25 | | |
| Mitch Donahue | LB | 6'2" | 254 | 26 | | |
| Richard Harvey | LB | 6'1" | 242 | 27 | | |
| Ray Jacobs | LB | 6'2" | 244 | 22 | | |
| Karl Mecklenburg | LB | 6'3" | 235 | 34 | | |
| Glenall Sanders | LB | 6'1" | 237 | 27 | | |
| Dave Wyman | LB | 6'2" | 248 | 30 | | |
| Steve Atwater | DB | 6'3" | 217 | 27 | 1 | |
| Ronnie Bradford | DB | 5'10" | 188 | 23 | | |
| Butler By'not'e | DB | 5'9" | 190 | 21 | | |
| Ray Crockett | DB | 5'10" | 185 | 27 | 2 | |
| Randy Fuller | DB | 5'9" | 173 | 24 | | |
| Darryl Hall | DB | 6'2" | 210 | 28 | | |
| Randy Hilliard | DB | 5'11" | 165 | 27 | 2 | |
| Rondell Jones | DB | 6'2" | 210 | 23 | 2 | |
| Ben Smith | DB | 5'11" | 185 | 27 | 1 | |
| Dennis Smith | DB | 6'3" | 200 | 35 | | |
| Charles Swann | DB | 6'1" | 188 | 23 | | |

| Use Name | Pos. | Hgt. | Wgt. | Age | Int | Pts |
|---|---|---|---|---|---|---|
| John Elway | QB | 6'3" | 215 | 34 | | 24 |
| Will Furrer | QB | 6'3" | 210 | 26 | | |
| Hugh Millen | QB | 6'5" | 216 | 30 | | |
| Rod Bernstine | HB-FB | 6'3" | 238 | 29 | | |
| Glyn Milburn | HB | 5'8" | 177 | 23 | | 24 |
| Leonard Russell | HB | 6'2" | 235 | 24 | | 54 |
| Deon Strother | HB | 5'11" | 213 | 22 | | |
| Derrick Clark | FB | 6'1" | 235 | 23 | | 18 |
| Reggie Rivers | FB | 6'1" | 215 | 26 | | 12 |
| Jeff Campbell | WR | 5'8" | 167 | 26 | | 6 |
| Tony Kimbrough | WR | 6'2" | 192 | 23 | | |
| Anthony Miller | WR | 5'11" | 190 | 29 | | 32 |
| Mike Pritchard | WR | 5'10" | 190 | 24 | | 6 |
| Derek Russell | WR | 6' | 195 | 25 | | 6 |
| Cedric Tillman | WR | 6'2" | 204 | 24 | | 6 |
| Dwayne Carswell | TE | 6'3" | 261 | 22 | | |
| Jerry Evans | TE | 6'4" | 250 | 25 | | 12 |
| Shannon Sharpe | TE | 6'2" | 230 | 26 | | 28 |
| Jason Elam | K | 5'11" | 192 | 24 | | 119 |
| Tom Rouen | K | 6'3" | 215 | 26 | | |

Melvin Bonner — Leg injury

## SEATTLE SEAHAWKS 6-10 Tom Flores

| Scores of Each Game | | |
|---|---|---|
| 28 | Washington | 7 |
| 38 | L.A. Raiders | 9 |
| 10 | SAN DIEGO | 24 |
| 30 | PITTSBURGH | 13 |
| 15 | Indianapolis | 17 |
| 9 | DENVER | 16 |
| 23 | Kansas City | 38 |
| 15 | San Diego | 35 |
| 17 | CINCINNATI | *20 |
| 10 | Denver | 17 |
| 22 | TAMPA BAY | 21 |
| 10 | KANSAS CITY | 9 |
| 19 | INDIANAPOLIS | 31 |
| 16 | Houston | 14 |
| 16 | L.A. RAIDERS | 17 |
| 9 | Cleveland | 35 |

| Use Name | Pos. | Hgt. | Wgt. | Age | Int | Pts |
|---|---|---|---|---|---|---|
| James Atkins | OT | 6'6" | 303 | 24 | | |
| Howard Ballard | OT | 6'6" | 332 | 30 | | |
| Mike Keim | OT | 6'7" | 302 | 28 | | |
| Ray Roberts | OT | 6'6" | 308 | 25 | | |
| Jeff Blackshear | OG | 6'6" | 323 | 25 | | |
| Bill Hitchcock | OG | 6'6" | 306 | 29 | | |
| Kevin Mawae | OG | 6'4" | 288 | 23 | | |
| Ray Donaldson | C | 6'3" | 300 | 36 | | |
| Joe Tofflemire | C | 6'3" | 277 | 29 | | |
| Antonio Edwards | DE | 6'3" | 271 | 24 | | |
| Michael McCrary | DE | 6'4" | 267 | 24 | | |
| Mike Sinclair | DE | 6'4" | 271 | 26 | | |
| Brent Williams | DE | 6'4" | 283 | 29 | | |
| Sam Adams | DT | 6'3" | 285 | 21 | | |
| Mike Frier (from CIN) | DT | 6'5" | 299 | 25 | | |
| Cortez Kennedy | DT | 6'3" | 293 | 26 | | |
| Joe Nash | DT | 6'2" | 278 | 33 | | |
| Tyrone Rodgers | DT | 6'3" | 276 | 25 | | |
| Team | | | | | | 2 |

Mitch Frerotte — Neck injury

| Use Name | Pos. | Hgt. | Wgt. | Age | Int | Pts |
|---|---|---|---|---|---|---|
| Duane Bickett | DB | 6'5" | 245 | 31 | | |
| David Brandon | LB | 6'4" | 240 | 29 | | |
| Rufus Porter | LB | 6'1" | 231 | 29 | 1 | |
| Bob Spitulski | LB | 6'3" | 246 | 24 | 1 | |
| Rod Stephens | LB | 6'1" | 237 | 28 | | |
| Dean Wells | LB | 6'3" | 242 | 24 | | |
| Terry Wooden | LB | 6'3" | 239 | 27 | 3 | 6 |
| Jay Bellamy | DB | 5'11" | 193 | 22 | | |
| Robert Blackmon | DB | 6' | 203 | 27 | 1 | |
| Tony Brown | DB | 5'9" | 183 | 24 | | |
| Carlton Gray | DB | 6' | 196 | 23 | 2 | |
| Patrick Hunter | DB | 5'11" | 184 | 29 | 3 | |
| Dion Lambert | DB | 6'1" | 190 | 25 | | |
| Dave McCloughan | DB | 6'1" | 186 | 27 | | |
| Eugene Robinson | DB | 6' | 195 | 31 | 3 | |
| Rafael Robinson | DB | 5'11" | 195 | 25 | 1 | |
| Terry Taylor | DB | 5'10" | 185 | 33 | 1 | |
| Orlando Watters | DB | 5'11" | 173 | 22 | 3 | 6 |

Kirby Jackson — Knee injury
Nate Odomes — Knee injury

| Use Name | Pos. | Hgt. | Wgt. | Age | Int | Pts |
|---|---|---|---|---|---|---|
| Stan Gelbaugh | QB | 6'3" | 215 | 31 | | |
| Dan McGwire | QB | 6'8" | 239 | 26 | | |
| Rick Mirer | QB | 6'2" | 211 | 24 | | |
| Beno Bryant | HB | 5'9" | 175 | 23 | | |
| Lamar Smith | HB | 5'11" | 224 | 23 | | |
| Mack Strong | HB-FB | 6' | 222 | 22 | | 12 |
| Jon Vaughn (to KC) | HB | 5'9" | 203 | 24 | | 26 |
| Chris Warren | HB | 6'2" | 225 | 27 | | 68 |
| Tracy Johnson | FB | 6' | 242 | 27 | | 12 |
| Steve Smith | FB | 6'1" | 242 | 30 | | 18 |
| Michael Bates | WR | 5'10" | 196 | 24 | | 6 |
| Brian Blades | WR | 5'11" | 186 | 29 | | 26 |
| Ronnie Harris (from NE) | WR | 5'11" | 180 | 24 | | |
| Kelvin Martin | WR | 5'9" | 171 | 29 | | 6 |
| James McKnight | WR | 6' | 186 | 22 | | 6 |
| Robb Thomas | WR | 5'11" | 175 | 28 | | |
| Terrence Warren | WR | 6'1" | 205 | 25 | | |
| Carlester Crumpler | TE | 6'6" | 254 | 29 | | |
| Ferrell Edmunds | TE | 6'6" | 254 | 28 | | |
| Paul Green | TE | 6'3" | 230 | 27 | | 6 |
| Trey Junkin | TE | 6'2" | 241 | 32 | | 6 |
| John Kasay | K | 5'10" | 197 | 24 | | 85 |
| Rick Tuten | K | 6'2" | 218 | 29 | | 2 |

Reggie Barrett — Knee injury

## SAN DIEGO CHARGERS

### RUSHING

| Last Name | No. | Yds | Avg | TD |
|---|---|---|---|---|
| Means | 343 | 1350 | 3.9 | 12 |
| Bieniemy | 73 | 295 | 4.0 | 0 |
| Harmon | 25 | 94 | 3.8 | 1 |
| Culver | 8 | 63 | 7.9 | 0 |
| Jefferson | 3 | 40 | 13.3 | 0 |
| Humphries | 19 | 19 | 1.0 | 0 |
| Hendrickson | 1 | 3 | 3.0 | 0 |
| Gilbert | 8 | -3 | -0.4 | 0 |
| Martin | 2 | -9 | -4.5 | 0 |

### RECEIVING

| Last Name | No. | Yds | Avg | TD |
|---|---|---|---|---|
| Seay | 58 | 645 | 11.1 | 6 |
| Harmon | 58 | 615 | 10.6 | 1 |
| Martin | 50 | 885 | 17.7 | 7 |
| Jefferson | 43 | 627 | 14.6 | 3 |
| Means | 39 | 235 | 6.0 | 0 |
| Pupunu | 21 | 214 | 10.2 | 2 |
| D. Young | 17 | 217 | 12.8 | 1 |
| Mitchell | 11 | 105 | 9.5 | 0 |
| Bieniemy | 5 | 48 | 9.6 | 0 |
| May | 2 | 22 | 11.0 | 0 |
| Barnes | 1 | 6 | 6.0 | 0 |

### PUNT RETURNS

| Last Name | No. | Yds | Avg | TD |
|---|---|---|---|---|
| Gordon | 36 | 475 | 13.2 | 2 |

### KICKOFF RETURNS

| Last Name | No. | Yds | Avg | TD |
|---|---|---|---|---|
| Coleman | 49 | 1293 | 26.4 | 2 |
| Harmon | 9 | 157 | 17.4 | 0 |
| Martin | 8 | 167 | 20.9 | 0 |
| Mitchell | 1 | 18 | 18.0 | 0 |
| Parker | 1 | 1 | 1.0 | 0 |

### PASSING — PUNTING — KICKING — Statistics

**PASSING**

| Last Name | Att | Cmp | % | Yds | Yd/Att | TD | Int— | % | RK |
|---|---|---|---|---|---|---|---|---|---|
| Humphries | 453 | 264 | 58.3 | 3209 | 7.08 | 17 | 12— | 2.6 | 5 |
| Gilbert | 67 | 41 | 61.2 | 410 | 6.33 | 3 | 1— | 1.5 | |
| Martin | 1 | 1 | 100 | 6 | 6.00 | 0 | 1— | 100.0 | |
| Means | 1 | 0 | 0.0 | 0 | 0.00 | 0 | 0— | 0.0 | |

**PUNTING**

| Last Name | No. | Avg. |
|---|---|---|
| Wagner | 65 | 41.6 |

**KICKING**

| Last Name | XP | ATT | % | FG | ATT | % |
|---|---|---|---|---|---|---|
| Carney | 33 | 33 | 100 | 34 | 38 | 89 |

**2 POINT XP**
Harmon (3)

## KANSAS CITY CHIEFS

### RUSHING

| Last Name | No. | Yds | Avg | TD |
|---|---|---|---|---|
| Allen | 189 | 709 | 3.8 | 7 |
| Hill | 141 | 574 | 4.1 | 1 |
| Anders | 62 | 231 | 3.7 | 2 |
| Bennett | 46 | 178 | 3.9 | 2 |
| Dawson | 3 | 24 | 8.0 | 0 |
| Montana | 18 | 17 | 0.9 | 0 |
| Dickerson | 1 | 0 | 0.0 | 0 |
| Bono | 4 | -1 | -0.3 | 0 |

### RECEIVING

| Last Name | No. | Yds | Avg | TD |
|---|---|---|---|---|
| Anders | 67 | 525 | 7.8 | 1 |
| W. Davis | 51 | 822 | 16.1 | 5 |
| Birden | 48 | 637 | 13.3 | 4 |
| Allen | 42 | 349 | 8.3 | 0 |
| Dawson | 37 | 537 | 14.5 | 2 |
| D. walker | 36 | 382 | 10.6 | 2 |
| Martin | 21 | 307 | 14.6 | 1 |
| Cash | 19 | 192 | 10.1 | 2 |
| Hill | 16 | 92 | 5.8 | 0 |
| Hughes | 7 | 80 | 11.4 | 0 |
| Bennett | 7 | 53 | 7.6 | 0 |
| Greene | 6 | 69 | 11.5 | 1 |
| Penn | 3 | 24 | 8.0 | 0 |
| Dickerson | 2 | 11 | 5.5 | 0 |
| Johnson | 2 | 7 | 3.5 | 0 |
| Valerio | 2 | 5 | 2.5 | 2 |

### PUNT RETURNS

| Last Name | No. | Yds | Avg | TD |
|---|---|---|---|---|
| Hughes | 27 | 192 | 7.1 | 0 |
| Carter | 16 | 124 | 7.8 | 0 |

### KICKOFF RETURNS

| Last Name | No. | Yds | Avg | TD |
|---|---|---|---|---|
| Dickerson | 21 | 472 | 22.5 | 0 |
| Hughes | 15 | 386 | 25.7 | 1 |
| Penn | 9 | 194 | 21.6 | 0 |
| Anders | 2 | 36 | 18.0 | 0 |
| Booker | 2 | 10 | 5.0 | 0 |
| Bennett | 1 | 12 | 12.0 | 0 |

### PASSING — PUNTING — KICKING

**PASSING**

| Last Name | Att | Cmp | % | Yds | Yd/Att | TD | Int— | % | RK |
|---|---|---|---|---|---|---|---|---|---|
| Montana | 493 | 299 | 60.6 | 3283 | 6.66 | 16 | 9— | 1.8 | 4 |
| Bono | 117 | 66 | 56.4 | 796 | 6.80 | 4 | 4— | 3.4 | |
| Blundin | 5 | 1 | 20.0 | 13 | 2.60 | 0 | 1— | 20.0 | |

**PUNTING**

| Last Name | No. | Avg. |
|---|---|---|
| Aguiar | 85 | 42.1 |

**KICKING**

| Last Name | XP | ATT | % | FG | ATT | % |
|---|---|---|---|---|---|---|
| Elliott | 30 | 30 | 100 | 25 | 30 | 83 |

**2 POINT XP**
Allen (1)
Birden (1)
W. Davis (1)

## LOS ANGELES RAIDERS

### RUSHING

| Last Name | No. | Yds | Avg | TD |
|---|---|---|---|---|
| H. Williams | 282 | 983 | 3.5 | 4 |
| Hostetler | 46 | 159 | 3.5 | 2 |
| Rathman | 28 | 118 | 4.2 | 0 |
| Montgomery | 36 | 97 | 2.7 | 0 |
| C. Jones | 22 | 93 | 4.2 | 0 |
| Ismail | 4 | 31 | 7.8 | 0 |
| Evans | 6 | 24 | 4.0 | 0 |
| McCallum | 3 | 5 | 1.7 | 1 |
| K. Smith | 1 | 2 | 2.0 | 0 |

### RECEIVING

| Last Name | No. | Yds | Avg | TD |
|---|---|---|---|---|
| Brown | 89 | 1309 | 14.7 | 9 |
| H. Williams | 47 | 391 | 8.3 | 3 |
| Ismail | 34 | 513 | 15.1 | 5 |
| Glover | 33 | 371 | 11.2 | 2 |
| Rathman | 26 | 194 | 7.5 | 0 |
| Wright | 16 | 294 | 18.4 | 2 |
| Jett | 15 | 253 | 16.9 | 0 |
| Montgomery | 8 | 126 | 15.8 | 1 |
| Hobbs | 5 | 52 | 10.4 | 0 |
| J. Williams | 3 | 25 | 8.3 | 0 |
| Bender | 2 | 14 | 7.0 | 0 |
| C. Jones | 2 | 6 | 3.0 | 0 |
| K. Smith | 1 | 8 | 8.0 | 0 |

### PUNT RETURNS

| Last Name | No. | Yds | Avg | TD |
|---|---|---|---|---|
| T. Brown | 40 | 487 | 12.2 | 0 |

### KICKOFF RETURNS

| Last Name | No. | Yds | Avg | TD |
|---|---|---|---|---|
| Ismail | 43 | 923 | 21.5 | 0 |
| Wright | 10 | 282 | 28.2 | 0 |
| H. Williams | 8 | 153 | 19.1 | 0 |
| J. Williams | 1 | 0 | 0.0 | 0 |

### PASSING — PUNTING — KICKING

**PASSING**

| Last Name | Att | Cmp | % | Yds | Yd/Att | TD | Int— | % | RK |
|---|---|---|---|---|---|---|---|---|---|
| Hostetler | 454 | 263 | 57.9 | 3334 | 7.34 | 20 | 16— | 3.5 | 6 |
| Evans | 33 | 18 | 54.5 | 222 | 6.73 | 2 | 0— | 0.0 | |

**PUNTING**

| Last Name | No. | Avg. |
|---|---|---|
| Gossett | 77 | 43.9 |

**KICKING**

| Last Name | XP | ATT | % | FG | ATT | % |
|---|---|---|---|---|---|---|
| Jaeger | 31 | 31 | 100 | 22 | 28 | 79 |

**2 POINT XP**
H. Williams (1)

## DENVER BRONCOS

### RUSHING

| Last Name | No. | Yds | Avg | TD |
|---|---|---|---|---|
| L. Russell | 190 | 620 | 3.3 | 9 |
| Elway | 58 | 235 | 4.1 | 4 |
| Milbum | 58 | 201 | 3.5 | 1 |
| Clark | 56 | 168 | 3.0 | 3 |
| Bernstine | 17 | 91 | 5.4 | 0 |
| Rivers | 43 | 83 | 1.9 | 2 |
| Millen | 5 | 57 | 11.4 | 0 |
| Campbell | 2 | 6 | 3.0 | 0 |
| D. Russell | 1 | 6 | 6.0 | 0 |
| Miller | 1 | 3 | 3.0 | 0 |

### RECEIVING

| Last Name | No. | Yds | Avg | TD |
|---|---|---|---|---|
| Sharpe | 87 | 1010 | 11.6 | 4 |
| Milbum | 77 | 549 | 7.1 | 3 |
| Miller | 60 | 1107 | 18.5 | 5 |
| L. Russell | 38 | 227 | 6.0 | 0 |
| Tillman | 28 | 455 | 16.3 | 1 |
| D. Russell | 25 | 342 | 13.7 | 1 |
| Rivers | 20 | 136 | 6.8 | 0 |
| Pritchard | 19 | 271 | 14.3 | 1 |
| Evans | 13 | 127 | 9.8 | 2 |
| Bernstine | 9 | 70 | 7.8 | 0 |
| Clark | 9 | 47 | 5.2 | 0 |
| Kimbrough | 2 | 20 | 10.0 | 0 |
| Campbell | 1 | 22 | 22.0 | 1 |

### PUNT RETURNS

| Last Name | No. | Yds | Avg | TD |
|---|---|---|---|---|
| Milburn | 41 | 379 | 9.2 | 0 |

### KICKOFF RETURNS

| Last Name | No. | Yds | Avg | TD |
|---|---|---|---|---|
| Milbum | 37 | 793 | 21.4 | 0 |
| By'not'e | 24 | 545 | 22.7 | 0 |
| D. Russell | 5 | 105 | 21.0 | 0 |
| Campbell | 3 | 24 | 8.0 | 0 |
| Clark | 3 | 34 | 11.3 | 0 |
| Swann | 1 | 16 | 16.0 | 0 |
| Evans | 1 | 6 | 6.0 | 0 |
| Carswell | 1 | 0 | 0.0 | 0 |

### PASSING — PUNTING — KICKING

**PASSING**

| Last Name | Att | Cmp | % | Yds | Yd/Att | TD | Int— | % | RK |
|---|---|---|---|---|---|---|---|---|---|
| Elway | 494 | 307 | 62.1 | 3490 | 7.06 | 16 | 10— | 2.0 | 2 |
| Millen | 131 | 81 | 61.8 | 893 | 6.82 | 2 | 3— | 2.3 | |
| Rivers | 1 | 0 | 0.0 | 0 | 0.00 | 0 | 0— | 0.0 | |

**PUNTING**

| Last Name | No. | Avg. |
|---|---|---|
| Rouen | 75 | 42.9 |

**KICKING**

| Last Name | XP | ATT | % | FG | ATT | % |
|---|---|---|---|---|---|---|
| Elam | 29 | 29 | 100 | 30 | 37 | 81 |

**2 POINT XP**
Sharpe (2)
Miller (1)

## SEATTLE SEAHAWKS

### RUSHING

| Last Name | No. | Yds | Avg | TD |
|---|---|---|---|---|
| C. Warren | 333 | 1545 | 4.6 | 9 |
| Mirer | 34 | 153 | 4.5 | 0 |
| Strong | 27 | 114 | 4.2 | 2 |
| Vaughn | 27 | 96 | 3.6 | 1 |
| S. Smith | 26 | 80 | 3.1 | 2 |
| Johnson | 12 | 44 | 3.7 | 2 |
| Blades | 2 | 32 | 16.0 | 0 |
| T. Warren | 3 | 15 | 5.0 | 0 |
| Gelbaugh | 1 | 10 | 10.0 | 0 |
| B. Bryant | 1 | 6 | 6.0 | 0 |
| L. Smith | 2 | -1 | -0.5 | 0 |
| Bates | 2 | -4 | -2.0 | 0 |
| McGwire | 10 | -6 | -0.6 | 0 |

### RECEIVING

| Last Name | No. | Yds | Avg | TD |
|---|---|---|---|---|
| Blades | 81 | 1086 | 13.4 | 4 |
| Martin | 56 | 681 | 12.2 | 1 |
| C. Warren | 41 | 323 | 7.9 | 2 |
| Green | 30 | 208 | 6.9 | 1 |
| Johnson | 10 | 91 | 9.1 | 0 |
| Edmunds | 7 | 43 | 6.1 | 0 |
| Bates | 5 | 112 | 22.4 | 1 |
| Thomas | 4 | 70 | 17.5 | 0 |
| Strong | 3 | 3 | 1.0 | 0 |
| Crumpler | 2 | 19 | 9.5 | 0 |
| McKnight | 1 | 25 | 25.0 | 1 |
| Vaughn | 1 | 5 | 5.0 | 1 |
| Junkin | 1 | 1 | 1.0 | 1 |

### PUNT RETURNS

| Last Name | No. | Yds | Avg | TD |
|---|---|---|---|---|
| Martin | 33 | 280 | 8.5 | 0 |
| McCloughan | 3 | 26 | 8.7 | 0 |
| B. Bryant | 1 | 31 | 31.0 | 0 |

### KICKOFF RETURNS

| Last Name | No. | Yds | Avg | TD |
|---|---|---|---|---|
| Vaughn | 33 | 829 | 25.1 | 2 |
| Bates | 26 | 508 | 19.5 | 0 |
| T. Warren | 14 | 350 | 25.0 | 0 |
| B. Bryant | 7 | 136 | 19.4 | 0 |
| Martin | 2 | 30 | 15.0 | 0 |

### PASSING — PUNTING — KICKING

**PASSING**

| Last Name | Att | Cmp | % | Yds | Yd/Att | TD | Int— | % | RK |
|---|---|---|---|---|---|---|---|---|---|
| Mirer | 381 | 195 | 51.2 | 2151 | 5.65 | 11 | 7— | 1.8 | 12 |
| McGwire | 105 | 51 | 48.6 | 578 | 5.65 | 1 | 2— | 1.9 | |
| Gelbaugh | 11 | 7 | 63.6 | 80 | 7.27 | 1 | 0— | 0.0 | |
| Tuten | 1 | 0 | 0.0 | 0 | 0.00 | 0 | 0— | 0.0 | |

**PUNTING**

| Last Name | No. | Avg. |
|---|---|---|
| Tuten | 91 | 42.9 |

**KICKING**

| Last Name | XP | ATT | % | FG | ATT | % |
|---|---|---|---|---|---|---|
| Kasay | 25 | 26 | 96 | 20 | 24 | 83 |

**2 POINT XP**
C. Warren (1)
Blades (1)
Vaughn (1)
Tuten (1)

December 31, 1994 at Miami, Fla. (Attendance 67,487)

**SCORING**

| | | | | | | |
|---|---|---|---|---|---|---|
| KANSAS CITY | 14 | 3 | 0 | 0 | - | 17 |
| MIAMI | 7 | 10 | 10 | 0 | - | 27 |

**First Quarter**
K.C.    D. Walker, 1 yard pass from Montana
    PAT — Elliott (kick)
Mia.    Parmalee, 1 yard run
    PAT — Stoyanovich (kick)
K.C.    Anders, 57 yard pass from Montana
    PAT — Elliott (kick)

**Second Quarter**
Mia.    Stoyanovich, 40 yard field goal
K.C.    Elliott, 21 yard field goal
Mia.    R. Williams, 1 yard pass from Marino
    PAT — Stoyanovich (kick)

**Third Quarter**
Mia.    Fryar, 7 yard pass from Marino
    PAT — Stoyanovich (kick)
Mia.    Stoyanovich, 40 yard field goal

January 1, 1995 at Cleveland, Ohio (Attendance 77,452)

**SCORING**

| | | | | | | |
|---|---|---|---|---|---|---|
| NEW ENGLAND | 0 | 10 | 0 | 3 | - | 13 |
| CLEVELAND | 13 | 7 | 7 | 3 | - | 20 |

**First Quarter**
Clev.    Stover, 30 yard field goal

**Second Quarter**
N.E.    Thompson, 13 yard pass from Bledsoe
    PAT — Bahr (kick)
Clev.    Carrier, 5 yard pass from Testaverde
    PAT — Stover (kick)
N.E.    Bahr, 23 yard field goal

**Third Quarter**
Clev.    Hoard, 10 yard run
    PAT — Stover (kick)

**Fourth Quarter**
Clev.    Stover, 21 yard field goal
N.E.    Bahr, 33 yard field goal

## TEAM STATISTICS

| K.C. | | MIA. |
|---|---|---|
| 24 | First Downs- Total | 22 |
| 7 | First Downs- Rushing | 7 |
| 17 | First Downs- Passing | 13 |
| 0 | First Downs- Penalty | 2 |
| 3 | Fumbles- Number | 0 |
| 1 | Fumbles- Lost Ball | 0 |
| 4 | Penalties- Number | 6 |
| 15 | Yards Penalized | 50 |
| 0 | Missed Field Goals | 0 |
| 60 | Offensive Plays | 61 |
| 414 | Net Yards | 381 |
| 6.9 | Average Gain | 6.2 |
| 3 | Giveaways | 0 |
| 0 | Takeaways | 3 |
| - 3 | Difference | + 3 |

## TEAM STATISTICS

| N.E. | | CLEV. |
|---|---|---|
| 20 | First Downs- Total | 22 |
| 6 | First Downs- Rushing | 8 |
| 14 | First Downs- Passing | 14 |
| 0 | First Downs- Penalty | 0 |
| 0 | Fumbles- Number | 2 |
| 0 | Fumbles- Lost Ball | 1 |
| 3 | Penalties- Number | 4 |
| 21 | Yards Penalized | 25 |
| 0 | Missed Field Goals | 2 |
| 68 | Offensive Plays | 66 |
| 303 | Net Yards | 379 |
| 4.5 | Average Gain | 5.7 |
| 3 | Giveaways | 1 |
| 1 | Takeaways | 3 |
| - 2 | Difference | + 2 |

## INDIVIDUAL STATISTICS

**KANSAS CITY** / **MIAMI**

### RUSHING

| | No. | Yds. | Avg. | | No. | Yds. | Avg. |
|---|---|---|---|---|---|---|---|
| M. Allen | 14 | 64 | 4.6 | Parmalee | 18 | 57 | 3.2 |
| Anders | 5 | 17 | 3.4 | Spikes | 9 | 49 | 5.4 |
| Hill | 2 | 14 | 7.0 | McDuffie | 1 | 19 | 19.0 |
| Montana | 2 | 5 | 2.5 | Marino | 2 | 4 | 2.0 |
| | 23 | 100 | 4.3 | Craver | 1 | 3 | 3.0 |
| | | | | | 31 | 132 | 4.3 |

### RECEIVING

| | No. | Yds. | Avg. | | No. | Yds. | Avg. |
|---|---|---|---|---|---|---|---|
| Anders | 6 | 103 | 17.2 | Fryar | 6 | 71 | 11.8 |
| M. Allen | 5 | 49 | 9.8 | Craver | 4 | 35 | 8.8 |
| Birden | 4 | 56 | 14.0 | Parmalee | 2 | 34 | 17.0 |
| Cash | 3 | 38 | 12.7 | K. Jackson | 2 | 29 | 14.5 |
| D. Walker | 3 | 27 | 9.0 | M. Williams | 2 | 28 | 14.0 |
| Dawson | 3 | 21 | 7.0 | McDuffie | 2 | 25 | 12.5 |
| Hill | 1 | 11 | 11.0 | Saxon | 2 | 24 | 12.0 |
| W. Davis | 1 | 9 | 9.0 | S. Miller | 1 | 10 | 10.0 |
| | 26 | 314 | 12.1 | R. Williams | 1 | 1 | 1.0 |
| | | | | | 22 | 257 | 11.7 |

### PUNTING

| | | | | | |
|---|---|---|---|---|---|
| Aguiar | 2 | 40.0 | Kidd | 3 | 43.3 |

### PUNT RETURNS

| | | | | | |
|---|---|---|---|---|---|
| D. Carter | 1 | 7 | 7.0 | McDuffie | 2FC |

### KICKOFF RETURNS

| | | | | | | | |
|---|---|---|---|---|---|---|---|
| Vaughn | 4 | 67 | 16.8 | McDuffie | 2 | 57 | 28.5 |
| Hughes | 1 | 14 | 14.0 | Spikes | 1 | 38 | 38.0 |
| | 5 | 81 | 16.2 | | 3 | 95 | 31.7 |

### INTERCEPTION RETURNS

| | | | | | | |
|---|---|---|---|---|---|---|
| None | | | | Brown | 1 | 24 | 24.0 |

### PASSING

**KANSAS CITY**

| | Att. | Comp. | Comp. Pct. | Yds. | Int. | Yds./ Att. | Yds./ Comp. |
|---|---|---|---|---|---|---|---|
| Montana | 37 | 26 | 70.3 | 314 | 1 | 8.5 | 12.1 |

**MIAMI**

| | Att. | Comp. | Comp. Pct. | Yds. | Int. | Yds./ Att. | Yds./ Comp. |
|---|---|---|---|---|---|---|---|
| Marino | 29 | 22 | 75.9 | 257 | 0 | 8.9 | 11.7 |

## INDIVIDUAL STATISTICS

**NEW ENGLAND** / **CLEVELAND**

### RUSHING

| | No. | Yds. | Avg. | | No. | Yds. | Avg. |
|---|---|---|---|---|---|---|---|
| Croom | 9 | 35 | 3.9 | Hoard | 17 | 66 | 3.9 |
| Thompson | 4 | 16 | 4.0 | Byner | 10 | 30 | 3.0 |
| Turner | 1 | 4 | 4.0 | Testaverde | 5 | 19 | 3.8 |
| Bledsoe | 2 | 2 | 1.0 | Metcalf | 2 | 10 | 5.0 |
| | 16 | 57 | 3.6 | | 34 | 125 | 3.7 |

### RECEIVING

| | No. | Yds. | Avg. | | No. | Yds. | Avg. |
|---|---|---|---|---|---|---|---|
| Brisby | 6 | 83 | 13.8 | M. Jackson | 7 | 122 | 17.4 |
| Coates | 6 | 79 | 13.2 | Alexander | 5 | 69 | 13.8 |
| Thompson | 4 | 33 | 8.3 | Hartley | 2 | 17 | 8.5 |
| Timpson | 2 | 20 | 10.0 | Byner | 2 | 16 | 8.0 |
| C. Brown | 1 | 21 | 21.0 | Carrier | 2 | 13 | 6.5 |
| Burke | 1 | 8 | 8.0 | Hoard | 1 | 25 | 25.0 |
| Turner | 1 | 7 | 7.0 | Kinchen | 1 | 6 | 6.0 |
| Croom | 1 | 5 | 5.0 | | 20 | 268 | 13.4 |
| | 22 | 256 | 11.6 | | | | |

### PUNTING

| | | | | | |
|---|---|---|---|---|---|
| O'Neill | 4 | 42.3 | Tupa | 3 | 37.7 |

### PUNT RETURNS

| | | | | | | |
|---|---|---|---|---|---|---|
| T. Brown | 2 | 5 | 2.5 | Metcalf | 1 | 1 | 1.0 |
| | | | | Metcalf | 1FC | | |

### KICKOFF RETURNS

| | | | | | | | |
|---|---|---|---|---|---|---|---|
| Thompson | 4 | 71 | 17.8 | Metcalf | 2 | 46 | 23.0 |
| Crittenden | 1 | 28 | 28.0 | Kinchen | 1 | 24 | 24.0 |
| C. Brown | 0 | 0 | 0.0 | | 3 | 70 | 23.3 |
| | 5 | 99 | 19.8 | | | | |

### INTERCEPTION RETURNS

| | | | | | | |
|---|---|---|---|---|---|---|
| None | | | E. Turner | 1 | 28 | 28.0 |
| | | | Riddick | 1 | 16 | 16.0 |
| | | | P. Johnson | 1 | 3 | 3.0 |
| | | | | 3 | 47 | 22.3 |

### PASSING

**NEW ENGLAND**

| | Att. | Comp. | Comp. Pct. | Yds. | Int. | Yds./ Att. | Yds./ Comp. |
|---|---|---|---|---|---|---|---|
| Bledsoe | 50 | 21 | 42.0 | 235 | 3 | 4.7 | 11.2 |
| O'Neill | 1 | 1 | 100.0 | 21 | 0 | 21.0 | 21.0 |
| | 51 | 22 | 43.1 | 256 | 3 | 5.0 | 11.6 |

**CLEVELAND**

| | Att. | Comp. | Comp. Pct. | Yds. | Int. | Yds./ Att. | Yds./ Comp. |
|---|---|---|---|---|---|---|---|
| Testaverde | 30 | 20 | 66.7 | 268 | 0 | 8.9 | 13.4 |

December 31, 1994 at Green Bay, Wis. (Attendance 58,125)

### SCORING

| | | | | | |
|---|---|---|---|---|---|
| DETROIT | 0 | 0 | 3 | 9 | - 12 |
| GREEN BAY | 7 | 3 | 3 | 3 | - 16 |

First Quarter
G.B.     Levens, 3 yard run
           PAT — Jacke (kick)

Second Quarter
G.B.     Jacke, 51 yard field goal

Third Quarter
Det.     Hanson, 38 yard field goal
G.B.     Jacke, 32 yard field goal

Fourth Quarter
Det.     Perriman, 3 yard pass from Krieg
           PAT — Hanson (kick)
G.B.     Jacke, 28 yard field goal
Det.     Team safety — Hentrich out of end zone

### TEAM STATISTICS

| DET. | | G.B. |
|---|---|---|
| 9 | First Downs- Total | 18 |
| 1 | First Downs- Rushing | 6 |
| 8 | First Downs- Passing | 11 |
| 0 | First Downs- Penalty | 1 |
| 1 | Fumbles- Number | 0 |
| 0 | Fumbles- Lost Ball | 0 |
| 4 | Penalties- Number | 3 |
| 30 | Yards Penalized | 35 |
| 1 | Missed Field Goals | 1 |
| 54 | Offensive Plays | 74 |
| 171 | Net Yards | 336 |
| 3.2 | Average Gain | 4.5 |
| 0 | Giveaways | 0 |
| 0 | Takeaways | 0 |
| 0 | Difference | 0 |

### INDIVIDUAL STATISTICS

**DETROIT**       **GREEN BAY**

#### RUSHING

| | No. | Yds. | Avg. | | No. | Yds. | Avg. |
|---|---|---|---|---|---|---|---|
| Krieg | 1 | 1 | 1.0 | Bennett | 22 | 70 | 3.2 |
| Sanders | 13 | -1 | -0.1 | Brooks | 1 | 13 | 13.0 |
| Perriman | 1 | -4 | -4.0 | Cobb | 8 | 12 | 1.5 |
| | 15 | -4 | -0.3 | Favre | 2 | 5 | 2.5 |
| | | | | Levens | 1 | 3 | 3.0 |
| | | | | Hentrich | 1 | -22 | -22.0 |
| | | | | | 35 | 81 | 2.3 |

#### RECEIVING

| | No. | Yds. | Avg. | | No. | Yds. | Avg. |
|---|---|---|---|---|---|---|---|
| Perriman | 4 | 62 | 15.5 | Brooks | 7 | 88 | 12.6 |
| Holman | 4 | 30 | 7.5 | Bennett | 6 | 31 | 5.2 |
| Matthews | 3 | 36 | 12.0 | Chmura | 5 | 75 | 15.0 |
| Sanders | 3 | 4 | 1.3 | A. Morgan | 3 | 33 | 11.0 |
| H. Moore | 2 | 52 | 26.0 | Cobb | 1 | 18 | 18.0 |
| Hallock | 1 | 15 | 15.0 | Mickens | 1 | 17 | 17.0 |
| | 17 | 199 | 11.7 | | 23 | 262 | 11.4 |

#### PUNTING

| | No. | | Avg. | | No. | | Avg. |
|---|---|---|---|---|---|---|---|
| Montgomery | 8 | | 36.5 | Hentrich | 5 | | 39.0 |

#### PUNT RETURNS

| | No. | Yds. | Avg. | | No. | Yds. | Avg. |
|---|---|---|---|---|---|---|---|
| Gray | 1 | 17 | 17.0 | Brooks | 3 | 15 | 5.0 |
| Gray | 1FC | | | Brooks | 2FC | | |

#### KICKOFF RETURNS

| | No. | Yds. | Avg. | | No. | Yds. | Avg. |
|---|---|---|---|---|---|---|---|
| Gray | 4 | 159 | 39.8 | C. Harris | 1 | 17 | 17.0 |
| Lynch | 1 | 27 | 27.0 | C. Jordan | 1 | 15 | 15.0 |
| | 5 | 186 | 37.2 | Levens | 1 | 13 | 13.0 |
| | | | | | 3 | 45 | 15.0 |

#### INTERCEPTION RETURNS

None            None

#### PASSING

**DETROIT**

| | Att. | Comp. | Comp. Pct. | Yds. | Int. | Yds./ Att. | Yds./ Comp. |
|---|---|---|---|---|---|---|---|
| Krieg | 35 | 17 | 48.6 | 199 | 0 | 5.7 | 11.7 |

**GREEN BAY**

| | Att. | Comp. | Comp. Pct. | Yds. | Int. | Yds./ Att. | Yds./ Comp. |
|---|---|---|---|---|---|---|---|
| Favre | 38 | 23 | 60.5 | 262 | 0 | 6.9 | 11.4 |

---

January 1, 1995 at Minneapolis, Minn. (Attendance 60,347)

### SCORING

| | | | | | |
|---|---|---|---|---|---|
| CHICAGO | 0 | 14 | 7 | 14 | - 35 |
| MINNESOTA | 3 | 6 | 3 | 6 | - 18 |

First Quarter
Minn.     Reveiz, 29 yard field goal

Second Quarter
Chi.     Tillman, 1 yard run
           PAT — Butler (kick)
Chi.     K. Jennings, 9 yard pass from Walsh
           PAT — Butler (kick)
Minn.     C. Carter, 4 yard pass from Moon
           PAT — 2-point attempt failed

Third Quarter
Chi.     R. Harris, 29 yard run
           PAT — Butler (kick)
Minn.     Reveiz, 48 yard field goal

Fourth Quarter
Chi.     Graham, 21 yard pass from Walsh
           PAT — Butler (kick)
Minn.     A. Lee, 11 yard pass from Moon
           PAT — 2-point attempt failed
Chi.     Miniefield, 48 yard fumble return
           PAT — Butler (kick)

### TEAM STATISTICS

| CHI. | | MINN. |
|---|---|---|
| 18 | First Downs- Total | 22 |
| 5 | First Downs- Rushing | 3 |
| 11 | First Downs- Passing | 18 |
| 2 | First Downs- Penalty | 1 |
| 1 | Fumbles- Number | 3 |
| 1 | Fumbles- Lost Ball | 2 |
| 6 | Penalties- Number | 11 |
| 30 | Yards Penalized | 85 |
| 0 | Missed Field Goals | 0 |
| 54 | Offensive Plays | 82 |
| 308 | Net Yards | 389 |
| 5.7 | Average Gain | 4.7 |
| 2 | Giveaways | 4 |
| 4 | Takeaways | 2 |
| + 2 | Difference | - 2 |

### INDIVIDUAL STATISTICS

**CHICAGO**       **MINNESOTA**

#### RUSHING

| | No. | Yds. | Avg. | | No. | Yds. | Avg. |
|---|---|---|---|---|---|---|---|
| R. Harris | 13 | 67 | 5.2 | T. Allen | 12 | 27 | 2.3 |
| Tillman | 11 | 19 | 1.7 | Graham | 4 | 13 | 3.3 |
| S. Walsh | 5 | 5 | 1.0 | Moon | 2 | 9 | 4.5 |
| J. Graham | 1 | 3 | 3.0 | R. Smith | 1 | 0 | 0.0 |
| | 30 | 94 | 3.1 | | 19 | 49 | 2.6 |

#### RECEIVING

| | No. | Yds. | Avg. | | No. | Yds. | Avg. |
|---|---|---|---|---|---|---|---|
| J. Graham | 4 | 108 | 27.0 | A. Lee | 11 | 159 | 14.4 |
| Conway | 4 | 56 | 14.0 | C. Carter | 8 | 61 | 7.6 |
| R. Harris | 3 | 20 | 6.7 | A. Jordan | 4 | 35 | 8.8 |
| T. Carter | 1 | 16 | 16.0 | J. Reed | 3 | 39 | 13.0 |
| K. Jennings | 1 | 9 | 9.0 | Ismail | 3 | 29 | 9.7 |
| L. Tillman | 1 | 7 | 7.0 | S. Jordan | 2 | 16 | 8.0 |
| R. Green | 1 | 5 | 5.0 | D. Palmer | 1 | 11 | 11.0 |
| | 15 | 221 | 14.7 | T. Allen | 1 | 1 | 1.0 |
| | | | | | 33 | 351 | 10.6 |

#### PUNTING

| | No. | | Avg. | | No. | | Avg. |
|---|---|---|---|---|---|---|---|
| Gardocki | 3 | | 38.7 | Saxon | 4 | | 32.8 |

#### PUNT RETURNS

| | No. | Yds. | Avg. | | No. | Yds. | Avg. |
|---|---|---|---|---|---|---|---|
| J. Graham | 1 | 1 | 1.0 | D. Palmer | 3FC | | |
| J. Graham | 2FC | | | | | | |

#### KICKOFF RETURNS

| | No. | Yds. | Avg. | | No. | Yds. | Avg. |
|---|---|---|---|---|---|---|---|
| N. Lewis | 2 | 47 | 23.5 | R. Smith | 6 | 132 | 22.0 |
| R. Green | 1 | 18 | 18.0 | | | | |
| Waddle | 0 | 0 | 0.0 | | | | |
| | 3 | 65 | 21.7 | | | | |

#### INTERCEPTIONS

| | No. | Yds. | Avg. | | No. | Yds. | Avg. |
|---|---|---|---|---|---|---|---|
| Lincoln | 1 | 12 | 12.0 | A. Parker | 1 | 10 | 10.0 |
| B. Minter | 1 | 7 | 7.0 | | | | |
| | 2 | 19 | 9.5 | | | | |

#### PASSING

**CHICAGO**

| | Att. | Comp. | Comp. Pct. | Yds. | Int. | Yds./ Att. | Yds./ Comp. |
|---|---|---|---|---|---|---|---|
| Walsh | 23 | 15 | 65.2 | 221 | 1 | 9.6 | 14.7 |

**MINNESOTA**

| | Att. | Comp. | Comp. Pct. | Yds. | Int. | Yds./ Att. | Yds./ Comp. |
|---|---|---|---|---|---|---|---|
| Moon | 52 | 29 | 55.8 | 292 | 2 | 5.6 | 10.1 |
| Salisbury | 9 | 4 | 44.4 | 59 | 0 | 6.6 | 14.8 |
| | 61 | 33 | 54.1 | 351 | 2 | 5.8 | 10.6 |

January 7, 1995 at Pittsburgh, Pa. (Attendance 58,185)

## SCORING

| | | | | | | |
|---|---|---|---|---|---|---|
| CLEVELAND | 0 | 3 | 0 | 6 | - | 9 |
| PITTSBURGH | 3 | 21 | 3 | 2 | - | 29 |

**First Quarter**
Pitt.    Anderson, 39 yard field goal

**Second Quarter**
Pitt.    E. Green, 2 yard pass from O'Donnell
         PAT — Anderson (kick)
Pitt.    J.L. Williams, 26 yard run
         PAT — Anderson (kick)
Clev.    Stover, 22 yard field goal
Pitt.    Thigpen, 9 yard pass from O'Donnell
         PAT — Anderson (kick)

**Third Quarter**
Pitt.    Anderson, 40 yard field goal

**Fourth Quarter**
Clev.    McCardell, 20 yard pass from O'Donnell
         PAT — 2-point attempt failed
Pitt.    Testaverde sacked by C. Lake for safety

## TEAM STATISTICS

| CLEV. | | PITT. |
|---|---|---|
| 10 | First Downs- Total | 23 |
| 3 | First Downs- Rushing | 14 |
| 6 | First Downs- Passing | 9 |
| 1 | First Downs- Penalty | 0 |
| 0 | Fumbles- Number | 2 |
| 0 | Fumbles- Lost Ball | 1 |
| 2 | Penalties- Number | 4 |
| 17 | Yards Penalized | 50 |
| 0 | Missed Field Goals | 0 |
| 50 | Offensive Plays | 74 |
| 186 | Net Yards | 424 |
| 3.7 | Average Gain | 5.7 |
| 2 | Giveaways | 1 |
| 1 | Takeaways | 2 |
| - 1 | Difference | + 1 |

## INDIVIDUAL STATISTICS

**CLEVELAND**      **PITTSBURGH**

### RUSHING

| | No. | Yds. | Avg. | | No. | Yds. | Avg. |
|---|---|---|---|---|---|---|---|
| Byner | 9 | 43 | 4.8 | Foster | 24 | 133 | 5.5 |
| Hoard | 3 | 8 | 2.7 | Morris | 22 | 60 | 2.7 |
| Metcalf | 5 | 4 | 0.8 | J.L. Williams | 2 | 43 | 21.5 |
| | 17 | 55 | 3.2 | Tomczak | 3 | 2 | 0.7 |
| | | | | | 51 | 238 | 4.7 |

### RECEIVING

| | No. | Yds. | Avg. | | No. | Yds. | Avg. |
|---|---|---|---|---|---|---|---|
| M. Jackson | 3 | 47 | 15.7 | Mills | 5 | 117 | 23.4 |
| McCardell | 3 | 47 | 15.7 | J.L. Williams | 4 | 20 | 5.0 |
| Metcalf | 2 | 18 | 9.0 | E. Green | 3 | 21 | 7.0 |
| Carrier | 2 | 8 | 4.0 | Hastings | 2 | 18 | 9.0 |
| Byner | 1 | 14 | 14.0 | Thigpen | 1 | 10 | 5.0 |
| Hoard | 1 | 5 | 5.0 | | 16 | 186 | 11.6 |
| Kinchen | 1 | 5 | 5.0 | | | | |
| | 13 | 144 | 11.1 | | | | |

### PUNTING

| | | | | | | | |
|---|---|---|---|---|---|---|---|
| Tupa | 5 | | 38.0 | Royals | 5 | | 38.2 |

### PUNT RETURNS

| | No. | Yds. | Avg. | | No. | Yds. | Avg. |
|---|---|---|---|---|---|---|---|
| Carrier | 3 | 40 | 13.3 | Woodson | 1 | 0 | 0.0 |
| | | | | Woodson | 1FC | | |

### KICKOFF RETURNS

| | No. | Yds. | Avg. | | No. | Yds. | Avg. |
|---|---|---|---|---|---|---|---|
| Metcalf | 4 | 69 | 17.3 | C. Johnson | 2 | 28 | 14.0 |
| Baldwin | 1 | 32 | 32.0 | Woodson | 1 | 2 | 2.0 |
| Dixon | 1 | 0 | 0.0 | E. Green | 0 | 0 | 0.0 |
| | 6 | 101 | 16.8 | | 3 | 30 | 10.0 |

### INTERCEPTION RETURNS

| | No. | Yds. | Avg. | | No. | Yds. | Avg. |
|---|---|---|---|---|---|---|---|
| None | | | | McKyer | 1 | 21 | 21.0 |
| | | | | D. Perry | 1 | 0 | 0.0 |
| | | | | | 2 | 21 | 10.5 |

### PASSING

**CLEVELAND**

| | Att. | Comp. | Comp. Pct. | Yds. | Int. | Yds./ Att. | Yds./ Comp. |
|---|---|---|---|---|---|---|---|
| Testaverde | 31 | 13 | 41.9 | 144 | 2 | 4.6 | 11.1 |

**PITTSBURGH**

| | Att. | Comp. | | Yds. | | Yds./ Att. | Yds./ Comp. |
|---|---|---|---|---|---|---|---|
| O'Donnell | 23 | 16 | 7.0 | 186 | 0 | 8.1 | 11.6 |

---

January 8, 1995 at San Diego, Calif. (Attendance 63,381)

## SCORING

| | | | | | | |
|---|---|---|---|---|---|---|
| MIAMI | 7 | 14 | 0 | 0 | - | 21 |
| SAN DIEGO | 0 | 6 | 9 | 7 | - | 22 |

**First Quarter**
Mia.    K. Jackson, 8 yard pass from Marino
        PAT — Stoyanovich (kick)

**Second Quarter**
S.D.    Carney, 20 yard field goal
Mia.    K. Jackson, 9 yard pass from Marino
        PAT — Stoyanovich (kick)
S.D.    Carney, 21 yard field goal
Mia.    M. Williams, 16 yard pass from Marino
        PAT — Stoyanovich (kick)

**Third Quarter**
S.D.    Parmalee tackled by R. Davis for safety
S.D.    Means, 24 yard run
        PAT — Carney (kick)

**Fourth Quarter**
S.D.    Seay, 8 yard pass from Humphries
        PAT — Carney (kick)

## TEAM STATISTICS

| MIA. | | S.D. |
|---|---|---|
| 17 | First Downs- Total | 28 |
| 2 | First Downs- Rushing | 12 |
| 12 | First Downs- Passing | 15 |
| 3 | First Downs- Penalty | 1 |
| 1 | Fumbles- Number | 2 |
| 0 | Fumbles- Lost Ball | 1 |
| 7 | Penalties- Number | 5 |
| 47 | Yards Penalized | 67 |
| 1 | Missed Field Goals | 0 |
| 47 | Offensive Plays | 85 |
| 282 | Net Yards | 466 |
| 6.0 | Average Gain | 5.5 |
| 0 | Giveaways | 3 |
| 3 | Takeaways | 0 |
| + 3 | Difference | - 3 |

## INDIVIDUAL STATISTICS

**MIAMI**      **SAN DIEGO**

### RUSHING

| | No. | Yds. | Avg. | | No. | Yds. | Avg. |
|---|---|---|---|---|---|---|---|
| Parmalee | 7 | 16 | 2.3 | Means | 24 | 139 | 5.8 |
| Craver | 1 | 10 | 10.0 | Bieniemy | 4 | 33 | 8.3 |
| | 8 | 26 | 3.3 | Culver | 6 | 14 | 2.3 |
| | | | | Harmon | 3 | 12 | 4.0 |
| | | | | Jefferson | 1 | 3 | 3.0 |
| | | | | Humphries | 2 | 1 | 0.5 |
| | | | | | 40 | 202 | 5.1 |

### RECEIVING

| | No. | Yds. | Avg. | | No. | Yds. | Avg. |
|---|---|---|---|---|---|---|---|
| K. Jackson | 8 | 109 | 13.6 | Harmon | 7 | 57 | 8.1 |
| Fryar | 5 | 70 | 14.0 | Seay | 6 | 61 | 10.2 |
| McDuffie | 5 | 46 | 9.2 | T. Martin | 5 | 62 | 12.4 |
| Craver | 2 | 8 | 4.0 | Jefferson | 3 | 44 | 14.7 |
| Parmalee | 2 | 8 | 4.0 | Means | 3 | 16 | 5.3 |
| M. Williams | 1 | 16 | 16.0 | Culver | 2 | 23 | 11.5 |
| Saxon | 1 | 5 | 5.0 | Pupunu | 2 | 13 | 6.5 |
| | 24 | 262 | 10.9 | | 28 | 276 | 9.9 |

### PUNTING

| | | | | | | | |
|---|---|---|---|---|---|---|---|
| Kidd | 5 | | 45.2 | Wagner | 2 | | 43.5 |

### PUNT RETURNS

| | No. | Yds. | Avg. | | No. | Yds. | Avg. |
|---|---|---|---|---|---|---|---|
| McDuffie | 1 | 14 | 14.0 | Coleman | 1 | 14 | 14.0 |
| McDuffie | 1FC | | | Gordon | 1 | 0 | 0.0 |
| | | | | Gordon | 1FC | | |
| | | | | | 2 | 14 | 7.0 |

### KICKOFF RETURNS

| | No. | Yds. | Avg. | | No. | Yds. | Avg. |
|---|---|---|---|---|---|---|---|
| McDuffie | 3 | 87 | 29.0 | Coleman | 3 | 57 | 19.0 |
| Spikes | 1 | 18 | 18.0 | Harmon | 1 | 18 | 18.0 |
| R. Williams | 1 | 7 | 7.0 | Bieniemy | 1 | 13 | 13.0 |
| | 5 | 112 | 22.4 | | 5 | 88 | 17.6 |

### INTERCEPTION RETURNS

| | No. | Yds. | Avg. | |
|---|---|---|---|---|
| F. Smith | 1 | 14 | 14.0 | None |
| Stewart | 1 | 0 | 0.0 | |
| | 2 | 14 | 7.0 | |

### PASSING

**MIAMI**

| | Att. | Comp. | Comp. Pct. | Yds. | Int. | Yds./ Att. | Yds./ Comp. |
|---|---|---|---|---|---|---|---|
| Marino | 38 | 24 | 63.2 | 262 | 0 | 6.9 | 10.9 |

**SAN DIEGO**

| | Att. | Comp. | Comp. Pct. | Yds. | Int. | Yds./ Att. | Yds./ Comp. |
|---|---|---|---|---|---|---|---|
| Humphries | 43 | 28 | 65.1 | 276 | 2 | 6.4 | 9.9 |

# 1994 N.F.C. DIVISIONAL PLAYOFFS

January 7, 1995 at San Francisco (Attendance 64,644)

## SCORING

| | | | | | |
|---|---|---|---|---|---|
| CHICAGO | 3 | 0 | 0 | 12 | - 15 |
| SAN FRANCISCO | 7 | 23 | 7 | 7 | - 44 |

**First Quarter**
Chi.    Butler, 39 yard field goal
S.F.    Floyd, 2 yard run
     PAT — Brien (kick)

**Second Quarter**
S.F.    Jones, 8 yard pass from Young
     PAT — Brien kick failed
S.F.    Floyd, 4 yard run
     PAT — Brien (kick)
S.F.    Brien, 36 yard field goal
S.F.    Young, 6 yard run
     PAT — Brien (kick)

**Third Quarter**
S.F.    Floyd, 1 yard run
     PAT — Brien (kick)

**Fourth Quarter**
Chi.    Flanigan, 2 yard pass from Walsh
     PAT — 2 point attempt failed
S.F.    Walker, 1 yard run
     PAT — Brien (kick)
Chi.    Tillman, 1 yard run
     PAT — 2 point attempt failed

## TEAM STATISTICS

| CHI. | | S.F. |
|---|---|---|
| 20 | First Downs- Total | 27 |
| 4 | First Downs- Rushing | 13 |
| 13 | First Downs- Passing | 11 |
| 3 | First Downs- Penalty | 3 |
| 2 | Fumbles- Number | 3 |
| 0 | Fumbles- Lost Ball | 1 |
| 4 | Penalties- Number | 3 |
| 32 | Yards Penalized | 16 |
| 0 | Missed Field Goals | 0 |
| 69 | Offensive Plays | 64 |
| 247 | Net Yards | 330 |
| 3.6 | Average Gain | 5.2 |
| 2 | Giveaways | 1 |
| 1 | Takeaways | 2 |
| - 1 | Difference | + 1 |

## INDIVIDUAL STATISTICS

### CHICAGO / SAN FRANCISCO

**RUSHING**

| | No. | Yds. | Avg. | | No. | Yds. | Avg. |
|---|---|---|---|---|---|---|---|
| R. Harris | 8 | 26 | 3.3 | Watters | 11 | 55 | 5.0 |
| Green | 2 | 8 | 4.0 | Young | 5 | 32 | 6.4 |
| Tillman | 6 | 5 | 0.8 | Floyd | 10 | 25 | 2.5 |
| Walsh | 1 | 0 | 0.0 | D. Carter | 3 | 20 | 6.7 |
| T. Carter | 1 | 0 | 0.0 | Taylor | 1 | 15 | 15.0 |
| | 18 | 39 | 2.2 | Walker | 3 | 3 | 1.0 |
| | | | | Grbac | 4 | -5 | -1.3 |
| | | | | | 37 | 145 | 3.9 |

**RECEIVING**

| | No. | Yds. | Avg. | | No. | Yds. | Avg. |
|---|---|---|---|---|---|---|---|
| Green | 5 | 43 | 8.6 | Jones | 5 | 26 | 5.2 |
| Wetnight | 5 | 39 | 7.8 | Taylor | 4 | 51 | 12.8 |
| R. Harris | 5 | 24 | 4.8 | Rice | 4 | 48 | 12.0 |
| J. Graham | 4 | 33 | 8.3 | Watters | 3 | 18 | 6.0 |
| Waddle | 3 | 49 | 16.3 | D. Carter | 1 | 44 | 44.0 |
| Conway | 3 | 25 | 8.3 | Popson | 1 | 3 | 3.0 |
| Jennings | 2 | 20 | 10.0 | | 18 | 190 | 10.6 |
| Tillman | 1 | 4 | 4.0 | | | | |
| Flanigan | 1 | 2 | 2.0 | | | | |
| | 29 | 239 | 8.2 | | | | |

**PUNTING**

| | No. | | Avg. | | No. | | Avg. |
|---|---|---|---|---|---|---|---|
| Gardocki | 4 | | 36.8 | Wilmsmeyer | 2 | | 38.5 |

**PUNT RETURNS**

| | No. | Yds. | Avg. | | No. | Yds. | Avg. |
|---|---|---|---|---|---|---|---|
| J. Graham 1FC | | | | D. Carter | 2 | 6 | 3.0 |
| | | | | D. Carter 1FC | | | |

**KICKOFF RETURNS**

| | No. | Yds. | Avg. | | No. | Yds. | Avg. |
|---|---|---|---|---|---|---|---|
| Lewis | 5 | 125 | 25.0 | Walker | 1 | 14 | 14.0 |
| Green | 1 | 12 | 12.0 | D. Carter | 1 | 10 | 10.0 |
| | 6 | 137 | 22.8 | | 2 | 24 | 12.0 |

**INTERCEPTION RETURNS**

| | No. | Yds. | Avg. | | No. | Yds. | Avg. |
|---|---|---|---|---|---|---|---|
| None | | | | Hanks | 1 | 31 | 31.0 |
| | | | | Davis | 1 | 0 | 0.0 |
| | | | | | 2 | 31 | 15.5 |

**PASSING**

**CHICAGO**

| | Att. | Comp. | Comp. Pct. | Yds. | Int. | Yds./ Att. | Yds./ Comp. |
|---|---|---|---|---|---|---|---|
| Walsh | 19 | 10 | 52.6 | 78 | 2 | 4.1 | 7.8 |
| Kramer | 28 | 19 | 67.9 | 161 | 0 | 5.8 | 8.5 |
| | 47 | 29 | 61.7 | 239 | 2 | 5.1 | 8.2 |

**SAN FRANCISCO**

| | Att. | Comp. | Comp. Pct. | Yds. | Int. | Yds./ Att. | Yds./ Comp. |
|---|---|---|---|---|---|---|---|
| Young | 22 | 16 | 72.7 | 143 | 0 | 6.5 | 8.9 |
| Grbac | 4 | 2 | 50.0 | 47 | 0 | 11.8 | 23.5 |
| | 26 | 18 | 69.2 | 190 | 0 | 7.3 | 10.6 |

---

January 8, 1995 at Irving, Texas (Attendance 64,745)

## SCORING

| | | | | | |
|---|---|---|---|---|---|
| GREEN BAY | 3 | 6 | 0 | 0 | - 9 |
| DALLAS | 14 | 14 | 0 | 7 | - 35 |

**First Quarter**
Dall.    Smith, 5 yard run
     PAT — Boniol (kick)
G.B.    Jacke, 50 yard field goal
Dall.    Harper, 94 yard pass from Aikman
     PAT — Boniol (kick)

**Second Quarter**
Dall.    Thomas, 1 yard run
     PAT — Boniol (kick)
G.B.    Bennett, 1 yard run
     PAT — 2 point attempt failed
Dall.    Galbraith, 1 yard pass from Aikman
     PAT — Boniol (kick)

**Fourth Quarter**
Dall.    Thomas, 2 yard run
     PAT — Boniol (kick)

## TEAM STATISTICS

| G.B. | | DAL. |
|---|---|---|
| 18 | First Downs- Total | 27 |
| 6 | First Downs- Rushing | 11 |
| 11 | First Downs- Passing | 13 |
| 1 | First Downs- Penalty | 3 |
| 0 | Fumbles- Number | 1 |
| 0 | Fumbles- Lost Ball | 1 |
| 8 | Penalties- Number | 7 |
| 43 | Yards Penalized | 46 |
| 1 | Missed Field Goals | 0 |
| 70 | Offensive Plays | 65 |
| 327 | Net Yards | 450 |
| 4.7 | Average Gain | 6.9 |
| 1 | Giveaways | 2 |
| 2 | Takeaways | 1 |
| +1 | Difference | -1 |

## INDIVIDUAL STATISTICS

### GREEN BAY / DALLAS

**RUSHING**

| | No. | Yds. | Avg. | | No. | Yds. | Avg. |
|---|---|---|---|---|---|---|---|
| Bennett | 11 | 34 | 3.1 | B. Thomas | 23 | 70 | 3.0 |
| Brunell | 4 | 26 | 6.5 | Smith | 7 | 44 | 6.3 |
| R. Brooks | 2 | 23 | 11.5 | Johnston | 1 | 4 | 4.0 |
| Cobb | 4 | 14 | 3.5 | Aikman | 1 | 2 | 2.0 |
| Favre | 2 | 2 | 1.0 | | 32 | 120 | 3.8 |
| | 23 | 99 | 4.3 | | | | |

**RECEIVING**

| | No. | Yds. | Avg. | | No. | Yds. | Avg. |
|---|---|---|---|---|---|---|---|
| R. Brooks | 8 | 138 | 17.3 | Novacek | 11 | 104 | 9.5 |
| A. Morgan | 5 | 52 | 10.4 | Irvin | 6 | 111 | 18.5 |
| Bennett | 3 | 11 | 3.7 | A. Harper | 2 | 108 | 54.0 |
| Chmura | 2 | 13 | 6.5 | Johnston | 1 | 8 | 8.0 |
| Cobb | 1 | 12 | 12.0 | Smith | 1 | 3 | 3.0 |
| R. Johnson | 1 | 9 | 9.0 | B. Thomas | 1 | 2 | 2.0 |
| Levens | 1 | 1 | 1.0 | Galbraith | 1 | 1 | 1.0 |
| | 21 | 236 | 11.2 | | 23 | 337 | 14.6 |

**PUNTING**

| | No. | | Avg. | | No. | | Avg. |
|---|---|---|---|---|---|---|---|
| Hentrich | 4 | | 44.0 | Jett | 4 | | 45.8 |

**PUNT RETURNS**

| | No. | Yds. | Avg. | | No. | Yds. | Avg. |
|---|---|---|---|---|---|---|---|
| R. Brooks | 2 | 23 | 11.5 | K. Williams 2FC | | | |

**KICKOFF RETURNS**

| | No. | Yds. | Avg. | | No. | Yds. | Avg. |
|---|---|---|---|---|---|---|---|
| C. Harris | 5 | 132 | 26.4 | K. Williams | 3 | 88 | 29.3 |
| C. Jordan | 1 | 12 | 12.0 | | | | |
| | 6 | 144 | 24.0 | | | | |

**INTERCEPTION RETURNS**

| | No. | Yds. | Avg. | | No. | Yds. | Avg. |
|---|---|---|---|---|---|---|---|
| Paup | 1 | 34 | 34.0 | K. Smith | 1 | 2 | 2.0 |

**PASSING**

**GREEN BAY**

| | Att. | Comp. | Comp. Pct. | Yds. | Int. | Yds./ Att. | Yds./ Comp. |
|---|---|---|---|---|---|---|---|
| Favre | 35 | 18 | 51.4 | 211 | 1 | 6.0 | 11.7 |
| Brunell | 11 | 3 | 27.3 | 25 | 0 | 2.3 | 8.3 |
| | 46 | 21 | 45.7 | 236 | 1 | 5.1 | 11.2 |

**DALLAS**

| | Att. | Comp. | Comp. Pct. | Yds. | Int. | Yds./ Att. | Yds./ Comp. |
|---|---|---|---|---|---|---|---|
| Aikman | 30 | 23 | 76.7 | 337 | 1 | 11.2 | 14.7 |
| Peete | 2 | 0 | 0.0 | 0 | 0 | 0.0 | 0.0 |
| | 32 | 23 | 71.9 | 337 | 1 | 10.5 | 14.7 |

# 1994 Championship Games

## A.F.C. CHAMPIONSHIP GAME
January 15, 1995 at Pittsburgh, Pa.
(Attendance 61,545)

The San Diego Chargers won their first AFC championship when they defeated the Pittsburgh Steelers 17-13 on the road. Trailing 13-3, the Chargers scored the final 14 points of the game on a pair of 43-yard touchdown passes from Stan Humphries to Alfred Pupunu and Tony Martin.

It was the second straight week the Chargers had come from behind to win a playoff game.

Pittsburgh had a chance to win the game and marched from its own 17-yard line in the waning minutes of the fourth quarter. But a fourth-down pass from Neil O'Donnell to Barry Foster was batted away at the goal line by Chargers linebacker Dennis Gibson.

San Diego linebacker Junior Seau, who made 16 tackles, said, "We've been underdogs all the way through the season. You have to do something rare to get respect in this league."

The Chargers did just that, winning their first title since 1963, when they were champions of the AFL.

Pittsburgh jumped out to a 7-0 lead on a 16-yard pass from O'Donnell to John L. Williams, but the Steelers could manage only two more field goals by Gary Anderson.

Pittsburgh coach Bill Cowher said, "It's a very empty feeling right now. I guess you can say the further you come, the harder it is to fall."

O'Donnell completed 32 of 54 passes for 349 yards, as the Steelers controlled the clock. But, when it counted, it was the Chargers and a couple of 43-yard TD passes that decided the game.

## SCORING

| | | | | | |
|---|---|---|---|---|---|
| SAN DIEGO | 0 | 3 | 7 | 7 | - 17 |
| PITTSBURGH | 7 | 3 | 3 | 0 | - 13 |

**First Quarter**
Pitt.  J.L. Williams, 16 yard pass from O'Donnell
PAT — Anderson (kick)

**Second Quarter**
S.D.  Carney, 20 yard field goal
Pitt.  Anderson, 39 yard field goal

**Third Quarter**
Pitt.  Anderson, 23 yard field goal
S.D.  Pupunu, 43 yard pass from Humphries
PAT — Carney (kick)

**Fourth Quarter**
S.D.  T. Martin, 43 yard pass from Humphries
PAT — Carney (kick)

### TEAM STATISTICS

| S.D. | | PITT. |
|---|---|---|
| 13 | First Downs- Total | 22 |
| 4 | First Downs- Rushing | 4 |
| 8 | First Downs- Passing | 17 |
| 1 | First Downs- Penalty | 1 |
| 0 | Fumbles- Number | 3 |
| 0 | Fumbles- Lost Ball | 1 |
| 3 | Penalties- Number | 8 |
| 15 | Yards Penalized | 111 |
| 0 | Missed Field Goals | 0 |
| 47 | Offensive Plays | 80 |
| 226 | Net Yards | 415 |
| 4.8 | Average Gain | 5.2 |
| 1 | Giveaways | 2 |
| 2 | Takeaways | 1 |
| +1 | Difference | -1 |

## INDIVIDUAL STATISTICS

| SAN DIEGO | | | | PITTSBURGH | | |
|---|---|---|---|---|---|---|
| | No. | Yds. | Avg. | | No. | Yds. | Avg. |

**RUSHING**

| SAN DIEGO | No. | Yds. | Avg. | PITTSBURGH | No. | Yds. | Avg. |
|---|---|---|---|---|---|---|---|
| Means | 20 | 69 | 3.5 | Foster | 20 | 47 | 2.4 |
| Humphries | 4 | -3 | -0.8 | J.L. Williams | 3 | 16 | 5.3 |
| | 24 | 66 | 2.8 | Morris | 2 | 2 | 1.0 |
| | | | | O'Donnell | 1 | 1 | 1.0 |
| | | | | | 26 | 66 | 2.5 |

**RECEIVING**

| SAN DIEGO | No. | Yds. | Avg. | PITTSBURGH | No. | Yds. | Avg. |
|---|---|---|---|---|---|---|---|
| Pupunu | 4 | 76 | 19.0 | Mills | 8 | 106 | 13.3 |
| Means | 2 | 19 | 9.5 | J.L. Williams | 7 | 45 | 6.4 |
| Jefferson | 2 | 16 | 8.0 | Hastings | 5 | 55 | 11.0 |
| T. Martin | 1 | 43 | 43.0 | Green | 4 | 80 | 20.0 |
| S. Mitchell | 1 | 19 | 19.0 | Thigpen | 3 | 35 | 11.7 |
| Harmon | 1 | -8 | -8.0 | Foster | 3 | 12 | 4.0 |
| | 11 | 165 | 15.0 | Hayes | 1 | 16 | 16.0 |
| | | | | Morris | 1 | 0 | 0.0 |
| | | | | | 32 | 349 | 10.9 |

**PUNTING**

| SAN DIEGO | No. | | Avg. | PITTSBURGH | No. | | Avg. |
|---|---|---|---|---|---|---|---|
| Wagner | 5 | | 38.4 | Royals | 5 | | 44.4 |

**PUNT RETURNS**

| SAN DIEGO | No. | Yds. | Avg. | PITTSBURGH | No. | Yds. | Avg. |
|---|---|---|---|---|---|---|---|
| Gordon | 2 | 2 | 1.0 | Woodson | 2 | 10 | 5.0 |
| | | | | Woodson | 1FC | | |
| | | | | C. Johnson | 1FC | | |

**KICKOFF RETURNS**

| SAN DIEGO | No. | Yds. | Avg. | PITTSBURGH | No. | Yds. | Avg. |
|---|---|---|---|---|---|---|---|
| Coleman | 2 | 49 | 24.5 | C. Johnson | 4 | 73 | 18.3 |
| Harmon | 1 | 23 | 23.0 | | | | |
| | 3 | 72 | 24.0 | | | | |

**INTERCEPTION RETURNS**

| SAN DIEGO | No. | Yds. | Avg. | PITTSBURGH | No. | Yds. | Avg. |
|---|---|---|---|---|---|---|---|
| None | | | | Woodson | 1 | 6 | 6.0 |

**PASSING**

| SAN DIEGO | Att. | Comp. | Comp. Pct. | Yds. | Int. | Yds./ Att. | Yds./ Comp. |
|---|---|---|---|---|---|---|---|
| Humphries | 22 | 11 | 50.0 | 165 | 1 | 7.5 | 15.0 |

| PITTSBURGH | Att. | Comp. | Comp. Pct. | Yds. | Int. | Yds./ Att. | Yds./ Comp. |
|---|---|---|---|---|---|---|---|
| O'Donnell | 54 | 32 | 59.3 | 349 | 0 | 9.5 | 10.9 |

---

## N.F.C. CHAMPIONSHIP GAME
January 15, 1995 at San Francisco, Calif.
(Attendance 69,125)

For the third consecutive year, the Dallas Cowboys and San Francisco 49ers faced off for the NFC championship, the game that seems to be the "real" Super Bowl in the last decade.

The 49ers jumped out to a 21-0 lead before the first quarter was half over and rolled to a 38-28 victory. Three Dallas turnovers led to the three San Francisco touchdowns. After that, every time the Cowboys tried to close the gap, the 49ers counterpunched.

The 49ers scored first on a 44-yard interception return by Eric Davis. Then Davis stripped Dallas' Michael Irvin of the ball and, five plays later, Steve Young threw a 29-yard touchdown pass to Ricky Watters. On the ensuing kickoff, Adam Walker stripped Kevin Williams of the ball, and seven plays later William Floyd scored a one-yard touchdown.

Dallas quarterback Troy Aikman lost for the first time in eight playoff starts, but he passed for 380 yards. He connected with Irvin on a 44-yard TD pass for Dallas' first score and later hit Irvin on a 10-yard scoring pass for the game's final score. Emmitt Smith, who played with a pulled hamstring, scored two touchdowns and rushed for 74 yards.

"I give them a lot of credit for fighting back," said Young.

Dallas closed the gap to 24-14 late in the first half but was unable to kill the clock. Just before halftime, Young hit Jerry Rice with a 28-yard touchdown pass.

Dallas won the battle of statistics, outgaining San Francisco 451-294, but the Cowboys lost the ball on five turnovers.

After the game, Aikman spoke to Young. "This is your year," he said. "This is your turn in the Super Bowl. Make the most of it."

## SCORING

| | | | | | |
|---|---|---|---|---|---|
| DALLAS | 7 | 7 | 7 | 7 | - 28 |
| SAN FRANCISCO | 21 | 10 | 7 | 0 | - 38 |

**First Quarter**
S.F.  Davis, 44 yard interception return
PAT — Brien (kick)
S.F.  Watters, 29 yard pass from Young
PAT — Brien (kick)
S.F.  Floyd, 1 yard run
PAT — Brien (kick)
Dall.  Irvin, 44 yard pass from Aikman
PAT — Boniol (kick)

**Second Quarter**
S.F.  Brien, 34 yard field goal
Dall.  Smith, 4 yard run
PAT — Boniol (kick)
S.F.  Rice, 28 yard pass from Young
PAT — Brien (kick)

**Third Quarter**
Dall.  Smith, 1 yard run
PAT — Boniol (kick)
S.F.  Young, 3 yard run
PAT — Brien (kick)

**Fourth Quarter**
Dall.  Irvin, 10 yard pass from Aikman
PAT — Boniol (kick)

### TEAM STATISTICS

| DALL. | | S.F. |
|---|---|---|
| 29 | First Downs- Total | 19 |
| 8 | First Downs- Rushing | 9 |
| 18 | First Downs- Passing | 9 |
| 3 | First Downs- Penalty | 1 |
| 2 | Fumbles- Number | 1 |
| 2 | Fumbles- Lost Ball | 1 |
| 9 | Penalties- Number | 4 |
| 98 | Yards Penalized | 30 |
| 1 | Missed Field Goals | 0 |
| 81 | Offensive Plays | 60 |
| 451 | Net Yards | 294 |
| 5.6 | Average Gain | 4.9 |
| 5 | Giveaways | 1 |
| 1 | Takeaways | 5 |
| - 4 | Difference | + 4 |

## INDIVIDUAL STATISTICS

**RUSHING**

| DALLAS | No. | Yds. | Avg. | SAN FRANCISCO | No. | Yds. | Avg. |
|---|---|---|---|---|---|---|---|
| Smith | 20 | 74 | 3.7 | Watters | 14 | 72 | 5.1 |
| Williams | 2 | 12 | 6.0 | Young | 10 | 47 | 4.7 |
| Aikman | 1 | 9 | 9.0 | Floyd | 7 | 20 | 2.9 |
| Johnston | 1 | 4 | 4.0 | | 31 | 139 | 4.5 |
| | 24 | 99 | 4.1 | | | | |

**RECEIVING**

| DALLAS | No. | Yds. | Avg. | SAN FRANCISCO | No. | Yds. | Avg. |
|---|---|---|---|---|---|---|---|
| Irvin | 12 | 192 | 16.0 | Jones | 3 | 37 | 12.3 |
| Williams | 6 | 78 | 13.0 | Floyd | 3 | 16 | 5.3 |
| Novacek | 5 | 72 | 14.4 | Rice | 2 | 36 | 18.0 |
| Johnston | 3 | 19 | 6.3 | Taylor | 2 | 31 | 15.5 |
| Smith | 3 | 5 | 1.7 | Popson | 2 | 6 | 3.0 |
| Harper | 1 | 14 | 14.0 | Watters | 1 | 29 | 29.0 |
| | 30 | 380 | 12.7 | | 13 | 155 | 11.9 |

**PUNTING**

| DALLAS | No. | | Avg. | SAN FRANCISCO | No. | | Avg. |
|---|---|---|---|---|---|---|---|
| Jett | | | 23.0 | Wilmsmeyer | 5 | | 35.6 |

**PUNT RETURNS**

| DALLAS | No. | Yds. | Avg. | SAN FRANCISCO | No. | Yds. | Avg. |
|---|---|---|---|---|---|---|---|
| Williams | 1 | 10 | 10.0 | None | | | |
| Williams | 1FC | | | | | | |

**KICKOFF RETURNS**

| DALLAS | No. | Yds. | Avg. | SAN FRANCISCO | No. | Yds. | Avg. |
|---|---|---|---|---|---|---|---|
| Williams | 6 | 130 | 21.7 | Carter | 3 | 65 | 21.7 |
| Marion | 1 | 14 | 14.0 | Sanders | 1 | 25 | 25.0 |
| | 7 | 144 | 20.6 | Walker | 1 | 0 | 0.0 |
| | | | | | 5 | 90 | 19.0 |

**INTERCEPTION RETURNS**

| DALLAS | No. | Yds. | Avg. | SAN FRANCISCO | No. | Yds. | Avg. |
|---|---|---|---|---|---|---|---|
| None | | | | E. Davis | 2 | 44 | 22.0 |
| | | | | Sanders | 1 | 0 | 0.0 |
| | | | | | 3 | 44 | 14.7 |

**PASSING**

| DALLAS | Att. | Comp. | Comp. Pct. | Yds. | Int. | Yds./ Att. | Yds./ Comp. |
|---|---|---|---|---|---|---|---|
| Aikman | 53 | 30 | 56.6 | 380 | 3 | 7.2 | 12.7 |

| SAN FRANCISCO | Att. | Comp. | Comp. Pct. | Yds. | Int. | Yds./ Att. | Yds./ Comp. |
|---|---|---|---|---|---|---|---|
| Young | 29 | 13 | 44.8 | 155 | 0 | 5.3 | 11.9 |

# 49ers Win Record Fifth Super Bowl

The San Diego Chargers knew they had their work cut out for them. They went into Super Bowl XXIX as 18.5-point underdogs, the biggest pointspread ever. For San Diego to win, it would have to avoid falling behind. That didn't happen. On the third play of the game, San Francisco's Steve Young hit Jerry Rice with a 44-yard touchdown pass — the fastest scoring pass in Super Bowl history. After that, the outcome was never in doubt, as San Francisco won its fifth Super Bowl 49-26.

Actually, San Diego was down by only a touchdown. But the Chargers went three-and-out on their first offensive series. Four plays later, Young hooked up with Ricky Watters over the middle for a 51-yard TD pass. Fourteen-zip and game over.

The 49ers scripted the first 15 plays of the game, scoring almost at will. Young threw a Super Bowl-record six touchdown passes, three of them to Rice and two to Watters, who also scored a third touchdown on the ground.

The 49ers averaged 43.7 points per game in their three postseason victories. While they were able to score 26 points on San Francisco, the Chargers never really mounted much of a threat.

"I can't say I'm surprised," admitted 49ers head coach George Seifert. "We've got a wonderful football team, a great offense."

And a great quarterback. Young completed 24 of 36 passes for 325 yards and six TD's and led all rushers with 49 yards on five carries. He was unanimously voted the game's Most Valuable Player. And, with a Super Bowl victory, he erased all doubts about his talents and ended the knock that he wasn't as good as Joe Montana, the former 49ers quarterback who won four Super Bowls.

The Chargers closed the lead to 14-7 on Natrone Means' one-yard touchdown run in the first quarter. But the 49ers answered with two passing TD's by Young in the second quarter — a five-yarder to rookie fullback William Floyd and an eight-yarder to Watters.

The Chargers were forced to abandon their ground game in the second half, when they scored two more touchdowns — a 98-yard kickoff return by Andre Coleman and a 30-yard pass from Stan Humphries to Tony Martin. And San Diego scored the first two two-point conversions in Super Bowl history, both on passes from Humphries.

But the Chargers were helpless in trying to stop the 49ers. "I don't know if anybody has," admitted San Diego head coach Bobby Ross. "Control the ball — that's what we wanted to do — but we weren't able to do that. They have great players. You're not talking about Pro Bowl players — you're talking about potential Hall of Fame players."

The 75 points scored were the most in a Super Bowl game. But Super Bowl XXIX was the 10th blowout in 12 years and the 11th consecutive Super Bowl victory for an NFC team. San Diego's 26 points was the second-most for a Super Bowl loser.

Rice caught 10 passes for 149 yards, giving him Super Bowl career records of 30 receptions, 407 yards and seven touchdowns.

Still, the lopsided game could have been worse. "We put up 49 points, but it could have been way worse than that," said the 49ers' Floyd.

## LINEUPS

| S.D. | | S.F. |
|---|---|---|
| **OFFENSE** | | |
| Jefferson | WR | Taylor |
| Swayne | LT | Wallace |
| I. Davis | LG | Sapolu |
| Hall | C | Oates |
| Cocozzo | RG | Deese |
| Brock | RT | Barton |
| Young | TE | Jones |
| Seay | WR | Rice |
| Humphries | QB | S. Young |
| Pupunu | TE-RB | Watters |
| Means | RB | Floyd |
| **DEFENSE** | | |
| Mims | LE | Brown |
| Lee | LT | B. Young |
| R. Davis | RT | Stubblefield |
| O'Neal | RE | R. Jackson |
| Griggs | OLB/LLB | Woodall |
| Gibson | ILB/MLB | Plummer |
| Seau | ILB/RLB | Norton |
| Gordon | LCB | E. Davis |
| Harper | RCB | Sanders |
| Carrington | SS | McDonald |
| Richard | FS | Hanks |

### SUBSTITUTES

**SAN DIEGO**
**OFFENSE**
| | |
|---|---|
| Gilbert | Bieniemy | Harmon |
| Hendrickson | Culver | Binn |
| Parker | Jonassen | T. Martin |
| Coleman | Mitchell | |
| | **DEFENSE** | |
| Van Horse | W. Clark | R. Harrison |
| Castle | D. Miller | Bush |
| L. Miller | Parrella | R. Johnson |
| | **KICKERS** | |
| Carney | Wagner | |

**SAN FRANCISCO**
**OFFENSE**
| | |
|---|---|
| Musgrave | Grbac | Loville |
| A. Walker | D. Carter | Logan |
| Tamm | Dalman | Pollack |
| McCaffrey | Popson | Singleton |
| | **DEFENSE** | |
| Drakeford | D. Hall | Cook |
| Mitchell | Mann | D. Jordan |
| R. Hall | T. Wilson | Goss |
| T. Harris | | |
| | **KICKERS** | |
| Brien | Wilmsmeyer | |

## SCORING

| | | | | | |
|---|---|---|---|---|---|
| SAN DIEGO | 7 | 3 | 8 | 8 | - 26 |
| SAN FRANCISCO | 14 | 14 | 14 | 7 | - 49 |

**First Quarter**
S.F. — Rice, 44 yard pass from Young
PAT — Brien (kick)
S.F. — Watters, 51 yard pass from Young
PAT — Brien (kick)
S.D. — Means, 1 yard run
PAT — Carney (kick)

**Second Quarter**
S.F. — Floyd, 5 yard pass from Young
PAT — Brien (kick)
S.F. — Watters, 8 yard pass from Young
PAT — Brien (kick)
S.D. — Carney, 31 yard field goal

**Third Quarter**
S.F. — Watters, 9 yard run
PAT — Brien (kick)
S.F. — Rice, 15 yard pass from Young
PAT — Brien (kick)
S.D. — Coleman, 98 yard kickoff return
PAT — Seay (pass from Humphries)

**Fourth Quarter**
S.F. — Rice, 7 yard pass from Young
PAT — Brien (kick)
S.D. — T. Martin, 30 yard pass from Humphries
PAT — Pupunu (pass from Humphries)

## TEAM STATISTICS

| S.D. | | S.F. |
|---|---|---|
| 20 | First Downs-Total | 28 |
| 5 | First Downs-Rushing | 10 |
| 14 | First Downs-Passing | 17 |
| 1 | First Downs-Penalty | 1 |
| 1 | Fumbles-Number | 2 |
| 0 | Fumbles-Lost Ball | 0 |
| 6 | Penalties-Number | 3 |
| 63 | Yards Penalized | 18 |
| 0 | Missed Field Goals | 1 |
| 76 | Offensive Plays | 73 |
| 354 | Net Yards | 449 |
| 4.7 | Average Gain | 6.2 |
| 3 | Giveaways | 0 |
| 0 | Takeaways | 3 |
| - 3 | Difference | + 3 |

## INDIVIDUAL STATISTICS

### RUSHING

| SAN DIEGO | No. | Yds. | Avg. | SAN FRANCISCO | No. | Yds. | Avg. |
|---|---|---|---|---|---|---|---|
| Means | 13 | 33 | 2.5 | Young | 5 | 49 | 9.8 |
| Harmon | 2 | 10 | 5.0 | Watters | 15 | 47 | 3.1 |
| Jefferson | 1 | 10 | 10.0 | Floyd | 9 | 32 | 3.6 |
| Gilbert | 1 | 8 | 8.0 | Rice | 1 | 10 | 10.0 |
| Bieniemy | 1 | 3 | 3.0 | D. Carter | 2 | -5 | -2.5 |
| Humphries | 1 | 3 | 3.0 | | 32 | 133 | 4.2 |
| | 19 | 67 | 3.5 | | | | |

### RECEIVING

| SAN DIEGO | No. | Yds. | Avg. | SAN FRANCISCO | No. | Yds. | Avg. |
|---|---|---|---|---|---|---|---|
| Harmon | 8 | 68 | 8.5 | Rice | 10 | 149 | 14.9 |
| Seay | 7 | 75 | 10.7 | Taylor | 4 | 43 | 10.8 |
| Pupunu | 4 | 48 | 12.0 | Floyd | 4 | 26 | 6.5 |
| T. Martin | 3 | 59 | 19.7 | Watters | 3 | 61 | 20.3 |
| Jefferson | 2 | 15 | 7.5 | B. Jones | 2 | 41 | 20.5 |
| Bieniemy | 1 | 33 | 33.0 | Popson | 1 | 6 | 6.0 |
| Means | 1 | 4 | 4.0 | McCaffrey | 1 | 5 | 5.0 |
| Young | 1 | 3 | 3.0 | | 25 | 331 | 13.2 |
| | 27 | 305 | 11.3 | | | | |

### PUNTING

| | | | | | | | |
|---|---|---|---|---|---|---|---|
| Wagner | 4 | | 48.8 | Wilmsmeyer | 5 | | 39.8 |

### PUNT RETURNS

| | | | | | | | |
|---|---|---|---|---|---|---|---|
| Gordon | 3 | 1 | 1.0 | D. Carter | 2 | 12 | 6.0 |
| Gordon | 2 FC | | | | | | |

### KICKOFF RETURNS

| | | | | | | | |
|---|---|---|---|---|---|---|---|
| Coleman | 8 | 242 | 30.3 | D. Carter | 4 | 48 | 12.0 |
| | | | | McCaffrey | 0 | 0 | 0.0 |
| | | | | | 4 | 48 | 12.0 |

### INTERCEPTION RETURNS

| | | | | | | | |
|---|---|---|---|---|---|---|---|
| None | | | | D. Sanders | 1 | 15 | 15.0 |
| | | | | Cook | 1 | 1 | 1.0 |
| | | | | E. Davis | 1 | 0 | 0.0 |
| | | | | | 3 | 16 | 5.3 |

### PASSING

| SAN DIEGO | Att. | Comp. | Comp. Pct. | Yds. | Int. | Yds./ Att. | Yds./ Comp. | Yards Lost Tackled |
|---|---|---|---|---|---|---|---|---|
| Humphries | 49 | 24 | 49.0 | 275 | 2 | 5.6 | 11.4 | 18 |
| Gilbert | 6 | 3 | 50.0 | 30 | 1 | 5.0 | 10.0 | 0 |
| | 55 | 27 | 49.1 | 305 | 3 | 5.5 | 11.3 | 18 |
| **SAN FRANCISCO** | | | | | | | | |
| Young | 36 | 24 | 66.7 | 325 | 0 | 9.0 | 13.5 | 15 |
| Musgrave | 1 | 1 | 100.0 | 6 | 0 | 6.0 | 6.0 | 0 |
| Grbac | 1 | 0 | 0.0 | 0 | 0 | 0.0 | 0.0 | 0 |
| | 38 | 25 | 65.8 | 331 | 0 | 8.7 | 13.2 | 15 |

# 1995 N.F.C. NFL Expands to Carolina and Jacksonville

The NFL added two teams in 1995 for the first time in 19 years, with the Carolina Panthers and Jacksonville Jaguars beginning play. Both teams broke the previous record for victories by an expansion team. The Panthers were the surprise of the league, going 7-9 and flirting with a .500 until the final game. The Jaguars, meanwhile, finished 4-12, starting out 3-5 before losing seven straight.

There were several reasons for the success of the new teams. Free agency gave them unlimited access to an enormous pool of talent and the expansion draft was filled with a solid group of players (as compared to the injured and over-the-hill players made available in 1976 when Seattle and Tampa Bay joined the league). In addition, both teams were given double the normal allotment of draft choices. And, because Carolina and Jacksonville were starting from nothing, they had a lot of money to spend just to get up to the league minimum that teams had to spend under the salary cap.

Both teams pulled off major upsets. First the Jaguars defeated the Steelers, who would go on to become AFC champions, and then the Panthers upset the defending Super Bowl champion 49ers.

In Miami, an era ended at the end of the season when Don Shula resigned following 33 years of coaching. If that wasn't a big-enough bombshell, the very next week the Dolphins hired former Cowboys coach Jimmy Johnson, who replaced another legend. Shula's final season was filled with turmoil, as his heavily favored Dolphins fell apart, but many felt Shula deserved a better fate.

## EASTERN DIVISION

**Dallas Cowboys** — They did it again. Oft-criticized in 1995 and with head coach Barry Switzer trying to prove he could do what Jimmy Johnson did twice, the Cowboys won their third Super Bowl in four years. Dallas won 12 regular-season games, a fifth consecutive NFC East title and stretched its playoff record over the past four seasons to 10-1. Again, the offensive "triplets" did it again. QB Troy Aikman started all 16 games and passed for 3,304 yards and 16 TD's, RB Emmitt Smith ran for 1,773 yards and an NFL-record 25 touchdowns, and WR Michael Irvin caught 111 passes for 1,603 yards and 10 scores. Although the defense took backseat to the offensive stars, it held seven of its final nine opponents to 21 points or fewer. And it had Deion Sanders, who signed with Dallas as a free agent.

**Philadelphia Eagles** — Philadelphia was outscored by 20 points during the regular season and lost five games by 12 or more points (playoffs included). They had the second-worst passing attack in the NFL and the league's worst special teams since 1976. Their defensive backs scored more touchdowns than their top wide receiver, and they beat only one team with a winning record all year. Somehow, the Eagles won 10 games and advanced to the second round of the playoffs. Randall Cunningham was replaced at quarterback by Rodney Peete, who was not good himself. Ricky Watters was the star on offense, rushing for 1,273 yards and 11 TD's after being signed as a free agent from San Francisco.

**Washington Redskins** — The Redskins started 1995 with a victory and ended it with two wins, but in between were too many losses. The Redskins did develop a running game, as Terry Allen gained 1,309 yards, the second-best season ever for a Washington back. And WR Henry Ellard had another 1,000-yard receiving season. But a season-long quarterback controversy plagued the team. Heath Shuler started the year but suffered an injury in the first game. Gus Frerotte took over, but the team went only 2-8 under him. Enter Shuler again, and he did defeat Dallas, but then he was injured again. The most consistent player was Brian Mitchell, who gained 1,408 yards on kickoffs, 315 on punt returns, 324 on receptions and 301 rushing.

**New York Giants** — The Giants didn't come close to expectations in 1995, going 5-11 in a season that began with a 35-0 loss to Dallas and two other losses. The Giants were 5-0 against teams that were under .500 and 0-11 against .500 or better clubs. RB Rodney Hampton ran for a career-high 1,182 yards and 10 TD's and kept Herschel Walker and rookie Tyrone Wheatley on the bench. But QB Dave Brown didn't

progress, even though he was the leader of a low-risk offense that finished dead-last in passing yards. He threw for 2,814 yards and 11 scores, but otherwise didn't impress. No one else — on offense or defense — seemed to be able to make big plays. The defense allowed more rushing yards than all but three teams.

**Arizona Cardinals** — Buddy Ryan failed to turn the Cardinals into winners, and he was fired following a 4-12 season. Arizona started off 1-5 and never got anything going. Again., the biggest problem was a lousy offense. QB Dave Krieg threw 21 interceptions and was sacked 53 times. RB Garrison Hearst surpassed 1,000 yards for his first time as a pro (1,070 yards), but Larry Centers was the back who stole the show, as he broke Roger Craig's NFL record for pass receptions by a running back (101) en route to a Pro Bowl season. Once again Ryan was loaded with defensive talent, but Eric Swann, Aeneas Williams, Seth Joyner and Clyde Simmons couldn't make up for the lack of offense.

## CENTRAL DIVISION

**Green Bay Packers** — With victories in the first two rounds of the playoffs, the Packers were on the brink of their first Super Bowl since the 1960s. Only a loss to Dallas ended those hopes for the Packers faithful. Still, 1995 was Green Bay's best season since the Lombardi era. Brett Favre was the NFL's Most Valuable Player, after he passed for 4,413 yards and 38 TD's to a corps of receivers that was unproven before the start of the season. Robert Brooks was the biggest playmaker, catching 102 balls for 1,497 yards and 13 scores. RB Edgar Bennett was a two-way threat, with 1,067 yards rushing and 61 catches. The defense yielded the fourth-fewest points in the NFL, though it was its most since 1990.

**Detroit Lions** — A season if many highs ended with the usual low — the Lions lost their wild-card game for the third consecutive year. A seven-game winning streak at the end of the season and a 10-6 record helped head coach Wayne Fontes keep his job again. The offense was explosive. QB Scott Mitchell threw for 4,338 yards and 32 touchdowns, Barry Sanders ran for 1,500 yards and 11 TD's, Herman Moore set an NFL record with 123 receptions for 1,686 yards and 14 scores, and Brett Perriman added 108 catches and nine TD's. The problem was a bad defense that allowed 20 or more points the first nine weeks of the season when Detroit started out 3-6.

**Chicago Bears** — The 1995 Bears were a team unlike any other Chicago team. The offense was record-setting and the defense was lousy. QB Erik Kramer had the best season by a quarterback in team history, passing for a team-record 3,838 yards and breaking Sid Luckman's record for TD passes with 29. Rookie RB Rashaan Salaam ran for 1,074 yards and WR's Jeff Graham and Curtis Conway each had 1,000-yard seasons and combined for 16 touchdowns. But the usual strong Chicago defense fell apart, allowing 360 points, fourth worst in the NFC. The Bears won six of their first eight games and appeared headed for the playoffs. Then came a losing streak, and only two wins to end the season gave them a winning record.

**Minnesota Vikings** — Minnesota slumped to an 8-8 record in 1995, losing five of its first eight games before a late-season winning streak. Quarterback Warren Moon had an impressive season, tying his career-best with 33 TD passes and topping 4,000 yards for the fourth time. He also became the first Vikings quarterback since 1979 to start all 16 games. RB Robert Smith showed flashes was the leading rusher with 632 yards, but he was extremely inconsistent and injury-prone. WR Cris Carter repeated his 122 catches of 1994 but lost his NFL record by one catch to Detroit's Herman Moore. But defense was the overriding reason the '95 Vikings fell out of the playoff picture, because DT John Randle was the only stellar player.

**Tampa Bay Buccaneers** — The Buccaneers finished in last place once again, but at least they stopped their streak of 12 consecutive seasons with 10 or more losses. They started out 5-2, but eventually mediocrity caught up to them again. Trent Dilfer (4 TD's, 18 intercep-

FINAL TEAM STATISTICS

**OFFENSE**

| | ARIZ | ATL | CAR | CHI | DAL | DET | G.B. | MINN | N.O. | NYG | PHIL | ST.L. | S.F. | T.B. | WASH |
|---|---|---|---|---|---|---|---|---|---|---|---|---|---|---|---|
| FIRST DOWNS: | | | | | | | | | | | | | | | |
| Total | 285 | 317 | 250 | 340 | 364 | 349 | 339 | 342 | 294 | 288 | 290 | 292 | 355 | 283 | 297 |
| by Rushing | 65 | 85 | 74 | 116 | 141 | 91 | 84 | 91 | 75 | 113 | 126 | 77 | 109 | 101 | 105 |
| by Passing | 184 | 216 | 157 | 201 | 195 | 230 | 235 | 223 | 202 | 150 | 145 | 199 | 231 | 159 | 169 |
| by Penalty | 36 | 16 | 19 | 23 | 28 | 28 | 20 | 28 | 17 | 25 | 19 | 16 | 15 | 23 | 23 |
| RUSHING: | | | | | | | | | | | | | | | |
| Number | 387 | 337 | 454 | 492 | 495 | 387 | 410 | 433 | 383 | 478 | 508 | 392 | 415 | 398 | 469 |
| Yards | 1363 | 1393 | 1573 | 1930 | 2201 | 1753 | 1428 | 1733 | 1390 | 1833 | 2121 | 1431 | 1479 | 1587 | 1956 |
| Average Yards | 3.5 | 4.1 | 3.5 | 3.9 | 4.4 | 4.5 | 3.5 | 4.0 | 3.6 | 3.8 | 4.2 | 3.7 | 3.6 | 4.0 | 4.2 |
| Touchdowns | 3 | 8 | 10 | 15 | 29 | 16 | 9 | 10 | 11 | 17 | 19 | 5 | 19 | 19 | 15 |
| PASSING: | | | | | | | | | | | | | | | |
| Attempts | 560 | 603 | 537 | 523 | 494 | 605 | 593 | 642 | 573 | 479 | 496 | 632 | 644 | 507 | 521 |
| Completions | 327 | 364 | 263 | 315 | 322 | 362 | 373 | 402 | 349 | 260 | 284 | 366 | 432 | 267 | 265 |
| Completion Pct. | 58.4 | 60.4 | 49.0 | 60.2 | 65.2 | 59.8 | 62.7 | 62.6 | 60.9 | 54.3 | 57.3 | 57.9 | 67.1 | 52.7 | 50.9 |
| Passing Yards | 3893 | 4456 | 3304 | 3838 | 3741 | 4510 | 4539 | 4500 | 4002 | 2863 | 2931 | 4113 | 4779 | 3341 | 3496 |
| Avg. Yds per Att. | 5.70 | 6.48 | 5.30 | 6.96 | 7.08 | 6.84 | 6.90 | 6.17 | 6.30 | 5.05 | 4.96 | 5.64 | 6.81 | 5.25 | 5.80 |
| Avg. Yds per Comp. | 11.91 | 12.24 | 12.56 | 12.18 | 11.62 | 12.46 | 12.20 | 11.19 | 11.47 | 11.01 | 10.32 | 11.24 | 11.06 | 12.51 | 13.19 |
| Times Tackled | 55 | 43 | 38 | 15 | 18 | 32 | 33 | 40 | 28 | 46 | 46 | 43 | 33 | 56 | 36 |
| Yds Lost Tackled | 390 | 270 | 258 | 95 | 118 | 150 | 217 | 295 | 214 | 213 | 245 | 308 | 171 | 386 | 268 |
| Net Yards | 3503 | 4186 | 3046 | 3743 | 3623 | 4360 | 4322 | 4205 | 3788 | 2650 | 2686 | 3805 | 4608 | 2955 | 3228 |
| Touchdowns | 17 | 26 | 16 | 29 | 18 | 33 | 39 | 33 | 26 | 11 | 11 | 27 | 29 | 5 | 16 |
| Interceptions | 24 | 12 | 25 | 10 | 10 | 12 | 15 | 16 | 14 | 13 | 19 | 23 | 16 | 20 | 20 |
| Pct. Intercepted | 4.3 | 2.0 | 4.7 | 1.9 | 2.0 | 2.0 | 2.5 | 2.5 | 2.4 | 2.7 | 3.8 | 3.6 | 2.5 | 3.9 | 3.8 |
| PUNTS: | | | | | | | | | | | | | | | |
| Number | 72 | 67 | 96 | 58 | 55 | 60 | 67 | 72 | 74 | 73 | 86 | 83 | 57 | 78 | 74 |
| Average | 43.8 | 41.2 | 41.0 | 37.4 | 40.8 | 40.5 | 40.9 | 40.9 | 40.1 | 42.2 | 42.8 | 44.3 | 40.6 | 42.3 | 42.4 |
| PUNT RETURNS | | | | | | | | | | | | | | | |
| Number | 23 | 39 | 49 | 24 | 23 | 24 | 61 | 35 | 29 | 31 | 29 | 55 | 27 | 29 | 26 |
| Yards | 172 | 383 | 500 | 179 | 255 | 189 | 515 | 414 | 268 | 218 | 293 | 587 | 272 | 293 | 315 |
| Average Yards | 7.5 | 9.8 | 10.2 | 7.5 | 11.1 | 7.9 | 8.4 | 11.8 | 9.2 | 7.0 | 10.1 | 10.7 | 10.1 | 10.1 | 12.1 |
| Touchdowns | 0 | 1 | 1 | 0 | 0 | 0 | 0 | 1 | 0 | 0 | 0 | 0 | 1 | 0 | 1 |
| KICKOFF RET.: | | | | | | | | | | | | | | | |
| Number | 73 | 70 | 55 | 71 | 58 | 67 | 61 | 72 | 73 | 70 | 71 | 73 | 58 | 76 | 69 |
| Yards | 1519 | 1506 | 1163 | 1459 | 1276 | 1367 | 1282 | 1612 | 1690 | 1448 | 1487 | 1618 | 1183 | 1443 | 1646 |
| Average Yards | 20.8 | 21.5 | 21.1 | 20.5 | 22.0 | 20.4 | 21.0 | 22.4 | 23.2 | 20.7 | 20.9 | 22.2 | 20.4 | 19.0 | 23.9 |
| Touchdowns | 0 | 0 | 0 | 0 | 0 | 0 | 0 | 0 | 0 | 1 | 1 | 0 | 0 | 0 | 0 |
| INTERCEPT RET.: | | | | | | | | | | | | | | | |
| Number | 19 | 18 | 21 | 16 | 19 | 22 | 13 | 25 | 17 | 16 | 19 | 22 | 26 | 14 | 16 |
| Yards | 259 | 304 | 319 | 146 | 261 | 270 | 253 | 326 | 195 | 269 | 239 | 245 | 425 | 137 | 250 |
| Average Yards | 13.6 | 16.9 | 15.2 | 9.1 | 13.7 | 12.3 | 19.5 | 13.0 | 11.5 | 16.8 | 12.6 | 11.1 | 16.3 | 9.8 | 15.6 |
| Touchdowns | 4 | 2 | 2 | 1 | 4 | 0 | 0 | 2 | 1 | 2 | 1 | 2 | 5 | 1 | 2 |
| PENALTIES: | | | | | | | | | | | | | | | |
| Number | 119 | 96 | 94 | 71 | 90 | 134 | 85 | 105 | 86 | 92 | 112 | 117 | 88 | 113 | 78 |
| Yards | 835 | 737 | 683 | 601 | 695 | 1032 | 604 | 797 | 688 | 772 | 838 | 916 | 711 | 882 | 563 |
| FUMBLES: | | | | | | | | | | | | | | | |
| Number | 41 | 21 | 28 | 26 | 24 | 21 | 22 | 29 | 19 | 27 | 31 | 27 | 21 | 25 | 24 |
| Number Lost | 19 | 9 | 16 | 16 | 13 | 13 | 6 | 13 | 11 | 15 | 17 | 16 | 12 | 14 | 10 |
| POINTS: | | | | | | | | | | | | | | | |
| Total | 275 | 362 | 289 | 392 | 435 | 436 | 404 | 412 | 319 | 290 | 318 | 309 | 457 | 238 | 326 |
| 1-PT PAT/ATT. | 19/19 | 29/30 | 27/28 | 45/45 | 46/48 | 48/48 | 48/48 | 44/44 | 27/29 | 28/28 | 32/33 | 30/31 | 51/54 | 25/25 | 33/33 |
| 2-PT PAT/Att. | 5/6 | 3/8 | 2/2 | 0/2 | 1/2 | 1/2 | 1/1 | 1/1 | 2/9 | 1/4 | 2/3 | 2/6 | 2/3 | 0/1 | 0/1 |
| FG Attempts | 39 | 40 | 33 | 31 | 28 | 34 | 28 | 36 | 31 | 28 | 30 | 28 | 28 | 26 | 36 |
| FG Made | 30 | 33 | 26 | 23 | 27 | 28 | 20 | 26 | 20 | 20 | 22 | 17 | 20 | 19 | 27 |
| Percent FG Made | 76.9 | 82.5 | 78.8 | 74.2 | 96.4 | 82.4 | 71.4 | 72.2 | 64.5 | 71.4 | 73.3 | 60.7 | 71.4 | 73.1 | 75.0 |
| Safeties | 0 | 0 | 0 | 1 | 0 | 1 | 0 | 0 | 0 | 1 | 0 | 1 | 0 | 0 | 1 |

**DEFENSE**

| | ARIZ | ATL | CAR | CHI | DAL | DET | G.B. | MINN | N.O. | NYG | PHIL | ST.L. | S.F. | T.B. | WASH |
|---|---|---|---|---|---|---|---|---|---|---|---|---|---|---|---|
| FIRST DOWNS: | | | | | | | | | | | | | | | |
| Total | 310 | 340 | 288 | 316 | 303 | 350 | 303 | 312 | 320 | 335 | 281 | 301 | 264 | 336 | 323 |
| by Rushing | 105 | 96 | 99 | 81 | 113 | 110 | 99 | 75 | 107 | 120 | 102 | 101 | 57 | 104 | 127 |
| by Passing | 180 | 230 | 175 | 212 | 165 | 201 | 188 | 212 | 195 | 187 | 154 | 178 | 192 | 202 | 182 |
| by Penalty | 25 | 14 | 14 | 23 | 25 | 39 | 16 | 25 | 18 | 28 | 25 | 22 | 15 | 30 | 14 |
| RUSHING: | | | | | | | | | | | | | | | |
| Number | 503 | 404 | 450 | 405 | 442 | 409 | 374 | 352 | 469 | 500 | 466 | 410 | 348 | 449 | 483 |
| Yards | 2249 | 1547 | 1576 | 1441 | 1772 | 1795 | 1515 | 1329 | 1838 | 2109 | 1822 | 1677 | 1061 | 1754 | 2132 |
| Average Yards | 4.5 | 3.8 | 3.5 | 3.6 | 4.0 | 4.4 | 4.1 | 3.8 | 3.9 | 4.2 | 3.9 | 4.1 | 3.0 | 3.9 | 4.4 |
| Touchdowns | 14 | 12 | 17 | 9 | 13 | 15 | 12 | 11 | 13 | 17 | 14 | 14 | 5 | 14 | 18 |
| PASSING: | | | | | | | | | | | | | | | |
| Attempts | 461 | 650 | 586 | 595 | 523 | 580 | 616 | 620 | 543 | 508 | 499 | 534 | 611 | 557 | 546 |
| Completions | 264 | 405 | 310 | 374 | 293 | 354 | 351 | 369 | 329 | 299 | 268 | 320 | 330 | 346 | 338 |
| Completion Pct. | 57.3 | 62.3 | 52.9 | 62.9 | 56.0 | 61.0 | 57.0 | 59.5 | 60.6 | 58.9 | 53.7 | 59.9 | 54.0 | 62.1 | 61.9 |
| Passing Yards | 3655 | 4751 | 3716 | 4240 | 3491 | 4121 | 3915 | 4416 | 3998 | 3361 | 3121 | 3699 | 3577 | 4098 | 3403 |
| Avg. Yds per Att. | 7.02 | 6.68 | 5.55 | 6.35 | 5.85 | 6.12 | 5.56 | 6.21 | 6.34 | 5.93 | 5.15 | 6.04 | 5.13 | 6.80 | 5.67 |
| Avg. Yds per Comp. | 13.84 | 11.73 | 11.99 | 11.34 | 11.91 | 11.64 | 11.15 | 11.97 | 12.15 | 11.24 | 11.65 | 11.56 | 10.84 | 11.84 | 10.07 |
| Times Tackled | 31 | 30 | 36 | 35 | 36 | 42 | 39 | 44 | 44 | 29 | 48 | 36 | 40 | 25 | 30 |
| Yds Lost Tackled | 200 | 210 | 265 | 239 | 219 | 317 | 275 | 294 | 275 | 177 | 305 | 258 | 240 | 140 | 135 |
| Net Yards | 3455 | 4541 | 3451 | 4001 | 3272 | 3804 | 3640 | 4122 | 3723 | 3184 | 2816 | 3441 | 3337 | 3958 | 3268 |
| Touchdowns | 33 | 28 | 15 | 27 | 17 | 17 | 25 | 29 | 23 | 17 | 14 | 27 | 19 | 19 | 20 |
| Interceptions | 19 | 18 | 21 | 16 | 19 | 22 | 13 | 25 | 17 | 16 | 19 | 22 | 26 | 14 | 16 |
| Pct. Intercepted | 4.1 | 2.8 | 3.6 | 4.5 | 3.6 | 3.8 | 2.1 | 4.0 | 3.1 | 3.1 | 3.8 | 4.1 | 4.3 | 2.5 | 2.9 |
| PUNTS: | | | | | | | | | | | | | | | |
| Number | 62 | 70 | 94 | 62 | 65 | 61 | 88 | 68 | 66 | 63 | 74 | 79 | 70 | 59 | 72 |
| Average | 43.5 | 43.3 | 40.4 | 37.3 | 42.7 | 42.7 | 42.6 | 42.2 | 41.8 | 42.2 | 41.3 | 43.5 | 41.7 | 40.0 | 41.4 |
| PUNT RETURNS | | | | | | | | | | | | | | | |
| Number | 32 | 28 | 39 | 28 | 22 | 29 | 36 | 41 | 36 | 34 | 38 | 38 | 26 | 41 | 26 |
| Yards | 242 | 236 | 342 | 257 | 216 | 442 | 279 | 446 | 233 | 297 | 527 | 393 | 292 | 335 | 173 |
| Average Yards | 7.6 | 8.4 | 8.8 | 9.2 | 9.8 | 15.2 | 7.8 | 10.9 | 6.5 | 8.7 | 13.9 | 10.3 | 11.2 | 8.2 | 6.7 |
| Touchdowns | 0 | 0 | 0 | 1 | 0 | 1 | 0 | 1 | 0 | 1 | 2 | 1 | 0 | 0 | 0 |
| KICKOFF RET.: | | | | | | | | | | | | | | | |
| Number | 65 | 59 | 62 | 72 | 85 | 80 | 74 | 74 | 68 | 54 | 61 | 59 | 82 | 46 | 70 |
| Yards | 1593 | 1323 | 1159 | 1570 | 1661 | 1828 | 1581 | 1581 | 1348 | 1129 | 1576 | 1247 | 1857 | 856 | 1434 |
| Average Yards | 24.5 | 22.4 | 18.7 | 21.8 | 19.5 | 22.9 | 21.4 | 21.4 | 19.8 | 20.9 | 25.8 | 21.1 | 22.6 | 18.6 | 20.5 |
| Touchdowns | 2 | 0 | 0 | 0 | 0 | 0 | 0 | 0 | 0 | 0 | 0 | 0 | 0 | 0 | 1 |
| INTERCEPT RET.: | | | | | | | | | | | | | | | |
| Number | 24 | 12 | 25 | 10 | 10 | 12 | 15 | 16 | 14 | 13 | 19 | 23 | 16 | 20 | 20 |
| Yards | 307 | 49 | 221 | 203 | 155 | 219 | 243 | 172 | 273 | 241 | 240 | 497 | 247 | 204 | 338 |
| Average Yards | 12.8 | 4.1 | 8.8 | 20.3 | 15.5 | 18.3 | 16.2 | 10.8 | 19.5 | 18.5 | 12.6 | 11.1 | 15.4 | 10.2 | 16.9 |
| Touchdowns | 4 | 2 | 3 | 1 | 1 | 2 | 0 | 1 | 2 | 1 | 2 | 5 | 2 | 0 | 3 |
| PENALTIES: | | | | | | | | | | | | | | | |
| Number | 117 | 94 | 112 | 104 | 112 | 120 | 98 | 100 | 109 | 94 | 87 | 87 | 74 | 87 | 100 |
| Yards | 860 | 688 | 808 | 821 | 913 | 1001 | 738 | 707 | 830 | 662 | 727 | 681 | 556 | 698 | 780 |
| FUMBLES: | | | | | | | | | | | | | | | |
| Number | 39 | 21 | 28 | 25 | 16 | 24 | 12 | 30 | 29 | 29 | 30 | 27 | 23 | 26 | 31 |
| Number Lost | 23 | 12 | 16 | 13 | 6 | 13 | 3 | 15 | 12 | 15 | 19 | 14 | 8 | 16 | 19 |
| POINTS: | | | | | | | | | | | | | | | |
| Total | 422 | 349 | 325 | 360 | 291 | 336 | 314 | 385 | 348 | 340 | 338 | 418 | 258 | 335 | 359 |
| 1-PT PAT/ATT. | 50/51 | 38/38 | 38/38 | 40/40 | 29/29 | 32/32 | 35/35 | 29/32 | 33/33 | 32/33 | 32/32 | 47/48 | 17/18 | 30/31 | 39/40 |
| 2-PT PAT/Att. | 0/0 | 0/5 | 0/0 | 1/1 | 1/3 | 2/3 | 0/2 | 7/8 | 3/5 | 1/4 | 2/4 | 1/3 | 2/8 | 1/4 | 1/2 |
| FG Attempts | 25 | 22 | 26 | 29 | 27 | 42 | 21 | 35 | 35 | 35 | 37 | 27 | 32 | 40 | 27 |
| FG Made | 18 | 17 | 19 | 24 | 22 | 28 | 19 | 26 | 27 | 28 | 28 | 21 | 27 | 31 | 22 |
| Percent FG Made | 72.0 | 77.3 | 73.1 | 82.8 | 81.5 | 66.7 | 90.5 | 74.3 | 77.1 | 80.0 | 75.7 | 77.8 | 84.4 | 77.5 | 81.5 |
| Safeties | 0 | 1 | 1 | 0 | 1 | 0 | 0 | 0 | 0 | 0 | 1 | 0 | 0 | 0 | 0 |

tions) and the Bucs had the lowest passer rating in the league, which hindered the performance of the wide receivers. Errict Rhett ran for 1,207 yards and 11 touchdowns and PK Michael Husted had winning kicks in three games. Perhaps the NFL's worst free-agent signing was that of WR Alvin Harper, who caught only 46 passes for 633 yards). After the season, Sam Wyche was fired and replaced by Tony Dungy.

## WESTERN DIVISION

**San Francisco 49ers** — The defending champions came down to earth quickly, going only 5-4 in the first nine weeks before a big win over Dallas in mid-November. But, even though the offense got untracked late in the season, the 49ers were shocked by Green Bay in the first round of the playoffs, losing 27-17. Still, San Francisco had an NFL-record 13th consecutive winning season and won the NFC West for the 12th time in 15 years. Steve Young passed for 3,200 yards and 20 TD's — mild numbers by his standards — but Jerry Rice was the offensive star with 122 receptions for a league-record 1,848 yards and 15 scores. Journeyman RB Derek Loville scored 13 times but wasn't good enough to help the 49ers over the top.

**Atlanta Falcons** — The Falcons went 9-7 and made the playoffs for only the fifth time in the franchise's 30 years. Atlanta was 7-1 at home, showing marked improvement in June Jones' second season as head coach. The Falcons allowed 4,541 yards — the most in NFL history. But they posted a team-record 4,186 yards passing and they had Morten Andersen. The former Saints kicker scored 122 points and set NFL records for most 50-yarders in a game (three) and season (eight) and three times set team records for longest field goals. Four players gained 1,000-yards — RB Craig Heyward (1,083 rushing) and WR's Eric Metcalf (104 receptions, 1,189 yards), Terance Mathis (1,039 yards) and Bert Emanuel (1,039).

**St. Louis Rams** — In their first season in St. Louis, the Rams started out as the surprise of the league and ended it as the same old Rams. They sprang out of the gate to a 5-1 mark, but losses in five of the final six games ended any hopes of making the playoffs. An unproven player entering the season, WR Isaac Bruce had a great season with 119 receptions for 1,781 yards and 13 touchdowns. QB Chris Miller was plagued with concussions again and missed too much time and threw too many interceptions. RB Jerome Bettis was even more disappointing, with only 637 rushing yards and three TD's. The defense allowed a franchise-record and league-worst 418 points, though the team did let up 10 TD's on returns.

**Carolina Panthers** — Carolina started out 0-5, then won seven of its final 11 games to set the league record for most victories by an expansion team. Dom Capers' blitzing defense set the stage, and Sam Mills was the ringleader. The 36-year-old linebacker created 14 turnovers and led the team in tackles. On offense, rookie Kerry Collins took over at quarterback a month into the season and passed for 14 touchdowns, though he had 19 interceptions. Derrick Moore was the leading ball carrier (740 yards) and WR Willie Green led the NFC with an 18.8-yard average on 47 receptions.

**New Orleans Saints** — The Saints started out with five losses and finished behind the expansion Panthers, but coach Jim Mora was spared of his job because the team rallied to a 7-4 mark over the last three months. The team has, however, slid from playoff contention. The 1995 Saints lost some key players and got no help from their draft class. QB Jim Everett did pass for almost 4,000 yards and 26 touchdowns. WR Quinn Early benefited the most, with 81 receptions for 1,0867 yards and eight scores. RB Mario Bates had 951 yards, but New Orleans mostly failed the run the ball with any consistency.

## DALLAS COWBOYS 12-4 Barry Switzer

| Scores of Each Game | | |
|---|---|---|
| 35 | New York Giants | 0 |
| 31 | DENVER | 21 |
| 23 | Minnesota | 17 |
| 34 | ARIZONA | 20 |
| 23 | Washington | 27 |
| 34 | GREEN BAY | 24 |
| 23 | San Diego | 9 |
| 28 | Atlanta | 13 |
| 34 | PHILADELPHIA | 12 |
| 20 | SAN FRANCISCO | 38 |
| 34 | Oakland | 21 |
| 24 | KANSAS CITY | 12 |
| 17 | WASHINGTON | 24 |
| 17 | Philadelphia | 20 |
| 21 | NEW YORK GIANTS | 20 |
| 37 | Arizona | 13 |

| Use Name | Pos. | Hgt. | Wgt. | Age | Int | Pts |
|---|---|---|---|---|---|---|
| George Hegamin | OT | 6'7" | 331 | 22 | | |
| Ron Stone | OT-OG | 6'5" | 310 | 24 | | |
| Mark Tuinei | OT | 6'5" | 314 | 25 | | |
| Erik Williams | OT | 6'6" | 324 | 26 | | |
| Larry Allen | OT | 6'3" | 326 | 23 | | |
| Michael Batiste | OG-DT | 6'3" | 305 | 24 | | |
| Dale Hellestrae | OG-C | 6'5" | 286 | 33 | | |
| Derek Kennard | OG | 6'3" | 333 | 32 | | |
| Nate Newton | OG | 6'3" | 320 | 33 | | |
| Ray Donaldson | C | 6'3" | 311 | 37 | | |
| Shante Carver | DE | 6'5" | 253 | 24 | | |
| Charles Haley | DE | 6'5" | 255 | 31 | | |
| Oscar Sturgis | DE | 6'5" | 278 | 24 | | |
| Tony Tolbert | DE | 6'6" | 263 | 27 | | |
| Darren Benson | DT | 6'7" | 308 | 22 | | |
| Chad Hennings | DT | 6'6" | 295 | 29 | | |
| Leon Lett | DT | 6'6" | 291 | 26 | | |
| Russell Maryland | DT | 6'1" | 282 | 26 | | |
| Hurvin McCormack | DT | 6'5" | 278 | 23 | | |
| Reggie Barnes | LB | 6'1" | 240 | 25 | | |
| Dixon Edwards | LB | 6'1" | 225 | 27 | | |
| Anthony Fieldings | LB | 6'1" | 237 | 24 | | |
| Darryl Hardy (from ARZ) | LB | 6'2" | 230 | 26 | | |
| Robert Jones | LB | 6'2" | 244 | 25 | | |
| Godfrey Myles | LB | 6'1" | 240 | 26 | 1 | |
| Jim Schwantz | LB | 6'2" | 240 | 25 | | |
| Darrin Smith | LB | 6'1" | 230 | 25 | | |
| Robert Bailey | DB | 5'9" | 176 | 26 | | |
| Bill Bates | DB | 6'1" | 211 | 34 | | |
| Alundis Brice | DB | 5'10" | 178 | 25 | 1 | |
| Greg Briggs | DB | 6'3" | 212 | 26 | | |
| Larry Brown | DB | 5'11" | 186 | 25 | 6 | 12 |
| Scott Case | DB | 6'1" | 188 | 33 | | |
| Clayton Holmes | DB | 5'10" | 181 | 26 | 1 | |
| Brock Marion | DB | 5'11" | 193 | 25 | 6 | 6 |
| Deion Sanders | DB-WR | 6'1" | 190 | 28 | 2 | |
| Kevin Smith | DB | 5'11" | 188 | 25 | | |
| Greg Tremble (to PHIL) | DB | 5'1" | 188 | 23 | | |
| Charlie Williams | DB | 6' | 189 | 23 | | |
| Darren Woodson | DB | 6'1" | 216 | 26 | 2 | 6 |
| Troy Aikman | QB | 6'4" | 223 | 28 | | 6 |
| Jason Garrett | QB | 6'2" | 195 | 29 | | |
| Wade Wilson | QB | 6'3" | 206 | 36 | | |
| David Lang | HB | 5'11" | 210 | 27 | | |
| Dominique Ross | HB | 6' | 203 | 23 | | |
| Emmitt Smith | HB | 5'9" | 209 | 26 | | 150 |
| Sherman Williams | HB | 5'8" | 191 | 22 | | 6 |
| Daryl Johnston | FB | 6'2" | 242 | 29 | | 18 |
| Billy Davis | WR | 6'1" | 197 | 23 | | |
| Cory Fleming | WR | 6'1" | 216 | 24 | | |
| Michael Irvin | WR | 6'2" | 207 | 29 | | 60 |
| Kevin Williams | WR | 5'9" | 194 | 24 | | 12 |
| Eric Bjornson | TE | 6'4" | 236 | 23 | | |
| Jay Novacek | TE | 6'4" | 234 | 32 | | 32 |
| Kendall Watkins | TE | 6'1" | 282 | 22 | | |
| Jon Baker | K | 6'1" | 170 | 23 | | |
| Chris Boniol | K | 5'11" | 167 | 23 | | 127 |
| John Jett | K | 6' | 199 | 26 | | |

## PHILADELPHIA EAGLES 10-6 Ray Rhodes

| Scores of Each Game | | |
|---|---|---|
| 6 | TAMPA BAY | 21 |
| 31 | Arizona | 19 |
| 21 | SAN DIEGO | 27 |
| 17 | Oakland | 48 |
| 15 | New Orleans | 10 |
| 37 | WASHINGTON | *34 |
| 17 | New York Giants | 14 |
| 20 | ST. LOUIS | 9 |
| 12 | Dallas | 34 |
| 31 | DENVER | 13 |
| 28 | NEW YORK GIANTS | 19 |
| 14 | Washington | 7 |
| 14 | Seattle | 26 |
| 20 | DALLAS | 17 |
| 21 | ARIZONA | 20 |
| 14 | Chicago | 20 |

| Use Name | Pos. | Hgt. | Wgt. | Age | Int | Pts |
|---|---|---|---|---|---|---|
| Harry Boatswain | OT | 6'4" | 295 | 26 | | |
| Barrett Brooks | OT | 6'4" | 309 | 23 | | |
| Antone Davis | OT | 6'4" | 335 | 28 | | |
| Troy Drake | OT | 6'6" | 289 | 23 | | |
| Mo Elewonibi | OT | 6'4" | 302 | 29 | | |
| Theo Adams | OG | 6'5" | 300 | 29 | | |
| Lester Holmes | OG | 6'3" | 305 | 25 | | |
| Guy McIntyre | OG | 6'3" | 290 | 34 | | |
| Joe Panos | OG-C | 6'2" | 293 | 24 | | |
| Joe Rudolph | OG | 6'1" | 285 | 23 | | |
| Frank Cornish (from JAX) | C | 6'4" | 315 | 27 | | |
| John Hudson | C | 6'2" | 276 | 27 | | |
| Raleigh Mckenzie | C | 6'2" | 283 | 32 | | |
| William Fuller | DE | 6'3" | 280 | 33 | | |
| Greg Jefferson | DE | 6'3" | 257 | 24 | | |
| Mike Mamula | DE-LB | 6'4" | 252 | 22 | | |
| Danny Stubbs | DE | 6'4" | 272 | 30 | | |
| Mike Chalenski | DT | 6'5" | 285 | 25 | | |
| Ronnie Dixon | DT | 6'3" | 292 | 24 | | |
| Mark Gunn | DT | 6'5" | 297 | 27 | | |
| Rhett Hall | DT | 6'2" | 276 | 26 | | |
| Andy Harmon | DT | 6'4" | 278 | 26 | | |
| Kevin Johnson | DT | 6'1" | 306 | 24 | | 6 |
| Nate Dingle | LB | 6'2" | 242 | 22 | | |
| Kurt Gouveia | LB | 6'1" | 240 | 30 | 1 | |
| Derrick Oden | LB | 5'11" | 237 | 24 | | |
| Bill Romanowski | LB | 6'4" | 241 | 29 | 2 | |
| William Thomas | LB | 6'2" | 223 | 27 | 7 | 6 |
| James Willis | LB | 6'2" | 237 | 22 | | |
| Marc Woodard | LB | 6' | 238 | 25 | | |
| Sylvester Wright | LB | 6'2" | 258 | 23 | | |
| Derrick Frazier | DB | 5'10" | 172 | 25 | 1 | |
| Jerome Henderson | DB | 5'10" | 188 | 26 | | 6 |
| Greg Jackson | DB | 6'1" | 204 | 29 | 1 | 6 |
| Mark McMillian | DB | 5'7" | 148 | 25 | 3 | |
| Bobby Taylor | DB | 6'3" | 216 | 21 | 2 | |
| David Whitmore | DB | 6' | 232 | 28 | | |
| Barry Wilburn | DB | 6'2" | 195 | 31 | 1 | |
| Eric Zomalt | DB | 5'11" | 201 | 23 | | |
| Mike Zordich | DB | 6'1" | 212 | 31 | 1 | 6 |
| Randall Cunningham | QB | 6'4" | 205 | 32 | | |
| Rodney peete | QB | 6' | 225 | 29 | | 6 |
| Charlie Garner | HB | 5'9" | 187 | 23 | | 36 |
| Ricky Waters | HB | 6'1" | 217 | 26 | | 72 |
| Derrick Witherspoon | HB | 5'10" | 196 | 24 | | 6 |
| Fred McCrary | FB | 6' | 219 | 22 | | 6 |
| Dexter McNabb | FB | 6'2" | 250 | 26 | | |
| James Saxon | FB | 5'11" | 239 | 29 | | |
| Kevin Turner | FB | 6'1" | 231 | 26 | | |
| Fred Barnett | WR | 6' | 200 | 29 | | 32 |
| Rob Carpenter | WR | 6'2" | 190 | 27 | | |
| Chris T. Jones | WR | 6'3" | 209 | 24 | | |
| Kelvin Martin | WR | 5'9" | 162 | 30 | | |
| Art Monk | WR | 6'3" | 207 | 37 | | |
| Calvin Williams | WR | 5'11" | 187 | 28 | | 14 |
| Jimmie Johnson | TE | 6'2" | 257 | 29 | | |
| Reggie Johnson | TE | 6'2" | 255 | 27 | | 12 |
| Frank Wainright | TE | 6'3" | 245 | 27 | | |
| Ed West | TE | 6'1" | 250 | 34 | | 6 |
| Gary Anderson | K | 5'11" | 178 | 36 | | 98 |
| Tom Hutton | K | 6'1" | 193 | 23 | | |

Bernard Williams — Suspended by Commissioner
Tommy Jeter — Eye Injury

Vaughn Hebron — Knee Injury

## WASHINGTON REDSKINS 6-10 Norv Turner

| Scores of Each Game | | |
|---|---|---|
| 27 | ARIZONA | 7 |
| 8 | OAKLAND | 20 |
| 31 | Denver | 38 |
| 6 | Tampa Bay | 14 |
| 27 | DALLAS | 23 |
| 34 | Philadelphia | *37 |
| 20 | Arizona | 24 |
| 36 | DETROIT | *30 |
| 15 | NEW YORK GIANTS | 24 |
| 3 | Kansas City | 24 |
| 20 | SEATTLE | 27 |
| 7 | PHILADELPHIA | 14 |
| 24 | Dallas | 17 |
| 13 | New York Giants | 20 |
| 35 | St. Louis | 23 |
| 20 | CAROLINA | 17 |

| Use Name | Pos. | Hgt. | Wgt. | Age | Int | Pts |
|---|---|---|---|---|---|---|
| Tré Johnson | OT-OG | 6'2" | 338 | 24 | | |
| Jim Lachey | OT | 6'6" | 294 | 32 | | |
| Joe Patton | OT | 6'5" | 288 | 23 | | |
| Ed Simmons | OT | 6'5" | 325 | 31 | | |
| Brian Thure | OT | 6'5" | 300 | 21 | | |
| Ray Brown | OG | 6'5" | 312 | 32 | | |
| Ron Lewis | OG | 6'3" | 299 | 22 | | |
| Vernice Smith | OG | 6'3" | 298 | 29 | | |
| John Gesek | C-OG | 6'5" | 282 | 32 | | |
| Trevor Matich | C | 6'4" | 297 | 33 | | |
| Cory Raymer | C | 6'2" | 293 | 22 | | |
| Terry Crews | DE | 6'2" | 245 | 27 | | |
| Mike Flores | DE | 6'3" | 256 | 28 | | |
| Dexter Nottage | DE | 6'4" | 290 | 24 | | |
| Rich Owens | DE | 6'6" | 255 | 23 | | |
| Sterling Palmer | DE | 6'5" | 256 | 24 | | |
| Tony Woods | DE | 6'4" | 282 | 29 | | 6 |
| Romeo Bandison | DT | 6'5" | 290 | 24 | | |
| Mark Boutte | DT | 6'4" | 311 | 26 | | |
| William Gaines | DT | 6'5" | 294 | 24 | | |
| Tim Johnson | DT | 6'3" | 286 | 30 | | |
| Darrick Brownlow | LB | 6' | 243 | 26 | | 2 |
| Dion Foxx (from MIA) | LB | 6'3" | 250 | 24 | | |
| Ken Harvey | LB | 6'2" | 245 | 30 | | |
| Marvcus Patton | LB | 6'2" | 240 | 28 | 2 | |
| Rod Stephens | LB | 6'1" | 237 | 29 | | |
| Matt Vanderbeek | LB | 6'3" | 243 | 28 | | |
| Tom Carter | DB | 5'11" | 181 | 22 | 4 | 6 |
| Darrell Green | DB | 5'8" | 180 | 35 | 3 | 6 |
| Darryl Morrison | DB | 5'11" | 200 | 24 | | |
| Muhammad Oliver | DB | 5'11" | 185 | 26 | | |
| Darryl Pounds | DB | 5'11" | 177 | 23 | 1 | |
| Stanley Richard | DB | 6'2" | 197 | 27 | 3 | |
| Sebastian Savage | DB | 5'10" | 187 | 25 | | |
| Keith Taylor | DB | 5'11" | 212 | 30 | | |
| Scott Turner | DB | 5'10" | 178 | 23 | 1 | |
| James Washington | DB | 6'1" | 209 | 30 | 2 | |
| Gus Frerotte | QB | 6'2" | 221 | 24 | | 6 |
| Trent Green | QB | 6'3" | 212 | 25 | | |
| Heath Shuler | QB | 6'2" | 221 | 23 | | |
| Terry Allen | HB | 5'10" | 208 | 27 | | 66 |
| William Bell | HB | 5'11" | 212 | 24 | | |
| Reggie Brooks | HB | 5'8" | 211 | 24 | | |
| Marc Logan | FB | 6' | 212 | 30 | | 18 |
| Brian Mitchell | FB-HB | 5'10" | 221 | 27 | | 18 |
| Cedric Smith | FB | 5'10" | 222 | 27 | | |
| Henry Ellard | WR | 5'11" | 185 | 34 | | 30 |
| Jeff Query (from CIN) | WR | 6' | 165 | 28 | | |
| Leslie Shepherd | WR | 5'11" | 189 | 25 | | 18 |
| Olanda Truitt | WR | 6' | 186 | 24 | | 6 |
| Michael Westbrook | WR | 6'3" | 215 | 23 | | 12 |
| Tydus Winans | WR | 5'11" | 180 | 23 | | |
| Jamie Asher | TE | 6'3" | 243 | 22 | | |
| Coleman Bell | TE | 6'2" | 243 | 25 | | 6 |
| Scott Galbraith | TE | 6'2" | 255 | 28 | | 12 |
| James Jenkins | TE | 6'2" | 241 | 28 | | |
| Eddie Murray | K | 5'11" | 195 | 39 | | 114 |
| Matt Turk | K | 6'5" | 230 | 27 | | |

Bobby Wilson — Back Injury

## NEW YORK GIANTS 5-11 Dan Reeves

| Scores of Each Game | | |
|---|---|---|
| 0 | DALLAS | 35 |
| 17 | Kansas City | *20 |
| 6 | Green Bay | 14 |
| 45 | NEW ORLEANS | 29 |
| 6 | San Francisco | 20 |
| 27 | ARIZONA | *21 |
| 14 | PHILADELPHIA | 17 |
| 24 | Washington | 15 |
| 28 | Seattle | 30 |
| 13 | OAKLAND | 17 |
| 19 | Philadelphia | 28 |
| 24 | CHICAGO | 27 |
| 10 | Arizona | 6 |
| 20 | WASHINGTON | 13 |
| 20 | Dallas | 21 |
| 17 | SAN DIEGO | 27 |

| Use Name | Pos. | Hgt. | Wgt. | Age | Int | Pts |
|---|---|---|---|---|---|---|
| Greg Bishop | OT | 6'5" | 296 | 24 | | |
| John Elliott | OT | 6'7" | 308 | 30 | | |
| Scott Gragg | OT | 6'8" | 316 | 23 | | |
| Doug Riesenberg | OT | 6'5" | 280 | 30 | | |
| Derek Allen | OG | 6'4" | 290 | 24 | | |
| Lance Smith | OG | 6'3" | 290 | 32 | | |
| Rob Zatechka | OG | 6'4" | 307 | 23 | | |
| Adam Schrieber | C | 6'4" | 290 | 33 | | |
| Brian Williams | C | 6'5" | 300 | 29 | | |
| Chad Bratzke | DE | 6'4" | 270 | 23 | | |
| Jamal Duff | DE | 6'7" | 259 | 23 | | |
| Robert Harris | DE | 6'4" | 290 | 26 | | |
| Coleman Rudolph | DE | 6'4" | 270 | 24 | | |
| Mike Strahan | DE | 6'4" | 270 | 23 | 2 | 2 |
| Ray Agnew | DT | 6'3" | 286 | 27 | | |
| Stacey Dillard | DT | 6'5" | 290 | 26 | | |
| Keith Hamilton | DT | 6'6" | 290 | 24 | | |
| Jessie Armstead | LB | 6'1" | 232 | 24 | 1 | 6 |
| Michael Brooks | LB | 6'1" | 236 | 30 | | |
| Marcus Buckley | LB | 6'3" | 240 | 24 | | |
| Mike Croel | LB | 6'3" | 240 | 26 | | |
| Corey Miller | LB | 6'2" | 247 | 26 | | |
| Ben Talley | LB | 6'3" | 248 | 23 | | |
| Corey Widmer | LB | 6'3" | 250 | 26 | | |
| Willie Beamon | DB | 5'11" | 178 | 25 | | |
| Jesse Campbell | DB | 6'1" | 215 | 26 | | |
| Maurice Douglass | DB | 5'11" | 203 | 31 | | |
| Vencie Glenn | DB | 6' | 189 | 30 | 5 | 6 |
| Thomas Randolph | DB | 5'9" | 176 | 24 | 2 | |
| Jason Sehorn | DB | 6'2" | 217 | 24 | | |
| Phillippi Sparks | DB | 5'11" | 190 | 26 | 5 | |
| Tim Watson (from KC) | DB | 6'1" | 215 | 25 | | |
| Tito Wooten | DB | 6' | 188 | 23 | 1 | 6 |
| Rodney Young | DB | 6'1" | 206 | 22 | | |
| Dave Brown | QB | 6'5" | 224 | 25 | | 24 |
| Tommy Maddox | QB | 6'4" | 205 | 23 | | |
| Stan White | QB | 6'2" | 214 | 24 | | |
| Keith Elias | HB | 5'9" | 200 | 23 | | |
| Rodney Hampton | HB | 5'11" | 230 | 26 | | 62 |
| Herschel Walker | HB | 6'1" | 225 | 33 | | 6 |
| Tyrone Wheatley | HB | 6' | 227 | 23 | | 18 |
| Charles Way | FB | 6' | 236 | 22 | | 6 |
| Chris Calloway | WR | 5'10" | 188 | 27 | | 18 |
| Omar Douglas | WR | 5'10" | 180 | 23 | | 6 |
| Gary Harrell | WR | 5'7" | 170 | 23 | | |
| Thomas Lewis | WR | 6'1" | 195 | 23 | | 12 |
| Arthur Marshall | WR | 5'11" | 178 | 26 | | 6 |
| Mike Sherrard | WR | 6'2" | 187 | 32 | | 24 |
| Howard Cross | TE | 6'5" | 260 | 28 | | |
| Brian Kozlowski | TE | 6'3" | 247 | 24 | | |
| Aaron Pierce | TE | 6'5" | 245 | 25 | | |
| Brad Daluiso | K | 6'2" | 215 | 27 | | 88 |
| Mike Horan | K | 5'11" | 188 | 36 | | |

Scott Davis — Knee Injury

## ARIZONA CARDINALS 4-12 Buddy Ryan

| Scores of Each Game | | |
|---|---|---|
| 7 | Washington | 27 |
| 19 | PHILADELPHIA | 31 |
| 20 | Detroit | 17 |
| 20 | Dallas | 34 |
| 3 | KANSAS CITY | 24 |
| 21 | New York Giants | *27 |
| 24 | WASHINGTON | 20 |
| 20 | SEATTLE | *14 |
| 6 | Denver | 38 |
| 24 | MINNESOTA | *30 |
| 7 | Carolina | 27 |
| 40 | ATLANTA | *37 |
| 6 | NEW YORK GIANTS | 10 |
| 25 | San Diego | 28 |
| 20 | Philadelphia | 21 |
| 13 | DALLAS | 37 |

| Use Name | Pos. | Hgt. | Wgt. | Age | Int | Pts |
|---|---|---|---|---|---|---|
| Bernard Dafney | OT | 6'5" | 329 | 26 | | |
| Ernest Dye | OT | 6'6" | 325 | 24 | | |
| Cecil Gray | OT | 6'4" | 300 | 27 | | |
| Larry Tharpe | OT | 6'4" | 299 | 24 | | |
| Eric Floyd | OG | 6'5" | 310 | 29 | | |
| Duval Love | OG | 6'3" | 288 | 32 | | |
| Anthony Redmon | OG | 6'4" | 308 | 24 | | |
| Rob Selby | OG | 6'3" | 286 | 27 | | |
| Joe Wolf | OG | 6'6" | 296 | 28 | | |
| Ed Cunningham | C | 6'3" | 285 | 26 | | |
| Jamie Dukes | C | 6'1" | 285 | 31 | | |
| Michael Bankston | DE-DT | 6'2" | 280 | 25 | 1 | |
| Chad Brown | DE | 6'7" | 265 | 24 | | |
| Jerry Drake | DE | 6'4" | 292 | 26 | | |
| Karl Dunbar | DE | 6'4" | 275 | 28 | | |
| Eric England | DE | 6'2" | 283 | 24 | | |
| Keith McCants | DE | 6'3" | 265 | 27 | | 6 |
| Clyde Simmons | DE | 6'6" | 280 | 31 | 1 | 6 |
| Chris Maumalanga | DT | 6'2" | 292 | 23 | | |
| Eric Swann | DT | 6'4" | 295 | 25 | | |
| Bernard Wilson | DT | 6'2" | 295 | 25 | | |
| Eric Hill | LB | 6'1" | 255 | 28 | | |
| Terry Irving | LB | 6' | 224 | 24 | | |
| Garth Jax | LB | 6'2" | 250 | 31 | | |
| Seth Joyner | LB | 6'2" | 235 | 30 | 3 | |
| Randy Kirk | LB | 6'2" | 231 | 30 | | |
| Wesley Leasy | LB | 6'2" | 234 | 23 | | |
| David Merritt | LB | 6'1" | 237 | 23 | | |
| Jamir Miller | LB | 6'4" | 242 | 21 | | |
| Simon Shanks | LB | 6'1" | 215 | 23 | | |
| Melvin Aldridge | DB | 6'2" | 195 | 25 | | |
| Brent Alexander | DB | 5'10" | 184 | 24 | 1 | |
| Carlos Brooks | DB | 6' | 200 | 24 | | |
| Lance Brown | DB | 6' | 200 | 23 | | |
| Terry Hoage | DB | 6'2" | 201 | 33 | 2 | |
| Patrick Hunter | DB | 5'11" | 186 | 30 | 2 | |
| Tony Jones | DB | 6'4" | 200 | 23 | | |
| Kwamie Lassiter | DB | 5'11" | 180 | 25 | | |
| Lorenzo Lynch | DB | 5'9" | 200 | 32 | 1 | 6 |
| Tito Paul | DB | 6' | 195 | 23 | 1 | |
| C.J. Richardson | DB | 5'10" | 209 | 23 | | |
| Ben Smith | DB | 5'11" | 185 | 28 | | |
| Andre Waters | DB | 5'11" | 200 | 33 | | |
| Aeneas Williams | DB | 5'10" | 190 | 27 | 6 | 18 |
| Mike Buck | QB | 6'3" | 227 | 28 | | |
| Stoney Case | QB | 6'2" | 206 | 23 | | |
| Dave Krieg | QB | 6'1" | 202 | 36 | | |
| Larry Centers | HB | 5'11" | 215 | 27 | | 24 |
| Garrison Hearst | HB | 5'11" | 215 | 24 | | 12 |
| Mark Higgs | HB | 5'7" | 199 | 29 | | |
| LeShon Johnson (from GB) | HB | 5'11" | 195 | 24 | | |
| Ryan Terry | HB | 5'11" | 203 | 23 | | |
| Stevie Anderson | WR | 6'5" | 215 | 25 | | 10 |
| Marcus Dowdell | WR | 5'10 | 179 | 25 | | |
| Anthony Edwards | WR | 5'10" | 190 | 29 | | 12 |
| Rob Moore | WR | 6'3" | 205 | 26 | | 32 |
| Bryan Reeves | WR | 5'11" | 195 | 25 | | |
| Frank Sanders | WR | 6'2" | 201 | 23 | | 16 |
| Chad Fann | TE | 6'3" | 250 | 25 | | |
| Wendall Gaines | TE | 6'4" | 293 | 23 | | 12 |
| Oscar McBride | TE | 6'5" | 266 | 23 | | 12 |
| Terry Samuels | TE | 6'2" | 254 | 24 | | |
| Greg Davis | K | 6' | 205 | 29 | | 109 |
| Jeff Feagles | K | 6'1" | 205 | 29 | | |

## RUSHING

### DALLAS COWBOYS

| Last Name | No. | Yds | Avg | TD |
|---|---|---|---|---|
| E. Smith | 377 | 1773 | 4.7 | 25 |
| S. Williams | 48 | 205 | 4.3 | 1 |
| Johnston | 25 | 111 | 4.4 | 2 |
| K. Williams | 10 | 53 | 5.3 | 0 |
| Aikman | 21 | 32 | 1.5 | 1 |
| Wilson | 10 | 12 | 1.2 | 0 |
| Sanders | 2 | 9 | 4.5 | 0 |
| Lang | 1 | 7 | 7.0 | 0 |
| Garrett | 1 | -1 | -1.0 | 0 |

### PHILADELPHIA EAGLES

| Last Name | No. | Yds | Avg | TD |
|---|---|---|---|---|
| Watters | 337 | 1273 | 3.8 | 11 |
| Garner | 108 | 588 | 5.4 | 6 |
| Peete | 32 | 147 | 4.6 | 1 |
| Cunningham | 21 | 98 | 4.7 | 0 |
| Turner | 2 | 9 | 4.5 | 0 |
| Witherspoon | 2 | 7 | 3.5 | 0 |
| McCrary | 3 | 1 | 0.3 | 1 |
| Hutton | 1 | 0 | 0.0 | 0 |
| Saxon | 1 | 0 | 0.0 | 0 |
| C. Williams | 1 | -2 | -2.0 | 0 |

### WASHINGTON REDSKINS

| Last Name | No. | Yds | Avg | TD |
|---|---|---|---|---|
| Allen | 338 | 1309 | 3.9 | 10 |
| Mitchell | 46 | 301 | 6.5 | 1 |
| Westbrook | 6 | 114 | 19.0 | 1 |
| Logan | 23 | 72 | 3.1 | 1 |
| Shepherd | 7 | 63 | 9.0 | 1 |
| Shuler | 18 | 57 | 3.2 | 0 |
| Frerotte | 22 | 16 | 0.7 | 1 |
| W. Bell | 4 | 13 | 3.3 | 0 |
| C. Smith | 3 | 13 | 4.3 | 0 |
| Brooks | 2 | -2 | -1.0 | 0 |

### NEW YORK GIANTS

| Last Name | No. | Yds | Avg | TD |
|---|---|---|---|---|
| Hampton | 306 | 1182 | 3.9 | 10 |
| Wheatley | 78 | 245 | 3.1 | 3 |
| Brown | 45 | 228 | 5.1 | 4 |
| Walker | 31 | 126 | 4.1 | 0 |
| Elias | 10 | 44 | 4.4 | 0 |
| Pierce | 1 | 6 | 6.0 | 0 |
| Way | 2 | 6 | 3.0 | 0 |
| Maddox | 1 | 4 | 4.0 | 0 |
| Marshall | 1 | 1 | 1.0 | 0 |
| Horan | 1 | 0 | 0.0 | 0 |
| Calloway | 2 | -9 | -4.5 | 0 |

### ARIZONA CARDINALS

| Last Name | No. | Yds | Avg | TD |
|---|---|---|---|---|
| Hearst | 284 | 1070 | 3.8 | 1 |
| Centers | 78 | 254 | 3.3 | 2 |
| Krieg | 19 | 29 | 1.5 | 0 |
| Case | 1 | 4 | 4.0 | 0 |
| Feagles | 2 | 4 | 2.0 | 0 |
| Lassiter | 1 | 1 | 1.0 | 0 |
| Sanders | 1 | 1 | 1.0 | 0 |
| Buck | 1 | 0 | 0.0 | 0 |
| Johnson | 2 | -2 | -1.0 | 0 |

## RECEIVING

### DALLAS COWBOYS

| Last Name | No. | Yds | Avg | TD |
|---|---|---|---|---|
| Irvin | 111 | 1603 | 14.4 | 10 |
| Novacek | 62 | 705 | 11.4 | 5 |
| E. Smith | 62 | 375 | 6.0 | 0 |
| K. Williams | 38 | 613 | 16.1 | 2 |
| Johnston | 30 | 248 | 8.3 | 1 |
| Bjornson | 7 | 53 | 7.6 | 0 |
| Fleming | 6 | 83 | 13.8 | 0 |
| S. Williams | 3 | 28 | 9.3 | 0 |
| Sanders | 2 | 25 | 12.5 | 0 |
| Watkins | 1 | 8 | 8.0 | 0 |

### PHILADELPHIA EAGLES

| Last Name | No. | Yds | Avg | TD |
|---|---|---|---|---|
| C. Williams | 63 | 768 | 12.2 | 2 |
| Watters | 62 | 434 | 7.0 | 1 |
| Barnett | 48 | 585 | 12.2 | 5 |
| Carpenter | 29 | 318 | 11.0 | 0 |
| West | 20 | 190 | 9.5 | 1 |
| Martin | 17 | 206 | 12.1 | 0 |
| Garner | 10 | 61 | 6.1 | 0 |
| McCrary | 9 | 60 | 6.7 | 0 |
| Monk | 6 | 114 | 19.0 | 0 |
| J. Johnson | 6 | 37 | 6.2 | 0 |
| R. Johnson | 5 | 68 | 13.6 | 2 |
| Jones | 5 | 61 | 12.2 | 0 |
| Turner | 4 | 29 | 7.3 | 0 |

### WASHINGTON REDSKINS

| Last Name | No. | Yds | Avg | TD |
|---|---|---|---|---|
| Ellard | 56 | 1005 | 17.9 | 5 |
| Mitchell | 38 | 324 | 8.5 | 1 |
| Westbrook | 34 | 522 | 15.4 | 1 |
| Allen | 31 | 232 | 7.5 | 1 |
| Shepherd | 29 | 486 | 16.8 | 2 |
| Logan | 25 | 276 | 11.0 | 2 |
| Asher | 14 | 172 | 12.3 | 0 |
| C. Bell | 14 | 166 | 11.9 | 1 |
| Galbraith | 10 | 80 | 8.0 | 2 |
| Truitt | 9 | 154 | 17.1 | 1 |
| Winans | 4 | 77 | 19.3 | 0 |
| Jenkins | 1 | 2 | 2.0 | 0 |

### NEW YORK GIANTS

| Last Name | No. | Yds | Avg | TD |
|---|---|---|---|---|
| Calloway | 56 | 796 | 14.2 | 3 |
| Sherrard | 44 | 577 | 13.1 | 4 |
| Pierce | 33 | 310 | 9.4 | 0 |
| Walker | 31 | 234 | 7.5 | 1 |
| Hampton | 24 | 142 | 5.9 | 0 |
| Cross | 18 | 197 | 10.9 | 0 |
| Marshall | 17 | 195 | 11.5 | 1 |
| Lewis | 12 | 208 | 17.3 | 1 |
| Elias | 9 | 69 | 7.7 | 0 |
| Way | 7 | 76 | 10.9 | 1 |
| Wheatley | 5 | 27 | 5.4 | 0 |
| Kozlowski | 2 | 17 | 8.5 | 0 |
| Douglas | 2 | 15 | 7.5 | 0 |

### ARIZONA CARDINALS

| Last Name | No. | Yds | Avg | TD |
|---|---|---|---|---|
| Centers | 101 | 962 | 9.5 | 2 |
| R. Moore | 63 | 907 | 14.4 | 5 |
| Sanders | 52 | 883 | 17.0 | 2 |
| Edwards | 29 | 417 | 14.4 | 2 |
| Hearst | 29 | 243 | 8.4 | 1 |
| Gaines | 14 | 117 | 8.4 | 2 |
| McBride | 13 | 112 | 8.6 | 2 |
| Dowdell | 10 | 96 | 9.6 | 0 |
| Reeves | 6 | 62 | 10.3 | 0 |
| Fann | 5 | 41 | 8.2 | 0 |
| Anderson | 3 | 34 | 11.3 | 1 |
| Samuels | 2 | 19 | 9.5 | 0 |

## PUNT RETURNS

### DALLAS COWBOYS

| Last Name | No. | Yds | Avg | TD |
|---|---|---|---|---|
| K. Williams | 18 | 166 | 9.2 | 0 |
| Holmes | 4 | 35 | 8.8 | 0 |
| Sanders | 1 | 54 | 54.0 | 0 |

### PHILADELPHIA EAGLES

| Last Name | No. | Yds | Avg | TD |
|---|---|---|---|---|
| Martin | 17 | 214 | 12.6 | 0 |
| Carpenter | 12 | 79 | 6.6 | 0 |

### WASHINGTON REDSKINS

| Last Name | No. | Yds | Avg | TD |
|---|---|---|---|---|
| Mitchell | 25 | 315 | 12.6 | 1 |
| Turner | 1 | 0 | 0.0 | 0 |

### NEW YORK GIANTS

| Last Name | No. | Yds | Avg | TD |
|---|---|---|---|---|
| Harrell | 12 | 76 | 6.3 | 0 |
| Marshall | 12 | 96 | 8.0 | 0 |
| Lewis | 6 | 46 | 7.7 | 0 |
| Young | 1 | 0 | 0.0 | 0 |

### ARIZONA CARDINALS

| Last Name | No. | Yds | Avg | TD |
|---|---|---|---|---|
| Edwards | 18 | 131 | 7.3 | 0 |
| Reeves | 4 | 41 | 10.3 | 0 |
| Dowdell | 1 | 0 | 0.0 | 0 |

## KICKOFF RETURNS

### DALLAS COWBOYS

| Last Name | No. | Yds | Avg | TD |
|---|---|---|---|---|
| K. Williams | 49 | 1108 | 22.6 | 0 |
| Holmes | 5 | 134 | 26.8 | 0 |
| Marion | 1 | 16 | 16.0 | 0 |
| Sanders | 1 | 15 | 15.0 | 0 |
| Schwantz | 1 | 9 | 9.0 | 0 |
| Watkins | 1 | -6 | -6.0 | 0 |

### PHILADELPHIA EAGLES

| Last Name | No. | Yds | Avg | TD |
|---|---|---|---|---|
| Garner | 29 | 590 | 20.3 | 0 |
| Martin | 20 | 388 | 19.4 | 0 |
| Witherspoon | 18 | 459 | 25.5 | 1 |
| Jones | 2 | 46 | 23.0 | 0 |
| Saxon | 1 | 3 | 3.0 | 0 |
| McCrary | 1 | 1 | 1.0 | 0 |

### WASHINGTON REDSKINS

| Last Name | No. | Yds | Avg | TD |
|---|---|---|---|---|
| Mitchell | 55 | 1408 | 25.6 | 0 |
| W. Bell | 8 | 121 | 15.1 | 0 |
| Shepherd | 3 | 85 | 28.3 | 0 |
| Asher | 1 | 13 | 13.0 | 0 |
| Jenkins | 1 | 12 | 12.0 | 0 |
| Vanderbeek | 1 | 7 | 7.0 | 0 |

### NEW YORK GIANTS

| Last Name | No. | Yds | Avg | TD |
|---|---|---|---|---|
| Walker | 41 | 881 | 21.5 | 0 |
| Wheatley | 10 | 186 | 18.6 | 0 |
| Lewis | 9 | 257 | 28.6 | 1 |
| Kozlowski | 5 | 75 | 15.0 | 0 |
| Harrell | 1 | 23 | 23.0 | 0 |
| Douglas | 1 | 13 | 13.0 | 0 |
| Way | 1 | 8 | 8.0 | 0 |
| Zatechka | 1 | 5 | 5.0 | 0 |
| Widmer | 1 | 0 | 0.0 | 0 |

### ARIZONA CARDINALS

| Last Name | No. | Yds | Avg | TD |
|---|---|---|---|---|
| Terry | 37 | 808 | 21.8 | 0 |
| Dowdell | 18 | 344 | 19.1 | 0 |
| Johnson | 11 | 259 | 23.5 | 0 |
| Edwards | 3 | 50 | 16.7 | 0 |
| Higgs | 2 | 26 | 13.0 | 0 |
| Anderson | 1 | 17 | 17.0 | 0 |
| Centers | 1 | 15 | 15.0 | 0 |

## PASSING — PUNTING — KICKING

### DALLAS COWBOYS

**PASSING**

| Last Name | Att | Cmp | % | Yds | Yd/Att | TD | Int— | % | RK |
|---|---|---|---|---|---|---|---|---|---|
| Aikman | 432 | 280 | 64.8 | 3304 | 7.65 | 16 | 7— | 1.6 | |

**PUNTING**

| Last Name | No. | Avg. |
|---|---|---|
| Jett | 53 | 40.9 |
| Boniol | 2 | 38.5 |

**KICKING**

| Last Name | XP | ATT | % | FG | ATT | % |
|---|---|---|---|---|---|---|
| Boniol | 46 | 48 | 96 | 27 | 28 | 96 |

**2 POINT XP**
Novacek (1)

### PHILADELPHIA EAGLES

**PASSING**

| Last Name | Att | Cmp | % | Yds | Yd/Att | TD | Int— | % | RK |
|---|---|---|---|---|---|---|---|---|---|
| Peete | 375 | 215 | 57.3 | 2326 | 6.20 | 8 | 14— | 3.7 | |
| Cunningham | 121 | 69 | 57.0 | 605 | 5.00 | 3 | 5— | 4.1 | |

**PUNTING**

| Last Name | No. | Avg. |
|---|---|---|
| Hutton | 86 | 42.8 |

**KICKING**

| Last Name | XP | ATT | % | FG | ATT | % |
|---|---|---|---|---|---|---|
| G. Anderson | 32 | 33 | 97 | 22 | 30 | 73 |

**2 POINT XP**
Barnett (1)
C. Williams (1)

### WASHINGTON REDSKINS

**PASSING**

| Last Name | Att | Cmp | % | Yds | Yd/Att | TD | Int— | % | RK |
|---|---|---|---|---|---|---|---|---|---|
| Frerotte | 396 | 199 | 50.3 | 2751 | 6.95 | 13 | 13— | 3.3 | |
| Shuler | 125 | 66 | 745 | 52.8 | 5.96 | 3 | 7— | 5.6 | |

**PUNTING**

| Last Name | No. | Avg. |
|---|---|---|
| Turk | 74 | 42.4 |

**KICKING**

| Last Name | XP | ATT | % | FG | ATT | % |
|---|---|---|---|---|---|---|
| Murray | 33 | 33 | 100 | 27 | 36 | 75 |

**2 POINT XP**
None

### NEW YORK GIANTS

**PASSING**

| Last Name | Att | Cmp | % | Yds | Yd/Att | TD | Int— | % | RK |
|---|---|---|---|---|---|---|---|---|---|
| Da. Brown | 456 | 254 | 55.7 | 2814 | 6.17 | 11 | 10— | 2.2 | |
| Maddox | 23 | 6 | 26.1 | 49 | 2.13 | 0 | 3— | 13.0 | |

**PUNTING**

| Last Name | No. | Avg. |
|---|---|---|
| Horan | 72 | 42.5 |
| Brown | 1 | 15.0 |

**KICKING**

| Last Name | XP | ATT | % | FG | ATT | % |
|---|---|---|---|---|---|---|
| Daluiso | 28 | 28 | 100 | 20 | 28 | 71 |

**2 POINT XP**
Hampton (1)

### ARIZONA CARDINALS

**PASSING**

| Last Name | Att | Cmp | % | Yds | Yd/Att | TD | Int— | % | RK |
|---|---|---|---|---|---|---|---|---|---|
| Krieg | 521 | 304 | 58.3 | 3554 | 6.82 | 16 | 21— | 4.0 | |
| Buck | 32 | 20 | 62.5 | 271 | 8.47 | 1 | 0— | 0.0 | |
| Case | 2 | 1 | 50.0 | 19 | 9.50 | 0 | 1— | 50.0 | |
| Hearst | 2 | 1 | 50.0 | 16 | 8.00 | 0 | 0— | 0.0 | |
| R. Moore | 2 | 1 | 50.0 | 33 | 16.50 | 0 | 1— | 50.0 | |
| Centers | 1 | 0 | 0.0 | 0 | 0.00 | 0 | 1— | 100.0 | |

**PUNTING**

| Last Name | No. | Avg. |
|---|---|---|
| Feagles | 72 | 43.8 |

**KICKING**

| Last Name | XP | ATT | % | FG | ATT | % |
|---|---|---|---|---|---|---|
| Davis | 19 | 19 | 100 | 30 | 39 | 77 |

**2 POINT XP**
Anderson (2)
Sanders (2)
R. Moore (1)

## GREEN BAY PACKERS 11-5 Mike Holmgren

| Scores of Each Game | | |
|---|---|---|
| 14 | ST. LOUIS | 17 |
| 27 | Chicago | 24 |
| 14 | NEW YORK GIANTS | 6 |
| 24 | Jacksonville | 14 |
| 24 | Dallas | 34 |
| 30 | DETROIT | 21 |
| 38 | MINNESOTA | 21 |
| 16 | Detroit | 24 |
| 24 | Minnesota | 27 |
| 35 | CHICAGO | 28 |
| 31 | Cleveland | 20 |
| 35 | TAMPA BAY | 13 |
| 24 | CINCINNATI | 10 |
| 10 | Tampa Bay | *13 |
| 34 | New Orleans | 23 |
| 24 | PITTSBURGH | 19 |

| Use Name | Pos. | Hgt. | Wgt. | Age | Int | Pts |
|---|---|---|---|---|---|---|
| Gary Brown | OT | 6'4" | 315 | 24 | | |
| Earl Dotson | OT | 6'4" | 310 | 24 | | |
| Ken Ruettgers | OT | 6'5" | 292 | 33 | | |
| Joe Sims | OT | 6'3" | 310 | 26 | | |
| Harry Galbreath | OG | 6'1" | 295 | 30 | | |
| Aaron Taylor | OG | 6'4" | 305 | 22 | | |
| Adam Timmerman | OG | 6'4" | 288 | 24 | | |
| Mike Arthur | C | 6'3" | 280 | 27 | | |
| Frank Winters | C-OG | 6'3" | 295 | 31 | | |
| Shannon Clavelle | DE | 6'2" | 287 | 22 | | |
| Sean Jones | DE | 6'7" | 283 | 32 | | 6 |
| Matt LaBounty | DE | 6'4" | 278 | 26 | | |
| Reggie White | DE-DT | 6'5" | 300 | 33 | | |
| Gabe Wilkins | DT-DE | 6'5" | 310 | 24 | | |
| Gilbert Brown | DT | 6'2" | 325 | 24 | | |
| Darius Holland | DT | 6'5" | 305 | 21 | | |
| John Jurkovic | NT | 6'2" | 295 | 28 | | |
| Bob Kuberski | NT | 6'5" | 300 | 24 | | |

Paul Hutchins — Back Injury

| Use Name | Pos. | Hgt. | Wgt. | Age | Int | Pts |
|---|---|---|---|---|---|---|
| Bernardo Harris | LB | 6'2" | 243 | 23 | | |
| Joe Kelly | LB | 6'2" | 235 | 30 | 1 | |
| George Koonce | LB | 6'1" | 243 | 26 | 1 | |
| Wayne Simmons | LB | 6'3" | 248 | 25 | | |
| Fred Strickland | LB | 6'2" | 250 | 29 | | |
| Brian Williams | LB | 6'2" | 240 | 22 | | |
| LeRoy Butler | DB | 6' | 200 | 27 | 5 | |
| Keith Crawford | DB | 6'2" | 198 | 24 | | |
| Matthew Dorsett | DB | 5'11" | 187 | 22 | | |
| Doug Evans | DB | 6'1" | 190 | 25 | 2 | |
| Lenny McGill | DB | 6'2" | 198 | 24 | | |
| Roderick Mullen | DB | 6'1" | 204 | 22 | | |
| Craig Newsome | DB | 6' | 188 | 24 | 1 | |
| Mike Prior | DB | 6' | 208 | 31 | 1 | |
| George Teague | DB | 6'1" | 195 | 24 | 2 | |

| Use Name | Pos. | Hgt. | Wgt. | Age | Int | Pts |
|---|---|---|---|---|---|---|
| Ty Detmer | QB | 6' | 194 | 27 | | |
| Brett Favre | QB | 6'2" | 220 | 25 | | 18 |
| Jim McMahon | QB | 6'1" | 195 | 36 | | |
| T.J. Rubley | QB | 6'4" | 212 | 26 | | |
| Marcus Wilson | HB | 6'1" | 215 | 27 | | |
| Edgar Bennett | HB | 6' | 217 | 26 | | 42 |
| William Henderson | FB | 6'2" | 248 | 24 | | |
| Travis Jervey | FB | 6' | 225 | 23 | | |
| Dorsey Levens | FB | 6'1" | 240 | 25 | | 42 |
| Robert Brooks | WR | 6' | 180 | 25 | | 78 |
| Antonio Freeman | WR | 6'1" | 187 | 23 | | 6 |
| Mark Ingram | WR | 5'11" | 194 | 30 | | 18 |
| Charles Jordan | WR | 5'10" | 183 | 25 | | 12 |
| Terry Mickens | WR | 6'1" | 198 | 24 | | |
| Anthony Morgan | WR | 6'1" | 200 | 27 | | 24 |
| Mike Bartrum | TE-FB | 6'5" | 243 | 25 | | |
| Mark Chmura | TE | 6'5" | 250 | 26 | | 44 |
| Keith Jackson | TE | 6'2" | 258 | 30 | | 6 |
| Jeff Thomason | TE | 6'5" | 250 | 25 | | |
| Jeff Wilner | TE | 6'5" | 250 | 23 | | |
| Dirk Borgognone | K | 6'2" | 221 | 27 | | |
| Craig Hentrich | K | 6'3" | 200 | 24 | | 14 |
| Chris Jacke | K | 6' | 205 | 29 | | 94 |

## DETROIT LIONS 10-6 Wayne Fontes

| Scores of Each Game | | |
|---|---|---|
| 20 | Pittsburgh | 23 |
| 10 | Minnesota | 20 |
| 17 | ARIZONA | 20 |
| 17 | SAN FRANCISCO | 24 |
| 38 | CLEVELAND | 20 |
| 21 | Green Bay | 30 |
| 30 | Washington | *36 |
| 24 | GREEN BAY | 16 |
| 22 | Atlanta | 34 |
| 27 | TAMPA BAY | 24 |
| 24 | Chicago | 17 |
| 44 | MINNESOTA | 38 |
| 27 | CHICAGO | 7 |
| 24 | Houston | 17 |
| 44 | JACKSONVILLE | 0 |
| 17 | Tampa Bay | 10 |

| Use Name | Pos. | Hgt. | Wgt. | Age | Int | Pts |
|---|---|---|---|---|---|---|
| Lomas Brown | OT | 6'4" | 275 | 32 | | |
| Scott Conover | OT | 6'4" | 285 | 26 | | |
| Jeff Jones | OT | 6'6" | 310 | 23 | | |
| Zefross Moss | OT | 6'6" | 324 | 29 | | |
| Mike Compton | OG-OT | 6'6" | 297 | 24 | | |
| Hessley Hempstead | OG | 6'1" | 295 | 23 | | |
| David Lutz | OT | 6'6" | 305 | 35 | | |
| Tony Semple | OG | 6'4" | 286 | 24 | | |
| Doug Widell | OG | 6'4" | 280 | 28 | | |
| Kevin Glover | C | 6'2" | 282 | 32 | | |
| Shane Bonham | DE | 6'4" | 275 | 24 | | |
| Luther Elliss | DE | 6'5" | 291 | 22 | | |
| Dan Owens | DE | 6'3" | 280 | 28 | | |
| Mike Wells | DE | 6'3" | 287 | 24 | | |
| Robert Porcher | DT | 6'3" | 270 | 26 | | |
| Henry Thomas | DT | 6'2" | 277 | 30 | | |

| Use Name | Pos. | Hgt. | Wgt. | Age | Int | Pts |
|---|---|---|---|---|---|---|
| Stephen Boyd | LB | 6' | 247 | 23 | | |
| Tracy Hayworth | LB | 6'3" | 260 | 27 | | |
| Mike Johnson | LB | 6'1" | 230 | 32 | 2 | |
| Scott Kowalkowski | LB | 6'2" | 228 | 27 | | |
| Antonio London | LB | 6'2" | 234 | 24 | | |
| Tracy Scroggins | LB | 6'2" | 255 | 25 | | 6 |
| Chris Spielman | LB | 6' | 247 | 29 | 1 | |
| Bennie Blades | DB | 6'1" | 221 | 28 | 1 | 2 |
| Willie Clay | DB | 5'9" | 184 | 24 | 8 | |
| Greg Jeffries | DB | 5'9" | 184 | 23 | | |
| Van Malone | DB | 5'11" | 186 | 25 | 1 | |
| Robert Massey | DB | 5'11" | 195 | 28 | | |
| Ryan McNeil | DB | 6' | 192 | 24 | 2 | |
| Corey Raymond | DB | 5'11" | 185 | 26 | 6 | |
| Sean Vanhorse | DB | 5'10" | 180 | 27 | 1 | |

| Use Name | Pos. | Hgt. | Wgt. | Age | Int | Pts |
|---|---|---|---|---|---|---|
| Kent Graham | QB | 6'5" | 242 | 26 | | |
| Don Majkowski | QB | 6'3" | 208 | 31 | | |
| Scott Mitchell | QB | 6'6" | 230 | 27 | | 24 |
| Eric Lynch | HB | 5'10" | 224 | 25 | | |
| Ron Rivers | HB | 5'8" | 205 | 23 | | 6 |
| Barry Sanders | HB-FB | 5'8" | 203 | 27 | | 72 |
| Allen Williams | HB | 5'10" | 205 | 22 | | |
| Tom Beer | FB | 6'1" | 237 | 26 | | |
| Cory Schlesinger | FB | 6'2" | 255 | 23 | | |
| Anthony Carter | WR | 5'11" | 181 | 34 | | |
| Aubrey Matthews | WR | 5'7" | 165 | 32 | | |
| Kez McCorvey | WR | 6' | 180 | 23 | | |
| Herman Moore | WR | 6'3" | 210 | 25 | | 84 |
| Johnnie Morton | WR | 6' | 190 | 23 | | 48 |
| Brett Perriman | WR | 5'9" | 180 | 29 | | 56 |
| Vernon Turner | WR | 5'8" | 185 | 28 | | |
| Ron Hall | TE | 6'4" | 245 | 31 | | |
| Kevin Hickman | TE | 6'4" | 258 | 24 | | |
| Rodney Holman | TE | 6'3" | 238 | 35 | | |
| David Sloan | TE | 6'6" | 254 | 24 | | 6 |
| Jason Hanson | K | 5'11" | 183 | 25 | | 132 |
| Mark Royals | K | 6'5" | 215 | 23 | | |

## CHICAGO BEARS 9-7 Dave Wannstedt

| Scores of Each Game | | |
|---|---|---|
| 31 | MINNESOTA | 14 |
| 24 | GREEN BAY | 27 |
| 25 | Tampa Bay | 6 |
| 28 | St. Louis | 34 |
| 31 | CAROLINA | 27 |
| 30 | Jacksonville | 27 |
| 35 | HOUSTON | 32 |
| 14 | Minnesota | 6 |
| 34 | PITTSBURGH | *37 |
| 28 | Green Bay | 35 |
| 17 | DETROIT | 24 |
| 27 | New York Giants | 24 |
| 7 | Detroit | 27 |
| 10 | Cincinnati | 16 |
| 31 | TAMPA BAY | 10 |
| 20 | PHILADELPHIA | 14 |

| Use Name | Pos. | Hgt. | Wgt. | Age | Int | Pts |
|---|---|---|---|---|---|---|
| Scott Adams | OT | 6'5" | 305 | 28 | | |
| Troy Auzenne | OT | 6'7" | 305 | 26 | | |
| Andy Heck | OT | 6'6" | 296 | 28 | | |
| James Williams | OT | 6'7" | 335 | 27 | | |
| Todd Burger | OG | 6'3" | 301 | 25 | | |
| Jay Leeuwenburg | OG | 6'2" | 295 | 26 | | |
| Todd Perry | OG | 6'5" | 310 | 24 | | |
| Jerry Fontenot | C | 6'3" | 290 | 28 | | |
| Richard Dent | DE | 6'5" | 265 | 34 | | |
| Albert Fontenot | DE | 6'4" | 275 | 24 | | 2 |
| Garland Hawkins | DE | 6'3" | 265 | 25 | | |
| Pat Riley | DE | 6'5" | 286 | 23 | | |
| Alonzo Spellman | DE | 6'4" | 290 | 23 | | |
| John Thierry | DE | 6'4" | 260 | 23 | | |
| Jim Flanigan | DT-FB | 6'2" | 280 | 24 | | 12 |
| Carl Simpson | DT | 6'2" | 295 | 25 | | |
| Chris Zorich | DT | 6'1" | 280 | 26 | | |

| Use Name | Pos. | Hgt. | Wgt. | Age | Int | Pts |
|---|---|---|---|---|---|---|
| Myron Baker | LB | 6'1" | 232 | 24 | | |
| Robert Bass | LB | 6'1" | 239 | 24 | | |
| Joe Cain | LB | 6'1" | 237 | 29 | | |
| Ron Cox | LB | 6'2" | 240 | 27 | 1 | |
| Sean Harris | LB | 6'3" | 244 | 23 | | |
| Darwin Ireland | LB | 5'11" | 240 | 24 | | |
| Barry Minter | LB | 6'2" | 240 | 25 | 1 | 6 |
| Vinson Smith | LB | 6'2" | 247 | 30 | | |
| James Burton | DB | 5'9" | 181 | 24 | | |
| Mark Carrier | DB | 6'1" | 190 | 27 | | |
| Marty Carter | DB | 6'1" | 209 | 25 | 2 | |
| Pat Eilers | DB | 5'11" | 195 | 28 | | |
| Keshon Johnson | DB | 5'10" | 177 | 25 | | |
| Dwayne Joseph | DB | 5'9" | 180 | 23 | 2 | |
| Jeremy Lincoln | DB | 5'10" | 180 | 26 | 1 | |
| John Mangum | DB | 5'10" | 186 | 28 | 1 | |
| Anthony Marshall | DB | 6'1" | 205 | 24 | 1 | 6 |
| Kevin Miniefield | DB | 5'9" | 180 | 25 | 3 | |
| Donnell Woolford | DB | 5'9" | 188 | 29 | 4 | |

| Use Name | Pos. | Hgt. | Wgt. | Age | Int | Pts |
|---|---|---|---|---|---|---|
| Erik Kramer | QB | 6'1" | 200 | 30 | | 6 |
| Steve Walsh | QB | 6'3" | 205 | 28 | | |
| Robert Green | HB | 5'8" | 212 | 24 | | 18 |
| Rashaan Salaam | HB | 6'1" | 226 | 20 | | 60 |
| Lewis Tillman | HB | 6' | 204 | 29 | | |
| Tony Carter | FB | 5'11" | 232 | 23 | | 6 |
| Mike Faulkerson | FB | 6' | 237 | 24 | | |
| Raymont Harris | FB | 6' | 225 | 24 | | |
| Fabien Bownes | WR | 5'11" | 180 | 23 | | |
| Curtis Conway | WR | 6' | 193 | 24 | | 72 |
| Jeff Graham | WR | 6'2" | 200 | 26 | | 24 |
| Nate Lewis | WR | 5'11" | 189 | 28 | | |
| Greg Primus | WR | 5'11" | 190 | 24 | | |
| -Michael Timpson | WR | 5'10" | 180 | 28 | | 18 |
| Chris Gedney | TE | 6'5" | 265 | 25 | | |
| Keith Jennings | TE | 6'4" | 270 | 29 | | 36 |
| Andre President (from NE) | TE | 6'3" | 255 | 24 | | |
| Ryan Wetnight | TE | 6'2" | 240 | 24 | | 12 |
| Kevin Butler | K | 6'1" | 205 | 33 | | 114 |
| Todd Sauerbrun | K | 5'10" | 206 | 22 | | |

## MINNESOTA VIKINGS 8-8 Dennis Green

| Scores of Each Game | | |
|---|---|---|
| 14 | Chicago | 31 |
| 20 | DETROIT | 10 |
| 17 | DALLAS | *23 |
| 44 | Pittsburgh | 24 |
| 23 | HOUSTON | *17 |
| 17 | Tampa Bay | *20 |
| 21 | Green Bay | 38 |
| 6 | CHICAGO | 14 |
| 27 | GREEN BAY | 24 |
| 30 | Arizona | *24 |
| 43 | NEW ORLEANS | 24 |
| 38 | Detroit | 44 |
| 31 | TAMPA BAY | 17 |
| 27 | CLEVELAND | 11 |
| 30 | San Francisco | 37 |
| 24 | Cincinnati | 27 |

| Use Name | Pos. | Hgt. | Wgt. | Age | Int | Pts |
|---|---|---|---|---|---|---|
| Rick Cunningham | OT | 6'6" | 306 | 28 | | |
| Todd Steussie | OT | 6'6" | 313 | 24 | | |
| Korey Stringer | OT | 6'4" | 339 | 21 | | |
| David Dixon | OG | 6'5" | 359 | 26 | | |
| John Gerak | OG-TE | 6'3" | 269 | 25 | | |
| Chris Hinton | OG | 6'4" | 306 | 34 | | |
| Everett Lindsay | PG-C | 6'4" | 305 | 24 | | |
| Randall McDaniel | OG | 6'3" | 277 | 30 | | |
| Jeff Christy | C | 6'3" | 284 | 26 | | |
| Mike Morris | C | 6'5" | 275 | 34 | | |
| Derrick Alexander | DE | 6'4" | 265 | 21 | | |
| Roy Barker | DE | 6'4" | 289 | 26 | 1 | |
| James Harris | DE | 6'4" | 255 | 27 | | |
| Martin Harrison | DE | 6'5" | 251 | 27 | 1 | |
| Fernando Smith | DE | 6'6" | 283 | 24 | | |
| Jason Fisk | DT | 6'3" | 284 | 22 | | |
| John Randle | DT | 6'1" | 277 | 27 | | |
| Esera Tuaolo | DT | 6'2" | 276 | 27 | | |

| Use Name | Pos. | Hgt. | Wgt. | Age | Int | Pts |
|---|---|---|---|---|---|---|
| Tuineau Alipate | LB | 6'2" | 239 | 28 | | |
| Pete Bercich | LB | 6'1" | 237 | 23 | | |
| Jeff Brady | LB | 6'1" | 238 | 26 | 2 | |
| Richard Brown | LB | 6'3" | 240 | 29 | | |
| Jack Del Rio | LB | 6'4" | 245 | 32 | 1 | |
| Ed McDaniel | LB | 5'11" | 230 | 26 | 1 | |
| Broderick Thomas | LB | 6'4" | 242 | 28 | | |
| Harlon Barnett | DB | 5'11" | 203 | 28 | | |
| Donald Frank | DB | 6' | 192 | 29 | 3 | |
| Corey Fuller | DB | 5'10" | 198 | 24 | 1 | 6 |
| Robert Griffith | DB | 5'11" | 193 | 24 | | |
| Shelly Hammonds | DB | 5'10" | 189 | 24 | | |
| Alfred Jackson | DB | 6' | 183 | 28 | 2 | 6 |
| Charles Mincy | DB | 5'11" | 198 | 25 | 3 | |
| Orlando Thomas | DB | 6'1" | 210 | 22 | **9** | 12 |
| Dewayne Washington | DB | 5'11" | 191 | 22 | 1 | |

| Use Name | Pos. | Hgt. | Wgt. | Age | Int | Pts |
|---|---|---|---|---|---|---|
| Brad Johnson | QB | 6'5" | 223 | 26 | | |
| Chad May | QB | 6'1" | 219 | 23 | | |
| Warren Moon | QB | 6'3" | 213 | 38 | | |
| Chuck Evans | HB | 6'1" | 240 | 28 | | 12 |
| Scottie Graham | HB | 5'9" | 222 | 26 | | 12 |
| Amp Lee | HB | 5'11" | 197 | 23 | | 18 |
| Bobby Phillips | HB | 5'9" | 187 | 25 | | |
| Robert Smith | HB | 6' | 205 | 23 | | 32 |
| James Stewart | HB-FB | 6'2" | 238 | 23 | | |
| Cris Carter | WR | 6'3" | 206 | 29 | | 102 |
| Qadry Ismail | WR | 6' | 196 | 24 | | 18 |
| David Palmer | WR | 5'8" | 169 | 22 | | 6 |
| Jake Reed | WR | 6'3" | 216 | 27 | | 54 |
| Chris Walsh | WR | 6'1" | 194 | 26 | | |
| Adrian Cooper | TE | 6'5" | 255 | 27 | | |
| Greg DeLong | TE | 6'4" | 245 | 22 | | |
| Andrew Jordan | TE | 6'4" | 258 | 23 | | 12 |
| Mike Tice | TE | 6'7" | 266 | 36 | | |
| Fuad Reveiz | K | 5'11" | 225 | 32 | | 122 |
| Mike Saxon | K | 6'3" | 205 | 33 | | |

## TAMPA BAY BUCCANEERS 7-9 Sam Wyche

| Scores of Each Game | | |
|---|---|---|
| 21 | Philadelphia | 6 |
| 6 | Cleveland | 22 |
| 6 | CHICAGO | 25 |
| 14 | WASHINGTON | 6 |
| 20 | Carolina | 13 |
| 19 | CINCINNATI | 16 |
| 20 | MINNESOTA | *17 |
| 21 | ATLANTA | 24 |
| 7 | Houston | 19 |
| 24 | Detroit | 27 |
| 17 | JACKSONVILLE | 16 |
| 13 | Green Bay | 35 |
| 17 | Minnesota | 31 |
| 13 | GREEN BAY | *10 |
| 10 | Chicago | 31 |
| 10 | DETROIT | 37 |

| Use Name | Pos. | Hgt. | Wgt. | Age | Int | Pts |
|---|---|---|---|---|---|---|
| Scott Dill | OT-OG | 6'5" | 295 | 29 | | |
| Paul Gruber | OT | 6'5" | 296 | 30 | | |
| Stephen Ingram | OT-OG | 6'4" | 311 | 24 | | |
| Pete Pierson | OT | 6'5" | 295 | 24 | | |
| Ian Beckles | OG | 6'1" | 304 | 28 | | |
| Charles McRae | OG-OT | 6'7" | 294 | 26 | | |
| Jim Pyne | OG | 6'2" | 282 | 23 | | |
| Mike Sullivan | OG-OT-C | 6'3" | 292 | 27 | | |
| Tony Mayberry | C | 6'4" | 292 | 27 | | |
| Chidi Ahanotu | DE-DT | 6'2" | 283 | 24 | | |
| Eric Curry | DE | 6'5" | 270 | 25 | | |
| Keith Powe | DE | 6'3" | 265 | 26 | | |
| Herman Smith | DE | 6'5" | 261 | 24 | | |
| Brad Culpepper | DT | 6'1" | 270 | 26 | | |
| Santana Dotson | DT-DE | 6'5" | 276 | 25 | | |
| Toddrick McIntosh | DT-DE | 6'3" | 277 | 23 | | |
| Warren Sapp | DT | 6'2" | 281 | 22 | 1 | 6 |
| Mark Wheeler | DT | 6'2" | 290 | 25 | | |

| Use Name | Pos. | Hgt. | Wgt. | Age | Int | Pts |
|---|---|---|---|---|---|---|
| Ed Brady | LB | 6'2" | 238 | 33 | | |
| Derrick Brooks | LB | 6' | 225 | 22 | | |
| Demetrious DuBose | LB | 6'1" | 235 | 24 | | |
| Lonnie Marts | LB | 6'1" | 236 | 26 | 1 | |
| Hardy Nickerson | LB | 6'2" | 229 | 30 | | |
| Wardell Rouse | LB | 6'2" | 235 | 23 | | |
| Darnell Stephens | LB | 5'11" | 243 | 22 | | |
| Clifton Abraham | DB | 5'9" | 184 | 23 | | |
| John Booty | DB | 6' | 180 | 29 | 1 | |
| Tony Bouie | DB | 5'10" | 187 | 23 | 1 | |
| Curtis Buckley | DB | 6' | 191 | 24 | | |
| Barney Bussey | DB-LB | 6' | 215 | 33 | | |
| Charles Dimry | DB | 6' | 176 | 29 | 1 | |
| Thomas Everett | DB | 5'9" | 185 | 30 | | |
| Kenneth Gant | DB | 5'11" | 195 | 28 | | |
| Melvin Johnson | DB | 6' | 191 | 23 | 1 | |
| John Lynch | DB | 6'2" | 216 | 23 | 3 | |
| Martin Mayhew | DB | 5'8" | 178 | 29 | 5 | 6 |
| Michael McGruder | DB | 5'10" | 178 | 31 | | |
| Tony Stargell | DB | 5'11" | 186 | 29 | | |

| Use Name | Pos. | Hgt. | Wgt. | Age | Int | Pts |
|---|---|---|---|---|---|---|
| Trent Dilfer | QB | 6'4" | 235 | 23 | | 12 |
| Todd Philcox | QB | 6'4" | 225 | 28 | | |
| Casey Weldon | QB | 6'1" | 206 | 26 | | 6 |
| Bobby Joe Edmonds | HB | 5'11" | 190 | 30 | | |
| Jerry Ellison | HB-FB | 5'10" | 198 | 23 | | 30 |
| Errict Rhett | HB | 5'11" | 211 | 24 | | 66 |
| Dave Moore | FB-TE | 6'2" | 243 | 25 | | |
| Horace Copeland | WR | 6'2" | 202 | 24 | | 12 |
| Tyree Davis | WR | 5'9" | 175 | 24 | | |
| Lawrence Dawsey | WR | 6' | 192 | 27 | | |
| Alvin Harper | WR | 6'4" | 218 | 27 | | 12 |
| Courtney Hawkins | WR | 5'9" | 183 | 25 | | |
| Lamar Thomas | WR | 6'1" | 173 | 25 | | |
| Tyji Armstrong | TE | 6'4" | 277 | 24 | | |
| Jackie Harris | TE | 6'4" | 239 | 27 | | 6 |
| Cedric Saunders | TE | 6'3" | 240 | 22 | | |
| Michael Husted | K | 6' | 195 | 25 | | 82 |
| Reggie Roby | K | 6'3" | 253 | 34 | | |

## GREEN BAY PACKERS

### RUSHING
| Last Name | No. | Yds | Avg | TD |
|---|---|---|---|---|
| E. Bennett | 316 | 1067 | 3.4 | 3 |
| Favre | 39 | 181 | 4.6 | 3 |
| Levens | 36 | 120 | 3.3 | 3 |
| Henderson | 7 | 35 | 5.0 | 0 |
| R. Brooks | 4 | 21 | 5.3 | 0 |
| Rubley | 2 | 6 | 3.0 | 0 |
| Detmer | 3 | 3 | 1.0 | 0 |
| Ingram | 1 | -3 | -3.0 | 0 |

### RECEIVING
| Last Name | No. | Yds | Avg | TD |
|---|---|---|---|---|
| Brooks | 102 | 1497 | 14.7 | 13 |
| Bennett | 61 | 648 | 10.6 | 4 |
| Chmura | 54 | 679 | 12.6 | 7 |
| Levens | 48 | 434 | 9.0 | 4 |
| Ingram | 39 | 469 | 12.0 | 3 |
| Morgan | 31 | 344 | 11.1 | 4 |
| Jackson | 13 | 142 | 10.9 | 1 |
| Freeman | 8 | 106 | 13.3 | 1 |
| Jordan | 7 | 117 | 16.7 | 2 |
| Mickens | 3 | 50 | 16.7 | 0 |
| Thomason | 3 | 32 | 10.7 | 0 |
| Henderson | 3 | 21 | 7.0 | 0 |

### PUNT RETURNS
| Last Name | No. | Yds | Avg | TD |
|---|---|---|---|---|
| Freeman | 37 | 292 | 7.9 | 0 |
| Jordan | 21 | 213 | 10.1 | 0 |
| Prior | 1 | 2 | 2.0 | 0 |
| Evans | 1 | 0 | 0.0 | 0 |
| Ingram | 1 | 0 | 0.0 | 0 |

### KICKOFF RETURNS
| Last Name | No. | Yds | Avg | TD |
|---|---|---|---|---|
| Freeman | 24 | 556 | 23.2 | 0 |
| Jordan | 21 | 444 | 21.1 | 0 |
| Jervey | 8 | 165 | 20.6 | 0 |
| Morgan | 3 | 46 | 15.3 | 0 |
| R. Brooks | 1 | 28 | 28.0 | 0 |
| Jurkovic | 1 | 17 | 17.0 | 0 |
| Thomason | 1 | 16 | 16.0 | 0 |
| Arthur | 1 | 10 | 10.0 | 0 |
| Mickens | 1 | 0 | 0.0 | 0 |

### PASSING — PUNTING — KICKING
| PASSING | Att | Cmp | % | Yds | Yd/Att | TD | Int— | % | RK |
|---|---|---|---|---|---|---|---|---|---|
| Favre | 570 | 359 | 63.0 | 4413 | 7.74 | 38 | 13— | 2.3 | |
| Detmer | 16 | 8 | 50.0 | 81 | 5.06 | 1 | 1— | 6.3 | |
| Rubley | 6 | 4 | 66.7 | 39 | 6.50 | 0 | 1— | 16.7 | |
| McMahon | 1 | 1 | 100.0 | 6 | 6.00 | 0 | 0— | 0.0 | |

| PUNTING | No. | Avg. |
|---|---|---|
| Hentrich | 67 | 40.9 |

| KICKING | XP | ATT | % | FG | ATT | % |
|---|---|---|---|---|---|---|
| Jacke | 43 | 43 | 100 | 17 | 23 | 74 |

2 POINT XP
Chmura(1)

## DETROIT LIONS

### RUSHING
| Last Name | No. | Yds | Avg | TD |
|---|---|---|---|---|
| Sanders | 314 | 1500 | 4.8 | 11 |
| S. Mitchell | 36 | 104 | 2.9 | 4 |
| Rivers | 18 | 73 | 4.1 | 1 |
| Perriman | 5 | 48 | 9.6 | 0 |
| Morton | 3 | 33 | 11.0 | 0 |
| Schlesinger | 1 | 1 | 1.0 | 0 |
| Majkowski | 9 | 1 | 0.1 | 0 |
| Royals | 1 | -7 | -7.0 | 0 |

### RECEIVING
| Last Name | No. | Yds | Avg | TD |
|---|---|---|---|---|
| H. Moore | 123 | 1686 | 13.7 | 14 |
| Perriman | 108 | 1488 | 13.8 | 9 |
| Sanders | 48 | 398 | 8.3 | 1 |
| Morton | 44 | 590 | 13.4 | 8 |
| Sloan | 17 | 184 | 10.8 | 1 |
| Hall | 11 | 81 | 7.4 | 0 |
| Holman | 5 | 35 | 7.0 | 0 |
| Matthews | 4 | 41 | 10.3 | 0 |
| Rivers | 1 | 5 | 5.0 | 0 |
| Schlesinger | 1 | 2 | 2.0 | 0 |

### PUNT RETURNS
| Last Name | No. | Yds | Avg | TD |
|---|---|---|---|---|
| Morton | 7 | 48 | 6.9 | 0 |
| Turner | 6 | 39 | 6.5 | 0 |
| Perriman | 5 | 50 | 10.0 | 0 |
| Clay | 5 | 49 | 9.8 | 0 |
| Carter | 1 | 3 | 3.0 | 0 |

### KICKOFF RETURNS
| Last Name | No. | Yds | Avg | TD |
|---|---|---|---|---|
| Rivers | 19 | 420 | 22.1 | 0 |
| Morton | 18 | 390 | 21.7 | 0 |
| Turner | 17 | 323 | 19.0 | 0 |
| Perriman | 5 | 65 | 13.0 | 0 |
| Williams | 4 | 100 | 25.0 | 0 |
| Carter | 2 | 46 | 23.0 | 0 |
| Sloan | 1 | 14 | 14.0 | 0 |
| Owens | 1 | 9 | 9.0 | 0 |

### PASSING — PUNTING — KICKING
| PASSING | Att | Cmp | % | Yds | Yd/Att | TD | Int— | % | RK |
|---|---|---|---|---|---|---|---|---|---|
| Mitchell | 583 | 346 | 59.3 | 4338 | 7.44 | 32 | 12— | 2.1 | |
| Majkowski | 20 | 15 | 75.0 | 161 | 8.05 | 1 | 0— | 0.0 | |
| Sanders | 2 | 1 | 50.0 | 11 | 5.50 | 0 | 0— | 0.0 | |

| PUNTING | No. | Avg. |
|---|---|---|
| Royals | 59 | 40.6 |
| Hanson | 1 | 34 | 34.0 | 0 |

| KICKING | XP | ATT | % | FG | ATT | % |
|---|---|---|---|---|---|---|
| Hanson | 48 | 48 | 100 | 28 | 34 | 82 |

2 POINT XP
Perriman (1)

## CHICAGO BEARS

### RUSHING
| Last Name | No. | Yds | Avg | TD |
|---|---|---|---|---|
| Salaam | 296 | 1074 | 3.6 | 10 |
| Green | 107 | 570 | 5.3 | 3 |
| Tillman | 29 | 79 | 2.7 | 0 |
| Conway | 5 | 77 | 15.4 | 1 |
| Kramer | 35 | 39 | 1.1 | 1 |
| T. Carter | 10 | 34 | 3.4 | 0 |
| Timpson | 3 | 28 | 9.3 | 1 |
| Flanigan | 1 | 0 | 0.0 | 0 |

### RECEIVING
| Last Name | No. | Yds | Avg | TD |
|---|---|---|---|---|
| Graham | 82 | 1301 | 15.9 | 4 |
| Conway | 62 | 1037 | 16.7 | 12 |
| T. carter | 40 | 329 | 8.2 | 1 |
| Green | 28 | 246 | 8.8 | 0 |
| Jennings | 25 | 217 | 8.7 | 6 |
| Timpson | 24 | 289 | 12.0 | 2 |
| Wetnight | 24 | 193 | 8.0 | 2 |
| Salaam | 7 | 56 | 8.0 | 0 |
| Gedney | 5 | 52 | 10.4 | 0 |
| Faulkerson | 2 | 22 | 11.0 | 0 |
| Flanigan | 2 | 6 | 3.0 | 2 |
| R. Harris | 1 | 4 | 4.0 | 0 |

### PUNT RETURNS
| Last Name | No. | Yds | Avg | TD |
|---|---|---|---|---|
| Graham | 23 | 183 | 8.0 | 0 |
| Lundy | 1 | -4 | -4.0 | 0 |

### KICKOFF RETURNS
| Last Name | No. | Yds | Avg | TD |
|---|---|---|---|---|
| Lewis | 42 | 904 | 21.5 | 0 |
| Timpson | 18 | 420 | 23.3 | 0 |
| T. Carter | 3 | 24 | 8.0 | 0 |
| Green | 3 | 29 | 9.7 | 0 |
| Primus | 2 | 39 | 19.5 | 0 |
| Tillman | 1 | 20 | 20.0 | 0 |
| Graham | 1 | 12 | 12.0 | 0 |

### PASSING — PUNTING — KICKING
| PASSING | Att | Cmp | % | Yds | Yd/Att | TD | Int— | % | RK |
|---|---|---|---|---|---|---|---|---|---|
| Kramer | 522 | 315 | 60.3 | 3838 | 7.35 | 29 | 10— | 1.9 | |
| Conway | 1 | 0 | 0.0 | 0 | 0.00 | 0 | 0— | 0.0 | |

| PUNTING | No. | Avg. |
|---|---|---|
| Sauerbrun | 55 | 37.8 |

| KICKING | XP | ATT | % | FG | ATT | % |
|---|---|---|---|---|---|---|
| Butler | 45 | 45 | 100 | 23 | 31 | 74 |

2 POINT XP
None

## MINNESOTA VIKINGS

### RUSHING
| Last Name | No. | Yds | Avg | TD |
|---|---|---|---|---|
| R. Smith | 139 | 632 | 4.5 | 5 |
| Graham | 110 | 406 | 3.7 | 2 |
| Lee | 69 | 371 | 5.4 | 2 |
| Stewart | 31 | 144 | 4.6 | 0 |
| Moon | 33 | 82 | 2.5 | 0 |
| Evans | 19 | 59 | 3.1 | 1 |
| Phillips | 14 | 26 | 1.9 | 0 |
| Palmer | 7 | 15 | 2.1 | 0 |
| Ismail | 1 | 7 | 7.0 | 0 |
| Carter | 1 | 0 | 0.0 | 0 |
| Johnson | 9 | -9 | -1.0 | 0 |

### RECEIVING
| Last Name | No. | Yds | Avg | TD |
|---|---|---|---|---|
| C. Carter | 122 | 1371 | 11.2 | 17 |
| Reed | 72 | 1167 | 16.2 | 9 |
| Lee | 71 | 558 | 7.9 | 1 |
| Ismail | 32 | 597 | 18.7 | 3 |
| Jordan | 27 | 185 | 6.9 | 2 |
| Cooper | 18 | 207 | 11.5 | 0 |
| Evans | 18 | 119 | 6.6 | 1 |
| Palmer | 12 | 100 | 8.3 | 0 |
| Walsh | 7 | 66 | 9.4 | 0 |
| R. Smith | 7 | 35 | 5.0 | 0 |
| DeLong | 6 | 38 | 6.3 | 0 |
| Graham | 4 | 30 | 7.5 | 0 |
| Tice | 3 | 22 | 7.3 | 0 |
| Gerak | 1 | 3 | 3.0 | 0 |
| Stewart | 1 | 3 | 3.0 | 0 |
| Stringer | 1 | -1 | -1.0 | 0 |

### PUNT RETURNS
| Last Name | No. | Yds | Avg | TD |
|---|---|---|---|---|
| Palmer | 26 | 342 | 13.2 | 1 |
| Lee | 5 | 50 | 10.0 | 0 |
| Mincy | 4 | 22 | 5.5 | 0 |

### KICKOFF RETURNS
| Last Name | No. | Yds | Avg | TD |
|---|---|---|---|---|
| Ismail | 42 | 1037 | 24.7 | 0 |
| Palmer | 17 | 354 | 20.8 | 0 |
| Lee | 5 | 100 | 20.0 | 0 |
| Phillips | 4 | 60 | 15.0 | 0 |
| Walsh | 3 | 42 | 14.0 | 0 |
| Gerak | 1 | 19 | 19.0 | 0 |

### PASSING — PUNTING — KICKING
| PASSING | Att | Cmp | % | Yds | Yd/Att | TD | Int— | % | RK |
|---|---|---|---|---|---|---|---|---|---|
| Moon | 606 | 377 | 62.2 | 4228 | 6.98 | 33 | 14— | 2.3 | |
| Johnson | 36 | 25 | 69.4 | 272 | 7.56 | 0 | 2— | 5.6 | |

| PUNTING | No. | Avg. |
|---|---|---|
| Saxon | 72 | 40.9 |

| KICKING | XP | ATT | % | FG | ATT | % |
|---|---|---|---|---|---|---|
| Reveiz | 44 | 44 | 100 | 26 | 36 | 72 |

2 POINT XP
R. Smith (1)

## TAMPA BAY BUCCANEERS

### RUSHING
| Last Name | No. | Yds | Avg | TD |
|---|---|---|---|---|
| Rhett | 332 | 1207 | 3.6 | 11 |
| Ellison | 26 | 218 | 8.4 | 5 |
| Dilfer | 5 | 28 | 5.6 | 0 |
| Edmonds | 5 | 28 | 5.6 | 0 |
| Hawkins | 4 | 5 | 1.3 | 0 |
| Thomas | 1 | 5 | 5.0 | 0 |
| Weldon | 5 | 5 | 1.0 | 0 |
| Moore | 1 | 4 | 4.0 | 0 |
| Roby | 1 | 0 | 0.0 | 0 |

### RECEIVING
| Last Name | No. | Yds | Avg | TD |
|---|---|---|---|---|
| Harris | 62 | 751 | 12.1 | 1 |
| Harper | 46 | 633 | 13.8 | 2 |
| Hawkins | 41 | 493 | 12.0 | 0 |
| Copeland | 35 | 605 | 17.3 | 2 |
| Dawsey | 30 | 372 | 12.4 | 0 |
| Rhett | 14 | 110 | 7.9 | 0 |
| Moore | 13 | 102 | 7.8 | 0 |
| Thomas | 10 | 107 | 10.7 | 0 |
| Armstrong | 7 | 68 | 9.7 | 0 |
| Ellison | 7 | 44 | 6.3 | 0 |
| Booty | 1 | 48 | 48.0 | 0 |
| Edmonds | 1 | 8 | 8.0 | 0 |

### PUNT RETURNS
| Last Name | No. | Yds | Avg | TD |
|---|---|---|---|---|
| Edmonds | 29 | 293 | 10.1 | 0 |

### KICKOFF RETURNS
| Last Name | No. | Yds | Avg | TD |
|---|---|---|---|---|
| Edmonds | 58 | 1147 | 19.8 | 0 |
| Ellison | 15 | 261 | 17.4 | 0 |
| Buckley | 2 | 29 | 14.5 | 0 |
| Armstrong | 1 | 6 | 6.0 | 0 |

### PASSING — PUNTING — KICKING
| PASSING | Att | Cmp | % | Yds | Yd/Att | TD | Int— | % | RK |
|---|---|---|---|---|---|---|---|---|---|
| Dilfer | 415 | 224 | 54.0 | 2774 | 6.68 | 4 | 18— | 4.3 | |
| Weldon | 91 | 42 | 46.2 | 519 | 5.70 | 1 | 2— | 2.2 | |
| Roby | 1 | 1 | 100.0 | 48 | 48.00 | 0 | 0— | 0.0 | |

| PUNTING | No. | Avg. |
|---|---|---|
| Roby | 78 | 42.3 |

| KICKING | XP | ATT | % | FG | ATT | % |
|---|---|---|---|---|---|---|
| Husted | 25 | 25 | 100 | 19 | 26 | 73 |

2 POINT XP
None

## SAN FRANCISCO 49ERS 11-5 George Seifert

| Scores of Each Game | | |
|---|---|---|
| 24 | New Orleans | 22 |
| 41 | ATLANTA | 10 |
| 28 | NEW ENGLAND | 3 |
| 24 | Detroit | 27 |
| 20 | NEW YORK GIANTS | 6 |
| 17 | Indianapolis | 18 |
| 44 | St. Louis | 10 |
| 7 | NEW ORLEANS | 11 |
| 7 | CAROLINA | 13 |
| 38 | Dallas | 20 |
| 44 | Miami | 20 |
| 41 | ST. LOUIS | 13 |
| 27 | BUFFALO | 17 |
| 31 | Carolina | 10 |
| 37 | MINNESOTA | 30 |
| 27 | Atlanta | 28 |

| Use Name | Pos. | Hgt. | Wgt. | Age | Int | Pts |
|---|---|---|---|---|---|---|
| Harris Barton | OT | 6'4" | 286 | 31 | | |
| Frank Pollack | OT | 6'5" | 285 | 27 | | |
| Kirk Scrafford | OT | 6'6" | 275 | 28 | | |
| Steve Wallace | OT | 6'5" | 280 | 30 | | |
| Chris Dalman | OG-C | 6'3" | 285 | 25 | | |
| Derrick Deese | OG | 6'3" | 270 | 25 | | |
| Rod Milstead | OG | 6'2" | 278 | 25 | | |
| Jesse Sapolu | OG | 6'4" | 278 | 34 | | |
| Bart Oates | C | 6'3" | 275 | 36 | | |
| Oliver Barnett | DE | 6'3" | 285 | 29 | | |
| Michael Brandon | DE | 6'4" | 290 | 27 | | |
| Dennis Brown | DE | 6'4" | 285 | 27 | | |
| Jamal Fountaine | DE | 6'3" | 240 | 24 | | |
| Tim Harris | DE | 6'6" | 265 | 30 | | |
| Rickey Jackson | DE | 6'2" | 245 | 37 | 1 | |
| Alfred Williams | DE | 6'6" | 240 | 26 | | |
| Junior Bryant | DT-DE | 6'4" | 275 | 24 | | |
| Dana Stubblefield | DT | 6'2" | 290 | 24 | 1 | |
| Bryant Young | DT | 6'2" | 276 | 23 | | |
| Antonio Goss | LB | 6'4" | 228 | 29 | | |
| Kevin Mitchell | LB | 6'1" | 260 | 24 | | |
| Ken Norton | LB | 6'2" | 241 | 28 | 3 | 12 |
| Anthony Peterson | LB | 6' | 223 | 23 | | |
| Gary Plummer | LB | 6'2" | 247 | 35 | | |
| Lee Woodall | LB | 6' | 220 | 25 | 2 | 6 |
| Toi Cook | DB | 5'11" | 188 | 30 | | |
| Eric Davis | DB | 5'11" | 178 | 27 | 3 | 6 |
| Dedrick Dodge | DB | 6'2" | 184 | 28 | 1 | |
| Tyronne Drakeford | DB | 5'9" | 185 | 24 | 5 | |
| Darryl Hall | DB | 6'2" | 210 | 29 | | |
| Merton Hanks | DB | 6'2" | 185 | 27 | 5 | 6 |
| Steve Israel | DB | 5'11" | 186 | 26 | | |
| Tim McDonald | DB | 6'2" | 215 | 30 | 4 | 12 |
| Marquez Pope | DB | 5'11" | 193 | 24 | 1 | |
| Michael Williams | DB | 5'10" | 185 | 25 | | |
| Jeff Brohm | QB | 6'1" | 205 | 24 | | |
| Cary Conklin | QB | 6'4" | 225 | 27 | | |
| Elvis Grbac | QB | 6'5" | 232 | 25 | | 12 |
| Steve Young | QB | 6'2" | 205 | 33 | | 18 |
| Dexter Carter | HB | 5'9" | 170 | 27 | | 6 |
| Ricky Ervins | HB | 5'7" | 195 | 26 | | |
| Derek Loville | HB | 5'10" | 205 | 27 | | 80 |
| Adam Walker | HB | 6'1 | 210 | 27 | | 6 |
| Jamal Willis | HB | 6'2" | 218 | 22 | | |
| William Floyd | FB | 6'1" | 242 | 23 | | 18 |
| Anthony Lynn | FB | 6'3" | 230 | 26 | | |
| Brian O'Neal | FB | 6' | 233 | 25 | | |
| Mike Caldwell | WR | 6'2" | 200 | 24 | | |
| Jerry Rice | WR | 6'2" | 200 | 32 | | 104 |
| Nate Singleton | WR | 5'11" | 190 | 27 | | 6 |
| J.J. Stokes | WR | 6'4" | 217 | 22 | | 24 |
| John Taylor | WR | 6'1" | 185 | 33 | | 12 |
| Chris Thomas | WR | 6'1" | 180 | 24 | | |
| Terrence Warren | WR | 6'1" | 205 | 26 | | |
| Brett Carolan | TE | 6'3" | 241 | 24 | | |
| Brent Jones | TE | 6'4" | 230 | 32 | | 18 |
| Ted Popson | LB | 6'4" | 250 | 28 | | |
| Tommy Thompson | K | 5'10" | 192 | 23 | | |
| Jeff Wilkins | K | 6'2" | 192 | 23 | | 63 |
| Tony Zendejas (from ATL) | K | 5'8" | 165 | 35 | | 14 |

## ATLANTA FALCONS 9-7 June Jones

| Scores of Each Game | | |
|---|---|---|
| 23 | CAROLINA | *20 |
| 10 | San Francisco | 41 |
| 27 | New Orleans | *24 |
| 13 | NEW YORK JETS | 3 |
| 30 | NEW ENGLAND | 17 |
| 19 | St. Louis | 21 |
| 24 | Tampa Bay | 21 |
| 13 | DALLAS | 28 |
| 34 | DETROIT | 22 |
| 17 | Buffalo | 23 |
| 31 | ST. LOUIS | 6 |
| 37 | Arizona | *40 |
| 20 | Miami | 21 |
| 19 | NEW ORLEANS | 14 |
| 17 | Carolina | 21 |
| 28 | SAN FRANCISCO | 27 |

| Use Name | Pos. | Hgt. | Wgt. | Age | Int | Pts |
|---|---|---|---|---|---|---|
| Lincoln Kennedy | OT-OG | 6'6" | 325 | 24 | | |
| Bob Whitfield | OT | 6'5" | 300 | 23 | | |
| Jeff Pahukoa | OG-OT | 6'2" | 298 | 26 | | |
| David Richards | OG | 6'5" | 315 | 29 | | |
| Jim Ritcher | OG | 6'3" | 273 | 37 | | |
| Robbie Tobeck | OG-C | 6'4" | 292 | 25 | | |
| Gene Williams | OG-OT | 6'2" | 305 | 26 | | |
| Mike Zandofsky | OG | 6'2" | 305 | 29 | | |
| Roman Fortin | C | 6'5" | 295 | 28 | | |
| Lester Archambeau | DE | 6'5" | 275 | 28 | | |
| Chris Doleman | DE | 6'5" | 275 | 33 | | |
| Travis Hall | DE | 6'5" | 278 | 23 | | |
| Chuck Smith | DE | 6'2" | 257 | 25 | | |
| Mel Agee | DT | 6'5" | 300 | 26 | | |
| John Burrough | DT | 6'5" | 265 | 23 | | |
| James Geathers | DT | 6'7" | 300 | 35 | | |
| Pierce Holt | DT | 6'4" | 275 | 33 | | |
| Moe Gardner | NT | 6'2" | 265 | 27 | | |
| Ron George | LB | 6'2" | 235 | 25 | | |
| Clay Matthews | LB | 6'2" | 245 | 39 | 2 | |
| Lorenzo Styles | LB | 6'1" | 244 | 21 | | |
| Darryl Talley | LB | 6'4" | 235 | 35 | | |
| Ken Tippins | LB | 6'1" | 235 | 29 | 1 | |
| Jessie Tuggle | LB | 5'11" | 230 | 30 | 3 | 6 |
| Devin Bush | DB | 5'11" | 205 | 22 | 1 | |
| Ronald Davis | DB | 5'10" | 190 | 23 | | |
| Brad Edwards | DB | 6'2" | 207 | 29 | | |
| Roger Harper | DB | 6'2" | 225 | 24 | 1 | |
| D.J. Johnson | DB | 6' | 193 | 29 | 2 | |
| Rich Miano | DB | 6'1" | 200 | 32 | | |
| Alton Montgomery | DB | 6' | 209 | 27 | 1 | 6 |
| Anthony Phillips | DB | 6'2" | 207 | 24 | 1 | |
| Kevin Ross | DB | 5'9" | 185 | 33 | 3 | 6 |
| Elbert Shelley | DB | 5'11" | 190 | 30 | | |
| Terry Taylor | DB | 5'10" | 185 | 34 | 3 | |
| Darnell Walker | DB | 5'8" | 168 | 25 | | |
| Jeff George | QB | 6'4" | 215 | 27 | | |
| Bobby Hebert | QB | 6'4" | 215 | 35 | | |
| Perry Klein | QB | 6'2" | 218 | 24 | | |
| Browning Nagle | QB | 6'3" | 225 | 27 | | |
| Jamal Anderson | HB-FB | 5'10" | 240 | 23 | | 6 |
| Craig Heyward | HB-FB | 5'11" | 260 | 28 | | 48 |
| J.J. Birden | WR | 5'9" | 170 | 30 | | 6 |
| Tyrone Brown | WR | 5'11" | 164 | 22 | | |
| Bert Emanuel | WR | 5'10" | 180 | 24 | | 30 |
| Terance Mathis | WR | 5'10" | 180 | 28 | | 60 |
| Eric Metcalf | WR-HB | 5'10" | 188 | 27 | | 60 |
| Roell Preston | WR | 5'10" | 187 | 23 | | 6 |
| Ricky Sanders | WR | 5'11" | 180 | 33 | | |
| Darryl Spencer | WR | 5'8" | 172 | 25 | | |
| Harper LeBel | TE | 6'4" | 255 | 32 | | |
| Mitch Lyons | TE | 6'4" | 265 | 25 | | |
| Morten Andersen | K | 6'2" | 221 | 35 | | 122 |
| Dan Stryzinski | K | 6'2" | 200 | 30 | | |

Eric Jack — Knee Injury

## ST. LOUIS RAMS 7-9 Rich Brooks

| Scores of Each Game | | |
|---|---|---|
| 17 | Green Bay | 14 |
| 17 | NEW ORLEANS | 13 |
| 31 | Carolina | 10 |
| 34 | CHICAGO | 28 |
| 18 | Indianapolis | 21 |
| 21 | ATLANTA | 19 |
| 10 | SAN FRANCISCO | 44 |
| 9 | Philadelphia | 20 |
| 10 | New Orleans | 19 |
| 28 | CAROLINA | 17 |
| 6 | Atlanta | 31 |
| 13 | San Francisco | 41 |
| 23 | New York Jets | 20 |
| 27 | BUFFALO | 45 |
| 23 | WASHINGTON | 35 |
| 22 | MIAMI | 41 |

| Use Name | Pos. | Hgt. | Wgt. | Age | Int | Pts |
|---|---|---|---|---|---|---|
| Darryl Ashmore | OT | 6'7" | 310 | 25 | | |
| Wayne Gandy | OT | 6'4" | 292 | 24 | | |
| Clarence Jones | OT | 6'6" | 295 | 27 | | |
| Jackie Slater | OT | 6'4" | 285 | 41 | | |
| Zack Wiegert | OT | 6'4" | 305 | 23 | | |
| Chuck Belin | OG | 6'2" | 305 | 24 | | |
| Leo Goeas | OG | 6'4" | 300 | 29 | | |
| Keith Loneker | OG | 6'3" | 325 | 24 | | |
| Dwayne White | OG | 6'2" | 315 | 28 | | |
| Bern Brostek | C | 6'3" | 300 | 28 | | |
| Jesse James | C | 6'4" | 311 | 23 | | |
| Kevin Carter | DE | 6'5" | 274 | 21 | | 2 |
| Sean Gilbert | DE | 6'4" | 305 | 25 | | |
| Fred Stokes | DE | 6'3" | 274 | 31 | | |
| Alberto White | DE | 6'3" | 245 | 24 | | |
| Robert Young | DE | 6'6" | 273 | 26 | | |
| Brad Ottis | DE | 6'4" | 272 | 23 | | |
| D'Marco Farr | DT | 6'1" | 270 | 24 | 1 | |
| Jay Williams | DT | 6'3" | 270 | 23 | | |
| Jimmie Jones | NT-DT | 6'4" | 285 | 29 | | |
| Shane Conlan | LB | 6'3" | 235 | 31 | 1 | |
| Paschall Davis | LB | 6'2" | 225 | 26 | | |
| Cedric Figaro | LB | 6'3" | 242 | 29 | | |
| Thomas Homco | LB | 6' | 245 | 25 | | |
| Dana Howard | LB | 6' | 238 | 23 | | |
| Carlos Jenkins | LB | 6'3" | 217 | 27 | | |
| Roman Phifer | LB | 6'2" | 235 | 27 | 3 | |
| Ashley Sheppard (from JAX) | LB | 6'3" | 240 | 26 | | |
| Dexter Davis | DB | 5'10" | 184 | 25 | | |
| Torin Dorn | DB | 6' | 190 | 27 | 1 | 12 |
| Todd Lyght | DB | 6' | 186 | 26 | 4 | 6 |
| Keith Lyle | DB | 6'2" | 204 | 23 | 3 | |
| Gerald McBurrows | DB | 5'11" | 195 | 21 | | |
| Anthony Parker | DB | 5'10" | 181 | 29 | 2 | 6 |
| John Reece | DB | 6' | 203 | 24 | | |
| Mike Scurlock | DB | 5'10" | 197 | 23 | 1 | |
| Toby Wright | DB | 5'11" | 203 | 24 | 6 | 6 |
| Dave Barr | QB | 6'3" | 210 | 23 | | |
| Chris Miller | QB | 6'2" | 212 | 30 | | |
| Mark Rypien | QB | 6'4" | 231 | 32 | | |
| Johnny Bailey | HB | 5'8" | 190 | 28 | | 14 |
| Jerome Bettis | HB-FB | 5'11" | 243 | 23 | | 18 |
| Brent Moss | HB | 5'8" | 211 | 23 | | |
| Greg Robinson | HB | 5'10" | 205 | 26 | | |
| Leonard Russell | HB | 6'2" | 235 | 25 | | |
| Ron Wolfley | FB | 6' | 224 | 32 | | |
| Isaac Bruce | WR | 6' | 180 | 22 | | 80 |
| Jessie Hester | WR | 5'11" | 175 | 32 | | 18 |
| Todd Kinchen | WR | 6' | 187 | 26 | | 24 |
| J.T. Thomas | WR | 5'10" | 173 | 24 | | |
| Alexander Wright | WR | 6' | 195 | 28 | | 12 |
| Pat Carter | TE | 6'4" | 258 | 29 | | |
| Marv Cook | TE | 6'4" | 234 | 29 | | 6 |
| Troy Drayton | TE | 6'3" | 255 | 25 | | 24 |
| Lovell Pinkney | TE | 6'4" | 248 | 23 | | |
| Jim Price | TE | 6'4" | 247 | 28 | | |
| Dean Biasucci | K | 6' | 190 | 33 | | 40 |
| Sean Landeta | K | 6' | 210 | 33 | | |
| Steve McLaughlin | K | 6' | 167 | 23 | | 41 |

Jermaine Ross — Knee Injury

## CAROLINA PANTHERS 7-9 Dom Capers

| Scores of Each Game | | |
|---|---|---|
| 20 | Atlanta | *23 |
| 9 | Buffalo | 31 |
| 10 | ST. LOUIS | 31 |
| 13 | TAMPA BAY | 20 |
| 27 | Chicago | 31 |
| 26 | NEW YORK JETS | 15 |
| 20 | NEW ORLEANS | 3 |
| 20 | New England | *17 |
| 13 | San Francisco | 7 |
| 17 | St. Louis | 28 |
| 27 | ARIZONA | 7 |
| 26 | New Orleans | 34 |
| 13 | INDIANAPOLIS | 10 |
| 10 | SAN FRANCISCO | 31 |
| 21 | ATLANTA | 17 |
| 17 | Washington | 20 |

| Use Name | Pos. | Hgt. | Wgt. | Age | Int | Pts |
|---|---|---|---|---|---|---|
| Blake Brockermeyer | OT | 6'4" | 300 | 22 | | |
| Mark Dennis | OT | 6'6" | 288 | 30 | | |
| Derrick Graham | OT | 6'4" | 315 | 28 | | |
| Matt Elliott | OG | 6'3" | 295 | 26 | | |
| Frank Garcia | OG | 6'1" | 295 | 23 | | |
| Sean Love | OG | 6'3" | 304 | 26 | | |
| Emerson Martin | OG | 6'2" | 297 | 25 | | |
| Andrew Peterson | OG-OT | 6'5" | 308 | 23 | | |
| Mark Rodenhauser | C | 6'5" | 280 | 34 | | |
| Curtis Whitley | C | 6'1" | 295 | 26 | | |
| Mike Fox | DE | 6'8" | 295 | 28 | | |
| Shawn King | DE | 6'3" | 278 | 23 | | |
| Shawn Price | DE | 6'5" | 275 | 25 | | |
| Mark Thomas | DE | 6'5" | 275 | 26 | | |
| Gerald Williams | DE | 6'3" | 290 | 31 | | |
| Jeff Fields | NT | 6'3" | 320 | 28 | | |
| Greg Kragen | NT | 6'3" | 267 | 33 | 1 | 6 |
| Jeff Zgonina | NT | 6'2" | 305 | 29 | | |
| Carlton Bailey | LB | 6'3" | 242 | 30 | | |
| Paul Butcher | LB | 6' | 233 | 31 | | |
| Darion Conner | LB | 6'2" | 250 | 27 | | |
| Brett Faryniarz | LB | 6'3" | 230 | 30 | | |
| Lamar Lathon | LB | 6'3" | 260 | 27 | | |
| Sam Mills | LB | 5'9" | 232 | 36 | 5 | 6 |
| Andre Royal | LB | 6'2" | 220 | 22 | | |
| Butler By'not'e | DB | 5'9" | 190 | 22 | | |
| Chad Cota | DB | 6'1" | 195 | 24 | | |
| Alan Haller | DB | 5'11" | 185 | 25 | | |
| Steve Lofton | DB | 5'9" | 177 | 26 | | |
| Brett Maxie | DB | 6'2" | 210 | 33 | 6 | |
| Bubba McDowell | DB | 6'1" | 206 | 28 | 1 | |
| Tim McKyer | DB | 6' | 184 | 31 | 3 | 6 |
| Tyrone Poole | DB | 5'8" | 188 | 23 | 2 | |
| Michael Reed | DB | 5'9" | 180 | 23 | | |
| Rod Smith | DB | 5'11" | 194 | 25 | | |
| Pat Terrell | DB | 6'2" | 210 | 27 | 3 | |
| Kerry Collins | QB | 6'5" | 240 | 22 | | 18 |
| Frank Reich | QB | 6'4" | 210 | 33 | | |
| Jack Trudeau | QB | 6'3" | 220 | 32 | | |
| Randy Baldwin (to SF) | HB | 5'10" | 216 | 28 | | |
| Howard Griffith | HB-FB | 6' | 240 | 27 | | 12 |
| Anthony Johnson (from CHI) | HB | 6' | 225 | 27 | | 6 |
| Derrick Moore | HB | 6'1" | 227 | 27 | | 24 |
| Dino Philyaw | HB | 5'10" | 199 | 24 | | |
| Blair Thomas | HB | 5'10" | 202 | 27 | | |
| Vince Workman | HB | 5'10" | 205 | 27 | | 6 |
| Bob Christian | FB | 5'10" | 230 | 26 | | 8 |
| Nate Turner | FB | 6'1" | 255 | 26 | | |
| Don Beebe | WR | 5'11" | 185 | 30 | | 6 |
| Mark Carrier | WR | 6' | 186 | 29 | | 18 |
| Willie Green | WR | 6'4" | 185 | 29 | | 36 |
| Eric Guliford | WR | 5'8" | 173 | 25 | | 12 |
| Reggie Jones | WR | 6' | 175 | 24 | | |
| Dwight Stone | WR | 6' | 195 | 31 | | |
| Matthew Campbell | TE | 6'4" | 270 | 23 | | |
| Pete Metzelaars | TE | 6'7" | 250 | 35 | | 18 |
| Walter Rasby | TE | 6'3" | 247 | 22 | | 2 |
| Lawyer Tillman | TE | 6'5" | 252 | 29 | | |
| Tommy Barnhardt | K | 6'2" | 218 | 32 | | |
| John Kasay | K | 5'10" | 198 | 25 | | 105 |

Jeremy Nunley — Knee Injury
Mike Teeter — Shoulder Injury
Dewell Brewer — Knee Injury
Tony Smith — Broken Leg

## NEW ORLEANS SAINTS 7-9 Jim Mora

| Scores of Each Game | | |
|---|---|---|
| 22 | SAN FRANCISCO | 24 |
| 13 | St. Louis | 17 |
| 24 | ATLANTA | *27 |
| 29 | New York Giants | 45 |
| 10 | PHILADELPHIA | 15 |
| 33 | MIAMI | 30 |
| 3 | Carolina | 20 |
| 11 | San Francisco | 7 |
| 19 | ST. LOUIS | 10 |
| 17 | INDIANAPOLIS | 14 |
| 24 | Minnesota | 43 |
| 34 | CAROLINA | 26 |
| 31 | New England | 17 |
| 14 | Atlanta | 19 |
| 23 | GREEN BAY | 34 |
| 12 | New York Jets | 0 |

| Use Name | Pos. | Hgt. | Wgt. | Age | Int | Pts |
|---|---|---|---|---|---|---|
| Richard Cooper | OT | 6'4" | 290 | 30 | | |
| Alan Kline | OT | 6'5" | 290 | 24 | | |
| Craig Novitsky | OT | 6'5" | 295 | 24 | | |
| Willie Roaf | OT | 6'4" | 300 | 25 | | |
| Jim Dombrowski | OG | 6'5" | 300 | 31 | | |
| Ed King | OG | 6'4" | 300 | 26 | | |
| Chris Port | OG-OT | 6'5" | 295 | 27 | | |
| Andy McCollum | C-OG | 6'4" | 295 | 25 | | |
| Jeff Uhlenhake | C | 6'3" | 284 | 29 | | |
| Dameian Jeffries | DE | 6'4" | 277 | 22 | | |
| Joe Johnson | DE-NT | 6'4" | 270 | 23 | | |
| Ernest Jones | DE | 6'2" | 255 | 24 | | |
| Israel Stanley | DE | 6'3" | 260 | 25 | | |
| Renaldo Turnbull | DE | 6'4" | 250 | 29 | | |
| Tory Epps | DT | 6'1" | 280 | 29 | | |
| Wayne Martin | DE | 6'5" | 275 | 29 | 1 | |
| Willie Broughton | NT-DE-DT | 6'5" | 285 | 30 | | |
| Ron Childs | LB | 5'11" | 212 | 23 | | |
| Ernest Dixon | LB-DE | 6'1" | 240 | 23 | 2 | |
| Mark Fields | LB | 6'2" | 244 | 22 | | |
| Richard Harvey | LB | 6'1" | 242 | 28 | | |
| John Johnson | LB | 6'3" | 247 | 27 | | |
| Brian Jones | LB | 6'1" | 250 | 27 | | |
| Rufus Porter | LB | 6'1" | 230 | 30 | | |
| Winfred Tubbs | LB | 6'4" | 250 | 24 | 1 | |
| Eric Allen | DB | 5'10" | 180 | 29 | 2 | |
| Vince Buck | DB | 6' | 198 | 27 | | |
| Israel Byrd | DB | 5'11" | 184 | 24 | | |
| Tyrone Hughes | DB | 5'9" | 175 | 25 | 2 | |
| Tyrone Legette | DB | 5'9" | 177 | 25 | 1 | |
| Sean Lumpkin | DB | 6' | 206 | 25 | 1 | 6 |
| J.J. McCleskey | DB | 5'7" | 177 | 25 | 1 | |
| Anthony Newman | DB | 6' | 200 | 29 | | |
| Shane Pahukoa | DB | 6'2" | 202 | 24 | 2 | |
| Jimmy Spencer | DB | 5'9" | 180 | 26 | 4 | |
| Jim Everett | QB | 6'5" | 212 | 32 | | |
| Tommy Hodson | QB | 6'3" | 195 | 28 | | |
| Doug Nussmeier | QB | 6'3" | 211 | 24 | | |
| Mario Bates | HB | 6'1" | 217 | 22 | | 42 |
| Derek Brown | HB | 5'9" | 205 | 24 | | 12 |
| Lorenzo Neal | FB | 5'10" | 240 | 24 | | 6 |
| Derrick Ned | FB | 6'1" | 230 | 26 | | |
| Ray Zellars | FB | 5'11" | 233 | 22 | | 12 |
| Lee DeRamus | WR | 6' | 191 | 23 | | |
| Quinn Early | WR | 6' | 190 | 30 | | 48 |
| Michael Haynes | WR | 6' | 184 | 29 | | 24 |
| Steve Rhem | WR | 6'2" | 212 | 23 | | |
| Torrance Small | WR | 6'3" | 201 | 24 | | 36 |
| Kirk Botkin | TE | 6'3" | 245 | 24 | | |
| Irv Smith | TE | 6'3" | 246 | 23 | | 20 |
| Wesley Walls | TE | 6'5" | 250 | 29 | | 26 |
| Doug Brien (from SF) | K | 6' | 180 | 24 | | 92 |
| Chip Lohmiller | K | 6'3" | 215 | 29 | | 35 |
| Klaus Wilmsmeyer | K | 6'1" | 210 | 27 | | |

Timm Rosenbach — Back Injury

## SAN FRANCISCO 49ERS

### RUSHING

| Last Name | No. | Yds | Avg | TD |
|---|---|---|---|---|
| Loville | 218 | 723 | 3.3 | 10 |
| Young | 50 | 250 | 5.0 | 3 |
| Floyd | 64 | 237 | 3.7 | 2 |
| Ervins | 23 | 88 | 3.8 | 0 |
| Walker | 14 | 44 | 3.1 | 1 |
| Rice | 5 | 36 | 7.2 | 1 |
| Willis | 12 | 35 | 2.9 | 0 |
| Grbac | 20 | 33 | 1.7 | 2 |
| Carter | 7 | 22 | 3.1 | 0 |
| Lynn | 2 | 11 | 5.5 | 0 |

### RECEIVING

| Last Name | No. | Yds | Avg | TD |
|---|---|---|---|---|
| Rice | 122 | 1848 | 15.1 | 15 |
| Loville | 87 | 662 | 7.6 | 3 |
| Jones | 60 | 595 | 9.9 | 3 |
| Floyd | 47 | 348 | 7.4 | 1 |
| Stokes | 38 | 517 | 13.6 | 4 |
| Taylor | 29 | 387 | 13.3 | 2 |
| Popson | 16 | 128 | 8.0 | 0 |
| Walker | 11 | 78 | 7.1 | 0 |
| Singleton | 8 | 108 | 13.5 | 1 |
| Thomas | 6 | 73 | 12.2 | 0 |
| Willis | 3 | 8 | 2.7 | 0 |
| Ervins | 2 | 21 | 10.5 | 0 |
| Carter | 2 | 4 | 2.0 | 0 |
| Carolan | 1 | 3 | 3.0 | 0 |
| Dalman | 1 | -1 | -1.0 | 0 |

### PUNT RETURNS

| Last Name | No. | Yds | Avg | TD |
|---|---|---|---|---|
| Carter | 30 | 309 | 10.3 | 1 |
| Taylor | 11 | 56 | 5.1 | 0 |
| Singleton | 5 | 27 | 5.4 | 0 |
| Thomas | 1 | 25 | 25.0 | 0 |
| Hanks | 1 | 0 | 0.0 | 0 |

### KICKOFF RETURNS

| Last Name | No. | Yds | Avg | TD |
|---|---|---|---|---|
| Carter | 56 | 1227 | 21.9 | 0 |
| Willis | 17 | 427 | 25.1 | 0 |
| Ervins | 5 | 32 | 6.4 | 0 |
| Warren | 4 | 67 | 16.8 | 0 |
| Dalman | 3 | 29 | 9.7 | 0 |
| Thomas | 3 | 49 | 16.3 | 0 |
| Caldwell | 2 | 40 | 20.0 | 0 |
| Walker | 1 | 17 | 17.0 | 0 |

### PASSING — PUNTING — KICKING — Statistics

| PASSING | Att | Cmp | % | Yds | Yd/Att | TD | Int— | % | RK |
|---|---|---|---|---|---|---|---|---|---|
| Young | 447 | 299 | 66.9 | 3200 | 7.16 | 20 | 11— | 2.5 | |
| Grbac | 183 | 127 | 69.4 | 1469 | 8.03 | 8 | 5— | 2.7 | |
| Conklin | 12 | 4 | 33.3 | 48 | 4.00 | 0 | 0— | 0.0 | |
| Rice | 1 | 1 | 100.0 | 41 | 41.00 | 1 | 0— | 0.0 | |
| Taylor | 1 | 1 | 100.0 | 21 | 21.00 | 0 | 0— | 0.0 | |

| PUNTING | No. | Avg. |
|---|---|---|
| Thompson | 57 | 40.6 |

| KICKING | XP | ATT | % | FG | ATT | % |
|---|---|---|---|---|---|---|
| Wilkins | 27 | 29 | 93 | 12 | 13 | 92 |
| Zendejas | 5 | 6 | 83 | 3 | 6 | 50 |

**2 POINT XP**
Loville (1)
Rice (1)

## ATLANTA FALCONS

### RUSHING

| Last Name | No. | Yds | Avg | TD |
|---|---|---|---|---|
| Heyward | 236 | 1083 | 4.6 | 6 |
| Anderson | 39 | 161 | 4.1 | 1 |
| Metcalf | 28 | 133 | 4.8 | 1 |
| J. George | 27 | 17 | 0.6 | 0 |
| Emanuel | 1 | 0 | 0.0 | 0 |
| Stryzinski | 1 | 0 | 0.0 | 0 |
| Hebert | 5 | -1 | -0.2 | 0 |

### RECEIVING

| Last Name | No. | Yds | Avg | TD |
|---|---|---|---|---|
| Metcalf | 104 | 1189 | 11.4 | 8 |
| Mathis | 78 | 1039 | 13.3 | 9 |
| Emanuel | 74 | 1039 | 14.0 | 5 |
| Heyward | 37 | 350 | 9.5 | 2 |
| Birden | 31 | 303 | 9.8 | 1 |
| Brown | 17 | 198 | 11.6 | 0 |
| Preston | 7 | 129 | 18.4 | 1 |
| Lyons | 5 | 83 | 16.6 | 0 |
| Spencer | 5 | 60 | 12.0 | 0 |
| Anderson | 4 | 42 | 10.5 | 0 |
| Sanders | 2 | 24 | 12.0 | 0 |

### PUNT RETURNS

| Last Name | No. | Yds | Avg | TD |
|---|---|---|---|---|
| Metcalf | 39 | 383 | 9.8 | 1 |

### KICKOFF RETURNS

| Last Name | No. | Yds | Avg | TD |
|---|---|---|---|---|
| Preston | 30 | 627 | 20.9 | 0 |
| Anderson | 24 | 541 | 22.5 | 0 |
| Metcalf | 12 | 278 | 23.2 | 0 |
| R. George | 3 | 45 | 15.0 | 0 |
| Tippins | 1 | 15 | 15.0 | 0 |

### PASSING — PUNTING — KICKING

| PASSING | Att | Cmp | % | Yds | Yd/Att | TD | Int— | % | RK |
|---|---|---|---|---|---|---|---|---|---|
| George | 557 | 336 | 60.3 | 4143 | 7.44 | 24 | 11— | 2.0 | |
| Hebert | 45 | 28 | 62.2 | 313 | 6.96 | 2 | 1— | 2.2 | |
| Metcalf | 1 | 0 | 0.0 | 0 | 0.00 | 0 | 0— | 0.0 | |

| PUNTING | No. | Avg. |
|---|---|---|
| Stryzinski | 67 | 41.2 |

| KICKING | XP | ATT | % | FG | ATT | % |
|---|---|---|---|---|---|---|
| Andersen | 29 | 30 | 97 | 31 | 37 | 84 |

**2 POINT XP**
Mathis (3)

## ST. LOUIS RAMS

### RUSHING

| Last Name | No. | Yds | Avg | TD |
|---|---|---|---|---|
| Bettis | 183 | 637 | 3.5 | 3 |
| Russell | 66 | 203 | 3.1 | 0 |
| Bailey | 36 | 182 | 5.1 | 2 |
| Robinson | 40 | 165 | 4.1 | 0 |
| Moss | 22 | 90 | 4.1 | 0 |
| Miller | 23 | 67 | 3.0 | 0 |
| Bruce | 3 | 17 | 5.7 | 0 |
| Wright | 1 | 17 | 17.0 | 0 |
| Kinchen | 4 | 16 | 4.0 | 0 |
| Rypien | 9 | 10 | 1.1 | 0 |
| Wolfley | 3 | 9 | 3.0 | 0 |
| T. Wright | 1 | 9 | 9.0 | 0 |
| Barr | 1 | 5 | 5.0 | 0 |
| Lyle | 1 | 4 | 4.0 | 0 |

### RECEIVING

| Last Name | No. | Yds | Avg | TD |
|---|---|---|---|---|
| Bruce | 119 | 1781 | 15.0 | 13 |
| Drayton | 47 | 458 | 9.7 | 4 |
| Bailey | 38 | 265 | 7.0 | 0 |
| Kinchen | 36 | 419 | 11.6 | 4 |
| Hester | 30 | 399 | 13.3 | 3 |
| Cook | 26 | 135 | 5.2 | 1 |
| Wright | 23 | 368 | 16.0 | 2 |
| Bettis | 18 | 106 | 5.9 | 0 |
| Russell | 16 | 89 | 5.6 | 0 |
| Thomas | 5 | 42 | 8.4 | 0 |
| Price | 4 | 29 | 7.3 | 0 |
| Robinson | 2 | 12 | 6.0 | 0 |
| Pinkney | 1 | 13 | 13.0 | 0 |
| Moss | 1 | -3 | -3.0 | 0 |

### PUNT RETURNS

| Last Name | No. | Yds | Avg | TD |
|---|---|---|---|---|
| Kinchen | 53 | 416 | 7.8 | 0 |
| Bailey | 2 | 42 | 21.0 | 0 |
| Thomas | 0 | 61 | — | 0 |
| Bruce | 0 | 52 | — | 0 |
| Lyght | 0 | 16 | — | 0 |

### KICKOFF RETURNS

| Last Name | No. | Yds | Avg | TD |
|---|---|---|---|---|
| Kinchen | 35 | 743 | 21.2 | 0 |
| Thomas | 32 | 752 | 23.5 | 0 |
| Bailey | 5 | 97 | 19.4 | 0 |
| Pinkney | 1 | 26 | 26.0 | 0 |

### PASSING — PUNTING — KICKING

| PASSING | Att | Cmp | % | Yds | Yd/Att | TD | Int— | % | RK |
|---|---|---|---|---|---|---|---|---|---|
| Miller | 405 | 232 | 57.3 | 2623 | 6.48 | 18 | 15— | 3.7 | |
| Rypien | 217 | 129 | 59.4 | 1448 | 6.67 | 9 | 8— | 3.7 | |
| Barr | 9 | 5 | 55.6 | 42 | 4.67 | 0 | 0— | 0.0 | |
| Kinchen | 1 | 0 | 0.0 | 0 | 0.00 | 0 | 0— | 0.0 | |

| PUNTING | No. | Avg. |
|---|---|---|
| Landeta | 83 | 44.3 |

| KICKING | XP | ATT | % | FG | ATT | % |
|---|---|---|---|---|---|---|
| McLaughlin | 17 | 17 | 100 | 8 | 16 | 50 |
| Biasucci | 13 | 14 | 93 | 9 | 12 | 75 |

**2 POINT XP**
Bailey (1)
Bruce (1)

## CAROLINA PANTHERS

### RUSHING

| Last Name | No. | Yds | Avg | TD |
|---|---|---|---|---|
| Moore | 195 | 740 | 3.8 | 4 |
| Griffith | 65 | 197 | 3.0 | 1 |
| Christian | 41 | 158 | 3.9 | 0 |
| Johnson | 30 | 140 | 4.7 | 1 |
| Workman | 35 | 139 | 4.0 | 1 |
| B. Thomas | 22 | 90 | 4.1 | 0 |
| Collins | 42 | 74 | 1.8 | 3 |
| Baldwin | 23 | 61 | 2.7 | 0 |
| Reich | 1 | 3 | 3.0 | |
| OStone | 1 | 3 | 3.0 | 0 |
| Guliford | 2 | 2 | 1.0 | 0 |
| Carrier | 3 | -4 | -1.3 | 0 |

### RECEIVING

| Last Name | No. | Yds | Avg | TD |
|---|---|---|---|---|
| Carrier | 66 | 1002 | 15.2 | 3 |
| Green | 47 | 882 | 18.8 | 6 |
| Guliford | 29 | 444 | 15.3 | 1 |
| Christian | 29 | 255 | 8.8 | 1 |
| Johnson | 29 | 207 | 7.1 | 0 |
| Metzelaars | 20 | 171 | 8.6 | 3 |
| Beebe | 14 | 152 | 10.9 | 1 |
| Workman | 13 | 74 | 5.7 | 0 |
| Griffith | 11 | 63 | 5.7 | 1 |
| Rasby | 5 | 47 | 9.4 | 0 |
| Moore | 4 | 12 | 3.0 | 0 |
| Campbell | 3 | 32 | 10.7 | 0 |
| B. Thomas | 3 | 24 | 8.0 | 0 |
| Tillman | 2 | 22 | 11.0 | 0 |
| Dennis | 1 | 3 | 3.0 | 0 |

### PUNT RETURNS

| Last Name | No. | Yds | Avg | TD |
|---|---|---|---|---|
| Guliford | 43 | 475 | 11.0 | 1 |
| Carrier | 6 | 25 | 4.2 | 0 |

### KICKOFF RETURNS

| Last Name | No. | Yds | Avg | TD |
|---|---|---|---|---|
| By'not'e | 18 | 335 | 18.6 | 0 |
| Baldwin | 14 | 316 | 22.6 | 0 |
| Stone | 12 | 269 | 22.4 | 0 |
| Beebe | 9 | 215 | 23.9 | 0 |
| Philyaw | 1 | 23 | 23.0 | 0 |
| Butcher | 1 | 5 | 5.0 | 0 |

### PASSING — PUNTING — KICKING

| PASSING | Att | Cmp | % | Yds | Yd/Att | TD | Int— | % | RK |
|---|---|---|---|---|---|---|---|---|---|
| Collins | 433 | 214 | 49.4 | 2717 | 6.27 | 14 | 19— | 4.4 | |
| Reich | 84 | 37 | 44.0 | 441 | 5.25 | 2 | 2— | 2.4 | |
| Trudeau | 17 | 11 | 64.7 | 100 | 5.88 | 0 | 3— | 17.6 | |
| Guliford | 2 | 1 | 50.0 | 23 | 23.00 | 0 | 1— | 50.0 | |
| Workman | 1 | 0 | 0.0 | 0 | 0.00 | 0 | 0— | 0.0 | |

| PUNTING | No. | Avg. |
|---|---|---|
| Barnhardt | 95 | 41.1 |

| KICKING | XP | ATT | % | FG | ATT | % |
|---|---|---|---|---|---|---|
| Kasay | 27 | 28 | 96 | 26 | 33 | 79 |

**2 POINT XP**
Christian (1)
Rasby (1)

## NEW ORLEANS SAINTS

### RUSHING

| Last Name | No. | Yds | Avg | TD |
|---|---|---|---|---|
| Bates | 244 | 951 | 3.9 | 7 |
| Zellars | 50 | 162 | 3.2 | 2 |
| Brown | 49 | 159 | 3.2 | 1 |
| Small | 6 | 75 | 12.5 | 1 |
| Everett | 24 | 42 | 1.8 | 0 |
| Neal | 5 | 3 | 0.6 | 0 |
| Ned | 3 | 1 | 0.3 | 0 |
| Early | 2 | -3 | -1.5 | 0 |

### RECEIVING

| Last Name | No. | Yds | Avg | TD |
|---|---|---|---|---|
| Early | 81 | 1087 | 13.4 | 8 |
| Walls | 57 | 694 | 12.2 | 4 |
| Smith | 45 | 466 | 10.4 | 3 |
| Haynes | 41 | 597 | 14.6 | 4 |
| Small | 38 | 461 | 12.1 | 5 |
| Brown | 35 | 266 | 7.6 | 1 |
| Bates | 18 | 114 | 6.3 | 0 |
| Neal | 12 | 123 | 10.3 | 1 |
| Zellars | 7 | 33 | 4.7 | 0 |
| DeRamus | 6 | 76 | 12.7 | 0 |
| Rhem | 4 | 50 | 12.5 | 0 |
| Ned | 3 | 9 | 3.0 | 0 |
| Newman | 1 | 18 | 18.0 | 0 |
| Botkin | 1 | 8 | 8.0 | 0 |

### PUNT RETURNS

| Last Name | No. | Yds | Avg | TD |
|---|---|---|---|---|
| Hughes | 28 | 262 | 9.4 | 0 |
| Legette | 1 | 6 | 6.0 | 0 |

### KICKOFF RETURNS

| Last Name | No. | Yds | Avg | TD |
|---|---|---|---|---|
| Hughes | 66 | 1617 | 24.5 | 0 |
| Ned | 2 | 33 | 16.5 | 0 |
| Neal | 2 | 28 | 14.0 | 0 |
| Smith | 1 | 6 | 6.0 | 0 |
| Walls | 1 | 6 | 6.0 | 0 |
| McClesky | 1 | 0 | 0.0 | 0 |

### PASSING — PUNTING — KICKING

| PASSING | Att | Cmp | % | Yds | Yd/Att | TD | Int— | % | RK |
|---|---|---|---|---|---|---|---|---|---|
| Everett | 567 | 345 | 60.8 | 3970 | 7.00 | 26 | 14— | 2.5 | |
| Hodson | 5 | 3 | 60.0 | 14 | 2.80 | 0 | 0— | 0.0 | |
| Wilmsmeyer | 1 | 1 | 100.0 | 18 | 18.00 | 0 | 0— | 0.0 | |

| PUNTING | No. | Avg. |
|---|---|---|
| Wilmsmeyer | 74 | 40.1 |

| KICKING | XP | ATT | % | FG | ATT | % |
|---|---|---|---|---|---|---|
| Brien | 35 | 35 | 100 | 19 | 29 | 66 |
| Lohmiller | 11 | 13 | 85 | 8 | 14 | 57 |

**2 POINT XP**
Smith (1)
Walls (1)

# 1995 A.F.C. Who's Coming and Who's Going?

Franchise free agency was the big story in the NFL in 1995. On November 6, the Browns — after 50 years in Cleveland where they had a fanatical following — announced that they would move to Baltimore at the end of the season. A looming court battle and intervention by the league office paved the way for a move that mean the Cleveland franchise would move to Baltimore and become the Ravens, and the NFL promised an NFL franchise for Cleveland in 1999 that would be named the Browns.

The Houston Oilers were talking move themselves, this time to Nashville, Tenn. However, with plans for a new stadium in Nashville moving slowly, the team announced first it would play in Memphis for 1996 and '97, and then that it would remain in Houston until 1998.

And, at season's end, the Seattle Seahawks announced a move to Los Angeles, a city without a market because, in 1995, the Rams moved to St. Louis and the Raiders went back to Oakland. The NFL stepped in this time and promised a protracted court fight with the Seahawks.

In Tampa, the Buccaneers were threatening to move somewhere, and the Bengals were claiming they might, too, if the voters of Cincinnati didn't pass a referendum for a new stadium (they did in March 1996).

Owners almost universally cited financial difficulties for their teams, clamoring for skyboxes, club seats and better stadium leases.

On another legal front, Cowboys owner Jerry Jones violated the NFL's marketing agreement by signing exclusive marketing deals with Nike, Pepsi and American Express.

## EASTERN DIVISION

**Buffalo Bills** — After being dismissed by most experts after their stumble to 7-9 in 1994, the Bills won another division title. QB Jim Kelly got a lot out of an attack short on wide receivers, but he still passed for 3,130 yards and 22 touchdowns, and RB Thurman Thomas rushed for 1,005 yards. On defense, free-agent acquisition Bryce Paup led the NFL with 17.5 sacks and was second on the team in tackles and interceptions. He was named the NFL Defensive Player of the Year. Bruce Smith (10.5 sacks) and Phil Hansen (10 sacks) helped Buffalo lead the league in QB sacks. With top WR Andre Reed injured much of the season, Bill Brooks picked up the slack and set a club record for receiving TD's (11).

**Indianapolis Colts** — The Colts were one of the surprise teams of the NFL, advancing to the AFC championship game and coming within a dropped "Hail Mary" pass in the end zone on the last play of the game of going to the Super Bowl. During the regular season, they finished 9-7. QB Jim Harbaugh had the best season of his career, as he led the NFL in passing. Harbaugh, who had lost his starting job to Craig Erickson at the start of the season, guided the team to three fourth-quarter come-backs. Marshall Faulk had his second straight 1,000-yard rushing season, and he also paced the club with 56 receptions. However, stellar season or not, shortly after it ended, head coach Ted Marchibroda was let go and replaced by offensive coordinator Lindy Infante.

**Miami Dolphins** — Don Shula's last season as the Dolphins' head coach was one of failure. Picked by most observers to win the AFC, Shula's Dolphins started off the season with four victories, but then they blew a 21-point lead and lost to the Colts in overtime on October 8. After that, they never were the same, finishing 9-7 and out of the playoffs. Dan Marino, however, became the most prolific passer in NFL history, as he set all-time records for attempts, completions, yards and touchdowns during the course of the season. Ironically, the Dolphins lost three of the games in which he set those marks. On defense, LB Bryan Cox continued to demonstrate immaturity off the field, but he dominated on it, leading the team in tackles and sacks.

**New England Patriots** — Bill Parcells could not manage to take the Patriots to the next level, as they slipped to a 6-10 mark. In fact, after five games, the Patriots had scored only 43 points, managing only a field goal in three outings. Parcells admitted that he erred by going with an inexperienced receiving corps and a defensive line of backup quality. The subpar wideouts and a shoulder injury were the main reasons QB Drew Bledsoe dropped to second-to-last in the conference in passing,

throwing only 13 TD passes. The Patriots did find a star in running back Curtis Martin, a third-round draft pick who broke Jim Nance's team rushing record with an AFC-leading 1,487 yards. He also scored 15 touchdowns and was named Rookie of the Year.

**New York Jets** — The Jets were the NFL's worst team in 1995, finishing 3-13 and defeating only expansion Jacksonville, downtrodden Miami and Seattle. The offense scored a league-worst 14.6 points per game. Third-year RB Adrian Murrell came into his own, leading the club in rushing (795 yards) and receiving (71 catches for 465 yards), but the receivers were weak (free-agent rookie Wayne Crebet had 66 receptions) and Boomer Esiason's quarterbacking was subpar. The Jets did have a decent defense that ranked respectable in yards allowed, but that was mainly because opponents took early leads and let the clock run out. Rookie DE Hugh Douglas did manage 10 sacks.

## CENTRAL DIVISION

**Pittsburgh Steelers** — After starting out 4-4, the Steelers won seven straight games to go 11-5, and they defeated Buffalo and Indianapolis in the playoffs before falling to Dallas in Super Bowl XXX. QB Neil O'Donnell turned the Steelers into a passing team, as he threw for 2,970 yards and 17 touchdowns. Yancey Thigpen set club records with 85 receptions and 1,307 yards. RB's Erric Pegram (813 yards) and Bam Morris (559 yards, nine TD's) paced the ground attack. The Steelers were without star CB Rod Woodson, who was injured in the opener, but LB Greg Lloyd and CB Willie Williams (AFC-leading seven interceptions) led the defense. Kordell Stewart was the big story, as the rookie quarterback also played wide receiver and running back.

**Cincinnati Bengals** — The Bengals climbed to second place behind a 7-9 record that included five losses by three points. Ki-Jana Carter, the rookie running back who was the first overall pick in the draft, was injured in training camp and missed the entire season, so QB Jeff Blake (3,822 yards, 28 TD's) and WR Carl Pickens (99 receptions, 1,234 yards, league-leading 17 TD's) starred on an explosive offense. Both players went to the Pro Bowl. However, the defense was the NFL's lowest-ranked unit, unable to rush passers and cover receivers and allowing 374 points. Third-year DE John Copeland did have a break-through season with nine sacks.

**Houston Oilers** — Jeff Fisher solidified himself as the Oilers' head coach by leading the team back to a 7-9 record after its miserable 1994 campaign. The Oilers, however, did it with mirrors, because the offense had little excitement. There was, however, lots of promise. QB Chris Chandler had the best season of his career, but he was replaced in December by No. 1 draft pick Steve McNair. Another rookie, RB Rodney Thomas, ran for 947 yards but had trouble holding on to the ball. And third-round WR Frank Sanders led the NFL with a 23.5-yard average and made the All-Rookie team. Rookie DL's Anthony Cook and Gary Walker also played well. Mostly, though, the team was distracted by news of a possible move to Nashville, Tenn.

**Cleveland Browns** — The Browns were struggling along with a 4-5 record when owner Art Modell announced they would move to Baltimore. Six losses followed in the final seven games, as fans stayed away from Cleveland Stadium by the thousands. QB Vinny Testaverde had a fine year, finishing as the third-rated AFC passer, with 17 TD's and 2,893 yards and only 10 interceptions. Veteran RB Earnest Byner led the team with 61 catches, as heralded free-agent signee Andre Rison was disappointing (47 receptions, three TD's). RB Lorenzo White was another free-agent bust. The aging defense, which allowed 204 points a year earlier, was not the same, letting up 356.

**Jacksonville Jaguars** — The Jaguars broke the previous record for victories for an expansion team, going 4-12 despite seven consecutive losses in the second half of the season when the defense fell apart. Coach Tom Coughlin, going mostly with young players, gained his first victory in the fifth week at Houston, and then the Jaguars upset Pittsburgh a week

**OFFENSE**

| | BUFF | CIN | CLEV | DEN | HOU | IND | JAX | K.C. | MIA | N.E. | NYJ | OAK | PITT | S.D. | SEA |
|---|---|---|---|---|---|---|---|---|---|---|---|---|---|---|---|
| FIRST DOWNS: | | | | | | | | | | | | | | | |
| Total | 300 | 288 | 293 | 344 | 295 | 281 | 283 | 295 | 345 | 335 | 254 | 317 | 344 | 314 | 311 |
| by Rushing | 130 | 76 | 83 | 114 | 109 | 110 | 100 | 113 | 98 | 106 | 78 | 104 | 117 | 108 | 121 |
| by Passing | 142 | 184 | 189 | 205 | 157 | 147 | 154 | 164 | 225 | 207 | 159 | 189 | 193 | 185 | 171 |
| by Penalty | 28 | 28 | 21 | 25 | 29 | 24 | 29 | 18 | 22 | 22 | 17 | 24 | 34 | 21 | 19 |
| RUSHING: | | | | | | | | | | | | | | | |
| Number | 521 | 364 | 398 | 440 | 478 | 478 | 410 | 507 | 413 | 474 | 365 | 463 | 494 | 479 | 477 |
| Yards | 1993 | 1439 | 1482 | 1995 | 1664 | 1855 | 1705 | 2222 | 1506 | 1866 | 1279 | 1932 | 1852 | 1747 | 2178 |
| Average Yards | 3.8 | 4.0 | 3.7 | 4.5 | 3.5 | 3.9 | 4.2 | 4.4 | 3.6 | 3.9 | 3.5 | 4.2 | 3.7 | 3.6 | 4.6 |
| Touchdowns | 10 | 7 | 5 | 14 | 12 | 14 | 9 | 14 | 16 | 16 | 2 | 10 | 17 | 14 | 20 |
| PASSING: | | | | | | | | | | | | | | | |
| Attempts | 506 | 586 | 555 | 594 | 536 | 434 | 495 | 531 | 592 | 686 | 589 | 543 | 592 | 540 | 511 |
| Completions | 279 | 334 | 324 | 350 | 314 | 270 | 275 | 300 | 384 | 351 | 330 | 317 | 348 | 318 | 273 |
| Completion Pct. | 55.1 | 57.0 | 58.4 | 58.9 | 58.6 | 62.2 | 55.6 | 56.5 | 64.9 | 51.2 | 56.0 | 58.4 | 58.8 | 58.9 | 53.4 |
| Passing Yards | 3348 | 3915 | 3772 | 4260 | 3512 | 3373 | 3144 | 3178 | 4398 | 3789 | 3129 | 3787 | 4093 | 3706 | 3359 |
| Avg. Yds per Att. | 5.81 | 6.14 | 6.12 | 6.52 | 5.71 | 6.34 | 5.05 | 5.47 | 6.78 | 5.04 | 4.38 | 6.17 | 6.36 | 6.06 | 5.56 |
| Avg. Yds per Comp. | 12.00 | 11.72 | 11.64 | 12.17 | 11.18 | 12.49 | 11.43 | 10.59 | 11.45 | 10.79 | 9.48 | 11.95 | 11.76 | 11.65 | 12.30 |
| Times Tackled | 32 | 25 | 32 | 26 | 32 | 49 | 57 | 21 | 29 | 27 | 47 | 36 | 24 | 32 | 45 |
| Yds Lost Tackled | 224 | 162 | 178 | 215 | 271 | 309 | 354 | 158 | 188 | 198 | 341 | 214 | 176 | 240 | 267 |
| Net Yards | 3124 | 3753 | 3594 | 4045 | 3241 | 3064 | 2790 | 3020 | 4210 | 3591 | 2788 | 3573 | 3917 | 3466 | 3092 |
| Touchdowns | 24 | 29 | 21 | 27 | 22 | 20 | 19 | 21 | 28 | 14 | 20 | 25 | 21 | 17 | 19 |
| Interceptions | 14 | 18 | 20 | 14 | 18 | 11 | 15 | 10 | 20 | 16 | 24 | 21 | 21 | 18 | 23 |
| Pct. Intercepted | 2.8 | 3.1 | 3.6 | 2.4 | 3.4 | 2.5 | 3.0 | 1.9 | 3.4 | 2.3 | 4.1 | 3.9 | 3.5 | 3.3 | 4.5 |
| PUNTS: | | | | | | | | | | | | | | | |
| Number | 88 | 70 | 65 | 54 | 79 | 63 | 82 | 91 | 57 | 79 | 105 | 76 | 59 | 72 | 83 |
| Average | 40.4 | 41.6 | 43.6 | 40.9 | 40.3 | 42.6 | 43.8 | 43.8 | 42.7 | 39.2 | 41.2 | 40.6 | 40.1 | 44.7 | 45.0 |
| PUNT RETURNS | | | | | | | | | | | | | | | |
| Number | 47 | 21 | 25 | 31 | 35 | 29 | 29 | 58 | 24 | 45 | 38 | 37 | 48 | 31 | 40 |
| Yards | 476 | 103 | 255 | 358 | 339 | 192 | 243 | 561 | 163 | 383 | 323 | 374 | 474 | 338 | 384 |
| Average Yards | 10.1 | 4.9 | 10.2 | 11.5 | 9.7 | 6.6 | 8.4 | 9.7 | 6.8 | 8.5 | 8.5 | 10.1 | 9.9 | 10.9 | 9.6 |
| Touchdowns | 0 | 0 | 1 | 0 | 0 | 0 | 0 | 1 | 0 | 0 | 0 | 0 | 1 | 1 | 1 |
| KICKOFF RET.: | | | | | | | | | | | | | | | |
| Number | 70 | 80 | 74 | 60 | 64 | 63 | 74 | 55 | 59 | 75 | 77 | 64 | 69 | 70 | 72 |
| Yards | 1302 | 1788 | 1455 | 1392 | 1277 | 1332 | 1532 | 1306 | 1338 | 1691 | 1613 | 1390 | 1530 | 1502 | 1620 |
| Average Yards | 18.6 | 22.4 | 19.7 | 23.2 | 20.0 | 21.1 | 20.7 | 23.7 | 22.7 | 22.5 | 20.9 | 21.7 | 22.2 | 21.5 | 22.5 |
| Touchdowns | 0 | 0 | 0 | 0 | 0 | 1 | 1 | 2 | 0 | 0 | 0 | 1 | 0 | 2 | 0 |
| INTERCEPT RET.: | | | | | | | | | | | | | | | |
| Number | 17 | 12 | 17 | 8 | 21 | 13 | 13 | 16 | 14 | 15 | 17 | 11 | 22 | 17 | 16 |
| Yards | 233 | 175 | 230 | 114 | 317 | 248 | 155 | 303 | 161 | 143 | 261 | 110 | 361 | 220 | 127 |
| Average Yards | 13.7 | 14.6 | 13.5 | 14.3 | 15.1 | 12.5 | 11.9 | 18.9 | 11.5 | 9.5 | 15.4 | 10.0 | 16.4 | 12.9 | 12.3 |
| Touchdowns | 2 | 1 | 2 | 0 | 4 | 1 | 1 | 2 | 1 | 0 | 3 | 2 | 3 | 1 | 0 |
| PENALTIES: | | | | | | | | | | | | | | | |
| Number | 89 | 103 | 107 | 109 | 98 | 97 | 121 | 116 | 110 | 84 | 121 | 134 | 109 | 107 | 100 |
| Yards | 672 | 835 | 966 | 851 | 791 | 943 | 970 | 851 | 907 | 676 | 1078 | 1059 | 839 | 953 | 852 |
| FUMBLES: | | | | | | | | | | | | | | | |
| Number | 25 | 23 | 25 | 25 | 36 | 21 | 23 | 17 | 24 | 32 | 38 | 25 | 24 | 30 | 24 |
| Number Lost | 12 | 14 | 11 | 16 | 20 | 11 | 13 | 11 | 12 | 20 | 18 | 13 | 13 | 12 | 9 |
| POINTS: | | | | | | | | | | | | | | | |
| Total | 350 | 349 | 289 | 388 | 348 | 331 | 275 | 358 | 398 | 294 | 233 | 348 | 407 | 321 | 363 |
| 1-PT PAT/ATT. | 33/35 | 34/34 | 26/26 | 39/39 | 33/33 | 34/34 | 27/28 | 34/37 | 37/37 | 27/27 | 24/24 | 39/40 | 39/39 | 32/33 | 40/40 |
| 2-PT PAT/Att. | 1/2 | 1/3 | 0/2 | 2/3 | 2/5 | 2/3 | 1/3 | 0/3 | 2/9 | 3/5 | 0/2 | 0/1 | 1/5 | 1/4 | 0/2 |
| FG Attempts | 40 | 36 | 33 | 38 | 31 | 33 | 27 | 30 | 34 | 33 | 21 | 27 | 41 | 26 | 28 |
| FG Made | 31 | 29 | 29 | 31 | 27 | 23 | 20 | 24 | 27 | 23 | 17 | 21 | 34 | 21 | 23 |
| Percent FG Made | 77.5 | 80.6 | 87.9 | 81.6 | 87.1 | 69.7 | 74.1 | 80.0 | 79.4 | 69.7 | 81.0 | 77.8 | 82.9 | 80.8 | 82.1 |
| Safeties | 0 | 2 | 0 | 0 | 1 | 1 | 0 | 0 | 0 | 0 | 1 | 0 | 0 | 1 | 1 |

**DEFENSE**

| | BUFF | CIN | CLEV | DEN | HOU | IND | JAX | K.C. | MIA | N.E. | NYJ | OAK | PITT | S.D. | SEA |
|---|---|---|---|---|---|---|---|---|---|---|---|---|---|---|---|
| FIRST DOWNS: | | | | | | | | | | | | | | | |
| Total | 287 | 354 | 342 | 322 | 267 | 304 | 320 | 289 | 309 | 308 | 301 | 293 | 272 | 313 | 321 |
| by Rushing | 93 | 117 | 112 | 114 | 85 | 92 | 121 | 83 | 93 | 106 | 123 | 90 | 67 | 112 | 116 |
| by Passing | 180 | 215 | 200 | 186 | 157 | 182 | 177 | 178 | 192 | 181 | 149 | 177 | 181 | 178 | 181 |
| by Penalty | 14 | 22 | 30 | 22 | 25 | 30 | 22 | 28 | 24 | 21 | 29 | 26 | 24 | 23 | 24 |
| RUSHING: | | | | | | | | | | | | | | | |
| Number | 453 | 483 | 480 | 451 | 400 | 418 | 504 | 404 | 415 | 448 | 526 | 446 | 370 | 441 | 496 |
| Yards | 1626 | 2104 | 1826 | 1895 | 1526 | 1457 | 2003 | 1327 | 1675 | 1878 | 2016 | 1794 | 1321 | 1691 | 2130 |
| Average Yards | 3.6 | 4.4 | 3.8 | 4.2 | 3.8 | 3.5 | 4.0 | 3.3 | 4.0 | 4.2 | 3.8 | 4.0 | 3.6 | 3.8 | 4.3 |
| Touchdowns | 16 | 10 | 15 | 19 | 11 | 8 | 17 | 7 | 7 | 12 | 15 | 15 | 9 | 15 | 11 |
| PASSING: | | | | | | | | | | | | | | | |
| Attempts | 582 | 602 | 573 | 529 | 553 | 569 | 509 | 596 | 556 | 549 | 497 | 527 | 531 | 543 | 554 |
| Completions | 310 | 364 | 360 | 297 | 289 | 336 | 304 | 329 | 327 | 342 | 263 | 301 | 314 | 321 | 310 |
| Completion Pct. | 53.3 | 60.5 | 62.8 | 56.1 | 52.3 | 59.1 | 59.7 | 55.2 | 58.8 | 62.3 | 52.9 | 57.1 | 59.1 | 59.1 | 56.0 |
| Passing Yards | 3864 | 4512 | 4013 | 3518 | 3325 | 3739 | 3584 | 3569 | 3756 | 4107 | 3055 | 3642 | 3512 | 3605 | 3706 |
| Avg. Yds per Att. | 5.55 | 65.9 | 6.35 | 5.90 | 5.36 | 5.97 | 6.68 | 5.01 | 6.10 | 6.63 | 5.07 | 5.81 | 5.65 | 5.84 | 6.08 |
| Avg. Yds per Comp. | 12.46 | 12.40 | 11.15 | 11.85 | 11.51 | 11.13 | 11.79 | 10.85 | 11.49 | 12.01 | 11.62 | 12.10 | 11.18 | 11.23 | 11.95 |
| Times Tackled | 49 | 42 | 29 | 30 | 30 | 29 | 17 | 47 | 29 | 37 | 43 | 43 | 42 | 36 | 28 |
| Yds Lost Tackled | 362 | 267 | 191 | 220 | 200 | 169 | 72 | 347 | 187 | 221 | 315 | 332 | 272 | 222 | 167 |
| Net Yards | 3502 | 4245 | 3822 | 3298 | 3125 | 3570 | 3512 | 3222 | 3569 | 3886 | 2740 | 3310 | 3240 | 3383 | 3539 |
| Touchdowns | 14 | 25 | 23 | 20 | 24 | 23 | 28 | 16 | 30 | 29 | 21 | 14 | 24 | 16 | 26 |
| Interceptions | 17 | 12 | 17 | 8 | 21 | 13 | 13 | 16 | 14 | 15 | 17 | 11 | 22 | 17 | 16 |
| Pct. Intercepted | 2.9 | 2.0 | 3.0 | 1.5 | 3.8 | 2.3 | 2.6 | 2.7 | 2.5 | 2.7 | 3.4 | 2.1 | 4.1 | 3.1 | 2.9 |
| PUNTS: | | | | | | | | | | | | | | | |
| Number | 90 | 64 | 59 | 76 | 86 | 63 | 61 | 102 | 59 | 86 | 85 | 70 | 85 | 73 | 81 |
| Average | 42.8 | 38.4 | 41.7 | 42.8 | 42.4 | 41.0 | 42.0 | 41.8 | 41.0 | 38.8 | 41.1 | 43.5 | 43.3 | 43.4 | 42.6 |
| PUNT RETURNS | | | | | | | | | | | | | | | |
| Number | 23 | 27 | 34 | 25 | 35 | 37 | 45 | 42 | 35 | 40 | 62 | 38 | 22 | 35 | 48 |
| Yards | 224 | 154 | 296 | 137 | 288 | 436 | 323 | 433 | 265 | 342 | 753 | 294 | 186 | 429 | 549 |
| Average Yards | 9.7 | 5.7 | 8.7 | 5.5 | 8.2 | 11.8 | 7.2 | 10.3 | 7.6 | 8.6 | 12.1 | 7.7 | 8.5 | 12.3 | 11.4 |
| Touchdowns | 1 | 0 | 0 | 0 | 1 | 0 | 0 | 0 | 0 | 0 | 0 | 0 | 0 | 1 | 0 |
| KICKOFF RET.: | | | | | | | | | | | | | | | |
| Number | 73 | 65 | 63 | 77 | 78 | 68 | 54 | 71 | 85 | 67 | 42 | 68 | 88 | 63 | 70 |
| Yards | 1615 | 1475 | 1172 | 1671 | 1467 | 1546 | 1278 | 1448 | 1782 | 1405 | 987 | 1469 | 1544 | 1496 | 1669 |
| Average Yards | 22.1 | 22.7 | 18.6 | 21.7 | 18.8 | 22.7 | 23.7 | 20.4 | 21.0 | 21.0 | 23.5 | 21.6 | 17.5 | 23.7 | 23.8 |
| Touchdowns | 0 | 0 | 0 | 2 | 0 | 1 | 1 | 0 | 0 | 0 | 0 | 0 | 0 | 0 | 2 |
| INTERCEPT RET.: | | | | | | | | | | | | | | | |
| Number | 17 | 12 | 17 | 8 | 21 | 13 | 13 | 16 | 14 | 15 | 17 | 11 | 22 | 17 | 16 |
| Yards | 233 | 175 | 230 | 114 | 317 | 248 | 155 | 303 | 161 | 143 | 261 | 110 | 361 | 220 | 127 |
| Average Yards | 13.4 | 17.1 | 13.8 | 7.4 | 14.7 | 14.2 | 11.9 | 12.3 | 10.5 | 10.1 | 16.8 | 16.4 | 11.2 | 9.1 | 16.7 |
| Touchdowns | 2 | 1 | 2 | 0 | 4 | 1 | 1 | 2 | 1 | 0 | 3 | 2 | 3 | 1 | 0 |
| PENALTIES: | | | | | | | | | | | | | | | |
| Number | 115 | 116 | 108 | 103 | 118 | 111 | 102 | 108 | 82 | 104 | 97 | 94 | 101 | 117 | 114 |
| Yards | 890 | 1143 | 736 | 848 | 962 | 935 | 958 | 828 | 739 | 816 | 759 | 730 | 931 | 951 | 901 |
| FUMBLES: | | | | | | | | | | | | | | | |
| Number | 23 | 27 | 20 | 20 | 28 | 24 | 22 | 35 | 30 | 24 | 27 | 37 | 30 | 24 | 17 |
| Number Lost | 11 | 12 | 7 | 13 | 17 | 13 | 11 | 17 | 16 | 14 | 17 | 22 | 12 | 10 | 9 |
| POINTS: | | | | | | | | | | | | | | | |
| Total | 335 | 374 | 356 | 345 | 324 | 316 | 404 | 241 | 332 | 377 | 384 | 332 | 327 | 323 | 366 |
| 1-PT PAT/ATT. | 29/29 | 34/34 | 34/36 | 42/42 | 35/35 | 29/29 | 45/45 | 25/25 | 31/33 | 40/41 | 40/41 | 27/29 | 34/34 | 28/29 | 36/37 |
| 2-PT PAT/Att. | 2/4 | 2/3 | 2/4 | 0/2 | 0/2 | 3/5 | 0/1 | 0/3 | 1/5 | 2/3 | 0/1 | 3/3 | 1/3 | 2/5 | 0/5 |
| FG Attempts | 43 | 49 | 34 | 19 | 24 | 38 | 31 | 19 | 31 | 32 | 41 | 41 | 25 | 32 | 35 |
| FG Made | 34 | 38 | 26 | 13 | 19 | 25 | 27 | 16 | 23 | 23 | 30 | 33 | 23 | 27 | 24 |
| Percent FG Made | 79.1 | 77.6 | 76.5 | 68.4 | 79.2 | 65.8 | 87.1 | 84.2 | 74.2 | 71.9 | 73.2 | 80.5 | 92.0 | 84.4 | 68.6 |
| Safeties | 1 | 0 | 0 | 0 | 2 | 1 | 1 | 0 | 1 | 0 | 1 | 1 | 0 | 0 | 0 |

later. The Jaguars also beat Cleveland twice, the first expansion team to sweep an opponent since 1966, and they became the first expansion team to go .500 in its division in its inaugural year. Mark Brunell led Jacksonville to all four wins, and he became the highest-rated quarterback ever for an expansion team. Rookies OT Tony Boselli and MLB Bryan Schwartz were star performers.

## WESTERN DIVISION

**Kansas City Chiefs** — Kansas City had the best record in the NFL in 1995, finishing with a franchise-record 13 victories and losses only to Cleveland, Dallas and Miami. However, the season went down as a disappointment, as the Chiefs lost in their first playoff game, 10-7 to Indianapolis. QB Steve Bono threw three interceptions in that game after having had only 10 all season (Lin Elliott also missed three field goals in that game). Bono also passed for 3,121 yards and 21 touchdowns for the season. Marcus Allen was the most consistent offensive performer as the ageless wonder rushed for 890 yards and five touchdowns. Kansas City had the league's No. 1 scoring defense, No. 1 rushing offense and topped the league in turnover ratio.

**San Diego Chargers** — The defending AFC champions struggled out of the gate in '95, losing four of its first seven games. Only victories in their final five games put the Chargers back in the playoffs, but there a first-round loss to Indianapolis awaited. WR Tony Martin had a club-record 90 receptions, but the team went only as far as QB Stan Humphries could take them — and he threw four interceptions in the playoff loss. Natrone Means held out then, when he was leading the conference in rushing, pulled a groin and had only 730 yards, eventually being replaced by rookie Aaron Hayden. The Chargers' biggest problem all season was turnovers — 30, leading to 115 points by their opponents. On defense, All-Pro LB Junior Seau led the club with 129 tackles.

**Denver Broncos** — Mike Shanahan had the same problems previous Broncos coaches have had — no defense. The offense was stellar: John Elway set team records for most TD passes in a season, rookie RB Terrell Davis became the Broncos' first 1,000-yard rusher since 1991, WR Anthony Miller tied the franchise record for TD's in a season, the offensive line allowed the fewest number of sacks since 1982, more Broncos were selected to the Pro Bowl than any other AFC team and the team racked up a club-record 6,240 yards. But the run defense was among the league's worst, the pass rush was nil and few players made big plays.

**Seattle Seahawks** — The Seahawks struggled early in 1995, then finished strong, going 8-8, with six victories over the second half of the season under new head coach Dennis Erickson. It was Seattle's first non-losing season since 1990. The offense featured the league's third-best rushing attack, led by Chris Warren's 1,346 yards and 15 TD's. But QB Rick Mirer had a subpar third season, with an AFC-high 20 interceptions. He ranked last in passing. Rookie WR Joey Galloway provided big plays, becaming the 10th NFL rookie with a 1,000-yard receiving season (67 catches). He averaged 45 yards on his nine scores.

**Oakland Raiders** — Back in Oakland after 13 seasons in Los Angeles, the Raiders weren't the same old Raiders. The started out 8-2 but then collapsed, losing their final six games. In his first year as head coach, Mike White saw the Raiders finish out of the playoffs for the seventh time in 10 years. WR Tim Brown was the best player, with 89 receptions for 1,342 yards and 10 TD's — all career highs. RB Harvey Williams had an excellent season with 1,114 yards rushing and nine scores. But QB Jeff Hostetler was very inconsistent, passing for only 12 touchdowns.

## BUFFALO BILLS 10-6 Marv Levy

| Scores of Each Game | | |
|---|---|---|
| 7 | Denver | 22 |
| 31 | CAROLINA | 9 |
| 20 | INDIANAPOLIS | 14 |
| 22 | at Cleveland | 19 |
| 29 | NEW YORK JETS | 10 |
| 27 | SEATTLE | 21 |
| 14 | New England | 27 |
| 6 | Miami | 23 |
| 16 | Indianapolis | 10 |
| 23 | ATLANTA | 17 |
| 28 | New York Jets | 26 |
| 25 | NEW ENGLAND | 35 |
| 17 | San Francisco | 27 |
| 45 | St. Louis | 27 |
| 23 | MIAMI | 20 |
| 17 | HOUSTON | 28 |

| Use Name | Pos. | Hgt. | Wgt. | Age | Int | Pts |
|---|---|---|---|---|---|---|
| John Fina | OT | 6'4" | 285 | 26 | | |
| Corey Louchiey | OT | 6'7" | 305 | 23 | | |
| Glenn Parker | OT-OG | 6'5" | 305 | 29 | | |
| Ruben Brown | OG | 6'3" | 304 | 25 | | |
| Mike Devlin | OG-C | 6'1" | 305 | 25 | | |
| Corbin Lacina | OG | 6'4" | 297 | 24 | | |
| Jerry Ostroski | OG | 6'2" | 310 | 25 | | |
| Kent Hull | C | 6'4" | 284 | 34 | | |
| Adam Lingner | C | 6'4" | 268 | 34 | | |
| Tom Nutten | C | 6'4" | 295 | 24 | | |
| Phil Hansen | DE | 6'5" | 278 | 27 | | |
| Mark Pike | DE | 6'4" | 272 | 31 | | |
| Bruce Smith | DE | 6'4" | 273 | 32 | | |
| Karl Wilson | DE | 6'5" | 277 | 30 | | |
| Jim Jeffcoat | DT-DE | 6'5" | 280 | 34 | | |
| Ed Philion | NT | 6'2" | 277 | 25 | | |
| Ted Washington | NT | 6'4" | 325 | 27 | | |
| Cornelius Bennett | LB | 6'2" | 238 | 30 | 1 | 6 |
| Monty Brown | LB | 6' | 235 | 25 | | |
| Damien Covington | LB | 5'11" | 236 | 22 | | |
| John Holecek | LB | 6'2" | 238 | 23 | | |
| Mark Maddox | LB | 6'1" | 233 | 27 | | |
| Bryce Paup | LB | 6'5" | 247 | 27 | 2 | |
| Mario Perry | LB | 6'4" | 250 | 23 | | |
| Sam Rogers | LB | 6'3" | 245 | 25 | | |
| David White | LB | 6'2" | 235 | 25 | 1 | |
| Jeff Burris | DB | 6' | 204 | 23 | 1 | |
| Matt Darby | DB | 6'1" | 200 | 26 | 2 | |
| Greg Evans | DB | 6'1" | 208 | 24 | | |
| Chris Green | DB | 5'11" | 198 | 27 | | |
| Ken Irvin | DB | 5'10" | 182 | 23 | | |
| Filmel Johnson | DB | 5'10" | 187 | 24 | | |
| Henry Jones | DB | 5'11" | 197 | 27 | 1 | |
| Marlon Kerner | DB | 5'10" | 187 | 22 | | |
| Kurt Schulz | DB | 6'1" | 208 | 26 | 6 | 6 |
| Thomas Smith | DB | 5'11" | 188 | 24 | 2 | |
| Todd Collins | QB | 6'4" | 224 | 23 | | |
| Jim Kelly | QB | 6'3" | 226 | 35 | | |
| Alex Van Pelt | QB | 6' | 220 | 25 | | |
| Darick Holmes | HB-FB | 6' | 226 | 24 | | 24 |
| Yonel Jourdain | HB | 5'11" | 204 | 24 | | |
| Thurman Thomas | HB | 5'10" | 198 | 29 | | 48 |
| Carwell Gardner | FB | 6'2" | 244 | 28 | | 8 |
| Tim Tindale | FB | 5'10" | 220 | 24 | | |
| Justin Armour | WR | 6'4" | 209 | 22 | | 18 |
| Bill Brooks | WR | 6' | 188 | 31 | | 66 |
| Russell Copeland | WR | 6' | 200 | 23 | | 6 |
| Andre Reed | WR | 6' | 190 | 31 | | 18 |
| Steve Tasker | WR | 5'9" | 181 | 33 | | 18 |
| Damon Thomas | WR | 6'2" | 208 | 24 | | |
| Tony Cline | TE | 6'4" | 247 | 23 | | |
| Robert Coons | TE | 6'5" | 249 | 25 | | |
| Lonnie Johnson | TE | 6'3" | 240 | 24 | | 6 |
| Steve Christie | K | 6' | 185 | 27 | | 126 |
| Chris Mohr | K | 6'5" | 215 | 29 | | |

## INDIANAPOLIS COLTS 9-7 Ted Marchibroda

| Scores of Each Game | | |
|---|---|---|
| 21 | CINCINNATI | *24 |
| 27 | New York Jets | *24 |
| 14 | Buffalo | 20 |
| 21 | ST. LOUIS | 18 |
| 27 | Miami | *24 |
| 18 | SAN FRANCISCO | 17 |
| 17 | Oakland | 30 |
| 10 | NEW YORK JETS | 10 |
| 10 | BUFFALO | 16 |
| 14 | New Orleans | 17 |
| 24 | New England | 10 |
| 36 | MIAMI | 28 |
| 10 | Carolina | 13 |
| 41 | Jacksonville | 31 |
| 24 | SAN DIEGO | 27 |
| 10 | NEW ENGLAND | 7 |

| Use Name | Pos. | Hgt. | Wgt. | Age | Int | Pts |
|---|---|---|---|---|---|---|
| Shawn Harper | OT | 6'3" | 290 | 27 | | |
| Jason Mathews | OT | 6'5" | 288 | 24 | | |
| Kipp Vickers | OT | 6'2" | 296 | 26 | | |
| Derek West | OT | 6'8" | 303 | 23 | | |
| Will Wolford | OT | 6'5" | 295 | 31 | | |
| Randy Dixon | OG | 6'3" | 290 | 30 | | |
| Eric Mahlum | OG | 6'4" | 290 | 24 | | |
| Garin Patrick | OG | 6'3" | 269 | 24 | | |
| Joe Staysniak | OG | 6'4" | 292 | 28 | | |
| Kirk Lowdermilk | C | 6'4" | 284 | 32 | | |
| Tony Bennett | DE | 6'2" | 242 | 28 | | 8 |
| Freddie Joe Nunn | DE | 6'5" | 258 | 33 | | |
| Bernard Whittington | DE | 6'6" | 278 | 24 | | |
| Ellis Johnson | DT-DE | 6'2" | 298 | 21 | | |
| Tony McCoy | DT | 6' | 282 | 26 | | |
| Tony Siragusa | DT-NT | 6'3" | 315 | 28 | | |
| Trev Alberts | LB | 6'4" | 245 | 25 | | |
| Quentin Coryatt | LB | 6'3" | 246 | 25 | 1 | |
| Steve Grant | LB | 6' | 240 | 25 | 1 | |
| Jeff Herrod | LB | 6' | 245 | 29 | | |
| Devon McDonald | LB | 6'4" | 228 | 25 | | |
| Steve Morrison | LB | 6'3" | 246 | 23 | | |
| Scott Radecic | LB | 6'3" | 243 | 33 | | |
| Glenell Sanders | LB | 6'1" | 236 | 28 | | |
| Trevor Wilmot | LB | 6'2" | 215 | 22 | | |
| Ashley Ambrose | DB | 5'10" | 192 | 24 | 3 | |
| Jason Belser | DB | 5'9" | 185 | 25 | 1 | |
| Ray Buchanan | DB | 5'9" | 189 | 23 | 2 | |
| Conrad Clarks | DB | 5'10" | 200 | 26 | | |
| Eugene Daniel | DB | 5'11" | 180 | 34 | 3 | 6 |
| Derwin Gray | DB | 5'10" | 203 | 24 | 1 | |
| Ray McElroy | DB | 5'11" | 195 | 23 | | |
| David Tate | DB | 6'1" | 212 | 30 | | |
| Damon Watts | DB | 5'10" | 173 | 23 | 1 | |
| Craig Erickson | QB | 6'2" | 205 | 26 | | |
| Jim Harbaugh | QB | 6'3" | 215 | 31 | | 12 |
| Paul Justin | QB | 6'4" | 215 | 27 | | |
| Marshall Faulk | HB | 5'10" | 205 | 22 | | 84 |
| Ronald Humphrey | HB | 5'10" | 211 | 26 | | |
| Lamont Warren | HB | 5'11" | 211 | 22 | | 6 |
| Zack Crockett | FB | 6'2" | 241 | 22 | | |
| Clif Groce | FB | 5'11" | 242 | 23 | | |
| Roosevelt Potts | FB-HB | 6' | 260 | 24 | | 6 |
| Willie Anderson | WR | 6' | 176 | 30 | | 12 |
| Aaron Bailey | WR | 5'10" | 184 | 23 | | 24 |
| Ben Bronson | WR | 5'10" | 165 | 22 | | |
| Sean Dawkins | WR | 6'4" | 211 | 24 | | 18 |
| Bobby Olive | WR | 5'11" | 170 | 26 | | |
| Brian Stablein | WR | 6'1" | 190 | 25 | | |
| Floyd Turner | WR | 5'11" | 199 | 29 | | 28 |
| Charles Arbuckle | TE | 6'3" | 248 | 26 | | |
| Bradford Banta | TE | 6'6" | 257 | 24 | | |
| Ken Dilger | TE | 6'5" | 256 | 24 | | 24 |
| Thomas McLemore | TE | 6'5" | 250 | 25 | | |
| Marcus Pollard | TE | 6'4" | 245 | 23 | | |
| Cary Blanchard | K | 6'1" | 225 | 26 | | 82 |
| Mike Cofer | K | 6'1" | 195 | 31 | | 21 |
| Chris Gardocki | K | 6'1" | 199 | 25 | | |

## MIAMI DOLPHINS 9-7 Don Shula

| Scores of Each Game | | |
|---|---|---|
| 52 | NEW YORK JETS | 14 |
| 20 | New England | 3 |
| 23 | PITTSBURGH | 10 |
| 26 | Cincinnati | 23 |
| 24 | INDIANAPOLIS | *27 |
| 30 | New Orleans | 33 |
| 16 | New York Jets | 17 |
| 23 | BUFFALO | 6 |
| 24 | San Diego | 14 |
| 17 | NEW ENGLAND | 34 |
| 20 | SAN FRANCISCO | 44 |
| 28 | Indianapolis | 36 |
| 21 | ATLANTA | 20 |
| 13 | KANSAS CITY | 6 |
| 20 | Buffalo | 23 |
| 41 | St. Louis | 22 |

| Use Name | Pos. | Hgt. | Wgt. | Age | Int | Pts |
|---|---|---|---|---|---|---|
| Ethan Albright | OT | 6'5" | 292 | 24 | | |
| Ron Heller | OT | 6'6" | 293 | 33 | | |
| Tom McHale | OT | 6'4" | 290 | 32 | | |
| Billy Milner | OT | 6'5" | 293 | 23 | | |
| Eric Moore (from CLEV) | OT | 6'6" | 290 | 30 | | |
| Richmond Webb | OT | 6'6" | 303 | 28 | | |
| Chris Gray | OG-OT | 6'4" | 292 | 25 | | |
| Andrew Greene | OG | 6'3" | 304 | 25 | | |
| Keith Sims | OG | 6'2" | 309 | 28 | | |
| Bert Weidner | OG | 6'3" | 295 | 29 | | |
| Tim Ruddy | C | 6'3" | 290 | 23 | | |
| Trace Armstrong | DE | 6'4" | 260 | 29 | | |
| Marco Coleman | DE | 6'3" | 267 | 25 | | |
| Jeff Cross | DE | 6'4" | 280 | 29 | | |
| Tim Bowens | DT | 6'4" | 310 | 22 | | |
| Steve Emtman | DT | 6'4" | 284 | 25 | | |
| Chuck Klingbeil | DT-NT | 6'1" | 288 | 29 | | |
| Ed Hawthorne | NT | 6'1" | 305 | 25 | | |
| Antonio Armstrong | LB | 6'1" | 234 | 21 | | |
| Aubrey Beavers | LB | 6'3" | 231 | 24 | 1 | |
| Bryan Cox | LB | 6'3" | 248 | 27 | 1 | |
| Dewayne Dotson | LB | 6'1" | 256 | 24 | | |
| Dwight Hollier | LB | 6'2" | 250 | 26 | | |
| Jeff Kopp | LB | 6'3" | 243 | 24 | | |
| Chris Singleton | LB | 6'2" | 246 | 28 | 1 | |
| Gene Atkins | DB | 5'11" | 201 | 30 | 1 | |
| J.B. Brown | DB | 6' | 191 | 28 | 2 | |
| Terrell Buckley | DB | 5'9" | 176 | 24 | 1 | |
| Sean Hill | DB | 5'10" | 179 | 24 | | |
| Calvin Jackson | DB | 5'10" | 185 | 22 | 1 | |
| Pat Johnson | DB | 6'1" | 204 | 23 | | 6 |
| Louis Oliver | DB | 6'2" | 224 | 29 | | |
| Frankie Smith | DB | 5'9" | 182 | 26 | | |
| Michael Stewart | DB | 5'11" | 202 | 30 | 1 | |
| Troy Vincent | DB | 6' | 195 | 25 | 5 | 6 |
| Bernie Kosar | QB | 6'5" | 214 | 31 | | 6 |
| Dan Marino | QB | 6'4" | 224 | 33 | | |
| Dan McGwire | QB | 6'8" | 240 | 27 | | |
| Terry Kirby | HB | 6'1" | 218 | 25 | | 42 |
| Bernie Parmalee | HB | 5'11" | 196 | 27 | | 60 |
| Irving Spikes | HB | 5'8" | 206 | 24 | | 12 |
| Keith Byars | FB | 6'1" | 255 | 31 | | 18 |
| Robert Wilson | FB | 6' | 255 | 26 | | |
| Gary Clark | WR | 5'9" | 175 | 33 | | 12 |
| Kirby DarDar | WR | 5'9" | 183 | 23 | | |
| Irving Fryar | WR | 6' | 200 | 32 | | 48 |
| Randal Hill | WR | 5'10" | 180 | 25 | | |
| O.J. McDuffie | WR | 5'10" | 188 | 25 | | 50 |
| Mike Williams | WR | 5'10" | 183 | 28 | | |
| Eric Green | TE | 6'5" | 280 | 28 | | 20 |
| Joe Planansky | TE | 6'4" | 250 | 24 | | |
| Ronnie Williams | TE | 6'3" | 258 | 29 | | |
| John Kidd | K | 6'3" | 214 | 34 | | |
| Pete Stoyonovich | K | 5'10" | 195 | 28 | | 118 |

Scott Miller — Knee Injury

## NEW ENGLAND PATRIOTS 6-10 Bill Parcells

| Scores of Each Game | | |
|---|---|---|
| 17 | CLEVELAND | 14 |
| 3 | MIAMI | 20 |
| 3 | San Francisco | 28 |
| 17 | Atlanta | 30 |
| 3 | DENVER | 37 |
| 26 | Kansas City | 31 |
| 27 | BUFFALO | 14 |
| 17 | CAROLINA | *20 |
| 20 | New York Jets | 7 |
| 34 | Miami | 17 |
| 10 | INDIANAPOLIS | 24 |
| 35 | Buffalo | 25 |
| 17 | NEW ORLEANS | 31 |
| 31 | NEW YORK JETS | 28 |
| 27 | Pittsburgh | 41 |
| 7 | Indianapolis | 10 |

| Use Name | Pos. | Hgt. | Wgt. | Age | Int | Pts |
|---|---|---|---|---|---|---|
| Bruce Armstrong | OT | 6'4" | 295 | 29 | | |
| Pat Harlow | OT | 6'6" | 290 | 26 | | |
| Max Lane | OT | 6'6" | 295 | 24 | | |
| Brandon Moore | OT | 6'6" | 295 | 25 | | |
| Mike Gisler | OG-C | 6'4" | 300 | 26 | | |
| Bob Kratch | OG | 6'3" | 288 | 29 | | |
| Williams Roberts | OG | 6'5" | 292 | 33 | | |
| Todd Rucci | OG | 6'5" | 291 | 25 | | |
| Jeff Dellenbach | C | 6'6' | 300 | 32 | | |
| Dave Wohlabaugh | C-OG | 6'3" | 304 | 23 | | |
| Troy Barnett | DE | 6'4" | 293 | 24 | | |
| Ferric Collons | DE | 6'6" | 285 | 25 | | |
| Aaron Jones | DE | 6'5" | 267 | 28 | | |
| Mike Jones | DE | 6'4" | 295 | 26 | | |
| Tim Roberts | DE | 6'6" | 318 | 26 | | |
| Bruce Walker | NT | 6'4" | 310 | 23 | | |
| Bobby Abrams | LB | 6'3" | 240 | 28 | | |
| Vincent Brown | LB | 6'2" | 245 | 30 | 4 | |
| Alcides Catanho | LB | 6'3" | 216 | 23 | | |
| Steve DeOssie | LB | 6'2" | 248 | 32 | | |
| Ted Johnson | LB | 6'3" | 240 | 22 | | |
| Willie McGinest | LB | 6'5" | 255 | 23 | | |
| Marty Moore | LB | 6'1" | 244 | 24 | | |
| Dwayne Sabb | LB | 6'4" | 248 | 25 | | |
| Chris Slade | LB | 6'4" | 242 | 24 | | 6 |
| Corwin Brown | DB | 6' | 200 | 25 | | |
| Eddie Cade | DB | 6'1" | 206 | 22 | | |
| Myron Guyton | DB | 6'1" | 205 | 28 | 3 | |
| Jimmy Hitchcock | DB | 5'10" | 188 | 23 | | |
| Maurice Hurst | DB | 5'10" | 185 | 27 | 1 | |
| Ty Law | DB | 5'11" | 196 | 21 | 3 | |
| Vernon Lewis | DB | 5'10" | 192 | 24 | | |
| Terry Ray | DB | 6'1" | 205 | 25 | 1 | |
| Ricky Reynolds | DB | 5'11" | 190 | 30 | 3 | |
| Larry Whigham | DB | 6'2" | 202 | 23 | | |
| Reggie White | NT | 6'4" | 315 | 25 | | |
| Carlos Yancy | DB | 6' | 185 | 25 | | |
| Jay Barker | QB | 6'3" | 215 | 23 | | |
| Drew Bledsoe | QB | 6'5" | 233 | 23 | | |
| Scott Zolak | QB | 6'5" | 222 | 27 | | |
| Corey Croom | HB | 5'11" | 208 | 24 | | |
| David Green | HB | 5'11" | 193 | 23 | | |
| Curtis Martin | HB | 5'11" | 203 | 22 | | 92 |
| David Meggett | HB | 5'7" | 195 | 29 | | 16 |
| Sam Gash | FB | 5'11" | 224 | 26 | | 6 |
| Rupert Grant | FB | 6'1" | 233 | 21 | | |
| Vincent Brisby | WR | 6'1" | 188 | 24 | | 18 |
| Troy Brown | WR | 5'9" | 190 | 24 | | 6 |
| Hason Graham | WR | 5'10" | 176 | 24 | | 12 |
| Kevin Lee | WR | 6'1" | 194 | 24 | | |
| Will Moore | WR | 6'2" | 180 | 25 | | 6 |
| John Burke | TE | 6'2" | 255 | 23 | | |
| Ben Coates | TE | 6'4" | 245 | 26 | | 36 |
| David Frisch | TE | 6'7" | 260 | 25 | | |
| Matt Bahr | K | 5'10" | 175 | 39 | | 96 |
| Pat O'Neill (to CHI) | K | 6'1" | 200 | 24 | | |
| Bryan Wagner | K | 6'2" | 200 | 33 | | |

## NEW YORK JETS 3-13 Rich Kotite

| Scores of Each Game | | |
|---|---|---|
| 14 | Miami | 52 |
| 24 | INDIANAPOLIS | *27 |
| 27 | JACKSONVILLE | 10 |
| 3 | Atlanta | 13 |
| 10 | OAKLAND | 47 |
| 10 | Buffalo | 29 |
| 15 | Carolina | 26 |
| 17 | MIAMI | 16 |
| 10 | Indianapolis | 17 |
| 7 | NEW ENGLAND | 20 |
| 26 | BUFFALO | 28 |
| 16 | Seattle | 10 |
| 20 | ST. LOUIS | 23 |
| 28 | New England | 31 |
| 6 | Houston | 23 |
| 0 | NEW ORLEANS | 12 |

| Use Name | Pos. | Hgt. | Wgt. | Age | Int | Pts |
|---|---|---|---|---|---|---|
| James Brown | OT | 6'6" | 329 | 25 | | |
| Melvin Hayes | OT | 6'6" | 329 | 22 | | |
| Siupeli Malamala | OT-OG | 6'5" | 315 | 26 | | |
| Matt Willig | OT | 6'8" | 317 | 26 | | |
| Roger Duffy | OG | 6'3" | 311 | 28 | | |
| Carlton Haselrig | G | 6'1" | 293 | 29 | | |
| Everett McIver | OG | 6'6" | 315 | 25 | | |
| Matt O'Dwyer | OG | 6'5" | 308 | 23 | | |
| Terrence Wisdom | OG-C | 6'4" | 300 | 23 | | |
| John Bock | C-OG | 6'3" | 285 | 24 | | |
| Cal Dixon | C-OG | 6'4" | 302 | 25 | | |
| Kurt Barber | DE | 6'4" | 260 | 26 | | |
| Hugh Douglas | DE | 6'2" | 265 | 24 | | |
| Donald Evans | DE | 6'2" | 282 | 31 | | |
| Marvin Washington | DE-DT | 6'6" | 280 | 29 | | |
| Lou Benfatti | DT | 6'4" | 278 | 24 | | |
| Matt Brock | DT-DE | 6'5" | 290 | 29 | 1 | 6 |
| Tony Casillas | DT | 6'3" | 278 | 31 | | |
| Erik Howard | DT-DE | 6'4" | 275 | 30 | | 2 |
| Marc Spindler | DT-DE | 6'5" | 290 | 25 | | |
| Chad Cascadden | LB | 6'1" | 225 | 23 | | |
| Kyle Clifton | LB | 6'4" | 236 | 33 | | |
| Bobby Houston | LB | 6'2" | 245 | 27 | | |
| Marvin Jones | LB | 6'2" | 249 | 23 | | |
| Mo Lewis | LB | 6'3" | 250 | 25 | 2 | 6 |
| Wilber Marshall | LB | 6'1" | 231 | 33 | 2 | |
| Eddie Mason | LB | 6' | 230 | 23 | | |
| Ron Carpenter | DB | 6'1" | 189 | 25 | | |
| Aaron Glenn | DB | 5'9" | 185 | 23 | 1 | |
| Victor Green | DB | 5'9" | 195 | 25 | 1 | |
| Carl Greenwood | DB | 5'11" | 186 | 23 | | |
| Gary Jones | DB | 6'1" | 217 | 27 | 2 | 1 |
| Vance Joseph | DB | 6' | 202 | 22 | 2 | |
| Anthony Prior | DB | 5'11" | 185 | 25 | | |
| Todd Scott | DB | 5'10" | 207 | 27 | | |
| Otis Smith | DB | 5'11" | 190 | 29 | 6 | 6 |
| Marcus Turner | DB | 6' | 190 | 29 | | |
| Lonnie Young | DB | 6'1" | 196 | 32 | | |
| Bubby Brister | QB | 6'3" | 207 | 33 | | |
| Boomer Esiason | QB | 6'5" | 224 | 34 | | |
| Glenn Foley | QB | 6'2" | 210 | 24 | | |
| Erik Wilhelm (from CIN) | QB | 6'3" | 217 | 29 | | |
| Ronald Moore | HB | 5'10" | 225 | 25 | | |
| Adrian Murrell | HB | 5'11" | 214 | 24 | | 18 |
| Richie Anderson | FB-HB | 6'2" | 225 | 23 | | |
| Brad Baxter | FB | 6'1" | 235 | 28 | | 6 |
| Sherriden May | FB | 6' | 215 | 22 | | |
| Kenyon Rasheed | FB | 5'10" | 235 | 25 | | |
| Curtis Ceaser | WR | 6'2" | 190 | 23 | | |
| Wayne Crebet | WR | 5'10" | 180 | 22 | | 24 |
| Tyrone Davis | WR | 6'4" | 229 | 23 | | |
| Jeff Sydner | WR | 5'6" | 177 | 25 | | |
| Charles Wilson | WR | 5'10" | 185 | 27 | | 24 |
| Ryan Yarborough | WR | 6'2" | 195 | 24 | | 12 |
| Fred Baxter | TE | 6'3" | 260 | 24 | | 6 |
| Kyle Brady | TE | 6'6" | 260 | 23 | | 12 |
| Johnny Mitchell | TE | 6'3" | 241 | 24 | | 30 |
| Brian Hansen | K | 6'4" | 215 | 34 | | |
| Nick Lowery | K | 6'4" | 215 | 39 | | 75 |
| Don Silvestri | K | 6'4" | 210 | 26 | | |

Dave Alexander — Knee Injury

## BUFFALO BILLS

### RUSHING

| Last Name | No. | Yds | Avg | TD |
|---|---|---|---|---|
| T. Thomas | 267 | 1005 | 3.8 | 6 |
| Holmes | 172 | 698 | 4.1 | 4 |
| Gardner | 20 | 77 | 3.9 | 0 |
| Tasker | 8 | 74 | 9.3 | 0 |
| Reed | 7 | 48 | 6.9 | 0 |
| Jourdain | 8 | 31 | 3.9 | 0 |
| Collins | 9 | 23 | 2.6 | 0 |
| Kelly | 17 | 20 | 1.2 | 0 |
| Tindale | 5 | 16 | 3.2 | 0 |
| Brooks | 3 | 7 | 2.3 | 0 |
| Copeland | 1 | -1 | -1.0 | 0 |
| Armour | 4 | -5 | -1.2 | 0 |

### RECEIVING

| Last Name | No. | Yds | Avg | TD |
|---|---|---|---|---|
| Brooks | 53 | 763 | 14.4 | 11 |
| L. Johnson | 49 | 504 | 10.3 | 1 |
| Copeland | 42 | 646 | 15.4 | 1 |
| Armour | 26 | 300 | 11.5 | 3 |
| T. Thomas | 26 | 220 | 8.5 | 2 |
| Reed | 24 | 312 | 13.0 | 3 |
| Holmes | 24 | 214 | 8.9 | 0 |
| Tasker | 20 | 255 | 12.8 | 3 |
| Cline | 8 | 64 | 8.0 | 0 |
| Coons | 3 | 28 | 9.3 | 0 |
| Gardner | 2 | 17 | 8.5 | 0 |
| D. Thomas | 1 | 18 | 18.0 | 0 |
| Jourdain | 1 | 7 | 7.0 | 0 |

### PUNT RETURNS

| Last Name | No. | Yds | Avg | TD |
|---|---|---|---|---|
| Burris | 20 | 229 | 11.5 | 0 |
| Tasker | 17 | 204 | 12.0 | 0 |
| Brooks | 6 | 35 | 5.8 | 0 |
| Copeland | 2 | 8 | 4.0 | 0 |
| Jourdain | 1 | 0 | 0.0 | 0 |
| D. Thomas | 1 | 0 | 0.0 | 0 |

### KICKOFF RETURNS

| Last Name | No. | Yds | Avg | TD |
|---|---|---|---|---|
| Holmes | 39 | 799 | 20.5 | 0 |
| Jourdain | 19 | 348 | 18.3 | 0 |
| Tindale | 6 | 62 | 10.3 | 0 |
| Green | 2 | 37 | 18.5 | 0 |
| Pike | 1 | 20 | 20.0 | 0 |
| Louchiey | 1 | 13 | 13.0 | 0 |
| Irvin | 1 | 12 | 12.0 | 0 |
| Cline | 1 | 11 | 1.0 | 0 |

### PASSING — PUNTING — KICKING Statistics

| Last Name | Att | Cmp | % | Yds | Yd/Att | TD | Int— | % RK |
|---|---|---|---|---|---|---|---|---|
| **PASSING** | | | | | | | | |
| Kelly | 458 | 255 | 55.7 | 3130 | 6.83 | 22 | 13— | 2.8 |
| Collins | 29 | 14 | 48.3 | 112 | 3.86 | 0 | 1— | 3.4 |
| Van Pelt | 18 | 10 | 55.6 | 106 | 5.89 | 2 | 0— | 0.0 |
| Armour | 1 | 0 | 0.0 | 0 | 0.00 | 0 | 0— | 0.0 |

| **PUNTING** | No. | Avg. |
|---|---|---|
| Mohr | 86 | 40.4 |

| **KICKING** | XP | ATT | % | FG | ATT | % |
|---|---|---|---|---|---|---|
| Christie | 33 | 35 | 94 | 31 | 40 | 78 |

**2 POINT XP**
Gardner (1)

## INDIANAPOLIS COLTS

### RUSHING

| Last Name | No. | Yds | Avg | TD |
|---|---|---|---|---|
| Faulk | 289 | 1078 | 3.7 | 11 |
| Potts | 65 | 309 | 4.8 | 0 |
| Harbaugh | 52 | 235 | 4.5 | 2 |
| Warren | 47 | 152 | 3.2 | 1 |
| Bailey | 1 | 34 | 34.0 | 0 |
| Erickson | 9 | 14 | 1.6 | 0 |
| Humphrey | 2 | 6 | 3.0 | 0 |
| Justin | 3 | 1 | 0.3 | 0 |
| Crockett | 1 | 0 | 0.0 | 0 |

### RECEIVING

| Last Name | No. | Yds | Avg | TD |
|---|---|---|---|---|
| Faulk | 56 | 475 | 8.5 | 3 |
| Dawkins | 52 | 784 | 15.1 | 3 |
| Dilger | 42 | 635 | 15.1 | 4 |
| Turner | 35 | 431 | 12.3 | 4 |
| Bailey | 21 | 379 | 18.0 | 3 |
| Potts | 21 | 228 | 10.9 | 1 |
| Warren | 17 | 159 | 9.4 | 0 |
| Anderson | 8 | 111 | 13.9 | 2 |
| Stablein | 8 | 95 | 11.9 | 0 |
| Arbuckle | 4 | 33 | 8.3 | 0 |
| Crockett | 2 | 35 | 17.5 | 0 |
| Humphrey | 2 | 11 | 5.5 | 0 |
| Banta | 1 | 6 | 6.0 | 0 |
| Harbaugh | 1 | -9 | -9.0 | 0 |

### PUNT RETURNS

| Last Name | No. | Yds | Avg | TD |
|---|---|---|---|---|
| Buchanan | 16 | 113 | 7.1 | 0 |
| Bronson | 13 | 79 | 6.1 | 0 |

### KICKOFF RETURNS

| Last Name | No. | Yds | Avg | TD |
|---|---|---|---|---|
| Bailey | 21 | 495 | 23.6 | 1 |
| Humphrey | 21 | 453 | 21.6 | 0 |
| Warren | 15 | 315 | 21.0 | 0 |
| Morrison | 2 | 6 | 3.0 | 0 |
| Bronson | 1 | 31 | 31.0 | 0 |
| Buchanan | 1 | 22 | 22.0 | 0 |
| Belser | 1 | 15 | 15.0 | 0 |
| Radecic | 1 | -5 | -5.0 | 0 |

### PASSING — PUNTING — KICKING Statistics

| Last Name | Att | Cmp | % | Yds | Yd/Att | TD | Int— | % RK |
|---|---|---|---|---|---|---|---|---|
| **PASSING** | | | | | | | | |
| Harbaugh | 314 | 200 | 63.7 | 2575 | 8.20 | 17 | 5— | 1.6 |
| Erickson | 83 | 50 | 60.2 | 586 | 7.06 | 3 | 4— | 4.8 |
| Juston | 36 | 20 | 55.6 | 212 | 5.89 | 0 | 2— | 5.6 |
| Gardocki | 1 | 0 | 0.0 | 0 | 0.00 | 0 | 0— | 0.0 |

| **PUNTING** | No. | Avg. |
|---|---|---|
| Gardocki | 63 | 42.6 |

| **KICKING** | XP | ATT | % | FG | ATT | % |
|---|---|---|---|---|---|---|
| Blanchard | 25 | 25 | **100** | 19 | 24 | 79 |
| Cofer | 9 | 9 | 100 | 4 | 9 | 44 |

**2 POINT XP**
Turner (2)

## MIAMI DOLPHINS

### RUSHING

| Last Name | No. | Yds | Avg | TD |
|---|---|---|---|---|
| Parmalee | 236 | 878 | 3.7 | 9 |
| Kirby | 108 | 414 | 3.8 | 4 |
| Spikes | 32 | 126 | 3.9 | 1 |
| Byars | 15 | 44 | 2.9 | 1 |
| Kosar | 7 | 19 | 2.7 | 1 |
| Marino | 11 | 14 | 1.3 | 0 |
| McDuffie | 3 | 6 | 2.0 | 0 |
| Wilson | 1 | 5 | 5.0 | 0 |

### RECEIVING

| Last Name | No. | Yds | Avg | TD |
|---|---|---|---|---|
| Kirby | 66 | 618 | 9.4 | 3 |
| Fryar | 62 | 910 | 14.7 | 8 |
| McDuffie | 62 | 819 | 13.2 | 8 |
| Byars | 51 | 362 | 7.1 | 2 |
| Green | 43 | 499 | 11.6 | 3 |
| Parmalee | 39 | 345 | 8.8 | 1 |
| Clark | 37 | 525 | 14.2 | 2 |
| R. Hill | 12 | 260 | 21.7 | 0 |
| Spikes | 5 | 18 | 3.6 | 1 |
| R. Williams | 3 | 28 | 9.3 | 0 |
| M. Williams | 2 | 17 | 8.5 | 0 |
| Wilson | 1 | 3 | 3.0 | 0 |
| Marino | 1 | -3 | -3.0 | 0 |

### PUNT RETURNS

| Last Name | No. | Yds | Avg | TD |
|---|---|---|---|---|
| McDuffie | 24 | 163 | 6.8 | 0 |

### KICKOFF RETURNS

| Last Name | No. | Yds | Avg | TD |
|---|---|---|---|---|
| McDuffie | 23 | 564 | 24.5 | 0 |
| Spikes | 18 | 378 | 21.0 | 0 |
| R. Hill | 12 | 287 | 23.9 | 0 |
| R. Williams | 2 | 20 | 10.0 | 0 |
| S. Hill | 1 | 38 | 38.0 | 0 |
| DarDar | 1 | 22 | 22.0 | 0 |
| Buckley | 1 | 16 | 16.0 | 0 |
| Miler | 1 | 13 | 13.0 | 0 |

### PASSING — PUNTING — KICKING Statistics

| Last Name | Att | Cmp | % | Yds | Yd/Att | TD | Int— | % RK |
|---|---|---|---|---|---|---|---|---|
| **PASSING** | | | | | | | | |
| Marino | 482 | 309 | 64.1 | 3668 | 7.61 | 24 | 15— | 3.1 |
| Kosar | 108 | 74 | 68.5 | 699 | 6.47 | 3 | 5— | 4.6 |
| Kirby | 1 | 1 | 100.0 | 31 | 31.00 | 1 | 0— | 0.0 |
| McGwire | 1 | 0 | 0.00 | 0 | 0.00 | 0 | 0— | 0.0 |

| **PUNTING** | No. | Avg. |
|---|---|---|
| Kidd | 57 | 42.7 |

| **KICKING** | XP | ATT | % | FG | ATT | % |
|---|---|---|---|---|---|---|
| Stoyonovich | 37 | 37 | 100 | 27 | 34 | 79 |

**2 POINT XP**
Green (1)
McDuffie (1)

## NEW ENGLAND PATRIOTS

### RUSHING

| Last Name | No. | Yds | Avg | TD |
|---|---|---|---|---|
| Martin | **368** | **1487** | 4.0 | 14 |
| Meggett | 60 | 250 | 4.2 | 2 |
| Croom | 13 | 54 | 4.2 | 0 |
| Bledsoe | 20 | 28 | 1.4 | 0 |
| Gash | 8 | 24 | 3.0 | 0 |
| Zolak | 4 | 19 | 4.8 | 0 |
| Lee | 1 | 4 | 4.0 | 0 |

### RECEIVING

| Last Name | No. | Yds | Avg | TD |
|---|---|---|---|---|
| Coates | 84 | 915 | 10.9 | 6 |
| Brisby | 66 | 974 | 14.8 | 3 |
| Meggett | 52 | 334 | 6.4 | 0 |
| W. Moore | 43 | 502 | 11.7 | 1 |
| Martin | 30 | 261 | 8.7 | 1 |
| Gash | 26 | 242 | 9.3 | 1 |
| Burke | 15 | 136 | 9.1 | 0 |
| T. Brown | 14 | 159 | 11.4 | 0 |
| Graham | 10 | 156 | 15.6 | 2 |
| Lee | 8 | 107 | 13.4 | 0 |
| Croom | 1 | 8 | 8.0 | 0 |
| Grant | 1 | 4 | 4.0 | 0 |
| Bledsoe | 1 | -9 | -9.0 | 0 |

### PUNT RETURNS

| Last Name | No. | Yds | Avg | TD |
|---|---|---|---|---|
| Meggett | 45 | 383 | 8.5 | 0 |

### KICKOFF RETURNS

| Last Name | No. | Yds | Avg | TD |
|---|---|---|---|---|
| Meggett | 38 | 964 | 25.4 | 0 |
| T. Brown | 31 | 672 | 21.7 | 0 |
| Gisler | 2 | 19 | 9.5 | 0 |
| Lee | 1 | 14 | 14.0 | 0 |
| Frisch | 1 | 8 | 8.0 | 0 |
| Burke | 1 | 7 | 7.0 | 0 |
| Grant | 1 | 7 | 7.0 | 0 |

### PASSING — PUNTING — KICKING Statistics

| Last Name | Att | Cmp | % | Yds | Yd/Att | TD | Int— | % RK |
|---|---|---|---|---|---|---|---|---|
| **PASSING** | | | | | | | | |
| Bledsoe | 636 | 323 | 50.8 | 3507 | 5.51 | 13 | 16— | 2.5 |
| Zolak | 49 | 28 | 57.1 | 282 | 5.76 | 1 | 0— | 0.0 |
| Meggett | 1 | 0 | 0.0 | 0 | 0.00 | 0 | 0— | 0.0 |

| **PUNTING** | No. | Avg. |
|---|---|---|
| O'Neill | 44 | 36.4 |
| Wagner | 37 | 42.1 |
| Bahr | 1 | 29.0 |

| **KICKING** | XP | ATT | % | FG | ATT | % |
|---|---|---|---|---|---|---|
| Bahr | 27 | 27 | 100 | 23 | 33 | 70 |

**2 POINT XP**
Meggett (2)
Martin (1)

## NEW YORK JETS

### RUSHING

| Last Name | No. | Yds | Avg | TD |
|---|---|---|---|---|
| Murrell | 192 | 795 | 4.1 | 1 |
| B. Baxter | 85 | 296 | 3.5 | 1 |
| Moore | 43 | 121 | 2.8 | 0 |
| Brister | 16 | 18 | 1.1 | 0 |
| Anderson | 5 | 17 | 3.4 | 0 |
| Esiason | 19 | 14 | 0.7 | 0 |
| Foley | 1 | 9 | 9.0 | 0 |
| May | 2 | 5 | 2.5 | 0 |
| Rasheed | 1 | 3 | 3.0 | 0 |
| Crebet | 1 | 1 | 1.0 | 0 |

### RECEIVING

| Last Name | No. | Yds | Avg | TD |
|---|---|---|---|---|
| Murrell | 71 | 465 | 6.5 | 2 |
| Crebet | 66 | 726 | 11.0 | 4 |
| Mitchell | 45 | 497 | 11.0 | 5 |
| Wilson | 41 | 484 | 11.8 | 4 |
| Brady | 26 | 252 | 9.7 | 2 |
| B. Baxter | 26 | 160 | 6.2 | 0 |
| Yarborough | 18 | 230 | 12.8 | 2 |
| F. Baxter | 18 | 122 | 12.3 | 1 |
| Moore | 8 | 50 | 6.3 | 0 |
| Anderson | 5 | 26 | 5.2 | 0 |
| Rasheed | 2 | 15 | 7.5 | 0 |
| Davis | 1 | 9 | 9.0 | 0 |
| Brister | 1 | 2 | 2.0 | 0 |
| Foley | 1 | -9 | -9.0 | 0 |

### PUNT RETURNS

| Last Name | No. | Yds | Avg | TD |
|---|---|---|---|---|
| Sydner | 17 | 178 | 10.5 | 0 |

### KICKOFF RETURNS

| Last Name | No. | Yds | Avg | TD |
|---|---|---|---|---|
| Carpenter | 20 | 553 | **27.7** | 0 |
| Moore | 8 | 166 | 20.8 | 0 |
| F. Baxter | 6 | 36 | 6.0 | 0 |
| Sydner | 3 | 45 | 15.0 | 0 |
| Brady | 2 | 25 | 12.5 | 0 |
| Benfatti | 1 | 25 | 25.0 | 0 |
| Glenn | 1 | 12 | 12.0 | 0 |
| Smith | 1 | 6 | 6.0 | 0 |
| Murrell | 1 | 5 | 5.0 | 0 |

### PASSING — PUNTING — KICKING Statistics

| Last Name | Att | Cmp | % | Yds | Yd/Att | TD | Int— | % RK |
|---|---|---|---|---|---|---|---|---|
| **PASSING** | | | | | | | | |
| Esiason | 389 | 221 | 56.8 | 2275 | 5.85 | 16 | 15— | 3.9 |
| Brister | 170 | 93 | 54.7 | 726 | 4.27 | 4 | 8— | 4.7 |
| Foley | 29 | 16 | 55.2 | 128 | 4.41 | 0 | 1— | 3.4 |
| Anderson | 1 | 0 | 0.0 | 0 | 0.00 | 0 | 0— | 0.0 |

| **PUNTING** | No. | Avg. |
|---|---|---|
| Hansen | 100 | 40.9 |
| Silvestri | 5 | 47.6 |

| **KICKING** | XP | ATT | % | FG | ATT | % |
|---|---|---|---|---|---|---|
| Lowery | 24 | 24 | 100 | 17 | 21 | 81 |

**2 POINT XP**
None

## PITTSBURGH STEELERS 11-5 Bill Cowher

| Scores of Each Game | | |
|---|---|---|
| 23 | DETROIT | 20 |
| 34 | Houston | 17 |
| 10 | Miami | 23 |
| 24 | MINNESOTA | 44 |
| 31 | SAN DIEGO | 16 |
| 16 | Jacksonville | 20 |
| 9 | CINCINNATI | 27 |
| 24 | JACKSONVILLE | 7 |
| 37 | Chicago | *34 |
| 20 | CLEVELAND | 3 |
| 49 | Cincinnati | 31 |
| 20 | Cleveland | 17 |
| 21 | HOUSTON | 7 |
| 29 | Oakland | 10 |
| 41 | NEW ENGLAND | 27 |
| 19 | Green Bay | 24 |

| Use Name | Pos. | Hgt. | Wgt. | Age | Int | Pts |
|---|---|---|---|---|---|---|
| John Jackson | OT | 6'6" | 297 | 30 | | |
| James Parrish | OT | 6'6" | 310 | 27 | | |
| Leon Searcy | OT | 6'3" | 304 | 25 | | |
| Tom Newberry | OG | 6'2" | 285 | 32 | | |
| Lonnie Palelei | OG | 6'3" | 320 | 24 | | |
| Brenden Stai | OT | 6'4" | 297 | 23 | | |
| Justin Strzelczyk | OG-OT | 6'5" | 302 | 27 | | |
| Dermontti Dawson | C | 6'2" | 288 | 30 | | |
| Kendall Gammon | C | 6'4" | 288 | 26 | | |
| Ariel Solomon | C-OG | 6'5" | 290 | 27 | | |
| Brentson Buckner | DE | 6'2" | 305 | 23 | 1 | |
| Taase Faumui | DE | 6'3" | 278 | 24 | | |
| Kevin Henry | DE | 6'4" | 282 | 26 | | |
| Ray Seals | DE | 6'3" | 306 | 30 | 1 | |
| Oliver Gibson | DT | 6'2" | 283 | 23 | | |
| Bill Johnson | NT | 6'4" | 300 | 26 | | |
| Joel Steed | NT | 6'2" | 300 | 26 | | |
| Chad Brown | LB | 6'2" | 240 | 25 | | |
| Jason Gildon | LB | 6'3" | 245 | 23 | | |
| Kevin Greene | LB | 6'3" | 247 | 33 | 1 | |
| Donta Jones | LB | 6'2" | 226 | 23 | | |
| Levon Kirkland | LB | 6' | 264 | 26 | | |
| Greg Lloyd | LB | 6'2" | 228 | 30 | 3 | |
| Jerry Olsavsky | LB | 6'1" | 224 | 28 | | |
| Eric Ravotti | LB | 6'3" | 246 | 24 | | |
| Myron Bell | DB | 5'11" | 203 | 23 | 2 | |
| Deon Figures | DB | 6' | 192 | 25 | | |
| Lethon Flowers | DB | 6' | 207 | 22 | | |
| Randy Fuller | DB | 5'10" | 175 | 25 | | |
| Carnell Lake | DB | 6'1" | 210 | 28 | 1 | 6 |
| Alvoid Mays | DB | 5'9" | 180 | 29 | 2 | 6 |
| Chris Oldham | DB | 5'9" | 193 | 26 | 1 | 6 |
| Darren Perry | DB | 5'10" | 196 | 26 | 4 | |
| Willie Williams | DB | 5'9" | 180 | 24 | 7 | 6 |
| Rod Woodson | DB | 6' | 200 | 30 | | |
| Jim Miller | QB | 6'2" | 210 | 24 | | |
| Neil O'Donnell | QB | 6'3" | 227 | 29 | | |
| Kordell Stewart | QB-WR-HB | 6'1" | 212 | 22 | | 12 |
| Mike Tomczak | QB | 6'1" | 201 | 32 | | |
| Fred McAfee | HB | 5'10" | 193 | 27 | | 6 |
| Bam Morris | HB | 6' | 246 | 23 | | 54 |
| Erric Pegram | HB | 5'10" | 195 | 26 | | 38 |
| Steve Avery | FB | 6'2" | 229 | 29 | | 6 |
| Tim Lester | FB | 5'9" | 227 | 27 | | 6 |
| John L. Williams | FB | 5'11" | 235 | 30 | | 6 |
| Johnnie Barnes | WR | 6'1" | 185 | 27 | | |
| Andre Hastings | WR | 6' | 190 | 24 | | 12 |
| Corey Holliday | WR | 6'2" | 208 | 24 | | |
| Charles Johnson | WR | 6' | 193 | 23 | | |
| Ernie Mills | WR | 5'11" | 192 | 26 | | 48 |
| Yancey Thigpen | WR | 6'1" | 202 | 26 | | 30 |
| Mark Bruener | TE | 6'4" | 254 | 22 | | 18 |
| Tracy Greene | TE | 6'5" | 270 | 22 | | |
| Jonathan Hayes | TE | 6'5" | 248 | 33 | | |
| Norm Johnson | K | 6'2" | 202 | 35 | | 141 |
| Rohn Stark | K | 6'3" | 203 | 36 | | |

Damon Mays — Shoulder Injury

## CINCINNATI BENGALS 7-9 Dave Shula

| Scores of Each Game | | |
|---|---|---|
| 24 | Indianapolis | *21 |
| 24 | JACKSONVILLE | 17 |
| 21 | Seattle | 24 |
| 28 | HOUSTON | 38 |
| 23 | MIAMI | 26 |
| 16 | Tampa Bay | 19 |
| 27 | Pittsburgh | 9 |
| 26 | CLEVELAND | *29 |
| 17 | OAKLAND | 20 |
| 32 | Houston | 25 |
| 31 | PITTSBURGH | 49 |
| 17 | Jacksonville | 13 |
| 10 | Green Bay | 24 |
| 16 | CHICAGO | 10 |
| 10 | Cleveland | 26 |
| 27 | MINNESOTA | 24 |

| Use Name | Pos. | Hgt. | Wgt. | Age | Int | Pts |
|---|---|---|---|---|---|---|
| Anthony Brown | OT | 6'5" | 310 | 22 | | |
| Kevin Sargent | OT | 6'6" | 284 | 26 | | |
| Scott Brumfield | OT | 6'8" | 320 | 25 | | |
| Melvin Tuten | OT | 6'6" | 305 | 23 | | 6 |
| Joe Walter | OT | 6'7" | 292 | 32 | | |
| Dan Jones | OG-C | 6'7" | 298 | 25 | | |
| Todd Kalis | OG | 6'6" | 296 | 30 | | |
| Bruce Kozerski | OG-OT | 6'4" | 287 | 33 | | |
| Trent Pollard | OG | 6'4" | 330 | 22 | | |
| Darrick Brilz | C | 6'3" | 287 | 31 | | |
| Greg Truitt | C | 6' | 235 | 29 | | |
| John Copeland | DE | 6'3" | 286 | 24 | | |
| Todd Kelly | DE | 6'2" | 259 | 24 | | |
| Ty Parten | DE | 6'4" | 272 | 25 | | |
| Artie Smith | DE-DT | 6'4" | 285 | 25 | | |
| Ramondo Stallings | DE | 6'7" | 285 | 23 | | |
| Alfred Oglesby (from NYJ) | DT | 6'4" | 290 | 28 | | |
| Keith Rucker | DT | 6'4" | 332 | 26 | | |
| Kimo Von Oelhoffen | DT | 6'4" | 300 | 24 | | |
| Dan Wilkinson | DT | 6'5" | 313 | 22 | | |
| Andre Collins | LB | 6'1" | 231 | 27 | 2 | |
| Gerald Collins | HB | 6'2" | 250 | 24 | | |
| James Francis | LB | 6'5" | 252 | 27 | | |
| Kevin Jefferson | LB | 6'2" | 232 | 31 | | |
| Ricardo McDonald | LB | 6'2" | 235 | 25 | | |
| Randy Neal | LB | 6'3" | 236 | 22 | | |
| Steve Tovar | LB | 6'3" | 244 | 25 | 1 | |
| Brett Wallerstedt | LB | 6'1" | 240 | 24 | | |
| Michael Brim | DB | 6' | 192 | 29 | | |
| Adrian Hardy | DB | 5'11" | 194 | 25 | | |
| Rod Jones | DB | 6' | 185 | 31 | 1 | |
| Roger Jones | DB | 5'9" | 175 | 26 | 1 | 6 |
| Corey Sawyer | DB | 5'11" | 171 | 23 | 2 | |
| Sam Shade | DB | 6'1" | 191 | 22 | | |
| Chris Shelling | DB | 5'10" | 180 | 22 | | |
| Bracey Walker | DB | 5'10" | 200 | 24 | 4 | |
| Leonard Wheeler | DB | 5'11" | 189 | 26 | | |
| Darryl Williams | DB | 6' | 191 | 25 | 1 | 2 |
| Jeff Blake | QB | 6' | 202 | 24 | | 14 |
| David Klingler | QB | 6'2" | 205 | 26 | | |
| John Walsh | QB | 6'4" | 215 | 22 | | |
| Erik Wilhelm | QB | 6'3" | 217 | 29 | | |
| Eric Bieniemy | HB | 5'7" | 198 | 26 | | 18 |
| Jason Burns | HB | 5'7" | 195 | 22 | | |
| Harold Green | HB | 6'2" | 222 | 27 | | 18 |
| Jeff Cothran | FB | 6'1" | 249 | 24 | | |
| James Joseph | FB | 6'2" | 222 | 27 | | |
| Thomas Bailey | WR | 6' | 196 | 23 | | |
| David Dunn | WR | 6'3" | 210 | 23 | | 6 |
| Jeff Hill | WR | 5'11" | 178 | 22 | | |
| Carl Pickens | WR | 6'2" | 206 | 25 | | 102 |
| Darnay Scott | WR | 6'1" | 180 | 23 | | 30 |
| Tony McGee | TE | 6'3" | 246 | 24 | | 24 |
| Troy Sadowski | TE | 6'5" | 250 | 29 | | |
| Derek Ware | TE | 6'2" | 255 | 27 | | |
| Lee Johnson | K | 6'2" | 200 | 33 | | |
| Doug Pelfrey | K | 5'11" | 185 | 24 | | 121 |

Rich Braham — Ankle Injury

Tim McGee — Neck Injury

## HOUSTON OILERS 7-9 Jeff Fisher

| Scores of Each Game | | |
|---|---|---|
| 10 | Houston | 3 |
| 17 | PITTSBURGH | 34 |
| 7 | CLEVELAND | 14 |
| 38 | Cincinnati | 28 |
| 16 | JACKSONVILLE | 17 |
| 17 | Minnesota | *23 |
| 32 | Chicago | 35 |
| 19 | TAMPA BAY | 7 |
| 37 | Cleveland | 10 |
| 25 | CINCINNATI | 32 |
| 13 | Kansas City | 20 |
| 42 | DENVER | 33 |
| 7 | Pittsburgh | 21 |
| 17 | DETROIT | 24 |
| 23 | NEW YORK JETS | 6 |
| 28 | Buffalo | 17 |

| Use Name | Pos. | Hgt. | Wgt. | Age | Int | Pts |
|---|---|---|---|---|---|---|
| Irv Eatman | OT | 6'7" | 305 | 34 | | |
| Brad Hopkins | OT | 6'3" | 306 | 24 | | |
| Jim Reid | OT-OG | 6'6" | 306 | 24 | | |
| David Williams | OT | 6'5" | 292 | 29 | | |
| Kevin Donnalley | OG | 6'5" | 305 | 27 | | |
| Bruce Matthews | OG-C | 6'4" | 299 | 34 | | |
| Erik Norgard | OG-C | 6'1" | 282 | 29 | | |
| Hicham El-Mashtoub | C-OG | 6'2" | 288 | 23 | | |
| Mark Stepnoski | C | 6'2" | 269 | 28 | | |
| Anthony Cook | DE-DT | 6'3" | 293 | 23 | | 2 |
| Kenny Davidson | DE | 6'5" | 288 | 28 | 1 | |
| Henry Ford | DE | 6'3" | 284 | 23 | | |
| Kanavis McGhee | DE | 6'4" | 257 | 26 | | |
| Natu Tuatagaloa | DE-DT | 6'4" | 275 | 29 | | |
| Ray Childress | DT | 6'6" | 272 | 32 | | |
| Josh Evans | DT-DE | 6' | 280 | 22 | | |
| Glenn Montgomery | DT | 6' | 282 | 28 | | |
| Craig Veasey | DT-DE | 6'2" | 285 | 29 | | |
| Gary Walker | DT-DE | 6'2" | 285 | 22 | | |
| Micheal Barrow | LB | 6'1" | 236 | 25 | | |
| Joe Bowden | LB | 5'11" | 230 | 25 | | |
| Lemanski Hall | LB | 6' | 229 | 24 | | |
| Eddie Robinson | LB | 6'1" | 245 | 25 | 1 | 6 |
| Al Smith | LB | 6'1" | 244 | 30 | | |
| Baron Wortham | LB | 5'11" | 244 | 25 | | |
| Tomur Barnes | DB | 5'10" | 188 | 24 | 2 | |
| Blaine Bishop | DB | 5'8" | 197 | 25 | 1 | 6 |
| Chuck Cecil | DB | 6' | 185 | 30 | 3 | 6 |
| Cris Dishman | DB | 6' | 188 | 30 | 3 | |
| Odie Harris | DB | 6' | 190 | 29 | 2 | |
| Torey Hunter | DB | 5'9" | 176 | 23 | | |
| Steve Jackson | DB | 5'8" | 182 | 26 | 2 | |
| Darryll Lewis | DB | 5'9" | 183 | 26 | 6 | 6 |
| Marcus Robertson | DB | 5'11" | 197 | 25 | | |
| Chris Chandler | QB | 6'4" | 225 | 29 | | 14 |
| Will Furrer | QB | 6'3" | 210 | 27 | | |
| Steve McNair | QB | 6'2" | 224 | 22 | | |
| Gary Brown | HB | 5'11" | 233 | 26 | | |
| Marion Butts | HB-FB | 6'1" | 248 | 29 | | 24 |
| Dennis Lundy (to CHI) | HB | 5'9" | 190 | 23 | | |
| Todd McNair | HB | 6'1" | 202 | 29 | | 6 |
| Rodney Thomas | HB | 5'10" | 213 | 22 | | 44 |
| Steve Hendrickson (from PHIL) | FB | 6' | 250 | 29 | | |
| Mel Gray | WR | 5'9" | 171 | 34 | | |
| Travis Hannah | WR | 5'7" | 161 | 25 | | |
| Haywood Jeffires | WR | 6'2" | 201 | 30 | | 48 |
| Derek Russell | WR | 6' | 195 | 26 | | |
| Chris Sanders | WR | 6' | 184 | 23 | | 54 |
| Malcolm Seabron | WR | 6' | 194 | 22 | | 6 |
| Roderick Lewis | TE | 6'5" | 254 | 24 | | |
| John Henry Mills | TE | 6' | 222 | 25 | | |
| Michael Roan | TE | 6'3" | 251 | 23 | | |
| James Thornton | TE | 6'2" | 242 | 30 | | |
| Frank Wycheck | TE | 6'3" | 247 | 23 | | |
| Rich Camarillo | K | 5'11" | 202 | 35 | | |
| Al Del Greco | K | 5'10" | 200 | 33 | | 114 |

## CLEVELAND BROWNS 5-11 Bill Belichick

| Scores of Each Game | | |
|---|---|---|
| 14 | New England | 17 |
| 22 | TAMPA BAY | 6 |
| 14 | Houston | 7 |
| 35 | KANSAS CITY | 17 |
| 19 | BUFFALO | 22 |
| 20 | Detroit | 38 |
| 15 | JACKSONVILLE | 23 |
| 29 | Cincinnati | *26 |
| 10 | HOUSTON | 37 |
| 3 | Pittsburgh | 20 |
| 20 | GREEN BAY | 31 |
| 17 | PITTSBURGH | 20 |
| 13 | San Diego | 31 |
| 11 | Minnesota | 27 |
| 26 | CINCINNATI | 10 |
| 21 | Jacksonville | 24 |

| Use Name | Pos. | Hgt. | Wgt. | Age | Int | Pts |
|---|---|---|---|---|---|---|
| Herman Arvie | OT | 6'4" | 305 | 24 | | |
| Orlando Brown | OT | 6'7" | 340 | 24 | | |
| Jed Devries | OT | 6'6" | 282 | 24 | | |
| Tony Jones | OT | 6'5" | 295 | 29 | | |
| Bob Dahl | OG | 6'5" | 310 | 26 | | |
| Wally Williams | OG-C | 6'2" | 300 | 24 | | |
| Steve Everitt | C | 6'5" | 290 | 25 | | |
| Rob Burnett | DE | 6'4" | 280 | 28 | | |
| Mike Frederick | DE | 6'5" | 280 | 23 | | |
| Rich McKenzie | DE | 6'2" | 258 | 24 | | |
| Anthony Pleasant | DE | 6'5" | 280 | 27 | | |
| Dan Footmann | DT | 6'5" | 290 | 26 | | |
| Tim Goad | DT | 6'3" | 280 | 29 | | |
| Pio Sagapolutele | DT | 6'6" | 297 | 25 | | |
| Larry Webster | DT | 6'5" | 288 | 26 | | |
| Carl Banks | LB | 6'4" | 235 | 33 | | |
| Mike Caldwell | LB | 6'2" | 235 | 24 | 2 | 6 |
| Gerald Dixon | LB | 6'3" | 250 | 26 | 2 | 6 |
| Travis Hill | LB | 6'2" | 240 | 25 | | |
| Pepper Johnson | LB | 6'3" | 248 | 31 | 2 | |
| Craig Powell | LB | 6'4" | 230 | 23 | | |
| Frank Stams (from KC) | LB | 6'2" | 230 | 29 | | |
| Eddie Sutter | LB | 6'3" | 235 | 25 | | |
| Vashone Adams | DB | 5'10" | 196 | 21 | | |
| Isaac Booth | DB | 6'3" | 190 | 24 | 1 | |
| Donny Brady | DB | 6'2" | 195 | 21 | | |
| Michael Davis | DB | 6' | 195 | 23 | | |
| Don Griffin | DB | 6' | 176 | 31 | 1 | |
| Dana Hall | DB | 6'2" | 206 | 26 | 2 | |
| Tim Jacobs | DB | 5'10" | 185 | 25 | | |
| Antonio Langham | DB | 6' | 180 | 23 | 2 | |
| Stevon Moore | DB | 5'11" | 210 | 28 | 5 | |
| Louis Riddick | DB | 6'2" | 215 | 26 | | |
| Johnny Thomas | DB | 5'9" | 191 | 31 | | |
| Bennie Thompson | DB | 6' | 214 | 32 | | |
| Eric Turner | DB | 6'1" | 207 | 26 | | |
| Vinny Testaverde | QB | 6'5" | 227 | 31 | | |
| Eric Zeier | QB | 6' | 205 | 22 | | 2 |
| Earnest Byner | HB | 5'10" | 215 | 32 | | 24 |
| Earnest Hunter | HB | 5'8" | 201 | 24 | | |
| Ricky Powers | HB | 6' | 213 | 24 | | |
| Lorenzo White | HB | 5'11" | 222 | 29 | | 6 |
| Leroy Hoard | FB-HB | 5'11" | 225 | 27 | | |
| Tommy Vardell | FB | 6'2" | 230 | 26 | | |
| Derrick Alexander | WR | 6'2" | 195 | 23 | | 6 |
| Michael Bates | WR | 5'10" | 189 | 25 | | |
| Michael Jackson | WR | 6'4" | 195 | 26 | | 54 |
| Keenan McCardell | WR | 6'1" | 175 | 25 | | 24 |
| Andre Rison | WR | 6'1" | 188 | 28 | | 18 |
| Rico Smith | WR | 6' | 185 | 26 | | 6 |
| Harold Bishop | TE | 6'4" | 250 | 25 | | |
| Frank Hartley | TE | 6'2" | 268 | 27 | | 6 |
| Brian Kinchen | TE | 6'2" | 240 | 30 | | |
| Walter Reeves | TE | 6'4" | 270 | 29 | | 6 |
| Matt Stover | K | 5'11" | 178 | 27 | | 113 |
| Tom Tupa | K | 6'4" | 230 | 29 | | |

Rick Lyle — Back Injury

## JACKSONVILLE JAGUARS 4-12 Tom Coughlin

| Scores of Each Game | | |
|---|---|---|
| 3 | HOUSTON | 10 |
| 17 | Cincinnati | 24 |
| 10 | New York Jets | 27 |
| 14 | GREEN BAY | 24 |
| 17 | Houston | 16 |
| 20 | PITTSBURGH | 16 |
| 27 | CHICAGO | 30 |
| 23 | Cleveland | 15 |
| 7 | Pittsburgh | 24 |
| 30 | SEATTLE | 47 |
| 16 | Tampa Bay | 17 |
| 13 | CINCINNATI | 17 |
| 23 | Denver | 31 |
| 31 | INDIANAPOLIS | 41 |
| 0 | Detroit | 44 |
| 24 | CLEVELAND | 21 |

| Use Name | Pos. | Hgt. | Wgt. | Age | Int | Pts |
|---|---|---|---|---|---|---|
| Tony Boselli | OT | 6-7 | 323 | 23 | | |
| Brian DeMarco | OT | 6'7" | 321 | 23 | | |
| Jeff Novak | OT-OG | 6'5" | 296 | 28 | | |
| Bruce Wilkerson | OT | 6'5" | 295 | 31 | | |
| Shawn Bouwens | OG | 6'5" | 293 | 27 | | |
| Eugene Chung | OG-OT | 6'5" | 311 | 26 | | |
| Ben Coleman (from ARZ) | OG-OT | 6'5" | 315 | 24 | | |
| Greg Huntington | OG | 6'4" | 293 | 24 | | |
| Tom Myslinski | OG | 6'3" | 287 | 26 | | |
| dave Widell | C | 6'7" | 308 | 30 | | |
| Paul Frase | DE-DT | 6'5" | 276 | 30 | | |
| Jeff Lageman | DE | 6'6" | 268 | 28 | | |
| Ernie Logan | DE | 6'3" | 283 | 27 | | |
| Bronzell Miller | DE | 6'4" | 245 | 23 | | |
| Joel Smeenge | DE-LB | 6'6" | 260 | 27 | 1 | |
| Don Davey | DT-DE | 6'4" | 275 | 27 | | |
| Ray Hall | DT | 6'4" | 294 | 24 | | |
| Corey Mayfield | DT | 6'3" | 302 | 25 | | |
| Kelvin Pritchett | DT | 6'3" | 290 | 25 | | |
| Mike Thompson | DT | 6'3" | 279 | 22 | | |
| Brant Boyer | LB | 6'1" | 235 | 24 | | |
| Bernard Carter | LB | 6'3" | 238 | 24 | | |
| Reggie Clark | LB | 6'3" | 245 | 27 | | |
| Keith Goganious | LB | 6'3" | 244 | 26 | 2 | |
| Tom McManus | LB | 6'2" | 252 | 25 | | |
| Bryan Schwartz | LB | 6'4" | 250 | 23 | | |
| Santo Stephens | LB | 6'4" | 244 | 26 | | |
| James Williams | LB | 6' | 243 | 26 | 2 | |
| Mark Williams | LB | 6'3" | 243 | 24 | | |
| Deral Boykin | DB | 5'11" | 198 | 24 | | |
| Darren Carrington | DB | 6'2" | 204 | 29 | 1 | |
| Vinnie Clark | DB | 6' | 204 | 26 | 1 | |
| Harry Colon | DB | 6' | 203 | 26 | 3 | |
| Travis Davis | DB | 6' | 200 | 22 | | |
| Mike Dumas | DB | 5'11" | 198 | 26 | 1 | |
| Rogerick Green | DB | 5'11" | 187 | 25 | | |
| Monty Grow | DB | 6'4" | 214 | 23 | 1 | |
| Chris Hudson | DB | 5'10" | 203 | 23 | | |
| Tommy Johnson | DB | 5'10" | 183 | 23 | | |
| Darren Studstill | DB | 6'1" | 186 | 25 | | |
| Dave Thomas | DB | 6'3" | 213 | 27 | | |
| Mickey Washington | DB | 5'10" | 191 | 27 | 1 | 6 |
| Steve Beuerlein | QB | 6'3" | 220 | 30 | | |
| Mark Brunell | QB | 6' | 217 | 24 | | 24 |
| Rob Johnson | QB | 6'3" | 222 | 22 | | |
| Reggie Cobb | HB | 6'1" | 221 | 27 | | |
| Vaughn Dunbar | HB | 5'10" | 204 | 26 | | 12 |
| Randy Jordan | HB | 5'10" | 216 | 25 | | 6 |
| James Stewart | HB | 6'1" | 221 | 23 | | 18 |
| Ryan Christopherson | FB | 5'11" | 237 | 23 | | 6 |
| Le'Shai Maston | FB | 6' | 229 | 24 | | |
| Ernest Givins | WR | 5'10" | 181 | 30 | | 18 |
| Desmond Howard | WR | 5'10" | 180 | 25 | | 6 |
| Willie Jackson | WR | 6'1" | 203 | 24 | | 32 |
| Curtis Marsh | WR | 6'2" | 201 | 24 | | |
| Jimmy Smith | WR | 6'1" | 207 | 26 | | 30 |
| Cedric Tillman | WR | 6'2" | 219 | 25 | | 18 |
| Rich Griffith | TE | 6'5" | 256 | 26 | | |
| Craig Keith | TE | 6'3" | 262 | 24 | | |
| Gordon Laro | TE | 6'3" | 253 | 23 | | |
| Pete Mitchell | TE | 6'2" | 243 | 23 | | 12 |
| Bryan Barker | K | 6'2" | 189 | 31 | | |
| Mike Hollis | K | 5'8" | 180 | 23 | | 87 |

Al Jackson — Knee Injury

Derek Brown — Broken Rib

## PITTSBURGH STEELERS

### RUSHING

| Last Name | No. | Yds | Avg | TD |
|---|---|---|---|---|
| Pegram | 213 | 813 | 3.8 | 5 |
| Morris | 148 | 559 | 3.8 | 9 |
| McAfee | 39 | 156 | 4.0 | 1 |
| J. Williams | 29 | 110 | 3.8 | 0 |
| Stewart | 15 | 86 | 5.7 | 1 |
| O'Donnell | 24 | 45 | 1.9 | 0 |
| Mills | 5 | 39 | 7.8 | 0 |
| Tomczak | 11 | 25 | 2.3 | 0 |
| Hastings | 1 | 14 | 14.0 | 0 |
| Lester | 5 | 9 | 1.8 | 1 |
| Avery | 1 | 3 | 3.0 | 0 |
| Miller | 1 | 2 | 2.0 | 0 |
| Thigpen | 1 | 1 | 1.0 | 0 |
| C. Johnson | 1 | -10 | -10.0 | 0 |

### RECEIVING

| Last Name | No. | Yds | Avg | TD |
|---|---|---|---|---|
| Thigpen | 85 | 1307 | 15.4 | 5 |
| Hastings | 48 | 502 | 10.5 | 1 |
| Mills | 39 | 679 | 17.4 | 8 |
| C. Johnson | 38 | 432 | 11.4 | 0 |
| Bruener | 26 | 238 | 9.2 | 3 |
| Pegram | 26 | 206 | 7.9 | 1 |
| J. Williams | 24 | 127 | 5.3 | 1 |
| McAfee | 15 | 88 | 5.9 | 0 |
| Stewart | 14 | 235 | 16.8 | 1 |
| Hayes | 11 | 113 | 10.3 | 0 |
| Avery | 11 | 82 | 7.5 | 1 |
| Morris | 8 | 36 | 4.5 | 0 |
| Barnes | 3 | 48 | 16.0 | 0 |

### PUNT RETURNS

| Last Name | No. | Yds | Avg | TD |
|---|---|---|---|---|
| Hastings | 48 | 474 | 9.9 | 1 |

### KICKOFF RETURNS

| Last Name | No. | Yds | Avg | TD |
|---|---|---|---|---|
| Mills | 54 | 1306 | 24.2 | 0 |
| McAfee | 5 | 56 | 11.2 | 0 |
| Pegram | 4 | 85 | 21.3 | 0 |
| Bruener | 2 | 19 | 9.5 | 0 |
| C. Johnson | 2 | 47 | 23.5 | 0 |
| Gibson | 1 | 10 | 10.0 | 0 |
| T. Greene | 1 | 7 | 7.0 | 0 |

### PASSING — PUNTING — KICKING

| PASSING | Att | Cmp | % | Yds | Yd/Att | TD | Int— | % | RK |
|---|---|---|---|---|---|---|---|---|---|
| O'Donnell | 416 | 246 | 59.1 | 2970 | 7.14 | 17 | 7— | 1.7 | |
| Tomczak | 113 | 65 | 57.5 | 666 | 5.89 | 1 | 9— | 8.0 | |
| Miller | 56 | 32 | 57.1 | 397 | 7.09 | 2 | 5— | 8.9 | |
| Stewart | 7 | 5 | 71.4 | 60 | 8.57 | 1 | 0— | 0.0 | |

| PUNTING | No. | Avg. |
|---|---|---|
| Stark | 59 | 40.1 |

| KICKING | XP | ATT | % | FG | ATT | % |
|---|---|---|---|---|---|---|
| N. Johnson | 39 | 39 | 100 | 34 | 41 | 83 |

**2 POINT XP**
Pegram (1)

## CINCINNATI BENGALS

### RUSHING

| Last Name | No. | Yds | Avg | TD |
|---|---|---|---|---|
| Green | 171 | 661 | 3.9 | 2 |
| Bieniemy | 98 | 381 | 3.9 | 3 |
| Blake | 53 | 309 | 5.8 | 2 |
| Cothran | 16 | 62 | 3.9 | 0 |
| Joseph | 16 | 40 | 2.5 | 0 |
| Scott | 5 | 11 | 2.2 | 0 |
| Pickens | 1 | 6 | 6.0 | 0 |
| Burns | 1 | 1 | 1.0 | 0 |
| Hill | 1 | -3 | -3.0 | 0 |
| Dunn | 1 | -13 | -13.0 | 0 |
| Johnson | 1 | -16 | -16.0 | 0 |

### RECEIVING

| Last Name | No. | Yds | Avg | TD |
|---|---|---|---|---|
| Pickens | 99 | 1234 | 12.5 | 17 |
| To. McGee | 55 | 754 | 13.7 | 4 |
| Scott | 52 | 821 | 15.8 | 5 |
| Bieniemy | 43 | 424 | 9.9 | 0 |
| Green | 27 | 182 | 6.7 | 1 |
| Joseph | 20 | 118 | 5.9 | 0 |
| Dunn | 17 | 209 | 12.3 | 1 |
| Cothran | 8 | 44 | 5.5 | 0 |
| Sadowski | 5 | 37 | 7.4 | 0 |
| Hill | 4 | 44 | 11.0 | 0 |
| Ware | 2 | 36 | 18.0 | 0 |
| Tuten | 2 | 12 | 6.0 | 1 |

### PUNT RETURNS

| Last Name | No. | Yds | Avg | TD |
|---|---|---|---|---|
| Sawyer | 9 | 58 | 6.4 | 0 |
| Bieniemy | 7 | 47 | 6.7 | 0 |
| Pickens | 5 | -2 | -0.4 | 0 |

### KICKOFF RETURNS

| Last Name | No. | Yds | Avg | TD |
|---|---|---|---|---|
| Dunn | 50 | 1092 | 21.8 | 0 |
| Hill | 17 | 454 | 26.7 | 0 |
| Bieniemy | 8 | 168 | 21.0 | 0 |
| Sawyer | 2 | 50 | 25.0 | 0 |
| Joseph | 1 | 17 | 17.0 | 0 |
| Von Oelhoffen | 1 | 10 | 10.0 | 0 |
| A. Collins | 1 | -3 | -3.0 | 0 |

### PASSING — PUNTING — KICKING

| PASSING | Att | Cmp | % | Yds | Yd/Att | TD | Int— | % | RK |
|---|---|---|---|---|---|---|---|---|---|
| Blake | 567 | 326 | 57.5 | 3822 | 6.74 | 28 | 17— | 3.0 | |
| Klingler | 15 | 7 | 46.7 | 88 | 5.87 | 1 | 1— | 6.7 | |
| Bieniemy | 2 | 0 | 0.0 | 0 | 0.00 | 0 | 0— | 0.0 | |
| Johnson | 1 | 1 | 100.0 | 5 | 5.00 | 0 | 0— | 0.0 | |
| Dunn | 1 | 0 | 0.0 | 0 | 0.00 | 0 | 0— | 0.0 | |

| PUNTING | No. | Avg. |
|---|---|---|
| Johnson | 68 | 42.1 |
| Pelfrey | 2 | 26.0 |

| KICKING | XP | ATT | % | FG | ATT | % |
|---|---|---|---|---|---|---|
| Pelfrey | 34 | 34 | 100 | 29 | 36 | 81 |

**2 POINT XP**
Blake (1)

## HOUSTON OILERS

### RUSHING

| Last Name | No. | Yds | Avg | TD |
|---|---|---|---|---|
| Thomas | 251 | 947 | 3.8 | 5 |
| Brown | 86 | 293 | 3.4 | 0 |
| Butts | 71 | 185 | 2.6 | 4 |
| T. McNair | 19 | 136 | 7.2 | 0 |
| Chandler | 28 | 58 | 2.1 | 2 |
| S. McNair | 11 | 38 | 3.5 | 0 |
| Furrer | 8 | 20 | 2.5 | 0 |
| Hannah | 1 | 5 | 5.0 | 0 |
| Wycheck | 1 | 1 | 1.0 | 0 |
| Sanders | 2 | -19 | -9.5 | 0 |

### RECEIVING

| Last Name | No. | Yds | Avg | TD |
|---|---|---|---|---|
| Jeffires | 61 | 684 | 11.2 | 8 |
| T. McNair | 60 | 501 | 8.4 | 1 |
| Wycheck | 40 | 471 | 11.8 | 1 |
| R. Thomas | 39 | 204 | 5.2 | 2 |
| Sanders | 35 | 823 | 23.5 | 9 |
| Russell | 24 | 321 | 13.4 | 0 |
| R. Lewis | 16 | 116 | 7.3 | 0 |
| Seabron | 12 | 167 | 13.9 | 1 |
| Hannah | 10 | 142 | 14.2 | 0 |
| Roan | 8 | 46 | 5.8 | 0 |
| Brown | 6 | 16 | 2.7 | 0 |
| Butts | 2 | 10 | 5.0 | 0 |
| Lundy | 1 | 11 | 11.0 | 0 |

### PUNT RETURNS

| Last Name | No. | Yds | Avg | TD |
|---|---|---|---|---|
| Gray | 30 | 303 | 10.1 | 0 |
| Hannah | 5 | 36 | 7.2 | 0 |

### KICKOFF RETURNS

| Last Name | No. | Yds | Avg | TD |
|---|---|---|---|---|
| Gray | 53 | 1183 | 22.3 | 0 |
| Lundy | 5 | 67 | 13.4 | 0 |
| R. Thomas | 3 | 48 | 16.0 | 0 |
| Butts | 2 | 14 | 7.0 | 0 |
| Bowden | 1 | 6 | 6.0 | 0 |
| R. Lewis | 1 | 5 | 5.0 | 0 |
| Barnes | 1 | -4 | -4.0 | 0 |
| Worthan | 1 | -3 | -3.0 | 0 |

### PASSING — PUNTING — KICKING

| PASSING | Att | Cmp | % | Yds | Yd/Att | TD | Int— | % | RK |
|---|---|---|---|---|---|---|---|---|---|
| Chandler | 356 | 225 | 63.2 | 2460 | 6.91 | 17 | 10— | 2.8 | |
| Furrer | 99 | 48 | 48.5 | 483 | 4.88 | 2 | 7— | 7.1 | |
| McNair | 80 | 41 | 51.3 | 569 | 7.11 | 3 | 1— | 1.3 | |
| Camarillo | 1 | 0 | 0.0 | 0 | 0.00 | 0 | 0— | 0.0 | |

| PUNTING | No. | Avg. |
|---|---|---|
| Camarillo | 78 | 40.6 |
| Del Greco | 1 | 15.0 |

| KICKING | XP | ATT | % | FG | ATT | % |
|---|---|---|---|---|---|---|
| Del Greco | 33 | 33 | 100 | 27 | 31 | 87 |

**2 POINT XP**
Chandler (1)
R. Thomas (1)

## CLEVELAND BROWNS

### RUSHING

| Last Name | No. | Yds | Avg | TD |
|---|---|---|---|---|
| Hoard | 136 | 547 | 4.0 | 0 |
| Byner | 115 | 432 | 3.8 | 2 |
| White | 62 | 163 | 2.6 | 1 |
| Hunter | 30 | 100 | 3.3 | 0 |
| Zeier | 15 | 80 | 5.3 | 0 |
| Testaverde | 18 | 62 | 3.4 | 2 |
| Powers | 14 | 51 | 3.6 | 0 |
| Alexander | 1 | 29 | 29.0 | 0 |
| Tupa | 1 | 9 | 9.0 | 0 |
| Vardell | 4 | 9 | 2.3 | 0 |
| Rison | 2 | 0 | 0.0 | 0 |

### RECEIVING

| Last Name | No. | Yds | Avg | TD |
|---|---|---|---|---|
| Byner | 61 | 494 | 8.1 | 2 |
| McCardell | 56 | 709 | 12.7 | 4 |
| Rison | 47 | 701 | 14.9 | 3 |
| Jackson | 44 | 714 | 16.2 | 9 |
| Kinchen | 20 | 216 | 10.8 | 0 |
| Bishop | 16 | 135 | 8.4 | 0 |
| Alexander | 15 | 216 | 14.4 | 0 |
| Smith | 13 | 173 | 13.3 | 1 |
| Hoard | 13 | 103 | 7.9 | 0 |
| Hartley | 11 | 137 | 12.5 | 1 |
| White | 8 | 64 | 8.0 | 0 |
| Vardell | 6 | 18 | 3.0 | 0 |
| Reeves | 6 | 12 | 2.0 | 0 |
| Hunter | 5 | 42 | 8.4 | 0 |
| Riddick | 1 | 25 | 25.0 | 0 |
| Testaverde | 1 | 7 | 7.0 | 0 |
| Powers | 1 | 6 | 6.0 | 0 |

### PUNT RETURNS

| Last Name | No. | Yds | Avg | TD |
|---|---|---|---|---|
| McCardell | 13 | 93 | 7.2 | 0 |
| Alexander | 9 | 122 | 13.6 | 1 |
| Hunter | 3 | 40 | 13.3 | 0 |

### KICKOFF RETURNS

| Last Name | No. | Yds | Avg | TD |
|---|---|---|---|---|
| Hunter | 23 | 508 | 22.1 | 0 |
| Alexander | 21 | 419 | 20.0 | 0 |
| Bates | 9 | 176 | 19.6 | 0 |
| McCardell | 9 | 161 | 17.9 | 0 |
| Byner | 5 | 98 | 19.6 | 0 |
| Powers | 3 | 54 | 18.0 | 0 |
| Frederick | 2 | 16 | 8.0 | 0 |
| Hoard | 1 | 13 | 13.0 | 0 |
| Dixon | 1 | 10 | 10.0 | 0 |

### PASSING — PUNTING — KICKING

| PASSING | Att | Cmp | % | Yds | Yd/Att | TD | Int— | % | RK |
|---|---|---|---|---|---|---|---|---|---|
| Testaverde | 392 | 241 | 61.5 | 2883 | 7.35 | 17 | 10— | 2.6 | |
| Zeier | 161 | 82 | 50.9 | 864 | 5.37 | 4 | 9— | 5.6 | |
| Tupa | 1 | 1 | 100.0 | 25 | 25.00 | 0 | 0— | 0.0 | |
| Jackson | 1 | 0 | 0 | 0 | 0.00 | 0 | 1—100.0 | | |

| PUNTING | No. | Avg. |
|---|---|---|
| Tupa | 65 | 43.6 |

| KICKING | XP | ATT | % | FG | ATT | % |
|---|---|---|---|---|---|---|
| Stover | 26 | 26 | 100 | 29 | 33 | 88 |

**2 POINT XP**
Zeier (1)

## JACKSONVILLE JAGUARS

### RUSHING

| Last Name | No. | Yds | Avg | TD |
|---|---|---|---|---|
| Stewart | 137 | 525 | 3.8 | 2 |
| Brunell | 67 | 480 | 7.2 | 4 |
| Dunbar | 110 | 361 | 3.3 | 4 |
| Maston | 41 | 186 | 4.5 | 0 |
| Jordan | 21 | 62 | 3.0 | 0 |
| Beuerlein | 5 | 32 | 6.4 | 0 |
| Cobb | 9 | 18 | 2.0 | 0 |
| R. Johnson | 3 | 17 | 5.7 | 0 |
| Christopherson | 16 | 16 | 1.0 | 1 |
| Howard | 1 | 8 | 8.0 | 0 |

### RECEIVING

| Last Name | No. | Yds | Avg | TD |
|---|---|---|---|---|
| W. Jackson | 53 | 589 | 11.1 | 5 |
| Mitchell | 41 | 527 | 12.9 | 2 |
| Tillman | 30 | 368 | 12.3 | 3 |
| Givins | 29 | 280 | 9.7 | 3 |
| Howard | 26 | 276 | 10.6 | 1 |
| Smith | 22 | 288 | 13.1 | 3 |
| Stewart | 21 | 190 | 9.0 | 1 |
| Maston | 18 | 131 | 7.3 | 0 |
| Griffith | 16 | 243 | 15.2 | 0 |
| Marsh | 7 | 127 | 18.1 | 0 |
| Jordan | 5 | 89 | 17.8 | 1 |
| Keith | 3 | 20 | 6.7 | 0 |
| Dunbar | 2 | 11 | 5.5 | 0 |
| Laro | 1 | 6 | 6.0 | 0 |
| Christopherson | 1 | -1 | -1.0 | 0 |

### PUNT RETURNS

| Last Name | No. | Yds | Avg | TD |
|---|---|---|---|---|
| Howard | 24 | 246 | 10.3 | 0 |
| Tillman | 2 | 6 | 3.0 | 0 |
| Givins | 2 | -7 | -3.5 | 0 |
| W. Jackson | 1 | -2 | -2.0 | 0 |

### KICKOFF RETURNS

| Last Name | No. | Yds | Avg | TD |
|---|---|---|---|---|
| Smith | 24 | 540 | 22.5 | 1 |
| W. Jackson | 19 | 404 | 21.3 | 0 |
| Marsh | 15 | 323 | 21.5 | 0 |
| Howard | 10 | 178 | 17.8 | 0 |
| Dunbar | 2 | 32 | 16.0 | 0 |
| Jordan | 2 | 41 | 20.5 | 0 |
| Griffith | 1 | 9 | 9.0 | 0 |
| Maston | 1 | 5 | 5.0 | 0 |

### PASSING — PUNTING — KICKING

| PASSING | Att | Cmp | % | Yds | Yd/Att | TD | Int— | % | RK |
|---|---|---|---|---|---|---|---|---|---|
| Brunell | 346 | 201 | 58.1 | 2168 | 6.27 | 15 | 7— | 2.0 | |
| Beuerlein | 142 | 71 | 50.0 | 952 | 6.70 | 4 | 7— | 4.9 | |
| R. Johnson | 7 | 3 | 42.9 | 24 | 3.43 | 0 | 1—14.3 | | |

| PUNTING | No. | Avg. |
|---|---|---|
| Barker | 82 | 43.8 |

| KICKING | XP | ATT | % | FG | ATT | % |
|---|---|---|---|---|---|---|
| Hollis | 27 | 28 | 96 | 20 | 27 | 74 |

**2 POINT XP**
Jackson (1)

## KANSAS CITY CHIEFS 13-3 Marty Schottenheimer

| Scores of Each Game | | |
|---|---|---|
| 34 | Seattle | 10 |
| 20 | NEW YORK GIANTS | *17 |
| 23 | OAKLAND | *17 |
| 17 | Cleveland | 35 |
| 24 | Arizona | 3 |
| 29 | SAN DIEGO | *23 |
| 31 | NEW ENGLAND | 26 |
| 21 | Denver | 7 |
| 24 | WASHINGTON | 3 |
| 22 | San Diego | 7 |
| 20 | HOUSTON | 13 |
| 12 | Dallas | 24 |
| 29 | Oakland | 23 |
| 6 | Miami | 13 |
| 20 | DENVER | 17 |
| 26 | SEATTLE | 3 |

| Use Name | Pos. | Hgt. | Wgt. | Age | Int | Pts |
|---|---|---|---|---|---|---|
| John Alt | OT | 6'7" | 307 | 33 | | |
| Jeff Criswell | OT | 6'7" | 294 | 31 | | |
| Trezelle Jenkins | OT | 6'7" | 294 | 22 | | |
| Ricky Siglar | OT | 6'7" | 316 | 29 | | |
| Will Shields | OG | 6'2" | 308 | 23 | | |
| Dave Szott | OG | 6'4" | 290 | 27 | | |
| Danny Villa | OG | 6'5" | 308 | 30 | | |
| Tim Grunhard | C | 6'2" | 299 | 27 | | |
| Joe Valerio | C-OT | 6'5" | 295 | 26 | | 6 |
| Vaughn Booker | DE | 6'5" | 293 | 27 | | 6 |
| Pellom McDaniels | DE | 6'3" | 292 | 27 | | |
| Darren Mickell | DE | 6'4" | 291 | 25 | | |
| Brian Proby | DE | 6'5" | 285 | 23 | | |
| Neil Smith | DE | 6'4" | 273 | 29 | | |
| Joe Phillips | DT | 6'5" | 310 | 32 | 1 | |
| Dan Saleaumua | DT | 6' | 315 | 30 | 1 | |
| Keith Traylor | DT | 6'2" | 295 | 25 | | |
| Anthony Davis | LB | 6' | 231 | 26 | 1 | |
| George Jamison | LB | 6'1" | 235 | 32 | | |
| Greg Manusky | LB | 6'1" | 243 | 29 | | |
| Tracy Rogers | LB | 6'2" | 244 | 28 | | |
| Tracy Simien | LB | 6'1" | 255 | 28 | | |
| Derrick Thomas | LB-DE | 6'3" | 247 | 28 | | |
| Darren Anderson | DB | 5'10" | 187 | 26 | | |
| Martin Bayless | DB | 6'2" | 219 | 32 | | |
| Dale Carter | DB | 6'1" | 188 | 25 | 4 | |
| Perry Carter | DB | 5'11" | 206 | 24 | | |
| Mark Collins | DB | 5'10" | 196 | 31 | 1 | 6 |
| James Hasty | DB | 6' | 207 | 30 | 3 | 6 |
| Doug Terry | DB | 5'11" | 204 | 25 | | |
| Brian Washington | DB | 6'1" | 210 | 29 | 3 | 6 |
| Tim Watson (to NYG) | DB | 6'1" | 215 | 25 | | |
| William White | DB | 5'10" | 205 | 29 | 2 | |
| Matt Blundin | QB | 6'6" | 233 | 26 | | |
| Steve Bono | QB | 6'4" | 215 | 33 | | 30 |
| Rich Gannon | QB | 6'3" | 205 | 29 | | 6 |
| Marcus Allen | HB | 6'2" | 210 | 35 | | 30 |
| Greg Hill | HB | 5'11" | 207 | 23 | | 6 |
| Leroy Thompson | HB | 5'11" | 217 | 27 | | |
| Kimble Anders | FB | 5'11" | 230 | 28 | | 18 |
| Donnell Bennett | FB | 6' | 241 | 22 | | |
| Tony Richardson | FB | 6'1" | 232 | 23 | | |
| Willie Davis | WR | 6' | 181 | 27 | | 30 |
| Lake Dawson | WR | 6'1" | 207 | 23 | | 30 |
| Danan Hughes | WR | 6'1" | 211 | 24 | | 6 |
| Chris Penn | WR | 6' | 198 | 24 | | |
| Webster Slaughter | WR | 6'1" | 175 | 30 | | 24 |
| Tamarick Vanover | WR | 5'11" | 213 | 21 | | 30 |
| Keith Cash | TE | 6'4" | 242 | 26 | | 6 |
| Derrick Walker | TE | 6' | 249 | 28 | | 6 |
| Louie Aguiar | K | 6'2" | 219 | 29 | | |
| Lin Elliott | K | 6' | 182 | 26 | | 106 |

Jaime Fields — Leg Injury
Jay Taylor — Achilles Injury

## SAN DIEGO CHARGERS 9-7 Bobby Ross

| Scores of Each Game | | |
|---|---|---|
| 7 | Oakland | 17 |
| 14 | SEATTLE | 10 |
| 27 | Philadelphia | 21 |
| 17 | DENVER | 6 |
| 16 | Pittsburgh | 31 |
| 23 | Kansas City | *29 |
| 9 | DALLAS | 23 |
| 35 | Seattle | 25 |
| 14 | MIAMI | 24 |
| 7 | KANSAS CITY | 22 |
| 27 | Denver | 30 |
| 12 | OAKLAND | 6 |
| 31 | CLEVELAND | 13 |
| 28 | ARIZONA | 25 |
| 27 | Indianapolis | 24 |
| 27 | New York Giants | 17 |

| Use Name | Pos. | Hgt. | Wgt. | Age | Int | Pts |
|---|---|---|---|---|---|---|
| Tony Berti | OT | 6'5" | 287 | 23 | | |
| Stan Brock | OT | 6'6" | 295 | 37 | | |
| Vaughn Parker | OT-OG | 6'3" | 296 | 24 | | |
| Harry Swayne | OT | 6'5" | 295 | 30 | | |
| Joe Cocozzo | OG | 6'4" | 300 | 25 | | |
| Isaac Davis | OG | 6'3" | 320 | 23 | | |
| Eric Moten | OG | 6'2" | 306 | 27 | | |
| David Binn | C | 6'3" | 240 | 23 | | |
| Greg Engel | C | 6'3" | 285 | 24 | | |
| Courtney Hall | C | 6'2" | 281 | 27 | | |
| Raylee Johnson | DE-DT | 6'3" | 265 | 25 | | |
| Chris Mims | DE | 6'5" | 290 | 24 | | |
| Leslie O'Neal | DE | 6'4" | 265 | 31 | | |
| Sebastian Barrie | DT | 6'2" | 280 | 25 | | |
| Reuben Davis | DT | 6'5" | 320 | 30 | | 2 |
| Shawn Lee | DT | 6'2" | 300 | 28 | | |
| John Parrella | DT | 6'3" | 290 | 25 | | |
| Don Sasa | DT | 6'3" | 286 | 22 | | |
| David Brandon | LB | 6'4" | 230 | 30 | | |
| Lewis Bush | LB | 6'2" | 245 | 25 | 1 | |
| Dennis Gibson | LB | 6'2" | 240 | 31 | | |
| Dwayne Gordon | LB | 6'1" | 240 | 25 | | |
| Junior Seau | LB | 6'3" | 250 | 26 | 2 | 6 |
| Glen Young | LB | 6'3" | 235 | 26 | | |
| Eric Castle | DB | 6'3" | 212 | 25 | | |
| Willie Clark | DB | 5'10" | 186 | 23 | 2 | |
| Shaun Gayle | DB | 5'11" | 202 | 33 | 2 | 12 |
| Dwayne Harper | DB | 5'11" | 175 | 29 | 4 | |
| Rodney Harrison | DB | 6' | 201 | 22 | 5 | |
| David Hendrix | DB | 6'1" | 213 | 23 | | |
| A.J. Johnson | DB | 5'8" | 175 | 28 | | |
| Mark Montreuil | DB | 6'2" | 200 | 23 | | |
| Bo Orlando | DB | 5'10" | 180 | 29 | | |
| Terrance Shaw | DB | 5'11" | 190 | 21 | 1 | |
| Gale Gilbert | QB | 6'3" | 209 | 33 | | |
| Stan Humphries | QB | 6'2" | 223 | 30 | | 6 |
| Rodney Culver | HB | 5'9" | 224 | 25 | | 18 |
| Terrell Fletcher | HB | 5'8" | 196 | 21 | | 6 |
| Ronnie Harmon | HB | 5'11" | 207 | 31 | | 36 |
| Aaron Hayden | HB-FB | 6 | 218 | 22 | | 18 |
| Natrone Means | HB-FB | 5'10" | 245 | 23 | | 30 |
| Andre Coleman | WR | 5'9" | 165 | 24 | | 18 |
| 'OMar Ellison | WR | 6'1" | 200 | 23 | | |
| Shawn Jefferson | WR | 5'11" | 180 | 26 | | 12 |
| Tony Martin | WR | 6' | 181 | 29 | | 36 |
| Mark Seay | WR | 6' | 175 | 28 | | 20 |
| Deems May | TE | 6'4" | 263 | 26 | | |
| Ron Middleton | TE | 6'2" | 262 | 30 | | |
| Shannon Mitchell | TE | 6'2" | 245 | 23 | | 6 |
| Alfred Pupunu | TE | 6'2" | 265 | 25 | | |
| Duane Young | TE | 6'1" | 270 | 27 | | |
| Darren Bennett | K | 6'5" | 235 | 30 | | |
| John Carney | K | 5'11" | 170 | 31 | | 95 |

## DENVER BRONCOS 8-8 Mike Shanahan

| Scores of Each Game | | |
|---|---|---|
| 22 | BUFFALO | 7 |
| 21 | Dallas | 31 |
| 38 | WASHINGTON | 31 |
| 6 | San Diego | 17 |
| 10 | Seattle | 27 |
| 37 | New England | 3 |
| 29 | OAKLAND | 0 |
| 7 | KANSAS CITY | 21 |
| 38 | ARIZONA | 6 |
| 13 | Philadelphia | 31 |
| 30 | SAN DIEGO | 27 |
| 33 | Houston | 42 |
| 31 | JACKSONVILLE | 23 |
| 27 | SEATTLE | 31 |
| 17 | Kansas City | 20 |
| 31 | Oakland | 28 |

| Use Name | Pos. | Hgt. | Wgt. | Age | Int | Pts |
|---|---|---|---|---|---|---|
| Jamie Brown | OT | 6'8" | 320 | 23 | | |
| Mike Lodish | OT | 6'3" | 280 | 28 | | |
| Reggie McElroy | OT | 6'6" | 290 | 35 | | |
| Bill Schultz | OT | 6'5" | 305 | 28 | | |
| Broderick Thompson | OT | 6'5" | 295 | 35 | | |
| Gary Zimmerman | OT | 6'6" | 294 | 33 | | |
| Brian Habib | OG | 6'7" | 299 | 30 | | |
| Mark Schlereth | OG | 6'3" | 278 | 29 | | |
| Ralph Tamm | OG | 6'4" | 280 | 29 | | |
| Tom Nalen | C | 6'2" | 280 | 24 | | |
| Shane Dronett | DE-DT | 6'6" | 275 | 24 | | |
| Simon Fletcher | DE | 6'5" | 240 | 33 | | |
| Harald Hasselbach | DE | 6'6" | 280 | 27 | | |
| Willie Oshodin | DE | 6'4" | 260 | 25 | | |
| Jeff Robinson | DE | 6'4" | 265 | 25 | | |
| Dan Williams | DE | 6'4" | 290 | 25 | | |
| Troy Wilson | DE | 6'4" | 250 | 24 | | |
| James Jones | DT | 6'2" | 290 | 26 | | |
| Michael Dean Perry | DT | 6'1" | 285 | 30 | | |
| Maa Tanuvasa | DT | 6'2" | 277 | 24 | | |
| Allen Aldridge | LB | 6'1" | 245 | 23 | | |
| Elijah Alexander | LB | 6'2" | 230 | 25 | 2 | |
| Ken Brown | LB | 6'1" | 235 | 24 | | |
| Keith Burns | LB | 6'2" | 245 | 23 | | |
| Glenn Cadrez (from NYJ) | LB | 6'3" | 245 | 25 | | |
| Dave Garnett | LB | 6'2" | 219 | 24 | | |
| Britt Hager | LB | 6'1" | 225 | 29 | 1 | |
| Ray Jacobs | LB | 6'2" | 244 | 23 | | |
| Dante Jones | LB | 6'2" | 235 | 30 | | |
| Dave Wyman | LB | 6'2" | 248 | 31 | | |
| Steve Atwater | DB | 6'3" | 217 | 28 | 3 | |
| Ronnie Bradford | DB | 5'10" | 188 | 24 | | |
| Tyrone Braxton | DB | 5'11" | 185 | 30 | 2 | |
| Ray Crockett | DB | 5'10" | 185 | 28 | | 6 |
| Tim Hauck | DB | 5'10" | 185 | 28 | | |
| Cliff Hicks | DB | 5'9" | 190 | 31 | | |
| Randy Hilliard | DB | 5'11" | 165 | 28 | | |
| Rondell Jones | DB | 6'2" | 210 | 24 | | |
| Eric Thomas | DB | 5'11" | 184 | 30 | | |
| Lionel Washington | DB | 6' | 185 | 34 | | |
| John Elway | QB | 6'3" | 215 | 35 | | 8 |
| Hugh Millen | QB | 6'5" | 216 | 31 | | |
| Bill Musgrave | QB | 6'3" | 215 | 27 | | |
| Aaron Craver | HB | 6' | 220 | 26 | | 36 |
| Terrell Davis | HB | 5'11" | 200 | 22 | | 48 |
| Glyn Milburn | HB | 5'8" | 177 | 24 | | |
| Rod Bernstine | FB | 6'3" | 238 | 30 | | 6 |
| Gary Downs | FB | 6' | 212 | 24 | | |
| Reggie Rivers | FB | 6'1" | 215 | 27 | | |
| Byron Chamberlain | WR | 6'1" | 240 | 23 | | |
| -Vance Johnson | WR | 5'11" | 185 | 32 | | |
| Ed McCaffrey | WR | 6'5" | 215 | 27 | | 14 |
| Anthony Miller | WR | 5'11" | 190 | 30 | | 84 |
| Mike Pritchard | WR | 5'10" | 190 | 25 | | 18 |
| Rod Smith | WR | 6' | 183 | 25 | | 6 |
| Dwayne Carswell | TE | 6'3" | 261 | 23 | | |
| Jerry Evans | TE | 6'4" | 250 | 26 | | 6 |
| Shannon Sharpe | TE | 6'2" | 230 | 27 | | 24 |
| Jason Elam | K | 5'11" | 192 | 25 | | 132 |
| Tom Rouen | K | 6'3" | 215 | 27 | | |

## SEATTLE SEAHAWKS 8-8 Dennis Erickson

| Scores of Each Game | | |
|---|---|---|
| 10 | KANSAS CITY | 34 |
| 10 | San Diego | 14 |
| 24 | CINCINNATI | 21 |
| 27 | DENVER | 10 |
| 14 | Oakland | 34 |
| 21 | Buffalo | 27 |
| 25 | SAN DIEGO | 35 |
| 14 | Arizona | *20 |
| 30 | NEW YORK GIANTS | 28 |
| 47 | Jacksonville | 30 |
| 27 | Washington | 20 |
| 10 | NEW YORK JETS | 16 |
| 26 | PHILADELPHIA | 14 |
| 31 | Denver | 27 |
| 44 | OAKLAND | 10 |
| 3 | Kansas City | 26 |

| Use Name | Pos. | Hgt. | Wgt. | Age | Int | Pts |
|---|---|---|---|---|---|---|
| James Atkins | OT | 6'6" | 303 | 25 | | |
| Howard Ballard | OT | 6'6" | 325 | 31 | | |
| Mike Keim | OT | 6'7" | 302 | 29 | | |
| Ray Roberts | OT | 6'6" | 311 | 26 | | |
| Jeff Blackshear | OG | 6'6" | 323 | 26 | | |
| Matt Joyce | OG | 6'7" | 316 | 23 | | |
| Kevin Mawae | OG | 6'4" | 288 | 24 | | |
| Jim Sweeney | C | 6'4" | 295 | 33 | | |
| Antonio Edwards | DE | 6'3" | 271 | 25 | | 6 |
| Michael McCrary | DE | 6'4" | 267 | 25 | | |
| Mike Sinclair | DE | 6'4" | 267 | 27 | | |
| Brent Williams | DE | 6'4" | 276 | 30 | | |
| Sam Adams | DT | 6'3" | 297 | 22 | | 2 |
| Cortez Kennedy | DT | 6'3" | 293 | 27 | | |
| Henry McMillian | DT | 6'3" | 275 | 23 | | |
| Joe Nash | DT | 6'2" | 278 | 34 | | |
| Michael Barber | LB | 6'1" | 252 | 23 | | |
| Duane Bickett | DB | 6'5" | 244 | 32 | | |
| Jason Kyle | LB | 6'3" | 242 | 23 | | |
| James Logan (from HOU & CIN) | LB | 6'2" | 214 | 22 | | |
| Winston Moss | LB | 6'3" | 245 | 29 | 1 | |
| Tyronne Stowe | LB | 6'2" | 239 | 30 | | |
| Dean Wells | LB | 6'3" | 244 | 25 | | |
| Terry Wooden | LB | 6'3" | 239 | 28 | 1 | |
| Jay Bellamy | DB | 5'11" | 198 | 23 | | |
| Robert Blackmon | DB | 6' | 208 | 28 | 5 | |
| Tony Brown | DB | 5'9" | 183 | 25 | | |
| Tony Covington | DB | 5'11" | 197 | 27 | | |
| Carlton Gray | DB | 6' | 200 | 24 | 4 | |
| Corey Harris | DB | 5'11" | 199 | 25 | 3 | 6 |
| Selwyn Jones | DB | 6' | 185 | 25 | 1 | |
| Eugene Robinson | DB | 6' | 195 | 32 | 1 | |
| Rafael Robinson | DB | 5'11" | 199 | 26 | | |
| John Friesz | QB | 6'4" | 211 | 28 | | |
| Stan Gelbaugh | QB | 6'3" | 215 | 32 | | |
| Rick Mirer | QB | 6'2" | 214 | 25 | | 6 |
| Steve Broussard | HB | 5'7" | 201 | 28 | | 6 |
| Lamar Smith | HB | 5'11" | 223 | 24 | | |
| Mack Strong | HB-FB | 6' | 224 | 23 | | 24 |
| Chris Warren | HB | 6'2" | 225 | 27 | | 96 |
| Tracy Johnson | FB | 6' | 242 | 28 | | 6 |
| Steve Smith | FB | 6'1" | 242 | 31 | | 6 |
| Brian Blades | WR | 5'11 | 188 | 30 | | 24 |
| Joey Galloway | WR | 5'11" | 188 | 23 | | 54 |
| Ronnie Harris (from NE) | WR | 5'11" | 175 | 25 | | |
| James McKnight | WR | 6' | 186 | 23 | | |
| Ricky Proehl | WR | 6' | 189 | 27 | | |
| Robb Thomas | WR | 5'11" | 175 | 29 | | 6 |
| Carlester Crumpler | TE | 6'6" | 260 | 23 | | 6 |
| Christian Fauria | TE | 6'4" | 245 | 23 | | 6 |
| Trey Junkin | TE | 6'2" | 241 | 34 | | |
| Todd Peterson | K | 5'10" | 173 | 25 | | 109 |
| Rick Tuten | K | 6'2" | 221 | 30 | | |

Bob Spitulski — Knee Injury
Nate Odomes — Knee Injury

## OAKLAND RAIDERS 8-8 Mike White

| Scores of Each Game | | |
|---|---|---|
| 17 | SAN DIEGO | 7 |
| 20 | Washington | 8 |
| 17 | Kansas City | *23 |
| 48 | PHILADELPHIA | 17 |
| 47 | New York Jets | 10 |
| 34 | SEATTLE | 14 |
| 0 | Denver | 27 |
| 30 | INDIANAPOLIS | 17 |
| 20 | Cincinnati | 17 |
| 17 | New York Giants | 13 |
| 21 | DALLAS | 34 |
| 6 | San Diego | 12 |
| 23 | KANSAS CITY | 29 |
| 10 | PITTSBURGH | 29 |
| 10 | Seattle | 44 |
| 28 | DENVER | 31 |

| Use Name | Pos. | Hgt. | Wgt. | Age | Int | Pts |
|---|---|---|---|---|---|---|
| Russell Freeman | OT | 6'7" | 295 | 25 | | |
| Robert Jenkins | OT | 6'5" | 295 | 31 | | |
| Jeff Kysar | OT | 6'7" | 330 | 23 | | |
| Gerald Perry | OT | 6'6" | 310 | 30 | | |
| Greg Skrepenak | OT | 6'6" | 325 | 25 | | |
| Rich Stephens | OT | 6'7" | 320 | 30 | | |
| Kevin Gogan | OG | 6'7" | 325 | 30 | | |
| Steve Wisniewski | OG | 6'4" | 295 | 28 | | |
| Barret Robbins | C | 6'3" | 300 | 22 | | |
| Dan Turk | C | 6'4" | 290 | 33 | | |
| Aundray Bruce | DE | 6'5" | 265 | 29 | 1 | 6 |
| Nolan Harrison | DE | 6'5" | 280 | 26 | | |
| Anthony Smith | DE | 6'3" | 265 | 28 | | |
| Pat Swilling | DE | 6'3" | 245 | 30 | | |
| Jerry Ball | DT | 6'1" | 325 | 30 | | |
| Matt Dyson | DT | 6'3" | 275 | 23 | | |
| Chester McGlockton | DT | 6'4" | 320 | 25 | | |
| Austin Robbins | DT | 6'6" | 285 | 24 | | 6 |
| Greg Biekert | LB | 6'2" | 240 | 26 | | |
| James Folston | LB | 6'3" | 235 | 24 | | |
| Keith Franklin | LB | 6'2" | 230 | 25 | | |
| Rob Fredrickson | LB | 6'4" | 240 | 24 | 1 | 6 |
| Rob Holmberg | LB | 6'3" | 230 | 24 | | |
| Mike Jones | LB | 6'1" | 230 | 26 | 1 | 6 |
| Mike Morton | LB | 6'4" | 230 | 23 | | |
| Aaron Wallace | LB | 6'3" | 240 | 28 | | |
| Eddie Anderson | DB | 6'1" | 210 | 32 | 1 | |
| Derrick Hoskins | DB | 6'2" | 210 | 24 | 1 | |
| Carl Kidd | DB | 6'1" | 200 | 22 | | |
| Joe King | DB | 6'2" | 200 | 27 | | |
| Dan Land | DB | 6' | 195 | 30 | | |
| Albert Lewis | DB | 6'2" | 204 | 34 | | |
| Terry McDaniel | DB | 5'10" | 180 | 30 | 6 | 6 |
| Najee Mustafaa | DB | 6'1" | 190 | 31 | | |
| Bruce Pickens | DB | 5'11" | 190 | 27 | | |
| James Trapp | DB | 6' | 185 | 25 | | |
| Vince Evans | QB | 6'2" | 215 | 40 | | |
| Billy Joe Hobert | QB | 6'3" | 230 | 24 | | |
| Jeff Hostetler | QB | 6'3" | 215 | 34 | | |
| Joe Aska | HB | 5'11" | 235 | 23 | | |
| Eric Ball | HB | 6'2" | 230 | 29 | | |
| Derrick Fenner | HB | 6'3" | 240 | 28 | | 18 |
| Calvin Jones | HB | 5'11" | 205 | 23 | | |
| Napoleon Kaufman | HB | 5'9" | 180 | 22 | | 12 |
| Harvey Williams | HB | 6'2" | 215 | 28 | | 54 |
| Tim Brown | WR | 6' | 195 | 29 | | 60 |
| Daryl Hobbs | WR | 6'2" | 175 | 27 | | 18 |
| Raghib Ismail | WR | 5'10" | 180 | 25 | | 18 |
| James Jett | WR | 5'10" | 165 | 24 | | 6 |
| Kerry Cash | TE | 6'4" | 245 | 26 | | 12 |
| Andrew Glover | TE | 6'6" | 250 | 28 | | 18 |
| Cole Ford | K | 6'2" | 205 | 22 | | 41 |
| Jeff Gossett | K | 6'2" | 195 | 38 | | |
| Jeff Jaeger | K | 5'11" | 195 | 30 | | 61 |

Dan Mosebar — Eye Injury

## KANSAS CITY CHIEFS

### RUSHING

| Last Name | No. | Yds | Avg | TD |
|---|---|---|---|---|
| Allen | 207 | 890 | 4.3 | 5 |
| Hill | 155 | 667 | 4.3 | 1 |
| Anders | 58 | 396 | 6.9 | 2 |
| Bono | 28 | 113 | 4.0 | 5 |
| Thompson | 28 | 73 | 2.6 | 0 |
| Vanover | 6 | 31 | 5.2 | 0 |
| Gannon | 8 | 25 | 3.1 | 1 |
| Richardson | 8 | 18 | 2.3 | 0 |
| Bennett | 7 | 11 | 1.6 | 0 |
| Hughes | 1 | 5 | 5.0 | 0 |
| Dawson | 1 | -9 | -9.0 | 0 |

### RECEIVING

| Last Name | No. | Yds | Avg | TD |
|---|---|---|---|---|
| Anders | 55 | 349 | 6.3 | 1 |
| Cash | 42 | 419 | 10.0 | 1 |
| Dawson | 40 | 513 | 12.8 | 5 |
| Slaughter | 34 | 514 | 15.1 | 4 |
| W. Davis | 33 | 527 | 16.0 | 5 |
| Allen | 27 | 210 | 7.8 | 0 |
| Walker | 25 | 205 | 8.2 | 1 |
| Hughes | 14 | 103 | 7.4 | 1 |
| Vanover | 11 | 231 | 21.0 | 2 |
| Thompson | 9 | 37 | 4.1 | 0 |
| Hill | 7 | 45 | 6.4 | 0 |
| Bennett | 1 | 12 | 12.0 | 0 |
| Penn | 1 | 12 | 12.0 | 0 |
| Valerio | 1 | 1 | 1.0 | 1 |

### PUNT RETURNS

| Last Name | No. | Yds | Avg | TD |
|---|---|---|---|---|
| Vanover | 51 | 540 | 10.6 | 1 |
| Penn | 4 | 12 | 3.0 | 0 |
| Hughes | 3 | 9 | 3.0 | 0 |

### KICKOFF RETURNS

| Last Name | No. | Yds | Avg | TD |
|---|---|---|---|---|
| Vanover | 43 | 1095 | 25.5 | 2 |
| Thompson | 6 | 152 | 25.3 | 0 |
| Penn | 2 | 36 | 18.0 | 0 |
| Valerio | 2 | 15 | 7.5 | 0 |
| Hughes | 1 | 18 | 18.0 | 0 |
| McDaniels | 1 | 0 | 0.0 | 0 |

### PASSING

| Last Name | Att | Cmp | % | Yds | Yd/Att | TD | Int— % | RK |
|---|---|---|---|---|---|---|---|---|
| Bono | 520 | 293 | 56.3 | 3121 | 6.00 | 21 | 10— 1.9 | |
| Gannon | 11 | 7 | 63.6 | 57 | 5.18 | 0 | 0— 0.0 | |

### PUNTING

| Last Name | No. | Avg. |
|---|---|---|
| Aguiar | 91 | 43.8 |

### KICKING

| Last Name | XP | ATT | % | FG | ATT | % |
|---|---|---|---|---|---|---|
| Elliott | 34 | 37 | 92 | 24 | 30 | 80 |

**2 POINT XP**
None

## SAN DIEGO CHARGERS

### RUSHING

| Last Name | No. | Yds | Avg | TD |
|---|---|---|---|---|
| Means | 186 | 730 | 3.9 | 5 |
| Hayden | 128 | 470 | 3.7 | 3 |
| Harmon | 51 | 187 | 3.7 | 1 |
| Culver | 47 | 155 | 3.3 | 3 |
| Fletcher | 26 | 140 | 5.4 | 1 |
| Humphries | 33 | 53 | 1.6 | 1 |
| Gilbert | 6 | 11 | 1.8 | 0 |
| Jefferson | 2 | 1 | 0.5 | 0 |

### RECEIVING

| Last Name | No. | Yds | Avg | TD |
|---|---|---|---|---|
| Martin | 90 | 1224 | 13.6 | 6 |
| Harmon | 62 | 662 | 10.7 | 5 |
| Jefferson | 48 | 621 | 12.9 | 2 |
| Seay | 45 | 537 | 11.9 | 3 |
| Pupunu | 35 | 315 | 9.0 | 0 |
| D. Young | 9 | 90 | 10.0 | 0 |
| Means | 7 | 46 | 6.6 | 0 |
| Hayden | 5 | 53 | 10.6 | 0 |
| Culver | 5 | 21 | 4.2 | 0 |
| Coleman | 4 | 78 | 19.5 | 0 |
| Mitchell | 3 | 31 | 10.3 | 1 |
| Fletcher | 3 | 26 | 8.7 | 0 |
| Ellison | 1 | 6 | 6.0 | 0 |
| Humphries | 1 | -4 | -4.0 | 0 |

### PUNT RETURNS

| Last Name | No. | Yds | Avg | TD |
|---|---|---|---|---|
| Coleman | 28 | 326 | 11.6 | 1 |
| Fletcher | 3 | 12 | 4.0 | 0 |

### KICKOFF RETURNS

| Last Name | No. | Yds | Avg | TD |
|---|---|---|---|---|
| Coleman | 62 | 1411 | 22.8 | 2 |
| Fletcher | 4 | 65 | 16.3 | 0 |
| Harmon | 4 | 25 | 6.3 | 0 |
| Engel | 0 | 1 | — | 0 |

### PASSING

| Last Name | Att | Cmp | % | Yds | Yd/Att | TD | Int— % | RK |
|---|---|---|---|---|---|---|---|---|
| Humphries | 478 | 282 | 59.0 | 3381 | 7.07 | 17 | 14— 2.9 | |
| Gilbert | 61 | 36 | 59.0 | 325 | 5.33 | 0 | 4— 6.6 | |
| Martin | 1 | 0 | 0.0 | 0 | 0.00 | 0 | 0— 0.0 | |

### PUNTING

| Last Name | No. | Avg. |
|---|---|---|
| Bennett | 72 | 44.7 |

### KICKING

| Last Name | XP | ATT | % | FG | ATT | % |
|---|---|---|---|---|---|---|
| Carney | 32 | 33 | 97 | 21 | 26 | 81 |

**2 POINT XP**
Seay (1)

## DENVER BRONCOS

### RUSHING

| Last Name | No. | Yds | Avg | TD |
|---|---|---|---|---|
| Davis | 237 | 1117 | 4.7 | 7 |
| Craver | 73 | 333 | 4.6 | 5 |
| Milburn | 49 | 266 | 5.4 | 0 |
| Elway | 41 | 176 | 4.3 | 1 |
| Bernstine | 23 | 76 | 3.3 | 1 |
| Pritchard | 6 | 17 | 2.8 | 0 |
| Millen | 3 | 8 | 2.7 | 0 |
| Miller | 1 | 5 | 5.0 | 0 |
| Rivers | 2 | 2 | 1.0 | 0 |
| McCaffrey | 1 | -1 | -1.0 | 0 |
| Musgrave | 4 | -4 | -1.0 | 0 |

### RECEIVING

| Last Name | No. | Yds | Avg | TD |
|---|---|---|---|---|
| Sharpe | 63 | 756 | 12.0 | 4 |
| Miller | 59 | 1079 | 18.3 | 14 |
| Davis | 49 | 367 | 7.5 | 1 |
| Craver | 43 | 369 | 8.6 | 1 |
| McCaffrey | 39 | 477 | 12.2 | 2 |
| Pritchard | 33 | 441 | 13.4 | 3 |
| Milburn | 22 | 191 | 8.7 | 0 |
| Johnson | 12 | 170 | 14.2 | 0 |
| Evans | 12 | 124 | 10.3 | 1 |
| Smith | 6 | 152 | 25.3 | 1 |
| Bernstine | 5 | 54 | 10.8 | 0 |
| Carswell | 3 | 37 | 12.3 | 0 |
| Rivers | 3 | 32 | 10.7 | 0 |
| Chamberlain | 1 | 11 | 11.0 | 0 |

### PUNT RETURNS

| Last Name | No. | Yds | Avg | TD |
|---|---|---|---|---|
| Milburn | 31 | 354 | 11.4 | 0 |
| Crockett | 0 | 4 | — | 0 |

### KICKOFF RETURNS

| Last Name | No. | Yds | Avg | TD |
|---|---|---|---|---|
| Milburn | 47 | 1269 | 27.0 | 0 |
| Craver | 7 | 50 | 7.1 | 0 |
| Smith | 4 | 54 | 13.5 | 0 |
| Robinson | 1 | 14 | 14.0 | 0 |
| Burns | 1 | 5 | 5.0 | 0 |

### PASSING

| Last Name | Att | Cmp | % | Yds | Yd/Att | TD | Int— % | RK |
|---|---|---|---|---|---|---|---|---|
| Elway | 542 | 316 | 58.3 | 3970 | 7.32 | 26 | 14— 2.6 | |
| Millen | 40 | 26 | 65.0 | 197 | 4.93 | 1 | 0— 0.0 | |
| Musgrave | 12 | 8 | 66.7 | 93 | 7.75 | 0 | 0— 0.0 | |

### PUNTING

| Last Name | No. | Avg. |
|---|---|---|
| Rouen | 53 | 41.4 |
| Elam | 1 | 17.0 |

### KICKING

| Last Name | XP | ATT | % | FG | ATT | % |
|---|---|---|---|---|---|---|
| Elam | 39 | 39 | 100 | 31 | 38 | 81 |

**2 POINT XP**
Elway (1)
McCaffrey (1)

## SEATTLE SEAHAWKS

### RUSHING

| Last Name | No. | Yds | Avg | TD |
|---|---|---|---|---|
| C. Warren | 310 | 1346 | 4.3 | 15 |
| Broussard | 46 | 222 | 4.8 | 1 |
| L. Smith | 36 | 215 | 6.0 | 0 |
| Mirer | 43 | 193 | 4.5 | 1 |
| Galloway | 11 | 154 | 14.0 | 1 |
| Strong | 8 | 23 | 2.9 | 1 |
| S. Smith | 9 | 19 | 2.1 | 0 |
| Blades | 2 | 4 | 2.0 | 0 |
| Johnson | 1 | 2 | 2.0 | 0 |
| Friesz | 11 | 0 | 0.0 | 0 |

### RECEIVING

| Last Name | No. | Yds | Avg | TD |
|---|---|---|---|---|
| Blades | 77 | 1001 | 13.0 | 4 |
| Galloway | 67 | 1039 | 15.5 | 7 |
| Warren | 35 | 247 | 7.1 | 1 |
| Crumpler | 23 | 254 | 11.0 | 1 |
| Fauria | 17 | 181 | 10.6 | 1 |
| Thomas | 12 | 239 | 19.9 | 1 |
| Strong | 12 | 117 | 9.8 | 3 |
| Broussard | 10 | 94 | 9.4 | 0 |
| S. Smith | 7 | 59 | 8.4 | 1 |
| McKnight | 6 | 91 | 15.2 | 0 |
| Proehl | 5 | 29 | 5.8 | 0 |
| L. Smith | 1 | 10 | 10.0 | 0 |
| Johnson | 1 | -2 | -2.0 | 0 |

### PUNT RETURNS

| Last Name | No. | Yds | Avg | TD |
|---|---|---|---|---|
| Galloway | 36 | 360 | 10.0 | 1 |
| R. Harris | 3 | 23 | 7.7 | 0 |
| E. Robinson | 1 | 1 | 1.0 | 0 |

### KICKOFF RETURNS

| Last Name | No. | Yds | Avg | TD |
|---|---|---|---|---|
| Broussard | 43 | 1064 | 24.7 | 0 |
| C. Harris | 19 | 397 | 20.9 | 0 |
| Strong | 4 | 65 | 16.3 | 0 |
| Galloway | 2 | 30 | 15.0 | 0 |
| R. Harris | 1 | 29 | 29.0 | 0 |
| L. Smith | 1 | 20 | 20.0 | 0 |
| S. Smith | 1 | 11 | 11.0 | 0 |
| McKnight | 1 | 4 | 4.0 | 0 |

### PASSING

| Last Name | Att | Cmp | % | Yds | Yd/Att | TD | Int— % | RK |
|---|---|---|---|---|---|---|---|---|
| Mirer | 391 | 209 | 53.5 | 2564 | 6.56 | 13 | 20— 5.1 | |
| Friesz | 120 | 64 | 53.3 | 795 | 6.63 | 6 | 3— 2.5 | |

### PUNTING

| Last Name | No. | Avg. |
|---|---|---|
| Tuten | 83 | 45.0 |

### KICKING

| Last Name | XP | ATT | % | FG | ATT | % |
|---|---|---|---|---|---|---|
| Peterson | 40 | 40 | 100 | 23 | 28 | 82 |

**2 POINT XP**
None

## OAKLAND RAIDERS

### RUSHING

| Last Name | No. | Yds | Avg | TD |
|---|---|---|---|---|
| H. Williams | 255 | 1114 | 4.4 | 9 |
| Kaufman | 108 | 490 | 4.5 | 1 |
| Hostetler | 31 | 119 | 3.8 | 0 |
| Fenner | 39 | 110 | 2.8 | 0 |
| Evans | 14 | 36 | 2.6 | 0 |
| Ismail | 6 | 29 | 4.8 | 0 |
| C. Jones | 5 | 19 | 3.8 | 0 |
| E. Ball | 2 | 10 | 5.0 | 0 |
| Hobert | 3 | 5 | 5.0 | 0 |

### RECEIVING

| Last Name | No. | Yds | Avg | TD |
|---|---|---|---|---|
| Brown | 89 | 1342 | 15.1 | 10 |
| Williams | 54 | 375 | 6.9 | 0 |
| Hobbs | 38 | 612 | 16.1 | 3 |
| Fenner | 35 | 252 | 7.2 | 3 |
| Ismail | 28 | 491 | 17.5 | 3 |
| Glover | 26 | 220 | 8.5 | 3 |
| Cash | 25 | 254 | 10.2 | 2 |
| Jett | 13 | 179 | 13.8 | 1 |
| Kaufman | 9 | 62 | 6.9 | 0 |

### PUNT RETURNS

| Last Name | No. | Yds | Avg | TD |
|---|---|---|---|---|
| T. Brown | 36 | 364 | 10.1 | 0 |
| Hobbs | 1 | 10 | 10.0 | 0 |

### KICKOFF RETURNS

| Last Name | No. | Yds | Avg | TD |
|---|---|---|---|---|
| Ismail | 36 | 706 | 19.6 | 0 |
| Kaufman | 22 | 572 | 26.0 | 1 |
| C. Jones | 5 | 92 | 18.4 | 0 |
| Hobbs | 1 | 20 | 20.0 | 0 |

### PASSING

| Last Name | Att | Cmp | % | Yds | Yd/Att | TD | Int— % | RK |
|---|---|---|---|---|---|---|---|---|
| Hostetler | 286 | 172 | 60.1 | 1998 | 6.99 | 12 | 9— 3.1 | |
| Evans | 175 | 100 | 57.1 | 1236 | 7.06 | 6 | 8— 4.6 | |
| Hobert | 80 | 44 | 55.0 | 540 | 6.75 | 4 | 5— 5.0 | |
| Williams | 1 | 1 | 100.0 | 13 | 13.00 | 1 | 0— 0.0 | |
| Hobbs | 1 | 0 | 0.0 | 0 | 0.00 | 0 | 0— 0.0 | |

### PUNTING

| Last Name | No. | Avg. |
|---|---|---|
| Gossett | 76 | 40.6 |

### KICKING

| Last Name | XP | ATT | % | FG | ATT | % |
|---|---|---|---|---|---|---|
| Jaeger | 22 | 22 | 100 | 13 | 18 | 72 |

**2 POINT XP**
None

December 30, 1995 at Buffalo, N.Y. (Attendance 73,103)

## SCORING

|  | | | | | |
|---|---|---|---|---|---|
| MIAMI | 0 | 0 | 0 | 22 | — 22 |
| BUFFALO | 10 | 14 | 3 | 10 | — 37 |

**First Quarter**
Buff.   Thomas, 1 yard run
   PAT — Christie (kick)
Buff.   Christie, 48 yard field goal

**Second Quarter**
Buff.   Holmes, 21 yard run
   PAT — Christie (kick)
Buff.   Tasker, 37 yard pass from Kelly
   PAT — Christie (kick)

**Third Quarter**
Buff.   Christie, 23 yard field goal

**Fourth Quarter**
Mia.   McDuffie, 5 yard pass from Marino
   PAT — Stoyanovich (kick)
Buff.   Tindale, 44 yard run
   PAT — Christie (kick)
Mia.   Hill, 45 yard pass from Marino
   PAT — Stoyanovich (kick)
Buff.   Christie, 42 yard field goal
Mia.   Kirby, 1 yard run
   PAT — McDuffie (pass reception)

December 31, 1995 at San Diego, Calif. (Attendance 61,182)

## SCORING

|  | | | | | |
|---|---|---|---|---|---|
| INDIANAPOLIS | 0 | 14 | 7 | 14 | — 35 |
| SAN DIEGO | 3 | 7 | 7 | 3 | — 20 |

**First Quarter**
S.D.   Carney, 54 yard field goal

**Second Quarter**
Ind.   Dilger, 2 yard pass from Harbaugh
   PAT — Blanchard (kick)
S.D.   Pupunu, 6 yard pass from Humphries
   PAT — Carney (kick)
Ind.   Crockett, 33 yard run
   PAT — Blanchard (kick)

**Third Quarter**
S.D.   Jefferson, 11 yard pass from Humphries
   PAT — Carney (kick)
Ind.   Dawkins, 42 yard pass from Harbaugh
   PAT — Blanchard (kick)

**Fourth Quarter**
S.D.   Carney, 30 yard field goal
Ind.   Crockett, 66 yard run
   PAT — Blanchard (kick)
Ind.   Harbaugh, 3 yard run
   PAT — Blanchard (kick)

## TEAM STATISTICS

| MIA. | | BUFF. |
|---|---|---|
| 26 | First Downs- Total | 27 |
| 5 | First Downs- Rushing | 18 |
| 20 | First Downs- Passing | 9 |
| 1 | First Downs- Penalty | 0 |
| 2 | Fumbles- Number | 1 |
| 1 | Fumbles- Lost Ball | 0 |
| 4 | Penalties- Number | 5 |
| 15 | Yards Penalized | 29 |
| 1 | Missed Field Goals | 0 |
| 80 | Offensive Plays | 74 |
| 502 | Net Yards | 536 |
| 6.3 | Average Gain | 7.2 |
| 4 | Giveaways | 2 |
| 2 | Takeaways | 4 |
| - 2 | Difference | + 2 |

## TEAM STATISTICS

| IND. | | S.D. |
|---|---|---|
| 19 | First Downs- Total | 27 |
| 10 | First Downs- Rushing | 7 |
| 9 | First Downs- Passing | 20 |
| 0 | First Downs- Penalty | 0 |
| 2 | Fumbles- Number | 0 |
| 0 | Fumbles- Lost Ball | 0 |
| 4 | Penalties- Number | 4 |
| 30 | Yards Penalized | 24 |
| 0 | Missed Field Goals | 0 |
| 58 | Offensive Plays | 80 |
| 333 | Net Yards | 429 |
| 5.7 | Average Gain | 5.4 |
| 1 | Giveaways | 4 |
| 4 | Takeaways | 1 |
| + 3 | Difference | - 3 |

## INDIVIDUAL STATISTICS

### MIAMI / BUFFALO

**RUSHING**

| | No. | Yds. | Avg. | | No. | Yds. | Avg. |
|---|---|---|---|---|---|---|---|
| Byars | 4 | 22 | 5.5 | Thomas | 25 | 158 | 6.3 |
| Kidd | 1 | 18 | 18.0 | Holmes | 15 | 87 | 5.8 |
| Parmalee | 5 | 13 | 2.6 | Tindale | 4 | 68 | 17.0 |
| McDuffie | 1 | 9 | 9.0 | Brooks | 2 | 28 | 14.0 |
| Kirby | 2 | 8 | 4.0 | Tasker | 2 | 7 | 3.5 |
| Marino | 1 | 0 | 0.0 | Kelly | 3 | -3 | -1.0 |
| | 14 | 70 | 5.0 | Copeland | 1 | -4 | -4.0 |
| | | | | | 52 | 341 | 6.6 |

**RECEIVING**

| | No. | Yds. | Avg. | | No. | Yds. | Avg. |
|---|---|---|---|---|---|---|---|
| McDuffie | 11 | 154 | 14.0 | Tasker | 5 | 108 | 21.6 |
| Kirby | 8 | 68 | 8.5 | Thomas | 3 | 42 | 14.0 |
| Parmalee | 4 | 51 | 12.8 | Cline | 2 | 32 | 16.0 |
| Byars | 4 | 30 | 7.5 | Brooks | 2 | 13 | 6.5 |
| Fryar | 3 | 29 | 9.7 | | 12 | 195 | 16.3 |
| Hill | 2 | 59 | 29.5 | | | | |
| Clark | 2 | 41 | 20.5 | | | | |
| | 34 | 432 | 12.7 | | | | |

**PUNTING**

| | | Yds. | Avg. | | No. | | Avg. |
|---|---|---|---|---|---|---|---|
| Kidd | | | 38.3 | Mohr | 4 | | 34.5 |

**PUNT RETURNS**

| | No. | Yds. | Avg. |
|---|---|---|---|
| McDuffie | 1 | 12 | 12.0 |
| McDuffie | 1FC | | |

**KICKOFF RETURNS**

| | No. | Yds. | Avg. | | No. | Yds. | Avg. |
|---|---|---|---|---|---|---|---|
| McDuffie | 5 | 105 | 21.0 | Holmes | 1 | 27 | 27.0 |
| Spikes | 2 | 32 | 16.0 | Thomas | 1 | 10 | 10.0 |
| Stewart | 1 | 0 | 0.0 | | 2 | 37 | 18.5 |
| | 8 | 137 | 17.1 | | | | |

**INTERCEPTION RETURNS**

| | No. | Yds. | Avg. | | No. | Yds. | Avg. |
|---|---|---|---|---|---|---|---|
| Atkins | 1 | 26 | 26.0 | Perry | 1 | 3 | 3.0 |
| Vincent | 1 | 0 | 0.0 | F. Johnson | 1 | 2 | 2.0 |
| | 2 | 26 | 13.0 | Irvin | 1 | 0 | 0.0 |
| | | | | | 3 | 5 | 1.7 |

**PASSING**

**MIAMI**

| | Att. | Comp. | Comp. Pct. | Yds. | Int. | Yds./ Att. | Yds./ Comp. |
|---|---|---|---|---|---|---|---|
| Marino | 64 | 33 | 51.6 | 422 | 3 | 6.6 | 12.8 |

**BUFFALO**

| | Att. | Comp. | Comp. Pct. | Yds. | Int. | Yds./ Att. | Yds./ Comp. |
|---|---|---|---|---|---|---|---|
| Kelly | 22 | 12 | 54.5 | 195 | 2 | 8.9 | 16.3 |

## INDIVIDUAL STATISTICS

### INDIANAPOLIS / SAN DIEGO

**RUSHING**

| | No. | Yds. | Avg. | | No. | Yds. | Avg. |
|---|---|---|---|---|---|---|---|
| Crockett | 13 | 147 | 11.3 | Hayden | 18 | 80 | 4.4 |
| Faulk | 1 | 16 | 16.0 | Humphries | 4 | 32 | 8.0 |
| Harbaugh | 5 | 10 | 2.0 | Fletcher | 3 | 23 | 7.7 |
| Warren | 10 | 5 | 0.5 | Means | 6 | 11 | 1.8 |
| | 29 | 178 | 6.1 | Harmon | 1 | -1 | -1.0 |
| | | | | | 32 | 145 | 4.5 |

**RECEIVING**

| | No. | Yds. | Avg. | | No. | Yds. | Avg. |
|---|---|---|---|---|---|---|---|
| Turner | 5 | 64 | 12.8 | Harmon | 10 | 133 | 13.3 |
| Warren | 4 | 45 | 11.3 | Martin | 3 | 39 | 13.0 |
| Dawkins | 2 | 49 | 24.5 | Jefferson | 3 | 33 | 11.0 |
| Crockett | 2 | 10 | 5.0 | Pupunu | 3 | 26 | 8.7 |
| Dilger | 2 | 9 | 4.5 | Fletcher | 2 | 42 | 21.0 |
| Humphrey | 1 | -2 | -2.0 | Seay | 2 | 19 | 9.5 |
| | 16 | 175 | 10.9 | | 23 | 292 | 12.7 |

**PUNTING**

| | No. | | Avg. | | No. | | Avg. |
|---|---|---|---|---|---|---|---|
| Gardocki | 5 | | 37.4 | Bennett | 2 | | 54.5 |

**PUNT RETURNS**

| | No. | Yds. | Avg. | | No. | | |
|---|---|---|---|---|---|---|---|
| Buchanan | 2 | 52 | 26.0 | Coleman | 2FC | | |

**KICKOFF RETURNS**

| | No. | Yds. | Avg. | | No. | Yds. | Avg. |
|---|---|---|---|---|---|---|---|
| Bailey | 2 | 44 | 22.0 | Coleman | 6 | 133 | 22.2 |
| Warren | 2 | 38 | 19.0 | | | | |
| Humphrey | 1 | 28 | 28.0 | | | | |
| | 5 | 110 | 22.0 | | | | |

**INTERCEPTION RETURNS**

| | No. | Yds. | Avg. | | No. | Yds. | Avg. |
|---|---|---|---|---|---|---|---|
| Belser | 2 | 68 | 34.0 | Seau | 1 | 0 | 0.0 |
| Grant | 1 | 13 | 13.0 | | | | |
| McElroy | 1 | 0 | 0.0 | | | | |
| | 4 | 81 | 20.3 | | | | |

**PASSING**

**INDIANAPOLIS**

| | Att. | Comp. | Comp. Pct. | Yds. | Int. | Yds./ Att. | Yds./ Comp. |
|---|---|---|---|---|---|---|---|
| Harbaugh | 27 | 16 | 59.3 | 175 | 1 | 6.5 | 10.9 |

**SAN DIEGO**

| | Att. | Comp. | Comp. Pct. | Yds. | Int. | Yds./ Att. | Yds./ Comp. |
|---|---|---|---|---|---|---|---|
| Humphries | 47 | 23 | 48.9 | 292 | 4 | 6.2 | 12.7 |

# 1995 N.F.C. — WILD-CARD PLAYOFFS

December 30, 1995 at Philadelphia, Pa. (Attendance 66,492)

## SCORING

| | | | | | | |
|---|---|---|---|---|---|---|
| DETROIT | 7 | 0 | 14 | 16 | — | 37 |
| PHILADELPHIA | 7 | 31 | 13 | 7 | — | 58 |

**First Quarter**
Phil.   Garner, 15 yard run
  PAT — Anderson (kick)
Det.   Sloan, 32 yard pass from Mitchell
  PAT — Hanson (kick)

**Second Quarter**
Phil.   Anderson, 21 yard field goal
Phil.   Barnett, 22 yard pass from Peete
  PAT — Anderson (kick)
Phil.   Wilburn, 24 yard interception return
  PAT — Anderson (kick)
Phil.   Watters, 1 yard run
  PAT — Anderson (kick)
Phil.   Carpenter, 43 yard pass from Peete
  PAT — Anderson (kick)

**Third Quarter**
Phil.   Watters, 45 yard pass from Peete
  PAT — Anderson (kick)
Phil.   Anderson, 31 yard field goal
Phil.   Anderson, 39 yard field goal
Det.   Moore, 68 yard pass from Majkowski
  PAT — Hanson (kick)
det.   Morton, 7 yard pass from Majkowski
  PAT — Hanson (kick)

**Fourth Quarter**
Phil.   Thomas, 30 yard interception return
  PAT — Anderson (kick)
Det.   Sloan, 2 yard pass from Majkowski
  PAT — Rivers (run)
Det.   Rivers, 1 yard run
  PAT — Moore (pass from Majkowski)

### TEAM STATISTICS

| DET. | | PHIL. |
|---|---|---|
| 26 | First Downs- Total | 22 |
| 5 | First Downs- Rushing | 7 |
| 20 | First Downs- Passing | 12 |
| 1 | First Downs- Penalty | 3 |
| 2 | Fumbles- Number | 1 |
| 1 | Fumbles- Lost Ball | 1 |
| 7 | Penalties- Number | 8 |
| 65 | Yards Penalized | 80 |
| 0 | Missed Field Goals | 1 |
| 70 | Offensive Plays | 69 |
| 422 | Net Yards | 452 |
| 6.0 | Average Gain | 6.6 |
| 7 | Giveaways | 1 |
| 1 | Takeaways | 7 |
| - 6 | Difference | + 6 |

### INDIVIDUAL STATISTICS

**DETROIT**      **PHILADELPHIA**

**RUSHING**

| | No. | Yds. | Avg. | | No. | Yds. | Avg. |
|---|---|---|---|---|---|---|---|
| Sanders | 10 | 40 | 4.0 | Garner | 12 | 78 | 6.5 |
| Majkowski | 3 | 16 | 5.3 | Watters | 18 | 49 | 2.7 |
| Rivers | 3 | 16 | 5.3 | Witherspoon | 5 | 21 | 4.2 |
| | 16 | 72 | 4.5 | Peete | 2 | 17 | 8.5 |
| | | | | Cunningham | 2 | 15 | 7.5 |
| | | | | Saxon | 4 | 9 | 2.3 |
| | | | | | 43 | 189 | 4.4 |

**RECEIVING**

| | No. | Yds. | Avg. | | No. | Yds. | Avg. |
|---|---|---|---|---|---|---|---|
| Moore | 7 | 133 | 19.0 | Barnett | 8 | 109 | 13.6 |
| Matthews | 7 | 73 | 10.4 | Watters | 3 | 64 | 21.3 |
| Sloan | 5 | 67 | 13.4 | Carpenter | 2 | 45 | 22.5 |
| Perriman | 3 | 26 | 8.7 | West | 2 | 19 | 9.5 |
| Rivers | 2 | 36 | 18.0 | Johnson | 1 | 22 | 22.0 |
| Sanders | 2 | 19 | 9.5 | C. Williams | 1 | 11 | 11.0 |
| Morton | 1 | 7 | 7.0 | | 17 | 270 | 15.9 |
| | 27 | 361 | 13.4 | | | | |

**PUNTING**

| | No. | | Avg. | | No. | | Avg. |
|---|---|---|---|---|---|---|---|
| Royals | 5 | | 37.4 | Hutton | 4 | | 42.8 |

**PUNT RETURNS**

| | | | | | No. | Yds. | Avg. |
|---|---|---|---|---|---|---|---|
| Perriman | 1FC | | | Carpenter | 2 | 13 | 6.5 |
| | | | | Carpenter | 2FC | | |

**KICKOFF RETURNS**

| | No. | Yds. | Avg. | | No. | Yds. | Avg. |
|---|---|---|---|---|---|---|---|
| Rivers | 6 | 108 | 18.0 | Witherspoon | 2 | 25 | 12.5 |
| A. Williams | 3 | 31 | 10.3 | Cornish | 1 | 0 | 0.0 |
| Clay | 1 | 9 | 9.0 | McMillian | 1 | 0 | 0.0 |
| | 10 | 148 | 14.8 | | 4 | 25 | 6.3 |

**INTERCEPTION RETURNS**

| | | | | | No. | Yds. | Avg. |
|---|---|---|---|---|---|---|---|
| None | | | | Jackson | 1 | 31 | 31.0 |
| | | | | Thomas | 1 | 30 | 30.0 |
| | | | | Wilburn | 1 | 24 | 24.0 |
| | | | | McMillian | 1 | 16 | 16.0 |
| | | | | Zordich | 1 | 15 | 15.0 |
| | | | | Gouveia | 1 | 3 | 3.0 |
| | | | | | 6 | 119 | 19.8 |

**PASSING**

**DETROIT**

| | Att. | Comp. | Comp. Pct. | Yds. | Int. | Yds./ Att. | Yds./ Comp. |
|---|---|---|---|---|---|---|---|
| Mitchell | 29 | 13 | 44.8 | 155 | 4 | 5.3 | 11.9 |
| Majkowski | 23 | 14 | 60.9 | 206 | 2 | 9.0 | 14.7 |
| | 52 | 27 | 51.9 | 361 | 6 | 7.0 | 13.4 |

**PHILADELPHIA**

| | Att. | Comp. | Comp. Pct. | Yds. | Int. | Yds./ Att. | Yds./ Comp. |
|---|---|---|---|---|---|---|---|
| Peete | 25 | 17 | 68.0 | 270 | 0 | 10.8 | 15.9 |

---

Dece,ber 31, 1995 at Green Bay, Wis. (Attendance 60,453)

## SCORING

| | | | | | | |
|---|---|---|---|---|---|---|
| ATLANTA | 7 | 3 | 0 | 10 | — | 20 |
| GREEN BAY | 14 | 13 | 0 | 10 | — | 37 |

**First Quarter**
Atl.   Metcalf, 65 yard pass from J. George
  PAT — Andersen (kick)
G.B.   Bennett, 8 yard run
  PAT — Jacke (kick)
G.B.   Brooks, 14 yard pass from Favre
  PAT — Jacke (kick)

**Second Quarter**
Atl.   Andersen, 31 yard field goal
G.B.   Freeman, 76 yard punt return
  PAT — Two-point attempt failed
G.B.   Chmura, 2 yard pass from Favre
  PAT — Jacke (kick)

**Fourth Quarter**
Atl.   Birden, 27 yard pass from J. George
  PAT — Andersen (kick)
Atl.   Andersen, 22 yard field goal
G.B.   Jacke, 25 yard field goal

### TEAM STATISTICS

| ATL. | | G.B. |
|---|---|---|
| 18 | First Downs- Total | 23 |
| 1 | First Downs- Rushing | 6 |
| 17 | First Downs- Passing | 14 |
| 0 | First Downs- Penalty | 3 |
| 1 | Fumbles- Number | 0 |
| 0 | Fumbles- Lost Ball | 0 |
| 5 | Penalties- Number | 5 |
| 67 | Yards Penalized | 36 |
| 0 | Missed Field Goals | 1 |
| 67 | Offensive Plays | 65 |
| 360 | Net Yards | 307 |
| 5.4 | Average Gain | 4.7 |
| 2 | Giveaways | 0 |
| 0 | Takeaways | 2 |
| - 2 | Difference | + 2 |

### INDIVIDUAL STATISTICS

**ATLANTA**      **GREEN BAY**

**RUSHING**

| | No. | Yds. | Avg. | | No. | Yds. | Avg. |
|---|---|---|---|---|---|---|---|
| Heyward | 9 | 21 | 2.3 | Bennett | 24 | 108 | 4.5 |
| J. George | 1 | 0 | 0.0 | Levens | 2 | 12 | 6.0 |
| | 10 | 21 | 2.1 | Favre | 3 | -3 | -1.0 |
| | | | | | 29 | 117 | 4.0 |

**RECEIVING**

| | No. | Yds. | Avg. | | No. | Yds. | Avg. |
|---|---|---|---|---|---|---|---|
| Metcalf | 8 | 114 | 14.3 | Brooks | 7 | 73 | 10.4 |
| Birden | 6 | 64 | 10.7 | Morgan | 4 | 36 | 9.0 |
| Emanuel | 6 | 62 | 10.3 | K. Jackson | 3 | 23 | 7.7 |
| Mathis | 5 | 93 | 18.6 | Bennett | 3 | 11 | 3.7 |
| Heyward | 3 | 20 | 6.7 | Levens | 2 | 19 | 9.5 |
| T. Brown | 1 | 14 | 14.0 | Chmura | 2 | 15 | 7.5 |
| Lyons | 1 | -1 | -1.0 | Freeman | 1 | 14 | 14.0 |
| | 30 | 366 | 12.2 | Henderson | 1 | 4 | 4.0 |
| | | | | Ingram | 1 | 4 | 4.0 |
| | | | | | 24 | 199 | 8.3 |

**PUNTING**

| | No. | | Avg. | | No. | | Avg. |
|---|---|---|---|---|---|---|---|
| Stryzinski | 5 | | 36.6 | Hentrich | 4 | | 42.5 |

**PUNT RETURNS**

| | No. | Yds. | Avg. | | No. | Yds. | Avg. |
|---|---|---|---|---|---|---|---|
| Metcalf | 2 | 6 | 3.0 | Freeman | 3 | 72 | 24.0 |
| Metcalf | 1FC | | | Prior | 2FC | | |

**KICKOFF RETURNS**

| | No. | Yds. | Avg. | | No. | Yds. | Avg. |
|---|---|---|---|---|---|---|---|
| Metcalf | 6 | 107 | 17.8 | Freeman | 2 | 54 | 27.0 |
| | | | | Jervey | 2 | 33 | 16.5 |
| | | | | | 4 | 87 | 21.8 |

**INTERCEPTIONS**

| | | | | | No. | Yds. | Avg. |
|---|---|---|---|---|---|---|---|
| None | | | | Teague | 1 | 30 | 30.0 |
| | | | | Evans | 1 | 0 | 0.0 |
| | | | | | 2 | 30 | 15.0 |

**PASSING**

**ATLANTA**

| | Att. | Comp. | Comp. Pct. | Yds. | Int. | Yds./ Att. | Yds./ Comp. |
|---|---|---|---|---|---|---|---|
| J. George | 54 | 30 | 55.6 | 366 | 2 | 6.8 | 12.2 |

**GREEN BAY**

| | Att. | Comp. | Comp. Pct. | Yds. | Int. | Yds./ Att. | Yds./ Comp. |
|---|---|---|---|---|---|---|---|
| Favre | 35 | 24 | 68.6 | 199 | 0 | 5.7 | 8.3 |

733

## Left Game

January 6, 1996 at Pittsburgh, Pa. (Attendance 59,072)

### SCORING

| | | | | |
|---|---|---|---|---|
| BUFFALO | 0 | 7 | 7 | 7 — 21 |
| PITTSBURGH | 7 | 16 | 3 | 14 — 40 |

**First Quarter**
Pitt.  J.L. Williams, 1 yard run
  PAT — Johnson (kick)

**Second Quarter**
Pitt.  Mills, 10 yard pass from O'Donnell
  PAT — Johnson (kick)
Pitt.  Johnson, 45 yard field goal
Pitt.  Johnson, 38 yard field goal
Buff.  Thomas, 1 yard run
  PAT — Christie (kick)

**Third Quarter**
Pitt.  Johnson, 39 yard field goal
Buff.  Cline, 2 yard pass from Van Pelt
  PAT — Christie (kick)

**Fourth Quarter**
Buff.  Thomas, 9 yard pass from Kelly
  PAT — Christie (kick)
Pitt.  Morris, 13 yard run
  PAT — Johnson (kick)
Pitt.  Morris, 2 yard run
  PAT — Johnson (kick)

### TEAM STATISTICS

| BUFF. | | PITT. |
|---|---|---|
| 18 | First Downs- Total | 23 |
| 6 | First Downs- Rushing | 8 |
| 11 | First Downs- Passing | 15 |
| 1 | First Downs- Penalty | 0 |
| 3 | Fumbles- Number | 1 |
| 1 | Fumbles- Lost Ball | 0 |
| 5 | Penalties- Number | 5 |
| 25 | Yards Penalized | 41 |
| 1 | Missed Field Goals | 0 |
| 62 | Offensive Plays | 78 |
| 250 | Net Yards | 409 |
| 4.0 | Average Gain | 5.2 |
| 4 | Giveaways | 2 |
| 2 | Takeaways | 4 |
| - 2 | Difference | + 2 |

### INDIVIDUAL STATISTICS

**BUFFALO** / **PITTSBURGH**

#### RUSHING

| | No. | Yds. | Avg. | | No. | Yds. | Avg. |
|---|---|---|---|---|---|---|---|
| Thomas | 13 | 46 | 3.5 | Morris | 25 | 106 | 4.2 |
| Tasker | 1 | 40 | 40.0 | Pegram | 8 | 33 | 4.1 |
| Holmes | 4 | 14 | 3.5 | Stewart | 1 | 5 | 5.0 |
| Van Pelt | 2 | 8 | 4.0 | J.L. Williams | 4 | 3 | 0.8 |
| Mohr | 1 | -14 | -14.0 | Mills | 1 | 3 | 3.0 |
| | 21 | 94 | 4.5 | O'Donnell | 4 | -3 | -0.8 |
| | | | | | 43 | 147 | 3.4 |

#### RECEIVING

| | No. | Yds. | Avg. | | No. | Yds. | Avg. |
|---|---|---|---|---|---|---|---|
| L. Johnson | 5 | 28 | 5.6 | Mills | 5 | 66 | 13.2 |
| Cline | 3 | 36 | 12.0 | Thigpen | 3 | 77 | 25.7 |
| Brooks | 3 | 28 | 9.3 | Hastings | 3 | 39 | 13.0 |
| Thomas | 3 | 12 | 4.0 | Stewart | 2 | 27 | 13.5 |
| Tasker | 2 | 38 | 19.0 | Pegram | 2 | 21 | 10.5 |
| Reed | 2 | 20 | 10.0 | Morris | 2 | 7 | 3.5 |
| | 18 | 162 | 9.0 | Hayes | 1 | 17 | 17.0 |
| | | | | J.L. Williams | 1 | 8 | 8.0 |
| | | | | | 19 | 262 | 13.8 |

#### PUNTING

| | No. | | Avg. | | No. | | Avg. |
|---|---|---|---|---|---|---|---|
| Mohr | 5 | | 39.8 | Stark | 4 | | 30.8 |
| | | | | Stewart | 1 | | 41.0 |
| | | | | | 5 | | 32.8 |

#### PUNT RETURNS

| | No. | Yds. | Avg. | | No. | Yds. | Avg. |
|---|---|---|---|---|---|---|---|
| Tasker | 3 | 4 | 1.3 | Hastings | 2 | 13 | 6.5 |
| Tasker | 1FC | | | Hastings | 1FC | | |

#### KICKOFF RETURNS

| | No. | Yds. | Avg. | | No. | Yds. | Avg. |
|---|---|---|---|---|---|---|---|
| Holmes | 7 | 110 | 15.7 | Mills | 3 | 51 | 17.0 |
| Tindale | 1 | 23 | 23.0 | McAfee | 1 | 20 | 20.0 |
| | 8 | 133 | 16.6 | | 4 | 71 | 17.8 |

#### INTERCEPTION RETURNS

| | No. | Yds. | Avg. | | No. | Yds. | Avg. |
|---|---|---|---|---|---|---|---|
| Evans | 1 | 19 | 19.0 | Olsavsky | 1 | 5 | 5.0 |
| Darby | 1 | 3 | 3.0 | Kirkland | 1 | 4 | 4.0 |
| | 2 | 22 | 11.0 | Lake | 1 | 3 | 3.0 |
| | | | | | 3 | 12 | 4.0 |

#### PASSING

**BUFFALO**

| | Att. | Comp. | Comp. Pct. | Yds. | Int. | Yds./ Att. | Yds./ Comp. |
|---|---|---|---|---|---|---|---|
| Kelly | 29 | 14 | 48.3 | 135 | 3 | 4.7 | 9.6 |
| Van Pelt | 14 | 4 | 40.0 | 27 | 0 | 1.9 | 6.8 |
| | 39 | 18 | 50.0 | 162 | 3 | 4.1 | 9.0 |

**PITTSBURGH**

| | Att. | Comp. | Comp. Pct. | Yds. | Int. | Yds./ Att. | Yds./ Comp. |
|---|---|---|---|---|---|---|---|
| O'Donnell | 35 | 19 | 54.3 | 262 | 2 | 7.5 | 13.8 |

## Right Game

January 7, 1996 at Kansas City, Mo. (Attendance 77,594)

### SCORING

| | | | | |
|---|---|---|---|---|
| INDIANAPOLIS | 0 | 7 | 3 | 0 — 10 |
| KANSAS CITY | 7 | 0 | 0 | 0 — 7 |

**First Quarter**
K.C.  Dawson, 20 yard pass from Bono
  PAT — Elliott (kick)

**Second Quarter**
Ind.  Turner, 5 yard pass from Harbaugh
  PAT — Blanchard (kick)

**Third Quarter**
Ind.  Blanchard, 30 yard field goal

### TEAM STATISTICS

| IND. | | K.C. |
|---|---|---|
| 16 | First Downs- Total | 15 |
| 7 | First Downs- Rushing | 5 |
| 8 | First Downs- Passing | 9 |
| 1 | First Downs- Penalty | 1 |
| 4 | Fumbles- Number | 1 |
| 0 | Fumbles- Lost Ball | 1 |
| 6 | Penalties- Number | 3 |
| 38 | Yards Penalized | 29 |
| 2 | Missed Field Goals | 3 |
| 68 | Offensive Plays | 61 |
| 249 | Net Yards | 281 |
| 3.7 | Average Gain | 4.6 |
| 1 | Giveaways | 4 |
| 4 | Takeaways | 1 |
| + 3 | Difference | - 3 |

### INDIVIDUAL STATISTICS

**INDIANAPOLIS** / **KANSAS CITY**

#### RUSHING

| | No. | Yds. | Avg. | | No. | Yds. | Avg. |
|---|---|---|---|---|---|---|---|
| Warren | 20 | 76 | 3.8 | Allen | 21 | 94 | 4.5 |
| Harbaugh | 9 | 48 | 5.3 | Gannon | 2 | 19 | 9.5 |
| Crockett | 6 | 12 | 2.0 | Anders | 5 | 16 | 5.3 |
| Humphrey | 4 | 11 | 2.8 | | 28 | 129 | 4.6 |
| | 39 | 147 | 3.8 | | | | |

#### RECEIVING

| | No. | Yds. | Avg. | | No. | Yds. | Avg. |
|---|---|---|---|---|---|---|---|
| Dawkins | 4 | 37 | 9.3 | Anders | 7 | 44 | 6.3 |
| Bailey | 2 | 37 | 18.5 | Dawson | 4 | 70 | 17.5 |
| Warren | 2 | 18 | 9.0 | Allen | 2 | 21 | 10.5 |
| Turner | 2 | 15 | 7.5 | Slaughter | 2 | 10 | 5.0 |
| Crockett | 2 | 5 | 2.5 | Walker | 1 | 7 | 7.0 |
| | 12 | 112 | 9.3 | | 16 | 152 | 9.5 |

#### PUNTING

| | No. | | Avg. | | No. | | Avg. |
|---|---|---|---|---|---|---|---|
| Gardocki | 6 | | 36.5 | Aguiar | 4 | | 36.8 |

#### PUNT RETURNS

| | No. | Yds. | Avg. | | No. | Yds. | Avg. |
|---|---|---|---|---|---|---|---|
| Buchanan | 2 | 10 | 5.0 | Vanover | 4 | 34 | 8.5 |
| Buchanan | 1FC | | | Vanover | 2FC | | |

#### KICKOFF RETURNS

| | No. | Yds. | Avg. | | No. | Yds. | Avg. |
|---|---|---|---|---|---|---|---|
| Humphrey | 2 | 22 | 11.0 | Vanover | 2 | 45 | 22.5 |
| Spikes | 1 | 18 | 18.0 | Thompson | 1 | 21 | 21.0 |
| | | | | | 3 | 66 | 22.0 |

#### INTERCEPTION RETURNS

| | No. | Yds. | Avg. | | No. | Yds. | Avg. |
|---|---|---|---|---|---|---|---|
| Daniel | 1 | 13 | 13.0 | Collins | 1 | 0 | 0.0 |
| Coryatt | 1 | 10 | 10.0 | | | | |
| Ambrose | 1 | 2 | 2.0 | | | | |
| | 3 | 25 | 8.3 | | | | |

#### PASSING

**INDIANAPOLIS**

| | Att. | Comp. | Comp. Pct. | Yds. | Int. | Yds./ Att. | Yds./ Comp. |
|---|---|---|---|---|---|---|---|
| Harbaugh | 27 | 12 | 44.4 | 112 | 1 | 4.1 | 9.3 |

**KANSAS CITY**

| | Att. | Comp. | Comp. Pct. | Yds. | Int. | Yds./ Att. | Yds./ Comp. |
|---|---|---|---|---|---|---|---|
| Bono | 25 | 11 | 44.0 | 122 | 3 | 4.9 | 11.1 |
| Gannon | 8 | 5 | 62.5 | 30 | 0 | 3.8 | 6.0 |
| | 33 | 16 | 48.5 | 152 | 3 | 4.6 | 9.5 |

January 6, 1996 at San Francisco (Attendance 69,311)

## SCORING

| | | | | | |
|---|---|---|---|---|---|
| **GREEN BAY** | 14 | 7 | 3 | 3 | — 27 |
| **SAN FRANCISCO** | 0 | 3 | 7 | 7 | — 17 |

**First Quarter**
G.B.    Newsome, 31 yard fumble return
     PAT — Jacke (kick)
G.B.    Jackson, 3 yard pass from Favre
     PAT — Jacke (kick)

**Second Quarter**
G.B.    Chmura, 13 yard pass from Favre
     PAT — Jacke (kick)
S.F.    Wilkins, 21 yard field goal

**Third Quarter**
S.F.    Young, 1 yard run
     PAT — Wilkins (kick)
S.F.    Jacke, 27 yard field goal

**Fourth Quarter**
G.B.    Jacke, 26 yard field goal
S.F.    Loville, 2 yard run
     PAT — Wilkins (kick)

January 7, 1996 at Irving, Texas (Attendance 64,371)

## SCORING

| | | | | | |
|---|---|---|---|---|---|
| **PHILADELPHIA** | 0 | 3 | 0 | 8 | — 11 |
| **DALLAS** | 3 | 14 | 6 | 7 | — 30 |

**First Quarter**
Dall.    Boniol, 24 yard field goal

**Second Quarter**
Phil.    Anderson, 26 yard field goal
Dall.    Sanders, 21 yard run
     PAT — Boniol (kick)
Dall.    Smith, 1 yard run
     PAT — Boniol (kick)

**Third Quarter**
Dall.    Boniol, 18 yard field goal
Dall.    Boniol, 51 yard field goal

**Fourth Quarter**
Dall.    Irvin, 9 yard pass from Aikman
     PAT — Boniol (kick)
Phil.    Cunningham, 4 yard run
     PAT — R. Johnson pass from Cunningham)

## TEAM STATISTICS

| G.B. | | S.F. |
|---|---|---|
| 18 | First Downs- Total | 25 |
| 3 | First Downs- Rushing | 7 |
| 13 | First Downs- Passing | 16 |
| 2 | First Downs- Penalty | 2 |
| 0 | Fumbles- Number | 2 |
| 0 | Fumbles- Lost Ball | 2 |
| 5 | Penalties- Number | 8 |
| 35 | Yards Penalized | 72 |
| 1 | Missed Field Goals | 0 |
| 57 | Offensive Plays | 86 |
| 368 | Net Yards | 395 |
| 6.5 | Average Gain | 4.6 |
| 0 | Giveaways | 4 |
| 4 | Takeaways | 0 |
| + 4 | Difference | - 4 |

## TEAM STATISTICS

| PHIL. | | DAL. |
|---|---|---|
| 13 | First Downs- Total | 21 |
| 4 | First Downs- Rushing | 10 |
| 8 | First Downs- Passing | 11 |
| 1 | First Downs- Penalty | 0 |
| 1 | Fumbles- Number | 0 |
| 0 | Fumbles- Lost Ball | 0 |
| 3 | Penalties- Number | 7 |
| 21 | Yards Penalized | 89 |
| 0 | Missed Field Goals | 0 |
| 58 | Offensive Plays | 63 |
| 227 | Net Yards | 397 |
| 3.9 | Average Gain | 4.0 |
| 1 | Giveaways | 1 |
| 1 | Takeaways | 1 |
| 0 | Difference | 0 |

## INDIVIDUAL STATISTICS

**GREEN BAY**      **SAN FRANCISCO**

### RUSHING

| | No. | Yds. | Avg. | | No. | Yds. | Avg. |
|---|---|---|---|---|---|---|---|
| Bennett | 23 | 51 | 2.2 | Young | 9 | 77 | 8.6 |
| Brooks | 1 | 15 | 15.0 | Loville | 8 | 5 | 0.6 |
| Favre | 3 | 11 | 3.7 | Rice | 1 | 5 | 5.0 |
| Levens | 1 | -3 | -3.0 | | 18 | 87 | 4.8 |
| | 28 | 74 | 2.6 | | | | |

### RECEIVING

| | No. | Yds. | Avg. | | No. | Yds. | Avg. |
|---|---|---|---|---|---|---|---|
| Brooks | 4 | 103 | 25.8 | Rice | 11 | 117 | 10.6 |
| Jackson | 4 | 101 | 25.3 | Jones | 8 | 112 | 14.0 |
| Chmura | 3 | 19 | 6.3 | Loville | 7 | 70 | 10.0 |
| Levens | 3 | 17 | 5.7 | Stokes | 3 | 24 | 8.0 |
| Ingram | 3 | 10 | 3.3 | Taylor | 1 | 7 | 7.0 |
| Morgan | 2 | 30 | 15.0 | D. Carter | 1 | 1 | 1.0 |
| Freeman | 2 | 19 | 9.5 | A. Walker | 1 | -3 | -3.0 |
| | 21 | 299 | 14.2 | | 32 | 328 | 10.3 |

### PUNTING

| | | | | | | |
|---|---|---|---|---|---|---|
| Hentrich | 5 | | 39.2 | Thompson | 5 | 44.0 |

### PUNT RETURNS

| | | | | | | | |
|---|---|---|---|---|---|---|---|
| Freeman | 3 | 17 | 5.7 | D. Carter | 3 | 14 | 4.7 |
| Freeman | 2FC | | | | | | |

### KICKOFF RETURNS

| | | | | | | | |
|---|---|---|---|---|---|---|---|
| Freeman | 2 | 53 | 26.5 | D. Carter | 3 | 63 | 21.0 |
| Jervey | 1 | 2 | 2.0 | | | | |
| | 3 | 55 | 18.3 | | | | |

### INTERCEPTION RETURNS

| | | | | | |
|---|---|---|---|---|---|
| Prior | 1 | 4 | 4.0 | None | |
| Newsome | 1 | 0 | 0.0 | | |
| | 2 | 4 | 2.0 | | |

### PASSING

**GREEN BAY**

| | Att. | Comp. | Comp. Pct. | Yds. | Int. | Yds./ Att. | Yds./ Comp. |
|---|---|---|---|---|---|---|---|
| Favre | 28 | 21 | 75.0 | 299 | 0 | 10.7 | 14.2 |

**SAN FRANCISCO**

| | Att. | Comp. | Comp. Pct. | Yds. | Int. | Yds./ Att. | Yds./ Comp. |
|---|---|---|---|---|---|---|---|
| Young | 65 | 32 | 49.2 | 328 | 2 | 5.0 | 10.3 |

## INDIVIDUAL STATISTICS

**PHILADELPHIA**      **DALLAS**

### RUSHING

| | No. | Yds. | Avg. | | No. | Yds. | Avg. |
|---|---|---|---|---|---|---|---|
| Watters | 13 | 39 | 3.0 | E. Smith | 21 | 99 | 4.7 |
| Cunningham | 3 | 19 | 6.3 | S. Williams | 10 | 30 | 3.0 |
| Garner | 5 | 13 | 2.6 | Sanders | 1 | 21 | 21.0 |
| Peete | 1 | 3 | 3.0 | Aikman | 1 | 3 | 3.0 |
| | 22 | 74 | 3.4 | Johnston | 3 | 2 | 0.7 |
| | | | | W. Wilson | 2 | -2 | -1.0 |

### RECEIVING

| | No. | Yds. | Avg. | | No. | Yds. | Avg. |
|---|---|---|---|---|---|---|---|
| C. Williams | 5 | 56 | 11.2 | K. Williams | 6 | 124 | 20.7 |
| Watters | 4 | 45 | 11.3 | Johnston | 3 | 40 | 13.3 |
| Carpenter | 2 | 43 | 21.5 | E. Smith | 3 | 40 | 13.3 |
| Barnett | 2 | 28 | 14.0 | Novacek | 3 | 27 | 9.0 |
| C. Jones | 1 | 17 | 17.0 | Sanders | 1 | 13 | 13.0 |
| | 14 | 189 | 13.5 | Irvin | 1 | 9 | 9.0 |
| | | | | | 17 | 253 | 14.9 |

### PUNTING

| | | | | | | |
|---|---|---|---|---|---|---|
| Hutton | 8 | | 41.4 | Jett | 4 | 42.3 |

### PUNT RETURNS

| | | | | | | | |
|---|---|---|---|---|---|---|---|
| Carpenter | 2 | 8 | 4.0 | Sanders | 2 | 21 | 10.5 |
| Carpenter | 2FC | | | Sanders | 1FC | | |

### KICKOFF RETURNS

| | | | | | | | |
|---|---|---|---|---|---|---|---|
| Garner | 4 | 36 | 9.0 | K. Williams | 2 | 45 | 22.5 |
| C. Jones | 2 | 18 | 9.0 | | | | |
| Saxon | 1 | 9 | 9.0 | | | | |
| | 7 | 63 | 9.0 | | | | |

### INTERCEPTION RETURNS

| | | | | | | | |
|---|---|---|---|---|---|---|---|
| McMillian | 1 | 34 | 34.0 | Sanders | 1 | 12 | 12.0 |

### PASSING

**PHILADELPHIA**

| | Att. | Comp. | Comp. Pct. | Yds. | Int. | Yds./ Att. | Yds./ Comp. |
|---|---|---|---|---|---|---|---|
| Cunningham | 26 | 11 | 42.3 | 161 | 1 | 6.2 | 14.6 |
| Peete | 5 | 3 | 60.0 | 28 | 0 | 5.6 | 9.3 |
| | 31 | 14 | 45.2 | 189 | 1 | 6.1 | 13.5 |

**DALLAS**

| | Att. | Comp. | Comp. Pct. | Yds. | Int. | Yds./ Att. | Yds./ Comp. |
|---|---|---|---|---|---|---|---|
| Aikman | 24 | 17 | 70.8 | 253 | 1 | 10.5 | 14.9 |

# 1995 Championship Games

## A.F.C. CHAMPIONSHIP GAME
January 14, 1996 at Pittsburgh, Pa.
(Attendance 61,062)

**SCORING**

| | | | | | |
|---|---|---|---|---|---|
| INDIANAPOLIS | 3 | 3 | 3 | 7 — 16 |
| PITTSBURGH | 3 | 7 | 3 | 7 — 20 |

**First Quarter**
Ind.    Blanchard, 34 yard field goal
Pitt.    Johnson, 31 yard field goal

**Second Quarter**
Ind.    Blanchard, 36 yard field goal
Pitt.    Stewart, 5 yard pass from O'Donnell
          PAT — Johnson (kick)

**Third Quarter**
Ind.    Blanchard, 37 yard field goal
Pitt.    Johnson, 36 yard field goal

**Fourth Quarter**
Ind.    Turner, 47 yard pass from Harbaugh
          PAT — Blanchard (kick)
Pitt.    Morris, 1 yard run
          PAT — Anderson (kick)

**TEAM STATISTICS**

| IND. | | PITT. |
|---|---|---|
| 16 | First Downs- Total | 21 |
| 4 | First Downs- Rushing | 6 |
| 12 | First Downs- Passing | 12 |
| 0 | First Downs- Penalty | 3 |
| 1 | Fumbles- Number | 0 |
| 0 | Fumbles- Lost Ball | 0 |
| 5 | Penalties- Number | 4 |
| 57 | Yards Penalized | 25 |
| 1 | Missed Field Goals | 1 |
| 60 | Offensive Plays | 66 |
| 328 | Net Yards | 285 |
| 5.5 | Average Gain | 4.3 |
| 0 | Giveaways | 1 |
| 1 | Takeaways | 0 |
| + 1 | Difference | - 1 |

Almost, but not quite.

The Pittsburgh Steelers defeated the Indianapolis Colts 20-16 to win the AFC championship, but only after Colts WR Aaron Bailey failed to hold on to a "Hail Mary" pass in the end zone on the final play of the game.

The Steelers had taken the lead on a one-yard run by Bam Morris with 1:34 left in the game before Indianapolis QB Jim Harbaugh attempted to pull off his fifth comeback victory of the season.

"All I know is we played our hearts out," said Harbaugh. "We just ran out of miracles."

On the other hand, Steelers QB Neil O'Donnell had a couple of his own. He hit WR Andre Hastings with a nine-yard pass on a 4th-and-3 play at midfield, then connected on a 37-yard floater down the right sideline with Ernie Mills, who looked like a ballet dancer when he went out of bounds on the Colts' one-yard line.

The game was one of field goals, with the Colts holding a 6-3 lead until just before halftime. That's when O'Donnell threw a five-yard TD pass to Kordell Stewart with 13 seconds remaining in the half. However, replays showed that Stewart had stepped out of the end zone just prior to the catch, but the officials missed it.

The teams traded field goals again in the third quarter, and then Indianapolis, which was playing without leading rusher Marshall Faulk, took the lead on a 47-yard pass from Harbaugh to Floyd Turner in the fourth quarter.

For the Steelers, it was their first AFC championship since 1979.

## INDIVIDUAL STATISTICS

### INDIANAPOLIS     PITTSBURGH

**RUSHING**

| | No. | Yds. | Avg. | | No. | Yds. | Avg. |
|---|---|---|---|---|---|---|---|
| Warren | 15 | 53 | 3.5 | Pegram | 10 | 46 | 4.6 |
| Harbaugh | 6 | 29 | 4.8 | Stewart | 4 | 12 | 3.0 |
| Crockett | 1 | 2 | 2.0 | Morris | 7 | 9 | 1.3 |
| Humphrey | 1 | -1 | -1.0 | Williams | 1 | 6 | 6.0 |
| | 23 | 83 | 3.6 | Mills | 1 | 5 | 5.0 |
| | | | | | 24 | 80 | 3.3 |

**RECEIVING**

| | No. | Yds. | Avg. | | No. | Yds. | Avg. |
|---|---|---|---|---|---|---|---|
| Dawkins | 7 | 96 | 13.7 | Thigpen | 6 | 65 | 10.8 |
| Warren | 7 | 37 | 5.3 | J.L. Williams | 4 | 21 | 5.3 |
| Turner | 3 | 73 | 24.2 | Morris | 4 | 11 | 2.8 |
| Crockett | 2 | 22 | 11.0 | Mills | 3 | 52 | 17.3 |
| Dilger | 1 | 30 | 30.0 | Hastings | 3 | 21 | 7.0 |
| Bailey | 1 | 9 | 9.0 | Stewart | 2 | 18 | 9.0 |
| | 21 | 267 | 12.7 | Holliday | 1 | 8 | 8.0 |
| | | | | Bruener | 1 | 6 | 6.0 |
| | | | | Pegram | 1 | 3 | 3.0 |
| | | | | | 25 | 205 | 8.2 |

**PUNTING**

| | No. | Yds. | Avg. | | No. | Yds. | Avg. |
|---|---|---|---|---|---|---|---|
| Gardocki | 4 | | 50.0 | Stark | 4 | | 38.8 |

**PUNT RETURNS**

| | No. | Yds. | Avg. | | No. | Yds. | Avg. |
|---|---|---|---|---|---|---|---|
| Buchanan | 1 | 5 | 5.0 | Hastings | 3 | 53 | 17.7 |
| Buchanan | 1FC | | | | | | |

**KICKOFF RETURNS**

| | No. | Yds. | Avg. | | No. | Yds. | Avg. |
|---|---|---|---|---|---|---|---|
| Bailey | 4 | 70 | 17.5 | Mills | 4 | 96 | 24.0 |

**INTERCEPTION RETURNS**

| | No. | Yds. | Avg. | | |
|---|---|---|---|---|---|
| Herrod | 1 | 17 | 17.0 | None | |

**PASSING**

**INDIANAPOLIS**

| | Att. | Comp. | Comp. Pct. | Yds. | Int. | Yds./ Att. | Yds./ Comp. |
|---|---|---|---|---|---|---|---|
| Harbaugh | 33 | 21 | 63.6 | 267 | 0 | 8.1 | 12.7 |
| Warren | 1 | 0 | 0.0 | 0 | 0 | 0.0 | 0.0 |
| | 34 | 21 | 61.8 | 267 | 0 | 7.9 | 7.9 |

**PITTSBURGH**

| | Att. | Comp. | Comp. Pct. | Yds. | Int. | Yds./ Att. | Yds./ Comp. |
|---|---|---|---|---|---|---|---|
| O'Donnell | 41 | 25 | 60.9 | 205 | 1 | 5.0 | 8.2 |

---

## N.F.C. CHAMPIONSHIP GAME
January 14, 1996 at Irving, Texas
(Attendance 65,135)

The Green Bay Packers made it to the NFC championship game for the first time since the Vince Lombardi era, but they could have used some of the Lombardi magic, as they were defeated by the Dallas Cowboys 38-27.

Green Bay held a 27-24 lead heading into the fourth quarter, but Emmitt Smith scored two touchdowns in the final period to give the Cowboys the victory.

Smith was unstoppable, as he ran 35 times for 150 yards and three TD's. Michael Irwin scored Dallas' other two touchdowns in the first quarter, on six- and four-yard passes from Troy Aikman.

Green Bay opened the scoring on a Chris Jacke field goal. Following Irvin's two TD's, Brett Favre — the NFL's top quarterback in 1995 — threw a 73-yard TD pass to Robert Brooks in the first quarter. Favre later connected with TE Keith Jackson on a 24-yard scoring pass and again with Brooks on a one-yarder.

However, with Dallas holding a slim 31-27 lead in the fourth quarter, Favre was intercepted by Dallas CB Larry Brown, who redeemed himself after being beat by Brooks on the 73-yard TD. Two plays later, Smith scored for the final time and Dallas advanced to its third Super Bowl in four years.

Packers coach Mike Holmgren tipped his hat to the Cowboys. "With Emmitt Smith, Troy Aikman and Michael Irvin, the Cowboys have as fine an offensive team as I've ever seen. Boy, they are tough."

Dallas coach Barry Switzer, with the victory finally silencing his critics, added, "Our great players played great. Emmitt Smith made great plays."

**SCORING**

| | | | | | |
|---|---|---|---|---|---|
| GREEN BAY | 10 | 7 | 10 | 0 — 27 |
| DALLAS | 14 | 10 | 0 | 14 — 38 |

**First Quarter**
G.B.    Jacke, 46 yard field goal
Dall.    Irvin, 6 yard pass from Aikman
          PAT — Boniol (kick)
Dall.    Irvin, 4 yard pass from Aikman
          PAT — Boniol (kick)
G.B.    Brooks, 73 yard pass from Favre
          PAT — Jacke (kick)

**Second Quarter**
G.B.    Jackson, 24 yard pass from Favre
          PAT — Jacke (kick)
Dall.    Boniol, 34 yard field goal
Dall.    Smith, 1 yard run
          PAT — Boniol (kick)

**Third Quarter**
G.B.    Jacke, 37 yard field goal
G.B.    Brooks, 1 yard pass from Favre
          PAT — Jacke (kick)

**Fourth Quarter**
Dall.    Smith, 5 yard run
          PAT — Boniol (kick)
Dall.    Smith, 16 yard run
          PAT — Boniol (kick)

**TEAM STATISTICS**

| G.B. | | DAL. |
|---|---|---|
| 17 | First Downs- Total | 27 |
| 3 | First Downs- Rushing | 12 |
| 11 | First Downs- Passing | 13 |
| 3 | First Downs- Penalty | 2 |
| 0 | Fumbles- Number | 0 |
| 0 | Fumbles- Lost Ball | 0 |
| 11 | Penalties- Number | 6 |
| 84 | Yards Penalized | 65 |
| 0 | Missed Field Goals | 1 |
| 55 | Offensive Plays | 77 |
| 328 | Net Yards | 419 |
| 6.0 | Average Gain | 5.4 |
| 2 | Giveaways | 0 |
| 0 | Takeaways | 2 |
| - 2 | Difference | + 2 |

## INDIVIDUAL STATISTICS

### GREEN BAY     DALLAS

**RUSHING**

| | No. | Yds. | Avg. | | No. | Yds. | Avg. |
|---|---|---|---|---|---|---|---|
| Bennett | 9 | 46 | 5.1 | E. Smith | 35 | 150 | 4.3 |
| Henderson | 1 | 2 | 2.0 | Johnston | 2 | 8 | 4.0 |
| Levens | 1 | 1 | 1.0 | Aikman | 3 | 6 | 2.0 |
| Favre | 1 | -1 | -1.0 | S. Williams | 1 | 3 | 3.0 |
| | 12 | 48 | 4.0 | Sanders | 2 | 2 | 1.0 |
| | | | | | 43 | 169 | 3.9 |

**RECEIVING**

| | No. | Yds. | Avg. | | No. | Yds. | Avg. |
|---|---|---|---|---|---|---|---|
| Brooks | 6 | 105 | 17.5 | Irvin | 7 | 100 | 14.3 |
| Jackson | 5 | 99 | 19.8 | Novacek | 5 | 56 | 11.2 |
| Bennett | 3 | 20 | 6.7 | K. Williams | 3 | 32 | 10.7 |
| Mickens | 2 | 38 | 19.0 | Johnston | 3 | 15 | 5.0 |
| Levens | 2 | 11 | 5.5 | E. Smith | 2 | 17 | 8.5 |
| Chmura | 1 | 16 | 16.0 | Sanders | 1 | 35 | 35.0 |
| Freeman | 1 | 10 | 10.0 | | 21 | 255 | 12.1 |
| Ingram | 1 | 8 | 8.0 | | | | |
| | 21 | 307 | 14.6 | | | | |

**PUNTING**

| | No. | Yds. | Avg. | | No. | Yds. | Avg. |
|---|---|---|---|---|---|---|---|
| Hentrich | 3 | | 48.0 | Jett | 5 | | 36.6 |

**PUNT RETURNS**

| | No. | Yds. | Avg. | | No. | Yds. | Avg. |
|---|---|---|---|---|---|---|---|
| Freeman | 4 | 54 | 13.5 | Sanders | 1 | 6 | 6.0 |
| | | | | Sanders | 1FC | | |

**KICKOFF RETURNS**

| | No. | Yds. | Avg. | | No. | Yds. | Avg. |
|---|---|---|---|---|---|---|---|
| Freeman | 7 | 148 | 21.1 | K. Williams | 4 | 90 | 22.5 |

**INTERCEPTION RETURNS**

| | | | | | No. | Yds. | Avg. |
|---|---|---|---|---|---|---|---|
| None | | | | L. Brown | 1 | 28 | 28.0 |
| | | | | Lett | 1 | -1 | -1.0 |
| | | | | | 2 | 27 | 13.5 |

**PASSING**

**GREEN BAY**

| | Att. | Comp. | Comp. Pct. | Yds. | Int. | Yds./ Att. | Yds./ Comp. |
|---|---|---|---|---|---|---|---|
| Favre | 39 | 21 | 53.8 | 307 | 2 | 7.9 | 14.6 |

**DALLAS**

| | Att. | Comp. | Comp. Pct. | Yds. | Int. | Yds./ Att. | Yds./ Comp. |
|---|---|---|---|---|---|---|---|
| Aikman | 33 | 21 | 63.6 | 255 | 0 | 7.7 | 12.1 |

# Cowboys Win For Third Time in Four Years

The Dallas Cowboys won their third Super Bowl in four years when they defeated the Pittsburgh Steelers 27-17. It was the Steelers' first Super Bowl loss after four victories in the 1970s.

While Dallas usually relies on its offensive troika of Troy Aikman, Emmitt Smith and Michael Irvin for most of its exploits, It was CB Larry Brown who was the star of the day.

Brown was named the game's Most Valuable Player after he intercepted Pittsburgh QB Neil O'Donnell twice in the second half. The first came in the third quarter with the Cowboys clinging to a 13-7 lead and Pittsburgh driving. O'Donnell threw a pass so poorly — he says it slipped out of his hand — that Brown looked as if he was the intended receiver. He picked it off at the Dallas 38-yard line returned it 44 yards. Two plays later, Smith scored a touchdown to put Dallas up 20-7.

The Steelers came back in the fourth quarter, scoring on a 46-yard field goal by Norm Johnson and a one-yard run by Bam Morris to make the score 20-17 and give the Super Bowl a close game for the first time in five years.

However, O'Donnell then delivered Gift No. 2 to Brown. Apparently there was miscommunication on the play, as a rookie receiver ran the wrong route. But O'Donnell threw another pass seemingly intended for Brown, who returned it 33 yards to the six-yard line. Two plays later, Smith scored again, and the game was all but over.

"I can't worry about how they throw them," said Brown. "All I do is catch them. My job is to catch the ball. My job isn't to question how the throw comes."

Smith scored the two touchdowns, but he hardly had a typical game, rushing for only 49 yards on 18 carries. However, Aikman was his usual efficient self, as he completed 15 of 23 passes for 209 yards, a touchdown and no interceptions. And Irvin caught five of those passes for 75 yards.

So with the Pittsburgh defense holding Dallas' superstars mostly in check, it was Brown and the Cowboys' other cornerback, Deion Sanders, who did the damage. Sanders' blanket-like coverage on defense allowed the Steelers only half of the field to play with, forcing O'Donnell to look the other way most of the game. Sanders, playing offense on occasion, also caught a 47-yard pass on the Cowboys' second possession to set up a three-yard TD pass from Aikman to Jay Novacek that give Dallas a 10-0 lead.

Pittsburgh, meanwhile, never led, though they did outplay Dallas most of the game and certainly the second half. O'Donnell completed 28 of 49 passes for 239 yards, including a six-yard scoring pass to Yancey Thigpen in the second quarter. Steelers receivers played well, as Hastings caught 10 passes for 98 yards and Ernie Mills added eight receptions for 78 yards.

"The two interceptions led to their only scored in the second half," said Steelers coach Bill Cowher. "Other than that, I thought we played an excellent football game in the second half. That's the game of football — big plays. They made them, and we didn't."

And the Cowboys won … again.

## LINEUPS

| DAL. | OFFENSE | PIT. |
|---|---|---|
| K. Williams | WR | Thigpen |
| Tuinei | LT | Jackson |
| Newton | LG | Newberry |
| Kennard | C | Dawson |
| Allen | RG | Stai |
| E. Williams | RT | Searcy |
| Novacek | TE | Bruener |
| Irvin | WR | Mills |
| Aikman | QB | O'Donnell |
| E. Smith | RB | Pegrams |
| Johnston | RB | J.L. Williams |
| | DEFENSE | |
| Tolbert | LE | Buckner |
| Maryland | LT/NT | Steed |
| Lett | RT/RE | Seals |
| Haley | RE/LOLB | Greene |
| Edwards | SLB/LILB | Kirkland |
| R. Jones | MLB/RILB | C. Brown |
| D. Smith | WLB/ROLB | Lloyd |
| Sanders | LCB | W. Williams |
| L. Brown | RCB | Lake |
| D. Woodson | SS | Bell |
| Marion | FS | Perry |

### SUBSTITUTES

**DALLAS**

| OFFENSE | |
|---|---|
| Lang | R. Stone |
| Fleming | Watkins |
| D. Davis | |

| DEFENSE | |
|---|---|
| Bailey | Case |
| Bates | C. Williams |
| Schwantz | Hennings |
| Myles | McCormack |

| KICKERS | |
|---|---|
| Boniol | Jett |

**PITTSBURGH**

| OFFENSE | |
|---|---|
| Stewart | McAfee | Morris |
| Lester | Gammon | Strzelczyk |
| Holliday | Hayes | Hastings |

| DEFENSE | | |
|---|---|---|
| Figures | Oldham | Woodson |
| Fuller | Flowers | D. Jones |
| Olsavsky | Henry | Parrish |
| B. Johnson | Gildon | |

| KICKERS | |
|---|---|
| Stark | N. Johnson |

| | | | | | | |
|---|---|---|---|---|---|---|
| **DALLAS** | 10 | 3 | 7 | 7 | — | 27 |
| **PITTSBURGH** | 0 | 7 | 0 | 10 | — | 17 |

**SCORING**

**First Quarter**
Dall. Boniol 42 yard field goal
Dall. Novacek, 3 yard pass from Aikman
　PAT — Brien (kick)

**Second Quarter**
Dall. Boniol, 35 yard field goal
Pitt. Thigpen, 6 yard pass from O'Donnell
　PAT — Johnson (kick)

**Third Quarter**
Dall. E. Smith, 1 yard run
　PAT — Brien (kick)

**Fourth Quarter**
Pitt. Johnson, 46 yard field goal
Pitt. Morris, 1 yard run
　PAT — Johnson (kick)
Dall. E. Smith, 4 yard run
　PAT — Brien (kick)

### TEAM STATISTICS

| DAL. | | PIT. |
|---|---|---|
| 15 | First Downs-Total | 25 |
| 5 | First Downs-Rushing | 9 |
| 10 | First Downs-Pasing | 15 |
| 0 | First Downs-Penalty | 1 |
| 0 | Fumbles-Number | 2 |
| 0 | Fumbles-Lost Ball | 0 |
| 5 | Penalties-Number | 2 |
| 25 | Yards Penalized | 15 |
| 0 | Missed Field Goals | 0 |
| 50 | Offensive Plays | 84 |
| 254 | Net Yards | 310 |
| 5.1 | Average Gain | 3.7 |
| 0 | Giveaways | 3 |
| 3 | Takeaways | 0 |
| +3 | Difference | -3 |

## INDIVIDUAL STATISTICS

**DALLAS**

| | No. | Yds. | Avg. |
|---|---|---|---|
| **RUSHING** | | | |
| E. Smith | 18 | 49 | 2.7 |
| Johnston | 2 | 8 | 4.0 |
| K. Williams | 1 | 2 | 2.0 |
| Aikman | 4 | -3 | -0.8 |
| | 25 | 56 | 2.2 |
| **RECEIVING** | | | |
| Irvin | 5 | 75 | 15.2 |
| Novacek | 5 | 50 | 10.0 |
| K. Williams | 2 | 29 | 14.5 |
| Sanders | 1 | 47 | 47.0 |
| Johnston | 1 | 4 | 4.0 |
| E. Smith | 1 | 3 | 3.0 |
| | 15 | 209 | 13.9 |
| **PUNTING** | | | |
| Jett | 5 | | 38.2 |
| **PUNT RETURNS** | | | |
| Sanders | 1 | 11 | 11.0 |
| **KICKOFF RETURNS** | | | |
| K. Williams | 2 | 24 | 12.0 |
| Marion | 1 | 13 | 13.0 |
| | 3 | 37 | 12.3 |
| **INTERCEPTION RETURNS** | | | |
| L. Brown | 2 | 24 | 12.0 |
| Marion | 1 | 13 | 13.0 |
| | 3 | 37 | 12.3 |

**PITTSBURGH**

| | No. | Yds. | Avg. |
|---|---|---|---|
| **RUSHING** | | | |
| Morris | 19 | 73 | 3.8 |
| Pegram | 6 | 15 | 2.5 |
| Stewart | 4 | 15 | 3.8 |
| O'Donnell | 1 | 0 | 0.0 |
| J.L. Williams | 1 | 0 | 0.0 |
| | 31 | 103 | 3.3 |
| **RECEIVING** | | | |
| Hastings | 10 | 98 | 9.8 |
| Mills | 8 | 78 | 9.8 |
| Thigpen | 3 | 19 | 6.3 |
| Morris | 3 | 18 | 6.0 |
| Holliday | 2 | 19 | 9.5 |
| J.L. Williams | 2 | 7 | 3.5 |
| | 28 | 239 | 8.5 |
| **PUNTING** | | | |
| Starl | 4 | | 44.8 |
| **PUNT RETURNS** | | | |
| Hastings | 2 | 18 | 9.0 |
| **KICKOFF RETURNS** | | | |
| Mills | 4 | 79 | 19.8 |
| McAfee | 1 | 17 | 17.0 |
| | 5 | 96 | 19.2 |
| **INTERCEPTION RETURNS** | | | |
| None | | | |

### PASSING

**DALLAS**

| | Att. | Comp. | Comp. Pct. | Yds. | Int. | Yds./ Att. | Yds./ Comp. | Yards Lost Tackled |
|---|---|---|---|---|---|---|---|---|
| Aikman | 23 | 15 | 65.2 | 209 | 0 | 9.1 | 13.9 | 2/11 |

**PITTSBURGH**

| | Att. | Comp. | Comp. Pct. | Yds. | Int. | Yds./ Att. | Yds./ Comp. | Yards Lost Tackled |
|---|---|---|---|---|---|---|---|---|
| O'Donnell | 49 | 28 | 57.1 | 239 | 3 | 4.9 | 8.5 | 4/32 |

| Use Name (Nickname) - Positions | Team by Year | See Section | Hgt. | Wgt. | College | Int | Pts |
|---|---|---|---|---|---|---|---|
| Abbott, Vince K | 87-88SD | 5 | 6' | 207 | Washington, Fullerton State | | 100 |
| Abercrombie, Walter HB | 82-87Pit 88Phi | 23 | 6' | 207 | Baylor | | 174 |
| Abraham, Clifton DB | 95TB | | 5'9" | 184 | Florida State | | |
| Abraham, Robert LB | 82-86Hou | | 6'1" | 226 | N. Carolina State | 2 | |
| Abramowitz, Sid OT-OG | 83Bal 84Sea 85NYJ 87Ind | | 6'6" | 281 | Air Force, Tulsa | | |
| Abrams, Bobby LB | 90-91NYG 92Dal 92Cle 92NYG 93Dal 93Mia 94Min 95NE | | 6'3" | 232 | Michigan | | |
| Ache, Steve LB | 87Min | | 6'3" | 229 | SW Missouri State | | |
| Achica, George DT | 83-85USFL 85Ind | | 6'5" | 260 | Southern Calif. | | |
| Acker, Bill NT-DT | 80-81StL 82KC 83-84Buf 87KC | | 6'3" | 255 | Texas | | |
| Ackerman, Richard DT | 82-84SD 84,87Raid | | 6'4" | 258 | Memphis State | | |
| Acorn, Fred DB | 84TB | | 5'10" | 185 | Texas | 1 | |
| Adams, Curtis HB | 86-87SD | 2 | 6'0" | 194 | Central Michigan | | 30 |
| Adams, David HB | 87Dal | | 5'6" | 170 | Arizona | | 6 |
| Adams, Ernie LB | 87Det | | 6'2" | 226 | Illinois | | |
| Adams, George FB | 85NYG 86KJ 87-89NYG 90-91NE | 2 | 6'1" | 225 | Kentucky | | 42 |
| Adams, Michael DB | 87-88NO 89Phx | | 5'10" | 195 | Arkansas State | | |
| Adams, Sam DT | 94-95Sea | | 6'3" | 285 | Texas A&M | | 2 |
| Adams, Scott OT-OG | 92-93Min 94NO 95Chi | | 6'5" | 295 | Georgia | | |
| Adams, Stanley LB | 84Raid | | 6'2" | 215 | Memphis State | | |
| Adams, Stefon DB | 86-90Raid 90Cle 90Mia | 3 | 5'10" | 189 | East Carolina | 2 | 2 |
| Adams, Theo OT | 92Sea 93TB 95Phi | | 6'4" | 298 | Hawaii | | |
| Adams, Vashone DB | 95Cle | | 5'10" | 196 | Eastern Michigan | | |
| Adams, Willis WR | 79-85Cle | 2 | 6'2" | 196 | Houston | | 12 |
| Adickes, John C | 87-88Chi 89Min | | 6'3" | 264 | Baylor | | |
| Adickes, Mark OG | 84-85USFL 86-89KC 90-91Was 92XJ | | 6'4" | 278 | Baylor | | 6 |
| Adkins, Kevin C | 87KC | | 6'1" | 250 | Oklahoma | | |
| Adkins, Sam QB | 77-83Sea | 1 | 6'2" | 214 | Wichita State | | |
| Affholter, Erik WR | 91GB | | 6' | 183 | Southern Calif. | | |
| Age, Louis OT | 92Chi | | 6'7" | 350 | Southwestern La. | | |
| Agee, Mel DE-DT | 91Ind 92-95Atl | | 6'5" | 294 | Illinois | | |
| Agee, Tommie FB | 88Sea 89KC 90-94Dal | 2 | 6' | 218 | Auburn | | 12 |
| Agnew, Ray DE-DT | 90-94NE 95NYG | | 6'3" | 276 | N. Carolina State | | |
| Aguiar, Louis K | 91-93NYJ 94-95KC | 4 | 6'2" | 212 | Utah State | | 3 |
| Ahanotu, Chidi DE-DT | 93-95TB | | 6'2" | 284 | California | | |
| Ahrens, Dave LB | 81-84StL 85-87Ind 88Det 89Mia 90Sea | | 6'3" | 238 | Wisconsin | 1 | 6 |
| Aikens, Carl WR | 87Raid | | 6'1" | 185 | Northern Illinois | | 18 |
| Aikman, Troy QB | 89-95Dal | 12 | 6'4" | 218 | Oklahoma, U.C.L.A. | | 18 |
| Akiu, Mike WR | 85-86Hou | | 5'9" | 182 | Hawaii | | 6 |
| Alberts, Trev LB | 94-95Ind | | 6'4" | 243 | Nebraska | | |
| Albright, Ethan OT | 95Mia | | 6'5" | 292 | North Carolina | | |
| Albright, Ira NT-FB | 87Buf | | 6' | 285 | Northeastern Okla. | | |
| Albritton, Vince DB | 84-91Dal | | 6'2" | 215 | Washington | 1 | |
| Aldridge, Allen LB | 94-95Den | | 6'1" | 245 | Houston | | |
| Aldridge, Jerry FB | 80SF | | 6'2" | 220 | Angelo State | | |
| Aldridge, Melvin DB | 93Hou 95Arz | | 6'2" | 195 | Murray State | | |
| Ale, Arnold LB | 94KC | | 6'3" | 234 | U.C.L.A. | | |
| Alex, Keith OG | 93Atl | | 6'4" | 307 | Texas A&M | | |
| Alexander, Brent DB | 94-95Arz | | 5'10" | 184 | Tennessee State | 2 | |
| Alexander, Bruce DB | 89-91Det 92-93Mia | | 5'9" | 171 | Stephen F. Austin | 2 | |
| Alexander, Charles HB-FB | 79-85Cin | 2 | 6'1" | 224 | Louisiana State | | 90 |
| Alexander, Dan OG-OT | 77-89NYJ | | 6'4" | 261 | Louisiana State | | |
| Alexander, David OT-OG-C | 87-94Phi 95KJ | | 6'3" | 276 | Tulsa | | |
| Alexander, Derrick WR | 94-95Cle | 2 | 6'2" | 195 | Michigan | | 20 |
| Alexander, Derrick DE | 95Mia | | 6'4" | 265 | Florida State | | |
| Alexander, Elijah LB | 92TB 93-95Den | | 6'2" | 230 | Kansas State | 3 | |
| Alexander, Harold K | 93-94Atl | 4 | 6'2" | 224 | Appalachian State | | |
| Alexander, Jeff FB | 89,92Den | 2 | 6' | 232 | Southern U. | | 12 |
| Alexander, Mike WR | 89Raid 90KJ 91Buf | 2 | 6'3" | 195 | Penn State | | 6 |
| Alexander, Ray WR | 84Den 85-86CFL 87HJ 88-89Dal | | 6'4" | 195 | Florida A&M | | 42 |
| Alexander, Robert HB | 82-83LA 85USFL | | 6' | 185 | West Virginia | | |
| Alexander, Rogers LB | 86NYJ 87NE | | 6'3" | 222 | Penn State | | |
| Alexander, Vincent FB | 87NO | | 5'10" | 205 | Southern Miss. | | 6 |
| Alexis, Alton WR | 80Cin | | 6' | 184 | Tulane | | |
| Alford, Lynwood LB | 87NO | | 6'3" | 220 | Syracuse | | |
| Alipate, Tuineau LB | 94NYJ 95Min | | 6'1" | 242 | Washington State | | |
| Allegre, Raul K | 83Bal 84-85Ind 86-91NYG 91NYJ | 5 | 5'10" | 167 | Montana, Texas | | 594 |
| Allen, Anthony WR | 83-85USFL 85-86Atl 87-88Was 89SD | 2 | 5'11" | 182 | Washington | | 48 |
| Allen, Carl DB | 77-82StL 83-85USFL | | 6' | 186 | Southern Miss. | 16 | 6 |
| Allen, Derek OG | 95NYG | | 6'4" | 290 | Illinois | | |
| Allen, Earl DB | 87Hou | | 5'11" | 193 | Houston | | |
| Allen, Egypt DB | 87Chi | | 6' | 203 | Texas Christian | | |
| Allen, Eric DB | 88-94Phi 95NO | | 5'10" | 183 | Arizona State | 36 | 30 |
| Allen, Gary HB | 82Hou 83-84Dal | 23 | 5'10" | 183 | Hawaii | | 12 |
| Allen, Greg HB | 85Cle 86TB | | 5'11" | 200 | Florida State | | |
| Allen, Harvey DB | 87SD | | 6'3" | 215 | Nevada-Las Vegas | | |
| Allen, Jeff DB | 80Mia 82SD | | 5'11' | 190 | Cal.-Davis | 1 | |
| Allen, Kevin OT | 85Phi | | 6'5" | 284 | Indiana | | |
| Allen, Larry OT-OG | 94-95Dal | | 6'3" | 325 | Sonoma (Calif.) | | |
| Allen, Marcus HB | 82-92Raid 93-95KC | 2 | 6'2" | 205 | Southern Calif. | | 752 |
| Allen, Marvin HB | 88-91NE | 23 | 5'10" | 215 | Tulane | | 12 |
| Allen, Patrick DB | 84-90Hou | 3 | 5'10" | 180 | Utah State | 7 | |
| Allen, Terry HB | 91-912in 93KJ 94Min 95Was | 2 | 5'10" | 194 | Clemson | | 224 |
| Allerman, Kurt LB | 77-79StL 80-81GB 82-84StL 85Det | | 6'3" | 222 | Penn State | | |
| Allert, Ty LB | 86-87SD 87-89Phi 90Den 90Sea | | 6'2" | 233 | Texas | | |
| Allred, Brian DB | 93Sea | | 5'10" | 175 | Sacramento State | | |
| Alm, Jeff DT | 90-93Hou | | 6'6" | 284 | Notre Dame | | |
| December 13, 1993 — Committed suicide | | | | | | | |
| Almodobar, Beau WR | 87NYG | | 5'9" | 180 | Norwich | | |
| Alphin, Gerald WR | 90-91 | | 6'3" | 220 | Kansas State | | |
| Alston, Lyneal WR | 87Pit | | 6'1" | 205 | Southern Miss. | | 12 |
| Alston, O'Brien LB | 88-89Ind 90KJ | | 6'6" | 246 | Maryland | | |
| Alt, John OT | 84-95KC | | 6'8" | 299 | Iowa | | |
| Althoff, Jim DT | 87Chi | | 6'3" | 278 | Winona State | | |
| Alvarez, Wilson K | 81Sea | 5 | 6' | 165 | Southeastern La. | | 23 |
| Alvers, Steve TE-C | 81Buf 82NYJ | | 6'4" | 240 | Miami (Fla.) | | |
| Alvord, Steve DT | 87StL 88Phx | | 6'4" | 272 | Washington | | |
| Ambrose, Ashley DB | 92-95Ind | | 5'10" | 177 | Miss. Valley St. | 5 | 6 |
| Anders, Kimble HB-FB | 91-95KC | 2 | 5'11" | 219 | Houston | | 36 |
| Andersen, Morten K | 82-95NO | 5 | 6'2" | 214 | Michigan State | | 1440 |
| Anderson, Alfred FB | 84-91Min | 23 | 6'1" | 219 | Baylor | | 162 |
| Anderson, Aric LB | 87GB | | 6'2" | 200 | Millikin | | |
| Anderson, Anthony HB | 79Pit 80Atl 83,85USFL | | 6' | 197 | Temple | | 6 |
| Anderson, Anthony DB | 87SD | | 6'2" | 205 | Grambling | | |
| Anderson, Brad WR | 84-85Chi | | 6'2" | 197 | Arizona | | 6 |
| Anderson, Curtis DE | 79KC 83-85USFL | | 6'6" | 250 | Central St.-Ohio | | |
| Anderson, Darren DB | 92NE 92-93TB 94-95KC | | 5'10" | 180 | Toledo | 1 | |
| Anderson, Don DB | 85Ind 87TB | | 5'10" | 196 | Purdue | 1 | |
| Anderson, Dunstan DE | 94Atl | | 6'4" | 254 | Tulsa | | |
| Anderson, Dwayne DB | 87StL | | 6' | 205 | S.M.U. | | |
| Anderson, Eddie DB | 86Sea 88-94Raid 95Oak | | 6'1" | 199 | Fort Valley State | 19 | 18 |
| Anderson, Erick LB | 93KC 94Was | | 6'1" | 235 | Michigan | | |
| Anderson, Fred DE-DT | 78Pit 79BH 80-82Sea 84USFL | | 6'4" | 238 | Oregon State, Prairie View | | |
| Anderson, Gary HB-WR | 83-85USFL 85-88SD 89HO 90-93TB 93Det | 23 | 6'1" | 185 | Arkansas | | 192 |
| Anderson, Gary K | 82-94Pit 95Phi | 5 | 5'11' | 171 | Syracuse | | 1441 |
| Anderson, Herbie DB | 91Hou | | 5'9" | 183 | Texas A&I | | |
| Anderson, Jamal HB-FB | 94-95Atl | 23 | 5'10" | 240 | Utah | | 6 |
| Anderson, Jesse TE | 90-92TB 92Pit 93NO | | 6'2" | 245 | Mississippi State | | 12 |
| Anderson, John LB | 78-89GB | | 6'3" | 226 | Michigan | 23 | 10 |
| Anderson, Kim DB | 80-83Bal 84Ind 85USFL | 3 | 5'11" | 183 | Arizona State | 7 | 6 |
| Anderson, Larry DB | 78-81Pit 82-83Bal 84Ind | 3 | 5'11" | 183 | Louisiana Tech | 2 | 6 |
| Anderson, Marcus WR | 81Chi 83-85USFL | | 6' | 178 | Tulane | | 12 |
| Anderson, Melvin WR | 87Pit | | 5'11" | 175 | Minnesota | | |
| Anderson, Neal HB | 86-93Chi | 2 | 5'11" | 210 | Florida | | 426 |
| Anderson Ottis (O.J.) HB-FB | 79-86StL 86-92NYG | 2 | 6'2" | 220 | Miami (Fla.) | | 518 |
| Anderson, Richie FB-HB | 93-95NYJ | 2 | 6'2" | 220 | Penn State | | 12 |
| Anderson, Stevie WR | 94NYJ 95Arz | 2 | 6'5" | 215 | Grambling | | 10 |
| Anderson, Stuart LB | 82-83Was 84Cle 85Was | | 6'1" | 238 | Virginia | | |
| Anderson, Vickey Ray FB | 80GB 83USFL | | 6' | 205 | Oklahoma | | |
| Anderson, Willie (Flipper) WR | 88-94LA 95Ind | 2 | 6' | 169 | U.C.L.A. | | 168 |
| Andolsek, Eric OG | 88-91Det | | 6'2" | 284 | Louisiana State | | |
| June 1992 — killed in accident | | | | | | | |
| Andrews, George LB | 79-84LA | | 6'3" | 224 | Nebraska | 2 | |
| Andrews, Ricky LB | 90Sea | | 6'2" | 236 | Washington | | |
| Angelo, Jim OG | 87Phi | | 6'3" | 275 | Indiana (Pa.) | | |
| Andrews, Mitch TE | 87Den | | 6'2" | 239 | Louisiana State | | |
| Andrews, Tom OT-C-OG | 84-85Chi 87Sea | | 6'4" | 265 | Louisville | | |
| Andrews, William FB | 79-83Atl 84-85KJ 86Atl | 2 | 6' | 206 | Auburn | | 246 |
| Andrus, Sheldon DT-NT | 86-87NO | | 6'1" | 271 | Nicholls State | | |
| Ankrom, Scott DB | 89Dal 90KJ | | 6'1" | 194 | Texas Christian | | |
| Anno, Sam LB | 87LA 87-88Min 89-91TB 92-93SD | | 6'2" | 236 | Southern Calif. | | |
| Anthony, Terrence DB | 87StL | | 5'10" | 183 | Iowa State | | |
| Anthony, Terry WR | 90-91TB | | 6' | 200 | Florida State | | |
| Anthony, Tyrone HB-FB | 84-85NO | 23 | 5'11" | 212 | North Carolina | | 6 |
| Antrum, Glenn WR | 89NE | | 5'1" | 175 | Connecticut | | |
| Apke, Steve LB | 87Pit | | 6'1' | 222 | Pittsburgh | | |
| Apuna, Ben LB | 80NYG 83-84USFL | | 6'1" | 222 | Arizona State | | |
| Arapostathis, Evan K | 86StL | 4 | 5'9" | 160 | Eastern Illinois | | |
| Arbubakrr, Hasson DE | 83TB 84Min | | 6'4" | 250 | Texas Tech | | |
| Arbuckle, Charles TE | 92-95Ind | 2 | 6'2" | 248 | U.C.L.A. | | 6 |
| Archambeau, Lester DE | 90-92GB 93-95Atl | | 6'4" | 274 | Stanford | | |
| Archer, David QB | 84-87Atl 88Was 89SD 92Phi | 12 | 6'2" | 207 | Iowa State | | 12 |
| Ard, Billy OG | 81-88NYG 89-91GB | | 6'3" | 265 | Wake Forest | | |
| Ariey, Mike OT | 89GB | | 6'5" | 285 | San Diego State | | |
| Ariri, Obed K | 83USFL 84TB 87Was | 5 | 5'8" | 168 | Clemson | | 110 |
| Armour, Justin WR | 95Buf | 2 | 6'4" | 209 | Stanford | | 18 |
| Armstead, Jessie LB | 93-95NYG | | 6'1" | 233 | Miami (Fla.) | 3 | 6 |
| Armstrong, Adger FB | 80-82Hou 83-85TB | 2 | 6' | 213 | Texas A&I | | 54 |
| Armstrong, Antonio LB | 95Mia | | 6'1" | 234 | Texas A&M | | |
| Armstrong, Bruce OT-OG | 87-95NE | | 6'4" | 286 | Louisville | | |
| Armstrong, Harvey NT | 82-84Phi 86-90Ind | | 6'3" | 265 | S.M.U. | 1 | |
| Armstrong, Jimmy DB | 87Dal | | 5'8" | 166 | Appalachian State | | |
| Armstrong, John DB | 87Buf | | 5'9" | 190 | Richmond | | |
| Armstrong, Trace DE | 89-94Chi 95Mia | | 6'4" | 266 | Arizona State, Florida | | |
| Armstrong, Tyji TE | 92-95TB | 2 | 6'4" | 259 | Mississippi | | 18 |
| Arnold, David DB | 89Pit | | 6'3" | 208 | Michigan | | |
| Arnold, Jim K | 83-85KC 86-93Det 94Mia | 4 | 6'2" | 215 | Vanderbilt | | |
| Arnold, John WR | 79-80Det 84-85USFL | | 5'10" | 175 | Wyoming | | |
| Arnold, Walt TE | 80-81LA 82-83Hou 84Was 84-87KC | 2 | 6'3" | 228 | New Mexico | | 48 |
| Aronson, Doug OG | 87Cin | | 6'3" | 293 | San Diego State | | |
| Arp, John OT | 87Chi | | 6'5" | 275 | Lincoln | | |
| Arthur, Mike C | 91-92Cin 93-94NE 95GB | | 6'3" | 278 | Texas A&M | | |
| Arvie, Herman OT | 93-95Cle | | 6'4" | 310 | Grambling | | |
| Ashe, Richard DE | 90LA | | 6'4" | 260 | Humboldt State | | |
| Asher, Jamie TE | 95Was | 2 | 6'3" | 243 | Louisville | | |
| Ashley, Walker Lee LB | 83-84Min 85LJ 86-88Min 89KC | | 6' | 236 | Penn State | 2 | 6 |
| Ashmore, Darryl OT | 93-94LA 95StL | | 6'7" | 303 | Northwestern | | |
| Aska, Joe HB | 95Oak | | 5'1" | 235 | Central St.-Okla. | | |
| Asmus, Jim K | 87SF | | 6'2" | 195 | Hawaii | | |
| Atkins, Gene DB | 87-93NO 94-95Mia | 3 | 6'1" | 200 | Florida A&M | 21 | |
| Atkins, James OT | 94-95Sea | | 6'6" | 303 | Southwestern La. | | |
| Atkins, Kelvin LB | 83Chi | | 6'3" | 235 | Illinois | | |
| Atkins, Steve FB-HB | 79-81GB 81Phi | 2 | 6' | 216 | Maryland | | 18 |
| Atkinson, Jess K | 85NYG 85StL 86-87Was 88Ind | 5 | 5'9" | 167 | Maryland | | 60 |
| Atkinson, Ricky DB | 87NE | | 6' | 175 | Southern Conn. St. | | |
| Atwater, Steve DB | 89-95Den | | 6'3" | 217 | Arkansas | 18 | |
| Audick, Dan OT-OG | 77StL 78-80SD 81-82SF 83-84StL | | 6'3" | 252 | Hawaii | | |
| Auer, Jim DE | 87Phi | | 6'7" | 275 | Georgia | | |
| Auer, Scott OT-OG | 84-85KC | | 6'5" | 255 | Michigan State | | |
| Auer, Todd LB | 87GB | | 6'1" | 230 | Western Illinois | | |
| Aughtman, Dowe DE | 84Dal | | 6'3" | 260 | Auburn | | |
| August, Steve OT | 77-84Sea 84Pit | | 6'5" | 265 | Tulsa | | |
| Augustyniak, Mike FB | 81-83NYJ 84KJ | 2 | 5'11" | 225 | Purdue | | 48 |
| Aupiu, David LB | 87LA | | 6'2" | 235 | Brigham Young | | |
| Austin, Cliff HB | 83NO 84-86Atl 87TB | 23 | 6' | 203 | Clemson | | 12 |
| Austin, Kent QB | 86StL | | 6'1" | 195 | Mississippi | | |
| Auzenne, Troy OT | 92-95Chi | | 6'7" | 296 | California | | |
| Avery, Steve FB | 89Hou 91GB 94-95Pit | 2 | 6'1" | 216 | Northern Michigan | | 6 |
| Awalt, Rob TE | 87StL 88-89Phx 90-91Dal 92-93Buf | 2 | 6'5" | 248 | Nevada-Reno, San Diego State | | 60 |
| Aydelette, Buddy OT | 80GB 81KJ 83-85USFL 87Pit 88KJ | | 6'4" | 256 | Alabama | | |
| Ayers, John OG-OT | 77-86SF 87Den | | 6'5" | 258 | Texas, West Texas State | | |
| Ayers, Marvin DE | 87Phi | | 6'5" | 265 | Grambling | | |
| Azelby, Joe LB | 84Buf | | 6'1" | 225 | Harvard | | |
| Baab, Mike C | 82-87Cle 88-89NE 90-91Cle 92KC | | 6'4" | 270 | Texas | | |
| Baack, Steve DE-DT-NT-OG | 84-87Det 88PJ | | 6'4" | 264 | Oregon | | |
| Badanjek, Rick FB | 86Was 87-88Atl | 2 | 5'8" | 217 | Maryland | | 6 |
| Baham, Curtis DB | 87Sea | | 5'11" | 180 | Tulane | | |
| Bahr, Chris K | 76-79Cin 80-81Oak 82-88Raid 89SD | 5 | 5'10" | 172 | Penn State | | 1213 |
| Bahr, Matt K | 79-80Pit 81SF 81-89Cle 90-92NYG 93Phi 93-95NE | 5 | 5'10" | 173 | Penn State | | 1422 |
| Bailey, Aaron WR | 94-95Ind | 23 | 5'10" | 184 | Louisville | | 24 |
| Bailey, Carlton LB | 88-92Buf 93-94NYG 95Car | | 6'2" | 239 | North Carolina | 1 | |

| Use Name (Nickname) - Positions | Team by Year | See Section | Hgt. | Wgt. | College | Int | Pts |
|---|---|---|---|---|---|---|---|
| Bailey, Clarence FB | 87Mia | | 5'11" | 220 | Hampton Institute | | |
| Bailey, David DE | 90Phi | | 6'4" | 240 | Oklahoma State | | |
| Bailey, Don C | 84-85 Ind | | 6'3" | 264 | Miami (Fla.) | | |
| Bailey, Edwin OG | 81-91Sea | | 6'4" | 271 | S. Carolina State | | |
| Bailey, Elmer WR | 80-81Mia 82Bal 84USFL | | 6' | 195 | Lincoln (Mo.), Macalester, Minnesota | | |
| Bailey, Eric TE | 87Phi 88XJ | | 6'5" | 240 | Kansas State | | |
| Bailey, Harold WR | 81-82Hou 83KJ | | 6'2" | 195 | Oklahoma State | | |
| Bailey, Johnny HB | 90-91Chi 92-93Phx 94Arz 95StL | 23 | 5'8" | 180 | Texas A&I | | 56 |
| Bailey, Robert DB | 91-94LA 95Was 95Dal | | 5'9" | 176 | Miami (Fla.) | 5 | 12 |
| Bailey, Stacey WR | 82-90Atl | 2 | 6' | 158 | San Jose State | | 78 |
| Bailey, Thomas WR | 95Cin | | 6' | 196 | Auburn | | |
| Bailey, Tom HB-FB | 71-74Phi 75KJ | 2 | 6'2" | 211 | Florida State | | 12 |
| Bailey, Victor WR | 93-94Phi 95KC | 2 | 6'2" | 196 | Texas-El Paso, Missouri | | 6 |
| Bain, Bill OG-OT | 75GB 76Den 77KJ 78Den 78NYG 79-85LA 86NYJ 86NE | | 6'4" | 279 | Colorado, Southern Calif. | | |
| Baker, Al (Bubba) DE | 78-82Det 83-86StL 87Cle 88Min 89-90Cle | | 6'6" | 265 | Colorado State | 4 | |
| Baker, Charlie LB | 80-87StL | | 6'2" | 226 | New Mexico | | |
| Baker, Jerry DT | 83Den | | 6'2" | 297 | Tulane | | |
| Baker, Jesse DE | 79-85Hou 86Dal 86-87Hou | | 6'5" | 269 | Jacksonville State | | 8 |
| Baker, Jon K | 95Dal | | 6'1" | 170 | Arizona State | | |
| Baker, Keith WR | 85Phi | | 5'10" | 185 | Texas A&M, Texas Southern | | |
| Baker, Myron LB | 93-95Chi | | 6'1" | 230 | Louisiana Tech | | 12 |
| Baker, Ron OG | 78-79Bal 80-88Phi | | 6'4" | 260 | Oklahoma State | | |
| Baker, Shannon WR | 94Ind | | 5'9" | 185 | Florida State | | |
| Baker, Stan WR | 87Det | | 5'10" | 165 | Olivet | | |
| Baker, Stephen WR | 87-92NYG | 2 | 5'8" | 160 | Fresno State | | 126 |
| Baker, Tony HB | 86Atl 86Cle 87BW 88Cle 89Phx | | 5'10" | 182 | East Carolina | | |
| Baldinger, Brian C-OG-OT | 82-84Dal 85KJ 86-87Dal 88-91Ind 92-93Phi | | 6'4" | 271 | Duke | | |
| Baldinger, Gary DE-NT | 86-88KC 90-92Buf | | 6'2" | 264 | Wake Forest | | |
| Baldinger, Rich OT-OG | 82-83NYG 83-92KC 93NE | | 6'4" | 288 | Wake Forest | | |
| Baldischwiler, Karl OT | 78-82Det 83Bal 84ZJ 85-86Ind | | 6'5" | 267 | Oklahoma | | |
| Baldwin, Keith DE | 82-85Cle 86KJ 87-88SD | | 6'4" | 263 | Texas A&M | | |
| Baldwin, Don DE | 87NYJ | | 6'3" | 263 | Purdue | | |
| Baldwin, Randy FB-HB | 91Min 92-94Cle 95Ca 95SF | 23 | 5'10" | 216 | Mississippi | | 12 |
| Baldwin, Tom DT-NT-DE | 84-86NYJ 87FJ 88NYJ | | 6'4" | 274 | Wisonsin, Tulsa | | |
| Ball, Eric HB-FB | 89-94Cin 95Oak | 23 | 6'2" | 219 | U.C.L.A. | | 66 |
| Ball, Jerry NT-DT | 87-93Det 94Raid 95Oak | | 6'1" | 306 | S.M.U. | | 8 |
| Ball, Michael DB | 88-93Ind | | 6' | 216 | Southern U. | 1 | 6 |
| Ballage, Pat DB | 86-87Ind | | 6'1" | 204 | Notre Dame | | |
| Ballard, Howard (House) OT | 88-93Buf 94-95Sea | | 6'6" | 326 | Alabama A&M | | |
| Ballard, Quinton DT | 83Bal | | 6'3" | 289 | Elon | | |
| Bandison, Romeo DT | 95Was | | 6'5" | 290 | Oregon | | |
| Banes, Joey OT | 90Ind | | 6'7" | 282 | Houston | | |
| Banker, Ted OG-C-OT | 84-88NYJ 89Cle 90KJ | | 6'2" | 270 | SE Missouri St. | | |
| Banks, Carl LB | 84-92NYG 93Was 94-95Cle | | 6'4" | 238 | Michigan State | 3 | 6 |
| Banks, Chip LB | 82-86 Cle 87SD 88HO 89-92Ind 93SJ | | 6'4" | 243 | Southern Calif. | 9 | 14 |
| Banks, Chuck FB | 86Hou 87Ind | 2 | 6'2" | 226 | West Virginia Tech | | |
| Banks, Fred WR | 85Cle 87-93Mia 93Chi | 2 | 5'10" | 179 | Liberty | | 60 |
| Banks, Gordon WR | 80-81NO 83-85USFL 85-87Dal | 23 | 5'10" | 174 | Stanford | | 6 |
| Banks, Robert DE | 88 Hou 89-90Cle | | 6'5" | 259 | Notre Dame | | |
| Banks, Roy WR | 87-88Ind | | 5'10" | 192 | Eastern Illinois | | |
| Bankston, Michael NT-DT | 92-93Phx 94-95Arz | | 6'2" | 285 | Sam Houston State | 1 | |
| Banta, Bradford TE | 94-95Ind | | 6'6" | 255 | Southern Calif. | | |
| Barbaro, Gary DB | 76-83KC 84-85USFL | | 6'4" | 203 | Nicholls State | 42 | 24 |
| Barbay, Roland NT | 87Sea 88KJ | | 260 | 260 | Louisiana State | | |
| Barber, Chris DB | 87Cin 88AJ 89Cin 92TB | | 6' | 187 | North Carolina A&T | | |
| Barber, Kurt LB-DE | 92-95NYJ | | 6'4" | 245 | Southern Calif. | | |
| Barber, Marion FB | 82-88NYJ | 2 | 6'3" | 226 | Minnesota | | 24 |
| Barber, Michael LB | 95Sea | | 6'1" | 252 | Clemson | | |
| Barber, Mike TE-WR | 76-81Hou 82-85LA 85Den | 2 | 6'3" | 236 | Louisiana Tech | | 102 |
| Barber, Mike WR | 89SF 89Phx 89SF 90-91Cin 92TB | 2 | 5'10" | 172 | Marshall | | 12 |
| Barker, Bryan K | 90-93KC 94Phi 95Jax | 4 | 6'1" | 187 | Santa Clara | | |
| Barker, Jay QB | 95NE | | 6'3" | 215 | Alabama | | |
| Barker, Leo LB | 84-91Cin | | 6'2" | 226 | New Mexico State | 3 | 6 |
| Barker, Roy DT-DE | 92-95Min | | 6'4" | 286 | North Carolina | 1 | |
| Barker, Tony LB | 92Was | | 6'2" | 230 | Rice | | |
| Barksdale, Rod WR | 86Raid 87Dal 88KJ | 2 | 6' | 189 | Arizona | | 18 |
| Barlow, Corey DB | 93Phi 94KJ | | 5'9" | 182 | Auburn | | |
| Barnes, Earnest DE | 83Bal | | 6'4" | 260 | Mississippi State | | |
| Barnes, Jeff LB | 77-81Oak 82-87Raid | | 6'2" | 223 | California | 5 | |
| Barnes, Johnnie WR | 92-94SD 95Pit | 2 | 6'1" | 180 | Hampton U. | | |
| Barnes, Lew WR | 86Chi 87BL 88Atl 89KC | 3 | 5'8" | 163 | Oregon | | 6 |
| Barnes, Reggie LB | 93,95Pit | | 6'1" | 235 | Oklahoma | | |
| Barnes, Roosevelt LB | 82-85Det | | 6'2" | 224 | Purdue | 3 | |
| Barnes, Tomur DB | 94-95Hou | | 5'10" | 188 | North Texas | 2 | |
| Barnett, Bill DE-NT | 80-85Mia | | 6'4" | 258 | Nebraska | | |
| Barnett, Buster TE | 81-84Buf | | 6'5" | 228 | Jackson State | | 6 |
| Barnett, Dean TE | 83Den | | 6'2" | 225 | Nevada-Las Vegas | | |
| Barnett, Doug DE-C | 82-83LA 84KJ 85Was 87Atl | | 6'3" | 253 | Azusa Pacific | | |
| Barnett, Fred WR | 90-95Phi | 2 | 6' | 203 | Arkansas State | | 170 |
| Barnett, Harlon DB | 90-92Cle 93-94NE 95Min | | 5'11" | 200 | Michigan State | 4 | |
| Barnett, Oliver DE-DT-NT | 90-92Atl 93-94Buf 95SF | | 6'3" | 288 | Kentucky | | 6 |
| Barnett, Tim WR | 91-93KC | 2 | 6'1" | 209 | Jackson State | | 60 |
| Barnett, Troy DE | 94-95NE | | 6'4" | 287 | North Carolina | | |
| Barnett, Vincent DB | 87Cle | | 6'1" | 200 | Arkansas State | | |
| Barney, Milton WR | 87Atl | 2 | 5'9" | 156 | Alcorn State | | 12 |
| Barnhardt, Tommy K | 87NO 87Chi 88Was 89-94NO 95Car | 4 | 6'3" | 205 | East Carolina, North Carolina | | |
| Barnwell, Malcolm WR | 81Oak 82-84Raid 85Was 85NO | 2 | 5'11" | 184 | Virginia Union | | 24 |
| Barr, Dave QB | 95StL | | 6'3" | 210 | California | | |
| Barrett, Dave FB | 82TB 83KJ | | 6' | 230 | Houston | | |
| Barrett, Reggie WR | 91-93Det 94KJ | | 6'3" | 215 | Texas-El Paso | | 6 |
| Barrie, Sebastian DE-DT | 92GB 94Arz 95SD | | 6'3" | 275 | Liberty | | |
| Barrow, Micheal LB | 93-95Hou | | 6'1" | 236 | Miami (Fla.) | | |
| Barrows, Scott OG-C | 86-88Det | | 6'2" | 278 | West Virginia | | |
| Bartalo, Steve HB | 87TB 88SF | | 5'9" | 200 | Colorado State | | 6 |
| Bartkowski, Steve QB | 75-85Atl 85Was 86LA | 12 | 6'4" | 215 | California | | 66 |
| Bartlett, Doug DE-DT | 88Phi | | 6'2" | 255 | Northern Illinois | | |
| Bartlewski, Rich TE | 90Raid 91Atl | | 6'5" | 250 | Fresno State | | |
| Bartley, Ephesians LB | 92Phi | | 6'2" | 213 | Florida | | |
| Barton, Harris OT | 87-95SF | | 6'4" | 282 | North Carolina | | |
| Bartrum, Mike TE-FB | 93KC 95GB | | 6'4" | 234 | Marshall | | |
| Baschnagel, Brian WR-DB | 76-84Chi 85KJ | 23 | 5'11" | 187 | Ohio State | | 60 |
| Bass, Don WR-TE | 78-81Cin 82NO | 2 | 6'2" | 219 | Houston | | 84 |

| Use Name (Nickname) - Positions | Team by Year | See Section | Hgt. | Wgt. | College | Int | Pts |
|---|---|---|---|---|---|---|---|
| Bass, Robert LB | 95Chi | | 6'1" | 239 | Miami (Fla.) | | |
| Bates, Bill DB | 83-95Dal | | 6'1" | 200 | Tennessee | 14 | |
| Bates, Mario HB | 94-95NO | 2 | 6'1" | 217 | Arizona State | | 78 |
| Bates, Michael WR | 93-94Sea 95Cle | 3 | 5'10" | 189 | Arizona | | 6 |
| Bates, Patrick DB | 93-94Raid | | 6'3" | 220 | Texas A&M | 1 | |
| Batiste, Michael OG-DT | 95Dal | | 6'3" | 305 | Tulane | | |
| Battaglia, Matt LB | 87Phi | | 6'2" | 225 | Louisville | | |
| Battle, Ralph DB | 84Cin | | 6'2" | 205 | Jacksonville State | | |
| Battle, Ron TE | 81-82LA | | 6'3" | 220 | North Texas State | | 6 |
| Batton, Bobby HB | 80NYJ | 1 | 5'11" | 185 | Nev.-Las Vegas | | |
| Baty, Greg TE | 86-87NE 87LA 88Phx 90-94Mia | 2 | 6'5" | 241 | Stanford | | 48 |
| Bauer, Hank HB-FB | 77-83SD | 2 | 5'10" | 200 | Cal. Lutheran | | 120 |
| Baugh, Tom C | 86-88KC 89Cle | | 6'3" | 274 | Southern Illinois | | |
| Baumann, Charlie K | 91Mia 91-92NE | 5 | 6'1" | 203 | West Virginia | | 97 |
| Baumhower, Bob NT | 77-84Mia 85KJ 86Mia | | 6'5" | 261 | Alabama | 1 | 12 |
| Bavaro, David LB | 90Phx 91Buf 92Min 93-94NE | | 6' | 234 | Syracuse | | |
| Bavaro, Mark TE | 85-90NYG 92Cle 93-94Phi | 2 | 6'4" | 245 | Notre Dame | | 234 |
| Bax, Carl OG-OT | 89-90TB | | 6'4" | 290 | Missouri | | |
| Baxley, Rob OT | 92Phx 93KJ | | 6'5" | 287 | Iowa | | |
| Baxter, Brad FB | 89-95NYJ | 2 | 6'1" | 233 | Alabama State | | 210 |
| Baxter, Fred TE | 93-95NYJ | 2 | 6'3" | 255 | Auburn | | 18 |
| Bayless, Martin DB | 84StL 84-86Buf 87-91SD 92-93KC 94Was 95KC | | 6'2" | 208 | Bowling Green | 12 | 6 |
| Bayless, Rick FB | 89Min | | 6' | 202 | Iowa | | |
| Baylor, John DB | 89-93Ind | | 6' | 203 | Southern Miss. | 8 | |
| Beach, Pat TE | 82-83Bal 84NJ 85-91Ind 92Phi 93Phx | 2 | 6'4" | 247 | Washington State | | 84 |
| Beach, Sanjay WR | 89NYJ 91SF 92GB 93SF | 2 | 6' | 189 | Colorado State | | 12 |
| Beals, Shawn WR | 88Phi | 3 | 5'10" | 178 | Idaho State | | |
| Bealles, Bill OT | 87Mia | | 6'7" | 290 | Northern Iowa | | |
| Beamon, Willie DB | 93-95NYG | | 5'11" | 175 | Northern Iowa | 1 | |
| Beasley, Tom DT-DE-NT | 78-83Pit 84-86Was | | 6'5" | 250 | Virginia Tech | | |
| Beauford, Clayton WR | 87Cle | | 5'11" | 190 | Auburn | | |
| Beavers, Aubrey LB | 94-95Mia | | 6'3" | 233 | Oklahoma | 3 | |
| Beavers, Scott OG | 90Den | | 6'4" | 277 | Georgia Tech | | |
| Becker, Dave DB | 80Chi | | 6'2" | 190 | Iowa | | |
| Becker, Kurt OG | 82-88Chi 89LA 90Chi | | 6'5" | 271 | Michigan | | |
| Beckles, Ian OG | 90-95TB | | 6'1" | 299 | Indiana | | |
| Beckman, Brad TE | 88NYG 89Atl | 2 | 6'3" | 238 | Nebraska-Omaha | | 6 |
| | Dec. 18, 1989 — Died in Automobile Accident | | | | | | |
| Beckman, Ed TE | 77-84KC | 2 | 6'4" | 229 | Florida State | | 8 |
| Beebe, Don WR | 89-94Buf 95Car | 23 | 5'11" | 177 | Western Illinois, Aurora, Chadron St. | | 114 |
| Beecham, Earl HB | 87NYG | | 5'8" | 180 | Bucknell | | |
| Beecher, Willie K | 87Mia | 5 | 5'10" | 170 | Utah State | | 21 |
| Beekley, Bruce LB | 80GB 83USFL | | 6'2" | 225 | Oregon | | |
| Beemer, Bob DE | 87Det | | 6'5" | 231 | Toledo | | |
| Beer, Tom LB-FB | 94-95Det | | 6'1" | 237 | Wayne State | | |
| Beeson, Terry LB | 77-81Sea 82SF 84-85USFL | | 6'3" | 239 | Kansas | 1 | |
| Behning, Mark OT | 86Pit 87FJ | | 6'6" | 290 | Nebraska | | |
| Belcher, Kevin OG | 83-84NYG | | 6'3" | 266 | Texas-El Paso | | |
| Belcher, Kevin OT | 85Raid 87Den | | 6'6" | 310 | Wisconsin Wesleyan | | |
| Belichick, Bill | HC91-95Cle | | | | | | |
| Belin, Chuck OG | 94LA 95StL | | 6'2" | 309 | Wisconsin | | |
| Belk, Rocky WR | 83Cle | | 6' | 187 | Miami (Fla.) | | |
| Belk, Veno TE | 87Buf | | 6'3" | 233 | Michigan State | | |
| Bell, Albert WR | 88GB | | 6' | 170 | Alabama | | |
| Bell, Anthony LB | 86-87StL 88-90Phx 91Det 92Raid | | 6'3" | 235 | Michigan State | 2 | |
| Bell, Billy DB | 89Hou 91KC | | 5'10" | 170 | Lamar | 1 | |
| Bell, Bobby LB | 84NYJ 87Chi | | 6'3" | 217 | Missouri | | |
| Bell, Coleman TE | 95Was | 2 | 6'2" | 243 | Miami (Fla.) | | 6 |
| Bell, Greg HB | 84-87Buf 87-89LA 90Raid | 2 | 5'10" | 210 | Notre Dame | | 348 |
| Bell, Jerry TE | 82-86TB | 2 | 6'5" | 230 | Arizona State | | 42 |
| Bell, Ken HB-WR | 86-89Den | 23 | 5'10" | 190 | Boston College | | |
| Bell, Kerwin QB | 88Atl 89TB | | 6'2" | 205 | Florida | | |
| Bell, Mark DE | 79-80Sea 81KJ 82Sea 83Bal 84Ind | | 6'5" | 241 | Colorado State | | |
| Bell, Mark WR | 80-81StL | | 5'9" | 175 | Colorado State | | |
| Bell, Mike DE | 79-85KC 86SL 87-91KC | | 6'4" | 257 | Colorado State | | |
| Bell, Myron DB | 94-95Pit | | 5'11" | 203 | Michigan State | 2 | |
| Bell, Nick HB | 91-93Raid | 2 | 6'2" | 255 | Iowa | | 42 |
| Bell, Richard HB | 90Pit | 2 | 6' | 200 | Nebraska | | 6 |
| Bell, Rick HB | 83Min | | 6' | 205 | St. John's | | |
| Bell, Ricky FB-HB | 77-81TB 82-83SD | 2 | 6'2" | 218 | Southern Calif. | | 114 |
| Bell, Theo WR | 76Pit 77FJ 78-80Pit 81-85TB | 23 | 6-0 | 185 | Arizona | | 48 |
| Bell, Todd DB | 81-84Chi 85HO 86-87Chi 88-89Phi | | 6'1" | 208 | Ohio State | 7 | 12 |
| Bell, William HB | 94-95Was | | 5'11" | 203 | Georgia Tech | | |
| Bellamy, Jay DB | 94-95Sea | | 5'11" | 193 | Rutgers | | |
| Bellamy, Mike WR | 90Phi | | 6' | 195 | Illinois | | |
| Bellamy, Victor DB | 87Phi | | 6'1" | 195 | Syracuse | | |
| Bellinger, Rodney DB | 84-86Buf | | 5'8" | 186 | Miami (Fla.) | 4 | 6 |
| Bellini, Mark WR | 87-88Ind | | 5'11" | 184 | Brigham Young | | |
| Belser, Jason DB | 92-95Ind | | 5'9" | 187 | Oklahoma | 6 | |
| Belway, Brian DE | 87Raid | | 6'6" | 265 | Calgary | | |
| Bender, Wes FB | 94Raid | | 5'10" | 235 | Southern Calif. | | |
| Bendross, Jesse WR | 84-85SD 87Phi | 2 | 6' | 196 | Alabama | | |
| Benfatti, Lou DT | 94-95NYJ | | 6'4" | 278 | Penn State | | |
| Bengen, Brant WR | 87Sea | | 5'8" | 172 | Idaho | | |
| Benirschke, Rolf K | 77-86SD | 5 | 6' | 171 | Cal.-Davis | | 766 |
| Benish, Dan DT | 83-86Atl 87Was 88KJ | | 6'5" | 273 | Clemson | | |
| Benjamin, Guy QB | 78-79Mia 80NO 81-83SF | 1 | 6'4" | 210 | Stanford | | |
| Benjamin, Ryan HB | 93Cin | | 5'7" | 183 | U. of Pacific | | |
| Benjamin, Bill LB | 87Ind | | 6'3" | 226 | San Jose State | | |
| Bennett, Antoine DB | 91-92Cin | | 5'11" | 185 | New Mexico State | | |
| Bennett, Barry DT-NT-DE | 78-81NO 82-88NYJ 88Min | | 6'4" | 258 | Concordia (Minn.) | | |
| Bennett, Ben QB | 84USFL 87Cin 88Chi | | 6'1" | 200 | Duke | | |
| Bennett, Charles DE | 87Mia | | 6'5" | 257 | Southwestern La. | | |
| Bennett, Cornelius LB | 87-95Buf | | 6'2" | 235 | Alabama | 11 | 18 |
| Bennett, Darren P | 95SD | 4 | 6'5" | 235 | none | | |
| Bennett, Donnell FB | 94-95KC | 2 | 6' | 241 | Miami (Fla.) | | 12 |
| Bennett, Edgar FB-HB | 92-95GB | 2 | 6' | 223 | Florida State | | 156 |
| Bennett, Leeman | HC77-82Atl HC85-86TB | | | | Kentucky | | |
| Bennett, Lewis WR | 87NO | 2 | 5'11" | 175 | Florida A&M | | 6 |
| Bennett, Monte NT-DE | 81NO 83-85USFL 87SD | | 6'5" | 265 | Kansas State | | |
| Bennett, Roy DB | 88-89SD | | 6'2" | 195 | Jackson State | 4 | 6 |
| Bennett, Tony LB | 90-93GB 94-95Ind | | 6'2" | 240 | Mississippi | | 20 |
| Bennett, Woody FB | 79-80NYJ 80-88Mia | 23 | 6'2" | 227 | Miami (Fla.) | | 78 |
| Benson, Brad OT-OG-C | 77-87NYG | | 6'3" | 262 | Penn State | | |
| Benson, Charles DE | 83-84Mia 85Ind 87Det | | 6'3" | 267 | Baylor | 1 | |
| Benson, Cliff TE | 84-85Atl 87Was 87-88NO | 2 | 6'4" | 238 | Purdue | | |

| Use Name (Nickname) - Positions | Team by Year | See Section | Hgt. | Wgt. | College | Int | Pts |
|---|---|---|---|---|---|---|---|
| Benson, Darren DT | 95Dal | | 6'7" | 308 | Trinity Valley C.C. | | |
| Benson, Mitchell NT-DT | 89-90Ind 91SD | | 6'4" | 302 | Texas Christian | | |
| Benson, Thomas LB | 84-85Atl 86-87SD 88NE 89-92Raid | | 6'2" | 238 | Oklahoma | 1 | |
| Benson, Troy LB | 86-89NYJ 90ZJ | | 6'2" | 235 | Pittsburgh | 1 | |
| Bentley, Albert HB | 84-85USFL 85-91Ind 92Pit | 23 | 5'11" | 213 | Miami (Fla.) | | 168 |
| Bentley, Ray LB | 86-92Buf 92Cin | | 6'2" | 240 | Central Michigan | 3 | 6 |
| Benyola, George K | 87NYG | | 5'10" | 195 | Louisiana Tech | | 12 |
| Bercich, Pete LB | 95Min | | 6'1" | 237 | Notre Dame | | |
| Berger, Mitch K | 94Phi | 4 | 6'2" | 231 | Colorado | | |
| Bergeson, Eric DB | 90LA | | 5'11" | 192 | Brigham Young | | |
| Bergold, Scott OT | 85StL 86XJ | | 6'7" | 263 | Wisconsin | | |
| Bernard, Karl HB | 87Det 88KJ | 2 | 5'11" | 205 | Southwestern La. | | 12 |
| Berns, Rick HB | 79-80 TB 82-83Raid | 2 | 6'2" | 206 | Nebraska | | |
| Bernstine, Rod TE-FB-HB | 87-92SD 93-95Den | 2 | 6'3" | 237 | Texas A&M | | 144 |
| Berry, Ed DB | 86GB 87SD | | 5'10" | 183 | Utah State | | |
| Berry, Latin DB | 90LA 91-92Cle | | 5'10" | 196 | Oregon | | |
| Berry, Louis K | 87Atl | | 6' | 193 | Florida State | | |
| Berry, Ray LB | 87-92Min 93Sea | | 6'2" | 227 | Baylor | 1 | 2 |
| Berthusen, Bill DE | 87Cin 87NYG | | 6'5" | 290 | Iowa State | | |
| Berti, Tony OT | 95SD | | 6'5" | 287 | Colorado | | |
| Bess, Gerald DB | 87Min | | 6' | 188 | Tuskegee Inst. | | |
| Bess, Rufus DB | 79Oak 80-81Buf 82-87Min | | 5'9" | 184 | S. Carolina State | 11 | |
| Bessillieu, Don DB | 79-81Mia 82StL 83Raid 84-85USFL | 3 | 6'1" | 200 | Georgia Tech | 5 | 6 |
| Best, Greg DB | 83Pit 84Cle | | 5'10" | 185 | Kansas State | | 6 |
| Bethea, Larry DT-DE | 78-83Dal 84-85USFL | | 6'5" | 251 | Michigan State | | |
| Bethune, George LB | 89-90LA | | 6'4" | 240 | Alabama | | |
| Betters, Doug DE | 78-87Mia | | 6'7" | 262 | Montana, Nevada-Reno | | |
| Bettis, Jerome HB-FB | 93-94LA 95StL | 2 | 5'11" | 243 | Notre Dame | | 88 |
| Beuerlein, Steve QB | 88-90Raid 91-92Dal 93Phx 94Arz 95Jax | 12 | 6'2" | 205 | Notre Dame | | 6 |
| Beverly, Dwight HB | 87NO | 2 | 5'11" | 205 | Illinois | | 12 |
| Bianchini, Frank HB | 87NE | | 5'8" | 190 | Hofstra | | |
| Biasucci, Dean K | 84,86-94Ind 95StL | 5 | 6' | 192 | Stanford | | 823 |
| Bickett, Duane LB | 85-93Ind 94-95Sea | | 6'5" | 247 | Southern Calif. | 9 | |
| Biekert, Greg LB | 93-94Raid 95Oak | | 6'2" | 236 | Colorado | 1 | |
| Bieniemy, Eric HB-FB | 91-94SD 95Cin | 23 | 5'7" | 210 | Colorado | | 42 |
| Bigby, Keiron WR | 87Was | | 5'10" | 177 | Brown | | |
| Biles, Ed | HC81-83Hou | | | | Miami-Ohio | | |
| Billups, Lewis DB | 86-91Cin 92GB | | 5'11" | 190 | North Alabama | 9 | 6 |
| Bingham, Craig LB | 82-84Pit 85SD 87Pit | | 6'2" | 218 | Syracuse | | |
| Bingham, Dwight DE | 87Atl | | 6'6" | 265 | Mississippi | | |
| Bingham, Guy C-OG-OT | 80-88NYJ 89-91Atl 92-93Was | | 6'3" | 257 | Montana | | |
| Binn, David TE-C | 94-95SD | | 6'3" | 240 | California | | |
| Bird, Steve WR | 83-84StL 84SD | | 5'11" | 171 | Eastern Kentucky | | |
| Birden, J.J. WR | 90-94KC 95Atl | 2 | 5'9" | 160 | Oregon | | 92 |
| Birdsong, Carl K | 81-85StL | 4 | 6' | 192 | Southwestern Okla. | | |
| Birdsong, Craig DB | 87Hou | | 6'2" | 217 | North Texas State | | |
| Bishop, Blaine DB | 93-95Hou | | 5'8" | 197 | St. Joseph's-Ind., Ball State | 3 | 6 |
| Bishop, Greg OT-OG | 93-95NYG | | 6'5" | 298 | U. of Pacific | | |
| Bishop, Harold TE | 94TB 95Cle | 2 | 6'4" | 252 | Louisiana State | | |
| Bishop, Keith C-OG | 80Den 81FJ 82-89Den | | 6'3" | 263 | Nebraska, Baylor | | |
| Bjornson, Eric TE | 95Dal | | 6'4" | 236 | Washington | | |
| Black, Barry OG | 87Raid | | 6'2" | 280 | Boise State | | |
| Black, James DE | 87KC | | 6'4" | 280 | S. Carolina State | | |
| Black, James HB | 84Cle | | 5'11" | 198 | Akron | | |
| Black, Mel LB | 86-87NE | | 6'2" | 228 | Eastern Illinois | | |
| Black, Mike K | 83-87Det | 4 | 6'1" | 197 | Arizona State | | |
| Black, Mike OT-OG | 86Phi 87NYG | | 6'4" | 285 | Sacramento State | | |
| Black, Todd WR | 87Chi | | 5'11" | 174 | Concordia | | |
| Blackledge, Todd QB | 83-87KC 88-89Pit | 12 | 6'3" | 224 | Penn State | | 12 |
| Blackmon, Don LB | 81-87NE | | 6'3" | 235 | Tulsa | 5 | 4 |
| Blackmon, Robert DB | 90-95Sea | | 6' | 202 | Baylor | 12 | 6 |
| Blackmore, Richard DB | 79-82Phi 83SF | | 5'10" | 174 | Mississippi State | 5 | 6 |
| Blackshear, Jeff OG | 93-95Sea | | 6'6" | 324 | Northeast La. | | |
| Blackwell, Kelly TE | 92Chi 93Dal | | 6'1" | 255 | Texas Christian | | |
| Blackwood, Glenn DB | 79-87Mia 88KJ | | 6' | 187 | Texas | 29 | 6 |
| Blackwood, Lyle DB | 73-75Cin 76Sea 77-80Bal 82-86Mia | 3 | 6'1" | 190 | Texas Christian | 35 | 12 |
| Blades, Bennie DB | 88-95Det | | 6'1" | 221 | Miami (Fla.) | 10 | 8 |
| Blades, Brian WR | 88-95Sea | 2 | 5'11" | 185 | Miami (Fla.) | | 182 |
| Blados, Brian OT | 84-90Cin 91Ind 92TB | | 6'5" | 300 | North Carolina | | |
| Blair, Paul OT | 86-87Ch 88KJ 90Mini | | 6'4" | 295 | Oklahoma State | | |
| Blair, Stanley DB | 90Phx | | 6' | 192 | Oklahoma State, Southeastern Okla. | | |
| Blake, Jeff QB | 92-93NYJ 94-95Cin | 12 | 6' | 202 | East Carolina | | 22 |
| Blake, Ricky FB | 91Dal | | 6'2" | 244 | Alabama A&M | | 6 |
| Blanchard, Cary K | 92-93NYJ 95Ind | 5 | 6'1" | 225 | Oklahoma State | | 229 |
| Bland, Carl WR | 84-88Det 89-90GB | 23 | 5'11" | 182 | Michigan | | 42 |
| Blankenship, Brian OG | 87-91Pit | | 6'1" | 277 | Nebraska-Omaha | | |
| Blanton, Jerry LB | 79-85KC | | 6'1" | 231 | Kentucky | 1 | |
| Blaylock, Anthony DB | 88-91Cle 91-92SD 93Chi | | 5'11" | 190 | Winston-Salem St. | 6 | 6 |
| Bledsoe, Curtis HB-FB | 81-82KC 83-85USFL | | 5'11" | 215 | San Diego State | | |
| Bledsoe, Drew QB | 93-95NE | 12 | 6'5" | 233 | Washington State | | |
| Bleier, Bob QB | 87NE | 1 | 6'3" | 210 | Richmond | | 6 |
| Bligen, Dennis HB | 84-86NYJ 86TB 87NYJ | 2 | 5'11" | 214 | St. John's (N.Y.) | | 12 |
| Blinka, Stan LB | 79-83NYJ 85USFL | | 6'2" | 230 | Sam Houston St. | 3 | |
| Blount, Alvin HB | 87Dal | 2 | 5'9" | 197 | Maryland | | 18 |
| Blount, Ed QB | 87SF | | 6' | 195 | Washington State | | |
| Blount, Eric HB | 92-93Phx | | 5'9" | 190 | North Carolina | | 6 |
| Blount, Tony DB | 80NYG 83USFL | | 6'1" | 195 | Virginia | | |
| Blue, Anthony DB | 87Sea | | 5'9 | 185 | Nevada-Las Vegas | | |
| Blundin, Matt QB | 92-95KC | | 6'6" | 230 | Virginia | | |
| Boadway, Steve LB | 87Det | | 6'4" | 240 | Arizona | | |
| Board, Dwaine DE | 79-88SF 88NO | | 6'5" | 248 | N. Carolina A&T | | 6 |
| Boatner, Mack HB | 83-85USFL 86TB | | 6' | 220 | Southeastern La. | | |
| Boatswain, Harry OT | 92-94SF 95Phi | | 6'4" | 295 | New Haven | | |
| Bob, Adam LB | 89NYJ | | 6'2" | 240 | Texas A&M | | |
| Bock, Joe C | 87StL 87Buf | | 6'4" | 254 | Virginia | | |
| Bock, John C-OG | 95NYJ | | 6'3" | 285 | Indiana State | | |
| Boddie, Tony HB | 86-87Den | | 5'11" | 198 | Montana State | | 6 |
| Boggs, Mark OT | 87Ind | | 6'5" | 301 | Ball State | | |
| Bohannon, Fred DB | 82-83Pit 84USFL | | 6' | 201 | Miss. Valley St. | | |
| Bohm, Ron DT | 87StL | | 6'3" | 250 | Illinois | | |
| Bojovic, Novo K | 83-84USFL 85StL | 5 | 5'10" | 172 | Central Michigan | | 20 |
| Bokamper, Kim LB-DE | 77-85Mia | | 6'6" | 250 | Concordia (Minn.), San Jose State | 6 | 8 |
| Bolcar, Ned LB | 90Sea 91Mia 92KJ | | 6'1" | 240 | Notre Dame | 1 | |
| Bolden, Gary (The Mule) DT | 87Phi | | 6'1" | 275 | Southwestern Okla. | | |

| Use Name (Nickname) - Positions | Team by Year | See Section | Hgt. | Wgt. | College | Int | Pts |
|---|---|---|---|---|---|---|---|
| Bolden, Rickey OT-TE | 84Cle 85USFL 86-89Cle | | 6'6" | 274 | S.M.U. | | 6 |
| Bolinger, Russ OG-OT | 76-77Det 78KJ 79-82Det 83-84LA 85USFL 85LA | | 6'5" | 255 | Cal.-Riverside, Long Beach State | | |
| Bollinger, Brian OG | 92-94SF | | 6'5" | 285 | North Carolina | | |
| Bolton, Scott WR | 88GB | | 6' | 188 | Auburn | | |
| Bolzan, Scott OG | 85USFL 85Cle | | 6'3" | 280 | Northern Illinois | | |
| Bone, Warren DE | 87GB | | 6'4" | 260 | Texas Southern | | |
| Bonham, Shane DE | 94-95Det | | 6'4" | 268 | Air Force, Tennessee | | |
| Boniol, Chris K | 94-95Dal | 5 | 5'11" | 169 | Louisiana Tech | | 241 |
| Bonner, Brian LB | 89Was | | 6'2" | 225 | Wisconsin, Minnesota | | |
| Bonner, Melvin WR | 93Den 94LJ | | 6'3" | 207 | Baylor | | |
| Bono, Steve QB | 85-86Min 87-88Pit 89-93SF 94-95KC | 12 | 6'4" | 215 | U.C.L.A. | | 42 |
| Booker, Vaughn DE | 94-95KC | | 6'5" | 288 | Cincinnati | | 6 |
| Boone, Greg HB | 87TB | | 5'9" | 196 | Duke | | |
| Booth, Isaac DB | 94-95Cle | | 6'3" | 190 | California | 2 | |
| Booty, John DB | 88-90NYJ 91-92Phi 93Phx 94NYG 95TB | | 6' | 179 | Texas Christian | 14 | |
| Borchardt, Jon OT-OG | 79-84Buf 85-87Sea | | 6'5" | 260 | Montana State | | |
| Borgella, Jocelyn DB | 94Det | | 5'10" | 180 | Cincinnati | | |
| Borgognone, Dirk K | 95GB | | 6'2" | 221 | U. of Pacific | | |
| Borcky, Dennis DT | 87NYG | | 6'4" | 284 | Memphis State | | |
| Borders, Nate DB | 87Cin | | 5'10" | 190 | Indiana | | |
| Borland, Kyle LB | 87LA | | 6'3" | 232 | Wisconsin | | |
| Borresen, Rich TE | 87Dal | | 6'5" | 252 | Northwestern | | |
| Bortz, Mark OG | 83-94Chi | | 6'6" | 279 | Iowa | | |
| Bosa, John DE | 87-90Mia 90KJ | | 6'4" | 270 | Boston College | | |
| Boselli, Tony OT | 95Jax | | 6'7" | 323 | Southern Calif. | | |
| Bosley, Keith OT | 87Cle | | 6'5" | 320 | Eastern Kentucky | | |
| Boso, Cap TE | 86StL 87-91Chi | 2 | 6'3" | 232 | Illinois | | 24 |
| Bostic, Jeff C | 80-93Was | | 6'2" | 268 | Clemson | | |
| Bostic, Joe OG-OT | 79-87StL 88Phx 89KJ | | 6'3" | 266 | Clemson | | |
| Bostic, John DB | 85-87Det | | 5'10" | 178 | Bethune-Cookman | 1 | |
| Bostic, Keith DB | 83-88Hou 90Cle | | 6'1" | 216 | Michigan | 13 | 6 |
| Bosworth, Brian LB | 87-89Sea | | 6'2" | 248 | Oklahoma | | |
| Botkin, Kirk TE | 94-95NO | | 6'3" | 245 | Arkansas | | |
| Boucher, Scott OG | 84-85USFL 87Hou | | 6'3" | 260 | Northeastern Okla. | | |
| Bouie, Tony DB | 95TB | | 5'10" | 187 | Arizona | 1 | |
| Boures, Emil C-OG | 82-86Pit | | 6'1" | 258 | Pittsburgh | | |
| Boutte, Marc DT | 92-93LA 94-95Was | | 6'4" | 303 | Louisiana State | | |
| Bouwens, Shawn OG | 91-94Det 95Jax | | 6'4" | 291 | Nebraska Wesleyan | | |
| Bouyer, Willie WR | 89Sea | | 6'3" | 200 | Michigan State | | |
| Bouza, Matt WR | 81SF 82-83Bal 84-89Ind | 2 | 6'2" | 211 | California | | 102 |
| Bowden, Joe LB | 92-95Hou | | 5'11" | 229 | Oklahoma | | |
| Bowen, Ken LB | 87Atl | | 6'1" | 220 | East Tennesee St. | | |
| Bowens, Tim DT | 94-95Mia | | 6'4" | 314 | Mississippi | | |
| Bowers, Sam TE | 87Chi | | 6'4" | 250 | Fordham | | |
| Bowick, Tony NT | 89Atl | | 6'2" | 265 | Tenn.-Chattanooga | | |
| Bowles, Todd DB | 86-90Was 91-92SF 93Was | | 6'2" | 203 | Temple | 15 | |
| Bowman, Barry P | 87Sea | | 5'11" | 180 | Louisiana Tech | | |
| Bowman, Jim DB | 85-89NE | | 6'2" | 210 | Central Michigan | 3 | |
| Bowman, Kevin WR | 87Phi | | 6'3" | 205 | San Jose State | | 6 |
| Bownes, Fabien WR | 95Chi | | 5'11" | 180 | Western Illinois | | |
| Bowser, Charles LB | 82-85Mia 86NJ | | 6'3" | 231 | Duke | | |
| Bowyer, Walt DE | 83-84,87-88Den | | 6'4" | 254 | Arizona State | 1 | |
| Boyarsky, Jerry NT | 81NO 82-85Cin 86Buf 86-89GB | | 6'3" | 290 | Pittsburgh | | |
| Boyd, Brent OG | 80-83Min 84LJ 85-86Min | | 6'3" | 268 | U.C.L.A. | | |
| Boyd, Dennis DE-DT-OT-C | 77-79Sea 80BA 81-82Sea | | 6'6" | 255 | Oregon State | | 6 |
| Boyd, Greg DE | 77-78NE 80-82Den 83GB 84SF 84Raid | | 6'6" | 274 | San Diego State | | 4 |
| Boyd, Jerome LB | 83Sea | | 6'2" | 225 | Oregon State | | |
| Boyd, Malik DB | 94Min | | 5'10" | 176 | Southern U. | 1 | |
| Boyd, Thomas LB | 87Det | | 6'3" | 210 | Alabama | | |
| Boyd, Stephen LB | 95Det | | 6' | 247 | Boston College | | |
| Boyer, Brant LB | 94Mia 95Jax | | 6' | 237 | Arizona | | |
| Boyer, Mark TE-HB | 85-89Ind 90-92NYJ | 2 | 6'4" | 239 | Southern Calif. | | 36 |
| Boykin, Deral DB | 93LA 94Was 95Jax | | 5'11" | 196 | Louisville | | 6 |
| Boyle, Jim OT | 87Pit | | 6'5" | 270 | Tulane | | |
| Brabham, Cary DB | 94Raid | | 6' | 195 | Southern Methodist | | |
| Bracelin, Greg LB | 80Den 81Oak 82Raid 83Bal 84Ind | | 6'1" | 214 | California | 3 | |
| Bracken, Don K | 85-90GB 92KC 93LA | 4 | 6' | 210 | Michigan | | |
| Bradey, Rickey TE | 94LA | | 6'4" | 246 | Oklahoma | | |
| Bradford, Ronnie DB | 93-95Den | | 5'10" | 188 | Colorado | 1 | |
| Bradley, Carlos LB | 81-85SD 87Phi | | 6' | 224 | Wake Forest | 2 | |
| Bradley, Chuck LB | 93Cin | | 6'5" | 296 | Kentucky | | |
| Bradley, Danny WR | 87Det | | 5'9" | 175 | Oklahoma | | 12 |
| Bradley, Henry NT-DT | 79-83Cle | | 6'2" | 261 | Alcorn State | | |
| Bradley, Luther DB | 78-81Det 83-85USFL | | 6'2" | 194 | Notre Dame | 9 | |
| Bradley, Steve QB | 87Chi | | 6'2" | 216 | Indiana | | |
| Bradshaw, Craig QB | 80Hou | | 6'5" | 215 | Utah State | | |
| Brady, Donny DB | 95Cle | | 6'2" | 195 | Wisconsin | | |
| Brady, Ed LB | 84-85LA 86-91Cin 92-95TB | | 6'2" | 234 | Illinois | | |
| Brady, Jeff LB | 91Pit 92GB 93LA 93SD 94TB 95Min | | 6'1" | 228 | Kentucky | 2 | |
| Brady, Kerry K | 87Dal 88Ind 89Buf | | 6'1" | 208 | Hawaii | | 1 |
| Brady, Kyle TE | 95NYJ | 2 | 6'6" | 260 | Penn State | | 12 |
| Braggs, Byron DE | 81-83GB 84TB | | 6'4" | 290 | Alabama | | |
| Braggs, Stephen DB | 87-91Cle 92-93Mia | | 5'10" | 178 | Texas | 5 | |
| Braham, Rich OT | 94Cin 95NJ | | 6'4" | 280 | West Virginia | | |
| Brammer, Mark TE | 80-84Buf | 2 | 6'3" | 236 | Michigan State | | 60 |
| Bramlett, Don NT | 87Min | | 6'2" | 270 | Carson-Newman | | |
| Branch, Reggie FB | 85-89Was 90NJ | | 5'11" | 232 | West Virginia St., East Carolina | | 6 |
| Brandes, John TE | 87-89Ind 90-92Was 92NYG 93SF | | 6'2" | 249 | Cameron | | |
| Brandon, David LB | 87-89SD 90KJ 91-93Cle 93-94Sea 95SD | | 6'4" | 231 | Memphis State | 4 | 24 |
| Brandon, Michael DE | 93Ind 94Arz 95SF | | 6'4" | 290 | Florida | | |
| Brannon, Robert DE | 87Cle 87NO | | 6'7" | 245 | Arkansas | | |
| Brantley, Chris WR | 94LA | | 5'10" | 180 | Rutgers | | |
| Brantley, John LB | 89Hou 92Was | | 6'2" | 245 | Georgia | | |
| Bransletter, Kent OT | 73GB | | 6'3" | 260 | Houston | | |
| Brantley, Scot LB | 80-87TB | | 6'1" | 230 | Florida | 8 | |
| Branton, Gene WR | 83TB 84LJ 85TB 86JJ | | 6'4" | 223 | Texas Southern | | |
| Bratton, Melvin FB | 89-90Den | 2 | 6'1" | 225 | Miami (Fla.) | | 48 |
| Bratzke, Chad DE | 94-95NYG | | 6'4" | 266 | Eastern Kentucky | | |
| Braxton, David LB | 89-90Min 90-93Phx 94Cin | | 6'1" | 236 | Wake Forest | | |
| Braxton, Tyrone DB | 87-93Den 94Mia 95Den | | 5'11" | 179 | N. Dakota State | 22 | 12 |
| Bravyak, Jack DE | 87Buf | | 6'3" | 255 | Temple | | |
| Braziel, Larry DB | 79-81Bal 82-85Cle | | 6' | 187 | Southern Calif. | 11 | 12 |
| Brazley, Carl DB | 87SD | | 6' | 180 | Western Kentucky | 1 | |
| Breech, Jim K | 78-79Oak 80-92Cin | 5 | 5'6" | 160 | California | | 1246 |

| Use Name (Nickname) - Positions | Team by Year | See Section | Hgt. | Wgt. | College | Int | Pts |
|---|---|---|---|---|---|---|---|
| Breeden, Louis DB | 78-87Cin | | 5'11" | 185 | N. Car. Central | 33 | 12 |
| Breen, Adrian QB | 87Cin | | 6'4" | 183 | Morehead State | | |
| Brennan, Brian WR | 84-91Cle 92Cin 92SD | 23 | 5'9" | 179 | Boston College | | 132 |
| Brennan, Mike OT | 90-91Cin 91Phx 91Buf | | 6'5" | 274 | Notre Dame | | |
| Brenner, Hoby TE | 81-93NO | 2 | 6'4" | 242 | Southern Calif. | | 126 |
| Brewer, Chris HB-FB | 84Den 87Chi | 2 | 6'1" | 203 | Arizona | | 18 |
| Brewer, Dewell HB | 94Ind 95KJ | 3 | 5'8" | 199 | Oklahoma | | 6 |
| Brice, Alundis DB | 95Dal | | 5'10" | 178 | Mississippi | 1 | |
| Briehl, Tom LB | 85Hou 86NJ 87Hou | | 6'3" | 247 | Illinois | | |
| Brien, Doug K | 94-95SF 95NO | 5 | 5'11" | 177 | California | | 197 |
| Briggs, Greg DB | 95Dal | | 6'3" | 212 | Texas Southern | | |
| Briggs, Walter QB | 87NYJ | | 6'1" | 205 | Montclair State | | |
| Bright, Greg DB | 80-81Cin | | 6' | 208 | Morehead State | 1 | |
| Bright, Leon HB | 81-83NYG 84-85TB | 23 | 5'9" | 192 | Florida State | | 12 |
| Brilz, Darrick OG-C | 87Was 88SD 89-93Sea 94-95Cin | | 6'3" | 281 | Oregon | | |
| Brim, James WR | 87Min | 2 | 6'3" | 187 | Wake Forest | | 18 |
| Brim, Michael DB | 88Phx 89Det 89-90Min 91-92NYJ 93-95Cin | | 6' | 188 | Virginia Union | 17 | 12 |
| Brinkley, Lester DE | 90Dal | | 6'6" | 270 | Mississippi | | |
| Brinson, Dana WR | 89SD | 2 | 5'9" | 167 | Nebraska | | |
| Brisby, Vincent WR | 93-95NE | 2 | 6'1" | 186 | Northeast La. | | 60 |
| Brister, Bubby QB | 86-92Pit 93-94Phi 95NYJ | 12 | 6'2" | 203 | Tulane, Northeast La. | | 42 |
| Britt, James DB | 84Atl 85BL 86-87Atl | | 6' | 185 | Louisiana State | 3 | 6 |
| Britt, Jessie WR | 86Pit | | 6'4" | 198 | N. Carolina A&T | | |
| Britt, Ralph TE | 87Pit | | 6'3" | 240 | N. Carolina State | | |
| Brock, Lou DB | 88Sea 88Det | | 5'10" | 175 | Southern Calif. | | |
| Brock, Dieter QB | 85LA 86XJ | 1 | 6' | 195 | Auburn, Jacksonville St. | | |
| Brock, Matt DE-DT | 89-94GB 95NYJ | | 6'5" | 284 | Oregon | 2 | 6 |
| Brock, Pete C-OT-OG-TE | 76-87NE | | 6'5" | 267 | Colorado | | 6 |
| Brock, Stan OT | 80-92NO 93-95SD | | 6'6" | 289 | Colorado | | |
| Brockemeyer, Stan OT | 95Car | | 6'4" | 300 | Texas | | |
| Brockhaus, Jeff K | 87SF | 5 | 6'2" | 218 | Missouri | | 20 |
| Brohm, Jeff QB | 94SD 95SF | | 6'1" | 200 | Louisville | | |
| Bronson, Ben WR | 95Ind | | 5'10" | 165 | Baylor | | |
| Brookins, Mitchell WR | 84-85Buf 86KJ | 2 | 5'11" | 196 | Illinois | | 6 |
| Brooks, Barrett OT | 95Phi | | 6'4" | 309 | Kansas State | | |
| Brooks, Bill WR | 86-92Ind 93-95Buf | 23 | 6' | 192 | Boston U. | | 276 |
| Brooks, Bucky WR | 94Buf | | 6' | 190 | North Carolina | | |
| Brooks, Carlos DB | 95Arz | | 6' | 200 | Bowling Green | | |
| Brooks, Chet DB | 88-90SF | | 5'11" | 191 | Texas A&M | 3 | |
| Brooks, Derrick LB | 95TB | | 6' | 225 | Florida State | | |
| Brooks, James HB | 81-83SD 84-91Cin 92Cle 92TB | 23 | 5'10" | 181 | Auburn | | 474 |
| Brooks, Jon LB | 79Det 80StL 80Atl 83-84USFL | | 6'2" | 215 | Clemson | | |
| Brooks, Kevin DT | 85-88Dal 89-90Det | | 6'6" | 277 | Michigan | | |
| Brooks, Michael LB | 87-92Den 93-95NYG | | 6'1" | 235 | Louisiana State | 4 | 8 |
| Brooks, Michael DB | 89-90SD 90Dal 91KJ | | 6' | 195 | N. Carolina State | | |
| Brooks, Perry DT | 78-84Was | | 6'3" | 264 | Southern U. | | |
| Brooks, Reggie HB | 93-95Was | 2 | 5'8" | 208 | Notre Dame | | 30 |
| Brooks, Rich | HC95StL | | | | Oregon State | | |
| Brooks, Robert WR | 92-95GB | 23 | 6' | 176 | South Carolina | | 126 |
| Brooks, Tony HB | 92Phi 93XJ | | 6' | 230 | Notre Dame | | |
| Brophy, Jay LB | 84-86Mia 87NYJ | | 6'3" | 233 | Miami (Fla.) | 1 | |
| Brostek, Bern C-OG | 90-94LA 95StL | | 6'3" | 300 | Washington | | |
| Brotzki, Bob OT | 86-88Ind 88Dal | | 6'5" | 281 | Syracuse | | |
| Broughton, Walter WR | 84-85USFL 86-88Buf | | 5'10" | 180 | Jacksonville St. | | 6 |
| Broughton, Willie DE-DT-NT | 85-86Ind 87KJ 89-90Dal 92-93Raid 95NO | | 6'5" | 279 | Miami (Fla.) | | |
| Broussard, Steve HB-WR | 90-93Atl 94Cin 95Sea | 23 | 5'7" | 201 | Washington State | | 92 |
| Brown, A.B. HB | 89-92NYJ | 2 | 5'9" | 212 | Pittsburgh | 6 | |
| Brown, Aaron LB | 78-80TB 82-84CFL 85Phi 86-87Atl | | 6'2" | 236 | Ohio State | 1 | |
| Brown, Andre WR | 89-90Mia | 2 | 6'3" | 210 | Miami (Fla.) | | 30 |
| Brown, Anthony OT | 95Cin | | 6'5" | 310 | Utah | | |
| Brown, Arnold DB | 85Det 86BA 87Sea | | 5'11" | 185 | N. Car. Central | | |
| Brown, Bud DB | 84-88Mia | | 6' | 194 | Southern Miss. | 5 | |
| Brown, Cedric DB | 77-84TB | | 6'1" | 199 | Kent State | 29 | 18 |
| Brown, Cedrick DB | 87Phi | | 5'10" | 178 | Washington State | 1 | |
| Brown, Chad LB | 93-95Pit | | 6'2" | 240 | Colorado | 1 | |
| Brown, Chad DE | 93Phx 94-95Arz | | 6'7" | 265 | Mississippi | | |
| Brown, Charlie WR | 82-84Was 85-87Atl | 2 | 5'10" | 182 | South Carolina | | 150 |
| Brown, Chris DB | 84-85Pit | | 6' | 200 | Notre Dame | 1 | |
| Brown, Chris OT | 87NYJ | | 6'1 | 295 | Lamar | | |
| Brown, Clay TE | 82Atl 83Den 84USFL | | 6'3" | 225 | Brigham Young | | |
| Brown, Corwin DB | 93-95NE | | 6' | 192 | Michigan | | |
| Brown, Curtis FB-HB | 77-82Buf 83Hou | 23 | 5'10" | 203 | Missouri | | 90 |
| Brown, Dave DB | 75Pit 76-86Sea 87-89GB 90LJ | 3 | 6'1" | 192 | Michigan | 62 | 32 |
| Brown, Dave LB | 87Phi | | 6'2" | 215 | Miami-Ohio | | |
| Brown, Dave QB | 92-95NYG | 12 | 6'5" | 215 | Duke | | 36 |
| Brown, Dennis DE | 90-95SF | | 6'4" | 290 | Washington | 1 | |
| Brown, Derek TE | 92-94NYG 95TJ | 2 | 6'6" | 252 | Notre Dame | | |
| Brown, Derek HB | 93-95NO | 2 | 5'9" | 198 | Nebraska | | 54 |
| Brown, Don OT | 83SD | | 6'6" | 262 | Santa Clara | | |
| Brown, Don DB | 87NYG | | 5'11" | 189 | Maryland | 1 | |
| Brown, Donald DB | 86SD 86Mia | | 5'11" | 189 | Oklahoma, Maryland | 1 | |
| Brown, Eddie WR | 85-91Cin 92ZJ | 2 | 6' | 185 | Miami (Fla.) | | 246 |
| Brown, Eric WR | 87KC | | 6'2" | 180 | Tulsa | | |
| Brown, Eric DB | 89Dal | | 5'11" | 177 | Savannah State | | |
| Brown, Gary HB-FB | 91-95Hou | 2 | 5'11" | 227 | Penn State | | 90 |
| Brown, Gary OT | 94-95GB | | 6'4" | 303 | Georgia Tech | | |
| Brown, Gilbert NT-DT | 93-95GB | | 6'2" | 327 | Kansas | | |
| Brown, Gordon HB | 87Ind | | 5'11" | 220 | Tulsa | | 6 |
| Brown, Greg DE-DT | 81-86Phi 87-88Atl | | 6'5" | 254 | Kansas State, Eastern Illinois | | 14 |
| Brown, Guy LB | 77-82Dal | | 6'4" | 223 | Houston | 1 | |
| Brown, Ivory Lee HB | 92Phx | 2 | 6'2" | 245 | Ark.-Pine Bluff | | |
| Brown, J.B. DB | 89-95Mia | | 6' | 192 | Maryland | 15 | 6 |
| Brown, James OT | 93Cle 94-95NYJ | | 6'6" | 325 | Virginia State | | |
| Brown, Jamie OT | 95Den | | 6'8" | 320 | Florida A&M | | |
| Brown, Jerome DT | 87-91Phi | | 6'2" | 291 | Miami (Fla.) | 1 | 2 |
| June 1992 — Died in Automobile Accident | | | | | | | |
| Brown, Ken WR | 87Cin | | 5'8" | 175 | Southern Arkansas | | |
| Brown, Ken LB | 95Den | | 6'1" | 235 | Virginia Tech | | |
| Brown, Kevin K | 87Chi | | 6'2" | 178 | West Texas State | | |
| Brown, Lance DB | 95Arz | | 6' | 200 | Indiana | | |
| Brown, Laron WR | 87Den | | 5'9" | 172 | Texas | | |
| Brown, Larry WR | 87Min | | 5'11" | 180 | Mankato State | | |
| Brown, Larry DB | 91-95Dal | | 5'11" | 184 | Texas Christian | 13 | 12 |
| Brown, Lomas OT | 85-95Det | | 6'4" | 281 | Florida | | |
| Brown, Marc WR | 87Buf | | 6'2" | 195 | Towson State | | 6 |
| Brown, Mark LB | 83-88Mia 89-91Det | | 6'2" | 230 | Purdue | 4 | |

| Use Name (Nickname) - Positions | Team by Year | See Section | Hgt. | Wgt. | College | Int | Pts |
|---|---|---|---|---|---|---|---|
| Brown, Monty LB | 93-95Buf | | 6' | 232 | Ferris State | | |
| Brown, Norris TE | 83Min 84-85USFL | | 6'3" | 220 | Southern Calif. | | |
| Brown, Orlando OT | 94-95Cle | | 6'7" | 332 | S. Carolina State | | |
| Brown, Preston WR | 80NE 81XJ 82NE 83NYJ 84Cle | 3 | 5'10" | 186 | Vanderbilt | | 6 |
| Brown, Ray OT-OG | 86-87StL 88Phx 89Was 90KJ 91EJ 92-95Was | | 6'5" | 295 | Memphis State, Arizona State, Arkansas State | | |
| Brown, Ray HB | 87SF | | 5'9" | 185 | South Carolina | | |
| Brown, Reggie FB | 82-83Atl 84-85USFL 87Phi | 23 | 5'11" | 211 | Oregon | | |
| Brown, Reggie WR | 93-94Hou | | 6'1" | 195 | Alabama State | | 2 |
| Brown, Richard LB | 87,89LA 90SD 91-92Cle 93KJ 94-95Min | | 6'3" | 240 | San Diego State | 1 | |
| Brown, Robert DE | 82-92GB | | 6'2" | 268 | Virginia Tech | 2 | 8 |
| Brown, Roger DB | 90-91NYG 92NE | | 6' | 196 | Virginia Tech | | |
| Brown, Ron WR-DB | 84-89LA 90Raid 91LA | 23 | 5'11" | 181 | Arizona State | | 84 |
| Brown, Ron DE | 88Raid | | 6'4" | 225 | Southern Calif. | | |
| Brown, Ron WR | 87StL | | 5'10" | 186 | Colorado | | |
| Brown, Rufus OG | 95Buf | | 6'3" | 304 | Pittsburgh | | |
| Brown, Rufus OG | 87TB | | 6'2" | 295 | Florida A&M | | |
| Brown, Rush DE-NT-DT | 80-83StL 84-85USFL | | 6'2" | 259 | Ball State | 1 | |
| Brown, Selwyn DB | 88TB | | 5'11" | 205 | Miami (Fla.) | | |
| Brown, Sonny DB | 87Hou | | 6'2" | 200 | Oklahoma | | |
| Brown, Steve DB | 83-87Hou | 3 | 5'11" | 189 | Oregon | 19 | 12 |
| Brown, Ted FB-HB | 79-86Min | 2 | 5'10" | 206 | N. Carolina State | | 318 |
| Brown, Theotis FB-HB | 79-81StL 81-83Sea 83-84KC | 2 | 6'3" | 225 | U.C.L.A. | | 198 |
| Brown, Thomas DE-NT | 80Phi 81,83Cle | | 6'4" | 247 | Baylor | | |
| Brown, Tim WR | 88-94Raid 95Oak | 23 | 6' | 195 | Notre Dame | | 300 |
| Brown, Tom FB | 87Mia 88KJ 89Mia 90KJ | 2 | 6'1" | 223 | Pittsburgh | | |
| Brown, Tom WR | 87Cin | | 6'4" | 190 | Augustana (S.D.) | | |
| Brown, Tony OT | 87Buf 88JJ | | 6'5" | 285 | Pittsburgh | | |
| Brown, Tony DB | 92-93Hou 94-95Sea | | 5'9" | 183 | Fresno State | | |
| Brown, Troy WR | 93-95NE | 23 | 5'9" | 183 | Marshall | | 6 |
| Brown, Tyrone WR | 95Atl | 2 | 5'11" | 164 | Toledo | | |
| Brown, Vincent LB | 89-95NE | | 6'2" | 245 | Miss. Valley St. | 10 | 12 |
| Browne, Jim HB | 87Raid | | 6'1" | 215 | Boston College | | |
| Browner, Jim DB | 79-80Cin | | 6'1" | 208 | Notre Dame | 1 | |
| Browner, Joey DB | 83-91Min | | 6'2" | 221 | Southern Calif. | 37 | 18 |
| Browner, Keith LB | 84-86TB 87SF 87Raid 88SD | | 6'6" | 245 | Southern Calif. | 4 | 6 |
| Browner, Ross DE | 78-84Cin 85USFL 85-86Cin 87GB | | 6'3" | 262 | Notre Dame | 1 | 3 |
| Browning, Dave DE | 78-81Oak 82Raid 83NE 84-85USFL | | 6'5" | 245 | Washington | 1 | |
| Brownlow, Darrick LB | 91Dal 92-93TB 94Dal 95Was | | 5'10" | 237 | Illinois | | 2 |
| Bruce, Aundray LB-TE-DE | 88-91Atl 92-94Raid 95Oak | | 6'5" | 265 | Auburn | 4 | 6 |
| Bruce, Isaac WR | 94LA 95StL | 2 | 6' | 178 | Memphis State | | 98 |
| Bruckner, Nick WR | 83-85NYJ 86SJ | | 5'11" | 185 | Syracuse | | |
| Brudzinski, Bob LB | 77-80LA 81-89Mia | | 6'4" | 229 | Ohio State | 9 | 12 |
| Bruener, Mark TE | 95Pit | 2 | 6'4" | 254 | Washington | | 18 |
| Bruer, Bob TE | 76Chi 77-78CFL 79-80SF 80-83Min 84KJ | 2 | 6'5" | 235 | Mankato State | | 60 |
| Bruhin, John OG | 88-91TB | | 6'3" | 282 | Tennessee | | |
| Brumfield, Scott OT-OG | 93-95Cin | | 6'8" | 320 | Brigham Young | | |
| Brune, Larry DB | 80Min | | 6'2" | 202 | Rice | 2 | |
| Brunell, Mark QB | 93-94GB 95Jax | 12 | 6'0" | 214 | Washington | | 30 |
| Brunner, Scott QB | 80-83NYG 84KJ 85StL | 1 | 6'5" | 203 | Delaware | | 6 |
| Bruno, Dave K | 87Min | | 6'1" | 235 | Moraine Valley | | |
| Bruno, John K | 87Pit | | 6'2" | 190 | Penn State | | |
| Bryan, Billy C-OG | 77-88Den 89KJ | | 6'2" | 251 | Duke | | |
| Bryan, Rick DT-DE-NT-LB | 84-91Atl 92ZJ 93Atl | | 6'4" | 265 | Oklahoma | | 3 |
| Bryan, Steve DE--NT-LB | 87-88Den | | 6'2" | 256 | Oklahoma | | |
| Bryant, Beno HB | 94Sea | | 5'9" | 175 | Washington | | |
| Bryant, Cullen FB-HB | 73-82LA 83-84Sea 87LA | 23 | 6'1" | 234 | Colorado | | 156 |
| Bryant, Domingo DB | 87-88Hou | | 6'4" | 176 | Texas A&M | 3 | 6 |
| Bryant, Jeff DE | 82-93Sea | | 6'5" | 276 | Clemson | 1 | 2 |
| Bryant, Junior DE-DT | 95SF | | 6'4" | 275 | Notre Dame | | |
| Bryant, Kelvin HB | 86-88Was 89KJ 90Was | 2 | 6'2" | 195 | North Carolina | | 120 |
| Bryant, Steve WR | 82-85Hou 87Ind | 2 | 6'2" | 195 | Purdue | | |
| Bryant, Tim LB | 87Min | | 6'2" | 217 | Southern Miss. | | |
| Bryant, Trent DB | 81Was 82-83KC 84-85USFL 87KC | | 5'10" | 180 | Arkansas | 2 | |
| Bryant, Warren OT | 77-84Atl 84Raid | | 6'6" | 273 | Kentucky | | |
| Buben, Mark DE-NT | 79NE 80JJ 81NE 82Cle 83-85USFL | | 6'3" | 260 | Tufts | 1 | |
| Buchanan, Charles DE | 88Cle | | 6'3" | 245 | Tennessee State | | 2 |
| Buchanan, Ray DB | 93-95Ind | | 5'9" | 193 | Louisville | 14 | 18 |
| Buchanan, Richard WR | 93-94LA | | 5'10" | 178 | Northwestern | | |
| Buck, Jason DE | 87-90Cin 91-93Was | | 6'5" | 268 | Brigham Young | | |
| Buck, Mike QB | 90-93NO 95Arz | 1 | 6'3" | 227 | Maine | | |
| Buck, Vince DB | 90-95NO | 3 | 6' | 198 | Central St.-Ohio | 10 | 6 |
| Buckley, Curtis DB-WR | 93-95TB | | 6' | 185 | East Texas State | | |
| Buckley, Marcus LB | 93-95NYG | | 6'3" | 237 | Texas A&M | | |
| Buckley, Terrell DB | 92-94GB 95Mia | 3 | 5'9" | 174 | Florida State | 11 | 12 |
| Buckner, Brentson DE | 94-95Pit | | 6'2" | 305 | Clemson | | 6 |
| Buczkowski, Bob DE | 87Raid 89Phx 90Cle | | 6'5" | 260 | Pittsburgh | | |
| Budde, Brad OG | 80-86KC 87TJ | | 6'4" | 262 | Southern Calif. | | |
| Buddenberg, John OG | 92Atl | | 6'6" | 270 | Akron | | |
| Buford, Maury K | 82-84SD 85-86Chi 88NYG 89-91Chi | 4 | 6'1" | 191 | Texas Tech | | |
| Buford, Tony LB | 87StL | | 6'2" | 222 | Tulsa | | |
| Bugel, Joe | HC90-93Phx | | | | Western Kentucky | | |
| Bujnoch, Glenn OG | 76-82Cin 83-84TB | | 6'5" | 259 | Texas A&M | | 6 |
| Bullard, Louis OT | 78-80Sea 83-85USFL | | 6'6" | 265 | Jackson State | | |
| Bullough, Chuck LB | 93-94Mia | | 6'1" | 238 | Michigan State | | |
| Bulluck, Brian LB | 87Ind | | 6'3" | 236 | N. Carolina State | | |
| Bunch, Derrick LB | 87Was | | 6'3" | 215 | Michigan State | | |
| Bunch, Jarrod FB | 91-93NYG 94Raid | 2 | 5'2" | 248 | Michigan | | 42 |
| Bungarda, Ken OT | 80SF 81KJ | | 6'6" | 270 | Missouri | | |
| Bunz, Dan LB | 78-84SF 85Det | | 6'4" | 226 | Long Beach State | 4 | |
| Burbage, Cornell WR | 87-89Dal | 2 | 5'10" | 186 | Kentucky | | 12 |
| Burger, Todd OG | 94-95Chi | | 6'3" | 299 | Penn State | | |
| Burgess, Charlie LB | 87NYG | | 6' | 230 | Carson-Newman | | |
| Burgess, Fernanza WR | 84NYJ 84Mia | | 6'1" | 210 | Miami (Fla.) | | |
| Burgess, Marvell DB | 87Mia | | 6'3" | 195 | Henderson State | | |
| Burgess, Ronnie DB | 85GB | | 5'11' | 175 | Wake Forest | | |
| Burke, Anthony DT | 87StL | | 6'3" | 262 | Minnesota | | |
| Burke, Joe HB | 87NYJ | | 6' | 200 | Rutgers | | |
| Burke, John TE | 94-95NE | 2 | 6'3" | 255 | Virginia Tech | | |
| Burke, Randy WR | 78-81Bal 84USFL | 2 | 6'2" | 190 | Kentucky | | 18 |
| Burkett, Chris WR | 85-89Buf 89-93NYJ | 2 | 6'4" | 205 | Jackson State | | 120 |
| Burks, Shawn LB | 86Was | | 6'1" | 230 | Louisiana State | | |
| Burley, Gary DE | 76-83Cin 84Atl | | 6'3" | 272 | Pittsburgh | | |
| Burmeister, Danny DB | 87Was | | 6'2" | 201 | North Carolina | | |
| Burnett, Rob DE | 90-95Cle | | 6'4" | 276 | Syracuse | | |
| Burnett, Victor DE | 87StL | | 6'5" | 250 | Fresno State | | |

| Use Name (Nickname) - Positions | Team by Year | See Section | Hgt. | Wgt. | College | Int | Pts |
|---|---|---|---|---|---|---|---|
| Burnette, Dave OT | 87Dal | | 6'6" | 278 | Arkansas, Central Arkansas | | |
| Burnette, Reggie LB | 91GB 92-93TB | | 6'2" | 240 | Houston | | |
| Burnham, Tim OT | 87-88Sea | | 6'5" | 280 | Washington | | |
| Burns, Jason HB | 95Cin | | 5'7" | 195 | Wisconsin | | |
| Burns, Jerry | HC86-91Min | | | | Michigan | | |
| Burns, Keith LB | 94-95Den | | 6'2" | 245 | Oklahoma State | | |
| Burrell, Clinton DB | 79-84Cle 85JJ | | 6'2" | 192 | Louisiana State | 8 | 6 |
| Burris, Jeff DB | 94-95Buf | 3 | 6' | 204 | Notre Dame | 3 | |
| Burrough, John DT | 95Atl | | 6'5" | 265 | Wyoming | | |
| Burroughs, Derrick DB | 85-89Buf | | 6'1" | 180 | Memphis State | 6 | |
| Burroughs, James DB | 82-83Bal 84Ind | | 6'1" | 192 | Michigan State | 6 | 6 |
| Burrow, Curtis K | 88GB | | 5'11" | 185 | Central Arkansas | | 2 |
| Burruss, Lloyd DB | 81-91KC | | 6' | 204 | Maryland | 22 | 30 |
| Burse, Tony FB | 87Sea | | 6' | 220 | Middle Tenn. St. | | |
| Burt, Jim NT-DT | 81-88NYG 88-91SF | | 6'1" | 260 | Miami (Fla.) | | 6 |
| Burton, Derek OG | 87Min | | 6'2" | 270 | Oklahoma State | | |
| Burton, James DB | 94-95Chi | | 5'9" | 181 | Fresno State | | |
| Burton, Leonard C | 86-89Buf 90KJ 91Cle 92,94Det | | 6'3" | 269 | South Carolina | | |
| Burton, Ron LB | 87-89Dal 89Phx 90Raid | | 6'1" | 247 | North Carolina | 1 | |
| Busch, Mike QB | 87NYG | 1 | 6'4" | 214 | S. Dakota State | | |
| Bush, Blair C | 78-82Cin 83-88Sea 89-91GB 92-94LA | | 6'3" | 268 | Washington | | |
| Bush, Devin DB | 95Atl | | 5'11" | 205 | Florida State | 1 | |
| Bush, Frank LB | 85-86Hou | | 6'1" | 218 | N. Carolina State | | |
| Bush, Lewis LB | 93-95SD | | 6'2" | 245 | Washington State | 1 | |
| Busick, Steve LB | 81-85Den 86LA 87SD | | 6'4" | 227 | Southern Calif. | 2 | |
| Bussey, Barney DB-LB | 84-85USFL 86-92Cin 93-95TB | 3 | 6' | 195 | S. Carolina State | 10 | 12 |
| Butcher, Paul LB | 86-88Det 89GJ 90-92LA 93-94Ind 95Car | | 6' | 228 | Wayne State | | |
| Butler, Bobby DB | 81-92Atl | | 5'11" | 174 | Florida State | 28 | 18 |
| Butler, Chuck LB | 84Sea | | 6' | 220 | Boise State | | |
| Butler, Dave LB | 87Cle | | 6'4" | 225 | Notre Dame | | |
| Butler, Jerry WR | 79-83Buf 84KJ 85-86Buf 87KJ | 2 | 6' | 178 | Clemson | | 174 |
| Butler, Jerry HB | 87Atl | | 5'11" | 193 | East Tennessee St. | | |
| Butler, John DB | 87SF | | 6'1" | 200 | Principia (Ill.) | | |
| Butler, Keith LB | 78-87Sea | | 6'4" | 230 | Memphis State | 8 | |
| Butler, Kevin K | 85-95Chi | 5 | 6'1" | 195 | Georgia | | 1116 |
| Butler, LeRoy DB | 90-95GB | | 6' | 192 | Florida State | 21 | 6 |
| Butler, Mike DE | 77-82GB 84-85USFL 85GB | | 6'5" | 265 | Kansas | | 6 |
| Butler, Ray WR | 80-83Bal 84-85Ind 85-88Sea | 2 | 6'3" | 200 | Southern Calif. | | 198 |
| Buttle, Greg LB | 76-84NYJ | | 6'3" | 232 | Penn State | 15 | 20 |
| Butts, Marion FB | 89-93SD 94NE 95Hou | 2 | 6'1" | 248 | Florida State | | 264 |
| Butz, Dave DT-DE | 73-74StL 75-88Was | | 6'7" | 291 | Purdue | 2 | |
| Byars, Keith HB | 86-92Phi 93-95Mia | 2 | 6'1 | 234 | Ohio State | | 276 |
| Byers, Scott DB | 84SD | | 5'11" | 170 | Long Beach State | | |
| Byner Earnest FB | 84-88Cle 89-93Was 94-95Cle | 23 | 5'10" | 215 | East Carolina | | 396 |
| By'not'e, Butler DB | 94Den 95Car | 3 | 5'9" | 190 | Ohio State | | |
| Bynum, Reggie WR | 87Buf | | 6'1" | 185 | Oregon State | | |
| Byrd, Boris DB | 87NYG | | 6' | 210 | Austin Peay | | |
| Byrd, Darryl LB | 83-84,87Raid | | 6'1" | 222 | Illinois | | |
| Byrd, Dennis DE-DT | 89-92NYJ | | 6'5" | 270 | Tulsa | | 2 |
| November 1992 — Paralyzed in Game | | | | | | | |
| Byrd, Gill DB | 83-92SD 93KJ | | 5'11" | 195 | San Jose State | 42 | 12 |
| Byrd, Israel DB | 94-95NO | | 5'11" | 184 | Utah State | | |
| Byrd, Richard DE | 85-89Hou | | 6'3" | 264 | Southern Miss. | | |
| Byrd, Sylvester TE | 87Atl | | 6'2" | 225 | Kansas | | |
| Byrum, Carl FB | 86-88Buf | 2 | 6' | 234 | Miss. Valley State | | 6 |
| Cabral, Brian LB | 79Atl 80GB 81-85Chi | | 6'1" | 223 | Colorado | | |
| Caesar, Ivan LB | 91Min | | 6'1" | 241 | Boston College | | |
| Cade, Eddie DB | 95NE | | 6'1" | 206 | Arizona State | | |
| Cade, Mossy DB | 83USFL 85-86GB 87SL | | 6'1" | 197 | Texas | 5 | |
| Cadigan, Dave OT-OG | 88-93NYJ 94Cin | | 6'4" | 285 | Southern Calif. | | |
| Cadrez, Glenn LB | 92-95NYJ 95Den | | 6'3" | 240 | Houston | | |
| Cain, Joe LB | 89-92Sea 93-95Chi | | 6'1" | 235 | Stanford, Oregon Tech | 3 | |
| Cain, Lynn HB | 79-84Atl 85LA | 2 | 6'1" | 205 | Southern Calif. | | 150 |
| Cain, Patrick C-OG | 87Det | | 6'2" | 260 | Wichita State | | |
| Caldwell, Bryan DE | 84Dal 84Hou | | 6'4" | 248 | Arizona State | | |
| Caldwell, Darryl OT | 83Buf | | 6'5" | 245 | Tennessee State | | |
| Caldwell, David NT | 87GB | | 6'1" | 261 | Texas Christian | | |
| Caldwell, Mike LB | 93-95Cle | | 6'2" | 231 | Middle Tenn. State | 3 | 6 |
| Caldwell, Mike WR | 95SF | | 6'2" | 200 | California | | |
| Caldwell, Ravin LB | 87-92Was | | 6'3" | 233 | Arkansas | | 2 |
| Caldwell, Scott HB | 87Den | | 5'10" | 196 | Texas-Arlington | | |
| Caldwell, Tony LB | 83-85Raid 87Sea | | 6'1" | 223 | Washington | | |
| Calhoun, Mike DT-DE | 80TB 80SF | | 6'4" | 260 | Notre Dame | | |
| Calhoun, Rick HB | 87Raid | | 5'7" | 190 | Fullerton State | | 6 |
| Caliguire, Dean OG-C | 91SF 91Pit | | 6'2" | 280 | Pittsburgh | | |
| Call, Kevin OT | 84-93Ind | | 6'7" | 302 | Colorado State | | |
| Callahan, Bill DB | 87Buf | | 6' | 200 | Pittsburgh | | |
| Callicut, Ken HB | 78-82Det | 3 | 6' | 191 | Clemson | | |
| Calloway, Chris WR | 90-91Pit 92-95NYG | 2 | 5'10" | 185 | Michigan | | 66 |
| Camarillo, Rich K | 81-87NE 88LA 89-93Phx 94-95Hou | 4 | 5'11" | 188 | Washington | | |
| Cameron, Glenn LB | 75-85Cin | | 6'2" | 226 | Florida | 5 | |
| Cameron, Jack DB | 84Chi | | 6' | 182 | Winston-Salem | | |
| Camp, Reggie DE | 83-87Cle 88Atl | | 6'4" | 274 | California | | |
| Campbell, Arnold DE | 87Buf | | 6'3" | 260 | Akron State | | |
| Campbell, Earl HB-FB | 78-83Hou 84-85NO | 2 | 5'11" | 232 | Texas | | 444 |
| Campbell, Gary LB | 77-83Chi | | 6'1" | 220 | Colorado | 4 | |
| Campbell, Glen OT | 87Buf | | 6'4" | 280 | Wake Forest | | |
| Campbell, Hugh | HC84-85Hou | | | | Washington State | | |
| Campbell, Jack OT | 82-83Sea | | 6'5" | 277 | Southern Calif., Utah | | |
| Campbell, Jeff WR | 90-93Det 94Den | 23 | 5'8" | 169 | Colorado | | 24 |
| Campbell, Jesse DB | 92-95NYG | | 6'1" | 215 | N. Carolina State | 3 | |
| Campbell, Joe LB | 88-89SD | | 6'4" | 245 | New Mexico State | | |
| Campbell, Matthew TE | 95Car | | 6'4" | 270 | South Carolina | | |
| Campbell, Rich QB | 81-84GB | 1 | 6'4" | 224 | California | | |
| Campbell, Russ TE | 92Pit | | 6'5" | 259 | Kansas State | | |
| Campbell, Scott QB | 84-86Pit 86-87Atl 88KJ 89-90Atl | 12 | 6' | 196 | Purdue | | 12 |
| Campen, James C | 87-88NO 89-93GB | | 6'3" | 269 | Tulane | | |
| Campfield, Billy HB-FB | 78-82Phi 83NYG 84-85USFL | 23 | 5'11" | 200 | Kansas | | 78 |
| Cancik, Phil LB | 80NYG 81Den 83USFL | | 6'1" | 228 | Northern Arizona | | |
| Canley, Sheldon HB | 92NYJ | | 5'9" | 195 | San Jose State | | |
| Cannon, Billy LB | 84Dal | | 6'4" | 231 | Texas A&M | | |
| Cannon, John DE-NT | 82-90TB | | 6'5" | 260 | William & Mary | 1 | |
| Cannon, Mark C | 84-89GB 89KC 91Ind | | 6'3" | 258 | Texas-Arlington | | |
| Capece, Bill K | 81-83TB | 5 | 5'7 | 170 | Florida State | | 196 |
| Capers, Dom | HC95Car | | | | Mount Union | | |

| Use Name (Nickname) - Positions | Team by Year | See Section | Hgt. | Wgt. | College | Int | Pts |
|---|---|---|---|---|---|---|---|
| Capers, James LB | 87Cle | | 6'4" | 232 | Central Michigan | | |
| Capers, Wayne WR | 83-84Pit 85-86Ind | 2 | 6'2" | 198 | Kansas | | 30 |
| Carano, Glenn QB | 77-83Dal 84USFL | 1 | 6'3" | 201 | Nevada-Las Vegas | | |
| Caravello, Joe TE | 87-88Was 89-90SD | 2 | 6'3" | 270 | Tulane | | 6 |
| Carey, Brian WR | 87NE | | 6' | 200 | American Inter. | | |
| Carey, Richard DB | 89Cin 90Buf | | 5'9" | 185 | Idaho | 1 | |
| Carlson, Cody QB | 87-94Hou | 12 | 6'3" | 200 | Baylor | | 24 |
| Carlson, Jeff QB | 90-91TB 92NE | 1 | 6'3" | 215 | Weber State | | |
| Carlson, Mark OT | 87Was | | 6'6" | 284 | Southern Conn. St. | | |
| Carney, John K | 88-89TB 90LA 91-95SD | 5 | 5'11" | 160 | Notre Dame | | 651 |
| Carolan, Brett TE | 94-95SF | | 6'3" | 241 | Washington State | | |
| Caron, Roger OT | 85-86Ind | | 6'5" | 282 | Harvard | | |
| Carpenter, Brian DB | 82NYG 83-84Was 84Buf | | 5'10" | 167 | Michigan | 4 | |
| Carpenter, Rob FB-HB | 77-81Hou 81-85NYG 86LA | 2 | 6'1" | 224 | Miami-Ohio | | 204 |
| Carpenter, Rob WR | 91NE 92-94NYJ 95Phi | 23 | 6'2" | 215 | Notre Dame, Syracuse | | 6 |
| Carpenter, Ron DB | 93Min 93Cin 95NYJ | | 6'1" | 188 | Miami (Ohio) | | |
| Carpenter, Steve DB | 80NYJ 81StL | | 6'2" | 195 | Western Illinois | | |
| Carr, Carl LB | 87Det | | 6'3" | 230 | North Carolina | | |
| Carr, Chetti DB | 87Raid | | 5'9" | 185 | Northwestern Okla. | | |
| Carr, Gregg LB | 85-88Pit | | 6'1" | 220 | Auburn | 1 | 2 |
| Carr, Lydell FB | 89Phx | | 6'1" | 228 | Oklahoma | | |
| Carr, Reggie DT | 87NYG | | 6'3" | 300 | Jackson State | | |
| Carreker, Alphonso DE | 84-88GB 89Den 90KJ 91Den | | 6'6" | 268 | Florida State | 1 | |
| Carreker, Vince DB | 87Cle | | 6' | 183 | Cincinnati | | |
| Carrier, Mark WR | 87-92TB 93-94Cle 95Car | 2 | 6' | 184 | Nicholls State | | 246 |
| Carrier, Mark DB | 90-95Chi | | 6'1" | 188 | Southern Calif. | 18 | 6 |
| Carrington, Darren DB | 89Den 90Det 91-94SD 95Jax | | 6'1" | 189 | Pittsburgh, Northern Arizona | 21 | 6 |
| Carroll, Herman DE | 94NO | | 6'4" | 265 | Mississippi State | | |
| Carroll, Jay TE | 84TB 85Min | | 6'4" | 231 | Minnesota | | 6 |
| Carroll, Pete | HC94NYJ | | | | U. of Pacific | | |
| Carroll, Wesley WR | 91-92NO 93Cin | 2 | 6' | 183 | Miami (Fla.) | | 18 |
| Carruth, Paul Ott FB | 85USFL 86-88GB 89KC | 2 | 6'1" | 220 | Alabama | | 48 |
| Carson, Bud | HC89-90Cle | | | | North Carolina | | |
| Carson, Carlos WR | 80-89KC 89Phi | 23 | 5'11" | 180 | Louisiana State | | 198 |
| Carson, Harry LB | 76-88NYG | | 6'2" | 237 | S. Carolina State | 11 | 12 |
| Carson, Howard LB | 81-83LA 84-85USFL | | 6'2" | 231 | Howard Payne | | |
| Carson, Malcolm OG | 84Min | | 6'2" | 260 | Tenn.-Chattanooga | | |
| Carswell, Dwayne TE | 94-95Den | | 6'3" | 261 | Liberty | | |
| Carter, Alex DE | 87Cle | | 6'3" | 255 | Tennessee State | | |
| Carter, Anthony WR | 83-85USFL 85-93Min 94-95Det | 2 | 5'11" | 174 | Michigan | | 342 |
| Carter, Bernard LB | 95Jax | | 6'3" | 238 | East Carolina | | |
| Carter, Carl DB | 86-87StL 88-89Phx 90Cin 91TB 92GB | | 5'11" | 180 | Texas Tech | 5 | |
| Carter, Cris WR | 87-89Phi 90-95Min | 2 | 6'3" | 196 | Ohio State | | 406 |
| Carter, Dale DB | 92-95KC | 3 | 6'1" | 188 | Tennessee | 14 | 18 |
| Carter, David C-OG | 77-83Hou 84-85NO | | 6'2" | 250 | Western Kentucky | | |
| Carter, Dexter HB | 90-94SF 95NYJ 95SF | 23 | 5'9" | 170 | Florida State | | 60 |
| Carter, Gerald WR | 80NYJ 80-86TB | 2 | 6'1" | 190 | Texas A&M | | 102 |
| Carter, Jimmie LB | 87StL | | 6'1" | 220 | New Mexico | | |
| Carter, Joe HB | 84-86Mia | 2 | 5'11" | 198 | Alabama | | 6 |
| Carter, Jon DT | 89Dal | | 6'4" | 273 | Pittsburgh | | |
| Carter, Kevin DE | 95StL | | 6'5" | 224 | Florida | | 2 |
| Carter, Larry DB | 80Buf | | 5'11" | 185 | Kentucky | | |
| Carter, Marty DB | 91-94TB 95Chi | | 6'1" | 200 | Middle Tenn. St. | 6 | |
| Carter, Michael NT | 84-92SF | | 6'2" | 285 | S.M.U. | 1 | |
| Carter, M.L. DB | 79-81KC 82CFL 83USFL | | 5'9" | 173 | Fullerton State, San Jose State | 3 | |
| Carter, Pat TE | 88Det 89-93LA 94Hou 95StL | 2 | 6'4" | 252 | Florida State | | 42 |
| Carter, Perry DB | 95KC | | 5'11" | 206 | Southern Mississippi | | |
| Carter, Rodney HB | 87-89Pit | 2 | 6' | 218 | Purdue | | 72 |
| Carter, Rubin NT-DT | 75-86Den | | 6' | 255 | Miami (Fla.) | | 6 |
| Carter, Russell DB | 84-87NYJ 88-89Raid | | 6'2" | 197 | S.M.U. | 4 | |
| Carter, Steve WR | 87TB | | 5'10" | 170 | Albany State | | |
| Carter, Tom DB | 93-95Was | | 5'11" | 181 | Notre Dame | 13 | 6 |
| Carter, Tony FB | 94-95Chi | 2 | 5'11" | 216 | Minnesota | | 6 |
| Carter, Walter DE | 87TB | | 6'4" | 276 | Florida State | | |
| Carthen, Jason LB | 93-94NE | | 6'3" | 255 | Ohio U. | | |
| Carthens, Milt OT | 87Ind | | 6'4" | 305 | Michigan | | |
| Carthon, Maurice FB | 83-85USFL 85-91NYG 92Ind | 2 | 6'1" | 225 | Arkansas State | | 18 |
| Carver, Dale LB | 83Cle | | 6'2" | 225 | Georgia | | |
| Carver, Melvin FB | 82-85TB 87Ind | 2 | 5'11" | 221 | Nevada-Las Vegas | | 18 |
| Carver, Shante DE | 94-95Dal | | 6'5" | 248 | Arizona State | | |
| Cascadden, Chad LB | 95NYJ | | 6'1" | 225 | Wisconsin | | |
| Case, Frank DE | 81KC 83-84USFL | | 6'4" | 243 | Penn State | | |
| Case, Scott DB | 84-94Atl 95Dal | | 6' | 178 | Oklahoma | 30 | 8 |
| Case, Stoney QB | 95Arz | | 6'2" | 206 | New Mexico | | |
| Cash, Keith TE | 91Pit 93-95KC | 2 | 6'4" | 235 | Texas | | 60 |
| Cash, Kerry TE | 91-94Ind 95Oak | 2 | 6'4" | 247 | Texas | | 54 |
| Casillas, Tony NT-DT | 86-90Atl 91-93Dal 94-95NYJ | | 6'3" | 280 | Oklahoma | | |
| Cason, Wendell DB | 85-87Atl | | 5'11" | 191 | Oregon | 4 | |
| Cassidy, Ron WR | 79-81GB 82SJ 83-84GB | 2 | 6' | 184 | Utah State | | |
| Castille, Jeremiah DB | 83-86TB 87-88Den | | 5'10" | 175 | Alabama | 14 | 6 |
| Castle, Eric DB | 93-95SD | | 6'3" | 212 | Oregon | | |
| Caston, Toby LB | 87-88Hou 89-93Det | | 6'1" | 240 | Louisiana State | | |
| Castor, Chris WR | 83-84Sea | 2 | 6' | 170 | Duke | | |
| Catanho, Alcides LB | 95NE | | 6'3" | 216 | Rutgers | | |
| Catano, Mark OT | 84-85Pit 86Buf | | 6'3" | 266 | Valdosta State | | |
| Catchings, Toney LB | 87Cin | | 6'3" | 236 | Cincinnati | | |
| Cater, Greg K | 80-83Buf 85USFL 86-87StL | 4 | 6' | 193 | Tenn.-Chattanooga | | |
| Caterbone, Mike WR | 87Mia | | 5'11" | 175 | Franklin & Marshall | | |
| Caterbone, Thomas DB | 87Phi | | 5'8" | 175 | Franklin & Marshall | | |
| Cavanaugh, Matt QB | 78-82NE 83-85SF 86-89Phi 90-91NYG | 12 | 6'2" | 211 | Pittsburgh | | 18 |
| Caver, James DB | 83Det 85USFL | | 5'9" | 175 | Missouri | | |
| Ceaser, Curtis WR | 95NYJ | | 6'2" | 190 | Grambling | | |
| Cecil, Chuck DB | 88-92GB 93Phx 95Hou | | 6' | 186 | Arizona | 16 | 6 |
| Cefalo, Jimmy WR | 78-84Mia | 23 | 5'11" | 189 | Penn State | | 78 |
| Celotto, Mario LB | 78Buf 80-81Oak 81Bal 81LA | | 6'3" | 228 | Southern Calif. | | |
| Centers, Larry HB-FB | 90-93Phx 94-95Arz | 23 | 5'11" | 211 | Stephen F. Austin | | 96 |
| Cephous, Frank HB | 84NYG | | 5'10" | 205 | U.C.L.A. | | |
| Cesare, Billy DB | 78-79TB 80Mia 81-82Det 83-84USFL | | 5'11" | 191 | Miami (Fla.) | | |
| Cesario, Sal OG | 87Dal | | 6'4" | 255 | Cal. Poly.-S.L.O. | | |
| Chadwick, Jeff WR | 83-89Det 89-91Sea 92LA | 2 | 6'3" | 189 | Grand Valley St. | | 168 |
| Chaffey, Pat FB | 91Atl 92-93NYJ | 2 | 6'1" | 218 | Oregon State | | 18 |
| Chalenski, Mike DE-DT | 93Phi 94KJ 95Phi | | 6'4" | 272 | Pittsburgh, U.C.L.A. | | |
| Chamberlain, Byron WR | 95Den | | 6'1" | 240 | Wayne State-Neb. | | |
| Chamblee, Al DE | 91-92TB | | 6'1" | 240 | Virginia Tech | | |

| Use Name (Nickname) - Positions | Team by Year | See Section | Hgt. | Wgt. | College | Int | Pts |
|---|---|---|---|---|---|---|---|
| Chandler, Chris QB | 88-89Ind 90-91TB 91-93Phx 94LA 95Hou | 12 | 6'4" | 210 | Washington | | 56 |
| Chandler, Thornton TE | 86-89Dal | 2 | 6'5" | 243 | Florida A&M, Alabama | | 24 |
| Chandler, Wes WR | 78-81NO 81-87SD 88SF | 23 | 6' | 184 | Florida | | 336 |
| Chapman, Mike C-OG | 84Atl | | 6'4" | 250 | Texas | | |
| Chapman, Ted DE | 87Raid | | 6'3" | 260 | Maryland | | |
| Chapura, Dick DT | 87-89Chi 90Phi 90Phx | | 6'3" | 277 | Missouri | | |
| Charles, Mike NT-DT | 83-86Mia 87-89SD 90Raid 91LA | | 6'4" | 292 | Syracuse | 1 | 2 |
| Charlton, Clifford LB | 88-89Cle | | 6'3" | 240 | Florida | | |
| Chatman, Cliff FB | 82NYG 84USFL | 2 | 6'2" | 225 | Central St.-Okla. | | 12 |
| Chatman, Ricky LB | 87Ind | | 6'2" | 230 | Louisiana State | | |
| Chavez, Laz LB | 87Mia | | 6' | 220 | Iowa | | |
| Chavis, Eddie WR | 87Mia | | 6' | 182 | Montclair State | | |
| Cheek, Louis OT-OG | 88-89Mia 90Dal 90Phx 91GB | | 6'6" | 295 | Texas A&M | | |
| Cherry, Bill C-OG | 86-87GB | | 6'4" | 277 | Middle Tenn. St. | | |
| Cherry, Deron DB | 81-91KC | | 5'11" | 197 | Rutgers | 50 | 18 |
| Cherry, Raphel DB | 85Was 88Det | | 6' | 192 | Hawaii | 5 | |
| Cherry, Tony HB | 86-87SF | | 5'7" | 187 | Oregon | | 6 |
| Chesley, Al LB | 79-81Phi 82Chi | | 6'3" | 240 | Pittsburgh | 4 | |
| Chesley, John TE | 84Mia | | 6'5" | 225 | Oklahoma State | | |
| Chetti, Joseph HB | 87Buf | | 5'9" | 205 | C.W. Post | | |
| Chickillo, Tony NT-DE-OG | 84-85SD 87NYJ | | 6'2" | 262 | Miami (Fla.) | | |
| Childress, Freddie OG-OT | 91NE 92Cle | | 6'4" | 331 | Arkansas | | 6 |
| Childress, Ray DE-DT-NT | 85-95Hou | | 6'6" | 274 | Texas A&M | | 14 |
| Childs, Jason OT | 93Sea | | 6'4" | 285 | North Dakota | | |
| Childs, Ron LB | 95NO | | 5'11" | 212 | Washington State | | |
| Chilton, Gene C-OT | 86-87StL 89KC 90-92NE | | 6'3" | 281 | Texas | | |
| Chmura, Mark TE | 93-95GB | 2 | 6'5" | 242 | Boston College | | 44 |
| Chirico, John FB | 87NYJ | | 6' | 220 | Columbia | | 6 |
| Choate, Putt LB | 87GB | | 6' | 225 | S.M.U. | | |
| Choma, John OG-OT-C | 79KC 81-83SF | | 6'5" | 256 | Virginia | | |
| Chrebet, Wayne WR | 95NYJ | 2 | 5'10" | 180 | Hofstra | | 24 |
| Christiansen, Jeff QB | 83Cin 84-85Phi 87Cle | 1 | 6'3" | 202 | Eastern Illinois | | |
| Christensen, Todd FB-TE | 79NYG 79-81Oak 82-88Raid | 2 | 6'3" | 230 | Brigham Young | | 254 |
| Christian, Bob FB | 92-94Chi 95Car | 2 | 5'10" | 225 | Northwestern | | 8 |
| Christie, Steve K | 90-91TB 92-95Buf | 5 | 6' | 180 | William & Mary | | 619 |
| Christopher, Herb DB | 79-82KC | | 5'10" | 195 | Morris Brown | 4 | |
| Christopherson, Ryan FB | 95Jax | | 5'11" | 237 | Wyoming | | 6 |
| Christy, Greg OT | 85Buf 86-87ZJ | | 6'4" | 285 | Pittsburgh | | |
| Christy, Jeff C | 93-95Min | | 6'3" | 284 | Pittsburgh | | |
| Chung, Eugene OT-OG | 92-94NE 95Jax | | 6'4" | 299 | Virginia Tech | | |
| Churchman, Ricky DB | 80-81SF | | 6'1" | 193 | Texas | 4 | |
| Cisowski, Steve OT | 87Dal | | 6'5" | 275 | Santa Clara | | |
| Clack, Darryl FB | 86-89Dal | 23 | 5'10" | 219 | Arizona State | | 18 |
| Claiborne, Robert WR | 92SD 93TB | | 5'10" | 175 | San Diego State | | |
| Claitt, Rickey HB-FB | 80-81Was 82KJ 83-85USFL | 2 | 5'10" | 206 | Bethune-Cookman | | 12 |
| Clancy, Sam DE-DT | 83Sea 84-85USFL 85-88Cle 89-93Ind | | 6'6" | 288 | Pittsburgh | | |
| Clanton, Chuck DB | 84-85USFL 85GB | | 6'6" | 280 | Oklahoma | | |
| Claphan, Sam OT-OG | 81-87SD | | 6'7" | 285 | Oklahoma | | |
| Clark, Allan HB | 79-80NE 81KJ 82GB 82Buf 84-85USFL | 23 | 5'10" | 186 | Northern Arizona | | 24 |
| Clark, Bernard LB | 90-91Cin 91Sea 91Cin | | 6'2" | 248 | Miami (Fla.) | | |
| Clark, Bret DB | 85USFL 86-88Atl | | 6'3" | 198 | Nebraska | 9 | |
| Clark, Brian OT | 82Den | | 6'6" | 260 | Clemson | | |
| Clark, Brian K | 82TB | | 6'2" | 190 | Florida | | |
| Clark, Bruce DE | 82-88NO 89KC | | 6'3" | 273 | Penn State | 1 | 2 |
| Clark, Bryan QB | 82SF 83SJ 84Cin | | 6'2" | 196 | Michigan State | | |
| Clark, Calvin DE | 81Was 83-85USFL | | 6'4" | 260 | Purdue | | |
| Clark, Dan LB | 87LA | | 6'2" | 233 | San Jose State | | |
| Clark, Darryl HB | 87Chi | | 5'11" | 204 | Texas | | |
| Clark, Derrick FB | 94Den | 2 | 6'1" | 234 | Evangel | | |
| Clark, Dexter DB | 87Det | | 6' | 190 | Toledo | | |
| Clark, Dwight WR | 79-87SF | 2 | 6'4" | 211 | Clemson | | 288 |
| Clark, Gary WR | 84-85USFL 85-92Was 93Phx 94Arz 95Mia | 2 | 5'9" | 173 | James Madison | | 390 |
| Clark, Greg LB | 88Chi 89Mia 90LA 91GB 91SD 92Sea | | 6'1" | 228 | Arizona State | | |
| Clark, Jessie FB | 83-87GB 88Det 88-89Phx 89-90Min | 2 | 6' | 231 | Arkansas | | 90 |
| Clark, Ken FB-HB | 90-92Ind | 2 | 5'9" | 203 | Nebraska | | |
| Clark, Kevin (K.C.) DB | 87-88,90-91Den | | 5'10" | 185 | San Jose State | 3 | 6 |
| Clark, Kelvin OT-OG | 79-81Den 82-85NO | | 6'3" | 260 | Nebraska | | 6 |
| Clark, Louis WR | 87-92Sea | 2 | 6'1" | 193 | Mississippi State | | 30 |
| Clark, Mario DB | 76-83Buf 84SF | | 6'2" | 194 | Oregon | 26 | |
| Clark, Mike DE | 81Was 82SF 84-85USFL 87TB | | 6'4" | 253 | Florida | | |
| Clark, Randy C-DT-OG | 80-86StL 87Atl | | 6'3" | 260 | Northern Illinois | | |
| Clark, Randy DB | 84TB | | 6' | 204 | Florida | | |
| Clark, Reggie LB | 94Pit 95Jax | | 6'2" | 238 | North Carolina | | |
| Clark, Robert WR | 88NO 89-91Det 92Mia | 2 | 5'11" | 175 | N. Car. Central | | 108 |
| Clark, Spark HB | 87Pit | | 5'7" | 182 | Akron | | |
| Clark, Steve OT | 81NE 82NJ | | 6'5" | 258 | Kansas State | | |
| Clark, Steve DT-OG | 82-86Mia | | 6'4" | 255 | Utah | | |
| Clark, Steve DB | 87Buf | | 6'2" | 190 | Liberty | 1 | |
| Clark, Torin DB | 87TB | | 6'1" | 175 | West Virginia St. | | |
| Clark, Vinnie DB | 91-92GB 93-94Atl 94NO 95Jax | | 6' | 194 | Ohio State | 12 | 6 |
| Clark, Willie DB | 94-95SD | | 5'10" | 186 | Notre Dame | 2 | |
| Clarke, Ken NT-DT | 78-87Phi 88Sea 89-91Min | | 6'2" | 268 | Syracuse | | 2 |
| Clarks, Conrad DB | 95Ind | | 5'10" | 200 | Northeast La. | | |
| Clavelle, Shannon DE | 95GB | | 6'2" | 287 | Colorado | | |
| Clasby, Bob DE-DT | 84-85USFL 86-87StL 88-90Phx | | 6'5" | 260 | Notre Dame | 1 | |
| Clay, John OT | 87Raid 88SD | | 6'5" | 300 | Missouri | | |
| Clay, Willie DB | 92-95Det | | 5'9" | 184 | Georgia Tech | 11 | 18 |
| Clayborn, Raymond DB | 77-89NE 90Cle 91LJ | 3 | 6' | 187 | Texas | 36 | 32 |
| Clayton, Harvey DB | 83-86Pit 87NYG | | 5'9" | 179 | Florida | 6 | 6 |
| Clayton, Mark WR | 83-92Mia 93GB | 23 | 5'9" | 177 | Louisville | | 510 |
| Clayton, Ralph WR-FB | 81StL | | 6'3" | 222 | Michigan | | |
| Clayton, Stan OG-OT | 88-89Atl 90-91NE | | 6'3" | 265 | Penn State | | |
| Clements, Tom QB | 80KC | | 6' | 183 | Notre Dame | | |
| Clemons, Michael HB | 87KC | | 5'5" | 166 | William & Mary | | |
| Clemons, Topper HB | 87Phi | | 5'11" | 205 | Wake Forest | | 6 |
| Clendenen, Mike K | 87Den | | 5'11" | 191 | Houston | | 16 |
| Cleveland, Greg OT | 87Mia | | 6'5" | 295 | Florida | | |
| Clifton, Gregory WR | 93Was | | 5'11" | 175 | V.M.I., Johnson C. Smith | | |
| Clifton, Kyle LB | 84-95NYJ | | 6'4" | 234 | Texas Christian | 12 | |
| Cline, Jackie DE-NT | 87Pit 87-89Mia | | 6'5" | 279 | Alabama | | |
| Cline, Tony TE | 95Buf | | 6'4" | 247 | Stanford | | |
| Clinkscale, Dexter DB | 80Dal 81FJ 82-85Dal 86Ind | | 5'11" | 192 | S. Carolina State | 9 | 6 |
| Clinkscales, Joey WR | 87-88Pit 88TB | 2 | 6' | 201 | Tennessee | | 6 |
| Coates, Ben TE | 91-95NE | 2 | 6'4" | 245 | Livingstone | | 150 |
| Cobb, Bob DE | 81LA 82TB 83-84USFL | | 6'4" | 248 | Arizona | | |
| Cobb, Garry LB | 79-84Det 85-87Phi 88-89Dal | | 6'2" | 227 | Southern Calif. | 10 | |
| Cobb, Reggie HB | 90-93TB 94GB 95Jax | 2 | 6' | 225 | Tennessee | | 156 |
| Cobb, Robert OT-OG | 84Min | | 6'2" | 260 | Texas | | |
| Cobb, Trevor HB | 94Chi | | 5'9" | 209 | Rice | | |
| Cobble, Eric HB | 87Hou | | 5'10" | 205 | SW Texas State | | |
| Cobbs, Duffy DB | 87NE | | 5'11" | 178 | Penn State | | |
| Cochran, Mark OT | 87SF 88KJ | | 6'5" | 284 | Baylor | | |
| Cocozzo, Joe OG | 93Sea 94-95SD | | 6'4" | 300 | Michigan | | |
| Cocroft, Sherman DB | 85-87KC 88Buf 89TB | | 6'1" | 195 | San Jose State | 7 | 2 |
| Cofer, Joe DB | 87Was | | 6' | 200 | Tennessee | | |
| Cofer, Mike LB-DE | 83-92Det 93KJ | | 6'5" | 245 | Tennessee | 1 | |
| Cofer, Mike K | 87NO 88-93SF 95Ind | 5 | 6'2" | 192 | N. Carolina State | | 711 |
| Coffey, Ken DB | 83-84Was 85KJ 86Was | | 6' | 193 | SW Texas State | 7 | |
| Coffey, Wayne WR | 87NE | | 5'7" | 158 | SW Texas State | | |
| Coffman, Paul TE | 78-85GB 86-87KC 88Min | 2 | 6'3" | 222 | Kansas State | | 252 |
| Cofield, Tim LB | 86-88KC 89NYJ 89Buf | | 6'2" | 245 | Elizabeth City St. | | |
| Cokeley, Will LB | 87Buf | | 6'2" | 220 | Kansas State | 1 | |
| Colbert, Darrell WR | 87-88KC | | 5'10" | 174 | Texas Southern | | |
| Colbert, Lewis K | 86-87KC 89SD | 4 | 5'11" | 182 | Auburn | | |
| Cole, Robin LB-DE | 77-87Pit 88NYJ | | 6'2" | 222 | New Mexico | 5 | |
| Coleman, Andre WR | 94-95SD | 3 | 5'9" | 165 | Kansas State | | 30 |
| Coleman, Anthony DB | 87Dal | | 6' | 185 | Baylor | | |
| Coleman, Ben OT-OG | 93Phx 94-95Arz 95Jax | | 6'6" | 335 | Wake Forest | | |
| Coleman, Charles TE | 87NYG | | 6'4" | 222 | Alcorn State | | |
| Coleman, Daniel DE | 87Min | | 6'4" | 249 | Murray State | | |
| Coleman, Eric DB | 89-90NE | | 6' | 190 | Wyoming | 1 | |
| Coleman, Greg K | 77Cle 78-87Min 88Was | 4 | 6' | 182 | Florida A&M | | |
| Coleman, Keo LB | 92NYJ 93GB | | 6'1" | 255 | Mississippi State | | |
| Coleman, Leonard DB | 85USFL 85-87Ind 88-89SD | | 6'2" | 203 | Vanderbilt | 6 | |
| Coleman, Lincoln FB-HB | 93-94Dal | 2 | 6'1" | 249 | Notre Dame, Baylor | | 18 |
| Coleman, Marco DE-LB | 92-95Mia | | 6'3" | 264 | Georgia Tech | | |
| Coleman, Monte LB | 79-94Was | | 6'3" | 237 | Central Arkansas | 17 | 24 |
| Coleman, Pat WR | 90NE 91-94Hou | 23 | 5'7" | 173 | Mississippi | | 12 |
| Coleman, Sidney LB | 88-90TB 91Phx 92TB | | 6'2" | 250 | Southern Miss. | | |
| Coley, James TE | 90Chi 91Ind | | 6'3" | 270 | Clemson | | |
| Collie, Bruce OT-OG | 85-89SF 90-91Phi | | 6'6" | 275 | Texas-Arlington | | |
| Collier, Reggie QB | 83-85USFL 86Dal 87Pit | | 6'3" | 207 | Southern Miss. | | |
| Collier, Steve OT-NT | 87GB | | 6'7" | 342 | Bethune-Cookman | | |
| Collier, Tim DB | 76-79KC 80-82StL 82-83SF 84LJ | | 6' | 172 | East Texas State | 15 | 12 |
| Collins, Andre LB | 90-94Was 95Cin | | 6'1" | 232 | Central Arkansas | 10 | 18 |
| Collins, Brett LB | 92-93GB 93LA | | 6'1" | 226 | Washington | | |
| Collins, Clarence WR | 87StL | | 6'1" | 180 | Illinois | | |
| Collins, Dwight WR | 84Min | 2 | 6'1" | 215 | Pittsburgh | | 6 |
| Collins, Fabray LB | 87Min | | 6'2" | 215 | Southern Illinois | | |
| Collins, George OG-OT | 78-82StL 84-85USFL | | 6'2" | 257 | Georgia | | |
| Collins, Gerald LB | 95Cin | | 6'2" | 250 | Vanderbilt | | |
| Collins, Glen DE | 82-85Cin 87SF | | 6'6" | 265 | Mississippi | | |
| Collins, Jim LB | 81-85LA 86SJ 87-88LA 89SD | | 6'2" | 231 | Syracuse | | |
| Collins, Kerry QB | 95Car | 12 | 6'5" | 240 | Penn State | | 18 |
| Collins, Kirk DB | 81-83LA 1984 — Died from cancer | | 5'11" | 182 | Baylor | 5 | |
| Collins, Mark DB | 86-93NYG 94-95KC | | 5'10" | 190 | Fullerton State | 20 | 20 |
| Collins, Patrick HB | 88GB | | 5'9" | 177 | Oklahoma | | |
| Collins, Roosevelt LB | 92Mia | | 6'4" | 235 | Texas Christian | | |
| Collins, Shawn WR | 89-91Atl 92Cle 93GB | 2 | 6'2" | 207 | Northern Arizona | | 30 |
| Collins, Shane DE | 92-94Was | | 6'3" | 267 | Arizona State | | |
| Collins, Todd LB | 92-94NE | | 6'2" | 242 | Georgia, Tennessee, Carson-Newman | | |
| Collins, Todd QB | 95Buf | 1 | 6'4" | 224 | Michigan | | |
| Collins, Tony HB | 81-87NE 88-89DR 90Mia | 23 | 5'11" | 208 | East Carolina | | 264 |
| Collins, Trent DB | 87NYJ | | 6'1" | 187 | San Diego State | | |
| Collinsworth, Cris WR | 81-88Cin | 2 | 6'5" | 192 | Florida | | 216 |
| Collons, Ferric DE | 95NE | | 6'6" | 285 | California | | |
| Colon, Harry DB | 91NE 92Dal 93-94Det 95Jax | | 5'11" | 203 | Missouri | 6 | |
| Colorito, Tony NT | 86Den 87KJ | | 6'5" | 260 | Southern Calif. | | |
| Colquitt, Craig K | 78-81Pit 82LJ 83-84Pit | 4 | 6'2" | 183 | Tennessee | | |
| Colquitt, Jimmy K | 85Sea | | 6'4" | 208 | Tennessee | | |
| Colter, Jeff DB | 84Min 87KC | | 5'10" | 171 | Kansas | | |
| Colton, George OT | 87NE | | 6'4" | 279 | Maryland | | |
| Combs, Chris TE-OT | 80-81StL 83-84USFL | | 6'4" | 238 | New Mexico | | 6 |
| Comeaux, Darren LB | 82-86Den 87SF 88-91Sea | | 6'1" | 229 | Arizona State | 3 | |
| Commiskey, Chuck OG | 83-84USFL 86-88NO | | 6'4" | 290 | Mississippi | | |
| Compton, Chuck DB | 87GB | | 5'10" | 190 | Boise State | | |
| Compton, Mike C-OG-OT | 93-95Det | | 6'6" | 297 | West Virginia | | |
| Conklin, Cary QB | 92-93Was 95SF | 1 | 6'4" | 220 | Washington | | |
| Conlan, Shane LB | 87-92Buf 93-94LA 95StL | | 6'3" | 233 | Penn State | 5 | |
| Conlin, Chris OG | 87Mia 88KJ 90-91Ind | | 6'4" | 290 | Penn State | | |
| Conlin, Ray DT | 87Phi | | 6'2" | 258 | Ohio State | | |
| Connell, Mike K | 78SF 80-81Was | 4 | 6'1' | 200 | Cincinnati | | |
| Conner, Darion LB | 90-93Atl 94NO 95Car | | 6'2" | 250 | Jackson State | 1 | |
| Conover, Frank DT | 91Cle | | 6'5" | 317 | Syracuse | | |
| Conover, Scott OG-OT | 91-95Det | | 6'4" | 285 | Purdue | | 6 |
| Contz, Bill OT | 83-86Cle 86-88NO | | 6'5" | 268 | Penn State | | |
| Conway, Curtis WR | 93-95Chi | 23 | 6' | 188 | Southern Calif. | | 90 |
| Conwell, Joe OT | 84-85USFL 86-87Phi | | 6'5" | 275 | North Carolina | | |
| Cook, Anthony DE-DT | 95Hou | | 6'3" | 293 | S. Carolina State | | 2 |
| Cook, Charles DT | 83NYG 85USFL | | 6'3" | 255 | Miami (Fla.) | | |
| Cook, Kelly FB | 87GB | | 5'11" | 225 | Oklahoma State | | |
| Cook, Marv TE | 89-93NE 94Chi 95StL | 2 | 6'4" | 234 | Iowa | | 72 |
| Cook, Toi DB | 87-93NO 94-95SF | | 5'11" | 188 | Stanford | 17 | 12 |
| Cooks, Johnie LB | 82-83Bal 84-88Ind 88-90NYG 91Cle | | 6'4" | 247 | Mississippi State | 4 | 6 |
| Cooks, Rayford DE | 87Hou | | 6'3" | 245 | North Texas State | | |
| Cooks, Terrence LB | 89NE | | 6' | 230 | Nicholls State | | |
| Coombs, Larry OG-C | 80NO | | 6'4" | 260 | Idaho | | |
| Coombs, Tom TE | 82-83NYJ | | 6'3" | 234 | Idaho | | |
| Coons, Robert TE | 95Buf | | 6'5" | 249 | Pittsburgh | | |
| Cooper, Adrian TE | 91-93Pit 94-95Min | 2 | 6'5" | 259 | Oklahoma | | 30 |
| Cooper, Earl FB-TE | 80-85SF 86Raid | 2 | 6'2" | 228 | Rice | | 108 |
| Cooper, Evan DB | 84-87Phi 88-89Atl | 3 | 5'11" | 185 | Michigan | 11 | |
| Cooper, George LB | 87SF | | 6'2" | 225 | Michigan State | | |
| Cooper, Jim OT-C-OG | 77-86Dal | | 6'5" | 262 | Temple | | |
| Cooper, Joe K | 84Hou 86NYG | 5 | 5'10" | 175 | Tulsa | | 56 |
| Cooper, Louis LB | 85-90KC 91Mia 93Phi | | 6'2" | 240 | Western Carolina | 1 | |
| Cooper, Mark OT | 83-87Den 87-89TB | | 6'5" | 271 | Miami (Fla.) | | |
| Cooper, Reggie LB | 91Dal | | 6'2" | 215 | Nebraska | | |
| Cooper, Richard OT | 90-95NO | | 6'4" | 288 | Tennessee | | |
| Cooper, Scott DE | 87Cle | | 6'5" | 285 | Kearney State | | |

| Use Name (Nickname) - Positions | Team by Year | See Section | Hgt. | Wgt. | College | Int | Pts |
|---|---|---|---|---|---|---|---|
| Copeland, Anthony LB | 87Was | | 6'2" | 250 | Wichita State, Louisville | | |
| Copeland, Danny DB | 89-90KC 91-93Was | 3 | 6'2" | 210 | Eastern Kentucky | 2 | 6 |
| Copeland, Horace WR | 93-95TB | 2 | 6'2" | 195 | Miami (Fla.) | | 38 |
| Copeland, John DT | 93-95Cin | | 6'3" | 286 | Alabama | | |
| Copeland, Russell WR | 93-95Buf | 23 | 6' | 200 | Memphis State | | 18 |
| Corker, John LB | 80-82Hou 83-85USFL 88GB | | 6'5" | 240 | Oklahoma State | | 6 |
| Corley, Anthony FB | 84Pit 85SD | | 6' | 210 | Nevada-Reno | | |
| Corley, Chris TE | 87Sea | | 6'4" | 285 | South Carolina | | |
| Cormier, Joe LB | 87Raid | | 6'6" | 230 | Southern Calif. | | |
| Cornish, Frank C-OG | 90-91SD 92-93Dal 94Min 95Jax 95Phi | | 6'4" | 292 | U.C.L.A. | | |
| Cornelson, Martin C | 87NYJ | | 6'1" | 230 | N. Carolina State | | |
| Cornwell, Fred TE | 84-85Dal | | 6'6" | 236 | Southern Calif. | | 6 |
| Corral, Frank K | 78-81LA 83-85USFL | 45 | 6'2" | 224 | U.C.L.A. | | 379 |
| Correal, Chuck C | 79-80Atl 81Cle 84USFL | | 6'3" | 247 | Penn State | | |
| Corrington, Kip DB | 89-90Den | | 6' | 175 | Texas A&M | 1 | |
| Corsetti, Rico LB | 87NE | | 6'1" | 225 | Bates | | |
| Cortes, Julio LB | 87Sea | | 6' | 226 | Miami (Fla.) | | |
| Corvino, Anthony OG-OT | 87NYJ | | 6'1" | 262 | Southern Conn. St. | | |
| Coryatt, Quentin LB | 92-95Ind | | 6'3" | 250 | Texas A&M | 1 | 6 |
| Coryell, Don | HC73-77StL HC78-86SD | | | | Washington | | |
| Cosbie, Doug TE | 79-88Dal | 2 | 6'6" | 235 | Santa Clara | | 180 |
| Coss, Eric C | 87NYJ | | 6'3" | 270 | Temple | | |
| Costello, Joe LB | 84-85USFL 86-88Atl 89Raid | | 6'3" | 245 | Central Conn. St. | | |
| Cota, Chad DB | 95Car | | 6'1" | 195 | Oregon | | |
| Cothran, Jeff FB | 94-95Cin | 2 | 6'1" | 249 | Ohio State | | 6 |
| Cotney, Mark DB | 75Hou 76-80TB 81KJ 82-84TB | | 6' | 204 | N. Mex. Highlands, Cameron | 17 | |
| Cotton, Barney OG | 79Cin 80-81StL 82KJ | | 6'5" | 264 | Nebraska | | |
| Cotton, Marcus LB | 88-90Atl 90Cle 91Sea 92KJ | | 6'3" | 225 | Southern Calif. | | |
| Coughlin, Tom | HC95Jax | | | | Syracuse | | |
| Courson, Steve OG | 78-83Pit 84-85TB | | 6'1" | 274 | South Carolina | | |
| Courtney, Matt DB | 87SF | | 5'11" | 194 | Idaho State | 1 | |
| Courville, Vince WR | 84-85USFL 87Dal | | 5'9" | 170 | Texas Southern, Rice | | |
| Cousineau, Tom LB | 79-81CFL 82-85Cle 86-87SF | | 6'3" | 225 | Ohio State | 10 | |
| Covert, Jim OT | 83-90Chi 91XJ | | 6'4" | 277 | Pittsburgh | | |
| Covington, Damien LB | 95Buf | | 5'11" | 236 | N. Carolina State | | |
| Covington, Jamie FB | 87NYG | | 6'1" | 234 | Syracuse | | |
| Covington, John DB | 94Ind | | 6' | 198 | Notre Dame | | |
| Covington, Tony DB | 91-92TB 93XJ 94TB 95Sea | | 5'11" | 190 | Virginia | 4 | |
| Cowan, Larry HB | 82Mia 82NE | | 5'11" | 194 | Jackson State | | |
| Cowher, Bill LB | 80Cle 81KJ 82Cle 83-84Phi HC92-95Pit | | 6'3" | 226 | N. Carolina State | | |
| Cowne, John C | 87Was | | 6'2" | 245 | Virginia Tech | | |
| Cox, Aaron WR | 88-92LA 93Ind | 2 | 5'9" | 174 | Arizona State | | 48 |
| Cox, Arthur TE | 83-87Atl 88-91SD 91Mia 91Cle | 2 | 6'3" | 262 | Texas Southern | | 60 |
| Cox, Bryan LB | 91-95Mia | | 6'3" | 244 | Western Illinois | 3 | |
| Cox, Greg DB | 88SF 89NYG 90-91SF | | 6' | 223 | San Jose State | | |
| Cox, Ron LB | 90-95Chi | | 6'2" | 240 | Fresno State | 1 | |
| Cox, Steve K | 81-84Cle 85-88Was | 45 | 6'4" | 195 | Arkansas | | 21 |
| Cox, Tom C | 87LA | | 6'5" | 260 | Southern Calif. | | |
| Crable, Bob LB | 82-87NYJ 88KJ | | 6'3" | 230 | Notre Dame | 3 | |
| Craft, Donnie FB | 82-84Hou | 2 | 6' | 206 | Louisville | | 24 |
| Crafts, Jerry OT | 92-94Buf | | 6'6" | 345 | Oklahoma, Louisville | | |
| Craig, Paco WR | 88Det | | 5'10" | 173 | U.C.L.A. | | |
| Craig, Roger FB-HB | 83-90SF 91Raid 92-93Min | 2 | 6' | 224 | Nebraska | | 438 |
| Craver, Aaron HB | 91-92Mia 93KJ 94Mia 95Den | 23 | 5'11" | 217 | Fresno State | | 42 |
| Crawford, Charles FB | 86-87Phi | 23 | 6'2" | 235 | Oklahoma State | | 6 |
| Crawford, Derrick WR | 86SF 87FJ | | 5'10" | 185 | Memphis State | | |
| Crawford, Elbert OG-C | 90-91NE | | 6'3" | 280 | Arkansas | | |
| Crawford, Keith WR | 93NYG 95GB | | 6'2" | 180 | Howard Payne | | |
| Crawford, Mike HB | 87Cle | | 5'10" | 215 | Arizona State | | |
| Crawford, Tim LB | 87Cle 87Ind | | 6'4" | 245 | Texas Tech | | |
| Creswell, Smiley DE | 85Phi | | 6'4" | 251 | Michigan State | | |
| Crews, Ron NT-DE | 80Cle | | 6'3" | 256 | Nevada-Las Vegas | | |
| Crews, Terry LB-DE | 91LA 93SD 95Was | | 6'2" | 244 | Western Michigan | | |
| Cribbs, James DE | 89Det | | 6'3" | 269 | Memphis State | | |
| Cribbs, Joe HB | 80-83Buf 84-85USFL 85Buf 86-87SF 88Ind 88Mia | 23 | 5'11" | 191 | Auburn | | 258 |
| Crissy, Cris DB | 81Was 82JJ | | 5'11" | 195 | Princeton | | |
| Criswell, Jeff OG-OT | 87Ind 88-94NYJ 95KC | | 6'7" | 289 | Graceland | | |
| Criswell, Kirby DE-LB | 80-81StL | | 6'5" | 238 | Kansas | | |
| Criswell, Ray K | 87-88TB | 4 | 6' | 192 | Florida | | 1 |
| Crittenden, Ray WR | 93-94NE | 23 | 6' | 188 | Virginia Tech | | 24 |
| Crocicchia, Jim QB | 87NYG | | 6'2" | 209 | Pennsylvania | | |
| Crockett, Ray DB | 89-93Det 94-95Den | | 5'9" | 183 | Baylor | 18 | 18 |
| Crockett, Willis LB | 90Dal | | 6'3" | 234 | Georgia Tech | | |
| Crockett, Zack FB | 95Ind | | 6'2" | 241 | Florida State | | |
| Croel, Mike LB | 91-94Den 95NYG | | 6'3" | 237 | Nebraska | 1 | 6 |
| Cromwell, Nolan DB | 77-87LA | | 6'1" | 199 | Kansas | 37 | 49 |
| Cronan, Pete LB | 77-79Sea 80ZJ 81Sea 81-85Was | | 6'2" | 238 | Boston College | 2 | |
| Croom, Corey HB | 93-95NE | 2 | 5'11" | 212 | Ball State | | |
| Crooms, Chris DB | 92LA | | 6'2" | 211 | Texas A&M | | |
| Crosby, Cleveland DE | 80Cle 82Bal 84-85USFL | | 6'4" | 251 | Purdue, Arizona | | |
| Crosby, Ron LB | 78NO 79-83NYJ 84-85USFL | | 6'3" | 224 | Penn State | 2 | |
| Cross, Howard TE | 89-95NYG | 2 | 6'5" | 245 | Alabama | | 84 |
| Cross, Jeff DE | 88-95Mia | | 6'4" | 275 | Missouri | 1 | |
| Cross, Justin OT | 82-86Buf | | 6'6" | 263 | Western St. (Colo.) | | |
| Cross, Randy OG-C | 76-88SF | | 6'3" | 259 | U.C.L.A. | | |
| Croston, Dave OT | 88GB 89SJ | | 6'5" | 280 | Iowa | | |
| Crouch, Terry OG | 82Bal 84USFL | | 6'2" | 278 | Oklahoma | | |
| Croudip, David DB | 83-84USFL 84LA 85SD 85-88Atl | | 5'8" | 183 | San Diego State | 4 | |
| October 10, 1988 — Died of drug overdose | | | | | | | |
| Crouse, Ray FB | 84GB | 2 | 5'11" | 214 | Oregon State | | 6 |
| Crudup, Derrick DB-FB | 89,91Raid | | 6'2" | 225 | Florida, Oklahoma | | |
| Crump, George DE | 82-83NE 84KJ | | 6'4" | 260 | East Carolina | | 2 |
| Crumpler, Carlester TE | 94-95Sea | | 6'6" | 255 | East Carolina | | 6 |
| Crutchfield, Dwayne FB | 82-83NYJ 83Hou 84LA | 2 | 6' | 235 | Iowa State | | 36 |
| Cryder, Bob OG-OT | 78-83NE 84-86Sea 87KJ | | 6'4" | 275 | Alabama | | |
| Cullity, Dave OT | 89SF 90SJ | | 6'7" | 275 | Utah | | |
| Culpepper, Brad DT | 92-93Min 94-95TB | | 6'1" | 268 | Florida | | |
| Culpepper, Willie WR | 92TB | | 5'11" | 155 | Southwestern La. | | |
| Culver, Rodney HB | 92-93Ind 94-95SD | 2 | 5'9" | 224 | Notre Dame | | 102 |
| Cumby, George LB | 80-85GB 86Buf 87Phi | | 6' | 220 | Oklahoma | 5 | |
| Cummings, Mack WR | 87NYG | | 6' | 195 | East Tennessee St. | | |
| Cunningham, Bennie TE | 76-85Pit | 2 | 6'4" | 254 | Clemson | | 120 |
| Cunningham, Ed C | 92-93Phx 94-95Arz | | 6'3" | 288 | Washington | | |
| Cunningham, Eric OG | 79NYJ 80StL 80NYJ | | 6'3" | 257 | Penn State | | |
| Cunningham, Pat OT | 90Ind | | 6'6" | 295 | Texas A&M | | |

| Use Name (Nickname) - Positions | Team by Year | See Section | Hgt. | Wgt. | College | Int | Pts |
|---|---|---|---|---|---|---|---|
| Cunningham, Randall QB | 85-95Phi | 12 | 6'4" | 196 | Nevada-Las Vegas | | 192 |
| Cunningham, Rick OT | 92-93Phx 94Arz 95Min | | 6'6" | 312 | Texas A&M | | |
| Cupp, Keith OT | 87Cin | | 6'6" | 301 | Findlay | | |
| Curcio, Mike LB | 81Phi 82NYG 82Phi 83GB | | 6'1" | 235 | Temple | | |
| Curley, August LB | 83-86Det | | 6'3" | 226 | Southern Calif. | | |
| Curran, Willie WR | 82-84Atl | | 5'10" | 175 | California | | |
| Currie, Herschel DB | 94Arz | | 6' | 189 | Oregon State | | |
| Currier, Bill DB | 77-79Hou 80NE 81-85NYG | | 6' | 196 | South Carolina | 11 | 6 |
| Curry, Buddy LB | 80-87Atl | | 6'4" | 224 | North Carolina | 7 | 12 |
| Curry, Craig DB | 84-86TB 87Ind | | 6' | 189 | Texas | 3 | |
| Curry, Eric DE | 93-95TB | | 6'5" | 270 | Alabama | | |
| Curry, Ivory DB | 87TB | | 5'11" | 185 | Florida | | |
| Curry, Shane DE | 91Ind | | 6'5' | 270 | Georgia Tech, Miami (Fla.) | | |
| 1992 — Killed in shooting | | | | | | | |
| Curtis, Bobby LB | 87Was 88JJ | | 6'3" | 235 | Savannah State | | |
| Curtis, Scott LB | 88Phi 89-90Den | | 6'1" | 230 | New Hampshire | | |
| Curtis, Travis DB | 87StL 88Phx 88Was 89Min 90NYJ 91Was | | 5'10" | 181 | West Virginia | 6 | |
| Cuthbert, Randy FB | 93-94Pit | | 6'3" | 225 | Duke | | |
| D'Addio, Dave FB | 84Det 85NJ 87KJ | | 6'2" | 235 | Maryland | | |
| Dafney, Bernard OG-OT | 92-94Min 95Arz | | 6'5" | 324 | Tennessee | | |
| Dahl, Bob OG-OT | 92-95Cle | | 6'5" | 303 | Notre Dame | | |
| Daigle, Anthony FB | 94Pit | | 5'10" | 203 | Arizona State | | |
| Dale, Jeff DB | 85-86SD 87XJ 88SD | | 6'3" | 211 | Louisiana State | 6 | 6 |
| Dallafior, Ken OG-OT-C | 84USFL 85-88SD 89-92Det | | 6'4" | 276 | Minnesota | | |
| Dalman, Chris OG-C | 93-95SF | | 6'3" | 285 | Stanford | | |
| Daluiso, Brad K | 91Atl 91Buf 92Den 93-95NYG | 5 | 6'2" | 208 | San Diego St., UCLA | | 137 |
| Daniel, Eugene DB | 84-95Ind | | 5'11" | 181 | Louisiana State | 32 | 18 |
| Daniel, Kenny DB | 83-84USFL 84NYG 85BH 86-87Ind | | 5'10" | 180 | San Jose State | 2 | |
| Daniels, Calvin LB | 82-85KC 86Was | | 6'3" | 238 | North Carolina | 3 | |
| Daniels, David WR | 91-92Sea | | 6'1" | 190 | Penn State | | |
| Danielson, Gary QB | 76-78Det 79KJ 80-84Det 85Cle 86NJ 87-88Cle | 12 | 6'2" | 195 | Purdue | | 48 |
| Danmeier, Rick K | 78-82Min 83XJ | 5 | 6' | 194 | Sioux Falls | | 364 |
| Darby, Byron DE-NT-TE | 83-86Phi 87-88Ind 89Det | | 6'4" | 260 | Southern Calif. | | |
| Darby, Matt DB | 92-95Buf | | 6'1" | 200 | U.C.L.A. | 8 | |
| Dardar, Ramsey OG-OT | 84StL | | 6'2" | 264 | Louisiana State | | |
| DarDar, Kirby WR | 95Min | | 5'9" | 183 | Syracuse | | |
| Darns, Phil DE | 84TB | | 6'3" | 245 | Miss. Valley St. | | |
| Darrington, Chris WR | 87Hou | | 5'10" | 180 | Weber State | | |
| Darwin, Matt OT-C | 86-89Phi | | 6'4" | 268 | Texas A&M | | |
| Daugherty, Ron WR | 87Min | | 6'3" | 185 | Northeastern | | |
| Daum, Mike OT | 81Was 84USFL | | 6'6" | 256 | Cal. Poly.-S.L.O. | | |
| Daum, Mitch TE | 87Hou | | 6'5" | 250 | Wyoming | | |
| Davenport, Charles WR | 92-94Pit | 2 | 6'3" | 210 | N. Carolina State | | 6 |
| Davenport, Ron FB | 85-89Mia | 2 | 6'2" | 230 | Louisville | | 102 |
| Davey, Don DE-NT-DT | 91-94GB 95Jax | | 6'4" | 274 | Wisconsin | | |
| David, Stan LB | 84Buf 85XJ | | 6'3" | 210 | Texas Tech | | 6 |
| Davidson, Chy WR | 84-85NYJ | | 5'11" | 175 | Rhode Island | | |
| Davidson, Greg C | 80-82Hou 84USFL | | 6'2" | 250 | North Texas | | |
| Davidson, Jeff OG-OT | 90-92Den 94SJ | | 6'5" | 309 | Ohio State | | |
| Davidson, Kenny DE-DT | 90-93Pit 94-95Hou | | 6'5" | 281 | Louisiana State | 2 | 6 |
| Davis, Anthony LB | 93Sea 94-95KC | | 6' | 231 | Utah | 1 | |
| Davis, Antone OT | 91-95Phi | | 6'4" | 327 | Tennessee | | |
| Davis, Billy LB | 84StL | | 6'4" | 210 | Clemson | | |
| Davis, Billy WR | 95Dal | | 6'1" | 197 | Pittsburgh | | |
| Davis, Brian DB | 87-90Was 91-92Sea 93SD 94Min | | 6'2" | 190 | Nebraska | 9 | 6 |
| Davis, Bruce OT-OG | 79-81Oak 82-87Raid 87-89Hou | | 6'6" | 287 | U.C.L.A. | | |
| Davis, Bruce WR | 84Cle | | 5'8" | 160 | Baylor | | 12 |
| Davis, Chris LB | 87NYG | | 6'1" | 225 | San Diego State | | |
| Davis, Darrell DE | 90-91NYJ | | 6'2" | 258 | Texas Christian | | 6 |
| Davis, Dexter DB | 91-92Phx 93-94LA 95StL | 3 | 5'10" | 190 | Clemson | 2 | |
| Davis, Eric DB | 90-95SF | | 5'11" | 178 | Jacksonville State | 12 | 18 |
| Davis, Elgin HB | 87-88NE | | 5'10" | 192 | Central Florida | | |
| Davis, Fred DB | 87Sea | | 5'10" | 182 | Western Carolina | | |
| Davis, Greg K | 87-88Atl 89NE 89-90Atl 91-93Phx 94-95Arz | 5 | 5'11" | 197 | The Citadel | | 733 |
| Davis, Isaac OG | 94-95SD | | 6'3" | 320 | Arkansas | | |
| Davis, James DB | 82-87Raid | | 6' | 193 | Southern U. | 4 | 6 |
| Davis, Jeff LB | 82-87TB | | 6' | 230 | Clemson | 3 | |
| Davis, Jerome NT | 87Det | | 6'1" | 260 | Ball State | | |
| Davis, John OT-OG-C | 87-88Hou 89-94Buf | | 6'4" | 306 | Georgia Tech | | |
| Davis, Johnny FB | 78-80TB 81SF 82-87Cle | 2 | 6'1" | 235 | Alabama | | 90 |
| Davis, Kelvin OG | 87NYG | | 6'2" | 260 | Johnson C. Smith | | |
| Davis, Kenneth HB | 86-88GB 89-94Buf | 23 | 5'10" | 209 | Texas Christian | | 192 |
| Davis, Lee DB | 85Cin 87Ind | | 5'11" | 200 | Mississippi | 1 | |
| Davis, Lorenzo WR | 90Pit | | 5'11" | 185 | Youngstown State | | |
| Davis, Michael DB | 94Hou 95Cle | | 6'1" | 192 | Cincinnati | | |
| Davis, Mike DB | 78-81Oak 82-85Raid 86JJ | | 6'3" | 203 | Colorado | 11 | 6 |
| Davis, Oliver DB | 77-80Cle 81-82Cin 83-85USFL | | 6'" | 203 | Tennessee State | 11 | 6 |
| Davis, Paschall LB | 95StL | | 6'2" | 225 | Texas A&I | | |
| Davis, Paul LB | 81-82Atl 83NYG 83StL | | 6'2" | 221 | North Carolina | 1 | |
| Davis, Preston DB | 84-86Ind | | 5'11" | 180 | Baylor | 3 | |
| Davis, Reuben DE-DT | 88-92TB 92-93Phx 94-95SD | | 6'4" | 301 | North Carolina | 1 | 8 |
| Davis, Ron DB | 95Atl | | 5'10" | 190 | Tennessee | | |
| Davis, Russell FB | 80-83Pit | 2 | 6'1" | 227 | Michigan | | 12 |
| Davis, Scott DE-LB-DT | 88-91,94Raid | | 6'7" | 276 | Illinois | | |
| Davis, Scott OG | 93-94NYG 95KJ | | 6'3" | 289 | Iowa | | |
| Davis, Terrell HB | 95Den | 2 | 5'11" | 200 | Georgia | | 48 |
| Davis, Travis NT | 90NO 91Ind | | 6'2" | 279 | Michigan State | | |
| Davis, Travis DB | 95Jax | | 6' | 200 | Notre Dame | | |
| Davis, Tyree WR | 95TB | | 5'9" | 175 | Central Arkansas | | |
| Davis, Tyrone DB | 85NYG 86XJ | | 6'1" | 190 | Clemson | | |
| Davis, Tyrone WR | 95NYJ | | 6'4" | 229 | Virginia | | |
| Davis, Wayne DB | 85-86SD 87-89Buf 89-90Was | | 5'11" | 177 | Indiana State | 3 | |
| Davis, Wayne LB | 87StL 88Phx | | 6'1" | 213 | Alabama | | |
| Davis, Wendell WR | 88-93Chi | 2 | 5'11" | 188 | Louisiana State | | 84 |
| Davis, Willie WR | 91-95KC | 2 | 6' | 174 | Central Arkansas | | 122 |
| Dawkins, Dale WR | 90-93NYJ | | 6'1" | 190 | Miami (Fla.) | | |
| Dawkins, Julius WR | 83-84Buf | 2 | 6'1" | 196 | Pittsburgh | | 18 |
| Dawkins, Sean WR | 93-95Ind | 2 | 6'4" | 213 | California | | 54 |
| Dawkins, Tommy DE | 87Pit | | 6'3" | 260 | Appalachian State | | |
| Dawsey, Lawrence WR | 91-95TB | 2 | 6' | 195 | Florida State | | 36 |
| Dawsey, Stacey WR | 87NO | 2 | 5'9" | 154 | Indiana | | |
| Dawson, Dale K | 87Min 88Phi 88GB | | 6' | 213 | Eastern Kentucky | | 20 |
| Dawson, Dermontti C-OG | 88-95Pit | | 6'2" | 282 | Kentucky | | |
| Dawson, Doug OG | 84-86StL 90-93Hou 94Cle | | 6'3" | 279 | Texas | | |
| Dawson, Lake WR | 94-95KC | | 6'1" | 204 | Notre Dame | | 42 |

| Use Name (Nickname) - Positions | Team by Year | See Section | Hgt. | Wgt. | College | Int | Pts |
|---|---|---|---|---|---|---|---|
| Dawson, Lin TE | 81-85NE 86KJ 87-90NE | 2 | 6'3" | 240 | N. Carolina State | | 48 |
| Dawson, Mike NT-DT-DE | 76-82StL 83Det 84KC | | 6'4" | 269 | Arizona | 1 | |
| Dean, Fred DE | 75-81SD 81-85SF | | 6'3" | 230 | Louisiana Tech | 1 | 12 |
| Dean, Kevin LB | 87SF | | 6'1" | 235 | Texas Christian | | |
| Dean, Vernon DB | 82-87Was 88Sea | | 5'11" | 178 | U.S. International, San Diego State | 22 | 24 |
| Dean, Walter FB | 91GB | | 5'10" | 216 | Grambling | | |
| DeAyala, Kiki LB | 84-85USFL 86-87Cin | | 6'1" | 225 | Texas | | |
| DeForest, Joe LB | 87NO | | 6'1" | 240 | Southwestern La. | | |
| DeBerg, Steve QB | 77-80SF 81-83Den 84-87TB 88-91KC 92-93TB 93Mia | 12 | 6'2" | 207 | San Jose State | | 42 |
| deBruijn, Case K | 82KC 84-85USFL | 4 | 6'1" | 176 | Idaho State | | |
| Dee, Donnie TE | 88-89Ind 89Sea | | 6'4" | 247 | Tulsa | | |
| Deese, Derrick OG | 94-95SF | | 6'3" | 270 | Southern Calif. | | |
| DeGraffenreid, Allen WR | 93Cin | | 6'3" | 200 | Ohio State | | |
| Degrate, Tony DE | 85GB | | 6'4" | 280 | Texas | | |
| DeJurnett, Charles DE-DT-NT | 76-80SD 81FJ 82-86LA | | 6'4" | 263 | San Jose State | | |
| Delaney, Jeff DB | 80LA 81Det 81TB 82-83Bal 84-85USFL | | 6' | 195 | Pittsburgh | 4 | |
| Delaney, Joe HB | 81-82KC | 2 | 5'10" | 184 | Northwestern La. | | 18 |
| 1983 — died in swimming accident | | | | | | | |
| Del Greco, Al K | 84-87GB 87StL 88-90Phx 91-95Hou | 5 | 5'10" | 191 | Auburn | | 980 |
| DeLine, Steve K | 88SD 89Phi | 5 | 5'11" | 185 | Colorado State | | 42 |
| Dellenbach, Jeff OT-C | 85-94Mia 95NE | | 6'6" | 288 | Wisconsin | | |
| DeLoach, Ralph DE | 81NYJ | | 6'5" | 245 | California | | |
| DeLong, Greg TE | 95Min | | 6'4" | 245 | North Carolina | | |
| DeLong, Keith LB | 89-93SF | | 6'2" | 245 | Tennessee | 2 | |
| Delpino, Robert FB-HB | 88-92LA 93Den | 23 | 6' | 205 | Missouri | | 162 |
| Del Rio, Jack LB | 85-86NO 87-88KC 89-91Dal 92-95Min | | 6'4" | 240 | Southern Calif. | 13 | 6 |
| DeMarco, Brian OT | 95Jax | | 6'7" | 321 | Michigan State | | |
| Dennard, Mark C | 79-83Mia 84-85Phi 86Cle | | 6'1" | 253 | Texas A&M | | |
| Dennard, Preston WR | 78-83LA 84Buf 85GB | 2 | 6'1" | 184 | New Mexico | | 180 |
| Dennis, Mark OT | 87-93Mia 94Cin 95Car | | 6'6" | 292 | Illinois | | |
| Dennis, Mike DB | 80-83NYG 84SD 84NYJ | | 5'10" | 190 | Wyoming | 6 | 6 |
| Dennison, Glenn TE | 84NYJ 85XJ 87Was | 2 | 6'3" | 225 | Miami (Fla.) | | 6 |
| Dennison, Rick LB | 82-90Den | | 6'3" | 219 | Colorado State | 4 | |
| Dent, Burnell LB | 86-92GB | | 6'1" | 236 | Tulane | 1 | |
| Dent, Richard DE | 83-93Chi 94SF 95Chi | | 6'5" | 264 | Tennessee State | 8 | 12 |
| DeOssie, Steve LB | 84-88Dal 89-93NYG 93NYJ 94-95NE | | 6'2" | 247 | Boston College | 1 | |
| DeRamus, Lee WR | 95NO | | 6' | 191 | Wisconsin | | |
| Derby, Glenn OT-OG | 89-90NO | | 6'6" | 290 | Wisconsin | | |
| Derby, John LB | 92Det | | 6' | 232 | Iowa | | |
| DeRiggi, Fred NT | 90NE | | 6'2" | 268 | Syracuse | | |
| DeRoo, Brian WR | 79-81Bal | | 6'3" | 193 | Redlands | | 6 |
| DeRose, Dan LB | 87NYG | | 6' | 230 | Southern Colorado | 1 | |
| Detmer, Ty QB | 92-95GB | | 6' | 184 | Brigham Young | | |
| DeVaughn, Dennis DB | 82-83Phi 85USFL | | 5'10" | 175 | Bishop | | |
| Devlin, Joe OT-OG | 76-82Buf 83BN 84-89Buf | | 6'5" | 261 | Iowa | | |
| Devlin, Mike C-OG | 93-95Buf | | 6'1" | 298 | Iowa | | |
| DeVita, Rob LB | 87Sea | | 6'2" | 222 | Illinois, Benedictine | | |
| Devries, Jed OT | 95Cle | | 6'6" | 282 | Utah State | | |
| Dial, Alan DB | 89Phi | | 6'1" | 188 | U.C.L.A. | | |
| Diana, Rich FB | 82Mia | | 5'9" | 220 | Yale | | |
| Diaz-Infante, David C-OG | 87SD | | 6'2" | 272 | San Jose State | | |
| DiBernardo, Rick LB | 86StL 87LA | | 6'3" | 230 | Notre Dame | | |
| Dick, Jim LB | 87Min | | 6'1" | 230 | N. Dakota State | | |
| Dickerson, Andy OG | 87Raid | | 6'5" | 260 | Cal. Lutheran | | |
| Dickerson, Anthony LB | 80-84Dal 85Buf | | 6'2" | 220 | S.M.U. | 5 | 2 |
| Dickerson, Eric HB-FB | 83-87LA 87-91Ind 92Raid 93Atl | 2 | 6'3" | 220 | S.M.U. | | 576 |
| Dckerson, Ron HB-WR | 93-94KC | 3 | 6' | 211 | Arkansas | | |
| Dickey, Charlie OG | 87Pit | | 6'3" | 270 | Arizona | | |
| Dickey, Curtis HB-FB | 80-83Bal 84-85Ind85-86Cle | 2 | 6'1" | 213 | Texas A&M | | 240 |
| Didier, Clint TE | 82-87Was 88-89GB | 2 | 6'5" | 240 | Portland State | | 132 |
| Didio, Mark WR | 92Pit | | 5'11" | 181 | Connecticut | | |
| Dierking, Scott HB-FB | 77-83NYJ 84TB | 2 | 5'10" | 218 | Purdue | | 138 |
| Dieterich, Chris OT-OG | 80-86Det | | 6'3" | 262 | N. Carolina State | | |
| Diettrich, John K | 87Hou | | 6'2" | 190 | Ball State | | 23 |
| DiGiacomo, Curt OG-C | 86SD 88KC | | 6'4" | 270 | Arizona | | |
| Dilfer, Trent QB | 94-95TB | 12 | 6'4" | 235 | Fresno State | | 12 |
| Dilger, Ken TE | 95Ind | 2 | 6'5" | 256 | Illinois | | 24 |
| Dill, Scott OG-OT | 88-89Phx 90-95TB | | 6'5" | 289 | Memphis State | | |
| Dillard, Stacey DE-NT-DT | 92-95NYG | | 6'5" | 290 | Oklahoma | | |
| Dils, Steve QB | 79-84Min 84-87LA 88Atl 89LA | 12 | 6'1" | 191 | Stanford | | |
| Dilweg, Anthony QB | 89-90GB | 12 | 6'3" | 215 | Duke | | |
| Dimler, Rich NT-DT | 79Cle 80GB 83-84USFL | | 6'6" | 260 | Southern Calif. | | |
| Dimry, Charles DB | 88-90Atl 91-93Den 94-95TB | | 6' | 175 | Nevada-Las Vegas | 12 | 6 |
| Dingle, Mike FB | 91Cin | 2 | 6'2" | 240 | South Carolina | | 6 |
| Dingle, Nate LB | 95Phi | | 6'2" | 242 | Cincinnati | | |
| Dinkel, Tom LB | 78-83Cin 84-85USFL 85Cin | | 6'3" | 240 | Kansas | 1 | |
| Dinkins, Howard LB | 93Atl | | 6'1" | 230 | Florida State | | |
| Dion, Terry DE | 80Sea | | 6'6" | 254 | Oregon | | |
| Diorio, Jerry TE | 87Det | | 6'3" | 245 | Michigan | | |
| DiRenzo, Fred FB | 87NYG | | 5'11" | 234 | New Haven | | |
| DiRico, Robert HB | 87NYG | 2 | 5'10" | 202 | Kutztown | | |
| Dishman, Cris DB | 88-95Hou | | 6' | 183 | Purdue | 30 | 30 |
| Dixon, Al TE | 77-79NYG 79-82KC 83Phi 84SD 84SF | 2 | 6'5" | 230 | Iowa State | | 48 |
| Dixon, Cal C-OG | 92-95NYJ | | 6'4" | 287 | Florida | | |
| Dixon, David OG | 94-95Min | | 6'5" | 354 | Arizona State | | |
| Dixon, Dwayne WR | 84,87TB | | 6'1" | 204 | Florida | | |
| Dixon, Ernest LB-DE | 94-95NO | | 6'1" | 245 | South Carolina | 2 | |
| Dixon, Floyd WR | 86-91Atl 92Phi | 23 | 5'9" | 170 | S.F. Austin State | | 96 |
| Dixon, Gerald LB | 93-95Cle | | 6'3" | 252 | South Carolina | 2 | 6 |
| Dixon, Hanford DB | 81-89Cle | | 5'11" | 186 | Southern Miss. | 26 | |
| Dixon, James WR-HB | 89-91Dal | 23 | 5'10" | 181 | Houston | | 18 |
| Dixon, Joe NT | 87Hou | | 6'3" | 275 | Tulsa | | |
| Dixon, Randy OT-OG | 87-95Ind | | 6'3" | 297 | Pittsburgh | | 6 |
| Dixon, Rich LB | 83Atl 85USFL | | 6'2" | 235 | California | | |
| Dixon, Rickey DB | 88-92Cin 93Raid | | 5'11" | 183 | Oklahoma | 3 | |
| Dixon, Ronnie NT-DT | 93NO 95Phi | | 6'2" | 292 | Cincinnati | | |
| Dixon, Titus WR | 89NYJ 89Ind | | 5'6" | 152 | Troy State | | |
| Dixon, Zachary HB | 79Den 79NYG 80Phi 80-83Bal 83-84Sea 85KJ | 23 | 6' | 203 | Temple | | 30 |
| Dodge, Dedrick DB | 91-92Sea 94-95SF | | 6'2" | 184 | Florida State | 2 | |
| Dodge, Kirk LB | 84Det 85SJ 86Hou 87Den | | 6'1" | 232 | Nevada-Las Vegas | | |
| Doerger, Jerry OT-C | 82Chi 84-85USFL 85SD | | 6'5" | 270 | Wisconsin | | |
| Dohring, Tom OT | 92KC | | 6'6" | 290 | Michigan | | |
| Doig, Steve LB | 82-84Det 86-87NE | | 6'2" | 242 | New Hampshire | | |
| Doleman, Chris DE-LB | 85-93Min 94-95Atl | | 6'5" | 267 | Pittsburgh | 9 | 16 |
| Dollinger, Tony FB | 87Det | | 5'11" | 205 | Evangel | | |
| Dombroski, Paul DB | 80KC 81-84NE 85TB | | 6' | 185 | Linfield | 2 | |

| Use Name (Nickname) - Positions | Team by Year | See Section | Hgt. | Wgt. | College | Int | Pts |
|---|---|---|---|---|---|---|---|
| Dombrowski, Jim OT-OG | 86-95NO | | 6'5" | 298 | Virginia | | |
| Donahue, Mitch LB | 91-92SF 93-94Den | | 6'2" | 254 | Wyoming | | |
| Donaldson, Jeff DB | 84-89Hou 90KC 91-93Atl | | 6' | 192 | Colorado | 12 | 6 |
| Donaldson, Ray C-OG | 80-83Bal 84-92Ind 93-94Sea 95Dal | | 6'3" | 291 | Georgia | | |
| Donley, Doug WR | 81-84Dal | 2 | 6' | 175 | Ohio State | | 24 |
| Donnalley, Kevin OT-OG | 91-95Hou | | 6'5" | 302 | Davidson, North Carolina | | |
| Donnalley, Rick C-OG | 82-83Pit 84-85Was 86-87KC | | 6'2" | 261 | North Carolina | | |
| Donnelly, Rick K | 85-88Atl 89XJ 90-91Sea | 4 | 6' | 190 | Wyoming | | 1 |
| D'Onofrio, Mark LB | 92GB 93LJ | | 6'2" | 235 | Penn State | | |
| Donovan, Tom WR | 80NO 83-85USFL | | 5'11" | 179 | Penn State | | |
| Doornink, Dan FB-HB | 78NYG 79-85Sea | 2 | 6'3" | 210 | Washington State | | 156 |
| Dorn, Torin DB | 90-93Raid 95StL | | 6' | 190 | North Carolina | 2 | 14 |
| Dornbrook, Thom OG-C | 79Pit 80Mia 83-85USFL | | 6'2" | 240 | Kentucky | | |
| Dorney, Keith OT-OG | 79-87Det | | 6'5" | 268 | Penn State | | |
| Dorning, Dale DE | 87Sea | | 6'5" | 260 | Oregon | | |
| Dorsett, Matthew DB | 95GB | | 5'11" | 187 | Southern-B.R. | | |
| Dorsett, Tony HB | 77-87Dal 88Den 89KJ | 2 | 5'11" | 190 | Pittsburgh | | 552 |
| Dorsey, Dean K | 88Phi 88GB | 5 | 5'11" | 190 | Toronto | | 27 |
| Dorsey, Eric DE | 86-92NYG | | 6'5" | 280 | Notre Dame | | |
| Dorsey, John LB | 84-88GB 89KJ | | 6'3" | 240 | Connecticut | | |
| Doss, Reggie DE-DT | 78-87LA | | 6'4" | 265 | Hampton U. | | |
| Dotson, Dewayne LB | 95Mia | | 6'1" | 256 | Mississippi | | |
| Dotson, Earl OT | 93-95GB | | 6'4" | 312 | Texas A&I | | |
| Dotson, Santana DE-DT | 92-95TB | | 6'5" | 272 | Baylor | | 6 |
| Doubiago, Dan OT | 87KC | | 6'5" | 283 | Utah | | |
| Douglas, David OT-OG-C | 86-88Cin 89-90NE | | 6'4" | 280 | Tennessee | | |
| Douglas, Derrick FB | 91Cle 92KJ | | 5'10" | 222 | Louisiana Tech | | |
| Douglas, Hugh DE | 95NYJ | | 6'2" | 265 | Central St.-Ohio | | |
| Douglas, Leland WR | 87Mia | | 6' | 179 | Baylor | | 6 |
| Douglas, Omar WR | 94-95NYG | | 5'10" | 170 | Minnesota | | 6 |
| Douglass, Mike LB | 78-85GB 86SD | | 6' | 220 | Arizona State, San Diego State | 10 | 18 |
| Douglass, Maurice DB | 86-94Chi 95NYG | | 5'11" | 200 | Kentucky | 5 | |
| Dove, Wes DE | 87Sea | | 6'7" | 270 | Syracuse | | |
| Dowdell, Marcus WR | 92-93NO 95Arz | 2 | 5'10" | 179 | Tennessee State, San Diego State | | 6 |
| Dowhower, Rod | HC85-86Ind | | | | | | |
| Dowling, Sean OG-OT | 87Buf | | 6'4" | 280 | C.W. Post | | |
| Downing, Walt OG-C | 78-83SF 85USFL | | 6'3" | 259 | Michigan | | |
| Downs, Gary FB | 94NYG 95Den | | 6' | 212 | N. Carolina State | | |
| Downs, Michael DB | 81-88Dal | | 6'3" | 205 | Rice | 35 | 18 |
| Dozier, Cornelius DB | 87KC | | 6'2" | 190 | S.M.U. | | |
| Dozier, D.J. HB-FB | 87-90Min 91Det | 2 | 6' | 198 | Penn State | | 54 |
| 92 played major league baseball | | | | | | | |
| Drake, Jerry DE | 95Arz | | 6'4" | 292 | Hastings | | |
| Drake, Joe NT | 85Phi 87SF | | 6'2" | 290 | Arizona | | |
| Drake, Troy OT | 95Phi | | 6'6" | 289 | Indiana | | |
| Drakeford, Tyronne DB | 94-95SF | | 5'9" | 185 | Virginia Tech | 6 | |
| Drane, Dwight DB | 84-85USFL 86-91Buf | | 6'2" | 204 | Oklahoma | 1 | |
| Drayton, Troy TE | 93-94LA 95StL | 2 | 6'3" | 255 | Penn State | | 84 |
| Dreschler, Dave OG | 83-84GB | | 6'3" | 264 | North Carolina | | |
| Dressel, Chris TE | 83-86Hou 87SF 89KC 89-91NYJ 92SF | 2 | 6'4" | 239 | Stanford | | 42 |
| Drewrey, Willie WR | 85-88Hou 89-92TB 93Hou | 23 | 5'7" | 164 | West Virginia | | 42 |
| Driver, Stacey HB | 87Cle | | 5'7" | 190 | Clemson | | |
| Dronett, Shane DE-DT | 92-95Den | | 6'6" | 275 | Texas | 2 | |
| Drost, Jeff NT | 87GB | | 6'5" | 286 | Iowa | | |
| Drozdov, Darren NT-DT | 93Den 94KJ | | 6'3" | 280 | Maryland | | |
| Drummond, Robert HB | 89-91Phi | 2 | 6'1" | 205 | Syracuse | | 24 |
| Duarte, George DB | 87Chi | | 5'9" | 172 | Northern Arizona | | |
| Dubois, Phil TE | 79-80Was 81LA 83USFL | | 6'2" | 220 | San Diego State | | |
| DuBose, Demetrious LB | 93-95TB | | 6'1" | 238 | Notre Dame | | |
| DuBose, Doug HB | 87-88SF | 23 | 5'11" | 190 | Nebraska | | 12 |
| Duckens, Mark DE | 89NYG 90Det 92TB | | 6'4" | 270 | Wichita State, Arizona State | | |
| Duckett, Forey DB | 94Cin 94GB 94Sea | | 6'3" | 195 | Nevada-Reno | | |
| Duckett, Kenny WR | 82-85NO 85Dal | 23 | 6' | 184 | Wake Forest | | 24 |
| Duckworth, Bobby WR | 82-84SD 85-86LA 86Phi | 2 | 6'3" | 197 | Arkansas | | 78 |
| Ducksworth, Robert DB | 86NYJ | | 5'11" | 200 | Southern Miss. | | |
| Duda, Mark DT | 83-87StL | | 6'3" | 273 | Maryland | | |
| Dudek, Joe HB | 87Den | | 6' | 181 | Plymouth State | | 12 |
| Dudley, Brian DB | 87Cle | | 6'1" | 180 | Bethune-Cookman | | |
| Duerson, Dave DB | 83-89Chi 90NYG 91-93Phx | | 6'1" | 207 | Notre Dame | 20 | 6 |
| Dufault, Paul C | 87Raid | | 6'4" | 255 | New Hampshire | | |
| Dufek, Don DB | 76-77Sea 78KJ 79-84Sea | | 6' | 195 | Michigan | 3 | |
| Dufek, Joe QB | 83-85Buf 85SD | | 6'4" | 215 | Yale | | 6 |
| Duff, Jamal DE | 95NYG | | 6'7" | 259 | San Diego State | | |
| Duff, John TE | 93-94Raid | | 6'7" | 250 | New Mexico | | |
| Duffy, Roger C-OG | 90-95NYJ | | 6'3" | 295 | Penn State | | |
| Dufour, Dan OG | 83-84Atl | | 6'5" | 280 | U.C.L.A. | | |
| Dugan, Bill OG-OT | 81-83Sea 84Min 85USFL 87NYG | | 6'4" | 275 | Penn State | | |
| Duhe, A.J. DE-LB | 77-84Mia | | 6'4" | 247 | Louisiana State | 3 | 2 |
| Dukes, Jamie OG-C | 86-93Atl 94GB 95Arz | | 6'1" | 285 | Florida State | | |
| Duliban, Chris LB | 87Dal | | 6'2" | 216 | Texas | | |
| Dulin, Gary DT-DE | 86-87StL | | 6'4" | 275 | Ohio State | | |
| Dumas, Mike DB | 91-92Hou 93FJ 94Buf 95Jax | | 5'11" | 178 | Indiana | 3 | 6 |
| Dumbauld, Jonathan DE | 86NO 87-88Phi 88NO | | 6'4" | 259 | Kentucky | | |
| Dumont, Jim LB | 84Cle 85USFL | | 6'1" | 224 | Rutgers | | |
| Dunaway, Craig TE | 83Pit | | 6'2" | 233 | Michigan | | |
| Dunbar, Karl DE-DT | 93NO 94-95Arz | | 6'4" | 275 | Louisiana State | | |
| Dunbar, Vaughn HB | 92NO 93KJ 94-95NO 95Jax | 2 | 5'10" | 204 | Indiana | | 30 |
| Duncan, Clyde WR | 84-85StL | | 6'1" | 202 | Tennessee | 6 | |
| Duncan, Curtis WR | 87-93Hou | 23 | 5'11" | 185 | Northwestern | | 120 |
| Duncan, Frank DB | 79-81SD 83-85USFL | | 6'1" | 188 | San Fran. State | 1 | |
| Dunek, Ken TE | 80Phi 83-85USFL | | 6'6" | 235 | Memphis State | | |
| Dunn, David WR | 95Cin | 23 | 6'3" | 210 | Fresno State | | 6 |
| Dunn, Gary DT-NT-DE | 76Pit 77KJ 78-87Pit | | 6'3" | 258 | Miami (Fla.) | | |
| Dunn, K.D. TE | 85-86TB 87Was 88NYJ | 2 | 6'3" | 235 | Clemson | | |
| Dunsmore, Pat TE | 83-84Chi 85LJ | 2 | 6'3" | 237 | Drake | | 6 |
| Dupard, Reggie HB-TE | 86-89NE 89-90Was | 2 | 5'11" | 205 | S.M.U. | | 66 |
| Duper, Mark WR | 82-92Mia | 2 | 5'9" | 188 | Northwestern La. | | 354 |
| Dupree, Marcus HB | 90-91LA | 2 | 6'2" | 225 | Oklahoma, Southern Miss. | | 6 |
| Dupree, Myron DB | 83Den | | 5'11" | 180 | N. Car. Central | | |
| Durham, Darius WR | 83SF | | 6'2" | 185 | San Diego State | | |
| Durham, Steve DE | 82Bal | | 6'5" | 256 | Clemson | | |
| Durrette, Michael OG | 86-87SF | | 6'4" | 280 | West Virginia | | |
| Dusbabek, Mark LB | 89-91Min | | 6'3" | 230 | Minnesota | 1 | 2 |
| Dutton, John DE-DT | 74-78Bal 79-87Dal | | 6'7" | 266 | Nebraska | 1 | 10 |
| Dwyer, Mike DT | 87Dal | | 6'3" | 280 | Massachusetts | | |

| Use Name (Nickname) - Positions | Team by Year | See Section | Hgt. | Wgt. | College | Int | Pts |
|---|---|---|---|---|---|---|---|
| Dyal, Mike TE | 89-90Raid 91LJ 92-93KC 93SD | 2 | 6'2" | 240 | Texas A&I | | 12 |
| Dye, Ernest OT-OG | 93Phx 94-95Arz | | 6'6" | 325 | South Carolina | | |
| Dykes, Donald DB | 79-81NYJ 82SD 84-85USFL | | 5'11" | 183 | Southeastern La. | 5 | |
| Dykes, Hart Lee WR | 89-90NE 91-92KJ | 2 | 6'4" | 218 | Oklahoma State | | 42 |
| Dykes, Sean DB | 87NYJ | | 5'10" | 170 | Bowling Green | | |
| Dyson, Matt DT | 95Oak | | 6'3" | 275 | Michigan | | |
| Eaddy, James NT | 87Cin | | 6'2" | 280 | New York Tech | | |
| Earl, Robin FB-TE | 77-82Chi 84-85USFL | 2 | 6'5" | 242 | Washington | | 30 |
| Early, Quinn WR | 88-90SD 91-95NO | 2 | 6' | 188 | Iowa | | 180 |
| Easley, Kenny DB | 81-87Sea | 3 | 6'3" | 206 | U.C.L.A. | 32 | 18 |
| Easley, Walt FB | 81-82SF 83-84USFL | 2 | 6'1" | 226 | West Virginia | | 6 |
| Easmon, Ricky DB | 85Dal 85-86TB 87KJ | | 5'10" | 160 | Florida | 1 | |
| Eason, Bo DB | 84-87Hou | | 6'2" | 200 | Cal.-Davis | 6 | |
| Eason, Tony QB | 83-89NE 89-90NYJ | 12 | 6'4" | 212 | Illinois | | 36 |
| Eatman, Irv OT | 83-85USFL 86-90KC 91-92NYJ 93LA 94Atl 95Hou | | 6'7" | 296 | U.C.L.A. | | |
| Eaton, Tracey DB | 89Hou 90Phx 91Atl 92KJ 93Atl | | 6'1" | 195 | Portland State | 4 | |
| Eccles, Scott TE | 87Hou | | 6'5" | 245 | Eastern New Mexico | | |
| Echols, Donnie TE | 87Cle | | 6'3" | 240 | Oklahoma State | | |
| Echols, Terry LB | 84Pit | | 6' | 220 | Marshall | | |
| Eckwood, Jerry HB-FB | 79-81TB | 2 | 6' | 198 | Arkansas | | 42 |
| Eddings, Floyd WR | 82-83NYG | 2 | 5'11" | 177 | California | | |
| Edelman, Brad OG | 82-89NO | | 6'6" | 265 | Missouri | | |
| Edmonds, Bobby Joe HB | 86-88Sea 89Raid 95TB | 3 | 5'11" | 186 | Arkansas | | 6 |
| Edmunds, Ferrell TE | 88-92Mia 93-94Sea | 2 | 6'6" | 252 | Maryland | | 72 |
| Edwards, Al WR | 90-92Buf 93SJ | 23 | 5'8" | 168 | Northwestern La. | | 12 |
| Edwards, Anthony WR | 89-90Phi 91-93Phx 94KJ 95Arz | 23 | 5'11" | 195 | N. Mex. Highlands | | 24 |
| Edwards, Antonio DE | 93-95Sea | | 6'3" | 270 | Valdosta State | | 8 |
| Edwards, Brad DB | 88-89Min 90-93Was 94-95Atl | | 6'1" | 205 | South Carolina | 16 | 12 |
| Edwards, Dave DB | 85-87Pit | | 6' | 196 | Illinois | 1 | 2 |
| Edwards, Dennis DE | 87LA | | 6'4" | 253 | Southern Calif. | | |
| Edwards, Dixon LB | 91-95Dal | | 6'1" | 224 | Michigan State | 1 | 6 |
| Edwards, Eddie DT-DE | 77-88Cin | | 6'5" | 256 | Miami (Fla.) | 1 | 6 |
| Edwards, Herman DB | 77-85Phi 86Atl | | 6' | 192 | California, San Diego State | 30 | 6 |
| Edwards, Kelvin WR | 86NO 87-88Dal | 2 | 6'2" | 202 | Liberty | | 24 |
| Edwards, Randy DE-NT | 84-87Sea | | 6'4" | 264 | Alabama | | |
| Edwards, Stan FB-HB | 82-86Hou 87Det | 2 | 6' | 210 | Michigan | | 18 |
| Edwards, Tim DE | 92NE | | 6'1" | 270 | Delta State | | |
| Egloff, Ron TE | 77-83Den 84SD | 2 | 6'5" | 230 | Wisconsin | | 24 |
| Egu, Patrick HB | 89NE 90AJ 91KJ | | 5'11" | 205 | Nevada-Reno | | 6 |
| Ehin, Chuck DE-NT-LB | 83-87SD | | 6'4" | 261 | Brigham Young | | |
| Eilers, Pat DB | 90-91Min 92-94Was 95Chi | | 5'11" | 195 | Notre Dame | | |
| Eisenhooth, Stan C-OT | 87-88Sea | | 6'5" | 287 | Towson State | | |
| Ekern , Andy OT | 84Ind | | 6'6" | 265 | Missouri | | |
| Ekern, Carl LB | 76-78LA 79KJ 80-88LA | | 6'3" | 223 | San Jose State | 6 | |
| Elam, Jason K | 93-95Den | 5 | 5'11" | 192 | Hawaii | | 370 |
| Elam, Onzy LB | 87-88NYJ 89Dal | | 6'2" | 225 | Tennessee State | | |
| Elder, Donnie DB | 85NYJ 86Pit 86Det 88-89TB 90-91SD | 3 | 5'9" | 175 | Memphis State | 6 | |
| Elewonibi, Mohammed OT | 92-93Was 95Phi | | 6'4" | 299 | Brigham Young | | |
| Eley, Clifton TE | 87Min | | 6'5" | 230 | Mississippi State | | |
| Elias, Homer OG-OT | 78-84Det | | 6'3" | 255 | Tennessee State | | |
| Elias, Keith HB | 94-95NYG | | 5'9" | 196 | Princeton | | |
| Eliopulos, Jim LB | 83StL 83-85NYJ | | 6'2" | 229 | Westminster (Mo.), Wyoming | | |
| Elkins, Mike QB | 89-90KC 92Hou | | 6'3" | 225 | Wake Forest | | |
| Elko, Bill OG-NT | 83-84SD 87Ind | | 6'5" | 279 | Arizona State, Louisiana State | | |
| Ellard, Henry WR | 83-93LA 94-95Was | 23 | 5'11" | 174 | Fresno State | | 378 |
| Ellerson, Gary FB-HB | 85-86GB 87Det | 2 | 5'11" | 219 | Wisconsin | | 54 |
| Elliott, John (Jumbo) OT | 88-95NYG | | 6'7" | 305 | Michigan | | |
| Elliott, Lin K | 92-93Dal 93Atl 94-95KC | 5 | 6' | 182 | Texas Tech | | 338 |
| Elliott, Matt C-OG | 92Was 93KJ 95Car | | 6'1" | 285 | Michigan | | |
| Elliott, Ted NT | 87NO | | 6'6" | 275 | Mankato State | | |
| Elliott, Tony DB | 87GB | | 5'10" | 195 | Central Michigan | | |
| Elliott, Tony NT | 82-88NO | | 6'2" | 282 | Wisconsin, North Texas | | |
| Ellis, Craig HB | 86Mia 87Raid | 23 | 5'11" | 185 | San Diego State | | 12 |
| Ellis, Gerry FB | 80-86GB | 2 | 5'11" | 221 | Missouri | | 210 |
| Ellis, Jim LB | 87Raid | | 6'3" | 240 | Boise State | | |
| Ellis, Ray DB | 81-85Phi 86-87Cle | | 6'1" | 194 | Ohio State | 14 | 6 |
| Ellison, Jerry HB-FB | 95TB | 2 | 5'10" | 198 | Tenn.-Chattanooga | | 30 |
| Ellison, 'OMar WR | 95SD | | 6'1" | 200 | Florida State | | |
| Ellison, Riki LB | 83-88SF 89KJ 90-92Raid | | 6'2" | 225 | Southern Calif. | | |
| Elliss, Luther DE | 95Det | | 6'5" | 291 | Utah | | |
| El-Mastoub, Hicham C-OG | 95Hou | | 6'2" | 288 | Arizona | | |
| Elshire, Neil DE | 81-86Min | | 6'6" | 260 | Oregon | | 2 |
| Elway, John QB | 83-95Den | 12 | 6'3" | 210 | Stanford | | 170 |
| Emanuel, Bert WR | 94-95Atl | 2 | 5'10" | 175 | Rice | | 54 |
| Embree, Jon TE | 87-88LA | | 6'2" | 234 | Colorado | | |
| Emery, Larry HB | 87Atl | | 5'9" | 195 | Wisconsin | | |
| Emtman, Steve DE-DT | 92-94Ind 95Mia | | 6'4" | 290 | Washington | 1 | 6 |
| Engel, Greg C | 95SD | | 6'3" | 285 | Illinois | | |
| England, Eric DE | 94-95Arz | | 6'2" | 283 | Texas A&M | | |
| English, Doug DT-NT | 75-79Det 80VR 81-85Det | | 6'5" | 255 | Texas | | 8 |
| English, Keith K | 90LA | | 6'3" | 220 | Colorado | | |
| Epps, Jack DB | 87KC | | 6' | 197 | Kansas State | | |
| Epps, Phillip WR | 82-88GB 89NYJ | 23 | 5'10" | 165 | Texas Christian | | 84 |
| Epps, Tory NT-DT | 90-93Atl 93-94Chi 95NO | | 6' | 278 | Memphis State | | |
| Erenberg, Rich HB | 84-86Pit 87KJ | 23 | 5'10" | 200 | Colgate | | 60 |
| Erhardt, Ron | HC78-81NE | | | | Jamestown | | |
| Erickson, Craig QB | 92-94TB 95Ind | 12 | 6'2" | 200 | Miami (Fla.) | | 6 |
| Erickson, Dennis | HC95Sea | | | | Montana State | | |
| Erlandson, Tom LB | 88Buf | | 6'1" | 220 | Washington | | |
| Ervins, Ricky HB | 91-94Was 95SF | 2 | 5'7" | 200 | Southern Calif. | | 60 |
| Erxleben, Russell K | 79-83NO 87Det | 4 | 6'4" | 223 | Texas | | 19 |
| Esiason, Boomer QB | 84-92Cin 93-95NYJ | 12 | 6'4" | 222 | Maryland | | 36 |
| Espinoza, Alex QB | 87KC | | 6'1" | 193 | Iowa State | | |
| Essink, Ron OT-TE | 80-85Sea 86BA | | 6'6" | 260 | Grand Valley St. | | 6 |
| Estell, Richard WR | 87KC | | 6'2" | 210 | Kansas | | |
| Estep, Mike OG-OT | 87Buf 87GB | | 6'4" | 270 | Bowling Green | | |
| Etheredge, Carlos TE | 94Ind | | 6'5" | 236 | Miami (Fla.) | | |
| Etienne, Larry LB | 90SF | | 6'2" | 245 | Nebraska | | |
| Etherly, David DB | 87Was | | 6'1" | 190 | Portland State | | |
| Evans, Byron LB | 87-94Phi | | 6'2" | 233 | Arizona | 13 | 12 |
| Evans, Chuck LB | 80-81NO | 2 | 6'3" | 233 | Stanford | | 12 |
| Evans, Chuck HB-FB | 93-95Min | | 6'1" | 229 | Clark-Atlanta | | |
| Evans, David DB | 83-85USFL 86-87Min | | 6' | 178 | Central Arkansas | | |
| Evans, Donald DE-DT-FB | 87LA 88Phi 90-93Pit 94-95NYJ | | 6'2" | 275 | Winston-Salem St. | | |

| Use Name (Nickname) - Positions | Team by Year | See Section | Hgt. | Wgt. | College | Int | Pts |
|---|---|---|---|---|---|---|---|
| Evans, Doug DB | 93-95GB | | 6'1" | 188 | Louisiana Tech | 3 | |
| Evans, Greg DB | 95Buf | | 6'1" | 208 | Texas Christian | 1 | |
| Evans, James FB | 87KC | | 6' | 220 | Southern U. | | |
| Evans, Jerry TE | 93-95Den | 2 | 6'4" | 250 | Toledo | | 18 |
| Evans, John TE | 87Atl | | 6'2" | 243 | S.F. Austin State | | |
| Evans, Josh DT-DE | 95Hou | | 6' | 280 | Ala.-Birmingham | | |
| Evans, Leon DE | 85-86Phi 87KJ | | 6'5" | 282 | Miami (Fla.) | | |
| Evans, Mike DT-DE | 92KC | | 6'3" | 269 | Michigan | | |
| Evans, Reggie HB | 83Was 85USFL | | 5'11" | 201 | Richmond | | 24 |
| Evans, Scott DE | 91Phx | | 6'3" | 261 | Oklahoma | | |
| Evans, Russell WR | 87Sea | | 5'8" | 165 | NE Missouri State | | |
| Evans, Vince QB | 77-83Chi 84-85USFL 87-94Raid 95Oak | 12 | 6'2" | 211 | Southern Calif. | | 84 |
| Everett, Eric DB | 88-89Phi 90TB 91-92KC | | 5'10" | 163 | Texas Tech | 8 | 6 |
| Everett, Jim QB | 86-93LA 94-95NO | 12 | 6'5" | 212 | Purdue | | 24 |
| Everett, Major FB-HB | 83-85Phi 86-87Cle 87Atl | 2 | 5'10" | 215 | Mississippi | | |
| Everett, Thomas DB | 87-91Pit 92-93Dal 94-95TB | | 5'9" | 183 | Baylor | 21 | |
| Everitt, Steve C-OG | 93-95Cle | | 6'5" | 292 | Michigan | | |
| Evers, William DB | 90-91Atl | | 5'10" | 175 | Florida A&M | | |
| Eyre, Nick OT | 81Hou 83USFL | | 6'5" | 274 | Brigham Young | | |
| Ezor, Blake HB | 90Den | | 5'9" | 183 | Michigan State | | |
| Faaola, Nuu HB-FB | 86-89NYJ 89Mia | | 5'11" | 216 | Hawaii | | 12 |
| Fada, Rob OG | 83-84Chi 85KC | | 6'2" | 265 | Pittsburgh | | |
| Fagan, Kevin DE | 87-93SF | | 6'4" | 260 | Miami (Fla.) | | |
| Fahnhorst, Jim LB | 83-84USFL 84-90SF | | 6'4" | 230 | Minnesota | 3 | |
| Fahnhorst, Keith OT | 74-87SF | | 6'6" | 266 | Minnesota | | |
| Fain, Richard DB | 91Cin 91Phx 92Chi | | 5'10" | 183 | Florida | 1 | |
| Fairbanks, Don DE | 87Sea | | 6'3" | 253 | Colorado | | |
| Fairchild, Paul OG-C | 84-90NE | | 6'4" | 270 | Kansas | | |
| Fairs, Eric LB | 86-91Hou 92Atl | | 6'3" | 240 | Memphis State | | 2 |
| Faison, Derrick WR | 90LA | | 6'4" | 200 | Howard | | 6 |
| Fann, Chad TE | 93Phx 94-95Arz | 2 | 6'3" | 250 | Mississippi, Florida A&M | | |
| Fantetti, Ken LB | 79-85Det | | 6'2" | 230 | Wyoming | 6 | |
| Farley, John HB | 84Cin | | 5'10" | 202 | Sacramento State | | |
| Farmer, George WR | 82-84LA 87Mia | 2 | 5'10" | 175 | Southern U. | | 42 |
| Farr, D'Marco DT | 94LA 95StL | | 6'1" | 270 | Washington | 1 | |
| Farr, Mel Jr. FB | 89LA | | 6' | 223 | U.C.L.A. | | |
| Farr, Mike WR | 90-92Det | 2 | 5'10" | 192 | U.C.L.A. | | 6 |
| Farrell, Sean OG | 82-86TB 87-89NE 90-91Den 92Sea | | 6'3" | 260 | Penn State | | |
| Farren, Paul OT-OG | 83-91Cle 92XJ | | 6'5" | 272 | Boston U. | | |
| Faryniarz, Brett LB | 88-91LA 93SF 94Hou 95Car | | 6'3" | 225 | San Diego State | | |
| Faucette, Chuck LB | 88SD | | 6'3" | 242 | Maryland | 1 | |
| Faulk, Marshall HB | 94-95Ind | 2 | 5'10" | 200 | San Diego State | | 156 |
| Faulkerson, Mike FB | 95Chi | | 6' | 237 | North Carolina | | |
| Faulkner, Chris OG-TE | 84LA 85SD | | 6'4" | 255 | Florida | | |
| Faulkner, Jeff NT-DE | 87KC 90Ind 91-92Phx 93NO 93Was | | 6'3" | 295 | Southern U. | | |
| Faumui, Taase DE | 94-95Pit | | 6'3" | 278 | Hawaii | | |
| Fauria, Christian TE | 95Sea | 2 | 6'4" | 245 | Colorado | | 6 |
| Faurot, Ron DT-DE | 84-85NYJ | | 6'7" | 262 | Arkansas | | |
| Favre, Brett QB | 91Atl 92-95GB | 12 | 6'2" | 220 | Southern Miss. | | 42 |
| Favron, Calvin LB | 79-82StL 83BL | | 6'1" | 225 | Southeastern La. | 1 | |
| Faylor, John DB | 87SF | | 6'1" | 197 | Santa Clara | | |
| Fazio, Ron TE | 87Phi | | 6'4" | 242 | Maryland | | |
| Feacher, Ricky WR | 76NE 76-84Cle | 23 | 5'10" | 175 | Miss. Valley St. | | 90 |
| Feagles, Jeff K | 88-89NE 90-93Phi 94-95Arz | 4 | 6' | 198 | Miami (Fla.) | | |
| Fears, Willie DE | 87Cin 88-89CFL 90Min | | 6'3" | 278 | Northeast La. | | |
| Feasel, Grant C | 83Bal 84Ind 84Min 85KJ 87-92Sea 93KJ | | 6'7" | 278 | Abilene Christian | | |
| Feasel, Greg OT | 83-85USFL 86GB 87SD | | 6'7" | 301 | Abilene Christian | | |
| Federico, Craig DB | 87Det | | 6'2" | 205 | Illinois State | | |
| Feehery, Gerry C-OG | 83-87Phi 88KC | | 6'2" | 269 | Syracuse | | |
| Feggins, Howard DB | 89NE | | 5'10" | 190 | North Carolina | 1 | |
| Feldman, Todd WR | 87Mia | | 5'10" | 184 | Kent State | | |
| Fellows, Mark LB | 86SD | | 6'2" | 233 | Montana State | | |
| Fellows, Ron DB | 81-86Dal 87-88Raid | 3 | 6' | 175 | Missouri | 19 | 18 |
| Felton, Joe OG | 87Det | | 6'2" | 266 | Albion | | |
| Fencik, Gary DB | 76-87Chi | | 6'1" | 194 | Yale | 38 | 6 |
| Fenerty, Gill HB | 90-91NO | 23 | 6' | 205 | Holy Cross | | 42 |
| Fenner, Derrick HB | 89-91Sea 92-94Cin 95Oak | 2 | 6'3" | 232 | North Carolina | | 204 |
| Fenney, Rick FB | 87-91Min | 2 | 6'1" | 235 | Washington | | 78 |
| Ferguson, Joe QB | 73-84Buf 85-87Det 88-89TB 90Ind | 12 | 6'1" | 192 | Arkansas | | 66 |
| Ferguson, Keith DE | 81-85SD 85-90Det | | 6'5" | 252 | Ohio State | 1 | |
| Ferguson, Kevin TE | 87SD | | 6'2" | 223 | Virginia | | |
| Ferguson, Vagas HB-FB | 80-82NE 83Cle 83Hou 84USFL | 2 | 6'1" | 204 | Notre Dame | | 30 |
| Fernandez, Mervyn WR | 82-86CFL 87-92Raid | 2 | 6'3" | 200 | San Jose State | | 114 |
| Ferragamo, Vince QB | 77-80LA 81CFL 82-84LA 85Buf 85-86GB | 12 | 6'3" | 212 | California, Nebraska | | 12 |
| Ferrari, Ron LB | 82-86SF | | 6' | 213 | Lakeland, Illinois | | |
| Ferrell, Earl FB | 82-87StL 88-89Phx | 2 | 6' | 225 | East Tennessee St. | | 156 |
| Fichtel, Brad C | 94LA | | 6'2" | 285 | Eastern Illinois | | |
| Fiedler, Don DE | 83-85USFL 85TB 86KJ | | 6'3" | 240 | Kentucky | | |
| Fiedler, Jay QB | 94-95Phi | | 6'1" | 215 | Dartmouth | | |
| Field, Amod WR | 91Phx | | 5'11" | 181 | Montclair State | | |
| Field, Doak LB | 81StL 83-85USFL | | 6'2" | 228 | Baylor | | |
| Fieldings, Anthony LB | 95Dal | | 6'1" | 237 | Morningside | | |
| Fields, Angelo OT | 80-81Hou 82GB | | 6'6" | 321 | Michigan State | | |
| Fields, Anthony DB | 87Det | | 6'1" | 192 | Eastern Michigan | | |
| Fields, Floyd DB | 91-93SD | | 6' | 208 | Arizona State | 1 | |
| Fields, Greg DE | 79-80Bal 83-85USFL | | 6'7" | 259 | Grambling | | |
| Fields, Jaime LB | 93-94KC 95LJ | | 5'11" | 233 | Washington | | |
| Fields, Jeff NT | 95Car | | 6'3" | 320 | Arkansas State | | |
| Fields, Jitter DB | 84NO 87Ind 87KC | | 5'8" | 184 | Texas | | 6 |
| Fields, Joe C-OG | 75-87NYJ 88NYG | | 6'2" | 250 | Rutgers-Camden, Widener | | |
| Fields, Mark LB | 95NO | | 6'2" | 244 | Washington State | | |
| Figaro, Cedric LB | 88-90SD 91Ind 91-92Cle 95StL | | 6'2" | 250 | Notre Dame | 2 | |
| Figures, Deon DB | 93-95Pit | | 6' | 198 | Colorado | 1 | |
| Fike, Dan OG-OT | 84-85USFL 85-92Cle 93Pit | | 6'7" | 282 | Florida | | |
| Fina, John OG-OT | 92-95Buf | | 6'4" | 284 | Arizona | | 6 |
| Finch, Steve WR | 87Min | | 6' | 200 | Elmhurst | | |
| Finzer, Dave K | 84Chi 85Sea | 4 | 6'1" | 195 | Illinois, DePauw | | |
| Fishback, Joe DB | 91Atl 92NYJ 92Atl 93-94Dal | | 5'11" | 198 | Carson-Newman | | 6 |
| Fisher, Bob TE | 80-81Chi 84USFL | 2 | 6'3" | 240 | S.M.U. | | 12 |
| Fisher, Jeff DB | 81-84Chi HC94-95Hou | 3 | 5'11" | 190 | Southern Calif. | 5 | 6 |
| Fisher, Mike WR | 81StL 83-84USFL | | 5'11" | 172 | Baylor | | |
| Fisk, Jason DT | 95Min | | 6'3" | 284 | Stanford | | |
| Fitzgerald, Greg DT | 87Chi | | 6'4" | 265 | Iowa | | |
| Fitzgerald, Jamie DB | 87Min | | 6' | 180 | Idaho State | | |
| Fitzgerald, Kevin TE | 87GB | | 6'3" | 235 | Wis.-Eau Claire | | |

| Use Name (Nickname) - Positions | Team by Year | See Section | Hgt. | Wgt. | College | Int | Pts |
|---|---|---|---|---|---|---|---|
| Fitzgerald, Mickey FB | 81Atl 81Phi 84USFL | | 6'2" | 235 | Virginia Tech | | |
| Fitzhugh, Steve DB | 87Den | | 5'11" | 188 | Miami-Ohio | | |
| Fitzkee, Scott WR | 79-80Phi 81-82SD 83-85USFL | 2 | 6' | 187 | Penn State | | 24 |
| FitzPatrick, James OT-OG | 86-89SD 90-91Raid 92KJ | | 6'8" | 305 | Southern Calif. | | |
| Flagler, Terrence HB | 87-89SF 90-91Phx | 23 | 6' | 200 | Clemson | | 18 |
| Flaherty, Harry LB | 87Dal | | 6'1" | 232 | Holy Cross | | |
| Flaherty, Tom LB | 87Cin | | 6'3" | 223 | Northwestern | | |
| Flanigan, Jim DT-FB | 94-95Chi | | 6'2" | 280 | Notre Dame | | 12 |
| Flannery, John OG-C | 91-93Hou | | 6'3" | 304 | Syracuse | | |
| Fleming, Cory WR | 94-95Dal | | 6'1" | 216 | Tennessee | | |
| Fletcher, John OG | 87Cin | | 6'3" | 293 | Texas A&I | | |
| Fletcher, Simon DE-LB | 85-95Den | | 6'5" | 240 | Houston | 2 | 2 |
| Fletcher, Terrell HB | 95SD | 2 | 5'8" | 196 | Wisconsin | | 6 |
| Flick, Tom QB | 81Was 82NE 84Cle 86SD 87NYJ | 1 | 6'3" | 190 | Washington | | 6 |
| Flint, Judson DB | 80-82Cle 83Buf | | 6' | 201 | California (Pa.), | 3 | |
| Flones, Brian LB | 81-82Sea 83KJ | | 6'1" | 228 | Washington State | | |
| Florence, Anthony DB | 91Cle | | 6' | 185 | Bethune-Cookman | | |
| Flores, Mike DE | 91-94Phi 95Was | | 6'3" | 256 | Louisville | | 2 |
| Flowers, Kenny HB | 87Atl 88KJ 89Atl | 2 | 6' | 210 | Clemson | | 6 |
| Flowers, Larry DB | 81-85NYG 85NYJ | | 6'1" | 192 | Texas Tech | 2 | |
| Flowers, Lethon DB | 95Pit | | 6' | 207 | Georgia Tech | | |
| Floyd, Eric OT-OG | 90-91SD 92-93Phi 95Arz | | 6'5" | 305 | Auburn | | |
| Floyd, George DB | 82NYJ 83KJ 84NYJ | | 5'11" | 190 | Eastern Kentucky | | |
| Floyd, John WR | 79-80SD 81StL | 2 | 6'1" | 195 | Northeast La. | | 12 |
| Floyd, Victor HB | 89SD | | 6'1" | 201 | Florida State | | |
| Floyd, William FB | 94-95SF | 2 | 6'1" | 242 | Florida State | | 54 |
| Flutie, Darren WR | 88SD 90FJ | 2 | 5'10" | 184 | Boston College | | 12 |
| Flutie, Doug QB | 85USFL 86-87Chi 87-89NE | 12 | 5'9" | 176 | Boston College | | 12 |
| Flynn, Tom DB | 84-86GB 86-88NYG | | 6' | 195 | Pittsburgh | 10 | 18 |
| Flythce, Mark DE | 93NYG | | 6'7" | 290 | Penn State | | |
| Foggie, Fred DB | 92Cle 94Pit | | 6' | 200 | Minnesota | | |
| Foley, Glenn QB | 94-95NYJ | 1 | 6'2" | 205 | Boston College | | |
| Foley, Steve DB | 76-86Den | | 6'2" | 189 | Tulane | 44 | 12 |
| Foley, Tim OT | 81Bal 82LJ | | 6'6" | 275 | Notre Dame | | |
| Folmar, Brendon QB | 87Det | | 6'1" | 200 | California (Pa.) | | |
| Folsom, Steve TE | 81Phi 82NYG 83-85USFL 87-90Dal | 2 | 6'5" | 235 | Long Beach State, Utah | | 24 |
| Folston, James LB | 94Raid 95Oak | | 6'3" | 235 | Northeast La. | | |
| Fontenot, Albert DE | 93-95Chi | | 6'4" | 271 | Baylor | | 2 |
| Fontenot, Herman HB-FB | 85-88Cle 89-90GB | 23 | 6' | 206 | Louisiana State | | 54 |
| Fontenot, Jerry C-OG | 89-95Chi | | 6'3" | 285 | Texas A&M | | |
| Foote, Chris C-OG | 80-81Bal 82-83NYG 84-85USFL 87-91Min | | 6'3" | 253 | Southern Calif. | | |
| Footman, Dan DE-DT | 93-95Cle | | 6'5" | 288 | Florida State | | |
| Ford, Bernard WR | 89Dal 90Hou | 2 | 5'9" | 168 | Central Florida | | 12 |
| Ford, Chris WR | 90TB | | 6'1" | 185 | Lamar | | |
| Ford, Cole K | 95Oak | 5 | 6'2" | 205 | Southern Calif. | | 41 |
| Ford, Darryl LB | 92Pit 92-93Det 94Atl | | 6'1" | 227 | New Mexico State | | |
| Ford, Henry DE | 94-95Hou | | 6'3" | 284 | Arkansas | | |
| Ford, John WR | 89Det | | 6'2" | 204 | Virginia | | |
| Ford, Mike QB | 81TB 84USFL | | 6'3" | 220 | S.M.U. | | |
| Ford, Moses WR | 87Pit | | 6'2" | 220 | Fayetteville St. | | |
| Forde, Brian LB | 88-91NO | | 6'2" | 230 | Washington State | | 2 |
| Forney, Phil LB | 87StL | | 6'2" | 230 | East Tennessee St. | | |
| Fortin, Roman OT-OG-C | 91Det 92-95Atl | | 6'5" | 292 | Oregon, San Diego State | | |
| Fortune, Hosea WR | 83SD | | 6' | 176 | Rice | | |
| Foster, Barry HB | 90-94Pit | 2 | 5'10" | 223 | Arkansas | | 168 |
| Foster, Derrick HB | 87NYJ | | 5'11" | 205 | Will. Patterson | | |
| Foster, Jerome DE-DT | 83-84Hou 86Mia 86-87NYJ | | 6'2" | 266 | Ohio State | | |
| Foster, Ron DB | 87Raid | | 6' | 200 | Northridge State | | |
| Foster, Roy OG-OT | 82-90Mia 91-93SF | | 6'4" | 282 | Southern Calif. | | |
| Foules, Elbert DB | 83-87Phi | | 5'11" | 185 | Alcorn State | 10 | |
| Fountaine, Jamal DE | 95SF | | 6'3" | 240 | Washington | | |
| Fourcade, John QB | 87-90NO | 12 | 6'1" | 208 | Mississippi | | 12 |
| Fourcade, Keith LB | 87NO | | 5'11" | 225 | Mississippi | | |
| Fouts, Dan QB | 73-87SD | 12 | 6'3" | 204 | Oregon | | 78 |
| Fowler, Amos C-OG | 78-84Det | | 6'3" | 251 | Southern Miss. | | |
| Fowler, Bobby FB | 85NO 86KJ | | 6'2" | 230 | Texas-El Paso, Louisiana Tech | | |
| Fowler, Todd FB | 83-84USFL 85-88Dal | 2 | 6'3" | 222 | S.F. Austin State | | |
| Fowlkes, Dennis LB | 84-85Min 87Mia | | 6'2" | 238 | West Virginia | | |
| Fox, Chas WR | 86StL 87JJ | | 5'11" | 180 | Furman | | 6 |
| Fox, Mike DE-DT | 90-94NYG 95Car | | 6'6" | 288 | West Virginia | | |
| Fox, Scott LB | 87Hou | | 6'2" | 222 | Austin Peay | | |
| Fox, Tim DB | 76-81NE 82-84SD 85-86LA | | 5'11" | 188 | Ohio State | 26 | |
| Foxx, Dion LB | 94-95Mia 95Was | | 6'3" | 254 | James Madison | | |
| Frain, Todd TE | 87NE | | 6'3" | 240 | Nebraska | | |
| Fralic, Bill OG-OT | 85-92Atl 93Det | | 6'5" | 280 | Pittsburgh | | |
| Francis, James LB | 90-95Cin | | 6'5" | 252 | Baylor | 7 | 14 |
| Francis, Jeff QB | 90Cle 91SJ 92Cle | | 6'4" | 225 | Tennessee | | |
| Francis, Jon HB | 87LA | 2 | 5'11" | 207 | Colorado State, Boise State | | 12 |
| Francis, Phil FB-HB | 79-80SF 81KJ | 2 | 6'1" | 205 | Stanford | | 6 |
| Francis, Ron DB | 87-90Dal | | 5'9" | 200 | Baylor | 4 | 6 |
| Francis, Russ TE | 75-80NE 81VR 82-87SF 87-88NE 89KJ | 2 | 6'6" | 242 | Oregon | | 240 |
| Franco, Brian K | 87Cle | | 5'8" | 165 | Penn State | | 11 |
| Frank, Donald DB | 90-93SD 94Raid 95Min | | 6' | 197 | Winston-Salem St. | 14 | 12 |
| Frank, John TE | 84-88SF | 2 | 6'3" | 225 | Ohio State | | 60 |
| Frank, Malcolm DB | 92Sea | | 5'8" | 182 | Baylor | | |
| Franklin, Andra FB | 81-84Mia | 2 | 5'10" | 225 | Nebraska | | 138 |
| Franklin, Arnold TE | 87NE | | 6'3" | 246 | North Carolina | | |
| Franklin, Byron WR | 81Buf 82XJ 83-84Buf 85-87Sea | 2 | 6'1" | 181 | Auburn | | 60 |
| Franklin, Jerrell OT | 87Hou | | 6'3" | 287 | Southern U. | | |
| Franklin, Jethro DE | 89Sea | | 6'1" | 258 | Fresno State | | |
| Franklin, Keith LB | 95Oak | | 6'2" | 230 | South Carolina | | |
| Franklin, Pat FB | 86TB 87Cin | | 6'1" | 230 | Houston, SW Texas State | | 12 |
| Franklin, Tony K | 79-83Phi 84-87NE 88Mia | 5 | 5'8" | 182 | Texas A&M | | 872 |
| Franks, Elvis DE | 80-84Cle 85-86Raid 86NYJ | | 6'4" | 252 | Morgan State | | |
| Franz, Nolan WR | 86GB | | 6'2" | 183 | Tulane | | |
| Franz, Tracy OG | 87SF | | 6'5" | 270 | San Jose State | | |
| Frase, Paul DE-NT-DT | 88-89NYJ 90IL 91-94NYJ 95Jax | | 6'5" | 272 | Syracuse | | |
| Frazier, Derrick DB | 94-95Phi | | 5'10" | 175 | Texas A&M | 1 | |
| Frazier, Frank OG | 87Was | | 6'5" | 290 | Miami (Fla.) | | |
| Frazier, Guy LB | 81-84Cin 85-86Buf | | 6'2" | 217 | Wyoming | 1 | |
| Frazier, Leslie DB | 81-85Chi 86KJ | | 6' | 189 | Alcorn State | 20 | 12 |
| Frazier, Paul HB | 89NO | 2 | 5'8" | 188 | Southwestern La. | | 6 |
| Frazier, Randy LB | 87KC | | 6'3" | 235 | Morehead State | | |
| Frederick, Andy OT | 77-81Dal 82Cle 83-85Chi 86FJ | | 6'6" | 257 | New Mexico | | |

| Use Name (Nickname) - Positions | Team by Year | See Section | Hgt. | Wgt. | College | Int | Pts |
|---|---|---|---|---|---|---|---|
| Frederick, Mike DE | 95Cle | | 6'5" | 280 | Virginia | | |
| Fredrickson, Rob LB | 94Raid 95Oak | | 6'4" | 240 | Michigan State | 1 | 6 |
| Freeman, Antonio WR | 95GB | 3 | 6'1" | 187 | Virginia Tech | | 6 |
| Freeman, Lorenzo NT-DT | 87-90Pit 91NYG 92KJ | | 6'5" | 298 | Pittsburgh | | |
| Freeman, Mike OG-C | 84Den 85KJ 86-87Den 88Raid | | 6'3" | 256 | Arizona | | |
| Freeman, Phil WR | 85-87TB | 23 | 5'11" | 185 | Arizona | | 24 |
| Freeman, Reggie LB | 93NO | | 6'1" | 233 | Florida State | | |
| Freeman, Russell OT | 92-94Den 95Oak | | 6'7" | 292 | Georgia Tech | | |
| Freeman, Steve DB | 75-86Buf 87Min | | 5'11" | 185 | Mississippi State | 23 | 18 |
| French, Ernest DB | 82Pit 83KJ | | 5'11" | 195 | Alabama A&M | | |
| Frerotte, Gus QB | 94-95Was | 12 | 6'2" | 221 | Tulsa | | 6 |
| Frerotte, Mitch OG | 87Buf 89XJ 90-92Buf 93-94ZJ | | 6'3" | 281 | Penn State | | 12 |
| Friday, Larry DB | 87Buf | | 6'4" | 215 | Mississippi State | | |
| Friede, Mike WR | 80Det 80-81NYG 83USFL | 2 | 6'3" | 203 | Indiana | | 6 |
| Frier, Mike DE | 92-94Cin 94Sea | | 6'5" | 299 | Appalachian State | | |
| December 1, 1994 — Paralyzed in auto accident | | | | | | | |
| Friesz, John QB | 90-91SD 92KJ 93SD 94Was 95Sea | 12 | 6'4" | 209 | Idaho | | |
| Frisch, David TE | 93-94Cin 95NE | | 6'7" | 260 | Colorado State | | |
| Fritzche, Jim OT-OG | 83Phi | | 6'8" | 265 | Purdue | | |
| Frizzell, William DB | 84-85Det 86-93Phi | | 6'3" | 203 | N. Car. Central | 11 | 6 |
| Fryar, Irving WR | 84-92NE 93-95Mia | 23 | 6' | 200 | Nebraska | | 376 |
| Frye, David LB | 83-85Atl 86-89Mia | | 6'2" | 223 | Purdue | 1 | |
| Frye, Phil HB | 87Min | | 5'11" | 180 | Cal. Lutheran | | |
| Fulcher, David DB | 86-92Cin 93Raid | | 6'3" | 236 | Arizona State | 31 | 14 |
| Fulhage, Scott K | 87-88Cin 89-92Atl | 4 | 5'11" | 191 | Kansas State | | |
| Fuller, Corey DB | 95Min | | 5'10" | 198 | Florida State | 1 | 6 |
| Fuller, Eddie FB | 91-93Buf | | 5'9" | 201 | Louisiana Tech | | |
| Fuller, James DB | 93SD | | 6' | 208 | Portland State | | |
| Fuller, Jeff DB-LB | 84-89SF | | 6'2" | 216 | Texas A&M | 10 | 2 |
| Fuller, Joe DB | 90SD 91GB | | 5'11" | 180 | Northern Iowa | 1 | |
| Fuller, Randy DB | 94Den 95Pit | | 5'9" | 174 | Tennessee State | | |
| Fuller, Steve QB | 79-82KC 83LA 84-86Chi 87SJ 88SD | 12 | 6'4" | 197 | Clemson | | 66 |
| Fuller, William DE | 84-85USFL 86-93Hou 94-95Phi | | 6'3" | 267 | North Carolina | 1 | 8 |
| Fullington, Darrell DB | 88-90Min 91NE 91-92TB | | 6'1" | 197 | Miami (Fla.) | 10 | |
| Fullwood, Brent FB-HB | 87-90GB 90Cle | 23 | 5'11" | 209 | Auburn | | 114 |
| Fulton, Dan WR | 79Buf 81-82Cle 84USFL | | 6'2" | 184 | Nebraska, Nebraska-Omaha | | |
| Furjanic, Tony LB | 86-87Buf | | 6'1" | 228 | Notre Dame | | |
| Furrer, Will QB | 92Chi 93Phx 94Den 95Hou | 1 | 6'3" | 208 | Virginia Tech | | |
| Fusina, Chuck QB | 79-81TB 83-85USFL 86GB | 1 | 6'1" | 197 | Penn State | | |
| Futrell, Bobby DB | 84-85USFL 86-90TB | 3 | 5'11" | 190 | Elizabeth City St. | 4 | |
| Gabbard, Steve OT | 91GB | | 6'4" | 297 | Florida State | | |
| Gadbois, Dennis WR | 87-88NE | | 6'1" | 183 | Boston U. | | |
| Gaffney, Derrick WR | 78-84,87NYJ | 2 | 6'1" | 181 | Florida | | 42 |
| Gaffney, Jeff K | 87SD | | 6'2" | 195 | Virginia | | 13 |
| Gage, Steve DB | 87-88Was | | 6'3" | 210 | Tulsa | 1 | |
| Gagliano, Bob QB | 82-83KC 84-85USFL 86-87SF 88Ind 89-90Det 91-92SD 93Atl | 12 | 6'3" | 195 | U.S. International, Utah State | | |
| Gainer, Derrick FB | 90Cle 92Raid 92Det 93Dal | 2 | 5'11" | 235 | Texas A&M | | 6 |
| Gaines, Chris LB | 88Mia | | 6' | 238 | Vanderbilt | | |
| Gaines, Greg LB | 81Sea 82KJ 83-88Sea | | 6'3" | 220 | Tennessee | 2 | |
| Gaines, Sheldon WR | 87Buf | | 5'9" | 155 | Long Beach State | | |
| Gaines, Wendall TE | 95Arz | 2 | 6'4" | 293 | Oklahoma State | | 12 |
| Gaines, William DT | 94Mia 95Was | | 6'5" | 300 | Florida | | |
| Gaison, Blane DB | 81-84Atl | | 6' | 185 | Hawaii | 2 | 6 |
| Gajan, Hokie FB | 82-85NO 86-87KJ | 2 | 5'11" | 220 | Louisiana State | | 78 |
| Galbraith, Scott TE | 90-92Cle 93-94Dal 95Was | 2 | 6'3" | 260 | Southern Calif. | | 24 |
| Galbreath, Harry OG | 88-92Mia 93-95GB | | 6'1" | 279 | Tennessee | | |
| Galbreath, Tony FB-HB | 76-80NO 81-83Min 84-87NYG | 23 | 6' | 228 | Missouri | | 265 |
| Gallery, Jim K | 87StL 89Cin 90Min | 5 | 6'1" | 190 | Minnesota | | 76 |
| Galloway, David DT-DE | 82-87StL 88-89Phx 90Den | | 6'3" | 279 | Florida | 1 | 2 |
| Galloway, Duane DB | 85-87Det | | 5'8" | 181 | Arizona State | 7 | |
| Galloway, Joey WR | 95Sea | 23 | 5'11" | 188 | Ohio State | | 54 |
| Galvin, John LB | 88NYJ 89Min 90-91NYJ | | 6'3" | 226 | Boston College | | |
| Gamache, Vince K | 86Sea 87Raid | 4 | 5'11" | 170 | Fullerton State | | |
| Gamble, Kenny HB-DB | 88-90KC | | 5'10" | 197 | Colgate | 1 | 6 |
| Gambol, Chris OT-OG | 88Ind 88SD 89Det 90NE | | 6'6" | 303 | Iowa | | |
| Gammon, Kendall C | 92-95Pit | | 6'4" | 285 | Pittsburg State | | |
| Gandy, Wayne OT | 94LA 95StL | | 6'4" | 291 | Auburn | | |
| Gann, Mike DE | 85-93Atl | | 6'5" | 271 | Notre Dame | 1 | 14 |
| Gannon, Chris DE-TE | 89SD 90-93NE | | 6'6" | 263 | Southwestern La. | | |
| Gannon, Rich QB | 87-92Min 93Was 95KC | 12 | 6'3" | 198 | Delaware | | 30 |
| Gansz, Frank | HC87-88KC | | | | Navy | | |
| Gant, Brian LB | 87TB | | 6' | 235 | Illinois State | 1 | |
| Gant, Earl HB | 79-80KC 83-85USFL | 2 | 6' | 207 | Missouri | | 6 |
| Gant, Kenneth DB | 90-94Dal 95TB | | 5'11" | 189 | Albany State | 7 | |
| Garalczyk, Mark DT-DE | 87StL 88Phx 88NYJ 89NJ 91ZJ | | 6'5" | 272 | Western Michigan | | |
| Garbarczyk, Tony DE | 87NYJ | | 6'4" | 275 | Wake Forest | | |
| Garcia, Bubba WR | 80-81KC 83USFL | | 5'11" | 185 | Texas-El Paso | | 6 |
| Garcia, Eddie K | 83-84GB | 5 | 5'8" | 178 | S.M.U. | | 23 |
| Garcia, Frank K | 81Sea 83USFL 83-87TB | 4 | 6' | 205 | Arizona State, Arizona | | |
| Garcia, Frank OG | 95Car | | 6'1" | 295 | Washington | | |
| Garcia, Teddy K | 88NE 89Min 90Hou | 5 | 5'10" | 190 | Northeast La. | | 108 |
| Gardner, Carwell FB | 90-95Buf | 2 | 6'2" | 239 | Kentucky, Louisville | | 74 |
| Gardner, Donnie DE | 91Mia | | 6'3" | 260 | Kentucky | | |
| Gardner, Ellis OT-OG | 83KC 84Ind | | 6'5" | 257 | Georgia Tech | | |
| Gardner, Moe NT-DE | 91-95Atl | | 6'2" | 261 | Illinois | | |
| Gardocki, Chris K | 91-94Chi 95Ind | 4 | 6'1" | 194 | Clemson | | |
| Garner, Charlie HB | 94-95Phi | 23 | 5'9" | 181 | Tennessee | | 54 |
| Garner, Dwight HB | 86Was | | 5'8" | 183 | California | | |
| Garner, Hal LB | 85-86Buf 87KJ 88Buf 89DR 90-91Buf | | 6'4" | 228 | Utah State | | |
| Garnett, Dave LB | 93-94Min 95Den | | 6'2" | 216 | Stanford | | |
| Garnett, Scott NT-DE | 84Den 85SF 85SD 87Buf | | 6'2" | 269 | Washington | | |
| Garrett, Alvin HB-WR | 80-81NYG 81-84Was | 3 | 5'7" | 179 | Angelo State | | 12 |
| Garrett, Curtis DE | 87NYG | | 6'5" | 302 | Illinois State | | |
| Garrett, Jason QB | 93-95Dal | 1 | 6'2" | 195 | Princeton | | |
| Garrett, John WR | 89Cin | | 5'11" | 180 | Columbia, Princeton | | |
| Garrett, Mike K | 81Bal | 4 | 6'1" | 184 | Georgia | | |
| Garrett, Shane WR | 91Cin 92AJ | | 5'11" | 185 | Texas A&M | | |
| Garrity, Gregg WR | 83-84Pit 84-89Phi | 23 | 5'10" | 170 | Penn State | | 42 |
| Gary, Cleveland HB | 89-93LA 94Mia | 2 | 6' | 226 | Georgia, Miami (Fla.) | | 174 |
| Gary, Keith DE | 83-88Pit | | 6'3" | 263 | Oklahoma | | |
| Gary, Russell DB | 81-86NO 86-87Phi | | 5'11" | 196 | Nebraska | 7 | |
| Garza, Sammy QB | 87StL | | 6'1" | 184 | Texas-El Paso | | 6 |
| Gash, Sam FB | 92-95NE | 2 | 5'11" | 224 | Penn State | | 18 |
| Gash, Thane DB | 88-90Cle 91ZJ 92SF 93KJ | | 6' | 200 | East Tennessee St. | 4 | 12 |
| Gastineau, Mark DE | 79-88NYJ | | 6'5" | 266 | Arizona State, E.C. Oklahoma | | 12 |
| Gault, Willie WR | 83-87Chi 88-93Raid | 23 | 6'1" | 181 | Tennessee | | 270 |

| Use Name (Nickname) - Positions | Team by Year | See Section | Hgt. | Wgt. | College | Int | Pts |
|---|---|---|---|---|---|---|---|
| Gay, Everett WR | 88Dal 89TB | 2 | 6'2" | 209 | Texas | | 6 |
| Gay, Matt DB | 94KC | | 6' | 197 | Kansas | | |
| Gay, William DT-DE-TE | 78-87Det 88Min | | 6'5" | 250 | Southern Calif. | 2 | 6 |
| Gayle, Shaun DB | 84-94Chi 95SD | | 5'11" | 198 | Ohio State | 16 | 18 |
| Gaynor, Doug QB | 86Cin | | 6'2" | 205 | Long Beach State | | |
| Geater, Ron NT | 92Den | | 6'6" | 270 | Iowa | | |
| Geathers, James (Jumpy) DE-NT-DT | 84-89NO 90-92Was 93-95Atl | | 6'7" | 283 | Wichita State | | |
| Gedney, Chris TE | 93-95Chi | 2 | 6'5" | 262 | Syracuse | | 18 |
| Gehring, Mark TE | 87Hou | | 6'4" | 235 | Eastern Washington | | 6 |
| Geile, Chris OG | 87Det | | 6'4" | 305 | Eastern Illinois | | |
| Gelbaugh, Stan QB | 86Buf 87EJ 88-89Buf 91Phx 92-95Sea | 12 | 6'3" | 207 | Maryland | | |
| Gentry, Dennis HB-WR | 82-92Chi | 23 | 5'8" | 180 | Baylor | | 96 |
| George, Jeff DB | 87TB | | 6'1" | 185 | Illinois State | | |
| George, Jeff QB | 90-93Ind 94-95Atl | 12 | 6'4" | 221 | Purdue, Illinois | | 12 |
| George, Ron LB | 93-95Atl | | 6' | 229 | Air Force, Stanford | | |
| Gerak, John OG-TE | 93-95Min | | 6'3" | 280 | Penn State | | |
| Gerhard, Chris DB | 87Phi | | 5'10" | 185 | East Stroudsburg | | |
| Gerhart, Tom DB | 92Phi | | 6'1" | 195 | Ohio U. | | |
| Gervais, Rick DB | 81-83SF | | 5'11" | 190 | Stanford | | |
| Gesek, John OG-C | 87-89Raid 90-94Dal 95Was | | 6'5" | 279 | Sacramento State | | |
| Getz, Lee OG | 87KC | | 6'3" | 250 | Rutgers | | |
| Giacomarro, Ralph K | 83-85Atl | 4 | 6'1" | 192 | Penn State | | |
| Giannetti, Frank NT | 91Ind | | 6'2" | 267 | Penn State | | |
| Giaquinto, Nick HB-FB | 80-81Mia 81-83Was | 23 | 5'11" | 204 | Bridgeport, Connecticut | | 30 |
| Gibbs, Joe | HC81-92Was | | | | San Diego State | | |
| Gibler, Andy TE | 83Cin | | 6'4" | 234 | Missouri | | |
| Gibson, Alec DE | 87Was | | 6'4" | 270 | Illinois | | |
| Gibson, Antonio DB | 83-85USFL 86-89,92NO | | 6'3" | 204 | Cincinnati | 3 | |
| Gibson, Dennis LB | 87-93Det 94-95SD | | 6'2" | 240 | Iowa State | 3 | |
| Gibson, Ernest DB | 84-88NE 89Mia | | 5'10" | 185 | Furman | 4 | |
| Gibson, Oliver DT | 95Pit | | 6'2" | 283 | Notre Dame | | |
| Gibson, Tom DE-DT | 89-90Cle 91LA | | 6'7" | 257 | Northern Arizona | | |
| Giddens, Frank OT | 81-82Phi 84USFL | | 6'7" | 300 | New Mexico | | |
| Giesler, Jon OT | 79-88Mia 89KJ | | 6'5" | 262 | Michigan | | |
| Gilbert, Daren OT | 85-88NO | | 6'6" | 289 | Fullerton State | | |
| Gilbert, Freddie DE | 84-85USFL 86-88Den 89Phx | | 6'4" | 275 | Georgia | | |
| Gilbert, Gale QB | 85-86Sea 87KJ 90-93Buf 94-95SD | 1 | 6'3" | 206 | California | | |
| Gilbert, Lewis TE | 78-79Atl 80Phi 80SF 81LA 83-85USFL | 1 | 6'4" | 225 | Florida | | |
| Gilbert, Sean DT-DE | 92-94LA 95StL | | 6'4" | 312 | Pittsburgh | | 2 |
| Gildon, Jason LB | 94-95Pit | | 6'3" | 241 | Oklahoma State | | |
| Giles, Jimmie TE | 77Hou 78-86TB 86-87Det 87-89Phi | 2 | 6'3" | 239 | Alcorn State | | 246 |
| Gill, Owen FB | 85-86Ind 87LA | 2 | 6'1" | 232 | Iowa | | 18 |
| Gillen, John LB | 81-82StL 83NE 84-85USFL | | 6'3" | 227 | Illinois | | |
| Gillespie, Fernandars (Scoop) HB | 84Pit | | 5'10" | 185 | William Jewell | | |
| Gillespie, Willie WR | 86TB 87Min | | 5'9" | 170 | Tenn.-Chattanooga | | |
| Gilmore, Jim OT-OG | 86Phi 87Mia | | 6'5" | 269 | Ohio State | | |
| Gillus, Willie QB | 87GB | | 6'4" | 215 | Norfolk State | | |
| Ginn, Tomie OG-C | 80-81Det 82KJ | | 6'3" | 253 | Arkansas | | |
| Gisler, Mike OG-C | 93-95NE | | 6'4" | 300 | Houston | | |
| Gissinger, Andrew OT | 82-84SD 85JJ | | 6'5" | 279 | Syracuse | | |
| Givins, Ernest WR | 86-94Hou 95Jax | 23 | 5'9" | 172 | Louisville | | 306 |
| Gladman, Charles HB | 87TB | | 5'11" | 205 | Pittsburgh | | |
| Gladney, Tony WR | 87SF | | 6'3" | 200 | Nevada-Las Vegas | | |
| Glanville, Jerry | HC85-89Hou 90-93Atl | | | | Montana State, Northern Michigan | | |
| Glasgow, Brian TE | 87Chi | | 6'2" | 230 | Northern Illinois | | |
| Glasgow, Nesby DB | 79-83Bal 84-87Ind 88-92Sea | 3 | 5'10" | 185 | Washington | 15 | 12 |
| Glass, Bill OG | 80Cin | | 6'4" | 261 | Baylor | | |
| Glaze, Charles DB | 87Sea | | 5'11" | 200 | S. Carolina State | 2 | |
| Glazebrook, Bob DB | 78-83Atl | | 6'1" | 200 | Fresno State | 8 | 6 |
| Glenn, Aaron DB | 94-95NYJ | 3 | 5'9" | 185 | Texas A&M | 1 | |
| Glenn, Kerry DB | 85-87NYJ 88KJ 89NYJ 90-92Mia | | 5'9" | 175 | Minnesota | 7 | 12 |
| Glenn, Vencie DB | 86SD 86NE 87-90SD 91NO 92-94Min 95NYG | | 6' | 191 | Indiana State | 35 | 18 |
| Glover, Andrew TE | 91-94Raid 95Oak | 2 | 6'6" | 245 | Grambling | | 60 |
| Glover, Clyde DE | 87SF | | 6'6" | 280 | Fresno State | | |
| Glover, Kevin C-OG | 85-95Det | | 6'2" | 276 | Maryland | | |
| Goad, Tim NT-DT | 88-94NE 95Cle | | 6'3" | 280 | North Carolina | | 6 |
| Godfrey, Chris OG-OT-DE-DT | 80NYJ 81KJ 83USFL 84-87NYG 88Sea | | 6'3" | 263 | Michigan | | |
| Goeas, Leo OT-OG | 90-92SD 93-94LA 95StL | | 6'4" | 295 | Hawaii | | |
| Goebel, Brad QB | 91Phi 92-94Cle | 1 | 6'3" | 198 | Baylor | | |
| Goebel, Hank OT | 87LA | | 6'7" | 270 | Fullerton State | | |
| Goff, Robert (Pig) DE-NT | 88-89TB 90-95NO | | 6'3" | 272 | Auburn | | 12 |
| Goff, Willard DT | 85Atl | | 6'4" | 265 | Illinois, West Texas State | | |
| Gogan, Kevin OT-OG | 87-93Dal 94Raid 95Oak | | 6'7" | 315 | Washington | | |
| Goganious, Keith LB | 92-94Buf 95Jax | | 6'2" | 237 | Penn State | 2 | |
| Goldberg, Bill NT-DT | 92-94Atl | | 6'2" | 272 | Georgia | | |
| Golden, Tim LB | 82-84NE 85Phil | | 6'1" | 220 | Florida | | |
| Golic, Bob NT-LB-DE | 79-82NE 83-88Cle 89-92Raid | | 6'2" | 264 | Notre Dame | 1 | 6 |
| Golic, Mike DT-NT-DE | 86-87Hou 87-92Phi 93Mia | | 6'5" | 274 | Notre Dame | 3 | |
| Golsteyn, Jerry QB | 77-78NYG 79Det 79Bal 82-83TB 84Raid 85USFL | 1 | 6'4" | 207 | Northern Illinois | | |
| Goltz, Rick DE | 87Raid | | 6'4" | 255 | Simon Fraser | | |
| Gonzales, Leon WR | 85Dal 87Atl | | 5'10" | 161 | Bethune-Cookman | | |
| Goodburn, Kelly K | 87-90KC 90-93Was | 4 | 6'2" | 197 | Iowa State, Emporia State | | |
| Goode, Conrad OT-OG-C | 84-85NYG 87TB | | 6'6" | 285 | Missouri | | |
| Goode, Chris DB | 87-93Ind | | 6' | 195 | North Alabama, Alabama | 7 | 6 |
| Goode, John TE | 84StL 85Phi | | 6'2" | 233 | Youngstown State | | |
| Goode, Kerry HB | 88TB 89Mia | 2 | 5'11" | 200 | Alabama | | 2 |
| Goodlow, Darryl LB | 87Raid | | 6'2" | 235 | Arizona | | |
| Goodlow, Eugene WR | 83-86NO | 2 | 6'2" | 185 | Kansas State | | 60 |
| Goodman, Don FB | 87StL | | 5'11" | 214 | Cincinnati | | |
| Goodman, John DE-DT-NT | 81-85Pit | | 6'6" | 253 | Oklahoma | | |
| Goodson, John K | 82Pit | 5 | 6'3" | 204 | Texas | | 52 |
| Goodspeed, Mark OT | 80StL 83USFL | | 6'5" | 270 | Nebraska | | |
| Gordon, Alex LB | 87-89NYJ 90Raid 91-93Cin | | 6'5" | 246 | Cincinnati | 1 | 2 |
| Gordon, Darrien DB | 93-95SD | 3 | 5'11" | 182 | Stanford | 5 | 12 |
| Gordon, Dwayne LB | 93-94Atl 95SD | | 6'1" | 236 | New Hampshire | | |
| Gordon, Sonny DB | 87TB | | 5'11" | 192 | Ohio State | | |
| Gordon, Tim DB | 88-90Atl 91-92NE | | 6' | 188 | Tulsa | 8 | |
| Gore, Stacy K | 87Mia | | 6' | 200 | Arkansas State | | |
| Gorecki, Chuck LB | 87Phi | | 6'4" | 237 | Boston College | | |
| Goss, Antonio LB | 89,91-95SF | | 6'4" | 228 | North Carolina | | |
| Gossett, Jeff K | 81-82KC 83Cle 84-85USFL 85-87Cle 87Hou 88-94Raid 95Oak | 4 | 6'2" | 197 | Eastern Illinois | | |
| Gothard, Preston TE | 85-88Pit | 2 | 6'4" | 239 | Alabama | | 18 |
| Gottschalk, Darren TE | 87NO | | 6'4" | 225 | Cal. Lutheran | | |
| Gouveia, Kurt LB | 87-94Was 95Phi | | 6'1" | 229 | Brigham Young | 8 | 12 |
| Gowdy, Cornell DB | 86Dal 87-88Pit | | 6'1" | 196 | Morgan State | 3 | 6 |
| Graddy, Sam WR | 87-88Den 89BL 90-92Raid | 23 | 5'10" | 165 | Tennessee | | 18 |
| Graf, Rick LB | 87-90Mia 91-92Hou 93Was | | 6'5" | 246 | Wisconsin | 2 | |
| Gragg, Scott OT | 95NYG | | 6'8" | 316 | Montana | | |
| Graham, Dan C | 89TB | | 6'2" | 270 | Northern Illinois | | |
| Graham, David DE-NT | 82Sea 84-85USFL 87Sea | | 6'6" | 250 | Morehouse | | |
| Graham, Derrick OT | 90-94KC 95Car | | 6'4" | 309 | Appalachian State | | |
| Graham, Don LB | 87TB 88Buf 89Was | | 6'2" | 244 | Penn State | | |
| Graham, Hason WR | 95NE | 2 | 5'10" | 176 | Georgia | | 12 |
| Graham, Jeff WR | 91-93Pit 94-95Chi | 23 | 6'1" | 195 | Ohio State | | 62 |
| Graham, Kent QB | 92-94NYG 95Det | 1 | 6'5" | 220 | Notre Dame, Ohio State | | |
| Graham, Scottie HB | 92NYJ 93-95Min | 2 | 5'9" | 220 | Ohio State | | 42 |
| Graham, William DB | 82-87Det | | 5'11" | 191 | Texas | 6 | |
| Granby, John DB | 92Den | | 6'1" | 198 | Virginia Tech | | |
| Granger, Norm FB | 84Dal 86KJ 87Atl | | 5'19' | 225 | Iowa | | |
| Grant, African DB | 90Mia | | 6' | 200 | Illinois | | |
| Grant, Alan DB | 90-91Ind 92-93SF 93Cin 94Was | 3 | 5'10" | 187 | Stanford | 3 | 6 |
| Grant, Darryl DT-OG-C-OT | 81-91Was | | 6'1" | 269 | Rice | 2 | 6 |
| Grant, David NT-DE-LB | 88-91Cin 92TB 93GB | | 6'4" | 277 | West Virginia | | |
| Grant, Otis WR | 83-84LA 87Phi | 2 | 6'3" | 197 | Michigan State | | 6 |
| Grant, Rupert FB | 95NE | | 6'1" | 233 | Howard | | |
| Grant, Steve LB | 92-95Ind | | 6' | 236 | West Virginia | 1 | |
| Grant, Will C | 78-85Buf 86Sea 87Buf | | 6'3" | 254 | Idaho State, Kentucky | | |
| Graves, Marsharne OT | 84Den 87Ind | | 6'4" | 268 | Arizona | | |
| Graves, Rory OT | 88-91Raid | | 6'6" | 288 | Ohio State | | |
| Gray, Carlton DB | 93-95Sea | | 6' | 191 | U.C.L.A. | 9 | |
| Gray, Cecil OG-DT-OT | 90-91Phi 92GB 93-94Ind 95Arz | | 6'4" | 288 | North Carolina | | |
| Gray, Chris OT-OG | 93-95Mia | | 6'4" | 290 | Auburn | | |
| Gray, Derwin DB | 93-95Ind | | 5'10" | 190 | Brigham Young | 1 | |
| Gray, Earnest WR | 79-84NYG 85StL | 2 | 6'3" | 195 | Memphis State | | 162 |
| Gray, Hector DB | 81-83Det | | 6'1" | 192 | Florida State | 2 | |
| Gray, Jerry DB | 85-91LA 92Hou 93TB | | 6' | 185 | Texas | 28 | 24 |
| Gray, Kevin DB | 82NO | | 5'11" | 179 | Eastern Illinois | | |
| Gray, Mel HB-WR | 84-85USFL 86-88NO 89-94Det 95Hou | 3 | 5'9" | 166 | Purdue | | 60 |
| Gray, Paul LB | 87Atl | | 6'2" | 231 | Western Kentucky | | |
| Graybill, Mike OT | 89Cle | | 6'7" | 275 | Boston U. | | |
| Grayson, David LB | 87-90Cle 91SD 92LJ | | 6'2" | 230 | Cal. Poly.-Pomona, Fresno State | 3 | 18 |
| Grbac, Elvis QB | 93-95SF | 12 | 6'5" | 232 | Michigan | | 12 |
| Greco, Don OG | 82-85Det | | 6'3" | 260 | Western Illinois | | |
| Green, Alex DB | 87Dal | | 6'1" | 194 | Indiana | 1 | |
| Green, Boyce FB-HB | 83-85Cle 86KC 87Sea | 2 | 5'11" | 215 | Carson-Newman | | 54 |
| Green, Bubba DT | 81Bal | | 6'4" | 278 | N. Carolina State | 1 | |
| Green, Chris DB | 91-94Mia 95Buf | | 5'11" | 191 | Illinois | 2 | |
| Green, Cleveland OT | 79-86Mia | | 6'3" | 263 | Southern U. | | |
| Green, Curtis DT-DE-NT | 81-89Det | | 6'3" | 260 | Alabama State | | |
| Green, Darrell DB | 83-95Was | 3 | 5'8" | 172 | Texas A&I | 40 | 36 |
| Green, David HB | 82Cle | | 5'10" | 200 | Edinboro | | |
| Green, David HB | 95NE | | 5'11" | 193 | Boston College | | |
| Green, Dennis | HC92-95Min | | | | Iowa | | |
| Green, Eric TE | 90-94Pit 95Mia | 2 | 6'5" | 274 | Liberty | | 164 |
| Green, Gary DB | 77-83KC 84-85LA | | 5'11" | 187 | Baylor | 33 | 12 |
| Green, Gaston HB | 88-90LA 92Den | 23 | 5'10" | 189 | U.C.L.A. | | 48 |
| Green, Harold HB | 90-95Cin | 2 | 6'2" | 222 | South Carolina | | 66 |
| Green, Hugh LB | 81-85TB 85-91Mia | | 6'2" | 225 | Pittsburgh | 6 | 12 |
| Green, Jacob DE | 80-91Sea 92SF | | 6'3" | 253 | Texas A&M | 3 | 24 |
| Green, Mark HB | 89-92Chi | 23 | 5'11" | 184 | Notre Dame | | 42 |
| Green, Mike LB | 83-85SD | | 6' | 235 | Oklahoma State | 3 | |
| Green, Paul TE | 92-94Sea | 2 | 6'3" | 230 | Southern Calif. | | 18 |
| Green, Robert HB | 92Was 93-95Chi | 2 | 5'8" | 207 | William & Mary | | 30 |
| Green, Rogerick DB | 92TB 93KJ 94TB 95Jax | | 5'10" | 180 | Kansas State | | |
| Green, Roy WR-DB | 79-87StL 88-90Phx 91-92Phi | 23 | 6' | 193 | Henderson State | 4 | 414 |
| Green, Tim LB-DE-DT | 86-93Atl | | 6'2" | 246 | Syracuse | | 2 |
| Green, Trent QB | 93SD 95Was | | 6'3" | 211 | Indiana | | |
| Green, Victor DB | 93-95NYJ | | 5'9" | 195 | Akron | 1 | |
| Green, Willie WR | 91-93Det 94TB 95Car | 2 | 6'2" | 179 | Mississippi | | 120 |
| Greene, Andrew OG | 95Mia | | 6'3" | 304 | Indiana | | |
| Greene, A.J. DB | 91NYG | | 5'8" | 167 | Wake Forest | | |
| Greene, Danny WR | 85Sea 86BG | | 5'11" | 190 | Washington | | |
| Greene, Doug DB | 78StL 79-80Buf 83-84USFL | | 6'2" | 205 | Texas A&I | 1 | |
| Greene, George (Tiger) DB | 85Atl 86-90GB | | 6' | 194 | Western Carolina | 5 | 6 |
| Greene, Ken DB | 78-82StL 83-84SD | | 6'3" | 203 | Washington State | 15 | |
| Greene, Kevin LB-DE | 85-92LA 93-95Pit | | 6'3" | 242 | Auburn | 3 | 12 |
| Greene, Marcellus DB | 84Min | | 6' | 185 | Arizona | | |
| Greene, Tracy TE | 94KC 95Pit | | 6'5" | 282 | Grambling | | 6 |
| Greenwood, Carl DB | 95NYJ | | 5'11" | 186 | U.C.L.A. | | |
| Greenwood, David DB | 83-85USFL 85TB 86GB 87GJ 88Raid | | 6'3" | 210 | Wisconsin | 5 | |
| Greer, Curtis DE | 80-85StL 86XJ 87StL 88XJ | | 6'4" | 255 | Michigan | | |
| Greer, Terry WR | 86Cle 87-89SF 90Det | 2 | 6'1" | 192 | Alabama State | | 24 |
| Gregor, Bob DB | 81-84SD | | 6'2" | 192 | Washington State | 4 | |
| Gregory, Ted NT | 88NO | | 6'1" | 260 | Syracuse | | |
| Griffin, Courtney DB | 93LA | | 5'10" | 180 | Fresno State | | |
| Griffin, Don DB | 86-93SF 94-95Cle | 3 | 6' | 176 | Middle Tenn. St. | 25 | 12 |
| Griffin, James DB | 83-85Cin 86-89Det | | 6'2" | 197 | Middle Tenn. St. | 19 | 18 |
| Griffin, Jeff DB | 81-85StL 87Phi | | 6' | 185 | Utah | 4 | |
| Griffin, Keith HB | 84-88Was 88Atl | 23 | 5'8" | 185 | Miami (Fla.) | | 30 |
| Griffin, Larry DB | 86Hou 87-92Pit | | 6' | 195 | North Carolina | 13 | 6 |
| Griffin, Leonard DE-NT | 86-93KC | | 6'4" | 268 | Grambling | | |
| Griffin, Ray DB | 78-84Cin | 3 | 5'10" | 186 | Ohio State | 11 | 18 |
| Griffin, Steve HB | 87Atl | | 5'10" | 185 | Clemson | | |
| Griffin, Steve WR | 87Atl | | 5'11" | 198 | Purdue | | |
| Griffith, Howard HB-FB | 93-94LA 95Car | 2 | 6' | 226 | Illinois | | 18 |
| Griffith, Rich TE | 93NE 95Jax | 2 | 6'5" | 256 | Arizona | | |
| Griffith, Robert DB | 94-95Min | | 5'11" | 189 | San Diego State | | |
| Griffith, Russell K | 87Sea | | 5'11" | 175 | Weber State | | |
| Groce, Clif FB | 95Ind | | 5'11" | 242 | Texas A&M | | |
| Griggs, Anthony LB | 82-85Phi 86-88Cle | | 6'3" | 227 | Villanova, Ohio State | 3 | |
| Griggs, Billy TE | 85-89NYJ | 2 | 6'3" | 232 | Virginia | | 6 |
| Griggs, David LB-DE | 89-93Mia 94SD | | 6'3" | 245 | Virginia | 1 | |
| Grimes, Randy C-OG | 83-90TB 91EJ 92TB | | 6'4" | 270 | Baylor | | |
| Grimm, Russ OG-C | 81-91Was | | 6'3" | 275 | Pittsburgh | | |
| Grimsley, John LB | 84-90Hou 91KJ 92-93Mia | | 6'2" | 235 | Kentucky | 1 | |
| Grogan, Steve QB | 75-90NE | 12 | 6'4" | 207 | Kansas State | | 210 |
| Grooms, Elois DE-DT | 75-81NO 82-85StL 87Phi | | 6'4" | 249 | Tennessee Tech | 3 | 14 |

| Use Name (Nickname) - Positions | Team by Year | See Section | Hgt. | Wgt. | College | Int | Pts |
|---|---|---|---|---|---|---|---|
| Gross, Al DB | 83-87Cle | | 6'3" | 191 | Arizona | 11 | 12 |
| Grossart, Kyle QB | 80Oak 81NYJ | | 6'4" | 210 | Oregon State | | |
| Grossman, Burt DE | 89-93SD 94Phi | | 6'6" | 269 | Pittsburgh | | 6 |
| Groth, Jeff WR | 79Mia 79-80Hou 81-85NO | 23 | 5'10" | 176 | Bowling Green | | 18 |
| Grow, Monty DB | 94KC 95Jax | | 6'3" | 214 | Florida | 2 | |
| Gruber, Bob OT | 84-85USFL 86Cle 87GB | | 6'5" | 275 | Pittsburgh | | |
| Gruber, Paul OT | 88-95TB | | 6'5" | 293 | Wisconsin | | |
| Grunhard, Tim C | 90-95KC | | 6'2" | 301 | Notre Dame | | |
| Grupp, Bob K | 79-81KC 83-85USFL | 4 | 5'11" | 193 | Duke | | |
| Grymes, Darrell WR | 87Det | | 6'2" | 182 | Central St.-Ohio | | 12 |
| Guendling, Mike LB | 85SD | | 6'3" | 238 | Northwestern | | |
| Guggemos, Neal DB | 86-87Min 88NYG | 3 | 6'1" | 189 | St. Thomas | 1 | |
| Guidry, Kevin DB | 88Den 89Phx | | 6' | 176 | Louisiana State | | |
| Guilbeau, Rusty LB-DE | 82-86NYJ 87Cle | | 6'4" | 242 | McNeese State | | |
| Guliford, Eric WR | 93-94Min 95Car | 23 | 5'8" | 167 | Arizona State | | 12 |
| Gulledge, David DB | 92Was | | 6'1" | 203 | Jacksonville State | | |
| Guman, Mike FB-HB | 80-88LA | 2 | 6'2" | 216 | Penn State | | 96 |
| Gunn, Lance DB | 93Cin | | 6'3" | 222 | Texas | | |
| Gunn, Mark DE-DT | 91-94NYJ 95Phi | | 6'5" | 291 | Pittsburgh | | |
| Gunter, Mike FB | 84KC | | 5'11" | 206 | Tulsa | | |
| Gustafson, Jim WR | 86-89Min 90ZJ | 2 | 6'1" | 177 | St. Thomas | | 30 |
| Guthrie, Keith NT | 84SD | | 6'4" | 264 | Texas A&M | | |
| Guyton, Myron DB | 89-93NYG 94-95NE | | 6'1" | 205 | Eastern Kentucky | 10 | |
| Guzik, John NT-DE | 87NE | | 6'4" | 270 | Ohio U. | | |
| Habib, Brian OT-OG | 89,91-92Min 93-95Den | | 6'7" | 296 | Washington | | |
| Hackett, Dino LB | 86-91KC 92IL 93Sea | | 6'3" | 228 | Appalachian State | 1 | 2 |
| Hackett, Joey TE | 83-85USFL 86Den 87-88GB | | 6'5" | 267 | Elon | | 6 |
| Hadd, Gary DT-NT | 88Det 89Phx | | 6'4" | 274 | Minnesota | | |
| Haddix, Michael FB | 83-87Phi 89-90GB | 2 | 6'2" | 226 | Memphis State | | 30 |
| Haddix, Wayne DB | 87-88NYG 90-91TB 91Cin | | 6'1" | 203 | Liberty | 7 | 18 |
| Haden, Nick OG-C | 86Phi 87NJ | | 6'2" | 270 | Penn State | | |
| Hadley, Ron LB | 87-88SF | | 6'2" | 240 | Washington | | |
| Hadnot, Jim FB | 80-83KC 85USFL | 2 | 6'2" | 244 | Texas Tech | | 30 |
| Hagen, Mike FB | 87Sea | | 6' | 240 | Montana | | |
| Hager, Britt LB | 89-94Phi 95Den | | 6'1" | 223 | Texas | 3 | |
| Haggins, Odell NT | 91Buf | | 6'2" | 278 | Florida State | | |
| Hagler, Scott K | 87Sea | | 5'8" | 160 | South Carolina | | 10 |
| Hagood, Rickey NT | 84SD | | 6'2" | 286 | South Carolina | | |
| Hagy, John DB | 88-90Buf | | 5'11" | 190 | Texas | 2 | |
| Haight, Mike OG-OT | 86-91NYJ 92Was | | 6'4" | 281 | Iowa | | |
| Haines, John NT-DE-DT | 84Min 86Ind | | 6'6" | 266 | Texas | | |
| Haines, Kris WR | 79Was 79-81Chi 83-85USFL 87Buf | | 5'11" | 181 | Notre Dame | | |
| Hairston, Carl DE-DT-LB | 76-83Phi 84-89Cle 90Phx | | 6'3" | 260 | Md. Eastern Shore | 1 | |
| Hairston, Russell WR | 87Pit | | 6'3" | 208 | Kentucky | | 6 |
| Hairston, Stacey DB | 93-94Cle | | 5'9" | 180 | Ohio Northern | | |
| Haji-Sheikh, Ali K | 83-85NYG 86Atl 87Was | 5 | 6' | 172 | Michigan | | 323 |
| Hakel, Chris QB | 93Atl | | 6'2" | 230 | William & Mary | | |
| Hale, Chris DB | 90-92Buf | 3 | 5'7" | 163 | Nebraska, Southern Calif. | 1 | 2 |
| Haley, Charles DE-LB | 86-91SF 92-95Dal | | 6'5" | 245 | James Madison | 2 | 8 |
| Haley, Darryl OT-OG | 82-84NE 85IL 86NE 87Cle 88GB | | 6'4" | 269 | Utah | | |
| Haliburton, Ronnie LB | 90-91Den 92ZJ | | 6'4" | 230 | Louisiana State | | |
| Hall, Alvin DB | 81-85,87Det | 3 | 5'10" | 185 | Miami-Ohio | 7 | 12 |
| Hall, Chris DB | 93Dal | | 6'2" | 184 | East Carolina | | |
| Hall, Courtney C-OG | 89-95SD | | 6'2" | 277 | Rice | | |
| Hall, Dana DB | 92-95SF | | 6'2" | 206 | Washington | 6 | |
| Hall, Darryl DB | 93-94Den 95SF | | 6'2" | 210 | Washington | 1 | |
| Hall, Delton DB | 87-91Pit 92SD | | 6'1" | 202 | Clemson | 5 | 12 |
| Hall, Dino HB | 79-83Cle 85USFL | 23 | 5'7" | 165 | Rowan | | 12 |
| Hall, James LB | 87Atl | | 6'1" | 252 | Northwestern La. | | |
| Hall, Lemanski LB | 95Hou | | 6' | 229 | Alabama | | |
| Hall, Mark DE | 89-90GB | | 6'4" | 285 | Louisiana State, Southwestern La. | | |
| Hall, Ray DT | 95Jax | | 6'4" | 294 | Washington State | | |
| Hall, Rhett DT | 91-93TB 94SF 95Phi | | 6'2" | 268 | California | | |
| Hall, Ron TE | 87-93TB 94-95Det | 2 | 6'4" | 243 | Cal. Poly.-Pomona, Hawaii | | 60 |
| Hall, Travis DE | 95Atl | | 6'5" | 278 | Brigham Young | | |
| Haller, Alan DB | 92Pit 92Cle 93Pit 95Car | | 5'11" | 185 | Michigan State | | |
| Hallock, Ty TE | 93-94Det | 2 | 6'3" | 249 | Michigan State | | 12 |
| Halloran, Shawn QB | 87StL | 1 | 6'4" | 217 | Boston College | | |
| Hallstrom, Ron OT-OG | 82-92GB 93Phi | | 6'6" | 299 | Iowa | | |
| Hamel, Dean DT | 85-88Was 89-90Dal | | 6'3" | 279 | Tulsa | | |
| Hamilton, Darrell OT | 89-91Den | | 6'5" | 298 | North Carolina | | |
| Hamilton, Harry DB | 84-87NYJ 88-91TB | | 6' | 194 | Penn State | 23 | |
| Hamilton, Keith DE | 92-95NYG | | 6'6" | 285 | Pittsburgh | | 2 |
| Hamilton, Rick LB | 93-94Was 94KC | | 6'2" | 241 | Central Florida | | |
| Hamilton, Ruffin LB | 94GB | | 6'1" | 230 | Tulane | | |
| Hamilton, Skip DT | 87Phi | | 6'2" | 265 | Southern | | |
| Hamilton, Wes OG | 76-84Min 85XJ | | 6'3" | 261 | Tulsa | | |
| Hamilton, Steve DE-DT | 85-88Was | | 6'4" | 263 | East Carolina | | |
| Hamm, Bob DE | 83-85Hou 87Ind | | 6'4" | 260 | Nevada-Reno | | |
| Hammerstein, Mike DE-NT | 86-87Cin 88KJ 89-90Cin | | 6'4" | 270 | Michigan | | |
| Hammond, Steve LB | 88NYJ | | 6'4" | 225 | Wake Forest | | |
| Hammonds, Shelly DB | 95Min | | 5'10" | 189 | Penn State | | |
| Hampton, Alonzo DB | 90Min 91TB | | 5'10" | 191 | Pittsburgh | 1 | |
| Hampton, Dan DE-DT | 79-90Chi | | 6'5" | 264 | Arkansas | | 2 |
| Hampton, Kwante WR | 87Atl | | 6'1" | 182 | Long Beach State | | |
| Hampton, Lorenzo HB | 85-89Mia | 23 | 6' | 209 | Florida | | 168 |
| Hampton, Rodney HB | 90-95NYG | 23 | 5'11" | 215 | Georgia | | 298 |
| Hamrick, James K | 87KC | | 5'11" | 177 | Rice | | 10 |
| Hancock, Anthony WR | 82-86KC | 23 | 6' | 200 | Tennessee | | 30 |
| Hancock, Kevin LB | 87Ind | | 6'2" | 225 | Baylor | | |
| Hand, Jon DE | 86-94Ind | | 6'7" | 297 | Alabama | 1 | |
| Handley, Ray | HC91-92NYG | | | | Stanford | | |
| Hanifan, Jim | HC80-85StL HC89Atl | | | | California | | |
| Hanks, Merton DB | 91-95SF | | 6'2" | 185 | Iowa | 17 | 18 |
| Hanna, Jim NT | 94NO | | 6'4" | 255 | Louisville | | |
| Hannah, Charley OG-OT-DE | 77-82TB 83-88Raid | | 6'5" | 260 | Alabama | | |
| Hannah, Travis WR | 93-95Hou | 2 | 5'7" | 161 | Southern Calif. | | |
| Hanneman, Cliff LB | 87Cle | | 6'2" | 235 | Fresno State | | |
| Hannon, Tom DB | 77-84Min | | 5'11" | 192 | Michigan | 15 | 10 |
| Hannula, Jim OT | 83Cin | | 6'6" | 264 | Northern Illinois | | |
| Hanousek, Matt OG-OT | 87Sea | | 6'4" | 265 | Drake, Utah State | | |
| Hansen, Brian K | 84-88NO 90NE 91-93Cle 94-95NYJ | 4 | 6'3" | 213 | Sioux Falls | | |
| Hansen, Bruce FB | 87NE 88AJ | | 6'1" | 225 | Brigham Young | | |
| Hansen, Phil DE | 91-95Buf | | 6'5" | 276 | N. Dakota State | | |
| Hanson, Jason K | 92-95Det | 5 | 5'11" | 183 | Washington State | | 448 |
| Hanson, Mark OG | 87Min | | 6'2" | 260 | Mankato State | | |
| Harbaugh, Jim QB | 87-93Chi 94-95Ind | 12 | 6'3" | 203 | Michigan | | 102 |
| Harbour, Dave C | 88-89Was | | 6'4" | 265 | Illinois | | |
| Harbour, James WR | 86Ind | | 6'1" | 192 | Mississippi | | |
| Harden, Bobby DB | 90-93Mia | | 6' | 192 | Miami (Fla.) | | 2 |
| Harden, Derrick WR | 87GB | | 6'1" | 175 | Eastern New Mexico | | |
| Harden, Mike DB | 80-88Den 89-90Raid | 3 | 6'1" | 192 | Michigan | 39 | 30 |
| Harding, Greg DB | 84NO 87Phi | | 6'2" | 197 | Nicholls State | | |
| Hardison, Dee DE-DT-OT-NT | 78-80Buf 81-85NYG 86-87SD 88KC | | 6'4" | 274 | North Carolina | | |
| Hardy, Adrian DB | 93-94SF 94-95Cin | | 5'11" | 194 | NW State-La. | | |
| Hardy, Andre FB | 84Phi 85Sea 87SF | 2 | 6'1" | 232 | Weber State, St. Mary's | | |
| Hardy, Bruce TE-QB | 78-89Mia | 2 | 6'5" | 232 | Arizona State | | 150 |
| Hardy, Darryl LB | 95Arz 95Dal | | 6'2" | 230 | Tennessee | | |
| Hardy, David K | 87Raid | | 5'7" | 180 | Texas A&M | | 7 |
| Hardy, John DB | 91Chi | | 5'10" | 166 | California | | |
| Hardy, Larry TE | 78-85NO | 2 | 6'3" | 234 | Jackson State | | 42 |
| Hardy, Robert DT | 79-82Sea 83BL | | 6'2" | 250 | Jackson State | | |
| Hardy, Robert HB | 91TB | | 5'10" | 210 | Carson-Newman | | |
| Hargain, Tony WR | 92KC | 2 | 6' | 194 | Oregon | | |
| Hargrove, Jim FB | 81Cin 83-84USFL 87GB | | 6'2" | 230 | Wake Forest | | 12 |
| Hargrove, Marvin WR | 90Phi | | 5'10" | 178 | Richmond | | 6 |
| Harkey, Lance DB | 87Raid | | 5'10" | 180 | Illinois | | |
| Harlow, Pat OT | 91-95NE | | 6'6" | 290 | Southern Calif. | | |
| Harmon, Andy DE-DT | 91-95Phi | | 6'4" | 269 | Kent State | 1 | |
| Harmon, Clarence HB-FB | 77-82Was84-85USFL | 2 | 5'11" | 204 | Mississippi State | | 96 |
| Harmon, Derrick HB | 84-86SF | 23 | 5'10" | 202 | Cornell | | 12 |
| Harmon, Kevin HB | 88-89Sea | | 6' | 190 | Iowa | | |
| Harmon, Mike WR | 83NYJ | | 6' | 185 | Mississippi | | |
| Harmon, Ronnie HB | 86-89Buf 90-95SD | 23 | 5'11" | 199 | Iowa | | 192 |
| Harper, Alvin WR | 91-94Dal 95TB | 2 | 6'3" | 203 | Tennessee | | 120 |
| Harper, Bruce HB-WR | 77-84NYJ | 23 | 5'8" | 176 | Kutztown | | 126 |
| Harper, Dave LB | 90Dal | | 6'1" | 220 | Humboldt State | | |
| Harper, Dwayne DB | 88-93Sea 94-95SD | | 5'11" | 169 | S. Carolina State | 20 | 6 |
| Harper, John LB | 83Atl 85USFL | | 6'3" | 230 | Southern Illinois | | |
| Harper, LaSalle LB | 89NYG 89Chi | | 6'1" | 235 | Arkansas | | |
| Harper, Mark DB | 84-85USFL 86-90Cle 91FJ | | 5'9" | 170 | Alcorn State | 8 | |
| Harper, Michael WR | 86-89NYJ | 2 | 5'10" | 180 | Southern Calif. | | 12 |
| Harper, Roger DB | 93-95Atl | | 6'2" | 223 | Ohio State | 2 | |
| Harper, Shawn OT | 95Ind | | 6'3" | 290 | Indiana | | |
| Harrah, Dennis OG-C | 75-87LA | | 6'5" | 260 | Miami (Fla.) | | |
| Harrell, Gary WR | 95NYG | | 5'7" | 170 | Howard | | |
| Harrell, James LB | 79-83Det 84USFL 85-86Det 87KC | | 6'1" | 224 | Florida | 1 | |
| Harrell, Sam FB | 81-82Min 84-85USFL 87Min | | 6'2" | 217 | East Carolina | | |
| Harrington, LaRue FB | 80SD 83-84USFL | | 6' | 210 | Norfolk State | | |
| Harrington, Perry FB-HB | 80-83Phi 84-85StL | 2 | 5'11" | 210 | Jackson State | | 36 |
| Harris, Al DE-LB | 79-84Chi 85HO 86-88Chi 89-90Phi | | 6'5" | 253 | Arizona State | 4 | 8 |
| Harris, Archie OT-OG | 87Den | | 6'6" | 270 | William & Mary | | |
| Harris, Bernardo LB | 95GB | | 6'2" | 243 | North Carolina | | |
| Harris, Bob LB | 83-85StL 86NJ 87KC | | 6'2" | 219 | Auburn | 3 | 6 |
| Harris, Corey WR-CB | 92Hou 92-94GB 95Sea | 3 | 5'11" | 195 | Vanderbilt | 3 | 6 |
| Harris, Darryl HB | 88Min | 23 | 5'10" | 178 | Arizona State | | 6 |
| Harris, Duriel WR | 76-83Mia 84Cle 84Dal | 23 | 5'11" | 179 | New Mexico State | | 120 |
| Harris, Elroy FB | 89Sea | | 5'9" | 218 | Eastern Kentucky | | |
| Harris, Eric DB | 80-82KC 83-85LA | | 6'3" | 198 | Memphis State | 21 | 6 |
| Harris, Frank HB | 87Chi | | 6'1" | 196 | N. Carolina State | | |
| Harris, Herbert WR | 86-87NO | 2 | 6'1" | 206 | Lamar | | |
| Harris, Jackie TE | 90-93GB 94-95TB | 2 | 6'3" | 240 | Northeastern La. | | 80 |
| Harris, James DE | 93-95Min | | 6'4" | 262 | Temple | 1 | 6 |
| Harris, John DB | 78-85Sea 86-88Min | | 6'2" | 200 | Arizona State | 47 | 12 |
| Harris, Leonard WR | 84-85USFL 86TB 87-93Hou 94Atl | 23 | 5'8" | 161 | Austin, Texas Tech | | 48 |
| Harris, Leotis OG | 78-83GB 84KJ | | 6'1" | 267 | Arkansas | | |
| Harris, Marshall DE-NT | 80-82Cle 83NE 84USFL | | 6'6" | 261 | Texas Christian | | |
| Harris, Michael C-OG | 89KC | | 6'4" | 306 | Grambling | | |
| Harris, M.L. TE | 80-85Cin | 2 | 6'5" | 238 | Tampa, Kansas St. | | 60 |
| Harris, Odie DB | 88-90TB 91-92Cle 92-93Phx 94-95Arz | | 6' | 190 | Sam Houston St. | 5 | |
| Harris, Raymont FB | 94-95Chi | 2 | 6' | 225 | Ohio State | | 6 |
| Harris, Robert DE | 92-94Min 95NYG | | 6'4" | 285 | Southern U. | | |
| Harris, Ronnie WR | 93-94NE 94-95Sea | | 5'10" | 170 | Oregon | | |
| Harris, Rod WR | 89NO 90Dal 90-91Phi | 3 | 5'10" | 183 | Texas A&M | | |
| Harris, Roy DE-NT | 84-85Atl 87TB | | 6'2" | 264 | Florida | | |
| Harris, Rudy FB | 93-94TB | | 6'1" | 255 | Clemson | | |
| Harris, Shawn LB | 95Chi | | 6'3" | 244 | Arizona | | |
| Harris, Steve HB | 87Min | | 5'11" | 194 | Northern Iowa | | |
| Harris, Tim HB | 83Pit | | 5'9" | 206 | Washington State | | |
| Harris, Tim LB-DE | 86-90GB 91-92SF 93Phi 94-95SF | | 6'5" | 251 | Memphis State | | 10 |
| Harris, Walter DB | 87SD | | 6'1" | 195 | Stanford | | |
| Harris, William TE | 87StL 89TB 90GB | | 6'4" | 239 | Texas, Bishop | | 6 |
| Harrison, Anthony DB | 87GB | | 6'1" | 195 | Georgia Tech | 1 | |
| Harrison, Dennis DE | 78-84Phi 85LA 86SF 86-87Atl | | 6'8" | 277 | Vanderbilt | 1 | |
| Harrison, Martin LB-DE | 90,92-93SF 94-95Min | | 6'5" | 244 | Washington | 1 | |
| Harrison, Nolan NT-DT-DE | 91-94Raid 95Oak | | 6'5" | 284 | Indiana | | 2 |
| Harrison, Rob FB | 87Raid | | 6'2" | 220 | Sacramento State | 1 | |
| Harrison, Rodney DB | 94-95SD | | 6' | 201 | Western Illinois | 5 | |
| Harrison, Todd TE | 92TB | | 6'4" | 260 | N. Carolina State | | |
| Harrison, Vic WR | 87NO | | 5'9" | 184 | North Carolina | | |
| Harry, Carl WR | 89,92Was | | 5'9" | 168 | Utah | | |
| Harry, Emile WR | 86KC 87SJ 88-92KC 92LA | 2 | 5'11" | 175 | Stanford | | 36 |
| Hart, Roy NT-DT | 89Sea 91Raid | | 6'1" | 280 | South Carolina | | |
| Hartenstine, Mike DE | 75-86Chi 87Min | | 6'3" | 251 | Penn State | | 14 |
| Hartley, Frank TE | 94-95Cle | 2 | 6'2" | 268 | Illinois | | 12 |
| Hartley, Ken K | 81NE 84-85USFL | | 6'2" | 200 | Catawba | | |
| Hartnett, Perry OG | 82-83Chi 84USFL 87GB | | 6'5" | 278 | S.M.U. | | |
| Hartwig, Carter DB | 79-84Hou | | 6' | 203 | Southern Calif. | 9 | |
| Harty, John NT-DE | 81-83SF 84FJ 85-86SF | | 6'4" | 260 | Iowa | | 2 |
| Harvey, Frank FB | 94Arz | | 6' | 245 | Georgia | | |
| Harvey, James OG-OT | 87-88KC | | 6'3" | 265 | Jackson State | | |
| Harvey, John HB | 90TB | 2 | 5'11" | 185 | Texas-El Paso | | 6 |
| Harvey, Ken LB | 88-93Phx 94-95Was | | 6'2" | 236 | California | | |
| Harvey, Marvin TE-WR | 81KC 84-85USFL | | 6'3" | 220 | Southern Miss. | | |
| Harvey, Maurice DB | 78 Den 79KJ 80Den 81-83GB 83Det 84TB | | 5'10" | 190 | Ball State | 9 | 6 |
| Harvey, Richard LB | 90-91NE 92-93Buf 94Den 95NO | | 6'1" | 233 | Tulane | | |
| Harvey, Stacy LB | 89KC | | 6'4" | 245 | Arizona State | | |
| Harvin, Allen FB | 87Det 87Was | | 5'9" | 200 | Cincinnati | | |
| Haselrig, Carlton OG | 90-93Pit 95NYJ | | 6'1" | 293 | Pittsburgh-Johnstown | | |
| Hasselbach, Harald DE | 94-95Den | | 6'6" | 280 | Washington | | |

| Use Name (Nickname) - Positions | Team by Year | See Section | Hgt. | Wgt. | College | Int | Pts |
|---|---|---|---|---|---|---|---|
| Hasselbeck, Don TE | 77-83NE 83Raid 84Min 85NYG | 2 | 6'7" | 245 | Colorado | | 108 |
| Haslett, Jim LB | 79-85Buf 86KJ 87NYG | | 6'3" | 233 | Indiana (Pa.) | 6 | |
| Hastings, Andre WR | 93-95Pit | 23 | 6' | 188 | Georgia | | 24 |
| Hasty, James DB | 88-94NYJ 95KC | | 6' | 200 | Central Washington, Washington State | 27 | 12 |
| Hatcher, Dale K | 85-89,91LA 93Mia | 4 | 6'2" | 204 | Clemson | | |
| Hatchett, Derrick DB | 80-83Bal 83Hou | | 5'11" | 183 | Texas | 7 | |
| Hathaway, Steve LB | 84Ind | | 6'4" | 238 | West Virginia | | |
| Hauck, Tim DB | 90NE 91-94GB 95Den | | 5'11" | 183 | Pacific (Ore.), Montana | | |
| Haverdink, Kevin OT | 89-91NO | | 6'5" | 285 | Western Michigan | | |
| Hawkins, Andy LB | 80-83TB 84-85USFL 86-87SD 88KC | | 6'2" | 225 | Texas A&I | 1 | |
| Hawkins, Courtney WR | 92-95TB | 23 | 5'9" | 180 | Michigan State | | 72 |
| Hawkins, Bill DT-DE | 89-92LA | | 6'6" | 268 | Miami (Fla.) | | |
| Hawkins, Frank FB-HB | 81Oak 82-87Raid | 2 | 5'9" | 210 | Nevada-Reno | | 108 |
| Hawkins, Garland DE | 95Chi | | 6'3" | 253 | Syracuse | | |
| Hawkins, Mike LB | 78-81NE 82Raid 84-85USFL | | 6'2" | 235 | Texas A&I | 5 | 6 |
| Hawkins, Steve WR | 94NE | | 6'5" | 210 | Western Michigan | | |
| Haworth, Steve DB | 84Atl | | 5'11" | 190 | Oklahoma | | |
| Haws, Kurt TE | 94Was | | 6'5" | 248 | Utah | | |
| Hawthorne, Ed NT | 95Mia | | 6'1" | 305 | Minnesota | | |
| Hawthorne, Greg HB-FB-TE-WR | 79-83Pit 84-86NE 87Ind | 2 | 6'2" | 228 | Baylor | | 66 |
| Hayden, Aaron HB-FB | 95SD | 2 | 6' | 218 | Tennessee | | 18 |
| Hayes, Gary DB | 84-86GB | | 5'10" | 180 | Fresno State | | |
| Hayes, Eric DT | 90-91Sea 92LA 93TB | | 6'3" | 292 | Florida State | | |
| Hayes, Jeff K | 82-85Was 86Cin 87Mia | 4 | 5'11" | 175 | North Carolina | | 6 |
| Hayes, Joe HB-WR | 84Phi | | 5'9" | 185 | Texas A&I, Central State-Okla. | | |
| Hayes, Jonathan TE | 85-93KC 94-95Pit | 2 | 6'5" | 242 | Iowa | | 78 |
| Hayes, Lester DB | 77-81Oak 82-86Raid 87FJ | | 6' | 200 | Texas A&M | 39 | 30 |
| Hayes, Melvin OT | 95NYJ | | 6'6" | 329 | Mississippi State | | |
| Haynes, James LB | 84-89NO | | 6'2" | 232 | Miss. Valley St. | 1 | 6 |
| Haynes, Louis LB | 82-83KC | | 6' | 227 | Bishop, North Texas | | |
| Haynes, Mark DB | 80-85NYG 86-89Den | | 5'11" | 194 | Colorado | 17 | 6 |
| Haynes, Michael WR | 88-93Atl 94-95NO | 2 | 6' | 180 | Northern Arizona | | 228 |
| Haynes, Mike DB | 76-82NE 83-89Raid | 3 | 6'2" | 192 | Arizona State | 46 | 30 |
| Haynes, Tommy DB | 87Dal | | 6' | 190 | Southern Calif. | 3 | |
| Hayworth, Tracy LB | 90-95Det | | 6'3" | 257 | Tennessee | 1 | 6 |
| Headen, Andy LB | 83-88NYG | | 6'5" | 240 | Clemson | 5 | 6 |
| Heard, Herman HB | 84-89KC | 2 | 5'10" | 186 | Fort Lewis, Southern Colorado | | 96 |
| Hearst, Garrison HB | 93Phx 94-95Arz | 2 | 5'11" | 215 | Georgia | | 24 |
| Heater, Larry HB | 80NYG 81BG 82-83NYG | 2 | 5'11" | 205 | Arizona | | 18 |
| Heath, JoJo DB | 80Cin 81Phi 83CFL 84USFL 87NYJ | | 5'10" | 181 | Pittsburgh | 1 | |
| Hebert, Bobby QB | 83-85USFL 85-89NO 90HO 91-92NO 93-95Atl | 12 | 6'4" | 215 | Northwestern La. | | 6 |
| Hebert, Bud DB | 80NYG | | 6' | 190 | Oklahoma | 1 | |
| Hebron, Vaughn HB | 93-94Phi 95KJ | 23 | 5'8" | 196 | Virginia Tech | | 30 |
| Heck, Andy OT-OG | 89-93Sea 94-95Chi | | 6'6" | 296 | Notre Dame | | |
| Hector, Johnny HB-FB | 83-92NYJ | 23 | 5'11" | 204 | Texas A&M | | 264 |
| Heffernan, Dave OT | 87TB | | 6'4" | 255 | Miami (Fla.) | | |
| Heflin, Victor DB | 83-84StL | | 6' | 184 | Central St.-Ohio | 1 | |
| Heflin, Vince WR | 82-85Mia 86TB | | 6' | 185 | Arizona State | | 6 |
| Hegamin, George OT | 94-95Dal | | 6'7" | 335 | N. Carolina State | | |
| Hegman, Mike LB | 76-87Dal | | 6'1" | 227 | Alabama A&M, Tennessee State | 7 | 12 |
| Heimkreiter, Steve LB | 80Bal | | 6'2" | 226 | Notre Dame | | |
| Heimuli, Lakei FB | 87Chi | 2 | 5'11" | 219 | Brigham Young | | 6 |
| Heller, Ron OT | 84-87TB 88-92Phi 93-95Mia | | 6'6" | 284 | Penn State | | 6 |
| Heller, Ron TE | 87-88SF 89Atl 90,92Sea | 2 | 6'3" | 236 | Oregon State | | 30 |
| Hellestrae, Dale OT-OG-C | 85-86Buf 87PJ 88Buf 89BL 90-95Dal | | 6'5" | 279 | S.M.U. | | |
| Helton, Barry K | 88-90SF 91LA | 4 | 6'3" | 205 | Colorado | | |
| Hemphill, Darryl DB | 82Bal 84-85USFL | | 6' | 195 | West Texas State | | |
| Hempstead, Hessley OG | 95Det | | 6'1" | 295 | Kansas | | |
| Hendel, Andy LB | 84USFL 86Mia 87LJ | | 6'1" | 230 | North Carolina State | | |
| Henderson, Jerome DB | 91-93NE 93-94Buf 95Phi | 3 | 5'10" | 189 | Clemson | 5 | 6 |
| Henderson, Keith FB | 89-92SF 92Min | 2 | 6'1" | 220 | Georgia | | 24 |
| Henderson, Othello DB | 93-94NO | | 6' | 204 | U.C.L.A. | | |
| Henderson, Rueben DB | 81-82Chi 83-84SD | | 6'1" | 196 | Oklahoma State, San Diego State | 4 | |
| Henderson, William FB | 95GB | | 6'2" | 248 | North Carolina | | |
| Henderson, Wyatt DB | 81SD 83-84USFL | | 5'10" | 180 | Fresno State | | |
| Henderson, Wymon DB | 87-88Min 89-92Den 93-94LA | | 5'10" | 186 | Nevada-Las Vegas | 16 | 12 |
| Henderson, Zac DB | 78-79CFL 80Phi 82-83CFL 84-85USFL | | 6'1" | 190 | Oklahoma | | |
| Hendley, David DB | 87NE | | 6' | 188 | Southern Conn. St. | | |
| Hendley, James C | 87Atl | | 6'3" | 257 | Florida State | | |
| Hendrickson, Steve LB-TE-FB | 89SF 89Dal 90-94SD 95Hou | | 6' | 251 | California | 1 | 12 |
| Hendrix, David DB | 95SD | | 6'1" | 213 | Georgia Tech | | |
| Hendrix, Manny DB | 86-91Dal | | 5'10" | 180 | Utah | 2 | 2 |
| Hendrix, Tim TE | 87Dal | | 6'5" | 241 | Tennessee | | |
| Hendy, John DB | 85SD 86KJ | | 5'10" | 196 | Long Beach State | 4 | 6 |
| Henesey, Brian FB | 94Arz | | 5'10" | 215 | Bucknell | | |
| Henke, Brad DE-NT | 89Den | | 6'3" | 275 | Iowa State, Arizona | | |
| Henley, Darryl DB | 89-94LA | 3 | 5'9" | 170 | U.C.L.A. | 12 | |
| Henley, Thomas WR | 87SF | | 5'11" | 185 | Stanford | | |
| Henning, Dan | HC83-86Atl 89-91SD | | | | William & Mary | | |
| Hennings, Chad DT | 92-95Dal | | 6'6" | 287 | Air Force | | |
| Henry, Bernard WR | 82-83Bal 84-85Ind 87LA | 2 | 6'1" | 182 | Arizona State | | 36 |
| Henry, Kevin DE | 93-95Pit | | 6'4" | 276 | Mississippi State | 1 | |
| Henry, Maurice LB | 90Phi | | 5'11" | 220 | Kansas State | | |
| Henry, Charles TE | 91Mia | | 6'4" | 230 | Miami (Fla.) | | |
| Henry, Steve DB | 79StL 80NYG 81Bal | | 6'2" | 190 | Emporia State | 1 | |
| Henry, Wally WR | 77-82Phi 83USFL | 23 | 5'8" | 175 | U.C.L.A. | | 18 |
| Henson, Luther NT | 82-84NE | | 6' | 275 | Ohio State | | |
| Henton, Anthony LB | 86Pit 87KJ 88Pit | | 6'1" | 224 | Troy State | | |
| Hentrich, Craig K | 94-95GB | 4 | 6'3" | 200 | Notre Dame | | 14 |
| Herkenhoff, Matt OT | 76-85KC | | 6'4" | 267 | Minnesota | | |
| Herline, Alan K | 87NE | 4 | 6' | 168 | Vanderbilt | | |
| Herman, Chuck OG | 80Atl | | 6'3" | 250 | Arkansas | | |
| Hernandez, Matt OT | 83Sea 84Min | | 6'6" | 260 | Purdue | | |
| Herrmann, Mark QB | 81-82Den 83Bal 84Ind 85-87SD 89LA 90-92Ind | 12 | 6'4" | 199 | Purdue | | 6 |
| Hernandez, Scott NT | 87Buf | | 6' | 250 | Kent State | | |
| Herrod, Jeff LB | 88-95Ind | | 6' | 246 | Mississippi | 4 | 6 |
| Herron, Bruce LB | 78-82Chi | | 6'2" | 220 | New Mexico | | |
| Hester, Jessie WR | 85-87Raid 88Atl 90-93Ind 94LA 95StL | 2 | 5'11" | 171 | Florida State | | 180 |
| Hester, Ron LB | 82Mia 83-84KJ | | 6'2" | 222 | Florida State | | |
| Hewko, Bob QB | 83TB | | 6'3" | 195 | Florida | | |
| Heyward, Craig (Ironhead) FB | 88-92NO 93Chi 94-95Atl | 2 | 5'11" | 254 | Pittsburgh | | 180 |
| Hickman, Kevin TE | 95Det | | 6'4" | 258 | Navy | | |
| Hicks, Bryan DB | 80-82Cin 83SJ | | 6' | 192 | McNeese State | 1 | |

| Use Name (Nickname) - Positions | Team by Year | See Section | Hgt. | Wgt. | College | Int | Pts |
|---|---|---|---|---|---|---|---|
| Hicks, Cliff DB | 87-90LA 90-92Buf 93-94NYJ 95Den | 3 | 5'10" | 189 | Oregon | 5 | |
| Hicks, Dwight DB | 79-85SF 86Ind | 3 | 6'1" | 190 | Michigan | 32 | 24 |
| Hicks, Ivan DB | 87Det | | 6'2" | 185 | Michigan | | |
| Hicks, Mark LB | 83Sea 87Det | | 6'2" | 235 | Arizona State | | |
| Hicks, Victor TE | 80LA 81FJ 83-84USFL | 2 | 6'3" | 250 | Oklahoma | | 18 |
| Higdon, Alex TE | 88Atl | | 6'5" | 247 | Ohio State | | 12 |
| Higgs, Mark HB-FB | 88Dal 89Phi 90-94Mia 94-95Arz | 23 | 5'7" | 198 | Kentucky | | 90 |
| Highsmith, Alonzo FB | 87-89Hou 90-91Dal 91-92TB | 2 | 6'1" | 235 | Miami (Fla.) | | 60 |
| Hilgenberg, Jay C-OG | 81-91Chi 92Cle 93NO | | 6'3" | 259 | Iowa | | |
| Hilgenberg, Joel C-OG | 84-93NO | | 6'3" | 251 | Iowa | | |
| Hilger, Rusty QB | 85-87Raid 88Det 90-91Ind 92Sea | 12 | 6'4" | 205 | Oklahoma State | | |
| Hill, Bill DB | 87Dal | | 5'9" | 172 | Rutgers | | |
| Hill, Bruce WR | 87-91TB | 2 | 6' | 178 | Arizona State | | 138 |
| Hill, David TE | 76-82Det 83-87LA | 2 | 6'2" | 229 | Texas A&I | | 168 |
| Hill, Derek WR | 89-90Pit | 2 | 6'1" | 193 | Arizona | | 6 |
| Hill, Drew WR | 79-82LA 83XJ 84LA 85-91Hou 92-93Atl | 23 | 5'9" | 171 | Georgia Tech | | 366 |
| Hill, Eddie HB | 79-80LA 81-84Mia | 2 | 6'2" | 205 | Memphis State | | 24 |
| Hill, Eric LB | 89-93Phx 94-95Arz | | 6'1" | 253 | Louisiana State | | 6 |
| Hill, Greg DB | 83Hou 84-86KC 87Raid 87-88KC | | 6'1" | 196 | Oklahoma State | 9 | 6 |
| Hill, Greg HB | 94-95KC | 2 | 5'11" | 205 | Texas A&M | | 12 |
| Hill, Jeff WR | 94-95Cin | | 5'11" | 178 | Purdue | | |
| Hill, Kenny DB | 81Oak 82-83Raid 84-88NYG 89KC | 3 | 6' | 194 | Yale | 6 | |
| Hill, Kent OG-OT | 79-86LA 87Hou | | 6'5" | 260 | Georgia Tech | | |
| Hill, Lonzell (Mo) WR | 87-90NO | 2 | 6' | 189 | Washington | | 78 |
| Hill, Nate DE | 88GB 88Mia | | 6'4" | 273 | Auburn | | |
| Hill, Randal WR | 91Mia 91-93Phx 94Arz 95Mia | 2 | 5'10" | 177 | Miami (Fla.) | | 48 |
| Hill, Rod DB | 82-83Dal 84-86Buf 86Det 87Raid | 3 | 6' | 186 | Kentucky State | 4 | |
| Hill, Sean DB | 94-95Mia | | 5'10" | 176 | Montana State | | |
| Hill, Tony WR | 77-86Dal | 23 | 6'2" | 199 | Stanford | | 306 |
| Hill, Tony DE | 91-92Dal | | 6'6" | 248 | Tenn.-Chattanooga | | |
| Hill, Travis LB | 94Cle 95Car 95Cle | | 6'2" | 240 | Nebraska | | 6 |
| Hill, Will DB | 88Cle | | 6' | 200 | Bishop | | |
| Hillary, Ira WR | 87-89Cin 90Min | 23 | 5'11" | 190 | South Carolina | | 12 |
| Hilliard, Dalton HB-FB | 86-93NO | 2 | 5'8" | 204 | Louisiana State | | 318 |
| Hilliard, Randy DB | 90-93Cle 94-95Den | | 5'11" | 162 | Northwestern La. | 4 | |
| Hilton, Carl TE | 86-89Min | | 6'3" | 232 | Houston | | 18 |
| Hines, Andre TE | 80Sea 83USFL | | 6'6" | 275 | Stanford | | |
| Hinkle, Bryan LB | 82-93Pit | | 6'1" | 222 | Oregon | 15 | 18 |
| Hinkle, George DE-NT-DT | 88-91SD 92Min 93Cin | | 6'5" | 273 | Arizona | | |
| Hinnant, Mike TE | 88-89Pit 92Det | | 6'3" | 268 | Temple | | |
| Hinton, Chris OG-OT | 83Bal 84-89Ind 90-93Atl 94-95Min | | 6'4" | 296 | Northwestern | | |
| Hintz, Mike DB | 87Chi | | 6'1" | 190 | Wis.-Platteville | | |
| Hipp, I.M. HB | 80Oak | | 5'10" | 200 | Nebraska | | |
| Hipple, Eric QB | 80-86Det 87RJ 88-89Det | 12 | 6'2" | 197 | Utah State | | 78 |
| Hire, Doug C | 87Sea | | 6'2" | 245 | Linfield | | |
| Hirsch, Steve DB | 87Det | | 6' | 195 | Northern Illinois | | |
| Hitchcock, Bill OT-OG | 91-94Sea | | 6'6" | 296 | Purdue | | |
| Hitchcock, Jimmy DB | 95NE | | 5'10" | 188 | North Carolina | | |
| Hitchcock, Ray C-OG | 87Was 88KJ | | 6'2" | 289 | Minnesota | | |
| Hoage, Terry DB | 84-85NO 86-90Phi 91Was 92AJ 93SF 93Hou 94-95Arz | | 6'3" | 199 | Georgia | 21 | 12 |
| Hoard, Leroy FB | 90-95Cle | 2 | 5'11" | 230 | Michigan | | 138 |
| Hobbs, Daryl WR | 93-94Raid 95Oak | 2 | 6'2" | 180 | U. of Pacific | | 18 |
| Hobbs, Stephen WR | 90-92Was 93TJ | | 5'11" | 195 | North Alabama | | 6 |
| Hobby, Marion DE | 90-92NE | | 6'4" | 277 | Tennessee | | |
| Hobbins, Jim OG | 87GB | | 6'6" | 275 | Minnesota | | |
| Hobert, Billy Joe QB | 93Raid 95Oak | 1 | 6'3" | 225 | Washington | | |
| Hobley, Liffort DB | 85StL 88-93Mia | | 6' | 204 | Louisiana State | 5 | 12 |
| Hodge, Floyd WR | 82-84Atl | 2 | 6' | 193 | Utah | | 24 |
| Hodge, Milford DE-NT | 86NO 86-89NE | | 6'3" | 275 | Washington State | | |
| Hodges, Eric WR | 87KC | | 6'1" | 189 | Florida | | |
| Hodson, Tom QB | 90-92NE 95NO | 1 | 6'3" | 195 | Louisiana State | | |
| Hoffman, Dave LB | 93Pit | | 6'2" | 233 | Washington | | |
| Hoffman, Gary OT | 84GB 87SF | | 6'7" | 284 | Santa Clara | | |
| Hogan, Mark DB | 87NYJ | | 6' | 180 | Baruch | 1 | |
| Hoge, Merril HB-FB | 87-93Pit 94Chi | 2 | 6'2" | 224 | Idaho State | | 204 |
| Hogeboom, Gary QB | 80-85Dal 86-88Ind 89Phx 90Was | 12 | 6'4" | 204 | Central Michigan | | 24 |
| Hoggard, D.D. DB | 84USFL 85-87Cle | | 6' | 188 | N. Carolina State | | |
| Hohensee, Mike QB | 87Chi | 1 | 6' | 205 | Minnesota | | |
| Hoke, Jonathan DB | 80Chi | | 5'11" | 175 | Ball State | | |
| Hold, Mike QB | 87TB | | 6' | 190 | South Carolina | | |
| Holecek, John LB | 95Buf | | 6'2" | 238 | Illinois | | |
| Holifield, John HB | 89Cin | | 6' | 202 | West Virginia | | |
| Holland, Darius DT | 95GB | | 6'5" | 305 | Colorado | | |
| Holland, Jamie WR-HB | 87-89SD 90-91Raid 92Cle | 23 | 6'2" | 192 | Ohio State | | 12 |
| Holland, Johnny LB | 87-93GB | | 6'2" | 231 | Texas A&M | 7 | |
| Hollas, Donald QB | 91-92Cin 93IL 94Cin | 12 | 6'3" | 215 | Rice | | |
| Holle, Eric DE-NT | 84-87KC | | 6'5" | 260 | Texas | | |
| Holliday, Corey WR | 95Pit | | 6'2" | 208 | North Carolina | | |
| Hollie, Doug DE | 87-88Sea | | 6'4" | 265 | S.M.U. | | |
| Hollier, Dwight LB | 92-95Mia | | 6'2" | 249 | North Carolina | 1 | |
| Hollinquest, Lamont LB | 94Was | | 6'3" | 245 | Southern Calif. | 1 | |
| Hollis, David DB | 87-88Sea 88KC 88-89Sea | 3 | 5'11" | 178 | Nevada-Las Vegas | 2 | |
| Hollis, Mike K | 95Jax | 5 | 5'7" | 180 | Idaho | | 87 |
| Hollingsworth, Shawn OT | 83Den | | 6'2" | 260 | New Mexico | | |
| Hollinquest, Lamont LB | 93Was | | 6'3" | 245 | Southern Calif. | | |
| Holloway, Brian OT-OG | 81-86NE 87-88Raid | | 6'7" | 284 | Stanford | | |
| Holloway, Cornell DB | 90-92Ind | | 5'11" | 182 | Pittsburgh | 1 | |
| Holloway, Derek WR | 83-85USFL 86Was 87FB | | 5'7" | 166 | Arkansas | | |
| Holloway, Johnny DB | 86Dal 87StL | | 5'11" | 182 | Kansas | 1 | |
| Holloway, Randy DE | 78-84Min 84StL 85USFL | | 6'5" | 250 | Pittsburgh | 1 | 8 |
| Holloway, Steve TE | 87TB | 2 | 6'3" | 235 | Tennessee State | | |
| Holloway, Stan LB | 80NO | | 6'2" | 218 | California | | |
| Holloway, Tony DE-LB | 87KC | | 6'2" | 222 | Nebraska | | |
| Holly, Bob QB | 82-83Was 84Phi 84-85Atl | 1 | 6'2" | 197 | Princeton | | 6 |
| Holman, Rodney TE | 82-92Cin 93-95Det | 2 | 6'3" | 235 | Tulane | | 216 |
| Holman, Scott WR | 86StL 87NYJ | 2 | 6'2" | 194 | Oregon | | |
| Holman, Walter FB | 87Was | | 5'10" | 208 | West Virginia State | | |
| Holmberg, Rob LB | 94Raid 95Oak | | 6'3" | 228 | Penn State | | |
| Holmes, Bruce LB | 87KC 93Min | | 6'2" | 235 | Minnesota | | |
| Holmes, Clayton DB | 92Dal 93KJ 94Det 95Dal | | 5'10" | 181 | Carson-Newman | 1 | |
| Holmes, Darick HB-FB | 95Buf | 23 | 6' | 226 | Portland State | | 24 |
| Holmes, Darryl DB | 87-89NE | | 6'2" | 190 | Ft. Valley State | 1 | |
| Holmes, Don WR | 86-87StL 88-90Phx | 2 | 5'10" | 180 | Colorado, Mesa | | 6 |
| Holmes, Jack FB-HB | 78-82NO 83USFL | 2 | 5'11" | 210 | Texas Southern | | 30 |
| Holmes, Jerry DB | 80-83NYJ 84-85USFL 86-87NYJ 88-89Det 90-91GB | | 6'2" | 175 | West Virginia | 25 | 18 |

| Use Name (Nickname) - Positions | Team by Year | See Section | Hgt. | Wgt. | College | Int | Pts |
|---|---|---|---|---|---|---|---|
| Holmes, Lester OG | 93-95Phi | | 6'3" | 302 | Jackson State | | |
| Holmes, Ron DE | 85-88TB 89-92Den | | 6'4" | 261 | Washington | | |
| Holmgren, Mike | HC92-95GB | | | | Southern Calif. | | |
| Holmoe, Tom DB | 83-84SF 85SJ 86-89SF | | 6'2" | 190 | Brigham Young | 7 | 12 |
| Holohan, Pete TE | 81-87SD 88-90LA 91KC 92Cle | 2 | 6'4" | 237 | Notre Dame | | 96 |
| Holston, Mike WR | 81-85Hou 86KC | 2 | 6'3" | 189 | Morgan State | | 24 |
| Holt, Harry TE | 83-86Cle 87SD | 2 | 6'4" | 236 | Arizona | | 36 |
| Holt, Issiac DB | 85-89Min 89-92Dal | | 6'2" | 200 | Alcorn State | 23 | 22 |
| Holt, John DB | 81-85TB 86-88Ind | 3 | 5'11" | 179 | West Texas State | 7 | |
| Holt, Pierce DE-DT | 88-92SF 93-95Atl | | 6'4" | 280 | Angelo State | | |
| Holt, Robert WR | 82Buf 83KJ | | 6'1" | 182 | Baylor | | |
| Homco, Thomas LB | 93-94LA 95StL | | 6' | 245 | Northwestern | 1 | |
| Hons, Todd QB | 87Det | 1 | 6'1" | 195 | Arizona State | | |
| Hood, Estus DB | 78-84GB | | 5'11" | 183 | Illinois State | 11 | 6 |
| Hood, Winford OG-OT | 84-88Den | | 6'3" | 262 | Georgia | | |
| Hooks, Alvin HB | 81Phi 83USFL | | 5'11" | 170 | Northridge State | | |
| Hooper, Trell DB | 87Mia | | 5'11" | 182 | Memphis State | 2 | 6 |
| Hoover, Houston OT-OG | 88-92Atl 93Cle 94Mia | | 6'2" | 293 | Jackson State | | |
| Hoover, Melvin WR | 82-84Phi 87Det | 2 | 6' | 185 | Arizona State | | 12 |
| Hope, Charles OG-C | 94GB | | 6'3" | 303 | Central St.-Ohio | | |
| Hope, Neil LB | 87LA | | 6'2" | 235 | Southern Calif. | | |
| Hopkins, Brad OT | 93-95Hou | | 6'3" | 306 | Illinois | | |
| Hopkins, Thomas OT | 83Cle | | 6'6" | 260 | Alabama A&M | | |
| Hopkins, Wes DB | 83-86Phi 87KJ 88-93Phi | | 6'1" | 213 | S.M.U. | 30 | 6 |
| Hopper, Darrel DB | 87SD | | 6'1" | 196 | Southern Calif. | | |
| Hoppock, Doug OT-OG | 87KC | | 6'4" | 280 | Kansas State | | |
| Horan, Mike K | 84-85Phi 86-92Den 93-95NYG | 4 | 5'11" | 188 | Long Beach State | | |
| Horn, Alvin DB | 87Cle | | 5'11" | 185 | Nevada-Las Vegas | 1 | |
| Horn, Bob LB | 76-81SD 82-83SF 84USFL | | 6'3" | 233 | Oregon State | 7 | |
| Horn, Marty QB | 87Phi | | 6'2" | 206 | Lehigh | | |
| Horn, Rod NT | 80-81Cin | | 6'4" | 268 | Nebraska | | |
| Horne, Greg K | 87Cin 87StL 88Phx | | 6' | 188 | Arkansas | | |
| Horton, Ethan FB-TE | 85KC 87,89-93Raid 94Was | 2 | 6'4" | 233 | North Carolina | | 120 |
| Horton, Ray DB | 83-88Cin 89-92Dal | | 5'11" | 190 | Washington | 19 | 30 |
| Hoskins, Derrick DB | 92-94Raid 95Oak | | 6'2" | 200 | Southern Miss. | 3 | |
| Hostetler, Jeff QB | 84-92NYG 93-94Raid 95Oak | 12 | 6'3" | 212 | West Virginia | | 96 |
| Hough, Jim OG-C | 78-86Min | | 6'2" | 268 | Utah State | | |
| House, Kevin WR | 80-86TB 86-87LA | 2 | 6'1" | 181 | Southern Illinois | | 204 |
| Housman, Walter OT-OG | 87NO | | 6'5" | 285 | Iowa, Upsala | | |
| Houston, Bobby LB | 90GB 92-95NYJ | | 6'2" | 239 | N. Carolina State | 2 | 6 |
| Howard, Anthony NT | 87NYG | | 6'3" | 267 | Tennessee | | |
| Howard, Bobby HB-FB | 86-88TB | 2 | 6' | 213 | Indiana | | 12 |
| Howard, Bryan DB | 82Min 84-85USFL | | 6' | 200 | Tennessee State | | |
| Howard, Carl DB | 84Dal 85TB 85-90NYJ | | 6'2" | 190 | Rutgers | 5 | |
| Howard, Dana LB | 95StL | | 6' | 238 | Illinois | | |
| Howard, David LB | 84-85USFL 85-89Min 89-90Dal 91-92NE | | 6'1" | 231 | Oregon State, Long Beach State | 5 | |
| Howard, Desmond WR | 92-94Was 95Jax | 23 | 5'9" | 182 | Michigan | | 44 |
| Howard, Erik NT-DT-DE | 86-94NYG 95NYJ | | 6'4" | 269 | Washington State | | 2 |
| Howard, Joey OT | 89SD | | 6'6" | 305 | Tennessee | | |
| Howard, Paul OG | 73-75Den 76JJ 77-86Den | | 6'3" | 260 | Brigham Young | | |
| Howard, Todd LB | 87-88KC | | 6'2" | 235 | Texas A&M | | |
| Howard, Tom LB | 77-83KC 84-85StL | | 6'2" | 213 | Texas Tech | 7 | 18 |
| Howard, William FB-HB | 88-89TB | 2 | 6' | 240 | Tennessee | | 18 |
| Howe, Garry NT | 92Pit 93Cin 94Ind | | 6'1" | 298 | Drake, Colorado | | |
| Howe, Glen OT | 85Pit 85-86Atl | | 6'7" | 295 | Southern Miss. | | |
| Howell, Pat OG | 79-83Atl 83-85Hou | | 6'5" | 257 | Southern Calif. | | |
| Howell, Steve FB-TE | 79-81Mia 83USFL | 2 | 6'2" | 227 | Baylor | | 6 |
| Howfield, Ian K | 91Hou | 5 | 6'2" | 196 | Tennessee | | 64 |
| Hoyem, Steve OT | 94Buf | | 6'7" | 287 | Stanford | | |
| Hubach, Mike K | 80-81NE | 4 | 5'10" | 185 | Kansas | | |
| Huckleby, Harlan HB | 80-85GB | 23 | 6'1" | 200 | Michigan | | 84 |
| Huddleston, Jim OG-OT | 87TB 87Mia | | 6'4" | 280 | Virginia | | |
| Hudson, Chris DB | 95Jax | | 5'10" | 203 | Colorado | | |
| Hudson, Doug QB | 87KC | | 6'2" | 201 | Nicholls State | | |
| Hudson, Gordon TE | 84-85USFL 86Sea | 2 | 6'4" | 241 | Brigham Young | | 6 |
| Hudson, John OG-C | 91-95Phi | | 6'2" | 275 | Auburn | | |
| Hudson, Mike DB | 87SD | | 6' | 202 | Oklahoma State | | |
| Hudson, Nat OG | 81NO 82Bal 84-85USFL | | 6'3" | 268 | Georgia | | |
| Huff, Alan NT | 87Pit | | 6'4" | 265 | Marshall | | |
| Huff, Charles DB | 87Atl | | 5'11" | 195 | Presbyterian | 2 | |
| Huff, Ken OG | 75-82Bal 83-85Was | | 6'4" | 260 | North Carolina | | |
| Huffman, Darvell WR | 91Ind | | 5'8" | 158 | Boston U. | | |
| Huffman, Dave OG-C-OT | 79-83Min 84-85USFL 85-90Min | | 6'6" | 271 | Notre Dame | | |
| Huffman, Tim OT-OG | 81-85GB | | 6'5" | 279 | Notre Dame | | |
| Hugger, Keith WR | 83NYG | | 5'11" | 175 | Connecticut | | |
| Hughes, Danan WR | 93-95KC | 23 | 6'1" | 201 | Iowa | | 6 |
| Hughes, David FB | 81-85Sea 86Pit | 2 | 6' | 220 | Boise State | | 42 |
| Hughes, Ernie OG-C | 78SF 79KJ 80SF 81-83NYG | | 6'3" | 259 | Notre Dame | | |
| Hughes, Tyrone DB | 93-95NO | 3 | 5'9" | 175 | Nebraska | 4 | 42 |
| Hughes, Van DE | 84-85USFL 86StL 87Sea | | 6'3" | 280 | SW Texas State | | |
| Hull, Kent C | 83-85USFL 86-95Buf | | 6'4" | 279 | Mississippi State | | |
| Humiston, Mike LB | 81Buf 82Bal 83NJ 84Ind 87SD | | 6'3" | 240 | Weber State | | 2 |
| Humphery, Bobby WR-DB | 84-89NYJ 90LA | 23 | 5'10" | 178 | New Mexico State | 5 | 32 |
| Humphrey, Bobby HB | 89-91Den 92Mia 93KJ | 2 | 6'1" | 201 | Alabama | | 102 |
| Humphrey, Donnie DE | 84-86GB | | 6'3" | 282 | Auburn | | |
| Humphrey, Ronald HB | 94-95Ind | 3 | 5'10" | 211 | Miss. Valley St. | | 6 |
| Humphrey, Tom OG-OT | 87NYJ | | 6'3" | 280 | Iowa | | |
| Humphries, Leonard DB | 94Ind | | 5'9" | 180 | Penn State | 1 | |
| Humphries, Stan QB | 89-91Was 92-95SD | 12 | 6'2" | 223 | Louisiana State, Northeast La. | | 42 |
| Humphries, Stefan OG | 84-86Chi 87-88Den | | 6'3" | 266 | Michigan | | |
| Hunley, Lamonte LB | 85-86Ind | | 6'2" | 240 | Arizona | | |
| Hunley, Ricky LB | 84-87Den 88Phx 89-90Raid | | 6'2" | 242 | Arizona | 3 | 6 |
| Hunt, Byron LB | 81-88NYG | | 6'5" | 238 | S.M.U. | 2 | |
| Hunt, Daryl LB | 79-84Hou | | 6'3" | 229 | Oklahoma | | |
| Hunt, Gary DB | 87Cin | | 5'11" | 175 | Memphis | | |
| Hunt, John OG | 87TB | | 6'5" | 245 | Florida | | |
| Hunt, John OT | 84Dal | | 6'4" | 254 | Florida | | |
| Hunter, Daniel DB | 85-86Den 86-87SD | | 5'11" | 178 | Henderson State | 1 | |
| Hunter, Earnest HB | 95Cle | 2 | 5'8" | 201 | Southeastern Okla. | | |
| Hunter, Eddie HB | 87NYJ 87TB | 2 | 5'11" | 205 | Virginia Tech | | 12 |
| Hunter, Hal | HC84Ind | | | | Pittsburgh | | |
| Hunter, Herman HB | 85Phi 86Det 87Hou | 23 | 6'1" | 197 | Tennessee State | | 18 |
| Hunter, Ivy Joe FB-HB | 89-91Ind 92KJ | 2 | 6' | 237 | Kentucky | | |
| Hunter, James NT-DE | 82Bal | | 6'5" | 251 | Southern Calif. | | |
| Hunter, Jeff DE | 90Buf 90-92Det 92-93Mia 94TB | | 6'2" | 285 | Albany State | | |
| Hunter, John OT | 89-91Atl 92Sea | | 6'8" | 296 | Brigham Young | | |

| Use Name (Nickname) - Positions | Team by Year | See Section | Hgt. | Wgt. | College | Int | Pts |
|---|---|---|---|---|---|---|---|
| Hunter, Monty DB | 82Dal 83StL | | 6' | 202 | Salem | | |
| Hunter, Patrick DB | 86-94Sea 95Arz | | 5'11" | 185 | Nevada-Reno | 14 | 6 |
| Hunter, Stan WR | 87NYJ | | 6'2" | 184 | Bowling Green | | 6 |
| Hunter, Tony TE | 83-84Buf 85-86LA | 2 | 6'4' | 237 | Notre Dame | | 54 |
| Hunter, Tony FB | 87GB | | 5'9" | 215 | Minnesota | | |
| Hunter, Torey DB | 95Hou | | 5'9" | 176 | Washington State | | |
| Huntington, Greg C-OG | 93Was 95Was | | 6'3" | 287 | Penn State | | |
| Hurd, Jeff LB | 87Dal 88-89KJ | | 6'2" | 245 | Kansas State | | |
| Hurley, Bill DB | 81-83NO 83Buf | | 5'11" | 195 | Syracuse | 1 | 6 |
| Hurst, Maurice DB | 89-95NE | | 5'10" | 185 | Southern U. | 27 | 6 |
| Hurt, Eric DB | 80Dal | | 5'11" | 171 | San Jose State | | |
| Husted, Michael K | 93-95TB | 5 | 6' | 190 | Virginia | | 246 |
| Hutchins, Paul OT | 93-94GB 95XJ | | 6'5" | 335 | Western Michigan | | |
| Hutchinson, Anthony HB | 83-84Chi | | 5'10" | 186 | Texas Tech | | 12 |
| Hutchinson, Scott DE | 78-80Buf 81TB 83Buf 85USFL | | 6'4" | 246 | Florida | | |
| Huther, Bruce LB | 77-80Dal 81Cle 82Chi 83Dal 84USFL | | 6'1" | 221 | New Hampshire | | |
| Hutson, Brian DB | 90NE | | 6'1" | 198 | Mississippi State | | |
| Hutton, Tom K | 95Phi | 4 | 6'1" | 193 | Tennessee | | |
| Hyche, Steve LB | 89Chi 91-93Phx | | 6'3" | 241 | Livingston | | |
| Hyde, Glenn OT-OG-C | 74-75WFL 76-81Den 82Bal 83USFL 85Den 86Sea 87KC | | 6'3" | 253 | Pittsburgh | | |
| Iaquiniello, Mike DB | 91Mia | | 6'3" | 208 | Michigan State | | |
| Igwebuike, Donald K | 85-89TB 90Min | 5 | 5'9" | 181 | Clemson | | 477 |
| Ilesic, Hank K | 89SD | 4 | 6'1" | 210 | none | | |
| Ilkin, Tunch OT-OG-C | 80-92Pit 93GB | | 6'3" | 263 | Indiana State | | |
| Infante, Lindy | HC88-91GB | | | | Florida | | |
| Inglis, Tim LB | 87-88Cin | | 6'3" | 232 | Toledo | | |
| Ingram, Brian LB | 82-85NE 86KJ 87SD | | 6'4" | 236 | Tennessee | | |
| Ingram, Byron OG | 87-88KC 89TB | | 6'2" | 295 | Eastern Kentucky | | |
| Ingram, Darryl TE | 89Min 91Cle 92-93GB | | 6'2" | 240 | California | | 6 |
| Ingram, Kevin QB | 87NO | | 6' | 178 | East Carolina | | |
| Ingram, Mark WR | 87-92NYG 93-94Mia 95GB | 23 | 5'10" | 188 | Michigan State | | 156 |
| Ingram, Stephen Ot-OG | 95TB | | 6'4" | 311 | Maryland | | |
| Inverso, Glenn QB | 84NYJ | | 6'1" | 199 | Liberty | | |
| Ireland, Darwin LB | 94-95Chi | | 5'11" | 240 | Arkansas | | |
| Irvin, Darrell DE | 80-82Buf 83Sea | | 6'4" | 259 | Oklahoma | | |
| Irvin, Ken DB | 95Buf | | 5'10" | 182 | Memphis | | |
| Irvin, LeRoy DB | 80-89LA 90Det | 3 | 5'11" | 183 | Kansas | 35 | 66 |
| Irvin, Mark DB | 87Mia | | 5'10" | 190 | Bethune-Cookman | | |
| Irvin, Michael WR | 88-95Dal | 2 | 6'2" | 202 | Miami (Fla.) | | 300 |
| Irving, Terry LB | 94-95Arz | | 6' | 224 | McNeese State | | |
| Irwin, Tim OT | 81-93Min 94Mia | | 6'6" | 292 | Tennessee | | |
| Ismail, Qadry WR | 93-95Min | 23 | 6' | 192 | Syracuse | | 54 |
| Ismail, Raghib (Rocket) WR | 93-94Raid 95Oak | 23 | 5'10" | 180 | Notre Dame | | 54 |
| Isom, Ray DB | 87-88TB | | 5'9" | 190 | Penn State | 2 | |
| Isom, Rickey FB | 87Mia | | 6' | 224 | N. Carolina State | | 6 |
| Israel, Steve DB | 92-94LA 95SF | | 5'10" | 186 | Pittsburgh | | |
| Ivery, Eddie Lee HB-FB | 79-86GB 87XJ | 2 | 6'1" | 210 | Georgia Tech | | 180 |
| Ivlow, John FB | 93Chi | | 5'11" | 226 | Northwestern, Colorado State | | |
| Jack, Eric DB | 94Atl | | 5'10" | 177 | New Mexico | | 6 |
| Jacke, Chris K | 89-95GB | 5 | 6' | 197 | Texas-El Paso | | 706 |
| Jackson, Al DB | 94Phi 95KJ | | 6' | 182 | Georgia | | |
| Jackson, Alfred WR | 78-84Atl | 2 | 5'11" | 176 | Texas | | 132 |
| Jackson, Alfred DB | 89-90LA 91-92Cle 95Min | | 6' | 179 | San Diego State | 3 | 6 |
| Jackson, Andrew HB | 87Hou | 2 | 5'10" | 190 | Iowa State | | 6 |
| Jackson, Bill DB | 82Cle | | 6'1" | 202 | North Carolina | | |
| Jackson, Billy FB-HB | 81-84KC | 2 | 5'10" | 217 | Alabama | | 108 |
| Jackson, Bo HB | 87-90Raid | 2 | 6'1" | 227 | Auburn | | 108 |
| 86-90,93 played major league baseball | | | | | | | |
| Jackson, Bobby DB | 78-85NYJ | | 5'9" | 178 | Florida State | 21 | 18 |
| Jackson, Calvin DB | 94-95Mia | | 5'10" | 179 | Auburn | 1 | |
| Jackson, Charles LB | 78-84KC 85-86NYJ | | 6'2" | 225 | Washington | 1 | 6 |
| Jackson, Charles DB | 87Was | | 6'4" | 210 | Texas Tech | | |
| Jackson, Cedric HB-FB | 91Det | | 5'11" | 229 | Texas Christian | | |
| Jackson, Cleveland TE | 79NYG 84USFL | | 6'4" | 230 | Nevada-Las Vegas | | |
| Jackson, David WR | 87TB | | 5'8" | 175 | SE Missouri St. | | |
| Jackson, Earnest HB-FB | 83-84SD 85Phi 86-88Pit | 2 | 5'9" | 213 | Texas A&M | | 144 |
| Jackson, Enis DB | 87Cle | | 5'9" | 180 | Memphis State | | |
| Jackson, Greg DB | 89-93NYG 94-95Phi | | 6'1" | 200 | Louisiana State | 21 | 12 |
| Jackson, Jeff LB | 84-85Atl 87-88SD | | 6'1" | 232 | Auburn | 1 | 6 |
| Jackson, Joe LB | 87Sea | | 6'1" | 225 | San Fran. State | | |
| Jackson, John OT | 88-95Pit | | 6'6" | 292 | Eastern Kentucky | | |
| Jackson, John WR | 90-92Phx | 3 | 5'10" | 175 | Southern Calif. | | 6 |
| Jackson, Johnny DB | 89-92SF 92GB | | 6'1" | 204 | Houston | 3 | 6 |
| Jackson, Keith TE | 88-91Phi 92-94Mia 95GB | 2 | 6'2" | 250 | Oklahoma | | 236 |
| Jackson, Kenny WR | 84-88Phi 89Hou 90-91Phi | 2 | 6' | 180 | Penn State | | 66 |
| Jackson, Kirby DB | 87LA 88-92Buf 93-94KJ | | 5'10" | 179 | Mississippi State | 6 | 12 |
| Jackson, Lawrence OG | 87Atl | | 6'1" | 275 | Presbyterian | | |
| Jackson, Leonard LB | 87Chi 87Raid | | 6' | 240 | Oklahoma State | | |
| Jackson, Louis HB | 81NYG 83-85USFL | 2 | 5'11" | 195 | Cal. Poly.-S.L.O. | | 6 |
| Jackson, Marcus DE-NT | 87Ind | | 6'5" | 260 | Purdue | | |
| Jackson, Mark WR | 86-92Den 93-94NYG 94Ind | 2 | 5'9" | 177 | Purdue | | 180 |
| Jackson, Mark DB | 87StL | | 5'9" | 180 | Abilene Christian | | 6 |
| Jackson, Michael LB | 79-86Sea | | 6'1" | 222 | Washington | 6 | |
| Jackson, Michael WR | 91-95Cle | 2 | 6'4" | 195 | Southern Miss. | | 168 |
| Jackson, Rickey LB-DE | 81-93NO 94SF | | 6'2" | 239 | Pittsburgh | 8 | 2 |
| Jackson, Robert LB | 78-81Cle 82Atl | | 6'1" | 230 | Texas A&M | 2 | |
| Jackson, Robert DB | 82-87Cin 88HO 89Cin | | 5'10" | 186 | Central Michigan | 15 | 12 |
| Jackson, Robert OG-OT-C | 75-85Cle | | 6'5" | 255 | Duke | | |
| Jackson, Roger DB | 82-85,87Den | | 6' | 186 | Bethune-Cookman | 2 | |
| Jackson, Steve DB | 91-95Hou | | 5'8" | 185 | Purdue | 11 | 6 |
| Jackson, Terry DB | 78-83NYG 84-85Sea | | 5'10" | 197 | San Diego State | 28 | 30 |
| Jackson, Tim DB | 89Dal | | 5'11" | 192 | Kansas State, Nebraska | | |
| Jackson, Tyoka DE | 94Mia | | 6'1" | 266 | Penn State | | |
| Jackson, Vestee DB | 86-90Chi 91-93Mia | | 6' | 189 | Washington | 18 | 12 |
| Jackson, Victor DB | 86Ind 87Raid | | 6' | 205 | Bowie State | | |
| Jackson, Willie WR | 95Jax | 2 | 6'1" | 203 | Florida | | 32 |
| Jacobs, Cam LB | 87TB | | 6'2" | 230 | Kentucky | | |
| Jacobs, Dave K | 79NYJ 81Cle 83USFL 87Phi | 5 | 5'7" | 152 | Syracuse | | 57 |
| Jacobs, Ray LB | 94-95Den | | 6'2" | 244 | North Carolina | | |
| Jacobs, Tim DB | 93-95Cle | | 5'10" | 185 | Delaware | 2 | |
| Jacobson, Steve OG | 87Mia | | 6'3" | 255 | Abilene Christian | | |
| Jacoby, Joe OT-OG | 81-93Was | | 6'7" | 305 | Louisville | | 6 |
| Jaeger, Jeff K | 87Cle 88FJ 89-94Raid 95Oak | 5 | 5'11" | 192 | Washington | | 742 |
| Jakes, Van DB | 83-84KC 85USFL 86-88NO 89GB | | 6' | 188 | Kent State | 8 | |
| James, Angelo DB | 87Phi | | 6' | 180 | Sacramento State | | |
| James, Arrike TE | 87Hou | | 6'4" | 238 | Delta State | | |

| Use Name (Nickname) - Positions | Team by Year | See Section | Hgt. | Wgt. | College | Int | Pts |
|---|---|---|---|---|---|---|---|
| James, Craig FB-HB | 83-84USFL 84-88NE | 2 | 6' | 215 | S.M.U. | | 114 |
| James, Garry HB | 86-88Det | 2 | 5'10" | 214 | Louisiana State | | 84 |
| James, Jesse C | 95StL | | 6'4" | 311 | Mississippi State | | |
| James, June LB | 85Det 87Ind | | 6'1" | 227 | Texas | | |
| James, Lionel WR-HB | 84-88SD | 23 | 5'7" | 170 | Auburn | | 96 |
| James, Lynn WR | 90-91Cin 91Cle | 2 | 6' | 191 | S.M.U., Arizona St. | | 6 |
| James, Phillip C-OG | 87NO | | 6'2" | 265 | Southern U. | | |
| James, Roland DB | 80-90NE | 3 | 6'2" | 190 | Tennessee | 29 | 8 |
| Jamison, George LB | 87-93Det 94-95KC | | 6'1" | 230 | Cincinnati | 8 | 20 |
| Janata, John OT | 83Chi | | 6'7" | 274 | Illinois | | |
| January, Mike LB | 87Chi | | 6'1" | 234 | Texas | | |
| Jarostchuk, Ilia LB | 87StL 88Mia 89Phx 90NE 91AJ | | 6'3" | 231 | New Hampshire | | |
| Jarvis, Curt DE-NT | 87-90TB | | 6'2" | 265 | Alabama | | |
| Jarvis, Ralph DE | 90Ind | | 6'4" | 255 | Temple | | |
| Jasper, Vince OG | 87NYJ | | 6'4" | 270 | Iowa State | | |
| Jaworski, Matt LB | 91Ind | | 6'1" | 226 | Colgate | | |
| Jaworski, Ron QB | 74-76LA 77-86Phi 87-88Mia 89KC | 12 | 6'2" | 195 | Youngstown State | | 96 |
| Jax, Garth LB | 86-88Dal 89-93Phx 94-95Arz | | 6'2" | 244 | Florida State | 2 | |
| Jay, Craig TE | 87GB | | 6'4" | 257 | Mt. Senario | | |
| Jean-Batiste, Garland FB | 87NO | | 6' | 208 | Louisiana State | | |
| Jeffcoat, Jim DE-DT | 83-94Dal 95Buf | | 6'5" | 271 | Arizona State | 2 | 18 |
| Jefferson, Ben OG | 90Cle | | 6'9" | 330 | Maryland | | |
| Jefferson, Greg DE | 95Phi | | 6'3" | 257 | Central Florida | | |
| Jefferson, James DB | 89-93Sea | 3 | 6'1" | 199 | Texas A&I | 2 | 6 |
| Jefferson, John (J.J.) WR | 78-80SD 81-84GB 85Cle | 2 | 6'1" | 198 | Arizona State | | 282 |
| Jefferson, Kevin LB | 94-95Cin | | 6'2" | 232 | Lehigh | | |
| Jefferson, Norman DB | 87-88GB | | 5'10" | 183 | Louisiana State | | |
| Jefferson, Shawn WR | 91-95SD | 2 | 5'11" | 172 | Central Florida | | 60 |
| Jefferson, Thad LB | 87Hou | | 5'11" | 225 | Hawaii | | |
| Jeffery, Tony HB | 88Phx | | 5'11" | 208 | Texas Christian | | |
| Jeffires, Haywood WR | 87-95Hou | 2 | 6'2" | 199 | N. Carolina State | | 288 |
| Jeffries, Curtis TE | 87Cin | | 6'4" | 236 | Louisville | | |
| Jeffries, Dameian DE | 95NO | | 6'4" | 277 | Alabama | | |
| Jeffries, Eric DB | 87Chi | | 5'10" | 161 | Texas | | |
| Jeffries, Greg DB | 93-95Det | | 5'9" | 184 | Virginia | | |
| Jelesky, Tom OT | 85-86Phi | | 6'6" | 275 | Purdue | | |
| Jenkins, A.J. LB-DE | 89-90Pit | | 6'2" | 237 | Fullerton State | | |
| Jenkins, Carlos LB | 91-94Min 95StL | | 6'3" | 220 | Michigan State | 3 | 12 |
| Jenkins, Fletcher DE-NT | 82Bal 84-85USFL | | 6'2" | 258 | Washington | | |
| Jenkins, Izel DB | 88-92Phi 93Min 93NYG | | 5'10" | 191 | N. Carolina State | 4 | 2 |
| Jenkins, James TE | 91-95Was | | 6'2" | 238 | Rutgers | | 24 |
| Jenkins, Ken HB | 83-84Det 85-86Was | 23 | 5'8" | 184 | Bucknell | | 6 |
| Jenkins, Keyvan HB | 87SD 88KC | | 5'10" | 191 | Nevada-Las Vegas | | |
| Jenkins, Melvin DB | 87-90Sea 91-92Det 93Atl 93Det | | 5'10" | 172 | Cincinnati | 11 | 6 |
| Jenkins, Robert OT | 87-93LA 94Raid 95Oak | | 6'5" | 285 | U.C.L.A. | | |
| (changed name from Robert Cox in 1991) | | | | | | | |
| Jenkins, Trezelle OT | 95KC | | 6'7" | 322 | Michigan | | |
| Jennings, Dave K | 74-84NYG 85-87NYJ | 4 | 6'4" | 203 | St. Lawrence | | |
| Jennings, Keith TE | 89Dal 91-95Chi | 2 | 6'4" | 251 | Clemson | | 60 |
| Jennings, Stanford HB-FB | 84-90Cin 91NO 92TB | 23 | 6'1" | 205 | Furman | | 120 |
| Jensen, Derrick FB-TE-HB | 79-81Oak 82-86Raid | 2 | 6'1" | 221 | Texas-Arlington | | 54 |
| Jensen, Jim WR-QB-FB-TE | 81-92Mia | 2 | 6'4" | 215 | Boston U. | | 114 |
| Jensen, Russ QB | 83-85USFL 85Raid | | 6'2" | 215 | San Fran. State, Cal. Lutheran | | |
| Jerue, Mark LB | 83-89LA | | 6'3" | 231 | Washington | 2 | |
| Jervey, Travis HB | 95GB | | 6' | 225 | The Citadel | | |
| Jessie, Tim HB | 87Was | | 5'11" | 190 | Auburn | | 6 |
| Jeter, Gary DE-DT | 77-82NYG 83-88LA 89NE | | 6'4" | 259 | Southern Calif. | 2 | |
| Jeter, Tommy DT | 92-94Phi 95IJ | | 6'5" | 282 | Texas | | |
| Jett, James WR | 93-94Raid 95Oak | 2 | 5'10" | 165 | West Virginia | | 24 |
| Jett, John K | 93-95Dal | 4 | 6' | 189 | East Carolina | | |
| Jetton, Paul OG-C | 89-91Cin 92-93NO | | 6'4" | 292 | Texas | | |
| Jiles, Dwayne LB | 85-89Phi 89NYG | | 6'4" | 244 | Texas Tech | | |
| Jimerson, A.J. LB | 90-91Raid | | 6'3" | 233 | Norfolk State | | |
| Jodat, Jim FB-HB | 77-79LA 80-81Sea 82-83SD | 23 | 5'11" | 211 | Carthage | | 60 |
| Joelson, Greg DE | 91SF | | 6'3" | 270 | Willamette, Arizona State | | |
| Johns, Paul WR | 81-84Sea | 23 | 5'11" | 173 | Tulsa | | 56 |
| Johnson, A.J. DB | 89-94Was 95SD | 3 | 5'8" | 176 | SW Texas State | 9 | 12 |
| Johnson, Alex WR | 91Hou | | 5'9" | 167 | Miami (Fla.) | | |
| Johnson, Alonzo LB | 86-87Phi | | 6'3" | 222 | Florida | 3 | |
| Johnson, Anthony FB-HB | 90-93Ind 94NYJ 95Chi 95Car | 2 | 6' | 222 | Notre Dame | | 42 |
| Johnson, Barry WR | 91Cle | | 6'2" | 197 | Maryland | | |
| Johnson, Bill FB | 84-85USFL 85-87Cin | 2 | 6'2" | 230 | Arkansas State | | 6 |
| Johnson, Bill DT | 92-94Cle 95Pit | | 6'4" | 303 | Michigan State | | |
| Johnson, Billy (White Shoes) WR | 74-80Hou 81CFL 82-87Atl 88Was | 23 | 5'9" | 170 | Widener | | 210 |
| Johnson, Bobby DB | 83-84NO 85-86StL 86NO | | 6' | 190 | Texas | 3 | 6 |
| Johnson, Bobby WR | 84-86NYG | 2 | 5'11" | 171 | Kansas | | 120 |
| Johnson, Brad QB | 93-95Min | 1 | 6'5" | 221 | Florida State | | |
| Johnson, Brent C | 87Chi | | 6'2" | 255 | Tenn.-Chattanooga | | |
| Johnson, Butch WR | 76-83Dal 84-85Den | 23 | 6'1" | 189 | Cal.-Riverside | | 168 |
| Johnson, Byron LB | 87Hou | | 6'1" | 220 | Baylor | | |
| Johnson, Cecil LB | 77-85TB | | 6'2" | 230 | Pittsburgh | 9 | |
| Johnson, Charles NT | 77-81Phi 82-84Min | | 6'3" | 266 | Colorado | 5 | 12 |
| Johnson, Charles DB | 79-80SF 81StL | | 5'10" | 180 | Grambling | 2 | |
| Johnson, Charles DT-NT | 79-80GB 82LJ 83GB | | 6'1" | 263 | Maryland | 1 | |
| Johnson, Charles WR | 94-95Pit | 2 | 6' | 189 | Colorado | | 18 |
| Johnson, Christopher DB | 87Phi | | 6'4" | 225 | Millersville | | |
| Johnson, Chuck OT | 92Den | | 6'5" | 275 | Texas | | |
| Johnson, Chuckie DT | 93Phx | | 6'4" | 310 | Auburn | | |
| Johnson, Damian OT-OG | 86-89NYG 90NE | | 6'5" | 290 | Kansas State | | |
| Johnson, Damone TE | 86-92LA | 2 | 6'4" | 230 | Cal.Poly.-S.L.O. | | 108 |
| Johnson, Dan TE | 83-87Mia 88XJ | 2 | 6'3" | 239 | Iowa State | | 96 |
| Johnson, David (D.J.) DB | 89-93Pit 94-95Atl | | 6' | 185 | Kentucky | 19 | 6 |
| Johnson, Demetrious DB | 83-86Det 87Mia 88LJ | | 5'11" | 190 | Missouri | 5 | |
| Johnson, Dennis LB | 80-85Min 85TB | | 6'3" | 233 | Southern Calif. | | |
| Johnson, Donnell OT | 93Cin | | 6'7" | 310 | Johnson C. Smith | | |
| Johnson, Earl DB | 85NO 87Den | | 6' | 195 | South Carolina | | |
| Johnson, Eddie LB | 81-90Cle | | 6'1" | 220 | Louisville | 6 | |
| Johnson, Ellis DT-DE | 95Ind | | 6'2" | 298 | Florida | | |
| Johnson, Filmel DB | 95Buf | | 5'10" | 187 | Illinois | | |
| Johnson, Ezra DE | 77-87GB 88-89Ind 90-91Hou | | 6'4" | 250 | Morris Brown | | |
| Johnson, Flip WR | 88-89Buf | 2 | 5'10" | 185 | McNeese State | | 12 |
| Johnson, Gary (Big Hands) DT-NT | 75-84SD 84-85SF | | 6'2" | 256 | Grambling | 2 | 22 |
| Johnson, Gary Don DT | 80Bal 84USFL | | 6'4" | 263 | Baylor | | |
| Johnson, Gilvanni WR | 87Det | | 6'1" | 195 | Michigan | | |
| Johnson, Greg OG | 88Mia 89KJ | | 6'4" | 295 | Oklahoma | | |

| Use Name (Nickname) - Positions | Team by Year | See Section | Hgt. | Wgt. | College | Int | Pts |
|---|---|---|---|---|---|---|---|
| Johnson, Greggory DB | 81-83Sea 84-85USFL 86Sea 87StL | | 6'1" | 191 | Oklahoma State | | 6 |
| Johnson, Henry LB | 80-83Min | | 6'1" | 235 | Georgia Tech | | |
| Johnson, Herbert WR | 87Chi | | 5'11" | 182 | Missouri | | |
| Johnson, Holbert DB | 87LA | | 5'9" | 180 | New Mexico State | 1 | |
| Johnson, Hoss OT | 87TB | | 6'4" | 295 | Alabama | | |
| Johnson, James LB | 86Det 87SF 87SD | | 6'2" | 236 | San Diego State | | |
| Johnson, Jason WR | 88Den 89Pit | | 5'10" | 179 | Illinois State | | |
| Johnson, Jesse DB | 80-83NYJ 84USFL | | 6'3" | 185 | Colorado | | |
| Johnson, Jimmie TE | 89-91Was 92-93Det 94KC 95Phi | 2 | 6'2" | 246 | Howard | | 24 |
| Johnson, Jimmy | HC89-93Dal | | | | Arkansas | | |
| Johnson, Joe WR | 89-91Was 92Min | 23 | 5'8" | 170 | Notre Dame | | 6 |
| (changed name from Joe Howard in 1991) | | | | | | | |
| Johnson, Joe DE-NT | 94-95NO | | 6'4" | 285 | Louisville | | |
| Johnson, John LB | 91-93SF 94Cin 95NO | | 6'3" | 230 | Clemson | 2 | 6 |
| Johnson, Johnnie DB | 80-88LA 89Sea | | 6'1" | 183 | Texas | 22 | 30 |
| Johnson, Johnny HB | 90-92Phx 93-94NYJ | 2 | 6'2" | 218 | San Jose State | | 156 |
| Johnson, Kelly WR | 87Ind | | 5'8" | 168 | Colorado | | |
| Johnson, Ken DE | 79-84Buf 87KC | | 6'5" | 254 | Knoxville | | 2 |
| Johnson, Ken DB | 89-90Min | | 6'2" | 197 | Florida A&M | | |
| Johnson, Ken DB | 90NYJ | | 6'2" | 208 | Florida A&M | | |
| Johnson, Kenneth DB | 87GB 88XJ | | 6' | 185 | Mississippi State | 1 | |
| Johnson, Kenny DB | 80-86Atl 86-89Hou | 3 | 5'10" | 174 | Mississippi State | 17 | 24 |
| Johnson, Keshon DB | 93-94Chi 94GB 95Chi | | 5'10" | 179 | Arizona | 1 | |
| Johnson, Kevin DT | 95Phi | | 6'1" | 306 | Texas Southern | | 6 |
| Johnson, Lawrence DB | 79-84Cle 84-85Buf 86KJ 87Buf | | 5'11" | 204 | Wisconsin | 9 | |
| Johnson, Lee K | 85-87Hou 87-88Cle 88-95Cin | 4 | 6'2" | 199 | Brigham Young | | 6 |
| Johnson, LeShon HB | 94-95GB 95Arz | 2 | 5'11" | 200 | Northern Illinois | | |
| Johnson, Lonnie TE | 94-95Buf | 2 | 6'3" | 235 | Florida State | | 6 |
| Johnson, M.L. LB | 87-89Sea | | 6'3" | 228 | Hawaii | | |
| Johnson, Mario DT | 92NYJ 93NE | | 6'3" | 292 | Missouri | | |
| Johnson, Mark DB | 87Cin | | 6'1" | 194 | Western Kentucky | | |
| Johnson, Maurice TE | 91-94Phi | 2 | 6'2" | 243 | Temple | | 24 |
| Johnson, Melvin DB | 95TB | | 6' | 191 | Kentucky | 1 | |
| Johnson, Mike DE | 84Hou | | 6'5" | 253 | Illinois | | |
| Johnson, Mike LB | 84-85USFL 86-93Cle 94-95Det | | 6'1" | 227 | Virginia Tech | 10 | 18 |
| Johnson, Nate WR | 80NYG | | 5'11" | 192 | Hillsdale | | |
| Johnson, Nate HB | 87NO | | 6'2" | 224 | Texas Southern | | |
| Johnson, Norm K | 82-90Sea 91-94Atl 95Pit | 5 | 6'2" | 195 | California | | 1346 |
| Johnson, Pat DB | 95Mia | | 6'1" | 204 | Purdue | | 6 |
| Johnson, Pepper LB | 86-92NYG 93-95Cle | | 6'3" | 248 | Ohio State | 12 | 12 |
| Johnson, Pete FB | 77-83Cin 84SD 84Mia | 2 | 6' | 252 | Ohio State | | 492 |
| Johnson, Raylee DE-DT | 93-95SD | | 6'3" | 258 | Arkansas | | |
| Johnson, Reggie TE | 91-93Den 94GB 95Phi | 2 | 6'2" | 256 | Florida State | | 30 |
| Johnson, Richard DB | 85-92Hou | | 6'1" | 192 | Wisconsin | 15 | 6 |
| Johnson, Richard WR | 87Was 89-90Det | 2 | 5'7" | 182 | Colorado | | 84 |
| Johnson, Rick OT | 87Det | | 6'6" | 255 | Grand Valley St. | | |
| Johnson, Rob QB | 95Jax | | 6'3" | 222 | Southern Calif. | | |
| Johnson, Ron WR | 82-84CFL 85USFL 86-89Phi 90VR | 2 | 6'3" | 186 | Long Beach State | | 24 |
| Johnson, Ron DB | 78-84Pit | | 5'10" | 200 | Eastern Michigan | 13 | 6 |
| Johnson, Samuel WR | 87LA | | 5'11" | 180 | Prairie View | | |
| Johnson, Sidney DB | 88KC 90-92Was | | 5'9" | 175 | California | 3 | |
| Johnson, Steve TE | 88NE | | 6'6" | 245 | Virginia Tech | | |
| Johnson, Ted LB | 95NE | | 6'3" | 240 | Colorado | | |
| Johnson, Tim DE-DT | 87-89Pit 90-95Was | | 6'3" | 276 | Penn State | 1 | |
| Johnson, Tommy DB | 95Jax | | 5'10" | 183 | Alabama | | |
| Johnson, Tracy FB | 89Hou 90-91Atl 92-95Sea | 2 | 6' | 229 | Clemson | | 48 |
| Johnson, Tré OT-OG | 94-95Was | | 6'2" | 329 | Temple | | |
| Johnson, Troy WR | 85USFL 86-87StL 88Pit 89Det | 2 | 6'1" | 180 | Southern U. | | 12 |
| Johnson, Troy LB-DE | 88-89Chi 90-91NYJ 92Det 94XJ | | 6' | 236 | Oklahoma | | |
| Johnson, Trumaine WR | 83-84USFL 85-86SD 87-88Buf | 2 | 6'1" | 195 | Grambling | | 24 |
| Johnson, Tyrone WR | 94NO | | 5'11" | 171 | Western St. (Colo.) | | |
| Johnson, Undra HB | 89NO 89Atl | | 5'9" | 199 | West Virginia | | |
| Johnson, Vance WR | 85-93,95Den | 23 | 5'11" | 185 | Arizona | | 222 |
| Johnson, Vaughan LB | 84-85USFL 86-93NO 94Phi | | 6'3" | 237 | N. Carolina State | 4 | |
| Johnson, Walter LB | 87-88Hou 89NO | | 6' | 240 | Louisiana Tech | | |
| Johnson, Walter DT | 87Dal | | 6'1" | 250 | Pittsburgh | | |
| Johnson, Wayne QB | 89Ind | | 6'4" | 221 | Georgia | | |
| Johnson, Will LB | 87Chi | | 6'4" | 242 | Northeast La. | | |
| Johnston, Brian C | 86NYG | | 6'3" | 275 | North Carolina | | |
| Johnston, Daryl FB | 89-95Dal | 2 | 6'2" | 236 | Syracuse | | 114 |
| Joiner, Tim LB | 83-84Hou 87Den | | 6'4" | 235 | Louisiana Tech | | |
| Joines, Vernon WR | 89-90Cle | | 6'2" | 200 | Maryland | | |
| Jolly, Ken LB | 84-85KC | | 6'2" | 220 | Mid-Amer. Nazarene | | |
| Jolly, Mike DB | 80GB 81KJ 82-83GB | | 6'3" | 188 | Michigan | 3 | |
| Jonassen, Eric OT | 93-94SD | | 6'5" | 310 | Penn St., Bloomsburg | | |
| Jones, A.J. FB-HB | 82-85LA 85Det | | 6'1" | 202 | Texas | | |
| Jones, Aaron DE-LB | 88-92Pit 93-95NE | | 6'5" | 263 | Eastern Kentucky | 1 | |
| Jones, Andre LB | 92Det | | 6'2" | 248 | Notre Dame | | |
| Jones, Anthony TE | 84-87Was | | 6'3" | 248 | Md.-Eastern Shore, Wichita State | | |
| Jones, Arrington HB | 81SF | | 6' | 225 | Winston-Salem St. | | |
| Jones, Bill HB | 90-92KC | 2 | 5'11" | 228 | S.M.U., SW Texas State | | 36 |
| Jones, Bobby WR | 78-82NYJ 83Cle | 2 | 5'11" | 182 | none | | 42 |
| Jones, Boyd OT | 84GB | | 6'3" | 265 | Texas Southern | | |
| Jones, Brent TE | 87-95SF | 2 | 6'4" | 230 | Santa Clara | | 182 |
| Jones, Brian LB | 91Ind 95NO | | 6'1" | 240 | U.C.L.A., Texas | | |
| Jones, Bruce DB | 87Pit | | 6'1" | 197 | North Alabama | | |
| Jones, Bryant DB | 87Ind | | 5'11" | 186 | Toledo | 2 | |
| Jones, Calvin HB | 94Raid 95Oak | 2 | 5'11" | 205 | Nebraska | | |
| Jones, Cedric WR | 82-90NE | 2 | 6'1" | 184 | Duke | | 108 |
| Jones, Clarence OT | 91-93NYG 94LA 95StL | | 6'6" | 285 | Maryland | | |
| Jones, Chris C | 87NYG | | 6'3" | 263 | Delaware State | | |
| Jones, Chris T. WR | 95Phi | | 6'3" | 209 | Miami (Fla.) | | |
| Jones, Dale LB | 87Dal | | 6'1" | 234 | Tennessee | | |
| Jones, Dan OT-OG-C | 93-95Cin | | 6'7" | 294 | Maine | | |
| Jones, Dante LB | 88-94Chi 95Den | | 6'1" | 236 | Oklahoma | 4 | 6 |
| Jones, David C-OG | 84-85Det 87Den | | 6'3" | 262 | Texas | | |
| Jones, David TE | 92Raid | | 6'2" | 220 | Delaware State | | |
| Jones, Darryll DB | 84-85GB 86ZJ 87Den | | 6'1" | 191 | Georgia | | |
| Jones, Don LB | 92-93NYJ 94KJ | | 6' | 231 | Washington | | |
| Jones, Donta LB | 95Pit | | 6'2" | 226 | Nebraska | | |
| Jones, E.J. HB-FB | 85KC 87Dal | | 5'11" | 216 | Kansas | | |
| Jones, Earl DB | 80-83Atl | | 6' | 178 | Norfolk State | 4 | |
| Jones, Ernest DE | 95NO | | 6'2" | 255 | Oregon | | |
| Jones, Ernie WR | 88-92Phx 93LA | 2 | 5'11" | 186 | Indiana | | 120 |
| Jones, Fred LB | 87KC | | 6'3" | 240 | Florida State | | |

| Use Name (Nickname) - Positions | Team by Year | See Section | Hgt. | Wgt. | College | Int | Pts |
|---|---|---|---|---|---|---|---|
| Jones, Fred WR | 90-93KC | 2 | 5'9" | 175 | Grambling | | |
| Jones, Gary DB | 90-91Pit 92KJ 93-94Pit 95NYJ | | 6'1" | 209 | Texas A&M | 6 | 6 |
| Jones, Gordon WR | 79-82TB 83LA | 2 | 6' | 190 | Pittsburgh | | 48 |
| Jones, Hassan WR | 86-92Min 93KC | 2 | 6' | 194 | Florida State | | 144 |
| Jones, Henry DB | 91-95Buf | | 5'11" | 197 | Illinois | 13 | 20 |
| Jones, James HB-FB | 80-82Dal 83KJ 84-85Dal | 23 | 5'10" | 201 | Mississippi State | | 12 |
| Jones, James FB-TE | 83-88Det 89-92Sea | 2 | 6'2" | 229 | Florida | | 216 |
| Jones, James DT-NT | 91-94Cle 95Den | | 6'2" | 292 | Northern Iowa | 1 | 20 |
| Jones, Jeff OT | 95Det | | 6'6" | 310 | Texas A&M | | |
| Jones, Jimmie DT-NT | 90-93Dal 94LA 95StL | | 6'4" | 279 | Miami (Fla.) | | |
| Jones, Jock LB | 90-91Cle 91-93Phx | | 6'2" | 235 | Virginia Tech | 1 | |
| Jones, Joe TE | 87Ind | | 6'5" | 255 | Virginia Tech | | 6 |
| Jones, Joey WR | 84-85USFL 86Atl 87KJ | | 5'8" | 165 | Alabama | | |
| Jones, Johnny (Lam) WR | 80-84NYJ 85RJ 86LJ | 2 | 5'11" | 180 | Texas | | 78 |
| Jones, Keith HB | 89Cle 90KJ | | 5'10" | 190 | Nebraska | | 6 |
| Jones, Keith HB-FB | 89-92Atl | 23 | 6'1" | 210 | Illinois | | 42 |
| Jones, Ken OT-DE | 76-86Buf 87NYJ | | 6'5" | 260 | Arkansas State | | |
| Jones, Lyndell DB | 87Atl | | 5'9" | 175 | Hawaii | | |
| Jones, Marlon DE-DT | 87-89Cle 90FJ | | 6'4" | 263 | Central State-Ohio | | |
| Jones, Marvin LB | 93-95NYJ | | 6'2" | 247 | Florida State | | |
| Jones, Melvin OG | 81Was | | 6'2" | 260 | Houston | | |
| Jones, Mike WR | 83-85Min 86-87,89NO | 2 | 5'11" | 181 | Tennessee State | | 66 |
| Jones, Mike LB | 87Buf | | 6'4" | 224 | Brockport State | | |
| Jones, Mike TE | 90-91Min 92Sea | | 6'3" | 255 | Michigan, Texas A&M | | 12 |
| Jones, Mike LB | 91-94Raid 95Oak | | 6'1" | 228 | Missouri | 1 | 6 |
| Jones, Mike DE | 91-93Phx 94-95NE | | 6'4" | 289 | N. Carolina State | | |
| Jones, Preston QB | 93Phi | | 6'3" | 223 | Georgia | | |
| Jones, Quinn FB | 80Atl | | 6'1" | 215 | Tulsa | | |
| Jones, Quintin DB | 88,90Hou | | 5'11" | 193 | Pittsburgh | | |
| Jones, Reggie DB | 91-94NO | | 6'1" | 202 | Memphis State | 4 | |
| Jones, Reggie WR | 95Car | | 6' | 175 | Louisiana State | | |
| Jones, Ricky DB-LB | 77-79Cle 80-83Bal 84JJ | | 6'1" | 211 | Tuskegee | | |
| Jones, Robbie LB | 84-87NYG | | 6'2" | 230 | Alabama | | |
| Jones, Robert LB | 92-95Dal | | 6'2" | 239 | East Carolina | | |
| Jones, Rod DB | 86-90TB 91-95Cin | | 6' | 180 | S.M.U. | 8 | |
| Jones, Rod TE | 87-88KC 89Sea | | 6'4" | 242 | Washington | | 6 |
| Jones, Roger DB | 91-93TB 94-95Cin | | 5'9" | 175 | Tennessee State | 1 | 12 |
| Jones, Rondell DB | 93-95Den | | 6'2" | 210 | North Carolina | 2 | |
| Jones, Rulon DE | 80-88Den | | 6'6" | 260 | Utah State | | 10 |
| Jones, Scott OT | 89Cin 90NYJ 91GB 91Cin | | 6'5" | 281 | Washington | | |
| Jones, Sean DE | 84-87Raid 88-93Hou 94-95GB | | 6'7" | 272 | Northeastern | 1 | 6 |
| Jones, Selwyn DB | 93Cle 94NO 95Sea | | 6' | 185 | Colorado State | 4 | |
| Jones, Shawn DB | 93Min | | 6'1" | 200 | Georgia Tech | | |
| Jones, Terry NT-DT | 78-84GB | | 6'2" | 257 | Alabama | | |
| Jones, Todd OT | 93NE | | 6'3" | 295 | Arkansas, Henderson State | | |
| Jones, Tony OT-OG | 88-95Cle | | 6'5" | 289 | Western Carolina | | |
| Jones, Tony WR | 90-91Hou 92Atl 93Hou | 2 | 5'7" | 139 | Texas | | 54 |
| Jones, Tony DB | 95Arz | | 6'4" | 200 | Syracuse | | |
| Jones, Ed (Too Tall) DE | 74-78Dal 79VR 80-89Dal | | 6'9" | 271 | Tennessee State | 3 | |
| Jones, Tyrone LB | 88Phx | | 6' | 220 | Southern U. | | |
| Jones, Tyrone DB | 89Phi | | 6'4" | 223 | Arkansas State | | |
| Jones, Victor LB | 88TB 89-94Det | | 6'2" | 244 | Virginia Tech | 1 | |
| Jones, Victor HB-FB | 90-91Hou 92Den 93-94Pit 94KC | | 5'8" | 214 | Louisiana State | | |
| Jones, Wayne OG | 87Min | | 6'4" | 270 | Utah | | |
| Jones, Willie DE | 79-81Oak 82KJ | | 6'4" | 244 | Florida State | | 12 |
| Jordan, Andrew TE | 94-95Min | 2 | 6'4" | 260 | Western Carolina | | 14 |
| Jordan, Brian DB | 89-91Atl | | 5'11" | 202 | Richmond | 5 | 4 |
| Jordan, Buford FB | 84-85USFL 86-92NO | 2 | 6' | 223 | McNeese State | | 60 |
| Jordan, Charles WR | 94-95GB | 3 | 5'10" | 175 | Long Beach City Coll | | 12 |
| Jordan, Curtis DB | 76-80TB 81-86Was | | 6'2" | 200 | Texas Tech | 17 | 12 |
| Jordan, Darin LB-DE | 88Pit 91-93SF | | 6'1" | 239 | Northeastern | 1 | 8 |
| Jordan, David OG | 84-85NYG 86BN 87TB | | 6'6" | 274 | Auburn | | |
| Jordan, Donald FB | 84Chi | 2 | 6' | 210 | Houston | | |
| Jordan, Homer QB | 87Cle | | 6' | 183 | Clemson | | |
| Jordan, Kenneth LB | 87GB | | 6'2" | 235 | Tuskegee | | |
| Jordan, Randy FB-HB | 93Raid 95Jax | 2 | 5'10" | 205 | North Carolina | | 6 |
| Jordan, Shelby OT | 75,77NE 83-86Raid 87AJ | | 6'7" | 275 | Washington-St.L. | | |
| 1976 — Ineligible to play pro football | | | | | | | |
| Jordan, Steve TE | 82-94Min | 2 | 6'4" | 236 | Brown | | 174 |
| Jordan, Steve K | 87Ind | | 5'10" | 205 | Southern Calif. | | 16 |
| Jordan, Tony HB | 88-89Phx | 2 | 6'2" | 220 | Kansas State | | 30 |
| Jordan, Tim LB | 87-89NE | | 6'3" | 226 | Wisconsin | 1 | |
| Jorden, Tim TE | 90-91Phx 92-93Pit | 2 | 6'2" | 235 | Indiana | | 12 |
| Joseph, Dwayne DB | 95Chi | | 5'9" | 180 | Syracuse | 2 | |
| Joseph, James HB-FB | 91-94Phi 95Cin | 2 | 6' | 222 | Auburn | | 42 |
| Joseph, Vance DB | 95NYJ | | 6' | 202 | Colorado | 2 | |
| Jourdain, Yonel HB | 94-95Buf | 23 | 5'11" | 204 | Southern Illinois | | |
| Joyce, Matt OG | 95Sea | | 6'7" | 316 | Richmond | | |
| Joyner, Seth LB | 86-93Phi 94-95Arz | | 6'2" | 240 | Texas-El Paso | 23 | 30 |
| Joyner, Willie HB | 84Hou | | 5'10" | 200 | Maryland | | |
| Jozwiak, Brian OG-OT | 86-88KC | | 6'5" | 304 | West Virginia | | |
| Judie, Ed LB | 82-83SF 83TB 84Mia | | 6'2" | 232 | Northern Arizona | | |
| Judson, William DB | 82-89Mia 90Det | | 6'1" | 189 | S. Carolina State | 24 | 12 |
| Juma, Kevin WR | 87Sea | | 6'2" | 195 | Idaho | | |
| Junior, E.J. LB | 81-87StL 88Phx 89-91Mia 92TB 92-93Sea | | 6'3" | 237 | Alabama | 12 | 6 |
| Junkin, Mike LB | 87-88Cle 89KC | | 6'3" | 241 | Duke | | |
| Junkin, Trey LB-TE | 83-84Buf 84Was 85-89Raid 90-95Sea | 2 | 6'2" | 229 | Louisiana Tech | | 42 |
| Juriga, Jim OT-OG | 88-90Den 91XJ | | 6'6" | 269 | Illinois | | |
| Jurkovic, John NT | 91-95GB | | 6'2" | 297 | Eastern Illinois | | |
| Justin, Kerry DB | 78-83Sea 84-85USFL 86-87Sea | | 5'11" | 176 | Oregon State | 7 | |
| Justin, Paul QB | 95Ind | 1 | 6'4" | 215 | Arizona State | | |
| Justin, Sid DB | 79LA 81JJ 82Bal | | 5'10" | 170 | California | 1 | 6 |
| Kab, Vyto TE | 82-85Phi 85NYG 87Det 88KJ | 2 | 6'5" | 243 | Penn State | | 30 |
| Kackerski, John LB | 92Den | | 6'3" | 240 | Ohio State | | |
| Kacmarek, Jeff NT | 87Det | | 6'2" | 240 | Western Michigan | | |
| Kafentzis, Kurt DB | 87Hou | | 6'2" | 190 | Hawaii | | |
| Kafentzis, Mark DB | 82Cle 83Bal 84Ind | | 5'10" | 190 | Hawaii | 1 | 6 |
| Kaiser, John LB | 84-86Sea 87Buf | | 6'3" | 227 | Arizona | | |
| Kalafat, Jim LB | 87LA | | 6' | 235 | Montana State | | |
| Kalis, Todd OG | 88-91Min 92KJ 93-94Min 95Cin | | 6'5" | 289 | Arizona State | | |
| Kamana, John LB-TE | 84LA 87Atl | | 6' | 223 | Southern Calif. | | 6 |
| Kane, Rick HB-FB | 77-83Det 84Was 85Det | 23 | 5'11" | 200 | Oregon, San Jose State | | 84 |
| Kane, Tommy WR | 88-92Sea | 2 | 5'11" | 180 | Dawson (Que.), Syracuse | | 54 |
| Kaplan, Ken OT | 84-85TB 87NO | | 6'4" | 272 | New Hampshire | | |

| Use Name (Nickname) - Positions | Team by Year | See Section | Hgt. | Wgt. | College | Int | Pts |
|---|---|---|---|---|---|---|---|
| Karcher, Ken QB | 87-88Den | 1 | 6'3" | 205 | Notre Dame, Tulane | | |
| Karlis, Rich K | 82-88Den 89Min 90Det | 5 | 6' | 180 | Cincinnati | | 799 |
| Karpinski, Keith LB | 89Det | | 6'3" | 225 | Penn State | | |
| Kartz, Keith OT-OG-C | 87-93Den 94KJ | | 6'4" | 270 | California | | |
| Kasay, John K | 91-95Sea | 5 | 5'10" | 189 | Georgia | | 446 |
| Katolin, Mike C | 84-85USFL 87Cle | | 6'3" | 255 | San Jose State | | |
| Kattus, Eric TE | 86-91Cin 92NYJ | 2 | 6'5" | 240 | Michigan | | 30 |
| Kauahi, Kani C | 82-86Sea 88GB 89-91Phx 92KC 93Phx | | 6'2" | 268 | Arizona State, Hawaii | | |
| Kaufman, Mel LB | 81-88Was | | 6'2" | 221 | Cal. Poly.-S.L.O. | 7 | 12 |
| Kaufman, Napoleon HB | 95Oak | 2 | 5'9" | 180 | Washington | | 12 |
| Kaufusi, Steve DE-DT | 89-90Phi | | 6'4" | 274 | Brigham Young | | |
| Kaumeyer, Thom DB | 89-90Sea 91-92KJ | | 5'11" | 187 | Oregon | | |
| Kauric, Jerry K | 90Cle | 5 | 6' | 210 | Kennedy (Ontario) | | 66 |
| Kay, Bill DB | 81-83Hou 84Stl 84SD | | 6'1" | 190 | Purdue | 4 | |
| Kay, Clarence TE | 84-92Den | 2 | 6'2" | 237 | Georgia | | 78 |
| Kearse, Tim WR | 87Ind | | 5'11" | 186 | San Jose State | | |
| Keating, Chris LB | 79-84Buf 85Was | | 6'2" | 223 | Maine | 3 | 6 |
| Keeble, Jerry LB | 87SF | | 6'3" | 230 | Minnesota | | |
| Keel, Mark TE | 87Sea 87KC | | 6'4" | 228 | Arizona | | |
| Keever, Carl LB | 87SF | | 6'2" | 236 | Oregon State, Boise State | | |
| Kehoe, Scott OT | 87Mia | | 6'4" | 282 | Illinois | | |
| Kehr, Rick OG | 87Was 88KJ | | 6'3" | 285 | Carthage | | |
| Keim, Mike DT-OT | 91NO 92-95Sea | | 6'7" | 299 | Brigham Young | | |
| Keith, Craig TE | 93-94Pit 95Jax | | 6'3" | 262 | Lenoir-Rhyne | | |
| Kellar, Bill WR | 78KC 79SJ | | 5'11" | 187 | Stanford | | |
| Kellar, Scott NT | 86-87Ind | | 6'3" | 282 | Northern Illinois | | |
| Kellermeyer, Doug OG-OT | 87Hou | | 6'3" | 275 | Brigham Young | | |
| Kelley, Chris TE | 87Cle | | 6'4" | 239 | Akron | | 1 |
| Kelley, Mike C-OG-OT | 85Hou 86ZJ 87Hou | | 6'5" | 273 | Notre Dame | | |
| Kelley, Mike QB | 87SD | | 6'3" | 195 | Georgia Tech | | |
| Kellin, Kevin DE | 86-88TB | | 6'6" | 267 | Minnesota | | |
| Kelly, Jim QB | 83-85USFL 86-95Buf | 12 | 6'3" | 217 | Miami (Fla.) | | 30 |
| Kelly, Joe LB | 86-89Cin 90-92NYJ 93Raid 94LA 95GB | | 6'2" | 231 | Washington | 6 | |
| Kelly, Paul QB | 87NYG | | 6'1" | 205 | New Haven | | |
| Kelly, Pat TE | 88-89Den 90-91NYJ | | 6'6" | 252 | Syracuse | | |
| Kelly, Todd DE | 93-94SF 95Cin | | 6'2" | 259 | Tennessee | | |
| Kelm, Larry LB | 87-92LA 93SF | | 6'4" | 236 | Texas A&M | 3 | |
| Kelso, Mark DB | 86-93Buf | | 5'11" | 181 | William & Mary | 30 | 18 |
| Kemp, Bobby DB | 81-86Cin 87TB | | 6' | 189 | Fullerton State | 10 | |
| Kemp, Jeff QB | 81-85LA 86SF 87-91Sea 91Phi | 12 | 6' | 200 | Dartmouth | | 6 |
| Kemp, Perry WR | 87Cle 88-91GB | 2 | 5'11" | 170 | California (Pa.) | | 48 |
| Kempf, Florian K | 82-84Hou 87NO | 5 | 5'9" | 170 | Pennsylvania | | 151 |
| Kenn, Mike OT | 78-94Atl | | 6'7" | 273 | Michigan | | |
| Kennard, Derek OG-C | 84-85USFL 86-87StL 88-90Phx 91-93NO 94-95Dal | | 6'3" | 297 | Nevada-Reno | | |
| Kennard, Ken NT-DE | 77-83Hou | | 6'2" | 248 | Angelo State | | 2 |
| Kennedy, Allan OT | 81SF 82NJ 83-84SF 85KJ | | 6'7" | 273 | Washington State | | |
| Kennedy, Cortez DT | 90-95Sea | | 6'3" | 293 | Miami (Fla.) | | |
| Kennedy, Lincoln OG-OT | 93-95Atl | | 6'6" | 339 | Washington | | |
| Kennedy, Mike DB | 83Buf 84Hou | | 6' | 195 | Toledo | 1 | 6 |
| Kennedy, Sam LB | 88SF | | 6'3" | 235 | San Jose State | | |
| Kenney, Bill QB | 79-88KC | 12 | 6'4" | 211 | Arizona State, Northern Colorado | | 30 |
| Ker, Crawford OG | 85-90Dal 91Den | | 6'3" | 288 | Florida | | |
| Kern, Don TE | 84-85Cin 86Buf | | 6'4" | 228 | Arizona State | | |
| Kerner, Marlon DB | 95Buf | | 5'10" | 187 | Ohio State | | |
| Kerrigan, Mike QB | 83-84NE | | 6'3" | 205 | Northwestern | | |
| Kersten, Wally OT | 82LA | | 6'5" | 270 | Minnesota | | |
| Keseday, Bob TE | 87StL | | 6'4" | 225 | Texas-El Paso | | |
| Key, David DB | 91NE | | 5'10" | 190 | Michigan | | |
| Keys, Tyrone DE | 83-85Chi 86-87TB 88SD | | 6'7" | 272 | Mississippi State | | |
| Kidd, Billy C | 87Hou | | 6'4" | 270 | Houston | | |
| Kidd, Carl DB | 95Oak | | 6'1" | 200 | Arkansas | | |
| Kidd, John K | 84-89Buf 90-94SD 94-95Mia | 4 | 6'3" | 207 | Northwestern | | 6 |
| Kidd, Keith WR | 87Min | | 6'1" | 195 | Arkansas | | |
| Kiel, Blair QB | 84TB 86-87Ind 88-91GB | 1 | 6' | 209 | Notre Dame | | 6 |
| Kiewel, Jeff OG | 83-84USFL 85Atl 86KJ 87Atl | | 6'4" | 271 | Arizona | | |
| Kilson, David DB | 83Buf | | 6'1" | 200 | Nevada-Reno | | 6 |
| Kimball, Bruce OG | 82NYG 83-84Was | | 6'2" | 260 | Massachusetts | | |
| Kimble, Garry DB | 87Was | | 5'11" | 184 | Sam Houston St. | | |
| Kimbrough, Tony WR | 93-94Den | 2 | 6'2" | 192 | Jackson State | | |
| Kimmel, Jamie LB | 86-87Raid 88KJ | | 6'3" | 235 | Syracuse | | |
| Kimmel, Jerry LB | 87NYG | | 6'2" | 240 | Syracuse | | |
| Kimmel, Jon LB | 85Phi 87Was | | 6'4" | 240 | Colgate | | |
| Kinard, Terry DB | 83-89NYG 90Hou | | 6'1" | 199 | Clemson | 31 | 18 |
| Kinchen, Brian TE | 88-90Mia 91-95Cle | 2 | 6'2" | 236 | Louisiana State | | 18 |
| Kinchen, Todd WR | 92-94LA 95StL | 23 | 6' | 187 | Louisiana State | | 66 |
| Kindt, Don TE | 87Chi | | 6'6" | 242 | Wis.-LaCrosse | | 6 |
| King, Angelo LB | 81-83Dal 84-87Det | | 6'1" | 224 | S. Carolina State | | 6 |
| King, Bruce FB | 85-86KC 86-87Buf | 2 | 6'1" | 221 | Purdue | | |
| King, David DB | 87GB | | 5'9" | 175 | Auburn | | |
| King, Don DB | 87GB | | 6' | 200 | S.M.U. | | |
| King, Ed OG-OT | 91-93Cle 95NO | | 6'4" | 303 | Auburn | | |
| King, Emanuel LB | 85-88Cin 89Raid | | 6'4" | 250 | Alabama | | |
| King, Gordon OT-OG | 78-83NYG 84BA 85NYG 86-87NYJ | | 6'6" | 274 | Stanford | | |
| King, Jerome DB | 79-80Atl 80NYG 83USFL | | 5'10" | 173 | Purdue | | |
| King, Joe DB | 91Cin 91Cle 92-93TB 95Oak | | 6'2" | 212 | Oklahoma State | 5 | |
| King, Kenny HB-FB | 79Hou 80-81Oak 82-85Raid | 2 | 5'11" | 205 | Oklahoma | | 48 |
| King, Linden LB | 82-85SD 86-89Raid | | 6'4" | 247 | Colorado State | 8 | 6 |
| King, Tim DB | 87TB | | 6'2" | 190 | Delaware State | | |
| Kinlaw, Reggie NT | 79-81Oak 82-84Raid 85-86Sea | | 6'2" | 245 | Oklahoma | | |
| Kinnebrew, Larry FB | 83-87Cin 89-90Buf | 2 | 6'1" | 255 | Tennessee State | | 282 |
| Kinney, Steve OT-OG | 80-85Phi 86Det | | 6'4" | 265 | Clemson | | |
| Kinzer, Matt K | 87Det | | 6'3" | 225 | Purdue | | |
| 87,90 played major league baseball | | | | | | | |
| Kirby, Terry HB | 93-95Mia | 2 | 6'1" | 221 | Virginia | | 92 |
| Kirchbaum, Kelly LB | 80KC 83-85USFL 87Phi | | 6'2" | 240 | Kentucky | | |
| Kirchner, Mark OT-OG | 83Pit 83KC 84Ind 85FJ 86Ind | | 6'3" | 262 | Baylor | | |
| Kirk, Randy LB | 87-88SD 89-90Phx 91Cle 91SD 92-93Cin 94-95Arz | | 6'2" | 231 | San Diego State | | |
| Kirkland, Levon LB | 92-95Pit | | 6' | 252 | Clemson | 2 | 6 |
| Kirksey, William LB | 90Min 92FJ | | 6'2" | 221 | Southern Miss. | | |
| Kirtman, Mike WR | 80Buf | | 6'1" | 180 | San Jose State | | |
| Kiser, Paul OG | 87Det | | 6'4" | 270 | Wake Forest | | |
| Kitson, Syd OG-OT | 80-81GB 82SJ 83-84GB 84Dal | | 6'4" | 258 | Wake Forest | | |
| Klecko, Joe DE-DT-NT | 77-87NYJ 88Ind | | 6'3" | 263 | Temple | | |
| Klein, Perry QB | 94-95Atl | | 6'2" | 218 | C.W. Post | | |
| Klever, Rocky TE-FB | 83-87NYJ 88XJ | | 6'3" | 227 | Montana | | 18 |

| Use Name (Nickname) - Positions | Team by Year | See Section | Hgt. | Wgt. | College | Int | Pts |
|---|---|---|---|---|---|---|---|
| Kline, Alan OT | 95NO | | 6'5" | 290 | Ohio State | | |
| Klingbeil, Chuck NT | 91-95Mia | | 6'1" | 269 | Northern Michigan | | 6 |
| Klingel, John DE | 87-88Phi | | 6'4" | 267 | Kentucky | | |
| Klingler, David QB | 92-95Cin | 12 | 6'2" | 205 | Houston | | |
| Klostermann, Bruce LB | 87-90Den | | 6'4" | 230 | Iowa, S. Dakota St. | | |
| Klug, Dave LB | 81-83KC | | 6'4" | 230 | Concordia (Minn.) | | 6 |
| Knafelc, Greg QB | 83NO | | 6'4" | 220 | Notre Dame | | |
| Knapczyk, Ken WR | 87Chi | | 5'11" | 190 | Northern Iowa | | |
| Knapp, Lindsay OG-OT | 94KC | | 6'6" | 290 | Notre Dame | | |
| Knapple, Jeff QB | 80Den 81CFL 83-84USFL | | 6'2" | 200 | Northern Colorado | | |
| Knight, Leander DB | 87-88Atl 89NYJ 90Hou | | 6'1" | 194 | Ferrum, | 1 | |
| | | | | | Montclair State | | |
| Knight, Marion DE | 87LA | | 6'2" | 265 | Nevada-Las Vegas | | |
| Knight, Shawn DE | 87NO 88Den 89Phx | | 6'6" | 288 | Brigham Young | | |
| Knight, Steve OG | 87Ind 88-89KJ | | 6'4" | 298 | Tennessee | | |
| Knox, Chuck | HC73-77LA HC78-82Buf HC83-91Sea | | | | Juniata | | |
| | HC92-94LA | | | | | | |
| Knox, Darryl LB | 87Pit | | 6'3" | 220 | Nevada-Las Vegas | | |
| Knox, Kevin WR | 94Arz | | 6'3" | 195 | Florida State | | |
| Knox, Mike LB | 87Den | | 6'2" | 240 | Nebraska | | |
| Koart, Matt DE | 86GB | | 6'5" | 258 | Southern Calif. | | |
| Koch, Greg OT-OG | 77-85GB 86-87Mia 87Min | | 6'4" | 270 | Arkansas | | |
| Koch, Markus DE | 86-91Was | | 6'5" | 270 | Boise State | | |
| Koch, Pete NT-DT | 84Cin 85-87KC 88BW 89Raid | | 6'6" | 269 | Maryland | | |
| Kofler, Matt QB | 82-84Buf 85Ind | 12 | 6'3" | 194 | San Diego State | | |
| Kohlbrand, Joe LB | 85-89NO | | 6'4" | 242 | Miami (Fla.) | | |
| Kohrs, Bob DE-LB | 81-85Pit | | 6'3" | 239 | Arizona State | | 2 |
| Kolic, Larry LB | 86-88Mia | | 6'1" | 240 | Ohio State | | |
| Kolodziejski, Chris TE | 84Pit | | 6'3" | 231 | Wyoming | | |
| Komlo, Jeff QB | 79-81Det 82Atl 83TB 84BJ | 12 | 6'2" | 200 | Delaware | | 12 |
| Konecny, Mark HB | 87Mia 88Phi 89KJ | 2 | 5'11" | 199 | Alma | | |
| Konopasek, Ed OT | 87GB | | 6'6" | 289 | Ball State | | |
| Koonce, George LB | 92-95GB | | 6'1" | 238 | East Carolina | 1 | |
| Kopp, Jeff LB | 95Mia | | 6'3" | 243 | Southern Calif. | | |
| Korff, Mark LB | 87SF | | 6'1" | 230 | Florida | | |
| Kors, R.J. DB | 91-92NYJ 93Cin | | 6' | 195 | Southern Calif., | 2 | |
| | | | | | Long Beach State | | |
| Korte, Steve OG-C | 83-90NO | | 6'2" | 265 | Arkansas | | 6 |
| Kosar, Bernie QB | 85-93Cle 93Dal 94-95Mia | 12 | 6'5" | 210 | Miami (Fla.) | | 30 |
| Koss, Stein TE | 87KC | | 6'2" | 225 | Arizona State | | |
| Kotite, Rich | HC91-94Phi HC95NYJ | | | | Wagner | | |
| Kovach, Jim LB | 79-85NO 85SF | | 6'2" | 229 | Kentucky | 4 | |
| Kovaleski, Mike LB | 87Cle | | 6'2" | 225 | Notre Dame | | |
| Kowalkowski, Scott LB | 91-92Phi 94-95Det | | 6'2" | 228 | Notre Dame | | |
| Kowalski, Gary OT-OG | 83LA 84KJ 85-88SD | | 6'6" | 280 | Boston College | | |
| Kowgios, Nick FB | 87Det | | 6' | 216 | Lafayette | | |
| Kozak, Scott LB | 89-93Hou | | 6'3" | 225 | Oregon | | |
| Kozerski, Bruce C-OG-OT | 84-95Cin | | 6'4" | 281 | Holy Cross | | |
| Kozlowski, Brian TE | 94-95NYG | | 6'3" | 250 | Connecticut | | |
| Kozlowski, Glen WR | 87-92Chi 93KJ | 2 | 6'1" | 200 | Brigham Young | | 18 |
| Kozlowski, Mike DB | 79Mia 80NJ 81-86Mia | 3 | 6' | 196 | San Diego State, | 8 | 18 |
| | | | | | Brigham Young, | | |
| | | | | | Colorado | | |
| Kragen, Greg NT | 85-93Den 94KC 95Den | | 6'3" | 261 | Utah State | 1 | 12 |
| Krakoski, Joe LB | 86Was | | 6'1" | 224 | Washington | | |
| Kramer, Erik QB | 87Atl 91-93Det 94-95Chi | 12 | 6' | 192 | N. Carolina State | | 12 |
| Kramer, Kyle DB | 89Cle 90SJ | | 6'3" | 190 | Bowling Green | 1 | |
| Kramer, Tommy QB | 77-89Min 90NO | 12 | 6'2" | 202 | Rice | | 48 |
| Kratch, Bob OG-OT | 89-93NYG 94-95NE | | 6'3" | 288 | Iowa | | |
| Krauss, Barry LB | 79-83Bal 84-88Ind 89Mia 90KJ | | 6'3" | 245 | Alabama | 6 | 6 |
| Kraynak, Rich LB | 83-86Phi 87Atl | | 6'1" | 227 | Pittsburgh | 1 | 6 |
| Kreider, Steve WR | 79-86Cin | 2 | 6'3" | 192 | Lehigh | | 56 |
| Kremer, Ken NT-DE | 79-84KC | | 6'4" | 252 | Ball State | 1 | |
| Krenk, Mitch TE | 84Chi | | 6'2" | 225 | Nebraska | | |
| Krerowicz, Mark OG | 87Cle | | 6'3" | 285 | Ohio State | | |
| Krieg, Dave QB | 80-91Sea 92-93KC 94Det 95Arz | 12 | 6'1" | 190 | Milton | | 72 |
| Krimm, John DB | 82NO 83KJ | | 6'1" | 190 | Notre Dame | | |
| Krueger, Todd QB | 87Min | | 6'4" | 200 | Northern Michigan | | |
| Krumm, Todd DB | 88Chi | | 6' | 189 | Michigan State | 2 | |
| Krumrie, Tim NT-DT | 83-94Cin | | 6'2" | 267 | Wisconsin | | |
| Kuberski, Bob NT | 95GB | | 6'5" | 300 | Navy | | |
| Kubiak, Gary QB | 83-91Den | 12 | 6' | 192 | Texas A&M | | 12 |
| Kubin, Larry LB | 82-84Was 85Buf 85TB | | 6'2" | 235 | Penn State | | |
| Kuehn, Art C | 76-82Sea 83NE 84-85USFL | | 6'3" | 257 | U.C.L.A. | | |
| Kugler, Pete NT-DE | 81-83SF 84-85USFL 86-90SF | | 6'4" | 255 | Penn State | | |
| Kuhlmann, Hank | HC89Phx | | | | Missouri | | |
| Kullman, Michael DB | 87Phi | | 6'1" | 185 | Kutztown | 2 | |
| Kumerow, Eric DE-LB | 88-90Mia 91BN | | 6'7" | 264 | Ohio State | 1 | |
| Kunz, Lee LB | 79-81Chi | | 6'2" | 224 | Nebraska | | |
| Kupp, Craig QB | 91Phx 91Dal | | 6'4" | 215 | Montana Tech, | | |
| | | | | | Pacific Lutheran | | |
| Kurisko, Jamie TE | 87NYJ 88LJ | | 6'4" | 236 | Southern Conn. St. | | 6 |
| Kush, Frank | HC82-83Bal HC84Ind | | | | Michigan State | | |
| Kush, Rod DB | 80-84Buf 85Hou 86KJ | | 6' | 189 | Nebraska-Omaha | 4 | |
| Kuykendall, Fulton (Captain Crazy) LB | 75-84Atl 85SF | | 6'5" | 225 | U.C.L.A. | 3 | 6 |
| Kyle, Jason LB | 95Sea | | 6'3" | 242 | Arizona State | | |
| Kyles, Troy WR | 90NYG | | 6' | 180 | Howard | | |
| Kysar, Jeff OT | 95Oak | | 6'7" | 330 | Arizona State | | |
| Laakso, Eric OT-OG | 78-84Mia | | 6'4" | 265 | Tulane | | |
| LaBeaux, Sandy DB | 83TB 85USFL | | 6'3" | 210 | Hayward State | | |
| LaBounty, Matt DE | 93SF 94XJ 95GB | | 6'4" | 266 | Oregon | | |
| LaChapelle, Sean WR | 93LA | | 6'3" | 205 | U.C.L.A. | | |
| Lachey, Jim OT | 85-87SD 88Raid 88-92Was 93KJ | | 6'6" | 289 | Ohio State | | |
| | 94-95Was | | | | | | |
| Lacina, Corbin OT-OG | 94-95Buf | | 6'4" | 297 | Augustana (S.D.) | | |
| Lacy, Ken FB | 83-84USFL 84-85,87KC | 2 | 6' | 222 | Tulsa | | 24 |
| Lafary, Dave OT-OG | 77-85NO | | 6'7" | 280 | Purdue | | |
| LaFleur, Greg TE | 81-86StL 86Ind | 2 | 6'4" | 236 | Louisiana State | | 18 |
| Lageman, Jeff LB-DE | 89-94NYJ 95Jax | | 6'5" | 265 | Virginia | 1 | |
| Laing, Aaron TE | 94SD | | 6'3" | 264 | New Mexico State | | |
| Lake, Carnell DB | 89-95Pit | | 6'1" | 206 | UCLA | 8 | 6 |
| Lamar, Kevin OG | 87Buf | | 6'4" | 260 | Stanford | | |
| Lamb, Brad WR | 92-93Buf | | 5'10" | 171 | Anderson | | |
| Lambert, Dion DB | 92-93NE 94Sea | | 6' | 185 | U.C.L.A. | 1 | |
| Lambrecht, Mike NT | 87-89Mia | | 6'1" | 273 | St. Cloud State | | |
| Land, Dan DB-HB | 87TB 89-94Raid 95Oak | | 6' | 191 | Albany State (Ga.) | 2 | |
| Land, Mel DE-LB | 79Mia 80SF 82CFL 83USFL | | 6'3" | 243 | Michigan State | | |
| Landeta, Sean K | 83-85USFL 85-93NYG 93-94LA 95StL | 4 | 6' | 200 | Towson State | | |
| Landrum, Mike TE | 84Atl 85-86KJ | | 6'2" | 231 | Southern Miss. | | |
| Landsee, Bob C-OG | 86-87Phi 88KJ | | 6'4" | 273 | Wisconsin | | |
| Lane, Eric HB-FB | 81-87Sea | 2 | 6' | 197 | Brigham Young | | 42 |

| Use Name (Nickname) - Positions | Team by Year | See Section | Hgt. | Wgt. | College | Int | Pts |
|---|---|---|---|---|---|---|---|
| Lane, Garcia DB | 84-85USFL 85,87KC | 3 | 5'9" | 180 | Ohio State | | |
| Lane, Max OT | 94-95NE | | 6'6" | 295 | Navy | | |
| Lane, Skip DB | 84NYJ 84KC 87Was | | 6'1" | 209 | Mississippi | | |
| Lang, David HB | 91-94LA 95Dal | 23 | 5'11" | 206 | Northern Arizona | | 36 |
| Lang, Gene HB | 84-87Den 88-90Atl | 23 | 5'10" | 196 | Louisiana State | | 120 |
| Lang, Le-Lo DB | 90-93Den | | 5'11" | 185 | Washington | 5 | |
| Langham, Antonio DB | 94-95Cle | | 6' | 180 | Alabama | 4 | |
| Langhorne, Reggie WR | 85-91Cle 92-93Ind | 2 | 6'2" | 200 | Elizabeth City St. | | 114 |
| Lanier, Ken OT | 81-92Den 93Raid 94Den | | 6'3" | 281 | Florida State | | |
| Lankford, Paul DB | 82-91Mia | | 6'1" | 185 | Penn State | 13 | |
| Lansford, Mike K | 82-90LA | 5 | 6' | 183 | Washington | | 789 |
| Lanza, Chuck C | 88-89Pit 90LJ | | 6'2" | 263 | Notre Dame | | |
| Lapka, Myron NT-DE-DT | 80NYG 81KJ 82-83LA | | 6'4" | 258 | Southern Calif. | | |
| LaPoint, Ron TE | 80Bal | | 6'2" | 235 | Penn State | | |
| Largent, Steve WR | 76-89Sea | 2 | 5'11" | 187 | Tulsa | | 608 |
| Larkin, Eric DE | 87Hou | | 6'4" | 265 | Miami (Fla.) | | |
| Laro, Gordon TE | 95Jax | | 6'3" | 253 | Boston College | | |
| Larson, Kurt LB | 89-90Ind 91GB | | 6'4" | 236 | Michigan State | | |
| Lasher, Tim K | 87Chi | 5 | 5'9" | 160 | Oklahoma | | 19 |
| Lasker, Greg DB | 86-88NYG 88Chi 88Phx | | 6' | 200 | Arkansas | | |
| Lassic, Derrick HB | 93Dal 94KJ | 2 | 5'10" | 188 | Alabama | | 18 |
| Lassiter, Kwamie DB | 95Arz | | 5'11" | 180 | Kansas | | |
| Laster, Donald OT | 82Was 83ZJ 84Det 85JJ | | 6'5" | 285 | Tennessee State | | |
| Lathan, Greg WR | 87Raid | | 6'1" | 195 | Cincinnati | | |
| Lathon, Lamar LB-DE | 90-94Hou 95Car | | 6'3" | 256 | Houston | 3 | 8 |
| Lathrop, Kit DE-NT | 79Den 79-80GB 83-84USFL | | 6'5" | 257 | Arizona State | | |
| | 86KC 87Was | | | | | | |
| Latimer, Al DB | 79Phi 80SF 82-84Det | | 5'11" | 176 | Clemson | 1 | |
| Lattimore, Brian HB-FB | 91Ind | | 6'1" | 202 | SE Missouri St. | | |
| Laufenberg, Babe QB | 83Was 84SJ 85SD 85Was | 12 | 6'2" | 198 | Stanford, Missouri, | | |
| | 86NO 87Was 88SD 89-90Dal | | | | Indiana | | |
| Laughlin, Jim LB | 80-82Atl 83GB 84-86LA 87Atl | | 6'1" | 222 | Ohio State | 2 | |
| Laughton, Jim TE | 86Sea | | 6'5" | 225 | San Diego State | | |
| Lavette, Robert HB | 85-87Dal 87Phi | 3 | 5'11" | 190 | Georgia Tech | | 6 |
| Lavine, Paul LB | 87Sea | | 6'2" | 207 | Utah State | | |
| Law, Ty DB | 95NE | | 5'11" | 196 | Michigan | 3 | |
| Lawrence, Amos (Famous Amos) HB | 81-82SF 84USFL | 3 | 5'11" | 180 | North Carolina | | 12 |
| Lawrence, Ben OG | 87Pit | | 6'1" | 325 | Indiana (Pa.) | | |
| Lawrence, Henry OT-OG | 74-81Oak 82-86Raid | | 6'4" | 272 | Florida A&M | | |
| Lawson, Jamie FB | 89-90TB 90NE | | 5'10" | 240 | Louisiana State, | | |
| | | | | | Nicholls State | | |
| Lawrence, Reggie WR | 93Phi | | 6' | 178 | Carolina State | | |
| Leach, Scott LB | 87NO | | 6'2" | 221 | Ohio State | 1 | |
| Leach, Bill OG-OT | 87NO | | 6'5" | 280 | Kentucky, | | |
| | | | | | N. Carolina State | | |
| Leahy, Pat K | 74-91NYJ | 5 | 6' | 194 | St. Louis | | 1470 |
| Leasy, Wesley LB | 95Arz | | 6'2" | 234 | Mississippi State | | |
| LeBel, Harper TE | 89Sea 90Phi 91-95Atl | | 6'4" | 251 | Colorado State | | |
| LeBlanc, Bob LB | 87Buf | | 6'2" | 243 | Elon | | |
| LeBlanc, Michael HB | 87NE | 2 | 5'11" | 199 | S.F. Austin State | | 6 |
| LeCount, Terry WR | 78-79SF 79-84,87Min | 2 | 5'10" | 178 | Florida | | 36 |
| Lee, Amp HB | 92-93SF 94-95Min | 23 | 5'11" | 200 | Florida State | | 72 |
| Lee, Byron LB | 86-87Phi | | 6'2" | 230 | Ohio State | | |
| Lee, Carl DB | 83-93Min 94NO | | 6' | 185 | Marshall | 31 | 12 |
| Lee, Danzell TE | 87Pit 88Atl | 2 | 6'2" | 235 | Lamar | | |
| Lee, Gary WR | 87-88Det | 23 | 6'1" | 202 | Georgia Tech | | 6 |
| Lee, Greg DB | 88Pit | | 6'1" | 207 | Arkansas State | | |
| Lee, Jeff WR | 80StL | | 6'2" | 195 | Nebraska | | |
| Lee, John K | 86StL | 5 | 5'11" | 182 | U.C.L.A. | | 38 |
| Lee, Keith DB | 81-84NE 85Ind | | 5'11" | 194 | Colorado State | 1 | |
| Lee, Kevin WR | 95NE | | 6'1" | 194 | Alabama | | |
| Lee, Larry OG-C | 81-85Det 85-86Mia 87-88Den | | 6'2" | 265 | U.C.L.A. | | |
| Lee, Mark DB | 80-90GB 91SF 91NO | 3 | 5'11" | 188 | Washington | 32 | 6 |
| Lee, Oudious NT | 80StL 83-84USFL | | 6'1" | 253 | Nebraska | | |
| Lee, Ronnie TE-OT-OG | 79-82Mia 83Atl 84-89Mia | 2 | 6'3" | 266 | Baylor | | 18 |
| | 90-92Sea | | | | | | |
| Lee, Shawn NT-DT | 88-89TB 90-91Mia 92-95SD | | 6'2" | 295 | North Alabama | 1 | |
| Lee, Zeph DB-FB | 87Den 87-89Raid | | 6'3" | 208 | Southern Calif. | 1 | |
| Leewenburg, Jay C-OT-OG | 92-95Chi | | 6'2" | 293 | Colorado | | |
| Legette, Burnie FB | 93-94NE | | 6' | 243 | Michigan | | |
| Legette, Tyrone DB | 92-95NO | | 5'9" | 177 | Nebraska | 1 | |
| Leggett, Brad C | 91NO 92Det | | 6'4" | 270 | Southern Calif. | | |
| Leggett, Scott OG-OT | 87Phi | | 6'3" | 285 | Central State-Okla. | | |
| Leiding, Jeff LB | 86Ind | | 6'3" | 232 | Texas | | 4 |
| Leiker, Tony DE | 87GB | | 6'5" | 250 | Stanford | | |
| Leonard, Jim C-OG | 80-82TB 83-85USFL 85SF 85-86SD | | 6'3" | 258 | Santa Clara | | |
| Leopold, Bobby LB | 80-83SF 84-85USFL 86GB 87XJ | | 6'1" | 217 | Notre Dame | 5 | |
| Lester, Keith TE | 87Ind | | 6'5" | 235 | Murray State | | |
| Lester, Tim FB-HB | 92-94LA 95Pit | 2 | 5'9" | 215 | Eastern Kentucky | | 6 |
| Lett, Leon DT | 91-95Dal | | 6'6" | 290 | Emporia State | | |
| Levenick, Dave LB | 83-84Atl | | 6'3" | 220 | Wisconsin | | |
| Levens, Dorsey HB-FB | 94-95GB | 2 | 6'1" | 235 | Georgia Tech | | 42 |
| Levy, Chuck HB-WR | 94Arz | 3 | 6' | 197 | Arizona | | |
| Levy, Marv | HC78-82KC HC86-95Buf | | | | Coe | | |
| Lewis, Albert DB | 83-93KC 94Raid 95Oak | | 6'2" | 193 | Grambling | 38 | 14 |
| Lewis, Bill C-OG | 86-88Raid 90-92Phx 93NE | | 6'7" | 285 | Nebraska | | |
| Lewis, Cliff LB | 81-84GB | | 6'1" | 226 | Southern Miss. | | |
| Lewis, Darryl TE | 84Cle | | 6'6" | 232 | Texas-Arlington | | |
| Lewis, Darren HB-FB | 91-93Chi | 23 | 5'10" | 230 | Texas A&M | | 30 |
| Lewis, Darryll DB | 91-95Hou | | 5'9" | 188 | Arizona | 13 | 18 |
| Lewis, Dave LB | 77-81TB 82SD 83LA | | 6'4" | 240 | Southern Calif. | 10 | 6 |
| Lewis, David TE | 84-86Det 87Mia | 2 | 6'3" | 234 | California | | 48 |
| Lewis, Gary TE-WR | 81-83GB 84USFL 84GB | 2 | 6'5" | 234 | Texas-Arlington | | 12 |
| Lewis, Gary NT | 83NO 84IL | | 6'3" | 260 | Oklahoma State | | |
| Lewis, Garry DB | 90-91Raid 92TB 93KC | | 5'11" | 185 | Alcorn State | 1 | |
| Lewis, Greg HB-FB | 91-92Den | 2 | 5'10" | 214 | Washington | | 48 |
| Lewis, John DB | 87Buf | | 5'10" | 175 | Pittsburgh | | |
| Lewis, Kenny HB-FB | 80-81NYJ 82USFL 83NYJ | | 6' | 192 | Virginia Tech | | |
| Lewis, Kevin DB | 90-91SF 92ZJ | | 5'11" | 173 | Northhwestern La. | 1 | |
| Lewis, Leo WR | 81-89Min 90Cle 90-91Min | 23 | 5'8" | 170 | Missouri | | 102 |
| Lewis, Mark TE | 85-87GB 87-88Det | | 6'2" | 239 | Texas A&M | | 18 |
| Lewis, Mo LB | 91-95NYJ | | 6'3" | 248 | Georgia | 9 | 18 |
| Lewis, Nate WR | 90-93SD 94-95Chi | 23 | 5'11" | 189 | Oregon Tech | | 96 |
| Lewis, Marvin FB | 82NO | | 6'3" | 208 | Tulane | | |
| Lewis, Reggie DE-NT | 79-80TB 83USFL | | 6'3" | 258 | North Texas | 1 | 6 |
| Lewis, Reggie DE | 82-84NO | | 6'2" | 252 | Oregon, | | |
| | | | | | San Diego State | | |
| Lewis, Roderick TE | 94-95Hou | 2 | 6'5" | 254 | Arizona | | |
| Lewis, Rodney DB | 82-84NO | | 5'11" | 189 | Nebraska | 1 | |
| Lewis, Ron WR | 90SF 91XJ 92SF 92-94GB | 2 | 5'11" | 173 | Florida State | | |
| Lewis, Ron OG | 95Was | | 6'3" | 299 | Washington State | | |

| Use Name (Nickname) - Positions | Team by Year | See Section | Hgt. | Wgt. | College | Int | Pts |
|---|---|---|---|---|---|---|---|
| Lewis, Sid DB | 87NYJ | | 5'11" | 180 | Penn State | | |
| Lewis, Tahaun DB | 92KC | | 5'10" | 175 | Nebraska | | |
| Lewis, Terry DB | 85SD | | 5'11" | 193 | Michigan State | | |
| Lewis, Thomas WR | 94-95NYG | 23 | 6'1" | 185 | Indiana | | 12 |
| Lewis, Tim DB | 83-86GB | | 5'11" | 192 | Pittsburgh | 16 | 6 |
| Lewis, Vernon DB | 93-95NE | | 5'10" | 192 | Pittsburgh | | |
| Lewis, Will DB | 80-81Sea 81KC 83-85USFL | 3 | 5'9" | 185 | Millersville | 6 | |
| Lick, Dennis OT | 78-82Chi | | 6'3" | 266 | Wisconsin | | |
| Liebenstein, Todd DE | 82-85Was | | 6'6" | 253 | Nevada-Las Vegas | | |
| Liles, Alva NT-DT | 80Oak 80Det 83USFL | | 6'3" | 255 | Boise State | | |
| Lilja, George C-OG-OT | 82LA 83-84NYJ 84-86Cle 87Dal | | 6'4" | 264 | Michigan | | |
| Lilly, Kevin DE-NT-DT | 88SF 89Dal 89SF | | 6'4" | 265 | Tulsa | | |
| Lilly, Sammy DB | 89-90Phi 90SD 91-92LA | | 5'9" | 178 | Georgia Tech | | |
| Lilly, Tony DB | 84-87Den 89Dal | | 6' | 199 | Florida | 9 | |
| Limbrick, Garrett FB | 90Mia 91SJ | | 6'2" | 240 | Oklahoma State | | |
| Lincoln, Jeremy DB | 93-95Chi | | 5'10" | 180 | Tennessee | 5 | 6 |
| Lindley, David QB | 87Sea | | 6' | 190 | Linfield | | |
| Lindsay, Everett OT-OG-C | 93Min 94SJ 95Min | | 6'4" | 295 | Mississippi | | |
| Lindstrom, Chris DE | 83Cin 84USFL 85TB 87KC | | 6'7" | 260 | Boston U. | | |
| Lindstrom, Dave DE | 78-85KC | | 6'6" | 255 | Boston U. | | |
| Lingmerth Goran K | 87Cle | | 5'8" | 160 | Northern Arizona | | |
| Lingner, Adam C-OG | 83-86KC 87Buf 88KC 89-95Buf | | 6'4" | 265 | Illinois | | |
| Linn, Jack OT-OG | 91Ind 92-93Det 93Cin | | 6'5" | 290 | West Virginia | | |
| Linne, Larry WR | 87NE | 2 | 6'1" | 185 | Texas-El Paso | | 12 |
| Linnin, Chris DE | 80NYG 84USFL | | 6'4" | 255 | Washington | | |
| Lippett, Ronnie DB | 83-88NE 89LJ 90-91NE | | 5'11" | 180 | Miami (Fla.) | 24 | 12 |
| Lipps, Louis WR | 84-91Pit 92NO | 23 | 5'10" | 188 | Southern Miss. | | 276 |
| Lisch, Rusty QB | 80-83StL 84Chi | 1 | 6'3" | 214 | Notre Dame | | |
| Liter, Greg DE | 87SF 87Phi | | 6'6" | 275 | Iowa State | | |
| Little, Dave TE | 84KC 85-89Phi 90Phx 91Det | 2 | 6'2" | 233 | Middle Tenn. St. | | 12 |
| Little, David LB | 81-92Pit | | 6'1" | 232 | Florida | 10 | |
| Little, George DE-NT | 85-87Mia | | 6'4" | 275 | Iowa | | |
| Livingston, Bruce DB | 87Dal | | 5'10" | 169 | Arkansas Tech | | |
| Lloyd, Doug FB | 91Raid | | 6'1" | 220 | N. Dakota State | | |
| Lloyd, Greg LB | 88-95Pit | | 6'2" | 225 | Ft. Valley State | 10 | |
| Lobenstein, Bill DE-NT | 87Den | | 6'3" | 261 | Wis.-Whitewater | | |
| Loberg, Greg OG-OT | 87NO | | 6'4" | 264 | California | | |
| Lockett, Charles WR | 87-88Pit 90LJ | 2 | 6' | 178 | Long Beach State | | 12 |
| Lockett, Danny LB | 87-88Det | | 6'2" | 239 | Arizona | | |
| Lockett, Frank WR | 83-85USFL 85Mia | | 6' | 200 | Nebraska | | |
| Lockett, Wade WR | 87Raid | | 6'1" | 190 | Fullerton State | | |
| Lockhart, Eugene LB | 84-90Dal 91-92NE | | 6'2" | 234 | Houston | 6 | 6 |
| Locklin, Kerry TE | 82LA 84USFL 87Den | | 6'3" | 230 | New Mexico State | | |
| Lockwood, Scott HB | 92-93NE | 2 | 5'10" | 196 | Southern Cal | | |
| Lodish, Mike DE-NT-DT | 90-94Buf 95Den | | 6'3" | 274 | U.C.L.A. | | 12 |
| Loewen, Chuck OT-OG | 80-82SD 83XJ 84SD | | 6'3" | 263 | S. Dakota State | | |
| Lofton, Steve DB | 91-93Phx 95Car | | 5'9" | 180 | Texas A&M | | |
| Lofton, James WR-DB | 78-86GB 87-88Raid 89-92Buf 93LA 93Phi | 2 | 6'3" | 192 | Stanford | | 456 |
| Logan, Dave WR-DB | 76-83Cle 84Den | 2 | 6'4" | 219 | Colorado | 1 | 144 |
| Logan, David NT-DE | 79-86TB 87GB | | 6'2" | 250 | Pittsburgh | 1 | 24 |
| Logan, Ernie DE | 91-92Cle 93Atl 95Jax | | 6'3" | 276 | East Carolina | | |
| Logan, James LB | 95Hou 95Cin 95Sea | | 6'2" | 214 | Memphis | | |
| Logan, Marc HB-FB | 87-88Cin 89-91Mia 92-94SF 95Was | 23 | 5'11" | 210 | Kentucky | | 102 |
| Lohmiller, Chip K | 88-94Was 95NO | 5 | 6'3" | 213 | Minnesota | | 822 |
| Lomack, Tony WR | 90LA 91Phx | | 5'8" | 180 | Florida | | |
| Lomax, Neil QB | 81-87StL 88Phx 89PJ | 12 | 6'3" | 215 | Portland State | | 60 |
| London, Antonio LB | 93-95Det | | 6'2" | 234 | Alabama | | |
| Loneker, Keith OG | 93-94LA 95StL | | 6'3" | 328 | Kansas | | |
| Long, Chuck QB | 86-89Det 90LA 91Det 92SJ 94Det | 12 | 6'4" | 216 | Iowa | | |
| Long, Darren TE | 86LA | | 6'3" | 240 | Long Beach State | | |
| Long, Howie DE-NT | 81Oak 82-93Raid | | 6'5" | 268 | Villanova | 1 | |
| Long, Matt C | 87Phi | | 6'3" | 270 | San Diego State | | |
| Long, Terry OG | 84-91Pit | | 5'11" | 273 | East Carolina | | |
| Long, Tim C | 87SF | | 6'6" | 295 | Memphis State | | |
| Looney, Jim LB | 81SF 83-84USFL | | 6' | 225 | Purdue | | |
| Lott, John C-OG | 87Pit | | 6'2" | 260 | North Texas | | |
| Lott, Ronnie DB | 81-90SF 92Raid 93-94NYJ | | 6' | 200 | Southern Calif. | 63 | 30 |
| Louallen, Fletcher DB | 87Min | | 6' | 195 | Livingston | 1 | |
| Louchiey, Corey OT | 95Buf | | 6'8" | 305 | South Carolina | | |
| Love, Duval OG-OT | 85-92LA 93-94Pit 95Arz | | 6'3" | 284 | Southern Calif., U.C.L.A. | | |
| Love, Randy HB-FB | 79-85StL 86XJ | 2 | 6'1" | 208 | Houston | | 30 |
| Love, Sean OG | 93-94TB 95Car | | 6'3" | 300 | Penn State | | |
| Love, Terry DB | 87Min | | 6'2" | 205 | Murray State | | |
| Loveall, Calvin DB | 88Hou 88KC 88Atl | | 5'9" | 180 | Idaho | | |
| Lovelady, Edwin WR | 87NYG | 2 | 5'9" | 180 | Memphis State | | 12 |
| Loville, Derek HB | 90-91Sea 94-95SF | 23 | 5'9" | 199 | Oregon | | 80 |
| Loving, Warren FB | 87Buf | | 6'1" | 230 | William Penn | | |
| Lowdermilk, Kirk C | 85-92Min 93-95Ind | | 6'3" | 275 | Ohio State | | |
| Lowe, Woodrow LB | 76-86SD 87KJ | | 6' | 227 | Alabama | 21 | 24 |
| Lowery, Nick K | 78NE 80-93KC 94-95NYJ | 5 | 6'4" | 189 | Dartmouth | | 1634 |
| Lowry, Orlando LB | 85-89Ind 89NE | | 6'4" | 237 | Ohio State | | |
| Lowry, Quentin LB | 81-83Was 83TB | | 6'3" | 232 | Youngstown State | | |
| Loyd, Mike QB | 79-80StL 84USFL | 1 | 6'2" | 216 | Missouri Southern | | |
| Lubischer, Steve LB | 87Mia | | 6'3" | 240 | Boston College | | |
| Lucas, Jeff OT | 87Pit | | 6'7" | 288 | West Virginia | | |
| Lucas, Tim LB | 87-93Den | | 6'3" | 230 | California | 1 | |
| Luck, Oliver QB | 82-86Hou | 12 | 6'2" | 196 | West Virginia | | 6 |
| Luckhurst, Mick K | 81-87Atl | 5 | 6' | 181 | St. Cloud State, California | | 558 |
| Lumpkin, Joey LB | 82-83Buf | | 6'2" | 230 | Arizona State | | |
| Lumpkin, Sean DB | 92-95NO | | 6' | 206 | Minnesota | 2 | 6 |
| Lundy, Dennis HB | 95Hou 95Chi | | 5'9" | 190 | Northwestern | | |
| Luscinski, Jim OT-OG | 82NYJ 83XJ | | 6'5" | 275 | Norwich | | |
| Lush, Mike DB | 83-85USFL 86Min 87Atl | | 6'1" | 195 | East Stroudsburg | | |
| Luther, Ed QB | 80-84SD 85USFL 86Ind | 12 | 6'3" | 207 | San Jose State | | |
| Lutz, David OT-OG | 83-92KC 93-95Det | | 6'6" | 299 | Georgia Tech | | |
| Lyday, Allen DB | 84-87Hou | | 5'10" | 190 | Texas Southern, Nebraska | 4 | |
| Lyght, Todd DB | 91-94LA 95StL | | 6' | 186 | Notre Dame | 11 | 12 |
| Lyle, Keith DB | 94LA 95StL | | 6'2" | 204 | Virginia | 5 | |
| Lyle, Rick DE | 94Cle 95XJ | | 6'5" | 275 | Missouri | | |
| Lyles, Lester DB-LB | 85-87NYJ 88Phx 89-90SD | | 6'3" | 210 | Virginia | 10 | |
| Lyles, Robert LB | 84-90Hou 90-91Atl | | 6'1" | 226 | Texas Christian | 10 | 12 |
| Lynch, Eric FB-HB | 92-95Det | 2 | 5'10" | 224 | Grand Valley St. | | 12 |
| Lynch, John DB | 93-95TB | | 6'2" | 220 | Stanford | 3 | |
| Lynch, Lorenzo DB | 87-89Chi 90-93Phx 94-95Arz | | 5'9" | 198 | Sacramento State | 12 | 18 |

| Use Name (Nickname) - Positions | Team by Year | See Section | Hgt. | Wgt. | College | Int | Pts |
|---|---|---|---|---|---|---|---|
| Lynch, Tom OG | 77-80Sea 81-84Buf | | 6'5" | 256 | Boston College | | |
| Lynn, Anthony FB | 93Den 95SF | | 6'3" | 230 | Texas Tech | | |
| Lynn, Johnny DB | 79NYJ 80KJ 81-86NYJ | | 6' | 196 | U.C.L.A. | 17 | 12 |
| Lyons, Marty DT-DE-NT | 79-89NYJ 90AJ | | 6'5" | 265 | Alabama | | 4 |
| Lyons, Mitch TE | 93-95Atl | 2 | 6'4" | 260 | Michigan State | | |
| Lyons, Robert DB | 89Cle | | 6'1" | 195 | Akron | 1 | |
| Lytle, Rob HB-FB | 77-83Den | 2 | 6'1" | 196 | Michigan | | 84 |
| Maarleveld, J.D. OT | 86-87TB | | 6'6" | 300 | Notre Dame, Maryland | | |
| Maas, Bill NT-DE | 84-92KC 93GB | | 6'5" | 270 | Pittsburgh | | 16 |
| Macaulay, John C | 84SF | | 6'3" | 254 | Stanford | | |
| MacDonald, Dan LB | 87Den | | 6'2" | 230 | Idaho State | | |
| MacDonald, Mark OG | 85-88Min 88Phx | | 6'4" | 266 | Boston College | | |
| Macek, Don C-OG | 76-89SD | | 6'3" | 261 | Boston College | | |
| Machurek, Mike QB | 82-84Det | | 6'1" | 205 | Idaho State | | |
| Mack, Cedric DB-WR | 83-87StL 88-90Phx 91SD 92KC 92-93NO | | 6' | 193 | Baylor | 20 | 6 |
| Mack, Kevin FB-HB | 84USFL 85-93Cle | 2 | 6' | 224 | Clemson | | 324 |
| Mack, Kim DB | 87Sea | | 6' | 190 | Florida State | | |
| Mack, Milton DB | 87-91NO 92-93TB 94Det | | 5'11" | 187 | Alcorn State | 9 | 6 |
| Mack, Rico LB | 93Pit 94NJ | | 6'4" | 239 | Appalachian State | | |
| Mack, Terence LB | 87StL | | 6'3" | 240 | Clemson | | |
| Mackey, Kyle QB | 84StL 86Phi 87Mia 88SJ 89NYJ | 1 | 6'3" | 217 | East Texas State | | 12 |
| Mackie, Doug OT | 87Atl | | 6'4" | 280 | Ohio State | | |
| Mackovic, John | HC83-86KC | | | | Wake Forest | | |
| MacPherson, Dick | HC91-92NE | | | | Springfield | | |
| Maddox, Mark LB | 92-95Buf | | 6'1" | 233 | Northern Michigan | 1 | |
| Maddox, Tommy QB | 92-93Den 94LA 95NYG | 1 | 6'4" | 200 | U.C.L.A. | | |
| Madsen, Lynn DE | 84-85USFL 86Hou | | 6'4" | 260 | Washington | | |
| Magee, Calvin TE | 85-88TB | 2 | 6'3" | 240 | Southern U. | | 66 |
| Maggs, Don OT-OG-TE | 84-85USFL 86,88-92Hou 93-94Den | | 6'5" | 287 | Tulane | | |
| Mahlum, Eric OG | 94-95Ind | | 6'4" | 288 | California | | |
| Maidlow, Steve LB | 83-84Cin 85,87Buf | | 6'2" | 235 | Michigan State | | |
| Majkowski, Don QB | 87-92GB 93-94Ind 95Det | 12 | 6'2" | 197 | Virginia | | 72 |
| Malamala, Siupeli OT-OG | 92-95NYJ | | 6'5" | 313 | Washington | | |
| Malancon, Rydell LB | 84Atl 85KJ 87GB | | 6'2" | 227 | Louisiana State | | |
| Malone, Darrell DB | 92KC 92-94Mia | | 5'10" | 177 | Jacksonville St. | 11 | |
| Malone, Ralph DE | 86Cle | | 6'5" | 225 | Georgia Tech | | |
| Mallory, Rick OG | 85-88TB | | 6'2" | 264 | Washington | | |
| Malone, Mark QB-WR | 80-87Pit 89NYJ | 12 | 6'4" | 221 | Arizona State | | 114 |
| Malone, Van DB | 94-95Det | | 5'11" | 186 | Texas | 1 | |
| Mamula, Mike DE-LB | 95Phi | | 6'4" | 252 | Boston College | | |
| Manca, Massimo K | 87Cin | | 5'10" | 211 | Penn State | 6 | |
| Mandarich, Tony OT | 89-91GB 92IL | | 6'5" | 304 | Michigan State | | |
| Mandeville, Chris DB | 87GB 89Was | | 6'1" | 213 | Cal.-Davis | | |
| Mandley, Pete WR | 84-88Det 89-90KC | 23 | 5'10" | 192 | Northern Arizona | | 84 |
| Maness, James WR | 85Chi | | 6'1" | 174 | Texas Christian | | |
| Mangiero, Dino NT-DE | 80-83KC 84Sea 87NE | | 6'2" | 266 | Rutgers | 1 | |
| Mangum, John DB | 90-95Chi | | 5'10" | 185 | Alabama | 3 | |
| Manley, Dexter DE | 81-89Was 90Phx 91TB | | 6'3" | 252 | Oklahoma State | 2 | 8 |
| Mann, Charles DE | 83-93Was 94SF | | 6'6" | 268 | Nevada-Reno | | 2 |
| Manning, Aaron DB | 87Cin | | 5'10" | 178 | Iowa State | | |
| Manning, Wade DB-WR | 79-80Dal 81-82Den | 3 | 5'11" | 190 | Ohio State | | |
| Manoa, Tim FB | 87-89Cle 90EJ 91Ind | 2 | 6'1" | 227 | Penn State | | 48 |
| Manor, Brison DE | 77-84Den 84TB | | 6'4" | 248 | Arkansas | 1 | |
| Manos, Sam C | 87Cin | | 6'3" | 265 | Marshall | | |
| Mansfield, Von DB | 82Phi 84-85USFL 87GB | | 5'11" | 184 | Wisconsin | | |
| Manucci, Dan QB | 79-80Buf 81CFL 83USFL 87Buf | | 6'2" | 196 | Kansas State | | |
| Manuel, Lionel WR | 84-90NYG | 2 | 5'11" | 178 | Pacific | | 138 |
| Manumaleuga, Frank LB | 79-81KC 83-85USFL | | 6'2" | 245 | U.C.L.A., San Jose State | 6 | 6 |
| Manusky, Greg LB | 88-90Was 91-93Min 94-95KC | | 6'1" | 240 | Colgate | | |
| Marchiol, Ken LB | 87NO | | 6'2" | 248 | Mesa | | |
| Margerum, Ken WR | 81-83Chi 84KJ 85Chi 86-87SF | 2 | 6' | 176 | Stanford | | 48 |
| Marino, Dan QB | 83-95Mia | 12 | 6'4" | 216 | Pittsburgh | | 48 |
| Marinovich, Todd QB | 91-92Raid | 1 | 6'4" | 215 | Southern Calif. | | |
| Marion, Brock DB | 93-95Dal | | 5'11" | 191 | Nevada-Reno | 8 | 6 |
| Marion, Frank LB | 77-83NYG | | 6'3" | 227 | Florida A&M | 1 | |
| Marion, Fred DB | 82-91NE | | 6'2" | 192 | Miami (Fla.) | 29 | 6 |
| Mark, Greg DE-LB | 90Mia 90Phi | | 6'3" | 252 | Miami (Fla.) | | |
| Markham, Dale OT-DE | 80NYG 81StL 83-85USFL | | 6'8" | 280 | North Dakota | | |
| Markland, Jeff TE | 88Pit | | 6'3" | 245 | Illinois | | |
| Marrone, Doug OG-C-OT | 87Mia 89NO | | 6'5" | 269 | Syracuse | | |
| Marrow, Vince TE | 94Buf | | 6'3" | 251 | Toledo | | |
| Marsh, Curt OG | 81Oak 82Raid 83XJ 84-86Raid 87NJ | | 6'5" | 273 | Washington | | |
| Marsh, Curtis WR | 95Jax | | 6'2" | 201 | Utah | | |
| Marsh, Doug TE | 80-86StL | 2 | 6'3" | 238 | Michigan | | 114 |
| Marshall, Anthony DB | 94-95Chi | | 6'1" | 205 | Louisiana State | 1 | 6 |
| Marshall, Arthur WR | 92-93Den 94-95NYG | 23 | 5'11" | 174 | Georgia | | 24 |
| Marshall, David LB | 84Cle 87Mia | | 6'3" | 220 | Eastern Michigan | | |
| Marshall, Henry WR | 76-87KC | 2 | 6'2" | 214 | Missouri | | 210 |
| Marshall, James DB | 80NO | | 6' | 187 | Jackson State | 2 | |
| Marshall, Leonard DE | 83-92NYG 93NYJ 94Was | | 6'3" | 285 | Louisiana State | 2 | 4 |
| Marshall, Warren FB | 87Den | | 6' | 216 | James Madison | | |
| Marshall, Wilber LB | 84-87Chi 88-92Was 93Hou 94Arz 95NYJ | | 6'1" | 228 | Florida | 23 | 24 |
| Martin, Charles NT-DE | 83USFL 84-87GB 87Hou 88Atl | | 6'4" | 276 | Livingston | | |
| Martin, Chris LB | 83NO 84-88Min 88-92KC 93-94LA | | 6'2" | 236 | Auburn | 1 | 24 |
| Martin, Curtis HB | 95NE | 2 | 5'11" | 203 | Pittsburgh | | 92 |
| Martin, David DB | 83-85USFL 86SD 87Buf | | 5'9" | 191 | Villanova | | |
| Martin, Derrick DB | 87SF | | 6' | 185 | San Jose State | 1 | |
| Martin, Doug DE-NT | 80-89Min | | 6'3" | 260 | Washington | 1 | |
| Martin, Emanuel DB | 93Hou | | 5'11" | 184 | Alabama State | | |
| Martin, Emerson OG | 95Car | | 6'2" | 297 | Hampton | | |
| Martin, Eric WR | 85-93NO 94KC | 23 | 6'1" | 205 | Louisiana State | | 294 |
| Martin, George DE-TE | 75-88NYG | | 6'4" | 247 | Oregon | 3 | 36 |
| Martin, Jamie QB | 93-94LA 95StL | | 6'2" | 215 | Weber State | | |
| Martin, Kelvin WR | 87-92Dal 93-94Sea 95Phi | 23 | 5'9" | 163 | Boston College | | 102 |
| Martin, Mike WR | 83-89Cin | 23 | 5'10" | 186 | Illinois | | 36 |
| Martin, Robbie WR | 81-84Det 85-86Ind | 3 | 5'8" | 181 | Cal. Poly.-S.L.O. | | 18 |
| Martin, Rod LB | 77-81Oak 82-88Raid | | 6'2" | 218 | Southern Calif. | 15 | 38 |
| Martin, Saladin DB | 80NYJ 81SF 83USFL | | 6' | 180 | San Diego State | 1 | |
| Martin, Sammy WR | 88-91NE 91Ind | 23 | 5'11" | 175 | Louisiana State | | 12 |
| Martin, Steve DE | 87Was | | 6'3" | 260 | Jackson State | | |
| Martin, Tony WR | 90-93Mia 94-95SD | 23 | 6' | 180 | Bishop, Mesa | | 132 |
| Martin , Tracy WR | 87NYJ 88LJ | | 6'3" | 205 | North Dakota | | |
| Martin, Wayne DE | 89-95NO | | 6'5" | 275 | Arkansas | 1 | |
| Martini, Rich WR | 79-80Oak 81NO | 2 | 6'2" | 185 | Cal.-Davis | | 12 |

| Use Name (Nickname) - Positions | Team by Year | See Section | Hgt. | Wgt. | College | Int | Pts |
|---|---|---|---|---|---|---|---|
| Marts, Lonnie LB | 91-93KC 94-95TB | | 6'1" | 239 | Tulane | 3 | 6 |
| Marve, Eugene LB | 82-87Buf 88-91TB 92SD | | 6'2" | 237 | Saginaw Valley St. | 3 | |
| Marvin, Mickey OG | 77-81Oak 82-86Raid 87KJ | | 6'4" | 269 | Tennessee | | |
| Maryland, Russell DT-DE | 91-95Dal | | 6'1" | 279 | Miami (Fla.) | | 6 |
| Mason, Eddie LB | 95NYJ | | 6' | 230 | North Carolina | | |
| Mason, Larry HB-FB | 87Cle 88GB | 2 | 5'11" | 205 | Troy State | | 18 |
| Mason, Lindsey OT | 78Oak 79KJ 80-81Oak 82SF 83Bal 84-85USFL | | 6'5" | 265 | Kansas | | |
| Massey, Robert DB | 89-90NO 91-93Phx 94-95Det | | 5'10" | 191 | N. Car. Central | 14 | 18 |
| Massie, Rick WR | 87-88Den | | 6'1" | 190 | Kentucky | | 24 |
| Maston, Le'Shai FB-HB-TE | 93-94Hou 95Jax | 2 | 6'1" | 225 | Baylor | | |
| Mataele, Stan NT | 87GB | | 6'2" | 278 | Arizona | | |
| Matau, Christopher OG | 87LA | | 6'3" | 310 | Brigham Young | | |
| Mathews, Jason OT | 94-95Ind | | 6'5" | 286 | Texas A&M | | |
| Mathis, Mark DB | 87StL | | 5'9" | 178 | Liberty | 1 | |
| Mathis, Reggie LB | 79-80NO 85USFL | | 6'2" | 220 | Oklahoma | 1 | |
| Mathis, Terance WR | 90-93NYJ 94-95Atl | 23 | 5'10" | 170 | New Mexico | | 172 |
| Mathison, Bruce QB | 83-84SD 85Buf 86SD 87-88Sea | 12 | 6'3" | 205 | Nebraska | | 6 |
| Matich, Trevor C-OG-TE-OT | 85-88NE 89Det 90-91NYJ 92-93Ind 94-95Was | | 6'4" | 286 | Brigham Young | | 6 |
| Mattes, Ron OT | 86-90Sea 91Chi 92Ind | | 6'6" | 304 | Virginia | | |
| Matthews, Allama TE-FB | 83-85Atl | 2 | 6'3" | 230 | Vanderbilt | | 6 |
| Matthews, Aubrey WR | 86-88Atl 88-89GB 90-95Det | 2 | 5'7" | 165 | Delta State | | 54 |
| Matthews, Bill LB | 79-81NE 82KJ 84USFL | | 6'2" | 235 | S. Dakota State | 1 | |
| Matthews, Bruce OG-OT-C | 83-95Hou | | 6'4" | 290 | Southern Calif. | | |
| Matthews, Clay LB | 78-93Cle 94-95Atl | | 6'2" | 239 | Southern Calif. | 16 | 12 |
| Matthews, Ira HB-WR | 79-81Oak 83USFL | 23 | 5'8" | 175 | Wisconsin | | 6 |
| Matthews, Shane QB | 93-94Chi | | 6'3" | 197 | Florida | | |
| Mattiace, Frank DE-NT | 87Ind | | 6'1" | 264 | Holy Cross | | |
| Maumalanga, Chris DT | 94NYG 95Arz | | 6'2" | 288 | Kansas | | |
| Mauti, Rich WR | 77-80NO 81AJ 82-83NO 84Was | 23 | 6' | 190 | Penn State | | 12 |
| Mawae, Kevin OG | 94-95Sea | | 6'4" | 288 | Louisiana State | | |
| Maxey, Curtis DE-NT | 88Cin 89Atl | | 6'3" | 298 | Grambling | | |
| Maxie, Brett DB | 85-93NO 94Atl 95Car | | 6'2" | 193 | Texas Southern | 21 | 20 |
| Maxwell, Vernon LB | 83Bal 84Ind 85-87Det 89Sea | | 6'2" | 233 | Arizona State | 1 | |
| May, Chad QB | 95Min | | 6'1" | 219 | Kansas State | | |
| May, Dean QB | 84Phi 87Den | | 6'5" | 220 | Louisville | | |
| May, Deems TE | 92-95SD | | 6'4" | 259 | North Carolina | | |
| May, Marc TE | 87Min | | 6'4" | 230 | Purdue | | |
| May, Mark OT-OG | 81-89Was 90KJ 91SD 92-93Phx | | 6'6" | 295 | Pittsburgh | | |
| May, Sherriden FB | 95NYJ | | 6' | 215 | Idaho | | |
| Mayberry, James FB-HB | 79-81Atl 83-85USFL | 2 | 5'11" | 210 | Colorado | 1 | 12 |
| Mayberry, Tony C | 90-95TB | | 6'4" | 290 | Wake Forest | | |
| Mayes, Michael DB | 89NO 90NYJ 91Min | | 5'10" | 182 | Louisiana State | 1 | |
| Mayes, Rueben HB | 86-88NO 89KJ 90NO 92-93Sea | 23 | 5'11" | 200 | Washington State | | 138 |
| Mayes, Tony DB | 87StL | | 6' | 200 | Kentucky | | |
| Mayfield, Corey NT-DT | 92TB 95Jax | | 6'3" | 291 | Oklahoma | | |
| Mayhew, Martin DB | 89-92Was 93-95TB | | 5'8" | 176 | Florida State | 20 | 12 |
| Mayock, Mike DB | 82-83NYG | | 6'2" | 195 | Boston College | | |
| Mays, Alvoid DB | 90-94Was 95Pit | | 5'9" | 180 | West Virginia | 5 | 6 |
| Mays, Damon WR | 92Hou 95SJ | | 5'9" | 170 | Missouri | | |
| Mays, Jerry HB | 90SD | | 5'7" | 176 | Georgia Tech | | |
| Mays, Stafford DE-NT | 80-86StL 87-88Min | | 6'2" | 252 | Washington | | |
| McAdoo, Derrick HB | 87StL 88TB 88Phx 94Arz 94Pit | 2 | 5'10" | 197 | Baylor | | 36 |
| McAfee, Fred HB | 91-93NO 94Arz 94-95Pit | 23 | 5'10" | 193 | Mississippi Coll. | | 42 |
| McAlister, Ken LB-DB | 82-83Sea 83SF 84KC 85KJ 86-87KC | | 6'5" | 220 | San Francisco | 2 | |
| McArthur, Kevin LB | 86-89NYJ | | 6'2" | 244 | Lamar | 1 | |
| McBride, Adrian WR | 87StL | | 6' | 195 | Missouri | | |
| McBride, Oscar TE | 95Arz | 2 | 6'5" | 266 | Notre Dame | | 12 |
| McBurrows, Gerald DB | 95StL | | 5'11" | 195 | Kansas | | |
| McCabe, Jerry LB | 87NE 88KC 89GA | | 6'1" | 225 | Holy Cross | | |
| McCaffrey, Ed WR | 91-93NYG 94SF 95Den | 2 | 6'5" | 215 | Stanford | | 68 |
| McCall, Joe HB-FB | 84Raid | | 6' | 200 | Pittsburgh | | |
| McCall, Reese TE | 78-82Bal 83-85Det | 2 | 6'7" | 239 | Auburn | | 78 |
| McCallister, Fred LB | 87TB | | 6'1" | 250 | Florida | | |
| McCallum, Napoleon HB | 86Raid 87-89MS 90-94Raid | 23 | 6'2" | 215 | Navy | | 36 |
| McCants, Keith LB-DE | 90-92TB 93-94Hou 94-95Arz | | 6'3" | 260 | Alabama | 1 | 12 |
| McCardell, Keenan WR | 92-95Cle | 2 | 6'1" | 185 | Nevada-Las Vegas | | 48 |
| McCarthy, John QB | 87GB | | 6'4" | 212 | Williams | | |
| McCarthy, Shawn K | 91-92NE | 4 | 6'6" | 227 | Purdue | | |
| McCartney, Pete OG | 87NYJ | | 6'6" | 260 | Louisville | | |
| McClendon, Skip DE | 87-91Cin 91SD 92Min 92-93Ind | | 6'6" | 282 | Northwestern, Arizona State | | |
| McClendon, Willie HB-FB | 79-82Chi 84USFL | 2 | 6'1" | 205 | Georgia | | 12 |
| McClesky, J.J. DB | 94NO | | 5'7" | 177 | Tennessee | | |
| McCloskey, Mike TE | 83-85Hou 87Phi | 2 | 6'5" | 245 | Penn State | | 18 |
| McCloughan, Dave DB | 91Ind 92GB 93-94Sea | | 6'1" | 180 | Colorado | | |
| McClure, Brian QB | 87Buf | 1 | 6'6" | 222 | Bowling Green | | |
| McCluskey, David FB | 87Cin | 2 | 6'1" | 227 | Georgia | | 6 |
| McColl, Milt LB | 81-87SF 88Raid | | 6'6" | 248 | Stanford | 2 | 6 |
| McCollum, Andy C-OG | 95NO | | 6'4" | 295 | Toledo | | |
| McConkey, Phil WR | 84-85NYG 86GB 86-88NYG 89Phx 89SD | 23 | 5'10" | 170 | Navy | | 18 |
| McCormack, Hurvin DT | 94-95Dal | | 6'5" | 276 | Indiana | | |
| McCorvey, Kez WR | 95Det | | 6' | 180 | Florida State | | |
| McCoy, Larry LB | 83USFL 84Raid 85USFL 87NO | | 6'2" | 240 | Lamar | | |
| McCoy, Mike (M.C.) DB | 76-83GB 84LJ | 3 | 5'11" | 183 | Colorado | 9 | |
| McCoy, Tony NT | 92-95Ind | | 6' | 279 | Florida | | |
| McCrary, Fred FB | 95Phi | | 6' | 219 | Mississippi State | | 6 |
| McCrary, Michael DE | 93-95Sea | | 6'4" | 263 | Wake Forest | | |
| McCray, Bruce DB | 87Chi | | 5'9" | 181 | Western Illinois | 1 | 6 |
| McCullough, Jake DE | 89-90Den | | 6'5" | 270 | Clemson | | |
| McCurry, Mike OG | 87Min | | 6'3" | 258 | Indiana | | |
| McDaniel, Ed LB | 92-95Min | | 5'11" | 232 | Clemson | 2 | |
| McDaniel, LeCharls DB | 81-82Was 83NYG | | 5'9" | 183 | Cal. Poly.-S.L.O. | | 1 |
| McDaniel, Orlando WR | 82Den | | 6' | 180 | Louisiana State | | |
| McDaniel, Randall OG | 88-95Min | | 6'3" | 274 | Arizona State | | |
| McDaniel, Terry DB | 88-94Raid 95Oak | | 5'10" | 177 | Tennessee | 28 | 36 |
| McDaniels, Pellom DE | 93-95KC | | 6'3" | 285 | Oregon State | | |
| McDole, Mardye WR | 81-83Min | | 5'11" | 198 | Mississippi State | | |
| McDonald, Devon LB | 93-95Ind | | 6'4" | 234 | Notre Dame | | |
| McDonald, James TE | 83-84LA 85Det 85,87LA | 2 | 6'5" | 234 | Southern Calif. | | 18 |
| McDonald, Keith WR | 87Hou 89Det | 2 | 5'9" | 170 | San Jose State | | 6 |
| McDonald, Mike LB | 84,86-91LA 92Det | | 6'1" | 238 | Southern Calif. | | |
| McDonald, Paul QB | 80-85Cle 86-87Dal | 12 | 6'2" | 185 | Southern Calif. | | 6 |
| McDonald, Quintus LB | 89-91Ind | | 6'3" | 259 | Penn State | | |
| McDonald, Ricardo LB | 92-95Cin | | 6'2" | 235 | Pittsburgh | 1 | |
| McDonald, Tim DB | 87StL 88-92Phx 93-95SF | | 6'2" | 212 | Southern Calif. | 29 | 30 |
| McDonough, Bob DB | 87Det | | 6'1" | 170 | California (Pa.) | | |

| Use Name (Nickname) - Positions | Team by Year | See Section | Hgt. | Wgt. | College | Int | Pts |
|---|---|---|---|---|---|---|---|
| McDowell, Anthony FB | 92-94TB | 2 | 5'11" | 233 | Texas Tech | | 24 |
| McDowell, Bubba DB | 89-94Hou 95Car | | 6'1" | 196 | Miami (Fla.) | 17 | 14 |
| McDuffie, George DE | 87Det | | 6'6" | 270 | Findlay | | |
| McDuffie, O.J. WR | 93-95Mia | 23 | 5'10" | 191 | Penn State | | 80 |
| McDouguld, Doug DE | 80NE | | 6'5" | 271 | Virginia Tech | | |
| McElroy, Ray DB | 95Ind | | 5'11" | 195 | Eastern Illinois | | |
| McElroy, Reggie OT-OG | 83-89NYJ 91-92Raid 93KC 94Min 95Den | | 6'6" | 285 | West Texas State | | |
| McElroy, Vann DB | 82-90Raid 90Sea 91-92NJ | | 6'2" | 193 | Baylor | 31 | 6 |
| McEwen, Craig TE | 87-88Was 89-91SD | 2 | 6'1" | 222 | Utah | | 36 |
| McFadden, Paul K | 84-87Phi 88NYG 89Atl | 5 | 5'11" | 163 | Youngstown State | | 520 |
| McFadden, Thad WR | 87Buf | | 6'2" | 200 | Wisconsin | | 6 |
| McGarry, John OG | 87GB | | 6'5" | 288 | St. Joseph's | | |
| McGee, Buford HB-FB | 84-86SD 87-91LA 92GB | 2 | 6' | 205 | Mississippi | | 180 |
| McGee, Carl LB | 80SD 83USFL | | 6'3" | 228 | Duke | | |
| McGee, Tim WR | 86-92Cin 93Was 94Cin 95ZJ | 23 | 5'10" | 176 | Tennessee | | 168 |
| McGee, Tony TE | 93-95Cin | 2 | 6'3" | 246 | Michigan | | 30 |
| McGhee, Kanavis LB | 91-93NYG 94Cin 95Hou | | 6'4" | 257 | Colorado | | |
| McGill, Eddie TE | 82-83StL 84KJ | | 6'6" | 225 | Western Carolina | | |
| McGill, Lenny DB | 94-95GB | | 6'2" | 194 | Arizona State | 2 | |
| McGill, Karmeeleyah LB | 93Cin | | 6'3" | 224 | Notre Dame | | |
| McGinest, Willie LB | 94-95NE | | 6'5" | 254 | Southern Calif. | | |
| McGlasson, Ed C | 79NYJ 80LA 81NYG | | 6'4" | 248 | Youngstown State | | |
| McGlockton, Chester DT | 92-94Raid 95Oak | | 6'4" | 317 | Clemson | 1 | |
| McGonnigal, Bruce TE | 91Cle | | 6'4" | 230 | Virginia | | |
| McGovern, Rob LB | 89-90KC 91Pit 92NE | | 6'2" | 223 | Holy Cross | | 2 |
| McGowan, Reggie WR | 87NYG | | 5'8" | 165 | Abilene Christian | | 6 |
| McGrail, Joe NT | 87Buf | | 6'3" | 280 | Delaware | | |
| McGrath, Mark WR | 81Sea 83-85Was | 2 | 5'11" | 175 | Montana State | | 6 |
| McGregor, Keli TE | 85Den 85Ind | | 6'6" | 250 | Colorado State | | |
| McGrew, Larry LB | 80NE 81KJ 82-89NE 90NYG | | 6'5" | 233 | Southern Calif. | 6 | |
| McGrew, Sylvester DE | 87GB | | 6'4" | 257 | Tulane | | |
| McGriff, Curtis DE-NT | 80-85NYG 86LJ 87Was | | 6'5" | 271 | Alabama | | |
| McGriff, Tyrone OG | 80-82Pit 83-85USFL | | 6' | 269 | Florida A&M | | |
| McGriggs, Lamar DB | 91-92NYG 93-94Min | | 6'3" | 213 | Oklahoma State, Western Illinois | 2 | 6 |
| McGruder, Michael DB | 89GB 90-91Mia 92-93SF 94-95TB | | 5'11" | 186 | Kent State | 6 | 6 |
| McGuire, Gene C | 92NO 93Chi | | 6'2" | 285 | Notre Dame | | |
| McGuire, Monte QB | 87Den | | 6'4" | 202 | Texas Tech | | |
| McGwire, Dan QB | 91-94Sea 95Mia | 1 | 6'8" | 243 | Iowa, San Diego St. | | |
| McHale, Joe LB | 87NE | | 6'2" | 227 | Delaware | | |
| McHale, Tom DE-OG-OT | 87-92TB 93-94Phi 95Mia | | 6'4" | 284 | Cornell | | |
| McInally, Pat WR-K | 76-85Cin | 2 4 | 6'6" | 210 | Harvard | | 30 |
| McInerney, Sean DE | 87Chi | | 6'3" | 255 | Frostburg State | | |
| McIntosh, Joe HB | 87Atl | | 5'10" | 192 | N. Carolina State | | 6 |
| McIntosh, Toddrick DT-DE | 94-95TB | | 6'3" | 277 | Florida State | | |
| McIntyre, Guy OG | 84-93SF 94GB 95Phi | | 6'3" | 271 | Georgia | | 12 |
| McIntyre, Jeff LB | 79SF 80StL 83-84USFL | | 6'3" | 232 | Arizona State | | |
| McIver, Everett OG | 94-95NYJ | | 6'6" | 315 | Elizabeth City St. | | |
| McIvor, Rick QB | 84-85StL | | 6'4" | 210 | Texas | | |
| McJulien, Paul K | 91-92GB 93LA | 4 | 5'10" | 190 | Jackson State | | |
| McKeever, Vito DB | 86-87TB | | 6' | 180 | Florida | 3 | |
| McKeller, Keith TE | 87-93Buf | 2 | 6'6" | 240 | Jacksonville St. | | 66 |
| McKenzie, Raleigh OG-C | 85-94Was 95Phi | | 6'2" | 276 | Tennessee | | |
| McKenzie, Reggie LB | 85-88Raid 89KJ 92SF | | 6'1" | 239 | Tennessee | 2 | |
| McKenzie, Rich DE | 95Cle | | 6'2" | 258 | Penn State | | |
| McKibben, Mike LB | 79-80NYJ 81KJ | | 6'3" | 228 | Kent State | 1 | |
| McKinney, Odis DB | 78-79NYG 80-81Oak 82-84Raid 85KC 85-86Raid | | 6'2" | 189 | Colorado | 11 | |
| McKinney, Zion WR | 80Was | | 6' | 200 | South Carolina | | |
| McKinnon, Dennis WR | 83-85Chi 86KJ 87-89Chi 90Dal 90Mia | 23 | 6'1" | 182 | Florida State | | 156 |
| McKnight, Dennis C-OG | 82-88SD 90KJ 90Det 91Phi 92Det | | 6'3" | 271 | Drake | | |
| McKnight, James WR | 94-95Sea | | 6' | 186 | Liberty | | 6 |
| McKyer, Tim DB | 86-89SF 90Mia 91-92Atl 93Det 94Pit 95Car | | 6' | 174 | Texas-Arlington | 32 | 12 |
| McLaughlin, Joe LB | 79GB 80-84NYG | | 6'1" | 235 | Massachusetts | | |
| McLaughlin, Steve K | 95StL | 5 | 6' | 167 | Arizona | | 41 |
| McLean, Ron NT-DE | 87Den 88KC | | 6'3" | 267 | Fullerton State | | |
| McLean, Scott LB | 83Dal | | 6'4" | 233 | Florida State | | |
| McLemore, Chris FB | 87Ind 87-88Raid | | 6'1" | 232 | Colorado, Arizona | | |
| McLemore, Dana DB | 82-86SF 86NO 87SF | 3 | 5'10" | 183 | Hawaii | 5 | 30 |
| McLemore, Thomas TE | 92Det 93-94Cle 95Ind | | 6'5" | 245 | Southern U. | | |
| McLeod, Mike DB | 84-85GB | | 6' | 180 | Minnesota | 1 | |
| McMahon, Jim QB | 82-88Chi 89SD 90-92Phi 93Min 94Arz 95GB | 12 | 6'1" | 191 | Brigham Young | | 108 |
| McManus, Danny QB | 88KC | | 6' | 200 | Florida State | | |
| McManus, Tom LB | 95Jax | | 6'2" | 252 | Boston College | | |
| McMichael, Steve (Mongo) DT-NT | 80NE 81-93Chi 94GB | | 6'2" | 263 | Texas | 2 | 6 |
| McMillan, Erik DB | 88-92NYJ 93Cle 93KC | | 6'2" | 197 | Missouri | 22 | 42 |
| McMillan, Randy FB | 81-83Bal 84-86Ind | 2 | 6' | 219 | Pittsburgh | | 156 |
| McMillian, Audray DB | 85-87Hou 88KJ 89-93Min | | 6' | 190 | Houston | 19 | 18 |
| McMillian, Henry DT | 95Sea | | 6'3" | 275 | Florida | | |
| McMillian, Mark DB | 92-95Phi | | 5'7" | 162 | Alabama | 8 | |
| McMillen, Dan LB | 87Phi87Raid | | 6'5" | 240 | Colorado | | |
| McMurtry, Greg WR | 90-93NE 94Chi | 2 | 6'2" | 207 | Michigan | | 24 |
| McNabb, Dexter FB | 92-93GB 95Phi | | 6'2" | 245 | Florida | | |
| McNair, Steve (Air) QB | 95Hou | 1 | 6'2" | 224 | Alcorn State | | |
| McNair, Todd HB | 89-93KC 94-95Hou | 23 | 6'1" | 185 | Temple | | 54 |
| McNanie, Sean DE | 84-87Buf 88Phx 90Ind | | 6'5" | 265 | Arizona State, San Diego State | | 6 |
| McNeal, Don DB | 80-82Mia 83LJ 84-89Mia | | 5'11" | 192 | Alabama | 18 | 12 |
| McNeal, Travis TE | 89-91Sea 91-93LA | 2 | 6'3" | 248 | Tenn.-Chattanooga | | 12 |
| McNeil, Emanuel NT | 89NE 90NYJ | | 6'3" | 285 | Tennessee-Martin | | |
| McNeil, Gerald (Ice Cube) WR | 86-89Cle 90Hou | 23 | 5'7" | 145 | Baylor | | 24 |
| McNeil, Freeman HB | 81-92NYJ | 2 | 5'11" | 214 | U.C.L.A. | | 300 |
| McNeil, Ryan DB | 93-95Det | | 6' | 188 | Miami (Fla.) | 5 | |
| McNorton, Bruce DB | 82-90Det 91BW | | 5'11" | 175 | Georgetown (Ky.) | 16 | |
| McPherson, Don QB | 88-89Phi 90Hou | | 6'1" | 183 | Syracuse | | |
| McPherson, Miles DB | 82-85SD | | 5'11" | 184 | New Haven | 2 | |
| McQuaid, Dan OT-OG | 85-87Was 88Min 88Ind | | 6'7" | 278 | Nevada-Las Vegas | | |
| McRae, Charles OT-OG | 91-95TB | | 6'7" | 298 | Tennessee | | |
| McSwain, Chuck HB | 83-84Dal 87NE | | 6' | 193 | Clemson | 2 | |
| McSwain, Rod DB | 84-90NE | | 6'1" | 198 | Clemson | 4 | 6 |
| McVeigh, John LB | 87Sea | | 6'1" | 226 | Kentucky, Miami (Fla.) | | |
| Meade, Mike FB | 82-83GB 84-85Det | 2 | 5'11" | 226 | Penn State | | 18 |
| Meadows, Darryl DB | 83-84Hou | | 6'1" | 199 | Toledo | | |
| Meads, Johnny LB | 84-92Hou 92Was | | 6'2" | 231 | Nicholls State | 1 | 6 |
| Meamber, Tim LB | 85Min | | 6'3" | 231 | Washington | | |

| Use Name (Nickname) - Positions | Team by Year | See Section | Hgt. | Wgt. | College | Int | Pts |
|---|---|---|---|---|---|---|---|
| Means, Natrone FB-HB | 93-95SD | 2 | 5'10" | 245 | North Carolina | | 150 |
| Mecklenburg, Karl LB-DE | 83-94Den | | 6'3" | 236 | Augustana (S.D.), Minnesota | 5 | 14 |
| Meehan, Greg WR | 87Cin | | 6' | 191 | Bowling Green | | |
| Meeks, Bob C | 93Den 94ZJ | | 6'2" | 279 | Auburn | | |
| Meggett, Dave HB | 89-94NYG 95NE | 23 | 5'7" | 180 | Morgan State, Towson State | | 148 |
| Mehl, Lance LB | 80-87NYJ | | 6'3" | 233 | Penn State | 15 | 6 |
| Meisner, Greg NT-DE | 81-88LA 89-90KC 91NYG | | 6'3" | 257 | Pittsburgh | 1 | |
| Melander, Jon OT-OG | 91NE 92Cin 93-94Den | | 6'7" | 280 | Minnesota | | |
| Melka, James LB | 87GB | | 6'1" | 235 | Wisconsin | 1 | |
| Melontree, Andre LB | 80Cin 83-85USFL | | 6'4" | 228 | Baylor | | |
| Mendenhall, Mat DE | 81-82Was 83IL | | 6'6" | 254 | Brigham Young | | |
| Mendoza, Ruben OT | 86GB | | 6'4" | 290 | Wayne State-Neb. | | |
| Merkens, Guido WR-DB-QB | 78-80Hou 80-85NO 87Phi | 12 | 6'1" | 200 | Sam Houston St. | | 18 |
| Merrill, Casey DE-DT | 79-83GB 83-85NYG 86NO | | 6'4" | 255 | Cal.-Davis | | |
| Merrill, Mark LB | 78-79NYJ 79Chi 81-82Den 82GB 83-84Buf 84Raid | | 6'4" | 236 | Minnesota | | |
| Merriman, Sam LB | 83-87Sea 88KJ | | 6'3" | 229 | Idaho | | 6 |
| Merrits, Jim DE-NT | 87Ind | | 6'3" | 255 | West Virginia | | |
| Merritt, David LB | 93Mia 93Phx 94-95Arz | | 6'1" | 237 | N. Carolina State | | |
| Merriweather, Mike LB | 82-87Pit 88HO 89-92Min 93NYJ | | 6'2" | 219 | Pacific | 18 | 32 |
| Mersereau, Scott NT-DE-DT | 87-93NYJ | | 6'3" | 275 | Southern Conn. St. | 3 | |
| Mesner, Bruce NT | 87Buf 88-89KJ | | 6'5" | 280 | Maryland | | |
| Mesner, Mark LB | 89LA | | 6'2" | 256 | Michigan | | |
| Metcalf, Bo DB | 84Ind | | 6'2" | 193 | Baylor | | |
| Metcalf, Eric HB-WR | 89-94Cle 95Atl | 23 | 5'10" | 187 | Texas | | 258 |
| Metzelaars, Pete TE | 82-84Sea 85-89-94Buf 95Car | 2 | 6'7" | 245 | Wabash | | 180 |
| Meuth, Kevin OT | 87NYG | | 6'5" | 270 | SW Texas State | | |
| Meyer, Jim OT | 87GB | | 6'5" | 290 | Illinois State | | |
| Meyer, Ron | HC82-84NE HC86-91Ind | | | | Purdue | | |
| Miano, Rich DB | 85-89NYJ 91-94Phi 95Atl | | 6' | 200 | Hawaii | 15 | 6 |
| Micech, Phil DE | 87Min | | 6'5" | 265 | Wis.-Platteville | | |
| Micho, Bobby TE-FB | 84SD 85FJ 86-87Den | 2 | 6'3" | 236 | Texas | | 12 |
| Mickel, Jeff OT | 90LA | | 6'6" | 300 | Eastern Washington | | |
| Mickell, Darren DE | 92-95KC | | 6'4" | 278 | Florida | | |
| Mickens, Terry WR | 94-95GB | | 6'1" | 200 | Florida A&M | | |
| Mickey, Joey TE | 93Dal | | 6'5" | 274 | Oklahoma | | |
| Mickles, Joe FB | 89Was 90SD | | 5'10" | 221 | Mississippi | | |
| Middleton, Frank HB | 84-85Ind 87SD | 2 | 5'11" | 204 | Florida A&M | | 18 |
| Middleton, Kelvin DB | 87Pit | | 6' | 186 | Wichita State | | |
| Middleton, Ron TE | 86-87Atl 88Was 89Cle 90-93Was 94LA 95SD | 2 | 6'2" | 262 | Auburn | | 18 |
| Middleton, Terdell HB | 77-81GB 82-83TB 84USFL | 2 | 6' | 198 | Memphis State | | 114 |
| Migliazzo, Paul LB | 87Chi | | 6'1" | 228 | Oklahoma | | |
| Mikeska, Russ TE | 79-83Atl | | 6'3" | 225 | Texas A&M | | |
| Mikolas, Doug NT | 87-88SF 88Hou | | 6'1" | 270 | Portland State | | |
| Milburn, Darryl DE | 91Det | | 6'3" | 260 | Grambling | | |
| Milburn, Glyn HB | 93-95Den | 23 | 5'8" | 177 | Oklahoma, Stanford | | 42 |
| Miles, Eddie LB | 90Pit | | 6'1" | 233 | Minnesota | | |
| Miles, Ostell HB | 92-93Cin | 2 | 6' | 236 | Houston | | 6 |
| Milinichik, Joe OG-OT | 87-89Det 90-92LA 93-94SD | | 6'5" | 288 | N. Carolina State | | |
| Millard, Bryan OG-OT | 83-84USFL 84-91Sea 92XJ | | 6'5" | 283 | Texas | | |
| Millard, Keith DT-DE | 85USFL 85-90Min 91KJ 92Sea 92GB 93Phi | | 6'5" | 262 | Washington State | 2 | 6 |
| Millen, Hugh QB | 87LA 88-90Atl 91-92NE 93Mia 94-95Den | 12 | 6'5" | 216 | Washington | | 6 |
| Millen, Matt LB | 80-81Oak 82-88Raid 89-90SF 91Was | | 6'2" | 250 | Penn State | 9 | |
| Miller, Anthony WR | 88-93SD 94-95Den | 23 | 5'11" | 185 | San Diego State, Tennessee | | 356 |
| Miller, Blake C | 92Det | | 6'1" | 282 | Louisiana State | | |
| Miller, Brett OT | 83-88Atl 89SD 90-92NYJ | | 6'7" | 293 | Iowa | | |
| Miller, Bronzell DE | 95Jax | | 6'4" | 245 | Utah | | |
| Miller, Chris QB | 87-93Atl 94LA 95Stl | 12 | 6'2" | 200 | Oregon | | 15 |
| Miller, Chuckie DB | 88Ind | | 5'10" | 180 | U.C.L.A. | | |
| Miller, Clay OT-OG | 87Hou | | 6'4" | 273 | Michigan | | |
| Miller, Corey LB | 91-95NYG | | 6'2" | 255 | South Carolina | 6 | |
| Miller, Danny K | 82NE 82Bal 84-85USFL | 5 | 5'10" | 172 | Miami (Fla.) | | 27 |
| Miller, Darrin LB | 88-89Sea | | 6'1" | 227 | Tennessee | 1 | |
| Miller, Donald LB | 90Sea | | 6'2" | 223 | Idaho State | | |
| Miller, Doug LB | 93-94SD | | 6'3" | 237 | S. Dakota State | | |
| Miller, Eddie WR | 92-93Ind | | 6' | 185 | South Carolina | | |
| Miller, Jamir LB | 94-95Arz | | 6'4" | 242 | U.C.L.A. | | |
| Miller, Jim K | 80-82SF 83-84Dal 87NYG | 4 | 5'11" | 183 | Mississippi | | |
| Miller, Jim QB | 94-95Pit | 1 | 6'2" | 226 | Michigan State | | |
| Miller, John LB | 87GB | | 6'2" | 218 | Mississippi State | | |
| Miller, John DB | 89-90Det | | 6'1" | 195 | Michigan State | | |
| Miller, Junior TE | 80-83Atl 84NO | 2 | 6'4" | 239 | Nebraska | | 84 |
| Miller, Larry QB | 87Min | | 6'4" | 220 | Northern Iowa | | |
| Miller, Les DE-NT | 87-90SD 91-94NO 94SD | | 6'7' | 290 | Kansas State, Ft. Hays State | | 18 |
| Miller, Mark QB | 87Buf | | 6'2" | 210 | Mesa | | |
| Miller, Matt OT-OG | 79Cle 80KJ 81-82Cle 84-85USFL | | 6'6" | 270 | Colorado | | |
| Miller, Mike WR | 83NYG 85NO 86LJ | | 6' | 182 | Tennessee | | |
| Miller, Nick LB | 87Cle | | 6'2" | 238 | Arkansas | | |
| Miller, Pat DB | 88SD | | 6'1" | 206 | Florida | | |
| Miller, Scott WR | 91-94Mia 95KJ | 23 | 5'10" | 179 | U.C.L.A. | | 6 |
| Miller, Shawn NT-DE-DT | 84-89LA | | 6'4" | 255 | Utah State | 1 | |
| Miller, Soloman WR | 86NYG 87TB | 2 | 6'1" | 185 | Utah State | | 12 |
| Miller, Terry HB | 78-80Buf 81Sea 83-84USFL | 23 | 5'10" | 196 | Oklahoma State | | 48 |
| Milling, James WR | 88,90,92Atl 93CJ | 2 | 5'9" | 156 | Maryland | | 6 |
| Million, Ted OT | 87Min | | 6'4" | 260 | Duke | | |
| Mills, Ernie WR | 91-95Pit | 23 | 5'11" | 185 | Florida | | 90 |
| Mills, Jeff LB | 90SD 90-93Den | | 6'3" | 244 | Nebraska | | |
| Mills, Jim OT | 83Bal 84Ind | | 6'9" | 276 | Hawaii | | |
| Mills, John Henry TE | 93-95Hou | 3 | 6' | 222 | Wake Forest | | |
| Mills, Lamar DE | 94Was | | 6'5" | 270 | Indiana | | |
| Mills, Sam LB | 83-85USFL 86-94NO 95Car | | 5'9" | 227 | Montclair State | 9 | 18 |
| Milner, Billy OT | 95Mia | | 6'5" | 293 | Houston | | |
| Milot, Rich LB | 79-87Was | | 6'4" | 234 | Penn State | 12 | |
| Milstead, Rod OG | 94-95SF | | 6'2" | 284 | Delaware State | | |
| Milton, Eldridge LB | 87Chi | | 6'1" | 235 | Clemson | | |
| Mims, Chris DE-DT | 92-95SD | | 6'5" | 283 | Tennessee | | 2 |
| Mims, David WR | 93-94Atl | 2 | 5'8" | 191 | Baylor | | 6 |
| Mincy, Charles DB | 92-94KC 95Min | | 5'11" | 197 | Washington | 15 | 18 |
| Miniefield, Kevin DB | 93-95Chi | | 5'9" | 178 | Arizona State | 3 | |
| Minnifield, Frank DB | 83-84USFL 84-92Cle | | 5'9" | 182 | Louisville | 20 | 12 |
| Minor, Vic DB | 80-81Sea 84-85USFL | | 6' | 198 | Northeast La. | 1 | |
| Minter, Barry LB | 93-95Chi | | 6'2" | 242 | Tulsa | 1 | 6 |
| Minter, Cedric HB | 84-85NYJ | 2 | 5'10" | 200 | Boise State | | 12 |
| Miotke, Frank WR | 91Hou | | 6' | 175 | Grand Valley State | | |
| Miraldi, Dean OG-OT | 81-84Phi 85Den 87Raid | | 6'5" | 266 | Long Beach State, Utah | | |
| Mirer, Rick QB | 93-95Sea | 12 | 6'2" | 216 | Notre Dame | | 24 |
| Misko, John K | 82-84LA 87Det | 4 | 6'5" | 207 | Oregon State | | |
| Mistler, John WR | 81-83NYG 84Buf 84NYG 85USFL | 2 | 6'2" | 186 | Arizona State | | 18 |
| Mitchell, Aaron DB | 79-80Dal 81TB 83-84USFL | | 6'1" | 196 | Morris Brown, Nevada-Las Vegas | 4 | |
| Mitchell, Alvin FB | 89TB | | 6' | 235 | Auburn | | |
| Mitchell, Brian HB-QB | 90-95Was | 23 | 5'10" | 199 | Southwestern La. | | 80 |
| Mitchell, Brian DB | 91-93Atl | | 5'9" | 164 | Brigham Young | 1 | |
| Mitchell, Derrell WR | 94NO | | 5'9" | 190 | Texas Tech | | |
| Mitchell, Devon DB | 86Det 87KJ 88Det | | 6'1" | 194 | Iowa | 8 | 6 |
| Mitchell, Johnny TE | 92-95NYJ | 2 | 6'3" | 247 | Nebraska | | 96 |
| Mitchell, Kevin LB | 94-95SF | | 6'1" | 260 | Syracuse | | |
| Mitchell, Leonard DE | 81-86Phi 87Atl | | 6'7" | 290 | Houston | | |
| Mitchell, Michael DB | 87Was 88PJ 89NJ | | 5'10" | 180 | Howard Payne | 1 | |
| Mitchell, Pete TE | 95Jax | 2 | 6'2" | 243 | Boston College | | 12 |
| Mitchell, Randall DT | 87Phi | | 6'1" | 275 | Tenn.-Chattanooga | | |
| Mitchell, Roland DB-LB | 87-88Buf 88-89Phx 90Atl 91-94GB | | 5'11" | 180 | Texas Tech | 6 | |
| Mitchell, Russell C | 87NYG | | 6'5" | 288 | Mississippi | | |
| Mitchell, Scott QB | 91-93Mia 94-95Det | 12 | 6'6" | 236 | Utah | | 30 |
| Mitchell, Shannon TE | 94-95SD | 2 | 6'2" | 245 | Georgia | | 6 |
| Mitchell, Stump HB | 81-87StL 88-89Phx 91KJ | 23 | 5'9" | 188 | The Citadel | | 252 |
| Mitz, Alonzo DE-LB | 86-89Sea 91-92Cin | | 6'3" | 274 | Florida | 2 | |
| Mobley, Orson TE | 86-90Den 90Ind | 2 | 6'5" | 256 | Florida State, Salem | | 24 |
| Mobley, Stacey WR | 87LA 89Det | 2 | 5'8" | 168 | Jackson State | | 6 |
| Modesitt, Jeff TE | 87TB 88SJ | | 6'5" | 245 | Delaware | | |
| Moffett, Tim WR | 85-86Raid 87SD | 2 | 6'2" | 180 | Mississippi | | 6 |
| Moffitt, Mike TE | 86GB | | 6'4" | 211 | Fresno State | | |
| Mohr, Chris K | 89TB 91-95Buf | 4 | 6'4" | 220 | Alabama | | 1 |
| Mohring, John LB | 80Det 80Cle | | 6'3" | 240 | C.W. Post | | |
| Mojsiejenko, Ralf K | 85-88SD 89-90Was 91SF | 4 | 6'3" | 209 | Michigan State | | |
| Molden, Fred DT | 87Min | | 6'2" | 272 | Jackson State | | |
| Monaco, Rob C | 85StL 86IL | | 6'3" | 283 | Vanderbilt | | |
| Monaco, Ron LB | 86StL | | 6'1" | 225 | South Carolina | | |
| Monger, Matt LB | 85-87NYJ 88AJ 89-90Buf | | 6'1" | 238 | Oklahoma State | | |
| Monk, Art WR | 80-93Was 94NYJ 95Phi | 2 | 6'3" | 210 | Syracuse | | 408 |
| Monroe, Carl HB-WR | 83-87SF | 23 | 5'8" | 164 | Utah | | 12 |
| Montagne, David WR | 87KC | | 6'2" | 184 | Oregon State | | |
| Montana, Joe QB | 79-90SF 91EJ 92SF 93-94KC | 12 | 6'2" | 197 | Notre Dame | | 120 |
| Montgomery, Alton DB | 90-92Den 93-95Atl | 3 | 6' | 195 | Houston | 3 | 6 |
| Montgomery, Blanchard LB | 83-84SF | | 6'2" | 236 | U.C.L.A. | | |
| Montgomery, Cle WR | 80Cin 81Cle 81Oak 82-85Raid | 3 | 5'8" | 183 | Abilene Christian | | 6 |
| Montgomery, Glenn NT-DT | 89-95Hou | | 6' | 277 | Houston | | |
| Montgomery, Greg K | 88-93Hou 94Det | 4 | 6'3" | 213 | Penn State, Michigan State | | |
| Montgomery, Tyrone HB | 93-94Raid | 2 | 6' | 190 | Mississippi | | 6 |
| Montgomery, Wilbert HB | 77-84Phi 85Det | 23 | 5'10" | 195 | Jackson State, Abilene Christian | | 348 |
| Montoute, Sankar LB | 87TB | | 6'3" | 230 | St. Leo | 1 | |
| Montoya, Max OG-OT | 79-89Cin 90-94Raid | | 6'5" | 282 | U.C.L.A. | | |
| Montreuil, Mark DB | 95SD | | 6'2" | 200 | Concordia (Quebec) | | |
| Moog, Aaron DE | 87Cle | | 6'4" | 260 | Nevada-Las Vegas | | |
| Moon, Warren QB | 84-93Hou 94-95Min | 12 | 6'3" | 210 | Washington | | 126 |
| Mooney, Mike OT | 93SD | | 6'6" | 320 | Georgia Tech | | |
| Mooney, Tim DE | 87Phi | | 6'2" | 265 | Western Kentucky | | |
| Moor, Buddy DE | 87Atl | | 6'5" | 250 | Eastern Kentucky | | 2 |
| Moore, Alvin HB | 83Bal 84Ind 85-86Det 87Sea | 2 | 6' | 194 | Arizona State | | 48 |
| Moore, Blake C-OT-OG | 80-83Cin 84-85GB | | 6'5" | 267 | Wooster | | 6 |
| Moore, Brent LB | 87GB 88KJ | | 6'5" | 242 | Southern Calif. | | |
| Moore, Booker FB | 82-85Buf | 2 | 5'11" | 224 | Pennsylvania | | 12 |
| Moore, Brandon OT | 93-95NE | | 6'6" | 290 | Duke | | |
| Moore, Dana K | 87NYG | | 5'10" | 180 | Mississippi State | | |
| Moore, Darryl OG | 93Was | | 6'2" | 292 | Texas-El Paso | | |
| Moore, Dave TE-FB | 92Mia 92-95TB | 2 | 6'2" | 245 | Pittsburgh | | 6 |
| Moore, Derrick HB-FB | 93-94Det 95Car | 2 | 6'1" | 227 | Troy State, Northeastern Okla. | | 72 |
| Moore, Eric OT-OG | 88-93NYG 94Cin 95Cle 95Mia | | 6'5" | 293 | Indiana | | |
| Moore, Greg LB | 87NE | | 6'1" | 240 | Tenn.-Chattanooga | | |
| Moore, Herman WR | 91-95Det | 2 | 6'3" | 208 | Virginia | | 210 |
| Moore, Jeff HB | 79-81Sea 82-83SF 84Was | 23 | 6' | 195 | Jackson State | | 78 |
| Moore, Jeff WR | 80-81LA | 2 | 6'1" | 194 | Tennessee | | 6 |
| Moore, Jimmy OG | 81Bal | | 6'5" | 268 | Ohio State | | |
| Moore, Leonard FB | 87Min | | 6' | 222 | Jackson State | | |
| Moore, Mack DE | 85-86Mia 86SD | | 6'4" | 258 | Texas A&M | | |
| Moore, Malcolm TE | 87LA | | 6'3" | 240 | Southern Calif. | | 6 |
| Moore, Mark DB | 87Sea | | 6' | 194 | Oklahoma State | | |
| Moore, Marty LB | 94-95NE | | 6'1" | 244 | Kentucky | | |
| Moore, Nat WR-HB | 74-86Mia | 23 | 5'9" | 184 | Tennessee-Martin, Florida | | 450 |
| Moore, Ricky FB | 86Buf 87Hou 88Phx | 2 | 5'11" | 234 | Alabama | | 6 |
| Moore, Rob WR | 90-94NYJ 95Arz | 2 | 6'3" | 205 | Syracuse | | 168 |
| Moore, Robert DB | 86-89Atl | | 5'11" | 190 | Northwestern La. | 7 | 12 |
| Moore, Rocca OG-OT | 80Chi | | 6'5" | 276 | Western Michigan | | |
| Moore, Ronald HB | 93Phx 94Arz 95NYJ | 2 | 5'10" | 220 | Pittsburg State | | 86 |
| Moore, Shawn QB | 92-93Den | 1 | 6'2" | 214 | Virginia | | |
| Moore, Steve (Big House) OT-OG | 83-87NE 88KJ | | 6'4" | 293 | Tennessee State | | |
| Moore, Stevon DB | 90Mia 91KJ 92-95Cle | | 5'11" | 204 | Mississippi | 5 | 12 |
| Moore, Will WR | 95NE | 2 | 6'2" | 180 | Texas Southern | | 6 |
| Moorehead, Emery TE-WR-HB-FB | 77-79NYG 80Den 81-88Chi | 23 | 6'2" | 218 | Colorado | | 90 |
| Mora, Jim | HC86-95NO | | | | Occidental | | |
| Moran, Eric OT-OG | 83USFL 84-86Hou | | 6'5" | 285 | Washington | | |
| Moran, Rich OG-C | 85-93GB | | 6'3" | 276 | San Diego State | | |
| Morgan, Anthony WR | 91-93Chi 93-95GB | 2 | 6'1" | 195 | Tennessee | | 60 |
| Morgan, Dan OG | 87NYG | | 6'6" | 285 | Penn State | | |
| Morgan, Karl DE-DT | 84-86TB | | 6'1" | 255 | U.C.L.A. | | |
| Morgan, Stanley WR | 77-89NE 90Ind | 23 | 5'11" | 180 | Tennessee | | 438 |
| Moriarty, Larry FB | 83-86Hou 86-88KC | 2 | 6'1" | 240 | Notre Dame | | 90 |
| Moroski, Mike QB | 79-84Atl 85Hou 86SF | 12 | 6'4" | 200 | Cal.-Davis | | 12 |
| Morrell, Kyle DB | 86Min | | 6'1" | 189 | Brigham Young | | |
| Morris, Bam HB | 94-95Pit | 2 | 6' | 241 | Texas Tech | | 96 |
| Morris, Dwaine NT-DT | 85Phi 87Atl | | 6'2" | 260 | Southwestern La. | | |
| Morris, Jamie HB | 88-90Was | 23 | 5'7" | 188 | Michigan | | 24 |
| Morris, Jim Bob DB | 87GB | | 6'3" | 211 | Kansas State | 3 | |
| Morris, Joe HB | 82-88NYG 89FJ 91Cle | 23 | 5'7" | 195 | Syracuse | | 312 |
| Morris, Larry HB | 87GB | | 5'7" | 207 | Syracuse | | |
| Morris, Lee WR | 87GB | 2 | 5'11" | 180 | Oklahoma | | 6 |
| Morris, Michael OG-C | 87StL 88KJ 89KC 89NE 90Sea 90Cle 91-95Min | | 6'5" | 278 | NE Missouri St. | | |

| Use Name (Nickname) - Positions | Team by Year | See Section | Hgt. | Wgt. | College | Int | Pts |
|---|---|---|---|---|---|---|---|
| Morris, Mitchell DE | 87KC | | 6'4" | 255 | Wichita State | | |
| Morris, Randall HB | 84-88Sea 88Det | 23 | 6' | 195 | Tennessee | | 6 |
| Morris, Raymond LB | 87Chi | | 5'10" | 222 | Texas-El Paso | | |
| Morris, Ron WR | 87-92Chi | 2 | 6'1" | 187 | S.M.U. | | 54 |
| Morris, Thomas DB | 82-83TB | | 5'11" | 175 | Michigan State | | |
| Morris, Victor LB | 87Mia | | 6'1" | 243 | Miami-Ohio | | |
| Morris, Wayne FB-HB | 76-83StL 84SD | 2 | 6' | 207 | S.M.U. | | 258 |
| Morrison, Darryl DB | 93-95Was | | 5'11" | 185 | Arizona | | 6 |
| Morrison, Pat DB | 87NYG | | 6'2" | 194 | Southern Conn. St. | | |
| Morrison, Steve LB | 95Ind | | 6'3" | 246 | Michigan | | |
| Morrison, Tim DB | 86-87Was | | 6'1" | 195 | North Carolina | | |
| Morriss, Guy C-OG | 73-83Phi 84-87NE | | 6'4" | 257 | Texas Christian | | |
| Morrissey, Jim LB | 85-93Chi 93GB | | 6'3" | 223 | Michigan State | 9 | |
| Morse, Bobby HB | 87Phi 89-91NO | 3 | 5'10" | 207 | Michigan State | | 6 |
| Morse, Steve FB | 85Pit | | 5'11" | 211 | Virginia | | |
| Morton, Johnnie WR | 94-95Det | 2 | 6' | 190 | Southern Calif. | | 60 |
| Morton, Michael HB | 82-84TB 85Was 87Sea | 2 | 5'8" | 179 | Nevada-Las Vegas | | 12 |
| Morton, Mike LB | 95Oak | | 6'4" | 230 | North Carolina | | |
| Mosebar, Don C-OT-OG | 83-94Raid 95IJ | | 6'6" | 288 | Southern Calif. | | |
| Moser, Rick HB | 78-79Pit 80Mia 81KC 81-82Pit 82TB | 2 | 6' | 210 | Rhode Island | | 12 |
| Mosley, Anthony HB | 87Chi | | 5'9" | 204 | Fresno State | | 6 |
| Mosley, Mike WR | 82-84Buf | 2 | 6'2" | 192 | Texas A&M | | 18 |
| Moss, Brent HB | 95StL | | 5'8" | 211 | Wisconsin | | |
| Moss, Gary DB | 87Atl | | 5'10" | 192 | Georgia | 1 | |
| Moss, Martin DT | 82-85Det | | 6'4" | 252 | U.C.L.A. | | |
| Moss, Winston LB | 87-90TB 91-94Raid 95Sea | | 6'3" | 238 | Miami (Fla.) | 2 | 6 |
| Moss, Zefross, OT | 89-94Ind 95Det | | 6'6" | 330 | Alabama State | | |
| Moten, Eric OG | 91-93SD 94KJ 95Sea | | 6'2" | 306 | Michigan State | | |
| Moten, Gary LB | 83SF 85USFL 87KC | | 6'1" | 210 | S.M.U. | | |
| Mott, Joe LB | 89-90NYJ 91KJ 93GB | | 6'4" | 253 | Iowa | | |
| Mott, Steve C | 83-88Det 89ZJ | | 6'3" | 266 | Alabama | | |
| Mowatt, Zeke TE | 83-84NYG 85KJ 86-89NYG 90NE 91NYG | 2 | 6'3" | 239 | Florida State | | 72 |
| Moyer, Alex LB | 85-86Mia | | 6'1" | 221 | Northwestern | 1 | |
| Moyer, Ken OT-OG | 89-91Cin 92FJ 93-94Cin | | 6'6" | 294 | Toledo | | |
| Moyer, Paul DB | 83-89Sea | | 6'1" | 200 | Fullerton State | 11 | 12 |
| Mraz, Mark DE | 87Atl 89Raid | | 6'4" | 258 | Utah State | | |
| Mrosko, Bob TE | 89Hou 90NYG 91Ind | 2 | 6'6" | 265 | Penn State | | 6 |
| Mueller, Jamie FB | 87-90Buf 91JJ | 2 | 6'1" | 225 | Benedictine | | 30 |
| Mueller, Vance FB-HB | 86-90Raid 91KJ | 23 | 6' | 211 | Occidental | | 30 |
| Muhammad, Calvin WR | 82-83Raid 84-85Was 87SD | 2 | 6' | 190 | Texas Southern | | 48 |
| Mularkey, Mike TE | 83-88Min 89-91Pit | 2 | 6'4" | 240 | Florida | | 54 |
| Mullady, Tom TE | 79-84NYG | 2 | 6'3" | 232 | Rhodes | | 24 |
| Mullaney, Mark DE | 75-86Min 87ZJ | | 6'6" | 243 | Colorado State | 1 | 2 |
| Mullen, Davlin DB | 83-86NYJ | | 6'1" | 177 | Western Kentucky | 4 | |
| Mullen, Gary WR | 87Chi | | 5'11" | 174 | West Virginia | | |
| Mullen, Roderick DB | 95GB | | 6'1" | 204 | Grambling | | |
| Mullins, Eric WR | 84Hou | | 5'11" | 181 | Stanford | | 6 |
| Mumford, Tony HB | 85StL | | 6' | 215 | Penn State | | |
| Mumphrey, Lloyd DE | 87KC | | 6'3" | 260 | Miss. Valley St. | | |
| Munchak, Mike OG | 82-93Hou | | 6'3" | 281 | Penn State | | 6 |
| Muncie, Chuck FB-HB | 76-80NO 80-84SD | 2 | 6'3" | 227 | California | | 444 |
| Munford, Marc LB | 87-90Den | | 6'2" | 231 | Nebraska | 2 | |
| Munoz, Anthony OT | 80-92Cin 93SJ | | 6'6" | 278 | Southern Calif. | | 24 |
| Muransky, Ed OT | 82-84Raid 85USFL | | 6'7" | 277 | Michigan | | |
| Murphy, James WR | 81Atl 81KC | | 5'10" | 177 | Utah State | | |
| Murphy, Kevin LB | 86-91TB 92SD 93Sea | | 6'2" | 233 | Oklahoma | 1 | 6 |
| Murphy, Mark DB | 77-84Was | | 6'4" | 210 | Colgate | | 27 |
| Murphy, Mark DB | 80-85GB 86FJ 87-91GB | | 6'2" | 200 | W. Liberty State | 18 | |
| Murphy, Phil DT | 80-81LA 83USFL | | 6'5" | 290 | S. Carolina State | | |
| Murray, Calvin HB | 81-82Phi 83-84USFL | 3 | 5'11" | 185 | Ohio State | | |
| Murray, Dan LB | 89Ind 90NYJ | | 6'1" | 240 | East Stroudsburg | | |
| Murray, Eddie K | 80-91Det 92KC 92TB 93Dal 94Phi 95Was | 5 | 5'10" | 173 | Tulane | | 1464 |
| Murray, Joe OG | 87LA | | 6'4" | 265 | Southern Calif. | | |
| Murray, Mark LB | 90Den | | 6'2" | 240 | Florida | | |
| Murray, Walter WR | 86-87Ind | 2 | 6'4" | 200 | Hawaii | | 18 |
| Murrell, Adrian HB | 93-95NYJ | 2 | 5'11" | 209 | West Virginia | | 24 |
| Murtha, Greg OT | 82Bal 83-84USFL | | 6'6" | 268 | Minnesota | | |
| Musgrave, Bill QB | 91-93SF 95Den | | 6'2" | 196 | Oregon | | |
| Musser, Neal LB | 81-83Atl | | 6'2" | 220 | N. Carolina State | 1 | |
| Mustafaa, Najee DB (changed name from Reggie Rutland in 1992) | 87-91Min 92XJ 93Cle 95Oak | | 6'1" | 194 | Georgia Tech | 11 | 18 |
| Muster, Brad FB | 88-92Chi 93-94NO | 2 | 6'3" | 231 | Stanford | | 186 |
| Myers, Wilbur DB | 83Den | | 5'11" | 195 | Delta State | | |
| Myles, Godfrey LB | 91-95Dal | | 6'1" | 241 | Florida | 2 | |
| Myles, Jesse HB-FB | 83-84Den | 2 | 5'10" | 210 | Louisiana State | | 6 |
| Myslinski, Tom OG | 92Was 93Buf 93-94Chi 95Jax | | 6'3" | 290 | Tennessee | | |
| Nagle, Browning | 91-93NYJ 94Ind 95Atl | 12 | 6'3" | 225 | West Virginia, Louisville | | |
| Najarian, Peter LB | 87Min 88-89TB | | 6'2" | 231 | Minnesota | | |
| Nairne, Rob LB | 77-80Den 81-83NO | | 6'4" | 223 | Oregon State | 3 | 6 |
| Nalen, Tom C-OG | 94-95Den | | 6'2" | 280 | Boston College | | |
| Naposki, Eric LB | 88-89NE 89Ind | | 6'2" | 230 | Connecticut | | |
| Nash, Joe NT-DT | 82-95Sea | | 6'2" | 270 | Boston College | 1 | 12 |
| Nash, Kenny WR | 87KC | | 6'2" | 195 | San Jose State | | |
| Nattiel, Ricky WR | 87-92Den | 23 | 5'9" | 180 | Florida | | 48 |
| Nathan, Tony HB-FB | 79-87Mia | 23 | 6' | 206 | Alabama | | 198 |
| Nave, Stevan LB | 87Cle | | 6'2" | 250 | Kansas | | |
| Neal, Frankie WR | 87GB | 2 | 6'1" | 202 | Ft. Hays State, Florida | | 18 |
| Neal, Lorenzo HB-FB | 93-95NO | 2 | 5'10" | 234 | Fresno State | | 18 |
| Neal, Randy LB | 95Cin | | 6'3" | 236 | Virginia | | |
| Neal, Speedy FB | 84Buf | 2 | 6'2" | 254 | Miami (Fla.) | | 6 |
| Nease, Mike OG | 87Phi | | 6'3" | 272 | Tenn.-Chattanooga | | |
| Ned, Derrick FB | 93-95NO | 2 | 6'1" | 220 | Grambling | | 6 |
| Nehemiah, Renaldo WR | 82-84SF | 2 | 6'1" | 181 | Maryland | | 24 |
| Neil, Kenny DE-DT | 81-83NYJ 85USFL 87Hou | | 6'4" | 245 | Iowa State | | |
| Neill, Bill NT | 81-83NYG 84GB | | 6'4" | 258 | Pittsburgh | | |
| Nelms, Mike DB | 80-84Was | 3 | 6'1" | 188 | Sam Houston St., Baylor | 1 | 12 |
| Nelson, Bob LB | 75-77Buf 78JJ 79SF 80Oak 81SJ 82-84Raid 85KJ | | 6'4" | 233 | Nebraska | 1 | |
| Nelson, Bob NT | 83-85USFL 86TB 88-90GB | | 6'4" | 272 | Miami (Fla.) | | |
| Nelson, Chuck K | 83LA 84Buf 86-88Min | 5 | 6' | 174 | Washington | | 364 |
| Nelson, Darrell TE | 84-85Pit | | 6'2" | 235 | Memphis State | | |
| Nelson, Darrin HB | 82-89Min 89-90SD 91-92Min | 23 | 5'9" | 184 | Stanford | | 138 |
| Nelson, David FB | 84Min | | 6'2" | 230 | Heidelberg | | |
| Nelson, Derrie LB | 83-86SD | | 6'2" | 236 | Nebraska | | 6 |
| Nelson, Edmund DE-NT-DT | 82-87Pit 88NE | | 6'3" | 272 | Auburn | | |
| Nelson, Karl OT | 84-86NYG 87IL 88NYG | | 6'6" | 285 | Iowa State | | |

| Use Name (Nickname) - Positions | Team by Year | See Section | Hgt. | Wgt. | College | Int | Pts |
|---|---|---|---|---|---|---|---|
| Nelson, Lee DB | 76-85StL 86XJ | | 5'10" | 185 | Florida State | 7 | 6 |
| Nelson, Mark OT | 87KC | | 6'4" | 270 | Bowling Green | | |
| Nelson, Steve LB | 74-87NE | | 6'2" | 230 | Augsburg, N. Dakota State | 18 | |
| Nelson, Ted DB | 87KC | | 5'10" | 203 | Nevada-Las Vegas | | |
| Neubert, Keith TE | 88-89NYJ | 2 | 6'5" | 250 | Nebraska | | 6 |
| Neuheisel, Rick QB | 87SD | 1 | 6'1" | 190 | U.C.L.A. | | 7 |
| Neville, Tom OT-OG | 86-88GB 91SF 92GB 93LJ | | 6'5" | 306 | Weber State, Fresno State | | |
| Newberry, Tom OG-C | 86-94LA 95Pit | | 6'2" | 282 | Wis.-La Crosse | | 6 |
| Newbill, Richard LB | 90Min 90-92Sea | | 6'1" | 240 | Miami (Fla.) | | |
| Newman, Anthony DB | 88-94LA 95NO | | 6' | 199 | Oregon | 11 | 12 |
| Newman, Pat WR | 90Min 91-93NO 94Cle | 23 | 5'11" | 189 | Utah State | | 6 |
| Newman, Tim HB | 87NYJ | | 6' | 220 | Johnson C. Smith | | |
| Newsom, Tony DB | 87Hou | | 5'8" | 175 | S.F. Austin State | 1 | |
| Newsome, Craig DB | 95GB | | 6' | 188 | Arizona State | 1 | |
| Newsome, Harry K | 85-89Pit 90-93Min | 4 | 6' | 187 | Wake Forest | | |
| Newsome, Ozzie TE | 78-90Cle | 2 | 6'2" | 232 | Alabama | | 294 |
| Newsome, Timmy FB | 80-88Dal | 23 | 6'1" | 232 | Winston-Salem St. | | 180 |
| Newsome, Vince DB | 83-90LA 91-92Cle | | 6'1" | 180 | Washington | 16 | 12 |
| Newton, Nate OG-OT | 84-85USFL 86-95Dal | | 6'3" | 318 | Florida A&M | | |
| Newton, Tim DT-NT | 85-89Min 90-91TB 93KC 94ZJ | | 6' | 280 | Florida | | 6 |
| Newton, Tom FB | 77-82NYJ 84-85USFL | 2 | 6' | 212 | California | | 54 |
| Nicholas, Calvin WR | 88SF | | 6'4" | 208 | Grambling | | |
| Nichols, Gerald NT-DT-DE | 87-90NYJ 91TB 93Phi 93Was | | 6'2" | 265 | Florida State | | |
| Nichols, Mark WR | 81-85Det 86KJ 87Det | 2 | 6'2" | 210 | San Jose State | | 54 |
| Nichols, Ricky WR | 85Ind | | 5'10" | 176 | East Carolina | | |
| Nicholson, Calvin DB | 89,91NO | | 5'9" | 183 | Oregon State | | |
| Nicholson, Frank LB | 87NYG | | 6'2" | 205 | Delaware State | | |
| Nickerson, Hardy LB | 87-92Pit 93-95TB | | 6'2" | 228 | California | 4 | |
| Niehoff, Rob DB | 87Cin | | 6'2" | 205 | Cincinnati | 1 | |
| Nies, John K | 90Buf | | 6'2" | 199 | Arizona | | |
| Nicolas, Scott LB | 82-86Cle 87Mia 88KJ | | 6'3" | 226 | Miami (Fla.) | | |
| Nielsen, Gifford QB | 78-83Hou | 12 | 6'4" | 207 | Brigham Young | | |
| Nielsen, Hans K | 81Chi | | 5'11" | 165 | Michigan State | | 8 |
| Nittmo, Bjorn K | 89NYG | | 5'11" | 185 | Appalachian State | | 39 |
| Nix, Roosevelt DE | 92-93Cin 94Min | | 6'6" | 299 | Central St.-Ohio | | |
| Nixon, Fred WR | 80-81GB 82KJ | 3 | 5'11" | 191 | Oklahoma | | |
| Nixon, Jeff DB | 79-82Buf 83KJ | | 6'3" | 190 | Richmond | 11 | 6 |
| Nixon, Tory DB | 86-88SF | | 5'11" | 186 | Arizona, San Diego State | 3 | 6 |
| Niziolek, Bob TE | 81Det 83-85USFL | | 6'4" | 220 | Colorado | | |
| Noble, Brian LB | 85-93GB | | 6'3" | 250 | Arizona State | 3 | 6 |
| Noble, Don TE | 87LA | | 6'2" | 253 | California | | |
| Noble, James WR | 86Was 87Ind | 2 | 6' | 195 | S.F. Austin State | | 12 |
| Noble, Mike LB | 87Raid | | 6'4" | 220 | Stanford | | |
| Noga, Al DT-DE | 88-92Min 93Was 94Ind | | 6'1" | 265 | Hawaii | 1 | 2 |
| Noga, Niko LB | 84-87StL 88Phx 89-91Det | | 6'1" | 234 | Hawaii | 1 | 6 |
| Noga, Peter LB | 87StL | | 6' | 212 | Hawaii | 1 | 6 |
| Noonan, Danny DT | 87-92Dal 92GB | | 6'4" | 270 | Nebraska | 1 | 8 |
| Nord, Keith DB | 79-83Min 84LJ 85Min | | 6' | 195 | St. Cloud State | 1 | 6 |
| Nordgren, Fred NT | 87TB | | 6' | 240 | Portland State | | |
| Norgard, Erik C-OG | 90Hou 91SJ 92-95Hou | | 6'1" | 278 | Colorado | | |
| Norman, Ben HB | 80Den | | 6' | 212 | Colorado State | | |
| Norman, Chris K | 84-86Den | 4 | 6'2" | 198 | South Carolina | | |
| Norman, Joe LB | 79-81Sea 82KJ 83Sea 84KJ | | 6'1" | 220 | Indiana | 1 | |
| Norman, Tim OG | 83Chi | | 6'6" | 270 | Illinois | | |
| Norman, Tony DE | 87Min | | 6'5" | 270 | Iowa State | | |
| Norrie, David QB | 87NYJ | 1 | 6'4" | 220 | U.C.L.A. | | |
| Norris, Jerome DB | 87Atl | | 6' | 187 | Furman | | |
| Norris, Jimmy DB | 87NYG | | 5'11" | 188 | Upsala | | |
| Norris, Jon DT | 87Chi | | 6'3" | 260 | American Inter. | 1 | |
| Norseth, Mike QB | 87-88Cin 90GB | | 6'2" | 200 | Kansas | | |
| Norris, Ulysses TE | 79-83Det 84-85Buf | 2 | 6'4" | 230 | Georgia | | 48 |
| Norton, Ken LB | 88-94Dal 95SF | | 6'2" | 238 | U.C.L.A. | 5 | 12 |
| Norwood, Ralph OT (Died Nov. 24, 1989 in automobile accident) | 89Atl | | 6'7" | 285 | Louisiana State | | |
| Norwood, Scott K | 83-84USFL 85-91Buf | 5 | 6' | 207 | James Madison | | 670 |
| Norvell, Jay LB | 87Chi | | 6'2" | 232 | Iowa | | |
| Nottage, Dexter DE | 94-95Was | | 6'4" | 273 | Florida A&M | | |
| Novacek, Jay TE-WR | 85-87StL 88-89Phx 90-95Dal | 2 | 6'4" | 229 | Wyoming | | 188 |
| Novak, Jeff OG-OT | 94Mia 95Jax | | 6'5" | 295 | SW Texas State | | |
| Novitsky, Craig C-OT | 94-95NO | | 6'5" | 295 | U.C.L.A. | | |
| Novoselsky, Brent TE | 88Chi 89-94Min | 2 | 6'3" | 232 | Pennsylvania | | 12 |
| Nugent, Terry QB | 84Cle 87Ind | | 6'4" | 216 | Colorado State | | |
| Nunley, Jeremy DE | 94Hou 95KJ | | 6'5" | 278 | Alabama | | |
| Nunn, Freddie Joe DE-LB | 85-87StL 88-93Phx 94-95Ind | | 6'4" | 249 | Mississippi | 2 | |
| Nussmeier, Doug QB | 94-95NO | | 6'3" | 211 | Idaho | | |
| Nutten, Tom C-OG | 95Buf | | 6'4" | 276 | Western Michigan | | |
| Nuzzo, Chip DB | 87Buf | | 5'11" | 190 | Princeton | | |
| Oates, Bart C | 83-85USFL 85-93NYG 94-95SF | | 6'3" | 268 | Brigham Young | | |
| Oatis, Victor WR | 83Bal | | 6' | 177 | Northwestern La. | | |
| O'Bard, Ronnie DB | 85SD | | 5'9" | 190 | Idaho, Brigham Young | | |
| Obee, Terry WR | 91Min 93Chi 94BN | 23 | 5'10" | 190 | Oregon | | 18 |
| O'Brien, Ken QB | 83-92NYJ 93Phi | 12 | 6'4" | 206 | Sacramento State, Cal.-Davis | | |
| Obrovac, Mike OT-OG | 81-83Cin | | 6'6" | 275 | Bowling Green | | |
| O'Callaghan, John TE | 87Sea | | 6'4" | 245 | San Diego State | | |
| O'Connor, Paul OG | 87TB | | 6'3" | 270 | Miami (Fla.) | | |
| O'Connor, Tom K | 87NYJ | | 6'1" | 190 | South Carolina | | |
| Odegard, Don DB | 90-91NYJ | | 6' | 180 | Oregon State, Nevada-Las Vegas | | |
| Oden, Derrick LB | 93-95Phi | | 5'11" | 230 | Alabama | | |
| Oden, McDonald TE | 80-82Cle 83-84USFL | | 6'4" | 234 | Tennessee State | | |
| Odom, Cliff LB | 80Cle 82-83Bal 84-89Ind 90-93Mia | | 6'2" | 237 | Texas-Arlington | 1 | 6 |
| Odom, Henry HB | 83Pit 85USFL | 3 | 5'10" | 200 | S. Carolina State | | |
| Odomes, Nate DB | 87-93Buf 94-95KJ | | 5'10" | 188 | Wisconsin | 26 | 18 |
| O'Donnell, Neil QB | 90-95Pit | 12 | 6'3" | 224 | Maryland | | 18 |
| O'Donoghue, Neil K | 77Buf 78-79TB 80-85StL | 5 | 6'6" | 208 | St. Bernard, Auburn | | 576 |
| O'Dwyer, Matt OG | 95NYJ | | 6'5" | 308 | Northwestern | | |
| Offerdahl, John LB | 86-93Mia | | 6'3" | 235 | Western Michigan | 4 | |
| Office, Anthony LB | 87Det | | 6'2" | 250 | Illinois State | | |
| Oglesby, Alfred NT-DT | 90-92Mia 92GB 94-95NYJ 95Cin | | 6'3" | 278 | Houston | | |
| Ogletree, Craig LB | 90Cin | | 6'2" | 236 | Auburn | | |
| Ogrin, Pat DE-DT | 81-82Was 84-85USFL | | 6'5" | 265 | Wyoming | | |
| Okoye, Christian FB | 87-92KC | 2 | 6'1" | 255 | Azusa Pacific | | 240 |
| Olderman, Bob OG | 85KC | | 6'5" | 262 | Virginia | | |
| Oldham, Chris DB | 90Det 91Buf 91-93Phx 94Arz 95Pit | | 5'9" | 188 | Oregon | 3 | 6 |
| Olenchalk, John LB-C | 81-82KC | | 6' | 228 | Stanford | | |
| Oliphant, Mike HB | 88Was 89Cle 90LJ 91Cle | 2 | 5'10" | 183 | Puget Sound | | 6 |
| Olive, Bobby WR | 95Ind | | 5'11" | 170 | Ohio State | | |

| Use Name (Nickname) - Positions | Team by Year | See Section | Hgt. | Wgt. | College | Int | Pts |
|---|---|---|---|---|---|---|---|
| Oliver, Darryl HB | 87Atl | | 5'10" | 194 | Miami (Fla.) | | |
| Oliver, Hubie FB | 81-85Phi 86Ind 86Hou | 2 | 5'10" | 215 | Arizona | | 24 |
| Oliver, Jack OT | 87Chi | | 6'3" | 281 | Texas-El Paso, Memphis State | | |
| Oliver, Jeff OT-OG | 89NYJ | | 6'4" | 292 | Boston College | | |
| Oliver, Louis DB | 89-93Mia 94Cin 95Mia | | 6'2" | 226 | Florida | 24 | 12 |
| Oliver, Maurice LB | 91TB | | 6'3" | 235 | Southern Miss. | | |
| Oliver, Muhammad DB | 92Den 93KC 93GB 94Mia 95Was | | 5'11" | 170 | Oregon | 1 | |
| Olkewicz, Neal LB | 79-89Was | | 6' | 230 | Maryland | 6 | 6 |
| Olsavsky, Jerry LB | 89-95Pit | | 6'1" | 222 | Pittsburgh | | |
| O'Neal, Brian FB | 94Phi 95SF | | 6' | 233 | Penn State | | |
| O'Neal, Leslie DE-LB | 86SD 87KJ 88-95SD | | 6'4" | 258 | Oklahoma State | 1 | 6 |
| O'Neal, Ken TE | 87NO | | 6'3" | 240 | Idaho State | | 6 |
| O'Neal, Robert DB | 94Ind | | 6'1" | 199 | Clemson | | |
| O'Neill, Pat K | 94-95NE 95Chi | 4 | 6'1" | 200 | Syracuse | | |
| Ontko, Bob LB | 87Ind | | 6'3" | 237 | Penn State | | |
| Opfar, David NT | 87Pit | | 6'4" | 270 | Penn State | | |
| Ori, Frank OG | 87Min | | 6'2" | 255 | Northern Iowa | | |
| Orlando, Bo DB | 90-94Hou | | 5'10" | 180 | West Virginia | 7 | 6 |
| Orns, Fred LB | 87Sea | | 6'2" | 230 | Chapman | | |
| Orosz, Tom K | 82Mia 83-84SF | 4 | 6'1" | 204 | Ohio State | | |
| Orr, Terry TE | 86-90Was 90SD 91-93Was | 2 | 6'3" | 229 | Texas | | 60 |
| Orton, Greg OG | 87Det | | 6'1" | 265 | Nebraska | | |
| Ortego, Keith WR | 85-87Chi | 2 | 6' | 180 | McNeese State | | 6 |
| Osbourne, Eldonta LB | 90Phx | | 6' | 226 | Louisiana Tech | | |
| Osby, Vince LB | 84-85SD | | 5'11" | 220 | Illinois | | |
| O'Shea, Terry TE | 89-90Pit | | 6'4" | 236 | California (Pa.) | | |
| Oshodin, Willie DE | 93-95Den | | 6'4" | 265 | Villanova | | |
| Osiecki, Sandy QB | 84KC | | 6'5" | 202 | Arizona State | | |
| O'Steen, Dwayne DB | 78-79LA 80-81Oak 82Bal 82-83TB 83-84GB | | 6'1" | 193 | California, San Jose State | 8 | |
| Ostroski, Jerry OG | 94-95Buf | | 6'2" | 310 | Tulsa | | |
| Oswald, Paul C-OG | 87Pit 88Dal 88Atl | | 6'3" | 274 | Kansas | | |
| Ottis, Brad DE-DT | 94LA 95StL | | 6'4" | 272 | Wayne St.-Neb. | | |
| Otto, Bob DE | 86Dal 87Hou | | 6'6" | 253 | Idaho State | | |
| Oubre, Louis OG | 82-84NO 87Mia | | 6'4" | 268 | Oklahoma | | |
| Ours, Greg C | 87Mia | | 6'5" | 279 | Muskingum | | |
| Overstreet, David HB-FB | 83Mia | 2 | 5'11" | 208 | Oklahoma | | 18 |
| June 1984 — Killed in automobile accident | | | | | | | |
| Overton, Don HB | 90NE 91-92Det | | 6' | 221 | Fairmont State | | |
| Owens, Billy DB | 88Dal | | 6'1" | 207 | Pittsburgh | | |
| Owens, Dan DE-NT | 90-95Det | | 6'3" | 277 | Southern Calif. | 1 | |
| Owens, Darrick WR | 92Pit | | 6'2" | 195 | Mississippi | | |
| Owens, Dennis NT | 82-86NE | | 6'1" | 257 | N. Carolina State | | |
| Owens, James WR-HB-DB | 79-80SF 81-84TB | 23 | 5'11" | 192 | U.C.L.A. | | 78 |
| Owens, Mel LB | 81-89LA 90XJ | | 6'2" | 224 | Michigan | 4 | |
| Owens, Rich DE | 95Was | | 6'6" | 255 | Lehigh | | |
| Pacella, Dave C-OG | 83-84USFL 84Phi | | 6'3" | 266 | Maryland | | |
| Pacheco, Chris NT | 87LA | | 6' | 250 | Fresno State | | |
| Padjen, Gary LB | 82-83Bal 84,87Ind | | 6'2" | 244 | Arizona State | | |
| Pagel, Mike QB | 82-83Bal 84-85Ind 86-90Cle 91-93LA | 12 | 6'2" | 206 | Arizona State | | 24 |
| Pahukoa, Jeff OG-OT | 91-93LA 95Atl | | 6'2" | 298 | Washington | | |
| Pahukoa, Shane DB | 95NO | | 6'2" | 202 | Washington | 2 | 0 |
| Paige, Lee DB | 87TB | | 6' | 197 | Florida State | | |
| Paige, Stephone WR | 83-91KC | 23 | 6'2" | 184 | Fresno State | | 294 |
| Paige, Tony FB | 84-86NYJ 87-89Det 90-92Mia | 2 | 5'10" | 228 | Virginia Tech | | 174 |
| Paine, Jeff LB | 84-85KC 86 Was 87StL | | 6'2" | 224 | Texas A&M | | |
| Painter, Carl HB | 88-89Det | 3 | 5'9" | 185 | Hampton U. | | |
| Palelei, Lonnie OG | 93,95Pit | | 6'3" | 311 | Purdue, Nevada-Las Vegas | | |
| Palmer, David HB-WR | 94-95Min | 23 | 5'8" | 167 | Alabama | | 6 |
| Palmer, Paul HB | 87-88KC 89Det 89Dal | 23 | 5'9" | 182 | Temple | | 60 |
| Palmer, Sterling DE | 93-95Was | | 6'5" | 265 | Florida State | | |
| Panepinto, Mike HB | 87Buf | | 5'7" | 180 | Canisius | | |
| Pankey, Irv OT | 80-82LA 83LJ 84-90LA 91-92Ind | | 6'4" | 277 | Penn State | | |
| Panos, Joe OG-C | 94-95Phi | | 6'2" | 296 | Wisconsin | | |
| Parcells, Bill | HC83-90NYG HC93-95NE | | | | Wichita State | | |
| Pardridge, Curt WR | 87Sea | | 5'10" | 175 | Northern Illinois | | 6 |
| Paris, Bubba OT | 83-90SF 91Ind 91Det | | 6'6" | 300 | Michigan | | |
| Park, Kaulana FB | 87NYG | | 6'2" | 230 | Stanford | | |
| Parker, Andy TE | 84-88Raid 89SD 90Raid | | 6'5" | 244 | Utah | | 12 |
| Parker, Anthony DB | 89Ind 91KC 92-94Min 95StL | 3 | 5'10" | 181 | Arizona State | 10 | 30 |
| Parker, Carl WR | 88-89Cin | | 6'2" | 201 | Vanderbilt | | |
| Parker, Daren K | 92Den | | 6' | 185 | South Carolin | | |
| Parker, Ervin LB | 80-83Buf | | 6'4" | 236 | S. Carolina State | | |
| Parker, Freddie FB | 87GB | | 5'10" | 215 | Miss. Valley St. | | |
| Parker, Glenn OT-OG | 90-95Buf | | 6'5" | 303 | Arizona | | |
| Parker, Jerry LB | 87Cle | | 6' | 227 | Central St.-Ohio | | |
| Parker, Jeff WR | 92TB | | 5'10" | 185 | Bethune-Cookman | | |
| Parker, Kerry DB | 84KC 87Buf | | 6'1" | 192 | Grambling | | |
| Parker, Orlando WR | 94NYJ | | 5'11" | 190 | Troy State | | |
| Parker, Robert RB | 87KC | 2 | 6'1" | 201 | Brigham Young | | 6 |
| Parker, Rodney WR | 80-81Phi 83-84USFL | | 6'1" | 190 | Tennessee State | | 18 |
| Parker, Steve DE | 80NO | | 6'6" | 265 | Idaho | | |
| Parker, Steve DE | 83Bal 84Ind | | 6'4" | 256 | Tennessee State | | |
| Parker, Vaughn OT-OG | 94-95SD | | 6'3" | 296 | U.C.L.A. | | |
| Parks, Jeff TE | 86-87Hou 88TB | | 6'4" | 239 | Auburn | | |
| Parks, Limbo OG | 87SF | | 6'3" | 265 | Arkansas | | |
| Parks, Rickey WR | 87Min | | 6'1" | 179 | Ark.-Pine Bluff | | |
| Parlavecchio, Chet DB | 83GB 83StL | | 6'2" | 225 | Penn State | | |
| Parmalee, Bernie HB | 92-95Mia | 2 | 5'11" | 193 | Ball State | | 104 |
| Parrella, John DE-DT | 93Buf 94-95SD | | 6'3" | 293 | Nebraska | | |
| Parrish, James OT | 93SF 95Pit | | 6'6" | 315 | Temple | | |
| Parrish, Don NT-DE | 78-82KC | | 6'2" | 257 | Pittsburgh | | |
| Parros, Rick FB-HB | 81-84Den 87Sea | 2 | 5'11" | 200 | Utah State | | 72 |
| Parten, Ty DT | 93-95Cin | | 6'4" | 272 | Arizona | | |
| Partridge, Rick K | 79NO 80SD 83-85USFL 87Buf | 4 | 6'1" | 175 | Utah | | |
| Paschal, Doug FB | 80Min 81KJ | | 6'2" | 219 | North Carolina | | 6 |
| Paskett, Keith WR | 87GB | 2 | 5'11" | 180 | Western Kentucky | | 6 |
| Pasquale, Ron OG | 87StL | | 6'2" | 266 | Akron | | |
| Paterra, Greg FB | 89Atl | | 5'11" | 211 | Slippery Rock | | |
| Patrick, Garin OG | 95Ind | | 6'3" | 269 | Louisville | | |
| Patten, Joel OT | 80Cle 81KJ 83-85USFL 87-88Ind 89-90SD 91Raid | | 6'7" | 289 | Duke | | |
| Patterson, Craig NT | 90-91Phx | | 6'5" | 314 | Brigham Young | 1 | |
| Patterson, Elvis DB | 84-87NYG 87-89SD 90-93Raid 93Dal | | 5'11" | 193 | Kansas | 10 | 24 |
| Patterson, Reno NT | 87SF | | 6'3" | 275 | Bethune-Cookman | | |
| Patterson, Shawn DE-NT | 88-91GB 92KJ 93GB | | 6'5" | 265 | Arizona State | 1 | 6 |
| Pattillo, Darrell DB | 83SD 84-85USFL | | 5'10" | 194 | Long Beach State | | |
| Pattison, Mark WR | 86LA86Raid 87-88NO | 2 | 6'2" | 190 | Washington | | |

| Use Name (Nickname) - Positions | Team by Year | See Section | Hgt. | Wgt. | College | Int | Pts |
|---|---|---|---|---|---|---|---|
| Patton, James NT-DE | 93-94Buf | | 6'3" | 287 | Texas | | |
| Patton, Joe C-OT | 94-95Was | | 6'5" | 288 | Alabama A&M | | |
| Patton, Marvcus LB | 90-94Buf 95Was | | 6'2" | 229 | U.C.L.A. | 6 | |
| Patton, Ricky HB | 78-79Atl 79GB 80-82SF | 2 | 5'11" | 190 | Jackson State | | 42 |
| Paul, Markus DB | 89-93Chi 93TB | | 6'2" | 199 | Syracuse | 7 | |
| Paul, Tito DB | 95Arz | | 6' | 195 | Ohio State | 1 | |
| Paul, Whitney LB-DE | 76-81KC 82-85NO 86KC | | 6'3" | 220 | Colorado | 11 | 12 |
| Paup, Bryce LB | 90-94GB 95Buf | | 6'5" | 245 | Northern Iowa | 6 | 8 |
| Pawlawski, Mike QB | 92TB | | 6'1" | 205 | California | | |
| Paye, John QB | 88SF | | 6'3" | 205 | Stanford | | |
| Payne, Russell TE | 87Den | | 6'1" | 240 | Appalachian State | | |
| Payton, Eddie (Sweet P) HB | 77Cle 77Det 78KC 80-82Min | 3 | 5'8" | 176 | Jackson State | | 18 |
| Payton, Sean QB | 87Chi | | 5'11" | 200 | Eastern Illinois | | |
| Payton, Walter (Sweetness) HB | 75-87Chi | 12 | 5'11" | 203 | Jackson State | | 750 |
| Peacock, Elvis HB-FB | 79-80LA 81Cin | 2 | 6'1" | 212 | Oklahoma | | 54 |
| Pearson, Aaron LB | 86-88KC | | 6'0" | 239 | Mississippi State | | |
| Pearson, J.C. (Jayice) DB | 86-92KC 93Min | | 5'11" | 187 | Cal. Poly.-Pomona, Washington | 4 | 6 |
| Pease, Brent QB | 87-88Hou | 12 | 6'2" | 200 | Montana | | 12 |
| Peat, Todd OG-TE | 87StL 88-89Phx 90,92-93Raid | | 6'2" | 300 | Northern Illinois | | |
| Peavey, Jack C | 87Den | | 6'2" | 260 | Troy State | | |
| Pederson, Doug QB | 93-94Mia 95GB | | 6'3" | 209 | Northeast La. | | |
| Peebles, Danny WR | 89-90TB 91Cle | 23 | 5'11" | 180 | N. Carolina State | | 6 |
| Peete, Rodney QB | 89-93Det 94Dal 95Phi | 12 | 6' | 193 | Southern Calif. | | 78 |
| Pegram, Erric HB | 91-94Atl 95Pit | 23 | 5'9" | 188 | North Texas | | 68 |
| Peguese, Willis DE | 90-92Hou 92-93Ind | | 6'4" | 269 | Miami (Fla.) | | |
| Pelfrey, Doug K | 93-95Cin | 5 | 5'11" | 185 | Kentucky | | 314 |
| Pellegrini, Joe OG-C | 82-83NYJ 84-86Atl | | 6'4" | 258 | Harvard | | |
| Pelluer, Scott LB | 81-85NO | | 6'2" | 219 | Washington State | | |
| Pelluer, Steve QB | 84-88Dal 89-90KC | 12 | 6'4" | 209 | Washington | | 36 |
| Penaranda, Jairo FB | 81LA 83-84USFL 85Phi | | 5'11" | 217 | U.C.L.A. | | |
| Penn, Chris WR | 94-95KC | | 6' | 198 | Tulsa | | |
| Penn, Jesse LB | 85-87Dal | | 6'3" | 220 | Virginia Tech | 1 | 6 |
| Pennington, Leon LB | 87TB | | 6'1" | 225 | Florida | | |
| Pennison, Jay C | 85USFL 86-90Hou | | 6'1" | 276 | Nicholls State | | |
| Peoples, George FB-HB | 82Dal 83NE 84-85TB | | 6' | 214 | Auburn | | |
| Perkins, Bruce FB | 90TB 91Ind | 2 | 6'2" | 230 | Arizona State | | 12 |
| Perkins, Johnny WR | 77-83NYG | 2 | 6'2" | 205 | Abilene Christian | | 108 |
| Perkins, Ray DE | 87Dal | | 6'5" | 242 | Virginia | | |
| Perko, Mike NT | 82-83Atl 84-85USFL | | 6'4" | 235 | Gonzaga, Utah St. | | |
| Perot, Petey OG | 79-82Phi 83SJ 84Phi 85NO | | 6'2" | 261 | Northwestern La. | | |
| Perriman, Brett WR | 88-90NO 91-95Det | 2 | 5'9" | 175 | Miami (Fla.) | | 150 |
| Perrin, Benny DB | 82-85StL | | 6'2" | 178 | Alabama | 9 | 6 |
| Perrino, Mike OT | 87Phi | | 6'5" | 285 | Notre Dame | | |
| Perry, Darren DB | 92-95Pit | | 5'10" | 194 | Penn State | 21 | |
| Perry, Gerald OT | 88-90Den 91-92LA 93-94Raid 95Oak | | 6'6" | 305 | Southern U. | | |
| Perry, Leon FB | 80NYG 84-85USFL | 2 | 5'11" | 225 | Mississippi | | 18 |
| Perry, Mario TE | 87Raid | | 6'6" | 240 | Mississippi | | 6 |
| Perry, Mario LB | 94-95Buf | | 6'4" | 250 | Jackson State | | |
| Perry, Michael Dean DT-DE-NT | 88-94Cle 95Den | | 6'1" | 285 | Clemson | | |
| Perry, Todd OG | 93-95Chi | | 6'5" | 306 | Kentucky | | |
| Perry, Vernon DB | 79-82Hou 83NO | | 6'2" | 211 | Jackson State | 11 | |
| Perry, Victor OT | 87StL | | 6'5" | 278 | Georgia | | |
| Perry, William (The Refrigerator) DT-DE-FB | 85-93Chi 93-94Phi | | 6'2" | 328 | Clemson | | 18 |
| Perryman, Bob FB | 87-90NE 90Dal 91-92Den | 2 | 6'1" | 233 | Michigan | | 54 |
| Perryman, Dean C | 87Sea | | 6'3" | 260 | Washington | | |
| Perryman, Jim DB | 84USFL 85Buf 87Ind | | 6'0" | 181 | Millikin | 1 | |
| Pete, Lawrence NT | 89-93Det | | 6' | 285 | Nebraska | | |
| Peterson, Andrew OG-OT | 95Car | | 6'5" | 308 | Washington | | |
| Peterson, Anthony LB | 94-95SF | | 6' | 223 | Notre Dame | | |
| Petersen, Kurt OG | 80-85Dal 86-87KJ | | 6'4" | 264 | Missouri | | |
| Petersen, Ted OT-C-OG | 77-83Pit 84Cle 84Ind 87Pit | | 6'5" | 245 | Eastern Illinois | | |
| Peterson, Todd K | 94Arz 95Sea | 5 | 5'10" | 176 | Georgia | | 119 |
| Petersmark, Brett C | 87Hou | | 6'3" | 280 | Eastern Michigan | | |
| Peterson, Joe DB | 87NE | | 5'10" | 185 | Nevada-Reno | 1 | |
| Petry, Stan DB | 89-90KC 91NO | | 5'11" | 175 | Texas Christian | 3 | 6 |
| Pettey, Phil OG | 87Was | | 6'4" | 274 | Missouri | | |
| Pettitt, Duane DE | 87SD | | 6'4" | 265 | San Diego State | | |
| Pettyjohn, Barry OT-C | 87Hou | | 6'5" | 285 | Pittsburgh | | |
| Petway, David DB | 81GB | | 6'1" | 207 | Northern Illinois | | |
| Phifer, Roman LB | 91-94LA 95StL | | 6'2" | 232 | U.C.L.A. | 6 | |
| Philcox, Todd QB | 90Cin 91-93Cle 94Cin 95TB | 1 | 6'4" | 217 | Syracuse | | 6 |
| Philion, Ed DT | 94-95Buf | | 6'2" | 273 | Ferris State | | |
| Phillips, Anthony DB | 94-95Atl | | 6'2" | 207 | Texas A&M | 2 | |
| Phillips, Bobby HB | 95Min | | 5'9" | 187 | Virginia Union | | |
| Phillips, Bum | HC75-80Hou HC81-85NO | | | | S.F. Austin State | | |
| Phillips, Irvin DB | 81SD 83Raid | | 6'1" | 191 | Arkansas Tech | | |
| Phillips, Jason WR | 89-90Det 91-93Atl | 2 | 5'7" | 168 | Houston | | 12 |
| Phillips, Joe DE-NT-DT | 86Min 87-91SD 92-95KC | | 6'5" | 293 | Oregon St., S.M.U. | 1 | |
| Phillips, Joe WR | 85,87Was | | 5'9" | 188 | Kentucky | | |
| Phillips, Kim DB | 89NO 90Buf | | 5'9" | 188 | North Texas | | |
| Phillips, Kirk WR | 84Dal | | 6'1" | 202 | Tulsa | | |
| Phillips, Ray LB-DE | 86Atl 87Phi | | 6'3" | 243 | N. Carolina State | | |
| Phillips, Reggie DB | 85-87Chi 88Phx | | 5'10" | 171 | S.M.U. | 3 | |
| Phillips, Wade | HC85NO HC93-94Den | | | | Houston | | |
| Philyaw, Dino HB | 95Car | | 5'10" | 199 | Oregon | | |
| Pickel, Bill NT-DE-DT | 83-90Raid 91-94NYJ | | 6'5" | 263 | Rutgers | | |
| Pickering, Clay WR | 84-85Cin 86Chi | | 6'5" | 215 | Maine | | |
| Pickens, Bruce DB | 91-93Atl 93GB 93KC 95Oak | | 5'11" | 190 | Nebraska | 2 | |
| Pickens, Carl WR | 92-95Cin | 23 | 6'2" | 206 | Tennessee | | 216 |
| Pickens, Lyle DB | 87Den | | 5'10" | 175 | Colorado | | |
| Pidgeon, Tim LB | 87Mia | | 6' | 233 | Syracuse | | |
| Piel, Mike DT | 89-92LA | | 6'4" | 268 | Illinois | | |
| Pierce, Aaron TE | 92-95NYG | 2 | 6'5" | 246 | Washington | | 24 |
| Pierce, Steve WR | 87Cle | | 5'10" | 190 | Illinois | | |
| Pieri, Damon DB | 93NYJ | | 6' | 186 | San Diego State | | |
| Pierson, Pete OT | 95TB | | 6'5" | 295 | Washington | | |
| Pike, Chris DT | 89-90Cle 91LA | | 6'8" | 290 | North Carolina, Tulsa | | |
| Pike, Mark DE-LB | 87-95Buf | | 6'4" | 269 | Georgia Tech | | |
| Pillers, Lawrence DE-DT-NT | 76-80NYJ 80-84SF 85Atl | | 6'3" | 255 | Alcorn State | 1 | |
| Pillman, Brian LB | 84Cin | | 5'10" | 228 | Miami-Ohio | | |
| Pillow, Frank WR | 88-90TB | 2 | 5'10" | 170 | Tennessee State | | 6 |
| Pinkett, Allen HB | 86-91Hou 92KJ | 23 | 5'9" | 189 | Notre Dame | | 156 |
| Pinkney, Lovell TE | 95StL | | 6'4" | 248 | Texas | | |
| Pinney, Ray OT-C-OG | 76-78Pit 79IL 80-82Pit 83-85USFL 85-87Pit | | 6'4" | 251 | Washington | | |

| Use Name (Nickname) - Positions | Team by Year | See Section | Hgt. | Wgt. | College | Int | Pts |
|---|---|---|---|---|---|---|---|
| Pippens, Woodie FB | 87KC | | 5'11" | 225 | Thiel | | |
| Pisarcik, Joe QB | 77-79NYG 80-84Phi | 12 | 6'4" | 220 | New Mexico State | | 30 |
| Pitcock, Charles C | 87TB | | 6'4" | 272 | Tulane | | |
| Pittman, Danny WR | 80-83NYG 83-84StL | 23 | 6'2" | 205 | Wyoming | | 6 |
| Pitts, Mike DE-DT | 83-86Atl 87-92Phi 93-94NE | | 6'5" | 276 | Alabama | 1 | 6 |
| Pitts, Ron DB | 86-87Buf 88-90GB | 3 | 5'10" | 175 | U.C.L.A. | 7 | 12 |
| Planansky, Joe TE | 95Mia | | 6'4" | 250 | Chadron State | | |
| Plantz, Ron C | 87Ind | | 6'4" | 272 | Notre Dame | | |
| Pleasant, Anthony DE | 90-95Cle | | 6'5" | 274 | Tennessee State | | 2 |
| Pleasant, Marquis WR | 87Cin | | 6'2" | 172 | S.M.U. | | |
| Pleasant, Mike HB | 84LA | | 6'1" | 195 | Oklahoma | | |
| Pleasant, Reggie DB | 85Atl | | 5'9" | 175 | Clemson | | |
| Ploeger, Kurt DE-DT | 86Dal 86GB 87Min | | 6'5" | 259 | Gustavus Adolphus | | |
| Plummer, Bruce DB | 87-88Den 88Mia 89Ind 90Den 90SF 91Phi | | 6'1" | 199 | Mississippi | 2 | |
| Plummer, Gary LB | 83-85USFL 86-94SD 95SF | | 6'2" | 242 | California | 6 | 12 |
| Plunkett, Art OT | 81-84StL 85NE 86KJ 87NE 88KJ | | 6'7" | 269 | Nevada-Las Vegas | | |
| Poe, Bill OG | 87Cin | | 6'3" | 280 | Morehead State | | |
| Poe, Johnnie DB | 81-87NO | | 6'1" | 190 | Missouri | 17 | 18 |
| Pointer, John LB | 87GB | | 6'2" | 225 | Vanderbilt | | |
| Pokorny, Frank WR | 85Pit | | 6' | 198 | Youngstown State | | |
| Pollack, Frank OT-OG | 90-91SF 92XJ 94-95SF | | 6'4" | 281 | Northern Arizona | | |
| Pollard, Darryl DB | 87-90SF 91AJ 92TB 93ZJ | | 5'11" | 187 | Weber State | 4 | |
| Pollard, Frank HB-FB | 80-88Pit | 2 | 5'10" | 218 | Baylor | | 120 |
| Pollard, Marcus TE | 95Ind | | 6'4" | 245 | Bradley | | |
| Pollard, Trent OT-OG | 94-95Cin | | 6'4" | 318 | Eastern Washington | | |
| Polley, Tom LB | 85Phi 87Cle | | 6'3" | 246 | Nevada-Las Vegas | | |
| Ponder, David DT | 85Dal | | 6'3" | 250 | Florida State | | |
| Pool, David DB | 90Buf 91-92NE 93Buf 94Mia | | 5'9" | 186 | Tennessee, Carson-Newman | 3 | 6 |
| Poole, Ken DE | 81Mia 82XJ | | 6'3" | 251 | Northeast La. | | |
| Poole, Nathan FB-HB | 79-80Cin 82-83,85,87Den | 2 | 5'9" | 210 | Louisville | | 30 |
| Poole, Shelley FB | 87Atl | | 5'7" | 219 | Temple | | |
| Poole, Tyrone DB | 95Car | | 5'8" | 188 | Ft. Valley State | 2 | |
| Pope, Marquez DB | 92-93SD 94LA 95SF | | 5'10" | 188 | Fresno State | 6 | |
| Popson, Ted TE | 94-95SF | 2 | 6'4" | 250 | Portland State | | |
| Porcher, Robert DE-DT | 92-95Det | | 6'3" | 280 | Tennessee, State, S. Carolina State | | |
| Porell, Tom NT | 87NE | | 6'3" | 275 | Boston College | | |
| Port, Chris OG-OT | 91-95NO | | 6'5" | 292 | Duke | | |
| Porter, Kevin DB | 88-92KC 92NYJ 93KJ | | 5'10" | 215 | Auburn | 1 | |
| Porter, Kerry HB-FB | 87Buf 89Raid 90Den | | 6'1" | 215 | Washington State | | |
| Porter, Ricky HB | 82Det 83Bal 85USFL 87Buf | 23 | 5'10" | 198 | Slippery Rock | | |
| Porter, Robert DB | 87NYG | | 6'2" | 210 | Holy Cross | | |
| Porter, Rufus LB-DE | 88-94Sea 95NO | | 6'1" | 223 | Southern | 1 | |
| Porter, Tracy WR | 81-82Det 83Bal 84Ind | 2 | 6'2" | 198 | Louisiana State | | 18 |
| Potter, Kevin DB | 84Chi | | 5'10" | 186 | Missouri | | |
| Potter, Steve LB | 81-82Mia 83KC 84Buf | | 6'3" | 235 | Virginia | 1 | |
| Potts, Roosevelt FB-HB | 93-95Ind | 2 | 6' | 251 | Northeast La. | | 18 |
| Pounds, Darryl DB | 95Was | | 5'10" | 177 | Nicholls State | 1 | |
| Powe, Karl WR | 85-86Dal | | 6'2" | 177 | Alabama State | | |
| Powe, Keith DE | 94-95TB | | 6'3" | 265 | Texas-El Paso | | |
| Powell, Alvin OG | 87-88Sea 89Mia | | 6'5" | 294 | Winston-Salem St. | | |
| Powell, Andre LB | 93-94NYG | | 6'1" | 226 | Penn State | | |
| Powell, Craig LB | 95Cle | | 6'4" | 230 | Ohio State | | |
| Powell, Jeff HB | 87SD | | 5'10" | 185 | Tennessee | | |
| Powell, Marvin OT | 77-85NYJ 86-87TB | | 6'5" | 268 | Southern Calif. | | |
| Powers, Ricky HB | 95Cle | | 6' | 213 | Michigan | | |
| Powers, Warren DE | 89-91Den 91LA | | 6'6" | 287 | Maryland | | 6 |
| Pozderac, Phil OT | 82-87Dal | | 6'9" | 277 | Notre Dame | | |
| Prater, Dean DE | 83KC 84-88Buf | | 6'4' | 255 | Oklahoma State | | |
| Prather, Guy LB | 81-85GB | | 6'2" | 230 | Grambling | | |
| President, Andre TE | 95NE 95Chi | | 6'3" | 255 | Angelo State | | |
| Preston, Dave HB | 78-83Den 84USFL | 23 | 5'10" | 195 | Bowling Green | | 78 |
| Preston, John DB | 87StL | | 6' | 207 | Central St.-Okla. | | |
| Preston, Ray LB | 76-84SD | | 6' | 218 | Syracuse | 6 | |
| Preston, Roell WR | 95Atl | 3 | 5'10" | 187 | Mississippi | | 6 |
| Prestridge, Luke K | 79-83Den 84NE | 4 | 6'4" | 235 | Baylor | | |
| Price, Art LB | 87Atl | | 6'3" | 227 | Wisconsin | | |
| Price, Dennis DB | 88-89Raid 90SJ 91KJ 92NYJ | | 6'1" | 175 | U.C.L.A. | 3 | |
| Price, Jim TE-WR | 91-93LA 93Dal 95StL | 2 | 6'4' | 247 | Stanford | | 24 |
| Price, Mitchell DB | 90-92Cin 92Phx 92-93Cin 93LA | 3 | 5'9" | 181 | S.M.U., Tulane | 2 | 12 |
| Price, Shawn DE | 93-94TB 95Car | | 6'5" | 271 | U. of Pacific | | |
| Price, Terry DE | 90Chi 91EJ | | 6'4" | 272 | Texas A&M | | |
| Pridemore, Tom DB | 78-85Atl | | 5'10" | 186 | West Virginia | 21 | 6 |
| Primus, Greg WR | 94-95Chi | | 5'11" | 190 | Colorado State | | |
| Primus, James HB | 88-89Atl | 2 | 5'11" | 196 | U.C.L.A. | | 6 |
| Prindle, Mike K | 87Det | | 5'9" | 160 | Western Michigan | | 24 |
| Pringle, Mike HB | 90Atl | | 5'8" | 186 | Washington State, Fullerton State | | |
| Prior, Anthony DB | 93-95NYJ | 3 | 5'11" | 185 | Washington State | | |
| Prior, Mike DB | 85TB 87-92Ind 93-95GB | 3 | 6' | 202 | Illinois State | 29 | 6 |
| Pritchard, Mike WR | 91-93Atl 94-95Den | 2 | 5'11" | 180 | Colorado | | 108 |
| Pritchett, Kelvin DE-DT | 91-94Det 95Jax | | 6'3" | 286 | Mississippi | | |
| Pritchett, Wes LB | 91Atl | | 6'2" | 234 | Notre Dame | | |
| Proby, Bryan DE | 95KC | | 6'5" | 285 | Arizona State | | |
| Proehl, Ricky WR | 90-93Phx 94Arz 95Sea | 2 | 5'10" | 185 | Wake Forest | | 126 |
| Profit, Eugene DB | 86-88NE 89LJ | | 5'10" | 168 | Yale | | |
| Prokop, Joe K | 85GB 87SD 88-90NYJ 91SF 92Mia 92NYG | 4 | 6'3" | 227 | Cal. Poly.-Pomona | | 6 |
| Provence, Andrew DT-DE | 83-87Atl 88FJ 89PJ | | 6'3" | 265 | South Carolina | | |
| Pruitt, James WR | 86-88Mia 88-89Ind 90-91Mia | 2 | 6'3" | 199 | Fullerton State | | 60 |
| Pruitt, Mickey LB-DB | 88-90Chi 91-92Dal | | 6'1" | 206 | Colorado | | |
| Pruitt, Mike FB | 76-84Cle 85Buf 85-86KC | 2 | 6' | 222 | Purdue | | 336 |
| Puki, Craig LB | 80-81SF 82StL | | 6'1" | 231 | Tennessee | 1 | |
| Pumphrey, Donald OT | 87TB | | 6'4" | 275 | Valdosta State | | |
| Pupunu, Alfred TE | 92-95SD | 2 | 6'2" | 261 | Weber State | | 12 |
| Purling, Dave DE | 87LA | | 6'5" | 240 | Southern Calif. | | |
| Putzier, Rollin DT-NT | 88Pit 89SF | | 6'4" | 280 | Oregon | | |
| Puzzuoli, Dave NT | 83-87Cle | | 6'3" | 260 | Pittsburgh | | |
| Pyles, David OT | 87Raid | | 6'5" | 275 | Miami-Ohio | | |
| Pyne, Jim OG | 95TB | | 6'2" | 282 | Virginia Tech | | |
| Quaerna, Jerry OT | 87Det | | 6'6" | 275 | Michigan | | |
| Quarles, Bernard QB | 87LA | | 6'2" | 215 | Hawaii | | |
| Query, Jeff WR | 89-91GB 92-95Cin 95Was | 23 | 6' | 165 | Millikin | | 72 |
| Quick, Greg OT | 87Atl | | 6'4" | 280 | Catawba | | |
| Quick, Jerry OT | 87Pit | | 6'5" | 279 | Wichita State | | |
| Quick, Mike WR | 82-90Phi | 2 | 6'2" | 190 | N. Carolina State | | 366 |
| Quillan, Fred C | 78-87SF | | 6'5" | 261 | Oregon | | |
| Quinn, Jeff QB | 82Pit 82TB 84USFL | | 6'3" | 205 | Nebraska | | |

| Use Name (Nickname) - Positions | Team by Year | See Section | Hgt. | Wgt. | College | Int | Pts |
|---|---|---|---|---|---|---|---|
| Quinn, Kelly DE | 87Min | | 6'1" | 220 | Michigan | | |
| Raab, Marc C | 93Was | | 6'3" | 265 | Southern Calif. | | |
| Rackley, David DB | 85NO | | 5'9" | 172 | Texas Southern | | |
| Radachowsky, George DB | 84-85Ind 87-89NYJ | | 5'11" | 186 | Boston College | 2 | 6 |
| Rade, John LB | 83-91Atl | | 6'1" | 232 | Boise State | 3 | 12 |
| Radecic, Keith C | 87StL | | 6'1" | 260 | Penn State | | |
| Radecic, Scott LB | 84-86KC 87-89Buf 90-91-95Ind | | 6'3" | 241 | Penn State | 8 | 6 |
| Radford, Bruce NT-DE | 79Den 80TB 81StL | | 6'5" | 257 | Grambling | | |
| Radloff, Wayne C-OG | 83-84USFL 85-89Atl 90KJ | | 6'5" | 274 | Georgia | | |
| Rafferty, Tom OG-C | 76-89Dal | | 6'3" | 256 | Penn State | | |
| Rafferty, Vince C-OG | 87GB | | 6'4" | 285 | Colorado | | |
| Raglin, Floyd DB | 87Mia | | 5'9" | 180 | Southern U. | | |
| Ragusa, Pat K | 87NYJ | | 5'8" | 180 | St. John's (N.Y.) | | 13 |
| Rains, Dan LB | 82-84Chi 85KJ 86Chi | | 6'1" | 224 | Cincinnati | | |
| Rakoczy, Gregg C-OT-OG | 87-90Cle 91-92NE | | 6'6" | 286 | Miami (Fla.) | | |
| Ralph, Dan DT | 84StL 85XJ | | 6'4" | 260 | Colorado, Oregon | | |
| Ramey, Jim DE | 79StL 80-81CFL83-85USFL 87TB | | 6'4" | 261 | Kentucky | | |
| Ramsey, Chuck K | 77-84NYJ | 4 | 6'2" | 191 | Wake Forest | | |
| Ramsey, Derrick TE | 78-81Oak 82-83Raid 83-85NE 87Det | 2 | 6'5" | 230 | Kentucky | | 126 |
| Ramsey, Greg DE | 87Sea | | 6'3" | 244 | Fresno State | | |
| Ramsey, Tom QB | 85-88NE 89Ind | 1 | 6'1" | 189 | U.C.L.A. | | 6 |
| Ramson, Eason TE | 78StL 79-83SF 85Buf | 2 | 6'2" | 232 | Washington State | | 30 |
| Randle, John DE-DT | 90-95Min | | 6'1" | 269 | Texas A&I | | |
| Randle, Ervin LB | 85-90TB 91-92KC | | 6'1" | 250 | Baylor | 1 | |
| Randle, Tate DB | 82-83Hou 83Bal 84-86Ind 87Mia | | 6' | 202 | Texas Tech | 7 | 2 |
| Randolph, Thomas DB | 94-95NYG | | 5'9" | 176 | Kansas State | 3 | |
| Ransdell, Bill QB | 88Ind | | 6'2" | 212 | Kentucky | | |
| Ransom, Brian QB | 83-85Hou | | 6'3" | 203 | Tennessee State | | |
| Rasby, Walter TE | 94Pit 95Car | | 6'3" | 247 | Wake Forest | | 2 |
| Rash, Lou DB | 84Phi 87GB | | 5'9" | 180 | Miss. Valley St. | | |
| Rasheed, Kenyon FB | 93-94NYG 95NYJ | 2 | 5'10" | 245 | Oklahoma | | 6 |
| Rasmussen, Randy C-OG | 84-86Pit 87-88Min | | 6'2" | 254 | Minnesota | | |
| Rathman, Tom FB | 86-93SF 94Raid | 2 | 6'1" | 232 | Nebraska | | 204 |
| Ratigan, Brian LB | 94Ind | | 6'4" | 241 | Notre Dame | | |
| Ravotti, Eric LB | 94-95Pit | | 6'3" | 254 | Penn State | | |
| Ray, Darrol DB | 80-84NYJ | | 6'1" | 200 | Oklahoma | 21 | 24 |
| Ray, John OT | 93Ind | | 6'8" | 350 | West Virginia | | |
| Ray, Ricky DB | 79-81NO 81Mia 82-83CFL 84USFL | | 5'11" | 180 | Norfolk State | 1 | |
| Ray, Terry DB | 92Atl 93-95NE | | 6'1" | 187 | Oklahoma | 3 | |
| Rayam, Thomas OT | 92-93Cin | | 6'6" | 297 | Alabama | | |
| Raye, Jimmy WR | 91LA | | 5'9" | 165 | San Diego State | | |
| Raymer, Cory C | 95Was | | 6'2" | 293 | Wisconsin | | |
| Raymond, Corey DB | 92-94NYG 95Det | | 5'11" | 180 | Louisiana State | 9 | |
| Razzano, Rick LB | 80-84Cin | | 5'11" | 227 | Virginia Tech | 1 | |
| Reach, Kevin OG-C | 87SF | | 6'3" | 270 | Utah | | |
| Readon, Ike NT | 87Mia | | 6' | 273 | Hampton U. | | |
| Reasons, Gary LB | 84-91NYG 92Cin | | 6'4" | 234 | Northwestern La. | 10 | 2 |
| Reaves, Willard HB | 89Mia 89Was | | 5'11" | 200 | Northern Arizona | | |
| Redd, Glen LB | 81NO 82KJ 83-86NO 86Ind | | 6'1" | 228 | Brigham Young | 2 | |
| Redden, Barry HB-FB | 82-86LA 87-88SD 89-90Cle | 23 | 5'10" | 210 | Richmond | | 66 |
| Redding, Reggie OT-OG | 91Atl 92NE | | 6'3" | 298 | Fullerton State | | |
| Redick, Cornelius WR | 87GB | | 6' | 185 | Fullerton State | | |
| Redmon, Anthony OG | 94-95Arz | | 6'4" | 308 | Auburn | | |
| Redwine, Jarvis HB | 81-83Min | 23 | 5'10" | 203 | Oregon State, Nebraska | | |
| Reece, Beasley DB | 76Dal 77-83NYG 83-84TB | 3 | 6'1" | 193 | North Texas | 19 | 6 |
| Reece, John DB | 95StL | | 6' | 203 | Nebraska | | |
| Reed, Andre WR | 85-95Buf | 2 | 6' | 188 | Kutztown | | 420 |
| Reed, Ben DE | 87NE | | 6'5" | 265 | Mississippi | | |
| Reed, Doug DE-DT | 84-90LA | | 6'3" | 254 | San Diego State | | |
| Reed, Jake WR | 91-95Min | 2 | 6'3" | 216 | Grambling | | 78 |
| Reed, Mark QB | 82NYG 83Bal 84NYJ | | 6'3" | 201 | Moorhead State | | |
| Reed, Michael DB | 95Car | | 5'9" | 180 | Boston College | | |
| Reeder, Dan FB | 86-87Pit | | 5'11" | 235 | Delaware | | |
| Reese, Archie DE-DT-NT | 78-81SF 82-83Raid 84USFL | | 6'3" | 267 | Clemson | | |
| Reese, Booker DE | 82-84TB 84-85LA | | 6'6" | 260 | Bethune-Cookman | 2 | |
| Reese, Jerry DE | 88Pit | | 6'2" | 267 | Kentucky | | |
| Reese, Jerry DB | 79-80KC 83USFL | | 6'3" | 192 | Oklahoma | | |
| Reeves, Bryan WR | 94-95Arz | 2 | 5'11" | 195 | Nevada-Reno | | 6 |
| Reeves, Ken OG-OT | 85-89Phi 90Cle | | 6'5" | 272 | Texas A&M | | |
| Reeves, Walter TE | 89-93Phx 94-95Cle | 2 | 6'4" | 255 | Auburn | | 18 |
| Regent, Shawn C | 87Raid | | 6'5" | 280 | Boston College | | |
| Rehage, Steve DB | 87NYG | | 6'1" | 190 | Louisiana State | 1 | |
| Rehder, Tom OT-OG | 88-89NE 90NYG | | 6'7" | 282 | Notre Dame | | |
| Reich, Frank QB | 85-94Buf 95Car | 12 | 6'3" | 209 | Maryland | | |
| Reichenbach, Mike LB | 84-89Phi 90-91Mia | | 6'2" | 236 | East S troudsburg | 2 | |
| Reid, Alan HB | 87Phi | | 5'8" | 190 | Minnesota | | |
| Reid, Jim OT-OG | 95Hou | | 6'6" | 306 | Virginia | | |
| Reid, Michael LB | 87-92Atl | | 6'2" | 228 | Wisconsin | | |
| Reid, Mike DB | 93-94Phi | | 6'1" | 218 | Clemson | | |
| Reilly, Dameon WR | 87Mia | | 5'11" | 180 | Rhode Island | | |
| Reilly, Mike LB | 82LA 83SL | | 6'4" | 219 | Oklahoma | | |
| Reimers, Bruce OT-OG | 84-91Cin 92-93TB | | 6'7" | 285 | Iowa State | | |
| Reinke, Jeff DE | 87Cin | | 6'4" | 262 | Mankato State | | |
| Rembert, Johnny LB | 83-92NE | | 6'3" | 234 | Clemson | 7 | 12 |
| Rembert, Reggie WR | 91-93Cin | 2 | 6'5" | 200 | West Virginia | | 6 |
| Remo, Roger LB | 87Ind | | 6'3" | 237 | Syracuse | | |
| Remsberg, Dan OT | 86-87Den | | 6'6" | 275 | Abilene Christian | | |
| Renfro, Mike WR | 78-83Hou 84-87Dal | 2 | 6' | 185 | Texas Christian | | 150 |
| Renfro, Leonard DT | 93-94Phi | | 6'2" | 291 | Colorado | | |
| Rennaker, Terry LB | 80Sea | | 6'6" | 225 | Stanford | | |
| Renner, Bill K | 86-87GB | | 6' | 198 | Virginia Tech | | |
| Rentie, Caesar OT | 88Chi | | 6'3" | 291 | Oklahoma | | |
| Repko, Jay TE | 87Phi | | 6'3" | 240 | Ursinus | | |
| Reveiz, Fuad K | 85-88Mia 90SD 90-95Min | 5 | 5'11" | 220 | Tennessee | | 921 |
| Reynolds, Ed LB | 83-91NE 92NYG | | 6'5" | 238 | Virginia | | |
| Reynolds, Ricky DB | 87-93TB 94-95NE | | 5'11" | 187 | Washington State | 21 | 30 |
| Rhem, Steve WR | 94-95NO | | 6'2" | 212 | Minnesota | | |
| Rhett, Errict HB | 94-95TB | 2 | 5'11" | 211 | Florida | | 110 |
| Rhodes, Ray | HC95Phi | | | | Texas Christian | | |
| Rhymes, Buster WR | 85-86Min | 3 | 6'2" | 217 | Oklahoma | | |
| Ricardo, Benny K | 76Buf 76Det 77SJ 78-79Det 80-81NO 83Min 84SD | 5 | 5'10" | 172 | San Diego State | | 447 |
| Rice, Allen HB-FB | 84-90Min 91GB | 23 | 5'10" | 203 | Baylor | | 114 |
| Rice, Dan FB | 87Cin | | 6'1" | 241 | Michigan | | |
| Rice, Jerry WR | 85-95SF | 2 | 6'2" | 200 | Miss. Valley St. | | 940 |
| Rice, Rodney DB | 89NE 90TB | | 5'8" | 180 | Brigham Young | 2 | |

| Use Name (Nickname) - Positions | Team by Year | See Section | Hgt. | Wgt. | College | Int | Pts |
|---|---|---|---|---|---|---|---|
| Richard, Gary DB | 88GB | | 5'9" | 171 | Pittsburgh | | |
| Richard, Stanley DB | 91-94SD 95Was | | 6'2" | 197 | Texas | 13 | 12 |
| Richards, Curvin HB | 91-92Dal 93Det | | 5'9" | 195 | Pittsburgh | | 6 |
| Richards, David OT-OG | 88-92SD 93Det 94-95Atl | | 6'5" | 310 | S.M.U., U.C.L.A. | | |
| Richards, Howard OG-OT | 81-86Dal 87Sea | | 6'6" | 263 | Missouri | | |
| Richardson, Al LB | 80-85Atl | | 6'2" | 211 | Georgia Tech | 9 | 6 |
| Richardson, Bucky QB | 92-94Hou | 12 | 6'1" | 221 | Texas A&M | | 6 |
| Richardson, C.J. DB | 95Arz | | 5'10" | 209 | Miami (Fla.) | | |
| Richardson, Eric WR | 85-86Buf | 2 | 6'1" | 185 | San Jose State | | |
| Richardson, Greg WR | 87Min 88TB | | 5'7" | 171 | Alabama | | |
| Richardson, Huey LB-DE | 91Pit 92Was 92NYJ | | 6'5" | 233 | Pittsburgh | | |
| Richardson, Mike DB | 83-88Chi | | 6' | 187 | Arizona State | 20 | 6 |
| Richardson, Paul WR | 93Phi | | 6'3" | 204 | U.C.L.A. | | |
| Richardson, Reggie DB | 87LA | | 6' | 180 | Utah | | |
| Richardson, Tony FB | 95KC | | 6'1" | 232 | Auburn | | |
| Richey, Tom OT | 87Cin | | 6'4" | 274 | Kentucky | | |
| Richmond, Rock DB | 87Pit | | 5'10" | 180 | Oregon | | |
| Ricketts, Tom OG-OT | 89-91Pit 92Ind 93KC | | 6'5" | 294 | Pittsburgh | | |
| Ricks, Harold HB | 87TB | | 5'10" | 200 | Tenn.-Chattanooga | | 6 |
| Ricks, Lawrence HB | 83-84KC | | 5'9" | 194 | Michigan | | |
| Riddick, Louis DB | 92Atl 93-95Cle | | 6'2" | 216 | Pittsburgh | | 2 |
| Riddick, Robb HB | 81Buf 82KJ 83-84Buf 85KJ 86-88Buf 89-90KJ | 23 | 6' | 195 | Millersville | | 164 |
| Ridgle, Elston DE | 87SF 88NJ 89Buf 89Sea 90Phx 92Cin | | 6'6" | 265 | Northern Arizona, Nevada-Reno | | |
| Riehm, Chris OT-OG | 84-85USFL 86Raid 87KJ 88Raid | | 6'6" | 278 | Ohio State | | |
| Rienstra, John OG | 86-90Pit 91-92Cle | | 6'5" | 271 | Temple | | |
| Riesenberg, Doug OT | 87-95NYG | | 6'5" | 276 | California | | |
| Riggins, Charles DE | 87TB | | 6'5" | 295 | Bethune-Cookman | | |
| Riggs, Gerald FB-HB | 82-88Atl 89-91Was | 2 | 6'1" | 231 | Arizona State | | 414 |
| Riggs, Jim TE | 87-92Cin 93Was | 2 | 6'5" | 245 | Clemson | | |
| Riley, Avon LB | 81-86Hou 87Pit | | 6'3" | 230 | U.C.L.A. | 3 | |
| Riley, Bob OT | 87Cin | | 6'5" | 276 | Indiana | | |
| Riley, Cameron DB | 87Pit | | 6'1" | 195 | Missouri | | |
| Riley, Eric TE | 87NYJ | | 6'3" | 230 | Eastern Washington | | |
| Riley, Eugene TE | 90Ind 91Det | | 6'2" | 236 | Ball State | | |
| Riley, Pat DE | 95Chi | | 6'5" | 286 | Miami (Fla.) | | |
| Rimington, Dave C | 83-87Cin 88-89Phi | | 6'3" | 288 | Nebraska | | |
| Rindy, Stuart OT-OG | 87Chi | | 6'5" | 266 | Wis.-Whitewater | | |
| Riordan, Tim QB | 87NO | | 6'1" | 185 | Temple | | |
| Ring, Bill HB-FB | 81-86SF | 2 | 5'10" | 208 | Brigham Young | | 48 |
| Risher, Alan QB | 83-85USFL 85TB 87GB | 1 | 6'2" | 190 | Louisiana State | | 6 |
| Risien, Cody OT-OG | 79-83Cle 84KJ 85-89Cle | | 6'7" | 269 | Texas A&M | | |
| Rison, Andre WR | 89Ind 90-94Atl 95Cle | 2 | 5'10" | 185 | Michigan State | | 380 |
| Ritcher, Jim OG-C | 80-93Buf 94-95Atl | | 6'3" | 267 | N. Carolina State | | |
| Rivera, Gabe NT | 83Pit | | 6'2" | 293 | Texas Tech | | |
| 1984 — Injured in automobile accident | | | | | | | |
| Rivera, Ron LB | 84-92Chi | | 6'3" | 239 | California | 8 | 6 |
| Rivers, Nate FB | 80NYG | | 6'3" | 215 | S. Carolina State | | |
| Rivers, Garland DB | 87Chi | | 6'1" | 181 | Michigan | | |
| Rivers, Reggie FB | 91-95Den | 2 | 6'1" | 215 | Southwest Texas | | 50 |
| Rivers, Ron HB | 95Det | | 5'8" | 205 | Fresno State | | 6 |
| Roaches, Carl WR | 80-84Hou | 3 | 5'8" | 168 | Texas A&M | | 12 |
| Roaf, Willie OT | 93-95NO | | 6'4" | 299 | Louisiana Tech | | |
| Roan, Michael TE | 95Hou | | 6'3" | 251 | Wisconsin | | |
| Robbins, Austin DT | 94Raid 95Oak | | 6'6" | 288 | North Carolina | | 6 |
| Robbins, Barret C | 95Oak | | 6'3" | 300 | Texas Christian | | |
| Robbins, Kevin OT-OG | 89-90Cle 93LA | | 6'6" | 287 | Wichita State, Michigan State | | |
| Robbins, Randy DB | 84-91Den 92NE | | 6'2" | 189 | Arizona | 13 | 12 |
| Robbins, Tootie OT | 82-87StL 88-91Phx 92-93GB | | 6'5" | 303 | East Carolina | | |
| Roberts, Alfredo TE | 88-90KC 91-92Dal 93FJ | 2 | 6'3" | 250 | Miami (Fla.) | | 12 |
| Roberts, Bill OT | 84NYG | | 6'5" | 280 | Ohio State | | |
| Roberts, George K | 78-80Mia 81SD 82Atl | 4 | 6' | 181 | Virginia Tech | | |
| Roberts, Greg OG | 79-82TB 84USFL | | 6'3" | 260 | Oklahoma | | |
| Roberts, Larry DE | 86-93SF | | 6'3" | 270 | Alabama | 1 | |
| Roberts, Ray OT | 92-95Sea | | 6'6" | 307 | Virginia | | |
| Roberts, Tim DT-DE | 92-94Hou 95NE | | 6'6" | 311 | Southern Miss. | | |
| Roberts, Wes DE | 80NYJ 83USFL | | 6'6" | 253 | Texas Christian | | |
| Roberts, William OT-OG | 86-94NYG 95NE | | 6'5" | 286 | Ohio State | | |
| Robertson, Marcus DB | 91-95Hou | | 5'11" | 197 | Iowa State | 11 | 6 |
| Robinson, Billy DB | 47Cle | | 6'1" | 200 | Arizona State | | |
| Robinson, Bo FB-TE | 79-80Det 81-83Atl 84NE 85GJ | 2 | 6'2" | 228 | West Texas State | | 30 |
| Robinson, DeJuan DB | 87Cle | | 5'10" | 185 | Northern Arizona | 1 | |
| Robinson, Don OT | 87Atl | | 6'5" | 280 | Baylor | | |
| Robinson, Ed LB | 94Pit | | 6' | 228 | Florida | | |
| Robinson, Eddie LB | 92-95Hou | | 6'1" | 242 | Alabama State | 1 | 6 |
| Robinson, Eugene DB | 85-95Sea | | 6' | 185 | Colgate | 42 | 12 |
| Robinson, Frank DB | 92Cin 92-93Den | | 5'11" | 174 | Boise State | 1 | |
| Robinson, Fred DE-LB | 84-86SD 86Mia | | 6'4" | 240 | Miami (Fla.) | | |
| Robinson, Freddie DB | 87-88Ind | | 6'1" | 191 | Alabama | 2 | |
| Robinson, Gerald DE-DT | 86-87Min 89-90SD 91-94LA | | 6'3" | 266 | Auburn | | |
| Robinson, Greg OT | 86TB 87NE | | 6'5" | 280 | Nevada-Reno, Sacramento State | | |
| Robinson, Greg HB | 93Raid 94KJ 95StL | 2 | 5'10" | 202 | Northeast La. | | 6 |
| Robinson, Jacque FB | 87Phi | | 5'11" | 215 | Washington | | |
| Robinson, Jeff DE | 93-95Den | | 6'4" | 265 | Idaho | | |
| Robinson, Jeroy LB | 90Den 90Phx | | 6'1" | 241 | Texas A&M | | |
| Robinson, Jerry LB | 79-84Phi 85-91Raid | | 6'2" | 223 | U.C.L.A. | 12 | 24 |
| Robinson, John | HC83-91LA | | | | Oregon | | |
| Robinson, Johnny NT | 81Oak 82-83Raid | | 6'2" | 258 | Louisiana Tech | | 2 |
| Robinson, Junior DB | 90NE 92Det | | 5'9" | 181 | East Carolina | | |
| Robinson, Larry DB | 87NYJ | | 5'9" | 194 | Northwestern La. | 1 | |
| Robinson, Lybrant DE | 89Was | | 6'4" | 250 | Delaware State | | |
| Robinson, Mark DB | 84-87KC 88-90TB 91SJ | | 5'11" | 204 | Penn State | 15 | |
| Robinson, Matt QB | 77-79NYJ 80Den 81-82Buf 84-85USFL | 12 | 6'2" | 196 | Georgia | | 24 |
| Robinson, Mike DE | 81-82Cle 84-85USFL | | 6'5" | 265 | Oklahoma State, Arizona | | |
| Robinson, Patrick WR | 93Cin 94Arz | 3 | 5'8" | 176 | Tennessee State | | |
| Robinson, Rafael DB | 92-95Sea | | 5'11" | 200 | Wisconsin | 1 | |
| Robinson, Rex K | 82NE | | 5'11" | 205 | Georgia | | 8 |
| Robinson, Shelton LB | 82-85Sea 86-88Det | | 6'2" | 235 | North Carolina | 1 | 12 |
| Robinson, Stacy WR | 85-90NYG | 2 | 5'11" | 186 | Prairie View, N. Dakota State | | 42 |
| Robinson, Tony QB | 87Was | | 6'3" | 200 | Tennessee | | |
| Robison, Tommy OT-OG | 87GB 88GJ 89Atl | | 6'4" | 290 | Texas A&M | | |
| Roby, Reggie K | 83-92Mia 93-94Was 95TB | 4 | 6'2" | 248 | Iowa | | |
| Rocker, David DT | 91-94LA | | 6'4" | 267 | Auburn | | |
| Rocker, Tracy DT | 89-90Was | | 6'3" | 288 | Auburn | | |
| Rockford, Jim DB | 85SD | | 5'10" | 180 | Oklahoma | | |
| Rockins, Chris DB | 84-87Cle | | 6' | 195 | Oklahoma State | 6 | |
| Rodenhauser, Mark C | 87Chi 89Min 90-91SD 92Chi 93-94Det 95Car | | 6'5" | 269 | Illinois State | | |
| Rodenberger, Jeff FB | 87NO | | 6'3" | 235 | Maryland | | |
| Rodgers, Del HB | 82GB 83NJ 84GB 87-88SF | 23 | 5'10" | 201 | Utah | | 30 |
| Rodgers, John TE | 82-84Pit | | 6'2" | 226 | Louisiana Tech | | |
| Rodgers, Tyrone DT | 92-94Sea | | 6'3" | 271 | Oklahoma, Washington | | |
| Rodriguez, Mike NT | 87Raid | | 6'1" | 275 | Alabama | | |
| Rodriguez, Ruben K | 87-89Sea 92Den 92NYG | 4 | 6'2" | 209 | Arizona | | |
| Roe, Bill LB | 80Dal 81BA 83-85USFL 87NO | | 6'3" | 233 | Colorado | | |
| Roehlk, Jon OG | 87Chi | | 6'2" | 257 | Iowa | | |
| Rogers, Darryl | HC85-88Det | | | | Fresno State | | |
| Rogers, Don DB | 84-85Cle | | 6'1" | 206 | U.C.L.A. | 2 | |
| 1986 — Died of cocaine overdose | | | | | | | |
| Rogers, Doug DE | 82-83Atl 83-84NE 85SJ 86SF | | 6'5" | 266 | Stanford | | |
| Rogers, George HB-FB | 81-84NO 85-87Was | 2 | 6'2" | 228 | South Carolina | | 324 |
| Rogers, Glenn DB | 91TB | | 6' | 185 | Memphis State | | |
| Rogers, Jimmy HB | 80-84NO | 2 | 5'10" | 191 | Oklahoma | | 30 |
| Rogers, Lamar DE | 91-92Cin | | 6'4" | 292 | Auburn | | |
| Rogers, Reggie DE | 87-88Det 91Buf 92TB | | 6'6" | 278 | Washington | | |
| Rogers, Sam LB | 94-95Buf | | 6'3" | 245 | Colorado | | |
| Rogers, Steve OT | 87KC | | 6'5" | 260 | Oregon State, Brigham Young | | |
| Rogers, Tracy LB | 90-95KC | | 6'2" | 241 | Fresno State | | 6 |
| Rohrer, Jeff LB | 82-87Dal 88XJ | | 6'3" | 228 | Yale | | |
| Roland, Benji DE | 90TB | | 6'3" | 260 | Auburn | | |
| Rolle, Butch TE | 86-91Buf 92-93Phx | 2 | 6'3" | 242 | Michigan State | | 66 |
| Rolling, Henry LB | 88-89TB 90-92SD 93-94LA | | 6'2" | 232 | Nevada-Reno | 5 | |
| Romano, Jim C | 82-84Raid 84-86Hou | | 6'3" | 258 | Penn State | | |
| Romanowski, Bill LB | 88-93SF 94-95Phi | | 6'4" | 237 | Boston College | 6 | |
| Romasko, Dave TE | 87Cin | | 6'3" | 241 | Carroll (Wis.) | | |
| Rome, Stan WR | 79-82KC 83USFL | 2 | 6'5" | 212 | Clemson | | 6 |
| Rome, Tag WR | 87SD | | 5'9" | 175 | Northwestern La. | | |
| Romer, Rich LB | 88-89Cin | | 6'3" | 222 | Union (N.Y.) | | |
| Romes, Charles DB | 77-86Buf 87SD | | 6'1" | 190 | N. Carolina State | 28 | 12 |
| Roopenian, Mark NT | 82-83Buf | | 6'5" | 254 | Boston College | | |
| Roper, John LB | 89-92Chi 93Dal 93Phi | | 6'1" | 232 | Texas A&M | 2 | |
| Roquemore, Durwood DB | 82-83KC 85USFL 87Buf | | 6'1" | 183 | Texas A&I | 5 | 6 |
| Rosado, Dan OG-C | 87-88SD | | 6'3" | 280 | Northern Illinois | | |
| Rose, Barry WR | 93Den | | 6' | 185 | Wis.-Stevens Point | | |
| Rose, Carlton LB | 87Was | | 6'2" | 220 | Michigan | | |
| Rose, Donovan DB | 80KC 81-85CFL 86-87Mia | | 6'1" | 187 | Hampton U. | 2 | |
| Rose, Ken LB | 87-89NYJ 90Cle 90-94Phi | | 6'1" | 211 | Nevada-Las Vegas | 1 | 6 |
| Rose, Joe TE | 80-85Mia 86LJ 87LA | 2 | 6'3" | 228 | California | | 54 |
| Rosenbach, Timm QB | 89-90Phx 91KJ 92Phx 95XJ | 12 | 6'2" | 210 | Washington State | | 18 |
| Rosenmeier, Eric C | 87Buf | | 6'4" | 240 | Colgate | | |
| Rosnagle, Ted DB | 85,87Min | | 6'3" | 205 | Portland State | | |
| Ross, Alvin FB | 87Phi | | 5'11" | 235 | Central St.-Okla. | | 6 |
| Ross, Bobby | HC92-95SD | | | | V.M.I. | | |
| Ross, Dan TE | 79-83Cin 84USFL 85Cin 85Sea 86GB | 2 | 6'4" | 236 | Northeastern | | 114 |
| Ross, Dominique HB | 95Dal | | 6' | 203 | Valdosta State | | |
| Ross, Jermaine WR | 94LA 95KJ | | 5'11" | 192 | Purdue | | 6 |
| Ross, Kevin DB | 84-93KC 94-95Atl | | 5'9" | 182 | Temple | 36 | 36 |
| Ross, Scott LB | 91NO | | 6'1" | 235 | Southern Calif. | | |
| Ross, Tom LB | 87Det | | 6'5" | 225 | Bowling Green | | |
| Rostosky, Pete OT-OG-C | 84-86Pit | | 6'4" | 259 | Connecticut | | |
| Roth, Pete FB | 87Mia | | 5'11" | 210 | Northern Illinois | | |
| Rother, Tim OT | 89-90Raid | | 6'7" | 285 | Nebraska | | |
| Rothschild, Doug LB | 87Chi | | 6'2" | 231 | Wheaton | | |
| Rouen, Tom K | 93-95Den | 4 | 6'3" | 215 | Colorado State, Colorado | | |
| Roundtree, Ray WR | 88Det | | 6' | 180 | Penn State | | |
| Rourke, Jim OG-OT-C | 80-84KC 85NO 86KC | | 6'5" | 265 | Boston College | | |
| Rouse, Curtis OG-OT | 82-86Min 87SD | | 6'3" | 316 | Tenn.-Chattanooga | | |
| Rouse, James FB-HB | 90-91Chi | 2 | 6' | 220 | Arkansas | | |
| Rouse, Wardell LB | 95TB | | 6'2" | 235 | Clemson | | |
| Rouson, Lee FB-HB | 85-90NYG 91Cle | 23 | 6'1" | 220 | Colorado | | 24 |
| Roveto, John K | 81-82Chi 83USFL | 5 | 5'11" | 178 | Southwestern La. | | 71 |
| Rowe, Patrick WR | 93Cle | | 6'1" | 195 | San Diego State | | |
| Rowe, Ray TE | 92-93Was | | 6'2" | 256 | San Diego State | | |
| Rowell, Eugene DT | 87Chi | | 6'3" | 265 | Dubuque | | |
| Rowell, Eugene WR | 90Cle | | 6'1" | 180 | Southern Miss. | | |
| Royal, Andre LB | 95Car | | 6'2" | 220 | Alabama | | |
| Royal, Ricky DB | 90Atl | | 5'9" | 187 | Sam Houston St. | | |
| Royals, Mark K | 87StL 87Phi 90-91TB 92-94Pit 95Det | | 6'5" | 216 | Appalachian State | | |
| Royster, Mazio FB | 92-94TB | 2 | 6'1" | 205 | Southern Calif. | | 6 |
| Rozier, Mike HB | 84-85USFL 85-90Hou 90-91Atl | 2 | 5'10" | 209 | Nebraska | | 186 |
| Rubbert, Ed QB | 87Was | 1 | 6'5" | 225 | Louisville | | |
| Rubens, Larry C | 82-83GB 85USFL 86Chi 87KJ | | 6'1" | 255 | Montana State | | |
| Rubick, Rob TE | 82-88Det | 2 | 6'3" | 232 | Grand Valley St. | | 24 |
| Rubley, T.J. QB | 93LA 95GB | 12 | 6'3" | 205 | Tulsa | | |
| Rucker, Keith NT-DT | 92-93Phx 94-95Cin | | 6'3" | 332 | Eastern Michigan, Ohio Wesleyan | | |
| Rucci, Todd OG | 93-95NE | | 6'5" | 291 | Penn State | | |
| Ruddy, Tim C | 94-95Mia | | 6'3" | 288 | Notre Dame | | |
| Rudolph, Ben DT-DE | 81-84NYJ 85USFL 85-86NYJ | | 6'5" | 270 | Long Beach State | | |
| Rudolph, Coleman DE-DT | 93NYJ 94-95NYG | | 6'4" | 270 | Georgia Tech | | |
| Rudolph, Joe OG | 95Phi | | 6'1" | 285 | Wisconsin | | |
| Rudolph, Martin DB | 87Den | | 5'10" | 183 | Arizona | | |
| Ruether, Mike C-OG-TE | 84-85USFL 86-87StL 88-89Den 90-93Atl | | 6'4" | 279 | Texas | | |
| Ruettgers, Ken OT | 85-95GB | | 6'5" | 285 | Southern Calif. | | |
| Ruff, Guy LB | 82Pit 84USFL | | 6'1" | 215 | Syracuse | | |
| Runager, Max K | 79-83Phi 84-88SF 88Cle 89Phi | 4 | 6'1" | 189 | South Carolina | | |
| Rush, Bob C-OT | 77SD 78KJ 79-82SD 83-85KC | | 6'5" | 265 | Memphis State | | |
| Rush, Tyrone HB | 94Was | | 5'11" | 196 | North Alabama | | |
| Rusinek, Mike NT | 87Cle | | 6'3" | 250 | California | | |
| Russell, Booker FB | 78-79Oak 80SD 81Phi 83-84USFL | 2 | 6'2" | 233 | SW Texas State | | 48 |
| Russell, Damien DB | 93SF | | 6'1" | 204 | Virginia Tech | | |
| Russell, Darryle DB | 87Den | | 6' | 190 | Appalachian State | | |
| Russell, Derek WR | 91-94Den 95Hou | 23 | 6' | 186 | Arkansas | | 36 |
| Russell, Leonard HB | 91-93NE 94Den 95StL | 2 | 6'2" | 235 | Arizona State | | 132 |
| Russell, Rusty OT | 84Phi | | 6'5" | 295 | South Carolina | | |
| Russell, Wade TE | 87Cin | | 6'4" | 250 | Taylor | | 6 |
| Rust, Rod | HC90NE | | | | Iowa State | | |
| Ruth, Mike NT | 86-87NE | | 6'1" | 266 | Boston College | | |
| Rutigliano, Sam | HC78-84Cle | | | | Tulsa | | |
| Rutledge, Craig DB | 87LA | | 6' | 190 | U.C.L.A. | | |
| Rutledge, Jeff QB | 79-81LA 82-89NYG 90-92Was | 12 | 6'1" | 196 | Alabama | | 6 |
| Ruzek, Roger K | 87-89Dal 89-93Phi | 5 | 6'1" | 195 | Weber State | | 566 |
| Ryan, Buddy | HC86-90Phi HC94-95Arz | | | | Oklahoma State | | |

| Use Name (Nickname) - Positions | Team by Year | See Section | Hgt. | Wgt. | College | Int | Pts |
|---|---|---|---|---|---|---|---|
| Ryan, Jim LB | 79-88Den | | 6'1" | 217 | William & Mary | 5 | 2 |
| Ryan, Pat QB | 78-89NYJ 91Phi | 12 | 6'3" | 208 | Tennessee | | 8 |
| Ryan, Tim DE-DT | 90-93Chi | | 6'4" | 268 | Southern Calif. | | |
| Ryan, Tim OG | 91-93TB | | 6'2" | 280 | Notre Dame | | |
| Rypien, Mark QB | 87-93Was 94Cle 95StL | 12 | 6'4" | 234 | Washington State | | 48 |
| Saalfield, Kelly C | 80NYG | | 6'3" | 246 | Nebraska | | |
| Saar, Brad LB | 87Ind | | 6'1" | 220 | Ball State | | |
| Sabb, Dwayne LB | 92-95NE | | 6'4" | 248 | New Hampshire | 2 | |
| Sacca, Tony QB | 92-93Phx | | 6'5" | 230 | Penn State | | |
| Sacco, Frank LB | 87NE | | 6'4" | 240 | Fordham | | |
| Saddler, Rod DE | 87StL 88-91Phx 91Cin | | 6'5" | 276 | Texas A&M | 1 | 12 |
| Sadowski, Troy TE | 90Atl 91KC 92-93NYJ 94-95Cin | 2 | 6'5" | 255 | Georgia | | |
| Sagapolutele, Pio DE-DT | 91-95Cle | | 6'6" | 297 | San Diego State | | |
| Sager, Ken TE | 87Sea | | 6'4" | 228 | Western Washington | | |
| Sagnella, Anthony DT | 87Was | | 6'5" | 260 | Rutgers | | |
| Saindon, Pat OG | 86NO 87Atl | | 6'3" | 273 | Vanderbilt | | |
| Salaam, Rashaan HB | 95Chi | 2 | 6'1" | 226 | Colorado | | 60 |
| Saldi, Jay TE-WR | 76-82Dal 83-84Chi | 2 | 6'3" | 225 | South Carolina | | 48 |
| Saleaumua, Dan NT-DT | 87-88Det 89-95KC | | 6' | 299 | Arizona State | 3 | 14 |
| Salem, Harvey OT-OG | 83-86Hou 86-90Det 91Den 92GB | | 6'6" | 283 | California | | |
| Salisbury, Sean QB | 86Sea 87Ind 88-89CFL 90-94Min | 1 | 6'5" | 215 | Southern Calif. | | |
| Sally, Jerome NT | 82-86NYG 87Ind 88KC | | 6'3" | 267 | Missouri | | |
| Salonen, Brian LB-TE | 84-85Dal 86-87GJ | | 6'3" | 227 | Montana | | |
| Sampleton, Lawrence TE | 82-84Phi 87Mia | | 6'5" | 233 | Texas | | |
| Sampson, Clint WR | 83-86Den 87KJ | 2 | 5'11" | 183 | San Diego State | | 48 |
| Sams, Ron OG | 83GB 84Min | | 6'3" | 262 | Pittsburgh | | |
| Samuels, Chris HB-FB | 91SD | | 5'10" | 202 | Texas | | |
| Samuels, Terry TE | 94-95Arz | 2 | 6'2" | 254 | Kentucky | | |
| Sanchez, Lupe DB | 84-85USFL 86-88Pit | 3 | 5'10" | 193 | U.C.L.A. | 4 | 6 |
| Sander, Mark LB | 92Mia | | 6'2" | 232 | Louisville | | |
| Sanders, Barry HB-FB | 89-95Det | 2 | 5'8" | 203 | Oklahoma State | | 480 |
| Sanders, Chris WR | 95Hou | 2 | 6' | 184 | Ohio State | | 54 |
| Sanders, Chuck FB | 86-87Pit | | 6'1" | 233 | Slippery Rock | | 6 |
| Sanders, Deion (Neon Deion) DB | 89-93Atl 94SF 95Dal | 23 | 6' | 187 | Florida State | 32 | 78 |
| 89-94 played major league baseball | | | | | | | |
| Sanders, Eric OT-OG-C | 81-86Atl 86-92Det | | 6'7" | 282 | Nevada-Reno | | |
| Sanders, Frank WR | 95Arz | 2 | 6'1" | 202 | Auburn | | 16 |
| Sanders, Gene OT-OG-DE-NT | 79-85TB | | 6'3" | 273 | Washington, Texas A&M | | |
| Sanders, Glenell LB | 90Chi 91LA 94Den 95Ind | | 6' | 224 | Louisiana Tech | | |
| Sanders, Ricky WR-HB | 86-93Was 94-95Atl | 23 | 5'11" | 182 | SW Texas State | | 228 |
| Sanders, Thomas HB | 85-89Chi 90-91Phi | 23 | 5'11" | 203 | Texas A&M | | 84 |
| Sanford, Lucius LB | 78-86Buf 87Cle | | 6'2" | 217 | Georgia Tech | 5 | 18 |
| Sanford, Rick DB | 79-84NE 85Sea | | 6'1" | 192 | South Carolina | 16 | 18 |
| Santos, Todd QB | 88SF | | 6'2" | 207 | San Jose State | | |
| Sandham, Todd OG | 87NE | | 6'3" | 255 | Northeastern | | |
| Sapolu, Jesse OG-C | 83-84SF 85BN 86LJ 87-95SF | | 6'4" | 269 | Hawaii | | |
| Sapp, Warren DT | 95TB | | 6'2" | 281 | Miami (Fla.) | 1 | 6 |
| Sargent, Broderick FB | 86-87StL 89Dal | 2 | 5'10" | 217 | Baylor | | 6 |
| Sargent, Kevin OT | 92-95Cin | | 6'6" | 284 | Eastern Washington | | |
| Sartin, Martin HB | 87SD | | 5'10" | 202 | Long Beach State | | 6 |
| Sasa, Don DT | 95SD | | 6'3" | 286 | Washington State | | |
| Sauerbrun, Todd K | 95Chi | 4 | 5'10" | 206 | West Virginia | | |
| Saunders, Al | HC86-88SD | | | | San Jose State | | |
| Saunders, Cedric TE | 95TB | | 6'3" | 240 | Ohio State | | |
| Savage, Sebastian DB | 94-95Was | | 5'10" | 187 | N. Carolina St. | | |
| Savage, Tony NT | 90SD 91KJ 92SD 92Cin | | 6'3" | 300 | Washington State | | |
| Sawyer, Buzz K | 87Dal | | 6'1" | 201 | Baylor | | |
| Sawyer, Corey DB | 94-95Cin | 3 | 5'11" | 171 | Florida State | 4 | 6 |
| Sawyer, John TE | 75-76Hou 77-78Sea 79LJ 80-82Sea 83Was 83-84Den | 2 | 6'2" | 230 | Southern Miss. | | 12 |
| Sawyer, Jon DB | 87NE | | 5'9" | 175 | Cincinnati | | |
| Saxon, James HB-FB | 88-91KC 92-94Mia 95Phi | 2 | 5'11" | 225 | San Jose State | | 30 |
| Saxon, Mike K | 85-92Dal 93NE 94-95Min | 4 | 6'3" | 193 | San Diego State | | |
| Scales, Dwight WR | 76-78LA 79NYG 81-83SD 84Sea | 2 | 6'2" | 178 | Grambling | | 30 |
| Scales, Greg TE | 88-91NO | 2 | 6'4" | 253 | Wake Forest | | 12 |
| Scanlon, Jerry OT-OG | 80-81Was | | 6'5" | 270 | Hawaii | | |
| Scardina, John OT | 87Min | | 6'4" | 265 | Lincoln (Mo.) | | |
| Schad, Mike OG | 88LA 89-90Phi 91XJ 92-93Phi 94LJ | | 6'5" | 290 | Queens (Ont.) | | |
| Schamel, Duke LB | 87Mia | | 6'3" | 235 | South Dakota | | |
| Schankweiler, Scott LB | 87Buf | | 6' | 225 | Maryland | 1 | |
| Schenk, Ed TE | 87Min | | 6'4" | 230 | Central Florida | | |
| Schippang, Gary OT | 86Min | | 6'4" | 279 | West Chester | | |
| Schlichter, Art QB | 82Bal 83SL 84-85Ind | | 6'2" | 210 | Ohio State | | 6 |
| Schillinger, Andy WR | 88Phx 89KJ | | 5'1" | 179 | Miami-Ohio | | |
| Schlesinger, Cory FB | 95Det | | 6' | 230 | Nebraska | | |
| Schlereth, Mark C-OG | 89-94Was 95Den | | 6'3" | 280 | Idaho | | |
| Schlopy, Todd K | 87Buf | | 5'10" | 165 | Michigan | | 7 |
| Schmitt, George DB | 83StL 84XJ | | 5'11" | 193 | Delaware | | |
| Scholtz, Bruce LB | 82-88Sea 89NE | | 6'6" | 241 | Texas | 5 | 6 |
| Schonert, Turk QB | 80-85Cin 86Atl 87-89Cin | 12 | 6'1" | 191 | Stanford | | 24 |
| Schreiber, Adam OG-C | 84Sea 85NO 86-88Phi 88-89NYJ 90-93Min 94-95NYG | | 6'4" | 283 | Texas | | |
| Schroeder, Jay QB | 84-87Was 88-92Raid 93Cin 94Arz | 12 | 6'4" | 215 | U.C.L.A. | | 30 |
| Schroy, Ken DB | 77-84NYJ 85SJ | | 6'2" | 196 | Maryland | 16 | 6 |
| Schubert, Eric K | 84USFL 85NYG 86StL 87NE | 5 | 5'8" | 193 | Pittsburgh | | 94 |
| Schuh, Jeff LB | 81-85Cin 86GB 86Min | | 6'2" | 230 | Minnesota | 1 | |
| Schuhmacher, John OG-OT | 78Hou 79-80XJ 81-85Hou | | 6'3" | 272 | Southern Calif. | | |
| Schulte, Rick OG-OT | 87Buf | | 6'2" | 270 | Illinois | | |
| Schultz, Chris OT | 83Dal 84KJ 85Dal | | 6'8" | 277 | Arizona | | |
| Schulz, Jody LB | 83-84Phi 85KJ 86-87Phi | | 6'3" | 235 | East Carolina | 1 | |
| Schultz, Kurt DB | 92-95Buf | | 6'1" | 206 | Eastern Washington | 6 | 6 |
| Schultz, William OT-OG | 90-93Ind 94Hou 95Den | | 6'5" | 303 | Southern Calif. | | 6 |
| Schutt, Scott LB | 87Cin | | 6'4" | 218 | N. Dakota State | | 2 |
| Schwantz, Jim LB | 92Chi 94-95Dal | | 6'2" | 235 | Purdue | | |
| Schwartz, Bryan LB | 95Jax | | 6'4" | 250 | Augustana (S.D.) | | |
| Schwartz, Don DB | 78-80NO 81StL 83-84USFL | | 6'1" | 191 | Washington State | 2 | |
| Schwedes, Scott WR | 87-90Mia 90SD 90Mia | 23 | 6' | 182 | Syracuse | | 12 |
| Sciarra, John DB-QB | 78-83Phi | 3 | 5'11" | 185 | U.C.L.A. | 4 | 12 |
| Scissum, Willard OT-OG | 87Was | | 6'3" | 275 | Alabama | | |
| Scoggins, Eric LB | 82SF 83-84USFL | | 6'2" | 235 | Southern Calif. | | |
| Scoggins, Ron OT | 87Sea | | 6'6" | 305 | Nevada-Las Vegas | | |
| Scott, Carlos C-OT | 83-85StL | | 6'4" | 295 | Texas-El Paso | | |
| Scott, Chris DE | 84-85,87Ind 88KJ | | 6'5" | 260 | Purdue | | |
| Scott, Chuck WR | 86LA 87Dal | | 6'2" | 198 | Vanderbilt | | |
| Scott, Darnay WR | 94-95Cin | 2 | 6'1" | 180 | San Diego State | | 60 |
| Scott, Ed DB | 87StL | | 5'10" | 182 | Grambling | | |
| Scott, Kevin HB | 88SD 89Dal | | 5'9" | 179 | Stanford | | |
| Scott, Kevin DB | 91-93Det 94KJ | | 5'9" | 175 | Stanford | 4 | |
| Scott, Lindsay WR | 82-85NO | 2 | 6'1" | 195 | Georgia | | 6 |
| Scott, Malcolm TE | 83NYG 87NO | 2 | 6'5" | 243 | Louisiana State | | |
| Scott, Patrick WR | 87-88GB | 2 | 5'10" | 170 | Grambling | | 6 |
| Scott, Randy LB | 81-86GB 87Min | | 6'1" | 223 | Alabama | 3 | |
| Scott, Ronald HB | 87Mia | 2 | 5'11" | 200 | Southern U. | | 18 |
| Scott, Sean LB | 88Dal | | 6'1" | 226 | Maryland | | |
| Scott, Stanley DE | 87Mia | | 6'3" | 255 | Florida State | | |
| Scott, Todd DB | 91-94Min 95NYJ 95TB | | 5'10" | 190 | Southwestern La. | 7 | 6 |
| Scott, Tom OT | 93Cin | | 6'6" | 330 | East Carolina | | |
| Scott, Victor DB | 84-88Dal | | 6' | 200 | Colorado | 5 | 6 |
| Scott, Willie TE | 81-85KC 86-88NE | 2 | 6'4" | 245 | South Carolina | | 96 |
| Scotts, Colin DT | 87StL 88SJ | | 6'5" | 263 | Hawaii | | |
| Scrafford, Kirk OT-OG | 90-92Cin 93-94Den 95SF | | 6'6" | 267 | Montana | | |
| Scribner, Bucky K | 83-84GB 87-89Min | 4 | 6' | 207 | Kansas | | |
| Scroggins, Tracy LB | 92-95Det | | 6'2" | 255 | Tulsa | 1 | 6 |
| Scully, John C-OG | 81-88Atl 89HO 90Atl | | 6'6" | 262 | Notre Dame | | |
| Scully, Mike C | 88Was | | 6'5" | 280 | Illinois | | |
| Scurlock, Mike DB | 95StL | | 5'10" | 197 | Arizona | 1 | |
| Seabaugh, Todd LB | 84Pit | | 6'4" | 225 | San Diego State | | |
| Seabron, Malcolm WR | 94-95Hou | 2 | 6' | 194 | Fresno State | | 6 |
| Seale, Eugene LB | 87-92Hou | | 5'10" | 247 | Lamar | 2 | 8 |
| Seale, Sam DB-WR | 84-87Raid 88-91SD 92Raid 93LA | | 5'9" | 182 | Western St. (Colo.) | 11 | 12 |
| Sealby, Randy LB | 87NE | | 6'2" | 230 | Missouri | | |
| Seals, Leon DE | 87-91Buf 92Phi | | 6'4" | 266 | Jackson State | 1 | 6 |
| Seals, Ray NT-DE | 89-90TB 90Ind 91-93TB 94-95Pit | | 6'3" | 294 | none | 2 | 6 |
| Searcey, Bill OG-C | 83-84USFL 85SD | | 6'1" | 281 | Alabama | | |
| Searcy, Leon OT | 92-95Pit | | 6'3" | 304 | Miami (Fla.) | | |
| Seau, Junior LB | 90-95SD | | 6'3" | 250 | Southern Calif. | 5 | 6 |
| Seay, Mark WR | 93-95SD | 2 | 6' | 175 | Long Beach State | | 56 |
| Seay, Virgil WR | 81-84Was 84Atl | 2 | 5'8" | 175 | Troy State | | 30 |
| Secules, Scott QB | 88Dal 89-91Mia 92SJ 93NE | 12 | 6'3" | 219 | Virginia | | 6 |
| Sehorn, Jason DB | 94-95NYG | | 6'2" | 212 | Southern Calif. | | |
| Seifert, George | HC89-95SF | | | | Utah | | |
| Seitz, Warren TE-WR | 86Pit 87NYG | | 6'4" | 217 | Missouri | | |
| Selby, Rob OG-OT | 91-94Phi 95Arz | | 6'3" | 286 | Auburn | | |
| Selesky, Ron C | 87Min | | 6'1" | 266 | North Central | | |
| Sellers, Lance LB | 87Cin | | 6'1" | 230 | Boise State | | |
| Selmon, Lee Roy DE | 76-84TB | | 6'3" | 256 | Oklahoma | | 6 |
| Semple, Tony OG | 95Det | | 6'4" | 286 | Memphis | | |
| Sendlein, Robin LB | 81-84Min 85Mia 86KJ 87IJ | | 6'3" | 225 | Texas | | |
| Sensor, Joe TE | 80-82Min 83KJ 84Min | | 6'4" | 237 | West Chester | | 96 |
| Septien, Rafael K | 77LA 78-86Dal | 5 | 5'10" | 176 | Southwestern La. | | 960 |
| Settle, John FB-HB | 87-90Atl 91TJ 92KJ | 2 | 5'9" | 209 | Appalachian State | | 78 |
| Settles, Tony LB | 87Was | | 6'3" | 210 | Elon | | |
| Seurer, Frank QB | 84-85USFL 86-87KC | 1 | 6'1" | 195 | Kansas | | |
| Sewell, Steve FB-WR | 86-91Den 92NJ | 2 | 6'3" | 210 | Oklahoma | | 126 |
| Shade, Sam DB | 95Cin | | 6'1" | 191 | Alabama | | |
| Shaffer, Craig LB | 82-84StL | | 6' | 230 | Indiana State | | |
| Shakespeare, Stanley WR | 87TB | | 5'11" | 190 | Miami (Fla.) | | |
| Shanahan, Mike | HC88-89Raid HC95Den | | | | Eastern Illinois | | |
| Shanks, Simon LB | 95Arz | | 6'1" | 215 | Coahoma J.C. (Miss.) | | |
| Shannon, John DT-DE | 88-89Chi | | 6'3" | 269 | Kentucky | | |
| Shannon, Randy LB | 89-90Dal | | 6'1" | 221 | Miami (Fla.) | | |
| Sharp, Dan TE | 87Atl | | 6'2" | 235 | Texas Christian | | |
| Sharpe, Luis OT | 82-84StL 85USFL 85-87StL 88-93Phx 94Arz | | 6'4" | 275 | U.C.L.A. | | 6 |
| Sharpe, Shannon TE-WR | 90-95Den | 2 | 6'2" | 228 | Savannah State | | 130 |
| Sharpe, Sterling WR | 88-94GB | 2 | 5'11" | 202 | South Carolina | | 396 |
| Shavers, Tyrone WR | 91Cle | | 6'3" | 210 | Lamar | | |
| Shaw, Eric LB | 92-94Cin | | 6'3" | 248 | Florida State, Louisiana Tech | | |
| Shaw, Rickie OT | 93Sea | | 6'4" | 294 | North Carolina | | |
| Shaw, Pete DB | 77-81SD 82-84NYG | | 5'10" | 181 | Northwestern | 12 | |
| Shaw, Ricky LB | 88-89NYG 89-90Phi | | 6'4" | 240 | Oklahoma State | | |
| Shaw, Robert C-OG | 79-81Dal 82KJ | | 6'4" | 245 | Tennessee | | |
| Shaw, Terrance DB | 95SD | | 5'11" | 190 | S.F. Austin State | 1 | |
| Shearer, Brad DT | 78Chi 79KJ 80-81Chi | | 6'3" | 249 | Texas | | |
| Shearin, Joe OG-C | 83-84LA 85TB 87Dal | | 6'4" | 254 | Texas | | |
| Sheffield, Chris DB | 86-87Pit 87Det | | 6'1" | 193 | Albany State (Ga.) | 1 | |
| Shegog, Ron DB | 87NE | | 5'11" | 190 | Austin Peay | 1 | |
| Shell, Donnie DB | 74-87Pit | | 5'11" | 192 | S. Carolina State | 55 | 18 |
| Shell, Todd LB | 84-87SF 88ZJ | | 6'4" | 225 | Brigham Young | 5 | 6 |
| Shelley, Elbert DB | 87-95Atl | | 5'11" | 184 | Arkansas State | 1 | |
| Shelley, Jonathan DB | 87SF | | 6' | 176 | Mississippi | | |
| Shelling, Chris DB | 95Cin | | 5'10" | 180 | Auburn | | |
| Shelton, Anthony DB | 90-91SD | | 6'1" | 195 | Tennessee State | 1 | |
| Shelton, Richard DB | 89Den 90-93Pit | | 5'10" | 180 | Liberty | 3 | 6 |
| Shepard, Derrick WR | 87-88Was 89NO 89-91Dal | 23 | 5'10" | 186 | Oklahoma | | 12 |
| Shepherd, Leslie WR | 94-95Was | 2 | 5'11" | 189 | Temple | | 18 |
| Sheppard, Ashley LB | 93-94Min 94-95Jax 95StL | | 6'3" | 242 | Clemson | | |
| Sheppard, Johnny HB | 87Buf | | 5'10" | 185 | Livingston | | |
| Sherman, Heath FB-HB | 89-93Phi | 2 | 6' | 195 | Texas A&I | | 84 |
| Sherrard, Mike WR | 86Dal 87-89BL 90-92SF 93-95NYG | 2 | 6'2" | 187 | U.C.L.A. | | 132 |
| Sherwin, Tim TE | 81-83Bal 84-87Ind | 2 | 6'6" | 243 | Boston College | | 18 |
| Shibest, James WR | 87Atl | | 5'10" | 187 | Arkansas | | |
| Shield, Joe QB | 86GB | | 6'1" | 185 | Trinity (Texas) | | |
| Shields, Billy OT | 75-83SD 84SF 85KC | | 6'7" | 272 | Georgia Tech | | |
| Shields, Jon OG | 87Dal | | 6'5 | 293 | Portland State | | |
| Shields, Will OG | 93-95KC | | 6'2" | 305 | Nebraska | | |
| Shipp, Jackie LB | 84-88Mia 89Raid | | 6'2" | 236 | Oklahoma | 1 | |
| Shiver, Sanders LB | 76-83Bal 84Mia | | 6'2" | 227 | Carson-Newman | 5 | 6 |
| Short, Laval NT | 80Den 81TB 83-84USFL | | 6'3" | 250 | Colorado | | |
| Shorthose, George WR | 85KC | | 6' | 198 | Missouri | | |
| Shorts, Peter DE | 89NE | | 6'8" | 278 | Illinois State | | |
| Shoulders, Darin OT | 91Ind | | 6'3" | 288 | Tulane | | |
| Shufelt, Pete LB | 94NYG | | 6'3" | 240 | Texas-El Paso | | |
| Shugarts, Bret DE | 87Pit | | 6'2" | 250 | Indiana (Pa.) | | |
| Shula, David WR | 81Bal HC92-95Cin | | 5'11" | 182 | Dartmouth | | |
| Shuler, Heath QB | 94-95Was | 12 | 6'2" | 221 | Tennessee | | |
| Shuler, Mickey TE | 78-89NYJ 90-91Phi | 2 | 6'3" | 232 | Penn State | | 222 |
| Shull, Steve LB | 80-82Mia 83KJ | | 6'1" | 219 | William & Mary | | |
| Shumann, Mike WR | 78-79SF 80TB 81SF 82-83StL | 2 | 6' | 178 | Florida State | | 30 |
| Shumate, Mark DE | 85NYJ 85GB | | 6'5" | 265 | Wisconsin | | |
| Shupe, Mark C | 87Buf | | 6'5" | 285 | Arizona State | | |
| Siano, Mike WR | 87Phi | | 6'4" | 220 | Syracuse | | |
| Sievers, Eric TE | 81-88SD 88LA 89-90NE | 2 | 6'4" | 235 | Maryland | | 60 |
| Siglar, Ricky OG-OT | 90SF 94-95KC | | 6'7" | 305 | San Jose State | | |

| Use Name (Nickname) - Positions | Team by Year | See Section | Hgt. | Wgt. | College | Int | Pts |
|---|---|---|---|---|---|---|---|
| Sikahema, Vai HB | 86-87StL 88-90Phx 91GB 92-93Phi | 23 | 5'9" | 191 | Brigham Young | | 30 |
| Sikora, Robert OT | 84Cle | | 6'8" | 285 | Indiana | | |
| Siler, Rich TE | 87Mia | | 6'4" | 240 | Texas A&M | | |
| Sileo, Dan NT | 87TB | | 6'2" | 282 | Miami (Fla.) | | |
| Silipo, Joe C | 87Buf | | 6'3" | 295 | Tulane | | |
| Silvestri, Don K | 95NYJ | | 6'4" | 210 | Pittsburgh | | |
| Simien, Tracy LB | 91-95KC | | 6'1" | 249 | Texas Christian | 3 | |
| Simmonds, Mike OG | 89TB 90KJ | | 6'4" | 285 | Indiana State | | |
| Simmons, Bob OG-OT | 77-83KC 84USFL | | 6'4" | 260 | Texas | | |
| Simmons, Cleo TE | 83Dal | | 6'2" | 225 | Jackson State | | |
| Simmons, Clyde DE-DT | 86-93Phi 94-95Arz | | 6'6" | 276 | Western Carolina | 3 | 32 |
| Simmons, Dave LB | 79GB 80Det 82Bal 83Chi 84-85USFL | | 6'4" | 221 | North Carolina | | |
| Simmons, Ed OT-OG | 87-95Was | | 6'5" | 299 | Eastern Washington | | |
| Simmons, Jeff WR | 83LA | | 6'3" | 195 | Southern Calif. | | |
| Simmons, John DB | 81-86Cin 86GB 87Ind | 3 | 5'11" | 192 | S.M.U. | 2 | 12 |
| Simmons, King DB | 87SD | | 6'2" | 199 | Texas Tech | | |
| Simmons, Marcello DB | 93Cin | | 6'1" | 180 | S.M.U. | | |
| Simmons, Michael DE | 89-90NO | | 6'4" | 269 | Mississippi State | | |
| Simmons, Roy OG | 79-81NYG 82VR 83Was 85USFL | | 6'3" | 264 | Georgia Tech | | |
| Simmons, Stacy WR | 90Ind | | 5'9" | 183 | Florida | | |
| Simmons, Tony DE | 85SD 86KJ 87SD | | 6'5" | 269 | Tennessee | | |
| Simmons, Victor LB | 87Dal | | 6'2" | 230 | Central St.-Ohio | | |
| Simmons, Wayne LB | 93-95GB | | 6'3" | 245 | Clemson | 2 | |
| Simms, Phil QB | 79-81NYG 82KJ 83-93NYG | 12 | 6'3" | 215 | Morehead State | | 30 |
| Simons, Kevin OT | 89Cle | | 6'3" | 315 | Tennessee | | |
| Simpkins, Ron LB | 80Cin 81LJ 82-86Cin 88GB | | 6'1" | 235 | Michigan | | |
| Simpson, Carl DT | 93-95Chi | | 6'2" | 289 | Florida State | | |
| Simpson, Keith DB | 78-85Sea | | 6'1" | 195 | Memphis State | 19 | 18 |
| Simpson, Tim OG-C | 94Pit | | 6'2" | 284 | Illinois | | |
| Simpson, Travis OG | 87GB | | 6'3" | 272 | Oklahoma | | |
| Sims, Billy HB | 80-84Det 85KJ | 2 | 6' | 212 | Oklahoma | | 282 |
| Sims, Darryl DE-NT | 85-86Pit 87-88Cle 89KJ | | 6'3" | 278 | Wisconsin | | |
| Sims, Jack OG | 87Sea | | 6'3" | 260 | Hawaii | | |
| Sims, Joe OT-OG | 91Atl 92-95GB | | 6'3" | 302 | Nebraska | | |
| Sims, Keith OG | 90-95Mia | | 6'2" | 308 | Iowa State | | |
| Sims, Ken DB | 87StL | | 5'9" | 177 | Iowa | | |
| Sims, Kenneth DE | 82-89NE | | 6'5" | 272 | Texas | | |
| Sims, Marvin FB | 80-81Bal | 2 | 6'4" | 236 | Clemson | | |
| Sims, Reggie TE | 87Cin | | 6'4" | 253 | Northern Illinois | | |
| Sims, Tom NT-DT | 91-92KC 93-94Ind | | 6'2" | 294 | Western Michigan, Pittsburgh | | |
| Sims, Tommy DB | 86Ind | | 6' | 190 | Tennessee | | |
| Sims, William LB | 94Min | | 6'3" | 258 | Southwestern La. | | |
| Sinclair, Mike DE | 92-95Sea | | 6'4" | 268 | Eastern New Mexico | | |
| Singer, Curt OT | 86Sea 87NJ 88Det 89NYJ 91Sea | | 6'5" | 278 | Tennessee | | |
| Singletary, Mike LB | 81-92Chi | | 6' | 230 | Baylor | 7 | |
| Singletary, Reggie OT-OG-DT | 86-90Phi | | 6'3" | 279 | N. Carolina State | | |
| Singleton, Chris LB | 90-93NE 93-95Mia | | 6'2" | 247 | Arizona | 2 | 6 |
| Singleton, Nate WR | 93-95SF | 2 | 5'11" | 190 | Grambling | | 24 |
| Sinnott, Greg OT | 87LA | | 6'7" | 280 | Utah State | | |
| Sinnott, John OG-OT | 80NYG 82Bal 83XJ | | 6'4" | 275 | Brown | | |
| Siragusa, Tony NT-LB-DT | 90-95Ind | | 6'3" | 308 | Pittsburgh | | |
| Sisley, Brian DE | 87NYG | | 6'4" | 235 | S. Dakota State | | |
| Sisson, Scott K | 93NE | 5 | 6' | 197 | Georgia Tech | | 57 |
| Skansi, Paul WR | 83Pit 84-91Sea | 23 | 5'11" | 186 | Washington | | 60 |
| Skaugstad, Daryle NT | 81-82Hou 83SF 83GB | | 6'5" | 254 | California | | |
| Skene, Doug OG | 94NE | | 6'6" | 295 | Michigan | | |
| Skibinski, John FB | 78-81Chi 83USFL | | 6' | 222 | Purdue | | |
| Skladany, Tom K | 78-82Det 83Phi | 4 | 6' | 192 | Ohio State | | |
| Skow, Jim DE | 86-89Cin 90TB 91Sea 92SD 92LA | | 6'3" | 253 | Nebraska | | |
| Skrepenak, Greg OT-OG | 92Raid 93NJ 94Raid 95Oak | | 6'6" | 311 | Michigan | | |
| Slack, Reggie QB | 90Hou | | 6'1" | 221 | Auburn | | |
| Slade, Chris LB | 93-95NE | | 6'4" | 232 | Virginia | | 6 |
| Slater, Jackie OT-OG | 76-94LA 95StL | | 6'4" | 278 | Jackson State | | |
| Slater, Mark C | 78SD 79-83Phi | | 6'2" | 256 | Minnesota | | |
| Slaton, Mike DB | 87Min | | 6'2" | 194 | South Dakota | | |
| Slaton, Tony C-OG | 85-90LA | | 6'3" | 265 | Southern Calif. | | |
| Slaughter, Chuck OT | 82NO 84USFL | | 6'5" | 260 | South Carolina | | |
| Slaughter, Webster WR | 86-91Cle 92-94Hou 95KC | 23 | 6' | 170 | San Diego State | | 258 |
| Slayden, Steve QB | 88Cle | | 6'1" | 185 | Duke | | |
| Sloan, David TE | 95Det | 2 | 6'6" | 254 | New Mexico | | 6 |
| Slovacek, Emil OT | 87SD | | 6'3" | 300 | S.F. Austin State | | |
| Smagala, Stan DB | 90-91Dal | | 5'10" | 184 | Notre Dame | | |
| Small, Donovan DB | 87Hou | | 5'11" | 190 | Minnesota | 1 | |
| Small, Fred LB | 85Pit | | 5'1" | 230 | Washington | | |
| Small, George NT | 80NYG | | 6'2" | 260 | N. Carolina A&T | | |
| Small, Gerald DB | 78-83Mia 84Atl | | 5'11" | 190 | San Jose State | 24 | 6 |
| Small, Jessie LB | 89-91Phi 92Phx | | 6'3" | 239 | Eastern Kentucky | | |
| Small, Torrance WR | 92-95NO | 2 | 6'3" | 201 | Alcorn State | | 92 |
| Smalls, Fred LB | 87Phi | | 6'3" | 225 | West Virginia | | |
| Smeenge, Joel LB-DE | 90-94NO 95Jax | | 6'6" | 255 | Western Michigan | 1 | |
| Smerek, Don DT-DE | 81-87Dal | | 6'7" | 258 | Nevada-Reno | | |
| Smerlas, Fred NT-DT | 79-89Buf 90SF 91-92NE | | 6'3" | 277 | Boston College | 2 | 6 |
| Smigelsky, Dave K | 82-83Atl 84USFL | 4 | 5"11" | 180 | Virginia Tech | | |
| Smith, Aaron LB | 84Den | | 6'2" | 223 | Utah State | | |
| Smith, Al LB | 87-95Hou | | 6'1" | 244 | Cal. Poly.-Pomona, Utah State | 2 | 6 |
| Smith, Anthony DE-DT | 91-94Raid 95Oak | | 6'3" | 264 | Alabama, Arizona | | 6 |
| Smith, Art LB | 80Den | | 6'1" | 222 | Hawaii | | |
| Smith, Artie DE-DT | 93-94SF 94-95Cin | | 6'4" | 291 | Louisiana Tech | | |
| Smith, Ben DB | 90-91Phi 92KJ 93Phi 94Den 95Arz | | 5'11" | 184 | Georgia | 6 | |
| Smith, Billy Ray LB | 83-92SD | | 6'3" | 235 | Arkansas | 14 | 6 |
| Smith, Blane DB | 87KC | | 5'10" | 190 | S.M.U. | | |
| Smith, Brad LB | 93Cin | | 6'2" | 228 | Texas Christian | | |
| Smith, Brian LB-DT-DE | 89-90LA | | 6'6" | 242 | Auburn | | |
| Smith, Bruce DE | 85-95Buf | | 6'4" | 281 | Virginia Tech | 2 | 8 |
| Smith, Byron DE | 84-85Ind | | 6'5" | 278 | California | | |
| Smith, Cedric FB | 90Min 91NO 94-95Was | 2 | 5'10" | 223 | Florida | | 6 |
| Smith, Chris FB | 86-87KC | 2 | 6' | 232 | Notre Dame | | 6 |
| Smith, Chuck DE-LB | 92-95Atl | | 6'2" | 252 | Tennessee | 1 | 6 |
| Smith, Dallis DB | 87Sea | | 5'11" | 170 | Valdosta State | | |
| Smith, Darrin LB | 93-95Dal | | 6'1" | 229 | Miami (Fla.) | 2 | 9 |
| Smith, Daryl DB | 87-88Cin 89Min | | 5'9" | 186 | North Alabama | 2 | |
| Smith, Daryle OT | 87-88Dal 89Cle 90-92Phi | | 6'5" | 277 | Tennessee | | |
| Smith, Dave OT | 88Cin | | 6'7" | 290 | Southern Illinois | | |
| Smith, Dennis DB | 81-94Den | | 6'3" | 200 | Southern Calif. | 30 | 6 |
| Smith, Dennis HB | 90Phx | | 6' | 235 | Utah | | |
| Smith, Don NT-DE-DT | 79-84Atl 85-86Buf 87NYJ | | 6'5" | 256 | Miami (Fla.) | | |

| Use Name (Nickname) - Positions | Team by Year | See Section | Hgt. | Wgt. | College | Int | Pts |
|---|---|---|---|---|---|---|---|
| Smith, Don HB-WR-FB | 87KJ 88-89TB 90Buf | 2 | 5'11" | 195 | Mississippi State | | 18 |
| Smith, Donald DB | 91Dal | | 5'11" | 189 | Liberty | | |
| Smith, Doug NT-DT | 84USFL 85-92Hou | | 6'4" | 294 | Auburn | 1 | |
| Smith, Doug C-OG-OT | 78-91LA | | 6'3" | 259 | Bowling Green | | |
| Smith, Doug DB | 87NYG | | 6' | 192 | Ohio State | | |
| Smith, Ed LB | 80-81Bal 83-85USFL | | 6'2" | 217 | Vanderbilt | 2 | |
| Smith, Elliot DB | 89SD 90Den | | 6'2" | 192 | Alcorn State | | |
| Smith, Emmitt HB | 90-95Dal | 2 | 5'9" | 205 | Florida | | 600 |
| Smith, Fernando DE | 94-95Min | | 6'6" | 279 | Jackson State | | |
| Smith, Frankie DB | 93-95Mia | | 5'9" | 186 | Baylor | | |
| Smith, Franky OT | 80KC 81-83CFL 84-85USFL | | 6'6" | 279 | Alabama A&M | | |
| Smith, Gary OG | 84Cin | | 6'2" | 265 | Virginia Tech | | |
| Smith, Gregory NT | 84Min | | 6'3" | 261 | Kansas | | |
| Smith, Herman DE | 95TB | | 6'5" | 261 | Portland State | | |
| Smith, Holden WR | 82Bal 84USFL | | 6'1" | 191 | California | | |
| Smith, Irv TE | 93-95NO | 2 | 6'3" | 246 | Notre Dame | | 50 |
| Smith, Jeff HB | 85-86KC 88TB | 23 | 5'9" | 202 | Nebraska | | 72 |
| Smith, Jeff DE | 87Cin | | 6'4" | 248 | Earlham | | |
| Smith, Jeff TE | 87NYG | | 6'3" | 240 | Tennessee | | |
| Smith, Jerry TE-WR | 65-77Was | 2 | 6'2" | 209 | Arizona State | | 360 |
| Smith, Jim WR | 77-82Pit 83-85USFL 85 Raid | 23 | 6'2" | 205 | Michigan | | 150 |
| Smith, Jimmy HB | 84Was 84Raid | | 6' | 205 | Elon | | |
| Smith, Jimmy HB | 87Min | | 5'11" | 190 | Purdue | | |
| Smith, Jimmy WR | 92Dal 93IL 95Jax | 23 | 6'1" | 206 | Jackson State | | 30 |
| Smith, Joey WR | 91-92NYG | 3 | 5'10" | 177 | Louisville | | |
| Smith, Johnny Ray DB | 82-83TB 84SD | | 5'9" | 183 | Lamar | | |
| Smith, J.T. WR | 78Was 78-84KC 85-87StL 88-90Phx | 23 | 6'2" | 185 | North Texas | | 234 |
| Smith, Ken OG | 87Cin | | 6'1" | 285 | Miami-Ohio | | |
| Smith, Kendal WR | 89-90Cin | 2 | 5'9" | 189 | Utah State | | 6 |
| Smith, Kevin DB | 91Pit | | 5'11" | 204 | Rhode Island | | |
| Smith, Kevin TE | 92-94Raid | | 6'4" | 255 | U.C.L.A. | | |
| Smith, Kevin DB | 92-95Dal | | 5'11" | 177 | Texas A&M | 10 | 6 |
| Smith, Lamar FB | 94-95Sea | 2 | 5'11" | 224 | Houston | | |
| Smith, Lance OG-OT | 86-87StL 88-93Phx 94-95NYG | | 6'2" | 283 | Louisiana State | | |
| Smith, Larry LB | 87Hou | | 6'1" | 210 | Kentucky | | |
| Smith, Leonard DB | 83-87StL 88Phx 88-91Buf | | 5'11" | 200 | McNeese State | 15 | 18 |
| Smith, Lucious DB | 80-82LA 83KC 84Buf 84-85SD | | 5'10" | 190 | San Diego State, Fullerton State | 4 | 6 |
| Smith, Matt LB | 87Den | | 6'2" | 234 | West Virginia | | |
| Smith, Michael WR | 92KC | | 5'8" | 160 | Kansas State | | |
| Smith, Mike WR | 80Atl 83USFL | | 5'10" | 194 | Grambling | | |
| Smith, Mike DB | 85-87Mia | | 6' | 172 | Texas-El Paso | | |
| Smith, Monte OG | 89Den 90FJ | | 6'5" | 270 | North Dakota | | |
| Smith, Neil DE | 88-95KC | | 6'4" | 271 | Nebraska | 3 | 12 |
| Smith, Otis DB | 91-94Phi 95NYJ | | 5'11" | 187 | Missouri | 10 | 12 |
| Smith, Phil WR | 83Bal 84Ind 86Phi | 3 | 6'3" | 188 | San Diego State | | 6 |
| Smith, Quintin WR | 90Chi 91LJ | | 5'10" | 172 | Kansas | | |
| Smith, Reggie WR | 80-81Atl 83USFL 87NYJ | 3 | 5'4" | 168 | N.Car. Central | | |
| Smith, Reggie OT | 87TB | | 6'5" | 295 | Kansas | | |
| Smith, Ricky DB-WR | 82-84NE 84Was 87Det | 3 | 6' | 182 | Alabama State | 2 | 12 |
| Smith, Rico WR | 92-95Cle | 2 | 6' | 185 | Colorado | | 6 |
| Smith, Robert DE | 84USFL 85Min 87AJ | | 6'5" | 255 | Grambling | | |
| Smith, Robert HB | 93-95Min | 2 | 6' | 196 | Ohio State | | 50 |
| Smith, Rod DB | 92-94NE 95Car | | 5'11" | 187 | Notre Dame | 1 | |
| Smith, Rod WR | 95Den | | 6' | 183 | Missouri Southern | | 6 |
| Smith, Ron WR | 78-79LA 80-81SD 81-83Phi 84USFL | 2 | 6' | 185 | San Diego State | | 24 |
| Smith, Sammie HB | 89-91Mia 92Den | 2 | 6'2" | 226 | Florida State | | 96 |
| Smith, Sean DE-DT | 87-88Chi 89Dal 89TB 89LA 90-91NE | | 6'4" | 280 | Grambling | | 2 |
| Smith, Struggy DB | 87Atl | | 6'2" | 190 | Appalachian State | | |
| Smith, Steve OT-DE-TE | 66Pit 68-70Min 71-74Phi | | 6'5" | 246 | Michigan | | 6 |
| Smith, Steve FB | 87-93Raid 94-95Sea | 2 | 6'1" | 235 | Penn State | | 132 |
| Smith, Thomas DB | 93-95Buf | | 5'11" | 188 | North Carolina | 3 | |
| Smith, Tim WR | 80-86Hou | 2 | 6'2" | 201 | Nebraska | | 72 |
| Smith, Timmy FB-HB | 87-88Was 90Dal | 2 | 5'11" | 216 | Texas Tech | | 18 |
| Smith, Tony HB | 92-94Atl 95BL | 23 | 6'1" | 214 | Southern Miss. | | 18 |
| Smith, Torin DE | 87NYG | | 6'4" | 320 | Mesa J.C. | | |
| Smith, Vernice OG-OT-C | 90-92Phx 93Chi 93-95Was | | 6'2" | 296 | Florida A&M | | |
| Smith, Vinson LB | 88Atl 89FJ 90-92Dal 93-95Chi | | 6'2" | 239 | East Carolina | | |
| Smith, Waddell WR | 84Dal | | 6'2" | 180 | Kansas | | |
| Smith, Wayne DB | 80-83Det 83-86StL 87Min | | 6' | 171 | Wis.-LaCrosse, Purdue | 9 | |
| Smith, Wes WR | 87GB | | 6' | 190 | East Texas State | | |
| Smith, Willie TE | 87Mia | | 6'2" | 235 | Miami (Fla.) | | 6 |
| Smoot, Raymond OG-OT | 93SD | | 6'4" | 305 | Louisiana State | | |
| Snell, Donald WR | 87Sea | | 6'2" | 177 | Virginia Tech | | |
| Snell, Ray OG-OT | 80-83TB 84-85Pit 85Det | | 6'4" | 262 | Wisconsin | | |
| Snipes, Angelo LB | 85USFL 86Was 86-87SD 87-89KC | | 6' | 222 | West Georgia | 1 | |
| Snow, Percy LB | 90KC 91BN 92KC 93Chi | | 6'2" | 248 | Michigan State | 1 | |
| Snyder, Loren QB | 87Dal | | 6'4" | 207 | Northern Colorado | | |
| Snyder, Pat LB | 91Ind | | 6'1" | 225 | Purdue | | |
| Sochia, Brian NT-DE | 83-85Hou 86-91Mia 91-92Den | | 6'3" | 270 | Northwestern Okla. | | 6 |
| Sohn, Kurt WR | 81-82NYJ 83KJ 84-88NYJ | 23 | 5'11" | 179 | N. Carolina State, Fordham | | 60 |
| Solomon, Ariel OG-OT-C | 91-95Pit | | 6'5" | 285 | Colorado | | |
| Solomon, Freddie WR-QB-HB | 75-77Mia 78-85SF | 23 | 5'11" | 185 | Tampa | | 342 |
| Solomon, Roland DB | 80Dal 80Buf 81Den | | 6' | 193 | Utah | | |
| Solomon, Jesse LB | 86-89Min 89-90Dal 91TB 92-93Atl 94Mia | | 6' | 235 | Florida State | 8 | 6 |
| Solt, Ron OG | 84-88Ind 88-91Phi 92Ind 93SJ | | 6'3" | 279 | Maryland | | |
| Sommer, Don OT | 87Buf | | 6'4" | 290 | Texas-El Paso | | |
| Songy, Treg DB | 87NYJ | | 6'2" | 200 | Tulane | | |
| Sowell, Robert DB | 83-85,87Mia | 3 | 5'11" | 176 | Howard | 2 | |
| Spagnola, John TE | 79-82Phi 83XJ 84-87Phi 88Sea 89GB | 2 | 6'4" | 241 | Yale | | 120 |
| Spani, Gary LB | 78-86KC | | 6'2" | 229 | Kansas State | 2 | 18 |
| Spann, Gary LB | 87KC | | 6'1" | 218 | Texas Christian | | |
| Sparenberg, Dave OG | 87Cle | | 6'3" | 267 | Western Ontario | | |
| Sparks, Phillipi DB | 92-95NYG | | 5'11" | 188 | Arizona State | 9 | |
| Spears, Anthony DE | 89Hou | | 6'5" | 260 | Portland State | | |
| Spears, Ernest DB | 90NO | | 5'11" | 192 | Southern Calif. | | |
| Spears, Ron DE | 82-83NE 83GB | | 6'6" | 255 | San Diego State | | |
| Speer, Del DB | 93-94Cle 94Sea | | 6' | 196 | Florida | 1 | |
| Spek, Jeff TE | 86TB | | 6'3" | 240 | San Diego State | | |
| Spellman, Alonzo DE-DT | 92-95Chi | | 6'4" | 286 | Ohio State | 1 | |
| Spencer, Darryl WR | 94-95Atl | | 5'8" | 172 | Miami (Fla.) | | |
| Spencer, Herb LB | 87Atl | | 6'3" | 230 | Newberry | | |
| Spencer, Jimmy DB | 92-95NO | | 5'9" | 180 | Florida | 9 | |
| Spencer, Tim FB | 83-85USFL 85-90SD | 2 | 6'2" | 224 | Ohio State | | 114 |
| Spencer, Todd HB | 84-85Pit 87SD | 23 | 6' | 203 | Southern Calif. | | |
| Spielman, Chris LB | 88-95Det | | 6' | 247 | Ohio State | 4 | 6 |

| Use Name (Nickname) - Positions | Team by Year | See Section | Hgt. | Wgt. | College | Int | Pts |
|---|---|---|---|---|---|---|---|
| Spikes, Irving HB | 94-95Mia | 23 | 5'8" | 215 | Northeast La. | | 24 |
| Spindler, Marc DT-DE-NT | 90-94Det 95NYJ | | 6'5" | 286 | Pittsburgh | | |
| Spitulski, Bob LB | 92-94Sea 95KJ | | 6'3" | 239 | Central Florida | 1 | |
| Spivey, Mike DB | 77-79Chi 80Oak 80-81NO 82Atl | | 6' | 197 | Colorado | | 6 |
| Spivey, Sebron WR | 87Dal | | 5'11" | 180 | Southern Illinois | | |
| Spradlin, Danny LB | 81-82Dal 83-84TB 85StL | | 6'1" | 235 | Tennessee | | |
| Springs, Kirk DB | 81-85NYJ 86KJ | 23 | 6' | 193 | Miami-Ohio | 4 | 6 |
| Springs, Ron FB-HB | 79-84Dal 85-86TB | 23 | 6'1" | 213 | Ohio State | | 228 |
| Squirek, Jack LB | 82-85Raid 86Mia | | 6'4" | 230 | Illinois | 1 | |
| Stablein, Brian WR | 95Ind | | 6'1" | 190 | Ohio State | | |
| Stachowicz, Ray K | 81-82GB 83Chi | 4 | 5'11" | 187 | Michigan State | | |
| Stachowski, Rich NT | 83Den | | 6'4" | 245 | California | | |
| Stacy, Siran HB | 92Phi | | 5'11" | 203 | Alabama | | |
| Stadnik, John C | 87SD | | 6'4" | 275 | Western Illinois | | |
| Stai, Brenden OG | 95Pit | | 6'4" | 297 | Nebraska | | |
| Stallings, Gene | HC 86-87StL HC88-89Phx | | | | Texas A&M | | |
| Stallings, Ramondo DE | 94-95Cin | | 6'7" | 285 | San Diego State | | |
| Stallings, Robert TE | 86StL 87NJ | | 6'6" | 250 | Southern Miss. | | |
| Stalls, David DE-DT-NT | 77-79Dal 80-83TB 83Raid 84USFL 85Raid | | 6'4" | 247 | Northern Colorado | | |
| Stallworth, John WR | 74-87Pit | 2 | 6'2" | 190 | Alabama A&M | | 384 |
| Stallworth, Ron DE | 89-90NYJ | | 6'5" | 262 | Auburn | | |
| Stallworth, Tim WR | 90Den | | 5'10" | 185 | Washington State | | |
| Stamps, Sylvester HB-WR | 84-88Atl 89TB | 23 | 5'7" | 172 | Jackson State | | 42 |
| Stams, Frank LB | 89-91LA 92-94Cle 95KC 95Cle | | 6'2" | 236 | Notre Dame | 2 | |
| Stanback, Harry DE | 82 Bal | | 6'5" | 255 | North Carolina | | |
| Stankavage, Scott QB | 84Den 87Mia | 1 | 6'1" | 192 | Florida A&M | | |
| Stanley, Israel DE | 95NO | | 6'3" | 260 | Arizona State | | |
| Stanley, Jack QB | 87Was | | 6'3" | 207 | Nevada-Reno | | |
| Stanley, Sylvester NT | 94NE | | 6'2" | 286 | Michigan | | |
| Stanley, Walter WR | 85-88GB 89Det 90Was 92SD 92NE | 23 | 5'9" | 179 | Colorado, Mesa | | 36 |
| Stargell, Tony DB | 90-91NYJ 92-93Ind 94-95TB | | 5'11" | 190 | Tennessee State | 5 | |
| Stark, Chad FB | 87Sea | | 6'1" | 220 | N. Dakota State | | |
| Stark, Rohn K | 82-83Bal 84-94Ind 95Pit | 4 | 6'3" | 203 | Florida State | | |
| Starks, Timothy DB | 87Min | | 5'9" | 175 | Kent State | | |
| Starnes, John K | 87Atl | | 6'3" | 185 | North Texas | | |
| Starring, Stephen WR | 83-87NE 88TB 88Det | 23 | 5'10" | 172 | McNeese State | | 66 |
| Station, Larry LB | 86Pit | | 5'11" | 227 | Iowa | | |
| Staurovsky, Jason K | 87StL 88-91NE 92NYJ | 5 | 5'9" | 169 | Tulsa | | 223 |
| Staubach, Scott HB | 81NO | | 5'11" | 204 | U.C.L.A. | | |
| Staysniak, Joe OT-OG | 91Buf 92KC 93-95Ind | | 6'5" | 296 | Ohio State | | |
| Steckel, Les | HC84Min | | | | Navy | | |
| Stedman, Troy LB | 88KC | | 6'3" | 243 | Washburn | | |
| Steed, Joel NT | 92-95Pit | | 6'2" | 294 | Colorado | | |
| Steele, Chuck C | 87Det | | 6'1" | 255 | California | | |
| Steels, Anthony HB-FB | 83-84USFL 85SD 85Buf 87SD | 3 | 5'9" | 200 | Nebraska | | |
| Stegall, Milt WR | 92-94Cin | 3 | 6' | 184 | Miami-Ohio | | 6 |
| Steinfeld, Al C-OG-OT | 82KC 83Hou 83NYG | | 6'5" | 256 | C.W. Post | | |
| Steinkuhler, Dean OT | 84Hou 85KJ 86-91Hou | | 6'3" | 283 | Nebraska | | |
| Stensrud, Mike NT-DT-DE | 79-85Hou 86Min 87TB 88KC 89Was | | 6'5" | 280 | Iowa State | 2 | |
| Stenstrom, Steve QB | 95Chi | | 6'1" | 200 | Stanford | | |
| Stepanek, Joe DT | 87Min | | 6'5" | 268 | Minnesota | | 2 |
| Stephen, Scott LB | 87-91GB 92LA | | 6'2" | 237 | Arizona State | 5 | |
| Stephens, Calvin OG | 92NE | | 6'2" | 285 | South Carolina | | |
| Stephens, Darnell LB | 95TB | | 5'11" | 143 | Clemson | | |
| Stephens, Hal DE | 85Det 85KC | | 6'4" | 252 | East Carolina | | |
| Stephens, John HB-FB | 88-92NE 93GB 93KC | 2 | 6'1" | 220 | Northwestern La. | | 114 |
| Stephens, Mac LB | 90NYJ 91Min | | 6'3" | 220 | Minnesota | | |
| Stephens, Rich OG-OT | 93Raid 95Oak | | 6'7" | 310 | Tulsa | | |
| Stephens, Rod LB | 89-94Sea 95Was | | 6'1" | 237 | Georgia Tech | | 10 |
| Stephens, Santo LB | 93KC 94Cin 95Jax | | 6'4" | 238 | Temple | | |
| Stephens, Steve TE | 81NYJ 83USFL | | 6'3" | 227 | Oklahoma State | | |
| Stephenson, Dwight C-OT | 80-87Mia 88KJ | | 6'2" | 255 | Alabama | | |
| Stepnoski, Mark OG-C | 89-94Dal 95Hou | | 6'2" | 269 | Pittsburgh | | |
| Sterling, John HB | 87GB | | 6'2" | 203 | Central St.-Okla. | | |
| Steussie, Todd OT | 94-95Min | | 6'6" | 309 | California | | |
| Stevens, Mark QB | 87SF | | 6'1" | 190 | Utah | | 6 |
| Stevens, Matt QB | 87KC | 1 | 6' | 190 | U.C.L.A. | | |
| Stevenson, Mark OG-C | 83USFL 85Det | | 6'3" | 285 | Missouri, Western Illinois | | |
| Stewart, Andrew DE | 89Cle 91KJ | | 6'5" | 265 | Cincinnati | | |
| Stewart, Curtis HB | 89Dal | | 5'11" | 208 | Auburn | | |
| Stewart, James HB | 95Jax | 2 | 6'1" | 221 | Tennessee | | 18 |
| Stewart, James HB-FB | 95Min | 2 | 6'2" | 238 | Miami (Fla.) | | |
| Stewart, Kordell QB-WR-HB | 95Pit | 2 | 6'1" | 212 | Colorado | | 12 |
| Stewart, Mark LB | 84Min | | 6'3" | 232 | Washington | | |
| Stewart, Michael DB | 87-93LA 94-95Mia | | 5'11" | 195 | Fresno State | 11 | 8 |
| Stief, Dave WR-DB | 78-82StL 83Was 84USFL | 2 | 6'3" | 195 | Portland State | | 30 |
| Stieve, Terry OG | 76-77NO 78-79StL 80KJ 81-84StL | | 6'2" | 256 | Wisconsin | | |
| Still, Art DE | 78-87KC 88-89Buf | | 6'7" | 253 | Kentucky | 1 | |
| Stills, Ken DB | 85-89GB 90Min | | 5'10" | 186 | Wisconsin | 7 | 6 |
| Stinson, Lemuel DB | 88-92Chi | | 5'9" | 159 | Texas Tech | 16 | 12 |
| Stock, Mark WR | 89Pit 92LJ 93Was 94KJ | | 5'11" | 177 | V.M.I. | | |
| Stockemer, Ralph FB | 87KC | | 6'1" | 212 | Baylor | | |
| Stokes, Eric C-OG | 87NE | | 6'4" | 255 | Northeastern | | |
| Stokes, Fred DE | 87-88LA 89-92Was 93-94LA 95StL | | 6'3" | 269 | Georgia Southern | | 2 |
| Stokes, J.J. WR | 95SF | 2 | 6'4" | 217 | U.C.L.A. | | 24 |
| Stone, Dwight HB-WR | 87-94Pit 95Car | 23 | 6' | 188 | Middle Tenn. St. | | 86 |
| Stone, Ron OT-OG | 93-95Dal | | 6'5" | 309 | Boston College | | |
| Stonebreaker, Mike LB | 91Chi 94NO | | 6' | 226 | Notre Dame | | |
| Stoops, Mike DB | 87Chi | | 6'1" | 185 | Iowa | | |
| Storr, Greg LB | 87Mia | | 6'2" | 225 | Boston College | | |
| Stoudt, Cliff QB | 77-83Pit 84-85USFL 86-87StL 88Phx 89Mia 90Dal | 12 | 6'4" | 215 | Youngstown State | | 24 |
| Stouffer, Kelly QB | 88-92Sea | 12 | 6'3" | 210 | Colorado State | | |
| Stover, Jeff DE | 82-88SF | | 6'5" | 275 | Oregon | | |
| Stover, Matt K | 91-95Cle | 5 | 5'11" | 178 | Louisiana Tech | | 480 |
| Stowe, Tyronne LB | 87-90Pit 91-93Phx 94Was 95Sea | | 6'1" | 243 | Rutgers | 1 | 2 |
| Stowers, Tommie TE | 92-93NO 94KC | | 6'3" | 240 | Missouri | | |
| Stoyanovich, Pete K | 89-95Mia | 5 | 5'10" | 180 | Indiana | | 774 |
| Strachan, Steve HB-FB | 85-89Raid | 2 | 6'1" | 221 | Boston College | | 6 |
| Stracka, Tim TE | 83-84Cle | | 6'3" | 225 | Wisconsin | | |
| Stradford, Troy HB-WR | 87-90Mia 91-92KC 92Det | 23 | 5'9" | 192 | Boston College | | 72 |
| Strahan, Mike DE | 93-95NYG | | 6'4" | 275 | Texas Southern | 2 | 2 |
| Strauthers, Thomas DE-DT | 83-86Phi 88Det 89-91Min | | 6'4" | 262 | Jackson State | | |
| Streater, Eric WR | 87TB | | 5'11" | 165 | North Carolina | | 12 |
| Strenger, Rich OT | 83-87Det 88KJ | | 6'7" | 278 | Michigan | | |
| Streeter, George DB | 89Chi 90Ind | | 6'2" | 212 | Notre Dame | | |

| Use Name (Nickname) - Positions | Team by Year | See Section | Hgt. | Wgt. | College | Int | Pts |
|---|---|---|---|---|---|---|---|
| Strickland, Fred LB | 88-92LA 93Min 94-95GB | | 6'2" | 244 | Purdue | 3 | |
| Stringer, Korey OT | 95Min | | 6'4" | 339 | Ohio State | | |
| Strock, Don QB | 74-87Mia 88Cle 89Ind | 12 | 6'5" | 220 | Virginia Tech | | 12 |
| Strom, Rick QB | 89-93Pit 94Buf | | 6'2" | 210 | Georgia Tech | | |
| Strong, Mack FB | 94-95Sea | 2 | 6' | 222 | Georgia | | 36 |
| Strong, Ray HB | 78-82Atl | 23 | 5'9" | 184 | Nevada-Las Vegas | | 18 |
| Stroth, Vince OT-OG-TE | 83-85USFL 85SF 87-88Hou | | 6'4" | 267 | Brigham Young | | |
| Strother, Deon HB | 94Den | | 5'11" | 213 | Southern Calif. | | |
| Strozier, Wilbur TE | 87Sea 88SD | | 6'4" | 255 | Georgia | | |
| Stryzinski, Dan K | 90-91Pit 92-94TB 95Atl | 4 | 6'1" | 193 | Indiana | | |
| Strzelczyk, Justin OT-C-OG | 90-95Pit | | 6'5" | 299 | Maine | | |
| Stubblefield, Dana DT | 93-95SF | | 6'2" | 298 | Kansas | 1 | |
| Stubbs, Danny DE-LB | 88-89SF 90-91Dal 91-93Cin 95Phi | | 6'4" | 264 | Miami (Fla.) | | |
| Stuckey, Jim DE | 80-86SF | | 6'4" | 252 | Clemson | | 2 |
| Studaway, Mark DE | 84Hou 85TB 87Atl | | 6'3" | 273 | Tennessee | | |
| Studdard, Dave OT-OG-TE | 79-88Den | | 6'4" | 258 | Texas | | 12 |
| Studdard, Les C | 82KC 83Hou | | 6'4" | 260 | Texas | | |
| Studley, Chuck | HC83Hou | | | | Illinois | | |
| Studstill, Darren DB | 94Dal 95Jax | | 6'1" | 186 | West Virginia | | |
| Studwell, Scott LB | 77-90Min | | 6'2" | 228 | Illinois | 11 | |
| Sturgis, Oscar DE | 95Dal | | 6'5" | 278 | North Carolina | | |
| Styles, Lorenzo LB | 95Atl | | 6'1" | 244 | Ohio State | | |
| Subis, Nick OT-C | 91Den | | 6'4" | 278 | Northwestern Okla. | | |
| Suhey, Matt FB | 80-89Chi | 23 | 5'11" | 215 | Penn State | | 150 |
| Sullins, John LB | 92Den | | 6'1" | 225 | Alabama | | |
| Sullivan, Carl DE | 87GB | | 6'4" | 248 | San Jose State | | |
| Sullivan, John DB | 86GB 86SD 87SF | | 6'1" | 190 | California | | |
| Sullivan, Kent K | 91Hou 92KC 93SD 93Hou | | 5'10" | 197 | Cal. Lutheran | | |
| Sullivan, Mike OG-C-OT | 92-95TB | | 6'3" | 290 | Miami (Fla.) | | |
| Sully, Ivory DB | 79-84LA 85-86TB 87Det | | 6' | 198 | Delaware | 1 | 2 |
| Summers, Don TE | 84-85Den 87GB | | 6'4" | 230 | Oregon Tech, Boise State | | 6 |
| Sunter, Ian K | 80Cin | 5 | 6'1" | 215 | none | | 48 |
| Superick, Steve K | 87Hou | | 5'11" | 204 | West Virginia | | |
| Sutter, Ed LB | 93-95Cle | | 6'3" | 240 | Northwestern | | |
| Sutton, Frank OT | 87NYG | | 6'3" | 280 | Jackson State | | |
| Sutton, John DB | 87NO | | 6'1" | 195 | New Mexico | | |
| Sutton, Mickey DB | 83CFL 84-85USFL 86-88LA 89GB 89Buf 90LA | 3 | 5'8" | 167 | Montana | 5 | |
| Sutton, Reggie DB | 87-88NO | | 5'10" | 180 | Miami (Fla.) | 8 | 6 |
| Sutton, Ricky DE | 93Pit | | 6'2" | 281 | Auburn | | |
| Sverchek, Paul NT | 84Min | | 6'3" | 252 | Cal. Poly.-S.L.O. | | |
| Swain, John DB | 81-84Min 85Mia 85-86Pit 87Mia | | 6'1" | 194 | Miami (Fla.) | 14 | |
| Swanke, Karl OT-C-OG | 80-86GB | | 6'6" | 257 | Boston College | | 6 |
| Swann, Charles DB | 94Den | | 6'1" | 188 | Indiana State | | |
| Swann, Eric DE-NT-DT | 91-93Phx 94-95Arz | | 6'4" | 303 | none | 1 | 4 |
| Swanson, Eric WR | 86StL | | 5'11" | 186 | Tennessee | | |
| Swanson, Shane WR | 87Den | | 5'9" | 200 | Nebraska | | 6 |
| Swarn, George HB | 87Cle 88NJ 90AJ | | 5'10" | 205 | Miami-Ohio | | |
| Swartwoudt, Gregg OT | 87NYG | | 6'3" | 275 | North Dakota | | |
| Swayne, Harry OT-DE | 87-90TB 91-95SD | | 6'5" | 289 | Rutgers | | |
| Sweeney, Calvin WR | 80-87Pit | 2 | 6'2" | 190 | Southern Calif. | | 42 |
| Sweeney, Jim OT-OG-C | 84-94NYJ 95Sea | | 6'4" | 282 | Pittsburgh | | |
| Sweeney, Kevin QB | 87-88Dal | 1 | 6' | 192 | Fresno State | | |
| Sweet, Tony TE | 87NYJ | | 6'4" | 230 | Montclair State | | |
| Swider, Larry K | 79Det 80StL 81-82TB 84-85USFL | 4 | 6'2" | 195 | Pittsburgh | | |
| Swilley, Dennis C-OG-OT | 77-83Min 84VR 85-87Min | | 6'3" | 248 | Texas A&M, North Texas | | |
| Swilling, Pat LB | 86-92NO 93-94Det 95Oak | | 6'3" | 242 | Georgia Tech | 6 | 6 |
| Switzer, Barry | HC94-95Dal | | | | Arkansas | | |
| Swoope, Craig DB | 86-87TB 87-88Ind | | 6'1" | 205 | Illinois | 1 | |
| Swoopes, Patrick NT | 87NO 88CFL 89NO 91KC 91Mia | | 6'4" | 280 | Mississippi State | | |
| Sydner, Jeff WR | 92-94Phi 95NYJ | 3 | 5'6" | 170 | Hawaii | | |
| Sydney, Harry FB | 87-91SF 92GB | 2 | 6' | 217 | Kansas | | 78 |
| Sydnor, Willie WR | 82Pit | | 5'11" | 170 | Northwestern, Villanova, Syracuse | | |
| Sytsma, Stan LB | 80Atl | | 6'2" | 200 | Minnesota | | |
| Szott, David OG | 90-95KC | | 6'4" | 287 | Penn State | | |
| Szymanski, Jim DE | 90-91Den | | 6'5" | 268 | Michigan State | | |
| Tabor, Paul C-OG | 80Chi 81KJ | | 6'4" | 241 | Oklahoma | | |
| Tabor, Phil DE-NT-DT | 79-82NYG | | 6'4" | 255 | Oklahoma | | |
| Tagliaferri, John HB | 87Mia | 2 | 5'11" | 195 | Cornell | | 6 |
| Taibi, Joe DE | 87NYG | | 6'5" | 265 | Idaho | | |
| Talley, Ben LB | 95NYG | | 6'3" | 248 | Tennessee | | |
| Talley, Darryl LB | 83-94Buf 95Atl | | 6'4" | 231 | West Virginia | 11 | 12 |
| Talley, John TE | 90-91Cle | | 6'5" | 245 | West Virginia | | |
| Talley, Stan K | 87Raid | 4 | 6'5" | 220 | Texas Christian | | |
| Talton, Ken HB | 80KC 83-84USFL | | 6' | 205 | Cornell | | |
| Tamburello, Ben OG-C | 87-90Phi 91KJ | | 6'3" | 278 | Auburn | | |
| Tamm, Ralph OG-C | 90-91Cle 91Was 91Cin 92-94SF 95Den | | 6'4" | 280 | West Chester | | 6 |
| Tanuvasa, Maa DT | 95Den | | 6'2" | 277 | Hawaii | | |
| Tardits, Richard LB | 90-92NE | | 6'2" | 228 | Georgia | | |
| Tasker, Steve WR | 85-86Hou 86-95Buf | 23 | 5'9" | 185 | Northwestern | | 38 |
| Tate, David DB | 88-92Chi 93NYG 94-95Ind | | 6'1" | 177 | Colorado | 11 | |
| Tate, Lars HB | 88-89TB 90Chi | 2 | 6'2" | 215 | Georgia | | 102 |
| Tate, Rodney HB | 82-83Cin 84Atl | 23 | 5'11" | 190 | Texas | | |
| Tatupu, Mosi FB | 78-90NE 91LA | 2 | 6' | 227 | Southern Calif. | | 120 |
| Tausch, Terry OT-OG | 82-88Min 89SF | | 6'5" | 275 | Texas | | |
| Tautalatasi, Junior HB-FB | 86-88Phi 89Dal | 2 | 5'10" | 207 | Washington State | | 12 |
| Tautolo, John OG-OT | 82-83NYG 85-86USFL 87Raid | | 6'3" | 267 | U.C.L.A. | | |
| Tautolo, Terry LB | 76-79Phi 80-81SF 81-82Det 83Mia 84Det | | 6'2" | 232 | U.C.L.A. | 1 | |
| Taylor, Aaron OG | 94KJ 95GB | | 6'4" | 305 | Notre Dame | | |
| Taylor, Alphonso DT | 93Den | | 6'3" | 350 | Temple | | |
| Taylor, Billy HB-FB | 78-81NYG 81NYJ 83-84USFL | 2 | 6' | 215 | Texas Tech | | 102 |
| Taylor, Bobby DB | 95Phi | | 6'3" | 216 | Notre Dame | 2 | |
| Taylor, Brian DB-HB | 89Chi 91Buf 93KJ | | 5'10" | 185 | Oregon State | | |
| Taylor, Craig FB | 89-91Cin | 2 | 5'11" | 224 | West Virginia | | 60 |
| Taylor, Derrick DB | 87NO | | 5'11" | 186 | N. Carolina State | | |
| Taylor, Gene WR | 87-88TB 89CFL 91NE | | 6'2" | 189 | Fresno State | | |
| Taylor, Greg HB | 82NE | | 5'8" | 175 | Virginia | | |
| Taylor, Hosea DE | 81Bal 82JJ 83Bal 84-85USFL | | 6'5" | 255 | Houston | | 2 |
| Taylor, Jay DB | 89-91Phx 92LJ 93-94KC 95LJ | | 5'9" | 170 | San Jose State | 5 | |
| Taylor, Jim Bob QB | 83Bal | | 6'2" | 197 | S.M.U. | | |
| Taylor, John WR | 87-95SF | 23 | 6'1" | 185 | Delaware State | | 276 |
| Taylor, Johnny LB | 84-86Atl 86Mia 87SD | | 6'4" | 237 | Hawaii | | |
| Taylor, J.T. OT | 78-81NO 84USFL | | 6'4" | 265 | Missouri | | |
| Taylor, Keith DB | 88-91Ind 92-93NO 94-95Was | | 5'11" | 193 | Illinois | 13 | 6 |
| Taylor, Ken DB | 85Chi 86SD | 3 | 6'1" | 186 | Oregon State | 4 | |
| Taylor, Kitrick WR | 88KC 89NE 90-91SD 92GB 93Den | 23 | 5'10" | 194 | Washington State | | 12 |

| Use Name (Nickname) - Positions | Team by Year | See Section | Hgt. | Wgt. | College | Int | Pts |
|---|---|---|---|---|---|---|---|
| Taylor, Lawrence (L.T.) LB | 81-93NYG | | 6'3" | 241 | North Carolina | 9 | 12 |
| Taylor, Lenny WR | 84GB 87Atl | | 5'10" | 181 | Tennessee | | 6 |
| Taylor, Malcolm DE-NT | 82-83Hou 84-85USFL 86Hou 87-88Raid 89Atl | | 6'6" | 281 | Tennessee State | | |
| Taylor, Rob OT | 83-85USFL 86-93TB | | 6'6" | 293 | Northwestern | | |
| Taylor, Roger OT | 81KC | | 6'6" | 271 | Oklahoma State | | |
| Taylor, Terry DB | 84-88Sea 89-91Det 92-93Cle 94Sea 95Atl | | 5'10" | 188 | Southern Illinois | 25 | 18 |
| Taylor, Tom OG | 87LA | | 6'3" | 265 | Georgia Tech | | |
| Taylor, Troy QB | 90-91NYJ | | 6'4" | 200 | California | | 6 |
| Teafatiller, Guy DT | 87Chi | | 6'2" | 260 | Illinois | | |
| Teague, George DB | 93-95GB | | 6'1" | 189 | Alabama | 6 | |
| Teague, Matthew DE | 80-81Atl | | 6'5" | 240 | Prairie View | | |
| Teague, Pat LB | 87TB | | 6'1" | 225 | N. Carolina State | | |
| Teal, Jimmy WR | 85-86Buf 87-88Sea | 2 | 5'10" | 171 | Texas A&M | | 18 |
| Teal, Willie DB | 80-86Min 87Raid | | 5'10" | 193 | Louisiana State | 12 | 6 |
| Teeter, Mike DT-NT | 91Min 93-94Hou 95SJ | | 6'2" | 269 | Michigan | | |
| Teichelman, Lance | 94Ind | | 6'4" | 276 | Texas A&M | | |
| Teifke, Mike C | 87Cle | | 6'4" | 255 | Akron | | |
| Teltschik, John K | 86-89Phi 90LJ | 4 | 6'2" | 212 | Texas | | |
| Tennell, Derek TE | 87-89Cle 91Det 92-93Min | 2 | 6'5" | 245 | U.C.L.A. | | 30 |
| Terrell, Pat DB | 90-93LA 94NYJ 95Car | | 6' | 199 | Notre Dame | 7 | |
| Terry, Doug DB | 92-95KC | | 5'11" | 192 | Kansas | 2 | |
| Terry, Joe LB | 87Sea | | 6'2" | 230 | Hayward State | | |
| Terry, Ryan HB | 95Arz | 3 | 5'11" | 203 | Iowa | | |
| Testaverde, Vinny QB | 87-92TB 93-95Cle | 12 | 6'5" | 217 | Miami (Fla.) | | 54 |
| Tharpe, Larry OT | 92-94Det 95Arz | | 6'4" | 299 | Tennessee State | | |
| Tharpe, Richard DE-NT | 87Buf | | 6'3" | 255 | Louisville | | |
| Thaxton, Galand LB | 89Atl 90AJ 91SD | | 6'1" | 242 | Wyoming | | |
| Thayer, Tom OG-C | 83-85USFL 85-92Ch 93Miai | | 6'4" | 271 | Notre Dame | | |
| Theismann, Joe QB | 74-85Was | 12 | 6' | 192 | Notre Dame | | 122 |
| Thielemann, R.C. OG-C | 77-84Atl 85-88Was | | 6'4" | 255 | Arkansas | | |
| Thierry, John DE | 94-95Chi | | 6'4" | 260 | Alcorn State | | |
| Thigpen, Yancey WR | 91SD 92-95Pit | 2 | 6'1" | 208 | Winston-Salem St. | | 72 |
| Thomas, Andre HB | 87Min | | 6' | 205 | Mississippi | | |
| Thomas, Ben DE-NT | 85-86NE 86GB 87KJ 88Pit 89Atl 91LA | | 6'4" | 276 | Auburn | | |
| Thomas, Blair HB | 90-93NYJ 94NE 94Dal 95Car | 2 | 5'10" | 195 | Penn State | | 48 |
| Thomas, Bob K | 75-81Chi 82Det 82-84Chi 85SD 86NYG | 5 | 5'10" | 175 | Notre Dame | | 756 |
| Thomas, Broderick LB-DE | 89-93TB 94Det 95Min | | 6'4" | 248 | Nebraska | 2 | 6 |
| Thomas, Carlton DB | 87KC | | 6' | 200 | Elizabeth City St. | | |
| Thomas, Calvin FB | 82-88Chi 88Den | 2 | 5'11" | 239 | Illinois | | 30 |
| Thomas, Chris WR | 95SF | | 6'1" | 180 | Cal. Poly.-SLO | | |
| Thomas, Chuck C-OG | 85Atl 87-92SF | | 6'3" | 277 | Oklahoma | | |
| Thomas, Curtland WR | 87NO | | 6' | 183 | Missouri | | |
| Thomas, Damon WR | 94-95Buf | | 6'2" | 215 | Wayne State | | |
| Thomas, Dave DB | 93-94Dal 95Jax | | 6'2" | 210 | Tennessee | | |
| Thomas, Dee DB | 90Hou | | 5'10" | 176 | Nicholls State | | |
| Thomas, Derrick FB | 87TB | | 6' | 232 | Arkansas | | |
| Thomas, Derrick LB | 89-95KC | | 6'3" | 239 | Alabama | | 20 |
| Thomas, Doug WR | 91-93Sea | 2 | 5'10" | 178 | Clemson | | |
| Thomas, Ed TE | 90-91TB 92KJ | | 6'3" | 240 | Houston | | |
| Thomas, Eric DB | 87-92Cin 93-94NYJ 95Den | | 5'11" | 181 | Tulane | 16 | 6 |
| Thomas, Garth OG | 87Sea | | 6'3" | 260 | Washington | | |
| Thomas, George WR-FB-TE | 89-92Atl 92TB | 2 | 5'9" | 169 | Nevada-Las Vegas | | 18 |
| Thomas, Henry DT | 87-94Min 95Det | | 6'2" | 274 | Louisiana State | 1 | 14 |
| Thomas, Henry OG | 87NO | | 6'2" | 275 | SW Texas State | | |
| Thomas, J.T. WR | 95StL | 3 | 5'10" | 173 | Arizona State | | |
| Thomas, Jewerl FB-HB | 80-82LA 83KC 84SD | 2 | 5'10" | 229 | San Jose State | | 30 |
| Thomas, Joe WR | 87NO | | 5'11" | 175 | Miss. Valley St. | | |
| Thomas, John OT | 87NYJ | | 6'4" | 280 | Toledo | | |
| Thomas, Johnny DB | 88Was 89SD 90,92-94Was 95Cle | | 5'9" | 188 | Baylor | | |
| Thomas, Kelly OT | 83-84TB 87LA | | 6'6" | 268 | Southern Calif. | | |
| Thomas, Ken HB | 83KC 84KJ | 2 | 5'9" | 211 | San Jose State | | |
| Thomas, Kevin C | 88TB | | 6'2" | 265 | Arizona State | | 6 |
| Thomas, Lamar WR | 93-95TB | 2 | 6'1" | 172 | Miami (Fla.) | | 12 |
| Thomas, Lavale HB | 87-88GB | | 6' | 205 | Fresno State | | 6 |
| Thomas, Lynn DB | 81-82SF 84-85USFL | | 5'11" | 181 | Pittsburgh | | |
| Thomas, Mark DE-LB | 93-94SF 95Car | | 6'5" | 274 | N. Carolina State | | |
| Thomas, Norris DB | 77-79Mia 80-84TB | | 5'11" | 179 | Southern Miss. | 9 | 6 |
| Thomas, Orlando DB | 95Min | | 6'1" | 210 | Southwestern La. | 9 | 12 |
| Thomas, Ricky DB | 87Sea | | 6' | 185 | Alabama | | |
| Thomas, Robb WR | 89-91KC 92-95Sea | 2 | 5'11" | 174 | Oregon State | | 48 |
| Thomas, Rodell LB | 81Mia 81-82Sea 83-84Mia | | 6'2" | 225 | Alabama State | | 6 |
| Thomas, Rodney DB | 88-90Mia 91LA 92KJ | | 5'10" | 190 | Brigham Young | 3 | |
| Thomas, Rodney HB | 95Hou | 2 | 5'10" | 213 | Texas A&M | | 44 |
| Thomas, Sean DB | 85Cin 85Atl 87NJ | | 5'11" | 190 | Texas Christian | | |
| Thomas, Stan OT | 91-92Chi 93-94Hou | | 6'5" | 296 | Texas | | |
| Thomas, Thurman HB | 88-95Buf | 2 | 5'10" | 198 | Oklahoma State | | 442 |
| Thomas, Todd C | 81KC 83-84USFL | | 6'5" | 262 | North Dakota | | |
| Thomas, William LB | 91-95Phi | | 6'2" | 219 | Texas A&M | 12 | 6 |
| Thomas, Zach WR | 83-84Den 84TB | 23 | 6' | 182 | S. Carolina State | | 6 |
| Thomaselli, Rich FB-HB | 81-82Hou | | 6'1" | 199 | West Va. Weslyan | | |
| Thomason, Jeff TE | 92-93Cin 95GB | | 6'4" | 233 | Oregon | | |
| Thomasson, Leon DB | 87Atl | | 5'11" | 190 | Texas Southern | | |
| Thome, Chris C | 91-92Cle 92NYG | | 6'4" | 280 | Minnesota | | |
| Thompson, Anthony HB | 90-92Phx 92LA | 2 | 5'11" | 207 | Indiana | | 36 |
| Thompson, Anthony LB | 90Den | | 6'1" | 227 | East Carolina | | |
| Thompson, Arland OG | 80Den 81GB 82Bal 83-85USFL 87KC | | 6'3" | 265 | Baylor | | |
| Thompson, Aundra WR-HB | 77-81GB 81SD 81-82NO | 23 | 6'1" | 186 | East Texas State | | 54 |
| Thompson, Bennie DB | 89-91NO 92-93KC 94-95Cle | | 6' | 200 | Grambling | 4 | |
| Thompson, Broderick OG-OT | 85USFL 85Dal 87-92SD 93-94Phi 95Den | | 6'5" | 291 | Kansas | | |
| Thompson, Craig TE | 92-93Cin | 2 | 6'2" | 244 | N. Carolina A&T | | 18 |
| Thompson, Darrell FB-HB | 90-94GB | 2 | 6' | 215 | Minnesota | | 54 |
| Thompson, Del HB | 82KC 83JJ | | 6' | 203 | Texas-El Paso, Texas | | |
| Thompson, Donnell DE | 81-83Bal 84-91Ind | | 6'4" | 270 | North Carolina | | 8 |
| Thompson, Emmuel DB | 87Hou | | 5'11" | 180 | Texas A&I | | |
| Thompson, Ernie FB | 91LA 93KC | | 5'11" | 230 | Indiana | | 6 |
| Thompson, Gary DB | 83-84Buf 87Was | | 6' | 180 | San Jose State | | |
| Thompson, Jack QB | 79-82Cin 83-84TB | 12 | 6'3" | 218 | Washington State | | 36 |
| Thompson, John TE | 79-82GB 84USFL | | 6'3" | 228 | Weber State, Utah State | | 12 |
| Thompson, Ken WR | 82-83StL | | 6'1" | 178 | West Texas State, Utah State | | |
| Thompson, Leonard WR-HB | 75-86Det | 23 | 5'11" | 190 | Oklahoma State | | 228 |
| Thompson, Leroy HB | 91-93Pit 94NE 95KC | 23 | 5'10" | 215 | Penn State | | 66 |
| Thompson, Marty DE | 93Det | | 6'3" | 243 | Fresno State | | |
| Thompson, Mike DT | 95Jax | | 6'3" | 279 | Wisconsin | | |

| Use Name (Nickname) - Positions | Team by Year | See Section | Hgt. | Wgt. | College | Int | Pts |
|---|---|---|---|---|---|---|---|
| Thompson, Reyna DB | 86-88Mia 89-92NYG 93NE | | 6' | 194 | Baylor | 3 | 6 |
| Thompson, Robert LB | 83-84TB 87Det | | 6'3" | 227 | Michigan | | |
| Thompson, Robert WR | 87Den | | 5'9" | 168 | Youngstown State | | |
| Thompson, Steve DT | 87Was | | 6'2" | 275 | Minnesota | | |
| Thompson, Tommy K | 95SF | | 5'120" | 192 | Oregon | | |
| Thompson, Vince FB | 81Det 82JJ 83Det | 2 | 6' | 228 | Villanova | | 12 |
| Thompson, Warren LB | 87NYG | | 6'3" | 241 | Oklahoma State | | |
| Thompson, Weegie WR | 84-89Pit | 2 | 6'6" | 212 | Florida State | | 66 |
| Thornton, Bruce DE-DT | 79-81Dal 82StL 84-85USFL | | 6'5" | 265 | Illinois | 1 | |
| Thornton, George DE-DT | 91-92SD 93NYG | | 6'3" | 300 | Alabama | | |
| Thornton, Jim (Robocop) TE | 88-91Chi 92FJ 93-94NYJ 95Hou | 2 | 6'2" | 242 | Fullerton State | | 42 |
| Thornton, John DE-DT | 91Cle 92LJ | | 6'3" | 303 | Cincinnati | | |
| Thornton, Reggie WR | 91Ind 93Cin | | 5'10" | 170 | Bowling Green | | |
| Thornton, Sidney HB-FB | 77-82Pit 84USFL | 2 | 5'11" | 230 | Northwestern La. | | 144 |
| Thorp, Don NT-DE | 84NO 87-88Ind 88KC | | 6'4" | 260 | Illinois | | |
| Thrift, Cliff LB | 79-84SD 85Chi 86LA | | 6'2" | 232 | E. C. Oklahoma | 3 | |
| Thure, Brian OT | 95Was | | 6'5" | 300 | California | | |
| Thurman, Dennis DB | 78-85Dal 86StL | | 5'11" | 176 | Southern Calif. | 36 | 30 |
| Thurman, Junior DB | 87NO | | 6' | 180 | Southern Calif. | | |
| Tice, John TE | 83-92NO | 2 | 6'5" | 246 | Maryland | | 90 |
| Tice, Mike TE | 81-88Sea 89Was 90-91Sea 92-93,95Min | 2 | 6'7" | 246 | Maryland | | 66 |
| Tiffin, Van K | 87TB 87Mia | | 5'9" | 155 | Alabama | | 26 |
| Tigges, Mark OT | 87Cin | | 6'3" | 290 | Western Illinois | | |
| Tiggle, Calvin LB | 91-92TB | | 6'1" | 235 | Georgia Tech | | |
| Tilley, Emmett LB | 83Mia | | 5'11" | 240 | Duke | | |
| Tilley, Pat WR | 76-86StL | 23 | 5'10" | 176 | Louisiana Tech | | 222 |
| Tillison, Ed FB | 92Det 93KJ | | 6' | 225 | NW Missouri St. | | |
| Tillman, Cedric WR | 92-94Den 95Jax | 2 | 6'2" | 204 | Alcorn State | | 42 |
| Tillman, Lawyer WR | 89Cle 90LJ 91-93Cle 95Car | 2 | 6'5" | 230 | Auburn | | 24 |
| Tillman, Lewis HB | 89-93NYG 94-95Chi | 2 | 6' | 199 | Jackson State | | 72 |
| Tillman, Spencer HB | 87-88Hou 89-91SF 92-94Hou | 23 | 5'11" | 206 | Oklahoma | | 12 |
| Tillmon, Tony DB | 87Raid | | 5'10" | 170 | Texas | | |
| Tilton, Ron OG | 86Was 88NYJ | | 6'4" | 250 | Tulane | | |
| Times, Ken NT-DT | 80SF 81StL | | 6'2" | 246 | Southern U. | | |
| Timmer, Kirk LB | 87Dal | | 6'3" | 242 | Montana State | | |
| Timmerman, Adam OG | 95GB | | 6'4" | 288 | S. Dakota State | | |
| Timpson, Michael WR | 89-94NE 95Chi | 23 | 5'10" | 175 | Kent State | | 66 |
| Tindale, Tim FB | 95Buf | | 5'10" | 220 | Western Ontario | | |
| Tinsley, Keith WR | 87Cle | | 5'9" | 184 | Pittsburgh | | |
| Tinsley, Scott QB | 87Phi | 1 | 6'2" | 195 | Southern Calif. | | |
| Tippett, Andre LB | 82-88NE 89SJ 90-93NE | | 6'3" | 240 | Iowa | 1 | 12 |
| Tippins, Ken LB | 89Dal 90-95Atl | | 6'1" | 233 | Middle Tenn. St. | 2 | 6 |
| Tipton, Gregg QB | 87StL | | 6'3" | 191 | Hawaii | | |
| Tipton, Rico LB | 87Sea | | 6'2" | 240 | Washington State | | |
| Titensor, Glen OG-C | 81-86Dal 87KJ 88Dal | | 6'4" | 263 | U.C.L.A., Brigham Young | | |
| Tiumalu, Casey FB | 87LA | | 5'8" | 206 | Brigham Young | | |
| Tobeck, Robbie C | 94-95Atl | | 6'4" | 289 | Middle Tenn. St. | | |
| Tobin, Steve C | 80NYG 83USFL | | 6'4" | 258 | Minnesota | | |
| Todd, Richard QB | 76-83NYJ 84-85NO 86NYJ | 12 | 6'2" | 207 | Alabama | | 84 |
| Toews, Jeff OG-C | 79-85Mia | | 6'3" | 255 | Washington | | |
| Toews, Loren LB | 78-83Pit | | 6'3" | 221 | California | 4 | 4 |
| Tofflemire, Joe C | 89-90Sea 91XJ 92-94Sea | | 6'2" | 274 | Arizona | | |
| Toibin, Brendan K | 87Was | | 6' | 205 | Richmond | | 4 |
| Tolbert, Tony DE | 89-95Dal | | 6'6" | 268 | Texas-El Paso | 1 | 6 |
| Toler, Ken WR | 81-82NE 84-85USFL | | 6'2" | 193 | Mississippi | | 12 |
| Toles, Alvin LB | 85-88NO | | 6'1" | 223 | Tennessee | | 6 |
| Tolle, Stuart NT | 87Det | | 6'3" | 245 | Bowling Green | | |
| Tolliver, Billy Joe QB | 89-90SD 91-93Atl 94Hou | 12 | 6'1" | 218 | Texas Tech | | 12 |
| Tomberlin, Pat OT-OG | 90Ind 91LJ 93TB | | 6'2" | 312 | Florida State | | |
| Tomczak, Mike QB | 85-90Chi 91GB 92Cle 93-95Pit | 12 | 6'1" | 199 | Ohio State | | 42 |
| Toner, Ed FB | 92-94Ind | | 6' | 240 | Boston College | | |
| Toney, Anthony FB-HB | 86-90Phi | 2 | 6' | 227 | Texas A&M | | 114 |
| Tongue, Marco DB | 83Bal 84Buf | | 5'9" | 177 | Bowie State | | |
| Toon, Al WR | 85-92NYJ | 2 | 6'4" | 205 | Wisconsin | | 186 |
| Toran, Stacey DB — Died in automobile accident — 1989 | 84-88Raid | | 6'2" | 200 | Notre Dame | 6 | 12 |
| Torretta, Gino QB | 93-94Min | | 6'2" | 215 | Miami (Fla.) | | |
| Toth, Tom OG-OT | 86-89Mia 90SD | | 6'5" | 279 | Western Michigan | | |
| Totten, Willie QB | 87Buf | 1 | 6'2" | 195 | Miss. Valley St. | | |
| Toussaint, Darrel DB | 87NO | | 6' | 175 | Northwestern La. | | |
| Tovar, Steve LB | 93-95Cin | | 6'3" | 244 | Ohio State | 2 | |
| Towns, Morris OT-OG | 77-83Hou 84Was | | 6'4" | 270 | Missouri | | |
| Townsell, JoJo WR | 83-85USFL 85-90NYJ | 23 | 5'9" | 180 | U.C.L.A. | | 42 |
| Townsend, Andre DE-NT | 84-90Den | | 6'3" | 265 | Mississippi | | 6 |
| Townsend, Brian LB | 92Cin | | 6'3" | 242 | Michigan | | |
| Townsend, Greg DE-NT-LB | 83-93Raid 94Phi | | 6'3" | 265 | Texas Christian | 3 | 32 |
| Trahan, John WR | 87KC | | 5'9" | 160 | Southern Colorado | | |
| Traylor, Keith LB | 91-92Den 93GB 95KC | | 6'2" | 260 | Oklahoma, Central St.-Okla. | | |
| Trapilo, Steve OG | 87-90NO 91KJ 92NO | | 6'5" | 290 | Boston College | | |
| Trapp, James DB | 93-94Raid 95Oak | | 6' | 180 | Clemson | 1 | |
| Travis, Mack NT | 93Det | | 6'1" | 280 | California | | |
| Traynowicz, Mark OG-C | 85-88Buf 88-89Phx | | 6'5" | 277 | Nebraska | | |
| Treadwell, David K | 89-92Den 93-94NYG | 5 | 6'1" | 175 | Clemson | | 587 |
| Treggs, Brian WR | 92Sea | | 5'9" | 161 | California | | |
| Tremble, Greg DB | 95Dal 95Phi | | 5'11" | 188 | Georgia | | |
| Trimble, Steve DB | 81-83Den 84-85USFL 87Chi | | 5'10" | 183 | Maryland | | |
| Tripoli, Paul DB | 87TB | | 6' | 197 | Alabama | 3 | 6 |
| Trocano, Rick QB-DB | 81-83Cle | | 6' | 188 | Pittsburgh | | |
| Trout, David K | 81Pit 83-85USFL 87Pit | 5 | 5'6" | 167 | Pittsburgh | | 84 |
| Trudeau, Jack QB | 86-93Ind 94NYJ 95Car | 12 | 6'3" | 213 | Illinois | | 18 |
| Truitt, Dave TE | 87Was | | 6'4" | 232 | North Carolina | | |
| Truitt, Greg DB-C | 94-95Cin | | 6' | 235 | Penn State | | |
| Truitt, Olanda WR | 93Min 94-95Was | | 6' | 186 | Mississippi State | | 12 |
| Truvillion, Eric WR | 83-85USFL 87Det | 2 | 6'4" | 205 | Florida A&M | | 6 |
| Tuaolo, Esera NT-DT | 91-92GB 92-95Min | | 6'2" | 272 | Oregon State | 1 | |
| Tuatagaloa, Natu NT-DE-LB | 89-91Cin 92-93Sea 95Hou | | 6'4" | 274 | California | 1 | |
| Tubbs, Winfred LB | 94-95NO | | 6'4" | 250 | Texas | 2 | |
| Tucker, Errol DB | 88-89Buf 89NE | 3 | 5'8" | 170 | Utah | | |
| Tucker, Mark OG | 94Arz | | 6'3" | 290 | Southern Calif. | | |
| Tucker, Travis TE | 85-86Cle | | 6'3" | 234 | Southern Conn. St. | | |
| Tuggle, Anthony DB | 87Pit | | 6'1" | 211 | Southern U., Nicholls State | | |
| Tuggle, Jessie LB | 87-95Atl | | 5'11" | 227 | Valdosta State | 6 | 30 |
| Tuggle, John FB | 83NYG 84KJ | | 6'1" | 210 | California | | 6 |
| Tuiasosopo, Manu NT-DT-DE | 79-83Sea 84-86SF | | 6'3" | 255 | U.C.L.A. | 1 | |
| Tuiasosopo, Navy C | 87LA | | 6'2" | 285 | Utah State | | |
| Tuinei, Mark OT-C-DT | 83-95Dal | | 6'5" | 297 | U.C.L.A., Hawaii | | |

| Use Name (Nickname) - Positions | Team by Year | See Section | Hgt. | Wgt. | College | Int | Pts |
|---|---|---|---|---|---|---|---|
| Tuinei, Tom DT | 80Det | | 6'4" | 250 | Hawaii | | |
| Tuipulotu, Peter HB-FB | 92SD | | 5'11" | 210 | Brigham Young | | |
| Tullis, Willie DB | 81-84Hou 85-86NO 87-88Ind | 3 | 6' | 193 | Southern Miss., Troy State | 18 | 6 |
| Tupa, Tom QB-K | 88-91Phx 92Ind 94-95Cle | 12 | 6'4" | 220 | Ohio State | | 12 |
| Tupper, Jeff DE | 86Phi 87Den | | 6'5" | 269 | Oklahoma | | |
| Turk, Dan C-OG | 86Pit 87-88TB 89-94Raid 95Oak | | 6'4" | 287 | Drake, Wisconsin | | |
| Turk, Matt K | 95Was | 4 | 6'5" | 230 | Wis.-Whitewater | | |
| Turnbull, Renaldo DE-LB | 90-95NO | | 6'4" | 252 | West Virginia | 1 | |
| Turner, Bill DE | 87NE | | 6'4" | 245 | Boston College | | |
| Turner, Daryl WR | 84-87Sea | 2 | 6'3" | 194 | Michigan State | | 216 |
| Turner, Dwain NT | 87Hou | | 6' | 290 | Rice | | |
| Turner, Eric DB | 91-95Cle | | 6'1" | 207 | U.C.L.A. | 17 | 12 |
| Turner, Floyd WR | 89-93NO 94-95Ind | 2 | 5'11" | 188 | Northwestern La. | | 112 |
| Turner, Jimmie LB | 84Dal | | 6'2" | 220 | Presbyterian | | |
| Turner, Jimmy DB | 83-86Cin 86-87Atl | | 6' | 187 | U.C.L.A. | 2 | |
| Turner, John DB | 78-83Min 84SD 85,87Min | | 6' | 197 | Miami (Fla.) | 24 | 6 |
| Turner, J.T. OG-DT | 77-83NYG 84Was 85USFL | | 6'3" | 253 | Duke | | |
| Turner, Keena LB | 80-90SF | | 6'2" | 221 | Purdue | 11 | 8 |
| Turner, Kevin LB | 80NYG 81Was 81Sea 82Cle 84-85USFL | | 6'2" | 225 | U. of Pacific | | |
| Turner, Kevin FB | 92-94NE 95Phi | 2 | 6' | 224 | Alabama | | 42 |
| Turner, Maurice HB-FB | 84-85Min 85GB 87NYJ | | 5'11" | 202 | Utah State | | |
| Turner, Mike OG | 87Min | | 6'3" | 255 | Louisiana State | | |
| Turner, Marcus DB | 89-91Phx 92-95NYJ | | 6' | 190 | U.C.L.A. | 8 | 18 |
| Turner, Nate FB | 93-94Buf | | 6'1" | 255 | Nebraska | | 6 |
| Turner, Norv | HC94Was 95-95Car | | | | Oregon | | |
| Turner, Odessa WR | 87-91NYG 92-93SF | 2 | 6'3" | 205 | Northwestern La. | | 48 |
| Turner, Richard NT | 81-83GB | | 6'2" | 260 | Oklahoma | | |
| Turner, Ricky QB | 88Ind | | 6' | 190 | Washington State | | 6 |
| Turner, Scott DB | 95Was | | 5'10" | 178 | Illinois | 1 | |
| Turner, T.J. DE-NT | 86-92Mia | | 6'4" | 276 | Houston | | |
| Turner, Vernon WR-HB | 90Buf 91-92LA 93Det 93-94TB 95Det | 3 | 5'8" | 185 | Carson-Newman | | 12 |
| Turnure, Tom C-OG | 80-83Det 84USFL 85-86Det | | 6'4" | 250 | Washington | | |
| Turpin, Miles LB | 86GB 87TB | | 6'4" | 232 | California | | |
| Turrall, Willie HB | 87Phi | | 5'10" | 190 | New Mexico | | |
| Tuten, Melvin OT | 95Cin | | 6'6" | 305 | Syracuse | | 6 |
| Tuten, Rick K | 89Phi 90Buf 91-95Sea | 4 | 6'2" | 220 | Miami (Fla.), Florida State | | 2 |
| Tutson, Tom DB | 83Atl | | 6'1" | 180 | S. Carolina State | | |
| Tuttle, Perry WR | 82-83Buf 84TB 84Atl | 2 | 6' | 178 | Clemson | | 18 |
| Tweet, Rodney WR | 87Cin | | 6'1" | 195 | South Dakota | | |
| Twombly, Darren C | 87NE | | 6'4" | 270 | Boston College | | |
| Tyler, Andre WR | 83TB | | 6' | 180 | Stanford | | |
| Tyler, Robert TE | 89Sea | 2 | 6'5" | 257 | S. Carolina State | | |
| Tyler, Toussaint FB | 81-82NO 84USFL | 2 | 6'2" | 220 | Washington | | |
| Tyler, Wendell HB | 77-82LA 83-86SF | 23 | 5'10" | 197 | U.C.L.A. | | 396 |
| Tyner, Scott K | 94Atl | | 6'1" | 189 | Oklahoma State | | |
| Tyrrell, Tim HB-FB | 84-86Atl 86-88LA 89Pit | | 6'1" | 204 | Northern Illinois | | |
| Uecker, Keith OT-OG | 82-83Den 84-85GB 86KJ 87-88GB 89KJ 90-91GB | | 6'5" | 276 | Auburn | | |
| Uhlenhake, Jeff C | 89-93Mia 94-95NO | | 6'3" | 282 | Ohio State | | |
| Ulmer, Mike DB | 80Chi 81CFL 84-85USFL 87Phi | | 6' | 196 | Doane | | |
| Umphrey, Rich C-OG | 82-84NYG 85SD | | 6'3" | 263 | Utah, Colorado | | |
| Unrein, Terry NT-DE | 86-87SD | | 6'5" | 281 | Colorado State | | |
| Urch, Scott OG | 87NYG | | 6'2" | 270 | Virginia | | |
| Usher, Darryl WR | 89SD 89Phx | 3 | 5'8" | 170 | Illinois | | |
| Utley, Mike OG-OT | 89-91Det | | 6'6" | 288 | Washington State | | |
| November 1991 — Paralyzed in game | | | | | | | |
| Utt, Ben OG | 82-83Bal 84-88Ind | | 6'5" | 275 | Georgia Tech | | |
| Valentine, Ira HB | 87Hou | | 6' | 212 | Marshall (Tex.) | | |
| Valentine, Zack LB | 79-81Pit 82Phi 83KJ | | 6'2" | 222 | East Carolina | | |
| Valerio, Joe OT-OG | 92-95KC | | 6'5" | 293 | Pennsylvania | | 24 |
| Vanderbeek, Matt LB-DE | 90-92Ind 93-94Dal 95Was | | 6'3" | 249 | Michigan State | | |
| Vander Poel, Mark OT | 91-92Ind 93TJ 94Arz | | 6'7" | 303 | Colorado | | |
| Van Divier, Randy OT-OG | 81Bal 82Raid 84-85USFL | | 6'5" | 274 | Washington | | |
| Van Dyke, Ralph OT | 87Cle | | 6'6" | 273 | Southern Illinois | | |
| Van Horne, Keith OT | 81-93Chi | | 6'6" | 281 | Southern Calif. | | |
| Van Horse, Sean DB | 92-94SD 95Det | | 5'10" | 180 | Howard | 6 | 6 |
| Vanover, Tamarick WR | 95KC | 23 | 5'11" | 213 | Florida State | | 30 |
| Van Pelt, Alex QB | 95Buf | | 6' | 220 | Pittsburgh | | |
| Van Raaphorst, Jeff QB | 87Atl | 1 | 6'1" | 210 | Arizona State | | |
| Vann, Norwood LB | 84-87LA 88Raid | | 6'1" | 228 | East Carolina | | |
| Varajon, Mike FB | 87SF | | 6'1" | 232 | Toledo | | |
| Vardell, Tommy FB | 92-95Cle | 2 | 6'2" | 238 | Stanford | | 30 |
| Vatterott, Charles OG-OT | 87StL | | 6'4" | 263 | SW Texas State | | |
| Vaughn, Clarence DB | 87-91Was 92KJ | | 6' | 202 | Northern Illinois | | |
| Vaughn, Jon HB | 91-92NE 93-94Sea 94KC | 23 | 5'9" | 203 | Michigan | | 56 |
| Vaughn, Ruben DT-NT-DE | 79SF 82Raid 84Min 85USFL | | 6'2" | 261 | Colorado | | |
| Veals, Elton FB | 84Pit | 2 | 5'11" | 230 | Tulane | | |
| Veasey, Craig DE-NT | 90-91Pit 92-93Hou 93-94Mia 95Hou | | 6'2" | 283 | Houston | 1 | |
| Veingrad, Alan OT-OG | 86-87GB 88PJ 89-90GB 91-92Dal | | 6'5" | 277 | East Texas State | | |
| Venturi, Rick | HC91Ind | | | | Northwestern | | |
| Venuto, Jay QB | 81Bal 83USFL | | 6'1" | 195 | Wake Forest | | |
| Verdin, Clarence WR | 86-87Was 88-93Ind 94Atl | 23 | 5'8" | 162 | Southwestern La. | | 72 |
| Verhulst, Chris TE | 88-89Hou 90Den | | 6'2" | 249 | Chico State | | |
| Veris, Garin DE | 85-88NE 89KJ 90-91NE 92SF | | 6'4" | 255 | Stanford | | |
| Verser, David WR | 81-84Cin 85TB 87Cle | 23 | 6'1" | 200 | Kansas | | 18 |
| Viaene, David OT | 89-90NE 91KJ 92GB | | 6'5" | 300 | Wis.-Platteville, Minnesota-Duluth | | |
| Vick, Roger FB | 87-89NYJ 90Phi | 2 | 6'3" | 239 | Texas A&M | | 72 |
| Vickers, Kipp OT | 95Ind | | 6'2" | 295 | Miami (Fla.) | | |
| Vigorito, Tommy HB-WR | 81-83Mia 84KJ 85Mia | 23 | 5'10" | 193 | Virginia | | 36 |
| Villa, Danny OT-C-OG | 87-91NE 92Phx 93-95KC | | 6'5" | 305 | Arizona State | | |
| Villanucci, Vince NT | 87GB | | 6'2" | 265 | Bowling Green | | |
| Vincent, Shawn DB | 91Pit | | 5'10" | 180 | Akron | 2 | |
| Vincent, Troy DB | 92-95Mia | | 6' | 191 | Wisconsin | 14 | 12 |
| Vinson, Fernandus DB | 91-94Cin | | 5'10" | 197 | N. Carolina State | | 6 |
| Virkus, Scott DE | 83-84Buf 84NE 84-85Ind | | 6'5" | 260 | Purdue | | |
| Visger, George DT | 80SF 81KJ | | 6'4" | 250 | Colorado | | |
| Vital, Lionel HB | 87Was | 2 | 5'9" | 195 | Nicholls State | | 12 |
| Vitiello, Sandro K | 80Cin 83-84USFL | | 6'2" | 197 | Massachusetts | | 1 |
| Vlasic, Mark QB | 87-88SD 89KJ 90SD 91-92KC 93TB | 1 | 6'3" | 205 | Iowa | | |
| Vogel, Paul LB | 87Hou | | 6'1" | 220 | South Carolina | | |
| Vogler, Tim C-OG | 79-88Buf 89KJ | | 6'3" | 259 | Ohio State | | |
| Von Oelhoffen, Kimo DT | 94-95Cin | | 6'4" | 300 | Boise State | | |
| von Schamann, Uwe K | 79-84Mia | 5 | 6' | 190 | Oklahoma | | 540 |
| Waddle, Tom WR | 89-94Chi | 2 | 6' | 181 | Boston College | | 54 |
| Waddy, Billy WR | 77-82LA 84Min | 23 | 5'11" | 187 | Colorado | | 60 |
| Waddy, Ray DB | 79-80Was 81LJ 84USFL | | 5'11" | 175 | Texas A&I | 1 | |

| Use Name (Nickname) - Positions | Team by Year | See Section | Hgt. | Wgt. | College | Int | Pts |
|---|---|---|---|---|---|---|---|
| Waechter, Henry DE-DT | 82Chi 83Bal 84Ind 84-86Chi 87Was | | 6'5" | 271 | Nebraska | | 2 |
| Wagner, Barry WR | 92Chi | | 6'3" | 213 | Alabama A&M | | |
| Wagner, Bryan K | 87-88Chi 89-90Cle 91NE 92-93GB 94SD 95NE | 4 | 6'2" | 198 | Cal. Lutheran, Northridge State | | |
| Wagner, Ray OT | 82Cin 84-85USFL | | 6'3" | 290 | Kent State | | |
| Wagoner, Dan DB | 82-84Det 84Min 85Atl 86KJ | | 5'10" | 180 | Kansas | | |
| Wahler, Jim DT-NT | 89-91Phx 92-93Was | | 6'4" | 272 | U.C.L.A. | 1 | |
| Wainright, Frank TE | 91-93NO 94FJ 95Phi 95Mia | 2 | 6'3" | 236 | Northern Colorado | | |
| Waiters, Van LB | 88-91Cle 92Min | | 6'4" | 243 | Indiana | 1 | 6 |
| Waits, Alex K | 91Sea | | 6'2" | 208 | Texas | | |
| Walczak, Mark TE | 87Buf 87Ind 88Phx 89,91SD | | 6'6" | 246 | Arizona | | |
| Waldemore, Stan OG-C-OT | 78-84NYJ 85-86KJ | | 6'4" | 263 | Nebraska | | |
| Waldrop, Rob DT | 94KC | | 6'1" | 276 | Arizona | | |
| Walen, Mark DT-DE | 87-88Dal 89KJ | | 6'5" | 266 | U.C.L.A. | | |
| Walker, Adam FB | 87Min | | 5'11" | 220 | Carthage | | |
| Walker, Adam HB-FB | 92-95SF | 2 | 6'1" | 210 | Pittsburgh | | 12 |
| Walker, Bracey DB | 94KC 94-95Cin | | 5'10" | 200 | North Carolina | 4 | |
| Walker, Bruce NT | 95NE | | 6'4" | 310 | U.C.L.A. | | |
| Walker, Byron WR | 82-86Sea | 2 | 6'4" | 190 | The Citadel | | 48 |
| Walker, Darnell DB | 93-95Atl | | 5'8" | 166 | Oklahoma | 3 | 6 |
| Walker, Derrick TE-FB | 90-93SD 94-95KC | 2 | 6'1" | 244 | Michigan | | 30 |
| Walker, Dwight HB-WR | 82-84Cle 87NO | 23 | 5'10" | 186 | Nicholls State | | 6 |
| Walker, Fulton DB | 81-85Mia 85-86Raid | 3 | 5'10" | 195 | West Virginia | 5 | 12 |
| Walker, Gary OG | 87Dal | | 6'3" | 283 | Boston U. | | |
| Walker, Gary DE-DT | 95Hou | | 6'2" | 285 | Auburn | | |
| Walker, Herschel HB-FB | 83-85USFL 86-89Dal 90-91Min 92-94Phi 95NE | 23 | 6'1" | 225 | Georgia | | 486 |
| Walker, Jackie LB-TE | 86-89TB | | 6'5" | 250 | Jackson State | | |
| Walker, James LB | 83KC | | 6'1" | 250 | Kansas State | | |
| Walker, Jay QB | 94NE | | 6'3" | 232 | Howard | | |
| Walker, Jeff OT-OG | 86SD 87KJ 88-89NO 90KJ | | 6'4" | 295 | Memphis State | | |
| Walker, Jimmy DT | 87Min | | 6'2" | 265 | Arkansas | | |
| Walker, John DE-DT | 87KC | | 6'6" | 270 | Nebraska-Omaha | | |
| Walker, Kenny LB-DE | 91-92Den | | 6'3" | 260 | Nebraska | | |
| Walker, Kevin DB | 86-87TB | | 5'11" | 180 | East Carolina | | |
| Walker, Kevin LB | 88-92Cin | | 6'2" | 238 | Maryland | | |
| Walker, Quentin FB | 84StL 87LJ | | 6'1" | 205 | Virginia | | |
| Walker, Rick TE | 77-79Cin 80-85Was | 2 | 6'3" | 236 | U.C.L.A. | | 54 |
| Walker, Sammy DB | 91-92Pit 93GB 93EJ | | 5'11" | 197 | Texas Tech | | |
| Walker, Tim LB | 80Sea | | 6'1" | 230 | Savannah State | | |
| Walker, Tony LB | 90-91Ind | | 6'3" | 235 | SE Missouri St. | | |
| Walker, Wayne (Bug) WR | 89SD 90KJ | 2 | 5'8" | 162 | Texas Tech | | 6 |
| Walker, Wesley WR | 77-89NYJ | 2 | 6' | 178 | California | | 428 |
| Wallace, Aaron LB | 90-94Raid 95Oak | | 6'3" | 237 | Texas A&M | | |
| Wallace, Calvin DE | 87GB | | 6'3" | 230 | West Virginia Tech | | |
| Wallace, Ray FB | 86-87Hou 88NJ 89Pit | 2 | 6' | 224 | Purdue | | 36 |
| Wallace, Steve OT-OG | 86-95SF | | 6'5" | 276 | Auburn | | |
| Wallerstedt, Brett LB | 93Phx 94-95Cin | | 6'1" | 240 | Arizona State | | |
| Walls, Craig LB | 87Buf | | 6'1" | 215 | Indiana | | |
| Walls, Everson DB | 81-89Dal 90-92NYG 92-93Cle | | 6'1" | 194 | Grambling | 57 | 6 |
| Walls, Henry LB | 87NYJ | | 6'2" | 220 | Clemson | | |
| Walls, Herkie WR | 83-85Hou 87TB | 23 | 5'8" | 159 | Texas | | 12 |
| Walls, Wesley TE | 89-91SF 92SJ 93SF 94-95NO | 2 | 6'5" | 246 | Mississippi | | 58 |
| Walsh, Bill | HC79-88SF | | | | San Jose State | | |
| Walsh, Chris WR | 92-93Buf 94-95Min | | 6'1" | 189 | Stanford | | |
| Walsh, Jim FB | 80Sea | | 5'11" | 220 | San Jose State | | |
| Walsh, John QB | 95Cin | | 6'4" | 215 | Brigham Young | | |
| Walsh, Steve QB | 89-90Dal 90-93NO 94-95Chi | 12 | 6'2" | 200 | Miami (Fla.) | | 6 |
| Walter, Dave QB | 87Cin | | 6'3" | 230 | Michigan Tech | | |
| Walter, Joe OT-OG | 85-93Cin 94KJ 95Cin | | 6'6" | 290 | Texas Tech | | |
| Walter, Michael LB | 83Dal 84-93SF | | 6'3" | 240 | Oregon | 2 | |
| Walters, Dale K | 87Cle | | 6' | 200 | Rice | | |
| Walters, Danny DB | 83-87SD | | 6'1" | 189 | Arkansas | 12 | |
| Walters, Joey WR | 87Hou | | 5'11" | 175 | Clemson | | |
| Walters, Pete OG | 87Phi | | 6'2" | 265 | Western Kentucky | | |
| Walterscheid, Len DB | 77-82Chi 83-84Buf | 3 | 5'11" | 189 | Southern Utah | 7 | 6 |
| Walton, Alvin DB | 86-91Was | | 6' | 180 | Kansas | 12 | 12 |
| Walton, Riley TE | 87KC | | 6'4" | 245 | Tennessee State | | |
| Walton, Whip LB | 80NYG | | 6'2" | 225 | San Diego State | | |
| Wannstedt, Dave | HC93-95Chi | | | | Pittsburgh | | |
| Ward, Chris OT | 78-83NYJ 84NO | | 6'3" | 269 | Ohio State | | |
| Ward, David LB | 87Cin 88SJ 89NE | | 6'2" | 231 | Southern Arkansas | | |
| Ware, Andre QB | 90-93Det | 12 | 6'2" | 205 | Houston | | |
| Ware, Derek TE | 92-93Phx 94Arz 94-95Cin | 2 | 6'2" | 255 | Texas A&M, Central St.-Iowa | | 6 |
| Ware, Timmie WR | 86-87SD 89Raid | | 5'10" | 171 | Southern Calif. | | |
| Warne, Jim OT | 87Det | | 6'7" | 315 | Arizona State | | |
| Warner, Curt HB | 83-89Sea 90LA | 2 | 5'11" | 205 | Penn State | | 378 |
| Warnke, David K | 83TB | 5 | 5'11" | 185 | Augsburg | | 1 |
| Warren, Chris HB | 90-95Sea | 23 | 6'2" | 225 | Virginia, Ferrum | | 236 |
| Warren, Don TE | 79-92Was | 2 | 6'4" | 240 | San Diego State | | 42 |
| Warren, Frank DE-NT | 81-89NO 90SL 91-94NO | | 6'4" | 285 | Auburn | 1 | 14 |
| Warren, John K | 83-84Dal | 4 | 6' | 207 | Tennessee | | |
| Warren, Lamont HB | 94-95Ind | 2 | 5'11" | 194 | Colorado | | 6 |
| Warren, Terrence WR | 93-94Sea 95SF | | 6'1" | 200 | Hampton U. | | |
| Warren, Vince WR | 86NYG | | 6' | 180 | San Diego State | | |
| Warren, Xavier DE | 87Pit | | 6'1" | 250 | Tulsa | | |
| Watters, Scott LB | 87Buf | | 6'2" | 230 | Wittenberg | | |
| Washington, Al LB | 81NYJ | | 6'3" | 235 | Ohio State | | |
| Washington, Anthony DB | 81-82Pit 83-84Was | | 6'1" | 204 | California, Fresno State | 8 | |
| Washington, Brian DB | 88Cle 90VR 90-94NYJ 95KC | | 6' | 210 | Nebraska | 24 | 24 |
| Washington, Charles DB | 89Ind 90-91KC 92-94Atl | | 6'1" | 208 | Texas, Cameron | 1 | |
| Washington, Chris LB | 84-88TB 89BL 90Phx | | 6'4" | 231 | Iowa State | 1 | |
| Washington, Chuck DB | 87GB | | 5'11" | 186 | Arkansas | | |
| Washington, Dewayne DB | 94-95Min | | 5'11" | 189 | N. Carolina St. | 4 | 18 |
| Washington, Fred DT | 90Chi | | 6'2" | 277 | Texas Christian | | |
| Dec. 21, 1990 — Died in automobile accident | | | | | | | |
| Washington, James DB | 88-89LA 90-94Dal 95Was | | 6'1" | 201 | U.C.L.A. | 17 | |
| Washington, Joe HB | 77SD 78-80Bal 81-84Was 85Atl | 2 | 5'10" | 180 | Oklahoma | | 186 |
| Washington, John DE-NT | 86-92NYG 92Atl 93NE | | 6'4" | 280 | Oklahoma State | | |
| Washington, Lionel DB | 83-86StL 87-94Raid 95Den | | 6' | 186 | Tulane | 33 | 24 |
| Washington, Marvin DE-DT | 90-95NYJ | | 6'6" | 272 | Texas-El Paso, Idaho | 1 | 2 |
| Washington, Mickey DB | 90-91NE 92Was 93-94Buf 95Jax | | 5'10" | 191 | Texas A&M | 7 | 12 |
| Washington, Mike DB | 76-84TB | | 6'3" | 200 | Alabama | 28 | 24 |
| Washington, Robert OT | 87Pit | | 6'4" | 251 | Alcorn State | | |
| Washington, Ronnie LB | 85Atl 87Raid 89Ind | | 6'1" | 244 | Northeast La. | | |
| Washington, Sam DB | 82-85Pit 85Cin | | 5'8" | 180 | Miss. Valley St. | 7 | 12 |
| Washington, Ted NT-DE-DT | 91-93SF 94Den 95Buf | | 6'4" | 306 | Louisville | 1 | |

| Use Name (Nickname) - Positions | Team by Year | See Section | Hgt. | Wgt. | College | Int | Pts |
|---|---|---|---|---|---|---|---|
| Washington, Tim DB | 82SF | | 5'9" | 184 | California, Fresno State | | |
| Waters, Andre DB | 84-93Phi 94-95Arz | | 5'11" | 189 | Cheyney State | 15 | 12 |
| Waters, Mike FB-TE | 86Phi 87NO 88XJ | | 6'2" | 228 | San Diego State | | 6 |
| Watkins, Bobby DB | 82-88Det | | 5'10" | 184 | SW Texas State | 20 | |
| Watkins, Kendall TE | 95Dal | | 6'1" | 282 | Mississippi State | | |
| Watson, Louis WR | 87Cle | | 5'11" | 175 | Miss. Valley St. | | |
| Watson, Remi WR | 87Cle | | 6' | 174 | Bethune-Cookman | | |
| Watson, Steve WR | 79-87Den 88ZJ | 2 | 6'4" | 195 | Temple | | 216 |
| Watson, Tim DB | 93-95KC 95NYG | | 6'1" | 213 | Howard | | |
| Wattelet, Frank DB | 81-87NO 87-88LA | | 6' | 186 | Kansas | 12 | 12 |
| Watters, Orlando DB | 94Sea | | 5'11" | 173 | Arkansas | 3 | 6 |
| Watters, Ricky HB | 91FJ 92-94SF 95Phi | 2 | 6'1" | 212 | Notre Dame | | 270 |
| Watts, Damon DB | 94-95Ind | | 5'10" | 173 | Indiana | 2 | |
| Watts, Elbert DB | 86GB 87KJ | | 6'1" | 205 | Oklahoma, Southern Calif. | 1 | |
| Watts, Randy DE-DT | 87Dal | | 6'6" | 275 | East Carolina, Catawba | | |
| Watts, Rickey WR | 79-83Chi 84JJ | 2 | 6'1" | 205 | Tulsa | | 54 |
| Watts, Ted DB | 81Oak 82-84Raid 85NYG 87SD | 3 | 6' | 193 | Texas Tech | 5 | 6 |
| Way, Charles FB | 95NYG | | 6' | 236 | Virginia | | 6 |
| Waymer, Dave DB | 80-89NO 90-91SF 92Raid | | 6'1" | 191 | Notre Dame | 48 | 6 |
| Weathers, Clarence WR | 83-84NE 85-88Cle 89Ind 89KC 90-91GB | 23 | 5'9" | 170 | Delaware State | | 102 |
| Weathers, Curtis LB-TE | 79-85Cle 86KJ | | 6'5" | 224 | Mississippi | 1 | |
| Weathers, Robert FB | 82-84NE | 2 | 6'2" | 220 | Arizona State | | 24 |
| Weatherspoon, Chuck FB | 91TB | | 5'7" | 230 | Houston | | |
| Weaver, Emanuel DT | 82Cin 83KJ 85USFL 87Atl | | 6'4" | 262 | South Carolina | | |
| Webb, Chuck FB | 91GB | | 5'9" | 201 | Tennessee | | |
| Webb, Richmond OT | 90-95Mia | | 6'6" | 299 | Texas A&M | | |
| Webster, Elnardo LB | 92Pit | | 6'2" | 243 | Rutgers | | |
| Webster, Kevin C | 87Min | | 6'2" | 260 | Northern Iowa | | |
| Webster, Larry DE-DT | 92-94Mia 95Cle | | 6'5" | 291 | Maryland | | |
| Webster, Mike C-OG | 74-88Pit 89-90KC | | 6'1" | 252 | Wisconsin | | |
| Weddington, Mike LB | 86-90GB | | 6'4" | 245 | Oklahoma | | |
| Weigel, Lee FB | 87GB | | 5'11" | 220 | Wis.-Eau Claire | | |
| Weidner, Bert C-OG | 90-95Mia | | 6'3" | 289 | Kent State | | |
| Weil, Jack K | 86Den 87Was | | 5'11" | 175 | Temple | | |
| Weishuhn, Clayton LB | 82-84NE 85KJ 86NE 87GB | | 6'2" | 220 | Angelo State | | 6 |
| Weissenhofer, Ron LB | 87NO | | 6'3" | 235 | Notre Dame | | |
| Welbourme, Tripp DB | 92Min | | 6' | 205 | Michigan | | |
| Welch, Herb DB | 85-87NYG 88LJ 89Was 90-91Det | | 5'11" | 180 | U.C.L.A. | 7 | |
| Weldon, Casey QB | 92-95TB | 1 | 6'1" | 200 | Florida State | | 6 |
| Wellman, Gary WR | 92-94Hou | 2 | 5'9" | 168 | Southern Calif. | | 6 |
| Wells, Arthur TE | 87TB | | 6'4" | 235 | Grambling | | 6 |
| Wells, Dana NT | 89Cin | | 6' | 270 | Arizona | | |
| Wells, Dean LB | 93-95Sea | | 6'3" | 242 | Kentucky | | |
| Wells, Kent DT | 90NYG | | 6'4" | 295 | Nebraska | | |
| Wells, Mike TE | 87SF | | 6'3" | 233 | San Diego State | | 6 |
| Wells, Mike DE | 94-95Det | | 6'3" | 287 | Iowa | | |
| Wells, Norm OG | 80Dal 81-82KJ | | 6'5" | 261 | Northwestern | | |
| Wellsandt, Doug TE | 90NYJ | | 6'3" | 248 | Washington State | | |
| Welter, Tom OT-OG | 87StL | | 6'5" | 280 | Nebraska | | |
| Wenglikowski, Al LB | 84,87Buf | | 6'1" | 215 | Pittsburgh | | |
| Wenzel, Jeff OT | 87Phi | | 6'7" | 270 | Tulane | | |
| Werner, Greg TE | 89NYJ | | 6'4" | 236 | DePauw | | |
| Wersching, Ray K | 73-76SD 77-87SF | 5 | 5'11" | 213 | California | | 1122 |
| West, Derek OT | 95Ind | | 6'8" | 303 | Colorado | | |
| West, Ed TE | 84-94GB 95Phi | 2 | 6'1" | 244 | Auburn | | 158 |
| West, Jeff TE-K | 75StL 76-79SD 81-85Sea | 4 | 6'3" | 212 | Cincinnati | | |
| West, Ronnie WR | 92Min 93LJ | | 6'1" | 215 | Valdosta State, Pittsburg State | | |
| West, Troy DB | 87Phi | | 6'1" | 205 | Southern Calif. | 1 | |
| Westbrook, Joey WR | 95Was | 2 | 6'3" | 215 | Colorado | | 12 |
| Wester, Cleve HB | 87Det | 2 | 5'8" | 188 | Concordia (Minn.) | | |
| Weston, Jeff OT-DT | 79-82NYG | | 6'5" | 259 | Notre Dame | | |
| Weston, Rhondy DE | 89TB 90KJ | | 6'5" | 275 | Florida | | |
| Wetnight, Ryan TE | 93-95Chi | 2 | 6'2" | 236 | Stanford | | 24 |
| Wetzel, Marty LB | 81NYJ | | 6'3" | 235 | Tulane | | |
| Wetzel, Ron TE | 83KC 84-85USFL | | 6'5" | 242 | Arizona State | | |
| Wheat, Warren OG | 89,91Sea | | 6'6" | 274 | Brigham Young | | |
| Wheatley, Tyrone HB | 95NYG | 2 | 6' | 227 | Michigan | | 18 |
| Wheeler, Dwight OT-C-OG | 78-83NE 84,87Raid 87SD 88Raid | | 6'3" | 266 | Tennessee State | | |
| Wheeler, Leonard DB | 92-93Cin 94BW 95Cin | | 5'11" | 189 | Mississippi, Troy State | 1 | |
| Wheeler, Mark TE | 87Det | | 6'2" | 232 | Kentucky | | |
| Wheeler, Mark DT-NT | 92-95TB | | 6'2" | 282 | Texas A&M | | |
| Wheeler, Ron TE | 87Raid | | 6'5" | 235 | Washington | | |
| Whigham, Larry DB | 94-95NE | | 6'2" | 202 | Northeast La. | 1 | |
| Whisenhunt, Ken TE | 85-88Atl 89LJ 90Was 91-92NYJ | 2 | 6'3" | 237 | Georgia Tech | | 30 |
| Whitaker, Bill DB | 81-82GB 83-84StL | | 6' | 182 | Missouri | | |
| Whitaker, Danta TE-WR | 90KC 92Min 93Chi | 2 | 6'4" | 248 | Miss. Valley St. | | 6 |
| White, Adrian DB | 87-89NYG 90KJ 91NYG 92GB 93NE | | 6' | 200 | Southern Illinois, Florida | 3 | |
| White, Alberto DE | 94Raid 95StL | | 6'3" | 245 | Texas Southern | | |
| White, Bob C-OG | 87-89Dal 90KJ | | 6'5" | 272 | Rhode Island | | |
| White, Brad NT-DT | 81-83TB 84-85Ind 87Min | | 6'2" | 256 | Tennessee | | |
| White, Charles HB | 80-82Cle 83BN 84Cle 85-88LA | 23 | 5'10" | 188 | Southern Calif. | | 144 |
| White, Chris DB | 87Sea | | 6'3" | 200 | Tennessee | | |
| White, Craig WR | 84Buf | | 6'1" | 194 | Missouri | | |
| White, Danny QB | 76-88Dal | 12 4 | 6'2" | 194 | Arizona State | | 60 |
| White, David LB | 93NE 95Buf | | 6'2" | 235 | Nebraska | 1 | |
| White, Dwayne OG | 90-94NYJ 95StL | | 6'2" | 312 | Alcorn State | | |
| White, Gerald FB | 87Dal | | 5'11" | 223 | Michigan | | |
| White, Lawrence WR | 87Chi | | 6'2" | 187 | Dana | | |
| White, Leon LB | 86-91Cin 91-93LA | | 6'3" | 240 | Brigham Young | 4 | 8 |
| White, Lorenzo HB | 88-94Hou 95Cle | 23 | 5'11" | 218 | Michigan State | | 220 |
| White, Lyman LB | 81-82Atl | | 6' | 217 | Louisiana State | | |
| White, Mike DE-DT-NT | 79-80Cin 81-82Sea | | 6'5" | 266 | Albany State (Ga.) | | |
| White, Mike | HC95Oak | | | | California | | |
| White, Randy DT-LB-DE | 75-88Dal | | 6'4" | 257 | Maryland | 1 | |
| White, Reggie DE-DT | 84-85USFL 85-92Phi 93-95GB | | 6'5" | 289 | Tennessee | 2 | 12 |
| White, Reggie DT-NT | 92-95SD | | 6'4" | 299 | N. Carolina A&T | | |
| White, Robb DE-NT | 88-89NYG 90TB | | 6'4" | 270 | South Dakota | | |
| White, Robert DB | 87Hou | | 6'2" | 180 | Lamar | | |
| White, Russell HB | 93LA | | 5'11" | 216 | California | | |
| White, Sammy WR | 76-85Min | 2 | 5'11" | 192 | Grambling | | 300 |
| White, Sheldon DB | 88-89NYG 90-92Det 93Cin | | 5'11" | 188 | Miami-Ohio | 11 | 6 |
| White, Stan QB | 94-95NYG | | 6'2" | 202 | Auburn | | |
| White, William DB | 88-93Det 94-95KC | | 5'10" | 196 | Ohio State | 17 | 18 |

| Use Name (Nickname) - Positions | Team by Year | See Section | Hgt. | Wgt. | College | Int | Pts |
|---|---|---|---|---|---|---|---|
| Whited, Mike OT | 80Det | | 6'4" | 250 | U. of Pacific | | |
| Whitfield, Bob OT | 92-95Atl | | 6'5" | 298 | Stanford | | |
| Whitehurst, David QB | 77-83GB 84KC | 12 | 6'2" | 204 | Furman | | 42 |
| Whitley, Curtis C | 92-94SD 95Car | | 6'1" | 291 | Clemson | | |
| Whitley, Wilson DT-NT | 77-82Cin | | 6'3" | 265 | Houston | 1 | |
| Whitmore, David DB | 90-91NYG 92SF 93-94KC 95Phi | | 6' | 235 | S.F. Austin State | 2 | |
| Whitten, Bobby OG | 81Cin | | 6'3" | 265 | Kansas | | |
| Whitten, Todd QB | 87NE | | 6' | 185 | S.F. Austin State | | |
| Whittington, Art HB | 78-81Oak 82Buf 83-84USFL | 23 | 5'11" | 182 | S.M.U. | | 96 |
| Whittington, Bernard DE | 94-95Ind | | 6'6" | 268 | Indiana | | |
| Whittingham, Cary LB | 87LA | | 6'2" | 230 | Brigham Young | | |
| Whittingham, Kyle LB | 87LA | | 6' | 232 | Brigham Young | | |
| Whittington, Mike LB | 80-83NYG 84-85USFL | | 6'2" | 220 | Notre Dame | | |
| Whitwell, Mike WR-DB | 82-83Cle 84KJ | | 6' | 175 | Texas A&M | 3 | |
| Wichard, Murray NT-DE | 87NE | | 6'2" | 260 | Frostburg State | | |
| Widell, Dave OT-OG-C | 88-89Dal 90-94Den 95Jax | | 6'7" | 299 | Boston College | | |
| Widell, Doug OG | 89-92Den 93GB 94-95Det | | 6'4" | 285 | Boston College | | |
| Widmer, Corey DT-LB | 92-95NYG | | 6'3" | 256 | Montana State | | |
| Wiegand, Eric C | 87Atl | | 6'2" | 260 | Missouri-Rolla | | |
| Wiegert, Zach OT | 95StL | | 6'4" | 305 | Nebraska | | |
| Wilburn, Barry DB | 86-89Was 92Cle 95Phi | | 6'3" | 186 | Mississippi | 19 | 6 |
| Wilburn, Steve DE | 87NE | | 6'4" | 266 | Illinois State | | |
| Wilcher, Mike LB | 83-90LA 91SD | | 6'3" | 238 | North Carolina | 4 | 6 |
| Wilcots, Solomon DB | 87-90Cin 91Min 92Pit | | 5'11" | 189 | Colorado | 2 | |
| Wilder, James FB-HB | 81-89TB 90Was 90Det | 2 | 6'3" | 224 | Missouri | | 282 |
| Wiley, Charles NT | 87Sea | | 6'2" | 268 | Nevada-Las Vegas | | |
| Wilhelm, Erik QB | 89-91,93-95Cin 95NYJ | 1 | 6'3" | 213 | Oregon State | | |
| Wilkerson, Bruce OG-OT | 87-94Raid 95Jax | | 6'5" | 291 | Tennessee | | |
| Wilkerson, Daryl DE | 81Bal 83-85USFL | | 6'4" | 255 | Houston | | |
| Wilkerson, Eric HB-WR | 89Pit | | 5'9" | 185 | Kent State | | |
| Wilkes, Reggie LB | 78-85Phi 86-87Atl | | 6'4" | 235 | Georgia Tech | 8 | 1 |
| Wilkins, David LB | 92SF | | 6'4" | 240 | Eastern Kentucky | | |
| Wilkins, Gabe DE-DT | 94-95GB | | 6'5" | 300 | Gardner-Webb | | |
| Wilkins, Gary FB-TE | 86-87Buf 88-91Atl | 2 | 6'1" | 235 | Georgia Tech | | 36 |
| Wilkins, Jeff K | 94Phi 95SF | 5 | 6'1" | 180 | Youngstown State | | 63 |
| Wilkinson, Dan DT | 94-95Cin | | 6'5" | 313 | Ohio State | | |
| Wilkinson, Jerry DE | 79LA 80Cle 80SF 83USFL | | 6'9" | 248 | Oregon State | | |
| Wilks, Jim DE-NT | 81-93NO | | 6'5" | 269 | California, San Diego State | | |
| Willhite, Gerald FB-HB | 82-88Den | 23 | 5'10" | 200 | San Jose State | | 138 |
| Willhite, Kevin HB | 87GB | 2 | 5'11" | 208 | Oregon | | |
| Williams, Aeneas DB | 91-93Phx 94-95Arz | | 5'10" | 188 | Southern | 26 | 30 |
| Williams, Al WR | 87SD | 2 | 5'10" | 180 | Nevada-Reno | | 6 |
| Williams, Albert LB | 87Pit | | 6'3" | 229 | Texas-El Paso | | |
| Williams, Alfred LB-DE | 91-94Cin 95SF | | 6'6" | 250 | Colorado | | 4 |
| Williams, Allen HB | 95Det | | 5'10" | 205 | Maryland | | |
| Williams, Alonzo HB | 87LA | | 5'9" | 190 | Mesa | | |
| Williams, Ben DE-NT | 76-85Buf | | 6'3" | 251 | Mississippi | 2 | 2 |
| Williams, Bernard OT | 94Phi 95SL | | 6'8" | 317 | Georgia | | |
| Williams, Brent DE-NT | 86-93NE 94-95Sea | | 6'3" | 278 | Toledo | | 12 |
| Williams, Brian TE | 82NE 84-85USFL | | 6'5" | 240 | Southern U. | | |
| Williams, Brian OG-C | 89-95NYG | | 6'5" | 300 | Minnesota | | |
| Williams, Brian LB | 95GB | | 6'2" | 240 | Southern Calif. | | |
| Williams, Brooks TE | 78-81NO 81-82Chi 83NE | 2 | 6'4" | 226 | North Carolina | | 12 |
| Williams, Byron WR | 83-85NYG | 2 | 6'2" | 182 | Texas-Arlington | | 72 |
| Williams, Calvin WR | 90-95Phi | 2 | 5'11" | 181 | Purdue | | 206 |
| Williams, Charlie DB | 95Dal | | 6' | 189 | Bowling Green | | |
| Williams, Chris DB | 82-83Buf | | 6' | 197 | Louisiana Tech | 3 | |
| Williams, Chris NT | 91Phx | | 6'3" | 304 | American Inter. | | |
| Williams, Clarence HB-FB | 93Cle | | 6'2" | 240 | Washington State | | |
| Williams, Dan DE | 93-95Den | | 6'4" | 290 | Tennessee State, Toledo | 1 | |
| Williams, Darryl DB | 92-95Cin | | 6' | 191 | Miami (Fla.) | 9 | 8 |
| Williams, David WR | 86TB 87Raid | | 6'3" | 190 | Illinois | | |
| Williams, David OT | 89-95Hou | | 6'5" | 292 | Florida | | |
| Williams, Demise DB | 87Raid | | 6'1" | 225 | Oklahoma | | |
| Williams, Derwin WR | 85-87NE | 2 | 6'1" | 180 | New Mexico | | |
| Williams, Dokie WR | 83-87Raid | 23 | 5'11" | 180 | U.C.L.A. | | 150 |
| Williams, Doug QB | 78-82TB 84-85USFL 86-89Was | 12 | 6'4" | 218 | Grambling | | 90 |
| Williams, Doug OT-OG | 86-87Hou 88LJ | | 6'5" | 286 | Texas A&M | | |
| Williams, Ed LB | 84-87NE 88-89KJ 90NE | | 6'4" | 244 | Texas | 1 | |
| Williams, Eric LB | 77-81StL 82-83LA 84SD 85USFL | | 6'2" | 227 | Southern Calif. | 5 | |
| Williams, Eric T. DB | 83-86Pit 87Det | | 6'1" | 188 | N. Carolina State | 10 | |
| Williams, Eric DT-NT-DT | 84-89Det 90-93Was | | 6'4" | 282 | Washington State | | |
| Williams, Erik OT | 91-95Dal | | 6'6" | 321 | Central St.-Ohio | | |
| Williams, Eugene LB | 82-83Sea | | 6'1" | 220 | Texas | 1 | |
| Williams, Gardner DB | 84Det | | 6'2" | 199 | St. Mary's | | |
| Williams, Gary WR | 84Cin | | 6'2" | 215 | Ohio State | | |
| Williams, Gene OG-OT | 91-92Mia 93-94Cle 95Atl | | 6'2" | 308 | Iowa State | | |
| Williams, Gerald NT-DE-DT | 86-94Pit 95Car | | 6'3" | 285 | Auburn | | 6 |
| Williams, Greg DB | 82-85Was | | 5'11" | 185 | Mississippi State | 2 | |
| Williams, Harvey HB | 91-93KC 94Raid 95Oak | 23 | 6'2" | 226 | Louisiana State | | 122 |
| Williams, Henry (Gizmo) WR | 89Phi | 3 | 5'6" | 185 | East Carolina | | |
| Williams, Henry DB | 79Oak 81CFL 83LA 83SD 85USFL | | 5'10" | 180 | San Diego State | 3 | |
| Williams, Herb DB | 80SF 81-82StL 84USFL | | 6' | 199 | Southern U. | | |
| Williams, James FB | 87Sea | | 5'10" | 210 | Fresno State | | |
| Williams, James LB | 90-94NO 95Jax | | 6' | 230 | Mississippi State | 4 | 6 |
| Williams, James (J.D.) DB | 90-93Buf 94Arz | | 5'10" | 174 | Fresno State | 11 | 6 |
| Williams, James (Big Cat) OT-DE | 91-95Chi | | 6'7" | 320 | Cheyney | | |
| Williams, Jamie TE | 83StL 84TB 84-88Hou 89-93SF 94Raid | 2 | 6'4" | 243 | Nebraska | | 66 |
| Williams, Jarvis DB | 88-93Mia 94NYG | | 5'11" | 196 | Florida | 16 | 6 |
| Williams, Jay DT | 95StL | | 6'3" | 270 | Wake Forest | | |
| Williams, Jerrol LB | 89-92Pit 93SD 94KC | | 6'5" | 240 | Purdue | 1 | 6 |
| Williams, Jimmy LB | 82-90Det 90-91Min 92-93TB | | 6'3" | 228 | Nebraska | 11 | 6 |
| Williams, Joe LB | 87Pit | | 6'4" | 237 | Grambling | | |
| Williams, Joel LB | 79-82Atl 83-85Phi 86-89Atl | | 6'1" | 222 | Wis.-La Crosse | 5 | 20 |
| Williams, Joel TE | 87Mia | | 6'3" | 242 | Notre Dame | | |
| Williams, John FB | 83-85USFL 85Dal 85Sea 86NO 87Ind | | 5'11" | 213 | Wisconsin | | |
| Williams, John L. FB | 86-93Sea 94-95Pit | 2 | 5'11" | 228 | Florida | | 222 |
| Williams, Jonathan HB | 84NE 85KJ | | 5'9" | 205 | Penn State | | |
| Williams, Keith WR-HB | 86Atl 87KJ | | 5'10" | 173 | SW Missouri St. | | 6 |
| Williams, Kendall DB | 83Bal | | 5'9" | 189 | Arizona State | 1 | |
| Williams, Kevin WR | 81Bal 83-85USFL | | 5'8" | 164 | Southern Calif. | | |
| Williams, Kevin DB | 85Was 86Buf 88Was | | 5'9" | 170 | Iowa State | | |
| Williams, Kevin WR | 93-95Dal | 23 | 5'9" | 194 | Miami (Fla.) | | 60 |
| Williams, Larry OG-C | 86-88Cle 89SJ 91NO 92NE | | 6'5" | 290 | Notre Dame | | |
| Williams, Lee DE-DT | 84USFL 84-90SD 91-93Hou | | 6'6" | 269 | Bethune-Cookman | 1 | 2 |

| Use Name (Nickname) - Positions | Team by Year | See Section | Hgt. | Wgt. | College | Int | Pts |
|---|---|---|---|---|---|---|---|
| Williams, Leonard HB | 87Buf | | 6' | 205 | Western Carolina | | |
| Williams, Lester NT-DE | 82-85NE 86SD 87Sea | | 6'3" | 275 | Miami (Fla.) | | |
| Williams, Mark LB | 94GB 95Jax | | 6'3" | 242 | Ohio State | | |
| Williams, Marvin TE | 87Was | | 6'3" | 235 | Fullerton State | | |
| Williams, Michael FB | 83-84Phi 87Atl | 2 | 6'2" | 220 | Mississippi Coll. | | |
| Williams, Michael DB | 95SF | | 5'10" | 185 | U.C.L.A. | | |
| Williams, Mike FB-TE | 79-81KC | 2 | 6'3" | 222 | New Mexico | | 24 |
| Williams, Mike TE | 82-84Was | | 6'4" | 249 | Alabama A&M | | |
| Williams, Mike WR | 89Det 91-95Mia | 23 | 5'10" | 177 | Northeastern | | |
| Williams, Newton HB-FB | 82SF 83Bal | | 5'10" | 204 | Arizona State | | |
| Williams, Oliver WR | 83-85USFL 85Ind 87Hou | 2 | 6'3" | 194 | Illinois | | 12 |
| Williams, Perry DB | 87NE | | 6'1" | 200 | Clemson | 1 | |
| Williams, Perry DB | 84-93NYG | | 6'2" | 203 | N. Carolina State | 18 | |
| Williams, Ray WR | 80Det 81KJ | 23 | 5'9" | 170 | Washington State | | 18 |
| Williams, Ray DB | 87Pit | | 5'11" | 180 | Rhode Island | 1 | |
| Williams, Ralph OT-OG | 82-83Hou 84-85USFL 85-86NO | | 6'3" | 280 | Southern U. | | |
| Williams, Reggie LB | 76-89Cin | | 6'1" | 228 | Dartmouth | 16 | 24 |
| Williams, Richard HB | 84Atl | | 6' | 205 | Memphis State | | |
| Williams, Ricky DB | 85,87Raid | | 6'1" | 195 | Langston | | |
| Williams, Robert DB | 84Pit | | 5'11" | 202 | Eastern Illinois | | |
| Williams, Robert DB | 87-92Dal | | 5'10" | 188 | Baylor | 4 | 12 |
| Williams, Ronnie TE | 91,93-95Mia | | 6'3" | 261 | Oklahoma State | | |
| Williams, Scott FB | 86-88Det | 2 | 6'2" | 234 | Georgia | | 24 |
| Williams, Sherman HB | 95Dal | 2 | 5'8" | 191 | Alabama | | 6 |
| Williams, Terry DB | 88-89NYJ 90KJ | | 5'11" | 197 | Bethune-Cookman | | |
| Williams, Toby DE-NT | 83-88NE | | 6'3" | 264 | Nebraska | | |
| Williams, Tyrone WR | 93Dal | | 6'5" | 220 | Western Ontario | | |
| Williams, Van HB | 83-85Buf 87NYG | 23 | 6' | 210 | East Tennessee St., Carson-Newman | | 6 |
| Williams, Vaughn DB | 84Ind | | 6'2" | 193 | Stanford | | |
| Williams, Vince FB | 82-83SF 85USFL | 2 | 6' | 231 | Oregon | | |
| Williams, Wally C-OG | 93-95Cle | | 6'2" | 300 | Florida A&M | | |
| Williams, Walt DB | 77-80Det 81-82Min 82-83Chi | | 6' | 185 | Ashland, New Mexico State | 4 | 2 |
| Williams, Warren HB | 88-92Pit 93Ind | 2 | 6' | 209 | Miami (Fla.) | | 60 |
| Williams, Willie OT | 91Phx 92KJ 94NO | | 6'6" | 300 | Louisiana State | | 6 |
| Williams, Willie DB | 93-95Pit | | 5'9" | 183 | Western Carolina | 7 | 6 |
| Williamson, Carlton DB | 81-87SF 88KJ | | 6' | 204 | Pittsburgh | 17 | 6 |
| Williamson, Greg DB | 87LA | | 5'11" | 185 | Fresno State | 1 | |
| Williamson, Richard | HC90-91TB | | | | Alabama | | |
| Willig, Matt OT-OG | 93-95NYJ | | 6'8" | 309 | Southern Calif. | | |
| Willis, Chester HB | 81Oak 82-84Raid | 2 | 5'11" | 196 | Auburn | | 6 |
| Willis, Jamal HB | 95SF | | 6'2" | 218 | Brigham Young | | |
| Willis, James LB | 93-94GB 95Phi | | 6'2" | 235 | Auburn | 2 | |
| Willis, Keith DE-NT-DT | 82-87Pit 88ZJ 89-91Pit 92Buf 93Was 93NYJ | | 6'1" | 260 | Northwestern | 1 | |
| Willis, Ken K | 90-91Dal 92TB 92NYG | 5 | 5'11" | 189 | Kentucky | | 255 |
| Willis, Mitch NT | 85-88Raid 88Atl 90Dal | | 6'8" | 278 | S.M.U. | | |
| Willis, Peter Tom QB | 90-92Chi | 1 | 6'2" | 188 | Florida State | | |
| Wills, Ladell LB | 87NYJ | | 6'3" | 240 | Jackson State | | |
| Wilmer, Ray DB | 84Sea | | 6'2" | 190 | Colorado | | |
| Wilmot, Trevor LB | 95Ind | | 6'2" | 215 | Indiana | | |
| Wilmsmeyer, Klaus K | 92-94SF 95NO | 4 | 6'1" | 210 | Louisville | | |
| Wilner, Jeff TE | 94-95GB | | 6'5" | 250 | Wesleyan (Conn.) | | |
| Wilson, Bobby DT | 91-94Was 95XJ | | 6'2" | 293 | Michigan State | | |
| Wilson, Bernard DT | 93-94TB 94-95Arz | | 6'2" | 295 | Tennessee State | | |
| Wilson, Brenard DB | 79-87Phi 87Atl | | 6' | 178 | Vanderbilt | 17 | |
| Wilson, Brett FB | 87Min | | 6' | 220 | Illinois | | |
| Wilson, Charles WR | 90-91GB 92-94TB 95NYJ | 23 | 5'9" | 174 | Memphis State | | 72 |
| Wilson, Darrell DB | 81NE | | 5'11" | 180 | Connecticut | | |
| Wilson, Darryal WR | 83NE 84KJ | | 6' | 182 | Tennessee | | |
| Wilson, Dave QB | 81NO 82KJ 83-89NO | 12 | 6'3" | 206 | Illinois | | 12 |
| Wilson, David DB | 92NE 92Min | | 5'10" | 192 | California | | |
| Wilson, Don DB | 84-85Buf | 3 | 6'2" | 190 | N. Carolina State | 2 | 6 |
| Wilson, Earl DE | 85-87SD | | 6'4" | 276 | Kentucky | | |
| Wilson, Eric LB | 85Buf 87Was | | 6'1" | 246 | Maryland | | |
| Wilson, Frank TE-FB | 82Pit | | 6'2" | 233 | Rice | | |
| Wilson, J.C. DB | 78-83Hou | | 6' | 178 | Tampa, Pittsburgh | 11 | 6 |
| Wilson, Karl DE-LB-DT | 87-88SD 89Phx 90Mia 91LA 92-93NYJ 93Mia 93SF 94TB 95Buf | | 6'4" | 273 | Louisiana State | | 2 |
| Wilson, Marc QB | 80-81Oak 82-87Raid 89-90NE | 12 | 6'6" | 207 | Brigham Young | | 30 |
| Wilson, Marcus HB | 91Raid 92-95GB | | 6'1" | 200 | Virginia | | |
| Wilson, Mike OT | 78-85Cin 86-89Sea | | 6'5" | 275 | Georgia | | |
| Wilson, Mike WR-HB | 81-90SF | 2 | 6'3" | 213 | Washington State | | 90 |
| Wilson, Otis LB | 80-87Chi 88KJ 89Raid | | 6'2" | 227 | Syracuse, Louisville | 10 | 14 |
| Wilson, Ray DB | 94NO 94GB | | 6'1" | 204 | New Mexico | | |
| Wilson, Robert FB | 91TB 94Dal 94-95Mia | 2 | 6' | 240 | Texas A&M | | 12 |
| Wilson, Stanley FB-HB | 83-84,86,88Cin 85,87,89SL | 2 | 5'10" | 210 | Oklahoma | | 78 |
| Wilson, Steve C-OG-OT | 76-85TB | | 6'3" | 267 | Georgia | | |
| Wilson, Steve DB-WR | 79-81Dal 82-88Den | 3 | 5'10" | 194 | Howard | 22 | 6 |
| Wilson, Ted WR | 87Was | | 5'9" | 170 | Central Florida | | 12 |
| Wilson, Tim FB | 77-82Hou 83-84NO | 2 | 6'3" | 226 | Maryland | | 54 |
| Wilson, Troy DB | 87Cle | | 5'10" | 170 | Notre Dame | 1 | |
| Wilson, Troy DE | 93-94SF 95Den | | 6'4" | 235 | Pittsburg State | | |
| Wilson, Wade QB | 81-91Min 91-92Atl 93-94NO 95Dal | 12 | 6'3" | 211 | East Texas State | | 54 |
| Wilson, Walter WR | 90SD | 2 | 5'10" | 185 | East Carolina | | |
| Wilson, Wayne FB-HB | 79-85NO 86Min 86NO 87Was | 23 | 6'3" | 215 | Shepherd | | 192 |
| Wimberly, Derek DE | 87Mia | | 6'4" | 270 | Purdue | | |
| Wimmer, Gary LB | 83Sea | | 6'2" | 225 | Stanford | | |
| Winans, Tydus WR | 94-95Was | 2 | 5'11" | 180 | Fresno State | | 14 |
| Winder, Sammy HB-FB | 82-90Den | 2 | 5'11" | 203 | Southern Miss. | | 288 |
| Windham, David LB | 87Was | | 6'2" | 240 | Jackson State | | |
| Wingate, Leonard DE | 87Atl | | 6'3" | 265 | S. Carolina State | | |
| Wingle, Blake OG | 83-85Pit 85GB 87Cle | | 6'2" | 265 | Cal. Poly.-S.L.O., U.C.L.A. | | |
| Wingo, Rich LB | 79GB 80XJ 81-84GB | | 6'1" | 230 | Alabama | 4 | 1 |
| Winn, Bryant LB | 87Den | | 6'4" | 231 | Houston | | |
| Winslow, George K | 87Cle 89NO | 4 | 6'4" | 203 | Villanova | | |
| Winslow, Kellen TE | 79-87SD | 2 | 6'5" | 250 | Missouri | | 270 |
| Winston, DeMond LB | 90NO 91KJ 92-94NO | | 6'2" | 239 | Vanderbilt | | |
| Winston, Dennis (Dirt) LB | 77-81Pit 82-85NO 85-86Pit | | 6' | 230 | Arkansas | 13 | ,24 |
| Winter, Blaise DE-NT | 84Ind 85SJ 86-87SD 88-90GB 92-94SD | | 6'3" | 279 | Syracuse | | |
| Winters, Chet HB | 83GB | | 5'11" | 204 | Oklahoma | | |
| Winters, Frank C-OG | 87-88Cle 89NYG 90-91KC 92-95GB | | 6'3" | 288 | Western Illinois | | |
| Wisdom, Terrence OG-C | 95NYJ | | 6'4" | 300 | Syracuse | | |
| Wise, Mike DE-DT | 86-90Raid 91Cle | | 6'7" | 271 | Cal.-Davis | | |
| Wiska, Jeff OG | 84-85USFL 86Cle 87Mia | | 6'3" | 263 | Michigan State | | |
| Wisniewski, Leo NT | 82-83Bal 84Ind 85KJ | | 6'1" | 262 | Penn State | | |
| Wisniewski, Steve OG | 89-94Raid 95Oak | | 6'4" | 288 | Penn State | | |
| Witherspoon, Derrick HB | 95Phi | | 5'10" | 196 | Clemson | | 6 |
| Withycombe, Mike OG-OT | 88-89NYJ 91Pit 91-92Cin | | 6'5" | 295 | Fresno State | | |
| Witkowski, John QB | 84Det 86-87Hou 88Det | 1 | 6'1 | 201 | Columbia | | |
| Witte, Mark TE | 83-85TB 87Det | | 6'3" | 236 | North Texas | | |
| Witteck, Mike LB | 87NYJ | | 6'2" | 225 | Northwestern | | |
| Woerner, Scott DB | 81Atl 83-85USFL 87NO | 3 | 6' | 190 | Georgia | | |
| Wohlabaugh, Dave C | 95NE | | 6'3" | 304 | Syracuse | | |
| Wojciechowski, John OG-OT | 87-93Chi | | 6'4" | 271 | Michigan State | | |
| Wolden, Al FB | 87Chi | | 6'3" | 232 | Bemidji State | | |
| Wolf, Joe OG-OT | 89-93Phx 94-95Arz | | 6'5" | 290 | Boston College | | |
| Wolfley, Craig OG-OT | 80-89Pit 90-91Min | | 6'1" | 269 | Syracuse | | |
| Wolfley, Ron FB | 85-87StL 88-91Phx 92-93Cle 95StL | 2 | 6' | 224 | West Virginia | | 24 |
| Wolford, Will OT-OG | 86-92Buf 93-95Ind | | 6'5" | 291 | Vanderbilt | | |
| Womack, Jeff HB | 87Min | | 5'9" | 188 | Memphis State | | 6 |
| Wonsley, George HB-FB | 84-88Ind 89NE | 2 | 5'10" | 218 | Mississippi State | | 54 |
| Wonsley, Nathan HB | 86TB 87ZJ | 2 | 5'10" | 190 | Mississippi | | 18 |
| Wonsley, Otis FB-HB | 81-85Was | 2 | 5'10" | 212 | Alcorn State | | 30 |
| Wood, Mike K | 78Min 78-79StL 79-80SD 81-82Bal 83JJ | 45 | 5'11" | 199 | SE Missouri St. | | 156 |
| Wood, Richard (Batman) LB | 75NYJ 76-84TB 85USFL | | 6'2" | 224 | Southern Calif. | 9 | 18 |
| Woodall, Lee LB | 94-95SF | | 6' | 220 | West Chester St. | 2 | 6 |
| Woodard, Ken LB | 82-86Den 87Pit 88-89SD | | 6'1" | 218 | Tuskegee | 3 | 12 |
| Woodard, Marc LB | 94-95Phi | | 6' | 236 | Mississippi State | | |
| Woodard, Ray DE | 87Den 87KC | | 6'6" | 290 | Texas | | |
| Woodberry, Dennis DB | 86Atl 87-88Was | | 5'10" | 183 | Southern Arkansas | 2 | |
| Wooden, Terry LB | 90-95Sea | | 6'3" | 236 | Syracuse | 5 | 6 |
| Woodley, David QB | 80-83Mia 84-85Pit | 12 | 6'2" | 204 | Louisiana State | | 72 |
| Woodring, John LB | 81-85NYJ | | 6'2" | 232 | Brown | | |
| Woodruff, Dwayne DB | 79-85Pit 86KJ 87-90Pit | | 5'11" | 195 | Louisville | 37 | 30 |
| Woodruff, Tony WR | 82-84Phi | 2 | 6' | 178 | Fresno State | | 30 |
| Woods, Carl HB | 87NE | | 5'11" | 200 | Vanderbilt | | 6 |
| Woods, Chris WR | 84-86CFL 87-88Raid 89Den | 3 | 5'11" | 190 | Auburn | | |
| Woods, Ickey FB-HB | 88-91Cin | 2 | 6'2" | 232 | Nevada-Las Vegas | | 162 |
| Woods, Jerry DB | 89Det 90GB | | 5'10" | 187 | Northern Michigan | | |
| Woods, Pete QB | 80Mia | | 6'3" | 214 | Missouri | | |
| Woods, Rick DB | 82-86Pit 87TB | 3 | 6' | 195 | Boise State | 13 | 6 |
| Woods, Rob OT | 91Cle | | 6'5" | 295 | Eastern Washington, Cal.-Santa Barbara, Arizona | | |
| Woods, Tony LB-DE | 87-92Sea 93LA 94-95Was | | 6'4" | 268 | Pittsburgh | | 6 |
| Woods, Tony DE-DT | 89Chi | | 6'4" | 274 | Oklahoma | | |
| Woodside, Keith HB | 88-91GB | 2 | 5'11" | 203 | Texas A&M | | 48 |
| Woodson, Darren DB | 92-95Dal | | 6'1" | 215 | Arizona State | 7 | 12 |
| Woodson, Rod DB | 87-95Pit | 3 | 6' | 198 | Purdue | 31 | 48 |
| Woolf, Scott QB | 87Raid | | 6'1" | 190 | Mt. Union | | |
| Woolford, Donnell DB | 89-95Chi | | 5'9" | 187 | Clemson | 26 | |
| Woolfolk, Butch FB-HB | 82-84NYG 85-86Hou 87-88Det | 23 | 6'1" | 210 | Michigan | | 96 |
| Woolford, Gary DB | 80NYG | | 6' | 182 | Florida State | 2 | |
| Wooten, Mike C | 87Was | | 6'3" | 260 | V.M.I. | | |
| Wooten, Ron OG | 82-88NE | | 6'4" | 274 | North Carolina | | |
| Wooten, Tito DB | 94-95NYG | | 6' | 186 | Northeast La. | 1 | 6 |
| Word, Barry FB-HB | 87-88NO 90-92KC 93Min 94Arz | 2 | 6'2" | 240 | Virginia | | 96 |
| Workman, Vince HB | 89-92GB 93-94TB 95Car 95Ind | 23 | 5'10" | 193 | Ohio State | | 120 |
| Worley, Tim HB | 89-91Pit 92SL 93Pit 93-94Chi | 2 | 6'2" | 228 | Georgia | | 42 |
| Wortham, Barron LB | 94-95Hou | | 5'11" | 244 | Texas-El Paso | | |
| Worthen, Naz WR | 89-90KC | 3 | 5'8" | 177 | N. Carolina State | | |
| Wren, Darryl DB | 93-94NE | | 6' | 188 | Pittsburg State | 3 | |
| Wright, Adrian FB | 87TB | 2 | 6'1" | 230 | Virginia Union | | 6 |
| Wright, Alexander WR | 90-92Dal 92-94Raid 95StL | 23 | 6' | 189 | Auburn | | 72 |
| Wright, Alvin NT-DE-DT | 86-92LA 92Cle | | 6'2" | 270 | Jacksonville St. | | |
| Wright, Brad QB | 82Dal | | 6'2" | 209 | New Mexico | | |
| Wright, Charles DB | 87StL 88TB 88Dal | | 5'9" | 178 | Tulsa | | |
| Wright, Dana HB | 87Cin | | 6'1" | 219 | Kent State, Findlay | | |
| Wright, Eric DB | 81-90SF | | 6'1" | 183 | Missouri | 18 | 12 |
| Wright, Eric WR | 92Chi | | 6' | 196 | S.F. Austin State | | |
| Wright, Felix DB | 85-90Cle 91-92Min | | 6'2" | 190 | Drake | 28 | 18 |
| Wright, James TE | 78Atl 79KJ 80-85Den | 2 | 6'3" | 240 | Texas Christian | | 24 |
| Wright, Jeff NT | 88-94Buf | | 6'2" | 270 | Tulsa, Central Missouri St. | 1 | |
| Wright, Johnnie FB | 82Bal 84USFL | | 6'2" | 210 | South Carolina | | |
| Wright, Louis DB | 75-86Den | | 6'2" | 198 | Arizona State, San Jose State | 26 | 24 |
| Wright, Randy QB | 84-88GB | 12 | 6'2" | 200 | Wisconsin | | 18 |
| Wright, Steve OT-OG-TE | 81-82Dal 83Bal 84Ind 85USFL 87-92Raid 93KJ | | 6'6" | 269 | Northern Iowa | | |
| Wright, Sylvester LB | 95Phi | | 6'2" | 258 | Kansas | | |
| Wright, Terry DB | 87-88Ind | | 6' | 195 | Temple | | |
| Wright, Toby DB | 94LA 95StL | | 5'11" | 203 | Nebraska | 6 | 12 |
| Wright, Willie TE | 92Phx | | 6'4" | 240 | Wyoming | | |
| Wrightman, Tim TE | 83-84USFL 85-86Chi 87KJ | 2 | 6'3" | 237 | U.C.L.A. | | 6 |
| Wyatt, Kervin LB | 80NYJ 81JJ | | 6'2" | 235 | Maryland | | |
| Wyatt, Kevin DB | 86SD 87KC | | 5'10" | 199 | Arkansas | | |
| Wyatt, Willie NT | 90TB | | 5'1" | 275 | Alabama | | |
| Wycheck, Frank TE | 93-94Was 95Hou | 2 | 6'3" | 235 | Maryland | | 12 |
| Wyman, David LB-DE | 87-92Sea 93-95Den | | 6'2" | 245 | Stanford | 3 | 6 |
| Yakavonis, Ray NT | 81-82Min 83KC | | 6'4" | 248 | East Stroudsburg | | |
| Yancy, Carlos DB | 95NE | | 6' | 185 | Georgia | | |
| Yarber, Eric WR | 86-87Was 88KJ | | 5'8" | 156 | Idaho | 3 | |
| Yarborough, Ryan WR | 94-95NYJ | 2 | 6'2" | 190 | Wyoming | | 18 |
| Yarbrough, Jim DB | 87NYG | | 6' | 195 | Murray State | | |
| Yarno, George OG-C-OT | 79-83TB 84-85USFL 85-87TB 88Atl 89Hou | | 6'2" | 261 | Washington State | | 1 |
| Yano, John C | 77-82Sea 84Den | | 6'5" | 251 | Idaho | | |
| Young, Almon OG | 87Hou 88HJ | | 6'3" | 290 | Bethune-Cookman | | |
| Young, Andre DB | 82-84SD | | 6' | 199 | Louisiana Tech | 6 | 6 |
| Young, Anthony DB | 85Ind 86ZJ | | 5'11" | 187 | Temple | 1 | 6 |
| Young, Ben TE | 83Atl | | 6'4" | 225 | Texas-Arlington | | 6 |
| Young, Bryant DT | 94-95SF | | 6'2" | 276 | Notre Dame | | |
| Young, Dave TE | 81NYG 83Bal 84Ind | 2 | 6'5" | 242 | Purdue | | 18 |
| Young, Duane TE | 91-95SD | 2 | 6'1" | 266 | Michigan State | | 18 |
| Young, Fredd LB | 84-87Sea 88-90Ind | | 6'1" | 233 | New Mexico State | 3 | 6 |
| Young, Glen WR | 83Phi 84-85,87-88Cle | 3 | 6'2" | 205 | Mississippi State | | 12 |
| Young, Glen LB | 95SD | | 6'3" | 235 | Syracuse | | |
| Young, Kevin DE | 87NO | | 6'5" | 265 | Utah State | | |
| Young, Lonnie DB | 85-87StL 88-90Phx 91-93NYJ 94SD 95NYJ | | 6'1" | 186 | Michigan State | 10 | |
| Young, Michael WR | 85-88LA 89-92Den 93Phi 94KC | 2 | 6'1" | 184 | U.C.L.A. | | 84 |
| Young, Mitchell DE | 87Atl | | 6'4" | 260 | Arkansas State | | |
| Young, Renard DB | 87Sea | | 5'10" | 184 | Nevada-Las Vegas, San Diego State | | |
| Young, Robert DE-DT | 91-94LA 95StL | | 6'6" | 275 | Mississippi State | | |

| Use Name (Nickname) - Positions | Team by Year | See Section | Hgt. | Wgt. | College | Int | Pts |
|---|---|---|---|---|---|---|---|
| Young, Rodney DB | 95NYG | | 6'1" | 206 | Louisiana State | | |
| Young, Roynell DB | 80-88Phi | | 6'1" | 183 | Alcorn State | 23 | |
| Young, Steve QB | 84-85USFL 85-86TB 87-95SF | 12 | 6'2" | 200 | Brigham Young | | 180 |
| Young, Theo TE | 87Pit | | 6'2" | 237 | Arkansas | | |
| Young, Tyrone WR | 83-84NO | 2 | 6'6" | 190 | Florida | | 36 |
| | | | | | | | |
| Zachary, Ken FB | 87SD | | 6' | 222 | Oklahoma State | | |
| Zackery, Tony DB | 89Atl 90-91NE | | 6'2" | 195 | Washington | 1 | |
| Zamberlin, John LB | 79-82NE 83-84KC | | 6'2" | 228 | Pacific Lutheran | 1 | |
| Zander, Carl LB | 85-91Cin | | 6'2" | 235 | Tennessee State | 3 | |
| Zandofsky, Mike OG-C | 89Phx 90-93SD 94-95Atl | | 6'2" | 299 | Washington | | |
| | | | | | | | |
| Zatechka, Rob OG | 95NYG | | 6'4" | 307 | Nebraska | | |
| Zawatson, Dave OG-OT | 89Chi 90NYJ 91Mia | | 6'4" | 275 | California | | |
| Zeier, Eric QB | 95Cle | 1 | 6' | 205 | Georgia | | 2 |
| Zellars, Ray FB | 95NO | 2 | 5'11" | 233 | Notre Dame | | 12 |
| Zele, Mike NT-DT | 79-83Atl | | 6'3" | 239 | Kent State | | |
| Zeman, Ed DB | 87LA | | 6'1" | 195 | Fort Lewis | | |
| Zendejas, Joaquin K | 83NE | 5 | 5'11" | 176 | La Verne | | 3 |
| Zendejas, Luis K | 87-88Dal 88-89Phi 89Dal | 5 | 5'9" | 160 | Arizona State | | 189 |

| Use Name (Nickname) - Positions | Team by Year | See Section | Hgt. | Wgt. | College | Int | Pts |
|---|---|---|---|---|---|---|---|
| Zendejas, Max K | 86Was 87-88GB | 5 | 5'11" | 184 | Arizona | | 155 |
| Zendejas, Tony K | 84-85USFL 85-90Hou 91-94LA 95Atl | 5 | 5'8" | 164 | Nevada-Reno | | 874 |
| Zeno, Lance C | 92-93Cle 93GB | | 6'4" | 279 | U.C.L.A. | | |
| Zentic, Mike C | 87Dal | | 6'3" | 255 | Oklahoma State | | |
| Zgonina, Jeff DT | 93-94Pit 95Car | | 6'1" | 284 | Purdue | | |
| | | | | | | | |
| Zimmerlink, Geno TE | 87Atl | | 6'3" | 222 | Virginia | | |
| Zimmerman, Gary OT | 84-85USFL 86-92Min 93-95Den | | 6'6" | 292 | Oregon | | |
| Zimmerman, Jeff OG | 87-90Dal | | 6'3" | 320 | Florida | | |
| Zogg, Jon OG | 87Raid | | 6'4" | 290 | Boise State | | |
| Zolak, Scott QB | 92-95NE | 1 | 6'5" | 222 | Maryland | | |
| | | | | | | | |
| Zomalt, Eric DB | 94-95Phi | | 5'11" | 197 | California | | |
| Zordich, Mike DB | 87-88NYJ 89-93Phx 94-95Phi | | 5'11" | 201 | Penn State | 13 | 24 |
| Zorich, Chris DT | 91-95Chi | | 6'1" | 275 | Notre Dame | | 6 |
| Zorn, Jim QB | 76-84Sea 85GB 87TB | 12 | 6'2" | 200 | Cal. Poly.-Pomona | | 102 |

Lifetime Statistics- 1980- 1995 Players Section 1 — **PASSING**
(All men with 25 or more passing attempts)

| Name | Years | Att. | Comp. | Comp. Pct. | Yards | Yds./ Att. | TD | Int. | Pct. Int. |
|---|---|---|---|---|---|---|---|---|---|
| Sam Adkins | 77-82 | 39 | 17 | 43.6 | 232 | 5.9 | 2 | 4 | 10.3 |
| Troy Aikman | 89-95 | 2713 | 1704 | 62.8 | 19607 | 7.2 | 98 | 88 | 3.2 |
| David Archer | 84-89 | 661 | 336 | 50.8 | 4337 | 6.6 | 18 | 30 | 4.5 |
| Steve Bartkowski | 75-86 | 3456 | 1932 | 55.9 | 24124 | 7.0 | 156 | 144 | 4.2 |
| Guy Benjamin | 78-83 | 68 | 39 | 57.4 | 439 | 6.5 | 3 | 3 | 4.4 |
| Steve Beuerlein | 88-95 | 1425 | 752 | 52.8 | 10042 | 7.0 | 53 | 52 | 3.6 |
| Todd Blackledge | 83-89 | 881 | 424 | 48.1 | 5286 | 6.0 | 29 | 38 | 4.3 |
| Jeff Blake | 92-95 | 882 | 486 | 55.1 | 6016 | 6.8 | 42 | 27 | 3.1 |
| Drew Bledsoe | 93-95 | 1756 | 937 | 53.3 | 10556 | 6.0 | 53 | 58 | 3.3 |
| Bob Bleier | 87 | 39 | 14 | 35.9 | 181 | 4.6 | 1 | 1 | 2.6 |
| Steve Bono | 85-95 | 1116 | 625 | 56.0 | 7034 | 6.3 | 45 | 24 | 2.2 |
| Bubby Brister | 86-95 | 2032 | 1101 | 54.2 | 13242 | 6.5 | 71 | 71 | 3.5 |
| Dieter Brock | 85 | 365 | 218 | 59.7 | 2658 | 7.3 | 16 | 13 | 3.6 |
| Dave Brown | 92-95 | 813 | 459 | 56.4 | 5371 | 6.6 | 23 | 26 | 3.2 |
| Mark Brunell | 93-95 | 373 | 213 | 57.1 | 2263 | 6.1 | 15 | 7 | 1.9 |
| Scott Brunner | 80-85 | 1046 | 512 | 48.9 | 6457 | 6.2 | 29 | 54 | 5.2 |
| Mike Buck | 90-93,95 | 90 | 54 | 60.0 | 729 | 8.1 | 5 | 3 | 3.3 |
| Mike Busch | 87 | 47 | 17 | 36.2 | 378 | 5.9 | 3 | 2 | 4.3 |
| Rich Campbell | 81-84 | 68 | 31 | 45.6 | 386 | 5.7 | 3 | 9 | 13.2 |
| Scott Campbell | 84-87,89-90 | 454 | 224 | 49.3 | 2983 | 6.6 | 19 | 25 | 5.5 |
| Glenn Carano | 77-83 | 57 | 21 | 36.8 | 304 | 5.3 | 3 | 1 | 1.8 |
| Cody Carlson | 87-94 | 659 | 370 | 56.1 | 4469 | 6.8 | 21 | 28 | 4.2 |
| Jeff Carlson | 90-92 | 114 | 49 | 43.0 | 636 | 5.6 | 2 | 9 | 7.9 |
| Matt Cavanaugh | 78-90 | 580 | 305 | 52.6 | 4332 | 7.5 | 28 | 30 | 5.2 |
| Chris Chandler | 88-95 | 1598 | 918 | 57.4 | 10581 | 6.6 | 58 | 60 | 3.8 |
| Jeff Christensen | 83-85,87 | 58 | 24 | 41.4 | 297 | 5.1 | 1 | 3 | 5.2 |
| Kerry Collins | 95 | 433 | 214 | 49.4 | 2717 | 6.3 | 14 | 19 | 4.4 |
| Todd Collins | 95 | 29 | 14 | 48.3 | 112 | 3.9 | 0 | 1 | 3.4 |
| Cary Conklin | 92-93,95 | 101 | 52 | 51.5 | 560 | 5.5 | 5 | 3 | 3.4 |
| Randall Cunningham | 85-95 | 3362 | 1874 | 55.7 | 22874 | 6.8 | 150 | 105 | 3.0 |
| Gary Danielson | 76-78,80-85,87-88 | 1932 | 1105 | 57.2 | 13764 | 7.1 | 81 | 78 | 4.0 |
| Steve DeBerg | 77-93 | 4965 | 2844 | 57.3 | 33872 | 6.8 | 193 | 203 | 4.1 |
| Trent Dilfer | 94-95 | 497 | 262 | 52.7 | 3207 | 6.4 | 5 | 24 | 4.8 |
| Steve Dils | 79-88 | 972 | 504 | 51.9 | 5816 | 6.0 | 27 | 32 | 3.3 |
| Anthony Dilweg | 89-90 | 193 | 102 | 52.8 | 1274 | 6.6 | 8 | 7 | 3.6 |
| Joe Dufek | 83-85 | 150 | 74 | 49.3 | 829 | 5.5 | 4 | 8 | 5.3 |
| Tony Eason | 83-90 | 1564 | 911 | 58.2 | 11142 | 7.1 | 61 | 51 | 3.3 |
| John Elway | 83-95 | 5926 | 3346 | 56.5 | 41706 | 7.0 | 225 | 191 | 3.2 |
| Craig Erickson | 92-95 | 965 | 523 | 54.2 | 6680 | 6.9 | 37 | 35 | 3.6 |
| Boomer Esiason | 84-95 | 4680 | 2661 | 56.9 | 34149 | 7.3 | 223 | 168 | 3.6 |
| Vince Evans | 77-83,87-95 | 1390 | 703 | 50.6 | 9485 | 6.8 | 52 | 75 | 5.4 |
| Jim Everett | 86-95 | 4384 | 2538 | 57.9 | 31583 | 7.2 | 190 | 155 | 3.5 |
| Brett Favre | 91-95 | 2150 | 1342 | 62.4 | 14825 | 6.9 | 108 | 66 | 3.1 |
| Joe Ferguson | 73-90 | 4519 | 2369 | 52.4 | 29817 | 6.6 | 196 | 209 | 4.6 |
| Vince Ferragamo | 77-80,82-86 | 1615 | 902 | 55.9 | 11336 | 7.0 | 76 | 91 | 5.6 |
| Tom Flick | 81-82,84,86 | 106 | 47 | 44.3 | 506 | 4.8 | 2 | 10 | 9.4 |
| Doug Flutie | 86-89 | 341 | 166 | 46.9 | 2203 | 6.5 | 14 | 16 | 4.7 |
| Glenn Foley | 94-95 | 37 | 21 | 56.8 | 173 | 4.7 | 0 | 2 | 5.4 |
| John Fourcade | 87-90 | 313 | 159 | 50.8 | 2312 | 7.4 | 14 | 15 | 4.8 |
| Dan Fouts | 73-87 | 5604 | 3297 | 58.8 | 43040 | 7.7 | 254 | 242 | 4.3 |
| Gus Frerotte | 94-95 | 496 | 245 | 49.1 | 3351 | 6.8 | 18 | 18 | 3.6 |
| John Friesz | 90-91-95 | 1047 | 570 | 54.4 | 6457 | 6.2 | 35 | 32 | 3.1 |
| Steve Fuller | 79-86,88 | 1066 | 605 | 56.8 | 7156 | 6.7 | 28 | 41 | 3.8 |
| Will Furrer | 92-95 | 124 | 57 | 46.0 | 572 | 4.6 | 2 | 10 | 8.1 |
| Chuck Fusina | 79-81,86 | 37 | 22 | 59.5 | 198 | 5.4 | 1 | 2 | 5.4 |
| Rich Gannon | 87-93,95 | 1144 | 642 | 56.1 | 7218 | 6.3 | 43 | 43 | 3.8 |
| Bob Gagliano | 82-83,86-93 | 486 | 249 | 51.2 | 3431 | 7.1 | 17 | 27 | 5.6 |
| Jason Garrett | 93-95 | 55 | 29 | 52.7 | 430 | 7.8 | 3 | 1 | 1.8 |
| Stan Gelbaugh | 86,88-89,92-95 | 389 | 192 | 49.3 | 2100 | 5.4 | 10 | 22 | 5.6 |
| Jeff George | 90-95 | 2613 | 1532 | 58.6 | 17429 | 6.7 | 88 | 75 | 2.9 |
| Gale Gilbert | 85-86,90-95 | 259 | 146 | 56.4 | 1544 | 6.0 | 9 | 12 | 4.6 |
| Brad Goebel | 91-94 | 59 | 32 | 54.2 | 299 | 5.1 | 0 | 6 | 10.2 |
| Jerry Golsteyn | 77-79,82-83 | 217 | 92 | 42.4 | 1077 | 5.0 | 2 | 13 | 6.0 |
| Kent Graham | 92-95 | 172 | 74 | 43.0 | 844 | 4.9 | 4 | 6 | 3.5 |
| Elvis Grbac | 93-95 | 223 | 162 | 72.6 | 1862 | 8.3 | 10 | 6 | 2.7 |
| Steve Grogan | 75-90 | 3593 | 1879 | 52.3 | 26886 | 7.5 | 182 | 208 | 5.8 |
| Shawn Halloran | 87 | 42 | 18 | 42.9 | 263 | 6.3 | 0 | 1 | 2.4 |
| Jim Harbaugh | 87-95 | 2275 | 1348 | 59.3 | 15582 | 6.8 | 76 | 67 | 2.9 |
| Bobby Hebert | 85-89,91-95 | 2633 | 1545 | 58.7 | 18531 | 7.0 | 113 | 99 | 3.8 |
| Mark Herrmann | 82-92 | 561 | 334 | 59.5 | 4015 | 7.2 | 16 | 36 | 6.4 |
| Rusty Hilger | 85-88,90-91 | 464 | 202 | 43.5 | 2584 | 5.6 | 11 | 19 | 4.1 |
| Eric Hipple | 80-86,88-89 | 1546 | 830 | 53.7 | 10711 | 6.9 | 55 | 70 | 4.5 |
| Billy Joe Hobert | 93,95 | 80 | 44 | 55.0 | 540 | 6.8 | 6 | 4 | 5.0 |
| Tom Hodson | 90-92,95 | 320 | 174 | 54.4 | 1823 | 5.7 | 7 | 11 | 3.4 |
| Gary Hogeboom | 80-89 | 1325 | 743 | 56.1 | 9436 | 7.1 | 49 | 60 | 4.5 |
| Mike Hohensee | 87 | 52 | 28 | 53.8 | 343 | 6.6 | 4 | 1 | 1.9 |
| Donald Hollas | 91-92,94 | 115 | 67 | 58.3 | 645 | 5.6 | 3 | 5 | 4.3 |
| Bob Holly | 82-85 | 40 | 25 | 62.5 | 300 | 7.5 | 1 | 2 | 5.0 |
| Todd Hons | 87 | 92 | 43 | 46.7 | 552 | 6.0 | 5 | 5 | 5.4 |
| Jeff Hostetler | 84-95 | 1791 | 1036 | 57.8 | 12983 | 7.2 | 66 | 47 | 2.6 |
| Stan Humphries | 89-95 | 1875 | 1078 | 57.5 | 13033 | 7.0 | 66 | 65 | 3.5 |
| Ron Jaworski | 74-89 | 4117 | 2187 | 53.1 | 28190 | 6.8 | 179 | 164 | 4.0 |
| Brad Johnson | 93-95 | 73 | 47 | 64.4 | 422 | 5.8 | 0 | 2 | 2.7 |
| Paul Justin | 95 | 36 | 20 | 55.6 | 212 | 5.9 | 0 | 2 | 5.6 |
| Ken Karcher | 87-88 | 114 | 62 | 54.4 | 756 | 6.6 | 6 | 4 | 3.5 |
| Jim Kelly | 86-95 | 4400 | 2652 | 60.3 | 32657 | 7.4 | 223 | 156 | 3.5 |
| Jeff Kemp | 81-91 | 916 | 479 | 52.3 | 6230 | 6.8 | 39 | 40 | 4.4 |
| Bill Kenney | 79-88 | 2430 | 1330 | 54.7 | 17277 | 7.1 | 105 | 86 | 3.5 |
| Mike Kerrigan | 83 | 14 | 6 | 42.9 | 72 | 5.1 | 0 | 1 | 7.1 |
| Blair Kiel | 84,86-87,89-91 | 193 | 108 | 55.9 | 1296 | 6.7 | 8 | 7 | 3.6 |
| David Klingler | 92-95 | 687 | 375 | 54.6 | 3880 | 5.6 | 16 | 21 | 3.1 |
| Matt Kofler | 83-85 | 202 | 91 | 45.0 | 1156 | 5.7 | 7 | 11 | 5.4 |
| Jeff Komlo | 79-81,83 | 437 | 218 | 49.9 | 2603 | 6.0 | 12 | 28 | 6.4 |
| Bernie Kosar | 85-95 | 3333 | 1970 | 59.1 | 23093 | 6.9 | 122 | 87 | 2.6 |
| Erik Kramer | 87,91-95 | 1281 | 740 | 57.8 | 8934 | 7.0 | 64 | 42 | 3.3 |
| Tommy Kramer | 77-90 | 3651 | 2012 | 55.1 | 24777 | 6.8 | 159 | 158 | 4.3 |
| Dave Krieg | 80-95 | 4911 | 2866 | 58.4 | 35668 | 7.3 | 247 | 187 | 3.8 |
| Gary Kubiak | 83-91 | 298 | 173 | 58.1 | 1928 | 6.4 | 14 | 16 | 5.4 |
| Babe Laufenberg | 83,85-88,90 | 211 | 93 | 44.1 | 1057 | 5.0 | 5 | 11 | 5.2 |
| Rusty Lisch | 80-84 | 115 | 55 | 47.8 | 547 | 4.8 | 1 | 11 | 9.6 |
| Neil Lomax | 81-88 | 3153 | 1817 | 57.6 | 22771 | 7.2 | 136 | 90 | 2.9 |
| Chuck Long | 86-90 | 607 | 331 | 54.5 | 3747 | 6.2 | 19 | 28 | 4.6 |
| Oliver Luck | 83-86 | 413 | 233 | 56.4 | 2544 | 6.2 | 13 | 21 | 5.1 |
| Ed Luther | 80-84,86 | 460 | 245 | 53.3 | 3187 | 6.9 | 12 | 23 | 5.0 |
| Mike Machurek | 84 | 43 | 14 | 32.6 | 193 | 4.5 | 0 | 0 | 0.0 |
| Kyle Mackey | 84,86-87,89 | 134 | 68 | 50.7 | 729 | 5.4 | 3 | 6 | 4.5 |
| Tommy Maddox | 92-95 | 164 | 83 | 50.6 | 948 | 5.8 | 6 | 14 | 8.5 |
| Don Majkowski | 87-95 | 1839 | 1001 | 54.4 | 12146 | 6.6 | 63 | 64 | 3.5 |
| Mark Malone | 80-89 | 1648 | 839 | 50.9 | 10175 | 6.2 | 60 | 81 | 4.8 |
| Dan Marino | 83-95 | 6531 | 3913 | 59.9 | 48841 | 7.5 | 352 | 200 | 3.1 |
| Todd Marinovich | 91-92 | 205 | 104 | 50.7 | 1345 | 6.6 | 8 | 9 | 4.4 |
| Bruce Mathison | 83-87 | 309 | 152 | 49.2 | 2177 | 7.0 | 7 | 20 | 6.5 |
| Brian McClure | 87 | 38 | 20 | 52.6 | 181 | 4.8 | 0 | 3 | 7.9 |
| Paul McDonald | 80-87 | 767 | 411 | 53.6 | 5269 | 6.9 | 24 | 37 | 4.8 |
| Dan McGwire | 91-95 | 148 | 74 | 50.0 | 745 | 5.0 | 2 | 6 | 4.1 |
| Jim McMahon | 82-95 | 2569 | 1489 | 58.0 | 18108 | 7.0 | 100 | 90 | 3.5 |
| Steve McNair | 95 | 80 | 41 | 51.3 | 569 | 7.1 | 3 | 1 | 1.3 |
| Guido Merkens | 78-85,87 | 66 | 27 | 41.0 | 283 | 4.3 | 2 | 2 | 3.0 |
| Hugh Millen | 87-95 | 928 | 560 | 60.3 | 6440 | 6.9 | 22 | 35 | 3.8 |
| Chris Miller | 87-95 | 2811 | 1534 | 54.6 | 18793 | 6.7 | 121 | 101 | 3.6 |
| Jim Miller | 94-95 | 56 | 32 | 57.1 | 397 | 7.1 | 2 | 5 | 8.9 |
| Rick Mirer | 93-95 | 1258 | 678 | 53.9 | 7548 | 6.0 | 36 | 44 | 3.5 |
| Scott Mitchell | 91-95 | 1070 | 600 | 56.1 | 7599 | 7.1 | 54 | 32 | 3.0 |
| Joe Montana | 79-90,92-94 | 5391 | 3409 | 63.2 | 40551 | 7.5 | 273 | 139 | 2.6 |
| Warren Moon | 84-95 | 5753 | 3380 | 58.9 | 42177 | 7.3 | 247 | 199 | 3.5 |
| Shawn Moore | 92 | 34 | 17 | 50.0 | 232 | 6.8 | 0 | 3 | 8.8 |
| Mike Moroski | 79-86 | 425 | 241 | 56.7 | 2864 | 6.7 | 8 | 18 | 4.2 |
| Browning Nagle | 91-95 | 424 | 207 | 48.8 | 2430 | 5.7 | 7 | 18 | 4.2 |
| Rick Neuheisel | 87 | 59 | 40 | 67.8 | 367 | 6.2 | 1 | 1 | 1.7 |
| Gifford Nielsen | 78-83 | 498 | 273 | 54.8 | 3255 | 6.5 | 20 | 22 | 4.4 |
| David Norrie | 87 | 68 | 35 | 51.5 | 376 | 5.5 | 1 | 4 | 5.9 |
| Ken O'Brien | 83-93 | 3602 | 2110 | 58.6 | 25094 | 7.0 | 128 | 98 | 2.7 |
| Neil O'Donnell | 90-95 | 1871 | 1069 | 57.1 | 12867 | 6.9 | 68 | 39 | 2.1 |
| Mike Pagel | 82-93 | 1509 | 756 | 50.0 | 9414 | 6.2 | 49 | 63 | 4.2 |
| Walter Payton | 75-87 | 34 | 11 | 32.3 | 331 | 9.7 | 8 | 4 | 11.8 |
| Brent Pease | 87-88 | 135 | 62 | 45.9 | 792 | 5.9 | 3 | 9 | 6.7 |
| Rodney Peete | 89-95 | 1556 | 889 | 57.1 | 10960 | 7.0 | 50 | 64 | 4.1 |
| Steve Pelluer | 84-90 | 974 | 548 | 56.3 | 6870 | 7.1 | 29 | 39 | 4.0 |
| Todd Philcox | 90-93 | 145 | 69 | 47.6 | 965 | 6.7 | 7 | 10 | 6.9 |
| Joe Pisarcik | 77-84 | 898 | 425 | 47.3 | 5552 | 6.2 | 24 | 48 | 5.3 |
| Tom Ramsey | 85-89 | 214 | 108 | 50.5 | 1275 | 6.0 | 7 | 10 | 4.7 |
| Frank Reich | 85-95 | 461 | 259 | 56.2 | 2981 | 6.5 | 20 | 14 | 3.0 |
| Bucky Richardson | 92-94 | 185 | 97 | 52.4 | 1257 | 6.8 | 6 | 6 | 3.2 |
| Alan Risher | 85,87 | 74 | 44 | 59.5 | 564 | 7.6 | 3 | 3 | 4.1 |
| Matt Robinson | 77-82 | 523 | 244 | 46.7 | 3347 | 6.4 | 18 | 38 | 7.3 |
| Timm Rosenbach | 89-90,92 | 551 | 295 | 53.5 | 3676 | 6.7 | 16 | 24 | 4.4 |
| Ed Rubbert | 87 | 49 | 26 | 53.1 | 532 | 10.9 | 4 | 1 | 2.0 |
| T.J. Rubley | 93,95 | 195 | 112 | 57.4 | 1377 | 7.1 | 8 | 7 | 3.6 |
| Jeff Rutledge | 79-81,83-92 | 526 | 274 | 52.1 | 3628 | 6.9 | 16 | 29 | 5.5 |
| Pat Ryan | 78-89,91 | 657 | 364 | 55.4 | 4320 | 6.6 | 31 | 35 | 5.3 |
| Mark Rypien | 87-95 | 2552 | 1432 | 56.1 | 18070 | 7.1 | 114 | 86 | 3.4 |
| Sean Salisbury | 86-87,90-94 | 416 | 236 | 56.7 | 2840 | 6.8 | 14 | 11 | 2.6 |
| Art Schlichter | 82,84 | 202 | 91 | 45.0 | 1006 | 5.0 | 3 | 11 | 5.4 |
| Turk Schonert | 81-89 | 504 | 311 | 61.7 | 3788 | 7.5 | 11 | 20 | 4.0 |
| Jay Schroeder | 84-94 | 2807 | 1426 | 50.8 | 20063 | 7.1 | 114 | 108 | 3.8 |
| Scott Secules | 88-91,93 | 204 | 108 | 52.9 | 1311 | 6.4 | 4 | 14 | 6.0 |
| Frank Seurer | 86-87 | 55 | 26 | 47.3 | 340 | 6.2 | 0 | 4 | 7.3 |
| Heath Shuler | 94-95 | 390 | 186 | 47.7 | 2403 | 6.2 | 13 | 19 | 4.9 |
| Phil Simms | 79-81,83-93 | 4647 | 2576 | 55.4 | 33462 | 7.2 | 199 | 157 | 3.4 |
| Scott Stankavage | 84,86-87 | 25 | 8 | 32.0 | 66 | 2.6 | 0 | 2 | 8.0 |
| Matt Stevens | 87 | 57 | 32 | 56.1 | 315 | 5.5 | 1 | 1 | 1.8 |
| Cliff Stoudt | 77-83,86-90 | 684 | 359 | 52.5 | 4506 | 6.6 | 23 | 43 | 6.3 |
| Kelly Stouffer | 88-92 | 437 | 225 | 51.5 | 2333 | 5.3 | 7 | 19 | 4.3 |
| Don Strock | 74-89 | 779 | 443 | 56.9 | 5349 | 6.9 | 45 | 42 | 5.4 |
| Kevin Sweeney | 87-88 | 106 | 47 | 44.3 | 605 | 5.7 | 7 | 6 | 5.7 |
| Vinny Testaverde | 87-95 | 3158 | 1704 | 54.0 | 22075 | 7.0 | 124 | 149 | 4.7 |
| Joe Theismann | 74-85 | 3602 | 2044 | 56.7 | 25206 | 7.0 | 160 | 138 | 3.8 |
| Jack Thompson | 79-84 | 845 | 449 | 53.1 | 5315 | 6.3 | 33 | 45 | 5.3 |
| Scott Tinsley | 87 | 86 | 48 | 55.8 | 637 | 7.4 | 3 | 4 | 4.7 |
| Richard Todd | 76-86 | 2967 | 1610 | 54.3 | 20610 | 6.9 | 124 | 161 | 5.4 |
| Billy Joe Tolliver | 89-94 | 1124 | 578 | 51.4 | 6740 | 6.0 | 39 | 43 | 3.8 |
| Mike Tomczak | 85-95 | 1624 | 850 | 52.3 | 11298 | 7.0 | 58 | 77 | 4.7 |
| Willie Totten | 87 | 33 | 13 | 39.4 | 155 | 4.7 | 2 | 2 | 6.1 |
| Jack Trudeau | 86-95 | 1644 | 873 | 53.1 | 10243 | 6.2 | 42 | 69 | 4.2 |
| Tom Tupa | 88-92,94-95 | 489 | 252 | 51.5 | 3256 | 6.7 | 10 | 24 | 4.9 |
| Jeff Van Raaphorst | 87 | 34 | 18 | 52.9 | 174 | 5.1 | 1 | 2 | 5.9 |
| Mark Vlasic | 87-88,90-93 | 142 | 75 | 52.8 | 762 | 5.4 | 4 | 5 | 3.5 |
| Steve Walsh | 89-95 | 1191 | 658 | 55.2 | 7368 | 6.2 | 40 | 39 | 3.3 |
| Andre Ware | 90-93 | 161 | 83 | 51.6 | 1112 | 6.9 | 5 | 8 | 5.0 |
| Casey Weldon | 92-95 | 111 | 55 | 49.5 | 637 | 5.7 | 1 | 3 | 2.7 |
| Danny White | 76-88 | 2950 | 1761 | 59.7 | 21959 | 7.4 | 155 | 132 | 4.4 |
| David Whitehurst | 77-84 | 980 | 504 | 51.4 | 6205 | 6.3 | 28 | 51 | 5.2 |
| Erik Wilhelm | 89-91,93-95 | 123 | 70 | 56.9 | 822 | 6.7 | 4 | 4 | 3.2 |
| Doug Williams | 78-82,86-89 | 2507 | 1240 | 49.5 | 16998 | 6.8 | 100 | 93 | 3.7 |
| Peter Tom Willis | 90-93 | 183 | 104 | 56.8 | 1261 | 6.9 | 6 | 15 | 8.2 |
| Dave Wilson | 81,83-89 | 1039 | 551 | 53.1 | 6987 | 6.7 | 36 | 55 | 5.3 |
| Marc Wilson | 80-87,89-90 | 2081 | 1085 | 52.1 | 14391 | 6.9 | 86 | 102 | 4.9 |
| Wade Wilson | 81-95 | 2301 | 1319 | 57.3 | 16523 | 7.2 | 92 | 97 | 4.2 |
| John Witkowski | 84-86,88 | 35 | 13 | 37.1 | 210 | 6.0 | 0 | 0 | 0.0 |
| David Woodley | 80-85 | 1300 | 687 | 52.8 | 8558 | 6.6 | 48 | 63 | 4.8 |
| Randy Wright | 84-88 | 1119 | 602 | 53.8 | 7106 | 6.4 | 31 | 57 | 5.1 |
| Steve Young | 85-95 | 2876 | 1845 | 64.1 | 23069 | 8.0 | 160 | 79 | 2.7 |
| Eric Zeier | 95 | 161 | 82 | 50.9 | 864 | 5.4 | 4 | 9 | 5.6 |
| Scott Zolak | 92-95 | 159 | 85 | 53.5 | 871 | 5.5 | 3 | 4 | 2.5 |
| Jim Zorn | 76-85,87 | 3149 | 1669 | 53.0 | 21115 | 6.7 | 111 | 141 | 4.5 |

Lifetime Statistics- 1980-1995 Players Section 2 - **RUSHING and RECEIVING**
(All men with 25 or more rushing attempts or 10 or more receptions)

| Name | Years | RUSHING Att. | Yards | Avg. | TD | RECEIVING Rec. | Yards | Avg. | TD |
|---|---|---|---|---|---|---|---|---|---|
| Walter Abercrombie | 82-88 | 847 | 3357 | 4.0 | 22 | 139 | 1351 | 9.7 | 7 |
| Curtis Adams | 86-88 | 246 | 858 | 3.4 | 6 | 8 | 64 | 8.0 | 0 |
| George Adams | 85-91 | 257 | 886 | 3.4 | 3 | 111 | 1014 | 9.1 | 4 |
| Willie Adams | 79-85 | 5 | 13 | 2.6 | 0 | 61 | 962 | 15.8 | 2 |
| Tommie Agee | 88-94 | 91 | 319 | 3.5 | 1 | 44 | 366 | 8.3 | 1 |
| Troy Aikman | 89-95 | 214 | 803 | 3.8 | 5 | 2 | -19 | -9.5 | 0 |
| Charles Alexander | 79-85 | 748 | 2645 | 3.5 | 13 | 165 | 1130 | 6.8 | 2 |
| Derrick Alexander | 94-95 | 5 | 67 | 13.4 | 0 | 63 | 1044 | 16.6 | 2 |
| Jeff Alexander | 89 | 45 | 146 | 3.2 | 2 | 8 | 84 | 10.5 | 0 |
| Mike Alexander | 89,91 | | | | | 16 | 302 | 18.9 | 1 |
| Ray Alexander | 84,88-89 | | | | | 63 | 936 | 14.9 | 7 |
| Anthony Allen | 85-89 | | | | | 44 | 667 | 15.2 | 8 |
| Marcus Allen | 82-95 | 2692 | 10908 | 4.1 | 103 | 549 | 5055 | 9.2 | 21 |
| Marvin Allen | 88-91 | 94 | 378 | 4.0 | 2 | 7 | 57 | 8.1 | 0 |
| Terry Allen | 91-92,94-95 | 979 | 4104 | 4.2 | 33 | 103 | 907 | 8.8 | 4 |
| Kimble Anders | 91-95 | 196 | 919 | 4.7 | 4 | 169 | 1295 | 7.7 | 3 |
| Alfred Anderson | 84-91 | 626 | 2374 | 3.8 | 22 | 114 | 1044 | 9.2 | 5 |
| Gary Anderson | 85-88,90-93 | 869 | 3409 | 3.9 | 16 | 302 | 2999 | 9.9 | 15 |
| Jamal Anderson | 94-95 | 41 | 160 | 3.9 | 1 | 4 | 42 | 10.5 | 0 |
| Jesse Anderson | 90-91 | | | | | 11 | 150 | 13.6 | 2 |
| Ottis Anderson | 79-92 | 2562 | 10273 | 4.0 | 81 | 376 | 3062 | 8.1 | 5 |
| Neal Anderson | 86-93 | 1515 | 6166 | 4.1 | 51 | 302 | 2763 | 9.1 | 20 |
| Richie Anderson | 93-95 | 48 | 224 | 4.7 | 1 | 30 | 238 | 7.9 | 1 |
| Stevie Anderson | 94-95 | | | | | 12 | 124 | 10.3 | 1 |
| Willie Anderson | 88-95 | 3 | 23 | 7.7 | 0 | 267 | 5357 | 20.1 | 28 |
| William Andrews | 79-86 | 1315 | 5986 | 4.6 | 30 | 277 | 2647 | 9.6 | 11 |
| Tyrone Anthony | 84-85 | 37 | 170 | 4.6 | 1 | 40 | 298 | 7.5 | 0 |
| Charles Arbuckle | 92-95 | | | | | 33 | 282 | 8.5 | 1 |
| David Archer | 84-89,92 | 135 | 706 | 5.2 | 2 | | | | |
| Justin Armour | 95 | 4 | -5 | -1.2 | 0 | 26 | 300 | 11.5 | 3 |
| Adger Armstrong | 80-85 | 58 | 231 | 4.0 | 2 | 80 | 710 | 9.0 | 7 |
| Tyji Armstrong | 92-95 | 3 | 4 | 1.3 | 0 | 45 | 557 | 12.4 | 3 |
| Walt Arnold | 80-87 | | | | | 99 | 1053 | 10.6 | 8 |
| Jamie Asher | 95 | | | | | 14 | 172 | 12.3 | 0 |
| Steve Atkins | 79-81 | 121 | 488 | 4.0 | 2 | 18 | 138 | 7.7 | 1 |
| Mike Augustyniak | 81-83 | 153 | 567 | 3.7 | 7 | 52 | 404 | 7.8 | 1 |
| Cliff Austin | 83-87 | 109 | 445 | 4.1 | 2 | 11 | 118 | 10.7 | 0 |
| Steve Avery | 91,94-95 | 3 | 7 | 2.3 | 0 | 12 | 84 | 7.0 | 1 |
| Rob Awalt | 87-93 | 2 | -9 | -4.5 | 0 | 138 | 1583 | 11.5 | 10 |
| Rick Badanjek | 86-87 | 29 | 87 | 3.0 | 1 | 6 | 35 | 5.8 | 0 |
| Aaron Bailey | 94-95 | 1 | 34 | 34.0 | 0 | 23 | 409 | 17.8 | 3 |
| Harold Bailey | 81-82 | 1 | 13 | 13.0 | 0 | 26 | 367 | 14.1 | 0 |
| Johnny Bailey | 90-95 | 189 | 832 | 4.4 | 6 | 161 | 1355 | 8.4 | 1 |
| Stacey Bailey | 82-90 | 4 | -2 | -0.5 | 0 | 208 | 3422 | 16.5 | 18 |
| Victor Bailey | 93-95 | | | | | 61 | 856 | 14.0 | 2 |
| Stephen Baker | 87-92 | 2 | 21 | 10.5 | 0 | 141 | 2587 | 18.3 | 21 |
| Tony Baker | 68-75 | 536 | 2087 | 3.9 | 15 | 82 | 685 | 8.4 | 2 |
| Randy Baldwin | 91-95 | 74 | 231 | 3.1 | 0 | 6 | 50 | 8.3 | 1 |
| Eric Ball | 89-95 | 158 | 586 | 3.7 | 8 | 22 | 216 | 9.8 | 3 |
| Chuck Banks | 86-87 | 79 | 325 | 4.1 | 0 | 16 | 121 | 7.6 | 0 |
| Fred Banks | 85,87-93 | | | | | 105 | 1636 | 15.6 | 10 |
| Gordon Banks | 80-81,85-87 | | | | | 35 | 458 | 13.1 | 1 |
| Marion Barber | 82-88 | 74 | 317 | 4.3 | 3 | 25 | 209 | 8.4 | 1 |
| Mike Barber | 76-85 | 5 | 19 | 8.9 | 0 | 222 | 2788 | 12.6 | 17 |
| Mike Barber | 89-92 | 1 | -13 | -13.0 | 0 | 38 | 483 | 12.7 | 2 |
| Rod Barksdale | 86-87 | | | | | 30 | 599 | 20.0 | 3 |
| Johnnie Barnes | 92-95 | | | | | 14 | 191 | 13.6 | 0 |
| Buster Barnett | 81-84 | | | | | 26 | 236 | 9.1 | 1 |
| Fred Barnett | 90-95 | 4 | -2 | -0.5 | 0 | 308 | 4634 | 15.0 | 28 |
| Tim Barnett | 91-93 | 1 | 3 | 3.0 | 0 | 82 | 1188 | 14.5 | 10 |
| Milton Barney | 87 | | | | | 10 | 175 | 17.5 | 2 |
| Malcolm Barnwell | 81-85 | 3 | 30 | 10.0 | 0 | 115 | 1969 | 17.1 | 4 |
| Steve Bartkowski | 75-86 | 178 | 259 | 1.5 | 11 | | | | |
| Brian Baschnagel | 76-84 | 8 | 0 | 0.0 | 0 | 134 | 2024 | 15.1 | 9 |
| Don Bass | 78-82 | 6 | 40 | 6.7 | 0 | 117 | 1580 | 13.5 | 13 |
| Mario Bates | 94-95 | 395 | 1530 | 3.9 | 13 | 26 | 176 | 6.7 | 0 |
| Greg Baty | 86-88,90-94 | | | | | 85 | 883 | 10.4 | 8 |
| Hank Bauer | 77-83 | 123 | 377 | 3.1 | 18 | 12 | 97 | 8.1 | 2 |
| Mark Bavaro | 85-90,92-94 | | | | | 351 | 4733 | 13.5 | 39 |
| Brad Baxter | 89-95 | 779 | 2928 | 3.8 | 35 | 80 | 587 | 7.3 | 0 |
| Fred Baxter | 93-95 | | | | | 24 | 281 | 11.7 | 3 |
| Pat Beach | 82-93 | | | | | 163 | 1558 | 9.6 | 14 |
| Sanjay Beach | 89,91-93 | | | | | 26 | 224 | 8.6 | 2 |
| Ed Beckman | 77-84 | | | | | 23 | 198 | 8.6 | 1 |
| Brad Beckman | 88-89 | | | | | 11 | 102 | 9.3 | 1 |
| Don Beebe | 89-95 | 4 | 28 | 7.0 | 0 | 178 | 2689 | 15.1 | 19 |
| Coleman Bell | 95 | | | | | 14 | 166 | 11.9 | 1 |
| Greg Bell | 84-90 | 1204 | 4959 | 4.1 | 51 | 157 | 1307 | 8.3 | 6 |
| Jerry Bell | 82-86 | | | | | 101 | 1218 | 12.1 | 7 |
| Ken Bell | 86-89 | 31 | 96 | 3.1 | 0 | 3 | 18 | 6.0 | 0 |
| Nick Bell | 91-93 | 226 | 853 | 3.8 | 7 | 21 | 213 | 10.1 | 0 |
| Richard Bell | 90 | 5 | 18 | 3.6 | 0 | 12 | 137 | 11.4 | 1 |
| Ricky Bell | 77-83 | 822 | 3063 | 3.7 | 16 | 97 | 842 | 8.7 | 3 |
| Theo Bell | 76-85 | 2 | 12 | 6.0 | 0 | 136 | 2375 | 17.5 | 8 |
| Mark Bellini | 86-88 | | | | | 10 | 133 | 13.3 | 0 |
| Jesse Bendross | 84-86 | | | | | 27 | 369 | 13.7 | 2 |
| Donnell Bennett | 94-95 | 53 | 189 | 3.6 | 2 | 8 | 65 | 8.1 | 0 |
| Edgar Bennett | 92-95 | 714 | 2454 | 3.4 | 17 | 211 | 1744 | 8.3 | 9 |
| Lewis Bennett | 87 | | | | | 10 | 184 | 18.4 | 1 |
| Woody Bennett | 79-88 | 424 | 1761 | 4.2 | 10 | 41 | 304 | 7.4 | 3 |
| Albert Bentley | 85-92 | 526 | 2355 | 4.4 | 19 | 226 | 2245 | 9.9 | 8 |
| Cliff Benson | 84-85,87-88 | 3 | 8 | 2.7 | 0 | 39 | 298 | 7.6 | 0 |
| Karl Bernard | 87 | 45 | 187 | 4.2 | 2 | 13 | 91 | 7.0 | 0 |
| Rick Berns | 79-83 | 68 | 255 | 3.8 | 0 | 6 | 46 | 7.7 | 0 |
| Rod Bernstine | 87-95 | 670 | 2990 | 4.5 | 22 | 149 | 1384 | 9.3 | 2 |
| Jerome Bettis | 93-95 | 796 | 3091 | 3.9 | 13 | 75 | 643 | 8.6 | 1 |
| Steve Beuerlein | 88-95 | 106 | 169 | 1.6 | 1 | 1 | 21 | 21.0 | 0 |
| Dwight Beverly | 87 | 62 | 217 | 3.5 | 2 | 1 | 8 | 8.0 | 0 |
| Eric Bieniemy | 91-95 | 281 | 1092 | 3.9 | 7 | 54 | 521 | 9.6 | 0 |
| J.J. Birden | 90-95 | | | | | 214 | 3122 | 14.6 | 15 |
| Harold Bishop | 94-95 | | | | | 16 | 135 | 8.4 | 0 |
| Todd Blackledge | 83-89 | 81 | 325 | 4.0 | 2 | | | | |
| Brian Blades | 88-95 | 25 | 156 | 6.2 | 0 | 483 | 6561 | 13.6 | 30 |
| Jeff Blake | 92-95 | 92 | 511 | 5.6 | 3 | | | | |
| Carl Bland | 84-90 | | | | | 90 | 1153 | 12.8 | 4 |

| Name | Years | RUSHING Att. | Yards | Avg. | TD | RECEIVING Rec. | Yards | Avg. | TD |
|---|---|---|---|---|---|---|---|---|---|
| Drew Bledsoe | 93-95 | 96 | 150 | 1.6 | 0 | 1 | -9 | -9.0 | 0 |
| Dennis Bligen | 84-87 | 73 | 300 | 4.1 | 2 | 18 | 130 | 7.2 | 0 |
| Alvin Blount | 87 | 46 | 125 | 2.7 | 3 | 1 | 5 | 5.0 | 0 |
| Steve Bono | 85-95 | 84 | 222 | 2.6 | 7 | | | | |
| Cap Boso | 86-91 | | | | | 54 | 591 | 10.9 | 4 |
| Matt Bouza | 81-89 | 1 | 12 | 12.0 | 0 | 234 | 3064 | 13.1 | 17 |
| Mark Boyer | 85-92 | | | | | 170 | 1534 | 9.0 | 6 |
| Kyle Brady | 95 | | | | | 26 | 252 | 9.7 | 2 |
| Mark Brammer | 80-84 | 3 | 25 | 8.3 | 0 | 116 | 1137 | 9.8 | 10 |
| Melvin Bratton | 89-90 | 57 | 190 | 3.3 | 4 | 39 | 345 | 8.8 | 4 |
| Brian Brennan | 84-92 | | | | | 334 | 4336 | 13.0 | 20 |
| Hoby Brenner | 81-93 | | | | | 267 | 3849 | 14.4 | 21 |
| Chris Brewer | 84,87 | 34 | 83 | 2.4 | 2 | 7 | 76 | 10.9 | 1 |
| Leon Bright | 81-85 | 53 | 204 | 3.9 | 2 | 32 | 343 | 10.7 | 0 |
| James Brim | 87 | 2 | 36 | 180 | 1 | 18 | 282 | 15.7 | 2 |
| Dana Brinson | 89 | 17 | 64 | 3.8 | 0 | 12 | 71 | 5.9 | 0 |
| Vincent Brisby | 93-95 | | | | | 169 | 2504 | 14.8 | 10 |
| Bubby Brister | 86-95 | 161 | 405 | 2.5 | 7 | 2 | -8 | -4.0 | 0 |
| Mitch Brookins | 84 | 2 | 27 | 13.5 | 0 | 18 | 318 | 17.7 | 1 |
| Bill Brooks | 86-95 | 21 | 113 | 5.8 | 0 | 566 | 7777 | 13.7 | 46 |
| James Brooks | 81-92 | 1685 | 7962 | 4.7 | 49 | 383 | 3621 | 9.5 | 30 |
| Reggie Brooks | 93-95 | 325 | 1358 | 4.2 | 5 | 34 | 254 | 7.5 | 0 |
| Robert Brooks | 92-95 | 10 | 52 | 5.2 | 0 | 192 | 2451 | 12.8 | 18 |
| Steve Broussard | 90-95 | 488 | 2097 | 4.3 | 13 | 92 | 692 | 7.5 | 2 |
| A.B. Brown | 89-92 | 40 | 117 | 2.9 | 1 | 8 | 40 | 5.0 | 0 |
| Andre Brown | 89-90 | | | | | 27 | 459 | 17.0 | 5 |
| Charlie Brown | 82-87 | 4 | 53 | 13.3 | 0 | 220 | 3548 | 16.1 | 25 |
| Curtis Brown | 77-83 | 567 | 2171 | 3.8 | 9 | 102 | 772 | 7.6 | 5 |
| Dave Brown | 92-95 | 110 | 419 | 3.8 | 6 | | | | |
| Derek Brown | 92-94 | | | | | 11 | 87 | 7.9 | 0 |
| Derek Brown | 93-95 | 375 | 1353 | 3.6 | 6 | 100 | 864 | 8.6 | 3 |
| Eddie Brown | 85-91 | 25 | 164 | 6.6 | 0 | 363 | 6134 | 16.9 | 41 |
| Gary Brown | 91-95 | 477 | 2115 | 4.4 | 12 | 48 | 456 | 9.5 | 3 |
| Ivory Lee Brown | 92 | 68 | 194 | 2.9 | 2 | 7 | 54 | 7.7 | 0 |
| Reggie Brown | 82-83,87 | 39 | 136 | 3.5 | 0 | | | | |
| Ron Brown | 84-91 | 21 | 127 | 6.0 | 0 | 98 | 1791 | 18.3 | 13 |
| Ted Brown | 79-86 | 1117 | 4546 | 4.1 | 40 | 339 | 2850 | 8.4 | 13 |
| Theotis Brown | 79-84 | 549 | 2046 | 3.7 | 30 | 172 | 1558 | 9.1 | 3 |
| Tim Brown | 88-95 | 24 | 69 | 2.9 | 1 | 405 | 6076 | 15.0 | 46 |
| Tom Brown | 87,89 | 13 | 26 | 2.0 | 0 | 13 | 117 | 9.0 | 0 |
| Troy Brown | 93-95 | | | | | 16 | 181 | 10.3 | 0 |
| Tyrone Brown | 95 | | | | | 17 | 198 | 11.6 | 0 |
| Isaac Bruce | 94-95 | 4 | 19 | 4.8 | 0 | 140 | 2053 | 14.7 | 16 |
| Bob Bruer | 76, 79-83 | 5 | -4 | -0.8 | 0 | 72 | 709 | 9.9 | 8 |
| Mark Bruener | 95 | | | | | 26 | 238 | 9.2 | 3 |
| Mark Brunell | 93-95 | 73 | 487 | 6.7 | 5 | | | | |
| Scott Brunner | 80-83 | 69 | 129 | 1.9 | 1 | | | | |
| Cullen Bryant | 73-84,87 | 849 | 3264 | 3.8 | 20 | 148 | 1176 | 8.0 | 3 |
| Kelvin Bryant | 86-88,90 | 260 | 1186 | 4.6 | 6 | 154 | 1634 | 10.6 | 14 |
| Stephen Bryant | 82-85 | | | | | 35 | 489 | 14.0 | 0 |
| Jarrod Bunch | 91-94 | 138 | 629 | 4.6 | 5 | 26 | 156 | 6.0 | 2 |
| Cornell Burbage | 87-89 | | | | | 26 | 352 | 13.5 | 2 |
| John Burke | 94-95 | | | | | 24 | 222 | 9.3 | 0 |
| Randy Burke | 78-81 | | | | | 30 | 489 | 16.3 | 3 |
| Chris Burkett | 85-93 | 2 | -6 | -3.0 | 0 | 292 | 4352 | 14.9 | 19 |
| Jerry Butler | 79-83 | 4 | 32 | 8.0 | 0 | 278 | 4301 | 15.5 | 29 |
| Ray Butler | 80-88 | 4 | 9 | 2.3 | 0 | 239 | 3948 | 16.6 | 37 |
| Marion Butts | 89-95 | 1345 | 5185 | 3.9 | 43 | 68 | 471 | 6.9 | 0 |
| Keith Byars | 86-95 | 848 | 3049 | 3.6 | 23 | 532 | 4925 | 9.3 | 22 |
| Earnest Byner | 84-95 | 1852 | 7314 | 3.9 | 52 | 461 | 4207 | 9.1 | 14 |
| Carl Byrum | 86-88 | 132 | 527 | 4.0 | 0 | 18 | 127 | 7.1 | 1 |
| Lynn Cain | 79-85 | 615 | 2309 | 3.8 | 19 | 127 | 1061 | 8.4 | 6 |
| Chris Calloway | 90-95 | 10 | 68 | 6.8 | 0 | 186 | 2688 | 14.4 | 11 |
| Earl Campbell | 79-85 | 2187 | 9407 | 4.3 | 74 | 121 | 806 | 6.7 | 0 |
| Jeff Campbell | 90-94 | 2 | 6 | 3.0 | 0 | 37 | 517 | 14.0 | 4 |
| Scott Campbell | 84-87,89-90 | 43 | 170 | 4.0 | 2 | | | | |
| Billy Campfield | 78-82 | 167 | 649 | 3.9 | 5 | 107 | 958 | 9.0 | 6 |
| Wayne Capers | 83-86 | 5 | 26 | 5.2 | 1 | 51 | 822 | 164 | 5 |
| Joe Caravello | 87-90 | 1 | 0 | 0.0 | 0 | 16 | 160 | 10.0 | 1 |
| Cody Carlson | 87-94 | 81 | 217 | 2.7 | 4 | | | | |
| Rob Carpenter | 77-86 | 1172 | 4363 | 3.7 | 29 | 215 | 1707 | 7.9 | 5 |
| Rob Carpenter | 91-95 | 1 | 2 | 2.0 | 0 | 51 | 607 | 11.9 | 1 |
| Mark Carrier | 87-95 | 8 | 36 | 4.5 | 2 | 459 | 7218 | 15.7 | 38 |
| Wesley Carroll | 91-93 | | | | | 42 | 519 | 12.4 | 3 |
| Paul Ott Carruth | 86-89 | 194 | 614 | 3.2 | 5 | 59 | 426 | 7.2 | 3 |
| Carlos Carson | 80-89 | 12 | 62 | 5.2 | 0 | 353 | 6372 | 18.1 | 33 |
| Anthony Carter | 85-95 | 47 | 289 | 6.1 | 2 | 486 | 7732 | 15.9 | 55 |
| Cris Carter | 87-95 | 11 | 38 | 3.5 | 0 | 571 | 7177 | 12.6 | 66 |
| Dexter Carter | 90-95 | 228 | 976 | 4.3 | 4 | 61 | 656 | 10.8 | 2 |
| Gerald Carter | 80-87 | 4 | 24 | 6.0 | 0 | 239 | 3443 | 14.4 | 17 |
| Joe Carter | 84-86 | 118 | 589 | 5.0 | 1 | 11 | 66 | 6.0 | 0 |
| Pat Carter | 88-95 | | | | | 74 | 744 | 10.0 | 7 |
| Rodney Carter | 87-89 | 52 | 244 | 4.6 | 4 | 86 | 810 | 9.4 | 8 |
| Tony Carter | 94-95 | 10 | 34 | 3.4 | 0 | 41 | 353 | 8.6 | 1 |
| Maurice Carthon | 85-92 | 300 | 950 | 3.2 | 2 | 90 | 745 | 8.3 | 1 |
| Melvin Carver | 82-84,87 | 197 | 624 | 3.2 | 1 | 39 | 335 | 8.6 | 2 |
| Keith Cash | 91-95 | 1 | 0 | 0.0 | 0 | 104 | 1056 | 10.2 | 10 |
| Kerry Cash | 91-95 | | | | | 128 | 1385 | 10.8 | 9 |
| Ron Cassidy | 79-84 | | | | | 14 | 233 | 16.6 | 0 |
| Matt Cavanaugh | 78-89 | 60 | 213 | 3.6 | 3 | 1 | 9 | 9.0 | 0 |
| Jimmy Cefalo | 78-84 | | | | | 93 | 1739 | 18.7 | 13 |
| Larry Centers | 90-95 | 269 | 925 | 3.4 | 7 | 313 | 2805 | 9.0 | 9 |
| Jeff Chadwick | 83-92 | 3 | 3 | 1.0 | 1 | 292 | 4549 | 15.6 | 27 |
| Pat Chaffey | 91-93 | 61 | 330 | 5.4 | 2 | 11 | 111 | 10.1 | 1 |
| Chris Chandler | 88-95 | 177 | 648 | 3.7 | 9 | | | | |
| Thornton Chandler | 86-89 | | | | | 29 | 268 | 9.2 | 4 |
| Wes Chandler | 78-88 | 16 | 84 | 5.3 | 0 | 559 | 8966 | 16.0 | 56 |
| Mark Chmura | 93-95 | | | | | 70 | 857 | 12.2 | 7 |
| Wayne Crebet | 95 | 1 | 1 | 1.0 | 0 | 66 | 726 | 11.0 | 4 |
| Todd Christensen | 79-88 | 1 | -6 | -6.0 | 0 | 461 | 5872 | 12.7 | 41 |
| Bob Christian | 92-95 | 56 | 206 | 3.7 | 0 | 47 | 445 | 9.5 | 1 |
| Darryl Clack | 86-89 | 29 | 113 | 3.9 | 2 | 22 | 213 | 9.7 | 1 |
| Rickey Claitt | 80-81 | 60 | 234 | 3.9 | 1 | 3 | 34 | 11.3 | 1 |
| Allan Clark | 79-81 | 28 | 140 | 5.0 | 3 | 2 | 35 | 17.5 | 0 |
| Derrick Clark | 94 | 56 | 168 | 3.0 | 0 | 9 | 47 | 5.2 | 0 |

Lifetime Statistics- 1980-1995 Players Section 2 - **RUSHING and RECEIVING** 772

(All men with 25 or more rushing attempts or 10 or more receptions)

| | | RUSHING | | | | RECEIVING | | | |
|---|---|---|---|---|---|---|---|---|---|
| **Name** | **Years** | **Att.** | **Yards** | **Avg.** | **TD** | **Rec.** | **Yards** | **Avg.** | **TD** |
| Dwight Clark | 79-87 | 6 | 50 | 8.3 | 0 | 506 | 6750 | 13.3 | 48 |
| Gary Clark | 85-95 | 11 | 54 | 4.9 | 0 | 699 | 10856 | 15.5 | 65 |
| Jessie Clark | 83-90 | 415 | 1736 | 4.2 | 9 | 102 | 943 | 9.2 | 6 |
| Ken Clark | 90-92 | 161 | 510 | 3.2 | 0 | 43 | 314 | 7.3 | 0 |
| Louis Clark | 87-92 | | | | | 67 | 798 | 11.9 | 3 |
| Robert Clark | 88-92 | | | | | 163 | 2624 | 16.1 | 18 |
| Mark Clayton | 83-93 | 14 | 108 | 7.7 | 0 | 582 | 8974 | 15.4 | 84 |
| Joey Clinkscales | 87 | | | | | 13 | 240 | 18.5 | 1 |
| Ben Coates | 91-95 | 3 | -4 | -1.3 | 0 | 263 | 3014 | 11.5 | 25 |
| Reggie Cobb | 90-95 | 1040 | 3658 | 3.5 | 24 | 119 | 926 | 7.8 | 2 |
| Paul Coffman | 78-87 | 1 | 3 | 3.0 | 0 | 339 | 4340 | 12.8 | 42 |
| Lincoln Coleman | 93-94 | 98 | 312 | 3.2 | 3 | 12 | 70 | 5.8 | 0 |
| Pat Coleman | 90-94 | 2 | 3 | 1.5 | 0 | 42 | 575 | 13.7 | 2 |
| Kerry Collins | 95 | 42 | 74 | 1.8 | 3 | | | | |
| Dwight Collins | 84 | 3 | -14 | -4.7 | 0 | 11 | 143 | 13.0 | 1 |
| Shawn Collins | 89-93 | | | | | 98 | 1433 | 14.6 | 5 |
| Tony Collins | 81-87,90 | 1191 | 4647 | 3.9 | 32 | 261 | 2356 | 9.0 | 12 |
| Cris Collinsworth | 81-88 | 7 | -15 | -2.6 | 0 | 417 | 6698 | 16.1 | 36 |
| Curtis Conway | 93-95 | 16 | 152 | 9.5 | 0 | 120 | 1814 | 15.1 | 16 |
| Marv Cook | 89-95 | | | | | 257 | 2190 | 8.5 | 12 |
| Adrian Cooper | 91-95 | | | | | 86 | 1026 | 11.9 | 5 |
| Earl Cooper | 80-86 | 298 | 1152 | 3.9 | 6 | 213 | 1908 | 9.0 | 12 |
| Horace Copeland | 93-95 | 3 | 34 | 11.3 | 0 | 82 | 1546 | 18.9 | 6 |
| Russell Copeland | 93-95 | 2 | -8 | -4.0 | 0 | 76 | 1143 | 15.0 | 2 |
| Doug Cosbie | 79-88 | 7 | 35 | 5.0 | 0 | 300 | 3728 | 12.4 | 30 |
| Jeff Cothran | 94-95 | 42 | 147 | 3.5 | 0 | 12 | 68 | 5.7 | 1 |
| Aaron Cox | 88-93 | | | | | 102 | 1732 | 17.0 | 8 |
| Arthur Cox | 83-91 | | | | | 170 | 1758 | 10.3 | 10 |
| Donnie Craft | 82-83 | 73 | 189 | 2.6 | 3 | 35 | 329 | 9.4 | 1 |
| Roger Craig | 83-93 | 1991 | 8189 | 4.1 | 56 | 566 | 4911 | 8.7 | 17 |
| Aaron Craver | 91-92,94-95 | 102 | 443 | 4.3 | 6 | 75 | 673 | 9.0 | 1 |
| Charles Crawford | 86 | 28 | 88 | 3.1 | 1 | | | | |
| Joe Cribbs | 80-83, 85-88 | 1299 | 5356 | 4.1 | 27 | 224 | 2199 | 9.8 | 15 |
| Ray Crittenden | 93-94 | 1 | -3 | -3.0 | 0 | 44 | 672 | 15.3 | 4 |
| Corey Croom | 93-95 | 73 | 252 | 3.5 | 1 | 9 | 100 | 11.1 | 0 |
| Howard Cross | 89-95 | | | | | 131 | 1686 | 12.9 | 14 |
| Ray Crouse | 84 | 53 | 169 | 3.2 | 0 | 9 | 93 | 10.3 | 1 |
| Carlester Crumpler | 94-95 | | | | | 25 | 273 | 10.9 | 1 |
| Dwayne Crutchfield | 82-85 | 235 | 993 | 4.3 | 5 | 21 | 144 | 6.9 | 1 |
| Rodney Culver | 92-95 | 241 | 689 | 2.9 | 13 | 42 | 343 | 8.2 | 3 |
| Bennie Cunningham | 76-85 | | | | | 202 | 2879 | 14.3 | 20 |
| Randall Cunningham | 85-95 | 677 | 4482 | 6.6 | 32 | 1 | -3 | -3.0 | 0 |
| Gary Danielson | 76-78, 80-85,88 | 186 | 857 | 4.6 | 7 | 1 | 22 | 22.0 | 1 |
| Charles Davenport | 92-94 | | | | | 13 | 187 | 14.4 | 0 |
| Ron Davenport | 85-89 | 274 | 1127 | 4.1 | 13 | 93 | 801 | 8.6 | 4 |
| Johnny Davis | 78-87 | 314 | 1094 | 3.5 | 15 | 22 | 106 | 4.8 | 0 |
| Kenneth Davis | 86-94 | 820 | 3513 | 4.3 | 27 | 135 | 878 | 6.5 | 5 |
| Russell Davis | 80-83 | 104 | 474 | 4.6 | 2 | 5 | 45 | 9.0 | 0 |
| Terrell Davis | 95 | 237 | 1117 | 4.7 | 7 | 49 | 367 | 7.5 | 1 |
| Wendell Davis | 88-93 | 5 | 45 | 9.0 | 0 | 207 | 3000 | 14.5 | 14 |
| Willie Davis | 91-95 | 1 | -11 | -11.0 | 0 | 172 | 3014 | 17.5 | 20 |
| Julius Dawkins | 83-84 | | | | | 32 | 418 | 13.1 | 3 |
| Sean Dawkins | 93-95 | | | | | 129 | 1956 | 15.2 | 9 |
| Lawrence Dawsey | 91-95 | 1 | 9 | 9.0 | 0 | 206 | 2842 | 13.8 | 5 |
| Stacey Dawsey | 87 | | | | | 13 | 142 | 10.9 | 0 |
| Lake Dawson | 94-95 | 4 | 15 | 3.8 | 0 | 77 | 1050 | 13.6 | 7 |
| Lin Dawson | 81-85,88-89 | | | | | 117 | 1233 | 10.5 | 8 |
| Steve DeBerg | 77-93 | 196 | 210 | 1.1 | 7 | | | | |
| Joe Delaney | 81-82 | 329 | 1501 | 4.6 | 3 | 33 | 299 | 9.1 | 0 |
| Robert Delpino | 88-93 | 502 | 1815 | 3.6 | 18 | 178 | 1769 | 9.9 | 9 |
| Preston Dennard | 78-85 | 12 | 81 | 6.8 | 0 | 232 | 3665 | 15.8 | 30 |
| Glenn Dennison | 84,87 | 1 | 4 | 4.0 | 0 | 20 | 149 | 7.5 | 1 |
| Eric Dickerson | 83-93 | 2996 | 13259 | 4.4 | 90 | 281 | 2137 | 7.6 | 6 |
| Curtis Dickey | 80-86 | 937 | 4019 | 4.3 | 32 | 134 | 1577 | 11.8 | 8 |
| Clint Didier | 82-89 | | | | | 141 | 1923 | 13.6 | 21 |
| Scott Dierking | 77-84 | 734 | 2915 | 4.0 | 18 | 124 | 1028 | 8.3 | 5 |
| Trent Dilfer | 94-95 | 25 | 142 | 5.7 | 2 | | | | |
| Ken Dilger | 95 | | | | | 42 | 635 | 15.1 | 4 |
| Steve Dils | 80-88 | 45 | 71 | 1.6 | 1 | | | | |
| Anthony Dilweg | 89-90 | 21 | 114 | 5.4 | 0 | | | | |
| Mike Dingle | 91 | 21 | 91 | 4.3 | 0 | 5 | 23 | 4.6 | 1 |
| Robert DiRico | 87 | 25 | 90 | 3.6 | 0 | 2 | 22 | 11.0 | 0 |
| Al Dixon | 77-84 | 1 | -5 | -5.0 | 0 | 80 | 1194 | 14.9 | 8 |
| Floyd Dixon | 86-92 | 23 | 110 | 11.8 | 0 | 184 | 2523 | 13.7 | 16 |
| James Dixon | 89-91 | 14 | 73 | 5.2 | 0 | 26 | 503 | 19.3 | 2 |
| Zachary Dixon | 79-84 | 197 | 732 | 3.7 | 3 | 41 | 367 | 9.0 | 1 |
| Doug Donley | 81-86 | 2 | 5 | 2.5 | 0 | 55 | 898 | 16.3 | 4 |
| Dan Doornink | 78-85 | 523 | 1836 | 3.5 | 15 | 209 | 2006 | 9.6 | 11 |
| Tony Dorsett | 77-88 | 2936 | 12739 | 4.3 | 77 | 398 | 3554 | 8.9 | 13 |
| Marcus Dowdell | 92-93,95 | | | | | 17 | 148 | 8.7 | 1 |
| D.J. Dozier | 87-91 | 172 | 691 | 4.0 | 7 | 33 | 301 | 9.1 | 2 |
| Troy Drayton | 93-95 | 2 | 11 | 5.5 | 0 | 106 | 1053 | 9.9 | 14 |
| Chris Dressel | 83-91 | 1 | 3 | 3.0 | 0 | 111 | 1098 | 9.9 | 8 |
| Willie Drewrey | 85-93 | 2 | -4 | -2.0 | 0 | 106 | 1601 | 15.1 | 7 |
| Robert Drummond | 89-91 | 52 | 187 | 3.6 | 3 | 22 | 219 | 10.0 | 1 |
| Doug DuBose | 87-88 | 34 | 149 | 4.4 | 2 | 10 | 94 | 9.4 | 0 |
| Kenny Duckett | 82-85 | 3 | -19 | -6.3 | 0 | 34 | 503 | 14.8 | 4 |
| Bobby Duckworth | 82-86 | | | | | 82 | 1784 | 21.7 | 13 |
| Joe Dudek | 87 | 35 | 154 | 4.4 | 2 | 7 | 41 | 5.9 | 0 |
| Vaughn Dunbar | 92,94-95 | 267 | 935 | 3.5 | 5 | 11 | 73 | 6.6 | 0 |
| Curtis Duncan | 87-93 | | | | | 322 | 3935 | 12.2 | 20 |
| David Dunn | 95 | 1 | -13 | -13.0 | 0 | 17 | 209 | 12.3 | 1 |
| K.D. Dunn | 85-89 | | | | | 11 | 163 | 14.8 | 0 |
| Pat Dunsmore | 83-84 | | | | | 17 | 208 | 12.2 | 1 |
| Reggie Dupard | 86-90 | 217 | 704 | 3.2 | 6 | 43 | 303 | 7.0 | 0 |
| Mark Duper | 82-92 | 1 | -10 | -10.0 | 0 | 511 | 8869 | 17.3 | 59 |
| Marcus Dupree | 90-91 | 68 | 251 | 3.7 | 1 | 6 | 46 | 7.7 | 0 |
| Hart Lee Dykes | 89-90 | | | | | 83 | 1344 | 16.2 | 7 |
| Mike Dyal | 89-90,92-93 | | | | | 38 | 640 | 16.8 | 2 |
| Robin Earl | 77-82 | 94 | 382 | 4.1 | 1 | 47 | 486 | 10.3 | 4 |
| Quinn Early | 88-95 | 20 | 133 | 6.7 | 0 | 325 | 4497 | 13.8 | 30 |
| Walt Easley | 81-82 | 76 | 224 | 2.9 | 1 | 9 | 62 | 6.9 | 0 |
| Tony Eason | 83-90 | 134 | 503 | 3.8 | 6 | | | | |
| Jerry Eckwood | 79-81 | 515 | 1845 | 3.6 | 6 | 93 | 956 | 10.3 | 1 |
| Floyd Eddings | 82-83 | 3 | 15 | 5.0 | 0 | 28 | 506 | 18.1 | 0 |
| Ferrell Edmunds | 88-94 | 1 | -8 | -8.0 | 0 | 148 | 1894 | 12.8 | 12 |
| Al Edwards | 90-92 | 2 | 25 | 12.5 | 0 | 26 | 264 | 10.2 | 2 |
| Anthony Edwards | 89-93,95 | | | | | 58 | 964 | 16.6 | 4 |
| Kelvin Edwards | 86-88 | 3 | 67 | 22.3 | 1 | 49 | 746 | 15.2 | 3 |
| Stan Edwards | 82-87 | 149 | 533 | 3.6 | 2 | 52 | 436 | 8.4 | 1 |
| Ron Egloff | 77-84 | | | | | 75 | 839 | 11.2 | 4 |
| Donnie Elder | 85-86 | | | | | 25 | 477 | 19.1 | 0 |
| Henry Ellard | 83-95 | 19 | 50 | 2.6 | 0 | 723 | 12163 | 16.8 | 59 |
| Gary Ellerson | 85-87 | 169 | 688 | 4.1 | 8 | 21 | 216 | 10.3 | 1 |
| Craig Ellis | 86-87 | 26 | 144 | 4.0 | 2 | 5 | 39 | 7.8 | 0 |
| Gerry Ellis | 80-86 | 836 | 3826 | 4.6 | 25 | 267 | 2514 | 9.4 | 10 |
| Jerry Ellison | 95 | 26 | 218 | 8.4 | 5 | 7 | 44 | 6.3 | 0 |
| John Elway | 83-95 | 636 | 2849 | 4.5 | 28 | 2 | 47 | 23.5 | 1 |
| Bert Emanuel | 94-95 | 3 | 4 | 1.3 | 0 | 120 | 1688 | 14.1 | 9 |
| Phillip Epps | 82-89 | 11 | 135 | 12.3 | 1 | 200 | 2992 | 15.0 | 14 |
| Rich Erenberg | 84-86 | 174 | 642 | 3.7 | 3 | 98 | 901 | 9.2 | 7 |
| Craig Erickson | 92-95 | 62 | 177 | 2.9 | 0 | | | | |
| Ricky Ervins | 91-95 | 534 | 2114 | 4.0 | 8 | 115 | 849 | 7.4 | 2 |
| Boomer Esiason | 84-95 | 425 | 1535 | 3.6 | 6 | 1 | -8 | -8.0 | 0 |
| Chuck Evans | 93-95 | 39 | 111 | 2.8 | 1 | 23 | 160 | 7.0 | 1 |
| Jerry Evans | 93-95 | | | | | 25 | 251 | 10.0 | 3 |
| Vince Evans | 77-83,87-95 | 212 | 1129 | 5.3 | 14 | | | | |
| Jim Everett | 86-95 | 230 | 587 | 2.5 | 4 | | | | |
| Major Everett | 83-87 | 55 | 158 | 2.9 | 0 | 14 | 84 | 6.0 | 0 |
| Chad Fann | 93-95 | | | | | 17 | 137 | 8.1 | 0 |
| George Farmer | 82-84,87 | 1 | -9 | -9.0 | 0 | 65 | 980 | 15.1 | 7 |
| Mike Farr | 90-92 | | | | | 69 | 716 | 10.4 | 1 |
| Marshall Faulk | 94-95 | 603 | 2360 | 3.9 | 22 | 108 | 997 | 9.2 | 4 |
| Christian Fauria | 95 | | | | | 17 | 181 | 10.6 | 1 |
| Brett Favre | 91-95 | 186 | 797 | 4.3 | 7 | 1 | -7 | -7.0 | 0 |
| Ricky Feacher | 76-84 | 2 | -2 | -1.0 | 0 | 113 | 2084 | 18.4 | 15 |
| Gill Fenerty | 90-91 | 212 | 832 | 3.9 | 5 | 44 | 444 | 10.1 | 2 |
| Derrick Fenner | 89-95 | 730 | 2727 | 3.7 | 28 | 157 | 1234 | 7.9 | 6 |
| Rick Fenney | 87-91 | 358 | 1508 | 4.2 | 11 | 71 | 628 | 8.8 | 2 |
| Joe Ferguson | 73-90 | 351 | 1210 | 3.4 | 11 | 2 | -9 | -4.5 | 0 |
| Vagas Ferguson | 80-83 | 290 | 1163 | 4.0 | 5 | 26 | 212 | 8.2 | 0 |
| Mervyn Fernandez | 87-92 | 6 | 35 | 5.8 | 0 | 209 | 3764 | 18.0 | 19 |
| Vince Ferragamo | 77-86 | 75 | 134 | 1.8 | 2 | | | | |
| Earl Ferrell | 82-89 | 682 | 2937 | 4.3 | 24 | 186 | 1628 | 8.8 | 8 |
| Robert Fisher | 80-81 | | | | | 12 | 203 | 16.9 | 3 |
| Scott Fitzkee | 79-82 | 1 | 15 | 15.0 | 0 | 17 | 321 | 18.9 | 4 |
| Terrence Flagler | 87-91 | 56 | 237 | 4.2 | 2 | 33 | 366 | 11.1 | 1 |
| Terrell Fletcher | 95 | 26 | 140 | 5.4 | 1 | 3 | 26 | 8.7 | 0 |
| Kenny Flowers | 87,89 | 27 | 85 | 3.1 | 1 | 7 | 50 | 7.1 | 0 |
| John Floyd | 79-81 | | | | | 14 | 215 | 15.4 | 2 |
| William Floyd | 94-95 | 151 | 542 | 3.6 | 8 | 66 | 493 | 7.5 | 1 |
| Darren Flutie | 88 | | | | | 18 | 208 | 11.6 | 2 |
| Doug Flutie | 86-89 | 59 | 281 | 4.8 | 2 | | | | |
| Steve Folsom | 81-82,87-89 | | | | | 37 | 349 | 9.4 | 2 |
| Herman Fontenot | 85-90 | 102 | 370 | 3.6 | 2 | 143 | 1453 | 10.2 | 6 |
| Bernard Ford | 89-90 | | | | | 17 | 176 | 10.4 | 2 |
| Barry Foster | 90-94 | 915 | 3943 | 4.3 | 26 | 93 | 804 | 8.6 | 2 |
| John Fourcade | 87-90 | 48 | 302 | 6.3 | 2 | | | | |
| Dan Fouts | 73-87 | 224 | 476 | 2.1 | 13 | | | | |
| Todd Fowler | 86-88 | 16 | 36 | 2.3 | 0 | 17 | 113 | 7.6 | 0 |
| Jon Francis | 87 | 35 | 138 | 3.9 | 0 | 8 | 38 | 4.8 | 2 |
| Phil Francis | 79-80 | 38 | 154 | 4.1 | 1 | 35 | 221 | 6.3 | 0 |
| Russ Francis | 75-80,82-88 | 2 | 12 | 6.0 | 0 | 393 | 5262 | 13.4 | 40 |
| John Frank | 84-88 | 2 | -1 | -0.5 | 0 | 65 | 662 | 10.2 | 10 |
| Andra Franklin | 81-84 | 622 | 2232 | 3.6 | 22 | 6 | 15 | 2.5 | 1 |
| Byron Franklin | 81,83-87 | 5 | -8 | -1.6 | 0 | 145 | 2016 | 13.9 | 10 |
| Paul Frazier | 89 | 25 | 112 | 4.5 | 1 | 3 | 25 | 8.3 | 0 |
| Phil Freeman | 85-87 | 1 | 1 | 1.0 | 0 | 22 | 370 | 16.8 | 4 |
| Gus Frerotte | 94-95 | 26 | 17 | 0.6 | 1 | | | | |
| Mike Friede | 80-81 | | | | | 40 | 621 | 15.5 | 1 |
| John Friesz | 90-91,93-95 | 33 | 25 | 0.8 | 0 | | | | |
| Irving Fryar | 84-95 | 36 | 188 | 5.2 | 1 | 562 | 8916 | 15.9 | 58 |
| Steve Fuller | 79-86 | 186 | 908 | 4.8 | 11 | | | | |
| Brent Fullwood | 87-90 | 433 | 1702 | 3.9 | 18 | 44 | 370 | 8.4 | 1 |
| Bob Gagliano | 82-83,86-93 | 93 | 352 | 3.8 | 4 | | | | |
| Derrick Gaffney | 78-84,87 | 2 | -2 | -1.0 | 0 | 156 | 2613 | 16.8 | 7 |
| Derrick Gainer | 90,92-93 | 41 | 120 | 2.9 | 1 | 13 | 122 | 9.4 | 0 |
| Wendell Gaines | 95 | | | | | 14 | 117 | 8.4 | 2 |
| Hokie Gajan | 82-85 | 252 | 1358 | 5.4 | 11 | 63 | 515 | 8.2 | 2 |
| Scott Galbraith | 90-95 | | | | | 50 | 565 | 11.3 | 4 |
| Tony Galbreath | 76-87 | 1031 | 4072 | 3.9 | 34 | 490 | 4066 | 8.3 | 9 |
| Joey Galloway | 95 | 11 | 154 | 14.0 | 1 | 67 | 1039 | 15.5 | 7 |
| Rich Gannon | 87-93,95 | 173 | 833 | 4.8 | 5 | 1 | 0 | 0.0 | 0 |
| Earl Gant | 79-80 | 65 | 228 | 3.5 | 1 | 24 | 169 | 7.0 | 0 |
| Carwell Gardner | 91-95 | 178 | 621 | 3.5 | 10 | 27 | 243 | 9.0 | 1 |
| Charlie Garner | 94-95 | 217 | 987 | 4.5 | 9 | 18 | 135 | 7.5 | 0 |
| Alvin Garrett | 80-84 | 12 | 33 | 2.8 | 0 | 32 | 412 | 12.9 | 2 |
| Gregg Garrity | 83-89 | | | | | 82 | 1329 | 16.2 | 6 |
| Cleveland Gary | 89-94 | 684 | 2645 | 3.9 | 14 | 135 | 876 | 6.5 | 5 |
| Sam Gash | 92-95 | 91 | 266 | 2.9 | 2 | 49 | 396 | 8.1 | 1 |
| Willie Gault | 83-93 | 21 | 154 | 7.3 | 0 | 333 | 6635 | 19.9 | 44 |
| Everett Gay | 88-89 | | | | | 15 | 205 | 13.7 | 1 |
| Chris Gedney | 93-95 | | | | | 28 | 307 | 11.0 | 3 |
| Stan Gelbaugh | 86,88-89,91-95 | 28 | 108 | 3.9 | 0 | | | | |
| Dennis Gentry | 82-92 | 137 | 764 | 5.6 | 5 | 171 | 2076 | 12.1 | 7 |
| Jeff George | 90-95 | 111 | 187 | 1.7 | 2 | | | | |
| Nick Giaquinto | 80-83 | 40 | 178 | 4.5 | 1 | 65 | 722 | 11.1 | 3 |
| Jimmie Giles | 77-89 | 5 | -3 | -0.6 | 0 | 350 | 5084 | 14.5 | 41 |
| Ernest Givins | 86-95 | 35 | 345 | 9.9 | 1 | 571 | 8215 | 14.4 | 49 |
| Andrew Glover | 91-95 | | | | | 83 | 869 | 10.5 | 10 |
| Kerry Goode | 88-89 | 63 | 231 | 3.7 | 0 | 7 | 68 | 9.7 | 0 |
| Eugene Goodlow | 83-86 | 2 | 8 | 4.0 | 0 | 115 | 1677 | 14.6 | 10 |
| Preston Gothard | 85-88 | | | | | 41 | 459 | 11.2 | 3 |
| Sam Graddy | 87-88,90-92 | | | | | 18 | 477 | 26.5 | 3 |
| Hason Graham | 95 | | | | | 10 | 156 | 15.6 | 2 |
| Jeff Graham | 91-95 | | | | | 239 | 3556 | 14.9 | 9 |
| Scottie Graham | 91-95 | 306 | 1129 | 3.7 | 7 | 12 | 77 | 6.4 | 1 |
| Otis Grant | 83-84,87 | 3 | 10 | 3.3 | 0 | 37 | 565 | 15.3 | 1 |
| Earnest Gray | 79-85 | 2 | 2 | 1.0 | 0 | 246 | 3790 | 15.4 | 27 |
| Elvis Grbac | 93-95 | 33 | 34 | 1.0 | 2 | | | | |

| | | RUSHING | | | | RECEIVING | | | |
|---|---|---|---|---|---|---|---|---|---|
| **Name** | **Years** | **Att.** | **Yards** | **Avg.** | **TD** | **Rec.** | **Yards** | **Avg.** | **TD** |
| Boyce Green | 83-87 | 417 | 1561 | 3.7 | 6 | 56 | 428 | 7.6 | 2 |
| Eric Green | 90-95 | | | | | 241 | 3180 | 13.2 | 27 |
| Gaston Green | 88-92 | 551 | 2136 | 3.9 | 6 | 32 | 232 | 7.3 | 1 |
| Harold Green | 90-95 | 968 | 3727 | 3.9 | 8 | 145 | 1004 | 6.9 | 3 |
| Mark Green | 89-92 | 116 | 496 | 4.3 | 6 | 22 | 213 | 9.7 | 1 |
| Paul Green | 92-94 | | | | | 62 | 453 | 7.3 | 3 |
| Robert Green | 92-95 | 155 | 767 | 4.9 | 3 | 66 | 513 | 7.8 | 2 |
| Roy Green | 79-92 | 23 | 140 | 6.1 | 1 | 559 | 8965 | 16.0 | 66 |
| Willie Green | 91-95 | | | | | 156 | 2672 | 17.1 | 20 |
| Terry Greer | 86-90 | 3 | 51 | 17.0 | 0 | 38 | 640 | 16.8 | 4 |
| Keith Griffin | 84-88 | 329 | 1343 | 4.1 | 3 | 61 | 460 | 7.5 | 2 |
| Howard Griffith | 93-95 | 74 | 227 | 3.1 | 1 | 27 | 176 | 6.5 | 2 |
| Rich Griffith | 93,95 | | | | | 16 | 243 | 15.2 | 0 |
| Billy Griggs | 85-89 | | | | | 25 | 262 | 10.5 | 1 |
| Steve Grogan | 75-90 | 445 | 2176 | 4.9 | 35 | 3 | 19 | 6.3 | 0 |
| Jeff Groth | 79-85 | 4 | 43 | 10.8 | 0 | 152 | 2126 | 14.0 | 5 |
| Eric Guliford | 93-95 | 2 | 2 | 1.0 | 0 | 30 | 489 | 16.3 | 1 |
| Mike Guman | 80-88 | 333 | 1286 | 3.9 | 11 | 150 | 1433 | 9.6 | 4 |
| Jim Gustafson | 85-89 | 1 | -2 | -2.0 | 0 | 38 | 491 | 12.9 | 5 |
| Michael Haddix | 83-90 | 543 | 1635 | 3.0 | 3 | 172 | 1310 | 7.6 | 3 |
| James Hadnot | 80-83 | 266 | 1029 | 3.9 | 5 | 54 | 426 | 7.9 | 0 |
| Dino Hall | 79-83 | 27 | 194 | 7.2 | 1 | 11 | 125 | 11.4 | 1 |
| Ron Hall | 87-95 | | | | | 230 | 2609 | 11.3 | 10 |
| Ty Hallock | 93-94 | | | | | 15 | 163 | 10.9 | 2 |
| Lorenzo Hampton | 85-89 | 503 | 1949 | 3.9 | 22 | 123 | 954 | 7.8 | 6 |
| Rodney Hampton | 90-95 | 1547 | 5989 | 3.9 | 47 | 159 | 1227 | 7.7 | 2 |
| Anthony Hancock | 82-86 | | | | | 73 | 1266 | 17.3 | 5 |
| Travis Hannah | 93-95 | 1 | 5 | 5.0 | 0 | 13 | 166 | 12.8 | 0 |
| Jim Harbaugh | 87-95 | 387 | 2067 | 5.3 | 17 | | | | |
| Andre Hardy | 84-85,87 | 26 | 94 | 3.6 | 0 | 6 | 36 | 6.0 | 0 |
| Bruce Hardy | 78-89 | 1 | 2 | 2.0 | 0 | 256 | 2455 | 9.6 | 25 |
| Larry Hardy | 78-85 | | | | | 71 | 960 | 13.5 | 7 |
| Tony Hargain | 92 | | | | | 17 | 205 | 12.1 | 0 |
| Clarence Harmon | 77-82 | 360 | 1374 | 3.8 | 5 | 133 | 1383 | 10.4 | 11 |
| Derrick Harmon | 84-86 | 94 | 361 | 3.8 | 2 | 23 | 203 | 8.8 | 0 |
| Ronnie Harmon | 86-95 | 576 | 2607 | 4.5 | 9 | 541 | 5380 | 9.9 | 22 |
| Alvin Harper | 91-95 | 1 | 15 | 15.0 | 0 | 170 | 3119 | 18.3 | 12 |
| Bruce Harper | 77-84 | 374 | 1829 | 4.9 | 8 | 220 | 2409 | 11.0 | 12 |
| Michael Harper | 86-89 | 1 | 3 | 3.0 | 0 | 25 | 352 | 14.1 | 1 |
| Perry Harrington | 80-85 | 155 | 683 | 4.4 | 6 | 26 | 144 | 5.5 | 0 |
| Darryl Harris | 88 | 34 | 151 | 4.4 | 1 | 6 | 30 | 5.0 | 0 |
| Duriel Harris | 76-85 | 3 | 33 | 11.0 | 0 | 302 | 5055 | 16.7 | 20 |
| Herbert Harris | 86 | | | | | 11 | 148 | 13.5 | 0 |
| Jackie Harris | 90-95 | 1 | 1 | 1.0 | 0 | 221 | 2708 | 12.3 | 13 |
| Leonard Harris | 86-94 | 2 | 25 | 12.5 | 0 | 105 | 1428 | 13.6 | 8 |
| M.L. Harris | 80-85 | 3 | -5 | -1.7 | 0 | 99 | 1369 | 13.8 | 10 |
| Raymont Harris | 94-95 | 123 | 464 | 3.8 | 1 | 40 | 240 | 6.0 | 0 |
| William Harris | 87,89 | | | | | 12 | 110 | 7.6 | 1 |
| Emile Harry | 86,88-92 | 2 | 36 | 18.0 | 0 | 150 | 2011 | 13.4 | 9 |
| Frank Hartley | 94-95 | | | | | 11 | 137 | 12.5 | 1 |
| John Harvey | 90 | 27 | 113 | 4.2 | 0 | 11 | 86 | 7.8 | 1 |
| Don Hasselbeck | 77-85 | | | | | 107 | 1542 | 14.4 | 18 |
| Andre Hastings | 93-95 | 1 | 14 | 14.0 | 0 | 71 | 827 | 11.6 | 3 |
| Courtney Hawkins | 92-95 | 4 | 5 | 1.3 | 0 | 160 | 2200 | 13.8 | 12 |
| Frank Hawkins | 81-86 | 427 | 1635 | 3.8 | 15 | 96 | 685 | 7.1 | 4 |
| Greg Hawthorne | 79-86 | 137 | 527 | 3.8 | 7 | 89 | 1071 | 12.0 | 4 |
| Aaron Hayden | 95 | 128 | 470 | 3.7 | 3 | 5 | 53 | 10.6 | 0 |
| Jonathan Hayes | 85-95 | | | | | 151 | 1704 | 11.3 | 13 |
| Michael Haynes | 88-95 | 8 | 78 | 9.8 | 0 | 372 | 5648 | 15.2 | 42 |
| Herman Heard | 83-89 | 651 | 2694 | 4.1 | 13 | 132 | 1125 | 8.5 | 3 |
| Garrison Hearst | 93-95 | 397 | 1503 | 3.8 | 3 | 41 | 310 | 7.6 | 1 |
| Larry Heater | 80,82-83 | 114 | 373 | 3.3 | 3 | 12 | 154 | 12.8 | 0 |
| Bobby Hebert | 85-89,91-95 | 180 | 543 | 3.0 | 0 | 4 | 8 | 2.0 | 1 |
| Vaughn Hebron | 93-94 | 166 | 622 | 3.7 | 5 | 29 | 219 | 7.6 | 0 |
| Johnny Hector | 83-92 | 1051 | 4280 | 4.1 | 41 | 188 | 1661 | 8.8 | 3 |
| Lakei Heimuli | 87 | 34 | 128 | 3.8 | 0 | 5 | 51 | 10.2 | 1 |
| Ron Heller | 87-90,92 | | | | | 84 | 871 | 10.4 | 5 |
| Keith Henderson | 89-92 | 194 | 755 | 3.9 | 4 | 42 | 532 | 12.7 | 0 |
| Bernard Henry | 82-85 | | | | | 50 | 695 | 13.9 | 6 |
| Wally Henry | 77-82 | 2 | -4 | -2.0 | 0 | 15 | 229 | 15.3 | 2 |
| Mark Herrmann | 81-92 | 35 | -2 | -0.1 | 1 | | | | |
| Jessie Hester | 85-88,90-95 | 8 | 53 | 6.6 | 1 | 373 | 5850 | 15.7 | 29 |
| Craig Heyward | 88-95 | 919 | 3881 | 4.2 | 26 | 152 | 1305 | 8.6 | 4 |
| Victor Hicks | 80 | 1 | 19 | 19.0 | 0 | 23 | 318 | 13.4 | 3 |
| Mark Higgs | 88-95 | 792 | 2959 | 3.7 | 14 | 40 | 303 | 7.6 | 0 |
| Alonzo Highsmith | 87-92 | 283 | 1195 | 4.2 | 6 | 42 | 428 | 10.2 | 3 |
| Rusty Hilger | 85-88,90-91 | 35 | 91 | 2.6 | 0 | | | | |
| Bruce Hill | 87-91 | 6 | -8 | -1.3 | 0 | 190 | 2942 | 15.5 | 23 |
| David Hill | 76-87 | 8 | 37 | 4.6 | 0 | 358 | 4212 | 11.8 | 28 |
| Derek Hill | 89-90 | | | | | 53 | 846 | 16.0 | 1 |
| Drew Hill | 79-93 | 3 | 19 | 6.3 | 0 | 634 | 9831 | 15.5 | 60 |
| Eddie Hill | 79-84 | 120 | 443 | 3.7 | 2 | 26 | 171 | 6.6 | 2 |
| Greg Hill | 94-95 | 296 | 1241 | 4.2 | 2 | 23 | 137 | 6.0 | 0 |
| Tony Hill | 77-86 | 14 | 84 | 6.0 | 0 | 479 | 7988 | 16.7 | 51 |
| Lonzell Hill | 87-90 | 4 | -9 | -2.3 | 0 | 136 | 1696 | 12.5 | 13 |
| Randal Hill | 91-95 | 1 | 4 | 4.0 | 0 | 186 | 2679 | 14.4 | 8 |
| Ira Hillary | 87-90 | 1 | -2 | -2.0 | 0 | 27 | 303 | 11.2 | 2 |
| Dalton Hilliard | 86-93 | 1126 | 4164 | 3.7 | 39 | 249 | 2233 | 9.0 | 14 |
| Eric Hipple | 80-86,88-89 | 145 | 550 | 3.8 | 13 | | | | |
| Leroy Hoard | 90-95 | 550 | 2203 | 4.0 | 10 | 177 | 1849 | 10.4 | 14 |
| Daryl Hobbs | 93-95 | | | | | 43 | 664 | 15.4 | 3 |
| Floyd Hodge | 82-84 | 4 | 28 | 7.0 | 0 | 63 | 674 | 10.7 | 4 |
| Merril Hoge | 87-94 | 825 | 3139 | 3.8 | 21 | 254 | 2133 | 8.4 | 23 |
| Gary Hogeboom | 80-89 | 83 | 181 | 2.2 | 4 | | | | |
| Jamie Holland | 87-92 | 9 | 65 | 7.2 | 0 | 73 | 1037 | 14.2 | 1 |
| Donald Hollas | 91-92,94 | 32 | 175 | 5.5 | 0 | | | | |
| Steve Holloway | 87 | | | | | 10 | 127 | 12.7 | 0 |
| Rodney Holman | 82-95 | | | | | 365 | 4771 | 13.1 | 36 |
| Scott Holman | 86-87 | | | | | 18 | 196 | 10.9 | 0 |
| Darick Holmes | 95 | 172 | 698 | 4.1 | 4 | 24 | 214 | 8.9 | 0 |
| Don Holmes | 86-90 | | | | | 25 | 413 | 16.5 | 1 |
| Jack Holmes | 78-82 | 117 | 393 | 3.4 | 4 | 71 | 453 | 6.4 | 1 |
| Pete Holohan | 81-92 | 1 | 3 | 3.0 | 0 | 363 | 3981 | 11.0 | 16 |
| Mike Holston | 81-85 | | | | | 74 | 1111 | 15.0 | 4 |
| Harry Holt | 83-87 | 5 | 36 | 5.0 | 1 | 70 | 895 | 12.8 | 5 |
| Melvin Hoover | 82-84 | 1 | 5 | 5.0 | 0 | 16 | 364 | 22.8 | 2 |
| Ethan Horton | 85,87,89-94 | 79 | 241 | 3.1 | 3 | 212 | 2360 | 11.1 | 16 |
| Jeff Hostetler | 84-95 | 264 | 1184 | 4.5 | 16 | | | | |
| Kevin House | 80-87 | 7 | 41 | 5.9 | 0 | 299 | 5169 | 17.3 | 34 |
| Bobby Howard | 86-87 | 60 | 210 | 3.5 | 2 | 15 | 183 | 12.2 | 0 |
| Desmond Howard | 92-95 | 7 | 43 | 6.1 | 0 | 92 | 1309 | 14.2 | 6 |
| William Howard | 88-89 | 223 | 809 | 3.6 | 2 | 41 | 285 | 7.0 | 1 |
| Steve Howell | 79-81 | 68 | 235 | 3.5 | 1 | 10 | 70 | 7.0 | 0 |
| Harlan Huckleby | 80-85 | 242 | 779 | 3.2 | 10 | 53 | 411 | 7.8 | 3 |
| Gordon Hudson | 86 | | | | | 13 | 131 | 10.1 | 1 |
| Danan Hughes | 92-95 | 1 | 5 | 5.0 | 0 | 21 | 183 | 8.7 | 1 |
| David Hughes | 81-86 | 308 | 1041 | 3.4 | 2 | 107 | 864 | 8.1 | 5 |
| Bobby Humphery | 84-90 | 1 | 10 | 10.0 | 0 | 14 | 206 | 14.7 | 1 |
| Bobby Humphrey | 89-92 | 695 | 2857 | 4.1 | 15 | 100 | 815 | 8.2 | 2 |
| Stan Humphries | 89-95 | 116 | 304 | 2.6 | 7 | 1 | -4 | -4.0 | 0 |
| Earnest Hunter | 95 | 30 | 100 | 3.3 | 0 | 5 | 42 | 8.4 | 0 |
| Eddie Hunter | 87 | 56 | 209 | 3.7 | 0 | 7 | 28 | 4.0 | 2 |
| Herman Hunter | 85-87 | 64 | 287 | 4.5 | 1 | 56 | 646 | 11.5 | 2 |
| Tony Hunter | 83-86 | 4 | 28 | 7.0 | 0 | 134 | 1501 | 11.2 | 9 |
| Mark Ingram | 87-95 | 3 | 2 | 0.7 | 0 | 263 | 3893 | 14.8 | 26 |
| Michael Irvin | 88-95 | 5 | 5 | 1.0 | 0 | 527 | 8538 | 16.2 | 50 |
| Qadry Ismail | 93-95 | 4 | 21 | 5.3 | 0 | 96 | 1505 | 15.7 | 9 |
| Raghib Ismail | 93-95 | 14 | 55 | 3.9 | 0 | 88 | 1357 | 15.4 | 9 |
| Eddie Lee Ivery | 79-86 | 667 | 2933 | 4.4 | 23 | 162 | 1612 | 9.9 | 7 |
| Alfred Jackson | 79-84 | 3 | 9 | 3.0 | 0 | 188 | 3010 | 16.0 | 21 |
| Andrew Jackson | 87 | 50 | 208 | 4.2 | 1 | 5 | 14 | 2.8 | 0 |
| Billy Jackson | 81-84 | 399 | 1365 | 3.4 | 16 | 58 | 416 | 7.2 | 2 |
| Bo Jackson | 87-90 | 515 | 2782 | 5.4 | 16 | 40 | 352 | 8.8 | 2 |
| Earnest Jackson | 83-88 | 1059 | 4167 | 3.9 | 22 | 87 | 695 | 8.0 | 2 |
| Keith Jackson | 88-95 | | | | | 401 | 4778 | 11.9 | 39 |
| Kenny Jackson | 84-91 | 8 | 51 | 6.4 | 0 | 126 | 2170 | 17.2 | 11 |
| Louis Jackson | 81 | 27 | 68 | 2.5 | 1 | 3 | 25 | 8.3 | 0 |
| Mark Jackson | 86-94 | 21 | 94 | 4.5 | 0 | 342 | 5551 | 16.2 | 29 |
| Michael Jackson | 91-95 | 2 | 22 | 11.0 | 0 | 170 | 2797 | 16.4 | 28 |
| Willie Jackson | 95 | | | | | 53 | 589 | 11.1 | 5 |
| Craig James | 84-88 | 589 | 2479 | 4.2 | 11 | 81 | 819 | 10.1 | 2 |
| Garry James | 86-88 | 422 | 1502 | 3.6 | 12 | 89 | 816 | 9.2 | 2 |
| Lionel James | 84-88 | 231 | 1062 | 4.6 | 4 | 209 | 2278 | 10.9 | 10 |
| Lynn James | 90-91 | 1 | 11 | 11.0 | 0 | 10 | 139 | 13.9 | 1 |
| Ron Jaworski | 74-89 | 257 | 859 | 3.3 | 16 | | | | |
| John Jefferson | 78-85 | 6 | 61 | 10.2 | 0 | 351 | 5714 | 16.3 | 47 |
| Shawn Jefferson | 91-95 | 11 | 121 | 11.0 | 0 | 162 | 2141 | 13.2 | 10 |
| Haywood Jeffires | 87-95 | | | | | 515 | 6119 | 11.9 | 47 |
| Ken Jenkins | 83-86 | 80 | 397 | 5.0 | 1 | 21 | 246 | 11.7 | 0 |
| Keith Jennings | 89,91-95 | | | | | 87 | 862 | 9.9 | 10 |
| Stanford Jennings | 84-92 | 313 | 1250 | 4.0 | 9 | 116 | 1096 | 9.4 | 10 |
| Derrick Jensen | 79-86 | 224 | 780 | 3.5 | 5 | 44 | 384 | 8.7 | 3 |
| Jim Jensen | 81-92 | 26 | 142 | 5.5 | 0 | 229 | 2171 | 9.5 | 19 |
| James Jett | 93-95 | 1 | 0 | 0.0 | 0 | 61 | 1203 | 19.7 | 4 |
| Jim Jodat | 77-83 | 226 | 866 | 3.8 | 7 | 35 | 265 | 7.6 | 2 |
| Paul Johns | 81-84 | 3 | 11 | 3.7 | 0 | 74 | 1058 | 14.3 | 7 |
| Anthony Johnson | 90-95 | 330 | 1469 | 4.5 | 2 | 185 | 1574 | 8.5 | 0 |
| Bill Johnson | 85-87 | 86 | 475 | 5.5 | 1 | 16 | 122 | 7.6 | 0 |
| Billy "White Shoes" Johnson | 74-87 | 56 | 316 | 5.6 | 2 | 337 | 4211 | 12.5 | 25 |
| Bobby Johnson | 84-86 | 2 | 28 | 14.0 | 0 | 112 | 1862 | 13.2 | 15 |
| Butch Johnson | 76-85 | 5 | 22 | 4.4 | 0 | 193 | 3091 | 16.0 | 28 |
| Charles Johnson | 94-95 | 5 | -11 | -2.3 | 0 | 76 | 1009 | 13.3 | 3 |
| Damone Johnson | 87-92 | | | | | 132 | 1015 | 7.7 | 18 |
| Dan Johnson | 83-87 | | | | | 94 | 1012 | 10.8 | 16 |
| Flip Johnson | 88-89 | | | | | 34 | 473 | 13.9 | 2 |
| Jimmie Johnson | 89-95 | | | | | 38 | 405 | 10.7 | 44 |
| Joe Johnson | 89-92 | 4 | 26 | 6.5 | 0 | 24 | 247 | 10.3 | 1 |
| Johnny Johnson | 90-94 | 1046 | 4078 | 3.9 | 21 | 177 | 1513 | 8.5 | 5 |
| LeShon Johnson | 94-95 | 28 | 97 | 3.5 | 0 | 13 | 168 | 12.9 | 0 |
| Lonnie Johnson | 94-95 | | | | | 52 | 546 | 10.5 | 0 |
| Maurice Johnson | 91-94 | | | | | 39 | 371 | 9.5 | 4 |
| Pete Johnson | 77-84 | 1489 | 5626 | 3.8 | 76 | 175 | 1334 | 7.6 | 6 |
| Reggie Johnson | 91-95 | 2 | 7 | 3.5 | 0 | 48 | 602 | 12.5 | 5 |
| Richard Johnson | 87,89-90 | 12 | 38 | 3.2 | 0 | 135 | 1823 | 13.5 | 14 |
| Ron Johnson | 86-89 | 1 | 3 | 3.0 | 0 | 61 | 1105 | 18.1 | 4 |
| Tracy Johnson | 89-95 | 60 | 228 | 3.8 | 5 | 28 | 218 | 7.8 | 2 |
| Troy Johnson | 86-89 | | | | | 41 | 777 | 19.0 | 2 |
| Trumaine Johnson | 85-88 | | | | | 86 | 1150 | 13.4 | 4 |
| Vance Johnson | 85-93,95 | 17 | 44 | 2.6 | 0 | 415 | 5695 | 13.7 | 37 |
| Daryl Johnston | 89-95 | 200 | 685 | 3.4 | 8 | 214 | 1727 | 8.1 | 11 |
| Bill Jones | 90-92 | 10 | 47 | 4.7 | 0 | 35 | 240 | 6.9 | 6 |
| Bobby Jones | 78-83 | 2 | 23 | 11.5 | 0 | 89 | 1368 | 15.4 | 6 |
| Brent Jones | 87-95 | | | | | 355 | 4384 | 12.3 | 30 |
| Calvin Jones | 94-95 | 27 | 112 | 4.1 | 0 | 2 | 6 | 3.0 | 0 |
| Cedric Jones | 82-90 | 2 | 10 | 5.0 | 0 | 191 | 2703 | 14.1 | 16 |
| Ernie Jones | 88-93 | 12 | 76 | 6.3 | 0 | 215 | 3630 | 16.9 | 20 |
| Fred Jones | 90-93 | 6 | 33 | 5.5 | 0 | 36 | 466 | 12.9 | 0 |
| Gordon Jones | 79-83 | 2 | 2 | 1.0 | 0 | 97 | 1402 | 14.5 | 8 |
| Hassan Jones | 86-93 | 5 | 52 | 10.4 | 0 | 229 | 3824 | 16.7 | 24 |
| James Jones | 80-82,84-85 | 84 | 331 | 3.9 | 1 | 42 | 312 | 7.4 | 1 |
| James Jones | 83-92 | 1010 | 3626 | 3.6 | 26 | 318 | 2641 | 8.3 | 10 |
| Johnny "Lam" Jones | 80-84 | 9 | 17 | 1.9 | 0 | 138 | 2322 | 16.8 | 13 |
| Keith Jones | 89-92 | 180 | 665 | 3.7 | 6 | 66 | 593 | 9.0 | 0 |
| Keith Jones | 89 | 43 | 160 | 3.7 | 1 | 15 | 126 | 8.4 | 0 |
| Mike Jones | 83-89 | 7 | 60 | 8.6 | 0 | 123 | 2372 | 19.3 | 11 |
| Tony Jones | 90-93 | | | | | 63 | 798 | 12.7 | 9 |
| Andrew Jordan | 94 | | | | | 35 | 336 | 9.6 | 0 |
| Buford Jordon | 86-91 | 184 | 687 | 3.7 | 8 | 37 | 355 | 9.6 | 2 |
| Randy Jordan | 93,95 | 33 | 95 | 2.9 | 0 | 62 | 521 | 8.4 | 2 |
| Steve Jordan | 82-94 | 1 | 4 | 4.0 | 1 | 498 | 6307 | 12.7 | 28 |
| Tony Jordan | 88-89 | 144 | 371 | 2.6 | 5 | 10 | 44 | 4.4 | 0 |
| Tim Jorden | 90-92 | | | | | 23 | 165 | 7.2 | 2 |
| James Joseph | 91-95 | 250 | 823 | 3.3 | 4 | 102 | 817 | 8.0 | 3 |
| Yonel Jourdain | 94-95 | 25 | 87 | 3.5 | 0 | 11 | 63 | 5.7 | 0 |
| Trey Junkin | 83-95 | | | | | 17 | 144 | 8.5 | 7 |
| Vyto Kab | 82-85,87 | | | | | 36 | 386 | 10.7 | 5 |
| Rick Kane | 77-85 | 409 | 1486 | 3.6 | 12 | 77 | 767 | 10.0 | 2 |
| Tommy Kane | 88-92 | | | | | 142 | 2034 | 14.3 | 9 |
| Eric Kattus | 86-92 | | | | | 66 | 698 | 10.6 | 5 |
| Napoleon Kaufman | 95 | 108 | 490 | 4.5 | 1 | 9 | 62 | 6.9 | 0 |

Lifetime Statistics- 1980-1995 Players Section 2 - **RUSHING and RECEIVING**
(All men with 25 or more rushing attempts or 10 or more receptions)
774

| Name | Years | RUSHING Att. | Yards | Avg. | TD | RECEIVING Rec. | Yards | Avg. | TD |
|---|---|---|---|---|---|---|---|---|---|
| Clarence Kay | 84-92 | | | | | 193 | 2136 | 11.1 | 3 |
| Jim Kelly | 86-95 | 285 | 983 | 3.4 | 5 | 2 | 40 | 20.0 | 0 |
| Jeff Kemp | 83-91 | 109 | 448 | 4.1 | 1 | | | | |
| Perry Kemp | 87-91 | 7 | 41 | 5.9 | 0 | 194 | 2565 | 13.2 | 8 |
| Bill Kenney | 79-88 | 123 | 191 | 1.6 | 5 | 2 | 0 | 0.0 | 0 |
| Tony Kimbrough | 93-94 | | | | | 10 | 99 | 9.9 | 0 |
| Brian Kinchen | 88-95 | | | | | 75 | 810 | 10.8 | 3 |
| Todd Kinchen | 92-95 | 7 | 70 | 10.0 | 1 | 67 | 908 | 13.6 | 7 |
| Bruce King | 85-87 | 41 | 121 | 3.0 | 0 | 8 | 48 | 6.0 | 0 |
| Kenny King | 79-85 | 579 | 2477 | 4.3 | 7 | 89 | 715 | 8.0 | 1 |
| Larry Kinnebrew | 83-87,89-90 | 779 | 3133 | 4.0 | 44 | 70 | 660 | 9.4 | 3 |
| Terry Kirby | 93-95 | 287 | 1037 | 3.6 | 9 | 155 | 1646 | 10.6 | 6 |
| Rocky Klever | 83-87 | | | | | 46 | 514 | 11.1 | 3 |
| David Klingler | 92-95 | 69 | 420 | 6.1 | 0 | 1 | -6 | -6.0 | 0 |
| Jeff Komlo | 79-83 | 38 | 121 | 3.2 | 2 | | | | |
| Bernie Kosar | 85-95 | 179 | 259 | 1.4 | 5 | 3 | -5 | -1.2 | 0 |
| Glen Kozlowski | 87-92 | 1 | 3 | 3.0 | 0 | 31 | 471 | 15.2 | 3 |
| Erik Kramer | 87,91-95 | 99 | 107 | 1.1 | 2 | | | | |
| Tommy Kramer | 77-90 | 214 | 531 | 2.5 | 8 | 1 | 23 | 23.0 | 1 |
| Steve Kreider | 79-86 | 4 | 23 | 5.8 | 0 | 150 | 2119 | 14.1 | 9 |
| Dave Krieg | 80-95 | 394 | 1252 | 3.2 | 12 | 2 | 5 | 2.5 | 0 |
| Gary Kubiak | 83-91 | 65 | 238 | 3.7 | 2 | | | | |
| Ken Lacy | 84-85,87 | 56 | 235 | 3.6 | 2 | 13 | 87 | 6.7 | 2 |
| Greg LaFleur | 81-86 | | | | | 64 | 729 | 11.4 | 3 |
| Eric Lane | 81-87 | 129 | 405 | 3.1 | 4 | 42 | 357 | 8.5 | 2 |
| David Lang | 91-95 | 49 | 273 | 5.6 | 5 | 30 | 388 | 12.9 | 1 |
| Gene Lang | 84-90 | 319 | 1148 | 3.6 | 11 | 134 | 1244 | 9.3 | 9 |
| Reggie Langhorne | 85-93 | 9 | 27 | 3.0 | 1 | 411 | 5446 | 13.2 | 19 |
| Steve Largent | 76-89 | 17 | 83 | 4.9 | 1 | 819 | 13089 | 16.0 | 100 |
| Derrick Lassic | 93 | 75 | 269 | 3.6 | 3 | 9 | 37 | 4.1 | 0 |
| Babe Laufenberg | 83,85-90 | 33 | 126 | 3.6 | 0 | | | | |
| Michael LeBlanc | 87 | 49 | 170 | 3.5 | 1 | 2 | 3 | 1.5 | 0 |
| Terry LeCount | 78-84 | 6 | 90 | 15.0 | 0 | 89 | 1354 | 15.2 | 7 |
| Amp Lee | 92-95 | 261 | 1067 | 4.1 | 5 | 152 | 1143 | 7.5 | 7 |
| Danzell Lee | 87 | | | | | 12 | 124 | 10.3 | 0 |
| Gary Lee | 87-88 | 41 | 569 | 13.9 | 1 | | | | |
| Ronnie Lee | 79-89 | | | | | 25 | 167 | 6.7 | 3 |
| Tim Lester | 92-95 | 23 | 97 | 4.2 | 1 | 19 | 155 | 8.2 | 0 |
| Dorsey Levens | 94-95 | 41 | 135 | 3.3 | 3 | 49 | 443 | 9.0 | 4 |
| Darren Lewis | 91-93 | 112 | 431 | 3.8 | 4 | 22 | 201 | 9.1 | 0 |
| David Lewis | 84-87 | | | | | 60 | 731 | 12.2 | 8 |
| Gary Lewis | 81-84 | 4 | 16 | 4.0 | 1 | 21 | 285 | 13.6 | 1 |
| Greg Lewis | 91-92 | 172 | 644 | 3.7 | 8 | 6 | 39 | 6.5 | 0 |
| Leo Lewis | 81-91 | 16 | 19 | 0.8 | 0 | 182 | 2924 | 16.1 | 16 |
| Nate Lewis | 90-95 | 12 | 44 | 3.7 | 1 | 130 | 1802 | 13.9 | 13 |
| Roderick Lewis | 94-95 | | | | | 20 | 164 | 8.2 | 0 |
| Ron Lewis | 90,92-94 | | | | | 27 | 315 | 11.7 | 0 |
| Thomas Lewis | 94-95 | | | | | 16 | 254 | 15.9 | 1 |
| Louis Lipps | 84-92 | 29 | 388 | 13.4 | 4 | 359 | 6019 | 16.8 | 39 |
| Dave Little | 84-91 | | | | | 25 | 243 | 9.7 | 1 |
| Larry Linne | 87 | | | | | 11 | 158 | 14.4 | 2 |
| Charles Lockett | 87-88 | | | | | 29 | 481 | 16.6 | 2 |
| Scott Lockwood | 92 | 35 | 162 | 4.6 | 0 | | | | |
| James Lofton | 78-93 | 32 | 246 | 7.7 | 1 | 764 | 14004 | 18.3 | 75 |
| Dave Logan | 76-84 | | | | | 263 | 4250 | 16.2 | 24 |
| Marc Logan | 87-95 | 301 | 1275 | 4.2 | 13 | 97 | 860 | 8.9 | 3 |
| Neil Lomax | 81-88 | 222 | 969 | 4.4 | 10 | 1 | 10 | 10.0 | 0 |
| Chuck Long | 86-90 | 34 | 88 | 2.6 | 0 | | | | |
| Randy Love | 79-86 | 65 | 211 | 3.2 | 3 | 15 | 95 | 6.3 | 2 |
| Edwin Lovelady | 87 | 2 | 11 | 5.5 | 0 | 10 | 125 | 12.5 | 2 |
| Derek Loville | 90-91,94-95 | 278 | 903 | 3.2 | 10 | 2 | 26 | 13.0 | 0 |
| Oliver Luck | 83-86 | 44 | 237 | 5.4 | 10 | 2 | 26 | 13.0 | 0 |
| Ed Luther | 80-84 | 20 | -19 | -1.0 | 0 | | | | |
| Eric Lynch | 92-95 | 54 | 207 | 3.8 | 2 | 15 | 100 | 6.7 | 0 |
| Mitch Lyons | 93-95 | | | | | 20 | 200 | 10.0 | 0 |
| Rob Lytle | 77-83 | 376 | 1451 | 3.9 | 12 | 61 | 562 | 9.2 | 2 |
| Kevin Mack | 85-93 | 1291 | 5123 | 4.0 | 46 | 197 | 1602 | 8.1 | 8 |
| Calvin Magee | 85-88 | | | | | 114 | 1379 | 12.1 | 11 |
| Don Majkowski | 87-95 | 222 | 964 | 4.3 | 12 | | | | |
| Mark Malone | 80-89 | 159 | 628 | 3.9 | 18 | 1 | 90 | 90.0 | 1 |
| Pete Mandley | 84-90 | 9 | 48 | 5.3 | 1 | 172 | 2370 | 13.8 | 12 |
| Tim Manoa | 87-89,91 | 236 | 938 | 4.0 | 6 | 40 | 308 | 7.7 | 2 |
| Lionel Manuel | 84-90 | 9 | 44 | 4.9 | 0 | 232 | 3941 | 17.0 | 23 |
| Ken Margerum | 81-87 | 2 | 18 | 9.0 | 0 | 94 | 1336 | 14.2 | 8 |
| Dan Marino | 83-95 | 246 | 111 | 0.5 | 8 | 1 | -6 | -6.0 | 0 |
| Doug Marsh | 80-86 | 2 | 0 | 0.0 | 0 | 166 | 2129 | 12.8 | 19 |
| Arthur Marshall | 92-95 | 14 | 65 | 4.6 | 0 | 87 | 1269 | 14.6 | 4 |
| Henry Marshall | 76-87 | 24 | 257 | 10.7 | 2 | 416 | 6545 | 15.7 | 33 |
| Curtis Martin | 95 | 368 | 1487 | 4.0 | 14 | 30 | 261 | 8.7 | 1 |
| Eric Martin | 85-94 | 4 | 11 | 2.8 | 0 | 553 | 8161 | 14.8 | 49 |
| Kelvin Martin | 87-95 | 11 | 7 | 0.6 | 0 | 342 | 4388 | 12.8 | 14 |
| Mike Martin | 83-89 | 3 | 24 | 8.0 | 0 | 67 | 1017 | 15.2 | 6 |
| Sammy Martin | 88-91 | 2 | 20 | 10.0 | 0 | 27 | 424 | 15.7 | 1 |
| Tony Martin | 90-95 | 5 | 3 | 0.6 | 0 | 249 | 3831 | 15.4 | 22 |
| Rich Martini | 79-81 | | | | | 33 | 367 | 11.1 | 2 |
| Larry Mason | 87-88 | 104 | 401 | 3.9 | 2 | 13 | 110 | 8.5 | 1 |
| Rick Massie | 87 | | | | | 13 | 244 | 18.8 | 4 |
| Le'Shai Maston | 93-95 | 41 | 186 | 4.5 | 0 | 21 | 157 | 7.5 | 0 |
| Terance Mathis | 90-95 | 8 | 73 | 9.1 | 2 | 282 | 3623 | 12.8 | 24 |
| Ira Matthews | 79-81 | 7 | 14 | 2.0 | 0 | 18 | 125 | 6.9 | 0 |
| Bruce Mathison | 83-87 | 34 | 245 | 7.2 | 1 | | | | |
| Allama Matthews | 83-85 | | | | | 11 | 101 | 9.2 | 1 |
| Aubrey Matthews | 86-95 | 6 | 6 | 1.0 | 0 | 157 | 2071 | 13.2 | 9 |
| Rich Mauti | 77-83 | 1 | 2 | 2.0 | 0 | 21 | 314 | 15.0 | 2 |
| James Mayberry | 79-81 | 81 | 347 | 4.3 | 1 | 13 | 53 | 4.1 | 0 |
| Rueben Mayes | 86-88,90,92-93 | 866 | 3484 | 4.0 | 23 | 57 | 401 | 7.0 | 0 |
| Derrick McAdoo | 87-88 | 53 | 230 | 4.3 | 3 | 2 | 12 | 6.0 | 0 |
| Fred McAfee | 91-95 | 256 | 975 | 3.8 | 6 | 19 | 119 | 6.3 | 0 |
| Oscar McBride | 95 | | | | | 13 | 112 | 8.6 | 2 |
| Ed McCaffrey | 91-95 | 1 | -1 | -1.0 | 0 | 142 | 1699 | 12.0 | 11 |
| Reece McCall | 78-85 | | | | | 94 | 1366 | 14.5 | 12 |
| Napoleon McCallum | 86,90-94 | 223 | 790 | 3.5 | 3 | 16 | 121 | 7.6 | 0 |
| Keenan McCardell | 92-95 | | | | | 80 | 1133 | 14.2 | 8 |
| Willie McClendon | 79-82 | 94 | 369 | 3.9 | 2 | 9 | 38 | 4.2 | 0 |
| Mike McCloskey | 83-85 | | | | | 29 | 318 | 11.0 | 3 |

| Name | Years | RUSHING Att. | Yards | Avg. | TD | RECEIVING Rec. | Yards | Avg. | TD |
|---|---|---|---|---|---|---|---|---|---|
| David McCluskey | 87 | 29 | 94 | 3.2 | 1 | 1 | 8 | 8.0 | 0 |
| Phil McConkey | 84-89 | | | | | 67 | 1118 | 16.6 | 2 |
| James McDonald | 83-85,87 | | | | | 14 | 168 | 12.0 | 3 |
| Keith McDonald | 87,89 | 1 | -2 | -2.0 | 0 | 16 | 194 | 12.1 | 1 |
| Paul McDonald | 82-87 | 37 | 10 | 0.3 | 1 | 1 | -4 | -4.0 | 0 |
| Anthony McDowell | 92-95 | 9 | 34 | 3.8 | 0 | 118 | 1504 | 12.7 | 11 |
| O.J. McDuffie | 93-94 | 6 | 28 | 4.7 | 0 | 56 | 685 | 12.2 | 3 |
| Craig McEwen | 87-91 | | | | | 108 | 1310 | 12.1 | 6 |
| Buford McGee | 84-92 | 289 | 1086 | 3.8 | 17 | 155 | 1264 | 8.2 | 13 |
| Tim McGee | 86-94 | 8 | 18 | 2.3 | 0 | 321 | 5203 | 16.2 | 28 |
| Tony McGee | 93-95 | | | | | 139 | 1771 | 12.7 | 5 |
| Mark McGrath | 81-85 | | | | | 15 | 171 | 11.4 | 1 |
| Keith McKeller | 87-93 | | | | | 115 | 1384 | 12.0 | 11 |
| Dennis McKinnon | 83-85,87-90 | 10 | 34 | 3.4 | 1 | 196 | 2925 | 14.9 | 22 |
| Jim McMahon | 82-95 | 335 | 1632 | 4.9 | 16 | 5 | 72 | 14.4 | 2 |
| Randy McMillan | 81-86 | 990 | 3876 | 3.9 | 24 | 164 | 1356 | 8.3 | 2 |
| Greg McMurtry | 90-94 | 2 | 3 | 1.5 | 0 | 128 | 1631 | 12.7 | 5 |
| Todd McNair | 89-95 | 138 | 771 | 5.6 | 3 | 233 | 2254 | 9.7 | 6 |
| Travis McNeal | 89-93 | 1 | 2 | 2.0 | 0 | 48 | 652 | 13.6 | 2 |
| Freeman McNeil | 81-92 | 1798 | 8074 | 4.5 | 38 | 295 | 2961 | 10.0 | 12 |
| Gerald McNeil | 86-90 | 4 | 61 | 15.3 | 0 | 29 | 380 | 13.1 | 2 |
| Mike Meade | 82-85 | 72 | 261 | 3.6 | 1 | 21 | 126 | 6.0 | 2 |
| Natrone Means | 93-95 | 689 | 2725 | 4.0 | 25 | 56 | 340 | 6.1 | 0 |
| Dave Meggett | 89-95 | 331 | 1480 | 4.5 | 7 | 283 | 2528 | 8.9 | 10 |
| Guido Merkens | 78-85,87 | 15 | 37 | 2.5 | 0 | 36 | 559 | 15.8 | 3 |
| Eric Metcalf | 89-95 | 620 | 2362 | 3.8 | 12 | 401 | 3921 | 9.8 | 23 |
| Pete Metzelaars | 82-95 | | | | | 349 | 3396 | 9.7 | 29 |
| Bobby Micho | 84,86-87 | 4 | 8 | 2.0 | 0 | 25 | 242 | 9.7 | 2 |
| Frank Middleton | 84-85,87 | 133 | 384 | 2.9 | 3 | 28 | 209 | 7.5 | 1 |
| Ron Middleton | 86-94 | | | | | 42 | 266 | 6.3 | 2 |
| Terdell Middleton | 77-83 | 561 | 2048 | 3.7 | 15 | 78 | 659 | 8.4 | 3 |
| Glyn Milburn | 93-95 | 159 | 698 | 4.4 | 1 | 137 | 1040 | 7.6 | 6 |
| Ostell Miles | 92-93 | 30 | 78 | 2.6 | 1 | 6 | 89 | 14.8 | 0 |
| Hugh Millen | 87-95 | 65 | 260 | 4.0 | 1 | | | | |
| Anthony Miller | 88-95 | 18 | 86 | 4.8 | 0 | 493 | 7768 | 15.8 | 56 |
| Chris Miller | 87-95 | 142 | 660 | 4.6 | 1 | | | | |
| Junior Miller | 80-84 | 3 | 0 | 0.0 | 0 | 122 | 1409 | 11.5 | 14 |
| Scott Miller | 91-94 | | | | | 12 | 158 | 13.2 | 1 |
| Solomon Miller | 86-87 | 1 | 3 | 3.0 | 0 | 14 | 241 | 17.2 | 2 |
| Terry Miller | 78-81 | 391 | 1583 | 4.0 | 8 | 35 | 382 | 10.9 | 0 |
| James Milling | 88,90,92 | | | | | 26 | 252 | 9.7 | 0 |
| Ernie Mills | 91-95 | 12 | 89 | 7.4 | 0 | 120 | 1911 | 15.9 | 14 |
| David Mims | 93-94 | 1 | 3 | 3.0 | 0 | 15 | 121 | 8.1 | 1 |
| Cedric Minter | 84-85 | 42 | 159 | 3.8 | 1 | 11 | 122 | 11.1 | 1 |
| Rick Mirer | 93-95 | 145 | 689 | 4.8 | 4 | | | | |
| John Mistler | 81-84 | | | | | 72 | 737 | 10.2 | 3 |
| Brian Mitchell | 90-95 | 211 | 1023 | 4.8 | 5 | 89 | 752 | 8.4 | 2 |
| Johnny Mitchell | 92-95 | | | | | 158 | 2086 | 13.2 | 16 |
| Pete Mitchell | 95 | | | | | 41 | 527 | 12.9 | 2 |
| Scott Mitchell | 91-95 | 80 | 227 | 2.8 | 5 | | | | |
| Shannon Mitchell | 94-95 | | | | | 14 | 136 | 9.7 | 1 |
| Stump Mitchell | 81-89 | 986 | 4649 | 4.7 | 32 | 209 | 1955 | 9.4 | 9 |
| Orson Mobley | 86-90 | 1 | -1 | -1.0 | 0 | 84 | 1019 | 12.1 | 4 |
| Stacey Mobley | 87,89 | | | | | 21 | 265 | 12.6 | 1 |
| Tim Moffett | 85-87 | 1 | 1 | 1.0 | 0 | 16 | 247 | 15.4 | 1 |
| Art Monk | 80-95 | 63 | 332 | 5.3 | 0 | 940 | 12721 | 13.5 | 68 |
| Carl Monroe | 83-87 | 15 | 62 | 4.1 | 0 | 28 | 323 | 11.5 | 2 |
| Joe Montana | 79-90,92-94 | 458 | 1676 | 3.7 | 20 | | | | |
| Tyrone Montgomery | 93-94 | 73 | 203 | 2.8 | 0 | 18 | 169 | 9.4 | 1 |
| Wilbert Montgomery | 77-85 | 1540 | 6789 | 4.4 | 45 | 273 | 2502 | 9.2 | 12 |
| Warren Moon | 84-95 | 499 | 1678 | 3.4 | 21 | | | | |
| Alvin Moore | 83-86 | 194 | 626 | 3.2 | 7 | 42 | 291 | 6.9 | 1 |
| Booker Moore | 82-85 | 115 | 420 | 3.7 | 1 | 75 | 423 | 5.6 | 1 |
| Dave Moore | 92-95 | 1 | 4 | 4.0 | 0 | 22 | 216 | 9.8 | 1 |
| Derrick Moore | 93-95 | 310 | 1197 | 3.9 | 11 | 26 | 191 | 7.3 | 1 |
| Herman Moore | 91-95 | | | | | 318 | 4895 | 15.4 | 35 |
| Jeff Moore | 79-83 | 208 | 722 | 3.5 | 7 | 115 | 1103 | 9.6 | 6 |
| Jeff Moore | 80-81 | | | | | 17 | 273 | 16.1 | 1 |
| Nat Moore | 74-86 | 40 | 249 | 6.2 | 1 | 510 | 7546 | 14.8 | 74 |
| Ricky Moore | 86-88 | 40 | 126 | 3.2 | 1 | 26 | 220 | 8.5 | 0 |
| Rob Moore | 90-95 | 5 | 8 | 1.6 | 0 | 369 | 5165 | 14.0 | 27 |
| Ronald Moore | 93-95 | 538 | 1919 | 3.6 | 13 | 19 | 118 | 6.2 | 1 |
| Will Moore | 95 | | | | | 43 | 502 | 11.7 | 1 |
| Emery Moorehead | 77-88 | 47 | 114 | 2.4 | 0 | 224 | 2980 | 13.3 | 15 |
| Anthony Morgan | 91-95 | 6 | 86 | 14.3 | 0 | 87 | 1283 | 14.7 | 12 |
| Stanley Morgan | 77-90 | 21 | 127 | 6.1 | 0 | 557 | 10716 | 19.2 | 72 |
| Larry Moriarty | 83-88 | 500 | 1908 | 3.8 | 13 | 77 | 494 | 6.4 | 2 |
| Mike Moroski | 79-86 | 37 | 182 | 4.9 | 2 | | | | |
| Bam Morris | 94-95 | 346 | 1395 | 4.0 | 16 | 30 | 240 | 8.0 | 0 |
| Jamie Morris | 88-90 | 252 | 777 | 3.1 | 4 | 9 | 68 | 7.6 | 0 |
| Joe Morris | 82-88,91 | 1411 | 5585 | 4.0 | 50 | 111 | 960 | 8.2 | 2 |
| Lee Morris | 87 | 2 | 2 | 1.0 | 0 | 16 | 259 | 16.2 | 1 |
| Randall Morris | 84-88 | 156 | 651 | 4.2 | 1 | 9 | 61 | 6.8 | 0 |
| Ron Morris | 87-92 | 6 | 52 | 8.7 | 0 | 121 | 1991 | 16.4 | 9 |
| Wayne Morris | 76-84 | 899 | 3387 | 3.8 | 38 | 157 | 1201 | 7.6 | 5 |
| Johnnie Morton | 94-95 | 3 | 33 | 11.0 | 0 | 47 | 629 | 13.4 | 9 |
| Michael Morton | 82-85,87 | 50 | 110 | 2.2 | 2 | 2 | 14 | 7.0 | 0 |
| Rick Moser | 78-82 | 54 | 190 | 3.5 | 1 | 3 | 10 | 3.3 | 1 |
| Mike Moseley | 82-84 | | | | | 27 | 314 | 11.6 | 3 |
| Zeke Mowatt | 83-84,86-91 | | | | | 135 | 1765 | 13.1 | 12 |
| Bob Mrosko | 89-91 | | | | | 14 | 145 | 10.4 | 1 |
| Calvin Muhammad | 82-85,87 | | | | | 69 | 1276 | 18.5 | 8 |
| Mike Mularkey | 84-91 | 1 | -6 | -6.0 | 0 | 102 | 1222 | 12.0 | 9 |
| Jamie Mueller | 87-90 | 238 | 901 | 3.8 | 4 | 28 | 169 | 6.0 | 1 |
| Vance Mueller | 86-90 | 128 | 469 | 3.7 | 3 | 40 | 452 | 11.3 | 2 |
| Tom Mullady | 79-84 | | | | | 84 | 1033 | 12.3 | 4 |
| Chuck Muncie | 76-84 | 1561 | 6702 | 4.3 | 71 | 263 | 2323 | 8.8 | 3 |
| Walter Murray | 86-87 | | | | | 22 | 373 | 17.0 | 3 |
| Adrian Murrell | 93-95 | 259 | 1112 | 4.3 | 2 | 83 | 553 | 6.7 | 2 |
| Brad Muster | 88-94 | 520 | 2231 | 4.3 | 23 | 202 | 1906 | 9.4 | 7 |
| Browning Nagle | 91-95 | 26 | 68 | 2.6 | 0 | | | | |
| Tony Nathan | 79-87 | 732 | 3543 | 4.8 | 16 | 383 | 3592 | 9.4 | 16 |
| Ricky Nattiel | 87-91 | 7 | 64 | 9.1 | 0 | 121 | 1972 | 16.3 | 8 |
| Frankie Neal | 87 | 1 | 0 | 0.0 | 0 | 36 | 420 | 11.7 | 3 |
| Lorenzo Neal | 93-95 | 56 | 268 | 4.8 | 2 | 14 | 132 | 9.4 | 1 |

775

Lifetime Statistics- 1980-1995 Players Section 2 - **RUSHING and RECEIVING**
(All men with 25 or more rushing attempts or 10 or more receptions)

| | | RUSHING | | | | RECEIVING | | | |
|---|---|---|---|---|---|---|---|---|---|
| **Name** | **Years** | **Att.** | **Yards** | **Avg.** | **TD** | **Rec.** | **Yards** | **Avg.** | **TD** |
| Speedy Neal | 84 | 49 | 175 | 3.6 | 1 | 9 | 76 | 8.4 | 0 |
| Derrick Ned | 93-95 | 23 | 108 | 4.7 | 1 | 25 | 149 | 6.0 | 0 |
| Renaldo Nehemiah | 82-84 | 1 | -1 | -1.0 | 0 | 43 | 754 | 17.5 | 4 |
| Darrin Nelson | 82-92 | 1020 | 4442 | 4.4 | 18 | 286 | 2559 | 8.9 | 5 |
| Keith Neubert | 88-89 | 28 | 302 | 10.8 | 1 | | | | |
| Pat Newman | 90-94 | | | | | 14 | 175 | 12.5 | 1 |
| Ozzie Newsome | 78-90 | 18 | 135 | 7.5 | 2 | 662 | 7980 | 12.1 | 47 |
| Timmy Newsome | 80-88 | 342 | 1226 | 3.6 | 19 | 212 | 1966 | 9.3 | 11 |
| Tom Newton | 77-82 | 188 | 722 | 4.1 | 9 | 52 | 369 | 7.1 | 0 |
| Mark Nichols | 81-87 | 4 | 108 | 12.0 | 0 | 124 | 2228 | 18.0 | 9 |
| Gifford Nielsen | 78-83 | 29 | 89 | 3.1 | 0 | | | | |
| James Noble | 86-87 | | | | | 10 | 78 | 7.8 | 2 |
| Ulysses Norris | 79-85 | | | | | 43 | 547 | 12.7 | 8 |
| Jay Novacek | 85-95 | 2 | 12 | 6.0 | 1 | 422 | 4630 | 11.0 | 30 |
| Brent Novoselsky | 88-94 | | | | | 14 | 108 | 7.7 | 2 |
| Terry Obee | 91,93 | | | | | 26 | 351 | 13.5 | 3 |
| Ken O'Brien | 83-93 | 174 | 394 | 2.3 | 0 | 1 | 27 | 27.0 | 0 |
| Neil O'Donnell | 90-95 | 126 | 323 | 2.6 | 3 | | | | |
| Christian Okoye | 87-92 | 1246 | 4897 | 3.9 | 40 | 42 | 294 | 7.0 | 0 |
| Mike Oliphant | 88-89,91 | 23 | 127 | 5.5 | 1 | 18 | 133 | 7.4 | 0 |
| Hubert Oliver | 81-86 | 270 | 1030 | 3.8 | 2 | 93 | 602 | 6.5 | 2 |
| Terry Orr | 86-93 | | | | | 52 | 939 | 18.1 | 10 |
| Keith Ortego | 85-87 | | | | | 23 | 430 | 18.7 | 1 |
| David Overstreet | 83 | 85 | 392 | 4.6 | 1 | 8 | 55 | 6.9 | 2 |
| James Owens | 79-84 | 271 | 944 | 3.5 | 8 | 56 | 535 | 9.6 | 3 |
| Mike Pagel | 82-93 | 136 | 831 | 6.1 | 4 | | | | |
| Stephone Paige | 83-91 | 6 | 32 | 5.3 | 0 | 377 | 6341 | 16.8 | 49 |
| Tony Paige | 84-92 | 272 | 853 | 3.1 | 20 | 197 | 1515 | 7.7 | 9 |
| Carl Painter | 88-89 | 32 | 106 | 3.3 | 0 | 4 | 42 | 10.5 | 0 |
| David Palmer | 94-95 | 8 | 16 | 2.0 | 0 | 18 | 190 | 10.6 | 0 |
| Paul Palmer | 87-89 | 280 | 1053 | 3.7 | 4 | 74 | 731 | 9.9 | 4 |
| Robert Parker | 87 | 47 | 150 | 3.2 | 1 | 7 | 44 | 6.3 | 0 |
| Rodney Parker | 80-81 | | | | | 17 | 316 | 18.6 | 3 |
| Bernie Parmalee | 92-95 | 462 | 1800 | 3.9 | 6 | 74 | 595 | 8.0 | 2 |
| Rick Parros | 81-85,87 | 350 | 1381 | 3.9 | 7 | 82 | 660 | 8.0 | 5 |
| Keith Paskett | 87 | | | | | 12 | 188 | 15.7 | 1 |
| Mark Pattison | 86-88 | | | | | 12 | 152 | 12.7 | 0 |
| Rickey Patton | 78-81 | 261 | 885 | 3.4 | 5 | 43 | 326 | 7.6 | 2 |
| Walter Payton | 75-87 | 3838 | 16726 | 4.4 | 110 | 492 | 4538 | 9.2 | 15 |
| Elvis Peacock | 79-81 | 216 | 1001 | 4.6 | 7 | 46 | 473 | 10.3 | 2 |
| Danny Peebles | 89-91 | 2 | -6 | -3.0 | 0 | 17 | 230 | 13.5 | 1 |
| Rodney Peete | 89-95 | 213 | 1031 | 4.8 | 14 | | | | |
| Erric Pegram | 91-95 | 730 | 2794 | 3.8 | 10 | 78 | 631 | 8.1 | 1 |
| Steve Pelluer | 84-90 | 143 | 858 | 6.0 | 6 | | | | |
| Bruce Perkins | 90-91 | 17 | 47 | 2.8 | 0 | 11 | 83 | 7.5 | 0 |
| Johnny Perkins | 77-82 | 3 | 2 | 0.7 | 0 | 163 | 2611 | 16.0 | 18 |
| Brett Perriman | 88-95 | 26 | 167 | 6.4 | 0 | 406 | 5176 | 12.7 | 24 |
| Leon Perry | 80-82 | 134 | 543 | 4.1 | 1 | 22 | 223 | 10.1 | 2 |
| Bob Perryman | 87-92 | 393 | 1338 | 3.4 | 9 | 83 | 616 | 7.4 | 0 |
| Jason Phillips | 89-93 | | | | | 49 | 578 | 11.8 | 2 |
| Carl Pickens | 92-95 | 1 | 6 | 6.0 | 0 | 239 | 3252 | 13.6 | 35 |
| Aaron Pierce | 92-95 | 1 | 6 | 6.0 | 0 | 65 | 736 | 11.3 | 4 |
| Frank Pillow | 88-90 | | | | | 23 | 324 | 14.1 | 1 |
| Allen Pinkett | 86-91 | 561 | 2324 | 4.1 | 21 | 119 | 921 | 7.7 | 5 |
| Joe Pisarcik | 77-84 | 65 | 147 | 2.3 | 5 | | | | |
| Danny Pittman | 80-84 | 1 | -7 | -7.0 | 0 | 46 | 657 | 14.3 | 1 |
| Frank Pollard | 80-88 | 953 | 3989 | 4.2 | 20 | 104 | 872 | 8.4 | 0 |
| Nathan Poole | 79-83,85,87 | 126 | 423 | 3.4 | 5 | 24 | 179 | 7.5 | 0 |
| Ted Popson | 94-95 | | | | | 29 | 269 | 9.3 | 0 |
| Ricky Porter | 82-83,87 | 47 | 177 | 3.8 | 0 | 9 | 70 | 7.8 | 0 |
| Tracy Porter | 81-84 | | | | | 79 | 1161 | 14.7 | 3 |
| Roosevelt Potts | 93-95 | 321 | 1356 | 4.2 | 1 | 73 | 668 | 9.2 | 2 |
| Jim Price | 91-93,95 | | | | | 74 | 767 | 10.4 | 4 |
| Dave Preston | 78-83 | 479 | 1793 | 3.7 | 10 | 161 | 1423 | 8.8 | 3 |
| James Primus | 88 | 35 | 95 | 2.7 | 1 | 8 | 42 | 5.3 | 0 |
| Mike Pritchard | 91-95 | 13 | 58 | 4.5 | 0 | 253 | 2899 | 11.5 | 18 |
| Ricky Proehl | 90-95 | 15 | 95 | 6.4 | 0 | 292 | 3869 | 13.3 | 21 |
| James Pruitt | 86-91 | | | | | 63 | 1013 | 16.1 | 10 |
| Mike Pruitt | 76-86 | 1846 | 7378 | 4.0 | 51 | 270 | 1860 | 6.9 | 5 |
| Alfred Pupunu | 92-95 | | | | | 69 | 671 | 9.7 | 2 |
| Jeff Query | 89-94 | 6 | 53 | 8.8 | 0 | 141 | 1865 | 13.2 | 11 |
| Mike Quick | 82-90 | 1 | -5 | -5.0 | 0 | 363 | 6464 | 17.8 | 61 |
| Derrick Ramsey | 78-85 | | | | | 188 | 2364 | 12.6 | 21 |
| Eason Ramson | 78-83,85 | 5 | 9 | 1.8 | 0 | 104 | 983 | 9.5 | 5 |
| Kenyon Rasheed | 93-95 | 27 | 89 | 3.3 | 1 | 13 | 115 | 8.8 | 0 |
| Tom Rathman | 86-94 | 544 | 2020 | 3.7 | 26 | 320 | 2684 | 8.4 | 8 |
| Barry Redden | 82-90 | 396 | 1735 | 4.4 | 10 | 10 | 88 | 8.8 | 1 |
| Jarvis Redwine | 81-83 | 17 | 70 | 4.1 | 0 | 1 | 4 | 4.0 | 0 |
| Andre Reed | 85-95 | 64 | 477 | 7.4 | 1 | 700 | 9848 | 14.1 | 69 |
| Jake Reed | 91-95 | | | | | 168 | 2549 | 15.2 | 13 |
| Bryan Reeves | 94-95 | 1 | -1 | -1.0 | 0 | 20 | 264 | 13.2 | 1 |
| Walter Reeves | 89-95 | | | | | 54 | 344 | 6.4 | 3 |
| Frank Reich | 85-95 | 63 | 48 | 0.8 | 0 | | | | |
| Reggie Rembert | 91-93 | | | | | 36 | 437 | 12.1 | 1 |
| Mike Renfro | 78-87 | 3 | 24 | 8.0 | 0 | 323 | 4708 | 14.6 | 28 |
| Errict Rhett | 94-95 | 616 | 2218 | 3.6 | 18 | 36 | 229 | 6.4 | 0 |
| Allen Rice | 84-91 | 337 | 1034 | 3.1 | 13 | 100 | 1067 | 10.7 | 6 |
| Jerry Rice | 85-95 | 69 | 547 | 7.9 | 9 | 944 | 15123 | 16.0 | 146 |
| Curvin Richards | 91-92 | 51 | 180 | 3.5 | 1 | 3 | 8 | 2.7 | 0 |
| Bucky Richardson | 92-94 | 33 | 225 | 6.8 | 1 | | | | |
| Eric Richardson | 85-86 | | | | | 15 | 250 | 16.7 | 0 |
| Robb Riddick | 81,83-84,86-88 | 330 | 1341 | 4.1 | 21 | 120 | 1165 | 9.7 | 5 |
| Gerald Riggs | 82-91 | 1989 | 8188 | 4.1 | 69 | 201 | 1516 | 7.5 | 0 |
| Jim Riggs | 87-93 | | | | | 37 | 274 | 7.4 | 0 |
| Bill Ring | 81-86 | 183 | 732 | 4.0 | 7 | 45 | 336 | 7.5 | 1 |
| Andre Rison | 89-95 | 6 | 9 | 1.5 | 0 | 522 | 7156 | 13.7 | 63 |
| Reggie Rivers | 91-95 | 136 | 422 | 3.1 | 6 | 74 | 676 | 9.1 | 2 |
| Alfredo Roberts | 88-92 | | | | | 48 | 450 | 9.4 | 2 |
| Bo Robinson | 79-85 | 121 | 445 | 3.7 | 2 | 37 | 305 | 8.2 | 3 |
| Greg Robinson | 93,95 | 196 | 756 | 3.9 | 1 | 17 | 154 | 9.1 | 0 |
| Matt Robinson | 77-82 | 58 | 117 | 2.0 | 4 | | | | |
| Stacy Robinson | 85-90 | | | | | 48 | 649 | 13.5 | 7 |
| Del Rodgers | 82-84,87-88 | 82 | 315 | 3.8 | 2 | 10 | 124 | 12.4 | 0 |
| George Rogers | 81-87 | 1692 | 7176 | 4.2 | 54 | 55 | 368 | 6.7 | 0 |
| Jimmy Rogers | 80-83 | 175 | 661 | 3.8 | 3 | 33 | 296 | 9.0 | 2 |

| | | RUSHING | | | | RECEIVING | | | |
|---|---|---|---|---|---|---|---|---|---|
| **Name** | **Years** | **Att.** | **Yards** | **Avg.** | **TD** | **Rec.** | **Yards** | **Avg.** | **TD** |
| Butch Rolle | 86-93 | | | | | 38 | 213 | 5.6 | 11 |
| Stan Rome | 79-82 | 1 | -5 | -5.0 | 0 | 20 | 261 | 13.1 | 1 |
| Joe Rose | 80-85 | | | | | 112 | 1493 | 13.3 | 13 |
| Timm Rosenbach | 89-90,92 | 101 | 507 | 5.0 | 3 | | | | |
| Dan Ross | 79-83,85-86 | | | | | 290 | 3419 | 11.8 | 19 |
| James Rouse | 90-91 | 43 | 130 | 3.0 | 0 | 15 | 93 | 6.2 | 0 |
| Mazio Royster | 92-94 | 42 | 122 | 2.9 | 1 | 13 | 62 | 4.8 | 0 |
| Lee Rouson | 85-91 | 114 | 415 | 3.6 | 2 | 33 | 453 | 13.7 | 2 |
| Mike Rozier | 85-91 | 1159 | 4462 | 3.8 | 30 | 90 | 715 | 8.1 | 1 |
| Robb Rubick | 82-88 | 1 | 1 | 1.0 | 1 | 44 | 511 | 11.6 | 3 |
| T.J. Rubley | 93,95 | 31 | 108 | 3.5 | 0 | | | | |
| Booker Russell | 78-81 | 90 | 419 | 4.7 | 8 | 7 | 74 | 10.6 | 0 |
| Derek Russell | 91-95 | 1 | 6 | 6.0 | 0 | 126 | 1839 | 14.6 | 5 |
| Leonard Russell | 91-95 | 945 | 3260 | 3.4 | 22 | 109 | 666 | 6.1 | 0 |
| Jeff Rutledge | 79-92 | 52 | 93 | 1.8 | 1 | | | | |
| Pat Ryan | 78-89,91 | 53 | 156 | 2.9 | 1 | | | | |
| Mark Rypien | 87-95 | 126 | 163 | 1.3 | 5 | | | | |
| Troy Sadowski | 90-95 | | | | | 19 | 125 | 6.6 | 0 |
| Rashaan Salaam | 95 | 296 | 1074 | 3.6 | 10 | 19 | 125 | 6.6 | 0 |
| Jay Saldi | 76-84 | 2 | 18 | 9.0 | 0 | 84 | 913 | 10.9 | 7 |
| Lawrence Sampleton | 82-84,87 | | | | | 11 | 116 | 10.5 | 0 |
| Clint Sampson | 83-86 | | | | | 66 | 1014 | 15.4 | 8 |
| Terry Samuels | 94-95 | | | | | 10 | 76 | 7.6 | 0 |
| Barry Sanders | 89-95 | 2077 | 10172 | 4.9 | 73 | 257 | 2180 | 8.5 | 4 |
| Chris Sanders | 95 | 2 | -19 | -9.5 | 0 | 35 | 823 | 23.5 | 9 |
| Deion Sanders | 89-95 | 3 | 5 | 1.7 | 0 | 13 | 185 | 14.2 | 2 |
| Frank Sanders | 95 | 1 | 1 | 1.0 | 0 | 52 | 883 | 17.0 | 2 |
| Ricky Sanders | 86-94 | 23 | 94 | 4.1 | 1 | 481 | 6453 | 13.4 | 37 |
| Thomas Sanders | 85-91 | 321 | 1237 | 3.8 | 12 | 28 | 284 | 10.1 | 1 |
| Broderick Sargent | 86-87,89 | 38 | 177 | 4.7 | 1 | 9 | 77 | 8.6 | 0 |
| John Sawyer | 75-84 | | | | | 129 | 1496 | 11.6 | 2 |
| James Saxon | 88-95 | 145 | 533 | 3.7 | 5 | 69 | 515 | 7.5 | 0 |
| Dwight Scales | 76-79,81-84 | | | | | 56 | 1120 | 20.0 | 4 |
| Greg Scales | 88-91 | | | | | 21 | 196 | 9.3 | 2 |
| Art Schlichter | 82,84-85 | 22 | 161 | 7.3 | 1 | | | | |
| Turk Schonert | 81-88 | 73 | 288 | 3.9 | 4 | | | | |
| Jay Schroeder | 84-94 | 242 | 761 | 3.1 | 5 | | | | |
| Scott Schwedes | 87-90 | | | | | 19 | 370 | 19.5 | 2 |
| Darnay Scott | 94-95 | 15 | 117 | 7.8 | 0 | 98 | 1687 | 17.2 | 10 |
| Lindsay Scott | 82-85 | 1 | -4 | -4.0 | 0 | 69 | 864 | 12.5 | 1 |
| Malcolm Scott | 83,87 | | | | | 23 | 241 | 10.5 | 0 |
| Patrick Scott | 87-88 | | | | | 28 | 354 | 12.6 | 1 |
| Ronald Scott | 87 | 47 | 199 | 4.2 | 3 | 2 | 7 | 3.5 | 0 |
| Willie Scott | 81-88 | 1 | 1 | 1.0 | 0 | 89 | 766 | 8.6 | 15 |
| Malcolm Seabron | 94-95 | | | | | 12 | 167 | 13.9 | 1 |
| Mark Seay | 93-95 | | | | | 103 | 1182 | 11.5 | 9 |
| Virgil Seay | 81-84 | | | | | 43 | 792 | 8.4 | 5 |
| Scott Secules | 88-91,93 | 24 | 136 | 5.7 | 1 | | | | |
| Joe Senser | 80-84 | 2 | 1 | 0.5 | 0 | 165 | 1822 | 11.0 | 16 |
| John Settle | 87-90 | 439 | 1801 | 4.1 | 10 | 118 | 1039 | 8.8 | 3 |
| Steve Sewell | 86-91 | 148 | 642 | 4.3 | 9 | 163 | 2160 | 13.3 | 12 |
| Shannon Sharpe | 90-95 | 3 | 9 | 3.0 | 0 | 313 | 3822 | 12.2 | 21 |
| Sterling Sharpe | 88-94 | 23 | 72 | 3.1 | 0 | 595 | 8134 | 13.7 | 65 |
| Derrick Shepard | 87-90 | 3 | 12 | 4.0 | 0 | 20 | 304 | 15.2 | 1 |
| Leslie Shepherd | 94-95 | 7 | 63 | 9.0 | 1 | 30 | 494 | 16.5 | 2 |
| Heath Sherman | 89-93 | 537 | 2130 | 4.0 | 10 | 75 | 608 | 8.1 | 4 |
| Mike Sherrard | 86,90-95 | 3 | 1 | 0.3 | 0 | 241 | 3746 | 15.5 | 21 |
| Tim Sherwin | 81-87 | | | | | 76 | 1002 | 13.2 | 2 |
| Heath Shuler | 94-95 | 44 | 160 | 3.6 | 0 | | | | |
| Mickey Shuler | 78-91 | | | | | 462 | 5100 | 11.0 | 37 |
| Mike Shumann | 78-83 | 1 | 19 | 19.0 | 0 | 62 | 760 | 12.3 | 5 |
| Eric Sievers | 81-90 | 1 | -7 | -7.0 | 0 | 214 | 2485 | 11.6 | 16 |
| Vai Sikahema | 86-93 | 59 | 217 | 3.7 | 0 | 53 | 537 | 10.1 | 1 |
| Phil Simms | 79-81, 83-93 | 349 | 1252 | 3.6 | 6 | 2 | 7 | 3.5 | 0 |
| Billy Sims | 80-84 | 1131 | 5106 | 4.5 | 42 | 186 | 2072 | 11.1 | 5 |
| Marvin Sims | 80-81 | 54 | 186 | 3.4 | 2 | 9 | 64 | 7.1 | 0 |
| Nate Singleton | 93-95 | | | | | 37 | 528 | 14.3 | 4 |
| Paul Skansi | 83-91 | | | | | 166 | 1950 | 11.7 | 10 |
| Webster Slaughter | 86-95 | 9 | 50 | 5.5 | 0 | 523 | 7584 | 14.5 | 42 |
| David Sloan | 95 | | | | | 17 | 184 | 10.8 | 1 |
| Torrance Small | 92-95 | 6 | 75 | 12.5 | 1 | 126 | 1622 | 12.9 | 14 |
| Cedric Smith | 90-91,94-95 | 22 | 70 | 3.2 | 0 | 15 | 118 | 7.9 | 1 |
| Chris Smith | 86-87 | 26 | 114 | 4.4 | 0 | 2 | 21 | 10.5 | 0 |
| Don Smith | 88-90 | 40 | 165 | 4.1 | 3 | 40 | 473 | 11.8 | 0 |
| Emmitt Smith | 90-95 | 2007 | 8956 | 4.5 | 96 | 301 | 1951 | 6.5 | 4 |
| Irv Smith | 93-95 | | | | | 102 | 976 | 9.6 | 8 |
| Jeff Smith | 85-88 | 204 | 752 | 3.7 | 5 | 87 | 718 | 8.3 | 7 |
| Jim Smith | 77-82,85 | 2 | 27 | 13.5 | 0 | 113 | 2103 | 18.6 | 25 |
| Jimmy Smith | 92,95 | | | | | 22 | 288 | 13.1 | 3 |
| J.T. Smith | 78-90 | 7 | 76 | 10.9 | 0 | 544 | 6974 | 12.8 | 35 |
| Kendal Smith | 89-90 | | | | | 17 | 185 | 10.9 | 1 |
| Lamar Smith | 94-95 | 38 | 214 | 5.6 | 0 | 1 | 10 | 10.0 | 0 |
| Rico Smith | 92-95 | | | | | 24 | 353 | 14.7 | 1 |
| Robert Smith | 93-95 | 252 | 1137 | 4.5 | 7 | 46 | 251 | 5.5 | 0 |
| Ron Smith | 78-83 | 1 | 7 | 7.0 | 0 | 62 | 1006 | 16.2 | 4 |
| Sammie Smith | 89-92 | 532 | 1881 | 3.5 | 15 | 32 | 310 | 9.7 | 1 |
| Steve Smith | 87-95 | 429 | 1627 | 3.8 | 9 | 131 | 1250 | 9.5 | 13 |
| Tim Smith | 83-86 | 2 | 16 | 8.0 | 0 | 206 | 3107 | 15.1 | 12 |
| Timmy Smith | 87-88,90 | 190 | 602 | 3.2 | 3 | 9 | 51 | 5.7 | 0 |
| Tony Smith | 92-94 | 87 | 329 | 3.8 | 2 | 2 | 14 | 7.0 | 0 |
| Kurt Sohn | 81-82,84-88 | 3 | 1 | 0.3 | 0 | 79 | 1016 | 12.9 | 10 |
| Freddie Solomon | 75-85 | 61 | 519 | 8.5 | 4 | 371 | 5846 | 15.8 | 48 |
| John Spagnola | 79-89 | | | | | 263 | 2886 | 11.0 | 15 |
| Tim Spencer | 85-89 | 474 | 1792 | 3.8 | 19 | 53 | 432 | 8.2 | 0 |
| Todd Spencer | 84-85,87 | 28 | 80 | 2.9 | 0 | 5 | 72 | 14.4 | 0 |
| Irving Spikes | 94-95 | 102 | 438 | 4.3 | 3 | 9 | 34 | 3.8 | 1 |
| Ron Springs | 79-84 | 694 | 2519 | 3.6 | 28 | 249 | 2259 | 7.1 | 10 |
| John Stallworth | 74-87 | 9 | 64 | 7.1 | 0 | 537 | 8723 | 16.2 | 63 |
| Sylvester Stamps | 84-89 | 66 | 382 | 5.8 | 1 | 48 | 413 | 8.6 | 1 |
| Walter Stanley | 85-90,92 | 6 | 58 | 9.7 | 0 | 130 | 2213 | 17.0 | 5 |
| Stephen Starring | 83-88 | 5 | -3 | -0.6 | 0 | 120 | 2029 | 16.9 | 11 |
| John Stephens | 88-93 | 945 | 3438 | 3.6 | 18 | 105 | 812 | 7.7 | 1 |
| James Stewart (Minn.) | 95 | 31 | 144 | 4.6 | 0 | 1 | 3 | 3.0 | 0 |
| James Stewart (Jax.) | 95 | 137 | 525 | 3.8 | 2 | 21 | 190 | 9.0 | 1 |
| Kordell Stewart | 95 | 15 | 86 | 5.7 | 1 | 14 | 235 | 16.8 | 1 |

Lifetime Statistics- 1980-1995 Players Section 2 - **RUSHING and RECEIVING**
(All men with 25 or more rushing attempts or 10 or more receptions)
776

| | | RUSHING | | | | RECEIVING | | | |
|---|---|---|---|---|---|---|---|---|---|
| **Name** | **Years** | **Att.** | **Yards** | **Avg.** | **TD** | **Rec.** | **Yards** | **Avg.** | **TD** |
| Dave Stief | 78-81 | 2 | 0 | 0.0 | 0 | 67 | 1043 | 15.6 | 5 |
| J.J. Stokes | 95 | | | | | 38 | 517 | 13.6 | 4 |
| Dwight Stone | 87-95 | 97 | 560 | 5.8 | 1 | 152 | 2460 | 16.2 | 12 |
| Cliff Stoudt | 82-83,86,88 | 122 | 661 | 5.4 | 4 | | | | |
| Kelly Stouffer | 88-92 | 30 | 75 | 2.5 | 0 | | | | |
| Mike Strachan | 75-80 | 472 | 1902 | 4.0 | 14 | 57 | 392 | 6.9 | 0 |
| Troy Stradford | 87-92 | 356 | 1370 | 3.8 | 10 | 170 | 1479 | 8.7 | 2 |
| Don Strock | 74-88 | 57 | 18 | 0.3 | 2 | | | | |
| Mack Strong | 94-95 | 35 | 137 | 3.9 | 3 | 15 | 120 | 8.0 | 3 |
| Ray Strong | 78-82 | 45 | 163 | 3.6 | 3 | 9 | 71 | 7.9 | 0 |
| Matt Suhey | 80-89 | 828 | 2946 | 3.6 | 20 | 260 | 2113 | 8.1 | 5 |
| Don Summers | 84-85,87 | | | | | 10 | 115 | 11.5 | 1 |
| Calvin Sweeney | 80-87 | 1 | -2 | -2.0 | 0 | 113 | 1775 | 15.7 | 7 |
| Harry Sydney | 87-92 | 190 | 805 | 4.2 | 9 | 84 | 682 | 8.1 | 4 |
| John Tagliaferri | 87 | 13 | 45 | 3.5 | 1 | 12 | 117 | 9.8 | 0 |
| Steve Tasker | 85-95 | 8 | 74 | 9.3 | 0 | 30 | 407 | 13.6 | 6 |
| Lars Tate | 88-90 | 292 | 1061 | 3.6 | 15 | 16 | 98 | 6.2 | 1 |
| Rodney Tate | 82-84 | 27 | 79 | 2.9 | 0 | 18 | 142 | 7.9 | 0 |
| Mosi Tatupu | 78-90 | 612 | 2415 | 3.9 | 18 | 96 | 843 | 8.8 | 2 |
| Junior Tautalatasi | 86-89 | 97 | 275 | 2.8 | 0 | 88 | 706 | 8.0 | 2 |
| Billy Taylor | 78-81 | 456 | 1641 | 3.6 | 13 | 78 | 647 | 8.3 | 4 |
| Craig Taylor | 89-91 | 114 | 480 | 4.2 | 7 | 28 | 188 | 6.7 | 2 |
| John Taylor | 87-95 | 6 | 31 | 5.2 | 0 | 347 | 5598 | 16.1 | 43 |
| Kitrick Taylor | 88-93 | 1 | 2 | 2.0 | 0 | 36 | 414 | 11.5 | 1 |
| Lenny Taylor | 84,87 | 1 | -13 | -13.0 | 0 | 13 | 179 | 13.8 | 1 |
| Jimmy Teal | 85-87 | | | | | 21 | 282 | 13.4 | 3 |
| Derek Tennell | 87-89,91-93 | | | | | 40 | 371 | 9.3 | 5 |
| Vinny Testaverde | 87-95 | 229 | 1078 | 4.7 | 9 | 2 | 10 | 5.0 | 0 |
| Joe Theismann | 74-85 | 355 | 1815 | 5.1 | 17 | | | | |
| Yancey Thigpen | 91-95 | 1 | 1 | 1.0 | 0 | 131 | 2009 | 15.3 | 12 |
| Blair Thomas | 90-95 | 533 | 2236 | 4.2 | 7 | 71 | 513 | 7.2 | 2 |
| Calvin Thomas | 82-88 | 171 | 672 | 3.9 | 5 | 20 | 115 | 5.8 | 0 |
| Charley Thomas | 82-84 | 53 | 215 | 4.1 | 1 | 11 | 52 | 4.7 | 0 |
| Doug Thomas | 91-93 | 4 | 11 | 2.8 | 0 | 22 | 207 | 9.4 | 0 |
| George Thomas | 89-92 | | | | | 56 | 848 | 15.1 | 3 |
| Jewerl Thomas | 80-84 | 173 | 783 | 4.5 | 4 | 28 | 167 | 6.0 | 0 |
| Ken Thomas | 83 | 15 | 55 | 3.7 | 0 | 28 | 236 | 8.4 | 1 |
| Lamar Thomas | 93-95 | 1 | 5 | 5.0 | 0 | 25 | 397 | 15.9 | 2 |
| Robb Thomas | 89-95 | 1 | -1 | -1.0 | 0 | 126 | 1610 | 12.8 | 6 |
| Rodney Thomas | 95 | 251 | 947 | 3.8 | 5 | 39 | 204 | 5.2 | 2 |
| Thurman Thomas | 88-95 | 2285 | 9729 | 4.3 | 54 | 371 | 3622 | 9.8 | 20 |
| Zach Thomas | 83-84 | | | | | 12 | 182 | 15.2 | 0 |
| Anthony Thompson | 90-92 | 251 | 831 | 3.3 | 6 | 14 | 74 | 5.3 | 0 |
| Aundra Thompson | 77-82 | 13 | 16 | 1.2 | 0 | 109 | 1792 | 16.4 | 8 |
| Craig Thompson | 92-93 | | | | | 36 | 281 | 7.8 | 3 |
| Darrell Thompson | 90-94 | 464 | 1642 | 3.5 | 7 | 41 | 330 | 8.0 | 1 |
| Jack Thompson | 79-84 | 70 | 262 | 3.7 | 6 | | | | |
| Leonard Thompson | 75-86 | 64 | 327 | 5.1 | 3 | 277 | 4682 | 16.9 | 35 |
| Leroy Thompson | 91-95 | 390 | 1365 | 3.5 | 5 | 148 | 1157 | 7.8 | 5 |
| Vince Thompson | 81, 83 | 75 | 349 | 4.7 | 2 | 8 | 56 | 7.0 | 0 |
| Weegie Thompson | 84-89 | | | | | 79 | 1377 | 17.4 | 11 |
| Jim Thornton | 88-91,93-95 | 1 | 4 | 4.0 | 0 | 107 | 1338 | 12.5 | 7 |
| Sidney Thornton | 77-82 | 356 | 1512 | 4.2 | 18 | 46 | 515 | 11.2 | 6 |
| John Tice | 83-92 | | | | | 158 | 1603 | 10.1 | 15 |
| Mike Tice | 81-93,95 | | | | | 107 | 894 | 8.4 | 11 |
| Pat Tilley | 76-86 | 1 | 32 | 32.0 | 0 | 468 | 7005 | 15.0 | 37 |
| Cedric Tillman | 92-95 | | | | | 87 | 1227 | 14.1 | 7 |
| Lawyer Tillman | 89,91-93,95 | 2 | 15 | 7.5 | 0 | 38 | 648 | 17.1 | 3 |
| Lewis Tillman | 89-95 | 659 | 2383 | 3.6 | 12 | 43 | 315 | 7.3 | 0 |
| Spencer Tillman | 87-94 | 40 | 181 | 4.5 | 1 | 3 | 7 | 2.3 | 0 |
| Michael Timpson | 89-95 | 6 | 38 | 6.3 | 1 | 196 | 2745 | 14.0 | 10 |
| Richard Todd | 76-86 | 259 | 932 | 3.6 | 14 | 1 | 1 | 1.0 | 0 |
| Billy Joe Tolliver | 89-94 | 53 | 128 | 2.4 | 2 | | | | |
| Mike Tomczak | 85-95 | 153 | 501 | 3.3 | 7 | 1 | 5 | 5.0 | 0 |
| Anthoney Toney | 86-90 | 639 | 2294 | 3.6 | 14 | 122 | 1031 | 8.5 | 5 |
| Al Toon | 85-92 | 4 | 7 | 1.8 | 0 | 517 | 6605 | 12.8 | 31 |
| JoJo Townsell | 85-89 | 2 | 0 | 0.0 | 0 | 66 | 1012 | 15.3 | 5 |
| Jack Trudeau | 86-95 | 97 | 186 | 1.9 | 3 | | | | |
| Olanda Truitt | 93-95 | | | | | 15 | 283 | 18.9 | 2 |
| Eric Truvillion | 87 | | | | | 10 | 184 | 18.4 | 1 |
| Tom Tupa | 89-92,94-95 | 48 | 190 | 4.0 | 1 | | | | |
| Daryl Turner | 84-87 | | | | | 101 | 1872 | 18.5 | 36 |
| Floyd Turner | 89-95 | 5 | 5 | 1.0 | 0 | 211 | 2832 | 13.4 | 24 |
| Kevin Turner | 92-95 | 98 | 391 | 4.0 | 1 | 102 | 885 | 8.7 | 6 |
| Odessa Turner | 87-93 | 2 | 11 | 5.5 | 0 | 97 | 1479 | 15.2 | 8 |
| Perry Tuttle | 82-84 | | | | | 25 | 375 | 15.0 | 3 |
| Robert Tyler | 89 | | | | | 14 | 148 | 10.6 | 0 |
| Toussaint Tyler | 81-82 | 46 | 204 | 4.4 | 0 | 27 | 166 | 6.2 | 0 |
| Wendell Tyler | 77-86 | 1344 | 6378 | 4.7 | 50 | 202 | 1816 | 9.0 | 16 |
| Tamarick Vanover | 95 | 6 | 31 | 5.2 | 0 | 11 | 231 | 21.0 | 2 |
| Tommy Vardell | 92-95 | 289 | 1070 | 3.7 | 3 | 54 | 434 | 8.0 | 2 |
| Jon Vaughn | 91-94 | 207 | 846 | 4.1 | 4 | 23 | 178 | 7.7 | 0 |
| Elton Veals | 84 | 31 | 87 | 2.8 | 0 | | | | |
| Clarence Verdin | 86-94 | 17 | 167 | 9.8 | 0 | 82 | 1329 | 16.2 | 6 |
| David Verser | 81-85 | 7 | 48 | 6.9 | 2 | 23 | 454 | 19.7 | 3 |
| Roger Vick | 87-90 | 333 | 1289 | 3.9 | 10 | 66 | 469 | 7.1 | 2 |
| Tommy Vigorito | 81-83, 85 | 54 | 215 | 4.0 | 2 | 59 | 439 | 7.4 | 2 |
| Lionel Vital | 87 | 80 | 346 | 4.3 | 2 | | | | |
| Tom Waddle | 89-94 | | | | | 173 | 2109 | 12.2 | 9 |
| Billy Waddy | 77-82,84 | 10 | 53 | 5.3 | 0 | 120 | 1963 | 16.4 | 10 |
| Frank Wainright | 91-92 | | | | | 10 | 146 | 14.6 | 0 |
| Adam Walker | 92-95 | 32 | 115 | 3.6 | 2 | 12 | 82 | 6.8 | 0 |
| Byron Walker | 82-86 | | | | | 54 | 925 | 17.1 | 7 |
| Derrick Walker | 90-95 | | | | | 159 | 1566 | 9.8 | 7 |
| Dwight Walker | 82-84,87 | 20 | 92 | 4.6 | 0 | 49 | 546 | 11.1 | 1 |
| Herschel Walker | 86-95 | 1938 | 8122 | 4.2 | 60 | 491 | 4621 | 9.4 | 19 |
| Rick Walker | 77-85 | 10 | 36 | 3.6 | 0 | 70 | 673 | 9.6 | 9 |
| Wayne Walker | 89 | 1 | 9 | 9.0 | 0 | 24 | 395 | 16.5 | 1 |
| Wesley Walker | 77-89 | 6 | 35 | 5.8 | 0 | 438 | 8306 | 19.0 | 71 |
| Ray Wallace | 86-87,89 | 76 | 330 | 4.3 | 4 | 24 | 211 | 8.8 | 2 |

| | | RUSHING | | | | RECEIVING | | | |
|---|---|---|---|---|---|---|---|---|---|
| **Name** | **Years** | **Att.** | **Yards** | **Avg.** | **TD** | **Rec.** | **Yards** | **Avg.** | **TD** |
| Herkie Walls | 83-85,87 | 9 | 64 | 7.1 | 0 | 32 | 587 | 18.3 | 2 |
| Wesley Walls | 89-91,93-95 | | | | | 106 | 1167 | 11.0 | 9 |
| Steve Walsh | 89-95 | 68 | 41 | 0.6 | 1 | | | | |
| Andre Ware | 90-93 | 38 | 217 | 5.7 | 0 | | | | |
| Derek Ware | 92-95 | | | | | 23 | 265 | 11.5 | 1 |
| Curt Warner | 83-90 | 1698 | 6844 | 4.0 | 56 | 193 | 1467 | 7.6 | 7 |
| Chris Warren | 90-95 | 1156 | 5004 | 4.3 | 35 | 109 | 812 | 7.4 | 3 |
| Don Warren | 79-92 | 1 | 5 | 5.0 | 0 | 244 | 2536 | 10.4 | 7 |
| Lamont Warren | 94-95 | 65 | 232 | 3.6 | 1 | 20 | 206 | 10.3 | 0 |
| Joe Washington | 76-85 | 1195 | 4839 | 4.0 | 12 | 395 | 3413 | 8.6 | 18 |
| Steve Watson | 79-87 | 6 | 19 | 3.2 | 0 | 353 | 6112 | 17.3 | 36 |
| Ricky Watters | 92-95 | 990 | 4113 | 4.2 | 36 | 202 | 1884 | 9.3 | 9 |
| Ricky Watts | 79-82 | 3 | -23 | -7.7 | 0 | 81 | 1547 | 19.1 | 8 |
| Clarence Weathers | 83-91 | 2 | 46 | 23.0 | 0 | 160 | 2426 | 15.2 | 17 |
| Robert Weathers | 82-86 | 159 | 733 | 4.6 | 4 | 29 | 268 | 9.2 | 0 |
| Gary Wellman | 92-94 | 3 | 3 | 1.0 | 0 | 41 | 542 | 13.2 | 1 |
| Ed West | 84-95 | 2 | 2 | 1.0 | 0 | 222 | 2511 | 11.3 | 26 |
| Joey Westbrook | 95 | 6 | 114 | 19.0 | 1 | 34 | 522 | 15.4 | 1 |
| Cleve Wester | 87 | 33 | 113 | 3.4 | 0 | | | | |
| Ryan Wetnight | 93-95 | | | | | 44 | 390 | 8.9 | 4 |
| Tyrone Wheatley | 95 | 78 | 245 | 3.1 | 3 | 5 | 27 | 5.4 | 0 |
| Danta Whitaker | 90,92-93 | | | | | 9 | 74 | 8.2 | 1 |
| Ken Whisenhunt | 85-88,90-92 | 2 | 23 | 11.5 | 0 | 62 | 596 | 9.6 | 5 |
| Charles White | 80-88 | 780 | 3075 | 3.9 | 23 | 114 | 860 | 7.5 | 1 |
| Danny White | 76-88 | 159 | 482 | 3.0 | 8 | 3 | 18 | 6.0 | 2 |
| Lorenzo White | 88-95 | 1062 | 4242 | 4.0 | 31 | 192 | 1738 | 9.1 | 6 |
| Sammy White | 76-85 | 18 | 97 | 5.4 | 0 | 393 | 6400 | 16.3 | 50 |
| David Whitehurst | 77-83 | 77 | 242 | 3.1 | 7 | | | | |
| Art Whittington | 78-82 | 448 | 1592 | 3.6 | 13 | 84 | 764 | 9.1 | 2 |
| James Wilder | 81-90 | 1586 | 6008 | 3.8 | 37 | 431 | 3500 | 8.1 | 10 |
| Gary Wilkins | 86-91 | 3 | 18 | 6.0 | 0 | 42 | 584 | 13.9 | 6 |
| Gerald Willhite | 82-88 | 380 | 1688 | 4.4 | 17 | 207 | 1767 | 8.5 | 5 |
| Kevin Willhite | 87 | 53 | 251 | 4.7 | 0 | 6 | 37 | 6.2 | 0 |
| Al Williams | 87 | 1 | 11 | 11.0 | 0 | 12 | 247 | 20.6 | 1 |
| Brooks Williams | 78-83 | | | | | 37 | 455 | 12.3 | 2 |
| Byron Williams | 83-85 | | | | | 84 | 1693 | 18.6 | 3 |
| Calvin Williams | 90-95 | 5 | 29 | 5.8 | 0 | 293 | 3832 | 13.1 | 34 |
| David Williams | 86-87 | | | | | 10 | 195 | 19.5 | 0 |
| Derwin Williams | 85-86 | | | | | 11 | 198 | 18.0 | 0 |
| Dokie Williams | 83-87 | 3 | 27 | 9.0 | 0 | 148 | 2886 | 19.4 | 25 |
| Doug Williams | 78-82,86-89 | 220 | 884 | 4.0 | 15 | | | | |
| Harvey Williams | 91-95 | 754 | 2955 | 3.9 | 15 | 129 | 979 | 7.6 | 5 |
| Jamie Williams | 84-94 | | | | | 181 | 1980 | 10.9 | 11 |
| John L. Williams | 86-95 | 1245 | 5006 | 4.0 | 18 | 546 | 4656 | 8.5 | 19 |
| Keith Williams | 86 | 3 | 18 | 6.0 | 0 | 12 | 164 | 13.7 | 1 |
| Kevin Williams | 93-95 | 23 | 99 | 4.3 | 2 | 71 | 945 | 13.3 | 4 |
| Mike Williams | 83-84,87 | 150 | 517 | 3.4 | 0 | 33 | 259 | 7.8 | 0 |
| Mike Williams | 79-81 | 71 | 261 | 3.7 | 1 | 19 | 141 | 7.4 | 3 |
| Mike Williams | 89,91-95 | | | | | 21 | 293 | 14.0 | 0 |
| Newton Williams | 83 | 28 | 77 | 2.8 | 0 | 4 | 46 | 11.5 | 0 |
| Oliver Williams | 87 | | | | | 20 | 340 | 17.0 | 2 |
| Ray Williams | 80 | 2 | 17 | 8.5 | 1 | 10 | 146 | 14.6 | 1 |
| Scott Williams | 86-88 | 30 | 73 | 2.4 | 3 | 9 | 71 | 7.9 | 1 |
| Sherman Williams | 95 | 48 | 205 | 4.3 | 1 | 3 | 28 | 9.3 | 0 |
| Van Williams | 83-85,87 | 50 | 170 | 3.4 | 0 | 10 | 82 | 8.2 | 0 |
| Vince Williams | 82-84 | 41 | 130 | 3.2 | 0 | 9 | 79 | 8.8 | 1 |
| Warren Williams | 88-93 | 258 | 1191 | 4.6 | 8 | 37 | 295 | 8.0 | 1 |
| Chester Willis | 81-83 | 32 | 73 | 2.3 | 1 | 1 | 24 | 24.0 | 0 |
| Charles Wilson | 90-95 | 7 | 25 | 3.6 | 0 | 113 | 1750 | 15.5 | 11 |
| Dave Wilson | 81,83-89 | 45 | 23 | 0.5 | 2 | | | | |
| Marc Wilson | 80-87,89-90 | 141 | 551 | 3.9 | 5 | | | | |
| Mike Wilson | 81-90 | | | | | 158 | 2199 | 13.9 | 15 |
| Robert Wilson | 91,94-95 | 44 | 183 | 4.2 | 0 | 21 | 124 | 5.9 | 2 |
| Stanley Wilson | 83-85,86,88 | 253 | 1118 | 4.4 | 11 | 28 | 277 | 9.6 | 2 |
| Tim Wilson | 77-84 | 398 | 1414 | 3.6 | 6 | 99 | 609 | 6.2 | 3 |
| Wade Wilson | 81-95 | 222 | 998 | 4.5 | 8 | | | | |
| Walter Wilson | 90 | 1 | 0 | 0.0 | 0 | 10 | 87 | 8.7 | 0 |
| Wayne Wilson | 79-87 | 684 | 2531 | 3.7 | 19 | 181 | 1533 | 8.5 | 14 |
| Tydus Winans | 94-95 | 1 | 5 | 5.0 | 0 | 23 | 421 | 18.3 | 2 |
| Sammy Winder | 82-90 | 1495 | 5427 | 3.6 | 39 | 197 | 1302 | 6.6 | 9 |
| Kellen Winslow | 79-87 | | | | | 541 | 6741 | 12.5 | 45 |
| Ron Wolfley | 85-93,95 | 86 | 263 | 3.1 | 2 | 26 | 200 | 7.7 | 1 |
| George Wonsley | 84-89 | 281 | 1158 | 4.1 | 9 | | | | |
| Nate Wonsley | 86 | 73 | 339 | 4.6 | 3 | 8 | 57 | 7.1 | 0 |
| Otis Wonsley | 81-85 | 61 | 181 | 3.0 | 4 | 2 | 6 | 3.0 | 1 |
| David Woodley | 80-85 | 201 | 856 | 4.3 | 11 | 2 | 21 | 10.5 | 1 |
| Tony Woodruff | 82-84 | | | | | 36 | 554 | 15.4 | 5 |
| Keith Woodside | 88-91 | 259 | 976 | 3.8 | 6 | 144 | 1248 | 8.7 | 2 |
| Ickey Woods | 88-91 | 332 | 1525 | 4.8 | 27 | 47 | 397 | 8.4 | 0 |
| Butch Woolfolk | 82-88 | 537 | 1923 | 3.6 | 8 | 187 | 1939 | 10.4 | 8 |
| Barry Word | 87-88,90-94 | 705 | 2897 | 4.1 | 16 | 30 | 280 | 9.3 | 0 |
| Vince Workman | 89-95 | 443 | 1667 | 3.8 | 13 | 175 | 1258 | 7.2 | 6 |
| Tim Worley | 89-91,93-94 | 455 | 1792 | 3.9 | 8 | 35 | 253 | 7.2 | 0 |
| Adrian Wright | 87 | 37 | 112 | 3.0 | 0 | 13 | 98 | 7.5 | 0 |
| Alexander Wright | 90-95 | 6 | 42 | 7.0 | 0 | 99 | 1573 | 15.9 | 10 |
| James Wright | 78-85 | 3 | -4 | -1.3 | 0 | 66 | 666 | 10.1 | 4 |
| Randy Wright | 84-88 | 55 | 173 | 3.5 | 3 | | | | |
| Tim Wrightman | 85-86 | | | | | 46 | 648 | 14.0 | 1 |
| Frank Wycheck | 93-95 | 1 | 1 | 1.0 | 0 | 63 | 639 | 10.1 | 2 |
| Ryan Yarborough | 94-95 | | | | | 24 | 272 | 11.3 | 3 |
| Dave Young | 81-84 | | | | | 19 | 213 | 11.2 | 3 |
| Duane Young | 91-95 | | | | | 38 | 405 | 10.7 | 3 |
| Michael Young | 85-94 | | | | | 144 | 2034 | 14.1 | 14 |
| Steve Young | 85-95 | 539 | 3219 | 6.0 | 30 | 2 | 2 | 1.0 | 0 |
| Tyrone Young | 83-84 | | | | | 36 | 682 | 18.9 | 6 |
| Ray Zellars | 95 | 50 | 162 | 3.2 | 2 | 7 | 33 | 4.7 | 0 |
| Jim Zorn | 76-85,87 | 322 | 1504 | 4.7 | 17 | 1 | 27 | 27.0 | 0 |

(All men with 25 or more punt returns or 25 or more kickoff returns)

| | | PUNT RETURNS | | | | KICKOFF RETURNS | | | |
|---|---|---|---|---|---|---|---|---|---|
| **Name** | **Years** | **No.** | **Yards** | **Avg.** | **TD** | **No.** | **Yards** | **Avg.** | **TD** |
| Stefon Adams | 86-90 | 43 | 321 | 7.5 | 0 | 65 | 1240 | 19.1 | 0 |
| Anthony Allen | 85-89 | 35 | 216 | 6.2 | 0 | 8 | 140 | 17.5 | 0 |
| Gary Allen | 82-84 | 63 | 599 | 9.5 | 1 | 56 | 1136 | 20.3 | 0 |
| Marvin Allen | 88-91 | | | | | 43 | 844 | 19.6 | 0 |
| Alfred Anderson | 84-91 | | | | | 42 | 803 | 19.1 | 0 |
| Gary Anderson | 85-88,90-93 | 48 | 385 | 8.0 | 0 | 143 | 2779 | 19.4 | 1 |
| Jamal Anderson | 94-95 | | | | | 25 | 552 | 22.1 | 0 |
| Kim Anderson | 80-81 | 5 | 7 | 1.4 | 0 | 40 | 779 | 19.5 | 0 |
| Larry Anderson | 78-84 | 75 | 582 | 7.8 | 0 | 189 | 4217 | 22.3 | 1 |
| Tyrone Anthony | 84-85 | | | | | 45 | 966 | 21.5 | 0 |
| Gene Atkins | 87-92 | | | | | 71 | 1508 | 21.2 | 0 |
| Cliff Austin | 83-87 | | | | | 57 | 1047 | 18.4 | 1 |
| Aaron Bailey | 94-95 | | | | | 21 | 495 | 23.6 | 1 |
| Johnny Bailey | 90-95 | 148 | 1420 | 9.6 | 2 | 115 | 2420 | 21.0 | 0 |
| Randy Baldwin | 91-95 | | | | | 97 | 2202 | 22.7 | 1 |
| Eric Ball | 89-94 | | | | | 115 | 2474 | 21.5 | 0 |
| Gordon Banks | 85-87 | 37 | 220 | 5.9 | 0 | 1 | 56 | 56.0 | 0 |
| Lew Barnes | 86,88-89 | 93 | 830 | 8.9 | 0 | 9 | 236 | 26.2 | 1 |
| Brian Baschnagel | 76-84 | 6 | 58 | 9.7 | 0 | 89 | 2102 | 23.6 | 1 |
| Michael Bates | 93-95 | | | | | 65 | 1287 | 19.8 | 0 |
| Shawn Beals | 88 | | | | | 34 | 625 | 18.4 | 0 |
| Don Beebe | 89-95 | | | | | 60 | 1198 | 20.0 | 0 |
| Ken Bell | 86-89 | 25 | 147 | 5.9 | 0 | 104 | 2218 | 21.3 | 0 |
| Theo Bell | 76-85 | 189 | 1511 | 8.0 | 0 | 3 | 50 | 16.7 | 0 |
| Albert Bentley | 85-92 | | | | | 149 | 3192 | 21.4 | 0 |
| Rufus Bess | 79-87 | 55 | 432 | 7.9 | 0 | 48 | 998 | 20.8 | 0 |
| Don Bessillieu | 79-83 | 2 | 12 | 6.0 | 0 | 47 | 1024 | 21.6 | 0 |
| Eric Bieniemy | 91-95 | 37 | 276 | 7.5 | 0 | 30 | 535 | 17.8 | 0 |
| Lyle Blackwood | 73-86 | 69 | 319 | 4.6 | 0 | 19 | 388 | 20.4 | 0 |
| Carl Bland | 84-90 | 5 | 59 | 11.8 | 0 | 36 | 697 | 19.4 | 0 |
| Brian Brennan | 84-92 | 56 | 438 | 7.8 | 1 | 1 | 10 | 10.0 | 0 |
| Dewell Brewer | 94 | 42 | 339 | 8.1 | 1 | 18 | 358 | 19.9 | 0 |
| Leon Bright | 81-85 | 141 | 1149 | 8.1 | 0 | 77 | 1544 | 20.1 | 0 |
| Bill Brooks | 86-95 | 50 | 330 | 6.6 | 0 | 8 | 143 | 17.9 | 0 |
| James Brooks | 81-92 | 52 | 565 | 10.9 | 0 | 130 | 2762 | 21.2 | 0 |
| Robert Brooks | 92-95 | 67 | 589 | 8.8 | 1 | 51 | 1237 | 24.3 | 1 |
| Steve Broussard | 90-95 | | | | | 53 | 1224 | 23.1 | 0 |
| Bobby Brown | 68-70 | 69 | 404 | 5.9 | 0 | 22 | 437 | 19.9 | 0 |
| Curtis Brown | 77-83 | 1 | 0 | 0.0 | 0 | 41 | 874 | 21.3 | 1 |
| Dave Brown | 75-90 | 35 | 291 | 8.3 | 0 | 6 | 126 | 21.0 | 0 |
| Preston Brown | 80-84 | 10 | 42 | 4.2 | 0 | 46 | 937 | 20.4 | 0 |
| Reggie Brown | 82-83,87 | | | | | 25 | 486 | 19.4 | 0 |
| Ron Brown | 84-91 | | | | | 199 | 4493 | 22.6 | 4 |
| Tim Brown | 88-95 | 269 | 2811 | 10.4 | 2 | 47 | 1204 | 25.6 | 1 |
| Troy Brown | 93-95 | 49 | 426 | 8.7 | 0 | 47 | 929 | 19.8 | 0 |
| Steve Brown | 83-86 | | | | | 36 | 857 | 23.8 | 1 |
| Vince Buck | 90-92 | 70 | 569 | 8.1 | 0 | 3 | 38 | 12.7 | 0 |
| Terrell Buckley | 92-95 | 21 | 211 | 10.0 | 1 | 1 | 16 | 16.0 | 0 |
| Jeff Burris | 94-95 | 52 | 561 | 10.8 | 0 | | | | |
| Barney Bussey | 86-92 | | | | | 29 | 507 | 17.5 | 0 |
| Earnest Byner | 94-95 | | | | | 28 | 515 | 18.4 | 0 |
| Butler By'not'e | 94-95 | | | | | 42 | 880 | 21.0 | 0 |
| Ken Callicutt | 78-81 | 5 | 25 | 5.0 | 0 | 44 | 742 | 16.9 | 0 |
| Jack Cameron | 84 | | | | | 26 | 485 | 18.7 | 0 |
| Jeff Campbell | 90-94 | 4 | 15 | 3.8 | 0 | 28 | 408 | 14.6 | 0 |
| Billy Campfield | 78-83 | | | | | 74 | 1566 | 21.2 | 1 |
| Rob Carpenter | 91-95 | 40 | 287 | 7.2 | 0 | | | | |
| Carlos Carson | 80-89 | | | | | 57 | 1241 | 21.9 | 0 |
| Dale Carter | 92-94 | 81 | 769 | 9.5 | 2 | 11 | 190 | 17.3 | 0 |
| Dexter Carter | 90-95 | 102 | 1041 | 10.2 | 2 | 209 | 4503 | 21.5 | 2 |
| Jimmy Cefalo | 78-84 | 30 | 242 | 8.1 | 0 | 2 | 40 | 20.0 | 0 |
| Larry Centers | 90-95 | 5 | 30 | 6.0 | 0 | 33 | 617 | 18.7 | 0 |
| Wes Chandler | 78-88 | 67 | 428 | 6.4 | 0 | 47 | 1021 | 21.7 | 0 |
| Darryl Clack | 86-89 | | | | | 83 | 1802 | 21.7 | 0 |
| Allan Clark | 79-82 | | | | | 44 | 912 | 20.7 | 0 |
| Kevin Clark | 87-88,90-91 | 59 | 575 | 9.7 | 0 | 22 | 550 | 25.0 | 0 |
| Andre Coleman | 94-95 | 28 | 326 | 11.6 | 1 | 111 | 2704 | 24.4 | 4 |
| Charles Crawford | 86 | | | | | 27 | 497 | 18.4 | 0 |
| Raymond Clayborn | 77-88 | | | | | 57 | 1538 | 27.0 | 3 |
| Mark Clayton | 83-93 | 52 | 485 | 9.3 | 1 | 3 | 40 | 13.3 | 0 |
| Pat Coleman | 90-94 | 31 | 186 | 6.0 | 0 | 32 | 601 | 18.8 | 0 |
| Tony Collins | 81-87,90 | 3 | 15 | 5.0 | 0 | 67 | 1365 | 20.4 | 0 |
| Curtis Conway | 93-95 | 8 | 63 | 7.9 | 0 | 31 | 678 | 21.9 | 0 |
| Evan Cooper | 84-88 | 101 | 763 | 7.6 | 0 | 43 | 790 | 18.4 | 0 |
| Danny Copeland | 89 | | | | | 26 | 466 | 17.9 | 0 |
| Russell Copeland | 93-95 | 34 | 293 | 8.6 | 1 | 36 | 668 | 18.6 | 0 |
| Aaron Craver | 91-92,94-95 | | | | | 47 | 839 | 17.9 | 0 |
| Joe Cribbs | 80-83,85-88 | 29 | 154 | 5.3 | 0 | 56 | 1229 | 21.9 | 1 |
| Ray Crittenden | 93-94 | 21 | 192 | 9.1 | 0 | 47 | 938 | 20.0 | 0 |
| Kenneth Davis | 86-94 | | | | | 42 | 707 | 16.8 | 0 |
| Robert Delpino | 88-93 | | | | | 68 | 1339 | 19.7 | 0 |
| Ron Dickerson | 93-94 | | | | | 32 | 709 | 22.2 | 0 |
| Floyd Dixon | 86-91 | 26 | 151 | 5.8 | 0 | 2 | 13 | 6.5 | 0 |
| James Dixon | 89-91 | | | | | 101 | 2315 | 22.9 | 1 |
| Zachary Dixon | 79-84 | 1 | 5 | 5.0 | 0 | 128 | 2634 | 20.6 | 1 |
| Willie Drewrey | 85-93 | 192 | 1597 | 8.3 | 0 | 102 | 2097 | 20.6 | 0 |
| Doug DuBose | 87-88 | | | | | 32 | 608 | 19.0 | 0 |
| Kenny Duckett | 82-85 | | | | | 73 | 1511 | 20.7 | 0 |
| Curtis Duncan | 87-93 | 13 | 67 | 5.1 | 0 | 29 | 580 | 20.0 | 0 |
| Jim Duncan | 69-71 | | | | | 42 | 1369 | 32.6 | 2 |
| David Dunn | 95 | | | | | 50 | 1092 | 21.8 | 0 |
| Kenny Easley | 81-87 | 26 | 302 | 11.6 | 0 | | | | |
| Bobby Joe Edmonds | 86-89,95 | 134 | 1471 | 11.0 | 1 | 173 | 3696 | 21.4 | 0 |
| Al Edwards | 90-91 | 27 | 161 | 6.0 | 0 | 42 | 879 | 20.9 | 1 |
| Anthony Edwards | 88-93,95 | 37 | 274 | 7.4 | 0 | 33 | 564 | 17.1 | 0 |
| Donnie Elder | 85-86,89-91 | 1 | 0 | 0.0 | 0 | 150 | 3040 | 20.3 | 0 |
| Henry Ellard | 83-95 | 135 | 1527 | 11.3 | 4 | 19 | 364 | 19.2 | 0 |
| Craig Ellis | 86 | 24 | 149 | 6.2 | 0 | 25 | 541 | 21.6 | 0 |
| Phillip Epps | 82-89 | 100 | 819 | 8.2 | 1 | 34 | 686 | 20.2 | 0 |
| Rich Erenberg | 84 | | | | | 28 | 575 | 20.5 | 0 |
| Ricky Feacher | 76-84 | 15 | 157 | 10.5 | 0 | 37 | 821 | 22.2 | 0 |
| Ron Fellows | 81-87 | 48 | 325 | 6.8 | 0 | 73 | 1478 | 20.2 | 0 |
| Gill Fenerty | 90-91 | 12 | 55 | 4.6 | 0 | 30 | 600 | 20.0 | 0 |
| Jitter Fields | 84 | 27 | 236 | 8.7 | 0 | 19 | 356 | 18.7 | 0 |
| Jeff Fisher | 81-84 | 120 | 1125 | 9.4 | 1 | 14 | 204 | 14.6 | 0 |

| | | PUNT RETURNS | | | | KICKOFF RETURNS | | | |
|---|---|---|---|---|---|---|---|---|---|
| **Name** | **Years** | **No.** | **Yards** | **Avg.** | **TD** | **No.** | **Yards** | **Avg.** | **TD** |
| Terrence Flagler | 87-91 | | | | | 57 | 1049 | 18.4 | 0 |
| Herman Fontenot | 85-90 | | | | | 50 | 997 | 19.9 | 0 |
| Antonio Freeman | 95 | 37 | 292 | 7.9 | 0 | 24 | 556 | 23.2 | 0 |
| Phil Freeman | 85-87 | | | | | 79 | 1667 | 21.1 | 0 |
| Irving Fryar | 84-95 | 206 | 2055 | 10.0 | 3 | 27 | 505 | 18.7 | 0 |
| Brent Fullwood | 87-90 | | | | | 62 | 1293 | 20.9 | 0 |
| Bobby Futrell | 86-90 | 77 | 639 | 8.3 | 0 | 42 | 820 | 19.5 | 0 |
| Tony Galbreath | 76-87 | 5 | 9 | 1.8 | 0 | 27 | 501 | 18.6 | 0 |
| Joey Galloway | 95 | 36 | 360 | 10.0 | 1 | 2 | 30 | 15.0 | 0 |
| Charlie Garner | 94-95 | | | | | 29 | 590 | 20.3 | 0 |
| Gregg Garrity | 83-89 | 21 | 203 | 9.7 | 1 | | | | |
| Alvin Garrett | 80-84 | 43 | 344 | 8.0 | 0 | 50 | 1013 | 20.3 | 0 |
| Willie Gault | 83-93 | | | | | 45 | 1088 | 24.2 | 1 |
| Dennis Gentry | 82-92 | 15 | 77 | 5.1 | 1 | 192 | 4353 | 22.7 | 3 |
| Ernest Givins | 86-95 | 58 | 390 | 6.7 | 1 | 1 | 27 | 27.0 | 0 |
| Nesby Glasgow | 79-90 | 80 | 651 | 8.1 | 1 | 85 | 1906 | 22.4 | 0 |
| Aaron Glenn | 94-95 | | | | | 28 | 594 | 21.2 | 0 |
| Darrien Gordon | 93 | 31 | 395 | 12.7 | 0 | | | | |
| Sam Graddy | 87-88,90-92 | | | | | 27 | 458 | 17.0 | 0 |
| Jeff Graham | 91-95 | 46 | 369 | 8.0 | 1 | 4 | 60 | 15.0 | 0 |
| Alan Grant | 90-92 | 33 | 261 | 7.9 | 0 | 21 | 370 | 17.6 | 0 |
| Mel Gray | 86-95 | 211 | 2387 | 11.3 | 3 | 362 | 8833 | 24.4 | 6 |
| Boyce Green | 83-87 | | | | | 30 | 644 | 21.5 | 1 |
| Darrell Green | 83-95 | 51 | 576 | 11.3 | 0 | | | | |
| Gaston Green | 88-92 | | | | | 47 | 981 | 20.9 | 1 |
| Mark Green | 89-92 | 19 | 150 | 7.9 | 0 | 33 | 644 | 19.5 | 0 |
| Roy Green | 80-92 | 27 | 230 | 8.5 | 1 | 89 | 2002 | 22.5 | 1 |
| Don Griffin | 86-95 | 74 | 667 | 9.1 | 1 | 41 | 848 | 20.7 | 0 |
| Keith Griffin | 84-88 | | | | | 52 | 985 | 18.9 | 0 |
| Jeff Groth | 79-85 | 105 | 887 | 8.4 | 0 | 16 | 287 | 17.9 | 0 |
| Neal Guggemos | 86-88 | | | | | 53 | 1152 | 21.7 | 0 |
| Eric Guliford | 93-95 | 77 | 701 | 9.1 | 1 | 5 | 101 | 20.2 | 0 |
| Chris Hale | 90-92 | 24 | 251 | 10.4 | 0 | | | | |
| Alvin Hall | 81-85,87 | 15 | 139 | 9.3 | 0 | 128 | 2819 | 22.0 | 1 |
| Dino Hall | 79-83 | 111 | 901 | 8.1 | 0 | 151 | 3185 | 21.1 | 0 |
| Lorenzo Hampton | 85-89 | | | | | 96 | 2025 | 21.1 | 0 |
| Rodney Hampton | 90-94 | | | | | 30 | 544 | 18.1 | 0 |
| Anthony Hancock | 82-86 | 29 | 198 | 6.8 | 0 | 64 | 1281 | 20.0 | 0 |
| Mike Harden | 80-89 | 6 | 102 | 14.6 | 1 | 28 | 425 | 15.2 | 0 |
| Derrick Harmon | 84-87 | | | | | 40 | 906 | 22.7 | 0 |
| Ronnie Harmon | 86-95 | | | | | 71 | 1330 | 18.7 | 0 |
| Bruce Harper | 77-84 | 183 | 1784 | 9.8 | 1 | 243 | 5407 | 22.3 | 0 |
| Corey Harris | 92-95 | 6 | 17 | 2.8 | 0 | 97 | 2188 | 22.6 | 0 |
| Darryl Harris | 88 | | | | | 39 | 833 | 21.4 | 0 |
| Duriel Harris | 76-85 | 18 | 152 | 8.4 | 0 | 56 | 1416 | 25.3 | 0 |
| Leonard Harris | 86-94 | | | | | 59 | 1240 | 21.0 | 0 |
| Rod Harris | 89-91 | 108 | 826 | 7.6 | 0 | 49 | 897 | 18.3 | 0 |
| Andre Hastings | 93-95 | 50 | 489 | 9.8 | 1 | 12 | 177 | 14.8 | 0 |
| Courtney Hawkins | 92-95 | 33 | 247 | 7.5 | 0 | 9 | 118 | 13.1 | 0 |
| Mike Haynes | 76-88 | 112 | 1168 | 10.4 | 2 | | | | |
| Vaughn Hebron | 93-94 | | | | | 24 | 478 | 19.9 | 0 |
| Johnny Hector | 83-92 | | | | | 34 | 735 | 21.6 | 0 |
| Jerome Henderson | 91 | 27 | 201 | 7.4 | 0 | | | | |
| Darryl Henley | 89-93 | 61 | 579 | 9.5 | 0 | | | | |
| Wally Henry | 77-82 | 148 | 1231 | 8.3 | 1 | 87 | 1950 | 22.4 | 0 |
| Cliff Hicks | 87-95 | 138 | 1284 | 9.3 | 0 | 7 | 154 | 22.0 | 0 |
| Dwight Hicks | 79-86 | 54 | 403 | 7.7 | 0 | 3 | 58 | 19.3 | 0 |
| Mark Higgs | 88-95 | | | | | 32 | 585 | 18.3 | 0 |
| Drew Hill | 79-93 | 3 | 22 | 7.3 | 0 | 172 | 3460 | 20.1 | 1 |
| Kenny Hill | 81-88 | | | | | 50 | 1220 | 24.4 | 1 |
| Rod Hill | 82-87 | 51 | 391 | 7.7 | 0 | 14 | 243 | 17.4 | 0 |
| Tony Hill | 77-86 | 27 | 268 | 9.9 | 0 | 4 | 96 | 24.0 | 0 |
| Ira Hillary | 87-90 | 31 | 230 | 7.4 | 0 | 28 | 439 | 15.7 | 0 |
| Jamie Holland | 87-92 | | | | | 133 | 2806 | 21.1 | 0 |
| David Hollis | 87-89 | 27 | 225 | 8.3 | 0 | 38 | 771 | 18.7 | 1 |
| Darick Holmes | 95 | | | | | 39 | 799 | 20.5 | 0 |
| John Holt | 81-87 | 36 | 241 | 6.7 | 0 | 11 | 274 | 24.9 | 0 |
| Desmond Howard | 92-95 | 34 | 355 | 10.4 | 1 | 53 | 1045 | 19.7 | 0 |
| Harlan Huckleby | 80-85 | | | | | 70 | 1300 | 18.6 | 0 |
| Danan Hughes | 93-95 | 33 | 250 | 7.6 | 0 | 24 | 474 | 19.8 | 0 |
| David Hughes | 81-86 | | | | | 32 | 663 | 20.7 | 0 |
| Tyrone Hughes | 93-95 | 86 | 908 | 10.6 | 2 | 159 | 3926 | 24.7 | 3 |
| Ronald Humphrey | 94-95 | | | | | 56 | 1236 | 22.1 | 1 |
| Bobby Humphrey | 84-90 | 1 | 0 | 0.0 | 0 | 130 | 2974 | 22.9 | 2 |
| Herman Hunter | 85-87 | 1 | 6 | 6.0 | 0 | 100 | 2133 | 21.3 | 0 |
| Ivy Joe Hunter | 89-91 | 31 | 100 | 3.2 | 0 | 11 | 97 | 8.8 | 0 |
| Mark Ingram | 87-95 | 9 | 49 | 5.4 | 0 | 48 | 742 | 15.5 | 0 |
| LeRoy Irvin | 80-89 | 146 | 1451 | 9.9 | 4 | 4 | 60 | 15.0 | 0 |
| Qadry Ismail | 93-95 | | | | | 119 | 2746 | 23.1 | 0 |
| Raghib Ismail | 93-95 | | | | | 104 | 2234 | 21.5 | 0 |
| John Jackson | 90-92 | 31 | 244 | 7.9 | 0 | 3 | 58 | 19.3 | 0 |
| Lionel James | 84-88 | 124 | 1193 | 9.6 | 2 | 99 | 2094 | 21.2 | 0 |
| Roland James | 80-89 | 42 | 400 | 9.5 | 1 | | | | |
| James Jefferson | 89-90 | 20 | 155 | 7.8 | 0 | 26 | 607 | 23.3 | 1 |
| Ken Jenkins | 83-86 | 78 | 773 | 9.9 | 0 | 108 | 2427 | 22.5 | 0 |
| Stanford Jennings | 84-92 | | | | | 148 | 2965 | 20.0 | 1 |
| Jim Jodat | 77-83 | | | | | 35 | 685 | 19.6 | 0 |
| Paul Johns | 81-84 | 74 | 843 | 11.4 | 2 | 8 | 138 | 17.3 | 0 |
| A.J. Johnson | 89-90 | | | | | 24 | 504 | 21.0 | 0 |
| Billy "White Shoes" Johnson | 74-88 | 282 | 3317 | 11.8 | 6 | 123 | 2941 | 23.9 | 2 |
| Butch Johnson | 76-85 | 146 | 1313 | 9.0 | 1 | 79 | 1832 | 23.2 | 0 |
| Joe Johnson | 89-92 | 31 | 209 | 9.7 | 0 | 53 | 1111 | 21.0 | 1 |
| Kenny Johnson | 80-89 | 110 | 854 | 7.8 | 0 | 60 | 1156 | 19.3 | 0 |
| Vance Johnson | 85-93,95 | 81 | 689 | 8.5 | 0 | 59 | 1312 | 22.2 | 0 |
| James Jones | 80-82,84-85 | 87 | 736 | 8.5 | 0 | 70 | 1444 | 20.6 | 0 |
| Keith Jones | 89-92 | | | | | 37 | 790 | 21.3 | 1 |
| Charles Jordan | 94-95 | 22 | 213 | 9.7 | 0 | 26 | 459 | 17.7 | 0 |
| Yonel Jourdain | 94-95 | 1 | 0 | 0.0 | 0 | 46 | 949 | 20.6 | 0 |
| Rick Kane | 77-85 | 1 | 13 | 13.0 | 0 | 64 | 1370 | 21.4 | 0 |
| Todd Kinchen | 92-95 | 80 | 709 | 8.7 | 2 | 66 | 1412 | 21.4 | 0 |
| Mark Konecny | 87-89 | 33 | 233 | 7.1 | 0 | 17 | 276 | 16.2 | 0 |
| Eric Lane | 81-86 | | | | | 27 | 442 | 16.4 | 0 |
| Garcia Lane | 85 | 43 | 381 | 8.9 | 0 | 13 | 269 | 20.7 | 0 |
| David Lang | 91-95 | | | | | 52 | 1048 | 20.2 | 0 |
| Gene Lang | 84-90 | | | | | 63 | 1353 | 21.5 | 0 |

| | | PUNT RETURNS | | | | KICKOFF RETURNS | | | |
|---|---|---|---|---|---|---|---|---|---|
| **Name** | **Years** | **No.** | **Yards** | **Avg.** | **TD** | **No.** | **Yards** | **Avg.** | **TD** |
| Robert Lavette | 85-87 | 18 | 92 | 5.1 | 0 | 76 | 1490 | 19.6 | 0 |
| Amos Lawrence | 81-82 | | | | | 26 | 627 | 24.1 | 1 |
| Amp Lee | 92-95 | 5 | 50 | 10.0 | 0 | 32 | 578 | 18.1 | 0 |
| Gary Lee | 87-88 | | | | | 50 | 1074 | 21.5 | 0 |
| Mark Lee | 80-89 | 26 | 220 | 8.5 | 1 | 45 | 859 | 19.1 | 0 |
| Chuck Levy | 94 | | | | | 26 | 513 | 19.7 | 0 |
| Darren Lewis | 91-92 | | | | | 25 | 524 | 21.0 | 1 |
| Leo Lewis | 81-91 | 202 | 1868 | 9.2 | 1 | 6 | 81 | 13.5 | 0 |
| Nate Lewis | 90-95 | 35 | 327 | 9.3 | 0 | 169 | 3825 | 22.6 | 1 |
| Thomas Lewis | 94-95 | 11 | 110 | 10.0 | 0 | 35 | 766 | 21.9 | 1 |
| Will Lewis | 80-81 | 56 | 449 | 8.0 | 1 | 45 | 963 | 21.4 | 0 |
| Louis Lipps | 84-92 | 112 | 1234 | 11.0 | 3 | 14 | 246 | 17.6 | 0 |
| Marc Logan | 87-95 | | | | | 85 | 1760 | 20.7 | 1 |
| Derek Loville | 90-91,94-95 | 3 | 16 | 5.3 | 0 | 38 | 805 | 21.2 | 0 |
| Vaughn Lusby | 80-81 | 36 | 274 | 7.6 | 0 | 6 | 92 | 15.3 | 0 |
| Pete Mandley | 84-90 | 165 | 1514 | 9.2 | 1 | 35 | 630 | 18.0 | 0 |
| Wade Manning | 79-82 | 51 | 433 | 8.5 | 0 | 48 | 1005 | 20.9 | 0 |
| Arthur Marshall | 92-95 | 46 | 446 | 9.7 | 0 | 23 | 381 | 16.6 | 0 |
| Eric Martin | 85-94 | 46 | 368 | 8.0 | 0 | 22 | 495 | 22.5 | 0 |
| Kelvin Martin | 87-95 | 220 | 2194 | 10.0 | 3 | 76 | 1453 | 19.1 | 0 |
| Mike Martin | 83-89 | 140 | 1381 | 9.9 | 0 | 75 | 1563 | 20.8 | 0 |
| Robbie Martin | 81-86 | 175 | 1670 | 9.5 | 2 | 113 | 2084 | 18.4 | 0 |
| Sammy Martin | 88-91 | 20 | 165 | 8.3 | 0 | 100 | 2317 | 23.2 | 1 |
| Tony Martin | 90-95 | 28 | 150 | 5.3 | 0 | 8 | 167 | 20.9 | 0 |
| Terance Mathis | 90-95 | 50 | 445 | 8.9 | 1 | 107 | 1980 | 18.5 | 0 |
| Ira Matthews | 79-81 | 80 | 586 | 7.3 | 0 | 71 | 1602 | 22.6 | 1 |
| Rich Mauti | 77-84 | 75 | 610 | 8.1 | 0 | 124 | 2836 | 22.9 | 0 |
| Rueben Mayes | 86-88,90,92-93 | | | | | 38 | 695 | 18.3 | 0 |
| Derrick McAdoo | 87-88 | 1 | 0 | 0.0 | 0 | 36 | 755 | 21.0 | 0 |
| Fred McAfee | 91-95 | | | | | 60 | 1156 | 19.3 | 0 |
| Napoleon McCallum | 86,90-94 | 11 | 63 | 5.7 | 0 | 29 | 574 | 19.8 | 0 |
| Phil McConkey | 84-89 | 218 | 1832 | 8.4 | 0 | 69 | 1324 | 19.2 | 0 |
| Mike McCoy | 76-83 | | | | | 54 | 1187 | 22.0 | 0 |
| O.J. McDuffie | 93-95 | 84 | 708 | 8.4 | 2 | 91 | 2086 | 22.9 | 0 |
| Tim McGee | 86-94 | | | | | 58 | 1249 | 21.5 | 0 |
| Willie McGee | 73-78 | 6 | 56 | 9.3 | 0 | 50 | 1115 | 22.3 | 0 |
| Dennis McKinnon | 83-85,87-90 | 129 | 1191 | 9.2 | 3 | 3 | 58 | 19.3 | 0 |
| Dana McLemore | 82-87 | 152 | 1598 | 10.5 | 4 | 56 | 1147 | 20.5 | 0 |
| Todd McNair | 89-95 | | | | | 57 | 1079 | 18.9 | 0 |
| Gerald McNeil | 86-90 | 191 | 1717 | 9.0 | 1 | 91 | 1852 | 20.4 | 1 |
| Dave Meggett | 89-95 | 249 | 2613 | 10.5 | 6 | 184 | 3953 | 21.5 | 1 |
| Eric Metcalf | 89-95 | 166 | 1724 | 10.4 | 5 | 151 | 3084 | 20.4 | 2 |
| Glyn Milburn | 93-95 | 112 | 1158 | 10.3 | 0 | 96 | 2250 | 23.4 | 0 |
| Hugh Millen | 87-94 | 62 | 252 | 4.1 | 1 | | | | |
| Anthony Miller | 88-95 | | | | | 50 | 1269 | 25.4 | 2 |
| Scott Miller | 91-94 | 53 | 436 | 8.2 | 0 | 3 | 35 | 11.7 | 0 |
| Terry Miller | 78-81 | | | | | 25 | 480 | 19.2 | 0 |
| Ernie Mills | 91-95 | | | | | 68 | 1607 | 23.6 | 0 |
| John Henry Mills | 93-95 | | | | | 26 | 512 | 19.7 | 0 |
| Brian Mitchell | 90-95 | 172 | 1938 | 11.3 | 6 | 216 | 5002 | 23.2 | 0 |
| Stump Mitchell | 81-89 | 156 | 1377 | 8.8 | 1 | 177 | 4007 | 22.6 | 0 |
| Carl Monroe | 83-87 | | | | | 76 | 1660 | 21.8 | 1 |
| Alton Montgomery | 90-93 | | | | | 63 | 1293 | 20.5 | 0 |
| Cle Montgomery | 80-85 | 70 | 622 | 8.9 | 1 | 132 | 2706 | 20.5 | 0 |
| Wilbert Montgomery | 77-85 | | | | | 32 | 814 | 25.4 | 1 |
| Jeff Moore | 79-83 | 10 | 90 | 9.0 | 0 | 40 | 784 | 19.6 | 0 |
| Nat Moore | 74-86 | 27 | 297 | 11.0 | 0 | 33 | 858 | 26.0 | 0 |
| Emory Moorehead | 77-88 | | | | | 31 | 627 | 20.2 | 0 |
| Stanley Morgan | 77-90 | 92 | 960 | 10.4 | 1 | 2 | 29 | 14.5 | 0 |
| Jamie Morris | 88-90 | | | | | 32 | 615 | 19.2 | 0 |
| Joe Morris | 82-88,91 | | | | | 40 | 659 | 16.5 | 0 |
| Randall Morris | 84-88 | | | | | 84 | 1662 | 19.8 | 0 |
| Bobby Morse | 87,89-91 | 39 | 247 | 6.3 | 0 | 41 | 780 | 19.0 | 0 |
| Michael Morton | 82-85 | | | | | 89 | 1885 | 21.2 | 0 |
| Mike Mosley | 82-83 | 11 | 61 | 5.5 | 0 | 27 | 723 | 26.8 | 0 |
| Vance Mueller | 86-90 | | | | | 39 | 878 | 22.5 | 0 |
| Adrian Murrell | 93-95 | | | | | 37 | 610 | 16.5 | 0 |
| Tony Nathan | 79-87 | 51 | 484 | 9.5 | 1 | 50 | 1118 | 22.4 | 0 |
| Ricky Nattiel | 87-91 | 54 | 416 | 7.7 | 0 | 11 | 202 | 18.4 | 0 |
| Mike Nelms | 80-84 | 212 | 1948 | 9.2 | 2 | 175 | 4128 | 23.6 | 0 |
| Darrin Nelson | 82-92 | 42 | 357 | 8.5 | 0 | 163 | 3659 | 22.4 | 0 |
| Pat Newman | 90-94 | 24 | 158 | 6.6 | 0 | 3 | 62 | 20.7 | 0 |
| Timmy Newsome | 80-88 | | | | | 33 | 677 | 20.5 | 0 |
| Fred Nixon | 80-81 | 26 | 203 | 7.8 | 0 | 18 | 382 | 21.2 | 0 |
| Terry Obee | 91,93 | 35 | 289 | 8.3 | 0 | 9 | 159 | 17.7 | 0 |
| Henry Odom | 83 | | | | | 39 | 756 | 19.4 | 0 |
| James Owens | 79-84 | | | | | 127 | 2801 | 22.1 | 2 |
| Stephone Paige | 84-91 | | | | | 29 | 580 | 20.0 | 0 |
| David Palmer | 94-95 | 56 | 535 | 9.6 | 1 | 17 | 354 | 20.8 | 0 |
| Paul Palmer | 87-89 | | | | | 72 | 1542 | 21.4 | 2 |
| Anthony Parker | 89,91-93 | 42 | 400 | 9.5 | 0 | 2 | 30 | 15.0 | 0 |
| Eddie Payton | 77-78,80-82 | 156 | 1387 | 8.9 | 1 | 156 | 2676 | 17.1 | 2 |
| Danny Peebles | 89-91 | | | | | 26 | 518 | 19.9 | 0 |
| Erric Pegram | 91-95 | | | | | 42 | 714 | 16.8 | 0 |
| Carl Pickens | 92-95 | 36 | 305 | 8.5 | 1 | | | | |
| Allen Pinkett | 86-91 | 1 | -1 | -1.0 | 0 | 54 | 1069 | 19.8 | 0 |
| Danny Pittman | 80-84 | 10 | 50 | 5.0 | 0 | 37 | 778 | 21.0 | 0 |
| Ron Pitts | 86-90 | 50 | 436 | 8.7 | 1 | 2 | 24 | 12.0 | 0 |
| Ricky Porter | 82-83,87 | 14 | 104 | 7.4 | 0 | 26 | 559 | 21.5 | 0 |
| Dave Preston | 78-81 | 18 | 155 | 8.6 | 0 | 26 | 597 | 23.0 | 0 |
| Roell Preston | 95 | | | | | 30 | 627 | 20.9 | 0 |
| Mitchell Price | 90-93 | 50 | 498 | 10.0 | 2 | 25 | 446 | 17.8 | 0 |
| Anthony Prior | 93-94 | | | | | 25 | 442 | 17.7 | 0 |
| Mike Prior | 85,87-94 | 42 | 368 | 8.8 | 0 | 13 | 178 | 13.7 | 0 |
| Jeff Query | 89-95 | 76 | 712 | 9.4 | 0 | 7 | 138 | 19.7 | 0 |
| Barry Redden | 82-90 | | | | | 66 | 1392 | 21.1 | 0 |
| Jarvis Redwine | 81-83 | | | | | 50 | 1124 | 22.5 | 0 |
| Beasley Reece | 76-84 | 5 | 18 | 3.6 | 0 | 40 | 775 | 19.4 | 0 |
| Buster Rhymes | 85-86 | | | | | 62 | 1558 | 25.1 | 0 |
| Allen Rice | 84-91 | 1 | 0 | 0.0 | 0 | 31 | 417 | 13.5 | 0 |
| Robb Riddick | 81,83-84,86-88 | 46 | 289 | 6.3 | 0 | 63 | 1276 | 20.3 | 0 |
| Carl Roaches | 80-85 | 155 | 1116 | 7.2 | 0 | 154 | 3352 | 21.8 | 2 |
| Patrick Robinson | 93-94 | 84 | 590 | 7.0 | 0 | 42 | 798 | 19.0 | 0 |
| Del Rodgers | 82-84,87-88 | | | | | 68 | 1445 | 21.3 | 1 |
| Jimmy Rogers | 80-84 | | | | | 77 | 1678 | 21.8 | 0 |

| | | PUNT RETURNS | | | | KICKOFF RETURNS | | | |
|---|---|---|---|---|---|---|---|---|---|
| **Name** | **Years** | **No.** | **Yards** | **Avg.** | **TD** | **No.** | **Yards** | **Avg.** | **TD** |
| Lee Rouson | 85-91 | | | | | 36 | 686 | 19.1 | 0 |
| Derek Russell | 91-95 | | | | | 37 | 753 | 20.4 | 0 |
| Lupe Sanchez | 86-88 | 2 | 11 | 5.5 | 0 | 35 | 778 | 22.2 | 0 |
| Deion Sanders | 89-95 | 94 | 843 | 9.0 | 2 | 148 | 3405 | 23.0 | 3 |
| Ricky Sanders | 86-95 | 2 | 12 | 6.0 | 0 | 36 | 619 | 17.2 | 0 |
| Thomas Sanders | 85-91 | | | | | 103 | 1946 | 18.9 | 1 |
| Corey Sawyer | 94-95 | 35 | 365 | 10.4 | 1 | 3 | 64 | 21.3 | 0 |
| Scott Schwedes | 87-90 | 80 | 765 | 9.6 | 1 | 17 | 302 | 17.8 | 0 |
| John Sciarra | 78-83 | 117 | 909 | 7.8 | 0 | | | | |
| Pete Shaw | 77-83 | 41 | 322 | 7.9 | 0 | 1 | 0 | 0.0 | 0 |
| Derrick Shepard | 87-91 | 75 | 679 | 9.1 | 1 | 51 | 1007 | 19.7 | 0 |
| Vai Sikahema | 86-93 | 292 | 3169 | 10.9 | 4 | 235 | 4933 | 21.0 | 0 |
| John Simmons | 83-87 | 46 | 307 | 6.7 | 0 | 17 | 342 | 20.1 | 0 |
| Paul Skansi | 83-91 | 91 | 863 | 9.5 | 0 | 20 | 379 | 19.0 | 0 |
| Webster Slaughter | 86-95 | 38 | 256 | 6.7 | 0 | 1 | 21 | 21.0 | 0 |
| Don Smith | 88-90 | | | | | 41 | 831 | 20.3 | 0 |
| Jeff Smith | 85-88 | 37 | 290 | 7.8 | 0 | 77 | 1475 | 19.2 | 0 |
| Jim Smith | 77-82,85 | 98 | 737 | 7.5 | 0 | 17 | 397 | 23.4 | 0 |
| Jimmy Smith | 92,95 | | | | | 24 | 540 | 22.5 | 1 |
| Joey Smith | 91-92 | | | | | 33 | 598 | 17.0 | 0 |
| J.T. Smith | 78-90 | 267 | 2764 | 10.4 | 4 | 25 | 473 | 18.9 | 0 |
| Phil Smith | 83-84,86-87 | 6 | 23 | 3.8 | 0 | 32 | 651 | 20.3 | 1 |
| Reggie Smith | 80-81 | 39 | 361 | 9.3 | 0 | 72 | 1655 | 23.0 | 0 |
| Ricky Smith | 82-84 | 54 | 537 | 9.9 | 0 | 67 | 1505 | 22.5 | 1 |
| Tony Smith | 92-94 | 56 | 485 | 8.7 | 0 | 61 | 1453 | 23.8 | 1 |
| Kurt Sohn | 81-88 | 68 | 519 | 7.6 | 0 | 63 | 1164 | 18.5 | 0 |
| Freddie Solomon | 75-85 | 177 | 1614 | 9.1 | 4 | 32 | 694 | 21.7 | 0 |
| Todd Spencer | 84-85,87 | | | | | 45 | 990 | 22.0 | 0 |
| Irving Spikes | 94-95 | | | | | 37 | 812 | 21.9 | 0 |
| Kirk Springs | 81-84 | 51 | 534 | 10.5 | 1 | 49 | 885 | 18.1 | 0 |
| Ron Springs | 79-86 | | | | | 44 | 905 | 20.6 | 0 |
| Sylvester Stamps | 84-89 | 1 | 8 | 8.0 | 0 | 92 | 2079 | 22.6 | 1 |
| Walter Stanley | 85-90,92 | 175 | 1619 | 9.3 | 1 | 89 | 1658 | 18.6 | 0 |
| Stephen Starring | 83-88 | 19 | 108 | 5.7 | 0 | 115 | 2389 | 20.8 | 0 |
| Anthony Steels | 85,87 | 8 | 45 | 5.6 | 0 | 30 | 561 | 18.7 | 0 |
| Milt Stegall | 92-94 | | | | | 26 | 446 | 17.2 | 0 |
| Dwight Stone | 87-95 | | | | | 109 | 2136 | 19.6 | 1 |
| Troy Stradford | 87-92 | 40 | 284 | 7.1 | 0 | 38 | 700 | 18.4 | 0 |
| Ray Strong | 78-81 | | | | | 28 | 561 | 20.0 | 0 |
| Matt Suhey | 80-89 | 1 | 4 | 4.0 | 0 | 26 | 508 | 19.5 | 0 |
| Mickey Sutton | 86-90 | 76 | 695 | 9.1 | 0 | 9 | 169 | 18.8 | 0 |
| Jeff Sydner | 92-95 | 64 | 611 | 9.5 | 0 | 49 | 963 | 19.7 | 0 |
| Steve Tasker | 85-95 | 18 | 204 | 11.3 | 0 | 43 | 898 | 20.9 | 0 |
| Rodney Tate | 82-84 | | | | | 36 | 680 | 18.9 | 0 |
| John Taylor | 87-95 | 149 | 1517 | 10.2 | 2 | 14 | 276 | 19.7 | 0 |
| Ken Taylor | 85-86 | 25 | 198 | 7.9 | 0 | 1 | 18 | 18.0 | 0 |
| Kitrick Taylor | 88-93 | 63 | 568 | 9.0 | 1 | 8 | 132 | 16.5 | 0 |
| Ryan Terry | 95 | | | | | 37 | 808 | 21.8 | 0 |
| J.T. Thomas | 95 | 0 | 61 | 0.0 | 0 | 32 | 752 | 23.5 | 0 |
| Zach Thomas | 83-84 | 54 | 493 | 9.1 | 1 | 46 | 924 | 20.1 | 0 |
| Aundra Thompson | 77-83 | | | | | 52 | 1090 | 21.0 | 1 |
| Leonard Thompson | 75-86 | 12 | 136 | 11.3 | 0 | 36 | 799 | 22.2 | 0 |
| Leroy Thompson | 91-95 | | | | | 31 | 664 | 21.4 | 0 |
| Pat Tilley | 76-86 | 31 | 264 | 8.5 | 0 | | | | |
| Spencer Tillman | 87-94 | | | | | 41 | 670 | 16.3 | 0 |
| Michael Timpson | 89-95 | | | | | 28 | 588 | 21.0 | 0 |
| JoJo Townsell | 85-90 | 127 | 1360 | 10.7 | 1 | 98 | 2048 | 20.9 | 1 |
| Erroll Tucker | 88-89 | 29 | 245 | 8.4 | 0 | 38 | 746 | 19.6 | 0 |
| Willie Tullis | 81-88 | 6 | 56 | 9.3 | 0 | 32 | 779 | 24.3 | 1 |
| Vernon Turner | 90-95 | 95 | 817 | 8.6 | 1 | 134 | 2626 | 19.6 | 0 |
| Andre Tyler | 83 | 27 | 208 | 7.7 | 0 | | | | |
| Wendell Tyler | 77-86 | | | | | 27 | 570 | 21.1 | 0 |
| Darryl Usher | 89 | 4 | 25 | 6.3 | 0 | 27 | 506 | 18.7 | 0 |
| Tamarick Vanover | 95 | 51 | 540 | 10.6 | 1 | 43 | 1095 | 25.5 | 2 |
| Jon Vaughn | 91-94 | | | | | 103 | 2390 | 23.2 | 2 |
| Clarence Verdin | 86-94 | 178 | 1650 | 9.3 | 5 | 253 | 5252 | 20.8 | 1 |
| David Verser | 81-85 | | | | | 65 | 1371 | 21.1 | 0 |
| Tommy Vigorito | 81-83,85 | 79 | 830 | 10.5 | 2 | 4 | 84 | 21.0 | 0 |
| Billy Waddy | 77-82,84 | 43 | 274 | 6.4 | 0 | | | | |
| Dwight Walker | 82-84,87 | 28 | 177 | 6.3 | 0 | 42 | 922 | 22.0 | 0 |
| Fulton Walker | 81-86 | 145 | 1439 | 9.9 | 1 | 167 | 3769 | 22.6 | 1 |
| Herschel Walker | 86-95 | | | | | 138 | 3138 | 22.7 | 2 |
| Herkie Walls | 83-85,87 | 4 | 12 | 3.0 | 0 | 42 | 769 | 18.3 | 0 |
| Len Walterscheid | 77-84 | 57 | 424 | 7.4 | 0 | 34 | 833 | 24.5 | 0 |
| Chris Warren | 90-94 | 94 | 819 | 8.7 | 0 | 86 | 1794 | 20.9 | 0 |
| Rickey Watts | 79-84 | | | | | 34 | 710 | 20.9 | 1 |
| Ted Watts | 81-85 | 35 | 284 | 8.1 | 1 | | | | |
| Clarence Weathers | 83-91 | 63 | 454 | 7.2 | 0 | 4 | 75 | 18.8 | 0 |
| Charles White | 80-88 | 1 | 14 | 14.0 | 0 | 52 | 970 | 18.7 | 0 |
| Lorenzo White | 88-95 | | | | | 33 | 666 | 20.2 | 1 |
| Art Whittington | 78-82 | 2 | 4 | 2.0 | 0 | 76 | 1513 | 19.9 | 1 |
| Gerald Willhite | 82-88 | 101 | 1054 | 10.4 | 1 | 26 | 521 | 20.0 | 0 |
| Dokie Williams | 83-87 | | | | | 44 | 949 | 21.6 | 0 |
| Harvey Williams | 91-95 | | | | | 56 | 1135 | 20.3 | 0 |
| Henry Williams | 89 | 30 | 267 | 8.9 | 0 | 14 | 249 | 17.8 | 0 |
| Kevin Williams | 93-95 | 93 | 896 | 9.6 | 3 | 123 | 2945 | 23.9 | 1 |
| Mike Williams | 89,91-95 | | | | | 29 | 517 | 17.8 | 0 |
| Ray Williams | 80 | 27 | 259 | 9.6 | 0 | 9 | 228 | 25.3 | 1 |
| Van Williams | 83-85,87 | 1 | 0 | 0.0 | 0 | 62 | 1334 | 21.5 | 0 |
| Charles Wilson | 90-95 | | | | | 92 | 2048 | 22.3 | 1 |
| Don Wilson | 84-85 | 49 | 458 | 9.3 | 1 | 56 | 1041 | 18.6 | 0 |
| Steve Wilson | 79-86 | 36 | 236 | 6.6 | 0 | 58 | 1107 | 19.1 | 0 |
| Wayne Wilson | 79-87 | | | | | 72 | 1630 | 22.6 | 0 |
| Scott Woerner | 81 | 33 | 278 | 8.4 | 0 | 10 | 210 | 21.0 | 0 |
| Chris Woods | 87-89 | 28 | 125 | 7.0 | 0 | 5 | 92 | 18.4 | 0 |
| Rick Woods | 82-86 | 70 | 568 | 8.1 | 0 | 1 | 17 | 17.0 | 0 |
| Rod Woodson | 87-95 | 256 | 2362 | 9.2 | 2 | 220 | 4894 | 22.2 | 2 |
| Butch Woolfolk | 82-88 | | | | | 53 | 1029 | 19.4 | 0 |
| Vince Workman | 89-95 | 1 | 0 | 0.0 | 0 | 61 | 980 | 16.1 | 0 |
| Naz Worthen | 89-90 | 44 | 313 | 7.1 | 0 | 16 | 339 | 21.2 | 0 |
| Alexander Wright | 90-95 | | | | | 79 | 1681 | 21.3 | 2 |
| Eric Yarber | 86-87 | 46 | 416 | 9.0 | 0 | | | | |
| Glen Young | 83-85,87-88 | 14 | 93 | 6.6 | 0 | 113 | 2626 | 23.2 | 0 |

Lifetime Statistics - 1980- 1995    Section 4 - **PUNTING**
(All men with 25 or more punts)

| Name | Years | No. | Avg. | Name | Years | No. | Avg. | Name | Years | No. | Avg. | Name | Years | No. | Avg. |
|---|---|---|---|---|---|---|---|---|---|---|---|---|---|---|---|
| Louie Aguiar | 91-95 | 386 | 41.2 | Dave Finzer | 84-85 | 153 | 39.9 | Sean Landeta | 85-95 | 733 | 43.4 | Mike Saxon | 85-95 | 820 | 41.0 |
| Harold Alexander | 93-94 | 143 | 41.6 | Scott Fulhage | 87-92 | 401 | 41.1 | Shawn McCarthy | 91-92 | 171 | 40.1 | Bucky Scribner | 83-84,87-89 | 342 | 39.5 |
| Evan Arapostathis | 86 | 30 | 38.0 | Vince Gamache | 86-87 | 93 | 38.4 | Pat McInally | 76-85 | 709 | 41.3 | Tom Skladany | 78-83 | 295 | 42.2 |
| Jim Arnold | 83-94 | 871 | 42.0 | Frank Garcia | 81,83-87 | 384 | 40.8 | Paul McJulien | 91-93 | 145 | 39.0 | Dave Smigelsky | 82 | 26 | 38.5 |
| Bryan Barker | 90-95 | 422 | 41.6 | Chris Gardocki | 91-95 | 298 | 40.5 | Jim Miller | 80-82 | 214 | 40.6 | Ray Stachowicz | 81-83 | 136 | 40.2 |
| | | | | | | | | | | | | | | | |
| Tommy Barnhardt | 87-95 | 551 | 42.4 | Ralph Giacomarro | 83-85,87 | 188 | 40.4 | John Misko | 82-84,87 | 207 | 40.4 | Rohn Stark | 82-95 | 1051 | 43.4 |
| Darren Bennett | 95 | 72 | 44.7 | Kelly Goodburn | 87-93 | 355 | 39.5 | Chris Mohr | 89,91-95 | 427 | 40.2 | Dan Stryzinski | 90-95 | 448 | 39.8 |
| Mitch Berger | 94 | 25 | 38.0 | John Goodson | 82 | 49 | 40.4 | Ralf Mojsiejenko | 85-91 | 418 | 42.0 | Larry Swider | 79-82 | 284 | 41.3 |
| Carl Birdsong | 81-85 | 369 | 41.1 | Jeff Gossett | 81-83,85-95 | 929 | 41.2 | Greg Montgomery | 88-94 | 380 | 42.9 | Stan Talley | 87 | 57 | 39.9 |
| Mike Black | 83-87 | 274 | 40.9 | Bob Grupp | 79-81 | 214 | 40.9 | Harry Newsome | 85-93 | 697 | 42.3 | John Teltschik | 86-89 | 350 | 39.5 |
| | | | | | | | | | | | | | | | |
| Don Bracken | 85-90,92-93 | 466 | 39.6 | Brian Hansen | 84-88,90-95 | 880 | 41.7 | Chris Norman | 84-86 | 220 | 39.9 | Tommy Thompson | 95 | 57 | 40.6 |
| Maury Buford | 82-86,88-91 | 586 | 40.7 | Dale Hatcher | 85-89,91,93 | 494 | 39.7 | Pat O'Neill | 94-95 | 113 | 39.3 | Tom Tupa | 88-92,94-95 | 86 | 40.6 |
| Rich Camarillo | 81-95 | 1033 | 42.5 | Jeff Hayes | 82-87 | 279 | 37.5 | Tom Orosz | 81-84 | 188 | 39.9 | Matt Turk | 95 | 74 | 42.4 |
| Greg Cater | 80-83,86-87 | 379 | 38.5 | Barry Helton | 88-91 | 217 | 38.2 | Rick Partridge | 79-80,87 | 136 | 39.4 | Rick Tuten | 89-95 | 482 | 43.3 |
| Lewis Colbert | 86-87,89 | 117 | 40.0 | Craig Hentrich | 94-95 | 148 | 41.0 | Luke Prestridge | 79-84 | 421 | 41.9 | Bryan Wagner | 87-95 | 511 | 40.3 |
| | | | | | | | | | | | | | | | |
| Greg Coleman | 77-88 | 823 | 40.4 | Alan Herline | 87 | 26 | 33.1 | Joe Prokop | 85,87-92 | 376 | 39.1 | John Warren | 83-84 | 50 | 39.5 |
| Craig Colquitt | 78-84 | 429 | 41.2 | Mike Horan | 84-95 | 765 | 42.0 | Chuck Ramsey | 77-84 | 553 | 40.0 | Jack Weil | 86 | 34 | 39.5 |
| Mike Connell | 78,80-81 | 254 | 38.7 | Greg Horne | 87-88 | 123 | 40.3 | Bill Renner | 86-87 | 38 | 35.1 | Jeff West | 75-79, 81-85 | 625 | 37.9 |
| Frank Corral | 78-81 | 165 | 40.8 | Mike Hubach | 80-81 | 82 | 38.0 | George Roberts | 78-82 | 306 | 41.0 | Danny White | 78-86 | 612 | 39.8 |
| Steve Cox | 81-88 | 393 | 41.2 | Tom Hutton | 95 | 86 | 42.8 | Reggie Roby | 83-95 | 796 | 42.3 | Ron Widby | 68-73 | 368 | 42.0 |
| | | | | | | | | | | | | | | | |
| Ray Criswell | 87-88 | 94 | 37.5 | Hank Ilesic | 89 | 76 | 40.1 | Ruben Rodriguez | 87-89,92 | 239 | 40.4 | Klaus Wilmsmeyer | 92-95 | 219 | 40.4 |
| Rick Donnelly | 85-88,91 | 377 | 42.0 | Dave Jennings | 74-87 | 1163 | 40.9 | Tom Rouen | 93-95 | 196 | 43.2 | George Winslow | 87,89 | 34 | 35.6 |
| Keith English | 90 | 68 | 39.2 | John Jett | 93-95 | 179 | 41.6 | Mark Royals | 87,90-95 | 486 | 40.9 | Mike Wood | 78-81 | 82 | 36.8 |
| Russell Erxleben | 79-83,87 | 280 | 40.6 | Lee Johnson | 85-95 | 757 | 41.8 | Max Runager | 79-89 | 668 | 39.8 | | | | |
| Jeff Feagles | 88-95 | 652 | 40.6 | John Kidd | 84-95 | 792 | 40.7 | Todd Sauerbrun | 95 | 55 | 37.8 | | | | |

Lifetime Statistics - 1980-1995    Section 5 - **KICKING**
(All men with 10 or more PAT or field goal attempts)

| Name | Years | PAT | PAT Att. | PAT Pct. | FG | FG Att. | FG Pct. |
|------|-------|-----|----------|----------|-----|---------|---------|
| Vince Abbott | 87-88 | 37 | 38 | 97 | 21 | 34 | 62 |
| Raul Allegre | 83-91 | 183 | 190 | 96 | 137 | 186 | 74 |
| Wilson Alvarez | 81 | 14 | 15 | 93 | 3 | 7 | 30 |
| Morten Andersen | 82-95 | 441 | 448 | 98 | 333 | 426 | 78 |
| Gary Anderson | 82-95 | 448 | 453 | 99 | 331 | 425 | 78 |
| Obed Ariri | 84,87 | 44 | 46 | 96 | 22 | 31 | 71 |
| Jess Atkinson | 85-87 | 21 | 22 | 95 | 11 | 19 | 58 |
| Chris Bahr | 76-89 | 490 | 519 | 94 | 241 | 381 | 63 |
| Matt Bahr | 79-95 | 522 | 534 | 98 | 300 | 415 | 72 |
| Charlie Baumann | 91-92 | 37 | 40 | 93 | 20 | 29 | 69 |
| Willie Beecher | 87-88 | 12 | 12 | 100 | 3 | 4 | 75 |
| Rolf Benirschke | 77-86 | 328 | 353 | 93 | 146 | 208 | 70 |
| Dean Biasucci | 84,86-95 | 268 | 275 | 97 | 185 | 262 | 71 |
| Cary Blanchard | 92-93,95 | 73 | 73 | 100 | 52 | 72 | 72 |
| Novo Bojovic | 85 | 11 | 12 | 92 | 3 | 7 | 43 |
| Chris Boniol | 94-95 | 94 | 96 | 98 | 49 | 57 | 86 |
| Jim Breech | 79-92 | 517 | 539 | 96 | 243 | 340 | 71 |
| Doug Brien | 94-95 | 95 | 97 | 98 | 34 | 49 | 69 |
| Jeff Brockhaus | 87 | 11 | 13 | 85 | 3 | 6 | 50 |
| Kevin Butler | 85-95 | 387 | 397 | 97 | 243 | 333 | 73 |
| Bill Capece | 81-83 | 67 | 72 | 93 | 43 | 70 | 61 |
| John Carney | 88-95 | 195 | 199 | 98 | 152 | 191 | 80 |
| Steve Christie | 90-95 | 199 | 203 | 98 | 140 | 177 | 79 |
| Mike Cofer | 87-93,95 | 303 | 312 | 97 | 133 | 201 | 66 |
| Joe Cooper | 84,86 | 17 | 17 | 100 | 13 | 17 | 76 |
| Frank Corral | 78-81 | 154 | 160 | 96 | 75 | 124 | 61 |
| Steve Cox | 81-87 | 3 | 3 | 100 | 6 | 12 | 50 |
| Brad Daluiso | 91-95 | 35 | 35 | 100 | 34 | 46 | 74 |
| Rick Danmeier | 78-82 | 154 | 165 | 93 | 70 | 106 | 66 |
| Greg Davis | 87-95 | 216 | 221 | 98 | 172 | 250 | 69 |
| Al Del Greco | 84-95 | 368 | 376 | 98 | 204 | 279 | 73 |
| Steve DeLine | 88-89 | 15 | 15 | 100 | 9 | 15 | 60 |
| Dean Dorsey | 88 | 12 | 13 | 92 | 5 | 10 | 50 |
| Jason Elam | 93-95 | 109 | 110 | 99 | 87 | 110 | 79 |
| Lin Elliott | 92-95 | 113 | 118 | 96 | 75 | 99 | 76 |
| Cole Ford | 95 | 17 | 18 | 94 | 8 | 9 | 89 |
| Tony Franklin | 79-88 | 341 | 355 | 96 | 177 | 264 | 67 |
| Jim Gallery | 87,89-90 | 43 | 44 | 98 | 11 | 25 | 44 |
| Edgar Garcia | 84 | 14 | 15 | 93 | 3 | 9 | 33 |
| Teddy Garcia | 88-90 | 45 | 52 | 87 | 21 | 38 | 55 |
| Ali Haji-Sheikh | 83-87 | 95 | 103 | 92 | 76 | 111 | 68 |
| Jason Hanson | 92-95 | 145 | 146 | 99 | 101 | 130 | 78 |
| Mike Hollis | 95 | 27 | 28 | 96 | 20 | 27 | 74 |
| Ian Howfield | 91 | 25 | 29 | 86 | 13 | 18 | 72 |
| Michael Husted | 93-95 | 72 | 72 | 100 | 58 | 83 | 70 |
| Donald Igwebuike | 85-90 | 153 | 160 | 96 | 108 | 143 | 76 |
| Chris Jacke | 89-95 | 250 | 253 | 99 | 152 | 197 | 77 |
| Dave Jacobs | 79,81,87 | 21 | 25 | 84 | 12 | 26 | 46 |
| Jeff Jaeger | 87,89-95 | 244 | 250 | 98 | 166 | 226 | 73 |
| Norm Johnson | 82-95 | 515 | 521 | 99 | 277 | 366 | 76 |

| Name | Years | PAT | PAT Att. | PAT Pct. | FG | FG Att. | FG Pct. |
|------|-------|-----|----------|----------|-----|---------|---------|
| Rich Karlis | 82-90 | 283 | 294 | 96 | 172 | 239 | 72 |
| John Kasay | 91-95 | 122 | 125 | 96 | 108 | 138 | 78 |
| Jerry Kauric | 90 | 24 | 27 | 89 | 14 | 20 | 70 |
| Florian Kempf | 82-84,87 | 64 | 67 | 96 | 29 | 38 | 76 |
| Mike Lansford | 82-90 | 315 | 325 | 97 | 158 | 217 | 73 |
| Tim Lashar | 87 | 10 | 10 | 100 | 3 | 4 | 75 |
| Pat Leahy | 74-91 | 558 | 584 | 96 | 304 | 426 | 71 |
| John Lee | 86 | 14 | 17 | 82 | 8 | 13 | 62 |
| Chip Lohmiller | 88-95 | 273 | 280 | 98 | 183 | 259 | 71 |
| Nick Lowery | 78,80-95 | 536 | 541 | 99 | 366 | 455 | 80 |
| Mick Luckhurst | 81-87 | 213 | 216 | 99 | 115 | 164 | 70 |
| Paul McFadden | 84-89 | 160 | 164 | 98 | 120 | 163 | 74 |
| Steve McLaughlin | 95 | 17 | 17 | 100 | 8 | 16 | 50 |
| Eddie Murray | 80-95 | 498 | 503 | 99 | 325 | 428 | 76 |
| Chuck Nelson | 83-84,86-88 | 175 | 184 | 95 | 63 | 93 | 68 |
| Bjorn Nittmo | 89 | 12 | 13 | 92 | 9 | 12 | 75 |
| Scott Norwood | 85-91 | 271 | 278 | 97 | 133 | 184 | 72 |
| Neil O'Donoghue | 77-85 | 240 | 257 | 93 | 112 | 189 | 59 |
| Doug Pelfrey | 93-95 | 71 | 75 | 95 | 81 | 100 | 81 |
| Todd Peterson | 94-95 | 44 | 44 | 100 | 25 | 32 | 78 |
| Fuad Reveiz | 85-88,90-95 | 367 | 378 | 97 | 188 | 250 | 75 |
| Benny Ricardo | 76-84 | 171 | 180 | 95 | 92 | 142 | 65 |
| John Roveto | 81-82 | 29 | 30 | 97 | 14 | 31 | 45 |
| Roger Ruzek | 87-93 | 206 | 219 | 94 | 120 | 166 | 72 |
| Eric Schubert | 85-87 | 36 | 38 | 95 | 18 | 36 | 50 |
| Rafael Septien | 77-86 | 420 | 433 | 97 | 180 | 256 | 70 |
| Scott Sisson | 93 | 15 | 15 | 100 | 14 | 26 | 54 |
| Jason Staurovsky | 87-92 | 69 | 71 | 97 | 54 | 80 | 68 |
| Matt Stover | 91-95 | 156 | 158 | 99 | 108 | 134 | 81 |
| Pete Stoyanovich | 89-95 | 246 | 250 | 98 | 176 | 222 | 79 |
| Ian Sunter | 80 | 15 | 15 | 100 | 11 | 20 | 55 |
| Bob Thomas | 75-86 | 303 | 330 | 92 | 151 | 239 | 63 |
| David Treadwell | 89-94 | 182 | 188 | 97 | 135 | 175 | 77 |
| David Trout | 81,87 | 48 | 56 | 86 | 12 | 19 | 63 |
| Uwe von Schamann | 79-84 | 237 | 250 | 95 | 101 | 149 | 68 |
| Ray Wersching | 73-87 | 456 | 477 | 96 | 222 | 329 | 67 |
| Jeff Wilkins | 94-95 | 27 | 29 | 93 | 12 | 13 | 92 |
| Ken Willis | 90-92 | 90 | 90 | 100 | 55 | 80 | 69 |
| Mike Wood | 78-82 | 69 | 77 | 90 | 29 | 49 | 59 |
| Luis Zendejas | 87-89 | 78 | 79 | 99 | 37 | 55 | 67 |
| Max Zendejas | 86-88 | 53 | 62 | 85 | 34 | 49 | 69 |
| Tony Zendejas | 85-95 | 316 | 327 | 97 | 186 | 252 | 74 |

# Leaders and Features

The mention of any sport bring certain images to mind. When it comes to pro football the pictures are vivid and swift. Mostly, though, it is an extreme of functions. For those in love with risk and the dramatics of suddenness, there is nothing more serene than the aerial ballet of a 50-yard pass play. And for those who like to chew their fantasy in small, but certain chunks of yardage, there is nothing more pleasurable than the fullback who eludes a mammoth of flesh in search of four yards of daylight. Yet these two simplified illustrations have not always held true for pro football. If nothing else, football is a game of constant change. Unlike any other major sport, there is no way to compare the football athletes of today's two-platoon game with those men who needed a double set of talents in which to sustain their playing careers. This point, for example, could not be any sharper than when one considers Joe Namath attempting to play in the 1940's. But fortunately for Namath, and perhaps even the fans of today who would have been denied the excitement of his precision arm, football is no longer a game of one man for sixty minutes.

It is for this reason that many of the records which appear on the following pages have no continuity with the players of yesteryear and those of the modern game. Field goals, for example, are a modern phenomenon with no pre-1960 player on the list of the top single-season leaders. On the other hand, in the category of punters, Yale Lary, with a 48.9 average, is the only post-1960 player among the top single-season leaders. Of course, the changing hash marks and goal post positions are greatly responsible for these records.

Yet, beyond the comparison of any era, more important are the achievements of the men who made up their time, and the fact that whatever the criteria, each contributed the fullest and the best of his talents. It is on this basis that each must be measured and appreciated in the light of pro football's changing game.

## Section Explanations

The following is an explanation of certain statistical matter which may be unfamiliar:

Yards per Game— In the category of Yards per Game for individuals, "per game" refers to games played by the team, because there is no available statistical information of the games played by the individual.

Passing Ranks— These ranks are determined by the formula used by the National Football League for its official rankings from 1960 to 1971. Each passer who qualifies by having a minimum number of passing attempts is ranked in four categories: Percent Completed, Percent Intercepted, Average Yards per Attempt, and Touchdowns. The four ranks are then added for each passer, and the totals are then ranked. This ranking of the sum of the four ranks is the passer's rank.

# YEARLY CHAMPIONSHIP GAMES

## NATIONAL FOOTBALL LEAGUE (CONFERENCE)

| Year | Winner | Loser | Score |
|---|---|---|---|
| 1933 | CHICAGO BEARS | New York Giants | 23-21 |
| 1934 | NEW YORK GIANTS | Chicago Bears | 30-13 |
| 1935 | DETROIT LIONS | New York Giants | 26- 7 |
| 1936 | Green Bay Packers | Boston Redskins | 21- 6 |
| | (at New York) | | |
| 1937 | Washington Redskins | CHICAGO BEARS | 28-21 |
| 1938 | NEW YORK GIANTS | Green Bay Packers | 23-17 |
| 1939 | GREEN BAY PACKERS | New York Giants | 27- 0 |
| | (at Milwaukee) | | |
| 1940 | Chicago Bears | WASHINGTON REDSKINS | 73- 0 |
| 1941 | CHICAGO BEARS | New York Giants | 37- 9 |
| 1942 | WASHINGTON REDSKINS | Chicago Bears | 14- 6 |
| 1943 | CHICAGO BEARS | Washington Redskins | 41-21 |
| 1944 | Green Bay Packers | NEW YORK GIANTS | 14- 7 |
| 1945 | CLEVELAND RAMS | Washington Redskins | 15-14 |
| 1946 | Chicago Bears | NEW YORK GIANTS | 24-14 |
| 1947 | CHICAGO CARDINALS | Philadelphia Eagles | 28-21 |
| 1948 | PHILADELPHIA EAGLES | Chicago Cardinals | 7- 0 |
| 1949 | Philadelphia Eagles | LOS ANGELES RAMS | 14- 0 |
| | | | |
| 1950 | CLEVELAND BROWNS | Los Angeles Rams | 30-28 |
| 1951 | LOS ANGELES RAMS | Cleveland Browns | 24-17 |
| 1952 | Detroit Lions | CLEVELAND BROWNS | 17- 7 |
| 1953 | DETROIT LIONS | Cleveland Browns | 17-16 |
| 1954 | CLEVELAND BROWNS | Detroit Lions | 56-10 |
| 1955 | Cleveland Browns | LOS ANGELES RAMS | 38-14 |
| 1956 | NEW YORK GIANTS | Chicago Bears | 47- 7 |
| 1957 | DETROIT LIONS | Cleveland Browns | 59-14 |
| 1958 | Baltimore Colts | NEW YORK GIANTS | 23-17 |
| 1959 | BALTIMORE COLTS | New York Giants | 31-16 |
| | | | |
| 1960 | PHILADELPHIA EAGLES | Green Bay Packers | 17-13 |
| 1961 | GREEN BAY PACKERS | New York Giants | 37- 0 |
| 1962 | Green Bay Packers | NEW YORK GIANTS | 16- 7 |
| 1963 | CHICAGO BEARS | New York Giants | 14-10 |
| 1964 | CLEVELAND BROWNS | Baltimore Colts | 27- 0 |
| 1965 | GREEN BAY PACKERS | Cleveland Browns | 23-12 |
| 1966 | Green Bay Packers | DALLAS COWBOYS | 34-27 |
| 1967 | GREEN BAY PACKERS | Dallas Cowboys | 21-17 |
| 1968 | Baltimore Colts | CLEVELAND BROWNS | 34- 0 |
| 1969 | MINNESOTA VIKINGS | Cleveland Browns | 27- 7 |
| | | | |
| 1970 | Dallas Cowboys | SAN FRANCISCO 49ERS | 17-10 |
| 1971 | DALLAS COWBOYS | San Francisco 49ers | 14- 3 |
| 1972 | WASHINGTON REDSKINS | Dallas Cowboys | 26- 3 |
| 1973 | Minnesota Vikings | DALLAS COWBOYS | 27-10 |
| 1974 | MINNESOTA VIKINGS | Los Angeles Rams | 14-10 |
| 1975 | Dallas Cowboys | LOS ANGELES RAMS | 37- 7 |
| 1976 | MINNESOTA VIKINGS | Los Angeles Rams | 24-13 |
| 1977 | DALLAS COWBOYS | Minnesota Vikings | 23- 6 |
| 1978 | Dallas Cowboys | LOS ANGELES RAMS | 28- 0 |
| 1979 | Los Angeles Rams | TAMPA BAY BUCCANEERS | 9- 0 |
| | | | |
| 1980 | PHILADELPHIA EAGLES | Dallas Cowboys | 20- 7 |
| 1981 | SAN FRANCISCO 49ERS | Dallas Cowboys | 28-27 |
| 1982 | WASHINGTON REDSKINS | Dallas Cowboys | 31-17 |
| 1983 | WASHINGTON REDSKINS | San Francisco 49ers | 24-21 |
| 1984 | SAN FRANCISCO 49ERS | Chicago Bears | 23- 0 |
| 1985 | CHICAGO BEARS | Los Angeles Rams | 24- 0 |
| 1986 | NEW YORK GIANTS | Washington Redskins | 17- 0 |
| 1987 | WASHINGTON REDSKINS | Minnesota Vikings | 17-10 |
| 1988 | San Francisco 49ers | CHICAGO BEARS | 28- 3 |
| 1989 | SAN FRANCISCO 49ERS | Los Angeles Rams | 30- 3 |
| | | | |
| 1990 | New York Giants | SAN FRANCISCO 49ERS | 15-13 |
| 1991 | WASHINGTON REDSKINS | Detroit Lions | 41-10 |
| 1992 | Dallas Cowboys | SAN FRANCISCO 49ERS | 30-20 |
| 1993 | DALLAS COWBOYS | San Francisco 49ers | 38-21 |
| 1994 | SAN FRANCISCO 49ERS | Dallas Cowboys | 38-28 |
| 1995 | DALLAS COWBOYS | Green Bay Packers | 39-27 |

## ALL-AMERICAN FOOTBALL CONFERENCE

| Year | Winner | Loser | Score |
|---|---|---|---|
| 1946 | CLEVELAND BROWNS | New York Yankees | 14- 9 |
| 1947 | Cleveland Browns | NEW YORK YANKEES | 14- 3 |
| 1948 | CLEVELAND BROWNS | Buffalo Bills | 49- 7 |
| 1949 | CLEVELAND BROWNS | San Francisco 49ers | 21- 7 |

## AMERICAN FOOTBALL LEAGUE (CONFERENCE)

| Year | Winner | Loser | Score |
|---|---|---|---|
| 1960 | HOUSTON OILERS | Los Angeles Chargers | 24-16 |
| 1961 | Houston Oilers | SAN DIEGO CHARGERS | 10- 3 |
| 1962 | Dallas Chiefs | HOUSTON OILERS | 20-17 |
| 1963 | SAN DIEGO CHARGERS | Boston Patriots | 51-10 |
| 1964 | BUFFALO BILLS | San Diego Chargers | 20- 7 |
| 1965 | Buffalo Bills | SAN DIEGO CHARGERS | 23- 0 |
| 1966 | Kansas City Chiefs | BUFFALO BILLS | 31- 7 |
| 1967 | OAKLAND RAIDERS | Houston Oilers | 40- 7 |
| 1968 | NEW YORK JETS | Oakland Raiders | 27-23 |
| 1969 | Kansas City Chiefs | OAKLAND RAIDERS | 17- 7 |
| | | | |
| 1970 | BALTIMORE COLTS | Oakland Raiders | 27-17 |
| 1971 | MIAMI DOLPHINS | Baltimore Colts | 21- 0 |
| 1972 | Miami Dolphins | PITTSBURGH STEELERS | 21-17 |
| 1973 | MIAMI DOLPHINS | Oakland Raiders | 27-10 |
| 1974 | Pittsburgh Steelers | OAKLAND RAIDERS | 24-13 |
| 1975 | PITTSBURGH STEELERS | Oakland Raiders | 16-10 |
| 1976 | OAKLAND RAIDERS | Pittsburgh Steelers | 24- 7 |
| 1977 | DENVER BRONCOS | Oakland Raiders | 20-17 |
| 1978 | PITTSBURGH STEELERS | Houston Oilers | 34- 5 |
| 1979 | PITTSBURGH STEELERS | Houston Oilers | 27-13 |
| | | | |
| 1980 | Oakland Raiders | SAN DIEGO CHARGERS | 34-27 |
| 1981 | CINCINNATI BENGALS | San Diego Chargers | 27- 7 |
| 1982 | MIAMI DOLPHINS | New York Jets | 14- 0 |
| 1983 | LOS ANGELES RAIDERS | Seattle Seahawks | 30-14 |
| 1984 | MIAMI DOLPHINS | Pittsburgh Steelers | 45-28 |
| 1985 | New England Patriots | MIAMI DOLPHINS | 31-14 |
| 1986 | Denver Broncos | CLEVELAND BROWNS | 23-20 |
| 1987 | DENVER BRONCOS | Cleveland Browns | 38-33 |
| 1988 | CINCINNATI BENGALS | Buffalo Bills | 21-10 |
| 1989 | DENVER BRONCOS | Cleveland Browns | 37-21 |
| | | | |
| 1990 | BUFFALO BILLS | Los Angeles Raiders | 51- 3 |
| 1991 | BUFFALO BILLS | Denver Broncos | 10- 7 |
| 1992 | Buffalo Bills | MIAMI DOLPHINS | 29-10 |
| 1993 | BUFFALO BILLS | Kansas City Chiefs | 30-13 |
| 1994 | San Diego Chargers | PITTSBURGH STEELERS | 17-13 |
| 1995 | PITTSBURGH STEELERS | Indianapolis Colts | 20-16 |

## COMPOSITE STANDINGS
### (All Leagues) Championship Games Only

| Team | Games | Wins | Losses | Pct. |
|---|---|---|---|---|
| Cincinnati Bengals | 2 | 2 | 0 | 1.000 |
| Denver Broncos | 5 | 4 | 1 | .800 |
| Philadelphia Eagles | 5 | 4 | 1 | .800 |
| Buffalo Bills | 8 | 6 | 2 | .750 |
| Kansas City Chiefs | 3 | 3 | 1 | .750 |
| Green Bay Packers | 11 | 8 | 3 | .727 |
| Miami Dolphins | 7 | 5 | 2 | .714 |
| Detroit Lions | 6 | 4 | 2 | .667 |
| Minnesota Vikings | 6 | 4 | 2 | .667 |
| Washington Redskins | 12 | 7 | 5 | .583 |
| Indianapolis Colts | 7 | 4 | 3 | .571 |
| Pittsburgh Steelers | 9 | 5 | 4 | .556 |
| Chicago Bears | 13 | 7 | 6 | .538 |
| Dallas Cowboys | 16 | 8 | 8 | .500 |
| Chicago Cardinals | 2 | 1 | 1 | .500 |
| New York Jets | 2 | 1 | 1 | .500 |
| New England Patriots | 2 | 1 | 1 | .500 |
| Cleveland Browns | 18 | 8 | 10 | .471 |
| San Francisco 49ers | 11 | 5 | 6 | .454 |
| Oakland/L. A. Raiders | 12 | 4 | 8 | .333 |
| Houston Oilers | 6 | 2 | 4 | .333 |
| New York Giants | 16 | 5 | 11 | .313 |
| Los Angeles Rams | 12 | 3 | 9 | .250 |
| San Diego Chargers | 8 | 2 | 6 | .250 |
| New York Yankees (AAFC) | 2 | 0 | 2 | .000 |
| Buffalo Bills (AAFC) | 1 | 0 | 1 | .000 |
| Tampa Bay Buccaneers | 1 | 0 | 1 | .000 |
| Seattle Seahawks | 1 | 0 | 1 | .000 |

Home Team in Upper Case
*—Sudden Death Game

**SUPER BOWL**

| Game | Team | Q1 | Q2 | Q3 | Q4 | | Total |
|---|---|---|---|---|---|---|---|
| I at Los Angeles | Green Bay | 7 | 7 | 14 | 7 | - | 35 |
| | Kansas City | 0 | 10 | 0 | 0 | - | 10 |
| II at Miami | Green Bay | 3 | 13 | 10 | 7 | - | 33 |
| | Oakland | 0 | 7 | 0 | 7 | - | 14 |
| III at Miami | N.Y. Jets | 0 | 7 | 6 | 3 | - | 16 |
| | Baltimore | 0 | 0 | 0 | 7 | - | 7 |
| V at New Orleans | Kansas City | 3 | 13 | 7 | 0 | - | 23 |
| | Minnesota | 0 | 0 | 7 | 0 | - | 7 |
| V at Miami | Baltimore | 0 | 6 | 0 | 10 | - | 16 |
| | Dallas | 3 | 10 | 0 | 0 | - | 13 |
| VI at New Orleans | Dallas | 3 | 7 | 7 | 7 | - | 24 |
| | Miami | 0 | 3 | 0 | 0 | - | 3 |
| VII at Los Angeles | Miami | 7 | 7 | 0 | 0 | - | 14 |
| | Washington | 0 | 0 | 0 | 7 | - | 7 |
| VIII at Houston | Miami | 14 | 3 | 7 | 0 | - | 24 |
| | Minnesota | 0 | 0 | 0 | 7 | - | 7 |
| IX at New Orleans | Pittsburgh | 0 | 2 | 7 | 7 | - | 16 |
| | Minnesota | 0 | 0 | 0 | 6 | - | 6 |
| X at Miami | Pittsburgh | 7 | 0 | 0 | 14 | - | 21 |
| | Dallas | 7 | 3 | 0 | 7 | - | 17 |
| XI at Pasadena | Oakland | 0 | 16 | 3 | 13 | - | 32 |
| | Minnesota | 0 | 0 | 7 | 7 | - | 14 |
| XII at New Orleans | Dallas | 10 | 3 | 7 | 7 | - | 27 |
| | Denver | 0 | 0 | 10 | 0 | - | 10 |
| XIII at Miami | Pittsburgh | 7 | 14 | 0 | 14 | - | 35 |
| | Dallas | 7 | 7 | 3 | 14 | - | 31 |
| XIV at Los Angeles | Pittsburgh | 3 | 7 | 7 | 14 | - | 31 |
| | Los Angeles | 7 | 6 | 6 | 0 | - | 19 |
| XV at New Orleans | Oakland | 14 | 0 | 10 | 3 | - | 27 |
| | Philadelphia | 0 | 3 | 0 | 7 | - | 10 |
| XVI at Detroit | San Francisco | 7 | 13 | 0 | 6 | - | 26 |
| | Cincinnati | 0 | 0 | 7 | 14 | - | 21 |
| XVII at Pasadena | Washington | 0 | 10 | 3 | 14 | - | 27 |
| | Miami | 7 | 10 | 0 | 0 | - | 17 |
| XVIII at Tampa | L.A. Raiders | 7 | 14 | 14 | 3 | - | 38 |
| | Washington | 0 | 3 | 6 | 0 | - | 9 |
| XIX at Stanford | San Francisco | 7 | 21 | 10 | 0 | - | 38 |
| | Miami | 10 | 6 | 0 | 0 | - | 16 |
| XX at New Orleans | Chicago | 13 | 10 | 21 | 2 | - | 46 |
| | New England | 3 | 0 | 0 | 7 | - | 10 |
| XXI at Pasadena | N.Y. Giants | 7 | 2 | 17 | 13 | - | 39 |
| | Denver | 10 | 0 | 0 | 10 | - | 20 |
| XXII at San Diego | Washington | 0 | 35 | 0 | 7 | - | 42 |
| | Denver | 10 | 0 | 0 | 0 | - | 10 |
| XXIII at Miami | Cincinnati | 0 | 3 | 10 | 3 | - | 16 |
| | San Francisco | 3 | 0 | 3 | 14 | - | 20 |
| XXIV at New Orleans | San Francisco | 13 | 14 | 14 | 14 | - | 55 |
| | Denver | 3 | 0 | 7 | 0 | - | 10 |
| XXV at Tampa | Buffalo | 3 | 9 | 0 | 7 | - | 19 |
| | New York Giants | 3 | 7 | 7 | 3 | - | 20 |
| XXVI at Minneapolis | Washington Redskins | 0 | 17 | 14 | 6 | - | 37 |
| | Buffalo Bills | 0 | 0 | 10 | 14 | - | 24 |
| XXVII at Pasadena | Buffalo Bills | 7 | 3 | 7 | 0 | - | 17 |
| | Dallas Cowboys | 14 | 14 | 3 | 21 | - | 52 |
| XXVIII at Atlanta | Dallas Cowboys | 6 | 0 | 14 | 10 | - | 30 |
| | Buffalo Bills | 3 | 10 | 0 | 0 | - | 13 |
| XXIX at Miami | San Diego Chargers | 7 | 3 | 8 | 8 | - | 26 |
| | San Francisco 49ers | 14 | 14 | 14 | 7 | - | 49 |
| XXX at Phoenix | Dallas Cowboys | 10 | 3 | 7 | 7 | - | 27 |
| | Pittsburgh Steelers | 0 | 7 | 0 | 10 | - | 17 |

**SUPER BOWL COMPOSITE STANDINGS**

| Team | Games | Wins | Losses | Pct. |
|---|---|---|---|---|
| San Francisco 49ers | 5 | 5 | 0 | 1.000 |
| Green Bay Packers | 2 | 2 | 0 | 1.000 |
| New York Giants | 2 | 2 | 0 | 1.000 |
| Chicago Bears | 1 | 1 | 0 | 1.000 |
| New York Jets | 1 | 1 | 0 | 1.000 |
| Pittsburgh Steelers | 5 | 4 | 1 | .800 |
| Oakland/L.A. Raiders | 4 | 3 | 1 | .750 |
| Dallas Cowboys | 8 | 5 | 3 | .625 |
| Washington Redskins | 5 | 3 | 2 | .600 |
| Kansas City Chiefs | 2 | 1 | 1 | .500 |
| Baltimore Colts | 2 | 1 | 1 | .500 |
| Miami Dolphins | 5 | 2 | 3 | .400 |
| Cincinnati Bengals | 1 | 0 | 1 | .000 |
| Los Angeles Rams | 1 | 0 | 1 | .000 |
| New England Patriots | 1 | 0 | 1 | .000 |
| Philadelphia Eagles | 1 | 0 | 1 | .000 |
| San Diego Chargers | 1 | 0 | 1 | .000 |
| Buffalo Bills | 4 | 0 | 4 | .000 |
| Denver Broncos | 4 | 0 | 4 | .000 |
| Minnesota Vikings | 4 | 0 | 4 | .000 |

# YEARLY TEAM LEADERS

## OFFENSE

|YEAR|LGUE|POINTS - PTS/G| | |FIRST DOWNS| |RUSH YARDS| |YDS/ GAME|RUSH AVERAGE| |RUSH TD| |PASS COMPLETION PERCENTAGE| |PASS YARDS| |YDS/ GAME|PASS YARDS/ ATTEMPT| |PASS TD| |FEWEST INT.| |LEAST INT.%| |PUNTING AVERAGE| |PUNT RETURN AVERAGE| |KICKOFF RETURN AVERAGE| |YEAR|LGUE|
|---|---|---|---|---|---|---|---|---|---|---|---|---|---|---|---|---|---|---|---|---|---|---|---|---|---|---|---|---|---|---|---|---|---|---|
|1933|NFL|NY G|244|17.4| | | | | | | | | |Bkn.|46.7| | | | | | | | | | | | | | | | | |1933|NFL|
|1934|NFL|ChiB|286|22.0| | | | | | | | | |NY G|40.9| | | | | | | | | | | | | | | | | |1934|NFL|
|1935|NFL|ChiB|192|16.0|ChiB|140|ChiB|2096|175| | |Det.|15|NY G|44.8|G.B.|1545|129|G.B.|6.72|ChiB|13| | | | | | | | | | |1935|NFL|
|1936|NFL|G.B.|248|20.7|Det.|170|Det.|2883|240|Det.|4.73|Det.|22|G.B.|42.4|G.B.|1629|136|ChiB|6.46|ChiB|17| | | | | | | | | | |1936|NFL|
| | | | | | | | | | | | | | | | | | | | | |G.B.|17| | | | | | | | | | | | |
|1937|NFL|G.B.|220|20.0|Was.|149|Det.|2074|189|Det.|4.30|Det.|12|Was.|44.6|G.B.|1397|127|ChiB|6.97|ChiB|16|NY G|11|NY G|5.42| | | | | | |1937|NFL|
| | | | | | | | | | | | | | | | | | | | | |G.B.|16| | | | | | | | | | | | |
|1938|NFL|G.B.|223|20.7|Was.|147|Det.|1893|172|Det.|4.01|NY G|12|NY G|48.9|Was.|1536|140|G.B.|6.98|G.B.|20|Bkn.|8|Bkn.|4.73| | | | | | |1938|NFL|
|1939|NFL|ChiB|298|27.1|G.B.|149|ChiB|2043|186|ChiB|4.66|ChiB|21|Was.|58.2|ChiB|1965|179|Was.|8.93|Was.|18|NY G|11|NY G|6.21| | | | | | |1939|NFL|
|1940|NFL|Was.|245|22.2|G.B.|154|ChiB|1818|165|Bkn.|3.92|ChiB|16|Was.|59.0|Was.|1887|172|ChiB|8.19|G.B.|18|Bkn.|13|Phi.|5.52| | | | | | |1940|NFL|
| | | | | | | | | | | | | | | | | | | | | |Was.|18| | | | | | | | | | | | |
|1941|NFL|ChiB|396|36.0|ChiB|181|ChiB|2290|208|ChiB|4.63|ChiB|30|G.B.|52.6|ChiB|2002|182|**ChiB**|**10.21**|ChiB|19|ChiB|11|G.B.|5.14|Was.|45.9|**ChiB**|**20.2**|Det.|26.5|1941|NFL|
|1942|NFL|ChiB|376|34.2|G.B.|176|ChiB|1911|174|ChiB|4.07|ChiB|23|Was.|53.3|G.B.|2407|219|ChiB|10.18|G.B.|28|Pit.|11|G.B.|5.45|Was.|44.3|Pit.|15.4|Was.|27.8|1942|NFL|
|1943|NFL|ChiB|303|30.3|ChiB|161|P-P|1730|173|ChiB|3.89|P-P|18|Was.|54.7|ChiB|2310|231|ChiB|10.09|ChiB|28|NY G|9|NY G|6.04|Was.|43.1|Det.|13.6|Det.|24.9|1943|NFL|
|1944|NFL|Phi.|267|26.7|G.B.|147|Phi.|1661|166|Phi.|3.92|Phi.|23|Was.|56.9|Was.|2021|202|ChiB|7.45|ChiB|21|Phi.|12|Was.|5.69|Det.|40.5|Det.|14.2|NY G|27.4|1944|NFL|
|1945|NFL|Phi.|272|27.2|ChiB|164|Cle.|1714|171|Cle.|4.61|Phi.|26|Was.|64.0|ChiB|1857|186|Cle.|8.88|Cle.|16|Was.|11|Was.|4.82|Was.|43.3|Det.|14.4|Phi.|24.5|1945|NFL|
|1946|NFL|ChiB|289|26.3|L.A.|214|G.B.|1765|160|L.A.|4.17|ChiB|19|Phi.|53.5|L.A.|2080|189|ChiB|7.71|L.A.|19|Pit.|13|L.A.|7.36|L.A.|44.4|Pit.|13.5|NY G|26.0|1946|NFL|
|1946|AAFC|Cle.|423|30.2|L.A.|183|S.F.|2175|155|Buf.|4.08|Cle.|27|L.A.|54.7|Cle.|2266|162|Cle.|9.56|Cle.|22|Cle.|7|Cle.|2.95|Bkn.|46.5|N.Y.|15.3|Chi.|24.5|1946|AAFC|
|1947|NFL|ChiB|363|30.3|ChiB|263|L.A.|2171|181|L.A.|4.73|ChiB|21|Was.|55.5|Was.|3336|278|ChiB|8.18|ChiB|29|Was.|18|Was.|4.33|G.B.|43.6|Bos.|15.1|Was.|22.1|1947|NFL|
| | | | | | | | | | | | |Phi.|21| | | | | | | | | | | | | | | | | | | | | |
|1947|AAFC|Cle.|410|29.8|S.F.|218|N.Y.|2930|209|N.Y.|5.49|N.Y.|27|Cle.|58.8|Cle.|2990|214|Cle.|10.10|Cle.|26|Cle.|12|Cle.|4.05|L.A.|45.0|Bal.|16.5|Buf.|25.6|1947|AAFC|
|1948|NFL|ChiC|395|32.9|ChiB|242|ChiC|2560|213|ChiC|4.82|ChiC|25|Was.|56.1|Was.|2861|238|Was.|7.95|L.A.|28|ChiC|12|ChiC|4.21|Phi.|45.9|ChiC|19.1|ChiB|25.9|1948|NFL|
|1948|AAFC|S.F.|495|35.4|Cle.|243|**S.F.**|**3663**|**262**|**S.F.**|**6.07**|S.F.|35|S.F.|56.3|Bal.|2899|207|Bal.|8.53|S.F.|30|Bal.|13|Bal.|3.82|L.A.|47.2|Buf.|16.9|S.F.|24.4|1948|AAFC|
|1949|NFL|Phi.|364|30.3|ChiB|248|Phi.|2607|217|ChiC|4.56|Phi.|25|L.A.|52.5|ChiB|3055|255|ChiB|7.94|ChiB|24|Phi.|14|Phi.|5.56|L.A.|44.4|ChiC|18.2|NY G|26.0|1949|NFL|
|1949|AAFC|S.F.|416|34.7|Buf.|184|S.F.|2798|233|S.F.|5.53|S.F.|26|Buf.|57.1|Cle.|2929|244|Cle.|9.90|S.F.|28|Cle.|12|Cle.|4.05|S.F.|45.5|S.F.|15.5|L.A.|23.7|1949|AAFC|
|1950|NFL|**L.A.**|466|**38.8**|L.A.|278|NY G|2336|195|NY Y|4.56|L.A.|28|L.A.|55.8|L.A.|3709|309|L.A.|8.19|L.A.|31|NY G|10|NY G|5.35|Cle.|43.2|G.B.|16.6|Det.|26.7|1950|NFL|
|1951|NFL|L.A.|392|32.7|L.A.|272|ChiB|2408|201|L.A.|5.19|ChiB|24|Cle.|55.7|L.A.|3296|275|L.A.|8.84|Det.|29|Cle.|7|L.A.|5.90|Cle.|45.5|Det.|15.1|NY G|25.9|1951|NFL|
|1952|NFL|L.A.|349|29.1|Cle.|228|S.F.|1905|159|Cle.|4.53|L.A.|17|S.F.|51.8|Cle.|2839|237|G.B.|7.98|G.B.|26|Phi.|19|Phi.|5.26|Cle.|45.7|Det.|14.9|Pit.|28.9|1952|NFL|
|1953|NFL|S.F.|372|31.0|Phi.|256|S.F.|2230|186|L.A.|5.04|S.F.|26|Cle.|63.0|Phi.|3357|280|Cle.|10.10|Phi.|25|Cle.|9|Cle.|2.97|Pit.|46.9|G.B.|8.9|NY G|26.3|1953|NFL|
|1954|NFL|Det.|337|28.1|L.A.|255|S.F.|2498|208|S.F.|5.65|S.F.|28|Cle.|59.0|ChiB|3299|275|L.A.|9.91|Phi.|33|S.F.|12|S.F.|3.53|Pit.|43.2|G.B.|9.9|Cle.|25.3|1954|NFL|
|1955|NFL|Cle.|349|29.1|ChiB|235|ChiB|2388|199|ChiB|4.90|Cle.|20|Cle.|55.6|Phi.|2696|225|Cle.|9.51|Cle.|21|Cle.|11|Cle.|4.70|L.A.|44.6|ChiC|12.0|Pit.|26.3|1955|NFL|
|1956|NFL|ChiB|363|30.3|Det.|247|ChiB|2468|206|L.A.|5.15|ChiB|22|Bal.|56.6|L.A.|2601|217|ChiB|8.77|G.B.|21|ChiC|14|NY G|5.09|L.A.|43.1|ChiC|9.5|Pit.|26.1|1956|NFL|
|1957|NFL|L.A.|307|25.6|L.A.|235|L.A.|2142|179|L.A.|4.52|Cle.|19|S.F.|62.6|Bal.|2608|217|Cle.|9.61|Bal.|25|NY G|12|NY G|4.46|S.F.|44.7|Was.|10.5|S.F.|26.1|1957|NFL|
|1958|NFL|Bal.|381|31.8|Bal.|253|Cle.|2526|211|Cle.|5.32|Bal.|24|S.F.|58.2|L.A.|2909|242|Pit.|8.62|Bal.|26|Bal.|11|Bal.|3.11|Was.|45.4|Cle.|8.2|ChiB|25.8|1958|NFL|
| | | | | | | | | | | | |Cle.|24| | | | | | | | | | | | | | | | | | | | | |
|1959|NFL|Bal.|374|31.2|Bal.|267|Cle.|2149|179|L.A.|4.79|Cle.|20|Cle.|57.6|Bal.|2938|245|NY G|8.72|Bal.|33|Cle.|9|Cle.|3.26|NY G|46.6|ChiC|9.8|L.A.|24.5|1959|NFL|
|1960|NFL|Cle.|362|30.2|G.B.|237|St.L.|2356|196|Cle.|5.04|G.B.|29|Cle.|60.6|Bal.|3164|264|Phi.|8.93|Phi.|29|**Cle.**|**5**|Cle.|1.89|St.L.|44.9|Cle.|9.9|S.F.|27.1|1960|NFL|
|1960|AFL|N.Y.|382|27.3|N.Y.|286|Dal.|1814|130|Dal.|3.76|Dal.|24|L.A.|51.9|Hou.|3371|241|Hou.|7.39|NY T|32|Dal.|19|Dal.|4.37|L.A.|39.7|Dal.|15.0|Hou.|25.5|1960|AFL|
|1961|NFL|G.B.|391|27.9|NY G|275|G.B.|2350|168|G.B.|4.96|G.B.|27|G.B.|57.8|Phi.|3824|273|Phi.|8.91|Phi.|34|Cle.|13|Cle.|4.06|**Det.**|**47.6**|G.B.|17.8|S.F.|26.6|1961|NFL|
| | | | | | | | | | | | |S.F.|27| | | | | | | | | | | | | | | | | | | | | |
|1961|AFL|Hou.|513|36.6|Hou.|293|Dal.|2183|156|Dal.|4.97|S.D.|24|Hou.|51.0|**Hou.**|4568|**326**|Hou.|9.17|Hou.|48|Bos.|21|Bos.|5.00|Buf.|44.5|N.Y.|17.8|Dal.|27.6|1961|AFL|
|1962|NFL|G.B.|415|29.6|G.B.|281|G.B.|2460|176|G.B.|4.75|**G.B.**|**36**|G.B.|60.1|Phi.|3632|259|hi.|8.49|NY G|35|G.B.|13|G.B.|4.18|S.F.|45.6|Det.|12.9|Was.|28.2|1962|NFL|
|1962|AFL|Dal.|389|27.8|Den.|270|Buf.|2480|177|Buf.|4.95|Dal.|21|Dal.|60.6|Den.|3739|267|Dal.|8.77|Hou.|32|Bos.|13|Bos.|3.40|Den.|42.9|N.Y.|12.3|Hou.|25.9|1962|AFL|
|1963|NFL|NY G|448|32.0|NY G|278|Cle.|2639|189|Cle.|5.74|G.B.|22|Bal.|57.3|Bal.|3605|258|NY G|8.35|NY G|39|Bal.|12|Bal.|2.77|Chi.|46.5|Was.|13.0|Was.|26.8|1963|NFL|
|1963|AFL|S.D.|399|28.5|N/A| |S.D.|2201|157|S.D.|5.57|Buf.|21|S.D.|56.4|Hou.|3478|248|Oak.|7.69|Oak.|31|K.C.|22|K.C.|5.01|Den.|44.3|Den.|12.9|Hou.|26.4|1963|AFL|
|1964|NFL|Bal.|428|30.6|St.L.|275|G.B.|2276|163|Cle.|4.97|Bal.|29|G.B.|57.9|Was.|3071|219|Bal.|8.83|Cle.|28|G.B.|6|G.B.|1.87|Min.|46.4|Cle.|15.2|G.B.|25.8|1964|NFL|
|1964|AFL|Buf.|400|28.6|Hou.|284|Buf.|2040|146|Oak.|4.47|Buf.|25|K.C.|55.3|Oak.|3886|276|Buf.|8.62|K.C.|32|K.C.|21|Hou.|4.90|Den.|43.4|Oak.|13.5|Oak.|25.0|1964|AFL|
|1965|NFL|S.F.|421|30.1|S.F.|292|Cle.|2331|167|Cle.|4.90|ChiB|27|S.F.|59.9|S.F.|3633|260|Chi.|8.37|S.F.|35|Min.|12|Min.|3.23|S.F.|45.8|Cle.|11.9|Det.|27.2|1965|NFL|
|1965|AFL|S.D.|340|24.3|S.D.|268|S.D.|1998|143|K.C.|4.19|Buf.|16|S.D.|50.6|S.D.|3379|241|S.D.|8.43|Hou.|25|Oak.|17|Oak.|3.94|NY J|45.3|S.D.|13.4|Den.|23.4|1965|AFL|
|1966|NFL|Dal.|445|31.8|Dal.|287|Cle.|2166|155|Cle.|5.22|Dal.|24|G.B.|60.7|Dal.|3331|238|G.B.|8.90|Cle.|33|**G.B.**|**5**|**G.B.**|**1.57**|Bal.|45.6|Det.|10.4|Chi.|27.9|1966|NFL|
|1966|AFL|K.C.|448|32.0|K.C.|266|K.C.|2274|162|K.C.|5.18|Buf.|19|K.C.|52.8|NY J|3556|254|K.C.|8.28|K.C.|31|K.C.|15|S.D.|3.46|Den.|45.2|S.D.|12.2|Den.|26.9|1966|AFL|
| | | | | | | | | | | | |K.C.|19| | | | | | | | | |S.D.|15| | | | | | | | | | |
|1967|NFL|L.A.|398|28.4|Bal.|289|Cle.|2139|153|Cle.|4.82|Bal.|21|Bal.|58.0|Was.|3887|278|G.B.|8.33|NY G|33|L.A.|16|Was.|3.23|Atl.|43.7|Cle.|10.2|G.B.|27.0|1967|NFL|
|1967|AFL|Oak.|468|33.4|NY J|282|Hou.|2122|152|Hou.|4.46|Oak.|19|K.C.|55.8|NY J|4128|295|NY J|8.02|Oak.|33|Den.|18|Den.|4.81|Den.|44.9|Den.|13.5|Den.|25.3|1967|AFL|
|1968|NFL|Dal.|431|30.8|Dal.|297|Chi.|2377|170|Chi.|4.75|Dal.|22|G.B.|59.1|Dal.|3295|235|Bal.|8.62|Bal.|28|Det.|15|Det.|3.98|Atl.|44.3|Dal.|13.5|Bal.|26.4|1968|NFL|
| | | | | | | | | | | | | | | | | | | | | | | |G.B.|15| | | | | | | | | | |
|1968|AFL|Oak.|453|32.4|Oak.|287|K.C.|2227|159|Oak.|4.64|NY J|22|K.C.|57.8|S.D.|3813|272|K.C.|9.23|Oak.|31|Cin.|11|Cin.|3.51|K.C.|45.3|K.C.|14.5|Hou.|23.3|1968|AFL|
|1969|NFL|Min.|379|27.1|N.O.|282|Dal.|2276|163|Atl.|4.52|Cle.|17|Was.|61.9|S.F.|3379|241|Dal.|9.05|L.A.|25|L.A.|7|L.A.|1.68|Bal.|45.3|Det.|11.0|Bal.|25.3|1969|NFL|
| | | | | | | | | | | | |Dal.|17| | | | | | | | | | | | | | | | | | | | | |
| | | | | | | | | | | | |St.L.|17| | | | | | | | | | | | | | | | | | | | | |
|1969|AFL|Oak.|377|26.9|S.D.|275|K.C.|2220|159|S.D.|4.36|K.C.|19|K.C.|55.8|Oak.|3375|241|Cin.|8.83|Oak.|36|Cin.|15|S.D.|4.73|S.D.|44.6|Den.|12.2|K.C.|26.6|1969|AFL|
|1970|NFC|S.F.|352|25.1|NY G|257|Dal.|2300|164|St.L.|4.66|St.L.|18|Was.|59.4|S.F.|2990|214|Dal.|8.23|S.F.|25|S.F.|10|S.F.|2.61|N.O.|42.5|S.F.|11.5|L.A.|26.3|1970|NFC|
|1970|AFC|Bal.|321|22.9|Oak.|270|Mia.|2082|149|Cin.|4.46|Den.|17|K.C.|53.3|Bal.|3087|221|Mia.|7.64|Oak.|28|Cin.|11|Cin.|3.24|Cin.|46.2|K.C.|12.0|Bal.|25.8|1970|AFC|
|1971|NFC|Dal.|406|29.0|Dal.|288|Det.|2376|170|L.A.|4.65|Dal.|25|Atl.|58.6|NY G|3062|219|Atl.|8.75|Dal.|22|L.A.|11|L.A.|2.97|Phi.|41.9|Was.|9.5|Dal.|27.5|1971|NFC|
|1971|AFC|Oak.|344|24.6|S.D.|264|Mia.|2429|174|Mia.|5.00|Bal.|23|Cin.|58.6|S.D.|3305|236|K.C.|7.99|S.D.|23|Mia.|10|Cin.|3.01|K.C.|44.8|Mia.|10.5|Mia.|25.2|1971|AFC|
|1972|NFC|S.F.|353|25.2|NY G|265|Chi.|2360|169|L.A.|4.68|Det.|20|NY G|59.9|S.F.|2888|206|Was.|8.03|S.F.|27|G.B.|9|Min.|3.37|L.A.|44.2|G.B.|14.6|**Chi.**|**29.4**|1972|NFC|
|1972|AFC|Mia.|385|27.5|Oak.|297|Mia.|2960|211|Pit.|5.07|Mia.|26|Cin.|57.0|NY J|2930|209|Mia.|8.63|Oak.|23|Cin.|11|Cin.|2.86|K.C.|44.8|Den.|11.1|Bal.|28.1|1972|AFC|
|1973|NFC|L.A.|388|27.7|L.A.|294|L.A.|2925|209|Dal.|4.46|Atl|18|Min.|60.1|Phi.|3236|231|Dal.|8.11|Dal.|26|Min.|9|Phi.|2.71|S.F.|43.8|S.F.|10.6|Was.|26.0|1973|NFC|
| | | | | | | | | | | | |L.A.|18| | | | | | | | | | | | | | | | | | | | | |
|1973|AFC|Den.|354|25.3|Oak.|288|Buf.|3088|221|Buf.|5.10|Buf.|20|Oak.|58.1|Den.|2706|193|Oak.|7.40|Den.|22|Cin.|12|Cin.|3.61|K.C.|45.6|S.D.|12.4|N.E.|24.1|1973|AFC|
| | | | | | | | | | | | | | | | | | | | | | | |Mia.|12| | | | | | | | | | |
|1974|NFC|Was.|320|22.9|Dal.|295|Dal.|2454|175|Dal.|4.53|Dal.|22|Was.|61.5|Was.|2978|213|Dal.|7.42|Min.|22|St.L.|8|St.L.|2.05|N.O.|41.8|Det.|12.6|Was.|25.9|1974|NFC|
| | | | | | | | | | | | | | | | | | | | | |Was.|22| | | | | | | | | | | | |
|1974|AFC|Oak.|355|25.4|Pit.|284|Pit.|2417|173|Cin.|4.44|Mia.|25|Cin.|63.5|Cin.|2804|200|Mia.|8.17|Oak.|28|Cin.|13|Cin.|3.68|Oak.|42.2|N.E.|13.3|Cle.|22.9|1974|AFC|
|1975|NFC|Min.|377|26.9|Min.|314|Dal.|2432|174|St.L.|4.33|St.L.|19|Min.|63.0|Min.|3121|223|Dal.|7.54|Was.|28|Det.|12|Min.|3.14|S.F.|41.9|St.L.|10.3|St.L.|24.3|1975|NFC|
|1975|AFC|Buf.|420|30.0|Buf.|318|Buf.|2974|212|Buf.|5.06|Bal.|28|Mia.|60.9|Cin.|3497|250|Cin.|8.08|Buf.|28|Bal.|8|Bal.|2.26|Oak.|43.8|Hou.|14.4|Oak.|26.0|1975|AFC|
| | | | | | | | | | | | |Oak.|28| | | | | | | | | | | | | | | | | | | | | |

**Bold - designates all-time leader**

# YEARLY TEAM LEADERS
## OFFENSE

| YEAR | LGUE | POINTS - PTS/G | FIRST DOWNS | RUSH YARDS / YDS/GAME | RUSH AVERAGE | RUSH TD | PASS COMPLETION PERCENTAGE | PASS YARDS / YDS/GAME | PASS YARDS/ ATTEMPT | PASS TD | FEWEST INT | LEAST INT% | PUNTING AVERAGE | PUNT RETURN AVERAGE | KICKOFF RETURN AVERAGE | YEAR | LGUE |
|---|---|---|---|---|---|---|---|---|---|---|---|---|---|---|---|---|---|
| 1976 | NFC | L.A. 351 25.1 | St.L. 307 | L.A. 2523 180 | Det. 4.29 | L.A. 23 | Min. 61.1 | Min. 2855 204 | L.A. 8.35 | Det. 20<br>Was. 20 | Min. 10 | Min. 2.26 | Atl. 42.1 | Was. 13.2 | Dal. 24.5 | 1976 | NFC |
| 1976 | AFC | Bal. 417 29.8 | Oak. 302 | Pit. 2971 212 | N.E. 4.99 | Pit. 33 | Oak. 63.3 | K.C. 2929 209 | Bal. 8.92 | Oak. 33 | Bal. 10 | Bal. 2.77 | Buf. 42.2 | N.E. 13.1 | Mia. 24.5 | 1976 | AFC |
| 1977 | NFC | Dal. 345 24.6 | Dal. 272 | Chi. 2811 201 | Chi. 4.7 | Chi. 21 | Min. 58.8 | Min. 2692 192 | Dal. 7.23 | Min. 19 | Dal. 10 | Dal. 2.69 | Atl. 41.2 | Phi. 10.4 | L.A. 18.9 | 1977 | NFC |
| 1977 | AFC | Oak. 351 25.1 | Oak. 305 | Oak. 2627 188 | Mia. 4.6 | Oak. 20<br>Pit. 20 | Mia. 58.5 | Buf. 2803 200 | Pit. 7.72 | Sea. 23 | Bal. 12<br>Den. 12 | Bal. 3.01 | Oak. 43.3 | Hou. 15.0 | N.E. 26.9 | 1977 | AFC |
| 1978 | NFC | Dal. 384 24.0 | Dal. 342 | Dal. 2783 174 | Dal. 4.5 | Dal. 22 | N.O. 61.4 | Min. 3528 221 | Dal. 7.58 | Dal. 25<br>Min. 25 | N.O. 16 | N.O. 3.34 | NY G 42.1 | L.A. 10.6 | Was. 23.3 | 1978 | NFC |
| 1978 | AFC | Mia. 372 23.3 | Sea. 345 | N.E. 3165 198 | N.E. 4.7 | N.E. 30 | Mia. 59.6 | S.D. 3566 223 | Pit. 7.79 | Pit. 28 | K.C. 16 | K.C. 4.32 | Cin. 42.4 | NY J 12.5 | K.C. 23.9 | 1978 | AFC |
| 1979 | NFC | Dal. 371 23.2 | Dal. 339 | St.L. 2582 161 | St.L. 4.6 | N.O. 28 | N.O. 60.0<br>S.F. 60.0 | Dal. 3883 243 | Dal. 7.72 | Dal. 29 | Dal. 13<br>Phi. 13 | Dal. 2.58 | NY G 42.7 | Phi. 9.5 | St.L. 22.7 | 1979 | NFC |
| 1979 | AFC | Pit. 416 26.0 | Cle. 350 | NY J 2646 165 | Pit. 4.6 | Pit. 25<br>S.D. 25 | S.D. 62.5 | S.D. 4138 259 | Pit. 7.88 | Cle. 28 | Buf. 15<br>Cin. 15 | Buf. 3.22 | K.C. 43.1 | K.C. 10.6 | Oak. 22.7 | 1979 | AFC |
| 1980 | NFC | Dal. 454 28.4 | Dal. 337 | L.A. 2799 175 | L.A. 4.6 | Dal. 26 | S.F. 60.8 | N.O. 4010 251 | Phi. 7.91 | Atl. 31<br>L.A. 31 | Det. 12<br>Phi. 12 | Atl. 2.51 | NY G 44.8 | Was. 10.1 | N.O. 22.4 | 1980 | NFC |
| 1980 | AFC | N.E. 441 27.6 | S.D. 372 | Hou. 2635 165 | Hou. 4.6 | Bal. 20 | Hou. 63.9 | S.D. 4741 296 | N.E. 8.22 | Cle. 30<br>S.D. 30 | Cle. 14<br>K.C. 14 | Cle. 2.52 | Den. 43.9 | K.C. 14.5 | N.E. 22.9 | 1980 | AFC |
| 1981 | NFC | Atl. 426 26.6 | Min. 343 | Det. 2795 175 | Det. 4.7 | Det. 26 | S.F. 63.4 | Min. 4567 285 | Det. 7.97 | Atl. 30 | S.F. 13 | S.F. 2.51 | Det. 43.5 | L.A. 13.8 | Was. 25.0 | 1981 | NFC |
| 1981 | AFC | S.D. 478 29.9 | Cle. 364 | K.C. 2633 165 | K.C. 4.3 | S.D. 26 | Cin. 60.4 | S.D. 4873 305 | Den. 8.23 | S.D. 34 | Cin. 12 | Cin. 2.18 | Cin. 44.8 | S.D. 12.2 | Hou. 23.9 | 1981 | AFC |
| 1982 | NFC | Dal. 226 25.1<br>G.B. 226 25.1 | Atl. 190 | Dal. 1313 146 | Dal. 4.4 | Dal. 13 | Atl. 64.0<br>Was. 64.0 | S.F. 2502 278 | Dal. 8.33 | S.F. 17 | St.L. 6 | St.L. 2.50 | St.L. 43.8 | Atl. 11.4 | N.O. 22.2 | 1982 | NFC |
| 1982 | AFC | S.D. 288 25.3 | S.D. 233 | Buf. 1371 152 | Buf. 4.3<br>NY J 4.3 | Buf. 15<br>S.D. 15 | S.D. 61.5 | S.D. 2927 325 | S.D. 8.94 | S.D. 19 | K.C. 8 | Cin. 2.90 | Den. 45.0 | Den. 14.5 | N.E. 23.1 | 1982 | AFC |
| 1983 | NFC | **Was. 541 33.8** | Was. 353 | Chi. 2727 170 | Chi. 4.7 | Was. 30 | **S.F. 64.2** | G.B. 4365 272 | G.B. 8.91 | G.B. 33 | Atl. 10 | Atl. 1.97 | T.B. 41.8 | Det. 11.3 | Min. 21.6 | 1983 | NFC |
| 1983 | AFC | Raid. 442 27.6 | Raid. 356 | Balt. 2695 168 | N.E. 4.8 | Cin. 24 | Cin. 63.9 | Raid. 4661 291 | Raid. 7.76 | Buf. 30 | Mia. 11 | Mia. 2.49 | Bal. 45.3 | Raid. 11.5 | Mia. 23.1 | 1983 | AFC |
| 1984 | NFC | S.F. 475 29.7 | S.F. 356 | Chi. 2974 186 | Chi. 5.3 | Chi. 22 | S.F. 62.9 | St.L. 4257 266 | S.F. 8.32 | S.F. 32 | S.F. 10 | S.F. 2.01 | N.O. 43.1 | L.A. 12.2 | S.F. 22.1 | 1984 | NFC |
| 1984 | AFC | Mia. 513 32.1 | **Mia. 387** | NY J 2189 137 | NY J 4.3 | Raid. 19 | **Mia. 64.2** | Mia. 5018 314 | Mia. 9.00 | **Mia. 49** | N.E. 14 | N.E. 2.80 | K.C. 44.9 | Cin. 12.4 | NY J 23.0 | 1984 | AFC |
| 1985 | NFC | Chi. 456 28.5 | NY G 356 | Chi. 2761 173 | G.B. 4.7<br>St.L. 4.7<br>S.F. 4.7 | Chi. 27 | S.F. 60.2 | Dal. 3861 241 | NY G 7.70 | S.F. 28 | L.A. 14<br>S.F. 14 | S.F. 2.54 | NY G 42.9 | L.A. 13.2 | Chi. 25.3 | 1985 | NFC |
| 1985 | AFC | S.D. 467 29.2 | S.D. 380 | N.E. 2331 146 | Ind. 5.0 | Ind. 22 | S.D. 61.1 | S.D. 4870 304 | S.D. 8.19 | S.D. 37 | NY J 8 | NY J 1.61 | NY J 44.8 | Ind. 11.1 | Den. 23.1 | 1985 | AFC |
| 1986 | NFC | Min. 398 24.9 | S.F. 346 | Chi. 2700 169 | Chi. 4.5 | Was. 23 | Dal. 58.3 | S.F. 4096 256 | Min. 8.06 | Min. 31 | L.A. 15<br>Min. 15 | Min. 2.89 | NY G 44.8 | St.L. 11.7 | N.O. 24.2 | 1986 | NFC |
| 1986 | AFC | Mia. 430 26.9 | S.D. 380 | Cin. 2533 158 | Cin. 4.9 | Cin. 24 | NY J 62.2 | Mia. 4779 299 | Cin. 8.37 | Mia. 46 | Cle. 11 | Cle. 2.04 | Ind. 44.7 | Sea. 11.7 | Cin. 22.0 | 1986 | AFC |
| 1987 | NFC | S.F. 459 30.6 | S.F. 357 | S.F. 2237 149 | S.F. 4.3 | Min. 20<br>N.O. 20 | Min. 64.3 | S.F. 3750 250 | S.F. 7.89 | S.F. 44 | S.F. 12 | S.F. 2.79 | Det. 41.8 | St.L. 12.5 | Atl. 21.5 | 1987 | NFC |
| 1987 | AFC | Cle. 390 26.0 | Den. 331<br>Mia. 331 | Raid. 2197 146 | Raid. 4.6 | Den. 18 | Cle. 60.4 | Mia. 3876 258 | Cle. 7.52 | Sea. 31 | Cle. 12 | Cle. 2.49 | S.D. 42.0 | NY J 11.8 | Den. 20.7 | 1987 | AFC |
| 1988 | NFC | L.A. 407 25.4 | Phx. 336 | S.F. 2523 158 | S.F. 4.8 | Chi. 25 | L.A. 59.8 | Wash. 4136 259 | L.A. 6.92 | Wash. 33 | NYG 14<br>S.F. 14 | S.F. 2.67 | Det. 42.4 | N.O. 11.8 | T.B. 21.0 | 1988 | NFC |
| 1988 | AFC | Cin. 448 28.0 | Cin. 351 | Cin. 2710 169 | Cin. 4.8 | Cin. 27 | Buf. 59.7 | Mia. 4516 282 | Cin. 7.93 | Mia. 29 | NYJ 11 | NYJ 1.85 | Den. 43.8 | NYJ 11.0 | S.D. 25.2 | 1988 | AFC |
| 1989 | NFC | S.F. 442 27.6 | S.F. 350 | Chi. 2287 143 | Det. 4.9 | Det. 23 | S.F. 70.2 | S.F. 4302 269 | S.F. 8.15 | S.F. 35 | S.F. 11 | S.F. 2.08 | Phx. 43.6 | NYG 12.7 | Pitt. 23.3 | 1989 | NFC |
| 1989 | AFC | Buf. 409 25.6 | Cin. 348 | Cin. 2483 155 | Cin. 4.7 | K.C. 18 | Hou. 59.5<br>K.C. 59.5 | Mia. 4216 264 | Buf. 7.00 | Buf. 32 | Cin. 13<br>Pit. 13 | Cin. 2.53 | Ind. 42.4 | Ind. 12.4 | Pitt. 23.3 | 1989 | AFC |
| 1990 | NFC | Phi. 396 24.8 | Was. 327 | Phi. 2556 160 | Det. 5.3 | Chi. 22 | S.F. 61.7 | S.F. 4177 261 | S.F. 6.74 | Phi. 34 | NYG 5 | NYG 1.3 | NYG 44.1 | Chi. 11.1 | Atl. 21.2 | 1990 | NFC |
| 1990 | AFC | Buf. 428 26.8 | Hou. 376 | S.D. 2257 141 | S.D. 4.7 | S.D. 20<br>Raid. 20 | Hou. 62.4 | Hou. 4805 300 | Raid. 7.36 | Hou. 37 | K.C. 5 | K.C. 1.1 | Hou. 45.0 | Ind. 11.2 | S.D. 21.6 | 1990 | AFC |
| 1991 | NFC | Wash. 485 30.3 | S.F. 336 | Minn. 2201 138 | Minn. 4.7 | Wash. 21 | S.F. 62.3 | S.F. 3997 250 | Wash. 8.02 | Wash. 30<br>Atl. 30 | NYG 8 | NYG 1.9 | Minn. 45.5 | Det. 14.8 | Dall. 21.7 | 1991 | NFC |
| 1991 | AFC | Buff. 458 28.6 | Buff. 359 | Buff. 2381 149 | S.D. 4.8 | NYJ 17 | Buff. 64.3 | Hou. 4621 289 | Buff. 7.03 | Buff. 39 | Clev. 10 | Clev. 2.0 | Mia. 44.8 | L.A.Rd. 11.4 | S.D. 21.3<br>Sea. 21.3 | 1991 | AFC |
| 1992 | NFC | S.F. 431 26.9 | S.F. 344 | Phil. 2388 149 | S.F. 4.8 | S.F. 22 | S.F. 66.5 | S.F. 3880 243 | S.F. 7.58 | Atl. 33 | S.F. 9 | S.F. 1.9 | Minn. 44.4 | Dall. 12.5 | Atl. 23.9 | 1992 | NFC |
| 1992 | AFC | Buff. 381 23.8 | Buff. 350 | Buff. 2436 152 | Hou. 4.6 | Buff. 18<br>S.D. 18 | Hou. 65.1 | Hou. 4029 252 | Mia. 6.73 | Hou. 27 | K.C. 12 | K.C. 2.9 | Hou. 45.2 | Cin. 11.9 | N.E. 21.5 | 1992 | AFC |
| 1993 | NFC | S.F. 473 29.5 | S.F. 372 | NYG 2210 138 | S.F. 4.6 | S.F. 22 | S.F. 67.6 | S.F. 4302 269 | S.F. 8.55 | S.F. 29 | Dall. 6 | Dall. 1.3 | Det. 44.5 | N.O. 13.6 | G.B. 24.7 | 1993 | NFC |
| 1993 | AFC | Den. 373 23.3 | Hou. 330 | Sea. 2015 126 | Hou. 4.6 | Hou. 14<br>K.C. 14<br>NYJ 14<br>S.D. 14 | Den. 63.3 | Mia. 4353 272 | Mia. 7.86 | Den. 27<br>Mia. 27 | Den. 10<br>Mia. 10 | Den. 1.8 | Hou. 45.4 | Cle. 13.4 | Mia. 21.8 | 1993 | AFC |
| 1994 | NFC | S.F. 505 31.6 | S.F. 362 | Det. 2080 130 | Det. 5.1 | Dall. 26 | S.F. 70.3 | Minn. 4324 270 | S.F. 8.54 | S.F. 37 | S.F. 11 | S.F. 2.2 | L.A. 44.8 | Wash. 14.1 | Dall. 25.7 | 1994 | NFC |
| 1994 | AFC | Mia. 389 24.3 | N.E. 348 | Pitt. 2180 136 | Sea. 4.3 | Den. 19 | Buff. 63.1 | N.E. 4444 278 | Raid. 7.30 | Mia. 31 | Pitt. 9<br>Sea. 9 | Sea. 1.8 | Raid. 43.8 | S.D. 13.2 | Clev. 24.5 | 1994 | AFC |
| 1995 | NFC | S.F. 457 28.6 | Dall. 364 | Dall. 2201 138 | Dall. 4.5 | Dlal. 29 | S.F. 67.1 | S.F. 4608 288 | Dal. 7.08 | G.B. 39 | Chi. 10<br>Dall. 10 | Chi. 1.9 | St.L. 44.3 | Wash. 12.1 | Wash. 23.9 | 1995 | NFC |
| 1995 | AFC | Pitt. 407 25.4 | Mia. 345 | K.C. 2222 139 | Sea. 4.6 | Sea. 20 | Mia. 64.9 | Mia. 4210 263 | Mia. 6.78 | Cin. 29 | K.C. 10 | K.C. 1.9 | Sea. 45.0 | Den. 11.5 | K.C. 23.7 | 1995 | AFC |

Bold - designates all-time leader

# YEARLY TEAM LEADERS
## DEFENSE

| YEAR | LGUE | POINTS-PT/G | FIRST DOWNS | RUSH YARDS | YARDS GAME | RUSH AVERAGE | RUSH TD | PASS COMPLETION PERCENTAGE | PASS YARDS | YARDS GAME | PASS YARDS/ATTEMPT | PASS TD | MOST INT. | HIGHEST INT.% | PUNT RETURN AVERAGE | KICKOFF RETURN AVERAGE | TEAM | LGUE |
|---|---|---|---|---|---|---|---|---|---|---|---|---|---|---|---|---|---|---|
| 1933 | NFL | **Bkn. 54** 5.4 | | | | | | | | | | | | | | | 1933 | NFL |
| 1934 | NFL | Det. 59 **4.5** | | | | | | | | | | | | | | | 1934 | NFL |
| 1935 | NFL | G.B. 96 8.0 / NY G 96 8.0 | | | | | | ChiB 30.4 | | | | | ChiB 37 | ChiB 19.1 | | | 1935 | NFL |
| 1936 | NFL | ChiB 94 7.8 | | | | | | Bos. 31.5 | | | | | ChiB 35 | ChiB 15.4 | | | 1936 | NFL |
| 1937 | NFL | ChiB 100 9.1 | | | | | | Pit. 32.4 | | | | | NY G 30 | NY G 16.5 | | | 1937 | NFL |
| 1938 | NFL | NY G 79 7.2 | | | | | | NY G 34.1 | | | | | NY G 34 | NY G 15.0 | | | 1938 | NFL |
| 1939 | NFL | NY G 85 7.7 | | | | | | Was. 37.0 | | | | | NY G 35 | NY G 15.8 | | | 1939 | NFL |
| 1940 | NFL | Bkn. 120 10.9 | | | | | | ChiC 37.1 | | | | | G.B. 40 | Det. 16.4 | | | 1940 | NFL |
| 1941 | NFL | NY G 114 10.3 | Bkn. 110 / ChiC 110 | ChiB 1076 | 98 | Was. 2.71 | Bkn. 6 / ChiB 6 | ChiB 40.0 | Pit. 1168 | 106 | ChiB 5.5 | Bkn. 6 / NY G 6 | ChiB 34 | NY G 13.3 | Cle. 8.2 | Was. 19.4 | 1941 | NFL |
| 1942 | NFL | ChiB 84 7.6 | ChiB 98 | ChiB 519 | 47 | ChiB 1.77 | ChiB 3 | Was 37.5 | Was 1093 | 99 | NY G 4.2 | NY G 4 | ChiB 33 / G.B. 33 | G.B. 13.6 | Det. 10.2 | Pit. 18.5 | 1942 | NFL |
| 1943 | NFL | Was. 137 13.7 | P-P 96 | P-P 793 | 79 | P-P 2.54 | NY G 8 | ChiB 31.5 | ChiB 980 | 98 | ChiB 4.8 | ChiB 8 | G.B. 42 | G.B. 17.4 | Was. 9.5 | NY G 19.3 | 1943 | NFL |
| 1944 | NFL | NY G 75 7.5 | **Phi. 86** | **Phi. 558** | 56 | Phi. 1.74 | NY G 6 | ChiB 33.2 | NY G 1052 | 105 | NY G 5.0 | **NY G 3** | NY G 34 | Phi. 14.3 | C-P 9.9 | Phi. 18.0 | 1944 | NFL |
| 1945 | NFL | Was. 121 12.1 | Phi. 104 | Phi. 817 | 82 | Det. 2.56 | Det. 7 | Cle. 39.1 | Was. 1121 | 112 | Was. 5.4 | NY G 6 | Bos. 30 | Bos. 13.2 | Det. 9.8 | Det. 16.6 | 1945 | NFL |
| 1946 | NFL | Pit. 117 10.6 | ChiB 138 | ChiB 1044 | 95 | Phi. 2.69 | Pit. 9 | Pit. 39.5 | **Pit. 939** | 85 | Pit. 5.8 | G.B. 8 / Pit. 6 | ChiB 27 | Phi. 11.8 | Pit. 7.7 | ChiB 16.0 | 1946 | NFL |
| 1946 | AAFC | Cle. 137 9.8 | N.Y. 119 | S.F. 873 | 62 | S.F. 2.05 | S.F. 7 | Cle. 41.8 | Cle. 1317 | 94 | Cle. 4.4 | Cle. 8 | Cle. 41 | Cle. 13.7 | N.Y. 10.8 | Mia. 18.5 | 1946 | AAFC |
| 1947 | NFL | G.B. 210 17.5 | Pit. 170 | Phi. 1329 | 111 | L.A. 3.41 | ChiB 6 | Pit. 40.2 | G.B. 1790 | 149 | G.B. 6.5 | G.B. 14 / L.A. 14 | G.B. 30 | G.B. 10.8 | ChiC 9.4 | ChiB 17.5 | 1947 | NFL |
| 1947 | AAFC | Cle. 185 13.2 | N.Y. 140 | N.Y. 1237 | 88 | N.Y. 3.33 | L.A. 9 | Cle. 42.6 | Cle. 1707 | 122 | Cle. 5.6 | Cle. 11 | Cle. 32 | Cle. 10.6 | L.A. 10.8 | L.A. 17.0 | 1947 | AAFC |
| 1948 | NFL | ChiB 151 12.6 | Phi. 158 | Phi. 1209 | 101 | Phi. 3.22 | Phi. 5 | Phi. 41.1 | G.B. 1626 | 135 | ChiB 4.9 | ChiB 12 | NY G 39 | NY G 12.5 | ChiB 9.2 | Pit. 17.8 | 1948 | NFL |
| 1948 | AAFC | Cle. 190 13.6 | Cle. 171 | Cle. 1519 | 108 | Cle. 3.48 | Cle. 10 | Cle. 44.9 | Bkn. 1985 | 142 | Cle. 5.9 | Cle. 14 | S.F. 32 | S.F. 8.6 | Bal. 10.3 | Chi. 17.5 | 1948 | AAFC |
| 1949 | NFL | Cle. 134 11.2 | Phi. 148 | ChiB 1196 | 100 | ChiB 2.79 | Phi. 5 | Phi. 39.9 | Pit. 1607 | 134 | Phi. 5.3 | Pit. 9 | ChiC 33 | Det. 10.3 | L.A. 8.3 | Det. 18.7 | 1949 | NFL |
| 1949 | AAFC | Cle. 171 14.2 | N.Y. 129 | N.Y. 1134 | 94 | N.Y. 3.15 | N.Y. 8 | Cle. 39.5 | Cle. 1677 | 140 | Cle. 5.5 | Cle. 9 | S.F. 32 | S.F. 10.1 | N.Y. 11.0 | L.A. 19.2 | 1949 | AAFC |
| 1950 | NFL | Phi. 141 11.7 | Phi. 141 | Det. 1367 | 114 | NY G 2.93 | Phi. 5 | Phi. 36.8 | Cle. 1581 | 132 | Cle. 5.4 | Cle. 8 | Bal. 34 | Phi. 11.2 | Cle. 6.6 | Pit. 19.2 | 1950 | NFL |
| 1951 | NFL | Cle. 152 12.7 | NY G 174 | NY G 913 | 76 | NY G 2.33 | Cle. 8 / NY G 8 | Phi. 41.5 | Pit. 1687 | 141 | Cle. 6.0 | Cle. 10 | NY G 41 | NY G 10.9 | S.F. 6.7 | G.B. 18.5 | 1951 | NFL |
| 1952 | NFL | Det. 192 16.0 | S.F. 167 | Det. 1145 | 95 | NY G 3.23 | ChiC 8 / Det. 8 / NY G 8 / Pit. 8 | Was. 40.5 | Was. 1817 | 151 | S.F. 5.6 | Was. 12 | L.A. 38 | L.A. 10.6 | NY G 6.7 | Pit. 18.3 | 1952 | NFL |
| 1953 | NFL | Cle. 162 13.5 | Pit. 184 | Phi. 1117 | 93 | Pit. 3.07 | Phi. 6 | Phi. 42.2 | Was. 1950 | 162 | Was. 5.6 | Was. 8 | Det. 38 | Det. 10.7 | ChiC 1.5 | Pit. 16.3 | 1953 | NFL |
| 1954 | NFL | Cle. 162 13.5 | Cle. 147 | Cle. 1050 | 88 | Cle. 2.82 | Cle. 4 | Phi. 41.4 | Cle. 1784 | 149 | Phi. 5.9 | Det. 10 | NY G 33 | Pit. 10.2 | **ChiC 1.2** | G.B. 18.5 | 1954 | NFL |
| 1955 | NFL | Cle. 218 18.2 | Cle. 171 | Cle. 1189 | 99 | Was. 3.26 | Was. 8 | Cle. 39.0 | Pit. 1530 | 127 | Cle. | S.F. 10 | G.B. 31 / L.A. 31 | G.B. 12.0 | Bal. 1.9 | L.A. 19.7 | 1955 | NFL |
| 1956 | NFL | Cle. 177 14.7 | Pit. 167 | NY G 1443 | 120 | NY G 3.48 | Det. 9 | ChiC 44.9 | Cle. 1215 | 101 | Cle. 5.4 | Cle. 7 | ChiC 33 | ChiC 11.5 | S.F. 3.5 | Pit. 19.0 | 1956 | NFL |
| 1957 | NFL | Cle. 172 14.3 | Pit. 156 | Bal. 1174 | 98 | Bal. 3.13 | Cle. 6 | Cle. 43.4 | Cle. 1511 | 126 | Cle. 6.2 | Cle. 8 | G.B. 30 | G.B. 9.6 | Det. 1.6 | Det. 20.1 | 1957 | NFL |
| 1958 | NFL | NY G 183 15.2 | ChiB 168 | Bal. 1291 | 108 | NY G 3.61 | Cle. 6 | NY G 45.7 | NY G 2130 | 177 | L.A. 6.0 | Bal. 9 | Bal. 35 | Bal. 9.6 | S.F. 2.5 | S.F. 17.6 | 1958 | NFL |
| 1959 | NFL | NY G 170 14.2 | NY G 167 | NY G 1261 | 105 | NY G 3.33 | NY G 6 | Pit. 44.9 | NY G 1811 | 151 | NY G 6.0 | NY G 11 | Bal. 40 | Bal. 11.4 | Cle. 1.2 | Pit. 17.5 | 1959 | NFL |
| 1960 | NFL | S.F. 205 17.1 | St.L. 158 | St.L. 1212 | 101 | NY G 3.20 | G.B. 7 | S.F. 47.8 | Chi. 1808 | 151 | Chi. 6.2 | Bal. 8 | Cle. 31 | Phi. 10.6 | Bal. 3.2 | Was. 17.1 | 1960 | NFL |
| 1960 | AFL | Dal. 253 18.1 | Buf. 225 | Dal. 980 | 70 | Dal. 2.32 | Hou. 6 | Buf. 43.1 | Buf. 2461 | 176 | Buf. 5.7 | Bos. 19 / Buf. 19 / Dal. 19 | Buf. 33 | Buf. 7.7 | Buf. 5.8 | Den. 20.1 | 1960 | AFL |
| 1961 | NFL | NY G 220 15.7 | NY G 212 | Pit. 1463 | 104 | St.L. 3.51 | NY G 6 | NY G 45.6 | Bal. 2320 | 166 | G.B. 6.4 | Det. 11 | NY G 33 | NY G 8.5 | Min. 6.0 | St.L. 20.1 | 1961 | NFL |
| 1961 | AFL | S.D. 219 15.6 | Buf. 200 | Bos. 1041 | 74 | Bos. 2.97 | S.D. 7 | Hou. 43.0 | S.D. 2736 | 195 | Hou. 5.6 | Hou. 13 | **S.D. 49** | S.D. 10.1 | Buf. 6.5 | Den. 17.1 | 1961 | AFL |
| 1962 | NFL | G.B. 148 10.6 | Det. 180 | Det. 1231 | 88 | Det. 3.51 | Chi. 4 | G.B. 46.8 | G.B. 2084 | 149 | G.B. 5.9 | G.B. 10 | G.B. 31 | G.B. 8.7 | St.L. 4.7 | G.B. 20.1 | 1962 | NFL |
| 1962 | AFL | Dal. 233 16.6 | Hou. 217 | Dal. 1250 | 89 | Dal. 3.56 | Buf. 10 | Buf. 43.8 | Oak. 2517 | 180 | Hou. 5.9 | Dal. 13 | Buf. 36 | Buf. 8.2 | Bos. 4.9 | Hou. 21.0 | 1962 | AFL |
| 1963 | NFL | Chi. 144 10.3 | G.B. 193 | Chi. 1442 | 103 | Chi. 3.50 | Chi. 7 | Chi. 46.5 | Chi. 2045 | 146 | Chi. 5.8 | G.B. 9 | ChiB 36 | ChiB 10.2 | Dal. 4.9 | G.B. 19.3 | 1963 | NFL |
| 1963 | AFL | S.D. 256 18.3 | N/A | N/A | | N/A | N/A | N/A | N/A | | N/A | N/A | N/A | N/A | N/A | N/A | 1963 | AFL |
| 1964 | NFL | Bal. 225 16.1 | Bal. 197 | L.A. 1501 | 107 | Dal. 3.43 | Bal. 6 | Dal. 45.6 | G.B. 1980 | 141 | G.B. 6.0 | G.B. 11 | Was. 34 | Was. 8.4 | Dal. 2.7 | Min. 20.2 | 1964 | NFL |
| 1964 | AFL | Buf. 242 17.3 | Buf. 206 | Buf. 913 | 65 | Buf. 3.04 | Buf. 4 | Buf. 46.6 | K.C. 2910 | 208 | S.D. 6.0 | Oak. 21 | NY T 34 | Den. 7.3 | Oak. 6.6 | Hou. 18.5 | 1964 | AFL |
| 1965 | NFL | L.A. 224 16.0 | L.A. 208 | L.A. 1409 | 101 | L.A. 3.38 | Det. 9 | Det. 48.1 | G.B. 2316 | 165 | G.B. 6.0 | G.B. 11 | G.B. 27 / Was. 27 | Was. 8.5 | Was. 4.6 | Dal. 19.5 | 1965 | NFL |
| 1965 | AFL | Buf. 226 16.1 | S.D. 190 | S.D. 1094 | 78 | Buf. 3.09 | Buf. 5 | Hou. 42.5 | S.D. 2480 | 177 | S.D. 5.2 | Bos. 17 | Buf. 32 | Hou. 6.5 | Bos. 7.0 | Oak. 19.8 | 1965 | AFL |
| 1966 | NFL | G.B. 163 11.6 | L.A. 196 | Dal. 1176 | 84 | St.L. 3.16 | Dal. 6 | St.L. 44.5 | G.B. 2316 | 165 | G.B. 5.9 | G.B. 7 | Cle. 30 | Cle. 7.4 | Det. 3.6 | St.L. 20.4 | 1966 | NFL |
| 1966 | AFL | Buf. 255 18.2 | Buf. 192 | Buf. 1051 | 75 | Buf. 3.06 | Buf. 6 | Buf. 44.0 | S.D. 2386 | 170 | S.D. 5.8 | S.D. 13 | K.C. 33 | Mia. 7.3 | NY J 5.0 | Mia. 20.4 | 1966 | AFL |
| 1967 | NFL | L.A. 196 14.0 | G.B. 183 | Dal. 1081 | 77 | L.A. 3.10 | Bal. 5 | Chi. 42.7 | G.B. 1644 | 117 | G.B. 4.9 | Det. 11 | Bal. 32 / L.A. 32 | Bal. 8.1 | G.B. 1.7 | Chi. 20.5 | 1967 | NFL |
| 1967 | AFL | Hou. 199 14.2 | Oak. 182 | Oak. 1129 | 81 | Oak. 3.21 | Hou. 7 | Oak. 41.2 | Buf. 2191 | 156 | Hou. 5.7 | Hou. 10 | K.C. 31 | Mia. 8.0 | Mia. 6.5 | Hou. 18.6 | 1967 | AFL |
| 1968 | NFL | Bal. 144 10.3 | L.A. 190 | Dal. 1195 | 85 | Dal. 3.24 | **Dal. 2** | N.O. 41.8 | G.B. 2031 | 145 | Bal. 5.6 | Bal. 9 | Cle. 32 | Cle. 7.3 | Chi. 3.3 | Chi. 17.9 | 1968 | NFL |
| 1968 | AFL | K.C. 170 12.1 | N.Y. 178 | NY J 1195 | 85 | NY J 3.25 | K.C. 4 | Buf. 42.1 | Hou. 2003 | 143 | Hou. 5.6 | Hou. 13 | K.C. 37 | K.C. 8.0 | Oak. 5.3 | K.C. 19.3 | 1968 | AFL |
| 1969 | NFL | Min. 133 9.5 | Min. 158 | Dal. 1050 | 75 | Min. 3.23 | Dal. 3 | L.A. 47.0 | Min. 2035 | 145 | Min. 5.0 | Min. 8 | Min. 30 | Min. 7.3 | G.B. 3.4 | Dal. 19.4 | 1969 | NFL |
| 1969 | AFL | K.C. 177 12.6 | K.C. 181 | K.C. 1091 | 78 | K.C. 3.47 | Oak. 6 | Oak. 38.9 | K.C. 2491 | 178 | K.C. 5.8 | K.C. 10 | K.C. 32 | K.C. 7.5 | Oak. 4.1 | Bos. 19.1 | 1969 | AFL |
| 1970 | NFC | Min. 143 10.2 | Min. 168 | Det. 1152 | 82 | Det. 3.18 | Min. 4 | St.L. 47.9 | Min. 1798 | 128 | Min. 4.9 | Min. 6 | Det. 28 / Min. 28 | Min. 7.6 | NY G 2.9 | L.A. 18.1 | 1970 | NFC |
| 1970 | AFC | Mia. 228 16.3 | Den. 199 | NY J 1283 | 92 | NY J 3.14 | Bal. 6 | NY J 43.1 | K.C. 2280 | 163 | K.C. 5.6 | S.D. 13 | K.C. 31 | K.C. 7.6 | Cle. 3.6 | Bos. 20.5 | 1970 | AFC |
| 1971 | NFC | Min. 139 9.9 | Min. 194 | Dal. 1144 | 82 | Dal. 3.24 | **Min. 2** | S.F. 44.6 | Atl. 1895 | 135 | Atl. 5.0 | Atl. 9 | Was. 29 | Det. 7.2 | S.F. 2.3 | Was. 17.5 | 1971 | NFC |
| 1971 | AFC | Bal. 140 10.0 | Bal. 196 | Bal. 1113 | 80 | Bal. 3.16 | Bal. 8 | Den. 42.1 | Bal. 2027 | 145 | Bal. 5.6 | Bal. 9 | Bal. 28 | Cin. 8.1 | S.D. 2.0 | Mia. 20.0 | 1971 | AFC |
| 1972 | NFC | Was. 218 15.6 | Min. 200 | Dal. 1515 | 108 | G.B. 3.42 | Dal. 7 | Atl. 45.5 | Min. 1791 | 128 | Min. 5.4 | Min. 8 | Min. 26 | Min. 7.9 | Was. 2.1 | L.A. 18.5 | 1972 | NFC |
| 1972 | AFC | Mia. 171 12.2 | Mia. 186 | Mia. 1548 | 111 | Oak. 3.76 | Pit. 7 | Buf. 42.5 | Cle. 1994 | 142 | Cin. 5.8 | Pit. 9 | Pit. 28 | Buf. 7.5 | Mia. 3.9 | Hou. 19.5 | 1972 | AFC |
| 1973 | NFC | Min. 168 12.0 | L.A. 173 | Dal. 1471 | 105 | Was. 3.34 | Dal. 5 / L.A. 5 / Min. 5 | Atl. 46.6 | Atl. 1619 | 116 | Atl. 5.0 | Min. 8 | Was. 26 | NY G 7.3 | Dal. 5.2 | Min. 19.1 | 1973 | NFC |
| 1973 | AFC | Mia. 150 10.7 | Min. 168 | Oak. 1470 | 105 | Oak. 3.38 | Oak. 8 | Buf. 45.1 | N.E. 1600 | 114 | Mia. 5.0 | Mia. 6 | Pit. 37 | Pit. 10.3 | Cin. 4.6 | Den. 20.4 | 1973 | AFC |
| 1974 | NFC | L.A. 181 12.9 | L.A. 186 | L.A. 1308 | 93 | Dal. 3.23 | L.A. 4 | Atl. 45.0 | Atl. 1847 | 132 | Was. 5.3 | Min. 8 | Was. 25 | Was. 6.4 | Phi. 6.8 | Min. 17.4 | 1974 | NFC |
| 1974 | AFC | Pit. 189 13.5 | Pit. 200 | N.E. 1587 | 113 | Pit. 3.41 | Mia. 7 | Pit. 43.4 | Pit. 1872 | 134 | Pit. 5.5 | Buf. 11 | K.C. 28 | Cle. 7.8 | Mia. 6.2 | Min. 19.1 | 1974 | AFC |
| 1975 | NFC | L.A. 135 9.6 | Min. 190 | Min. 1532 | 109 | S.F. 3.53 | L.A. 4 | Dal. 43.4 | Min. 1994 | 142 | L.A. 5.5 | L.A. 11 | Min. 28 | G.B. 7.8 | G.B. 4.9 | Min. 19.5 | 1975 | NFC |
| 1975 | AFC | Pit. 162 11.6 | Pit. 214 | Hou. 1680 | 120 | Hou. 3.38 | Pit. 8 | Oak. 43.0 | Cin. 2001 | 143 | Cin. 5.1 | Oak. 9 / Pit. 9 | Oak. 35 | Oak. 8.8 | Pit. 5.5 | Oak. 18.6 | 1975 | AFC |

Bold - designates all-time leader

# YEARLY TEAM LEADERS
## DEFENSE

| YEAR | LGUE | POINTS-PT/G | FIRST DOWNS | RUSH YARDS | YARDS GAME | RUSH AVERAGE | RUSH TD | PASS COMPLETION PECENTAGE | PASS YARDS | YARDS GAME | PASS YARDS/ ATTEMPT | PASS TD | MOST INT. | HIGHEST INT.% | PUNT RETURN AVERAGE | KICKOFF RETURN AVERAGE | TEAM | LGUE |
|---|---|---|---|---|---|---|---|---|---|---|---|---|---|---|---|---|---|---|
| 1976 | NFC | Min. 176 12.6 | Det. 191 | L.A. 1564 | 112 L.A. | 3.6 | Chi. 10 | Was. 41.2 | Min. 1575 | 113 | Dal. 5.7 | Min. 8 | L.A. 32 | L.A. 8.1 | G.B. 5.6 | Was. 16.4 | 1976 | NFC |
| 1976 | AFC | Pit. 138 9.9 | Pit. 182 | Pit. 1457 | 104 Pit. | 3.2 | Pit. 5 | Pit. 42.4 | Cin. 1758 | 126 | Den. 5.8 | Den. 8 | Cin. 26 | Cin. 7.1 | Pit. 5.7 | Oak. 18.4 | 1976 | AFC |
| 1977 | NFC | Atl. 129 9.2 | Atl. 192 | Dal. 1651 | 118 NY G | 3.4 | Atl. 5 | Atl. 41.5 | Atl. 1775 | 127 | Dal. 5.4 | Chi. 7 | Atl. 26 | Atl. 8.1 | L.A. 4.0 | Was. 19.1 | 1977 | NFC |
| 1977 | AFC | Den. 148 10.6 | Oak. 204 | Den. 1531 | 109 Den. | 3.3 | Den. 5 | Pit. 44.0 | S.D. 2088 | 149 | Mia. 5.8 | Bal. 10, Mia. 10 | Pit. 31 | Pit. 8.7 | Cin. 6.8 | Oak. 15.8 | 1977 | AFC |
| 1978 | NFC | Dal. 208 13.0 | L.A. 229 | Dal. 1721 | 108 T.B. | 3.4 | N.O. 9 | Dal. 46.8 | L.A. 2449 | 153 | NY G 6.0 | NY G 10 | T.B. 29 | L.A. 5.5 | G.B. 5.6 | Was. 17.5 | 1978 | NFC |
| 1978 | AFC | Pit. 195 12.2 | Den. 251 | Pit. 1774 | 111 Pit. | 3.5 | Pit. 11 | Cin. 48.7 | Buf. 2156 | 135 | Den. 6.2 | Den. 9 | Mia. 32 | Mia. 7.3 | Den. 4.7 | Oak. 19.5 | 1978 | AFC |
| 1979 | NFC | T.B. 237 4.8 | T.B. 247 | T.B. 1873 | 117 T.B. | 3.5 | Chi. 9 | Dal. 47.6 | T.B. 2405 | 150 | T.B. 5.5 | Min. 14, T.B. 14 | Chi. 29 | Chi. 6.3 | Was. 4.7 | Was. 16.8 | 1979 | NFC |
| 1979 | AFC | S.D. 246 15.4 | Mia. 238 | Den. 1693 | 106 Den. | 3.4 | K.C. 8 | Pit. 47.1 | Buf. 2713 | 170 | Pit. 6.1 | Den. 11, S.D. 11 | Hou. 34 | Hou. 7.3 | Mia. 5.2 | Sea. 17.7 | 1979 | AFC |
| 1980 | NFC | Phi. 222 13.9 | Det. 265 | Det. 1599 | 100 Det. | 3.6 | Atl. 8, Phi. 8 | Was. 47.7 | Was. 2504 | 157 | Phi. 5.9 | Det. 14 | Was. 33 | Was. 8.4 | Min. 6.2 | Min. 16.9 | 1980 | NFC |
| 1980 | AFC | Hou. 251 15.7 | Buf. 251 | Cin. 1680 | 105 Oak. | 3.4 | Hou. 8 | Pit. 52.6 | Buf. 2561 | 160 | Buf. 5.9 | Buf. 15 | Oak. 35 | Oak. 6.7 | Buf. 6.0 | **Cle. 14.3** | 1980 | AFC |
| 1981 | NFC | Phi. 221 13.9 | Phi. 266 | Det. 1623 | 101 NY G | 3.4 | Atl. 10, NY G 10, S.F. 10 | Chi. 44.4 | Phi. 3050 | 191 | Phi. 6.0 | T.B. 10 | Dal. 37 | Dal. 7.2 | Dal. 6.1 | G.B. 16.9 | 1981 | NFC |
| 1981 | AFC | Mia. 275 17.2 | Den. 268 | K.C. 1747 | 109 K.C. | 3.4 | Buf. 7 | K.C. 51.3 | N.E. 3052 | 191 | Den. 6.4 | Den. 13 | Pit. 30 | Pit. 5.5 | Sea. 4.6 | S.D. 17.4 | 1981 | AFC |
| 1982 | NFC | Was. 128 14.2 | N.O. 151, Was. 151 | Det. 854 | 95 Det. | 3.2 | Chi. 4 | Dal. 52.6 | T.B. 1384 | 154 | G.B. 6.0 | Was. 8 | Det. 18 | Det. 6.3 | Was. 3.5 | Was. 17.3 | 1982 | NFC |
| 1982 | AFC | Mia. 131 14.6 | Mia. 147 | Pit. 762 | 85 Den. | 3.2, Pit. 3.2 | NY J 5, Pit. 5 | Buf. 44.5 | Mia. 1027 | 114 | Buf. 5.4 | Sea. 4 | Mia. 19 | Mia. 8.4 | Buf. 3.0 | Sea. 15.0 | 1982 | AFC |
| 1983 | NFC | Det. 286 17.9 | Chi. 286, Dal. 286, St.L. 286 | Was. 1289 | 81 NY G | 3.5 | Was. 9 | Chi. 50.8 | N.O. 2691 | 168 | N.O. 6.3 | Chi. 15, T.B. 15 | Was. 34 | Was. 6.0 | Atl. 5.3 | Det. 16.1 | 1983 | NFC |
| 1983 | AFC | Mia. 250 15.6 | Cin. 276 | Cin. 1499 | 94 Cin. | 3.5 | N.E. 9 | K.C. 52.2 | Cin. 2828 | 179 | Cin. 6.3 | Cin. 17 | K.C. 30 | K.C. 6.0 | Sea. 5.1 | Sea. 16.1 | 1983 | AFC |
| 1984 | NFC | S.F. 227 14.2 | Chi. 216 | Chi. 1377 | 86 Det. | 3.5 | Dal. 8 | Chi. 45.5 | N.O. 2453 | 153 | Dal. 6.1 | Chi. 14, S.F. 14 | Dal. 28 | Dal. 5.3 | Dal. 4.2 | G.B. 16.0 | 1984 | NFC |
| 1984 | AFC | Den. 241 15.1 | Cle. 270 | Pit. 1617 | 101 Ind. | 3.6, Pit. 3.6 | Cle. 10, Den. 10, K.C. 10 | Raid. 50.0 | Cle. 2696 | 169 | Raid. 6.4 | Cin. 15, Cle. 15 | Sea. 38 | Sea. 7.3 | Sea. 6.4 | Sea. 16.7 | 1984 | AFC |
| 1985 | NFC | Chi. 198 12.4 | Chi. 236 | Chi. 1319 | 82 NY G | 3.5 | Chi. 6 | Chi. 47.7 | Was. 2746 | 172 | NY G 6.3 | S.F. 11 | Chi. 34 | Chi. 6.5 | Dal. 6.5 | Atl. 18.3 | 1985 | NFC |
| 1985 | AFC | NY J 264 16.5 | Raid. 273, Pit. 273 | NY J 1516 | 95 Raid. | 3.5, NY J 3.5 | Raid. 7 | Raid. 49.1 | Pit. 2783 | 174 | Pit. 6.4 | N.E. 14 | K.C. 27 | Sea. 4.8 | Raid. 6.1 | Cin. 17.3 | 1985 | AFC |
| 1986 | NFC | Chi. 187 11.7 | Chi. 241 | NY G 1284 | 80 N.O. | 3.2 | Chi. 4 | Chi. 47.4 | St.L. 2637 | 165 | L.A. 5.5 | Chi. 12 | S.F. 39 | S.F. 6.5 | Chi. 4.8 | St.L. 17.7 | 1986 | NFC |
| 1986 | AFC | Cle. 310 19.4 | Raid. 283 | Cle. 1651 | 103 S.D. | 3.5 | Pit. 10 | Hou. 46.5 | N.E. 2978 | 186 | K.C. 6.2 | N.E. 15 | K.C. 31 | K.C. 5.4 | NY J 4.6 | Raid. 16.9 | 1986 | AFC |
| 1987 | NFC | S.F. 253 16.9 | S.F. 250 | Chi. 1413 | 94 Chi. | 3.4 | S.F. 6 | S.F. 48.0 | S.F. 2484 | 166 | S.F. 5.9 | S.F. 13 | N.O. 30 | N.O. 6.1 | Det. 5.2 | St.L. 18.0 | 1987 | NFC |
| 1987 | AFC | Ind. 238 15.9 | Cle. 251 | Cle. 1433 | 96 Raid. | 3.5 | Ind. 6 | Ind. 49.9 | Raid. 2727 | 182 | Ind. 6.1 | Cle. 15, Den. 15 | Den. 28 | Den. 6.1 | NY J 4.9 | Buf. 15.8 | 1987 | AFC |
| 1988 | NFC | Chi. 215 13.4 | Min. 243 | Chi. 1326 | 83 T.B. | 3.2 | Chi. 5 | Chi. 45.0 | Min. 2489 | 156 | Min. 4.8 | G.B. 12, Min. 12 | Min. 36 | Min. 7.5 | Atl. 5.8 | NYG 17.4 | 1988 | NFC |
| 1988 | AFC | Buf. 237 14.8 | N.E. 272 | Hou. 1592 | 100 Pit. | 3.6 | Cle. 13 | NYJ 51.3 | K.C. 2434 | 152 | Buf. 5.5 | K.C. 12 | NYJ 24 | NYJ 5.0 | Sea. 5.6 | Buf. 16.2 | 1988 | AFC |
| 1989 | NFC | NYG 252 15.8 | Min. 266, NYG 266 | N.O. 1326 | 83 Det. | 3.5, NYG 3.5 | Phi. 8 | Phi. 48.8 | Min. 2501 | 156 | Min. 4.5 | S.F. 15 | Phi. 30 | Phi. 5.7 | Phi. 5.8 | Det. 16.0 | 1989 | NFC |
| 1989 | AFC | Den. 226 14.1 | Den. 246 | Den. 1580 | 99 Den. | 3.7 | Cle. 8 | Cle. 49.8 | K.C. 2527 | 158 | K.C. 5.0 | Den. 13 | Cle. 27 | Cle. 5.0 | Raid. 7.3 | Buff. 15.8 | 1989 | AFC |
| 1990 | NFC | NYG 211 13.2 | NYG 245 | Phi. 1169 | 73 Atl. | 3.6 | S.F. 7 | Phi. 48.2 | Dal. 2639 | 165 | NYG 5.2, Dal. 5.2 | Dal. 12, NYG 12 | Chi. 31 | Chi. 6.3 | Phx. 6.3 | N.O. 16.2 | 1990 | NFC |
| 1990 | AFC | Pit. 240 15.0 | Pit. 257 | S.D. 1515 | 95 Pit. | 3.6, S.D. 3.6 | Raid. 4 | Pit. 51.3 | Pit. 2500 | 156 | Pit. 5.1 | Pit. 9 | Pit. 24 | Pit. 5.2 | S.D. 4.7 | Buf. 15.5 | 1990 | AFC |
| 1991 | NFC | N.O. 211 13.2 | N.O. 214 | Phil. 1136 | 71 Phil. | 3.0 | Phil. 4 | Phil. 44.1 | Phil. 2413 | 151 | Phil. 4.6 | N.O. 12, Phx. 12 | N.O. 29 | N.O. 5.9 | Wash. 6.1 | Dall. 16.9 | 1991 | NFC |
| 1991 | AFC | Den. 235 14.7 | Den. 242 | NYJ 1442 | 99 N.E. | 3.4, Pitt. 3.4 | Sea. 4 | Den. 51.7 | Den. 2755 | 172 | Den. 5.2 | Buff. 12, Den. 12 | Buff. 23, Den. 23 | Den. 4.8 | Buff. 3.5 | NYJ 15.4 | 1991 | AFC |
| 1992 | NFC | N.O. 202 12.6 | Phil. 242 | Dall. 1244 | 78 Dall. | 3.6 | Phil. 4 | Phil. 50.9 | N.O. 2470 | 154 | N.O. 4.3 | Minn. 12 | Minn. 28 | Minn. 5.5 | T.B. 5.3 | G.B. 15.8 | 1992 | NFC |
| 1992 | AFC | Pitt. 225 14.1 | Sea. 247 | Buff. 1395 87, S.D. 1395 87 | 87 Clev. | 3.3 | Pitt. 5 | Pitt. 52.7 | K.C. 2537 | 159 | K.C. 5.0 | Raid. 11, Sea. 11 | S.D. 25 | K.C. 5.2 | Ind. 7.0 | Hou. 15.7 | 1992 | AFC |
| 1993 | NFC | NYG 205 12.8 | Minn. 259 | Minn. 1534 | 96 Minn. | 3.7, S.F. 3.7 | G.B. 6, Minn. 6, S.F. 6 | Phil. 54.2 | N.O. 2606 | 163 | Dall. 6.0 | Minn. 11 | Minn. 24 | Minn. 5.0 | Chi. 5.2 | Chi. 17.3 | 1993 | NFC |
| 1993 | AFC | Hou. 238 14.8 | NYJ 266 | Hou. 1273 | 80 S.D. | 3.2 | Den. 6, Pitt. 6 | Hou. 51.9 | N.E. 2845 | 178 | Clev. 6.4 | NYJ 15 | Hou. 26 | Pitt. 4.6 | NYJ 6.0 | Ind. 14.9 | 1993 | AFC |
| 1994 | NFC | Dall. 248 15.5 | Ariz. 245 | Minn. 1090 | 68 Minn. | 3.1 | Ariz. 7 | Ariz. 50.3 | Dall. 2752 | 172 | Dall. 5.8 | S.F. 15 | Ariz. 23, S.F. 23 | Ariz. 4.9 | T.B. 5.4 | G.B. 18.4 | 1994 | NFC |
| 1994 | AFC | Clev. 204 12.8 | Pitt. 262 | S.D. 1404 | 88 Buff. | 3.4, Pitt. 3.4 | Pitt. 7 | Pitt. 52.6 | Hou. 2795 | 175 | Clev. 5.8 | Pitt. 12 | Mia. 23 | Pitt. 4.3 | Clev. 5.8 | Hou. 17.3 | 1994 | AFC |
| 1995 | NFC | S.F. 258 16.1 | S.F. 264 | S.F. 1061 | 66 S.F. | 3.0 | S.F. 5 | Car. 52.9 | Phil. 2816 | 176 | S.F. 5.1 | Phil. 14 | S.F. 26 | S.F. 4.3 | N.O. 6.5 | T.B. 18.6 | 1995 | NFC |
| 1995 | AFC | K.C. 241 15.1 | Hou. 267 | Pitt. 1321 | 83 K.C. | 3.3 | K.C. 7, Mia. 7 | Hou. 52.3 | NYJ 2740 | 171 | K.C. 5.0 | Buff. 14, Oak. 14 | Pitt. 22 | Pitt. 4.1 | Den. 5.5 | Pitt. 17.5 | 1995 | AFC |

Bold - designates all-time leader

787

# YEARLY PASSING LEADERS

| YEAR | LGUE | RANK NAME | TEAM | YARDS NAME | TEAM | | COMPLETIONS NAME | TEAM | | COMP. PCT. NAME | TEAM | | TOUCHDOWNS NAME | TEAM | | YARDS/ATT. NAME | TEAM | | FEWEST PCT. INT. NAME | TEAM | | YEAR | LGUE |
|---|---|---|---|---|---|---|---|---|---|---|---|---|---|---|---|---|---|---|---|---|---|---|---|
| 1933 | NFL | Friedman | Bkn. | Newman | NY G | 973 | Newman | NY G | 53 | Friedman | Bkn. | 52.5 | Newman | NY G | 9 | Molesworth | ChiB | 8.4 | Monnett | G.B. | 6.5 | 1933 | NFL |
| 1934 | NFL | Herber | G.B. | Herber | G.B. | 799 | Herber | G.B. | 42 | Clark | Det. | 46.9 | Herber | G.B. | 8 | Clark | Det. | 7.8 | Newman | NY G | 5.5 | 1934 | NFL |
| 1935 | NFL | Danowski | NY G | Danowski | NY G | 795 | Danowski | NY G | 57 | Danowski | NY G | 50.4 | Danowski | NY G | 11 | Masterson | ChiB | 10.4 | N/A | | | 1935 | NFL |
| 1936 | NFL | Herber | G.B. | Herber | G.B. | 1239 | Herber | G.B. | 77 | Clark | Det. | 53.5 | Herber | G.B. | 11 | Herber | G.B. | 7.2 | Monnett | G.B. | 3.8 | 1936 | NFL |
| 1937 | NFL | Monnett | G.B. | Baugh | Was. | 1127 | Baugh | Was. | 81 | Monnett | G.B. | 50.7 | Monnett | G.B. | 9 | Masterson | ChiB | 8.5 | Danowski | NY G | 3.7 | 1937 | NFL |
| 1938 | NFL | Monnett | G.B. | Parker | Bkn. | 865 | Danowski | NY G | 70 | Monnett | G.B. | 54.4 | Monnett | G.B. | 9 | Monnett | G.B. | 8.2 | Parker | Bkn. | 4.7 | 1938 | NFL |
| 1939 | NFL | Filchock | Was. | O'Brien | Phi. | 1324 | Hall | Cle. | 106 | Filchock | Was. | 61.8 | Filchock | Was. | 11 | Filchock | Was. | 12.3 | Sloan | Det. | 2.8 | 1939 | NFL |
| 1940 | NFL | Baugh | Was. | Baugh | Was. | 1367 | O'Brien | Phi. | 124 | Baugh | Was. | 62.7 | Baugh | Was. | 12 | Luckman | ChiB | 9.0 | Watkins | Phi. | 3.5 | 1940 | NFL |
| 1941 | NFL | Luckman | ChiB. | Isbell | G.B. | 1479 | Isbell | G.B. | 117 | Luckman | ChiB | 57.1 | Isbell | G.B. | 15 | Luckman | ChiB | 9.9 | Mallouf | ChiC | 4.2 | 1941 | NFL |
| 1942 | NFL | Baugh | Was. | Isbell | G.B. | 2021 | Isbell | G.B. | 146 | Baugh | Was. | 58.7 | Isbell | G.B. | 24 | O'Rourke | ChiB | 10.8 | Baugh | Was. | 4.9 | 1942 | NFL |
| 1943 | NFL | Luckman | ChiB | Luckman | ChiB | 2194 | Baugh | Was. | 133 | Baugh | Was. | 56.2 | Luckman | ChiB | 28 | Luckman | ChiB | 10.9 | Comp. | G.B. | 4.3 | 1943 | NFL |
| 1944 | NFL | Filchock | Was. | Comp | G.B. | 1159 | Filchock | Was. | 84 | Filchock | Was. | 57.1 | Filchock | Was. | 13 | Ronzani | ChiB | 8.0 | Baugh | Was. | 5.5 | 1944 | NFL |
| 1945 | NFL | Baugh | Was. | Luckman | ChiB | 1725 | Baugh | Was. | 128 | Baugh | Was. | 70.3 | Luckman / Waterfield | ChiB / Cle. | 14 / 14 | Waterfield | Cle. | 9.4 | Baugh | Was. | 2.2 | 1945 | NFL |
| 1946 | NFL | Luckman | ChiB | Luckman | ChiB | 1826 | Waterfield | L.A. | 127 | Thompson | Phi. | 55.3 | Waterfield | L.A. | 18 | Luckman | ChiB | 8.0 | Governali | Bos. | 5.2 | 1946 | NFL |
| 1946 | AAFC | Graham | Cle. | Dobbs | Bkn. | 1886 | Dobbs | Bkn. | 135 | O'Rourke | L.A. | 57.7 | Graham | Cle. | 17 | Graham | Cle. | 10.5 | Parker | N.Y. | 2.6 | 1946 | AAFC |
| 1947 | NFL | Baugh | Was. | Baugh | Was. | 2938 | Baugh | Was. | 210 | Baugh | Was. | 59.3 | Baugh | Was. | 25 | Luckman | ChiB | 8.4 | Baugh | Was. | 4.2 | 1947 | NFL |
| 1947 | AAFC | Graham | Cle. | Graham | Cle. | 2753 | Schwenk | Bal. | 168 | Graham | Cle. | 60.6 | Graham | Cle. | 25 | Graham | Cle. | 10.2 | Graham | Cle. | 4.1 | 1947 | AAFC |
| 1948 | NFL | Baugh | Was. | Baugh | Was. | 2599 | Baugh | Was. | 185 | Baugh | Was. | 58.7 | Thompson | Phi. | 25 | LeForce | Det. | 9.0 | Hardy | L.A. | 3.3 | 1948 | NFL |
| 1948 | AAFC | Tittle | Bal. | Graham | Cle. | 2713 | Dobbs | L.A. | 185 | Albert | S.F. | 58.3 | Albert | S.F. | 29 | Tittle | Bal. | 8.7 | Tittle | Bal. | 3.1 | 1948 | AAFC |
| 1949 | NFL | Baugh | Was. | Lujack | ChiB | 2658 | Lujack | ChiB | 162 | Baugh | Was. | 56.9 | Lujack | ChiB | 23 | Lujack | ChiB | 8.7 | Enke | Det. | 3.5 | 1949 | NFL |
| 1949 | AAFC | Graham | Cle. | Graham | Cle. | 2785 | Graham | Cle. | 161 | Ratterman | Buf. | 57.9 | Albert | S.F. | 27 | Graham | Cle. | 9.8 | Graham | Cle. | 3.5 | 1949 | AAFC |
| 1950 | NFL | Van Brocklin | L.A. | Layne | Det. | 2323 | Tittle | Bal. | 161 | Waterfield | L.A. | 57.3 | Ratterman | NY Y | 22 | Van Brocklin | L.A. | 8.8 | Conerly | NY G | 5.3 | 1950 | NFL |
| 1951 | NFL | Graham | Cle. | Layne | Det. | 2403 | Layne | Det. | 152 | Graham | Cle. | 56.6 | Layne | Det. | 26 | Waterfield | L.A. | 8.9 | Thomason | G.B. | 4.1 | 1951 | NFL |
| 1952 | NFL | Rote | G.B. | Graham | Cle. | 2816 | Graham | Cle. | 181 | Van Brocklin | L.A. | 55.1 | Finks / Graham | Pit. / Cle. | 20 / 20 | Van Brocklin | L.A. | 8.5 | Thomason | Phi. | 4.2 | 1952 | NFL |
| 1953 | NFL | Graham | Cle. | Graham | Cle. | 2722 | Blanda | ChiB | 169 | Graham | Cle. | 64.7 | Thomason | Phi. | 21 | Graham | Cle. | 10.6 | Graham | Cle. | 3.5 | 1953 | NFL |
| 1954 | NFL | Layne | Det. | Van Brocklin | L.A. | 2637 | Rote | G.B. | 180 | Graham | Cle. | 59.2 | Burk | Phi. | 23 | Van Brocklin | L.A. | 10.1 | Tittle | S.F. | 3.1 | 1954 | NFL |
| 1955 | NFL | Graham | Cle. | Finks | Pit. | 2270 | Finks | Pit. | 165 | Graham | Cle. | 53.0 | Rote / Tittle | G.B. / S.F. | 17 / 17 | Graham | Cle. | 9.3 | Gilmer | Det. | 3.3 | 1955 | NFL |
| 1956 | NFL | Brown | ChiB | Rote | G.B. | 2203 | Rote | G.B. | 146 | Brown | ChiB | 57.1 | Rote | G.B. | 18 | Brown | ChiB | 9.9 | Conerly | NY G | 4.0 | 1956 | NFL |
| 1957 | NFL | Unitas | Bal. | Unitas | Bal. | 2550 | Tittle | S.F. | 176 | Tittle | S.F. | 63.1 | Unitas | Bal. | 24 | O'Connell | Cle. | 11.2 | Morrall | Pit. | 4.2 | 1957 | NFL |
| 1958 | NFL | Unitas | Bal. | Wade | L.A. | 2875 | Van Brocklin | Phi. | 198 | Brodie | S.F. | 59.9 | Unitas | Bal. | 19 | LeBaron | Was. | 9.4 | Unitas | Bal. | 2.7 | 1958 | NFL |
| 1959 | NFL | Conerly | NY G | Unitas | Bal. | 2899 | Unitas | Bal. | 193 | Wade | L.A. | 58.6 | Unitas | Bal. | 32 | Conerly | NY G | 8.8 | Conerly | NY G | 2.1 | 1959 | NFL |
| 1960 | NFL | Plum | Cle. | Unitas | Bal. | 3099 | Unitas | Bal. | 190 | Plum | Cle. | 60.4 | Unitas | Bal. | 25 | Plum | Cle. | 9.2 | Plum | Cle. | 2.0 | 1960 | NFL |
| 1960 | AFL | Kemp | L.A. | Tripucka | Den. | 3038 | Tripucka | Den. | 248 | Flores | Oak. | 54.0 | Dorow | NY T | 26 | Kemp | L.A. | 7.4 | Songin | Bos. | 3.8 | 1960 | AFL |
| 1961 | NFL | Plum | Cle. | Jurgensen | Phi. | 3723 | Jurgensen | Phi. | 235 | Plum | Cle. | 58.6 | Jurgensen | Phi. | 32 | Brodie | S.F. | 9.1 | Plum | Cle. | 3.3 | 1961 | NFL |
| 1961 | AFL | Blanda | Hou. | Blanda | Hou. | 3330 | Dorow | NY T | 197 | Parilli | Bos. | 52.5 | Blanda | Hou. | 36 | Blanda | Hou. | 9.2 | Songin | Bos. | 4.3 | 1961 | AFL |
| 1962 | NFL | Starr | G.B. | Jurgensen | Phi. | 3261 | Wade | Chi. | 225 | Starr | G.B. | 62.4 | Tittle | NY G | 33 | Jurgensen | Phi. | 8.9 | Starr | G.B. | 3.2 | 1962 | NFL |
| 1962 | AFL | Dawson | Dal. | Tripucka | Den. | 2917 | Tripucka | Den. | 240 | Dawson | Dal. | 61.0 | Dawson | Dal. | 29 | Dawson | Dal. | 8.9 | Parilli | Bos. | 3.2 | 1962 | AFL |
| 1963 | NFL | Tittle | NY G | Unitas | Bal. | 3481 | Unitas | Bal. | 237 | Tittle | NY G | 60.2 | Tittle | NY G | 36 | Tittle | NY G | 8.6 | Unitas | Bal. | 2.9 | 1963 | NFL |
| 1963 | AFL | Rote | S.D. | Blanda | Hou. | 3003 | Blanda | Hou. | 224 | Rote | S.D. | 59.4 | Dawson | Dal. | 26 | Rote | S.D. | 8.7 | Wood | NY T | 5.1 | 1963 | AFL |
| 1964 | NFL | Starr | G.B. | Johnson | St.L. | 3045 | Johnson | St.L. | 223 | Bukich | Chi. | 61.9 | Ryan | Cle. | 25 | Unitas | Bal. | 9.3 | Starr | G.B. | 1.5 | 1964 | NFL |
| 1964 | AFL | Dawson | K.C. | Parilli | Bos. | 3465 | Blanda | Hou. | 262 | Dawson | K.C. | 56.2 | Parilli | Bos. | 31 | Kemp | Buf. | 8.5 | Dawson | K.C. | 5.1 | 1964 | AFL |
| 1965 | NFL | Bukich | ChiB | Brodie | S.F. | 3112 | Brodie | S.F. | 242 | Brodie | S.F. | 61.9 | Brodie | S.F. | 30 | Unitas | Bal. | 9.0 | Bukich | Chi. | 2.9 | 1965 | NFL |
| 1965 | AFL | Dawson | K.C. | Hadl | S.D. | 2798 | Blanda | Hou. | 186 | Dawson | K.C. | 53.4 | Dawson | K.C. | 21 | Hadl | S.D. | 8.0 | Wood | Oak. | 3.8 | 1965 | AFL |
| 1966 | NFL | Starr | G.B. | Jurgensen | Was. | 3209 | Jurgensen | Was. | 254 | Starr | G.B. | 62.2 | Ryan | Cle. | 29 | Starr | G.B. | 9.0 | Starr | G.B. | 1.2 | 1966 | NFL |
| 1966 | AFL | Dawson | K.C. | Namath | NY J | 3379 | Namath | NY J | 232 | Dawson | K.C. | 56.0 | Dawson | K.C. | 26 | Dawson | K.C. | 8.9 | Trull | Hou. | 2.9 | 1966 | AFL |
| 1967 | NFL | Jurgensen | Was. | Jurgensen | Was. | 3747 | Jurgensen | Was. | 288 | Unitas | Bal. | 58.5 | Jurgensen | Was. | 31 | Starr | G.B. | 8.7 | Jurgensen | Was. | 3.2 | 1967 | NFL |
| 1967 | AFL | Lamonica | Oak. | Namath | NY J | 4007 | Namath | NY J | 258 | Dawson | K.C. | 57.7 | Lamonica | Oak. | 30 | Namath | NY J | 8.2 | Lamonica | Oak. | 4.7 | 1967 | AFL |
| 1968 | NFL | Morrall | Bal. | Brodie | S.F. | 3020 | Brodie | S.F. | 234 | Starr | G.B. | 63.7 | Morrall | Bal. | 26 | Starr | G.B. | 9.5 | Munson | Det. | 2.4 | 1968 | NFL |
| 1968 | AFL | Dawson | K.C. | Hadl | S.D. | 3473 | Hadl | S.D. | 208 | Dawson | K.C. | 58.5 | Hadl | S.D. | 27 | Dawson | K.C. | 9.4 | Stofa | Cin. | 2.8 | 1968 | AFL |
| 1969 | NFL | Jurgensen | Was. | Jurgensen | Was. | 3102 | Jurgensen | Was. | 274 | Starr | G.B. | 62.2 | Gabriel | L.A. | 24 | Horn | L.A. | 9.0 | Gabriel | L.A. | 1.8 | 1969 | NFL |
| 1969 | AFL | Cook | Cin. | Lamonica | Oak. | 3302 | Lamonica | Oak. | 221 | Dawson | K.C. | 59.0 | Lamonica | Oak. | 34 | Cook | Cin. | 9.0 | Hadl | S.D. | 3.4 | 1969 | AFL |
| 1970 | NFC | Brodie | S.F. | Brodie | S.F. | 2941 | Brodie | S.F. | 223 | Jurgensen | Was. | 59.9 | Brodie | S.F. | 24 | Morton | Dal. | 8.8 | Brodie | S.F. | 2.7 | 1970 | NFC |
| 1970 | AFC | Lamonica | Oak. | Lamonica | Oak. | 2516 | Lamonica | Oak. | 179 | Griese | Mia. | 58.0 | Hadl / Lamonica | S.D. / Oak. | 22 / 22 | Griese | Mia. | 8.2 | Carter | Cin. | 3.2 | 1970 | AFC |
| 1971 | NFC | Staubach | Dal. | Brodie | S.F. | 2642 | Tarkenton | NY G | 226 | Berry | Atl. | 60.2 | Brodie | S.F. | 18 | Staubach | Dal. | 8.9 | Staubach | Dal. | 1.9 | 1971 | NFC |
| 1971 | AFC | Griese | Mia. | Hadl | S.D. | 3075 | Hadl | S.D. | 233 | Carter | Cin. | 62.2 | Hadl | S.D. | 21 | Dawson | K.C. | 8.3 | Carter | Cin. | 3.2 | 1971 | AFC |
| 1972 | NFC | Tarkenton | Min. | Manning | N.O. | 2781 | Manning | N.O. | 230 | Snead | NY G | 60.3 | Kilmer | Was. | 19 | Berry | Atl. | 7.8 | Tarkenton | Min. | 3.4 | 1972 | NFC |
| 1972 | AFC | Morrall | Mia. | Namath | NY J | 2816 | Hadl | S.D. | 190 | Dawson | K.C. | 57.4 | Namath | NY J | 19 | Morrall | Mia. | 9.1 | Anderson | Cin. | 2.3 | 1972 | AFC |
| 1973 | NFC | Gabriel | Phi. | Gabriel | Phi. | 3219 | Gabriel | Phi. | 270 | Staubach | Dal. | 62.6 | Gabriel / Staubach | Phi. / Dal. | 23 / 23 | Staubach | Dal. | 8.5 | Tarkenton | Min. | 2.6 | 1973 | NFC |
| 1973 | AFC | Anderson | Cin. | Plunkett | N.E. | 2550 | Plunkett | N.E. | 193 | Stabler | Oak. | 62.7 | Johnson | Den. | 20 | Stabler | Oak. | 7.7 | Anderson | Cin. | 3.6 | 1973 | AFC |
| 1974 | NFC | Jurgensen | Was. | Tarkenton | Min. | 2598 | Hart | St.L. | 200 | Jurgensen | Was. | 64.1 | Hart | St.L. | 20 | Harris | L.A. | 7.8 | Hart | St.L. | 2.1 | 1974 | NFC |
| 1974 | AFC | Anderson | Cin. | Anderson | Cin. | 2667 | Anderson | Cin. | 213 | Anderson | Cin. | 64.9 | Stabler | Oak. | 26 | Anderson | Cin. | 8.1 | Anderson | Cin. | 2.0 | 1974 | AFC |
| 1975 | NFC | Tarkenton | Min. | Tarkenton | Min. | 2994 | Tarkenton | Min. | 273 | Tarkenton | Min. | 64.2 | Tarkenton | Min. | 25 | Staubach | Dal. | 7.7 | Tarkenton | Min. | 3.1 | 1975 | NFC |
| 1975 | AFC | Anderson | Cin. | Anderson | Cin. | 3169 | Anderson | Cin. | 228 | Dawson | K.C. | 66.4 | Ferguson | Buf. | 25 | Griese | Mia. | 8.9 | Jones | Bal. | 2.3 | 1975 | AFC |

788

# YEARLY PASSING LEADERS

| YEAR | LGUE | RANK NAME | TEAM | YARDS NAME | TEAM |  | COMPLETIONS NAME | TEAM |  | COMP. PCT. NAME | TEAM |  | TOUCHDOWNS NAME | TEAM |  | YARDS/ATT. NAME | TEAM |  | FEWEST PCT. INT. NAME | TEAM |  | YEAR | LGUE |
|---|---|---|---|---|---|---|---|---|---|---|---|---|---|---|---|---|---|---|---|---|---|---|---|
| 1976 | NFC | Harris | L.A. | Tarkenton | Min. | 2961 | Tarkenton | Min. | 255 | Tarkenton | Min. | 61.9 | Hart | St.L. | 18 | Harris | L.A. | 9.2 | Tarkenton | Min. | 1.9 | 1976 | NFC |
| 1976 | AFC | Stabler | Oak. | Jones | Bal. | 3014 | Fouts | S.D. | 208 | Stabler | Oak. | 66.7 | Stabler | Oak. | 27 | Stabler | Oak. | 9.4 | Ferguson | Buf. | 0.7 | 1976 | AFC |
| 1977 | NFC | Staubach | Dal. | Staubach | Dal. | 2620 | Staubach | Dal. | 210 | Tarkenton | Min. | 60.1 | Jaworski / Staubach | Phi. / Dal. | 18 / 18 | Staubach | Dal. | 7.3 | Staubach | Dal. | 2.5 | 1977 | NFC |
| 1977 | AFC | Griese | Mia. | Ferguson | Buf. | 2803 | Jones | Bal. | 224 | Griese | Mia. | 58.6 | Griese | Mia. | 22 | Bradshaw | Pit. | 8.0 | Jones | Bal. | 2.8 | 1977 | AFC |
| 1978 | AFC | Bradshaw | Pit. | Zom | Sea. | 3283 | Zom | Sea. | 248 | Griese | Mia. | 63.0 | Bradshaw | Pit. | 28 | Bradshaw | Pit. | 7.9 | Morton | Den. | 3.0 | 1978 | AFC |
| 1978 | NFC | Staubach | Dal. | Tarkenton | Min. | 3468 | Tarkenton | Min. | 345 | Manning | N.O. | 61.8 | Staubach / Tarkenton | Dal. / Min. | 25 / 25 | Staubach | Dal. | 7.7 | Manning | N.O. | 3.4 | 1978 | NFC |
| 1979 | AFC | Fouts | S.D. | Fouts | S.D. | 4082 | Fouts | S.D. | 332 | Fouts | S.D. | 62.6 | Grogan / Sipe | N.E. / Cle. | 28 / 28 | Todd | N.Y.J. | 8.0 | Anderson | Cin. | 2.9 | 1979 | AFC |
| 1979 | NFC | Staubach | Dal. | DeBerg | S.F. | 3652 | DeBerg | S.F. | 347 | DeBerg | S.F. | 60.0 | Staubach | Dal. | 27 | Staubach | Dal. | 7.8 | Staubach | Dal. | 2.4 | 1979 | NFC |
| 1980 | AFC | Sipe | Cle. | Fouts | S.D. | 4715 | Fouts | S.D. | 348 | Stabler | Hou. | 64.1 | Fouts / Sipe | S.D. / Cle. | 30 / 30 | Grogan | N.E. | 8.1 | Sipe | Cle. | 2.5 | 1980 | AFC |
| 1980 | NFC | Jaworski | Phi. | Manning | N.O. | 3716 | Manning | N.O. | 309 | Montana | S.F. | 64.5 | Bartkowski | Atl. | 31 | Ferragamo | L.A. | 7.9 | Danielson | Det. | 2.6 | 1980 | NFC |
| 1981 | AFC | Anderson | Cin. | Fouts | S.D. | 4802 | Fouts | S.D. | 360 | Anderson | Cin. | 62.6 | Fouts | S.D. | 33 | Grogan | N.E. | 8.6 | Anderson | Cin. | 2.1 | 1981 | AFC |
| 1981 | NFC | Montana | S.F. | Kramer | Min. | 3912 | Kramer | Min. | 322 | Montana | S.F. | 63.7 | Bartkowski | Atl. | 30 | Hipple | Det. | 8.5 | Montana | S.F. | 2.5 | 1981 | NFC |
| 1982 | NFC | Theismann | Was. | Montana | S.F. | 2613 | Montana | S.F. | 213 | Theismann | Was. | 63.9 | Montana / White | S.F. / Dal. | 17 / 17 | White | Dal. | 8.4 | Lomax | St.L. | 2.9 | 1982 | NFC |
| 1982 | AFC | Anderson | Cin. | Fouts | S.D. | 2883 | Anderson | Cin. | 218 | Anderson | Cin. | 70.6 | Bradshaw / Fouts | Pit. / S.D. | 17 / 17 | Fouts | S.D. | 8.7 | Anderson | Cin. | 2.9 | 1982 | AFC |
| 1983 | NFC | Bartkowski | Atl. | Dickey | G.B. | 4458 | White | Dal. | 334 | Montana | S.F. | 64.5 | Dickey | G.B. | 32 | Dickey | G.B. | 9.2 | Bartkowski | Atl. | 1.2 | 1983 | NFC |
| 1983 | AFC | Marino | Mia. | Kenney | K.C. | 4348 | Kenney | K.C. | 346 | Anderson | Cin. | 66.7 | Ferguson / Sipe | Buf. / Cle. | 26 / 26 | Krieg | Sea. | 8.8 | Marino | Mia. | 2.0 | 1983 | AFC |
| 1984 | NFC | Montana | S.F. | Lomax | St.L. | 4614 | Lomax | St.L. | 345 | Bartkowski | Atl. | 67.3 | Lomax / Montana | St.L. / S.F. | 28 / 28 | Montana | S.F. | 8.4 | Montana | S.F. | 2.3 | 1984 | NFC |
| 1984 | AFC | Marino | Mia. | Marino | Mia. | 5084 | Marino | Mia. | 362 | Marino | Mia. | 64.2 | Marino | Mia. | 48 | Marino | Mia. | 9.0 | Eason | N.E. | 1.9 | 1984 | AFC |
| 1985 | NFC | Montana | S.F. | Simms | NY G | 3829 | Montana | S.F. | 303 | Montana | S.F. | 61.3 | Montana | S.F. | 27 | Simms | NY G | 7.7 | Lomax | St.L. | 2.5 | 1985 | NFC |
| 1985 | AFC | O'Brien | NY J | Marino | Mia. | 4137 | Marino | Mia. | 336 | O'Brien | NY J | 60.9 | Marino | Mia. | 30 | Fouts | S.D. | 8.5 | O'Brien | NY J | 1.6 | 1985 | AFC |
| 1986 | NFC | Kramer | Min. | Schroeder | Was. | 4109 | Schroeder | Was. | 276 | Hipple | Det. | 63.0 | Kramer | Min. | 24 | Kramer | Min. | 8.1 | Jaworski | Phi. | 2.4 | 1986 | NFC |
| 1986 | AFC | Marino | Mia. | Marino | Mia. | 4746 | Marino | Mia. | 378 | O'Brien | NY J | 62.2 | Marino | Mia. | 44 | Esiason | Cin. | 8.4 | Kosar | Cle. | 1.9 | 1986 | AFC |
| 1987 | NFC | Montana | S.F. | Lomax | St.L. | 3387 | Lomax | St.L. | 275 | Montana | S.F. | 66.8 | Montana | S.F. | 31 | Wilson | Min. | 8.0 | DeBerg | T.B. | 2.5 | 1987 | NFC |
| 1987 | AFC | Kosar | Cle. | Esiason | Cin. | 3321 | Marino | Mia. | 263 | Kosar | Cle. | 62.0 | Marino | Mia. | 26 | Elway | Den. | 7.8 | O'Brien | NY J | 2.0 | 1987 | AFC |
| 1988 | NFC | W. Wilson | Min. | Everett | L.A. | 3964 | Everett | L.A. | 308 | W. Wilson | Min. | 61.4 | Everett | L.A. | 31 | W. Wilson | Min. | 8.3 | Simms | NYG | 2.3 | 1988 | NFC |
| 1988 | AFC | Esiason | Cin. | Marino | Mia. | 4434 | Marino | Mia. | 354 | Marino | Mia. | 60.2 | Esiason / Marino | Cin. / Mia. | 28 / 28 | Esiason | Cin. | 9.2 | O'Brien | NYJ | 1.7 | 1988 | AFC |
| 1989 | NFC | Montana | S.F. | Majkowski | G.B. | 4318 | Majkowski | G.B. | 353 | Montana | S.F. | 70.2 | Everett | L.A. | 29 | Montana | S.F. | 9.1 | Miller | Atl. | 1.9 | 1989 | NFC |
| 1989 | AFC | Esiason | Cin. | Marino | Mia. | 3997 | Marino | Mia. | 308 | DeBerg | K.C. | 60.5 | Esiason | Cin. | 28 | Kelly | Buff. | 8.0 | Esiason | Cin. | 2.4 | 1989 | AFC |
| 1990 | NFC | Simms | NYG | Everett | L.A. | 3989 | Montana | S.F. | 321 | Montana | S.F. | 61.7 | Cunningham | Phi. | 30 | Simms | NYG | 7.7 | Simms | NYG | 1.3 | 1990 | NFC |
| 1990 | AFC | Kelly | Buf. | Moon | Hou. | 4689 | Moon | Hou. | 362 | Kelly | Buf. | 63.3 | Moon | Hou. | 33 | Schroeder | Raid. | 8.5 | DeBerg | K.C. | 0.9 | 1990 | AFC |
| 1991 | NFC | Young | S.F. | Rypien | Wash. | 3564 | Everett | L.A. | 277 | Aikman | Dall. | 65.3 | Rypien | Wash. | 28 | Young | S.F. | 9.0 | Hostetler | NYG | 1.4 | 1991 | NFC |
| 1991 | AFC | Kelly | Buf. | Moon | Hou. | 4690 | Moon | Hou. | 404 | Krieg | Sea. | 65.6 | Kelly | Buff. | 33 | Kelly | Buff. | 8.1 | Kosar | Clev. | 1.8 | 1991 | AFC |
| 1992 | NFC | Young | S.F. | Young. | S.F. | 3465 | Aikman / Favre | Dall. / G.B. | 302 / 302 | Young | S.F. | 66.7 | Young | S.F. | 25 | Young | S.F. | 8.6 | Young. | S.F. | 1.7 | 1992 | NFC |
| 1992 | AFC | Moon | Hou. | Marino | Mia. | 4116 | Marino | Mia. | 330 | Carlson | Hou. | 65.6 | Marino | Mia. | 24 | Krieg | K.C. | 7.5 | O'Donnell | Pitt. | 2.9 | 1992 | AFC |
| 1993 | NFC | Young | S.F. | Young | S.F. | 4023 | Favre | G.B. | 318 | Young | S.F. | 68.0 | Young | S.F. | 29 | Young | S.F. | 8.71 | Aikman | Dall. | 1.5 | 1993 | NFC |
| 1993 | AFC | Elway | Den. | Elway | Den. | 4030 | Elway | Den. | 348 | Elway | Den. | 63.2 | Elway | Den. | 25 | Testaverde | Clev. | 7.81 | O'Donnell | Pitt. | 1.4 | 1993 | AFC |
| 1994 | NFC | Young | S.F. | Moon | Minn. | 4264 | Moon | Minn. | 371 | Young | S.F. | 70.3 | Young | S.F. | 35 | Young | S.F. | 8.61 | Young | S.F. | 2.2 | 1994 | NFC |
| 1994 | AFC | Marino | Mia. | Bledsoe | N.E. | 4555 | Bledsoe | N.E. | 400 | Kelly | Buff. | 63.6 | Marino | Mia. | 30 | Hostetler | Raid. | 7.34 | Montana / Mirer | K.C. / Sea. | 1.8 / 1.8 | 1994 | AFC |
| 1995 | NFC | Favre | G.B. | Favre | G.B. | 4413 | Moon | Minn. | 377 | Young | S.F. | 66.9 | Favre | G.B. | 38 | Favre | G.B. | 7.74 | Aikman | Dall. | 1.6 | 1995 | NFC |
| 1995 | AFC | Harbaugh | Ind. | Elway | Den. | 3970 | Blake | Cin. | 326 | Marino | Mia. | 64.1 | Blake | Cin. | 28 | Harbaugh | Ind. | 8.20 | Harbaugh | Ind. | 1.6 | 1995 | AFC |

# YEARLY RUSHING LEADERS

|  |  | ATTEMPTS | | | YARDS | | | AVERAGE YARDS | | | TOUCHDOWNS | | |  |  |
|---|---|---|---|---|---|---|---|---|---|---|---|---|---|---|---|
| YEAR | LGUE | NAME | TEAM | | NAME | TEAM | | NAME | TEAM | | NAME | TEAM | | YEAR | LGUE |
| 1933 | NFL | Jim Musick | Bos. | 173 | Jim Musick | Bos. | 809 | Kink Richards | NY | 6.2 | Glenn Presnell | Det. | 6 | 1933 | NFL |
| 1934 | NFL | Swede Hanson | Phi. | 147 | Beattie Feathers | ChiB | 1004 | Beattie Feathers | ChiB | 9.9 | Dutch Clark | Det. | 8 | 1934 | NFL |
|  |  |  |  |  |  |  |  |  |  |  | Beattie Feathers | ChiB | 8 |  |  |
| 1935 | NFL | Kink Richards | NY G | 149 | Doug Russell | ChiC | 499 | Ernie Caddel | Det. | 5.2 | Ernie Caddel | Det. | 6 | 1935 | NFL |
| 1936 | NFL | Tuffy Leemans | NY G | 206 | Tuffy Leemans | NY G | 830 | Ernie Caddel | Det. | 6.4 | Dutch Clark | Det. | 7 | 1936 | NFL |
| 1937 | NFL | Cliff Battles | Was. | 216 | Cliff Battles | Was. | 874 | Ernie Caddel | Det. | 5.6 | Cliff Battles | Was. | 5 | 1937 | NFL |
|  |  |  |  |  |  |  |  |  |  |  | Dutch Clark | Det. | 5 |  |  |
|  |  |  |  |  |  |  |  |  |  |  | Clarke Hinkle | G.B. | 5 |  |  |
| 1938 | NFL | Whizzer White | Pit. | 152 | Whizzer White | Pit. | 567 | Cecil Isbell | G.B. | 5.2 | Andy Farkas | Was. | 6 | 1938 | NFL |
| 1939 | NFL | Andy Farkas | Was. | 139 | Bill Osmanski | ChiB | 699 | Joe Maniaci | ChiB | 7.1 | Johnny Drake | Cle. | 9 | 1939 | NFL |
| 1940 | NFL | Whizzer White | Det. | 146 | Whizzer White | Det. | 514 | Banks McFadden | Bkn. | 6.3 | Johnny Drake | Cle. | 9 | 1940 | NFL |
| 1941 | NFL | Clarke Hinkle | G.B. | 129 | Pug Manders | Bkn. | 486 | George McAfee | ChiB | 7.3 | Hugh Gallameau | ChiB | 8 | 1941 | NFL |
| 1942 | NFL | Bill Dudley | Pit. | 162 | Bill Dudley | Pit. | 696 | Frank Maznicki | ChiB | 6.4 | Gary Famiglietti | ChiB | 8 | 1942 | NFL |
| 1943 | NFL | Bill Paschal | NY G | 147 | Bill Paschal | NY G | 572 | Ward Cuff | NY G | 6.5 | Bill Paschal | NY G | 10 | 1943 | NFL |
| 1944 | NFL | Bill Paschal | NY G | 196 | Bill Paschal | NY G | 737 | Al Grygo | ChiB | 6.1 | Bill Paschal | NY G | 9 | 1944 | NFL |
| 1945 | NFL | Frank Akins | Was. | 147 | Steve Van Buren | Phi. | 832 | Fred Gehrke | Cle. | 6.3 | Steve Van Buren | Phi. | 15 | 1945 | NFL |
| 1946 | NFL | Bill Dudley | Pit. | 146 | Bill Dudley | Pit. | 604 | Elmer Angsman | ChiC | 6.8 | Ted Fritsch | G.B. | 9 | 1946 | NFL |
| 1946 | AAFC | Spec Sanders | N.Y. | 140 | Spec Sanders | N.Y. | 709 | Chuck Fenenbock | L.A. | 8.4 | Len Eshmont | S.F. | 6 | 1946 | AAFC |
|  |  |  |  |  |  |  |  |  |  |  | Don Greenwood | Cle. | 6 |  |  |
|  |  |  |  |  |  |  |  |  |  |  | John Kimbrough | L.A. | 6 |  |  |
|  |  |  |  |  |  |  |  |  |  |  | Spec Sanders | N.Y. | 6 |  |  |
| 1947 | NFL | Steve Van Buren | Phi. | 217 | Steve Van Buren | Phi. | 1008 | Kenny Washington | L.A. | 7.4 | Steve Van Buren | Phi. | 13 | 1947 | NFL |
| 1947 | AAFC | Spec Sanders | N.Y. | 231 | Spec Sanders | N.Y. | 1432 | Special Delivery Jones | Cle. | 7.0 | Spec Sanders | N.Y. | 18 | 1947 | AAFC |
| 1948 | NFL | Steve Van Buren | Phi. | 201 | Steve Van Buren | Phi. | 945 | Charlie Trippi | ChiC | 5.4 | Steve Van Buren | Phi. | 10 | 1948 | NFL |
| 1948 | AAFC | Spec Sanders | N.Y. | 169 | Marion Motley | Cle. | 964 | Joe Perry | S.F. | 7.3 | Chet Mutryn | Buf. | 10 | 1948 | AAFC |
|  |  |  |  |  |  |  |  |  |  |  | Joe Perry | S.F. | 10 |  |  |
| 1949 | NFL | Steve Van Buren | Phi. | 263 | Steve Van Buren | Phi. | 1146 | Bosh Pritchard | Phi. | 6.0 | Steve Van Buren | Phi. | 11 | 1949 | NFL |
| 1949 | AAFC | Bob Hoernschemeyer | Chi. | 133 | Joe Perry | S.F. | 783 | Frankie Albert | S.F. | 7.1 | Marion Motley | Cle. | 8 | 1949 | AAFC |
|  |  |  |  |  |  |  |  |  |  |  | Joe Perry | S.F. | 8 |  |  |
| 1950 | NFL | Joe Geri | Pit. | 188 | Marion Motley | Cle. | 810 | Johnny Lujack | ChiB | 6.3 | Johnny Lujack | ChiB | 11 | 1950 | NFL |
|  |  | Steve Van Buren | Phi. | 188 |  |  |  |  |  |  |  |  |  |  |  |
| 1951 | NFL | Eddie Price | NY G | 271 | Eddie Price | NY G | 971 | Tobin Rote | G.B. | 6.9 | Rob Goode | Was. | 9 | 1951 | NFL |
| 1952 | NFL | Eddie Price | NY G | 183 | Dan Towler | L.A. | 894 | Hugh McElhenny | S.F. | 7.0 | Dan Towler | L.A. | 10 | 1952 | NFL |
| 1953 | NFL | Joe Perry | S.F. | 192 | Joe Perry | S.F. | 1018 | Skeets Quinlan | L.A. | 7.3 | Joe Perry | S.F. | 10 | 1953 | NFL |
| 1954 | NFL | Joe Perry | S.F. | 173 | Joe Perry | S.F. | 1049 | Hugh McElhenny | S.F. | 8.0 | Dan Towler | L.A. | 11 | 1954 | NFL |
| 1955 | NFL | Alan Ameche | Bal. | 213 | Alan Ameche | Bal. | 961 | Rick Casares | ChiB | 5.4 | Alan Ameche | Bal. | 9 | 1955 | NFL |
| 1956 | NFL | Rick Casares | ChiB | 234 | Rick Casares | ChiB | 1126 | Lenny Moore | Bal. | 7.5 | Rick Casares | ChiB | 12 | 1956 | NFL |
| 1957 | NFL | Rick Casares | ChiB | 204 | Jimmy Brown | Cle. | 942 | Lenny Moore | Bal. | 5.0 | Jimmy Brown | Cle. | 9 | 1957 | NFL |
| 1958 | NFL | Jimmy Brown | Cle. | 257 | Jimmy Brown | Cle. | 1527 | Lenny Moore | Bal. | 7.3 | Jimmy Brown | Cle. | 17 | 1958 | NFL |
| 1959 | NFL | Jimmy Brown | Cle. | 290 | Jimmy Brown | Cle. | 1329 | Johnny Olszewski | Was. | 6.6 | Jimmy Brown | Cle. | 14 | 1959 | NFL |
| 1960 | NFL | Jim Taylor | G.B. | 230 | Jimmy Brown | Cle. | 1257 | John David Crow | St.L. | 5.9 | Paul Hornung | G.B. | 13 | 1960 | NFL |
| 1960 | AFL | Abner Haynes | Dal. | 156 | Abner Haynes | Dal. | 875 | Paul Lowe | L.A. | 6.3 | Abner Haynes | Dal. | 9 | 1960 | AFL |
|  |  |  |  |  |  |  |  |  |  |  | Paul Lowe | L.A. | 9 |  |  |
| 1961 | NFL | Jimmy Brown | Cle. | 305 | Jimmy Brown | Cle. | 1408 | Lenny Moore | Bal. | 7.0 | Jim Taylor | G.B. | 15 | 1961 | NFL |
| 1961 | AFL | Bill Mathis | NY T | 202 | Billy Cannon | Hou. | 948 | Jack Spikes | Dal. | 8.6 | Abner Haynes | Dal. | 9 | 1961 | AFL |
|  |  |  |  |  |  |  |  |  |  |  | Paul Lowe | L.A. | 9 |  |  |
| 1962 | NFL | Jim Taylor | G.B. | 272 | Jim Taylor | G.B. | 1474 | Amos Marsh | Dal. | 5.6 | Jim Taylor | G.B. | 19 | 1962 | NFL |
| 1962 | AFL | Charley Tolar | Hou. | 244 | Cookie Gilchrist | Buf. | 1096 | Len Dawson | Dal. | 6.6 | Cookie Gilchrist | Buf. | 13 | 1962 | AFL |
|  |  |  |  |  |  |  |  |  |  |  | Abner Haynes | Dal. | 13 |  |  |
| 1963 | NFL | Jimmy Brown | Cle. | 291 | Jimmy Brown | Cle. | 1863 | Jimmy Brown | Cle. | 6.4 | Jimmy Brown | Cle. | 12 | 1963 | NFL |
| 1963 | AFL | Cookie Gilchrist | Buf. | 232 | Clem Daniels | Oak. | 1099 | Keith Lincoln | S.D. | 6.5 | Cookie Gilchrist | Buf. | 12 | 1963 | AFL |
| 1964 | NFL | Jimmy Brown | Cle. | 280 | Jimmy Brown | Cle. | 1446 | Jimmy Brown | Cle. | 5.2 | Lenny Moore | Bal. | 16 | 1964 | NFL |
| 1964 | AFL | Cookie Gilchrist | Buf. | 230 | Cookie Gilchrist | Buf. | 981 | Mack Lee Hill | K.C. | 5.5 | Sid Banks | Hou. | 6 | 1964 | AFL |
|  |  |  |  |  |  |  |  |  |  |  | Cookie Gilchrist | Buf. | 6 |  |  |
|  |  |  |  |  |  |  |  |  |  |  | Daryle Lamonica | Buf. | 6 |  |  |
| 1965 | NFL | Jimmy Brown | Cle. | 289 | Jimmy Brown | Cle. | 1544 | Timmy Brown | Phi. | 5.4 | Jimmy Brown | Cle. | 17 | 1965 | NFL |
| 1965 | AFL | Cookie Gilchrist | Buf. | 252 | Paul Lowe | S.D. | 1121 | Paul Lowe | S.D. | 5.1 | Paul Lowe | S.D. | 7 | 1965 | AFL |
| 1966 | NFL | Bill Brown | Min. | 251 | Gale Sayers | Chi. | 1231 | Leroy Kelly | Cle. | 5.5 | Leroy Kelly | Cle. | 15 | 1966 | NFL |
| 1966 | AFL | Jim Nance | Bos. | 299 | Jim Nance | Bos. | 1458 | Mike Garrett | K.C. | 5.5 | Jim Nance | Bos. | 11 | 1966 | AFL |
| 1967 | NFL | Leroy Kelly | Cle. | 235 | Leroy Kelly | Cle. | 1205 | Leroy Kelly | Cle. | 5.1 | Leroy Kelly | Cle. | 11 | 1967 | NFL |
| 1967 | AFL | Jim Nance | Bos. | 269 | Jim Nance | Bos. | 1216 | Brad Hubbert | S.D. | 5.5 | Emerson Boozer | NY J | 10 | 1967 | AFL |
| 1968 | NFL | Leroy Kelly | Cle. | 248 | Leroy Kelly | Cle. | 1239 | Gale Sayers | Chi. | 6.2 | Leroy Kelly | Cle. | 16 | 1968 | NFL |
| 1968 | AFL | Paul Robinson | Cin. | 238 | Paul Robinson | Cin. | 1023 | Dickie Post | S.D. | 5.0 | Paul Robinson | Cin. | 8 | 1968 | AFL |
| 1969 | NFL | Gale Sayers | Chi. | 236 | Gale Sayers | Chi. | 1032 | Tony Baker | N.O. | 4.8 | Tom Matte | Bal. | 11 | 1969 | NFL |
| 1969 | AFL | Jim Nance | Bos. | 193 | Dickie Post | S.D. | 873 | Carl Garrett | Bos. | 5.0 | Jim Kiick | Mia. | 9 | 1969 | AFL |
| 1970 | NFC | Ron Johnson | NY G | 263 | Larry Brown | Was. | 1125 | Duane Thomas | Dal. | 5.3 | MacArthur Lane | St.L. | 11 | 1970 | NFC |
| 1970 | AFC | Floyd Little | Den. | 209 | Floyd Little | Den. | 901 | John Fuqua | Pit. | 5.0 | John Fuqua | Pit. | 7 | 1970 | AFC |
|  |  |  |  |  |  |  |  |  |  |  | Jim Nance | Bos. | 7 |  |  |
|  |  |  |  |  |  |  |  |  |  |  | Bo Scott | Cle. | 7 |  |  |
| 1971 | NFC | Larry Brown | Was. | 253 | John Brockington | G.B. | 1105 | John Brockington | G.B. | 5.1 | Duane Thomas | Dal. | 11 | 1971 | NFC |
| 1971 | AFC | Floyd Little | Den. | 284 | Floyd Little | Den. | 1133 | Larry Csonka | Mia. | 5.4 | Leroy Kelly | Cle. | 10 | 1971 | AFC |
| 1972 | NFC | Ron Johnson | NY G | 298 | Larry Brown | Was. | 1216 | Bobby Douglass | Chi. | 6.9 | Ron Johnson | NY G | 9 | 1972 | NFC |
|  |  |  |  |  |  |  |  |  |  |  | Greg Landry | Det. | 9 |  |  |
| 1972 | AFC | O.J. Simpson | Buf. | 292 | O.J. Simpson | Buf. | 1251 | Franco Harris | Pit. | 5.6 | Mercury Morris | Mia. | 12 | 1972 | AFC |
| 1973 | NFC | Calvin Hill | Dal. | 273 | John Brockington | G.B. | 1144 | Bobby Douglass | Chi. | 5.6 | Donny Anderson | St.L. | 10 | 1973 | NFC |
| 1973 | AFC | O.J. Simpson | Buf. | 332 | O.J. Simpson | Buf. | 2003 | Mercury Morris | Mia. | 6.4 | Floyd Little | Den. | 12 | 1973 | AFC |
|  |  |  |  |  |  |  |  |  |  |  | O.J. Simpson | Buf. | 12 |  |  |
| 1974 | NFC | John Brockington | G.B. | 266 | Lawrence McCutcheon | L.A. | 1109 | Terry Metcalf | St.L. | 4.7 | Tom Sullivan | Phi. | 11 | 1974 | NFC |
| 1974 | AFC | O.J. Simpson | Buf. | 270 | Otis Armstrong | Den. | 1407 | Otis Armstrong | Den. | 5.3 | Jon Keyworth | Den. | 10 | 1974 | AFC |
| 1975 | NFC | Chuck Foreman | Min. | 280 | Jim Otis | St.L. | 1076 | Del Williams | S.F. | 5.4 | Chuck Foreman | Min. | 13 | 1975 | NFC |
| 1975 | AFC | O.J. Simpson | Buf. | 329 | O.J. Simpson | Oak. | 1817 | O.J. Simpson | Oak. | 5.5 | Pete Banaszak | Oak. | 16 | 1975 | AFC |
|  |  |  |  |  |  |  |  |  |  |  | O.J. Simpson | Buf. | 16 |  |  |
| 1976 | NFC | Walter Payton | Chi. | 311 | Walter Payton | Chi. | 1390 | Delvin Williams | S.F. | 4.9 | Chuck Foreman | Min. | 13 | 1976 | NFC |
|  |  |  |  |  |  |  |  |  |  |  | Walter Payton | Chi. | 13 |  |  |
| 1976 | AFC | O.J. Simpson | Buf. | 290 | O.J. Simpson | Buf. | 1503 | Don Calhoun | N.E. | 5.6 | Franco Harris | Pit. | 14 | 1976 | AFC |
| 1977 | NFC | Walter Payton | Chi. | 339 | Walter Payton | Chi. | 1852 | Walter Payton | Chi. | 5.5 | Walter Payton | Chi. | 14 | 1977 | NFC |
| 1977 | AFC | Mark van Eeghen | Oak. | 324 | Mark van Eeghen | Oak. | 1273 | Benny Malone | Mia. | 4.8 | Franco Harris | Pit. | 11 | 1977 | AFC |
| 1978 | AFC | Franco Harris | Pit. | 310 | Earl Campbell | Hou. | 1450 | Ted McKnight | K.C. | 6.0 | David Sims | Sea. | 14 | 1978 | AFC |
| 1978 | NFC | Walter Payton | Chi. | 333 | Walter Payton | Chi. | 1395 | Wilbert Montgomery | Phi. | 4.7 | Terdell Middleton | G.B. | 11 | 1978 | NFC |
|  |  |  |  |  |  |  |  |  |  |  | Walter Payton | Chi. | 11 |  |  |
| 1979 | AFC | Earl Campbell | Hou. | 368 | Earl Campbell | Hou. | 1697 | Sidney Thornton | Pit. | 5.0 | Earl Campbell | Hou. | 19 | 1979 | AFC |
| 1979 | NFC | Walter Payton | Chi. | 369 | Walter Payton | Chi. | 1610 | Wendell Tyler | L.A. | 5.1 | Walter Payton | Chi. | 14 | 1979 | NFC |

# YEARLY RUSHING LEADERS

| | | ATTEMPTS | | | YARDS | | | AVERAGE YARDS | | | TOUCHDOWNS | | | | |
|---|---|---|---|---|---|---|---|---|---|---|---|---|---|---|---|
| YEAR | LGUE | NAME | TEAM | | NAME | TEAM | | NAME | TEAM | | NAME | TEAM | | YEAR | LGUE |
| 1980 | AFC | Earl Campbell | Hou. | 373 | Earl Campbell | Hou. | 1934 | Earl Campbell | Hou. | 5.2 | Earl Campbell | Hou. | 13 | 1980 | AFC |
| 1980 | NFC | Walter Payton | Chi. | 317 | Walter Payton | Chi. | 1460 | Dexter Bussey | Det. | 5.0 | Billy Sims | Det. | 13 | 1980 | NFC |
| 1981 | AFC | Earl Campbell | Hou. | 361 | Earl Campbell | Hou. | 1376 | Tony Nathan | Mia. | 5.3 | Chuck Muncie | N.O. | 19 | 1981 | AFC |
| 1981 | NFC | George Rogers | N.O. | 378 | George Rogers | N.O. | 1674 | Wilbert Montgomery | Phi. | 4.9 | John Riggins | Was. | 13 | 1981 | NFC |
| | | | | | | | | | | | George Rogers | N.O. | 13 | | |
| | | | | | | | | | | | Billy Sims | Det. | 13 | | |
| 1982 | AFC | Andra Franklin | Mia. | 177 | Freeman McNeil | NY J | 786 | Freeman McNeil | NY J | 5.2 | Marcus Allen | Raid. | 11 | 1982 | AFC |
| 1982 | NFC | Tony Dorsett | Dal. | 177 | Tony Dorsett | Dal. | 745 | Wilbert Montgomery | Phi. | 4.5 | Eddie Lee Ivery | G.B. | 9 | 1982 | NFC |
| | | John Riggins | Was. | 177 | | | | | | | Wendell Tyler | L.A. | 9 | | |
| 1983 | AFC | Curt Warner | Sea. | 335 | Curt Warner | Sea. | 1449 | Mosi Tatupu | N.E. | 5.5 | Pete Johnson | Cin. | 24 | 1983 | AFC |
| 1983 | NFC | Eric Dickerson | L.A. | 390 | Eric Dickerson | L.A. | 1806 | Gerry Ellis | G.B. | 5.3 | John Riggins | Was. | 24 | 1983 | NFC |
| 1984 | AFC | Earnest Jackson | S.D. | 296 | Earnest Jackson | S.D. | 1179 | Joe Carter | Mia. | 5.0 | Marcus Allen | Raid. | 13 | 1984 | AFC |
| | | Sammy Winder | Den. | 296 | | | | | | | | | | | |
| 1984 | NFC | James Wilder | T.B. | 407 | Eric Dickerson | L.A. | 2105 | Hokie Gajan | N.O. | 6.0 | Eric Dickerson | L.A. | 14 | 1984 | NFC |
| | | | | | | | | | | | John Riggins | Was. | 14 | | |
| 1985 | AFC | Marcus Allen | Raid. | 380 | Marcus Allen | Raid. | 1759 | George Wonsley | Ind. | 5.2 | Marcus Allen | Raid. | 11 | 1985 | AFC |
| | | | | | | | | | | | Ron Davenport | Mia. | 11 | | |
| 1985 | NFC | Gerald Riggs | Atl. | 397 | Gerald Riggs | Atl. | 1719 | Stump Mitchell | St.L. | 5.5 | Joe Morris | NY G | 21 | 1985 | NFC |
| 1986 | AFC | Curt Warner | Sea. | 319 | Curt Warner | Sea. | 1481 | James Brooks | Cin. | 5.3 | Curt Warner | Sea. | 13 | 1986 | AFC |
| 1986 | NFC | Eric Dickerson | L.A. | 404 | Eric Dickerson | L.A. | 1821 | Herschel Walker | Dal. | 4.9 | George Rogers | Was. | 18 | 1986 | NFC |
| 1987 | AFC | Eric Dickerson | L.A.-Ind. | 283 | Eric Dickerson | L.A.-Ind. | 1288 | Eric Dickerson | L.A.-Ind. | 4.6 | Johnny Hector | NY J | 11 | 1987 | AFC |
| 1987 | NFC | Charles White | L.A. | 324 | Charles White | L.A. | 1374 | Darrin Nelson | Min. | 4.9 | Charles White | L.A. | 11 | 1987 | NFC |
| 1988 | AFC | Eric Dickerson | Ind. | 388 | Eric Dickerson | Ind. | 1659 | Ickey Woods | Cin. | 5.3 | Ickey Woods | Cin. | 15 | 1988 | AFC |
| 1988 | NFC | Herschel Walker | Dal. | 361 | Herschel Walker | Dal. | 1514 | Randall Cunningham | Phil. | 6.7 | Greg Bell | L.A. | 16 | 1988 | NFC |
| 1989 | NFC | Dalton Hilliard | N.O. | 344 | Barry Sanders | Det. | 1470 | Randall Cunningham | Phil. | 6.0 | Greg Bell | L.A. Rams | 15 | 1989 | NFC |
| 1989 | AFC | Christian Okoye | K.C. | 370 | Christian Okoye | K.C. | 1480 | James Brooks | Cin. | 5.6 | Christian Okoye | K.C. | 12 | 1989 | AFC |
| 1990 | NFC | Earnest Byner | Was. | 297 | Barry Sanders | Det. | 1304 | Randall Cunningham | Phil. | 8.0 | Cleveland Gary | L.A. | 14 | 1990 | NFC |
| 1990 | AFC | Bobby Humphrey | Den. | 288 | Thurman Thomas | Buf. | 1297 | Bo Jackson | Raid. | 5.6 | Derrick Fenner | Sea. | 14 | 1990 | NFC |
| 1991 | NFC | Emmitt Smith | Dall. | 365 | Emmitt Smith | Dall. | 1563 | Terry Allen | Minn. | 4.7 | Barry Sanders | Det. | 16 | 1991 | NFC |
| 1991 | AFC | Thurman Thomas | Buff. | 288 | Thurman Thomas | Buff. | 1407 | Thurman Thomas | Buff. | 4.9 | Brad Baxter | NYJ | 11 | 1991 | AFC |
| 1992 | NFC | Emmitt Smith | Dall. | 373 | Emmitt Smith | Dall. | 1713 | Heath Sherman | Phil. | 5.2 | Emmitt Smith | Dall. | 18 | 1992 | NFC |
| 1992 | AFC | Barry Foster | Pitt. | 390 | Barry Foster | Pitt. | 1690 | Thurman Thomas | Buff. | 4.8 | Barry Foster | Pitt. | 11 | 1992 | AFC |
| 1993 | NFC | Jerome Bettis | L.A. | 294 | Emmitt Smith | Dall. | 1486 | Steve Young | S.F. | 5.9 | Ricky Watters | S.F. | 10 | 1993 | NFC |
| 1993 | AFC | Thurman Thomas | Buff. | 355 | Thurman Thomas | Buff. | 1315 | Gary Brown | Hou. | 5.1 | Marcus Allen | K.C. | 12 | 1993 | AFC |
| 1994 | NFC | Emmitt Smith | Dall. | 368 | Barry Sanders | Det. | 1883 | Barry Sanders | Det. | 5.7 | Emmitt Smith | Dall. | 21 | 1994 | NFC |
| 1994 | AFC | Natrone Means | S.D. | 343 | Chris Warren | Sea. | 1545 | Chris Warren | Sea. | 4.6 | Natrone Means | S.D. | 12 | 1994 | AFC |
| 1995 | NFC | Emmitt Smith | Dall. | 377 | Emmitt Smith | Dall. | 1773 | Charlie Garner | Phil. | 5.4 | Emmitt Smith | Dall. | 25 | 1995 | NFC |
| 1995 | AFC | Curtis Martin | N.E. | 368 | Curtis Martin | N.E. | 1487 | Terrell Davis | Den. | 4.7 | Chris Warren | Sea. | 15 | 1995 | AFC |

# YEARLY LEADERS

## RECEIVING

### AVERAGE

| | | RECEPTIONS | | | YARDS | | | YARDS | | | TOUCHDOWNS | | | INTERCEPTIONS | | | | |
|---|---|---|---|---|---|---|---|---|---|---|---|---|---|---|---|---|---|---|
| YEAR | LGUE | NAME | TEAM | | NAME | TEAM | | NAME | TEAM | | NAME | TEAM | | NAME | TEAM | | YEAR | LGUE |
| 1933 | NFL | Shipwreck Kelly | Bkn. | 22 | Paul Moss | Pit. | 383 | Paul Moss | Pit. | 29.5 | 5 tied with 3 each | | | | | | 1933 | NFL |
| 1934 | NFL | Red Badgro | NY G | 20 | Harry Ebding | Det. | 257 | Harry Ebding | Det. | 28.6 | Bill Hewitt | ChiB | 5 | | | | 1934 | NFL |
| 1935 | NFL | Tod Goodwin | NY G | 26 | Charley Malone | Bos. | 433 | Joe Carter | Phi. | 23.6 | Don Hutson | G.B. | 7 | | | | 1935 | NFL |
| 1936 | NFL | Don Hutson | G.B. | 34 | Don Hutson | G.B. | 526 | Bill Hewitt | ChiB | 23.9 | Don Hutson | G.B. | 8 | | | | 1936 | NFL |
| 1937 | NFL | Don Hutson | G.B. | 41 | Gaynell Tinsley | ChiC | 675 | Jeff Barrett | Bkn. | 23.1 | Don Hutson | G.B. | 7 | | | | 1937 | NFL |
| 1938 | NFL | Gaynell Tinsley | ChiC | 41 | Don Hutson | G.B. | 548 | Jim Benton | Cle. | 19.9 | Don Hutson | G.B. | 9 | | | | 1938 | NFL |
| 1939 | NFL | Don Hutson | G.B. | 34 | Don Hutson | G.B. | 846 | Andy Farkas | Was. | 27.3 | Jim Benton | Cle. | 7 | | | | 1939 | NFL |
| 1940 | NFL | Don Looney | Phi. | 58 | Don Looney | Phi. | 707 | Paul McDonough | Cle. | 26.3 | Don Hutson | G.B. | 7 | Don Hutson<br>Ace Parker<br>Rip Ryan | G.B.<br>Bkn.<br>Det. | 6<br>6<br>6 | 1940 | NFL |
| 1941 | NFL | Don Hutson | G.B. | 58 | Don Hutson | G.B. | 738 | Ken Kavanaugh | ChiB | 28.5 | Don Hutson | G.B. | 10 | Marshall Goldberg<br>Art Jones | ChiC<br>Pit. | 7<br>7 | 1941 | NFL |
| 1942 | NFL | Don Hutson | G.B. | 74 | Don Hutson | G.B. | 1211 | Ray McLean | ChiB | 30.1 | Don Hutson | G.B. | 17 | Bulldog Turner | ChiB | 8 | 1942 | NFL |
| 1943 | NFL | Don Hutson | G.B. | 47 | Don Hutson | G.B. | 776 | Tony Bova | P-P | 24.6 | Don Hutson | G.B. | 11 | Sammy Baugh | Was. | 11 | 1943 | NFL |
| 1944 | NFL | Don Hutson | G.B. | 58 | Don Hutson | G.B. | 866 | Mel Bleeker | Phi. | 37.4 | Don Hutson | G.B. | 9 | Howie Livingston | NY G | 9 | 1944 | NFL |
| 1945 | NFL | Don Hutson | G.B. | 47 | Jim Benton | Cle. | 1067 | Frank Liebel | NY G | 27.0 | Frank Liebel | NY G | 10 | Roy Zimmerman | Phi. | 7 | 1945 | NFL |
| 1946 | NFL | Jim Benton | L.A. | 63 | Jim Benton | L.A. | 981 | Bill Dewell | ChiC | 23.8 | Bill Dewell | ChiC | 7 | Bill Dudley | Pit. | 10 | 1946 | NFL |
| 1946 | AAFC | Alyn Beals<br>Dante Lavelli | S.F.<br>Cle. | 40<br>40 | Dante Lavelli | Cle. | 843 | Jim McCarthy | Bkn. | 26.9 | Alyn Beals | S.F. | 10 | Tom Colella | Cle. | 10 | 1946 | AAFC |
| 1947 | NFL | Jim Keane | ChiB | 64 | Mal Kutner | ChiC | 944 | Dan Currivan | Bos. | 32.6 | Ken Kavanaugh | ChiB | 13 | Frank Reagan<br>Frank Seno | NY G<br>Bos. | 10<br>10 | 1947 | NFL |
| 1947 | AAFC | Mac Speedie | Cle. | 67 | Mac Speedie | Cle. | 1146 | Crazy Legs Hirsch | Chi. | 28.2 | Alyn Beals | S.F. | 10 | Tom Colella<br>Len Eshmont<br>Bill Killagher | Cle.<br>S.F.<br>Chi. | 6<br>6<br>6 | 1947 | AAFC |
| 1948 | NFL | Tom Fears | L.A. | 51 | Mal Kutner | ChiC | 943 | Frank Seno | Bos. | 24.8 | Mal Kutner | ChiC | 14 | Dan Sandifer | Was. | 13 | 1948 | NFL |
| 1948 | AAFC | Mac Speedie | Cle. | 58 | Billy Hillenbrand | Bal. | 970 | John North | Bal. | 26.0 | Alyn Beals | S.F. | 14 | Otto Schnellbacher | N.Y. | 11 | 1948 | AAFC |
| 1949 | NFL | Tom Fears | L.A. | 77 | Bob Mann | Det. | 1014 | Elbie Nickel | Pit. | 24.3 | Tom Fears<br>Ken Kavanaugh<br>Hugh Taylor | L.A.<br>ChiB<br>Was. | 9<br>9<br>9 | Bob Nussbaumer | ChiC | 12 | 1949 | NFL |
| 1949 | AAFC | Mac Speedie | Cle. | 62 | Mac Speedie | Cle. | 1028 | Bill Boedecker | Cle. | 33.7 | Alyn Beals | S.F. | 12 | Jim Cason | S.F. | 9 | 1949 | AAFC |
| 1950 | NFL | Tom Fears | L.A. | 84 | Tom Fears | L.A. | 1116 | Hugh Taylor | Was. | 21.4 | Bob Shaw | ChiC | 12 | Spec Sanders | NY Y | 13 | 1950 | NFL |
| 1951 | NFL | Crazy Legs Hirsch | L.A. | 66 | Crazy Legs Hirsch | L.A. | 1495 | Crazy Legs Hirsch | L.A. | 22.7 | Crazy Legs Hirsch | L.A. | 17 | Otto Schnellbacher | NY G | 11 | 1951 | NFL |
| 1952 | NFL | Mac Speedie | Cle. | 62 | Billy Howton | G.B. | 1231 | Hugh Taylor | Was. | 23.4 | Cloyce Box | Det. | 15 | Night Train Lane | L.A. | 14 | 1952 | NFL |
| 1953 | NFL | Pete Pihos | Phi. | 63 | Pete Pihos | Phi. | 1049 | Bob Boyd | L.A. | 22.8 | Pete Pihos<br>Billy Wilson | Phi.<br>S.F. | 10<br>10 | Jack Christiansen | Det. | 12 | 1953 | NFL |
| 1954 | NFL | Pete Pihos | Phi. | 60 | Bob Boyd | L.A. | 1212 | Harlon Hill | ChiB | 25.0 | Harlon Hill | ChiB | 12 | Night Train Lane | ChiC | 10 | 1954 | NFL |
| 1955 | NFL | Pete Pihos | Phi. | 62 | Pete Pihos | Phi. | 864 | Ray Renfro | Cle. | 20.8 | Harlon Hill | ChiB | 9 | Will Sherman | L.A. | 11 | 1955 | NFL |
| 1956 | NFL | Billy Wilson | S.F. | 60 | Billy Howton | G.B. | 1188 | Harlon Hill | ChiB | 24.0 | Billy Howton | G.B. | 12 | Linden Crow | ChiC | 11 | 1956 | NFL |
| 1957 | NFL | Billy Wilson | S.F. | 52 | Ray Berry | Bal. | 800 | Ray Renfro | Cle. | 28.0 | Jim Mutscheller | Bal. | 8 | Jack Butler<br>Jack Christiansen<br>Milt Davis | Pit.<br>Det.<br>Bal. | 10<br>10<br>10 | 1957 | NFL |
| 1958 | NFL | Ray Berry<br>Pete Retzlaff | Bal.<br>Phi. | 56<br>56 | Del Shofner | L.A. | 1097 | Jimmy Orr | Pit. | 27.6 | Ray Berry<br>Tommy McDonald | Bal.<br>Phi. | 9<br>9 | Jimmy Patton | NY G | 11 | 1958 | NFL |
| 1959 | NFL | Ray Berry | Bal. | 66 | Ray Berry | Bal. | 959 | Max McGee | G.B. | 23.2 | Ray Berry | Bal. | 14 | Milt Davis<br>Dean Derby<br>Don Shinnick | Bal.<br>Pit.<br>Bal. | 7<br>7<br>7 | 1959 | NFL |
| 1960 | NFL | Ray Berry | Bal. | 74 | Ray Berry | Bal. | 1298 | Buddy Dial | Pit. | 24.3 | Sonny Randle | St.L. | 15 | Dave Baker<br>Jerry Norton | S.F.<br>St.L. | 10<br>10 | 1960 | NFL |
| 1960 | AFL | Lionel Taylor | Den. | 92 | Bill Groman | Hou. | 1473 | Bill Groman | Hou. | 20.5 | Art Powell | NY T | 14 | Goose Gonsoulin | Den. | 11 | 1960 | AFL |
| 1961 | NFL | Jim Phillips | L.A. | 78 | Tommy McDonald | Phi. | 1144 | Frank Clarke | Dal. | 22.4 | Tommy McDonald | Phi. | 14 | Dick Lynch | NY G | 9 | 1961 | NFL |
| 1961 | AFL | Lionel Taylor | Den. | 100 | Charley Hennigan | Hou. | 1746 | Bill Groman | Hou. | 23.5 | Bill Groman | Hou. | 17 | Billy Atkins | Buf. | 10 | 1961 | AFL |
| 1962 | NFL | Bobby Mitchell | Was. | 72 | Bobby Mitchell | Was. | 1384 | Frank Clarke | Dal. | 22.2 | Frank Clarke | Dal. | 14 | Willie Wood | G.B. | 9 | 1962 | NFL |
| 1962 | AFL | Lionel Taylor | Den. | 77 | Art Powell | NY T | 1130 | Jim Colclough | Bos. | 21.7 | Chris Burford | Dal. | 12 | Lee Riley | NY T | 11 | 1962 | AFL |
| 1963 | NFL | Bobby Joe Conrad | St.L. | 73 | Bobby Mitchell | Was. | 1436 | Buddy Dial | Pit. | 21.6 | Terry Barr<br>Gary Collins | Det.<br>Cle. | 13<br>13 | Dick Lynch<br>Rosey Taylor | NY G<br>ChiB | 9<br>9 | 1963 | NFL |
| 1963 | AFL | Lionel Taylor | Den. | 78 | Art Powell | Oak. | 1304 | Clem Daniels | Oak. | 22.8 | Art Powell | Oak. | 16 | Freddie Glick | Hou. | 12 | 1963 | AFL |
| 1964 | NFL | Johnny Morris | Chi. | 93 | Johnny Morris | Chi. | 1200 | Gary Ballman | Pit. | 19.9 | Bobby Mitchell<br>Johnny Morris<br>Bucky Pope | Was.<br>Chi.<br>L.A. | 10<br>10<br>10 | Paul Krause | Was. | 12 | 1964 | NFL |
| 1964 | AFL | Charley Hennigan | Hou. | 101 | Charley Hennigan | Hou. | 1546 | Elbert Dubenion | Buf. | 27.1 | Lance Alworth | S.D. | 13 | Dainard Paulson | NY T | 12 | 1964 | AFL |
| 1965 | NFL | Dave Parks | S.F. | 80 | Dave Parks | S.F. | 1344 | Bob Hayes | Dal. | 21.8 | Bob Hayes<br>Dave Parks | Dal.<br>S.F. | 12<br>12 | Bobby Boyd | Bal. | 9 | 1965 | NFL |
| 1965 | AFL | Lionel Taylor | Den. | 85 | Lance Alworth | S.D. | 1602 | Lance Alworth | S.D. | 23.2 | Lance Alworth<br>Don Maynard | S.D.<br>NY J | 14<br>14 | W.K. Hicks | Hou. | 9 | 1965 | AFL |
| 1966 | NFL | Charley Taylor | Was. | 72 | Pat Studstill | Det. | 1266 | Homer Jones | NY G | 21.8 | Bob Hayes | Dal. | 13 | Larry Wilson | St.L. | 10 | 1966 | NFL |
| 1966 | AFL | Lance Alworth | S.D. | 73 | Lance Alworth | S.D. | 1383 | Otis Taylor | K.C. | 22.4 | Lance Alworth | S.D. | 13 | Bobby Hunt<br>Johnny Robinson | K.C.<br>K.C. | 10<br>10 | 1966 | AFL |
| 1967 | NFL | Charley Taylor | Was. | 70 | Ben Hawkins | Phi. | 1265 | Homer Jones | NY G | 24.7 | Homer Jones | NY G | 13 | Lem Barney<br>Dave Whitsell | Det.<br>N.O. | 10<br>10 | 1967 | NFL |
| 1967 | AFL | George Sauer | NY J | 75 | Don Maynard | NY J | 1434 | Don Maynard | NY J | 20.2 | Al Denson<br>Otis Taylor | Den.<br>K.C. | 11<br>11 | Miller Farr<br>Tom Janik<br>Dick Westmoreland | Hou.<br>Buf.<br>Mia. | 10<br>10<br>10 | 1967 | AFL |
| 1968 | NFL | Clifton McNeil | S.F. | 71 | Roy Jefferson | Pit. | 1074 | Homer Jones | NY G | 23.5 | Paul Warfield | Cle. | 12 | Willie Williams | NY G | 10 | 1968 | NFL |
| 1968 | AFL | Lance Alworth | S.D. | 68 | Lance Alworth | S.D. | 1312 | Don Maynard | NY J | 22.8 | Warren Wells | Oak. | 11 | Dave Grayson | Oak. | 10 | 1968 | AFL |
| 1969 | NFL | Dan Abramowicz | N.O. | 73 | Harold Jackson | Phi. | 1116 | Lance Rentzel | Dal. | 22.3 | Lance Rentzel | Dal. | 12 | Mel Renfro | Dal. | 10 | 1969 | NFL |
| 1969 | AFL | Lance Alworth | S.D. | 64 | Warren Wells | Oak. | 1260 | Warren Wells | Oak. | 26.8 | Warren Wells | Oak. | 14 | Emmitt Thomas | K.C. | 9 | 1969 | AFL |
| 1970 | NFL | Dick Gordon | Chi. | 71 | Gene Washington | S.F. | 1100 | John Gilliam | St.L. | 21.2 | Dick Gordon | Chi. | 13 | Dick LeBeau | Det. | 9 | 1970 | NFC |
| 1970 | AFC | Marlin Briscoe | Buf. | 57 | Marlin Briscoe | Buf. | 1036 | Gary Garrison | S.D. | 22.9 | Gary Garrison | S.D. | 12 | Johnny Robinson | K.C. | 10 | 1970 | AFC |
| 1971 | NFC | Bob Tucker | NY G | 59 | Gene Washington | S.F. | 884 | Bob Hayes | Dal. | 24.0 | Bob Hayes | Dal. | 8 | Bill Bradley | Phi. | 11 | 1971 | NFC |
| 1971 | AFC | Fred Biletnikoff | Oak. | 61 | Otis Taylor | K.C. | 1110 | Paul Warfield | Mia. | 23.2 | Paul Warfield | Mia. | 11 | Ken Houston | Hou. | 9 | 1971 | AFC |
| 1972 | NFC | Harold Jackson | Phi. | 62 | Harold Jackson | Phi. | 1048 | John Gilliam | Min. | 22.0 | Gene Washington | S.F. | 9 | Bill Bradley | Phi. | 9 | 1972 | NFC |
| 1972 | AFC | Fred Biletnikoff | Oak. | 58 | Rich Caster | NY J | 833 | Rich Caster | NY J | 21.4 | Rich Caster | NY J | 10 | Mike Sensibaugh | K.C. | 8 | 1972 | AFC |
| 1973 | NFC | Harold Carmichael | Phi. | 67 | Harold Carmichael | Phi. | 1116 | Harold Jackson | L.A. | 21.9 | Harold Jackson | L.A. | 13 | Bobby Bryant | Min. | 7 | 1973 | NFC |
| 1973 | AFC | Fred Willis | Hou. | 57 | Isaac Curtis | Cin. | 843 | Isaac Curtis | Cin. | 18.7 | Paul Warfield | Mia. | 11 | Dick Anderson<br>Mike Wagner | Mia.<br>Pit. | 8<br>8 | 1973 | AFC |

# YEARLY LEADERS

## RECEIVING

## INTERCEPTIONS

| YEAR | LGUE | RECEPTIONS NAME | TEAM | | YARDS NAME | TEAM | | AVERAGE YARDS NAME | TEAM | | TOUCHDOWNS NAME | TEAM | | INT NAME | TEAM | | YEAR | LGUE |
|---|---|---|---|---|---|---|---|---|---|---|---|---|---|---|---|---|---|---|
| 1974 | NFC | Charle Young | Phi. | 63 | Drew Pearson | Dal. | 1087 | Gene Washington | S.F. | 21.2 | Harold Carmichael | Phi. | 8 | Ray Brown | Atl. | 8 | 1974 | NFC |
| 1974 | AFC | Lydell Mitchell | Bal. | 72 | Cliff Branch | Oak. | 1092 | Isaac Curtis | Cin. | 21.1 | Cliff Branch | Oak. | 13 | Emmitt Thomas | K.C. | 12 | 1974 | AFC |
| 1975 | NFC | Chuck Foreman | Min. | 73 | Mel Gray | St.L. | 996 | Alfred Jenkins | Atl. | 20.2 | Mel Gray | St.L. | 11 | Paul Krause | Min. | 10 | 1975 | NFC |
| 1975 | AFC | Lydell Mitchell | Bal. | 60 | Ken Burrough | Hou. | 1063 | Isaac Curtis | Cin. | 21.2 | Lynn Swann | Pit. | 11 | Mel Blount | Pit. | 11 | 1975 | AFC |
| | | Reggie Rucker | Cle. | 60 | | | | | | | | | | | | | | |
| 1976 | NFC | Drew Pearson | Dal. | 58 | Sammy White | Min. | 906 | Ron Jessie | L.A. | 22.9 | Sammy White | Min. | 10 | Monte Jackson | L.A. | 10 | 1976 | NFC |
| 1976 | AFC | MacArthur Lane | K.C. | 66 | Roger Carr | Bal. | 1112 | Roger Carr | Bal. | 25.9 | Cliff Branch | Oak. | 12 | Ken Riley | Cin. | 9 | 1976 | AFC |
| 1977 | NFC | Ahmad Rashad | Min. | 51 | Drew Pearson | Dal. | 870 | Mel Gray | St.L. | 20.6 | Henry Childs | N.O. | 9 | Rolland Lawrence | Atl. | 7 | 1977 | NFC |
| | | | | | | | | | | | Sammy White | Min. | 9 | | | | | |
| 1977 | AFC | Lydell Mitchell | Bal. | 71 | Ken Burrough | Hou. | 816 | Wesley Walker | NY J | 21.1 | Nat Moore | Mia. | 12 | Lyle Blackwood | Bal. | 10 | 1977 | AFC |
| 1978 | AFC | Steve Largent | Sea. | 71 | Wesley Walker | NY J | 1169 | Wesley Walker | NY J | 24.4 | John Jefferson | S.D. | 13 | Thom Darden | Cle. | 10 | 1978 | AFC |
| 1978 | NFC | Rickey Young | Min. | 88 | Harold Carmichael | Phi. | 1072 | Morris Owens | T.B. | 20.0 | Billy Joe DuPree | Dal. | 9 | Willie Buchanon | G.B. | 9 | 1978 | NFC |
| | | | | | | | | | | | Sammy White | Min. | 9 | Ken Stone | St.L. | 9 | | |
| 1979 | AFC | Joe Washington | Bal. | 82 | Steve Largent | Sea. | 1237 | Stanley Morgan | N.E. | 22.8 | Stanley Morgan | N.E. | 12 | Mike Reinfeldt | Hou. | 12 | 1979 | AFC |
| 1979 | NFC | Ahmad Rashad | Min. | 80 | Ahmad Rashad | Min. | 1156 | Drew Pearson | Dal. | 18.7 | Harold Carmichael | Phi. | 11 | Lemar Parrish | Was. | 9 | 1979 | NFC |
| 1980 | AFC | Kellen Winslow | S.D. | 89 | John Jefferson | S.D. | 1340 | Stanley Morgan | N.E. | 22.0 | John Jefferson | S.D. | 13 | Lester Hayes | Oak. | 13 | 1980 | AFC |
| 1980 | NFC | Earl Cooper | S.F. | 83 | James Lofton | G.B. | 1226 | James Scott | Chi. | 19.3 | Earnest Gray | NY G | 10 | Nolan Cromwell | L.A. | 8 | 1980 | NFC |
| 1981 | AFC | Kellen Winslow | S.D. | 88 | Frank Lewis | Buf. | 1244 | Stanley Morgan | N.E. | 23.4 | Steve Watson | Den. | 13 | John Harris | Sea. | 10 | 1981 | AFC |
| | | | | | Steve Watson | Den. | 1244 | | | | | | | | | | | |
| 1981 | NFC | Dwight Clark | S.F. | 85 | Alfred Jenkins | Atl. | 1358 | Kevin House | T.B. | 21.0 | Alfred Jenkins | Atl. | 13 | Everson Walls | Dal. | 11 | 1981 | NFC |
| 1982 | AFC | Kellen Winslow | S.D. | 54 | Wes Chandler | S.D. | 1032 | Wes Chandler | S.D. | 21.1 | Wes Chandler | S.D. | 9 | 4 tied with 5 each | | | 1982 | AFC |
| 1982 | NFC | Dwight Clark | S.F. | 60 | Dwight Clark | S.F. | 913 | Charlie Brown | Was. | 21.6 | Charlie Brown | Was. | 8 | Everson Walls | Dal. | 7 | 1982 | NFC |
| 1983 | AFC | Todd Christensen | Raid. | 92 | Carlos Carson | K.C. | 1351 | Mark Duper | Mia. | 19.7 | Todd Christensen | Raid. | 12 | Vann McElroy | Raid. | 8 | 1983 | AFC |
| | | | | | | | | | | | | | | Ken Riley | Cin. | 8 | | |
| 1983 | NFC | Charlie Brown | Was. | 78 | Mike Quick | Phi. | 1409 | James Lofton | G.B. | 22.4 | Roy Green | St.L. | 14 | Mark Murphy | Was. | 9 | 1983 | NFC |
| | | Earnest Gray | NY G | 78 | | | | | | | | | | | | | | |
| | | Roy Green | St.L. | 78 | | | | | | | | | | | | | | |
| 1984 | AFC | Ozzie Newsome | Cle. | 89 | John Stallworth | Pit. | 1395 | Daryl Turner | Sea. | 20.4 | Mark Clayton | Mia. | 18 | Kenny Easley | Sea. | 10 | 1984 | AFC |
| 1984 | NFC | Art Monk | Was. | 106 | Roy Green | St.L. | 1555 | James Lofton | G.B. | 22.0 | Roy Green | St.L. | 12 | Tom Flynn | G.B. | 9 | 1984 | NFC |
| 1985 | AFC | Lionel James | S.D. | 86 | Steve Largent | Sea. | 1287 | Stephone Paige | K.C. | 21.9 | Daryl Turner | Sea. | 13 | Eugene Daniel | Ind. | 8 | 1985 | AFC |
| | | | | | | | | | | | | | | Albert Lewis | K.C. | 8 | | |
| 1985 | NFC | Roger Craig | S.F. | 92 | Mike Quick | Phi. | 1247 | Willie Gault | Chi. | 21.3 | Mike Quick | Phi. | 11 | Everson Walls | Dal. | 9 | 1985 | NFC |
| 1986 | AFC | Todd Christensen | Raid. | 95 | Stanley Morgan | NE | 1491 | Chris Burkett | Buf. | 22.9 | Wesley Walker | NY J | 12 | Deron Cherry | K.C. | 9 | 1986 | AFC |
| 1986 | NFC | Jerry Rice | S.F. | 86 | Jerry Rice | S.F. | 1570 | Walter Stanley | G.B. | 20.7 | Jerry Rice | S.F. | 15 | Ronnie Lott | S.F. | 10 | 1986 | NFC |
| 1987 | AFC | Al Toon | NY J | 68 | Carlos Carson | K.C. | 1044 | James Lofton | Raid. | 21.5 | Steve Largent | Sea. | 8 | Mike Prior | Ind. | 6 | 1987 | AFC |
| | | | | | | | | | | | Mark Duper | Mia. | 8 | Mark Kelso | Buf. | 6 | | |
| | | | | | | | | | | | | | | Keith Bostic | Hou. | 6 | | |
| 1987 | NFC | J.T. Smith | St.L. | 91 | J.T. Smith | St.L. | 1117 | Anthony Carter | Min. | 24.3 | Jerry Rice | S.F. | 22 | Barry Wilburn | Was. | 9 | 1987 | NFC |
| 1988 | AFC | Al Toon | NYJ | 93 | Eddie Brown | Cin. | 1273 | Eddie Brown | Cin. | 24.0 | Mark Clayton | Mia. | 14 | Erik McMillan | NYJ | 8 | 1988 | AFC |
| 1988 | NFC | Henry Ellard | L.A. | 86 | Henry Ellard | L.A. | 1414 | Jerry Rice | S.F. | 20.4 | Ricky Sanders | Was. | 12 | Scott Case | Atl. | 10 | 1988 | NFC |
| 1989 | NFC | Sterling Sharpe | G.B. | 90 | Jerry Rice | S.F. | 1483 | Willie Anderson | L.A. | 26.0 | Jerry Rice | S.F. | 17 | Eric Allen | Phi. | 8 | 1989 | NFC |
| 1989 | AFC | Andre Reed | Buf. | 88 | Andre Reed | Buf. | 1312 | Webster Slaughter | Cle. | 19.0 | Anthony Miller | S.D. | 10 | Felix Wright | Cle. | 9 | 1989 | AFC |
| 1990 | NFC | Jerry Rice | S.F. | 100 | Jerry Rice | S.F. | 1502 | Willie Anderson | L.A. | 21.5 | Jerry Rice | S.F. | 13 | Mark Carrier | Chi. | 10 | 1990 | NFC |
| 1990 | AFC | Drew Hill | Hou. | 74 | Haywood Jeffires | Hou. | 1048 | James Lofton | Buf. | 20.3 | Eddie Brown | Cin. | 9 | Richard Johnson | Hou. | 8 | 1990 | Hou. |
| | | Haywood Jeffires | Hou. | 74 | | | | | | | Ernest Givins | Hou. | 9 | | | | | |
| 1991 | NFC | Michael Irvin | Dall. | 93 | Michael Irvin | Dall. | 1523 | Michael Haynes | Atl. | 22.4 | Jerry Rice | S.F. | 14 | Ray Crockett | Det | 6 | 1991 | NFC |
| | | | | | | | | | | | | | | Tim McKyer | Atl. | 6 | | |
| | | | | | | | | | | | | | | Deion Sanders | Atl. | 6 | | |
| | | | | | | | | | | | | | | Aeneas Williams | Phx. | 6 | | |
| 1991 | AFC | Haywood Jeffires | Hou. | 100 | Haywood Jeffires | Hou. | 1181 | Dwight Stone | Pitt. | 20.3 | Mark Clayton | Mia. | 12 | Ronnie Lott | Raid. | 8 | 1991 | AFC |
| 1992 | NFC | Sterling Sharpe | G.B. | 108 | Sterling Sharpe | G.B. | 1461 | Herman Moore | Det. | 18.9 | Sterling Sharpe | G.B. | 13 | Audray McMillian | Minn. | 8 | 1992 | NFC |
| 1992 | AFC | Haywood Jeffires | Hou. | 90 | Anthony Miller | S.D. | 1060 | Willie Davis | K.C. | 21.0 | Ernest Givins | Hou. | 10 | Henry Jones | Buff. | 8 | 1992 | AFC |
| 1993 | NFC | Sterling Sharpe | G.B. | 112 | Jerry Rice | S.F. | 1503 | Alvin Harper | Dall. | 21.6 | Jerry Rice | S.F. | 15 | Deion Sanders | Atl. | 7 | 1993 | NFC |
| | | | | | | | | | | | Andre Rison | Atl. | 15 | | | | | |
| 1993 | AFC | Reggie Langhorne | Ind. | 85 | Tim Brown | L.A. | 1180 | James Jett | L.A. | 23.4 | Shannon Sharpe | Den. | 9 | Eugene Robinson | Sea. | 9 | 1993 | AFC |
| | | | | | | | | | | | | | | Nate Odomes | Buff. | 9 | | |
| 1994 | NFC | Cris Carter | Minn. | 122 | Jerry Rice | S.F. | 1499 | Willie Anderson | L.A. | 20.5 | Sterling Sharpe | G.B. | 18 | Aeneas Williams | Ariz. | 9 | 1994 | NFC |
| 1994 | AFC | Ben Coates | N.E. | 96 | Tim Brown | Raid. | 1309 | Darnay Scott | Cin. | 18.9 | Carl Pickens | Cin. | 11 | Eric Turner | Clev. | 9 | 1994 | AFC |
| 1995 | NFC | Herman Moore | Det. | 123 | Jerry Rice | S.F. | 1848 | Willie Green | Car. | 18.8 | Cris Carter | Minn. | 17 | Orlando Thomas | Minn. | 9 | 1995 | NFC |
| 1995 | AFC | Carl Pickens | Cin. | 99 | Tim Brown | Oak. | 1342 | Chris Sanders | Hou. | 23.5 | Carl Pickens | Cin. | 17 | Willie Williams | Pitt. | 7 | 1995 | AFC |

# YEARLY LEADERS

| YEAR | LGUE | PUNTING AVERAGE NAME | TEAM | | FIELD GOALS MADE NAME | TEAM | | FIELD GOALS PERCENTAGE NAME | TEAM | | PAT'S MADE NAME | TEAM | | POINTS SCORED NAME | TEAM | | YEAR | LGUE |
|---|---|---|---|---|---|---|---|---|---|---|---|---|---|---|---|---|---|---|
| 1933 | NFL | | | | Jack Manders | ChiB | 5 | | | | Jack Manders | ChiB | 14 | Glenn Presnell | Det. | 63 | 1933 | NFL |
| | | | | | Glenn Presnell | Det. | 5 | | | | Ken Strong | NY G | 14 | | | | | |
| | | | | | Ken Strong | NY G | 5 | | | | | | | | | | | |
| 1934 | NFL | | | | Jack Manders | ChiB | 10 | | | | Jack Manders | ChiB | 31 | Jack Manders | ChiB | 79 | 1934 | NFL |
| 1935 | NFL | | | | Armand Niccolai | Pit. | 6 | | | | Dutch Clark | Det. | 16 | Dutch Clark | Det. | 55 | 1935 | NFL |
| | | | | | Bill Smith | ChiC | 6 | | | | Jack Manders | ChiB | 16 | | | | | |
| 1936 | NFL | | | | Jack Manders | ChiB | 7 | | | | Dutch Clark | Det. | 19 | Dutch Clark | Det. | 73 | 1936 | NFL |
| | | | | | Armand Niccolai | Pit. | 7 | | | | | | | | | | | |
| 1937 | NFL | | | | Jack Manders | ChiB | 8 | | | | Riley Smith | Was. | 22 | Jack Manders | ChiB | 69 | 1937 | NFL |
| 1938 | NFL | | | | Ward Cuff | NY G | 5 | Regis Monohan | Det. | .80 | Ward Cuff | NY G | 18 | Clarke Hinkle | G.B. | 58 | 1938 | NFL |
| | | | | | Ralph Kercheval | Bkn. | 5 | | | | | | | | | | | |
| 1939 | NFL | George Faust | ChiC | 44 | Ward Cuff | NY G | 7 | Chuck Hanneman | Det. | .80 | Tiny Engebretsen | G.B. | 18 | Andy Farkas | Was. | 68 | 1939 | NFL |
| | | Sid Luckman | ChiB | 44 | | | | | | | | | | | | | | |
| 1940 | NFL | Sammy Baugh | Was. | 51.3 | Clarke Hinkle | G.B. | 9 | Clarke Hinkle | G.B. | .64 | Ace Parker | Bkn. | 19 | Don Hutson | G.B. | 57 | 1940 | NFL |
| 1941 | NFL | Sammy Baugh | Was. | 48.7 | Clarke Hinkle | G.B. | 6 | Andy Marefos | NY G | .80 | Don Hutson | G.B. | 20 | Don Hutson | G.B. | 95 | 1941 | NFL |
| | | | | | | | | | | | Bob Snyder | ChiB | 20 | | | | | |
| 1942 | NFL | Sammy Baugh | Was. | 46.6 | Bill Daddio | ChiC | 5 | Ted Fritsch | G.B. | .80 | Don Hutson | G.B. | 33 | Don Hutson | G.B. | 138 | 1942 | NFL |
| | | | | | | | | Frank Maznicki | ChiB | .80 | | | | | | | | |
| 1943 | NFL | Sammy Baugh | Was. | 45.9 | Ward Cuff | NY G | 3 | Don Hutson | G.B. | .60 | Bob Snyder | ChiB | 39 | Don Hutson | G.B. | 117 | 1943 | NFL |
| | | | | | Don Hutson | G.B. | 3 | | | | | | | | | | | |
| 1944 | NFL | Cecil Johnson | Bkn. | 42.6 | Ken Strong | NY G | 6 | Ken Strong | NY G | .50 | Pete Gudauskas | ChiB | 36 | Don Hutson | G.B. | 85 | 1944 | NFL |
| 1945 | NFL | Sammy Baugh | Was. | 43.3 | Joe Aguirre | Was. | 7 | Ben Agajanian | Phi. + Pit. | 1.00 | Don Hutson | G.B. | 31 | Steve Van Buren | Phi. | 110 | 1945 | NFL |
| | | | | | | | | | | | Bob Waterfield | Cle. | 31 | | | | | |
| 1946 | NFL | Bob Cifers | Det. | 45.6 | Ted Fritsch | G.B. | 9 | Bob Waterfield | L.A. | .67 | Bob Waterfield | L.A. | 37 | Ted Fritsch | G.B. | 100 | 1946 | NFL |
| 1946 | AAFC | Glenn Dobbs | Bkn. | 47.8 | Lou Groza | Cle. | 13 | Steve Nemeth | Chi. | .75 | Lou Groza | Cle. | 45 | Lou Groza | Cle. | 84 | 1946 | AAFC |
| 1947 | NFL | George Gulyanics | ChiB | 44.8 | Ward Cuff | G.B. | 7 | Pat Harder | ChiC | .70 | Ray McLean | ChiB | 44 | Pat Harder | ChiC | 102 | 1947 | NFL |
| | | | | | Pat Harder | ChiC | 7 | | | | | | | | | | | |
| | | | | | Bob Waterfield | L.A. | 7 | | | | | | | | | | | |
| 1947 | AAFC | Bob Reinhard | L.A. | 45.7 | Ben Agajanian | L.A. | 15 | Harvey Johnson | N.Y. | .88 | Harvey Johnson | N.Y. | 49 | Spec Sanders | N.Y. | 114 | 1947 | AAFC |
| 1948 | NFL | Joe Muha | Phi. | 47.2 | Cliff Patton | Phi. | 8 | Dick Poillon | Was. | .71 | Pat Harder | ChiC | 53 | Pat Harder | ChiC | 110 | 1948 | NFL |
| 1948 | AAFC | Glenn Dobbs | L.A. | 49.1 | Rex Grossman | Bal. | 10 | Joe Vetrano | S.F. | .63 | Joe Vetrano | S.F. | 62 | Chet Mutryn | Buf. | 96 | 1948 | AAFC |
| 1949 | NFL | George Gulyanics | ChiB | 47.2 | Cliff Patton | Phi. | 9 | Vinnie Yablonski | ChiC | .83 | Pat Harder | ChiC | 45 | Pat Harder | ChiC | 102 | 1949 | NFL |
| | | | | | Bob Waterfield | L.A. | 9 | | | | | | | Choo-Choo Roberts | NY G | 102 | | |
| 1949 | AAFC | Frankie Albert | S.F. | 48.2 | Harvey Johnson | N.Y. | 7 | Rex Grossman | Bal. | .55 | Joe Vetrano | S.F. | 56 | Alyn Beals | S.F. | 73 | 1949 | AAFC |
| 1950 | NFL | Curley Morrison | ChiB | 43.3 | Lou Groza | Cle. | 13 | Lou Groza | Cle. | .68 | Bob Waterfield | L.A. | 54 | Doak Walker | Det. | 128 | 1950 | NFL |
| 1951 | NFL | Horace Gillom | Cle. | 45.5 | Bob Waterfield | L.A. | 13 | Bill Dudley | Was. | .77 | Lou Groza | Cle. | 43 | Elroy Hirsch | L.A. | 102 | 1951 | NFL |
| | | | | | | | | | | | Doak Walker | Det. | 43 | | | | | |
| 1952 | NFL | Horace Gillom | Cle. | 45.7 | Lou Groza | Cle. | 19 | Bob Waterfield | L.A. | .61 | Bob Waterfield | L.A. | 44 | Gordy Soltau | S.F. | 94 | 1952 | NFL |
| 1953 | NFL | Pat Brady | Pit. | 46.9 | Lou Groza | Cle. | 23 | Lou Groza | Cle. | .88 | Gordy Soltau | S.F. | 48 | Gordy Soltau | S.F. | 114 | 1953 | NFL |
| 1954 | NFL | Pat Brady | Pit. | 43.2 | Lou Groza | Cle. | 16 | Lou Groza | Cle. | .67 | Doak Walker | Det. | 43 | Bobby Walston | Phi. | 114 | 1954 | NFL |
| 1955 | NFL | Norm Van Brocklin | L.A. | 44.6 | Fred Cone | G.B. | 16 | Fred Cone | G.B. | .67 | Lou Groza | Cle. | 44 | Doak Walker | Det. | 96 | 1955 | NFL |
| 1956 | NFL | Norm Van Brocklin | L.A. | 43.1 | Sam Baker | Was. | 17 | Bobby Layne | Det. | .80 | George Blanda | ChiB | 45 | Bobby Layne | Det. | 99 | 1956 | NFL |
| 1957 | NFL | Don Chandler | NY G | 44.6 | Lou Groza | Cle. | 15 | Bobby Walston | Phi. | .75 | Paige Cothren | L.A. | 38 | Sam Baker | Was. | 77 | 1957 | NFL |
| 1958 | NFL | Sam Baker | Was. | 45.4 | Paige Cothren | L.A. | 14 | Paige Cothren | L.A. | .56 | Steve Myhra | Bal. | 48 | Jim Brown | Cle. | 108 | 1958 | NFL |
| | | | | | Tom Miner | Pit. | 14 | | | | | | | | | | | |
| 1959 | NFL | Yale Lary | Det. | 47.1 | Pat Summerall | NY G | 20 | Pat Summerall | NY G | .69 | Steve Myhra | Bal. | 50 | Paul Hornung | G.B. | 94 | 1959 | NFL |
| 1960 | NFL | Jerry Norton | St.L. | 45.6 | Tommy Davis | S.F. | 19 | Bobby Walston | Phi. | .70 | Sam Baker | Cle. | 44 | Paul Hornung | G.B. | 176 | 1960 | NFL |
| 1960 | AFL | Paul Maguire | L.A. | 40.5 | Gene Mingo | Den.. | 18 | Gene Mingo | Den. | .64 | Bill Shockley | NY T | 47 | Gene Mingo | Den. | 123 | 1960 | AFL |
| 1961 | NFL | Yale Lary | Det. | 48.4 | Steve Myhra | Bal. | 21 | Lou Groza | Cle. | .70 | Pat Summerall | NY G | 46 | Paul Hornung | G.B. | 146 | 1961 | NFL |
| 1961 | AFL | Billy Atkins | Buf. | 45.0 | Gino Cappelletti | Bos. | 17 | George Blanda | Hou. | .62 | George Blanda | Hou. | 64 | Gino Cappelletti | Bos. | 147 | 1961 | AFL |
| 1962 | NFL | Tommy Davis | S.F. | 45.6 | Lou Michaels | Pit. | 26 | Don Chandler | NY G | .68 | Sam Baker | Dal. | 50 | Jim Taylor | G.B. | 114 | 1962 | NFL |
| 1962 | AFL | Jim Fraser | Den. | 44.4 | Gene Mingo | Den. | 27 | George Blair | S.D. | .85 | George Blanda | Hou. | 48 | Gene Mingo | Den. | 137 | 1962 | AFL |
| 1963 | NFL | Yale Lary | Det. | 48.9 | Jim Martin | Bal. | 24 | Lou Groza | Cle. | .65 | Don Chandler | NY G | 52 | Don Chandler | NY G | 106 | 1963 | NFL |
| 1963 | AFL | Jim Fraser | Den. | 46.1 | Gino Cappelletti | Bos. | 22 | George Blair | S.D. | .63 | Mike Mercer | Oak. | 47 | Gino Cappelletti | Bos. | 113 | 1963 | AFL |
| 1964 | NFL | Bobby Walden | Min. | 46.4 | Jim Bakken | St.L. | 25 | Bruce Gossett | L.A. | .75 | Lou Michaels | Bal. | 53 | Lenny Moore | Bal. | 120 | 1964 | NFL |
| 1964 | AFL | Jim Fraser | Den. | 44.7 | Gino Cappelletti | Bos. | 25 | Pete Gogolak | Buf. | .66 | Tommy Brooker | K.C. | 46 | Gino Cappelletti | Bos. | 155 | 1964 | AFL |
| 1965 | NFL | Gary Collins | Cle. | 46.7 | Fred Cox | Min. | 23 | Jim Bakken | St.L. | .68 | Tommy Davis | S.F. | 52 | Gale Sayers | ChiB | 132 | 1965 | NFL |
| | | | | | | | | | | | Roger Leclerc | ChiB | 52 | | | | | |
| 1965 | AFL | Jerrel Wilson | K.C. | 46.1 | Pete Gogolak | Buf. | 28 | Gino Cappelletti | Bos. | .63 | Herb Travenio | S.D. | 40 | Gino Cappelletti | Bos. | 132 | 1965 | AFL |
| 1966 | NFL | David Lee | Bal. | 45.6 | Bruce Gossett | L.A. | 28 | Sam Baker | Phi. | .72 | Danny Villanueva | Dal. | 56 | Bruce Gossett | L.A. | 113 | 1966 | NFL |
| 1966 | AFL | Bob Scarpitto | Den. | 45.8 | Mike Mercer | Oak. + K.C. | 21 | Mike Mercer | Oak. + K.C. | .70 | Booth Lusteg | Buf. | 41 | Gino Cappelletti | Bos. | 119 | 1966 | AFL |
| 1967 | NFL | Billy Lothridge | Atl. | 43.7 | Jim Bakken | St.L. | 27 | Jim Bakken | St.L. | .69 | Bruce Gossett | L.A. | 48 | Jim Bakken | St.L. | 117 | 1967 | NFL |
| 1967 | AFL | Bob Scarpitto | Den. | 44.9 | Jan Stenerud | K.C. | 21 | George Blanda | Hou. | .67 | George Blanda | Hou. | 56 | George Blanda | Hou. | 116 | 1967 | AFL |
| 1968 | NFL | Billy Lothridge | Atl. | 44.3 | Mac Percival | Chi. | 25 | Don Cockroft | Cle. | .75 | Mike Clark | Dal. | 54 | Leroy Kelly | Cle. | 120 | 1968 | NFL |
| 1968 | AFL | Jerrel Wilson | K.C. | 45.1 | Jim Turner | NY J | 34 | Jan Stenerud | K.C. | .75 | George Blanda | Hou. | 54 | Jim Turner | NY J | 145 | 1968 | AFL |
| 1969 | NFL | David Lee | Bal. | 45.3 | Fred Cox | Min. | 26 | Fred Cox | Min. | .70 | Don Cockroft | Cle. | 45 | Fred Cox | Min. | 121 | 1969 | NFL |
| 1969 | AFL | Dennis Partee | S.D. | 44.6 | Jim Turner | NY J | 32 | Jan Stenerud | K.C. | .77 | George Blanda | Oak. | 45 | Jim Turner | NY J | 129 | 1969 | AFL |
| 1970 | NFC | Julian Fagan | N.O. | 42.5 | Fred Cox | Min. | 30 | Curt Knight | Was. | .74 | Errol Mann | Det. | 41 | Fred Cox | Min. | 125 | 1970 | NFC |
| 1970 | AFC | Dave Lewis | Cin. | 46.2 | Jan Stenerud | K.C. | 30 | Garo Yepremian | Mia. | .76 | George Blanda | Oak. | 36 | Jan Stenerud | K.C. | 116 | 1970 | AFC |
| | | | | | | | | | | | Jim O'Brien | Bal. | 36 | | | | | |
| 1971' | NFC | Tom McNeill | Phi. | 42.0 | Curt Knight | Was. | 29 | Tom Dempsey | Phi. | .71 | Mike Clark | Dal. | 47 | Curt Knight | Was. | 114 | 1971 | NFC |
| 1971 | AFC | Dave Lewis | Cin. | 44.8 | Garo Yepremian | Mia. | 28 | Garo Yepremian | Mia. | .70 | George Blanda | Oak. | 41 | Garo Yepremian | Mia. | 117 | 1971 | AFC |
| 1972 | NFC | Dave Chapple | L.A. | 44.2 | Chester Marcol | G.B. | 33 | Errol Mann | Det. | .69 | Bruce Gossett | S.F. | 41 | Chester Marcol | G.B. | 128 | 1972 | NFC |
| 1972 | AFC | Jerrel Wilson | K.C. | 44.8 | Roy Gerela | Pit. | 28 | Don Cockroft | Cle. | .82 | George Blanda | Oak. | 44 | Bobby Howfield | NY J | 121 | 1972 | AFC |
| 1973 | NFC | Tom Wittum | S.F. | 43.7 | David Ray | L.A. | 30 | Bruce Gossett | S.F. | .79 | Toni Fritsch | Dal. | 43 | David Ray | L.A. | 130 | 1973 | NFC |
| 1973 | AFC | Jerrel Wilson | K.C. | 45.5 | Roy Gerela | Pit. | 29 | Don Cockroft | Cle. | .71 | Jim Turner | Den. | 40 | Roy Gerela | Pit. | 123 | 1973 | AFC |
| 1974 | NFC | Tom Blanchard | N.O. | 42.1 | Chester Marcol | G.B. | 25 | Errol Mann | Det. | .72 | Efren Herrara | Dal. | 33 | Chester Marcol | G.B. | 94 | 1974 | NFC |
| 1974 | AFC | Ray Guy | Oak. | 42.2 | Roy Gerela | Pit. | 20 | Don Cockroft | Cle. | .88 | George Blanda | Oak. | 44 | Roy Gerela | Pit. | 93 | 1974 | AFC |
| 1975 | NFC | Herman Weaver | Det. | 42.0 | Toni Fritsch | Dal. | 22 | Tom Dempsey | L.A. | .81 | Fred Cox | Min. | 46 | Chuck Foreman | Min. | 132 | 1975 | NFC |
| 1975 | AFC | Ray Guy | Oak. | 43.8 | Jan Stenerud | K.C. | 22 | Garo Yepremian | Mia. | .81 | John Leypoldt | Buf. | 51 | O.J. Simpson | Buf. | 138 | 1975 | AFC |
| | | | | | | | | | | | Toni Linhart | Bal. | 51 | | | | | |
| 1976 | NFC | John James | Atl. | 42.1 | Mark Moseley | Was. | 22 | Efren Herrera | Dal. | .78 | Tom Dempsey | L.A. | 36 | Mark Moseley | Was. | 97 | 1976 | NFC |
| | | | | | | | | Rick Szaro | N.O. | .78 | | | | | | | | |
| 1976 | AFC | Marv Bateman | Buf. | 42.8 | Jan Stenerud | K.C. | 21 | Toni Linhart | Bal. | .74 | Toni Linhart | Bal. | 49 | Toni Linhart | Bal. | 109 | 1976 | AFC |
| 1977 | NFC | Tom Blanchard | N.O. | 42.4 | Mark Moseley | Was. | 21 | Efren Herrera | Dal. | .62 | Efren Herrera | Dal. | 39 | Walter Payton | Chi. | 96 | 1977 | NFC |
| 1977 | AFC | Ray Guy | Oak. | 43.3 | Errol Mann | Oak. | 20 | Rolf Benirschke | S.D. | .74 | Errol Mann | Oak. | 39 | Errol Mann | Oak. | 99 | 1977 | AFC |
| | | | | | | | | Don Cockroft | Cle. | .74 | | | | | | | | |

# YEARLY LEADERS

## PUNTING — AVERAGE | FIELD GOALS — MADE | FIELD GOALS — PERCENTAGE | PAT'S MADE | POINTS SCORED

| YEAR | LGUE | NAME | TEAM | AVG | NAME | TEAM | MADE | NAME | TEAM | PCT | NAME | TEAM | MADE | NAME | TEAM | PTS | YEAR | LGUE |
|---|---|---|---|---|---|---|---|---|---|---|---|---|---|---|---|---|---|---|
| 1978 | AFC | Pat McInally | Cin. | 43.1 | Pat Leahy | NY J | 22 | Garo Yepremian | Mia. | .826 | Roy Gerela | Pit. | 44 | Pat Leahy | NY J | 107 | 1978 | AFC |
| 1978 | NFC | Tom Skladany | Det. | 42.5 | Frank Corral | L.A. | 29 | Tim Mazzetti | Atl. | .813 | Rafael Septien | Dal. | 46 | Frank Corral | L.A. | 118 | 1978 | NFC |
| 1979 | AFC | Bob Grupp | K.C. | 43.6 | John Smith | N.E. | 23 | Toni Fritsch | Hou. | .840 | Matt Bahr | Pit. | 50 | John Smith | N.E. | 115 | 1979 | AFC |
| 1979 | NFC | Dave Jennings | NY G | 42.7 | Mark Moseley | Was. | 25 | Ray Wersching | S.F. | .833 | Rafael Septien | Dal. | 40 | Mark Moseley | Was. | 114 | 1979 | NFC |
| 1980 | AFC | Luke Prestridge | Den. | 43.9 | John Smith | N.E. | 26 | Toni Fritsch | Hou. | .792 | John Smith | N.E. | 51 | John Smith | N.E. | 124 | 1980 | AFC |
|  |  |  |  |  | Fred Steinfort | Den. | 26 |  |  |  |  |  |  |  |  |  |  |  |
| 1980 | NFC | Dave Jennings | NY G | 44.8 | Ed Murray | Det. | 27 | Ray Wersching | S.F. | .789 | Rafael Septien | Dal. | 59 | Ed Murray | Det. | 116 | 1980 | NFC |
| 1981 | AFC | Pat McInally | Cin. | 45.4 | Nick Lowery | K.C. | 26 | Uwe von Schamann | Mia. | .779 | Rolf Benirschke | S.D. | 55 | Jim Breech | Cin. | 115 | 1981 | AFC |
|  |  |  |  |  |  |  |  |  |  |  |  |  |  | Nick Lowery | K.C. | 115 |  |  |
| 1981 | NFC | Tom Skladany | Det. | 43.5 | Rafael Septien | Dal. | 27 | Jan Stenerud | G.B. | .917 | Mick Luckhurst | Atl. | 51 | Ed Murray | Det. | 121 | 1981 | NFC |
|  |  |  |  |  |  |  |  |  |  |  |  |  |  | Rafael Septien | Dal. | 121 |  |  |
| 1982 | AFC | Luke Prestridge | Den. | 45.0 | Nick Lowery | K.C. | 19 | Nick Lowery | K.C. | 79.2 | Pat Leahy | NY J | 32 | Marcus Allen | Raid. | 84 | 1982 | AFC |
|  |  |  |  |  |  |  |  |  |  |  | Rolf Benirschke | S.D. | 32 |  |  |  |  |  |
| 1982 | NFC | Carl Birdsong | St.L. | 43.8 | Mark Moseley | Was. | 20 | Mark Moseley | Was. | 90.5 | Rafael Septien | Dal. | 28 | Wendell Tyler | L.A. | 78 | 1982 | NFC |
| 1983 | AFC | Rohn Stark | Bal. | 45.3 | Raul Allegre | Bal. | 30 | Matt Bahr | Cle. | 87.5 | Chris Bahr | Raid. | 51 | Gary Anderson | Pit. | 119 | 1983 | AFC |
| 1983 | NFC | Frank Garcia | T.B. | 42.2 | Ali Haji-Sheikh | NY G | 35 | Ray Wersching | S.F. | 83.3 | Mark Moseley | Was. | 62 | John Riggins | Was. | 144 | 1983 | NFC |
| 1984 | AFC | Jim Arnold | K.C. | 44.9 | Gary Anderson | Pit. | 24 | Norm Johnson | Sea. | 83.3 | Uwe von Schamann | Mia. | 66 | Gary Anderson | Pit. | 117 | 1984 | AFC |
| 1984 | NFC | Brian Hansen | N.O. | 43.8 | Paul McFadden | Phi. | 30 | Jan Stenerud | Min. | 87.0 | Ray Wersching | S.F. | 56 | Ray Wersching | S.F. | 131 | 1984 | NFC |
| 1985 | AFC | Rohn Stark | Ind. | 45.9 | Gary Anderson | Pit. | 31 | Nick Lowery | K.C. | 88.9 | Bob Thomas | S.D. | 51 | Gary Anderson | Pit. | 139 | 1985 | AFC |
| 1985 | NFC | Rick Donnelly | Atl. | 42.6 | Kevin Butler | Chi. | 33 | Morten Andersen | N.O. | 88.5 | Ray Wersching | S.F. | 52 | Kevin Butler | Chi. | 144 | 1985 | NFC |
| 1986 | AFC | Rohn Stark | Ind. | 45.2 | Tony Franklin | N.E. | 32 | Matt Bahr | Cle. | 76.9 | Fuad Reveiz | Mia. | 52 | Tony Franklin | N.E. | 140 | 1986 | AFC |
| 1986 | NFC | Sean Landeta | NY G | 44.8 | Kevin Butler | Chi. | 28 | Morten Andersen | N.O. | 86.7 | Chuck Nelson | Min. | 44 | Kevin Butler | Chi. | 120 | 1986 | NFC |
| 1987 | AFC | Ralf Mojsiejenko | S.D. | 42.9 | Jim Breech | Cin. | 24 | Dean Biasucci | Ind. | 88.9 | Norm Johnson | Sea. | 40 | Jim Breech | Cin. | 97 | 1987 | AFC |
|  |  |  |  |  | Dean Biasucci | Ind. | 24 |  |  |  |  |  |  |  |  |  |  |  |
| 1987 | NFC | Rick Donnelly | Atl. | 44.0 | Morten Andersen | N.O. | 28 | Roger Ruzek | Dal. | 88.0 | Ray Wersching | S.F. | 44 | Jerry Rice | S.F. | 138 | 1987 | NFC |
| 1988 | AFC | Mike Horan | Den. | 44.0 | Scott Norwood | Buf. | 32 | Scott Norwood | Buf. | 86.5 | Jim Breech | Cin. | 56 | Scott Norwood | Buf. | 129 | 1988 | AFC |
| 1988 | NFC | Jim Arnold | Det. | 44.4 | Mike Cofer | S.F. | 27 | Eddie Murray | Det. | 95.2 | Chuck Nelson | Min. | 48 | Mike Cofer | S.F. | 121 | 1988 | NFC |
| 1989 | NFC | Rich Camarillo | Phx. | 43.4 | Rich Karlis | Min. | 31 | Eddie Murray | Det. | 95.2 | Mike Lansford | L.A. | 51 | Mike Cofer | S.F. | 136 | 1989 | NFC |
| 1989 | AFC | Greg Montgomery | Hou. | 43.8 | David Treadwell | Den. | 27 | David Treadwell | Den. | 87.6 | Scott Norwood | Buf. | 46 | David Treadwell | Den. | 120 | 1989 | AFC |
| 1990 | NFC | Sean Landeta | NYG | 44.1 | Chip Lohmiller | Was. | 30 | Donald Igwebuike | Min. | 87.5 | Roger Ruzek | Phi. | 45 | Chip Lohmiller | Was. | 131 | 1990 | NFC |
| 1990 | AFC | Mike Horan | Den. | 44.4 | Nick Lowery | K.C. | 34 | Nick Lowery | K.C. | 91.9 | Scott Norwood | Buf. | 50 | Nick Lowery | K.C. | 139 | 1990 | AFC |
| 1991 | NFC | Harry Newsome | Minn. | 45.5 | Chip Lomiller | Wash. | 31 | Tony Zendejas | L.A. | 1.000 | Chip Lohmiller | Wash. | 56 | Chip Lohmiller | Wash. | 149 | 1991 | NFC |
| 1991 | AFC | Reggie Roby | Mia. | 45.7 | Pete Styanovich | Mia. | 31 | Jeff Jaeger | Raid. | 85.3 | Scott Norwood | Buff. | 56 | Pete Stoyanovich | Mia. | 121 | 1991 | Mia. |
| 1992 | NFC | Harry Newsome | Minn. | 45.0 | Chip Lohmiller | Wash. | 30 | Morten Andersen | N.O. | 85.3 | Mike Cofer | S.F. | 53 | Morten Andersen | N.O. | 120 | 1992 | NFC |
|  |  |  |  |  |  |  |  |  |  |  |  |  |  | Chip Lohmiller | Wash. | 120 |  |  |
| 1992 | AFC | Greg Montgomery | Hou. | 46.9 | Pete Stoyanovich | Mia. | 30 | Nick Lowery | K.C. | 91.7 | Steve Christie | Buff. | 43 | Pete Stoyanovich | Mia. | 124 | 1992 | AFC |
| 1993 | NFC | Jim Arnold | Det. | 44.5 | Jason Hanson | Det. | 34 | Norm Johnson | Atl. | 96.3 | Mike Cofer | S.F. | 59 | Jason Hanson | Det. | 130 | 1993 | NFC |
| 1993 | AFC | Greg Montgomery | Hou. | 45.6 | Jeff Jaeger | L.A.Rd. | 35 | Gary Anderson | Pitt. | 93.3 | Jason Elam | Den. | 41 | Jeff Jaeger | L.A.Rd. | 132 | 1993 | AFC |
| 1994 | NFC | Sean Landeta | L.A. | 44.8 | Fuad Reveiz | Minn. | 34 | Fuad Reveiz | Minn. | 87.2 | Doug Brien | S.F. | 60 | Emmitt Smith | Dall. | 132 | 1994 | NFC |
|  |  |  |  |  |  |  |  |  |  |  |  |  |  | Fuad Reveiz | Minn. | 132 |  |  |
| 1994 | AFC | Jeff Gossett | Raid. | 43.9 | John Carney | S.D. | 34 | Matt Stover | Clev. | 92.9 | Steve Christie | Buff. | 38 | John Carney | S.D. | 135 | 1994 | AFC |
| 1995 | NFC | Sean Landeta | StL. | 44.3 | Morten Andersen | Atl. | 31 | Chris Boniol | Dall. | 96.4 | Jason Hanson | Det. | 48 | Emmitt Smith | Dall. | 150 | 1995 | NFC |
| 1995 | AFC | Rick Tuten | Sea. | 45.0 | Norm Johnson | Pitt. | 34 | Matt Stover | Clev. | 87.9 | Todd Peterson | Sea. | 40 | Norm Johnson | Pitt. | 141 | 1995 | AFC |

# YEARLY RETURN LEADERS

**PUNT RETURNS** | **KICKOFF RETURNS**

| YEAR | LGUE | Returns Name | Tm | No | Yards Name | Tm | Yds | Avg Name | Tm | Avg | Returns Name | Tm | No | Yards Name | Tm | Yds | Avg Name | Tm | Avg | YEAR | LGUE |
|---|---|---|---|---|---|---|---|---|---|---|---|---|---|---|---|---|---|---|---|---|---|
| 1941 | NFL | Whizzer White | Det. | 19 | Whizzer White | Det. | 262 | | | | Marshall Goldberg | ChiC | 15 | Marshall Goldberg | ChiC | 393 | | | | 1941 | NFL |
| 1942 | NFL | Merl Condit | Bkn. | 21 | Bill Dudley | Pit. | 271 | Emie Steele | Phi. | 26.4 | Ken Heineman | Bkn. | 16 | Ken Heineman | Bkn. | 442 | Bill Dudley | Pit. | 27.1 | 1942 | NFL |
| 1943 | NFL | Andy Farkas | Was. | 15 | Frankie Sinkwich | Det. | 228 | Frankie Sinkwich | Det. | 20.7 | John Grigas | C-P | 23 | John Grigas | C-P | 471 | Ned Matthews | Det. | 35.1 | 1943 | NFL |
| 1944 | NFL | Bob Davis | Bos. | 22 | Bob Davis | Bos. | 271 | Emie Steele | Phi. | 16.5 | Frank Seno | ChiC | 19 | Frank Seno | ChiC | 408 | Steve Van Buren | Phi. | 33.3 | 1944 | NFL |
| 1945 | NFL | Steve Bagarus | Was. | 21 | Steve Bagarus | Was. | 251 | Fred Gehrke | Cle. | 15.0 | | | | | | | Ted Fritsch | G.B. | 34.9 | 1945 | NFL |
| 1946 | NFL | Bill Dudley | Pit. | 27 | Bill Dudley | Pit. | 385 | Gil Steinke | Phi. | 14.5 | Sonny Karnofsky | Bos. | 21 | Sonny Karnofsky | Bos. | 599 | Frank Seno | ChiC | 31.4 | 1946 | NFL |
| 1946 | AAFC | Ken Casanega; Bob Seymour | S.F.; L.A. | 18 | Chuck Fenenbock | L.A. | 299 | Chuck Fenenbock | L.A. | 18.7 | Steve Juzwik | Buf. | 21 | Chuck Fenenbock | L.A. | 479 | Monk Gafford | Bkn.-Mia. | 31.4 | 1946 | NFL |
| 1947 | NFL | Walt Slater | Pit. | 28 | Walt Slater | Pit. | 435 | Frank Seno | Bos. | 17.8 | Eddie Saenz | Was. | 29 | Eddie Saenz | Was. | 797 | Steve Van Buren | Phi. | 29.4 | 1947 | NFL |
| 1947 | AAFC | Glenn Dobbs | Bkn.-L.A. | 19 | Glenn Dobbs | Bkn.-L.A. | 215 | Spec Sanders | N.Y. | 27.3 | Spec Sanders | N.Y. | 22 | Chet Mutryn | Buf. | 691 | Chet Mutryn | Buf. | 32.9 | 1947 | AAFC |
| 1948 | NFL | George McAfee | ChiB | 30 | George McAfee | ChiB | 417 | Jerry Davis | ChiC | 20.9 | Dan Sandifer | Was. | 26 | Dan Sandifer | Was. | 594 | Frank Minini | G.B. | 30.8 | 1948 | NFL |
| 1948 | AAFC | Cliff Lewis | Cle. | 26 | Herm Wedermeyer | L.A. | 368 | Tom Casey | N.Y. | 25.4 | Monk Gafford | Bkn. | 23 | Monk Gafford | Bkn. | 559 | Forrest Hall | S.F. | 28.4 | 1948 | AAFC |
| 1949 | NFL | Vitamin Smith | L.A. | 27 | Vitamin Smith | L.A. | 427 | Red Cochran | ChiC | 20.9 | Eddie Saenz; Dan Sandifer | Was.; Was. | 24 | Don Doll | Det. | 536 | John Salscheider | NY G | 31.6 | 1949 | NFL |
| 1949 | AAFC | Pete Layden | N.Y. | 29 | Jim Cason | S.F. | 351 | Buddy Young | N.Y. | 19.0 | Herm Wedermeyer | Bal. | 30 | Herm Wedermeyer | Bal. | 602 | Ray Ramsey | Chi. | 29.2 | 1949 | AAFC |
| 1950 | NFL | George McAfee | ChiB | 33 | Billy Grimes | G.B. | 555 | Herb Rich | Bal. | 23.0 | Don Paul | ChiC | 28 | Vitamin Smith | L.A. | 742 | Vitamin Smith | L.A. | 33.7 | 1950 | NFL |
| 1951 | NFL | Em Tunnell | NY G | 34 | Em Tunnell | NY G | 489 | Buddy Young | NY Y | 19.3 | George Taliaferro | NY Y | 27 | George Taliaferro | NY Y | 622 | Lynn Chandnois | Pit. | 32.5 | 1951 | NFL |
| 1952 | NFL | Bibbles Bawel | Phi. | 34 | Em Tunnell | NY G | 411 | Jack Christiansen | Det. | 21.5 | Billy Baggett; Buddy Young | Dal.; Dal. | 23 | Buddy Young | Dal. | 643 | Lynn Chandnois | Pit. | 35.2 | 1952 | NFL |
| 1953 | NFL | Em Tunnell | NY G | 38 | Woodley Lewis | L.A. | 267 | Charlie Trippi | ChiC | 11.4 | Woodley Lewis | L.A. | 32 | Woodley Lewis | L.A. | 830 | Joe Arenas | S.F. | 34.4 | 1953 | NFL |
| 1954 | NFL | Chet Hanulak | Cle. | 27 | Veryl Switzer | G.B. | 306 | Veryl Switzer | G.B. | 12.8 | Woodley Lewis | L.A. | 34 | Woodley Lewis | L.A. | 836 | Billy Reynolds | Cle. | 29.5 | 1954 | NFL |
| 1955 | NFL | Bert Rechichar | Bal. | 30 | Ollie Matson | ChiC | 245 | Ollie Matson | ChiC | 18.8 | Sid Watson | Pit. | 27 | Sid Watson | Pit. | 716 | Al Carmichael | G.B. | 29.9 | 1955 | NFL |
| 1956 | NFL | Carl Taseff | Bal. | 30 | Carl Taseff | Bal. | 233 | Kenny Konz | Cle. | 14.4 | Al Carmichael | G.B. | 33 | Al Carmichael | G.B. | 927 | Tom Wilson | L.A. | 31.8 | 1956 | NFL |
| 1957 | NFL | Tommy McDonald | Phi. | 26 | Bert Zagers | Was. | 217 | Bert Zagers | Was. | 15.5 | Al Carmichael | G.B. | 31 | Al Carmichael | G.B. | 690 | Jon Arnett | L.A. | 28.0 | 1957 | NFL |
| 1958 | NFL | Carl Taseff | Bal. | 29 | Jon Arnett | L.A. | 223 | Jon Arnett | L.A. | 12.4 | Jimmy Sears | ChiC | 32 | Jimmy Sears | ChiC | 756 | Ollie Matson | ChiC | 35.5 | 1958 | NFL |
| 1959 | NFL | Bill Stacy | ChiC | 29 | Bill Stacy | ChiC | 281 | Johnny Morris | ChiB | 12.2 | Lenny Lyles | S.F. | 33 | Lenny Lyles | S.F. | 565 | Abe Woodson | S.F. | 34.9 | 1959 | NFL |
| 1960 | NFL | Bill Stits | NY G | 18 | Abe Woodson | S.F. | 174 | Abe Woodson | S.F. | 13.4 | Ted Dean; Tom Frankhouser | Phi.; Dal. | 26 | Ted Dean | Phi. | 533 | Tom Moore | G.B. | 33.1 | 1960 | NFL |
| 1960 | AFL | Al Carmichael | Den. | 15 | Abner Haynes | Dal. | 215 | Abner Haynes | Dal. | 15.4 | Leon Burton | NY T | 31 | Leon Burton | NY T | 897 | Ken Hall | Hou. | 31.3 | 1960 | AFL |
| 1961 | NFL | Johnny Sample | Pit. | 26 | Johnny Sample | Pit. | 283 | Willie Wood | G.B. | 16.1 | Timmy Brown; Jim Steffen | Phi.; Was. | 29 | Timmy Brown | Phi. | 811 | Dick Bass | L.A. | 30.3 | 1961 | NFL |
| 1961 | AFL | Fred Bruney | Bos. | 23 | Dick Christy | NY T | 383 | Dick Christy | NY T | 21.3 | George Fleming | Oak. | 29 | Frank Jackson | Dal. | 645 | Dave Grayson | Oak. | 28.3 | 1961 | AFL |
| 1962 | NFL | Pat Studstill | Det. | 29 | Pat Studstill | Det. | 457 | Pat Studstill | Det. | 15.8 | Abe Woodson | S.F. | 37 | Abe Woodson | S.F. | 1157 | Abe Woodson | S.F. | 31.3 | 1962 | NFL |
| 1962 | AFL | Leon Burton | Bos. | 21 | Dick Christy | NY T | 250 | Dick Christy | NY T | 16.7 | Dick Christy | NY T | 38 | Dick Christy | NY T | 824 | Bobby Jancik | Hou. | 30.3 | 1962 | AFL |
| 1963 | NFL | Tom Watkins | Det. | 32 | Tom Watkins | Det. | 399 | Dick James | Was. | 13.4 | Timmy Brown; Bill Butler | Phi.; Min. | 33 | Timmy Brown | Phi. | 945 | Abe Woodson | S.F. | 32.2 | 1963 | NFL |
| 1963 | AFL | Claude Gibson | Oak. | 26 | Claude Gibson | Oak. | 307 | Claude Gibson | Oak. | 11.8 | Bobby Jancik | Hou. | 45 | Bobby Jancik | Hou. | 1317 | Bobby Jancik | Hou. | 29.3 | 1963 | AFL |
| 1964 | NFL | Mel Renfro | Dal. | 32 | Mel Renfro | Dal. | 418 | Tom Watkins | Det. | 14.9 | Mel Renfro | Dal. | 40 | Mel Renfro | Dal. | 1017 | Clarence Childs | NY G | 29.0 | 1964 | NFL |
| 1964 | AFL | Hagood Clarke | Buf. | 33 | Claude Gibson | Oak. | 419 | Bobby Jancik | Hou. | 18.3 | Odell Barry | Den. | 47 | Odell Barry | Den. | 1245 | Bo Roberson | Oak. | 27.1 | 1964 | AFL |
| 1965 | NFL | Alvin Haymond | Bal. | 41 | Alvin Haymond | Bal. | 403 | Leroy Kelly | Cle. | 15.6 | Kermit Alexander | S.F. | 32 | Kermit Alexander | S.F. | 741 | Tom Watkins | Det. | 34.4 | 1965 | NFL |
| 1965 | AFL | Claude Gibson | Oak. | 31 | Speedy Duncan | S.D. | 464 | Speedy Duncan | S.D. | 15.5 | Abner Haynes | Den. | 34 | Abner Haynes | Den. | 901 | Abner Haynes | Den. | 26.5 | 1965 | AFL |
| 1966 | NFL | Alvin Haymond | Bal. | 40 | Alvin Haymond | Bal. | 347 | Johnny Roland | St.L. | 11.1 | Ron Smith | Atl. | 43 | Ron Smith | Atl. | 1013 | Gale Sayers | Chi. | 31.2 | 1966 | NFL |
| 1966 | AFL | Rodger Bird | Oak. | 37 | Rodger Bird | Oak. | 323 | Speedy Duncan | S.D. | 13.2 | Bobby Jancik | Hou. | 33 | Bobby Jancik | Hou. | 875 | Goldie Sellers | Den. | 28.5 | 1966 | AFL |
| 1967 | NFL | Doug Cunningham | S.F. | 27 | Bob Hayes | Dal. | 276 | Ben Davis | Cle. | 12.7 | Ron Smith | Atl. | 39 | Ron Smith | Atl. | 976 | Travis Williams | G.B. | 41.1 | 1967 | NFL |
| 1967 | AFL | Rodger Bird | Oak. | 46 | Rodger Bird | Oak. | 612 | Floyd Little | Den. | 16.9 | Noland Smith | K.C. | 33 | Noland Smith | K.C. | 1148 | Zeke Moore | Hou. | 28.9 | 1967 | AFL |
| 1968 | NFL | Roy Jefferson; Chuck Latourette | Pit.; St.L. | 28 | Chuck Latourette | St.L. | 345 | Bob Hayes | Dal. | 20.8 | Chuck Latourette | St.L. | 46 | Chuck Latourette | St.L. | 1237 | Preston Pearson | Bal. | 35.1 | 1968 | NFL |
| 1968 | AFL | Butch Atkinson | Oak. | 36 | Butch Atkinson | Oak. | 490 | Noland Smith | K.C. | 15.0 | Max Anderson | Buf. | 39 | Max Anderson | Buf. | 971 | Butch Atkinson | Oak. | 25.1 | 1968 | AFL |
| 1969 | NFL | Charlie West | Min. | 39 | Alvin Haymond | L.A. | 435 | Alvin Haymond | L.A. | 13.2 | Preston Pearson | Bal. | 31 | Bo Scott | Cle. | 722 | Bobby Williams | Det. | 33.1 | 1969 | NFL |
| 1969 | AFL | Jerry LeVias | Hou. | 35 | Jerry LeVias | Hou. | 292 | Bill Thompson | Den. | 11.5 | Mercury Morris | Mia. | 43 | Mercury Morris | Mia. | 1136 | Bill Thompson | Den. | 28.5 | 1969 | AFL |
| 1970 | NFC | Alvin Haymond | L.A. | 53 | Bruce Taylor | S.F. | 516 | Bruce Taylor | S.F. | 12.0 | Alvin Haymond | L.A. | 35 | Alvin Haymond | L.A. | 1022 | Cecil Turner | Chi. | 32.7 | 1970 | NFC |
| 1970 | AFC | Hubie Bryant | Pit. | 37 | Ron Gardin | Bal. | 330 | Ed Podolak | K.C. | 13.5 | Mike Battle | NY J | 39 | Mike Battle | NY J | 891 | Jim Duncan | Bal. | 35.4 | 1970 | AFC |
| 1971 | NFC | Bruce Taylor | S.F. | 34 | Bruce Taylor | S.F. | 235 | Speedy Duncan | Was. | 10.6 | Dave Hampton | G.B. | 46 | Dave Hampton | G.B. | 1314 | Travis Williams | L.A. | 29.7 | 1971 | NFC |
| 1971 | AFC | Jake Scott | Mia. | 33 | Jake Scott | Mia. | 318 | Leroy Kelly | Cle. | 9.7 | Linzy Cole | Hou. | 32 | Linzy Cole | Hou. | 834 | Mercury Morris | Mia. | 28.2 | 1971 | AFC |
| 1972 | NFC | Ron Smith | Chi. | 26 | Jim Bertelsen | L.A. | 232 | Margene Adkins | G.B. | 15.4 | Margene Adkins | N.O. | 43 | Margene Adkins | N.O. | 1020 | Ron Smith | Chi. | 30.8 | 1972 | NFC |
| 1972 | AFC | Bruce Laird | Bal. | 34 | Bruce Laird | Bal. | 303 | Chris Farasopoulos | NY J | 10.5 | Jesse Taylor | S.D. | 31 | Bruce Laird | Bal. | 843 | Bruce Laird | Bal. | 29.1 | 1972 | AFC |
| 1973 | NFC | Ray Brown | Atl. | 40 | Ray Brown | Atl. | 360 | Bruce Taylor | S.F. | 13.8 | Herb Mul-Key | Was. | 36 | Herb Mul-Key | Was. | 1011 | Carl Garrett | Chi. | 30.4 | 1973 | NFC |
| 1973 | AFC | Butch Atkinson; Mack Herron | Oak.; N.E. | 41 | Bill Thompson | Den. | 366 | Ron Smith | S.D. | 13.0 | | | | Mack Herron | N.E. | 1092 | Wallace Francis | Buf. | 29.9 | 1973 | AFC |
| 1974 | NFC | Howard Stevens | N.O. | 37 | Howard Stevens | N.O. | 376 | Dick Jauron | Det. | 16.8 | Jimmie Jones | Det. | 38 | Jimmie Jones | Det. | 927 | Terry Metcalf | St.L. | 31.2 | 1974 | NFC |
| 1974 | AFC | Donnie Walker | Buf. | 43 | Lynn Swann | Pit. | 577 | Lemar Parrish | Cin. | 18.8 | Lou Piccone | NY J | 39 | Lou Piccone | NY J | 961 | Greg Pruitt | Cle. | 27.5 | 1974 | AFC |
| 1975 | NFC | Larry Jones | Was. | 53 | Virgil Livers | Chi. | 456 | Terry Metcalf | St.L. | 12.4 | Larry Jones | Was. | 47 | Larry Jones | Was. | 1086 | Walter Payton | Chi. | 31.7 | 1975 | NFC |
| 1975 | AFC | Neal Colzie | Oak. | 48 | Neal Colzie | Oak. | 655 | Billy Johnson | Hou. | 15.3 | Rick Upchurch | Den. | 40 | Rick Upchurch | Den. | 1084 | Harold Hart | Oak. | 30.5 | 1975 | AFC |
| 1976 | NFC | Rolland Lawrence | Atl. | 54 | Eddie Brown | Was. | 646 | Eddie Brown | Was. | 13.5 | Eddie Brown; Larry Marshall; Oliver Ross | Was.; Phi.; Sea. | 30 | Brian Baschnagel | Chi. | 754 | Cullen Bryant | L.A. | 28.7 | 1976 | NFC |
| 1976 | AFC | Mike Haynes | N.E. | 45 | Mike Haynes | N.E. | 608 | Rick Upchurch | Den. | 13.7 | Lou Piccone | NY J | 31 | Willie Shelby | Cin. | 761 | Duriel Harris | Mia. | 32.9 | 1976 | AFC |
| 1977 | NFC | Eddie Brown | Was. | 57 | Larry Marshall | Phi. | 489 | Larry Marshall | Phi. | 10.6 | Paul Hofer | S.F. | 36 | Paul Hofer | S.F. | 871 | Wilbert Montgomery | Phi. | 26.9 | 1977 | NFC |
| | | | | | | | | | | | | | | Bruce Harper | NY J | 1035 | Ray Claybom | N.E. | 31.0 | 1977 | AFC |

# YEARLY RETURN LEADERS

## PUNT RETURNS

| YEAR | LGUE | RETURNS (Name, Team, No.) | YARDS (Name, Team, Yds) | AVERAGE YARDS (Name, Team, Avg) |
|---|---|---|---|---|
| 1977 | AFC | Rick Upchurch, Den., 51 | Rick Upchurch, Den., 653 | Billy Johnson, Hou., 15.4 |
| 1978 | AFC | Neal Colzie, Den., 47 | Rick Upchurch, Den., 493 | Rick Upchurch, Den., 13.7 |
| 1978 | NFC | Jackie Wallace, L.A., 52 | Jackie Wallace, L.A., 618 | Jackie Wallace, L.A., 11.9 |
| 1979 | AFC | J.T. Smith, K.C., 58 | J.T. Smith, K.C., 612 | Tony Nathan, Mia., 10.9 |
| 1979 | NFC | Danny Reece, T.B., 70 | Danny Reece, T.B., 431 | John Sciarra, Phi., 11.4 |
| 1980 | AFC | Ira Matthews, Oak., 48 | J.T. Smith, K.C., 581 | J.T. Smith, K.C., 14.5 |
| 1980 | NFC | Danny Reece, T.B., 57 | James Jones, Dal., 548 | Kenny Johnson, Atl., 12.2 |
| 1981 | AFC | J.T. Smith, K.C., 50 | J.T. Smith, K.C., 528 | James Brooks, S.D., 13.2 |
| 1981 | NFC | Wally Henry, Phi., 54 | LeRoy Irvin, L.A., 615 | LeRoy Irvin, L.A., 13.4 |
| 1982 | AFC | Greg Pruitt, Raid., 27 | Rick Upchurch, Den., 242 | Rick Upchurch, Den., 16.1 |
| 1982 | NFC | Leon Bright, NY G, 37 | Leon Bright, NY G, 325 | Billy Johnson, Atl., 11.4 |
| 1983 | AFC | Greg Pruitt, Raid., 58 | Greg Pruitt, Raid., 666 | Kirk Springs, NY J, 13.6 |
| 1983 | NFC | Billy Johnson, Atl., 46 | Billy Johnson, Atl., 489 | Henry Ellard, L.A., 13.6 |
| 1984 | AFC | Louis Lipps, Pit., 53; Greg Pruitt, Raid., 53 | Louis Lipps, Pit., 656 | Mike Martin, Cin., 15.7 |
| 1984 | NFC | Jeff Fisher, Chi., 57 | Dana McLemore, S.F., 521 | Henry Ellard, L.A., 13.4 |
| 1985 | AFC | Fulton Walker, Raid., 62 | Fulton Walker, Raid., 692 | Irving Fryar, N.E., 14.1 |
| 1985 | NFC | Phil McConkey, NY G, 53 | Henry Ellard, L.A., 501 | Henry Ellard, L.A., 13.5 |
| 1986 | AFC | Fulton Walker, Raid., 49 | Gerald Wilhite, Den., 468 | Bobby Joe Edmonds, Sea., 12.3 |
| 1986 | NFC | Lew Barnes, Chi., 57 | Vai Sikahema, St.L., 522 | Vai Sikahema, St.L., 12.1 |
| 1987 | AFC | Ice Cube McNeil, Cle., 34 | Bobby Joe Edmonds, Sea., 400 | Bobby Joe Edmonds, Sea., 12.6 |
| 1987 | NFC | Vai Sikahema, St.L., 44 | Vai Sikahema, St.L., 550 | Mel Gray, N.O., 14.7 |
| 1988 | AFC | Tim Brown, Raid., 49 | Tim Brown, Raid., 444 | JoJo Townsell, NYJ, 11.7 |
| 1988 | NFC | Leo Lewis, Min., 58 | John Taylor, S.F., 556 | John Taylor, S.F., 12.6 |
| 1989 | NFC | Dave Meggett, NYG, 46 | Dave Meggett, NYG, 582 | Walter Stanley, Det., 13.8 |
| 1989 | AFC | Gerald McNeil, Clev., 49 | Gerald McNeil, Clev., 496 | Clarence Verdin, Ind., 12.9 |
| 1990 | NFC | Dave Meggett, NYG, 43 | Dave Meggett, NYG, 467 | Johnny Bailey, Chi., 11.1 |
| 1990 | AFC | Rod Woodson, Pit., 38 | Rod Woodson, Pit., 398 | Clarence Verdin, Ind., 12.8 |
| 1991 | NFC | Rod Harris, Phil., 53 | Brian Mitchell, Wash., 600 | Mel Gray, Det., 15.4 |
| 1991 | AFC | Chris Warren, Sea., 32 | Tim Brown, Raid., 330 | Rod Woodson, Pitt., 11.4 |
| 1992 | NFC | Kelvin Martin, Dall., 42 | Kelvin Martin, Dall., 532 | Johnny Bailey, Phx., 13.2 |
| 1992 | AFC | Eric Metcalf, Clev., 44 | Eric Metcalf, Clev., 429 | Rod Woodson, Pitt., 11.4 |
| 1993 | NFC | Kevin Williams, Dall., 38 | Tyrone Hughes, N.O., 503 | Tyrone Hughes, N.O., 13.6 |
| 1993 | AFC | Patrick Robinson, Cin., 43 | Tim Brown, L.A.Rd., 465 | Eric Metcalf, Clev., 12.9 |
| 1994 | NFC | Patrick Robinson, Ariz., 41 | Brian Mitchell, Wash., 452 | Brian Mitchell, Wash., 14.1 |
| 1994 | AFC | Dewell Brewer, Ind., 42 | Tim Brown, Raid., 487 | Darrien Gordon, S.D., 13.2 |
| 1995 | NFC | Todd Kinchen, StL., 53 | Eric Guliford, Car., 475 | David Palmer, Minn., 13.2 |
| 1995 | AFC | Tamarick Vanover, K.C., 51 | Tamarick Vanover, K.C., 540 | Andre Coleman, S.D., 11.6 |

## KICKOFF RETURNS

| RETURNS (Name, Team, No.) | YARDS (Name, Team, Yds) | AVERAGE YARDS (Name, Team, Avg) | YEAR | LGUE |
|---|---|---|---|---|
| Bruce Harper, NY J, 42 | Bruce Harper, NY J, 1280 | Keith Wright, Cle., 26.3 | 1978 | AFC |
| Kevin Miller, Min., 40 | Tony Green, Was., 870 | Steve Odom, G.B., 27.1 | 1978 | NFC |
| Bruce Harper, NY J, 55; David Turner, Cin., 55 | Bruce Harper, NY J, 1158 | Larry Brunson, Oak., 25.9 | 1979 | AFC |
| Jimmy Edwards, Min., 40; Steve Odom, GB-NYG, 40 | Jimmy Edwards, Min., 1103 | Jimmy Edwards, Min., 25.1 | 1979 | NFC |
| Bruce Harper, NY J, 49 | Bruce Harper, NY J, 1070 | Horace Ivory, N.E., 27.6 | 1980 | AFC |
|  | Eddie Payton, Min., 1184 | Rich Mauti, N.O., 25.7 | 1980 | NFC |
| James Brooks, S.D., 40 | James Brooks, S.D., 949 | Carl Roaches, Hou., 27.5 | 1981 | AFC |
| Drew Hill, L.A., 60 | Stump Mitchell, St.L., 1292 | Mike Nelms, Was., 29.7 | 1981 | NFC |
| James Brooks, S.D., 33 | James Brooks, S.D., 749 | Mike Mosley, Buf., 27.1 | 1982 | AFC |
| Wally Henry, Phil., 24; Reggie Brown, Atl., 24 | Mike Nelms, Was., 557 | Alvin Hall, Det., 26.6 | 1982 | NFC |
| Zachary Dixon, Bal.-Sea., 51 | Zachary Dixon, Bal.-Sea., 1171 | Fulton Walker, Mia., 26.7 | 1983 | AFC |
| Ron Fellows, Dal., 43 | Ron Fellows, Dal., 855 | Darrin Nelson, Min., 24.7 | 1983 | NFC |
| Lionel James, S.D., 43 | Lionel James, S.D., 959 | Bobby Humphery, NY J, 30.7 | 1984 | AFC |
| Mike Nelms, Was., 42 | Darrin Nelson, Min., 891 | Barry Redden, L.A., 23.0 | 1984 | NFC |
| Mike Martin, Cin., 48; Stephen Starring, N.E., 48 | Mike Martin, Cin., 1104 | Glen Young, Cle., 25.7 | 1985 | AFC |
| Buster Rhymes, Min., 48 | Buster Rhymes, Min., 1345 | Ron Brown, L.A., 32.8 | 1985 | NFC |
| Gerald McNeil, Cle., 47 | Tim McGee, Cin., 1007 | Lupe Sanchez, Pit., 23.6 | 1986 | AFC |
| Herman Hunter, Det., 49 | Herman Hunter, Det., 1007 | Dennis Gentry, Chi., 28.8 | 1986 | NFC |
| Paul Palmer, K.C., 38 | Paul Palmer, K.C., 923 | Paul Palmer, K.C., 24.3 | 1987 | AFC |
| Neal Guggemos, Min., 36 | Neal Guggemos, Min., 808 | Sylvester Stamps, Atl., 27.5 | 1987 | NFC |
| Tim Brown, Raid., 41 | Tim Brown, Raid., 1098 | Tim Brown, Raid., 26.8 | 1988 | AFC |
| Daryl Harris, Min., 39 | Daryl Harris, Min., 833 | Donnie Elder, T.B., 22.7 | 1988 | NFC |
| James Dixon, Dall., 47; Ron Brown, L.A., 47 | James Dixon, Dall., 1181 | Mel Gray, Det, 26.7 | 1989 | NFC |
| Rod Woodson, Pitt., 36 | Rod Woodson, Pitt., 982 | Rod Woodson, Pitt., 27.3 | 1989 | AFC |
| Herschel Walker, Min., 44 | Herschel Walker, Min., 966 | Dave Meggett, NYG, 23.4 | 1990 | NFC |
| Eric Metcalf, Cle., 52 | Eric Metcalf, Cle., 1052 | Kevin Clark, Den., 25.3 | 1990 | AFC |
| Dexter Carter, S.F., 37 | Mel Gray, Det., 929 | Mel Gray, Det., 25.8 | 1991 | NFC |
| Rod Woodson, Pitt., 44 | Rod Woodson, Pitt., 880 | Nate Lewis, S.D., 25.1 | 1991 | AFC |
| Mel Gray, Det., 42 | Deion Sanders, Atl., 1067 | Deion Sanders, Atl., 26.7 | 1992 | NFC |
| Clarence Verdin, Ind., 39 | Clarence Verdin, Ind., 815 | Jon Vaughn, N.E., 28.2 | 1992 | AFC |
| Qadry Ismail, Minn., 42 | Tony Smith, Atl., 948 | Robert Brooks, G.B., 26.6 | 1993 | NFC |
| Clarence Verdin, Ind., 50 | Clarence Verdin, Ind., 1050 | Raghib Ismail, L.A.Rd., 24.2 | 1993 | AFC |
| Tyrone Hughes, N.O., 63 | Tyrone Hughes, N.O., 1556 | Mel Gray, Det., 28.4 | 1994 | NFC |
| Andre Coleman, S.D., 49 | Andre Coleman, S.D., 1293 | Randy Baldwin, Clev., 26.9 | 1994 | AFC |
| Tyrone Hughes, N.O., 66 | Tyrone Hughes, N.O., 1617 | Brian Mitchell, Wash., 25.6 | 1995 | NFC |
| Andre Coleman, S.D., 62 | Andre Coleman, S.D., 1411 | Ron Carpenter, NYJ, 27.7 | 1995 | AFC |

# SINGLE SEASON LEADERS

## PASSING

**Note:** (For all single season leaders)—Number after individual name indicates the number of times that individual appears within a specific category ; the bold indicates the individual appearing most within a specific category.

### COMPLETIONS

| | | | | | |
|---|---|---|---|---|---|
| 1 | Warren Moon-1 | Hou. | AFC | 91 | 404 |
| 2 | Drew Bledsoe | N.E. | AFC | 94 | 400 |
| 3 | Dan Marino-1 | Mia. | AFC | 94 | 385 |
| 4 | Dan Marino-2 | Mia. | AFC | 86 | 377 |
| | Warren Moon-2 | Minn. | NFC | 95 | 377 |
| 6 | Warren Moon-3 | Minn. | NFC | 94 | 371 |
| 7 | Brett Favre-1 | G.B. | NFC | 93 | 363 |
| 8 | Dan Marino-3 | Mia. | AFC | 84 | 362 |
| | Warren Moon-4 | Hou. | AFC | 90 | 362 |
| 10 | Dan Fouts-1 | S.D. | AFC | 81 | 360 |
| 11 | Brett Favre-2 | G.B. | NFC | 95 | 359 |
| 12 | Dan Marino-4 | Mia. | AFC | 88 | 354 |
| 13 | Don Majkowski-1 | G.B. | NFC | 89 | 353 |
| 14 | Dan Fouts-2 | S.D. | AFC | 80 | 348 |
| | John Elway-1 | Den. | AFC | 93 | 348 |
| 16 | Steve DeBerg-1 | S.F. | NFC | 79 | 347 |
| 17 | Bill Kenney | K.C. | AFC | 83 | 346 |
| | Jim Everett-1 | N.O. | NFC | 94 | 346 |
| | Scott Mitchell | Det. | NFC | 95 | 346 |
| 20 | Neil Lomax-1 | St.L. | NFC | 84 | 345 |
| | Fran Tarkenton | Min. | NFC | 78 | 345 |
| | Jim Everett-2 | N.O. | NFC | 95 | 345 |
| 23 | Brian Sipe-1 | Cle. | AFC | 80 | 337 |
| 24 | Dan Marino-5 | Mia. | AFC | 85 | 336 |
| | Jeff George-1 | Atl. | NFC | 95 | 336 |
| 26 | Danny White-1 | Dal. | NFC | 83 | 334 |
| 27 | Dan Fouts-3 | S.D. | AFC | 80 | 332 |
| | Joe Montana-1 | S.F. | NFC | 83 | 332 |
| | Dan Marino-6 | Mia. | AFC | 92 | 332 |
| 30 | John Elway-2 | Den. | AFC | 85 | 327 |
| 31 | Jeff Blake | Cin. | AFC | 95 | 326 |
| 32 | Steve Young-1 | S.F. | NFC | 94 | 324 |
| 33 | Drew Bledsoe | N.E. | AFC | 95 | 323 |
| 34 | Tommy Kramer-1 | Min. | NFC | 81 | 322 |
| | Jeff George-2 | Atl. | NFC | 94 | 322 |
| 36 | Joe Montana-2 | S.F. | NFC | 90 | 321 |
| 37 | Dan Marino-7 | Mia. | AFC | 91 | 318 |
| | Brett Favre-3 | G.B. | NFC | 93 | 318 |
| 39 | Dan Fouts-4 | S.D. | AFC | 83 | 317 |
| 40 | John Elway-3 | Den. | AFC | 95 | 316 |
| 41 | Tommy Kramer-2 | Min. | NFC | 79 | 315 |
| | Erik Kramer | Chi. | NFC | 95 | 315 |
| 43 | Steve Young-2 | S.F. | NFC | 93 | 314 |
| 44 | Brian Sipe-2 | Clev. | AFC | 81 | 313 |
| 45 | Joe Montana-2 | S.F. | NFC | 81 | 311 |
| 46 | Bernie Kosar-1 | Cle. | AFC | 86 | 310 |
| 47 | Archie Manning-1 | N.O. | NFC | 80 | 309 |
| | Dan Marino-8 | Mia. | AFC | 95 | 309 |
| 49 | Richard Todd | NYJ | AFC | 83 | 308 |
| | Steve DeBerg-2 | T.B. | NFC | 84 | 308 |
| | Jim Everett-3 | L.A. | NFC | 88 | 308 |
| | Dan Marino-9 | Mia. | AFC | 89 | 308 |
| 53 | Jim Everett-4 | L.A. | NFC | 90 | 307 |
| | Bernie Kosar-2 | Clev. | AFC | 91 | 307 |
| | John Elway-4 | Den. | AFC | 94 | 307 |
| 56 | Dan Marino-10 | Mia. | AFC | 90 | 306 |
| 57 | Ken Stabler-1 | Oak. | AFC | 79 | 304 |
| | Jim Everett-5 | L.A. | NFC | 89 | 304 |
| | Jim Kelly | Buff. | AFC | 91 | 304 |
| | Dave Krieg | Ariz. | NFC | 95 | 304 |
| 61 | Joe Montana-4 | S.F. | NFC | 85 | 303 |
| | Bernie Kosar-3 | Clev. | AFC | 89 | 303 |
| | Warren Moon-5 | Hou. | AFC | 93 | 303 |
| 64 | Troy Aikman | Dall. | NFC | 92 | 302 |
| | Brett Favre-4 | G.B. | NFC | 92 | 302 |
| 66 | R. Cunningham-1 | Phil. | NFC | 88 | 301 |
| 67 | Ken Anderson-1 | Cin. | AFC | 81 | 300 |
| | Ken O'Brien-1 | NYJ | AFC | 86 | 300 |
| 69 | Tommy Kramer-3 | Min. | NFC | 80 | 299 |
| | Joe Montana-5 | K.C. | AFC | 94 | 299 |
| 71 | Steve Bartkowski | Atl. | NFC | 81 | 297 |
| | Ken O'Brien-2 | NYJ | AFC | 85 | 297 |
| 73 | John Elway-5 | Den | AFC | 90 | 294 |
| 74 | Ken Stabler-2 | Hou. | AFC | 80 | 293 |
| | Joe Theismann | Was. | NFC | 81 | 293 |
| | Steve Bono | K.C. | AFC | 95 | 293 |
| 77 | Jeff George-2 | Ind. | AFC | 91 | 292 |
| 78 | Archie Manning-2 | N.O. | NFC | 78 | 291 |
| | Brian Sipe-3 | Cle. | AFC | 83 | 291 |
| 80 | R. Cunningham-2 | Phil. | NFC | 89 | 290 |
| 81 | Lynn Dickey | G.B. | NFC | 83 | 289 |

### COMPLETION PERCENTAGE

(Minimum 100 Attempts)

| | | | | | Att. | Comp. | Pct. |
|---|---|---|---|---|---|---|---|
| 1 | Ken Anderson-1 | Cin. | AFC | 82 | 309 | 218 | 70.6 |
| 2 | Sammy Baugh-1 | Was. | NFL | 45 | 182 | 128 | 70.3 |
| 3 | Steve Young-1 | S.F. | NFC | 94 | 461 | 324 | 70.3 |
| 4 | Joe Montana-1 | S.F. | NFC | 89 | 386 | 271 | 70.2 |
| 5 | Troy Aikman-1 | Dall. | NFC | 93 | 392 | 271 | 69.1 |
| 6 | Steve Young-2 | S.F. | NFC | 93 | 462 | 314 | 68.0 |
| 7 | Steve Bartkowski-1 | Atl. | NFC | 84 | 269 | 181 | 67.3 |
| 8 | Steve Young-3 | S.F. | NFC | 95 | 447 | 299 | 66.9 |
| 9 | Joe Montana-2 | S.F. | NFC | 87 | 398 | 266 | 66.8 |
| 10 | Ken Stabler-1 | Oak. | AFC | 76 | 291 | 194 | 66.7 |
| | Ken Anderson-2 | Cin | AFC | 83 | 297 | 198 | 66.7 |
| | Turk Schonert | Cin | AFC | 84 | 117 | 78 | 66.7 |
| | Steve Young-4 | S.F. | NFC | 92 | 402 | 268 | 66.7 |
| 14 | Dave Krieg | Sea. | AFC | 91 | 285 | 187 | 65.6 |
| | Cody Carlson | Hou. | AFC | 92 | 227 | 149 | 65.6 |
| 16 | Len Dawson-1 | K.C. | AFC | 75 | 140 | 93 | 66.4 |
| 17 | Len Dawson-2 | K.C. | AFC | 73 | 101 | 66 | 65.3 |
| | Troy Aikman-2 | Dall. | NFC | 91 | 363 | 237 | 65.3 |
| 19 | Ken Anderson-3 | Cin. | AFC | 74 | 328 | 213 | 64.9 |
| 20 | Troy Aikman-3 | Dall. | NFC | 95 | 432 | 280 | 64.8 |
| 21 | Otto Graham | Cle. | NFL | 53 | 258 | 167 | 64.7 |
| | Warren Moon-1 | Hou. | AFC | 92 | 346 | 224 | 64.7 |
| 23 | Joe Montana-3 | S.F. | NFC | 84 | 432 | 279 | 64.6 |
| 24 | Joe Montana-4 | S.F. | NFC | 80 | 273 | 176 | 64.5 |
| | Joe Montana-5 | S.F. | NFC | 83 | 515 | 332 | 64.5 |
| | Steve Young-5 | S.F. | NFC | 91 | 279 | 180 | 64.5 |
| | Troy Aikman-4 | Dall. | NFC | 94 | 361 | 233 | 64.5 |
| 28 | Fran Tarkenton-1 | Min. | NFC | 75 | 475 | 273 | 64.2 |
| | Dan Marino-1 | Mia. | AFC | 84 | 564 | 362 | 64.2 |
| 30 | Ken Stabler-2 | Hou. | AFC | 80 | 457 | 293 | 64.1 |
| | Sonny Jurgensen-1 | Was. | NFC | 74 | 167 | 107 | 64.1 |
| | Jim Kelly-1 | Buff. | AFC | 91 | 474 | 304 | 64.1 |
| | Troy Aikman-5 | Dall. | NFC | 92 | 473 | 302 | 64.1 |
| | Jim Everett | N.O. | NFC | 94 | 540 | 346 | 64.1 |
| | Dan Marino-2 | Mia. | AFC | 95 | 482 | 309 | 64.1 |
| 36 | Joe Theismann | Was. | NFC | 82 | 252 | 161 | 63.9 |
| 37 | Bart Starr-1 | G.B. | NFL | 68 | 171 | 109 | 63.7 |
| | Joe Montana-6 | S.F. | NFC | 81 | 488 | 311 | 63.7 |
| | Jim Harbaugh | Ind. | AFC | 95 | 314 | 200 | 63.7 |
| 40 | John Brodie-1 | S.F. | NFC | 72 | 110 | 70 | 63.6 |
| | Ken Anderson-4 | Cin. | AFC | 84 | 275 | 175 | 63.6 |
| | Jim Kelly-2 | Buff. | AFC | 94 | 448 | 285 | 63.6 |
| 43 | Steve Bartkowski-2 | Atl. | NFC | 82 | 262 | 166 | 63.4 |
| | Steve Bartkowski-3 | Atl. | NFC | 83 | 432 | 274 | 63.4 |
| 45 | Jim Kelly-3 | Buf. | AFC | 90 | 346 | 219 | 63.3 |
| 46 | Danny White-1 | Dal. | NFC | 82 | 247 | 156 | 63.2 |
| | Dan Fouts | S.D. | AFC | 83 | 340 | 215 | 63.2 |
| | John Elway-1 | Den. | AFC | 93 | 551 | 348 | 63.2 |
| | Chris Chandler | Hou. | AFC | 95 | 356 | 225 | 63.2 |
| 50 | Y.A. Tittle | S.F. | NFL | 57 | 279 | 176 | 63.1 |
| 51 | Bob Griese-1 | Mia. | AFC | 78 | 235 | 148 | 63.0 |
| | Eric Hipple | Det. | NFC | 86 | 305 | 192 | 63.0 |
| | Brett Favre-1 | G.B. | NFC | 95 | 570 | 359 | 63.0 |
| 54 | Bobby Hebert | N.O. | NFC | 89 | 353 | 222 | 62.9 |
| 55 | Jeff Hostetler | NYG | NFC | 91 | 285 | 179 | 62.8 |
| 56 | Sammy Baugh-2 | Was. | NFL | 40 | 177 | 111 | 62.7 |
| | Ken Stabler-3 | Oak. | AFC | 73 | 260 | 163 | 62.7 |
| | Danny White-2 | Dal. | NFC | 83 | 533 | 334 | 62.7 |
| 59 | Dan Fouts-2 | S.D. | AFC | 79 | 530 | 332 | 62.6 |
| | Ken Anderson-5 | Cin. | AFC | 81 | 479 | 300 | 62.6 |
| | Roger Staubach | Dal. | NFC | 73 | 286 | 179 | 62.6 |
| | Dan Marino-3 | Mia. | AFC | 94 | 615 | 385 | 62.6 |
| 63 | Bart Starr-2 | G.B. | NFL | 62 | 285 | 178 | 62.5 |
| | Dan Fouts-3 | S.D. | AFC | 84 | 507 | 317 | 62.5 |
| 65 | Brett Favre-2 | G.B. | NFC | 94 | 582 | 363 | 62.4 |
| | Rodney Peete | Det. | NFC | 93 | 252 | 157 | 62.3 |
| 67 | Bart Starr-3 | G.B. | NFL | 69 | 148 | 92 | 62.2 |
| | Virgil Carter | Chi. | NFC | 71 | 222 | 138 | 62.2 |
| | Bart Starr-4 | G.B. | NFL | 66 | 251 | 156 | 62.2 |
| | Joe Montana-7 | S.F. | NFC | 86 | 307 | 191 | 62.2 |
| | Warren Moon-2 | Minn. | NFC | 95 | 606 | 377 | 62.2 |
| 72 | Bernie Kosar-1 | Clev. | AFC | 91 | 494 | 307 | 62.1 |
| | John Elway-2 | Den. | AFC | 94 | 494 | 307 | 62.1 |
| 74 | Sonny Jurgensen-2 | Was. | NFL | 69 | 442 | 274 | 62.0 |
| | Bernie Kosar-2 | Cle. | AFC | 87 | 389 | 241 | 62.0 |
| | Warren Moon-3 | Hou. | AFC | 90 | 584 | 362 | 62.0 |
| 77 | John Brodie-2 | S.F. | NFL | 65 | 391 | 242 | 61.9 |
| | Fran Tarkenton-2 | Min. | NFC | 76 | 412 | 255 | 61.9 |
| | Rudy Bukich | Chi. | NFL | 64 | 160 | 99 | 61.9 |
| | Ken Stabler-4 | N.O. | NFC | 82 | 189 | 117 | 61.9 |
| 81 | Bob Griese-2 | Mia. | AFC | 76 | 191 | 118 | 61.8 |
| | Archie Manning | N.O. | NFC | 78 | 471 | 291 | 61.8 |
| | Dan Fouts-4 | S.D. | AFC | 82 | 330 | 204 | 61.8 |
| | Phil Simms | NYG | NFC | 93 | 400 | 247 | 61.8 |

### YARDS PASSING

| | | | | | |
|---|---|---|---|---|---|
| 1 | Dan Marino-1 | Mia. | AFC | 84 | 5084 |
| 2 | Dan Fouts-1 | S.D. | AFC | 81 | 4802 |
| 3 | Dan Marino-2 | Mia. | AFC | 86 | 4746 |
| 4 | Dan Fouts-2 | S.D. | AFC | 80 | 4715 |
| 5 | Warren Moon-1 | Hou. | AFC | 91 | 4690 |
| 6 | Warren Moon-2 | Hou. | AFC | 90 | 4689 |
| 7 | Neil Lomax-1 | St.L. | NFC | 84 | 4619 |
| 8 | Drew Bledsoe | N.E. | AFC | 94 | 4555 |
| 9 | Lynn Dickey | G.B. | NFC | 83 | 4458 |
| 10 | Dan Marino-3 | Mia. | AFC | 94 | 4453 |
| 11 | Dan Marino-4 | Mia. | AFC | 88 | 4434 |
| 12 | Brett Favre-1 | G.B. | NFC | 95 | 4413 |
| 13 | Bill Kenney | K.C. | AFC | 83 | 4348 |
| 14 | Scott Mitchell | Det. | NFC | 95 | 4338 |
| 15 | Don Majkowski | G.B. | NFC | 89 | 4318 |
| 16 | Jim Everett-1 | L.A. | NFC | 89 | 4310 |
| 17 | Warren Moon-3 | Minn. | NFC | 94 | 4264 |
| 18 | Warren Moon-4 | Minn. | NFC | 95 | 4228 |
| 19 | Jeff George | Atl. | NFC | 95 | 4143 |
| 20 | Dan Marino-5 | Mia. | AFC | 85 | 4137 |
| 21 | Brian Sipe-1 | Cle. | AFC | 80 | 4132 |
| 22 | Dan Marino-6 | Mia. | AFC | 92 | 4116 |
| 23 | Jay Schroeder | Was. | NFC | 86 | 4109 |
| 24 | Dan Fouts-3 | S.D. | AFC | 79 | 4082 |
| 25 | Joe Namath | NYJ | AFL | 67 | 4097 |
| 26 | Phil Simms-1 | NYG | NFC | 84 | 4044 |
| 27 | John Elway-1 | Den | AFC | 93 | 4030 |
| 28 | Steve Young | S.F. | NFC | 93 | 4023 |
| 29 | Dan Marino-7 | Mia. | AFC | 89 | 3997 |
| 30 | Jim Everett | L.A. | NFC | 90 | 3989 |
| 31 | Danny White | Dal | NFC | 83 | 3980 |
| 32 | Dan Marino-8 | Mia. | AFC | 91 | 3970 |
| | Jim Everett-4 | N.O. | NFC | 95 | 3970 |
| | John Elway-2 | Den. | AFC | 95 | 3970 |
| 35 | Steve Young | S.F. | NFC | 94 | 3969 |
| 36 | Jim Everett-3 | L.A. | NFC | 88 | 3964 |
| 37 | Boomer Esiason-1 | Cin. | AFC | 86 | 3959 |
| 38 | Joe Montana-1 | S.F. | NFC | 90 | 3944 |
| 39 | Tommy Kramer-1 | Min. | NFC | 81 | 3912 |
| 40 | Joe Montana-2 | S.F. | NFC | 83 | 3910 |
| 41 | John Elway-3 | Den. | AFC | 85 | 3891 |
| 42 | Ken O'Brien | NYJ | AFC | 85 | 3888 |
| 43 | Brett Favre-2 | G.B. | NFC | 94 | 3882 |
| 44 | Brian Sipe-2 | Cle. | AFC | 81 | 3876 |
| 45 | Jim Everett-5 | N.O. | NFC | 93 | 3855 |
| 46 | Bernie Kosar | Cle. | AFC | 86 | 3854 |
| 47 | Jim Kelly | Buff. | AFC | 91 | 3844 |
| 48 | Erik Kramer | Chi. | NFC | 95 | 3838 |
| 49 | Steve Bartkowski | Atl. | NFC | 81 | 3829 |
| | Phil Simms-2 | NYG | NFC | 85 | 3829 |
| 51 | Jeff Blake | Cin. | AFC | 95 | 3822 |
| 52 | R. Cunningham | Phil. | NFC | 88 | 3808 |
| 53 | Brian Sipe-3 | Cle. | AFC | 79 | 3793 |
| 54 | Mark Rypien | Wash. | NFC | 89 | 3768 |
| 55 | Ken Anderson | Cin. | AFC | 81 | 3754 |
| 56 | Sonny Jurgensen | Was. | NFL | 67 | 3747 |
| 57 | Dan Fouts-4 | S.D. | AFC | 84 | 3740 |
| 58 | Terry Bradshaw | Pit. | AFC | 79 | 3724 |
| 59 | Sonny Jurgensen-2 | Phi | NFL | 61 | 3723 |
| 60 | Archie Manning | N.O. | NFC | 80 | 3716 |
| 61 | Joe Theismann-1 | Was. | NFC | 83 | 3714 |
| 62 | Ken O'Brien-2 | NYJ | AFC | 86 | 3690 |
| 63 | Dave Krieg-1 | Sea. | AFC | 84 | 3671 |
| 64 | Dan Marino-9 | Mia. | AFC | 95 | 3668 |
| 65 | Jim Zorn | Sea. | AFC | 79 | 3661 |
| 66 | Joe Montana-3 | S.F. | NFC | 85 | 3653 |
| 67 | Steve DeBerg | S.F. | NFC | 79 | 3652 |
| | Joe Ferguson | Buf. | AFC | 81 | 3652 |
| 69 | Dan Fouts-5 | S.D. | AFC | 85 | 3638 |
| 70 | Warren Moon-5 | Hous. | AFC | 89 | 3631 |
| 71 | Joe Montana-4 | S.F. | NFC | 84 | 3630 |
| 72 | Ken Stabler | Oak | AFC | 79 | 3615 |
| 73 | Dave Krieg-2 | Sea. | AFC | 85 | 3602 |
| 74 | Jim Kelly-2 | Buf. | AFC | 86 | 3593 |
| 75 | Roger Staubach | Dal. | NFC | 79 | 3586 |
| 76 | Tommy Kramer-2 | Min. | NFC | 80 | 3582 |
| 77 | Joe Ferguson-2 | Buf. | AFC | 79 | 3572 |
| | Boomer Esiason-2 | Cin. | AFC | 88 | 3572 |
| 79 | Joe Theismann-2 | Was. | NFC | 81 | 3568 |

### YARDS PASSING PER SCHEDULED GAME

| | | | | | |
|---|---|---|---|---|---|
| 1 | Dan Fouts-1 | S.D. | AFC | 82 | 320 |
| 2 | Dan Marino-1 | Mia. | AFC | 84 | 318 |
| 3 | Dan Fouts-2 | S.D. | AFC | 81 | 300 |
| 4 | Dan Marino-2 | Mia. | AFC | 86 | 297 |
| 5 | Dan Fouts-3 | S.D. | AFC | 80 | 295 |
| 6 | Warren Moon-1 | Hou. | AFC | 90 | 293 |
| | Warren Moon-2 | Hou. | AFC | 91 | 293 |
| 8 | Joe Montana-1 | S.F. | NFC | 82 | 290 |
| 9 | Neil Lomax | St.L. | NFC | 84 | 289 |
| 10 | Joe Namath-1 | NYJ | AFL | 67 | 286 |
| 11 | Drew Bledsoe | N.E. | AFC | 94 | 285 |
| 12 | Lynn Dickey | G.B. | NFC | 83 | 279 |
| 13 | Ken Anderson | Cin. | AFC | 82 | 278 |
| | Dan Marino-3 | Mia. | AFC | 94 | 278 |
| 15 | Dan Marino-4 | Mia. | AFC | 88 | 277 |
| 16 | Brett Favre-1 | G.B. | NFC | 95 | 276 |
| 17 | Bill Kenney | K.C. | AFC | 83 | 272 |
| 18 | Scott Mitchell | Det. | NFC | 95 | 271 |
| 19 | Don Majkowski | G.B. | NFC | 89 | 270 |
| 20 | Jim Everett-1 | L.A. | NFC | 89 | 269 |
| 21 | Sonny Jurgensen-1 | Was. | NFL | 67 | 268 |
| 22 | Warren Moon-3 | Minn. | NFC | 94 | 267 |
| 23 | Sonny Jurgensen-2 | Phi. | NFL | 61 | 266 |
| 24 | Warren Moon-4 | Minn. | NFC | 95 | 264 |
| 25 | Dan Marino-5 | Mia. | AFC | 85 | 259 |
| | Jeff George | Atl. | NFC | 95 | 259 |
| 27 | Johnny Unitas-1 | Bal. | NFL | 60 | 258 |
| | Brian Sipe | Cle. | AFC | 80 | 258 |
| 29 | Dan Marino-6 | Mia. | AFC | 92 | 257 |
| 30 | Phil Simms | NYG | NFC | 84 | 253 |
| 31 | John Elway-1 | Den. | AFC | 93 | 252 |
| | Dan Fouts-4 | S.D. | AFC | 79 | 252 |
| 33 | Steve Young-1 | S.F. | NFC | 93 | 251 |
| 34 | Dan Marino-7 | Mia. | AFC | 89 | 250 |
| 35 | Johnny Unitas-2 | Bal. | NFL | 63 | 249 |
| | Danny White | Dal. | NFC | 83 | 249 |
| | Jim Everett-2 | L.A. | NFC | 90 | 249 |
| 38 | John Hadl-1 | S.D. | AFL | 68 | 248 |
| | Babe Parilli | Bos. | AFL | 64 | 248 |
| | Jim Everett-3 | L.A. | NFC | 88 | 248 |
| | Dan Marino-8 | Mia. | AFC | 91 | 248 |
| | Steve Young-2 | S.F. | NFC | 94 | 248 |
| | John Elway-2 | Den. | AFC | 95 | 248 |
| | Jim Everett-4 | N.O. | NFC | 95 | 248 |
| 45 | Boomer Esiason | Cin. | AFC | 86 | 247 |
| | Jay Schroeder | Was. | NFC | 86 | 247 |
| | Joe Montana-2 | S.F. | NFC | 90 | 247 |
| 48 | Johnny Unitas-3 | Bal. | NFL | 67 | 245 |
| | Sammy Baugh | Was. | NFL | 47 | 245 |
| | Tommy Kramer | Min. | NFC | 81 | 245 |
| 51 | Joe Montana-3 | S.F. | NFC | 83 | 244 |
| 52 | Norm Snead | Phi. | NFL | 67 | 243 |
| | John Elway-2 | Den. | AFC | 85 | 243 |
| | Ken O'Brien | NYJ | AFC | 85 | 243 |
| | Brett Favre | G.B. | NFC | 94 | 243 |

### YARDS PER ATTEMPT

(Minimum 100 Attempts)

| | | | | | Att. | Yards | Yd/A |
|---|---|---|---|---|---|---|---|
| 1 | Tom O'Connell | Cle. | NFL | 57 | 110 | 1229 | 11.2 |
| 2 | Sid Luckman-1 | ChiB | NFL | 43 | 202 | 2194 | 10.9 |
| 3 | Otto Graham-1 | Cle | NFL | 53 | 258 | 2722 | 10.6 |
| 4 | Otto Graham-2 | Cle. | AAFC | 46 | 174 | 1834 | 10.5 |
| 5 | Otto Graham-3 | Cle. | AAFC | 47 | 269 | 2753 | 10.2 |
| 6 | Norm Van Brocklin | L.A. | NFL | 54 | 260 | 2637 | 10.1 |
| 7 | Bill Nelsen | Pit. | NFL | 66 | 112 | 1122 | 10.0 |
| 8 | Sid Luckman-2 | ChiB | NFL | 41 | 119 | 1181 | 9.9 |
| | Ed Brown | ChiB | NFL | 56 | 168 | 1667 | 9.9 |
| 10 | Otto Graham-4 | Cle. | AAFC | 49 | 285 | 2785 | 9.8 |
| 11 | Sid Luckman-3 | ChiB | NFL | 42 | 105 | 1023 | 9.7 |
| 12 | Jacky Lee | Hou. | AFL | 61 | 127 | 1205 | 9.5 |
| 13 | Bart Starr | G.B. | NFL | 68 | 171 | 1617 | 9.5 |
| 14 | Len Dawson | K.C. | AFL | 68 | 224 | 2109 | 9.4 |
| | Eddie LeBaron | Was. | NFL | 58 | 145 | 1365 | 9.4 |
| | Greg Cook | Cin. | AFL | 69 | 197 | 1854 | 9.4 |
| | Bob Waterfield | Cle. | NFL | 45 | 171 | 1609 | 9.4 |
| | Ken Stabler | Oak. | AFC | 76 | 291 | 2737 | 9.4 |
| | Bob Berry | Atl. | NFL | 68 | 153 | 1433 | 9.4 |
| 20 | Otto Graham-5 | Cle. | NFL | 55 | 185 | 1721 | 9.3 |
| | Johnny Unitas | Bal. | NFL | 64 | 305 | 2824 | 9.3 |
| 22 | James Harris | L.A. | NFC | 76 | 158 | 1460 | 9.2 |
| | George Blanda | Hou. | AFL | 61 | 362 | 3330 | 9.2 |
| | Milt Plum | Cle. | NFL | 60 | 250 | 2297 | 9.2 |
| | Earl Morrall | Bal. | NFL | 68 | 317 | 2909 | 9.2 |
| | Sammy Baugh | Was. | NFL | 45 | 182 | 1669 | 9.2 |
| | Lynn Dickey | G.B. | NFC | 83 | 484 | 4458 | 9.2 |
| | Boomer Esiason | Cin. | AFC | 88 | 388 | 3572 | 9.2 |
| 29 | John Brodie | S.F. | NFL | 61 | 283 | 2588 | 9.1 |
| | Earl Morrall-2 | Mia. | AFC | 72 | 150 | 1360 | 9.1 |
| | Joe Montana | S.F. | NFC | 89 | 386 | 3521 | 9.1 |

# SINGLE SEASON LEADERS
# PASSING

### TOUCHDOWN PASSES

| | | | | | |
|---|---|---|---|---|---|
| 1 | Dan Marino-1 | Mia. | AFC | 84 | 48 |
| 2 | Dan Marino-2 | Mia. | AFC | 86 | 44 |
| 3 | Brett Favre | G.B. | NFC | 95 | 38 |
| 4 | George Blanda | Hou. | AFL | 61 | 36 |
| | Y.A. Tittle-1 | NYG | NFL | 63 | 36 |
| 6 | Steve Young-1 | S.F. | NFC | 94 | 35 |
| 7 | Daryle Lamonica-1 | Oak. | AFL | 69 | 34 |
| 8 | Y.A. Tittle-2 | NYG | NFL | 62 | 33 |
| | Dan Fouts-1 | S.D. | AFC | 81 | 33 |
| | Warren Moon-1 | Hou. | AFC | 90 | 33 |
| | Jim Kelly | Buff. | AFC | 91 | 33 |
| | Brett Favre | G.B. | NFC | 94 | 33 |
| | Warren Moon-2 | Minn. | NFC | 95 | 33 |
| 14 | Johnny Unitas | Bal. | NFL | 59 | 32 |
| | Lynn Dickey | G.B. | NFC | 83 | 32 |
| | Dave Krieg-1 | Sea. | AFC | 84 | 32 |
| | Scott Mitchell | Det. | NFC | 95 | 32 |
| 18 | Babe Parilli | Bos. | AFL | 64 | 31 |
| | Sonny Jurgensen-1 | Was. | NFL | 67 | 31 |
| | Steve Bartkowski-1 | Atl. | NFC | 80 | 31 |
| | Joe Montana-1 | S.F. | NFC | 87 | 31 |
| | Jim Everett-1 | L.A. | NFC | 88 | 31 |
| 23 | Len Dawson-1 | K.C. | AFL | 64 | 30 |
| | John Brodie | S.F. | NFL | 65 | 30 |
| | Daryle Lamonica-2 | Oak. | AFL | 67 | 30 |
| | Vince Ferragamo | L.A. | NFC | 80 | 30 |
| | Dan Fouts-2 | S.D. | AFC | 80 | 30 |
| | Brian Sipe-1 | Cle. | AFC | 80 | 30 |
| | Steve Bartkowski-2 | Atl. | NFC | 81 | 30 |
| | Dan Marino-3 | Mia. | AFC | 85 | 30 |
| | Randall Cunningham | Phi. | NFC | 90 | 30 |
| | Dan Marino-4 | Mia. | AFC | 94 | 30 |
| 33 | Frankie Albert-1 | S.F. | AAFC | 48 | 29 |
| | Len Dawson-2 | Dal. | AFL | 62 | 29 |
| | Frank Ryan | Cle. | NFL | 66 | 29 |
| | Norm Snead | Phi. | NFL | 67 | 29 |
| | Fran Tarkenton | NYG | NFL | 67 | 29 |
| | Ken Anderson | Cin. | AFC | 81 | 29 |
| | Joe Theismann | Was. | NFC | 83 | 29 |
| | Danny White-1 | Dal. | NFC | 83 | 29 |
| | Jim Everett-2 | L.A. | NFC | 89 | 29 |
| | Steve Young-2 | S.F. | NFC | 93 | 29 |
| | Erik Kramer | Chi. | NFC | 95 | 29 |
| 44 | Sid Luckman | ChiB | NFL | 43 | 28 |
| | Charley Johnson | St.L. | NFL | 63 | 28 |
| | Sonny Jurgensen-2 | Was. | NFL | 64 | 28 |
| | Terry Bradshaw | Pit. | AFC | 78 | 28 |
| | Steve Grogan | N.E. | AFC | 79 | 28 |
| | Brian Sipe-2 | Cle. | AFC | 79 | 28 |
| | Danny White-2 | Dal. | AFC | 80 | 28 |
| | Neil Lomax | St.L. | NFC | 84 | 28 |
| | Joe Montana-2 | S.F. | NFC | 84 | 28 |
| | Boomer Esiason-1 | Cin. | AFC | 88 | 28 |
| | Dan Marino-5 | Mia. | AFC | 88 | 28 |
| | Boomer Esiason-2 | Cin. | AFC | 89 | 28 |
| | Mark Rypien | Wash. | NFC | 91 | 28 |
| | Jeff Blake | Cin. | AFC | 95 | 28 |
| 58 | Frankie Albert-2 | S.F. | AAFC | 47 | 27 |
| | George Blanda-2 | Hou. | AFL | 62 | 27 |
| | John Hadl | S.D. | AFL | 68 | 27 |
| | Ken Stabler | Oak. | AFC | 76 | 27 |
| | Roger Staubach | Dal. | NFC | 79 | 27 |
| | Ron Jaworski | Phi. | NFC | 80 | 27 |
| | Dave Krieg-2 | Sea. | AFC | 85 | 27 |
| | Dan Fouts-3 | S.D. | AFC | 85 | 27 |
| | Boomer Esiason-3 | Cin. | AFC | 85 | 27 |
| | Joe Montana-3 | S.F. | NFC | 85 | 27 |
| | Don Majkowski | G.B. | NFC | 89 | 27 |

### LOWEST PASS INTERCEPTION PERCENTAGE

(MINIMUM 100 ATTEMPTS)

| | | | | | Att. | Int. | Pct. |
|---|---|---|---|---|---|---|---|
| 1 | Joe Ferguson | Buf. | AFC | 76 | 151 | 1 | 0.662 |
| 2 | Bill Nelsen | Pit. | NFL | 66 | 112 | 1 | 0.893 |
| 3 | Steve DeBerg | K.C. | AFC | 90 | 444 | 4 | 0.900 |
| 4 | Steve Bartkowski | Atl. | NFC | 83 | 432 | 5 | 1.157 |
| 5 | Bart Starr | G.B. | NFL | 66 | 251 | 3 | 1.195 |
| 6 | Phil Simms | N.Y. | NFC | 90 | 311 | 4 | 1.286 |
| 7 | Jim McMahon | Chi. | NFC | 84 | 143 | 2 | 1.399 |
| 8 | Jeff Hostetler | NYG | NFC | 91 | 285 | 4 | 1.408 |
| 9 | Neil O'Donnell-1 | Pitt. | AFC | 93 | 486 | 7 | 1.440 |
| 10 | Bart Starr-2 | G.B. | NFL | 64 | 272 | 4 | 1.471 |
| 11 | Jeff George | Ind. | AFC | 93 | 407 | 6 | 1.474 |
| 12 | Jim Harbaugh-1 | Ind. | AFC | 95 | 314 | 5 | 1.592 |
| 13 | Bob Berry | Atl. | NFL | 69 | 124 | 2 | 1.612 |
| 14 | Bubby Brister | Phil. | NFC | 93 | 309 | 5 | 1.618 |
| 15 | Troy Aikman | Dall. | NFC | 95 | 432 | 7 | 1.620 |
| 16 | Ken O'Brien-1 | NYJ | AFC | 85 | 488 | 8 | 1.639 |
| 17 | Ken O'Brien-2 | NYJ | AFC | 88 | 424 | 7 | 1.651 |
| 18 | John Friesz | S.D. | AFC | 93 | 238 | 4 | 1.681 |
| 19 | Neil O'Donnell-2 | Pitt. | AFC | 95 | 416 | 7 | 1.683 |
| 20 | Steve Bono-1 | S.F. | NFC | 91 | 237 | 4 | 1.688 |
| 21 | Rich Gannon | Minn. | NFC | 91 | 354 | 6 | 1.695 |
| 22 | Joe Pisarcik | Phi. | NFC | 84 | 176 | 3 | 1.705 |
| 23 | Steve Young-1 | S.F. | NFC | 92 | 402 | 7 | 1.741 |
| 24 | Roman Gabriel-1 | L.A. | NFL | 69 | 399 | 7 | 1.754 |
| 25 | John Elway-1 | Den. | AFC | 93 | 551 | 10 | 1.814 |
| 26 | Bernie Kosar-1 | Clev. | AFC | 91 | 494 | 9 | 1.821 |
| 27 | Joe Montana-1 | K.C. | AFC | 94 | 493 | 9 | 1.826 |
| 28 | Bill Munson-1 | Det. | NFC | 75 | 109 | 2 | 1.835 |
| 29 | Rick Mirer | Sea. | AFC | 94 | 381 | 7 | 1.837 |
| 30 | Tony Eason | N.E. | AFC | 84 | 431 | 8 | 1.856 |
| 31 | Bernie Kosar-2 | Cle. | AFC | 86 | 531 | 10 | 1.883 |
| 32 | Roger Staubach-1 | Dal. | NFC | 71 | 211 | 4 | 1.895 |
| 33 | Chris Miller | Atl. | NFC | 89 | 526 | 10 | 1.901 |
| 34 | Erik Kramer | Chi. | NFC | 95 | 522 | 10 | 1.916 |
| 35 | Jim Harbaugh-2 | Chi. | NFC | 90 | 312 | 6 | 1.923 |
| | Steve Bono-2 | K.C. | AFC | 95 | 520 | 10 | 1.923 |
| 37 | Fran Tarkenton-1 | Min. | NFC | 76 | 412 | 8 | 1.942 |
| 38 | Fran Tarkenton-2 | NYG | NFL | 69 | 409 | 8 | 1.955 |
| 39 | Steve Dils | Min. | NFC | 81 | 101 | 2 | 1.961 |
| 40 | Johnny Unitas | Bal. | NFL | 64 | 305 | 6 | 1.967 |
| 41 | Jeff George | Atl. | NFC | 95 | 557 | 11 | 1.975 |
| 42 | Roman Gabriel-2 | L.A. | NFL | 62 | 101 | 2 | 1.980 |
| | Steve Pelluer | Dal. | NFL | 87 | 101 | 2 | 1.980 |
| 44 | Scott Hunter | Atl. | NFC | 77 | 151 | 3 | 1.987 |
| | Ed Luther | S.D. | AFC | 84 | 151 | 3 | 1.987 |
| 46 | Milt Plum | Cle. | NFL | 60 | 250 | 5 | 2.000 |
| 47 | Mark Brunell | Jax. | AFC | 95 | 346 | 7 | 2.023 |
| 48 | John Elway-2 | Den. | AFC | 94 | 494 | 10 | 2.024 |
| 49 | Dan Marino-1 | Mia. | AFC | 83 | 296 | 6 | 2.027 |
| 50 | Ken O'Brien-3 | NYJ | AFC | 87 | 393 | 8 | 2.036 |
| 51 | Scott Mitchell | Det. | NFC | 95 | 583 | 12 | 2.058 |
| 52 | Charlie Conerly | NYG | NFL | 59 | 194 | 4 | 2.062 |
| | Jim Hart | St.L. | NFC | 74 | 388 | 8 | 2.062 |
| 54 | Dan Marino | Mia. | AFC | 90 | 531 | 11 | 2.071 |
| 55 | Joe Montana-2 | S.F. | NFC | 89 | 386 | 8 | 2.072 |
| 56 | Ken Anderson-1 | Cin. | AFC | 81 | 479 | 10 | 2.088 |
| 57 | Gary Wood | NYG | NFL | 64 | 143 | 3 | 2.098 |
| 58 | Steve Young-2 | S.F. | NFC | 94 | 461 | 10 | 2.169 |
| 59 | Dave Brown | NYG | NFC | 95 | 456 | 10 | 2.193 |
| 60 | Sammy Baugh | Was. | NFL | 45 | 182 | 4 | 2.198 |
| 61 | Warren Moon | Hou. | AFC | 90 | 584 | 13 | 2.222 |
| 62 | Tony Eason | N.E. | AFC | 86 | 448 | 10 | 2.232 |
| 63 | Ken O'Brien-4 | NYJ | AFC | 91 | 489 | 11 | 2.249 |
| 64 | Phil Simms-1 | NYG | NFC | 93 | 400 | 9 | 2.250 |
| 65 | Jim Zorn | Sea. | AFC | 81 | 397 | 7 | 2.267 |
| 66 | Brett Favre | G.B. | NFC | 95 | 570 | 13 | 2.281 |
| 67 | Phil Simms-2 | NYG | NFC | 88 | 479 | 11 | 2.296 |
| 68 | Warren Moon | Minn. | NFC | 95 | 606 | 14 | 2.310 |
| 69 | Bernie Kosar-3 | Cle. | AFC | 87 | 389 | 9 | 2.314 |
| 70 | Joe Montana-3 | S.F. | NFC | 84 | 432 | 10 | 2.315 |
| 71 | Ken Anderson-2 | Cin. | AFC | 72 | 301 | 7 | 2.325 |
| 72 | Steve Walsh | Chi. | NFC | 94 | 343 | 8 | 2.332 |
| 73 | Boomer Esiason | NYJ | AFC | 93 | 473 | 11 | 2.235 |
| 74 | Bert Jones | Bal. | AFC | 75 | 344 | 8 | 2.326 |
| 75 | Joe Montana-4 | S.F. | NFC | 83 | 515 | 12 | 2.330 |
| 76 | Joe Montana-5 | K.C. | AFC | 93 | 298 | 7 | 2.349 |
| 77 | Steve Walsh | N.O. | NFC | 91 | 255 | 6 | 2.353 |
| 78 | Y.A. Tittle | S.F. | NFL | 60 | 127 | 3 | 2.362 |
| | Don Majkowski | G.B. | NFC | 87 | 127 | 3 | 2.362 |
| 80 | Dan Marino-2 | Mia. | AFC | 91 | 549 | 13 | 2.368 |
| 81 | Chris Miller-2 | Atl. | NFC | 92 | 253 | 6 | 2.371 |
| 82 | Edd Hargett | N.O. | NFC | 71 | 210 | 5 | 2.380 |
| 83 | Roger Staubach-2 | Dal. | NFC | 79 | 461 | 11 | 2.386 |
| 84 | Jeff Hostetler | Phx. | NFC | 93 | 419 | 10 | 2.387 |

# INTERCEPTIONS

| | | | | | |
|---|---|---|---|---|---|
| 1 | Night Train Lane-1 | L.A. | NFL | 62 | 14 |
| 2 | Don Sandler | Was. | NFL | 48 | 13 |
| | Spec Sanders | NYY | NFL | 50 | 13 |
| | Lester Hayes | Oak. | AFC | 80 | 13 |
| 5 | Bob Nussbaumer | ChiC | NFL | 49 | 12 |
| | Don Doll-1 | Det. | NFL | 50 | 12 |
| | Woodley Lewis | L.A. | NFL | 50 | 12 |
| | Jack Christiansen | Det. | NFL | 53 | 12 |
| | Fred Glick | Hou. | AFL | 63 | 12 |
| | Paul Krause-1 | Min. | NFL | 64 | 12 |
| | Dainard Paulson | NYJ | AFL | 64 | 12 |
| | Emmitt Thomas | K.C. | AFC | 74 | 12 |
| | Mike Reinfeldt | Hou. | AFC | 79 | 12 |
| 14 | Sammy Baugh | Was. | NFL | 43 | 11 |
| | Don Doll-2 | Det. | NFL | 49 | 11 |
| | O. Schnellbacher-1 | N.Y. | AAFC | 48 | 11 |
| | O. Schnellbacher-2 | NYG | NFL | 51 | 11 |
| | Tom Keane-1 | Bal. | NFL | 53 | 11 |
| | Will Sherman | L.A. | NFL | 55 | 11 |
| | Lindon Crow | ChiC | NFL | 56 | 11 |
| | Jim Patton | NYG | NFL | 58 | 11 |
| | Goose Gonsoulin | Den. | AFL | 60 | 11 |
| | Lee Riley | NYT | AFL | 62 | 11 |
| | Ron Hall | Bos. | AFL | 63 | 11 |
| | Bill Bradley | Phi. | NFC | 71 | 11 |
| | Mel Blount | Pit. | AFC | 75 | 11 |
| | Everson Walls | Dal | NFC | 81 | 11 |
| 28 | Eddie Kotal | G.B. | NFL | 28 | 10 |
| | Irv Comp | G.B. | NFL | 43 | 10 |
| | Bill Dudley | Pit. | NFL | 46 | 10 |
| | Tom Colella | Cle. | AAFC | 46 | 10 |
| | Frank Seno | Bos. | NFL | 47 | 10 |
| | Frank Reagan | NYG | NFL | 47 | 10 |
| | Em Tunnell | NYG | NFL | 49 | 10 |
| | Howard Hartley | Pit. | NFL | 51 | 10 |
| | Tom Keane-2 | Dal. | NFL | 51 | 10 |
| | Don Doll-3 | Was. | NFL | 53 | 10 |
| | Ray Ramsey | ChiC | NFL | 53 | 10 |
| | Night Train Lane-2 | ChiC | NFL | 54 | 10 |
| | Jack Butler | Pit. | NFL | 57 | 10 |
| | Jack Christiansen | Det. | NFL | 57 | 10 |
| | Milt Davis | Bal. | NFL | 57 | 10 |
| | Dave Baker | S.F. | NFL | 60 | 10 |
| | Jerry Norton | St.L. | NFL | 60 | 10 |
| | Billy Atkins | Buf. | AFL | 61 | 10 |
| | Tommy Morrow | Oak. | AFL | 62 | 10 |
| | Pat Fischer | St.L. | NFL | 64 | 10 |
| | Bobby Hunt | K.C. | AFL | 66 | 10 |
| | Larry Wilson | St.L. | NFL | 66 | 10 |
| | Johnny Robinson | K.C. | AFL | 66 | 10 |
| | Lem Barney | Det. | NFL | 67 | 10 |
| | Miller Farr | Hou. | AFL | 67 | 10 |
| | Tom Janik | Buf. | AFL | 67 | 10 |
| | Dick Westmoreland | Mia. | AFL | 67 | 10 |
| | Dave Whitsell | N.O. | NFL | 67 | 10 |
| | Dave Grayson | Oak. | AFL | 68 | 10 |
| | Willie Williams | NYG | NFL | 68 | 10 |
| | Mel Renfro | Dal. | NFL | 69 | 10 |
| | Johnny Robinson | K.C. | AFC | 70 | 10 |
| | Paul Krause-2 | Min. | NFC | 75 | 10 |
| | Monte Jackson | L.A. | NFC | 76 | 10 |
| | Lyle Blackwood | Bal. | AFC | 77 | 10 |
| | Gary Barbaro | K.C. | AFC | 80 | 10 |
| | John Harris | Sea. | AFC | 81 | 10 |
| | Kenny Easley | Sea. | AFC | 84 | 10 |
| | Ronnie Lott | S.F. | NFC | 86 | 10 |
| | Scott Case | Atl. | NFC | 88 | 10 |
| | Mark Carrier | Chi. | NFC | 90 | 10 |

# PUNTING AVERAGE

(MINIMUM 30 PUNTS)

| | | | | | |
|---|---|---|---|---|---|
| 1 | Sammy Baugh-1 | Was. | NFL | 40 | 51.3 |
| 2 | Glenn Dobbs-1 | L.A. | AAFC | 48 | 49.1 |
| 3 | Yale Lary-1 | Det. | NFL | 63 | 48.9 |
| 4 | Sammy Baugh-2 | Was. | NFL | 41 | 48.7 |
| 5 | Yale Lary-2 | Det. | NFL | 61 | 48.4 |
| 6 | Frankie Albert | S.F. | AAFC | 49 | 48.2 |
| 7 | Glenn Dobbs-2 | Bkn. | AAFC | 46 | 47.8 |
| 8 | Joe Muha | Phi. | NFL | 48 | 47.2 |
| 9 | Yale Lary-3 | Det. | NFL | 59 | 47.1 |
| 10 | Bobby Joe Green-1 | Pit. | NFL | 61 | 47.0 |
| 11 | Pat Brady | Pit. | NFL | 53 | 46.9 |
| | Greg Montgomery-1 | Hou. | AFC | 92 | 46.9 |
| 13 | Gary Collins | Cle. | NFL | 65 | 46.7 |
| 14 | Sammy Baugh-3 | Was. | NFL | 42 | 46.6 |
| 16 | Don Chandler-1 | NYG | NFL | 59 | 46.6 |
| 15 | Bobby Joe Green-2 | Chi. | NFL | 63 | 46.5 |
| 17 | Bobby Walden-1 | Min. | NFL | 64 | 46.4 |
| 18 | Yale Lary-4 | Det | NFL | 64 | 46.3 |
| 19 | Dave Lewis | Cin. | AFC | 70 | 46.2 |
| 20 | Jim Fraser | Den. | AFL | 63 | 46.1 |
| | Jerrel Wilson-1 | K.C. | AFL | 65 | 46.1 |
| 22 | Sammy Baugh-4 | Was. | NFL | 43 | 45.9 |
| | Rohn Stark-1 | Ind. | AFC | 85 | 45.9 |
| 24 | Tommy Davis-1 | S.F. | NFL | 65 | 45.8 |
| | Bob Scarpitto | Den. | AFL | 66 | 45.8 |
| 26 | Horace Gillom-1 | Cle. | NFL | 52 | 45.7 |
| | Tommy Davis-2 | S.F. | NFL | 59 | 45.7 |
| | Reggie Roby | Mia. | AFC | 91 | 45.7 |
| 29 | Bob Cifers | Det. | NFL | 46 | 45.6 |
| | Jerry Norton | St.L. | NFL | 60 | 45.6 |
| | Tommy Davis-3 | S.F. | NFL | 62 | 45.6 |
| | Don Chandler-2 | NYG | NFL | 64 | 45.6 |
| | Tommy Davis-4 | S.F. | NFL | 64 | 45.6 |
| | David Lee-1 | Bal. | NFL | 66 | 45.6 |
| | Greg Montgomery-2 | Hou. | AFC | 93 | 45.6 |
| 35 | Horace Gillom-2 | Cle. | NFL | 51 | 45.5 |
| | Sam Baker-1 | Was. | NFL | 59 | 45.5 |
| | Danny Villanueva-1 | L.A. | NFL | 62 | 45.5 |
| | Jerrel Wilson-2 | K.C. | AFC | 73 | 45.5 |
| | Harry Newsome | Minn. | NFC | 91 | 45.5 |
| 39 | Bob Reinhard | L.A. | AAFC | 46 | 45.4 |
| | Sam Baker-2 | Was. | NFL | 58 | 45.4 |
| | Tommy Davis-5 | S.F. | NFL | 61 | 45.4 |
| | Sam Baker-3 | Dal. | NFL | 62 | 45.4 |
| | Danny Villanueva-2 | L.A. | NFL | 63 | 45.4 |
| | Tommy Davis-6 | S.F. | NFL | 63 | 45.4 |
| | Pat McInally | Cin. | AFC | 81 | 45.4 |
| 47 | Yale Lary-5 | Det. | NFL | 62 | 45.3 |
| | Curley Johnson | NYJ | AFL | 65 | 45.3 |
| | David Lee-2 | Bal. | NFL | 69 | 45.3 |
| | Ray Guy | Oak. | AFC | 73 | 45.3 |
| | Rohn Stark-2 | Bal. | AFC | 83 | 45.3 |
| | Rich Camarillo | Phx. | NFC | 91 | 45.3 |
| 53 | Bobby Walden-2 | Pit. | AFC | 70 | 45.2 |
| | Rohn Stark | Ind. | AFC | 83 | 45.2 |

# SINGLE SEASON LEADERS
# RUSHING

## RUSHING ATTEMPTS

| | | | | | |
|---|---|---|---|---|---|
| 1 | James Wilder-1 | T.B. | NFC | 84 | 407 |
| 2 | Eric Dickerson-1 | L.A. | NFC | 86 | 404 |
| 3 | Gerald Riggs-1 | Atl. | NFC | 85 | 397 |
| 4 | Eric Dickerson-2 | L.A. | NFC | 83 | 390 |
| | Barry Foster | Pitt. | AFC | 92 | 390 |
| 6 | Eric Dickerson-3 | Ind. | AFC | 88 | 388 |
| 7 | Walter Payton-1 | Chi. | NFC | 83 | 381 |
| 8 | Marcus Allen | L.A. | AFC | 85 | 380 |
| 9 | Eric Dickerson-4 | L.A. | NFC | 84 | 379 |
| 10 | George Rogers-1 | N.O. | NFC | 81 | 378 |
| 11 | Emmitt Smith-2 | Dall. | NFC | 95 | 377 |
| 12 | John Riggins-1 | Was. | NFC | 83 | 375 |
| 13 | Earl Campbell-1 | Hou. | AFC | 80 | 373 |
| | Emmitt Smith-1 | Dall. | NFC | 92 | 373 |
| 15 | Christian Okoye | K.C. | AFC | 89 | 370 |
| 16 | Walter Payton-2 | Chi. | NFC | 79 | 369 |
| 17 | Earl Campbell | Hou. | AFC | 79 | 368 |
| | Emmitt Smith-3 | Dall. | NFC | 94 | 368 |
| | Curtis Martin | N.E. | NFC | 95 | 368 |
| 20 | James Wilder-2 | T.B. | NFC | 85 | 365 |
| | Emmitt Smith-\4 | Dall. | NFC | 91 | 365 |
| 22 | Earl Campbell-3 | Hou. | AFC | 81 | 361 |
| | Herschel Walker | Dal. | NFC | 88 | 361 |
| 24 | Thurman Thomas-1 | Buff. | AFC | 93 | 355 |
| 25 | Gerald Riggs-2 | Atl. | NFC | 84 | 353 |
| 26 | Dalton Hilliard | N.O. | NFC | 89 | 344 |
| 27 | Gerald Riggs-3 | Atl. | NFC | 86 | 343 |
| | Natrone Means | S.D. | AFC | 94 | 343 |
| 29 | Tony Dorsett-1 | Dal. | NFC | 81 | 342 |
| | Barry Sanders-1 | Det. | NFC | 91 | 343 |
| 31 | Joe Morris-1 | NYG | NFC | 86 | 341 |
| 32 | Walter Payton-3 | Chi. | NFC | 77 | 339 |
| | Walter Payton-4 | Chi. | NFC | 81 | 339 |
| 34 | Wilb. Montgomery | Phi. | NFC | 79 | 338 |
| | Terry Allen | Wash. | NFC | 95 | 338 |
| 36 | Ricky Watters | Phil. | NFC | 95 | 337 |
| 37 | Curt Warner-1 | Sea. | AFC | 83 | 335 |
| 38 | Walter Payton-5 | Chi. | NFC | 78 | 333 |
| | Chris Warren | Sea. | AFC | 94 | 333 |
| 40 | O.J. Simpson-1 | Buf. | AFC | 73 | 332 |
| | Errict Rhett | T.B. | NFC | 95 | 332 |
| 42 | Ottis Anderson-1 | St.L. | NFC | 79 | 331 |
| | William Andrews | Atl. | NFC | 83 | 331 |
| | Barry Sanders-2 | Det. | NFC | 94 | 331 |
| 45 | O.J. Simpson-2 | Buf. | AFC | 75 | 329 |
| 46 | Ottis Anderson-2 | St.L. | NFC | 81 | 328 |
| 47 | John Riggins-2 | Was. | NFC | 84 | 327 |
| | Rodney Hampton-1 | NYG | NFC | 94 | 327 |
| 49 | Ottis Anderson-3 | NYG | NFC | 89 | 325 |
| 50 | Mark van Eeghen | Oak. | AFC | 77 | 324 |
| | Walter Payton-6 | Chi. | NFC | 85 | 324 |
| | Charles White | L.A. | NFC | 87 | 324 |
| 53 | Earl Campbell-4 | Hou. | AFC | 83 | 322 |
| 54 | Walter Payton-7 | Chi. | NFC | 86 | 321 |
| 55 | Curt Warner-2 | Sea. | AFC | 86 | 319 |
| | Jerome Bettis | L.A. | NFC | 94 | 319 |
| 57 | Walter Payton-8 | Chi. | NFC | 80 | 317 |
| 58 | Edgar Bennett | G.B. | NFC | 95 | 316 |
| 59 | Walter Payton-9 | Chi. | NFC | 83 | 314 |
| | Eric Dickerson-5 | Ind. | AFC | 89 | 314 |
| | Marshall Faulk | Ind. | AFC | 94 | 314 |
| | Barry Sanders-3 | Det. | NFC | 95 | 314 |
| 63 | Billy Sims-1 | Det. | NFC | 80 | 313 |
| 64 | Thurman Thomas-2 | Buff. | AFC | 92 | 312 |
| | Barry Sanders-4 | Det. | NFC | 92 | 312 |
| 66 | Walter Payton-10 | Chi. | NFC | 76 | 311 |
| 67 | Franco Harris-1 | Pit. | AFC | 78 | 310 |
| | Roger Craig | S.F. | NFC | 88 | 310 |
| | Reggie Cobb | T.B. | NFC | 92 | 310 |
| | Chris Warren | Sea. | AFC | 95 | 310 |
| 71 | Joe Morris-2 | NYG | NFC | 88 | 307 |
| 72 | Joe Cribbs | Buf. | AFC | 80 | 306 |
| | Rodney Hampton-2 | NYG | NFC | 95 | 306 |
| 74 | Jim Brown-1 | Cle. | NFL | 61 | 305 |
| | Tony Dorsett-2 | Dal. | NFC | 85 | 305 |
| 76 | George Rogers-2 | Was | NFC | 86 | 303 |
| 77 | Earl Campbell-5 | Hou. | AFC | 78 | 302 |
| | Tony Dorsett-3 | Dal. | NFC | 84 | 302 |
| 79 | Franco Harris-2 | Pit. | AFC | 77 | 301 |
| | Ottis Anderson-4 | St.L. | NFC | 80 | 301 |
| 81 | Lydell Mitchell | Bal. | AFC | 77 | 300 |
| | Leonard Russell | N.E. | AFC | 93 | 300 |
| 83 | Jim Nance | Bos. | AFL | 66 | 299 |
| 84 | Ron Johnson | NYG | NFC | 72 | 298 |
| | Thurman Thomas-3 | Buff. | AFC | 89 | 298 |
| 86 | John Stephens | N.E. | AFC | 88 | 297 |
| | Earnest Byner | Was. | NFC | 90 | 297 |
| 88 | Billy Sims-2 | Det. | NFC | 81 | 296 |
| | Ottis Anderson-5 | St.L. | NFC | 83 | 296 |
| | Sammy Winder | Den. | AFC | 84 | 296 |
| | Earnest Jackson | S.D. | AFC | 84 | 296 |
| | Rashaan Salaam | Chi. | NFC | 95 | 296 |

## YARDS

| | | | | | |
|---|---|---|---|---|---|
| 1 | Eric Dickerson-1 | L.A. | NFC | 84 | 2105 |
| 2 | O.J. Simpson | Buf. | AFC | 73 | 2003 |
| 3 | Earl Campbell-1 | Hou. | AFC | 80 | 1934 |
| 4 | Barry Sanders-1 | Det. | NFC | 94 | 1883 |
| 5 | Jim Brown-1 | Cle. | NFL | 63 | 1863 |
| 6 | Walter Payton-1 | Chi. | NFC | 77 | 1852 |
| 7 | Eric Dickerson-2 | L.A. | NFC | 86 | 1821 |
| 8 | O.J. Simpson-2 | Buf. | AFC | 75 | 1817 |
| 9 | Eric Dickerson-3 | L.A. | NFC | 83 | 1808 |
| 10 | Emmitt Smith-1 | Dall. | NFC | 95 | 1773 |
| 11 | Marcus Allen | Raid. | AFC | 85 | 1759 |
| 12 | Gerald Riggs | Atl. | NFC | 85 | 1719 |
| 13 | Emmitt Smith-2 | Dall. | NFC | 92 | 1713 |
| 14 | Earl Campbell-2 | Hou. | AFC | 79 | 1697 |
| 15 | Barry Foster | Pitt. | AFC | 92 | 1690 |
| 16 | Walter Payton-2 | Chi. | NFC | 84 | 1684 |
| 17 | George Rogers-1 | N.O. | NFC | 81 | 1674 |
| 18 | Eric Dickerson-4 | Ind. | AFC | 88 | 1659 |
| 19 | Tony Dorsett-1 | Dal. | NFC | 81 | 1646 |
| 20 | Walter Payton-3 | Chi. | NFC | 79 | 1610 |
| 21 | Ottis Anderson-1 | St.L. | NFC | 79 | 1605 |
| 22 | William Andrews | Atl. | NFC | 83 | 1567 |
| 23 | Emmitt Smith-3 | Dall. | NFC | 91 | 1563 |
| 24 | Walter Payton-4 | Chi. | NFC | 85 | 1551 |
| 25 | Barry Sanders-2 | Det. | NFC | 91 | 1548 |
| 26 | Chris Warren-1 | Sea. | AFC | 94 | 1545 |
| 27 | Jim Brown-2 | Cle. | NFL | 65 | 1544 |
| | James Wilder-1 | T.B. | NFC | 84 | 1544 |
| 29 | Jim Brown-3 | Cle. | NFL | 58 | 1527 |
| 30 | Joe Morris | NYG | NFC | 86 | 1516 |
| 31 | Herschel Walker | Dall. | NFC | 88 | 1514 |
| 32 | Wilb. Montgomery-1 | Phi. | NFC | 79 | 1512 |
| 33 | O.J. Simpson-3 | Buff. | AFC | 76 | 1503 |
| 34 | Roger Craig | S.F. | NFC | 88 | 1502 |
| 35 | Barry Sanders | Det. | NFC | 95 | 1500 |
| 36 | Thurman Thomas-1 | Buff. | AFC | 92 | 1487 |
| | Curtis Martin | N.E. | AFC | 95 | 1487 |
| 38 | Gerald Riggs | Atl. | NFC | 84 | 1486 |
| | Emmitt Smith-4 | Dall. | NFC | 93 | 1486 |
| 40 | Emmitt Smith-5 | Dall. | NFC | 94 | 1484 |
| 41 | Curt Warner-1 | Sea. | AFC | 86 | 1481 |
| 42 | Christian Okoye | K.C. | AFC | 89 | 1480 |
| 43 | Jim Taylor-1 | G.B. | NFL | 62 | 1474 |
| 44 | Barry Sanders-4 | Det. | NFC | 89 | 1470 |
| 45 | Walter Payton-5 | Chi. | NFC | 80 | 1460 |
| 46 | Jim Nance | Bos. | AFL | 66 | 1458 |
| 47 | Earl Campbell-3 | Hou. | AFC | 78 | 1450 |
| 48 | Curt Warner-2 | Sea. | AFC | 83 | 1449 |
| 49 | Jim Brown-4 | Cle. | NFL | 64 | 1446 |
| 50 | Billy Sims-1 | Det. | NFC | 81 | 1437 |
| 51 | Spec Sanders | N.Y. | AAFC | 47 | 1432 |
| 52 | Jerome Bettis | L.A. | NFC | 93 | 1429 |
| 53 | Walter Payton-6 | Chi. | NFC | 83 | 1421 |
| 54 | Jim Brown-5 | Cle. | NFL | 61 | 1408 |
| 55 | Otis Armstrong | Den. | AFC | 74 | 1407 |
| | Thurman Thomas-2 | Buff. | AFC | 91 | 1407 |
| 57 | Wilb. Montgomery-2 | Phi. | NFC | 81 | 1402 |
| 58 | Walter Payton-7 | Chi. | NFC | 78 | 1395 |
| 59 | Walter Payton-8 | Chi. | NFC | 76 | 1390 |
| 60 | Ottis Anderson-2 | St.L. | NFC | 81 | 1376 |
| | Earl Campbell-4 | Hou. | AFC | 81 | 1376 |
| 62 | Charles White | L.A. | NFC | 87 | 1374 |
| 63 | Rueben Mayes | N.O. | NFC | 86 | 1353 |
| 64 | Ottis Anderson-3 | St.L. | NFC | 80 | 1352 |
| | Barry Sanders-5 | Det. | NFC | 93 | 1352 |
| 66 | Natrone Means | S.D. | AFC | 94 | 1350 |
| 67 | John Riggins | Was. | NFC | 83 | 1347 |
| 68 | Chris Warren-2 | Sea. | AFC | 95 | 1346 |
| 69 | Joe Morris | NYG | NFC | 85 | 1336 |
| 70 | Walter Payton-9 | Chi. | NFC | 86 | 1333 |
| 71 | Freeman McNeil | NYJ | AFC | 85 | 1331 |
| 72 | Jim Brown-6 | Cle. | NFL | 59 | 1329 |
| 73 | Gerald Riggs-2 | Atl. | NFC | 86 | 1327 |
| 74 | Tony Dorsett-2 | Dal. | NFC | 78 | 1325 |
| 75 | Tony Dorsett-3 | Dal. | NFC | 83 | 1321 |
| 76 | Thurman Thomas-3 | Buff. | AFC | 93 | 1315 |
| 77 | Eric Dickerson-5 | Ind. | AFC | 89 | 1311 |
| 78 | Terry Allen | Wash. | NFC | 95 | 1309 |
| 79 | William Andrews-2 | Atl. | NFC | 80 | 1308 |
| 80 | Jim Taylor-2 | G.B. | NFL | 61 | 1307 |
| | Tony Dorsett-4 | Dal. | NFC | 85 | 1307 |
| 82 | Barry Sanders-6 | Det. | NFC | 90 | 1304 |
| 83 | Billy Sims-2 | Det. | NFC | 80 | 1303 |
| 84 | Williams Andrews-3 | Atl. | NFC | 81 | 1301 |
| | Earl Campbell-5 | Hou. | AFC | 83 | 1301 |
| 86 | James Wilder-2 | T.B. | NFC | 85 | 1300 |
| 87 | Thurman Thomas-4 | Buf. | AFC | 90 | 1297 |
| 88 | Mike Pruitt | Cle. | AFC | 79 | 1294 |
| 89 | Eric Dickerson-6 | L.A.-Ind | N/AFC | 87 | 1288 |
| 90 | Marshall Faulk | Ind. | AFC | 94 | 1282 |
| 91 | Neal Anderson | Chi. | NFC | 89 | 1275 |
| 92 | Mark van Eeghen | Oak. | AFC | 77 | 1273 |
| | Ricky Watters | Phil. | NFC | 95 | 1273 |
| 94 | Ottis Anderson-4 | St.L. | NFC | 83 | 1270 |
| 95 | Ricky Bell | T.B. | NFC | 79 | 1263 |
| 96 | Wendell Tyler | S.F. | NFC | 84 | 1262 |
| | Dalton Hilliard | N.O. | NFC | 89 | 1262 |
| 98 | Delvin Williams | Mia | AFC | 78 | 1258 |
| 99 | Jim Brown-7 | Cle. | NFL | 60 | 1257 |
| 100 | O.J. Simpson-4 | Buf. | AFC | 72 | 1251 |

## YARDS PER SCHEDULED GAME

| | | | | | |
|---|---|---|---|---|---|
| 1 | O.J. Simpson-1 | Buf. | AFC | 73 | 143 |
| 2 | Jim Brown-1 | Cle. | NFL | 63 | 133 |
| 3 | Walter Payton-1 | Chi. | NFC | 77 | 132 |
| | Eric Dickerson-1 | L.A. | NFC | 84 | 132 |
| 5 | O.J. Simpson-2 | Buf. | AFC | 75 | 130 |
| 6 | Jim Brown-2 | Cle. | NFL | 58 | 127 |
| 7 | Earl Campbell-1 | Hou. | AFC | 80 | 121 |
| 8 | Barry Sanders-1 | Det. | NFC | 94 | 118 |
| 9 | Eric Dickerson-2 | L.A. | NFC | 86 | 114 |
| 10 | Eric Dickerson-3 | L.A. | NFC | 83 | 113 |
| 11 | Jim Brown-3 | Cle. | NFL | 59 | 111 |
| | Emmitt Smith-1 | Dall. | NFC | 95 | 111 |
| 13 | Jim Brown-4 | Cle. | NFL | 65 | 110 |
| | Marcus Allen | Raid. | AFC | 85 | 110 |
| 15 | O.J. Simpson-3 | Buf. | AFC | 76 | 107 |
| | Emmitt Smith-2 | Dall. | NFC | 92 | 107 |
| 17 | Earl Campbell-2 | Hou. | AFC | 79 | 106 |
| | Barry Foster | Pitt. | AFC | 92 | 106 |
| 19 | JimTaylor-1 | G.B. | NFL | 62 | 105 |
| | Jim Brown-5 | Cle. | NFL | 60 | 105 |
| | Walter Payton-2 | Chi. | NFC | 84 | 105 |
| 22 | George Rogers | N.O. | NFC | 81 | 104 |
| | Jim Nance | Bos. | AFL | 66 | 104 |
| | Eric Dickerson-4 | Ind. | AFC | 88 | 104 |
| 25 | Jim Brown-6 | Cle. | NFL | 64 | 103 |
| | Tony Dorsett | Dal. | NFC | 81 | 103 |
| 27 | Spec Sanders | N.Y. | AAFC | 47 | 102 |
| 28 | Walter Payton-3 | Chi. | NFC | 79 | 101 |
| | Jim Brown-7 | Cle. | NFL | 61 | 101 |
| | Otis Armstrong | Den. | AFC | 74 | 101 |
| 31 | Ottis Anderson | St.L. | NFC | 79 | 100 |
| 32 | Walter Payton-4 | Chi. | NFC | 76 | 99 |
| 33 | William Andrews | Atl. | NFC | 83 | 98 |
| | Emmitt Smith-3 | Dall. | NFC | 91 | 98 |
| 35 | James Wilder | T.B. | NFC | 84 | 97 |
| | Walter Payton-5 | Chi. | NFC | 85 | 97 |
| | Barry Sanders-2 | Det. | NFC | 91 | 97 |
| | Chris Warren | Sea. | AFC | 94 | 97 |
| 39 | Steve Van Buren | Phi. | NFL | 47 | 96 |
| 40 | Wilb. Montgomery-1 | Phi. | NFC | 79 | 95 |
| | Joe Morris | NYG | NFC | 86 | 95 |
| | Herschel Walker | Dall. | NFC | 88 | 95 |
| 43 | Rick Casares | ChiB | NFL | 56 | 94 |
| | Roger Craig | S.F. | NFC | 88 | 94 |
| | Thurman Thomas | Buff. | AFC | 92 | 94 |
| | Barry Sanders-3 | Det. | NFC | 94 | 94 |
| 47 | Jim Taylor-2 | G.B. | NFL | 61 | 93 |
| | Gerald Riggs | Atl. | NFC | 84 | 93 |
| | Curt Warner | Sea. | AFC | 86 | 93 |
| | Christian Okoye | K.C. | AFC | 89 | 93 |
| | Emmitt Smith-4 | Dall. | NFC | 93 | 93 |
| | Emmitt Smith-5 | Dall. | NFC | 94 | 93 |
| 53 | Jim Taylor-3 | G.B. | NFL | 60 | 92 |
| | Charles White | L.A. | NFC | 87 | 92 |
| | Barry Sanders-4 | Det. | NFC | 89 | 92 |

## AVERAGE YARDS

(Minimum 100 Attempts)

| | | | | | Att. | Yards | Avg. |
|---|---|---|---|---|---|---|---|
| 1 | Beattie Feathers | ChiB | NFL | 34 | 101 | 1004 | 9.94 |
| 2 | Randall Cunningham | Phi. | NFC | 90 | 118 | 942 | 7.78 |
| 3 | Bobby Douglass | Chi | NFC | 72 | 141 | 948 | 6.87 |
| 4 | Joe Perry-1 | S.F. | AAFC | 49 | 115 | 783 | 6.81 |
| 5 | Dan Towler-1 | L.A. | NFL | 51 | 126 | 854 | 6.78 |
| 6 | Johnny Strzykalski-1 | S.F. | AAFC | 48 | 141 | 915 | 6.46 |
| 7 | Keith Lincoln | S.D. | NFL | 63 | 128 | 826 | 6.45 |
| 8 | Mercury Morris | Mia. | AFC | 73 | 149 | 954 | 6.40 |
| | Jim Brown-1 | Cle. | NFL | 63 | 291 | 1863 | 6.40 |
| 10 | Johnny Strzykalski-2 | S.F. | AAFC | 47 | 143 | 906 | 6.34 |
| 11 | Paul Lowe | L.A. | AFL | 60 | 136 | 855 | 6.29 |
| 12 | Dutch Clark | Det. | NFL | 34 | 122 | 763 | 6.25 |
| 13 | Gale Sayers | Chi. | NFL | 68 | 138 | 856 | 6.20 |
| | Chet Mutryn-1 | Buf. | AAFC | 47 | 140 | 868 | 6.20 |
| | Spec Sanders | N.Y. | AAFC | 47 | 231 | 1432 | 6.20 |
| 16 | Marion Motley-1 | Cle. | AAFC | 48 | 157 | 964 | 6.14 |
| | Buddy Young | N.Y. | AAFC | 47 | 116 | 712 | 6.14 |
| 18 | Marion Motley-2 | Cle. | AAFC | 47 | 146 | 889 | 6.09 |
| 19 | Joe Perry-2 | S.F. | NFL | 58 | 125 | 758 | 6.06 |
| | Joe Perry-3 | S.F. | NFL | 54 | 173 | 1049 | 6.06 |
| 21 | O.J. Simpson-1 | Buf. | AFC | 73 | 322 | 2003 | 6.03 |
| | Ted McKnight | K.C. | AFC | 78 | 104 | 627 | 6.03 |
| | Hokie Gajan | N.O. | NFC | 84 | 102 | 615 | 6.03 |
| 24 | Randall Cunningham | Phil. | NFC | 89 | 104 | 621 | 5.97 |
| 25 | Jim Brown-2 | Cle. | NFL | 60 | 215 | 1257 | 5.94 |
| 26 | John David Crow | St.L. | NFL | 60 | 183 | 1071 | 5.85 |
| | Jim Brown-3 | Cle. | NFL | 60 | 215 | 1257 | 5.85 |
| 28 | Steve Van Buren | Phi. | NFL | 45 | 143 | 832 | 5.82 |
| 29 | Marion Motley-3 | Cle. | NFL | 50 | 140 | 810 | 5.79 |
| 30 | Dan Towler-2 | L.A. | NFL | 53 | 152 | 879 | 5.78 |
| | Bill Osmanski | ChiB | NFL | 39 | 121 | 699 | 5.78 |
| 32 | Dan Towler-3 | L.A. | NFL | 52 | 156 | 894 | 5.73 |
| 33 | Paul Lowe-2 | S.D. | AFL | 63 | 177 | 1010 | 5.71 |
| 34 | Barry Sanders | Det. | AFC | 94 | 331 | 1883 | 5.69 |
| 35 | Bobby Mitchell | Cle. | NFL | 59 | 131 | 743 | 5.67 |
| 36 | Franco Harris | Pit | AFC | 72 | 188 | 1055 | 5.61 |
| | Abner Haynes | Dal. | AFL | 60 | 156 | 875 | 5.61 |
| | James Brooks | Cin. | AFC | 89 | 221 | 1239 | 5.61 |
| 39 | Chet Mutryn-2 | Buf. | AAFC | 48 | 147 | 823 | 5.60 |
| 40 | Don Calhoun | N.E. | AFC | 76 | 129 | 721 | 5.59 |
| 41 | Eddie Price | NYG | NFL | 50 | 126 | 703 | 5.58 |
| | Bo Jackson | L.A. | AFC | 90 | 125 | 698 | 5.58 |
| 43 | Amos Marsh | Dal. | NFL | 62 | 114 | 802 | 5.57 |
| 44 | Eric Dickerson | L.A. | NFC | 84 | 379 | 2105 | 5.55 |
| 45 | Brad Hubbert | S.D. | AFL | 67 | 116 | 643 | 5.54 |
| 46 | O.J. Simpson-2 | Buf. | AFC | 75 | 329 | 1817 | 5.52 |
| 47 | Stump Mitchell | St.L. | NFC | 85 | 183 | 1006 | 5.50 |
| 48 | Mack Lee Hill | K.C. | AFL | 64 | 105 | 576 | 5.49 |
| | Gerry Ellis | G.B. | NFC | 85 | 104 | 571 | 5.49 |
| | Bo Jackson | L.A. | AFC | 89 | 173 | 950 | 5.49 |
| 51 | Swede Hansen | Phi. | NFL | 34 | 147 | 805 | 5.48 |
| 52 | Walter Payton | Chi | NFC | 77 | 339 | 1852 | 5.46 |
| | Leroy Kelly | Cle. | NFL | 66 | 209 | 1141 | 5.46 |
| 54 | Timmy Brown | Phi. | NFL | 65 | 148 | 861 | 5.45 |
| | Greg Pruitt | Cle. | AFC | 78 | 176 | 960 | 5.45 |
| | Mike Garrett | K.C. | AFL | 66 | 147 | 801 | 5.45 |
| | Mosi Tatupu | N.E. | AFC | 83 | 106 | 578 | 5.45 |

## TOUCHDOWNS

| | | | | | |
|---|---|---|---|---|---|
| 1 | Emmitt Smith-1 | Dall. | NYG | 95 | 25 |
| 2 | John Riggins-1 | Was. | NFC | 83 | 24 |
| 3 | Joe Morris-1 | NYG | NFC | 85 | 21 |
| 4 | Emmitt Smith-2 | Dall. | NFC | 94 | 21 |
| 5 | Jim Taylor-1 | G.B. | NFL | 62 | 19 |
| | Earl Campbell-1 | Hou. | AFC | 79 | 19 |
| | Chuck Muncie-1 | N.O. | NFC | 81 | 19 |
| 8 | Spec Sanders | N.Y. | AAFC | 47 | 18 |
| | Eric Dickerson-1 | L.A. | NFC | 83 | 18 |
| | George Rogers-1 | Was. | NFC | 86 | 18 |
| | Emmitt Smith-3 | Dall. | NFC | 92 | 18 |
| 12 | Jim Brown-1 | Cle. | NFL | 58 | 17 |
| | Jim Brown-2 | Cle. | NFL | 65 | 17 |
| 14 | Lenny Moore | Bal. | NFL | 64 | 16 |
| | Leroy Kelly-1 | Cle. | NFL | 68 | 16 |
| | O.J. Simpson-1 | Buf. | AFC | 75 | 16 |
| | Pete Banaszek | Oak. | AFC | 75 | 16 |
| | Greg Bell | L.A. | NFC | 88 | 16 |
| | Barry Sanders-1 | Det. | NFC | 91 | 16 |
| 20 | Steve Van Buren-1 | Phi. | NFL | 45 | 15 |
| | Jim Taylor-2 | G.B. | NFL | 61 | 15 |
| | Leroy Kelly-2 | Cle. | NFL | 66 | 15 |
| | Pete Johnson-1 | S.D.,Mia | AFC | 84 | 15 |
| | Marcus Allen-1 | Raid. | NFL | 84 | 15 |
| | Ickey Woods | Cin. | AFC | 88 | 15 |
| | Greg Bell | L.A. | NFC | 89 | 15 |
| | Chris Warren | Sea. | AFC | 95 | 15 |
| 28 | Jim Brown-3 | Cle. | NFL | 59 | 14 |
| | John David Crow | St.L. | NFL | 62 | 14 |
| | Gale Sayers | Chi. | NFL | 65 | 14 |
| | Franco Harris-1 | Pit. | AFC | 76 | 14 |
| | Walter Payton-1 | Chi. | NFC | 77 | 14 |
| | David Sims | Sea. | AFC | 78 | 14 |
| | Pete Johnson-2 | Cin. | AFC | 79 | 14 |
| | Walter Payton-2 | Chi. | NFC | 79 | 14 |
| | Pete Johnson-3 | Cin. | AFC | 83 | 14 |
| | John Riggins-2 | Was. | NFC | 84 | 14 |
| | Eric Dickerson-2 | L.A. | NFC | 84 | 14 |
| | Joe Morris-2 | NYG | NFC | 86 | 14 |
| | Eric Dickerson-3 | Ind. | AFC | 88 | 14 |
| | Barry Sanders-2 | Det. | NFC | 89 | 14 |
| | Ottis Anderson | NYG | NFC | 89 | 14 |
| | Derrick Fenner | Sea. | AFC | 90 | 14 |
| | Cleveland Gary | L.A. | NFC | 90 | 14 |
| | Reggie Cobb | T.B. | NFC | 92 | 14 |
| | Curtis Martin | N.E. | AFC | 95 | 14 |
| 47 | Steve Van Buren-2 | Phi. | NFL | 47 | 13 |
| | Paul Hornung | G.B. | NFL | 60 | 13 |
| | Jim Brown-4 | Cle. | NFL | 62 | 13 |
| | Cookie Gilchrist-1 | Buf. | AFL | 62 | 13 |
| | Abner Haynes | Dal. | AFL | 62 | 13 |
| | Chuck Foreman-1 | Min. | NFC | 75 | 13 |
| | Chuck Foreman-2 | Min. | NFC | 76 | 13 |
| | Walter Payton-3 | Chi. | NFC | 76 | 13 |
| | Earl Campbell-2 | Hou. | AFC | 78 | 13 |
| | Earl Campbell-3 | Hou. | AFC | 80 | 13 |
| | Billy Sims | Det. | NFC | 80 | 13 |
| | John Riggins-3 | Was. | NFC | 81 | 13 |
| | George Rogers-2 | N.O. | NFC | 81 | 13 |
| | Billy Sims-2 | Det. | NFC | 81 | 13 |
| | Curt Warner-1 | Sea. | AFC | 83 | 13 |
| | James Wilder | T.B. | NFC | 84 | 13 |
| | Gerald Riggs | Atl. | NFC | 84 | 13 |
| | Curt Warner-2 | Sea | AFC | 86 | 13 |
| | Dalton Hilliard | N.O. | NFC | 89 | 13 |
| | Barry Sanders-3 | Det. | NFC | 90 | 13 |
| | Terry Allen | Minn. | NFC | 92 | 13 |

# SINGLE SEASON LEADERS

# RECEIVING

### RECEPTIONS

| | | | | | |
|---|---|---|---|---|---|
| 1 | Herman Moore | Det. | NFC | 95 | 123 |
| 2 | Cris Carter-1 | Minn. | NFC | 94 | 122 |
| | Jerry Rice-1 | S.F. | NFC | 95 | 122 |
| | Cris Carter-2 | Minn. | NFC | 95 | 122 |
| 5 | Isaac Bruce | StL. | NFC | 95 | 119 |
| 6 | Sterling Sharpe-1 | G.B. | NFC | 93 | 112 |
| | Jerry Rice-2 | S.F. | NFC | 94 | 112 |
| 8 | Terance Mathis | Atl. | NFC | 94 | 111 |
| | Michael Irvin-1 | Dall. | NFC | 95 | 111 |
| 10 | Sterling Sharpe-2 | G.B. | NFC | 92 | 108 |
| | Brett Perriman | Det. | NFC | 95 | 108 |
| 12 | Art Monk-1 | Was. | NFC | 84 | 106 |
| 13 | Eric Metcalf | Atl. | NFC | 95 | 104 |
| 14 | Robert Brooks | G.B. | NFC | 95 | 102 |
| 15 | Charley Hennigan | Hou. | AFL | 64 | 101 |
| | Larry Centers | Ariz. | NFC | 95 | 101 |
| 17 | Lionel Taylor-1 | Den. | AFL | 61 | 100 |
| | Jerry Rice-3 | S.F. | NFC | 90 | 100 |
| | Haywood Jeffires-1 | Hou. | AFC | 91 | 100 |
| 20 | Carl Pickens | Cin. | AFC | 95 | 99 |
| 21 | Jerry Rice-4 | S.F. | NFC | 93 | 98 |
| 22 | Ben Coates | N.E. | AFC | 94 | 96 |
| 23 | Todd Christensen-1 | Raid. | AFC | 86 | 95 |
| 24 | Sterling Sharpe-3 | G.B. | NFC | 94 | 94 |
| 25 | Johnny Morris | Chi. | NFL | 64 | 93 |
| | Al Toon-1 | NYJ | AFC | 88 | 93 |
| | Michael Irvin-2 | Dall. | NFC | 91 | 93 |
| | Andre Rison-1 | Atl. | NFC | 92 | 93 |
| 29 | Lionel Taylor-2 | Den. | AFL | 60 | 92 |
| | Todd Christensen | Raid. | AFC | 83 | 92 |
| | Roger Craig | S.F. | NFC | 85 | 92 |
| 32 | Art Monk-2 | Was. | NFC | 85 | 91 |
| | J.T. Smith | St.L. | NFC | 87 | 91 |
| 34 | Sterling Sharpe-4 | G.B. | NFC | 89 | 90 |
| | Drew Hill | Hou. | AFC | 91 | 90 |
| | Haywood Jeffires-2 | Hou. | AFC | 92 | 90 |
| | Andre Reed-2 | Buff. | AFC | 94 | 90 |
| | Tony Martin | S.D. | AFC | 95 | 90 |
| 39 | Kellen Winslow | S.D. | AFC | 80 | 89 |
| | Ozzie Newsome-1 | Cle. | AFC | 83 | 89 |
| | Ozzie Newsome-2 | Cle. | AFC | 84 | 89 |
| | Tim Brown-1 | Raid. | AFC | 94 | 89 |
| | Tim Brown-2 | Oak. | AFC | 95 | 89 |
| 44 | Rickey Young | Min. | NFC | 78 | 88 |
| | Kellen Winslow-2 | S.D. | AFC | 81 | 88 |
| | Kellen Winslow-3 | S.D. | AFC | 83 | 88 |
| | Andre Reed-1 | Buff. | AFC | 89 | 88 |
| | Michael Irvin-3 | Dall. | NFC | 93 | 88 |
| 49 | Shannon Sharpe | Den. | AFC | 94 | 87 |
| | Derek Loville | S.F. | NFC | 95 | 87 |
| 51 | Lionel James | S.D. | AFC | 85 | 86 |
| | Jerry Rice-5 | S.F. | NFC | 86 | 86 |
| | Mark Clayton | Mia. | AFC | 88 | 86 |
| | Henry Ellard | L.A. | NFC | 88 | 86 |
| | Mark Carrier | T.B. | NFC | 89 | 86 |
| | Art Monk-3 | Wash. | NFC | 89 | 86 |
| | Andre Rison-2 | Atl. | NFC | 93 | 86 |
| | Cris Carter | Minn. | NFC | 93 | 86 |
| 59 | Lionel Taylor-3 | Den. | AFL | 75 | 85 |
| | Dwight Clark | S.F. | NFC | 81 | 85 |
| | James Wilder | T.B. | NFC | 84 | 85 |
| | Al Toon-2 | NYJ | AFC | 86 | 85 |
| | Eric Martin | N.O. | NFC | 88 | 85 |
| | Reggie Langhorne | Ind. | AFC | 93 | 85 |
| | Jake Reed | Minn. | NFC | 94 | 85 |
| | Yancey Thigpen | Pitt. | AFC | 95 | 85 |

### YARDS

| | | | | | |
|---|---|---|---|---|---|
| 1 | Jerry Rice-1 | S.F. | NFC | 95 | 1848 |
| 2 | Isaac Bruce | StL. | NFC | 95 | 1781 |
| 3 | Charley Hennigan-1 | Hou. | AFL | 61 | 1746 |
| 4 | Herman Moore | Det. | NFC | 95 | 1686 |
| 5 | Michael Irvin-1 | Dall. | NFC | 95 | 1603 |
| 6 | Lance Alworth-1 | S.D. | AFL | 65 | 1602 |
| 7 | Jerry Rice-2 | S.F. | NFC | 86 | 1570 |
| 8 | Roy Green | St.L. | NFC | 84 | 1555 |
| 9 | Charley Hennigan-2 | Hou. | AFL | 64 | 1546 |
| 10 | Michael Irvin-2 | Dall. | NFC | 91 | 1523 |
| 11 | Jerry Rice-3 | S.F. | NFC | 93 | 1503 |
| 12 | Jerry Rice-4 | S.F. | NFC | 90 | 1502 |
| 13 | Jerry Rice-5 | S.F. | NFC | 94 | 1499 |
| 14 | Robert Brooks | G.B. | NFC | 95 | 1497 |
| 15 | Crazy Legs Hirsch | L.A. | NFL | 51 | 1495 |
| 16 | Stanley Morgan | N.E. | AFC | 86 | 1491 |
| 17 | Brett Perriman | Det. | NFC | 95 | 1488 |
| 18 | Jerry Rice-6 | S.F. | NFC | 89 | 1483 |
| 19 | Bill Groman | Hou. | AFL | 60 | 1473 |
| 20 | Sterling Sharpe-1 | G.B. | NFC | 92 | 1461 |
| 21 | Bobby Mitchell | Was. | NFL | 63 | 1436 |
| 22 | Don Maynard-1 | NYJ | AFL | 67 | 1434 |
| 23 | Sterling Sharpe-2 | G.B. | NFC | 89 | 1423 |
| 24 | Mark Carrier | T.B. | NFC | 89 | 1422 |
| 25 | Henry Ellard-1 | L.A. | NFC | 88 | 1414 |
| 26 | Mike Quick | Phi. | NFC | 83 | 1409 |
| 27 | Henry Ellard-2 | Wash. | NFC | 94 | 1397 |
| 28 | Michael Irvin-3 | Dall. | NFC | 92 | 1396 |
| 29 | John Stallworth | Pit. | AFC | 84 | 1395 |
| 30 | Mark Clayton | Mia. | AFC | 84 | 1389 |
| 31 | Bobby Mitchell-2 | Was. | NFL | 62 | 1384 |
| 32 | Lance Alworth-2 | S.D. | AFL | 66 | 1383 |
| 33 | Henry Ellard-3 | L.A. | NFC | 89 | 1382 |
| 34 | Art Monk | Was. | NFC | 84 | 1372 |
| 35 | Cris Carter-1 | Minn. | NFC | 95 | 1371 |
| 36 | Art Powell-1 | Oak. | AFL | 64 | 1361 |
| | James Lofton-1 | G.B. | NFC | 84 | 1361 |
| 38 | Alfred Jenkins | Atl. | NFC | 81 | 1358 |
| 39 | Carlos Carson | K.C. | AFC | 83 | 1351 |
| 40 | Dave Parks | S.F. | NFL | 65 | 1344 |
| 41 | Terance Mathis | Atl. | NFC | 94 | 1342 |
| | Tim Brown-2 | Oak. | AFC | 95 | 1342 |
| 43 | John Jefferson | S.D. | AFC | 80 | 1340 |
| | Gary Clark-1 | Wash. | NFC | 91 | 1340 |
| 45 | Michael Irvin-4 | Dall. | NFC | 93 | 1330 |
| 46 | Mark Duper-1 | Mia. | AFC | 86 | 1313 |
| 47 | Lance Alworth-3 | S.D. | AFL | 68 | 1312 |
| | Andre Reed-1 | Buff. | AFC | 89 | 1312 |
| 49 | Tim Brown-1 | Raid. | AFC | 94 | 1309 |
| 50 | Yancey Thigpen | Pitt. | AFC | 95 | 1307 |
| 51 | Mark Duper-2 | Mia. | AFC | 84 | 1306 |
| | Jerry Rice-7 | S.F. | NFC | 88 | 1306 |
| 53 | Art Powell-2 | Oak. | AFL | 63 | 1304 |
| 54 | Andre Reed-2 | Buff. | AFC | 94 | 1303 |
| 55 | Jeff Graham | Chi. | NFC | 95 | 1301 |
| 56 | James Lofton-2 | G.B. | NFC | 83 | 1300 |
| 57 | Raymond Berry | Bal. | NFL | 60 | 1298 |
| 58 | Otis Taylor | K.C. | AFL | 66 | 1297 |
| | Don Maynard-2 | NYJ | AFL | 68 | 1297 |
| 60 | Buddy Dial | Pit. | NFL | 63 | 1295 |
| 61 | James Lofton-3 | G.B. | NFC | 81 | 1294 |
| | Henry Ellard-4 | L.A. | NFC | 90 | 1294 |
| 63 | Kellen Winslow | S.D. | AFC | 80 | 1290 |
| 64 | Steve Largent-1 | Sea. | AFC | 85 | 1287 |
| 65 | Sterling Sharpe-3 | G.B. | NFC | 93 | 1274 |
| 66 | Eddie Brown | Cin. | AFC | 88 | 1273 |
| 67 | Irving Fryar | Mia. | AFC | 94 | 1270 |
| 68 | Pat Studstill | Det. | NFL | 66 | 1266 |
| 69 | Don Maynard-3 | NYJ | AFL | 60 | 1265 |
| | Ben Hawkins | Phi. | NFL | 67 | 1265 |
| | Gary Clark-2 | Was. | NFC | 86 | 1265 |
| 72 | Warren Wells | Oak. | AFL | 69 | 1260 |
| 73 | Cris Carter-2 | Minn. | AFC | 94 | 1256 |
| 74 | Anthony Miller | S.D. | AFC | 89 | 1252 |
| 75 | Todd Christensen | Raid. | AFC | 83 | 1247 |
| | Mike Quick | Phi. | NFC | 85 | 1247 |
| 77 | Frank Lewis | Buf. | AFC | 81 | 1244 |
| | Steve Watson | Den. | AFC | 81 | 1244 |
| 79 | Andre Rison | Atl. | NFC | 93 | 1242 |
| 80 | Michael Irvin-4 | Dall. | NFC | 94 | 1241 |
| 81 | Steve Largent-2 | Sea. | AFC | 79 | 1237 |
| 82 | Webster Slaughter | Clev. | AFC | 89 | 1236 |
| 83 | Lionel Taylor | Den. | AFL | 60 | 1235 |
| | Lance Alworth-4 | S.D. | AFL | 64 | 1235 |
| 85 | Carl Pickens | Cin. | AFC | 95 | 1234 |
| 86 | Bob Hayes | Dal. | NFL | 66 | 1232 |
| 87 | Billy Howton | G.B. | NFL | 52 | 1231 |
| 88 | Tony Martin | S.D. | AFC | 95 | 1224 |

### YARDS PER SCHEDULED GAME

| | | | | | |
|---|---|---|---|---|---|
| 1 | Charley Hennigan-1 | Hou. | AFL | 61 | 125 |
| | Crazy Legs Hirsch | L.A. | NFL | 51 | 125 |
| 3 | Jerry Rice-1 | S.F. | NFC | 95 | 116 |
| 4 | Wes Chandler | S.D. | AFC | 82 | 115 |
| 5 | Lance Alworth-1 | S.D. | AFL | 65 | 114 |
| 6 | Isaac Bruce | StL. | NFC | 95 | 111 |
| 7 | Charley Hennigan-2 | Hou. | AFL | 64 | 110 |
| | Don Hutson | G.B. | NFL | 42 | 110 |
| 9 | Raymond Berry | Bal. | NFL | 60 | 108 |
| 10 | Jim Benton-1 | Cle. | NFL | 45 | 107 |
| 11 | Bill Groman-1 | Hou. | AFL | 60 | 105 |
| | Herman Moore | Det. | NFC | 95 | 105 |
| 13 | Billy Howton-1 | G.B. | NFL | 52 | 103 |
| | Bobby Mitchell-1 | Was. | NFL | 63 | 103 |
| 15 | Don Maynard-1 | NYJ | AFL | 67 | 102 |
| 16 | Bob Boyd | L.A. | NFL | 54 | 101 |
| 17 | Michael Irvin-1 | Dall. | NFC | 95 | 100 |
| 18 | Billy Howton-2 | G.B. | NFL | 56 | 99 |
| | Bobby Mitchell-2 | Was. | NFL | 62 | 99 |
| | Lance Alworth-2 | S.D. | AFL | 66 | 99 |
| 21 | Jerry Rice-2 | S.F. | NFC | 86 | 98 |
| 22 | Art Powell-1 | Oak. | AFL | 64 | 97 |
| | Roy Green | St.L. | NFC | 84 | 97 |
| 24 | Dave Parks | S.F. | NFL | 65 | 96 |
| 25 | Michael Irvin-2 | Dall. | NFC | 91 | 95 |
| 26 | Harlon Hill-1 | ChiB | NFL | 56 | 94 |
| | Lance Alworth-3 | S.D. | AFL | 68 | 94 |
| | Harlon Hill-2 | ChiB | NFL | 54 | 94 |
| | Jerry Rice-3 | S.F. | NFC | 90 | 94 |
| | Jerry Rice-4 | S.F. | NFC | 93 | 94 |
| | Jerry Rice-5 | S.F. | NFC | 94 | 94 |
| | Robert Brooks | G.B. | NFC | 95 | 94 |
| 33 | Art Powell | NYT | AFL | 63 | 93 |
| | Tom Fears-1 | L.A. | NFL | 50 | 93 |
| | Otis Taylor | K.C. | AFL | 66 | 93 |
| | Don Maynard-2 | NYJ | AFL | 68 | 93 |
| | Buddy Dial | Pit. | NFL | 63 | 93 |
| | Jerry Rice-6 | S.F. | NFC | 89 | 93 |
| | Brett Perriman | Det. | NFC | 95 | 93 |
| 40 | Del Shofner-1 | L.A. | NFL | 58 | 91 |
| | Sterling Sharpe-1 | G.B. | NFC | 92 | 91 |
| 42 | Pat Studstill | Det. | NFL | 66 | 90 |
| | Don Maynard-3 | NYJ | AFL | 60 | 90 |
| | Ben Hawkins | Phi. | NFL | 67 | 90 |
| | Warren Wells | Oak. | AFL | 69 | 90 |
| 46 | Jim Benton-2 | L.A. | NFL | 46 | 89 |
| | Sterling Sharpe-2 | G.B. | NFC | 89 | 89 |
| | Mark Carrier | T.B. | NFC | 89 | 89 |
| 49 | Lionel Taylor-1 | Den. | AFL | 69 | 88 |
| | Lance Alworth-4 | S.D. | AFL | 64 | 88 |
| | Bob Hayes | Dal. | NFL | 66 | 88 |
| | Mike Quick | Phi. | NFC | 83 | 88 |
| | Henry Ellard-1 | L.A. | NFC | 88 | 88 |

### AVERAGE YARDS

(Minimum 400 Yards)

| | | | | | Rec. | Yards | Avg. |
|---|---|---|---|---|---|---|---|
| 1 | Don Currivan | Bos. | NFL | 47 | 24 | 782 | 32.6 |
| 2 | Bucky Pope | L.A. | NFL | 64 | 25 | 786 | 31.4 |
| 3 | Billy Cannon | Oak. | AFL | 66 | 14 | 436 | 31.1 |
| 4 | Ray McLean-1 | ChiB | NFL | 42 | 19 | 571 | 30.1 |
| 5 | Mel Gray | St.L. | NFC | 71 | 18 | 534 | 29.7 |
| 6 | Bobby Duckworth | S.D. | AFC | 84 | 25 | 715 | 28.6 |
| 7 | Ray Renfro | Cle. | NFL | 57 | 21 | 589 | 28.0 |
| 8 | Jimmy Orr-1 | Pit. | NFL | 58 | 33 | 910 | 27.6 |
| 9 | Jesse Hester | Raid. | AFC | 86 | 23 | 632 | 27.5 |
| 10 | Andy Farkas | Was. | NFL | 39 | 16 | 437 | 27.3 |
| | Homer Jones-1 | NYG | NFL | 65 | 26 | 709 | 27.3 |
| 12 | Elbert Dubenion | Buf. | AFL | 64 | 42 | 1139 | 27.1 |
| 13 | Frank Liebel | NYG | NFL | 45 | 22 | 593 | 27.0 |
| 14 | Leonard Thompson | Det. | NFC | 80 | 19 | 511 | 26.9 |
| 15 | Warren Wells | Oak. | AFL | 69 | 47 | 1260 | 26.8 |
| | Buddy Dial-1 | Pit. | NFL | 69 | 16 | 428 | 26.8 |
| 17 | Billy Van Heusen | Den. | AFC | 74 | 16 | 421 | 26.3 |
| | Earl McCullough | Det. | NFC | 71 | 21 | 552 | 26.3 |
| | Jack Snow | L.A. | NFL | 67 | 28 | 735 | 26.3 |
| 20 | Art Graham | Bos. | AFL | 63 | 21 | 550 | 26.2 |
| | Bob Hayes-1 | Dal. | NFC | 70 | 34 | 889 | 26.2 |
| 22 | Ron Sellers | Bos. | AFL | 69 | 27 | 705 | 26.1 |
| 23 | Mervyn Fernandez | Raid. | AFC | 88 | 31 | 805 | 26.0 |
| | Willie Anderson | L.A. | NFC | 89 | 44 | 1146 | 26.0 |
| 25 | Roger Carr | Bal. | AFC | 76 | 43 | 1112 | 25.9 |
| 26 | Theo Bell | Pit. | AFC | 80 | 29 | 748 | 25.8 |
| 27 | Jimmy Orr-2 | Bal. | NFL | 68 | 29 | 743 | 25.6 |
| | Ken Kavanaugh | ChiB | NFL | 47 | 32 | 818 | 25.6 |
| 29 | Cloyce Box | Det. | NFL | 53 | 16 | 403 | 25.2 |
| 30 | Paul Warfield | Mia. | AFC | 70 | 28 | 703 | 25.1 |
| 31 | Harlon Hill-1 | ChiB | NFL | 54 | 45 | 1124 | 25.0 |
| 32 | Don Hutson | G.B. | NFL | 39 | 34 | 846 | 24.9 |
| 33 | Wesley Walker-1 | NYJ | AFC | 79 | 23 | 569 | 24.7 |
| | Red Mack | Pit. | NFL | 63 | 25 | 618 | 24.7 |
| | Homer Jones-2 | NYG | NFL | 67 | 49 | 1209 | 24.7 |
| 36 | Tony Bowa | P-P | NFL | 43 | 17 | 419 | 24.6 |
| 37 | Wesley Walker-2 | NYJ | AFC | 78 | 48 | 1169 | 24.4 |
| 38 | Elbie Nickel-1 | Pit. | NFL | 49 | 26 | 633 | 24.3 |
| | Walter White | K.C. | AFC | 75 | 23 | 559 | 24.3 |
| | Buddy Dial-2 | Pit. | NFL | 60 | 40 | 972 | 24.3 |
| | Anthony Carter | Min. | NFC | 87 | 38 | 922 | 24.3 |
| 42 | Rick Upchurch | Den. | AFC | 75 | 18 | 436 | 24.2 |
| | Ray McLean-2 | ChiB | NFL | 43 | 18 | 435 | 24.2 |
| | Cliff Branch | Oak. | AFC | 76 | 46 | 1111 | 24.2 |
| 45 | Roy Jefferson | Pit. | NFL | 66 | 32 | 772 | 24.1 |
| | Stanley Morgan | N.E. | AFC | 78 | 34 | 820 | 24.1 |
| | Rod Barksdale | Raid. | AFC | 86 | 18 | 434 | 24.1 |
| 48 | Harlon Hill-2 | ChiB | NFL | 56 | 47 | 1128 | 24.0 |
| | Bob Hayes-2 | Dal. | NFC | 71 | 35 | 840 | 24.0 |
| | Elbie Nickel-2 | Pit. | NFL | 50 | 22 | 527 | 24.0 |
| | Eddie Brown | Cin. | AFC | 88 | 53 | 1273 | 24.0 |

### TOUCHDOWNS

| | | | | | |
|---|---|---|---|---|---|
| 1 | Jerry Rice-1 | S.F. | NFC | 87 | 22 |
| 2 | Mark Clayton-1 | Mia. | AFC | 84 | 18 |
| | Sterling Sharpe-1 | G.B. | NFC | 94 | 18 |
| 4 | Don Hutson | G.B. | NFL | 42 | 17 |
| | Crazy Legs Hirsch | L.A. | NFL | 51 | 17 |
| | Bill Groman | Hou. | AFL | 61 | 17 |
| | Jerry Rice-2 | S.F. | NFC | 89 | 17 |
| | Carl Pickens | Cin. | AFC | 95 | 17 |
| | Cris Carter | Minn. | NFC | 95 | 17 |
| 8 | Art Powell-1 | NYT | AFL | 63 | 16 |
| 9 | Cloyce Box | Det. | NFL | 52 | 15 |
| | Sonny Randle | St.L. | NFL | 60 | 15 |
| | Jerry Rice-3 | S.F. | NFC | 86 | 15 |
| | Jerry Rice-4 | S.F. | NFC | 93 | 15 |
| | Andre Rison | Atl. | NFC | 93 | 15 |
| | Jerry Rice-5 | S.F. | NFC | 95 | 15 |
| 14 | Mal Kutner | ChiC | NFL | 48 | 14 |
| | Alyn Beals | S.F. | AAFC | 48 | 14 |
| | Raymond Berry | Bal. | NFL | 59 | 14 |
| | Art Powell-2 | NYT | AFL | 60 | 14 |
| | Frank Clarke | Dal. | NFL | 62 | 14 |
| | Lance Alworth-1 | S.D. | AFL | 65 | 14 |
| | Don Maynard | NYJ | AFL | 65 | 14 |
| | Warren Wells | Oak. | AFL | 69 | 14 |
| | Roy Green | St.L. | NFC | 83 | 14 |
| | Mark Clayton-2 | Mia. | AFC | 88 | 14 |
| | Jerry Rice-6 | S.F. | NFC | 91 | 14 |
| | Anthony Miller | Den. | AFC | 95 | 14 |
| | Herman Moore | Det. | NFC | 95 | 14 |
| 25 | Ken Kavanaugh | ChiB | NFL | 47 | 13 |
| | Billy Howton | G.B. | NFL | 52 | 13 |
| | Tommy McDonald-1 | Phi. | NFL | 60 | 13 |
| | Tommy McDonald-2 | Phi. | NFL | 61 | 13 |
| | Terry Barr | Det. | NFL | 63 | 13 |
| | Gary Collins | Cle. | NFL | 63 | 13 |
| | Lance Alworth-2 | S.D. | AFL | 64 | 13 |
| | Lance Alworth-3 | S.D. | AFL | 66 | 13 |
| | Bob Hayes | Dal. | NFL | 66 | 13 |
| | Homer Jones | NYG | NFL | 67 | 13 |
| | Dick Gordon | Chi | NFC | 70 | 13 |
| | Harold Jackson | L.A. | NFC | 73 | 13 |
| | Cliff Branch | Oak. | AFC | 74 | 13 |
| | John Jefferson-1 | S.D. | AFC | 78 | 13 |
| | John Jefferson-2 | S.D. | AFC | 80 | 13 |
| | Alfred Jenkins | Atl. | NFC | 81 | 13 |
| | Steve Watson | Den. | AFC | 81 | 13 |
| | Mike Quick | Phi. | NFC | 83 | 13 |
| | Jerry Rice-7 | S.F. | NFC | 90 | 13 |
| | Sterling Sharpe-2 | G.B. | NFC | 92 | 13 |
| | Jerry Rice-8 | S.F. | NFC | 94 | 13 |
| | Isaac Bruce | StL. | NFC | 95 | 13 |
| | Robert Brooks | G.B. | NFC | 95 | 13 |

# SINGLE SEASON LEADERS

## PUNT RETURNS

| | | | | | |
|---|---|---|---|---|---|
| 1 | Danny Reece-1 | T.B. | NFC | 79 | 70 |
| 2 | Fulton Walker-1 | Raid. | AFC | 85 | 62 |
| 3 | Greg Pruitt-1 | Raid. | AFC | 83 | 58 |
| | Leo Lewis | Min. | NFC | 88 | 58 |
| 5 | Eddie Brown-1 | Was. | NFC | 77 | 57 |
| | Danny Reece-2 | T.B. | NFC | 80 | 57 |
| | Jeff Fisher-1 | Chi. | NFC | 84 | 57 |
| | Lew Barnes | Chi. | NFC | 86 | 57 |
| 9 | Eddie Brown-2 | L.A. | NFC | 79 | 56 |
| 10 | Rolland Lawrence-1 | Atl. | NFC | 76 | 54 |
| | James Jones | Dal. | NFC | 80 | 54 |
| | Wally Henry | Phi. | NFC | 81 | 54 |
| | Gary Allen | Dal. | NFC | 84 | 54 |
| 14 | Alvin Hammond-1 | L.A. | NFC | 70 | 53 |
| | Larry Jones | Was. | NFC | 75 | 53 |
| | Louis Lipps | Pit. | AFC | 84 | 53 |
| | Greg Pruitt-2 | Raid. | AFC | 84 | 53 |
| | Phil McConkey-1 | NYG | NFC | 85 | 53 |
| | Todd Kinchen | St.L. | NFC | 95 | 53 |
| 20 | Jackie Wallace | L.A. | NFC | 78 | 52 |
| | Leon Bright | NYG | NFC | 81 | 52 |
| | Bobby Martin | Det. | NFC | 81 | 52 |
| 23 | Rolland Lawrence-2 | Atl. | NFC | 77 | 51 |
| | Rick Upchurch-1 | Den. | AFC | 77 | 51 |
| | Butch Johnson-1 | Dal. | AFC | 78 | 51 |
| | Tamarick Vanover | K.C. | AFC | 95 | 51 |
| 27 | Butch Johnson-2 | Dal. | NFC | 77 | 50 |
| | J.T. Smith-1 | K.C. | AFC | 79 | 50 |
| | J.T. Smith-2 | K.C. | AFC | 81 | 50 |
| 30 | Mike Nelms-1 | Was. | NFC | 84 | 49 |
| | Fulton Walker-2 | Raid. | AFC | 86 | 49 |
| | Tim Brown | Raid. | AFC | 88 | 49 |
| | Gerald McNeil | Clev. | AFC | 89 | 49 |
| 34 | Neal Colzie-1 | Oak. | AFC | 75 | 48 |
| | Eddie Brown-3 | Was. | NFC | 76 | 48 |
| | Ira Matthews | Oak. | AFC | 80 | 48 |
| | Mike Nelms-2 | Was. | NFC | 80 | 48 |
| | Andre Hastings | Pitt. | AFC | 95 | 48 |
| 39 | Manfred Moore | Min. | NFC | 77 | 47 |
| | Neal Colzie-2 | Oak. | AFC | 78 | 47 |
| | Carl Roaches | Hou. | AFC | 80 | 47 |
| 42 | Rodger Bird | Oak. | AFL | 67 | 46 |
| | Larry Marshall | Phi. | NFC | 77 | 46 |
| | Mike Fuller | S.D. | AFC | 79 | 46 |
| | LeRoy Irvin | L.A. | NFC | 80 | 46 |
| | Butch Johnson-3 | Atl. | NFC | 83 | 46 |
| | Phil McConkey-2 | NYG | NFC | 84 | 46 |
| | Dave Meggett-1 | NYG | NFC | 89 | 46 |
| 49 | Mike Haynes | N.E. | AFC | 76 | 45 |
| | Butch Johnson-4 | Dal. | NFC | 76 | 45 |
| | Theo Bell | Pit. | AFC | 79 | 45 |
| | Mike Nelms-3 | Was. | NFC | 81 | 45 |
| | Dana McLemore | S.F. | NFC | 84 | 45 |
| | Brian Mitchell | Wash. | NFC | 91 | 45 |
| | Dave Meggett-2 | N.E. | AFC | 95 | 45 |

### YARDS

| | | | | | |
|---|---|---|---|---|---|
| 1 | Fulton Walker | Raid. | AFC | 85 | 692 |
| 2 | Greg Pruitt-1 | Raid. | AFC | 83 | 666 |
| 3 | Louis Lipps-1 | Pit. | AFC | 84 | 656 |
| 4 | Neal Colzie-1 | Oak. | AFC | 75 | 655 |
| 5 | Rick Upchurch-1 | Den. | AFC | 77 | 653 |
| 6 | Eddie Brown-1 | Was. | NFC | 76 | 646 |
| 7 | Jackie Wallace | L.A. | NFC | 78 | 618 |
| 8 | LeRoy Irvin | L.A. | NFC | 81 | 615 |
| 9 | Rodger Bird | Oak. | AFL | 67 | 612 |
| | J.T. Smith-1 | K.C. | AFC | 79 | 612 |
| 11 | Billy Johnson-1 | Hou. | AFC | 75 | 610 |
| 12 | Mike Haynes | N.E. | AFC | 76 | 608 |
| 13 | Brian Mitchell | Wash. | NFC | 91 | 600 |
| 14 | Charley Rogers-1 | Fra. | NFL | 27 | 589 |
| 15 | Dave Meggett | NYG | NFC | 89 | 582 |
| 16 | J.T. Smith-2 | K.C. | AFC | 80 | 581 |
| 17 | Lynn Swann | Pit. | AFC | 74 | 577 |
| 18 | John Taylor | S.F. | NFC | 88 | 556 |
| 19 | Billy Grimes | G.B. | NFL | 50 | 555 |
| 20 | Vai Sikahema-1 | St.L. | NFC | 87 | 550 |
| | Leo Lewis | Min. | NFC | 88 | 550 |
| 22 | James Jones | Dal. | NFC | 80 | 548 |
| 23 | Tamarick Vanover | K.C. | AFC | 95 | 540 |
| 24 | Billy Johnson-2 | Hou. | AFC | 77 | 539 |
| 25 | Rick Upchurch-2 | Den. | AFC | 76 | 536 |
| 26 | Kelvin Martin | Dall. | NFC | 92 | 532 |
| 27 | Charley Rogers-2 | Fra. | NFL | 28 | 528 |
| | J.T. Smith-3 | K.C. | AFC | 81 | 528 |
| 29 | Vai Sikahema-2 | St.L. | NFC | 86 | 522 |
| 30 | Dana McLemore | S.F. | NFC | 84 | 521 |
| 31 | Irving Fryar | N.E. | AFC | 85 | 520 |
| 32 | Mack Herron | N.E. | AFC | 74 | 517 |
| 33 | Bruce Taylor | S.F. | NFC | 70 | 516 |
| 34 | Jeff Fisher-1 | Chi. | NFC | 81 | 509 |
| 35 | Vai Sikahema-3 | Phil. | NFC | 92 | 503 |
| 36 | Tyrone Hughes | N.O. | NFC | 93 | 503 |
| 37 | Henry Ellard | L.A. | NFC | 85 | 501 |
| 38 | Walter Stanley | Det. | NFC | 89 | 496 |
| | Gerald McNeil | Clev. | AFC | 89 | 496 |
| 40 | Rick Upchurch-3 | Den. | AFC | 78 | 493 |
| 41 | Mike Nelms-1 | Was. | NFC | 81 | 492 |
| | Jeff Fisher-2 | Chi. | NFC | 84 | 492 |
| 43 | Butch Atkinson | Oak. | AFL | 68 | 490 |
| 44 | Emlen Tunnell | NYG | NFL | 51 | 489 |
| | Butch Johnson | Dal. | NFC | 76 | 489 |
| | Larry Marshall | Phi. | NFC | 77 | 489 |
| | Billy Johnson-3 | Atl. | NFC | 83 | 489 |
| 48 | Mike Nelms-2 | Was. | NFC | 80 | 487 |
| | Tim Brown-1 | Raid. | AFC | 94 | 487 |
| 50 | Ron Smith | Oak. | AFC | 74 | 486 |
| 51 | Lew Barnes | Chi. | NFC | 86 | 482 |
| 52 | Darrien Gordon | S.D. | AFC | 94 | 475 |
| | Eric Guliford | Car. | NFC | 95 | 475 |
| 54 | Andre Hastings | Pitt. | AFC | 95 | 474 |
| 55 | Greg Pruitt-2 | Raid. | AFC | 84 | 473 |
| 56 | Gerald Willhite | Den. | AFC | 86 | 468 |
| 57 | Dave Meggett | NYG | NFC | 90 | 467 |
| 58 | Tim Brown | L.A.Rd. | AFC | 93 | 465 |
| 59 | Speedy Duncan | S.D. | AFL | 65 | 464 |
| 60 | Eric Metcalf | Clev. | AFC | 93 | 464 |
| 61 | Pat Studstill | Det. | NFL | 62 | 457 |
| 62 | Virgil Livers | Chi. | NFC | 75 | 456 |
| 63 | Jack Ernst | Port. | NFL | 26 | 453 |
| 64 | Eddie Brown-2 | Was. | NFC | 77 | 452 |
| | Brian Mitchell | Wash. | NFC | 94 | 452 |
| 66 | Robbie Martin | Det. | NFC | 81 | 450 |
| 67 | Neal Colzie-2 | Oak. | AFC | 76 | 448 |
| | Mike Fuller | S.D. | AFC | 79 | 448 |
| 69 | Gary Allen | Dal. | NFC | 84 | 446 |
| | Leo Lewis | Minn. | NFC | 89 | 446 |
| 71 | Stump Mitchell | St.L. | NFC | 81 | 445 |
| 72 | Tim Brown-2 | Raid. | AFC | 88 | 444 |

### AVERAGE RETURNS

(Minimum — 1 Return per Game)

| | | | | | Ret. | Yds. | Avg. |
|---|---|---|---|---|---|---|---|
| 1 | Ernie Steele | Phi. | NFL | 42 | 10 | 264 | 26.40 |
| 2 | Herb Rich | Bal. | NFL | 50 | 12 | 276 | 23.00 |
| 3 | Jack Christiansen-1 | Det. | NFL | 52 | 15 | 322 | 21.47 |
| 4 | Dick Christy | NYT | AFL | 61 | 18 | 383 | 21.28 |
| 5 | Rex Baumgardner | Buf. | AAFC | 48 | 16 | 336 | 21.00 |
| 6 | Red Cochran | ChiC | NFL | 49 | 15 | 314 | 20.93 |
| 7 | Jerome Davis | ChiC | NFL | 48 | 16 | 334 | 20.88 |
| 8 | Bob Hayes | Dal. | NFL | 68 | 15 | 312 | 20.80 |
| 9 | Frank Sinkwich | Det. | NFL | 43 | 11 | 228 | 20.73 |
| 10 | Paddy Driscoll | ChiC | NFL | 21 | 8 | 154 | 19.25 |
| | Buddy Young | NYY | NFL | 51 | 12 | 231 | 19.25 |
| 12 | Billy Grimes | G.B. | NFL | 50 | 29 | 555 | 19.14 |
| 13 | Jack Christiansen-2 | Det. | NFL | 51 | 18 | 343 | 19.06 |
| 14 | Ollie Matson | ChiC | NFL | 55 | 13 | 245 | 18.85 |
| 15 | Lemar Parrish | Cin. | AFC | 74 | 18 | 338 | 18.78 |
| 16 | Chuck Fenenbock | L.A. | AAFC | 46 | 16 | 299 | 18.69 |
| 17 | Woodley Lewis | L.A. | NFL | 52 | 19 | 351 | 18.47 |
| 18 | Frank Seno | Bos. | NFL | 47 | 12 | 213 | 17.75 |

## KICKOFF RETURNS

| | | | | | |
|---|---|---|---|---|---|
| 1 | Tyrone Hughes-1 | N.O. | NFC | 95 | 66 |
| 2 | Tyrone Hughes-2 | N.O. | NFC | 94 | 63 |
| 3 | Andre Coleman | S.D. | AFC | 95 | 62 |
| 4 | Drew Hill-1 | L.A. | NFC | 81 | 60 |
| 5 | Brian Mitchell-1 | Wash. | NFC | 94 | 58 |
| | Bobby Joe Edmonds | T.B. | NFC | 95 | 58 |
| 7 | Dexter Carter | NYJ-SF | A/NFC | 95 | 56 |
| 8 | Bruce Harper-1 | NYJ | AFC | 78 | 55 |
| | Bruce Harper-2 | NYJ | AFC | 79 | 55 |
| | David Turner | Cin. | AFC | 79 | 55 |
| | Stump Mitchell | St.L. | NFC | 81 | 55 |
| | Brian Mitchell-2 | Wash. | NFC | 95 | 55 |
| 13 | Ernie Mills | Pitt. | AFC | 95 | 54 |
| 14 | Eddie Payton-1 | Min. | NFC | 80 | 53 |
| | Buster Rhymes | Min. | NFC | 85 | 53 |
| | Mel Gray-1 | Hou. | AFC | 95 | 53 |
| 17 | Eric Metcalf | Cle. | AFC | 90 | 52 |
| 18 | Zachary Dixon | Sea. | AFC | 83 | 51 |
| 19 | Nesby Glasgow | Bal. | AFC | 79 | 50 |
| | Clarence Verdin-1 | Ind. | AFC | 93 | 50 |
| | David Dunn | Cin. | AFC | 95 | 50 |
| 22 | Bruce Harper-3 | NYJ | AFC | 80 | 49 |
| | Herman Hunter-1 | Det. | NFC | 86 | 49 |
| | Andre Coleman-2 | S.D. | AFC | 94 | 49 |
| | Kevin Williams | Dall. | NFC | 95 | 49 |
| 26 | Mike Martin | Cin. | AFC | 85 | 48 |
| | Stephen Starring | N.E. | AFC | 85 | 48 |
| | Phil Freeman | T.B. | NFC | 85 | 48 |
| | Herman Hunter-2 | Phi. | NFC | 85 | 48 |
| | Dexter Carter | S.F. | NFC | 94 | 48 |
| 31 | Odell Barry | Den. | AFL | 64 | 47 |
| | Larry Jones | Was. | NFC | 75 | 47 |
| | Reggie Smith | Atl. | NFC | 81 | 47 |
| | Gerald McNeil | Cle. | AFC | 86 | 47 |
| | James Dixon | Dall. | NFC | 89 | 47 |
| | Ron Brown | L.A. | NFC | 89 | 47 |
| | Glyn Milburn | Den. | AFC | 95 | 47 |
| 38 | Chuck Latourette | St.L. | NFL | 68 | 46 |
| | Dave Hampton | G.B. | NFC | 71 | 46 |
| 40 | Bobby Jancik | Atl. | NFL | 68 | 45 |
| | Tony Nathan | Mia. | AFC | 79 | 45 |
| | Lorenzo Hampton | Mia. | AFC | 86 | 45 |
| | Mel Gray-2 | Det. | NFC | 94 | 45 |
| 44 | Jimmy Edwards | Min. | NFC | 79 | 44 |
| | Steve Odom | GB,NYG | NFC | 79 | 44 |
| | Gary Davis | T.B. | NFC | 80 | 44 |
| | Cle Montgomery | Cin. | AFC | 80 | 44 |
| | Herschel Walker | Min. | NFC | 90 | 44 |
| | Rod Woodson | Pitt. | AFC | 91 | 44 |
| | Clarence Verdin-2 | Atl. | NFC | 94 | 44 |
| 51 | Ron Smith-1 | Atl. | NFL | 66 | 43 |
| | Mercury Morris | Mia. | AFL | 69 | 43 |
| | Margene Adkins | N.O. | NFC | 72 | 43 |
| | Dino Hall | Cle. | AFC | 79 | 43 |
| | Drew Hill-2 | L.A. | NFC | 80 | 43 |
| | Ron Fellows | Dal. | NFC | 83 | 43 |
| | Lionel James | S.D. | AFC | 84 | 43 |
| | Tim McGee | Cin. | AFC | 86 | 43 |
| | Terance Mathis | NYJ | AFC | 90 | 43 |
| | Kevin Williams | Dall. | NFC | 94 | 43 |
| | Vernon Turner | T.B. | NFC | 94 | 43 |
| | Raghib Ismail | Raid. | AFC | 94 | 43 |
| | Steve Broussard | Sea. | AFC | 95 | 43 |
| | Tamarick Vanover | K.C. | AFC | 95 | 43 |

### YARDS

| | | | | | |
|---|---|---|---|---|---|
| 1 | Tyrone Hughes-1 | N.O. | NFC | 95 | 1617 |
| 2 | Tyrone Hughes-2 | N.O. | NFC | 94 | 1556 |
| 3 | Brian Mitchell-1 | Wash. | NFC | 94 | 1478 |
| 4 | Andre Coleman-1 | S.D. | AFC | 95 | 1411 |
| 5 | Brian Mitchell-2 | Wash. | NFC | 95 | 1408 |
| 6 | Buster Rhymes | Min. | NFC | 85 | 1345 |
| 7 | Bobby Jancik | Hou. | AFL | 63 | 1317 |
| 8 | Dave Hampton | G.B. | NFC | 71 | 1314 |
| 9 | Ernie Mills | Pitt. | AFC | 95 | 1306 |
| 10 | Andre Coleman-2 | S.D. | AFC | 94 | 1293 |
| 11 | Stump Mitchell | St.L. | NFC | 81 | 1292 |
| 12 | Bruce Harper-1 | NYJ | AFC | 78 | 1280 |
| 13 | Mel Gray-1 | Det. | NFC | 94 | 1276 |
| 14 | Glyn Milburn | Den. | AFC | 95 | 1269 |
| 15 | Odell Berry | Den. | AFL | 64 | 1245 |
| 16 | Chuck Latourette | St.L. | NFL | 68 | 1237 |
| 17 | Dexter Carter | NYJ-SF | A/NFC | 95 | 1227 |
| 18 | Eddie Payton | Min. | NFC | 80 | 1184 |
| 19 | Mel Gray-2 | Hou. | AFC | 95 | 1183 |
| 20 | James Dixon | Dall. | NFC | 89 | 1181 |
| 21 | Zachary Dixon | Sea. | AFC | 83 | 1171 |
| 22 | Drew Hill | L.A. | NFC | 81 | 1170 |
| 23 | Bruce Harper-2 | NYJ | AFC | 79 | 1158 |
| 24 | Abe Woodson | S.F. | NFL | 62 | 1157 |
| 25 | David Turner | Cin. | AFC | 79 | 1149 |
| 26 | Noland Smith | K.C. | AFL | 67 | 1148 |
| | Kevin Williams | Dall. | NFC | 94 | 1148 |
| 28 | Bobby Joe Edmonds | T.B. | NFC | 95 | 1147 |
| 29 | Reggie Smith | Atl. | NFC | 81 | 1143 |
| 30 | Mercury Morris | Mia. | AFC | 69 | 1136 |
| 31 | Nesby Glasgow | Bal. | AFC | 79 | 1126 |
| 32 | Kevin Williams-2 | Dall. | NFC | 95 | 1108 |
| 33 | Dexter Carter | S.F. | NFC | 94 | 1105 |
| 34 | Mike Martin | Cin. | AFC | 85 | 1104 |
| 35 | Jimmy Edwards | Min. | NFC | 79 | 1103 |
| 36 | Mike Nelms | Was. | NFC | 81 | 1099 |
| 37 | Tim Brown | Raid. | AFC | 88 | 1098 |
| 38 | Tamarick Vanover | K.C. | AFC | 95 | 1095 |
| 39 | Mack Herron | N.E. | AFC | 73 | 1092 |
| | David Dunn | Cin. | AFC | 95 | 1092 |
| 41 | Larry Jones | Was. | NFC | 75 | 1086 |
| 42 | Phil Freeman | T.B. | NFL | 85 | 1085 |
| 43 | Rick Upchurch | Den. | AFC | 75 | 1084 |
| 44 | Bruce Harper-3 | NYJ | AFC | 80 | 1070 |
| 45 | Deion Sanders | Atl. | NFC | 92 | 1067 |
| 46 | Steve Broussard | Sea. | AFC | 95 | 1064 |
| 47 | Eric Metcalf | Cle. | AFC | 90 | 1052 |
| 48 | Clarence Verdin | Ind. | AFC | 93 | 1050 |
| 49 | Herman Hunter-1 | Phi. | NFC | 85 | 1047 |
| 50 | Qadry Ismail | Minn. | NFC | 95 | 1037 |
| 51 | Bruce Harper-4 | NYJ | AFC | 77 | 1035 |
| 52 | Steve Odom-1 | G.B. | NFC | 75 | 1034 |
| 53 | Clarence Verdin-2 | Atl. | NFC | 94 | 1026 |
| 54 | Alvin Haymond | L.A. | NFC | 70 | 1022 |
| 55 | Margene Adkins | N.O. | NFC | 72 | 1020 |
| | Lorenzo Hampton | Mia. | AFC | 85 | 1020 |
| 57 | Ken Jenkins | Was. | NFC | 85 | 1018 |
| 58 | Mel Renfro | Dal. | NFL | 64 | 1017 |
| 59 | Tony Nathan | Mia. | AFC | 79 | 1016 |
| 60 | Ron Smith-1 | Atl. | NFL | 66 | 1013 |
| 61 | Stephen Starring | N.E. | AFC | 85 | 1012 |
| 62 | Herb Mul-Key | Was. | NFC | 73 | 1011 |
| 63 | Tim McGee | Cin | AFC | 86 | 1007 |
| | Herman Hunter-2 | Det. | NFC | 86 | 1007 |

### AVERAGE RETURNS

(Minimum — 1 Return per Game)

| | | | | | Ret. | Yds. | Avg. |
|---|---|---|---|---|---|---|---|
| 1 | Travis Williams | G.B. | NFL | 67 | 18 | 739 | 41.06 |
| 2 | Gale Sayers-1 | Chi. | NFL | 67 | 16 | 603 | 37.69 |
| 3 | Ollie Matson-1 | ChiC | NFL | 58 | 14 | 479 | 35.50 |
| 4 | Speedy Duncan | Bal. | AFC | 70 | 20 | 707 | 35.35 |
| 5 | Lynn Chandnois-1 | Pit. | NFL | 52 | 17 | 599 | 35.24 |
| 6 | Preston Pearson | Bal. | NFL | 68 | 15 | 527 | 35.13 |
| 7 | Joe Arenas | S.F. | NFL | 53 | 16 | 551 | 34.44 |
| 8 | Tom Watkins | Det. | NFL | 65 | 17 | 584 | 34.35 |
| 9 | Vitamin Smith | L.A. | NFL | 50 | 22 | 742 | 33.73 |
| 10 | Bobby Williams | Det. | NFL | 69 | 17 | 563 | 33.12 |
| 11 | Tom Moore | G.B. | NFL | 60 | 12 | 397 | 33.08 |
| 12 | Chet Mutryn | Buf. | AAFC | 47 | 21 | 691 | 32.90 |
| 13 | Duriel Harris | Mia. | AFC | 76 | 17 | 559 | 32.88 |
| 14 | Ron Brown | L.A. | NFC | 85 | 28 | 918 | 32.79 |
| 15 | Cecil Turner | Chi. | NFC | 70 | 23 | 752 | 32.70 |
| 16 | Lynn Chandnois-2 | Pit. | NFL | 51 | 23 | 752 | 32.70 |
| 17 | Abe Woodson-1 | S.F. | NFL | 63 | 29 | 935 | 32.24 |
| 18 | Tom Willson | L.A. | NFL | 56 | 15 | 477 | 31.80 |
| 19 | Gary Ballman | Pit. | NFL | 63 | 22 | 698 | 31.73 |
| 20 | Walter Payton | Chi. | NFC | 75 | 14 | 444 | 31.71 |
| 21 | Jack Salscheider | NYG | NFL | 49 | 15 | 474 | 31.60 |
| 22 | Gale Sayers-2 | Chi. | NFL | 65 | 21 | 660 | 31.43 |
| 23 | Frank Zeno | ChiC | NFL | 46 | 13 | 408 | 31.38 |
| 24 | Abe Woodson-2 | S.F. | NFL | 62 | 37 | 1157 | 31.27 |
| 25 | Ron Hall | Hou. | AFL | 60 | 19 | 594 | 31.26 |
| 26 | Gale Sayers-3 | Chi. | NFL | 66 | 23 | 718 | 31.22 |
| 27 | Ollie Matson-2 | ChiC | NFL | 52 | 20 | 624 | 31.20 |
| 28 | Terry Metcalf | St.L. | NFC | 74 | 20 | 623 | 31.15 |
| 29 | Ray Clayborn | N.E. | AFC | 77 | 28 | 869 | 31.04 |
| 30 | Lenny Lyles | S.F. | NFL | 60 | 19 | 526 | 30.94 |
| 31 | Frank Minini | ChiB | NFL | 48 | 12 | 370 | 30.83 |
| 32 | Ron Smith | Chi. | NFC | 72 | 30 | 924 | 30.80 |
| 33 | Alvin Haymond | Bal. | NFL | 65 | 20 | 614 | 30.70 |
| 34 | Bobby Humphery | NYJ | AFC | 84 | 22 | 675 | 30.68 |
| 35 | Buddy Young | NYY | NFL | 51 | 14 | 427 | 30.50 |
| 36 | Harold Hart | Oak. | AFC | 75 | 17 | 518 | 30.47 |
| 37 | Carl Garrett | Chi. | NFC | 73 | 16 | 486 | 30.38 |
| 38 | Dick Bass | L.A. | NFL | 61 | 23 | 698 | 30.35 |
| 39 | Bobby Jancik | Hou. | AFL | 62 | 24 | 726 | 30.25 |
| 40 | Johnny Counts | NYG | NFL | 62 | 26 | 784 | 30.15 |
| 41 | Lemar Parrish | Cin. | AFC | 70 | 16 | 482 | 30.13 |
| 42 | John Gilliam | N.O. | NFL | 67 | 16 | 431 | 30.01 |
| 43 | Mel Renfro | Dal. | NFL | 65 | 21 | 630 | 30.00 |

# SINGLE SEASON LEADERS

## POINTS

| | | | | | |
|---|---|---|---|---|---|
| 1 | Paul Hornung-1 | G.B. | NFL | 60 | 176 |
| 2 | Mark Moseley- 1 | Was. | NFC | 83 | 161 |
| 3 | Gino Cappelletti-1 | Bos. | AFL | 64 | 155 |
| 4 | Emmitt Smith-1 | Dall. | NFC | 95 | 150 |
| 5 | Chip Lohmiller-1 | Wash. | NFC | 91 | 149 |
| 6 | Gino Cappelletti-2 | Bos. | AFL | 61 | 147 |
| 7 | Paul Hornung-2 | G.B. | NFL | 61 | 146 |
| 8 | Jim Turner-1 | NY J | AFL | 68 | 145 |
| 9 | John Riggins | Was. | NFC | 83 | 144 |
| | Kevin Butler | Chi. | NFL | 85 | 144 |
| 11 | Norm Johnson | Pitt. | AFC | 95 | 141 |
| 12 | Tony Franklin | NE | AFC | 85 | 140 |
| 13 | Gary Anderson | Pit. | AFC | 85 | 139 |
| | Nick Lowery | K.C. | AFC | 90 | 139 |
| 15 | Don Hutson-1 | G.B. | NFL | 42 | 138 |
| | O.J. Simpson | Buf. | AFC | 75 | 138 |
| | Jerry Rice | S.F. | NFC | 87 | 138 |
| 18 | Gene Mingo-1 | Den. | AFL | 62 | 137 |
| 19 | Mike Cofer-1 | S.F. | NFC | 89 | 136 |
| 20 | John Carney-1 | S.D. | AFC | 94 | 135 |
| 21 | Gale Sayers | Chi. | NFL | 65 | 132 |
| | Gino Cappelletti- 3 | Bos. | AFL | 65 | 132 |
| | Chuck Foreman | Min. | NFC | 75 | 132 |
| | Jeff Jaeger | L.A.Rd. | AFC | 93 | 132 |
| | Fuad Reveiz-1 | Minn. | NFC | 94 | 132 |
| | Emmitt Smith-2 | Dall. | NFC | 94 | 132 |
| | Jason Hanson-1 | Det. | NFC | 95 | 132 |
| | Jason Elam | Den. | AFC | 95 | 132 |
| 29 | Ray Wersching- 1 | S.F. | NFC | 84 | 131 |
| | Chip Lohmiller-2 | Was. | NFC | 90 | 131 |
| 31 | Dave Ray- 1 | L.A. | NFC | 73 | 130 |
| | Jason Hanson-2 | Det. | NFC | 93 | 130 |
| 33 | Jan Stenerud | K.C. | AFL | 68 | 129 |
| | Jim Turner- 2 | NY J | AFL | 69 | 129 |
| | John Smith- | NE | AFC | 80 | 129 |
| | Scott Norwood | Buf. | AFC | 88 | 129 |
| 37 | Doak Walker | Det. | NFL | 50 | 128 |
| | Gino Cappelletti- 4 | Bos. | AFL | 62 | 128 |
| | Cookie Gilchrist | Buf. | AFL | 62 | 128 |
| | Chester Marcol | G.B. | NFC | 72 | 128 |
| | Chip Lohmiller-2 | Wash. | NFC | 89 | 128 |
| | Chris Jacke | G.B. | NFC | 93 | 128 |
| 43 | Ali Haji - Sheikh | NY G | NFC | 83 | 127 |
| | Chris Boniol | Dall. | NFC | 95 | 127 |
| 45 | Jimmy Brown | Cle. | NFC | 65 | 126 |
| | Ray Wersching- 2 | S.F. | NFC | 83 | 126 |
| | Joe Morris | NY G | NFC | 85 | 126 |
| | Al Del Greco | Hou. | AFC | 93 | 126 |
| | Steve Christie | Buff. | AFC | 95 | 126 |
| 50 | Fred Cox- 1 | Min. | NFC | 70 | 125 |
| 51 | Pete Stoyanovich | Mia. | AFC | 92 | 124 |
| 52 | John Carney-2 | S.D. | AFC | 93 | 124 |
| 53 | Gene Mingo- 2 | Den. | AFL | 60 | 123 |
| | Roy Gerela | Pit. | AFC | 73 | 123 |
| | Rafael Septien- 1 | Dal. | NFC | 83 | 123 |
| 56 | Eddie Murray-1 | Dall. | NFC | 93 | 122 |
| | Morten Andersen-1 | Atl. | NFC | 95 | 122 |
| | Fuad reveiz-2 | Minn. | NFC | 95 | 122 |
| 59 | Fred Cox- 2 | Min. | NFL | 64 | 121 |
| | Dave Ray- 2 | L.A. | NFC | 70 | 121 |
| | Bobby Howfield | NY J | AFC | 72 | 121 |
| | Eddie Murray- 2 | Det. | NFC | 81 | 121 |
| | Rafael Septien- 2 | Dal. | NFC | 81 | 121 |
| | Pat Leahy | NY J | AFC | 85 | 121 |
| | Morten Andersen-2 | N.O. | NFC | 87 | 121 |
| | Mike Cofer-2 | S.F. | NFC | 88 | 121 |
| | Pete Stoyanovich | Mia. | AFC | 91 | 121 |
| | Doug Pelfrey | Cin. | AFC | 95 | 121 |
| 69 | Lenny Moore | Bal. | NFC | 64 | 120 |
| | Leroy Kelly | Cle. | NFC | 68 | 120 |
| | Eric Dickerson | L.A. | NFC | 83 | 120 |
| | Mark Moseley- 2 | Was. | NFC | 84 | 120 |
| | Morten Andersen-3 | N.O. | NFC | 85 | 120 |
| | Jim Breech | Cin. | AFC | 85 | 120 |
| | Kevin Butler- 2 | Chi. | NFC | 86 | 120 |
| | David Treadwell | Den. | AFC | 89 | 120 |
| | Rich Karlis | Minn. | NFC | 89 | 120 |
| | Mike Lansford | L.A. | NFC | 89 | 120 |
| | Chip Lohmiller-3 | Wash. | NFC | 92 | 120 |
| | Morten Andersen-4 | N.O. | NFC | 92 | 120 |

### POINTS PER SCHEDULED GAME

| | | | | | |
|---|---|---|---|---|---|
| 1 | Paul Hornung- 1 | G.B. | NFL | 60 | 14.7 |
| 2 | Don Hutson- 1 | G.B. | NFL | 42 | 12.5 |
| 3 | Don Hutson- 2 | G.B. | NFL | 43 | 11.7 |
| 4 | Gino Cappelletti- 1 | Bos. | AFL | 64 | 11.1 |
| 5 | Steve Van Buren | Phi. | NFL | 45 | 11.0 |
| 6 | Doak Walker- 1 | Det. | NFL | 50 | 10.7 |
| 7 | Gino Cappelletti- 2 | Bos. | AFL | 61 | 10.5 |
| 8 | Paul Hornung- 2 | G.B. | NFL | 61 | 10.4 |
| | Jim Turner- 1 | NY J | AFL | 68 | 10.4 |
| 10 | Mark Moseley | Was. | NFC | 83 | 10.1 |
| 11 | O.J. Simpson | Buf. | AFC | 75 | 9.9 |
| 12 | Gene Mingo- 1 | Den. | AFL | 62 | 9.8 |
| 13 | Don Hutson- 3 | G.B. | NFL | 45 | 9.7 |
| 14 | Gordon Soltau | S.F. | NFL | 53 | 9.5 |
| | Bobby Walston- 1 | Phi. | NFL | 54 | 9.5 |
| 16 | Gale Sayers | Chi. | NFL | 65 | 9.4 |
| | Gino Cappelletti- 3 | Bos. | AFL | 65 | 9.4 |
| | Chuck Foreman | Min. | NFC | 75 | 9.4 |
| | Emmitt Smith | Dall. | NFC | 95 | 9.4 |
| 20 | Dave Ray- 1 | L.A. | NFC | 73 | 9.3 |
| | Marcus Allen | Raid. | AFC | 82 | 9.3 |
| | Chip Lohmiller | Wash. | NFC | 91 | 9.3 |
| 23 | Jan Stenerud- | K.C. | AFL | 68 | 9.2 |
| | Jim Turner- 2 | NY J | AFL | 69 | 9.2 |
| | Pat Harder | ChiC | NFL | 48 | 9.2 |
| | Jerry Rice | S.F. | NFC | 87 | 9.2 |
| 27 | Gino Cappelletti- 4 | Bos. | AFL | 62 | 9.1 |
| | Cookie Gilchrist | Buf. | AFL | 62 | 9.1 |
| | Chester Marcol | G.B. | NFC | 72 | 9.1 |
| | Johnny Lujack | ChiB | NFL | 50 | 9.1 |
| 31 | Lou Groza | Cle. | NFL | 53 | 9.0 |
| | Jimmy Brown- 1 | Cle. | NFL | 58 | 9.0 |
| | Jimmy Brown- 2 | Cle. | NFL | 65 | 9.0 |
| | John Riggins | Was. | NFC | 83 | 9.0 |
| | Kevin Butler | Chi. | NFC | 85 | 9.0 |
| 36 | Fred Cox- 1 | Min. | NFC | 70 | 8.9 |
| | Rolf Benirschke | S.D. | AFC | 82 | 8.9 |
| 38 | Doak Walker- 2 | Det. | NFL | 54 | 8.8 |
| | Gene Mingo- 2 | Den. | AFL | 60 | 8.8 |
| | Roy Gerela- | Pit. | AFC | 73 | 8.8 |
| | Bobby Walston- 2 | Phi. | NFL | 60 | 8.8 |
| | Tony Franklin | NE | AFC | 86 | 8.8 |
| | Norm Johnson | Pitt. | AFC | 95 | 8.8 |
| 44 | Gary Anderson | Pit. | AFC | 85 | 8.7 |
| | Nick Lowery | K.C. | AFC | 90 | 8.7 |
| 46 | Fred Cox- 2 | Min. | NFL | 69 | 8.6 |
| | Dave Ray- 2 | L.A. | NFC | 70 | 8.6 |
| | Bobby Howfield | NY J | AFC | 72 | 8.6 |
| | Don Hutson- 4 | G.B. | NFL | 41 | 8.6 |
| | Lenny Moore | Bal. | NFL | 64 | 8.6 |
| | Leroy Kelly | Cle. | NFL | 68 | 8.6 |

## FIELD GOALS

| | | | | | |
|---|---|---|---|---|---|
| 1 | Ali Haji - Sheikh | NY G | NFC | 83 | 35 |
| | Jeff Jaeger-1 | L.A.Rd. | AFC | 93 | 35 |
| 3 | Jim Turner- 1 | NY J | AFL | 68 | 34 |
| | Nick Lowery-1 | K.C. | AFC | 90 | 34 |
| | Jason Hanson-1 | Det. | NFC | 93 | 34 |
| | John Carney-1 | S.D. | AFC | 94 | 34 |
| | Fuad Reveiz | Minn. | NFC | 94 | 34 |
| | Norm Johnson | Pitt. | AFC | 95 | 34 |
| 9 | Chester Marcol- 1 | G.B. | NFC | 72 | 33 |
| | Mark Moseley-1 | Was. | NFC | 83 | 33 |
| | Gary Anderson- 1 | Pit. | AFC | 85 | 33 |
| 12 | Jim Turner- 2 | NY J | AFL | 69 | 32 |
| | Tony Franklin | NE | AFC | 86 | 32 |
| | Scott Norwood | Buf. | AFC | 88 | 32 |
| 15 | Morten Andersen- 1 | N.O. | NFC | 85 | 31 |
| | Kevin Butler- 1 | Chi. | NFC | 85 | 31 |
| | Rich Karlis | Minn. | NFC | 89 | 31 |
| | Chip Lohmiller-1 | Wash. | NFC | 91 | 31 |
| | Pete Stoyanovich-1 | Mia. | AFC | 91 | 31 |
| | John Carney-2 | S.D. | AFC | 93 | 31 |
| | Chris Jacke | G.B. | NFC | 93 | 31 |
| | Jason Elam-1 | Den. | AFC | 95 | 31 |
| | Steve Christie-1 | Buff. | AFC | 95 | 31 |
| | Morten Andersen-2 | Atl. | NFC | 95 | 31 |
| 25 | Jan Stenerud- 1 | K.C. | AFL | 68 | 30 |
| | Jan Stenerud- 2 | K.C. | AFC | 70 | 30 |
| | Fred Cox - | Min. | NFC | 70 | 30 |
| | Dave Ray- 1 | L.A. | NFC | 73 | 30 |
| | Raul Allegre | Bal. | AFC | 83 | 30 |
| | Paul McFadden- 1 | Phil. | NFC | 84 | 30 |
| | Chip Lohmiller-2 | Wash. | NFC | 90 | 30 |
| | Chip Lohmiller-3 | Wash. | NFC | 92 | 30 |
| | Pete Stoyanovich-2 | Mia. | AFC | 92 | 30 |
| | Jason Elam-2 | Den. | AFC | 94 | 30 |
| | Greg Davis | Ariz. | NFC | 95 | 30 |
| 36 | David Ray- 2 | L.A. | NFC | 70 | 29 |
| | Curt Knight | Was. | NFC | 71 | 29 |
| | Roy Gerela- 1 | Pitt. | AFC | 73 | 29 |
| | Frank Corral | L.A. | NFC | 78 | 29 |
| | Mike Cofer | S.F. | NFC | 89 | 29 |
| | Chip Lohmiller-4 | Wash. | NFC | 89 | 29 |
| | Jeff Jaeger-2 | L.A. | AFC | 91 | 29 |
| | Morten Andersen-3 | N.O. | NFC | 92 | 29 |
| | Al Del Greco | Hou. | AFC | 93 | 29 |
| 45 | Pete Gogolak- 1 | Buf. | AFL | 65 | 28 |
| | Kevin Butler- 2 | Chi. | AFC | 86 | 28 |
| | Bruce Gossett- | L.A. | NFL | 66 | 28 |
| | Garo Yepremian- 1 | Mia. | AFC | 71 | 28 |
| | Roy Gerela- 2 | Pit. | AFC | 72 | 28 |
| | Morten Andersen-4 | N.O. | NFC | 87 | 28 |
| | Gary Anderson-2 | Pit. | AFC | 88 | 28 |
| | Roger Ruzek | Phil. | NFC | 91 | 28 |
| | Gary Anderson-3 | Pitt. | AFC | 92 | 28 |
| | Gary Anderson-4 | Pitt. | AFC | 93 | 28 |
| | Eddie Murray-1 | Dall. | NFC | 93 | 28 |
| | Morten Andersen-5 | N.O. | NFC | 93 | 28 |
| | Steve Christie-2 | Buff. | AFC | 94 | 28 |
| | Morten Andersen-6 | N.O. | NFC | 94 | 28 |
| | Jason Hanson-2 | Det. | NFC | 95 | 28 |

### PERCENTAGE—FIELD GOALS MADE

(Minimum Attempts: to 1949=5, 1950-59=10, 1960-91=20)

| | | | | | Made | Att. | Pct. |
|---|---|---|---|---|---|---|---|
| 1 | Chris Boniol | Dall. | NFC | 95 | 27 | 28 | 96.4 |
| 2 | Norm Johnson-1 | Atl. | NFC | 93 | 26 | 27 | 96.3 |
| 2 | Mark Moseley- 1 | Was. | NFC | 82 | 20 | 21 | 95.2 |
| 3 | Eddie Murray-1 | Det. | NFC | 88 | 20 | 21 | 95.2 |
| | Eddie Murray-2 | Det. | NFC | 89 | 20 | 21 | 95.2 |
| 6 | Gary Anderson-1 | Pitt. | AFC | 93 | 28 | 30 | 93.3 |
| 7 | Matt Stover-1 | Clev. | AFC | 94 | 26 | 28 | 92.9 |
| 8 | Nick Lowery-1 | K.C. | AFC | 90 | 34 | 37 | 91.9 |
| 9 | Jan Stenerud-1 | G.B. | NFC | 81 | 22 | 24 | 91.7 |
| | Nick Lowery-2 | K.C. | AFC | 92 | 22 | 24 | 91.7 |
| 11 | John Carney-1 | S.D. | AFC | 90 | 19 | 21 | 90.5 |
| 12 | John Carney-2 | S.D. | AFC | 94 | 34 | 38 | 89.5 |
| 13 | Nick Lowery- 3 | K.C. | AFC | 85 | 24 | 27 | 88.9 |
| | Dean Biasucci-1 | Ind. | AFC | 87 | 24 | 27 | 88.9 |
| 15 | Morten Andersen- 1 | N.O. | NFC | 85 | 31 | 35 | 88.6 |
| 16 | Lou Groza | Cle. | NFL | 53 | 23 | 26 | 88.5 |
| | Pat Leahy-1 | NYJ | AFC | 90 | 23 | 26 | 88.5 |
| 18 | Roger Ruzek | Dal. | NFC | 87 | 22 | 25 | 88.0 |
| 19 | Matt Stover-2 | Clev. | AFC | 95 | 29 | 33 | 87.9 |
| 20 | Tony Zendejas | Hous. | AFC | 89 | 25 | 27 | 87.6 |
| 21 | Jack Manders | ChiB | NFL | 36 | 7 | 8 | 87.5 |
| | Matt Bahr- 1 | Cle. | AFC | 83 | 21 | 24 | 87.5 |
| 23 | Fuad Reveiz | Minn. | NFC | 94 | 34 | 39 | 87.2 |
| 24 | Gary Anderson- 2 | Pit. | AFC | 83 | 27 | 31 | 87.1 |
| | Al Del Greco-1 | Hou. | AFC | 95 | 27 | 31 | 87.1 |
| 26 | Jan Stenerud- 2 | Min. | NFC | 84 | 20 | 23 | 87.0 |
| 27 | Nick Lowery | NYJ | AFC | 94 | 20 | 23 | 87.0 |
| 28 | Morten Andersen- 2 | N.O. | NFC | 86 | 26 | 30 | 86.7 |
| 29 | Scott Norwood | Buf. | AFC | 88 | 32 | 37 | 86.5 |
| 30 | David Treadwell-1 | NYG | NFC | 93 | 25 | 29 | 86.2 |
| 31 | Raul Allegre | Bal. | AFC | 83 | 30 | 35 | 85.7 |
| | Steve Christie | Buff. | AFC | 94 | 24 | 28 | 85.7 |
| 33 | Jeff Jaeger | L.A. | AFC | 91 | 29 | 34 | 85.3 |
| | Morten Andersen-3 | N.O. | NFC | 92 | 29 | 34 | 85.3 |
| | Al Del Greco-2 | Hou. | AFC | 93 | 29 | 34 | 85.3 |
| 36 | Steve Christie | T.B. | NFC | 90 | 23 | 27 | 85.2 |
| 37 | Roger Ruzek | Phil. | NFC | 91 | 28 | 33 | 84.9 |
| | Eddie Murray-3 | Dall. | NFC | 93 | 28 | 33 | 84.9 |
| | Doug Pelfrey | Cin. | AFC | 94 | 28 | 33 | 84.9 |
| 40 | Nick Lowery-4 | K.C. | AFC | 88 | 27 | 32 | 84.4 |
| 41 | Toni Fritsch- 1 | Hou. | AFC | 79 | 21 | 25 | 84.0 |
| | Rick Danmeier | Min. | NFC | 81 | 21 | 25 | 84.0 |
| | Rich Karlis-1 | Den. | AFC | 83 | 21 | 25 | 84.0 |
| | Pete Stoyanovich-1 | Mia. | AFC | 90 | 21 | 25 | 84.0 |
| | Eddie Murray4 | Phil. | NFC | 94 | 21 | 25 | 84.0 |
| | Norm Johnson-2 | Atl. | NFC | 94 | 21 | 25 | 84.0 |
| 47 | Eddie Murray-5 | Det. | NFC | 85 | 26 | 31 | 83.9 |
| | Dean Biasucci-2 | Ind. | AFC | 93 | 26 | 31 | 83.9 |
| 49 | Kevin Butler | Chi. | NFC | 85 | 31 | 37 | 83.8 |
| | Pete Stoyanovich | Mia. | AFC | 91 | 31 | 37 | 83.8 |
| | Chris Jacke | G.B. | NFC | 93 | 31 | 37 | 83.8 |
| | Morten Anderson-4 | Atl. | NFC | 95 | 31 | 37 | 83.8 |
| 53 | Ray Wersching- | S.F. | NFC | 79 | 20 | 24 | 83.3 |
| | Ali Haji-Sheikh | NY G | NFC | 83 | 35 | 42 | 83.3 |
| | Ray Wersching-2 | S.F. | NFC | 83 | 25 | 30 | 83.3 |
| | Norm Johnson-3 | Sea. | AFC | 84 | 20 | 24 | 83.3 |
| | Paul McFadden-1 | Phi. | NFC | 85 | 25 | 30 | 83.3 |
| | Nick Lowery-6 | K.C. | AFC | 91 | 25 | 30 | 83.3 |
| | David Treadwell-2 | Den. | AFC | 92 | 20 | 24 | 83.3 |
| | Lin Elliott | K.C. | AFC | 94 | 25 | 30 | 83.3 |
| | John Kasay-1 | Sea. | AFC | 94 | 20 | 24 | 83.3 |
| 62 | Norm Johnson-4 | Pitt. | AFC | 95 | 34 | 41 | 82.9 |
| 63 | Matt Bahr-2 | Clev. | AFC | 88 | 24 | 29 | 82.8 |
| | Gary Anderson-3 | Pitt. | AFC | 94 | 24 | 29 | 82.8 |
| 65 | Garo Yepremian | Mia. | AFC | 78 | 19 | 23 | 82.6 |
| | Efren Herrera | Sea. | AFC | 79 | 19 | 23 | 82.6 |
| | Nick Lowery-7 | K.C. | AFC | 87 | 19 | 23 | 82.6 |
| | Norm Johnson-5 | Atl. | NFC | 91 | 19 | 23 | 82.6 |
| 69 | Jason Hanson | Det. | NFC | 95 | 28 | 34 | 82.4 |
| 70 | Pat Leahy-2 | NYJ | AFC | 88 | 23 | 28 | 82.1 |
| | John Kasay-2 | Sea. | AFC | 93 | 23 | 28 | 82.1 |
| | Todd Peterson | Sea. | AFC | 95 | 23 | 28 | 82.1 |
| 73 | Rolf Benirschke | S.D. | AFC | 78 | 18 | 22 | 81.8 |
| | Pat Leahy-3 | NYJ | AFC | 87 | 18 | 22 | 81.8 |
| | David Treadwell-3 | Den. | AFC | 89 | 27 | 33 | 81.8 |
| | Norm Johnson-6 | Atl. | NFC | 92 | 18 | 22 | 81.8 |
| 77 | Jason Elam | Den. | AFC | 95 | 31 | 38 | 81.6 |
| 78 | Don Cockroft | Cle. | AFC | 72 | 22 | 27 | 81.5 |
| | Rafael Septien | Dal. | NFC | 83 | 22 | 27 | 81.5 |
| | Fuad Reveiz-2 | Mia. | AFC | 85 | 22 | 27 | 81.5 |
| | Tony Zendejas- 2 | Hou. | AFC | 86 | 22 | 27 | 81.5 |
| | Gary Anderson- 4 | Pit. | AFC | 87 | 22 | 27 | 81.5 |

## POINTS AFTER TOUCHDOWN

| | | | | | |
|---|---|---|---|---|---|
| 1 | Uwe von Schamann | Mia. | AFC | 84 | 66 |
| 2 | George Blanda- 1 | Hou. | AFL | 61 | 64 |
| 3 | Joe Vetrano- 1 | S.F. | AAFC | 48 | 62 |
| | Mark Moseley- | Was. | NFC | 83 | 62 |
| 5 | Doug Brien | S.F. | NFC | 94 | 60 |
| 6 | Rafael Septien- 1 | Dal. | NFC | 80 | 59 |
| | Mike Cofer | S.F. | NFC | 93 | 59 |
| 8 | Rafael Septien- 2 | Dal. | NFC | 81 | 57 |
| 9 | Joe Vetrano- 2 | S.F. | AAFC | 49 | 56 |
| | Danny Villanueva | Dal. | NFL | 66 | 56 |
| | George Blanda- 2 | Oak. | AFL | 67 | 56 |
| | Ray Wersching- 1 | S.F. | NFC | 84 | 56 |
| | Jim Breech-1 | Cin. | AFC | 88 | 56 |
| | Chip Lohmiller | Wash. | NFC | 91 | 56 |
| | Scott Norwood | Buff. | AFC | 91 | 56 |
| 16 | Rolf Benirschke | S.D. | AFC | 81 | 55 |
| 17 | Bob Waterfield | L.A. | NFL | 50 | 54 |
| | George Blanda- 3 | Oak. | AFL | 68 | 54 |
| | Mike Clark- 1 | Dal. | NFL | 68 | 54 |
| 20 | Pat Harder | ChiC | NFL | 48 | 53 |
| | Lou Michaels- | Bal. | NFL | 64 | 53 |
| | Mike Cofer | S.F. | NFC | 92 | 53 |
| 23 | Don Chandler- 1 | NY G | NFL | 63 | 52 |
| | Tommy Davis | S.F. | NFL | 65 | 52 |
| | Roger LeClerc | Chi. | NFL | 65 | 52 |
| | Jan Stenerud | G.B. | NFC | 83 | 52 |
| | Ray Wersching- 2 | S.F. | NFC | 85 | 52 |
| | Fuad Reveiz- 1 | Mia. | AFC | 86 | 52 |
| 29 | Lou Groza- 1 | Cle. | AAFC | 48 | 51 |
| | Lou Groza- 2 | Cle. | NFL | 66 | 51 |
| | John Leypoldt | Buf. | AFC | 75 | 51 |
| | Toni Linhart- 1 | Bal. | AFC | 75 | 51 |
| | Frank Corral | L.A. | NFC | 80 | 51 |
| | John Smith | NE | AFC | 80 | 51 |
| | Mick Luckhurst | Atl. | NFC | 81 | 51 |
| | Chris Bahr | Raid. | AFC | 83 | 51 |
| | Bob Thomas | S.D. | AFC | 85 | 51 |
| | Kevin Butler | Chi. | NFC | 85 | 51 |
| | Ray Wersching- 3 | S.F. | NFC | 83 | 51 |
| | Mike Lansford | L.A. | NFC | 89 | 51 |
| 41 | Cliff Patton | Phi. | NFL | 48 | 50 |
| | Steve Myrha- | Bal. | NFL | 59 | 50 |
| | Sam Baker | Dal. | NFL | 62 | 50 |
| | Matt Bahr | Pit. | AFC | 79 | 50 |
| | Norm Johnson- 1 | Sea. | AFC | 84 | 50 |
| | Fuad Reveiz- 2 | Mia. | AFC | 85 | 50 |
| | Jim Breech- 2 | Cin. | AFC | 86 | 50 |
| | Scott Norwood | Buf. | AFC | 90 | 50 |
| 48 | Harvey Johnson | N.Y. | AAFC | 47 | 49 |
| | Lou Groza- 3 | Cle. | NFL | 64 | 49 |
| | Toni Linhart- 2 | Bal. | AFC | 76 | 49 |
| | Jim Breech- 3 | Cin. | AFC | 81 | 49 |
| | Norm Johnson- 2 | Sea. | AFC | 83 | 49 |
| | Mike Cofer-2 | S.F. | NFC | 89 | 49 |
| | Mike Cofer-3 | S.F. | NFC | 91 | 49 |

### MOST PAT'S—NO MISSES

| | | | | | |
|---|---|---|---|---|---|
| 1 | Joe Vetrano | S.F. | AAFC | 49 | 56 |
| | Danny Villanueva | Dal. | NFL | 66 | 56 |
| | Ray Wersching- 1 | S.F. | NFC | 84 | 56 |
| 4 | George Blanda-1 | Oak. | AFL | 68 | 54 |
| | Mike Clark- 1 | Dal. | NFL | 68 | 54 |
| 6 | Pat Harder | ChiC | NFL | 48 | 53 |
| 7 | Roger LeClerc | Chi. | NFL | 65 | 52 |
| | Jan Stenerud- 1 | G.B. | NFC | 83 | 52 |
| 9 | Mick Luckhurst | Atl. | NFC | 81 | 51 |
| | John Smith | NE | AFC | 80 | 51 |
| | Ray Wersching- 2 | S.F. | NFC | 83 | 51 |
| | Kevin Butler-1 | Chi. | NFC | 85 | 51 |
| | Mike Lansford | L.A. | NFC | 89 | 51 |
| 14 | Cliff Paxton | Phi. | NFL | 48 | 50 |
| 15 | Jim Bakken- 1 | St.L. | NFL | 65 | 48 |
| | Bruce Gossett | L.A. | NFL | 67 | 48 |
| | Tony Franklin | Phi. | NFC | 80 | 48 |
| | Chris Boniol | Dall. | NFC | 94 | 48 |
| | Jason Hanson | Det. | NFC | 95 | 48 |
| 20 | Mike Mercer | Oak. | AFL | 63 | 47 |
| | Mike Clark-2 | Dal. | NFC | 71 | 47 |
| 22 | Pat Summerall | NYG | NFL | 61 | 46 |
| | Tom Brocker | K.C. | AFL | 64 | 46 |
| | Eddie Murray | Det. | NFC | 81 | 46 |
| 25 | Lou Groza-1 | Cle. | NFL | 65 | 45 |
| | Sam Baker | Phi. | NFL | 67 | 45 |
| | Jan Stenerud-2 | K.C. | AFL | 67 | 45 |
| | Dick Van Raaphorst | S.D. | AFL | 67 | 45 |
| | George Blanda-2 | Oak. | AFL | 69 | 45 |
| | Don Cockroft | Cle. | NFL | 69 | 45 |
| | Gary Anderson-1 | Pit. | AFC | 84 | 45 |
| | Fuad Reveiz-1 | Minn. | NFC | 92 | 45 |
| | Kevin Butler-2 | Chi. | NFC | 95 | 45 |
| 34 | Tommy Davis | S.F. | NFL | 61 | 44 |
| | Jim Bakken- 2 | St.L. | NFL | 63 | 44 |
| | Fred Cox- 1 | Min. | NFL | 65 | 44 |
| | George Blanda- 3 | Oak. | AFC | 72 | 44 |
| | Pat Leahy | NY J | AFC | 86 | 44 |
| | Fuad Reveiz-2 | Minn. | NFC | 95 | 44 |

# LIFETIME LEADERS
# PASSING

### ATTEMPTS (1975)

| | | | |
|---|---|---|---|
| 1 | **Dan Marino** | **1983-** | **6531** |
| 2 | Fran Tarkenton | 1961-78 | 6467 |
| 3 | **John Elway** | **1983-** | **5926** |
| 4 | **Warren Moon** | **1984-** | **5753** |
| 5 | Dan Fouts | 1973-87 | 5604 |
| 6 | Joe Montana | 1979-94 | 5391 |
| 7 | Johnny Unitas | 1956-73 | 5186 |
| 8 | Jim Hart | 1966-84 | 5076 |
| 9 | Steve DeBerg | 1977-93 | 4965 |
| 10 | **Dave Krieg** | **1980-** | **4911** |
| 11 | John Hadl | 1962-77 | 4687 |
| 12 | **Boomer Esiason** | **1984-** | **4680** |
| 13 | Phil Simms | 1979-81,83-93 | 4647 |
| 14 | Joe Ferguson | 1973-90 | 4519 |
| 15 | Roman Gabriel | 1962-77 | 4498 |
| 16 | John Brodie | 1957-73 | 4491 |
| 17 | Ken Anderson | 1971-86 | 4475 |
| 18 | **Jim Kelly** | **1986-** | **4400** |
| 19 | Y. A. Tittle | 1948-64 | 4395 |
| 20 | **Jim Everett** | **1986-** | **4384** |
| 21 | Norm Snead | 1961-76 | 4353 |
| 22 | Sonny Jurgensen | 1957-74 | 4262 |
| 23 | Ron Jaworski | 1974-89 | 4117 |
| 24 | George Blanda | 1949-58,60-75 | 4007 |
| 25 | Terry Bradshaw | 1970-83 | 3901 |
| 26 | Ken Stabler | 1970-84 | 3793 |
| 27 | Craig Morton | 1965-82 | 3786 |
| 28 | Joe Namath | 1965-77 | 3762 |
| 29 | Len Dawson | 1957-75 | 3741 |
| 30 | Jim Plunkett | 1971-86 | 3701 |
| 31 | Bobby Layne | 1948-62 | 3700 |
| 32 | Tommy Kramer | 1977-90 | 3651 |
| 33 | Archie Manning | 1971-84 | 3642 |
| 34 | Joe Theismann | 1971-85 | 3602 |
| | Ken O'Brien | 1983-93 | 3602 |
| 36 | Steve Grogan | 1975-90 | 3593 |
| 37 | Steve Bartkowski | 1975-86 | 3456 |
| 38 | Brian Sipe | 1974-83 | 3439 |
| 39 | Bob Griese | 1967-80 | 3429 |
| 40 | Charley Johnson | 1961-75 | 3392 |
| 41 | **R. Cunningham** | **1985-** | **3362** |
| 42 | **Bernie Kosar** | **1985-** | **3333** |
| 43 | Babe Parilli | 1952-53,56-58,60-69 | 3330 |
| 44 | **Vinny Testaverde** | **1987-** | **3158** |
| 45 | Neil Lomax | 1981-88 | 3153 |
| 46 | Bart Starr | 1956-71 | 3149 |
| | Jim Zorn | 1976-85,87 | 3149 |
| 48 | Lynn Dickey | 1971-77,79-85 | 3125 |
| 49 | Jack Kemp | 1957,60-67,69 | 3073 |
| 50 | Dan Pastorini | 1971-83 | 3055 |
| 51 | Sammy Baugh | 1937-52 | 2995 |
| 52 | Billy Kilmer | 1961-62,64,66-78 | 2984 |
| 53 | Richard Todd | 1976-86 | 2967 |
| 54 | Roger Staubach | 1969-79 | 2958 |
| 55 | Danny White | 1976-88 | 2950 |
| 56 | Tobin Rote | 1950-59,63-64,66 | 2907 |
| 57 | Norm Van Brocklin | 1949-60 | 2895 |
| 58 | **Steve Young** | **1985-** | **2876** |
| 59 | Charlie Conerly | 1948-61 | 2833 |
| 60 | **Chris Miller** | **1987-** | **2811** |
| 61 | Jay Schroeder | 1984-94 | 2807 |
| 62 | **Troy Aikman** | **1989-** | **2713** |
| 63 | Earl Morrall | 1956-76 | 2689 |
| 64 | **Bobby Hebert** | **1985-89,91-** | **2633** |
| 65 | Otto Graham | 1946-55 | 2626 |
| 66 | **Jeff George** | **1990-** | **2613** |
| 67 | Daryle Lamonica | 1963-74 | 2601 |
| 68 | **Jim McMahon** | **1982-** | **2569** |
| 69 | **Mark Rypien** | **1987-** | **2552** |
| 70 | Bert Jones | 1973-82 | 2551 |
| 71 | Billy Wade | 1954-66 | 2523 |
| 72 | Doug Williams | 1978-82,86-89 | 2507 |
| 73 | Bill Kenney | 1979-88 | 2430 |
| 74 | Milt Plum | 1957-69 | 2419 |
| 75 | Don Meredith | 1960-68 | 2308 |
| 76 | **Wade Wilson** | **1981-** | **2301** |
| 77 | Greg Landry | 1968-81,84 | 2300 |
| 78 | **Jim Harbaugh** | **1987-** | **2275** |
| 79 | **Brett Favre** | **1991-** | **2150** |
| 80 | Frank Ryan | 1958-70 | 2133 |
| 81 | Marc Wilson | 1980-87,89-90 | 2081 |
| 82 | **Bubby Brister** | **1986-** | **2032** |
| 83 | Ed Brown | 1954-65 | 1987 |
| 84 | Bill Munson | 1964-79 | 1982 |

### COMPLETIONS (1090)

| | | | |
|---|---|---|---|
| 1 | **Dan Marino** | **1983-** | **3913** |
| 2 | Fran Tarkenton | 1961-78 | 3686 |
| 3 | Joe Montana | 1979-94 | 3409 |
| 4 | **Warren Moon** | **1984-** | **3380** |
| 5 | **John Elway** | **1983-** | **3346** |
| 6 | Dan Fouts | 1973-87 | 3297 |
| 7 | **Dave Krieg** | **1980-** | **2866** |
| 8 | Steve DeBerg | 1978-93 | 2844 |
| 9 | Johnny Unitas | 1956-73 | 2830 |
| 10 | **Boomer Esiason** | **1984-** | **2661** |
| 11 | Ken Anderson | 1971-84 | 2654 |
| 12 | **Jim Kelly** | **1986-** | **2652** |
| 13 | Jim Hart | 1966-84 | 2593 |
| 14 | Phil Simms | 1979-81,83-93 | 2576 |
| 15 | **Jim Everett** | **1986-** | **2538** |
| 16 | John Brodie | 1957-73 | 2469 |
| 17 | Sonny Jurgensen | 1957-74 | 2433 |
| 18 | Y. A. Tittle | 1948-64 | 2427 |
| 19 | Joe Ferguson | 1973-90 | 2369 |
| 20 | Roman Gabriel | 1962-77 | 2366 |
| 21 | John Hadl | 1962-77 | 2363 |
| 22 | Norm Snead | 1961-76 | 2276 |
| 23 | Ken Stabler | 1970-84 | 2270 |
| 24 | Ron Jaworski | 1974-89 | 2187 |
| 25 | Len Dawson | 1957-75 | 2136 |
| 26 | Ken O'Brien | 1983-93 | 2110 |
| 27 | Craig Morton | 1965-82 | 2053 |
| 28 | Joe Theismann | 1974-85 | 2044 |
| 29 | Terry Bradshaw | 1970-83 | 2025 |
| 30 | Tommy Kramer | 1977-90 | 2012 |
| 31 | Archie Manning | 1971-75,77-84 | 2011 |
| 32 | **Bernie Kosar** | **1985** | **1970** |
| 33 | Brian Sipe | 1974-83 | 1944 |
| 34 | Jim Plunkett | 1971-86 | 1943 |
| 35 | Steve Bartkowski | 1975-86 | 1932 |
| 36 | Bob Griese | 1967-80 | 1926 |
| 37 | George Blanda | 1949-58,60-75 | 1911 |
| 38 | Joe Namath | 1965-77 | 1886 |
| 39 | Steve Grogan | 1975-90 | 1879 |
| 40 | **R. Cunningham** | **1985-** | **1874** |
| 41 | **Steve Young** | **1985-** | **1845** |
| 42 | Neil Lomax | 1981-88 | 1817 |
| 43 | Bobby Layne | 1948-62 | 1814 |
| 44 | Bart Starr | 1956-71 | 1808 |
| 45 | Danny White | 1976-88 | 1761 |
| 46 | Lynn Dickey | 1971-77,79-85 | 1747 |
| 47 | Charley Johnson | 1961-75 | 1737 |
| 48 | **Troy Aikman** | **1989-** | **1704** |
| | **Vinny Testaverde** | **1987-** | **1704** |
| 50 | Sammy Baugh | 1937-52 | 1693 |
| 51 | Roger Staubach | 1969-79 | 1685 |
| 52 | Jim Zorn | 1976-85,87 | 1669 |
| 53 | Richard Todd | 1976-86 | 1610 |
| 54 | Billy Kilmer | 1961-62,64,66-78 | 1585 |
| 55 | Dan Pastorini | 1971-83 | 1556 |
| 56 | Norm Van Brocklin | 1949-60 | 1553 |
| 57 | Babe Parilli | 1952-53,56-58,60-69 | 1552 |
| 58 | **Bobby Hebert** | **1985-89,91** | **1545** |
| 59 | **Chris Miller** | **1987-** | **1534** |
| 60 | **Jeff George** | **1990-** | **1532** |
| 61 | **Jim McMahon** | **1982-** | **1489** |
| 62 | Otto Graham | 1946-55 | 1464 |
| 63 | Jack Kemp | 1957,60-67,69 | 1436 |
| 64 | **Mark Rypien** | **1987-** | **1432** |
| 65 | Bert Jones | 1973-82 | 1430 |
| 66 | Jay Schroeder | 1984-94 | 1426 |
| 67 | Charlie Conerly | 1948-61 | 1418 |
| 68 | Earl Morrall | 1956-76 | 1379 |
| 69 | Billy Wade | 1954-66 | 1370 |
| 70 | **Jim Harbaugh** | **1987-** | **1348** |
| 71 | Bill Kenney | 1979-88 | 1330 |
| 72 | Tobin Rote | 1950-52,63-64,66 | 1329 |
| 73 | **Wade Wilson** | **1981-** | **1319** |
| 74 | **Jeff Hostetler** | **1984-** | **1306** |
| | Milt Plum | 1957-69 | 1306 |
| 76 | Daryle Lamonica | 1963-74 | 1288 |
| 77 | Greg Landry | 1968-81,84 | 1276 |
| 78 | Doug Williams | 1978-82,86-89 | 1240 |
| 79 | Don Meredith | 1960-68 | 1170 |
| 80 | Gary Danielson | 1976-85,87-88 | 1105 |
| 81 | Frank Ryan | 1958-70 | 1090 |
| 82 | **Stan Humphries** | **1989-** | **1078** |
| 83 | **Neil O'Donnell** | **1090-** | **1069** |
| 84 | **Bubby Brister** | **1986-** | **1001** |

### COMPLETION PERCENTAGE
(All with over 1975 attempts)

| | | Att. | Comp. | Pct. |
|---|---|---|---|---|
| 1 | **Steve Young** | **2876** | **1845** | **64.15** |
| 2 | Joe Montana | 5391 | 3409 | 63.24 |
| 3 | **Troy Aikman** | **2713** | **1704** | **62.81** |
| 4 | **Brett Favre** | **2150** | **1342** | **62.42** |
| 5 | **Jim Kelly** | **4400** | **2652** | **60.27** |
| 6 | **Dan Marino** | **6531** | **3913** | **59.91** |
| 7 | Ken Stabler | 3793 | 2270 | 59.85 |
| 8 | Danny White | 2950 | 1761 | 59.70 |
| 9 | Ken Anderson | 4475 | 2654 | 59.31 |
| 10 | **Jim Harbaugh** | **2275** | **1348** | **59.25** |
| 11 | **Bernie Kosar** | **3333** | **1970** | **59.11** |
| 12 | Dan Fouts | 5604 | 3297 | 58.83 |
| 13 | **Warren Moon** | **5753** | **3380** | **58.75** |
| 14 | **Bobby Hebert** | **2633** | **1545** | **58.68** |
| 15 | **Jeff George** | **2613** | **1532** | **58.63** |
| 16 | Ken O'Brien | 3602 | 2110 | 58.58 |
| 17 | **Dave Krieg** | **4911** | **2866** | **58.36** |
| 18 | **Jim McMahon** | **2569** | **1489** | **57.96** |
| 19 | **Jim Everett** | **4384** | **2538** | **57.89** |
| 20 | Neil Lomax | 3153 | 1817 | 57.63 |
| 21 | Bart Starr | 3149 | 1808 | 57.42 |
| 22 | **Wade Wilson** | **2301** | **1319** | **57.32** |
| 23 | Steve DeBerg | 4965 | 2844 | 57.28 |
| 24 | Len Dawson | 3741 | 2136 | 57.10 |
| 25 | Sonny Jurgensen | 4262 | 2433 | 57.09 |
| 26 | Fran Tarkenton | 6467 | 3686 | 57.00 |
| 27 | Roger Staubach | 2958 | 1685 | 56.96 |
| 28 | **Boomer Esiason** | **4680** | **2661** | **56.86** |
| 29 | Joe Theismann | 3602 | 2044 | 56.75 |
| 30 | Brian Sipe | 3439 | 1944 | 56.53 |
| | Sammy Baugh | 2995 | 1693 | 56.53 |
| 32 | **John Elway** | **5926** | **3346** | **56.46** |
| 33 | Bob Griese | 3429 | 1926 | 56.17 |
| 34 | **Mark Rypien** | **2552** | **1432** | **56.11** |
| 35 | Bert Jones | 2551 | 1430 | 56.06 |
| 36 | Lynn Dickey | 3125 | 1747 | 55.90 |
| | Steve Bartkowski | 3456 | 1932 | 55.90 |
| 38 | Otto Graham | 2626 | 1464 | 55.75 |
| 39 | **Randall Cunningham** | **3362** | **1874** | **55.74** |
| 40 | Greg Landry | 2300 | 1276 | 55.48 |
| 41 | Phil Simms | 4647 | 2576 | 55.43 |
| 42 | Y. A. Tittle | 4395 | 2427 | 55.22 |
| | Archie Manning | 3642 | 2011 | 55.22 |
| 44 | Tommy Kramer | 3651 | 2012 | 55.10 |
| 45 | John Brodie | 4491 | 2469 | 54.98 |
| 46 | Bill Kenney | 2430 | 1330 | 54.73 |
| 47 | **Chris Miller** | **2811** | **1534** | **54.57** |
| 48 | Johnny Unitas | 5186 | 2830 | 54.47 |
| 49 | Billy Wade | 2523 | 1370 | 54.30 |
| 50 | Richard Todd | 2967 | 1610 | 54.26 |
| 51 | Craig Morton | 3786 | 2053 | 54.23 |
| 52 | Bubby Brister | 2032 | 1101 | 54.18 |
| 53 | Milt Plum | 2419 | 1306 | 53.99 |
| | Bill Munson | 1982 | 1070 | 53.99 |
| 55 | **Vinny Testaverde** | **3158** | **1704** | **53.96** |
| 56 | Norm Van Brocklin | 2895 | 1553 | 53.64 |
| 57 | Billy Kilmer | 2984 | 1585 | 53.12 |
| | Ron Jaworski | 4117 | 2187 | 53.12 |
| 59 | Jim Zorn | 3149 | 1669 | 53.00 |
| 60 | Roman Gabriel | 4498 | 2366 | 52.60 |
| 61 | Jim Plunkett | 3701 | 1943 | 52.50 |
| 62 | Joe Ferguson | 4511 | 2367 | 52.47 |
| 63 | Steve Grogan | 3593 | 1879 | 52.29 |
| 64 | Norm Snead | 4353 | 2373 | 52.21 |
| 65 | Marc Wilson | 2081 | 1085 | 52.13 |
| 66 | Terry Bradshaw | 3901 | 2025 | 51.91 |
| 67 | Earl Morrall | 2689 | 1379 | 51.28 |
| 68 | Charley Johnson | 3392 | 1737 | 51.21 |
| 69 | Frank Ryan | 2133 | 1090 | 51.10 |
| 70 | Jim Hart | 5076 | 2593 | 51.08 |
| 71 | Dan Pastorini | 3055 | 1556 | 50.93 |
| 72 | Jay Schroeder | 2807 | 1426 | 50.80 |
| 73 | Don Meredith | 2308 | 1170 | 50.69 |
| 74 | John Hadl | 4687 | 2363 | 50.42 |
| 75 | Joe Namath | 3762 | 1886 | 50.13 |
| 76 | Charlie Conerly | 2833 | 1418 | 50.05 |
| 77 | Daryle Lamonica | 2601 | 1288 | 49.52 |
| 78 | Doug Williams | 2507 | 1240 | 49.46 |
| 79 | Bobby Layne | 3700 | 1814 | 49.03 |
| 80 | Ed Brown | 1987 | 949 | 47.77 |
| 81 | George Blanda | 4007 | 1911 | 47.69 |
| 82 | Jack Kemp | 3073 | 1436 | 46.73 |
| 83 | Babe Parilli | 3330 | 1552 | 46.61 |
| 84 | Tobin Rote | 2907 | 1329 | 45.72 |

### YARDS (13,500)

| | | | |
|---|---|---|---|
| 1 | **Dan Marino** | **1983-** | **48841** |
| 2 | Fran Tarkenton | 1961-78 | 47003 |
| 3 | Dan Fouts | 1973-87 | 43040 |
| 4 | **Warren Moon** | **1984-** | **42177** |
| 5 | **John Elway** | **1983-** | **41706** |
| 6 | Joe Montana | 1979-94 | 40551 |
| 7 | Johnny Unitas | 1956-73 | 40239 |
| 8 | **Dave Krieg** | **1980-** | **35668** |
| 9 | Jim Hart | 1966-84 | 34665 |
| 10 | **Boomer Esiason** | **1984-** | **34149** |
| 11 | Steve DeBerg | 1978-93 | 33872 |
| 12 | John Hadl | 1962-77 | 33503 |
| 13 | Phil Simms | 1979-93 | 33462 |
| 14 | Y. A. Tittle | 1948-64 | 33070 |
| 15 | Ken Anderson | 1971-84 | 32838 |
| 16 | **Jim Kelly** | **1986-** | **32657** |
| 17 | Sonny Jurgensen | 1957-74 | 32224 |
| 18 | **Jim Everett** | **1986-** | **31583** |
| 19 | John Brodie | 1957-73 | 31548 |
| 20 | Norm Snead | 1961-76 | 30797 |
| 21 | Joe Ferguson | 1973-89 | 29817 |
| 22 | Roman Gabriel | 1962-77 | 29444 |
| 23 | Len Dawson | 1957-75 | 28711 |
| 24 | Ron Jaworski | 1974-89 | 28190 |
| 25 | Terry Bradshaw | 1970-83 | 27989 |
| 26 | Ken Stabler | 1970-84 | 27938 |
| 27 | Craig Morton | 1965-82 | 27908 |
| 28 | Joe Namath | 1965-77 | 27663 |
| 29 | George Blanda | 1949-58,60-75 | 26920 |
| 30 | Steve Grogan | 1975-90 | 26886 |
| 31 | Bobby Layne | 1948-62 | 25967 |
| 32 | Jim Plunkett | 1971-86 | 25882 |
| 33 | Joe Theismann | 1974-85 | 25206 |
| 34 | Ken O'Brien | 1983-93 | 25094 |
| 35 | Bob Griese | 1967-80 | 25092 |
| 36 | Tommy Kramer | 1977-90 | 24776 |
| 37 | Bart Starr | 1956-71 | 24718 |
| 38 | Charley Johnson | 1961-75 | 24410 |
| 39 | Steve Bartkowski | 1975-86 | 24124 |
| 40 | Archie Manning | 1971-75,77-84 | 23911 |
| 41 | Brian Sipe | 1974-83 | 23713 |
| 42 | Norm Van Brocklin | 1949-60 | 23611 |
| 43 | Otto Graham | 1946-55 | 23584 |
| 44 | Lynn Dickey | 1971-77,79-85 | 23322 |
| 45 | **Bernie Kosar** | **1985-** | **23093** |
| 46 | **Steve Young** | **12985-** | **23069** |
| 47 | **R. Cunningham** | **1985-** | **22874** |
| 48 | Neil Lomax | 1981-88 | 22771 |
| 49 | Roger Staubach | 1969-79 | 22700 |
| 50 | Babe Parilli | 1952-53,56-58,60-69 | 22681 |
| 51 | **Vinny Testaverde** | **1987-** | **22075** |
| 52 | Danny White | 1976-88 | 21959 |
| 53 | Sammy Baugh | 1937-52 | 21886 |
| 54 | Jack Kemp | 1957,60-67,69 | 21218 |
| 55 | Jim Zorn | 1976-85,87 | 21115 |
| 56 | Earl Morrall | 1956-76 | 20809 |
| 57 | Richard Todd | 1976-86 | 20610 |
| 58 | Billy Kilmer | 1961-62,64,66-78 | 20495 |
| 59 | Jay Schroeder | 1984-94 | 20063 |
| 60 | **Troy Aikman** | **1989-** | **19607** |
| 61 | Charlie Conerly | 1948-61 | 19488 |
| 62 | Daryle Lamonica | 1963-74 | 19154 |
| 63 | Tobin Rote | 1950-59,63-64,66 | 18850 |
| 64 | **Chris Miller** | **1987-** | **18793** |
| 65 | **Bobby Hebert** | **1985-89,91** | **18531** |
| 66 | Billy Wade | 1954-66 | 18530 |
| 67 | Dan Pastorini | 1971-83 | 18515 |
| 68 | Bert Jones | 1973-82 | 18190 |
| 69 | **Jim McMahon** | **1982-** | **18108** |
| 70 | **Mark Rypien** | **1987-** | **18070** |
| 71 | Milt Plum | 1957-69 | 17536 |
| 72 | **Jeff George** | **1990-** | **17429** |
| 73 | Bill Kenney | 1980-88 | 17277 |
| 74 | Don Meredith | 1960-68 | 17199 |
| 75 | Doug Williams | 1978-82,86-89 | 16998 |
| 76 | **Wade Wilson** | **1981-** | **16523** |
| 77 | Greg Landry | 1968-81,84 | 16052 |
| 78 | Frank Ryan | 1958-70 | 16042 |
| 79 | Ed Brown | 1954-65 | 15600 |
| 80 | **Jim Harbaugh** | **1987-** | **15582** |
| 81 | **Brett Favre** | **1991-** | **14825** |
| 82 | Sid Luckman | 1939-50 | 14683 |
| 83 | Marc Wilson | 1980-87,89-90 | 14391 |
| 84 | Bill Nelsen | 1963-72 | 14165 |
| 85 | Gary Danielson | 1976-85,87-88 | 13764 |
| 86 | **Bubby Brister** | **1986-** | **13242** |

Players active at the end of **1995** are shown in **bold face**.

# LIFETIME LEADERS
# PASSING

### YARDS PER ATTEMPT

(All with over 1975 Attempts)

| | | Yards | Att. | Y/A |
|---|---|---|---|---|
| 1 | Otto Graham | 23584 | 2626 | 8.98 |
| 2 | Norm Van Brocklin | 23611 | 2895 | 8.16 |
| 3 | **Steve Young** | **23069** | **2876** | **8.02** |
| 4 | Ed Brown | 15600 | 1987 | 7.85 |
| | Bart Starr | 24718 | 3149 | 7.85 |
| 6 | Johnny Unitas | 40239 | 5186 | 7.76 |
| 7 | Earl Morrall | 20809 | 2689 | 7.74 |
| 8 | Len Dawson | 28711 | 3741 | 7.68 |
| | Dan Fouts | 43040 | 5604 | 7.68 |
| 10 | Roger Staubach | 22700 | 2958 | 7.67 |
| 11 | Sonny Jurgensen | 32224 | 4262 | 7.56 |
| 12 | Joe Montana | 40551 | 5391 | 7.52 |
| | Y.A. Tittle | 33070 | 4395 | 7.52 |
| | Frank Ryan | 16042 | 2133 | 7.52 |
| 15 | Steve Grogan | 26886 | 3593 | 7.48 |
| | **Dan Marino** | **48841** | **6531** | **7.48** |
| 17 | Lynn Dickey | 23322 | 3125 | 7.47 |
| 18 | Don Meredith | 17199 | 2308 | 7.45 |
| 19 | Danny White | 21959 | 2950 | 7.44 |
| 20 | **Jim Kelly** | **32657** | **4400** | **7.42** |
| 21 | Craig Morton | 27908 | 3786 | 7.37 |
| | Ken Stabler | 27938 | 3793 | 7.37 |
| 23 | Daryle Lamonica | 19154 | 2601 | 7.36 |
| 24 | Joe Namath | 27663 | 3762 | 7.35 |
| 25 | Ken Anderson | 32838 | 4475 | 7.34 |
| | Billy Wade | 18530 | 2523 | 7.34 |
| 27 | **Warren Moon** | **42177** | **5753** | **7.33** |
| 28 | Bob Griese | 25092 | 3426 | 7.32 |

| | | Yards | Att. | Y/A |
|---|---|---|---|---|
| 29 | Sammy Baugh | 21886 | 2995 | 7.31 |
| 30 | **Boomer Esiason** | **34149** | **4680** | **7.30** |
| 31 | Fran Tarkenton | 47003 | 6467 | 7.27 |
| 32 | **Dave Krieg** | **35668** | **4911** | **7.26** |
| 33 | Milt Plum | 17536 | 2419 | 7.25 |
| 34 | Bobby Layne | 25967 | 3700 | 7.24 |
| | **Troy Aikman** | **19607** | **2713** | **7.23** |
| 36 | Neil Lomax | 22771 | 3153 | 7.22 |
| 37 | Charley Johnson | 24410 | 3392 | 7.20 |
| | Phil Simms | 33462 | 4647 | 7.20 |
| | **Jim Everett** | **31583** | **4384** | **7.20** |
| 40 | **Wade Wilson** | **16523** | **2301** | **7.18** |
| 41 | Terry Bradshaw | 27989 | 3901 | 7.17 |
| 42 | John Hadl | 33503 | 4687 | 7.15 |
| | Jay Schroeder | 20063 | 2807 | 7.15 |
| 44 | Bert Jones | 18190 | 2551 | 7.13 |
| 45 | Bill Kenney | 17277 | 2430 | 7.11 |
| 46 | **Mark Rypien** | **18070** | **2552** | **7.08** |
| 47 | Norm Snead | 30797 | 4353 | 7.07 |
| 48 | **Jim McMahon** | **18108** | **2569** | **7.05** |
| 49 | **Bobby Hebert** | **18531** | **2633** | **7.04** |
| | **John Elway** | **41706** | **5926** | **7.04** |
| 51 | John Brodie | 31548 | 4491 | 7.03 |
| 52 | Joe Theismann | 25206 | 3602 | 7.00 |
| 53 | Jim Plunkett | 25882 | 3701 | 6.99 |
| | **Vinny Testaverde** | **22075** | **3158** | **6.99** |
| 55 | Steve Bartkowski | 24124 | 3456 | 6.98 |
| 56 | Ken O'Brien | 25094 | 3602 | 6.97 |

| | | Yards | Att. | Y/A |
|---|---|---|---|---|
| 57 | Greg Landry | 15853 | 2280 | 6.95 |
| 58 | Richard Todd | 20610 | 2967 | 6.95 |
| 59 | **Bernie Kosar** | **23093** | **3333** | **6.93** |
| 60 | Marc Wilson | 14391 | 2081 | 6.91 |
| 61 | Brian Sipe | 23713 | 3439 | 6.90 |
| | Jack Kemp | 21218 | 3073 | 6.90 |
| | **Brett Favre** | **14825** | **2150** | **6.90** |
| 64 | Charlie Conerly | 19488 | 2833 | 6.88 |
| 65 | Billy Kilmer | 20495 | 2984 | 6.87 |
| 66 | **Jim Harbaugh** | **15582** | **2275** | **6.85** |
| | Ron Jaworski | 28190 | 4117 | 6.85 |
| 68 | Jim Hart | 34665 | 5076 | 6.83 |
| 69 | Steve DeBerg | 33872 | 4965 | 6.82 |
| 70 | Babe Parilli | 22681 | 3330 | 6.81 |
| 71 | **Randall Cunningham** | **22874** | **3362** | **6.80** |
| 72 | Tommy Kramer | 24776 | 3651 | 6.78 |
| | Doug Williams | 16998 | 2507 | 6.78 |
| 74 | George Blanda | 26920 | 4007 | 6.72 |
| 75 | Jim Zorn | 21115 | 3149 | 6.71 |
| 76 | **Jeff George** | **17429** | **2613** | **6.67** |
| 77 | **Chris Miller** | **18793** | **2811** | **6.69** |
| 78 | Joe Ferguson | 29816 | 4519 | 6.59 |
| 79 | Archie Manning | 23911 | 3642 | 6.57 |
| 80 | Roman Gabriel | 29444 | 4498 | 6.55 |
| 81 | **Bubby Brister** | **13242** | **2032** | **6.52** |
| 82 | Bill Munson | 12896 | 1982 | 6.51 |
| 83 | Tobin Rote | 18850 | 2907 | 6.45 |
| 84 | Dan Pastorini | 18515 | 3055 | 6.06 |

### TOUCHDOWNS (125)

| | | | |
|---|---|---|---|
| 1 | **Dan Marino** | **1983-** | **352** |
| 2 | Fran Tarkenton | 1961-78 | 342 |
| 3 | Johnny Unitas | 1956-73 | 290 |
| 4 | Joe Montana | 1979-94 | 273 |
| 5 | Sonny Jurgensen | 1957-74 | 255 |
| 6 | Dan Fouts | 1973-87 | 254 |
| 7 | **Warren Moon** | **1984-** | **247** |
| | **Dave Krieg** | **1980-** | **247** |
| 9 | John Hadl | 1962-77 | 244 |
| 10 | Y.A. Tittle | 1948-64 | 242 |
| 11 | Len Dawson | 1957-75 | 239 |
| 12 | George Blanda | 1948-58,60-75 | 236 |
| 13 | **John Elway** | **1983-** | **225** |
| 14 | **Jim Kelly** | **1986-** | **223** |
| | **Boomer Esiason** | **1984-** | **223** |
| 16 | John Brodie | 1957-73 | 214 |
| 17 | Terry Bradshaw | 1970-83 | 212 |
| 18 | Jim Hart | 1966-84 | 209 |
| 19 | Roman Gabriel | 1962-77 | 201 |
| 20 | Phil Simms | 1979-93 | 199 |
| 21 | Ken Anderson | 1971-84 | 197 |
| 22 | Bobby Layne | 1948-62 | 196 |
| | Joe Ferguson | 1973-90 | 196 |
| | Norm Snead | 1961-76 | 196 |
| 25 | Ken Stabler | 1970-84 | 194 |
| 26 | Steve DeBerg | 1977-93 | 193 |
| 27 | Bob Griese | 1967-80 | 192 |
| 28 | **Jim Everett** | **1986-** | **190** |
| 29 | Sammy Baugh | 1937-52 | 186 |
| 30 | Craig Morton | 1965-82 | 183 |
| 31 | Steve Grogan | 1975-90 | 182 |
| 32 | Babe Parilli | 1952-53,56-58,60-69 | 178 |
| 33 | Ron Jaworski | 1974-89 | 179 |
| 34 | Otto Graham | 1946-55 | 174 |
| 35 | Charlie Conerly | 1948-81 | 173 |
| | Norm Van Brocklin | 1949-60 | 173 |
| | Joe Namath | 1965-77 | 173 |
| 38 | Charley Johnson | 1961-75 | 170 |
| 39 | Daryle Lamonica | 1963-74 | 164 |
| | Jim Plunkett | 1971-86 | 164 |
| 41 | Earl Morrall | 1956-76 | 161 |
| 42 | Joe Theismann | 1974-85 | 160 |
| | **Steve Young** | **1985-** | **160** |
| 44 | Tommy Kramer | 1977-90 | 159 |
| 45 | Steve Bartkowski | 1975-86 | 156 |
| 46 | Danny White | 1976-88 | 155 |
| 47 | Brian Sipe | 1974-83 | 154 |
| 48 | Roger Staubach | 1969-79 | 153 |
| 49 | Bart Starr | 1956-71 | 152 |
| | Billy Kilmer | 1961-62,64,66-78 | 152 |
| 51 | **Randall Cunningham** | **1985-** | **150** |
| 52 | Frank Ryan | 1958-70 | 149 |
| 53 | Tobin Rote | 1950-59,63,64,66 | 148 |
| 54 | Lynn Dickey | 1971-85 | 141 |
| 55 | Sid Luckman | 1939-50 | 137 |
| 56 | Neil Lomax | 1981-88 | 136 |
| 57 | Don Meredith | 1960-68 | 135 |
| 58 | Ken O'Brien | 1983-93 | 128 |
| 59 | Archie Manning | 1971-75,77-84 | 125 |

### INTERCEPTIONS (158)

| | | | |
|---|---|---|---|
| 1 | George Blanda | 1949-58,60-75 | 277 |
| 2 | John Hadl | 1962-77 | 268 |
| 3 | Fran Tarkenton | 1961-78 | 266 |
| 4 | Norm Snead | 1961-76 | 257 |
| 5 | Johnny Unitas | 1956-73 | 253 |
| 6 | Y.A. Tittle | 1948-64 | 248 |
| 7 | Jim Hart | 1966-84 | 247 |
| 8 | Bobby Layne | 1948-62 | 245 |
| 9 | Dan Fouts | 1973-87 | 242 |
| 10 | John Brodie | 1957-73 | 224 |
| 11 | Ken Stabler | 1970-84 | 222 |
| 12 | Babe Parilli | 1952-53,56-58,60-69 | 220 |
| | Joe Namath | 1965-77 | 220 |
| 14 | Terry Bradshaw | 1970-83 | 210 |
| 15 | Joe Ferguson | 1973-90 | 209 |
| 16 | Steve Grogan | 1975-90 | 208 |
| 17 | Sammy Baugh | 1937-52 | 203 |
| 18 | Steve DeBerg | 1978-93 | 203 |
| 19 | **Dan Marino** | **1983-** | **200** |
| 20 | **Warren Moon** | **1984-** | **199** |
| 21 | Jim Plunkett | 1971-86 | 198 |
| 22 | **John Elway** | **1983-** | **191** |
| | Tobin Rote | 1950-59,63-64,66 | 191 |
| 24 | Sonny Jurgensen | 1957-74 | 189 |
| 25 | **Dave Krieg** | **1980-** | **187** |
| | Craig Morton | 1965-82 | 187 |
| 27 | Len Dawson | 1957-75 | 183 |
| | Jack Kemp | 1957,60-67,69 | 183 |
| 29 | Charley Johnson | 1949-60 | 181 |
| 30 | Lynn Dickey | 1971-85 | 179 |
| 31 | Norm Van Brocklin | 1949-60 | 178 |
| 32 | Archie Manning | 1972-75,77-84 | 173 |
| 33 | Bob Griese | 1967-80 | 172 |
| 34 | **Boomer Esiason** | **1984-** | **168** |
| 35 | Charlie Conerly | 1948-61 | 167 |
| 36 | Ron Jaworski | 1974-89 | 164 |
| 37 | Dan Pastorini | 1971-83 | 161 |
| | Richard Todd | 1976-86 | 161 |
| 39 | Ken Anderson | 1971-84 | 160 |
| 40 | Tommy Kramer | 1977-90 | 158 |

### PERCENT INTERCEPTED

(All with over 1975 attempts)

| | | Att. | Int. | Pct. |
|---|---|---|---|---|
| 1 | Joe Montana | 5391 | 139 | 2.58 |
| 2 | **Bernie Kosar** | **3333** | **87** | **2.61** |
| 3 | Ken O'Brien | 3602 | 98 | 2.72 |
| 4 | **Steve Young** | **2876** | **79** | **2.75** |
| 5 | Neil Lomax | 3153 | 90 | 2.85 |
| 6 | **Jeff George** | **2613** | **75** | **2.87** |
| 7 | **Jim Harbaugh** | **2275** | **67** | **2.95** |
| 8 | **Dan Marino** | **6531** | **200** | **3.06** |
| 9 | **Brett Favre** | **2150** | **66** | **3.07** |
| 10 | **Randall Cunningham** | **3362** | **105** | **3.12** |
| 11 | **John Elway** | **5926** | **191** | **3.22** |
| 12 | **Troy Aikman** | **2713** | **88** | **3.24** |
| 13 | Roman Gabriel | 4498 | 149 | 3.31 |
| 14 | **Mark Rypien** | **2552** | **86** | **3.37** |
| 15 | Phil Simms | 4647 | 157 | 3.38 |
| 16 | **Warren Moon** | **5753** | **199** | **3.46** |
| 17 | **Bubby Brister** | **2032** | **71** | **3.49** |
| 18 | **Jim McMahon** | **2569** | **90** | **3.50** |
| 19 | Bill Kenney | 2430 | 86 | 3.54 |
| | **Jim Everett** | **4384** | **155** | **3.54** |
| 21 | **Jim Kelly** | **4400** | **156** | **3.55** |
| 22 | Ken Anderson | 4475 | 160 | 3.58 |
| 23 | **Chris Miller** | **2811** | **101** | **3.59** |
| | **Boomer Esiason** | **4680** | **168** | **3.59** |
| 25 | Roger Staubach | 2958 | 109 | 3.68 |
| 26 | Doug Williams | 2507 | 93 | 3.71 |
| 27 | **Bobby Hebert** | **2633** | **99** | **3.76** |
| 28 | **Dave Krieg** | **4911** | **187** | **3.81** |

| | | Att. | Int. | Pct. |
|---|---|---|---|---|
| 29 | Joe Theismann | 3602 | 138 | 3.83 |
| 30 | Jay Schroeder | 2807 | 108 | 3.85 |
| 31 | Bert Jones | 2551 | 101 | 3.96 |
| 32 | Ron Jaworski | 4117 | 164 | 3.98 |
| 33 | Bill Munson | 1982 | 80 | 4.04 |
| 34 | Steve DeBerg | 4965 | 203 | 4.09 |
| 35 | Fran Tarkenton | 6467 | 266 | 4.11 |
| 36 | Steve Bartkowski | 3456 | 144 | 4.17 |
| 37 | **Wade Wilson** | **2301** | **97** | **4.22** |
| 38 | Tommy Kramer | 3651 | 158 | 4.32 |
| | Dan Fouts | 5604 | 242 | 4.32 |
| 40 | Brian Sipe | 3439 | 149 | 4.33 |
| 41 | Bart Starr | 3149 | 138 | 4.38 |
| 42 | Greg Landry | 2280 | 100 | 4.39 |
| 43 | Sonny Jurgensen | 4262 | 189 | 4.44 |
| 44 | Danny White | 2950 | 132 | 4.47 |
| 45 | Jim Zorn | 3149 | 141 | 4.48 |
| 46 | Joe Ferguson | 4519 | 209 | 4.62 |
| 47 | **Vinny Testaverde** | **3158** | **149** | **4.72** |
| 48 | Archie Manning | 3642 | 173 | 4.75 |
| 49 | Don Meredith | 2308 | 111 | 4.81 |
| 50 | Jim Hart | 5076 | 247 | 4.87 |
| 51 | Johnny Unitas | 5186 | 253 | 4.88 |
| 52 | Len Dawson | 3741 | 183 | 4.89 |
| | Billy Kilmer | 2984 | 146 | 4.89 |
| 54 | Marc Wilson | 2081 | 102 | 4.90 |
| 55 | Craig Morton | 3786 | 187 | 4.94 |

| | | Att. | Int. | Pct. |
|---|---|---|---|---|
| 56 | John Brodie | 4491 | 224 | 4.99 |
| 57 | Bob Griese | 3429 | 172 | 5.02 |
| 58 | Otto Graham | 2626 | 135 | 5.14 |
| 59 | Frank Ryan | 2133 | 111 | 5.20 |
| 60 | Milt Plum | 2410 | 127 | 5.27 |
| | Dan Pastorini | 3055 | 161 | 5.27 |
| 62 | Daryle Lamonica | 2601 | 138 | 5.31 |
| | Billy Wade | 2523 | 134 | 5.31 |
| 64 | Charley Johnson | 3392 | 181 | 5.34 |
| 65 | Jim Plunkett | 3701 | 198 | 5.35 |
| 66 | Terry Bradshaw | 3901 | 210 | 5.38 |
| 67 | Richard Todd | 2967 | 161 | 5.43 |
| 68 | Earl Morrall | 2689 | 148 | 5.50 |
| 69 | Y.A. Tittle | 4395 | 248 | 5.51 |
| 70 | John Hadl | 4687 | 268 | 5.72 |
| 71 | Lynn Dickey | 3125 | 179 | 5.73 |
| 72 | Steve Grogan | 3593 | 208 | 5.78 |
| 73 | Joe Namath | 3762 | 220 | 5.85 |
| | Ken Stabler | 3793 | 222 | 5.85 |
| 75 | Charlie Conerly | 2833 | 167 | 5.90 |
| 76 | Norm Snead | 4353 | 257 | 5.94 |
| 77 | Norm Van Brocklin | 2895 | 178 | 6.15 |
| 78 | Jack Kemp | 2973 | 183 | 6.16 |
| 79 | Bobby Layne | 3700 | 243 | 6.57 |
| | Tobin Rote | 2907 | 191 | 6.57 |
| 81 | Babe Parilli | 3330 | 220 | 6.61 |
| 82 | Sammy Baugh | 2995 | 203 | 6.78 |
| 83 | George Blanda | 4057 | 277 | 6.91 |
| 84 | Ed Brown | 1987 | 138 | 6.94 |

### RANK

(All with over 1975 attempts)

| | | Comp. Pct. | Yds./ Att. | Pct. Int. | Pct. TD Passes | | Total |
|---|---|---|---|---|---|---|---|
| 1 | Steve Young | 1 | 3 | 4 | 14 | — | 22 |
| 2 | Joe Montana | 2 | 12 | 1 | 29 | — | 44 |
| 3 | Dan Marino | 6 | 15 | 8 | 16 | — | 45 |
| 4 | Jim Kelly | 5 | 20 | 21 | 28 | — | 74 |
| 5 | Roger Staubach | 27 | 10 | 25 | 22 | — | 84 |
| 6 | Len Dawson | 24 | 8 | 52 | 3 | — | 87 |
| | Sonny Jurgensen | 25 | 11 | 43 | 8 | — | 87 |
| 8 | Bart Starr | 21 | 4 | 41 | 24 | — | 90 |
| 9 | Danny White | 8 | 19 | 44 | 20 | — | 91 |
| 10 | Otto Graham | 38 | 1 | 58 | 2 | — | 99 |
| 11 | Dan Fouts | 12 | 8 | 38 | 42 | — | 100 |
| 12 | Brett Favre | 5 | 61 | 9 | 33 | — | 108 |
| | Ken Anderson | 9 | 25 | 22 | 52 | — | 108 |
| 14 | Dave Krieg | 17 | 32 | 28 | 32 | — | 109 |
| 15 | Fran Tarkenton | 26 | 31 | 35 | 19 | — | 111 |
| 16 | Warren Moon | 13 | 27 | 16 | 61 | — | 117 |
| 17 | Neil Lomax | 20 | 36 | 5 | 58 | — | 119 |
| 18 | Boomer Esiason | 28 | 30 | 23 | 39 | — | 120 |
| | Johnny Unitas | 48 | 6 | 51 | 13 | — | 120 |
| 20 | Ken Stabler | 7 | 21 | 73 | 24 | — | 125 |
| 21 | Troy Aikman | 3 | 34 | 12 | 77 | — | 127 |
| 22 | Bob Griese | 33 | 28 | 57 | 12 | — | 130 |
| 23 | Jim Everett | 19 | 37 | 19 | 56 | — | 131 |
| 24 | Y.A. Tittle | 42 | 12 | 69 | 15 | — | 138 |
| 25 | Frank Ryan | 69 | 12 | 59 | 1 | — | 141 |
| 26 | Mark Rypien | 34 | 46 | 14 | 48 | — | 142 |
| 27 | Norm Van Brocklin | 56 | 2 | 77 | 8 | — | 143 |
| 28 | Bert Jones | 35 | 44 | 31 | 36 | — | 146 |

| | | Comp. Pct. | Yds./ Att. | Pct. Int. | Pct. TD Passes | | Total |
|---|---|---|---|---|---|---|---|
| | Sammy Baugh | 30 | 29 | 82 | 5 | — | 146 |
| 30 | Bernie Kosar | 11 | 59 | 2 | 76 | — | 148 |
| 31 | Earl Morrall | 67 | 7 | 68 | 7 | — | 149 |
| 32 | Bobby Hebert | 14 | 49 | 27 | 61 | — | 151 |
| | Don Meredith | 73 | 18 | 49 | 11 | — | 151 |
| 34 | Ken O'Brien | 16 | 56 | 3 | 78 | — | 153 |
| 35 | Jim McMahon | 41 | 37 | 15 | 63 | — | 156 |
| | Phil Simms | 41 | 37 | 15 | 63 | — | 156 |
| 37 | Joe Theismann | 29 | 52 | 29 | 50 | — | 160 |
| 38 | Randall Cunningham | 39 | 71 | 10 | 41 | — | 161 |
| 39 | Craig Morton | 51 | 21 | 55 | 37 | — | 164 |
| 40 | Daryle Lamonica | 77 | 23 | 62 | 4 | — | 166 |
| | John Elway | 32 | 49 | 11 | 74 | — | 166 |
| 42 | Bill Kenney | 46 | 45 | 19 | 57 | — | 167 |
| | Jim Harbaugh | 10 | 66 | 7 | 84 | — | 167 |
| 44 | Lynn Dickey | 36 | 17 | 71 | 44 | — | 168 |
| | Wade Wilson | 22 | 40 | 37 | 69 | — | 168 |
| 46 | Steve Bartkowski | 36 | 55 | 36 | 44 | — | 171 |
| | Bill Wade | 49 | 25 | 62 | 35 | — | 171 |
| 48 | Milt Plum | 53 | 33 | 60 | 31 | — | 177 |
| 49 | Brian Sipe | 30 | 61 | 40 | 47 | — | 178 |
| 50 | Steve Grogan | 63 | 15 | 72 | 29 | — | 179 |
| | Jeff George | 15 | 76 | 6 | 82 | — | 179 |
| 52 | John Brodie | 45 | 51 | 56 | 38 | — | 190 |
| 53 | Ed Brown | 80 | 4 | 84 | 23 | — | 191 |
| 54 | Steve DeBerg | 23 | 69 | 34 | 72 | — | 198 |
| | Greg Landry | 40 | 57 | 42 | 59 | — | 198 |
| 56 | Bill Kilmer | 57 | 65 | 52 | 26 | — | 200 |

| | | Comp. Pct. | Yds./ Att. | Pct. Int. | Pct. TD Passes | | Total |
|---|---|---|---|---|---|---|---|
| 57 | Roman Gabriel | 60 | 80 | 13 | 48 | — | 201 |
| 58 | Charlie Johnson | 68 | 37 | 64 | 34 | — | 203 |
| 59 | Chris Miller | 47 | 77 | 23 | 59 | — | 206 |
| 60 | Tommy Kramer | 44 | 72 | 38 | 53 | — | 207 |
| | John Hadl | 74 | 42 | 70 | 21 | — | 207 |
| 62 | Ron Jaworski | 57 | 66 | 32 | 53 | — | 208 |
| 63 | Bobby Layne | 79 | 34 | 79 | 18 | — | 210 |
| 64 | Jay Schroeder | 72 | 42 | 30 | 67 | — | 211 |
| 65 | Joe Namath | 75 | 24 | 73 | 40 | — | 212 |
| 66 | Terry Bradshaw | 66 | 41 | 66 | 42 | — | 215 |
| 67 | Charlie Conerly | 76 | 64 | 75 | 6 | — | 221 |
| 68 | Vinny Testaverde | 55 | 53 | 47 | 71 | — | 226 |
| 69 | Jim Plunkett | 61 | 53 | 65 | 51 | — | 230 |
| | Bubby Brister | 52 | 81 | 17 | 80 | — | 230 |
| 71 | Bill Munson | 53 | 82 | 33 | 63 | — | 231 |
| 72 | Norm Snead | 64 | 47 | 76 | 46 | — | 233 |
| 73 | Richard Todd | 50 | 58 | 67 | 65 | — | 240 |
| 74 | Joe Ferguson | 62 | 78 | 46 | 55 | — | 241 |
| 75 | Marc Wilson | 65 | 60 | 54 | 66 | — | 245 |
| 76 | Doug Williams | 78 | 72 | 26 | 70 | — | 246 |
| 77 | George Blanda | 81 | 74 | 83 | 10 | — | 248 |
| 78 | Archie Manning | 42 | 79 | 48 | 81 | — | 250 |
| 79 | Babe Parilli | 83 | 70 | 81 | 17 | — | 251 |
| 80 | Jim hart | 70 | 68 | 50 | 67 | — | 255 |
| 81 | Jim Zorn | 59 | 75 | 45 | 79 | — | 258 |
| 82 | Tobin Rote | 84 | 83 | 79 | 26 | — | 272 |
| 83 | Jack Kemp | 82 | 61 | 78 | 75 | — | 296 |
| 84 | Dan Pastorini | 71 | 84 | 60 | 82 | — | 297 |

Players Active at the end of **1995** are shown in **bold face.**

# LIFETIME LEADERS
# RUSHING

## ATTEMPTS (1157)

| | | | |
|---|---|---|---|
| 1 | Walter Payton | 1975-87 | 3838 |
| 2 | Eric Dickerson | 1983-93 | 2996 |
| 3 | Franco Harris | 1972-84 | 2949 |
| 4 | Tony Dorsett | 1977-88 | 2936 |
| 5 | John Riggins | 1971-79, 81-85 | 2740 |
| **6** | **Marcus Allen** | **1982-** | **2692** |
| 7 | Ottis Anderson | 1979-92 | 2562 |
| 8 | O.J. Simpson | 1969-79 | 2404 |
| 9 | Jimmy Brown | 1957-65 | 2359 |
| **10** | **Thurman Thomas** | **1988-** | **2285** |
| 11 | Earl Campbell | 1978-85 | 2187 |
| **12** | **Barry Sanders** | **1989-** | **2077** |
| **13** | **Emmitt Smith** | **1990-** | **2007** |
| 14 | Roger Craig | 1983-93 | 1991 |
| 15 | Gerald Riggs | 1982-91 | 1989 |
| 16 | Jim Taylor | 1958-67 | 1941 |
| **17** | **Herschel Walker** | **1986-** | **1938** |
| 18 | Joe Perry | 1948-63 | 1929 |
| 19 | Larry Csonka | 1968-74,76-79 | 1891 |
| **20** | **Ernest Byner** | **1984-** | **1852** |
| 21 | Mike Pruitt | 1976-86 | 1846 |
| 22 | Freeman McNeil | 1981-92 | 1798 |
| 23 | Leroy Kelly | 1964-73 | 1727 |
| 24 | Curt Warner | 1983-90 | 1698 |
| 25 | George Rogers | 1981-87 | 1692 |
| 26 | James Brooks | 1981-92 | 1685 |
| 27 | Lydell Mitchell | 1972-80 | 1675 |
| 28 | Mark van Eeghen | 1974-83 | 1652 |
| 29 | Bill Brown | 1961-74 | 1649 |
| 30 | Floyd Little | 1967-75 | 1641 |
| 31 | Ken Willard | 1965-74 | 1622 |
| 32 | James Wilder | 1981-90 | 1586 |
| 33 | John Henry Johnson | 1954-66 | 1571 |
| 34 | Chuck Muncie | 1976-84 | 1561 |
| 35 | Chuck Foreman | 1973-80 | 1556 |
| **36** | **Rodney Hampton** | **1990-** | **1547** |
| 37 | Wilbert Montgomery | 1977-85 | 1540 |
| 38 | Larry Brown | 1969-76 | 1530 |
| 39 | Lawrence McCutcheon | 1972-81 | 1521 |
| 40 | Neal Anderson | 1986-93 | 1515 |
| 41 | Don Perkins | 1961-68 | 1500 |
| 42 | Sammy Winder | 1982-90 | 1495 |
| 43 | Pete Johnson | 1977-84 | 1489 |
| 44 | Calvin Hill | 1969-74,76-81 | 1452 |
| 45 | Rick Casares | 1955-66 | 1431 |
| 46 | Sam Cunningham | 1973-79,81-82 | 1385 |
| 47 | John Brockington | 1971-77 | 1347 |
| 48 | Wendell Tyler | 1977-86 | 1344 |
| 49 | Jim Nance | 1965-71,73 | 1341 |
| 50 | Steve Van Buren | 1944-51 | 1320 |
| 51 | Joe Morris | 1982-88,91 | 1411 |
| **52** | **Marion Butts** | **1989-** | **1345** |
| 53 | William Andrews | 1979-83,86 | 1315 |
| 54 | Delvin Williams | 1974-81 | 1312 |
| 55 | Mike Garrett | 1966-73 | 1308 |
| 56 | Joe Cribbs | 1980-83,85-88 | 1299 |
| 57 | Emerson Boozer | 1966-75 | 1291 |
| | Kevin Mack | 1985-93 | 1291 |
| 59 | Christian Okoye | 1987-92 | 1246 |
| **60** | **John L. Williams** | **1986-** | **1245** |
| 61 | Dick Bass | 1960-69 | 1218 |
| 62 | MacArthur Lane | 1968-78 | 1206 |
| 63 | Greg Bell | 1984-90 | 1204 |
| 64 | Ron Johnson | 1969-75 | 1203 |
| | Dexter Bussey | 1974-84 | 1203 |
| 66 | Tom Matte | 1961-71 | 1200 |
| 67 | Donny Anderson | 1966-74 | 1197 |
| 68 | Alex Webster | 1955-64 | 1196 |
| | Greg Pruitt | 1973-84 | 1196 |
| 70 | Joe Washington | 1977-85 | 1195 |
| 71 | Tony Collins | 1981-87,90 | 1191 |
| 72 | Dave Osborn | 1965-76 | 1179 |
| 73 | Rob Carpenter | 1977-86 | 1172 |
| 74 | Ollie Matson | 1952, 54-66 | 1170 |
| | Altie Taylor | 1969-76 | 1170 |
| 76 | Jim Otis | 1970-78 | 1160 |
| | Robert Newhouse | 1972-83 | 1160 |
| 78 | Mike Rozier | 1985-91 | 1159 |
| 79 | John David Crow | 1958-68 | 1157 |
| | Ed Podolak | 1969-77 | 1157 |

## YARDS (3850)

| | | | |
|---|---|---|---|
| 1 | Walter Payton | 1975-87 | 16726 |
| 2 | Eric Dickerson | 1983-93 | 13259 |
| 3 | Tony Dorsett | 1977-88 | 12739 |
| 4 | Jimmy Brown | 1957-65 | 12312 |
| 5 | Franco Harris | 1972-84 | 12120 |
| 6 | John Riggins | 1974-79,81-85 | 11352 |
| 7 | O.J. Simpson | 1969-79 | 11236 |
| **8** | **Marcus Allen** | **1982-** | **10908** |
| 9 | Ottis Anderson | 1979-92 | 10273 |
| **10** | **Barry Sanders** | **1989-** | **10172** |
| **11** | **Thurman Thomas** | **1988-** | **9729** |
| 12 | Joe Perry | 1948-63 | 9723 |
| **13** | **Emmitt Smith** | **1990-** | **8956** |
| 14 | Earl Campbell | 1978-85 | 9407 |
| 15 | Jim Taylor | 1958-67 | 8597 |
| 16 | Roger Craig | 1983-93 | 8189 |
| 17 | Gerald Riggs | 1982-91 | 8188 |
| **18** | **Herschel Walker** | **1986-** | **8122** |
| 19 | Larry Csonka | 1968-74,76-79 | 8081 |
| 20 | Freeman McNeil | 1981-92 | 8074 |
| 21 | James Brooks | 1981-92 | 7962 |
| 22 | Mike Pruitt | 1976-86 | 7378 |
| **23** | **Ernest Byner** | **1984-** | **7314** |
| 24 | Leroy Kelly | 1964-73 | 7274 |
| 25 | George Rogers | 1982-87 | 7176 |
| 26 | Curt Warner | 1983-90 | 6844 |
| 27 | John Henry Johnson | 1954-66 | 6803 |
| 28 | Wilbert Montgomery | 1977-85 | 6789 |
| 29 | Chuck Muncie | 1976-84 | 6702 |
| 30 | Mark van Eeghen | 1974-83 | 6651 |
| 31 | Lawrence McCutcheon | 1972-81 | 6578 |
| 32 | Lydell Mitchell | 1972-80 | 6534 |
| 33 | Wendell Tyler | 1977-86 | 6378 |
| 34 | Floyd Little | 1965-75 | 6323 |
| 35 | Don Perkins | 1961-68 | 6217 |
| 36 | Neal Anderson | 1986-93 | 6166 |
| 37 | Ken Willard | 1965-74 | 6105 |
| 38 | Calvin Hill | 1969-74,76-81 | 6083 |
| 39 | James Wilder | 1981-90 | 6008 |
| **40** | **Rodney Hampton** | **1990-** | **5989** |
| 41 | William Andrews | 1979-83,86 | 5986 |
| 42 | Chuck Foreman | 1973-80 | 5950 |
| 43 | Larry Brown | 1969-76 | 5875 |
| 44 | Steve Van Buren | 1944-51 | 5860 |
| 45 | Bill Brown | 1961-74 | 5838 |
| 46 | Rick Casares | 1955-66 | 5797 |
| 47 | Greg Pruitt | 1973-84 | 5672 |
| 48 | Pete Johnson | 1977-84 | 5626 |
| 49 | Delvin Williams | 1974-81 | 5598 |
| 50 | Joe Morris | 1982-88,91 | 5585 |
| 51 | Mike Garrett | 1966-73 | 5481 |
| 52 | Sam Cunningham | 1973-79,81-82 | 5453 |
| 53 | Sammy Winder | 1982-90 | 5427 |
| 54 | Dick Bass | 1960-69 | 5417 |
| 55 | Jim Nance | 1965-71,73 | 5401 |
| 56 | Joe Cribbs | 1980-83,85-88 | 5356 |
| 57 | Hugh McElhenny | 1952-64 | 5281 |
| 58 | John Brockington | 1971-77 | 5185 |
| | **Marion Butts** | **1989-** | **5185** |
| 60 | Lenny Moore | 1956-67 | 5174 |
| 61 | Ollie Matson | 1952-66 | 5173 |
| 62 | Clem Daniels | 1960-68 | 5138 |
| 63 | Emerson Boozer | 1966-75 | 5135 |
| 64 | Kevin Mack | 1985-93 | 5123 |
| 65 | Billy Sims | 1980-84 | 5106 |
| 66 | Dexter Bussey | 1974-84 | 5105 |
| **67** | **John L. Williams** | **1986-** | **5006** |
| **68** | **Chris Warren** | **1990-** | **5004** |
| 69 | Paul Lowe | 1960-61,63-69 | 4995 |
| 70 | John David Crow | 1958-68 | 4963 |
| 71 | Greg Bell | 1984-90 | 4959 |
| 72 | Gale Sayers | 1965-71 | 4956 |
| 73 | Christian Okoye | 1987-92 | 4897 |
| 74 | Joe Washington | 1977-85 | 4839 |
| 75 | Robert Newhouse | 1972-83 | 4784 |
| 76 | Marion Motley | 1946-53,55 | 4720 |
| 77 | Donny Anderson | 1966-74 | 4696 |
| 78 | J.D. Smith | 1955-66 | 4672 |
| 79 | MacArthur Lane | 1968-78 | 4656 |
| 80 | Stump Mitchell | 1981-89 | 4649 |
| 81 | Tony Collins | 1981-87,90 | 4647 |
| 82 | Tom Matte | 1961-71 | 4646 |
| 83 | Alex Webster | 1955-64 | 4638 |
| 84 | Abner Haynes | 1960-67 | 4630 |
| 85 | Bob Hoernschemeyer | 1946-55 | 4548 |
| 86 | Ted Brown | 1979-86 | 4546 |
| 87 | Marv Hubbard | 1969-75,77 | 4544 |
| 88 | Dave Hampton | 1969-76 | 4536 |
| **89** | **Randall Cunningham** | **1985-** | **4482** |
| 90 | Mike Rozier | 1985-91 | 4462 |
| 91 | Otis Armstrong | 1973-80 | 4453 |
| 92 | Ed Podolak | 1969-77 | 4451 |
| 93 | Rob Carpenter | 1977-86 | 4363 |
| 94 | Jim Otis | 1970-78 | 4350 |
| 95 | Dave Osborn | 1965-76 | 4336 |
| 96 | Altie Taylor | 1969-76 | 4308 |
| 97 | Ron Johnson | 1969-75 | 4307 |
| 98 | Cookie Gilchrist | 1962-67 | 4293 |
| 99 | Matt Snell | 1964-72 | 4285 |
| 100 | Darrin Nelson | 1982-92 | 4442 |
| 101 | Johnny Hector | 1983-92 | 4280 |
| **102** | **Lorenzo White** | **1988-** | **4242** |
| 103 | Tommy Mason | 1961-71 | 4203 |
| 104 | Tony Canadeo | 1941-44,46-52 | 4197 |
| | Carl Garrett | 1969-77 | 4197 |
| 106 | Mike Thomas | 1975-80 | 4196 |
| 107 | Earnest Jackson | 1983-88 | 4167 |
| 108 | Dalton Hilliard | 1986-93 | 4164 |
| 109 | Mercury Morris | 1969-76 | 4133 |
| **110** | **Terry Allen** | **1991-92,94-** | **4104** |
| 111 | Johnny Johnson | 1990-94 | 4078 |
| 112 | Tony Galbreath | 1976-87 | 4072 |
| 113 | Alan Ameche | 1955-60 | 4045 |
| 114 | Nick Pietrosante | 1959-67 | 4026 |
| 115 | Curtis Dickey | 1980-86 | 4019 |
| 116 | Frank Pollard | 1980-88 | 3989 |
| 117 | Dick Hoak | 1961-70 | 3965 |
| 118 | Barry Foster | 1990-94 | 3943 |
| 119 | Walt Garrison | 1966-74 | 3886 |
| **120** | **Craig Heyward** | **1988-** | **3881** |
| 121 | Randy McMillan | 1981-86 | 3876 |
| 122 | Rocky Bleier | 1968-69,71-80 | 3864 |
| 123 | Timmy Brown | 1959-68 | 3862 |
| 124 | Wilbur Jackson | 1974-82 | 3852 |

## AVERAGE YARDS (4.24)
(Minimum 700 rushes)

| | | | Att. | Yards | Avg. |
|---|---|---|---|---|---|
| 1 | Marion Motley | 1946-53,55 | 828 | 4720 | 5.70 |
| 2 | Jimmy Brown | 1957-65 | 2359 | 12312 | 5.22 |
| 3 | Mercury Morris | 1969-76 | 804 | 4133 | 5.14 |
| 4 | Joe Perry | 1948-63 | 1929 | 9723 | 5.04 |
| 5 | Gale Sayers | 1965-71 | 991 | 4956 | 5.00 |
| **6** | **Barry Sanders** | **1989-** | **2077** | **10172** | **4.90** |
| 7 | Paul Lowe | 1960-61,63-69 | 1026 | 4995 | 4.87 |
| 8 | Lenny Moore | 1956-67 | 1069 | 5174 | 4.84 |
| 9 | Tony Nathan | 1979-87 | 732 | 3543 | 4.84 |
| 10 | Marv Hubbard | 1965-75,77 | 951 | 4544 | 4.78 |
| 11 | Wendell Tyler | 1977-86 | 1344 | 6378 | 4.75 |
| 12 | Greg Pruitt | 1973-84 | 1196 | 5672 | 4.74 |
| 13 | Tank Younger | 1949-58 | 770 | 3640 | 4.73 |
| | James Brooks | 1981-92 | 1685 | 7962 | 4.73 |
| 15 | Stump Mitchell | 1981-89 | 986 | 4699 | 4.71 |
| 16 | Hugh McElhenny | 1952-64 | 1124 | 5281 | 4.70 |
| 17 | O.J. Simpson | 1969-79 | 2404 | 11236 | 4.67 |
| 18 | Dutch Clark | 1931-32,34-38 | 706 | 3272 | 4.63 |
| 19 | Gerry Ellis | 1980-86 | 836 | 3826 | 4.58 |
| 20 | Terry Metcalf | 1973-77,81 | 766 | 3498 | 4.57 |
| 21 | William Andrews | 1979-83,86-87 | 1315 | 5986 | 4.55 |
| 22 | Bronko Nagurski | 1930-37,43 | 738 | 3353 | 4.54 |
| | Hoyle Granger | 1966-72 | 805 | 3653 | 4.54 |
| 24 | Clarence Davis | 1971-78 | 804 | 3640 | 4.53 |
| 25 | Billy Sims | 1980-84 | 1131 | 5106 | 4.51 |
| | Freeman McNeil | 1981-92 | 1798 | 8074 | 4.49 |
| 27 | Clem Daniels | 1960-68 | 1146 | 5138 | 4.48 |
| | Essex Daniels | 1968-76 | 722 | 3236 | 4.48 |
| 29 | Abner Haynes | 1960-67 | 1036 | 4630 | 4.47 |
| 30 | Keith Lincoln | 1961-68 | 758 | 3386 | 4.46 |
| | **Emmitt Smith** | **1990-** | **2007** | **8956** | **4.46** |
| 32 | Dick Bass | 1960-69 | 1218 | 5417 | 4.45 |
| 33 | Steve Van Buren | 1944-51 | 1320 | 5860 | 4.44 |
| 34 | Jim Taylor | 1958-67 | 1941 | 8597 | 4.43 |
| | Eric Dickerson | 1983-92 | 2996 | 13259 | 4.43 |
| 36 | Ollie Matson | 1952,54-66 | 1170 | 5173 | 4.42 |
| 37 | Wilbert Montgomery | 1977-85 | 1540 | 6789 | 4.41 |
| 38 | Walter Payton | 1975-87 | 3838 | 16726 | 4.36 |
| 39 | Otis Armstrong | 1973-80 | 1023 | 4453 | 4.35 |
| | Darrin Nelson | 1982-92 | 1020 | 4442 | 4.35 |
| 41 | Tony Dorsett | 1977-88 | 2936 | 12739 | 4.34 |
| | Timmy Brown | 1959-68 | 889 | 3862 | 4.34 |
| 43 | John Henry Johnson | 1954-66 | 1571 | 6803 | 4.33 |
| | **Chris Warren** | **1990-** | **1156** | **5004** | **4.33** |
| 45 | Walt Garrison | 1966-74 | 899 | 3886 | 4.32 |
| | Lawrence McCutcheon | 1972-81 | 1521 | 6578 | 4.32 |
| 47 | Barry Foster | 1990-94 | 915 | 3943 | 4.31 |
| 48 | Earl Campbell | 1978-85 | 2187 | 9407 | 4.30 |
| | Frank Gifford | 1952-60,62-64 | 840 | 3609 | 4.30 |
| | Amos Marsh | 1961-67 | 750 | 3222 | 4.30 |
| 51 | Bob Hoernschemeyer | 1946-55 | 1059 | 4548 | 4.29 |
| | John David Crow | 1958-68 | 1157 | 4963 | 4.29 |
| | Curtis Dickey | 1980-86 | 937 | 4019 | 4.29 |
| | Chuck Muncie | 1976-84 | 1561 | 6702 | 4.29 |
| 55 | Tom Woodeschick | 1963-72 | 1836 | 3577 | 4.28 |
| | Willie Ellison | 1967-74 | 801 | 3426 | 4.28 |
| | Kenneth Davis | 1986-94 | 820 | 3513 | 4.28 |
| 58 | Les Josephson | 1964-67,69-74 | 797 | 3407 | 4.27 |
| | Larry Csonka | 1968-74,76-79 | 1891 | 8081 | 4.27 |
| **60** | **Thurman Thomas** | **1988-** | **2285** | **9729** | **4.26** |
| 61 | Cookie Gilchrist | 1962-67 | 1010 | 4293 | 4.25 |
| | J.D. Smith | 1956-66 | 1100 | 4672 | 4.25 |
| | Dexter Bussey | 1974-84 | 1203 | 5105 | 4.25 |
| 64 | George Rogers | 1981-87 | 1692 | 7176 | 4.24 |

## TOUCHDOWNS (35)

| | | | |
|---|---|---|---|
| 1 | Walter Payton | 1975-87 | 110 |
| 2 | Jimmy Brown | 1957-65 | 106 |
| 3 | John Riggins | 1971-79,81-85 | 104 |
| **4** | **Marcus Allen** | **1982-** | **103** |
| **5** | **Emmitt Smith** | **1990-** | **96** |
| 6 | Franco Harris | 1972-84 | 91 |
| 7 | Eric Dickerson | 1983-93 | 90 |
| 8 | Jim Taylor | 1958-67 | 83 |
| 9 | Ottis Anderson | 1979-92 | 81 |
| 10 | Tony Dorsett | 1977-88 | 77 |
| 11 | Pete Johnson | 1977-84 | 76 |
| 12 | Leroy Kelly | 1964-73 | 74 |
| | Earl Campbell | 1978-85 | 74 |
| **14** | **Barry Sanders** | **1989-** | **73** |
| 15 | Joe Perry | 1948-63 | 71 |
| | Chuck Muncie | 1976-84 | 71 |
| 17 | Steve Van Buren | 1944-51 | 69 |
| | Gerald Riggs | 1982-91 | 69 |
| 19 | Larry Csonka | 1968-74,76-79 | 64 |
| 20 | Lenny Moore | 1956-67 | 63 |
| 21 | O.J. Simpson | 1969-79 | 61 |
| **22** | **Herschel Walker** | **1986-** | **60** |
| 23 | Curt Warner | 1983-90 | 56 |
| | Roger Craig | 1983-93 | 56 |
| 25 | George Rogers | 1981-87 | 54 |
| | **Thurman Thomas** | **1988-** | **54** |
| 27 | Chuck Foreman | 1973-80 | 53 |
| 28 | Bill Brown | 1961-74 | 52 |
| | Emerson Boozer | 1966-75 | 52 |
| | **Earnest Byner** | **1984-** | **52** |
| 31 | Mike Pruitt | 1976-86 | 51 |
| | Greg Bell | 1984-90 | 51 |
| | Neal Anderson | 1986-93 | 51 |
| | Paul Hornung | 1957-62,64-66 | 50 |
| | Wendell Tyler | 1977-86 | 50 |
| | Joe Morris | 1982-88,91 | 50 |
| 37 | Rick Casares | 1955-66 | 49 |
| | James Brooks | 1981-92 | 49 |
| | John Henry Johnson | 1954-66 | 48 |
| **40** | **Rodney Hampton** | **1990-** | **47** |
| | Pete Banaszak | 1966-78 | 47 |
| 42 | Abner Haynes | 1960-67 | 46 |
| | Kevin Mack | 1985-93 | 46 |
| 44 | Tom Matte | 1961-72 | 45 |
| | Jim Nance | 1965-71,73 | 45 |
| | Ken Willard | 1965-74 | 45 |
| | Wilbert Montgomery | 1977-85 | 45 |
| 48 | Otto Graham | 1946-55 | 44 |
| | Larry Kinnebrew | 1983-87,89-90 | 44 |
| 50 | Dan Towler | 1950-55 | 43 |
| | Floyd Little | 1967-75 | 43 |
| | Sam Cunningham | 1973-79,81 | 43 |
| | **Marion Butts** | **1989-** | **43** |
| 54 | Don Perkins | 1961-68 | 42 |
| | Calvin Hill | 1969-74,76-81 | 42 |
| | Billy Sims | 1980-84 | 42 |
| 57 | Donny Anderson | 1966-74 | 41 |
| | Johnny Hector | 1983-92 | 41 |
| 59 | Vern Lewellen | 1924-32 | 40 |
| | Alan Ameche | 1955-60 | 40 |
| | Ollie Matson | 1952,54-66 | 40 |
| | J.D. Smith | 1955-66 | 40 |
| | Jack Kemp | 1957,60-67,69 | 40 |
| | Paul Lowe | 1960-61,63-69 | 40 |
| | Ron Johnson | 1969-75 | 40 |
| | Ted Brown | 1979-86 | 40 |
| | Don McCauley | 1971-81 | 40 |
| | Christian Okoye | 1987-92 | 40 |
| 69 | Alex Webster | 1955-64 | 39 |
| | Gale Sayers | 1965-71 | 39 |
| | Y.A. Tittle | 1948-64 | 39 |
| | Sammy Winder | 1982-90 | 39 |
| | Dalton Hilliard | 1986-93 | 39 |
| 74 | Hugh McElhenny | 1952-64 | 38 |
| | John David Crow | 1958-68 | 38 |
| | Freeman McNeil | 1981-92 | 38 |
| 77 | Ernie Nevers | 1926-27,29-31 | 37 |
| | Tobin Rote | 1950-59,63-64,66 | 37 |
| | Bill Mathis | 1960-69 | 37 |
| | Cookie Gilchrist | 1962-67 | 37 |
| | Mark van Eeghen | 1974-83 | 37 |
| | Wayne Morris | 1976-84 | 37 |
| | James Wilder | 1981-90 | 37 |
| 84 | Dutch Clark | 1931-32,34-38 | 36 |
| | Pug Manders | 1939- 47 | 36 |
| | **Ricky Watters** | **1992-** | **36** |
| 87 | Clarke Hinkle | 1932- 41 | 35 |
| | Mike Garrett | 1966-73 | 35 |
| | Larry Brown | 1969-76 | 35 |
| | Steve Grogan | 1975-90 | 35 |
| | **Brad Baxter** | **1989-** | **35** |
| | **Chris Warren** | **1990-** | **35** |

Players active at the end of **1995** are shown in **bold face.**

# LIFETIME LEADERS
# RECEIVING

## RECEPTIONS (400)

| | | | |
|---|---|---|---|
| 1 | **Jerry Rice** | **1985-** | **944** |
| 2 | **Art Monk** | **1980-** | **940** |
| 3 | Steve Largent | 1976-89 | 819 |
| 4 | James Lofton | 1978-93 | 764 |
| 5 | Charlie Joiner | 1969-86 | 750 |
| 6 | **Henry Ellard** | **1983-** | **723** |
| 7 | **Andre Reed** | **1985-** | **700** |
| 8 | **Gary Clark** | **1985-** | **699** |
| 9 | Ozzie Newsome | 1978-90 | 662 |
| 10 | Charley Taylor | 1964-75,77 | 649 |
| 11 | Drew Hill | 1979-93 | 634 |
| 12 | Don Maynard | 1958, 60-73 | 633 |
| 13 | Raymond Berry | 1955-67 | 631 |
| 14 | Sterling Sharpe | 1988-94 | 595 |
| 15 | Harold Carmichael | 1971-84 | 590 |
| 16 | Fred Biletnikoff | 1965-78 | 589 |
| 17 | Mark Clayton | 1983-93 | 582 |
| 18 | Harold Jackson | 1968-83 | 579 |
| 19 | **Cris Carter** | **1987-** | **571** |
| | **Ernest Givins** | **1986-** | **571** |
| 21 | Lionel Taylor | 1959-68 | 567 |
| 22 | Roger Craig | 1983-93 | 566 |
| | **Bill Brooks** | **1986-** | **566** |
| 24 | **Irving Fryar** | **1984-** | **562** |
| 25 | Wes Chandler | 1978-88 | 559 |
| 26 | Roy Green | 1979-92 | 559 |
| 27 | Stanley Morgan | 1977-90 | 557 |
| 28 | Eric Martin | 1985-94 | 553 |
| | **Marcus Allen** | **1982-** | **549** |
| 30 | **John L. Williams** | **1986-** | **546** |
| 31 | J.T. Smith | 1978-90 | 544 |
| 32 | Lance Alworth | 1962-72 | 542 |
| 33 | Kellen Winslow | 1979-87 | 541 |
| | **Ronnie Harmon** | **1986-** | **541** |
| 35 | John Stallworth | 1974-87 | 537 |
| 36 | **Keith Byars** | **1986-** | **532** |
| 37 | **Michael Irvin** | **1988-** | **527** |
| 38 | **Webster Slaughter** | **1986-** | **523** |
| 39 | **Andre Rison** | **1989-** | **522** |
| 40 | Bobby Mitchell | 1958-68 | 521 |
| 41 | Al Toon | 1985-92 | 517 |
| 42 | **Haywood Jeffires** | **1987-** | **515** |
| 43 | Mark Duper | 1982-92 | 511 |
| 44 | Nat Moore | 1974-86 | 510 |
| 45 | Dwight Clark | 1979-87 | 506 |
| 46 | Billy Howton | 1952-63 | 503 |
| 47 | Cliff Branch | 1972-85 | 501 |
| 48 | Steve Jordan | 1982-94 | 498 |
| 49 | Tommy McDonald | 1957-68 | 495 |
| | Ahmad Rashad | 1972-74,76-82 | 495 |
| 51 | **Anthony Miller** | **1988-** | **493** |
| 52 | Walter Payton | 1975-87 | 492 |
| 53 | **Herschel Walker** | **1986-** | **491** |
| 54 | Tony Galbreath | 1976-88 | 490 |
| 55 | Drew Pearson | 1973-83 | 489 |
| 56 | Don Hutson | 1935-45 | 488 |
| 57 | Anthony Carter | 1985-95 | 486 |
| 58 | **Brian Blades** | **1988-** | **483** |
| 59 | Ricky Sanders | 1986-94 | 481 |
| 60 | Jackie Smith | 1963-78 | 480 |
| 61 | Art Powell | 1959-68 | 479 |
| | Tony Hill | 1977-86 | 479 |
| 63 | Boyd Dowler | 1959-69,71 | 474 |
| 64 | Pat Tilley | 1976-86 | 468 |
| 65 | Mickey Shuler | 1978-91 | 462 |
| 66 | Todd Christensen | 1979-88 | 461 |
| | **Earnest Byner** | **1984-** | **461** |
| 68 | **Mark Carrier** | **1987-** | **459** |
| 69 | Pete Retzlaff | 1956-66 | 452 |
| 70 | Roy Jefferson | 1965-76 | 451 |
| 71 | Haven Moses | 1968-81 | 448 |
| 72 | Reggie Rucker | 1970-81 | 447 |
| 73 | Carroll Dale | 1960-73 | 438 |
| | Wesley Walker | 1977-89 | 438 |
| 75 | James Wilder | 1981-90 | 431 |
| 76 | Mike Ditka | 1961-72 | 427 |
| | Paul Warfield | 1964-74,76-77 | 427 |
| 78 | Bobby Joe Conrad | 1958-69 | 422 |
| | Bob Tucker | 1970-80 | 422 |
| | **Jay Novacek** | **1985-** | **422** |
| 81 | Jerry Smith | 1965-77 | 421 |
| | Ken Burrough | 1970-82 | 421 |
| 83 | Charle Young | 1973-85 | 418 |
| 84 | Cris Collinsworth | 1981-88 | 417 |
| 85 | Isaac Curtis | 1973-84 | 416 |
| | Henry Marshall | 1976-87 | 416 |
| 87 | **Vance Johnson** | **1985-93,95-** | **415** |
| 88 | Reggie Langhorne | 1985-93 | 411 |
| 89 | Charley Hennigan | 1960-66 | 410 |
| | Otis Taylor | 1965-74 | 410 |
| 91 | Rickey Young | 1975-83 | 408 |
| 92 | Billy Wilson | 1951-60 | 407 |
| 93 | **Brett Perriman** | **1988-** | **406** |
| 94 | Gary Garrison | 1966-77 | 405 |
| | **Tim Brown** | **1988-** | **405** |
| 96 | Vance Johnson | 1985-93 | 403 |
| 97 | Jim Phillips | 1958-67 | 401 |
| | **Keith Jackson** | **1988-** | **401** |
| | **Eric Metcalf** | **1989-** | **401** |
| 100 | Tom Fears | 1948-56 | 400 |
| | Jimmy Orr | 1958-70 | 400 |

## YARDS (6100)

| | | | |
|---|---|---|---|
| 1 | **Jerry Rice** | **1985-** | **15123** |
| 2 | James Lofton | 1978-93 | 14004 |
| 3 | Steve Largent | 1976-89 | 13089 |
| 4 | **Art Monk** | **1980-** | **12721** |
| 5 | **Henry Ellard** | **1983-** | **12163** |
| 6 | Charlie Joiner | 1969-86 | 12146 |
| 7 | Don Maynard | 1958,1960-73 | 11834 |
| 8 | **Gary Clark** | **1985-** | **10856** |
| 9 | Stanley Morgan | 1977-90 | 10716 |
| 10 | Harold Jackson | 1968-83 | 10372 |
| 11 | Lance Alworth | 1962-72 | 10266 |
| 12 | **Andre Reed** | **1985-** | **9848** |
| 13 | Drew Hill | 1979-93 | 9831 |
| 14 | Raymond Berry | 1955-67 | 9275 |
| 15 | Charley Taylor | 1964-75, 77 | 9110 |
| 16 | Harold Carmichael | 1971-84 | 8985 |
| 17 | Fred Biletnikoff | 1965-78 | 8974 |
| | Mark Clayton | 1983-93 | 8974 |
| 19 | Wes Chandler | 1978-88 | 8966 |
| 20 | Roy Green | 1979-92 | 8965 |
| 21 | **Irving Fryar** | **1984-** | **8916** |
| 22 | Mark Duper | 1982-92 | 8869 |
| 23 | John Stallworth | 1974-87 | 8723 |
| 24 | Cliff Branch | 1972-85 | 8685 |
| 25 | Paul Warfield | 1964-74,76-77 | 8565 |
| 26 | **Michael Irvin** | **1988-** | **8538** |
| 27 | Billy Howton | 1952-63 | 8459 |
| 28 | Tommy McDonald | 1957-68 | 8410 |
| 29 | Wesley Walker | 1977-89 | 8306 |
| 30 | Carroll Dale | 1960-73 | 8277 |
| 31 | **Ernest Givins** | **1986-** | **8215** |
| 32 | Eric Martin | 1985-94 | 8161 |
| 33 | Sterling Sharpe | 1988-94 | 8134 |
| 34 | Haven Moses | 1968-81 | 8091 |
| 35 | Art Powell | 1959-68 | 8046 |
| 36 | Tony Hill | 1977-86 | 7988 |
| 37 | Don Hutson | 1935-45 | 7981 |
| 38 | Bobby Mitchell | 1958-68 | 7954 |
| 39 | Jimmy Orr | 1958-70 | 7914 |
| 40 | Drew Pearson | 1973-83 | 7822 |
| 41 | Ozzie Newsome | 1978-90 | 7980 |
| 42 | **Bill Brooks** | **1986-** | **7777** |
| 43 | **Anthony Miller** | **1988-** | **7768** |
| 44 | Anthony Carter | 1985-95 | 7732 |
| 45 | **Webster Slaughter** | **1986-** | **7584** |
| 46 | Nat Moore | 1974-86 | 7546 |
| 47 | Roy Jefferson | 1965-76 | 7539 |
| 48 | Gary Garrison | 1966-77 | 7538 |
| 49 | Jackie Smith | 1963-78 | 7418 |
| 50 | Bob Hayes | 1965-75 | 7414 |
| 51 | Pete Retzlaff | 1956-66 | 7412 |
| 52 | Otis Taylor | 1965-74 | 7306 |
| 53 | Boyd Dowler | 1959-69,71 | 7270 |
| 54 | **Mark Carrier** | **1987-** | **7218** |
| 55 | Lionel Taylor | 1959-68 | 7195 |
| 56 | **Cris Carter** | **1987-** | **7177** |
| 57 | **Andre Rison** | **1989-** | **7156** |
| 58 | Ken Burrough | 1970-81 | 7102 |
| 59 | Isaac Curtis | 1973-84 | 7101 |
| 60 | Reggie Rucker | 1970-81 | 7065 |
| 61 | John Gilliam | 1967-77 | 7056 |
| 62 | Elroy Hirsch | 1946-57 | 7029 |
| 63 | Pat Tilley | 1976-86 | 7005 |
| 64 | J.T. Smith | 1978-90 | 6974 |
| 65 | Gene Washington | 1968-77,79 | 6856 |
| 66 | Ahmad Rashad | 1972-74,76-82 | 6831 |
| 67 | Charley Hennigan | 1960-66 | 6823 |
| 68 | Dwight Clark | 1979-87 | 6750 |
| 69 | Kellen Winslow | 1979-87 | 6741 |
| 70 | Frank Lewis | 1971-83 | 6724 |
| 71 | Cris Collinsworth | 1981-88 | 6698 |
| 72 | Mel Gray | 1971-82 | 6644 |
| 73 | Willie Gault | 1983-93 | 6635 |
| 74 | Al Toon | 1985-92 | 6605 |
| 75 | **Brian Blades** | **1988-** | **6561** |
| 76 | Henry Marshall | 1976-87 | 6545 |
| 77 | Dante Lavelli | 1946-56 | 6488 |
| 78 | Del Shofner | 1957-67 | 6470 |
| 79 | Mike Quick | 1982-90 | 6464 |
| 80 | Ricky Sanders | 1986-94 | 6453 |
| 81 | Sammy White | 1976-85 | 6400 |
| 82 | Carlos Carson | 1980-89 | 6372 |
| 83 | Max McGee | 1954,57-67 | 6346 |
| 84 | Stephone Paige | 1983-91 | 6341 |
| 85 | Steve Jordan | 1982-94 | 6307 |
| 86 | Alfred Jenkins | 1975-83 | 6258 |
| 87 | Eddie Brown | 1985-91 | 6134 |
| 88 | Steve Watson | 1979-88 | 6112 |

## AVERAGE YARDS (16.20)

(Minimum 200 receptions)

| | | | | | |
|---|---|---|---|---|---|
| 1 | Homer Jones | 1964-70 | 224 | 4986 | 22.26 |
| 2 | Buddy Dial | 1959-66 | 261 | 5436 | 20.83 |
| 3 | Harlon Hill | 1954-62 | 233 | 4717 | 20.25 |
| 4 | **Willie Anderson** | **1988-** | **267** | **5357** | **20/06** |
| | Paul Warfield | 1964-74,76-77 | 427 | 8656 | 20.06 |
| 6 | Bob Hayes | 1965-75 | 371 | 7414 | 19.98 |
| 7 | Willie Gault | 1983-93 | 333 | 6635 | 19.92 |
| 8 | Jimmy Orr | 1958-70 | 400 | 7914 | 19.79 |
| 9 | Ray Renfro | 1952-63 | 281 | 5508 | 19.60 |
| 10 | Stanley Morgan | 1977-90 | 557 | 10716 | 19.24 |
| | Hugh Taylor | 1947-54 | 272 | 5233 | 19.24 |
| 12 | Wesley Walker | 1977-89 | 438 | 8306 | 18.96 |
| 13 | Lance Alworth | 1962-72 | 542 | 10267 | 18.94 |
| 14 | Mel Gray | 1971-83 | 351 | 6644 | 18.93 |
| 15 | Carroll Dale | 1960-73 | 438 | 8277 | 18.90 |
| 16 | Roger Carr | 1974-84 | 254 | 4770 | 18.78 |
| 17 | Don Maynard | 1958,60-73 | 633 | 11834 | 18.70 |
| 18 | Frank Clarke | 1957-67 | 291 | 5426 | 18.65 |
| 19 | Gary Garrison | 1966-77 | 405 | 7538 | 18.61 |
| 20 | Del Shofner | 1957-67 | 349 | 6470 | 18.54 |
| 21 | John Gilliam | 1967-77 | 382 | 7056 | 18.47 |
| 22 | Max McGee | 1954,57-67 | 345 | 6346 | 18.39 |
| 23 | James Lofton | 1978-93 | 764 | 14004 | 18.33 |
| 24 | Ben Hawkins | 1966-73 | 261 | 4764 | 18.25 |
| 25 | Elroy Hirsch | 1946-57 | 387 | 7029 | 18.16 |
| 26 | Haven Moses | 1968-81 | 448 | 8091 | 18.06 |
| 27 | Carlos Carson | 1980-89 | 353 | 6372 | 18.05 |
| 28 | Lance Rentzel | 1965-72,74 | 268 | 4826 | 18.01 |
| 29 | Mervyn Fernandez | 1987-92 | 209 | 3764 | 18.01 |
| 30 | Elbert Dubenion | 1960-68 | 295 | 5305 | 17.98 |
| 31 | Harold Jackson | 1968-83 | 579 | 10372 | 17.92 |
| 32 | Darrell Brewster | 1952-60 | 210 | 3798 | 17.90 |
| 33 | Otis Taylor | 1965-74 | 410 | 7302 | 17.82 |
| 34 | Gene Washington | 1968-77,79 | 385 | 6856 | 17.81 |
| | Jack Snow | 1965-75 | 340 | 6012 | 17.81 |
| 36 | Mike Quick | 1982-90 | 363 | 6464 | 17.80 |
| 37 | Jim Colclough | 1960-68 | 283 | 5001 | 17.67 |
| 38 | Alfred Jenkins | 1975-83 | 359 | 6258 | 17.43 |
| 39 | Aaron Thomas | 1961-70 | 262 | 4554 | 17.38 |
| | Bob Schnelker | 1953-61 | 211 | 3667 | 17.38 |
| 41 | Mark Duper | 1982-92 | 511 | 8869 | 17.36 |
| 42 | Cliff Branch | 1972-85 | 501 | 8685 | 17.34 |
| 43 | Steve Watson | 1979-87 | 353 | 6112 | 17.31 |
| 44 | Jim Doran | 1951-61 | 212 | 3667 | 17.30 |
| 45 | Kevin House | 1980-87 | 299 | 5169 | 17.29 |
| 46 | Bobby Walston | 1951-62 | 311 | 5363 | 17.24 |
| 47 | Rich Caster | 1970-81 | 322 | 5515 | 17.13 |
| 48 | Ray Mathews | 1951-60 | 233 | 3963 | 17.01 |
| 49 | Tommy McDonald | 1957-68 | 495 | 8410 | 16.99 |
| 50 | Frank Lewis | 1971-83 | 397 | 6724 | 16.94 |
| 51 | Isaac Curtis | 1973-84 | 420 | 7106 | 16.92 |
| 52 | Leonard Thompson | 1975-86 | 277 | 4682 | 16.90 |
| | Eddie Brown | 1985-91 | 363 | 6134 | 16.90 |
| 54 | Ernie Jones | 1988-93 | 215 | 3630 | 16.88 |
| 55 | Ken Burrough | 1970-81 | 421 | 7102 | 16.87 |
| 56 | Billy Howton | 1952-63 | 503 | 8549 | 16.82 |
| | Stephone Paige | 1983-91 | 377 | 6341 | 16.82 |
| 58 | Dante Lavelli | 1946-56 | 386 | 6488 | 16.81 |
| 59 | Art Powell | 1959-68 | 479 | 8046 | 16.80 |
| 60 | Lionel Manuel | 1984-90 | 232 | 3898 | 16.80 |
| 61 | Terry Barr | 1957-65 | 227 | 3810 | 16.78 |
| 62 | Louis Lipps | 1984-92 | 359 | 6019 | 16.77 |
| 63 | Jim Mutscheller | 1954-61 | 220 | 3864 | 16.75 |
| 64 | Duriel Harris | 1976-84 | 302 | 5055 | 16.74 |
| 65 | Roy Jefferson | 1956-76 | 451 | 7539 | 16.72 |
| 66 | Hassan Jones | 1986-93 | 229 | 3824 | 16.70 |
| 67 | Tony Hill | 1977-86 | 479 | 7988 | 16.68 |
| 68 | Jim Benton | 1938-40,42-47 | 288 | 4801 | 16.67 |
| | **Michael Irvin** | **1988-** | **416** | **6935** | **16.67** |
| 70 | Charley Hennigan | 1960-66 | 410 | 6823 | 16.64 |
| | Lenny Moore | 1956-67 | 363 | 6039 | 16.64 |
| 72 | Gary Ballman | 1962-73 | 323 | 5366 | 16.61 |
| 73 | Charley Frazier | 1962-70 | 209 | 3461 | 16.56 |
| 74 | Ray Butler | 1980-88 | 239 | 3948 | 16.52 |
| 75 | Jackie Smith | 1963-78 | 480 | 7418 | 16.50 |
| 76 | Stacey Bailey | 1982-90 | 208 | 3422 | 16.45 |
| 77 | Al Denson | 1964-71 | 260 | 4278 | 16.44 |
| 78 | Sonny Randle | 1959-68 | 365 | 5996 | 16.43 |
| | Dave Kocourek | 1960-68 | 249 | 4090 | 16.43 |
| 80 | Pete Retzlaff | 1956-66 | 452 | 7412 | 16.40 |
| 81 | Don Hutson | 1935-45 | 488 | 7981 | 16.36 |
| | Rick Upchurch | 1975-83 | 267 | 4369 | 16.36 |
| 83 | Clem Daniels | 1960-68 | 203 | 3314 | 16.33 |
| 84 | Jeff Chadwick | 1983-90 | 241 | 3932 | 16.31 |
| 85 | Freddie Scott | 1974-83 | 257 | 4199 | 16.30 |
| 86 | Sammy White | 1976-85 | 393 | 6400 | 16.28 |
| | John Jefferson | 1978-85 | 351 | 5714 | 16.28 |
| 88 | Lynn Swann | 1974-82 | 336 | 5462 | 16.26 |
| 89 | John Stallworth | 1974-87 | 537 | 8723 | 16.24 |
| 90 | Mark Jackson | 1986-94 | 342 | 5551 | 16.23 |
| 91 | Tim McGee | 1986-94 | 321 | 5203 | 16.21 |
| | **Henry Ellard** | **1983-** | **527** | **8538** | **16.20** |

## TOUCHDOWNS (49)

| | | | |
|---|---|---|---|
| 1 | **Jerry Rice** | **1985-** | **131** |
| 2 | Don Hutson | 1935-45 | 100 |
| | Steve Largent | 1976-89 | 100 |
| 4 | Don Maynard | 1958,60-73 | 88 |
| 5 | Lance Alworth | 1962-72 | 85 |
| | Paul Warfield | 1964-74,76-77 | 85 |
| 7 | Tommy McDonald | 1957-68 | 84 |
| 8 | Art Powell | 1959-68 | 81 |
| | Mark Clayton | 1983-93 | 84 |
| 10 | Charley Taylor | 1964-75,77 | 79 |
| | Harold Carmichael | 1971-84 | 79 |
| 12 | Fred Biletnikoff | 1965-78 | 76 |
| | Harold Jackson | 1968-83 | 76 |
| 14 | James Lofton | 1978-93 | 75 |
| 15 | Nat Moore | 1974-86 | 74 |
| 16 | Stanley Morgan | 1977-90 | 72 |
| 17 | Bob Hayes | 1965-75 | 71 |
| 18 | Wesley Walker | 1977-89 | 71 |
| 19 | Gary Collins | 1962-71 | 70 |
| 20 | **Andre Reed** | **1985-** | **69** |
| 21 | Raymond Berry | 1955-67 | 68 |
| | **Art Monk** | **1980-** | **68** |
| 23 | Cliff Branch | 1972-85 | 67 |
| 24 | Jimmy Orr | 1958-70 | 66 |
| | Roy Green | 1979-92 | 66 |
| | **Cris Carter** | **1987-** | **66** |
| 27 | Bobby Mitchell | 1958-68 | 65 |
| | Sonny Randle | 1959-68 | 65 |
| | Charley Joiner | 1969-86 | 65 |
| | Sterling Sharpe | 1988-94 | 65 |
| | **Gary Clark** | **1985-** | **65** |
| 32 | John Stallworth | 1974-87 | 63 |
| | **Andre Rison** | **1989-** | **63** |
| 34 | Dante Lavelli | 1946-56 | 62 |
| 35 | Pete Pihos | 1947-55 | 61 |
| | Billy Howton | 1952-63 | 61 |
| | Mike Quick | 1982-90 | 61 |
| 38 | Elroy Hirsch | 1946-57 | 60 |
| | Jerry Smith | 1965-77 | 60 |
| | Gene Washington | 1969-77,79 | 60 |
| | Drew Hill | 1979-93 | 60 |
| 42 | Mark Duper | 1982-92 | 59 |
| | **Henry Ellard** | **1983-** | **59** |
| 44 | Hugh Taylor | 1947-54 | 58 |
| | Gary Garrison | 1966-77 | 58 |
| | **Irving Fryar** | **1984-** | **58** |
| 47 | Otis Taylor | 1965-74 | 57 |
| 48 | Haven Moses | 1968-81 | 56 |
| | Wes Chandler | 1978-88 | 56 |
| | **Anthony Miller** | **1988-** | **56** |
| 51 | Chris Burford | 1960-67 | 55 |
| | Anthony Carter | 1985-95 | 55 |
| 53 | Isaac Curtis | 1973-84 | 53 |
| 54 | Carroll Dale | 1960-73 | 52 |
| | Roy Jefferson | 1965-76 | 52 |
| | Dave Casper | 1974-84 | 52 |
| 57 | Del Shofner | 1957-67 | 51 |
| | Charley Hennigan | 1960-66 | 51 |
| | Lynn Swann | 1974-82 | 51 |
| | Tony Hill | 1977-86 | 51 |
| 61 | Ken Kavanaugh | 1940-41, 45-50 | 50 |
| | Ray Renfro | 1952-63 | 50 |
| | Max McGee | 1954, 57-67 | 50 |
| | Frank Clarke | 1957-67 | 50 |
| | Sammy White | 1976-85 | 50 |
| | **Michael Irvin** | **1988-** | **50** |
| 67 | Alyn Beals | 1946-51 | 49 |
| | Billy Wilson | 1951-60 | 49 |
| | Ken Burrough | 1970-81 | 49 |
| | Stephone Paige | 1983-91 | 49 |
| | Eric Martin | 1985-94 | 49 |
| | Ernest Givins | 1986- | 49 |

Players active at the end of 1995 are shown in **bold face.**

# LIFETIME LEADERS
# PUNT RETURNS

**(146)**

| | | | |
|---|---|---|---|
| 1 | Vai Sikahema | 1986-93 | 292 |
| 2 | Billy Johnson | 1974-87 | 282 |
| 3 | **Tim Brown** | **1988-** | **269** |
| 4 | J.T. Smith | 1978-90 | 267 |
| 5 | Emlen Tunnell | 1948-61 | 258 |
| 6 | **Rod Woodson** | **1987-** | **256** |
| 7 | Alvin Haymond | 1964-73 | 253 |
| 8 | Mike Fuller | 1975-82 | 252 |
| 9 | **Dave Meggett** | **1989-** | **249** |
| 10 | Rick Upchurch | 1975-83 | 248 |
| 11 | Ron Smith | 1965-74 | 235 |
| 12 | Danny Reece | 1976-80 | 222 |
| 13 | **Kelvin Martin** | **1987-** | **220** |
| 14 | Phil McConkey | 1984-89 | 218 |
| 15 | Mike Nelms | 1980-84 | 212 |
| 16 | **Mel Gray** | **1986** | **211** |
| 17 | **Irving Fryar** | **1984-** | **206** |
| 18 | Speedy Duncan | 1964-74 | 202 |
| | Leo Lewis | 1981-91 | 202 |
| 20 | Greg Pruitt | 1973-84 | 194 |
| 21 | Willie Drewrey | 1985-93 | 192 |
| 22 | Gerald McNeil | 1986-90 | 191 |
| 23 | Theo Bell | 1976-85 | 189 |
| 24 | Willie Wood | 1960-71 | 187 |
| 25 | Bruce Harper | 1977-84 | 183 |
| 26 | Clarence Verdin | 1986-94 | 178 |
| 27 | Freddie Solomon | 1975-85 | 177 |
| 28 | Robbie Martin | 1981-86 | 175 |
| | Walter Stanley | 1985-90,92 | 175 |
| 30 | Eddie Brown | 1974-79 | 172 |
| | **Brian Mitchell** | **1990-** | **172** |
| 32 | Neal Colzie | 1975-83 | 170 |
| 33 | **Eric Metcalf** | **1989-** | **166** |
| 34 | Pete Mandley | 1984-90 | 165 |
| 35 | Howard Stevens | 1973-77 | 163 |
| 36 | Larry Marshall | 1972-78 | 162 |
| 37 | Charlie West | 1968-79 | 158 |
| 38 | Bill Thompson | 1969-81 | 157 |
| 39 | Eddie Payton | 1977-78,80-82 | 156 |
| | Stump Mitchell | 1981-89 | 156 |
| 41 | Carl Roaches | 1980-85 | 155 |
| 42 | Dana McLemore | 1982-87 | 152 |
| 43 | **John Taylor** | **1987-** | **149** |
| 44 | Butch Atkinson | 1968-77,79 | 148 |
| | Wally Henry | 1977-82 | 148 |
| | **Johnny Bailey** | **1990-** | **148** |
| 47 | Butch Johnson | 1976-85 | 146 |
| | LeRoy Irvin | 1980-90 | 146 |

**YARDS (1350)**

| | | | |
|---|---|---|---|
| 1 | Billy Johnson | 1974-88 | 3317 |
| 2 | Vai Sikahema | 1986-93 | 3169 |
| 3 | Rick Upchurch | 1975-83 | 3008 |
| 4 | **Tim Brown** | **1988-** | **2811** |
| 5 | J.T. Smith | 1978-90 | 2764 |
| 6 | Mike Fuller | 1975-82 | 2660 |
| 7 | **Dave Meggett** | **1989-** | **2613** |
| 8 | **Mel Gray** | **1986-** | **2387** |
| 9 | **Rod Woodson** | **1987-** | **2362** |
| 10 | Emlen Tunnell | 1948-61 | 2209 |
| 11 | Speedy Duncan | 1964-74 | 2201 |
| 12 | **Kelvin Martin** | **1987-** | **2194** |
| 13 | Alvin Haymond | 1964-73 | 2148 |
| 14 | **Irving Fryar** | **1984-** | **2055** |
| 15 | Greg Pruitt | 1973-84 | 2007 |
| 16 | Mike Nelms | 1980-84 | 1948 |
| 17 | **Brian Mitchell** | **1990-** | **1938** |
| 18 | Leo Lewis | 1981-91 | 1868 |
| 19 | Phil McConkey | 1984-89 | 1832 |
| 20 | Bill Thompson | 1969-81 | 1814 |
| 21 | Ron Smith | 1965-74 | 1788 |
| 22 | Bruce Harper | 1977-84 | 1784 |
| 23 | Neal Colzie | 1975-82 | 1759 |
| 24 | **Eric Metcalf** | **1989-** | **1724** |
| 25 | Gerald McNeil | 1986-90 | 1717 |
| 26 | Robbie Martin | 1981-86 | 1670 |
| 27 | Clarence Verdin | 1986-94 | 1650 |
| 28 | Walter Stanley | 1985-90,92 | 1619 |
| 29 | Freddie Solomon | 1975-85 | 1614 |
| 30 | Dana McLemore | 1982-87 | 1598 |
| 31 | Willie Drewrey | 1985-93 | 1597 |
| 32 | Howard Stevens | 1973-77 | 1559 |
| 33 | Danny Reece | 1976-80 | 1554 |
| 34 | **Henry Ellard** | **1983-** | **1527** |
| 35 | **John Taylor** | **1987-** | **1517** |
| 36 | Bill Dudley | 1942,45-51,53 | 1515 |
| 37 | Pete Mandley | 1984-90 | 1514 |
| 38 | Eddie Brown | 1974-79 | 1511 |
| 39 | Theo Bell | 1976,78-85 | 1511 |
| 40 | **Bobby J. Edmonds** | **1986-89,95-** | **1471** |
| 41 | Larry Marshall | 1972-78 | 1466 |
| 42 | LeRoy Irvin | 1980-90 | 1451 |
| 43 | Fulton Walker | 1981-86 | 1439 |
| 44 | George McAfee | 1940-41,45-50 | 1431 |
| 45 | **Johnny Bailey** | **1990-** | **1420** |
| 46 | Willie Wood | 1960-71 | 1391 |
| 47 | Eddie Payton | 1977-78,80-82 | 1387 |
| 48 | Claude Gibson | 1961-65 | 1381 |
| | Mike Martin | 1983-89 | 1381 |
| 50 | Stump Mitchell | 1981-89 | 1377 |
| 51 | JoJo Townsell | 1985-90 | 1360 |
| 52 | Jake Scott | 1970-78 | 1357 |

**AVERAGE RETURN (10.5)**

(Minimum 75 returns)

| | | | Ret. | Yards | Avg. |
|---|---|---|---|---|---|
| 1 | Two Bits Homan | 1925-30 | 76 | 1009 | 13.28 |
| 2 | Charley Rogers | 1927-29 | 92 | 1199 | 13.03 |
| 3 | George McAfee | 1940-41,45-50 | 112 | 1431 | 12.78 |
| 4 | Jack Christiansen | 1951-58 | 85 | 1084 | 12.75 |
| 5 | Ken Strong | 1929-35,39-44,47 | 88 | 1112 | 12.64 |
| 6 | Claude Gibson | 1961-65 | 110 | 1381 | 12.56 |
| 7 | Bill Dudley | 1942,45-51,53 | 124 | 1515 | 12.22 |
| 8 | Rick Upchurch | 1975-83 | 248 | 3008 | 12.13 |
| 9 | Jack Ernst | 1925-30 | 89 | 1060 | 11.91 |
| 10 | Billy Johnson | 1974-88 | 282 | 3317 | 11.76 |
| 11 | Mack Herron | 1973-75 | 84 | 982 | 11.69 |
| 12 | Bill Thompson | 1969-81 | 157 | 1814 | 11.55 |
| 13 | **Mel Gray** | **1986-** | **181** | **2084** | **11.51** |
| 14 | **Henry Ellard** | **1983-** | **135** | **1527** | **11.31** |
| | Rodger Bird | 1961-68 | 94 | 1063 | 11.31 |
| 16 | Bosh Pritchard | 1942,46-49,51 | 95 | 1072 | 11.28 |
| 17 | Bobby Joe Edmonds | 1986-89 | 105 | 1178 | 11.22 |
| 18 | Terry Metcalf | 1973-77,81 | 84 | 936 | 11.14 |
| 19 | Bob Hayes | 1965-75 | 104 | 1158 | 11.13 |
| 20 | Floyd Little | 1967-75 | 81 | 893 | 11.02 |
| | Louis Lipps | 1984-92 | 112 | 1234 | 11.02 |
| 22 | Speedy Duncan | 1964-74 | 202 | 2201 | 10.90 |
| 23 | Vitamin Smith | 1949-53 | 75 | 814 | 10.85 |
| 24 | Vai Sikahema | 1986-93 | 292 | 3169 | 10.85 |
| 25 | **Dave Meggett** | **1989-** | **204** | **2230** | **10.93** |
| 26 | JoJo Townsell | 1985-90 | 127 | 1360 | 10.71 |
| 27 | **John Taylor** | **1987-** | **138** | **1461** | **10.59** |
| 28 | **Eric Metcalf** | **1989-** | **127** | **1341** | **10.56** |
| | Mike Fuller | 1975-82 | 252 | 2660 | 10.56 |
| 30 | Leroy Kelly | 1964-73 | 94 | 990 | 10.53 |
| 31 | Tommy Vigorito | 1981-83,85 | 79 | 830 | 10.51 |
| 32 | Dana McLemore | 1982-87 | 152 | 1598 | 10.51 |
| 33 | **Tim Brown** | **1988-** | **233** | **2447** | **10.50** |
| 34 | Keith Moody | 1976-80 | 88 | 920 | 10.45 |
| 35 | Jake Scott | 1970-78 | 130 | 1357 | 10.44 |
| 36 | Gerald Wilhite | 1982-88 | 101 | 1054 | 10.44 |
| 37 | Mike Haynes | 1976-88 | 112 | 1168 | 10.43 |
| | Stanley Morgan | 1977-90 | 92 | 960 | 10.43 |
| 39 | **Brian Mitchell** | **1980-** | **147** | **1623** | **10.40** |
| 40 | Neal Colzie | 1975-82 | 170 | 1759 | 10.35 |
| | Greg Pruitt | 1973-84 | 194 | 2007 | 10.35 |
| | J.T. Smith | 1978-90 | 267 | 2764 | 10.35 |

**TOUCHDOWNS (3)**

| | | | |
|---|---|---|---|
| 1 | Jack Christiansen | 1951-58 | 8 |
| | Rick Upchurch | 1975-83 | 8 |
| 3 | Billy Johnson | 1974-88 | 6 |
| | **Dave Meggett** | **1989-** | **6** |
| | **Brian Mitchell** | **1990-** | **6** |
| 6 | Em Tunnell | 1948-61 | 5 |
| | Clarence Verdin | 1986-94 | 5 |
| | **Eric Metcalf** | **1989-** | **5** |
| 9 | Curly Oden | 1925-28,30-32 | 4 |
| | Speedy Duncan | 1964-74 | 4 |
| | Dick Christy | 1958,60-62 | 4 |
| | Lemar Parrish | 1970-81 | 4 |
| | Freddie Solomon | 1975-85 | 4 |
| | J.T. Smith | 1978-90 | 4 |
| | LeRoy Irvin | 1980-90 | 4 |
| | Dana McLemore | 1982-87 | 4 |
| | **Henry Ellard** | **1983-** | **4** |
| | Vai Sikahema | 1986-93 | 4 |
| 19 | Dick Todd | 1939-40,42,45-48 | 3 |
| | Ray McLean | 1940,42-47 | 3 |
| | Bill Dudley | 1942,45-51,53 | 3 |
| | Woodley Lewis | 1950-60 | 3 |
| | Ray Mathews | 1951-60 | 3 |
| | Yale Lary | 1952-53,56-64 | 3 |
| | Ollie Matson | 1952,54-66 | 3 |
| | Bert Zagers | 1955,57-58 | 3 |
| | Bobby Mitchell | 1958-68 | 3 |
| | Claude Gibson | 1961-65 | 3 |
| | Tom Watkins | 1961-65,67-68 | 3 |
| | Leroy Kelly | 1964-73 | 3 |
| | Bob Hayes | 1965-75 | 3 |
| | Rickie Harris | 1965-72 | 3 |
| | Butch Atkinson | 1968-77,79 | 3 |
| | John Staggers | 1970-75 | 3 |
| | Steve Schubert | 1974-79 | 3 |
| | Keith Moody | 1976-80 | 3 |
| | Dennis McKinnon | 1983-85,87-90 | 3 |
| | **Irving Fryar** | **1984-** | **3** |
| | Louis Lipps | 1984-92 | 3 |
| | **Mel Gray** | **1986-** | **3** |
| | **Kelvin Martin** | **1987-** | **3** |
| | **Kevin Williams** | **1993-** | **3** |

# KICKOFF RETURNS

**(148)**

| | | | |
|---|---|---|---|
| 1 | **Mel Gray** | **1986-** | **362** |
| 2 | Ron Smith | 1965-74 | 275 |
| 3 | Clarence Verdin | 1986-94 | 253 |
| 4 | Bruce Harper | 1977-84 | 243 |
| 5 | Vai Sikahema | 1986-93 | 235 |
| 6 | **Rod Woodson** | **1987-** | **220** |
| 7 | **Brian Mitchell** | **1990-** | **216** |
| 8 | **Dexter Carter** | **1990-** | **209** |
| 9 | Ron Brown | 1984-91 | 199 |
| 10 | Steve Odom | 1974-79 | 194 |
| 11 | Abe Woodson | 1958-68 | 193 |
| 12 | Dennis Gentry | 1982-92 | 192 |
| 13 | Al Carmichael | 1953-58,60-61 | 191 |
| 14 | Dick James | 1956-61 | 189 |
| | Larry Anderson | 1978-84 | 189 |
| 16 | Timmy Brown | 1959-68 | 184 |
| 17 | **Dave Meggett** | **1989-** | **184** |
| 18 | Speedy Duncan | 1964-74 | 180 |
| 19 | Stump Mitchell | 1981-89 | 177 |
| 20 | Mike Nelms | 1980-84 | 175 |
| 21 | **Bobby J. Edmonds** | **1986-89,95-** | **173** |
| 22 | Drew Hill | 1979-93 | 172 |
| 23 | Alvin Haymond | 1963-73 | 170 |
| 24 | **Nate Lewis** | **1990-** | **169** |
| 25 | Fulton Walker | 1981-86 | 167 |
| 26 | Darrin Nelson | 1982-92 | 163 |
| 27 | **Tyrone Hughes** | **1993-** | **159** |
| 28 | Eddie Payton | 1977-78,80-82 | 156 |
| 29 | Bobby Jancik | 1962-67 | 158 |
| 30 | Carl Garrett | 1969-77 | 154 |
| | Carl Roaches | 1980-85 | 154 |
| 32 | Kermit Alexander | 1963-73 | 153 |
| 33 | Bruce Laird | 1972-83 | 152 |
| 34 | Dino Hall | 1979-83 | 151 |
| | **Eric Metcalf** | **1989-** | **151** |
| 36 | Donnie Elder | 1985-86,89-91 | 150 |
| 37 | Albert Bentley | 1985-92 | 149 |
| 38 | Stanford Jennings | 1984-92 | 148 |
| 39 | **Deion Sanders** | **1989-** | **148** |

**YARDS (2950)**

| | | | |
|---|---|---|---|
| 1 | **Mel Gray** | **1986-** | **8833** |
| 2 | Ron Smith | 1965-74 | 6922 |
| 3 | Abe Woodson | 1958-66 | 5538 |
| 4 | Bruce Harper | 1977-84 | 5407 |
| 5 | Clarence Verdin | 1986-94 | 5252 |
| 6 | **Brian Mitchell** | **1990-** | **5002** |
| 7 | Vai Sikahema | 1986-93 | 4933 |
| 8 | **Rod Woodson** | **1987-** | **4894** |
| 9 | Al Carmichael | 1953-58,60-61 | 4798 |
| 10 | Timmy Brown | 1959-68 | 4781 |
| 11 | Dick James | 1956-61 | 4676 |
| 12 | Speedy Duncan | 1964-74 | 4539 |
| 13 | **Dexter Carter** | **1990-** | **4503** |
| 14 | Ron Brown | 1981-91 | 4493 |
| 15 | Alvin Haymond | 1963-73 | 4438 |
| 16 | Dennis Gentry | 1982-92 | 4353 |
| 17 | Steve Odom | 1974-79 | 4251 |
| 18 | Larry Anderson | 1978-84 | 4217 |
| 19 | Bobby Jancik | 1962-67 | 4185 |
| 20 | Mike Nelms | 1980-84 | 4128 |
| 21 | Stump Mitchell | 1981-89 | 4007 |
| 22 | **Dave Meggett** | **1989-** | **3953** |
| 23 | **Tyrone Hughes** | **1993-** | **3926** |
| 24 | **Nate Lewis** | **1990-** | **3825** |
| 25 | Joe Arenas | 1951-57 | 3798 |
| 26 | Fulton Walker | 1981-86 | 3769 |
| 27 | Ollie Matson | 1952, 54-66 | 3746 |
| 28 | Bruce Laird | 1972-83 | 3728 |
| 29 | Carl Garrett | 1969-77 | 3704 |
| 30 | **Bobby J. Edmonds** | **1986-89,95-** | **3696** |
| 31 | Darrin Nelson | 1982-92 | 3659 |
| 32 | Kermit Alexander | 1963-73 | 3586 |
| 33 | Buddy Young | 1947-55 | 3465 |
| 34 | Drew Hill | 1979-93 | 3460 |
| 35 | Clarence Childs | 1964-68 | 3454 |
| 36 | **Deion Sanders** | **1989-** | **3405** |
| 37 | Larry Marshall | 1972-78 | 3396 |
| 38 | Carl Roaches | 1980-85 | 3352 |
| 39 | Vic Washington | 1971-76 | 3341 |
| 40 | Woodley Lewis | 1950-60 | 3325 |
| 41 | Dino Hall | 1979-83 | 3185 |
| 42 | Albert Bentley | 1985-92 | 3192 |
| 43 | **Herschel Walker** | **1986-** | **3138** |
| 44 | Jon Arnett | 1957-66 | 3110 |
| 45 | Terry Metcalf | 1973-77,81 | 3087 |
| 46 | **Eric Metcalf** | **1989-** | **3084** |
| 47 | Herb Adderley | 1961-72 | 3080 |
| 48 | Bo Roberson | 1961-66 | 3057 |
| 49 | Donnie Elder | 1985-86,89-91 | 3040 |
| 50 | Abner Haynes | 1960-67 | 3025 |
| 51 | Bobby Humphery | 1981-90 | 2974 |
| 52 | Stanford Jennings | 1984-92 | 2965 |

**AVERAGE RETURNS (25.5)**

(Minimum 75 returns)

| | | | Ret. | Yards | Avg. |
|---|---|---|---|---|---|
| 1 | Gale Sayers | 1965-71 | 91 | 2781 | 30.56 |
| 2 | Lynn Chandnois | 1950-56 | 92 | 2720 | 29.57 |
| 3 | Abe Woodson | 1958-66 | 193 | 5538 | 28.69 |
| 4 | Buddy Young | 1947-55 | 125 | 3465 | 27.72 |
| 5 | Travis Williams | 1967-71 | 102 | 2801 | 27.46 |
| 6 | Joe Arenas | 1951-57 | 139 | 3798 | 27.32 |
| 7 | Clarence Davis | 1971-78 | 79 | 2140 | 27.09 |
| 8 | Steve Van Buren | 1944-51 | 76 | 2030 | 26.71 |
| 9 | Lenny Lyles | 1958-69 | 81 | 2161 | 26.68 |
| 10 | Mercury Morris | 1969-76 | 111 | 2947 | 26.55 |
| 11 | Bobby Jancik | 1962-67 | 158 | 4185 | 26.49 |
| 12 | Mel Renfro | 1964-77 | 85 | 2246 | 26.42 |
| 13 | Bobby Mitchell | 1958-68 | 102 | 2690 | 26.37 |
| 14 | Ollie Matson | 1952,54-66 | 143 | 3746 | 26.20 |
| 15 | Alvin Haymond | 1963-73 | 170 | 4438 | 26.11 |
| 16 | Noland Smith | 1967-69 | 82 | 2137 | 26.06 |
| 17 | Al Nelson | 1965-73 | 101 | 2625 | 25.99 |
| 18 | Timmy Brown | 1959-68 | 184 | 4781 | 25.98 |
| 19 | Vic Washington | 1971-76 | 129 | 3341 | 25.90 |
| 20 | Dave Hampton | 1966-76 | 113 | 2923 | 25.87 |
| 21 | Larry Garron | 1960-68 | 89 | 2299 | 25.83 |
| 22 | Clarence Childs | 1964-68 | 134 | 3454 | 25.78 |
| 23 | Terry Metcalf | 1973-77,81 | 120 | 3087 | 25.73 |
| 24 | Herb Adderley | 1961-72 | 120 | 3080 | 25.67 |
| 25 | Pat Studstill | 1961-62,64-72 | 75 | 1924 | 25.65 |
| 26 | Walter Roberts | 1964-67,69-70 | 107 | 2728 | 25.50 |

**TOUCHDOWNS (3)**

| | | | |
|---|---|---|---|
| 1 | Ollie Matson | 1952,54-66 | 6 |
| | Gale Sayers | 1965-71 | 6 |
| | Travis Williams | 1967-71 | 6 |
| | **Mel Gray** | **1986-** | **6** |
| 5 | Bobby Mitchell | 1958-68 | 5 |
| | Abe Woodson | 1958-66 | 5 |
| | Timmy Brown | 1959-68 | 5 |
| 8 | Buddy Young | 1947-55 | 4 |
| | Cecil Turner | 1968-73 | 4 |
| | Steve Van Buren | 1944-51 | 4 |
| | Ron Brown | 1984-91 | 4 |
| | **Andre Coleman** | **1994-** | **4** |
| 12 | Vitamin Smith | 1949-53 | 3 |
| | Lynn Chandnois | 1950-56 | 3 |
| | Lenny Lyles | 1958-69 | 3 |
| | Charley Warner | 1963-66 | 3 |
| | Ron Smith | 1965-74 | 3 |
| | Dave Hampton | 1969-76 | 3 |
| | Mercury Morris | 1969-76 | 3 |
| | Cullen Bryant | 1969-76 | 3 |
| | **Ray Clayborn** | **1977-88** | **3** |
| | Dave Williams | 1977-81 | 3 |
| | Dennis Gentry | 1982-92 | 3 |
| | **Deion Sanders** | **1989-** | **3** |
| | **Tyrone Hughes** | **1993-** | **3** |

Players active at the end of **1995** are shown in **bold face**.

# LIFETIME LEADERS
# POINTS AFTER TOUCHDOWNS

### ATTEMPTS (280)

| | | | |
|---|---|---|---|
| 1 | George Blanda | 1949-58,60-75 | 959 |
| 2 | Lou Groza | 1946-59,61-67 | 834 |
| 3 | Jan Stenerud | 1967-85 | 601 |
| 4 | Pat Leahy | 1974-91 | 584 |
| 5 | Jim Bakken | 1962-78 | 553 |
| 6 | Jim Turner | 1964-79 | 544 |
| 7 | **Nick Lowery** | **1978,80-** | **541** |
| 8 | Fred Cox | 1963-77 | 539 |
| | Jim Breech | 1979-92 | 539 |
| 10 | **Matt Bahr** | **1979-** | **534** |
| 11 | **Norm Johnson** | **1982-** | **521** |
| 12 | Chris Bahr | 1976-89 | 519 |
| 13 | Mark Moseley | 1970-86 | 511 |
| 14 | **Eddie Murray** | **1980-** | **503** |
| 15 | Ray Wersching | 1973-87 | 477 |
| 16 | Garo Yepremian | 1966-67,70-81 | 464 |
| 17 | Don Cockroft | 1968-80 | 457 |
| 18 | **Gary Anderson** | **1982-** | **453** |
| 19 | **Morten Andersen** | **1982-** | **448** |
| 20 | Sam Baker | 1953,56-69 | 444 |
| 21 | Rafael Septien | 1977-86 | 433 |
| 22 | Lou Michaels | 1958-69,71 | 402 |
| 23 | **Kevin Butler** | **1985-** | **397** |
| 24 | Bobby Walston | 1951-62 | 384 |
| 25 | Bruce Gossett | 1964-74 | 383 |
| 26 | **Fuad Reveiz** | **1985-88,90-** | **378** |
| 27 | **Al Del Greco** | **1984-** | **376** |
| 28 | Roy Gerela | 1969-79 | 365 |
| 29 | Tony Franklin | 1979-88 | 355 |
| 30 | Pete Gogolak | 1964-74 | 354 |
| 31 | Gino Cappelletti | 1960-70 | 353 |
| | Rolf Benirschke | 1977-86 | 353 |
| 33 | Ben Agajanian | 1945,47-49,53-57,60-62,64 | 351 |
| 34 | Tommy Davis | 1959-69 | 350 |
| 35 | Mike Clark | 1963-71,73 | 338 |
| 36 | Bob Waterfield | 1945-52 | 336 |
| 37 | Errol Mann | 1968-78 | 333 |
| 38 | Bob Thomas | 1975-86 | 330 |
| 39 | **Tony Zendejas** | **1985-** | **327** |
| 40 | John Smith | 1974-83 | 326 |
| 41 | Mike Lansford | 1982-90 | 315 |
| 42 | Mike Cofer | 1987-93,95 | 312 |
| 43 | Gordy Soltau | 1945-52 | 302 |
| 44 | Mike Mercer | 1950-58 | 295 |
| 45 | Rich Karlis | 1982-90 | 294 |
| 46 | Toni Fritsch | 1971-73,75-81 | 291 |
| 47 | Tom Dempsey | 1969-79 | 282 |
| 48 | Chip Lohmiller | 1988-95 | 280 |

### GOOD (270)

| | | | |
|---|---|---|---|
| 1 | George Blanda | 1949-58,60-75 | 943 |
| 2 | Lou Groza | 1946-59,61-67 | 810 |
| 3 | Jan Stenerud | 1967-85 | 580 |
| 4 | Pat Leahy | 1974-91 | 558 |
| 5 | **Nick Lowery** | **1978-** | **536** |
| 6 | Jim Bakken | 1962-78 | 534 |
| 7 | **Matt Bahr** | **1979-** | **522** |
| 8 | Jim Turner | 1964-79 | 521 |
| 9 | Fred Cox | 1963-77 | 519 |
| 10 | Jim Breech | 1979-92 | 517 |
| 11 | **Norm Johnson** | **1982-** | **515** |
| 12 | Mark Moseley | 1970-86 | 511 |
| 13 | **Eddie Murray** | **1980-** | **498** |
| 14 | Chris Bahr | 1976-89 | 490 |
| 15 | Ray Wersching | 1973-87 | 456 |
| 16 | **Gary Anderson** | **1982-** | **448** |
| 17 | Garo Yepremian | 1966-67,70-81 | 444 |
| 18 | **Morten Andersen** | **1982** | **441** |
| 19 | Don Cockroft | 1968-80 | 432 |
| 20 | Sam Baker | 1953,56-59 | 428 |
| 21 | Rafael Septien | 1977-86 | 420 |
| 22 | **Kevin Butler** | **1985-** | **387** |
| 23 | Lou Michaels | 1958-69,71 | 386 |
| 24 | Bruce Gossett | 1964-74 | 374 |
| 25 | **Fuad Reveiz** | **1985-88,90-** | **367** |
| 26 | **Al Del Greco** | **1984-** | **368** |
| 27 | Bobby Walston | 1951-62 | 365 |
| 28 | Roy Gerela | 1969-79 | 351 |
| 29 | Tommy Davis | 1959-69 | 348 |
| 30 | Pete Gogolak | 1969-74 | 344 |
| 31 | Ben Agajanian | 1945,47-49,53-57,60-62,64 | 343 |
| 32 | Gino Cappelletti | 1960-70 | 342 |
| 33 | Tony Franklin | 1979-88 | 341 |
| 34 | Rolf Benirschke | 1977-86 | 328 |
| 35 | Mike Clark | 1968-71,73 | 325 |
| 36 | **Tony Zendejas** | **1985-** | **316** |
| 37 | Bob Waterfield | 1945-52 | 315 |
| | Errol Mann | 1968-78 | 315 |
| | Mike Lansford | 1982-90 | 315 |
| 40 | John Smith | 1974-83 | 308 |
| 41 | Bob Thomas | 1975-86 | 303 |
| 42 | Mike Cofer | 1987-93,95 | 303 |
| 43 | Mike Mercer | 1950-58 | 288 |
| 44 | Gordy Soltau | 1945-52 | 284 |
| 45 | Rich Karlis | 1982-90 | 283 |
| 46 | Toni Fritsch | 1971-73,75-81 | 279 |
| 47 | Chip Lohmiller | 1988-95 | 273 |
| 48 | Scott Norwood | 1985-91 | 271 |

### PERCENT MADE (96.02)
(Minimum 200 attempts)

| | | | Good | Att. | Pct. |
|---|---|---|---|---|---|
| 1 | Tommy Davis | 1959-69 | 348 | 350 | 99.43 |
| 2 | **Nick Lowery** | **1978-** | **536** | **541** | **99.08** |
| 3 | **Eddie Murray** | **1980-** | **498** | **503** | **99.01** |
| 4 | **Gary Anderson** | **1982-** | **448** | **453** | **98.90** |
| 5 | **Norm Johnson** | **1982-** | **515** | **521** | **98.85** |
| 6 | **Chris Jacke** | **1989-** | **250** | **253** | **98.81** |
| 7 | Mick Luckhurst | 1981-87 | 213 | 216 | 98.61 |
| 8 | **Morten Andersen** | **1982-** | **441** | **448** | **98.44** |
| 9 | **Pete Stoyanovich** | **1989-** | **246** | **250** | **98.40** |
| 10 | George Blanda | 1949-58,60-75 | 943 | 959 | 98.33 |
| 11 | **Steve Christie** | **1990-** | **199** | **203** | **98.03** |
| 12 | Danny Villanueva | 1960-67 | 236 | 241 | 97.92 |
| 13 | **Al Del Greco** | **1984-** | **368** | **376** | **97.87** |
| 14 | **Matt Bahr** | **1979-** | **522** | **534** | **97.75** |
| 15 | **Greg Davis** | **1987-** | **216** | **221** | **97.74** |
| 16 | Ben Agajanian | 1945,47-49,53-57,60-62,64 | 343 | 351 | 97.72 |
| 17 | Bruce Gossett | 1964-74 | 374 | 383 | 97.65 |
| 18 | Mike Mercer | 1950-58 | 288 | 295 | 97.62 |
| 19 | **Jeff Jaeger** | **1987,89-** | **244** | **250** | **97.60** |
| 20 | Chip Lohmiller | 1988-95 | 273 | 280 | 97.50 |
| 21 | Scott Norwood | 1985-91 | 271 | 278 | 97.48 |
| | **Kevin Butler** | **1985-** | **387** | **397** | **97.48** |
| 23 | **Dean Biasucci** | **1984,86-** | **268** | **275** | **97.45** |
| 24 | Pete Gogolak | 1964-74 | 344 | 354 | 97.18 |
| 25 | Lou Groza | 1946-59,61-69 | 810 | 834 | 97.12 |
| 26 | **Fuad Reveiz** | **1985-88,90-91** | **367** | **378** | **97.09** |
| 27 | Pat Harder | 1946-53 | 198 | 204 | 97.05 |
| 28 | Mike Cofer | 1987-93 | 294 | 303 | 97.03 |
| 29 | Rafael Septien | 1977-86 | 420 | 433 | 97.00 |
| 30 | Pat Summerall | 1952-61 | 257 | 265 | 96.98 |
| 31 | Mike Lansford | 1982-90 | 315 | 325 | 96.92 |
| 32 | Gino Cappelletti | 1960-70 | 342 | 353 | 96.88 |
| 33 | **Tony Zendejas** | **1985-** | **316** | **327** | **96.64** |
| 34 | Nick Mike-Mayer | 1973-82 | 226 | 234 | 96.58 |
| 35 | Jim Bakken | 1962-78 | 534 | 553 | 96.56 |
| 36 | Jan Stenerud | 1967-85 | 580 | 601 | 96.51 |
| 37 | Gene Mingo | 1960-67,69-70 | 215 | 223 | 96.41 |
| 38 | Sam Baker | 1953,56-59 | 428 | 444 | 96.39 |
| 39 | Fred Cox | 1963-77 | 519 | 539 | 96.28 |
| 40 | Rich Karlis | 1982-90 | 283 | 294 | 96.26 |
| 41 | Roy Gerela | 1969-79 | 351 | 365 | 96.16 |
| 42 | Mike Clark | 1963-71,73 | 325 | 338 | 96.15 |
| 43 | Don Chandler | 1956-67 | 248 | 258 | 96.12 |
| 44 | Tony Franklin | 1978-88 | 341 | 355 | 96.06 |
| 45 | Bobby Howfield | 1968-74 | 193 | 201 | 96.02 |

# FIELD GOALS

### ATTEMPTS (170)

| | | | |
|---|---|---|---|
| 1 | George Blanda | 1949-58,60-75 | 638 |
| 2 | Jan Stenerud | 1967-85 | 558 |
| 3 | Jim Turner | 1964-79 | 488 |
| 4 | Lou Groza | 1946-59,61-67 | 481 |
| 5 | Mark Moseley | 1970-86 | 457 |
| 6 | Fred Cox | 1963-77 | 455 |
| 7 | **Nick Lowery** | **1978-** | **455** |
| 8 | Jim Bakken | 1962-78 | 447 |
| 9 | **Eddie Murray** | **1980-** | **428** |
| 10 | **Morten Andersen** | **1982-** | **426** |
| | Pat Leahy | 1974-91 | 426 |
| 12 | **Gary Anderson** | **1982-** | **425** |
| 13 | **Matt Bahr** | **1979-** | **415** |
| 14 | Chris Bahr | 1976-89 | 381 |
| 15 | **Norm Johnson** | **1982-** | **366** |
| 16 | Bruce Gossett | 1964-74 | 360 |
| 17 | Lou Michaels | 1958-69,71 | 341 |
| 18 | Jim Breech | 1979-92 | 340 |
| 19 | Gino Cappelletti | 1960-70 | 333 |
| | **Kevin Butler** | **1985-** | **333** |
| 21 | Ray Wersching | 1973-87 | 329 |
| 22 | Don Cockroft | 1968-80 | 328 |
| 23 | Sam Baker | 1953,56-69 | 316 |
| 24 | Garo Yepremian | 1966-67,70-81 | 313 |
| 25 | Roy Gerela | 1969-79 | 306 |
| 26 | Pete Gogolak | 1964-74 | 294 |
| 27 | **Al Del Greco** | **1984-** | **279** |
| 28 | Tommy Davis | 1959-69 | 276 |
| | Errol Mann | 1968-78 | 276 |
| 30 | Tony Franklin | 1979-88 | 264 |
| 31 | **Dean Biasucci** | **1984,86-** | **262** |
| 32 | Chip Lohmiller | 1988-95 | 259 |
| 33 | Tom Dempsey | 1969-79 | 258 |
| 34 | Rafael Septien | 1977-86 | 256 |
| 35 | **Tony Zendejas** | **1985-** | **252** |
| 36 | **Fuad Reveiz** | **1985-88,90-** | **250** |
| | **Greg Davis** | **1987-** | **250** |
| 38 | Horst Muhlmann | 1969-77 | 239 |
| | Bob Thomas | 1975-86 | 239 |
| | Rich Karlis | 1982-90 | 239 |
| 41 | Mike Clark | 1963-71,73 | 232 |
| 42 | Joe Danelo | 1975-84 | 228 |
| 43 | **Jeff Jaeger** | **1987,89-** | **226** |
| 44 | Toni Fritsch | 1971-73,75-81 | 224 |
| 45 | **Pete Stoyanovich** | **1989-** | **222** |
| 46 | Gene Mingo | 1960-67,69-70 | 219 |
| 47 | Mike Lansford | 1982-90 | 217 |
| 48 | Pat Summerall | 1952-61 | 212 |
| 49 | Rolf Benirschke | 1977-86 | 208 |
| 50 | Ben Agajanian | 1945,47-49,53-57,60-62,64 | 204 |
| | Nick Mike-Mayer | 1973-82 | 204 |
| 52 | Mike Cofer | 1987-93,95 | 201 |
| 53 | **Chris Jacke** | **1989-** | **197** |
| 54 | Chester Marcol | 1972-80 | 196 |
| 55 | Mike Mercer | 1961-70 | 193 |
| 56 | Jim Martin | 1950-61,63-64 | 192 |
| 57 | **John Carney** | **1988-** | **191** |
| | John Smith | 1974-83 | 191 |
| 59 | Mac Percival | 1967-74 | 190 |
| 60 | Neil O' Donoghue | 1977-85 | 189 |
| 61 | Raul Allegre | 1983-91 | 186 |
| 62 | Scott Norwood | 1985-91 | 184 |
| 63 | David Ray | 1969-74 | 178 |
| 64 | Curt Knight | 1969-73 | 175 |
| | David Treadwell | 1989-94 | 175 |
| 66 | Efren Herrera | 1974,76-82 | 171 |
| 67 | Bobby Howfield | 1968-74 | 166 |
| | Roger Ruzek | 1987-93 | 166 |

### GOOD (121)

| | | | |
|---|---|---|---|
| 1 | Jan Stenerud | 1967-85 | 373 |
| 2 | **Nick Lowery** | **1978-** | **366** |
| 3 | George Blanda | 1949-58,60-75 | 335 |
| 4 | **Morten Andersen** | **1982-** | **333** |
| 5 | **Gary Anderson** | **1982-** | **331** |
| 6 | **Eddie Murray** | **1960-** | **325** |
| 7 | Pat Leahy | 1974-91 | 304 |
| 8 | Jim Turner | 1964-79 | 304 |
| 9 | Mark Moseley | 1970-86 | 300 |
| | **Matt Bahr** | **1979-** | **300** |
| 11 | Jim Bakken | 1962-78 | 282 |
| | Fred Cox | 1963-77 | 282 |
| 13 | **Norm Johnson** | **1982-** | **277** |
| 14 | Lou Groza | 1946-59,61-67 | 264 |
| 15 | Jim Breech | 1979-92 | 243 |
| | **Kevin Butler** | **1985-** | **243** |
| 17 | Chris Bahr | 1976-89 | 241 |
| 18 | Ray Wersching | 1973-87 | 222 |
| 19 | Bruce Gossett | 1964-74 | 219 |
| 20 | Don Cockroft | 1968-80 | 216 |
| 21 | Garo Yepremian | 1966-67,70-81 | 210 |
| 22 | **Al Del Greco** | **1984-** | **204** |
| 23 | **Fuad Reveiz** | **1985-88,90** | **188** |
| 24 | Lou Michaels | 1958-69,71 | 187 |
| 25 | **Tony Zendejas** | **1985-** | **186** |
| 26 | **Dean Biasucci** | **1984,86-** | **185** |
| 27 | Roy Gerela | 1969-79 | 184 |
| 28 | Chip Lohmiller | 1988-95 | 183 |
| 29 | Rafael Septien | 1977-86 | 180 |
| 30 | Sam Baker | 1953,56-69 | 179 |
| 31 | Errol Mann | 1968-78 | 177 |
| | Tony Franklin | 1979-88 | 177 |
| 33 | Gino Cappelletti | 1960-70 | 176 |
| | **Pete Stoyanovich** | **1989-** | **176** |
| 35 | Pete Gogolak | 1964-74 | 173 |
| 36 | Rich Karlis | 1982-90 | 172 |
| | **Greg Davis** | **1987-** | **172** |
| 38 | **Jeff Jaeger** | **1987,89-91** | **166** |
| 39 | Tom Dempsey | 1968-79 | 159 |
| 40 | Mike Lansford | 1982-90 | 158 |
| 41 | Horst Muhlmann | 1969-77 | 154 |
| 42 | Toni Fritsch | 1971-73,75-81 | 153 |
| 43 | **Chris Jacke** | **1989-** | **152** |
| | **John Carney** | **1988-** | **152** |
| 45 | Bob Thomas | 1975-86 | 151 |
| 46 | Rolf Benirschke | 1977-86 | 146 |
| 47 | **Steve Christie** | **1990-** | **140** |
| 48 | Raul Allegre | 1983-91 | 137 |
| 49 | David Treadwell | 1989-94 | 135 |
| 50 | Mike Clark | 1963-71,73 | 133 |
| | Joe Danelo | 1975-84 | 133 |
| | Scott Norwood | 1985-91 | 133 |
| 53 | Tommy Davis | 1959-69 | 130 |
| 54 | Mike Cofer | 1987-93,95 | 133 |
| 55 | John Smith | 1974-83 | 128 |
| 56 | Chester Marcol | 1972-80 | 121 |

### PERCENT MADE (58.38)
(Minimum 100 attempts)

| | | | Good | Att. | Pct. |
|---|---|---|---|---|---|
| 1 | **Matt Stover** | **1991-** | **108** | **134** | **80.60** |
| 2 | **Nick Lowery** | **1978-** | **366** | **455** | **80.44** |
| 3 | **John Carney** | **1988-** | **152** | **191** | **79.59** |
| 4 | **Pete Stoyanovich** | **1989-** | **176** | **222** | **79.28** |
| 5 | **Steve Christie** | **1990-** | **140** | **177** | **79.10** |
| 6 | **Jason Elam** | **1993-** | **87** | **110** | **79.09** |
| 7 | **John Kasay** | **1991-** | **108** | **138** | **78.26** |
| 8 | **Morten Andersen** | **1982-** | **333** | **426** | **78.17** |
| 9 | **Gary Anderson** | **1982-** | **331** | **425** | **77.88** |
| 10 | **Jason Hanson** | **1992-** | **101** | **130** | **77.69** |
| 11 | **Chris Jacke** | **1989-** | **152** | **197** | **77.16** |
| 12 | David Treadwell | 1989-94 | 135 | 175 | 77.14 |
| 13 | **Eddie Murray** | **1980-** | **325** | **428** | **75.93** |
| 14 | **Norm Johnson** | **1982-** | **277** | **366** | **75.68** |
| 15 | Donald Igwebuike | 1985-90 | 108 | 143 | 75.52 |
| 16 | **Fuad Reveiz** | **1985-88,90-** | **188** | **250** | **75.20** |
| 17 | **Tony Zendejas** | **1985-** | **186** | **252** | **73.81** |
| 18 | Raul Allegre | 1983-91 | 137 | 186 | 73.66 |
| 19 | Paul McFadden | 1984-89 | 120 | 163 | 73.62 |
| 20 | **Jeff Jaeger** | **1987,89-** | **166** | **226** | **73.45** |
| 21 | **Al Del Greco** | **1984-** | **204** | **279** | **73.12** |
| 22 | **Kevin Butler** | **1985-** | **243** | **333** | **72.97** |
| 23 | Mike Lansford | 1982-90 | 158 | 217 | 72.81 |
| 24 | **Matt Bahr** | **1979-** | **300** | **415** | **72.29** |
| | Roger Ruzek | 1987-93 | 120 | 166 | 72.29 |
| 26 | Scott Norwood | 1985-91 | 133 | 184 | 72.28 |
| 27 | Rich Karlis | 1982-90 | 172 | 239 | 71.96 |
| 28 | Jim Breech | 1979-92 | 243 | 340 | 71.47 |
| 29 | Chip Lohmiller | 1988-95 | 183 | 259 | 70.66 |
| 30 | Pat Leahy | 1974-91 | 304 | 426 | 71.36 |
| 31 | **Dean Biasucci** | **1984,86-** | **185** | **262** | **70.61** |
| 32 | Rafael Septien | 1977-86 | 180 | 256 | 70.31 |
| 33 | Rolf Benirschke | 1977-86 | 146 | 208 | 70.19 |
| 34 | Mick Luckhurst | 1981-87 | 115 | 164 | 70.12 |
| 35 | **Greg Davis** | **1987-** | **172** | **250** | **68.80** |
| 36 | Ali Haji-Sheikh | 1983-87 | 76 | 111 | 68.47 |
| 37 | Toni Fritsch | 1971-73,75-81 | 153 | 224 | 68.30 |
| 38 | Efren Herrera | 1974,76-82 | 116 | 171 | 67.84 |
| 39 | Uwe von Schamann | 1979-84 | 101 | 149 | 67.79 |
| 40 | Ray Wersching | 1973-87 | 222 | 329 | 67.48 |
| 41 | Mike Cofer | 1987-93,95 | 133 | 201 | 66.17 |
| 42 | Garo Yepremian | 1966-67,70-81 | 210 | 313 | 67.09 |
| 43 | Tony Franklin | 1979-88 | 177 | 264 | 67.05 |
| 44 | John Smith | 1974-83 | 128 | 191 | 67.02 |
| 45 | Jan Stenerud | 1967-85 | 373 | 558 | 66.85 |
| 46 | Don Cockroft | 1968-80 | 216 | 328 | 65.85 |
| 47 | Mark Moseley | 1970-86 | 300 | 457 | 65.65 |
| 48 | Rick Danmeier | 1978-82 | 78 | 120 | 65.00 |
| 49 | Benny Ricardo | 1976-84 | 92 | 142 | 64.79 |
| 50 | Horst Muhlmann | 1969-77 | 154 | 239 | 64.44 |
| 51 | Errol Mann | 1968-78 | 177 | 276 | 64.13 |
| 52 | Chris Bahr | 1976-89 | 241 | 381 | 63.25 |
| 53 | Bob Thomas | 1975-86 | 151 | 239 | 63.18 |
| 54 | Jim Bakken | 1962-78 | 282 | 447 | 63.09 |
| 55 | Jim Turner | 1964-79 | 304 | 488 | 62.30 |
| 56 | Fred Cox | 1963-77 | 282 | 455 | 61.98 |
| 57 | David Ray | 1969-74 | 110 | 178 | 61.80 |
| 58 | Chester Marcol | 1972-80 | 121 | 196 | 61.73 |
| 59 | Tom Dempsey | 1968-79 | 159 | 258 | 61.63 |
| 60 | Bruce Gossett | 1964-74 | 219 | 360 | 60.83 |
| 61 | Frank Corral | 1978-81 | 75 | 124 | 60.48 |
| 62 | John Leypoldt | 1971-78 | 93 | 154 | 60.39 |
| 63 | Roy Gerela | 1969-79 | 184 | 306 | 60.13 |
| 64 | Neil O' Donoghue | 1977-85 | 112 | 189 | 59.26 |
| 65 | Toni Linhart | 1972,74-79 | 75 | 127 | 59.06 |
| 66 | Bobby Howfield | 1968-74 | 98 | 166 | 59.04 |
| 67 | Pete Gogolak | 1964-74 | 173 | 294 | 58.84 |
| 68 | Dennis Partee | 1968-75 | 71 | 121 | 58.68 |
| 69 | Don Chandler | 1956-67 | 94 | 161 | 58.38 |

Players active at the end of 1995 are shown in **bold face.**

# LIFETIME LEADERS

## POINTS

**(392)**

| | | | |
|---|---|---|---|
| 1 | George Blanda | 1949-58, 60-75 | 2002 |
| 2 | Jan Stenerud | 1967-85 | 1699 |
| **3** | **Nick Lowery** | **1978-** | **1634** |
| 4 | Lou Groza | 1946-59, 61-67 | 1608 |
| 5 | Pat Leahy | 1974-91 | 1470 |
| **6** | **Eddie Murray** | **1980-** | **1464** |
| **7** | **Gary Anderson** | **1982-** | **1441** |
| **8** | **Morten Andersen** | **1982-** | **1440** |
| 9 | Jim Turner | 1964-79 | 1439 |
| **10** | **Matt Bahr** | **1979-** | **1422** |
| 11 | Mark Moseley | 1970-86 | 1382 |
| 12 | Jim Bakken | 1962-78 | 1380 |
| 13 | Fred Cox | 1963-77 | 1365 |
| **14** | **Norm Johnson** | **1982-** | **1346** |
| 15 | Jim Breech | 1979-92 | 1246 |
| 16 | Chris Bahr | 1976-89 | 1213 |
| 17 | Gino Cappelletti | 1960-70 | 1130 |
| 18 | Ray Wersching | 1973-87 | 1122 |
| **19** | **Kevin Butler** | **1985-** | **1116** |
| 20 | Don Cockroft | 1968-80 | 1080 |
| 21 | Garo Yepremian | 1966-67, 70-81 | 1074 |
| 22 | Bruce Gossett | 1964-74 | 1031 |
| **23** | **Al Del Greco** | **1984-** | **980** |
| 24 | Sam Baker | 1953, 56-69 | 977 |
| 25 | Rafael Septien | 1977-86 | 960 |
| 26 | Lou Michaels | 1958-69, 71 | 955 |
| **27** | **Jerry Rice** | **1985-** | **940** |
| **28** | **Fuad Reveiz** | **1985-88,90-** | **921** |
| 29 | Roy Gerela | 1969-79 | 903 |
| 30 | Bobby Walston | 1951-62 | 881 |
| **31** | **Tony Zendejas** | **1985-** | **874** |
| 32 | Tony Franklin | 1979-88 | 872 |
| 33 | Pete Gogolak | 1964-74 | 863 |
| 34 | Errol Mann | 1968-78 | 846 |
| 35 | Don Hutson | 1935-45 | 823 |
| | **Dean Biasucci** | **1984,86-** | **823** |
| 37 | Chip Lohmiller | 1988-95 | 822 |
| 38 | Rich Karlis | 1982-90 | 799 |
| 39 | Mike Lansford | 1982-90 | 789 |
| **40** | **Pete Stoyanovich** | **1989-** | **774** |
| 41 | Rolf Benirschke | 1977-86 | 766 |
| 42 | Paul Hornung | 1957-62, 64-66 | 760 |
| 43 | Toni Fritsch | 1971-73, 75-82 | 758 |
| 44 | Jim Brown | 1957-65 | 756 |
| | Bob Thomas | 1975-86 | 756 |
| 46 | **Marcus Allen** | **1982-** | **752** |
| 47 | Walter Payton | 1975-87 | 750 |
| **48** | **Jeff Jaeger** | **1987-** | **742** |
| 49 | Tommy Davis | 1959-69 | 738 |
| **50** | **Greg Davis** | **1987-** | **733** |
| 51 | Tom Dempsey | 1969-79 | 729 |
| 52 | Mike Clark | 1963-71,73 | 724 |
| 53 | Mike Cofer | 1987-93,95 | 711 |
| 54 | Horst Muhlmann | 1967-77 | 707 |
| **55** | **Chris Jacke** | **1989-** | **706** |
| 56 | John Riggins | 1971-79,81-85 | 696 |
| 57 | John Smith | 1974-83 | 692 |
| 58 | Lenny Moore | 1956-67 | 678 |
| 59 | Scott Norwood | 1985-91 | 670 |
| 60 | Ben Agajanian | 1945,47-49,53-57, 60-62,64 | 655 |
| **61** | **John Carney** | **1988-** | **651** |
| 62 | Gordy Soltau | 1950-58 | 644 |
| 63 | Joe Danelo | 1975-84 | 639 |
| 64 | Gene Mingo | 1960-67,69-70 | 629 |
| **65** | **Steve Christie** | **1990-** | **619** |
| 66 | Steve Largent | 1976-89 | 608 |
| 67 | Efren Herrera | 1974,76-82 | 604 |
| 68 | Franco Harris | 1972-84 | 600 |
| | **Emmitt Smith** | **1990-** | **600** |
| 70 | Mike Mercer | 1961-70 | 594 |
| 71 | Raul Allegre | 1983-91 | 594 |
| 72 | David Treadwell | 1989-94 | 587 |
| 73 | Neil O'Donoghue | 1977-85 | 576 |
| | Eric Dickerson | 1983-93 | 576 |
| 75 | Bob Waterfield | 1945-52 | 573 |
| 76 | Nick Mike-Mayer | 1973-82 | 571 |
| 77 | Roger Ruzek | 1987-93 | 566 |
| 78 | Pat Summerall | 1952-61 | 563 |
| 79 | Jim Taylor | 1958-67 | 558 |
| | Mick Luckhurst | 1981-87 | 558 |
| 81 | Tony Dorsett | 1977-88 | 552 |
| 82 | Bobby Mitchell | 1958-68 | 546 |
| 83 | Leroy Kelly | 1964-73 | 540 |
| | Charley Taylor | 1964-75,77 | 540 |
| | Uwe von Schamann | 1979-84 | 540 |
| 86 | Doak Walker | 1950-55 | 534 |
| 87 | Don Maynard | 1958, 60-67 | 532 |
| 88 | Chester Marcol | 1972-80 | 525 |
| 89 | Lance Alworth | 1962-72 | 524 |
| 90 | Paul McFadden | 1984-89 | 520 |
| 91 | Ottis Anderson | 1979-92 | 518 |
| 92 | Paul Warfield | 1964-74, 76-77 | 516 |
| 93 | Joe Perry | 1948-63 | 513 |
| 94 | Tommy McDonald | 1957-68 | 510 |
| | Pete Johnson | 1977-84 | 510 |
| | Mark Clayton | 1983-93 | 510 |
| 97 | David Ray | 1969-74 | 497 |
| 98 | Fred Cone | 1951-57, 60 | 494 |
| 99 | Art Powell | 1959-67 | 492 |
| 100 | Danny Villanueva | 1960-67 | 491 |
| 101 | Bobby Howfield | 1968-74 | 487 |
| **102** | **Herschel Walker** | **1986-** | **486** |
| 103 | Bill Dudley | 1942, 45-51, 53 | 484 |
| | Frank Gifford | 1952-60, 62-64 | 484 |
| 105 | John Leypoldt | 1971-78 | 482 |
| **106** | **Barry Sanders** | **1989-** | **480** |
| 107 | Ken Strong | 1929-35, 39, 44-47 | 479 |
| 108 | Donald Igwebuike | 1985-90 | 477 |
| 109 | Curt Knight | 1969-73 | 475 |
| 110 | Harold Carmichael | 1971-84 | 474 |
| | James Brooks | 1981-92 | 474 |
| 112 | Mac Percival | 1967-74 | 466 |
| 113 | Steve Van Buren | 1944-51 | 464 |
| 114 | Fred Biletnikoff | 1965-78 | 462 |
| 115 | Bill Brown | 1961-74 | 456 |
| | Bob Hayes | 1965-75 | 456 |
| | O.J. Simpson | 1969-79 | 456 |
| | Chuck Foreman | 1973-80 | 456 |
| | Harold Jackson | 1968-83 | 456 |
| | James Lofton | 1978-93 | 456 |
| 121 | Nat Moore | 1974-86 | 450 |
| **122** | **Jason Hanson** | **1992-** | **448** |
| 123 | Benny Ricardo | 1976, 78-84 | 447 |
| **124** | **John Kasay** | **1991-** | **446** |
| 125 | John David Crow | 1958-68 | 444 |
| | Chuck Muncie | 1976-84 | 444 |
| | Earl Campbell | 1978-85 | 444 |
| **128** | **Thurman Thomas** | **1988-** | **442** |
| 129 | Ollie Matson | 1952, 54-66 | 438 |
| | Stanley Morgan | 1977-90 | 438 |
| | Roger Craig | 1983-93 | 438 |
| 132 | Jim Martin | 1950-61, 63-64 | 434 |
| 133 | Wesley Walker | 1977-89 | 428 |
| | Neal Anderson | 1986-93 | 426 |
| 135 | Toni Linhart | 1972, 74-79 | 425 |
| 136 | Gary Collins | 1962-71 | 420 |
| | **Andre Reed** | **1985-** | **420** |
| 138 | Paddy Driscoll | 1920-29 | 418 |
| 139 | Ward Cuff | 1937-47 | 417 |
| 140 | Abner Haynes | 1960-67 | 414 |
| | Roy Green | 1979-92 | 414 |
| | Gerald Riggs | 1982-91 | 414 |
| 143 | Raymond Berry | 1955-67 | 408 |
| | Larry Csonka | 1968-74, 76-79 | 408 |
| | **Art Monk** | **1980-** | **408** |
| **146** | **Cris Carter** | **1987-** | **406** |
| 147 | Elroy Hirsch | 1946-57 | 405 |
| 148 | Cliff Branch | 1972-85 | 402 |
| 149 | Jimmy Orr | 1958-70 | 396 |
| | Wendell Tyler | 1977-86 | 396 |
| | Sterling Sharpe | 1988-94 | 396 |
| | **Earnest Byner** | **1984-** | **396** |
| 153 | Billy Cannon | 1960-70 | 392 |

## INTERCEPTIONS

**(32)**

| | | | |
|---|---|---|---|
| 1 | Paul Krause | 1964-79 | 81 |
| 2 | Emlen Tunnell | 1948-61 | 79 |
| 3 | Night Train Lane | 1952-65 | 68 |
| 4 | Ken Riley | 1969-83 | 65 |
| **5** | **Ronnie Lott** | **1981-** | **63** |
| 6 | Dick LeBeau | 1959-72 | 62 |
| | Dave Brown | 1975-89 | 62 |
| 8 | Emmitt Thomas | 1966-81 | 58 |
| 9 | Bobby Boyd | 1960-68 | 57 |
| | Mel Blount | 1970-83 | 57 |
| | Everson Walls | 1981-93 | 57 |
| 12 | Pat Fischer | 1961-77 | 56 |
| | Lem Barney | 1967-77 | 56 |
| 14 | Donnie Shell | 1974-87 | 55 |
| 15 | Willie Brown | 1963-78 | 54 |
| 16 | Jack Butler | 1951-59 | 52 |
| | Bobby Dillon | 1952-59 | 52 |
| | Jimmy Patton | 1955-66 | 52 |
| | Larry Wilson | 1960-72 | 52 |
| | Mel Renfro | 1964-77 | 52 |
| 21 | Bobby Bryant | 1968-80 | 51 |
| 22 | Yale Lary | 1952-53, 56-64 | 50 |
| | Don Burroughs | 1955-64 | 50 |
| | Deron Cherry | 1981-91 | 50 |
| 25 | Ken Houston | 1967-80 | 49 |
| | Jake Scott | 1970-78 | 49 |
| 27 | Richie Petitbon | 1959-73 | 48 |
| | Willie Wood | 1960-70 | 48 |
| | Herb Adderley | 1961-72 | 48 |
| | Dave Grayson | 1961-70 | 48 |
| | Dave Waymer | 1980-92 | 48 |
| 32 | Jimmy Johnson | 1961-76 | 47 |
| | Lemar Parrish | 1970-82 | 47 |
| | John Harris | 1978-88 | 47 |
| 35 | Jack Christiansen | 1951-58 | 46 |
| | Dave Whitsell | 1958-69 | 46 |
| | Ed Meador | 1959-70 | 46 |
| | Goose Gonsoulin | 1960-67 | 46 |
| | Mike Haynes | 1976-89 | 46 |
| 40 | Erich Barnes | 1958-71 | 45 |
| | Jim Norton | 1960-68 | 45 |
| | Thom Darden | 1972-74, 76-81 | 45 |
| 43 | Warren Lahr | 1949-59 | 44 |
| | Steve Foley | 1976-86 | 44 |
| 45 | Kermit Alexander | 1963-73 | 43 |
| 46 | Bobby Hunt | 1962-69 | 42 |
| | Gill Byrd | 1983-93 | 42 |
| | **Eugene Robinson** | **1985-** | **42** |
| 49 | Don Doll | 1949-54 | 41 |
| | Johnny Sample | 1958-68 | 41 |
| | Spider Lockhart | 1965-75 | 41 |
| | Charlie Waters | 1970-81 | 41 |
| 53 | Tom Keane | 1948-55 | 40 |
| | Ed Sharockman | 1962-72 | 40 |
| | Butch Byrd | 1964-71 | 40 |
| | W.K. Hicks | 1964-72 | 40 |
| | Bill Thompson | 1969-81 | 40 |
| | Roger Wehrli | 1969-82 | 40 |
| | **Darrell Green** | **1983-** | **40** |
| 60 | Glen Edwards | 1971-81 | 39 |
| | Rolland Lawrence | 1973-80 | 39 |
| | Gary Barbaro | 1976-82 | 39 |
| | Clarence Scott | 1971-83 | 39 |
| | Lester Hayes | 1977-87 | 39 |
| | Mike Harden | 1980-90 | 39 |
| 66 | Linden Crow | 1955-64 | 38 |
| | Rick Volk | 1965-78 | 38 |
| | Ray Brown | 1971-80 | 38 |
| | Gary Fencik | 1976-87 | 38 |
| | **Albert Lewis** | **1983-** | **38** |
| 71 | Don Shinnick | 1957-69 | 37 |
| | Dick Lynch | 1958-66 | 37 |
| | Ken Reaves | 1966-77 | 37 |
| | Bob Howard | 1967-79 | 37 |
| | Tony Greene | 1971-79 | 37 |
| | Jack Tatum | 1971-80 | 37 |
| | Nolan Cromwell | 1977-87 | 37 |
| | Joey Browner | 1983-91 | 37 |
| | Dwayne Woodruff | 1979-90 | 37 |
| 80 | Jim David | 1952-59 | 36 |
| | Fred Williamson | 1960-67 | 36 |
| | Brig Owens | 1966-77 | 36 |
| | Mike Wagner | 1971-80 | 36 |
| | Tom Myers | 1972-81 | 36 |
| | Dennis Thurman | 1978-86 | 36 |
| | Raymond Clayborn | 1977-91 | 36 |
| | **Kevin Ross** | **1984-** | **36** |
| | **Eric Allen** | **1988-** | **36** |
| 89 | Frank Reagan | 1941,1946-51 | 35 |
| | Ray Ramsey | 1947-53 | 35 |
| | Jerry Norton | 1954-64 | 35 |
| | Miller Farr | 1965-73 | 35 |
| | Willie Williams | 1965-73 | 35 |
| | Nate Wright | 1969-80 | 35 |
| | Ron Bolton | 1972-82 | 35 |
| | Lyle Blackwood | 1973-86 | 35 |
| | Michael Downs | 1981-88 | 35 |
| | LeRoy Irvin | 1980-90 | 35 |
| 99 | Tommy James | 1947-56 | 34 |
| | Jim Cason | 1948-52, 54-56 | 34 |
| | Otto Schnellbacher | 1948-51 | 34 |
| | Don Paul | 1950-58 | 34 |
| | Bill Baird | 1963-69 | 34 |
| | Jerry Logan | 1963-72 | 34 |
| | Cornell Green | 1962-74 | 34 |
| | Dick Anderson | 1968-74, 76-77 | 34 |
| | Bill Bradley | 1969-77 | 34 |
| | Clarence Scott | 1971-81 | 34 |
| | Stan White | 1972-82 | 34 |
| | Bill Simpson | 1974-78, 80-82 | 34 |
| 111 | Irv Comp | 1943-49 | 33 |
| | Jim Smith | 1948-53 | 33 |
| | Andy Nelson | 1957-64 | 33 |
| | Gary Green | 1977-85 | 33 |
| | Herman Edwards | 1977-86 | 33 |
| | Norm Thompson | 1971-79 | 33 |
| | Joe Lavender | 1973-82 | 33 |
| | Louis Breeden | 1978-87 | 33 |
| | **Lionel Washington** | **1983-** | **33** |
| 120 | Lowell Wagner | 1946-53, 55 | 32 |
| | Tom Landry | 1949-55 | 32 |
| | Roosevelt Taylor | 1961-72 | 32 |
| | Nick Buoniconti | 1962-64, 66-76 | 32 |
| | Lee Roy Jordan | 1963-75 | 32 |
| | Charlie Stukes | 1967-74 | 32 |
| | Jack Ham | 1971-82 | 32 |
| | Dwight Hicks | 1979-86 | 32 |
| | Kenny Easley | 1981-87 | 32 |
| | Mark Lee | 1980-91 | 32 |
| | **Eugene Daniel** | **1984-** | **32** |
| | **Deion Sanders** | **1989-** | **32** |

## PUNTING

**PUNTS (380)**

| | | | |
|---|---|---|---|
| 1 | Dave Jennings | 1974-87 | 1168 |
| 2 | Jerrel Wilson | 1963-78 | 1069 |
| 3 | Ray Guy | 1974-86 | 1052 |
| **4** | **Rohn Stark** | **1982-** | **1051** |
| **5** | **Rich Camarillo** | **1981-** | **1033** |
| 6 | John James | 1972-83 | 995 |
| 7 | Mike Bragg | 1968-80 | 978 |
| 8 | Bobby Walden | 1964-77 | 974 |
| 9 | Bobby Joe Green | 1960-73 | 970 |
| **10** | **Jeff Gossett** | **1981-83,85-** | **929** |
| 11 | Bob Parsons | 1972-83 | 884 |
| **12** | **Brian Hansen** | **1984-88,90-93** | **880** |
| 13 | Jim Arnold | 1983-94 | 871 |
| 14 | David Lee | 1966-78 | 838 |
| 15 | Greg Coleman | 1977-88 | 823 |
| **16** | **Mike Saxon** | **1985-** | **820** |
| 17 | Tom Blanchard | 1971-81 | 819 |
| **18** | **Reggie Roby** | **1983-** | **796** |
| 19 | Paul Maguire | 1960-70 | 794 |
| **20** | **John Kidd** | **1984-** | **792** |
| **21** | **Mike Horan** | **1984-** | **765** |
| **22** | **Lee Johnson** | **1985-** | **757** |
| **23** | **Sean Landeta** | **1985-** | **733** |
| 24 | Sam Baker | 1953, 56-69 | 701 |
| 25 | Pat McInally | 1976-85 | 700 |
| 26 | Harry Newsome | 1985-93 | 697 |
| 27 | Verne Lewellyn | 1924-32 | 679 |
| 28 | Max Runager | 1979-89 | 668 |
| 29 | Don Chandler | 1956-67 | 660 |
| **30** | **Jeff Feagles** | **1988-** | **652** |
| 31 | Don Cockroft | 1968-80 | 651 |
| 32 | Herman Weaver | 1970-80 | 635 |
| 33 | Larry Seiple | 1968-77 | 633 |
| 34 | Jeff West | 1975-79, 81-85 | 625 |
| 35 | Danny White | 1976-88 | 612 |
| 36 | Spike Jones | 1970-77 | 592 |
| 37 | Dave Beverly | 1974-80 | 586 |
| 38 | Maury Buford | 1982-86,88-91 | 586 |
| 39 | Bill Van Heusen | 1968-76 | 574 |
| 40 | Mike Eischeid | 1966-74 | 564 |
| 41 | Pat Studstill | 1961-62, 64-72 | 560 |
| 42 | Curley Johnson | 1960-69 | 556 |
| 43 | Chuck Ramsey | 1977-84 | 553 |
| **44** | **Tommy Barnhardt** | **1987-** | **551** |
| 45 | Billy Lothridge | 1964-72 | 532 |
| 46 | Norm Van Brocklin | 1949-60 | 523 |
| 47 | Dennis Partee | 1968-75 | 519 |
| 48 | Jim Norton | 1960-68 | 518 |
| 49 | Tommy Davis | 1959-69 | 511 |
| | **Bryan Wagner** | **1987-** | **511** |
| 51 | Yale Lary | 1952-53, 56-64 | 503 |
| 52 | Dale Hatcher | 1985-89,91,93 | 494 |
| 53 | Ed Brown | 1954-65 | 493 |
| 54 | Horace Gillon | 1947-56 | 492 |
| 55 | Danny Villanueva | 1960-67 | 488 |
| **56** | **Mark Royals** | **1987,90-** | **486** |
| **57** | **Rick Tuten** | **1989-** | **482** |
| 58 | Adrian Burke | 1950-56 | 474 |
| 59 | Don Bracken | 1985-90,92-93 | 466 |
| **60** | **Dan Stryzinski** | **1990-** | **448** |
| 61 | Craig Colquitt | 1978-84 | 429 |
| **62** | **Chris Mohr** | **1989,91-** | **427** |
| 63 | Dave Green | 1973-78 | 424 |
| **64** | **Bryan Barker** | **1990-** | **422** |
| 65 | Luke Prestridge | 1979-84 | 421 |
| 66 | Ralf Mojsiejenko | 1985-91 | 418 |
| 67 | Cliff Parsley | 1977-81 | 407 |
| 68 | Marv Bateman | 1972-77 | 401 |
| | Scott Fulhage | 1987-92 | 401 |
| 70 | Jug Girard | 1948-57 | 397 |
| 71 | Steve Cox | 1981-88 | 393 |
| 72 | Tom Landry | 1949-55 | 389 |
| 73 | Donny Anderson | 1966-74 | 387 |
| **74** | **Louie Aguiar** | **1991-** | **386** |
| 75 | Frank Garcia | 1981,83-87 | 384 |
| 76 | Greg Montgomery | 1988-94 | 380 |

**PUNTING AVERAGE (42.3)**

(Minimum 250 punts)

| | | | |
|---|---|---|---|
| 1 | Sammy Baugh | 1937-52 | 44.9 |
| 2 | Tommy Davis | 1959-69 | 44.7 |
| 3 | Yale Lary | 1952-53, 56-64 | 44.3 |
| 4 | Bob Scarpitto | 1961-68 | 44.0 |
| 5 | Jerry Norton | 1954-64 | 43.8 |
| 6 | Dave Lewis | 1970-81 | 43.7 |
| 7 | Don Chandler | 1956-67 | 43.5 |
| **8** | **Rohn Stark** | **1982-** | **43.4** |
| | **Sean Landeta** | **1985-** | **43.4** |
| 10 | Jim Fraser | 1962-66, 68 | 43.3 |
| | **Rick Tuten** | **1989-** | **43.3** |
| 12 | Jerrel Wilson | 1963-78 | 43.2 |
| 13 | Horace Gillom | 1947-56 | 43.1 |
| 14 | Frankie Albert | 1946-52 | 43.0 |
| 15 | Norm Van Brocklin | 1949-60 | 42.9 |
| | Greg Montgomery | 1988-94 | 42.9 |
| 17 | Danny Villanueva | 1960-67 | 42.7 |
| **18** | **Rich Camarillo** | **1981-** | **42.5** |
| 19 | Bobby Joe Green | 1960-73 | 42.6 |
| | Curley Johnson | 1960-69 | 42.6 |
| **21** | **Tommy Barnhardt** | **1987-** | **42.4** |
| 22 | Harry Newsome | 1985-93 | 42.3 |
| | **Reggie Roby** | **1983-** | **42.3** |

Players active at the end of **1995** are shown in **bold face**.

# THE HALL OF FAME

## 1963

Sammy Baugh — Quarterback, Coach
Bert Bell — NFL Commissioner, Coach, Owner
Johnny Blood (McNally) — Halfback, Coach
Joe Carr — NFL President, Founder
Dutch Clark — Quarterback, Coach
Red Grange — Halfback
George Halas — End, Coach, Owner, Founder
Mel Hein — Center
Pete Henry — Tackle
Carl Hubbard — Tackle
Don Hutson — End
Curly Lambeau — Halfback, Coach, Founder
Tim Mara — Owner
George Preston Marshall — Owner
Bronko Nagurski — Fullback
Ernie Nevers — Fullback, Tailback, Coach
Jim Thorpe — Halfback, Coach, First NFL President

## 1964

Jimmy Conzelman — Quarterback, Coach, Owner
Ed Healey — Tackle
Clarke Hinkle — Fullback
Mike Michalske — Guard
Art Rooney — Owner
George Trafton — Center

## 1965

Guy Chamberlin — End, Coach
Paddy Driscoll — Quarterback
Danny Fortmann — Guard
Otto Graham — Quarterback
Sid Luckman — Quarterback
Steve Van Buren — Halfback
Bob Waterfield — Quarterback, Kicker

## 1966

Bill Dudley — Halfback, Tailback, Kicker
Joe Guyon — Fullback, Tailback
Arnie Herber — Quarterback
Walt Kiesling — Guard, Coach
George McAfee - Halfback
Steve Owen — Tackle, Coach
Shorty Ray — League Official

## 1967

Chuck Bednarik — Center, Linebacker
Charles Bidwell — Owner
Paul Brown — Coach, Owner
Bobby Layne — Quarterback
Dan Reeves — Owner
Ken Strong — Halfback, Kicker
Joe Stydahar — Tackle
Emlen Tunnell — Defensive Back

## 1968

Cliff Battles — Halfback, Tailback
Art Donovan — Defensive Tackle
Elroy "Crazy Legs" Hirsch — End
Wayne Millner — End
Marion Motley — Fullback
Charlie Trippi — Halfback, Quarterback
Alex Wojciechowicz — Center, Linebacker

## 1969

Turk Edwards — Tackle
Greasy Neale — Coach
Leo Nomellini — Defensive Tackle
Joe Perry — Fullback
Ernie Stautner — Defensive Tackle

## 1970

Jack Christiansen — Defensive Back
Tom Fears — End
Hugh McElhenny — Halfback
Pete Pihos — End

## 1971

Jim Brown — Fullback
Bill Hewitt — End
Bruiser Kinard — Tackle
Vince Lombardi — Coach
Andy Robustelli — Defensive End
Y.A. Tittle — Quarterback
Norm Van Brocklin — Quarterback

## 1972

Lamar Hunt — AFL Founder and Owner
Gino Marchetti — Defensive End
Ollie Matson — Halfback
Ace Parker — Tailback, Quarterback

## 1973

Raymond Berry — End
Jim Parker — Offensive Tackle, Offensive Guard
Joe Schmidt — Linebacker

## 1974

Tony Canadeo — Halfback, Fullback
Bill George — Guard, Linebacker, Tackle
Lou Groza — Kicker, Tackle
Dick "Night Train" Lane — Defensive Back

## 1975

Roosevelt Brown — Offensive Tackle
George Conner — Tackle, Guard, Linebacker
Dante Lavelli — End
Lenny Moore — Halfback, Flanker

## 1976

Ray Flaherty — End
Len Ford — End
Jim Taylor — Fullback

## 1977

Frank Gifford — Halfback, Flanker
Forrest Gregg — Offensive Tackle
Gale Sayers — Halfback
Bart Starr — Quarterback
Bill Willis — Guard

## 1978

Lance Alworth — Wide Receiver
Weeb Ewbank — Coach
Tuffy Leemans — Fullback
Ray Nitschke — Linebacker
Larry Wilson — Defensive Back

# THE HALL OF FAME (Continued)

### 1979

Dick Butkus — Linebacker
Yale Lary — Defensive Back, Punter
Ron Mix — Offensive Tackle
Johnny Unitas — Quarterback

### 1980

Herb Adderley — Cornerback
Deacon Jones — Defensive End
Bob Lilly — Defensive Tackle
Jim Otto — Center

### 1981

Red Badgro — End
George Blanda — Quarterback, Kicker
Willie Davis — Defensive End
Jim Ringo — Center

### 1982

Doug Atkins — Defensive End
Sam Huff — Linebacker
George Musso — Tackle, Guard
Merlin Olsen — Defensive Tackle

### 1983

Bobby Bell — Linebacker
Sid Gillman — Coach
Sonny Jurgensen — Quarterback
Bobby Mitchell — Halfback, Wide Receiver
Paul Warfield — Wide Receiver

### 1984

Willie Brown — Safety
Mike McCormack — Tackle
Charley Taylor — Wide Receiver
Arnie Weinmeister — Defensive Tackle

### 1985

Frank Gatski — Center
Joe Namath — Quarterback
Pete Rozelle — Commissioner
O.J. Simpson — Running Back
Roger Staubach — Quarterback

### 1986

Paul Hornung — Halfback, Kicker
Ken Houston — Safety
Willie Lanier — Linebacker
Fran Tarkenton — Quarterback
Doak Walker — Halfback, Kicker

### 1987

Larry Csonka — Fullback
Len Dawson — Quarterback
Joe Greene — Defensive Tackle
John Henry Johnson — Fullback
Jim Langer — Center
Don Maynard — Wide Receiver
Gene Upshaw — Offensive Guard

### 1988

Fred Biletnikoff — Wide Receiver
Mike Ditka — Tight End, Coach
Jack Ham — Linebacker
Alan Page — Defensive Tackle

### 1989

Mel Blount — Cornerback
Terry Bradshaw — Quarterback
Art Shell — Offensive Tackle
Willie Wood — Safety

### 1990

Buck Buchanan — Defensive Tackle
Bob Griese — Quarterback
Franco Harris — Running Back
Ted Hendricks — Linebacker
Jack Lambert — Linebacker
Tom Landry — Defensive Back, Coach
Bob St. Clair — Offensive Tackle

### 1991

Earl Campbell — Running Back
John Hannah — Offensive Guard
Stan Jones — Offensive Guard, Defensive Tackle
Tex Schramm — General Manager
Jan Stenerud — Kicker

### 1992

Lem Barney — Cornerback
Al Davis — Coach, Owner, Commissioner
John Mackey — Tight End
John Riggins — Running Back

### 1993

Dan Fouts — Quarterback
Larry Little — Offensive Guard
Chuck Noll — Coach
Walter Payton — Running Back
Bill Walsh — Coach

### 1994

Tony Dorsett — Running Back
Bud Grant — Coach
Jimmy Johnson — Cornerback
Leroy Kelly — Running Back
Jackie Smith — Tight End
Randy White — Defensive Tackle

### 1995

Jim Finks — General Manager
Henry Jordan — Defensive Tackle
Steve Largent — Wide Receiver
Lee Roy Selmon — Defensive End
Kellen Winslow — Tight End

### 1996

Lou Creekmur — Offensive Guard, Offensive Tackle
Dan Dierdorf — Offensive Tackle
Joe Gibbs — Head Coach
Charlie Joiner — Wide Receiver
Mel Renfro — Cornerback, Safety

# Football Caricatures by Bob Carroll
Reprinted by Permission

JIM THORPE

SAMMY BAUGH

JOE NAMATH

PETE ROZELLE

EMLEN TUNNELL

GEORGE HALAS

MARION MOTLEY

SID LUCKMAN

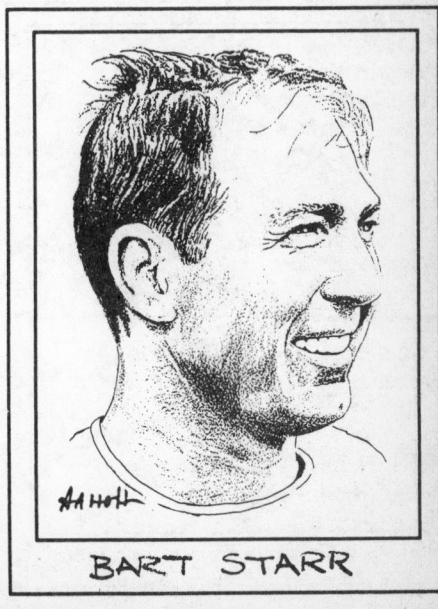

BART STARR

# Football Caricatures by Bob Carroll
Reprinted by Permission

ROGER STAUBACH

ERNIE NEVERS

ART DONOVAN

PAUL BROWN

PADDY DRISCOLL

OTTO GRAHAM

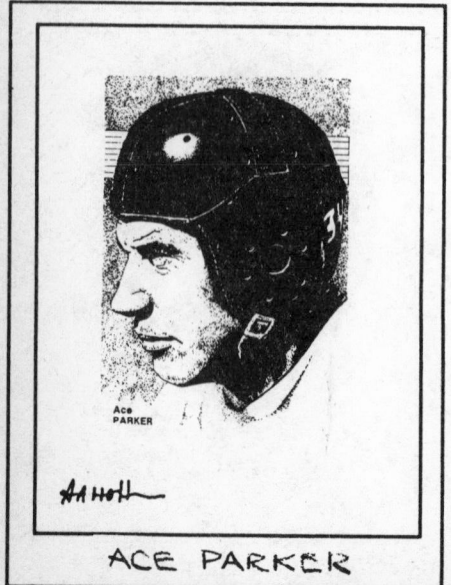

ACE PARKER

GALE SAYERS

GEORGE BLANDA

# Football Caricatures by Bob Carroll
Reprinted by Permission

DON HUTSON

RED GRANGE

JIM BROWN

CLIFF BATTLES

VINCE LOMBARDI

LOU GROZA

DICK BUTKUS

PAUL WARFIELD

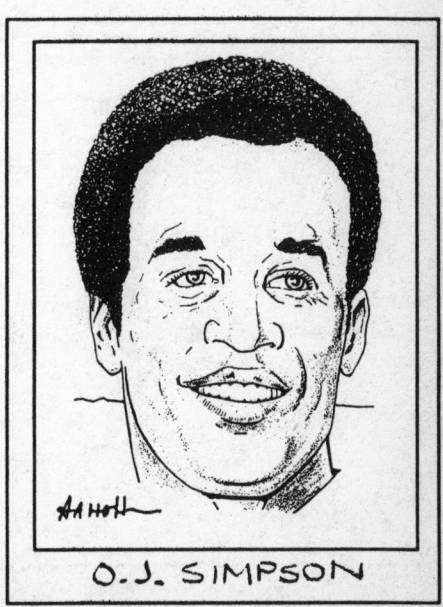

O.J. SIMPSON

# Football Caricatures by Bob Carroll
Reprinted by Permission

BOB LILLY

WILLIE LANIER

TERRY BRADSHAW

FRAN TARKENTON

LARRY CSONKA

ALAN PAGE

BOBBY LAYNE

FRANCO HARRIS

JIM TAYLOR

# MANAGEMENT
## AN INTEGRATED APPROACH

### SECOND EDITION

## GULATI
Harvard Business School

## MAYO
Harvard Business School

## NOHRIA
Harvard Business School

CENGAGE
Learning®

Australia • Brazil • Mexico • Singapore • United Kingdom • United States

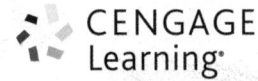

**Management**, Second Edition

Ranjay Gulati, Anthony J. Mayo,
Nitin Nohria

Vice President, General Manager, Social
Science & Qualitative Business: Erin Joyner

Product Director: Jason Fremder

Senior Product Manager: Person Scott

Content Developer: Tara Singer

Product Assistant: Brian Pierce

Marketing Director: Kristen Hurd

Marketing Manager: Emily Horowitz

Marketing Coordinator: Christopher Walz

Art and Cover Direction, Production
Management, and Composition:
Lumina Datamatics, Inc.

Intellectual Property Analyst: Diane Garrity

Project Manager: Sarah Shainwald

Manufacturing Planner: Ron Montgomery

Cover Image: ©Anita Ponne/Shutterstock

Internal Design Images: ©DeSerg/
Shutterstock, ©fonikum/iStockphoto.com,
Janos Levente/Shutterstock.com

For product information and technology assistance, contact us at
**Cengage Learning Customer & Sales Support, 1-800-354-9706**

For permission to use material from this text or product,
submit all requests online at **www.cengage.com/permissions**
Further permissions questions can be emailed to
**permissionrequest@cengage.com**

Library of Congress Control Number: 2015949125

Student Edition:
ISBN: 978-1-305-50208-6

Loose-leaf Edition:
ISBN: 978-1-305-50210-9

**Cengage Learning**
20 Channel Center Street
Boston, MA 02210
USA

Cengage Learning is a leading provider of customized learning solutions
with employees residing in nearly 40 different countries and sales in
more than 125 countries around the world. Find your local representative at
**www.cengage.com**.

Cengage Learning products are represented in Canada by Nelson Education, Ltd.

To learn more about Cengage Learning Solutions, visit **www.cengage.com**

Purchase any of our products at your local college store or at our preferred
online store **www.cengagebrain.com**

Unless otherwise noted, all items are © Cengage Learning

Printed in the United States of America
Print Number: 02   Print Year:  2016